INGENIX®

ingenix *e*solutions

Electronic coding, billing & reimbursement products

Electronic coding, billing and reimbursement products.

Ingenix provides a robust suite of eSolutions to solve a wide variety of coding, billing and reimbursement issues. As the industry moves to electronic products, you can rely on Ingenix to help support you through the transition.

← **Web-based applications for all markets**

← **Dedicated support**

← **Environmentally responsible**

Key Features and Benefits

Using eSolutions is a step in the right direction when it comes to streamlining your coding, billing and reimbursement practices. Ingenix eSolutions can help you save time and increase your efficiency with accurate and on-time content.

- **Rely on a leader in health care.** Ingenix has been producing quality coding products for over 25 years. All of the expert content that goes into our books goes into our electronic resources.

- **Save time and money.** Ingenix eSolutions combine the content of over 37 code books and data files.

- **Go Green.** Eco-friendly electronic products are not only faster and easier to use than books, they require less storage space, less paper and leave a lighter carbon footprint.

- **Increase accuracy.** Electronic solutions are updated regularly so you know you're always working with the most current content available.

- **Get the training and support you need.** Convenient, online training and customized training programs are available to meet your specific needs.

- **Take baby steps.** Transition at your pace with code book and solution packages that let you keep your books while you learn how to become a whiz with your electronic products.

- **Get Started.** Visit **shopingenix.com/ eSolutions** for product listing.

SAVE UP TO 20%

with source code FB10E

Visit **www.shopingenix.com** and enter the source code in the lower right-hand corner and save 20%.

Call toll-free **1-800-INGENIX** (464-3649), option 1 and save 15%.

Ingenix | Information is the Lifeblood of Health Care | Call toll-free 1-800-INGENIX (464-3649), option 1.

100% Money Back Guarantee If our merchandise ever fails to meet your expectations, please contact our Customer Service Department toll-free at 1-800-INGENIX (464-3649), option 1, for an immediate response. Software: Credit will be granted for unopened packages only.

Also available from your medical bookstore or distributor.

FB10E

2010

INGENIX®

ICD-9-CM Expert

for Hospitals
Volumes 1, 2, & 3

International Classification of Diseases
9th Revision
Clinical Modification

Sixth Edition

Edited by:
Anita C. Hart, RHIA, CCS, CCS-P
Melinda S. Stegman, MBA, CCS
Beth Ford, RHIT, CCS

Ingenix is committed to providing you with the ICD-9-CM code update information you need to code accurately and to be in compliance with HIPAA regulations. In case of adoption of additional ICD-9-CM code changes effective April 1, 2010, Ingenix will provide these code changes to you at no additional cost! Just check back at www.shopingenix.com/productalerts to review the latest information concerning any new code changes.

Codes Valid October 1, 2009, through September 30, 2010

PUBLISHER'S NOTICE

All codes, indexes, and other material in the ICD-9-CM are compiled from official ICD-9-CM codes and instructions as well as the Medicare regulations and manuals issued or authorized by the Centers for Medicare and Medicaid Services. The code book is designed to provide accurate and authoritative information in regard to the subject covered, and every reasonable effort has been made to ensure the accuracy of the information within these pages. However, the ultimate responsibility for correct coding lies with the provider of services.

Ingenix, its employees, agents and staff make no representation, warranty or guarantee that this compilation of codes and narratives is error-free or that the use of this code book will prevent differences of opinion or disputes with Medicare or other third-party payers as to the codes that are accepted or the amounts that will be paid to providers for services, and will bear no responsibility or liability for the results or consequences of the use of this code book.

OUR COMMITMENT TO ACCURACY

Ingenix is committed to producing accurate and reliable materials. To report corrections, please visit www.ingenixon-line.com/accuracy or email accuracy@ingenix.com. You can also reach customer service by calling 1.800.INGENIX (464.3649), option 1.

SPECIAL REPORTS AND ANNOUNCEMENTS

Purchase of this publication entitles you to Special Reports and announcements via email. Please call customer service at 800 INGENIX (464-3649) or contact your bookstore to take advantage of this exciting free service that will keep you abreast of important code changes and regulatory developments.

Review, download, and print the Special Reports in .pdf format. Log on to
www.shopingenix.com/productalerts

Preface

Since the federal government implemented diagnosis-related groups (DRGs) on October 1, 1983, medical record profes-sionals and others have had to refer to many sources for ICD-9-CM codes and coding and reimbursement principles.

ICD-9-CM for Hospitals, Volumes 1, 2 & 3, has been designed with the health information professional in mind. All three volumes of the most recent official government version of ICD-9-CM have been combined into one book.

Our technical experts have drawn upon their extensive hands-on experience to enhance the government's book with valuable features essential to correct coding and reimbursement. Without these enhancements, health information management departments would spend hours locating the information required to code each record accurately. Because of the thoroughness, accuracy, timeliness and ease of use of *ICD-9-CM for Hospitals*, health information departments nationwide have turned to them for their coding needs.

ICD-9-CM for Hospitals includes many of the enhancements described below in direct response to requests from our subscribers. As you review the content, you'll find the following:

- The complete ICD-9-CM official guidelines for coding and reporting, published by the U.S. Department of Health and Human Services and approved by the cooperating parties (American Hospital Association, American Health Information Management Association, Health Care Financing Administration and National Center for Health Statistics)
- All the official ICD-9-CM codes, indexes, notes, footnotes and symbols
- Color-highlighted illustrations and clearly worded definitions integrated in the tabular, provide important clinical information
- Exclusive color coding, symbols, and footnotes that alert coders to coding and reimbursement issues, including the majority of the Medicare code edits and identification of conditions that significantly affect DRG assignment of HIV cases.
- The complication and comorbidity (CC) exclusion list, integrated beneath the applicable codes makes it easier to determine complications and comorbidities excluded with a particular principal diagnosis
- The American Hospital Association (AHA's) *Coding Clinic for ICD-9-CM* references, integrated beneath the applicable codes to provide easy reference to official coding advice as designated by the four cooperating parties (AHA, AHIMA, CMS, and NCHS)
- Check fourth- and fifth-digit symbols identify codes that require the addition of a fourth or fifth digit for code specificity and validity
- Symbols identify new codes and text revisions and pages are dated to indicate when the changes were made
- Synopsis of the code changes for the current year
- Color coding and symbol legend at the bottom of each page
- Exclusive QuickFlip Color Tabs for quick, easy location of terms and codes in the index and Tabular List

Please review "How to Use *ICD-9-CM for Hospitals (Volumes 1, 2 & 3)*" in this section to learn about the features that will help you assign and report correct codes, ensuring appropriate reimbursement.

USE OF OFFICIAL SOURCES

The *ICD-9-CM for Hospitals* contains the official U.S. Department of Health and Human Services, Ninth Revision, Sixth Edition ICD-9-CM codes, effective for the current year.

The color-coding, footnotes and symbols, which identify coding and reimbursement issues, are derived from official federal government sources, including the Medicare Code Edits (MCE), Version 27.0.

The American Hospital Association's (AHA) *Coding Clinic for ICD-9-CM* references are used with permission of the AHA.

IMPORTANT INFORMATION ABOUT YOUR SUBSCRIPTION SERVICE

If you have purchased the updateable *ICD-9-CM Expert for Hospitals*, your subscription includes an updating service throughout the year to keep the code book current and accurate. The February update includes new illustrations and definitions, AHA's *Coding Clinic* references for third and fourth quarter, the latest MCEs, and official errata changes. In July you will receive a list of all new, revised, and invalid codes for the upcoming year.

TECHNICAL EDITORS

Anita C. Hart, RHIA, CCS, CCS-P, *Product Manager, Ingenix*
Ms. Hart's experience includes conducting and publishing research in clinical medicine and human genetics for Yale University, Massachusetts General Hospital, and Massachusetts Institute of Technology. In addition, Ms. Hart has supervised medical records management, health information management, coding and reimbursement, and worker's compensation issues as the office manager for a physical therapy rehabilitation clinic. Ms. Hart is an expert in physician and facility coding, reimbursement systems, and compliance issues. Ms. Hart has developed and has served as technical consultant for numerous other publications for hospital and physician practices. Currrenty, Ms. Hart is the Product Manager and Technical Editor for the ICD-9-CM and ICD-10-CM/PCS product lines.

Melinda S. Stegman, MBA, CCS, *Clinical/Technical Editor, Ingenix*
Ms. Stegman has more than 25 years of experience in the HIM profession and has been responsible for managing the clinical aspects of the HSS/Ingenix HIM Consulting practice in the Washington, DC area office. Her areas of specialization include training on inpatient and DRG coding, outpatient coding, and Ambulatory Payment Classifications (APCs) for HIM professionals, software developers, and other clients; developing an outpatient billing/coding compliance tool for a major accounting firm; and managing HIM consulting practices. Ms. Stegman is a regular contributing author for *Advance for Health Information Management Professionals* and for the *Journal of Health Care Compliance*. She has performed coding assessments and educational sessions throughout the country. Ms. Stegman is credentialed by the American Health Information Management Association (AHIMA) as a Certified Coding Specialist (CCS) and holds a Master of Business Administration degree with a concentration in health care management from the University of New Mexico—Albuquerque.

Beth Ford, RHIT, CCS, *Clinical/Technical Editor, Ingenix*
Ms. Ford is a clinical/technical editor for Ingenix. She has extensive background in both physician and facility ICD-9-CM and CPT/HCPCS coding. Ms. Ford has served as a coding specialist, coding manager, coding trainer/educator and coding consultant, as well as a health information management director. She is an active member of the American Heath Information Management Association (AHIMA).

In addition to the editors, the following people have contributed to this book:

Stacy Perry, Manager, Desktop Publishing
Tracy Betzler, Desktop Publishing Specialist
Hope Dunn, Desktop Publishing Specialist
Toni Stewart, Desktop Publishing Specialist
Kate Holden, Editor

WHAT TO DO IF YOU HAVE QUESTIONS

If you have any questions call our customer service department toll-free at 800-INGENIX (464-3649), option 1.

If you have comments on the content of this book, please email them to customerservice@ingenix.com or fax to 801-982-4033.

ADDITIONAL COPIES

Contact the customer service order department toll-free at 800-INGENIX (464-3649), option 1.

Introduction

HISTORY AND FUTURE OF ICD-9

The International Classification of Diseases, Ninth Revision, Clinical Modification (ICD-9-CM) is based on the official version of the World Health Organization's Ninth Revision, International Classification of Diseases (ICD-9). ICD-9 classifies morbidity and mortality information for statistical purposes, and for the indexing of hospital records by disease and operations, for data storage and retrieval.

This modification of ICD-9 supplants the Eighth Revision International Classification of Diseases, Adapted for Use in the United States (ICDA-8) and the Hospital Adaptation of ICDA (H-ICDA).

The concept of extending the International Classification of Diseases for use in hospital indexing was originally developed in response to a need for a more efficient basis for storage and retrieval of diagnostic data. In 1950, the U.S. Public Health Service and the Veterans Administration began independent tests of the International Classification of Diseases for hospital indexing purposes. The following year, the Columbia Presbyterian Medical Center in New York City adopted the International Classification of Diseases, Sixth Revision, with some modifications for use in its medical record department. A few years later, the Commission on Professional and Hospital Activities (CPHA) in Ann Arbor, Mich., adopted the International Classification of Diseases with similar modifications for use in hospitals participating in the Professional Activity Study.

The problem of adapting ICD for indexing hospital records was taken up by the U.S. National Committee on Vital and Health Statistics through its subcommittee on hospital statistics. The subcommittee reviewed the modifications made by the various users of ICD and proposed that uniform changes be made. This was done by a small working party.

In view of the growing interest in the use of the International Classification of Diseases for hospital indexing, a study was undertaken in 1956 by the American Hospital Association and the American Medical Record Association (then the American Association of Medical Record Librarians) of the relative efficiencies of coding systems for diagnostic indexing. This study indicated the International Classification of Diseases provided a suitable and efficient framework for indexing hospital records. The major users of the International Classification of Diseases for hospital indexing purposes then consolidated their experiences, and an adaptation was first published in December 1959. A revision was issued in 1962 and the first "Classification of Operations and Treatments" was included.

In 1966, the international conference for revising the International Classification of Diseases noted the eighth revision of ICD had been constructed with hospital indexing in mind and considered the revised classification suitable, in itself, for hospital use in some countries. However, it was recognized that the basic classification might provide inadequate detail for diagnostic indexing in other countries. A group of consultants was asked to study the eighth revision of ICD (ICD-8) for applicability to various users in the United States. This group recommended that further detail be provided for coding of hospital and morbidity data. The American Hospital Association was requested to develop the needed adaptation proposals. This was done by an advisory committee (the Advisory Committee to the Central Office on ICDA). In 1968 the United States Public Health Service published the product, Eighth Revision International Classification of Diseases, Adapted for Use in the United States. This became commonly known as ICDA-8, and beginning in 1968 it served as the basis for coding diagnostic data for both official morbidity and mortality statistics in the United States.

In 1968, the CPHA published the Hospital Adaptation of ICDA (H-ICDA) based on both the original ICD-8 and ICDA-8. In 1973, CPHA published a revision of H-ICDA, referred to as H-ICDA-2. Hospitals throughout the United States were divided in their use of these classifications until January 1979, when ICD-9-CM was made the single classification intended primarily for use in the United States, replacing these earlier related, but somewhat dissimilar, classifications.

Physicians have been required by law to submit diagnosis codes for Medicare reimbursement since the passage of the Medicare Catastrophic Coverage Act of 1988. This act requires physician offices to include the appropriate diagnosis codes when billing for services provided to Medicare beneficiaries on or after April 1, 1989. The Centers for Medicare and Medicaid Services (formerly known as Health Care Financing Administration) designated ICD-9-CM as the coding system physicians must use.

In 1993 the World Health Organization published the newest version of International Classification of Diseases, Tenth Revision, ICD-10. This version contains the greatest number of changes in the history of ICD. There are more codes (5,500 more than ICD-9) to allow more specific reporting of diseases and newly recognized conditions. ICD-10 consists of three volumes; Tabular List (volume I), instructions (volume 2) and the Alphabetic Index (volume 3). It contains 21 chapters including two supplementary ones. The codes are alphanumeric (A00–T98, V01–Y98 and Z00–Z99). Currently ICD-10 is being used in some European countries with implementation date of October 1, 2013, in the United States.

ICD-9-CM BACKGROUND

In February 1977, a steering committee was convened by the National Center for Health Statistics to provide advice and counsel in developing a clinical modification of ICD-9. The organizations represented on the steering committee included the following:

- American Association of Health Data Systems
- American Hospital Association
- American Medical Record Association
- Association for Health Records
- Council on Clinical Classifications
- Centers for Medicare and Medicaid Services, Department of Health and Human Services
- WHO Center for Classification of Diseases for North America, sponsored by the National Center for Health Statistics, Department of Health and Human Services

The Council on Clinical Classifications was sponsored by the following:

- American Academy of Pediatrics
- American College of Obstetricians and Gynecologists
- American College of Physicians
- American College of Surgeons
- American Psychiatric Association
- Commission on Professional and Hospital Activities

The steering committee met periodically in 1977. Clinical guidance and technical input were provided by task forces on classification from the Council on Clinical Classification's sponsoring organizations.

ICD-9-CM is a clinical modification of the World Health Organization's ICD-9. The term "clinical" is used to emphasize the modification's intent: to serve as a useful tool to classify morbidity data for indexing medical records, medical care review, and ambulatory and other medical care programs, as well as for basic health statistics. To describe the clinical picture of the patient, the codes must be more precise than those needed only for statistical groupings and trend analysis.

CHARACTERISTICS OF ICD-9-CM

ICD-9-CM far exceeds its predecessors in the number of codes provided. The disease classification has been expanded to include health-related conditions and to provide greater specificity at the fifth-digit level of detail. These fifth digits are not optional; they are intended for use in recording the information substantiated in the clinical record.

Volume I (Tabular List) of ICD-9-CM contains four appendixes:

Appendix A: Morphology of Neoplasms

Appendix B: Deleted Effective October 1, 2004

Appendix C: Classification of Drugs by American Hospital Formulary
                       Service List Number and Their ICD-9-CM Equivalents

Appendix D: Classification of Industrial Accidents According to
                       Agency

Appendix E: List of Three-Digit Categories

These appendixes are included as a reference to provide further information about the patient's clinical picture, to further define a diagnostic statement, to aid in classifying new drugs or to reference three-digit categories.

Volume 2 (Alphabetic Index) of ICD-9-CM contains many diagnostic terms that do not appear in Volume I since the index includes most diagnostic terms currently in use.

Volume 3 (Procedure Index and Procedure Tabular) of ICD-9-CM contains codes for operations and procedures. The format for the tabular is the same as Volume 1 disease tabular, except the codes consist of two digits with one or two digits following the decimal point. Conventions in the index follow Volume 2 conventions except some subterms appear immediately below the main term rather than following alphabetizing rules.

THE DISEASE CLASSIFICATION

ICD-9-CM is totally compatible with its parent system, ICD-9, thus meeting the need for comparability of morbidity and mortality statistics at the international level. A few fourth-digit codes were created in existing three-digit rubrics only when the necessary detail could not be accommodated by the use of a fifth-digit subclassification. To ensure that each rubric of ICD-9-CM collapses back to its ICD-9 counterpart the following specifications governed the ICD-9-CM disease classification:

Specifications for the Tabular List:

1. Three-digit rubrics and their contents are unchanged from ICD-9.

2. The sequence of three-digit rubrics is unchanged from ICD-9.

3. Three-digit rubrics are not added to the main body of the classification.

4. Unsubdivided three-digit rubrics are subdivided where necessary to
   - add clinical detail
   - isolate terms for clinical accuracy.

5. The modification in ICD-9-CM is accomplished by adding a fifth digit to existing ICD-9 rubrics, except as noted under #7 below.

6. The optional dual classification in ICD-9 is modified.
   - Duplicate rubrics are deleted:
     – four-digit manifestation categories duplicating etiology entries
     – manifestation inclusion terms duplicating etiology entries
   - Manifestations of disease are identified, to the extent possible, by creating five-digit codes in the etiology rubrics.
   - When the manifestation of a disease cannot be included in the etiology rubrics, provision for its identification is made by retaining the ICD-9 rubrics used for classifying manifestations of disease.

7. The format of ICD-9-CM is revised from that used in ICD-9.
   - American spelling of medical terms is used.
   - Inclusion terms are indented beneath the titles of codes.
   - Codes not to be used for primary tabulation of disease are printed in italics with the notation, "code first underlying disease."

Specifications for the Alphabetic Index:

1. The format of the Alphabetic Index follows that of ICD-9.

2. When two codes are required to indicate etiology and manifestation, the manifestation code appears in brackets (e.g., diabetic cataract 250.5 [366.41]).

THE ICD-9-CM COORDINATION AND MAINTENANCE COMMITTEE

The four cooperating parties involved in maintaining the ICD-9-CM classification system include representatives of the American Hospital Association (AHA), the Centers for Medicare and Medicaid Services (CMS), the National Center for Health Statistics (NCHS), and the American Health Information Management Association (AHIMA).

Proposals for changes to the ICD-9-CM classification system are submitted and discussed in two open forum meetings held in March and September of each year at the Headquarters of the Centers for Medicare and Medicaid Services, Baltimore, Maryland. Comments received during and after the meetings are then discussed by the Committee. A notice of the new codes and code revisions approved by the Committee are published in the *Federal Register* as part of the proposed and final rule for the changes to the inpatient prospective payment system. The complete official document of changes to the classification system is released as the Addenda for the International Classification of Diseases, Ninth Revision, Clinical Modification, Sixth Edition, Volumes 1, 2, and 3.

How to Use the ICD-9-CM for Hospitals (Volumes 1, 2 & 3)

ICD-9-CM for Hospitals is based on the official version of the International Classification of Diseases, Ninth Revision, Clinical Modification, Sixth Edition, issued by the U.S. Department of Health and Human Services. Annual code changes are implemented by the government and are effective Oct. 1 and valid through Sept. 30 of the following year.

The code book is totally compatible with its parent system, ICD-9, thus meeting the need for comparability of morbidity and mortality statistics at the international level.

This book is consistent with the content of the government's version of ICD-9-CM. However, to accommodate the coder's approach to coding, the Alphabetic Index has been placed before the Tabular List in both the disease and procedure classifications. This allows the user to locate the correct codes in a logical, natural manner by locating the term in the index, then confirming the accuracy of the code in the Tabular List.

STEPS TO CORRECT CODING

1. Look up the main term in the Alphabetic Index and scan the subterm entries as appropriate. Follow any cross-references such as *"see"* and *"see also."* Do not code from the Alphabetic Index without verifying the accuracy of the code in the Tabular List.

2. Locate the code in the numerically arranged Tabular List.

3. Observe the punctuation, footnotes, cross-references, color-coded prompts and other conventions described in the 'Conventions' section.

4. To determine the appropriateness of the code selection, read all instructional material:
   - "includes" and *"excludes"* notes
   - *"see," "see also"* and *"see category"* cross-references
   - "use additional code" and *"code first underlying disease"* instructions
   - "code also" and *"omit code"* notes
   - fourth- and fifth-digit requirements
   - CC exclusions

5. Consult definitions, relevant illustrations, CC exclusions, color coding and reimbursement prompts, the check fourth- and fifth-digit, age and sex symbols. Refer to the color/symbol legend at the bottom of each page for symbols. Refer to the list of footnotes that is included in the "Additional Conventions" section of this book for a full explanation of a footnote associated with a code.

6. Consult the official ICD-9-CM guidelines for coding and reporting, and refer to the AHA's *Coding Clinic for ICD-9-CM* for coding guidelines governing the use of specific codes.

7. Confirm and transcribe the correct code.

ORGANIZATION

Introduction
The introductory material in this book includes the history and future of ICD-9-CM as well as an overview of the classification system.

Official ICD-9-CM Conventions
This section provides a full explanation of all the official footnotes, symbols, instructional notes, and conventions found in the official government version.

Additional Conventions
Exclusive color-coding, symbols, and notations have been included in the *ICD-9-CM for Hospitals, Volumes 1, 2 & 3* to alert coders to important coding and reimbursement issues. This section provides a full explanation of the additional conventions used throughout this book.

Coding Guidelines
Included in this book are the official ICD-9-CM coding guidelines as approved by the four cooperating parties of the ICD-9-CM Coordination and Maintenance Committee. Failure to comply with the official coding guidelines may result in denied or delayed claims.

Summary of Code Changes
This section includes a complete listing of all new code changes for the current year.

Summary of AHA's *Coding Clinic for ICD-9-CM* Topics
This is a brief summary of the official advice concerning coding topics covered in the latest issues of AHA's *Coding Clinic for ICD-9-CM* and is found **only** in the *ICD-9-CM Expert for Hospitals Expert* updateable edition.

ICD-9-CM Code Changes for 2010: An Insider's View
Chapter by chapter detailed clinical and coding information with coding scenarios for all the new codes adopted for 2010 located in one resource for quick reference and training. This section is found **ONLY** in the Expert editions.

Disease Classification: Alphabetic Index to Diseases
The Alphabetic Index to Diseases is separated by tabs labeled with the letters of the alphabet, contains diagnostic terms for illnesses, injuries and reasons for encounters with health care professionals. The Table of Drugs and Chemicals is easily located with the tab in this section.

The warning statement at the bottom of every page of the index, ⚠ Subterms under main terms may continue to next column or page, is a reminder to always check for additional subterms before making final selection.

Disease Classification: Tabular List of Diseases
The Tabular List of Diseases arranges the ICD-9-CM codes and descriptors numerically. QuickFlip color tabs divide this section into chapters, identified by the code range on the tab.

The Tabular List includes two supplementary classifications:

- V Codes—Supplementary Classification of Factors Influencing Health Status and Contact with Health Services (V01–V89)
- E Codes—Supplementary Classification of External Causes of Injury and Poisoning (E000–E999)

ICD-9-CM includes four official appendixes.

- Appendix A   Morphology of Neoplasms
- Appendix B: Deleted Effective October 1, 2004
- Appendix C   Classification of Drugs by AHFS List
- Appendix D   Classification of Industrial Accidents According to Agency
- Appendix E   List of Three-digit Categories

These appendixes are included as a reference to provide further information about the patient's circumstances, help further define a diagnostic statement, maintain a tumor registry and aid in classifying new drugs.

Procedure Classification: Alphabetic Index to Procedures
The Alphabetic Index to Procedures lists common surgical and procedural terminology.

The warning statement at the bottom of every page of the index, ⚠ Subterms under main terms may continue to next column or page, is a reminder to always check for additional subterms before making a final selection.

Procedure Classification: Tabular List of Procedures
The Tabular List of Procedures numerically arranges the procedure codes and their descriptors.

Resources

Listed below are the exclusive resources found **ONLY** in the *ICD-9-CM Expert for Hospitals, Volumes 1, 2 & 3* books.

Mapping of CMS-DRG Version 24.0 to MS-DRG Version 25.0

This resource lists the official mapping of CMS-DRG Version 24.0 to the new MS-DRG Version 25.0 released by the Centers for Medicare and Medicaid Services (CMS) in 2005.

Dx/MDC/DRG List

Provides the complete list of principal diagnosis codes and the MDC and MS-DRG to which they group, with the exception of a combination of principal and secondary diagnosis affecting DRG assignment.

MCC Condition List

A complete list of all codes considered MCC (Major Complications and Comorbidities) that will affect DRG assignment. This is an essential auditing tool for assigning the most appropriate DRG.

CC Condition List

A complete list of all codes considered CC (Complications and Comorbidities) that will affect DRG assignment. This an essential auditing tool for assigning the most appropriate DRG.

Pharmacological Listings

The most common generic and brand names of drugs are linked with the disease processes to assist in the identification of CC, thereby improving DRG assignment practices.

Valid Three-digit Code Table

ICD-9-CM is composed of codes with either 3, 4, or 5 digits. A code is invalid if it has not been coded to the full number of digits required for that code. There are a certain number codes that are valid for reporting as three digit codes. A list of the valid three-digit code is included as a convenient reference when auditing claims.

Present on Admission (POA) Indicator Tutorial

This resource presents an in-depth explanation of guidelines for assigning the present on admission (POA) indicators with case scenarios and exemptions. A table of official guidelines is included for quick reference regarding the use of information documented in the medical record.

10 Steps to Correct Coding

This is a valuable resource that takes the coder step by step through the coding process with detailed explanations accompanied by coding examples that demonstrate the practical application of ICD-9-CM conventions and coding guidelines in 10 steps.

---

* Congenital conditions - Main term: Anomaly

* Complications of medical/surgical care - indexed under the term "Complications" rather than the name of the condition

* Late effects of an earlier condition - main term "late", effects of.

cc/mcc - causes patient's length of stay to increase, thus the cost of caring for the patient increases.(more resources are required). .

Principal Diagnosis:

- Admission following medical observation: principal diagnosis would be the medical condition that led to the hospital admission

- Admission following postoperative observation: the condition responsible for occasioning the admission to the hospital

- Admission from out patient surgery, if the condition is:

    - a complication, assign the complication as the diagnosis code
    - if no complication, assign the reason for the admission as the principal diagnosis
    - a condition unrelated to the surgery, assign the unrelated condition as the principal diagnosis.

ICD-9-CM Official Conventions

ICD-9-CM Footnotes, Symbols, Instructional Notes and Conventions

This *ICD-9-CM for Hospitals* preserves all the footnotes, symbols, instructional notes and conventions found in the government's official version. Accurate coding depends upon understanding the meaning of these elements.

The following appear in the disease Tabular List, unless otherwise noted.

Official Government Symbols

§   The section mark preceding a code denotes a footnote on the page. This symbol is used in the Tabular List of Diseases and in the Tabular List of Procedures.

ICD-9-CM Conventions Used in the Tabular List

In addition to the symbols and footnotes above, the ICD-9-CM disease tabular has certain abbreviations, punctuation, symbols and other conventions. Our *ICD-9-CM for Hospitals* preserves these conventions. Proper use of the conventions will lead to efficient and accurate coding.

Abbreviations

NEC   Not elsewhere classifiable
This abbreviation is used when the ICD-9-CM system does not provide a code specific for the patient's condition.

NOS   Not otherwise specified
This abbreviation is the equivalent of "unspecified" and is used only when the coder lacks the information necessary to code to a more specific four-digit subcategory.

[ ]   Brackets enclose synonyms, alternative terminology or explanatory phrases:

482.2   Pneumonia due to Hemophilus influenzae [H. influenzae]

Brackets that appear beneath a code indicate the fifth digits that are considered valid fifth digits for the code. This convention is applied for those instances in ICD-9-CM where not all common fifth digits are considered valid for each subcategory within a category.

715.0   Osteoarthrosis, generalized
[0,4,9]

Generalized arthrosis can only be assigned in cases for which the degenerative joint disease involves multiple joints. Therefore, this code is considered for arthrosis in the sites described as unspecified, hand (which consists of multiple joints), or multiple sites. Therefore, only fifth digits 0, 4, and 9 are valid with subcategory 715.0.

[]   Slanted brackets that appear in the Alphabetic Indexes indicate mandatory multiple coding. Both codes must be assigned to fully describe the condition and are sequenced in the order listed.

Tachycardia
ventricular (paroxysmal)
    psychogenic 316 *[427.1]*

Psychogenic paroxysmal tachycardia is reported using both 316, Psychogenic factors associated with diseases classified elsewhere, and 427.1, Paroxysmal ventricular tachydcardia.

Diversion
biliopancratic (BPD) 43.7 *[45.51] [45.91]*

Code assignment of biliopancratic diversion is reported using all three codes 43.7, Partial gastrectomy with anastomosis to jejunum, 45.51, Isolation of segment of small intestine, and 45.91, Small-to-small intestinal anastomosis.

( )   Parentheses enclose supplementary words, called nonessential modifiers, that may be present in the narrative description of a disease without affecting the code assignment:

198.4   Other parts of nervous system
Meninges (cerebral) (spinal)

:   Colons are used in the Tabular List after an incomplete term that needs one or more of the modifiers that follow in order to make it assignable to a given category:

021.1   Enteric tularemia
Tularemia:
    cryptogenic
    intestinal
    typhoidal

}   Braces enclose a series of terms, each of which is modified by the statement appearing to the right of the brace:

560.2   Volvulus
Knotting
Strangulation   } of intestine, bowel, or colon
Torsion
Twist

Other Conventions

Boldface   Boldface type is used for all codes and titles in the Tabular List.

Italicized   Italicized type is used for all exclusion notes and to identify codes that should not be used for describing the primary diagnosis.

General Notes Used in the Tabular

These notes appear only in the Tabular List of Diseases:

Includes: An includes note further defines or clarifies the content of the chapter, subchapter, category, subcategory or subclassification. The includes note in the example below applies only to category 461.

Excludes: Terms following the word "Excludes" are not classified to the chapter, subchapter, category, subcategory or specific subclassification code under which it is found. The note also may provide the location of the excluded diagnosis. Excludes notes are italicized.

461   Acute sinusitis
INCLUDES   abscess
    empyema   } acute, of sinus
    infection   (accessory)
    inflammation   (nasal)
    suppuration
EXCLUDES   *chronic or unspecified sinusitis (473.0-473.9)*

INSTRUCTIONAL NOTES

The following official instructional notes are critical to correct coding practices. The instructional notes appear in red type in the Tabular List.

Use additional code:

This instruction signals the coder that an additional code should be used if the information is available to provide a more complete picture of that diagnosis.

For emphasis this instructional note appears in red type in the tabular section.

362.13 **Changes in vascular appearance**
    Vascular sheathing of retina
    Use additional code for any associated
        atherosclerosis (440.8)

There are coding circumstances outside of the etiology/manifestation convention when multiple coding for a single condition is required. The "Use additional code" note will be found under the associated condition code in the tabular. In the index, the multiple coding requirement is indicated by the use of the slanted bracket. The two codes are to be sequenced as listed in the index. For example, retinal arteriosclerosis must be coded using two codes sequenced as listed in the index.

Arteriosclerosis, arteriosclerotic
    retinal (vascular) 440.8 *[362.13]*

Code first underlying disease:

The *"Code first underlying disease"* instructional note found under certain codes is a sequencing rule. Most often this sequencing rule applies to the etiology/manifestation convention and is found under the manifestation code. The manifestation code may never be used alone or as a primary diagnosis (i.e., sequenced first). The instructional note, the code and its descriptor appear in italics in the Tabular List.

590.81 **Pyelitis or pyelonephritis in diseases classified elsewhere**
    Code first underlying disease as:
        tuberculosis (016.0)

Not all codes with a "Code first underlying disease" instructional note are part of the etiology/manifestation convention. The "Code first" note will appear, but the title of the code and the instructional note are not in italics. These codes may be reported alone or as the secondary diagnosis. For example, disseminated chorioretinitis may be reported as a principal diagnosis. However, if the underlying condition that caused disseminated chorioretinitis is known, such as tuberculous disseminated chorioretinitis, two codes are required and sequenced as listed in the index.

363.13 **Disseminated choroiditis and chorioretinitis, generalized**
    Code first underlying disease as:
        tuberculosis (017.3)

For emphasis this instructional note appears in red type in the tabular section.

Code, if applicable, any causal condition first:

A code with this note indicates that this code may be assigned as a principal diagnosis when the causal condition is unknown or not applicable. If a causal condition is known, then the code for that condition should be sequenced as the principal or first-listed diagnosis.

590.0 **Chronic pyelonephritis**
    Chronic pyelitis
    Chronic pyonephrosis
    Code, if applicable, any causal condition first

For emphasis this instructional note appears in red type in the tabular section.

INSTRUCTIONAL NOTES USED IN THE INDEX

Omit code:

"Omit code" is used to instruct the coder that no code is to be assigned. When this instruction is found in the Alphabetic Index to Diseases the medical term should not be coded as a diagnosis.

Metaplasia
    cervix — *omit code*

When used in Volume 3, *omit code* is meant to indicate procedures that do not merit separate code assignments, such as minor procedures preformed in conjunction with more extensive procedures or procedures that represent an operative approach.

Arthrotomy 80.10
    as operative approach — *omit code*

See Condition:

The *"see* condition" note found in the Alphabetic Index to Disease instructs the coder to refer to a main term for the condition. This note will follow index terms that are nouns for anatomical sites or adjectival forms of disease term. In the example below, the index terms "Cervix" and "Diffuse" are followed by the — *see* condition. Coders should search the index using a condition term such as atrophy or prolapse.

Cervix — *see* condition
Diffuse — *see* condition

Morphology Codes

For each neoplastic disease listed in the index, a morphology code is provided that identifies histological type and behavior.

Example:

Myelolipoma (M8870/0) — *see* Neoplasm, by site, benign

The histology is identified by the first four digits and the behavior is identified by the digit following the slash. Appendix A of Volume 1 contains a listing of morphology codes. This appendix is helpful when the pathology report identifies the neoplasm by using an M code. The coder may refer to Appendix A to determine the nomenclature of the neoplasm that will be the main term to search in the Index. The behavior classification is as follows:

    0   Benign

    1   Uncertain behavior

    2   Carcinoma in situ

    3   Malignant, primary site

    6   Malignant, secondary site.

Additional Conventions

NEW AND REVISED TEXT SYMBOLS

●   A bullet at a code or line of text indicates that that the entry is new.

▲   A triangle in the Tabular List indicates that the code title is revised. In the Alphabetic Index the triangle indicates that a code has changed.

►◄   These symbols appear at the beginning and at the end of a section of new or revised text.

When these symbols appear on a page there will be a date on the lower outside corner of the page indicating the date of the change, (e.g., October 2009).

ADDITIONAL DIGITS REQUIRED

√3ʳᵈ   This symbol indicates that the code requires a third digit.

√4ᵗʰ   This symbol indicates that the code requires a fourth digit.

√5ᵗʰ   This symbol indicates that a code requires a fifth digit.

✔   This symbol found only in the Alphabetic Index sections and the Table of Drugs and Chemicals indicates that an additional digit is required. Referring to the tabular section is essential to locate the appropriate additional digit.

DEFINITIONS

DEF: This symbol indicates a definition of disease or procedure term. The definition will appear in blue type in the Disease and Procedure Tabular Lists.

AHA's *CODING CLINIC FOR ICD-9-CM* REFERENCES

The four cooperating parties have designated the AHA's *Coding Clinic for ICD-9-CM* as the official publication for coding guidelines. The references are identified by the notation **AHA:** followed by the issue, year and page number.

In the example below, AHA's *Coding Clinic for ICD-9-CM*, third quarter 1991, page 15, contains a discussion on code assignment for vitreous hemorrhage:

> **379.23 Vitreous hemorrhage**
> **AHA: 3Q, '91, 15**

The table below explains the abbreviations in the Coding Clinic references:

J-F	January/February
M-A	March/April
M-J	May/June
J-A	July/August
S-O	September/October
N-D	November/December
1Q	First quarter
2Q	Second quarter
3Q	Third quarter
4Q	Fourth quarter

AHA's *Coding Clinic for ICD-9-CM* references appear in blue type in the Tabular List.

MEDICARE CODE EDITS

Fiscal intermediaries use Medicare code edits (MCE) to check the coding accuracy on claims. The Medicare code edits are listed below:

- Invalid diagnosis or procedure code
- E-code as principal diagnosis
- Duplicate of principal diagnosis (PDx) (as applied to a secondary diagnosis)

- *Age conflict
- *Sex conflict
- *Manifestation code as principal diagnosis
- *Questionable admission
- *Unacceptable principal diagnosis
- *Noncovered procedure
- Open biopsy check
- *Bilateral procedure
- Invalid age
- Invalid sex
- Invalid discharge status
- *Limited coverage procedure
- *Wrong surgery

Starred edits are identified by colors, symbols or footnotes as described on the next page.

Age and Sex Edit Symbols

The age edits below address MCE edit 4 and are used to detect inconsistencies between the patient's age and diagnosis. They appear in the Tabular List of Diseases to the right of the code description.

Newborn Age: 0   N
     These diagnoses are intended for newborns and neonates and the patient's age must be 0 years.

Pediatric Age: 0-17   P
     These diagnoses are intended for children and the patient's age must between 0 and 17 years.

Maternity Age: 12-55   M
     These diagnoses are intended for the patients between the age of 12 and 55 years.

Adult Age: 15-124   A
     These diagnoses are intended for the patients between the age of 15 and 124 years.

The sex symbols below address MCE edit 5 and are used to detect inconsistencies between the patient's sex and diagnosis or procedure. They appear in the Tabular Lists to the right of the code description:

♂   **Male diagnosis or procedure only**
     This symbol appears to the right of the code description. This reference appears in the disease and procedure Tabular List.

♀   **Female diagnosis or procedure only**
     This symbol appears to the right of the code description. This reference appears in the disease and procedure Tabular List.

Color Coding

For a quick reference to the color codes and their meaning, refer to the color/symbol legend located at the bottom of each page.

To alert the coder to important reimbursement issues affected by the code assignment, color bars have been added. The colors represent Medicare code edits as well as other reimbursement issues.

Color coding appears in both Tabular Lists. Some codes carry more than one color. Please note that the same color may appear in the disease and procedure Tabular Lists, but with different meanings.

Disease Tabular List
Manifestation Code
     These codes will appear in italic type as well as with a blue color bar over the code title. A manifestation code is not allowed to be reported as a primary diagnosis because each describes a

manifestation of some other underlying disease, not the disease underlying disease codes identified. In the Alphabetic Index these codes are listed as the secondary code in slanted brackets with the code for the underlying disease listed first.

Unacceptable PDx

These codes will appear with a gray color bar over the code title. These codes do not describe a current illness or injury, but a circumstance which influences a patient's health status. These are considered an unacceptable principal diagnosis for inpatient admission.

Questionable Admission

These codes will also appear with a gray color bar over the code title. These codes identify a condition that usually is insufficient justification for hospital admission. Since these codes are considered an unacceptable principal diagnoses for inpatient admission, they are color coded in the same manner as the "unacceptable PDx codes".

Nonspecific PDx

Effective October 1, 2007 the Medicare code edit for Non-Specific Diagnoses was deactivated. Therefore, these codes will no longer be identified by a yellow color bar over the code title.

Hospital Acquired Condition (HAC)

These codes will appear with a yellow color bar over the code title. These codes identify conditions that are high cost or high volume or both, a complication or comorbidity (CC) or major complication or comorbidity (MCC) that as a secondary diagnosis would result in assignment of a case to a higher-paying MS-DRG, and reasonably preventable through the application of evidence-based guidelines. If the condition is not present on admission, the case would not group to the higher-paying MS-DRG based solely upon the reporting of the HAC.

Procedure Tabular List
Nonspecific OR Procedure

Effective October 1, 2007 the Medicare code edit for Non-Specific OR was deactivated. Therefore, these codes will no longer be identified by a yellow color bar over the code title.

Valid OR

A procedure that triggers a change in DRG assignment and is designated by a gray color bar over the code title.

Non-OR Procedure

A non-operating room procedure that affects DRG assignment and is designated by a blue color bar over the code title.

Adjunct Codes

These codes are not to be reported alone and are indicated by the red color bar over the code title. Adjunct codes are assigned only in addition to a principal procedure. Their purpose is to provide supplemental information about the principal procedure performed. Adjunct codes are not procedure codes, but serve to provide additional detail about the principal procedure.

Example:

PTCA balloon inflation of two vessels, with insertion of one intravascular coronary stent.

Code assignment:

00.66 Percutaneous transluminal coronary angioplasty [PTCA] or coronary atherectomy

00.41 Procedure on two vessels

00.45 Insertion of one vascular stent

In the above example, codes 00.41 and 00.45 are adjunct codes that provide specific detail about the PTCA procedure performed.

Footnotes

All footnotes are identified by a numerical superscript that appears to the upper left of the code:

[1] **427.41 Ventricular fibrillation**

The footnote 1 indicates "MCC = Only if patient is discharged alive." This means that ventricular fibrillation is considered a major complication or comorbidity that may affect DRG assignment only if the patient is discharged alive. Otherwise ventricular fibrillation is assigned as a non CC condition.

The following list identifies the meaning of each footnote number and the classification in which the footnote appears:

Disease Tabular

1   Major complication or comorbidity (MCC) that may affect DRG assignment only if the patient is discharged alive.

2   These V codes may be used as principal diagnosis on Medicare patients.

3   This V code, with the fourth digit of 1 or 2, is unacceptable as a principal diagnosis.

4   These codes, with the fourth digit of 0, may be used as a principal diagnosis for Medicare patients.

5   Rehabilitation codes acceptable as a principal diagnosis when accompanied by a secondary diagnosis reflecting the condition treated.

6   These V codes are acceptable as principal diagnosis when accompanied by a diagnosis of personal history of malignancy. These codes group to MS-DRG 949-950.

7   Diagnosis code with fifth digit of 0 is considered a "Questionable Admission" diagnosis when used as a principal diagnosis.

8   These codes are considered CC/MCC conditions that affect DRG assignment, except when reported in combination with diagnosis code 996.64 and the condition is not present on admission.

9   This condition is designated as a hospital acquired condition (HAC) that when reported as not present upon admission and when in combination with a procedure code from 36.10-36.19 will not solely group the case to a higher-paying MS-DRG.

10   The codes within the category or subcategory qualify as hospital acquired conditions when not present upon admission and only for the valid CC and MCC codes within that range.

*   Wrong Surgery edit applies to the E code which when reported will trigger the Wrong Surgery edit and the claim will be denied and returned to the provider.

Procedure Tabular

1   Valid OR procedure code if accompanied by one of the following codes: 37.80, 37.81, 37.82, 37.85, 37.86, 37.87.

2   Valid OR procedure code if accompanied by one of the following codes: 37.80, 37.83.

3   Valid OR procedure code if accompanied by one of the following codes: 37.80, 37.85, 37.86, 37.87.

4   Valid OR procedure code if accompanied by any one of the following codes: 37.80, 37.81, 37.82, 37.83, 37.85, 37.86, 37.87.

5   Valid OR procedure code if accompanied by any one of the following codes: 37.70, 37.71, 37.73, 37.74.

6   Valid OR procedure code if accompanied by one of the following codes: 37.72, 37.74.

7   Non-covered except when reported with procedure code 00.65, Percutaneous insertion of intracranial vascular stent(s).

8   Non-covered procedure only when the following diagnoses are present as either a principal or secondary diagnosis: 204.00, 205.00, 205.10, 205.11, 206.00, 207.00, 208.00.

9   Non-covered procedure only when the following diagnoses are present as either a principal or secondary diagnosis: 203.00, 203.01.

10   Non-covered procedure unless reported with code 55.69 and a diagnosis code from 250.x0 or 250.x2 with 403.x1, 404.x2, 404.x3, 585.x, V42.0 or V42.89; or reported with a diagnosis code 250.x1 or 250.x3.

11   Non-covered except when the patient is 60 years old or less.

12   Limited coverage for the procedure is provided only when reported in combination with diagnosis code V70.7. Medicare limits the coverage to a portion of the costs and only when certain criteria are met such as participation in a clinical study.

Other Notations

Alphabetic Indexes
▽ **Subterms under main terms may continue to next column or page.**

This warning statement is a reminder to always check for additional subterms and information that may continue onto the next page or column before making a final selection.

Disease Tabular
TIPS:

This symbol precedes official coding advice found in the official coding guidelines and AHA's [ital] Coding Clinic for ICD-9-CM. [end ital] Coding tips appear in blue type in the Tabular List.

I-10

In preparation for the transition to coding using the ICD-10-CM classification system, examples of ICD-10-CM codes have been provided for selected ICD-9-CM diagnosis codes. This symbol indicates that the code provided is an ICD-10-CM code to which the selected ICD-9-CM code is mapped.

Note: Coding professionals should keep in mind the following points when referring to the ICD-10-CM codes provided:

- ICD-10-CM codes are not currently valid for reporting purposes.
- The ICD-10-CM code may represent only one possible coding option. Since mappings between ICD-9-CM and ICD-10-CM are not always straightforward one-to-one correspondences due to the differences in terminology and clinical concepts, the mapping may result in a one-to-many code option. Not all code options for a particular ICD-9-CM code are provided. For cases in which many code alternatives are possible in ICD-10-CM, only one example is provided.
- The ICD-10-CM code examples are provided only for the most frequently reported ICD-9-CM codes in each chapter.
- The ICD-10-CM codes are examples only and are provided to ease the transition to the new classification system.

cc **CC Condition**

This symbol designates a complication or comorbidity diagnosis that may affect DRG assignment. A complication or comorbidity diagnosis, CC condition, is defined as a significant acute disease, a significant acute manifestation of a chronic disease, an advanced or end stage chronic disease, or a chronic disease associated with systemic physiological decompensation and debility that have consistently greater impact on hospital resources.

A CC listed with a digit or range of digits indicates that only the fifth-digit assignments stated for that code are to be considered CC conditions. For example, code 642.1 has a CC 3-4 which means that only codes 642.13 and 642.14 are considered CC

conditions. Codes 642.11 and 642.12 are considered major complications or comorbidity (MCC) conditions. Code 642.10 is not designated as CC or MCC.

mcc **MCC Condition**

This symbol designates a complication or comorbidity diagnosis that meets the criteria established for the revised CC list and was an AP-DRG major CC and was an APR-DRG default severity level 3 (major) or level 4 (extensive) with the exception of the newborn, maternity, and congenital anomalies which are APR-DRG default severity level 3 (major) or level 4 (extensive) only.

An MCC listed with a digit or range of digits indicates that only the fifth-digit assignments stated for that code are to be considered MCC conditions. For example; code 642.1 has a CC 3-4 which means that only codes 642.13 and 642.14 are considered CC conditions. Codes 642.11 and 642.12 are considered major complications or comorbidity (MCC) conditions and code 642.1 also has an MCC 1-2 designation. Code 642.10 is not designated as CC or MCC.

CC Exclusion List

A exclusive feature of *ICD-9-CM for Hospitals* is the integration of the government's CC exclusion list with each affected code. The CC exclusion list indicates secondary diagnosis codes that are excluded as CC or MCC conditions with certain principal diagnoses. This exclusion occurs because the cited conditions are inherent to the disease process of the principal diagnosis, conditions that could not coexist, nonspecific codes for the principal diagnosis, or conditions affecting proximal anatomical sites.

Listed below each code that is considered a complication or comorbidity (CC) or a major complication or comorbidity (MCC) are the codes or code ranges representing principal diagnoses for which the CC or MCC will not be recognized as such for DRG assignment.

In the example below, code 254.1 is considered a CC condition. However, the CC exclusion (CC Excl:) notation indicates that if a code from the listed code ranges is assigned as the principal diagnosis, the secondary diagnosis of 254.1 will not be recognized as a CC condition in DRG assignment.

254.1   Abscess of thymus   **cc**
         CC Excl: 254.0-254.9, 259.50-259.9

Please note that the same notation, CC Exclusion (**CC Excl:**), is used for both the MCC and CC conditions. Both MCC and CC are considered complication and comorbidity conditions. And for both, the same criteria are applied in determining which principal diagnosis for which the designated CC or MCC will not affect DRG assignment.

HIV **HIV**

This symbol indicates that the condition is considered a major HIV related diagnosis. When the condition is coded in combination with a diagnosis of human immunodeficiency virus (HIV), code 042, the case will move from MS-DRG 977 to MS-DRGs 974–976.

Medicare as Secondary Payer (MSP)
Note: This edit is no longer included in the official Medicare Code Editor (MCE) for the inpatient prospective payment system (IPPS).

Wrong Surgery Edit
The Wrong Surgery edit was created to identify cases in which wrong surgeries occurred. Any claim submitted with a code from the E876.5-E876.7 code range, whether they are in the principal or secondary diagnosis position, will trigger the Wrong Surgery edit. The claim will be denied and returned to the

provider. A surgical or other invasive procedure is considered to be a wrong procedure if:

- the procedure was performed on the wrong site
- the procedure was performed on the wrong patient, or
- the incorrect procedure was performed on a patient

V Code Table

Note: Please note that while the official guidelines [Section 1. C.18.e.] include the V Code Table the reporting designations indicated by the Table are often in conflict with the Medicare code edits (MCE) for the inpatient prospective payment system (IPPS). Therefore, only the inpatient prospective payment system code edits are represented in this edition.

Procedure Tabular
🄽🄲 Noncovered Procedure

A procedure not covered by Medicare. In some instances this procedure may also be identified as a valid operating room (OR) procedure that may trigger a DRG assignment. Even if a DRG

assignment is made, Medicare may not reimburse for the noncovered procedure.

🄻🄲 Limited Coverage Procedure

A procedure whose medical complexity and serious nature incur associated costs that are deemed extraordinary and Medicare limits coverage to a portion of the cost.

🄱🄸 Bilateral Edit

Due to the lack of laterality in ICD-9-CM, there are certain lower extremity joint procedure codes that do not accurately reflect procedures that are performed in one admission on two different bilateral joints. To group to MS-DRG 461 or 462, Bilateral or Multiple Joint Procedures of Lower Extremity with or without MCC, a case must be coded with a combination of two or more different major lower extremity joint procedures. The bilateral procedure symbol identifies those procedure codes that when coded twice represent the same procedure performed on both of the same bilateral joints of the lower extremity. Otherwise, a code edit will instruct the fiscal intermediary to verify that the two different procedures were performed on two different bilateral joints.

Summary of Code Changes

DIAGNOSIS TABULAR (VOLUME 1)

001-139	INFECTIOUS AND PARASITIC DISEASES
	Exclusion term revised
008.63	Inclusion note added
▲ 008.65	Calicivirus
035	Exclusion term revised
037	Exclusion term revised
▲ 041.3	~~Friedländer's bacillus~~ Klebsiella pneumoniae
	Inclusion note deleted
▲ 041.86	Helicobacter pylori ~~(H. pylori)~~ ►[H. pylori]◄
046.1	Use additional code note added
▲ 050-059	VIRAL DISEASES ►GENERALLY◄ ACCOMPANIED BY EXANTHEM
078.89	Inclusion note added
190	Exclusion notes added
196	Exclusion note added
197	Exclusion notes added
198	Exclusion note added
199	Exclusion note added
	Exclusion terms revised
199.2	Use additional code note revised
200-208	MALIGNANT NEOPLASM OF LYMPHATIC AND HEMATOPOIETIC TISSUE
	Exclusion note added
202.0	Inclusion term revised
202.1	Exclusion note added
209	Exclusion note added
	Exclusion term revised
209.30	Exclusion note added
● 209.31	Merkel cell carcinoma of the face
	Inclusion notes added
● 209.32	Merkel cell carcinoma of the scalp and neck
● 209.33	Merkel cell carcinoma of the upper limb
● 209.34	Merkel cell carcinoma of the lower limb
● 209.35	Merkel cell carcinoma of the trunk
● 209.36	Merkel cell carcinoma of other sites
	Inclusion notes added
● 209.7	Secondary neuroendocrine tumors
	Inclusion note added
● 209.70	Secondary neuroendocrine tumor, unspecified site
● 209.71	Secondary neuroendocrine tumor of distant lymph nodes
	Inclusion note added
● 209.72	Secondary neuroendocrine tumor of liver
● 209.73	Secondary neuroendocrine tumor of bone
● 209.74	Secondary neuroendocrine tumor of peritoneum
● 209.75	Secondary Merkel cell carcinoma
	Inclusion notes added
● 209.79	Secondary neuroendocrine tumor of other sites
	238.72 Inclusion note added
	238.73 Inclusion note deleted
● 239.81	Retina and choroid
	Inclusion notes added
● 239.89	Other specified sites
251.3	Use additional code notes added
	Exclusion notes added
269.8	Exclusion term revised
270	Exclusion term revised

272.2	Inclusion notes added
272.4	Inclusion note deleted
● 274.00	Gouty arthropathy, unspecified
● 274.01	Acute gouty arthropathy
	Inclusion notes added
● 274.02	Chronic gouty arthropathy without mention of tophus (tophi)
	Inclusion note added
● 274.03	Chronic gouty arthropathy with tophus (tophi)
	Inclusion notes added
274.82	Exclusion notes added
277.2	Exclusion term revised
● 277.88	Tumor lysis syndrome
	Inclusion notes added
	Use additional code note added
279.4	Inclusion note deleted
● 279.41	Autoimmune lymphoproliferative syndrome
	Inclusion note added
● 279.49	Autoimmune disease, not elsewhere classified
	Inclusion note added
279.5	Code first notes revised
285.2	Inclusion term revised
285.22	Exclusion note added
● 285.3	Antineoplastic chemotherapy induced anemia
	Inclusion note added
	Exclusion notes added
290.0	Exclusion term revised
294.1	Code first note revised
294.8	Exclusion term revised
307.0	Exclusion note added
	Exclusion term revised
310.1	Exclusion notes added
	Exclusion note deleted
310.8	Exclusion note added
331.7	Exclusion term revised
331.83	Exclusion note added
333.2	Inclusion note added
	Inclusion notes deleted
	Exclusion notes added
345	Fifth-digit subclassification inclusion notes added
	Exclusion notes added
345.1	Inclusion notes added
348.8	Inclusion notes deleted
● 348.81	Temporal sclerosis
	Inclusion notes added
● 348.89	Other conditions of brain
	Inclusion notes added
359.22	Inclusion note added
359.29	Inclusion note deleted
● 359.7	Inflammatory and immune myopathies, NEC
● 359.71	Inclusion body myositis
	Inclusion note added
● 359.79	Other inflammatory and immune myopathies, NEC
	Inclusion note added
● 372.06	Acute chemical conjunctivitis
	Inclusion note added
	Use additional code note added
	Exclusion notes added
372.34	Exclusion note added
372.51	Exclusion note added
403	Exclusion term revised
413.9	Inclusion note added
	Use additional code note added
415.1	Exclusion notes added

● 416.2	Chronic pulmonary embolism
	Use additional code note added
	Exclusion note added
● 438.13	Dysarthria
● 438.14	Fluency disorder
	Inclusion note added
445.81	Use additional code note revised
453	Exclusion note deleted
▲ 453.2	►Of inferior◄ vena cava
▲ 453.4	►Acute◄ venous embolism and thrombosis of deep vessels of lower extremity
▲ 453.40	►Acute◄ venous embolism and thrombosis of unspecified deep vessels of lower extremity
▲ 453.41	►Acute◄ venous embolism and thrombosis of deep vessels of proximal lower extremity
▲ 453.42	►Acute◄ venous embolism and thrombosis of deep vessels of distal lower extremity
● 453.5	Chronic venous embolism and thrombosis of deep vessels of lower extremity
	Use additional code note added
	Exclusion note added
● 453.50	Chronic venous embolism and thrombosis of unspecified deep vessels of lower extremity
● 453.51	Chronic venous embolism and thrombosis of deep vessels of proximal lower extremity
● 453.52	Chronic venous embolism and thrombosis of deep vessels of distal lower extremity
● 453.6	Venous embolism and thrombosis of superficial vessels of lower extremity
	Inclusion note added
● 453.7	Chronic venous embolism and thrombosis of other specified vessels
	Use additional code note added
	Exclusion note added
● 453.71	Chronic venous embolism and thrombosis of superficial veins of upper extremity
	Inclusion notes added
● 453.72	Chronic venous embolism and thrombosis of deep veins of upper extremity
	Inclusion notes added
● 453.73	Chronic venous embolism and thrombosis of upper extremity, unspecified
● 453.74	Chronic venous embolism and thrombosis of axillary veins
● 453.75	Chronic venous embolism and thrombosis of subclavian veins
● 453.76	Chronic venous embolism and thrombosis of internal jugular veins
● 453.77	Chronic venous embolism and thrombosis of other thoracic veins
	Inclusion notes added
● 453.79	Chronic venous embolism and thrombosis of other specified veins
▲ 453.8	►Acute venous embolism and thrombosis of◄ other specified veins

►◄ Revised Text　　　● New Code　　　▲ Revised Code Title

Code	Description
● 453.81	Acute venous embolism and thrombosis of superficial veins of upper extremity Inclusion notes added
● 453.82	Acute venous embolism and thrombosis of deep veins of upper extremity Inclusion notes added
● 453.83	Acute venous embolism and thrombosis of upper extremity, unspecified
● 453.84	Acute venous embolism and thrombosis of axillary veins
● 453.85	Acute venous embolism and thrombosis of subclavian veins
● 453.86	Acute venous embolism and thrombosis of internal jugular veins
● 453.87	Acute venous embolism and thrombosis of other thoracic veins Inclusion notes added
● 453.89	Acute venous embolism and thrombosis of other specified veins
487	Inclusion note added Exclusion notes added Exclusion term revised
▲ 488	Influenza due to ►certain◄ identified ~~avian~~ influenza ►viruses◄ Instructional note deleted Exclusion term revised
● 488.0	Influenza due to identified avian influenza virus Inclusion notes added
● 488.1	Influenza due to identified novel H1N1 influenza virus Inclusion notes added
536.2	Exclusion notes added
567	Exclusion term revised
● 569.7	Complications of intestinal pouch
● 569.71	Pouchitis Inclusion note added
● 569.79	Other complications of intestinal pouch
● 569.87	Vomiting of fecal matter
▲ 572.2	Hepatic ~~coma~~ ►encephalopathy◄ Inclusion note added Inclusion note deleted
▲ 584	Acute ~~renal~~ ►kidney◄ failure Inclusion note added
▲ 584.5	►Acute kidney failure◄ ~~With~~ with lesion of tubular necrosis
▲ 584.6	►Acute kidney failure◄ ~~With~~ with lesion of renal cortical necrosis
▲ 584.7	►Acute kidney failure◄ ~~With~~ with lesion of renal medullary [papillary] necrosis
▲ 584.8	►Acute kidney failure◄ ~~With~~ with other specified pathological lesion in kidney
▲ 584.9	►Acute kidney failure◄ ~~Acute renal failure~~, unspecified
587	Inclusion term revised Inclusion note deleted
611.82	Exclusion note added
614	Exclusion term revised
615	Exclusion terms revised
621.3	Inclusion notes deleted
621.30	Inclusion notes added
621.31	Exclusion note added
621.32	Exclusion note added
621.33	Exclusion note added
● 621.34	Benign endometrial hyperplasia
● 621.35	Endometrial intraepithelial neoplasia [EIN] Exclusion note added
624	Exclusion term revised
▲ 639.3	~~Renal~~ ►Kidney◄ failure Inclusion term revised
646.6	Exclusion term revised
649.3	Instructional note revised Use additional code note revised
▲ 669.3 [0, 2, 4]	Acute ~~renal~~ ►kidney◄ failure following labor and delivery
670	Major puerperal infection Use 0 as fourth digit note deleted Inclusion notes deleted
▲ 670.00	Major puerperal infection ►, unspecified,◄ unspecified as to episode of care or not applicable
▲ 670.02	Major puerperal infection ►, unspecified,◄ delivered with mention of postpartum complication
▲ 670.04	Major puerperal infection ►, unspecified,◄ postpartum condition or complication
● 670.10	Puerperal endometritis, unspecified as to episode of care or not applicable
● 670.12	Puerperal endometritis, delivered with mention of postpartum complication
● 670.14	Puerperal endometritis, postpartum condition or complication
● 670.20	Puerperal sepsis, unspecified as to episode of care or not applicable Inclusion note added
● 670.22	Puerperal sepsis , delivered with mention of postpartum complication Inclusion note added
● 670.24	Puerperal sepsis, postpartum condition or complication Inclusion note added
● 670.30	Puerperal septic thrombophlebitis, unspecified as to episode of care or not applicable
● 670.32	Puerperal septic thrombophlebitis, delivered with mention of postpartum complication
● 670.34	Puerperal septic thrombophlebitis, postpartum condition or complication
● 670.80	Other major puerperal infection, unspecified as to episode of care or not applicable Inclusion notes added
● 670.82	Other major puerperal infection, delivered with mention of postpartum complication Inclusion notes added
● 670.84	Other major puerperal infection, postpartum condition or complication Inclusion notes added
671	Exclusion notes added
671.2	Inclusion notes added
671.3	Use additional code notes added
671.4	Use additional code notes added
671.9	Inclusion notes deleted
680-686	INFECTIONS OF SKIN AND SUBCUTANEOUS TISSUE Exclusion term revised
707.03	Inclusion note added
712	Exclusion term revised
713.0	Exclusion term revised
727.01	Exclusion term revised
733.1	Inclusion note added
● 756.72	Omphalocele Inclusion note added
● 756.73	Gastroschisis
756.79	Inclusion notes deleted
▲ 757.6	Specified ►congenital◄ anomalies of breast Inclusion term revised Exclusion note added
762.3	Use additional code note revised
768.5	Exclusion term revised
768.6	Exclusion term revised
● 768.70	Hypoxic-ischemic encephalopathy, unspecified
● 768.71	Mild hypoxic-ischemic encephalopathy
● 768.72	Moderate hypoxic-ischemic encephalopathy
● 768.73	Severe hypoxic-ischemic encephalopathy
772	Exclusion note added
▲ 772.0	Fetal blood loss ►affecting newborn◄
776	Inclusion term revised
▲ 776.9	Unspecified hematological disorder specific to ~~fetus or~~ newborn
777.5	Inclusion note deleted
777.51	Inclusion note added
▲ 779.3	►Disorder of stomach function and ◄ feeding problems in newborn Inclusion notes deleted
● 779.31	Feeding problems in newborn Inclusion note added Exclusion note added
● 779.32	Bilious vomiting in newborn Exclusion note added
● 779.33	Other vomiting in newborn Inclusion note added Exclusion note added
● 779.34	Failure to thrive in newborn Exclusion note added
780.0	Exclusion notes added
780.93	Exclusion notes added Exclusion term revised
783.3	Exclusion term revised
783.41	Exclusion note added
▲ 784.4	Voice ~~disturbance~~ ►and resonance disorders◄
▲ 784.40	Voice ~~disturbance~~ ►and resonance disorder◄, unspecified
● 784.42	Dysphonia Inclusion note added
● 784.43	Hypernasality
● 784.44	Hyponasality
▲ 784.49	Other ►voice and resonance disorders◄ Inclusion notes deleted
784.5	Inclusion notes deleted Exclusion note added
● 784.51	Dysarthria Exclusion note added
● 784.59	Other speech disturbance Inclusion notes added
787.0	Exclusion notes added Exclusion term revised
● 787.04	Bilious emesis Inclusion note added Exclusion note added
789.00	Inclusion notes deleted Exclusion note deleted
789.01	Inclusion notes deleted Exclusion note deleted

Code	Description
789.02	Inclusion notes deleted
	Exclusion note deleted
789.03	Inclusion notes deleted
	Exclusion note deleted
789.04	Inclusion notes deleted
	Exclusion note deleted
789.05	Inclusion notes deleted
	Exclusion note deleted
789.06	Inclusion notes deleted
	Exclusion note deleted
789.07	Inclusion notes deleted
	Exclusion note deleted
789.09	Inclusion notes deleted
	Exclusion note deleted
● 789.7	Colic
	Inclusion notes added
	Exclusion notes added
790.01	Inclusion note added
▲ 793	Nonspecific ▶(abnormal)◀ findings on radiological and other examination of body structure
● 793.82	Inconclusive mammogram
	Inclusion notes added
▲ 793.89	Other ▶(abnormal)◀ findings on radiological examination of breast
▲ 793.99	Other nonspecific ▶(abnormal)◀ findings on radiological examination and other examinations of body structure
795.0	Exclusion term revised
795.39	Exclusion note added
796.7	Exclusion term revised
▲ 799.2	Nervousness ▶Signs and symptoms involving emotional state ◀
	Inclusion note deleted
	Exclusion notes added
● 799.21	Nervousness
	Inclusion note added
● 799.22	Irritability
	Inclusion note added
● 799.23	Impulsiveness
	Inclusion note added
	Exclusion note added
● 799.24	Emotional lability
● 799.25	Demoralization and apathy
	Inclusion note added
● 799.29	Other signs and symptoms involving emotional state
● 799.82	Apparent life threatening event in infant
	Inclusion notes added
	Exclusion notes added
	Use additional code note added
800-804	FRACTURE OF SKULL
	Inclusion note added
▲ 813.45	Torus fracture of radius ▶(alone)◀
	Exclusion note added
● 813.46	Torus fracture of ulna (alone)
	Exclusion note added
● 813.47	Torus fracture of radius and ulna
832	Fifth-digit subclassification note revised
● 832.2	Nursemaid's elbow
	Inclusion note added
850-854	INTRACRANIAL INJURY, EXCLUDING THOSE WITH SKULL FRACTURE
	Inclusion note added
854	Inclusion note added
	Inclusion terms revised
870-897	OPEN WOUNDS
	Use additional code note deleted
969.0	Inclusion notes deleted
● 969.00	Antidepressant, unspecified

● 969.01	Monoamine oxidase inhibitors
	Inclusion note added
● 969.02	Selective serotonin and norepinephrine reuptake inhibitors
	Inclusion note added
● 969.03	Selective serotonin reuptake inhibitors
	Inclusion note added
● 969.04	Tetracyclic antidepressants
● 969.05	Tricyclic antidepressants
● 969.09	Other antidepressants
969.7	Inclusion notes deleted
● 969.70	Psychostimulant, unspecified
● 969.71	Caffeine
● 969.72	Amphetamines
	Inclusion note added
● 969.73	Methylphenidate
● 969.79	Other psychostimulants
974.1	Exclusion term revised
● 995.24	Failed moderate sedation during procedure
	Inclusion note added
995.92	Use additional code note revised
995.94	Use additional code note revised
▲ 996.43	~~Prosthetic joint implant failure~~ ▶Broken prosthetic joint implant◀
996.47	Inclusion note added
996.7	Use additional code note added
997.31	Inclusion note added
997.4	Exclusion notes added
997.5	Inclusion term revised
999.6	Exclusion notes added
V07.52	Inclusion term revised
V10	Code first note deleted
V10.0	Exclusion notes added
V10.1	Exclusion notes added
V10.8	Exclusion notes added
▲ V10.9	▶Other and◀ ~~U~~unspecified personal history of malignant neoplasm
● V10.90	Personal history of unspecified malignant neoplasm
	Inclusion note added
	Exclusion notes added
● V10.91	Personal history of malignant neuroendocrine tumor
	Inclusion notes added
	Code first note added
V12.54	Exclusion note added
▲ V15.06	Allergy to insects ▶and arachnids◀
● V15.52	History of traumatic brain injury
	Exclusion note added
● V15.80	History of failed moderate sedation
	Inclusion note added
● V15.83	Underimmunization status
	Inclusion notes added
▲ V15.84	▶Contact with and (suspected)◀ exposure to asbestos
▲ V15.85	▶Contact with and (suspected)◀ exposure to potentially hazardous body fluids
▲ V15.86	▶Contact with and (suspected)◀ exposure to lead
V20.2	Inclusion note added
	Inclusion note deleted
	Exclusion notes added
● V20.3	Newborn health supervision
	Inclusion note added
	Exclusion note added
● V20.31	Health supervision for newborn under 8 days old
	Inclusion note added

Code	Description
● V20.32	Health supervision for newborn 8 to 28 days old
	Inclusion notes added
V23.86	Exclusion term revised
● V26.42	Encounter for fertility preservation counseling
	Inclusion notes added
● V26.82	Encounter for fertility preservation procedure
	Inclusion notes added
V45.71	Exclusion note added
▲ V53.5	Other ▶gastrointestinal◀ appliance ▶and device◀
● V53.50	Fitting and adjustment of intestinal appliance and device
● V53.51	Fitting and adjustment of gastric lap band
● V53.59	Fitting and adjustment of other gastrointestinal appliance and device
V54.1	Exclusion note added
V54.2	Exclusion note added
▲ V57.3	Speech ▶-language◀ therapy
● V60.81	Foster care (status)
● V60.89	Other specified housing or economic circumstances
V61.01	Exclusion note added
● V61.07	Family disruption due to death of family member
	Exclusion note added
● V61.08	Family disruption due to other extended absence of family member
	Exclusion note added
● V61.23	Counseling for parent-biological child problem
	Inclusion notes added
● V61.24	Counseling for parent-adopted child problem
	Inclusion notes added
● V61.25	Counseling for parent (guardian)-foster child problem
	Inclusion notes added
▲ V61.29	Other ▶parent-child problems◀
	Inclusion note deleted
● V61.42	Substance abuse in family
V62.82	Exclusion note added
▲ V65.11	Pediatric pre-birth visit for ▶expectant◀ ~~mother~~ ▶parent(s)◀
	Inclusion note added
V70.0	Exclusion notes added
	Exclusion term revised
V72	Exclusion notes added
	Exclusion term revised
V72.5	Exclusion note deleted
	Exclusion note added
V72.6	Inclusion note added
	Exclusion note deleted
● V72.60	Laboratory examination, unspecified
● V72.61	Antibody response examination
	Inclusion note added
	Exclusion note added
● V72.62	Laboratory examination ordered as part of a routine general medical examination
	Inclusion note added
● V72.63	Pre-procedural laboratory examination
	Inclusion notes added
● V72.69	Other laboratory examination
V72.8	Exclusion note added
V72.83	Inclusion note added
● V80.01	Traumatic brain injury

● V80.09   Other neurological conditions
● V87.32   Contact with and (suspected) exposure to algae bloom
● V87.43   Personal history of estrogen therapy
● V87.44   Personal history of inhaled steroid therapy
● V87.45   Personal history of systemic steroid therapy
            Inclusion note added
● V87.46   Personal history of immunosuppression therapy
            Exclusion note added
  E000-E999 SUPPLEMENTARY CLASSIFICATION OF EXTERNAL CAUSES OF INJURY AND POISONING ►(E000-E999)◄
            Revised section introduction
● EXTERNAL CAUSE STATUS (E000)
            Instructional note added
● E000   External cause status
● E000.0   Civilian activity done for income or pay
            Inclusion note added
            Exclusion note added
● E000.1   Military activity
            Exclusion note added
● E000.8   Other external cause status
            Inclusion notes added
            Exclusion notes added
● E000.9   Unspecified external cause status
● ACTIVITY (E001-E030)
            Instructional note added
● E001   Activities involving walking and running
            Exclusion notes added
● E001.0   Walking, marching and hiking
            Inclusion note added
            Exclusion note added
● E001.1   Running
● E002   Activities involving water and water craft
            Exclusion note added
● E002.0   Swimming
● E002.1   Springboard and platform diving
● E002.2   Water polo
● E002.3   Water aerobics and water exercise
● E002.4   Underwater diving and snorkeling
            Inclusion note added
● E002.5   Rowing, canoeing, kayaking, rafting and tubing
            Inclusion note added
● E002.6   Water skiing and wake boarding
● E002.7   Surfing, windsurfing and boogie boarding
● E002.8   Water sliding
● E002.9   Other activity involving water and watercraft
            Inclusion notes added
● E003   Activities involving ice and snow
            Exclusion note added
● E003.0   Ice skating
            Inclusion notes added
            Exclusion note added
● E003.1   Ice hockey
● E003.2   Snow (alpine) (downhill) skiing, snow boarding, sledding, tobogganing and snow tubing
            Exclusion note added
● E003.3   Cross country skiing
            Inclusion note added
● E003.9   Other activity involving ice and snow
            Inclusion note added

● E004   Activities involving climbing, rappelling and jumping off
            Exclusion notes added
● E004.0   Mountain climbing, rock climbing and wall climbing
● E004.1   Rappelling
● E004.2   BASE jumping
            Inclusion note added
● E004.3   Bungee jumping
● E004.4   Hang gliding
● E004.9   Other activity involving climbing, rappelling and jumping off
● E005   Activities involving dancing and other rhythmic movement
            Exclusion note added
● E005.0   Dancing
● E005.1   Yoga
● E005.2   Gymnastics
            Inclusion note added
            Exclusion note added
● E005.3   Trampoline
● E005.4   Cheerleading
● E005.9   Other activity involving dancing and other rhythmic movements
● E006   Activities involving other sports and athletics played individually
            Exclusion notes added
● E006.0   Roller skating (inline) and skateboarding
● E006.1   Horseback riding
● E006.2   Golf
● E006.3   Bowling
● E006.4   Bike riding
            Exclusion note added
● E006.5   Jumping rope
● E006.6   Non-running track and field events
            Exclusion note added
● E006.9   Other activity involving other sports and athletics played individually
            Exclusion notes added
● E007   Activities involving other sports and athletics played as a team or group
            Exclusion notes added
● E007.0   American tackle football
            Inclusion note added
● E007.1   American flag or touch football
● E007.2   Rugby
● E007.3   Baseball
            Inclusion note added
● E007.4   Lacrosse and field hockey
● E007.5   Soccer
● E007.6   Basketball
● E007.7   Volleyball (beach) (court)
● E007.8   Physical games generally associated with school recess, summer camp and children
            Inclusion notes added
● E007.9   Other activity involving other sports and athletics played as a team or group
            Inclusion note added
● E008   Activities involving other specified sports and athletics
● E008.0   Boxing
● E008.1   Wrestling
● E008.2   Racquet and hand sports
            Inclusion notes added
● E008.3   Frisbee
            Inclusion note added
● E008.4   Martial arts
            Inclusion note added

● E008.9   Other specified sports and athletics activity
            Exclusion note added
● E009   Activity involving other cardiorespiratory exercise
            Inclusion note added
● E009.0   Exercise machines primarily for cardiorespiratory conditioning
            Inclusion notes added
● E009.1   Calisthenics
            Inclusion notes added
● E009.2   Aerobic and step exercise
● E009.3   Circuit training
● E009.4   Obstacle course
            Inclusion notes added
● E009.5   Grass drills
            Inclusion note added
● E009.9   Other activity involving other cardiorespiratory exercise
            Exclusion note added
● E010   Activity involving other muscle strengthening exercises
● E010.0   Exercise machines primarily for muscle strengthening
● E010.1   Push-ups, pull-ups, sit-ups
● E010.2   Free weights
            Inclusion notes added
● E010.3   Pilates
● E010.9   Other activity involving other muscle strengthening exercises
            Exclusion note added
● E011 Activities involving computer technology and electronic devices
            Exclusion note added
● E011.0   Computer keyboarding
            Inclusion note added
● E011.1   Hand held interactive electronic device
            Inclusion notes added
            Exclusion notes added
● E011.9   Other activity involving computer technology and electronic devices
● E012   Activities involving arts and handcrafts
            Exclusion note added
● E012.0   Knitting and crocheting
● E012.1   Sewing
● E012.2   Furniture building and finishing
            Inclusion note added
● E012.9   Activity involving other arts and handcrafts
● E013   Activities involving personal hygiene and household maintenance
            Exclusion notes added
● E013.0   Personal bathing and showering
● E013.1   Laundry
● E013.2   Vacuuming
● E013.3   Ironing
● E013.4   Floor mopping and cleaning
● E013.5   Residential relocation
            Inclusion note added
● E013.8   Other personal hygiene activity
● E013.9   Other household maintenance
● E014   Activities involving person providing caregiving
● E014.0   Caregiving involving bathing
● E014.1   Caregiving involving lifting
● E014.9   Other activity involving person providing caregiving
● E015   Activities involving food preparation, cooking and grilling
● E015.0   Food preparation and clean up
            Inclusion note added
● E015.1   Grilling and smoking food

● E015.2   Cooking and baking
       Inclusion note added

● E015.9   Other activity involving cooking and grilling

● E016   Activities involving property and land maintenance, building and construction

● E016.0   Digging, shoveling and raking
       Inclusion notes added

● E016.1   Gardening and landscaping
       Inclusion note added

● E016.2   Building and construction

● E016.9   Other activity involving property and land maintenance, building and construction

● E017   Activities involving roller coasters and other types of external motion

● E017.0   Roller coaster riding

● E017.9   Other activity involving external motion

● E018   Activities involving playing musical instrument
       Inclusion note added

● E018.0   Piano playing
       Inclusion note added

● E018.1   Drum and other percussion instrument playing

● E018.2   String instrument playing

● E018.3   Wind and brass instrument playing

● E019   Activities involving animal care
       Exclusion note added

● E019.0   Walking an animal

● E019.1   Milking an animal

● E019.2   Grooming and shearing an animal

● E019.9   Other activity involving animal care

● E029   Other activity

● E029.0   Refereeing a sports activity

● E029.1   Spectator at an event

● E029.2   Rough housing and horseplay

● E029.9   Other activity

● E030   Unspecified activity

● TRANSPORT ACCIDENTS (E800-E848)
       Instructional note added

E830-E838 WATER TRANSPORT ACCIDENTS
       Fourth-digit subdivision added

● E830.7   Accident to watercraft causing submersion, Occupant of military watercraft, any type

● E831.7   Accident to watercraft causing other injury, Occupant of military watercraft, any type

● E832.7   Other accidental submersion or drowning in water transport accident, Occupant of military watercraft, any type

● E833.7   Fall on stairs or ladders in water transport, Occupant of military watercraft, any type

● E834.7   Other fall from one level to another in water transport, Occupant of military watercraft, any type

● E835.7   Other and unspecified fall in water transport, Occupant of military watercraft, any type

● E836.7   Machinery accident in water transport, Occupant of military watercraft, any type

● E837.7   Explosion, fire, or burning in watercraft, Occupant of military watercraft, any type

● E838.7   Other and unspecified water transport accident, Occupant of military watercraft, any type

▲ E876.5   Performance of inappropriate ►wrong◄ operation ►(procedure) on correct patient◄
       Inclusion note added
       Exclusion note added

● E876.6   Performance of operation (procedure) on patient not scheduled for surgery
       Inclusion notes added

● E876.7   Performance of correct operation (procedure) on wrong side/body part
       Inclusion notes added

E918   Exclusion note added

E919   Exclusion note added

E920   Exclusion note added

E922   Exclusion note added

E923   Exclusion note added

E927   Use additional code note added

● E928.7   Mechanism or component of firearm and air gun
       Inclusion notes added
       Exclusion note added

E930-E949 DRUGS, MEDICINAL AND BIOLOGICAL SUBSTANCES CAUSING ADVERSE EFFECTS IN THERAPEUTIC USE
       Exclusion term revised

E990-E999 INJURY RESULTING FROM OPERATIONS OF WAR
       Inclusion term revised

E990.0   Inclusion note added

● E990.1   From flamethrower

● E990.2   From incendiary bullet

● E990.3   From fire caused indirectly from conventional weapon
       Exclusion note added

E991   Exclusion notes added

● E991.4   Fragments from munitions
       Inclusion notes added

● E991.5   Fragments from person-borne improvised explosive device [IED]

● E991.6   Fragments from vehicle-borne improvised explosive device [IED]
       Inclusion note added

● E991.7   Fragments from other improvised explosive device [IED]
       Inclusion note added

● E991.8   Fragments from weapons
       Inclusion notes added

E991.9   Inclusion notes deleted
       Inclusion term revised

E992   Inclusion notes deleted
       Exclusion note added

● E992.0   Torpedo

● E992.1   Depth charge

● E992.2   Marine mines
       Inclusion notes added

● E992.3   Sea-based artillery shell

● E992.8   Other marine weapons

● E992.9   Unspecified marine weapon
       Inclusion note added

E993   Inclusion notes added
       Inclusion notes deleted
       Exclusion notes added

● E993.0   Aerial bomb

● E993.1   Guided missile

● E993.2   Mortar
       Inclusion notes added

● E993.3   Person-borne improvised explosive device [IED]

● E993.4   Vehicle-borne improvised explosive device [IED]
       Inclusion notes added

● E993.5   Other improvised explosive device [IED]
       Inclusion note added

● E993.6   Unintentional detonation of own munitions
       Inclusion notes added

● E993.7   Unintentional discharge of own munitions launch device
       Inclusion notes added

● E993.8   Other specified explosion
       Inclusion notes added

● E993.9   Unspecified explosion
       Inclusion notes added

E994   Inclusion notes deleted

● E994.0   Destruction of aircraft due to enemy fire or explosives
       Inclusion notes added

● E994.1   Unintentional destruction of aircraft due to own onboard explosives

● E994.2   Destruction of aircraft due to collision with other aircraft

● E994.3   Destruction of aircraft due to onboard fire

● E994.8   Other destruction of aircraft

● E994.9   Unspecified destruction of aircraft

E995   Inclusion notes deleted

● E995.0   Unarmed hand-to-hand combat
       Exclusion note added

● E995.1   Struck by blunt object
       Inclusion notes added

● E995.2   Piercing object
       Inclusion notes added

● E995.3   Intentional restriction of air and airway
       Inclusion notes added

● E995.4   Unintentional drowning due to inability to surface or obtain air
       Inclusion note added

● E995.8   Other forms of conventional warfare

● E995.9   Unspecified form of conventional warfare

E996   Inclusion notes deleted
       Inclusion note added
       Exclusion note added

● E996.0   Direct blast effect of nuclear weapon
       Inclusion notes added

● E996.1   Indirect blast effect of nuclear weapon
       Inclusion notes added

● E996.2   Thermal radiation effect of nuclear weapon
       Inclusion notes added

● E996.3   Nuclear radiation effects
       Inclusion notes added

● E996.8   Other effects of nuclear weapons

● E996.9   Unspecified effect of nuclear weapon

● E997.3   Weapon of mass destruction [WMD], unspecified

● E998.0   Explosion of mines

● E998.1   Explosion of bombs

● E998.8   Injury due to other war operations but occurring after cessation of hostilities

PROCEDURE TABULAR (VOLUME 3)

00.2	Inclusion note added
	Exclusion note added
▲ 00.56	Insertion or replacement of implantable pressure sensor [lead] for intracardiac ▶or great vessel◀ hemodynamic monitoring
▲ 00.57	Implantation or replacement of subcutaneous device for intracardiac ▶or great vessel◀ hemodynamic monitoring
01.59	Exclusion note added
06.31	Exclusion note added
13.2	Code also note added
13.3	Code also note added
13.4	Code also note added
● 17.5	Additional cardiovascular procedures
● 17.51	Implantation of rechargeable cardiac contractility modulation [CCM], total system
	Instructional note added
	Code also note added
	Exclusion note added
● 17.52	Implantation or replacement of cardiac contractility modulation [CCM] rechargeable pulse generator only
	Instructional note added
	Code also note added
● 17.6	Laser interstitial thermal therapy [LITT] under guidance
	Inclusion notes added
● 17.61	Laser interstitial thermal therapy [LITT] of lesion or tissue of brain under guidance
	Inclusion notes added
	Exclusion note added
● 17.62	Laser interstitial thermal therapy [LITT] of lesion or tissue of head and neck under guidance
	Inclusion notes added
	Exclusion note added
● 17.63	Laser interstitial thermal therapy [LITT] of lesion or tissue of liver under guidance
	Inclusion notes added
● 17.69	Laser interstitial thermal therapy [LITT] of lesion or tissue of other and unspecified site under guidance
	Inclusion notes added
	Exclusion notes added
● 17.7	Other diagnostic and therapeutic procedures

● 17.70	Intravenous infusion of clofarabine
	Exclusion note added
▲ 27.5	Plastic repair of ▶lip and◀ mouth
32.29	Exclusion note added
33.24	Inclusion note added
▲ 33.71	Endoscopic insertion or replacement of bronchial valve(s)▶, single lobe◀
	Exclusion note added
● 33.73	Endoscopic insertion or replacement of bronchial valve(s), multiple lobes
	Exclusion note added
34.1	Code also note added
34.22	Code also note revised
37.79	Inclusion term revised
37.94	Code also note revised
38.23	Inclusion term revised
	Exclusion terms revised
● 38.24	Intravascular imaging of coronary vessel(s) by optical coherence tomography [OCT]
● 38.25	Intravascular imaging of non-coronary vessel(s) by optical coherence tomography [OCT]
	Exclusion note added
39.50	Code also note added
	Code also note revised
▲ 39.7	Endovascular ~~repair~~ ▶procedures on◀ ~~of~~ ▶vessel(s)◀
	Inclusion notes added
▲ 39.72	Endovascular ~~repair~~ ▶embolization◀ or occlusion of head and neck vessels
	Inclusion note deleted
	Exclusion notes added
39.74	Exclusion notes added
	Exclusion terms revised
● 39.75	Endovascular embolization or occlusion of vessel(s) of head or neck using bare coils
	Inclusion notes added
● 39.76	Endovascular embolization or occlusion of vessel(s) of head or neck using bioactive coils
	Inclusion notes added
▲ 39.79	Other endovascular ~~repair~~ ▶procedures◀ ~~(of aneurysm) of~~ ▶on◀ other vessels
	Inclusion notes added
	Inclusion term revised
	Exclusion notes added
	Exclusion terms revised
▲ 39.90	Insertion of non-drug-eluting peripheral ▶(non-coronary)◀ vessel stent(s)
46.85	Exclusion note added

● 46.86	Endoscopic insertion of colonic stent(s)
	Inclusion notes added
	Exclusion note added
● 46.87	Other insertion of colonic stent(s)
	Inclusion notes added
	Code also note added
	Exclusion note added
50.29	Exclusion note added
60.61	Inclusion note deleted
	Exclusion note added
▲ 80.00	Arthrotomy for removal of prosthesis ▶without replacement,◀ unspecified site
▲ 80.01	Arthrotomy for removal of prosthesis ▶without replacement,◀ shoulder
▲ 80.02	Arthrotomy for removal of prosthesis ▶without replacement,◀ elbow
▲ 80.03	Arthrotomy for removal of prosthesis ▶without replacement,◀ wrist
▲ 80.04	Arthrotomy for removal of prosthesis ▶without replacement,◀ hand and finger
▲ 80.05	Arthrotomy for removal of prosthesis ▶without replacement,◀ hip
▲ 80.06	Arthrotomy for removal of prosthesis ▶without replacement,◀ knee
▲ 80.07	Arthrotomy for removal of prosthesis ▶without replacement,◀ ankle
▲ 80.08	Arthrotomy for removal of prosthesis ▶without replacement,◀ foot and toe
▲ 80.09	Arthrotomy for removal of prosthesis ▶without replacement,◀ other specified sites
81.5	Instructional note added
81.54	Inclusion note added
81.84	Inclusion note added
85.20	Exclusion note added
88.91	Exclusion note added
88.92	Exclusion notes added
88.95	Exclusion note added
88.97	Exclusion note added
99.25	Exclusion note added

ICD-9-CM Changes 2010: An Insider's View

Volume 1—Tabular List of Diseases and Injuries

Chapter 2: Neoplasms (140–239)

Merkel Cell Carcinoma (209.31–209.36)

- **209.31**   **Merkel cell carcinoma of the face**
- **209.32**   **Merkel cell carcinoma of the scalp and neck**
- **209.33**   **Merkel cell carcinoma of the upper limb**
- **209.34**   **Merkel cell carcinoma of the lower limb**
- **209.35**   **Merkel cell carcinoma of the trunk**
- **209.36**   **Merkel cell carcinoma of other sites**

Merkel cell carcinoma is an aggressive neuroendocrine skin cancer that arises from the uncontrolled growth of Merkel cells in the epidermal layer of the skin. Merkel cells are of unknown function, but they are suspected of being involved in the sense of touch. Merkel cell carcinoma is considered a neuroendocrine tumor because the affected Merkel cells have both sensory and hormonal functions. Merkel cell carcinoma has become the most common cause of nonmelanoma skin cancer fatalities in the United States. Characteristic signs include firm, flesh or red-violet-colored bumps that develop suddenly on sun-exposed skin and tend to grow rapidly over a period of weeks or months. Due to the aggressive nature of Merkel cell carcinoma, immediate identification is necessary to ensure optimal treatment. Surgical treatment may include sentinel lymph node biopsy followed by excision of the tumor. Radiation therapy is of vital importance to ensure optimal outcomes. Adjuvant chemotherapy has not been proven to improve the prognosis.

Coding Tips

Merkel cell carcinoma unknown primary site, documented using terminology such as nodal presentation or visceral metastatic, is reported using code 209.75.

Scenario

The patient presents with a lesion, which was identified by biopsy as Merkel cell carcinoma of the skin, right upper eyelid. Patient will be referred to a cosmetic surgeon to undergo Mohs micrographic surgery.

Code assignment:

209.31   Merkel cell carcinoma of the face

Secondary Neuroendocrine Tumors (209.70–209.79)

- **209.70**   **Secondary neuroendocrine tumor, unspecified site**
- **209.71**   **Secondary neuroendocrine tumor of distant lymph nodes**
- **209.72**   **Secondary neuroendocrine tumor of liver**
- **209.73**   **Secondary neuroendocrine tumor of bone**
- **209.74**   **Secondary neuroendocrine tumor of peritoneum**
- **209.75**   **Secondary Merkel cell carcinoma**
- **209.79**   **Secondary neuroendocrine tumor of other sites**

The most common metastatic sites for neuroendocrine tumor are the peritoneum, liver, lymph nodes, and bones. Liver metastasis is of particularly high incidence in certain primary neuroendocrine tumors (e.g., intestines, pancreas). The treatment of liver metastases may dominate the cancer treatment due to the prominent blood supply, risk for hepatic failure and surgical risk included in debulking of the tumor.

Although many neuroendocrine tumors are slow-growing by comparison to other pathologies, some manifestations present aggressively and are recalcitrant to conventional treatment. For example, an adenocarcinoma may be treated with cytotoxic chemotherapy, while a neuroendocrine tumor is likely to be more responsive to hormonal therapies due to the nature of the tumor.

Coding Tips

Neuroendocrine tumors are located in the index under the main term "Tumor," subterm "carcinoid." While these are considered malignant carcinoid tumors and are classified in the neoplasm chapter, they are not listed in the Neoplasm Table.

Scenario

A 68-year-old patient presents for evaluation of liver lesion. A biopsy-confirmed metastatic carcinoid lesions of the liver from her existing previously confirmed primary transverse carcinoid colon malignancy.

Code assignment:

209.72   Secondary neuroendocrine tumor of the liver

209.14   Malignant carcinoid tumor of the transverse colon

Retinal and Choroidal Neoplasms of Uncertain Behavior (239.81)

- **239.81**   **Retina and choroid**
- **239.89**   **Other specified sites**

Black or darkened spot, or other abnormal-appearing lesion of the retina and choroid, may be noted upon examination and considered suspicious melanomas. Due to the procedural risks involved, a biopsy is typically not indicated until the neoplasm has grown sufficiently for an adequate tissue sample to be obtained. Retinal and choroidal lesions may be characterized by size, appearance, or other factors that raise suspicion for malignancy. Dome- or mushroom-shaped choroidal tumors greater than and/or equal to 2.5 mm are commonly identified as melanomas. Retinal adenomas typically arise from the retinal pigment epithelium and are not usually associated with retinal detachment. Adenomas may present on angiography as dark or black lesions, or as choroid-adherent tuberous or dome-shaped lesions on ultrasound. Treatment depends on the size of the tumor and severity of associated symptoms.

Coding Tips

New codes 239.81 and 239.89 allow for classification of retinal and choroidal neoplasms in the absence of a histologic confirmation of the diagnosis. Assign code 239.81 for "suspected" melanoma of the retina or choroid.

Scenario

A patient presents with suspicious lesions of the choroid. Due to the small size of the lesion, biopsy is contraindicated, as adequate sample is not possible at this time.

Code assignment:

239.81   Neoplasm of unspecified nature, other specified sites, retina and choroid

Chapter 3: Endocrine, Nutritional and Metabolic Diseases, and Immunity Disorders (240–279)

Gouty Arthropathy (274.00–274.03)

- **274.00**   **Gouty arthropathy, unspecified**
- **274.01**   **Acute gouty arthropathy**
- **274.02**   **Chronic gouty arthropathy without mention of tophus (tophi)**
- **274.03**   **Chronic gouty arthropathy with tophus (tophi)**

The advent of new treatments (e.g., selective xanthine oxidase inhibitor; PEGylated uricase enzyme, interluekin-1 receptor antagonist, cyclooxygenase-2 inhibitors) has necessitated more clinically specific ICD-9-CM classifications. Gout is a disorder in which urate (uric acid) crystals are deposited in joints, synovial fluid, and soft tissues, causing inflammation and degenerative changes. Gout is characterized by hyperuricemia (excessive uric acid in the blood), although hyperuricemia does not always progress to gout. Uric acid is normally dissolved in the bloodstream and passes through the urinary system. However, if the body produces too much uric acid or the kidneys excrete too little uric acid, an abnormal accumulation of urate crystals form and become deposited in the joints and surrounding tissues.

Onset of symptoms includes typically nocturnal attacks of pain, burning, swelling, redness, and stiffness in a joint. Attacks (flares) typically persist for three to 10 days on average, then subside for a period of months, or perhaps years. Recurrent attacks are common if left untreated. Eventually, the urate deposits can cause debilitating damage to the joints, tendons, and other tissues.

Disease progression may be clinically categorized into four progressive stages:

- Stage I: Asymptomatic urate deposition or accumulation—uric acid accumulation in the tissues of a hyperuricemic patient, in the absence of a diagnosis of gout

- Stage II: Acute gout (a.k.a., gouty arthropathy, gout "attacks" or "flares")—an acute, intermittent and painfully debilitating inflammation caused by accumulation of urate crystals in one or more joints

- Stage III: Intercritical gout—The interval between gout attacks or flares during which joint symptoms lie dormant or quiescent although hyperuricemia may persist

- Stage IV: Chronic tophaceous gout—a stage of chronic gouty arthritis associated with accumulation of tophi (i.e., concentrated urate crystal deposits in and around joints and subcutaneous tissue), characterized by tender and swollen joints

Coding Tips

The terms "asymptomatic urate deposition" and "intercritical gout" are terms not generally found in the medical record. However, acute and chronic gout with and without tophi are current terms commonly used in the clinical environment and documented in the medical record.

Scenario

A 58-year-old male presents with a seven-year history of acute gout attacks and periods of relative remission. He is currently being monitored for hyperuricemia and intermittent joint swelling and stiffness due to tophi. Diagnosis is consistent with stage IV chronic tophaceous gout.

Code assignment:

274.03   Chronic gouty arthropathy with tophus (tophi)

Tumor Lysis Syndrome (277.88)

● **277.88   Tumor lysis syndrome**

Tumor lysis syndrome (TLS) is a potentially fatal metabolic complication of spontaneous or treatment-related tumor necrosis. TLS comprises a constellation of metabolic conditions caused by the accumulation of byproducts produced by dying cancer cells. The waste products rendered by tumor necrosis accumulate faster than the body can effectively eliminate them. Symptoms may include nausea and vomiting, shortness of breath, irregular heartbeat, abnormal urine, fatigue, and joint pain. With delayed treatment, symptoms may progress to acute kidney failure, arrhythmias, seizures, dyskinesia, and cardiorespiratory failure. The metabolic disturbances inherent in TLS may include hyperkalemia, hyperphosphatemia and hyperuricemia. As such, TLS is often associated with acute renal failure.

Antineoplastic therapy tumor lysis occurs most commonly after treatment of leukemia and lymphoma. However, spontaneous tumor lysis syndrome may occur prior to the initiation of chemotherapy may also be referred to as "pretreatment" TLS. This type of TLS is differentiated from post-therapeutic TLS in that the spontaneous forms are not typically associated with hyperphosphatemia. Preventative treatment may include intravenous hydration, allopurinol or Elitek (rasburicase) therapy and sodium bicarbonate. Once TLS has occurred, treatment is focused on correcting the specific resultant metabolic abnormality.

Coding Tips

Assign additional codes to report associated conditions. Use an additional E code to identify the cause, if drug-induced.

Scenario

A patient is admitted in acute renal failure associated with tumor lysis syndrome after initiation of chemotherapy for hairy cell leukemia. Laboratory blood tests indicate elevated serum phosphates and hyperuricemia.

Code assignment:

584.9   Acute kidney failure, unspecified

277.88   Tumor lysis syndrome

E933.1   Adverse effects; antineoplastic and immunosuppressive drugs

202.40   Leukemic reticuloendotheliosis, unspecified site, extranodal and solid organ sites

Autoimmune Lymphoproliferative Syndrome (279.41)

● **279.41   Autoimmune lymphoproliferative syndrome**
● **279.49   Autoimmune disease, not elsewhere classified**

Autoimmune lymphoproliferative syndrome (ALPS) is a rare disease that affects both children and adults. A genetic mutation in a gene that encodes a protein referred to as *Fas* has been associated with approximately 83 percent of ALPS patients. This protein plays an integral role in apoptosis, the normal process through which cells die. The genetically altered *Fas* protein does not allow the cells to die normally, resulting in an overabundance of lymphocytes in the tissues. As a result, ALPS exacerbates postinfection, when the lymphocytes continue producing excess T and B cells in the lymph glands, liver and spleen. The B cells continue to make antibodies, but since the infection has been eradicated, the cells make antibodies against platelets, red blood cells, or other healthy cells.

Clinical features of the syndrome present in early childhood or at birth and may include:

- Chronic multifocal lymphadenopathy
- Splenomegaly
- Autoimmune hemolytic anemia or other cytopenias
- Hepatomegaly
- Epistaxis
- Genetic mutations

The majority of patients improve with steroid therapy and blood transfusions. Complications may include various anemias, increased infection risk, hemorrhage, and organ damage. Splenectomy may be indicated in certain cases to regulate complications, although complications tend to lessen in severity with age. Some patients have a higher risk for developing lymphoma.

Coding Tips

Assign additional codes, as necessary, to report any associated complications of ALPS. ALPS can be located in the index under main term "ALPS" or "Autoimmune."

Scenario

A 9-year-old male presents for evaluation of multifocal lymphadenopathy, enlarged spleen and autoimmune neutropenia due to chronic otitis media. Upon investigation, the physician documents ALPS.

Code assignment:

279.41   Autoimmune lymphoproliferative disorder

382.9   Unspecified otitis media

Chapter 4: Diseases of the Blood and Blood-Forming Organs (280–289)

Antineoplastic Chemotherapy Induced Anemia (285.3)

● **285.3   Antineoplastic chemotherapy induced anemia**

Chemotherapy-induced anemia affects approximately 20 percent to 60 percent of cancer patients, resulting in fatigue and inability to perform daily tasks. Cancer and cancer-related treatment often inhibits the production of bone marrow, resulting in decreased red blood cell production. Red blood cells carry oxygen throughout the body. When the production of red blood cells is too low, the body receives inadequate oxygen. Oxygen is of vital importance to the health of tissues and organs. With insufficient oxygen supply, the heart works harder than normal in an attempt to oxygenate the body. As a result, the patient may feel weak, short of breath, dizzy, or fatigued. Anemia stresses the body and may exacerbate other existing medical conditions. As a result, anemia can cause treatment delays and dosage adjustments that can decrease the effectiveness of cancer therapy. Multiple treatment options are available, including dietary modifications, supplements, red blood cell transfusions, and erythropoiesis-stimulating agents (ESAs).

Coding Tip

The type of antineoplastic chemotherapy-induced anemia classifiable to new code 285.3 does not include, nor is it synonymous with, aplastic anemia. Cancer treatment anemia is typically short-term conditions, which do not routinely reduce the bone marrow cellularity to a point of aplasia. As a result, aplastic anemia due to chemotherapy is more appropriately classified to code 284.89. Similarly, anemia due to the neoplastic disease itself is excluded from code 285.3 and classified instead to code 285.22.

Scenario

A 54-year old breast cancer patient presents for treatment of antineoplastic chemotherapy-induced anemia.

Code assignment:

285.3	Antineoplastic chemotherapy-induced anemia
174.9	Malignant neoplasm of female breast, unspecified

Chapter 6: Diseases of the Nervous System and Sense Organs (320–389)

Temporal Sclerosis (348.81)

- **348.81 Temporal sclerosis**
- **348.89 Other conditions of brain**

Temporal sclerosis (a.k.a., mesial temporal sclerosis, hippocampal sclerosis) is a condition associated with certain brain injuries. Temporal sclerosis is caused by scarring or hardening of the tissues of the temporal lobe of the brain, with resultant loss of functional neurons. Additional contributing factors include structural changes due to conditions such as tumors, vascular or cortical malformations, and hypoxic or traumatic injury. These structural changes may affect the amygdale, hippocampus, and parahippocampal gyrus and are often readily identifiable on magnetic resonance imaging (MRI) scan. As the sclerosis progresses, brain damage is demonstrated radiographically by neuronal loss, fibrillary gliosis (scarring), and hippocampal atrophy (shrinkage).

Approximately 70 percent of patients with temporal lobe epilepsy also have associated mesial temporal sclerosis. Temporal lobe epilepsy is one of the most common forms of epilepsy occurring in adults, with onset of seizures in childhood or adolescence. Temporal seizures may be precipitated by certain situations or senses that trigger an emotional response. Treatment is focused on suppressing the seizures with antiepileptic medications. However, as scarring formation progresses and seizures persist, surgical measures may be indicated, such as temporal lobectomy, during which the scarred tissue is removed from the temporal lobe of the brain.

Coding Tips

An exclusion note has been added to 345 Epilepsy and recurrent seizures, for temporal sclerosis (348.81). An additional code should be reported for temporal sclerosis when the temporal sclerosis and temporal lobe epilepsy are documented.

Scenario

A 50 year old female with a long history of refractory temporal lobe epilepsy presents for follow up MRI to assess neurological changes. MRI reveals scarring consistent with mesial temporal sclerosis.

Code assignment:

345.41	Localization-related (focal) (partial) epilepsy and epileptic syndromes with complex partial seizures, with intractable epilepsy
348.81	Temporal lobe sclerosis

Inclusion Body Myositis (IBM) (359.71)

- **359.71 Inclusion body myositis**
- **359.79 Other inflammatory and immune myopathies, NEC**

Inclusion body myositis (IBM) is a progressive, debilitating inflammatory muscle disease characterized by chronic muscle swelling, weakness, and atrophy (wasting). IBM most commonly affects men over 50 years of age but can occur decades earlier. Onset is usually gradual, progressing over a period of months or years. Initial symptoms include excessive muscle weakness or falling and tripping. As the disease progresses, individuals commonly experience weakness and atrophy of the muscles of the extremities along with fine motor skill impairment. Approximately half of patients with IBM experience difficulty swallowing. Muscle biopsy is essential to diagnosis. Treatment for IBM is generally palliative, as it has proven unresponsive to corticosteroids and immunosuppressive drugs. Some patients have experienced short-term benefits from intravenous immunoglobulin.

Clinical trials are currently underway to explore the role of genetics and viral infection in IBM, and to examine the safety and efficacy of new proposed treatment regimens.

Coding Tips

New code 259.71 provides a unique code for reporting inclusion body myositis (IBM). Other inflammatory and immune myopathies previously classified to code 359.89 are now reported with new code 359.79.

Scenario

A 57-year-old male presents with a history of progressive muscle weakness, dysphagia and atrophy. Diagnostic muscle biopsy reveals inclusion body myositis.

Code assignment:

359.71	Inclusion body myositis

Acute Chemical Conjunctivitis (372.06)

- **372.06 Acute chemical conjunctivitis**

Acute conjunctivitis is an inflammation of the mucous membrane covering the anterior surface of the eyeball and the lining of the eyelids. Acute conjunctivitis is commonly due to exposure of the conjunctiva to contaminants or irritants such as detergents, airborne chemicals or solvents, smoke, industrial pollutants, and chlorine in swimming pools. In acute presentation, symptoms develop suddenly and typically run a short course. Symptoms include redness, pain, and excess tearing (i.e., pink eye) in milder presentations. Acute chemical conjunctivitis may progress to include a worsening of swelling, pain, and redness, with blurring of vision. Chemical conjunctivitis can damage to the surface of the eye and impair vision but typically does not pose as serious a threat to ocular structures as a chemical burn of the eye. Diagnostic tests include culture and sensitivity to rule out bacterial infection. Treatment includes irrigation and removal of chemical irritant, lubricant eye drops, topical analgesics, and antispasmodics.

Coding Tips

Code 372.06 should be not be assigned for exposure to chemicals that result in alkaline (940.2) or acid (940.3) eye burn. New code 372.06 should be reported with an additional E code to identify the causal chemical or toxic agent.

Scenario

A 10-year old female presents with bilateral conjunctival redness, inflammation, and pain consistent with acute conjunctivitis. Onset of symptoms coincides with irritation experienced after swimming. Diagnosis is consistent with chemical conjunctivitis due to excessive chlorine content in a local swimming pool.

Code assignment:

372.06   Acute chemical conjunctivitis

Chapter 7: Diseases of the Circulatory System (390–459)

Chronic Pulmonary Embolism (416.2)

- **416.2   Chronic pulmonary embolism**

Pulmonary embolism (PE) may present as an acute event (generally, within two weeks of onset) or as a chronic condition that can persist over many weeks, months, or years. In chronic PE, small blood clots travel to the lungs repeatedly over a period of time. Chronic PE is often closely associated with pulmonary hypertension, whereby the embolus blocks pulmonary circulation from the right side of the heart to the left, causing an increase in pulmonary arterial pressure. Pulmonary hypertension may initially lie relatively quiescent but progress to episodes of dizziness or syncope. As the pumping mechanism of the right heart is forced to work harder, it struggles to pump blood through the lungs and into the left heart. As a result, the patient may experience ischemic chest pain (angina) accompanied by peripheral edema or ascites. Patients with only mild elevations in their pulmonary artery pressures may be amenable to medical therapy; however, those who are limited by their symptoms and are qualified surgical candidates may be treated with interventions such as IVC filter or pulmonary thromboendarterectomy. Prognosis depends on the status of the affected lung and the presence of comorbid conditions.

Coding Tips

New code 416.2 distinguishes between chronic pulmonary embolism and acute pulmonary embolism (415.19). An old or chronic thrombus requires continuation of established therapy, as opposed to the initiation of aggressive anticoagulation to treat acute thrombus. Modifications to the index include the addition of new subterms under the main term Embolism to serve as a reminder to clearly establish whether the embolism is a new (acute) diagnosis or an old (chronic) diagnosis. An additional code should be assigned for associated long-term (current) use of anticoagulants (V58.61), where appropriate. Code 416.2 excludes personal history of pulmonary embolism (V12.51).

Scenario

A patient diagnosed with chronic pulmonary embolism who is on anticoagulation therapy presents for evaluation of the status of his condition.

Code assignment:

416.2   Chronic pulmonary embolism

V58.61   Long term (current) use of anticoagulants

Late Effects of Cerebrovascular Disease, Dysarthria (438.13) and Fluency Disorder (438.14)

- **438.13   Late effects of cerebrovascular disease, dysarthria**
- **438.14   Late effects of cerebrovascular disease, fluency disorder**

A fluency disorder may be defined as an interruption in the flow of speech that significantly interferes with communication. Stuttering is a specific type of fluency disorder in which the disruption in speech production is characterized by a primary sound and syllable repetitions, articulatory fixations (i.e., blocked speech), and abnormal prolongations of certain speech sounds. Stuttering results in speech that sounds fragmented or halting, with frequent interruptions. The term "neurogenic stuttering" may be used to describe stuttering that occurs as a result of injury or disease to the central nervous system (e.g., cerebrovascular accident). Neurogenic stuttering often presents as an overlapping or inter-related condition with some other form of fluency disorder (e.g., dysarthria, apraxia, aphasia), when due to neurological injury or impairment.

Dysarthria is a speech disorder due to disturbances of neuromuscular control (e.g., paralysis, spasticity). It is often caused by damage to the central or peripheral nervous system by illness or injury. The patient demonstrates difficulty expressing certain words or sounds, often resulting in slurring or interrupted rhythm of speech. In severe cases, distortion of vowel sound may be significantly impaired. Speech intelligibility varies on the severity of presentation and extent of neurological damage. Dysarthria is a common sequela of stroke and may be associated with dysphagia (difficulty swallowing) due to damage of the nerves that control both functions. Other causal conditions include neuromuscular disease (MS, myasthenia gravis), head trauma, Bell's palsy, post-surgical states, and effects of certain medications. Examination by a speech language pathologist can help establish a diagnosis and treatment plan. Speech therapy helps the patient improve breath support, strengthen muscles, and improve orofacial mobility and articulation. Other therapies include isometric exercises and feedback therapies (e.g., electromyographic, delayed auditory feedback). Depending on the severity and underlying pathology, prosthetic devices or surgical intervention may be indicated.

Coding Tips

Dysarthria (438.13) and fluency disorders (438.14) due to cerebrovascular accident are excluded from the newly expanded subcategory 785.5. New code 438.14 includes stuttering due to cerebrovascular accident. Stuttering, NOS is classified to default code 307.0 Category 307 is a unique category intended for a single (or group of) psychopathologic symptom not part of an organic illness or other mental disorder classified elsewhere.

Scenario

A patient presents for continuation of speech-language therapy for neurogenic stuttering and dysarthria due to late effects CVA.

Code assignment:

V57.3   Care involving use of rehabilitation procedures, speech-language therapy

438.13   Late effects of cerebrovascular disease, dysarthria

438.14   Late effects of cerebrovascular disease, fluency disorder

Acute and Chronic Venous Thrombosis and Embolism (453.50–453.79, 453.81–453.89)

- **453.50   Chronic venous embolism and thrombosis of unspecified deep vessels of lower extremity**
- **453.51   Chronic venous embolism and thrombosis of deep vessels of proximal lower extremity**
- **453.52   Chronic venous embolism and thrombosis of deep vessels of distal lower extremity**
- **453.6   Venous embolism and thrombosis of superficial vessels of lower extremity**
- **453.71   Chronic venous embolism and thrombosis of superficial veins of upper extremity**
- **453.72   Chronic venous embolism and thrombosis of deep veins of upper extremity**
- **453.73   Chronic venous embolism and thrombosis of upper extremity, unspecified**
- **453.74   Chronic venous embolism and thrombosis of axillary veins**
- **453.75   Chronic venous embolism and thrombosis of subclavian veins**
- **453.76   Chronic venous embolism and thrombosis of internal jugular veins**
- **453.77   Chronic venous embolism and thrombosis of other thoracic veins**
- **453.79   Chronic venous embolism and thrombosis of other specified veins**
- **453.81   Acute venous embolism and thrombosis of superficial veins of upper extremity**
- **453.82   Acute venous embolism and thrombosis of deep veins of upper extremity**
- **453.83   Acute venous embolism and thrombosis of upper extremity, unspecified**

- **453.84**   **Acute venous embolism and thrombosis of axillary veins**
- **453.85**   **Acute venous embolism and thrombosis of subclavian veins**
- **453.86**   **Acute venous embolism and thrombosis of internal jugular veins**
- **453.87**   **Acute venous embolism and thrombosis of other thoracic veins**
- **453.89**   **Acute venous embolism and thrombosis of other specified veins**

Patients with chronic venous thromboembolic disease often require prolonged medical therapy and follow-up for treatment of complications associated with the thrombus. These complications may include extension of the initial (acute phase) thrombosis, recurrence of thrombus, or anticoagulant-related hemorrhage or anemia. The increased use of invasive vascular devices (e.g., PICC lines, central catheters, tunneled dialysis catheters, wired cardiac devices) has resulted in an increased incidence of deep vein thrombosis of the major veins in the thorax and upper extremities. As such, axillary, jugular, and subclavian thrombi have become a common complication of care, necessitating vessel-specific coding classifications.

Coding Tips

Previously, patients with chronic thromboembolic disease were erroneously reported as having an "active" or acute thrombosis when the patient was actually maintained on anticoagulant therapy for a chronic condition. New codes were created to differentiate between acute (453.81–453.89) and chronic (453.50–453.52, 453.6, 453.71–453.79) disease and to identify specific anatomic sites previously classified to 453.8. No official definition exists for the terms "chronic" and "acute." In general, initial episode of care would indicate the acute phase, while "subsequent episode of care" would indicate the chronic phase.

Scenario

A patient presents with a recent subclavian vein PICC line in situ and with acute, complicating subclavian vein thrombus.

Code assignment:

996.74   Other complications of internal (biological) (synthetic) prosthetic device, implant and graft, Due to other vascular device, implant and graft

453.85   Acute venous embolism and thrombosis of subclavian veins

Diseases of the Respiratory System (460–519)

Influenza due to Identified Avian Influenza Virus (488.0)

- **488.0**   **Influenza due to identified avian influenza virus**

Avian influenza can cause infection in humans, even though the virus is predominately found in birds. Since these viruses do not typically infect humans, the risk from avian influenza is generally low to the majority of people. However, since 1997, various subtypes of avian influenza infection have been identified in humans. Most cases resulted from direct contact with infected domesticated poultry, or from contact with surfaces contaminated with the secretions or excretions of infected birds. In recent years, the United States reported incidents of H5 and H7 low pathogenic avian influenza (LPAI) and a highly pathogenic avian influenza (HPAI) that was restricted to one poultry farm. Symptoms of avian influenza in humans may vary according to the virulence of the causal influenza strain. Symptoms are generally similar to other influenza infections, such as fever, cough, sore throat and myalgia. Eye infections, pneumonia, lung diseases, or other severe and life-threatening complications have been reported in more severe cases.

Coding Tips

Code 488.0 reports only influenza that has been confirmed as being due to the avian influenza virus. Other forms of influenza may be reported more appropriately with codes from category 487.Category 488 codes are not reported when the diagnostic statement indicates that the infection is "suspected," "possible," "likely," "probable," or "questionable." This is an

exception to the hospital inpatient guideline to assign a code for a diagnosis qualified as suspected or probable as if it were established.

Scenario

A patient presents with an acute recent onset of fever, cough, sore throat, and myalgia. History notes the patient is a zoological worker who has been handling exotic avian species recently transported from Asia. Testing revealed that the patient had been infected with a low pathogenic avian influenza A (H7N2) virus.

Code assignment:

488.0   Influenza due to identified avian influenza virus

Influenza Due to Identified Novel H1N1 Influenza Virus (488.1)

- **488.1**   **Influenza due to identified novel H1N1 influenza virus**

Novel influenza A (H1N1) is a newly identified strain of influenza of swine origin, which has mutated as such to be transmissible from person to person. H1N1 is currently crowding out other, more common strains of influenza.

Novel influenza A (H1N1) flu is transmitted similarly to seasonal influenza: by contact with airborne or surface respiratory secretions of infected persons. General symptoms mimic those of other influenza infection, including fever, body aches, chills, and fatigue. Respiratory symptoms include cough and sore throat. Gastrointestinal symptoms may include diarrhea, nausea, and vomiting. Although most cases have been mild, requiring minimal treatment, approximately half of the H1N1 mortalities were previously young, healthy individuals. Because this is a new virus, the public has little or no immunity against it and severe or widespread outbreaks can result.

The CDC diagnostic test kit to detect novel H1N1 virus has been distributed nationally. Antiviral medications are typically reserved for use during outbreaks or to treat severe cases with risk for serious complications.

Coding Tips

Code 488.1 reports only influenza that has been confirmed as being due to the novel H1N2 virus. Other forms of influenza may be reported more appropriately with codes from category 487.

Category 488 codes are not reported when the diagnostic statement indicates that the infection is "suspected," "possible," "likely;" "probable," or "questionable." This is an exception to the hospital inpatient guideline to assign a code for a diagnosis qualified as suspected or probable as if it were established.

Scenario

A patient returns from a recent trip to Mexico with flu-like symptoms of fever, body aches, chills, cough, and fatigue. Diagnostic testing confirms novel H1N1 virus.

Code assignment:

488.1   Influenza due to identified novel H1N1 influenza virus

Chapter 9: Diseases of the Digestive System (520–579)

Pouchitis (569.71)

- **569.71**   **Pouchitis**
- **569.79**   **Other complications of intestinal pouch**

Pouchitis is an inflammation of a surgically created internal ileoanal pouch, which is commonly adjunct to resection of the colon or rectum. The internal pouch eliminates the need to wear an external device. In pouch creation, the patient's small intestine (ileum) is used to create an internal pouch for collection of stool. The surgery may be performed to treat ulcerative colitis or familial adenomatous polyposis. Inflammation of the pouch (pouchitis) is one a common post-procedural complication. Symptoms may mimic those of ulcerative colitis, with diarrhea, rectal bleeding, crampy abdominal pain, fecal urgency, or incontinence. Additional symptoms may include fever, loss of appetite, dehydration, joint pain, and malaise. Approximately one third of patients with an ileoanal pouch experience at least one episode of pouchitis. Patients with concomitant autoimmune or inflammatory disease have a higher incidence of occurrence.

Chronic pouchitis is relatively rare, although those patients may be effectively treated with surgical conversion to standard ileostomy.

Pouchitis may be treated successfully with a short course of antibiotics, suggesting an infectious etiology, although the cause of the inflammation may not be determined. Recent clinical research suggests that a genetic susceptibility, history of ulcerative colitis, and a trigger, such as bacteria, within the stool in the pouch may be contributory factors.

Coding Tips

New subcategory 569.7 classifies complications of surgically created internal intestinal pouch. New code 569.71 Pouchitis reports inflammation or infection of intestinal pouch. Other complications of intestinal pouch not classifiable to 569.71 may be reported with new code 569.79.

Scenario

A patient with a history of intestinal resection for Crohn's disease presents with acute onset of fever, bloody diarrhea, crampy abdominal pain, and fecal incontinence. Diagnostic endoscopy and biopsy of the site of inflammation confirms the diagnosis of pouchitis.

Code assignment:

569.71	Pouchitis
555.9	Regional enteritis, unspecified site

Vomiting Fecal Matter (569.87)

● **569.87   Vomiting of fecal matter**

Vomiting is a nonspecific complaint with many possible causal conditions. Certain types of vomiting can indicate very serious conditions, requiring a more extensive evaluation. The condition referred to as "vomiting of fecal matter" (a.k.a., copremesis, stercoraceous vomiting) is not the actual expulsion of fecal matter. Instead, it is a half-digested substance with a similar odor to fecal matter. This matter is expelled by spasmodic force from the intestines into the stomach and up into the esophagus through the mouth and possibly, the nasal passages. This type of vomitus often suggests bowel obstruction or abnormal fistula formation. Underlying causal pathology is routinely identified with diagnostic imaging or endoscopy. Treatment depends on the nature of the diagnosis. Surgical intervention is often indicated.

Coding Tips

Vomiting of fecal matter was previously indexed to code 569.89 Other disorders of intestine, other. Although this condition is largely a symptom, it is a specific gastrointestinal manifestation of an underlying pathology. Therefore, a unique code has been created in chapter 9, "Diseases of the Digestive System," instead of Chapter 16, "Symptoms, Signs and Ill-Defined Conditions." New code 569.87 helps improve data tracking of specific types of vomiting.

Scenario

A patient presents with vomiting of a malodorous, half-digested substance, resembling fecal matter. The patient is scheduled for diagnostic imaging to determine the cause.

Code assignment:

569.87	Vomiting of fecal matter

Chapter 10: Diseases of the Genitourinary System (580–629)

Benign Endometrial Hyperplasia (621.34) and Endometrial Intraepithelial Neoplasia [EIN] (621.35)

●	621.34	Benign endometrial hyperplasia
●	621.35	Endometrial intraepithelial neoplasia [EIN]

Endometrial intraepithelial neoplasia (EIN) is currently clinically classified into separate benign (benign endometrial hyperplasia) and premalignant (EIN) categories in accordance with histologic behavior and treatment indications. As such, a distinction is made between benign and neoplastic lesions. The pathogenesis of benign endometrial hyperplasia follows a sequence of primary hormonal changes that result in (i.e., polyclonal normal) secondary effects to the endometrial stroma and associated structures. Benign endometrial hyperplasia is an excessive cell growth often associated with the menopausal process when the cycle of sequentially regulated estrogen and progesterone is naturally physiologically altered. In contrast, endometrial epithelial neoplasia are abnormal neoplastic changes (i.e., genetically mutated monoclona) of the endometrial glands that are prone to malignant transformation. Although EIN is a premalignant lesion requiring a distinct classification due to the associated cancer risk, not all EIN lesions progress to carcinoma; some lesions spontaneously resolve. The progression of EIN to carcinoma occurs through acquisition of certain genetic mutations that precipitate local tissue invasion and metastatic growth. An important distinction between the two conditions is that EIN lesions have initiated the first step of the carcinogenesis process by clonal expansion of a mutated cell (monoclonus), whereas benign endometrial hyperplasia has not.

Coding Tips

When a malignant neoplasm of the endometrium is present with EIN, report only code 182.0 Malignant neoplasm of body of uterus. New code 621.35 Endometrial intraepithelial neoplasia [EIN] represents only premalignant changes that are prone to malignant transformation but have not genetically converted into a malignant phenotype.

Scenario

A 48-year-old female presents for follow-up biopsy of the endometrium. She has a history of abnormal Pap smear. Tissue samples demonstrate a monoclonal growth pattern and clonally distributed mutations consistent with the diagnosis of endometrial epithelial neoplasia.

Code assignment:

621.35	Endometrial intraepithelial neoplasia [EIN]

Chapter 11: Complications of Pregnancy, Childbirth and the Puerperium (630–379)

Major Puerperal Infection (670.10–670.84)

▲	✓5ᵗʰ	670.0 [0,2,4]	Major puerperal infection, unspecified
●	✓5ᵗʰ	670.1 [0,2,4]	Puerperal endometritis
●	✓5ᵗʰ	670.2 [0,2,4]	Puerperal sepsis
●	✓5ᵗʰ	670.3 [0,2,4]	Puerperal septic thrombophlebitis
●	✓5ᵗʰ	670.8 [0,2,4]	Other major puerperal infection

A puerperal infection (typically bacterial) follows childbirth. Risk of infection may be related to surgical intervention (e.g., cesarean section), complications of labor, maternal obesity, or other obstetric complicating conditions affecting her general health. In puerperal infection, causal organisms are normally found in the mother's genital tract but may be introduced from the woman's intestine and skin or from the practitioner. Symptoms may vary depending on the site and nature of the infection. The presence of fever between birth and 10 days postpartum is often the first sign of infection, which can spread to other parts of the body and be potentially fatal if not adequately treated. Of all puerperal infection, endometritis (670.10–670.14) is the most common, often occurring when a portion of the placenta is retained in the uterus.

Puerperal sepsis (670.20–670.24) is an infection that can spread from the point of origin to adjacent tissues, cavities, or into the bloodstream (septicemia, bacteremia), causing peritonitis, organ failure, and potentially uncontrolled and fatal sepsis. Puerperal septic thrombophlebitis (670.30–670.34)—is an inflammatory condition that affects the adnexa in the pelvis that follows delivery, especially after cesarean delivery. Puerperal septic thrombophlebitis may present as a late complication of a previous puerperal infection (e.g., endometritis) or as a septic ovarian vein thrombophlebitis secondary to pelvic inflammatory disease or progressive infection of the urinary tract. Antibiotic therapy is initiated in the event of puerperal fever to abate or prevent further infection.

Coding Tips

When reporting antepartum or postpartum deep phlebothrombosis, assign an additional code from category 453 Other venous embolism and thrombosis to identify the anatomic site of thrombosis. Report also any long-term (current use) of anticoagulants (V58.61).

Scenario

A patient presents two weeks postpartum with unremitting fever on antibiotic therapy and recurrent lower quadrant pelvic pain. Abdominal MRI revealed ovarian vein thrombosis. The physician documented puerperal septic ovarian vein thrombophlebitis.

Code assignment:

670.34   Puerperal septic thrombophlebitis

Chapter 14: Congenital Anomalies (740–759)

Omphalocele (756.72) and Gastroschisis (756.73)

- **756.72   Omphalocele**
- **756.73   Gastroschisis**

Omphalocele is a congenital ventral abdominal wall herniation of the infant's intestine or other abdominal organs from the navel. During development, the fetal umbilical ring muscles fail to close properly, and the intestine or other organs remain outside the umbilical cord. The intestines are usually covered by a protective membrane, with exposure of the herniated organs to amniotic fluid typically occurring only in the event of rupture. Omphalocele is often associated with other chromosomal (e.g., trisomy) or structural congenital anomalies (e.g., heart defects).

Gastroschisis is a congenital abnormal opening of the ventral abdominal wall. During development, the abdominal wall fails to close, allowing for the fetal intestines to herniate through the defect; usually to the right of the umbilical cord. The exposed intestines are not encased in a protective membrane, resulting in a prolonged exposure to amniotic fluid. Consequently, the intestines become swollen and inflamed, increasing the risk of dehydration, hypothermia, and infection at birth. Other associated congenital defects or syndromes are rare with gastroschisis, although other gastrointestinal anomalies such as intestinal atresia, stenosis, and malrotation may concomitantly occur.

Prenatal examination by ultrasonography often identifies these conditions. Surgical repair is necessary to reduce the hernia back into the abdominal cavity and close the defect. Medical therapies include IV antibiotics to help prevent infection, IV hydration for replacement of fluid and nutrients, and careful monitoring of the infant's body temperature to prevent hypothermia.

Coding Tips

Previously, both conditions were indexed and included in code 756.79 Other congenital anomalies of the abdominal wall. New code 756.72 Omphalocele also includes exophthalmos, previously classified to 756.79. Use additional codes as necessary to report any associated chromosomal or structural anomalies.

Scenario

Infant presents to the operating suite for closure of congenital gastroschisis defect. Exam reveals congenital herniation of a portion of intestine through a congenital right umbilical abdominal wall defect.

Code assignment:

756.73   Gastroschisis

Chapter 15: Certain Conditions Originating in the Perinatal Period (760–779)

Hypoxic-ischemic Encephalopathy (HIE) (768.70–768.73)

- **768.70   Hypoxic-ischemic encephalopathy, unspecified**
- **768.71   Mild hypoxic-ischemic encephalopathy**
- **768.72   Moderate hypoxic-ischemic encephalopathy**
- **768.73   Severe hypoxic-ischemic encephalopathy**

Neonatal encephalopathy is clinically defined based on various factors, including abnormalities in consciousness, tone, and reflexes, feeding, respirations, or seizures. These factors may result from many conditions, which may or may not affect permanent neurological impairment. However, poor outcomes may occur due to events before or after delivery. Two main clinical mechanisms can be used to deprive the brain of oxygen: hypoxia and ischemia. Hypoxic-ischemic encephalopathy (HIE) describes the resultant conditions due to a lack of oxygen supply to the brain. HIE has well-defined clinical definitions (mild, moderate, severe) based on clinical presentation and imaging findings. The most common staging system for HIE is the Sarnat scale, which combines clinical and EEG findings [mild (I), moderate (II), severe (III)]. A modified Sarnat score refers to grading based only on clinical findings, excluding EEG findings. Prognosis depends on the severity of HIE, ranging accordingly from return to normal function to death, in severe cases. However, even moderate HIE may result in death or disability. Disabilities are more common than fatalities in moderate HIE and may include cerebral palsy, cognitive deficits, and seizures. Disabilities associated with severe cases may include mental retardation, severe motor dysfunction, and seizures.

Coding Tips

Report HIE to the fifth-digit subclassification that accurately represents the clinical severity as documented in the medical record. In the absence of definitive documentation of clinical stage, query the physician for clarification if necessary.

Scenario

A 38-week-old male infant is delivered to a mother whose pregnancy has been uncomplicated. Delivery was complicated by sustained fetal bradycardia and late decelerations. Immediately following delivery, the infant became hypoxic. Apgar score at five minutes was 3; with physical exam demonstrating lethargy and reduced muscle tone of the extremities and/or trunk. Fetal umbilical cord arterial blood collected at delivery showed evidence of metabolic acidosis. The physician documented moderate HIE.

Code assignment:

V30.00   Single liveborn, born in hospital, delivered

768.72   Moderate hypoxic-ischemic encephalopathy

Disorder of Stomach Function and Feeding Problems in Newborn (779.31–779.34)

- **779.31   Feeding problems in newborn**
- **779.32   Bilious vomiting in newborn**
- **779.33   Other vomiting in newborn**
- **779.34   Failure to thrive in newborn**

Vomiting is a nonspecific complaint with many possible causal conditions. Certain types of vomiting can indicate very serious conditions, requiring a more extensive evaluation. Bile-stained vomitus in a newborn is commonly a sign of potentially fatal intestinal instruction. Diagnostic radiographic testing can confirm possible causal conditions such as intestinal malrotation, Hirschsprung's disease, or necrotizing enterocolitis. Premature infants are at high risk for necrotizing enterocolitis (NEC); therefore, protocols for suspended feeds are often necessary as a precautionary measure when bilious aspirates are identified. Alternately, some premature infants may suffer self-limiting bilious emesis due to an immature digestive system. Nonbilious vomiting in the newborn may indicate underlying congenital conditions classifiable elsewhere (e.g., gastroesophageal reflux, congenital pyloric stenosis). Diagnostic ultrasound or barium swallow can help establish causation and determine the course of treatment.

Nutritional intake is vital to the growth and development of the newborn. When feeding problems may herald a more serious underlying condition. Certain problems (e.g., poor latching, spitting up, weak suck) can be alleviated by using specialized feeding techniques. An oral sensorimotor feeding evaluation and barium swallow helps rule out underlying pathology.

In lieu of a precise definition, failure to thrive (FTT) (779.34) indicates an inability to receive, retain, or properly use nutrition to grow and develop as expected. It is important to determine whether the FTT is due to environmental factors (i.e., neglect) or underlying medical issues. FTT is a form of arrested growth that can affect long-term health and emotional development. The most common causes include feeding difficulties, gastroesophageal reflux, infection, and congenital metabolic or digestive disorders (i.e., malabsorption syndrome), although many other congenital systemic or structural anomalies can cause failure to thrive. A diagnostic work-up is indicated to identify causal pathology if an infant has not regained its birth weight within seven weeks with lactation and nutritional support. In the absence of apparent cause, screening lab tests and diagnostic radiological testing are often indicated.

Coding Tips

Symptom codes should be used in the absence of a more definitive diagnosis or the identification of underlying cause. New codes 779.31–779.34 report specific conditions in newborn patients (from birth to 28 days old). Check all exclusion notes to ensure code assignment is correct for the age of the patient. For example, new code 779.34 reports failure to thrive in a newborn. To report failure to thrive in patients greater than 28 days old, assign code 783.41 Lack of expected normal physiological development in childhood, Failure to thrive.

Scenario

Premature infant returns to the hospital for evaluation and observation of nonbilious vomiting. Diagnostic imaging reveals no pathology. The physician documents nonbilious vomiting probably due to immature digestive tract.

Code assignment:

779.33   Other vomiting in newborn

Chapter 16: Symptoms, Signs and Ill-Defined Conditions (780–779)

Voice and Resonance Disorders (784.42–784.44)

- **784.40   Voice and resonance disorder, unspecified**
- **784.42   Dysphonia**
- **784.43   Hypernasality**
- **784.44   Hyponasality**
- **784.49   Other voice and resonance disorders**

Dysphonia is a disorder of phonation (voice production), whereas hypernasality and hyponasality are disorders of resonance, the vibratory characteristics in amplitude (tone, pitch). Phonation occurs when air is expelled from the lungs through the glottis, creating a pressure drop across the larynx. This drop in pressures causes the focal folds of the larynx to vibrate. The vocal folds fail to vibrate if there is a lack or excess of tension, or if the pressure gradient across the larynx is insufficient. Dysphonia is often a symptom of a laryngeal disorder affecting the structure and/or function of the larynx.

Resonance disorders are often associated with an impairment affecting the structure and/or function of the oral cavity, nasal airway, and/or the velopharyngeal port. Such conditions include hypernasality and hyponasality. Common characteristics include impaired airway flow, reduced orolaryngeal pressure, and compensatory articulation. Structural anomalies or deficits (cleft palate), certain neurological disorders (cerebral palsy), and poor voice hygiene (improper learning) are often primary causes of voice resonance disorders. Diagnostic tests include acoustic analysis, nasometry and pressure gradient examinations, endoscopy, fluoroscopy, and cephalometric radiography.

Hypernasality is often caused by a dysfunction of the velopharyngeal mechanism; the soft palate (velum), and related musculature used to close the nasopharynx, which separates the oral and nasal cavities. Such structural abnormalities may be confirmed with diagnostic imaging and often require

surgical correction or prosthetics. Hyponasality is often associated with certain types of velopharyngeal incompetence (VPI) in which the nasopharynx is obstructed and cannot open sufficiently to produce certain consonant sounds. Causal conditions include hypertrophied adenoids or other structural abnormalities identifiable upon examination or diagnostic imaging. Speech therapy for phonation disorders often includes articulation therapy techniques, voice education, and vocal hygiene.

Coding Tips

Dysphonia and hoarseness (784.42), hypernasality (784.43), and hyponasality (784.44) were previously all included in code 784.49 Other voice disturbance. Separate, unique codes have been created to report each condition. Voice change remains indexed to 784.49, although coders are directed to "see dysphonia," which is now reported to code 784.42.

Scenario

A 7-year-old patient presents for speech therapy for resonance disorder with hypernasality. History is consistent with residual congenital velopharyngeal incompetence; status post cleft palate repair as an infant.

Code assignment:

V57.3   Speech-language therapy

784.43   Hypernasality

750.29   Other specified anomalies of pharynx

Dysarthria (785.51)

- **784.51   Dysarthria**
- **784.59   Other speech disturbance**

Dysarthria is a speech disorder due to disturbances of neuromuscular control (e.g., paralysis, spasticity), often caused by damage to the central or peripheral nervous system by illness or injury. Characterized by difficulty expressing certain words or sounds, dysarthria is often results in slurring or interrupted rhythm of speech. In severe cases, distortion of vowel sound may be significantly impaired. Speech intelligibility varies according to the severity of presentation and extent of neurological damage. Dysarthria is a common sequela of stroke and may be associated with dysphagia (difficulty swallowing) due to the damage of the nerves that control both functions. Other causal conditions include neuromuscular disease (MS, myasthenia gravis), head trauma, Bell's palsy, post-surgical states, and effects of certain medications.

Coding Tips

Dysarthria due to cerebrovascular accident is excluded from new code 784.51 and is reported with 438.13. New code 784.59 does not include stuttering, which is classified to default code 307.0. Dysphasia (784.59) is distinct from stuttering and requires separate classification codes.

Scenario

Patient presents for speech therapy evaluation for dysarthria due to Bell's palsy.

Code assignment:

V57.3   Speech-language therapy

785.51   Dysarthria

351.0   Bell's Palsy

Bilious Emesis (787.04)

- **787.04   Bilious emesis**

Vomiting (emesis) is a nonspecific complaint with many possible causal conditions. Certain types of vomiting can indicate very serious conditions, requiring a more extensive evaluation. The condition referred to as "bilious emesis" refers to emesis that contains bile and has been regurgitated from the duodenum; usually indicating ileus or obstruction distal to the junction of the duodenum and common bile duct. Certain causal conditions may initially present with nonbilious emesis and progress to bilious emesis as the condition worsens. Intestinal obstruction is a potentially serious, if not fatal, condition. Prompt examination followed by decompression or surgical correction of underlying causal pathology is required to prevent further complications, including necrotic bowel, perforation, sepsis, and death.

Coding Tips

New code 787.04 reports bilious emesis (vomiting) in an adult or child over 28 days old. To report bilious vomiting in a newborn, assign code 779.32.

Scenario

A 28-year-old patient presents for diagnostic work-up of cramping, RUQ abdominal pain, and bilious emesis.

Code assignment:

787.04	Bilious emesis
789.02	Abdominal pain, right upper quadrant

Colic (789.7)

● **789.7 Colic**

In neonates and infants, colic is often defined as crying for more than three hours a day, three days a week for more than three weeks in an otherwise well-fed, healthy baby. However, excessive crying or fussiness does not necessarily indicate colic. Colic is associated with intense, inconsolable crying that occurs in predictable episodes; nearly the same time every day, typically late afternoon or evening. The duration of these episodes may range from a few minutes to in excess of three hours or more. Posture changes are common in colic episodes; the infant will appear tense, with rigid abdomen, clenched fists or curled-up legs.

Colic generally affects newborns and infants between 3 and 12 weeks of age. Although distressing to parents, colic is a benign condition and typically ends by 9 months of age. The underlying cause is largely unknown, yet is thought to include allergies, lactose intolerance, immature digestive system, or other environmental stressors. In an otherwise healthy baby in whom underlying pathology has been ruled out, colic is treated palliatively, with methods to soothe the baby and provide support mechanisms to the parents.

Coding Tips

Report code 789.7 for colic in infants up to 12 months of age. Colic in adults and children over 12 months of age is reported with the appropriate site-specific code from subcategory 789.0.

Scenario

A 3-month-old infant presents for episodes of unrelenting, inconsolable crying. Examination reveals rigid abdomen and clenched fists, with no identifiable pathology. The physician documents "colic" as the primary diagnosis. The patient will be placed on alternate formula, with support resources provided to the parents.

Code assignment:

789.7	Colic

Inconclusive Mammogram (793.82)

● **793.82 Inconclusive mammogram**

A routine mammogram may be deemed inconclusive due to a finding documented as "dense breasts." This type of breast tissue is common in younger women and poses certain mammography challenges because the density of their breasts can hide a tumor. This is not considered an abnormal condition but one that requires further testing to confirm that no malignant condition exists. Digital mammography may be able to detect suspicious lesions in dense breast tissue by offering enhanced magnification and alternative viewing capabilities.

Coding Tips

The title of category 793 was modified to allow the term "abnormal" to be nonessential, therefore allowing the inclusion of inconclusive, but not necessarily abnormal, test findings in the category. The finding "dense breasts" is included in new code 793.82 and may be indexed under "Breast, dense," "Findings, dense breasts," or "Findings, inconclusive due to dense breasts."

Scenario

A 26-year old female presents for mammogram. Her sister has been diagnosed recently with breast cancer at the age of 29. Examination reveals dense breast tissue, obscuring certain views resulting in inconclusive results. Clinical correlation with the patient's history may necessitate repeat digital examination to assess tissue for changes.

Code assignment:

793.82	Inconclusive mammogram
V16.3	Family history of malignant neoplasm, breast

Signs and Symptoms Involving Emotional State (799.21–799.29)

● **799.21 Nervousness**
● **799.22 Irritability**
● **799.23 Impulsiveness**
● **799.24 Emotional lability**
● **799.25 Demoralization and apathy**
● **799.29 Other signs and symptoms involving emotional state**

Traumatic brain injury (TBI) includes the initial injury out of which manifestations may develop over variable time periods. Each person's injury can manifest itself in different ways, including a diverse constellation of cognitive, neurological, physical, sensory, and psychosocial conditions. In TBI, the normal control of emotions may be disrupted, resulting in emotional lability. These emotional changes may be experienced as rapidly changing and intense emotions. The area of the brain injured may also play a significant role in the nature of associated emotional or behavioral manifestations. Trauma to the brainstem can lead to disorientation, frustration, and anger. Damage to the temporal lobes may induce seizures and other behavioral disorders. The frontal lobe is a common area affected by TBI due to its size and prominence in cranial structure. Injury to the frontal lobe may manifest as cognitive dysfunction, impaired judgment, and increased impulsivity. These emotional effects are commonly managed with medical (e.g., SSRIs), behavioral, and other rehabilitative therapies.

Coding Tips

Coding guidelines allow the reporting of a symptom or condition code in conjunction with a late effect code when reporting such symptoms due to previous injury. Assign the new subcategory 799.2 codes, as appropriate, to report specific symptoms of organic cause in the absence of a documented mental disorder.

Scenario

A 29-year old male presents for review and adjustment of psychiatric medications for impulsive behavior and emotional lability related to late effects of previous traumatic intracranial brain injury.

Code assignment:

799.23	Impulsiveness
799.24	Emotional lability
907.0	Late effect of intracranial injury without mention of skull fracture

Apparent Life-Threatening Event in Infant (799.82)

● **799.82 Apparent life-threatening event in infant**

The term ALTE describes a clinical syndrome in which a variety of symptoms may occur, possibly as a result of identifiable diseases or conditions (e.g., gastroesophageal reflux, respiratory disease, or seizures). Due to the wide variety of possible causes, work-up may be extensive. In approximately one-half of the cases, despite extensive work-up, no cause for the episode can be identified. These events can occur during sleep, wakefulness, or feeding, although more than half of the episodes reported have occurred when the infant was awake. Infants particularly vulnerable to ATLE are those born at greater that 37 weeks of gestational age, and those on home cardiorespiratory monitoring. An ATLE event may manifest with cyanosis and apnea as predominant presenting symptoms, accompanied by syncope, apnea, altered or loss of consciousness, difficulty breathing, pallor, stiffness, floppiness, choking, red face, limb jerking, and vomiting. Once an underlying etiology is identified, further testing may not be indicated unless ALTEs continue or a risk for future ALTEs is established. Infants with idiopathic ALTE and certain underlying conditions have a greater risk of sudden infant death syndrome(SIDS), often necessitating home apnea/bradycardia monitoring.

Coding Tips

New code 779.82 may be reported as the principal or first-listed diagnosis when the underlying cause has not been determined. Additional codes should be assigned for associated symptoms reported as secondary diagnoses. When the underlying cause has been determined, that condition should be reported as the principal or first-listed diagnosis rather than ALTE. However, ALTE may be reported as a secondary diagnosis in this situation when ALTE is specifically documented.

Scenario

A newborn infant presents for observation and evaluation after an apparent life-threatening event (ATLE). The patient sustained an observed spontaneous episode of seizure followed by an apneic episode characterized by breathing cessation, cyanosis, and bradycardia.

Code assignment:

799.82	Apparent life-threatening event in infant
770.81	Primary apnea of newborn
779.81	Neonatal bradycardia
779.0	Convulsions in newborn

Chapter 17: Injury and Poisoning (800–999)

Torus Fracture of Ulna (813.46), Radius and Ulna (813.47)

▲ **813.45   Torus fracture of radius (alone)**
● **813.46   Torus fracture of ulna (alone)**

● **813.47   Torus fracture of radius and ulna**

Torus fractures (a.k.a., buckle fracture, incomplete fracture) are common injuries among the pediatric population. It is commonly a result of axial loading on a long bone of an extremity; such as falling on an outstretched hand. Torus (buckle) fractures of the radius are the most common; although they often occur in either or both of the long bones of the distal upper extremity (radius or ulna) or the humerus. This type of fracture is characterized by the buckling in on itself of one side of the bone without disrupting the other side. This characteristic "buckling" is due to the softer nature of the child's developing bone, allowing for the bone to compress, buckle, or "collapse" on one side, instead of break. Diagnostic imaging readily identifies torus fracture. These are generally quick-healing injuries treated with immobilization by casting or splinting.

Coding Tips

A new subterm "buckle" has been added to the main term "Fracture" in the Alphabetic Index. An instructional note directs the coder to "see Fracture, torus." Site-specific subterms have been added after the "Fracture, torus" listing. The code description for 813.45 Torus fracture of radius, (alone) was revised to designate this code as applicable to the radius only. New codes 813.46 and 813.47 have been created to expand the subclassification to include anatomic specificity.

Scenario

A 3-year-old female presents to the emergency department with right upper limb pain after falling from playground equipment. Diagnostic imaging reveals a buckle fracture of the distal radius and ulna.

Code assignment:

813.47	Torus fracture of radius and ulna

Nursemaid's Elbow (832.2)

● **832.2   Nursemaid's elbow**

A subluxation is a partial dislocation. Nursemaid's elbow is a common specific type of partial dislocation of the radial head whereby the head of the radius is dislocated from its encirclement by annular ligament, which slips or tears over the radial head. Subluxation of the radial head most commonly occurs in children under the age of five. The mechanism of injury is often one of a sudden pull on the upper limb. Upon presentation, the injured elbow is often pronated, partially flexed, and held by the side of the body with pain and tenderness over the anterolateral radial head. Manual reduction of the dislocation is often effectively performed in the emergency department, often with an immediate relief of pain. Immobilization may not be necessary if treatment is immediately sought. However, if treatment is delayed, immobilization and splinting are indicated.

Coding Tips

New code 832.2 provides a unique classification for this commonly occurring injury in young children. The Alphabetic Index entry for nursemaid's elbow was revised from code 832.0 to new code 832.2. Fifth-digit subclassifications applicable to 832.0 and 832.1 are not valid with code 832.2.

Scenario

A 3-year-old male presents to the emergency department with elbow pain following a jerking injury intended to prevent the child from running into a busy parking lot. Diagnostic imaging confirms dislocation of radial head consistent with nursemaid's elbow. Manual reduction of dislocation was performed with immediate pain relief.

Code assignment:

832.2	Nursemaid's elbow

Poisoning by Antidepressants (969.00–969.09) and Psychostimulants (969.70–969.71)

●	969.00	**Antidepressant, unspecified**
●	969.01	**Monoamine oxidase inhibitors**
●	969.02	**Selective serotonin and norepinephrine reuptake inhibitors**
●	969.03	**Selective serotonin reuptake inhibitors**
●	969.04	**Tetracyclic antidepressants**
●	969.05	**Tricyclic antidepressants**
●	969.09	**Other antidepressants**
●	969.70	**Psychostimulant, unspecified**
●	969.71	**Caffeine**
●	969.72	**Amphetamines**
●	969.73	**Methylphenidate**
●	969.79	**Other psychostimulants**

Psychotropic drugs and substances may be defined as those that affect or alter mental activity, behavior, perception, or mood. Common psychotropic substances include stimulants, tranquilizers, sedatives, and antidepressants. There are multiple types and classes of antidepressants widely available, including monoamine oxidase inhibitors (MAOIs), tricyclic antidepressants (TCAs), tetracyclic antidepressants (TeCAs), selective serotonin reuptake inhibitors (SSRIs), and serotonin-norepinephrine reuptake inhibitors (SNRIs).

As with all medicines, it is possible for a person to overdose on these medications. The overdose effects vary depending on a number of factors, including how much medication is taken and if it is taken in combination any other medicines or substances. Certain antidepressants can cause serious adverse drug interactions when taken in combination with other medications such as triptans taken with (SSRIs). These interactions include serotonin syndrome; a potentially fatal condition characterized by muscle spasm, muscle paralysis, neurological damage, and renal failure.

Caffeine is a CNS stimulant, a mild diuretic and acts as a mild antidepressant. In excess, it may disrupt behavior in certain substance sensitive individuals. Caffeinated beverages have become popular and are widely available in various forms, including coffee, soft drinks, and energy drinks. Symptoms of overdose and poisoning may vary according to individual tolerances, but may include dizziness, breathlessness, chest discomfort, nervousness, and irritability. Excessive doses may cause more severe multisystemic and potentially fatal symptoms such as arrhythmia, hypertension, seizure, respiratory failure, cerebral edema. Headache, irritability, and lethargy are commonly associated with caffeine withdrawal, which can be more effectively managed by slowly tapering off intake. Individuals who are particularly caffeine- or substance-sensitive seem to have a higher incidence of these symptoms.

Coding Tips

Subcategories 969.0 and 969.7 were expanded to fifth-digit subclassifications, creating unique codes to report specific substances. Accordingly, multiple subterms have been added to the Table of Drugs and Chemicals to assist in specific reporting. Report also any additional associated manifestations or substance abuse or dependence, as documented.

Scenario

A 19-year-old patient with a historically limited caffeine intake presents to the emergency department after losing track of the amount of Red Bull and coffee she drank in an attempt to stay awake to study for examinations. Symptoms of dizziness, breathlessness, chest discomfort, and tachycardia are consistent with caffeine overdose.

Code assignment:

969.71	Poisoning by psychostimulants, Caffeine
E854.2	Accidental poisoning by other psychotropic agents, Psychostimulants

Failed Moderate Sedation During Procedure (995.24)

● **995.24 Failed moderate sedation during procedure**

Many minor procedures do not require full anesthesia, and can be satisfactorily managed with moderate (conscious) sedation. However, in some situations, inadequate sedation can occur, resulting in unsafe conditions for the patient. A patient may exhibit an adverse or idiosyncratic response to the sedation, become under- or oversedated, be unable to maintain a patent airway, or experience hemodynamic compromise. These situations may extend beyond the capabilities of the provider administering the sedation. This often requires urgent intervention, such as enlisting the services of an anesthesiologist or other expert to ensure a safe outcome for the patient by administering deep sedation or anesthesia. Patients may have a history of such situations during previous procedures, which necessitates planned intervention during subsequent procedures to prevent a similar adverse sedation event.

Coding Tips

New code 995.24 includes failed moderate or conscious sedation. This code should be reported for oversedation, undersedation—including inadequate sedation, or for any adverse or idiosyncratic reaction to the agent administered. Assign secondary codes to further specify any associated symptoms or conditions, as appropriate.

Scenario

A pediatric patient with seizure disorder presents for lumbar puncture. Upon administration of moderate sedation (barbiturate), the patient became hypoxic and hypotensive. This was corrected satisfactorily with .01mg/ kg of Flumazenil.

Code assignment:

345.90	Epilepsy, unspecified
995.24	Failed moderate sedation during procedure
E937.0	Adverse effect, sedatives an hypnotics, Barbiturates
458.9	Hypotension, unspecified
786.03	Apnea

Supplementary Classification of Factors Influencing Health Status and Contact with Health Services (V01–V89)

Personal History of Tumors, Neuroendocrine (V10.91) and Unspecified Type (V10.90)

● **V10.90   Personal history of unspecified malignant neoplasm**
● **V10.91   Personal history of malignant neuroendocrine tumor**

Neuroendocrine cells produce and secrete regulatory hormones. Tumors comprising these cells are consequently capable of producing hormonal syndromes (e.g., carcinoid syndrome) in which the normal hormonal balance required to support body system functions is adversely affected. A patient with a history of neuroendocrine tumor may require specialized treatments and outcomes management, since some manifestations of neuroendocrine tumor present in a particularly aggressive manner and may be recalcitrant to conventional treatment. For this reason, management often includes hormonal therapies.

Coding Tips

New code V10.91 allows for the reporting of a history of primary malignant neuroendocrine tumor in those situations when that status may play a role or have an impact in the patient's health care. Assign an additional code first for any functional activity, such as carcinoid syndrome (259.2), as appropriate.

Scenario

A 68-year-old patient presents with biopsy-confirmed metastatic carcinoid lesions of the liver. She has a history of previously resected primary transverse carcinoid colon malignancy, resected two years previously.

Code assignment:

209.72	Secondary neuroendocrine tumor of the liver
V10.91	Personal history of malignant neuroendocrine tumor

Personal History of Traumatic Brain Injury (V15.52)

● **V15.52   History of traumatic brain injury**

Traumatic brain injury (TBI) includes the initial injury out of which manifestations may develop over variable time periods. Each person's injury can manifest itself in different ways, including a diverse constellation of cognitive, neurological, physical, sensory, and psychosocial conditions. A patient may present for services that are in some manner related to a previous old or healed injury.

Coding Tips

New code V15.52 represents the patient's post-TBI status. Assign this code to report a causal link to any associated complications or conditions resulting from the injury or its treatments.

Scenario

A 48-year-old patient presents for follow-up MRI to evaluate recurrent headaches. He has a history of traumatic brain injury in the remote past.

Code assignment:

784.0	Headache
V15.52	History of traumatic brain injury

Personal History of Failed Moderate Sedation (V15.80)

● **V15.80   History of failed moderate sedation**

A patient who has exhibited failed moderate sedation during past interventional episodes may require precautionary measures to ensure optimal outcome. Such past situations may have included over- or undersedation, adverse reactions to medications, or other respiratory or hemodynamic responses. In these cases, nonroutine services may be necessary to prevent another failed sedation episode (e.g., medication change, specialist services).

Coding Tips

New code V15.80 identifies patients with a history of failed sedation and provides a supportive rationale for preventative interventions and other measures performed due to the associated risks. Assign this code to assist in supporting medical necessity, where appropriate.

Scenario

A patient presents for carpal tunnel release under moderate sedation. An anesthetist has been called in to observe and assist as necessary, since the patient has a history of failed sedation during a previous surgical episode.

Code assignment:

354.0	Carpal tunnel syndrome
V15.80	History of failed moderate sedation

Personal History of Underimmunization Status (V15.83)

● **V15.83 Underimmunization status**

According to the U.S. recommended immunization schedule, a significant population has received part or only some of the recommended immunizations. This population includes families without immunization or consistent health insurance coverage, foreign adoptees, and other immigrating persons. The underimmunized population poses public health risks by allowing themselves to be in a state whereby they could contract otherwise preventable diseases and spread them to others.

Coding Tips

New code V15.83 identifies the status of the person who is at risk for underimmunization on the recommended schedule and includes both delinquent and lapsed immunization status.

Scenario

A 5-year-old adoptee presents for medical examination. Upon review of records, the physician documents underimmunization status and orders antibody testing.

Code assignment:

V70.3	Other medical examination for administrative purposes
V15.83	Underimmunization status

Health Supervision for Newborn under 8 Days Old (V20.31) and 8–28 Days Old (V20.32)

● **V20.31 Health supervision for newborn under 8 days old**
● **V20.32 Health supervision for newborn 8 to 28 days old**

The American Academy of Pediatrics (AAP) recommends that all newborns have a follow-up examination by their primary care provider within two days of discharge from the hospital or birthing center to assess health status, perform state-regulated tests as clinically indicated, and to identify potential parental support or future health care needs.

Coding Tips

New codes V20.31 and V20.32 have been created to specifically report newborn health supervision encounters. Classifications are separated by age; in the first seven days of life versus eight to 28 days of life, in accordance with AAP guidelines for post-hospital newborn care.

Scenario

A five-day-old infant presents to the pediatrician's office for a routine newborn check to assess health status.

Code assignment:

V20.31	Health supervision for newborn under 8 days old

Encounter for Fertility Preservation Counseling (V26.42) or Procedure (V26.82)

● **V26.42 Encounter for fertility preservation counseling**
● **V26.82 Encounter for fertility preservation procedure**

Patients may seek fertility preservation counseling or services following a diagnosis of certain illnesses such as cancer. The incidence of cancer and other diseases in younger populations, coupled with the increase in individuals who wish to start or expand their families later in life have resulted in many patients' seeking measures to preserve their ability to procreate. The effect of disease (including cancer) and its associated treatment on a patient's fertility may be temporary or permanent, depending on the factors involved. The impact of such factors may depend on the nature of the disease or type of tumor, the type and dosage of therapeutic regimens, the route of administration or anatomic site of treatment, and the patient's health and fertility status before diagnosis and treatment.

Fertility preservation counseling may include discussion regarding the timing of conception in relation to initiation of treatment, donation of reproductive products (i.e., eggs, sperm), and possible surgical modification options that would allow for physical fertility preservation (e.g., organ preservation). Fertility preservation procedures may include in vitro fertilization or cryopreservation; the harvesting and freezing of oocytes, sperm, testicular or ovarian tissue, and embryos for future use. In vitro fertilization may be used to harvest eggs for safekeeping before initiation of cancer therapy, with reimplantation upon disease remission. Similarly, male patients may donate sperm to preserve by freezing methods.

Coding Tips

New codes V26.42 and V26.82 report encounters for which a patient receives counseling or procedures for fertility preservation and are not to be confused with encounters for genetic or expectant parent counseling and testing classifiable elsewhere. The Alphabetic Index lists these encounters under the main term "Admission" and subterms "counseling" and "fertility preservation."

Scenario

A 32-year-old ovarian cancer patient presents for fertility preservation counseling to assess potential for cryopreservation of oocytes prior to initiation of chemotherapy.

Code assignment:

V26.42	Encounter for fertility preservation counseling
183.0	Malignant neoplasm, ovary

Fitting and Adjustment of Gastric Lap Band (V53.51)

● **V53.50 Fitting and adjustment of intestinal appliance and device**
● **V53.51 Fitting and adjustment of gastric lap band**
● **V53.59 Fitting and adjustment of other gastrointestinal appliance and device**

Gastric banding ("lap band") is a type of bariatric surgery to treat obesity. A restrictive inflatable silicone ring is placed around the top portion of the stomach, restricting the expansion of the stomach and slowing the passage of food. The silicone ring can be inflated or deflated as necessary to achieve desired weight loss. Tightening of the band is achieved by adding saline to inflate the band. If vomiting or difficulty in swallowing occurs, the band may need to be loosened by reducing the amount of saline. When adjusted optimally, the patient can achieve weight loss by feeling full with less food, slowing digestion and increasing the feeling of fullness after a meal, yet allowing adequate nutrition. A self-adjusting subcutaneous port is connected to the band, allowing adjustments to be made through the skin with a syringe; adding or releasing saline as necessary. Patients may be allowed to self-adjust the band; however, physician office visits may be necessary to optimal adjustment.

Coding Tips

Code V53.5 has been expanded to fifth-digit subclassifications to allow for creation of a unique code for gastric lab band (V53.51) encounters and to allow for classification of similar encounters specifically for fitting and adjustment of other gastrointestinal appliances or devices. The Alphabetic Index lists these encounters under the main term "Admission."

Scenario

A patient presents for a follow-up visit to the bariatric surgeon for the purpose of assessment and adjustment of gastric lap band. The band was assessed and adjusted with sterile saline injection.

Code assignment:

V53.51	Fitting and adjustment of gastric lap band
V45.86	Bariatric surgery status

Family Circumstances (V60.81–V60.89, V61.07–V61.08, V61.23–V61.25, V61.42)

- **V60.81** **Foster care (status)**
- **V60.89** **Other specified housing or economic circumstances**
- **V61.08** **Family disruption due to other extended absence of family member**
- **V61.23** **Counseling for parent-biological child problem**
- **V61.24** **Counseling for parent-adopted child problem**
- **V61.25** **Counseling for parent (guardian)-foster child problem**
- **V61.42** **Substance abuse in family**

Certain familial disruption circumstances can affect how care providers interact with patients or manage medical problems, or they may cause or exacerbate certain conditions for which the patient may seek counseling or other medical care. Disruptive or stressful situations (e.g., physical separation, death, deployment, foster care, adoption, substance abuse) can manifest as emotional, behavioral, or health problems and have adverse effects not only for the patient, but for family members as well.

Coding Tips

Assign new codes for foster care status (V60.81), substance abuse in family (V61.42), and the newly expanded counseling codes (V61.23–V61.25) to report those family circumstances for which individuals and families may seek health-related services. Sequencing depends on the circumstances of the encounter. Certain codes within these rubrics may be allowable only as first or additional use codes.

Scenario

A 10-year-old foster child presents for counseling for problems adjusting to his new foster home and foster parents.

Code assignment:

V61.25	Counseling for parent (guardian)-foster child problem
V60.81	Foster care (status)

Laboratory Examinations (V72.60–V72.69)

- **V72.60** **Laboratory examination, unspecified**
- **V72.61** **Antibody response examination**
- **V72.62** **Laboratory examination ordered as part of a routine general medical examination**
- **V72.63** **Pre-procedural laboratory examination**
- **V72.69** **Other laboratory examination**

Antibody response examinations ensure that persons in need of vaccines receive them and that adequately vaccinated patients are not overimmunized. In lieu of adequate vaccination documentation, prevaccination serologic testing helps determine immunity and eliminating unnecessary vaccinations. Similarly, serologic susceptibility testing may help reduce the cost of vaccinating adult populations that have an expected high prevalence of disease. Postvaccination testing for antibody response helps determine the appropriate postexposure prophylaxis, since medical management of exposures often depends on the patient's immune status.

Coding Tips

Code V72.6 has been expanded to fifth-digit subclassifications to provide specific codes to report laboratory service encounters for the specific purposes of antibody testing, general medical examinations, and pre-procedural circumstances. These codes are acceptable as first-listed or additional diagnoses.

Scenario

A foreign adoptee presents for antibody testing to assess immunization status needs.

Code assignment:

V72.61	Antibody response examination

Special Screening for Traumatic Brain Injury (V80.01) and Neurological Conditions (V80.09)

- **V80.01** **Traumatic brain injury**
- **V80.09** **Other neurological conditions**

Screening examinations are often indicated to assess and diagnose cognitive deficits related to traumatic brain injury (TBI) or other neurological conditions. Depending on the nature and scope of the testing, neurological and TBI screening exams help triage patients into evaluation, establishing diagnoses and treatment plans and obtaining appropriate education and clinical resources.

Coding Tips

Report new codes V80.01 and V80.09 to support referrals for comprehensive diagnostic testing, which may be required to establish or confirm a diagnosis. Screening codes may be reported as the first-listed diagnosis if the screening is the reason for the encounter, or as a secondary diagnosis if a screening examination is performed during an encounter for other health problems. History or status V codes may be used in conjunction with screening codes to explain the reason for the screening, if applicable.

Scenario

An enlisted military officer reports for routine post-tour of duty TBI screening examination. History reveals no known injury during recent tour in which he was engaged in combat.

Code assignment:

V80.01	Special screening for neurological, eye and ear diseases, Neurological conditions, Traumatic brain injury

Contact with and (Suspected) Exposure to Algae Bloom (V87.32)

- **V87.32** **Contact with and (suspected) exposure to algae bloom**

The term "algae bloom" describes the rapid multiplication and accumulation of algae, which presents as a scum or foam on the water's surface. Affected water sources may change in color to blue-green, neon green, or reddish brown. This accumulation may cause a bad odor or taste to the water. Certain types of algae (e.g., microcystis) secrete toxins into water sources. Blooms may consist of several species of algae. Health risks are associated with exposure, which includes contact, ingestion, or inhalation of algae bloom. Contact exposure to the skin may result in rashes, lesions, and blisters. Ingestion may cause headaches, nausea and vomiting, and muscular pains. Exposure by inhalation may cause asthma-like symptoms, sore throat, or irritated upper respiratory tract. Severe adverse reactions may include seizure, hepatic failure, and respiratory arrest, although these severe reactions are relatively rare. Children and those with weakened immune systems are at increased risk for severe reactions to exposure.

Coding Tips

New code V87.32 reports contact or exposure to algae bloom in the absence of associated signs or symptoms of illness for which health care services may be sought to assess health care risks.

This code identifies the possible contact and exposure to an algae bloom for a person who may have not yet developed symptoms. Similarly, this code may be used to report circumstances in which an individual may have symptoms suggesting that the person was in the vicinity of an algae bloom, but a definitive cause has not been confirmed.

Scenario

A park ranger presents for observation after occupational exposure to algae bloom in a local pond.

Code assignment:

V87.32   Contact with and (suspected) exposure to algae bloom

Personal History of Immunosuppression, (V87.46) Estrogen (V87.43), and Steroid (V87.44, V87.45) Therapy

- **V87.43   Personal history of estrogen therapy**
- **V87.44   Personal history of inhaled steroid therapy**
- **V87.45   Personal history of systemic steroid therapy**
- **V87.46   Personal history of immunosuppression therapy**

Patients may be initially asymptomatic following exposures to drugs, chemicals, and other substances but develop subsequent health concerns as a result. Adverse effects of exposures (whether occupational, environmental or therapeutic) include medical problems that persist for months or years after the initial exposure.

Coding Tips

Report a code from subcategory V87.4 when a history of past drug therapy is linked or otherwise related to current health problems, or is documented to present hazards to the patient's long term health.

Scenario

An otherwise healthy postmenopausal 60-year-old female with endometrial hyperplasia presents for repeat endometrial biopsy. She has a history of estrogen therapy, which as been discontinued in recent years but is documented as a significant risk factor, necessitating further testing.

Code assignment:

621.30   Endometrial hyperplasia, unspecified

V87.43   Personal history of estrogen therapy

Volume 3 Procedure Codes

Chapter 3A: Other Miscellaneous Diagnostic and Therapeutic Procedures (17)

Cardiac Contractility Modulation (CCM)

- **17.5   Additional Cardiovascular Procedures**
- **17.51   Implantation of rechargeable cardiac contractility modulation [CCM], total system**
- **17.52   Implantation or replacement of cardiac contractility modulation [CCM] rechargeable pulse generator only**

During the absolute refractory period (ARP), the heart muscle is incapable of responding to the next excitatory stimulus. Cardiac contractility modulation signals are nonexcitatory signals that enhance cardiac strength and performance rather than initiating a new heartbeat. Automatic implantable cardioverter/defibrillators (AICD) and pacemakers control and restore normal rhythm of the heart. The cardiac contractility modulation (CCM) system delivers nonexcitatory impulses to the right ventricular septum during the absolute refractory period to improve the strength and performance of the heart muscle. The implantable pulse generator delivers the CCM signals to the heart through standard pacemaker leads. Implantation of a CCM system includes formation of pocket, placement of a catheter and transvenous leads, and intraoperative evaluation of lead signals and sensing threshold and defibrillator threshold measurements. CCM systems are used for the treatment

of moderate to severe heart failure. The CCM system is used alone or in combination with AICD.

Coding Tips

Testing of the device is included in the code and should not be reported separately. In addition to the implantation of the total CCM system (17.51), code any concomitant coronary bypass (36.01–36.19), extracorporeal circulation (39.61), or insertion or replacement of automatic cardioverter/defibrillator — total system (37.94). When reporting the replacement of the pulse generator of the CCM system only (17.52), code also any revision of device pocket (37.79) or revision of leads or electrodes (37.75). Caution: The index lists CCM procedures under the main term "Implantation" rather than under "Insertion."

Scenario

A patient with chronic systolic and diastolic congestive heart failure with a pre-existing AICD is admitted for implantation of a cardiac contractility modulation system implantation to improve heart function. The patient received a total Optimizer III® system. During the procedure a catheter-based transducer was introduced for hemodynamic measurements during the positioning of three standard pacemaker leads — two placed in the right ventricular septum and one in the right atrium. The leads were connected to the implantable pulse generator which was placed in a subcutaneous pectoral pocket. Intraoperative testing of the device was performed to ensure appropriate function.

Code assignment:

428.42   Chronic combined systolic and diastolic heart failure

428.0   Congestive heart failure, unspecified

17.51   Implantation of rechargeable cardiac contractility modulation [CCM], total system

Laser Interstitial Thermal Therapy [LITT]

- **17.6   MRI-guided laser interstitial thermal therapy (LITT)**
- **17.61   Laser interstitial thermal therapy [LITT] of lesion or tissue of brain under guidance**
- **17.62   Laser interstitial thermal therapy [LITT] of lesion or tissue of head and neck under guidance**
- **17.63   Laser interstitial thermal therapy [LITT] of lesion or tissue of liver under guidance**
- **17.69   Laser interstitial thermal therapy [LITT] of lesion or tissue of other and unspecified site under guidance**

Treatment options for patients with brain cancer typically include a combination of surgical resection, stereotactic radiosurgery, external beam or intracranial radiation, and chemotherapy. Laser interstitial thermal therapy (LITT) under real time MRI guidance has been developed for ablation of brain tumors. LITT for tumor ablation uses a laser probe which focuses the laser's energy on the targeted tumor tissue reducing or avoiding damage to surrounding tissue. LITT under guidance such as MRI or ultrasound has been effective at destroying or reducing the size of tumors in the brain, head and neck, thyroid, lung, breast, liver, bone, prostate, uterus, and rectum. The treating physician visualizes the procedure in real time using a standard 1.5T MRI scanner with software and controls to remotely monitor and position devices allowing precise control of the thermal ablation. A thin, side-firing laser combined with gas cooling within the probe tip is inserted through a small burr hole in the skull. The laser energy discharged heats the targeted tissue while cooling all surrounding tissue allowing the physician to selectively treat the tumor tissue without damaging other tissue.

Coding Tip

A new subcategory was created in 2010 to include site-specific codes for LITT of the brain (17.61), the head and neck (17.62), and the liver (17.63). Prior to the creation of subcategory 17.6, MRI-guided LITT of a brain lesion or tissue was coded with 01.59 Other excision or destruction of lesion or tissue of brain.

Scenario

A patient is admitted for treatment of medulloblastoma in the fourth ventricle, between the brain stem and the cerebellum. After a 1 cm burr hole is drilled through the skull at the location of the tumor, the physician uses the AutoLITT™ workstation in the MRI control room to monitor and control the thermal ablation in real time. A standard MRI scanner guides the placement of the MRI-compatible laser probe through the transcranial burr hole. The laser is used to thermally ablate the tumor tissue while simultaneously cooling the surrounding tissue to prevent that tissue from being damaged. The physician repositions the probe to treat different areas of the tumor. After the treatment is completed, the physician withdraws the probe and the burr hole is closed.

Code assignment:

191.5	Malignant neoplasm of ventricles of brain
17.61	Laser interstitial thermal therapy [LITT] of lesion or tissue of brain under guidance

Intravenous Infusion Of Clofarabine

- **17.7   Other diagnostic and therapeutic procedures**
- **   17.70   Intravenous infusion of clofarabine**

Clofarabine is an antineoplastic treatment option for acute lymphoblastic leukemia (ALL) and acute myeloid leukemia (AML). Clofarabine is a purine nucleoside antimetabolite that interferes with cell division and the development of new cancer cells. Clofarabine was originally approved by the Food and Drug Administration to treat relapsed or refractory ALL in pediatric patients who have previously received at least two other types of treatment. Clofarabine has also proven effective in the treatment of adults 70 years or older with AML and an unfavorable prognosis factor such as poor performance status, advanced age, or an antecedent hematologic disorder. Myeloid leukemia is a rapid proliferation of malignant myeloblasts. Patients with AML typically present with symptoms resulting from bone marrow failure such as anemia, neutropenia, thrombocytopenia, or from organ infiltration with leukemic cells.

Coding Tips

Do not assign code 99.25 Injection or infusion of cancer chemotherapeutic substance, to report intravenous infusion of clofarabine. A new subcategory, 17.7 Other pharmaceuticals, and a unique code, 17.70 Intravenous infusion of clofarabine, were created specifically to report an intravenous infusion of clofarabine.

Scenario

A 75-year-old patient with myelodysplastic syndrome secondary to aggressive cancer treatment is admitted for the first cycle of CLOLAR® therapy for treatment of AML. The clofarabine is administered intravenously at a dose of 52 mg/m2, over a two-hour period. The initial dosing cycle is once daily for five consecutive days. This dosing cycle will be repeated in two to six weeks depending on the patient's response to treatment.

Code assignment:

V58.11	Encounter for antineoplastic chemotherapy
205.00	Myeloid leukemia, Acute, without mention of remission
238.75	Myelodysplastic syndrome, unspecified
17.70	Intravenous infusion of clofarabine

Chapter 6: Operations on the Respiratory system (30–34)

Endoscopic Bronchial Valve Insertion

- **33.73   Endoscopic insertion or replacement of bronchial valve(s), multiple lobes**

Bronchial valve insertion is typically performed to treat severe emphysema or to manage prolonged air leaks. Emphysema is a chronic, progressive disease characterized by the destruction of lung tissue in multiple lobes. Air leaks can be a result of traumatic, iatrogenic, or spontaneous causes, but air leaks most commonly occur following surgery (e.g., lobectomy, segmentectomy, or lung volume reduction surgery) as a result of lung tissue that has not completely closed and sealed. Endoscopic bronchial valve insertion is a minimally invasive

procedure because the valves are placed via a bronchoscopic procedure which does not require a surgical incision. Other treatments for air leaks include surgical intervention such as pleurodesis or insertion of drain tubes into the chest.

Bronchial valve insertion in multiple lobes of the lungs requires more clinical resources and time to perform than single lobe treatment. Consequently, a new code was created in subcategory 33.7 Other endoscopic procedures in bronchus or lung, for endoscopic insertion or replacement of bronchial valves in multiple lobes. New code 33.73 Endoscopic insertion or replacement of bronchial valve(s), multiple lobes, is used to report these situations. Prior to creation of this new code, endoscopic insertion or replacement of bronchial valves was reported with code 33.71 Endoscopic insertion or replacement of bronchial valve(s), which did not capture the extent of treatment for multiple lobes versus a single lobe.

Coding Tips

The Spiration ®IBV® Valve System is approved to control prolonged or significant air leaks of the lung. Clinical investigation of the IBV® Valve System as a new treatment option for patients with severe emphysema is currently underway.

Review the operative report for the time and clinical resources (e.g., length of anesthesia, number of valves) required to perform the procedure because valve insertion in multiple lobes during the same procedural episode involves more time and resources than a single lobe.

Scenario

A patient is admitted for endobronchial valve insertion for treatment of severe emphysema. Due to the severity of the patient's emphysema, multiple lobes require treatment during the operative session. The physician uses a CT scan to determine the location and number of valves to be placed based on the extent of the disease in each lobe. Using an airway sizing kit, a balloon is inflated with saline at the target implantation site to determine the appropriate valve size for each airway. A catheter is passed through the bronchoscope, and the small umbrella-shaped valves are deployed into the segmental and subsegmental bronchi.

Code assignment:

492.8	Other emphysema
33.73	Endoscopic insertion or replacement of bronchial valve(s), multiple lobes

Chapter 7: Operations on the Cardiovascular System (35–39)

Optical Coherence Tomography

- **38.24   Intravascular imaging of coronary vessel(s) by optical coherence tomography [OCT]**
- **38.25   Intravascular imaging of non-coronary vessel(s) by optical coherence tomography [OCT]**

Coronary angiography is a commonly performed, two-dimensional imaging technique used to visualize atherosclerotic disease. Due to its limited imaging aspect, coronary angiography cannot identify details of a particular lesion such as the presence and composition of coronary atherosclerotic plaques. Intravascular ultrasound (IVUS) is also frequently used to assess coronary vascular lesions; however, IVUS uses sound waves to view the lumen and is limited by its low resolution. Optical coherence tomography (OCT) is a new technology developed for coronary plaque characterization. Optical coherence tomography provides enhanced resolution imaging which enables better assessment of the vessel with the coronary atherosclerotic plaque. OCT produces cross-sectional images of coronary and peripheral vessels using fiber-optic catheter probes and near-infrared electromagnetic radiation light. Intravascular OCT high-resolution images can identify intraluminal thrombus, thin cap fibroatheromas, and can also quantify macrophages within the plaque. OCT provides images of the coronary and peripheral vessel lumen and wall structures to assist in stenting procedures and to assess endothelial growth over stented vessels in the treatment of late stent thrombosis and re-stenosis.

Two new codes were created for 2010 to report the use of intravascular OCT of coronary and non-coronary vessels: 38.24 Intravascular imaging of coronary vessel(s) by optical coherence tomography [OCT] and 38.25 Intravascular imaging of non-coronary vessel(s) by optical coherence tomography [OCT].

Coding Tips

Coronary angiography is performed using a variety of techniques, and careful review of the documentation for specific information regarding the procedure is necessary to ensure accurate code assignment. Intravascular ultrasound (IVUS) of the coronary vessels is a catheter-based ultrasound imaging technique reported with code 00.24. Similar to a rotational IVUS catheter, the inner portion of the OCT catheter is a rotating optical fiber with an imaging lens attached to it using, however, near-infrared light instead of ultrasound. Code 88.57 Other and unspecified coronary arteriography, describes an unspecified coronary angiography procedure that is not classified elsewhere. SPY angiography (88.59 SPY intraoperative fluorescence vascular angiography) is an imaging technology used to test cardiac graft patency and technical adequacy at the time of coronary artery bypass grafting (CABG).

Scenario

A patient with coronary artery disease (CAD) undergoes optical coherence tomography imaging of his coronary atherosclerotic plaque. The physician uses a catheter-based system to assess vascular morphology, the vessel lumen, and plaque components. After the imaging catheter has been placed in the coronary artery, the physician uses a power injector connected to a catheter to flush saline and contrast to clear the vessel and begins to acquire the images. The inner member of the catheter is a rotating optical fiber with an imaging lens attached. The lens is moved across the targeted area while the recording takes place. After the image acquisition, the physician reviews the images and analyzes various measurements to guide clinical decision making.

Code assignment:

414.00   Coronary atherosclerosis of unspecified type of vessel, native or graft

38.24   Intravascular imaging of coronary vessel(s) by optical coherence tomography [OCT]

Endovascular Coil Embolization

● **39.75   Endovascular embolization or occlusion of vessel(s) of head or neck using bare coils**

● **39.76   Endovascular embolization or occlusion of vessel(s) of head or neck using bioactive coils**

Endovascular coil embolization is a minimally invasive procedure used to treat brain aneurysms or artery wall weaknesses that result in dilation and ballooning of a blood vessel. Left untreated, an aneurysm may lead to stroke or death. Filling an aneurysm with coils initiates a healing response and prevents rupture of the aneurysm. ICD-9-CM code 39.72, Endovascular repair or occlusion of head and neck vessels, does not differentiate between the use of bare platinum coils (BPCs) and biodegradable polymer coils. Codes for endovascular treatment of vessel(s) of the head or neck using BPCs and bioactive coils were created in subcategory 39.7 Endovascular repair of vessel. Bioactive coils include an active biological agent to enhance occlusion and thrombus formation and have shown improved clinical outcomes for treating cerebral aneurysms.

Coding Tip

Endovascular procedures on vessels include embolization, implantation, occlusion, removal, and repair. Endovascular embolization or occlusion of head and neck vessels, other than the use of bare or bioactive coils e.g., adhesive glue or endografts is reported with code 39.72.

Scenario

A patient with a brain aneurysm is admitted for endovascular coiling. The physician inserts a catheter into the femoral artery and guides it to the aneurysm in the brain and places a Cerecyte® bioactive microcoil though the catheter into the aneurysm. Blood flow into the aneurysm is disrupted and rupture is prevented.

Code assignment:

437.3   Cerebral aneurysm, nonruptured

39.76   Endovascular embolization or occlusion of vessel(s) of head or neck using bioactive coils

Chapter 9: Operations on the Digestive System (42–54)

Colonic Stent Insertion

● **46.86   Endoscopic insertion of colonic stent(s)**
● **46.87   Other insertion of colonic stent(s)**

Colonic stents can be placed endoscopically, under fluoroscopic guidance, or using a combination of techniques. In a non-endoscopic, fluoroscopic stent insertion, an angiography catheter is inserted into the anus and advanced to the level of obstruction. Radiographic contrast is injected and a guidewire is placed. The stent delivery system is inserted over the guidewire and the stent is deployed. Contrast is injected to rule out any perforation.

Colonic stent insertion using self-expandable metal stents is an alternative to surgery in the treatment of patients with acute malignant colonic obstruction.

Prior to 2010, the Volume 3 procedure classification did not include a code to report an endoscopic insertion of a colonic stent. Coding guidance advised coders to report endoscopic colonic stenting with procedure code 46.85 Dilation of intestine. New codes for endoscopic and other insertion of colonic stent(s) were added to subcategory 46.8 Dilation and manipulation of intestine. Procedure code 46.85 Dilation of intestine, was revised with the addition of an exclusion term for the two new codes. Unique codes were created to report endoscopic and other insertion of colonic stent(s). Code 46.86 is assigned to report a colonoscopy through a stoma with transendoscopic stent insertion and code 46.87 Other insertion of colonic stent(s) reports non-endoscopic insertion and colonic stenting with fluoroscopic guidance only or by rectal guiding tube. In addition to code 46.87, code also any diagnostic procedure(s) performed synchronously.

Coding Tip

Currently three self-expandable colonic stents have been approved by the FDA: the Colonic Z-Stent®, the Enteral Wallstent®, and the Ultraflex™ Precision Colonic stent. Endoscopic insertion of these devices is reported using code 46.86.

Scenario

A patient is admitted for surgical treatment of an acute bowel obstruction. The physician inserts a colonic stent using endoscopic visualization with fluoroscopy. After the patient is sedated, the physician inserts the endoscope, visualizes the obstruction, and measures the length of the obstruction. Contrast is injected and a guidewire is placed through the scope beyond the level of the obstruction. A Colonic Z-Stent® stent designed to fit through the scope is inserted over the guidewire and deployed under endoscopic visualization with fluoroscopic confirmation.

Code assignment:

560.89   Other specified intestinal obstruction

46.86   Endoscopic insertion of colonic stent(s)

Coding Guidelines

Effective October 1, 2008
Note: The revised guidelines effective October 1, 2009 were not released in time to be included in this publication. The complete revised guidelines effective October 1, 2009 will be available on our Web site. Please log on to: www.ShopIngenix.com/productalerts to view and download the latest revisions to the official coding guidelines.

The Centers for Medicare and Medicaid Services (CMS) and the National Center for Health Statistics (NCHS), two departments within the U.S. Federal Government's Department of Health and Human Services (DHHS) provide the following guidelines for coding and reporting using the International Classification of Diseases, 9th Revision, Clinical Modification (ICD-9-CM). These guidelines should be used as a companion document to the official version of the ICD-9-CM as published on CD-ROM by the U.S. Government Printing Office (GPO).

These guidelines have been approved by the four organizations that make up the Cooperating Parties for the ICD-9-CM: the American Hospital Association (AHA), the American Health Information Management Association (AHIMA), CMS, and NCHS. These guidelines are included on the official government version of the ICD-9-CM, and also appear in "*Coding Clinic for ICD-9-CM*" published by the AHA.

These guidelines are a set of rules that have been developed to accompany and complement the official conventions and instructions provided within the ICD-9-CM itself. These guidelines are based on the coding and sequencing instructions in Volumes I, II and III of ICD-9-CM, but provide additional instruction. Adherence to these guidelines when assigning ICD-9-CM diagnosis and procedure codes is required under the Health Insurance Portability and Accountability Act (HIPAA). The diagnosis codes (Volumes 1-2) have been adopted under HIPAA for all healthcare settings. Volume 3 procedure codes have been adopted for inpatient procedures reported by hospitals. A joint effort between the healthcare provider and the coder is essential to achieve complete and accurate documentation, code assignment, and reporting of diagnoses and procedures. These guidelines have been developed to assist both the healthcare provider and the coder in identifying those diagnoses and procedures that are to be reported. The importance of consistent, complete documentation in the medical record cannot be overemphasized. Without such documentation accurate coding cannot be achieved. The entire record should be reviewed to determine the specific reason for the encounter and the conditions treated.

The term encounter is used for all settings, including hospital admissions. In the context of these guidelines, the term provider is used throughout the guidelines to mean physician or any qualified health care practitioner who is legally accountable for establishing the patient's diagnosis. Only this set of guidelines, approved by the Cooperating Parties, is official.

The guidelines are organized into sections. Section I includes the structure and conventions of the classification and general guidelines that apply to the entire classification, and chapter-specific guidelines that correspond to the chapters as they are arranged in the classification. Section II includes guidelines for selection of principal diagnosis for non-outpatient settings. Section III includes guidelines for reporting additional diagnoses in non-outpatient settings. Section IV is for outpatient coding and reporting.

Section I. Conventions, general coding guidelines and chapter specific guidelines

A. Conventions for the ICD-9-CM
1. Format:
2. Abbreviations
   a. Index abbreviations
   b. Tabular abbreviations
3. Punctuation
4. Includes and Excludes Notes and Inclusion terms
5. Other and Unspecified codes
   a. "Other" codes
   b. "Unspecified" codes
6. Etiology/manifestation convention ("code first", "use additional code" and "in diseases classified elsewhere" notes)
7. "And"
8. "With"
9. "See" and "See Also"

B. General Coding Guidelines
1. Use of Both Alphabetic Index and Tabular List
2. Locate each term in the Alphabetic Index
3. Level of Detail in Coding
4. Code or codes from 001.0 through V89
5. Selection of codes 001.0 through 999.9
6. Signs and symptoms
7. Conditions that are an integral part of a disease process
8. Conditions that are not an integral part of a disease process
9. Multiple coding for a single condition
10. Acute and Chronic Conditions
11. Combination Code
12. Late Effects
13. Impending or Threatened Condition
14. Reporting Same Diagnosis Code More than Once
15. Admissions/Encounters for Rehabilitation
16. Documentation for BMI and Pressure Ulcer Stages

C. Chapter-Specific Coding Guidelines
1. Chapter 1: Infectious and Parasitic Diseases (001-139)
   a. Human Immunodeficiency Virus (HIV) Infections
   b. Septicemia, Systemic Inflammatory Response Syndrome (SIRS), Sepsis, Severe Sepsis and Septic Shock
   c. Methicillin Resistant *Staphylococcus aureus* (MRSA) Conditions
2. Chapter 2: Neoplasms (140-239)
   a. Treatment directed at the malignancy
   b. Treatment of secondary site
   c. Coding and sequencing of complications
   d. Primary malignancy previously excised
   e. Admissions/Encounters involving chemotherapy, immunotherapy and radiation therapy
   f. Admission/encounter to determine extent of malignancy
   g. Symptoms, signs, and ill-defined conditions listed in Chapter 16 associated with neoplasms
   h. Admission/encounter for pain control/management
   i. Malignant neoplasm associated with transplanted organ
3. Chapter 3: Endocrine, Nutritional, and Metabolic Diseases and Immunity Disorders (240-279)
   a. Diabetes mellitus
4. Chapter 4: Diseases of Blood and Blood Forming Organs (280-289)
   a. Anemia of chronic disease
5. Chapter 5: Mental Disorders (290-319)
   Reserved for future guideline expansion
6. Chapter 6: Diseases of Nervous System and Sense Organs (320-389)
   a. Pain - Category 338
7. Chapter 7: Diseases of Circulatory System (390-459)
   a. Hypertension
   b. Cerebral infarction/stroke/cerebrovascular accident (CVA)
   c. Postoperative cerebrovascular accident
   d. Late Effects of Cerebrovascular Disease
   e. Acute myocardial infarction (AMI)
8. Chapter 8: Diseases of Respiratory System (460-519)
   a. Chronic Obstructive Pulmonary Disease [COPD] and Asthma
   b. Chronic Obstructive Pulmonary Disease [COPD] and Bronchitis
   c. Acute Respiratory Failure
   d. Influenza due to identified avian influenza virus (avian influenza)
9. Chapter 9: Diseases of Digestive System (520-579)
   Reserved for future guideline expansion
10. Chapter 10: Diseases of Genitourinary System (580-629)
    a. Chronic kidney disease
11. Chapter 11: Complications of Pregnancy, Childbirth, and the Puerperium (630-679)
    a. General Rules for Obstetric Cases
    b. Selection of OB Principal or First-listed Diagnosis
    c. Fetal Conditions Affecting the Management of the Mother
    d. HIV Infection in Pregnancy, Childbirth and the Puerperium
    e. Current Conditions Complicating Pregnancy
    f. Diabetes mellitus in pregnancy
    g. Gestational diabetes
    h. Normal Delivery, Code 650
    i. The Postpartum and Peripartum Periods
    j. Code 677, Late effect of complication of pregnancy
    k. Abortions
12. Chapter 12: Diseases Skin and Subcutaneous Tissue (680-709)
    a. Pressure ulcer stage codes

Appendix I: Present on Admission Reporting Guidelines

SECTION I. CONVENTIONS, GENERAL CODING GUIDELINES AND CHAPTER SPECIFIC GUIDELINES

The conventions, general guidelines and chapter-specific guidelines are applicable to all health care settings unless otherwise indicated.

A. Conventions for the ICD-9-CM

The conventions for the ICD-9-CM are the general rules for use of the classification independent of the guidelines. These conventions are incorporated within the index and tabular of the ICD-9-CM as instructional notes. The conventions are as follows:

1. **Format:**
   The ICD-9-CM uses an indented format for ease in reference

2. **Abbreviations**
   a. **Index abbreviations**
      NEC   "Not elsewhere classifiable"
      This abbreviation in the index represents "other specified" when a specific code is not available for a condition the index directs the coder to the "other specified" code in the tabular.

   b. **Tabular abbreviations**
      NEC   "Not elsewhere classifiable"
      This abbreviation in the tabular represents "other specified". When a specific code is not available for a condition the tabular includes an NEC entry under a code to identify the code as the "other specified" code.
      See Section I.A.5.a. "Other" codes

      NOS   "Not otherwise specified"
      This abbreviation is the equivalent of unspecified.
      See Section I.A.5.b., "Unspecified" codes

3. **Punctuation**
   [ ]   Brackets are used in the tabular list to enclose synonyms, alternative wording or explanatory phrases. Brackets are used in the index to identify manifestation codes.
   See Section I.A.6. "Etiology/manifestations"

   ( )   Parentheses are used in both the index and tabular to enclose supplementary words that may be present or absent in the statement of a disease or procedure without affecting the code number to which it is assigned. The terms within the parentheses are referred to as nonessential modifiers.

   :   Colons are used in the Tabular list after an incomplete term which needs one or more of the modifiers following the colon to make it assignable to a given category.

4. **Includes and Excludes Notes and Inclusion terms**
   Includes: This note appears immediately under a three-digit code title to further define, or give examples of, the content of the category.

   Excludes: An excludes note under a code indicates that the terms excluded from the code are to be coded elsewhere. In some cases the codes for the excluded terms should not be used in conjunction with the code from which it is excluded. An example of this is a congenital condition excluded from an acquired form of the same condition. The congenital and acquired codes should not be used together. In other cases, the excluded terms may be used together with an excluded code. An example of this is when fractures of different bones are coded to different codes. Both codes may be used together if both types of fractures are present.

Inclusion terms: List of terms is included under certain four and five digit codes. These terms are the conditions for which that code number is to be used. The terms may be synonyms of the code title, or, in the case of "other specified" codes, the terms are a list of the various conditions assigned to that code. The inclusion terms are not necessarily exhaustive. Additional terms found only in the index may also be assigned to a code.

5. **Other and Unspecified codes**

   a. **"Other" codes**

   Codes titled "other" or "other specified" (usually a code with a 4th digit 8 or fifth-digit 9 for diagnosis codes) are for use when the information in the medical record provides detail for which a specific code does not exist. Index entries with NEC in the line designate "other" codes in the tabular. These index entries represent specific disease entities for which no specific code exists so the term is included within an "other" code.

   b. **"Unspecified" codes**

   Codes (usually a code with a 4th digit 9 or 5th digit 0 for diagnosis codes) titled "unspecified" are for use when the information in the medical record is insufficient to assign a more specific code.

6. **Etiology/manifestation convention ("Code first," "Use additional code" and "In diseases classified elsewhere" notes)**

   Certain conditions have both an underlying etiology and multiple body system manifestations due to the underlying etiology. For such conditions, the ICD-9-CM has a coding convention that requires the underlying condition be sequenced first followed by the manifestation. Wherever such a combination exists, there is a "Use additional code" note at the etiology code, and a "Code first" note at the manifestation code. These instructional notes indicate the proper sequencing order of the codes, etiology followed by manifestation.

   In most cases the manifestation codes will have in the code title, "In diseases classified elsewhere." Codes with this title are a component of the etiology/manifestation convention. The code title indicates that it is a manifestation code. "In diseases classified elsewhere" codes are never permitted to be used as first listed or principal diagnosis codes. They must be used in conjunction with an underlying condition code and they must be listed following the underlying condition.

   There are manifestation codes that do not have "In diseases classified elsewhere" in the title. For such codes a "Use additional code" note will still be present and the rules for sequencing apply.

   In addition to the notes in the tabular, these conditions also have a specific index entry structure. In the index both conditions are listed together with the etiology code first followed by the manifestation codes in brackets. The code in brackets is always to be sequenced second.

   The most commonly used etiology/manifestation combinations are the codes for Diabetes mellitus, category 250. For each code under category 250 there is a use additional code note for the manifestation that is specific for that particular diabetic manifestation. Should a patient have more than one manifestation of diabetes, more than one code from category 250 may be used with as many manifestation codes as are needed to fully describe the patient's complete diabetic condition. The category 250 diabetes codes should be sequenced first, followed by the manifestation codes.

   "Code first" and "Use additional code" notes are also used as sequencing rules in the classification for certain codes that are not part of an etiology/manifestation combination.

   See - Section I.B.9. "Multiple coding for a single condition."

7. **"And"**

   The word "and" should be interpreted to mean either "and" or "or" when it appears in a title.

8. **"With"**

   The word "with" in the alphabetic index is sequenced immediately following the main term, not in alphabetical order.

9. **"See" and "See Also"**

   The "see" instruction following a main term in the index indicates that another term should be referenced. It is necessary to go to the main term referenced with the "see" note to locate the correct code.

   A "see also" instruction following a main term in the index instructs that there is another main term that may also be referenced that may provide additional index entries that may be useful. It is not necessary to follow the "see also" note when the original main term provides the necessary code.

B. **General Coding Guidelines**

1. **Use of Both Alphabetic Index and Tabular List**

   Use both the Alphabetic Index and the Tabular List when locating and assigning a code. Reliance on only the Alphabetic Index or the Tabular List leads to errors in code assignments and less specificity in code selection.

2. **Locate each term in the Alphabetic Index**

   Locate each term in the Alphabetic Index and verify the code selected in the Tabular List. Read and be guided by instructional notations that appear in both the Alphabetic Index and the Tabular List.

3. **Level of Detail in Coding**

   Diagnosis and procedure codes are to be used at their highest number of digits available.

   ICD-9-CM diagnosis codes are composed of codes with 3, 4, or 5 digits. Codes with three digits are included in ICD-9-CM as the heading of a category of codes that may be further subdivided by the use of fourth and/or fifth-digits, which provide greater detail.

   A three-digit code is to be used only if it is not further subdivided. Where fourth-digit subcategories and/or fifth-digit subclassifications are provided, they must be assigned. A code is invalid if it has not been coded to the full number of digits required for that code. For example, Acute myocardial infarction, code 410, has fourth-digits that describe the location of the infarction (e.g., 410.2, Of inferolateral wall), and fifth-digits that identify the episode of care. It would be incorrect to report a code in category 410 without a fourth and fifth-digit.

   ICD-9-CM Volume 3 procedure codes are composed of codes with either 3 or 4 digits. Codes with two digits are included in ICD-9-CM as the heading of a category of codes that may be further subdivided by the use of third and/or fourth-digits, which provide greater detail.

4. **Code or codes from 001.0 through V89.09**

   The appropriate code or codes from 001.0 through V89.09 must be used to identify diagnoses, symptoms, conditions, problems, complaints or other reason(s) for the encounter/visit.

5. **Selection of codes 001.0 through 999.9**

   The selection of codes 001.0 through 999.9 will frequently be used to describe the reason for the admission/encounter. These codes are from the section of ICD-9-CM for the classification of diseases and injuries (e.g., infectious and parasitic diseases; neoplasms; symptoms, signs, and ill-defined conditions, etc.).

6. **Signs and symptoms**

   Codes that describe symptoms and signs, as opposed to diagnoses, are acceptable for reporting purposes when a related definitive diagnosis has not been established (confirmed) by the provider. Chapter 16 of ICD-9-CM, Symptoms, Signs, and Ill-Defined conditions (codes 780.0 - 799.9) contain many, but not all codes for symptoms.

7. **Conditions that are an integral part of a disease process**

   Signs and symptoms that are associated routinely with a disease process should not be assigned as additional codes, unless otherwise instructed by the classification.

8. **Conditions that are not an integral part of a disease process**

   Additional signs and symptoms that may not be associated routinely with a disease process should be coded when present.

9. **Multiple coding for a single condition**

   In addition to the etiology/manifestation convention that requires two codes to fully describe a single condition that affects multiple body systems, there are other single conditions that also require more than one code. "Use additional code" notes are found in the tabular at codes that are not part of an etiology/manifestation pair where a secondary code is useful to fully describe a condition. The sequencing rule is the same as the etiology/manifestation pair - , "Use additional code" indicates that a secondary code should be added.

   For example, for infections that are not included in chapter 1, a secondary code from category 041, Bacterial infection in conditions classified elsewhere and of unspecified site, may be required to identify the bacterial organism causing the infection. A "Use additional code" note will normally be found at the infectious disease code, indicating a need for the organism code to be added as a secondary code.

   "Code first" notes are also under certain codes that are not specif- ically manifestation codes but may be due to an underlying cause. When a "Code first" note is present and an underlying condition is present the underlying condition should be sequenced first.

   "Code, if applicable, any causal condition first", notes indicate that this code may be assigned as a principal diagnosis when the causal condition is unknown or not applicable. If a causal condition is known, then the code for that condition should be sequenced as the principal or first-listed diagnosis. Multiple codes may be needed for late effects, complication codes and obstetric codes to more fully describe a condition. See the specific guidelines for these conditions for further instruction.

10. Acute and Chronic Conditions

If the same condition is described as both acute (subacute) and chronic, and separate subentries exist in the Alphabetic Index at the same indentation level, code both and sequence the acute (subacute) code first.

11. Combination Code

A combination code is a single code used to classify:

- Two diagnoses, or
- A diagnosis with an associated secondary process (manifestation)
- A diagnosis with an associated complication

Combination codes are identified by referring to subterm entries in the Alphabetic Index and by reading the inclusion and exclusion notes in the Tabular List.

Assign only the combination code when that code fully identifies the diagnostic conditions involved or when the Alphabetic Index so directs. Multiple coding should not be used when the classification provides a combination code that clearly identifies all of the elements documented in the diagnosis. When the combination code lacks necessary specificity in describing the manifestation or complication, an additional code should be used as a secondary code.

12. Late Effects

A late effect is the residual effect (condition produced) after the acute phase of an illness or injury has terminated. There is no time limit on when a late effect code can be used. The residual may be apparent early, such as in cerebrovascular accident cases, or it may occur months or years later, such as that due to a previous injury. Coding of late effects generally requires two codes sequenced in the following order: The condition or nature of the late effect is sequenced first. The late effect code is sequenced second.

An exception to the above guidelines are those instances where the code for late effect is followed by a manifestation code identified in the Tabular List and title, or the late effect code has been expanded (at the fourth and fifth-digit levels) to include the manifestation(s). The code for the acute phase of an illness or injury that led to the late effect is never used with a code for the late effect.

13. Impending or Threatened Condition

Code any condition described at the time of discharge as "impending" or "threatened" as follows:

If it did occur, code as confirmed diagnosis. If it did not occur, reference the Alphabetic Index to determine if the condition has a subentry term for "impending" or "threatened" and also reference main term entries for "Impending" and for "Threatened." If the subterms are listed, assign the given code. If the subterms are not listed, code the existing underlying condition(s) and not the condition described as impending or threatened.

14. Reporting Same Diagnosis Code More than Once

Each unique ICD-9-CM diagnosis code may be reported only once for an encounter. This applies to bilateral conditions or two different conditions classified to the same ICD-9-CM diagnosis code.

15. Admissions/Encounters for Rehabilitation

When the purpose for the admission/encounter is rehabilitation, sequence the appropriate V code from category V57, Care involving use of rehabilitation procedures, as the principal/first-listed diagnosis. The code for the condition for which the service is being performed should be reported as an additional diagnosis.

Only one code from category V57 is required. Code V57.89, Other specified rehabilitation procedures, should be assigned if more than one type of rehabilitation is performed during a single encounter. A procedure code should be reported to identify each type of rehabilitation therapy actually performed.

16. Documentation for BMI and Pressure Ulcer Stages

For the Body Mass Index (BMI) and pressure ulcer stage codes, code assignment may be based on medical record documentation from clinicians who are not the patient's provider (i.e., physician or other qualified healthcare practitioner legally accountable for establishing the patient's diagnosis), since this information is typically documented by other clinicians involved in the care of the patient (e.g., a dietitian often documents the BMI and nurses often documents the pressure ulcer stages). However, the associated diagnosis (such as overweight, obesity, or pressure ulcer) must be documented by the patient's provider. If there is conflicting medical record documentation, either from the same clinician or different clinicians, the patient's attending provider should be queried for clarification.

The BMI and pressure ulcer stage codes should only be reported as secondary diagnoses. As with all other secondary diagnosis codes, the BMI and pressure ulcer stage codes should only be assigned when they meet the definition of a reportable additional diagnosis.

See Section III, Reporting Additional Diagnoses.

C. Chapter-Specific Coding Guidelines

In addition to general coding guidelines, there are guidelines for specific diagnoses and/or conditions in the classification. Unless otherwise indicated, these guidelines apply to all health care settings. Please refer to Section II for guidelines on the selection of principal diagnosis.

1. Chapter 1: Infectious and Parasitic Diseases (001-139)

a. Human Immunodeficiency Virus (HIV) Infections

1) Code only confirmed cases

Code only confirmed cases of HIV infection/illness. This is an exception to the hospital inpatient guideline Section II, H.

In this context, "confirmation" does not require documentation of positive serology or culture for HIV; the provider's diagnostic statement that the patient is HIV positive, or has an HIV-related illness is sufficient.

2) Selection and sequencing of HIV codes

(a) Patient admitted for HIV-related condition

If a patient is admitted for an HIV-related condition, the principal diagnosis should be 042, followed by additional diagnosis codes for all reported HIV-related conditions.

(b) Patient with HIV disease admitted for unrelated condition

If a patient with HIV disease is admitted for an unrelated condition (such as a traumatic injury), the code for the unrelated condition (e.g., the nature of injury code) should be the principal diagnosis. Other diagnoses would be 042 followed by additional diagnosis codes for all reported HIV-related conditions.

(c) Whether the patient is newly diagnosed

Whether the patient is newly diagnosed or has had previous admissions/encounters for HIV conditions is irrelevant to the sequencing decision.

(d) Asymptomatic human immunodeficiency virus

V08 Asymptomatic human immunodeficiency virus [HIV] infection, is to be applied when the patient without any documentation of symptoms is listed as being "HIV positive," "known HIV," "HIV test positive," or similar terminology. Do not use this code if the term "AIDS" is used or if the patient is treated for any HIV-related illness or is described as having any condition(s) resulting from his/her HIV positive status; use 042 in these cases.

(e) Patients with inconclusive HIV serology

Patients with inconclusive HIV serology, but no definitive diagnosis or manifestations of the illness, may be assigned code 795.71, Inconclusive serologic test for Human Immunodeficiency Virus [HIV].

(f) Previously diagnosed HIV-related illness

Patients with any known prior diagnosis of an HIV-related illness should be coded to 042. Once a patient has developed an HIV-related illness, the patient should always be assigned code 042 on every subsequent admission/encounter. Patients previously diagnosed with any HIV illness (042) should never be assigned to 795.71 or V08.

(g) HIV Infection in Pregnancy, Childbirth and the Puerperium

During pregnancy, childbirth or the puerperium, a patient admitted (or presenting for a health care encounter) because of an HIV-related illness should receive a principal diagnosis code of 647.6x, Other specified infectious and parasitic diseases in the mother classifiable elsewhere, but complicating the pregnancy, childbirth or the puerperium, followed by 042 and the code(s) for the HIV-related illness(es). Codes from Chapter 15 always take sequencing priority.

Patients with asymptomatic HIV infection status admitted (or presenting for a health care encounter) during pregnancy, childbirth, or the puerperium should receive codes of 647.6x and V08.

(h) Encounters for testing for HIV

If a patient is being seen to determine his/her HIV status, use code V73.89, Screening for other specified viral disease. Use code V69.8, Other problems related to lifestyle, as a secondary code if an asymptomatic patient is in a known high risk group for HIV. Should a patient with signs or symptoms or illness, or a confirmed HIV related diagnosis be tested for HIV, code the signs and symptoms or the diagnosis. An additional counseling code V65.44 may be used if counseling is provided during the encounter for the test.

When a patient returns to be informed of his/her HIV test results use code V65.44, HIV counseling, if the results of the test are negative.

If the results are positive but the patient is asymptomatic use code V08, Asymptomatic HIV infection. If the results are positive and the patient is symptomatic use code 042, HIV infection, with codes for the HIV related symptoms or diagnosis. The HIV counseling code may also be used if counseling is provided for patients with positive test results.

b. **Septicemia, Systemic Inflammatory Response Syndrome (SIRS), Sepsis, Severe Sepsis, and Septic Shock**

1) **SIRS, Septicemia, and Sepsis**

   (a) The terms *septicemia* and *sepsis* are often used interchangeably by providers, however they are not considered synonymous terms. The following descriptions are provided for reference but do not preclude querying the provider for clarification about terms used in the documentation:

   (i) Septicemia generally refers to a systemic disease associated with the presence of pathological microorganisms or toxins in the blood, which can include bacteria, viruses, fungi or other organisms.

   (ii) Systemic inflammatory response syndrome (SIRS) generally refers to the systemic response to infection, trauma/burns, or other insult (such as cancer) with symptoms including fever, tachycardia, tachypnea, and leukocytosis.

   (iii) Sepsis generally refers to SIRS due to infection.

   (iv) Severe sepsis generally refers to sepsis with associated acute organ dysfunction.

   (b) **The coding of SIRS, sepsis and severe sepsis**
   The coding of SIRS, sepsis and severe sepsis requires a minimum of 2 codes: a code for the underlying cause (such as infection or trauma) and a code from subcategory 995.9 Systemic inflammatory response syndrome (SIRS).

   (i) The code for the underlying cause (such as infection or trauma) must be sequenced before the code from subcategory 995.9 Systemic inflammatory response syndrome (SIRS).

   (ii) Sepsis and severe sepsis require a code for the systemic infection (038.xx, 112.5, etc.) and either code 995.91, Sepsis, or 995.92, Severe sepsis. If the causal organism is not documented, assign code 038.9, Unspecified septicemia.

   (iii) Severe sepsis requires additional code(s) for the associated acute organ dysfunction(s).

   (iv) If a patient has sepsis with multiple organ dysfunctions, follow the instructions for coding severe sepsis.

   (v) Either the term sepsis or SIRS must be documented to assign a code from subcategory 995.9.

   (vi) *See Section I.C.17.g, Injury and poisoning, for information regarding systemic inflammatory response syndrome (SIRS) due to trauma/burns and other non-infectious processes.*

   (c) Due to the complex nature of sepsis and severe sepsis, some cases may require querying the provider prior to assignment of the codes.

2) **Sequencing sepsis and severe sepsis**

   (a) **Sepsis and severe sepsis as principal diagnosis**
   If sepsis or severe sepsis is present on admission, and meets the definition of principal diagnosis, the systemic infection code (e.g., 038.xx, 112.5, etc) should be assigned as the principal diagnosis, followed by code 995.91, Sepsis, or 995.92, Severe sepsis, as required by the sequencing rules in the Tabular List. Codes from subcategory 995.9 can never be assigned as a principal diagnosis. A code should also be assigned for any localized infection, if present.

   If the sepsis or severe sepsis is due to a postprocedural infection, *see Section I.C.10 for guidelines related to sepsis due to postprocedural infection.*

   (b) **Sepsis and severe sepsis as secondary diagnoses**
   When sepsis or severe sepsis develops during the encounter (it was not present on admission), the systemic infection code and code 995.91 or 995.92 should be assigned as secondary diagnoses.

   (c) **Documentation unclear as to whether sepsis or severe sepsis is present on admission**
   Sepsis or severe sepsis may be present on admission but the diagnosis may not be confirmed until sometime after admission. If the documentation is not clear whether the sepsis or severe sepsis was present on admission, the provider should be queried.

3) **Sepsis/SIRS with Localized Infection**
   If the reason for admission is both sepsis, severe sepsis, or SIRS and a localized infection, such as pneumonia or cellulitis, a code for the systemic infection (038.xx, 112.5, etc) should be assigned first, then code 995.91 or 995.92, followed by the code for the localized infection. If the patient is admitted with a localized infection, such as pneumonia, and sepsis/SIRS doesn't develop until after admission, see guideline I.C.1.b.2.b).

   If the localized infection is postprocedural, *see Section I.C.10 for guidelines related to sepsis due to postprocedural infection.*

   Note: The term urosepsis is a nonspecific term. If that is the only term documented then only code 599.0 should be assigned based on the default for the term in the ICD-9-CM index, in addition to the code for the causal organism if known.

4) **Bacterial Sepsis and Septicemia**
   In most cases, it will be a code from category 038, Septicemia, that will be used in conjunction with a code from subcategory 995.9 such as the following:

   (a) **Streptococcal sepsis**
   If the documentation in the record states streptococcal sepsis, codes 038.0, Streptococcal septicemia, and code 995.91 should be used, in that sequence.

   (b) **Streptococcal septicemia**
   If the documentation states streptococcal septicemia, only code 038.0 should be assigned, however, the provider should be queried whether the patient has sepsis, an infection with SIRS.

5) **Acute organ dysfunction that is not clearly associated with the sepsis**
   If a patient has sepsis and an acute organ dysfunction, but the medical record documentation indicates that the acute organ dysfunction is related to a medical condition other than the sepsis, do not assign code 995.92, Severe sepsis. An acute organ dysfunction must be associated with the sepsis in order to assign the severe sepsis code. If the documentation is not clear as to whether an acute organ dysfunction is related to the sepsis or another medical condition, query the provider.

6) **Septic shock**

   (a) **Sequencing of septic shock**
   Septic shock generally refers to circulatory failure associated with severe sepsis, and, therefore, it represents a type of acute organ dysfunction.

   For all cases of septic shock, the code for the systemic infection should be sequenced first, followed by codes 995.92 and 785.52. Any additional codes for other acute organ dysfunctions should also be assigned. As noted in the sequencing instructions in the Tabular List, the code for septic shock cannot be assigned as a principal diagnosis.

   (b) **Septic Shock without documentation of severe sepsis**
   Septic shock indicates the presence of severe sepsis.

   Code 995.92, Severe sepsis, must be assigned with code 785.52, Septic shock, even if the term severe sepsis is not documented in the record. The "Use additional code" note and the "Code first" note in the tabular support this guideline.

7) **Sepsis and septic shock complicating abortion and pregnancy**
Sepsis and septic shock complicating abortion, ectopic pregnancy, and molar pregnancy are classified to category codes in Chapter 11 (630-639).
See section I.C.11.

8) **Negative or inconclusive blood cultures**
Negative or inconclusive blood cultures do not preclude a diagnosis of septicemia or sepsis in patients with clinical evidence of the condition, however, the provider should be queried.

9) **Newborn sepsis**
See Section I.C.15.j for information on the coding of newborn sepsis.

10) **Sepsis due to a postprocedural infection**
   (a) **Documentation of causal relationship**
   As with all postprocedural complications, code assignment is based on the provider's documentation of the relationship between the infection and the procedure.

   (b) **Sepsis due to postprocedural infection**
   In cases of postprocedural sepsis, the complication code, such as code 998.59, Other postoperative infection, or 674.3x, Other complications of obstetrical surgical wounds should be coded first followed by the appropriate sepsis codes (systemic infection code and either code 995.91or 995.92). An additional code(s) for any acute organ dysfunction should also be assigned for cases of severe sepsis.

11) **External cause of injury codes with SIRS**
Refer to Section I.C.19.a.7 for instruction on the use of external cause of injury codes with codes for SIRS resulting from trauma.

12) **Sepsis and severe sepsis associated with noninfectious process**
In some cases, a non-infectious process, such as trauma, may lead to an infection which can result in sepsis or severe sepsis. If sepsis or severe sepsis is documented as associated with a non-infectious condition, such as a burn or serious injury, and this condition meets the definition for principal diagnosis, the code for the noninfectious condition should be sequenced first, followed by the code for the systemic infection and either code 995.91, Sepsis, or 995.92, Severe sepsis. Additional codes for any associated acute organ dysfunction(s) should also be assigned for cases of severe sepsis. If the sepsis or severe sepsis meets the definition of principal diagnosis, the systemic infection and sepsis codes should be sequenced before the non-infectious condition. When both the associated non-infectious condition and the sepsis or severe sepsis meet the definition of principal diagnosis, either may be assigned as principal diagnosis.

See Section I.C.1.b.2) (a) for guidelines pertaining to sepsis or severe sepsis as the principal diagnosis.

Only one code from subcategory 995.9 should be assigned. Therefore, when a non-infectious condition leads to an infection resulting in sepsis or severe sepsis, assign either code 995.91 or 995.92. Do not additionally assign code 995.93, Systemic inflammatory response syndrome due to non-infectious process without acute organ dysfunction, or 995.94, Systemic inflammatory response syndrome with acute organ dysfunction.

See Section I.C.17.g for information on the coding of SIRS due to trauma/burns or other non-infectious disease processes.

c. **Methicillin Resistant *Staphylococcus aureus* (MRSA) Conditions**
   1) **Selection and sequencing of MRSA codes**
      (a) **Combination codes for MRSA infection**
      When a patient is diagnosed with an infection that is due to methicillin resistant Staphylococcus aureus (MRSA), and that infection has a combination code that includes the causal organism (e.g., septicemia, pneumonia) assign the appropriate code for the condition (e.g., code 038.12, Methicillin resistant Staphylococcus aureus septicemia or code 482.42, Methicillin resistant pneumonia due to Staphylococcus aureus). Do not assign code 041.12, Methicillin resistant Staphylococcus aureus, as an additional code because the code includes the type of infection

and the MRSA organism. Do not assign a code from subcategory V09.0, Infection with microorganisms resistant to penicillins, as an additional diagnosis.
See Section C.1.b.1 for instructions on coding and sequencing of septicemia.

   (b) **Other codes for MRSA infection**
   When there is documentation of a current infection (e.g., wound infection, stitch abscess, urinary tract infection) due to MRSA, and that infection does not have a combination code that includes the causal organism, select the appropriate code to identify the condition along with code 041.12, Methicillin resistant Staphylococcus aureus, for the MRSA infection. Do not assign a code from subcategory V09.0, Infection with microorganisms resistant to penicillins.

   (c) **Methicillin susceptible *Staphylococcus aureus* (MSSA) and MRSA colonization**
   The condition or state of being colonized or carrying MSSA or MRSA is called colonization or carriage, while an individual person is described as being colonized or being a carrier. Colonization means that MSSA or MSRA is present on or in the body without necessarily causing illness. A positive MRSA colonization test might be documented by the provider as "MRSA screen positive" or "MRSA nasal swab positive".

   Assign code V02.54, Carrier or suspected carrier, Methicillin resistant Staphylococcus aureus, for patients documented as having MRSA colonization. Assign code V02.53, Carrier or suspected carrier, Methicillin susceptible Staphylococcus aureus, for patient documented as having MSSA colonization. Colonization is not necessarily indicative of a disease process or as the cause of a specific condition the patient may have unless documented as such by the provider.

   Code V02.59, Other specified bacterial diseases, should be assigned for other types of staphylococcal colonization (e.g., S. epidermidis, S. saprophyticus). Code V02.59 should not be assigned for colonization with any type of Staphylococcus aureus (MRSA, MSSA).

   (d) **MRSA colonization and infection**
   If a patient is documented as having both MRSA colonization and infection during a hospital admission, code V02.54, Carrier or suspected carrier, Methicillin resistant Staphylococcus aureus, and a code for the MRSA infection may both be assigned.

2. **Chapter 2: Neoplasms (140-239)**
   General guidelines
   Chapter 2 of the ICD-9-CM contains the codes for most benign and all malignant neoplasms. Certain benign neoplasms, such as prostatic adenomas, may be found in the specific body system chapters. To properly code a neoplasm it is necessary to determine from the record if the neoplasm is benign, in-situ, malignant, or of uncertain histologic behavior. If malignant, any secondary (metastatic) sites should also be determined.

   The neoplasm table in the Alphabetic Index should be referenced first. However, if the histological term is documented, that term should be referenced first, rather than going immediately to the Neoplasm Table, in order to determine which column in the Neoplasm Table is appropriate. For example, if the documentation indicates "adenoma," refer to the term in the Alphabetic Index to review the entries under this term and the instructional note to "see also neoplasm, by site, benign." The table provides the proper code based on the type of neoplasm and the site. It is important to select the proper column in the table that corresponds to the type of neoplasm. The tabular should then be referenced to verify that the correct code has been selected from the table and that a more specific site code does not exist.

   See Section I. C. 18.d.4. for information regarding V codes for genetic susceptibility to cancer.

a. Treatment directed at the malignancy

If the treatment is directed at the malignancy, designate the malignancy as the principal diagnosis.

The only exception to this guideline is if a patient admission/encounter is solely for the administration of chemotherapy, immunotherapy or radiation therapy, assign the appropriate V58.x code as the first-listed or principal diagnosis, and the diagnosis or problem for which the service is being performed as a secondary diagnosis.

b. Treatment of secondary site

When a patient is admitted because of a primary neoplasm with metastasis and treatment is directed toward the secondary site only, the secondary neoplasm is designated as the principal diagnosis even though the primary malignancy is still present.

c. Coding and sequencing of complications

Coding and sequencing of complications associated with the malignancies or with the therapy thereof are subject to the following guidelines:

1) Anemia associated with malignancy

When admission/encounter is for management of an anemia associated with the malignancy, and the treatment is only for anemia, the appropriate anemia code (such as code 285.22, Anemia in neoplastic disease) is designated as the principal diagnosis and is followed by the appropriate code(s) for the malignancy.

Code 285.22 may also be used as a secondary code if the patient suffers from anemia and is being treated for the malignancy.

2) Anemia associated with chemotherapy, immunotherapy and radiation therapy

When the admission/encounter is for management of an anemia associated with chemotherapy**,** immunotherapy or radiotherapy and the only treatment is for the anemia, the anemia is sequenced first followed by code E933.1. The appropriate neoplasm code should be assigned as an additional code.

3) Management of dehydration due to the malignancy

When the admission/encounter is for management of dehydration due to the malignancy or the therapy, or a combination of both, and only the dehydration is being treated (intravenous rehydration), the dehydration is sequenced first, followed by the code(s) for the malignancy.

4) Treatment of a complication resulting from a surgical procedure

When the admission/encounter is for treatment of a complication resulting from a surgical procedure, designate the complication as the principal or first-listed diagnosis if treatment is directed at resolving the complication.

d. Primary malignancy previously excised

When a primary malignancy has been previously excised or eradicated from its site and there is no further treatment directed to that site and there is no evidence of any existing primary malignancy, a code from category V10, Personal history of malignant neoplasm, should be used to indicate the former site of the malignancy. Any mention of extension, invasion, or metastasis to another site is coded as a secondary malignant neoplasm to that site. The secondary site may be the principal or first-listed with the V10 code used as a secondary code.

e. Admissions/Encounters involving chemotherapy, immunotherapy and radiation therapy

1) Episode of care involves surgical removal of neoplasm

When an episode of care involves the surgical removal of a neoplasm, primary or secondary site, followed by adjunct chemotherapy or radiation treatment during the same episode of care, the neoplasm code should be assigned as principal or first-listed diagnosis, using codes in the 140-198 series or where appropriate in the 200-203 series.

2) Patient admission/encounter solely for administration of chemotherapy, immunotherapy and radiation therapy

If a patient admission/encounter is solely for the administration of chemotherapy, immunotherapy or radiation therapy assign code V58.0, Encounter for radiation therapy, or V58.11, Encounter for antineoplastic chemotherapy, or V58.12, Encounter for antineoplastic immunotherapy as the first-listed or principal diagnosis. If a patient receives more than one of these therapies during the same admission more than one of these codes may be assigned, in any sequence.

The malignancy for which the therapy is being administered should be assigned as a secondary diagnosis.

3) Patient admitted for radiotherapy/chemotherapy and immunotherapy and develops complications

When a patient is admitted for the purpose of radiotherapy, immunotherapy or chemotherapy and develops complications such as uncontrolled nausea and vomiting or dehydration, the principal or first-listed diagnosis is V58.0, Encounter for radiotherapy, or V58.11, Encounter for antineoplastic chemotherapy, or V58.12, Encounter for antineoplastic immunotherapy followed by any codes for the complications.

f. Admission/encounter to determine extent of malignancy

When the reason for admission/encounter is to determine the extent of the malignancy, or for a procedure such as paracentesis or thoracentesis, the primary malignancy or appropriate metastatic site is designated as the principal or first-listed diagnosis, even though chemotherapy or radiotherapy is administered.

g. Symptoms, signs, and ill-defined conditions listed in Chapter 16 associated with neoplasms

Symptoms, signs, and ill-defined conditions listed in Chapter 16 characteristic of, or associated with, an existing primary or secondary site malignancy cannot be used to replace the malignancy as principal or first-listed diagnosis, regardless of the number of admissions or encounters for treatment and care of the neoplasm.

See section I.C.18.d.14, Encounter for prophylactic organ removal.

h. Admission/encounter for pain control/management

See Section I.C.6.a.5 for information on coding admission/encounter for pain control/management.

i. Malignant neoplasm associated with transplanted organ

A malignant neoplasm of a transplanted organ should be coded as a transplant complication. Assign first the appropriate code from subcategory 996.8, Complications of transplanted organ, followed by code 199.2, Malignant neoplasm associated with transplanted organ. Use an additional code for the specific malignancy.

3. Chapter 3: Endocrine, Nutritional, and Metabolic Diseases and Immunity Disorders (240-279)

a. Diabetes mellitus

Codes under category 250, Diabetes mellitus, identify complications/manifestations associated with diabetes mellitus. A fifth-digit is required for all category 250 codes to identify the type of diabetes mellitus and whether the diabetes is controlled or uncontrolled.

See I.C.3.a.7 for secondary diabetes

1) Fifth-digits for category 250:

The following are the fifth-digits for the codes under category 250:

0   type II or unspecified type, not stated as uncontrolled

1   type I, [juvenile type], not stated as uncontrolled

2   type II or unspecified type, uncontrolled

3   type I, [juvenile type], uncontrolled

The age of a patient is not the sole determining factor, though most type I diabetics develop the condition before reaching puberty. For this reason type I diabetes mellitus is also referred to as juvenile diabetes.

2) Type of diabetes mellitus not documented

If the type of diabetes mellitus is not documented in the medical record the default is type II.

3) Diabetes mellitus and the use of insulin

All type I diabetics must use insulin to replace what their bodies do not produce. However, the use of insulin does not mean that a patient is a type I diabetic. Some patients with type II diabetes mellitus are unable to control their blood sugar through diet and oral medication alone and do require insulin.

If the documentation in a medical record does not indicate the type of diabetes but does indicate that the patient uses insulin, the appropriate fifth-digit for type II must be used. For type II patients who routinely use insulin, code V58.67, Long-term (current) use of insulin, should also be assigned to indicate that the patient uses insulin. Code V58.67 should not be assigned if insulin is given temporarily to bring a type II patient's blood sugar under control during an encounter.

4) Assigning and sequencing diabetes codes and associated conditions

When assigning codes for diabetes and its associated conditions, the code(s) from category 250 must be sequenced before the codes for the associated conditions. The diabetes codes and the secondary codes that correspond to them are paired codes that follow the etiology/manifestation convention of the classification (*See Section I.A.6., Etiology/manifestation convention*). Assign as many codes from category 250 as needed to identify all of the associated conditions that the patient has. The corresponding secondary codes are listed under each of the diabetes codes.

(a) Diabetic retinopathy/diabetic macular edema
Diabetic macular edema, code 362.07, is only present with diabetic retinopathy. Another code from subcategory 362.0, Diabetic retinopathy, must be used with code 362.07. Codes under subcategory 362.0 are diabetes manifestation codes, so they must be used following the appropriate diabetes code.

5) Diabetes mellitus in pregnancy and gestational diabetes

(a) For diabetes mellitus complicating pregnancy, *see Section I.C.11.f., Diabetes mellitus in pregnancy.*

(b) For gestational diabetes, *see Section I.C.11, g., Gestational diabetes.*

6) Insulin pump malfunction

(a) Underdose of insulin due insulin pump failure
An underdose of insulin due to an insulin pump failure should be assigned 996.57, Mechanical complication due to insulin pump, as the principal or first listed code, followed by the appropriate diabetes mellitus code based on documentation.

(b) Overdose of insulin due to insulin pump failure
The principal or first listed code for an encounter due to an insulin pump malfunction resulting in an overdose of insulin, should also be 996.57, Mechanical complication due to insulin pump, followed by code 962.3, Poisoning by insulins and antidiabetic agents, and the appropriate diabetes mellitus code based on documentation.

7) Secondary Diabetes Mellitus
Codes under category 249, Secondary diabetes mellitus, identify complications/manifestations associated with secondary diabetes mellitus. Secondary diabetes is always caused by another condition or event (e.g., cystic fibrosis, malignant neoplasm of pancreas, pancreatectomy, adverse effect of drug, or poisoning).

(a) Fifth-digits for category 249:
A fifth-digit is required for all category 249 codes to identify whether the diabetes is controlled or uncontrolled.

(b) Secondary diabetes mellitus and the use of insulin
For patients who routinely use insulin, code V58.67, Long-term (current) use of insulin, should also be assigned. Code V58.67 should not be assigned if insulin is given temporarily to bring a patient's blood sugar under control during an encounter.

(c) Assigning and sequencing secondary diabetes codes and associated conditions
When assigning codes for secondary diabetes and its associated conditions (e.g. renal manifestations), the code(s) from category 249 must be sequenced before the codes for the associated conditions. The secondary diabetes codes and the diabetic manifestation codes that correspond to them are paired codes that follow the etiology/manifestation convention of the classification. Assign as many codes from category 249 as needed to identify all of the associated conditions that the patient has. The corresponding codes for the associated conditions are listed under each of the secondary diabetes codes. For example, secondary diabetes with diabetic nephrosis is assigned to code 249.40, followed by 581.81.

(d) Assigning and sequencing secondary diabetes codes and its causes
The sequencing of the secondary diabetes codes in relationship to codes for the cause of the diabetes is based on the reason for the encounter, applicable ICD-9-CM sequencing conventions, and chapter-specific guidelines.
If a patient is seen for treatment of the secondary diabetes or one of its associated conditions, a code from category 249 is sequenced as the principal or first-listed diagnosis, with the cause of the secondary diabetes (e.g. cystic fibrosis) sequenced as an additional diagnosis.
If, however, the patient is seen for the treatment of the condition causing the secondary diabetes (e.g., malignant

neoplasm of pancreas), the code for the cause of the secondary diabetes should be sequenced as the principal or first-listed diagnosis followed by a code from category 249.

(i) Secondary diabetes mellitus due to pancreatectomy
For postpancreatectomy diabetes mellitus (lack of insulin due to the surgical removal of all or part of the pancreas), assign code 251.3, Postsurgical hypoinsulinemia. A code from subcategory 249 should not be assigned for secondary diabetes mellitus due to pancreatectomy. Code also any diabetic manifestations (e.g. diabetic nephrosis 581.81).

(ii) Secondary diabetes due to drugs
Secondary diabetes may be caused by an adverse effect of correctly administered medications, poisoning or late effect of poisoning.
See Section I.C.17.e for coding of adverse effects and poisoning, and section I.C.19 for E code reporting.

4. Chapter 4: Diseases of Blood and Blood Forming Organs (280-289)

a. Anemia of chronic disease
Subcategory 285.2, Anemia in chronic illness, has codes for anemia in chronic kidney disease, code 285.21; anemia in neoplastic disease, code 285.22; and anemia in other chronic illness, code 285.29. These codes can be used as the principal/first listed code if the reason for the encounter is to treat the anemia. They may also be used as secondary codes if treatment of the anemia is a component of an encounter, but not the primary reason for the encounter. When using a code from subcategory 285 it is also necessary to use the code for the chronic condition causing the anemia.

1) Anemia in chronic kidney disease
When assigning code 285.21, Anemia in chronic kidney disease, it is also necessary to assign a code from category 585, Chronic kidney disease, to indicate the stage of chronic kidney disease.
See I.C.10.a. Chronic kidney disease (CKD).

2) Anemia in neoplastic disease
When assigning code 285.22, Anemia in neoplastic disease, it is also necessary to assign the neoplasm code that is responsible for the anemia. Code 285.22 is for use for anemia that is due to the malignancy, not for anemia due to antineoplastic chemotherapy drugs, which is an adverse effect.
See Section I.C.2.c.1 Anemia associated with malignancy. See Section I.C.2.c.2 Anemia associated with chemotherapy, immunotherapy and radiation therapy. See Section I.C.17.e.1. Adverse effects.

5. Chapter 5: Mental Disorders (290-319)
Reserved for future guideline expansion

6. Chapter 6: Diseases of Nervous System and Sense Organs (320-389)

a. Pain - Category 338

1) General coding information
Codes in category 338 may be used in conjunction with codes from other categories and chapters to provide more detail about acute or chronic pain and neoplasm- related pain, unless otherwise indicated below.

If the pain is not specified as acute or chronic, do not assign codes from category 338, except for post-thoracotomy pain, postoperative pain, neoplasm related pain, or central pain syndrome.

A code from subcategories 338.1 and 338.2 should not be assigned if the underlying (definitive) diagnosis is known, unless the reason for the encounter is pain control/ management and not management of the underlying condition.

(a) Category 338 codes as principal or first-listed diagnosis
Category 338 codes are acceptable as principal diagnosis or the first-listed code:

- When pain control or pain management is the reason for the admission/encounter (e.g., a patient with displaced intervertebral disc, nerve impingement and severe back pain presents for injection of steroid into the spinal canal). The underlying cause of the pain should be reported as an additional diagnosis, if known.
- When an admission or encounter is for a procedure aimed at treating the underlying condition (e.g., spinal fusion, kyphoplasty), a code for the underlying condition (e.g., vertebral fracture, spinal stenosis) should

be assigned as the principal diagnosis. No code from category 338 should be assigned.

- When a patient is admitted for the insertion of a neurostimulator for pain control, assign the appropriate pain code as the principal or first listed diagnosis. When an admission or encounter is for a procedure aimed at treating the underlying condition and a neurostimulator is inserted for pain control during the same admission/encounter, a code for the underlying condition should be assigned as the principal diagnosis and the appropriate pain code should be assigned as a secondary diagnosis.

(b) **Use of category 338 codes in conjunction with site specific pain codes**

(i) **Assigning category 338 codes and site-specific pain codes**

Codes from category 338 may be used in conjunction with codes that identify the site of pain (including codes from chapter 16) if the category 338 code provides additional information. For example, if the code describes the site of the pain, but does not fully describe whether the pain is acute or chronic, then both codes should be assigned.

(ii) **Sequencing of category 338 codes with site-specific pain codes**

The sequencing of category 338 codes with site-specific pain codes (including chapter 16 codes), is dependent on the circumstances of the encounter/admission as follows:

- If the encounter is for pain control or pain management, assign the code from category 338 followed by the code identifying the specific site of pain (e.g., encounter for pain management for acute neck pain from trauma is assigned code 338.11, Acute pain due to trauma, followed by code 723.1, Cervicalgia, to identify the site of pain).

- If the encounter is for any other reason except pain control or pain management, and a related definitive diagnosis has not been established (confirmed) by the provider, assign the code for the specific site of pain first, followed by the appropriate code from category 338.

2) **Pain due to devices, implants and grafts**

Pain associated with devices, implants or grafts left in a surgical site (for example painful hip prosthesis) is assigned to the appropriate code(s) found in Chapter 17, Injury and Poisoning. Use additional code(s) from category 338 to identify acute or chronic pain due to presence of the device, implant or graft (338.18- 338.19 or 338.28-338.29).

3) **Postoperative pain**

Post-thoracotomy pain and other postoperative pain are classified to subcategories 338.1 and 338.2, depending on whether the pain is acute or chronic. The default for post-thoracotomy and other postoperative pain not specified as acute or chronic is the code for the acute form.

Routine or expected postoperative pain immediately after surgery should not be coded.

(a) **Postoperative pain not associated with specific postoperative complication**

Postoperative pain not associated with a specific postoperative complication is assigned to the appropriate postoperative pain code in category 338.

(b) **Postoperative pain associated with specific postoperative complication**

Postoperative pain associated with a specific postoperative complication (such as painful wire sutures) is assigned to the appropriate code(s) found in Chapter 17, Injury and Poisoning. If appropriate, use additional code(s) from category 338 to identify acute or chronic pain (338.18 or 338.28). If pain control/management is the reason for the encounter, a code from category 338 should be assigned as the principal or first-listed diagnosis in accordance with *Section I.C.6.a.1.a above*.

(c) **Postoperative pain as principal or first-listed diagnosis**

Postoperative pain may be reported as the principal or first-listed diagnosis when the stated reason for the admission/encounter is documented as postoperative pain control/management.

(d) **Postoperative pain as secondary diagnosis**

Postoperative pain may be reported as a secondary diagnosis code when a patient presents for outpatient surgery and develops an unusual or inordinate amount of postoperative pain.

The provider's documentation should be used to guide the coding of postoperative pain, as well as *Section III. Reporting Additional Diagnoses* and *Section IV. Diagnostic Coding and Reporting in the Outpatient Setting*.

See Section II.I.2 for information on sequencing of diagnoses for patients admitted to hospital inpatient care following post-operative observation.

See Section II.J for information on sequencing of diagnoses for patients admitted to hospital inpatient care from outpatient surgery.

See Section IV.A.2 for information on sequencing of diagnoses for patients admitted for observation.

4) **Chronic pain**

Chronic pain is classified to subcategory 338.2. There is no time frame defining when pain becomes chronic pain. The provider's documentation should be used to guide use of these codes.

5) **Neoplasm related pain**

Code 338.3 is assigned to pain documented as being related, associated or due to cancer, primary or secondary malignancy, or tumor. This code is assigned regardless of whether the pain is acute or chronic.

This code may be assigned as the principal or first-listed code when the stated reason for the admission/encounter is documented as pain control/pain management. The underlying neoplasm should be reported as an additional diagnosis.

When the reason for the admission/encounter is management of the neoplasm and the pain associated with the neoplasm is also documented, code 338.3 may be assigned as an additional diagnosis.

See Section I.C.2 for instructions on the sequencing of neoplasms for all other stated reasons for the admission/encounter (except for pain control/pain management).

6) **Chronic pain syndrome**

This condition is different than the term "chronic pain," and therefore this code should only be used when the provider has specifically documented this condition.

7. **Chapter 7: Diseases of Circulatory System (390-459)**

a. **Hypertension**

Hypertension Table

The Hypertension Table, found under the main term, "Hypertension," in the Alphabetic Index, contains a complete listing of all conditions due to or associated with hypertension and classifies them according to malignant, benign, and unspecified.

1) **Hypertension, essential, or NOS**

Assign hypertension (arterial) (essential) (primary) (systemic) (NOS) to category code 401 with the appropriate fourth-digit to indicate malignant (.0), benign (.1), or unspecified (.9). Do not use either .0 malignant or .1 benign unless medical record documentation supports such a designation.

2) **Hypertension with heart disease**

Heart conditions (425.8, 429.0-429.3, 429.8, 429.9) are assigned to a code from category 402 when a causal relationship is stated (due to hypertension) or implied (hypertensive). Use an additional code from category 428 to identify the type of heart failure in those patients with heart failure. More than one code from category 428 may be assigned if the patient has systolic or diastolic failure and congestive heart failure.

The same heart conditions (425.8, 429.0-429.3, 429.8, 429.9) with hypertension, but without a stated causal relationship, are coded separately. Sequence according to the circumstances of the admission/encounter.

3) **Hypertensive chronic kidney disease**

Assign codes from category 403, Hypertensive chronic kidney disease, when conditions classified to categories 585-587 are present. Unlike hypertension with heart disease, ICD-9-CM presumes a cause-and-effect relationship and classifies chronic kidney disease (CKD) with hypertension as hypertensive chronic kidney disease.

Fifth-digits for category 403 should be assigned as follows:

- 0   with CKD stage I through stage IV, or unspecified.
- 1   with CKD stage V or end stage renal disease.

The appropriate code from category 585, Chronic kidney disease, should be used as a secondary code with a code from category 403 to identify the stage of chronic kidney disease.

See Section I.C.10.a for information on the coding of chronic kidney disease.

4) Hypertensive heart and chronic kidney disease

Assign codes from combination category 404, Hypertensive heart and chronic kidney disease, when both hypertensive kidney disease and hypertensive heart disease are stated in the diagnosis. Assume a relationship between the hypertension and the chronic kidney disease, whether or not the condition is so designated. Assign an additional code from category 428, to identify the type of heart failure. More than one code from category 428 may be assigned if the patient has systolic or diastolic failure and congestive heart failure.

Fifth-digits for category 404 should be assigned as follows:

- 0   without heart failure and with chronic kidney disease (CKD) stage I through stage IV, or unspecified
- 1   with heart failure and with CKD stage I through stage IV, or unspecified
- 2   without heart failure and with CKD stage V or end stage renal disease
- 3   with heart failure and with CKD stage V or end stage renal disease

The appropriate code from category 585, Chronic kidney disease, should be used as a secondary code with a code from category 404 to identify the stage of kidney disease.

See Section I.C.10.a for information on the coding of chronic kidney disease.

5) Hypertensive cerebrovascular disease

First assign codes from 430-438, Cerebrovascular disease, then the appropriate hypertension code from categories 401-405.

6) Hypertensive retinopathy

Two codes are necessary to identify the condition. First assign the code from subcategory 362.11, Hypertensive retinopathy, then the appropriate code from categories 401-405 to indicate the type of hypertension.

7) Hypertension, secondary

Two codes are required: one to identify the underlying etiology and one from category 405 to identify the hypertension. Sequencing of codes is determined by the reason for admission/encounter.

8) Hypertension, transient

Assign code 796.2, Elevated blood pressure reading without diagnosis of hypertension, unless patient has an established diagnosis of hypertension. Assign code 642.3x for transient hypertension of pregnancy.

9) Hypertension, controlled

Assign appropriate code from categories 401-405. This diagnostic statement usually refers to an existing state of hypertension under control by therapy.

10) Hypertension, uncontrolled

Uncontrolled hypertension may refer to untreated hypertension or hypertension not responding to current therapeutic regimen. In either case, assign the appropriate code from categories 401-405 to designate the stage and type of hypertension. Code to the type of hypertension.

11) Elevated blood pressure

For a statement of elevated blood pressure without further specificity, assign code 796.2, Elevated blood pressure reading without diagnosis of hypertension, rather than a code from category 401.

b. Cerebral infarction/stroke/cerebrovascular accident (CVA)

The terms stroke and CVA are often used interchangeably to refer to a cerebral infarction. The terms stroke, CVA, and cerebral infarction NOS are all indexed to the default code 434.91, Cerebral artery occlusion,

unspecified, with infarction. Code 436, Acute, but ill-defined, cerebrovascular disease, should not be used when the documentation states stroke or CVA.

See Section I.C.18.d.3 for information on coding status post administration of tPA in a different facility within the last 24 hours.

c. Postoperative cerebrovascular accident

A cerebrovascular hemorrhage or infarction that occurs as a result of medical intervention is coded to 997.02, Iatrogenic cerebrovascular infarction or hemorrhage. Medical record documentation should clearly specify the cause- and-effect relationship between the medical intervention and the cerebrovascular accident in order to assign this code. A secondary code from the code range 430-432 or from a code from subcategories 433 or 434 with a fifth-digit of "1" should also be used to identify the type of hemorrhage or infarct.

This guideline conforms to the use additional code note instruction at category 997. Code 436, Acute, but ill-defined, cerebrovascular disease, should not be used as a secondary code with code 997.02.

d. Late Effects of cerebrovascular disease

1) Category 438, late effects of cerebrovascular disease

Category 438 is used to indicate conditions classifiable to categories 430-437 as the causes of late effects (neurologic deficits), themselves classified elsewhere. These "late effects" include neurologic deficits that persist after initial onset of conditions classifiable to 430-437. The neurologic deficits caused by cerebrovascular disease may be present from the onset or may arise at any time after the onset of the condition classifiable to 430-437.

2) Codes from category 438 with codes from 430-437

Codes from category 438 may be assigned on a health care record with codes from 430-437, if the patient has a current cerebrovascular accident (CVA) and deficits from an old CVA.

3) Code V12.54

Assign code V12.54, Transient ischemic attack (TIA), and cerebral infarction without residual deficits (and not a code from category 438) as an additional code for history of cerebrovascular disease when no neurologic deficits are present.

e. Acute myocardial infarction (AMI)

1) ST elevation myocardial infarction (STEMI) and non ST elevation myocardial infarction (NSTEMI)

The ICD-9-CM codes for acute myocardial infarction (AMI) identify the site, such as anterolateral wall or true posterior wall. Subcategories 410.0-410.6 and 410.8 are used for ST elevation myocardial infarction (STEMI). Subcategory 410.7, Subendocardial infarction, is used for non ST elevation myocardial infarction (NSTEMI) and nontransmural MIs.

2) Acute myocardial infarction, unspecified

Subcategory 410.9 is the default for the unspecified term acute myocardial infarction. If only STEMI or transmural MI without the site is documented, query the provider as to the site, or assign a code from subcategory 410.9.

3) AMI documented as nontransmural or subendocardial but site provided

If an AMI is documented as nontransmural or subendocardial, but the site is provided, it is still coded as a subendocardial AMI. If NSTEMI evolves to STEMI, assign the STEMI code. If STEMI converts to NSTEMI due to thrombolytic therapy, it is still coded as STEMI.

See Section I.C.18.d.3 for information on coding status post administration of tPA in a different facility within the last 24 hours.

8.   Chapter 8: Diseases of Respiratory System (460-519)

See I.C.17.f. for ventilator-associated pneumonia.

a. Chronic obstructive pulmonary disease [COPD] and asthma

1) Conditions that comprise COPD and asthma

The conditions that comprise COPD are obstructive chronic bronchitis, subcategory 491.2, and emphysema, category 492. All asthma codes are under category 493, Asthma. Code 496, Chronic airway obstruction, not elsewhere classified, is a nonspecific code that should only be used when the documentation in a medical record does not specify the type of COPD being treated.

2) Acute exacerbation of chronic obstructive bronchitis and asthma

The codes for chronic obstructive bronchitis and asthma distinguish between uncomplicated cases and those in acute exacerbation. An acute exacerbation is a worsening or a decompensation of a chronic condition. An acute exacerbation is not equivalent to an infection superimposed on a chronic condition, though an exacerbation may be triggered by an infection.

3) Overlapping nature of the conditions that comprise COPD and asthma

Due to the overlapping nature of the conditions that make up COPD and asthma, there are many variations in the way these conditions are documented. Code selection must be based on the terms as documented. When selecting the correct code for the documented type of COPD and asthma, it is essential to first review the index, and then verify the code in the tabular list. There are many instructional notes under the different COPD subcategories and codes. It is important that all such notes are reviewed to assure correct code assignment.

4) Acute exacerbation of asthma and status asthmaticus
An acute exacerbation of asthma is an increased severity of the asthma symptoms, such as wheezing and shortness of breath. Status asthmaticus refers to a patient's failure to respond to therapy administered during an asthmatic episode and is a life threatening complication that requires emergency care. If status asthmaticus is documented by the provider with any type of COPD or with acute bronchitis, the status asthmaticus should be sequenced first. It supersedes any type of COPD including that with acute exacerbation or acute bronchitis. It is inappropriate to assign an asthma code with 5th digit 2, with acute exacerbation, together with an asthma code with 5th digit 1, with status asthmatics. Only the 5th digit 1 should be assigned.

b. Chronic obstructive pulmonary disease [COPD] and bronchitis

1) Acute bronchitis with COPD
Acute bronchitis, code 466.0, is due to an infectious organism. When acute bronchitis is documented with COPD, code 491.22, Obstructive chronic bronchitis with acute bronchitis, should be assigned. It is not necessary to also assign code 466.0. If a medical record documents acute bronchitis with COPD with acute exacerbation, only code 491.22 should be assigned. The acute bronchitis included in code 491.22 supersedes the acute exacerbation. If a medical record documents COPD with acute exacerbation without mention of acute bronchitis, only code 491.21 should be assigned.

c. Acute Respiratory Failure

1) Acute respiratory failure as principal diagnosis
Code 518.81, Acute respiratory failure, may be assigned as a principal diagnosis when it is the condition established after study to be chiefly responsible for occasioning the admission to the hospital, and the selection is supported by the Alphabetic Index and Tabular List. However, chapter-specific coding guidelines (such as obstetrics, poisoning, HIV, newborn) that provide sequencing direction take precedence.

2) Acute respiratory failure as secondary diagnosis
Respiratory failure may be listed as a secondary diagnosis if it occurs after admission, or if it is present on admission, but does not meet the definition of principal diagnosis.

3) Sequencing of acute respiratory failure and another acute condition
When a patient is admitted with respiratory failure and another acute condition, (e.g., myocardial infarction, cerebrovascular accident, aspiration pneumonia), the principal diagnosis will not be the same in every situation. This applies whether the other acute condition is a respiratory or nonrespiratory condition. Selection of the principal diagnosis will be dependent on the circumstances of admission. If both the respiratory failure and the other acute condition are equally responsible for occasioning the admission to the hospital, and there are no chapter-specific sequencing rules, the guideline regarding two or more diagnoses that equally meet the definition for principal diagnosis *(Section II, C.)* may be applied in these situations.

If the documentation is not clear as to whether acute respiratory failure and another condition are equally responsible for occasioning the admission, query the provider for clarification.

d. Influenza due to identified avian influenza virus (avian influenza)
Code only confirmed cases of avian influenza. This is an exception to the hospital inpatient guideline Section II, H. (Uncertain Diagnosis).

In this context, "confirmation" does not require documentation of positive laboratory testing specific for avian influenza. However, coding should be based on the provider's diagnostic statement that the patient has avian influenza.

If the provider records "suspected or possible or probable avian influenza," the appropriate influenza code from category 487 should be assigned. Code 488, Influenza due to identified avian influenza virus, should not be assigned.

9. Chapter 9: Diseases of Digestive System (520-579)
Reserved for future guideline expansion

10. Chapter 10: Diseases of Genitourinary System (580-629)

a. Chronic kidney disease

1) Stages of chronic kidney disease (CKD)
The ICD-9-CM classifies CKD based on severity. The severity of CKD is designated by stages I-V. Stage II, code 585.2, equates to mild CKD; stage III, code 585.3, equates to moderate CKD; and stage IV, code 585.4, equates to severe CKD. Code 585.6, End stage renal disease (ESRD), is assigned when the provider has documented end-stage-renal disease (ESRD).

If both a stage of CKD and ESRD are documented, assign code 585.6 only.

2) Chronic kidney disease and kidney transplant status
Patients who have undergone kidney transplant may still have some form of CKD, because the kidney transplant may not fully restore kidney function. Therefore, the presence of CKD alone does not constitute a transplant complication. Assign the appropriate 585 code for the patient's stage of CKD and code V42.0. If a transplant complication such as failure or rejection is documented, see section I.C.17.f.1.b for information on coding complications of a kidney transplant. If the documentation is unclear as to whether the patient has a complication of the transplant, query the provider.

3) Chronic kidney disease with other conditions
Patients with CKD may also suffer from other serious conditions, most commonly diabetes mellitus and hypertension. The sequencing of the CKD code in relationship to codes for other contributing conditions is based on the conventions in the tabular list.

See Section I.C.3.a.4 for sequencing instructions for diabetes.
See Section I.C.4.a.1 for anemia in CKD.
See Section I.C.7.a.3 for hypertensive chronic kidney disease.
See Section I.C.17.f.1.b, Kidney transplant complications, for instructions on coding of documented rejection or failure.

11. Chapter 11: Complications of Pregnancy, Childbirth, and the Puerperium (630-679)

a. General Rules for Obstetric Cases

1) Codes from chapter 11 and sequencing priority
Obstetric cases require codes from chapter 11, codes in the range 630-679, Complications of Pregnancy, Childbirth, and the Puerperium. Chapter 11 codes have sequencing priority over codes from other chapters. Additional codes from other chapters may be used in conjunction with chapter 11 codes to further specify conditions. Should the provider document that the pregnancy is incidental to the encounter, then code V22.2 should be used in place of any chapter 11 codes. It is the provider's responsibility to state that the condition being treated is not affecting the pregnancy.

2) Chapter 11 codes used only on the maternal record
Chapter 11 codes are to be used only on the maternal record, never on the record of the newborn.

3) Chapter 11 fifth-digits
Categories 640-648, 651-676 have required fifth-digits, which indicate whether the encounter is antepartum, postpartum and whether a delivery has also occurred.

4) Fifth-digits, appropriate for each code
The fifth-digits, which are appropriate for each code number, are listed in brackets under each code. The fifth-digits on each code should all be consistent with each other. That is, should a delivery occur all of the fifth-digits should indicate the delivery.

b. Selection of OB Principal or First-listed Diagnosis

1) Routine outpatient prenatal visits
For routine outpatient prenatal visits when no complications are present codes V22.0, Supervision of normal first pregnancy, and

V22.1, Supervision of other normal pregnancy, should be used as the first-listed diagnoses. These codes should not be used in conjunction with chapter 11 codes.

2) Prenatal outpatient visits for high-risk patients
For prenatal outpatient visits for patients with high-risk pregnancies, a code from category V23, Supervision of high-risk pregnancy, should be used as the first-listed diagnosis. Secondary Chapter 11 codes may be used in conjunction with these codes if appropriate.

3) Episodes when no delivery occurs
In episodes when no delivery occurs, the principal diagnosis should correspond to the principal complication of the pregnancy, which necessitated the encounter. Should more than one complication exist, all of which are treated or monitored, any of the complications codes may be sequenced first.

4) When a delivery occurs
When a delivery occurs, the principal diagnosis should correspond to the main circumstances or complication of the delivery. In cases of cesarean delivery, the selection of the principal diagnosis should correspond to the reason the cesarean delivery was performed unless the reason for admission/encounter was unrelated to the condition resulting in the cesarean delivery.

5) Outcome of delivery
An outcome of delivery code, V27.0-V27.9, should be included on every maternal record when a delivery has occurred. These codes are not to be used on subsequent records or on the newborn record.

c. Fetal conditions affecting the management of the mother

1) Codes from category 655
Known or suspected fetal abnormality affecting management of the mother, and category 656, Other fetal and placental problems affecting the management of the mother, are assigned only when the fetal condition is actually responsible for modifying the management of the mother, i.e., by requiring diagnostic studies, additional observation, special care, or termination of pregnancy. The fact that the fetal condition exists does not justify assigning a code from this series to the mother's record.
See I.C.18.d. for suspected maternal and fetal conditions not found

2) In utero surgery
In cases when surgery is performed on the fetus, a diagnosis code from category 655, Known or suspected fetal abnormalities affecting management of the mother, should be assigned identifying the fetal condition. Procedure code 75.36, Correction of fetal defect, should be assigned on the hospital inpatient record.
No code from Chapter 15, the perinatal codes, should be used on the mother's record to identify fetal conditions. Surgery performed in utero on a fetus is still to be coded as an obstetric encounter.

d. HIV infection in pregnancy, childbirth and the puerperium
During pregnancy, childbirth or the puerperium, a patient admitted because of an HIV-related illness should receive a principal diagnosis of 647.6x, Other specified infectious and parasitic diseases in the mother classifiable elsewhere, but complicating the pregnancy, childbirth or the puerperium, followed by 042 and the code(s) for the HIV-related illness(es).
Patients with asymptomatic HIV infection status admitted during pregnancy, childbirth, or the puerperium should receive codes of 647.6x and V08.

e. Current conditions complicating pregnancy
Assign a code from subcategory 648.x for patients that have current conditions when the condition affects the management of the pregnancy, childbirth, or the puerperium. Use additional secondary codes from other chapters to identify the conditions, as appropriate.

f. Diabetes mellitus in pregnancy
Diabetes mellitus is a significant complicating factor in pregnancy. Pregnant women who are diabetic should be assigned code 648.0x, Diabetes mellitus complicating pregnancy, and a secondary code from category 250, Diabetes mellitus, or category 249, Secondary diabetes to identify the type of diabetes.
Code V58.67, Long-term (current) use of insulin, should also be assigned if the diabetes mellitus is being treated with insulin.

g. Gestational diabetes
Gestational diabetes can occur during the second and third trimester of pregnancy in women who were not diabetic prior to pregnancy.

Gestational diabetes can cause complications in the pregnancy similar to those of pre-existing diabetes mellitus. It also puts the woman at greater risk of developing diabetes after the pregnancy. Gestational diabetes is coded to 648.8x, Abnormal glucose tolerance. Codes 648.0x and 648.8x should never be used together on the same record. Code V58.67, Long-term (current) use of insulin, should also be assigned if the gestational diabetes is being treated with insulin.

h. Normal delivery, Code 650

1) Normal delivery
Code 650 is for use in cases when a woman is admitted for a full-term normal delivery and delivers a single, healthy infant without any complications antepartum, during the delivery, or postpartum during the delivery episode. Code 650 is always a principal diagnosis. It is not to be used if any other code from chapter 11 is needed to describe a current complication of the antenatal, delivery, or perinatal period. Additional codes from other chapters may be used with code 650 if they are not related to or are in any way complicating the pregnancy.

2) Normal delivery with resolved antepartum complication
Code 650 may be used if the patient had a complication at some point during her pregnancy, but the complication is not present at the time of the admission for delivery.

3) V27.0, Single liveborn, outcome of delivery
V27.0, Single liveborn, is the only outcome of delivery code appropriate for use with 650.

i. The postpartum and peripartum periods

1) Postpartum and peripartum periods
The postpartum period begins immediately after delivery and continues for six weeks following delivery. The peripartum period is defined as the last month of pregnancy to five months postpartum.

2) Postpartum complication
A postpartum complication is any complication occurring within the six-week period.

3) Pregnancy-related complications after 6 week period
Chapter 11 codes may also be used to describe pregnancy-related complications after the six-week period should the provider document that a condition is pregnancy related.

4) Postpartum complications occurring during the same admission as delivery
Postpartum complications that occur during the same admission as the delivery are identified with a fifth-digit of "2." Subsequent admissions/encounters for postpartum complications should be identified with a fifth-digit of "4."

5) Admission for routine postpartum care following delivery outside hospital
When the mother delivers outside the hospital prior to admission and is admitted for routine postpartum care and no complications are noted, code V24.0, Postpartum care and examination immediately after delivery, should be assigned as the principal diagnosis.

6) Admission following delivery outside hospital with postpartum conditions
A delivery diagnosis code should not be used for a woman who has delivered prior to admission to the hospital. Any postpartum conditions and/or postpartum procedures should be coded.

j. Code 677, Late effect of complication of pregnancy

1) Code 677
Code 677, Late effect of complication of pregnancy, childbirth, and the puerperium is for use in those cases when an initial complication of a pregnancy develops a sequelae requiring care or treatment at a future date.

2) After the initial postpartum period
This code may be used at any time after the initial postpartum period.

3) Sequencing of Code 677
This code, like all late effect codes, is to be sequenced following the code describing the sequelae of the complication.

k. Abortions

1) Fifth-digits required for abortion categories
Fifth-digits are required for abortion categories 634-637.
Fifth-digit 1, incomplete, indicates that all of the products of

conception have not been expelled from the uterus. fifth-digit 2, complete, indicates that all products of conception have been expelled from the uterus prior to the episode of care.

2) Code from categories 640-648 and 651-659

A code from categories 640-648 and 651-659 may be used as additional codes with an abortion code to indicate the complication leading to the abortion.

Fifth-digit 3 is assigned with codes from these categories when used with an abortion code because the other fifth-digits will not apply. Codes from the 660-669 series are not to be used for complications of abortion.

3) Code 639 for complications

Code 639 is to be used for all complications following abortion. Code 639 cannot be assigned with codes from categories 634-638.

4) Abortion with liveborn fetus

When an attempted termination of pregnancy results in a liveborn fetus assign code 644.21, Early onset of delivery, with an appropriate code from category V27, Outcome of Delivery. The procedure code for the attempted termination of pregnancy should also be assigned.

5) Retained products of conception following an abortion

Subsequent admissions for retained products of conception following a spontaneous or legally induced abortion are assigned the appropriate code from category 634, Spontaneous abortion, or 635 Legally induced abortion, with a fifth-digit of "1" (incomplete). This advice is appropriate even when the patient was discharged previously with a discharge diagnosis of complete abortion.

12. Chapter 12: Diseases of Skin and Subcutaneous Tissue (680-709)

a. Pressure ulcer stage codes

1) Pressure ulcer stages

Two codes are needed to completely describe a pressure ulcer: A code from subcategory 707.0, Pressure ulcer, to identify the site of the pressure ulcer and a code from subcategory 707.2, Pressure ulcer stages.

The codes in subcategory 707.2, Pressure ulcer stages, are to be used as an additional diagnosis with a code(s) from subcategory 707.0, Pressure Ulcer. Codes from 707.2, Pressure ulcer stages, may not be assigned as a principal or first-listed diagnosis. The pressure ulcer stage codes should only be used with pressure ulcers and not with other types of ulcers (e.g., stasis ulcer).

The ICD-9-CM classifies pressure ulcer stages based on severity, which is designated by stages I-IV and unstageable.

2) Unstageable pressure ulcers

Assignment of code 707.25, Pressure ulcer, unstageable, should be based on the clinical documentation. Code 707.25 is used for pressure ulcers whose stage cannot be clinically determined (e.g., the ulcer is covered by eschar or has been treated with a skin or muscle graft) and pressure ulcers that are documented as deep tissue injury but not documented as due to trauma. This code should not be confused with code 707.20, Pressure ulcer, stage unspecified. Code 707.20 should be assigned when there is no documentation regarding the stage of the pressure ulcer.

3) Documented pressure ulcer stage

Assignment of the pressure ulcer stage code should be guided by clinical documentation of the stage or documentation of the terms found in the index. For clinical terms describing the stage that are not found in the index, and there is no documentation of the stage, the provider should be queried.

4) Bilateral pressure ulcers with same stage

When a patient has bilateral pressure ulcers (e.g., both buttocks) and both pressure ulcers are documented as being the same stage, only the code for the site and one code for the stage should be reported.

5) Bilateral pressure ulcers with different stages

When a patient has bilateral pressure ulcers at the same site (e.g., both buttocks) and each pressure ulcer is documented as being at a different stage, assign one code for the site and the appropriate codes for the pressure ulcer stage.

6) Multiple pressure ulcers of different sites and stages

When a patient has multiple pressure ulcers at different sites (e.g., buttock, heel, shoulder) and each pressure ulcer is documented as

being at different stages (e.g., stage 3 and stage 4), assign the appropriate codes for each different site and a code for each different pressure ulcer stage.

7) Patients admitted with pressure ulcers documented as healed

No code is assigned if the documentation states that the pressure ulcer is completely healed.

8) Patients admitted with pressure ulcers documented as healing

Pressure ulcers described as healing should be assigned the appropriate pressure ulcer stage code based on the documentation in the medical record. If the documentation does not provide information about the stage of the healing pressure ulcer, assign code 707.20, Pressure ulcer stage, unspecified.

If the documentation is unclear as to whether the patient has a current (new) pressure ulcer or if the patient is being treated for a healing pressure ulcer, query the provider.

9) Patient admitted with pressure ulcer evolving into another stage during the admission

If a patient is admitted with a pressure ulcer at one stage and it progresses to a higher stage, assign the code for highest stage reported for that site.

13. Chapter 13: Diseases of Musculoskeletal and Connective Tissue (710-739)

a. Coding of pathologic fractures

1) Acute fractures vs. aftercare

Pathologic fractures are reported using subcategory 733.1, when the fracture is newly diagnosed. Subcategory 733.1 may be used while the patient is receiving active treatment for the fracture. Examples of active treatment are: surgical treatment, emergency department encounter, evaluation and treatment by a new physician.

Fractures are coded using the aftercare codes (subcategories V54.0, V54.2, V54.8 or V54.9) for encounters after the patient has completed active treatment of the fracture and is receiving routine care for the fracture during the healing or recovery phase. Examples of fracture aftercare are: cast change or removal, removal of external or internal fixation device, medication adjustment, and follow up visits following fracture treatment.

Care for complications of surgical treatment for fracture repairs during the healing or recovery phase should be coded with the appropriate complication codes.

Care of complications of fractures, such as malunion and nonunion, should be reported with the appropriate codes.

See Section I. C. 17.b for information on the coding of traumatic fractures.

14. Chapter 14: Congenital Anomalies (740-759)

a. Codes in categories 740-759, congenital anomalies

Assign an appropriate code(s) from categories 740-759, Congenital Anomalies, when an anomaly is documented. A congenital anomaly may be the principal/first listed diagnosis on a record or a secondary diagnosis.

When a congenital anomaly does not have a unique code assignment, assign additional code(s) for any manifestations that may be present. When the code assignment specifically identifies the congenital anomaly, manifestations that are an inherent component of the anomaly should not be coded separately. Additional codes should be assigned for manifestations that are not an inherent component.

Codes from Chapter 14 may be used throughout the life of the patient. If a congenital anomaly has been corrected, a personal history code should be used to identify the history of the anomaly. Although present at birth, a congenital anomaly may not be identified until later in life. Whenever the condition is diagnosed by the physician, it is appropriate to assign a code from codes 740-759.

For the birth admission, the appropriate code from category V30, Liveborn infants, according to type of birth should be sequenced as the principal diagnosis, followed by any congenital anomaly codes, 740-759.

15. Chapter 15: Newborn (Perinatal) Guidelines (760-779)

For coding and reporting purposes the perinatal period is defined as before birth through the 28th day following birth. The following guidelines are provided for reporting purposes. Hospitals may record other diagnoses as needed for internal data use.

a. **General perinatal rules**
1) **Chapter 15 Codes**
   They are <u>never</u> for use on the maternal record. Codes from Chapter 11, the obstetric chapter, are never permitted on the newborn record. Chapter 15 code may be used throughout the life of the patient if the condition is still present.

2) **Sequencing of perinatal codes**
   Generally, codes from Chapter 15 should be sequenced as the principal/first-listed diagnosis on the newborn record, with the exception of the appropriate V30 code for the birth episode, followed by codes from any other chapter that provide additional detail. The "use additional code" note at the beginning of the chapter supports this guideline. If the index does not provide a specific code for a perinatal condition, assign code 779.89, Other specified conditions originating in the perinatal period, followed by the code from another chapter that specifies the condition. Codes for signs and symptoms may be assigned when a definitive diagnosis has not been established.

3) **Birth process or community acquired conditions**
   If a newborn has a condition that may be either due to the birth process or community acquired and the documentation does not indicate which it is, the default is due to the birth process and the code from Chapter 15 should be used. If the condition is community-acquired, a code from Chapter 15 should not be assigned.

4) **Code all clinically significant conditions**
   All clinically significant conditions noted on routine newborn examination should be coded. A condition is clinically significant if it requires:
   - clinical evaluation; or
   - therapeutic treatment; or
   - diagnostic procedures; or
   - extended length of hospital stay; or
   - increased nursing care and/or monitoring; or
   - has implications for future health care needs

   Note: The perinatal guidelines listed above are the same as the general coding guidelines for "additional diagnoses", except for the final point regarding implications for future health care needs. Codes should be assigned for conditions that have been specified by the provider as having implications for future health care needs. Codes from the perinatal chapter should not be assigned unless the provider has established a definitive diagnosis.

b. **Use of codes V30-V39**
   When coding the birth of an infant, assign a code from categories V30-V39, according to the type of birth. A code from this series is assigned as a principal diagnosis, and assigned only once to a newborn at the time of birth.

c. **Newborn transfers**
   If the newborn is transferred to another institution, the V30 series is not used at the receiving hospital.

d. **Use of category V29**
1) **Assigning a code from category V29**
   Assign a code from category V29, Observation and evaluation of newborns and infants for suspected conditions not found, to identify those instances when a healthy newborn is evaluated for a suspected condition that is determined after study not to be present. Do not use a code from category V29 when the patient has identified signs or symptoms of a suspected problem; in such cases, code the sign or symptom.

   A code from category V29 may also be assigned as a principal code for readmissions or encounters when the V30 code no longer applies. Codes from category V29 are for use only for healthy newborns and infants for which no condition after study is found to be present.

2) **V29 code on a birth record**
   A V29 code is to be used as a secondary code after the V30, Outcome of delivery, code.

e. **Use of other V codes on perinatal records**
   V codes other than V30 and V29 may be assigned on a perinatal or newborn record code. The codes may be used as a principal or first-listed diagnosis for specific types of encounters or for readmissions or encounters when the V30 code no longer applies.
   See Section I.C.18 for information regarding the assignment of V codes.

f. **Maternal causes of perinatal morbidity**
   Codes from categories 760-763, Maternal causes of perinatal morbidity and mortality, are assigned only when the maternal condition has actually affected the fetus or newborn. The fact that the mother has an associated medical condition or experiences some complication of pregnancy, labor or delivery does not justify the routine assignment of codes from these categories to the newborn record.

g. **Congenital anomalies in newborns**
   For the birth admission, the appropriate code from category V30, Liveborn infants according to type of birth, should be used, followed by any congenital anomaly codes, categories 740-759. Use additional secondary codes from other chapters to specify conditions associated with the anomaly, if applicable.
   Also, see Section I.C.14 for information on the coding of congenital anomalies.

h. **Coding additional perinatal diagnoses**
1) **Assigning codes for conditions that require treatment**
   Assign codes for conditions that require treatment or further investigation, prolong the length of stay, or require resource utilization.

2) **Codes for conditions specified as having implications for future health care needs**
   Assign codes for conditions that have been specified by the provider as having implications for future health care needs.
   Note: This guideline should not be used for adult patients.

3) **Codes for newborn conditions originating in the perinatal period**
   Assign a code for newborn conditions originating in the perinatal period (categories 760-779), as well as complications arising during the current episode of care classified in other chapters, only if the diagnoses have been documented by the responsible provider at the time of transfer or discharge as having affected the fetus or newborn.

i. **Prematurity and fetal growth retardation**
   Providers utilize different criteria in determining prematurity. A code for prematurity should not be assigned unless it is documented. The 5th digit assignment for codes from category 764 and subcategories 765.0 and 765.1 should be based on the recorded birth weight and estimated gestational age.

   A code from subcategory 765.2, Weeks of gestation, should be assigned as an additional code with category 764 and codes from 765.0 and 765.1 to specify weeks of gestation as documented by the provider in the record.

j. **Newborn sepsis**
   Code 771.81, Septicemia [sepsis] of newborn, should be assigned with a secondary code from category 041, Bacterial infections in conditions classified elsewhere and of unspecified site, to identify the organism. It is not necessary to use a code from subcategory 995.9, Systemic inflammatory response syndrome (SIRS), on a newborn record. Do not assign code 995.91, Sepsis, as code 771.81 describes the sepsis. If applicable, use additional codes to identify severe sepsis (995.92) and any associated acute organ dysfunction.

16. **Chapter 16: Signs, Symptoms and Ill-Defined Conditions (780-799)**
   Reserved for future guideline expansion

17. **Chapter 17: Injury and Poisoning (800-999)**
   a. **Coding of injuries**
   When coding injuries, assign separate codes for each injury unless a combination code is provided, in which case the combination code is assigned. Multiple injury codes are provided in ICD-9-CM, but should not be assigned unless information for a more specific code is not available. These codes are not to be used for normal, healing surgical wounds or to identify complications of surgical wounds.

   The code for the most serious injury, as determined by the provider and the focus of treatment, is sequenced first.

   1) **Superficial injuries**
   Superficial injuries such as abrasions or contusions are not coded when associated with more severe injuries of the same site.

   2) **Primary injury with damage to nerves/blood vessels**
   When a primary injury results in minor damage to peripheral nerves or blood vessels, the primary injury is sequenced first with additional code(s) from categories 950-957, Injury to nerves and spinal cord, and/or 900-904, Injury to blood vessels. When the primary injury is to the blood vessels or nerves, that injury should be sequenced first.

b. **Coding of traumatic fractures**

The principles of multiple coding of injuries should be followed in coding fractures. Fractures of specified sites are coded individually by site in accordance with both the provisions within categories 800-829 and the level of detail furnished by medical record content. Combination categories for multiple fractures are provided for use when there is insufficient detail in the medical record (such as trauma cases transferred to another hospital), when the reporting form limits the number of codes that can be used in reporting pertinent clinical data, or when there is insufficient specificity at the fourth-digit or fifth-digit level. More specific guidelines are as follows:

1) **Acute fractures vs. aftercare**

Traumatic fractures are coded using the acute fracture codes (800-829) while the patient is receiving active treatment for the fracture. Examples of active treatment are: surgical treatment, emergency department encounter, and evaluation and treatment by a new physician.

Fractures are coded using the aftercare codes (subcategories V54.0, V54.1, V54.8, or V54.9) for encounters after the patient has completed active treatment of the fracture and is receiving routine care for the fracture during the healing or recovery phase. Examples of fracture aftercare are: cast change or removal, removal of external or internal fixation device, medication adjustment, and follow up visits following fracture treatment.

Care for complications of surgical treatment for fracture repairs during the healing or recovery phase should be coded with the appropriate complication codes.

Care of complications of fractures, such as malunion and nonunion, should be reported with the appropriate codes.

Pathologic fractures are not coded in the 800-829 range, but instead are assigned to subcategory 733.1. *See Section I.C.13.a for additional information.*

2) **Multiple fractures of same limb**

Multiple fractures of same limb classifiable to the same three-digit or four-digit category are coded to that category.

3) **Multiple unilateral or bilateral fractures of same bone**

Multiple unilateral or bilateral fractures of same bone(s) but classified to different fourth-digit subdivisions (bone part) within the same three-digit category are coded individually by site.

4) **Multiple fracture categories 819 and 828**

Multiple fracture categories 819 and 828 classify bilateral fractures of both upper limbs (819) and both lower limbs (828), but without any detail at the fourth-digit level other than open and closed type of fractures.

5) **Multiple fractures sequencing**

Multiple fractures are sequenced in accordance with the severity of the fracture. The provider should be asked to list the fracture diagnoses in the order of severity.

c. **Coding of burns**

Current burns (940-948) are classified by depth, extent and by agent (E code). Burns are classified by depth as first degree (erythema), second degree (blistering), and third degree (full-thickness involvement).

1) **Sequencing of burn and related condition codes**

Sequence first the code that reflects the highest degree of burn when more than one burn is present.

a. When the reason for the admission or encounter is for treatment of external multiple burns, sequence first the code that reflects the burn of the highest degree.

b. When a patient has both internal and external burns, the circumstances of admission govern the selection of the principal diagnosis or first-listed diagnosis.

c. When a patient is admitted for burn injuries and other related conditions such as smoke inhalation and/or respiratory failure, the circumstances of admission govern the selection of the principal or first-listed diagnosis.

2) **Burns of the same local site**

Classify burns of the same local site (three-digit category level, 940-947) but of different degrees to the subcategory identifying the highest degree recorded in the diagnosis.

3) **Non-healing burns**

Non-healing burns are coded as acute burns.

Necrosis of burned skin should be coded as a non-healed burn.

4) **Code 958.3, posttraumatic wound infection**

Assign code 958.3, Posttraumatic wound infection, not elsewhere classified, as an additional code for any documented infected burn site.

5) **Assign separate codes for each burn site**

When coding burns, assign separate codes for each burn site. Category 946, Burns of Multiple specified sites, should only be used if the location of the burns are not documented. Category 949, Burn, unspecified, is extremely vague and should rarely be used.

6) **Assign codes from category 948, burns**

Burns classified according to extent of body surface involved, when the site of the burn is not specified or when there is a need for additional data. It is advisable to use category 948 as additional coding when needed to provide data for evaluating burn mortality, such as that needed by burn units. It is also advisable to use category 948 as an additional code for reporting purposes when there is mention of a third-degree burn involving 20 percent or more of the body surface.

In assigning a code from category 948:

Fourth-digit codes are used to identify the percentage of total body surface involved in a burn (all degree).

Fifth-digits are assigned to identify the percentage of body surface involved in third-degree burn.

Fifth-digit zero (0) is assigned when less than 10 percent or when no body surface is involved in a third-degree burn.

Category 948 is based on the classic "rule of nines" in estimating body surface involved: head and neck are assigned nine percent, each arm nine percent, each leg 18 percent, the anterior trunk 18 percent, posterior trunk 18 percent, and genitalia one percent. Providers may change these percentage assignments where necessary to accommodate infants and children who have proportionately larger heads than adults and patients who have large buttocks, thighs, or abdomen that involve burns.

7) **Encounters for treatment of late effects of burns**

Encounters for the treatment of the late effects of burns (i.e., scars or joint contractures) should be coded to the residual condition (sequelae) followed by the appropriate late effect code (906.5-906.9). A late effect E code may also be used, if desired.

8) **Sequelae with a late effect code and current burn**

When appropriate, both a sequelae with a late effect code, and a current burn code may be assigned on the same record (when both a current burn and sequelae of an old burn exist).

d. **Coding of debridement of wound, infection, or burn**

Excisional debridement involves surgical removal or cutting away, as opposed to a mechanical (brushing, scrubbing, washing) debridement. For coding purposes, excisional debridement is assigned to code 86.22. Nonexcisional debridement is assigned to code 86.28.

e. **Adverse effects, poisoning and toxic effects**

The properties of certain drugs, medicinal and biological substances or combinations of such substances, may cause toxic reactions. The occurrence of drug toxicity is classified in ICD-9-CM as follows:

1) **Adverse effect**

When the drug was correctly prescribed and properly administered, code the reaction plus the appropriate code from the E930-E949 series. Codes from the E930-E949 series must be used to identify the causative substance for an adverse effect of drug, medicinal and biological substances, correctly prescribed and properly administered. The effect, such as tachycardia, delirium, gastrointestinal hemorrhaging, vomiting, hypokalemia, hepatitis, renal failure, or respiratory failure, is coded and followed by the appropriate code from the E930-E949 series.

Adverse effects of therapeutic substances correctly prescribed and properly administered (toxicity, synergistic reaction, side effect, and idiosyncratic reaction) may be due to (1) differences among patients, such as age, sex, disease, and genetic factors, and (2) drug-related factors, such as type of drug, route of administration, duration of therapy, dosage, and bioavailability.

2) **Poisoning**

(a) **Error was made in drug prescription**

Errors made in drug prescription or in the administration of the drug by provider, nurse, patient, or other person, use the appropriate poisoning code from the 960-979 series.

(b) **Overdose of a drug intentionally taken**

If an overdose of a drug was intentionally taken or administered and resulted in drug toxicity, it would be coded as a poisoning (960-979 series).

(c) **Nonprescribed drug taken with correctly prescribed and properly administered drug**

If a nonprescribed drug or medicinal agent was taken in combination with a correctly prescribed and properly administered drug, any drug toxicity or other reaction resulting from the interaction of the two drugs would be classified as a poisoning.

(d) **Sequencing of poisoning**

When a reaction results from the interaction of a drug(s) and alcohol, this would be classified as poisoning.

(e) **Sequencing of poisoning**

When coding a poisoning or reaction to the improper use of a medication (e.g., wrong dose, wrong substance, wrong route of administration) the poisoning code is sequenced first, followed by a code for the manifestation. If there is also a diagnosis of drug abuse or dependence to the substance, the abuse or dependence is coded as an additional code.

See Section I.C.3.a.6.b. if poisoning is the result of insulin pump malfunctions and Section I.C.19 for general use of E-codes.

3) **Toxic effects**

(a) **Toxic effect codes**

When a harmful substance is ingested or comes in contact with a person, this is classified as a toxic effect. The toxic effect codes are in categories 980-989.

(b) **Sequencing toxic effect codes**

A toxic effect code should be sequenced first, followed by the code(s) that identify the result of the toxic effect.

(c) **External cause codes for toxic effects**

An external cause code from categories E860-E869 for accidental exposure, codes E950.6 or E950.7 for intentional self-harm, category E962 for assault, or categories E980-E982, for undetermined, should also be assigned to indicate intent.

f. **Complications of care**

1) **Complications of care**

(a) **Documentation of complications of care**

As with all procedural or postprocedural complications, code assignment is based on the provider's documentation of the relationship between the condition and the procedure.

2) **Transplant complications**

(a) **Transplant complications other than kidney**

Codes under subcategory 996.8, Complications of transplanted organ, are for use for both complications and rejection of transplanted organs. A transplant complication code is only assigned if the complication affects the function of the transplanted organ. Two codes are required to fully describe a transplant complication, the appropriate code from subcategory 996.8 and a secondary code that identifies the complication.

Pre-existing conditions or conditions that develop after the transplant are not coded as complications unless they affect the function of the transplanted organs.

See I.C.18.d.3) for transplant organ removal status

See I.C.2.i for malignant neoplasm associated with transplanted organ.

(b) **Chronic kidney disease and kidney transplant complications**

Patients who have undergone kidney transplant may still have some form of chronic kidney disease (CKD) because the kidney transplant may not fully restore kidney function. Code 996.81 should be assigned for documented complications of a kidney transplant, such as transplant failure or rejection or other transplant complication. Code 996.81 should not be assigned for post kidney transplant patients who have chronic kidney (CKD) unless a transplant complication such as transplant failure or rejection is documented. If the documentation is unclear as to whether the patient has a complication of the transplant, query the provider.

For patients with CKD following a kidney transplant, but who do not have a complication such as failure or rejection, see

section I.C.10.a.2, *Chronic kidney disease and kidney transplant status.*

3) **Ventilator associated pneumonia**

(a) **Documentation of Ventilator associated Pneumonia**

As with all procedural or postprocedural complications, code assignment is based on the provider's documentation of the relationship between the condition and the procedure.

Code 997.31, Ventilator associated pneumonia, should be assigned only when the provider has documented ventilator associated pneumonia (VAP). An additional code to identify the organism (e.g., Pseudomonas aeruginosa, code 041.7) should also be assigned. Do not assign an additional code from categories 480-484 to identify the type of pneumonia.

Code 997.31 should not be assigned for cases where the patient has pneumonia and is on a mechanical ventilator but the provider has not specifically stated that the pneumonia is ventilator-associated pneumonia.

If the documentation is unclear as to whether the patient has a pneumonia that is a complication attributable to the mechanical ventilator, query the provider.

(b) **Patient admitted with pneumonia and develops VAP**

A patient may be admitted with one type of pneumonia (e.g., code 481, Pneumococcal pneumonia) and subsequently develop VAP. In this instance, the principal diagnosis would be the appropriate code from categories 480-484 for the pneumonia diagnosed at the time of admission. Code 997.31, Ventilator associated pneumonia, would be assigned as an additional diagnosis when the provider has also documented the presence of ventilator associated pneumonia.

g. **SIRS due to non-infectious process**

The systemic inflammatory response syndrome (SIRS) can develop as a result of certain non-infectious disease processes, such as trauma, malignant neoplasm, or pancreatitis. When SIRS is documented with a noninfectious condition, and no subsequent infection is documented, the code for the underlying condition, such as an injury, should be assigned, followed by code 995.93, Systemic inflammatory response syndrome due to noninfectious process without acute organ dysfunction, or 995.94, Systemic inflammatory response syndrome due to non-infectious process with acute organ dysfunction. If an acute organ dysfunction is documented, the appropriate code(s) for the associated acute organ dysfunction(s) should be assigned in addition to code 995.94. If acute organ dysfunction is documented, but it cannot be determined if the acute organ dysfunction is associated with SIRS or due to another condition (e.g., directly due to the trauma), the provider should be queried.

When the non-infectious condition has led to an infection that results in SIRS, *see Section I.C.1.b.12 for the guideline for sepsis and severe sepsis associated with a non-infectious process.*

18. **Classification of Factors Influencing Health Status and Contact with Health Service (Supplemental V01-V89)**

Note: The chapter specific guidelines provide additional information about the use of V codes for specified encounters.

a. **Introduction**

ICD-9-CM provides codes to deal with encounters for circumstances other than a disease or injury. The Supplementary Classification of Factors Influencing Health Status and Contact with Health Services (V01.0 - V89.09) is provided to deal with occasions when circumstances other than a disease or injury (codes 001-V89.09) are recorded as a diagnosis or problem.

There are four primary circumstances for the use of V codes:

1) A person who is not currently sick encounters the health services for some specific reason, such as to act as an organ donor, to receive prophylactic care, such as inoculations or health screenings, or to receive counseling on health related issues.

2) A person with a resolving disease or injury, or a chronic, long-term condition requiring continuous care, encounters the health care system for specific aftercare of that disease or injury (e.g., dialysis for renal disease; chemotherapy for malignancy; cast change). A diagnosis/symptom code should be used whenever a current, acute, diagnosis is being treated or a sign or symptom is being studied.

3) Circumstances or problems influence a person's health status but are not in themselves a current illness or injury.

    4)   Newborns, to indicate birth status

b. V codes use in any healthcare setting

V codes are for use in any healthcare setting. V codes may be used as either a first listed (principal diagnosis code in the inpatient setting) or secondary code, depending on the circumstances of the encounter. Certain V codes may only be used as first listed, others only as secondary codes.

See Section I.C.18.e, V Code Table.

c. V Codes indicate a reason for an encounter

They are not procedure codes. A corresponding procedure code must accompany a V code to describe the procedure performed.

d. Categories of V codes

1) Contact/exposure

Category V01 indicates contact with or exposure to communicable diseases. These codes are for patients who do not show any sign or symptom of a disease but have been exposed to it by close personal contact with an infected individual or are in an area where a disease is epidemic. These codes may be used as a first listed code to explain an encounter for testing, or, more commonly, as a secondary code to identify a potential risk.

2) Inoculations and vaccinations

Categories V03-V06 are for encounters for inoculations and vaccinations. They indicate that a patient is being seen to receive a prophylactic inoculation against a disease. The injection itself must be represented by the appropriate procedure code. A code from V03-V06 may be used as a secondary code if the inoculation is given as a routine part of preventive health care, such as a well-baby visit.

3) Status

Status codes indicate that a patient is either a carrier of a disease or has the sequelae or residual of a past disease or condition. This includes such things as the presence of prosthetic or mechanical devices resulting from past treatment. A status code is informative, because the status may affect the course of treatment and its outcome. A status code is distinct from a history code. The history code indicates that the patient no longer has the condition.

A status code should not be used with a diagnosis code from one of the body system chapters, if the diagnosis code includes the information provided by the status code. For example, code V42.1, Heart transplant status, should not be used with code 996.83, Complications of transplanted heart. The status code does not provide additional information. The complication code indicates that the patient is a heart transplant patient.

The status V codes/categories are:

V02   Carrier or suspected carrier of infectious diseases
         Carrier status indicates that a person harbors the specific organisms of a disease without manifest symptoms and is capable of transmitting the infection.

V07.5x   Prophylactic use of agents affecting estrogen receptors and estrogen level
         This code indicates when a patient is receiving a drug that affects estrogen receptors and estrogen levels for prevention of cancer.

V08   Asymptomatic HIV infection status
         This code indicates that a patient has tested positive for HIV but has manifested no signs or symptoms of the disease.

V09   Infection with drug-resistant microorganisms
         This category indicates that a patient has an infection that is resistant to drug treatment. Sequence the infection code first.

V21   Constitutional states in development

V22.2   Pregnant state, incidental
         This code is a secondary code only for use when the pregnancy is in no way complicating the reason for visit. Otherwise, a code from the obstetric chapter is required.

V26.5x   Sterilization status

V42   Organ or tissue replaced by transplant

V43   Organ or tissue replaced by other means

V44   Artificial opening status

V45   Other postsurgical states

Assign code V45.87, Transplant organ removal status, to indicate that a transplanted organ has been previously removed. This code should not be assigned for the encounter in which the transplanted organ is removed. The complication necessitating removal of the transplant organ should be assigned for that encounter.

See section I.C17.f.2. for information on the coding of organ transplant complications.

Assign code V45.88, Status post administration of tPA (rtPA) in a different facility within the last 24 hours prior to admission to the current facility, as a secondary diagnosis when a patient is received by transfer into a facility and documentation indicates they were administered tissue plasminogen activator (tPA) within the last 24 hours prior to admission to the current facility.

This guideline applies even if the patient is still receiving the tPA at the time they are received into the current facility.

The appropriate code for the condition for which the tPA was administered (such as cerebrovascular disease or myocardial infarction) should be assigned first.

Code V45.88 is only applicable to the receiving facility record and not to the transferring facility record.

V46   Other dependence on machines

V49.6   Upper limb amputation status

V49.7   Lower limb amputation status
         Note: Categories V42-V46, and subcategories V49.6, V49.7 are for use only if there are no complications or malfunctions of the organ or tissue replaced, the amputation site or the equipment on which the patient is dependent.

V49.81   Postmenopausal status

V49.82   Dental sealant status

V49.83   Awaiting organ transplant status

V58.6x   Long-term (current) drug use
         Codes from this subcategory indicate a patient's continuous use of a prescribed drug (including such things as aspirin therapy) for the long-term treatment of a condition or for prophylactic use. It is not for use for patients who have addictions to drugs. This subcategory is not for use of medications for detoxification or maintenance programs to prevent withdrawal symptoms in patients with drug dependence (e.g., methadone maintenance for opiate dependence). Assign the appropriate code for the drug dependence instead.
         Assign a code from subcategory V58.6, Long-term (current) drug use, if the patient is receiving a medication for an extended period as a prophylactic measure (such as for the prevention of deep vein thrombosis) or as treatment of a chronic condition (such as arthritis) or a disease requiring a lengthy course of treatment (such as cancer). Do not assign a code from subcategory V58.6 for medication being administered for a brief period of time to treat an acute illness or injury (such as a course of antibiotics to treat acute bronchitis).

V83   Genetic carrier status
         Genetic carrier status indicates that a person carries a gene, associated with a particular disease, which may be passed to offspring who may develop that disease. The person does not have the disease and is not at risk of developing the disease.

V84   Genetic susceptibility status
         Genetic susceptibility indicates that a person has a gene that increases the risk of that person developing the disease.
         Codes from category V84, Genetic susceptibility to disease, should not be used as principal or first-listed codes. If the patient has the condition to which he/she is susceptible, and that condition is the reason for the encounter, the code for the current condition should

be sequenced first. If the patient is being seen for follow-up after completed treatment for this condition, and the condition no longer exists, a follow-up code should be sequenced first, followed by the appropriate personal history and genetic susceptibility codes. If the purpose of the encounter is genetic counseling associated with procreative management, a code from subcategory V26.3, Genetic counseling and testing, should be assigned as the first-listed code, followed by a code from category V84. Additional codes should be assigned for any applicable family or personal history. *See Section I.C. 18.d.14 for information on prophylactic organ removal due to a genetic susceptibility.*

| V86 | Estrogen receptor status |
| V88 | Acquired absence of other organs and tissue |

4) History (of)

There are two types of history V codes, personal and family. Personal history codes explain a patient's past medical condition that no longer exists and is not receiving any treatment, but that has the potential for recurrence, and therefore may require continued monitoring. The exceptions to this general rule are category V14, Personal history of allergy to medicinal agents, and subcategory V15.0, Allergy, other than to medicinal agents. A person who has had an allergic episode to a substance or food in the past should always be considered allergic to the substance.

Family history codes are for use when a patient has a family member(s) who has had a particular disease that causes the patient to be at higher risk of also contracting the disease.

Personal history codes may be used in conjunction with follow-up codes and family history codes may be used in conjunction with screening codes to explain the need for a test or procedure. History codes are also acceptable on any medical record regardless of the reason for visit. A history of an illness, even if no longer present, is important information that may alter the type of treatment ordered.

The history V code categories are:

V10	Personal history of malignant neoplasm
V12	Personal history of certain other diseases
V13	Personal history of other diseases
	Except: V13.4, Personal history of arthritis, and V13.6, Personal history of congenital malformations. These conditions are life-long so are not true history codes.
V14	Personal history of allergy to medicinal agents
V15	Other personal history presenting hazards to health
	Except: V15.7, Personal history of contraception.
V16	Family history of malignant neoplasm
V17	Family history of certain chronic disabling diseases
V18	Family history of certain other specific diseases
V19	Family history of other conditions
V87	Other specified personal exposures and history presenting hazards to health

5) Screening

Screening is the testing for disease or disease precursors in seemingly well individuals so that early detection and treatment can be provided for those who test positive for the disease. Screenings that are recommended for many subgroups in a population include: routine mammograms for women over 40, a fecal occult blood test for everyone over 50, an amniocentesis to rule out a fetal anomaly for pregnant women over 35, because the incidence of breast cancer and colon cancer in these subgroups is higher than in the general population, as is the incidence of Down's syndrome in older mothers.

The testing of a person to rule out or confirm a suspected diagnosis because the patient has some sign or symptom is a diagnostic examination, not a screening. In these cases, the sign or symptom is used to explain the reason for the test.

A screening code may be a first listed code if the reason for the visit is specifically the screening exam. It may also be used as an additional code if the screening is done during an office visit for other health problems. A screening code is not necessary if the screening is inherent to a routine examination, such as a pap smear done during a routine pelvic examination.

Should a condition be discovered during the screening then the code for the condition may be assigned as an additional diagnosis.

The V code indicates that a screening exam is planned. A procedure code is required to confirm that the screening was performed.

The screening V code categories:

| V28 | Antenatal screening |
| V73-V82 | Special screening examinations |

6) Observation

There are three observation V code categories. They are for use in very limited circumstances when a person is being observed for a suspected condition that is ruled out. The observation codes are not for use if an injury or illness or any signs or symptoms related to the suspected condition are present. In such cases the diagnosis/symptom code is used with the corresponding E code to identify any external cause.

The observation codes are to be used as principal diagnosis only. The only exception to this is when the principal diagnosis is required to be a code from the V30, Live born infant, category. Then the V29 observation code is sequenced after the V30 code. Additional codes may be used in addition to the observation code but only if they are unrelated to the suspected condition being observed.

Codes from subcategory V89.0, Suspected maternal and fetal conditions not found, may either be used as a first listed or as an additional code assignment depending on the case. They are for use in very limited circumstances on a maternal record when an encounter is for a suspected maternal or fetal condition that is ruled out during that encounter (for example, a maternal or fetal condition may be suspected due to an abnormal test result). These codes should not be used when the condition is confirmed. In those cases, the confirmed condition should be coded. In addition, these codes are not for use if an illness or any signs or symptoms related to the suspected condition or problem are present. In such cases the diagnosis/symptom code is used.

Additional codes may be used in addition to the code from subcategory V89.0, but only if they are unrelated to the suspected condition being evaluated.

Codes from subcategory V89.0 may not be used for encounters for antenatal screening of mother. *See Section I.C.18.d., Screening.*

For encounters for suspected fetal condition that are inconclusive following testing and evaluation, assign the appropriate code from category 655, 656, 657 or 658.

The observation V code categories:

V29	Observation and evaluation of newborns for suspected condition not found
	For the birth encounter, a code from category V30 should be sequenced before the V29 code.
V71	Observation and evaluation for suspected condition not found
V89	Suspected maternal and fetal conditions not found

7) Aftercare

Aftercare visit codes cover situations when the initial treatment of a disease or injury has been performed and the patient requires continued care during the healing or recovery phase, or for the long-term consequences of the disease. The aftercare V code should not be used if treatment is directed at a current, acute disease or injury. The diagnosis code is to be used in these cases. Exceptions to this rule are codes V58.0, Radiotherapy, and codes from subcategory V58.1, Encounter for chemotherapy and immunotherapy for neoplastic conditions. These codes are to be first listed, followed by the diagnosis code when a patient's encounter is solely to receive radiation therapy or chemotherapy for the treatment of a neoplasm. Should a patient receive both chemotherapy and radiation therapy during the same encounter code V58.0 and V58.1 may be used together on a record with either one being sequenced first.

The aftercare codes are generally first listed to explain the specific reason for the encounter. An aftercare code may be used as an additional code when some type of aftercare is provided in addition to the reason for admission and no diagnosis code is applicable. An example of this would be the closure of a colostomy during an encounter for treatment of another condition.

Aftercare codes should be used in conjunction with any other aftercare codes or other diagnosis codes to provide better detail on the specifics of an aftercare encounter visit, unless otherwise directed by the classification. The sequencing of multiple aftercare codes is discretionary.

Certain aftercare V code categories need a secondary diagnosis code to describe the resolving condition or sequelae, for others, the condition is inherent in the code title.

Additional V code aftercare category terms include, fitting and adjustment, and attention to artificial openings.

Status V codes may be used with aftercare V codes to indicate the nature of the aftercare. For example code V45.81, Aortocoronary bypass status, may be used with code V58.73, Aftercare following surgery of the circulatory system, NEC, to indicate the surgery for which the aftercare is being performed. Also, a transplant status code may be used following code V58.44, Aftercare following organ transplant, to identify the organ transplanted. A status code should not be used when the aftercare code indicates the type of status, such as using V55.0, Attention to tracheostomy with V44.0, Tracheostomy status.

See Section I. B.16 Admissions/Encounter for Rehabilitation

The aftercare V category/codes:

V51.0	Encounter for breast reconstruction following mastectomy
V52	Fitting and adjustment of prosthetic device and implant
V53	Fitting and adjustment of other device
V54	Other orthopedic aftercare
V55	Attention to artificial openings
V56	Encounter for dialysis and dialysis catheter care
V57	Care involving the use of rehabilitation procedures
V58.0	Radiotherapy
V58.11	Encounter for antineoplastic chemotherapy
V58.12	Encounter for antineoplastic immunotherapy
V58.3x	Attention to dressings and sutures
V58.41	Encounter for planned post-operative wound closure
V58.42	Aftercare, surgery, neoplasm
V58.43	Aftercare, surgery, trauma
V58.44	Aftercare involving organ transplant
V58.49	Other specified aftercare following surgery
V58.7x	Aftercare following surgery
V58.81	Fitting and adjustment of vascular catheter
V58.82	Fitting and adjustment of non-vascular catheter
V58.83	Monitoring therapeutic drug
V58.89	Other specified aftercare

8) **Follow-up**

The follow-up codes are used to explain continuing surveillance following completed treatment of a disease, condition, or injury. They imply that the condition has been fully treated and no longer exists. They should not be confused with aftercare codes that explain current treatment for a healing condition or its sequelae. Follow-up codes may be used in conjunction with history codes to provide the full picture of the healed condition and its treatment. The follow-up code is sequenced first, followed by the history code.

A follow-up code may be used to explain repeated visits. Should a condition be found to have recurred on the follow-up visit, then the diagnosis code should be used in place of the follow-up code.

The follow-up V code categories:

V24	Postpartum care and evaluation
V67	Follow-up examination

9) **Donor**

Category V59 is the donor codes. They are used for living individuals who are donating blood or other body tissue. These codes are only for individuals donating for others, not for self donations. They are not for use to identify cadaveric donations.

10) **Counseling**

Counseling V codes are used when a patient or family member receives assistance in the aftermath of an illness or injury, or when support is required in coping with family or social problems. They

are not necessary for use in conjunction with a diagnosis code when the counseling component of care is considered integral to standard treatment.

The counseling V categories/codes:

V25.0	General counseling and advice for contraceptive management
V26.3	Genetic counseling
V26.4	General counseling and advice for procreative management
V61.x	Other family circumstances
V65.1	Person consulted on behalf of another person
V65.3	Dietary surveillance and counseling
V65.4	Other counseling, not elsewhere classified

11) **Obstetrics and related conditions**

See Section I.C.11., the Obstetrics guidelines for further instruction on the use of these codes.

V codes for pregnancy are for use in those circumstances when none of the problems or complications included in the codes from the Obstetrics chapter exist (a routine prenatal visit or postpartum care). Codes V22.0, Supervision of normal first pregnancy, and V22.1, Supervision of other normal pregnancy, are always first listed and are not to be used with any other code from the OB chapter.

The outcome of delivery, category V27, should be included on all maternal delivery records. It is always a secondary code.

V codes for family planning (contraceptive) or procreative management and counseling should be included on an obstetric record either during the pregnancy or the postpartum stage, if applicable.

Obstetrics and related conditions V code categories:

V22	Normal pregnancy
V23	Supervision of high-risk pregnancy
	Except: V23.2, Pregnancy with history of abortion. Code 646.3, Habitual aborter, from the OB chapter is required to indicate a history of abortion during a pregnancy.
V24	Postpartum care and evaluation
V25	Encounter for contraceptive management
	Except V25.0x
	See Section I.C.18.d.11, Counseling
V26	Procreative management
	Except V26.5x, Sterilization status, V26.3 and V26.4
	See Section I.C.18.d.11, Counseling
V27	Outcome of delivery
V28	Antenatal screening
	See Section I.C.18.d.6., Screening

12) **Newborn, infant and child**

See Section I.C.15, the Newborn guidelines for further instruction on the use of these codes.

Newborn V code categories:

V20	Health supervision of infant or child
V29	Observation and evaluation of newborns for suspected condition not found
	See Section I.C.18.d.7, Observation
V30-V39	Liveborn infant according to type of birth

13) **Routine and administrative examinations**

The V codes allow for the description of encounters for routine examinations, such as, a general check-up, or, examinations for administrative purposes, such as, a pre-employment physical. The codes are not to be used if the examination is for diagnosis of a suspected condition or for treatment purposes. In such cases the diagnosis code is used. During a routine exam, should a diagnosis or condition be discovered, it should be coded as an additional code. Pre-existing and chronic conditions and history codes may also be included as additional codes as long as the examination is for administrative purposes and not focused on any particular condition.

Pre-operative examination V codes are for use only in those situations when a patient is being cleared for surgery and no treatment is given.

The V codes categories/code for routine and administrative examinations:

V20.2   Routine infant or child health check
Any injections given should have a corresponding procedure code.

V70   General medical examination

V72   Special investigations and examinations
Codes V72.5 and V72.6 may be used if the reason for the patient encounter is for routine laboratory/radiology testing in the absence of any signs, symptoms, or associated diagnosis. If routine testing is performed during the same encounter as a test to evaluate a sign, symptom, or diagnosis, it is appropriate to assign both the V code and the code describing the reason for the non-routine test.

14) Miscellaneous V codes

The miscellaneous V codes capture a number of other health care encounters that do not fall into one of the other categories. Certain of these codes identify the reason for the encounter, others are for use as additional codes that provide useful information on circumstances that may affect a patient's care and treatment.

Prophylactic organ removal

For encounters specifically for prophylactic removal of breasts, ovaries, or another organ due to a genetic susceptibility to cancer or a family history of cancer, the principal or first listed code should be a code from subcategory V50.4, Prophylactic organ removal, followed by the appropriate genetic susceptibility code and the appropriate family history code.

If the patient has a malignancy of one site and is having prophylactic removal at another site to prevent either a new primary malignancy or metastatic disease, a code for the malignancy should also be assigned in addition to a code from subcategory V50.4. A V50.4 code should not be assigned if the patient is having organ removal for treatment of a malignancy, such as the removal of the testes for the treatment of prostate cancer.

Miscellaneous V code categories/codes:

V07   Need for isolation and other prophylactic measures
Except V07.5, Prophylactic use of agents affecting estrogen receptors and estrogen levels

V50   Elective surgery for purposes other than remedying health states

V58.5   Orthodontics

V60   Housing, household, and economic circumstances

V62   Other psychosocial circumstances

V63   Unavailability of other medical facilities for care

V64   Persons encountering health services for specific procedures, not carried out

V66   Convalescence and palliative care

V68   Encounters for administrative purposes

V69   Problems related to lifestyle

V85   Body Mass Index

15) Nonspecific V codes

Certain V codes are so non-specific, or potentially redundant with other codes in the classification, that there can be little justification for their use in the inpatient setting. Their use in the outpatient setting should be limited to those instances when there is no further documentation to permit more precise coding. Otherwise, any sign or symptom or any other reason for visit that is captured in another code should be used.

Nonspecific V code categories/codes:

V11   Personal history of mental disorder A code from the mental disorders chapter, with an in remission fifth-digit, should be used.

V13.4   Personal history of arthritis

V13.6   Personal history of congenital malformations

V15.7   Personal history of contraception

V23.2   Pregnancy with history of abortion

V40   Mental and behavioral problems

V41   Problems with special senses and other special functions

V47   Other problems with internal organs

V48   Problems with head, neck, and trunk

V49   Problems with limbs and other problems
Exception:
V49.6   Upper limb amputation status
V49.7   Lower limb amputation status
V49.81   Postmenopausal status
V49.82   Dental sealant status
V49.83   Awaiting organ transplant status

V51.8   Other aftercare involving the use of plastic surgery

V58.2   Blood transfusion, without reported diagnosis

V58.9   Unspecified aftercare
See Section IV.K. and Section IV.L. of the Outpatient guidelines.

V CODE TABLE

October 1, 2008 (FY2009)

The following V code table contains columns for 1st listed, 1st or additional, additional only, and non-specific. Each code or category is listed on the left hand column and the allowable sequencing of the code or codes within the category is noted under the appropriate column.

As indicated by the footnote in the "1st Dx Only" column, the V codes designated as first-listed only are generally intended to be limited for use as a first-listed only diagnosis, but may be reported as an additional diagnosis in those situations when the patient has more than one encounter on a single day and the codes for the multiple encounters are combined, or when there is more than one V code that meets the definition of principal diagnosis (e.g., a patient is admitted to home healthcare for both aftercare and rehabilitation and they equally meet the definition of principal diagnosis). The V codes designated as first-listed only should not be reported if they do not meet the definition of principal or first-listed diagnosis.

See Section II and Section IV.A for information on selection of principal and first-listed diagnosis.

See Section II.C for information on two or more diagnoses that equally meet the definition for principal diagnosis.

Code(s)	Description	1st Dx Only[1]	1st or Add'l Dx[2]	Add'l Dx Only[3]	Non-Specific Diagnosis[4]
V01.X	Contact with or exposure to communicable diseases		X		
V02.X	Carrier or suspected carrier of infectious diseases		X		
V03.X	Need for prophylactic vaccination and inoculation against bacterial diseases		X		
V04.X	Need for prophylactic vaccination and inoculation against certain diseases		X		
V05.X	Need for prophylactic vaccination and inoculation against single diseases		X		
V06.X	Need for prophylactic vaccination and inoculation against combinations of diseases		X		
V07.0	Isolation		X		
V07.1	Desensitization to allergens		X		
V07.2	Prophylactic immunotherapy		X		
V07.3X	Other prophylactic chemotherapy		X		
V07.4	Hormone replacement therapy (postmenopausal)			X	
V07.5X	Prophylactic use of agents affecting estrogen receptors and estrogen levels			X	
V07.8	Other specified prophylactic measure		X		

1.   Generally for use as first listed only but may be used as additional if patient has more than one encounter on one day or there is more than one reason for the encounter
2.   These codes may be used as first listed or additional codes
3.   These codes are only for use as additional codes
4.   These codes are primarily for use in the nonacute setting and should be limited to encounters for which no sign or symptom or reason for visit is documented in the record. Their use may be as either a first listed or additional code.

Code(s)	Description	1st Dx Only[1]	1st or Add'l Dx[2]	Add'l Dx Only[3]	Non-Specific Diagnosis[4]
V07.9	Unspecified prophylactic measure				X
V08	Asymptomatic HIV infection status		X		
V09.X	Infection with drug resistant organisms			X	
V10.X	Personal history of malignant neoplasm		X		
V11.X	Personal history of mental disorder				X
V12.X	Personal history of certain other diseases		X		
V13.0X	Personal history of other disorders of urinary system		X		
V13.1	Personal history of trophoblastic disease		X		
V13.2X	Personal history of other genital system and obstetric disorders		X		
V13.3	Personal history of diseases of skin and subcutaneous tissue		X		
V13.4	Personal history of arthritis				X
V13.5X	Personal history of other musculoskeletal disorders		X		
V13.61	Personal history of hypospadias			X	
V13.69	Personal history of congenital malformations				X
V13.7	Personal history of perinatal problems		X		
V13.8	Personal history of other specified diseases		X		
V13.9	Personal history of unspecified disease				X
V14.X	Personal history of allergy to medicinal agents			X	
V15.0X	Personal history of allergy, other than to medicinal agents			X	
V15.1	Personal history of surgery to heart and great vessels			X	
V15.2X	Personal history of surgery to other organs			X	
V15.3	Personal history of irradiation			X	
V15.4X	Personal history of psychological trauma			X	
V15.5X	Personal history of injury			X	
V15.6	Personal history of poisoning			X	
V15.7	Personal history of contraception				X
V15.81	Personal history of noncompliance with medical treatment			X	
V15.82	Personal history of tobacco use			X	
V15.84	Personal history of exposure to asbestos			X	
V15.85	Personal history of exposure to potentially hazardous body fluids			X	
V15.86	Personal history of exposure to lead			X	
V15.87	Personal history of extracorporeal membrane oxygenation [ECMO]			X	
V15.88	History of fall		X		
V15.89	Other specified personal history presenting hazards to health			X	
V16.X	Family history of malignant neoplasm		X		
V17.X	Family history of certain chronic disabling diseases		X		
V18.X	Family history of certain other specific conditions		X		
V19.X	Family history of other conditions		X		
V20.X	Health supervision of infant or child	X			
V21.X	Constitutional states in development			X	
V22.0	Supervision of normal first pregnancy	X			
V22.1	Supervision of other normal pregnancy	X			
V22.2	Pregnancy state, incidental			X	
V23.X	Supervision of high-risk pregnancy		X		
V24.X	Postpartum care and examination	X			
V25.X	Encounter for contraceptive management		X		
V26.0	Tuboplasty or vasoplasty after previous sterilization		X		
V26.1	Artificial insemination		X		
V26.2X	Procreative management investigation and testing		X		
V26.3X	Procreative management, genetic counseling and testing		X		
V26.4X	Procreative management, genetic counseling and advice		X		
V26.5X	Procreative management, sterilization status			X	
V26.81	Encounter for assisted reproductive fertility procedure cycle	X			
V26.89	Other specified procreative management		X		
V26.9	Unspecified procreative management		X		
V27.X	Outcome of delivery			X	
V28.X	Encounter for antenatal screening of mother		X		
V29.X	Observation and evaluation of newborns for suspected condition not found		X		
V30.X	Single liveborn	X			

1. Generally for use as first listed only but may be used as additional if patient has more than one encounter on one day or there is more than one reason for the encounter
2. These codes may be used as first listed or additional codes
3. These codes are only for use as additional codes
4. These codes are primarily for use in the nonacute setting and should be limited to encounters for which no sign or symptom or reason for visit is documented in the record. Their use may be as either a first listed or additional code.

Code(s)	Description	1st Dx Only[1]	1st or Add'l Dx[2]	Add'l Dx Only[3]	Non-Specific Diagnosis[4]
V31.X	Twin, mate liveborn	X			
V32.X	Twin, mate stillborn	X			
V33.X	Twin, unspecified	X			
V34.X	Other multiple, mates all liveborn	X			
V35.X	Other multiple, mates all stillborn	X			
V36.X	Other multiple, mates live- and stillborn	X			
V37.X	Other multiple, unspecified	X			
V39.X	Unspecified	X			
V40.X	Mental and behavioral problems				X
V41.X	Problems with special senses and other special functions				X
V42.X	Organ or tissue replaced by transplant			X	
V43.0	Organ or tissue replaced by other means, eye globe			X	
V43.1	Organ or tissue replaced by other means, lens			X	
V43.21	Organ or tissue replaced by other means, heart assist device			X	
V43.22	Fully implantable artificial heart status		X		
V43.3	Organ or tissue replaced by other means, heart valve			X	
V43.4	Organ or tissue replaced by other means, blood vessel			X	
V43.5	Organ or tissue replaced by other means, bladder			X	
V43.6X	Organ or tissue replaced by other means, joint			X	
V43.7	Organ or tissue replaced by other means, limb			X	
V43.8X	Other organ or tissue replaced by other means			X	
V44.X	Artificial opening status			X	
V45.0X	Cardiac device in situ			X	
V45.1X	Renal dialysis status			X	
V45.2	Presence of cerebrospinal fluid drainage device			X	
V45.3	Intestinal bypass or anastomosis status			X	
V45.4	Arthrodesis status			X	
V45.5X	Presence of contraceptive device			X	
V45.6X	States following surgery of eye and adnexa			X	
V45.7X	Acquired absence of organ		X		
V45.8X	Other postprocedural status			X	
V46.0	Other dependence on machines, aspirator			X	
V46.11	Dependence on respiratory, status			X	
V46.12	Encounter for respirator dependence during power failure	X			
V46.13	Encounter for weaning from respirator [ventilator]	X			
V46.14	Mechanical complication of respirator [ventilator]		X		
V46.2	Other dependence on machines, supplemental oxygen			X	
V46.3	Wheelchair dependence			X	
V46.8	Other dependence on other enabling machines			X	
V46.9	Unspecified machine dependence				X
V47.X	Other problems with internal organs				X
V48.X	Problems with head, neck and trunk				X
V49.0	Deficiencies of limbs				X
V49.1	Mechanical problems with limbs				X
V49.2	Motor problems with limbs				X
V49.3	Sensory problems with limbs				X
V49.4	Disfigurements of limbs				X
V49.5	Other problems with limbs				X
V49.6X	Upper limb amputation status		X		
V49.7X	Lower limb amputation status		X		
V49.81	Asymptomatic postmenopausal status (age-related) (natural)		X		
V49.82	Dental sealant status			X	
V49.83	Awaiting organ transplant status			X	
V49.84	Bed confinement status		X		
V49.85	Dual sensory impairment			X	
V49.89	Other specified conditions influencing health status		X		
V49.9	Unspecified condition influencing health status				X
V50.X	Elective surgery for purposes other than remedying health states		X		
V51.0	Encounter for breast reconstruction following mastectomy	X			

1. Generally for use as first listed only but may be used as additional if patient has more than one encounter on one day or there is more than one reason for the encounter
2. These codes may be used as first listed or additional codes
3. These codes are only for use as additional codes
4. These codes are primarily for use in the nonacute setting and should be limited to encounters for which no sign or symptom or reason for visit is documented in the record. Their use may be as either a first listed or additional code.

Code(s)	Description	1st Dx Only[1]	1st or Add'l Dx[2]	Add'l Dx Only[3]	Non-Specific Diagnosis[4]
V51.8	Other aftercare involving the use of plastic surgery				X
V52.X	Fitting and adjustment of prosthetic device and implant		X		
V53.X	Fitting and adjustment of other device		X		
V54.X	Other orthopedic aftercare		X		
V55.X	Attention to artificial openings		X		
V56.0	Extracorporeal dialysis	X			
V56.1	Encounter for fitting and adjustment of extracorporeal dialysis catheter		X		
V56.2	Encounter for fitting and adjustment of peritoneal dialysis catheter		X		
V56.3X	Encounter for adequacy testing for dialysis		X		
V56.8	Encounter for other dialysis and dialysis catheter care		X		
V57.X	Care involving use of rehabilitation procedures	X			
V58.0	Radiotherapy	X			
V58.11	Encounter for antineoplastic chemotherapy	X			
V58.12	Encounter for antineoplastic immunotherapy	X			
V58.2	Blood transfusion without reported diagnosis				X
V58.3X	Attention to dressings and sutures		X		
V58.4X	Other aftercare following surgery		X		
V58.5	Encounter for orthodontics				X
V58.6X	Long term (current) drug use			X	
V58.7X	Aftercare following surgery to specified body systems, not elsewhere classified		X		
V58.8X	Other specified procedures and aftercare		X		
V58.9	Unspecified aftercare				X
V59.X	Donors	X			
V60.X	Housing, household, and economic circumstances			X	
V61.X	Other family circumstances		X		
V62.X	Other psychosocial circumstances			X	
V63.X	Unavailability of other medical facilities for care		X		
V64.X	Persons encountering health services for specified procedure, not carried out			X	
V65.X	Other persons seeking consultation without complaint or sickness		X		
V66.0	Convalescence and palliative care following surgery	X			
V66.1	Convalescence and palliative care following radiotherapy	X			
V66.2	Convalescence and palliative care following chemotherapy	X			
V66.3	Convalescence and palliative care following psychotherapy and other treatment for mental disorder	X			
V66.4	Convalescence and palliative care following treatment of fracture	X			
V66.5	Convalescence and palliative care following other treatment	X			
V66.6	Convalescence and palliative care following combined treatment	X			
V66.7	Encounter for palliative care			X	
V66.9	Unspecified convalescence	X			
V67.X	Follow-up examination		X		
V68.X	Encounters for administrative purposes	X			
V69.X	Problems related to lifestyle		X		
V70.0	Routine general medical examination at a health care facility	X			
V70.1	General psychiatric examination, requested by the authority	X			
V70.2	General psychiatric examination, other and unspecified	X			
V70.3	Other medical examination for administrative purposes	X			
V70.4	Examination for medicolegal reasons	X			
V70.5	Health examination of defined subpopulations	X			
V70.6	Health examination in population surveys	X			
V70.7	Examination of participant in clinical trial		X		
V70.8	Other specified general medical examinations	X			
V70.9	Unspecified general medical examination	X			
V71.X	Observation and evaluation for suspected conditions not found	X			
V72.0	Examination of eyes and vision		X		
V72.1X	Examination of ears and hearing		X		
V72.2	Dental examination		X		
V72.3X	Gynecological examination		X		
V72.4X	Pregnancy examination or test		X		
V72.5	Radiological examination, NEC		X		

1. Generally for use as first listed only but may be used as additional if patient has more than one encounter on one day or there is more than one reason for the encounter
2. These codes may be used as first listed or additional codes
3. These codes are only for use as additional codes
4. These codes are primarily for use in the nonacute setting and should be limited to encounters for which no sign or symptom or reason for visit is documented in the record. Their use may be as either a first listed or additional code.

Code(s)	Description	1st Dx Only[1]	1st or Add'l Dx[2]	Add'l Dx Only[3]	Non-Specific Diagnosis[4]
V72.6	Laboratory examination		X		
V72.7	Diagnostic skin and sensitization tests		X		
V72.81	Preoperative cardiovascular examination		X		
V72.82	Preoperative respiratory examination		X		
V72.83	Other specified preoperative examination		X		
V72.84	Preoperative examination, unspecified		X		
V72.85	Other specified examination		X		
V72.86	Encounter for blood typing		X		
V72.9	Unspecified examination				X
V73.X	Special screening examination for viral and chlamydial diseases		X		
V74.X	Special screening examination for bacterial and spirochetal diseases		X		
V75.X	Special screening examination for other infectious diseases		X		
V76.X	Special screening examination for malignant neoplasms		X		
V77.X	Special screening examination for endocrine, nutritional, metabolic and immunity disorders		X		
V78.X	Special screening examination for disorders of blood and blood-forming organs		X		
V79.X	Special screening examination for mental disorders and developmental handicaps		X		
V80.X	Special screening examination for neurological, eye, and ear diseases		X		
V81.X	Special screening examination for cardiovascular, respiratory, and genitourinary diseases		X		
V82.X	Special screening examination for other conditions		X		
V83.X	Genetic carrier status		X		
V84.X	Genetic susceptibility to disease			X	
V85	Body mass index			X	
V86	Estrogen receptor status			X	
V87.0X	Contact with and (suspected) exposure to hazardous metals		X		
V87.1X	Contact with and (suspected) exposure to hazardous aromatic compounds		X		
V87.2	Contact with and (suspected) exposure to other potentially hazardous chemicals		X		
V87.3X	Contact with and (suspected) exposure to other potentially hazardous substances		X		
V87.4X	Personal history of drug therapy			X	
V88.0X	Acquired absence of cervix and uterus			X	
V89.0X	Suspected maternal and fetal anomalies not found		X		

1.   Generally for use as first listed only but may be used as additional if patient has more than one encounter on one day or there is more than one reason for the encounter
2.   These codes may be used as first listed or additional codes
3.   These codes are only for use as additional codes
4.   These codes are primarily for use in the nonacute setting and should be limited to encounters for which no sign or symptom or reason for visit is documented in the record. Their use may be as either a first listed or additional code.

19. **Supplemental Classification of External Causes of Injury and Poisoning (E codes, E800-E999)**

Introduction: These guidelines are provided for those who are currently collecting E codes in order that there will be standardization in the process. If your institution plans to begin collecting E codes, these guidelines are to be applied. The use of E codes is supplemental to the application of ICD-9-CM diagnosis codes. E codes are never to be recorded as principal diagnoses (first-listed in non-inpatient setting) and are not required for reporting to CMS.

External causes of injury and poisoning codes (E codes) are intended to provide data for injury research and evaluation of injury prevention strategies. E codes capture how the injury or poisoning happened (cause), the intent (unintentional or accidental; or intentional, such as suicide or assault), and the place where the event occurred.

Some major categories of E codes include:

- transport accidents
- poisoning and adverse effects of drugs, medicinal substances and biologicals
- accidental falls
- accidents caused by fire and flames
- accidents due to natural and environmental factors
- late effects of accidents, assaults or self injury
- assaults or purposely inflicted injury
- suicide or self inflicted injury

These guidelines apply for the coding and collection of E codes from records in hospitals, outpatient clinics, emergency departments, other ambulatory care settings and provider offices, and nonacute care settings, except when other specific guidelines apply.

a. **General E code coding guidelines**

1) **Used with any code in the range of 001-V89**

An E code may be used with any code in the range of 001-V89, which indicates an injury, poisoning, or adverse effect due to an external cause.

2) **Assign the appropriate E code for all initial treatments**

Assign the appropriate E code for the initial encounter of an injury, poisoning, or adverse effect of drugs, not for subsequent treatment.

External cause of injury codes (E-codes) may be assigned while the acute fracture codes are still applicable.

See Section I.C.17.b.1 for coding of acute fractures.

3) **Use the full range of E codes**

Use the full range of E codes to completely describe the cause, the intent and the place of occurrence, if applicable, for all injuries, poisonings, and adverse effects of drugs.

4) **Assign as many E codes as necessary**

Assign as many E codes as necessary to fully explain each cause. If only one E code can be recorded, assign the E code most related to the principal diagnosis.

5) **The selection of the appropriate E code**

The selection of the appropriate E code is guided by the Index to External Causes, which is located after the alphabetical index to diseases and by Inclusion and Exclusion notes in the Tabular List.

6) **E code can never be a principal diagnosis**

An E code can never be a principal (first listed) diagnosis.

7) **External cause code(s) with systemic inflammatory response syndrome (SIRS)**

An external cause code is not appropriate with a code from subcategory 995.9, unless the patient also has an injury, poisoning, or adverse effect of drugs.

b. **Place of occurrence guideline**
Use an additional code from category E849 to indicate the Place of Occurrence for injuries and poisonings. The Place of Occurrence describes the place where the event occurred and not the patient's activity at the time of the event.
Do not use E849.9 if the place of occurrence is not stated.

c. **Adverse effects of drugs, medicinal and biological substances guidelines**
1) **Do not code directly from the Table of Drugs**
Do not code directly from the Table of Drugs and Chemicals. Always refer back to the Tabular List.
2) **Use as many codes as necessary to describe**
Use as many codes as necessary to describe completely all drugs, medicinal or biological substances.
3) **If the same E code would describe the causative agent**
If the same E code would describe the causative agent for more than one adverse reaction, assign the code only once.
4) **If two or more drugs, medicinal or biological substances**
If two or more drugs, medicinal or biological substances are reported, code each individually unless the combination code is listed in the Table of Drugs and Chemicals. In that case, assign the E code for the combination.
5) **When a reaction results from the interaction of a drug(s)**
When a reaction results from the interaction of a drug(s) and alcohol, use poisoning codes and E codes for both.
6) **If the reporting format limits the number of E codes**
If the reporting format limits the number of E codes that can be used in reporting clinical data, code the one most related to the principal diagnosis. Include at least one from each category (cause, intent, place) if possible.
If there are different fourth-digit codes in the same three digit category, use the code for "Other specified" of that category. If there is no "Other specified" code in that category, use the appropriate "Unspecified" code in that category.
If the codes are in different three digit categories, assign the appropriate E code for other multiple drugs and medicinal substances.
7) **Codes from the E930-E949 series**
Codes from the E930-E949 series must be used to identify the causative substance for an adverse effect of drug, medicinal and biological substances, correctly prescribed and properly administered. The effect, such as tachycardia, delirium, gastrointestinal hemorrhaging, vomiting, hypokalemia, hepatitis, renal failure, or respiratory failure, is coded and followed by the appropriate code from the E930-E949 series.

d. **Multiple cause E code coding guidelines**
If two or more events cause separate injuries, an E code should be assigned for each cause. The first listed E code will be selected in the following order:
E codes for child and adult abuse take priority over all other E codes.
See Section I.C.19.e., Child and Adult abuse guidelines.
E codes for terrorism events take priority over all other E codes except child and adult abuse.
E codes for cataclysmic events take priority over all other E codes except child and adult abuse and terrorism.
E codes for transport accidents take priority over all other E codes except cataclysmic events and child and adult abuse and terrorism.
The first-listed E code should correspond to the cause of the most serious diagnosis due to an assault, accident, or self-harm, following the order of hierarchy listed above.

e. **Child and adult abuse guideline**
1) **Intentional injury**
When the cause of an injury or neglect is intentional child or adult abuse, the first listed E code should be assigned from categories E960-E968, Homicide and injury purposely inflicted by other persons, (except category E967). An E code from category E967, Child and adult battering and other maltreatment, should be added as an additional code to identify the perpetrator, if known.
2) **Accidental intent**
In cases of neglect when the intent is determined to be accidental E code E904.0, Abandonment or neglect of infant and helpless person, should be the first listed E code.

f. **Unknown or suspected intent guideline**
1) **If the intent (accident, self-harm, assault) of the cause of an injury or poisoning is unknown**
If the intent (accident, self-harm, assault) of the cause of an injury or poisoning is unknown or unspecified, code the intent as undetermined E980-E989.
2) **If the intent (accident, self-harm, assault) of the cause of an injury or poisoning is questionable**
If the intent (accident, self-harm, assault) of the cause of an injury or poisoning is questionable, probable or suspected, code the intent as undetermined E980-E989.

g. **Undetermined cause**
When the intent of an injury or poisoning is known, but the cause is unknown, use codes: E928.9, Unspecified accident, E958.9, Suicide and self-inflicted injury by unspecified means, and E968.9, Assault by unspecified means.
These E codes should rarely be used, as the documentation in the medical record, in both the inpatient outpatient and other settings, should normally provide sufficient detail to determine the cause of the injury.

h. **Late effects of external cause guidelines**
1) **Late effect E codes**
Late effect E codes exist for injuries and poisonings but not for adverse effects of drugs, misadventures and surgical complications.
2) **Late effect E codes (E929, E959, E969, E977, E989, or E999.1)**
A late effect E code (E929, E959, E969, E977, E989, or E999.1) should be used with any report of a late effect or sequela resulting from a previous injury or poisoning (905-909).
3) **Late effect E code with a related current injury**
A late effect E code should never be used with a related current nature of injury code.
4) **Use of late effect E codes for subsequent visits**
Use a late effect E code for subsequent visits when a late effect of the initial injury or poisoning is being treated. There is no late effect E code for adverse effects of drugs. Do not use a late effect E code for subsequent visits for follow-up care (e.g., to assess healing, to receive rehabilitative therapy) of the injury or poisoning when no late effect of the injury has been documented.

i. **Misadventures and complications of care guidelines**
1) **Code range E870-E876**
Assign a code in the range of E870-E876 if misadventures are stated by the provider.
2) **Code range E878-E879**
Assign a code in the range of E878-E879 if the provider attributes an abnormal reaction or later complication to a surgical or medical procedure, but does not mention misadventure at the time of the procedure as the cause of the reaction.

j. **Terrorism guidelines**
1) **Cause of injury identified by the Federal Government (FBI) as terrorism**
When the cause of an injury is identified by the Federal Government (FBI) as terrorism, the first-listed E-code should be a code from category E979, Terrorism. The definition of terrorism employed by the FBI is found at the inclusion note at E979. The terrorism E-code is the only E-code that should be assigned. Additional E codes from the assault categories should not be assigned.
2) **Cause of an injury is suspected to be the result of terrorism**
When the cause of an injury is suspected to be the result of terrorism a code from category E979 should not be assigned. Assign a code in the range of E codes based circumstances on the documentation of intent and mechanism.
3) **Code E979.9, Terrorism, secondary effects**
Assign code E979.9, Terrorism, secondary effects, for conditions occurring subsequent to the terrorist event. This code should not be assigned for conditions that are due to the initial terrorist act.
4) **Statistical tabulation of terrorism codes**
For statistical purposes these codes will be tabulated within the category for assault, expanding the current category from E960-E969 to include E979 and E999.1.

SECTION II. SELECTION OF PRINCIPAL DIAGNOSIS

The circumstances of inpatient admission always govern the selection of principal diagnosis. The principal diagnosis is defined in the Uniform Hospital Discharge Data Set (UHDDS) as "that condition established after study to be chiefly responsible for occasioning the admission of the patient to the hospital for care."

The UHDDS definitions are used by hospitals to report inpatient data elements in a standardized manner. These data elements and their definitions can be found in the July 31, 1985, Federal Register (Vol. 50, No, 147), pp. 31038-40.

Since that time the application of the UHDDS definitions has been expanded to include all non-outpatient settings (acute care, short term, long term care and psychiatric hospitals; home health agencies; rehab facilities; nursing homes, etc).

In determining principal diagnosis the coding conventions in the ICD-9-CM, Volumes I and II take precedence over these official coding guidelines.

(See Section I.A., Conventions for the ICD-9-CM)

The importance of consistent, complete documentation in the medical record cannot be overemphasized. Without such documentation the application of all coding guidelines is a difficult, if not impossible, task.

A.   Codes for symptoms, signs, and ill-defined conditions
Codes for symptoms, signs, and ill-defined conditions from Chapter 16 are not to be used as principal diagnosis when a related definitive diagnosis has been established.

B.   Two or more interrelated conditions, each potentially meeting the definition for principal diagnosis
When there are two or more interrelated conditions (such as diseases in the same ICD-9-CM chapter or manifestations characteristically associated with a certain disease) potentially meeting the definition of principal diagnosis, either condition may be sequenced first, unless the circumstances of the admission, the therapy provided, the Tabular List, or the Alphabetic Index indicate otherwise.

C.   Two or more diagnoses that equally meet the definition for principal diagnosis
In the unusual instance when two or more diagnoses equally meet the criteria for principal diagnosis as determined by the circumstances of admission, diagnostic workup and/or therapy provided, and the Alphabetic Index, Tabular List, or another coding guidelines does not provide sequencing direction, any one of the diagnoses may be sequenced first.

D.   Two or more comparative or contrasting conditions
In those rare instances when two or more contrasting or comparative diagnoses are documented as "either/or" (or similar terminology), they are coded as if the diagnoses were confirmed and the diagnoses are sequenced according to the circumstances of the admission. If no further determination can be made as to which diagnosis should be principal, either diagnosis may be sequenced first.

E.   A symptom(s) followed by contrasting/comparative diagnoses
When a symptom(s) is followed by contrasting/comparative diagnoses, the symptom code is sequenced first. All the contrasting/comparative diagnoses should be coded as additional diagnoses.

F.   Original treatment plan not carried out
Sequence as the principal diagnosis the condition, which after study occasioned the admission to the hospital, even though treatment may not have been carried out due to unforeseen circumstances.

G.   Complications of surgery and other medical care
When the admission is for treatment of a complication resulting from surgery or other medical care, the complication code is sequenced as the principal diagnosis. If the complication is classified to the 996-999 series and the code lacks the necessary specificity in describing the complication, an additional code for the specific complication should be assigned.

H.   Uncertain diagnosis
If the diagnosis documented at the time of discharge is qualified as "probable", "suspected", "likely", "questionable", "possible", or "still to be ruled out", or other similar terms indicating uncertainty, code the condition as if it existed or was established. The bases for these guidelines are the diagnostic workup, arrangements for further workup or observation, and initial therapeutic approach that correspond most closely with the established diagnosis.
Note: This guideline is applicable only to inpatient admissions to short-term, acute, long-term care and psychiatric hospitals.

I.   Admission from observation unit
   1.   Admission following medical observation
   When a patient is admitted to an observation unit for a medical condition, which either worsens or does not improve, and is subsequently admitted as an inpatient of the same hospital for this same medical condition, the principal diagnosis would be the medical condition which led to the hospital admission.
   2.   Admission following post-operative observation
   When a patient is admitted to an observation unit to monitor a condition (or

complication) that develops following outpatient surgery, and then is subsequently admitted as an inpatient of the same hospital, hospitals should apply the Uniform Hospital Discharge Data Set (UHDDS) definition of principal diagnosis as "that condition established after study to be chiefly responsible for occasioning the admission of the patient to the hospital for care."

J.   Admission from outpatient surgery
When a patient receives surgery in the hospital's outpatient surgery department and is subsequently admitted for continuing inpatient care at the same hospital, the following guidelines should be followed in selecting the principal diagnosis for the inpatient admission:

   •   If the reason for the inpatient admission is a complication, assign the complication as the principal diagnosis.
   •   If no complication, or other condition, is documented as the reason for the inpatient admission, assign the reason for the outpatient surgery as the principal diagnosis.
   •   If the reason for the inpatient admission is another condition unrelated to the surgery, assign the unrelated condition as the principal diagnosis.

SECTION III. REPORTING ADDITIONAL DIAGNOSES

GENERAL RULES FOR OTHER (ADDITIONAL) DIAGNOSES

For reporting purposes the definition for "other diagnoses" is interpreted as additional conditions that affect patient care in terms of requiring:

   clinical evaluation; or
   therapeutic treatment; or
   diagnostic procedures; or
   extended length of hospital stay; or
   increased nursing care and/or monitoring.

The UHDDS item #11-b defines Other Diagnoses as "all conditions that coexist at the time of admission, that develop subsequently, or that affect the treatment received and/or the length of stay. Diagnoses that relate to an earlier episode which have no bearing on the current hospital stay are to be excluded." UHDDS definitions apply to inpatients in acute care, short-term, long term care and psychiatric hospital setting. The UHDDS definitions are used by acute care short-term hospitals to report inpatient data elements in a standardized manner. These data elements and their definitions can be found in the July 31, 1985, Federal Register (Vol. 50, No, 147), pp. 31038-40.

Since that time the application of the UHDDS definitions has been expanded to include all non-outpatient settings (acute care, short term, long term care and psychiatric hospitals; home health agencies; rehab facilities; nursing homes, etc).

The following guidelines are to be applied in designating "other diagnoses" when neither the Alphabetic Index nor the Tabular List in ICD-9-CM provide direction. The listing of the diagnoses in the patient record is the responsibility of the attending provider.

A.   Previous conditions
If the provider has included a diagnosis in the final diagnostic statement, such as the discharge summary or the face sheet, it should ordinarily be coded. Some providers include in the diagnostic statement resolved conditions or diagnoses and status-post procedures from previous admission that have no bearing on the current stay. Such conditions are not to be reported and are coded only if required by hospital policy.
However, history codes (V10-V19) may be used as secondary codes if the historical condition or family history has an impact on current care or influences treatment.

B.   Abnormal findings
Abnormal findings (laboratory, x-ray, pathologic, and other diagnostic results) are not coded and reported unless the provider indicates their clinical significance. If the findings are outside the normal range and the attending provider has ordered other tests to evaluate the condition or prescribed treatment, it is appropriate to ask the provider whether the abnormal finding should be added.
Please note: This differs from the coding practices in the outpatient setting for coding encounters for diagnostic tests that have been interpreted by a provider.

C.   Uncertain diagnosis
If the diagnosis documented at the time of discharge is qualified as "probable", "suspected", "likely", "questionable", "possible", or "still to be ruled out" or other similar terms indicating uncertainty, code the condition as if it existed or was established. The bases for these guidelines are the diagnostic workup, arrangements for further workup or observation, and initial therapeutic approach that correspond most closely with the established diagnosis.
Note: This guideline is applicable only to inpatient admissions to short-term, acute, long-term care and psychiatric hospitals.

SECTION IV. DIAGNOSTIC CODING AND REPORTING GUIDELINES FOR OUTPATIENT SERVICES

These coding guidelines for outpatient diagnoses have been approved for use by hospitals/ providers in coding and reporting hospital-based outpatient services and provider-based office visits.

Information about the use of certain abbreviations, punctuation, symbols, and other conventions used in the ICD-9-CM Tabular List (code numbers and titles), can be found in Section IA of these guidelines, under "Conventions Used in the Tabular List." Information about the correct sequence to use in finding a code is also described in Section I.

The terms encounter and visit are often used interchangeably in describing outpatient service contacts and, therefore, appear together in these guidelines without distinguishing one from the other.

Though the conventions and general guidelines apply to all settings, coding guidelines for outpatient and provider reporting of diagnoses will vary in a number of instances from those for inpatient diagnoses, recognizing that:

The Uniform Hospital Discharge Data Set (UHDDS) definition of principal diagnosis applies only to inpatients in acute, short-term, long-term care and psychiatric hospitals.

Coding guidelines for inconclusive diagnoses (probable, suspected, rule out, etc.) were developed for inpatient reporting and do not apply to outpatients.

A. Selection of first-listed condition

In the outpatient setting, the term first-listed diagnosis is used in lieu of principal diagnosis.

In determining the first-listed diagnosis the coding conventions of ICD-9-CM, as well as the general and disease specific guidelines take precedence over the outpatient guidelines.

Diagnoses often are not established at the time of the initial encounter/visit. It may take two or more visits before the diagnosis is confirmed.

The most critical rule involves beginning the search for the correct code assignment through the Alphabetic Index. Never begin searching initially in the Tabular List as this will lead to coding errors.

1. Outpatient surgery

When a patient presents for outpatient surgery, code the reason for the surgery as the first-listed diagnosis (reason for the encounter), even if the surgery is not performed due to a contraindication.

2. Observation stay

When a patient is admitted for observation for a medical condition, assign a code for the medical condition as the first-listed diagnosis.

When a patient presents for outpatient surgery and develops complications requiring admission to observation, code the reason for the surgery as the first reported diagnosis (reason for the encounter), followed by codes for the complications as secondary diagnoses.

B. Codes from 001.0 through V89

The appropriate code or codes from 001.0 through **V89** must be used to identify diagnoses, symptoms, conditions, problems, complaints, or other reason(s) for the encounter/visit.

C. Accurate reporting of ICD-9-CM diagnosis codes

For accurate reporting of ICD-9-CM diagnosis codes, the documentation should describe the patient's condition, using terminology which includes specific diagnoses as well as symptoms, problems, or reasons for the encounter. There are ICD-9-CM codes to describe all of these.

D. Selection of codes 001.0 through 999.9

The selection of codes 001.0 through 999.9 will frequently be used to describe the reason for the encounter. These codes are from the section of ICD-9-CM for the classification of diseases and injuries (e.g. infectious and parasitic diseases; neoplasms; symptoms, signs, and ill-defined conditions, etc.).

E. Codes that describe symptoms and signs

Codes that describe symptoms and signs, as opposed to diagnoses, are acceptable for reporting purposes when a diagnosis has not been established (confirmed) by the provider. Chapter 16 of ICD-9-CM, Symptoms, Signs, and Ill-defined conditions (codes 780.0-799.9) contain many, but not all codes for symptoms.

F. Encounters for circumstances other than a disease or injury

ICD-9-CM provides codes to deal with encounters for circumstances other than a disease or injury. The Supplementary Classification of factors Influencing Health Status and Contact with Health Services (V01.0-**V89**) is provided to deal with occasions when circumstances other than a disease or injury are recorded as diagnosis or problems. *See Section I.C. 18 for information on V-codes*

G. Level of detail in coding

1. ICD-9-CM codes with 3, 4, or 5 digits

ICD-9-CM is composed of codes with either 3, 4, or 5 digits. Codes with three digits are included in ICD-9-CM as the heading of a category of codes that may be further subdivided by the use of fourth and/or fifth-digits, which provide greater specificity.

2. Use of full number of digits required for a code

A three-digit code is to be used only if it is not further subdivided. Where fourth-digit subcategories and/or fifth-digit subclassifications are provided, they must be assigned. A code is invalid if it has not been coded to the full number of digits required for that code.

See also discussion under Section I.b.3., General Coding Guidelines, Level of Detail in Coding.

H. ICD-9-CM code for the diagnosis, condition, problem, or other reason for encounter/visit

List first the ICD-9-CM code for the diagnosis, condition, problem, or other reason for encounter/visit shown in the medical record to be chiefly responsible for the services provided. List additional codes that describe any coexisting conditions. In some cases the first-listed diagnosis may be a symptom when a diagnosis has not been established (confirmed) by the physician.

I. Uncertain diagnosis

Do not code diagnoses documented as "probable", "suspected", "questionable", "rule out", or "working diagnosis" or other similar terms indicating uncertainty. Rather, code the condition(s) to the highest degree of certainty for that encounter/visit, such as symptoms, signs, abnormal test results, or other reason for the visit.

Please note: This differs from the coding practices used by short-term, acute care, long-term care and psychiatric hospitals.

J. Chronic diseases

Chronic diseases treated on an ongoing basis may be coded and reported as many times as the patient receives treatment and care for the condition(s)

K. Code all documented conditions that coexist

Code all documented conditions that coexist at the time of the encounter/visit, and require or affect patient care treatment or management. Do not code conditions that were previously treated and no longer exist. However, history codes (V10-V19) may be used as secondary codes if the historical condition or family history has an impact on current care or influences treatment.

L. Patients receiving diagnostic services only

For patients receiving diagnostic services only during an encounter/visit, sequence first the diagnosis, condition, problem, or other reason for encounter/visit shown in the medical record to be chiefly responsible for the outpatient services provided during the encounter/visit. Codes for other diagnoses (e.g., chronic conditions) may be sequenced as additional diagnoses.

For encounters for routine laboratory/radiology testing in the absence of any signs, symptoms, or associated diagnosis, assign V72.5 and V72.6. If routine testing is performed during the same encounter as a test to evaluate a sign, symptom, or diagnosis, it is appropriate to assign both the V code and the code describing the reason for the non-routine test.

For outpatient encounters for diagnostic tests that have been interpreted by a physician, and the final report is available at the time of coding, code any confirmed or definitive diagnosis(es) documented in the interpretation. Do not code related signs and symptoms as additional diagnoses.

Please note: This differs from the coding practice in the hospital inpatient setting regarding abnormal findings on test results.

M. Patients receiving therapeutic services only

For patients receiving therapeutic services only during an encounter/visit, sequence first the diagnosis, condition, problem, or other reason for encounter/visit shown in the medical record to be chiefly responsible for the outpatient services provided during the encounter/visit. Codes for other diagnoses (e.g., chronic conditions) may be sequenced as additional diagnoses.

The only exception to this rule is that when the primary reason for the admission/encounter is chemotherapy, radiation therapy, or rehabilitation, the appropriate V code for the service is listed first, and the diagnosis or problem for which the service is being performed listed second.

N. Patients receiving preoperative evaluations only

For patients receiving preoperative evaluations only, sequence first a code from category V72.8, Other specified examinations, to describe the pre-op consultations. Assign a code for the condition to describe the reason for the surgery as an additional diagnosis. Code also any findings related to the pre-op evaluation.

O. Ambulatory surgery

For ambulatory surgery, code the diagnosis for which the surgery was performed. If the postoperative diagnosis is known to be different from the preoperative diagnosis at the time the diagnosis is confirmed, select the postoperative diagnosis for coding, since it is the most definitive.

P. Routine outpatient prenatal visits

For routine outpatient prenatal visits when no complications are present, codes V22.0, Supervision of normal first pregnancy, or V22.1, Supervision of other normal pregnancy, should be used as the principal diagnosis. These codes should not be used in conjunction with chapter 11 codes.

APPENDIX I. PRESENT ON ADMISSION REPORTING GUIDELINES

Introduction

These guidelines are to be used as a supplement to the *ICD-9-CM Official Guidelines for Coding and Reporting* to facilitate the assignment of the Present on Admission (POA) indicator for each diagnosis and external cause of injury code reported on claim forms (UB-04 and 837 Institutional).

These guidelines are not intended to replace any guidelines in the main body of the *ICD-9-CM Official Guidelines for Coding and Reporting*. The POA guidelines are not intended to provide guidance on when a condition should be coded, but rather, how to apply the POA indicator to the final set of diagnosis codes that have been assigned in accordance with Sections I, II, and III of the official coding guidelines. Subsequent to the assignment of the ICD-9-CM codes, the POA indicator should then be assigned to those conditions that have been coded.

As stated in the Introduction to the ICD-9-CM Official Guidelines for Coding and Reporting, a joint effort between the healthcare provider and the coder is essential to achieve complete and accurate documentation, code assignment, and reporting of diagnoses and procedures. The importance of consistent, complete documentation in the medical record cannot be overemphasized. Medical record documentation from any provider involved in the care and treatment of the patient may be used to support the determination of whether a condition was present on admission or not. In the context of the official coding guidelines, the term "provider" means a physician or any qualified healthcare practitioner who is legally accountable for establishing the patient's diagnosis.

These guidelines are not a substitute for the provider's clinical judgment as to the determination of whether a condition was/was not present on admission. The provider should be queried regarding issues related to the linking of signs/symptoms, timing of test results, and the timing of findings.

General Reporting Requirements

All claims involving inpatient admissions to general acute care hospitals or other facilities that are subject to a law or regulation mandating collection of present on admission information.

Present on admission is defined as present at the time the order for inpatient admission occurs. Conditions that develop during an outpatient encounter, including emergency department, observation, or outpatient surgery, are considered as present on admission.

POA indicator is assigned to principal and secondary diagnoses (as defined in Section II of the Official Guidelines for Coding and Reporting) and the external cause of injury codes.

Issues related to inconsistent, missing, conflicting or unclear documentation must still be resolved by the provider.

If a condition would not be coded and reported based on UHDDS definitions and current official coding guidelines, then the POA indicator would not be reported.

Reporting Options

Y - Yes

N - No

U - Unknown

W – Clinically undetermined

Unreported/Not used (or "1" for Medicare usage) – (Exempt from POA reporting)

For more specific instructions on Medicare POA indicator reporting options, refer to http://www.cms.hhs.gov/HospitalAcqCond/02_Statute_Regulations_Program_Instructions.asp#TopOfPage

Reporting Definitions

Y = present at the time of inpatient admission

N = not present at the time of inpatient admission

U = documentation is insufficient to determine if condition is present on admission

W = provider is unable to clinically determine whether condition was present on admission or not

Timeframe for POA Identification and Documentation

There is no required timeframe as to when a provider (per the definition of "provider" used in these guidelines) must identify or document a condition to be present on admission. In some clinical situations, it may not be possible for a provider to make a definitive diagnosis (or a condition may not be recognized or reported by the patient) for a period of time after admission. In some cases it may be several days before the provider arrives at a definitive diagnosis. This does not mean that the condition was not present on admission. Determination of whether the condition was present on admission or not will be based on the

applicable POA guideline as identified in this document, or on the provider's best clinical judgment.

If at the time of code assignment the documentation is unclear as to whether a condition was present on admission or not, it is appropriate to query the provider for clarification.

Assigning the POA Indicator

Condition is on the "Exempt from Reporting" list
Leave the "present on admission" field blank if the condition is on the list of ICD-9-CM codes for which this field is not applicable. This is the only circumstance in which the field may be left blank.

POA explicitly documented
Assign Y for any condition the provider explicitly documents as being present on admission.

Assign N for any condition the provider explicitly documents as not present at the time of admission.

Conditions diagnosed prior to inpatient admission
Assign "Y" for conditions that were diagnosed prior to admission (example: hypertension, diabetes mellitus, asthma)

Conditions diagnosed during the admission but clearly present before admission
Assign "Y" for conditions diagnosed during the admission that were clearly present but not diagnosed until after admission occurred.

Diagnoses subsequently confirmed after admission are considered present on admission if at the time of admission they are documented as suspected, possible, rule out, differential diagnosis, or constitute an underlying cause of a symptom that is present at the time of admission.

Condition develops during outpatient encounter prior to inpatient admission
Assign Y for any condition that develops during an outpatient encounter prior to a written order for inpatient admission.

Documentation does not indicate whether condition was present on admission
Assign "U" when the medical record documentation is unclear as to whether the condition was present on admission. "U" should not be routinely assigned and used only in very limited circumstances. Coders are encouraged to query the providers when the documentation is unclear.

Documentation states that it cannot be determined whether the condition was or was not present on admission
Assign "W" when the medical record documentation indicates that it cannot be clinically determined whether or not the condition was present on admission.

Chronic condition with acute exacerbation during the admission
If the code is a combination code that identifies both the chronic condition and the acute exacerbation, see POA guidelines pertaining to combination codes.

If the combination code only identifies the chronic condition and not the acute exacerbation (e.g., acute exacerbation of CHF), assign "Y."

Conditions documented as possible, probable, suspected, or rule out at the time of discharge
If the final diagnosis contains a possible, probable, suspected, or rule out diagnosis, and this diagnosis was suspected at the time of inpatient admission, assign "Y."

If the final diagnosis contains a possible, probable, suspected, or rule out diagnosis, and this diagnosis was based on symptoms or clinical findings that were not present on admission, assign "N".

Conditions documented as impending or threatened at the time of discharge
If the final diagnosis contains an impending or threatened diagnosis, and this diagnosis is based on symptoms or clinical findings that were present on admission, assign "Y".

If the final diagnosis contains an impending or threatened diagnosis, and this diagnosis is based on symptoms or clinical findings that were not present on admission, assign "N".

Acute and chronic conditions
Assign "Y" for acute conditions that are present at time of admission and N for acute conditions that are not present at time of admission.

Assign "Y" for chronic conditions, even though the condition may not be diagnosed until after admission.

If a single code identifies both an acute and chronic condition, see the POA guidelines for combination codes.

Combination codes
Assign "N" if any part of the combination code was not present on admission (e.g., obstructive chronic bronchitis with acute exacerbation and the exacerbation was not present on admission; gastric ulcer that does not

start bleeding until after admission; asthma patient develops status asthmaticus after admission)

Assign "Y" if all parts of the combination code were present on admission (e.g., patient with diabetic nephropathy is admitted with uncontrolled diabetes)

If the final diagnosis includes comparative or contrasting diagnoses, and both were present, or suspected, at the time of admission, assign "Y".

For infection codes that include the causal organism, assign "Y" if the infection (or signs of the infection) was present on admission, even though the culture results may not be known until after admission (e.g., patient is admitted with pneumonia and the provider documents pseudomonas as the causal organism a few days later).

Same Diagnosis Code for Two or More Conditions

When the same ICD-9-CM diagnosis code applies to two or more conditions during the same encounter (e.g. bilateral condition, or two separate conditions classified to the same ICD-9-CM diagnosis code):

Assign "Y" if all conditions represented by the single ICD-9-CM code were present on admission (e.g. bilateral fracture of the same bone, same site, and both fractures were present on admission)

Assign "N" if any of the conditions represented by the single ICD-9-CM code was not present on admission (e.g. dehydration with hyponatremia is assigned to code 276.1, but only one of these conditions was present on admission).

Obstetrical conditions

Whether or not the patient delivers during the current hospitalization does not affect assignment of the POA indicator. The determining factor for POA assignment is whether the pregnancy complication or obstetrical condition described by the code was present at the time of admission or not.

If the pregnancy complication or obstetrical condition was present on admission (e.g., patient admitted in preterm labor), assign "Y".

If the pregnancy complication or obstetrical condition was not present on admission (e.g., 2nd degree laceration during delivery, postpartum hemorrhage that occurred during current hospitalization, fetal distress develops after admission), assign "N".

If the obstetrical code includes more than one diagnosis and any of the diagnoses identified by the code were not present on admission (e.g., Code 642.7, Pre-eclampsia or eclampsia superimposed on preexisting hypertension) assign "N".

If the obstetrical code includes information that is not a diagnosis, do not consider that information in the POA determination. Example, code 652.1x, Breech or other malpresentation successfully converted to cephalic presentation, should be reported as present on admission if the fetus was breech on admission but was converted to cephalic presentation after admission. Since the conversion to cephalic presentation does not represent a diagnosis, the fact that the conversion occurred after admission has no bearing on the POA determination.

Perinatal conditions

Newborns are not considered to be admitted until after birth. Therefore, any condition present at birth or that developed in utero is considered present at admission and should be assigned "Y". This includes conditions that occur during delivery (e.g., injury during delivery, meconium aspiration, exposure to streptococcus B in the vaginal canal).

Congenital conditions and anomalies

Assign "Y" for congenital conditions and anomalies. Congenital conditions are always considered present on admission.

External cause of injury codes

Assign "Y" for any E code representing an external cause of injury or poisoning that occurred prior to inpatient admission (e.g., patient fell out of bed at home, patient fell out of bed in emergency room prior to admission)

Assign "N" for any E code representing an external cause of injury or poisoning that occurred during inpatient hospitalization (e.g., patient fell out of hospital bed during hospital stay, patient experienced an adverse reaction to a medication administered after inpatient admission)

Categories and Codes Exempt from Diagnosis Present on Admission Requirement

Note: *"Diagnosis present on admission" for these code categories are exempt because they represent circumstances regarding the healthcare encounter or factors influencing health status that do not represent a current disease or injury or are always present on admission*

137-139	Late effects of infectious and parasitic diseases
268.1	Rickets, late effect
326	Late effects of intracranial abscess or pyogenic infection
412	Old myocardial infarction
438	Late effects of cerebrovascular disease
650	Normal delivery
660.7	Failed forceps or vacuum extractor, unspecified
677	Late effect of complication of pregnancy, childbirth, and the puerperium
905-909	Late effects of injuries, poisonings, toxic effects, and other external causes
V02	Carrier or suspected carrier of infectious diseases
V03	Need for prophylactic vaccination and inoculation against bacterial diseases
V04	Need for prophylactic vaccination and inoculation against certain viral diseases
V05	Need for other prophylactic vaccination and inoculation against single diseases
V06	Need for prophylactic vaccination and inoculation against combinations of diseases
V07	Need for isolation and other prophylactic measures
V10	Personal history of malignant neoplasm
V11	Personal history of mental disorder
V12	Personal history of certain other diseases
V13	Personal history of other diseases
V14	Personal history of allergy to medicinal agents
V15.01-V15.09	Other personal history, Allergy, other than to medicinal agents
V15.1	Other personal history, Surgery to heart and great vessels
V15.2	Other personal history, Surgery to other major organs
V15.3	Other personal history, Irradiation
V15.4	Other personal history, Psychological trauma
V15.5	Other personal history, Injury
V15.6	Other personal history, Poisoning
V15.7	Other personal history, Contraception
V15.81	Other personal history, Noncompliance with medical treatment
V15.82	Other personal history, History of tobacco use
V15.88	Other personal history, History of fall
V15.89	Other personal history, Other
V15.9	Unspecified personal history presenting hazards to health
V16	Family history of malignant neoplasm
V17	Family history of certain chronic disabling diseases
V18	Family history of certain other specific conditions
V19	Family history of other conditions
V20	Health supervision of infant or child
V21	Constitutional states in development
V22	Normal pregnancy
V23	Supervision of high-risk pregnancy
V24	Postpartum care and examination
V25	Encounter for contraceptive management
V26	Procreative management
V27	Outcome of delivery
V28	Antenatal screening
V29	Observation and evaluation of newborns for suspected condition not found
V30-V39	Liveborn infants according to type of birth
V42	Organ or tissue replaced by transplant
V43	Organ or tissue replaced by other means
V44	Artificial opening status
V45	Other postprocedural states
V46	Other dependence on machines
V49.60-V49.77	Upper and lower limb amputation status
V49.81-V49.84	Other specified conditions influencing health status
V50	Elective surgery for purposes other than remedying health states
V51	Aftercare involving the use of plastic surgery
V52	Fitting and adjustment of prosthetic device and implant
V53	Fitting and adjustment of other device
V54	Other orthopedic aftercare
V55	Attention to artificial openings
V56	Encounter for dialysis and dialysis catheter care
V57	Care involving use of rehabilitation procedures
V58	Encounter for other and unspecified procedures and aftercare
V59	Donors
V60	Housing, household, and economic circumstances
V61	Other family circumstances
V62	Other psychosocial circumstances
V64	Persons encountering health services for specific procedures, not carried out
V65	Other persons seeking consultation
V66	Convalescence and palliative care
V67	Follow-up examination
V68	Encounters for administrative purposes
V69	Problems related to lifestyle

V70	General medical examination
V71	Observation and evaluation for suspected condition not found
V72	Special investigations and examinations
V73	Special screening examination for viral and chlamydial diseases
V74	Special screening examination for bacterial and spirochetal diseases
V75	Special screening examination for other infectious diseases
V76	Special screening for malignant neoplasms
V77	Special screening for endocrine, nutritional, metabolic, and immunity disorders
V78	Special screening for disorders of blood and blood-forming organs
V79	Special screening for mental disorders and developmental handicaps
V80	Special screening for neurological, eye, and ear diseases
V81	Special screening for cardiovascular, respiratory, and genitourinary diseases
V82	Special screening for other conditions
V83	Genetic carrier status
V84	Genetic susceptibility to disease
V85	Body Mass Index
V86	Estrogen receptor status
V87.4	Personal history of drug therapy
V88	Acquired absence of cervix and uterus
V89	Suspected maternal and fetal conditions not found
E800-E807	Railway accidents
E810-E819	Motor vehicle traffic accidents
E820-E825	Motor vehicle nontraffic accidents E826-E829, Other road vehicle accidents
E830-E838	Water transport accidents
E840-E845	Air and space transport accidents
E846-E848	Vehicle accidents not elsewhere classifiable
E849.0-E849.6	Place of occurrence
E849.8-E849.9	Place of occurrence
E883.1	Accidental fall into well
E883.2	Accidental fall into storm drain or manhole
E884.0	Fall from playground equipment
E884.1	Fall from cliff
E885.0	Fall from (nonmotorized) scooter
E885.1	Fall from roller skates
E885.2	Fall from skateboard
E885.3	Fall from skis
E885.4	Fall from snowboard
E886.0	Fall on same level from collision, pushing, or shoving, by or with other person, In sports
E890.0-E890.9	Conflagration in private dwelling
E893.0	Accident caused by ignition of clothing, from controlled fire in private dwelling
E893.2	Accident caused by ignition of clothing, from controlled fire not in building or structure
E894	Ignition of highly inflammable material
E895	Accident caused by controlled fire in private dwelling
E897	Accident caused by controlled fire not in building or structure
E898.0-E898.1	Accident caused by other specified fire and flames
E917.0	Striking against or struck accidentally by objects or persons, in sports without subsequent fall
E917.1	Striking against or struck accidentally by objects or persons, caused by a crowd, by collective fear or panic without subsequent fall
E917.2	Striking against or struck accidentally by objects or persons, in running water without subsequent fall
E917.5	Striking against or struck accidentally by objects or persons, object in sports with subsequent fall
E917.6	Striking against or struck accidentally by objects or persons, caused by a crowd, by collective fear or panic with subsequent fall
E919.0-E919.1	Accidents caused by machinery
E919.3-E919.9	Accidents caused by machinery
E921.0-E921.9	Accident caused by explosion of pressure vessel
E922.0-E922.9	Accident caused by firearm and air gun missile
E924.1	Caustic and corrosive substances
E926.2	Visible and ultraviolet light sources
E928.0-E928.8	Other and unspecified environmental and accidental causes
E929.0-E929.9	Late effects of accidental injury
E959	Late effects of self-inflicted injury
E970-E978	Legal intervention
E979	Terrorism

E981.0-E981.8	Poisoning by gases in domestic use, undetermined whether accidentally or purposely inflicted
E982.0-E982.9	Poisoning by other gases, undetermined whether accidentally or purposely inflicted
E985.0-E985.7	Injury by firearms, air guns and explosives, undetermined whether accidentally or purposely inflicted
E987.0	Falling from high place, undetermined whether accidentally or purposely inflicted, residential premises
E987.2	Falling from high place, undetermined whether accidentally or purposely inflicted, natural sites
E989	Late effects of injury, undetermined whether accidentally or purposely inflicted
E990-E999	Injury resulting from operations of war

POA Examples

General Medical Surgical

1. Patient is admitted for diagnostic work-up for cachexia. The final diagnosis is malignant neoplasm of lung with metastasis.

   Assign "Y" on the POA field for the malignant neoplasm. The malignant neoplasm was clearly present on admission, although it was not diagnosed until after the admission occurred.

2. A patient undergoes outpatient surgery. During the recovery period, the patient develops atrial fibrillation and the patient is subsequently admitted to the hospital as an inpatient.

   Assign "Y" on the POA field for the atrial fibrillation since it developed prior to a written order for inpatient admission.

3. A patient is treated in observation and while in Observation, the patient falls out of bed and breaks a hip. The patient is subsequently admitted as an inpatient to treat the hip fracture.

   Assign "Y" on the POA field for the hip fracture since it developed prior to a written order for inpatient admission.

4. A patient with known congestive heart failure is admitted to the hospital after he develops decompensated congestive heart failure.

   Assign "Y" on the POA field for the congestive heart failure. The ICD-9-CM code identifies the chronic condition and does not specify the acute exacerbation.

5. A patient undergoes inpatient surgery. After surgery, the patient develops fever and is treated aggressively. The physician's final diagnosis documents "possible postoperative infection following surgery."

   Assign "N" on the POA field for the postoperative infection since final diagnoses that contain the terms "possible", "probable", "suspected" or "rule out" and that are based on symptoms or clinical findings that were not present on admission should be reported as "N".

6. A patient with severe cough and difficulty breathing was diagnosed during his hospitalization to have lung cancer.

   Assign "Y" on the POA field for the lung cancer. Even though the cancer was not diagnosed until after admission, it is a chronic condition that was clearly present before the patient's admission.

7. A patient is admitted to the hospital for a coronary artery bypass surgery. Postoperatively he developed a pulmonary embolism.

   Assign "N" on the POA field for the pulmonary embolism. This is an acute condition that was not present on admission.

8. A patient is admitted with a known history of coronary atherosclerosis, status post myocardial infarction five years ago is now admitted for treatment of impending myocardial infarction. The final diagnosis is documented as "impending myocardial infarction."

   Assign "Y" to the impending myocardial infarction because the condition is present on admission.

9. A patient with diabetes mellitus developed uncontrolled diabetes on day 3 of the hospitalization.

   Assign "N" to the diabetes code because the "uncontrolled" component of the code was not present on admission.

10. A patient is admitted with high fever and pneumonia. The patient rapidly deteriorates and becomes septic. The discharge diagnosis lists sepsis and pneumonia. The documentation is unclear as to whether the sepsis was present on admission or developed shortly after admission.

    Query the physician as to whether the sepsis was present on admission, developed shortly after admission, or it cannot be clinically determined as to whether it was present on admission or not.

11. A patient is admitted for repair of an abdominal aneurysm. However, the aneurysm ruptures after hospital admission.

    Assign "N" for the ruptured abdominal aneurysm. Although the aneurysm was present on admission, the "ruptured" component of the code description did not occur until after admission.

12. A patient with viral hepatitis B progresses to hepatic coma after admission.

    Assign "N" for the viral hepatitis B with hepatic coma because part of the code description did not develop until after admission.

13. A patient with a history of varicose veins and ulceration of the left lower extremity strikes the area against the side of his hospital bed during an inpatient hospitalization. It bleeds profusely. The final diagnosis lists varicose veins with ulcer and hemorrhage.

    Assign "Y" for the varicose veins with ulcer. Although the hemorrhage occurred after admission, the code description for varicose veins with ulcer does not mention hemorrhage.

14. The nursing initial assessment upon admission documents the presence of a decubitus ulcer. There is no mention of the decubitus ulcer in the physician documentation until several days after admission.

    Query the physician as to whether the decubitus ulcer was present on admission, or developed after admission. Both diagnosis code assignment and determination of whether a condition was present on admission must be based on provider documentation in the medical record (per the definition of "provider" found at the beginning of these POA guidelines and in the introductory section of the ICD-9-CM Official Guidelines for Coding and Reporting). If it cannot be determined from the provider documentation whether or not a condition was present on admission, the provider should be queried.

15. A urine culture is obtained on admission. The provider documents urinary tract infection when the culture results become available a few days later.

    Assign "Y" to the urinary tract infection since the diagnosis is based on test results from a specimen obtained on admission. It may not be possible for a provider to make a definitive diagnosis for a period of time after admission. There is no required timeframe as to when a provider must identify or document a condition to be present on admission.

16. A patient tested positive for Methicillin resistant Staphylococcus (MRSA) on routine nasal culture on admission to the hospital. During the hospitalization, he underwent insertion of a central venous catheter and later developed an infection and was diagnosed with MRSA sepsis due to central venous catheter infection.

    Assign "Y" to the positive MRSA colonization. Assign "N" for the MRSA sepsis due to central venous catheter infection since the patient did not have a MRSA infection at the time of admission.

Obstetrics

1. A female patient was admitted to the hospital and underwent a normal delivery.

    Leave the "present on admission" (POA) field blank. Code 650, Normal delivery, is on the "exempt from reporting" list.

2. Patient admitted in late pregnancy due to excessive vomiting and dehydration. During admission patient goes into premature labor

    Assign "Y" for the excessive vomiting and the dehydration.
    Assign "N" for the premature labor

3. Patient admitted in active labor. During the stay, a breast abscess is noted when mother attempted to breast feed. Provider is unable to determine whether the abscess was present on admission

    Assign "W" for the breast abscess.

4. Patient admitted in active labor. After 12 hours of labor it is noted that the infant is in fetal distress and a Cesarean section is performed

    Assign "N" for the fetal distress.

5. Pregnant female was admitted in labor and fetal nuchal cord entanglement was diagnosed. Physician is queried, but is unable to determine whether the cord entanglement was present on admission or not.

    Assign "W" for the fetal nuchal cord entanglement.

Newborn

1. A single liveborn infant was delivered in the hospital via Cesarean section. The physician documented fetal bradycardia during labor in the final diagnosis in the newborn record.

    Assign " Y" because the bradycardia developed prior to the newborn admission (birth).

2. A newborn developed diarrhea which was believed to be due to the hospital baby formula.

    Assign " N" because the diarrhea developed after admission.

3. A newborn born in the hospital, birth complicated by nuchal cord entanglement.

    Assign "Y" for the nuchal cord entanglement on the baby's record. Any condition that is present at birth or that developed in utero is considered present at admission, including conditions that occur during delivery.

A

AAT (alpha-1 antitrypsin) deficiency 273.4
AAV (disease) (illness) (infection) — see Human immunodeficiency virus (disease) (illness) (infection)
Abactio — see Abortion, induced
Abactus venter — see Abortion, induced
Abarognosis 781.99
Abasia (-astasia) 307.9
   atactica 781.3
   choreic 781.3
   hysterical 300.11
   paroxysmal trepidant 781.3
   spastic 781.3
   trembling 781.3
   trepidans 781.3
Abderhalden-Kaufmann-Lignac syndrome (cystinosis) 270.0
Abdomen, abdominal — see also condition
   accordion 306.4
   acute 789.0 ☑
   angina 557.1
   burst 868.00
   convulsive equivalent (see also Epilepsy) 345.5 ☑
   heart 746.87
   muscle deficiency syndrome 756.79
   obstipum 756.79
Abdominalgia 789.0 ☑
   periodic 277.31
Abduction contracture, hip or other joint — see Contraction, joint
Abercrombie's syndrome (amyloid degeneration) 277.39
Aberrant (congenital) — see also Malposition, congenital
   adrenal gland 759.1
   blood vessel NEC 747.60
     arteriovenous NEC 747.60
     cerebrovascular 747.81
     gastrointestinal 747.61
     lower limb 747.64
     renal 747.62
     spinal 747.82
     upper limb 747.63
   breast 757.6
   endocrine gland NEC 759.2
   gastrointestinal vessel (peripheral) 747.61
   hepatic duct 751.69
   lower limb vessel (peripheral) 747.64
   pancreas 751.7
   parathyroid gland 759.2
   peripheral vascular vessel NEC 747.60
   pituitary gland (pharyngeal) 759.2
   renal blood vessel 747.62
   sebaceous glands, mucous membrane, mouth 750.26
   spinal vessel 747.82
   spleen 759.0
   testis (descent) 752.51
   thymus gland 759.2
   thyroid gland 759.2
   upper limb vessel (peripheral) 747.63
Aberratio
   lactis 757.6
   testis 752.51
Aberration — see also Anomaly
   chromosome — see Anomaly, chromosome(s)
   distantial 368.9
   mental (see also Disorder, mental, nonpsychotic) 300.9
Abetalipoproteinemia 272.5
Abionarce 780.79
Abiotrophy 799.89
Ablatio
   placentae — see Placenta, ablatio
   retinae (see also Detachment, retina) 361.9
Ablation
   pituitary (gland) (with hypofunction) 253.7
   placenta — see Placenta, ablatio
   uterus 621.8
Ablepharia, ablepharon, ablephary 743.62
Ablepsia — see Blindness
Ablepsy — see Blindness
Ablutomania 300.3

Abnormal, abnormality, abnormalities — see also Anomaly
acid-base balance 276.4
   fetus or newborn — see Distress, fetal
adaptation curve, dark 368.63
alveolar ridge 525.9
amnion 658.9 ☑
   affecting fetus or newborn 762.9
anatomical relationship NEC 759.9
apertures, congenital, diaphragm 756.6
auditory perception NEC 388.40
autosomes NEC 758.5
   13 758.1
   18 758.2
   21 or 22 758.0
   D_1 758.1
   E_3 758.2
   G 758.0
ballistocardiogram 794.39
basal metabolic rate (BMR) 794.7
biosynthesis, testicular androgen 257.2
blood level (of)
   cobalt 790.6
   copper 790.6
   iron 790.6
   lead 790.6
   lithium 790.6
   magnesium 790.6
   mineral 790.6
   zinc 790.6
blood pressure
   elevated (without diagnosis of hypertension) 796.2
   low (see also Hypotension) 458.9
     reading (incidental) (isolated) (nonspecific) 796.3
blood sugar 790.29
bowel sounds 787.5
breathing behavior — see Respiration
caloric test 794.19
cervix (acquired) NEC 622.9
   congenital 752.40
   in pregnancy or childbirth 654.6 ☑
     causing obstructed labor 660.2 ☑
       affecting fetus or newborn 763.1
chemistry, blood NEC 790.6
chest sounds 786.7
chorion 658.9 ☑
   affecting fetus or newborn 762.9
chromosomal NEC 758.89
   analysis, nonspecific result 795.2
   autosomes (see also Abnormal, autosomes NEC) 758.5
   fetal, (suspected) affecting management of pregnancy 655.1 ☑
   sex 758.81
clinical findings NEC 796.4
communication — see Fistula
configuration of pupils 379.49
coronary
   artery 746.85
   vein 746.9
cortisol-binding globulin 255.8
course, Eustachian tube 744.24
creatinine clearance 794.4
dentofacial NEC 524.9
   functional 524.50
   specified type NEC 524.89
development, developmental NEC 759.9
   bone 756.9
   central nervous system 742.9
direction, teeth 524.30
Dynia (see also Defect, coagulation) 286.9
Ebstein 746.2
echocardiogram 793.2
echoencephalogram 794.01
echogram NEC — see Findings, abnormal, structure
electrocardiogram (ECG) (EKG) 794.31
electroencephalogram (EEG) 794.02
electromyogram (EMG) 794.17
   ocular 794.14
electro-oculogram (EOG) 794.12
electroretinogram (ERG) 794.11
erythrocytes 289.9

Abnormal, abnormality, abnormalities — see also Anomaly — continued
erythrocytes — continued
   congenital, with perinatal jaundice 282.9 [774.0]
Eustachian valve 746.9
excitability under minor stress 301.9
fat distribution 782.9
feces 787.7
fetal heart rate — see Distress, fetal
fetus NEC
   affecting management of pregnancy — see Pregnancy, management affected by, fetal
   causing disproportion 653.7 ☑
     affecting fetus or newborn 763.1
     causing obstructed labor 660.1 ☑
       affecting fetus or newborn 763.1
findings without manifest disease — see Findings, abnormal
fluid
   amniotic 792.3
   cerebrospinal 792.0
   peritoneal 792.9
   pleural 792.9
   synovial 792.9
   vaginal 792.9
forces of labor NEC 661.9 ☑
   affecting fetus or newborn 763.7
form, teeth 520.2
function studies
   auditory 794.15
   bladder 794.9
   brain 794.00
   cardiovascular 794.30
   endocrine NEC 794.6
   kidney 794.4
   liver 794.8
   nervous system
     central 794.00
     peripheral 794.19
   oculomotor 794.14
   pancreas 794.9
   placenta 794.9
   pulmonary 794.2
   retina 794.11
   special senses 794.19
   spleen 794.9
   thyroid 794.5
   vestibular 794.16
gait 781.2
   hysterical 300.11
gastrin secretion 251.5
globulin
   cortisol-binding 255.8
   thyroid-binding 246.8
glucagon secretion 251.4
glucose 790.29
   in pregnancy, childbirth, or puerperium 648.8 ☑
     fetus or newborn 775.0
   non-fasting 790.29
gravitational (G) forces or states 994.9
hair NEC 704.2
hard tissue formation in pulp 522.3
head movement 781.0
heart
   rate
     fetus, affecting liveborn infant
       before the onset of labor 763.81
       during labor 763.82
       unspecified as to time of onset 763.83
     intrauterine
       before the onset of labor 763.81
       during labor 763.82
       unspecified as to time of onset 763.83
     newborn
       before the onset of labor 763.81
       during labor 763.82
       unspecified as to time of onset 763.83
   shadow 793.2
   sounds NEC 785.3

Abnormal, abnormality, abnormalities — see also Anomaly — continued
hemoglobin (see also Disease, hemoglobin) 282.7
   trait — see Trait, hemoglobin, abnormal
hemorrhage, uterus — see Hemorrhage, uterus
histology NEC 795.4
increase
   in
     appetite 783.6
     development 783.9
involuntary movement 781.0
jaw closure 524.51
karyotype 795.2
knee jerk 796.1
labor NEC 661.9 ☑
   affecting fetus or newborn 763.7
laboratory findings — see Findings, abnormal
length, organ or site, congenital — see Distortion
liver function test 790.6
loss of height 781.91
loss of weight 783.21
lung shadow 793.1
mammogram 793.80
   calcification 793.89
   calculus 793.89
   microcalcification 793.81
Mantoux test 795.5
membranes (fetal)
   affecting fetus or newborn 762.9
   complicating pregnancy 658.8 ☑
menstruation — see Menstruation
metabolism (see also condition) 783.9
movement 781.0
   disorder NEC 333.90
     sleep related, unspecified 780.58
     specified NEC 333.99
   head 781.0
   involuntary 781.0
   specified type NEC 333.99
muscle contraction, localized 728.85
myoglobin (Aberdeen) (Annapolis) 289.9
narrowness, eyelid 743.62
optokinetic response 379.57
organs or tissues of pelvis NEC
   in pregnancy or childbirth 654.9 ☑
     affecting fetus or newborn 763.89
     causing obstructed labor 660.2 ☑
       affecting fetus or newborn 763.1
origin — see Malposition, congenital
palmar creases 757.2
Papanicolaou (smear)
   anus 796.70
     with
       atypical squamous cells
         cannot exclude high grade squamous intraepithelial lesion (ASC-H) 796.72
         of undetermined significance (ASC-US) 796.71
       cytologic evidence of malignancy 796.76
       high grade squamous intraepithelial lesion (HGSIL) 796.74
       low grade squamous intraepithelial lesion (LGSIL) 796.73
     glandular 796.70
     specified finding NEC 796.79
   cervix 795.00
     with
       atypical squamous cells
         cannot exclude high grade squamous intraepithelial lesion (ASC-H) 795.02
         of undetermined significance (ASC-US) 795.01
       cytologic evidence of malignancy 795.06
       high grade squamous intraepithelial lesion (HGSIL) 795.04
       low grade squamous intraepithelial lesion (LGSIL) 795.03
       nonspecific finding NEC 795.09
   other site 796.9

Index

Abnormal, abnormality, abnormalities — Abortion

Abnormal, abnormality, abnormalities — see
also Anomaly — continued
Papanicolaou — continued
vagina 795.10
with
atypical squamous cells
cannot exclude high grade
squamous intraepithelial
lesion (ASC-H) 795.12
of undetermined significance
(ASC-US) 795.11
cytologic evidence of malignancy
795.16
high grade squamous intraepithelial lesion (HGSIL) 795.14
low grade squamous intraepithelial
lesion (LGSIL) 795.13
glandular 795.10
specified finding NEC 795.19
parturition
affecting fetus or newborn 763.9
mother — see Delivery, complicated
pelvis (bony) — see Deformity, pelvis
percussion, chest 786.7
periods (grossly) (see also Menstruation) 626.9
phonocardiogram 794.39
placenta — see Placenta, abnormal
plantar reflex 796.1
plasma protein — see Deficiency, plasma,
protein
pleural folds 748.8
position (see also Malposition)
gravid uterus 654.4 ☑
causing obstructed labor 660.2 ☑
affecting fetus or newborn 763.1
posture NEC 781.92
presentation (fetus) — see Presentation, fetus,
abnormal
product of conception NEC 631
puberty — see Puberty
pulmonary
artery 747.3
function, newborn 770.89
test results 794.2
ventilation, newborn 770.89
hyperventilation 786.01
pulsations in neck 785.1
pupil reflexes 379.40
quality of milk 676.8 ☑
radiological examination 793.99
abdomen NEC 793.6
biliary tract 793.3
breast 793.89
mammogram NOS 793.80
mammographic
calcification 793.89
calculus 793.89
microcalcification 793.81
gastrointestinal tract 793.4
genitourinary organs 793.5
head 793.0
image test inconclusive due to excess body
fat 793.91
intrathoracic organ NEC 793.2
lung (field) 793.1
musculoskeletal system 793.7
retroperitoneum 793.6
skin and subcutaneous tissue 793.99
skull 793.0
red blood cells 790.09
morphology 790.09
volume 790.09
reflex NEC 796.1
renal function test 794.4
respiration signs — see Respiration
response to nerve stimulation 794.10
retinal correspondence 368.34
rhythm, heart (see also Arrhythmia)
fetus — see Distress, fetal
saliva 792.4
scan
brain 794.09
kidney 794.4
liver 794.8
lung 794.2
thyroid 794.5

Abnormal, abnormality, abnormalities — see
also Anomaly — continued
secretion
gastrin 251.5
glucagon 251.4
semen 792.2
serum level (of)
acid phosphatase 790.5
alkaline phosphatase 790.5
amylase 790.5
enzymes NEC 790.5
lipase 790.5
shape
cornea 743.41
gallbladder 751.69
gravid uterus 654.4 ☑
affecting fetus or newborn 763.89
causing obstructed labor 660.2 ☑
affecting fetus or newborn 763.1
head (see also Anomaly, skull) 756.0
organ or site, congenital NEC — see Distortion
sinus venosus 747.40
size
fetus, complicating delivery 653.5 ☑
causing obstructed labor 660.1 ☑
gallbladder 751.69
head (see also Anomaly, skull) 756.0
organ or site, congenital NEC — see Distortion
teeth 520.2
skin and appendages, congenital NEC 757.9
soft parts of pelvis — see Abnormal, organs
or tissues of pelvis
spermatozoa 792.2
sputum (amount) (color) (excessive) (odor)
(purulent) 786.4
stool NEC 787.7
bloody 578.1
occult 792.1
bulky 787.7
color (dark) (light) 792.1
content (fat) (mucus) (pus) 792.1
occult blood 792.1
synchondrosis 756.9
test results without manifest disease — see
Findings, abnormal
thebesian valve 746.9
thermography — see Findings, abnormal,
structure
threshold, cones or rods (eye) 368.63
thyroid-binding globulin 246.8
thyroid product 246.8
toxicology (findings) NEC 796.0
tracheal cartilage (congenital) 748.3
transport protein 273.8
ultrasound results — see Findings, abnormal,
structure
umbilical cord
affecting fetus or newborn 762.6
complicating delivery 663.9 ☑
specified NEC 663.8 ☑
union
cricoid cartilage and thyroid cartilage 748.3
larynx and trachea 748.3
thyroid cartilage and hyoid bone 748.3
urination NEC 788.69
psychogenic 306.53
stream
intermittent 788.61
slowing 788.62
splitting 788.61
weak 788.62
urgency 788.63
urine (constituents) NEC 791.9
uterine hemorrhage (see also Hemorrhage,
uterus) 626.9
climacteric 627.0
postmenopausal 627.1
vagina (acquired) (congenital)
in pregnancy or childbirth 654.7 ☑
affecting fetus or newborn 763.89
causing obstructed labor 660.2 ☑
affecting fetus or newborn 763.1
vascular sounds 785.9
vectorcardiogram 794.39

Abnormal, abnormality, abnormalities — see
also Anomaly — continued
visually evoked potential (VEP) 794.13
vulva (acquired) (congenital)
in pregnancy or childbirth 654.8 ☑
affecting fetus or newborn 763.89
causing obstructed labor 660.2 ☑
affecting fetus or newborn 763.1
weight
gain 783.1
of pregnancy 646.1 ☑
with hypertension — see Toxemia,
of pregnancy
loss 783.21
x-ray examination — see Abnormal, radiological examination
Abnormally formed uterus — see Anomaly,
uterus
Abnormity (any organ or part) — see Anomaly
ABO
hemolytic disease 773.1
incompatibility reaction 999.6
Abocclusion 524.20
Abolition, language 784.69
Aborter, habitual or recurrent NEC
without current pregnancy 629.81
current abortion (see also Abortion, spontaneous) 634.9 ☑
affecting fetus or newborn 761.8
observation in current pregnancy 646.3 ☑
Abortion (complete) (incomplete) (inevitable)
(with retained products of conception)
637.9 ☑

> Note — Use the following fifth-digit subclas-
> sification with categories 634–637:
>
> 0   unspecified
>
> 1   incomplete
>
> 2   complete

with
complication(s) (any) following previous
abortion — see category 639 ☑
damage to pelvic organ (laceration) (rupture) (tear) 637.2 ☑
embolism (air) (amniotic fluid) (blood clot)
(pulmonary) (pyemic) (septic)
(soap) 637.6 ☑
genital tract and pelvic infection 637.0 ☑
hemorrhage, delayed or excessive 637.1 ☑
metabolic disorder 637.4 ☑
renal failure (acute) 637.3 ☑
sepsis (genital tract) (pelvic organ)
637.0 ☑
urinary tract 637.7 ☑
shock (postoperative) (septic) 637.5 ☑
specified complication NEC 637.7 ☑
toxemia 637.3 ☑
unspecified complication(s) 637.8 ☑
urinary tract infection 637.7 ☑
accidental — see Abortion, spontaneous
artificial — see Abortion, induced
attempted (failed) — see Abortion, failed
criminal — see Abortion, illegal
early — see Abortion, spontaneous
elective — see Abortion, legal
failed (legal) 638.9
with
damage to pelvic organ (laceration)
(rupture) (tear) 638.2
embolism (air) (amniotic fluid) (blood
clot) (pulmonary) (pyemic)
(septic) (soap) 638.6
genital tract and pelvic infection 638.0
hemorrhage, delayed or excessive
638.1
metabolic disorder 638.4
renal failure (acute) 638.3
sepsis (genital tract) (pelvic organ)
638.0
urinary tract 638.7
shock (postoperative) (septic) 638.5
specified complication NEC 638.7
toxemia 638.3
unspecified complication(s) 638.8

Abortion — continued
failed — continued
with — continued
urinary tract infection 638.7
fetal indication — see Abortion, legal
fetus 779.6
following threatened abortion — see Abortion,
by type
habitual or recurrent (care during pregnancy)
646.3 ☑
with current abortion (see also Abortion,
spontaneous) 634.9 ☑
affecting fetus or newborn 761.8
without current pregnancy 629.81
homicidal — see Abortion, illegal
illegal 636.9 ☑
with
damage to pelvic organ (laceration)
(rupture) (tear) 636.2 ☑
embolism (air) (amniotic fluid) (blood
clot) (pulmonary) (pyemic)
(septic) (soap) 636.6 ☑
genital tract and pelvic infection
636.0 ☑
hemorrhage, delayed or excessive
636.1 ☑
metabolic disorder 636.4 ☑
renal failure 636.3 ☑
sepsis (genital tract) (pelvic organ)
636.0 ☑
urinary tract 636.7 ☑
shock (postoperative) (septic) 636.5 ☑
specified complication NEC 636.7 ☑
toxemia 636.3 ☑
unspecified complication(s) 636.8 ☑
urinary tract infection 636.7 ☑
fetus 779.6
induced 637.9 ☑
illegal — see Abortion, illegal
legal indications — see Abortion, legal
medical indications — see Abortion, legal
therapeutic — see Abortion, legal
late — see Abortion, spontaneous
legal (legal indication) (medical indication)
(under medical supervision) 635.9 ☑
with
damage to pelvic organ (laceration)
(rupture) (tear) 635.2 ☑
embolism (air) (amniotic fluid) (blood
clot) (pulmonary) (pyemic)
(septic) (soap) 635.6 ☑
genital tract and pelvic infection
635.0 ☑
hemorrhage, delayed or excessive
635.1 ☑
metabolic disorder 635.4 ☑
renal failure (acute) 635.3 ☑
sepsis (genital tract) (pelvic organ)
635.0 ☑
urinary tract 635.7 ☑
shock (postoperative) (septic) 635.5 ☑
specified complication NEC 635.7 ☑
toxemia 635.3 ☑
unspecified complication(s) 635.8 ☑
urinary tract infection 635.7 ☑
fetus 779.6
medical indication — see Abortion, legal
mental hygiene problem — see Abortion, legal
missed 632
operative — see Abortion, legal
psychiatric indication — see Abortion, legal
recurrent — see Abortion, spontaneous
self-induced — see Abortion, illegal
septic — see Abortion, by type, with sepsis
spontaneous 634.9 ☑
with
damage to pelvic organ (laceration)
(rupture) (tear) 634.2 ☑
embolism (air) (amniotic fluid) (blood
clot) (pulmonary) (pyemic)
(septic) (soap) 634.6 ☑
genital tract and pelvic infection
634.0 ☑
hemorrhage, delayed or excessive
634.1 ☑

☑ Additional Digit Required — Refer to the Tabular List for Digit Selection   ▽ Subterms under main terms may continue to next column or page

2 — Volume 2   ▶◀ Revised Text   ● New Line   ▲ Revised Code   2010 ICD-9-CM

Abortion — *continued*
  spontaneous — *continued*
    with — *continued*
      metabolic disorder 634.4 ☑
      renal failure 634.3 ☑
      sepsis (genital tract) (pelvic organ) 634.0 ☑
      urinary tract 634.7 ☑
      shock (postoperative) (septic) 634.5 ☑
      specified complication NEC 634.7 ☑
      toxemia 634.3 ☑
      unspecified complication(s) 634.8 ☑
      urinary tract infection 634.7 ☑
    fetus 761.8
    threatened 640.0 ☑
      affecting fetus or newborn 762.1
  surgical — *see* Abortion, legal
  therapeutic — *see* Abortion, legal
  threatened 640.0 ☑
    affecting fetus or newborn 762.1
  tubal — *see* Pregnancy, tubal
  voluntary — *see* Abortion, legal
Abortus fever 023.9
Aboulomania 301.6
Abrachia 755.20
Abrachiatism 755.20
Abrachiocephalia 759.89
Abrachiocephalus 759.89
Abrami's disease (acquired hemolytic jaundice) 283.9
Abramov-Fiedler myocarditis (acute isolated myocarditis) 422.91
Abrasion — *see also* Injury, superficial, by site
  cornea 918.1
  dental 521.20
    extending into
      dentine 521.22
      pulp 521.23
    generalized 521.25
    limited to enamel 521.21
    localized 521.24
  teeth, tooth (dentifrice) (habitual) (hard tissues) (occupational) (ritual) (traditional) (wedge defect) (*see also* Abrasion, dental) 521.20
Abrikossov's tumor (M9580/0) — *see also* Neoplasm, connective tissue, benign
  malignant (M9580/3) — *see* Neoplasm, connective tissue, malignant
Abrism 988.8
Abruption, placenta — *see* Placenta, abruptio
Abruptio placentae — *see* Placenta, abruptio
Abscess (acute) (chronic) (infectional) (lymphangitic) (metastatic) (multiple) (pyogenic) (septic) (with lymphangitis) — *see also* Cellulitis 682.9
  abdomen, abdominal
    cavity 567.22
    wall 682.2
  abdominopelvic 567.22
  accessory sinus (chronic) (*see also* Sinusitis) 473.9
  adrenal (capsule) (gland) 255.8
  alveolar 522.5
    with sinus 522.7
  amebic 006.3
    bladder 006.8
    brain (with liver or lung abscess) 006.5
    liver (without mention of brain or lung abscess) 006.3
      with
        brain abscess (and lung abscess) 006.5
        lung abscess 006.4
    lung (with liver abscess) 006.4
      with brain abscess 006.5
    seminal vesicle 006.8
    specified site NEC 006.8
    spleen 006.8
  anaerobic 040.0
  ankle 682.6
  anorectal 566
  antecubital space 682.3
  antrum (chronic) (Highmore) (*see also* Sinusitis, maxillary) 473.0
  anus 566

Abscess — *see also* Cellulitis — *continued*
  apical (tooth) 522.5
    with sinus (alveolar) 522.7
  appendix 540.1
  areola (acute) (chronic) (nonpuerperal) 611.0
    puerperal, postpartum 675.1 ☑
  arm (any part, above wrist) 682.3
  artery (wall) 447.2
  atheromatous 447.2
  auditory canal (external) 380.10
  auricle (ear) (staphylococcal) (streptococcal) 380.10
  axilla, axillary (region) 682.3
    lymph gland or node 683
  back (any part) 682.2
  Bartholin's gland 616.3
    with
      abortion — *see* Abortion, by type, with sepsis
      ectopic pregnancy (*see also* categories 633.0–633.9) 639.0
      molar pregnancy (*see also* categories 630–632) 639.0
    complicating pregnancy or puerperium 646.6 ☑
    following
      abortion 639.0
      ectopic or molar pregnancy 639.0
  bartholinian 616.3
  Bezold's 383.01
  bile, biliary, duct or tract (*see also* Cholecystitis) 576.8
  bilharziasis 120.1
  bladder (wall) 595.89
    amebic 006.8
  bone (subperiosteal) (*see also* Osteomyelitis) 730.0 ☑
    accessory sinus (chronic) (*see also* Sinusitis) 473.9
    acute 730.0 ☑
    chronic or old 730.1 ☑
    jaw (lower) (upper) 526.4
    mastoid — *see* Mastoiditis, acute
    petrous (*see also* Petrositis) 383.20
    spinal (tuberculous) (*see also* Tuberculosis) 015.0 ☑ *[730.88]*
      nontuberculous 730.08
  bowel 569.5
  brain (any part) 324.0
    amebic (with liver or lung abscess) 006.5
    cystic 324.0
    late effect — *see* category 326
    otogenic 324.0
    tuberculous (*see also* Tuberculosis) 013.3 ☑
  breast (acute) (chronic) (nonpuerperal) 611.0
    newborn 771.5
    puerperal, postpartum 675.1 ☑
    tuberculous (*see also* Tuberculosis) 017.9 ☑
  broad ligament (chronic) (*see also* Disease, pelvis, inflammatory) 614.4
    acute 614.3
  Brodie's (chronic) (localized) (*see also* Osteomyelitis) 730.1 ☑
  bronchus 519.19
  buccal cavity 528.3
  bulbourethral gland 597.0
  bursa 727.89
    pharyngeal 478.29
  buttock 682.5
  canaliculus, breast 611.0
  canthus 372.20
  cartilage 733.99
  cecum 569.5
    with appendicitis 540.1
  cerebellum, cerebellar 324.0
    late effect — *see* category 326
  cerebral (embolic) 324.0
    late effect — *see* category 326
  cervical (neck region) 682.1
    lymph gland or node 683
    stump (*see also* Cervicitis) 616.0
  cervix (stump) (uteri) (*see also* Cervicitis) 616.0
  cheek, external 682.0
    inner 528.3

Abscess — *see also* Cellulitis — *continued*
  chest 510.9
    with fistula 510.0
    wall 682.2
  chin 682.0
  choroid 363.00
  ciliary body 364.3
  circumtonsillar 475
  cold (tuberculous) (*see also* Tuberculosis, abscess)
    articular — *see* Tuberculosis, joint
  colon (wall) 569.5
  colostomy or enterostomy 569.61
  conjunctiva 372.00
  connective tissue NEC 682.9
  cornea 370.55
    with ulcer 370.00
  corpus
    cavernosum 607.2
    luteum (*see also* Salpingo-oophoritis) 614.2
  Cowper's gland 597.0
  cranium 324.0
  cul-de-sac (Douglas') (posterior) (*see also* Disease, pelvis, inflammatory) 614.4
    acute 614.3
  dental 522.5
    with sinus (alveolar) 522.7
  dentoalveolar 522.5
    with sinus (alveolar) 522.7
  diaphragm, diaphragmatic 567.22
  digit NEC 681.9
  Douglas' cul-de-sac or pouch (*see also* Disease, pelvis, inflammatory) 614.4
    acute 614.3
  Dubois' 090.5
  ductless gland 259.8
  ear
    acute 382.00
    external 380.10
    inner 386.30
    middle — *see* Otitis media
  elbow 682.3
  endamebic — *see* Abscess, amebic
  entamebic — *see* Abscess, amebic
  enterostomy 569.61
  epididymis 604.0
  epidural 324.9
    brain 324.0
    late effect — *see* category 326
    spinal cord 324.1
  epiglottis 478.79
  epiploon, epiploic 567.22
  erysipelatous (*see also* Erysipelas) 035
  esophagostomy 530.86
  esophagus 530.19
  ethmoid (bone) (chronic) (sinus) (*see also* Sinusitis, ethmoidal) 473.2
  external auditory canal 380.10
  extradural 324.9
    brain 324.0
    late effect — *see* category 326
    spinal cord 324.1
  extraperitoneal — *see* Abscess, peritoneum
  eye 360.00
  eyelid 373.13
  face (any part, except eye) 682.0
  fallopian tube (*see also* Salpingo-oophoritis) 614.2
  fascia 728.89
  fauces 478.29
  fecal 569.5
  femoral (region) 682.6
  filaria, filarial (*see also* Infestation, filarial) 125.9
  finger (any) (intrathecal) (periosteal) (subcutaneous) (subcuticular) 681.00
  fistulous NEC 682.9
  flank 682.2
  foot (except toe) 682.7
  forearm 682.3
  forehead 682.0
  frontal (sinus) (chronic) (*see also* Sinusitis, frontal) 473.1
  gallbladder (*see also* Cholecystitis, acute) 575.0
  gastric 535.0 ☑
  genital organ or tract NEC
    female 616.9

Abscess — *see also* Cellulitis — *continued*
  genital organ or tract — *continued*
    female — *continued*
      with
        abortion — *see* Abortion, by type, with sepsis
        ectopic pregnancy (*see also* categories 633.0–633.9) 639.0
        molar pregnancy (*see also* categories 630–632) 639.0
      following
        abortion 639.0
        ectopic or molar pregnancy 639.0
      puerperal, postpartum, childbirth 670.8 ☑ ▲
    male 608.4
  genitourinary system, tuberculous (*see also* Tuberculosis) 016.9 ☑
  gingival 523.30
  gland, glandular (lymph) (acute) NEC 683
  glottis 478.79
  gluteal (region) 682.5
  gonorrheal NEC (*see also* Gonococcus) 098.0
  groin 682.2
  gum 523.30
  hand (except finger or thumb) 682.4
  head (except face) 682.8
  heart 429.89
  heel 682.7
  helminthic (*see also* Infestation, by specific parasite) 128.9
  hepatic 572.0
    amebic (*see also* Abscess, liver, amebic) 006.3
    duct 576.8
  hip 682.6
    tuberculous (active) (*see also* Tuberculosis) 015.1 ☑
  ileocecal 540.1
  ileostomy (bud) 569.61
  iliac (region) 682.2
    fossa 540.1
  iliopsoas 567.31
    nontuberculous 728.89
    tuberculous (*see also* Tuberculosis) 015.0 ☑ *[730.88]*
  infraclavicular (fossa) 682.3
  inguinal (region) 682.2
    lymph gland or node 683
  intersphincteric (anus) 566
  intestine, intestinal 569.5
    rectal 566
  intra-abdominal (*see also* Abscess, peritoneum) 567.22
    postoperative 998.59
  intracranial 324.0
    late effect — *see* category 326
  intramammary — *see* Abscess, breast
  intramastoid (*see also* Mastoiditis, acute) 383.00
  intraorbital 376.01
  intraperitoneal 567.22
  intraspinal 324.1
    late effect — *see* category 326
  intratonsillar 475
  iris 364.3
  ischiorectal 566
  jaw (bone) (lower) (upper) 526.4
    skin 682.0
  joint (*see also* Arthritis, pyogenic) 711.0 ☑
    vertebral (tuberculous) (*see also* Tuberculosis) 015.0 ☑ *[730.88]*
      nontuberculous 724.8
  kidney 590.2
    with
      abortion — *see* Abortion, by type, with urinary tract infection
      calculus 592.0
      ectopic pregnancy (*see also* categories 633.0–633.9) 639.8
      molar pregnancy (*see also* categories 630–632) 639.8
    complicating pregnancy or puerperium 646.6 ☑
      affecting fetus or newborn 760.1

☑ Additional Digit Required — Refer to the Tabular List for Digit Selection   ▽ Subterms under main terms may continue to next column or page

2010 ICD-9-CM   ▶◀ Revised Text   ● New Line   ▲ Revised Code   October 2009 • Volume 2 — 3

Abscess — *see also* Cellulitis — *continued*
  kidney — *continued*
    following
      abortion 639.8
      ectopic or molar pregnancy 639.8
  knee 682.6
    joint 711.06
    tuberculous (active) (*see also* Tuberculosis) 015.2 ☑
  labium (majus) (minus) 616.4
    complicating pregnancy, childbirth, or puerperium 646.6 ☑
  lacrimal (passages) (sac) (*see also* Dacryocystitis) 375.30
    caruncle 375.30
    gland (*see also* Dacryoadenitis) 375.00
  lacunar 597.0
  larynx 478.79
  lateral (alveolar) 522.5
    with sinus 522.7
  leg, except foot 682.6
  lens 360.00
  lid 373.13
  lingual 529.0
    tonsil 475
  lip 528.5
  Littre's gland 597.0
  liver 572.0
    amebic 006.3
      with
        brain abscess (and lung abscess) 006.5
        lung abscess 006.4
      due to Entamoeba histolytica 006.3
    dysenteric (*see also* Abscess, liver, amebic) 006.3
    pyogenic 572.0
    tropical (*see also* Abscess, liver, amebic) 006.3
  loin (region) 682.2
  lumbar (tuberculous) (*see also* Tuberculosis) 015.0 ☑ *[730.88]*
    nontuberculous 682.2
  lung (miliary) (putrid) 513.0
    amebic (with liver abscess) 006.4
      with brain abscess 006.5
  lymphangitic, acute — *see* Cellulitis
  lymph, lymphatic, gland or node (acute) 683
    any site, except mesenteric 683
    mesentery 289.2
  malar 526.4
  mammary gland — *see* Abscess, breast
  marginal (anus) 566
  mastoid (process) (*see also* Mastoiditis, acute) 383.00
    subperiosteal 383.01
  maxilla, maxillary 526.4
    molar (tooth) 522.5
      with sinus 522.7
    premolar 522.5
    sinus (chronic) (*see also* Sinusitis, maxillary) 473.0
  mediastinum 513.1
  meibomian gland 373.12
  meninges (*see also* Meningitis) 320.9
  mesentery, mesenteric 567.22
  mesosalpinx (*see also* Salpingo-oophoritis) 614.2
  milk 675.1 ☑
  Monro's (psoriasis) 696.1
  mons pubis 682.2
  mouth (floor) 528.3
  multiple sites NEC 682.9
  mural 682.2
  muscle 728.89
    psoas 567.31
  myocardium 422.92
  nabothian (follicle) (*see also* Cervicitis) 616.0
  nail (chronic) (with lymphangitis) 681.9
    finger 681.02
    toe 681.11
  nasal (fossa) (septum) 478.19
    sinus (chronic) (*see also* Sinusitis) 473.9
  nasopharyngeal 478.29
  nates 682.5
  navel 682.2

Abscess — *see also* Cellulitis — *continued*
  navel — *continued*
    newborn NEC 771.4
  neck (region) 682.1
    lymph gland or node 683
  nephritic (*see also* Abscess, kidney) 590.2
  nipple 611.0
    puerperal, postpartum 675.0 ☑
  nose (septum) 478.19
    external 682.0
  omentum 567.22
  operative wound 998.59
  orbit, orbital 376.01
  ossifluent — *see* Abscess, bone
  ovary, ovarian (corpus luteum) (*see also* Salpingo-oophoritis) 614.2
  oviduct (*see also* Salpingo-oophoritis) 614.2
  palate (soft) 528.3
    hard 526.4
  palmar (space) 682.4
  pancreas (duct) 577.0
  paradontal 523.30
  parafrenal 607.2
  parametric, parametrium (chronic) (*see also* Disease, pelvis, inflammatory) 614.4
    acute 614.3
  paranephric 590.2
  parapancreatic 577.0
  parapharyngeal 478.22
  pararectal 566
  parasinus (*see also* Sinusitis) 473.9
  parauterine (*see also* Disease, pelvis, inflammatory) 614.4
    acute 614.3
  paravaginal (*see also* Vaginitis) 616.10
  parietal region 682.8
  parodontal 523.30
  parotid (duct) (gland) 527.3
    region 528.3
  parumbilical 682.2
    newborn 771.4
  pectoral (region) 682.2
  pelvirectal 567.22
  pelvis, pelvic
    female (chronic) (*see also* Disease, pelvis, inflammatory) 614.4
      acute 614.3
    male, peritoneal (cellular tissue) — *see* Abscess, peritoneum
    tuberculous (*see also* Tuberculosis) 016.9 ☑
  penis 607.2
    gonococcal (acute) 098.0
      chronic or duration of 2 months or over 098.2
  perianal 566
  periapical 522.5
    with sinus (alveolar) 522.7
  periappendiceal 540.1
  pericardial 420.99
  pericecal 540.1
  pericemental 523.30
  pericholecystic (*see also* Cholecystitis, acute) 575.0
  pericoronal 523.30
  peridental 523.30
  perigastric 535.0 ☑
  perimetric (*see also* Disease, pelvis, inflammatory) 614.4
    acute 614.3
  perinephric, perinephritic (*see also* Abscess, kidney) 590.2
  perineum, perineal (superficial) 682.2
    deep (with urethral involvement) 597.0
    urethra 597.0
  periodontal (parietal) 523.31
    apical 522.5
  periosteum, periosteal (*see also* Periostitis) 730.3 ☑
    with osteomyelitis (*see also* Osteomyelitis) 730.2 ☑
      acute or subacute 730.0 ☑
      chronic or old 730.1 ☑
  peripleuritic 510.9
    with fistula 510.0
  periproctic 566

Abscess — *see also* Cellulitis — *continued*
  periprostatic 601.2
  perirectal (staphylococcal) 566
  perirenal (tissue) (*see also* Abscess, kidney) 590.2
  perisinuous (nose) (*see also* Sinusitis) 473.9
  peritoneum, peritoneal (perforated) (ruptured) 567.22
    with
      abortion — *see* Abortion, by type, with sepsis
      appendicitis 540.1
      ectopic pregnancy (*see also* categories 633.0–633.9) 639.0
      molar pregnancy (*see also* categories 630–632) 639.0
    following
      abortion 639.0
      ectopic or molar pregnancy 639.0
    pelvic, female (*see also* Disease, pelvis, inflammatory) 614.4
      acute 614.3
    postoperative 998.59
    puerperal, postpartum, childbirth 670.8 ☑ ▲
    tuberculous (*see also* Tuberculosis) 014.0 ☑
  peritonsillar 475
  perityphlic 540.1
  periureteral 593.89
  periurethral 597.0
    gonococcal (acute) 098.0
      chronic or duration of 2 months or over 098.2
  periuterine (*see also* Disease, pelvis, inflammatory) 614.4
    acute 614.3
  perivesical 595.89
  pernicious NEC 682.9
  petrous bone — *see* Petrositis
  phagedenic NEC 682.9
    chancroid 099.0
  pharynx, pharyngeal (lateral) 478.29
  phlegmonous NEC 682.9
  pilonidal 685.0
  pituitary (gland) 253.8
  pleura 510.9
    with fistula 510.0
  popliteal 682.6
  postanal 566
  postcecal 540.1
  postlaryngeal 478.79
  postnasal 478.19
  postpharyngeal 478.24
  posttonsillar 475
  posttyphoid 002.0
  Pott's (*see also* Tuberculosis) 015.0 ☑ *[730.88]*
  pouch of Douglas (chronic) (*see also* Disease, pelvis, inflammatory) 614.4
  premammary — *see* Abscess, breast
  prepatellar 682.6
  prostate (*see also* Prostatitis) 601.2
    gonococcal (acute) 098.12
      chronic or duration of 2 months or over 098.32
  psoas 567.31
    nontuberculous 728.89
    tuberculous (*see also* Tuberculosis) 015.0 ☑ *[730.88]*
  pterygopalatine fossa 682.8
  pubis 682.2
  puerperal — *see* Puerperal, abscess, by site
  pulmonary — *see* Abscess, lung
  pulp, pulpal (dental) 522.0
    finger 681.01
    toe 681.10
  pyemic — *see* Septicemia
  pyloric valve 535.0 ☑
  rectovaginal septum 569.5
  rectovesical 595.89
  rectum 566
  regional NEC 682.9
  renal (*see also* Abscess, kidney) 590.2
  retina 363.00
  retrobulbar 376.01
  retrocecal 567.22

Abscess — *see also* Cellulitis — *continued*
  retrolaryngeal 478.79
  retromammary — *see* Abscess, breast
  retroperineal 682.2
  retroperitoneal 567.38
    postprocedural 998.59
  retropharyngeal 478.24
    tuberculous (*see also* Tuberculosis) 012.8 ☑
  retrorectal 566
  retrouterine (*see also* Disease, pelvis, inflammatory) 614.4
    acute 614.3
  retrovesical 595.89
  root, tooth 522.5
    with sinus (alveolar) 522.7
  round ligament (*see also* Disease, pelvis, inflammatory) 614.4
    acute 614.3
  rupture (spontaneous) NEC 682.9
  sacrum (tuberculous) (*see also* Tuberculosis) 015.0 ☑ *[730.88]*
    nontuberculous 730.08
  salivary duct or gland 527.3
  scalp (any part) 682.8
  scapular 730.01
  sclera 379.09
  scrofulous (*see also* Tuberculosis) 017.2 ☑
  scrotum 608.4
  seminal vesicle 608.0
    amebic 006.8
  septal, dental 522.5
    with sinus (alveolar) 522.7
  septum (nasal) 478.19
  serous (*see also* Periostitis) 730.3 ☑
  shoulder 682.3
  side 682.2
  sigmoid 569.5
  sinus (accessory) (chronic) (nasal) (*see also* Sinusitis) 473.9
    intracranial venous (any) 324.0
      late effect — *see* category 326
  Skene's duct or gland 597.0
  skin NEC 682.9
    tuberculous (primary) (*see also* Tuberculosis) 017.0 ☑
  sloughing NEC 682.9
  specified site NEC 682.8
    amebic 006.8
  spermatic cord 608.4
  sphenoidal (sinus) (*see also* Sinusitis, sphenoidal) 473.3
  spinal
    cord (any part) (staphylococcal) 324.1
      tuberculous (*see also* Tuberculosis) 013.5 ☑
    epidural 324.1
  spine (column) (tuberculous) (*see also* Tuberculosis) 015.0 ☑ *[730.88]*
    nontuberculous 730.08
  spleen 289.59
    amebic 006.8
  staphylococcal NEC 682.9
  stitch 998.59
  stomach (wall) 535.0 ☑
  strumous (tuberculous) (*see also* Tuberculosis) 017.2 ☑
  subarachnoid 324.9
    brain 324.0
    cerebral 324.0
    late effect — *see* category 326
    spinal cord 324.1
  subareolar (*see also* Abscess, breast)
    puerperal, postpartum 675.1 ☑
  subcecal 540.1
  subcutaneous NEC 682.9
  subdiaphragmatic 567.22
  subdorsal 682.2
  subdural 324.9
    brain 324.0
    late effect — *see* category 326
    spinal cord 324.1
  subgaleal 682.8
  subhepatic 567.22
  sublingual 528.3
    gland 527.3

Abscess — see also Cellulitis — continued
  submammary — see Abscess, breast
  submandibular (region) (space) (triangle) 682.0
    gland 527.3
  submaxillary (region) 682.0
    gland 527.3
  submental (pyogenic) 682.0
    gland 527.3
  subpectoral 682.2
  subperiosteal — see Abscess, bone
  subperitoneal 567.22
  subphrenic (see also Abscess, peritoneum) 567.22
    postoperative 998.59
  subscapular 682.2
  subungual 681.9
  suburethral 597.0
  sudoriparous 705.89
  suppurative NEC 682.9
  supraclavicular (fossa) 682.3
  suprahepatic 567.22
  suprapelvic (see also Disease, pelvis, inflammatory) 614.4
    acute 614.3
  suprapubic 682.2
  suprarenal (capsule) (gland) 255.8
  sweat gland 705.89
  syphilitic 095.8
  teeth, tooth (root) 522.5
    with sinus (alveolar) 522.7
    supporting structures NEC 523.30
  temple 682.0
  temporal region 682.0
  temporosphenoidal 324.0
    late effect — see category 326
  tendon (sheath) 727.89
  testicle — see Orchitis
  thecal 728.89
  thigh (acquired) 682.6
  thorax 510.9
    with fistula 510.0
  throat 478.29
  thumb (intrathecal) (periosteal) (subcutaneous) (subcuticular) 681.00
  thymus (gland) 254.1
  thyroid (gland) 245.0
  toe (any) (intrathecal) (periosteal) (subcutaneous) (subcuticular) 681.10
  tongue (staphylococcal) 529.0
  tonsil(s) (lingual) 475
  tonsillopharyngeal 475
  tooth, teeth (root) 522.5
    with sinus (alveolar) 522.7
    supporting structure NEC 523.30
  trachea 478.9
  trunk 682.2
  tubal (see also Salpingo-oophoritis) 614.2
  tuberculous — see Tuberculosis, abscess
  tubo-ovarian (see also Salpingo-oophoritis) 614.2
  tunica vaginalis 608.4
  umbilicus NEC 682.2
    newborn 771.4
  upper arm 682.3
  upper respiratory 478.9
  urachus 682.2
  urethra (gland) 597.0
  urinary 597.0
  uterus, uterine (wall) (see also Endometritis) 615.9
    ligament (see also Disease, pelvis, inflammatory) 614.4
     acute 614.3
    neck (see also Cervicitis) 616.0
  uvula 528.3
  vagina (wall) (see also Vaginitis) 616.10
  vaginorectal (see also Vaginitis) 616.10
  vas deferens 608.4
  vermiform appendix 540.1
  vertebra (column) (tuberculous) (see also Tuberculosis) 015.0 ☑ [730.88]
    nontuberculous 730.0 ☑
  vesical 595.89
  vesicouterine pouch (see also Disease, pelvis, inflammatory) 614.4
  vitreous (humor) (pneumococcal) 360.04

Abscess — see also Cellulitis — continued
  vocal cord 478.5
  von Bezold's 383.01
  vulva 616.4
    complicating pregnancy, childbirth, or puerperium 646.6 ☑
  vulvovaginal gland (see also Vaginitis) 616.3
  web-space 682.4
  wrist 682.4

Absence (organ or part) (complete or partial)
  acoustic nerve 742.8
  adrenal (gland) (congenital) 759.1
    acquired V45.79
  albumin (blood) 273.8
  alimentary tract (complete) (congenital) (partial) 751.8
    lower 751.5
    upper 750.8
  alpha-fucosidase 271.8
  alveolar process (acquired) 525.8
    congenital 750.26
  anus, anal (canal) (congenital) 751.2
  aorta (congenital) 747.22
  aortic valve (congenital) 746.89
  appendix, congenital 751.2
  arm (acquired) V49.60
    above elbow V49.66
    below elbow V49.65
    congenital (see also Deformity, reduction, upper limb) 755.20
     lower — see Absence, forearm, congenital
     upper (complete) (partial) (with absence of distal elements, incomplete) 755.24
      with
       complete absence of distal elements 755.21
       forearm (incomplete) 755.23
  artery (congenital) (peripheral) NEC (see also Anomaly, peripheral vascular system) 747.60
    brain 747.81
    cerebral 747.81
    coronary 746.85
    pulmonary 747.3
    umbilical 747.5
  atrial septum 745.69
  auditory canal (congenital) (external) 744.01
  auricle (ear) (with stenosis or atresia of auditory canal), congenital 744.01
  bile, biliary duct (common) or passage (congenital) 751.61
  bladder (acquired) V45.74
    congenital 753.8
  bone (congenital) NEC 756.9
    marrow 284.9
     acquired (secondary) 284.89
     congenital 284.09
     hereditary 284.09
     idiopathic 284.9
    skull 756.0
  bowel sounds 787.5
  brain 740.0
    specified part 742.2
  breast(s) (acquired) V45.71
    congenital 757.6
  broad ligament (congenital) 752.19
  bronchus (congenital) 748.3
  calvarium, calvaria (skull) 756.0
  canaliculus lacrimalis, congenital 743.65
  carpal(s) (congenital) (complete) (partial) (with absence of distal elements, incomplete) (see also Deformity, reduction, upper limb) 755.28
    with complete absence of distal elements 755.21
  cartilage 756.9
  caudal spine 756.13
  cecum (acquired) (postoperative) (posttraumatic) V45.72
    congenital 751.2
  cementum 520.4
  cerebellum (congenital) (vermis) 742.2
  cervix (acquired) (uteri) V88.01
    with remaining uterus V88.03

Absence — continued
  cervix — continued
    and uterus V88.01
    congenital 752.49
  chin, congenital 744.89
  cilia (congenital) 743.63
    acquired 374.89
  circulatory system, part NEC 747.89
  clavicle 755.51
  clitoris (congenital) 752.49
  coccyx, congenital 756.13
  cold sense (see also Disturbance, sensation) 782.0
  colon (acquired) (postoperative) V45.72
    congenital 751.2
  congenital
    lumen — see Atresia
    organ or site NEC — see Agenesis
    septum — see Imperfect, closure
  corpus callosum (congenital) 742.2
  cricoid cartilage 748.3
  diaphragm (congenital) (with hernia) 756.6
    with obstruction 756.6
  digestive organ(s) or tract, congenital (complete) (partial) 751.8
    acquired V45.79
    lower 751.5
    upper 750.8
  ductus arteriosus 747.89
  duodenum (acquired) (postoperative) V45.72
    congenital 751.1
  ear, congenital 744.09
    acquired V45.79
    auricle 744.01
    external 744.01
    inner 744.05
    lobe, lobule 744.21
    middle, except ossicles 744.03
     ossicles 744.04
    ossicles 744.04
  ejaculatory duct (congenital) 752.89
  endocrine gland NEC (congenital) 759.2
  epididymis (congenital) 752.89
    acquired V45.77
  epiglottis, congenital 748.3
  epileptic (atonic) (typical) (see also Epilepsy) 345.0 ☑
  erythrocyte 284.9
  erythropoiesis 284.9
    congenital 284.01
  esophagus (congenital) 750.3
  Eustachian tube (congenital) 744.24
  extremity (acquired)
    congenital (see also Deformity, reduction) 755.4
    lower V49.70
    upper V49.60
  extrinsic muscle, eye 743.69
  eye (acquired) V45.78
    adnexa (congenital) 743.69
    congenital 743.00
    muscle (congenital) 743.69
  eyelid (fold), congenital 743.62
    acquired 374.89
  face
    bones NEC 756.0
    specified part NEC 744.89
  fallopian tube(s) (acquired) V45.77
    congenital 752.19
  femur, congenital (complete) (partial) (with absence of distal elements, incomplete) (see also Deformity, reduction, lower limb) 755.34
    with
     complete absence of distal elements 755.31
     tibia and fibula (incomplete) 755.33
  fibrin 790.92
  fibrinogen (congenital) 286.3
    acquired 286.6
  fibula, congenital (complete) (partial) (with absence of distal elements, incomplete) (see also Deformity, reduction, lower limb) 755.37

Absence — continued
  fibula, congenital (see also Deformity, reduction, lower limb) — continued
    with
     complete absence of distal elements 755.31
     tibia 755.35
      with
       complete absence of distal elements 755.31
       femur (incomplete) 755.33
        with complete absence of distal elements 755.31
  finger (acquired) V49.62
    congenital (complete) (partial) (see also Deformity, reduction, upper limb) 755.29
    meaning all fingers (complete) (partial) 755.21
    transverse 755.21
  fissures of lungs (congenital) 748.5
  foot (acquired) V49.73
    congenital (complete) 755.31
  forearm (acquired) V49.65
    congenital (complete) (partial) (with absence of distal elements, incomplete) (see also Deformity, reduction, upper limb) 755.25
    with
     complete absence of distal elements (hand and fingers) 755.21
     humerus (incomplete) 755.23
  fovea centralis 743.55
  fucosidase 271.8
  gallbladder (acquired) V45.79
    congenital 751.69
  gamma globulin (blood) 279.00
  genital organs
    acquired V45.77
    congenital
     female 752.89
      external 752.49
      internal NEC 752.89
     male 752.89
      penis 752.69
  genitourinary organs, congenital NEC 752.89
  glottis 748.3
  gonadal, congenital NEC 758.6
  hair (congenital) 757.4
    acquired — see Alopecia
  hand (acquired) V49.63
    congenital (complete) (see also Deformity, reduction, upper limb) 755.21
  heart (congenital) 759.89
    acquired — see Status, organ replacement
  heat sense (see also Disturbance, sensation) 782.0
  humerus, congenital (complete) (partial) (with absence of distal elements, incomplete) (see also Deformity, reduction, upper limb) 755.24
    with
     complete absence of distal elements 755.21
     radius and ulna (incomplete) 755.23
  hymen (congenital) 752.49
  ileum (acquired) (postoperative) (posttraumatic) V45.72
    congenital 751.1
  immunoglobulin, isolated NEC 279.03
    IgA 279.01
    IgG 279.03
    IgM 279.02
  incus (acquired) 385.24
    congenital 744.04
  internal ear (congenital) 744.05
  intestine (acquired) (small) V45.72
    congenital 751.1
    large 751.2
    large V45.72
     congenital 751.2
  iris (congenital) 743.45
  jaw — see Absence, mandible
  jejunum (acquired) V45.72

☑ Additional Digit Required — Refer to the Tabular List for Digit Selection   ▽ Subterms under main terms may continue to next column or page

2010 ICD-9-CM   ▶◀ Revised Text   ● New Line   ▲ Revised Code   **Volume 2 — 5**

Index

Absence — Absorption

Absence — continued

jejunum — continued
  congenital 751.1
joint, congenital NEC 755.8
kidney(s) (acquired) V45.73
  congenital 753.0
labium (congenital) (majus) (minus) 752.49
labyrinth, membranous 744.05
lacrimal apparatus (congenital) 743.65
larynx (congenital) 748.3
leg (acquired) V49.70
  above knee V49.76
  below knee V49.75
  congenital (partial) (unilateral) (see also
    Deformity, reduction, lower limb)
    755.31
    lower (complete) (partial) (with ab-
      sence of distal elements, incom-
      plete) 755.35
      with
        complete absence of distal ele-
          ments (foot and toes)
          755.31
        thigh (incomplete) 755.33
        with complete absence of
          distal elements
          755.31
    upper — see Absence, femur
lens (congenital) 743.35
  acquired 379.31
ligament, broad (congenital) 752.19
limb (acquired)
  congenital (complete) (partial) (see also
    Deformity, reduction) 755.4
    lower 755.30
      complete 755.31
      incomplete 755.32
      longitudinal — see Deficiency,
        lower limb, longitudinal
      transverse 755.31
    upper 755.20
      complete 755.21
      incomplete 755.22
      longitudinal — see Deficiency, up-
        per limb, longitudinal
      transverse 755.21
    lower NEC V49.70
    upper NEC V49.60
lip 750.26
liver (congenital) (lobe) 751.69
lumbar (congenital) (vertebra) 756.13
  isthmus 756.11
  pars articularis 756.11
lumen — see Atresia
lung (bilateral) (congenital) (fissure) (lobe)
  (unilateral) 748.5
  acquired (any part) V45.76
mandible (congenital) 524.09
maxilla (congenital) 524.09
menstruation 626.0
metacarpal(s), congenital (complete) (partial)
  (with absence of distal elements, incomplete) (see also Deformity, reduction, upper limb) 755.28
  with all fingers, complete 755.21
metatarsal(s), congenital (complete) (partial)
  (with absence of distal elements, incomplete) (see also Deformity, reduction, lower limb) 755.38
  with complete absence of distal elements
    755.31
muscle (congenital) (pectoral) 756.81
  ocular 743.69
musculoskeletal system (congenital) NEC 756.9
nail(s) (congenital) 757.5
neck, part 744.89
nerve 742.8
nervous system, part NEC 742.8
neutrophil 288.00
nipple (congenital) 757.6
  acquired V45.71
nose (congenital) 748.1
  acquired 738.0
nuclear 742.8
ocular muscle (congenital) 743.69

Absence — continued

organ
  of Corti (congenital) 744.05
  or site
    acquired V45.79
    congenital NEC 759.89
osseous meatus (ear) 744.03
ovary (acquired) V45.77
  congenital 752.0
oviduct (acquired) V45.77
  congenital 752.19
pancreas (congenital) 751.7
  acquired (postoperative) (posttraumatic)
    V45.79
parathyroid gland (congenital) 759.2
parotid gland(s) (congenital) 750.21
patella, congenital 755.64
pelvic girdle (congenital) 755.69
penis (congenital) 752.69
  acquired V45.77
pericardium (congenital) 746.89
perineal body (congenital) 756.81
phalange(s), congenital 755.4
  lower limb (complete) (intercalary) (partial)
    (terminal) (see also Deformity, reduc-
    tion, lower limb) 755.39
    meaning all toes (complete) (partial)
      755.31
    transverse 755.31
  upper limb (complete) (intercalary) (partial)
    (terminal) (see also Deformity, reduc-
    tion, upper limb) 755.29
    meaning all digits (complete) (partial)
      755.21
    transverse 755.21
pituitary gland (congenital) 759.2
postoperative — see Absence, by site, acquired
prostate (congenital) 752.89
  acquired V45.77
pulmonary
  artery 747.3
  trunk 747.3
  valve (congenital) 746.01
  vein 747.49
punctum lacrimale (congenital) 743.65
radius, congenital (complete) (partial) (with
  absence of distal elements, incomplete) 755.26
  with
    complete absence of distal elements
      755.21
    ulna 755.25
      with
        complete absence of distal ele-
          ments 755.21
        humerus (incomplete) 755.23
ray, congenital 755.4
  lower limb (complete) (partial) (see also
    Deformity, reduction, lower limb)
    755.38
    meaning all rays 755.31
    transverse 755.31
  upper limb (complete) (partial) (see also
    Deformity, reduction, upper limb)
    755.28
    meaning all rays 755.21
    transverse 755.21
rectum (congenital) 751.2
  acquired V45.79
red cell 284.9
  acquired (secondary) 284.81
  congenital 284.01
  hereditary 284.01
  idiopathic 284.9
respiratory organ (congenital) NEC 748.9
rib (acquired) 738.3
  congenital 756.3
roof of orbit (congenital) 742.0
round ligament (congenital) 752.89
sacrum, congenital 756.13
salivary gland(s) (congenital) 750.21
scapula 755.59
scrotum, congenital 752.89
seminal tract or duct (congenital) 752.89
  acquired V45.77

Absence — continued

septum (congenital) (see also Imperfect, closure, septum)
  atrial 745.69
    and ventricular 745.7
    between aorta and pulmonary artery 745.0
  ventricular 745.3
    and atrial 745.7
sex chromosomes 758.81
shoulder girdle, congenital (complete) (partial)
  755.59
skin (congenital) 757.39
skull bone 756.0
  with
    anencephalus 740.0
    encephalocele 742.0
    hydrocephalus 742.3
      with spina bifida (see also Spina bi-
        fida) 741.0 ☑
    microcephalus 742.1
spermatic cord (congenital) 752.89
spinal cord 742.59
spine, congenital 756.13
spleen (congenital) 759.0
  acquired V45.79
sternum, congenital 756.3
stomach (acquired) (partial) (postoperative)
  V45.75
  with postgastric surgery syndrome 564.2
  congenital 750.7
submaxillary gland(s) (congenital) 750.21
superior vena cava (congenital) 747.49
tarsal(s), congenital (complete) (partial) (with
  absence of distal elements, incomplete) (see also Deformity, reduction,
  lower limb) 755.38
teeth, tooth (congenital) 520.0
  with abnormal spacing 524.30
  acquired 525.10
    with malocclusion 524.30
    due to
      caries 525.13
      extraction 525.10
      periodontal disease 525.12
      trauma 525.11
tendon (congenital) 756.81
testis (congenital) 752.89
  acquired V45.77
thigh (acquired) 736.89
thumb (acquired) V49.61
  congenital 755.29
thymus gland (congenital) 759.2
thyroid (gland) (surgical) 246.8
  with hypothyroidism 244.0
  cartilage, congenital 748.3
  congenital 243
tibia, congenital (complete) (partial) (with absence of distal elements, incomplete)
  (see also Deformity, reduction, lower
  limb) 755.36
  with
    complete absence of distal elements
      755.31
    fibula 755.35
      with
        complete absence of distal ele-
          ments 755.31
        femur (incomplete) 755.33
          with complete absence of
            distal elements
            755.31
toe (acquired) V49.72
  congenital (complete) (partial) 755.39
    meaning all toes 755.31
    transverse 755.31
  great V49.71
tongue (congenital) 750.11
tooth, teeth (congenital) 520.0
  with abnormal spacing 524.30
  acquired 525.10
    with malocclusion 524.30
    due to
      caries 525.13
      extraction 525.10
      periodontal disease 525.12
      trauma 525.11

Absence — continued

trachea (cartilage) (congenital) (rings) 748.3
transverse aortic arch (congenital) 747.21
tricuspid valve 746.1
ulna, congenital (complete) (partial) (with absence of distal elements, incomplete)
  (see also Deformity, reduction, upper
  limb) 755.27
  with
    complete absence of distal elements
      755.21
    radius 755.25
      with
        complete absence of distal ele-
          ments 755.21
        humerus (incomplete) 755.23
umbilical artery (congenital) 747.5
ureter (congenital) 753.4
  acquired V45.74
urethra, congenital 753.8
  acquired V45.74
urinary system, part NEC, congenital 753.8
  acquired V45.74
uterus (acquired) V88.01
  with remaining cervical stump V88.02
  and cervix V88.01
  congenital 752.3
uvula (congenital) 750.26
vagina, congenital 752.49
  acquired V45.77
vas deferens (congenital) 752.89
  acquired V45.77
vein (congenital) (peripheral) NEC (see also
  Anomaly, peripheral vascular system)
  747.60
  brain 747.81
  great 747.49
  portal 747.49
  pulmonary 747.49
vena cava (congenital) (inferior) (superior)
  747.49
ventral horn cell 742.59
ventricular septum 745.3
vermis of cerebellum 742.2
vertebra, congenital 756.13
vulva, congenital 752.49
Absentia epileptica — see also Epilepsy 345.0 ☑
Absinthemia — see also Dependence 304.6 ☑
Absinthism — see also Dependence 304.6 ☑
Absorbent system disease 459.89
Absorption
  alcohol, through placenta or breast milk 760.71
  antibiotics, through placenta or breast milk
    760.74
  anticonvulsants, through placenta or breast
    milk 760.77
  antifungals, through placenta or breast milk
    760.74
  anti-infective, through placenta or breast milk
    760.74
  antimetabolics, through placenta or breast
    milk 760.78
  chemical NEC 989.9
    specified chemical or substance — see
      Table of Drugs and Chemicals
    through placenta or breast milk (fetus or
      newborn) 760.70
      alcohol 760.71
      anticonvulsants 760.77
      antifungals 760.74
      anti-infective agents 760.74
      antimetabolics 760.78
      cocaine 760.75
      "crack" 760.75
      diethylstilbestrol [DES] 760.76
      hallucinogenic agents 760.73
      medicinal agents NEC 760.79
      narcotics 760.72
      obstetric anesthetic or analgesic drug
        763.5
      specified agent NEC 760.79
      suspected, affecting management of
        pregnancy 655.5 ☑
  cocaine, through placenta or breast milk
    760.75
  drug NEC (see also Reaction, drug)

☑ Additional Digit Required — Refer to the Tabular List for Digit Selection   ⁿᵉʷ Subterms under main terms may continue to next column or page

6 — Volume 2   ▶◀ Revised Text   ● New Line   ▲ Revised Code   2010 ICD-9-CM

Absorption — continued
drug (see also Reaction, drug) — continued
through placenta or breast milk (fetus or newborn) 760.70
alcohol 760.71
anticonvulsants 760.77
antifungals 760.74
anti-infective agents 760.74
antimetabolics 760.78
cocaine 760.75
"crack" 760.75
diethylstilbestrol [DES] 760.76
hallucinogenic agents 760.73
medicinal agents NEC 760.79
narcotics 760.72
obstetric anesthetic or analgesic drug 763.5
specified agent NEC 760.79
suspected, affecting management of pregnancy 655.5 ☑
fat, disturbance 579.8
hallucinogenic agents, through placenta or breast milk 760.73
immune sera, through placenta or breast milk 760.79
lactose defect 271.3
medicinal agents NEC, through placenta or breast milk 760.79
narcotics, through placenta or breast milk 760.72
noxious substance — see Absorption, chemical
protein, disturbance 579.8
pus or septic, general — see Septicemia
quinine, through placenta or breast milk 760.74
toxic substance — see Absorption, chemical
uremic — see Uremia
Abstinence symptoms or syndrome
alcohol 291.81
drug 292.0
neonatal 779.5
Abt-Letterer-Siwe syndrome (acute histiocytosis X) (M9722/3) 202.5 ☑
Abulia 799.89
Abulomania 301.6
Abuse
adult 995.80
emotional 995.82
multiple forms 995.85
neglect (nutritional) 995.84
physical 995.81
psychological 995.82
sexual 995.83
alcohol — see also Alcoholism 305.0 ☑
dependent 303.9 ☑
non-dependent 305.0 ☑
child 995.50
counseling
perpetrator
non-parent V62.83
parent V61.22
victim V61.21
emotional 995.51
multiple forms 995.59
neglect (nutritional) 995.52
physical 995.54
shaken infant syndrome 995.55
psychological 995.51
sexual 995.53
drugs, nondependent 305.9 ☑

Note — Use the following fifth-digit subclassification with the following codes: 305.0, 305.2–305.9:
0   unspecified
1   continuous
2   episodic
3   in remission

amphetamine type 305.7 ☑
antidepressants 305.8 ☑
anxiolytic 305.4 ☑
barbiturates 305.4 ☑

Abuse — continued
drugs, nondependent — continued
caffeine 305.9 ☑
cannabis 305.2 ☑
cocaine type 305.6 ☑
hallucinogens 305.3 ☑
hashish 305.2 ☑
hypnotic 305.4 ☑
inhalant 305.9 ☑
LSD 305.3 ☑
marijuana 305.2 ☑
mixed 305.9 ☑
morphine type 305.5 ☑
opioid type 305.5 ☑
phencyclidine (PCP) 305.9 ☑
sedative 305.4 ☑
specified NEC 305.9 ☑
tranquilizers 305.4 ☑
spouse 995.80
tobacco 305.1
Acalcerosis 275.40
Acalcicosis 275.40
Acalculia 784.69
developmental 315.1
Acanthocheilonemiasis 125.4
Acanthocytosis 272.5
Acanthokeratodermia 701.1
Acantholysis 701.8
bullosa 757.39
Acanthoma (benign) (M8070/0) — see also Neoplasm, by site, benign
malignant (M8070/3) — see Neoplasm, by site, malignant
Acanthosis (acquired) (nigricans) 701.2
adult 701.2
benign (congenital) 757.39
congenital 757.39
glycogenic
esophagus 530.89
juvenile 701.2
tongue 529.8
Acanthrocytosis 272.5
Acapnia 276.3
Acarbia 276.2
Acardia 759.89
Acardiacus amorphus 759.89
Acardiotrophia 429.1
Acardius 759.89
Acariasis 133.9
sarcoptic 133.0
Acaridiasis 133.9
Acarinosis 133.9
Acariosis 133.9
Acarodermatitis 133.9
urticarioides 133.9
Acarophobia 300.29
Acatalasemia 277.89
Acatalasia 277.89
Acatamathesia 784.69
Acataphasia 784.59
Acathisia 781.0
due to drugs 333.99
Acceleration, accelerated
atrioventricular conduction 426.7
idioventricular rhythm 427.89
Accessory (congenital)
adrenal gland 759.1
anus 751.5
appendix 751.5
atrioventricular conduction 426.7
auditory ossicles 744.04
auricle (ear) 744.1
autosome(s) NEC 758.5
21 or 22 758.0
biliary duct or passage 751.69
bladder 753.8
blood vessels (peripheral) (congenital) NEC (see also Anomaly, peripheral vascular system) 747.60
cerebral 747.81
coronary 746.85
bone NEC 756.9
foot 755.67
breast tissue, axilla 757.6
carpal bones 755.56
cecum 751.5

Accessory — continued
cervix 752.49
chromosome(s) NEC 758.5
13-15 758.1
16-18 758.2
21 or 22 758.0
autosome(s) NEC 758.5
D₁ 758.1
E₃ 758.2
G 758.0
sex 758.81
coronary artery 746.85
cusp(s), heart valve NEC 746.89
pulmonary 746.09
cystic duct 751.69
digits 755.00
ear (auricle) (lobe) 744.1
endocrine gland NEC 759.2
external os 752.49
eyelid 743.62
eye muscle 743.69
face bone(s) 756.0
fallopian tube (fimbria) (ostium) 752.19
fingers 755.01
foreskin 605
frontonasal process 756.0
gallbladder 751.69
genital organ(s)
female 752.89
external 752.49
internal NEC 752.89
male NEC 752.89
penis 752.69
genitourinary organs NEC 752.89
heart 746.89
valve NEC 746.89
pulmonary 746.09
hepatic ducts 751.69
hymen 752.49
intestine (large) (small) 751.5
kidney 753.3
lacrimal canal 743.65
leaflet, heart valve NEC 746.89
pulmonary 746.09
ligament, broad 752.19
liver (duct) 751.69
lobule (ear) 744.1
lung (lobe) 748.69
muscle 756.82
navicular of carpus 755.56
nervous system, part NEC 742.8
nipple 757.6
nose 748.1
organ or site NEC — see Anomaly, specified type NEC
ovary 752.0
oviduct 752.19
pancreas 751.7
parathyroid gland 759.2
parotid gland (and duct) 750.22
pituitary gland 759.2
placental lobe — see Placenta, abnormal
preauricular appendage 744.1
prepuce 605
renal arteries (multiple) 747.62
rib 756.3
cervical 756.2
roots (teeth) 520.2
salivary gland 750.22
sesamoids 755.8
sinus — see condition
skin tags 757.39
spleen 759.0
sternum 756.3
submaxillary gland 750.22
tarsal bones 755.67
teeth, tooth 520.1
causing crowding 524.31
tendon 756.89
thumb 755.01
thymus gland 759.2
thyroid gland 759.2
toes 755.02
tongue 750.13
tragus 744.1
ureter 753.4

Accessory — continued
urethra 753.8
urinary organ or tract NEC 753.8
uterus 752.2
vagina 752.49
valve, heart NEC 746.89
pulmonary 746.09
vertebra 756.19
vocal cords 748.3
vulva 752.49
Accident, accidental — see also condition
birth NEC 767.9
cardiovascular (see also Disease, cardiovascular) 429.2
cerebral (see also Disease, cerebrovascular, acute) 434.91
cerebrovascular (current) (CVA) (see also Disease, cerebrovascular, acute) 434.91
aborted 434.91
embolic 434.11
healed or old V12.54
hemorrhagic — see Hemorrhage, brain
impending 435.9
ischemic 434.91
late effect — see Late effect(s) (of) cerebrovascular disease
postoperative 997.02
thrombotic 434.01
coronary (see also Infarct, myocardium) 410.9 ☑
craniovascular (see also Disease, cerebrovascular, acute) 436
during pregnancy, to mother, affecting fetus or newborn 760.5
heart, cardiac (see also Infarct, myocardium) 410.9 ☑
intrauterine 779.89
vascular — see Disease, cerebrovascular, acute
Accommodation
disorder of 367.51
drug-induced 367.89
toxic 367.89
insufficiency of 367.4
paralysis of 367.51
hysterical 300.11
spasm of 367.53
Accouchement — see Delivery
Accreta placenta (without hemorrhage) 667.0 ☑
with hemorrhage 666.0 ☑
Accretio cordis (nonrheumatic) 423.1
Accretions on teeth 523.6
Accumulation secretion, prostate 602.8
Acephalia, acephalism, acephaly 740.0
Acephalic 740.0
Acephalobrachia 759.89
Acephalocardia 759.89
Acephalocardius 759.89
Acephalochiria 759.89
Acephalochirus 759.89
Acephalogaster 759.89
Acephalostomus 759.89
Acephalothorax 759.89
Acephalus 740.0
Acetonemia 790.6
diabetic 250.1 ☑
due to secondary diabetes 249.1 ☑
Acetonglycosuria 982.8
Acetonuria 791.6
Achalasia 530.0
cardia 530.0
digestive organs congenital NEC 751.8
esophagus 530.0
pelvirectal 751.3
psychogenic 306.4
pylorus 750.5
sphincteral NEC 564.89
Achard-Thiers syndrome (adrenogenital) 255.2
Ache(s) — see Pain
Acheilia 750.26
Acheiria 755.21
Achillobursitis 726.71
Achillodynia 726.71
Achlorhydria, achlorhydric 536.0
anemia 280.9
diarrhea 536.0
neurogenic 536.0

☑ Additional Digit Required — Refer to the Tabular List for Digit Selection   ▶◄ Revised Text   ● New Line   ▲ Revised Code   ▽ Subterms under main terms may continue to next column or page

2010 ICD-9-CM   October 2009 • Volume 2 — 7

Index

Achlorhydria, achlorhydric — Adenitis

Achlorhydria, achlorhydric — *continued*
  postvagotomy 564.2
  psychogenic 306.4
  secondary to vagotomy 564.2
Achloroblepsia 368.52
Achloropsia 368.52
Acholia 575.8
Acholuric jaundice (familial) (splenomegalic) —
    see also Spherocytosis 282.0
  acquired 283.9
Achondroplasia 756.4
Achrestic anemia 281.8
Achroacytosis, lacrimal gland 375.00
  tuberculous (*see also* Tuberculosis) 017.3 ☑
Achroma, cutis 709.00
Achromate (congenital) 368.54
Achromatopia 368.54
Achromatopsia (congenital) 368.54
Achromia
  congenital 270.2
  parasitica 111.0
  unguium 703.8
Achylia
  gastrica 536.8
    neurogenic 536.3
    psychogenic 306.4
  pancreatica 577.1
Achylosis 536.8
Acid
  burn (*see also* Burn, by site)
    from swallowing acid — *see* Burn, internal
      organs
  deficiency
    amide nicotinic 265.2
    amino 270.9
    ascorbic 267
    folic 266.2
    nicotinic (amide) 265.2
    pantothenic 266.2
  intoxication 276.2
  peptic disease 536.8
  stomach 536.8
    psychogenic 306.4
Acidemia 276.2
  arginosuccinic 270.6
  fetal
    affecting management of pregnancy
      656.3 ☑
    before onset of labor, in liveborn infant
      768.2
    during labor and delivery in liveborn infant
      768.3
    intrauterine 656.3 ☑
    unspecified as to time of onset, in liveborn
      infant 768.4
  newborn 775.81
  pipecolic 270.7
Acidity, gastric (high) (low) 536.8
  psychogenic 306.4
Acidocytopenia 288.59
Acidocytosis 288.3
Acidopenia 288.59
Acidosis 276.2
  diabetic 250.1 ☑
    due to secondary diabetes 249.1 ☑
  fetal, affecting management of pregnancy
    756.8 ☑
  fetal, affecting newborn 775.81
  kidney tubular 588.89
    newborn 775.81
  lactic 276.2
  metabolic NEC 276.2
    with respiratory acidosis 276.4
      of newborn 775.81
    late, of newborn 775.7
  newborn 775.81
  renal
    hyperchloremic 588.89
    tubular (distal) (proximal) 588.89
  respiratory 276.2
    complicated by
      metabolic acidosis 276.4
        of newborn 775.81
      metabolic alkalosis 276.4
Aciduria 791.9
  arginosuccinic 270.6

Aciduria — *continued*
  beta-aminoisobutyric (BAIB) 277.2
  glutaric
    type I 270.7
    type II (type IIA, IIB, IIC) 277.85
    type III 277.86
  glycolic 271.8
  methylmalonic 270.3
    with glycinemia 270.7
  organic 270.9
  orotic (congenital) (hereditary) (pyrimidine
    deficiency) 281.4
Acladiosis 111.8
  skin 111.8
Aclasis
  diaphyseal 756.4
  tarsoepiphyseal 756.59
Acleistocardia 745.5
Aclusion 524.4
Acmesthesia 782.0
Acne (pustular) (vulgaris) 706.1
  agminata (*see also* Tuberculosis) 017.0 ☑
  artificialis 706.1
  atrophica 706.0
  cachecticorum (Hebra) 706.1
  conglobata 706.1
  conjunctiva 706.1
  cystic 706.1
  decalvans 704.09
  erythematosa 695.3
  eyelid 706.1
  frontalis 706.0
  indurata 706.1
  keloid 706.1
  lupoid 706.0
  necrotic, necrotica 706.0
    miliaris 704.8
  neonatal 706.1
  nodular 706.1
  occupational 706.1
  papulosa 706.1
  rodens 706.0
  rosacea 695.3
  scorbutica 267
  scrofulosorum (Bazin) (*see also* Tuberculosis)
    017.0 ☑
  summer 692.72
  tropical 706.1
  varioliformis 706.0
Acneiform drug eruptions 692.3
Acnitis (primary) — *see also* Tuberculosis
    017.0 ☑
Acomia 704.00
Acontractile bladder 344.61
Aconuresis — *see also* Incontinence 788.30
Acosta's disease 993.2
Acousma 780.1
Acoustic — *see* condition
Acousticophobia 300.29
Acquired — *see* condition
Acquired immune deficiency syndrome —
    see Human immunodeficiency virus (dis-
    ease) (illness) (infection)
Acquired immunodeficiency syndrome — *see*
    Human immunodeficiency virus (disease)
    (illness) (infection)
Acragnosis 781.99
Acrania 740.0
Acroagnosis 781.99
Acroasphyxia, chronic 443.89
Acrobrachycephaly 756.0
Acrobystiolith 608.89
Acrobystitis 607.2
Acrocephalopolysyndactyly 755.55
Acrocephalosyndactyly 755.55
Acrocephaly 756.0
Acrochondrohyperplasia 759.82
Acrocyanosis 443.89
  newborn 770.83
    meaning transient blue hands and feet —
      omit code
Acrodermatitis 686.8
  atrophicans (chronica) 701.8
  continua (Hallopeau) 696.1
  enteropathica 686.8
  Hallopeau's 696.1

Acrodermatitis — *continued*
  perstans 696.1
  pustulosa continua 696.1
  recalcitrant pustular 696.1
Acrodynia 985.0
Acrodysplasia 755.55
Acrohyperhidrosis — *see also* Hyperhidrosis
    780.8
Acrokeratosis verruciformis 757.39
Acromastitis 611.0
Acromegaly, acromegalia (skin) 253.0
Acromelalgia 443.82
Acromicria, acromikria 756.59
Acronyx 703.0
Acropachyderma 757.39
Acropachy, thyroid — *see also* Thyrotoxicosis
    242.9 ☑
Acroparesthesia 443.89
  simple (Schultz's type) 443.89
  vasomotor (Nothnagel's type) 443.89
Acropathy thyroid — *see also* Thyrotoxicosis
    242.9 ☑
Acrophobia 300.29
Acroposthitis 607.2
Acroscleriasis — *see also* Scleroderma 710.1
Acroscleroderma — *see also* Scleroderma 710.1
Acrosclerosis — *see also* Scleroderma 710.1
Acrosphacelus 785.4
Acrosphenosyndactylia 755.55
Acrospiroma, eccrine (M8402/0) — *see* Neo-
    plasm, skin, benign
Acrostealgia 732.9
Acrosyndactyly — *see also* Syndactylism 755.10
Acrotrophodynia 991.4
Actinic — *see also* condition
  cheilitis (due to sun) 692.72
    chronic NEC 692.74
    due to radiation, except from sun 692.82
  conjunctivitis 370.24
  dermatitis (due to sun) (*see also* Dermatitis,
    actinic) 692.70
  due to
    roentgen rays or radioactive substance
      692.82
    ultraviolet radiation, except from sun
      692.82
    sun NEC 692.70
  elastosis solare 692.74
  granuloma 692.73
  keratitis 370.24
  ophthalmia 370.24
  reticuloid 692.73
Actinobacillosis, general 027.8
Actinobacillus
  lignieresii 027.8
  mallei 024
  muris 026.1
Actinocutitis NEC — *see also* Dermatitis, actinic
    692.70
Actinodermatitis NEC — *see also* Dermatitis,
    actinic 692.70
Actinomyces
  israelii (infection) — *see* Actinomycosis
  muris-ratti (infection) 026.1
Actinomycosis, actinomycotic 039.9
  with
    pneumonia 039.1
    abdominal 039.2
    cervicofacial 039.3
    cutaneous 039.0
    pulmonary 039.1
    specified site NEC 039.8
    thoracic 039.1
Actinoneuritis 357.89
Action, heart
  disorder 427.9
    postoperative 997.1
  irregular 427.9
    postoperative 997.1
    psychogenic 306.2
Active — *see* condition
Activity decrease, functional 780.99
Acute — *see also* condition
  abdomen NEC 789.0 ☑
  gallbladder (*see also* Cholecystitis, acute) 575.0
Acyanoblepsia 368.53

Acyanopsia 368.53
Acystia 753.8
Acystinervia — *see* Neurogenic, bladder
Acystineuria — *see* Neurogenic, bladder
Adactylia, adactyly (congenital) 755.4
  lower limb (complete) (intercalary) (partial)
    (terminal) (*see also* Deformity, reduc-
    tion, lower limb) 755.39
    meaning all digits (complete) (partial)
      755.31
    transverse (complete) (partial) 755.31
  upper limb (complete) (intercalary) (partial)
    (terminal) (*see also* Deformity, reduc-
    tion, upper limb) 755.29
    meaning all digits (complete) (partial)
      755.21
    transverse (complete) (partial) 755.21
Adair-Dighton syndrome (brittle bones and
    blue sclera, deafness) 756.51
Adamantinoblastoma (M9310/0) — *see*
    Ameloblastoma
Adamantinoma (M9310/0) — *see* Ameloblas-
    toma
Adamantoblastoma (M9310/0) — *see*
    Ameloblastoma
**Adams-Stokes (-Morgagni) disease or syn-
    drome** (syncope with heart block) 426.9
Adaptation reaction — *see also* Reaction, adjust-
    ment 309.9
Addiction — *see also* Dependence
  absinthe 304.6 ☑
  alcoholic (ethyl) (methyl) (wood) 303.9 ☑
    complicating pregnancy, childbirth, or
      puerperium 648.4 ☑
      affecting fetus or newborn 760.71
    suspected damage to fetus affecting
      management of pregnancy
      655.4 ☑
  drug (*see also* Dependence) 304.9 ☑
  ethyl alcohol 303.9 ☑
  heroin 304.0 ☑
  hospital 301.51
  methyl alcohol 303.9 ☑
  methylated spirit 303.9 ☑
  morphine (-like substances) 304.0 ☑
  nicotine 305.1
  opium 304.0 ☑
  tobacco 305.1
  wine 303.9 ☑
Addison's
  anemia (pernicious) 281.0
  disease (bronze) (primary adrenal insufficiency)
    255.41
    tuberculous (*see also* Tuberculosis)
      017.6 ☑
  keloid (morphea) 701.0
  melanosis (adrenal cortical hypofunction)
    255.41
Addison-Biermer anemia (pernicious) 281.0
Addison-Gull disease — *see* Xanthoma
Addisonian crisis or melanosis (acute adreno-
    cortical insufficiency) 255.41
Additional — *see also* Accessory
  chromosome(s) 758.5
    13-15 758.1
    16-18 758.2
    21 758.0
    autosome(s) NEC 758.5
    sex 758.81
Adduction contracture, hip or other joint —
    see Contraction, joint
ADEM (acute disseminated encephalomyelitis)
    (postinfectious) 136.9 *[323.61]*
  infectious 136.9 *[323.61]*
  noninfectious 323.81
Adenasthenia gastrica 536.0
Aden fever 061
Adenitis — *see also* Lymphadenitis 289.3
  acute, unspecified site 683
    epidemic infectious 075
  axillary 289.3
    acute 683
    chronic or subacute 289.1
  Bartholin's gland 616.89
  bulbourethral gland (*see also* Urethritis) 597.89
  cervical 289.3

Adenitis — *see also* Lymphadenitis — *continued*
  cervical — *continued*
    acute 683
    chronic or subacute 289.1
  chancroid (Ducrey's bacillus) 099.0
  chronic (any lymph node, except mesenteric) 289.1
    mesenteric 289.2
  Cowper's gland (*see also* Urethritis) 597.89
  epidemic, acute 075
  gangrenous 683
  gonorrheal NEC 098.89
  groin 289.3
    acute 683
    chronic or subacute 289.1
  infectious 075
  inguinal (region) 289.3
    acute 683
    chronic or subacute 289.1
  lymph gland or node, except mesenteric 289.3
    acute 683
    chronic or subacute 289.1
    mesenteric (acute) (chronic) (nonspecific) (subacute) 289.2
  mesenteric (acute) (chronic) (nonspecific) (subacute) 289.2
    due to Pasteurella multocida (P. septica) 027.2
  parotid gland (suppurative) 527.2
  phlegmonous 683
  salivary duct or gland (any) (recurring) (suppurative) 527.2
  scrofulous (*see also* Tuberculosis) 017.2 ✓
  septic 289.3
  Skene's duct or gland (*see also* Urethritis) 597.89
  strumous, tuberculous (*see also* Tuberculosis) 017.2 ✓
  subacute, unspecified site 289.1
  sublingual gland (suppurative) 527.2
  submandibular gland (suppurative) 527.2
  submaxillary gland (suppurative) 527.2
  suppurative 683
  tuberculous — *see* Tuberculosis, lymph gland
  urethral gland (*see also* Urethritis) 597.89
  venereal NEC 099.8
  Wharton's duct (suppurative) 527.2

Adenoacanthoma (M8570/3) — *see* Neoplasm, by site, malignant

Adenoameloblastoma (M9300/0) 213.1
  upper jaw (bone) 213.0

Adenocarcinoma (M8140/3) — *see also* Neoplasm, by site, malignant

Note — The list of adjectival modifiers below is not exhaustive. A description of adenocarcinoma that does not appear in this list should be coded in the same manner as carcinoma with that description. Thus, "mixed acidophil-basophil adenocarcinoma," should be coded in the same manner as "mixed acidophil-basophil carcinoma," which appears in the list under "Carcinoma."

Except where otherwise indicated, the morphological varieties of adenocarcinoma in the list below should be coded by site as for "Neoplasm, malignant."

  with
    apocrine metaplasia (M8573/3)
    cartilaginous (and osseous) metaplasia (M8571/3)
    osseous (and cartilaginous) metaplasia (M8571/3)
    spindle cell metaplasia (M8572/3)
    squamous metaplasia (M8570/3)
  acidophil (M8280/3)
    specified site — *see* Neoplasm, by site, malignant
    unspecified site 194.3
  acinar (M8550/3)
  acinic cell (M8550/3)
  adrenal cortical (M8370/3) 194.0

Adenocarcinoma — *see also* Neoplasm, by site, malignant — *continued*
  alveolar (M8251/3)
    and
      epidermoid carcinoma, mixed (M8560/3)
      squamous cell carcinoma, mixed (M8560/3)
  apocrine (M8401/3)
    breast — *see* Neoplasm, breast, malignant
    specified site NEC — *see* Neoplasm, skin, malignant
    unspecified site 173.9
  basophil (M8300/3)
    specified site — *see* Neoplasm, by site, malignant
    unspecified site 194.3
  bile duct type (M8160/3)
    liver 155.1
    specified site NEC — *see* Neoplasm, by site, malignant
    unspecified site 155.1
  bronchiolar (M8250/3) — *see* Neoplasm, lung, malignant
  ceruminous (M8420/3) 173.2
  chromophobe (M8270/3)
    specified site — *see* Neoplasm, by site, malignant
    unspecified site 194.3
  clear cell (mesonephroid type) (M8310/3)
  colloid (M8480/3)
  cylindroid type (M8200/3)
  diffuse type (M8145/3)
    specified site — *see* Neoplasm, by site, malignant
    unspecified site 151.9
  duct (infiltrating) (M8500/3)
    with Paget's disease (M8541/3) — *see* Neoplasm, breast, malignant
    specified site — *see* Neoplasm, by site, malignant
    unspecified site 174.9
  embryonal (M9070/3)
  endometrioid (M8380/3) — *see* Neoplasm, by site, malignant
  eosinophil (M8280/3)
    specified site — *see* Neoplasm, by site, malignant
    unspecified site 194.3
  follicular (M8330/3)
    and papillary (M8340/3) 193
    moderately differentiated type (M8332/3) 193
    pure follicle type (M8331/3) 193
    specified site — *see* Neoplasm, by site, malignant
    trabecular type (M8332/3) 193
    unspecified type 193
    well differentiated type (M8331/3) 193
  gelatinous (M8480/3)
  granular cell (M8320/3)
  Hürthle cell (M8290/3) 193
  in
    adenomatous
      polyp (M8210/3)
      polyposis coli (M8220/3) 153.9
    polypoid adenoma (M8210/3)
    tubular adenoma (M8210/3)
    villous adenoma (M8261/3)
  infiltrating duct (M8500/3)
    with Paget's disease (M8541/3) — *see* Neoplasm, breast, malignant
    specified site — *see* Neoplasm, by site, malignant
    unspecified site 174.9
  inflammatory (M8530/3)
    specified site — *see* Neoplasm, by site, malignant
    unspecified site 174.9
  in situ (M8140/2) — *see* Neoplasm, by site, in situ
  intestinal type (M8144/3)
    specified site — *see* Neoplasm, by site, malignant
    unspecified site 151.9

Adenocarcinoma — *see also* Neoplasm, by site, malignant — *continued*
  intraductal (noninfiltrating) (M8500/2)
    papillary (M8503/2)
      specified site — *see* Neoplasm, by site, in situ
      unspecified site 233.0
    specified site — *see* Neoplasm, by site, in situ
    unspecified site 233.0
  islet cell (M8150/3)
    and exocrine, mixed (M8154/3) — *see* Neoplasm, by site, malignant
      unspecified site 157.9
    pancreas 157.4
    specified site NEC — *see* Neoplasm, by site, malignant
    unspecified site 157.4
  lobular (M8520/3)
    specified site — *see* Neoplasm, by site, malignant
    unspecified site 174.9
  medullary (M8510/3)
  mesonephric (M9110/3)
  mixed cell (M8323/3)
  mucinous (M8480/3)
  mucin-producing (M8481/3)
  mucoid (M8480/3) (*see also* Neoplasm, by site, malignant)
    cell (M8300/3)
      specified site — *see* Neoplasm, by site, malignant
      unspecified site 194.3
  nonencapsulated sclerosing (M8350/3) 193
  oncocytic (M8290/3)
  oxyphilic (M8290/3)
  papillary (M8260/3)
    and follicular (M8340/3) 193
    intraductal (noninfiltrating) (M8503/2)
      specified site — *see* Neoplasm, by site, in situ
      unspecified site 233.0
    serous (M8460/3)
      specified site — *see* Neoplasm, by site, malignant
      unspecified site 183.0
  papillocystic (M8450/3)
    specified site — *see* Neoplasm, by site, malignant
    unspecified site 183.0
  pseudomucinous (M8470/3)
    specified site — *see* Neoplasm, by site, malignant
    unspecified site 183.0
  renal cell (M8312/3) 189.0
  sebaceous (M8410/3)
  serous (M8441/3) (*see also* Neoplasm, by site, malignant)
    papillary
      specified site — *see* Neoplasm, by site, malignant
      unspecified site 183.0
  signet ring cell (M8490/3)
  superficial spreading (M8143/3)
  sweat gland (M8400/3) — *see* Neoplasm, skin, malignant
  trabecular (M8190/3)
  tubular (M8211/3)
  villous (M8262/3)
  water-clear cell (M8322/3) 194.1

Adenofibroma (M9013/0)
  clear cell (M8313/0) — *see* Neoplasm, by site, benign
  endometrioid (M8381/0) 220
    borderline malignancy (M8381/1) 236.2
    malignant (M8381/3) 183.0
  mucinous (M9015/0)
    specified site — *see* Neoplasm, by site, benign
    unspecified site 220
  prostate 600.20
    with
      other lower urinary tract symptoms (LUTS) 600.21

Adenofibroma — *continued*
  prostate — *continued*
    with — *continued*
      urinary
        obstruction 600.21
        retention 600.21
  serous (M9014/0)
    specified site — *see* Neoplasm, by site, benign
    unspecified site 220
  specified site — *see* Neoplasm, by site, benign
  unspecified site 220

Adenofibrosis
  breast 610.2
  endometrioid 617.0

Adenoiditis 474.01
  acute 463
  chronic 474.01
    with chronic tonsillitis 474.02

Adenoids (congenital) (of nasal fossa) 474.9
  hypertrophy 474.12
  vegetations 474.2

Adenolipomatosis (symmetrical) 272.8

Adenolymphoma (M8561/0)
  specified site — *see* Neoplasm, by site, benign
  unspecified site 210.2

Adenomatosis (M8220/0)
  endocrine (multiple) (M8360/1)
    single specified site — *see* Neoplasm, by site, uncertain behavior
    two or more specified sites 237.4
    unspecified site 237.4
  erosive of nipple (M8506/0) 217
  pluriendocrine — *see* Adenomatosis, endocrine
  pulmonary (M8250/1) 235.7
    malignant (M8250/3) — *see* Neoplasm, lung, malignant
  specified site — *see* Neoplasm, by site, benign
  unspecified site 211.3

Adenomatous
  cyst, thyroid (gland) — *see* Goiter, nodular
  goiter (nontoxic) (*see also* Goiter, nodular) 241.9
    toxic or with hyperthyroidism 242.3 ✓

Adenoma (sessile) (M8140/0) — *see also* Neoplasm, by site, benign

Note — Except where otherwise indicated, the morphological varieties of adenoma in the list below should be coded by site as for "Neoplasm, benign."

  acidophil (M8280/0)
    specified site — *see* Neoplasm, by site, benign
    unspecified site 227.3
  acinar (cell) (M8550/0)
  acinic cell (M8550/0)
  adrenal (cortex) (cortical) (functioning) (M8370/0) 227.0
    clear cell type (M8373/0) 227.0
    compact cell type (M8371/0) 227.0
    glomerulosa cell type (M8374/0) 227.0
    heavily pigmented variant (M8372/0) 227.0
    mixed cell type (M8375/0) 227.0
  alpha cell (M8152/0)
    pancreas 211.7
    specified site NEC — *see* Neoplasm, by site, benign
    unspecified site 211.7
  alveolar (M8251/0)
  apocrine (M8401/0)
    breast 217
    specified site NEC — *see* Neoplasm, skin, benign
    unspecified site 216.9
  basal cell (M8147/0)
  basophil (M8300/0)
    specified site — *see* Neoplasm, by site, benign
    unspecified site 227.3
  beta cell (M8151/0)
    pancreas 211.7
    specified site NEC — *see* Neoplasm, by site, benign
    unspecified site 211.7
  bile duct (M8160/0) 211.5

Adenoma — *see also* Neoplasm, by site, benign
— *continued*
black (M8372/0) 227.0
bronchial (M8140/1) 235.7
carcinoid type (M8240/3) — *see* Neoplasm, lung, malignant
cylindroid type (M8200/3) — *see* Neoplasm, lung, malignant
ceruminous (M8420/0) 216.2
chief cell (M8321/0) 227.1
chromophobe (M8270/0)
specified site — *see* Neoplasm, by site, benign
unspecified site 227.3
clear cell (M8310/0)
colloid (M8334/0)
specified site — *see* Neoplasm, by site, benign
unspecified site 226
cylindroid type, bronchus (M8200/3) — *see* Neoplasm, lung, malignant
duct (M8503/0)
embryonal (M8191/0)
endocrine, multiple (M8360/1)
single specified site — *see* Neoplasm, by site, uncertain behavior
two or more specified sites 237.4
unspecified site 237.4
endometrioid (M8380/0) (*see also* Neoplasm, by site, benign)
borderline malignancy (M8380/1) — *see* Neoplasm, by site, uncertain behavior
eosinophil (M8280/0)
specified site — *see* Neoplasm, by site, benign
unspecified site 227.3
fetal (M8333/0)
specified site — *see* Neoplasm, by site, benign
unspecified site 226
follicular (M8330/0)
specified site — *see* Neoplasm, by site, benign
unspecified site 226
hepatocellular (M8170/0) 211.5
Hürthle cell (M8290/0) 226
intracystic papillary (M8504/0)
islet cell (functioning) (M8150/0)
pancreas 211.7
specified site NEC — *see* Neoplasm, by site, benign
unspecified site 211.7
liver cell (M8170/0) 211.5
macrofollicular (M8334/0)
specified site NEC — *see* Neoplasm, by site, benign
unspecified site 226
malignant, malignum (M8140/3) — *see* Neoplasm, by site, malignant
mesonephric (M9110/0)
microfollicular (M8333/0)
specified site — *see* Neoplasm, by site, benign
unspecified site 226
mixed cell (M8323/0)
monomorphic (M8146/0)
mucinous (M8480/0)
mucoid cell (M8300/0)
specified site — *see* Neoplasm, by site, benign
unspecified site 227.3
multiple endocrine (M8360/1)
single specified site — *see* Neoplasm, by site, uncertain behavior
two or more specified sites 237.4
unspecified site 237.4
nipple (M8506/0) 217
oncocytic (M8290/0)
oxyphilic (M8290/0)
papillary (M8260/0) (*see also* Neoplasm, by site, benign)

Adenoma — *see also* Neoplasm, by site, benign
— *continued*
papillary (*see also* Neoplasm, by site, benign) — *continued*
intracystic (M8504/0)
papillotubular (M8263/0)
Pick's tubular (M8640/0)
specified site — *see* Neoplasm, by site, benign
unspecified site
female 220
male 222.0
pleomorphic (M8940/0)
polypoid (M8210/0)
prostate (benign) 600.20
with
other lower urinary tract symptoms (LUTS) 600.21
urinary
obstruction 600.21
retention 600.21
rete cell 222.0
sebaceous, sebaceum (gland) (senile) (M8410/0) (*see also* Neoplasm, skin, benign)
disseminata 759.5
Sertoli cell (M8640/0)
specified site — *see* Neoplasm, by site, benign
unspecified site
female 220
male 222.0
skin appendage (M8390/0) — *see* Neoplasm, skin, benign
sudoriferous gland (M8400/0) — *see* Neoplasm, skin, benign
sweat gland or duct (M8400/0) — *see* Neoplasm, skin, benign
testicular (M8640/0)
specified site — *see* Neoplasm, by site, benign
unspecified site
female 220
male 222.0
thyroid 226
trabecular (M8190/0)
tubular (M8211/0) (*see also* Neoplasm, by site, benign)
papillary (M8460/3)
Pick's (M8640/0)
specified site — *see* Neoplasm, by site, benign
unspecified site
female 220
male 222.0
tubulovillous (M8263/0)
villoglandular (M8263/0)
villous (M8261/1) — *see* Neoplasm, by site, uncertain behavior
water-clear cell (M8322/0) 227.1
wolffian duct (M9110/0)
Adenomyoma (M8932/0) — *see also* Neoplasm, by site, benign
prostate 600.20
with
other lower urinary tract symptoms (LUTS) 600.21
urinary
obstruction 600.21
retention 600.21
Adenomyometritis 617.0
Adenomyosis (uterus) (internal) 617.0
Adenopathy (lymph gland) 785.6
inguinal 785.6
mediastinal 785.6
mesentery 785.6
syphilitic (secondary) 091.4
tracheobronchial 785.6
tuberculous (*see also* Tuberculosis) 012.1 ☑
primary, progressive 010.8 ☑
tuberculous (*see also* Tuberculosis, lymph gland) 017.2 ☑
tracheobronchial 012.1 ☑
primary, progressive 010.8 ☑
Adenopharyngitis 462

Adenophlegmon 683
Adenosalpingitis 614.1
Adenosarcoma (M8960/3) 189.0
Adenosclerosis 289.3
Adenosis
breast (sclerosing) 610.2
vagina, congenital 752.49
Adentia (complete) (partial) — *see also* Absence, teeth 520.0
Adherent
labium (minus) 624.4
pericardium (nonrheumatic) 423.1
rheumatic 393
placenta 667.0 ☑
with hemorrhage 666.0 ☑
prepuce 605
scar (skin) NEC 709.2
tendon in scar 709.2
Adhesion(s), adhesive (postinfectional) (postoperative)
abdominal (wall) (*see also* Adhesions, peritoneum) 568.0
amnion to fetus 658.8 ☑
affecting fetus or newborn 762.8
appendix 543.9
arachnoiditis — *see* Meningitis
auditory tube (Eustachian) 381.89
bands (*see also* Adhesions, peritoneum)
cervix 622.3
uterus 621.5
bile duct (any) 576.8
bladder (sphincter) 596.8
bowel (*see also* Adhesions, peritoneum) 568.0
cardiac 423.1
rheumatic 398.99
cecum (*see also* Adhesions, peritoneum) 568.0
cervicovaginal 622.3
congenital 752.49
postpartal 674.8 ☑
old 622.3
cervix 622.3
clitoris 624.4
colon (*see also* Adhesions, peritoneum) 568.0
common duct 576.8
congenital (*see also* Anomaly, specified type NEC)
fingers (*see also* Syndactylism, fingers) 755.11
labium (majus) (minus) 752.49
omental, anomalous 751.4
ovary 752.0
peritoneal 751.4
toes (*see also* Syndactylism, toes) 755.13
tongue (to gum or roof of mouth) 750.12
conjunctiva (acquired) (localized) 372.62
congenital 743.63
extensive 372.63
cornea — *see* Opacity, cornea
cystic duct 575.8
diaphragm (*see also* Adhesions, peritoneum) 568.0
due to foreign body — *see* Foreign body
duodenum (*see also* Adhesions, peritoneum) 568.0
with obstruction 537.3
ear, middle — *see* Adhesions, middle ear
epididymis 608.89
epidural — *see* Adhesions, meninges
epiglottis 478.79
Eustachian tube 381.89
eyelid 374.46
postoperative 997.99
surgically created V45.69
gallbladder (*see also* Disease, gallbladder) 575.8
globe 360.89
heart 423.1
rheumatic 398.99
ileocecal (coil) (*see also* Adhesions, peritoneum) 568.0
ileum (*see also* Adhesions, peritoneum) 568.0
intestine (postoperative) (*see also* Adhesions, peritoneum) 568.0
with obstruction 560.81
with hernia (*see also* Hernia, by site, with obstruction)

Adhesion(s), adhesive — *continued*
intestine (*see also* Adhesions, peritoneum) — *continued*
with obstruction — *continued*
with hernia (*see also* Hernia, by site, with obstruction) — *continued*
gangrenous — *see* Hernia, by site, with gangrene
intra-abdominal (*see also* Adhesions, peritoneum) 568.0
iris 364.70
to corneal graft 996.79
joint (*see also* Ankylosis) 718.5 ☑
kidney 593.89
labium (majus) (minus), congenital 752.49
liver 572.8
lung 511.0
mediastinum 519.3
meninges 349.2
cerebral (any) 349.2
congenital 742.4
congenital 742.8
spinal (any) 349.2
congenital 742.59
tuberculous (cerebral) (spinal) (*see also* Tuberculosis, meninges) 013.0 ☑
mesenteric (*see also* Adhesions, peritoneum) 568.0
middle ear (fibrous) 385.10
drum head 385.19
to
incus 385.11
promontorium 385.13
stapes 385.12
specified NEC 385.19
nasal (septum) (to turbinates) 478.19
nerve NEC 355.9
spinal 355.9
root 724.9
cervical NEC 723.4
lumbar NEC 724.4
lumbosacral 724.4
thoracic 724.4
ocular muscle 378.60
omentum (*see also* Adhesions, peritoneum) 568.0
organ or site, congenital NEC — *see* Anomaly, specified type NEC
ovary 614.6
congenital (to cecum, kidney, or omentum) 752.0
parauterine 614.6
parovarian 614.6
pelvic (peritoneal)
female (postoperative) (postinfection) 614.6
male (postoperative) (postinfection) (*see also* Adhesions, peritoneum) 568.0
postpartal (old) 614.6
tuberculous (*see also* Tuberculosis) 016.9 ☑
penis to scrotum (congenital) 752.69
periappendiceal (*see also* Adhesions, peritoneum) 568.0
pericardium (nonrheumatic) 423.1
rheumatic 393
tuberculous (*see also* Tuberculosis) 017.9 ☑ [420.0]
pericholecystic 575.8
perigastric (*see also* Adhesions, peritoneum) 568.0
periovarian 614.6
periprostatic 602.8
perirectal (*see also* Adhesions, peritoneum) 568.0
perirenal 593.89
peritoneum, peritoneal (fibrous) (postoperative) 568.0
with obstruction (intestinal) 560.81
with hernia (*see also* Hernia, by site, with obstruction)
gangrenous — *see* Hernia, by site, with gangrene
duodenum 537.3
congenital 751.4

☑ Additional Digit Required — Refer to the Tabular List for Digit Selection   ▽ Subterms under main terms may continue to next column or page

2010 ICD-9-CM   ▶◀ Revised Text   ● New Line   ▲ Revised Code   October 2009 • Volume 2 — 11

Admission — *continued*
for — *continued*
counseling (*see also* Counseling) — *continued*
for — *continued*
pediatric — *continued*
pre-birth visit for expectant ●
parent(s) V65.11 ●
victim of abuse
child V61.21
partner or spouse V61.11
genetic V26.33
gonorrhea V65.45
HIV V65.44
human immunodeficiency virus V65.44
injury prevention V65.43
insulin pump training V65.46
natural family planning
procreative V26.41
to avoid pregnancy V25.04
procreative management V26.49
using natural family planning V26.41
sexually transmitted disease NEC V65.45
HIV V65.44
specified reason NEC V65.49
substance use and abuse V65.42
syphilis V65.45
victim of abuse
child V61.21
partner or spouse V61.11
desensitization to allergens V07.1
dialysis V56.0
catheter
fitting and adjustment
extracorporeal V56.1
peritoneal V56.2
removal or replacement
extracorporeal V56.1
peritoneal V56.2
extracorporeal (renal) V56.0
peritoneal V56.8
renal V56.0
dietary surveillance and counseling V65.3
drug monitoring, therapeutic V58.83
ear piercing V50.3
elective surgery V50.9
breast
augmentation or reduction V50.1
reconstruction following mastectomy V51.0
removal, prophylactic V50.41
circumcision, ritual or routine (in absence of medical indication) V50.2
cosmetic NEC V50.1
breast reconstruction following mastectomy V51.0
following healed injury or operation V51.8
ear piercing V50.3
face-lift V50.1
hair transplant V50.0
plastic
breast reconstruction following mastectomy V51.0
cosmetic NEC V50.1
following healed injury or operation V51.8
prophylactic organ removal V50.49
breast V50.41
ovary V50.42
repair of scarred tissue (following healed injury or operation) V51.8
specified type NEC V50.8
end-of-life care V66.7
examination (*see also* Examination) V70.9
administrative purpose NEC V70.3
adoption V70.3
allergy V72.7
antibody response V72.61 ●
at health care facility V70.0
athletic team V70.3
camp V70.3

Admission — *continued*
for — *continued*
examination (*see also* Examination) — *continued*
cardiovascular, preoperative V72.81
clinical research investigation (control) (participant) V70.7
dental V72.2
developmental testing (child) (infant) V20.2
donor (potential) V70.8
driver's license V70.3
ear V72.19
employment V70.5
eye V72.0
fertility preservation (prior to cancer ●
therapy) (prior to surgical re- ●
moval of gonads) V26.82 ●
follow-up (routine) — *see* Examination, follow-up
for admission to
old age home V70.3
school V70.3
general V70.9
specified reason NEC V70.8
gynecological V72.31
health supervision
child (over 28 days old) V20.2 ●
infant (over 28 days old) V20.2 ●
newborn
8 to 28 days old V20.32 ●
under 8 days old V20.31 ●
hearing V72.19
following failed hearing screening V72.11
immigration V70.3
infant
8 to 28 days old V20.32 ●
over 28 days old, routine V20.2 ●
under 8 days old V20.31 ●
insurance certification V70.3
laboratory V72.60 ▲
ordered as part of a routine gen- ●
eral medical examination ●
V72.62 ●
pre-operative V72.63 ●
pre-procedural V72.63 ●
specified NEC V72.69 ●
marriage license V70.3
medical (general) (*see also* Examination, medical) V70.9
medicolegal reasons V70.4
naturalization V70.3
pelvic (annual) (periodic) V72.31
postpartum checkup V24.2
pregnancy (possible) (unconfirmed) V72.40
negative result V72.41
positive result V72.42
preoperative V72.84
cardiovascular V72.81
respiratory V72.82
specified NEC V72.83
preprocedural V72.84
cardiovascular V72.81
general physical V72.83
respiratory V72.82
specified NEC V72.83
prior to chemotherapy V72.83 ●
prison V70.3
psychiatric (general) V70.2
requested by authority V70.1
radiological NEC V72.5
respiratory, preoperative V72.82
school V70.3
screening — *see* Screening
skin hypersensitivity V72.7
specified type NEC V72.85
sport competition V70.3
vision V72.0
well baby and child care V20.2
exercise therapy V57.1
face-lift, cosmetic reason V50.1
fertility preservation (prior to cancer ●
therapy) (prior to surgical re- ●
moval of gonads) V26.82 ●

Admission — *continued*
for — *continued*
fitting (of)
artificial
arm (complete) (partial) V52.0
eye V52.2
leg (complete) (partial) V52.1
biliary drainage tube V58.82
brain neuropacemaker V53.02
breast V52.4
implant V52.4
prosthesis V52.4
cardiac pacemaker V53.31
catheter
non-vascular V58.82
vascular V58.81
cerebral ventricle (communicating)
shunt V53.01
chest tube V58.82
colostomy belt V55.2
contact lenses V53.1
cystostomy device V53.6
dental prosthesis V52.3
device, unspecified type V53.90
abdominal V53.59 ▲
cerebral ventricle (communicating)
shunt V53.01
gastrointestinal NEC V53.59 ●
insulin pump V53.91
intestinal V53.50 ●
intrauterine contraceptive V25.1
nervous system V53.09
orthodontic V53.4
other device V53.99
prosthetic V52.9
breast V52.4
dental V52.3
eye V52.2
special senses V53.09
substitution
auditory V53.09
nervous system V53.09
visual V53.09
diaphragm (contraceptive) V25.02
fistula (sinus tract) drainage tube V58.82
gastric lap band V53.51 ●
gastrointestinal appliance and device ●
NEC V53.59 ●
growth rod V54.02
hearing aid V53.2
ileostomy device V55.2
intestinal appliance ►and◄ device
V53.50
intrauterine contraceptive device V25.1
neuropacemaker (brain) (peripheral nerve) (spinal cord) V53.02
orthodontic device V53.4
orthopedic (device) V53.7
brace V53.7
cast V53.7
shoes V53.7
pacemaker
brain V53.02
cardiac V53.31
carotid sinus V53.39
spinal cord V53.02
pleural drainage tube V58.82
portacath V58.81
prosthesis V52.9
arm (complete) (partial) V52.0
breast V52.4
dental V52.3
eye V52.2
leg (complete) (partial) V52.1
specified type NEC V52.8
spectacles V53.1
wheelchair V53.8
follow-up examination (routine) (following) V67.9
cancer chemotherapy V67.2
chemotherapy V67.2
high-risk medication NEC V67.51
injury NEC V67.59
psychiatric V67.3
psychotherapy V67.3

Admission — *continued*
for — *continued*
follow-up examination — *continued*
radiotherapy V67.1
specified surgery NEC V67.09
surgery V67.00
vaginal pap smear V67.01
treatment (for) V67.9
combined V67.6
fracture V67.4
involving high-risk medication NEC V67.51
mental disorder V67.3
specified NEC V67.59
hair transplant, for cosmetic reason V50.0
health advice, education, or instruction V65.4 ☑
hearing conservation and treatment V72.12
hormone replacement therapy (post-menopausal) V07.4
hospice care V66.7
immunizations (childhood) appropriate ●
for age V20.2 ●
immunotherapy, antineoplastic V58.12
insertion (of)
subdermal implantable contraceptive V25.5
insulin pump titration V53.91
insulin pump training V65.46
intrauterine device
insertion V25.1
management V25.42
investigation to determine further disposition V63.8
in vitro fertilization cycle V26.81
isolation V07.0
issue of
disability examination certificate V68.01
medical certificate NEC V68.09
repeat prescription NEC V68.1
contraceptive device NEC V25.49
kidney dialysis V56.0
lengthening of growth rod V54.02
mental health evaluation V70.2
requested by authority V70.1
natural family planning counseling and advice
procreative V26.41
to avoid pregnancy V25.04
nonmedical reason NEC V68.89
nursing care evaluation V63.8
observation (without need for further medical care) (*see also* Observation) V71.9
accident V71.4
alleged rape or seduction V71.5
criminal assault V71.6
following accident V71.4
at work V71.3
foreign body ingestion V71.89
growth and development variations, childhood V21.0
inflicted injury NEC V71.6
ingestion of deleterious agent or foreign body V71.89
injury V71.6
malignant neoplasm V71.1
mental disorder V71.09
newborn — *see* Observation, suspected, condition, newborn
rape V71.5
specified NEC V71.89
suspected
abuse V71.81
accident V71.4
at work V71.3
benign neoplasm V71.89
cardiovascular V71.7
disorder V71.9
exposure
anthrax V71.82
biological agent NEC V71.83
SARS V71.83
heart V71.7
inflicted injury NEC V71.6

Admission — *continued*
for — *continued*
observation (*see also* Observation) — *continued*
suspected — *continued*
malignant neoplasm V71.1
maternal and fetal problem not found
amniotic cavity and membrane V89.01
cervical shortening V89.05
fetal anomaly V89.03
fetal growth V89.04
oligohydramnios V89.01
other specified NEC V89.09
placenta V89.02
polyhydramnios V89.01
mental NEC V71.09
neglect V71.81
specified condition NEC V71.89
tuberculosis V71.2
tuberculosis V71.2
occupational therapy V57.21
organ transplant, donor — *see* Donor
ovary, ovarian removal, prophylactic V50.42
palliative care V66.7
Papanicolaou smear
cervix V76.2
for suspected malignant neoplasm V76.2
no disease found V71.1
routine, as part of gynecological examination V72.31
to confirm findings of recent normal smear following initial abnormal smear V72.32
vaginal V76.47
following hysterectomy for malignant condition V67.01
passage of sounds or bougie in artificial opening — *see* Attention to, artificial, opening
paternity testing V70.4
peritoneal dialysis V56.32
physical therapy NEC V57.1
plastic surgery
breast reconstruction following mastectomy V51.0
cosmetic NEC V50.1
following healed injury or operation V51.8
postmenopausal hormone replacement therapy V07.4
postpartum observation
immediately after delivery V24.0
routine follow-up V24.2
poststerilization (for restoration) V26.0
procreative management V26.9
assisted reproductive fertility procedure cycle V26.81
in vitro fertilization cycle V26.81
specified type NEC V26.89
prophylactic
administration of
antibiotics V07.39
antitoxin, any V07.2
antivenin V07.2
chemotherapeutic agent NEC V07.39
chemotherapy NEC V07.39
diphtheria antitoxin V07.2
fluoride V07.31
gamma globulin V07.2
immune sera (gamma globulin) V07.2
RhoGAM V07.2
tetanus antitoxin V07.2
breathing exercises V57.0
chemotherapy NEC V07.39
fluoride V07.31
measure V07.9
specified type NEC V07.8
organ removal V50.49
breast V50.41
ovary V50.42
psychiatric examination (general) V70.2

Admission — *continued*
for — *continued*
psychiatric examination — *continued*
requested by authority V70.1
radiation management V58.0
radiotherapy V58.0
reconstruction following mastectomy V51.0
reforming of artificial opening — *see* Attention to, artificial, opening
rehabilitation V57.9
multiple types V57.89
occupational V57.21
orthoptic V57.4
orthotic V57.81
physical NEC V57.1
specified type NEC V57.89
speech ▶(-language)◀ V57.3
vocational V57.22
→ removal of
breast tissue expander without synchronous insertion of permanent implant V52.4
cardiac pacemaker V53.31
cast (plaster) V54.89
catheter from artificial opening — *see* Attention to, artificial, opening
cerebral ventricle (communicating) shunt V53.01
cystostomy catheter V55.5
device
cerebral ventricle (communicating) shunt V53.01
fixation
external V54.89
internal V54.01
intrauterine contraceptive V25.42
traction, external V54.89
drains V58.49
dressing
wound V58.30
nonsurgical V58.30
surgical V58.31
fixation device
external V54.89
internal V54.01
intrauterine contraceptive device V25.42
Kirschner wire V54.89
neuropacemaker (brain) (peripheral nerve) (spinal cord) V53.02
nonsurgical wound dressing V58.30
orthopedic fixation device
external V54.89
internal V54.01
pacemaker device
brain V53.02
cardiac V53.31
carotid sinus V53.39
nervous system V53.02
plaster cast V54.89
plate (fracture) V54.01
rod V54.01
screw (fracture) V54.01
splint, traction V54.89
staples V58.32
Steinmann pin V54.89
subdermal implantable contraceptive V25.43
surgical wound dressing V58.31
sutures V58.32
traction device, external V54.89
ureteral stent V53.6
wound packing V58.30
nonsurgical V58.30
surgical V58.31
repair of scarred tissue (following healed injury or operation) V51.8
reprogramming of cardiac pacemaker V53.31
respirator [ventilator] dependence during
mechanical failure V46.14
power failure V46.12
for weaning V46.13

Admission — *continued*
for — *continued*
restoration of organ continuity (poststerilization) (tuboplasty) (vasoplasty) V26.0
Rh typing V72.86
routine infant and child vision and hearing testing V20.2 ●
●
sensitivity test (*see also* Test, skin)
allergy NEC V72.7
bacterial disease NEC V74.9
Dick V74.8
Kveim V82.89
Mantoux V74.1
mycotic infection NEC V75.4
parasitic disease NEC V75.8
Schick V74.3
Schultz-Charlton V74.8
social service (agency) referral or evaluation V63.8
speech ▶(-language)◀ therapy V57.3
sterilization V25.2
suspected disorder (ruled out) (without need for further care) — *see* Observation
terminal care V66.7
tests only — *see* Test
therapeutic drug monitoring V58.83
therapy
blood transfusion, without reported diagnosis V58.2
breathing exercises V57.0
chemotherapy, antineoplastic V58.11
prophylactic NEC V07.39
fluoride V07.31
dialysis (intermittent) (treatment)
extracorporeal V56.0
peritoneal V56.8
renal V56.0
specified type NEC V56.8
exercise (remedial) NEC V57.1
breathing V57.0
immunotherapy, antineoplastic V58.12
long-term (current) drug use NEC V58.69
antibiotics V58.62
anticoagulants V58.61
anti-inflammatories, non-steroidal (NSAID) V58.64
antiplatelets V58.63
antithrombotics V58.63
aspirin V58.66
high-risk medications NEC V58.69
insulin V58.67
methadone V58.69
opiate analgesic V58.69
steroids V58.65
occupational V57.21
orthoptic V57.4
physical NEC V57.1
radiation V58.0
speech ▶(-language)◀ V57.3
vocational V57.22
toilet or cleaning
of artificial opening — *see* Attention to, artificial, opening
of non-vascular catheter V58.82
of vascular catheter V58.81
tubal ligation V25.2
tuboplasty for previous sterilization V26.0
ultrasound, routine fetal V28.3
vaccination, prophylactic (against)
arthropod-borne virus, viral NEC V05.1
disease NEC V05.1
encephalitis V05.0
Bacille Calmette Guérin (BCG) V03.2
BCG V03.2
chickenpox V05.4
cholera alone V03.0
with typhoid-paratyphoid (cholera + TAB) V06.0
common cold V04.7
dengue V05.1
diphtheria alone V03.5
diphtheria-tetanus-pertussis (DTP) (DTaP) V06.1

Admission — *continued*
for — *continued*
vaccination, prophylactic — *continued*
diphtheria-tetanus-pertussis — *continued*
with
poliomyelitis (DTP + polio) V06.3
typhoid-paratyphoid (DTP + TAB) V06.2
diphtheria-tetanus [Td] [DT] without pertussis V06.5
disease (single) NEC V05.9
bacterial NEC V03.9
specified type NEC V03.89
combinations NEC V06.9
specified type NEC V06.8
specified type NEC V05.8
viral NEC V04.89
encephalitis, viral, arthropod-borne V05.0
Hemophilus influenzae, type B [Hib] V03.81
hepatitis, viral V05.3
human papillomavirus (HPV) V04.89
immune sera (gamma globulin) V07.2
influenza V04.81
with
Streptococcus pneumoniae [pneumococcus] V06.6
Leishmaniasis V05.2
measles alone V04.2
measles-mumps-rubella (MMR) V06.4
mumps alone V04.6
with measles and rubella (MMR) V06.4
not done because of contraindication V64.09
pertussis alone V03.6
plague V03.3
pneumonia V03.82
poliomyelitis V04.0
with diphtheria-tetanus-pertussis (DTP+ polio) V06.3
rabies V04.5
respiratory syncytial virus (RSV) V04.82
rubella alone V04.3
with measles and mumps (MMR) V06.4
smallpox V04.1
specified type NEC V05.8
Streptococcus pneumoniae [pneumococcus] V03.82
with
influenza V06.6
tetanus toxoid alone V03.7
with diphtheria [Td] [DT] V06.5
and pertussis (DTP) (DTaP) V06.1
tuberculosis (BCG) V03.2
tularemia V03.4
typhoid alone V03.1
with diphtheria-tetanus-pertussis (TAB + DTP) V06.2
typhoid-paratyphoid alone (TAB) V03.1
typhus V05.8
varicella (chicken pox) V05.4
viral encephalitis, arthropod-borne V05.0
viral hepatitis V05.3
yellow fever V04.4
vasectomy V25.2
vasoplasty for previous sterilization V26.0
vision examination V72.0
vocational therapy V57.22
waiting period for admission to other facility V63.2
undergoing social agency investigation V63.8
well baby and child care V20.2
x-ray of chest
for suspected tuberculosis V71.2
routine V72.5
Adnexitis (suppurative) — *see also* Salpingo-oophoritis 614.2
Adolescence NEC V21.2

Adoption
- agency referral V68.89
- examination V70.3
- held for V68.89

Adrenal gland — see condition

Adrenalism 255.9
- tuberculous (see also Tuberculosis) 017.6 ☑

Adrenalitis, adrenitis 255.8
- meningococcal hemorrhagic 036.3

Adrenarche, precocious 259.1

Adrenocortical syndrome 255.2

Adrenogenital syndrome (acquired) (congenital) 255.2
- iatrogenic, fetus or newborn 760.79

Adrenoleukodystrophy 277.86
- neonatal 277.86
- x-linked 277.86

Adrenomyeloneuropathy 277.86

Adventitious bursa — see Bursitis

Adynamia (episodica) (hereditary) (periodic) 359.3

Adynamic
- ileus or intestine (see also Ileus) 560.1
- ureter 753.22

Aeration lung, imperfect, newborn 770.5

Aerobullosis 993.3

Aerocele — see Embolism, air

Aerodermectasia
- subcutaneous (traumatic) 958.7
  - surgical 998.81
- surgical 998.81

Aerodontalgia 993.2

Aeroembolism 993.3

Aerogenes capsulatus infection — see also Gangrene, gas 040.0

Aero-otitis media 993.0

Aerophagy, aerophagia 306.4
- psychogenic 306.4

Aerosinusitis 993.1

Aerotitis 993.0

Affection, affections — see also Disease
- sacroiliac (joint), old 724.6
- shoulder region NEC 726.2

Afibrinogenemia 286.3
- acquired 286.6
- congenital 286.3
- postpartum 666.3 ☑

African
- sleeping sickness 086.5
- tick fever 087.1
- trypanosomiasis 086.5
  - Gambian 086.3
  - Rhodesian 086.4

Aftercare V58.9
- amputation stump V54.89
- artificial openings — see Attention to, artificial, opening
- blood transfusion without reported diagnosis V58.2
- breathing exercise V57.0
- cardiac device V53.39
  - defibrillator, automatic implantable V53.32
  - pacemaker V53.31
    - carotid sinus V53.39
- carotid sinus pacemaker V53.39
- cerebral ventricle (communicating) shunt V53.01
- chemotherapy ▶(oral) (intravenous)◀ session (adjunctive) (maintenance) V58.11
- defibrillator, automatic implantable cardiac V53.32
- exercise (remedial) (therapeutic) V57.1
  - breathing V57.0
- extracorporeal dialysis (intermittent) (treatment) V56.0
- following surgery NEC V58.49
  - for
    - injury V58.43
    - neoplasm V58.42
    - organ transplant V58.44
    - trauma V58.43
  - joint replacement V54.81
  - of
    - circulatory system V58.73
    - digestive system V58.75
    - genital organs V58.76

Aftercare — continued
- following surgery — continued
  - of — continued
    - genitourinary system V58.76
    - musculoskeletal system V58.78
    - nervous system V58.72
    - oral cavity V58.75
    - respiratory system V58.74
    - sense organs V58.71
    - skin V58.77
    - subcutaneous tissue V58.77
    - teeth V58.75
    - urinary system V58.76
  - spinal — see Aftercare, following surgery, of, specified body system
  - wound closure, planned V58.41
- fracture V54.9
  - healing V54.89
    - pathologic
      - ankle V54.29
      - arm V54.20
        - lower V54.22
        - upper V54.21
      - finger V54.29
      - foot V54.29
      - hand V54.29
      - hip V54.23
      - leg V54.24
        - lower V54.26
        - upper V54.25
      - pelvis V54.29
      - specified site NEC V54.29
      - toe(s) V54.29
      - vertebrae V54.27
      - wrist V54.29
    - traumatic
      - ankle V54.19
      - arm V54.10
        - lower V54.12
        - upper V54.11
      - finger V54.19
      - foot V54.19
      - hand V54.19
      - hip V54.13
      - leg V54.14
        - lower V54.16
        - upper V54.15
      - pelvis V54.19
      - specified site NEC V54.19
      - toe(s) V54.19
      - vertebrae V54.17
      - wrist V54.19
  - removal of
    - external fixation device V54.89
    - internal fixation device V54.01
  - specified care NEC V54.89
- gait training V57.1
  - for use of artificial limb(s) V57.81
- internal fixation device V54.09
- involving
  - dialysis (intermittent) (treatment)
    - extracorporeal V56.0
    - peritoneal V56.8
    - renal V56.0
  - gait training V57.1
    - for use of artificial limb(s) V57.81
  - growth rod
    - adjustment V54.02
    - lengthening V54.02
  - internal fixation device V54.09
  - orthoptic training V57.4
  - orthotic training V57.81
  - radiotherapy session V58.0
  - removal of
    - drains V58.49
    - dressings
      - wound V58.30
        - nonsurgical V58.30
        - surgical V58.31
    - fixation device
      - external V54.89
      - internal V54.01
    - fracture plate V54.01
    - nonsurgical wound dressing V58.30
    - pins V54.01
    - plaster cast V54.89

Aftercare — continued
- involving — continued
  - removal of — continued
    - rods V54.01
    - screws V58.32
    - staples V58.32
    - surgical wound dressings V58.31
    - sutures V58.32
    - traction device, external V54.89
    - wound packing V58.30
      - nonsurgical V58.30
      - surgical V58.31
  - neuropacemaker (brain) (peripheral nerve) (spinal cord) V53.02
  - occupational therapy V57.21
  - orthodontic V58.5
  - orthopedic V54.9
    - change of external fixation or traction device V54.89
    - following joint replacement V54.81
    - internal fixation device V54.09
    - removal of fixation device
      - external V54.89
      - internal V54.01
    - specified care NEC V54.89
  - orthoptic training V57.4
  - orthotic training V57.81
  - pacemaker
    - brain V53.02
    - cardiac V53.31
    - carotid sinus V53.39
    - peripheral nerve V53.02
    - spinal cord V53.02
  - peritoneal dialysis (intermittent) (treatment) V56.8
  - physical therapy NEC V57.1
    - breathing exercises V57.0
  - radiotherapy session V58.0
  - rehabilitation procedure V57.9
    - breathing exercises V57.0
    - multiple types V57.89
    - occupational V57.21
    - orthoptic V57.4
    - orthotic V57.81
    - physical therapy NEC V57.1
    - remedial exercises V57.1
    - specified type NEC V57.89
    - speech ▶(-language)◀ V57.3
    - therapeutic exercises V57.1
    - vocational V57.22
  - renal dialysis (intermittent) (treatment) V56.0
  - specified type NEC V58.89
    - removal of non-vascular catheter V58.82
    - removal of vascular catheter V58.81
  - speech ▶(-language)◀ therapy V57.3
  - stump, amputation V54.89
  - vocational rehabilitation V57.22

After-cataract 366.50
- obscuring vision 366.53
- specified type, not obscuring vision 366.52

Agalactia 676.4 ☑

Agammaglobulinemia 279.00
- with lymphopenia 279.2
- acquired (primary) (secondary) 279.06
- Bruton's X-linked 279.04
- infantile sex-linked (Bruton's) (congenital) 279.04
- Swiss-type 279.2

Aganglionosis (bowel) (colon) 751.3

Age (old) — see also Senile 797

Agenesis — see also Absence, by site, congenital
- acoustic nerve 742.8
- adrenal (gland) 759.1
- alimentary tract (complete) (partial) NEC 751.8
  - lower 751.2
  - upper 750.8
- anus, anal (canal) 751.2
- aorta 747.22
- appendix 751.2
- arm (complete) (partial) (see also Deformity, reduction, upper limb) 755.20
- artery (peripheral) NEC (see also Anomaly, peripheral vascular system) 747.60
  - brain 747.81
  - coronary 746.85
  - pulmonary 747.3

Agenesis — see also Absence, by site, congenital — continued
- artery (see also Anomaly, peripheral vascular system) — continued
  - umbilical 747.5
- auditory (canal) (external) 744.01
- auricle (ear) 744.01
- bile, biliary duct or passage 751.61
- bone NEC 756.9
- brain 740.0
  - specified part 742.2
- breast 757.6
- bronchus 748.3
- canaliculus lacrimalis 743.65
- carpus NEC (see also Deformity, reduction, upper limb) 755.28
- cartilage 756.9
- cecum 751.2
- cerebellum 742.2
- cervix 752.49
- chin 744.89
- cilia 743.63
- circulatory system, part NEC 747.89
- clavicle 755.51
- clitoris 752.49
- coccyx 756.13
- colon 751.2
- corpus callosum 742.2
- cricoid cartilage 748.3
- diaphragm (with hernia) 756.6
- digestive organ(s) or tract (complete) (partial) NEC 751.8
  - lower 751.2
  - upper 750.8
- ductus arteriosus 747.89
- duodenum 751.1
- ear NEC 744.09
  - auricle 744.01
  - lobe 744.21
- ejaculatory duct 752.89
- endocrine (gland) NEC 759.2
- epiglottis 748.3
- esophagus 750.3
- Eustachian tube 744.24
- extrinsic muscle, eye 743.69
- eye 743.00
  - adnexa 743.69
- eyelid (fold) 743.62
- face
  - bones NEC 756.0
  - specified part NEC 744.89
- fallopian tube 752.19
- femur NEC (see also Absence, femur, congenital) 755.34
- fibula NEC (see also Absence, fibula, congenital) 755.37
- finger NEC (see also Absence, finger, congenital) 755.29
- foot (complete) (see also Deformity, reduction, lower limb) 755.31
- gallbladder 751.69
- gastric 750.8
- genitalia, genital (organ)
  - female 752.89
    - external 752.49
    - internal NEC 752.89
  - male 752.89
    - penis 752.69
- glottis 748.3
- gonadal 758.6
- hair 757.4
- hand (complete) (see also Deformity, reduction, upper limb) 755.21
- heart 746.89
  - valve NEC 746.89
    - aortic 746.89
    - mitral 746.89
    - pulmonary 746.01
- hepatic 751.69
- humerus NEC (see also Absence, humerus, congenital) 755.24
- hymen 752.49
- ileum 751.1
- incus 744.04
- intestine (small) 751.1
  - large 751.2

Agenesis — *see also* Absence, by site, congenital
— *continued*
iris (dilator fibers) 743.45
jaw 524.09
jejunum 751.1
kidney(s) (partial) (unilateral) 753.0
labium (majus) (minus) 752.49
labyrinth, membranous 744.05
lacrimal apparatus (congenital) 743.65
larynx 748.3
leg NEC (*see also* Deformity, reduction, lower limb) 755.30
lens 743.35
limb (complete) (partial) (*see also* Deformity, reduction) 755.4
lower NEC 755.30
upper 755.20
lip 750.26
liver 751.69
lung (bilateral) (fissures) (lobe) (unilateral) 748.5
mandible 524.09
maxilla 524.09
metacarpus NEC 755.28
metatarsus NEC 755.38
muscle (any) 756.81
musculoskeletal system NEC 756.9
nail(s) 757.5
neck, part 744.89
nerve 742.8
nervous system, part NEC 742.8
nipple 757.6
nose 748.1
nuclear 742.8
organ
of Corti 744.05
or site not listed — *see* Anomaly, specified type NEC
osseous meatus (ear) 744.03
ovary 752.0
oviduct 752.19
pancreas 751.7
parathyroid (gland) 759.2
patella 755.64
pelvic girdle (complete) (partial) 755.69
penis 752.69
pericardium 746.89
perineal body 756.81
pituitary (gland) 759.2
prostate 752.89
pulmonary
artery 747.3
trunk 747.3
vein 747.49
punctum lacrimale 743.65
radioulnar NEC (*see also* Absence, forearm, congenital) 755.25
radius NEC (*see also* Absence, radius, congenital) 755.26
rectum 751.2
renal 753.0
respiratory organ NEC 748.9
rib 756.3
roof of orbit 742.0
round ligament 752.89
sacrum 756.13
salivary gland 750.21
scapula 755.59
scrotum 752.89
seminal duct or tract 752.89
septum
atrial 745.69
between aorta and pulmonary artery 745.0
ventricular 745.3
shoulder girdle (complete) (partial) 755.59
skull (bone) 756.0
with
anencephalus 740.0
encephalocele 742.0
hydrocephalus 742.3
with spina bifida (*see also* Spina bifida) 741.0 ☑
microcephalus 742.1
spermatic cord 752.89
spinal cord 742.59
spine 756.13

Agenesis — *see also* Absence, by site, congenital
— *continued*
spine — *continued*
lumbar 756.13
isthmus 756.11
pars articularis 756.11
spleen 759.0
sternum 756.3
stomach 750.7
tarsus NEC 755.38
tendon 756.81
testicular 752.89
testis 752.89
thymus (gland) 759.2
thyroid (gland) 243
cartilage 748.3
tibia NEC (*see also* Absence, tibia, congenital) 755.36
tibiofibular NEC 755.35
toe (complete) (partial) (*see also* Absence, toe, congenital) 755.39
tongue 750.11
trachea (cartilage) 748.3
ulna NEC (*see also* Absence, ulna, congenital) 755.27
ureter 753.4
urethra 753.8
urinary tract NEC 753.8
uterus 752.3
uvula 750.26
vagina 752.49
vas deferens 752.89
vein(s) (peripheral) NEC (*see also* Anomaly, peripheral vascular system) 747.60
brain 747.81
great 747.49
portal 747.49
pulmonary 747.49
vena cava (inferior) (superior) 747.49
vermis of cerebellum 742.2
vertebra 756.13
lumbar 756.13
isthmus 756.11
pars articularis 756.11
vulva 752.49
Ageusia — *see also* Disturbance, sensation 781.1
Aggressiveness 301.3
Aggressive outburst — *see also* Disturbance, conduct 312.0 ☑
in children or adolescents 313.9
Aging skin 701.8
Agitated — *see* condition
Agitation 307.9
catatonic (*see also* Schizophrenia) 295.2 ☑
Aglossia (congenital) 750.11
Aglycogenosis 271.0
Agnail (finger) (with lymphangitis) 681.02
Agnosia (body image) (tactile) 784.69
verbal 784.69
auditory 784.69
secondary to organic lesion 784.69
developmental 315.8
secondary to organic lesion 784.69
visual 368.16
object 368.16
Agoraphobia 300.22
with panic disorder 300.21
Agrammatism 784.69
Agranulocytopenia — *see also* Agranulocytosis 288.09
Agranulocytosis ▶ — *see also* Neutropenia ◄ 288.09
chronic 288.09
cyclical 288.02
due to infection 288.04
genetic 288.01
infantile 288.01
periodic 288.02
pernicious 288.09
Agraphia (absolute) 784.69
with alexia 784.61
developmental 315.39
Agrypnia — *see also* Insomnia 780.52
Ague — *see also* Malaria 084.6
brass-founders' 985.8
dumb 084.6

Ague — *see also* Malaria — *continued*
tertian 084.1
Agyria 742.2
Ahumada-del Castillo syndrome (nonpuerperal galactorrhea and amenorrhea) 253.1
AIDS 042
AIDS-associated retrovirus (disease) (illness) 042
infection — *see* Human immunodeficiency virus, infection
AIDS-associated virus (disease) (illness) 042
infection — *see* Human immunodeficiency virus, infection
AIDS-like disease (illness) (syndrome) 042
AIDS-related complex 042
AIDS-related conditions 042
AIDS-related virus (disease) (illness) 042
infection — *see* Human immunodeficiency virus, infection
AIDS virus (disease) (illness) 042
infection — *see* Human immunodeficiency virus, infection
Ailment, heart — *see* Disease, heart
Ailurophobia 300.29
Ainhum (disease) 136.0
AIN I [anal intraepithelial neoplasia I] (histologically confirmed) 569.44
AIN II [anal intraepithelial neoplasia II] (histologically confirmed) 569.44
AIN III [anal intraepithelial neoplasia III] 230.6
anal canal 230.5
Air
anterior mediastinum 518.1
compressed, disease 993.3
embolism (any site) (artery) (cerebral) 958.0
with
abortion — *see* Abortion, by type, with embolism
ectopic pregnancy (*see also* categories 633–633.9) 639.6
molar pregnancy (*see also* categories 630–632) 639.6
due to implanted device — *see* Complications, due to (presence of) any device, implant, or graft classified to 996.0–996.5 NEC
following
abortion 639.6
ectopic or molar pregnancy 639.6
infusion, perfusion, or transfusion 999.1
in pregnancy, childbirth, or puerperium 673.0 ☑
traumatic 958.0
hunger 786.09
psychogenic 306.1
leak (lung) (pulmonary) (thorax) 512.8
iatrogenic 512.1
postoperative 512.1
rarefied, effects of — *see* Effect, adverse, high altitude
sickness 994.6
Airplane sickness 994.6
Akathisia, acathisia 781.0
due to drugs 333.99
neuroleptic-induced acute 333.99
Akinesia algera 352.6
Akiyami 100.89
Akureyri disease (epidemic neuromyasthenia) 049.8
Alacrima (congenital) 743.65
Alactasia (hereditary) 271.3
Alagille syndrome 759.89
Alalia 784.3
developmental 315.31
receptive-expressive 315.32
secondary to organic lesion 784.3
Alaninemia 270.8
Alastrim 050.1
Albarrán's disease (colibacilluria) 791.9
Albers-Schönberg's disease (marble bones) 756.52
Albert's disease 726.71
Albinism, albino (choroid) (cutaneous) (eye) (generalized) (isolated) (ocular) (oculocutaneous) (partial) 270.2
Albinismus 270.2

Albright (-Martin) (-Bantam) disease (pseudohypoparathyroidism) 275.49
Albright (-McCune) (-Sternberg) syndrome (osteitis fibrosa disseminata) 756.59
Albuminous — *see* condition
Albuminuria, albuminuric (acute) (chronic) (subacute) 791.0
Bence-Jones 791.0
cardiac 785.9
complicating pregnancy, childbirth, or puerperium 646.2 ☑
with hypertension — *see* Toxemia, of pregnancy
affecting fetus or newborn 760.1
cyclic 593.6
gestational 646.2 ☑
gravidarum 646.2 ☑
with hypertension — *see* Toxemia, of pregnancy
affecting fetus or newborn 760.1
heart 785.9
idiopathic 593.6
orthostatic 593.6
postural 593.6
pre-eclamptic (mild) 642.4 ☑
affecting fetus or newborn 760.0
severe 642.5 ☑
affecting fetus or newborn 760.0
recurrent physiologic 593.6
scarlatinal 034.1
Albumosuria 791.0
Bence-Jones 791.0
myelopathic (M9730/3) 203.0 ☑
Alcaptonuria 270.2
Alcohol, alcoholic
abstinence 291.81
acute intoxication 305.0 ☑
with dependence 303.0 ☑
addiction (*see also* Alcoholism) 303.9 ☑
maternal
with suspected fetal damage affecting management of pregnancy 655.4 ☑
affecting fetus or newborn 760.71
amnestic disorder, persisting 291.1
anxiety 291.89
brain syndrome, chronic 291.2
cardiopathy 425.5
chronic (*see also* Alcoholism) 303.9 ☑
cirrhosis (liver) 571.2
delirium 291.0
acute 291.0
chronic 291.1
tremens 291.0
withdrawal 291.0
dementia NEC 291.2
deterioration 291.2
drunkenness (simple) 305.0 ☑
hallucinosis (acute) 291.3
induced
circadian rhythm sleep disorder 291.82
hypersomnia 291.82
insomnia 291.82
mental disorder 291.9
anxiety 291.89
mood 291.89
sexual 291.89
sleep 291.82
specified type 291.89
parasomnia 291.82
persisting
amnestic disorder 291.1
dementia 291.2
psychotic disorder
with
delusions 291.5
hallucinations 291.3
sleep disorder 291.82
insanity 291.9
intoxication (acute) 305.0 ☑
with dependence 303.0 ☑
pathological 291.4
jealousy 291.5
Korsakoff's, Korsakov's, Korsakow's 291.1
liver NEC 571.3
acute 571.1

☑ Additional Digit Required — Refer to the Tabular List for Digit Selection

⬝ Subterms under main terms may continue to next column or page

2010 ICD-9-CM

▶◀ Revised Text

● New Line

▲ Revised Code

October 2009 • Volume 2 — 15

Index

Alcohol, alcoholic — Amebiasis

Alcohol, alcoholic — *continued*
liver — *continued*
chronic 571.2
mania (acute) (chronic) 291.9
mood 291.89
paranoia 291.5
paranoid (type) psychosis 291.5
pellagra 265.2
poisoning, accidental (acute) NEC 980.9
specified type of alcohol — *see* Table of Drugs and Chemicals
psychosis (*see also* Psychosis, alcoholic) 291.9
Korsakoff's, Korsakov's, Korsakow's 291.1
polyneuritic 291.1
with
delusions 291.5
hallucinations 291.3
related disorder 291.9
withdrawal symptoms, syndrome NEC 291.81
delirium 291.0
hallucinosis 291.3
Alcoholism 303.9 ☑

Note — Use the following fifth-digit subclassification with category 303:

0 *unspecified*
1 *continuous*
2 *episodic*
3 *in remission*

with psychosis (*see also* Psychosis, alcoholic) 291.9
acute 303.0 ☑
chronic 303.9 ☑
with psychosis 291.9
complicating pregnancy, childbirth, or puerperium 648.4 ☑
affecting fetus or newborn 760.71
history V11.3
Korsakoff's, Korsakov's, Korsakow's 291.1
suspected damage to fetus affecting management of pregnancy 655.4 ☑
Alder's anomaly or syndrome (leukocyte granulation anomaly) 288.2
Alder-Reilly anomaly (leukocyte granulation) 288.2
Aldosteronism (primary) 255.10
congenital 255.10
familial type I 255.11
glucocorticoid-remediable 255.11
secondary 255.14
Aldosteronoma (M8370/1) 237.2
Aldrich (-Wiskott) syndrome (eczema-thrombocytopenia) 279.12
Aleppo boil 085.1
Aleukemic — *see* condition
Aleukia
congenital 288.09
hemorrhagica 284.9
acquired (secondary) 284.89
congenital 284.09
idiopathic 284.9
splenica 289.4
Alexia (congenital) (developmental) 315.01
secondary to organic lesion 784.61
Algoneurodystrophy 733.7
Algophobia 300.29
Alibert-Bazin disease (M9700/3) 202.1 ☑
Alibert's disease (mycosis fungoides) (M9700/3) 202.1 ☑
Alice in Wonderland syndrome 293.89
Alienation, mental — *see also* Psychosis 298.9
Alkalemia 276.3
Alkalosis 276.3
metabolic 276.3
with respiratory acidosis 276.4
respiratory 276.3
Alkaptonuria 270.2
Allen-Masters syndrome 620.6
Allergic bronchopulmonary aspergillosis 518.6
Allergy, allergic (reaction) 995.3
air-borne substance — *see also* Fever, hay 477.9
specified allergen NEC 477.8
alveolitis (extrinsic) 495.9

Allergy, allergic — *continued*
alveolitis — *continued*
due to
Aspergillus clavatus 495.4
cryptostroma corticale 495.6
organisms (fungal, thermophilic actinomycete, other) growing in ventilation (air conditioning systems) 495.7
specified type NEC 495.8
anaphylactic shock 999.4
due to food — *see* Anaphylactic shock, due to, food
angioneurotic edema 995.1
animal (cat) (dog) (epidermal) 477.8
dander 477.2
hair 477.2
arthritis (*see also* Arthritis, allergic) 716.2 ☑
asthma — *see* Asthma
bee sting (anaphylactic shock) 989.5
biological — *see* Allergy, drug
bronchial asthma — *see* Asthma
conjunctivitis (eczematous) 372.14
dander, animal (cat) (dog) 477.2
dandruff 477.8
dermatitis (venenata) — *see* Dermatitis
diathesis V15.09
drug, medicinal substance, and biological (any) (correct medicinal substance properly administered) (external) (internal) 995.27
wrong substance given or taken NEC 977.9
specified drug or substance — *see* Table of Drugs and Chemicals
dust (house) (stock) 477.8
eczema — *see* Eczema
endophthalmitis 360.19
epidermal (animal) 477.8
existing dental restorative material 525.66
feathers 477.8
food (any) (ingested) 693.1
atopic 691.8
in contact with skin 692.5
gastritis 535.4 ☑
gastroenteritis 558.3
gastrointestinal 558.3
grain 477.0
grass (pollen) 477.0
asthma (*see also* Asthma) 493.0 ☑
hay fever 477.0
hair, animal (cat) (dog) 477.2
hay fever (grass) (pollen) (ragweed) (tree) (*see also* Fever, hay) 477.9
history (of) V15.09
to
arachnid bite V15.06
eggs V15.03
food additives V15.05
insect bite V15.06
latex V15.07
milk products V15.02
nuts V15.05
peanuts V15.01
radiographic dye V15.08
seafood V15.04
specified food NEC V15.05
spider bite V15.06
horse serum — *see* Allergy, serum
inhalant 477.9
dust 477.8
pollen 477.0
specified allergen other than pollen 477.8
kapok 477.8
medicine — *see* Allergy, drug
migraine 339.00
milk protein 558.3
pannus 370.62
pneumonia 518.3
pollen (any) (hay fever) 477.0
asthma (*see also* Asthma) 493.0 ☑
primrose 477.0
primula 477.0
purpura 287.0
ragweed (pollen) (Senecio jacobae) 477.0
asthma (*see also* Asthma) 493.0 ☑
hay fever 477.0

Allergy, allergic — *continued*
respiratory (*see also* Allergy, inhalant) 477.9
due to
drug — *see* Allergy, drug
food — *see* Allergy, food
rhinitis (*see also* Fever, hay) 477.9
due to food 477.1
rose 477.0
Senecio jacobae 477.0
serum (prophylactic) (therapeutic) 999.5
anaphylactic shock 999.4
shock (anaphylactic) (due to adverse effect of correct medicinal substance properly administered) 995.0
food — *see* Anaphylactic shock, due to, food
from serum or immunization 999.5
anaphylactic 999.4
sinusitis (*see also* Fever, hay) 477.9
skin reaction 692.9
specified substance — *see* Dermatitis, due to
tree (any) (hay fever) (pollen) 477.0
asthma (*see also* Asthma) 493.0 ☑
upper respiratory (*see also* Fever, hay) 477.9
urethritis 597.89
urticaria 708.0
vaccine — *see* Allergy, serum
Allescheriosis 117.6
Alligator skin disease (ichthyosis congenita) 757.1
acquired 701.1
Allocheiria, allochiria — *see also* Disturbance, sensation 782.0
Almeida's disease (Brazilian blastomycosis) 116.1
Alopecia (atrophicans) (pregnancy) (premature) (senile) 704.00
adnata 757.4
areata 704.01
celsi 704.01
cicatrisata 704.09
circumscripta 704.01
congenital, congenitalis 757.4
disseminata 704.01
effluvium (telogen) 704.02
febrile 704.09
generalisata 704.09
hereditaria 704.09
marginalis 704.01
mucinosa 704.09
postinfectional 704.09
seborrheica 704.09
specific 091.82
syphilitic (secondary) 091.82
telogen effluvium 704.02
totalis 704.09
toxica 704.09
universalis 704.09
x-ray 704.09
Alpers' disease 330.8
Alpha-lipoproteinemia 272.4
Alpha thalassemia 282.49
Alphos 696.1
Alpine sickness 993.2
Alport's syndrome (hereditary hematuria-anephropathy-deafness) 759.89
ALPS (autoimmune lymphoproliferative syndrome) 279.41 ●
ALTE (apparent life threatening event) **in newborn and infant** 799.82 ●
Alteration (of), altered
awareness 780.09
transient 780.02
consciousness 780.09
persistent vegetative state 780.03
transient 780.02
mental status 780.97
amnesia (retrograde) 780.93
memory loss 780.93
Alternaria (infection) 118
Alternating — *see* condition
Altitude, high (effects) — *see* Effect, adverse, high altitude
Aluminosis (of lung) 503
Alvarez syndrome (transient cerebral ischemia) 435.9

Alveolar capillary block syndrome 516.3
Alveolitis
allergic (extrinsic) 495.9
due to organisms (fungal, thermophilic actinomycete, other) growing in ventilation (air conditioning systems) 495.7
specified type NEC 495.8
due to
Aspergillus clavatus 495.4
Cryptostroma corticale 495.6
fibrosing (chronic) (cryptogenic) (lung) 516.3
idiopathic 516.3
rheumatoid 714.81
jaw 526.5
sicca dolorosa 526.5
Alveolus, alveolar — *see* condition
Alymphocytosis (pure) 279.2
Alymphoplasia, thymic 279.2
Alzheimer's
dementia (senile)
with behavioral disturbance 331.0 *[294.11]*
without behavioral disturbance 331.0 *[294.10]*
disease or sclerosis 331.0
with dementia — *see* Alzheimer's, dementia
Amastia — *see also* Absence, breast 611.89
Amaurosis (acquired) (congenital) — *see also* Blindness 369.00
fugax 362.34
hysterical 300.11
Leber's (congenital) 362.76
tobacco 377.34
uremic — *see* Uremia
Amaurotic familial idiocy (infantile) (juvenile) (late) 330.1
Ambisexual 752.7
Amblyopia (acquired) (congenital) (partial) 368.00
color 368.59
acquired 368.55
deprivation 368.02
ex anopsia 368.00
hysterical 300.11
nocturnal 368.60
vitamin A deficiency 264.5
refractive 368.03
strabismic 368.01
suppression 368.01
tobacco 377.34
toxic NEC 377.34
uremic — *see* Uremia
Ameba, amebic (histolytica) — *see also* Amebiasis
abscess 006.3
bladder 006.8
brain (with liver and lung abscess) 006.5
liver 006.3
with
brain abscess (and lung abscess) 006.5
lung abscess 006.4
lung (with liver abscess) 006.4
with brain abscess 006.5
seminal vesicle 006.8
spleen 006.8
carrier (suspected of) V02.2
meningoencephalitis
due to Naegleria (gruberi) 136.29
primary 136.29
Amebiasis NEC 006.9
with
brain abscess (with liver or lung abscess) 006.5
liver abscess (without mention of brain or lung abscess) 006.3
lung abscess (with liver abscess) 006.4
with brain abscess 006.5
acute 006.0
bladder 006.8
chronic 006.1
cutaneous 006.6
cutis 006.6
due to organism other than Entamoeba histolytica 007.8

Amebiasis — continued
hepatic (see also Abscess, liver, amebic) 006.3
nondysenteric 006.2
seminal vesicle 006.8
specified
organism NEC 007.8
site NEC 006.8
Ameboma 006.8
Amelia 755.4
lower limb 755.31
upper limb 755.21
Ameloblastoma (M9310/0) 213.1
jaw (bone) (lower) 213.1
upper 213.0
long bones (M9261/3) — see Neoplasm, bone, malignant
malignant (M9310/3) 170.1
jaw (bone) (lower) 170.1
upper 170.0
mandible 213.1
tibial (M9261/3) 170.7
Amelogenesis imperfecta 520.5
nonhereditaria (segmentalis) 520.4
Amenorrhea (primary) (secondary) 626.0
due to ovarian dysfunction 256.8
hyperhormonal 256.8
Amentia — see also Retardation, mental 319
Meynert's (nonalcoholic) 294.0
alcoholic 291.1
nevoid 759.6
American
leishmaniasis 085.5
mountain tick fever 066.1
trypanosomiasis — see Trypanosomiasis, American
Ametropia — see also Disorder, accommodation 367.9
Amianthosis 501
Amimia 784.69
Amino acid
deficiency 270.9
anemia 281.4
metabolic disorder (see also Disorder, amino acid) 270.9
Aminoaciduria 270.9
imidazole 270.5
Amnesia (retrograde) 780.93
auditory 784.69
developmental 315.31
secondary to organic lesion 784.69
dissociative 300.12
hysterical or dissociative type 300.12
psychogenic 300.12
transient global 437.7
Amnestic (confabulatory) **syndrome** 294.0
alcohol-induced persisting 291.1
drug-induced persisting 292.83
posttraumatic 294.0
Amniocentesis screening (for) V28.2
alphafetoprotein level, raised V28.1
chromosomal anomalies V28.0
Amnion, amniotic — see also condition
nodosum 658.8 ☑
Amnionitis (complicating pregnancy) 658.4 ☑
affecting fetus or newborn 762.7
Amoral trends 301.7
Amotio retinae — see also Detachment, retina 361.9
Ampulla
lower esophagus 530.89
phrenic 530.89
Amputation
any part of fetus, to facilitate delivery 763.89
cervix (supravaginal) (uteri) 622.8
in pregnancy or childbirth 654.6 ☑
affecting fetus or newborn 763.89
clitoris — see Wound, open, clitoris
congenital
lower limb 755.31
upper limb 755.21
neuroma (traumatic) (see also Injury, nerve, by site)
surgical complication (late) 997.61
penis — see Amputation, traumatic, penis
status (without complication) — see Absence, by site, acquired

Amputation — continued
stump (surgical) (posttraumatic)
abnormal, painful, or with complication (late) 997.60
healed or old NEC (see also Absence, by site, acquired)
lower V49.70
upper V49.60
traumatic (complete) (partial)

Note — "Complicated" includes traumatic amputation with delayed healing, delayed treatment, foreign body, or infection.

arm 887.4
at or above elbow 887.2
complicated 887.3
below elbow 887.0
complicated 887.1
both (bilateral) (any level(s)) 887.6
complicated 887.7
complicated 887.5
finger(s) (one or both hands) 886.0
with thumb(s) 885.0
complicated 885.1
complicated 886.1
foot (except toe(s) only) 896.0
and other leg 897.6
complicated 897.7
both (bilateral) 896.2
complicated 896.3
complicated 896.1
toe(s) only (one or both feet) 895.0
complicated 895.1
genital organ(s) (external) NEC 878.8
complicated 878.9
hand (except finger(s) only) 887.0
and other arm 887.6
complicated 887.7
both (bilateral) 887.6
complicated 887.7
complicated 887.1
finger(s) (one or both hands) 886.0
with thumb(s) 885.0
complicated 885.1
complicated 886.1
thumb(s) (with fingers of either hand) 885.0
complicated 885.1
head 874.9
late effect — see Late, effects (of), amputation
leg 897.4
and other foot 897.6
complicated 897.7
at or above knee 897.2
complicated 897.3
below knee 897.0
complicated 897.1
both (bilateral) 897.6
complicated 897.7
complicated 897.5
lower limb(s) except toe(s) — see Amputation, traumatic, leg
nose — see Wound, open, nose
penis 878.0
complicated 878.1
sites other than limbs — see Wound, open, by site
thumb(s) (with finger(s) of either hand) 885.0
complicated 885.1
toe(s) (one or both feet) 895.0
complicated 895.1
upper limb(s) — see Amputation, traumatic, arm
Amputee (bilateral) (old) — see also Absence, by site, acquired V49.70
Amusia 784.69
developmental 315.39
secondary to organic lesion 784.69
Amyelencephalus 740.0
Amyelia 742.59
Amygdalitis — see Tonsillitis
Amygdalolith 474.8
Amyloid disease or degeneration 277.30
heart 277.39 [425.7]

Amyloidosis (familial) (general) (generalized) (genetic) (primary) 277.30
with lung involvement 277.39 [517.8]
cardiac, hereditary 277.39
heart 277.39 [425.7]
nephropathic 277.39 [583.81]
neuropathic (Portuguese) (Swiss) 277.39 [357.4]
pulmonary 277.39 [517.8]
secondary 277.39
systemic, inherited 277.39
Amylopectinosis (brancher enzyme deficiency) 271.0
Amylophagia 307.52
Amyoplasia, congenita 756.89
Amyotonia 728.2
congenita 358.8
Amyotrophia, amyotrophy, amyotrophic 728.2
congenita 756.89
diabetic 250.6 ☑ [353.5]
due to secondary diabetes 249.6 ☑ [353.5]
lateral sclerosis (syndrome) 335.20
neuralgic 353.5
sclerosis (lateral) 335.20
spinal progressive 335.21
Anacidity, gastric 536.0
psychogenic 306.4
Anaerosis of newborn 770.88
Analbuminemia 273.8
Analgesia — see also Anesthesia 782.0
Analphalipoproteinemia 272.5
Anaphylactic shock or reaction (correct substance properly administered) 995.0
due to
food 995.60
additives 995.66
crustaceans 995.62
eggs 995.68
fish 995.65
fruits 995.63
milk products 995.67
nuts (tree) 995.64
peanuts 995.61
seeds 995.64
specified NEC 995.69
tree nuts 995.64
vegetables 995.63
immunization 999.4
overdose or wrong substance given or taken 977.9
specified drug — see Table of Drugs and Chemicals
serum 999.4
following sting(s) 989.5
purpura 287.0
serum 999.4
Anaphylactoid shock or reaction — see Anaphylactic shock
Anaphylaxis — see Anaphylactic shock
Anaplasia, cervix 622.10
Anarthria 784.51 ▲
Anarthritic rheumatoid disease 446.5
Anasarca 782.3
cardiac (see also Failure, heart) 428.0
fetus or newborn 778.0
lung 514
nutritional 262
pulmonary 514
renal (see also Nephrosis) 581.9
Anaspadias 752.62
Anastomosis
aneurysmal — see Aneurysm
arteriovenous, congenital NEC (see also Anomaly, arteriovenous) 747.60
ruptured, of brain (see also Hemorrhage, subarachnoid) 430
intestinal 569.89
complicated NEC 997.4
involving urinary tract 997.5
retinal and choroidal vessels 743.58
acquired 362.17
Anatomical narrow angle (glaucoma) 365.02
Ancylostoma (infection) (infestation) 126.9
americanus 126.1
braziliense 126.2
caninum 126.8

Ancylostoma — continued
ceylanicum 126.3
duodenale 126.0
Necator americanus 126.1
Ancylostomiasis (intestinal) 126.9
ancylostoma
americanus 126.1
caninum 126.8
ceylanicum 126.3
duodenale 126.0
braziliense 126.2
Necator americanus 126.1
Anders' disease or syndrome (adiposis tuberosa simplex) 272.8
Andersen's glycogen storage disease 271.0
Anderson's disease 272.7
Andes disease 993.2
Andrews' disease (bacterid) 686.8
Androblastoma (M8630/1)
benign (M8630/0)
specified site — see Neoplasm, by site, benign
unspecified site
female 220
male 222.0
malignant (M8630/3)
specified site — see Neoplasm, by site, malignant
unspecified site
female 183.0
male 186.9
specified site — see Neoplasm, by site, uncertain behavior
tubular (M8640/0)
with lipid storage (M8641/0)
specified site — see Neoplasm, by site, benign
unspecified site
female 220
male 222.0
specified site — see Neoplasm, by site, benign
unspecified site
female 220
male 222.0
unspecified site
female 236.2
male 236.4
Android pelvis 755.69
with disproportion (fetopelvic) 653.3 ☑
affecting fetus or newborn 763.1
causing obstructed labor 660.1 ☑
affecting fetus or newborn 763.1
Anectasis, pulmonary (newborn or fetus) 770.5
Anemia 285.9
with
disorder of
anaerobic glycolysis 282.3
pentose phosphate pathway 282.2
koilonychia 280.9
6-phosphogluconic dehydrogenase deficiency 282.2
achlorhydric 280.9
achrestic 281.8
Addison's (pernicious) 281.0
Addison-Biermer (pernicious) 281.0
agranulocytic 288.09
amino acid deficiency 281.4
antineoplastic chemotherapy induced 285.3 ●
aplastic 284.9
acquired (secondary) 284.89
congenital 284.01
constitutional 284.01
due to
antineoplastic chemotherapy 284.89
chronic systemic disease 284.89
drugs 284.89
infection 284.89
radiation 284.89
idiopathic 284.9
myxedema 244.9
of or complicating pregnancy 648.2 ☑
red cell (acquired) (adult) (with thymoma) 284.81
congenital 284.01
pure 284.01

☑ Additional Digit Required — Refer to the Tabular List for Digit Selection   ⚑ Subterms under main terms may continue to next column or page

2010 ICD-9-CM   ►◄ Revised Text   ● New Line   ▲ Revised Code   **October 2009 · Volume 2 — 17**

Index

Anemia — Anemia

Anemia — *continued*
  aplastic — *continued*
    specified type NEC 284.89
    toxic (paralytic) 284.89
  aregenerative 284.9
    congenital 284.01
  asiderotic 280.9
  atypical (primary) 285.9
  autohemolysis of Selwyn and Dacie (type I) 282.2
  autoimmune hemolytic 283.0
  Baghdad Spring 282.2
  Balantidium coli 007.0
  Biermer's (pernicious) 281.0
  blood loss (chronic) 280.0
    acute 285.1
  bothriocephalus 123.4
  brickmakers' (*see also* Ancylostomiasis) 126.9
  cerebral 437.8
  childhood 282.9
  chlorotic 280.9
  chronica congenita aregenerativa 284.01
  chronic simple 281.9
  combined system disease NEC 281.0 [336.2]
    due to dietary deficiency 281.1 [336.2]
  complicating pregnancy or childbirth 648.2 ☑
  congenital (following fetal blood loss) 776.5
    aplastic 284.01
    due to isoimmunization NEC 773.2
    Heinz-body 282.7
    hereditary hemolytic NEC 282.9
    nonspherocytic
      Type I 282.2
      Type II 282.3
    pernicious 281.0
    spherocytic (*see also* Spherocytosis) 282.0
  Cooley's (erythroblastic) 282.49
  crescent — *see* Disease, sickle-cell
  cytogenic 281.0
  Dacie's (nonspherocytic)
    type I 282.2
    type II 282.3
  Davidson's (refractory) 284.9
  deficiency 281.9
    2, 3 diphosphoglycurate mutase 282.3
    2, 3 PG 282.3
    6-PGD 282.2
    6-phosphogluronic dehydrogenase 282.2
    amino acid 281.4
    combined B_{12} and folate 281.3
    enzyme, drug-induced (hemolytic) 282.2
    erythrocytic glutathione 282.2
    folate 281.2
      dietary 281.2
      drug-induced 281.2
    folic acid 281.2
      dietary 281.2
      drug-induced 281.2
    G-6-PD 282.2
    GGS-R 282.2
    glucose-6-phosphate dehydrogenase (G-6-PD) 282.2
    glucose-phosphate isomerase 282.3
    glutathione peroxidase 282.2
    glutathione reductase 282.2
    glyceraldehyde phosphate dehydrogenase 282.3
    GPI 282.3
    G SH 282.2
    hexokinase 282.3
    iron (Fe) 280.9
      specified NEC 280.8
    nutritional 281.9
      with
        poor iron absorption 280.9
        specified deficiency NEC 281.8
      due to inadequate dietary iron intake 280.1
      specified type NEC 281.8
    of or complicating pregnancy 648.2 ☑
    pentose phosphate pathway 282.2
    PFK 282.3
    phosphofructo-aldolase 282.3
    phosphofructokinase 282.3
    phosphoglycerate kinase 282.3
    PK 282.3

Anemia — *continued*
  deficiency — *continued*
    protein 281.4
    pyruvate kinase (PK) 282.3
    TPI 282.3
    triosephosphate isomerase 282.3
    vitamin B_{12} NEC 281.1
      dietary 281.1
      pernicious 281.0
  Diamond-Blackfan (congenital hypoplastic) 284.01
  dibothriocephalus 123.4
  dimorphic 281.9
  diphasic 281.8
  diphtheritic 032.89
  Diphyllobothrium 123.4
  drepanocytic (*see also* Disease, sickle-cell) 282.60
  due to
    antineoplastic chemotherapy 285.3 ●
    blood loss (chronic) 280.0
      acute 285.1
    chemotherapy, antineoplastic 285.3 ●
    defect of Embden-Meyerhof pathway glycolysis 282.3
    disorder of glutathione metabolism 282.2
    drug — *see* Anemia, by type (*see also* Table of Drugs and Chemicals)
      chemotherapy, antineoplastic 285.3 ●
    fetal blood loss 776.5
    fish tapeworm (D. latum) infestation 123.4
    glutathione metabolism disorder 282.2
    hemorrhage (chronic) 280.0
      acute 285.1
    hexose monophosphate (HMP) shunt deficiency 282.2
    impaired absorption 280.9
    loss of blood (chronic) 280.0
      acute 285.1
    myxedema 244.9
    Necator americanus 126.1
    prematurity 776.6
    selective vitamin B_{12} malabsorption with proteinuria 281.1
  Dyke-Young type (secondary) (symptomatic) 283.9
  dyserythropoietic (congenital) (types I, II, III) 285.8
  dyshemopoietic (congenital) 285.8
  Egypt (*see also* Ancylostomiasis) 126.9
  elliptocytosis (*see also* Elliptocytosis) 282.1
  enzyme deficiency, drug-induced 282.2
  epidemic (*see also* Ancylostomiasis) 126.9
  EPO resistant 285.21
  erythroblastic
    familial 282.49
    fetus or newborn (*see also* Disease, hemolytic) 773.2
      late 773.5
  erythrocytic glutathione deficiency 282.2
  erythropoietin-resistant (EPO resistant anemia) 285.21
  essential 285.9
  Faber's (achlorhydric anemia) 280.9
  factitious (self-induced blood letting) 280.0
  familial erythroblastic (microcytic) 282.49
  Fanconi's (congenital pancytopenia) 284.09
  favism 282.2
  fetal 678.0 ☑
    following blood loss, affecting newborn 776.5
  fetus or newborn
    due to
      ABO
        antibodies 773.1
        incompatibility, maternal/fetal 773.1
        isoimmunization 773.1
      Rh
        antibodies 773.0
        incompatibility, maternal/fetal 773.0
        isoimmunization 773.0
    following fetal blood loss 776.5
  fish tapeworm (D. latum) infestation 123.4
  folate (folic acid) deficiency 281.2

Anemia — *continued*
  folate deficiency — *continued*
    dietary 281.2
    drug-induced 281.2
  folate malabsorption, congenital 281.2
  folic acid deficiency 281.2
    dietary 281.2
    drug-induced 281.2
  G-6-PD 282.2
  general 285.9
  glucose-6-phosphate dehydrogenase deficiency 282.2
  glutathione-reductase deficiency 282.2
  goat's milk 281.2
  granulocytic 288.09
  Heinz-body, congenital 282.7
  hemoglobin deficiency 285.9
  hemolytic 283.9
    acquired 283.9
      with hemoglobinuria NEC 283.2
      autoimmune (cold type) (idiopathic) (primary) (secondary) (symptomatic) (warm type) 283.0
      due to
        cold reactive antibodies 283.0
        drug exposure 283.0
        warm reactive antibodies 283.0
      fragmentation 283.19
      idiopathic (chronic) 283.9
      infectious 283.19
        autoimmune 283.0
      non-autoimmune 283.10
      toxic 283.19
      traumatic cardiac 283.19
    acute 283.9
      due to enzyme deficiency NEC 282.3
      fetus or newborn (*see also* Disease, hemolytic) 773.2
        late 773.5
      Lederer's (acquired infectious hemolytic anemia) 283.19
    autoimmune (acquired) 283.0
    chronic 282.9
      idiopathic 283.9
    cold type (secondary) (symptomatic) 283.0
    congenital (spherocytic) (*see also* Spherocytosis) 282.0
      nonspherocytic — *see* Anemia, hemolytic, nonspherocytic, congenital
    drug-induced 283.0
      enzyme deficiency 282.2
    due to
      cardiac conditions 283.19
      drugs 283.0
      enzyme deficiency NEC 282.3
        drug-induced 282.2
      presence of shunt or other internal prosthetic device 283.19
      thrombotic thrombocytopenic purpura 446.6
    elliptocytotic (*see also* Elliptocytosis) 282.1
    familial 282.9
    hereditary 282.9
      due to enzyme deficiency NEC 282.3
      specified NEC 282.8
    idiopathic (chronic) 283.9
    infectious (acquired) 283.19
    mechanical 283.19
    microangiopathic 283.19
    non-autoimmune NEC 283.10
    nonspherocytic
      congenital or hereditary NEC 282.3
        glucose-6-phosphate dehydrogenase deficiency 282.2
        pyruvate kinase (PK) deficiency 282.3
        type I 282.2
        type II 282.3
      type I 282.2
      type II 282.3
    of or complicating pregnancy 648.2 ☑
    resulting from presence of shunt or other internal prosthetic device 283.19
    secondary 283.19
      autoimmune 283.0

Anemia — *continued*
  hemolytic — *continued*
    sickle-cell — *see* Disease, sickle-cell
    Stransky-Regala type (Hb-E) (*see also* Disease, hemoglobin) 282.7
    symptomatic 283.19
      autoimmune 283.0
    toxic (acquired) 283.19
    uremic (adult) (child) 283.11
    warm type (secondary) (symptomatic) 283.0
  hemorrhagic (chronic) 280.0
    acute 285.1
  HEMPAS 285.8
  hereditary erythroblast multinuclearity-positive acidified serum test 285.8
  Herrick's (hemoglobin S disease) 282.61
  hexokinase deficiency 282.3
  high A_2 282.49
  hookworm (*see also* Ancylostomiasis) 126.9
  hypochromic (idiopathic) (microcytic) (normoblastic) 280.9
    with iron loading 285.0
    due to blood loss (chronic) 280.0
      acute 285.1
    familial sex linked 285.0
    pyridoxine-responsive 285.0
  hypoplasia, red blood cells 284.81
    congenital or familial 284.01
  hypoplastic (idiopathic) 284.9
    congenital 284.01
    familial 284.01
    of childhood 284.09
  idiopathic 285.9
    hemolytic, chronic 283.9
  in ▶(due to) (with)◀
    chronic illness NEC 285.29
    chronic kidney disease 285.21
    end-stage renal disease 285.21
    neoplastic disease 285.22
  infantile 285.9
  infective, infectional 285.9
  intertropical (*see also* Ancylostomiasis) 126.9
  iron (Fe) deficiency 280.9
    due to blood loss (chronic) 280.0
      acute 285.1
    of or complicating pregnancy 648.2 ☑
    specified NEC 280.8
  Jaksch's (pseudoleukemia infantum) 285.8
  Joseph-Diamond-Blackfan (congenital hypoplastic) 284.01
  labyrinth 386.50
  Lederer's (acquired infectious hemolytic anemia) 283.19
  leptocytosis (hereditary) 282.49
  leukoerythroblastic 284.2
  macrocytic 281.9
    nutritional 281.2
    of or complicating pregnancy 648.2 ☑
    tropical 281.2
  malabsorption (familial), selective B_{12} with proteinuria 281.1
  malarial (*see also* Malaria) 084.6
  malignant (progressive) 281.0
  malnutrition 281.9
  marsh (*see also* Malaria) 084.6
  Mediterranean (with hemoglobinopathy) 282.49
  megaloblastic 281.9
    combined B_{12} and folate deficiency 281.3
    nutritional (of infancy) 281.2
    of infancy 281.2
    of or complicating pregnancy 648.2 ☑
    refractory 281.3
    specified NEC 281.3
  megalocytic 281.9
  microangiopathic hemolytic 283.19
  microcytic (hypochromic) 280.9
    due to blood loss (chronic) 280.0
      acute 285.1
    familial 282.49
    hypochromic 280.9
  microdrepanocytosis 282.49
  miners' (*see also* Ancylostomiasis) 126.9
  myelopathic 285.8
  myelophthisic (normocytic) 284.2

☑ Additional Digit Required — Refer to the Tabular List for Digit Selection
                            ▽ Subterms under main terms may continue to next column or page
18 — Volume 2 • October 2009   ▶◀ Revised Text   ● New Line   ▲ Revised Code   2010 ICD-9-CM

Anemia — *continued*
  newborn (*see also* Disease, hemolytic) 773.2
    due to isoimmunization (*see also* Disease, hemolytic) 773.2
    late, due to isoimmunization 773.5
    posthemorrhagic 776.5
  nonregenerative 284.9
  nonspherocytic hemolytic — *see* Anemia, hemolytic, nonspherocytic
  normocytic (infectional) (not due to blood loss) 285.9
    due to blood loss (chronic) 280.0
      acute 285.1
    myelophthisic 284.2
  nutritional (deficiency) 281.9
    with
      poor iron absorption 280.9
      specified deficiency NEC 281.8
    due to inadequate dietary iron intake 280.1
    megaloblastic (of infancy) 281.2
  of childhood 282.9
  of chronic
    disease NEC 285.29
    illness NEC 285.29
  of or complicating pregnancy 648.2 ☑
    affecting fetus or newborn 760.8
  of prematurity 776.6
  orotic aciduric (congenital) (hereditary) 281.4
  osteosclerotic 289.89
  ovalocytosis (hereditary) (*see also* Elliptocytosis) 282.1
  paludal (*see also* Malaria) 084.6
  pentose phosphate pathway deficiency 282.2
  pernicious (combined system disease) (congenital) (dorsolateral spinal degeneration) (juvenile) (myelopathy) (neuropathy) (posterior sclerosis) (primary) (progressive) (spleen) 281.0
    of or complicating pregnancy 648.2 ☑
  pleochromic 285.9
    of sprue 281.8
  portal 285.8
  posthemorrhagic (chronic) 280.0
    acute 285.1
    newborn 776.5
  postoperative
    due to (acute) blood loss 285.1
      chronic blood loss 280.0
    other 285.9
  postpartum 648.2 ☑
  pressure 285.9
  primary 285.9
  profound 285.9
  progressive 285.9
    malignant 281.0
    pernicious 281.0
  protein-deficiency 281.4
  pseudoleukemica infantum 285.8
  puerperal 648.2 ☑
  pure red cell 284.81
    congenital 284.01
  pyridoxine-responsive (hypochromic) 285.0
  pyruvate kinase (PK) deficiency 282.3
  refractoria sideroblastica 238.72
  refractory (primary) 238.72
    with
      excess
        blasts-1 (RAEB-1) 238.72 ▲
        blasts-2 (RAEB-2) 238.73
      hemochromatosis 238.72
      ringed sideroblasts (RARS) 238.72
    due to
      drug 285.0
      myelodysplastic syndrome 238.72
      toxin 285.0
    hereditary 285.0
    idiopathic 238.72
    megaloblastic 281.3
    sideroblastic 238.72
      hereditary 285.0
    sideropenic 280.9
  Rietti-Greppi-Micheli (thalassemia minor) 282.49
  scorbutic 281.8
  secondary (to) 285.9
    blood loss (chronic) 280.0

Anemia — *continued*
  secondary — *continued*
    blood loss — *continued*
      acute 285.1
    hemorrhage 280.0
      acute 285.1
    inadequate dietary iron intake 280.1
  semiplastic 284.9
  septic 285.9
  sickle-cell (*see also* Disease, sickle-cell) 282.60
  sideroachrestic 285.0
  sideroblastic (acquired) (any type) (congenital) (drug-induced) (due to disease) (hereditary) (primary) (secondary) (sex-linked hypochromic) (vitamin B$_6$ responsive) 285.0
    refractory 238.72
      congenital 285.0
      drug-induced 285.0
      hereditary 285.0
      sex-linked hypochromic 285.0
      vitamin B$_6$-responsive 285.0
  sideropenic (refractory) 280.9
    due to blood loss (chronic) 280.0
      acute 285.1
  simple chronic 281.9
  specified type NEC 285.8
  spherocytic (hereditary) (*see also* Spherocytosis) 282.0
  splenic 285.8
    familial (Gaucher's) 272.7
  splenomegalic 285.8
  stomatocytosis 282.8
  syphilitic 095.8
  target cell (oval) 282.49
  thalassemia 282.49
  thrombocytopenic (*see also* Thrombocytopenia) 287.5
  toxic 284.89
  triosephosphate isomerase deficiency 282.3
  tropical, macrocytic 281.2
  tuberculous (*see also* Tuberculosis) 017.9 ☑
  vegan's 281.1
  vitamin
    B$_6$-responsive 285.0
    B$_{12}$ deficiency (dietary) 281.1
      pernicious 281.0
  von Jaksch's (pseudoleukemia infantum) 285.8
  Witts' (achlorhydric anemia) 280.9
  Zuelzer (-Ogden) (nutritional megaloblastic anemia) 281.2
Anencephalus, anencephaly 740.0
  fetal, affecting management of pregnancy 655.0 ☑
Anergasia — *see also* Psychosis, organic 294.9
  senile 290.0
Anesthesia, anesthetic 782.0
  complication or reaction NEC 995.22
    due to
      correct substance properly administered 995.22
      overdose or wrong substance given 968.4
        specified anesthetic — *see* Table of Drugs and Chemicals
  cornea 371.81
  death from
    correct substance properly administered 995.4
    during delivery 668.9 ☑
    overdose or wrong substance given 968.4
    specified anesthetic — *see* Table of Drugs and Chemicals
  eye 371.81
  functional 300.11
  hyperesthetic, thalamic 338.0
  hysterical 300.11
  local skin lesion 782.0
  olfactory 781.1
  sexual (psychogenic) 302.72
  shock
    due to
      correct substance properly administered 995.4

Anesthesia, anesthetic — *continued*
  shock — *continued*
    due to —
      overdose or wrong substance given 968.4
      specified anesthetic — *see* Table of Drugs and Chemicals
  skin 782.0
  tactile 782.0
  testicular 608.9
  thermal 782.0
Anetoderma (maculosum) 701.3
Aneuploidy NEC 758.5
Aneurin deficiency 265.1
Aneurysm (anastomotic) (artery) (cirsoid) (diffuse) (false) (fusiform) (multiple) (ruptured) (saccular) (varicose) 442.9
  abdominal (aorta) 441.4
    ruptured 441.3
    syphilitic 093.0
  aorta, aortic (nonsyphilitic) 441.9
    abdominal 441.4
      dissecting 441.02
      ruptured 441.3
      syphilitic 093.0
    arch 441.2
      ruptured 441.1
    arteriosclerotic NEC 441.9
      ruptured 441.5
    ascending 441.2
      ruptured 441.1
    congenital 747.29
    descending 441.9
      abdominal 441.4
        ruptured 441.3
      ruptured 441.5
      thoracic 441.2
        ruptured 441.1
    dissecting 441.00
      abdominal 441.02
      thoracic 441.01
      thoracoabdominal 441.03
    due to coarctation (aorta) 747.10
    ruptured 441.5
    sinus, right 747.29
    syphilitic 093.0
    thoracoabdominal 441.7
      ruptured 441.6
    thorax, thoracic (arch) (nonsyphilitic) 441.2
      dissecting 441.01
      ruptured 441.1
      syphilitic 093.0
    transverse 441.2
      ruptured 441.1
    valve (heart) (*see also* Endocarditis, aortic) 424.1
  arteriosclerotic NEC 442.9
    cerebral 437.3
      ruptured (*see also* Hemorrhage, subarachnoid) 430
  arteriovenous (congenital) (peripheral) NEC (*see also* Anomaly, arteriovenous) 747.60
    acquired NEC 447.0
      brain 437.3
        ruptured (*see also* Hemorrhage, subarachnoid) 430
      coronary 414.11
      pulmonary 417.0
    brain (cerebral) 747.81
      ruptured (*see also* Hemorrhage, subarachnoid) 430
    coronary 746.85
    pulmonary 747.3
    retina 743.58
    specified site NEC 747.89
      acquired 447.0
    traumatic (*see also* Injury, blood vessel, by site) 904.9
  basal — *see* Aneurysm, brain
  berry (congenital) (ruptured) (*see also* Hemorrhage, subarachnoid) 430
  brain 437.3
    arteriosclerotic 437.3
      ruptured (*see also* Hemorrhage, subarachnoid) 430

Aneurysm — *continued*
  brain — *continued*
    arteriovenous 747.81
      acquired 437.3
        ruptured (*see also* Hemorrhage, subarachnoid) 430
      ruptured (*see also* Hemorrhage, subarachnoid) 430
    berry (congenital) (ruptured) (*see also* Hemorrhage, subarachnoid) 430
    congenital 747.81
      ruptured (*see also* Hemorrhage, subarachnoid) 430
    meninges 437.3
      ruptured (*see also* Hemorrhage, subarachnoid) 430
    miliary (congenital) (ruptured) (*see also* Hemorrhage, subarachnoid) 430
    mycotic 421.0
      ruptured (*see also* Hemorrhage, subarachnoid) 430
    nonruptured 437.3
    ruptured (*see also* Hemorrhage, subarachnoid) 430
    syphilitic 094.87
  syphilitic (hemorrhage) 094.87
  traumatic — *see* Injury, intracranial
  cardiac (false) (*see also* Aneurysm, heart) 414.10
  carotid artery (common) (external) 442.81
    internal (intracranial portion) 437.3
      extracranial portion 442.81
      ruptured into brain (*see also* Hemorrhage, subarachnoid) 430
    syphilitic 093.89
      intracranial 094.87
  cavernous sinus (*see also* Aneurysm, brain) 437.3
    arteriovenous 747.81
      ruptured (*see also* Hemorrhage, subarachnoid) 430
    congenital 747.81
      ruptured (*see also* Hemorrhage, subarachnoid) 430
  celiac 442.84
  central nervous system, syphilitic 094.89
  cerebral — *see* Aneurysm, brain
  chest — *see* Aneurysm, thorax
  circle of Willis (*see also* Aneurysm, brain) 437.3
    congenital 747.81
      ruptured (*see also* Hemorrhage, subarachnoid) 430
    ruptured (*see also* Hemorrhage, subarachnoid) 430
  common iliac artery 442.2
  congenital (peripheral) NEC 747.60
    brain 747.81
      ruptured (*see also* Hemorrhage, subarachnoid) 430
    cerebral — *see* Aneurysm, brain, congenital
    coronary 746.85
    gastrointestinal 747.61
    lower limb 747.64
    pulmonary 747.3
    renal 747.62
    retina 743.58
    specified site NEC 747.89
    spinal 747.82
    upper limb 747.63
  conjunctiva 372.74
  conus arteriosus (*see also* Aneurysm, heart) 414.10
  coronary (arteriosclerotic) (artery) (vein) (*see also* Aneurysm, heart) 414.11
    arteriovenous 746.85
    congenital 746.85
    syphilitic 093.89
  cylindrical 441.9
    ruptured 441.5
    syphilitic 093.9
  dissecting 442.9
    aorta 441.00
      abdominal 441.02
      thoracic 441.01
      thoracoabdominal 441.03

☑ Additional Digit Required — Refer to the Tabular List for Digit Selection   ⚐ Subterms under main terms may continue to next column or page

2010 ICD-9-CM   ►◄ Revised Text   ● New Line   ▲ Revised Code   **October 2009 · Volume 2 — 19**

Index

Aneurysm — Anhydremia

Aneurysm — *continued*
  dissecting — *continued*
    syphilitic 093.9
  ductus arteriosus 747.0
  embolic — *see* Embolism, artery
  endocardial, infective (any valve) 421.0
  femoral 442.3
  gastroduodenal 442.84
  gastroepiploic 442.84
  heart (chronic or with a stated duration of over 8 weeks) (infectional) (wall) 414.10
    acute or with a stated duration of 8 weeks or less (*see also* Infarct, myocardium) 410.9 ☑
    congenital 746.89
    valve — *see* Endocarditis
  hepatic 442.84
  iliac (common) 442.2
  infective (any valve) 421.0
  innominate (nonsyphilitic) 442.89
    syphilitic 093.89
  interauricular septum (*see also* Aneurysm, heart) 414.10
  interventricular septum (*see also* Aneurysm, heart) 414.10
  intracranial — *see* Aneurysm, brain
  intrathoracic (nonsyphilitic) 441.2
    ruptured 441.1
    syphilitic 093.0
  jugular vein 453.89   ▲
  lower extremity 442.3
  lung (pulmonary artery) 417.1
  malignant 093.9
  mediastinal (nonsyphilitic) 442.89
    syphilitic 093.89
  miliary (congenital) (ruptured) (*see also* Hemorrhage, subarachnoid) 430
  mitral (heart) (valve) 424.0
  mural (arteriovenous) (heart) (*see also* Aneurysm, heart) 414.10
  mycotic, any site 421.0
    without endocarditis — *see* Aneurysm by site
      ruptured, brain (*see also* Hemorrhage, subarachnoid) 430
  myocardium (*see also* Aneurysm, heart) 414.10
  neck 442.81
  pancreaticoduodenal 442.84
  patent ductus arteriosus 747.0
  peripheral NEC 442.89
    congenital NEC (*see also* Aneurysm, congenital) 747.60
  popliteal 442.3
  pulmonary 417.1
    arteriovenous 747.3
      acquired 417.0
    syphilitic 093.89
    valve (heart) (*see also* Endocarditis, pulmonary) 424.3
  racemose 442.9
    congenital (peripheral) NEC 747.60
  radial 442.0
  Rasmussen's (*see also* Tuberculosis) 011.2 ☑
  renal 442.1
  retinal (acquired) 362.17
    congenital 743.58
    diabetic 250.5 ☑ [362.01]
      due to secondary diabetes 249.5 ☑ [362.01]
  sinus, aortic (of Valsalva) 747.29
  specified site NEC 442.89
  spinal (cord) 442.89
    congenital 747.82
    syphilitic (hemorrhage) 094.89
  spleen, splenic 442.83
  subclavian 442.82
    syphilitic 093.89
  superior mesenteric 442.84
  syphilitic 093.9
    aorta 093.0
    central nervous system 094.89
    congenital 090.5
    spine, spinal 094.89
  thoracoabdominal 441.7
    ruptured 441.6
  thorax, thoracic (arch) (nonsyphilitic) 441.2

Aneurysm — *continued*
  thorax, thoracic — *continued*
    dissecting 441.01
    ruptured 441.1
    syphilitic 093.0
    traumatic (complication) (early) — *see* Injury, blood vessel, by site
    tricuspid (heart) (valve) — *see* Endocarditis, tricuspid
  ulnar 442.0
  upper extremity 442.0
  valve, valvular — *see* Endocarditis
  venous 456.8
    congenital NEC (*see also* Aneurysm, congenital) 747.60
  ventricle (arteriovenous) (*see also* Aneurysm, heart) 414.10
  visceral artery NEC 442.84
Angiectasis 459.89
Angiectopia 459.9
Angiitis 447.6
  allergic granulomatous 446.4
  hypersensitivity 446.20
    Goodpasture's syndrome 446.21
    specified NEC 446.29
  necrotizing 446.0
  Wegener's (necrotizing respiratory granulomatosis) 446.4
Angina (attack) (cardiac) (chest) (effort) (heart) (pectoris) (syndrome) (vasomotor) 413.9
  abdominal 557.1
  accelerated 411.1
  agranulocytic 288.03
  aphthous 074.0
  catarrhal 462
  crescendo 411.1
  croupous 464.4
  cruris 443.9
    due to atherosclerosis NEC (*see also* Arteriosclerosis, extremities) 440.20
  decubitus 413.0
  diphtheritic (membranous) 032.0
  equivalent 413.9   ●
  erysipelatous 034.0
  erythematous 462
  exudative, chronic 476.0
  faucium 478.29
  gangrenous 462
    diphtheritic 032.0
  infectious 462
  initial 411.1
  intestinal 557.1
  ludovici 528.3
  Ludwig's 528.3
  malignant 462
    diphtheritic 032.0
  membranous 464.4
    diphtheritic 032.0
  mesenteric 557.1
  monocytic 075
  nocturnal 413.0
  phlegmonous 475
    diphtheritic 032.0
  preinfarctional 411.1
  Prinzmetal's 413.1
  progressive 411.1
  pseudomembranous 101
  psychogenic 306.2
  pultaceous, diphtheritic 032.0
  scarlatinal 034.1
  septic 034.0
  simple 462
  stable NEC 413.9
  staphylococcal 462
  streptococcal 034.0
  stridulous, diphtheritic 032.3
  syphilitic 093.9
    congenital 090.5
  tonsil 475
  trachealis 464.4
  unstable 411.1
  variant 413.1
  Vincent's 101
Angioblastoma (M9161/1) — *see* Neoplasm, connective tissue, uncertain behavior

Angiocholecystitis — *see also* Cholecystitis, acute 575.0
Angiocholitis — *see also* Cholecystitis, acute 576.1
Angiodysgensis spinalis 336.1
Angiodysplasia (intestinalis) (intestine) 569.84
  with hemorrhage 569.85
  duodenum 537.82
    with hemorrhage 537.83
  stomach 537.82
    with hemorrhage 537.83
Angioedema (allergic) (any site) (with urticaria) 995.1
  hereditary 277.6
Angioendothelioma (M9130/1) — *see also* Neoplasm, by site, uncertain behavior
  benign (M9130/0) (*see also* Hemangioma, by site) 228.00
  bone (M9260/3) — *see* Neoplasm, bone, malignant
  Ewing's (M9260/3) — *see* Neoplasm, bone, malignant
  nervous system (M9130/0) 228.09
Angiofibroma (M9160/0) — *see also* Neoplasm, by site, benign
  juvenile (M9160/0) 210.7
    specified site — *see* Neoplasm, by site, benign
  unspecified site 210.7
Angiohemophilia (A) (B) 286.4
Angioid streaks (choroid) (retina) 363.43
Angiokeratoma (M9141/0) — *see also* Neoplasm, skin, benign
  corporis diffusum 272.7
Angiokeratosis
  diffuse 272.7
Angioleiomyoma (M8894/0) — *see* Neoplasm, connective tissue, benign
Angioleucitis 683
Angiolipoma (M8861/0) — *see also* Lipoma, by site 214.9
  infiltrating (M8861/1) — *see* Neoplasm, connective tissue, uncertain behavior
Angioma (M9120/0) — *see also* Hemangioma, by site 228.00
  capillary 448.1
  hemorrhagicum hereditaria 448.0
  malignant (M9120/3) — *see* Neoplasm, connective tissue, malignant
  pigmentosum et atrophicum 757.33
  placenta — *see* Placenta, abnormal
  plexiform (M9131/0) — *see* Hemangioma, by site
  senile 448.1
  serpiginosum 709.1
  spider 448.1
  stellate 448.1
Angiomatosis 757.32
  bacillary 083.8
  corporis diffusum universale 272.7
  cutaneocerebral 759.6
  encephalocutaneous 759.6
  encephalofacial 759.6
  encephalotrigeminal 759.6
  hemorrhagic familial 448.0
  hereditary familial 448.0
  heredofamilial 448.0
  meningo-oculofacial 759.6
  multiple sites 228.09
  neuro-oculocutaneous 759.6
  retina (Hippel's disease) 759.6
  retinocerebellosa 759.6
  retinocerebral 759.6
  systemic 228.09
Angiomyolipoma (M8860/0)
  specified site — *see* Neoplasm, connective tissue, benign
  unspecified site 223.0
Angiomyoliposarcoma (M8860/3) — *see* Neoplasm, connective tissue, malignant
Angiomyoma (M8894/0) — *see* Neoplasm, connective tissue, benign
Angiomyosarcoma (M8894/3) — *see* Neoplasm, connective tissue, malignant
Angioneurosis 306.2

Angioneurotic edema (allergic) (any site) (with urticaria) 995.1
  hereditary 277.6
Angiopathia, angiopathy 459.9
  diabetic (peripheral) 250.7 ☑ [443.81]
    due to secondary diabetes 249.7 ☑ [443.81]
  peripheral 443.9
    diabetic 250.7 ☑ [443.81]
      due to secondary diabetes 249.7 ☑ [443.81]
    specified type NEC 443.89
  retinae syphilitica 093.89
  retinalis (juvenilis) 362.18
    background 362.10
    diabetic 250.5 ☑ [362.01]
      due to secondary diabetes 249.5 ☑ [362.01]
    proliferative 362.29
    tuberculous (*see also* Tuberculosis) 017.3 ☑ [362.18]
Angiosarcoma (M9120/3) — *see* Neoplasm, connective tissue, malignant
Angiosclerosis — *see* Arteriosclerosis
Angioscotoma, enlarged 368.42
Angiospasm 443.9
  brachial plexus 353.0
  cerebral 435.9
  cervical plexus 353.2
  nerve
    arm 354.9
      axillary 353.0
      median 354.1
      ulnar 354.2
    autonomic (*see also* Neuropathy, peripheral, autonomic) 337.9
    axillary 353.0
    leg 355.8
      plantar 355.6
    lower extremity — *see* Angiospasm, nerve, leg
    median 354.1
    peripheral NEC 355.9
    spinal NEC 355.9
    sympathetic (*see also* Neuropathy, peripheral, autonomic) 337.9
    ulnar 354.2
    upper extremity — *see* Angiospasm, nerve, arm
  peripheral NEC 443.9
  traumatic 443.9
    foot 443.9
    leg 443.9
    vessel 443.9
Angiospastic disease or edema 443.9
Angle's
  class I 524.21
  class II 524.22
  class III 524.23
Anguillulosis 127.2
Angulation
  cecum (*see also* Obstruction, intestine) 560.9
  coccyx (acquired) 738.6
    congenital 756.19
  femur (acquired) 736.39
    congenital 755.69
  intestine (large) (small) (*see also* Obstruction, intestine) 560.9
  sacrum (acquired) 738.5
    congenital 756.19
  sigmoid (flexure) (*see also* Obstruction, intestine) 560.9
  spine (*see also* Curvature, spine) 737.9
  tibia (acquired) 736.89
    congenital 755.69
  ureter 593.3
  wrist (acquired) 736.09
    congenital 755.59
Angulus infectiosus 686.8
Anhedonia 780.99
Anhidrosis (lid) (neurogenic) (thermogenic) 705.0
Anhydration 276.51
  with
    hypernatremia 276.0
    hyponatremia 276.1
Anhydremia 276.52

☑ Additional Digit Required — Refer to the Tabular List for Digit Selection   ⱽ Subterms under main terms may continue to next column or page

20 — Volume 2 • October 2009   ►◄ Revised Text   ● New Line   ▲ Revised Code   2010 ICD-9-CM

Anhydremia — *continued*
with
    hypernatremia 276.0
    hyponatremia 276.1
Anidrosis 705.0
Aniridia (congenital) 743.45
Anisakiasis (infection) (infestation) 127.1
Anisakis larva infestation 127.1
Aniseikonia 367.32
Anisocoria (pupil) 379.41
    congenital 743.46
Anisocytosis 790.09
Anisometropia (congenital) 367.31
Ankle — *see* condition
Ankyloblepharon (acquired) (eyelid) 374.46
    filiforme (adnatum) (congenital) 743.62
    total 743.62
Ankylodactly — *see also* Syndactylism 755.10
Ankyloglossia 750.0
Ankylosis (fibrous) (osseous) 718.50
    ankle 718.57
    any joint, produced by surgical fusion V45.4
    cricoarytenoid (cartilage) (joint) (larynx) 478.79
    dental 521.6
    ear ossicle NEC 385.22
        malleus 385.21
    elbow 718.52
    finger 718.54
    hip 718.55
    incostapedial joint (infectional) 385.22
    joint, produced by surgical fusion NEC V45.4
    knee 718.56
    lumbosacral (joint) 724.6
    malleus 385.21
    multiple sites 718.59
    postoperative (status) V45.4
    sacroiliac (joint) 724.6
    shoulder 718.51
    specified site NEC 718.58
    spine NEC 724.9
    surgical V45.4
    teeth, tooth (hard tissues) 521.6
    temporomandibular joint 524.61
    wrist 718.53
Ankylostoma — *see* Ancylostoma
Ankylostomiasis (intestinal) — *see* Ancylostomiasis
Ankylurethria — *see also* Stricture, urethra 598.9
Annular — *see also* condition
    . detachment, cervix 622.8
    organ or site, congenital NEC — *See* Distortion
    pancreas (congenital) 751.7
Anodontia (complete) (partial) (vera) 520.0
    with abnormal spacing 524.30
    acquired 525.10
        causing malocclusion 524.30
        due to
            caries 525.13
            extraction 525.10
            periodontal disease 525.12
            trauma 525.11
Anomaly, anomalous (congenital) (unspecified type) 759.9
    abdomen 759.9
    abdominal wall 756.70
    acoustic nerve 742.9
    adrenal (gland) 759.1
    Alder (-Reilly) (leukocyte granulation) 288.2
    alimentary tract 751.9
        lower 751.5
        specified type NEC 751.8
        upper (any part, except tongue) 750.9
            tongue 750.10
                specified type NEC 750.19
    alveolar 524.70
        ridge (process) 525.8
        specified NEC 524.79
    ankle (joint) 755.69
    anus, anal (canal) 751.5
    aorta, aortic 747.20
        arch 747.21
        coarctation (postductal) (preductal) 747.10
        cusp or valve NEC 746.9
        septum 745.0
        specified type NEC 747.29
    aorticopulmonary septum 745.0

Anomaly, anomalous — *continued*
    apertures, diaphragm 756.6
    appendix 751.5
    aqueduct of Sylvius 742.3
        with spina bifida (*see also* Spina bifida) 741.0 ☑
    arm 755.50
        reduction (*see also* Deformity, reduction, upper limb) 755.20
    arteriovenous (congenital) (peripheral) NEC 747.60
        brain 747.81
        cerebral 747.81
        coronary 746.85
        gastrointestinal 747.61
            acquired — *see* Angiodysplasia
        lower limb 747.64
        renal 747.62
        specified site NEC 747.69
        spinal 747.82
        upper limb 747.63
    artery (*see also* Anomaly, peripheral vascular system) NEC 747.60
        brain 747.81
        cerebral 747.81
        coronary 746.85
        eye 743.9
        pulmonary 747.3
        renal 747.62
        retina 743.9
        umbilical 747.5
    arytenoepiglottic folds 748.3
    atrial
        bands 746.9
        folds 746.9
        septa 745.5
    atrioventricular
        canal 745.69
        common 745.69
        conduction 426.7
        excitation 426.7
        septum 745.4
    atrium — *see* Anomaly, atrial
    auditory canal 744.3
        specified type NEC 744.29
            with hearing impairment 744.02
    auricle
        ear 744.3
            causing impairment of hearing 744.02
        heart 746.9
            septum 745.5
    autosomes, autosomal NEC 758.5
    Axenfeld's 743.44
    back 759.9
    band
        atrial 746.9
        heart 746.9
        ventricular 746.9
    Bartholin's duct 750.9
    biliary duct or passage 751.60
        atresia 751.61
    bladder (neck) (sphincter) (trigone) 753.9
        specified type NEC 753.8
    blood vessel 747.9
        artery — *see* Anomaly, artery
        peripheral vascular — *see* Anomaly, peripheral vascular system
        vein — *see* Anomaly, vein
    bone NEC 756.9
        ankle 755.69
        arm 755.50
        chest 756.3
        cranium 756.0
        face 756.0
        finger 755.50
        foot 755.67
        forearm 755.50
        frontal 756.0
        head 756.0
        hip 755.63
        leg 755.60
        lumbosacral 756.10
        nose 748.1
        pelvic girdle 755.60
        rachitic 756.4
        rib 756.3

Anomaly, anomalous — *continued*
    bone — *continued*
        shoulder girdle 755.50
        skull 756.0
            with
                anencephalus 740.0
                encephalocele 742.0
                hydrocephalus 742.3
                    with spina bifida (*see also* Spina bifida) 741.0 ☑
                microcephalus 742.1
        toe 755.66
    brain 742.9
        multiple 742.4
        reduction 742.2
        specified type NEC 742.4
        vessel 747.81
    branchial cleft NEC 744.49
        cyst 744.42
        fistula 744.41
        persistent 744.41
        sinus (external) (internal) 744.41
    breast 757.6   ▲
    broad ligament 752.10
        specified type NEC 752.19
    bronchus 748.3
    bulbar septum 745.0
    bulbus cordis 745.9
        persistent (in left ventricle) 745.8
    bursa 756.9
    canal of Nuck 752.9
    canthus 743.9
    capillary NEC (*see also* Anomaly, peripheral vascular system) 747.60
    cardiac 746.9
        septal closure 745.9
            acquired 429.71
        valve NEC 746.9
            pulmonary 746.00
            specified type NEC 746.89
    cardiovascular system 746.9
        complicating pregnancy, childbirth, or puerperium 648.5 ☑
    carpus 755.50
    cartilage, trachea 748.3
    cartilaginous 756.9
    caruncle, lacrimal, lachrymal 743.9
    cascade stomach 750.7
    cauda equina 742.59
    cecum 751.5
    cerebral (*see also* Anomaly, brain vessels) 747.81
    cerebrovascular system 747.81
    cervix (uterus) 752.40
        with doubling of vagina and uterus 752.2
        in pregnancy or childbirth 654.6 ☑
            affecting fetus or newborn 763.89
            causing obstructed labor 660.2 ☑
                affecting fetus or newborn 763.1
    Chédiak-Higashi (-Steinbrinck) (congenital gigantism of peroxidase granules) 288.2
    cheek 744.9
    chest (wall) 756.3
    chin 744.9
        specified type NEC 744.89
    chordae tendineae 746.9
    choroid 743.9
        plexus 742.9
    chromosomes, chromosomal 758.9
        13 (13-15) 758.1
        18 (16-18) 758.2
        21 or 22 758.0
        autosomes NEC (*see also* Abnormal, autosomes) 758.5
            deletion 758.39
        Christchurch 758.39
        D_1 758.1
        E_3 758.2
        G 758.0
        mitochondrial 758.9
        mosaics 758.89
        sex 758.81
            complement, XO 758.6
            complement, XXX 758.81
            complement, XXY 758.7
            complement, XYY 758.81

Anomaly, anomalous — *continued*
    chromosomes, chromosomal — *continued*
        sex — *continued*
            gonadal dysgenesis 758.6
            Klinefelter's 758.7
            Turner's 758.6
        trisomy 21 758.0
    cilia 743.9
    circulatory system 747.9
        specified type NEC 747.89
    clavicle 755.51
    clitoris 752.40
    coccyx 756.10
    colon 751.5
    common duct 751.60
    communication
        coronary artery 746.85
        left ventricle with right atrium 745.4
    concha (ear) 744.3
    connection
        renal vessels with kidney 747.62
        total pulmonary venous 747.41
    connective tissue 756.9
        specified type NEC 756.89
    cornea 743.9
        shape 743.41
        size 743.41
        specified type NEC 743.49
    coronary
        artery 746.85
        vein 746.89
    cranium — *see* Anomaly, skull
    cricoid cartilage 748.3
    cushion, endocardial 745.60
        specified type NEC 745.69
    cystic duct 751.60
    dental arch 524.20
        specified NEC 524.29
    dental arch relationship 524.20
        angle's class I 524.21
        angle's class II 524.22
        angle's class III 524.23
        articulation
            anterior 524.27
            posterior 524.27
            reverse 524.27
        disto-occlusion 524.22
            division I 524.22
            division II 524.22
        excessive horizontal overlap 524.26
        interarch distance (excessive) (inadequate) 524.28
        mesio-occlusion 524.23
        neutro-occlusion 524.21
        open
            anterior occlusal relationship 524.24
            posterior occlusal relationship 524.25
        specified NEC 524.29
    dentition 520.6
    dentofacial NEC 524.9
        functional 524.50
        specified type NEC 524.89
    dermatoglyphic 757.2
    Descemet's membrane 743.9
        specified type NEC 743.49
    development
        cervix 752.40
        vagina 752.40
        vulva 752.40
    diaphragm, diaphragmatic (apertures) NEC 756.6
    digestive organ(s) or system 751.9
        lower 751.5
        specified type NEC 751.8
        upper 750.9
    distribution, coronary artery 746.85
    ductus
        arteriosus 747.0
        Botalli 747.0
    duodenum 751.5
    dura 742.9
        brain 742.4
        spinal cord 742.59
    ear 744.3
        causing impairment of hearing 744.00

☑ Additional Digit Required — Refer to the Tabular List for Digit Selection   ▽ Subterms under main terms may continue to next column or page

2010 ICD-9-CM   ▶◀ Revised Text   ● New Line   ▲ Revised Code   October 2009 • Volume 2 — 21

Index — Anomaly, anomalous — Anomaly, anomalous

Anomaly, anomalous — *continued*
  ear — *continued*
    causing impairment of hearing — *continued*
      specified type NEC 744.09
    external 744.3
      causing impairment of hearing 744.02
      specified type NEC 744.29
    inner (causing impairment of hearing) 744.05
    middle, except ossicles (causing impairment of hearing) 744.03
      ossicles 744.04
    ossicles 744.04
    prominent auricle 744.29
    specified type NEC 744.29
      with hearing impairment 744.09
  Ebstein's (heart) 746.2
    tricuspid valve 746.2
  ectodermal 757.9
  Eisenmenger's (ventricular septal defect) 745.4
  ejaculatory duct 752.9
    specified type NEC 752.89
  elbow (joint) 755.50
  endocardial cushion 745.60
    specified type NEC 745.69
  endocrine gland NEC 759.2
  epididymis 752.9
  epiglottis 748.3
  esophagus 750.9
    specified type NEC 750.4
  Eustachian tube 744.3
    specified type NEC 744.24
  eye (any part) 743.9
    adnexa 743.9
      specified type NEC 743.69
    anophthalmos 743.00
    anterior
      chamber and related structures 743.9
        angle 743.9
          specified type NEC 743.44
        specified type NEC 743.44
      segment 743.9
        combined 743.48
        multiple 743.48
        specified type NEC 743.49
    cataract (*see also* Cataract) 743.30
    glaucoma (*see also* Buphthalmia) 743.20
    lid 743.9
      specified type NEC 743.63
    microphthalmos (*see also* Microphthalmos) 743.10
    posterior segment 743.9
      specified type NEC 743.59
      vascular 743.58
      vitreous 743.9
        specified type NEC 743.51
    ptosis (eyelid) 743.61
    retina 743.9
      specified type NEC 743.59
    sclera 743.9
      specified type NEC 743.47
    specified type NEC 743.8
  eyebrow 744.89
  eyelid 743.9
    specified type NEC 743.63
  face (any part) 744.9
    bone(s) 756.0
    specified type NEC 744.89
  fallopian tube 752.10
    specified type NEC 752.19
  fascia 756.9
    specified type NEC 756.89
  femur 755.60
  fibula 755.60
  finger 755.50
    supernumerary 755.01
    webbed (*see also* Syndactylism, fingers) 755.11
  fixation, intestine 751.4
  flexion (joint) 755.9
    hip or thigh (*see also* Dislocation, hip, congenital) 754.30
  folds, heart 746.9
  foot 755.67

Anomaly, anomalous — *continued*
  foramen
    Botalli 745.5
    ovale 745.5
  forearm 755.50
  forehead (*see also* Anomaly, skull) 756.0
  form, teeth 520.2
  fovea centralis 743.9
  frontal bone (*see also* Anomaly, skull) 756.0
  gallbladder 751.60
  Gartner's duct 752.41
  gastrointestinal tract 751.9
    specified type NEC 751.8
    vessel 747.61
  genitalia, genital organ(s) or system
    female 752.9
      external 752.40
        specified type NEC 752.49
      internal NEC 752.9
    male (external and internal) 752.9
      epispadias 752.62
      hidden penis 752.65
      hydrocele, congenital 778.6
      hypospadias 752.61
      micropenis 752.64
      testis, undescended 752.51
        retractile 752.52
    specified type NEC 752.89
  genitourinary NEC 752.9
  Gerbode 745.4
  globe (eye) 743.9
  glottis 748.3
  granulation or granulocyte, genetic 288.2
    constitutional 288.2
    leukocyte 288.2
  gum 750.9
  gyri 742.9
  hair 757.9
    specified type NEC 757.4
  hand 755.50
  hard tissue formation in pulp 522.3
  head (*see also* Anomaly, skull) 756.0
  heart 746.9
    auricle 746.9
    bands 746.9
    fibroelastosis cordis 425.3
    folds 746.9
    malposition 746.87
    maternal, affecting fetus or newborn 760.3
    obstructive NEC 746.84
    patent ductus arteriosus (Botalli) 747.0
    septum 745.9
      acquired 429.71
      aortic 745.0
      aorticopulmonary 745.0
      atrial 745.5
      auricular 745.5
      between aorta and pulmonary artery 745.0
      endocardial cushion type 745.60
        specified type NEC 745.69
      interatrial 745.5
      interventricular 745.4
        with pulmonary stenosis or atresia, dextraposition of aorta, and hypertrophy of right ventricle 745.2
        acquired 429.71
      specified type NEC 745.8
      ventricular 745.4
        with pulmonary stenosis or atresia, dextraposition of aorta, and hypertrophy of right ventricle 745.2
        acquired 429.71
    specified type NEC 746.89
    tetralogy of Fallot 745.2
    valve NEC 746.9
      aortic 746.9
        atresia 746.89
        bicuspid valve 746.4
        insufficiency 746.4
        specified type NEC 746.89
        stenosis 746.3
          subaortic 746.81
          supravalvular 747.22

Anomaly, anomalous — *continued*
  heart — *continued*
    valve — *continued*
      mitral 746.9
        atresia 746.89
        insufficiency 746.6
        specified type NEC 746.89
        stenosis 746.5
      pulmonary 746.00
        atresia 746.01
        insufficiency 746.09
        stenosis 746.02
          infundibular 746.83
          subvalvular 746.83
      tricuspid 746.9
        atresia 746.1
        stenosis 746.1
    ventricle 746.9
  heel 755.67
  Hegglin's 288.2
  hemianencephaly 740.0
  hemicephaly 740.0
  hemicrania 740.0
  hepatic duct 751.60
  hip (joint) 755.63
  hourglass
    bladder 753.8
    gallbladder 751.69
    stomach 750.7
  humerus 755.50
  hymen 752.40
  hypersegmentation of neutrophils, hereditary 288.2
  hypophyseal 759.2
  ileocecal (coil) (valve) 751.5
  ileum (intestine) 751.5
  ilium 755.60
  integument 757.9
    specified type NEC 757.8
  interarch distance (excessive) (inadequate) 524.28
  intervertebral cartilage or disc 756.10
  intestine (large) (small) 751.5
    fixational type 751.4
  iris 743.9
    specified type NEC 743.46
  ischium 755.60
  jaw NEC 524.9
    closure 524.51
    size (major) NEC 524.00
    specified type NEC 524.89
  jaw-cranial base relationship 524.10
    specified NEC 524.19
  jejunum 751.5
  joint 755.9
    hip
      dislocation (*see also* Dislocation, hip, congenital) 754.30
      predislocation (*see also* Subluxation, congenital, hip) 754.32
      preluxation (*see also* Subluxation, congenital, hip) 754.32
      subluxation (*see also* Subluxation, congenital, hip) 754.32
    lumbosacral 756.10
      spondylolisthesis 756.12
      spondylosis 756.11
    multiple arthrogryposis 754.89
    sacroiliac 755.69
  Jordan's 288.2
  kidney(s) (calyx) (pelvis) 753.9
    vessel 747.62
  Klippel-Feil (brevicollis) 756.16
  knee (joint) 755.64
  labium (majus) (minus) 752.40
  labyrinth, membranous (causing impairment of hearing) 744.05
  lacrimal
    apparatus, duct or passage 743.9
      specified type NEC 743.65
    gland 743.9
      specified type NEC 743.64
  Langdon Down (mongolism) 758.0
  larynx, laryngeal (muscle) 748.3
    web, webbed 748.2
  leg (lower) (upper) 755.60

Anomaly, anomalous — *continued*
  leg — *continued*
    reduction NEC (*see also* Deformity, reduction, lower limb) 755.30
  lens 743.9
    shape 743.36
    specified type NEC 743.39
  leukocytes, genetic 288.2
    granulation (constitutional) 288.2
  lid (fold) 743.9
  ligament 756.9
    broad 752.10
    round 752.9
  limb, except reduction deformity 755.9
    lower 755.60
      reduction deformity (*see also* Deformity, reduction, lower limb) 755.30
      specified type NEC 755.69
    upper 755.50
      reduction deformity (*see also* Deformity, reduction, upper limb) 755.20
      specified type NEC 755.59
  lip 750.9
    harelip (*see also* Cleft, lip) 749.10
    specified type NEC 750.26
  liver (duct) 751.60
    atresia 751.69
  lower extremity 755.60
    vessel 747.64
  lumbosacral (joint) (region) 756.10
  lung (fissure) (lobe) NEC 748.60
    agenesis 748.5
    specified type NEC 748.69
  lymphatic system 759.9
  Madelung's (radius) 755.54
  mandible 524.9
    size NEC 524.00
  maxilla 524.9
    size NEC 524.00
  May (-Hegglin) 288.2
  meatus urinarius 753.9
    specified type NEC 753.8
  meningeal bands or folds, constriction of 742.8
  meninges 742.9
    brain 742.4
    spinal 742.59
  meningocele (*see also* Spina bifida) 741.9 ☑
    acquired 349.2
  mesentery 751.9
  metacarpus 755.50
  metatarsus 755.67
  middle ear, except ossicles (causing impairment of hearing) 744.03
    ossicles 744.04
  mitral (leaflets) (valve) 746.9
    atresia 746.89
    insufficiency 746.6
    specified type NEC 746.89
    stenosis 746.5
  mouth 750.9
    specified type NEC 750.26
  multiple NEC 759.7
    specified type NEC 759.89
  muscle 756.9
    eye 743.9
      specified type NEC 743.69
    specified type NEC 756.89
  musculoskeletal system, except limbs 756.9
    specified type NEC 756.9
  nail 757.9
    specified type NEC 757.5
  narrowness, eyelid 743.62
  nasal sinus or septum 748.1
  neck (any part) 744.9
    specified type NEC 744.89
  nerve 742.9
    acoustic 742.9
      specified type NEC 742.8
    optic 742.9
      specified type NEC 742.8
  nervous system NEC 742.9
    brain 742.9
      specified type NEC 742.4

☑ Additional Digit Required — Refer to the Tabular List for Digit Selection
▶◀ Revised Text   ● New Line   ▲ Revised Code
▽ Subterms under main terms may continue to next column or page
22 — Volume 2   2010 ICD-9-CM

Index

Anomaly, anomalous — *continued*
  specified type — *continued*
    round ligament 752.89
    sacrum 756.19
    salivary duct or gland 750.26
    scapula 755.59
    sclera 743.47
    scrotum 752.89
      transposition 752.81
    seminal duct or tract 752.89
    shoulder girdle 755.59
    site NEC 759.89
    skin 757.39
    skull (bone(s)) 756.0
      with
        anencephalus 740.0
        encephalocele 742.0
        hydrocephalus 742.3
          with spina bifida (*see also* Spina bifida) 741.0 ☑
        microcephalus 742.1
    specified organ or site NEC 759.89
    spermatic cord 752.89
    spinal cord 742.59
    spine 756.19
    spleen 759.0
    sternum 756.3
    stomach 750.7
    tarsus 755.67
    tendon 756.89
    testis 752.89
    thorax (wall) 756.3
    thymus 759.2
    thyroid (gland) 759.2
      cartilage 748.3
    tibia 755.69
    toe 755.66
    tongue 750.19
    trachea (cartilage) 748.3
    ulna 755.59
    urachus 753.7
    ureter 753.4
      obstructive 753.29
    urethra 753.8
      obstructive 753.6
    urinary tract 753.8
    uterus 752.3
    uvula 750.26
    vagina 752.49
    vascular NEC (*see also* Anomaly, peripheral vascular system) 747.60
      brain 747.81
    vas deferens 752.89
    vein(s) (peripheral) NEC (*see also* Anomaly, peripheral vascular system) 747.60
      brain 747.81
      great 747.49
      portal 747.49
      pulmonary 747.49
    vena cava (inferior) (superior) 747.49
    vertebra 756.19
    vulva 752.49
  spermatic cord 752.9
  spine, spinal 756.10
    column 756.10
    cord 742.9
      meningocele (*see also* Spina bifida) 741.9 ☑
      specified type NEC 742.59
      spina bifida (*see also* Spina bifida) 741.9 ☑
      vessel 747.82
    meninges 742.59
    nerve root 742.9
  spleen 759.0
  Sprengel's 755.52
  sternum 756.3
  stomach 750.9
    specified type NEC 750.7
  submaxillary gland 750.9
  superior vena cava 747.40
  talipes — *see* Talipes
  tarsus 755.67
    with complete absence of distal elements 755.31
  teeth, tooth NEC 520.9

Anomaly, anomalous — *continued*
  teeth, tooth — *continued*
    position 524.30
      crowding 524.31
      displacement 524.30
        horizontal 524.33
        vertical 524.34
      distance
        interocclusal
          excessive 524.37
          insufficient 524.36
        excessive spacing 524.32
      rotation 524.35
      specified NEC 524.39
    spacing 524.30
  tendon 756.9
    specified type NEC 756.89
  termination
    coronary artery 746.85
  testis 752.9
  thebesian valve 746.9
  thigh 755.60
    flexion (*see also* Subluxation, congenital, hip) 754.32
  thorax (wall) 756.3
  throat 750.9
  thumb 755.50
    supernumerary 755.01
  thymus gland 759.2
  thyroid (gland) 759.2
    cartilage 748.3
  tibia 755.60
    saber 090.5
  toe 755.66
    supernumerary 755.02
    webbed (*see also* Syndactylism, toes) 755.13
  tongue 750.10
    specified type NEC 750.19
  trachea, tracheal 748.3
    cartilage 748.3
    rings 748.3
  tragus 744.3
  transverse aortic arch 747.21
  trichromata 368.59
  trichromatopsia 368.59
  tricuspid (leaflet) (valve) 746.9
    atresia 746.1
    Ebstein's 746.2
    specified type NEC 746.89
    stenosis 746.1
  trunk 759.9
  Uhl's (hypoplasia of myocardium, right ventricle) 746.84
  ulna 755.50
  umbilicus 759.9
    artery 747.5
  union, trachea with larynx 748.3
  unspecified site 759.9
  upper extremity 755.50
    vessel 747.63
  urachus 753.7
    specified type NEC 753.7
  ureter 753.9
    obstructive 753.20
    specified type NEC 753.4
      obstructive 753.29
  urethra (valve) 753.9
    obstructive 753.6
    specified type NEC 753.8
  urinary tract or system (any part, except urachus) 753.9
    specified type NEC 753.8
    urachus 753.7
  uterus 752.3
    with only one functioning horn 752.3
    in pregnancy or childbirth 654.0 ☑
      affecting fetus or newborn 763.89
      causing obstructed labor 660.2 ☑
        affecting fetus or newborn 763.1
  uvula 750.9
  vagina 752.40
  valleculae 748.3
  valve (heart) NEC 746.9
    formation, ureter 753.29
    pulmonary 746.00

Anomaly, anomalous — *continued*
  valve — *continued*
    specified type NEC 746.89
    vascular NEC (*see also* Anomaly, peripheral vascular system) 747.60
    ring 747.21
  vas deferens 752.9
  vein(s) (peripheral) NEC (*see also* Anomaly, peripheral vascular system) 747.60
    brain 747.81
    cerebral 747.81
    coronary 746.89
    great 747.40
      specified type NEC 747.49
    portal 747.40
    pulmonary 747.40
    retina 743.9
  vena cava (inferior) (superior) 747.40
  venous — *see* Anomaly, vein
  venous return (pulmonary) 747.49
    partial 747.42
    total 747.41
  ventricle, ventricular (heart) 746.9
    bands 746.9
    folds 746.9
    septa 745.4
  vertebra 756.10
  vesicourethral orifice 753.9
  vessels NEC (*see also* Anomaly, peripheral vascular system) 747.60
    optic papilla 743.9
  vitelline duct 751.0
  vitreous humor 743.9
    specified type NEC 743.51
  vulva 752.40
  wrist (joint) 755.50
Anomia 784.69
Anonychia 757.5
  acquired 703.8
Anophthalmos, anophthalmus (clinical) (congenital) (globe) 743.00
  acquired V45.78
Anopsia (altitudinal) (quadrant) 368.46
Anorchia 752.89
Anorchism, anorchidism 752.89
Anorexia 783.0
  hysterical 300.11
  nervosa 307.1
Anosmia — *see also* Disturbance, sensation 781.1
  hysterical 300.11
  postinfectional 478.9
  psychogenic 306.7
  traumatic 951.8
Anosognosia 780.99
Anosphrasia 781.1
Anosteoplasia 756.50
Anotia 744.09
Anovulatory cycle 628.0
Anoxemia 799.02
  newborn 770.88
Anoxia 799.02
  altitude 993.2
  cerebral 348.1
    with
      abortion — *see* Abortion, by type, with specified complication NEC
      ectopic pregnancy (*see also* categories 633.0–633.9) 639.8
      molar pregnancy (*see also* categories 630–632) 639.8
    complicating
      delivery (cesarean) (instrumental) 669.4 ☑
      ectopic or molar pregnancy 639.8
      obstetric anesthesia or sedation 668.2 ☑
    during or resulting from a procedure 997.01
    following
      abortion 639.8
      ectopic or molar pregnancy 639.8
    newborn (*see also* Distress, fetal, liveborn infant) 770.88
  due to drowning 994.1
  fetal, affecting newborn 770.88
  heart — *see* Insufficiency, coronary

Anoxia — *continued*
  high altitude 993.2
  intrauterine
    fetal death (before onset of labor) 768.0
      during labor 768.1
    liveborn infant — *see* Distress, fetal, liveborn infant
  myocardial — *see* Insufficiency, coronary
  newborn 768.9
    mild or moderate 768.6
    severe 768.5
  pathological 799.02
Anteflexion — *see* Anteversion
Antenatal
  care, normal pregnancy V22.1
    first V22.0
  sampling
    chorionic villus V28.89
  screening of mother (for) V28.9
    based on amniocentesis NEC V28.2
      chromosomal anomalies V28.0
      raised alphafetoprotein levels V28.1
    chromosomal anomalies V28.0
    fetal growth retardation using ultrasonics V28.4
    genomic V28.89
    isoimmunization V28.5
    malformations using ultrasonics V28.3
    proteomic V28.89
    raised alphafetoprotein levels in amniotic fluid V28.1
    risk
      pre-term labor V28.82
    specified condition NEC V28.89
    Streptococcus B V28.6
  survey
    fetal anatomic V28.81
  testing
    nuchal translucency V28.89
Antepartum — *see* condition
Anterior — *see also* condition
  spinal artery compression syndrome 721.1
Antero-occlusion 524.24
Anteversion
  cervix — *see* Anteversion, uterus
  femur (neck), congenital 755.63
  uterus, uterine (cervix) (postinfectional) (postpartal, old) 621.6
    congenital 752.3
    in pregnancy or childbirth 654.4 ☑
      affecting fetus or newborn 763.89
      causing obstructed labor 660.2 ☑
        affecting fetus or newborn 763.1
Anthracosilicosis (occupational) 500
Anthracosis (lung) (occupational) 500
  lingua 529.3
Anthrax 022.9
  with pneumonia 022.1 *[484.5]*
  colitis 022.2
  cutaneous 022.0
  gastrointestinal 022.2
  intestinal 022.2
  pulmonary 022.1
  respiratory 022.1
  septicemia 022.3
  specified manifestation NEC 022.8
Anthropoid pelvis 755.69
  with disproportion (fetopelvic) 653.2 ☑
    affecting fetus or newborn 763.1
    causing obstructed labor 660.1 ☑
      affecting fetus or newborn 763.1
Anthropophobia 300.29
Antibioma, breast 611.0
Antibodies
  maternal (blood group) (*see also* Incompatibility) 656.2 ☑
    anti-D, cord blood 656.1 ☑
      fetus or newborn 773.0
Antibody deficiency syndrome
  agammaglobulinemic 279.00
  congenital 279.04
  hypogammaglobulinemic 279.00
Anticoagulant, ▶intrinsic,◄ circulating, ▶causing hemorrhagic disorder◄
  see also Circulating anticoagulants 286.5
Antimongolism syndrome 758.39

Anomaly, anomalous — Antimongolism syndrome

Antimonial cholera 985.4
Antisocial personality 301.7
Antithrombinemia — see also Circulating anti-
    coagulants 286.5
Antithromboplastinemia — see also Circulating
    anticoagulants 286.5
Antithromboplastinogenemia — see also Cir-
    culating anticoagulants 286.5
Antitoxin complication or reaction — see
    Complications, vaccination
Anton (-Babinski) syndrome (hemiasomatog-
    nosia) 307.9
Antritis (chronic) 473.0
    maxilla 473.0
        acute 461.0
    stomach 535.4 ☑
Antrum, antral — see condition
Anuria 788.5
    with
        abortion — see Abortion, by type, with
            renal failure
        ectopic pregnancy (see also categories
            633.0–633.9) 639.3
        molar pregnancy (see also categories
            630–632) 639.3
    calculus (impacted) (recurrent) 592.9
        kidney 592.0
        ureter 592.1
    congenital 753.3
    due to a procedure 997.5
    following
        abortion 639.3
        ectopic or molar pregnancy 639.3
    newborn 753.3
    postrenal 593.4
    puerperal, postpartum, childbirth 669.3 ☑
    specified as due to a procedure 997.5
    sulfonamide
        correct substance properly administered
            788.5
        overdose or wrong substance given or
            taken 961.0
    traumatic (following crushing) 958.5
Anus, anal — see also condition
    high risk human papillomavirus (HPV) DNA
        test positive 796.75
    low risk human papillomavirus (HPV) DNA test
        positive 796.79
Anusitis 569.49
Anxiety (neurosis) (reaction) (state) 300.00
    alcohol-induced 291.89
    depression 300.4
    drug-induced 292.89
    due to or associated with physical condition
        293.84
    generalized 300.02
    hysteria 300.20
    in
        acute stress reaction 308.0
        transient adjustment reaction 309.24
    panic type 300.01
    separation, abnormal 309.21
    syndrome (organic) (transient) 293.84
Aorta, aortic — see condition
Aortectasia 441.9
Aortitis (nonsyphilitic) 447.6
    arteriosclerotic 440.0
    calcific 447.6
    Döhle-Heller 093.1
    luetic 093.1
    rheumatic (see also Endocarditis, acute,
        rheumatic) 391.1
    rheumatoid — see Arthritis, rheumatoid
    specific 093.1
    syphilitic 093.1
        congenital 090.5
Apathetic 799.25 ▲
    thyroid storm (see also Thyrotoxicosis) ●
        242.9 ☑ ●
Apathy 799.25 ●
Apepsia 536.8
    achlorhydric 536.0
    psychogenic 306.4
Aperistalsis, esophagus 530.0
Apert-Gallais syndrome (adrenogenital) 255.2
Apertognathia 524.20

Apert's syndrome (acrocephalosyndactyly)
    755.55
Aphagia 787.20
    psychogenic 307.1
Aphakia (acquired) (bilateral) (postoperative)
    (unilateral) 379.31
    congenital 743.35
Aphalangia (congenital) 755.4
    lower limb (complete) (intercalary) (partial)
        (terminal) 755.39
        meaning all digits (complete) (partial)
            755.31
        transverse 755.31
    upper limb (complete) (intercalary) (partial)
        (terminal) 755.29
        meaning all digits (complete) (partial)
            755.21
        transverse 755.21
Aphasia (amnestic) (ataxic) (auditory) (Broca's)
    (choreatic) (classic) (expressive) (global)
    (ideational) (ideokinetic) (ideomotor) (jar-
    gon) (motor) (nominal) (receptive) (seman-
    tic) (sensory) (syntactic) (verbal) (visual)
    (Wernicke's) 784.3
    developmental 315.31
    syphilis, tertiary 094.89
    uremic — see Uremia
Aphemia 784.3
    uremic — see Uremia
Aphonia 784.41
    clericorum 784.49
    hysterical 300.11
    organic 784.41
    psychogenic 306.1
Aphthae, aphthous — see also condition
    Bednar's 528.2
    cachectic 529.0
    epizootic 078.4
    fever 078.4
    oral 528.2
    stomatitis 528.2
    thrush 112.0
    ulcer (oral) (recurrent) 528.2
        genital organ(s) NEC
            female 616.50
            male 608.89
        larynx 478.79
Apical — see condition
Apical ballooning syndrome 429.83
Aplasia — see also Agenesis
    alveolar process (acquired) 525.8
        congenital 750.26
    aorta (congenital) 747.22
    aortic valve (congenital) 746.89
    axialis extracorticalis (congenital) 330.0
    bone marrow (myeloid) 284.9
        acquired (secondary) 284.89
        congenital 284.01
        idiopathic 284.9
    brain 740.0
        specified part 742.2
    breast 757.6
    bronchus 748.3
    cementum 520.4
    cerebellar 742.2
    congenital (pure) red cell 284.01
    corpus callosum 742.2
    erythrocyte 284.81
        congenital 284.01
    extracortical axial 330.0
    eye (congenital) 743.00
    fovea centralis (congenital) 743.55
    germinal (cell) 606.0
    iris 743.45
    labyrinth, membranous 744.05
    limb (congenital) 755.4
        lower NEC 755.30
        upper NEC 755.20
    lung (bilateral) (congenital) (unilateral) 748.5
    nervous system NEC 742.8
    nuclear 742.8
    ovary 752.0
    Pelizaeus-Merzbacher 330.0
    prostate (congenital) 752.89
    red cell (with thymoma) (adult) 284.81
        acquired (secondary) 284.81

Aplasia — see also Agenesis — continued
    red cell — continued
        congenital 284.01
        hereditary 284.01
        of infants 284.01
        primary 284.01
        pure 284.01
    round ligament (congenital) 752.89
    salivary gland 750.21
    skin (congenital) 757.39
    spinal cord 742.59
    spleen 759.0
    testis (congenital) 752.89
    thymic, with immunodeficiency 279.2
    thyroid 243
    uterus 752.3
    ventral horn cell 742.59
Apleuria 756.3
Apnea, apneic (spells) 786.03
    newborn, neonatorum 770.81
        essential 770.81
        obstructive 770.82
        primary 770.81
        sleep 770.81
        specified NEC 770.82
    psychogenic 306.1
    sleep, unspecified 780.57
        with
            hypersomnia, unspecified 780.53
            hyposomnia, unspecified 780.51
            insomnia, unspecified 780.51
            sleep disturbance 780.57
        central, in conditions classified elsewhere
            327.27
        obstructive (adult) (pediatric) 327.23
        organic 327.20
        other 327.29
        primary central 327.21
Apneumatosis newborn 770.4
Apodia 755.31
Aponeurosis 726.90
Apophysitis (bone) — see also Osteochondrosis
    732.9
    calcaneus 732.5
    juvenile 732.6
Apoplectiform convulsions — see also Disease,
    cerebrovascular, acute 436
Apoplexia, apoplexy, apoplectic — see also
    Disease, cerebrovascular, acute 436
    abdominal 569.89
    adrenal 036.3
    attack 436
    basilar (see also Disease, cerebrovascular,
        acute) 436
    brain (see also Disease, cerebrovascular, acute)
        436
    bulbar (see also Disease, cerebrovascular,
        acute) 436
    capillary (see also Disease, cerebrovascular,
        acute) 436
    cardiac (see also Infarct, myocardium) 410.9 ☑
    cerebral (see also Disease, cerebrovascular,
        acute) 436
    chorea (see also Disease, cerebrovascular,
        acute) 436
    congestive (see also Disease, cerebrovascular,
        acute) 436
        newborn 767.4
    embolic (see also Embolism, brain) 434.1 ☑
    fetus 767.0
    fit (see also Disease, cerebrovascular, acute)
        436
    healed or old V12.54
    heart (auricle) (ventricle) (see also Infarct, my-
        ocardium) 410.9 ☑
    heat 992.0
    hemiplegia (see also Disease, cerebrovascular,
        acute) 436
    hemorrhagic (stroke) (see also Hemorrhage,
        brain) 432.9
    ingravescent (see also Disease, cerebrovascular,
        acute) 436
    late effect — see Late effect(s) (of) cerebrovas-
        cular disease
    lung — see Embolism, pulmonary

Apoplexia, apoplexy, apoplectic — see also
    Disease, cerebrovascular, acute —
    continued
    meninges, hemorrhagic (see also Hemorrhage,
        subarachnoid) 430
    neonatorum 767.0
    newborn 767.0
    pancreatitis 577.0
    placenta 641.2 ☑
    progressive (see also Disease, cerebrovascular,
        acute) 436
    pulmonary (artery) (vein) — see Embolism,
        pulmonary
    sanguineous (see also Disease, cerebrovascular,
        acute) 436
    seizure (see also Disease, cerebrovascular,
        acute) 436
    serous (see also Disease, cerebrovascular,
        acute) 436
    spleen 289.59
    stroke (see also Disease, cerebrovascular, acute)
        436
    thrombotic (see also Thrombosis, brain)
        434.0 ☑
    uremic — see Uremia
    uteroplacental 641.2 ☑
Appendage
    fallopian tube (cyst of Morgagni) 752.11
    intestine (epiploic) 751.5
    preauricular 744.1
    testicular (organ of Morgagni) 752.89
Appendicitis 541
    with
        perforation, peritonitis (generalized), or
            rupture 540.0
            with peritoneal abscess 540.1
        peritoneal abscess 540.1
    acute (catarrhal) (fulminating) (gangrenous)
        (inflammatory) (obstructive) (retroce-
        cal) (suppurative) 540.9
        with
            perforation, peritonitis, or rupture 540.0
                with peritoneal abscess 540.1
            peritoneal abscess 540.1
    amebic 006.8
    chronic (recurrent) 542
    exacerbation — see Appendicitis, acute
    fulminating — see Appendicitis, acute
    gangrenous — see Appendicitis, acute
    healed (obliterative) 542
    interval 542
    neurogenic 542
    obstructive 542
    pneumococcal 541
    recurrent 542
    relapsing 542
    retrocecal 541
    subacute (adhesive) 542
    subsiding 542
    suppurative — see Appendicitis, acute
    tuberculous (see also Tuberculosis) 014.8 ☑
Appendiclausis 543.9
Appendicolithiasis 543.9
Appendicopathia oxyurica 127.4
Appendix, appendicular — see also condition
    Morgagni (male) 752.89
        fallopian tube 752.11
Appetite
    depraved 307.52
    excessive 783.6
        psychogenic 307.51
    lack or loss (see also Anorexia) 783.0
        nonorganic origin 307.59
    perverted 307.52
        hysterical 300.11
Apprehension, apprehensiveness (abnormal)
    (state) 300.00
    specified type NEC 300.09
Approximal wear 521.10
Apraxia (classic) (ideational) (ideokinetic) (ideo-
    motor) (motor) 784.69
    oculomotor, congenital 379.51
    verbal 784.69
Aptyalism 527.7
Aqueous misdirection 365.83

☑ Additional Digit Required — Refer to the Tabular List for Digit Selection   ▽ Subterms under main terms may continue to next column or page

2010 ICD-9-CM   ▶◄ Revised Text   ● New Line   ▲ Revised Code   October 2009 · Volume 2 — 25

Arabicum elephantiasis — *see also* Infestation, filarial 125.9
Arachnidism 989.5
Arachnitis — *see* Meningitis
Arachnodactyly 759.82
Arachnoidism 989.5
Arachnoiditis (acute) (adhesive) (basic) (brain) (cerebrospinal) (chiasmal) (chronic) (spinal) — *see also* Meningitis 322.9
  meningococcal (chronic) 036.0
  syphilitic 094.2
  tuberculous (*see also* Tuberculosis, meninges) 013.0 ☑
Araneism 989.5
Arboencephalitis, Australian 062.4
Arborization block (heart) 426.6
Arbor virus, arbovirus (infection) NEC 066.9
ARC 042
Arches — *see* condition
Arcuatus uterus 752.3
Arcus (cornea)
  juvenilis 743.43
    interfering with vision 743.42
  senilis 371.41
Arc-welders' lung 503
Arc-welders' syndrome (photokeratitis) 370.24
Areflexia 796.1
Areola — *see* condition
Argentaffinoma (M8241/1) — *see also* Neoplasm, by site, uncertain behavior
  benign (M8241/0) — *see* Neoplasm, by site, benign
  malignant (M8241/3) — *see* Neoplasm, by site, malignant
  syndrome 259.2
Argentinian hemorrhagic fever 078.7
Arginosuccinicaciduria 270.6
Argonz-Del Castillo syndrome (nonpuerperal galactorrhea and amenorrhea) 253.1
Argyll-Robertson phenomenon, pupil, or syndrome (syphilitic) 094.89
  atypical 379.45
  nonluetic 379.45
  nonsyphilitic 379.45
  reversed 379.45
Argyria, argyriasis NEC 985.8
  conjunctiva 372.55
  cornea 371.16
  from drug or medicinal agent
    correct substance properly administered 709.09
    overdose or wrong substance given or taken 961.2
Arhinencephaly 742.2
Arias-Stella phenomenon 621.30
Ariboflavinosis 266.0
Arizona enteritis 008.1
Arm — *see* condition
Armenian disease 277.31
Arnold-Chiari obstruction or syndrome — *see also* Spina bifida 741.0 ☑
  type I 348.4
  type II (*see also* Spina bifida) 741.0 ☑
  type III 742.0
  type IV 742.2
Arousals
  confusional 327.41
Arrest, arrested
  active phase of labor 661.1 ☑
    affecting fetus or newborn 763.7
  any plane in pelvis
    complicating delivery 660.1 ☑
      affecting fetus or newborn 763.1
  bone marrow (*see also* Anemia, aplastic) 284.9
  cardiac 427.5
    with
      abortion — *see* Abortion, by type, with specified complication NEC
      ectopic pregnancy (*see also* categories 633.0–633.9) 639.8
      molar pregnancy (*see also* categories 630–632) 639.8
    complicating
      anesthesia
        correct substance properly administered 427.5

Arrest, arrested — *continued*
  cardiac — *continued*
    complicating — *continued*
      anesthesia — *continued*
        obstetric 668.1 ☑
        overdose or wrong substance given 968.4
        specified anesthetic — *see* Table of Drugs and Chemicals
      delivery (cesarean) (instrumental) 669.4 ☑
      ectopic or molar pregnancy 639.8
      surgery (nontherapeutic) (therapeutic) 997.1
    fetus or newborn 779.85
    following
      abortion 639.8
      ectopic or molar pregnancy 639.8
    personal history, successfully resuscitated V12.53
    postoperative (immediate) 997.1
      long-term effect of cardiac surgery 429.4
  cardiorespiratory (*see also* Arrest, cardiac) 427.5
  deep transverse 660.3 ☑
    affecting fetus or newborn 763.1
  development or growth
    bone 733.91
    child 783.40
    fetus 764.9 ☑
      affecting management of pregnancy 656.5 ☑
    tracheal rings 748.3
  epiphyseal 733.91
  granulopoiesis 288.09
  heart — *see* Arrest, cardiac
  respiratory 799.1
    newborn 770.87
  sinus 426.6
  transverse (deep) 660.3 ☑
    affecting fetus or newborn 763.1
Arrhenoblastoma (M8630/1)
  benign (M8630/0)
    specified site — *see* Neoplasm, by site, benign
    unspecified site
      female 220
      male 222.0
  malignant (M8630/3)
    specified site — *see* Neoplasm, by site, malignant
    unspecified site
      female 183.0
      male 186.9
  specified site — *see* Neoplasm, by site, uncertain behavior
  unspecified site
    female 236.2
    male 236.4
Arrhinencephaly 742.2
  due to
    trisomy 13 (13-15) 758.1
    trisomy 18 (16-18) 758.2
Arrhythmia (auricle) (cardiac) (cordis) (gallop rhythm) (juvenile) (nodal) (reflex) (sinus) (supraventricular) (transitory) (ventricle) 427.9
  bigeminal rhythm 427.89
  block 426.9
  bradycardia 427.89
  contractions, premature 427.60
  coronary sinus 427.89
  ectopic 427.89
  extrasystolic 427.60
  postoperative 997.1
  psychogenic 306.2
  vagal 780.2
Arrillaga-Ayerza syndrome (pulmonary artery sclerosis with pulmonary hypertension) 416.0
Arsenical
  dermatitis 692.4
  keratosis 692.4
  pigmentation 985.1

Arsenical — *continued*
  pigmentation — *continued*
    from drug or medicinal agent
      correct substance properly administered 709.09
      overdose or wrong substance given or taken 961.1
Arsenism 985.1
  from drug or medicinal agent
    correct substance properly administered 692.4
    overdose or wrong substance given or taken 961.1
Arterial — *see* condition
Arteriectasis 447.8
Arteriofibrosis — *see* Arteriosclerosis
Arteriolar sclerosis — *see* Arteriosclerosis
Arteriolith — *see* Arteriosclerosis
Arteriolitis 447.6
  necrotizing, kidney 447.5
  renal — *see* Hypertension, kidney
Arteriolosclerosis — *see* Arteriosclerosis
Arterionephrosclerosis — *see also* Hypertension, kidney 403.90
Arteriopathy 447.9
Arteriosclerosis, arteriosclerotic (artery) (deformans) (diffuse) (disease) (endarteritis) (general) (obliterans) (obliterative) (occlusive) (senile) (with calcification) 440.9
  with
    gangrene 440.24
    psychosis (*see also* Psychosis, arteriosclerotic) 290.40
    ulceration 440.23
  aorta 440.0
  arteries of extremities — *see* Arteriosclerosis, extremities
  basilar (artery) (*see also* Occlusion, artery, basilar) 433.0 ☑
  brain 437.0
  bypass graft
    coronary artery 414.05
      autologous artery (gastroepiploic) (internal mammary) 414.04
      autologous vein 414.02
      nonautologous biological 414.03
      of transplanted heart 414.07
    extremity 440.30
      autologous vein 440.31
      nonautologous biological 440.32
  cardiac — *see* Arteriosclerosis, coronary
  cardiopathy — *see* Arteriosclerosis, coronary
  cardiorenal (*see also* Hypertension, cardiorenal) 404.90
  cardiovascular (*see also* Disease, cardiovascular) 429.2
  carotid (artery) (common) (internal) (*see also* Occlusion, artery, carotid) 433.1 ☑
  central nervous system 437.0
  cerebral 437.0
    late effect — *see* Late effect(s) (of) cerebrovascular disease
  cerebrospinal 437.0
  cerebrovascular 437.0
  coronary (artery) 414.00
    due to lipid rich plaque 414.3
    graft — *see* Arteriosclerosis, bypass graft
    native artery 414.01
      of transplanted heart 414.06
  extremities (native artery) NEC 440.20
    bypass graft 440.30
      autologous vein 440.31
      nonautologous biological 440.32
    claudication (intermittent) 440.21
      and
        gangrene 440.24
        rest pain 440.22
          and
            gangrene 440.24
            ulceration 440.23
              and gangrene 440.24
        ulceration 440.23
          and gangrene 440.24
    gangrene 440.24
    rest pain 440.22

Arteriosclerosis, arteriosclerotic — *continued*
  extremities — *continued*
    rest pain — *continued*
      and
        gangrene 440.24
        ulceration 440.23
          and gangrene 440.24
    specified site NEC 440.29
    ulceration 440.23
      and gangrene 440.24
  heart (disease) (*see also* Arteriosclerosis, coronary)
    valve 424.99
      aortic 424.1
      mitral 424.0
      pulmonary 424.3
      tricuspid 424.2
  kidney (*see also* Hypertension, kidney) 403.90
  labyrinth, labyrinthine 388.00
  medial NEC (*see also* Arteriosclerosis, extremities) 440.20
  mesentery (artery) 557.1
  Mönckeberg's (*see also* Arteriosclerosis, extremities) 440.20
  myocarditis 429.0
  nephrosclerosis (*see also* Hypertension, kidney) 403.90
  peripheral (of extremities) — *see* Arteriosclerosis, extremities
  precerebral 433.9 ☑
    specified artery NEC 433.8 ☑
  pulmonary (idiopathic) 416.0
  renal (*see also* Hypertension, kidney) 403.90
    arterioles (*see also* Hypertension, kidney) 403.90
    artery 440.1
  retinal (vascular) 440.8 [362.13]
  specified artery NEC 440.8
    with gangrene 440.8 [785.4]
  spinal (cord) 437.0
  vertebral (artery) (*see also* Occlusion, artery, vertebral) 433.2 ☑
Arteriospasm 443.9
Arteriovenous — *see* condition
Arteritis 447.6
  allergic (*see also* Angiitis, hypersensitivity) 446.20
  aorta (nonsyphilitic) 447.6
    syphilitic 093.1
  aortic arch 446.7
  brachiocephalica 446.7
  brain 437.4
    syphilitic 094.89
  branchial 446.7
  cerebral 437.4
    late effect — *see* Late effect(s) (of) cerebrovascular disease
    syphilitic 094.89
  coronary (artery) (*see also* Arteriosclerosis, coronary)
    rheumatic 391.9
      chronic 398.99
    syphilitic 093.89
  cranial (left) (right) 446.5
  deformans — *see* Arteriosclerosis
  giant cell 446.5
  necrosing or necrotizing 446.0
  nodosa 446.0
  obliterans (*see also* Arteriosclerosis)
    subclaviocarotica 446.7
  pulmonary 417.8
  retina 362.18
  rheumatic — *see* Fever, rheumatic
  senile — *see* Arteriosclerosis
  suppurative 447.2
  syphilitic (general) 093.89
    brain 094.89
    coronary 093.89
    spinal 094.89
  temporal 446.5
  young female, syndrome 446.7
Artery, arterial — *see* condition
Arthralgia — *see also* Pain, joint 719.4 ☑
  allergic (*see also* Pain, joint) 719.4 ☑
  in caisson disease 993.3

Arthralgia — see also Pain, joint — continued
  psychogenic 307.89
  rubella 056.71
  Salmonella 003.23
  temporomandibular joint 524.62
Arthritis, arthritic (acute) (chronic) (subacute)
  716.9 ☑
  meaning Osteoarthritis — see Osteoarthrosis

> Note — Use the following fifth-digit subclas-
> sification with categories 711–712, 715–716:
>
> 0   site unspecified
> 1   shoulder region
> 2   upper arm
> 3   forearm
> 4   hand
> 5   pelvic region and thigh
> 6   lower leg
> 7   ankle and foot
> 8   other specified sites
> 9   multiple sites

  allergic 716.2 ☑
  ankylosing (crippling) (spine) 720.0
   sites other than spine 716.9 ☑
  atrophic 714.0
   spine 720.9
  back (see also Arthritis, spine) 721.90
  Bechterew's (ankylosing spondylitis) 720.0
  blennorrhagic 098.50
  cervical, cervicodorsal (see also Spondylosis,
   cervical) 721.0
  Charcôt's 094.0 [713.5]
   diabetic 250.6 ☑ [713.5]
    due to secondary diabetes
     249.6 ☑ [713.5]
   syringomyelic 336.0 [713.5]
   tabetic 094.0 [713.5]
  chylous (see also Filariasis) 125.9 [711.7] ☑
  climacteric NEC 716.3 ☑
  coccyx 721.8
  cricoarytenoid 478.79
  crystal (-induced) — see Arthritis, due to crystals
  deformans (see also Osteoarthrosis) 715.9 ☑
   spine 721.90
    with myelopathy 721.91
  degenerative (see also Osteoarthrosis) 715.9 ☑
   idiopathic 715.09
   polyarticular 715.09
   spine 721.90
    with myelopathy 721.91
  dermatoarthritis, lipoid 272.8 [713.0]
  due to or associated with
   acromegaly 253.0 [713.0]
   actinomycosis 039.8 [711.4] ☑
   amyloidosis 277.39 [713.7]
   bacterial disease NEC 040.89 [711.4] ☑
   Behçet's syndrome 136.1 [711.2] ☑
   blastomycosis 116.0 [711.6] ☑
   brucellosis (see also Brucellosis)
    023.9 [711.4] ☑
   caisson disease 993.3
   coccidioidomycosis 114.3 [711.6] ☑
   coliform (Escherichia coli) 711.0 ☑
   colitis, ulcerative (see also Colitis, ulcerative)
    556.9 [713.1]
   cowpox 051.01 [711.5] ☑
   crystals (see also Gout)
    dicalcium phosphate 275.49 [712.1] ☑
    pyrophosphate 275.49 [712.2] ☑
    specified NEC 275.49 [712.8] ☑
   dermatoarthritis, lipoid 272.8 [713.0]
   dermatological disorder NEC 709.9 [713.3]
   diabetes 250.6 ☑ [713.5]
    due to secondary diabetes
     249.6 ☑ [713.5]
   diphtheria 032.89 [711.4] ☑
   dracontiasis 125.7 [711.7] ☑
   dysentery 009.0 [711.3] ☑
   endocrine disorder NEC 259.9 [713.0]
   enteritis NEC 009.1 [711.3] ☑

Arthritis, arthritic — continued
  due to or associated with — continued
   enteritis — continued
    infectious (see also Enteritis, infectious)
     009.0 [711.3] ☑
    specified organism NEC
     008.8 [711.3] ☑
    regional (see also Enteritis, regional)
     555.9 [713.1]
    specified organism NEC
     008.8 [711.3] ☑
   epiphyseal slip, nontraumatic (old)
    716.8 ☑
   erysipelas 035 [711.4] ☑
   erythema
    epidemic 026.1
    multiforme 695.10 [713.3]
    nodosum 695.2 [713.3]
   Escherichia coli 711.0 ☑
   filariasis NEC 125.9 [711.7] ☑
   gastrointestinal condition NEC
    569.9 [713.1]
   glanders 024 [711.4] ☑
   Gonococcus 098.50
   gout 274.00 ▲
   helminthiasis NEC 128.9 [711.7] ☑
   hematological disorder NEC 289.9 [713.2]
   hemochromatosis 275.0 [713.0]
   hemoglobinopathy NEC (see also Disease,
    hemoglobin) 282.7 [713.2]
   hemophilia (see also Hemophilia)
    286.0 [713.2]
   Hemophilus influenzae (H. influenzae)
    711.0 ☑
   Henoch (-Schönlein) purpura 287.0 [713.6]
   H. influenzae 711.0 ☑
   histoplasmosis NEC (see also Histoplasmo-
    sis) 115.99 [711.6] ☑
   human parvovirus 079.83 [711.5] ☑
   hyperparathyroidism 252.00 [713.0]
   hypersensitivity reaction NEC 995.3 [713.6]
   hypogammaglobulinemia (see also Hy-
    pogamma-globulinemia)
    279.00 [713.0]
   hypothyroidism NEC 244.9 [713.0]
   infection (see also Arthritis, infectious)
    711.9 ☑
   infectious disease NEC 136.9 [711.8] ☑
   leprosy (see also Leprosy) 030.9 [711.4] ☑
   leukemia NEC (M9800/3) 208.9 [713.2]
   lipoid dermatoarthritis 272.8 [713.0]
   Lyme disease 088.81 [711.8] ☑
   Mediterranean fever, familial 277.31 [713.7]
   meningococcal infection 036.82
   metabolic disorder NEC 277.9 [713.0]
   multiple myelomatosis (M9730/3) 203.0
    [713.2]
   mumps 072.79 [711.5] ☑
   mycobacteria 031.8 [711.4] ☑
   mycosis NEC 117.9 [711.6] ☑
   neurological disorder NEC 349.9 [713.5]
   ochronosis 270.2 [713.0]
   O'Nyong Nyong 066.3 [711.5] ☑
   parasitic disease NEC 136.9 [711.8] ☑
   paratyphoid fever (see also Fever, paraty-
    phoid) 002.9 [711.3] ☑
   parvovirus B19 079.83 [711.5] ☑
   Pneumococcus 711.0 ☑
   poliomyelitis (see also Poliomyelitis)
    045.9 ☑ [711.5] ☑
   Pseudomonas 711.0 ☑
   psoriasis 696.0
   pyogenic organism (E. coli) (H. influenzae)
    (Pseudomonas) (Streptococcus)
    711.0 ☑
   rat-bite fever 026.1 [711.4] ☑
   regional enteritis (see also Enteritis, region-
    al) 555.9 [713.1]
   Reiter's disease 099.3 [711.1] ☑
   respiratory disorder NEC 519.9 [713.4]
   reticulosis, malignant (M9720/3) 202.3
    [713.2]
   rubella 056.71
   salmonellosis 003.23
   sarcoidosis 135 [713.7]

Arthritis, arthritic — continued
  due to or associated with — continued
   serum sickness 999.5 [713.6]
   Staphylococcus 711.0 ☑
   Streptococcus 711.0 ☑
   syphilis (see also Syphilis) 094.0 [711.4] ☑
   syringomyelia 336.0 [713.5]
   thalassemia 282.49 [713.2]
   tuberculosis (see also Tuberculosis, arthritis)
    015.9 ☑ [711.4] ☑
   typhoid fever 002.0 [711.3] ☑
   ulcerative colitis (see also Colitis, ulcerative)
    556.9 [713.1]
   urethritis
    nongonococcal (see also Urethritis,
     nongonococcal)
     099.40 [711.1] ☑
    nonspecific (see also Urethritis, non-
     gonococcal) 099.40 [711.1] ☑
    Reiter's 099.3
   viral disease NEC 079.99 [711.5] ☑
  erythema epidemic 026.1
  gonococcal 098.50
  gouty 274.00 ▲
   acute 274.01 ●
  hypertrophic (see also Osteoarthrosis) 715.9 ☑
   spine 721.90
    with myelopathy 721.91
  idiopathic, blennorrheal 099.3
  in caisson disease 993.3 [713.8]
  infectious or infective (acute) (chronic) (subacute) NEC 711.9 ☑
   nonpyogenic 711.9 ☑
   spine 720.9
  inflammatory NEC 714.9
  juvenile rheumatoid (chronic) (polyarticular)
   714.30
   acute 714.31
   monoarticular 714.33
   pauciarticular 714.32
  lumbar (see also Spondylosis, lumbar) 721.3
  meningococcal 036.82
  menopausal NEC 716.3 ☑
  migratory — see Fever, rheumatic
  neuropathic (Charcôt's) 094.0 [713.5]
   diabetic 250.6 ☑ [713.5]
    due to secondary diabetes
     249.6 ☑ [713.5]
   nonsyphilitic NEC 349.9 [713.5]
   syringomyelic 336.0 [713.5]
   tabetic 094.0 [713.5]
  nodosa (see also Osteoarthrosis) 715.9 ☑
   spine 721.90
    with myelopathy 721.91
  nonpyogenic NEC 716.9 ☑
   spine 721.90
    with myelopathy 721.91
  ochronotic 270.2 [713.0]
  palindromic (see also Rheumatism, palindromic) 719.3 ☑
  pneumococcal 711.0 ☑
  postdysenteric 009.0 [711.3] ☑
  postrheumatic, chronic (Jaccoud's) 714.4
  primary progressive 714.0
   spine 720.9
  proliferative 714.0
   spine 720.0
  psoriatic 696.0
  purulent 711.0 ☑
  pyogenic or pyemic 711.0 ☑
  rheumatic 714.0
   acute or subacute — see Fever, rheumatic
   chronic 714.0
   spine 720.9
  rheumatoid (nodular) 714.0
   with
    splenoadenomegaly and leukopenia
     714.1
    visceral or systemic involvement 714.2
   aortitis 714.89
   carditis 714.2
   heart disease 714.2
   juvenile (chronic) (polyarticular) 714.30
    acute 714.31
    monoarticular 714.33
    pauciarticular 714.32

Arthritis, arthritic — continued
  rheumatoid — continued
   spine 720.0
  rubella 056.71
  sacral, sacroiliac, sacrococcygeal (see also
   Spondylosis, sacral) 721.3
  scorbutic 267
  senile or senescent (see also Osteoarthrosis)
   715.9 ☑
   spine 721.90
    with myelopathy 721.91
  septic 711.0 ☑
  serum (nontherapeutic) (therapeutic)
   999.5 [713.6]
  specified form NEC 716.8 ☑
  spine 721.90
   with myelopathy 721.91
   atrophic 720.9
   degenerative 721.90
    with myelopathy 721.91
   hypertrophic (with deformity) 721.90
    with myelopathy 721.91
   infectious or infective NEC 720.9
   Marie-Strümpell 720.0
   nonpyogenic 721.90
    with myelopathy 721.91
   pyogenic 720.9
   rheumatoid 720.0
   traumatic (old) 721.7
   tuberculous (see also Tuberculosis)
    015.0 ☑ [720.81]
  staphylococcal 711.0 ☑
  streptococcal 711.0 ☑
  suppurative 711.0 ☑
  syphilitic 094.0 [713.5]
   congenital 090.49 [713.5]
  syphilitica deformans (Charcôt) 094.0 [713.5]
  temporomandibular joint 524.69
  thoracic (see also Spondylosis, thoracic) 721.2
  toxic of menopause 716.3 ☑
  transient 716.4 ☑
  traumatic (chronic) (old) (post) 716.1 ☑
   current injury — see nature of injury
  tuberculous (see also Tuberculosis, arthritis)
   015.9 ☑ [711.4] ☑
  urethritica 099.3 [711.1] ☑
  urica, uratic 274.00 ▲
  venereal 099.3 [711.1] ☑
  vertebral (see also Arthritis, spine) 721.90
  villous 716.8 ☑
  von Bechterew's 720.0
Arthrocele — see also Effusion, joint 719.0 ☑
Arthrochondritis — see Arthritis
Arthrodesis status V45.4
Arthrodynia — see also Pain, joint 719.4 ☑
  psychogenic 307.89
Arthrodysplasia 755.9
Arthrofibrosis joint — see also Ankylosis
  718.5 ☑
Arthrogryposis 728.3
  multiplex, congenita 754.89
Arthrokatadysis 715.35
Arthrolithiasis 274.00 ▲
Arthro-onychodysplasia 756.89
Arthro-osteo-onychodysplasia 756.89
Arthropathy — see also Arthritis 716.9 ☑

> Note — Use the following fifth-digit subclas-
> sification with categories 711–712, 716:
>
> 0   site unspecified
> 1   shoulder region
> 2   upper arm
> 3   forearm
> 4   hand
> 5   pelvic region and thigh
> 6   lower leg
> 7   ankle and foot
> 8   other specified sites
> 9   multiple sites

  Behçet's 136.1 [711.2] ☑
  Charcôt's 094.0 [713.5]

☑ Additional Digit Required — Refer to the Tabular List for Digit Selection   ▽ Subterms under main terms may continue to next column or page

Index

Arthropathy — Asthenospermia

Arthropathy — *see also* Arthritis — *continued*
  Charcôt's — *continued*
    diabetic 250.6 ☑ [713.5]
      due to secondary diabetes 249.6 ☑ [713.5]
    syringomyelic 336.0 [713.5]
    tabetic 094.0 [713.5]
  crystal (-induced) — *see* Arthritis, due to crystals
  gouty 274.00   ▲
    acute 274.01   ●
    chronic (without mention of tophus (tophi)) 274.02   ●
      with tophus (tophi) 274.03   ●
  neurogenic, neuropathic (Charcôt's) (tabetic) 094.0 [713.5]
    diabetic 250.6 ☑ [713.5]
      due to secondary diabetes 249.6 ☑ [713.5]
    nonsyphilitic NEC 349.9 [713.5]
    syringomyelic 336.0 [713.5]
  postdysenteric NEC 009.0 [711.3] ☑
  postrheumatic, chronic (Jaccoud's) 714.4
  psoriatic 696.0
  pulmonary 731.2
  specified NEC 716.8 ☑
  syringomyelia 336.0 [713.5]
  tabes dorsalis 094.0 [713.5]
  tabetic 094.0 [713.5]
  transient 716.4 ☑
  traumatic 716.1 ☑
  uric acid 274.00   ▲
Arthrophyte — *see also* Loose, body, joint 718.1 ☑
Arthrophytis 719.80
  ankle 719.87
  elbow 719.82
  foot 719.87
  hand 719.84
  hip 719.85
  knee 719.86
  multiple sites 719.89
  pelvic region 719.85
  shoulder (region) 719.81
  specified site NEC 719.88
  wrist 719.83
Arthropyosis — *see also* Arthritis, pyogenic 711.0 ☑
Arthroscopic surgical procedure converted to open procedure V64.43
Arthrosis (deformans) (degenerative) — *see also* Osteoarthrosis 715.9 ☑
  Charcôt's 094.0 [713.5]
  polyarticular 715.09
  spine (*see also* Spondylosis) 721.90
Arthus phenomenon 995.21
  due to
    correct substance properly administered 995.21
    overdose or wrong substance given or taken 977.9
      specified drug — *see* Table of Drugs and Chemicals
  serum 999.5
Articular — *see also* condition
  disc disorder (reducing or non-reducing) 524.63
  spondylolisthesis 756.12
Articulation
  anterior 524.27
  posterior 524.27
  reverse 524.27
Artificial
  device (prosthetic) — *see* Fitting, device
  insemination V26.1
  menopause (states) (symptoms) (syndrome) 627.4
  opening status (functioning) (without complication) V44.9
    anus (colostomy) V44.3
    colostomy V44.3
    cystostomy V44.50
      appendico-vesicostomy V44.52
      cutaneous-vesicostomy V44.51
      specified type NEC V44.59

Artificial — *continued*
  opening status — *continued*
    enterostomy V44.4
    gastrostomy V44.1
    ileostomy V44.2
    intestinal tract NEC V44.4
    jejunostomy V44.4
    nephrostomy V44.6
    specified site NEC V44.8
    tracheostomy V44.0
    ureterostomy V44.6
    urethrostomy V44.6
    urinary tract NEC V44.6
    vagina V44.7
  vagina status V44.7
ARV (disease) (illness) (infection) — *see* Human immunodeficiency virus (disease) (illness) (infection)
Arytenoid — *see* condition
Asbestosis (occupational) 501
Asboe-Hansen's disease (incontinentia pigmenti) 757.33
Ascariasis (intestinal) (lung) 127.0
Ascaridiasis 127.0
Ascaridosis 127.0
Ascaris 127.0
  lumbricoides (infestation) 127.0
  pneumonia 127.0
Ascending — *see* condition
ASC-H (atypical squamous cells cannot exclude high grade squamous intraepithelial lesion)
  anus 796.72
  cervix 795.02
  vagina 795.12
Aschoff's bodies — *see also* Myocarditis, rheumatic 398.0
Ascites 789.59
  abdominal NEC 789.59
  cancerous (M8000/6) 789.51
  cardiac 428.0
  chylous (nonfilarial) 457.8
    filarial (*see also* Infestation, filarial) 125.9
  congenital 778.0
  due to S. japonicum 120.2
  fetal, causing fetopelvic disproportion 653.7 ☑
  heart 428.0
  joint (*see also* Effusion, joint) 719.0 ☑
  malignant (M8000/6) 789.51
  pseudochylous 789.59
  syphilitic 095.2
  tuberculous (*see also* Tuberculosis) 014.0 ☑
Ascorbic acid (vitamin C) **deficiency** (scurvy) 267
ASC-US (atypical squamous cells of undetermined significance)
  anus 796.71
  cervix 795.01
  vagina 795.11
ASCVD (arteriosclerotic cardiovascular disease) 429.2
Aseptic — *see* condition
Asherman's syndrome 621.5
Asialia 527.7
Asiatic cholera — *see also* Cholera 001.9
Asocial personality or trends 301.7
Asomatognosia 781.8
Aspergillosis 117.3
  with pneumonia 117.3 [484.6]
  allergic bronchopulmonary 518.6
  nonsyphilitic NEC 117.3
Aspergillus (flavus) (fumigatus) (infection) (terreus) 117.3
Aspermatogenesis 606.0
Aspermia (testis) 606.0
Asphyxia, asphyxiation (by) 799.01
  antenatal — *see* Distress, fetal
  bedclothes 994.7
  birth (*see also* Asphyxia, newborn) 768.9
  bunny bag 994.7
  carbon monoxide 986
  caul (*see also* Asphyxia, newborn) 768.9
  cave-in 994.7
    crushing — *see* Injury, internal, intrathoracic organs
  constriction 994.7

Asphyxia, asphyxiation — *continued*
  crushing — *see* Injury, internal, intrathoracic organs
  drowning 994.1
  fetal, affecting newborn 768.9
  food or foreign body (in larynx) 933.1
    bronchioles 934.8
    bronchus (main) 934.1
    lung 934.8
    nasopharynx 933.0
    nose, nasal passages 932
    pharynx 933.0
    respiratory tract 934.9
      specified part NEC 934.8
    throat 933.0
    trachea 934.0
  gas, fumes, or vapor NEC 987.9
    specified — *see* Table of Drugs and Chemicals
  gravitational changes 994.7
  hanging 994.7
  inhalation — *see* Inhalation
  intrauterine
    fetal death (before onset of labor) 768.0
      during labor 768.1
    liveborn infant — *see* Distress, fetal, liveborn infant
  local 443.0
  mechanical 994.7
    during birth (*see also* Distress, fetal) 768.9
  mucus 933.1
    bronchus (main) 934.1
    larynx 933.1
    lung 934.8
    nasal passages 932
    newborn 770.18
    pharynx 933.0
    respiratory tract 934.9
      specified part NEC 934.8
    throat 933.0
    trachea 934.0
    vaginal (fetus or newborn) 770.18
  newborn 768.9
    with neurologic involvement 768.5
    blue 768.6
    livida 768.6
    mild or moderate 768.6
    pallida 768.5
    severe 768.5
    white 768.5
  pathological 799.01
  plastic bag 994.7
  postnatal (*see also* Asphyxia, newborn) 768.9
    mechanical 994.7
  pressure 994.7
  reticularis 782.61
  strangulation 994.7
  submersion 994.1
  traumatic NEC — *see* Injury, internal, intrathoracic organs
  vomiting, vomitus — *see* Asphyxia, food or foreign body
Aspiration
  acid pulmonary (syndrome) 997.39
    obstetric 668.0 ☑
  amniotic fluid 770.13
    with respiratory symptoms 770.14
  bronchitis 507.0
  clear amniotic fluid 770.13
    with
      pneumonia 770.14
      pneumonitis 770.14
      respiratory symptoms 770.14
  contents of birth canal 770.17
    with respiratory symptoms 770.18
  fetal 770.10
    blood 770.15
      with
        pneumonia 770.16
        pneumonitis 770.16
      pneumonitis 770.18
  food, foreign body, or gasoline (with asphyxiation) — *see* Asphyxia, food or foreign body
  meconium 770.11

Aspiration — *continued*
  meconium — *continued*
    with
      pneumonia 770.12
      pneumonitis 770.12
      respiratory symptoms 770.12
    below vocal cords 770.11
      with respiratory symptoms 770.12
  mucus 933.1
    into
      bronchus (main) 934.1
      lung 934.8
      respiratory tract 934.9
        specified part NEC 934.8
      trachea 934.0
    newborn 770.17
    vaginal (fetus or newborn) 770.17
  newborn 770.10
    with respiratory symptoms 770.18
    blood 770.15
      with
        pneumonia 770.16
        pneumonitis 770.16
        respiratory symptoms 770.16
    pneumonia 507.0
      fetus or newborn 770.18
      meconium 770.12
    pneumonitis 507.0
      fetus or newborn 770.18
      meconium 770.12
      obstetric 668.0 ☑
    postnatal stomach contents 770.85
      with
        pneumonia 770.86
        pneumonitis 770.86
        respiratory symptoms 770.86
    syndrome of newborn (massive) 770.18
      meconium 770.12
    vernix caseosa 770.12
Asplenia 759.0
  with mesocardia 746.87
Assam fever 085.0
Assimilation, pelvis
  with disproportion 653.2 ☑
    affecting fetus or newborn 763.1
    causing obstructed labor 660.1 ☑
      affecting fetus or newborn 763.1
Assmann's focus — *see also* Tuberculosis 011.0 ☑
Astasia (-abasia) 307.9
  hysterical 300.11
Asteatosis 706.8
  cutis 706.8
Astereognosis 780.99
Asterixis 781.3
  in liver disease 572.8
Asteroid hyalitis 379.22
Asthenia, asthenic 780.79
  cardiac (*see also* Failure, heart) 428.9
    psychogenic 306.2
  cardiovascular (*see also* Failure, heart) 428.9
    psychogenic 306.2
  heart (*see also* Failure, heart) 428.9
    psychogenic 306.2
  hysterical 300.11
  myocardial (*see also* Failure, heart) 428.9
    psychogenic 306.2
  nervous 300.5
  neurocirculatory 306.2
  neurotic 300.5
  psychogenic 300.5
  psychoneurotic 300.5
  psychophysiologic 300.5
  reaction, psychoneurotic 300.5
  senile 797
  Stiller's 780.79
  tropical anhidrotic 705.1
Asthenopia 368.13
  accommodative 367.4
  hysterical (muscular) 300.11
  psychogenic 306.7
Asthenospermia 792.2

Asthma, asthmatic (bronchial) (catarrh) (spasmodic) 493.9 ☑

> Note — Use the following fifth-digit subclassification with codes 493.0–493.2, 493.9:
>
> 0   without mention of status asthmaticus or acute exacerbation or unspecified
>
> 1   with status asthmaticus
>
> 2   with acute exacerbation

with
  chronic obstructive pulmonary disease (COPD) 493.2 ☑
  hay fever 493.0 ☑
  rhinitis, allergic 493.0 ☑
allergic 493.9 ☑
  stated cause (external allergen) 493.0 ☑
atopic 493.0 ☑
cardiac (see also Failure, ventricular, left) 428.1
cardiobronchial (see also Failure, ventricular, left) 428.1
cardiorenal (see also Hypertension, cardiorenal) 404.90
childhood 493.0 ☑
Colliers' 500
cough variant 493.82
croup 493.9 ☑
detergent 507.8
due to
  detergent 507.8
  inhalation of fumes 506.3
  internal immunological process 493.0 ☑
endogenous (intrinsic) 493.1 ☑
eosinophilic 518.3
exercise induced bronchospasm 493.81
exogenous (cosmetics) (dander or dust) (drugs) (dust) (feathers) (food) (hay) (platinum) (pollen) 493.0 ☑
extrinsic 493.0 ☑
grinders' 502
hay 493.0 ☑
heart (see also Failure, ventricular, left) 428.1
IgE 493.0 ☑
infective 493.1 ☑
intrinsic 493.1 ☑
Kopp's 254.8
late-onset 493.1 ☑
meat-wrappers' 506.9
Millar's (laryngismus stridulus) 478.75
millstone makers' 502
miners' 500
Monday morning 504
New Orleans (epidemic) 493.0 ☑
platinum 493.0 ☑
pneumoconiotic (occupational) NEC 505
potters' 502
psychogenic 316 [493.9] ☑
pulmonary eosinophilic 518.3
red cedar 495.8
Rostan's (see also Failure, ventricular, left) 428.1
sandblasters' 502
sequoiosis 495.8
stonemasons' 502
thymic 254.8
tuberculous (see also Tuberculosis, pulmonary) 011.9 ☑
Wichmann's (laryngismus stridulus) 478.75
wood 495.8
Astigmatism (compound) (congenital) 367.20
  irregular 367.22
  regular 367.21
Astroblastoma (M9430/3)
  nose 748.1
  specified site — see Neoplasm, by site, malignant
  unspecified site 191.9
Astrocytoma (cystic) (M9400/3)
  anaplastic type (M9401/3)
    specified site — see Neoplasm, by site, malignant
    unspecified site 191.9
  fibrillary (M9420/3)
    specified site — see Neoplasm, by site, malignant

Astrocytoma — continued
  fibrillary — continued
    unspecified site 191.9
  fibrous (M9420/3)
    specified site — see Neoplasm, by site, malignant
    unspecified site 191.9
  gemistocytic (M9411/3)
    specified site — see Neoplasm, by site, malignant
    unspecified site 191.9
  juvenile (M9421/3)
    specified site — see Neoplasm, by site, malignant
    unspecified site 191.9
  nose 748.1
  pilocytic (M9421/3)
    specified site — see Neoplasm, by site, malignant
    unspecified site 191.9
  piloid (M9421/3)
    specified site — see Neoplasm, by site, malignant
    unspecified site 191.9
  protoplasmic (M9410/3)
    specified site — see Neoplasm, by site, malignant
    unspecified site 191.9
  specified site — see Neoplasm, by site, malignant
  subependymal (M9383/1) 237.5
    giant cell (M9384/1) 237.5
  unspecified site 191.9
Astroglioma (M9400/3)
  nose 748.1
  specified site — see Neoplasm, by site, malignant
  unspecified site 191.9
Asymbolia 784.60
Asymmetrical breathing 786.09
Asymmetry — see also Distortion
  breast, between native and reconstructed 612.1
  chest 786.9
  face 754.0
  jaw NEC 524.12
    maxillary 524.11
  pelvis with disproportion 653.0 ☑
    affecting fetus or newborn 763.1
    causing obstructed labor 660.1 ☑
      affecting fetus or newborn 763.1
Asynergia 781.3
Asynergy 781.3
  ventricular 429.89
Asystole (heart) — see also Arrest, cardiac 427.5
Ataxia, ataxy, ataxic 781.3
  acute 781.3
  brain 331.89
  cerebellar 334.3
    hereditary (Marie's) 334.2
    in
      alcoholism 303.9 ☑ [334.4]
      myxedema (see also Myxedema) 244.9 [334.4]
      neoplastic disease NEC 239.9 [334.4]
  cerebral 331.89
  family, familial 334.2
    cerebral (Marie's) 334.2
    spinal (Friedreich's) 334.0
  Friedreich's (heredofamilial) (spinal) 334.0
  frontal lobe 781.3
  gait 781.2
    hysterical 300.11
  general 781.3
  hereditary NEC 334.2
    cerebellar 334.2
    spastic 334.1
    spinal 334.0
  heredofamilial (Marie's) 334.2
  hysterical 300.11
  locomotor (progressive) 094.0
    diabetic 250.6 ☑ [337.1]
      due to secondary diabetes 249.6 ☑ [337.1]
  Marie's (cerebellar) (heredofamilial) 334.2
  nonorganic origin 307.9

Ataxia, ataxy, ataxic — continued
  partial 094.0
  postchickenpox 052.7
  progressive locomotor 094.0
  psychogenic 307.9
  Sanger-Brown's 334.2
  spastic 094.0
    hereditary 334.1
    syphilitic 094.0
  spinal
    hereditary 334.0
    progressive locomotor 094.0
  telangiectasia 334.8
Ataxia-telangiectasia 334.8
Atelectasis (absorption collapse) (complete) (compression) (massive) (partial) (postinfective) (pressure collapse) (pulmonary) (relaxation) 518.0
  newborn (congenital) (partial) 770.5
    primary 770.4
  primary 770.4
  tuberculous (see also Tuberculosis, pulmonary) 011.9 ☑
Ateleiosis, ateliosis 253.3
Atelia — see Distortion
Ateliosis 253.3
Atelocardia 746.9
Atelomyelia 742.59
Athelia 757.6
Atheroembolism
  extremity
    lower 445.02
    upper 445.01
  kidney 445.81
  specified site NEC 445.89
Atheroma, atheromatous — see also Arteriosclerosis 440.9
  aorta, aortic 440.0
    valve (see also Endocarditis, aortic) 424.1
  artery — see Arteriosclerosis
  basilar (artery) (see also Occlusion, artery, basilar') 433.0 ☑
  carotid (artery) (common) (internal) (see also Occlusion, artery, carotid) 433.1 ☑
  cerebral (arteries) 437.0
  coronary (artery) — see Arteriosclerosis, coronary
  degeneration — see Arteriosclerosis
  heart, cardiac — see Arteriosclerosis, coronary
  mitral (valve) 424.0
  myocardium, myocardial — see Arteriosclerosis, coronary
  pulmonary valve (heart) (see also Endocarditis, pulmonary) 424.3
  skin 706.2
  tricuspid (heart) (valve) 424.2
  valve, valvular — see Endocarditis
  vertebral (artery) (see also Occlusion, artery, vertebral) 433.2 ☑
Atheromatosis — see also Arteriosclerosis
  arterial, congenital 272.8
Atherosclerosis — see Arteriosclerosis
Athetosis (acquired) 781.0
  bilateral 333.79
  congenital (bilateral) 333.6
  double 333.71
  unilateral 781.0
Athlete's
  foot 110.4
  heart 429.3
Athletic team examination V70.3
Athrepsia 261
Athyrea (acquired) — see also Hypothyroidism 244.9
  congenital 243
Athyreosis (congenital) 243
  acquired — see Hypothyroidism
Athyroidism (acquired) — see also Hypothyroidism 244.9
  congenital 243
Atmospheric pyrexia 992.0
Atonia, atony, atonic
  abdominal wall 728.2
  bladder (sphincter) 596.4
    neurogenic NEC 596.54
      with cauda equina syndrome 344.61

Atonia, atony, atonic — continued
  capillary 448.9
  cecum 564.89
    psychogenic 306.4
  colon 564.89
    psychogenic 306.4
  congenital 779.89
  dyspepsia 536.3
    psychogenic 306.4
  intestine 564.89
    psychogenic 306.4
  stomach 536.3
    neurotic or psychogenic 306.4
    psychogenic 306.4
  uterus 661.2 ☑
    with hemorrhage (postpartum) 666.1 ☑
    without hemorrhage
      intrapartum 661.2 ☑
      postpartum 669.8 ☑
  vesical 596.4
Atopy NEC V15.09
Atransferrinemia, congenital 273.8
Atresia, atretic (congenital) 759.89
  alimentary organ or tract NEC 751.8
    lower 751.2
    upper 750.8
  ani, anus, anal (canal) 751.2
  aorta 747.22
    with hypoplasia of ascending aorta and defective development of left ventricle (with mitral valve atresia) 746.7
    arch 747.11
    ring 747.21
  aortic (orifice) (valve) 746.89
    arch 747.11
  aqueduct of Sylvius 742.3
    with spina bifida (see also Spina bifida) 741.0 ☑
  artery NEC (see also Atresia, blood vessel) 747.60
    cerebral 747.81
    coronary 746.85
    eye 743.58
    pulmonary 747.3
    umbilical 747.5
  auditory canal (external) 744.02
  bile, biliary duct (common) or passage 751.61
    acquired (see also Obstruction, biliary) 576.2
  bladder (neck) 753.6
  blood vessel (peripheral) NEC 747.60
    cerebral 747.81
    gastrointestinal 747.61
    lower limb 747.64
    pulmonary artery 747.3
    renal 747.62
    spinal 747.82
    upper limb 747.63
  bronchus 748.3
  canal, ear 744.02
  cardiac
    valve 746.89
      aortic 746.89
      mitral 746.89
      pulmonary 746.01
      tricuspid 746.1
  cecum 751.2
  cervix (acquired) 622.4
    congenital 752.49
    in pregnancy or childbirth 654.6 ☑
      affecting fetus or newborn 763.89
      causing obstructed labor 660.2 ☑
        affecting fetus or newborn 763.1
  choana 748.0
  colon 751.2
  cystic duct 751.61
    acquired 575.8
      with obstruction (see also Obstruction, gallbladder) 575.2
  digestive organs NEC 751.8
  duodenum 751.1
  ear canal 744.02
  ejaculatory duct 752.89
  epiglottis 748.3
  esophagus 750.3

☑ Additional Digit Required — Refer to the Tabular List for Digit Selection   ▽ Subterms under main terms may continue to next column or page

2010 ICD-9-CM   ►◄ Revised Text   ● New Line   ▲ Revised Code   Volume 2 — 29

Atresia, atretic — *continued*
Eustachian tube 744.24
fallopian tube (acquired) 628.2
  congenital 752.19
follicular cyst 620.0
foramen of
  Luschka 742.3
    with spina bifida (*see also* Spina bifida)
      741.0 ☑
  Magendie 742.3
    with spina bifida (*see also* Spina bifida)
      741.0 ☑
gallbladder 751.69
genital organ
  external
    female 752.49
    male NEC 752.89
      penis 752.69
  internal
    female 752.89
    male 752.89
glottis 748.3
gullet 750.3
heart
  valve NEC 746.89
    aortic 746.89
    mitral 746.89
    pulmonary 746.01
    tricuspid 746.1
hymen 752.42
  acquired 623.3
  postinfective 623.3
ileum 751.1
intestine (small) 751.1
  large 751.2
iris, filtration angle (*see also* Buphthalmia)
  743.20
jejunum 751.1
kidney 753.3
lacrimal, apparatus 743.65
  acquired — *see* Stenosis, lacrimal
larynx 748.3
ligament, broad 752.19
lung 748.5
meatus urinarius 753.6
mitral valve 746.89
  with atresia or hypoplasia of aortic orifice
      or valve, with hypoplasia of ascend-
      ing aorta and defective develop-
      ment of left ventricle 746.7
nares (anterior) (posterior) 748.0
nasolacrimal duct 743.65
nasopharynx 748.8
nose, nostril 748.0
  acquired 738.0
organ or site NEC — *see* Anomaly, specified
    type NEC
osseous meatus (ear) 744.03
oviduct (acquired) 628.2
  congenital 752.19
parotid duct 750.23
  acquired 527.8
pulmonary (artery) 747.3
  valve 746.01
  vein 747.49
pulmonic 746.01
pupil 743.46
rectum 751.2
salivary duct or gland 750.23
  acquired 527.8
sublingual duct 750.23
  acquired 527.8
submaxillary duct or gland 750.23
  acquired 527.8
trachea 748.3
tricuspid valve 746.1
ureter 753.29
ureteropelvic junction 753.21
ureterovesical orifice 753.22
urethra (valvular) 753.6
urinary tract NEC 753.29
uterus 752.3
  acquired 621.8
vagina (acquired) 623.2
  congenital 752.49
    postgonococcal (old) 098.2

Atresia, atretic — *continued*
vagina — *continued*
  postinfectional 623.2
  senile 623.2
vascular NEC (*see also* Atresia, blood vessel)
  747.60
  cerebral 747.81
vas deferens 752.89
vein NEC (*see also* Atresia, blood vessel) 747.60
  cardiac 746.89
  great 747.49
  portal 747.49
  pulmonary 747.49
vena cava (inferior) (superior) 747.49
vesicourethral orifice 753.6
vulva 752.49
  acquired 624.8
Atrichia, atrichosis 704.00
  congenital (universal) 757.4
Atrioventricularis commune 745.69
At risk for falling V15.88
Atrophia — *see also* Atrophy
alba 709.09
cutis 701.8
  idiopathica progressiva 701.8
  senilis 701.8
dermatological, diffuse (idiopathic) 701.8
flava hepatis (acuta) (subacuta) (*see also*
  Necrosis, liver) 570
gyrata of choroid and retina (central) 363.54
  generalized 363.57
senilis 797
  dermatological 701.8
unguium 703.8
  congenita 757.5
Atrophoderma, atrophodermia 701.9
diffusum (idiopathic) 701.8
maculatum 701.3
  et striatum 701.3
    due to syphilis 095.8
  syphilitic 091.3
neuriticum 701.8
pigmentosum 757.33
reticulatum symmetricum faciei 701.8
senile 701.8
symmetrical 701.8
vermiculata 701.8
Atrophy, atrophic
adrenal (autoimmune) (capsule) (cortex)
  (gland) 255.41
  with hypofunction 255.41
alveolar process or ridge (edentulous) 525.20
  mandible 525.20
    minimal 525.21
    moderate 525.22
    severe 525.23
  maxilla 525.20
    minimal 525.24
    moderate 525.25
    severe 525.26
appendix 543.9
Aran-Duchenne muscular 335.21
arm 728.2
arteriosclerotic — *see* Arteriosclerosis
arthritis 714.0
  spine 720.9
bile duct (any) 576.8
bladder 596.8
blanche (of Milian) 701.3
bone (senile) 733.99
  due to
    disuse 733.7
    infection 733.99
    tabes dorsalis (neurogenic) 094.0
  posttraumatic 733.99
brain (cortex) (progressive) 331.9
  with dementia 290.10
  Alzheimer's 331.0
    with dementia — *see* Alzheimer's, de-
      mentia
  circumscribed (Pick's) 331.11
    with dementia
      with behavioral disturbance
        331.11 *[294.11]*
      without behavioral disturbance
        331.11 *[294.10]*

Atrophy, atrophic — *continued*
brain — *continued*
  congenital 742.4
  hereditary 331.9
  senile 331.2
breast 611.4
  puerperal, postpartum 676.3 ☑
buccal cavity 528.9
cardiac (brown) (senile) (*see also* Degeneration,
  myocardial) 429.1
cartilage (infectional) (joint) 733.99
cast, plaster of Paris 728.2
cerebellar — *see* Atrophy, brain
cerebral — *see* Atrophy, brain
cervix (endometrium) (mucosa) (myometrium)
  (senile) (uteri) 622.8
  menopausal 627.8
Charcôt-Marie-Tooth 356.1
choroid 363.40
  diffuse secondary 363.42
  hereditary (*see also* Dystrophy, choroid)
    363.50
  gyrate
    central 363.54
    diffuse 363.57
    generalized 363.57
  senile 363.41
ciliary body 364.57
colloid, degenerative 701.3
conjunctiva (senile) 372.89
corpus cavernosum 607.89
cortical (*see also* Atrophy, brain) 331.9
Cruveilhier's 335.21
cystic duct 576.8
dacryosialadenopathy 710.2
degenerative
  colloid 701.3
  senile 701.3
Déjérine-Thomas 333.0
diffuse idiopathic, dermatological 701.8
disuse
  bone 733.7
  muscle 728.2
  pelvic muscles and anal sphincter 618.83
Duchenne-Aran 335.21
ear 388.9
edentulous alveolar ridge 525.20
  mandible 525.20
    minimal 525.21
    moderate 525.22
    severe 525.23
  maxilla 525.20
    minimal 525.24
    moderate 525.25
    severe 525.26
emphysema, lung 492.8
endometrium (senile) 621.8
  cervix 622.8
enteric 569.89
epididymis 608.3
eyeball, cause unknown 360.41
eyelid (senile) 374.50
facial (skin) 701.9
facioscapulohumeral (Landouzy-Déjérine)
  359.1
fallopian tube (senile), acquired 620.3
fatty, thymus (gland) 254.8
gallbladder 575.8
gastric 537.89
gastritis (chronic) 535.1 ☑
gastrointestinal 569.89
genital organ, male 608.89
glandular 289.3
globe (phthisis bulbi) 360.41
gum (*see also* Recession, gingival) 523.20
hair 704.2
heart (brown) (senile) (*see also* Degeneration,
  myocardial) 429.1
hemifacial 754.0
  Romberg 349.89
hydronephrosis 591
infantile 261
  paralysis, acute (*see also* Poliomyelitis, with
    paralysis) 045.1 ☑
intestine 569.89

Atrophy, atrophic — *continued*
iris (generalized) (postinfectional) (sector
  shaped) 364.59
  essential 364.51
  progressive 364.51
  sphincter 364.54
kidney (senile) (*see also* Sclerosis, renal) 587
  with hypertension (*see also* Hypertension,
    kidney) 403.90
  congenital 753.0
  hydronephrotic 591
  infantile 753.0
lacrimal apparatus (primary) 375.13
  secondary 375.14
Landouzy-Déjérine 359.1
laryngitis, infection 476.0
larynx 478.79
Leber's optic 377.16
lip 528.5
liver (acute) (subacute) (*see also* Necrosis, liver)
  570
  chronic (yellow) 571.8
  yellow (congenital) 570
    with
      abortion — *see* Abortion, by type,
        with specified complication
        NEC
      ectopic pregnancy (*see also* cate-
        gories 633.0–633.9) 639.8
      molar pregnancy (*see also* cate-
        gories 630–632) 639.8
  chronic 571.8
  complicating pregnancy 646.7 ☑
  following
    abortion 639.8
    ectopic or molar pregnancy 639.8
  from injection, inoculation or transfu-
    sion (onset within 8 months af-
    ter administration) — *see* Hep-
    atitis, viral
  healed 571.5
  obstetric 646.7 ☑
  postabortal 639.8
  postimmunization — *see* Hepatitis, vi-
    ral
  posttransfusion — *see* Hepatitis, viral
  puerperal, postpartum 674.8 ☑
lung (senile) 518.89
  congenital 748.69
macular (dermatological) 701.3
  syphilitic, skin 091.3
    striated 095.8
muscle, muscular 728.2
  disuse 728.2
  Duchenne-Aran 335.21
  extremity (lower) (upper) 728.2
  familial spinal 335.11
  general 728.2
  idiopathic 728.2
  infantile spinal 335.0
  myelopathic (progressive) 335.10
  myotonic 359.21
  neuritic 356.1
  neuropathic (peroneal) (progressive) 356.1
  peroneal 356.1
  primary (idiopathic) 728.2
  progressive (familial) (hereditary) (pure)
    335.21
    adult (spinal) 335.19
    infantile (spinal) 335.0
    juvenile (spinal) 335.11
    spinal 335.10
      adult 335.19
      hereditary or familial 335.11
      infantile 335.0
  pseudohypertrophic 359.1
  spinal (progressive) 335.10
    adult 335.19
    Aran-Duchenne 335.21
    familial 335.11
    hereditary 335.11
    infantile 335.0
    juvenile 335.11
  syphilitic 095.6
myocardium (*see also* Degeneration, myocardial) 429.1

☑ Additional Digit Required — Refer to the Tabular List for Digit Selection   ▽ Subterms under main terms may continue to next column or page

30 — Volume 2   ▶◀ Revised Text   ● New Line   ▲ Revised Code   **2010 ICD-9-CM**

Atrophy, atrophic — *continued*
- myometrium (senile) 621.8
  - cervix 622.8
- myotatic 728.2
- myotonia 359.21
- nail 703.8
  - congenital 757.5
- nasopharynx 472.2
- nerve (*see also* Disorder, nerve)
  - abducens 378.54
  - accessory 352.4
  - acoustic or auditory 388.5
  - cranial 352.9
    - first (olfactory) 352.0
    - second (optic) (*see also* Atrophy, optic nerve) 377.10
    - third (oculomotor) (partial) 378.51
      - total 378.52
    - fourth (trochlear) 378.53
    - fifth (trigeminal) 350.8
    - sixth (abducens) 378.54
    - seventh (facial) 351.8
    - eighth (auditory) 388.5
    - ninth (glossopharyngeal) 352.2
    - tenth (pneumogastric) (vagus) 352.3
    - eleventh (accessory) 352.4
    - twelfth (hypoglossal) 352.5
  - facial 351.8
  - glossopharyngeal 352.2
  - hypoglossal 352.5
  - oculomotor (partial) 378.51
    - total 378.52
  - olfactory 352.0
  - peripheral 355.9
  - pneumogastric 352.3
  - trigeminal 350.8
  - trochlear 378.53
  - vagus (pneumogastric) 352.3
- nervous system, congenital 742.8
- neuritic (*see also* Disorder, nerve) 355.9
- neurogenic NEC 355.9
  - bone
    - tabetic 094.0
- nutritional 261
- old age 797
- olivopontocerebellar 333.0
- optic nerve (ascending) (descending) (infectional) (nonfamilial) (papillomacular bundle) (postretinal) (secondary NEC) (simple) 377.10
  - associated with retinal dystrophy 377.13
  - dominant hereditary 377.16
  - glaucomatous 377.14
  - hereditary (dominant) (Leber's) 377.16
  - Leber's (hereditary) 377.16
  - partial 377.15
  - postinflammatory 377.12
  - primary 377.11
  - syphilitic 094.84
    - congenital 090.49
    - tabes dorsalis 094.0
  - orbit 376.45
- ovary (senile), acquired 620.3
- oviduct (senile), acquired 620.3
- palsy, diffuse 335.20
- pancreas (duct) (senile) 577.8
- papillary muscle 429.81
- paralysis 355.9
- parotid gland 527.0
- patches skin 701.3
  - senile 701.8
- penis 607.89
- pharyngitis 472.1
- pharynx 478.29
- pluriglandular 258.8
- polyarthritis 714.0
- prostate 602.2
- pseudohypertrophic 359.1
- renal (*see also* Sclerosis, renal) 587
- reticulata 701.8
- retina (*see also* Degeneration, retina) 362.60
  - hereditary (*see also* Dystrophy, retina) 362.70
- rhinitis 472.0
- salivary duct or gland 527.0
- scar NEC 709.2

Atrophy, atrophic — *continued*
- sclerosis, lobar (of brain) 331.0
  - with dementia
    - with behavioral disturbance 331.0 *[294.11]*
    - without behavioral disturbance 331.0 *[294.10]*
- scrotum 608.89
- seminal vesicle 608.89
- senile 797
  - degenerative, of skin 701.3
- skin (patches) (senile) 701.8
- spermatic cord 608.89
- spinal (cord) 336.8
  - acute 336.8
  - muscular (chronic) 335.10
    - adult 335.19
    - familial 335.11
    - juvenile 335.10
  - paralysis 335.10
    - acute (*see also* Poliomyelitis, with paralysis) 045.1 ☑
- spine (column) 733.99
- spleen (senile) 289.59
- spots (skin) 701.3
  - senile 701.8
- stomach 537.89
- striate and macular 701.3
  - syphilitic 095.8
- subcutaneous 701.9
  - due to injection 999.9
- sublingual gland 527.0
- submaxillary gland 527.0
- Sudeck's 733.7
- suprarenal (autoimmune) (capsule) (gland) 255.41
  - with hypofunction 255.41
- tarso-orbital fascia, congenital 743.66
- testis 608.3
- thenar, partial 354.0
- throat 478.29
- thymus (fat) 254.8
- thyroid (gland) 246.8
  - with
    - cretinism 243
    - myxedema 244.9
  - congenital 243
- tongue (senile) 529.8
  - papillae 529.4
  - smooth 529.4
- trachea 519.19
- tunica vaginalis 608.89
- turbinate 733.99
- tympanic membrane (nonflaccid) 384.82
  - flaccid 384.81
- ulcer (*see also* Ulcer, skin) 707.9
- upper respiratory tract 478.9
- uterus, uterine (acquired) (senile) 621.8
  - cervix 622.8
  - due to radiation (intended effect) 621.8
- vagina (senile) 627.3
- vascular 459.89
- vas deferens 608.89
- vertebra (senile) 733.99
- vulva (primary) (senile) 624.1
- Werdnig-Hoffmann 335.0
- yellow (acute) (congenital) (liver) (subacute) (*see also* Necrosis, liver) 570
  - chronic 571.8
  - resulting from administration of blood, plasma, serum, or other biological substance (within 8 months of administration) — *see* Hepatitis, viral

Attack
- akinetic (*see also* Epilepsy) 345.0 ☑
- angina — *see* Angina
- apoplectic (*see also* Disease, cerebrovascular, acute) 436
- benign shuddering 333.93
- bilious — *see* Vomiting
- cataleptic 300.11
- cerebral (*see also* Disease, cerebrovascular, acute) 436
- coronary (*see also* Infarct, myocardium) 410.9 ☑
- cyanotic, newborn 770.83

Attack — *continued*
- epileptic (*see also* Epilepsy) 345.9 ☑
- epileptiform 780.39
- heart (*see also* Infarct, myocardium) 410.9 ☑
- hemiplegia (*see also* Disease, cerebrovascular, acute) 436
- hysterical 300.11
- jacksonian (*see also* Epilepsy) 345.5 ☑
- myocardium, myocardial (*see also* Infarct, myocardium) 410.9 ☑
- myoclonic (*see also* Epilepsy) 345.1 ☑
- panic 300.01
- paralysis (*see also* Disease, cerebrovascular, acute) 436
- paroxysmal 780.39
- psychomotor (*see also* Epilepsy) 345.4 ☑
- salaam (*see also* Epilepsy) 345.6 ☑
- schizophreniform (*see also* Schizophrenia) 295.4 ☑
- sensory and motor 780.39
- syncope 780.2
- toxic, cerebral 780.39
- transient ischemic (TIA) 435.9
- unconsciousness 780.2
  - hysterical 300.11
- vasomotor 780.2
- vasovagal (idiopathic) (paroxysmal) 780.2

Attention to
- artificial opening (of) V55.9
  - digestive tract NEC V55.4
  - specified site NEC V55.8
  - urinary tract NEC V55.6
  - vagina V55.7
- colostomy V55.3
- cystostomy V55.5
- dressing
  - wound V58.30
    - nonsurgical V58.30
    - surgical V58.31
- gastrostomy V55.1
- ileostomy V55.2
- jejunostomy V55.4
- nephrostomy V55.6
- surgical dressings V58.31
- sutures V58.32
- tracheostomy V55.0
- ureterostomy V55.6
- urethrostomy V55.6

Attrition
- gum (*see also* Recession, gingival) 523.20
- teeth (hard tissues) 521.10
  - excessive 521.10
    - extending into
      - dentine 521.12
      - pulp 521.13
    - generalized 521.15
    - limited to enamel 521.11
    - localized 521.14

Atypical — *see also* condition
- cells
  - endocervical 795.00
  - endometrial 795.00
  - glandular
    - anus 796.70
    - cervical 795.00
    - vaginal 795.10
  - distribution, vessel (congenital) (peripheral) NEC 747.60
  - endometrium 621.9
  - kidney 593.89

Atypism, cervix 622.10
Audible tinnitus — *see also* Tinnitus 388.30
Auditory — *see* condition
Audry's syndrome (acropachyderma) 757.39
Aujeszky's disease 078.89
Aura
- jacksonian (*see also* Epilepsy) 345.5 ☑
- persistent migraine 346.5 ☑
  - with cerebral infarction 346.6 ☑
  - without cerebral infarction 346.5 ☑

Aurantiasis, cutis 278.3
Auricle, auricular — *see* condition
Auriculotemporal syndrome 350.8
Australian
- Q fever 083.0
- X disease 062.4

Autism, autistic (child) (infantile) 299.0 ☑
Autodigestion 799.89
Autoerythrocyte sensitization 287.2
Autographism 708.3
Autoimmune
- cold sensitivity 283.0
- disease NEC 279.49 ▲
- hemolytic anemia 283.0
- lymphoproliferative syndrome (ALPS) 279.41 ●
- thyroiditis 245.2

Autoinfection, septic — *see* Septicemia
Autointoxication 799.89
Automatism 348.89 ▲
- epileptic (*see also* Epilepsy) 345.4 ☑
- paroxysmal, idiopathic (*see also* Epilepsy) 345.4 ☑

Autonomic, autonomous
- bladder 596.54
  - neurogenic 596.54
    - with cauda equina 344.61
- dysreflexia 337.3
- faciocephalalgia (*see also* Neuropathy, peripheral, autonomic) 337.9
- hysterical seizure 300.11
- imbalance (*see also* Neuropathy, peripheral, autonomic) 337.9

Autophony 388.40
Autosensitivity, erythrocyte 287.2
Autotopagnosia 780.99
Autotoxemia 799.89
Autumn — *see* condition
Avellis' syndrome 344.89
Aviators
- disease or sickness (*see also* Effect, adverse, high altitude) 993.2
- ear 993.0
- effort syndrome 306.2

Avitaminosis (multiple NEC) — *see also* Deficiency, vitamin 269.2
- A 264.9
- B 266.9
  - with
    - beriberi 265.0
    - pellagra 265.2
- B_1 265.1
- B_2 266.0
- B_6 266.1
- B_{12} 266.2
- C (with scurvy) 267
- D 268.9
  - with
    - osteomalacia 268.2
    - rickets 268.0
- E 269.1
- G 266.0
- H 269.1
- K 269.0
- multiple 269.2
- nicotinic acid 265.2
- P 269.1

Avulsion (traumatic) 879.8
- blood vessel — *see* Injury, blood vessel, by site
- cartilage (*see also* Dislocation, by site)
  - knee, current (*see also* Tear, meniscus) 836.2
  - symphyseal (inner), complicating delivery 665.6 ☑
- complicated 879.9
- diaphragm — *see* Injury, internal, diaphragm
- ear — *see* Wound, open, ear
- epiphysis of bone — *see* Fracture, by site
- external site other than limb — *see* Wound, open, by site
- eye 871.3
- fingernail — *see* Wound, open, finger
- fracture — *see* Fracture, by site
- genital organs, external — *see* Wound, open, genital organs
- head (intracranial) NEC (*see also* Injury, intracranial, with open intracranial wound)
  - complete 874.9
  - external site NEC 873.8
    - complicated 873.9
- internal organ or site — *see* Injury, internal, by site

☑ Additional Digit Required — Refer to the Tabular List for Digit Selection   🔰 Subterms under main terms may continue to next column or page

2010 ICD-9-CM   ▶◀ Revised Text   ● New Line   ▲ Revised Code   **October 2009 · Volume 2 — 31**

Bednar's aphthae 528.2
Bedsore (see also Ulcer, pressure) 707.00
  with gangrene 707.00 [785.4]
Bedwetting — see also Enuresis 788.36
Beer-drinkers' heart (disease) 425.5
Bee sting (with allergic or anaphylactic shock) 989.5
Begbie's disease (exophthalmic goiter) 242.0 ☑
Behavior disorder, disturbance — see also Disturbance, conduct
  antisocial, without manifest psychiatric disorder
    adolescent V71.02
    adult V71.01
    child V71.02
  dyssocial, without manifest psychiatric disorder
    adolescent V71.02
    adult V71.01
    child V71.02
  high risk — see Problem
Behçet's syndrome 136.1
Behr's disease 362.50
Beigel's disease or morbus (white piedra) 111.2
Bejel 104.0
Bekhterev's disease (ankylosing spondylitis) 720.0
Bekhterev-Strümpell-Marie syndrome (ankylosing spondylitis) 720.0
Belching — see also Eructation 787.3
Bell's
  disease (see also Psychosis, affective) 296.0 ☑
  mania (see also Psychosis, affective) 296.0 ☑
  palsy, paralysis 351.0
    infant 767.5
    newborn 767.5
    syphilitic 094.89
  spasm 351.0
Bence-Jones albuminuria, albuminosuria, or proteinuria 791.0
Bends 993.3
Benedikt's syndrome (paralysis) 344.89
Benign — see also condition
  cellular changes, cervix 795.09
  prostate
    with
      other lower urinary tract symptoms (LUTS) 600.21
      urinary
        obstruction 600.21
        retention 600.21
    hyperplasia 600.20
    neoplasm 222.2
Bennett's
  disease (leukemia) 208.9 ☑
  fracture (closed) 815.01
    open 815.11
Benson's disease 379.22
Bent
  back (hysterical) 300.11
  nose 738.0
    congenital 754.0
Bereavement V62.82
  as adjustment reaction 309.0
Bergeron's disease (hysteroepilepsy) 300.11
Berger's paresthesia (lower limb) 782.0
Beriberi (acute) (atrophic) (chronic) (dry) (subacute) (wet) 265.0
  with polyneuropathy 265.0 [357.4]
  heart (disease) 265.0 [425.7]
  leprosy 030.1
  neuritis 265.0 [357.4]
Berlin's disease or edema (traumatic) 921.3
Berloque dermatitis 692.72
Bernard-Horner syndrome — see also Neuropathy, peripheral, autonomic 337.9
Bernard-Sergent syndrome (acute adrenocortical insufficiency) 255.41
Bernard-Soulier disease or thrombopathy 287.1
Bernhardt's disease or paresthesia 355.1
Bernhardt-Roth disease or syndrome (paresthesia) 355.1
Bernheim's syndrome — see also Failure, heart 428.0
Bertielliasis 123.8

Bertolotti's syndrome (sacralization of fifth lumbar vertebra) 756.15
Berylliosis (acute) (chronic) (lung) (occupational) 503
Besnier's
  lupus pernio 135
  prurigo (atopic dermatitis) (infantile eczema) 691.8
Besnier-Boeck disease or sarcoid 135
Besnier-Boeck-Schaumann disease (sarcoidosis) 135
Best's disease 362.76
Bestiality 302.1
Beta-adrenergic hyperdynamic circulatory state 429.82
Beta-aminoisobutyric aciduria 277.2
Beta-mercaptolactate-cysteine disulfiduria 270.0
Beta thalassemia (major) (minor) (mixed) 282.49
Beurmann's disease (sporotrichosis) 117.1
Bezoar 938
  intestine 936
  stomach 935.2
Bezold's abscess — see also Mastoiditis 383.01
Bianchi's syndrome (aphasia-apraxia-alexia) 784.69
Bicornuate or bicornis uterus 752.3
  in pregnancy or childbirth 654.0 ☑
    with obstructed labor 660.2 ☑
      affecting fetus or newborn 763.1
    affecting fetus or newborn 763.89
Bicuspid aortic valve 746.4
Biedl-Bardet syndrome 759.89
Bielschowsky's disease 330.1
Bielschowsky-Jansky
  amaurotic familial idiocy 330.1
  disease 330.1
Biemond's syndrome (obesity, polydactyly, and mental retardation) 759.89
Biermer's anemia or disease (pernicious anemia) 281.0
Biett's disease 695.4
Bifid (congenital) — see also Imperfect, closure
  apex, heart 746.89
  clitoris 752.49
  epiglottis 748.3
  kidney 753.3
  nose 748.1
  patella 755.64
  scrotum 752.89
  toe 755.66
  tongue 750.13
  ureter 753.4
  uterus 752.3
  uvula 749.02
    with cleft lip (see also Cleft, palate, with cleft lip) 749.20
Biforis uterus (suprasimplex) 752.3
Bifurcation (congenital) — see also Imperfect, closure
  gallbladder 751.69
  kidney pelvis 753.3
  renal pelvis 753.3
  rib 756.3
  tongue 750.13
  trachea 748.3
  ureter 753.4
  urethra 753.8
  uvula 749.02
    with cleft lip (see also Cleft, palate, with cleft lip) 749.20
  vertebra 756.19
Bigeminal pulse 427.89
Bigeminy 427.89
Big spleen syndrome 289.4
Bilateral — see condition
Bile duct — see condition
Bile pigments in urine 791.4
Bilharziasis — see also Schistosomiasis 120.9
  chyluria 120.0
  cutaneous 120.3
  galacturia 120.0
  hematochyluria 120.0
  intestinal 120.1
  lipemia 120.9
  lipuria 120.0

Bilharziasis — see also Schistosomiasis — continued
  Oriental 120.2
  piarhemia 120.9
  pulmonary 120.2
  tropical hematuria 120.0
  vesical 120.0
Biliary — see condition
Bilious (attack) — see also Vomiting
  fever, hemoglobinuric 084.8
Bilirubinuria 791.4
Biliuria 791.4
Billroth's disease
  meningocele (see also Spina bifida) 741.9 ☑
Bilobate placenta — see Placenta, abnormal
Bilocular
  heart 745.7
  stomach 536.8
Bing-Horton syndrome (histamine cephalgia) 339.00
Binswanger's disease or dementia 290.12
Biörck (-Thorson) syndrome (malignant carcinoid) 259.2
Biparta, bipartite — see also Imperfect, closure
  carpal scaphoid 755.59
  patella 755.64
  placenta — see Placenta, abnormal
  vagina 752.49
Bird
  face 756.0
  fanciers' lung or disease 495.2
  flu 488.0 ●
Bird's disease (oxaluria) 271.8
Birth
  abnormal fetus or newborn 763.9
  accident, fetus or newborn — see Birth, injury
  complications in mother — see Delivery, complicated
  compression during NEC 767.9
  defect — see Anomaly
  delayed, fetus 763.9
  difficult NEC, affecting fetus or newborn 763.9
  dry, affecting fetus or newborn 761.1
  forced, NEC, affecting fetus or newborn 763.89
  forceps, affecting fetus or newborn 763.2
  hematoma of sternomastoid 767.8
  immature 765.1 ☑
    extremely 765.0 ☑
  inattention, after or at 995.52
  induced, affecting fetus or newborn 763.89
  infant — see Newborn
  injury NEC 767.9
    adrenal gland 767.8
    basal ganglia 767.0
    brachial plexus (paralysis) 767.6
    brain (compression) (pressure) 767.0
    cerebellum 767.0
    cerebral hemorrhage 767.0
    conjunctiva 767.8
    eye 767.8
    fracture
      bone, any except clavicle or spine 767.3
      clavicle 767.2
      femur 767.3
      humerus 767.3
      long bone 767.3
      radius and ulna 767.3
      skeleton NEC 767.3
      skull 767.3
      spine 767.4
      tibia and fibula 767.3
    hematoma 767.8
      liver (subcapsular) 767.8
      mastoid 767.8
      skull 767.8
      sternomastoid 767.8
      testes 767.8
      vulva 767.8
    intracranial (edema) 767.0
    laceration
      brain 767.0
      by scalpel 767.8
      peripheral nerve 767.7
      liver 767.8
    meninges
      brain 767.0

Birth — continued
  injury — continued
    meninges — continued
      spinal cord 767.4
    nerves (cranial, peripheral) 767.7
      brachial plexus 767.6
      facial 767.5
    paralysis 767.7
      brachial plexus 767.6
      Erb (-Duchenne) 767.6
      facial nerve 767.5
      Klumpke (-Déjérine) 767.6
      radial nerve 767.6
      spinal (cord) (hemorrhage) (laceration) (rupture) 767.4
    rupture
      intracranial 767.0
      liver 767.8
      spinal cord 767.4
      spleen 767.8
      viscera 767.8
    scalp 767.19
    scalpel wound 767.8
    skeleton NEC 767.3
    specified NEC 767.8
    spinal cord 767.4
    spleen 767.8
    subdural hemorrhage 767.0
    tentorial, tear 767.0
    testes 767.8
    vulva 767.8
  instrumental, NEC, affecting fetus or newborn 763.2
  lack of care, after or at 995.52
  multiple
    affected by maternal complications of pregnancy 761.5
    healthy liveborn — see Newborn, multiple
  neglect, after or at 995.52
  newborn — see Newborn
  palsy or paralysis NEC 767.7
  precipitate, fetus or newborn 763.6
  premature (infant) 765.1 ☑
  prolonged, affecting fetus or newborn 763.9
  retarded, fetus or newborn 763.9
  shock, newborn 779.89
  strangulation or suffocation
    due to aspiration of clear amniotic fluid 770.13
      with respiratory symptoms 770.14
    mechanical 767.8
  trauma NEC 767.9
  triplet
    affected by maternal complications of pregnancy 761.5
    healthy liveborn — see Newborn, multiple
  twin
    affected by maternal complications of pregnancy 761.5
    healthy liveborn — see Newborn, twin
  ventouse, affecting fetus or newborn 763.3
Birthmark 757.32
Birt-Hogg-Dube syndrome 759.89
Bisalbuminemia 273.8
Biskra button 085.1
Bite(s)
  with intact skin surface — see Contusion
  animal — see Wound, open, by site
    intact skin surface — see Contusion
  bedbug — see Injury, superficial, by site
  centipede 989.5
  chigger 133.8
  fire ant 989.5
  flea — see Injury, superficial, by site
  human (open wound) (see also Wound, open, by site)
    intact skin surface — see Contusion
  insect
    nonvenomous — see Injury, superficial, by site
    venomous 989.5
  mad dog (death from) 071
  open
    anterior 524.24
    posterior 524.25
  poisonous 989.5

☑ Additional Digit Required — Refer to the Tabular List for Digit Selection   Subterms under main terms may continue to next column or page

2010 ICD-9-CM   ▶◀ Revised Text   ● New Line   ▲ Revised Code   October 2009 • Volume 2 — 33

Bite(s) — continued
  red bug 133.8
  reptile 989.5
    nonvenomous — see Wound, open, by site
  snake 989.5
    nonvenomous — see Wound, open, by site
  spider (venomous) 989.5
    nonvenomous — see Injury, superficial, by site
  venomous 989.5
Biting
  cheek or lip 528.9
  nail 307.9
Black
  death 020.9
  eye NEC 921.0
  hairy tongue 529.3
  heel 924.20
  lung disease 500
  palm 923.20
Blackfan-Diamond anemia or syndrome
    (congenital hypoplastic anemia) 284.01
Blackhead 706.1
Blackout 780.2
Blackwater fever 084.8
Bladder — see condition
Blast
  blindness 921.3
  concussion — see Blast, injury
  injury 869.0
    with open wound into cavity 869.1
      abdomen or thorax — see Injury, internal, by site
      brain (see also Concussion, brain) 850.9
        with skull fracture — see Fracture, skull
      ear (acoustic nerve trauma) 951.5
        with perforation, tympanic membrane — see Wound, open, ear, drum
      lung (see also Injury, internal, lung) 861.20
      otitic (explosive) 388.11
Blastomycosis, blastomycotic (chronic) (cutaneous) (disseminated) (lung) (pulmonary) (systemic) 116.0
  Brazilian 116.1
  European 117.5
  keloidal 116.2
  North American 116.0
  primary pulmonary 116.0
  South American 116.1
Bleb(s) 709.8
  emphysematous (bullous) (diffuse) (lung) (ruptured) (solitary) 492.0
  filtering, eye (postglaucoma) (status) V45.69
    with complication 997.99
      postcataract extraction (complication) 997.99
  lung (ruptured) 492.0
    congenital 770.5
  subpleural (emphysematous) 492.0
Bleeder (familial) (hereditary) — see also Defect, coagulation 286.9
  nonfamilial 286.9
Bleeding — see also Hemorrhage 459.0
  anal 569.3
  anovulatory 628.0
  atonic, following delivery 666.1 ☑
  capillary 448.9
  due to subinvolution 621.1
    puerperal 666.2 ☑
  ear 388.69
  excessive, associated with menopausal onset 627.0
  familial (see also Defect, coagulation) 286.9
  following intercourse 626.7
  gastrointestinal 578.9
  gums 523.8
  hemorrhoids — see Hemorrhoids, bleeding
  intermenstrual
    irregular 626.6
    regular 626.5
  intraoperative 998.11
  irregular NEC 626.4
  menopausal 627.0
  mouth 528.9

Bleeding — see also Hemorrhage — continued
  nipple 611.79
  nose 784.7
  ovulation 626.5
  postclimacteric 627.1
  postcoital 626.7
  postmenopausal 627.1
    following induced menopause 627.4
  postoperative 998.11
  preclimacteric 627.0
  puberty 626.3
    excessive, with onset of menstrual periods 626.3
  rectum, rectal 569.3
  tendencies (see also Defect, coagulation) 286.9
  throat 784.8
  umbilical stump 772.3
  umbilicus 789.9
  unrelated to menstrual cycle 626.6
  uterus, uterine 626.9
    climacteric 627.0
    dysfunctional 626.8
    functional 626.8
    unrelated to menstrual cycle 626.6
  vagina, vaginal 623.8
    functional 626.8
  vicarious 625.8
Blennorrhagia, blennorrhagic — see Blennorrhea
Blennorrhea (acute) 098.0
  adultorum 098.40
  alveolaris 523.40
  chronic or duration of 2 months or over 098.2
  gonococcal (neonatorum) 098.40
  inclusion (neonatal) (newborn) 771.6
  neonatorum 098.40
Blepharelosis — see also Entropion 374.00
Blepharitis (eyelid) 373.00
  angularis 373.01
  ciliaris 373.00
    with ulcer 373.01
  marginal 373.00
    with ulcer 373.01
  scrofulous (see also Tuberculosis)
    017.3 ☑ [373.00]
  squamous 373.02
  ulcerative 373.01
Blepharochalasis 374.34
  congenital 743.62
Blepharoclonus 333.81
Blepharoconjunctivitis — see also Conjunctivitis 372.20
  angular 372.21
  contact 372.22
Blepharophimosis (eyelid) 374.46
  congenital 743.62
Blepharoplegia 374.89
Blepharoptosis 374.30
  congenital 743.61
Blepharopyorrhea 098.49
Blepharospasm 333.81
  due to drugs 333.85
Blessig's cyst 362.62
Blighted ovum 631
Blind
  bronchus (congenital) 748.3
  eye (see also Blindness)
    hypertensive 360.42
    hypotensive 360.41
  loop syndrome (postoperative) 579.2
  sac, fallopian tube (congenital) 752.19
  spot, enlarged 368.42
  tract or tube (congenital) NEC — see Atresia
Blindness (acquired) (congenital) (both eyes) 369.00
  with deafness V49.85
  blast 921.3
    with nerve injury — see Injury, nerve, optic
  Bright's — see Uremia
  color (congenital) 368.59
    acquired 368.55
    blue 368.53
    green 368.52
    red 368.51
    total 368.54

Blindness — continued
  concussion 950.9
  cortical 377.75
  day 368.10
    acquired 368.10
    congenital 368.10
    hereditary 368.10
    specified type NEC 368.10
  due to
    injury NEC 950.9
    refractive error — see Error, refractive
  eclipse (total) 363.31
  emotional 300.11
  face 368.16
  hysterical 300.11
  legal (both eyes) (USA definition) 369.4
    with impairment of better (less impaired) eye
      near-total 369.02
        with
          lesser eye impairment 369.02
          near-total 369.04
          total 369.03
      profound 369.05
        with
          lesser eye impairment 369.05
          near-total 369.07
          profound 369.08
          total 369.06
      severe 369.21
        with
          lesser eye impairment 369.21
          blind 369.11
          near-total 369.13
          profound 369.14
          severe 369.22
          total 369.12
      total
        with lesser eye impairment
          total 369.01
  mind 784.69
  moderate
    both eyes 369.25
      with impairment of lesser eye (specified as)
        blind, not further specified 369.15
        low vision, not further specified 369.23
        near-total 369.17
        profound 369.18
        severe 369.24
        total 369.16
    one eye 369.74
      with vision of other eye (specified as)
        near-normal 369.75
        normal 369.76
  near-total
    both eyes 369.04
      with impairment of lesser eye (specified as)
        blind, not further specified 369.02
        total 369.03
    one eye 369.64
      with vision of other eye (specified as)
        near-normal 369.65
        normal 369.66
  night 368.60
    acquired 368.62
    congenital (Japanese) 368.61
    hereditary 368.61
    specified type NEC 368.69
    vitamin A deficiency 264.5
  nocturnal — see Blindness, night
  one eye 369.60
    with low vision of other eye 369.10
  profound
    both eyes 369.08
      with impairment of lesser eye (specified as)
        blind, not further specified 369.05
        near-total 369.07
        total 369.06
    one eye 369.67
      with vision of other eye (specified as)
        near-normal 369.68
        normal 369.69

Blindness — continued
  psychic 784.69
  severe
    both eyes 369.22
      with impairment of lesser eye (specified as)
        blind, not further specified 369.11
        low vision, not further specified 369.21
        near-total 369.13
        profound 369.14
        total 369.12
    one eye 369.71
      with vision of other eye (specified as)
        near-normal 369.72
        normal 369.73
  snow 370.24
  sun 363.31
  temporary 368.12
  total
    both eyes 369.01
    one eye 369.61
      with vision of other eye (specified as)
        near-normal 369.62
        normal 369.63
  transient 368.12
  traumatic NEC 950.9
  word (developmental) 315.01
    acquired 784.61
    secondary to organic lesion 784.61
Blister — see also Injury, superficial, by site
  beetle dermatitis 692.89
  due to burn — see Burn, by site, second degree
  fever 054.9
  multiple, skin, nontraumatic 709.8
Bloating 787.3
Bloch-Siemens syndrome (incontinentia pigmenti) 757.33
Bloch-Stauffer dyshormonal dermatosis 757.33
Bloch-Sulzberger disease or syndrome (incontinentia pigmenti) (melanoblastosis) 757.33
Block
  alveolar capillary 516.3
  arborization (heart) 426.6
  arrhythmic 426.9
  atrioventricular (AV) (incomplete) (partial) 426.10
    with
      2:1 atrioventricular response block 426.13
      atrioventricular dissociation 426.0
      first degree (incomplete) 426.11
      second degree (Mobitz type I) 426.13
        Mobitz (type) II 426.12
      third degree 426.0
    complete 426.0
      congenital 746.86
    congenital 746.86
    Mobitz (incomplete)
      type I (Wenckebach's) 426.13
      type II 426.12
    partial 426.13
  auriculoventricular (see also Block, atrioventricular) 426.10
    complete 426.0
      congenital 746.86
    congenital 746.86
  bifascicular (cardiac) 426.53
  bundle branch (complete) (false) (incomplete) 426.50
    bilateral 426.53
    left (complete) (main stem) 426.3
      with right bundle branch block 426.53
      anterior fascicular 426.2
        with
          posterior fascicular block 426.3
          right bundle branch block 426.52
      hemiblock 426.2
      incomplete 426.2
        with right bundle branch block 426.53
      posterior fascicular 426.2

☑ Additional Digit Required — Refer to the Tabular List for Digit Selection   ▽ Subterms under main terms may continue to next column or page

34 — Volume 2   ▶◀ Revised Text   ● New Line   ▲ Revised Code   2010 ICD-9-CM

Block — *continued*
 bundle branch — *continued*
  left — *continued*
   posterior fascicular — *continued*
    with
     anterior fascicular block 426.3
     right bundle branch block 426.51
   right 426.4
    with
     left bundle branch block (incomplete) (main stem) 426.53
     left fascicular block 426.53
      anterior 426.52
      posterior 426.51
   Wilson's type 426.4
 cardiac 426.9
 conduction 426.9
  complete 426.0
 Eustachian tube (*see also* Obstruction, Eustachian tube) 381.60
 fascicular (left anterior) (left posterior) 426.2
 foramen Magendie (acquired) 331.3
  congenital 742.3
   with spina bifida (*see also* Spina bifida) 741.0 ☑
 heart 426.9
  first degree (atrioventricular) 426.11
  second degree (atrioventricular) 426.13
  third degree (atrioventricular) 426.0
  bundle branch (complete) (false) (incomplete) 426.50
   bilateral 426.53
   left (*see also* Block, bundle branch, left) 426.3
   right (*see also* Block, bundle branch, right) 426.4
  complete (atrioventricular) 426.0
  congenital 746.86
  incomplete 426.13
  intra-atrial 426.6
  intraventricular NEC 426.6
  sinoatrial 426.6
  specified type NEC 426.6
 hepatic vein 453.0
 intraventricular (diffuse) (myofibrillar) 426.6
  bundle branch (complete) (false) (incomplete) 426.50
   bilateral 426.53
   left (*see also* Block, bundle branch, left) 426.3
   right (*see also* Block, bundle branch, right) 426.4
 kidney (*see also* Disease, renal) 593.9
  postcystoscopic 997.5
 myocardial (*see also* Block, heart) 426.9
 nodal 426.10
 optic nerve 377.49
 organ or site (congenital) NEC — *see* Atresia
 parietal 426.6
 peri-infarction 426.6
 portal (vein) 452
 sinoatrial 426.6
 sinoauricular 426.6
 spinal cord 336.9
 trifascicular 426.54
 tubal 628.2
 vein NEC 453.9
Blocq's disease or syndrome (astasia-abasia) 307.9
Blood
 constituents, abnormal NEC 790.6
 disease 289.9
  specified NEC 289.89
 donor V59.01
  other blood components V59.09
  stem cells V59.02
  whole blood V59.01
 dyscrasia 289.9
  with
   abortion — *see* Abortion, by type, with hemorrhage, delayed or excessive
   ectopic pregnancy (*see also* categories 633.0–633.9) 639.1

Blood — *continued*
 dyscrasia — *continued*
  with — *continued*
   molar pregnancy (*see also* categories 630–632) 639.1
  following
   abortion 639.1
   ectopic or molar pregnancy 639.1
  newborn NEC 776.9 ●
  puerperal, postpartum 666.3 ☑
 flukes NEC (*see also* Infestation, Schistosoma) 120.9
 in
  feces (*see also* Melena) 578.1
   occult 792.1
  urine (*see also* Hematuria) 599.70
 mole 631
 occult 792.1
 poisoning (*see also* Septicemia) 038.9
 pressure
  decreased, due to shock following injury 958.4
  fluctuating 796.4
  high (*see also* Hypertension) 401.9
   incidental reading (isolated) (nonspecific), without diagnosis of hypertension 796.2
  low (*see also* Hypotension) 458.9
   incidental reading (isolated) (nonspecific), without diagnosis of hypotension 796.3
 spitting (*see also* Hemoptysis) 786.3
 staining cornea 371.12
 transfusion
  without reported diagnosis V58.2
  donor V59.01
   stem cells V59.02
  reaction or complication — *see* Complications, transfusion
 tumor — *see* Hematoma
 vessel rupture — *see* Hemorrhage
 vomiting (*see also* Hematemesis) 578.0
Blood-forming organ disease 289.9
Bloodgood's disease 610.1
Bloodshot eye 379.93
Bloom (-Machacek) (-Torre) syndrome 757.39
Blotch, palpebral 372.55
Blount-Barber syndrome (tibia vara) 732.4
Blount's disease (tibia vara) 732.4
Blue
 baby 746.9
 bloater 491.20
  with
   acute bronchitis 491.22
   exacerbation (acute) 491.21
 diaper syndrome 270.0
 disease 746.9
 dome cyst 610.0
 drum syndrome 381.02
 sclera 743.47
  with fragility of bone and deafness 756.51
 toe syndrome 445.02
Blueness — *see also* Cyanosis 782.5
Blurring, visual 368.8
Blushing (abnormal) (excessive) 782.62
BMI (body mass index)
 adult
  25.0-25.9 V85.21
  26.0-26.9 V85.22
  27.0-27.9 V85.23
  28.0-28.9 V85.24
  29.0-29.9 V85.25
  30.0-30.9 V85.30
  31.0-31.9 V85.31
  32.0-32.9 V85.32
  33.0-33.9 V85.33
  34.0-34.9 V85.34
  35.0-35.9 V85.35
  36.0-36.9 V85.36
  37.0-37.9 V85.37
  38.0-38.9 V85.38
  39.0-39.9 V85.39
  40 and over V85.4
  between 19-24 V85.1
  less than 19 V85.0

BMI — *continued*
 pediatric
  5th percentile to less than 85th percentile for age V85.52
  85th percentile to less than 95th percentile for age V85.53
  greater than or equal to 95th percentile for age V85.54
  less than 5th percentile for age V85.51
Boarder, hospital V65.0
 infant V65.0
Bockhart's impetigo (superficial folliculitis) 704.8
Bodechtel-Guttmann disease (subacute sclerosing panencephalitis) 046.2
Boder-Sedgwick syndrome (ataxia-telangiectasia) 334.8
Body, bodies
 Aschoff (*see also* Myocarditis, rheumatic) 398.0
 asteroid, vitreous 379.22
 choroid, colloid (degenerative) 362.57
  hereditary 362.77
 cytoid (retina) 362.82
 drusen (retina) (*see also* Drusen) 362.57
  optic disc 377.21
 fibrin, pleura 511.0
 foreign — *see* Foreign body
 Hassall-Henle 371.41
 loose
  joint (*see also* Loose, body, joint) 718.1 ☑
   knee 717.6
  knee 717.6
  sheath, tendon 727.82
 Mallory's 034.1
 mass index (BMI)
  adult
   25.0-25.9 V85.21
   26.0-26.9 V85.22
   27.0-27.9 V85.23
   28.0-28.9 V85.24
   29.0-29.9 V85.25
   30.0-30.9 V85.30
   31.0-31.9 V85.31
   32.0-32.9 V85.32
   33.0-33.9 V85.33
   34.0-34.9 V85.34
   36.0-36.9 V85.36
   37.0-37.9 V85.37
   38.0-38.9 V85.38
   39.0-39.9 V85.39
   40 and over V85.4
   between 19-24 V85.1
   less than 19 V85.0
  pediatric
   5th percentile to less than 85th percentile for age V85.52
   85th percentile to less than 95th percentile for age V85.53
   greater than or equal to 95th percentile for age V85.54
   less than 5th percentile for age V85.51
 Mooser 081.0
 Negri 071
 rice (joint) (*see also* Loose, body, joint) 718.1 ☑
  knee 717.6
 rocking 307.3
Boeck's
 disease (sarcoidosis) 135
 lupoid (miliary) 135
 sarcoid 135
Boerhaave's syndrome (spontaneous esophageal rupture) 530.4
Boggy
 cervix 622.8
 uterus 621.8
Boil — *see also* Carbuncle 680.9
 abdominal wall 680.2
 Aleppo 085.1
 ankle 680.6
 anus 680.5
 arm (any part, above wrist) 680.3
 auditory canal, external 680.0
 axilla 680.3
 back (any part) 680.2
 Baghdad 085.1
 breast 680.2
 buttock 680.5

Boil — *see also* Carbuncle — *continued*
 chest wall 680.2
 corpus cavernosum 607.2
 Delhi 085.1
 ear (any part) 680.0
 eyelid 373.13
 face (any part, except eye) 680.0
 finger (any) 680.4
 flank 680.2
 foot (any part) 680.7
 forearm 680.3
 Gafsa 085.1
 genital organ, male 608.4
 gluteal (region) 680.5
 groin 680.2
 hand (any part) 680.4
 head (any part, except face) 680.8
 heel 680.7
 hip 680.6
 knee 680.6
 labia 616.4
 lacrimal (*see also* Dacryocystitis) 375.30
  gland (*see also* Dacryoadenitis) 375.00
  passages (duct) (sac) (*see also* Dacryocystitis) 375.30
 leg, any part, except foot 680.6
 multiple sites 680.9
 natal 085.1
 neck 680.1
 nose (external) (septum) 680.0
 orbit, orbital 376.01
 partes posteriores 680.5
 pectoral region 680.2
 penis 607.2
 perineum 680.2
 pinna 680.0
 scalp (any part) 680.8
 scrotum 608.4
 seminal vesicle 608.0
 shoulder 680.3
 skin NEC 680.9
 specified site NEC 680.8
 spermatic cord 608.4
 temple (region) 680.0
 testis 608.4
 thigh 680.6
 thumb 680.4
 toe (any) 680.7
 tropical 085.1
 trunk 680.2
 tunica vaginalis 608.4
 umbilicus 680.2
 upper arm 680.3
 vas deferens 608.4
 vulva 616.4
 wrist 680.4
Bold hives — *see also* Urticaria 708.9
Bolivian hemorrhagic fever 078.7
Bombé, iris 364.74
Bomford-Rhoads anemia (refractory) 238.72
Bone — *see* condition
Bonnevie-Ullrich syndrome 758.6
Bonnier's syndrome 386.19
Bonvale Dam fever 780.79
Bony block of joint 718.80
 ankle 718.87
 elbow 718.82
 foot 718.87
 hand 718.84
 hip 718.85
 knee 718.86
 multiple sites 718.89
 pelvic region 718.85
 shoulder (region) 718.81
 specified site NEC 718.88
 wrist 718.83
BOOP (bronchiolitis obliterans organized pneumonia) 516.8
Borderline
 intellectual functioning V62.89
 osteopenia 733.90
 pelvis 653.1 ☑
  with obstruction during labor 660.1 ☑
   affecting fetus or newborn 763.1
 psychosis (*see also* Schizophrenia) 295.5 ☑

Block — Borderline

☑ Additional Digit Required — Refer to the Tabular List for Digit Selection   ▽ Subterms under main terms may continue to next column or page

2010 ICD-9-CM   ▶◀ Revised Text   ● New Line   ▲ Revised Code   October 2009 • Volume 2 — 35

Borderline — *continued*
  psychosis (*see also* Schizophrenia) — *continued*
    of childhood (*see also* Psychosis, childhood) 299.8 ☑
  schizophrenia (*see also* Schizophrenia) 295.5 ☑
Borna disease 062.9
Bornholm disease (epidemic pleurodynia) 074.1
Borrelia vincentii (mouth) (pharynx) (tonsils) 101
Bostock's catarrh — *see also* Fever, hay 477.9
Boston exanthem 048
Botalli, ductus (patent) (persistent) 747.0
Bothriocephalus latus infestation 123.4
Botulism 005.1
  food poisoning 005.1
  infant 040.41
  non-foodborne 040.42
  wound 040.42
Bouba — *see also* Yaws 102.9
Bouffée délirante 298.3
Bouillaud's disease or syndrome (rheumatic heart disease) 391.9
Bourneville's disease (tuberous sclerosis) 759.5
Boutonneuse fever 082.1
Boutonniere
  deformity (finger) 736.21
  hand (intrinsic) 736.21
Bouveret (-Hoffmann) disease or syndrome (paroxysmal tachycardia) 427.2
Bovine heart — *see* Hypertrophy, cardiac
Bowel — *see* condition
Bowen's
  dermatosis (precancerous) (M8081/2) — *see* Neoplasm, skin, in situ
  disease (M8081/2) — *see* Neoplasm, skin, in situ
  epithelioma (M8081/2) — *see* Neoplasm, skin, in situ
  type
    epidermoid carcinoma in situ (M8081/2) — *see* Neoplasm, skin, in situ
    intraepidermal squamous cell carcinoma (M8081/2) — *see* Neoplasm, skin, in situ
Bowing
  femur 736.89
    congenital 754.42
  fibula 736.89
    congenital 754.43
  forearm 736.09
    away from midline (cubitus valgus) 736.01
    toward midline (cubitus varus) 736.02
  leg(s), long bones, congenital 754.44
  radius 736.09
    away from midline (cubitus valgus) 736.01
    toward midline (cubitus varus) 736.02
  tibia 736.89
    congenital 754.43
Bowleg(s) 736.42
  congenital 754.44
  rachitic 268.1
Boyd's dysentery 004.2
Brachial — *see* condition
Brachman-de Lange syndrome (Amsterdam dwarf, mental retardation, and brachycephaly) 759.89
Brachycardia 427.89
Brachycephaly 756.0
Brachymorphism and ectopia lentis 759.89
Bradley's disease (epidemic vomiting) 078.82
Bradycardia 427.89
  chronic (sinus) 427.81
  newborn 779.81
  nodal 427.89
  postoperative 997.1
  reflex 337.09
  sinoatrial 427.89
    with paroxysmal tachyarrhythmia or tachycardia 427.81
    chronic 427.81
  sinus 427.89
    with paroxysmal tachyarrhythmia or tachycardia 427.81
    chronic 427.81
    persistent 427.81

Bradycardia — *continued*
  sinus — *continued*
    severe 427.81
    tachycardia syndrome 427.81
    vagal 427.89
Bradykinesia 781.0
Bradypnea 786.09
Brailsford's disease 732.3
  radial head 732.3
  tarsal scaphoid 732.5
Brailsford-Morquio disease or syndrome (mucopolysaccharidosis IV) 277.5
Brain — *see also* condition
  death 348.89 ▲
  syndrome (acute) (chronic) (nonpsychotic) (organic) (with neurotic reaction) (with behavioral reaction) (*see also* Syndrome, brain) 310.9
    with
      presenile brain disease 290.10
      psychosis, psychotic reaction (*see also* Psychosis, organic) 294.9
    congenital (*see also* Retardation, mental) 319
Branched-chain amino-acid disease 270.3
Branchial — *see* condition
Brandt's syndrome (acrodermatitis enteropathica) 686.8
Brash (water) 787.1
Brass-founders' ague 985.8
Bravais-Jacksonian epilepsy — *see also* Epilepsy 345.5 ☑
Braxton Hicks contractions 644.1 ☑
Braziers' disease 985.8
Brazilian
  blastomycosis 116.1
  leishmaniasis 085.5
BRBPR (bright red blood per rectum) 569.3
Break
  cardiorenal — *see* Hypertension, cardiorenal
  retina (*see also* Defect, retina) 361.30
Breakbone fever 061
Breakdown
  device, implant, or graft — *see* Complications, mechanical
  nervous (*see also* Disorder, mental, nonpsychotic) 300.9
  perineum 674.2 ☑
Breast — *see also* condition
  buds 259.1
    in newborn 779.89
  dense 793.82
  nodule 793.89
Breast feeding difficulties 676.8 ☑
Breath
  foul 784.99
  holder, child 312.81
  holding spells 786.9
  shortness 786.05
Breathing
  asymmetrical 786.09
  bronchial 786.09
  exercises V57.0
  labored 786.09
  mouth 784.99
    causing malocclusion 524.59
  periodic 786.09
    high altitude 327.22
  tic 307.20
Breathlessness 786.09
Breda's disease — *see also* Yaws 102.9
Breech
  delivery, affecting fetus or newborn 763.0
  extraction, affecting fetus or newborn 763.0
  presentation (buttocks) (complete) (frank) 652.2 ☑
    with successful version 652.1 ☑
    before labor, affecting fetus or newborn 761.7
    during labor, affecting fetus or newborn 763.0
Breisky's disease (kraurosis vulvae) 624.09
Brennemann's syndrome (acute mesenteric lymphadenitis) 289.2
Brenner's
  tumor (benign) (M9000/0) 220

Brenner's — *continued*
  tumor — *continued*
    borderline malignancy (M9000/1) 236.2
    malignant (M9000/3) 183.0
    proliferating (M9000/1) 236.2
● **Bretonneau's disease** (diphtheritic malignant angina) 032.0
Breus' mole 631
Brevicollis 756.16
Bricklayers' itch 692.89
Brickmakers' anemia 126.9
Bridge
  myocardial 746.85
Bright's
  blindness — *see* Uremia
  disease (*see also* Nephritis) 583.9
    arteriosclerotic (*see also* Hypertension, kidney) 403.90
Bright red blood per rectum (BRBPR) 569.3
Brill's disease (recrudescent typhus) 081.1
  flea-borne 081.0
  louse-borne 081.1
Brill-Symmers disease (follicular lymphoma) (M9690/3) 202.0 ☑
Brill-Zinsser disease (recrudescent typhus) 081.1
Brinton's disease (linitis plastica) (M8142/3) 151.9
Brion-Kayser disease — *see also* Fever, paratyphoid 002.9
Briquet's disorder or syndrome 300.81
Brissaud's
  infantilism (infantile myxedema) 244.9
  motor-verbal tic 307.23
Brissaud-Meige syndrome (infantile myxedema) 244.9
Brittle
  bones (congenital) 756.51
  nails 703.8
    congenital 757.5
Broad — *see also* condition
  beta disease 272.2
  ligament laceration syndrome 620.6
Brock's syndrome (atelectasis due to enlarged lymph nodes) 518.0
Brocq's disease 691.8
  atopic (diffuse) neurodermatitis 691.8
  lichen simplex chronicus 698.3
  parakeratosis psoriasiformis 696.2
  parapsoriasis 696.2
Brocq-Duhring disease (dermatitis herpetiformis) 694.0
▲ **Brodie's**
  abscess (localized) (chronic) (*see also* Osteomyelitis) 730.1 ☑
  disease (joint) (*see also* Osteomyelitis) 730.1 ☑
Broken
  arches 734
    congenital 755.67
  back — *see* Fracture, vertebra, by site
  bone — *see* Fracture, by site
  compensation — *see* Disease, heart
  heart syndrome 429.83
  implant or internal device — *see* listing under Complications, mechanical
  neck — *see* Fracture, vertebra, cervical
  nose 802.0
    open 802.1
  tooth, teeth 873.63
    complicated 873.73
Bromhidrosis 705.89
Bromidism, bromism
  acute 967.3
    correct substance properly administered 349.82
    overdose or wrong substance given or taken 967.3
  chronic (*see also* Dependence) 304.1 ☑
Bromidrosiphobia 300.23
Bromidrosis 705.89
Bronchi, bronchial — *see* condition
Bronchiectasis (cylindrical) (diffuse) (fusiform) (localized) (moniliform) (postinfectious) (recurrent) (saccular) 494.0
  with acute exacerbation 494.1
  congenital 748.61
  tuberculosis (*see also* Tuberculosis) 011.5 ☑

Bronchiolectasis — *see* Bronchiectasis
Bronchiolitis (acute) (infectious) (subacute) 466.19
  with
    bronchospasm or obstruction 466.19
    influenza, flu, or grippe 487.1
  catarrhal (acute) (subacute) 466.19
  chemical 506.0
    chronic 506.4
  chronic (obliterative) 491.8
  due to external agent — *see* Bronchitis, acute, due to
  fibrosa obliterans 491.8
  influenzal 487.1
  obliterans 491.8
    with organizing pneumonia (BOOP) 516.6
    status post lung transplant 996.84
  obliterative (chronic) (diffuse) (subacute) 491.8
    due to fumes or vapors 506.4
  respiratory syncytial virus 466.11
  vesicular — *see* Pneumonia, broncho-
Bronchitis (diffuse) (hypostatic) (infectious) (inflammatory) (simple) 490
  with
    emphysema — *see* Emphysema
    influenza, flu, or grippe 487.1
    obstruction airway, chronic 491.20
      with
        acute bronchitis 491.22
        exacerbation (acute) 491.21
    tracheitis 490
      acute or subacute 466.0
        with bronchospasm or obstruction 466.0
      chronic 491.8
  acute or subacute 466.0
    with
      bronchiectasis 494.1
      bronchospasm 466.0
      obstruction 466.0
      tracheitis 466.0
    chemical (due to fumes or vapors) 506.0
    due to
      fumes or vapors 506.0
      radiation 508.8
  allergic (acute) (*see also* Asthma) 493.9 ☑
  arachidic 934.1
  aspiration 507.0
    due to fumes or vapors 506.0
  asthmatic (acute) 493.90
    with
      acute exacerbation 493.92
      status asthmaticus 493.91
    chronic 493.2 ☑
  capillary 466.19
    with bronchospasm or obstruction 466.19
    chronic 491.8
  caseous (*see also* Tuberculosis) 011.3 ☑
  Castellani's 104.8
  catarrhal 490
    acute — *see* Bronchitis, acute
    chronic 491.0
  chemical (acute) (subacute) 506.0
    chronic 506.4
    due to fumes or vapors (acute) (subacute) 506.0
      chronic 506.4
  chronic 491.9
    with
      tracheitis (chronic) 491.8
    asthmatic 493.2 ☑
    catarrhal 491.0
    chemical (due to fumes and vapors) 506.4
    due to
      fumes or vapors (chemical) (inhalation) 506.4
      radiation 508.8
      tobacco smoking 491.0
    mucopurulent 491.1
    obstructive 491.20
      with
        acute bronchitis 491.22
        exacerbation (acute) 491.21
    purulent 491.1
    simple 491.0
    specified type NEC 491.8

Index

Borderline — Bronchitis

Bronchitis — *continued*
croupous 466.0
with bronchospasm or obstruction 466.0
due to fumes or vapors 506.0
emphysematous 491.20
with
acute bronchitis 491.22
exacerbation (acute) 491.21
exudative 466.0
fetid (chronic) (recurrent) 491.1
fibrinous, acute or subacute 466.0
with bronchospasm or obstruction 466.0
grippal 487.1
influenzal 487.1
membranous, acute or subacute 466.0
with bronchospasm or obstruction 466.0
moulders' 502
mucopurulent (chronic) (recurrent) 491.1
acute or subacute 466.0
obliterans 491.8
obstructive (chronic) 491.20
with
acute bronchitis 491.22
exacerbation (acute) 491.21
pituitous 491.1
plastic (inflammatory) 466.0
pneumococcal, acute or subacute 466.0
with bronchospasm or obstruction 466.0
pseudomembranous 466.0
purulent (chronic) (recurrent) 491.1
acute or subacute 466.0
with bronchospasm or obstruction 466.0
putrid 491.1
scrofulous (*see also* Tuberculosis) 011.3 ☑
senile 491.9
septic, acute or subacute 466.0
with bronchospasm or obstruction 466.0
smokers' 491.0
spirochetal 104.8
suffocative, acute or subacute 466.0
summer (*see also* Asthma) 493.9 ☑
suppurative (chronic) 491.1
acute or subacute 466.0
tuberculous (*see also* Tuberculosis) 011.3 ☑
ulcerative 491.8
Vincent's 101
Vincent's 101
viral, acute or subacute 466.0
Bronchoalveolitis 485
Bronchoaspergillosis 117.3
Bronchocele
meaning
dilatation of bronchus 519.19
goiter 240.9
Bronchogenic carcinoma 162.9
Bronchohemisporosis 117.9
Broncholithiasis 518.89
tuberculous (*see also* Tuberculosis) 011.3 ☑
Bronchomalacia 748.3
Bronchomoniliasis 112.89
Bronchomycosis 112.89
Bronchonocardiosis 039.1
Bronchopleuropneumonia — *see* Pneumonia, broncho-
Bronchopneumonia — *see* Pneumonia, broncho-
Bronchopneumonitis — *see* Pneumonia, broncho-
Bronchopulmonary — *see* condition
Bronchopulmonitis — *see* Pneumonia, broncho-
Bronchorrhagia 786.3
newborn 770.3
tuberculous (*see also* Tuberculosis) 011.3 ☑
Bronchorrhea (chronic) (purulent) 491.0
acute 466.0
Bronchospasm 519.11
with
asthma — *see* Asthma
bronchiolitis, acute 466.19
due to respiratory syncytial virus 466.11
bronchitis — *see* Bronchitis
chronic obstructive pulmonary disease (COPD) 496
emphysema — *see* Emphysema

Bronchospasm — *continued*
with — *continued*
emphysema — *see* Emphysema — *continued*
due to external agent — *see* Condition, respiratory, acute, due to
acute 519.11
exercise induced 493.81
Bronchospirochetosis 104.8
Bronchostenosis 519.19
Bronchus — *see* condition
Bronze, bronzed
diabetes 275.0
disease (Addison's) (skin) 255.41
tuberculous (*see also* Tuberculosis) 017.6 ☑
Brooke's disease or tumor (M8100/0) — *see* Neoplasm, skin, benign
Brown enamel of teeth (hereditary) 520.5
Brown-Séquard's paralysis (syndrome) 344.89
Brown's tendon sheath syndrome 378.61
Brow presentation complicating delivery 652.4 ☑
Brucella, brucellosis (infection) 023.9
abortus 023.1
canis 023.3
dermatitis, skin 023.9
melitensis 023.0
mixed 023.8
suis 023.2
Bruck-de Lange disease or syndrome (Amsterdam dwarf, mental retardation, and brachycephaly) 759.89
Bruck's disease 733.99
Brugada syndrome 746.89
Brug's filariasis 125.1
Brugsch's syndrome (acropachyderma) 757.39
Bruhl's disease (splenic anemia with fever) 285.8
Bruise (skin surface intact) — *see also* Contusion
with
fracture — *see* Fracture, by site
open wound — *see* Wound, open, by site
internal organ (abdomen, chest, or pelvis) — *see* Injury, internal, by site
umbilical cord 663.6 ☑
affecting fetus or newborn 762.6
Bruit 785.9
arterial (abdominal) (carotid) 785.9
supraclavicular 785.9
Brushburn — *see* Injury, superficial, by site
Bruton's X-linked agammaglobulinemia 279.01
Bruxism 306.8
sleep related 327.53
Bubbly lung syndrome 770.7
Bubo 289.3
blennorrhagic 098.89
chancroidal 099.0
climatic 099.1
due to Hemophilus ducreyi 099.0
gonococcal 098.89
indolent NEC 099.8
inguinal NEC 099.8
chancroidal 099.0
climatic 099.1
due to H. ducreyi 099.0
scrofulous (*see also* Tuberculosis) 017.2 ☑
soft chancre 099.0
suppurating 683
syphilitic 091.0
congenital 090.0
tropical 099.1
venereal NEC 099.8
virulent 099.0
Bubonic plague 020.0
Bubonocele — *see* Hernia, inguinal
Buccal — *see* condition
Buchanan's disease (juvenile osteochondrosis of iliac crest) 732.1
Buchem's syndrome (hyperostosis corticalis) 733.3
Buchman's disease (osteochondrosis, juvenile) 732.1
Bucket handle fracture (semilunar cartilage) — *see also* Tear, meniscus 836.2

Budd-Chiari syndrome (hepatic vein thrombosis) 453.0
Budgerigar-fanciers' disease or lung 495.2
Büdinger-Ludloff-Läwen disease 717.89
Buds
breast 259.1
in newborn 779.89
Buerger's disease (thromboangiitis obliterans) 443.1
Bulbar — *see* condition
Bulbus cordis 745.9
persistent (in left ventricle) 745.8
Bulging fontanels (congenital) 756.0
Bulimia 783.6
nervosa 307.51
nonorganic origin 307.51
Bulky uterus 621.2
Bulla(e) 709.8
lung (emphysematous) (solitary) 492.0
Bullet wound — *see also* Wound, open, by site
fracture — *see* Fracture, by site, open
internal organ (abdomen, chest, or pelvis) — *see* Injury, internal, by site, with open wound
intracranial — *see* Laceration, brain, with open wound
Bullis fever 082.8
Bullying — *see also* Disturbance, conduct 312.0 ☑
Bundle
branch block (complete) (false) (incomplete) 426.50
bilateral 426.53
left (*see also* Block, bundle branch, left) 426.3
hemiblock 426.2
right (*see also* Block, bundle branch, right) 426.4
of His — *see* condition
of Kent syndrome (anomalous atrioventricular excitation) 426.7
Bungpagga 040.81
Bunion 727.1
Bunionette 727.1
Bunyamwera fever 066.3
Buphthalmia, buphthalmos (congenital) 743.20
associated with
keratoglobus, congenital 743.22
megalocornea 743.22
ocular anomalies NEC 743.22
isolated 743.21
simple 743.21
Bürger-Grütz disease or syndrome (essential familial hyperlipemia) 272.3
Buried roots 525.3
Burke's syndrome 577.8
Burkitt's
tumor (M9750/3) 200.2 ☑
type malignant, lymphoma, lymphoblastic, or undifferentiated (M9750/3) 200.2 ☑
Burn (acid) (cathode ray) (caustic) (chemical) (electric heating appliance) (electricity) (fire) (flame) (hot liquid or object) (irradiation) (lime) (radiation) (steam) (thermal) (x-ray) 949.0

Note — Use the following fifth-digit subclassification with category 948 to indicate the percent of body surface with third degree burn:

0	Less than 10% or unspecified
1	10–19%
2	20–29%
3	30–39%
4	40–49%
5	50–59%
6	60–69%
7	70–79%
8	80–89%
9	90% or more of body surface

with
blisters — *see* Burn, by site, second degree

Burn — *continued*
with — *continued*
erythema — *see* Burn, by site, first degree
skin loss (epidermal) (*see also* Burn, by site, second degree)
full thickness (*see also* Burn, by site, third degree)
with necrosis of underlying tissues — *see* Burn, by site, third degree, deep
first degree — *see* Burn, by site, first degree
second degree — *see* Burn, by site, second degree
third degree — *see* Burn, by site, third degree
deep — *see* Burn, by site, third degree, deep
abdomen, abdominal (muscle) (wall) 942.03
with
trunk — *see* Burn, trunk, multiple sites
first degree 942.13
second degree 942.23
third degree 942.33
deep 942.43
with loss of body part 942.53
ankle 945.03
with
lower limb(s) — *see* Burn, leg, multiple sites
first degree 945.13
second degree 945.23
third degree 945.33
deep 945.43
with loss of body part 945.53
anus — *see* Burn, trunk, specified site NEC
arm(s) 943.00
first degree 943.10
second degree 943.20
third degree 943.30
deep 943.40
with loss of body part 943.50
lower — *see* Burn, forearm(s)
multiple sites, except hand(s) or wrist(s) 943.09
first degree 943.19
second degree 943.29
third degree 943.39
deep 943.49
with loss of body part 943.59
upper 943.03
first degree 943.13
second degree 943.23
third degree 943.33
deep 943.43
with loss of body part 943.53
auditory canal (external) — *see* Burn, ear
auricle (ear) — *see* Burn, ear
axilla 943.04
with
upper limb(s), except hand(s) or wrist(s) — *see* Burn, arm(s), multiple sites
first degree 943.14
second degree 943.24
third degree 943.34
deep 943.44
with loss of body part 943.54
back 942.04
with
trunk — *see* Burn, trunk, multiple sites
first degree 942.14
second degree 942.24
third degree 942.34
deep 942.44
with loss of body part 942.54
biceps
brachii — *see* Burn, arm(s), upper
femoris — *see* Burn, thigh
breast(s) 942.01
with
trunk — *see* Burn, trunk, multiple sites
first degree 942.11
second degree 942.21
third degree 942.31
deep 942.41
with loss of body part 942.51
brow — *see* Burn, forehead

☑ Additional Digit Required — Refer to the Tabular List for Digit Selection ⩔ Subterms under main terms may continue to next column or page

Burn — *continued*
- buttock(s) — *see* Burn, back
- canthus (eye) 940.1
  - chemical 940.0
- cervix (uteri) 947.4
- cheek (cutaneous) 941.07
  - with
    - face or head — *see* Burn, head, multiple sites
  - first degree 941.17
  - second degree 941.27
  - third degree 941.37
    - deep 941.47
      - with loss of body part 941.57
- chest wall (anterior) 942.02
  - with
    - trunk — *see* Burn, trunk, multiple sites
  - first degree 942.12
  - second degree 942.22
  - third degree 942.32
    - deep 942.42
      - with loss of body part 942.52
- chin 941.04
  - with
    - face or head — *see* Burn, head, multiple sites
  - first degree 941.14
  - second degree 941.24
  - third degree 941.34
    - deep 941.44
      - with loss of body part 941.54
- clitoris — *see* Burn, genitourinary organs, external
- colon 947.3
- conjunctiva (and cornea) 940.4
  - chemical
    - acid 940.3
    - alkaline 940.2
- cornea (and conjunctiva) 940.4
  - chemical
    - acid 940.3
    - alkaline 940.2
- costal region — *see* Burn, chest wall
- due to ingested chemical agent — *see* Burn, internal organs
- ear (auricle) (canal) (drum) (external) 941.01
  - with
    - face or head — *see* Burn, head, multiple sites
  - first degree 941.11
  - second degree 941.21
  - third degree 941.31
    - deep 941.41
      - with loss of a body part 941.51
- elbow 943.02
  - with
    - hand(s) and wrist(s) — *see* Burn, multiple specified sites
    - upper limb(s), except hand(s) or wrist(s) (*see also* Burn, arm(s), multiple sites)
  - first degree 943.12
  - second degree 943.22
  - third degree 943.32
    - deep 943.42
      - with loss of body part 943.52
- electricity, electric current — *see* Burn, by site
- entire body — *see* Burn, multiple, specified sites
- epididymis — *see* Burn, genitourinary organs, external
- epigastric region — *see* Burn, abdomen
- epiglottis 947.1
- esophagus 947.2
- extent (percent of body surface)
  - less than 10 percent 948.0 ☑
  - 10-19 percent 948.1 ☑
  - 20-29 percent 948.2 ☑
  - 30-39 percent 948.3 ☑
  - 40-49 percent 948.4 ☑
  - 50-59 percent 948.5 ☑
  - 60-69 percent 948.6 ☑
  - 70-79 percent 948.7 ☑
  - 80-89 percent 948.8 ☑
  - 90 percent or more 948.9 ☑

Burn — *continued*
- extremity
  - lower — *see* Burn, leg
  - upper — *see* Burn, arm(s)
- eye(s) (and adnexa) (only) 940.9
  - with
    - face, head, or neck 941.02
      - first degree 941.12
      - second degree 941.22
      - third degree 941.32
        - deep 941.42
          - with loss of body part 941.52
    - other sites (classifiable to more than one category in 940–945) — *see* Burn, multiple, specified sites
    - resulting rupture and destruction of eyeball 940.5
    - specified part — *see* Burn, by site
- eyeball (*see also* Burn, eye)
  - with resulting rupture and destruction of eyeball 940.5
- eyelid(s) 940.1
  - chemical 940.0
- face — *see* Burn, head
- finger (nail) (subungual) 944.01
  - with
    - hand(s) — *see* Burn, hand(s), multiple sites
    - other sites — *see* Burn, multiple, specified sites
    - thumb 944.04
      - first degree 944.14
      - second degree 944.24
      - third degree 944.34
        - deep 944.44
          - with loss of body part 944.54
  - first degree 944.11
  - second degree 944.21
  - third degree 944.31
    - deep 944.41
      - with loss of body part 944.51
  - multiple (digits) 944.03
    - with thumb — *see* Burn, finger, with thumb
    - first degree 944.13
    - second degree 944.23
    - third degree 944.33
      - deep 944.43
        - with loss of body part 944.53
- flank — *see* Burn, abdomen
- foot 945.02
  - with
    - lower limb(s) — *see* Burn, leg, multiple sites
  - first degree 945.12
  - second degree 945.22
  - third degree 945.32
    - deep 945.42
      - with loss of body part 945.52
- forearm(s) 943.01
  - with
    - upper limb(s), except hand(s) or wrist(s) — *see* Burn, arm(s), multiple sites
  - first degree 943.11
  - second degree 943.21
  - third degree 943.31
    - deep 943.41
      - with loss of body part 943.51
- forehead 941.07
  - with
    - face or head — *see* Burn, head, multiple sites
  - first degree 941.17
  - second degree 941.27
  - third degree 941.37
    - deep 941.47
      - with loss of body part 941.57
- fourth degree — *see* Burn, by site, third degree, deep
- friction — *see* Injury, superficial, by site
- from swallowing caustic or corrosive substance NEC — *see* Burn, internal organs

Burn — *continued*
- full thickness — *see* Burn, by site, third degree
- gastrointestinal tract 947.3
- genitourinary organs
  - external 942.05
    - with
      - trunk — *see* Burn, trunk, multiple sites
    - first degree 942.15
    - second degree 942.25
    - third degree 942.35
      - deep 942.45
        - with loss of body part 942.55
  - internal 947.8
- globe (eye) — *see* Burn, eyeball
- groin — *see* Burn, abdomen
- gum 947.0
- hand(s) (phalanges) (and wrist) 944.00
  - first degree 944.10
  - second degree 944.20
  - third degree 944.30
    - deep 944.40
      - with loss of body part 944.50
  - back (dorsal surface) 944.06
    - first degree 944.16
    - second degree 944.26
    - third degree 944.36
      - deep 944.46
        - with loss of body part 944.56
  - multiple sites 944.08
    - first degree 944.18
    - second degree 944.28
    - third degree 944.38
      - deep 944.48
        - with loss of body part 944.58
- head (and face) 941.00
  - first degree 941.10
  - second degree 941.20
  - third degree 941.30
    - deep 941.40
      - with loss of body part 941.50
  - eye(s) only 940.9
  - specified part — *see* Burn, by site
  - multiple sites 941.09
    - with eyes — *see* Burn, eyes, with face, head, or neck
    - first degree 941.19
    - second degree 941.29
    - third degree 941.39
      - deep 941.49
        - with loss of body part 941.59
- heel — *see* Burn, foot
- hip — *see* Burn, trunk, specified site NEC
- iliac region — *see* Burn, trunk, specified site NEC
- infected 958.3
- inhalation (*see also* Burn, internal organs) 947.9
- internal organs 947.9
  - from caustic or corrosive substance (swallowing) NEC 947.9
  - specified NEC (*see also* Burn, by site) 947.8
- interscapular region — *see* Burn, back
- intestine (large) (small) 947.3
- iris — *see* Burn, eyeball
- knee 945.05
  - with
    - lower limb(s) — *see* Burn, leg, multiple sites
  - first degree 945.15
  - second degree 945.25
  - third degree 945.35
    - deep 945.45
      - with loss of body part 945.55
- labium (majus) (minus) — *see* Burn, genitourinary organs, external
- lacrimal apparatus, duct, gland, or sac 940.1
  - chemical 940.0
- larynx 947.1
- late effect — *see* Late, effects (of), burn
- leg 945.00
  - first degree 945.10
  - second degree 945.20
  - third degree 945.30
    - deep 945.40
      - with loss of body part 945.50
  - lower 945.04

Burn — *continued*
- leg — *continued*
  - lower — *continued*
    - with other part(s) of lower limb(s) — *see* Burn, leg, multiple sites
    - first degree 945.14
    - second degree 945.24
    - third degree 945.34
      - deep 945.44
        - with loss of body part 945.54
  - multiple sites 945.09
    - first degree 945.19
    - second degree 945.29
    - third degree 945.39
      - deep 945.49
        - with loss of body part 945.59
  - upper — *see* Burn, thigh
- lightning — *see* Burn, by site
- limb(s)
  - lower (including foot or toe(s)) — *see* Burn, leg
  - upper (except wrist and hand) — *see* Burn, arm(s)
- lip(s) 941.03
  - with
    - face or head — *see* Burn, head, multiple sites
  - first degree 941.13
  - second degree 941.23
  - third degree 941.33
    - deep 941.43
      - with loss of body part 941.53
- lumbar region — *see* Burn, back
- lung 947.1
- malar region — *see* Burn, cheek
- mastoid region — *see* Burn, scalp
- membrane, tympanic — *see* Burn, ear
- midthoracic region — *see* Burn, chest wall
- mouth 947.0
- multiple (*see also* Burn, unspecified) 949.0
  - specified sites classifiable to more than one category in 940-945 ☑, 946.0
    - first degree 946.1
    - second degree 946.2
    - third degree 946.3
      - deep 946.4
        - with loss of body part 946.5
- muscle, abdominal — *see* Burn, abdomen
- nasal (septum) — *see* Burn, nose
- neck 941.08
  - with
    - face or head — *see* Burn, head, multiple sites
  - first degree 941.18
  - second degree 941.28
  - third degree 941.38
    - deep 941.48
      - with loss of body part 941.58
- nose (septum) 941.05
  - with
    - face or head — *see* Burn, head, multiple sites
  - first degree 941.15
  - second degree 941.25
  - third degree 941.35
    - deep 941.45
      - with loss of body part 941.55
- occipital region — *see* Burn, scalp
- orbit region 940.1
  - chemical 940.0
- oronasopharynx 947.0
- palate 947.0
- palm(s) 944.05
  - with
    - hand(s) and wrist(s) — *see* Burn, hand(s), multiple sites
  - first degree 944.15
  - second degree 944.25
  - third degree 944.35
    - deep 944.45
      - with loss of a body part 944.55
- parietal region — *see* Burn, scalp
- penis — *see* Burn, genitourinary organs, external
- perineum — *see* Burn, genitourinary organs, external

☑ Additional Digit Required — Refer to the Tabular List for Digit Selection   🖤 Subterms under main terms may continue to next column or page

38 — Volume 2   ▶◀ Revised Text   ● New Line   ▲ Revised Code   2010 ICD-9-CM

Burn — *continued*
  periocular area 940.1
    chemical 940.0
  pharynx 947.0
  pleura 947.1
  popliteal space — *see* Burn, knee
  prepuce — *see* Burn, genitourinary organs, external
  pubic region — *see* Burn, genitourinary organs, external
  pudenda — *see* Burn, genitourinary organs, external
  rectum 947.3
  sac, lacrimal 940.1
    chemical 940.0
  sacral region — *see* Burn, back
  salivary (ducts) (glands) 947.0
  scalp 941.06
    with
      face or neck — *see* Burn, head, multiple sites
      first degree 941.16
      second degree 941.26
      third degree 941.36
        deep 941.46
          with loss of body part 941.56
  scapular region 943.06
    with
      upper limb(s), except hand(s) or wrist(s) — *see* Burn, arm(s), multiple sites
      first degree 943.16
      second degree 943.26
      third degree 943.36
        deep 943.46
          with loss of body part 943.56
  sclera — *see* Burn, eyeball
  scrotum — *see* Burn, genitourinary organs, external
  septum, nasal — *see* Burn, nose
  shoulder(s) 943.05
    with
      hand(s) and wrist(s) — *see* Burn, multiple, specified sites
      upper limb(s), except hand(s) or wrist(s) — *see* Burn, arm(s), multiple sites
      first degree 943.15
      second degree 943.25
      third degree 943.35
        deep 943.45
          with loss of body part 943.55
  skin NEC (*see also* Burn, unspecified) 949.0
  skull — *see* Burn, head
  small intestine 947.3
  sternal region — *see* Burn, chest wall
  stomach 947.3
  subconjunctival — *see* Burn, conjunctiva
  subcutaneous — *see* Burn, by site, third degree
  submaxillary region — *see* Burn, head
  submental region — *see* Burn, chin
  sun — *see* Sunburn
  supraclavicular fossa — *see* Burn, neck
  supraorbital — *see* Burn, forehead
  temple — *see* Burn, scalp
  temporal region — *see* Burn, scalp
  testicle — *see* Burn, genitourinary organs, external
  testis — *see* Burn, genitourinary organs, external
  thigh 945.06
    with
      lower limb(s) — *see* Burn, leg, multiple sites
      first degree 945.16
      second degree 945.26
      third degree 945.36
        deep 945.46
          with loss of body part 945.56
  thorax (external) — *see* Burn, chest wall
  throat 947.0
  thumb(s) (nail) (subungual) 944.02
    with
      finger(s) — *see* Burn, finger, with other sites, thumb

Burn — *continued*
  thumb(s) — *continued*
    with — *continued*
      hand(s) and wrist(s) — *see* Burn, hand(s), multiple sites
      first degree 944.12
      second degree 944.22
      third degree 944.32
        deep 944.42
          with loss of body part 944.52
  toe (nail) (subungual) 945.01
    with
      lower limb(s) — *see* Burn, leg, multiple sites
      first degree 945.11
      second degree 945.21
      third degree 945.31
        deep 945.41
          with loss of body part 945.51
  tongue 947.0
  tonsil 947.0
  trachea 947.1
  trunk 942.00
    first degree 942.10
    second degree 942.20
    third degree 942.30
      deep 942.40
        with loss of body part 942.50
    multiple sites 942.09
      first degree 942.19
      second degree 942.29
      third degree 942.39
        deep 942.49
          with loss of body part 942.59
    specified site NEC 942.09
      first degree 942.19
      second degree 942.29
      third degree 942.39
        deep 942.49
          with loss of body part 942.59
  tunica vaginalis — *see* Burn, genitourinary organs, external
  tympanic membrane — *see* Burn, ear
  tympanum — *see* Burn, ear
  ultraviolet 692.82
  unspecified site (multiple) 949.0
    with extent of body surface involved specified
      less than 10 percent 948.0 ☑
      10-19 percent 948.1 ☑
      20-29 percent 948.2 ☑
      30-39 percent 948.3 ☑
      40-49 percent 948.4 ☑
      50-59 percent 948.5 ☑
      60-69 percent 948.6 ☑
      70-79 percent 948.7 ☑
      80-89 percent 948.8 ☑
      90 percent or more 948.9 ☑
    first degree 949.1
    second degree 949.2
    third degree 949.3
      deep 949.4
        with loss of body part 949.5
  uterus 947.4
  uvula 947.0
  vagina 947.4
  vulva — *see* Burn, genitourinary organs, external
  wrist(s) 944.07
    with
      hand(s) — *see* Burn, hand(s), multiple sites
      first degree 944.17
      second degree 944.27
      third degree 944.37
        deep 944.47
          with loss of body part 944.57
Burnett's syndrome (milk-alkali) 275.42
Burnier's syndrome (hypophyseal dwarfism) 253.3
Burning
  feet syndrome 266.2
  sensation (*see also* Disturbance, sensation) 782.0
  tongue 529.6

Burns' disease (osteochondrosis, lower ulna) 732.3
Bursa — *see also* condition
  pharynx 478.29
Bursitis NEC 727.3
  Achilles tendon 726.71
  adhesive 726.90
    shoulder 726.0
  ankle 726.79
  buttock 726.5
  calcaneal 726.79
  collateral ligament
    fibular 726.63
    tibial 726.62
  Duplay's 726.2
  elbow 726.33
  finger 726.8
  foot 726.79
  gonococcal 098.52
  hand 726.4
  hip 726.5
  infrapatellar 726.69
  ischiogluteal 726.5
  knee 726.60
  occupational NEC 727.2
  olecranon 726.33
  pes anserinus 726.61
  pharyngeal 478.29
  popliteal 727.51
  prepatellar 726.65
  radiohumeral 727.3
  scapulohumeral 726.19
    adhesive 726.0
  shoulder 726.10
    adhesive 726.0
  subacromial 726.19
    adhesive 726.0
  subcoracoid 726.19
  subdeltoid 726.19
    adhesive 726.0
  subpatellar 726.69
  syphilitic 095.7
  Thornwaldt's, Tornwaldt's (pharyngeal) 478.29
  toe 726.79
  trochanteric area 726.5
  wrist 726.4
Burst stitches or sutures (complication of surgery) (external) (*see also* Dehiscence) 998.32
  internal 998.31
Buruli ulcer 031.1
Bury's disease (erythema elevatum diutinum) 695.89
Buschke's disease or scleredema (adultorum) 710.1
Busquet's disease (osteoperiostitis) — *see also* Osteomyelitis 730.1 ☑
Busse-Buschke disease (cryptococcosis) 117.5
Buttock — *see* condition
Button
  Biskra 085.1
  Delhi 085.1
  oriental 085.1
Buttonhole hand (intrinsic) 736.21
Bwamba fever (encephalitis) 066.3
Byssinosis (occupational) 504
Bywaters' syndrome 958.5

C

Cacergasia 300.9
Cachexia 799.4
  cancerous (*see also* Neoplasm, by site, malignant) 799.4
  cardiac — *see* Disease, heart
  dehydration 276.51
    with
      hypernatremia 276.0
      hyponatremia 276.1
  due to malnutrition 799.4
  exophthalmic 242.0 ☑
  heart — *see* Disease, heart
  hypophyseal 253.2
  hypopituitary 253.2
  lead 984.9
    specified type of lead — *see* Table of Drugs and Chemicals

Cachexia — *continued*
  malaria 084.9
  malignant (*see also* Neoplasm, by site, malignant) 799.4
  marsh 084.9
  nervous 300.5
  old age 797
  pachydermic — *see* Hypothyroidism
  paludal 084.9
  pituitary (postpartum) 253.2
  renal (*see also* Disease, renal) 593.9
  saturnine 984.9
    specified type of lead — *see* Table of Drugs and Chemicals
  senile 797
  Simmonds' (pituitary cachexia) 253.2
  splenica 289.59
  strumipriva (*see also* Hypothyroidism) 244.9
  tuberculous NEC (*see also* Tuberculosis) 011.9 ☑
Café au lait spots 709.09
Caffey's disease or syndrome (infantile cortical hyperostosis) 756.59
Caisson disease 993.3
Caked breast (puerperal, postpartum) 676.2 ☑
Cake kidney 753.3
Calabar swelling 125.2
Calcaneal spur 726.73
Calcaneoapophysitis 732.5
Calcaneonavicular bar 755.67
Calcareous — *see* condition
Calcicosis (occupational) 502
Calciferol (vitamin D) **deficiency** 268.9
  with
    osteomalacia 268.2
    rickets (*see also* Rickets) 268.0
Calcification
  adrenal (capsule) (gland) 255.41
    tuberculous (*see also* Tuberculosis) 017.6 ☑
  aorta 440.0
  artery (annular) — *see* Arteriosclerosis
  auricle (ear) 380.89
  bladder 596.8
    due to S. hematobium 120.0
  brain (cortex) — *see* Calcification, cerebral
  bronchus 519.19
  bursa 727.82
  cardiac (*see also* Degeneration, myocardial) 429.1
  cartilage (postinfectional) 733.99
  cerebral (cortex) 348.89 ▲
    artery 437.0
  cervix (uteri) 622.8
  choroid plexus 349.2
  conjunctiva 372.54
  corpora cavernosa (penis) 607.89
  cortex (brain) — *see* Calcification, cerebral
  dental pulp (nodular) 522.2
  dentinal papilla 520.4
  disc, intervertebral 722.90
    cervical, cervicothoracic 722.91
    lumbar, lumbosacral 722.93
    thoracic, thoracolumbar 722.92
  fallopian tube 620.8
  falx cerebri — *see* Calcification, cerebral
  fascia 728.89
  gallbladder 575.8
  general 275.40
  heart (*see also* Degeneration, myocardial) 429.1
    valve — *see* Endocarditis
  intervertebral cartilage or disc (postinfectional) 722.90
    cervical, cervicothoracic 722.91
    lumbar, lumbosacral 722.93
    thoracic, thoracolumbar 722.92
  intracranial — *see* Calcification, cerebral
  intraspinal ligament 728.89
  joint 719.80
    ankle 719.87
    elbow 719.82
    foot 719.87
    hand 719.84
    hip 719.85
    knee 719.86
    multiple sites 719.89

☑ Additional Digit Required — Refer to the Tabular List for Digit Selection   ⤶ Subterms under main terms may continue to next column or page

Calcification — Carcinoma

Calcification — *continued*
  joint — *continued*
    pelvic region 719.85
    shoulder (region) 719.81
    specified site NEC 719.88
    wrist 719.83
  kidney 593.89
    tuberculous (*see also* Tuberculosis)
      016.0 ☑
  larynx (senile) 478.79
  lens 366.8
  ligament 728.89
    intraspinal 728.89
    knee (medial collateral) 717.89
  lung 518.89
    active 518.89
    postinfectional 518.89
    tuberculous (*see also* Tuberculosis, pulmonary) 011.9 ☑
  lymph gland or node (postinfectional) 289.3
    tuberculous (*see also* Tuberculosis, lymph gland) 017.2 ☑
  mammographic 793.89
  massive (paraplegic) 728.10
  medial NEC (*see also* Arteriosclerosis, extremities) 440.20
  meninges (cerebral) 349.2
  metastatic 275.40
  Mönckeberg's — *see* Arteriosclerosis
  muscle 728.10
    heterotopic, postoperative 728.13
  myocardium, myocardial (*see also* Degeneration, myocardial) 429.1
  ovary 620.8
  pancreas 577.8
  penis 607.89
  periarticular 728.89
  pericardium (*see also* Pericarditis) 423.8
  pineal gland 259.8
  pleura 511.0
    postinfectional 518.89
    tuberculous (*see also* Tuberculosis, pleura) 012.0 ☑
  pulp (dental) (nodular) 522.2
  renal 593.89
  Rider's bone 733.99
  sclera 379.16
  semilunar cartilage 717.89
  spleen 289.59
  subcutaneous 709.3
  suprarenal (capsule) (gland) 255.41
  tendon (sheath) 727.82
    with bursitis, synovitis or tenosynovitis 727.82
  trachea 519.19
  ureter 593.89
  uterus 621.8
  vitreous 379.29
Calcified — *see also* Calcification
  hematoma NEC 959.9
Calcinosis (generalized) (interstitial) (tumoral) (universalis) 275.49
  circumscripta 709.3
  cutis 709.3
  intervertebralis 275.49 [722.90]
  Raynaud's phenomenonsclerodactylytelangiectasis (CRST) 710.1
Calciphylaxis — *see also* Calcification, by site 275.49
Calcium
  blood
    high (*see also* Hypercalcemia) 275.42
    low (*see also* Hypocalcemia) 275.41
  deposits (*see also* Calcification, by site)
    in bursa 727.82
    in tendon (sheath) 727.82
      with bursitis, synovitis or tenosynovitis 727.82
  salts or soaps in vitreous 379.22
Calciuria 791.9
Calculi — *see* Calculus
Calculosis, intrahepatic — *see* Choledocholithiasis
Calculus, calculi, calculous 592.9
  ampulla of Vater — *see* Choledocholithiasis
  anuria (impacted) (recurrent) 592.0

Calculus, calculi, calculous — *continued*
  appendix 543.9
  bile duct (any) — *see* Choledocholithiasis
  biliary — *see* Cholelithiasis
  bilirubin, multiple — *see* Cholelithiasis
  bladder (encysted) (impacted) (urinary) 594.1
    diverticulum 594.0
  bronchus 518.89
  calyx (kidney) (renal) 592.0
    congenital 753.3
  cholesterol (pure) (solitary) — *see* Cholelithiasis
  common duct (bile) — *see* Choledocholithiasis
  conjunctiva 372.54
  cystic 594.1
    duct — *see* Cholelithiasis
  dental 523.6
    subgingival 523.6
    supragingival 523.6
  epididymis 608.89
  gallbladder (*see also* Cholelithiasis)
    congenital 751.69
  hepatic (duct) — *see* Choledocholithiasis
  intestine (impaction) (obstruction) 560.39
  kidney (impacted) (multiple) (pelvis) (recurrent) (staghorn) 592.0
    congenital 753.3
  lacrimal (passages) 375.57
  liver (impacted) — *see* Choledocholithiasis
  lung 518.89
  mammographic 793.89
  nephritic (impacted) (recurrent) 592.0
  nose 478.19
  pancreas (duct) 577.8
  parotid gland 527.5
  pelvis, encysted 592.0
  prostate 602.0
  pulmonary 518.89
  renal (impacted) (recurrent) 592.0
    congenital 753.3
  salivary (duct) (gland) 527.5
  seminal vesicle 608.89
  staghorn 592.0
  Stensen's duct 527.5
  sublingual duct or gland 527.5
    congenital 750.26
  submaxillary duct, gland, or region 527.5
  suburethral 594.8
  tonsil 474.8
  tooth, teeth 523.6
  tunica vaginalis 608.89
  ureter (impacted) (recurrent) 592.1
  urethra (impacted) 594.2
  urinary (duct) (impacted) (passage) (tract) 592.9
    lower tract NEC 594.9
      specified site 594.8
  vagina 623.8
  vesical (impacted) 594.1
  Wharton's duct 527.5
Caliectasis 593.89
California
  disease 114.0
  encephalitis 062.5
Caligo cornea 371.03
Callositas, callosity (infected) 700
Callus (infected) 700
  bone 726.91
  excessive, following fracture (*see also* Late, effect (of), fracture)
Calvé (-Perthes) disease (osteochondrosis, femoral capital) 732.1
Calvities — *see also* Alopecia 704.00
Cameroon fever — *see also* Malaria 084.6
Camptocormia 300.11
Camptodactyly (congenital) 755.59
Camurati-Engelmann disease (diaphyseal sclerosis) 756.59
Canal — *see* condition
Canaliculitis (lacrimal) (acute) 375.31
  Actinomyces 039.8
  chronic 375.41
Canavan's disease 330.0

Cancer (M8000/3) — *see also* Neoplasm, by site, malignant

> *Note* — The term *"cancer"* when modified by an adjective or adjectival phrase indicating a morphological type should be coded in the same manner as *"carcinoma"* with that adjective or phrase. Thus, *"squamous-cell cancer"* should be coded in the same manner as *"squamous-cell carcinoma,"* which appears in the list under *"Carcinoma."*

  bile duct type (M8160/3), liver 155.1
  hepatocellular (M8170/3) 155.0
Cancerous (M8000/3) — *see* Neoplasm, by site, malignant
Cancerphobia 300.29
Cancrum oris 528.1
Candidiasis, candidal 112.9
  with pneumonia 112.4
  balanitis 112.2
  congenital 771.7
  disseminated 112.5
  endocarditis 112.81
  esophagus 112.84
  intertrigo 112.3
  intestine 112.85
  lung 112.4
  meningitis 112.83
  mouth 112.0
  nails 112.3
  neonatal 771.7
  onychia 112.3
  otitis externa 112.82
  otomycosis 112.82
  paronychia 112.3
  perionyxis 112.3
  pneumonia 112.4
  pneumonitis 112.4
  skin 112.3
  specified site NEC 112.89
  systemic 112.5
  urogenital site NEC 112.2
  vagina 112.1
  vulva 112.1
  vulvovaginitis 112.1
Candidiosis — *see* Candidiasis
Candiru infection or infestation 136.8
Canities (premature) 704.3
  congenital 757.4
Canker (mouth) (sore) 528.2
  rash 034.1
Cannabinosis 504
Canton fever 081.9
Cap
  cradle 690.11
Capillariasis 127.5
Capillary — *see* condition
Caplan-Colinet syndrome 714.81
Caplan's syndrome 714.81
Capsule — *see* condition
Capsulitis (joint) 726.90
  adhesive (shoulder) 726.0
  hip 726.5
  knee 726.60
  labyrinthine 387.8
  thyroid 245.9
  wrist 726.4
Caput
  crepitus 756.0
  medusae 456.8
  succedaneum 767.19
Carapata disease 087.1
Carate — *see* Pinta
Carbohydrate-deficient glycoprotein syndrome (CGDS) 271.8
Carboxyhemoglobinemia 986
Carbuncle 680.9
  abdominal wall 680.2
  ankle 680.6
  anus 680.5
  arm (any part, above wrist) 680.3
  auditory canal, external 680.0
  axilla 680.3
  back (any part) 680.2
  breast 680.2
  buttock 680.5
  chest wall 680.2

Carbuncle — *continued*
  corpus cavernosum 607.2
  ear (any part) (external) 680.0
  eyelid 373.13
  face (any part, except eye) 680.0
  finger (any) 680.4
  flank 680.2
  foot (any part) 680.7
  forearm 680.3
  genital organ (male) 608.4
  gluteal (region) 680.5
  groin 680.2
  hand (any part) 680.4
  head (any part, except face) 680.8
  heel 680.7
  hip 680.6
  kidney (*see also* Abscess, kidney) 590.2
  knee 680.6
  labia 616.4
  lacrimal
    gland (*see also* Dacryoadenitis) 375.00
    passages (duct) (sac) (*see also* Dacryocystitis) 375.30
  leg, any part except foot 680.6
  lower extremity, any part except foot 680.6
  malignant 022.0
  multiple sites 680.9
  neck 680.1
  nose (external) (septum) 680.0
  orbit, orbital 376.01
  partes posteriores 680.5
  pectoral region 680.2
  penis 607.2
  perineum 680.2
  pinna 680.0
  scalp (any part) 680.8
  scrotum 608.4
  seminal vesicle 608.0
  shoulder 680.3
  skin NEC 680.9
  specified site NEC 680.8
  spermatic cord 608.4
  temple (region) 680.0
  testis 608.4
  thigh 680.6
  thumb 680.4
  toe (any) 680.7
  trunk 680.2
  tunica vaginalis 608.4
  umbilicus 680.2
  upper arm 680.3
  urethra 597.0
  vas deferens 608.4
  vulva 616.4
  wrist 680.4
Carbunculus — *see also* Carbuncle 680.9
Carcinoid (tumor) (M8240/1) — *see* Tumor, carcinoid
Carcinoidosis 259.2
Carcinomaphobia 300.29
Carcinomatosis
  peritonei (M8010/6) 197.6
  specified site NEC (M8010/3) — *see* Neoplasm, by site, malignant
  unspecified site (M8010/6) 199.0
Carcinoma (M8010/3) — *see also* Neoplasm, by site, malignant

> *Note* — *Except where otherwise indicated, the morphological varieties of carcinoma in the list below should be coded by site as for "Neoplasm, malignant."*

  with
    apocrine metaplasia (M8573/3)
    cartilaginous (and osseous) metaplasia (M8571/3)
    osseous (and cartilaginous) metaplasia (M8571/3)
    productive fibrosis (M8141/3)
    spindle cell metaplasia (M8572/3)
    squamous metaplasia (M8570/3)
  acidophil (M8280/3)
    specified site — *see* Neoplasm, by site, malignant
    unspecified site 194.3

☑ Additional Digit Required — Refer to the Tabular List for Digit Selection ▀̶ Subterms under main terms may continue to next column or page

40 — Volume 2   ▶◀ Revised Text   ● New Line   ▲ Revised Code   **2010 ICD-9-CM**

Carcinoma — *see also* Neoplasm, by site, malignant — *continued*
  acidophil-basophil, mixed (M8281/3)
    specified site — *see* Neoplasm, by site, malignant
    unspecified site 194.3
  acinar (cell) (M8550/3)
  acinic cell (M8550/3)
  adenocystic (M8200/3)
  adenoid
    cystic (M8200/3)
    squamous cell (M8075/3)
  adenosquamous (M8560/3)
  adnexal (skin) (M8390/3) — *see* Neoplasm, skin, malignant
  adrenal cortical (M8370/3) 194.0
  alveolar (M8251/3)
    cell (M8250/3) — *see* Neoplasm, lung, malignant
  anaplastic type (M8021/3)
  apocrine (M8401/3)
    breast — *see* Neoplasm, breast, malignant
    specified site NEC — *see* Neoplasm, skin, malignant
    unspecified site 173.9
  basal cell (pigmented) (M8090/3) (*see also* Neoplasm, skin, malignant)
    fibro-epithelial type (M8093/3) — *see* Neoplasm, skin, malignant
    morphea type (M8092/3) — *see* Neoplasm, skin, malignant
    multicentric (M8091/3) — *see* Neoplasm, skin, malignant
  basaloid (M8123/3)
  basal-squamous cell, mixed (M8094/3) — *see* Neoplasm, skin, malignant
  basophil (M8300/3)
    specified site — *see* Neoplasm, by site, malignant
    unspecified site 194.3
  basophil-acidophil, mixed (M8281/3)
    specified site — *see* Neoplasm, by site, malignant
    unspecified site 194.3
  basosquamous (M8094/3) — *see* Neoplasm, skin, malignant
  bile duct type (M8160/3)
    and hepatocellular, mixed (M8180/3) 155.0
    liver 155.1
    specified site NEC — *see* Neoplasm, by site, malignant
    unspecified site 155.1
  branchial or branchiogenic 146.8
  bronchial or bronchogenic — *see* Neoplasm, lung, malignant
  bronchiolar (terminal) (M8250/3) — *see* Neoplasm, lung, malignant
  bronchiolo-alveolar (M8250/3) — *see* Neoplasm, lung, malignant
  bronchogenic (epidermoid) 162.9
  C cell (M8510/3)
    specified site — *see* Neoplasm, by site, malignant
    unspecified site 193
  ceruminous (M8420/3) 173.2
  chorionic (M9100/3)
    specified site — *see* Neoplasm, by site, malignant
    unspecified site
      female 181
      male 186.9
  chromophobe (M8270/3)
    specified site — *see* Neoplasm, by site, malignant
    unspecified site 194.3
  clear cell (mesonephroid type) (M8310/3)
  cloacogenic (M8124/3)
    specified site — *see* Neoplasm, by site, malignant
    unspecified site 154.8
  colloid (M8480/3)
  cribriform (M8201/3)
  cylindroid type (M8200/3)
  diffuse type (M8145/3)
    specified site — *see* Neoplasm, by site, malignant

Carcinoma — *see also* Neoplasm, by site, malignant — *continued*
  diffuse type — *continued*
    unspecified site 151.9
  duct (cell) (M8500/3)
    with Paget's disease (M8541/3) — *see* Neoplasm, breast, malignant
    infiltrating (M8500/3)
      specified site — *see* Neoplasm, by site, malignant
      unspecified site 174.9
  ductal (M8500/3)
  ductular, infiltrating (M8521/3)
  embryonal (M9070/3)
    and teratoma, mixed (M9081/3)
    combined with choriocarcinoma (M9101/3) — *see* Neoplasm, by site, malignant
    infantile type (M9071/3)
    liver 155.0
    polyembryonal type (M9072/3)
  endometrioid (M8380/3)
  eosinophil (M8280/3)
    specified site — *see* Neoplasm, by site, malignant
    unspecified site 194.3
  epidermoid (M8070/3) (*see also* Carcinoma, squamous cell)
    and adenocarcinoma, mixed (M8560/3)
    in situ, Bowen's type (M8081/2) — *see* Neoplasm, skin, in situ
    intradermal — *see* Neoplasm, skin, in situ
  fibroepithelial type basal cell (M8093/3) — *see* Neoplasm, skin, malignant
  follicular (M8330/3)
    and papillary (mixed) (M8340/3) 193
    moderately differentiated type (M8332/3) 193
    pure follicle type (M8331/3) 193
    specified site — *see* Neoplasm, by site, malignant
    trabecular type (M8332/3) 193
    unspecified site 193
    well differentiated type (M8331/3) 193
  gelatinous (M8480/3)
  giant cell (M8031/3)
    and spindle cell (M8030/3)
  granular cell (M8320/3)
  granulosa cell (M8620/3) 183.0
  hepatic cell (M8170/3) 155.0
  hepatocellular (M8170/3) 155.0
    and bile duct, mixed (M8180/3) 155.0
  hepatocholangiolitic (M8180/3) 155.0
  Hürthle cell (thyroid) 193
  hypernephroid (M8311/3)
  in
    adenomatous
      polyp (M8210/3)
      polyposis coli (M8220/3) 153.9
    pleomorphic adenoma (M8940/3)
    polypoid adenoma (M8210/3)
    situ (M8010/3) — *see* Carcinoma, in situ
    tubular adenoma (M8210/3)
    villous adenoma (M8261/3)
  infiltrating duct (M8500/3)
    with Paget's disease (M8541/3) — *see* Neoplasm, breast, malignant
    specified site — *see* Neoplasm, by site, malignant
    unspecified site 174.9
  inflammatory (M8530/3)
    specified site — *see* Neoplasm, by site, malignant
    unspecified site 174.9
  in situ (M8010/2) (*see also* Neoplasm, by site, in situ)
    epidermoid (M8070/2) (*see also* Neoplasm, by site, in situ)
      with questionable stromal invasion (M8076/2)
      specified site — *see* Neoplasm, by site, in situ
      unspecified site 233.1
    Bowen's type (M8081/2) — *see* Neoplasm, skin, in situ

Carcinoma — *see also* Neoplasm, by site, malignant — *continued*
  in situ (*see also* Neoplasm, by site, in situ) — *continued*
    intraductal (M8500/2)
      specified site — *see* Neoplasm, by site, in situ
      unspecified site 233.0
    lobular (M8520/2)
      specified site — *see* Neoplasm, by site, in situ
      unspecified site 233.0
    papillary (M8050/2) — *see* Neoplasm, by site, in situ
    squamous cell (M8070/2) (*see also* Neoplasm, by site, in situ)
      with questionable stromal invasion (M8076/2)
      specified site — *see* Neoplasm, by site, in situ
      unspecified site 233.1
    transitional cell (M8120/2) — *see* Neoplasm, by site, in situ
  intestinal type (M8144/3)
    specified site — *see* Neoplasm, by site, malignant
    unspecified site 151.9
  intraductal (noninfiltrating) (M8500/2)
    papillary (M8503/2)
      specified site — *see* Neoplasm, by site, in situ
      unspecified site 233.0
    specified site — *see* Neoplasm, by site, in situ
    unspecified site 233.0
  intraepidermal (M8070/2) (*see also* Neoplasm, skin, in situ)
    squamous cell, Bowen's type (M8081/2) — *see* Neoplasm, skin, in situ
  intraepithelial (M8010/2) (*see also* Neoplasm, by site, in situ)
    squamous cell (M8072/2) — *see* Neoplasm, by site, in situ
  intraosseous (M9270/3) 170.1
    upper jaw (bone) 170.0
  islet cell (M8150/3)
    and exocrine, mixed (M8154/3)
      specified site — *see* Neoplasm, by site, malignant
      unspecified site 157.9
    pancreas 157.4
    specified site NEC — *see* Neoplasm, by site, malignant
    unspecified site 157.4
  juvenile, breast (M8502/3) — *see* Neoplasm, breast, malignant
  Kulchitsky's cell (carcinoid tumor of intestine) 259.2
  large cell (M8012/3)
    squamous cell, non-keratinizing type (M8072/3)
  Leydig cell (testis) (M8650/3)
    specified site — *see* Neoplasm, by site, malignant
    unspecified site 186.9
      female 183.0
      male 186.9
  liver cell (M8170/3) 155.0
  lobular (infiltrating) (M8520/3)
    non-infiltrating (M8520/3)
      specified site — *see* Neoplasm, by site, in situ
      unspecified site 233.0
    specified site — *see* Neoplasm, by site, malignant
    unspecified site 174.9
  lymphoepithelial (M8082/3)
  medullary (M8510/3)
    with
      amyloid stroma (M8511/3)
        specified site — *see* Neoplasm, by site, malignant
        unspecified site 193
      lymphoid stroma (M8512/3)
        specified site — *see* Neoplasm, by site, malignant

Carcinoma — *see also* Neoplasm, by site, malignant — *continued*
  medullary — *continued*
    with — *continued*
      lymphoid stroma — *continued*
        unspecified site 174.9
  Merkel cell 209.36 ●
    buttock 209.36 ●
    ear 209.31 ●
    eyelid, including canthus 209.31 ●
    face 209.31 ●
    genitals 209.36 ●
    lip 209.31 ●
    lower limb 209.34 ●
    neck 209.32 ●
    nodal presentation 209.75 ●
    scalp 209.32 ●
    secondary (any site) 209.75 ●
    specified site NEC 209.36 ●
    trunk 209.35 ●
    unknown primary site 209.75 ●
    upper limb 209.33 ●
    visceral metastatic presentation 209.75 ●
  mesometanephric (M9110/3)
  mesonephric (M9110/3)
  metastatic (M8010/6) — *see* Metastasis, cancer
  metatypical (M8095/3) — *see* Neoplasm, skin, malignant
  morphea type basal cell (M8092/3) — *see* Neoplasm, skin, malignant
  mucinous (M8480/3)
  mucin-producing (M8481/3)
  mucin-secreting (M8481/3)
  mucoepidermoid (M8430/3)
  mucoid (M8480/3)
    cell (M8300/3)
      specified site — *see* Neoplasm, by site, malignant
      unspecified site 194.3
  mucous (M8480/3)
  neuroendocrine
    high grade (M8240/3) 209.30
    malignant poorly differentiated (M8240/3) 209.30
  nonencapsulated sclerosing (M8350/3) 193
  noninfiltrating
    intracystic (M8504/2) — *see* Neoplasm, by site, in situ
    intraductal (M8500/2)
      papillary (M8503/2)
        specified site — *see* Neoplasm, by site, in situ
        unspecified site 233.0
      specified site — *see* Neoplasm, by site, in situ
      unspecified site 233.0
    lobular (M8520/2)
      specified site — *see* Neoplasm, by site, in situ
      unspecified site 233.0
  oat cell (M8042/3)
    specified site — *see* Neoplasm, by site, malignant
    unspecified site 162.9
  odontogenic (M9270/3) 170.1
    upper jaw (bone) 170.0
  onocytic (M8290/3)
  oxyphilic (M8290/3)
  papillary (M8050/3)
    and follicular (mixed) (M8340/3) 193
    epidermoid (M8052/3)
    intraductal (noninfiltrating) (M8503/2)
      specified site — *see* Neoplasm, by site, in situ
      unspecified site 233.0
    serous (M8460/3)
      specified site — *see* Neoplasm, by site, malignant
      surface (M8461/3)
        specified site — *see* Neoplasm, by site, malignant
        unspecified site 183.0
      unspecified site 183.0

☑ Additional Digit Required — Refer to the Tabular List for Digit Selection　　　　　　　　　▽ Subterms under main terms may continue to next column or page

2010 ICD-9-CM　　　▶◀ Revised Text　　　● New Line　　　▲ Revised Code　　　**October 2009 • Volume 2 — 41**

Carcinoma — see also Neoplasm, by site, malignant — continued
papillary — continued
squamous cell (M8052/3)
transitional cell (M8130/3)
papillocystic (M8450/3)
specified site — see Neoplasm, by site, malignant
unspecified site 183.0
parafollicular cell (M8510/3)
specified site — see Neoplasm, by site, malignant
unspecified site 193
pleomorphic (M8022/3)
polygonal cell (M8034/3)
prickle cell (M8070/3)
pseudoglandular, squamous cell (M8075/3)
pseudomucinous (M8470/3)
specified site — see Neoplasm, by site, malignant
unspecified site 183.0
pseudosarcomatous (M8033/3)
regaud type (M8082/3) — see Neoplasm, nasopharynx, malignant
renal cell (M8312/3) 189.0
reserve cell (M8041/3)
round cell (M8041/3)
Schmincke (M8082/3) — see Neoplasm, nasopharynx, malignant
Schneiderian (M8121/3)
specified site — see Neoplasm, by site, malignant
unspecified site 160.0
scirrhous (M8141/3)
sebaceous (M8410/3) — see Neoplasm, skin, malignant
secondary (M8010/6) — see Neoplasm, by site, malignant, secondary
secretory, breast (M8502/3) — see Neoplasm, breast, malignant
serous (M8441/3)
papillary (M8460/3)
specified site — see Neoplasm, by site, malignant
unspecified site 183.0
surface, papillary (M8461/3)
specified site — see Neoplasm, by site, malignant
unspecified site 183.0
Sertoli cell (M8640/3)
specified site — see Neoplasm, by site, malignant
unspecified site 186.9
signet ring cell (M8490/3)
metastatic (M8490/6) — see Neoplasm, by site, secondary
simplex (M8231/3)
skin appendage (M8390/3) — see Neoplasm, skin, malignant
small cell (M8041/3)
fusiform cell type (M8043/3)
squamous cell, non-keratinizing type (M8073/3)
solid (M8230/3)
with amyloid stroma (M8511/3)
specified site — see Neoplasm, by site, malignant
unspecified site 193
spheroidal cell (M8035/3)
spindle cell (M8032/3)
and giant cell (M8030/3)
spinous cell (M8070/3)
squamous (cell) (M8070/3)
adenoid type (M8075/3)
and adenocarcinoma, mixed (M8560/3)
intraepidermal, Bowen's type — see Neoplasm, skin, in situ
keratinizing type (large cell) (M8071/3)
large cell, non-keratinizing type (M8072/3)
microinvasive (M8076/3)
specified site — see Neoplasm, by site, malignant
unspecified site 180.9

Carcinoma — see also Neoplasm, by site, malignant — continued
squamous — continued
non-keratinizing type (M8072/3)
papillary (M8052/3)
pseudoglandular (M8075/3)
small cell, non-keratinizing type (M8073/3)
spindle cell type (M8074/3)
verrucous (M8051/3)
superficial spreading (M8143/3)
sweat gland (M8400/3) — see Neoplasm, skin, malignant
theca cell (M8600/3) 183.0
thymic (M8580/3) 164.0
trabecular (M8190/3)
transitional (cell) (M8120/3)
papillary (M8130/3)
spindle cell type (M8122/3)
tubular (M8211/3)
undifferentiated type (M8020/3)
urothelial (M8120/3)
ventriculi 151.9
verrucous (epidermoid) (squamous cell) (M8051/3)
villous (M8262/3)
water-clear cell (M8322/3) 194.1
wolffian duct (M9110/3)
Carcinosarcoma (M8980/3) — see also Neoplasm, by site, malignant
embryonal type (M8981/3) — see Neoplasm, by site, malignant
Cardiac — see also condition
death — see Disease, heart
device
defibrillator, automatic implantable V45.02
in situ NEC V45.00
pacemaker
cardiac
fitting or adjustment V53.31
in situ V45.01
carotid sinus
fitting or adjustment V53.39
in situ V45.09
pacemaker — see Cardiac, device, pacemaker
tamponade 423.3
Cardia, cardial — see condition
Cardialgia — see also Pain, precordial 786.51
Cardiectasis — see Hypertrophy, cardiac
Cardiochalasia 530.81
Cardiomalacia — see also Degeneration, myocardial 429.1
Cardiomegalia glycogenica diffusa 271.0
Cardiomegaly — see also Hypertrophy, cardiac 429.3
congenital 746.89
glycogen 271.0
hypertensive (see also Hypertension, heart) 402.90
idiopathic 429.3
Cardiomyoliposis — see also Degeneration, myocardial 429.1
Cardiomyopathy (congestive) (constrictive) (familial) (infiltrative) (obstructive) (restrictive) (sporadic) 425.4
alcoholic 425.5
amyloid 277.39 [425.7]
beriberi 265.0 [425.7]
cobalt-beer 425.5
congenital 425.3
due to
amyloidosis 277.39 [425.7]
beriberi 265.0 [425.7]
cardiac glycogenosis 271.0 [425.7]
Chagas' disease 086.0
Friedreich's ataxia 334.0 [425.8]
hypertension — see Hypertension, with, heart involvement
mucopolysaccharidosis 277.5 [425.7]
myotonia atrophica 359.21 [425.8]
progressive muscular dystrophy 359.1 [425.8]
sarcoidosis 135 [425.8]
glycogen storage 271.0 [425.7]
hypertensive — see Hypertension, with, heart involvement

Cardiomyopathy — continued
hypertrophic
nonobstructive 425.4
obstructive 425.1
congenital 746.84
idiopathic (concentric) 425.4
in
Chagas' disease 086.0
sarcoidosis 135 [425.8]
ischemic 414.8
metabolic NEC 277.9 [425.7]
amyloid 277.39 [425.7]
thyrotoxic (see also Thyrotoxicosis) 242.9 ☑ [425.7]
thyrotoxicosis (see also Thyrotoxicosis) 242.9 ☑ [425.7]
newborn 425.4
congenital 425.3
nutritional 269.9 [425.7]
beriberi 265.0 [425.7]
obscure of Africa 425.2
peripartum 674.5 ☑
postpartum 674.5 ☑
primary 425.4
secondary 425.9
stress inuced 429.83
takotsubo 429.83
thyrotoxic (see also Thyrotoxicosis) 242.9 ☑ [425.7]
toxic NEC 425.9
tuberculous (see also Tuberculosis) 017.9 ☑ [425.8]
Cardionephritis — see Hypertension, cardiorenal
Cardionephropathy — see Hypertension, cardiorenal
Cardionephrosis — see Hypertension, cardiorenal
Cardioneurosis 306.2
Cardiopathia nigra 416.0
Cardiopathy — see also Disease, heart 429.9
hypertensive (see also Hypertension, heart) 402.90
idiopathic 425.4
mucopolysaccharidosis 277.5 [425.7]
Cardiopericarditis — see also Pericarditis 423.9
Cardiophobia 300.29
Cardioptosis 746.87
Cardiorenal — see condition
Cardiorrhexis — see also Infarct, myocardium 410.9 ☑
Cardiosclerosis — see Arteriosclerosis, coronary
Cardiosis — see Disease, heart
Cardiospasm (esophagus) (reflex) (stomach) 530.0
congenital 750.7
Cardiostenosis — see Disease, heart
Cardiosymphysis 423.1
Cardiothyrotoxicosis — see Hyperthyroidism
Cardiovascular — see condition
Carditis (acute) (bacterial) (chronic) (subacute) 429.89
Coxsackie 074.20
hypertensive (see also Hypertension, heart) 402.90
meningococcal 036.40
rheumatic — see Disease, heart, rheumatic
rheumatoid 714.2
Care (of)
child (routine) V20.1
convalescent following V66.9
chemotherapy V66.2
medical NEC V66.5
psychotherapy V66.3
radiotherapy V66.1
surgery V66.0
surgical NEC V66.0
treatment (for) V66.5
combined V66.6
fracture V66.4
mental disorder NEC V66.3
specified type NEC V66.5
end-of-life V66.7
family member (handicapped) (sick)
creating problem for family V61.49
provided away from home for holiday relief V60.5

Care — continued
family member — continued
unavailable, due to
absence (person rendering care) (sufferer) V60.4
inability (any reason) of person rendering care V60.4
holiday relief V60.5
hospice V66.7
lack of (at or after birth) (infant) (child) 995.52
adult 995.84
lactation of mother V24.1
palliative V66.7
postpartum
immediately after delivery V24.0
routine follow-up V24.2
prenatal V22.1
first pregnancy V22.0
high-risk pregnancy V23.9
specified problem NEC V23.89
terminal V66.7
unavailable, due to
absence of person rendering care V60.4
inability (any reason) of person rendering care V60.4
well baby V20.1
Caries (bone) — see also Tuberculosis, bone 015.9 ☑ [730.8] ☑
arrested 521.04
cementum 521.03
cerebrospinal (tuberculous) 015.0 ☑ [730.88]
dental (acute) (chronic) (incipient) (infected) 521.00
with pulp exposure 521.03
extending to
dentine 521.02
pulp 521.03
other specified NEC 521.09
pit and fissure 521.06
primary
pit and fissure origin 521.06
root surface 521.08
smooth surface origin 521.07
root surface 521.08
smooth surface 521.07
dentin (acute) (chronic) 521.02
enamel (acute) (chronic) (incipient) 521.01
external meatus 380.89
hip (see also Tuberculosis) 015.1 ☑ [730.85]
initial 521.01
knee 015.2 ☑ [730.86]
labyrinth 386.8
limb NEC 015.7 ☑ [730.88]
mastoid (chronic) (process) 383.1
middle ear 385.89
nose 015.7 ☑ [730.88]
orbit 015.7 ☑ [730.88]
ossicle 385.24
petrous bone 383.20
sacrum (tuberculous) 015.0 ☑ [730.88]
spine, spinal (column) (tuberculous) 015.0 ☑ [730.88]
syphilitic 095.5
congenital 090.0 [730.8] ☑
teeth (internal) 521.00
initial 521.01
vertebra (column) (tuberculous) 015.0 ☑ [730.88]
Carini's syndrome (ichthyosis congenita) 757.1
Carious teeth 521.00
Carneous mole 631
Carnosinemia 270.5
Carotid body or sinus syndrome 337.01
Carotidynia 337.01
Carotinemia (dietary) 278.3
Carotinosis (cutis) (skin) 278.3
Carpal tunnel syndrome 354.0
Carpenter's syndrome 759.89
Carpopedal spasm — see also Tetany 781.7
Carpoptosis 736.05
Carrier (suspected) of
amebiasis V02.2
bacterial disease (meningococcal, staphylococcal) NEC V02.59
cholera V02.0
cystic fibrosis gene V83.81

Carrier (suspected) **of** — *continued*
  defective gene V83.89
  diphtheria V02.4
  dysentery (bacillary) V02.3
    amebic V02.2
  Endamoeba histolytica V02.2
  gastrointestinal pathogens NEC V02.3
  genetic defect V83.89
  gonorrhea V02.7
  group B streptococcus V02.51
  HAA (hepatitis Australian-antigen) V02.61
  hemophilia A (asymptomatic) V83.01
    symptomatic V83.02
  hepatitis V02.60
    Australian-antigen (HAA) V02.61
    B V02.61
    C V02.62
    serum V02.61
    specified type NEC V02.69
    viral V02.60
  infective organism NEC V02.9
  malaria V02.9
  paratyphoid V02.3
  Salmonella V02.3
    typhosa V02.1
  serum hepatitis V02.61
  Shigella V02.3
  Staphylococcus NEC V02.59
    methicillin
      resistant Staphylococcus aureus V02.54
      susceptible Staphylococcus aureus V02.53
  Streptococcus NEC V02.52
    group B V02.51
  typhoid V02.1
  venereal disease NEC V02.8
Carrión's disease (Bartonellosis) 088.0
Car sickness 994.6
Carter's
  relapsing fever (Asiatic) 087.0
Cartilage — *see* condition
Caruncle (inflamed)
  abscess, lacrimal (*see also* Dacryocystitis) 375.30
  conjunctiva 372.00
    acute 372.00
  eyelid 373.00
  labium (majus) (minus) 616.89
  lacrimal 375.30
  urethra (benign) 599.3
  vagina (wall) 616.89
Cascade stomach 537.6
Caseation lymphatic gland — *see also* Tuberculosis 017.2 ☑
Caseous
  bronchitis — *see* Tuberculosis, pulmonary
  meningitis 013.0 ☑
  pneumonia — *see* Tuberculosis, pulmonary
Cassidy (-Scholte) syndrome (malignant carcinoid) 259.2
Castellani's bronchitis 104.8
Castleman's tumor or lymphoma (mediastinal lymph node hyperplasia) 785.6
Castration, traumatic 878.2
  complicated 878.3
Casts in urine 791.7
Catalepsy 300.11
  catatonic (acute) (*see also* Schizophrenia) 295.2 ☑
  hysterical 300.11
  schizophrenic (*see also* Schizophrenia) 295.2 ☑
Cataphasia 307.0
Cataplexy (idiopathic) — *see* Narcolepsy
Cataract (anterior cortical) (anterior polar) (black) (capsular) (central) (cortical) (hypermature) (immature) (incipient) (mature) 366.9
  anterior
    and posterior axial embryonal 743.33
    pyramidal 743.31
    subcapsular polar
      infantile, juvenile, or presenile 366.01
      senile 366.13
  associated with
    calcinosis 275.40 *[366.42]*
    craniofacial dysostosis 756.0 *[366.44]*

Cataract — *continued*
  associated with — *continued*
    galactosemia 271.1 *[366.44]*
    hypoparathyroidism 252.1 *[366.42]*
    myotonic disorders 359.21 *[366.43]*
    neovascularization 366.33
  blue dot 743.39
  cerulean 743.39
  complicated NEC 366.30
  congenital 743.30
    capsular or subcapsular 743.31
    cortical 743.32
    nuclear 743.33
    specified type NEC 743.39
    total or subtotal 743.34
    zonular 743.32
  coronary (congenital) 743.39
    acquired 366.12
  cupuliform 366.14
  diabetic 250.5 ☑ *[366.41]*
    due to secondary diabetes 249.5 ☑ *[366.41]*
  drug-induced 366.45
  due to
    chalcosis 360.24 *[366.34]*
    chronic choroiditis (*see also* Choroiditis) 363.20 *[366.32]*
    degenerative myopia 360.21 *[366.34]*
    glaucoma (*see also* Glaucoma) 365.9 *[366.31]*
    infection, intraocular NEC 366.32
    inflammatory ocular disorder NEC 366.32
    iridocyclitis, chronic 364.10 *[366.33]*
    pigmentary retinal dystrophy 362.74 *[366.34]*
    radiation 366.46
  electric 366.46
  glassblowers' 366.46
  heat ray 366.46
  heterochromic 366.33
  in eye disease NEC 366.30
  infantile (*see also* Cataract, juvenile) 366.00
  intumescent 366.12
  irradiational 366.46
  juvenile 366.00
    anterior subcapsular polar 366.01
    combined forms 366.09
    cortical 366.03
    lamellar 366.03
    nuclear 366.04
    posterior subcapsular polar 366.02
    specified NEC 366.09
    zonular 366.03
  lamellar 743.32
    infantile, juvenile, or presenile 366.03
  morgagnian 366.18
  myotonic 359.21 *[366.43]*
  myxedema 244.9 *[366.44]*
  nuclear 366.16
  posterior, polar (capsular) 743.31
    infantile, juvenile, or presenile 366.02
    senile 366.14
  presenile (*see also* Cataract, juvenile) 366.00
  punctate
    acquired 366.12
    congenital 743.39
  secondary (membrane) 366.50
    obscuring vision 366.53
    specified type, not obscuring vision 366.52
  senile 366.10
    anterior subcapsular polar 366.13
    combined forms 366.19
    cortical 366.15
    hypermature 366.18
    immature 366.12
    incipient 366.12
    mature 366.17
    nuclear 366.16
    posterior subcapsular polar 366.14
    specified NEC 366.19
    total or subtotal 366.17
  snowflake 250.5 ☑ *[366.41]*
    due to secondary diabetes 249.5 ☑ *[366.41]*
  specified NEC 366.8
  subtotal (senile) 366.17

Cataract — *continued*
  subtotal — *continued*
    congenital 743.34
  sunflower 360.24 *[366.34]*
  tetanic NEC 252.1 *[366.42]*
  total (mature) (senile) 366.17
    congenital 743.34
    localized 366.21
    traumatic 366.22
  toxic 366.45
  traumatic 366.20
    partially resolved 366.23
    total 366.22
  zonular (perinuclear) 743.32
    infantile, juvenile, or presenile 366.03
Cataracta 366.10
  brunescens 366.16
  cerulea 743.39
  complicata 366.30
  congenita 743.30
  coralliformis 743.39
  coronaria (congenital) 743.39
    acquired 366.12
  diabetic 250.5 ☑ *[366.41]*
    due to secondary diabetes 249.5 ☑ *[366.41]*
  floriformis 360.24 *[366.34]*
  membranacea
    accreta 366.50
    congenita 743.39
  nigra 366.16
Catarrh, catarrhal (inflammation) — *see also* condition 460
  acute 460
  asthma, asthmatic (*see also* Asthma) 493.9 ☑
  Bostock's (*see also* Fever, hay) 477.9
  bowel — *see* Enteritis
  bronchial 490
    acute 466.0
    chronic 491.0
    subacute 466.0
  cervix, cervical (canal) (uteri) — *see* Cervicitis
  chest (*see also* Bronchitis) 490
  chronic 472.0
  congestion 472.0
  conjunctivitis 372.03
  due to syphilis 095.9
    congenital 090.0
  enteric — *see* Enteritis
  epidemic 487.1
  Eustachian 381.50
  eye (acute) (vernal) 372.03
  fauces (*see also* Pharyngitis) 462
  febrile 460
  fibrinous acute 466.0
  gastroenteric — *see* Enteritis
  gastrointestinal — *see* Enteritis
  gingivitis 523.00
  hay (*see also* Fever, hay) 477.9
  infectious 460
  intestinal — *see* Enteritis
  larynx (*see also* Laryngitis, chronic) 476.0
  liver 070.1
    with hepatic coma 070.0
  lung (*see also* Bronchitis) 490
    acute 466.0
    chronic 491.0
  middle ear (chronic) — *see* Otitis media, chronic
  mouth 528.00
  nasal (chronic) (*see also* Rhinitis) 472.0
    acute 460
  nasobronchial 472.2
  nasopharyngeal (chronic) 472.2
    acute 460
  nose — *see* Catarrh, nasal
  ophthalmia 372.03
  pneumococcal, acute 466.0
  pulmonary (*see also* Bronchitis) 490
    acute 466.0
    chronic 491.0
  spring (eye) 372.13
  suffocating (*see also* Asthma) 493.9 ☑
  summer (hay) (*see also* Fever, hay) 477.9
  throat 472.1
  tracheitis 464.10

Catarrh, catarrhal — *see also* condition — *continued*
  tracheitis — *continued*
    with obstruction 464.11
  tubotympanal 381.4
    acute (*see also* Otitis media, acute, nonsuppurative) 381.00
    chronic 381.10
  vasomotor (*see also* Fever, hay) 477.9
  vesical (bladder) — *see* Cystitis
Catarrhus aestivus — *see also* Fever, hay 477.9
Catastrophe, cerebral — *see also* Disease, cerebrovascular, acute 436
Catatonia, catatonic (acute) 781.99
  with
    affective psychosis — *see* Psychosis, affective
    agitation 295.2 ☑
    dementia (praecox) 295.2 ☑
    due to or associated with physical condition 293.89
    excitation 295.2 ☑
    excited type 295.2 ☑
    in conditions classified elsewhere 293.89
    schizophrenia 295.2 ☑
    stupor 295.2 ☑
Cat's ear 744.29
Cat-scratch — *see also* Injury, superficial disease or fever 078.3
Cauda equina — *see also* condition syndrome 344.60
Cauliflower ear 738.7
Caul over face 768.9
Causalgia 355.9
  lower limb 355.71
  upper limb 354.4
Cause
  external, general effects NEC 994.9
  not stated 799.9
  unknown 799.9
Caustic burn — *see also* Burn, by site
  from swallowing caustic or corrosive substance — *see* Burn, internal organs
Cavare's disease (familial periodic paralysis) 359.3
Cave-in, injury
  crushing (severe) (*see also* Crush, by site) 869.1
  suffocation 994.7
Cavernitis (penis) 607.2
  lymph vessel — *see* Lymphangioma
Cavernositis 607.2
Cavernous — *see* condition
Cavitation of lung — *see also* Tuberculosis 011.2 ☑
  nontuberculous 518.89
  primary, progressive 010.8 ☑
Cavity
  lung — *see* Cavitation of lung
  optic papilla 743.57
  pulmonary — *see* Cavitation of lung
  teeth 521.00
  vitreous (humor) 379.21
Cavovarus foot, congenital 754.59
Cavus foot (congenital) 754.71
  acquired 736.73
Cazenave's
  disease (pemphigus) NEC 694.4
  lupus (erythematosus) 695.4
CDGS (carbohydrate-deficient glycoprotein syndrome) 271.8
Cecitis — *see* Appendicitis
Cecocele — *see* Hernia
Cecum — *see* condition
Celiac
  artery compression syndrome 447.4
  disease 579.0
  infantilism 579.0
Cell, cellular — *see also* condition
  anterior chamber (eye) (positive aqueous ray) 364.04
Cellulitis (diffuse) (with lymphangitis) — *see also* Abscess 682.9
  abdominal wall 682.2
  anaerobic (*see also* Gas gangrene) 040.0
  ankle 682.6
  anus 566
  areola 611.0

☑ Additional Digit Required — Refer to the Tabular List for Digit Selection   Ⓥ Subterms under main terms may continue to next column or page

2010 ICD-9-CM   ▶◀ Revised Text   ● New Line   ▲ Revised Code   Volume 2 — 43

Cellulitis — *see also* Abscess — *continued*
- arm (any part, above wrist) 682.3
- auditory canal (external) 380.10
- axilla 682.3
- back (any part) 682.2
- breast 611.0
  - postpartum 675.1 ☑
- broad ligament (*see also* Disease, pelvis, inflammatory) 614.4
  - acute 614.3
- buttock 682.5
- cervical (neck region) 682.1
- cervix (uteri) (*see also* Cervicitis) 616.0
- cheek, external 682.0
  - internal 528.3
- chest wall 682.2
- chronic NEC 682.9
- colostomy 569.61
- corpus cavernosum 607.2
- digit 681.9
- Douglas' cul-de-sac or pouch (chronic) (*see also* Disease, pelvis, inflammatory) 614.4
  - acute 614.3
- drainage site (following operation) 998.59
- ear, external 380.10
- enterostomy 569.61
- erysipelar (*see also* Erysipelas) 035
- esophagostomy 530.86
- eyelid 373.13
- face (any part, except eye) 682.0
- finger (intrathecal) (periosteal) (subcutaneous) (subcuticular) 681.00
- flank 682.2
- foot (except toe) 682.7
- forearm 682.3
- gangrenous (*see also* Gangrene) 785.4
- genital organ NEC
  - female — *see* Abscess, genital organ, female
  - male 608.4
- glottis 478.71
- gluteal (region) 682.5
- gonococcal NEC 098.0
- groin 682.2
- hand (except finger or thumb) 682.4
- head (except face) NEC 682.8
- heel 682.7
- hip 682.6
- jaw (region) 682.0
- knee 682.6
- labium (majus) (minus) (*see also* Vulvitis) 616.10
- larynx 478.71
- leg, except foot 682.6
- lip 528.5
- mammary gland 611.0
- mouth (floor) 528.3
- multiple sites NEC 682.9
- nasopharynx 478.21
- navel 682.2
  - newborn NEC 771.4
- neck (region) 682.1
- nipple 611.0
- nose 478.19
  - external 682.0
- orbit, orbital 376.01
- palate (soft) 528.3
- pectoral (region) 682.2
- pelvis, pelvic
  - with
    - abortion — *see* Abortion, by type, with sepsis
    - ectopic pregnancy (*see also* categories 633.0–633.9) 639.0
    - molar pregnancy (*see also* categories 630–632) 639.0
  - female (*see also* Disease, pelvis, inflammatory) 614.4
    - acute 614.3
  - following
    - abortion 639.0
    - ectopic or molar pregnancy 639.0
  - male 567.21
  - puerperal, postpartum, childbirth 670.8 ☑ ▲

Cellulitis — *see also* Abscess — *continued*
- penis 607.2
- perineal, perineum 682.2
- perirectal 566
- peritonsillar 475
- periurethral 597.0
- periuterine (*see also* Disease, pelvis, inflammatory) 614.4
  - acute 614.3
- pharynx 478.21
- phlegmonous NEC 682.9
- rectum 566
- retromammary 611.0
- retroperitoneal (*see also* Peritonitis) 567.2 ☑, 567.38
- round ligament (*see also* Disease, pelvis, inflammatory) 614.4
  - acute 614.3
- scalp (any part) 682.8
  - dissecting 704.8
- scrotum 608.4
- seminal vesicle 608.0
- septic NEC 682.9
- shoulder 682.3
- specified sites NEC 682.8
- spermatic cord 608.4
- submandibular (region) (space) (triangle) 682.0
  - gland 527.3
- submaxillary 528.3
  - gland 527.3
- submental (pyogenic) 682.0
  - gland 527.3
- suppurative NEC 682.9
- testis 608.4
- thigh 682.6
- thumb (intrathecal) (periosteal) (subcutaneous) (subcuticular) 681.00
- toe (intrathecal) (periosteal) (subcutaneous) (subcuticular) 681.10
- tonsil 475
- trunk 682.2
- tuberculous (primary) (*see also* Tuberculosis) 017.0 ☑
- tunica vaginalis 608.4
- umbilical 682.2
  - newborn NEC 771.4
- vaccinal 999.39
- vagina — *see* Vaginitis
- vas deferens 608.4
- vocal cords 478.5
- vulva (*see also* Vulvitis) 616.10
- wrist 682.4

Cementoblastoma, benign (M9273/0) 213.1
- upper jaw (bone) 213.0

Cementoma (M9273/0) 213.1
- gigantiform (M9276/0) 213.1
  - upper jaw (bone) 213.0
- upper jaw (bone) 213.0

Cementoperiostitis 523.40
- acute 523.33
- apical 523.40

Cephalgia, cephalagia — *see also* Headache 784.0
- histamine 339.00
- nonorganic origin 307.81
- other trigeminal autonomic (TACS) 339.09
- psychogenic 307.81
- tension 307.81

Cephalhematocele, cephalematocele
- due to birth injury 767.19
- fetus or newborn 767.19
- traumatic (*see also* Contusion, head) 920

Cephalhematoma, cephalematoma (calcified)
- due to birth injury 767.19
- fetus or newborn 767.19
- traumatic (*see also* Contusion, head) 920

Cephalic — *see* condition

Cephalitis — *see* Encephalitis

Cephalocele 742.0

Cephaloma — *see* Neoplasm, by site, malignant

Cephalomenia 625.8

Cephalopelvic — *see* condition

Cercomoniasis 007.3

Cerebellitis — *see* Encephalitis

Cerebellum (cerebellar) — *see* condition

Cerebral — *see* condition

Cerebritis — *see* Encephalitis

Cerebrohepatorenal syndrome 759.89

Cerebromacular degeneration 330.1

Cerebromalacia — *see also* Softening, brain 434.9 ☑

Cerebrosidosis 272.7

Cerebrospasticity — *see* Palsy, cerebral

Cerebrospinal — *see* condition

Cerebrum — *see* condition

Ceroid storage disease 272.7

Cerumen (accumulation) (impacted) 380.4

Cervical — *see also* condition
- auricle 744.43
- high risk human papillomavirus (HPV) DNA test positive 795.05
- intraepithelial glandular neoplasia 233.1
- low risk human papillomavirus (HPV) DNA test positive 795.09
- rib 756.2
- shortening — *see* Short, cervical

Cervicalgia 723.1

Cervicitis (acute) (chronic) (nonvenereal) (subacute) (with erosion or ectropion) 616.0
- with
  - abortion — *see* Abortion, by type, with sepsis
  - ectopic pregnancy (*see also* categories 633.0–633.9) 639.0
  - molar pregnancy (*see also* categories 630–632) 639.0
  - ulceration 616.0
- chlamydial 099.53
- complicating pregnancy or puerperium 646.6 ☑
  - affecting fetus or newborn 760.8
- following
  - abortion 639.0
  - ectopic or molar pregnancy 639.0
- gonococcal (acute) 098.15
  - chronic or duration of 2 months or more 098.35
- senile (atrophic) 616.0
- syphilitic 095.8
- trichomonal 131.09
- tuberculous (*see also* Tuberculosis) 016.7 ☑

Cervicoaural fistula 744.49

Cervicocolpitis (emphysematosa) — *see also* Cervicitis 616.0

Cervix — *see* condition

Cesarean delivery, operation or section NEC 669.7 ☑
- affecting fetus or newborn 763.4
- post mortem, affecting fetus or newborn 761.6
- previous, affecting management of pregnancy 654.2 ☑

Céstan-Chenais paralysis 344.89

Céstan-Raymond syndrome 433.8 ☑

Céstan's syndrome 344.89

Cestode infestation NEC 123.9
- specified type NEC 123.8

Cestodiasis 123.9

CGF (congenital generalized fibromatosis) 759.89

Chabert's disease 022.9

Chacaleh 266.2

Chafing 709.8

Chagas' disease — *see also* Trypanosomiasis, American 086.2
- with heart involvement 086.0

Chagres fever 084.0

Chalasia (cardiac sphincter) 530.81

Chalazion 373.2

Chalazoderma 757.39

Chalcosis 360.24
- cornea 371.15
- crystalline lens 360.24 [366.34]
- retina 360.24

Chalicosis (occupational) (pulmonum) 502

Chancre (any genital site) (hard) (indurated) (infecting) (primary) (recurrent) 091.0
- congenital 090.0
- conjunctiva 091.2
- Ducrey's 099.0
- extragenital 091.2
- eyelid 091.2
- Hunterian 091.0
- lip (syphilis) 091.2

Chancre — *continued*
- mixed 099.8
- nipple 091.2
- Nisbet's 099.0
- of
  - carate 103.0
  - pinta 103.0
  - yaws 102.0
- palate, soft 091.2
- phagedenic 099.0
- Ricord's 091.0
- Rollet's (syphilitic) 091.0
- seronegative 091.0
- seropositive 091.0
- simple 099.0
- soft 099.0
  - bubo 099.0
- urethra 091.0
- yaws 102.0

Chancriform syndrome 114.1

Chancroid 099.0
- anus 099.0
- penis (Ducrey's bacillus) 099.0
- perineum 099.0
- rectum 099.0
- scrotum 099.0
- urethra 099.0
- vulva 099.0

Chandipura fever 066.8

Chandler's disease (osteochondritis dissecans, hip) 732.7

Change(s) (of) — *see also* Removal of
- arteriosclerotic — *see* Arteriosclerosis
- battery
  - cardiac pacemaker V53.31
- bone 733.90
  - diabetic 250.8 ☑ [731.8]
    - due to secondary diabetes 249.8 ☑ [731.8]
  - in disease, unknown cause 733.90
- bowel habits 787.99
- cardiorenal (vascular) (*see also* Hypertension, cardiorenal) 404.90
- cardiovascular — *see* Disease, cardiovascular
- circulatory 459.9
- cognitive or personality change of other type, nonpsychotic 310.1
- color, teeth, tooth
  - during formation 520.8
  - extrinsic 523.6
  - intrinsic posteruptive 521.7
- contraceptive device V25.42
- cornea, corneal
  - degenerative NEC 371.40
  - membrane NEC 371.30
  - senile 371.41
- coronary (*see also* Ischemia, heart) 414.9
- degenerative
  - chamber angle (anterior) (iris) 364.56
  - ciliary body 364.57
  - spine or vertebra (*see also* Spondylosis) 721.90
- dental pulp, regressive 522.2
- drains V58.49
- dressing
  - wound V58.30
    - nonsurgical V58.30
    - surgical V58.31
- fixation device V54.89
  - external V54.89
  - internal V54.01
- heart (*see also* Disease, heart)
- hip joint 718.95
- hyperplastic larynx 478.79
- hypertrophic
  - nasal sinus (*see also* Sinusitis) 473.9
  - turbinate, nasal 478.0
  - upper respiratory tract 478.9
- inflammatory — *see* Inflammation
- joint (*see also* Derangement, joint) 718.90
  - sacroiliac 724.6
- Kirschner wire V54.89
- knee 717.9
- macular, congenital 743.55

☑ Additional Digit Required — Refer to the Tabular List for Digit Selection   ⩔ Subterms under main terms may continue to next column or page

44 — Volume 2 · October 2009   ▶◀ Revised Text   ● New Line   ▲ Revised Code   2010 ICD-9-CM

Change(s) — *see also* Removal of — *continued*
  malignant (M — — /3) (*see also* Neoplasm, by site, malignant)

Note — *for malignant change occurring in a neoplasm, use the appropriate M code with behavior digit /3 e.g., malignant change in uterine fibroid — M8890/3. For malignant change occurring in a nonneo-plastic condition (e.g., gastric ulcer) use the M code M8000/3.*

  mental (status) NEC 780.97
    due to or associated with physical condition — *see* Syndrome, brain
  myocardium, myocardial — *see* Degeneration, myocardial
  of life (*see also* Menopause) 627.2
  pacemaker battery (cardiac) V53.31
  peripheral nerve 355.9
  personality (nonpsychotic) NEC 310.1
  plaster cast V54.89
  refractive, transient 367.81
  regressive, dental pulp 522.2
  retina 362.9
    myopic (degenerative) (malignant) 360.21
    vascular appearance 362.13
  sacroiliac joint 724.6
  scleral 379.19
    degenerative 379.16
  senile (*see also* Senility) 797
  sensory (*see also* Disturbance, sensation) 782.0
  skin texture 782.8
  spinal cord 336.9
  splint, external V54.89
  subdermal implantable contraceptive V25.5
  suture V58.32
  traction device V54.89
  trophic 355.9
    arm NEC 354.9
    leg NEC 355.8
    lower extremity NEC 355.8
    upper extremity NEC 354.9
  vascular 459.9
  vasomotor 443.9
  voice 784.49
    psychogenic 306.1
  wound packing V58.30
    nonsurgical V58.30
    surgical V58.31
Changing sleep-work schedule, affecting sleep 327.36
Changuinola fever 066.0
Chapping skin 709.8
Character
  depressive 301.12
Charcôt's
  arthropathy 094.0 [713.5]
  cirrhosis — *see* Cirrhosis, biliary
  disease 094.0
    spinal cord 094.0
  fever (biliary) (hepatic) (intermittent) — *see* Choledocholithiasis
  joint (disease) 094.0 [713.5]
    diabetic 250.6 ☑ [713.5]
      due to secondary diabetes 249.6 ☑ [713.5]
    syringomyelic 336.0 [713.5]
  syndrome (intermittent claudication) 443.9
    due to atherosclerosis 440.21
Charcôt-Marie-Tooth disease, paralysis, or syndrome 356.1
CHARGE association (syndrome) 759.89
Charleyhorse (quadriceps) 843.8
  muscle, except quadriceps — *see* Sprain, by site
Charlouis' disease — *see also* Yaws 102.9
Chauffeur's fracture — *see* Fracture, ulna, lower end
Cheadle (-Möller) (-Barlow) disease or syndrome (infantile scurvy) 267
Checking (of)
  contraceptive device (intrauterine) V25.42
  device
    fixation V54.89
      external V54.89
      internal V54.09

Checking — *continued*
  device — *continued*
    traction V54.89
    Kirschner wire V54.89
    plaster cast V54.89
    splint, external V54.89
Checkup
  following treatment — *see* Examination
  health V70.0
  infant ▶(over 28 days old)◀ (not sick) V20.2
  newborn, routine
    8 to 28 days old V20.32 ●
    over 28 days old, routine V20.2 ●
    under 8 days old V20.31 ●
    weight V20.32 ●
  pregnancy (normal) V22.1
    first V22.0
    high-risk pregnancy V23.9
      specified problem NEC V23.89
Chédiak-Higashi (-Steinbrinck) anomaly, disease, or syndrome (congenital gigantism of peroxidase granules) 288.2
Cheek — *see also* condition
  biting 528.9
Cheese itch 133.8
Cheese washers' lung 495.8
Cheilitis 528.5
  actinic (due to sun) 692.72
    chronic NEC 692.74
      due to radiation, except from sun 692.82
    due to radiation, except from sun 692.82
  acute 528.5
  angular 528.5
  catarrhal 528.5
  chronic 528.5
  exfoliative 528.5
  gangrenous 528.5
  glandularis apostematosa 528.5
  granulomatosa 351.8
  infectional 528.5
  membranous 528.5
  Miescher's 351.8
  suppurative 528.5
  ulcerative 528.5
  vesicular 528.5
Cheilodynia 528.5
Cheilopalatoschisis — *see also* Cleft, palate, with cleft lip 749.20
Cheilophagia 528.9
Cheiloschisis — *see also* Cleft, lip 749.10
Cheilosis 528.5
  with pellagra 265.2
  angular 528.5
  due to
    dietary deficiency 266.0
    vitamin deficiency 266.0
Cheiromegaly 729.89
Cheiropompholyx 705.81
Cheloid — *see also* Keloid 701.4
Chemical burn — *see also* Burn, by site
  from swallowing chemical — *see* Burn, internal organs
Chemodectoma (M8693/1) — *see* Paraganglioma, nonchromaffin
Chemoprophylaxis NEC V07.39
Chemosis, conjunctiva 372.73
Chemotherapy
  convalescence V66.2
  encounter (for) ▶(oral) (intravenous)◀ V58.11
  maintenance ▶(oral) (intravenous)◀ V58.11
  prophylactic NEC V07.39
    fluoride V07.31
Cherubism 526.89
Chest — *see* condition
Cheyne-Stokes respiration (periodic) 786.04
Chiari's
  disease or syndrome (hepatic vein thrombosis) 453.0
  malformation
    type I 348.4
    type II (*see also* Spina bifida) 741.0 ☑
    type III 742.0
    type IV 742.2
  network 746.89
Chiari-Frommel syndrome 676.6 ☑

Chicago disease (North American blastomycosis) 116.0
Chickenpox — *see also* Varicella 052.9
  exposure to V01.71
  vaccination and inoculation (prophylactic) V05.4
Chiclero ulcer 085.4
Chiggers 133.8
Chignon 111.2
  fetus or newborn (from vacuum extraction) 767.19
Chigoe disease 134.1
Chikungunya fever 066.3
Chilaiditi's syndrome (subphrenic displacement, colon) 751.4
Chilblains 991.5
  lupus 991.5
Child
  behavior causing concern V61.20
    adopted child V61.24 ●
    biological child V61.23 ●
    foster child V61.25 ●
Childbed fever 670.8 ☑ ▲
Childbirth — *see also* Delivery
  puerperal complications — *see* Puerperal
Childhood, period of rapid growth V21.0
Chill(s) 780.64
  with fever 780.60
  without fever 780.64
  congestive 780.99
    in malarial regions 084.6
  septic — *see* Septicemia
  urethral 599.84
Chilomastigiasis 007.8
Chin — *see* condition
Chinese dysentery 004.9
Chiropractic dislocation — *see also* Lesion, nonallopathic, by site 739.9
Chitral fever 066.0
Chlamydia, chlamydial — *see* condition
Chloasma 709.09
  cachecticorum 709.09
  eyelid 374.52
    congenital 757.33
    hyperthyroid 242.0 ☑
  gravidarum 646.8 ☑
  idiopathic 709.09
  skin 709.09
  symptomatic 709.09
Chloroma (M9930/3) 205.3 ☑
Chlorosis 280.9
  Egyptian (*see also* Ancylostomiasis) 126.9
  miners' (*see also* Ancylostomiasis) 126.9
Chlorotic anemia 280.9
Chocolate cyst (ovary) 617.1
Choked
  disk or disc — *see* Papilledema
  on food, phlegm, or vomitus NEC (*see also* Asphyxia, food) 933.1
  phlegm 933.1
  while vomiting NEC (*see also* Asphyxia, food) 933.1
Chokes (resulting from bends) 993.3
Choking sensation 784.99
Cholangiectasis — *see also* Disease, gallbladder 575.8
Cholangiocarcinoma (M8160/3)
  and hepatocellular carcinoma, combined (M8180/3) 155.0
  liver 155.1
  specified site NEC — *see* Neoplasm, by site, malignant
  unspecified site 155.1
Cholangiohepatitis 575.8
  due to fluke infestation 121.1
Cholangiohepatoma (M8180/3) 155.0
Cholangiolitis (acute) (chronic) (extrahepatic) (gangrenous) 576.1
  intrahepatic 575.8
  paratyphoid (*see also* Fever, paratyphoid) 002.9
  typhoidal 002.0
Cholangioma (M8160/0) 211.5
  malignant — *see* Cholangiocarcinoma

Cholangitis (acute) (ascending) (catarrhal) (chronic) (infective) (malignant) (primary) (recurrent) (sclerosing) (secondary) (stenosing) (suppurative) 576.1
  chronic nonsuppurative destructive 571.6
  nonsuppurative destructive (chronic) 571.6
Cholecystdocholithiasis — *see* Choledocholithiasis
Cholecystitis 575.10
  with
    calculus, stones in
      bile duct (common) (hepatic) — *see* Choledocholithiasis
      gallbladder — *see* Cholelithiasis
  acute 575.0
  acute and chronic 575.12
  chronic 575.11
  emphysematous (acute) (*see also* Cholecystitis, acute) 575.0
  gangrenous (*see also* Cholecystitis, acute) 575.0
  paratyphoidal, current (*see also* Fever, paratyphoid) 002.9
  suppurative (*see also* Cholecystitis, acute) 575.0
  typhoidal 002.0
Choledochitis (suppurative) 576.1
Choledocholith — *see* Choledocholithiasis
Choledocholithiasis 574.5 ☑

Note — *Use the following fifth-digit subclassification with category 574:*
0   without mention of obstruction
1   with obstruction

  with
    cholecystitis 574.4 ☑
      acute 574.3 ☑
      chronic 574.4 ☑
    cholelithiasis 574.9 ☑
      with
        cholecystitis 574.7 ☑
          acute 574.6 ☑
            and chronic 574.8 ☑
          chronic 574.7 ☑
Cholelithiasis (impacted) (multiple) 574.2 ☑

Note — *Use the following fifth-digit subclassification with category 574:*
0   without mention of obstruction
1   with obstruction

  with
    cholecystitis 574.1 ☑
      acute 574.0 ☑
      chronic 574.1 ☑
    choledocholithiasis 574.9 ☑
      with
        cholecystitis 574.7 ☑
          acute 574.6 ☑
            and chronic 574.8 ☑
          chronic cholecystitis 574.7 ☑
Cholemia — *see also* Jaundice 782.4
  familial 277.4
  Gilbert's (familial nonhemolytic) 277.4
Cholemic gallstone — *see* Cholelithiasis
Choleperitoneum, choleperitonitis — *see also* Disease, gallbladder 567.81
Cholera (algid) (Asiatic) (asphyctic) (epidemic) (gravis) (Indian) (malignant) (morbus) (pestilential) (spasmodic) 001.9
  antimonial 985.4
  carrier (suspected) of V02.0
  classical 001.0
  contact V01.0
  due to
    Vibrio
      cholerae (Inaba, Ogawa, Hikojima serotypes) 001.0
      El Tor 001.1
  El Tor 001.1
  exposure to V01.0
  vaccination, prophylactic (against) V03.0
Cholerine — *see also* Cholera 001.9
Cholestasis 576.8
  due to total parenteral nutrition (TPN) 573.8
Cholesteatoma (ear) 385.30
  attic (primary) 385.31

☑ Additional Digit Required — Refer to the Tabular List for Digit Selection   ▼ Subterms under main terms may continue to next column or page

2010 ICD-9-CM   ▶◀ Revised Text   ● New Line   ▲ Revised Code   October 2009 • Volume 2 — 45

Change(s) — Cholesteatoma

Index

Cholesteatoma — Cicatrix

Cholesteatoma — *continued*
  diffuse 385.35
  external ear (canal) 380.21
  marginal (middle ear) 385.32
    with involvement of mastoid cavity 385.33
      secondary (with middle ear involvement)
        385.33
  mastoid cavity 385.30
  middle ear (secondary) 385.32
    with involvement of mastoid cavity 385.33
  postmastoidectomy cavity (recurrent) 383.32
  primary 385.31
  recurrent, postmastoidectomy cavity 383.32
  secondary (middle ear) 385.32
    with involvement of mastoid cavity 385.33
Cholesteatosis (middle ear) — *see also*
  Cholesteatoma 385.30
  diffuse 385.35
Cholesteremia 272.0
Cholesterin
  granuloma, middle ear 385.82
  in vitreous 379.22
Cholesterol
  deposit
    retina 362.82
    vitreous 379.22
  elevated (high) 272.0
    with elevated (high) triglycerides 272.2
  imbibition of gallbladder (*see also* Disease,
    gallbladder) 575.6
Cholesterolemia 272.0
  essential 272.0
  familial 272.0
  hereditary 272.0
Cholesterosis, cholesterolosis (gallbladder)
  575.6
  with
    cholecystitis — *see* Cholecystitis
    cholelithiasis — *see* Cholelithiasis
  middle ear (*see also* Cholesteatoma) 385.30
Cholocolic fistula — *see also* Fistula, gallbladder
  575.5
Choluria 791.4
Chondritis (purulent) 733.99
  auricle 380.03
  costal 733.6
    Tietze's 733.6
  patella, posttraumatic 717.7
  pinna 380.03
  posttraumatica patellae 717.7
  tuberculous (active) (*see also* Tuberculosis)
    015.9 ☑
      intervertebral 015.0 ☑ *[730.88]*
Chondroangiopathia calcarea seu punctate
  756.59
Chondroblastoma (M9230/0) — *see also* Neoplasm, bone, benign
  malignant (M9230/3) — *see* Neoplasm, bone,
    malignant
Chondrocalcinosis (articular) (crystal deposition)
  (dihydrate) — *see also* Arthritis, due to,
    crystals 275.49 *[712.3]* ☑
  due to
    calcium pyrophosphate 275.49 *[712.2]* ☑
    dicalcium phosphate crystals
      275.49 *[712.1]* ☑
    pyrophosphate crystals 275.49 *[712.2]* ☑
Chondrodermatitis nodularis helicis 380.00
Chondrodysplasia 756.4
  angiomatose 756.4
  calcificans congenita 756.59
  epiphysialis punctata 756.59
  hereditary deforming 756.4
  rhizomelic punctata 277.86
Chondrodystrophia (fetalis) 756.4
  calcarea 756.4
  calcificans congenita 756.59
  fetalis hypoplastica 756.59
  hypoplastica calcinosa 756.59
  punctata 756.59
  tarda 277.5
Chondrodystrophy (familial) (hypoplastic) 756.4
  myotonic (congenital) 359.23
Chondroectodermal dysplasia 756.55
Cholerolysis 733.99

Chondroma (M9220/0) — *see also* Neoplasm
  cartilage, benign
  juxtacortical (M9221/0) — *see* Neoplasm,
    bone, benign
  periosteal (M9221/0) — *see* Neoplasm, bone,
    benign
Chondromalacia 733.92
  epiglottis (congenital) 748.3
  generalized 733.92
  knee 717.7
  larynx (congenital) 748.3
  localized, except patella 733.92
  patella, patellae 717.7
  systemic 733.92
  tibial plateau 733.92
  trachea (congenital) 748.3
Chondromatosis (M9220/1) — *see* Neoplasm,
  cartilage, uncertain behavior
Chondromyxosarcoma (M9220/3) — *see* Neoplasm, cartilage, malignant
Chondro-osteodysplasia (Morquio-Brailsford
  type) 277.5
Chondro-osteodystrophy 277.5
Chondro-osteoma (M9210/0) — *see* Neoplasm,
  bone, benign
Chondropathia tuberosa 733.6
Chondrosarcoma (M9220/3) — *see also* Neoplasm, cartilage, malignant
  juxtacortical (M9221/3) — *see* Neoplasm,
    bone, malignant
  mesenchymal (M9240/3) — *see* Neoplasm,
    connective tissue, malignant
Chordae tendineae rupture (chronic) 429.5
Chordee (nonvenereal) 607.89
  congenital 752.63
  gonococcal 098.2
Chorditis (fibrinous) (nodosa) (tuberosa) 478.5
Chordoma (M9370/3) — *see* Neoplasm, by site,
  malignant
Chorea (gravis) (minor) (spasmodic) 333.5
  with
    heart involvement — *see* Chorea with
      rheumatic heart disease
    rheumatic heart disease (chronic, inactive,
      or quiescent) (conditions classifi-
      able to 393–398) (*see* rheumatic
      heart condition involved)
      active or acute (conditions classifiable
        to 391) 392.0
  acute — *see* Chorea, Sydenham's
  apoplectic (*see also* Disease, cerebrovascular,
    acute) 436
  chronic 333.4
  electric 049.8
  gravidarum — *see* Eclampsia, pregnancy
  habit 307.22
  hereditary 333.4
  Huntington's 333.4
  posthemiplegic 344.89
  pregnancy — *see* Eclampsia, pregnancy
  progressive 333.4
    chronic 333.4
    hereditary 333.4
  rheumatic (chronic) 392.9
    with heart disease or involvement — *see*
      Chorea, with rheumatic heart dis-
      ease
  senile 333.5
  Sydenham's 392.9
    with heart involvement — *see* Chorea,
      with rheumatic heart disease
    nonrheumatic 333.5
  variabilis 307.23
Choreoathetosis (paroxysmal) 333.5
Chorioadenoma (destruens) (M9100/1) 236.1
Chorioamnionitis 658.4 ☑
  affecting fetus or newborn 762.7
Chorioangioma (M9120/0) 219.8
Choriocarcinoma (M9100/3)
  combined with
    embryonal carcinoma (M9101/3) — *see*
      Neoplasm, by site, malignant
    teratoma (M9101/3) — *see* Neoplasm, by
      site, malignant
  specified site — *see* Neoplasm, by site, malig-
    nant

Choriocarcinoma — *continued*
  unspecified site
    female 181
    male 186.9
Chorioencephalitis, lymphocytic (acute)
  (serous) 049.0
Chorioepithelioma (M9100/3) — *see* Choriocarcinoma
Choriomeningitis (acute) (benign) (lymphocytic)
  (serous) 049.0
Chorionepithelioma (M9100/3) — *see* Choriocarcinoma
Chorionitis — *see also* Scleroderma 710.1
Chorioretinitis 363.20
  disseminated 363.10
    generalized 363.13
    in
      neurosyphilis 094.83
      secondary syphilis 091.51
    peripheral 363.12
    posterior pole 363.11
    tuberculous (*see also* Tuberculosis)
      017.3 ☑ *[363.13]*
  due to
    histoplasmosis (*see also* Histoplasmosis)
      115.92
    toxoplasmosis (acquired) 130.2
      congenital (active) 771.2
  focal 363.00
    juxtapapillary 363.01
    peripheral 363.04
    posterior pole NEC 363.03
  juxtapapillaris, juxtapapillary 363.01
  progressive myopia (degeneration) 360.21
  syphilitic (secondary) 091.51
    congenital (early) 090.0 *[363.13]*
      late 090.5 *[363.13]*
    late 095.8 *[363.13]*
  tuberculous (*see also* Tuberculosis)
    017.3 ☑ *[363.13]*
Choristoma — *see* Neoplasm, by site, benign
Choroid — *see* condition
Choroideremia, choroidermia (initial stage)
  (late stage) (partial or total atrophy) 363.55
Choroiditis — *see also* Chorioretinitis 363.20
  leprous 030.9 *[363.13]*
  senile guttate 363.41
  sympathetic 360.11
  syphilitic (secondary) 091.51
    congenital (early) 090.0 *[363.13]*
    late 090.5 *[363.13]*
    late 095.8 *[363.13]*
  Tay's 363.41
  tuberculous (*see also* Tuberculosis)
    017.3 ☑ *[363.13]*
Choroidopathy NEC 363.9
  degenerative (*see also* Degeneration, choroid)
    363.40
  hereditary (*see also* Dystrophy, choroid) 363.50
  specified type NEC 363.8
Choroidoretinitis — *see* Chorioretinitis
Choroidosis, central serous 362.41
Choroidretinopathy, serous 362.41
Christian's syndrome (chronic histiocytosis X)
  277.89
Christian-Weber disease (nodular nonsuppura-
  tive panniculitis) 729.30
Christmas disease 286.1
Chromaffinoma (M8700/0) — *see also* Neo-
  plasm, by site, benign
  malignant (M8700/3) — *see* Neoplasm, by
    site, malignant
Chromatopsia 368.59
Chromhidrosis, chromidrosis 705.89
Chromoblastomycosis 117.2
Chromomycosis 117.2
Chromophytosis 111.0
Chromotrichomycosis 111.8
Chronic — *see* condition
Churg-Strauss syndrome 446.4
Chyle cyst, mesentery 457.8
Chylocele (nonfilarial) 457.8
  filarial (*see also* Infestation, filarial) 125.9
  tunica vaginalis (nonfilarial) 608.84
    filarial (*see also* Infestation, filarial) 125.9

Chylomicronemia (fasting) (with hyperprebetalipoproteinemia) 272.3
Chylopericardium (acute) 420.90
Chylothorax (nonfilarial) 457.8
  filarial (*see also* Infestation, filarial) 125.9
Chylous
  ascites 457.8
  cyst of peritoneum 457.8
  hydrocele 603.9
  hydrothorax (nonfilarial) 457.8
    filarial (*see also* Infestation, filarial) 125.9
Chyluria 791.1
  bilharziasis 120.0
  due to
    Brugia (malayi) 125.1
    Wuchereria (bancrofti) 125.0
      malayi 125.1
  filarial (*see also* Infestation, filarial) 125.9
  filariasis (*see also* Infestation, filarial) 125.9
  nonfilarial 791.1
Cicatricial (deformity) — *see* Cicatrix
Cicatrix (adherent) (contracted) (painful) (vicious)
  709.2
  adenoid 474.8
  alveolar process 525.8
  anus 569.49
  auricle 380.89
  bile duct (*see also* Disease, biliary) 576.8
  bladder 596.8
  bone 733.99
  brain 348.89   ▲
  cervix (postoperative) (postpartal) 622.3
    in pregnancy or childbirth 654.6 ☑
      causing obstructed labor 660.2 ☑
  chorioretinal 363.30
    disseminated 363.35
    macular 363.32
    peripheral 363.34
    posterior pole NEC 363.33
  choroid — *see* Cicatrix, chorioretinal
  common duct (*see also* Disease, biliary) 576.8
  congenital 757.39
  conjunctiva 372.64
  cornea 371.00
    tuberculous (*see also* Tuberculosis)
      017.3 ☑ *[371.05]*
  duodenum (bulb) 537.3
  esophagus 530.3
  eyelid 374.46
    with
      ectropion — *see* Ectropion
      entropion — *see* Entropion
  hypopharynx 478.29
  knee, semilunar cartilage 717.5
  lacrimal
    canaliculi 375.53
    duct
      acquired 375.56
      neonatal 375.55
    punctum 375.52
    sac 375.54
  larynx 478.79
  limbus (cystoid) 372.64
  lung 518.89
  macular 363.32
    disseminated 363.35
    peripheral 363.34
  middle ear 385.89
  mouth 528.9
  muscle 728.89
  nasolacrimal duct
    acquired 375.56
    neonatal 375.55
  nasopharynx 478.29
  palate (soft) 528.9
  penis 607.89
  prostate 602.8
  rectum 569.49
  retina 363.30
    disseminated 363.35
    macular 363.32
    peripheral 363.34
    posterior pole NEC 363.33
  semilunar cartilage — *see* Derangement,
    meniscus
  seminal vesicle 608.89

☑ Additional Digit Required — Refer to the Tabular List for Digit Selection   Subterms under main terms may continue to next column or page

Cicatrix — *continued*
  skin 709.2
    infected 686.8
    postinfectional 709.2
    tuberculous (*see also* Tuberculosis)
      017.0 ☑
  specified site NEC 709.2
  throat 478.29
  tongue 529.8
  tonsil (and adenoid) 474.8
  trachea 478.9
  tuberculous NEC (*see also* Tuberculosis)
    011.9 ☑
  ureter 593.89
  urethra 599.84
  uterus 621.8
  vagina 623.4
    in pregnancy or childbirth 654.7 ☑
      causing obstructed labor 660.2 ☑
  vocal cord 478.5
  wrist, constricting (annular) 709.2
CIDP (chronic inflammatory demyelinating polyneuropathy) 357.81
CIN I [cervical intraepithelial neoplasia I] 622.11
CIN II [cervical intraepithelial neoplasia II] 622.12
CIN III [cervical intraepithelial neoplasia III] 233.1
Cinchonism
  correct substance properly administered 386.9
  overdose or wrong substance given or taken 961.4
Circine herpes 110.5
Circle of Willis — *see* condition
Circular — *see also* condition
  hymen 752.49
Circulating, ▶intrinsic◀ anticoagulants ▶causing hemorrhagic disorder◀ 286.5
  following childbirth 666.3 ☑
  postpartum 666.3 ☑
Circulation
  collateral (venous), any site 459.89
  defective 459.9
    congenital 747.9
    lower extremity 459.89
  embryonic 747.9
  failure 799.89
    fetus or newborn 779.89
    peripheral 785.59
  fetal, persistent 747.83
  heart, incomplete 747.9
Circulatory system — *see* condition
Circulus senilis 371.41
Circumcision
  in absence of medical indication V50.2
  ritual V50.2
  routine V50.2
  status (post), female 629.20
Circumscribed — *see* condition
Circumvallata placenta — *see* Placenta, abnormal
Cirrhosis, cirrhotic 571.5
  with alcoholism 571.2
  alcoholic (liver) 571.2
  atrophic (of liver) — *see* Cirrhosis, portal
  Baumgarten-Cruveilhier 571.5
  biliary (cholangiolitic) (cholangitic) (cholestatic) (extrahepatic) (hypertrophic) (intrahepatic) (nonobstructive) (obstructive) (pericholangiolitic) (posthepatic) (primary) (secondary) (xanthomatous) 571.6
    due to
      clonorchiasis 121.1
      flukes 121.3
  brain 331.9
  capsular — *see* Cirrhosis, portal
  cardiac 571.5
    alcoholic 571.2
  central (liver) — *see* Cirrhosis, liver
  Charcôt's 571.6
  cholangiolitic — *see* Cirrhosis, biliary
  cholangitic — *see* Cirrhosis, biliary
  cholestatic — *see* Cirrhosis, biliary
  clitoris (hypertrophic) 624.2
  coarsely nodular 571.5
  congestive (liver) — *see* Cirrhosis, cardiac

Cirrhosis, cirrhotic — *continued*
  Cruveilhier-Baumgarten 571.5
  cryptogenic (of liver) 571.5
    alcoholic 571.2
  dietary (*see also* Cirrhosis, portal) 571.5
  due to
    bronzed diabetes 275.0
    congestive hepatomegaly — *see* Cirrhosis, cardiac
    cystic fibrosis 277.00
    hemochromatosis 275.0
    hepatolenticular degeneration 275.1
    passive congestion (chronic) — *see* Cirrhosis, cardiac
    Wilson's disease 275.1
    xanthomatosis 272.2
  extrahepatic (obstructive) — *see* Cirrhosis, biliary
  fatty 571.8
    alcoholic 571.0
  florid 571.2
  Glisson's — *see* Cirrhosis, portal
  Hanot's (hypertrophic) — *see* Cirrhosis, biliary
  hepatic — *see* Cirrhosis, liver
  hepatolienal — *see* Cirrhosis, liver
  hobnail — *see* Cirrhosis, portal
  hypertrophic (*see also* Cirrhosis, liver)
    biliary — *see* Cirrhosis, biliary
    Hanot's — *see* Cirrhosis, biliary
  infectious NEC — *see* Cirrhosis, portal
  insular — *see* Cirrhosis, portal
  intrahepatic (obstructive) (primary) (secondary) — *see* Cirrhosis, biliary
  juvenile (*see also* Cirrhosis, portal) 571.5
  kidney (*see also* Sclerosis, renal) 587
  Laennec's (of liver) 571.2
    nonalcoholic 571.5
  liver (chronic) (hepatolienal) (hypertrophic) (nodular) (splenomegalic) (unilobar) 571.5
    with alcoholism 571.2
    alcoholic 571.2
    congenital (due to failure of obliteration of umbilical vein) 777.8
    cryptogenic 571.5
      alcoholic 571.2
    fatty 571.8
      alcoholic 571.0
    macronodular 571.5
      alcoholic 571.2
    micronodular 571.5
      alcoholic 571.2
    nodular, diffuse 571.5
      alcoholic 571.2
    pigmentary 275.0
    portal 571.5
      alcoholic 571.2
    postnecrotic 571.5
      alcoholic 571.2
    syphilitic 095.3
  lung (chronic) (*see also* Fibrosis, lung) 515
  macronodular (of liver) 571.5
    alcoholic 571.2
  malarial 084.9
  metabolic NEC 571.5
  micronodular (of liver) 571.5
    alcoholic 571.2
  monolobular — *see* Cirrhosis, portal
  multilobular — *see* Cirrhosis, portal
  nephritis (*see also* Sclerosis, renal) 587
  nodular — *see* Cirrhosis, liver
  nutritional (fatty) 571.5
  obstructive (biliary) (extrahepatic) (intrahepatic) — *see* Cirrhosis, biliary
  ovarian 620.8
  paludal 084.9
  pancreas (duct) 577.8
  pericholangiolitic — *see* Cirrhosis, biliary
  periportal — *see* Cirrhosis, portal
  pigment, pigmentary (of liver) 275.0
  portal (of liver) 571.5
    alcoholic 571.2
  posthepatitic (*see also* Cirrhosis, postnecrotic) 571.5
  postnecrotic (of liver) 571.5
    alcoholic 571.2

Cirrhosis, cirrhotic — *continued*
  primary (intrahepatic) — *see* Cirrhosis, biliary
  pulmonary (*see also* Fibrosis, lung) 515
  renal (*see also* Sclerosis, renal) 587
  septal (*see also* Cirrhosis, postnecrotic) 571.5
  spleen 289.51
  splenomegalic (of liver) — *see* Cirrhosis, liver
  stasis (liver) — *see* Cirrhosis, liver
  stomach 535.4 ☑
  Todd's (*see also* Cirrhosis, biliary) 571.6
  toxic (nodular) — *see* Cirrhosis, postnecrotic
  trabecular — *see* Cirrhosis, postnecrotic
  unilobar — *see* Cirrhosis, liver
  vascular (of liver) — *see* Cirrhosis, liver
  xanthomatous (biliary) (*see also* Cirrhosis, biliary) 571.6
    due to xanthomatosis (familial) (metabolic) (primary) 272.2
Cistern, subarachnoid 793.0
Citrullinemia 270.6
Citrullinuria 270.6
Ciuffini-Pancoast tumor (M8010/3) (carcinoma, pulmonary apex) 162.3
Civatte's disease or poikiloderma 709.09
CJD (Creutzfeldt-Jakob disease) 046.19
  variant (vCJD) 046.11
Clam diggers' itch 120.3
Clap — *see* Gonorrhea
Clarke-Hadfield syndrome (pancreatic infantilism) 577.8
Clark's paralysis 343.9
Clastothrix 704.2
Claude Bernard-Horner syndrome — *see also* Neuropathy, peripheral, autonomic 337.9
Claude's syndrome 352.6
Claudication, intermittent 443.9
  cerebral (artery) (*see also* Ischemia, cerebral, transient) 435.9
  due to atherosclerosis 440.21
  spinal cord (arteriosclerotic) 435.1
    syphilitic 094.89
  spinalis 435.1
  venous (axillary) 453.89 ▲
Claudicatio venosa intermittens 453.89 ▲
Claustrophobia 300.29
Clavus (infected) 700
Clawfoot (congenital) 754.71
  acquired 736.74
Clawhand (acquired) 736.06
  congenital 755.59
Clawtoe (congenital) 754.71
  acquired 735.5
Clay eating 307.52
Clay shovelers' fracture — *see* Fracture, vertebra, cervical
Cleansing of artificial opening — *see also* Attention to artificial opening V55.9
Cleft (congenital) — *see also* Imperfect, closure
  alveolar process 525.8
  branchial (persistent) 744.41
    cyst 744.42
  clitoris 752.49
  cricoid cartilage, posterior 748.3
  facial (*see also* Cleft, lip) 749.10
  lip 749.10
    with cleft palate 749.20
      bilateral (lip and palate) 749.24
        with unilateral lip or palate 749.25
        complete 749.23
        incomplete 749.24
      unilateral (lip and palate) 749.22
        with bilateral lip or palate 749.25
        complete 749.21
        incomplete 749.22
    bilateral 749.14
      with cleft palate, unilateral 749.25
      complete 749.13
      incomplete 749.14
    unilateral 749.12
      with cleft palate, bilateral 749.25
      complete 749.11
      incomplete 749.12
  nose 748.1
  palate 749.00
    with cleft lip 749.20
      bilateral (lip and palate) 749.24

Cleft — *see also* Imperfect, closure — *continued*
  palate — *continued*
    with cleft lip — *continued*
      bilateral — *continued*
        with unilateral lip or palate 749.25
        complete 749.23
        incomplete 749.24
      unilateral (lip and palate) 749.22
        with bilateral lip or palate 749.25
        complete 749.21
        incomplete 749.22
    bilateral 749.04
      with cleft lip, unilateral 749.25
      complete 749.03
      incomplete 749.04
    unilateral 749.02
      with cleft lip, bilateral 749.25
      complete 749.01
      incomplete 749.02
  penis 752.69
  posterior, cricoid cartilage 748.3
  scrotum 752.89
  sternum (congenital) 756.3
  thyroid cartilage (congenital) 748.3
  tongue 750.13
  uvula 749.02
    with cleft lip (*see also* Cleft, lip, with cleft palate) 749.20
  water 366.12
Cleft hand (congenital) 755.58
Cleidocranial dysostosis 755.59
Cleidotomy, fetal 763.89
Cleptomania 312.32
Clérambault's syndrome 297.8
  erotomania 302.89
Clergyman's sore throat 784.49
Click, clicking
  systolic syndrome 785.2
Clifford's syndrome (postmaturity) 766.22
Climacteric — *see also* Menopause 627.2
  arthritis NEC (*see also* Arthritis, climacteric) 716.3 ☑
  depression (*see also* Psychosis, affective) 296.2 ☑
  disease 627.2
    recurrent episode 296.3 ☑
    single episode 296.2 ☑
  female (symptoms) 627.2
  male (symptoms) (syndrome) 608.89
  melancholia (*see also* Psychosis, affective) 296.2 ☑
    recurrent episode 296.3 ☑
    single episode 296.2 ☑
  paranoid state 297.2
  paraphrenia 297.2
  polyarthritis NEC 716.39
    male 608.89
  symptoms (female) 627.2
Clinical research investigation (control) (participant) V70.7
Clinodactyly 755.59
Clitoris — *see* condition
Cloaca, persistent 751.5
Clonorchiasis 121.1
Clonorchiosis 121.1
Clonorchis infection, liver 121.1
Clonus 781.0
Closed bite 524.20
Closed surgical procedure converted to open procedure
  arthroscopic V64.43
  laparoscopic V64.41
  thoracoscopic V64.42
Closure
  artificial opening (*see also* Attention to artificial opening) V55.9
  congenital, nose 748.0
  cranial sutures, premature 756.0
  defective or imperfect NEC — *see* Imperfect, closure
  fistula, delayed — *see* Fistula
  fontanelle, delayed 756.0
  foramen ovale, imperfect 745.5
  hymen 623.3
  interauricular septum, defective 745.5

Cicatrix — Closure

☑ Additional Digit Required — Refer to the Tabular List for Digit Selection   ▽ Subterms under main terms may continue to next column or page

2010 ICD-9-CM   ▶◀ Revised Text   ● New Line   ▲ Revised Code   October 2009 • Volume 2 — 47

Closure — *continued*
  interventricular septum, defective 745.4
  lacrimal duct 375.56
    congenital 743.65
    neonatal 375.55
  nose (congenital) 748.0
    acquired 738.0
  vagina 623.2
  valve — *see* Endocarditis
  vulva 624.8
Clot (blood)
  artery (obstruction) (occlusion) (*see also* Embolism) 444.9
  atrial appendage 429.89
  bladder 596.7
  brain (extradural or intradural) (*see also* Thrombosis, brain) 434.0 ☑
    late effect — *see* Late effect(s) (of) cerebrovascular disease
  circulation 444.9
  heart (*see also* Infarct, myocardium) 410.9 ☑
    without myocardial infarction 429.89
  vein (*see also* Thrombosis) 453.9
Clotting defect NEC — *see also* Defect, coagulation 286.9
Clouded state 780.09
  epileptic (*see also* Epilepsy) 345.9 ☑
  paroxysmal (idiopathic) (*see also* Epilepsy) 345.9 ☑
Clouding
  corneal graft 996.51
Cloudy
  antrum, antra 473.0
  dialysis effluent 792.5
Clouston's (hidrotic) ectodermal dysplasia 757.31
Clubbing of fingers 781.5
Clubfinger 736.29
  acquired 736.29
  congenital 754.89
Clubfoot (congenital) 754.70
  acquired 736.71
  equinovarus 754.51
  paralytic 736.71
Club hand (congenital) 754.89
  acquired 736.07
Clubnail (acquired) 703.8
  congenital 757.5
Clump kidney 753.3
Clumsiness 781.3
  syndrome 315.4
Cluttering 307.0
Clutton's joints 090.5
Coagulation, intravascular (diffuse) (disseminated) — *see also* Fibrinolysis 286.6
  newborn 776.2
Coagulopathy — *see also* Defect, coagulation 286.9
  consumption 286.6
  intravascular (disseminated) NEC 286.6
    newborn 776.2
Coalition
  calcaneoscaphoid 755.67
  calcaneus 755.67
  tarsal 755.67
Coal miners'
  elbow 727.2
  lung 500
Coal workers' lung or pneumoconiosis 500
Coarctation
  aorta (postductal) (preductal) 747.10
  pulmonary artery 747.3
Coated tongue 529.3
Coats' disease 362.12
Cocainism — *see also* Dependence 304.2 ☑
Coccidioidal granuloma 114.3
Coccidioidomycosis 114.9
  with pneumonia 114.0
  cutaneous (primary) 114.1
  disseminated 114.3
  extrapulmonary (primary) 114.1
  lung 114.5
    acute 114.0
    chronic 114.4
    primary 114.0
  meninges 114.2

Coccidioidomycosis — *continued*
  primary (pulmonary) 114.0
    acute 114.0
  prostate 114.3
  pulmonary 114.5
    acute 114.0
    chronic 114.4
    primary 114.0
  specified site NEC 114.3
Coccidioidosis 114.9
  lung 114.5
    acute 114.0
    chronic 114.4
    primary 114.0
  meninges 114.2
Coccidiosis (colitis) (diarrhea) (dysentery) 007.2
Cocciuria 791.9
Coccus in urine 791.9
Coccydynia 724.79
Coccygodynia 724.79
Coccyx — *see* condition
Cochin-China
  diarrhea 579.1
    anguilluliasis 127.2
  ulcer 085.1
Cockayne's disease or syndrome (microcephaly and dwarfism) 759.89
Cockayne-Weber syndrome (epidermolysis bullosa) 757.39
Cocked-up toe 735.2
Cock's peculiar tumor 706.2
Codman's tumor (benign chondroblastoma) (M9230/0) — *see* Neoplasm, bone, benign
Coenurosis 123.8
Coffee workers' lung 495.8
Cogan's syndrome 370.52
  congenital oculomotor apraxia 379.51
  nonsyphilitic interstitial keratitis 370.52
Coiling, umbilical cord — *see* Complications, umbilical cord
Coitus, painful (female) 625.0
  male 608.89
  psychogenic 302.76
Cold 460
  with influenza, flu, or grippe 487.1
  abscess (*see also* Tuberculosis, abscess)
    articular — *see* Tuberculosis, joint
  agglutinin
    disease (chronic) or syndrome 283.0
    hemoglobinuria 283.0
      paroxysmal (cold) (nocturnal) 283.2
  allergic (*see also* Fever, hay) 477.9
  bronchus or chest — *see* Bronchitis
    with grippe or influenza 487.1
  common (head) 460
    vaccination, prophylactic (against) V04.7
  deep 464.10
  effects of 991.9
    specified effect NEC 991.8
  excessive 991.9
    specified effect NEC 991.8
  exhaustion from 991.8
  exposure to 991.9
    specified effect NEC 991.8
  grippy 487.1
  head 460
  injury syndrome (newborn) 778.2
  intolerance 780.99
  on lung — *see* Bronchitis
  rose 477.0
  sensitivity, autoimmune 283.0
  virus 460
Coldsore — *see also* Herpes, simplex 054.9
Colibacillosis 041.4
  generalized 038.42
Colibacilluria 791.9
Colic (recurrent) 789.7 ▲
  abdomen 789.7 ▲
    psychogenic 307.89
  appendicular 543.9
  appendix 543.9
  bile duct — *see* Choledocholithiasis
  biliary — *see* Cholelithiasis
  bilious — *see* Cholelithiasis
  common duct — *see* Choledocholithiasis
  Devonshire NEC 984.9

Colic — *continued*
  Devonshire — *continued*
    specified type of lead — *see* Table of Drugs and Chemicals
  flatulent 787.3
  gallbladder or gallstone — *see* Cholelithiasis
  gastric 536.8
  hepatic (duct) — *see* Choledocholithiasis
  hysterical 300.11
  in   ●
    adult 789.0 ☑   ●
    child over 12 months old 789.0 ☑   ●
    infant 789.7   ●
  infantile 789.7   ▲
  intestinal 789.7   ▲
  kidney 788.0
  lead NEC 984.9
    specified type of lead — *see* Table of Drugs and Chemicals
  liver (duct) — *see* Choledocholithiasis
  mucous 564.9
    psychogenic 316 *[564.9]*
  nephritic 788.0
  painter's NEC 984.9
  pancreas 577.8
  psychogenic 306.4
  renal 788.0
  saturnine NEC 984.9
    specified type of lead — *see* Table of Drugs and Chemicals
  spasmodic 789.7   ▲
  ureter 788.0
  urethral 599.84
    due to calculus 594.2
  uterus 625.8
    menstrual 625.3
  vermicular 543.9
  virus 460
  worm NEC 128.9
Colicystitis — *see also* Cystitis 595.9
Colitis (acute) (catarrhal) (croupous) (cystica superficialis) (exudative) (hemorrhagic) (noninfectious) (phlegmonous) (presumed noninfectious) 558.9
  adaptive 564.9
  allergic 558.3
  amebic (*see also* Amebiasis) 006.9
    nondysenteric 006.2
  anthrax 022.2
  bacillary (*see also* Infection, Shigella) 004.9
  balantidial 007.0
  chronic 558.9
    ulcerative (*see also* Colitis, ulcerative) 556.9
  coccidial 007.2
  dietetic 558.9
  due to radiation 558.1
  eosinophilic 558.42   ▲
  functional 558.9
  gangrenous 009.0
  giardial 007.1
  granulomatous 555.1
  gravis (*see also* Colitis, ulcerative) 556.9
  infectious (*see also* Enteritis, due to, specific organism) 009.0
    presumed 009.1
  ischemic 557.9
    acute 557.0
    chronic 557.1
    due to mesenteric artery insufficiency 557.1
  membranous 564.9
    psychogenic 316 *[564.9]*
  mucous 564.9
    psychogenic 316 *[564.9]*
  necrotic 009.0
  polyposa (*see also* Colitis, ulcerative) 556.9
  protozoal NEC 007.9
  pseudomembranous 008.45
  pseudomucinous 564.9
  regional 555.1
  segmental 555.1
  septic (*see also* Enteritis, due to, specific organism) 009.0
  spastic 564.9
    psychogenic 316 *[564.9]*
  Staphylococcus 008.41

Colitis — *continued*
  Staphylococcus — *continued*
    food 005.0
  thromboulcerative 557.0
  toxic 558.2
  transmural 555.1
  trichomonal 007.3
  tuberculous (ulcerative) 014.8 ☑
  ulcerative (chronic) (idiopathic) (nonspecific) 556.9
    entero- 556.0
    fulminant 557.0
    ileo- 556.1
    left-sided 556.5
    procto- 556.2
    proctosigmoid 556.3
    psychogenic 316 *[556]* ☑
    specified NEC 556.8
    universal 556.6
Collagen disease NEC 710.9
  nonvascular 710.9
  vascular (allergic) (*see also* Angiitis, hypersensitivity) 446.20
Collagenosis — *see also* Collagen disease 710.9
  cardiovascular 425.4
  mediastinal 519.3
Collapse 780.2
  adrenal 255.8
  cardiorenal (*see also* Hypertension, cardiorenal) 404.90
  cardiorespiratory 785.51
    fetus or newborn 779.85
  cardiovascular (*see also* Disease, heart) 785.51
    fetus or newborn 779.85
  circulatory (peripheral) 785.59
    with
      abortion — *see* Abortion, by type, with shock
      ectopic pregnancy (*see also* categories 633.0–633.9) 639.5
      molar pregnancy (*see also* categories 630–632) 639.5
    during or after labor and delivery 669.1 ☑
    fetus or newborn 779.85
    following
      abortion 639.5
      ectopic or molar pregnancy 639.5
    during or after labor and delivery 669.1 ☑
    fetus or newborn 779.89
  external ear canal 380.50
    secondary to
      inflammation 380.53
      surgery 380.52
      trauma 380.51
  general 780.2
  heart — *see* Disease, heart
  heat 992.1
  hysterical 300.11
  labyrinth, membranous (congenital) 744.05
  lung (massive) (*see also* Atelectasis) 518.0
    pressure, during labor 668.0 ☑
  myocardial — *see* Disease, heart
  nervous (*see also* Disorder, mental, nonpsychotic) 300.9
  neurocirculatory 306.2
  nose 738.0
  postoperative (cardiovascular) 998.0
  pulmonary (see also Atelectasis) 518.0
    fetus or newborn 770.5
      partial 770.5
      primary 770.4
  thorax 512.8
    iatrogenic 512.1
    postoperative 512.1
  trachea 519.19
  valvular — *see* Endocarditis
  vascular (peripheral) 785.59
    with
      abortion — *see* Abortion, by type, with shock
      ectopic pregnancy (*see also* categories 633.0–633.9) 639.5
      molar pregnancy (*see also* categories 630–632) 639.5
    cerebral (*see also* Disease, cerebrovascular, acute) 436

☑ Additional Digit Required — Refer to the Tabular List for Digit Selection   ▽ Subterms under main terms may continue to next column or page

48 — Volume 2 • October 2009   ▶◀ Revised Text   ● New Line   ▲ Revised Code   2010 ICD-9-CM

Collapse — *continued*
vascular — *continued*
during or after labor and delivery 669.1 ☑
fetus or newborn 779.89
following
abortion 639.5
ectopic or molar pregnancy 639.5
vasomotor 785.59
vertebra 733.13
Collateral — *see also* condition
circulation (venous) 459.89
dilation, veins 459.89
Colles' fracture (closed) (reversed) (separation) 813.41
open 813.51
Collet-Sicard syndrome 352.6
Collet's syndrome 352.6
Colliculitis urethralis — *see also* Urethritis 597.89
Colliers'
asthma 500
lung 500
phthisis (*see also* Tuberculosis) 011.4 ☑
Collodion baby (ichthyosis congenita) 757.1
Colloid milium 709.3
Coloboma NEC 743.49
choroid 743.59
fundus 743.52
iris 743.46
lens 743.36
lids 743.62
optic disc (congenital) 743.57
acquired 377.23
retina 743.56
sclera 743.47
Coloenteritis — *see* Enteritis
Colon — *see* condition
Colonization
MRSA (methicillin resistant Staphylococcus aureus) V02.54
MSSA (methicillin susceptible Staphylococcus aureus) V02.53
Coloptosis 569.89
Color
amblyopia NEC 368.59
acquired 368.55
blindness NEC (congenital) 368.59
acquired 368.55
Colostomy
attention to V55.3
fitting or adjustment V55.3
malfunctioning 569.62
status V44.3
Colpitis — *see also* Vaginitis 616.10
Colpocele 618.6
Colpocystitis — *see also* Vaginitis 616.10
Colporrhexis 665.4 ☑
Colpospasm 625.1
Column, spinal, vertebral — *see* condition
Coma 780.01
apoplectic (*see also* Disease, cerebrovascular, acute) 436
diabetic (with ketoacidosis) 250.3 ☑
due to secondary diabetes 249.3 ☑
hyperosmolar 250.2 ☑
due to secondary diabetes 249.2 ☑
eclamptic (*see also* Eclampsia) 780.39
epileptic 345.3
hepatic 572.2
hyperglycemic 250.3 ☑
due to secondary diabetes 249.3 ☑
hyperosmolar (diabetic) (nonketotic) 250.2 ☑
due to secondary diabetes 249.2 ☑
hypoglycemic 251.0
diabetic 250.3 ☑
due to secondary diabetes 249.3 ☑
insulin 250.3 ☑
due to secondary diabetes 249.3 ☑
hyperosmolar 250.2 ☑
due to secondary diabetes 249.2 ☑
non-diabetic 251.0
organic hyperinsulinism 251.0
Kussmaul's (diabetic) 250.3 ☑
due to secondary diabetes 249.3 ☑
liver 572.2
newborn 779.2
prediabetic 250.2 ☑

Coma — *continued*
prediabetic — *continued*
due to secondary diabetes 249.2 ☑
uremic — *see* Uremia
Combat fatigue — *see also* Reaction, stress, acute 308.9
Combined — *see* condition
Comedo 706.1
Comedocarcinoma (M8501/3) — *see also* Neoplasm, breast, malignant
noninfiltrating (M8501/2)
specified site — *see* Neoplasm, by site, in situ
unspecified site 233.0
Comedomastitis 610.4
Comedones 706.1
lanugo 757.4
Comma bacillus, carrier (suspected) of V02.3
Comminuted fracture — *see* Fracture, by site
Common
aortopulmonary trunk 745.0
atrioventricular canal (defect) 745.69
atrium 745.69
cold (head) 460
vaccination, prophylactic (against) V04.7
truncus (arteriosus) 745.0
ventricle 745.3
Commotio (current)
cerebri (*see also* Concussion, brain) 850.9
with skull fracture — *see* Fracture, skull, by site
retinae 921.3
spinalis — *see* Injury, spinal, by site
Commotion (current)
brain (without skull fracture) (*see also* Concussion, brain) 850.9
with skull fracture — *see* Fracture, skull, by site
spinal cord — *see* Injury, spinal, by site
Communication
abnormal (*see also* Fistula)
between
base of aorta and pulmonary artery 745.0
left ventricle and right atrium 745.4
pericardial sac and pleural sac 748.8
pulmonary artery and pulmonary vein 747.3
congenital, between uterus and anterior abdominal wall 752.3
bladder 752.3
intestine 752.3
rectum 752.3
left ventricular — right atrial 745.4
pulmonary artery — pulmonary vein 747.3
Compartment syndrome — *see* Syndrome, compartment
Compensation
broken — *see* Failure, heart
failure — *see* Failure, heart
neurosis, psychoneurosis 300.11
Complaint — *see also* Disease
bowel, functional 564.9
psychogenic 306.4
intestine, functional 564.9
psychogenic 306.4
kidney (*see also* Disease, renal) 593.9
liver 573.9
miners' 500
Complete — *see* condition
Complex
cardiorenal (*see also* Hypertension, cardiorenal) 404.90
castration 300.9
Costen's 524.60
ego-dystonic homosexuality 302.0
Eisenmenger's (ventricular septal defect) 745.4
homosexual, ego-dystonic 302.0
hypersexual 302.89
inferiority 301.9
jumped process
spine — *see* Dislocation, vertebra
primary, tuberculosis (*see also* Tuberculosis) 010.0 ☑
regional pain syndrome 355.9
type I 337.20

Complex — *continued*
regional pain syndrome — *continued*
type I — *continued*
lower limb 337.22
specified site NEC 337.29
upper limb 337.21
type II
lower limb 355.71
upper limb 354.4
Taussig-Bing (transposition, aorta and overriding pulmonary artery) 745.11
Complications
abortion NEC — *see* categories 634-639 ☑
accidental puncture or laceration during a procedure 998.2
amniocentesis, fetal 679.1 ☑
amputation stump (late) (surgical) 997.60
traumatic — *see* Amputation, traumatic
anastomosis (and bypass) (*see also* Complications, due to (presence of) any device, implant, or graft classified to 996.0–996.5 NEC)
hemorrhage NEC 998.11
intestinal (internal) NEC 997.4
involving urinary tract 997.5
mechanical — *see* Complications, mechanical, graft
urinary tract (involving intestinal tract) 997.5
anesthesia, anesthetic NEC (*see also* Anesthesia, complication) 995.22
in labor and delivery 668.9 ☑
affecting fetus or newborn 763.5
cardiac 668.1 ☑
central nervous system 668.2 ☑
pulmonary 668.0 ☑
specified type NEC 668.8 ☑
aortocoronary (bypass) graft 996.03
atherosclerosis — *see* Arteriosclerosis, coronary
embolism 996.72
occlusion NEC 996.72
thrombus 996.72
arthroplasty (*see also* Complications, prosthetic joint) 996.49
artificial opening
cecostomy 569.60
colostomy 569.60
cystostomy 997.5
enterostomy 569.60
esophagostomy 530.87
infection 530.86
mechanical 530.87
gastrostomy 536.40
ileostomy 569.60
jejunostomy 569.60
nephrostomy 997.5
tracheostomy 519.00
ureterostomy 997.5
urethrostomy 997.5
bariatric surgery 997.4
bile duct implant (prosthetic) NEC 996.79
infection or inflammation 996.69
mechanical 996.59
bleeding (intraoperative) (postoperative) 998.11
blood vessel graft 996.1
aortocoronary 996.03
atherosclerosis — *see* Arteriosclerosis, coronary
embolism 996.72
occlusion NEC 996.72
thrombus 996.72
atherosclerosis — *see* Arteriosclerosis, extremities
embolism 996.74
occlusion NEC 996.74
thrombus 996.74
bone growth stimulator NEC 996.78
infection or inflammation 996.67
bone marrow transplant 996.85
breast implant (prosthetic) NEC 996.79
infection or inflammation 996.69
mechanical 996.54
bypass (*see also* Complications, anastomosis)
aortocoronary 996.03

Complications — *continued*
bypass (*see also* Complications, anastomosis) — *continued*
aortocoronary — *continued*
atherosclerosis — *see* Arteriosclerosis, coronary
embolism 996.72
occlusion NEC 996.72
thrombus 996.72
carotid artery 996.1
atherosclerosis — *see* Arteriosclerosis, extremities
embolism 996.74
occlusion NEC 996.74
thrombus 996.74
cardiac (*see also* Disease, heart) 429.9
device, implant, or graft NEC 996.72
infection or inflammation 996.61
long-term effect 429.4
mechanical (*see also* Complications, mechanical, by type) 996.00
valve prosthesis 996.71
infection or inflammation 996.61
postoperative NEC 997.1
long-term effect 429.4
cardiorenal (*see also* Hypertension, cardiorenal) 404.90
carotid artery bypass graft 996.1
atherosclerosis — *see* Arteriosclerosis, extremities
embolism 996.74
occlusion NEC 996.74
thrombus 996.74
cataract fragments in eye 998.82
catheter device NEC (*see also* Complications, due to (presence of) any device, implant, or graft classified to 996.0–996.5 NEC)
mechanical — *see* Complications, mechanical, catheter
cecostomy 569.60
cesarean section wound 674.3 ☑
chemotherapy (antineoplastic) 995.29
chin implant (prosthetic) NEC 996.79
infection or inflammation 996.69
mechanical 996.59
colostomy (enterostomy) 569.60
specified type NEC 569.69
contraceptive device, intrauterine NEC 996.76
infection 996.65
inflammation 996.65
mechanical 996.32
cord (umbilical) — *see* Complications, umbilical cord
cornea
due to
contact lens 371.82
coronary (artery) bypass (graft) NEC 996.03
atherosclerosis — *see* Arteriosclerosis, coronary
embolism 996.72
infection or inflammation 996.61
mechanical 996.03
occlusion NEC 996.72
specified type NEC 996.72
thrombus 996.72
cystostomy 997.5
delivery 669.9 ☑
procedure (instrumental) (manual) (surgical) 669.4 ☑
specified type NEC 669.8 ☑
dialysis (hemodialysis) (peritoneal) (renal) NEC 999.9
catheter NEC (*see also* Complications, due to (presence of) any device, implant, or graft classified to 996.0–996.5 NEC)
infection or inflammation 996.62
peritoneal 996.68
mechanical 996.1
peritoneal 996.56
drug NEC 995.29
due to (presence of) any device, implant, or graft classified to 996.0–996.5 NEC 996.70

☑ Additional Digit Required — Refer to the Tabular List for Digit Selection

🔱 Subterms under main terms may continue to next column or page

2010 ICD-9-CM

▶◀ Revised Text   ● New Line   ▲ Revised Code

Volume 2 — 49

Collapse — Complications

Complications — *continued*
  due to any device, implant, or graft classified to 996.0–996.5 — *continued*
    with infection or inflammation — *see* Complications, infection or inflammation, due to (presence of) any device, implant, or graft classified to 996.0–996.5 NEC
  arterial NEC 996.74
    coronary NEC 996.03
      atherosclerosis — *see* Arteriosclerosis, coronary
      embolism 996.72
      occlusion NEC 996.72
      specified type NEC 996.72
      thrombus 996.72
    renal dialysis 996.73
  arteriovenous fistula or shunt NEC 996.74
  bone growth stimulator 996.78
  breast NEC 996.79
  cardiac NEC 996.72
    defibrillator 996.72
    pacemaker 996.72
    valve prosthesis 996.71
  catheter NEC 996.79
    spinal 996.75
    urinary, indwelling 996.76
    vascular NEC 996.74
      renal dialysis 996.73
    ventricular shunt 996.75
  coronary (artery) bypass (graft) NEC 996.03
    atherosclerosis — *see* Arteriosclerosis, coronary
    embolism 996.72
    occlusion NEC 996.72
    thrombus 996.72
  electrodes
    brain 996.75
    heart 996.72
  esophagostomy 530.87
  gastrointestinal NEC 996.79
  genitourinary NEC 996.76
  heart valve prosthesis NEC 996.71
  infusion pump 996.74
  insulin pump 996.57
  internal
    joint prosthesis 996.77
    orthopedic NEC 996.78
    specified type NEC 996.79
  intrauterine contraceptive device NEC 996.76
  joint prosthesis, internal NEC 996.77
  mechanical — *see* Complications, mechanical
  nervous system NEC 996.75
  ocular lens NEC 996.79
  orbital NEC 996.79
  orthopedic NEC 996.78
    joint, internal 996.77
  renal dialysis 996.73
  specified type NEC 996.79
  urinary catheter, indwelling 996.76
  vascular NEC 996.74
  ventricular shunt 996.75
  during dialysis NEC 999.9
  ectopic or molar pregnancy NEC 639.9
  electroshock therapy NEC 999.9
  enterostomy 569.60
    specified type NEC 569.69
  esophagostomy 530.87
    infection 530.86
    mechanical 530.87
  external (fixation) device with internal component(s) NEC 996.78
    infection or inflammation 996.67
    mechanical 996.49
  extracorporeal circulation NEC 999.9
  eye implant (prosthetic) NEC 996.79
    infection or inflammation 996.69
    mechanical
      ocular lens 996.53
      orbital globe 996.59
  fetal, from amniocentesis 679.1 ☑
  gastrointestinal, postoperative NEC (*see also* Complications, surgical procedures) 997.4

Complications — *continued*
  gastrostomy 536.40
    specified type NEC 536.49
  genitourinary device, implant or graft NEC 996.76
    infection or inflammation 996.65
      urinary catheter, indwelling 996.64
    mechanical (*see also* Complications, mechanical, by type) 996.30
      specified NEC 996.39
  graft (bypass) (patch) (*see also* Complications, due to (presence of) any device, implant, or graft classified to 996.0–996.5 NEC)
    bone marrow 996.85
    corneal NEC 996.79
      infection or inflammation 996.69
      rejection or reaction 996.51
      mechanical — *see* Complications, mechanical, graft
    organ (immune or nonimmune cause) (partial) (total) 996.80
      bone marrow 996.85
      heart 996.83
      intestines 996.87
      kidney 996.81
      liver 996.82
      lung 996.84
      pancreas 996.86
      specified NEC 996.89
    skin NEC 996.79
      infection or inflammation 996.69
      rejection 996.52
        artificial 996.55
        decellularized allodermis 996.55
  heart (*see also* Disease, heart transplant (immune or nonimmune cause)) 996.83
  hematoma (intraoperative) (postoperative) 998.12
  hemorrhage (intraoperative) (postoperative) 998.11
  hyperalimentation therapy NEC 999.9
  immunization (procedure) — *see* Complications, vaccination
  implant (*see also* Complications, due to (presence of) any device, implant, or graft classified to 996.0–996.5 NEC)
    dental placement, hemorrhagic 525.71
    mechanical — *see* Complications, mechanical, implant
  infection and inflammation
    due to (presence of) any device, implant or graft classified to 996.0–996.5 NEC 996.60
      arterial NEC 996.62
        coronary 996.61
        renal dialysis 996.62
      arteriovenous fistula or shunt 996.62
      artificial heart 996.61
      bone growth stimulator 996.67
      breast 996.69
      cardiac 996.61
      catheter NEC 996.69
        central venous 999.31
        Hickman 999.31
        peripherally inserted central (PICC) 999.31
        peritoneal 996.68
        portacath (port-a-cath) 999.31
        spinal 996.63
        triple lumen 999.31
        umbilical venous 999.31
        urinary, indwelling 996.64
        vascular (arterial) (dialysis) (peripheral venous) NEC 996.62
        ventricular shunt 996.63
      central venous catheter 999.31
      coronary artery bypass 996.61
      electrodes
        brain 996.63
        heart 996.61
      gastrointestinal NEC 996.69
      genitourinary NEC 996.65
        indwelling urinary catheter 996.64
      heart assist device 996.61
      heart valve 996.61

Complications — *continued*
  infection and inflammation — *continued*
    due to any device, implant or graft classified to 996.0–996.5 — *continued*
      Hickman catheter 999.31
      infusion pump 996.62
      insulin pump 996.69
      intrauterine contraceptive device 996.65
      joint prosthesis, internal 996.66
      ocular lens 996.69
      orbital (implant) 996.69
      orthopedic NEC 996.67
        joint, internal 996.66
      peripherally inserted central catheter (PICC) 999.31
      portacath (port-a-cath) 999.31
      specified type NEC 996.69
      triple lumen catheter 999.31
      umbilical venous catheter 999.31
      urinary catheter, indwelling 996.64
      ventricular shunt 996.63
  infusion (procedure) 999.88
    blood — *see* Complications, transfusion
    infection NEC 999.39
    sepsis NEC 999.39
  inhalation therapy NEC 999.9
  injection (procedure) 999.9
    drug reaction (*see also* Reaction, drug) 995.27
    infection NEC 999.39
    sepsis NEC 999.39
    serum (prophylactic) (therapeutic) — *see* Complications, vaccination
    vaccine (any) — *see* Complications, vaccination
  inoculation (any) — *see* Complications, vaccination
  insulin pump 996.57
  internal device (catheter) (electronic) (fixation) (prosthetic) (*see also* Complications, due to (presence of) any device, implant, or graft classified to 996.0–996.5 NEC)
    mechanical — *see* Complications, mechanical
  intestinal pouch, specified NEC 569.79 ●
  intestinal transplant (immune or nonimmune cause) 996.87
  intraoperative bleeding or hemorrhage 998.11
  intrauterine contraceptive device (*see also* Complications, contraceptive device) 996.76
    with fetal damage affecting management of pregnancy 655.8 ☑
    infection or inflammation 996.65
  in utero procedure
    fetal 679.1 ☑
    maternal 679.0 ☑
  jejunostomy 569.60
  kidney transplant (immune or nonimmune cause) 996.81
  labor 669.9 ☑
    specified condition NEC 669.8 ☑
  liver transplant (immune or nonimmune cause) 996.82
  lumbar puncture 349.0
  mechanical
    anastomosis — *see* Complications, mechanical, graft
    artificial heart 996.09
    bypass — *see* Complications, mechanical, graft
    catheter NEC 996.59
      cardiac 996.09
      cystostomy 996.39
      dialysis (hemodialysis) 996.1
        peritoneal 996.56
      during a procedure 998.2
      urethral, indwelling 996.31
    colostomy 569.62
    device NEC 996.59
      balloon (counterpulsation), intra-aortic 996.1
      cardiac 996.00

Complications — *continued*
  mechanical — *continued*
    device — *continued*
      cardiac — *continued*
        automatic implantable defibrillator 996.04
        long-term effect 429.4
        specified NEC 996.09
      contraceptive, intrauterine 996.32
      counterpulsation, intra-aortic 996.1
      fixation, external, with internal components 996.49
      fixation, internal (nail, rod, plate) 996.40
      genitourinary 996.30
        specified NEC 996.39
      insulin pump 996.57
      nervous system 996.2
      orthopedic, internal 996.40
        prosthetic joint (*see also* Complications, mechanical, device, orthopedic, prosthetic, joint) 996.47
      prosthetic NEC 996.59
        joint 996.47
          articular bearing surface wear 996.46
          aseptic loosening 996.41
          breakage 996.43
          dislocation 996.42
          failure 996.47 ▲
          fracture 996.43
            around prosthetic 996.44
            peri-prosthetic 996.44
          instability 996.42
          loosening 996.41
          peri-prosthetic osteolysis 996.45
          subluxation 996.42
          wear 996.46
      umbrella, vena cava 996.1
      vascular 996.1
    dorsal column stimulator 996.2
    electrode NEC 996.59
      brain 996.2
      cardiac 996.01
      spinal column 996.2
    enterostomy 569.62
    esophagostomy 530.87
    fistula, arteriovenous, surgically created 996.1
    gastrostomy 536.42
    graft NEC 996.52
      aortic (bifurcation) 996.1
      aortocoronary bypass 996.03
      blood vessel NEC 996.1
      bone 996.49
      cardiac 996.00
      carotid artery bypass 996.1
      cartilage 996.49
      corneal 996.51
      coronary bypass 996.03
      decellularized allodermis 996.55
      genitourinary 996.30
        specified NEC 996.39
      muscle 996.49
      nervous system 996.2
      organ (immune or nonimmune cause) 996.80
        heart 996.83
        intestines 996.87
        kidney 996.81
        liver 996.82
        lung 996.84
        pancreas 996.86
        specified NEC 996.89
      orthopedic, internal 996.49
      peripheral nerve 996.2
      prosthetic NEC 996.59
      skin 996.52
        artificial 996.55
      specified NEC 996.59
      tendon 996.49
      tissue NEC 996.52
      tooth 996.59
      ureter, without mention of resection 996.39
      vascular 996.1

☑ Additional Digit Required — Refer to the Tabular List for Digit Selection
▽ Subterms under main terms may continue to next column or page
50 — Volume 2 • October 2009
▶◀ Revised Text ● New Line ▲ Revised Code
2010 ICD-9-CM

Complications — *continued*
mechanical — *continued*
heart valve prosthesis 996.02
long-term effect 429.4
implant NEC 996.59
cardiac 996.00
automatic implantable defibrillator 996.04
long-term effect 429.4
specified NEC 996.09
electrode NEC 996.59
brain 996.2
cardiac 996.01
spinal column 996.2
genitourinary 996.30
nervous system 996.2
orthopedic, internal 996.49
prosthetic NEC 996.59
in
bile duct 996.59
breast 996.54
chin 996.59
eye
ocular lens 996.53
orbital globe 996.59
vascular 996.1
insulin pump 996.57
nonabsorbable surgical material 996.59
→ pacemaker NEC 996.59
brain 996.2
<u>cardiac 996.01</u>
nerve (phrenic) 996.2
patch — *see* Complications, mechanical, graft
prosthesis NEC 996.59
bile duct 996.59
breast 996.54
chin 996.59
ocular lens 996.53
reconstruction, vas deferens 996.39
reimplant NEC 996.59
extremity (*see also* Complications, reattached, extremity) 996.90
organ (*see also* Complications, transplant, organ, by site) 996.80
repair — *see* Complications, mechanical, graft
respirator [ventilator] V46.14
shunt NEC 996.59
arteriovenous, surgically created 996.1
ventricular (communicating) 996.2
stent NEC 996.59
tracheostomy 519.02
vas deferens reconstruction 996.39
ventilator [respirator] V46.14
medical care NEC 999.9
cardiac NEC 997.1
gastrointestinal NEC 997.4
nervous system NEC 997.00
peripheral vascular NEC 997.2
respiratory NEC 997.39
urinary NEC 997.5
vascular
mesenteric artery 997.71
other vessels 997.79
peripheral vessels 997.2
renal artery 997.72
nephrostomy 997.5
nervous system
device, implant, or graft NEC 349.1
mechanical 996.2
postoperative NEC 997.00
obstetric 669.9 ☑
procedure (instrumental) (manual) (surgical) 669.4 ☑
specified NEC 669.8 ☑
surgical wound 674.3 ☑
ocular lens implant NEC 996.79
infection or inflammation 996.69
mechanical 996.53
organ transplant — *see* Complications, transplant, organ, by site
orthopedic device, implant, or graft
internal (fixation) (nail) (plate) (rod) NEC 996.78
infection or inflammation 996.67

Complications — *continued*
orthopedic device, implant, or graft — *continued*
internal — *continued*
joint prosthesis 996.77
infection or inflammation 996.66
mechanical 996.40
pacemaker (cardiac) 996.72
infection or inflammation 996.61
mechanical 996.01
pancreas transplant (immune or nonimmune cause) 996.86
perfusion NEC 999.9
perineal repair (obstetrical) 674.3 ☑
disruption 674.2 ☑
pessary (uterus) (vagina) — *see* Complications, contraceptive device
phototherapy 990
postcystoscopic 997.5
postmastoidectomy NEC 383.30
postoperative — *see* Complications, surgical procedures
pregnancy NEC 646.9 ☑
affecting fetus or newborn 761.9
prosthetic device, internal (*see also* Complications, due to (presence of) any device, implant or graft classified to 996.0–996.5 NEC)
mechanical NEC (*see also* Complications, mechanical) 996.59
puerperium NEC (*see also* Puerperal) 674.9 ☑
puncture, spinal 349.0
pyelogram 997.5
radiation 990
radiotherapy 990
reattached
body part, except extremity 996.99
extremity (infection) (rejection) 996.90
arm(s) 996.94
digit(s) (hand) 996.93
foot 996.95
finger(s) 996.93
foot 996.95
forearm 996.91
hand 996.92
leg 996.96
lower NEC 996.96
toe(s) 996.95
upper NEC 996.94
reimplant NEC (*see also* Complications, due to (presence of) any device, implant, or graft classified to 996.0–996.5 NEC)
bone marrow 996.85
extremity (*see also* Complications, reattached, extremity) 996.90
due to infection 996.90
mechanical — *see* Complications, mechanical, reimplant
organ (immune or nonimmune cause) (partial) (total) (*see also* Complications, transplant, organ, by site) 996.80
renal allograft 996.81
renal dialysis — *see* Complications, dialysis
respirator [ventilator], mechanical V46.14
respiratory 519.9
device, implant or graft NEC 996.79
infection or inflammation 996.69
mechanical 996.59
distress syndrome, adult, following trauma or surgery 518.5
insufficiency, acute, postoperative 518.5
postoperative NEC 997.39
therapy NEC 999.9
sedation during labor and delivery 668.9 ☑
affecting fetus or newborn 763.5
cardiac 668.1 ☑
central nervous system 668.2 ☑
pulmonary 668.0 ☑
specified type NEC 668.8 ☑
seroma (intraoperative) (postoperative) (noninfected) 998.13
infected 998.51
shunt (*see also* Complications, due to (presence of) any device, implant, or graft classified to 996.0–996.5 NEC)

Complications — *continued*
shunt (*see also* Complications, due to any device, implant, or graft classified to 996.0–996.5) — *continued*
mechanical — *see* Complications, mechanical, shunt
specified body system NEC
device, implant, or graft — *see* Complications, due to (presence of) any device, implant, or graft classified to 996.0–996.5 NEC
postoperative NEC 997.99
spinal puncture or tap 349.0
stomach banding 997.4
stomach stapling 997.4
stoma, external
gastrointestinal tract
colostomy 569.60
enterostomy 569.60
esophagostomy 530.87
infection 530.86
mechanical 530.87
gastrostomy 536.40
urinary tract 997.5
surgical procedures 998.9
accidental puncture or laceration 998.2
amputation stump (late) 997.60
anastomosis — *see* Complications, anastomosis
burst stitches or sutures (external) (*see also* Dehiscence) 998.32
internal 998.31
cardiac 997.1
long-term effect following cardiac surgery 429.4
cataract fragments in eye 998.82
catheter device — *see* Complications, catheter device
cecostomy malfunction 569.62
colostomy malfunction 569.62
cystostomy malfunction 997.5
dehiscence (of incision) (external) (*see also* Dehiscence) 998.32
internal 998.31
dialysis NEC (*see also* Complications, dialysis) 999.9
disruption (*see also* Dehiscence)
anastomosis (internal) — *see* Complications, mechanical, graft
internal suture (line) 998.31
wound (external) 998.32
internal 998.31
dumping syndrome (postgastrectomy) 564.2
elephantiasis or lymphedema 997.99
postmastectomy 457.0
emphysema (surgical) 998.81
enterostomy malfunction 569.62
esophagostomy malfunction 530.87
evisceration 998.32
fistula (persistent postoperative) 998.6
foreign body inadvertently left in wound (sponge) (suture) (swab) 998.4
from nonabsorbable surgical material (Dacron) (mesh) (permanent suture) (reinforcing) (Teflon) — *see* Complications, due to (presence of) any device, implant, or graft classified to 996.0–996.5 NEC
gastrointestinal NEC 997.4
gastrostomy malfunction 536.42
hematoma 998.12
hemorrhage 998.11
ileostomy malfunction 569.62
internal prosthetic device NEC (*see also* Complications, internal device) 996.70
hemolytic anemia 283.19
infection or inflammation 996.60
malfunction — *see* Complications, mechanical
mechanical complication — *see* Complications, mechanical
thrombus 996.70
jejunostomy malfunction 569.62
nervous system NEC 997.00

Complications — *continued*
surgical procedures — *continued*
obstruction, internal anastomosis — *see* Complications, mechanical, graft
other body system NEC 997.99
peripheral vascular NEC 997.2
postcardiotomy syndrome 429.4
postcholecystectomy syndrome 576.0
postcommissurotomy syndrome 429.4
postgastrectomy dumping syndrome 564.2
postmastectomy lymphedema syndrome 457.0
postmastoidectomy 383.30
cholesteatoma, recurrent 383.32
cyst, mucosal 383.31
granulation 383.33
inflammation, chronic 383.33
postvagotomy syndrome 564.2
postvalvulotomy syndrome 429.4
reattached extremity (infection) (rejection) (*see also* Complications, reattached, extremity) 996.90
respiratory NEC 997.39
seroma 998.13
shock (endotoxic) (hypovolemic) (septic) 998.0
shunt, prosthetic (thrombus) (*see also* Complications, due to (presence of) any device, implant, or graft classified to 996.0–996.5 NEC)
hemolytic anemia 283.19
specified complication NEC 998.89
stitch abscess 998.59
transplant — *see* Complications, graft
ureterostomy malfunction 997.5
urethrostomy malfunction 997.5
urinary NEC 997.5
vascular
mesenteric artery 997.71
other vessels 997.79
peripheral vessels 997.2
renal artery 997.72
wound infection 998.59
therapeutic misadventure NEC 999.9
surgical treatment 998.9
tracheostomy 519.00
transfusion (blood) (lymphocytes) (plasma) NEC 999.89
acute lung injury (TRALI) 518.7
atrophy, liver, yellow, subacute (within 8 months of administration) — *see* Hepatitis, viral
bone marrow 996.85
embolism
air 999.1
thrombus 999.2
hemolysis NEC 999.89
bone marrow 996.85
hepatitis (serum) (type B) (within 8 months after administration) — *see* Hepatitis, viral
incompatibility reaction
ABO 999.6   ●
minor blood group 999.89   ●
Rh (factor) 999.7
infection 999.39
jaundice (serum) (within 8 months after administration) — *see* Hepatitis, viral
sepsis 999.39
shock or reaction NEC 999.89
bone marrow 996.85
subacute yellow atrophy of liver (within 8 months after administration) — *see* Hepatitis, viral
thromboembolism 999.2
transplant NEC (*see also* Complications, due to (presence of) any device, implant, or graft classified to 996.0–996.5 NEC)
bone marrow 996.85
organ (immune or nonimmune cause) (partial) (total) 996.80
bone marrow 996.85
heart 996.83
intestines 996.87

Complications — *continued*
  transplant (*see also* Complications, due to any
      device, implant, or graft classified to
      996.0–996.5) — *continued*
    organ — *continued*
      kidney 996.81
      liver 996.82
      lung 996.84
      pancreas 996.86
      specified NEC 996.89
    trauma NEC (early) 958.8
    ultrasound therapy NEC 999.9
    umbilical cord
      affecting fetus or newborn 762.6
      complicating delivery 663.9 ☑
        affecting fetus or newborn 762.6
        specified type NEC 663.8 ☑
    urethral catheter NEC 996.76
      infection or inflammation 996.64
      mechanical 996.31
    urinary, postoperative NEC 997.5
    vaccination 999.9
      anaphylaxis NEC 999.4
      cellulitis 999.39
      encephalitis or encephalomyelitis 323.51
      hepatitis (serum) (type B) (within 8 months
          after administration) — *see* Hepati-
          tis, viral
      infection (general) (local) NEC 999.39
      jaundice (serum) (within 8 months after
          administration) — *see* Hepatitis,
          viral
      meningitis 997.09 *[321.8]*
      myelitis 323.52
      protein sickness 999.5
      reaction (allergic) 999.5
        Herxheimer's 995.0
        serum 999.5
      sepsis 999.39
      serum intoxication, sickness, rash, or other
          serum reaction NEC 999.5
      shock (allergic) (anaphylactic) 999.4
      subacute yellow atrophy of liver (within 8
          months after administration) — *see*
          Hepatitis, viral
      vaccinia (generalized) 999.0
        localized 999.39
    vascular
      device, implant, or graft NEC 996.74
        infection or inflammation 996.62
        mechanical NEC 996.1
          cardiac (*see also* Complications,
              mechanical, by type) 996.00
      following infusion, perfusion, or transfusion
          999.2
      postoperative NEC 997.2
        mesenteric artery 997.71
        other vessels 997.79
        peripheral vessels 997.2
        renal artery 997.72
    ventilation therapy NEC 999.9
    ventilator [respirator], mechanical V46.14
Compound presentation, complicating deliv-
    ery 652.8 ☑
  causing obstructed labor 660.0 ☑
Compressed air disease 993.3
Compression
  with injury — *see* specific injury
  arm NEC 354.9
  artery 447.1
    celiac, syndrome 447.4
  brachial plexus 353.0
  brain (stem) 348.4
    due to
      contusion, brain — *see* Contusion,
          brain
      injury NEC (*see also* Hemorrhage, brain,
          traumatic)
        birth — *see* Birth, injury, brain
      laceration, brain — *see* Laceration,
          brain
    osteopathic 739.0
  bronchus 519.19
  by cicatrix — *see* Cicatrix
  cardiac 423.9
  cauda equina 344.60

Compression — *continued*
  cauda equina — *continued*
    with neurogenic bladder 344.61
  celiac (artery) (axis) 447.4
  cerebral — *see* Compression, brain
  cervical plexus 353.2
  cord (umbilical) — *see* Compression, umbilical
      cord
  cranial nerve 352.9
    second 377.49
    third (partial) 378.51
      total 378.52
    fourth 378.53
    fifth 350.8
    sixth 378.54
    seventh 351.8
  divers' squeeze 993.3
  duodenum (external) (*see also* Obstruction,
      duodenum) 537.3
  during birth 767.9
  esophagus 530.3
    congenital, external 750.3
  Eustachian tube 381.63
  facies (congenital) 754.0
  fracture — *see* Fracture, by site
  heart — *see* Disease, heart
  intestine (*see also* Obstruction, intestine) 560.9
    with hernia — *see* Hernia, by site, with
        obstruction
  laryngeal nerve, recurrent 478.79
  leg NEC 355.8
  lower extremity NEC 355.8
  lumbosacral plexus 353.1
  lung 518.89
  lymphatic vessel 457.1
  medulla — *see* Compression, brain
  nerve NEC (*see also* Disorder, nerve)
    arm NEC 354.9
    autonomic nervous system (*see also* Neu-
        ropathy, peripheral, autonomic)
        337.9
    axillary 353.0
    cranial NEC 352.9
    due to displacement of intervertebral disc
        722.2
      with myelopathy 722.70
      cervical 722.0
        with myelopathy 722.71
      lumbar, lumbosacral 722.10
        with myelopathy 722.73
      thoracic, thoracolumbar 722.11
        with myelopathy 722.72
    iliohypogastric 355.79
    ilioinguinal 355.79
    leg NEC 355.8
    lower extremity NEC 355.8
    median (in carpal tunnel) 354.0
    obturator 355.79
    optic 377.49
    plantar 355.6
    posterior tibial (in tarsal tunnel) 355.5
    root (by scar tissue) NEC 724.9
      cervical NEC 723.4
      lumbar NEC 724.4
      lumbosacral 724.4
      thoracic 724.4
    saphenous 355.79
    sciatic (acute) 355.0
    sympathetic 337.9
    traumatic — *see* Injury, nerve
    ulnar 354.2
    upper extremity NEC 354.9
  peripheral — *see* Compression, nerve
  spinal (cord) (old or nontraumatic) 336.9
    by displacement of intervertebral disc —
        see Displacement, intervertebral
        disc
    nerve
      root NEC 724.9
        postoperative 722.80
          cervical region 722.81
          lumbar region 722.83
          thoracic region 722.82
        traumatic — *see* Injury, nerve,
            spinal
    traumatic — *see* Injury, nerve, spinal

Compression — *continued*
  spinal — *continued*
    spondylogenic 721.91
      cervical 721.1
      lumbar, lumbosacral 721.42
      thoracic 721.41
    traumatic (*see also* Injury, spinal, by site)
      with fracture, vertebra — *see* Fracture,
          vertebra, by site, with spinal
          cord injury
    spondylogenic — *see* Compression, spinal
        cord, spondylogenic
  subcostal nerve (syndrome) 354.8
  sympathetic nerve NEC 337.9
  syndrome 958.5
  thorax 512.8
    iatrogenic 512.1
    postoperative 512.1
  trachea 519.19
    congenital 748.3
  ulnar nerve (by scar tissue) 354.2
  umbilical cord
    affecting fetus or newborn 762.5
    cord prolapsed 762.4
    complicating delivery 663.2 ☑
      cord around neck 663.1 ☑
      cord prolapsed 663.0 ☑
  upper extremity NEC 354.9
  ureter 593.3
  urethra — *see* Stricture, urethra
  vein 459.2
  vena cava (inferior) (superior) 459.2
  vertebral NEC — *see* Compression, spinal
      (cord)
Compulsion, compulsive
  eating 307.51
  neurosis (obsessive) 300.3
  personality 301.4
  states (mixed) 300.3
  swearing 300.3
    in Gilles de la Tourette's syndrome 307.23
  tics and spasms 307.22
  water drinking NEC (syndrome) 307.9
Concato's disease (pericardial polyserositis) 423.2
  peritoneal 568.82
  pleural — *see* Pleurisy
Concavity, chest wall 738.3
Concealed
  hemorrhage NEC 459.0
  penis 752.65
Concentric fading 368.12
Concern (normal) **about sick person in family**
    V61.49
Concrescence (teeth) 520.2
Concretio cordis 423.1
  rheumatic 393
Concretion — *see also* Calculus
  appendicular 543.9
  canaliculus 375.57
  clitoris 624.8
  conjunctiva 372.54
  eyelid 374.56
  intestine (impaction) (obstruction) 560.39
  lacrimal (passages) 375.57
  prepuce (male) 605
    female (clitoris) 624.8
  salivary gland (any) 527.5
  seminal vesicle 608.89
  stomach 537.89
  tonsil 474.8
Concussion (current) 850.9
  with
    loss of consciousness 850.5
      brief (less than one hour)
        30 minutes or less 850.11
        31-59 minutes 850.12
      moderate (1-24 hours) 850.2
      prolonged (more than 24 hours) (with
          complete recovery) (with return
          to pre-existing conscious level)
          850.3
      without return to pre-existing con-
          scious level 850.4
    mental confusion or disorientation (with-
        out loss of consciousness) 850.0

Concussion — *continued*
  with — *continued*
    mental confusion or disorientation —
        continued
      with loss of consciousness — *see* Con-
          cussion, with, loss of conscious-
          ness
  without loss of consciousness 850.0
  blast (air) (hydraulic) (immersion) (underwater)
      869.0
    with open wound into cavity 869.1
    abdomen or thorax — *see* Injury, internal,
        by site
    brain — *see* Concussion, brain
    ear (acoustic nerve trauma) 951.5
      with perforation, tympanic membrane
          — *see* Wound, open, ear drum
    thorax — *see* Injury, internal, intrathoracic
        organs NEC
  brain or cerebral (without skull fracture) 850.9
    with
      loss of consciousness 850.5
        brief (less than one hour)
          30 minutes or less 850.11
          31-59 minutes 850.12
        moderate (1-24 hours) 850.2
        prolonged (more than 24 hours)
            (with complete recovery)
            (with return to pre-existing
            conscious level) 850.3
          without return to pre-existing
              conscious level 850.4
      mental confusion or disorientation
          (without loss of consciousness)
          850.0
        with loss of consciousness — *see*
            Concussion, brain, with, loss
            of consciousness
      skull fracture — *see* Fracture, skull, by
          site
    without loss of consciousness 850.0
  cauda equina 952.4
  cerebral — *see* Concussion, brain
  conus medullaris (spine) 952.4
  hydraulic — *see* Concussion, blast
  internal organs — *see* Injury, internal, by site
  labyrinth — *see* Injury, intracranial
  ocular 921.3
  osseous labyrinth — *see* Injury, intracranial
  spinal (cord) (*see also* Injury, spinal, by site)
    due to
      broken
        back — *see* Fracture, vertebra, by
            site, with spinal cord injury
        neck — *see* Fracture, vertebra, cer-
            vical, with spinal cord injury
      fracture, fracture dislocation, or com-
          pression fracture of spine or
          vertebra — *see* Fracture, verte-
          bra, by site, with spinal cord in-
          jury
  syndrome 310.2
  underwater blast — *see* Concussion, blast
Condition — *see also* Disease
  fetal hematologic 678.0 ☑
  psychiatric 298.9
  respiratory NEC 519.9
    acute or subacute NEC 519.9
      due to
        external agent 508.9
          specified type NEC 508.8
          fumes or vapors (chemical) (inhala-
              tion) 506.3
          radiation 508.0
    chronic NEC 519.9
      due to
        external agent 508.9
          specified type NEC 508.8
          fumes or vapors (chemical) (inhala-
              tion) 506.4
          radiation 508.1
    due to
      external agent 508.9
        specified type NEC 508.8
        fumes or vapors (chemical) (inhalation)
            506.9

Conduct disturbance — *see also* Disturbance, conduct 312.9
  adjustment reaction 309.3
  hyperkinetic 314.2
Condyloma NEC 078.11
  acuminatum 078.11
  gonorrheal 098.0
  latum 091.3
  syphilitic 091.3
    congenital 090.0
  venereal, syphilitic 091.3
Confinement — *see* Delivery
Conflagration — *see also* Burn, by site
  asphyxia (by inhalation of smoke, gases, fumes, or vapors) 987.9
    specified agent — *see* Table of Drugs and Chemicals
Conflict
  family V61.9
    specified circumstance NEC V61.8
  interpersonal NEC V62.81
  marital V61.10
    involving
      divorce V61.03
      estrangement V61.09
  parent ▶(guardian)◀-child V61.20
    adopted child V61.24
    biological child V61.23
    foster child V61.25
  partner V61.10
Confluent — *see* condition
Confusional arousals 327.41
Confusion, confused (mental) (state) — *see also* State, confusional 298.9
  acute 293.0
  epileptic 293.0
  postoperative 293.9
  psychogenic 298.2
  reactive (from emotional stress, psychological trauma) 298.2
  subacute 293.1
Congelation 991.9
Congenital — *see also* condition
  aortic septum 747.29
  generalized fibromatosis (CGF) 759.89
  intrinsic factor deficiency 281.0
  malformation — *see* Anomaly
Congestion, congestive
  asphyxia, newborn 768.9
  bladder 596.8
  bowel 569.89
  brain (*see also* Disease, cerebrovascular NEC) 437.8
    malarial 084.9
  breast 611.79
  bronchi 519.19
  bronchial tube 519.19
  catarrhal 472.0
  cerebral — *see* Congestion, brain
  cerebrospinal — *see* Congestion, brain
  chest 786.9
  chill 780.99
    malarial (*see also* Malaria) 084.6
  circulatory NEC 459.9
  conjunctiva 372.71
  due to disturbance of circulation 459.9
  duodenum 537.3
  enteritis — *see* Enteritis
  eye 372.71
  fibrosis syndrome (pelvic) 625.5
  gastroenteritis — *see* Enteritis
  general 799.89
  glottis 476.0
  heart (*see also* Failure, heart) 428.0
  hepatic 573.0
  hypostatic (lung) 514
  intestine 569.89
  intracranial — *see* Congestion, brain
  kidney 593.89
  labyrinth 386.50
  larynx 476.0
  liver 573.0
  lung 786.9
    active or acute (*see also* Pneumonia) 486
      congenital 770.0
    chronic 514

Congestion, congestive — *continued*
  lung — *continued*
    hypostatic 514
    idiopathic, acute 518.5
    passive 514
  malaria, malarial (brain) (fever) (*see also* Malaria) 084.6
  medulla — *see* Congestion, brain
  nasal 478.19
  nose 478.19
  orbit, orbital 376.33
    inflammatory (chronic) 376.10
      acute 376.00
  ovary 620.8
  pancreas 577.8
  pelvic, female 625.5
  pleural 511.0
  prostate (active) 602.1
  pulmonary — *see* Congestion, lung
  renal 593.89
  retina 362.89
  seminal vesicle 608.89
  spinal cord 336.1
  spleen 289.51
    chronic 289.51
  stomach 537.89
  trachea 464.11
  urethra 599.84
  uterus 625.5
    with subinvolution 621.1
  viscera 799.89
Congestive — *see* Congestion
Conical
  cervix 622.6
  cornea 371.60
  teeth 520.2
Conjoined twins 759.4
  causing disproportion (fetopelvic) 678.1 ☑
  fetal 678.1 ☑
Conjugal maladjustment V61.10
  involving
    divorce V61.03
    estrangement V61.09
Conjunctiva — *see* condition
Conjunctivitis (exposure) (infectious) (nondiphtheritic) (pneumococcal) (pustular) (staphylococcal) (streptococcal) NEC 372.30
  actinic 370.24
  acute 372.00
    atopic 372.05
    chemical 372.06
    contagious 372.03
    follicular 372.02
    hemorrhagic (viral) 077.4
    toxic 372.06
  adenoviral (acute) 077.3
  allergic (chronic) 372.14
    with hay fever 372.05
  anaphylactic 372.05
  angular 372.03
  Apollo (viral) 077.4
  atopic 372.05
  blennorrhagic (neonatorum) 098.40
  catarrhal 372.03
  chemical 372.06 ▲
    allergic 372.05
    meaning corrosion — *see* Burn, conjunctiva
  chlamydial 077.98
    due to
      Chlamydia trachomatis — *see* Trachoma
      paratrachoma 077.0
  chronic 372.10
    allergic 372.14
    follicular 372.12
    simple 372.11
    specified type NEC 372.14
    vernal 372.13
  diphtheritic 032.81
  due to
    dust 372.05
    enterovirus type 70 077.4
    erythema multiforme 695.10 [372.33]
    filariasis (*see also* Filariasis) 125.9 [372.15]

Conjunctivitis — *continued*
  due to — *continued*
    mucocutaneous
      disease NEC 372.33
      leishmaniasis 085.5 [372.15]
    Reiter's disease 099.3 [372.33]
    syphilis 095.8 [372.10]
    toxoplasmosis (acquired) 130.1
      congenital (active) 771.2
    trachoma — *see* Trachoma
  dust 372.05
  eczematous 370.31
  epidemic 077.1
    hemorrhagic 077.4
  follicular (acute) 372.02
    adenoviral (acute) 077.3
    chronic 372.12
  glare 370.24
  gonococcal (neonatorum) 098.40
  granular (trachomatous) 076.1
    late effect 139.1
  hemorrhagic (acute) (epidemic) 077.4
  herpetic (simplex) 054.43
    zoster 053.21
  inclusion 077.0
  infantile 771.6
  influenzal 372.03
  Koch-Weeks 372.03
  light 372.05
  medicamentosa 372.05
  membranous 372.04
  meningococcic 036.89
  Morax-Axenfeld 372.02
  mucopurulent NEC 372.03
  neonatal 771.6
    gonococcal 098.40
  Newcastle's 077.8
  nodosa 360.14
  of Beal 077.3
  parasitic 372.15
    filariasis (*see also* Filariasis) 125.9 [372.15]
    mucocutaneous leishmaniasis 085.5 [372.15]
  Parinaud's 372.02
  petrificans 372.39
  phlyctenular 370.31
  pseudomembranous 372.04
    diphtheritic 032.81
  purulent 372.03
  Reiter's 099.3 [372.33]
  rosacea 695.3 [372.31]
  serous 372.01
    viral 077.99
  simple chronic 372.11
  specified NEC 372.39
  sunlamp 372.04
  swimming pool 077.0
  toxic 372.06
  trachomatous (follicular) 076.1
    acute 076.0
    late effect 139.1
  traumatic NEC 372.39
  tuberculous (*see also* Tuberculosis) 017.3 ☑ [370.31]
  tularemic 021.3
  tularensis 021.3
  vernal 372.13
    limbar 372.13 [370.32]
  viral 077.99
    acute hemorrhagic 077.4
    specified NEC 077.8
Conjunctivochalasis 372.81
Conjunctoblepharitis — *see* Conjunctivitis
Connective tissue — *see* condition
Conn (-Louis) syndrome (primary aldosteronism) 255.12
Conradi (-Hünermann) syndrome or disease (chondrodysplasia calcificans congenita) 756.59
Consanguinity V19.7
Consecutive — *see* condition
Consolidated lung (base) — *see* Pneumonia, lobar
Constipation 564.00
  atonic 564.09

Constipation — *continued*
  drug induced
    correct substance properly administered 564.09
    overdose or wrong substance given or taken 977.9
      specified drug — *see* Table of Drugs and Chemicals
  neurogenic 564.09
  other specified NEC 564.09
  outlet dysfunction 564.02
  psychogenic 306.4
  simple 564.00
  slow transit 564.01
  spastic 564.09
Constitutional — *see also* condition
  arterial hypotension (*see also* Hypotension) 458.9
  obesity 278.00
    morbid 278.01
  psychopathic state 301.9
  short stature in childhood 783.43
  state, developmental V21.9
    specified development NEC V21.8
  substandard 301.6
Constitutionally substandard 301.6
Constriction
  anomalous, meningeal bands or folds 742.8
  aortic arch (congenital) 747.10
  asphyxiation or suffocation by 994.7
  bronchus 519.19
  canal, ear (*see also* Stricture, ear canal, acquired) 380.50
  duodenum 537.3
  gallbladder (*see also* Obstruction, gallbladder) 575.2
    congenital 751.69
  intestine (*see also* Obstruction, intestine) 560.9
  larynx 478.74
    congenital 748.3
  meningeal bands or folds, anomalous 742.8
  organ or site, congenital NEC — *see* Atresia
  prepuce (congenital) 605
  pylorus 537.0
    adult hypertrophic 537.0
    congenital or infantile 750.5
    newborn 750.5
  ring (uterus) 661.4 ☑
    affecting fetus or newborn 763.7
  spastic (*see also* Spasm)
    ureter 593.3
    urethra — *see* Stricture, urethra
  stomach 537.89
  ureter 593.3
  urethra — *see* Stricture, urethra
  visual field (functional) (peripheral) 368.45
Constrictive — *see* condition
Consultation
  without complaint or sickness V65.9
    feared complaint unfounded V65.5
    specified reason NEC V65.8
  medical (*see also* Counseling, medical)
    specified reason NEC V65.8
Consumption — *see* Tuberculosis
Contact
  with
    AIDS virus V01.79
    anthrax V01.81
    asbestos V15.84
    cholera V01.0
    communicable disease V01.9
      specified type NEC V01.89
      viral NEC V01.79
    Escherichia coli (E. coli) V01.83
    German measles V01.4
    gonorrhea V01.6
    HIV V01.79
    human immunodeficiency virus V01.79
    lead V15.86
    meningococcus V01.84
    parasitic disease NEC V01.89
    poliomyelitis V01.2
    potentially hazardous body fluids V15.85
    rabies V01.5
    rubella V01.4
    SARS-associated coronavirus V01.82

☑ Additional Digit Required — Refer to the Tabular List for Digit Selection   ▽ Subterms under main terms may continue to next column or page

2010 ICD-9-CM   ▶◀ Revised Text   ● New Line   ▲ Revised Code   October 2009 • Volume 2 — 53

COPD - 493.XX

Contact — continued
with — continued
smallpox V01.3
syphilis V01.6
tuberculosis V01.1
varicella V01.71
venereal disease V01.6
viral disease NEC V01.79
dermatitis — see Dermatitis
Contamination, food — see also Poisoning, food 005.9
Contraception, contraceptive
advice NEC V25.09
family planning V25.09
fitting of diaphragm V25.02
prescribing or use of
oral contraceptive agent V25.01
specified agent NEC V25.02
counseling NEC V25.09
emergency V25.03
family planning V25.09
fitting of diaphragm V25.02
prescribing or use of
oral contraceptive agent V25.01
emergency V25.03
postcoital V25.03
specified agent NEC V25.02
device (in situ) V45.59
causing menorrhagia 996.76
checking V25.42
complications 996.32
insertion V25.1
intrauterine V45.51
reinsertion V25.42
removal V25.42
subdermal V45.52
fitting of diaphragm V25.02
insertion
intrauterine contraceptive device V25.1
subdermal implantable V25.5
maintenance V25.40
examination V25.40
oral contraceptive V25.41
specified method NEC V25.49
subdermal implantable V25.43
intrauterine device V25.42
intrauterine device V25.42
oral contraceptive V25.41
specified method NEC V25.49
subdermal implantable V25.43
management NEC V25.49
prescription
oral contraceptive agent V25.01
emergency V25.03
postcoital V25.03
repeat V25.41
specified agent NEC V25.02
repeat V25.49
sterilization V25.2
surveillance V25.40
intrauterine device V25.42
oral contraceptive agent V25.41
subdermal implantable V25.43
specified method NEC V25.49
Contraction, contracture, contracted
Achilles tendon (see also Short, tendon, Achilles) 727.81
anus 564.89
axilla 729.90
bile duct (see also Disease, biliary) 576.8
bladder 596.8
neck or sphincter 596.0
bowel (see also Obstruction, intestine) 560.9
Braxton Hicks 644.1 ☑
breast implant, capsular 611.83
bronchus 519.19
burn (old) — see Cicatrix
capsular, of breast implant 611.83
cecum (see also Obstruction, intestine) 560.9
cervix (see also Stricture, cervix) 622.4
congenital 752.49
cicatricial — see Cicatrix
colon (see also Obstruction, intestine) 560.9
conjunctiva trachomatous, active 076.1
late effect 139.1
Dupuytren's 728.6

Contraction, contracture, contracted — continued
eyelid 374.41
eye socket (after enucleation) 372.64
face 729.90
fascia (lata) (postural) 728.89
Dupuytren's 728.6
palmar 728.6
plantar 728.71
finger NEC 736.29
congenital 755.59
joint (see also Contraction, joint) 718.44
flaccid, paralytic
joint (see also Contraction, joint) 718.4 ☑
muscle 728.85
ocular 378.50
gallbladder (see also Obstruction, gallbladder) 575.2
hamstring 728.89
tendon 727.81
heart valve — see Endocarditis
Hicks' 644.1 ☑
hip (see also Contraction, joint) 718.4 ☑
hourglass
bladder 596.8
congenital 753.8
gallbladder (see also Obstruction, gallbladder) 575.2
congenital 751.69
stomach 536.8
congenital 750.7
psychogenic 306.4
uterus 661.4 ☑
affecting fetus or newborn 763.7
hysterical 300.11
infantile (see also Epilepsy) 345.6 ☑
internal os (see also Stricture, cervix) 622.4
intestine (see also Obstruction, intestine) 560.9
joint (abduction) (acquired) (adduction) (flexion) (rotation) 718.40
ankle 718.47
congenital NEC 755.8
generalized or multiple 754.89
lower limb joints 754.89
hip (see also Subluxation, congenital, hip) 754.32
lower limb (including pelvic girdle) not involving hip 754.89
upper limb (including shoulder girdle) 755.59
elbow 718.42
foot 718.47
hand 718.44
hip 718.45
hysterical 300.11
knee 718.46
multiple sites 718.49
pelvic region 718.45
shoulder (region) 718.41
specified site NEC 718.48
wrist 718.43
kidney (granular) (secondary) (see also Sclerosis, renal) 587
congenital 753.3
hydronephritic 591
pyelonephritic (see also Pyelitis, chronic) 590.00
tuberculous (see also Tuberculosis) 016.0 ☑
ligament 728.89
congenital 756.89
liver — see Cirrhosis, liver
muscle (postinfectional) (postural) NEC 728.85
congenital 756.89
sternocleidomastoid 754.1
extraocular 378.60
eye (extrinsic) (see also Strabismus) 378.9
paralytic (see also Strabismus, paralytic) 378.50
flaccid 728.85
hysterical 300.11
ischemic (Volkmann's) 958.6
paralytic 728.85
posttraumatic 958.6
psychogenic 306.0
specified as conversion reaction 300.11

Contraction, contracture, contracted — continued
myotonic 728.85
neck (see also Torticollis) 723.5
congenital 754.1
psychogenic 306.0
ocular muscle (see also Strabismus) 378.9
paralytic (see also Strabismus, paralytic) 378.50
organ or site, congenital NEC — see Atresia
outlet (pelvis) — see Contraction, pelvis
palmar fascia 728.6
paralytic
joint (see also Contraction, joint) 718.4 ☑
muscle 728.85
ocular (see also Strabismus, paralytic) 378.50
pelvis (acquired) (general) 738.6
affecting fetus or newborn 763.1
complicating delivery 653.1 ☑
causing obstructed labor 660.1 ☑
generally contracted 653.1 ☑
causing obstructed labor 660.1 ☑
inlet 653.2 ☑
causing obstructed labor 660.1 ☑
midpelvic 653.8 ☑
causing obstructed labor 660.1 ☑
midplane 653.8 ☑
causing obstructed labor 660.1 ☑
outlet 653.3 ☑
causing obstructed labor 660.1 ☑
plantar fascia 728.71
premature
atrial 427.61
auricular 427.61
auriculoventricular 427.61
heart (junctional) (nodal) 427.60
supraventricular 427.61
ventricular 427.69
prostate 602.8
pylorus (see also Pylorospasm) 537.81
rectosigmoid (see also Obstruction, intestine) 560.9
rectum, rectal (sphincter) 564.89
psychogenic 306.4
ring (Bandl's) 661.4 ☑
affecting fetus or newborn 763.7
scar — see Cicatrix
sigmoid (see also Obstruction, intestine) 560.9
socket, eye 372.64
spine (see also Curvature, spine) 737.9
stomach 536.8
hourglass 536.8
congenital 750.7
psychogenic 306.4
tendon (sheath) (see also Short, tendon) 727.81
toe 735.8
ureterovesical orifice (postinfectional) 593.3
urethra 599.84
uterus 621.8
abnormal 661.9 ☑
affecting fetus or newborn 763.7
clonic, hourglass or tetanic 661.4 ☑
affecting fetus or newborn 763.7
dyscoordinate 661.4 ☑
affecting fetus or newborn 763.7
hourglass 661.4 ☑
affecting fetus or newborn 763.7
hypotonic NEC 661.2 ☑
affecting fetus or newborn 763.7
incoordinate 661.4 ☑
affecting fetus or newborn 763.7
inefficient or poor 661.2 ☑
affecting fetus or newborn 763.7
irregular 661.2 ☑
affecting fetus or newborn 763.7
tetanic 661.4 ☑
affecting fetus or newborn 763.7
vagina (outlet) 623.2
vesical 596.8
neck or urethral orifice 596.0
visual field, generalized 368.45
Volkmann's (ischemic) 958.6
Contusion (skin surface intact) 924.9

Contusion — continued
with
crush injury — see Crush
dislocation, by site — see Dislocation, by site
fracture — see Fracture, by site
internal injury (see also Injury, internal, by site)
heart — see Contusion, cardiac
kidney — see Contusion, kidney
liver — see Contusion, liver
lung — see Contusion, lung
spleen — see Contusion, spleen
intracranial injury — see Injury, intracranial
nerve injury — see Injury, nerve
open wound — see Wound, open, by site
abdomen, abdominal (muscle) (wall) 922.2
organ(s) NEC 868.00
adnexa, eye NEC 921.9
ankle 924.21
with other parts of foot 924.20
arm 923.9
lower (with elbow) 923.10
upper 923.03
with shoulder or axillary region 923.09
auditory canal (external) (meatus) (and other part(s) of neck, scalp, or face, except eye) 920
auricle, ear (and other part(s) of neck, scalp, or face except eye) 920
axilla 923.02
with shoulder or upper arm 923.09
back 922.31
bone NEC 924.9
brain (cerebral) (membrane) (with hemorrhage) 851.8 ☑

Note—Use the following fifth-digit subclassification with categories 851–854:

0   unspecified state of consciousness

1   with no loss of consciousness

2   with brief [less than one hour] loss of consciousness

3   with moderate [1–24 hours] loss of consciousness

4   with prolonged [more than 24 hours] loss of consciousness and return to pre–existing conscious level

5   with prolonged [more than 24 hours] loss of consciousness, without return to pre–existing conscious level

Use fifth–digit 5 to designate when a patient is unconscious and dies before regaining consciousness, regardless of the duration of the loss of consciousness

6   with loss of consciousness of unspecified duration

9   with concussion, unspecified

with
open intracranial wound 851.9 ☑
skull fracture — see Fracture, skull, by site
cerebellum 851.4 ☑
with open intracranial wound 851.5 ☑
cortex 851.0 ☑
with open intracranial wound 851.1 ☑
occipital lobe 851.4 ☑
with open intracranial wound 851.5 ☑
stem 851.4 ☑
with open intracranial wound 851.5 ☑
breast 922.0
brow (and other part(s) of neck, scalp, or face, except eye) 920
buttock 922.32
canthus 921.1
cardiac 861.01
with open wound into thorax 861.11
cauda equina (spine) 952.4
cerebellum — see Contusion, brain, cerebellum
cerebral — see Contusion, brain
cheek(s) (and other part(s) of neck, scalp, or face, except eye) 920

Contusion — continued
- chest (wall) 922.1
- chin and other part(s) of neck, scalp, or face, except eye) 920
- clitoris 922.4
- conjunctiva 921.1
- conus medullaris (spine) 952.4
- cornea 921.3
- corpus cavernosum 922.4
- cortex (brain) (cerebral) — see Contusion, brain, cortex
- costal region 922.1
- ear (and other part(s) of neck, scalp, or face except eye) 920
- elbow 923.11
  - with forearm 923.10
- epididymis 922.4
- epigastric region 922.2
- eye NEC 921.9
- eyeball 921.3
- eyelid(s) (and periocular area) 921.1
- face (and neck, or scalp, any part, except eye) 920
- femoral triangle 922.2
- fetus or newborn 772.6
- finger(s) (nail) (subungual) 923.3
- flank 922.2
- foot (with ankle) (excluding toe(s)) 924.20
- forearm (and elbow) 923.10
- forehead (and other part(s) of neck, scalp, or face, except eye) 920
- genital organs, external 922.4
- globe (eye) 921.3
- groin 922.2
- gum(s) (and other part(s) of neck, scalp, or face, except eye) 920
- hand(s) (except fingers alone) 923.20
- head (any part, except eye) (and face) (and neck) 920
- heart — see Contusion, cardiac
- heel 924.20
- hip 924.01
  - with thigh 924.00
- iliac region 922.2
- inguinal region 922.2
- internal organs (abdomen, chest, or pelvis) NEC — see Injury, internal, by site
- interscapular region 922.33
- iris (eye) 921.3
- kidney 866.01
  - with open wound into cavity 866.11
- knee 924.11
  - with lower leg 924.10
- labium (majus) (minus) 922.4
- lacrimal apparatus, gland, or sac 921.1
- larynx (and other part(s) of neck, scalp, or face, except eye) 920
- late effect — see Late, effects (of), contusion
- leg 924.5
  - lower (with knee) 924.10
- lens 921.3
- lingual (and other part(s) of neck, scalp, or face, except eye) 920
- lip(s) (and other part(s) of neck, scalp, or face, except eye) 920
- liver 864.01
  - with
    - laceration — see Laceration, liver
    - open wound into cavity 864.11
- lower extremity 924.5
  - multiple sites 924.4
- lumbar region 922.31
- lung 861.21
  - with open wound into thorax 861.31
- malar region (and other part(s) of neck, scalp, or face, except eye) 920
- mandibular joint (and other part(s) of neck, scalp, or face, except eye) 920
- mastoid region (and other part(s) of neck, scalp, or face, except eye) 920
- membrane, brain — see Contusion, brain
- midthoracic region 922.1
- mouth (and other part(s) of neck, scalp, or face, except eye) 920
- multiple sites (not classifiable to same three-digit category) 924.8

Contusion — continued
- multiple sites — continued
  - lower limb 924.4
  - trunk 922.8
  - upper limb 923.8
- muscle NEC 924.9
- myocardium — see Contusion, cardiac
- nasal (septum) (and other part(s) of neck, scalp, or face, except eye) 920
- neck (and scalp or face, any part, except eye) 920
- nerve — see Injury, nerve, by site
- nose (and other part(s) of neck, scalp, or face, except eye) 920
- occipital region (scalp) (and neck or face, except eye) 920
  - lobe — see Contusion, brain, occipital lobe
- orbit (region) (tissues) 921.2
- palate (soft) (and other part(s) of neck, scalp, or face, except eye) 920
- parietal region (scalp) (and neck, or face, except eye) 920
  - lobe — see Contusion, brain
- penis 922.4
- pericardium — see Contusion, cardiac
- perineum 922.4
- periocular area 921.1
- pharynx (and other part(s) of neck, scalp, or face, except eye) 920
- popliteal space (see also Contusion, knee) 924.11
- prepuce 922.4
- pubic region 922.4
- pudenda 922.4
- pulmonary — see Contusion, lung
- quadriceps femoralis 924.00
- rib cage 922.1
- sacral region 922.32
- salivary ducts or glands (and other part(s) of neck, scalp, or face, except eye) 920
- scalp (and neck, or face any part, except eye) 920
- scapular region 923.01
  - with shoulder or upper arm 923.09
- sclera (eye) 921.3
- scrotum 922.4
- shoulder 923.00
  - with upper arm or axillar regions 923.09
- skin NEC 924.9
- skull 920
- spermatic cord 922.4
- spinal cord (see also Injury, spinal, by site)
  - cauda equina 952.4
  - conus medullaris 952.4
- spleen 865.01
  - with open wound into cavity 865.11
- sternal region 922.1
- stomach — see Injury, internal, stomach
- subconjunctival 921.1
- subcutaneous NEC 924.9
- submaxillary region (and other part(s) of neck, scalp, or face, except eye) 920
- submental region (and other part(s) of neck, scalp, or face, except eye) 920
- subperiosteal NEC 924.9
- supraclavicular fossa (and other part(s) of neck, scalp, or face, except eye) 920
- supraorbital (and other part(s) of neck, scalp, or face, except eye) 920
- temple (region) (and other part(s) of neck, scalp, or face, except eye) 920
- testis 922.4
- thigh (and hip) 924.00
- thorax 922.1
  - organ — see Injury, internal, intrathoracic
- throat (and other part(s) of neck, scalp, or face, except eye) 920
- thumb(s) (nail) (subungual) 923.3
- toe(s) (nail) (subungual) 924.3
- tongue (and other part(s) of neck, scalp, or face, except eye) 920
- trunk 922.9
  - multiple sites 922.8
  - specified site — see Contusion, by site
- tunica vaginalis 922.4

Contusion — continued
- tympanum (membrane) (and other part(s) of neck, scalp, or face, except eye) 920
- upper extremity 923.9
  - multiple sites 923.8
- uvula (and other part(s) of neck, scalp, or face, except eye) 920
- vagina 922.4
- vocal cord(s) (and other part(s) of neck, scalp, or face, except eye) 920
- vulva 922.4
- wrist 923.21
  - with hand(s), except finger(s) alone 923.20
Conus (any type) (congenital) 743.57
- acquired 371.60
- medullaris syndrome 336.8
Convalescence (following) V66.9
- chemotherapy V66.2
- medical NEC V66.5
- psychotherapy V66.3
- radiotherapy V66.1
- surgery NEC V66.0
- treatment (for) NEC V66.5
  - combined V66.6
  - fracture V66.4
  - mental disorder NEC V66.3
  - specified disorder NEC V66.5
Conversion
- closed surgical procedure to open procedure
  - arthroscopic V64.43
  - laparoscopic V64.41
  - thoracoscopic V64.42
- hysteria, hysterical, any type 300.11
- neurosis, any 300.11
- reaction, any 300.11
Converter, tuberculosis (test reaction) 795.5
Convulsions (idiopathic) 780.39
- apoplectiform (see also Disease, cerebrovascular, acute) 436
- brain 780.39
- cerebral 780.39
- cerebrospinal 780.39
- due to trauma NEC — see Injury, intracranial
- eclamptic (see also Eclampsia) 780.39
- epileptic (see also Epilepsy) 345.9 ☑
- epileptiform (see also Seizure, epileptiform) 780.39
- epileptoid (see also Seizure, epileptiform) 780.39
- ether
  - anesthetic
    - correct substance properly administered 780.39
    - overdose or wrong substance given 968.2
    - other specified type — see Table of Drugs and Chemicals
- febrile (simple) 780.31
  - complex 780.32
- generalized 780.39
- hysterical 300.11
- infantile 780.39
  - epilepsy — see Epilepsy
- internal 780.39
- jacksonian (see also Epilepsy) 345.5 ☑
- myoclonic 333.2
- newborn 779.0
- paretic 094.1
- pregnancy (nephritic) (uremic) — see Eclampsia, pregnancy
- psychomotor (see also Epilepsy) 345.4 ☑
- puerperal, postpartum — see Eclampsia, pregnancy
- recurrent 780.39
  - epileptic — see Epilepsy
- reflex 781.0
- repetitive 780.39
  - epileptic — see Epilepsy
- salaam (see also Epilepsy) 345.6 ☑
- scarlatinal 034.1
- spasmodic 780.39
- tetanus, tetanic (see also Tetanus) 037
- thymic 254.8
- uncinate 780.39
- uremic 586
Convulsive — see also Convulsions

Convulsive — see also Convulsions — continued
- disorder or state 780.39
  - epileptic — see Epilepsy
- equivalent, abdominal (see also Epilepsy) 345.5 ☑
Cooke-Apert-Gallais syndrome (adrenogenital) 255.2
Cooley's anemia (erythroblastic) 282.49
Coolie itch 126.9
Cooper's
- disease 610.1
- hernia — see Hernia, Cooper's
Coordination disturbance 781.3
Copper wire arteries, retina 362.13
Copra itch 133.8
Coprolith 560.39
Coprophilia 302.89
Coproporphyria, hereditary 277.1
Coprostasis 560.39
- with hernia (see also Hernia, by site, with obstruction)
  - gangrenous — see Hernia, by site, with gangrene
Cor
- biloculare 745.7
- bovinum — see Hypertrophy, cardiac
- bovis (see also Hypertrophy, cardiac)
- pulmonale (chronic) 416.9
  - acute 415.0
- triatriatum, triatrium 746.82
- triloculare 745.8
  - biatriatum 745.3
  - biventriculare 745.69
Corbus' disease 607.1
Cord — see also condition
- around neck (tightly) (with compression)
  - affecting fetus or newborn 762.5
  - complicating delivery 663.1 ☑
    - without compression 663.3 ☑
      - affecting fetus or newborn 762.6
- bladder NEC 344.61
  - tabetic 094.0
- prolapse
  - affecting fetus or newborn 762.4
  - complicating delivery 663.0 ☑
Cord's angiopathy — see also Tuberculosis 017.3 ☑ [362.18]
Cordis ectopia 746.87
Corditis (spermatic) 608.4
Corectopia 743.46
Cori type glycogen storage disease — see Disease, glycogen storage
Cork-handlers' disease or lung 495.3
Corkscrew esophagus 530.5
Corlett's pyosis (impetigo) 684
Corn (infected) 700
Cornea — see also condition
- donor V59.5
- guttata (dystrophy) 371.57
- plana 743.41
Cornelia de Lange's syndrome (Amsterdam dwarf, mental retardation, and brachycephaly) 759.89
Cornual gestation or pregnancy — see Pregnancy, cornual
Cornu cutaneum 702.8
Coronary (artery) — see also condition
- arising from aorta or pulmonary trunk 746.85
Corpora — see also condition
- amylacea (prostate) 602.8
- cavernosa — see condition
Corpulence — see Obesity
Corpus — see condition
Corrigan's disease — see Insufficiency, aortic
Corrosive burn — see Burn, by site
Corsican fever — see also Malaria 084.6
Cortical — see also condition
- blindness 377.75
- necrosis, kidney (bilateral) 583.6
Corticoadrenal — see condition
Corticosexual syndrome 255.2
Coryza (acute) 460
- with grippe or influenza 487.1
- syphilitic 095.8
  - congenital (chronic) 090.0

☑ Additional Digit Required — Refer to the Tabular List for Digit Selection   ᵂ Subterms under main terms may continue to next column or page

2010 ICD-9-CM   ▶◀ Revised Text   ● New Line   ▲ Revised Code   Volume 2 — 55

Costen's syndrome or complex 524.60
Costiveness — *see also* Constipation 564.00
Costochondritis 733.6
Cotard's syndrome (paranoia) 297.1
Cot death 798.0
Cotia virus 059.8
Cotungo's disease 724.3
Cough 786.2
  with hemorrhage (*see also* Hemoptysis) 786.3
  affected 786.2
  bronchial 786.2
    with grippe or influenza 487.1
  chronic 786.2
  epidemic 786.2
  functional 306.1
  hemorrhagic 786.3
  hysterical 300.11
  laryngeal, spasmodic 786.2
  nervous 786.2
  psychogenic 306.1
  smokers' 491.0
  tea tasters' 112.89
Counseling NEC V65.40
  without complaint or sickness V65.49
  abuse victim NEC V62.89
    child V61.21
    partner V61.11
    spouse V61.11
  child abuse, maltreatment, or neglect V61.21
  contraceptive NEC V25.09
    device (intrauterine) V25.02
    maintenance V25.40
      intrauterine contraceptive device V25.42
      oral contraceptive (pill) V25.41
      specified type NEC V25.49
      subdermal implantable V25.43
    management NEC V25.9
    oral contraceptive (pill) V25.01
      emergency V25.03
      postcoital V25.03
    prescription NEC V25.02
      oral contraceptive (pill) V25.01
        emergency V25.03
        postcoital V25.03
        repeat prescription V25.41
      repeat prescription V25.40
      subdermal implantable V25.43
    surveillance NEC V25.40
  dietary V65.3
  exercise V65.41
  expectant ▶parent(s)◀
    pediatric pre-adoption visit V65.11 ●
    pediatric pre-birth visit V65.11 ●
  explanation of
    investigation finding NEC V65.49
    medication NEC V65.49
  family planning V25.09
    natural
      procreative V26.41
      to avoid pregnancy V25.04
  for nonattending third party V65.19
  genetic V26.33
  gonorrhea V65.45
  health (advice) (education) (instruction) NEC V65.49
  HIV V65.44
  human immunodeficiency virus V65.44
  injury prevention V65.43
  insulin pump training V65.46
  marital V61.10
  medical (for) V65.9
    boarding school resident V60.6
    condition not demonstrated V65.5
    feared complaint and no disease found V65.5
    institutional resident V60.6
    on behalf of another V65.19
    person living alone V60.3
  natural family planning
    procreative V26.41
    to avoid pregnancy V25.04
  parent ▶(guardian)◀-child conflict V61.20
    adopted child V61.24 ●
    biological child V61.23 ●
    foster child V61.25 ●

Counseling — *continued*
  parent -child conflict — *continued*
    specified problem NEC V61.29
  partner abuse
    perpetrator V61.12
    victim V61.11
  pediatric
    pre-adoption visit for adoptive parent(s) ●
      V65.11 ●
    pre-birth visit for expectant parents ●
      V65.11 ●
  perpetrator of
    child abuse V62.83
      parental V61.22
    partner abuse V61.12
    spouse abuse V61.12
  procreative V65.49
  sex NEC V65.49
    transmitted disease NEC V65.45
      HIV V65.44
  specified reason NEC V65.49
  spousal abuse
    perpetrator V61.12
    victim V61.11
  substance use and abuse V65.42
  syphilis V65.45
  victim (of)
    abuse NEC V62.89
    child abuse V61.21
    partner abuse V61.11
    spousal abuse V61.11
Coupled rhythm 427.89
Couvelaire uterus (complicating delivery) — *see* Placenta, separation
Cowper's gland — *see* condition
Cowperitis — *see also* Urethritis 597.89
  gonorrheal (acute) 098.0
    chronic or duration of 2 months or over 098.2
Cowpox (abortive) 051.01
  due to vaccination 999.0
  eyelid 051.01 *[373.5]*
    postvaccination 999.0 *[373.5]*
Coxa
  plana 732.1
  valga (acquired) 736.31
    congenital 755.61
    late effect of rickets 268.1
  vara (acquired) 736.32
    congenital 755.62
    late effect of rickets 268.1
Coxae malum senilis 715.25
Coxalgia (nontuberculous) 719.45 ●
  tuberculous (*see also* Tuberculosis) 015.1 ☑ *[730.85]*
Coxalgic pelvis 736.30
Coxitis 716.65
Coxsackie (infection) (virus) 079.2
  central nervous system NEC 048
  endocarditis 074.22
  enteritis 008.67
  meningitis (aseptic) 047.0
  myocarditis 074.23
  pericarditis 074.21
  pharyngitis 074.0
  pleurodynia 074.1
  specific disease NEC 074.8
Crabs, meaning pubic lice 132.2
Crack baby 760.75
Cracked
  nipple 611.2
    puerperal, postpartum 676.1 ☑
  tooth 521.81
Cradle cap 690.11
Craft neurosis 300.89
Craigiasis 007.8
Cramp(s) 729.82
  abdominal 789.0 ☑
  bathing 994.1
  colic 789.7
    infantile 789.7
    psychogenic 306.4
  due to immersion 994.1
  extremity (lower) (upper) NEC 729.82
  fireman 992.2
  heat 992.2

Cramp(s) — *continued*
  hysterical 300.11
  immersion 994.1
  intestinal 789.0 ☑
    psychogenic 306.4
  linotypist's 300.89
    organic 333.84
  muscle (extremity) (general) 729.82
    due to immersion 994.1
    hysterical 300.11
  occupational (hand) 300.89
    organic 333.84
  psychogenic 307.89
  salt depletion 276.1
  sleep related leg 327.52
  stoker 992.2
  stomach 789.0 ☑
  telegraphers' 300.89
    organic 333.84
  typists' 300.89
    organic 333.84
  uterus 625.8
    menstrual 625.3
  writers' 333.84
    organic 333.84
    psychogenic 300.89
Cranial — *see* condition
Cranioclasis, fetal 763.89
Craniocleidodysostosis 755.59
Craniofenestria (skull) 756.0
Craniolacunia (skull) 756.0
Craniopagus 759.4
Craniopathy, metabolic 733.3
Craniopharyngeal — *see* condition
Craniopharyngioma (M9350/1) 237.0
Craniorachischisis (totalis) 740.1
Cranioschisis 756.0
Craniostenosis 756.0
Craniosynostosis 756.0
Craniotabes (cause unknown) 733.3
  rachitic 268.1
  syphilitic 090.5
Craniotomy, fetal 763.89
Cranium — *see* condition
Craw-craw 125.3
CRBSI (catheter-related bloodstream infection) 999.31
Creaking joint 719.60
  ankle 719.67
  elbow 719.62
  foot 719.67
  hand 719.64
  hip 719.65
  knee 719.66
  multiple sites 719.69
  pelvic region 719.65
  shoulder (region) 719.61
  specified site NEC 719.68
  wrist 719.63
Creeping
  eruption 126.9
  palsy 335.21
  paralysis 335.21
Crenated tongue 529.8
Creotoxism 005.9
Crepitus
  caput 756.0
  joint 719.60
    ankle 719.67
    elbow 719.62
    foot 719.67
    hand 719.64
    hip 719.65
    knee 719.66
    multiple sites 719.69
    pelvic region 719.65
    shoulder (region) 719.61
    specified site NEC 719.68
    wrist 719.63
▲ **Crescent or conus choroid, congenital** 743.57
● **Cretin, cretinism** (athyrotic) (congenital) (endemic) (metabolic) (nongoitrous) (sporadic) 243
  goitrous (sporadic) 246.1
  pelvis (dwarf type) (male type) 243
    with disproportion (fetopelvic) 653.1 ☑
      affecting fetus or newborn 763.1

Cretin, cretinism — *continued*
  pelvis — *continued*
    with disproportion — *continued*
      causing obstructed labor 660.1 ☑
        affecting fetus or newborn 763.1
  pituitary 253.3
Cretinoid degeneration 243
Creutzfeldt-Jakob disease (CJD) (syndrome) 046.19
  with dementia
    with behavioral disturbance 046.19 *[294.11]*
    without behavioral disturbance 046.19 *[294.10]*
  familial 046.19
  iatrogenic 046.19
  specified NEC 046.19
  sporadic 046.19
  variant (vCJD) 046.11
    with dementia
      with behavioral disturbance 046.11 *[294.11]*
      without behavioral disturbance 046.11 *[294.10]*
Crib death 798.0
Cribriform hymen 752.49
Cri-du-chat syndrome 758.31
Crigler-Najjar disease or syndrome (congenital hyperbilirubinemia) 277.4
Crimean hemorrhagic fever 065.0
Criminalism 301.7
Crisis
  abdomen 789.0 ☑
  addisonian (acute adrenocortical insufficiency) 255.41
  adrenal (cortical) 255.41
  asthmatic — *see* Asthma
  brain, cerebral (*see also* Disease, cerebrovascular, acute) 436
  celiac 579.0
  Dietl's 593.4
  emotional NEC 309.29
    acute reaction to stress 308.0
    adjustment reaction 309.9
    specific to childhood or adolescence 313.9
  gastric (tabetic) 094.0
  glaucomatocyclitic 364.22
  heart (*see also* Failure, heart) 428.9
  hypertensive — *see* Hypertension
  nitritoid
    correct substance properly administered 458.29
    overdose or wrong substance given or taken 961.1
  oculogyric 378.87
    psychogenic 306.7
  Pel's 094.0
  psychosexual identity 302.6
  rectum 094.0
  renal 593.81
  sickle cell 282.62
  stomach (tabetic) 094.0
  tabetic 094.0
  thyroid (*see also* Thyrotoxicosis) 242.9 ☑
  thyrotoxic (*see also* Thyrotoxicosis) 242.9 ☑
  vascular — *see* Disease, cerebrovascular, acute
Crocq's disease (acrocyanosis) 443.89
Crohn's disease — *see also* Enteritis, regional 555.9
Cronkhite-Canada syndrome 211.3
Crooked septum, nasal 470
Cross
  birth (of fetus) complicating delivery 652.3 ☑
    with successful version 652.1 ☑
    causing obstructed labor 660.0 ☑
  bite, anterior or posterior 524.27
  eye (*see also* Esotropia) 378.00
Crossed ectopia of kidney 753.3
Crossfoot 754.50
Croup, croupous (acute) (angina) (catarrhal) (infective) (inflammatory) (laryngeal) (membranous) (nondiphtheritic) (pseudomembranous) 464.4
  asthmatic (*see also* Asthma) 493.9 ☑
  bronchial 466.0
  diphtheritic (membranous) 032.3

☑ Additional Digit Required — Refer to the Tabular List for Digit Selection   ⏷ Subterms under main terms may continue to next column or page

56 — Volume 2 • October 2009   ▶◀ Revised Text   ● New Line   ▲ Revised Code   **2010 ICD-9-CM**

Note — *In general, cysts are not neoplastic and are classified to the appropriate category for disease of the specified anatomical site. This generalization does not apply to certain types of cysts which are neoplastic in nature, for example, dermoid, nor does it apply to cysts of certain structures, for example, branchial cleft, which are classified as developmental anomalies.*

The following listing includes some of the most frequently reported sites of cysts as well as qualifiers which indicate the type of cyst. The latter qualifiers usually are not repeated under the anatomical sites. Since the code assignment for a given site may vary depending upon the type of cyst, the coder should refer to the listings under the specified type of cyst before consideration is given to the site.

☑ Additional Digit Required — Refer to the Tabular List for Digit Selection   ☝ Subterms under main terms may continue to next column or page

2010 ICD-9-CM   ▶◀ Revised Text   ● New Line   ▲ Revised Code   **October 2009 • Volume 2 — 57**

Cyst — *continued*
  bile duct (*see also* Disease, biliary) 576.8
  bladder (multiple) (trigone) 596.8
  Blessig's 362.62
  blood, endocardial (*see also* Endocarditis) 424.90
  blue dome 610.0
  bone (local) 733.20
    aneurysmal 733.22
    jaw 526.2
      developmental (odontogenic) 526.0
      fissural 526.1
      latent 526.89
    solitary 733.21
    unicameral 733.21
  brain 348.0
    congenital 742.4
    hydatid (*see also* Echinococcus) 122.9
    third ventricle (colloid) 742.4
  branchial (cleft) 744.42
  branchiogeneal 744.42
  breast (benign) (blue dome) (pedunculated) (solitary) (traumatic) 610.0
    involution 610.4
    sebaceous 610.8
  broad ligament (benign) 620.8
    embryonic 752.11
  bronchogenic (mediastinal) (sequestration) 518.89
    congenital 748.4
  buccal 528.4
  bulbourethral gland (Cowper's) 599.89
  bursa, bursal 727.49
    pharyngeal 478.26
  calcifying odontogenic (M9301/0) 213.1
    upper jaw (bone) 213.0
  canal of Nuck (acquired) (serous) 629.1
    congenital 752.41
  canthus 372.75
  carcinomatous (M8010/3) — *see* Neoplasm, by site, malignant
  cartilage (joint) — *see* Derangement, joint
  cauda equina 336.8
  cavum septi pellucidi NEC 348.0
  celomic (pericardium) 746.89
  cerebellopontine (angle) — *see* Cyst, brain
  cerebellum — *see* Cyst, brain
  cerebral — *see* Cyst, brain
  cervical lateral 744.42
  cervix 622.8
    embryonal 752.41
    nabothian (gland) 616.0
  chamber, anterior (eye) 364.60
    exudative 364.62
    implantation (surgical) (traumatic) 364.61
    parasitic 360.13
  chiasmal, optic NEC (*see also* Lesion, chiasmal) 377.54
  chocolate (ovary) 617.1
  choledochal (congenital) 751.69
    acquired 576.8
  choledochus 751.69
  chorion 658.8 ☑
  choroid plexus 348.0
  chyle, mesentery 457.8
  ciliary body 364.60
    exudative 364.64
    implantation 364.61
    primary 364.63
  clitoris 624.8
  coccyx (*see also* Cyst, bone) 733.20
  colloid
    third ventricle (brain) 742.4
    thyroid gland — *see* Goiter
  colon 569.89
  common (bile) duct (*see also* Disease, biliary) 576.8
  congenital NEC 759.89
    adrenal glands 759.1
    epiglottis 748.3
    esophagus 750.4
    fallopian tube 752.11
    kidney 753.10
      multiple 753.19
      single 753.11
    larynx 748.3

Cyst — *continued*
  congenital — *continued*
    liver 751.62
    lung 748.4
    mediastinum 748.8
    ovary 752.0
    oviduct 752.11
    pancreas 751.7
    periurethral (tissue) 753.8
    prepuce NEC 752.69
      penis 752.69
    sublingual 750.26
    submaxillary gland 750.26
    thymus (gland) 759.2
    tongue 750.19
    ureterovesical orifice 753.4
    vulva 752.41
  conjunctiva 372.75
  cornea 371.23
  corpora quadrigemina 348.0
  corpus
    albicans (ovary) 620.2
    luteum (ruptured) 620.1
  Cowper's gland (benign) (infected) 599.89
  cranial meninges 348.0
  craniobuccal pouch 253.8
  craniopharyngeal pouch 253.8
  cystic duct (*see also* Disease, gallbladder) 575.8
  Cysticercus (any site) 123.1
  Dandy-Walker 742.3
    with spina bifida (*see also* Spina bifida) 741.0 ☑
  dental 522.8
    developmental 526.0
    eruption 526.0
    lateral periodontal 526.0
    primordial (keratocyst) 526.0
    root 522.8
  dentigerous 526.0
    mandible 526.0
    maxilla 526.0
  dermoid (M9084/0) (*see also* Neoplasm, by site, benign)
    with malignant transformation (M9084/3) 183.0
    implantation
      external area or site (skin) NEC 709.8
      iris 364.61
      skin 709.8
      vagina 623.8
      vulva 624.8
    mouth 528.4
    oral soft tissue 528.4
    sacrococcygeal 685.1
      with abscess 685.0
  developmental of ovary, ovarian 752.0
  dura (cerebral) 348.0
    spinal 349.2
  ear (external) 706.2
  echinococcal (*see also* Echinococcus) 122.9
  embryonal
    cervix uteri 752.41
    genitalia, female external 752.41
    uterus 752.3
    vagina 752.41
  endometrial 621.8
    ectopic 617.9
  endometrium (uterus) 621.8
    ectopic — *see* Endometriosis
  enteric 751.5
  enterogenous 751.5
  epidermal (inclusion) (*see also* Cyst, skin) 706.2
  epidermoid (inclusion) (*see also* Cyst, skin) 706.2
    mouth 528.4
    not of skin — *see* Cyst, by site
    oral soft tissue 528.4
  epididymis 608.89
  epiglottis 478.79
  epiphysis cerebri 259.8
  epithelial (inclusion) (*see also* Cyst, skin) 706.2
  epoophoron 752.11
  eruption 526.0
  esophagus 530.89
  ethmoid sinus 478.19
  eye (retention) 379.8

Cyst — *continued*
  eye — *continued*
    congenital 743.03
    posterior segment, congenital 743.54
  eyebrow 706.2
  eyelid (sebaceous) 374.84
    infected 373.13
    sweat glands or ducts 374.84
  falciform ligament (inflammatory) 573.8
  fallopian tube 620.8
    congenital 752.11
  female genital organs NEC 629.89
  fimbrial (congenital) 752.11
  fissural (oral region) 526.1
  follicle (atretic) (graafian) (ovarian) 620.0
    nabothian (gland) 616.0
  follicular (atretic) (ovarian) 620.0
    dentigerous 526.0
  frontal sinus 478.19
  gallbladder or duct 575.8
  ganglion 727.43
  Gartner's duct 752.41
  gas, of mesentery 568.89
  gingiva 523.8
  gland of moll 374.84
  globulomaxillary 526.1
  graafian follicle 620.0
  granulosal lutein 620.2
  hemangiomatous (M9121/0) (*see also* Hemangioma) 228.00
  hydatid (*see also* Echinococcus) 122.9
    fallopian tube (Morgagni) 752.11
    liver NEC 122.8
    lung NEC 122.9
    Morgagni 752.89
      fallopian tube 752.11
    specified site NEC 122.9
  hymen 623.8
    embryonal 752.41
  hypopharynx 478.26
  hypophysis, hypophyseal (duct) (recurrent) 253.8
    cerebri 253.8
  implantation (dermoid)
    anterior chamber (eye) 364.61
    external area or site (skin) NEC 709.8
    iris 364.61
    vagina 623.8
    vulva 624.8
  incisor, incisive canal 526.1
  inclusion (epidermal) (epithelial) (epidermoid) (mucous) (squamous) (*see also* Cyst, skin) 706.2
    not of skin — *see* Neoplasm, by site, benign
  intestine (large) (small) 569.89
  intracranial — *see* Cyst, brain
  intraligamentous 728.89
    knee 717.89
  intrasellar 253.8
  iris (idiopathic) 364.60
    exudative 364.62
    implantation (surgical) (traumatic) 364.61
    miotic pupillary 364.55
    parasitic 360.13
  Iwanoff's 362.62
  jaw (bone) (aneurysmal) (extravasation) (hemorrhagic) (traumatic) 526.2
    developmental (odontogenic) 526.0
    fissural 526.1
  keratin 706.2
  kidney (congenital) 753.10
    acquired 593.2
    calyceal (*see also* Hydronephrosis) 591
    multiple 753.19
    pyelogenic (*see also* Hydronephrosis) 591
    simple 593.2
    single 753.11
    solitary (not congenital) 593.2
  labium (majus) (minus) 624.8
    sebaceous 624.8
  lacrimal
    apparatus 375.43
    gland or sac 375.12
  larynx 478.79
  lens 379.39

Cyst — *continued*
  lens — *continued*
    congenital 743.39
  lip (gland) 528.5
  liver 573.8
    congenital 751.62
    hydatid (*see also* Echinococcus) 122.8
      granulosis 122.0
      multilocularis 122.5
  lung 518.89
    congenital 748.4
    giant bullous 492.0
  lutein 620.1
  lymphangiomatous (M9173/0) 228.1
  lymphoepithelial
    mouth 528.4
    oral soft tissue 528.4
  macula 362.54
  malignant (M8000/3) — *see* Neoplasm, by site, malignant
  mammary gland (sweat gland) (*see also* Cyst, breast) 610.0
  mandible 526.2
    dentigerous 526.0
    radicular 522.8
  maxilla 526.2
    dentigerous 526.0
    radicular 522.8
  median
    anterior maxillary 526.1
    palatal 526.1
  mediastinum (congenital) 748.8
  meibomian (gland) (retention) 373.2
    infected 373.12
  membrane, brain 348.0
  meninges (cerebral) 348.0
    spinal 349.2
  meniscus knee 717.5
  mesentery, mesenteric (gas) 568.89
    chyle 457.8
    gas 568.89
  mesonephric duct 752.89
  mesothelial
    peritoneum 568.89
    pleura (peritoneal) 568.89
  milk 611.5
  miotic pupillary (iris) 364.55
  Morgagni (hydatid) 752.89
    fallopian tube 752.11
  mouth 528.4
  Müllerian duct 752.89
    appendix testis 608.89
    cervix (embryonal) 752.41
    fallopian tube 752.11
    prostatic utricle 599.89
    vagina (embryonal) 752.41
  multilocular (ovary) (M8000/1) 239.5
  myometrium 621.8
  nabothian (follicle) (ruptured) 616.0
  nasal sinus 478.19
  nasoalveolar 528.4
  nasolabial 528.4
  nasopalatine (duct) 526.1
    anterior 526.1
  nasopharynx 478.26
  neoplastic (M8000/1) (*see also* Neoplasm, by site, unspecified nature)
    benign (M8000/0) — *see* Neoplasm, by site, benign
    uterus 621.8
  nervous system — *see* Cyst, brain
  neuroenteric 742.59
  neuroepithelial ventricle 348.0
  nipple 610.0
  nose 478.19
    skin of 706.2
  odontogenic, developmental 526.0
  omentum (lesser) 568.89
    congenital 751.8
  oral soft tissue (dermoid) (epidermoid) (lymphoepithelial) 528.4
  ora serrata 361.19
  orbit 376.81
  ovary, ovarian (twisted) 620.2
    adherent 620.2
    chocolate 617.1

Cyst — *continued*
  ovary, ovarian — *continued*
    corpus
      albicans 620.2
      luteum 620.1
    dermoid (M9084/0) 220
    developmental 752.0
    due to failure of involution NEC 620.2
    endometrial 617.1
    follicular (atretic) (graafian) (hemorrhagic)
      620.0
    hemorrhagic 620.2
    in pregnancy or childbirth 654.4 ☑
      affecting fetus or newborn 763.89
      causing obstructed labor 660.2 ☑
        affecting fetus or newborn 763.1
    multilocular (M8000/1) 239.5
    pseudomucinous (M8470/0) 220
    retention 620.2
    serous 620.2
    theca lutein 620.2
    tuberculous (*see also* Tuberculosis)
      016.6 ☑
    unspecified 620.2
  oviduct 620.8
  palatal papilla (jaw) 526.1
  palate 526.1
    fissural 526.1
    median (fissural) 526.1
  palatine, of papilla 526.1
  pancreas, pancreatic 577.2
    congenital 751.7
    false 577.2
    hemorrhagic 577.2
    true 577.2
  paralabral
    hip 718.85
    shoulder 840.7
  paramesonephric duct — *see* Cyst, Müllerian
    duct
  paranephric 593.2
  para ovarian 752.11
  paraphysis, cerebri 742.4
  parasitic NEC 136.9
  parathyroid (gland) 252.8
  paratubal (fallopian) 620.8
  paraurethral duct 599.89
  paroophoron 752.11
  parotid gland 527.6
    mucous extravasation or retention 527.6
  parovarian 752.11
  pars planus 364.60
    exudative 364.64
    primary 364.63
  pelvis, female
    in pregnancy or childbirth 654.4 ☑
      affecting fetus or newborn 763.89
      causing obstructed labor 660.2 ☑
        affecting fetus or newborn 763.1
  penis (sebaceous) 607.89
  periapical 522.8
  pericardial (congenital) 746.89
    acquired (secondary) 423.8
  pericoronal 526.0
  perineural (Tarlov's) 355.9
  periodontal 522.8
    lateral 526.0
  peripancreatic 577.2
  peripelvic (lymphatic) 593.2
  peritoneum 568.89
    chylous 457.8
  pharynx (wall) 478.26
  pilonidal (infected) (rectum) 685.1
    with abscess 685.0
    malignant (M9084/3) 173.5
  pituitary (duct) (gland) 253.8
  placenta (amniotic) — *see* Placenta, abnormal
  pleura 519.8
  popliteal 727.51
  porencephalic 742.4
    acquired 348.0
  posterior segment of eye, congenital 743.54
  postmastoidectomy cavity 383.31
  preauricular 744.47

Cyst — *continued*
  prepuce 607.89
    congenital 752.69
  primordial (jaw) 526.0
  prostate 600.3
  pseudomucinous (ovary) (M8470/0) 220
  pudenda (sweat glands) 624.8
  pupillary, miotic 364.55
    sebaceous 624.8
  radicular (residual) 522.8
  radiculodental 522.8
  ranular 527.6
  Rathke's pouch 253.8
  rectum (epithelium) (mucous) 569.49
  renal — *see* Cyst, kidney
  residual (radicular) 522.8
  retention (ovary) 620.2
  retina 361.19
    macular 362.54
    parasitic 360.13
    primary 361.13
    secondary 361.14
  retroperitoneal 568.89
  sacrococcygeal (dermoid) 685.1
    with abscess 685.0
  salivary gland or duct 527.6
    mucous extravasation or retention 527.6
  Sampson's 617.1
  sclera 379.19
  scrotum (sebaceous) 706.2
    sweat glands 706.2
  sebaceous (duct) (gland) 706.2
    breast 610.8
    eyelid 374.84
    genital organ NEC
      female 629.89
      male 608.89
    scrotum 706.2
  semilunar cartilage (knee) (multiple) 717.5
  seminal vesicle 608.89
  serous (ovary) 620.2
  sinus (antral) (ethmoidal) (frontal) (maxillary)
    (nasal) (sphenoidal) 478.19
  Skene's gland 599.89
  skin (epidermal) (epidermoid, inclusion) (ep-
    ithelial) (inclusion) (retention) (seba-
    ceous) 706.2
    breast 610.8
    eyelid 374.84
    genital organ NEC
      female 629.89
      male 608.89
    neoplastic 216.3
    scrotum 706.2
    sweat gland or duct 705.89
  solitary
    bone 733.21
    kidney 593.2
  spermatic cord 608.89
  sphenoid sinus 478.19
  spinal meninges 349.2
  spine (*see also* Cyst, bone) 733.20
  spleen NEC 289.59
    congenital 759.0
    hydatid (*see also* Echinococcus) 122.9
  spring water (pericardium) 746.89
  subarachnoid 348.0
    intrasellar 793.0
  subdural (cerebral) 348.0
    spinal cord 349.2
  sublingual gland 527.6
    mucous extravasation or retention 527.6
  submaxillary gland 527.6
    mucous extravasation or retention 527.6
  suburethral 599.89
  suprarenal gland 255.8
  suprasellar — *see* Cyst, brain
  sweat gland or duct 705.89
  sympathetic nervous system 337.9
  synovial 727.40
    popliteal space 727.51
  Tarlov's 355.9
  tarsal 373.2
  tendon (sheath) 727.42
  testis 608.89
  theca-lutein (ovary) 620.2

Cyst — *continued*
  Thornwaldt's, Tornwaldt's 478.26
  thymus (gland) 254.8
  thyroglossal (duct) (infected) (persistent) 759.2
  thyroid (gland) 246.2
    adenomatous — *see* Goiter, nodular
    colloid (*see also* Goiter) 240.9
  thyrolingual duct (infected) (persistent) 759.2
  tongue (mucous) 529.8
  tonsil 474.8
  tooth (dental root) 522.8
  tubo-ovarian 620.8
    inflammatory 614.1
  tunica vaginalis 608.89
  turbinate (nose) (*see also* Cyst, bone) 733.20
  Tyson's gland (benign) (infected) 607.89
  umbilicus 759.89
  urachus 753.7
  ureter 593.89
  ureterovesical orifice 593.89
    congenital 753.4
  urethra 599.84
  urethral gland (Cowper's) 599.89
  uterine
    ligament 620.8
      embryonic 752.11
    tube 620.8
  uterus (body) (corpus) (recurrent) 621.8
    embryonal 752.3
  utricle (ear) 386.8
    prostatic 599.89
  utriculus masculinus 599.89
  vagina, vaginal (squamous cell) (wall) 623.8
    embryonal 752.41
    implantation 623.8
    inclusion 623.8
  vallecula, vallecular 478.79
  ventricle, neuroepithelial 348.0
  verumontanum 599.89
  vesical (orifice) 596.8
  vitreous humor 379.29
  vulva (sweat glands) 624.8
    congenital 752.41
    implantation 624.8
    inclusion 624.8
    sebaceous gland 624.8
  vulvovaginal gland 624.8
  wolffian 752.89
Cystadenocarcinoma (M8440/3) — *see also*
  Neoplasm, by site, malignant
  bile duct type (M8161/3) 155.1
  endometrioid (M8380/3) — *see* Neoplasm, by
    site, malignant
  mucinous (M8470/3)
    papillary (M8471/3)
      specified site — *see* Neoplasm, by site,
        malignant
      unspecified site 183.0
    specified site — *see* Neoplasm, by site,
      malignant
    unspecified site 183.0
  papillary (M8450/3)
    mucinous (M8471/3)
      specified site — *see* Neoplasm, by site,
        malignant
      unspecified site 183.0
    pseudomucinous (M8471/3)
      specified site — *see* Neoplasm, by site,
        malignant
      unspecified site 183.0
    serous (M8460/3)
      specified site — *see* Neoplasm, by site,
        malignant
      unspecified site 183.0
    specified site — *see* Neoplasm, by site,
      malignant
    unspecified 183.0
  pseudomucinous (M8470/3)
    papillary (M8471/3)
      specified site — *see* Neoplasm, by site,
        malignant
      unspecified site 183.0
    specified site — *see* Neoplasm, by site,
      malignant
    unspecified site 183.0

Cystadenocarcinoma — *see also* Neoplasm, by
  site, malignant — *continued*
  serous (M8441/3)
    papillary (M8460/3)
      specified site — *see* Neoplasm, by site,
        malignant
      unspecified site 183.0
    specified site — *see* Neoplasm, by site,
      malignant
    unspecified site 183.0
Cystadenofibroma (M9013/0)
  clear cell (M8313/0) — *see* Neoplasm, by site,
    benign
  endometrioid (M8381/0) 220
    borderline malignancy (M8381/1) 236.2
    malignant (M8381/3) 183.0
  mucinous (M9015/0)
    specified site — *see* Neoplasm, by site,
      benign
    unspecified site 220
  serous (M9014/0)
    specified site — *see* Neoplasm, by site,
      benign
    unspecified site 220
  specified site — *see* Neoplasm, by site, benign
  unspecified site 220
Cystadenoma (M8440/0) — *see also* Neoplasm,
  by site, benign
  bile duct (M8161/0) 211.5
  endometrioid (M8380/0) (*see also* Neoplasm,
    by site, benign)
    borderline malignancy (M8380/1) — *see*
      Neoplasm, by site, uncertain behav-
      ior
  malignant (M8440/3) — *see* Neoplasm, by
    site, malignant
  mucinous (M8470/0)
    borderline malignancy (M8470/1)
      specified site — *see* Neoplasm, uncer-
        tain behavior
      unspecified site 236.2
    papillary (M8471/0)
      borderline malignancy (M8471/1)
        specified site — *see* Neoplasm, by
          site, uncertain behavior
        unspecified site 236.2
      specified site — *see* Neoplasm, by site,
        benign
      unspecified site 220
    specified site — *see* Neoplasm, by site,
      benign
    unspecified site 220
  papillary (M8450/0)
    borderline malignancy (M8450/1)
      specified site — *see* Neoplasm, by site,
        uncertain behavior
      unspecified site 236.2
    lymphomatosum (M8561/0) 210.2
    mucinous (M8471/0)
      borderline malignancy (M8471/1)
        specified site — *see* Neoplasm, by
          site, uncertain behavior
        unspecified site 236.2
      specified site — *see* Neoplasm, by site,
        benign
      unspecified site 220
    pseudomucinous (M8471/0)
      borderline malignancy (M8471/1)
        specified site — *see* Neoplasm, by
          site, uncertain behavior
        unspecified site 236.2
      specified site — *see* Neoplasm, by site,
        benign
      unspecified site 220
    serous (M8460/0)
      borderline malignancy (M8460/1)
        specified site — *see* Neoplasm, by
          site, uncertain behavior
        unspecified site 236.2
      specified site — *see* Neoplasm, by site,
        benign
      unspecified site 220
    specified site — *see* Neoplasm, by site,
      benign
    unspecified site 220

☑ Additional Digit Required — Refer to the Tabular List for Digit Selection   ▽ Subterms under main terms may continue to next column or page

2010 ICD-9-CM   ▶◀ Revised Text   ● New Line   ▲ Revised Code   Volume 2 — 59

Cyst — Cystadenoma

Cystadenoma — *see also* Neoplasm, by site, benign — *continued*
pseudomucinous (M8470/0)
borderline malignancy (M8470/1)
specified site — *see* Neoplasm, by site, uncertain behavior
unspecified site 236.2
papillary (M8471/0)
borderline malignancy (M8471/1)
specified site — *see* Neoplasm, by site, uncertain behavior
unspecified site 236.2
specified site — *see* Neoplasm, by site, benign
unspecified site 220
specified site — *see* Neoplasm, by site, benign
unspecified site 220
serous (M8441/0)
borderline malignancy (M8441/1)
specified site — *see* Neoplasm, by site, uncertain behavior
unspecified site 236.2
papillary (M8460/0)
borderline malignancy (M8460/1)
specified site — *see* Neoplasm, by site, uncertain behavior
unspecified site 236.2
specified site — *see* Neoplasm, by site, benign
unspecified site 220
specified site — *see* Neoplasm, by site, benign
unspecified site 220
thyroid 226
Cystathioninemia 270.4
Cystathioninuria 270.4
Cystic — *see also* condition
breast, chronic 610.1
corpora lutea 620.1
degeneration, congenital
brain 742.4
kidney (*see also* Cystic, disease, kidney) 753.10
disease
breast, chronic 610.1
kidney, congenital 753.10
medullary 753.16
multiple 753.19
polycystic — *see* Polycystic, kidney
single 753.11
specified NEC 753.19
liver, congenital 751.62
lung 518.89
congenital 748.4

Cystic — *see also* condition — *continued*
disease — *continued*
pancreas, congenital 751.7
semilunar cartilage 717.5
duct — *see* condition
eyeball, congenital 743.03
fibrosis (pancreas) 277.00
with
manifestations
gastrointestinal 277.03
pulmonary 277.02
specified NEC 277.09
meconium ileus 277.01
pulmonary exacerbation 277.02
hygroma (M9173/0) 228.1
kidney, congenital 753.10
medullary 753.16
multiple 753.19
polycystic — *see* Polycystic, kidney
single 753.11
specified NEC 753.19
liver, congenital 751.62
lung 518.89
congenital 748.4
mass — *see* Cyst
mastitis, chronic 610.1
ovary 620.2
pancreas, congenital 751.7
Cysticerciasis 123.1
Cysticercosis (mammary) (subretinal) 123.1
Cysticercus 123.1
cellulosae infestation 123.1
Cystinosis (malignant) 270.0
Cystinuria 270.0
Cystitis (bacillary) (colli) (diffuse) (exudative) (hemorrhagic) (purulent) (recurrent) (septic) (suppurative) (ulcerative) 595.9
with
abortion — *see* Abortion, by type, with urinary tract infection
ectopic pregnancy (*see also* categories 633.0–633.9) 639.8
fibrosis 595.1
leukoplakia 595.1
malakoplakia 595.1
metaplasia 595.1
molar pregnancy (*see also* categories 630–632) 639.8
actinomycotic 039.8 *[595.4]*
acute 595.0
of trigone 595.3
allergic 595.89
amebic 006.8 *[595.4]*
bilharzial 120.9 *[595.4]*
blennorrhagic (acute) 098.11

Infection of the lower urinary tract (physicians sometimes use the term "UTI").

Cystitis — *continued*
blennorrhagic — *continued*
chronic or duration of 2 months or more 098.31
bullous 595.89
calculous 594.1
chlamydial 099.53
chronic 595.2
interstitial 595.1
of trigone 595.3
complicating pregnancy, childbirth, or puerperium 646.6 ☑
affecting fetus or newborn 760.1
cystic(a) 595.81
diphtheritic 032.84
echinococcal
granulosus 122.3 *[595.4]*
multilocularis 122.6 *[595.4]*
emphysematous 595.89
encysted 595.81
follicular 595.3
following
abortion 639.8
ectopic or molar pregnancy 639.8
gangrenous 595.89
glandularis 595.89
gonococcal (acute) 098.11
chronic or duration of 2 months or more 098.31
incrusted 595.89
interstitial 595.1
irradiation 595.82
irritation 595.89
malignant 595.89
monilial 112.2
of trigone 595.3
panmural 595.1
polyposa 595.89
prostatic 601.3
radiation 595.82
Reiter's (abacterial) 099.3
specified NEC 595.89
subacute 595.2
submucous 595.1
syphilitic 095.8
trichomoniasis 131.09
tuberculous (*see also* Tuberculosis) 016.1 ☑
ulcerative 595.1
Cystocele
female (without uterine prolapse) 618.01
with uterine prolapse 618.4
complete 618.3
incomplete 618.2
lateral 618.02
midline 618.01

Cystocele — *continued*
female — *continued*
paravaginal 618.02
in pregnancy or childbirth 654.4 ☑
affecting fetus or newborn 763.89
causing obstructed labor 660.2 ☑
affecting fetus or newborn 763.1
male 596.8
Cystoid
cicatrix limbus 372.64
degeneration macula 362.53
Cystolithiasis 594.1
Cystoma (M8440/0) — *see also* Neoplasm, by site, benign
endometrial, ovary 617.1
mucinous (M8470/0)
specified site — *see* Neoplasm, by site, benign
unspecified site 220
serous (M8441/0)
specified site — *see* Neoplasm, by site, benign
unspecified site 220
simple (ovary) 620.2
Cystoplegia 596.53
Cystoptosis 596.8
Cystopyelitis — *see also* Pyelitis 590.80
Cystorrhagia 596.8
Cystosarcoma phyllodes (M9020/1) 238.3
benign (M9020/0) 217
malignant (M9020/3) — *see* Neoplasm, breast, malignant
Cystostomy status V44.50
with complication 997.5
appendico-vesicostomy V44.52
cutaneous-vesicostomy V44.51
specified type NEC V44.59
Cystourethritis — *see also* Urethritis 597.89
Cystourethrocele — *see also* Cystocele
female (without uterine prolapse) 618.09
with uterine prolapse 618.4
complete 618.3
incomplete 618.2
male 596.8
Cytomegalic inclusion disease 078.5
congenital 771.1
Cytomycosis, reticuloendothelial — *see also* Histoplasmosis, American 115.00
Cytopenia 289.9
refractory
with
multilineage dysplasia (RCMD) 238.72
and ringed sideroblasts (RCMD-RS) 238.72

D

Daae (-Finsen) disease (epidemic pleurodynia) 074.1
Dabney's grip 074.1
Da Costa's syndrome (neurocirculatory asthenia) 306.2
Dacryoadenitis, dacryadenitis 375.00
  acute 375.01
  chronic 375.02
Dacryocystitis 375.30
  acute 375.32
  chronic 375.42
  neonatal 771.6
  phlegmonous 375.33
  syphilitic 095.8
    congenital 090.0
  trachomatous, active 076.1
    late effect 139.1
  tuberculous (see also Tuberculosis) 017.3 ☑
Dacryocystoblenorrhea 375.42
Dacryocystocele 375.43
Dacryolith, dacryolithiasis 375.57
Dacryoma 375.43
Dacryopericystitis (acute) (subacute) 375.32
  chronic 375.42
Dacryops 375.11
Dacryosialadenopathy, atrophic 710.2
Dacryostenosis 375.56
  congenital 743.65
Dactylitis
  bone (see also Osteomyelitis) 730.2 ☑
  sickle-cell 282.62
    Hb-C 282.64
    Hb-SS 282.62
    specified NEC 282.69
  syphilitic 095.5
  tuberculous (see also Tuberculosis) 015.5 ☑
Dactylolysis spontanea 136.0
Dactylosymphysis — see also Syndactylism 755.10
Damage
  arteriosclerotic — see Arteriosclerosis
  brain 348.9
    anoxic, hypoxic 348.1
      during or resulting from a procedure 997.01
      ischemic, in newborn 768.70 ▲
        mild 768.71 ●
        moderate 768.72 ●
        severe 768.73 ●
    child NEC 343.9
    due to birth injury 767.0
    minimal (child) (see also Hyperkinesia) 314.9
    newborn 767.0
  cardiac (see also Disease, heart)
  cardiorenal (vascular) (see also Hypertension, cardiorenal) 404.90
  central nervous system — see Damage, brain
  cerebral NEC — see Damage, brain
  coccyx, complicating delivery 665.6 ☑
  coronary (see also Ischemia, heart) 414.9
  eye, birth injury 767.8
  heart (see also Disease, heart)
    valve — see Endocarditis
  hypothalamus NEC 348.9
  liver 571.9
    alcoholic 571.3
  medication 995.20
  myocardium (see also Degeneration, myocardial) 429.1
  pelvic
    joint or ligament, during delivery 665.6 ☑
    organ NEC
      with
        abortion — see Abortion, by type, with damage to pelvic organs
        ectopic pregnancy (see also categories 633.0–633.9) 639.2
        molar pregnancy (see also categories 630–632) 639.2
      during delivery 665.5 ☑
      following
        abortion 639.2

Damage — continued
  pelvic — continued
    organ — continued
      following — continued
        ectopic or molar pregnancy 639.2
  renal (see also Disease, renal) 593.9
  skin, solar 692.79
    acute 692.72
    chronic 692.74
  subendocardium, subendocardial (see also Degeneration, myocardial) 429.1
  vascular 459.9
Dameshek's syndrome (erythroblastic anemia) 282.49
Dana-Putnam syndrome (subacute combined sclerosis with pernicious anemia) 281.0 [336.2]
Danbolt (-Closs) syndrome (acrodermatitis enteropathica) 686.8
Dandruff 690.18
Dandy fever 061
Dandy-Walker deformity or syndrome (atresia, foramen of Magendie) 742.3
  with spina bifida (see also Spina bifida) 741.0 ☑
Dangle foot 736.79
Danielssen's disease (anesthetic leprosy) 030.1
Danlos' syndrome 756.83
Darier's disease (congenital) (keratosis follicularis) 757.39
  due to vitamin A deficiency 264.8
  meaning erythema annulare centrifugum 695.0
Darier-Roussy sarcoid 135
Dark area on retina 239.81 ●
Darling's
  disease (see also Histoplasmosis, American) 115.00
  histoplasmosis (see also Histoplasmosis, American) 115.00
Dartre 054.9
Darwin's tubercle 744.29
Davidson's anemia (refractory) 284.9
Davies-Colley syndrome (slipping rib) 733.99
Davies' disease 425.0
Dawson's encephalitis 046.2
Day blindness — see also Blindness, day 368.60
Dead
  fetus
    retained (in utero) 656.4 ☑
      early pregnancy (death before 22 completed weeks gestation) 632
      late (death after 22 completed weeks gestation) 656.4 ☑
    syndrome 641.3 ☑
  labyrinth 386.50
  ovum, retained 631
Deaf and dumb NEC 389.7
Deaf mutism (acquired) (congenital) NEC 389.7
  endemic 243
  hysterical 300.11
  syphilitic, congenital 090.0
Deafness (acquired) (complete) (congenital) (hereditary) (middle ear) (partial) 389.9
  with
    blindness V49.85
    blue sclera and fragility of bone 756.51
  auditory fatigue 389.9
  aviation 993.0
    nerve injury 951.5
  boilermakers' 951.5
  central 389.14
    with conductive hearing loss 389.20
      bilateral 389.22
      unilateral 389.21
  conductive (air) 389.00
    with sensorineural hearing loss 389.20
      bilateral 389.22
      unilateral 389.21
    bilateral 389.06
    combined types 389.08
    external ear 389.01
    inner ear 389.04
    middle ear 389.03
    multiple types 389.08

Deafness — continued
  conductive — continued
    tympanic membrane 389.02
    unilateral 389.05
  emotional (complete) 300.11
  functional (complete) 300.11
  high frequency 389.8
  hysterical (complete) 300.11
  injury 951.5
  low frequency 389.8
  mental 784.69
  mixed conductive and sensorineural 389.20
    bilateral 389.22
    unilateral 389.21
  nerve
    with conductive hearing loss 389.20
      bilateral 389.22
      unilateral 389.21
    bilateral 389.12
    unilateral 389.13
  neural
    with conductive hearing loss 389.20
      bilateral 389.22
      unilateral 389.21
    bilateral 389.12
    unilateral 389.13
  noise-induced 388.12
    nerve injury 951.5
  nonspeaking 389.7
  perceptive 389.9
    with conductive hearing loss 389.20
      bilateral 389.22
      unilateral 389.21
    central 389.14
    neural
      bilateral 389.12
      unilateral 389.13
    sensorineural 389.10
      asymmetrical 389.16
      bilateral 389.18
      unilateral 389.15
    sensory
      bilateral 389.11
      unilateral 389.17
  psychogenic (complete) 306.7
  sensorineural (see also Deafness, perceptive) 389.10
    asymmetrical 389.16
    bilateral 389.18
    unilateral 389.15
  sensory
    with conductive hearing loss 389.20
      bilateral 389.22
      unilateral 389.21
    bilateral 389.11
    unilateral 389.17
  specified type NEC 389.8
  sudden NEC 388.2
  syphilitic 094.89
  transient ischemic 388.02
  transmission — see Deafness, conductive
  traumatic 951.5
  word (secondary to organic lesion) 784.69
    developmental 315.31
Death
  after delivery (cause not stated) (sudden) 674.9 ☑
  anesthetic
    due to
      correct substance properly administered 995.4
      overdose or wrong substance given 968.4
        specified anesthetic — see Table of Drugs and Chemicals
    during delivery 668.9 ☑
  brain 348.89 ▲
  cardiac (sudden) (SCD) — code to underlying condition
    family history of V17.41
    personal history of, successfully resuscitated V12.53
  cause unknown 798.2
  cot (infant) 798.0
  crib (infant) 798.0

Death — continued
  fetus, fetal (cause not stated) (intrauterine) 779.9
    early, with retention (before 22 completed weeks gestation) 632
    from asphyxia or anoxia (before labor) 768.0
      during labor 768.1
    late, affecting management of pregnancy (after 22 completed weeks gestation) 656.4 ☑
  from pregnancy NEC 646.9 ☑
  instantaneous 798.1
  intrauterine (see also Death, fetus) 779.9
    complicating pregnancy 656.4 ☑
  maternal, affecting fetus or newborn 761.6
  neonatal NEC 779.9
  sudden (cause unknown) 798.1
    cardiac (SCD)
      family history of V17.41
      personal history of, successfully resuscitated V12.53
    during delivery 669.9 ☑
      under anesthesia NEC 668.9 ☑
    infant, syndrome (SIDS) 798.0
    puerperal, during puerperium 674.9 ☑
  unattended (cause unknown) 798.9
  under anesthesia NEC
    due to
      correct substance properly administered 995.4
      overdose or wrong substance given 968.4
        specified anesthetic — see Table of Drugs and Chemicals
    during delivery 668.9 ☑
  violent 798.1
de Beurmann-Gougerot disease (sporotrichosis) 117.1
Debility (general) (infantile) (postinfectional) 799.3
  with nutritional difficulty 269.9
  congenital or neonatal NEC 779.9
  nervous 300.5
  old age 797
  senile 797
Débove's disease (splenomegaly) 789.2
Decalcification
  bone (see also Osteoporosis) 733.00
  teeth 521.89
Decapitation 874.9
  fetal (to facilitate delivery) 763.89
Decapsulation, kidney 593.89
Decay
  dental 521.00
  senile 797
  tooth, teeth 521.00
Decensus, uterus — see Prolapse, uterus
Deciduitis (acute)
  with
    abortion — see Abortion, by type, with sepsis
    ectopic pregnancy (see also categories 633.0–633.9) 639.0
    molar pregnancy (see also categories 630–632) 639.0
  affecting fetus or newborn 760.8
  following
    abortion 639.0
    ectopic or molar pregnancy 639.0
  in pregnancy 646.6 ☑
  puerperal, postpartum 670.1 ☑ ▲
Deciduoma malignum (M9100/3) 181
Deciduous tooth (retained) 520.6
Decline (general) — see also Debility 799.3
Decompensation
  cardiac (acute) (chronic) (see also Disease, heart) 429.9
    failure — see Failure, heart
  cardiorenal (see also Hypertension, cardiorenal) 404.90
  cardiovascular (see also Disease, cardiovascular) 429.2
  heart (see also Disease, heart) 429.9
    failure — see Failure, heart
  hepatic 572.2

☑ Additional Digit Required — Refer to the Tabular List for Digit Selection   ▽ Subterms under main terms may continue to next column or page

2010 ICD-9-CM   ►◄ Revised Text   ● New Line   ▲ Revised Code   October 2009 • Volume 2 — 61

Decompensation — *continued*
- myocardial (acute) (chronic) (*see also* Disease, heart) 429.9
- failure — *see* Failure, heart
- respiratory 519.9

Decompression sickness 993.3

Decrease, decreased
- blood
  - platelets (*see also* Thrombocytopenia) 287.5
  - pressure 796.3
    - due to shock following
      - injury 958.4
      - operation 998.0
  - white cell count 288.50
    - specified NEC 288.59
- cardiac reserve — *see* Disease, heart
- estrogen 256.39
  - postablative 256.2
- fetal movements 655.7 ☑
- fragility of erythrocytes 289.89
- function
  - adrenal (cortex) 255.41
    - medulla 255.5
  - ovary in hypopituitarism 253.4
  - parenchyma of pancreas 577.8
  - pituitary (gland) (lobe) (anterior) 253.2
    - posterior (lobe) 253.8
- functional activity 780.99
- glucose 790.29
- haptoglobin (serum) NEC 273.8
- leukocytes 288.50
- libido 799.81
- lymphocytes 288.51
- platelets (*see also* Thrombocytopenia) 287.5
- pulse pressure 785.9
- respiration due to shock following injury 958.4
- sexual desire 799.81
- tear secretion NEC 375.15
- tolerance
  - fat 579.8
  - salt and water 276.9
- vision NEC 369.9
- white blood cell count 288.50

Decubital gangrene — *see also* Ulcer, pressure 707.00 [785.4]

Decubiti — *see also* Ulcer, pressure 707.00

Decubitus (ulcer) — *see also* Ulcer, pressure 707.00
- with gangrene 707.00 [785.4]
- ankle 707.06
- back
  - lower 707.03
  - upper 707.02
- buttock 707.05
- coccyx 707.03
- elbow 707.01
- head 707.09
- heel 707.07
- hip 707.04
- other site 707.09
- sacrum 707.03
- shoulder blades 707.02

Deepening acetabulum 718.85

Defect, defective 759.9
- 3-beta-hydroxysteroid dehydrogenase 255.2
- 11-hydroxylase 255.2
- 21-hydroxylase 255.2
- abdominal wall, congenital 756.70
- aorticopulmonary septum 745.0
- aortic septal 745.0
- atrial septal (ostium secundum type) 745.5
  - acquired 429.71
  - ostium primum type 745.61
  - sinus venosus 745.8
- atrioventricular
  - canal 745.69
  - septum 745.4
    - acquired 429.71
- atrium secundum 745.5
  - acquired 429.71
- auricular septal 745.5
  - acquired 429.71
- bilirubin excretion 277.4
- biosynthesis, testicular androgen 257.2
- bridge 525.60

Defect, defective — *continued*
- bulbar septum 745.0
- butanol-insoluble iodide 246.1
- chromosome — *see* Anomaly, chromosome
- circulation (acquired) 459.9
  - congenital 747.9
  - newborn 747.9
- clotting NEC (*see also* Defect, coagulation) 286.9
- coagulation (factor) (*see also* Deficiency, coagulation factor) 286.9
  - with
    - abortion — *see* Abortion, by type, with hemorrhage
    - ectopic pregnancy (*see also* categories 634–638) 639.1
    - molar pregnancy (*see also* categories 630–632) 639.1
  - acquired (any) 286.7
  - antepartum or intrapartum 641.3 ☑
    - affecting fetus or newborn 762.1
  - causing hemorrhage of pregnancy or delivery 641.3 ☑
  - complicating pregnancy, childbirth, or puerperium 649.3 ☑
  - due to
    - liver disease 286.7
    - vitamin K deficiency 286.7
  - newborn, transient 776.3
  - postpartum 666.3 ☑
  - specified type NEC 286.9
- conduction (heart) 426.9
  - bone (*see also* Deafness, conductive) 389.00
- congenital, organ or site NEC (*see also* Anomaly)
  - circulation 747.9
  - Descemet's membrane 743.9
    - specified type NEC 743.49
  - diaphragm 756.6
  - ectodermal 757.9
  - esophagus 750.9
  - pulmonic cusps — *see* Anomaly, heart valve
  - respiratory system 748.9
    - specified type NEC 748.8
- crown 525.60
- cushion endocardial 745.60
- dental restoration 525.60
- dentin (hereditary) 520.5
- Descemet's membrane (congenital) 743.9
  - acquired 371.30
  - specific type NEC 743.49
- deutan 368.52
- developmental (*see also* Anomaly, by site)
  - cauda equina 742.59
  - left ventricle 746.9
    - with atresia or hypoplasia of aortic orifice or valve, with hypoplasia of ascending aorta 746.7
    - in hypoplastic left heart syndrome 746.7
  - testis 752.9
  - vessel 747.9
- diaphragm
  - with elevation, eventration, or hernia — *see* Hernia, diaphragm
  - congenital 756.6
    - with elevation, eventration, or hernia 756.6
    - gross (with elevation, eventration, or hernia) 756.6
- ectodermal, congenital 757.9
- Eisenmenger's (ventricular septal defect) 745.4
- endocardial cushion 745.60
  - specified type NEC 745.69
- esophagus, congenital 750.9
- extensor retinaculum 728.9
- fibrin polymerization (*see also* Defect, coagulation) 286.3
- filling
  - biliary tract 793.3
  - bladder 793.5
  - dental 525.60
  - gallbladder 793.3
  - kidney 793.5

Defect, defective — *continued*
- filling — *continued*
  - stomach 793.4
  - ureter 793.5
- fossa ovalis 745.5
- gene, carrier (suspected) of V83.89
- Gerbode 745.4
- glaucomatous, without elevated tension 365.89
- Hageman (factor) (*see also* Defect, coagulation) 286.3
- hearing (*see also* Deafness) 389.9
- high grade 317
- homogentisic acid 270.2
- interatrial septal 745.5
  - acquired 429.71
- interauricular septal 745.5
  - acquired 429.71
- interventricular septal 745.4
  - with pulmonary stenosis or atresia, dextraposition of aorta, and hypertrophy of right ventricle 745.2
  - acquired 429.71
  - in tetralogy of Fallot 745.2
- iodide trapping 246.1
- iodotyrosine dehalogenase 246.1
- kynureninase 270.2
- learning, specific 315.2
- major osseous 731.3
- mental (*see also* Retardation, mental) 319
- osseous, major 731.3
- osteochondral NEC 738.8
- ostium
  - primum 745.61
  - secundum 745.5
- pericardium 746.89
- peroxidase-binding 246.1
- placental blood supply — *see* Placenta, insufficiency
- platelet (qualitative) 287.1
  - constitutional 286.4
- postural, spine 737.9
- protan 368.51
- pulmonic cusps, congenital 746.00
- renal pelvis 753.9
  - obstructive 753.29
  - specified type NEC 753.3
- respiratory system, congenital 748.9
  - specified type NEC 748.8
- retina, retinal 361.30
  - with detachment (*see also* Detachment, retina, with retinal defect) 361.00
    - multiple 361.33
      - with detachment 361.02
    - nerve fiber bundle 362.85
    - single 361.30
      - with detachment 361.01
- septal (closure) (heart) NEC 745.9
  - acquired 429.71
  - atrial 745.5
  - specified type NEC 745.8
- speech NEC 784.59 ▲
  - developmental 315.39
  - late effect of cerebrovascular disease — ●
    - *see* Late effect(s) (of) cerebrovas- ●
    - cular disease, speech and lan- ●
    - guage deficit ●
  - secondary to organic lesion 784.59 ▲
- Taussig-Bing (transposition, aorta and overriding pulmonary artery) 745.11
- teeth, wedge 521.20
- thyroid hormone synthesis 246.1
- tritan 368.53
- ureter 753.9
  - obstructive 753.29
- vascular (acquired) (local) 459.9
  - congenital (peripheral) NEC 747.60
    - gastrointestinal 747.61
    - lower limb 747.64
    - renal 747.62
    - specified NEC 747.69
    - spinal 747.82
    - upper limb 747.63
- ventricular septal 745.4

Defect, defective — *continued*
- ventricular septal — *continued*
  - with pulmonary stenosis or atresia, dextraposition of aorta, and hypertrophy of right ventricle 745.2
  - acquired 429.71
  - atrioventricular canal type 745.69
  - between infundibulum and anterior portion 745.4
  - in tetralogy of Fallot 745.2
  - isolated anterior 745.4
- vision NEC 369.9
- visual field 368.40
  - arcuate 368.43
  - heteronymous, bilateral 368.47
  - homonymous, bilateral 368.46
  - localized NEC 368.44
  - nasal step 368.44
  - peripheral 368.44
  - sector 368.43
- voice ▶and resonance◀ 784.40
- wedge, teeth (abrasion) 521.20

Defeminization syndrome 255.2

Deferentitis 608.4
- gonorrheal (acute) 098.14
  - chronic or duration of 2 months or over 098.34

Defibrination syndrome — *see also* Fibrinolysis 286.6

Deficiency, deficient
- 3-beta-hydroxysteroid dehydrogenase 255.2
- 6-phosphogluconic dehydrogenase (anemia) 282.2
- 11-beta-hydroxylase 255.2
- 17-alpha-hydroxylase 255.2
- 18-hydroxysteroid dehydrogenase 255.2
- 20-alpha-hydroxylase 255.2
- 21-hydroxylase 255.2
- AAT (alpha-1 antitrypsin) 273.4
- abdominal muscle syndrome 756.79
- accelerator globulin (Ac G) (blood) (*see also* Defect, coagulation) 286.3
- AC globulin (congenital) (*see also* Defect, coagulation) 286.3
  - acquired 286.7
- activating factor (blood) (*see also* Defect, coagulation) 286.3
- adenohypophyseal 253.2
- adenosine deaminase 277.2
- aldolase (hereditary) 271.2
- alpha-1-antitrypsin 273.4
- alpha-1-trypsin inhibitor 273.4
- alpha-fucosidase 271.8
- alpha-lipoprotein 272.5
- alpha-mannosidase 271.8
- amino acid 270.9
- anemia — *see* Anemia, deficiency
- aneurin 265.1
  - with beriberi 265.0
- antibody NEC 279.00
- antidiuretic hormone 253.5
- antihemophilic
  - factor (A) 286.0
    - B 286.1
    - C 286.2
  - globulin (AHG) NEC 286.0
- antithrombin III 289.81
- antitrypsin 273.4
- argininosuccinate synthetase or lyase 270.6
- ascorbic acid (with scurvy) 267
- autoprothrombin
  - I (*see also* Defect, coagulation) 286.3
  - II 286.1
  - C (*see also* Defect, coagulation) 286.3
- bile salt 579.8
- biotin 266.2
- biotinidase 277.6
- bradykinase-1 277.6
- brancher enzyme (amylopectinosis) 271.0
- calciferol 268.9
  - with
    - osteomalacia 268.2
    - rickets (*see also* Rickets) 268.0
- calcium 275.40
  - dietary 269.3
- calorie, severe 261

Left margin: Index

Left margin: Decompensation — Deficiency, deficient

Deficiency, deficient — *continued*
carbamyl phosphate synthetase 270.6
cardiac (*see also* Insufficiency, myocardial) 428.0
carnitine 277.81
due to
hemodialysis 277.83
inborn errors of metabolism 277.82
valproic acid therapy 277.83
iatrogenic 277.83
palmitoyltransferase (CPT1, CPT2) 277.85
palmityl transferase (CPT1, CPT2) 277.85
primary 277.81
secondary 277.84
carotene 264.9
Carr factor (*see also* Defect, coagulation) 286.9
central nervous system 349.9
ceruloplasmin 275.1
cevitamic acid (with scurvy) 267
choline 266.2
Christmas factor 286.1
chromium 269.3
citrin 269.1
clotting (blood) (*see also* Defect, coagulation) 286.9
coagulation factor NEC 286.9
with
abortion — *see* Abortion, by type, with hemorrhage
ectopic pregnancy (*see also* categories 634–638) 639.1
molar pregnancy (*see also* categories 630–632) 639.1
acquired (any) 286.7
antepartum or intrapartum 641.3 ☑
affecting fetus or newborn 762.1
complicating pregnancy, childbirth, or puerperium 649.3 ☑
due to
liver disease 286.7
vitamin K deficiency 286.7
newborn, transient 776.3
postpartum 666.3 ☑
specified type NEC 286.3
color vision (congenital) 368.59
acquired 368.55
combined glucocorticoid and mineralocorticoid 255.41
combined, two or more coagulation factors (*see also* Defect, coagulation) 286.9
complement factor NEC 279.8
contact factor (*see also* Defect, coagulation) 286.3
copper NEC 275.1
corticoadrenal 255.41
craniofacial axis 756.0
cyanocobalamin (vitamin B₁₂) 266.2
debrancher enzyme (limit dextrinosis) 271.0
desmolase 255.2
diet 269.9
dihydrofolate reductase 281.2
dihydropteridine reductase 270.1
disaccharidase (intestinal) 271.3
disease NEC 269.9
ear(s) V48.8
edema 262
endocrine 259.9
enzymes, circulating NEC (*see also* Deficiency, by specific enzyme) 277.6
ergosterol 268.9
with
osteomalacia 268.2
rickets (*see also* Rickets) 268.0
erythrocytic glutathione (anemia) 282.2
eyelid(s) V48.8
factor (*see also* Defect, coagulation) 286.9
I (congenital) (fibrinogen) 286.3
antepartum or intrapartum 641.3 ☑
affecting fetus or newborn 762.1
newborn, transient 776.3
postpartum 666.3 ☑
II (congenital) (prothrombin) 286.3
V (congenital) (labile) 286.3
VII (congenital) (stable) 286.3
VIII (congenital) (functional) 286.0

factor (*see also* Defect, coagulation) — *continued*
VIII — *continued*
with
functional defect 286.0
vascular defect 286.4
IX (Christmas) (congenital) (functional) 286.1
X (congenital) (Stuart-Prower) 286.3
XI (congenital) (plasma thromboplastin antecedent) 286.2
XII (congenital) (Hageman) 286.3
XIII (congenital) (fibrin stabilizing) 286.3
Hageman 286.3
multiple (congenital) 286.9
acquired 286.7
fibrinase (*see also* Defect, coagulation) 286.3
fibrinogen (congenital) (*see also* Defect, coagulation) 286.3
acquired 286.6
fibrin-stabilizing factor (congenital) (*see also* Defect, coagulation) 286.3
finger — *see* Absence, finger
fletcher factor (*see also* Defect, coagulation) 286.9
fluorine 269.3
folate, anemia 281.2
folic acid (vitamin B꜀) 266.2
anemia 281.2
follicle-stimulating hormone (FSH) 253.4
fructokinase 271.2
fructose-1, 6-diphosphate 271.2
fructose-1-phosphate aldolase 271.2
FSH (follicle-stimulating hormone) 253.4
fucosidase 271.8
galactokinase 271.1
galactose-1-phosphate uridyl transferase 271.1
gamma globulin in blood 279.00
glass factor (*see also* Defect, coagulation) 286.3
glucocorticoid 255.41
glucose-6-phosphatase 271.0
glucose-6-phosphate dehydrogenase anemia 282.2
glucuronyl transferase 277.4
glutathione-reductase (anemia) 282.2
glycogen synthetase 271.0
growth hormone 253.3
Hageman factor (congenital) (*see also* Defect, coagulation) 286.3
head V48.0
hemoglobin (*see also* Anemia) 285.9
hepatophosphorylase 271.0
hexose monophosphate (HMP) shunt 282.2
HGH (human growth hormone) 253.3
HG-PRT 277.2
homogentisic acid oxidase 270.2
hormone (*see also* Deficiency, by specific hormone)
anterior pituitary (isolated) (partial) NEC 253.4
growth (human) 253.3
follicle-stimulating 253.4
growth (human) (isolated) 253.3
human growth 253.3
interstitial cell-stimulating 253.4
luteinizing 253.4
melanocyte-stimulating 253.4
testicular 257.2
human growth hormone 253.3
humoral 279.00
with
hyper-IgM 279.05
autosomal recessive 279.05
X-linked 279.05
increased IgM 279.05
congenital hypogammaglobulinemia 279.04
non-sex-linked 279.06
selective immunoglobulin NEC 279.03
IgA 279.01
IgG 279.03
IgM 279.02
increased 279.05
specified NEC 279.09
hydroxylase 255.2

Deficiency, deficient — *continued*
hypoxanthine-guanine phosphoribosyltransferase (HG-PRT) 277.2
ICSH (interstitial cell-stimulating hormone) 253.4
immunity NEC 279.3
cell-mediated 279.10
with
hyperimmunoglobulinemia 279.2
thrombocytopenia and eczema 279.12
specified NEC 279.19
combined (severe) 279.2
syndrome 279.2
common variable 279.06
humoral NEC 279.00
IgA (secretory) 279.01
IgG 279.03
IgM 279.02
immunoglobulin, selective NEC 279.03
IgA 279.01
IgG 279.03
IgM 279.02
inositol (B complex) 266.2
interferon 279.49 ▲
internal organ V47.0
interstitial cell-stimulating hormone (ICSH) 253.4
intrinsic factor (Castle's) (congenital) 281.0
intrinsic (urethral) sphincter (ISD) 599.82
invertase 271.3
iodine 269.3
iron, anemia 280.9
labile factor (congenital) (*see also* Defect, coagulation) 286.3
acquired 286.7
lacrimal fluid (acquired) 375.15
congenital 743.64
lactase 271.3
Laki-Lorand factor (*see also* Defect, coagulation) 286.3
lecithin-cholesterol acyltranferase 272.5
LH (luteinizing hormone) 253.4
limb V49.0
lower V49.0
congenital (*see also* Deficiency, lower limb, congenital) 755.30
upper V49.0
congenital (*see also* Deficiency, upper limb, congenital) 755.20
lipocaic 577.8
lipoid (high-density) 272.5
lipoprotein (familial) (high density) 272.5
liver phosphorylase 271.0
long chain 3-hydroxyacyl CoA dehydrogenase (LCHAD) 277.85
long chain/very long chain acyl CoA dehydrogenase (LCAD, VLCAD) 277.85
lower limb V49.0
congenital 755.30
with complete absence of distal elements 755.31
longitudinal (complete) (partial) (with distal deficiencies, incomplete) 755.32
with complete absence of distal elements 755.31
combined femoral, tibial, fibular (incomplete) 755.33
femoral 755.34
fibular 755.37
metatarsal(s) 755.38
phalange(s) 755.39
meaning all digits 755.31
tarsal(s) 755.38
tibia 755.36
tibiofibular 755.35
transverse 755.31
luteinizing hormone (LH) 253.4
lysosomal alpha-1, 4 glucosidase 271.0
magnesium 275.2
mannosidase 271.8
medium chain acyl CoA dehydrogenase (MCAD) 277.85
melanocyte-stimulating hormone (MSH) 253.4
menadione (vitamin K) 269.0

Deficiency, deficient — *continued*
menadione — *continued*
newborn 776.0
mental (familial) (hereditary) (*see also* Retardation, mental) 319
methylenetetrahydrofolate reductase (MTHFR) 270.4
mineral NEC 269.3
mineralocorticoid 255.42
molybdenum 269.3
moral 301.7
multiple, syndrome 260
myocardial (*see also* Insufficiency, myocardial) 428.0
myophosphorylase 271.0
NADH-diaphorase or reductase (congenital) 289.7
NADH (DPNH)-methemoglobin-reductase (congenital) 289.7
neck V48.1
niacin (amide) (-tryptophan) 265.2
nicotinamide 265.2
nicotinic acid (amide) 265.2
nose V48.8
number of teeth (*see also* Anodontia) 520.0
nutrition, nutritional 269.9
specified NEC 269.8
ornithine transcarbamylase 270.6
ovarian 256.39
oxygen (*see also* Anoxia) 799.02
pantothenic acid 266.2
parathyroid (gland) 252.1
phenylalanine hydroxylase 270.1
phosphoenolpyruvate carboxykinase 271.8
phosphofructokinase 271.2
phosphoglucomutase 271.0
phosphohexosisomerase 271.8
phosphomannomutase 271.8
phosphomannose isomerase 271.8
phosphomannosyl mutase 271.8
phosphorylase kinase, liver 271.0
pituitary (anterior) 253.2
posterior 253.5
placenta — *see* Placenta, insufficiency
plasma
cell 279.00
protein (paraproteinemia) (pyroglobulinemia) 273.8
gamma globulin 279.00
thromboplastin
antecedent (PTA) 286.2
component (PTC) 286.1
platelet NEC 287.1
constitutional 286.4
polyglandular 258.9
potassium (K) 276.8
proaccelerin (congenital) (*see also* Defect, coagulation) 286.3
acquired 286.7
proconvertin factor (congenital) (*see also* Defect, coagulation) 286.3
acquired 286.7
prolactin 253.4
protein 260
anemia 281.4
C 289.81
plasma — *see* Deficiency, plasma, protein
S 289.81
prothrombin (congenital) (*see also* Defect, coagulation) 286.3
acquired 286.7
Prower factor (*see also* Defect, coagulation) 286.3
PRT 277.2
pseudocholinesterase 289.89
psychobiological 301.6
PTA 286.2
PTC 286.1
purine nucleoside phosphorylase 277.2
pyracin (alpha) (beta) 266.1
pyridoxal 266.1
pyridoxamine 266.1
pyridoxine (derivatives) 266.1
pyruvate carboxylase 271.8
pyruvate dehydrogenase 271.8
pyruvate kinase (PK) 282.3

☑ Additional Digit Required — Refer to the Tabular List for Digit Selection ⯈◀ Revised Text ● New Line ▲ Revised Code ⯇ Subterms under main terms may continue to next column or page

2010 ICD-9-CM October 2009 • Volume 2 — 63

Deficiency, deficient — *continued*
riboflavin (vitamin B$_2$) 266.0
saccadic eye movements 379.57
salivation 527.7
salt 276.1
secretion
ovary 256.39
salivary gland (any) 527.7
urine 788.5
selenium 269.3
serum
antitrypsin, familial 273.4
protein (congenital) 273.8
short chain acyl CoA dehydrogenase (SCAD) 277.85
short stature homeobox gene (SHOX)
with
dyschondrosteosis 756.89
short stature (idiopathic) 783.43
Turner's syndrome 758.6
smooth pursuit movements (eye) 379.58
sodium (Na) 276.1
SPCA (*see also* Defect, coagulation) 286.3
specified NEC 269.8
stable factor (congenital) (*see also* Defect, coagulation) 286.3
acquired 286.7
Stuart (-Prower) factor (*see also* Defect, coagulation) 286.3
sucrase 271.3
sucrase-isomaltase 271.3
sulfite oxidase 270.0
syndrome, multiple 260
thiamine, thiaminic (chloride) 265.1
thrombokinase (*see also* Defect, coagulation) 286.3
newborn 776.0
thrombopoieten 287.39
thymolymphatic 279.2
thyroid (gland) 244.9
tocopherol 269.1
toe — *see* Absence, toe
tooth bud (*see also* Anodontia) 520.0
trunk V48.1
UDPG-glycogen transferase 271.0
upper limb V49.0
congenital 755.20
with complete absence of distal elements 755.21
longitudinal (complete) (partial) (with distal deficiencies, incomplete) 755.22
carpal(s) 755.28
combined humeral, radial, ulnar (incomplete) 755.23
humeral 755.24
metacarpal(s) 755.28
phalange(s) 755.29
meaning all digits 755.21
radial 755.26
radioulnar 755.25
ulnar 755.27
transverse (complete) (partial) 755.21
vascular 459.9
vasopressin 253.5
viosterol (*see also* Deficiency, calciferol) 268.9
vitamin (multiple) NEC 269.2
A 264.9
with
Bitôt's spot 264.1
corneal 264.2
with corneal ulceration 264.3
keratomalacia 264.4
keratosis, follicular 264.8
night blindness 264.5
scar of cornea, xerophthalmic 264.6
specified manifestation NEC 264.8
ocular 264.7
xeroderma 264.8
xerophthalmia 264.7
xerosis
conjunctival 264.0
with Bitôt's spot 264.1
corneal 264.2

Deficiency, deficient — *continued*
vitamin — *continued*
A — *continued*
with — *continued*
xerosis — *continued*
corneal — *continued*
with corneal ulceration 264.3
B (complex) NEC 266.9
with
beriberi 265.0
pellagra 265.2
specified type NEC 266.2
B$_1$ NEC 265.1
beriberi 265.0
B$_2$ 266.0
B$_6$ 266.1
B$_{12}$ 266.2
B$_c$ (folic acid) 266.2
C (ascorbic acid) (with scurvy) 267
D (calciferol) (ergosterol) 268.9
with
osteomalacia 268.2
rickets (*see also* Rickets) 268.0
E 269.1
folic acid 266.2
G 266.0
H 266.2
K 269.0
of newborn 776.0
nicotinic acid 265.2
P 269.1
PP 265.2
specified NEC 269.1
zinc 269.3
Deficient — *see also* Deficiency
blink reflex 374.45
craniofacial axis 756.0
number of teeth (*see also* Anodontia) 520.0
secretion of urine 788.5
Deficit
neurologic NEC 781.99
due to
cerebrovascular lesion (*see also* Disease, cerebrovascular, acute) 436
late effect — *see* Late effect(s) (of) cerebrovascular disease
transient ischemic attack 435.9
ischemic
reversible (RIND) 434.91
history of (personal) V12.54
prolonged (PRIND) 434.91
history of (personal) V12.54
oxygen 799.02
Deflection
radius 736.09
septum (acquired) (nasal) (nose) 470
spine — *see* Curvature, spine
turbinate (nose) 470
Defluvium
capillorum (*see also* Alopecia) 704.00
ciliorum 374.55
unguium 703.8
Deformity 738.9
abdomen, congenital 759.9
abdominal wall
acquired 738.8
congenital 756.70
muscle deficiency syndrome 756.79
acquired (unspecified site) 738.9
specified site NEC 738.8
adrenal gland (congenital) 759.1
alimentary tract, congenital 751.9
lower 751.5
specified type NEC 751.8
upper (any part, except tongue) 750.9
specified type NEC 750.8
tongue 750.10
specified type NEC 750.19
ankle (joint) (acquired) 736.70
abduction 718.47
congenital 755.69
contraction 718.47
specified NEC 736.79
anus (congenital) 751.5

Deformity — *continued*
anus — *continued*
acquired 569.49
aorta (congenital) 747.20
acquired 447.8
arch 747.21
acquired 447.8
coarctation 747.10
aortic
arch 747.21
acquired 447.8
cusp or valve (congenital) 746.9
acquired (*see also* Endocarditis, aortic) 424.1
ring 747.21
appendix 751.5
arm (acquired) 736.89
congenital 755.50
arteriovenous (congenital) (peripheral) NEC 747.60
gastrointestinal 747.61
lower limb 747.64
renal 747.62
specified NEC 747.69
spinal 747.82
upper limb 747.63
artery (congenital) (peripheral) NEC (*see also* Deformity, vascular) 747.60
acquired 447.8
cerebral 747.81
coronary (congenital) 746.85
acquired (*see also* Ischemia, heart) 414.9
retinal 743.9
umbilical 747.5
atrial septal (congenital) (heart) 745.5
auditory canal (congenital) (external) (*see also* Deformity, ear) 744.3
acquired 380.50
auricle
ear (congenital) (*see also* Deformity, ear) 744.3
acquired 380.32
heart (congenital) 746.9
back (acquired) — *see* Deformity, spine
Bartholin's duct (congenital) 750.9
bile duct (congenital) 751.60
acquired 576.8
with calculus, choledocholithiasis, or stones — *see* Choledocholithiasis
biliary duct or passage (congenital) 751.60
acquired 576.8
with calculus, choledocholithiasis, or stones — *see* Choledocholithiasis
bladder (neck) (sphincter) (trigone) (acquired) 596.8
congenital 753.9
bone (acquired) NEC 738.9
congenital 756.9
turbinate 738.0
boutonniere (finger) 736.21
brain (congenital) 742.9
acquired 348.89 ▲
multiple 742.4
reduction 742.2
vessel (congenital) 747.81
breast (acquired) 611.89
congenital 757.6 ▲
reconstructed 612.0
bronchus (congenital) 748.3
acquired 519.19
bursa, congenital 756.9
canal of Nuck 752.9
canthus (congenital) 743.9
acquired 374.89
capillary (acquired) 448.9
congenital NEC (*see also* Deformity, vascular) 747.60
cardiac — *see* Deformity, heart
cardiovascular system (congenital) 746.9
caruncle, lacrimal (congenital) 743.9
acquired 375.69
cascade, stomach 537.6
cecum (congenital) 751.5

Deformity — *continued*
cecum — *continued*
acquired 569.89
cerebral (congenital) 742.9
acquired 348.89 ▲
cervix (acquired) (uterus) 622.8
congenital 752.40
cheek (acquired) 738.19
congenital 744.9
chest (wall) (acquired) 738.3
congenital 754.89
late effect of rickets 268.1
chin (acquired) 738.19
congenital 744.9
choroid (congenital) 743.9
acquired 363.8
plexus (congenital) 742.9
acquired 349.2
cicatricial — *see* Cicatrix
cilia (congenital) 743.9
acquired 374.89
circulatory system (congenital) 747.9
clavicle (acquired) 738.8
congenital 755.51
clitoris (congenital) 752.40
acquired 624.8
clubfoot — *see* Clubfoot
coccyx (acquired) 738.6
congenital 756.10
colon (congenital) 751.5
acquired 569.89
concha (ear) (congenital) (*see also* Deformity, ear) 744.3
acquired 380.32
congenital, organ or site not listed (*see also* Anomaly) 759.9
cornea (congenital) 743.9
acquired 371.70
coronary artery (congenital) 746.85
acquired (*see also* Ischemia, heart) 414.9
cranium (acquired) 738.19
congenital (*see also* Deformity, skull, congenital) 756.0
cricoid cartilage (congenital) 748.3
acquired 478.79
cystic duct (congenital) 751.60
acquired 575.8
Dandy-Walker 742.3
with spina bifida (*see also* Spina bifida) 741.0 ☑
diaphragm (congenital) 756.6
acquired 738.8
digestive organ(s) or system (congenital) NEC 751.9
specified type NEC 751.8
ductus arteriosus 747.0
duodenal bulb 537.89
duodenum (congenital) 751.5
acquired 537.89
dura (congenital) 742.9
brain 742.4
acquired 349.2
spinal 742.59
acquired 349.2
ear (congenital) 744.3
acquired 380.32
auricle 744.3
causing impairment of hearing 744.02
causing impairment of hearing 744.00
external 744.3
causing impairment of hearing 744.02
internal 744.05
lobule 744.3
middle 744.03
ossicles 744.04
ossicles 744.04
ectodermal (congenital) NEC 757.9
specified type NEC 757.8
ejaculatory duct (congenital) 752.9
acquired 608.89
elbow (joint) (acquired) 736.00
congenital 755.50
contraction 718.42
endocrine gland NEC 759.2
epididymis (congenital) 752.9
acquired 608.89

Deformity — *continued*
  epididymis — *continued*
    torsion 608.24
  epiglottis (congenital) 748.3
    acquired 478.79
  esophagus (congenital) 750.9
    acquired 530.89
  Eustachian tube (congenital) NEC 744.3
    specified type NEC 744.24
  extremity (acquired) 736.9
    congenital, except reduction deformity 755.9
      lower 755.60
      upper 755.50
    reduction — *see* Deformity, reduction
  eye (congenital) 743.9
    acquired 379.8
    muscle 743.9
  eyebrow (congenital) 744.89
  eyelid (congenital) 743.9
    acquired 374.89
    specified type NEC 743.62
  face (acquired) 738.19
    congenital (any part) 744.9
      due to intrauterine malposition and pressure 754.0
  fallopian tube (congenital) 752.10
    acquired 620.8
  femur (acquired) 736.89
    congenital 755.60
  fetal
    with fetopelvic disproportion 653.7 ☑
      affecting fetus or newborn 763.1
    causing obstructed labor 660.1 ☑
      affecting fetus or newborn 763.1
    known or suspected, affecting management of pregnancy 655.9 ☑
  finger (acquired) 736.20
    boutonniere type 736.21
    congenital 755.50
    flexion contracture 718.44
    swan neck 736.22
  flexion (joint) (acquired) 736.9
    congenital NEC 755.9
    hip or thigh (acquired) 736.39
      congenital (*see also* Subluxation, congenital, hip) 754.32
  foot (acquired) 736.70
    cavovarus 736.75
      congenital 754.59
    congenital NEC 754.70
      specified type NEC 754.79
    valgus (acquired) 736.79
      congenital 754.60
        specified type NEC 754.69
    varus (acquired) 736.79
      congenital 754.50
        specified type NEC 754.59
  forearm (acquired) 736.00
    congenital 755.50
  forehead (acquired) 738.19
    congenital (*see also* Deformity, skull, congenital) 756.0
  frontal bone (acquired) 738.19
    congenital (*see also* Deformity, skull, congenital) 756.0
  gallbladder (congenital) 751.60
    acquired 575.8
  gastrointestinal tract (congenital) NEC 751.9
    acquired 569.89
    specified type NEC 751.8
  genitalia, genital organ(s) or system NEC
    congenital 752.9
    female (congenital) 752.9
      acquired 629.89
      external 752.40
      internal 752.9
    male (congenital) 752.9
      acquired 608.89
  globe (eye) (congenital) 743.9
    acquired 360.89
  gum (congenital) 750.9
    acquired 523.9
  gunstock 736.02
  hand (acquired) 736.00
    claw 736.06

Deformity — *continued*
  hand — *continued*
    congenital 755.50
    minus (and plus) (intrinsic) 736.09
    pill roller (intrinsic) 736.09
    plus (and minus) (intrinsic) 736.09
    swan neck (intrinsic) 736.09
  head (acquired) 738.10
    congenital (*see also* Deformity, skull congenital) 756.0
    specified NEC 738.19
  heart (congenital) 746.9
    auricle (congenital) 746.9
    septum 745.9
      auricular 745.5
      specified type NEC 745.8
      ventricular 745.4
    valve (congenital) NEC 746.9
      acquired — *see* Endocarditis
      pulmonary (congenital) 746.00
      specified type NEC 746.89
    ventricle (congenital) 746.9
  heel (acquired) 736.76
    congenital 755.67
  hepatic duct (congenital) 751.60
    acquired 576.8
      with calculus, choledocholithiasis, or stones — *see* Choledocholithiasis
  hip (joint) (acquired) 736.30
    congenital NEC 755.63
    flexion 718.45
      congenital (*see also* Subluxation, congenital, hip) 754.32
  hourglass — *see* Contraction, hourglass
  humerus (acquired) 736.89
    congenital 755.50
  hymen (congenital) 752.40
  hypophyseal (congenital) 759.2
  ileocecal (coil) (valve) (congenital) 751.5
    acquired 569.89
  ileum (intestine) (congenital) 751.5
    acquired 569.89
  ilium (acquired) 738.6
    congenital 755.60
  integument (congenital) 757.9
  intervertebral cartilage or disc (acquired) (*see also* Displacement, intervertebral disc)
    congenital 756.10
  intestine (large) (small) (congenital) 751.5
    acquired 569.89
  iris (acquired) 364.75
    congenital 743.9
    prolapse 364.89
  ischium (acquired) 738.6
    congenital 755.60
  jaw (acquired) (congenital) NEC 524.9
    due to intrauterine malposition and pressure 754.0
  joint (acquired) NEC 738.8
    congenital 755.9
    contraction (abduction) (adduction) (extension) (flexion) — *see* Contraction, joint
  kidney(s) (calyx) (pelvis) (congenital) 753.9
    acquired 593.89
    vessel 747.62
      acquired 459.9
  Klippel-Feil (brevicollis) 756.16
  knee (acquired) NEC 736.6
    congenital 755.64
  labium (majus) (minus) (congenital) 752.40
    acquired 624.8
  lacrimal apparatus or duct (congenital) 743.9
    acquired 375.69
  larynx (muscle) (congenital) 748.3
    acquired 478.79
    web (glottic) (subglottic) 748.2
  leg (lower) (upper) (acquired) NEC 736.89
    congenital 755.60
    reduction — *see* Deformity, reduction, lower limb
  lens (congenital) 743.9
    acquired 379.39
  lid (fold) (congenital) 743.9
    acquired 374.89

Deformity — *continued*
  ligament (acquired) 728.9
    congenital 756.9
  limb (acquired) 736.9
    congenital, except reduction deformity 755.9
      lower 755.60
        reduction (*see also* Deformity, reduction, lower limb) 755.30
      upper 755.50
        reduction (*see also* Deformity, reduction, upper limb) 755.20
    specified NEC 736.89
  lip (congenital) NEC 750.9
    acquired 528.5
    specified type NEC 750.26
  liver (congenital) 751.60
    acquired 573.8
    duct (congenital) 751.60
      acquired 576.8
        with calculus, choledocholithiasis, or stones — *see* Choledocholithi-asis
  lower extremity — *see* Deformity, leg
  lumbosacral (joint) (region) (congenital) 756.10
    acquired 738.5
  lung (congenital) 748.60
    acquired 518.89
    specified type NEC 748.69
  lymphatic system, congenital 759.9
  Madelung's (radius) 755.54
  maxilla (acquired) (congenital) 524.9
  meninges or membrane (congenital) 742.9
    brain 742.4
      acquired 349.2
    spinal (cord) 742.59
      acquired 349.2
  mesentery (congenital) 751.9
    acquired 568.89
  metacarpus (acquired) 736.00
    congenital 755.50
  metatarsus (acquired) 736.70
    congenital 754.70
  middle ear, except ossicles (congenital) 744.03
    ossicles 744.04
  mitral (leaflets) (valve) (congenital) 746.9
    acquired — *see* Endocarditis, mitral
    Ebstein's 746.89
    parachute 746.5
    specified type NEC 746.89
    stenosis, congenital 746.5
  mouth (acquired) 528.9
    congenital NEC 750.9
      specified type NEC 750.26
  multiple, congenital NEC 759.7
    specified type NEC 759.89
  muscle (acquired) 728.9
    congenital 756.9
      specified type NEC 756.89
      sternocleidomastoid (due to intrauterine malposition and pressure) 754.1
  musculoskeletal system, congenital NEC 756.9
    specified type NEC 756.9
  nail (acquired) 703.9
    congenital 757.9
  nasal — *see* Deformity, nose
  neck (acquired) NEC 738.2
    congenital (any part) 744.9
      sternocleidomastoid 754.1
  nervous system (congenital) 742.9
  nipple (congenital) 757.6 ▲
    acquired 611.89
  nose, nasal (cartilage) (acquired) 738.0
    bone (turbinate) 738.0
    congenital 748.1
      bent 754.0
      squashed 754.0
    saddle 738.0
      syphilitic 090.5
    septum 470
      congenital 748.1
    sinus (wall) (congenital) 748.1
      acquired 738.0
    syphilitic (congenital) 090.5

Deformity — *continued*
  nose, nasal — *continued*
    syphilitic — *continued*
      late 095.8
  ocular muscle (congenital) 743.9
    acquired 378.60
  opticociliary vessels (congenital) 743.9
  orbit (congenital) (eye) 743.9
    acquired NEC 376.40
      associated with craniofacial deformities 376.44
      due to
        bone disease 376.43
        surgery 376.47
        trauma 376.47
  organ of Corti (congenital) 744.05
  ovary (congenital) 752.0
    acquired 620.8
  oviduct (congenital) 752.10
    acquired 620.8
  palate (congenital) 750.9
    acquired 526.89
    cleft (congenital) (*see also* Cleft, palate) 749.00
    hard, acquired 526.89
    soft, acquired 528.9
  pancreas (congenital) 751.7
    acquired 577.8
  parachute, mitral valve 746.5
  parathyroid (gland) 759.2
  parotid (gland) (congenital) 750.9
    acquired 527.8
  patella (acquired) 736.6
    congenital 755.64
  pelvis, pelvic (acquired) (bony) 738.6
    with disproportion (fetopelvic) 653.0 ☑
      affecting fetus or newborn 763.1
      causing obstructed labor 660.1 ☑
        affecting fetus or newborn 763.1
    congenital 755.60
    rachitic (late effect) 268.1
  penis (glans) (congenital) 752.9
    acquired 607.89
  pericardium (congenital) 746.9
    acquired — *see* Pericarditis
  pharynx (congenital) 750.9
    acquired 478.29
  Pierre Robin (congenital) 756.0
  pinna (acquired) 380.32
    congenital 744.3
  pituitary (congenital) 759.2
  pleural folds (congenital) 748.8
  portal vein (congenital) 747.40
  posture — *see* Curvature, spine
  prepuce (congenital) 752.9
    acquired 607.89
  prostate (congenital) 752.9
    acquired 602.8
  pulmonary valve — *see* Endocarditis, pulmonary
  pupil (congenital) 743.9
    acquired 364.75
  pylorus (congenital) 750.9
    acquired 537.89
  rachitic (acquired), healed or old 268.1
  radius (acquired) 736.00
    congenital 755.50
    reduction — *see* Deformity, reduction, upper limb
  rectovaginal septum (congenital) 752.40
    acquired 623.8
  rectum (congenital) 751.5
    acquired 569.49
  reduction (extremity) (limb) 755.4
    brain 742.2
    lower limb 755.30
      with complete absence of distal elements 755.31
      longitudinal (complete) (partial) (with distal deficiencies, incomplete) 755.32
        with complete absence of distal elements 755.31
        combined femoral, tibial, fibular (incomplete) 755.33
        femoral 755.34

☑ Additional Digit Required — Refer to the Tabular List for Digit Selection   ⬗ Subterms under main terms may continue to next column or page

2010 ICD-9-CM   ▶◀ Revised Text   ● New Line   ▲ Revised Code   October 2009 • Volume 2 — 65

Deformity — Deformity

☑ Additional Digit Required — Refer to the Tabular List for Digit Selection ⩔ Subterms under main terms may continue to next column or page

2010 ICD-9-CM ▶◀ Revised Text ● New Line ▲ Revised Code Volume 2 — 67

Degeneration, degenerative — *continued*
  vascular (*see also* Arteriosclerosis) — *continued*
    hypertensive — *see* Hypertension
    vitreoretinal (primary) 362.73
      secondary 362.66
    vitreous humor (with infiltration) 379.21
    wallerian NEC — *see* Disorder, nerve
    waxy (any site) 277.39
    Wilson's hepatolenticular 275.1
Deglutition
  paralysis 784.99
    hysterical 300.11
  pneumonia 507.0
Degos' disease or syndrome 447.8
Degradation disorder, branched-chain amino acid 270.3
Dehiscence
  anastomosis — *see* Complications, anastomosis
  cesarean wound 674.1 ✓
  closure of
    cornea 998.32
    fascia, superficial or muscular 998.31
    internal organ 998.31
    mucosa 998.32
    muscle or muscle flap 998.31
    ribs or rib cage 998.31
    skin 998.32
    skull or craniotomy 998.31
    sternum or sternotomy 998.31
    subcutaneous tissue 998.32
    tendon or ligament 998.31
    traumatic laceration (external) (internal) 998.33
  episiotomy 674.2 ✓
  operation wound 998.32
    deep 998.31
    external 998.32
    internal 998.31
    superficial 998.32
  perineal wound (postpartum) 674.2 ✓
  postoperative 998.32
    abdomen 998.32
      internal 998.31
    internal 998.31
  traumatic injury wound repair 998.33
  uterine wound 674.1 ✓
Dehydration (cachexia) 276.51
  with
    hypernatremia 276.0
    hyponatremia 276.1
  newborn 775.5
Deiters' nucleus syndrome 386.19
Déjérine's disease 356.0
Déjérine-Klumpke paralysis 767.6
Déjérine-Roussy syndrome 338.0
Déjérine-Sottas disease or neuropathy (hypertrophic) 356.0
Déjérine-Thomas atrophy or syndrome 333.0
de Lange's syndrome (Amsterdam dwarf, mental retardation, and brachycephaly) 759.89
Delay, delayed
  adaptation, cones or rods 368.63
  any plane in pelvis
    affecting fetus or newborn 763.1
    complicating delivery 660.1 ✓
  birth or delivery NEC 662.1 ✓
    affecting fetus or newborn 763.89
    second twin, triplet, or multiple mate 662.3 ✓
  closure (*see also* Fistula)
    cranial suture 756.0
    fontanel 756.0
  coagulation NEC 790.92
  conduction (cardiac) (ventricular) 426.9
  delivery NEC 662.1 ✓
    second twin, triplet, etc. 662.3 ✓
      affecting fetus or newborn 763.89
  development
    in childhood 783.40
      physiological 783.40
    intellectual NEC 315.9
    learning NEC 315.2
    reading 315.00
    sexual 259.0

Delay, delayed — *continued*
  development — *continued*
    speech 315.39
      and language due to hearing loss 315.34
      associated with hyperkinesis 314.1
    spelling 315.09
  gastric emptying 536.8
  menarche 256.39
    due to pituitary hypofunction 253.4
  menstruation (cause unknown) 626.8
  milestone in childhood 783.42
  motility — *see* Hypomotility
  passage of meconium (newborn) 777.1
  primary respiration 768.9
  puberty 259.0
  separation of umbilical cord 779.83
  sexual maturation, female 259.0
  vaccination V64.00
Del Castillo's syndrome (germinal aplasia) 606.0
Déleage's disease 359.89
Deletion syndrome
  5p 758.31
  22q11.2 758.32
  autosomal NEC 758.39
  constitutional 5q deletion 758.39
Delhi (boil) (button) (sore) 085.1
Delinquency (juvenile) 312.9
  group (*see also* Disturbance, conduct) 312.2 ✓
  neurotic 312.4
Delirium, delirious 780.09
  acute (psychotic) 293.0
  alcoholic 291.0
    acute 291.0
    chronic 291.1
  alcoholicum 291.0
  chronic (*see also* Psychosis) 293.89
    due to or associated with physical condition — *see* Psychosis, organic
  drug-induced 292.81
  due to conditions classified elsewhere 293.0
  eclamptic (*see also* Eclampsia) 780.39
  exhaustion (*see also* Reaction, stress, acute) 308.9
  hysterical 300.11
  in
    presenile dementia 290.11
    senile dementia 290.3
  induced by drug 292.81
  manic, maniacal (acute) (*see also* Psychosis, affective) 296.0 ✓
    recurrent episode 296.1 ✓
    single episode 296.0 ✓
  puerperal 293.9
  senile 290.3
  subacute (psychotic) 293.1
  thyroid (*see also* Thyrotoxicosis) 242.9 ✓
  traumatic (*see also* Injury, intracranial)
    with
      lesion, spinal cord — *see* Injury, spinal, by site
      shock, spinal — *see* Injury, spinal, by site
  tremens (impending) 291.0
  uremic — *see* Uremia
  withdrawal
    alcoholic (acute) 291.0
      chronic 291.1
    drug 292.0

Delivery

> Note — Use the following fifth-digit subclassification with categories 640–649, 651–676:
>
> 0   unspecified as to episode of care
>
> 1   delivered, with or without mention of antepartum condition
>
> 2   delivered, with mention of postpartum complication
>
> 3   antepartum condition or complication
>
> 4   postpartum condition or complication

  breech (assisted) (buttocks) (complete) (frank) (spontaneous) 652.2 ✓

Delivery — *continued*
  breech — *continued*
    affecting fetus or newborn 763.0
    extraction NEC 669.6 ✓
  cesarean (for) 669.7 ✓
    abnormal
      cervix 654.6 ✓
      pelvic organs or tissues 654.9 ✓
      pelvis (bony) (major) NEC 653.0 ✓
      presentation or position 652.9 ✓
        in multiple gestation 652.6 ✓
      size, fetus 653.5 ✓
      soft parts (of pelvis) 654.9 ✓
      uterus, congenital 654.0 ✓
      vagina 654.7 ✓
      vulva 654.8 ✓
    abruptio placentae 641.2 ✓
    acromion presentation 652.8 ✓
    affecting fetus or newborn 763.4
    anteversion, cervix or uterus 654.4 ✓
    atony, uterus 661.2 ✓
      with hemorrhage 666.1 ✓
    bicornis or bicornuate uterus 654.0 ✓
    breech presentation (buttocks) (complete) (frank) 652.2 ✓
    brow presentation 652.4 ✓
    cephalopelvic disproportion (normally formed fetus) 653.4 ✓
    chin presentation 652.4 ✓
    cicatrix of cervix 654.6 ✓
    contracted pelvis (general) 653.1 ✓
      inlet 653.2 ✓
      outlet 653.3 ✓
    cord presentation or prolapse 663.0 ✓
    cystocele 654.4 ✓
    deformity (acquired) (congenital)
      pelvic organs or tissues NEC 654.9 ✓
      pelvis (bony) NEC 653.0 ✓
    displacement, uterus NEC 654.4 ✓
    disproportion NEC 653.9 ✓
    distress
      fetal 656.8 ✓
      maternal 669.0 ✓
    eclampsia 642.6 ✓
    face presentation 652.4 ✓
    failed
      forceps 660.7 ✓
      trial of labor NEC 660.6 ✓
      vacuum extraction 660.7 ✓
      ventouse 660.7 ✓
    fetal deformity 653.7 ✓
    fetal-maternal hemorrhage 656.0 ✓
    fetus, fetal
      distress 656.8 ✓
      prematurity 656.8 ✓
    fibroid (tumor) (uterus) 654.1 ✓
    footling 652.8 ✓
      with successful version 652.1 ✓
    hemorrhage (antepartum) (intrapartum) NEC 641.9 ✓
    hydrocephalic fetus 653.6 ✓
    incarceration of uterus 654.3 ✓
    incoordinate uterine action 661.4 ✓
    inertia, uterus 661.2 ✓
      primary 661.0 ✓
      secondary 661.1 ✓
    lateroversion, uterus or cervix 654.4 ✓
    mal lie 652.9 ✓
    malposition
      fetus 652.9 ✓
        in multiple gestation 652.6 ✓
      pelvic organs or tissues NEC 654.9 ✓
      uterus NEC or cervix 654.4 ✓
    malpresentation NEC 652.9 ✓
      in multiple gestation 652.6 ✓
    maternal
      diabetes mellitus (conditions classifiable to 249 and 250) 648.0 ✓
      heart disease NEC 648.6 ✓
    meconium in liquor 656.8 ✓
      staining only 792.3
    oblique presentation 652.3 ✓
    oversize fetus 653.5 ✓
    pelvic tumor NEC 654.9 ✓

Delivery — *continued*
  cesarean — *continued*
    placental insufficiency 656.5 ✓
    placenta previa 641.0 ✓
      with hemorrhage 641.1 ✓
    poor dilation, cervix 661.0 ✓
    pre-eclampsia 642.4 ✓
      severe 642.5 ✓
    previous
      cesarean delivery, section 654.2 ✓
      surgery (to)
        cervix 654.6 ✓
        gynecological NEC 654.9 ✓
        rectum 654.8 ✓
        uterus NEC 654.9 ✓
          previous cesarean delivery, section 654.2 ✓
        vagina 654.7 ✓
    prolapse
      arm or hand 652.7 ✓
      uterus 654.4 ✓
    prolonged labor 662.1 ✓
    rectocele 654.4 ✓
    retroversion, uterus or cervix 654.3 ✓
    rigid
      cervix 654.6 ✓
      pelvic floor 654.4 ✓
      perineum 654.8 ✓
      vagina 654.7 ✓
      vulva 654.8 ✓
    sacculation, pregnant uterus 654.4 ✓
    scar(s)
      cervix 654.6 ✓
      cesarean delivery, section 654.2 ✓
      uterus NEC 654.9 ✓
        due to previous cesarean delivery, section 654.2 ✓
    Shirodkar suture in situ 654.5 ✓
    shoulder presentation 652.8 ✓
    stenosis or stricture, cervix 654.6 ✓
    transverse presentation or lie 652.3 ✓
    tumor, pelvic organs or tissues NEC 654.4 ✓
    umbilical cord presentation or prolapse 663.0 ✓
  completely normal case — *see* category 650
  complicated (by) NEC 669.9 ✓
    abdominal tumor, fetal 653.7 ✓
      causing obstructed labor 660.1 ✓
    abnormal, abnormality of
      cervix 654.6 ✓
        causing obstructed labor 660.2 ✓
      forces of labor 661.9 ✓
      formation of uterus 654.0 ✓
      pelvic organs or tissues 654.9 ✓
        causing obstructed labor 660.2 ✓
      pelvis (bony) (major) NEC 653.0 ✓
        causing obstructed labor 660.1 ✓
      presentation or position NEC 652.9 ✓
        causing obstructed labor 660.0 ✓
      size, fetus 653.5 ✓
        causing obstructed labor 660.1 ✓
      soft parts (of pelvis) 654.9 ✓
        causing obstructed labor 660.2 ✓
      uterine contractions NEC 661.9 ✓
      uterus (formation) 654.0 ✓
        causing obstructed labor 660.2 ✓
      vagina 654.7 ✓
        causing obstructed labor 660.2 ✓
    abnormally formed uterus (any type) (congenital) 654.0 ✓
      causing obstructed labor 660.2 ✓
    acromion presentation 652.8 ✓
      causing obstructed labor 660.0 ✓
    adherent placenta 667.0 ✓
      with hemorrhage 666.0 ✓
    adhesions, uterus (to abdominal wall) 654.4 ✓
    advanced maternal age NEC 659.6 ✓
      multigravida 659.6 ✓
      primigravida 659.5 ✓
    air embolism 673.0 ✓
    amnionitis 658.4 ✓

Delivery — *continued*
  complicated — *continued*
    amniotic fluid embolism 673.1 ☑
    anesthetic death 668.9 ☑
    annular detachment, cervix 665.3 ☑
    antepartum hemorrhage — *see* Delivery, complicated, hemorrhage
    anteversion, cervix or uterus 654.4 ☑
      causing obstructed labor 660.2 ☑
    apoplexy 674.0 ☑
      placenta 641.2 ☑
    arrested active phase 661.1 ☑
    asymmetrical pelvis bone 653.0 ☑
      causing obstructed labor 660.1 ☑
    atony, uterus with hemorrhage (hypotonic) (inertia) 666.1 ☑
      hypertonic 661.4 ☑
    Bandl's ring 661.4 ☑
    battledore placenta — *see* Placenta, abnormal
    bicornis or bicornuate uterus 654.0 ☑
      causing obstructed labor 660.2 ☑
    birth injury to mother NEC 665.9 ☑
    bleeding (*see also* Delivery, complicated, hemorrhage) 641.9 ☑
    breech presentation (assisted) (buttocks) (complete) (frank) (spontaneous) 652.2 ☑
      with successful version 652.1 ☑
    brow presentation 652.4 ☑
    cephalopelvic disproportion (normally formed fetus) 653.4 ☑
      causing obstructed labor 660.1 ☑
    cerebral hemorrhage 674.0 ☑
    cervical dystocia 661.2 ☑
    chin presentation 652.4 ☑
      causing obstructed labor 660.0 ☑
    cicatrix
      cervix 654.6 ☑
        causing obstructed labor 660.2 ☑
      vagina 654.7 ☑
        causing obstructed labor 660.2 ☑
    coagulation defect 649.3 ☑
    colporrhexis 665.4 ☑
      with perineal laceration 664.0 ☑
    compound presentation 652.8 ☑
      causing obstructed labor 660.0 ☑
    compression of cord (umbilical) 663.2 ☑
      around neck 663.1 ☑
      cord prolapsed 663.0 ☑
    contraction, contracted pelvis 653.1 ☑
      causing obstructed labor 660.1 ☑
      general 653.1 ☑
        causing obstructed labor 660.1 ☑
      inlet 653.2 ☑
        causing obstructed labor 660.1 ☑
      midpelvic 653.8 ☑
        causing obstructed labor 660.1 ☑
      midplane 653.8 ☑
        causing obstructed labor 660.1 ☑
      outlet 653.3 ☑
        causing obstructed labor 660.1 ☑
    contraction ring 661.4 ☑
    cord (umbilical) 663.9 ☑
      around neck, tightly or with compression 663.1 ☑
        without compression 663.3 ☑
      bruising 663.6 ☑
      complication NEC 663.9 ☑
        specified type NEC 663.8 ☑
      compression NEC 663.2 ☑
      entanglement NEC 663.3 ☑
        with compression 663.2 ☑
      forelying 663.0 ☑
      hematoma 663.6 ☑
      marginal attachment 663.8 ☑
      presentation 663.0 ☑
      prolapse (complete) (occult) (partial) 663.0 ☑
      short 663.4 ☑
      specified complication NEC 663.8 ☑
      thrombosis (vessels) 663.6 ☑
      vascular lesion 663.6 ☑

Delivery — *continued*
  complicated — *continued*
    cord — *continued*
      velamentous insertion 663.8 ☑
    Couvelaire uterus 641.2 ☑
    cretin pelvis (dwarf type) (male type) 653.1 ☑
      causing obstructed labor 660.1 ☑
    crossbirth 652.3 ☑
      with successful version 652.1 ☑
      causing obstructed labor 660.0 ☑
    cyst (Gartner's duct) 654.7 ☑
    cystocele 654.4 ☑
      causing obstructed labor 660.2 ☑
    death of fetus (near term) 656.4 ☑
      early (before 22 completed weeks gestation) 632
    deformity (acquired) (congenital)
      fetus 653.7 ☑
        causing obstructed labor 660.1 ☑
      pelvic organs or tissues NEC 654.9 ☑
        causing obstructed labor 660.2 ☑
      pelvis (bony) NEC 653.0 ☑
        causing obstructed labor 660.1 ☑
    delay, delayed
      delivery in multiple pregnancy 662.3 ☑
      due to locked mates 660.5 ☑
      following rupture of membranes (spontaneous) 658.2 ☑
        artificial 658.3 ☑
    depressed fetal heart tones 659.7 ☑
    diastasis recti 665.8 ☑
    dilatation
      bladder 654.4 ☑
        causing obstructed labor 660.2 ☑
      cervix, incomplete, poor or slow 661.0 ☑
    diseased placenta 656.7 ☑
    displacement uterus NEC 654.4 ☑
      causing obstructed labor 660.2 ☑
    disproportion NEC 653.9 ☑
      causing obstructed labor 660.1 ☑
    disruptio uteri — *see* Delivery, complicated, rupture, uterus
    distress
      fetal 656.8 ☑
      maternal 669.0 ☑
    double uterus (congenital) 654.0 ☑
      causing obstructed labor 660.2 ☑
    dropsy amnion 657.0 ☑
    dysfunction, uterus 661.9 ☑
      hypertonic 661.4 ☑
      hypotonic 661.2 ☑
        primary 661.0 ☑
        secondary 661.1 ☑
      incoordinate 661.4 ☑
    dystocia
      cervical 661.2 ☑
      fetal — *see* Delivery, complicated, abnormal, presentation
      maternal — *see* Delivery, complicated, prolonged labor
      pelvic — *see* Delivery, complicated, contraction pelvis
      positional 652.8 ☑
      shoulder girdle 660.4 ☑
    eclampsia 642.6 ☑
    ectopic kidney 654.4 ☑
      causing obstructed labor 660.2 ☑
    edema, cervix 654.6 ☑
      causing obstructed labor 660.2 ☑
    effusion, amniotic fluid 658.1 ☑
    elderly multigravida 659.6 ☑
    elderly primigravida 659.5 ☑
    embolism (pulmonary) 673.2 ☑
      air 673.0 ☑
      amniotic fluid 673.1 ☑
      blood clot 673.2 ☑
      cerebral 674.0 ☑
      fat 673.8 ☑
      pyemic 673.3 ☑
      septic 673.3 ☑
    entanglement, umbilical cord 663.3 ☑

Delivery — *continued*
  complicated — *continued*
    entanglement, umbilical cord — *continued*
      with compression 663.2 ☑
      around neck (with compression) 663.1 ☑
    eversion, cervix or uterus 665.2 ☑
    excessive
      fetal growth 653.5 ☑
        causing obstructed labor 660.1 ☑
      size of fetus 653.5 ☑
        causing obstructed labor 660.1 ☑
    face presentation 652.4 ☑
      causing obstructed labor 660.0 ☑
      to pubes 660.3 ☑
    failure, fetal head to enter pelvic brim 652.5 ☑
      causing obstructed labor 660.0 ☑
    female genital mutilation 660.8 ☑
    fetal
      acid-base balance 656.8 ☑
      death (near term) NEC 656.4 ☑
        early (before 22 completed weeks gestation) 632
      deformity 653.7 ☑
        causing obstructed labor 660.1 ☑
      distress 656.8 ☑
      heart rate or rhythm 659.7 ☑
      reduction of multiple fetuses reduced to single fetus 651.7 ☑
    fetopelvic disproportion 653.4 ☑
      causing obstructed labor 660.1 ☑
    fever during labor 659.2 ☑
    fibroid (tumor) (uterus) 654.1 ☑
      causing obstructed labor 660.2 ☑
    fibromyomata 654.1 ☑
      causing obstructed labor 660.2 ☑
    forelying umbilical cord 663.0 ☑
    fracture of coccyx 665.6 ☑
    hematoma 664.5 ☑
      broad ligament 665.7 ☑
      ischial spine 665.7 ☑
      pelvic 665.7 ☑
      perineum 664.5 ☑
      soft tissues 665.7 ☑
      subdural 674.0 ☑
      umbilical cord 663.6 ☑
      vagina 665.7 ☑
      vulva or perineum 664.5 ☑
    hemorrhage (uterine) (antepartum) (intrapartum) (pregnancy) 641.9 ☑
      accidental 641.2 ☑
      associated with
        afibrinogenemia 641.3 ☑
        coagulation defect 641.3 ☑
        hyperfibrinolysis 641.3 ☑
        hypofibrinogenemia 641.3 ☑
      cerebral 674.0 ☑
      due to
        low-lying placenta 641.1 ☑
        placenta previa 641.1 ☑
        premature separation of placenta (normally implanted) 641.2 ☑
        retained placenta 666.0 ☑
        trauma 641.8 ☑
        uterine leiomyoma 641.8 ☑
      marginal sinus rupture 641.2 ☑
      placenta NEC 641.9 ☑
      postpartum (atonic) (immediate) (within 24 hours) 666.1 ☑
        with retained or trapped placenta 666.0 ☑
        delayed 666.2 ☑
        secondary 666.2 ☑
        third stage 666.0 ☑
    hourglass contraction, uterus 661.4 ☑
    hydramnios 657.0 ☑
    hydrocephalic fetus 653.6 ☑
      causing obstructed labor 660.1 ☑
    hydrops fetalis 653.7 ☑
      causing obstructed labor 660.1 ☑

Delivery — *continued*
  complicated — *continued*
    hypertension — *see* Hypertension, complicating pregnancy
    hypertonic uterine dysfunction 661.4 ☑
    hypotonic uterine dysfunction 661.2 ☑
    impacted shoulders 660.4 ☑
    incarceration, uterus 654.3 ☑
      causing obstructed labor 660.2 ☑
    incomplete dilation (cervix) 661.0 ☑
    incoordinate uterus 661.4 ☑
    indication NEC 659.9 ☑
      specified type NEC 659.8 ☑
    inertia, uterus 661.2 ☑
      hypertonic 661.4 ☑
      hypotonic 661.2 ☑
      primary 661.0 ☑
      secondary 661.1 ☑
    infantile
      genitalia 654.4 ☑
        causing obstructed labor 660.2 ☑
      uterus (os) 654.4 ☑
        causing obstructed labor 660.2 ☑
    injury (to mother) NEC 665.9 ☑
    intrauterine fetal death (near term) NEC 656.4 ☑
      early (before 22 completed weeks gestation) 632
    inversion, uterus 665.2 ☑
    kidney, ectopic 654.4 ☑
      causing obstructed labor 660.2 ☑
    knot (true), umbilical cord 663.2 ☑
    labor, premature (before 37 completed weeks gestation) 644.2 ☑
    laceration 664.9 ☑
      anus (sphincter) (healed) (old) 654.8 ☑
        with mucosa 664.3 ☑
          not associated with third-degree perineal laceration 664.6 ☑
      bladder (urinary) 665.5 ☑
      bowel 665.5 ☑
      central 664.4 ☑
      cervix (uteri) 665.3 ☑
      fourchette 664.0 ☑
      hymen 664.0 ☑
      labia (majora) (minora) 664.0 ☑
      pelvic
        floor 664.1 ☑
        organ NEC 665.5 ☑
      perineum, perineal 664.4 ☑
        first degree 664.0 ☑
        second degree 664.1 ☑
        third degree 664.2 ☑
        fourth degree 664.3 ☑
        central 664.4 ☑
        extensive NEC 664.4 ☑
        muscles 664.1 ☑
        skin 664.0 ☑
        slight 664.0 ☑
      peritoneum 665.5 ☑
      periurethral tissue 664.8 ☑
      rectovaginal (septum) (without perineal laceration) 665.4 ☑
        with perineum 664.2 ☑
          with anal or rectal mucosa 664.3 ☑
      skin (perineum) 664.0 ☑
      specified site or type NEC 664.8 ☑
      sphincter ani (healed) (old) 654.8 ☑
        with mucosa 664.3 ☑
          not associated with third-degree perineal laceration 664.6 ☑
      urethra 665.5 ☑
      uterus 665.1 ☑
        before labor 665.0 ☑
      vagina, vaginal (deep) (high) (sulcus) (wall) (without perineal laceration) 665.4 ☑
        with perineum 664.0 ☑
          muscles, with perineum 664.1 ☑
      vulva 664.0 ☑
    lateroversion, uterus or cervix 654.4 ☑
      causing obstructed labor 660.2 ☑
    locked mates 660.5 ☑

Delivery — *continued*
  complicated — *continued*
    low implantation of placenta — *see* Delivery, complicated, placenta, previa
    mal lie 652.9 ☑
    malposition
      fetus NEC 652.9 ☑
        causing obstructed labor 660.0 ☑
      pelvic organs or tissues NEC 654.9 ☑
        causing obstructed labor 660.2 ☑
      placenta 641.1 ☑
        without hemorrhage 641.0 ☑
      uterus NEC or cervix 654.4 ☑
        causing obstructed labor 660.2 ☑
    malpresentation 652.9 ☑
      causing obstructed labor 660.0 ☑
    marginal sinus (bleeding) (rupture) 641.2 ☑
    maternal hypotension syndrome 669.2 ☑
    meconium in liquor 656.8 ☑
    membranes, retained — *see* Delivery, complicated, placenta, retained
    mentum presentation 652.4 ☑
      causing obstructed labor 660.0 ☑
    metrorrhagia (myopathia) — *see* Delivery, complicated, hemorrhage
    metrorrhexis — *see* Delivery, complicated, rupture, uterus
    multiparity (grand) 659.4 ☑
    myelomeningocele, fetus 653.7 ☑
      causing obstructed labor 660.1 ☑
    Nägele's pelvis 653.0 ☑
      causing obstructed labor 660.1 ☑
    nonengagement, fetal head 652.5 ☑
      causing obstructed labor 660.0 ☑
    oblique presentation 652.3 ☑
      causing obstructed labor 660.0 ☑
    obstetric
      shock 669.1 ☑
      trauma NEC 665.9 ☑
    obstructed labor 660.9 ☑
      due to
        abnormality of pelvic organs or tissues (conditions classifiable to 654.0–654.9) 660.2 ☑
        deep transverse arrest 660.3 ☑
        impacted shoulders 660.4 ☑
        locked twins 660.5 ☑
        malposition and malpresentation of fetus (conditions classifiable to 652.0–652.9) 660.0 ☑
        persistent occipitoposterior 660.3 ☑
        shoulder dystocia 660.4 ☑
    occult prolapse of umbilical cord 663.0 ☑
    oversize fetus 653.5 ☑
      causing obstructed labor 660.1 ☑
    pathological retraction ring, uterus 661.4 ☑
    pelvic
      arrest (deep) (high) (of fetal head) (transverse) 660.3 ☑
      deformity (bone) (*see also* Deformity, pelvis, with disproportion)
        soft tissue 654.9 ☑
          causing obstructed labor 660.2 ☑
      tumor NEC 654.9 ☑
        causing obstructed labor 660.2 ☑
    penetration, pregnant uterus by instrument 665.1 ☑
    perforation — *see* Delivery, complicated, laceration
    persistent
      hymen 654.8 ☑
        causing obstructed labor 660.2 ☑
      occipitoposterior 660.3 ☑
    placenta, placental
      ablatio 641.2 ☑
      abnormality 656.7 ☑
        with hemorrhage 641.2 ☑
      abruptio 641.2 ☑
      accreta 667.0 ☑

Delivery — *continued*
  complicated — *continued*
    placenta, placental — *continued*
      accreta — *continued*
        with hemorrhage 666.0 ☑
      adherent (without hemorrhage) 667.0 ☑
        with hemorrhage 666.0 ☑
      apoplexy 641.2 ☑
      battledore placenta — *see* Placenta, abnormal
      detachment (premature) 641.2 ☑
      disease 656.7 ☑
      hemorrhage NEC 641.9 ☑
      increta (without hemorrhage) 667.0 ☑
        with hemorrhage 666.0 ☑
      low (implantation) 641.1 ☑
        without hemorrhage 641.0 ☑
      malformation 656.7 ☑
        with hemorrhage 641.2 ☑
      malposition 641.1 ☑
        without hemorrhage 641.0 ☑
      marginal sinus rupture 641.2 ☑
      percreta 667.0 ☑
        with hemorrhage 666.0 ☑
      premature separation 641.2 ☑
      previa (central) (lateral) (marginal) (partial) 641.1 ☑
        without hemorrhage 641.0 ☑
      retained (with hemorrhage) 666.0 ☑
        without hemorrhage 667.0 ☑
      rupture of marginal sinus 641.2 ☑
      separation (premature) 641.2 ☑
      trapped 666.0 ☑
        without hemorrhage 667.0 ☑
      vicious insertion 641.1 ☑
    polyhydramnios 657.0 ☑
    polyp, cervix 654.6 ☑
      causing obstructed labor 660.2 ☑
    precipitate labor 661.3 ☑
    premature
      labor (before 37 completed weeks gestation) 644.2 ☑
      rupture, membranes 658.1 ☑
        delayed delivery following 658.2 ☑
    presenting umbilical cord 663.0 ☑
    previous
      cesarean delivery, section 654.2 ☑
      surgery
        cervix 654.6 ☑
          causing obstructed labor 660.2 ☑
        gynecological NEC 654.9 ☑
          causing obstructed labor 660.2 ☑
        perineum 654.8 ☑
        rectum 654.8 ☑
        uterus NEC 654.9 ☑
          due to previous cesarean delivery, section 654.2 ☑
        vagina 654.7 ☑
          causing obstructed labor 660.2 ☑
        vulva 654.8 ☑
    primary uterine inertia 661.0 ☑
    primipara, elderly or old 659.5 ☑
    prolapse
      arm or hand 652.7 ☑
        causing obstructed labor 660.0 ☑
      cord (umbilical) 663.0 ☑
      fetal extremity 652.8 ☑
      foot or leg 652.8 ☑
        causing obstructed labor 660.0 ☑
      umbilical cord (complete) (occult) (partial) 663.0 ☑
      uterus 654.4 ☑
        causing obstructed labor 660.2 ☑
    prolonged labor 662.1 ☑
      first stage 662.0 ☑
      second stage 662.2 ☑
      active phase 661.2 ☑
      due to
        cervical dystocia 661.2 ☑
        contraction ring 661.4 ☑

Delivery — *continued*
  complicated — *continued*
    prolonged labor — *continued*
      due to — *continued*
        tetanic uterus 661.4 ☑
        uterine inertia 661.2 ☑
          primary 661.0 ☑
          secondary 661.1 ☑
      latent phase 661.0 ☑
    pyrexia during labor 659.2 ☑
    rachitic pelvis 653.2 ☑
      causing obstructed labor 660.1 ☑
    rectocele 654.4 ☑
      causing obstructed labor 660.2 ☑
    retained membranes or portions of placenta 666.2 ☑
      without hemorrhage 667.1 ☑
    retarded (prolonged) birth 662.1 ☑
    retention secundines (with hemorrhage) 666.2 ☑
      without hemorrhage 667.1 ☑
    retroversion, uterus or cervix 654.3 ☑
      causing obstructed labor 660.2 ☑
    rigid
      cervix 654.6 ☑
        causing obstructed labor 660.2 ☑
      pelvic floor 654.4 ☑
        causing obstructed labor 660.2 ☑
      perineum or vulva 654.8 ☑
        causing obstructed labor 660.2 ☑
      vagina 654.7 ☑
        causing obstructed labor 660.2 ☑
    Robert's pelvis 653.0 ☑
      causing obstructed labor 660.1 ☑
    rupture (*see also* Delivery, complicated, laceration)
      bladder (urinary) 665.5 ☑
      cervix 665.3 ☑
      marginal sinus 641.2 ☑
      membranes, premature 658.1 ☑
      pelvic organ NEC 665.5 ☑
      perineum (without mention of other laceration) — *see* Delivery, complicated, laceration, perineum
      peritoneum 665.5 ☑
      urethra 665.5 ☑
      uterus (during labor) 665.1 ☑
        before labor 665.0 ☑
    sacculation, pregnant uterus 654.4 ☑
    sacral teratomas, fetal 653.7 ☑
      causing obstructed labor 660.1 ☑
    scar(s)
      cervix 654.6 ☑
        causing obstructed labor 660.2 ☑
      cesarean delivery, section 654.2 ☑
        causing obstructed labor 660.2 ☑
      perineum 654.8 ☑
        causing obstructed labor 660.2 ☑
      uterus NEC 654.9 ☑
        causing obstructed labor 660.2 ☑
        due to previous cesarean delivery, section 654.2 ☑
      vagina 654.7 ☑
        causing obstructed labor 660.2 ☑
      vulva 654.8 ☑
        causing obstructed labor 660.2 ☑
    scoliotic pelvis 653.0 ☑
      causing obstructed labor 660.1 ☑
    secondary uterine inertia 661.1 ☑
    secundines, retained — *see* Delivery, complicated, placenta, retained
    separation
      placenta (premature) 641.2 ☑
      pubic bone 665.6 ☑
      symphysis pubis 665.6 ☑
    septate vagina 654.7 ☑
      causing obstructed labor 660.2 ☑
    shock (birth) (obstetric) (puerperal) 669.1 ☑
    short cord syndrome 663.4 ☑
    shoulder
      girdle dystocia 660.4 ☑
      presentation 652.8 ☑

Delivery — *continued*
  complicated — *continued*
    shoulder — *continued*
      presentation — *continued*
        causing obstructed labor 660.0 ☑
    Siamese twins 678.1 ☑
    slow slope active phase 661.2 ☑
    spasm
      cervix 661.4 ☑
      uterus 661.4 ☑
    spondylolisthesis, pelvis 653.3 ☑
      causing obstructed labor 660.1 ☑
    spondylolysis (lumbosacral) 653.3 ☑
      causing obstructed labor 660.1 ☑
    spondylosis 653.0 ☑
      causing obstructed labor 660.1 ☑
    stenosis or stricture
      cervix 654.6 ☑
        causing obstructed labor 660.2 ☑
      vagina 654.7 ☑
        causing obstructed labor 660.2 ☑
    sudden death, unknown cause 669.9 ☑
    tear (pelvic organ) (*see also* Delivery, complicated, laceration) 664.9 ☑
      anal sphincter (healed) (old) 654.8 ☑
        not associated with third-degree perineal laceration 664.6 ☑
    teratomas, sacral, fetal 653.7 ☑
      causing obstructed labor 660.1 ☑
    tetanic uterus 661.4 ☑
    tipping pelvis 653.0 ☑
      causing obstructed labor 660.1 ☑
    transverse
      arrest (deep) 660.3 ☑
      presentation or lie 652.3 ☑
        with successful version 652.1 ☑
        causing obstructed labor 660.0 ☑
    trauma (obstetrical) NEC 665.9 ☑
    tumor
      abdominal, fetal 653.7 ☑
        causing obstructed labor 660.1 ☑
      pelvic organs or tissues NEC 654.9 ☑
        causing obstructed labor 660.2 ☑
    umbilical cord (*see also* Delivery, complicated, cord) 663.9 ☑
      around neck tightly, or with compression 663.1 ☑
      entanglement NEC 663.3 ☑
        with compression 663.2 ☑
      prolapse (complete) (occult) (partial) 663.0 ☑
    unstable lie 652.0 ☑
      causing obstructed labor 660.0 ☑
    uterine
      inertia (*see also* Delivery, complicated, inertia, uterus) 661.2 ☑
      spasm 661.4 ☑
    vasa previa 663.5 ☑
    velamentous insertion of cord 663.8 ☑
    young maternal age 659.8 ☑
  delayed NEC 662.1 ☑
    following rupture of membranes (spontaneous) 658.2 ☑
      artificial 658.3 ☑
    second twin, triplet, etc. 662.3 ☑
  difficult NEC 669.9 ☑
    previous, affecting management of pregnancy or childbirth V23.49
    specified type NEC 669.8 ☑
  early onset (spontaneous) 644.2 ☑
  footling 652.8 ☑
    with successful version 652.1 ☑
  forceps NEC 669.5 ☑
    affecting fetus or newborn 763.2
  missed (at or near term) 656.4 ☑
  multiple gestation NEC 651.9 ☑
    with fetal loss and retention of one or more fetus(es) 651.6 ☑
    following (elective) fetal reduction 651.7 ☑
  specified type NEC 651.8 ☑
    with fetal loss and retention of one or more fetus(es) 651.6 ☑

Delivery — continued
  multiple gestation — continued
    specified type — continued
      following (elective) fetal reduction
        651.7 ✔
  nonviable infant 656.4 ✔
  normal — see category 650
  precipitate 661.3 ✔
    affecting fetus or newborn 763.6
  premature NEC (before 37 completed weeks
      gestation) 644.2 ✔
    previous, affecting management of preg-
      nancy V23.41
  quadruplet NEC 651.2 ✔
    with fetal loss and retention of one or more
      fetus(es) 651.5 ✔
    following (elective) fetal reduction
      651.7 ✔
  quintuplet NEC 651.8 ✔
    with fetal loss and retention of one or more
      fetus(es) 651.6 ✔
    following (elective) fetal reduction
      651.7 ✔
  sextuplet NEC 651.8 ✔
    with fetal loss and retention of one or more
      fetus(es) 651.6 ✔
    following (elective) fetal reduction
      651.7 ✔
  specified complication NEC 669.8 ✔
  stillbirth (near term) NEC 656.4 ✔
    early (before 22 completed weeks gesta-
      tion) 632
  term pregnancy (live birth) NEC — see catego-
    ry 650
    stillbirth NEC 656.4 ✔
  threatened premature 644.2 ✔
  triplets NEC 651.1 ✔
    with fetal loss and retention of one or more
      fetus(es) 651.4 ✔
    delayed delivery (one or more mates)
      662.3 ✔
    following (elective) fetal reduction
      651.7 ✔
    locked mates 660.5 ✔
  twins NEC 651.0 ✔
    with fetal loss and retention of one fetus
      651.3 ✔
    delayed delivery (one or more mates)
      662.3 ✔
    locked mates 660.5 ✔
  uncomplicated — see category 650
  vacuum extractor NEC 669.5 ✔
    affecting fetus or newborn 763.3
  ventouse NEC 669.5 ✔
    affecting fetus or newborn 763.3
Dellen, cornea 371.41
Delusions (paranoid) 297.9
  grandiose 297.1
  parasitosis 300.29
  systematized 297.1
Dementia 294.8
  alcohol-induced persisting (see also Psychosis,
    alcoholic) 291.2
  Alzheimer's — see Alzheimer's, dementia
  arteriosclerotic (simple type) (uncomplicated)
    290.40
    with
      acute confusional state 290.41
      delirium 290.41
      delusions 290.42
      depressed mood 290.43
    depressed type 290.43
    paranoid type 290.42
  Binswanger's 290.12
  catatonic (acute) (see also Schizophrenia)
    295.2 ✔
  congenital (see also Retardation, mental) 319
  degenerative 290.9
    presenile-onset — see Dementia, presenile
    senile-onset — see Dementia, senile
  developmental (see also Schizophrenia)
    295.9 ✔
  dialysis 294.8
    transient 293.9

Dementia — continued
  drug-induced persisting (see also Psychosis,
    drug) 292.82
  due to or associated with condition(s) classi-
    fied elsewhere
    Alzheimer's
      with behavioral disturbance
        331.0 [294.11]
      without behavioral disturbance
        331.0 [294.10]
    cerebral lipidoses
      with behavioral disturbance
        330.1 [294.11]
      without behavioral disturbance
        330.1 [294.10]
    epilepsy
      with behavioral disturbance
        345.9 ✔ [294.11]
      without behavioral disturbance
        345.9 ✔ [294.10]
    hepatolenticular degeneration
      with behavioral disturbance
        275.1 [294.11]
      without behavioral disturbance
        275.1 [294.10]
    HIV
      with behavioral disturbance
        042 [294.11]
      without behavioral disturbance
        042 [294.10]
    Huntington's chorea
      with behavioral disturbance
        333.4 [294.11]
      without behavioral disturbance
        333.4 [294.10]
    Jakob-Creutzfeldt disease (CJD)
      with behavioral disturbance
        046.19 [294.11]
      without behavioral disturbance
        046.19 [294.10]
      variant (vCJD) 046.11
        with dementia
          with behavioral disturbance
            046.11 [294.11]
          without behavioral disturbance
            046.11 [294.10]
    Lewy bodies
      with behavioral disturbance
        331.82 [294.11]
      without behavioral disturbance
        331.82 [294.10]
    multiple sclerosis
      with behavioral disturbance
        340 [294.11]
      without behavioral disturbance
        340 [294.10]
    neurosyphilis
      with behavioral disturbance
        094.9 [294.11]
      without behavioral disturbance
        094.9 [294.10]
    Parkinsonism
      with behavioral disturbance
        331.82 [294.11]
      without behavioral disturbance
        331.82 [294.10]
    Pelizaeus-Merzbacher disease
      with behavioral disturbance
        333.0 [294.11]
      without behavioral disturbance
        333.0 [294.10]
    Pick's disease
      with behavioral disturbance
        331.11 [294.11]
      without behavioral disturbance
        331.11 [294.10]
    polyarteritis nodosa
      with behavioral disturbance
        446.0 [294.11]
      without behavioral disturbance
        446.0 [294.10]
    syphilis
      with behavioral disturbance
        094.1 [294.11]
      without behavioral disturbance
        094.1 [294.10]

Dementia — continued
  due to or associated with condition(s) classified
    elsewhere — continued
    Wilson's disease
      with behavioral disturbance
        275.1 [294.11]
      without behavioral disturbance
        275.1 [294.10]
  frontal 331.19
    with behavioral disturbance
      331.19 [294.11]
    without behavioral disturbance
      331.19 [294.10]
  frontotemporal 331.19
    with behavioral disturbance
      331.19 [294.11]
    without behavioral disturbance
      331.19 [294.10]
  hebephrenic (acute) 295.1 ✔
  Heller's (infantile psychosis) (see also Psychosis,
    childhood) 299.1 ✔
  idiopathic 290.9
    presenile-onset — see Dementia, presenile
    senile-onset — see Dementia, senile
  in
    arteriosclerotic brain disease 290.40
    senility 290.0
  induced by drug 292.82
  infantile, infantilia (see also Psychosis, child-
    hood) 299.0 ✔
  Lewy body 331.82
    with behavioral disturbance
      331.82 [294.11]
    without behavioral disturbance
      331.82 [294.10]
  multi-infarct (cerebrovascular) (see also Demen-
    tia, arteriosclerotic) 290.40
  old age 290.0
  paralytica, paralytic 094.1
    juvenilis 090.40
    syphilitic 094.1
      congenital 090.40
      tabetic form 094.1
  paranoid (see also Schizophrenia) 295.3 ✔
  paraphrenic (see also Schizophrenia) 295.3 ✔
  paretic 094.1
  praecox (see also Schizophrenia) 295.9 ✔
  presenile 290.10
    with
      acute confusional state 290.11
      delirium 290.11
      delusional features 290.12
      depressive features 290.13
    depressed type 290.13
    paranoid type 290.12
    simple type 290.10
    uncomplicated 290.10
  primary (acute) (see also Schizophrenia)
    295.0 ✔
  progressive, syphilitic 094.1
  puerperal — see Psychosis, puerperal
  schizophrenic (see also Schizophrenia)
    295.9 ✔
  senile 290.0
    with
      acute confusional state 290.3
      delirium 290.3
      delusional features 290.20
      depressive features 290.21
    depressed type 290.21
    exhaustion 290.0
    paranoid type 290.20
  simple type (acute) (see also Schizophrenia)
    295.0 ✔
  simplex (acute) (see also Schizophrenia)
    295.0 ✔
  syphilitic 094.1
  uremic — see Uremia
  vascular 290.40
    with
      delirium 290.41
      delusions 290.42
      depressed mood 290.43
Demerol dependence — see also Dependence
  304.0 ✔

Demineralization, ankle — see also Osteoporosis 733.00
Demodex folliculorum (infestation) 133.8
Demoralization 799.25 ●
de Morgan's spots (senile angiomas) 448.1
Demyelinating
  polyneuritis, chronic inflammatory 357.81
Demyelination, demyelinization
  central nervous system 341.9
    specified NEC 341.8
  corpus callosum (central) 341.8
  global 340
Dengue (fever) 061
  sandfly 061
  vaccination, prophylactic (against) V05.1
  virus hemorrhagic fever 065.4
Dens
  evaginatus 520.2
  in dente 520.2
  invaginatus 520.2
Dense
  breast(s) — omit code
Density
  increased, bone (disseminated) (generalized)
    (spotted) 733.99
  lung (nodular) 518.89
Dental — see also condition
  examination only V72.2
Dentia praecox 520.6
Denticles (in pulp) 522.2
Dentigerous cyst 526.0
Dentin
  irregular (in pulp) 522.3
  opalescent 520.5
  secondary (in pulp) 522.3
  sensitive 521.89
Dentinogenesis imperfecta 520.5
Dentinoma (M9271/0) 213.1
  upper jaw (bone) 213.0
Dentition 520.7
  abnormal 520.6
  anomaly 520.6
  delayed 520.6
  difficult 520.7
  disorder of 520.6
  precocious 520.6
  retarded 520.6
Denture sore (mouth) 528.9
Dependence

Note — Use the following fifth-digit subclassification with category 304:

  0   unspecified

  1   continuous

  2   episodic

  3   in remission

  with
    withdrawal symptoms
      alcohol 291.81
      drug 292.0
  14-hydroxy-dihydromorphinone 304.0 ✔
  absinthe 304.6 ✔
  acemorphan 304.0 ✔
  acetanilid(e) 304.6 ✔
  acetophenetidin 304.6 ✔
  acetorphine 304.0 ✔
  acetyldihydrocodeine 304.0 ✔
  acetyldihydrocodeinone 304.0 ✔
  Adalin 304.1 ✔
  Afghanistan black 304.3 ✔
  agrypnal 304.1 ✔
  alcohol, alcoholic (ethyl) (methyl) (wood)
    303.9 ✔
    maternal, with suspected fetal damage af-
      fecting management of pregnancy
      655.4 ✔
  allobarbitone 304.1 ✔
  allonal 304.1 ✔
  allylisopropylacetylurea 304.1 ✔
  alphaprodine (hydrochloride) 304.0 ✔
  Alurate 304.1 ✔
  Alvodine 304.0 ✔
  amethocaine 304.6 ✔
  amidone 304.0 ✔

✔ Additional Digit Required — Refer to the Tabular List for Digit Selection   🔛 Subterms under main terms may continue to next column or page

2010 ICD-9-CM   ▶◀ Revised Text   ● New Line   ▲ Revised Code   October 2009 • Volume 2 — 71

Dependence — *continued*

amidopyrine 304.6 ☑
aminopyrine 304.6 ☑
amobarbital 304.1 ☑
amphetamine(s) (type) (drugs classifiable to 969.7) 304.4 ☑
amylene hydrate 304.6 ☑
amylobarbitone 304.1 ☑
amylocaine 304.6 ☑
Amytal (sodium) 304.1 ☑
analgesic (drug) NEC 304.6 ☑
    synthetic with morphine-like effect 304.0 ☑
anesthetic (agent) (drug) (gas) (general) (local) NEC 304.6 ☑
Angel dust 304.6 ☑
anileridine 304.0 ☑
antipyrine 304.6 ☑
anxiolytic 304.1 ☑
aprobarbital 304.1 ☑
aprobarbitone 304.1 ☑
atropine 304.6 ☑
Avertin (bromide) 304.6 ☑
barbenyl 304.1 ☑
barbital(s) 304.1 ☑
barbitone 304.1 ☑
barbiturate(s) (compounds) (drugs classifiable to 967.0) 304.1 ☑
barbituric acid (and compounds) 304.1 ☑
benzedrine 304.4 ☑
benzylmorphine 304.0 ☑
Beta-chlor 304.1 ☑
bhang 304.3 ☑
blue velvet 304.0 ☑
Brevital 304.1 ☑
bromal (hydrate) 304.1 ☑
bromide(s) NEC 304.1 ☑
bromine compounds NEC 304.1 ☑
bromisovalum 304.1 ☑
bromoform 304.1 ☑
Bromo-seltzer 304.1 ☑
bromural 304.1 ☑
butabarbital (sodium) 304.1 ☑
butabarpal 304.1 ☑
butallylonal 304.1 ☑
butethal 304.1 ☑
buthalitone (sodium) 304.1 ☑
Butisol 304.1 ☑
butobarbitone 304.1 ☑
butyl chloral (hydrate) 304.1 ☑
caffeine 304.4 ☑
cannabis (indica) (sativa) (resin) (derivatives) (type) 304.3 ☑
carbamazepine 304.6 ☑
Carbrital 304.1 ☑
carbromal 304.1 ☑
carisoprodol 304.6 ☑
Catha (edulis) 304.4 ☑
chloral (betaine) (hydrate) 304.1 ☑
chloralamide 304.1 ☑
chloralformamide 304.1 ☑
chloralose 304.1 ☑
chlordiazepoxide 304.1 ☑
Chloretone 304.1 ☑
chlorobutanol 304.1 ☑
chlorodyne 304.1 ☑
chloroform 304.6 ☑
Cliradon 304.0 ☑
coca (leaf) and derivatives 304.2 ☑
cocaine 304.2 ☑
    hydrochloride 304.2 ☑
    salt (any) 304.2 ☑
codeine 304.0 ☑
combination of drugs (excluding morphine or opioid type drug) NEC 304.8 ☑
    morphine or opioid type drug with any other drug 304.7 ☑
croton-chloral 304.1 ☑
cyclobarbital 304.1 ☑
cyclobarbitone 304.1 ☑
dagga 304.3 ☑
Delvinal 304.1 ☑
Demerol 304.0 ☑

Dependence — *continued*

desocodeine 304.0 ☑
desomorphine 304.0 ☑
desoxyephedrine 304.4 ☑
DET 304.5 ☑
dexamphetamine 304.4 ☑
dexedrine 304.4 ☑
dextromethorphan 304.0 ☑
dextromoramide 304.0 ☑
dextronorpseudoephedrine 304.4 ☑
dextrorphan 304.0 ☑
diacetylmorphine 304.0 ☑
Dial 304.1 ☑
diallylbarbituric acid 304.1 ☑
diamorphine 304.0 ☑
diazepam 304.1 ☑
dibucaine 304.6 ☑
dichloroethane 304.6 ☑
diethyl barbituric acid 304.1 ☑
diethylsulfone-diethylmethane 304.1 ☑
difencloxazine 304.0 ☑
dihydrocodeine 304.0 ☑
dihydrocodeinone 304.0 ☑
dihydrohydroxycodeinone 304.0 ☑
dihydroisocodeine 304.0 ☑
dihydromorphine 304.0 ☑
dihydromorphinone 304.0 ☑
dihydroxcodeinone 304.0 ☑
Dilaudid 304.0 ☑
dimenhydrinate 304.6 ☑
dimethylmeperidine 304.0 ☑
dimethyltriptamine 304.5 ☑
Dionin 304.0 ☑
diphenoxylate 304.6 ☑
dipipanone 304.0 ☑
d-lysergic acid diethylamide 304.5 ☑
DMT 304.5 ☑
Dolophine 304.0 ☑
DOM 304.2 ☑
Doriden 304.1 ☑
dormiral 304.1 ☑
Dormison 304.1 ☑
Dromoran 304.0 ☑
drug NEC 304.9 ☑
    analgesic NEC 304.6 ☑
    combination (excluding morphine or opioid type drug) NEC 304.8 ☑
        morphine or opioid type drug with any other drug 304.7 ☑
    complicating pregnancy, childbirth, or puerperium 648.3 ☑
        affecting fetus or newborn 779.5 ☑
    hallucinogenic 304.5 ☑
    hypnotic NEC 304.1 ☑
    narcotic NEC 304.9 ☑
    psychostimulant NEC 304.4 ☑
    sedative 304.1 ☑
    soporific NEC 304.1 ☑
    specified type NEC 304.6 ☑
    suspected damage to fetus affecting management of pregnancy 655.5 ☑
    synthetic, with morphine-like effect 304.0 ☑
    tranquilizing 304.1 ☑
duboisine 304.6 ☑
ectylurea 304.1 ☑
Endocaine 304.6 ☑
Equanil 304.1 ☑
Eskabarb 304.1 ☑
ethchlorvynol 304.1 ☑
ether (ethyl) (liquid) (vapor) (vinyl) 304.6 ☑
ethidene 304.6 ☑
ethinamate 304.1 ☑
ethoheptazine 304.6 ☑
ethyl
    alcohol 303.9 ☑
    bromide 304.6 ☑
    carbamate 304.6 ☑
    chloride 304.6 ☑
    morphine 304.0 ☑
ethylene (gas) 304.6 ☑
    dichloride 304.6 ☑

Dependence — *continued*

ethylidene chloride 304.6 ☑
etilfen 304.1 ☑
etorphine 304.0 ☑
etoval 304.1 ☑
eucodal 304.0 ☑
euneryl 304.1 ☑
Evipal 304.1 ☑
Evipan 304.1 ☑
fentanyl 304.0 ☑
ganja 304.3 ☑
gardenal 304.1 ☑
gardenpanyl 304.1 ☑
gelsemine 304.6 ☑
Gelsemium 304.6 ☑
Gemonil 304.1 ☑
glucochloral 304.1 ☑
glue (airplane) (sniffing) 304.6 ☑
glutethimide 304.1 ☑
hallucinogenics 304.5 ☑
hashish 304.3 ☑
headache powder NEC 304.6 ☑
Heavenly Blue 304.5 ☑
hedonal 304.1 ☑
hemp 304.3 ☑
heptabarbital 304.1 ☑
Heptalgin 304.0 ☑
heptobarbitone 304.1 ☑
heroin 304.0 ☑
    salt (any) 304.0 ☑
hexethal (sodium) 304.1 ☑
hexobarbital 304.1 ☑
Hycodan 304.0 ☑
hydrocodone 304.0 ☑
hydromorphinol 304.0 ☑
hydromorphinone 304.0 ☑
hydromorphone 304.0 ☑
hydroxycodeine 304.0 ☑
hypnotic NEC 304.1 ☑
Indian hemp 304.3 ☑
inhalant 304.6 ☑
intranarcon 304.1 ☑
Kemithal 304.1 ☑
ketobemidone 304.0 ☑
khat 304.4 ☑
kif 304.3 ☑
Lactuca (virosa) extract 304.1 ☑
lactucarium 304.1 ☑
laudanum 304.0 ☑
Lebanese red 304.3 ☑
Leritine 304.0 ☑
lettuce opium 304.1 ☑
Levanil 304.1 ☑
Levo-Dromoran 304.0 ☑
levo-iso-methadone 304.0 ☑
levorphanol 304.0 ☑
Librium 304.1 ☑
Lomotil 304.6 ☑
Lotusate 304.1 ☑
LSD (-25) (and derivatives) 304.5 ☑
Luminal 304.1 ☑
lysergic acid 304.5 ☑
    amide 304.5 ☑
maconha 304.3 ☑
magic mushroom 304.5 ☑
marihuana 304.3 ☑
MDA (methylene dioxyamphetamine) 304.4 ☑
Mebaral 304.1 ☑
Medinal 304.1 ☑
Medomin 304.1 ☑
megahallucinogenics 304.5 ☑
meperidine 304.0 ☑
mephobarbital 304.1 ☑
meprobamate 304.1 ☑
mescaline 304.5 ☑
methadone 304.0 ☑
methamphetamine(s) 304.4 ☑
methaqualone 304.1 ☑
metharbital 304.1 ☑
methitural 304.1 ☑
methobarbitone 304.1 ☑
methohexital 304.1 ☑

Dependence — *continued*

methopholine 304.6 ☑
methyl
    alcohol 303.9 ☑
    bromide 304.6 ☑
    morphine 304.0 ☑
    sulfonal 304.1 ☑
methylaparafynol 304.1 ☑
methylated spirit 303.9 ☑
methylbutinol 304.6 ☑
methyldihydromorphinone 304.0 ☑
methylene
    chloride 304.6 ☑
    dichloride 304.6 ☑
    dioxyamphetamine (MDA) 304.4 ☑
methylphenidate 304.4 ☑
methyprylone 304.1 ☑
metopon 304.0 ☑
Miltown 304.1 ☑
morning glory seeds 304.5 ☑
morphinan(s) 304.0 ☑
morphine (sulfate) (sulfite) (type) (drugs classifiable to 965.00–965.09) 304.0 ☑
morphine or opioid type drug (drugs classifiable to 965.00–965.09) with any other drug 304.7 ☑
morphinol(s) 304.0 ☑
morphinon 304.0 ☑
morpholinylethylmorphine 304.0 ☑
mylomide 304.1 ☑
myristicin 304.5 ☑
narcotic (drug) NEC 304.9 ☑
nealbarbital 304.1 ☑
nealbarbitone 304.1 ☑
Nembutal 304.1 ☑
Neonal 304.1 ☑
Neraval 304.1 ☑
Neravan 304.1 ☑
neurobarb 304.1 ☑
nicotine 305.1
Nisentil 304.0 ☑
nitrous oxide 304.6 ☑
Noctec 304.1 ☑
Noludar 304.1 ☑
nonbarbiturate sedatives and tranquilizers with similar effect 304.1 ☑
noptil 304.1 ☑
normorphine 304.0 ☑
noscapine 304.0 ☑
Novocaine 304.6 ☑
Numorphan 304.0 ☑
nunol 304.1 ☑
Nupercaine 304.6 ☑
Oblivon 304.1 ☑
on
    aspirator V46.0
    hemodialysis V45.11
    hyperbaric chamber V46.8
    iron lung V46.11
    machine (enabling) V46.9
        specified type NEC V46.8
    peritoneal dialysis V45.11
    Possum (Patient-Operated-Selector-Mechanism) V46.8
    renal dialysis machine V45.11
    respirator [ventilator] V46.11
        encounter
            during
                mechanical failure V46.14
                power failure V46.12
            for weaning V46.13
    supplemental oxygen V46.2
    wheelchair V46.3
opiate 304.0 ☑
opioids 304.0 ☑
opioid type drug 304.0 ☑
    with any other drug 304.7 ☑
opium (alkaloids) (derivatives) (tincture) 304.0 ☑
ortal 304.1 ☑
Oxazepam 304.1 ☑
oxycodone 304.0 ☑
oxymorphone 304.0 ☑
Palfium 304.0 ☑

Dependence — *continued*
- Panadol 304.6 ☑
- pantopium 304.0 ☑
- pantopon 304.0 ☑
- papaverine 304.0 ☑
- paracetamol 304.6 ☑
- paracodin 304.0 ☑
- paraldehyde 304.1 ☑
- paregoric 304.0 ☑
- Parzone 304.0 ☑
- PCP (phencyclidine) 304.6 ☑
- Pearly Gates 304.5 ☑
- pentazocine 304.0 ☑
- pentobarbital 304.1 ☑
- pentobarbitone (sodium) 304.1 ☑
- Pentothal 304.1 ☑
- Percaine 304.6 ☑
- Percodan 304.0 ☑
- Perichlor 304.1 ☑
- Pernocton 304.1 ☑
- Pernoston 304.1 ☑
- peronine 304.0 ☑
- pethidine (hydrochloride) 304.0 ☑
- petrichloral 304.1 ☑
- peyote 304.5 ☑
- Phanodron 304.1 ☑
- phenacetin 304.6 ☑
- phenadoxone 304.0 ☑
- phenaglycodol 304.1 ☑
- phenazocine 304.0 ☑
- phencyclidine 304.6 ☑
- phenmetrazine 304.4 ☑
- phenobal 304.1 ☑
- phenobarbital 304.1 ☑
- phenobarbitone 304.1 ☑
- phenomorphan 304.0 ☑
- phenonyl 304.1 ☑
- phenoperidine 304.0 ☑
- pholcodine 304.0 ☑
- piminodine 304.0 ☑
- Pipadone 304.0 ☑
- Pitkin's solution 304.6 ☑
- Placidyl 304.1 ☑
- polysubstance 304.8 ☑
- Pontocaine 304.6 ☑
- pot 304.3 ☑
- potassium bromide 304.1 ☑
- Preludin 304.4 ☑
- Prinadol 304.0 ☑
- probarbital 304.1 ☑
- procaine 304.6 ☑
- propanal 304.1 ☑
- propoxyphene 304.6 ☑
- psilocibin 304.5 ☑
- psilocin 304.5 ☑
- psilocybin 304.5 ☑
- psilocyline 304.5 ☑
- psilocyn 304.5 ☑
- psychedelic agents 304.5 ☑
- psychostimulant NEC 304.4 ☑
- psychotomimetic agents 304.5 ☑
- pyrahexyl 304.3 ☑
- Pyramidon 304.6 ☑
- quinalbarbitone 304.1 ☑
- racemoramide 304.0 ☑
- racemorphan 304.0 ☑
- Rela 304.6 ☑
- scopolamine 304.6 ☑
- secobarbital 304.1 ☑
- Seconal 304.1 ☑
- sedative NEC 304.1 ☑
  - nonbarbiturate with barbiturate effect 304.1 ☑
- Sedormid 304.1 ☑
- sernyl 304.1 ☑
- sodium bromide 304.1 ☑
- Soma 304.6 ☑
- Somnal 304.1 ☑
- Somnos 304.1 ☑
- Soneryl 304.1 ☑
- soporific (drug) NEC 304.1 ☑
- specified drug NEC 304.6 ☑
- speed 304.4 ☑

Dependence — *continued*
- spinocaine 304.6 ☑
- Stovaine 304.6 ☑
- STP 304.5 ☑
- stramonium 304.6 ☑
- Sulfonal 304.1 ☑
- sulfonethylmethane 304.1 ☑
- sulfonmethane 304.1 ☑
- Surital 304.1 ☑
- synthetic drug with morphine-like effect 304.0 ☑
- talbutal 304.1 ☑
- tetracaine 304.6 ☑
- tetrahydrocannabinol 304.3 ☑
- tetronal 304.1 ☑
- THC 304.3 ☑
- thebacon 304.0 ☑
- thebaine 304.0 ☑
- thiamil 304.1 ☑
- thiamylal 304.1 ☑
- thiopental 304.1 ☑
- tobacco 305.1
- toluene, toluol 304.6 ☑
- tranquilizer NEC 304.1 ☑
  - nonbarbiturate with barbiturate effect 304.1 ☑
- tribromacetaldehyde 304.6 ☑
- tribromethanol 304.6 ☑
- tribromomethane 304.6 ☑
- trichloroethanol 304.6 ☑
- trichloroethyl phosphate 304.1 ☑
- triclofos 304.1 ☑
- Trional 304.1 ☑
- Tuinal 304.1 ☑
- Turkish Green 304.3 ☑
- urethan(e) 304.6 ☑
- Valium 304.1 ☑
- Valmid 304.1 ☑
- veganin 304.0 ☑
- veramon 304.1 ☑
- Veronal 304.1 ☑
- versidyne 304.6 ☑
- vinbarbital 304.1 ☑
- vinbarbitone 304.1 ☑
- vinyl bitone 304.1 ☑
- vitamin B₆ 266.1
- wine 303.9 ☑
- Zactane 304.6 ☑

Dependency
- passive 301.6
- reactions 301.6

Depersonalization (episode, in neurotic state) (neurotic) (syndrome) 300.6

Depletion
- carbohydrates 271.9
- complement factor 279.8
- extracellular fluid 276.52
- plasma 276.52
- potassium 276.8
  - nephropathy 588.89
- salt or sodium 276.1
  - causing heat exhaustion or prostration 992.4
  - nephropathy 593.9
- volume 276.50
  - extracellular fluid 276.52
  - plasma 276.52

Deployment (military) ●
- personal history of V62.22 ●
- returned from V62.22 ●
- status V62.21 ●

Deposit
- argentous, cornea 371.16
- bone, in Boeck's sarcoid 135
- calcareous, calcium — *see* Calcification
- cholesterol
  - retina 362.82
  - skin 709.3
  - vitreous (humor) 379.22
- conjunctival 372.56
- cornea, corneal NEC 371.10
  - argentous 371.16
  - in
    - cystinosis 270.0 [371.15]

Deposit — *continued*
- cornea, corneal — *continued*
  - in — *continued*
    - mucopolysaccharidosis 277.5 [371.15]
- crystalline, vitreous (humor) 379.22
- hemosiderin, in old scars of cornea 371.11
- metallic, in lens 366.45
- skin 709.3
- teeth, tooth (betel) (black) (green) (materia alba) (orange) (soft) (tobacco) 523.6
- urate, in kidney (*see also* Disease, renal) 593.9

Depraved appetite 307.52

Depression 311
- acute (*see also* Psychosis, affective) 296.2 ☑
  - recurrent episode 296.3 ☑
  - single episode 296.2 ☑
- agitated (*see also* Psychosis, affective) 296.2 ☑
  - recurrent episode 296.3 ☑
  - single episode 296.2 ☑
- anaclitic 309.21
- anxiety 300.4
- arches 734
  - congenital 754.61
- autogenous (*see also* Psychosis, affective) 296.2 ☑
  - recurrent episode 296.3 ☑
  - single episode 296.2 ☑
- basal metabolic rate (BMR) 794.7
- bone marrow 289.9
- central nervous system 799.1
  - newborn 779.2
- cerebral 331.9
  - newborn 779.2
- cerebrovascular 437.8
  - newborn 779.2
- chest wall 738.3
- endogenous (*see also* Psychosis, affective) 296.2 ☑
  - recurrent episode 296.3 ☑
  - single episode 296.2 ☑
- functional activity 780.99
- hysterical 300.11
- involutional, climacteric, or menopausal (*see also* Psychosis, affective) 296.2 ☑
  - recurrent episode 296.3 ☑
  - single episode 296.2 ☑
- manic (*see also* Psychosis, affective) 296.80
- medullary 348.89 ▲
  - newborn 779.2
- mental 300.4
- metatarsal heads — *see* Depression, arches
- metatarsus — *see* Depression, arches
- monopolar (*see also* Psychosis, affective) 296.2 ☑
  - recurrent episode 296.3 ☑
  - single episode 296.2 ☑
- nervous 300.4
- neurotic 300.4
- nose 738.0
- postpartum 648.4 ☑
- psychogenic 300.4
  - reactive 298.0
- psychoneurotic 300.4
- psychotic (*see also* Psychosis, affective) 296.2 ☑
  - reactive 298.0
  - recurrent episode 296.3 ☑
  - single episode 296.2 ☑
- reactive 300.4
  - neurotic 300.4
  - psychogenic 298.0
  - psychoneurotic 300.4
  - psychotic 298.0
- recurrent 296.3 ☑
- respiratory center 348.89 ▲
  - newborn 770.89
- scapula 736.89
- senile 290.21
- situational (acute) (brief) 309.0
  - prolonged 309.1
- skull 754.0
- sternum 738.3
- visual field 368.40

Depressive reaction — *see also* Reaction, depressive

Depressive reaction — *see also* Reaction, depressive — *continued*
- acute (transient) 309.0
  - with anxiety 309.28
- prolonged 309.1
- situational (acute) 309.0
  - prolonged 309.1

Deprivation
- cultural V62.4
- emotional V62.89
  - affecting
    - adult 995.82
    - infant or child 995.51
- food 994.2
  - specific substance NEC 269.8
- protein (familial) (kwashiorkor) 260
- sleep V69.4
- social V62.4
  - affecting
    - adult 995.82
    - infant or child 995.51
- symptoms, syndrome
  - alcohol 291.81
  - drug 292.0
- vitamins (*see also* Deficiency, vitamin) 269.2
- water 994.3

de Quervain's
- disease (tendon sheath) 727.04
- syndrome 259.51
- thyroiditis (subacute granulomatous thyroiditis) 245.1

Derangement
- ankle (internal) 718.97
  - current injury (*see also* Dislocation, ankle) 837.0
  - recurrent 718.37
- cartilage (articular) NEC (*see also* Disorder, cartilage, articular) 718.0 ☑
  - knee 717.9
    - recurrent 718.36
  - recurrent 718.3 ☑
- collateral ligament (knee) (medial) (tibial) 717.82
  - current injury 844.1
    - lateral (fibular) 844.0
  - lateral (fibular) 717.81
    - current injury 844.0
- cruciate ligament (knee) (posterior) 717.84
  - anterior 717.83
    - current injury 844.2
  - current injury 844.2
- elbow (internal) 718.92
  - current injury (*see also* Dislocation, elbow) 832.00
  - recurrent 718.32
- gastrointestinal 536.9
- heart — *see* Disease, heart
- hip (joint) (internal) (old) 718.95
  - current injury (*see also* Dislocation, hip) 835.00
  - recurrent 718.35
- intervertebral disc — *see* Displacement, intervertebral disc
- joint (internal) 718.90
  - ankle 718.97
  - current injury (*see also* Dislocation, by site)
    - knee, meniscus or cartilage (*see also* Tear, meniscus) 836.2
  - elbow 718.92
  - foot 718.97
  - hand 718.94
  - hip 718.95
  - knee 717.9
  - multiple sites 718.99
  - pelvic region 718.95
  - recurrent 718.30
    - ankle 718.37
    - elbow 718.32
    - foot 718.37
    - hand 718.34
    - hip 718.35
    - knee 718.36
    - multiple sites 718.39
    - pelvic region 718.35
    - shoulder (region) 718.31
    - specified site NEC 718.38

☑ Additional Digit Required — Refer to the Tabular List for Digit Selection

▽ Subterms under main terms may continue to next column or page

►◄ Revised Text   ● New Line   ▲ Revised Code

Derangement — *continued*
  joint — *continued*
    recurrent — *continued*
      temporomandibular (old) 524.69
      wrist 718.33
     shoulder (region) 718.91
     specified site NEC 718.98
     spine NEC 724.9
     temporomandibular 524.69
     wrist 718.93
    knee (cartilage) (internal) 717.9
     current injury (*see also* Tear, meniscus) 836.2
     ligament 717.89
      capsular 717.85
      collateral — *see* Derangement, collateral ligament
      cruciate — *see* Derangement, cruciate ligament
      specified NEC 717.85
     recurrent 718.36
    low back NEC 724.9
    meniscus NEC (knee) 717.5
     current injury (*see also* Tear, meniscus) 836.2
     lateral 717.40
      anterior horn 717.42
      posterior horn 717.43
      specified NEC 717.49
     medial 717.3
      anterior horn 717.1
      posterior horn 717.2
     recurrent 718.3 ☑
     site other than knee — *see* Disorder, cartilage, articular
    mental (*see also* Psychosis) 298.9
    rotator cuff (recurrent) (tear) 726.10
     current 840.4
    sacroiliac (old) 724.6
     current — *see* Dislocation, sacroiliac
    semilunar cartilage (knee) 717.5
     current injury 836.2
      lateral 836.1
      medial 836.0
     recurrent 718.3 ☑
    shoulder (internal) 718.91
     current injury (*see also* Dislocation, shoulder) 831.00
     recurrent 718.31
    spine (recurrent) NEC 724.9
     current — *see* Dislocation, spine
    temporomandibular (internal) (joint) (old) 524.69
     current — *see* Dislocation, jaw
Dercum's disease or syndrome (adiposis dolorosa) 272.8
Derealization (neurotic) 300.6
Dermal — *see* condition
Dermaphytid — *see* Dermatophytosis
Dermatergosis — *see* Dermatitis
Dermatitis (allergic) (contact) (occupational) (venenata) 692.9
  ab igne 692.82
  acneiform 692.9
  actinic (due to sun) 692.70
   acute 692.72
   chronic NEC 692.74
   other than from sun NEC 692.82
  ambustionis
   due to
    burn or scald — *see* Burn, by site
    sunburn (*see also* Sunburn) 692.71
  amebic 006.6
  ammonia 691.0
  anaphylactoid NEC 692.9
  arsenical 692.4
  artefacta 698.4
   psychogenic 316 [698.4]
  asthmatic 691.8
  atopic (allergic) (intrinsic) 691.8
   psychogenic 316 [691.8]
  atrophicans 701.8
   diffusa 701.8
   maculosa 701.3
  autoimmune progesterone 279.49 ●
  berlock, berloque 692.72

Dermatitis — *continued*
  blastomycetic 116.0
  blister beetle 692.89
  Brucella NEC 023.9
  bullosa 694.9
   striata pratensis 692.6
  bullous 694.9
   mucosynechial, atrophic 694.60
    with ocular involvement 694.61
   seasonal 694.8
  calorica
   due to
    burn or scald — *see* Burn, by site
    cold 692.89
    sunburn (*see also* Sunburn) 692.71
  caterpillar 692.89
  cercarial 120.3
  combustionis
   due to
    burn or scald — *see* Burn, by site
    sunburn (*see also* Sunburn) 692.71
  congelationis 991.5
  contusiformis 695.2
  diabetic 250.8 ☑
  diaper 691.0
  diphtheritica 032.85
  due to
   acetone 692.2
   acids 692.4
   adhesive plaster 692.4
   alcohol (skin contact) (substances classifiable to 980.0–980.9) 692.4
    taken internally 693.8
   alkalis 692.4
   allergy NEC 692.9
   ammonia (household) (liquid) 692.4
   animal
    dander (cat) (dog) 692.84
    hair (cat) (dog) 692.84
   arnica 692.3
   arsenic 692.4
    taken internally 693.8
   blister beetle 692.89
   cantharides 692.3
   carbon disulphide 692.2
   caterpillar 692.89
   caustics 692.4
   cereal (ingested) 693.1
    contact with skin 692.5
   chemical(s) NEC 692.4
    internal 693.8
    irritant NEC 692.4
    taken internally 693.8
   chlorocompounds 692.2
   coffee (ingested) 693.1
    contact with skin 692.5
   cold weather 692.89
   cosmetics 692.81
   cyclohexanes 692.2
   dander, animal (cat) (dog) 692.84
   deodorant 692.81
   detergents 692.0
   dichromate 692.4
   drugs and medicinals (correct substance properly administered) (internal use) 693.0
    external (in contact with skin) 692.3
     wrong substance given or taken 976.9
      specified substance — *see* Table of Drugs and Chemicals
    wrong substance given or taken 977.9
     specified substance — *see* Table of Drugs and Chemicals
   dyes 692.89
    hair 692.89
   epidermophytosis — *see* Dermatophytosis
   esters 692.2
   external irritant NEC 692.9
    specified agent NEC 692.89
   eye shadow 692.81
   fish (ingested) 693.1
    contact with skin 692.5
   flour (ingested) 693.1
    contact with skin 692.5

Dermatitis — *continued*
  due to — *continued*
   food (ingested) 693.1
    in contact with skin 692.5
   fruit (ingested) 693.1
    contact with skin 692.5
   fungicides 692.3
   furs 692.84
   glycols 692.2
   greases NEC 692.1
   hair, animal (cat) (dog) 692.84
   hair dyes 692.89
   hot
    objects and materials — *see* Burn, by site
    weather or places 692.89
   hydrocarbons 692.2
   infrared rays, except from sun 692.82
    solar NEC (*see also* Dermatitis, due to, sun) 692.70
   ingested substance 693.9
    drugs and medicinals (*see also* Dermatitis, due to, drugs and medicinals) 693.0
    food 693.1
    specified substance NEC 693.8
   ingestion or injection of chemical 693.8
    drug (correct substance properly administered) 693.0
    wrong substance given or taken 977.9
     specified substance — *see* Table of Drugs and Chemicals
   insecticides 692.4
   internal agent 693.9
    drugs and medicinals (*see also* Dermatitis, due to, drugs and medicinals) 693.0
    food (ingested) 693.1
     in contact with skin 692.5
    specified agent NEC 693.8
   iodine 692.3
   iodoform 692.3
   irradiation 692.82
   jewelry 692.83
   keratolytics 692.3
   ketones 692.2
   lacquer tree (Rhus verniciflua) 692.6
   light (sun) NEC (*see also* Dermatitis, due to, sun) 692.70
    other 692.82
   low temperature 692.89
   mascara 692.81
   meat (ingested) 693.1
    contact with skin 692.5
   mercury, mercurials 692.3
   metals 692.83
   milk (ingested) 693.1
    contact with skin 692.5
   Neomycin 692.3
   nylon 692.4
   oils NEC 692.1
   paint solvent 692.2
   pediculocides 692.3
   petroleum products (substances classifiable to 981) 692.4
   phenol 692.3
   photosensitiveness, photosensitivity (sun) 692.72
    other light 692.82
   plants NEC 692.6
   plasters, medicated (any) 692.3
   plastic 692.4
   poison
    ivy (Rhus toxicodendron) 692.6
    oak (Rhus diversiloba) 692.6
    plant or vine 692.6
    sumac (Rhus venenata) 692.6
    vine (Rhus radicans) 692.6
   preservatives 692.89
   primrose (primula) 692.6
   primula 692.6
   radiation 692.82
    sun NEC (*see also* Dermatitis, due to, sun) 692.70
    tanning bed 692.82
   radioactive substance 692.82

Dermatitis — *continued*
  due to — *continued*
   radium 692.82
   ragweed (Senecio jacobae) 692.6
   Rhus (diversiloba) (radicans) (toxicodendron) (venenata) (verniciflua) 692.6
   rubber 692.4
   scabicides 692.3
   Senecio jacobae 692.6
   solar radiation — *see* Dermatitis, due to, sun
   solvents (any) (substances classifiable to 982.0–982.8) 692.2
    chlorocompound group 692.2
    cyclohexane group 692.2
    ester group 692.2
    glycol group 692.2
    hydrocarbon group 692.2
    ketone group 692.2
    paint 692.2
   specified agent NEC 692.89
   sun 692.70
    acute 692.72
    chronic NEC 692.74
    specified NEC 692.79
   sunburn (*see also* Sunburn) 692.71
   sunshine NEC (*see also* Dermatitis, due to, sun) 692.70
   tanning bed 692.82
   tetrachlorethylene 692.2
   toluene 692.2
   topical medications 692.3
   turpentine 692.2
   ultraviolet rays, except from sun 692.82
    sun NEC (*see also* Dermatitis, due to, sun) 692.70
   vaccine or vaccination (correct substance properly administered) 693.0
    wrong substance given or taken
     bacterial vaccine 978.8
      specified — *see* Table of Drugs and Chemicals
     other vaccines NEC 979.9
      specified — *see* Table of Drugs and Chemicals
   varicose veins (*see also* Varicose, vein, inflamed or infected) 454.1
   x-rays 692.82
  dyshydrotic 705.81
  dysmenorrheica 625.8
  eczematoid NEC 692.9
   infectious 690.8
  eczematous NEC 692.9
  epidemica 695.89
  erysipelatosa 695.81
  escharotica — *see* Burn, by site
  exfoliativa, exfoliative 695.89
   generalized 695.89
   infantum 695.81
   neonatorum 695.81
  eyelid 373.31
   allergic 373.32
   contact 373.32
   eczematous 373.31
   herpes (zoster) 053.20
    simplex 054.41
   infective 373.5
    due to
     actinomycosis 039.3 [373.5]
     herpes
      simplex 054.41
      zoster 053.20
     impetigo 684 [373.5]
     leprosy (*see also* Leprosy) 030.0 [373.4]
     lupus vulgaris (tuberculous) (*see also* Tuberculosis) 017.0 ☑ [373.4]
     mycotic dermatitis (*see also* Dermatomycosis) 111.9 [373.5]
     vaccinia 051.02 [373.5]
      postvaccination 999.0 [373.5]
     yaws (*see also* Yaws) 102.9 [373.4]
  facta, factitia 698.4
   psychogenic 316 [698.4]
  ficta 698.4

☑ Additional Digit Required — Refer to the Tabular List for Digit Selection
▽ Subterms under main terms may continue to next column or page
74 — Volume 2 • October 2009
►◄ Revised Text ● New Line ▲ Revised Code
2010 ICD-9-CM

Dermatitis — *continued*
 ficta — *continued*
  psychogenic 316 *[698.4]*
 flexural 691.8
 follicularis 704.8
 friction 709.8
 fungus 111.9
  specified type NEC 111.8
 gangrenosa, gangrenous (infantum) (*see also* Gangrene) 785.4
 gestationis 646.8 ☑
 gonococcal 098.89
 gouty 274.89
 harvest mite 133.8
 heat 692.89
 herpetiformis (bullous) (erythematous) (pustular) (vesicular) 694.0
  juvenile 694.2
  senile 694.5
 hiemalis 692.89
 hypostatic, hypostatica 454.1
  with ulcer 454.2
 impetiginous 684
 infantile (acute) (chronic) (intertriginous) (intrinsic) (seborrheic) 690.12
 infectiosa eczematoides 690.8
 infectious (staphylococcal) (streptococcal) 686.9
  eczematoid 690.8
 infective eczematoid 690.8
 Jacquet's (diaper dermatitis) 691.0
 leptus 133.8
 lichenified NEC 692.9
 lichenoid, chronic 701.0
 lichenoides purpurica pigmentosa 709.1
 meadow 692.6
 medicamentosa (correct substance properly administered) (internal use) (*see also* Dermatitis, due to, drugs or medicinals) 693.0
  due to contact with skin 692.3
 mite 133.8
 multiformis 694.0
  juvenile 694.2
  senile 694.5
 napkin 691.0
 neuro 698.3
 neurotica 694.0
 nummular NEC 692.9
 osteatosis, osteatotic 706.8
 papillaris capillitii 706.1
 pellagrous 265.2
 perioral 695.3
 perstans 696.1
 photosensitivity (sun) 692.72
  other light 692.82
 pigmented purpuric lichenoid 709.1
 polymorpha dolorosa 694.0
 primary irritant 692.9
 pruriginosa 694.0
 pruritic NEC 692.9
 psoriasiform nodularis 696.2
 psychogenic 316
 purulent 686.00
 pustular contagious 051.2
 pyococcal 686.00
 pyocyaneus 686.09
 pyogenica 686.00
 radiation 692.82
 repens 696.1
 Ritter's (exfoliativa) 695.81
 Schamberg's (progressive pigmentary dermatosis) 709.09
 schistosome 120.3
 seasonal bullous 694.8
 seborrheic 690.10
  infantile 690.12
 sensitization NEC 692.9
 septic (*see also* Septicemia) 686.00
  gonococcal 098.89
 solar, solare NEC (*see also* Dermatitis, due to, sun) 692.70
 stasis 454.1
  due to
   postphlebitic syndrome 459.12
    with ulcer 459.13

Dermatitis — *continued*
 stasis — *continued*
  due to — *continued*
   varicose veins — *see* Varicose
  ulcerated or with ulcer (varicose) 454.2
 sunburn (*see also* Sunburn) 692.71
 suppurative 686.00
 traumatic NEC 709.8
 trophoneurotica 694.0
 ultraviolet, except from sun 692.82
  due to sun NEC (*see also* Dermatitis, due to, sun) 692.82
 varicose 454.1
  with ulcer 454.2
 vegetans 686.8
 verrucosa 117.2
 xerotic 706.8
Dermatoarthritis, lipoid 272.8 *[713.0]*
Dermatochalasia, dermatochalasis 374.87
Dermatofibroma (lenticulare) (M8832/0) — *see also* Neoplasm, skin, benign
 protuberans (M8832/1) — *see* Neoplasm, skin, uncertain behavior
Dermatofibrosarcoma (protuberans) (M8832/3) — *see* Neoplasm, skin, malignant
Dermatographia 708.3
Dermatolysis (congenital) (exfoliativa) 757.39
 acquired 701.8
 eyelids 374.34
 palpebrarum 374.34
 senile 701.8
Dermatomegaly NEC 701.8
Dermatomucomyositis 710.3
Dermatomycosis 111.9
 furfuracea 111.0
 specified type NEC 111.8
Dermatomyositis (acute) (chronic) 710.3
Dermatoneuritis of children 985.0
Dermatophiliasis 134.1
Dermatophytide — *see* Dermatophytosis
Dermatophytosis (Epidermophyton) (infection) (microsporum) (tinea) (Trichophyton) 110.9
 beard 110.0
 body 110.5
 deep seated 110.6
 fingernails 110.1
 foot 110.4
 groin 110.3
 hand 110.2
 nail 110.1
 perianal (area) 110.3
 scalp 110.0
 scrotal 110.8
 specified site NEC 110.8
 toenails 110.1
 vulva 110.8
Dermatopolyneuritis 985.0
Dermatorrhexis 756.83
 acquired 701.8
Dermatosclerosis — *see also* Scleroderma 710.1
 localized 701.0
Dermatosis 709.9
 Andrews' 686.8
 atopic 691.8
 Bowen's (M8081/2) — *see* Neoplasm, skin, in situ
 bullous 694.9
  specified type NEC 694.8
 erythematosquamous 690.8
 exfoliativa 695.89
 factitial 698.4
 gonococcal 098.89
 herpetiformis 694.0
  juvenile 694.2
  senile 694.5
 hysterical 300.11
 linear IgA 694.8
 menstrual NEC 709.8
 neutrophilic, acute febrile 695.89
 occupational (*see also* Dermatitis) 692.9
 papulosa nigra 709.8
 pigmentary NEC 709.00
  progressive 709.09
  Schamberg's 709.09
  Siemens-Bloch 757.33
 progressive pigmentary 709.09

Dermatosis — *continued*
 psychogenic 316
 pustular subcorneal 694.1
 Schamberg's (progressive pigmentary) 709.09
 senile NEC 709.3
 specified NEC 702.8
 Unna's (seborrheic dermatitis) 690.10
Dermographia 708.3
Dermographism 708.3
Dermoid (cyst) (M9084/0) — *see also* Neoplasm, by site, benign
 with malignant transformation (M9084/3) 183.0
Dermopathy
 infiltrative, with thyrotoxicosis 242.0 ☑
 nephrogenic fibrosing 701.8
 senile NEC 709.3
Dermophytosis — *see* Dermatophytosis
Descemet's membrane — *see* condition
Descemetocele 371.72
Descending — *see* condition
Descensus uteri (complete) (incomplete) (partial) (without vaginal wall prolapse) 618.1
 with mention of vaginal wall prolapse — *see* Prolapse, uterovaginal
Desensitization to allergens V07.1
Desert
 rheumatism 114.0
 sore (*see also* Ulcer, skin) 707.9
Desertion (child) (newborn) 995.52
 adult 995.84
Desmoid (extra-abdominal) (tumor) (M8821/1) — *see also* Neoplasm, connective tissue, uncertain behavior
 abdominal (M8822/1) — *see* Neoplasm, connective tissue, uncertain behavior
Despondency 300.4
Desquamative dermatitis NEC 695.89
Destruction
 articular facet (*see also* Derangement, joint) 718.9 ☑
  vertebra 724.9
 bone 733.90
  syphilitic 095.5
 joint (*see also* Derangement, joint) 718.9 ☑
  sacroiliac 724.6
 kidney 593.89
 live fetus to facilitate birth NEC 763.89
 ossicles (ear) 385.24
 rectal sphincter 569.49
 septum (nasal) 478.19
 tuberculous NEC (*see also* Tuberculosis) 011.9 ☑
 tympanic membrane 384.82
 tympanum 385.89
 vertebral disc — *see* Degeneration, intervertebral disc
Destructiveness — *see also* Disturbance, conduct 312.9
 adjustment reaction 309.3
Detachment
 cartilage (*see also* Sprain, by site)
  knee — *see* Tear, meniscus
 cervix, annular 622.8
  complicating delivery 665.3 ☑
 choroid (old) (postinfectional) (simple) (spontaneous) 363.70
  hemorrhagic 363.72
  serous 363.71
 knee, medial meniscus (old) 717.3
  current injury 836.0
 ligament — *see* Sprain, by site
 placenta (premature) — *see* Placenta, separation
 retina (recent) 361.9
  with retinal defect (rhegmatogenous) 361.00
   giant tear 361.03
   multiple 361.02
   partial
    with
     giant tear 361.03
     multiple defects 361.02
     retinal dialysis (juvenile) 361.04
     single defect 361.01
    retinal dialysis (juvenile) 361.04

 retina — *continued*
  with retinal defect — *continued*
   single 361.01
   subtotal 361.05
   total 361.05
  delimited (old) (partial) 361.06
  old
   delimited 361.06
   partial 361.06
   total or subtotal 361.07
  pigment epithelium (RPE) (serous) 362.42
   exudative 362.42
   hemorrhagic 362.43
  rhegmatogenous (*see also* Detachment, retina, with retinal defect) 361.00
  serous (without retinal defect) 361.2
  specified type NEC 361.89
  traction (with vitreoretinal organization) 361.81
 vitreous humor 379.21
Detergent asthma 507.8
Deterioration
 epileptic
  with behavioral disturbance 345.9 ☑ *[294.11]*
  without behavioral disturbance 345.9 ☑ *[294.10]*
 heart, cardiac (*see also* Degeneration, myocardial) 429.1
 mental (*see also* Psychosis) 298.9
 myocardium, myocardial (*see also* Degeneration, myocardial) 429.1
 senile (simple) 797
 transplanted organ — *see* Complications, transplant, organ, by site
de Toni-Fanconi syndrome (cystinosis) 270.0
Deuteranomaly 368.52
Deuteranopia (anomalous trichromat) (complete) (incomplete) 368.52
Deutschländer's disease — *see* Fracture, foot
Development
 abnormal, bone 756.9
 arrested 783.40
  bone 733.91
  child 783.40
  due to malnutrition (protein-calorie) 263.2
  fetus or newborn 764.9 ☑
  tracheal rings (congenital) 748.3
 defective, congenital (*see also* Anomaly)
  cauda equina 742.59
  left ventricle 746.9
   with atresia or hypoplasia of aortic orifice or valve with hypoplasia of ascending aorta 746.7
   in hypoplastic left heart syndrome 746.7
 delayed (*see also* Delay, development) 783.40
  arithmetical skills 315.1
  language (skills) 315.31
   and speech due to hearing loss 315.34
   expressive 315.31
   mixed receptive-expressive 315.32
  learning skill, specified NEC 315.2
  mixed skills 315.5
  motor coordination 315.4
  reading 315.00
  specified
   learning skill NEC 315.2
   type NEC, except learning 315.8
  speech 315.39
   and language due to hearing loss 315.34
   associated with hyperkinesia 314.1
   phonological 315.39
  spelling 315.09
  written expression 315.2
 imperfect, congenital (*see also* Anomaly)
  heart 746.9
  lungs 748.60
 improper (fetus or newborn) 764.9 ☑
 incomplete (fetus or newborn) 764.9 ☑
  affecting management of pregnancy 656.5 ☑
  bronchial tree 748.3
  organ or site not listed — *see* Hypoplasia

☑ Additional Digit Required — Refer to the Tabular List for Digit Selection   ▽ Subterms under main terms may continue to next column or page

2010 ICD-9-CM   ▶◀ Revised Text   ● New Line   ▲ Revised Code   **Volume 2 — 75**

Dermatitis — Development

Development — continued

incomplete — *continued*
   respiratory system 748.9
sexual, precocious NEC 259.1
tardy, mental (*see also* Retardation, mental)
   319

Developmental — *see* condition

Devergie's disease (pityriasis rubra pilaris) 696.4

Deviation

conjugate (eye) 378.87
   palsy 378.81
   spasm, spastic 378.82
esophagus 530.89
eye, skew 378.87
mandible, opening and closing 524.53
midline (jaw) (teeth) 524.29
   specified site NEC — *see* Malposition
occlusal plane 524.76
organ or site, congenital NEC — *see* Malposition, congenital
septum (acquired) (nasal) 470
   congenital 754.0
sexual 302.9
   bestiality 302.1
   coprophilia 302.89
   ego-dystonic
      homosexuality 302.0
      lesbianism 302.0
   erotomania 302.89
      Clérambault's 297.8
   exhibitionism (sexual) 302.4
   fetishism 302.81
      transvestic 302.3
   frotteurism 302.89
   homosexuality, ego-dystonic 302.0
      pedophilic 302.2
   lesbianism, ego-dystonic 302.0
   masochism 302.83
   narcissism 302.89
   necrophilia 302.89
   nymphomania 302.89
   pederosis 302.2
   pedophilia 302.2
   sadism 302.84
   sadomasochism 302.84
   satyriasis 302.89
   specified type NEC 302.89
   transvestic fetishism 302.3
   transvestism 302.3
   voyeurism 302.82
   zoophilia (erotica) 302.1
teeth, midline 524.29
trachea 519.19
ureter (congenital) 753.4

Devic's disease 341.0

Device

cerebral ventricle (communicating) in situ
   V45.2
contraceptive — *see* Contraceptive, device
drainage, cerebrospinal fluid V45.2

Devil's

grip 074.1
pinches (purpura simplex) 287.2

Devitalized tooth 522.9

Devonshire colic 984.9

specified type of lead — *see* Table of Drugs
   and Chemicals

Dextraposition, aorta 747.21

with ventricular septal defect, pulmonary
   stenosis or atresia, and hypertrophy of
   right ventricle 745.2
in tetralogy of Fallot 745.2

Dextratransposition, aorta 745.11

Dextrinosis, limit (debrancher enzyme deficiency) 271.0

Dextrocardia (corrected) (false) (isolated) (secondary) (true) 746.87

with
   complete transposition of viscera 759.3
   situs inversus 759.3

Dextroversion, kidney (left) 753.3

Dhobie itch 110.3

Diabetes, diabetic (brittle) (congenital) (familial) (mellitus) (severe) (slight) (without compli-cation) 250.0 ☑

> Note — Use the following fifth-digit subclas-
> sification with category 250:
>
> 0   type II or unspecified type, not stated
>   as uncontrolled
>
> Fifth-digit 0 is for use for type II patients,
> even if the patient requires insulin
>
> 1   type I [juvenile type], not stated as
>   uncontrolled ·
>
> 2   type II or unspecified type, uncon-
>   trolled
>
> Fifth-digit 2 is for use for type II patients,
> even if the patient requires insulin
>
> 3   type I [juvenile type], uncontrolled

with
   coma (with ketoacidosis) 250.3 ☑
      due to secondary diabetes 249.3 ☑
      hyperosmolar (nonketotic) 250.2 ☑
         due to secondary diabetes 249.2 ☑
   complication NEC 250.9 ☑
      due to secondary diabetes 249.9 ☑
      specified NEC 250.8 ☑
         due to secondary diabetes 249.8 ☑
   gangrene 250.7 ☑ *[785.4]*
      due to secondary diabetes
         249.7 ☑ *[785.4]*
   hyperglycemia — code to Diabetes, by
      type, with 5th digit for not stated
      as uncontrolled
   hyperosmolarity 250.2 ☑
      due to secondary diabetes 249.2 ☑
   ketosis, ketoacidosis 250.1 ☑
      due to secondary diabetes 249.1 ☑
   osteomyelitis 250.8 ☑ *[731.8]*
      due to secondary diabetes
         249.8 ☑ *[731.8]*
   specified manifestations NEC 250.8 ☑
      due to secondary diabetes 249.8 ☑
acetonemia 250.1 ☑
   due to secondary diabetes 249.1 ☑
acidosis 250.1 ☑
   due to secondary diabetes 249.1 ☑
amyotrophy 250.6 ☑ *[353.5]*
   due to secondary diabetes 249.6 ☑ *[353.5]*
angiopathy, peripheral 250.7 ☑ *[443.81]*
   due to secondary diabetes
      249.7 ☑ *[443.81]*
asymptomatic 790.29
autonomic neuropathy (peripheral)
   250.6 ☑ *[337.1]*
   due to secondary diabetes 249.6 ☑ *[337.1]*
bone change 250.8 ☑ *[731.8]*
   due to secondary diabetes 249.8 ☑ *[731.8]*
bronze, bronzed 275.0
cataract 250.5 ☑ *[366.41]*
   due to secondary diabetes
      249.5 ☑ *[366.41]*
chemical induced — *see* Diabetes, secondary
complicating pregnancy, childbirth, or
   puerperium 648.0 ☑
coma (with ketoacidosis) 250.3 ☑
   due to secondary diabetes 249.3 ☑
   hyperglycemic 250.3 ☑
      due to secondary diabetes 249.3 ☑
   hyperosmolar (nonketotic) 250.2 ☑
      due to secondary diabetes 249.2 ☑
   hypoglycemic 250.3 ☑
      due to secondary diabetes 249.3 ☑
   insulin 250.3 ☑
      due to secondary diabetes 249.3 ☑
complicating pregnancy, childbirth, or puerperium (maternal) (conditions classifiable to 249 and 250) 648.0 ☑
   affecting fetus or newborn 775.0
complication NEC 250.9 ☑
   due to secondary diabetes 249.9 ☑
   specified NEC 250.8 ☑
      due to secondary diabetes 249.8 ☑

Diabetes, diabetic — continued

dorsal sclerosis 250.6 ☑ *[340]*
   due to secondary diabetes 249.6 ☑ *[340]*
drug-induced — *see also* Diabetes, secondary
   overdose or wrong substance given or
      taken — *see* Table of Drugs and
      Chemicals
due to
   cystic fibrosis — *see* Diabetes, secondary
   infection — *see* Diabetes, secondary
dwarfism-obesity syndrome 258.1
gangrene 250.7 ☑ *[785.4]*
   due to secondary diabetes 249.7 ☑ *[785.4]*
gastroparesis 250.6 ☑ *[536.3]*
   due to secondary diabetes 249.6 ☑ *[536.3]*
gestational 648.8 ☑
   complicating pregnancy, childbirth, or
      puerperium 648.8 ☑
glaucoma 250.5 ☑ *[365.44]*
   due to secondary diabetes
      249.5 ☑ *[365.44]*
glomerulosclerosis (intercapillary)
   250.4 ☑ *[581.81]*
   due to secondary diabetes
      249.4 ☑ *[581.81]*
glycogenosis, secondary 250.8 ☑ *[259.8]*
   due to secondary diabetes 249.8 ☑ *[259.8]*
hemochromatosis 275.0
hyperosmolar coma 250.2 ☑
   due to secondary diabetes 249.2 ☑
hyperosmolarity 250.2 ☑
   due to secondary diabetes 249.2 ☑
hypertension-nephrosis syndrome
   250.4 ☑ *[581.81]*
   due to secondary diabetes
      249.4 ☑ *[581.81]*
hypoglycemia 250.8 ☑
   due to secondary diabetes 249.8 ☑
hypoglycemic shock 250.8 ☑
   due to secondary diabetes 249.8 ☑
inadequately controlled — code to Diabetes,
   by type, with 5th digit for not stated as
   uncontrolled
insipidus 253.5
   nephrogenic 588.1
   pituitary 253.5
   vasopressin-resistant 588.1
intercapillary glomerulosclerosis
   250.4 ☑ *[581.81]*
   due to secondary diabetes
      249.4 ☑ *[581.81]*
iritis 250.5 ☑ *[364.42]*
   due to secondary diabetes
      249.5 ☑ *[364.42]*
ketosis, ketoacidosis 250.1 ☑
   due to secondary diabetes 249.1 ☑
Kimmelstiel (-Wilson) disease or syndrome
   (intercapillary glomerulosclerosis)
   250.4 ☑ *[581.81]*
   due to secondary diabetes
      249.4 ☑ *[581.81]*
Lancereaux's (diabetes mellitus with marked
   emaciation) 250.8 ☑ *[261]*
   due to secondary diabetes 249.8 ☑ *[261]*
latent (chemical) — *see* Diabetes, secondary
complicating pregnancy, childbirth, or
   puerperium 648.0 ☑
lipoidosis 250.8 ☑ *[272.7]*
   due to secondary diabetes 249.8 ☑ *[272.7]*
macular edema 250.5 ☑ *[362.07]*
   due to secondary diabetes
      249.5 ☑ *[362.07]*
maternal
   with manifest disease in the infant 775.1
   affecting fetus or newborn 775.0
microaneurysms, retinal 250.5 ☑ *[362.01]*
   due to secondary diabetes
      249.5 ☑ *[362.01]*
mononeuropathy 250.6 ☑ *[355.9]*
   due to secondary diabetes 249.6 ☑ *[355.9]*
neonatal, transient 775.1
nephropathy 250.4 ☑ *[583.81]*
   due to secondary diabetes
      249.4 ☑ *[583.81]*   ▲

Diabetes, diabetic — continued

nephrosis (syndrome) 250.4 ☑ *[581.81]*
   due to secondary diabetes
      249.4 ☑ *[581.81]*
neuralgia 250.6 ☑ *[357.2]*
   due to secondary diabetes 249.6 ☑ *[357.2]*
neuritis 250.6 ☑ *[357.2]*
   due to secondary diabetes 249.6 ☑ *[357.2]*
neurogenic arthropathy 250.6 ☑ *[713.5]*
   due to secondary diabetes 249.6 ☑ *[713.5]*
neuropathy 250.6 ☑ *[357.2]*
   autonomic (peripheral) 250.6 ☑ *[337.1]* ●
      due to secondary diabetes   ●
         249.6 ☑ *[337.1]*   ●
   due to secondary diabetes 249.6 ☑ *[357.2]*
nonclinical 790.29
osteomyelitis 250.8 ☑ *[731.8]*
   due to secondary diabetes 249.8 ☑ *[731.8]*
out of control — code to Diabetes, by type,
   with 5th digit for uncontrolled
peripheral autonomic neuropathy
   250.6 ☑ *[337.1]*
   due to secondary diabetes 249.6 ☑ *[337.1]*
phosphate 275.3
polyneuropathy 250.6 ☑ *[357.2]*
   due to secondary diabetes 249.6 ☑ *[357.2]*
poorly controlled — code to Diabetes, by type,
   with 5th digit for not stated as uncontrolled
renal (true) 271.4
retinal
   edema 250.5 ☑ *[362.07]*
      due to secondary diabetes
         249.5 ☑ *[362.07]*
   hemorrhage 250.5 ☑ *[362.01]*
      due to secondary diabetes
         249.5 ☑ *[362.01]*
   microaneurysms 250.5 ☑ *[362.01]*
      due to secondary diabetes
         249.5 ☑ *[362.01]*
retinitis 250.5 ☑ *[362.01]*
   due to secondary diabetes
      249.5 ☑ *[362.01]*
retinopathy 250.5 ☑ *[362.01]*
   background 250.5 ☑ *[362.01]*
      due to secondary diabetes
         249.5 ☑ *[362.01]*
   due to secondary diabetes
      249.5 ☑ *[362.01]*
   nonproliferative 250.5 ☑ *[362.03]*
      due to secondary diabetes
         249.5 ☑ *[362.03]*
      mild 250.5 ☑ *[362.04]*
         due to secondary diabetes
            249.5 ☑ *[362.04]*
      moderate 250.5 ☑ *[362.05]*
         due to secondary diabetes
            249.5 ☑ *[362.05]*
      severe 250.5 ☑ *[362.06]*
         due to secondary diabetes
            249.5 ☑ *[362.06]*
   proliferative 250.5 ☑ *[362.02]*
      due to secondary diabetes
         249.5 ☑ *[362.02]*
secondary (chemical-induced) (due to chronic
   condition) (due to infection) (drug-induced) 249.0 ☑
with
   coma (with ketoacidosis) 249.3 ☑
      hyperosmolar (nonketotic)
         249.2 ☑
   complication NEC 249.9 ☑
      specified NEC 249.8 ☑
   gangrene 249.7 ☑ *[785.4]*
   hyperosmolarity 249.2 ☑
   ketosis, ketoacidosis 249.1 ☑
   osteomyelitis 249.8 ☑ *[731.8]*
   specified manifestations NEC 249.8 ☑
acetonemia 249.1 ☑
acidosis 249.1 ☑
amyotrophy 249.6 ☑ *[353.5]*
angiopathy, peripheral 249.7 ☑ *[443.81]*
autonomic neuropathy (peripheral)
   249.6 ☑ *[337.1]*

☑ Additional Digit Required — Refer to the Tabular List for Digit Selection   ▽ Subterms under main terms may continue to next column or page

76 — Volume 2 • October 2009   ▶◀ Revised Text   ● New Line   ▲ Revised Code   2010 ICD-9-CM

Diabetes, diabetic — *continued*
secondary — *continued*
  bone change 249.8 ☑ [731.8]
  cataract 249.5 ☑ [366.41]
  coma (with ketoacidosis) 249.3 ☑
    hyperglycemic 249.3 ☑
    hyperosmolar (nonketotic) 249.2 ☑
    hypoglycemic 249.3 ☑
    insulin 249.3 ☑
  complicating pregnancy, childbirth, or
    puerperium (maternal) 648.0 ☑
    affecting fetus or newborn 775.0
  complication NEC 249.9 ☑
    specified NEC 249.8 ☑
  dorsal sclerosis 249.6 ☑ [340]
  due to overdose or wrong substance given
    or taken — *see* Table of Drugs and
    Chemicals
  gangrene 249.7 ☑ [785.4]
  gastroparesis 249.6 ☑ [536.3]
  glaucoma 249.5 ☑ [365.44]
  glomerulosclerosis (intercapillary)
    249.4 ☑ [581.81]
  glycogenosis, secondary 249.8 ☑ [259.8]
  hyperosmolar coma 249.2 ☑
  hyperosmolarity 249.2 ☑
  hypertension-nephrosis syndrome
    249.4 ☑ [581.81]
  hypoglycemia 249.8 ☑
  hypoglycemic shock 249.8 ☑
  intercapillary glomerulosclerosis
    249.4 ☑ [581.81]
  iritis 249.5 ☑ [364.42]
  ketosis, ketoacidosis 249.1 ☑
  Kimmelstiel (-Wilson) disease or syndrome
    (intercapillary glomerulosclerosis)
    249.4 ☑ [581.81]
  Lancereaux's (diabetes mellitus with
    marked emaciation) 249.8 ☑ [261]
  lipoidosis 249.8 ☑ [272.7]
  macular edema 249.5 ☑ [362.07]
  maternal
    with manifest disease in the infant
      775.1
    affecting fetus or newborn 775.0
  microaneurysms, retinal 249.5 ☑ [362.01]
  mononeuropathy 249.6 ☑ [355.9]
  nephropathy 249.4 ☑ [583.81] ▲
  nephrosis (syndrome) 249.4 ☑ [581.81]
  neuralgia 249.6 ☑ [357.2]
  neuritis 249.6 ☑ [357.2]
  neurogenic arthropathy 249.6 ☑ [713.5]
  neuropathy 249.6 ☑ [357.2]
    autonomic (peripheral)   ●
      249.6 ☑ [337.1]   ●
  osteomyelitis 249.8 ☑ [731.8]
  peripheral autonomic neuropathy
    249.6 ☑ [337.1]
  polyneuropathy 249.6 ☑ [357.2]
  retinal
    edema 249.5 ☑ [362.07]
    hemorrhage 249.5 ☑ [362.01]
    microaneurysms 249.5 ☑ [362.01]
  retinitis 249.5 ☑ [362.01]
  retinopathy 249.5 ☑ [362.01]
    background 249.5 ☑ [362.01]
    nonproliferative 249.5 ☑ [362.03]
      mild 249.5 ☑ [362.04]
      moderate 249.5 ☑ [362.05]
      severe 249.5 ☑ [362.06]
    proliferative 249.5 ☑ [362.02]
  ulcer (skin) 249.8 ☑ [707.9]
    lower extemity 249.8 ☑ [707.10]
      ankle 249.8 ☑ [707.13]
      calf 249.8 ☑ [707.12]
      foot 249.8 ☑ [707.15]
      heel 249.8 ☑ [707.14]
      knee 249.8 ☑ [707.19]
      specified site NEC 249.8 ☑ [707.19]
      thigh 249.8 ☑ [707.11]
      toes 249.8 ☑ [707.15]
    specified site NEC 249.8 ☑ [707.8]
  xanthoma 249.8 ☑ [272.2]

Diabetes, diabetic — *continued*
steroid induced — *see also* Diabetes, secondary
  overdose or wrong substance given or
    taken 962.0
stress 790.29
subclinical 790.29
subliminal 790.29
sugar 250.0 ☑
ulcer (skin) 250.8 ☑ [707.9]
  due to secondary diabetes 249.8 ☑ [707.9]
  lower extremity 250.8 ☑ [707.10]
    ankle 250.8 ☑ [707.13]
      due to secondary diabetes
        249.8 ☑ [707.13]
    calf 250.8 ☑ [707.12]
      due to secondary diabetes
        249.8 ☑ [707.12]
    due to secondary diabetes
      249.8 ☑ [707.10]
    foot 250.8 ☑ [707.15]
      due to secondary diabetes
        249.8 ☑ [707.15]
    heel 250.8 ☑ [707.14]
      due to secondary diabetes
        249.8 ☑ [707.14]
    knee 250.8 ☑ [707.19]
      due to secondary diabetes
        249.8 ☑ [707.19]
    specified site NEC 250.8 ☑ [707.19]
      due to secondary diabetes
        249.8 ☑ [707.19]
    thigh 250.8 ☑ [707.11]
      due to secondary diabetes
        249.8 ☑ [707.11]
    toes 250.8 ☑ [707.15]
      due to secondary diabetes
        249.8 ☑ [707.15]
  specified site NEC 250.8 ☑ [707.8]
    due to secondary diabetes
      249.8 ☑ [707.8]
xanthoma 250.8 ☑ [272.2]
  due to secondary diabetes 249.8 ☑ [272.2]
Diacyclothrombopathia 287.1
Diagnosis deferred 799.9
Dialysis (intermittent) (treatment)
  anterior retinal (juvenile) (with detachment)
    361.04
  extracorporeal V56.0
  hemodialysis V56.0
    status only V45.11
  peritoneal V56.8
    status only V45.11
  renal V56.0
    status only V45.11
  specified type NEC V56.8
Diamond-Blackfan anemia or syndrome
  (congenital hypoplastic anemia) 284.01
Diamond-Gardener syndrome (autoerythrocyte
  sensitization) 287.2
Diaper rash 691.0
Diaphoresis (excessive) NEC — *see also* Hyperhidrosis) 780.8
Diaphragm — *see* condition
Diaphragmalgia 786.52
Diaphragmitis 519.4
Diaphyseal aclasis 756.4
Diaphysitis 733.99
Diarrhea, diarrheal (acute) (autumn) (bilious)
  (bloody) (catarrhal) (choleraic) (chronic)
  (gravis) (green) (infantile) (lienteric) (noninfectious) (presumed noninfectious) (pu-
  trefactive) (secondary) (sporadic) (summer)
  (symptomatic) (thermic) 787.91
  achlorhydric 536.0
  allergic 558.3
  amebic (*see also* Amebiasis) 006.9
    with abscess — *see* Abscess, amebic
    acute 006.0
    chronic 006.1
    nondysenteric 006.2
  bacillary — *see* Dysentery, bacillary
  bacterial NEC 008.5
  balantidial 007.0
  bile salt-induced 579.8

Diarrhea, diarrheal — *continued*
cachectic NEC 787.91
chilomastix 007.8
choleriformis 001.1
coccidial 007.2
Cochin-China 579.1
  anguilluliasis 127.2
  psilosis 579.1
Dientamoeba 007.8
dietetic 787.91
due to
  achylia gastrica 536.8
  Aerobacter aerogenes 008.2
  Bacillus coli — *see* Enteritis, E. coli
  bacteria NEC 008.5
  bile salts 579.8
  Capillaria
    hepatica 128.8
    philippinensis 127.5
  Clostridium perfringens (C) (F) 008.46
  Enterobacter aerogenes 008.2
  enterococci 008.49
  Escherichia coli — *see* Enteritis, E. coli
  Giardia lamblia 007.1
  Heterophyes heterophyes 121.6
  irritating foods 787.91
  Metagonimus yokogawai 121.5
  Necator americanus 126.1
  Paracolobactrum arizonae 008.1
  Paracolon bacillus NEC 008.47
    Arizona 008.1
  Proteus (bacillus) (mirabilis) (Morganii)
    008.3
  Pseudomonas aeruginosa 008.42
  S. japonicum 120.2
  specified organism NEC 008.8
    bacterial 008.49
    viral NEC 008.69
  Staphylococcus 008.41
  Streptococcus 008.49
    anaerobic 008.46
  Strongyloides stercoralis 127.2
  Trichuris trichiuria 127.3
  virus NEC (*see also* Enteritis, viral) 008.69
dysenteric 009.2
  due to specified organism NEC 008.8
dyspeptic 787.91
endemic 009.3
  due to specified organism NEC 008.8
epidemic 009.2
  due to specified organism NEC 008.8
fermentative 787.91
flagellate 007.9
Flexner's (ulcerative) 004.1
functional 564.5
  following gastrointestinal surgery 564.4
  psychogenic 306.4
giardial 007.1
Giardia lamblia 007.1
hill 579.1
hyperperistalsis (nervous) 306.4
infectious 009.2
  due to specified organism NEC 008.8
  presumed 009.3
inflammatory 787.91
  due to specified organism NEC 008.8
malarial (*see also* Malaria) 084.6
mite 133.8
mycotic 117.9
nervous 306.4
neurogenic 564.5
parenteral NEC 009.2
postgastrectomy 564.4
postvagotomy 564.4
prostaglandin induced 579.8
protozoal NEC 007.9
psychogenic 306.4
septic 009.2
  due to specified organism NEC 008.8
specified organism NEC 008.8
  bacterial 008.49
  viral NEC 008.69
Staphylococcus 008.41
Streptococcus 008.49
  anaerobic 008.46
toxic 558.2

Diarrhea, diarrheal — *continued*
travelers' 009.2
  due to specified organism NEC 008.8
trichomonal 007.3
tropical 579.1
tuberculous 014.8 ☑
ulcerative (chronic) (*see also* Colitis, ulcerative)
  556.9
viral (*see also* Enteritis, viral) 008.8
zymotic NEC 009.2
Diastasis
cranial bones 733.99
  congenital 756.0
joint (traumatic) — *see* Dislocation, by site
muscle 728.84
  congenital 756.89
recti (abdomen) 728.84
  complicating delivery 665.8 ☑
  congenital 756.79
Diastema, teeth, tooth 524.30
Diastematomyelia 742.51
Diataxia, cerebral, infantile 343.0
Diathesis
allergic V15.09
bleeding (familial) 287.9
cystine (familial) 270.0
gouty 274.9
hemorrhagic (familial) 287.9
  newborn NEC 776.0
oxalic 271.8
scrofulous (*see also* Tuberculosis) 017.2 ☑
spasmophilic (*see also* Tetany) 781.7
ulcer 536.9
uric acid 274.9
Diaz's disease or osteochondrosis 732.5
Dibothriocephaliasis 123.4
  larval 123.5
Dibothriocephalus (infection) (infestation) (latus)
  123.4
  larval 123.5
Dicephalus 759.4
Dichotomy, teeth 520.2
Dichromat, dichromata (congenital) 368.59
Dichromatopsia (congenital) 368.59
Dichuchwa 104.0
Dicroceliasis 121.8
Didelphys, didelphic — *see also* Double uterus
  752.2
Didymitis — *see also* Epididymitis 604.90
Died — *see also* Death
  without
    medical attention (cause unknown) 798.9
    sign of disease 798.2
Dientamoeba diarrhea 007.8
Dietary
inadequacy or deficiency 269.9
surveillance and counseling V65.3
Dietl's crisis 593.4
Dieulafoy lesion (hemorrhagic)
  of
    duodenum 537.84
    esophagus 530.82
    intestine 569.86
    stomach 537.84
Difficult
birth, affecting fetus or newborn 763.9
delivery NEC 669.9 ☑
Difficulty
feeding 783.3
  adult 783.3
  breast 676.8 ☑
  child 783.3
  elderly 783.3
  infant 783.3
  newborn 779.31   ▲
  nonorganic (infant) NEC 307.59
mechanical, gastroduodenal stoma 537.89
reading 315.00
specific, spelling 315.09
swallowing (*see also* Dysphagia) 787.20
walking 719.7
Diffuse — *see* condition
Diffused ganglion 727.42
Di George's syndrome (thymic hypoplasia)
  279.11
Digestive — *see* condition

☑ Additional Digit Required — Refer to the Tabular List for Digit Selection   ▼ Subterms under main terms may continue to next column or page

2010 ICD-9-CM   ▶◀ Revised Text   ● New Line   ▲ Revised Code   October 2009 • Volume 2 — 77

Di Guglielmo's disease or syndrome (M9841/3)
207.0 ☑

Diktyoma (M9051/3) — *see* Neoplasm, by site,
malignant

Dilaceration, tooth 520.4

Dilatation
anus 564.89
venule — *see* Hemorrhoids
aorta (focal) (general) (*see also* Aneurysm,
aorta) 441.9
congenital 747.29
infectional 093.0
ruptured 441.5
syphilitic 093.0
appendix (cystic) 543.9
artery 447.8
bile duct (common) (cystic) (congenital)
751.69
acquired 576.8
bladder (sphincter) 596.8
congenital 753.8
in pregnancy or childbirth 654.4 ☑
causing obstructed labor 660.2 ☑
affecting fetus or newborn 763.1
blood vessel 459.89
bronchus, bronchi 494.0
with acute exacerbation 494.1
calyx (due to obstruction) 593.89
capillaries 448.9
cardiac (acute) (chronic) (*see also* Hypertrophy,
cardiac) 429.3
congenital 746.89
valve NEC 746.89
pulmonary 746.09
hypertensive (*see also* Hypertension, heart)
402.90
cavum septi pellucidi 742.4
cecum 564.89
psychogenic 306.4
cervix (uteri) (*see also* Incompetency, cervix)
incomplete, poor, slow
affecting fetus or newborn 763.7
complicating delivery 661.0 ☑
affecting fetus or newborn 763.7
colon 564.7
congenital 751.3
due to mechanical obstruction 560.89
psychogenic 306.4
common bile duct (congenital) 751.69
acquired 576.8
with calculus, choledocholithiasis, or
stones — *see* Choledocholithiasis
cystic duct 751.69
acquired (any bile duct) 575.8
duct, mammary 610.4
duodenum 564.89
esophagus 530.89
congenital 750.4
due to
achalasia 530.0
cardiospasm 530.0
Eustachian tube, congenital 744.24
fontanel 756.0
gallbladder 575.8
congenital 751.69
gastric 536.8
acute 536.1
psychogenic 306.4
heart (acute) (chronic) (*see also* Hypertrophy,
cardiac) 429.3
congenital 746.89
hypertensive (*see also* Hypertension, heart)
402.90
valve (*see also* Endocarditis)
congenital 746.89
ileum 564.89
psychogenic 306.4
inguinal rings — *see* Hernia, inguinal
jejunum 564.89
psychogenic 306.4
kidney (calyx) (collecting structures) (cystic)
(parenchyma) (pelvis) 593.89
lacrimal passages 375.69
lymphatic vessel 457.1
mammary duct 610.4

Dilatation — *continued*
Meckel's diverticulum (congenital) 751.0
meningeal vessels, congenital 742.8
myocardium (acute) (chronic) (*see also* Hypertrophy, cardiac) 429.3
organ or site, congenital NEC — *see* Distortion
pancreatic duct 577.8
pelvis, kidney 593.89
pericardium — *see* Pericarditis
pharynx 478.29
prostate 602.8
pulmonary
artery (idiopathic) 417.8
congenital 747.3
valve, congenital 746.09
pupil 379.43
rectum 564.89
renal 593.89
saccule vestibularis, congenital 744.05
salivary gland (duct) 527.8
sphincter ani 564.89
stomach 536.8
acute 536.1
psychogenic 306.4
submaxillary duct 527.8
trachea, congenital 748.3
ureter (idiopathic) 593.89
congenital 753.20
due to obstruction 593.5
urethra (acquired) 599.84
vasomotor 443.9
vein 459.89
ventricular, ventricle (acute) (chronic) (*see also*
Hypertrophy, cardiac) 429.3
cerebral, congenital 742.4
hypertensive (*see also* Hypertension, heart)
402.90
venule 459.89
anus — *see* Hemorrhoids
vesical orifice 596.8

Dilated, dilation — *see* Dilatation

Diminished
hearing (acuity) (*see also* Deafness) 389.9
pulse pressure 785.9
vision NEC 369.9
vital capacity 794.2

Diminuta taenia 123.6

Diminution, sense or sensation (cold) (heat)
(tactile) (vibratory) — *see also* Disturbance,
sensation 782.0

Dimitri-Sturge-Weber disease (encephalocutaneous angiomatosis) 759.6

Dimple
parasacral 685.1
with abscess 685.0
pilonidal 685.1
with abscess 685.0
postanal 685.1
with abscess 685.0

Dioctophyma renale (infection) (infestation)
128.8

Dipetalonemiasis 125.4

Diphallus 752.69

Diphtheria, diphtheritic (gangrenous) (hemorrhagic) 032.9
carrier (suspected) of V02.4
cutaneous 032.85
cystitis 032.84
faucial 032.0
infection of wound 032.85
inoculation (anti) (not sick) V03.5
laryngeal 032.3
myocarditis 032.82
nasal anterior 032.2
nasopharyngeal 032.1
neurological complication 032.89
peritonitis 032.83
specified site NEC 032.89

Diphyllobothriasis (intestine) 123.4
larval 123.5

Diplacusis 388.41

Diplegia (upper limbs) 344.2
brain or cerebral 437.8
congenital 343.0
facial 351.0
congenital 352.6

Diplegia — *continued*
infantile or congenital (cerebral) (spastic)
(spinal) 343.0
lower limbs 344.1
syphilitic, congenital 090.49

Diplococcus, diplococcal — *see* condition

Diplomyelia 742.59

Diplopia 368.2
refractive 368.15

Dipsomania — *see also* Alcoholism 303.9 ☑
with psychosis (*see also* Psychosis, alcoholic)
291.9

Dipylidiasis 123.8
intestine 123.8

Direction, teeth, abnormal 524.30

Dirt-eating child 307.52

Disability
heart — *see* Disease, heart
learning NEC 315.2
special spelling 315.09

Disarticulation — *see also* Derangement, joint
718.9 ☑
meaning
amputation
status — *see* Absence, by site
traumatic — *see* Amputation, traumatic
dislocation, traumatic or congenital — *see*
Dislocation

Disaster, cerebrovascular — *see also* Disease,
cerebrovascular, acute 436

Discharge
anal NEC 787.99
breast (female) (male) 611.79
conjunctiva 372.89
continued locomotor idiopathic (*see also*
Epilepsy) 345.5 ☑
diencephalic autonomic idiopathic (*see also*
Epilepsy) 345.5 ☑
ear 388.60
blood 388.69
cerebrospinal fluid 388.61
excessive urine 788.42
eye 379.93
nasal 478.19
nipple 611.79
patterned motor idiopathic (*see also* Epilepsy)
345.5 ☑
penile 788.7
postnasal — *see* Sinusitis
sinus, from mediastinum 510.0
umbilicus 789.9
urethral 788.7
bloody 599.84
vaginal 623.5

Discitis 722.90
cervical, cervicothoracic 722.91
lumbar, lumbosacral 722.93
thoracic, thoracolumbar 722.92

Discogenic syndrome — *see* Displacement, intervertebral disc

Discoid
kidney 753.3
meniscus, congenital 717.5
semilunar cartilage 717.5

Discoloration
mouth 528.9
nails 703.8
teeth 521.7
due to
drugs 521.7
metals (copper) (silver) 521.7
pulpal bleeding 521.7
during formation 520.8
extrinsic 523.6
intrinsic posteruptive 521.7

Discomfort
chest 786.59
visual 368.13

Discomycosis — *see* Actinomycosis

Discontinuity, ossicles, ossicular chain 385.23

Discrepancy
centric occlusion
maximum intercuspation 524.55
of teeth 524.55
leg length (acquired) 736.81

Discrepancy — *continued*
leg length — *continued*
congenital 755.30
uterine size-date 649.6 ☑

Discrimination
political V62.4
racial V62.4
religious V62.4
sex V62.4

Disease, diseased — *see also* Syndrome
Abrami's (acquired hemolytic jaundice) 283.9
absorbent system 459.89
accumulation — *see* Thesaurismosis
acid-peptic 536.8
Acosta's 993.2
Adams-Stokes (-Morgagni) (syncope with
heart block) 426.9
Addison's (bronze) (primary adrenal insufficiency) 255.41
anemia (pernicious) 281.0
tuberculous (*see also* Tuberculosis)
017.6 ☑
Addison-Gull — *see* Xanthoma
adenoids (and tonsils) (chronic) 474.9
adrenal (gland) (capsule) (cortex) 255.9
hyperfunction 255.3
hypofunction 255.41
specified type NEC 255.8
ainhum (dactylolysis spontanea) 136.0
akamushi (scrub typhus) 081.2
Akureyri (epidemic neuromyasthenia) 049.8
Albarrán's (colibacilluria) 791.9
Albers-Schönberg's (marble bones) 756.52
Albert's 726.71
Albright (-Martin) (-Bantam) 275.49
Alibert's (mycosis fungoides) (M9700/3)
202.1 ☑
Alibert-Bazin (M9700/3) 202.1 ☑
alimentary canal 569.9
alligator skin (ichthyosis congenita) 757.1
acquired 701.1
Almeida's (Brazilian blastomycosis) 116.1
Alpers' 330.8
alpine 993.2
altitude 993.2
alveoli, teeth 525.9
Alzheimer's — *see* Alzheimer's
amyloid (any site) 277.30
anarthritic rheumatoid 446.5
Anders' (adiposis tuberosa simplex) 272.8
Andersen's (glycogenosis IV) 271.0
Anderson's (angiokeratoma corporis diffusum)
272.7
Andes 993.2
Andrews' (bacterid) 686.8
angiospastic, angiospasmodic 443.9
cerebral 435.9
with transient neurologic deficit 435.9
vein 459.89
anterior
chamber 364.9
horn cell 335.9
specified type NEC 335.8
antral (chronic) 473.0
acute 461.0
anus NEC 569.49
aorta (nonsyphilitic) 447.9
syphilitic NEC 093.89
aortic (heart) (valve) (*see also* Endocarditis,
aortic) 424.1
apollo 077.4
aponeurosis 726.90
appendix 543.9
aqueous (chamber) 364.9
arc-welders' lung 503
Armenian 277.31
Arnold-Chiari (*see also* Spina bifida) 741.0 ☑
arterial 447.9
occlusive (*see also* Occlusion, by site)
444.22
with embolus or thrombus — *see* Occlusion, by site
due to stricture or stenosis 447.1
specified type NEC 447.8
arteriocardiorenal (*see also* Hypertension, cardiorenal) 404.90

Disease, diseased — *see also* Syndrome — *continued*

arteriolar (generalized) (obliterative) 447.9
  specified type NEC 447.8
arteriorenal — *see* Hypertension, kidney
arteriosclerotic (*see also* Arteriosclerosis)
  cardiovascular 429.2
  coronary — *see* Arteriosclerosis, coronary
  heart — *see* Arteriosclerosis, coronary
  vascular — *see* Arteriosclerosis
artery 447.9
  cerebral 437.9
  coronary — *see* Arteriosclerosis, coronary
  specified type NEC 447.8
arthropod-borne NEC 088.9
  specified type NEC 088.89
Asboe-Hansen's (incontinentia pigmenti) 757.33
atticoantral, chronic (with posterior or superior marginal perforation of ear drum) 382.2
auditory canal, ear 380.9
Aujeszky's 078.89
auricle, ear NEC 380.30
Australian X 062.4
autoimmune NEC 279.49 ▲
  hemolytic (cold type) (warm type) 283.0
  parathyroid 252.1
  thyroid 245.2
aviators' (*see also* Effect, adverse, high altitude) 993.2
ax(e)-grinders' 502
Ayala's 756.89
Ayerza's (pulmonary artery sclerosis with pulmonary hypertension) 416.0
Azorean (of the nervous system) 334.8
Babington's (familial hemorrhagic telangiectasia) 448.0
back bone NEC 733.90
bacterial NEC 040.89
  zoonotic NEC 027.9
  specified type NEC 027.8
Baehr-Schiffrin (thrombotic thrombocytopenic purpura) 446.6
Baelz's (cheilitis glandularis apostematosa) 528.5
Baerensprung's (eczema marginatum) 110.3
Balfour's (chloroma) 205.3 ☑
balloon (*see also* Effect, adverse, high altitude 993.2
Baló's 341.1
Bamberger (-Marie) (hypertrophic pulmonary osteoarthropathy) 731.2
Bang's (Brucella abortus) 023.1
Bannister's 995.1
Banti's (with cirrhosis) (with portal hypertension) — *see* Cirrhosis, liver
Barcoo (*see also* Ulcer, skin) 707.9
barium lung 503
Barlow (-Möller) (infantile scurvy) 267
barometer makers' 985.0
Barraquer (-Simons) (progressive lipodystrophy) 272.6
basal ganglia 333.90
  degenerative NEC 333.0
  specified NEC 333.89
Basedow's (exophthalmic goiter) 242.0 ☑
basement membrane NEC 583.89
  with
    pulmonary hemorrhage (Goodpasture's syndrome) 446.21 [583.81]
Bateman's 078.0
  purpura (senile) 287.2
Batten's 330.1 [362.71]
Batten-Mayou (retina) 330.1 [362.71]
Batten-Steinert 359.21
Battey 031.0
Baumgarten-Cruveilhier (cirrhosis of liver) 571.5
bauxite-workers' 503
Bayle's (dementia paralytica) 094.1
Bazin's (primary) (*see also* Tuberculosis) 017.1 ☑
Beard's (neurasthenia) 300.5
Beau's (*see also* Degeneration, myocardial) 429.1

Disease, diseased — *see also* Syndrome — *continued*

Bechterew's (ankylosing spondylitis) 720.0
Becker's
  idiopathic mural endomyocardial disease 425.2
  myotonia congenita, recessive form 359.22
Begbie's (exophthalmic goiter) 242.0 ☑
Behr's 362.50
Beigel's (white piedra) 111.2
Bekhterev's (ankylosing spondylitis) 720.0
Bell's (*see also* Psychosis, affective) 296.0 ☑
Bennett's (leukemia) 208.9 ☑
Benson's 379.22
Bergeron's (hysteroepilepsy) 300.11
Berlin's 921.3
Bernard-Soulier (thrombopathy) 287.1
Bernhardt (-Roth) 355.1
beryllium 503
Besnier-Boeck (-Schaumann) (sarcoidosis) 135
Best's 362.76
Beurmann's (sporotrichosis) 117.1
Bielschowsky (-Jansky) 330.1
Biermer's (pernicious anemia) 281.0
Biett's (discoid lupus erythematosus) 695.4
bile duct (*see also* Disease, biliary) 576.9
biliary (duct) (tract) 576.9
  with calculus, choledocholithiasis, or stones — *see* Choledocholithiasis
Billroth's (meningocele) (*see also* Spina bifida) 741.9 ☑
Binswanger's 290.12
Bird's (oxaluria) 271.8
bird fanciers' 495.2
black lung 500
bladder 596.9
  specified NEC 596.8
bleeder's 286.0
Bloch-Sulzberger (incontinentia pigmenti) 757.33
Blocq's (astasia-abasia) 307.9
blood (-forming organs) 289.9
  specified NEC 289.89
  vessel 459.9
Bloodgood's 610.1
blue 746.9
Blount's (tibia vara) 732.4
Bodechtel-Guttmann (subacute sclerosing panencephalitis) 046.2
Boeck's (sarcoidosis) 135
bone 733.90
  fibrocystic NEC 733.29
    jaw 526.2
  marrow 289.9
  Paget's (osteitis deformans) 731.0
  specified type NEC 733.99
  von Recklinghausen's (osteitis fibrosa cystica) 252.01
Bonfils' — *see* Disease, Hodgkin's
Borna 062.9
Bornholm (epidemic pleurodynia) 074.1
Bostock's (*see also* Fever, hay) 477.9
Bouchard's (myopathic dilatation of the stomach) 536.1
Bouillaud's (rheumatic heart disease) 391.9
Bourneville (-Brissaud) (tuberous sclerosis) 759.5
Bouveret (-Hoffmann) (paroxysmal tachycardia) 427.2
bowel 569.9
  functional 564.9
    psychogenic 306.4
Bowen's (M8081/2) — *see* Neoplasm, skin, in situ
Bozzolo's (multiple myeloma) (M9730/3) 203.0 ☑
Bradley's (epidemic vomiting) 078.82
Brailsford's 732.3
  radius, head 732.3
  tarsal, scaphoid 732.5
Brailsford-Morquio (mucopolysaccharidosis IV) 277.5
brain 348.9
  Alzheimer's 331.0
    with dementia — *see* Alzheimer's, dementia

Disease, diseased — *see also* Syndrome — *continued*

brain — *continued*
  arterial, artery 437.9
  arteriosclerotic 437.0
  congenital 742.9
  degenerative — *see* Degeneration, brain
  inflammatory (*see also* Encephalitis)
    late effect — *see* category 326
  organic 348.9
    arteriosclerotic 437.0
  parasitic NEC 123.9
  Pick's 331.11
    with dementia
      with behavioral disturbance 331.11 [294.11]
      without behavioral disturbance 331.11 [294.10]
  senile 331.2
braziers' 985.8
breast 611.9
  cystic (chronic) 610.1
  fibrocystic 610.1
  inflammatory 611.0
  Paget's (M8540/3) 174.0
  puerperal, postpartum NEC 676.3 ☑
  specified NEC 611.89
Breda's (*see also* Yaws) 102.9
Breisky's (kraurosis vulvae) 624.09
Bretonneau's (diphtheritic malignant angina) 032.0
Bright's (*see also* Nephritis) 583.9
  arteriosclerotic (*see also* Hypertension, kidney) 403.90
Brill's (recrudescent typhus) 081.1
  flea-borne 081.0
  louse-borne 081.1
Brill-Symmers (follicular lymphoma) (M9690/3) 202.0 ☑
Brill-Zinsser (recrudescent typhus) 081.1
Brinton's (leather bottle stomach) (M8142/3) 151.9
Brion-Kayser (*see also* Fever, paratyphoid) 002.9
broad
  beta 272.2
  ligament, noninflammatory 620.9
    specified NEC 620.8
Brocq's 691.8
  meaning
    atopic (diffuse) neurodermatitis 691.8
    dermatitis herpetiformis 694.0
    lichen simplex chronicus 698.3
    parapsoriasis 696.2
    prurigo 698.2
Brocq-Duhring (dermatitis herpetiformis) 694.0
Brodie's (joint) (*see also* Osteomyelitis) 730.1 ☑
bronchi 519.19
bronchopulmonary 519.19
bronze (Addison's) 255.41
  tuberculous (*see also* Tuberculosis) 017.6 ☑
Brown-Séquard 344.89
Bruck's 733.99
Bruck-de Lange (Amsterdam dwarf, mental retardation and brachycephaly) 759.89
Bruhl's (splenic anemia with fever) 285.8
Bruton's (X-linked agammaglobulinemia) 279.04
buccal cavity 528.9
Buchanan's (juvenile osteochondrosis, iliac crest) 732.1
Buchman's (osteochondrosis juvenile) 732.1
Budgerigar-Fanciers' 495.2
Büdinger-Ludloff-Läwen 717.89
Buerger's (thromboangiitis obliterans) 443.1
Bürger-Grütz (essential familial hyperlipemia) 272.3
Burns' (lower ulna) 732.3
bursa 727.9
Bury's (erythema elevatum diutinum) 695.89
Buschke's 710.1
Busquet's (*see also* Osteomyelitis) 730.1 ☑
Busse-Buschke (cryptococcosis) 117.5
C₂ (*see also* Alcoholism) 303.9 ☑
Caffey's (infantile cortical hyperostosis) 756.59

Disease, diseased — *see also* Syndrome — *continued*

caisson 993.3
calculous 592.9
California 114.0
Calvé (-Perthes) (osteochondrosis, femoral capital) 732.1
Camurati-Engelmann (diaphyseal sclerosis) 756.59
Canavan's 330.0
capillaries 448.9
Carapata 087.1
cardiac — *see* Disease, heart
cardiopulmonary, chronic 416.9
cardiorenal (arteriosclerotic) (hepatic) (hypertensive) (vascular) (*see also* Hypertension, cardiorenal) 404.90
cardiovascular (arteriosclerotic) 429.2
  congenital 746.9
  hypertensive (*see also* Hypertension, heart) 402.90
    benign 402.10
    malignant 402.00
  renal (*see also* Hypertension, cardiorenal) 404.90
  syphilitic (asymptomatic) 093.9
carotid gland 259.8
Carrión's (Bartonellosis) 088.0
cartilage NEC 733.90
  specified NEC 733.99
Castellani's 104.8
cat-scratch 078.3
Cavare's (familial periodic paralysis) 359.3
Cazenave's (pemphigus) 694.4
cecum 569.9
celiac (adult) 579.0
  infantile 579.0
cellular tissue NEC 709.9
central core 359.0
cerebellar, cerebellum — *see* Disease, brain
cerebral (*see also* Disease, brain) 348.9
  arterial, artery 437.9
  degenerative — *see* Degeneration, brain
cerebrospinal 349.9
cerebrovascular NEC 437.9
  acute 436
    embolic — *see* Embolism, brain
    late effect — *see* Late effect(s) (of) cerebrovascular disease
    puerperal, postpartum, childbirth 674.0 ☑
    thrombotic — *see* Thrombosis, brain
  arteriosclerotic 437.0
  embolic — *see* Embolism, brain
  ischemic, generalized NEC 437.1
  late effect — *see* Late effect(s) (of) cerebrovascular disease
  occlusive 437.1
  puerperal, postpartum, childbirth 674.0 ☑
  specified type NEC 437.8
  thrombotic — *see* Thrombosis, brain
ceroid storage 272.7
cervix (uteri)
  inflammatory 616.0
  noninflammatory 622.9
    specified NEC 622.8
Chabert's 022.9
Chagas' (*see also* Trypanosomiasis, American) 086.2
Chandler's (osteochondritis dissecans, hip) 732.7
Charcôt-Marie-Tooth 356.1
Charcôt's (joint) 094.0 [713.5]
  spinal cord 094.0
Charlouis' (*see also* Yaws) 102.9
Cheadle (-Möller) (-Barlow) (infantile scurvy) 267
Chédiak-Steinbrinck (-Higashi) (congenital gigantism of peroxidase granules) 288.2
cheek, inner 528.9
chest 519.9
Chiari's (hepatic vein thrombosis) 453.0
Chicago (North American blastomycosis) 116.0
chignon (white piedra) 111.2
chigoe, chigo (jigger) 134.1
childhood granulomatous 288.1

☑ Additional Digit Required — Refer to the Tabular List for Digit Selection   ▽ Subterms under main terms may continue to next column or page

2010 ICD-9-CM   ▶◀ Revised Text   ● New Line   ▲ Revised Code   October 2009 · Volume 2 — 79

Index

Disease, diseased — Disease, diseased

Disease, diseased — *see also* Syndrome — *continued*
- Chinese liver fluke 121.1
- chlamydial NEC 078.88
- cholecystic (*see also* Disease, gallbladder) 575.9
- choroid 363.9
  - degenerative (*see also* Degeneration, choroid) 363.40
  - hereditary (*see also* Dystrophy, choroid) 363.50
  - specified type NEC 363.8
- Christian's (chronic histiocytosis X) 277.89
- Christian-Weber (nodular nonsuppurative panniculitis) 729.30
- Christmas 286.1
- ciliary body 364.9
  - specified NEC 364.89
- circulatory (system) NEC 459.9
  - chronic, maternal, affecting fetus or newborn 760.3
  - specified NEC 459.89
  - syphilitic 093.9
    - congenital 090.5
- Civatte's (poikiloderma) 709.09
- climacteric 627.2
  - male 608.89
- coagulation factor deficiency (congenital) (*see also* Defect, coagulation) 286.9
- Coats' 362.12
- coccidioidal pulmonary 114.5
  - acute 114.0
  - chronic 114.4
  - primary 114.0
  - residual 114.4
- Cockayne's (microcephaly and dwarfism) 759.89
- Cogan's 370.52
- cold
  - agglutinin 283.0
    - or hemoglobinuria 283.0
      - paroxysmal (cold) (nocturnal) 283.2
  - hemagglutinin (chronic) 283.0
- collagen NEC 710.9
  - nonvascular 710.9
  - specified NEC 710.8
  - vascular (allergic) (*see also* Angiitis, hypersensitivity) 446.20
- colon 569.9
  - functional 564.9
    - congenital 751.3
  - ischemic 557.0
- combined system (of spinal cord) 266.2 *[336.2]*
  - with anemia (pernicious) 281.0 *[336.2]*
- compressed air 993.3
- Concato's (pericardial polyserositis) 423.2
  - peritoneal 568.82
  - pleural — *see* Pleurisy
- congenital NEC 799.89
- conjunctiva 372.9
  - chlamydial 077.98
    - specified NEC 077.8
  - specified type NEC 372.89
  - viral 077.99
    - specified NEC 077.8
- connective tissue, diffuse (*see also* Disease, collagen) 710.9
- Conor and Bruch's (boutonneuse fever) 082.1
- Conradi (-Hünermann) 756.59
- Cooley's (erythroblastic anemia) 282.49
- Cooper's 610.1
- Corbus' 607.1
- cork-handlers' 495.3
- cornea (*see also* Keratopathy) 371.9
- coronary (*see also* Ischemia, heart) 414.9
  - congenital 746.85
  - ostial, syphilitic 093.20
    - aortic 093.22
    - mitral 093.21
    - pulmonary 093.24
    - tricuspid 093.23
- Corrigan's — *see* Insufficiency, aortic
- Cotugno's 724.3
- Coxsackie (virus) NEC 074.8
- cranial nerve NEC 352.9
- Creutzfeldt-Jakob (CJD) 046.19

Disease, diseased — *see also* Syndrome — *continued*
- Creutzfeldt-Jakob — *continued*
  - with dementia
    - with behavioral disturbance 046.19 *[294.11]*
    - without behavioral disturbance 046.19 *[294.10]*
  - familial 046.19
  - iatrogenic 046.19
  - specified NEC 046.19
  - sporadic 046.19
  - variant (vCJD) 046.11
    - with dementia
      - with behavioral disturbance 046.11 *[294.11]*
      - without behavioral disturbance 046.11 *[294.10]*
- Crigler-Najjar (congenital hyperbilirubinemia) 277.4
- Crocq's (acrocyanosis) 443.89
- Crohn's (intestine) (*see also* Enteritis, regional) 555.9
- Crouzon's (craniofacial dysostosis) 756.0
- Cruchet's (encephalitis lethargica) 049.8
- Cruveilhier's 335.21
- Cruz-Chagas (*see also* Trypanosomiasis, American) 086.2
- crystal deposition (*see also* Arthritis, due to, crystals) 712.9 ☑
- Csillag's (lichen sclerosus et atrophicus) 701.0
- Curschmann's 359.21
- Cushing's (pituitary basophilism) 255.0
- cystic
  - breast (chronic) 610.1
  - kidney, congenital (*see also* Cystic, disease, kidney) 753.10
  - liver, congenital 751.62
  - lung 518.89
    - congenital 748.4
  - pancreas 577.2
    - congenital 751.7
  - renal, congenital (*see also* Cystic, disease, kidney) 753.10
  - semilunar cartilage 717.5
- cysticercus 123.1
- cystine storage (with renal sclerosis) 270.0
- cytomegalic inclusion (generalized) 078.5
  - with
    - pneumonia 078.5 *[484.1]*
  - congenital 771.1
- Daae (-Finsen) (epidemic pleurodynia) 074.1
- dancing 297.8
- Danielssen's (anesthetic leprosy) 030.1
- Darier's (congenital) (keratosis follicularis) 757.39
  - erythema annulare centrifugum 695.0
  - vitamin A deficiency 264.8
- Darling's (histoplasmosis) (*see also* Histoplasmosis, American) 115.00
- Davies' 425.0
- de Beurmann-Gougerot (sporotrichosis) 117.1
- Débove's (splenomegaly) 789.2
- deer fly (*see also* Tularemia) 021.9
- deficiency 269.9
- degenerative (*see also* Degeneration)
  - disc — *see* Degeneration, intervertebral disc
- Degos' 447.8
- Déjérine (-Sottas) 356.0
- Déleage's 359.89
- demyelinating, demyelinizating (brain stem) (central nervous system) 341.9
  - multiple sclerosis 340
  - specified NEC 341.8
- de Quervain's (tendon sheath) 727.04
  - thyroid (subacute granulomatous thyroiditis) 245.1
- Dercum's (adiposis dolorosa) 272.8
- Deutschländer's — *see* Fracture, foot
- Devergie's (pityriasis rubra pilaris) 696.4
- Devic's 341.0
- diaphorase deficiency 289.7
- diaphragm 519.4
- diarrheal, infectious 009.2
- diatomaceous earth 502

Disease, diseased — *see also* Syndrome — *continued*
- Diaz's (osteochondrosis astragalus) 732.5
- digestive system 569.9
- Di Guglielmo's (erythemic myelosis) (M9841/3) 207.0 ☑
- Dimitri-Sturge-Weber (encephalocutaneous angiomatosis) 759.6
- disc, degenerative — *see* Degeneration, intervertebral disc
- discogenic (*see also* Disease, intervertebral disc) 722.90
- diverticular — *see* Diverticula
- Down's (mongolism) 758.0
- Dubini's (electric chorea) 049.8
- Dubois' (thymus gland) 090.5
- Duchenne's 094.0
  - locomotor ataxia 094.0
  - muscular dystrophy 359.1
  - paralysis 335.22
  - pseudohypertrophy, muscles 359.1
- Duchenne-Griesinger 359.1
- ductless glands 259.9
- Duhring's (dermatitis herpetiformis) 694.0
- Dukes (-Filatov) 057.8
- duodenum NEC 537.9
  - specified NEC 537.89
- Duplay's 726.2
- Dupré's (meningism) 781.6
- Dupuytren's (muscle contracture) 728.6
- Durand-Nicolas-Favre (climatic bubo) 099.1
- Duroziez's (congenital mitral stenosis) 746.5
- Dutton's (trypanosomiasis) 086.9
- Eales' 362.18
- ear (chronic) (inner) NEC 388.9
  - middle 385.9
    - adhesive (*see also* Adhesions, middle ear) 385.10
    - specified NEC 385.89
- Eberth's (typhoid fever) 002.0
- Ebstein's
  - heart 746.2
  - meaning diabetes 250.4 ☑ *[581.81]*
    - due to secondary diabetes 249.4 ☑ *[581.81]*
- Echinococcus (*see also* Echinococcus) 122.9
- ECHO virus NEC 078.89
- Economo's (encephalitis lethargica) 049.8
- Eddowes' (brittle bones and blue sclera) 756.51
- Edsall's 992.2
- Eichstedt's (pityriasis versicolor) 111.0
- Ellis-van Creveld (chondroectodermal dysplasia) 756.55
- endocardium — *see* Endocarditis
- endocrine glands or system NEC 259.9
  - specified NEC 259.8
- endomyocardial, idiopathic mural 425.2
- Engelmann's (diaphyseal sclerosis) 756.59
- Engel-von Recklinghausen (osteitis fibrosa cystica) 252.01
- English (rickets) 268.0
- Engman's (infectious eczematoid dermatitis) 690.8
- enteroviral, enterovirus NEC 078.89
  - central nervous system NEC 048
- epidemic NEC 136.9
- epididymis 608.9
- epigastric, functional 536.9
  - psychogenic 306.4
- Erb (-Landouzy) 359.1
- Erb-Goldflam 358.00
- Erdheim-Chester (ECD) 277.89 ●
- Erichsen's (railway spine) 300.16
- esophagus 530.9
  - functional 530.5
  - psychogenic 306.4
- Eulenburg's (congenital paramyotonia) 359.29
- Eustachian tube 381.9
- Evans' (thrombocytopenic purpura) 287.32
- external auditory canal 380.9
- extrapyramidal NEC 333.90
- eye 379.90
  - anterior chamber 364.9
  - inflammatory NEC 364.3
  - muscle 378.9

Disease, diseased — *see also* Syndrome — *continued*
- eyeball 360.9
- eyelid 374.9
- eyeworm of Africa 125.2
- Fabry's (angiokeratoma corporis diffusum) 272.7
- facial nerve (seventh) 351.9
  - newborn 767.5
- Fahr-Volhard (malignant nephrosclerosis) 403.00
- fallopian tube, noninflammatory 620.9
  - specified NEC 620.8
- familial periodic 277.31
  - paralysis 359.3
- Fanconi's (congenital pancytopenia) 284.09
- Farber's (disseminated lipogranulomatosis) 272.8
- fascia 728.9
  - inflammatory 728.9
- Fauchard's (periodontitis) 523.40
- Favre-Durand-Nicolas (climatic bubo) 099.1
- Favre-Racouchot (elastoidosis cutanea nodularis) 701.8
- Fede's 529.0
- Feer's 985.0
- Felix's (juvenile osteochondrosis, hip) 732.1
- Fenwick's (gastric atrophy) 537.89
- Fernels' (aortic aneurysm) 441.9
- fibrocaseous, of lung (*see also* Tuberculosis, pulmonary) 011.9 ☑
- fibrocystic (*see also* Fibrocystic, disease)
  - newborn 277.01
- Fiedler's (leptospiral jaundice) 100.0
- fifth 057.0
- Filatoff's (infectious mononucleosis) 075
- Filatov's (infectious mononucleosis) 075
- file-cutters' 984.9
  - specified type of lead — *see* Table of Drugs and Chemicals
- filterable virus NEC 078.89
- fish skin 757.1
  - acquired 701.1
- Flajani (-Basedow) (exophthalmic goiter) 242.0 ☑
- Flatau-Schilder 341.1
- flax-dressers' 504
- Fleischner's 732.3
- flint 502
- fluke — *see* Infestation, fluke
- Følling's (phenylketonuria) 270.1
- foot and mouth 078.4
- foot process 581.3
- Forbes' (glycogenosis III) 271.0
- Fordyce's (ectopic sebaceous glands) (mouth) 750.26
- Fordyce-Fox (apocrine miliaria) 705.82
- Fothergill's
  - meaning scarlatina anginosa 034.1
  - neuralgia (*see also* Neuralgia, trigeminal) 350.1
- Fournier's 608.83
- fourth 057.8
- Fox (-Fordyce) (apocrine miliaria) 705.82
- Francis' (*see also* Tularemia) 021.9
- Franklin's (heavy chain) 273.2
- Frei's (climatic bubo) 099.1
- Freiberg's (flattening metatarsal) 732.5
- Friedländer's (endarteritis obliterans) — *see* Arteriosclerosis
- Friedreich's
  - combined systemic or ataxia 334.0
  - facial hemihypertrophy 756.0
  - myoclonia 333.2
- Fröhlich's (adiposogenital dystrophy) 253.8
- Frommel's 676.6 ☑
- frontal sinus (chronic) 473.1
  - acute 461.1
- Fuller's earth 502
- fungus, fungous NEC 117.9
- Gaisböck's (polycythemia hypertonica) 289.0
- gallbladder 575.9
  - congenital 751.60
- Gamna's (siderotic splenomegaly) 289.51
- Gamstorp's (adynamia episodica hereditaria) 359.3

Disease, diseased — *see also* Syndrome — *continued*
- Gandy-Nanta (siderotic splenomegaly) 289.51
- Gannister (occupational) 502
- Garré's (*see also* Osteomyelitis) 730.1 ☑
- gastric (*see also* Disease, stomach) 537.9
- gastroesophageal reflux (GERD) 530.81
- gastrointestinal (tract) 569.9
  - amyloid 277.39
  - functional 536.9
    - psychogenic 306.4
- Gaucher's (adult) (cerebroside lipidosis) (infantile) 272.7
- Gayet's (superior hemorrhagic polioencephalitis) 265.1
- Gee (-Herter) (-Heubner) (-Thaysen) (nontropical sprue) 579.0
- generalized neoplastic (M8000/6) 199.0
- genital organs NEC
  - female 629.9
    - specified NEC 629.89
  - male 608.9
- Gerhardt's (erythromelalgia) 443.82
- Gerlier's (epidemic vertigo) 078.81
- Gibert's (pityriasis rosea) 696.3
- Gibney's (perispondylitis) 720.9
- Gierke's (glycogenosis I) 271.0
- Gilbert's (familial nonhemolytic jaundice) 277.4
- Gilchrist's (North American blastomycosis) 116.0
- Gilford (-Hutchinson) (progeria) 259.8
- Gilles de la Tourette's (motor-verbal tic) 307.23
- Giovannini's 117.9
- gland (lymph) 289.9
- Glanzmann's (hereditary hemorrhagic thrombasthenia) 287.1
- glassblowers' 527.1
- Glénard's (enteroptosis) 569.89
- Glisson's (*see also* Rickets) 268.0
- glomerular
  - membranous, idiopathic 581.1
  - minimal change 581.3
- glycogen storage (Andersen's) (Cori types 1-7) (Forbes') (McArdle-Schmid-Pearson) (Pompe's) (types I-VII) 271.0
  - cardiac 271.0 *[425.7]*
  - generalized 271.0
  - glucose–6–phosphatase deficiency 271.0
  - heart 271.0 *[425.7]*
  - hepatorenal 271.0
  - liver and kidneys 271.0
  - myocardium 271.0 *[425.7]*
  - von Gierke's (glycogenosis I) 271.0
- Goldflam-Erb 358.00
- Goldscheider's (epidermolysis bullosa) 757.39
- Goldstein's (familial hemorrhagic telangiectasia) 448.0
- gonococcal NEC 098.0
- Goodall's (epidemic vomiting) 078.82
- Gordon's (exudative enteropathy) 579.8
- Gougerot's (trisymptomatic) 709.1
- Gougerot-Carteaud (confluent reticulate papillomatosis) 701.8
- Gougerot-Hailey-Hailey (benign familial chronic pemphigus) 757.39
- graft-versus-host 279.50
  - acute 279.51
    - on chronic 279.53
  - chronic 279.52
- grain-handlers' 495.8
- Grancher's (splenopneumonia) — *see* Pneumonia
- granulomatous (childhood) (chronic) 288.1
- graphite lung 503
- Graves' (exophthalmic goiter) 242.0 ☑
- Greenfield's 330.0
- green monkey 078.89
- Griesinger's (*see also* Ancylostomiasis) 126.9
- grinders' 502
- Grisel's 723.5
- Gruby's (tinea tonsurans) 110.0
- Guertin's (electric chorea) 049.8
- Guillain-Barré 357.0
- Guinon's (motor-verbal tic) 307.23
- Gull's (thyroid atrophy with myxedema) 244.8
- Gull and Sutton's — *see* Hypertension, kidney

Disease, diseased — *see also* Syndrome — *continued*
- gum NEC 523.9
- Günther's (congenital erythropoietic porphyria) 277.1
- gynecological 629.9
  - specified NEC 629.89
- H 270.0
- Haas' 732.3
- Habermann's (acute parapsoriasis varioliformis) 696.2
- Haff 985.1
- Hageman (congenital factor XII deficiency) (*see also* Defect, congenital) 286.3
- Haglund's (osteochondrosis os tibiale externum) 732.5
- Hagner's (hypertrophic pulmonary osteoarthropathy) 731.2
- Hailey-Hailey (benign familial chronic pemphigus) 757.39
- hair (follicles) NEC 704.9
  - specified type NEC 704.8
- Hallervorden-Spatz 333.0
- Hallopeau's (lichen sclerosus et atrophicus) 701.0
- Hamman's (spontaneous mediastinal emphysema) 518.1
- hand, foot, and mouth 074.3
- Hand-Schüller-Christian (chronic histiocytosis X) 277.89
- Hanot's — *see* Cirrhosis, biliary
- Hansen's (leprosy) 030.9
  - benign form 030.1
  - malignant form 030.0
- Harada's 363.22
- Harley's (intermittent hemoglobinuria) 283.2
- Hartnup (pellagra-cerebellar ataxia-renal aminoaciduria) 270.0
- Hart's (pellagra-cerebellar ataxia-renal aminoaciduria) 270.0
- Hashimoto's (struma lymphomatosa) 245.2
- Hb — *see* Disease, hemoglobin
- heart (organic) 429.9
  - with
    - acute pulmonary edema (*see also* Failure, ventricular, left) 428.1
    - hypertensive 402.91
      - with renal failure 404.93
      - benign 402.11
        - with renal failure 404.13
      - malignant 402.01
        - with renal failure 404.03
    - kidney disease — *see* Hypertension, cardiorenal
    - rheumatic fever (conditions classifiable to 390)
      - active 391.1
        - with chorea 392.0
      - inactive or quiescent (with chorea) 398.90
  - amyloid 277.39 *[425.7]*
  - aortic (valve) (*see also* Endocarditis, aortic) 424.1
  - arteriosclerotic or sclerotic (minimal) (senile) — *see* Arteriosclerosis, coronary
  - artery, arterial — *see* Arteriosclerosis, coronary
  - atherosclerotic — *see* Arteriosclerosis, coronary
  - beer drinkers' 425.5
  - beriberi 265.0 *[425.7]*
  - black 416.0
  - congenital NEC 746.9
    - cyanotic 746.9
    - maternal, affecting fetus or newborn 760.3
    - specified type NEC 746.89
  - congestive (*see also* Failure, heart) 428.0
  - coronary 414.9
  - cryptogenic 429.9
  - due to
    - amyloidosis 277.39 *[425.7]*
    - beriberi 265.0 *[425.7]*
    - cardiac glycogenosis 271.0 *[425.7]*
    - Friedreich's ataxia 334.0 *[425.8]*

Disease, diseased — *see also* Syndrome — *continued*
- heart — *continued*
  - due to — *continued*
    - gout 274.82
    - mucopolysaccharidosis 277.5 *[425.7]*
    - myotonia atrophica 359.21 *[425.8]*
    - progressive muscular dystrophy 359.1 *[425.8]*
    - sarcoidosis 135 *[425.8]*
  - fetal 746.9
    - inflammatory 746.89
  - fibroid (*see also* Myocarditis) 429.0
  - functional 427.9
    - postoperative 997.1
    - psychogenic 306.2
  - glycogen storage 271.0 *[425.7]*
  - gonococcal NEC 098.85
  - gouty 274.82
  - hypertensive (*see also* Hypertension, heart) 402.90
    - benign 402.10
    - malignant 402.00
  - hyperthyroid (*see also* Hyperthyroidism) 242.9 ☑ *[425.7]*
  - incompletely diagnosed — *see* Disease, heart
  - ischemic (chronic) (*see also* Ischemia, heart) 414.9
    - acute (*see also* Infarct, myocardium) 410.9 ☑
      - without myocardial infarction 411.89
      - with coronary (artery) occlusion 411.81
    - asymptomatic 412
    - diagnosed on ECG or other special investigation but currently presenting no symptoms 412
  - kyphoscoliotic 416.1
  - mitral (*see also* Endocarditis, mitral) 394.9
  - muscular (*see also* Degeneration, myocardial) 429.1
  - postpartum 674.8 ☑
  - psychogenic (functional) 306.2
  - pulmonary (chronic) 416.9
    - acute 415.0
    - specified NEC 416.8
  - rheumatic (chronic) (inactive) (old) (quiescent) (with chorea) 398.90
    - active or acute 391.9
      - with chorea (active) (rheumatic) (Sydenham's) 392.0
      - specified type NEC 391.8
    - maternal, affecting fetus or newborn 760.3
  - rheumatoid — *see* Arthritis, rheumatoid
  - sclerotic — *see* Arteriosclerosis, coronary
  - senile (*see also* Myocarditis) 429.0
  - specified type NEC 429.89
  - syphilitic 093.89
    - aortic 093.1
      - aneurysm 093.0
    - asymptomatic 093.89
    - congenital 090.5
  - thyroid (gland) (*see also* Hyperthyroidism) 242.9 ☑ *[425.7]*
  - thyrotoxic (*see also* Thyrotoxicosis) 242.9 ☑ *[425.7]*
  - tuberculous (*see also* Tuberculosis) 017.9 ☑ *[425.8]*
  - valve, valvular (obstructive) (regurgitant) (*see also* Endocarditis)
    - congenital NEC (*see also* Anomaly, heart, valve) 746.9
    - pulmonary 746.00
    - specified type NEC 746.89
  - vascular — *see* Disease, cardiovascular
- heavy-chain (gamma G) 273.2
- Heberden's 715.04
- Hebra's
  - dermatitis exfoliativa 695.89
  - erythema multiforme exudativum 695.19
  - pityriasis
    - maculata et circinata 696.3
    - rubra 695.89

Disease, diseased — *see also* Syndrome — *continued*
- Hebra's — *continued*
  - pityriasis — *continued*
    - rubra — *continued*
      - pilaris 696.4
    - prurigo 698.2
- Heerfordt's (uveoparotitis) 135
- Heidenhain's 290.10
  - with dementia 290.10
- Heilmeyer-Schöner (M9842/3) 207.1 ☑
- Heine-Medin (*see also* Poliomyelitis) 045.9 ☑
- Heller's (*see also* Psychosis, childhood) 299.1 ☑
- Heller-Döhle (syphilitic aortitis) 093.1
- hematopoietic organs 289.9
- hemoglobin (Hb) 282.7
  - with thalassemia 282.49
  - abnormal (mixed) NEC 282.7
    - with thalassemia 282.49
  - AS genotype 282.5
  - Bart's 282.49
  - C (Hb-C) 282.7
    - with other abnormal hemoglobin NEC 282.7
    - elliptocytosis 282.7
    - Hb-S (without crisis) 282.63
      - with
        - crisis 282.64
          - vaso-occlusive pain 282.64
    - sickle-cell (without crisis) 282.63
      - with
        - crisis 282.64
          - vaso-occlusive pain 282.64
    - thalassemia 282.49
  - constant spring 282.7
  - D (Hb-D) 282.7
    - with other abnormal hemoglobin NEC 282.7
    - Hb-S (without crisis) 282.68
      - with crisis 282.69
    - sickle-cell (without crisis) 282.68
      - with crisis 282.69
    - thalassemia 282.49
  - E (Hb-E) 282.7
    - with other abnormal hemoglobin NEC 282.7
    - Hb-S (without crisis) 282.68
      - with crisis 282.69
    - sickle-cell (without crisis) 282.68
      - with crisis 282.69
    - thalassemia 282.49
  - elliptocytosis 282.7
  - F (Hb-F) 282.7
  - G (Hb-G) 282.7
  - H (Hb-H) 282.49
  - hereditary persistence, fetal (HPFH) ("Swiss variety") 282.7
  - high fetal gene 282.7
  - I thalassemia 282.49
  - M 289.7
  - S (*see also* Disease, sickle-cell, Hb-S)
    - thalassemia (without crisis) 282.41
      - with
        - crisis 282.42
          - vaso-occlusive pain 282.42
  - spherocytosis 282.7
  - unstable, hemolytic 282.7
  - Zurich (Hb-Zurich) 282.7
- hemolytic (fetus) (newborn) 773.2
  - autoimmune (cold type) (warm type) 283.0
  - due to or with
    - incompatibility
      - ABO (blood group) 773.1
      - blood (group) (Duffy) (Kell) (Kidd) (Lewis) (M) (S) NEC 773.2
      - Rh (blood group) (factor) 773.0
        - Rh negative mother 773.0
  - unstable hemoglobin 282.7
- hemorrhagic 287.9
  - newborn 776.0
- Henoch (-Schönlein) (purpura nervosa) 287.0
- hepatic — *see* Disease, liver
- hepatolenticular 275.1
- heredodegenerative NEC
  - brain 331.89

☑ Additional Digit Required — Refer to the Tabular List for Digit Selection   ▽ Subterms under main terms may continue to next column or page

2010 ICD-9-CM   ▶◀ Revised Text   ● New Line   ▲ Revised Code   Volume 2 — 81

Disease, diseased — *see also* Syndrome — *continued*

heredodegenerative — *continued*
  spinal cord 336.8
Hers' (glycogenosis VI) 271.0
Herter (-Gee) (-Heubner) (nontropical sprue) 579.0
Herxheimer's (diffuse idiopathic cutaneous atrophy) 701.8
Heubner's 094.89
Heubner-Herter (nontropical sprue) 579.0
high fetal gene or hemoglobin thalassemia 282.49
Hildenbrand's (typhus) 081.9
hip (joint) NEC 719.95
  congenital 755.63
  suppurative 711.05
  tuberculous (*see also* Tuberculosis) 015.1 ☑ *[730.85]*
Hippel's (retinocerebral angiomatosis) 759.6
Hirschfeld's (acute diabetes mellitus) (*see also* Diabetes) 250.0 ☑
  due to secondary diabetes 249.0 ☑
Hirschsprung's (congenital megacolon) 751.3
His (-Werner) (trench fever) 083.1
HIV 042
Hodgkin's (M9650/3) 201.9 ☑

Note — Use the following fifth-digit sub-classification with category 201:

0   *unspecified site*
1   *lymph nodes of head, face, and neck*
2   *intrathoracic lymph nodes*
3   *intra-abdominal lymph nodes*
4   *lymph nodes of axilla and upper limb*
5   *lymph nodes of inguinal region and lower limb*
6   *intrapelvic lymph nodes*
7   *spleen*
8   *lymph nodes of multiple sites*

  lymphocytic
    depletion (M9653/3) 201.7 ☑
      diffuse fibrosis (M9654/3) 201.7 ☑
      reticular type (M9655/3) 201.7 ☑
    predominance (M9651/3) 201.4 ☑
  lymphocytic-histiocytic predominance (M9651/3) 201.4 ☑
  mixed cellularity (M9652/3) 201.6 ☑
  nodular sclerosis (M9656/3) 201.5 ☑
    cellular phase (M9657/3) 201.5 ☑
Hodgson's 441.9
  ruptured 441.5
Hoffa (-Kastert) (liposynovitis prepatellaris) 272.8
Holla (*see also* Spherocytosis) 282.0
homozygous-Hb-S 282.61
hoof and mouth 078.4
hookworm (*see also* Ancylostomiasis) 126.9
Horton's (temporal arteritis) 446.5
host-versus-graft (immune or nonimmune cause) 279.50
HPFH (hereditary persistence of fetal hemoglobin) ("Swiss variety") 282.7
Huchard's disease (continued arterial hypertension) 401.9
Huguier's (uterine fibroma) 218.9
human immunodeficiency (virus) 042
hunger 251.1
Hunt's
  dyssynergia cerebellaris myoclonica 334.2
  herpetic geniculate ganglionitis 053.11
Huntington's 333.4
Huppert's (multiple myeloma) (M9730/3) 203.0 ☑
Hurler's (mucopolysaccharidosis I) 277.5
Hutchinson-Boeck (sarcoidosis) 135
Hutchinson-Gilford (progeria) 259.8
Hutchinson's, meaning
  angioma serpiginosum 709.1
  cheiropompholyx 705.81
  prurigo estivalis 692.72
hyaline (diffuse) (generalized) 728.9

Disease, diseased — *see also* Syndrome — *continued*

hyaline — *continued*
  membrane (lung) (newborn) 769
hydatid (*see also* Echinococcus) 122.9
Hyde's (prurigo nodularis) 698.3
hyperkinetic (*see also* Hyperkinesia) 314.9
  heart 429.82
hypertensive (*see also* Hypertension) 401.9
hypophysis 253.9
  hyperfunction 253.1
  hypofunction 253.2
Iceland (epidemic neuromyasthenia) 049.8
I cell 272.7
ill-defined 799.89
immunologic NEC 279.9
immunoproliferative 203.8 ☑
inclusion 078.5
  salivary gland 078.5
infancy, early NEC 779.9
infective NEC 136.9
inguinal gland 289.9
internal semilunar cartilage, cystic 717.5
intervertebral disc 722.90
  with myelopathy 722.70
  cervical, cervicothoracic 722.91
    with myelopathy 722.71
  lumbar, lumbosacral 722.93
    with myelopathy 722.73
  thoracic, thoracolumbar 722.92
    with myelopathy 722.72
intestine 569.9
  functional 564.9
    congenital 751.3
    psychogenic 306.4
  lardaceous 277.39
  organic 569.9
  protozoal NEC 007.9
iris 364.9
  specified NEC 364.89
iron
  metabolism 275.0
  storage 275.0
Isambert's (*see also* Tuberculosis, larynx) 012.3 ☑
Iselin's (osteochondrosis, fifth metatarsal) 732.5
island (scrub typhus) 081.2
itai-itai 985.5
Jadassohn's (maculopapular erythroderma) 696.2
Jadassohn-Pellizari's (anetoderma) 701.3
Jakob-Creutzfeldt (CJD) 046.19
  with dementia
    with behavioral disturbance 046.19 *[294.11]*
    without behavioral disturbance 046.19 *[294.10]*
  familial 046.19
  iatrogenic 046.19
  specified NEC 046.19
  sporadic 046.19
  variant (vCJD) 046.11
    with dementia
      with behavioral disturbance 046.11 *[294.11]*
      without behavioral disturbance 046.11 *[294.10]*
Jaksch (-Luzet) (pseudoleukemia infantum) 285.8
Janet's 300.89
Jansky-Bielschowsky 330.1
jaw NEC 526.9
  fibrocystic 526.2
Jensen's 363.05
Jeune's (asphyxiating thoracic dystrophy) 756.4
jigger 134.1
Johnson-Stevens (erythema multiforme exudativum) 695.13
joint NEC 719.9 ☑
  ankle 719.97
  Charcôt 094.0 *[713.5]*
  degenerative (*see also* Osteoarthrosis) 715.9 ☑
    multiple 715.09
    spine (*see also* Spondylosis) 721.90

Disease, diseased — *see also* Syndrome — *continued*

joint — *continued*
  elbow 719.92
  foot 719.97
  hand 719.94
  hip 719.95
  hypertrophic (chronic) (degenerative) (*see also* Osteoarthrosis) 715.9 ☑
    spine (*see also* Spondylosis) 721.90
  knee 719.96
  Luschka 721.90
  multiple sites 719.99
  pelvic region 719.95
  sacroiliac 724.6
  shoulder (region) 719.91
  specified site NEC 719.98
  spine NEC 724.9
    pseudarthrosis following fusion 733.82
    sacroiliac 724.6
  wrist 719.93
Jourdain's (acute gingivitis) 523.00
Jüngling's (sarcoidosis) 135
Kahler (-Bozzolo) (multiple myeloma) (M9730/3) 203.0 ☑
Kalischer's 759.6
Kaposi's 757.33
  lichen ruber 697.8
    acuminatus 696.4
    moniliformis 697.8
  xeroderma pigmentosum 757.33
Kaschin-Beck (endemic polyarthritis) 716.00
  ankle 716.07
  arm 716.02
    lower (and wrist) 716.03
    upper (and elbow) 716.02
  foot (and ankle) 716.07
  forearm (and wrist) 716.03
  hand 716.04
  leg 716.06
    lower 716.06
    upper 716.05
  multiple sites 716.09
  pelvic region (hip) (thigh) 716.05
  shoulder region 716.01
  specified site NEC 716.08
Katayama 120.2
Kawasaki 446.1
Kedani (scrub typhus) 081.2
kidney (functional) (pelvis) (*see also* Disease, renal) 593.9
  chronic 585.9
    requiring chronic dialysis 585.6
    stage
      I 585.1
      II (mild) 585.2
      III (moderate) 585.3
      IV (severe) 585.4
      V 585.5
  cystic (congenital) 753.10
    multiple 753.19
    single 753.11
    specified NEC 753.19
  fibrocystic (congenital) 753.19
  in gout 274.10
  polycystic (congenital) 753.12
    adult type (APKD) 753.13
    autosomal dominant 753.13
    autosomal recessive 753.14
    childhood type (CPKD) 753.14
    infantile type 753.14
Kienböck's (carpal lunate) (wrist) 732.3
Kimmelstiel (-Wilson) (intercapillary glomerulosclerosis) 250.4 ☑ *[581.81]*
  due to secondary diabetes 249.4 ☑ *[581.81]*
Kinnier Wilson's (hepatolenticular degeneration) 275.1
kissing 075
Kleb's (*see also* Nephritis) 583.9
Klinger's 446.4
Klippel's 723.8
Klippel-Feil (brevicollis) 756.16
knight's 911.1
Köbner's (epidermolysis bullosa) 757.39
Koenig-Wichmann (pemphigus) 694.4

Disease, diseased — *see also* Syndrome — *continued*

Köhler's
  first (osteoarthrosis juvenilis) 732.5
  second (Freiberg's infraction, metatarsal head) 732.5
  patellar 732.4
  tarsal navicular (bone) (osteoarthrosis juvenilis) 732.5
Köhler-Freiberg (infraction, metatarsal head) 732.5
Köhler-Mouchet (osteoarthrosis juvenilis) 732.5
Köhler-Pellegrini-Stieda (calcification, knee joint) 726.62
Kok 759.89
König's (osteochondritis dissecans) 732.7
Korsakoff's (nonalcoholic) 294.0
  alcoholic 291.1
Kostmann's (infantile genetic agranulocytosis) 288.01
Krabbe's 330.0
Kraepelin-Morel (*see also* Schizophrenia) 295.9 ☑
Kraft-Weber-Dimitri 759.6
Kufs' 330.1
Kugelberg-Welander 335.11
Kühnt-Junius 362.52
Kümmell's (-Verneuil) (spondylitis) 721.7
Kundrat's (lymphosarcoma) 200.1 ☑
kuru 046.0
Kussmaul (-Meier) (polyarteritis nodosa) 446.0
Kyasanur Forest 065.2
Kyrle's (hyperkeratosis follicularis in cutem penetrans) 701.1
labia
  inflammatory 616.10
  noninflammatory 624.9
  specified NEC 624.8
labyrinth, ear 386.8
lacrimal system (apparatus) (passages) 375.9
  gland 375.00
  specified NEC 375.89
Lafora's 333.2
Lagleyze-von Hippel (retinocerebral angiomatosis) 759.6
Lancereaux-Mathieu (leptospiral jaundice) 100.0
Landry's 357.0
Lane's 569.89
lardaceous (any site) 277.39
Larrey-Weil (leptospiral jaundice) 100.0
Larsen (-Johansson) (juvenile osteopathia patellae) 732.4
larynx 478.70
Lasègue's (persecution mania) 297.9
Leber's 377.16
Lederer's (acquired infectious hemolytic anemia) 283.19
Legg's (capital femoral osteochondrosis) 732.1
Legg-Calvé-Perthes (capital femoral osteochondrosis) 732.1
Legg-Calvé-Waldenström (femoral capital osteochondrosis) 732.1
Legg-Perthes (femoral capital osteochondrosis) 732.1
Legionnaires' 482.84
Leigh's 330.8
Leiner's (exfoliative dermatitis) 695.89
Leloir's (lupus erythematosus) 695.4
Lenegre's 426.0
lens (eye) 379.39
Leriche's (osteoporosis, posttraumatic) 733.7
Letterer-Siwe (acute histiocytosis X) (M9722/3) 202.5 ☑
Lev's (acquired complete heart block) 426.0
Lewandowski's (*see also* Tuberculosis) 017.0 ☑
Lewandowski-Lutz (epidermodysplasia verruciformis) 078.19
Lewy body 331.82
  with dementia
    with behavioral disturbance 331.82 *[294.11]*
    without behavioral disturbance 331.82 *[294.10]*
Leyden's (periodic vomiting) 536.2

Disease, diseased — see also Syndrome — continued
Libman-Sacks (verrucous endocarditis) 710.0 [424.91]
Lichtheim's (subacute combined sclerosis with pernicious anemia) 281.0 [336.2]
ligament 728.9
light chain 203.0 ☑
Lightwood's (renal tubular acidosis) 588.89
Lignac's (cystinosis) 270.0
Lindau's (retinocerebral angiomatosis) 759.6
Lindau-von Hippel (angiomatosis retinocerebellosa) 759.6
lip NEC 528.5
lipidosis 272.7
lipoid storage NEC 272.7
Lipschütz's 616.50
Little's — see Palsy, cerebral
liver 573.9
    alcoholic 571.3
        acute 571.1
        chronic 571.3
    chronic 571.9
        alcoholic 571.3
    cystic, congenital 751.62
    drug-induced 573.3
    due to
        chemicals 573.3
        fluorinated agents 573.3
        hypersensitivity drugs 573.3
        isoniazids 573.3
    end stage NEC 572.8
        due to hepatitis — see Hepatitis
    fibrocystic (congenital) 751.62
    glycogen storage 271.0
    organic 573.9
    polycystic (congenital) 751.62
Lobo's (keloid blastomycosis) 116.2
Lobstein's (brittle bones and blue sclera) 756.51
locomotor system 334.9
Lorain's (pituitary dwarfism) 253.3
Lou Gehrig's 335.20
Lucas-Championnière (fibrinous bronchitis) 466.0
Ludwig's (submaxillary cellulitis) 528.3
luetic — see Syphilis
lumbosacral region 724.6
lung NEC 518.89
    black 500
    congenital 748.60
    cystic 518.89
        congenital 748.4
    fibroid (chronic) (see also Fibrosis, lung) 515
    fluke 121.2
        oriental 121.2
    in
        amyloidosis 277.39 [517.8]
        polymyositis 710.4 [517.8]
        sarcoidosis 135 [517.8]
        Sjögren's syndrome 710.2 [517.8]
        syphilis 095.1
        systemic lupus erythematosus 710.0 [517.8]
        systemic sclerosis 710.1 [517.2]
    interstitial (chronic) 515
        acute 136.3
    nonspecific, chronic 496
    obstructive (chronic) (COPD) 496
        with
            acute
                bronchitis 491.22
                exacerbation NEC 491.21
            alveolitis, allergic (see also Alveolitis, allergic) 495.9
            asthma (chronic) (obstructive) 493.2 ☑
            bronchiectasis 494.0
                with acute exacerbation 494.1
            bronchitis (chronic) 491.20
                with
                    acute bronchitis 491.22
                    exacerbation (acute) 491.21
            decompensated 491.21
                with exacerbation 491.21
            emphysema NEC 492.8

Disease, diseased — see also Syndrome — continued
lung — continued
    obstructive — continued
        diffuse (with fibrosis) 496
    polycystic 518.89
        asthma (chronic) (obstructive) 493.2 ☑
        congenital 748.4
    purulent (cavitary) 513.0
    restrictive 518.89
    rheumatoid 714.81
        diffuse interstitial 714.81
    specified NEC 518.89
Lutembacher's (atrial septal defect with mitral stenosis) 745.5
Lutz-Miescher (elastosis perforans serpiginosa) 701.1
Lutz-Splendore-de Almeida (Brazilian blastomycosis) 116.1
Lyell's (toxic epidermal necrolysis) 695.15
    due to drug
        correct substance properly administered 695.15
        overdose or wrong substance given or taken 977.9
            specific drug — see Table of Drugs and Chemicals
Lyme 088.81
lymphatic (gland) (system) 289.9
    channel (noninfective) 457.9
    vessel (noninfective) 457.9
    specified NEC 457.8
lymphoproliferative (chronic) (M9970/1) 238.79
Machado-Joseph 334.8
Madelung's (lipomatosis) 272.8
Madura (actinomycotic) 039.9
    mycotic 117.4
Magitot's 526.4
Majocchi's (purpura annularis telangiectodes) 709.1
malarial (see also Malaria) 084.6
Malassez's (cystic) 608.89
Malibu 919.8
    infected 919.9
malignant (M8000/3) (see also Neoplasm, by site, malignant)
    previous, affecting management of pregnancy V23.89
Manson's 120.1
maple bark 495.6
maple syrup (urine) 270.3
Marburg (virus) 078.89
Marchiafava (-Bignami) 341.8
Marfan's 090.49
    congenital syphilis 090.49
    meaning Marfan's syndrome 759.82
Marie-Bamberger (hypertrophic pulmonary osteoarthropathy) (secondary) 731.2
    primary or idiopathic (acropachyderma) 757.39
    pulmonary (hypertrophic osteoarthropathy) 731.2
Marie-Strümpell (ankylosing spondylitis) 720.0
Marion's (bladder neck obstruction) 596.0
Marsh's (exophthalmic goiter) 242.0 ☑
Martin's 715.27
mast cell 757.33
    systemic (M9741/3) 202.6 ☑
mastoid (see also Mastoiditis) 383.9
    process 385.9
maternal, unrelated to pregnancy NEC, affecting fetus or newborn 760.9
Mathieu's (leptospiral jaundice) 100.0
Mauclaire's 732.3
Mauriac's (erythema nodosum syphiliticum) 091.3
Maxcy's 081.0
McArdle (-Schmid-Pearson) (glycogenosis V) 271.0
mediastinum NEC 519.3
Medin's (see also Poliomyelitis) 045.9 ☑
Mediterranean (with hemoglobinopathy) 282.49
medullary center (idiopathic) (respiratory) 348.89

Disease, diseased — see also Syndrome — continued
Meige's (chronic hereditary edema) 757.0
Meleda 757.39
Ménétrier's (hypertrophic gastritis) 535.2 ☑
Ménière's (active) 386.00
    cochlear 386.02
    cochleovestibular 386.01
    inactive 386.04
    in remission 386.04
    vestibular 386.03
meningeal — see Meningitis
mental (see also Psychosis) 298.9
Merzbacher-Pelizaeus 330.0
mesenchymal 710.9
mesenteric embolic 557.0
metabolic NEC 277.9
metal polishers' 502
metastatic — see Metastasis
Mibelli's 757.39
microdrepanocytic 282.49
microvascular — code to condition
Miescher's 709.3
Mikulicz's (dryness of mouth, absent or decreased lacrimation) 527.1
Milkman (-Looser) (osteomalacia with pseudofractures) 268.2
Miller's (osteomalacia) 268.2
Mills' 335.29
Milroy's (chronic hereditary edema) 757.0
Minamata 985.0
Minor's 336.1
Minot's (hemorrhagic disease, newborn) 776.0
Minot-von Willebrand-Jürgens (angiohemophilia) 286.4
Mitchell's (erythromelalgia) 443.82
mitral — see Endocarditis, mitral
Mljet (mal de Meleda) 757.39
Möbius', Moebius' 346.2 ☑
Moeller's 267
Möller (-Barlow) (infantile scurvy) 267
Mönckeberg's (see also Arteriosclerosis, extremities) 440.20
Mondor's (thrombophlebitis of breast) 451.89
Monge's 993.2
Morel-Kraepelin (see also Schizophrenia) 295.9 ☑
Morgagni's (syndrome) (hyperostosis frontalis interna) 733.3
Morgagni-Adams-Stokes (syncope with heart block) 426.9
Morquio (-Brailsford) (-Ullrich) (mucopolysaccharidosis IV) 277.5
Morton's (with metatarsalgia) 355.6
Morvan's 336.0
motor neuron (bulbar) (mixed type) 335.20
Mouchet's (juvenile osteochondrosis, foot) 732.5
mouth 528.9
Moyamoya 437.5
Mucha's (acute parapsoriasis varioliformis) 696.2
mu-chain 273.2
mucolipidosis (I) (II) (III) 272.7
Münchmeyer's (exostosis luxurians) 728.11
Murri's (intermittent hemoglobinuria) 283.2
muscle 359.9
    inflammatory 728.9
    ocular 378.9
musculoskeletal system 729.90
mushroom workers' 495.5
Myà's (congenital dilation, colon) 751.3
mycotic 117.9
myeloproliferative (chronic) (M9960/1) 238.79
myocardium, myocardial (see also Degeneration, myocardial) 429.1
    hypertensive (see also Hypertension, heart) 402.90
    primary (idiopathic) 425.4
myoneural 358.9
Naegeli's 287.1
nail 703.9
    specified type NEC 703.8
Nairobi sheep 066.1
nasal 478.19
    cavity NEC 478.19

Disease, diseased — see also Syndrome — continued
nasal — continued
    sinus (chronic) — see Sinusitis
navel (newborn) NEC 779.89
    delayed separation of umbilical cord 779.83
nemaline body 359.0
neoplastic, generalized (M8000/6) 199.0
nerve — see Disorder, nerve
nervous system (central) 349.9
    autonomic, peripheral (see also Neuropathy, peripheral, autonomic) 337.9
    congenital 742.9
    inflammatory — see Encephalitis
    parasympathetic (see also Neuropathy, peripheral, autonomic) 337.9
    peripheral NEC 355.9
    prion NEC 046.79
    specified NEC 349.89
    sympathetic (see also Neuropathy, peripheral, autonomic) 337.9
    vegetative (see also Neuropathy, peripheral, autonomic) 337.9
Nettleship's (urticaria pigmentosa) 757.33
Neumann's (pemphigus vegetans) 694.4
neurologic (central) NEC (see also Disease, nervous system) 349.9
    peripheral NEC 355.9
neuromuscular system NEC 358.9
Newcastle 077.8
Nicolas (-Durand) — Favre (climatic bubo) 099.1
Niemann-Pick (lipid histiocytosis) 272.7
nipple 611.9
    Paget's (M8540/3) 174.0
Nishimoto (-Takeuchi) 437.5
nonarthropod-borne NEC 078.89
    central nervous system NEC 049.9
    enterovirus NEC 078.89
nonautoimmune hemolytic NEC 283.10
Nonne-Milroy-Meige (chronic hereditary edema) 757.0
Norrie's (congenital progressive oculoacoustic-ocerebral degeneration) 743.8
nose 478.19
nucleus pulposus — see Disease, intervertebral disc
nutritional 269.9
    maternal, affecting fetus or newborn 760.4
oasthouse, urine 270.2
obliterative vascular 447.1
Odelberg's (juvenile osteochondrosis) 732.1
Oguchi's (retina) 368.61
Ohara's (see also Tularemia) 021.9
Ollier's (chondrodysplasia) 756.4
Opitz's (congestive splenomegaly) 289.51
Oppenheim's 358.8
Oppenheim-Urbach (necrobiosis lipoidica diabeticorum) 250.8 ☑ [709.3]
    due to secondary diabetes 249.8 ☑ [709.3]
optic nerve NEC 377.49
orbit 376.9
    specified NEC 376.89
Oriental liver fluke 121.1
Oriental lung fluke 121.2
Ormond's 593.4
Osgood-Schlatter 732.4
Osgood's tibia (tubercle) 732.4
Osler (-Vaquez) (polycythemia vera) (M9950/1) 238.4
Osler-Rendu (familial hemorrhagic telangiectasia) 448.0
osteofibrocystic 252.01
Otto's 715.35
outer ear 380.9
ovary (noninflammatory) NEC 620.9
    cystic 620.2
    polycystic 256.4
    specified NEC 620.8
Owren's (congenital) (see also Defect, coagulation) 286.3
Paas' 756.59
Paget's (osteitis deformans) 731.0

▲

☑ Additional Digit Required — Refer to the Tabular List for Digit Selection   ▽ Subterms under main terms may continue to next column or page

2010 ICD-9-CM   ▶◀ Revised Text   ● New Line   ▲ Revised Code   October 2009 • Volume 2 — 83

Disease, diseased — *see also* Syndrome — *continued*

Paget's — *continued*
  with infiltrating duct carcinoma of the breast (M8541/3) — *see* Neoplasm, breast, malignant
  bone 731.0
    osteosarcoma in (M9184/3) — *see* Neoplasm, bone, malignant
  breast (M8540/3) 174.0
  extramammary (M8542/3) (*see also* Neoplasm, skin, malignant)
    anus 154.3
    skin 173.5
  malignant (M8540/3)
    breast 174.0
    specified site NEC (M8542/3) — *see* Neoplasm, skin, malignant
    unspecified site 174.0
  mammary (M8540/3) 174.0
  nipple (M8540/3) 174.0
palate (soft) 528.9
Paltauf-Sternberg 201.9 ☑
pancreas 577.9
  cystic 577.2
    congenital 751.7
  fibrocystic 277.00
Panner's 732.3
  capitellum humeri 732.3
  head of humerus 732.3
  tarsal navicular (bone) (osteochondrosis) 732.5
panvalvular — *see* Endocarditis, mitral
parametrium 629.9
parasitic NEC 136.9
  cerebral NEC 123.9
  intestinal NEC 129
  mouth 112.0
  skin NEC 134.9
  specified type — *see* Infestation
  tongue 112.0
parathyroid (gland) 252.9
  specified NEC 252.8
Parkinson's 332.0
parodontal 523.9
Parrot's (syphilitic osteochondritis) 090.0
Parry's (exophthalmic goiter) 242.0 ☑
Parson's (exophthalmic goiter) 242.0 ☑
Pavy's 593.6
Paxton's (white piedra) 111.2
Payr's (splenic flexure syndrome) 569.89
pearl-workers' (chronic osteomyelitis) (*see also* Osteomyelitis) 730.1 ☑
Pel-Ebstein — *see* Disease, Hodgkin's
Pelizaeus-Merzbacher 330.0
  with dementia
    with behavioral disturbance 330.0 [294.11]
    without behavioral disturbance 330.0 [294.10]
Pellegrini-Stieda (calcification, knee joint) 726.62
pelvis, pelvic
  female NEC 629.9
    specified NEC 629.89
  gonococcal (acute) 098.19
    chronic or duration of 2 months or over 098.39
  infection (*see also* Disease, pelvis, inflammatory) 614.9
  inflammatory (female) (PID) 614.9
    with
      abortion — *see* Abortion, by type, with sepsis
      ectopic pregnancy (*see also* categories 633.0–633.9) 639.0
      molar pregnancy (*see also* categories 630–632) 639.0
    acute 614.3
    chronic 614.4
    complicating pregnancy 646.6 ☑
      affecting fetus or newborn 760.8
    following
      abortion 639.0
      ectopic or molar pregnancy 639.0
    peritonitis (acute) 614.5

pelvis, pelvic — *continued*
  inflammatory — *continued*
    peritonitis — *continued*
      chronic NEC 614.7
      puerperal, postpartum, childbirth 670.8 ☑ ▲
      specified NEC 614.8
    organ, female NEC 629.9
      specified NEC 629.89
    peritoneum, female NEC 629.9
      specified NEC 629.89
  penis 607.9
    inflammatory 607.2
  peptic NEC 536.9
    acid 536.8
  periapical tissues NEC 522.9
  pericardium 423.9
    specified type NEC 423.8
  perineum
    female
      inflammatory 616.9
        specified NEC 616.89
      noninflammatory 624.9
        specified NEC 624.8
    male (inflammatory) 682.2
  periodic (familial) (Reimann's) NEC 277.31
    paralysis 359.3
  periodontal NEC 523.9
    specified NEC 523.8
  periosteum 733.90
  peripheral
    arterial 443.9
    autonomic nervous system (*see also* Neuropathy, autonomic) 337.9
    nerve NEC (*see also* Neuropathy) 356.9
      multiple — *see* Polyneuropathy
    vascular 443.9
      specified type NEC 443.89
  peritoneum 568.9
    pelvic, female 629.9
      specified NEC 629.89
Perrin-Ferraton (snapping hip) 719.65
persistent mucosal (middle ear) (with posterior or superior marginal perforation of ear drum) 382.2
Perthes' (capital femoral osteochondrosis) 732.1
Petit's (*see also* Hernia, lumbar) 553.8
Peutz-Jeghers 759.6
Peyronie's 607.85
Pfeiffer's (infectious mononucleosis) 075
pharynx 478.20
Phocas' 610.1
photochromogenic (acid-fast bacilli) (pulmonary) 031.0
  nonpulmonary 031.9
Pick's
  brain 331.11
    with dementia
      with behavioral disturbance 331.11 [294.11]
      without behavioral disturbance 331.11 [294.10]
  cerebral atrophy 331.11
    with dementia
      with behavioral disturbance 331.11 [294.11]
      without behavioral disturbance 331.11 [294.10]
  lipid histiocytosis 272.7
  liver (pericardial pseudocirrhosis of liver) 423.2
  pericardium (pericardial pseudocirrhosis of liver) 423.2
  polyserositis (pericardial pseudocirrhosis of liver) 423.2
Pierson's (osteochondrosis) 732.1
pigeon fanciers' or breeders' 495.2
pineal gland 259.8
pink 985.0
Pinkus' (lichen nitidus) 697.1
pinworm 127.4
pituitary (gland) 253.9
  hyperfunction 253.1

pituitary — *continued*
  hypofunction 253.2
pituitary snuff-takers' 495.8
placenta
  affecting fetus or newborn 762.2
  complicating pregnancy or childbirth 656.7 ☑
pleura (cavity) (*see also* Pleurisy) 511.0
Plummer's (toxic nodular goiter) 242.3 ☑
pneumatic
  drill 994.9
  hammer 994.9
policeman's 729.2
Pollitzer's (hidradenitis suppurativa) 705.83
polycystic (congenital) 759.89
  congenital 748.4
  kidney or renal 753.12
    adult type (APKD) 753.13
    autosomal dominant 753.13
    autosomal recessive 753.14
    childhood type (CPKD) 753.14
    infantile type 753.14
  liver or hepatic 751.62
  lung or pulmonary 518.89
  ovary, ovaries 256.4
  spleen 759.0
Pompe's (glycogenosis II) 271.0
Poncet's (tuberculous rheumatism) (*see also* Tuberculosis) 015.9 ☑
Posada-Wernicke 114.9
Potain's (pulmonary edema) 514
Pott's (*see also* Tuberculosis) 015.0 ☑ [730.88]
  osteomyelitis 015.0 ☑ [730.88]
  paraplegia 015.0 ☑ [730.88]
  spinal curvature 015.0 ☑ [737.43]
  spondylitis 015.0 ☑ [720.81]
Potter's 753.0
Poulet's 714.2
pregnancy NEC (*see also* Pregnancy) 646.9 ☑
Preiser's (osteoporosis) 733.09
Pringle's (tuberous sclerosis) 759.5
Profichet's 729.90
prostate 602.9
  specified type NEC 602.8
protozoal NEC 136.8
  intestine, intestinal NEC 007.9
pseudo-Hurler's (mucolipidosis III) 272.7
psychiatric (*see also* Psychosis) 298.9
psychotic (*see also* Psychosis) 298.9
Puente's (simple glandular cheilitis) 528.5
puerperal NEC (*see also* Puerperal) 674.9 ☑
pulmonary (*see also* Disease, lung)
  amyloid 277.39 [517.8]
  artery 417.9
  circulation, circulatory 417.9
    specified NEC 417.8
  diffuse obstructive (chronic) 496
    with
      acute bronchitis 491.22
      asthma (chronic) (obstructive) 493.2 ☑
      exacerbation NEC (acute) 491.21
  heart (chronic) 416.9
    specified NEC 416.8
  hypertensive (vascular) 416.0
    cardiovascular 416.0
  obstructive diffuse (chronic) 496
    with
      acute bronchitis 491.22
      asthma (chronic) (obstructive) 493.2 ☑
      bronchitis (chronic) 491.20
        with
          exacerbation (acute) 491.21
        acute 491.22
        exacerbation NEC (acute) 491.21
      decompensated 491.21
        with exacerbation 491.21
  valve (*see also* Endocarditis, pulmonary) 424.3
pulp (dental) NEC 522.9
pulseless 446.7

Putnam's (subacute combined sclerosis with pernicious anemia) 281.0 [336.2]
Pyle (-Cohn) (craniometaphyseal dysplasia) 756.89
pyramidal tract 333.90
Quervain's
  tendon sheath 727.04
  thyroid (subacute granulomatous thyroiditis) 245.1
Quincke's — *see* Edema, angioneurotic
Quinquaud (acne decalvans) 704.09
rag sorters' 022.1
Raynaud's (paroxysmal digital cyanosis) 443.0
reactive airway — *see* Asthma
Recklinghausen's (M9540/1) 237.71
  bone (osteitis fibrosa cystica) 252.01
Recklinghausen-Applebaum (hemochromatosis) 275.0
Reclus' (cystic) 610.1
rectum NEC 569.49
Refsum's (heredopathia atactica polyneuritiformis) 356.3
Reichmann's (gastrosuccorrhea) 536.8
Reimann's (periodic) 277.31
Reiter's 099.3
renal (functional) (pelvis) (*see also* Disease, kidney) 593.9
  with
    edema (*see also* Nephrosis) 581.9
    exudative nephritis 583.89
    lesion of interstitial nephritis 583.89
    stated generalized cause — *see* Nephritis
  acute 593.9
  basement membrane NEC 583.89
    with
      pulmonary hemorrhage (Goodpasture's syndrome) 446.21 [583.81]
  chronic (*see also* Disease, kidney, chronic) 585.9
  complicating pregnancy or puerperium NEC 646.2 ☑
    with hypertension — *see* Toxemia, of pregnancy
    affecting fetus or newborn 760.1
  cystic, congenital (*see also* Cystic, disease, kidney) 753.10
  diabetic 250.4 ☑ [583.81]
    due to secondary diabetes 249.4 ☑ [581.81]
  due to
    amyloidosis 277.39 [583.81]
    diabetes mellitus 250.4 ☑ [583.81]
      due to secondary diabetes 249.4 ☑ [581.81]
    systemic lupus erythematosus 710.0 [583.81]
  end-stage 585.6
  exudative 583.89
  fibrocystic (congenital) 753.19
  gonococcal 098.19 [583.81]
  gouty 274.10
  hypertensive (*see also* Hypertension, kidney) 403.90
  immune complex NEC 583.89
  interstitial (diffuse) (focal) 583.89
  lupus 710.0 [583.81]
  maternal, affecting fetus or newborn 760.1
    hypertensive 760.0
  phosphate-losing (tubular) 588.0
  polycystic (congenital) 753.12
    adult type (APKD) 753.13
    autosomal dominant 753.13
    autosomal recessive 753.14
    childhood type (CPKD) 753.14
    infantile type 753.14
  specified lesion or cause NEC (*see also* Glomerulonephritis) 583.89
  subacute 581.9
  syphilitic 095.4
  tuberculous (*see also* Tuberculosis) 016.0 ☑ [583.81]
  tubular (*see also* Nephrosis, tubular) 584.5

Disease, diseased — *see also* Syndrome — *continued*

Rendu-Osler-Weber (familial hemorrhagic telangiectasia) 448.0
renovascular (arteriosclerotic) (*see also* Hypertension, kidney) 403.90
respiratory (tract) 519.9
　acute or subacute (upper) NEC 465.9
　　due to fumes or vapors 506.3
　　multiple sites NEC 465.8
　　noninfectious 478.9
　　streptococcal 034.0
　chronic 519.9
　　arising in the perinatal period 770.7
　　due to fumes or vapors 506.4
　　due to
　　　aspiration of liquids or solids 508.9
　　　external agents NEC 508.9
　　　　specified NEC 508.8
　　　fumes or vapors 506.9
　　　　acute or subacute NEC 506.3
　　　　chronic 506.4
　fetus or newborn NEC 770.9
　obstructive 496
　specified type NEC 519.8
　upper (acute) (infectious) NEC 465.9
　　multiple sites NEC 465.8
　　noninfectious NEC 478.9
　　streptococcal 034.0
retina, retinal NEC 362.9
　Batten's or Batten-Mayou 330.1 [362.71]
　degeneration 362.89
　vascular lesion 362.17
rheumatic (*see also* Arthritis) 716.8 ☑
　heart — *see* Disease, heart, rheumatic
rheumatoid (heart) — *see* Arthritis, rheumatoid
rickettsial NEC 083.9
　specified type NEC 083.8
Riedel's (ligneous thyroiditis) 245.3
Riga (-Fede) (cachectic aphthae) 529.0
Riggs' (compound periodontitis) 523.40
Ritter's 695.81
Rivalta's (cervicofacial actinomycosis) 039.3
Robles' (onchocerciasis) 125.3 [360.13]
Roger's (congenital interventricular septal defect) 745.4
Rokitansky's (*see also* Necrosis, liver) 570
Romberg's 349.89
Rosenthal's (factor XI deficiency) 286.2
Rossbach's (hyperchlorhydria) 536.8
　psychogenic 306.4
Roth (-Bernhardt) 355.1
Runeberg's (progressive pernicious anemia) 281.0
Rust's (tuberculous spondylitis) (*see also* Tuberculosis) 015.0 ☑ [720.81]
Rustitskii's (multiple myeloma) (M9730/3) 203.0 ☑
Ruysch's (Hirschsprung's disease) 751.3
Sachs (-Tay) 330.1
sacroiliac NEC 724.6
salivary gland or duct NEC 527.9
　inclusion 078.5
　　streptococcal 034.0
　virus 078.5
Sander's (paranoia) 297.1
Sandhoff's 330.1
sandworm 126.9
Savill's (epidemic exfoliative dermatitis) 695.89
Schamberg's (progressive pigmentary dermatosis) 709.09
Schaumann's (sarcoidosis) 135
Schenck's (sporotrichosis) 117.1
Scheuermann's (osteochondrosis) 732.0
Schilder (-Flatau) 341.1
Schimmelbusch's 610.1
Schlatter-Osgood 732.4
Schlatter's tibia (tubercle) 732.4
Schmorl's 722.30
　cervical 722.39
　lumbar, lumbosacral 722.32
　specified region NEC 722.39
　thoracic, thoracolumbar 722.31
Scholz's 330.0

Disease, diseased — *see also* Syndrome — *continued*

Schönlein (-Henoch) (purpura rheumatica) 287.0
Schottmüller's (*see also* Fever, paratyphoid) 002.9
Schüller-Christian (chronic histiocytosis X) 277.89
Schultz's (agranulocytosis) 288.09
Schwalbe-Ziehen-Oppenheimer 333.6
Schwartz-Jampel 359.23
Schweninger-Buzzi (macular atrophy) 701.3
sclera 379.19
scrofulous (*see also* Tuberculosis) 017.2 ☑
scrotum 608.9
sebaceous glands NEC 706.9
Secretan's (posttraumatic edema) 782.3
semilunar cartilage, cystic 717.5
seminal vesicle 608.9
Senear-Usher (pemphigus erythematosus) 694.4
serum NEC 999.5
Sever's (osteochondrosis calcaneum) 732.5
sexually transmitted — *see* Disease, venereal
Sézary's (reticulosis) (M9701/3) 202.2 ☑
Shaver's (bauxite pneumoconiosis) 503
Sheehan's (postpartum pituitary necrosis) 253.2
shimamushi (scrub typhus) 081.2
shipyard 077.1
sickle cell 282.60
　with
　　crisis 282.62
　　Hb-S disease 282.61
　　other abnormal hemoglobin (Hb-D) (Hb-E) (Hb-G) (Hb-J) (Hb-K) (Hb-O) (Hb-P) (high fetal gene) (without crisis) 282.68
　　with crisis 282.69
　elliptocytosis 282.60
　Hb-C (without crisis) 282.63
　　with
　　　crisis 282.64
　　　vaso-occlusive pain 282.64
　Hb-S 282.61
　　with
　　　crisis 282.62
　　　Hb-C (without crisis) 282.63
　　　　with
　　　　　crisis 282.64
　　　　　vaso-occlusive pain 282.64
　　　other abnormal hemoglobin (Hb-D) (Hb-E) (Hb-G) (Hb-J) (Hb-K) (Hb-O) (Hb-P) (high fetal gene) (without crisis) 282.68
　　　with crisis 282.69
　spherocytosis 282.60
　thalassemia (without crisis) 282.41
　　with
　　　crisis 282.42
　　　vaso-occlusive pain 282.42
Siegal-Cattan-Mamou (periodic) 277.31
silo fillers' 506.9
Simian B 054.3
Simmonds' (pituitary cachexia) 253.2
Simons' (progressive lipodystrophy) 272.6
Sinding-Larsen (juvenile osteopathia patellae) 732.4
sinus (*see also* Sinusitis)
　brain 437.9
　specified NEC 478.19
Sirkari's 085.0
sixth (*see also* Exanthem subitum) 058.10
Sjögren (-Gougerot) 710.2
　with lung involvement 710.2 [517.8]
Skevas-Zerfus 989.5
skin NEC 709.9
　due to metabolic disorder 277.9
　specified type NEC 709.8
sleeping (*see also* Narcolepsy) 347.00
　meaning sleeping sickness (*see also* Trypanosomiasis) 086.5
small vessel 443.9
Smith-Strang (oasthouse urine) 270.2
Sneddon-Wilkinson (subcorneal pustular dermatosis) 694.1

Disease, diseased — *see also* Syndrome — *continued*

South African creeping 133.8
Spencer's (epidemic vomiting) 078.82
Spielmeyer-Stock 330.1
Spielmeyer-Vogt 330.1
spine, spinal 733.90
　combined system (*see also* Degeneration, combined) 266.2 [336.2]
　　with pernicious anemia 281.0 [336.2]
　cord NEC 336.9
　　congenital 742.9
　demyelinating NEC 341.8
　joint (*see also* Disease, joint, spine) 724.9
　　tuberculous 015.0 ☑ [730.8] ☑
spinocerebellar 334.9
　specified NEC 334.8
spleen (organic) (postinfectional) 289.50
　amyloid 277.39
　lardaceous 277.39
　polycystic 759.0
　specified NEC 289.59
sponge divers' 989.5
Stanton's (melioidosis) 025
Stargardt's 362.75
Startle 759.89
Steinert's 359.21
Sternberg's — *see* Disease, Hodgkin's
Stevens-Johnson (erythema multiforme exudativum) 695.13
Sticker's (erythema infectiosum) 057.0
Stieda's (calcification, knee joint) 726.62
Still's (juvenile rheumatoid arthritis) 714.30
　adult onset 714.2
Stiller's (asthenia) 780.79
Stokes' (exophthalmic goiter) 242.0 ☑
Stokes-Adams (syncope with heart block) 426.9
Stokvis (-Talma) (enterogenous cyanosis) 289.7
stomach NEC (organic) 537.9
　functional 536.9
　　psychogenic 306.4
　lardaceous 277.39
stonemasons' 502
storage
　glycogen (*see also* Disease, glycogen storage) 271.0
　lipid 272.7
　mucopolysaccharide 277.5
striatopallidal system 333.90
　specified NEC 333.89
Strümpell-Marie (ankylosing spondylitis) 720.0
Stuart's (congenital factor X deficiency) (*see also* Defect, coagulation) 286.3
Stuart-Prower (congenital factor X deficiency) (*see also* Defect, coagulation) 286.3
Sturge (-Weber) (-Dimitri) (encephalocutaneous angiomatosis) 759.6
Stuttgart 100.89
Sudeck's 733.7
supporting structures of teeth NEC 525.9
suprarenal (gland) (capsule) 255.9
　hyperfunction 255.3
　hypofunction 255.41
Sutton's 709.09
Sutton and Gull's — *see* Hypertension, kidney
sweat glands NEC 705.9
　specified type NEC 705.89
sweating 078.2
Sweeley-Klionsky 272.4
Swift (-Feer) 985.0
swimming pool (bacillus) 031.1
swineherd's 100.89
Sylvest's (epidemic pleurodynia) 074.1
Symmers (follicular lymphoma) (M9690/3) 202.0 ☑
sympathetic nervous system (*see also* Neuropathy, peripheral, autonomic) 337.9
synovium 727.9
syphilitic — *see* Syphilis
systemic tissue mast cell (M9741/3) 202.6 ☑
Taenzer's 757.4
Takayasu's (pulseless) 446.7
Talma's 728.85
Tangier (familial high-density lipoprotein deficiency) 272.5

Disease, diseased — *see also* Syndrome — *continued*

Tarral-Besnier (pityriasis rubra pilaris) 696.4
Taylor's 701.8
Tay-Sachs 330.1
tear duct 375.69
teeth, tooth 525.9
　hard tissues 521.9
　　specified NEC 521.89
　pulp NEC 522.9
tendon 727.9
　inflammatory NEC 727.9
terminal vessel 443.9
testis 608.9
Thaysen-Gee (nontropical sprue) 579.0
Thomsen's 359.22
Thomson's (congenital poikiloderma) 757.33
Thornwaldt's, Tornwaldt's (pharyngeal bursitis) 478.29
throat 478.20
　septic 034.0
thromboembolic (*see also* Embolism) 444.9
thymus (gland) 254.9
　specified NEC 254.8
thyroid (gland) NEC 246.9
　heart (*see also* Hyperthyroidism) 242.9 ☑ [425.7]
　lardaceous 277.39
　specified NEC 246.8
Tietze's 733.6
Tommaselli's
　correct substance properly administered 599.70
　overdose or wrong substance given or taken 961.4
tongue 529.9
tonsils, tonsillar (and adenoids) (chronic) 474.9
　specified NEC 474.8
tooth, teeth 525.9
　hard tissues 521.9
　　specified NEC 521.89
　pulp NEC 522.9
Tornwaldt's (pharyngeal bursitis) 478.29
Tourette's 307.23
trachea 519.19
tricuspid — *see* Endocarditis, tricuspid
triglyceride-storage, type I, II, III 272.7
triple vessel (coronary arteries) — *see* Arteriosclerosis, coronary
trisymptomatic, Gougerot's 709.1
trophoblastic (*see also* Hydatidiform mole) 630
　previous, affecting management of pregnancy V23.1
tsutsugamushi (scrub typhus) 081.2
tube (fallopian), noninflammatory 620.9
　specified NEC 620.8
tuberculous NEC (*see also* Tuberculosis) 011.9 ☑
tubo-ovarian
　inflammatory (*see also* Salpingo-oophoritis) 614.2
　noninflammatory 620.9
　　specified NEC 620.8
tubotympanic, chronic (with anterior perforation of ear drum) 382.1
tympanum 385.9
Uhl's 746.84
umbilicus (newborn) NEC 779.89
　delayed separation 779.83
Underwood's (sclerema neonatorum) 778.1
undiagnosed 799.9
Unna's (seborrheic dermatitis) 690.18
unstable hemoglobin hemolytic 282.7
Unverricht (-Lundborg) 345.1 ▲
Urbach-Oppenheim (necrobiosis lipoidica diabeticorum) 250.8 ☑ [709.3]
　due to secondary diabetes 249.8 ☑ [709.3]
Urbach-Wiethe (lipoid proteinosis) 272.8
ureter 593.9
urethra 599.9
　specified type NEC 599.84
urinary (tract) 599.9
　bladder 596.9
　　specified NEC 596.8
　maternal, affecting fetus or newborn 760.1

☑ Additional Digit Required — Refer to the Tabular List for Digit Selection　　　　　　　　　　▽ Subterms under main terms may continue to next column or page

2010 ICD-9-CM　　　▶◀ Revised Text　　　● New Line　　　▲ Revised Code　　　October 2009 • Volume 2 — 85

Disease, diseased — *see also* Syndrome — *continued*
Usher-Senear (pemphigus erythematosus) 694.4
uterus (organic) 621.9
infective (*see also* Endometritis) 615.9
inflammatory (*see also* Endometritis) 615.9
noninflammatory 621.9
specified type NEC 621.8
uveal tract
anterior 364.9
posterior 363.9
vagabonds' 132.1
vagina, vaginal
inflammatory 616.10
noninflammatory 623.9
specified NEC 623.8
Valsuani's (progressive pernicious anemia, puerperal) 648.2 ☑
complicating pregnancy or puerperium 648.2 ☑
valve, valvular — *see also* Endocarditis
congenital NEC (*see also* Anomaly, heart, valve) 746.9
pulmonary 746.00
specified type NEC 746.89
van Bogaert-Nijssen (-Peiffer) 330.0
van Creveld-von Gierke (glycogenosis I) 271.0
van den Bergh's (enterogenous cyanosis) 289.7
van Neck's (juvenile osteochondrosis) 732.1
Vaquez (-Osler) (polycythemia vera) (M9950/1) 238.4
vascular 459.9
arteriosclerotic — *see* Arteriosclerosis
hypertensive — *see* Hypertension
obliterative 447.1
peripheral 443.9
occlusive 459.9
peripheral (occlusive) 443.9
in ►(due to) (with)◄ diabetes mellitus 250.7 *[443.81]*
►in (due to) (with)◄ secondary diabetes 249.7 *[443.81]*
specified type NEC 443.89
vas deferens 608.9
vasomotor 443.9
vasospastic 443.9
vein 459.9
venereal 099.9
chlamydial NEC 099.50
anus 099.52
bladder 099.53
cervix 099.53
epididymis 099.54
genitourinary NEC 099.55
lower 099.53
specified NEC 099.54
pelvic inflammatory disease 099.54
perihepatic 099.56
peritoneum 099.56
pharynx 099.51
rectum 099.52
specified site NEC 099.59
testis 099.54
vagina 099.53
vulva 099.53
complicating pregnancy, childbirth, or puerperium 647.2 ☑
fifth 099.1
sixth 099.1
specified nature or type NEC 099.8
chlamydial — *see* Disease, venereal, chlamydial
Verneuil's (syphilitic bursitis) 095.7
Verse's (calcinosis intervertebralis) 275.49 *[722.90]*
vertebra, vertebral NEC 733.90
disc — *see* Disease, Intervertebral disc
vibration NEC 994.9
Vidal's (lichen simplex chronicus) 698.3
Vincent's (trench mouth) 101
Virchow's 733.99
virus (filterable) NEC 078.89
arbovirus NEC 066.9
arthropod-borne NEC 066.9
central nervous system NEC 049.9

Disease, diseased — *see also* Syndrome — *continued*
virus — *continued*
central nervous system — *continued*
specified type NEC 049.8
complicating pregnancy, childbirth, or puerperium 647.6 ☑
contact (with) V01.79
varicella V01.71
exposure to V01.79
varicella V01.71
Marburg 078.89
maternal
with fetal damage affecting management of pregnancy 655.3 ☑
nonarthropod-borne NEC 078.89
central nervous system NEC 049.9
specified NEC 049.8
vaccination, prophylactic (against) V04.89
vitreous 379.29
vocal cords NEC 478.5
Vogt's (Cecile) 333.71
Vogt-Spielmeyer 330.1
Volhard-Fahr (malignant nephrosclerosis) 403.0
Volkmann's
acquired 958.6
von Bechterew's (ankylosing spondylitis) 720.0
von Economo's (encephalitis lethargica) 049.8
von Eulenburg's (congenital paramyotonia) 359.29
von Gierke's (glycogenosis I) 271.0
von Graefe's 378.72
von Hippel's (retinocerebral angiomatosis) 759.6
von Hippel-Lindau (angiomatosis retinocerebellosa) 759.6
von Jaksch's (pseudoleukemia infantum) 285.8
von Recklinghausen's (M9540/1) 237.71
bone (osteitis fibrosa cystica) 252.01
von Recklinghausen-Applebaum (hemochromatosis) 275.0
von Willebrand (-Jürgens) (angiohemophilia) 286.4
von Zambusch's (lichen sclerosus et atrophicus) 701.0
Voorhoeve's (dyschondroplasia) 756.4
Vrolik's (osteogenesis imperfecta) 756.51
vulva
inflammatory 616.10
noninflammatory 624.9
specified NEC 624.8
Wagner's (colloid milium) 709.3
Waldenström's (osteochondrosis capital femoral) 732.1
Wallgren's (obstruction of splenic vein with collateral circulation) 459.89
Wardrop's (with lymphangitis) 681.9
finger 681.02
toe 681.11
Wassilieff's (leptospiral jaundice) 100.0
wasting NEC 799.4
due to malnutrition 261
paralysis 335.21
Waterhouse-Friderichsen 036.3
waxy (any site) 277.39
Weber-Christian (nodular nonsuppurative panniculitis) 729.30
Wegner's (syphilitic osteochondritis) 090.0
Weil's (leptospiral jaundice) 100.0
of lung 100.0
Weir Mitchell's (erythromelalgia) 443.82
Werdnig-Hoffmann 335.0
Werlhof's (*see also* Purpura, thrombocytopenic) 287.39
Wermer's 258.01
Werner's (progeria adultorum) 259.8
Werner-His (trench fever) 083.1
Werner-Schultz (agranulocytosis) 288.09
Wernicke's (superior hemorrhagic polioencephalitis) 265.1
Wernicke-Posadas 114.9
Whipple's (intestinal lipodystrophy) 040.2
whipworm 127.3
White's (congenital) (keratosis follicularis) 757.39

Disease, diseased — *see also* Syndrome — *continued*
white
blood cell 288.9
specified NEC 288.8
spot 701.0
Whitmore's (melioidosis) 025
Widal-Abrami (acquired hemolytic jaundice) 283.9
Wilkie's 557.1
Wilkinson-Sneddon (subcorneal pustular dermatosis) 694.1
Willis' (diabetes mellitus) (*see also* Diabetes) 250.0 ☑
due to secondary diabetes 249.0 ☑
Wilson's (hepatolenticular degeneration) 275.1
Wilson-Brocq (dermatitis exfoliativa) 695.89
winter vomiting 078.82
Wise's 696.2
Wohlfart-Kugelberg-Welander 335.11
Woillez's (acute idiopathic pulmonary congestion) 518.5
Wolman's (primary familial xanthomatosis) 272.7
wool-sorters' 022.1
Zagari's (xerostomia) 527.7
Zahorsky's (exanthem subitum) 058.10
Ziehen-Oppenheim 333.6
zoonotic, bacterial NEC 027.9
specified type NEC 027.8
Disfigurement (due to scar) 709.2
head V48.6
limb V49.4
neck V48.7
trunk V48.7
Disgerminoma — *see* Dysgerminoma
Disinsertion, retina 361.04
Disintegration, complete, of the body 799.89
traumatic 869.1
Disk kidney 753.3
Dislocatable hip, congenital — *see also* Dislocation, hip, congenital 754.30
Dislocation (articulation) (closed) (displacement) (simple) (subluxation) 839.8

Note — *"Closed" includes simple, complete, partial, uncomplicated, and unspecified dislocation.*

"Open" includes dislocation specified as infected or compound and dislocation with foreign body.

"Chronic," "habitual," "old," or "recurrent" dislocations should be coded as indicated under the entry "Dislocation, recurrent," and "pathological" as indicated under the entry "Dislocation, pathological."

For late effect of dislocation see Late, effect, dislocation.

with fracture — *see* Fracture, by site
acromioclavicular (joint) (closed) 831.04
open 831.14
anatomical site (closed)
specified NEC 839.69
open 839.79
unspecified or ill-defined 839.8
open 839.9
ankle (scaphoid bone) (closed) 837.0
open 837.1
arm (closed) 839.8
open 839.9
astragalus (closed) 837.0
open 837.1
atlanto-axial (closed) 839.01
open 839.11
atlas (closed) 839.01
open 839.11
axis (closed) 839.02
open 839.12
back (closed) 839.8
open 839.9
Bell-Daly 723.8
breast bone (closed) 839.61
open 839.71
capsule, joint — *see* Dislocation, by site
carpal (bone) — *see* Dislocation, wrist

Dislocation — *continued*
carpometacarpal (joint) (closed) 833.04
open 833.14
cartilage (joint) (*see also* Dislocation, by site)
knee — *see* Tear, meniscus
cervical, cervicodorsal, or cervicothoracic (spine) (vertebra) — *see* Dislocation, vertebra, cervical
chiropractic (*see also* Lesion, nonallopathic) 739.9
chondrocostal — *see* Dislocation, costochondral
chronic — *see* Dislocation, recurrent
clavicle (closed) 831.04
open 831.14
coccyx (closed) 839.41
open 839.51
collar bone (closed) 831.04
open 831.14
compound (open) NEC 839.9
congenital NEC 755.8
hip (*see also* Dislocation, hip, congenital) 754.30
lens 743.37
rib 756.3
sacroiliac 755.69
spine NEC 756.19
vertebra 756.19
coracoid (closed) 831.09
open 831.19
costal cartilage (closed) 839.69
open 839.79
costochondral (closed) 839.69
open 839.79
cricoarytenoid articulation (closed) 839.69
open 839.79
cricothyroid (cartilage) articulation (closed) 839.69
open 839.79
dorsal vertebrae (closed) 839.21
open 839.31
ear ossicle 385.23
elbow (closed) 832.00
anterior (closed) 832.01
open 832.11
congenital 754.89
divergent (closed) 832.09
open 832.19
lateral (closed) 832.04
open 832.14
medial (closed) 832.03
open 832.13
open 832.10
posterior (closed) 832.02
open 832.12
recurrent 718.32
specified type NEC 832.09
open 832.19
eye 360.81
lateral 376.36
eyeball 360.81
lateral 376.36
femur
distal end (closed) 836.50
anterior 836.52
open 836.62
lateral 836.54 ▲
open 836.64 ▲
medial 836.53 ▲
open 836.63 ▲
open 836.60
posterior 836.51
open 836.61
proximal end (closed) 835.00
anterior (pubic) 835.03
open 835.13
obturator 835.02
open 835.12
open 835.10
posterior 835.01
open 835.11
fibula
distal end (closed) 837.0
open 837.1
proximal end (closed) 836.59
open 836.69

Dislocation — continued
  finger(s) (phalanx) (thumb) (closed) 834.00
    interphalangeal (joint) 834.02
      open 834.12
    metacarpal (bone), distal end 834.01
      open 834.11
    metacarpophalangeal (joint) 834.01
      open 834.11
    open 834.10
    recurrent 718.34
  foot (closed) 838.00
    open 838.10
    recurrent 718.37
  forearm (closed) 839.8
    open 839.9
  fracture — see Fracture, by site
  glenoid (closed) 831.09
    open 831.19
  habitual — see Dislocation, recurrent
  hand (closed) 839.8
    open 839.9
  hip (closed) 835.00
    anterior 835.03
      obturator 835.02
        open 835.12
      open 835.13
    congenital (unilateral) 754.30
      with subluxation of other hip 754.35
      bilateral 754.31
    developmental 718.75
    open 835.10
    posterior 835.01
      open 835.11
    recurrent 718.35
  humerus (closed) 831.00
    distal end (see also Dislocation, elbow)
      832.00
    open 831.10
    proximal end (closed) 831.00
      anterior (subclavicular) (subcoracoid)
        (subglenoid) (closed) 831.01
        open 831.11
      inferior (closed) 831.03
        open 831.13
      open 831.10
      posterior (closed) 831.02
        open 831.12
  implant — see Complications, mechanical
  incus 385.23
  infracoracoid (closed) 831.01
    open 831.11
  innominate (pubic junction) (sacral junction)
    (closed) 839.69
    acetabulum (see also Dislocation, hip)
      835.00
    open 839.79
  interphalangeal (joint)
    finger or hand (closed) 834.02
      open 834.12
    foot or toe (closed) 838.06
      open 838.16
  jaw (cartilage) (meniscus) (closed) 830.0
    open 830.1
    recurrent 524.69
  joint NEC (closed) 839.8
    developmental 718.7 ☑
    open 839.9
    pathological — see Dislocation, patholog-
      ical
    recurrent — see Dislocation, recurrent
  knee (closed) 836.50
    anterior 836.51
      open 836.61
    congenital (with genu recurvatum) 754.41
    habitual 718.36
    lateral 836.54
      open 836.64
    medial 836.53
      open 836.63
    old 718.36
    open 836.60
    posterior 836.52
      open 836.62
    recurrent 718.36
    rotatory 836.59
      open 836.69

Dislocation — continued
  lacrimal gland 375.16
  leg (closed) 839.8
    open 839.9
  lens (crystalline) (complete) (partial) 379.32
    anterior 379.33
    congenital 743.37
    ocular implant 996.53
    posterior 379.34
    traumatic 921.3
  ligament — see Dislocation, by site
  lumbar (vertebrae) (closed) 839.20
    open 839.30
  lumbosacral (vertebrae) (closed) 839.20
    congenital 756.19
    open 839.30
  mandible (closed) 830.0
    open 830.1
  maxilla (inferior) (closed) 830.0
    open 830.1
  meniscus (knee) (see also Tear, meniscus)
    other sites — see Dislocation, by site
  metacarpal (bone)
    distal end (closed) 834.01
      open 834.11
    proximal end (closed) 833.05
      open 833.15
  metacarpophalangeal (joint) (closed) 834.01
    open 834.11
  metatarsal (bone) (closed) 838.04
    open 838.14
  metatarsophalangeal (joint) (closed) 838.05
    open 838.15
  midcarpal (joint) (closed) 833.03
    open 833.13
  midtarsal (joint) (closed) 838.02
    open 838.12
  Monteggia's — see Dislocation, hip
  multiple locations (except fingers only or toes
    only) (closed) 839.8
    open 839.9
  navicular (bone) foot (closed) 837.0
    open 837.1
  neck (see also Dislocation, vertebra, cervical)
    839.00
  Nélaton's — see Dislocation, ankle
  nontraumatic (joint) — see Dislocation,
    pathological
  nose (closed) 839.69
    open 839.79
  not recurrent, not current injury — see Dislo-
    cation, pathological
  occiput from atlas (closed) 839.01
    open 839.11
  old — see Dislocation, recurrent
  open (compound) NEC 839.9
  ossicle, ear 385.23
  paralytic (flaccid) (spastic) — see Dislocation,
    pathological
  patella (closed) 836.3
    congenital 755.64
    open 836.4
  pathological NEC 718.20
    ankle 718.27
    elbow 718.22
    foot 718.27
    hand 718.24
    hip 718.25
    knee 718.26
    lumbosacral joint 724.6
    multiple sites 718.29
    pelvic region 718.25
    sacroiliac 724.6
    shoulder (region) 718.21
    specified site NEC 718.28
    spine 724.8
      sacroiliac 724.6
    wrist 718.23
  pelvis (closed) 839.69
    acetabulum (see also Dislocation, hip)
      835.00
    open 839.79
  phalanx
    foot or toe (closed) 838.09
      open 838.19

Dislocation — continued
  phalanx — continued
    hand or finger (see also Dislocation, finger)
      834.00
  postpoliomyelitic — see Dislocation, patholog-
    ical
  prosthesis, internal — see Complications,
    mechanical
  radiocarpal (joint) (closed) 833.02
    open 833.12
  radioulnar (joint)
    distal end (closed) 833.01
      open 833.11
    proximal end (see also Dislocation, elbow)
      832.00
  radius
    distal end (closed) 833.00
      open 833.10
    proximal end (closed) 832.01
      open 832.11
    recurrent (see also Derangement, joint, recur-
      rent) 718.3 ☑
    elbow 718.32
    hip 718.35
    joint NEC 718.38
    knee 718.36
    lumbosacral (joint) 724.6
    patella 718.36
    sacroiliac 724.6
    shoulder 718.31
    temporomandibular 524.69
  rib (cartilage) (closed) 839.69
    congenital 756.3
    open 839.79
  sacrococcygeal (closed) 839.42
    open 839.52
  sacroiliac (joint) (ligament) (closed) 839.42
    congenital 755.69
    open 839.52
    recurrent 724.6
  sacrum (closed) 839.42
    open 839.52
  scaphoid (bone)
    ankle or foot (closed) 837.0
      open 837.1
    wrist (closed) (see also Dislocation, wrist)
      833.00
      open 833.10
  scapula (closed) 831.09
    open 831.19
  semilunar cartilage, knee — see Tear, meniscus
  septal cartilage (nose) (closed) 839.69
    open 839.79
  septum (nasal) (old) 470
  sesamoid bone — see Dislocation, by site
  shoulder (blade) (ligament) (closed) 831.00
    anterior (subclavicular) (subcoracoid)
      (subglenoid) (closed) 831.01
      open 831.11
    chronic 718.31
    inferior 831.03
      open 831.13
    open 831.10
    posterior (closed) 831.02
      open 831.12
    recurrent 718.31
  skull — see Injury, intracranial
  Smith's — see Dislocation, foot
  spine (articular process) (see also Dislocation,
    vertebra) (closed) 839.40
    atlanto-axial (closed) 839.01
      open 839.11
      recurrent 723.8
    cervical, cervicodorsal, cervicothoracic
      (closed) (see also Dislocation, verte-
      brae, cervical) 839.00
      open 839.10
      recurrent 723.8
    coccyx 839.41
      open 839.51
    congenital 756.19
    due to birth trauma 767.4
    open 839.50
    recurrent 724.9
    sacroiliac 839.42
      recurrent 724.6

Dislocation — continued
  spine (see also Dislocation, vertebra) — contin-
    ued
    sacrum (sacrococcygeal) (sacroiliac) 839.42
      open 839.52
  spontaneous — see Dislocation, pathological
  sternoclavicular (joint) (closed) 839.61
    open 839.71
  sternum (closed) 839.61
    open 839.71
  subastragalar — see Dislocation, foot
  subglenoid (closed) 831.01
    open 831.11
  symphysis
    jaw (closed) 830.0
      open 830.1
    mandibular (closed) 830.0
      open 830.1
    pubis (closed) 839.69
      open 839.79
  tarsal (bone) (joint) 838.01
    open 838.11
  tarsometatarsal (joint) 838.03
    open 838.13
  temporomandibular (joint) (closed) 830.0
    open 830.1
    recurrent 524.69
  thigh
    distal end (see also Dislocation, femur, dis-
      tal end) 836.50
    proximal end (see also Dislocation, hip)
      835.00
  thoracic (vertebrae) (closed) 839.21
    open 839.31
  thumb(s) (see also Dislocation, finger) 834.00
  thyroid cartilage (closed) 839.69
    open 839.79
  tibia
    distal end (closed) 837.0
      open 837.1
    proximal end (closed) 836.50
      anterior 836.51
        open 836.61
      lateral 836.54
        open 836.64
      medial 836.53
        open 836.63
      open 836.60
      posterior 836.52
        open 836.62
      rotatory 836.59
        open 836.69
  tibiofibular
    distal (closed) 837.0
      open 837.1
    superior (closed) 836.59
      open 836.69
  toe(s) (closed) 838.09
    open 838.19
  trachea (closed) 839.69
    open 839.79
  ulna
    distal end (closed) 833.09
      open 833.19
    proximal end — see Dislocation, elbow
  vertebra (articular process) (body) (closed)
    (traumatic) 839.40
    cervical, cervicodorsal or cervicothoracic
      (closed) 839.00
      first (atlas) 839.01
        open 839.11
      second (axis) 839.02
        open 839.12
      third 839.03
        open 839.13
      fourth 839.04
        open 839.14
      fifth 839.05
        open 839.15
      sixth 839.06
        open 839.16
      seventh 839.07
        open 839.17
      congential 756.19
      multiple sites 839.08
        open 839.18

☑ Additional Digit Required — Refer to the Tabular List for Digit Selection   ▽ Subterms under main terms may continue to next column or page

Index

Dislocation — Disorder

Dislocation — *continued*
  vertebra — *continued*
    cervical, cervicodorsal or cervicothoracic
      — *continued*
        open 839.10
      congenital 756.19
      dorsal 839.21
        open 839.31
        recurrent 724.9
      lumbar, lumbosacral 839.20
        open 839.30
      non-traumatic — *see* Displacement, inter-
        vertebral disc
      open NEC 839.50
      recurrent 724.9
      specified region NEC 839.49
        open 839.59
      thoracic 839.21
        open 839.31
    wrist (carpal bone) (scaphoid) (semilunar)
      (closed) 833.00
      carpometacarpal (joint) 833.04
        open 833.14
      metacarpal bone, proximal end 833.05
        open 833.15
      midcarpal (joint) 833.03
        open 833.13
      open 833.10
      radiocarpal (joint) 833.02
        open 833.12
      radioulnar (joint) 833.01
        open 833.11
      recurrent 718.33
      specified site NEC 833.09
        open 833.19
    xiphoid cartilage (closed) 839.61
      open 839.71

Dislodgement
  artificial skin graft 996.55
  decellularized allodermis graft 996.55

Disobedience, hostile (covert) (overt) — *see also*
  Disturbance, conduct 312.0 ☑

Disorder — *see also* Disease
  academic underachievement, childhood and
    adolescence 313.83
  accommodation 367.51
    drug-induced 367.89
    toxic 367.89
  adjustment (*see also* Reaction, adjustment)
    309.9
    with
      anxiety 309.24
      anxiety and depressed mood 309.28
      depressed mood 309.0
      disturbance of conduct 309.3
      disturbance of emotions and conduct
        309.4
  adrenal (capsule) (cortex) (gland) 255.9
    specified type NEC 255.8
  adrenogenital 255.2
  affective (*see also* Psychosis, affective) 296.90
    atypical 296.81
  aggressive, unsocialized (*see also* Disturbance,
    conduct) 312.0 ☑
  alcohol, alcoholic (*see also* Alcohol) 291.9
  allergic — *see* Allergy
  amino acid (metabolic) (*see also* Disturbance,
    metabolism, amino acid) 270.9
    albinism 270.2
    alkaptonuria 270.2
    argininosuccinicaciduria 270.6
    beta-amino-isobutyricaciduria 277.2
    cystathioninuria 270.4
    cystinosis 270.0
    cystinuria 270.0
    glycinuria 270.0
    homocystinuria 270.4
    imidazole 270.5
    maple syrup (urine) disease 270.3
    neonatal, transitory 775.89
    oasthouse urine disease 270.2
    ochronosis 270.2
    phenylketonuria 270.1
    phenylpyruvic oligophrenia 270.1
    purine NEC 277.2
    pyrimidine NEC 277.2

Disorder — *see also* Disease — *continued*
  amino acid (*see also* Disturbance, metabolism,
    amino acid) — *continued*
    renal transport NEC 270.0
    specified type NEC 270.8
    transport NEC 270.0
      renal 270.0
    xanthinuria 277.2
  amnestic (*see also* Amnestic syndrome) 294.8
    alcohol-induced persisting 291.1
    drug-induced persisting 292.83
    in conditions classified elsewhere 294.0
  anaerobic glycolysis with anemia 282.3
  anxiety (*see also* Anxiety) 300.00
    due to or associated with physical condi-
      tion 293.84
  arteriole 447.9
    specified type NEC 447.8
  artery 447.9
    specified type NEC 447.8
  articulation — *see* Disorder, joint
  Asperger's 299.8 ☑
  attachment of infancy or early childhood
    313.89
  attention deficit 314.00
    with hyperactivity 314.01
    predominantly
      combined hyperactive/inattentive
        314.01
      hyperactive/impulsive 314.01
      inattentive 314.00
    residual type 314.8
  auditory processing disorder 388.45
    acquired 388.45
    developmental 315.32
  autistic 299.0 ☑
  autoimmune NEC 279.49   ▲
    hemolytic (cold type) (warm type) 283.0
    parathyroid 252.1
    thyroid 245.2
  avoidant, childhood or adolescence 313.21
  balance
    acid-base 276.9
      mixed (with hypercapnia) 276.4
    electrolyte 276.9
    fluid 276.9
  behavior NEC (*see also* Disturbance, conduct)
    312.9
    disruptive 312.9
  bilirubin excretion 277.4
  bipolar (affective) (alternating) 296.80

Note — Use the following fifth-digit subclassification with categories 296.0–296.6:

  0   *unspecified*

  1   *mild*

  2   *moderate*

  3   *severe, without mention of psychotic*
      behavior

  4   *severe, specified as with psychotic*
      behavior

  5   *in partial or unspecified remission*

  6   *in full remission*

    atypical 296.7
    currently
      depressed 296.5 ☑
      hypomanic 296.4 ☑
      manic 296.4 ☑
      mixed 296.6 ☑
    specified type NEC 296.89
    type I 296.7
      most recent episode (or current)
        depressed 296.5 ☑
        hypomanic 296.4 ☑
        manic 296.4 ☑
        mixed 296.6 ☑
        unspecified 296.7
      single manic episode 296.0 ☑
    type II (recurrent major depressive
      episodes with hypomania) 296.89
  bladder 596.9
    functional NEC 596.59
    specified NEC 596.8

Disorder — *see also* Disease — *continued*
  bleeding 286.9
  bone NEC 733.90
    specified NEC 733.99
  brachial plexus 353.0
  branched-chain amino-acid degradation 270.3
  breast 611.9
    puerperal, postpartum 676.3 ☑
    specified NEC 611.89
  Briquet's 300.81
  bursa 727.9
    shoulder region 726.10
  carbohydrate metabolism, congenital 271.9
  cardiac, functional 427.9
    postoperative 997.1
    psychogenic 306.2
  cardiovascular, psychogenic 306.2
  cartilage NEC 733.90
    articular 718.00
      ankle 718.07
      elbow 718.02
      foot 718.07
      hand 718.04
      hip 718.05
      knee 717.9
      multiple sites 718.09
      pelvic region 718.05
      shoulder region 718.01
      specified
        site NEC 718.08
        type NEC 733.99
      wrist 718.03
  catatonic — *see* Catatonia
  central auditory processing 315.32
    acquired 388.45
    developmental 315.32
  cervical region NEC 723.9
  cervical root (nerve) NEC 353.2
  character NEC (*see also* Disorder, personality)
    301.9
  ciliary body 364.9
    specified NEC 364.89
  coagulation (factor) (*see also* Defect, coagula-
    tion) 286.9
    factor VIII (congenital) (functional) 286.0
    factor IX (congenital) (functional) 286.1
    neonatal, transitory 776.3
  coccyx 724.70
    specified NEC 724.79
  cognitive 294.9
  colon 569.9
    functional 564.9
      congenital 751.3
  communication 307.9
  conduct (*see also* Disturbance, conduct) 312.9
    adjustment reaction 309.3
    adolescent onset type 312.82
    childhood onset type 312.81
    compulsive 312.30
      specified type NEC 312.39
    hyperkinetic 314.2
    onset unspecified 312.89
    socialized (type) 312.20
      aggressive 312.23
      unaggressive 312.21
    specified NEC 312.89
  conduction, heart 426.9
    specified NEC 426.89
  conflict
    sexual orientation 302.0
  congenital
    glycosylation (CDG) 271.8
  convulsive (secondary) (*see also* Convulsions)
    780.39
    due to injury at birth 767.0
    idiopathic 780.39
  coordination 781.3
  cornea NEC 371.89
    due to contact lens 371.82
  corticosteroid metabolism NEC 255.2
  cranial nerve — *see* Disorder, nerve, cranial
  cyclothymic 301.13
  degradation, branched-chain amino acid 270.3
  delusional 297.1
  dentition 520.6
  depersonalization 300.6

Disorder — *see also* Disease — *continued*
  depressive NEC 311
    atypical 296.82
    major (*see also* Psychosis, affective)
      296.2 ☑
      recurrent episode 296.3 ☑
      single episode 296.2 ☑
  development, specific 315.9
    associated with hyperkinesia 314.1
    coordination 315.4
    language 315.31
      and speech due to hearing loss 315.34
    learning 315.2
      arithmetical 315.1
      reading 315.00
    mixed 315.5
    motor coordination 315.4
    specified type NEC 315.8
    speech 315.39
      and language due to hearing loss
        315.34
  diaphragm 519.4
  digestive 536.9
    fetus or newborn 777.9
      specified NEC 777.8
    psychogenic 306.4
  disintegrative, childhood 299.1 ☑
  dissociative 300.15
    identity 300.14
    nocturnal 307.47
  drug-related 292.9
  dysmorphic body 300.7
  dysthymic 300.4
  ear 388.9
    degenerative NEC 388.00
    external 380.9
      specified 380.89
    pinna 380.30
    specified type NEC 388.8
    vascular NEC 388.00
  eating NEC 307.50
  electrolyte NEC 276.9
    with
      abortion — *see* Abortion, by type, with
        metabolic disorder
      ectopic pregnancy (*see also* categories
        633.0–633.9) 639.4
      molar pregnancy (*see also* categories
        630–632) 639.4
    acidosis 276.2
      metabolic 276.2
      respiratory 276.2
    alkalosis 276.3
      metabolic 276.3
      respiratory 276.3
    following
      abortion 639.4
      ectopic or molar pregnancy 639.4
    neonatal, transitory NEC 775.5
  emancipation as adjustment reaction 309.22
  emotional (*see also* Disorder, mental, nonpsy-
    chotic) V40.9
  endocrine 259.9
    specified type NEC 259.8
  esophagus 530.9
    functional 530.5
    psychogenic 306.4
  explosive
    intermittent 312.34
    isolated 312.35
  expressive language 315.31
  eye 379.90
    globe — *see* Disorder, globe
    ill-defined NEC 379.99
    limited duction NEC 378.63
    specified NEC 379.8
  eyelid 374.9
    degenerative 374.50
    sensory 374.44
    specified type NEC 374.89
    vascular 374.85
  factitious (with combined psychological and
    physical signs and symptoms) (with
    predominantly physical signs and
    symptoms) 300.19

☑ Additional Digit Required — Refer to the Tabular List for Digit Selection

▽ Subterms under main terms may continue to next column or page

▶◀ Revised Text   ● New Line   ▲ Revised Code

Disorder — *see also* Disease — *continued*
factitious — *continued*
 with predominantly psychological signs and symptoms 300.16
 factor, coagulation (*see also* Defect, coagulation) 286.9
 IX (congenital) (funcitonal) 286.1
 VIII (congenital) (functional) 286.0
fascia 728.9
fatty acid oxidation 277.85
feeding — *see* Feeding
female sexual arousal 302.72
fluid NEC 276.9
gastric (functional) 536.9
 motility 536.8
 psychogenic 306.4
 secretion 536.8
gastrointestinal (functional) NEC 536.9
 newborn (neonatal) 777.9
 specified NEC 777.8
 psychogenic 306.4
gender (child) 302.6
 adult 302.85
gender identity (childhood) 302.6
 adolescents 302.85
 adults (-life) 302.85
genitourinary system, psychogenic 306.50
globe 360.9
 degenerative 360.20
 specified NEC 360.29
 specified type NEC 360.89
hearing (*see also* Deafness)
 conductive type (air) (*see also* Deafness, conductive) 389.00
 mixed conductive and sensorineural 389.20
 bilateral 389.22
 unilateral 389.21
 nerve
 bilateral 389.12
 unilateral 389.13
 perceptive (*see also* Deafness, perceptive) 389.10
 sensorineural type NEC (*see also* Deafness, sensorineural 389.10
heart action 427.9
 postoperative 997.1
hematological, transient neonatal 776.9
 specified type NEC 776.8
hematopoietic organs 289.9
hemorrhagic NEC 287.9
 due to intrinsic circulating anticoagulants 286.5
 specified type NEC 287.8
hemostasis (*see also* Defect, coagulation) 286.9
homosexual conflict 302.0
hypomanic (chronic) 301.11
identity
 childhood and adolescence 313.82
 gender 302.6
immune mechanism (immunity) 279.9
 single complement (C1-C9) 279.8
 specified type NEC 279.8
impulse control (*see also* Disturbance, conduct, compulsive) 312.30
infant sialic acid storage 271.8
integument, fetus or newborn 778.9
 specified type NEC 778.8
interactional psychotic (childhood) (*see also* Psychosis, childhood) 299.1 ☑
intermittent explosive 312.34
intervertebral disc 722.90
 cervical, cervicothoracic 722.91
 lumbar, lumbosacral 722.93
 thoracic, thoracolumbar 722.92
intestinal 569.9
 functional NEC 564.9
 congenital 751.3
 postoperative 564.4
 psychogenic 306.4
introverted, of childhood and adolescence 313.22
involuntary emotional expression (IEED) 310.8
iris 364.9
 specified NEC 364.89
iron, metabolism 275.0

Disorder — *see also* Disease — *continued*
isolated explosive 312.35
joint NEC 719.90
 ankle 719.97
 elbow 719.92
 foot 719.97
 hand 719.94
 hip 719.95
 knee 719.96
 multiple sites 719.99
 pelvic region 719.95
 psychogenic 306.0
 shoulder (region) 719.91
 specified site NEC 719.98
 temporomandibular 524.60
 sounds on opening or closing 524.64
 specified NEC 524.69
 wrist 719.93
kidney 593.9
 functional 588.9
 specified NEC 588.89
labyrinth, labyrinthine 386.9
 specified type NEC 386.8
lactation 676.9 ☑
language (developmental) (expressive) 315.31
 mixed receptive-expressive 315.32
learning 315.9
ligament 728.9
ligamentous attachments, peripheral (*see also* Enthesopathy)
 spine 720.1
limb NEC 729.90
 psychogenic 306.0
lipid
 metabolism, congenital 272.9
 storage 272.7
lipoprotein deficiency (familial) 272.5
low back NEC 724.9
 psychogenic 306.0
lumbosacral
 plexus 353.1
 root (nerve) NEC 353.4
lymphoproliferative (chronic) NEC (M9970/1) 238.79
 post-transplant (PTLD) 238.77
major depressive (*see also* Psychosis, affective) 296.2 ☑
 recurrent episode 296.3 ☑
 single episode 296.2 ☑
male erectile 607.84
 nonorganic origin 302.72
manic (*see also* Psychosis, affective) 296.0 ☑
 atypical 296.81
mathematics 315.1
meniscus NEC (*see also* Disorder, cartilage, articular) 718.0 ☑
menopausal 627.9
 specified NEC 627.8
menstrual 626.9
 psychogenic 306.52
 specified NEC 626.8
mental (nonpsychotic) 300.9
 affecting management of pregnancy, childbirth, or puerperium 648.4 ☑
 drug-induced 292.9
 hallucinogen persisting perception 292.89
 specified type NEC 292.89
 due to or associated with
 alcoholism 291.9
 drug consumption NEC 292.9
 specified type NEC 292.89
 physical condition NEC 293.9
 induced by drug 292.9
 specified type NEC 292.89
 neurotic (*see also* Neurosis) 300.9
 of infancy, childhood or adolescence 313.9
 persistent
 other
 due to conditions classified elsewhere 294.8
 unspecified
 due to conditions classified elsewhere 294.9
 presenile 310.1
 psychotic NEC 290.10

Disorder — *see also* Disease — *continued*
mental — *continued*
 previous, affecting management of pregnancy V23.89
 psychoneurotic (*see also* Neurosis) 300.9
 psychotic (*see also* Psychosis) 298.9
 brief 298.8
 senile 290.20
 specific, following organic brain damage 310.9
 cognitive or personality change of other type 310.1
 frontal lobe syndrome 310.0
 postconcussional syndrome 310.2
 specified type NEC 310.8
 transient
 in conditions classified elsewhere 293.9
metabolism NEC 277.9
 with
 abortion — *see* Abortion, by type, with metabolic disorder
 ectopic pregnancy (*see also* categories 633.0–633.9) 639.4
 molar pregnancy (*see also* categories 630–632) 639.4
 alkaptonuria 270.2
 amino acid (*see also* Disorder, amino acid) 270.9
 specified type NEC 270.8
 ammonia 270.6
 arginine 270.6
 argininosuccinic acid 270.6
 basal 794.7
 bilirubin 277.4
 calcium 275.40
 carbohydrate 271.9
 specified type NEC 271.8
 cholesterol 272.9
 citrulline 270.6
 copper 275.1
 corticosteroid 255.2
 cystine storage 270.0
 cystinuria 270.0
 fat 272.9
 fatty acid oxidation 277.85
 following
 abortion 639.4
 ectopic or molar pregnancy 639.4
 fructosemia 271.2
 fructosuria 271.2
 fucosidosis 271.8
 galactose-1-phosphate uridyl transferase 271.1
 glutamine 270.7
 glycine 270.7
 glycogen storage NEC 271.0
 hepatorenal 271.0
 hemochromatosis 275.0
 in labor and delivery 669.0 ☑
 iron 275.0
 lactose 271.3
 lipid 272.9
 specified type NEC 272.8
 storage 272.7
 lipoprotein (*see also* Hyperlipemia deficiency (familial)) 272.5
 lysine 270.7
 magnesium 275.2
 mannosidosis 271.8
 mineral 275.9
 specified type NEC 275.8
 mitochondrial 277.87
 mucopolysaccharide 277.5
 nitrogen 270.9
 ornithine 270.6
 oxalosis 271.8
 pentosuria 271.8
 phenylketonuria 270.1
 phosphate 275.3
 phosphorous 275.3
 plasma protein 273.9
 specified type NEC 273.8
 porphyrin 277.1
 purine 277.2
 pyrimidine 277.2
 serine 270.7

Disorder — *see also* Disease — *continued*
metabolism — *continued*
 sodium 276.9
 specified type NEC 277.89
 steroid 255.2
 threonine 270.7
 urea cycle 270.6
 xylose 271.8
micturition NEC 788.69
 psychogenic 306.53
misery and unhappiness, of childhood and adolescence 313.1
mitochondrial metabolism 277.87
mitral valve 424.0
mood (*see also* Disorder, bipolar) 296.90
 episodic 296.90
 specified NEC 296.99
 in conditions classified elsewhere 293.83
motor tic 307.20
 chronic 307.22
 transient (childhood) 307.21
movement NEC 333.90
 hysterical 300.11
 medication-induced 333.90
 periodic limb 327.51
 sleep related, unspecified 780.58
 other organic 327.59
 specified type NEC 333.99
 stereotypic 307.3
mucopolysaccharide 277.5
muscle 728.9
 psychogenic 306.0
 specified type NEC 728.3
muscular attachments, peripheral (*see also* Enthesopathy)
 spine 720.1
musculoskeletal system NEC 729.90
 psychogenic 306.0
myeloproliferative (chronic) NEC (M9960/1) 238.79
myoneural 358.9
 due to lead 358.2
 specified type NEC 358.8
 toxic 358.2
myotonic 359.29
neck region NEC 723.9
nerve 349.9
 abducens NEC 378.54
 accessory 352.4
 acoustic 388.5
 auditory 388.5
 auriculotemporal 350.8
 axillary 353.0
 cerebral — *see* Disorder, nerve, cranial
 cranial 352.9
 first 352.0
 second 377.49
 third
 partial 378.51
 total 378.52
 fourth 378.53
 fifth 350.9
 sixth 378.54
 seventh NEC 351.9
 eighth 388.5
 ninth 352.2
 tenth 352.3
 eleventh 352.4
 twelfth 352.5
 multiple 352.6
 entrapment — *see* Neuropathy, entrapment
 facial 351.9
 specified NEC 351.8
 femoral 355.2
 glossopharyngeal NEC 352.2
 hypoglossal 352.5
 iliohypogastric 355.79
 ilioinguinal 355.79
 intercostal 353.8
 lateral
 cutaneous of thigh 355.1
 popliteal 355.3
 lower limb NEC 355.8
 medial, popliteal 355.4
 median NEC 354.1

Disorder — *see also* Disease — *continued*
- nerve — *continued*
  - obturator 355.79
  - oculomotor
    - partial 378.51
    - total 378.52
  - olfactory 352.0
  - optic 377.49
    - hypoplasia 377.43
    - ischemic 377.41
    - nutritional 377.33
    - toxic 377.34
  - peroneal 355.3
  - phrenic 354.8
  - plantar 355.6
  - pneumogastric 352.3
  - posterior tibial 355.5
  - radial 354.3
  - recurrent laryngeal 352.3
  - root 353.9
    - specified NEC 353.8
  - saphenous 355.79
  - sciatic NEC 355.0
  - specified NEC 355.9
    - lower limb 355.79
    - upper limb 354.8
  - spinal 355.9
  - sympathetic NEC 337.9
  - trigeminal 350.9
    - specified NEC 350.8
  - trochlear 378.53
  - ulnar 354.2
  - upper limb NEC 354.9
  - vagus 352.3
- nervous system NEC 349.9
  - autonomic (peripheral) (*see also* Neuropathy, peripheral, autonomic) 337.9
  - cranial 352.9
  - parasympathetic (*see also* Neuropathy, peripheral, autonomic) 337.9
  - specified type NEC 349.89
  - sympathetic (*see also* Neuropathy, peripheral, autonomic) 337.9
  - vegetative (*see also* Neuropathy, peripheral, autonomic) 337.9
- neurohypophysis NEC 253.6
- neurological NEC 781.99
  - peripheral NEC 355.9
- neuromuscular NEC 358.9
  - hereditary NEC 359.1
  - specified NEC 358.8
  - toxic 358.2
- neurotic 300.9
  - specified type NEC 300.89
- neutrophil, polymorphonuclear (functional) 288.1
- nightmare 307.47
- night terror 307.46
- obsessive-compulsive 300.3
- oppositional defiant, childhood and adolescence 313.81
- optic
  - chiasm 377.54
    - associated with
      - inflammatory disorders 377.54
      - neoplasm NEC 377.52
        - pituitary 377.51
      - pituitary disorders 377.51
      - vascular disorders 377.53
  - nerve 377.49
  - radiations 377.63
  - tracts 377.63
- orbit 376.9
  - specified NEC 376.89
- orgasmic
  - female 302.73
  - male 302.74
- overanxious, of childhood and adolescence 313.0
- oxidation, fatty acid 277.85
- pancreas, internal secretion (other than diabetes mellitus) 251.9
  - specified type NEC 251.8
- panic 300.01
  - with agoraphobia 300.21
- papillary muscle NEC 429.81

Disorder — *see also* Disease — *continued*
- paranoid 297.9
  - induced 297.3
  - shared 297.3
- parathyroid 252.9
  - specified type NEC 252.8
- paroxysmal, mixed 780.39
- pentose phosphate pathway with anemia 282.2
- periodic limb movement 327.51
- peroxisomal 277.86
- personality 301.9
  - affective 301.10
  - aggressive 301.3
  - amoral 301.7
  - anancastic, anankastic 301.4
  - antisocial 301.7
  - asocial 301.7
  - asthenic 301.6
  - avoidant 301.82
  - borderline 301.83
  - compulsive 301.4
  - cyclothymic 301.13
  - dependent-passive 301.6
  - dyssocial 301.7
  - emotional instability 301.59
  - epileptoid 301.3
  - explosive 301.3
  - following organic brain damage 310.1
  - histrionic 301.50
  - hyperthymic 301.11
  - hypomanic (chronic) 301.11
  - hypothymic 301.12
  - hysterical 301.50
  - immature 301.89
  - inadequate 301.6
  - introverted 301.21
  - labile 301.59
  - moral deficiency 301.7
  - narcissistic 301.81
  - obsessional 301.4
  - obsessive-compulsive 301.4
  - overconscientious 301.4
  - paranoid 301.0
  - passive (-dependent) 301.6
  - passive-aggressive 301.84
  - pathological NEC 301.9
  - pseudosocial 301.7
  - psychopathic 301.9
  - schizoid 301.20
    - introverted 301.21
    - schizotypal 301.22
  - schizotypal 301.22
  - seductive 301.59
  - type A 301.4
  - unstable 301.59
- pervasive developmental 299.9 ☑
  - childhood-onset 299.8 ☑
  - specified NEC 299.8 ☑
- phonological 315.39
- pigmentation, choroid (congenital) 743.53
- pinna 380.30
  - specified type NEC 380.39
- pituitary, thalamic 253.9
  - anterior NEC 253.4
  - iatrogenic 253.7
  - postablative 253.7
  - specified NEC 253.8
- pityriasis-like NEC 696.8
- platelets (blood) 287.1
- polymorphonuclear neutrophils (functional) 288.1
- porphyrin metabolism 277.1
- postmenopausal 627.9
  - specified type NEC 627.8
- post-transplant lymphoproliferative (PTLD) 238.77
- posttraumatic stress 309.81
- post-traumatic stress (PTSD) 309.81
  - acute 309.81
  - brief 309.81
  - chronic 309.81
- premenstrual dysphoric (PMDD) 625.4
- psoriatic-like NEC 696.8
- psychic, with diseases classified elsewhere 316
- psychogenic NEC (*see also* condition) 300.9

Disorder — *see also* Disease — *continued*
- psychogenic (*see also* condition) — *continued*
  - allergic NEC
    - respiratory 306.1
  - anxiety 300.00
    - atypical 300.00
    - generalized 300.02
  - appetite 307.59
  - articulation, joint 306.0
  - asthenic 300.5
  - blood 306.8
  - cardiovascular (system) 306.2
  - compulsive 300.3
  - cutaneous 306.3
  - depressive 300.4
  - digestive (system) 306.4
  - dysmenorrheic 306.52
  - dyspneic 306.1
  - eczematous 306.3
  - endocrine (system) 306.6
  - eye 306.7
  - feeding 307.59
  - functional NEC 306.9
  - gastric 306.4
  - gastrointestinal (system) 306.4
  - genitourinary (system) 306.50
  - heart (function) (rhythm) 306.2
  - hemic 306.8
  - hyperventilatory 306.1
  - hypochondriacal 300.7
  - hysterical 300.10
  - intestinal 306.4
  - joint 306.0
  - learning 315.2
  - limb 306.0
  - lymphatic (system) 306.8
  - menstrual 306.52
  - micturition 306.53
  - monoplegic NEC 306.0
  - motor 307.9
  - muscle 306.0
  - musculoskeletal 306.0
  - neurocirculatory 306.2
  - obsessive 300.3
  - occupational 300.89
  - organ or part of body NEC 306.9
  - organs of special sense 306.7
  - paralytic NEC 306.0
  - phobic 300.20
  - physical NEC 306.9
  - pruritic 306.3
  - rectal 306.4
  - respiratory (system) 306.1
  - rheumatic 306.0
  - sexual (function) 302.70
    - specified type NEC 302.79
  - sexual orientation conflict 302.0
  - skin (allergic) (eczematous) (pruritic) 306.3
  - sleep 307.40
    - initiation or maintenance 307.41
      - persistent 307.42
      - transient 307.41
    - movement 780.58
    - sleep terror 307.46
    - specified type NEC 307.49
  - specified part of body NEC 306.8
  - stomach 306.4
- psychomotor NEC 307.9
  - hysterical 300.11
- psychoneurotic (*see also* Neurosis) 300.9
  - mixed NEC 300.89
- psychophysiologic (*see also* Disorder, psychosomatic) 306.9
- psychosexual identity (childhood) 302.6
  - adult-life 302.85
- psychosomatic NEC 306.9
  - allergic NEC
    - respiratory 306.1
  - articulation, joint 306.0
  - cardiovascular (system) 306.2
  - cutaneous 306.3
  - digestive (system) 306.4
  - dysmenorrheic 306.52
  - dyspneic 306.1
  - endocrine (system) 306.6

Disorder — *see also* Disease — *continued*
- psychosomatic — *continued*
  - eye 306.7
  - gastric 306.4
  - gastrointestinal (system) 306.4
  - genitourinary (system) 306.50
  - heart (functional) (rhythm) 306.2
  - hyperventilatory 306.1
  - intestinal 306.4
  - joint 306.0
  - limb 306.0
  - lymphatic (system) 306.8
  - menstrual 306.52
  - micturition 306.53
  - monoplegic NEC 306.0
  - muscle 306.0
  - musculoskeletal 306.0
  - neurocirculatory 306.2
  - organs of special sense 306.7
  - paralytic NEC 306.0
  - pruritic 306.3
  - rectal 306.4
  - respiratory (system) 306.1
  - rheumatic 306.0
  - sexual (function) 302.70
  - skin 306.3
  - specified part of body NEC 306.8
  - specified type NEC 302.79
  - stomach 306.4
- psychotic (*see also* Psychosis) 298.9
  - brief 298.8
- purine metabolism NEC 277.2
- pyrimidine metabolism NEC 277.2
- reactive attachment of infancy or early childhood 313.89
- reading, developmental 315.00
- reflex 796.1
- REM sleep behavior 327.42
- renal function, impaired 588.9
  - specified type NEC 588.89
- renal transport NEC 588.89
- respiration, respiratory NEC 519.9
  - due to
    - aspiration of liquids or solids 508.9
    - inhalation of fumes or vapors 506.9
  - psychogenic 306.1
- retina 362.9
  - specified type NEC 362.89
- rumination 307.53
- sacroiliac joint NEC 724.6
- sacrum 724.6
- schizo-affective (*see also* Schizophrenia) 295.7 ☑
- schizoid, childhood or adolescence 313.22
- schizophreniform 295.4 ☑
- schizotypal personality 301.22
- secretion, thyrocalcitonin 246.0
- seizure 345.9 ☑
  - recurrent 345.9 ☑
    - epileptic — *see* Epilepsy
- semantic pragmatic 315.39
  - with autism 299.0 ☑
- sense of smell 781.1
  - psychogenic 306.7
- separation anxiety 309.21
- sexual (*see also* Deviation, sexual) 302.9
  - aversion 302.79
  - desire, hypoactive 302.71
  - function, psychogenic 302.70
- shyness, of childhood and adolescence 313.21
- single complement (C1-C9) 279.8
- skin NEC 709.9
  - fetus or newborn 778.9
    - specified type 778.8
  - psychogenic (allergic) (eczematous) (pruritic) 306.3
  - specified type NEC 709.8
  - vascular 709.1
- sleep 780.50
  - with apnea — *see* Apnea, sleep
  - alcohol induced 291.82
  - arousal 307.46
    - confusional 327.41
  - circadian rhythm 327.30
    - advanced sleep phase type 327.32
    - alcohol induced 291.82

Disorder — see also Disease — continued

sleep — continued

  circadian rhythm — continued

    delayed sleep phase type 327.31

    drug induced 292.85

    free running type 327.34

    in conditions classified elsewhere 327.37

    irregular sleep-wake type 327.33

    jet lag type 327.35

    other 327.39

    shift work type 327.36

  drug induced 292.85

  initiation or maintenance (see also Insomnia) 780.52

    nonorganic origin (transient) 307.41

      persistent 307.42

  nonorganic origin 307.40

    specified type NEC 307.49

  organic specified type NEC 327.8

  periodic limb movement 327.51

  specified NEC 780.59

  wake

    cycle — see Disorder, sleep, circadian rhythm

    schedule — see Disorer, sleep, circadian rhythm

social, of childhood and adolescence 313.22

soft tissue 729.90

  specified type NEC 729.99

somatization 300.81

somatoform (atypical) (undifferentiated) 300.82

  severe 300.81

  specified type NEC 300.89

speech NEC 784.59 ▲

  nonorganic origin 307.9

spine NEC 724.9

  ligamentous or muscular attachments, peripheral 720.1

steroid metabolism NEC 255.2

stomach (functional) (see also Disorder, gastric) 536.9

  psychogenic 306.4

storage, iron 275.0

stress (see also Reaction, stress, acute) 308.3

  posttraumatic

    acute 309.81

    brief 309.81

    chronic 309.81

substitution 300.11

suspected — see Observation

synovium 727.9

temperature regulation, fetus or newborn 778.4

temporomandibular joint NEC 524.60

  sounds on opening or closing 524.64

  specified NEC 524.69

tendon 727.9

  shoulder region 726.10

thoracic root (nerve) NEC 353.3

thyrocalcitonin secretion 246.0

thyroid (gland) NEC 246.9

  specified type NEC 246.8

tic 307.20

  chronic (motor or vocal) 307.22

  motor-verbal 307.23

  organic origin 333.1

  transient (of childhood) 307.21

tooth NEC 525.9

  development NEC 520.9

    specified type NEC 520.8

  eruption 520.6

  specified type NEC 525.8

Tourette's 307.23

transport, carbohydrate 271.9

  specified type NEC 271.8

tubular, phosphate-losing 588.0

tympanic membrane 384.9

unaggressive, unsocialized (see also Disturbance, conduct) 312.1 ☑

undersocialized, unsocialized (see also Disturbance, conduct)

  aggressive (type) 312.0 ☑

  unaggressive (type) 312.1 ☑

vision, visual NEC 368.9

Disorder — see also Disease — continued

vision, visual — continued

  binocular NEC 368.30

  cortex 377.73

    associated with

      inflammatory disorders 377.73

      neoplasms 377.71

      vascular disorders 377.72

  pathway NEC 377.63

    associated with

      inflammatory disorders 377.63

      neoplasms 377.61

      vascular disorders 377.62

vocal tic

  chronic 307.22

wakefulness (see also Hypersomnia) 780.54

  nonorganic origin (transient) 307.43

    persistent 307.44

written expression 315.2

Disorganized globe 360.29

Displacement, displaced

Note — For acquired displacement of bones, cartilage, joints, tendons, due to injury, see also Dislocation.

Displacements at ages under one year should be considered congenital, provided there is no indication the condition was acquired after birth.

acquired traumatic of bone, cartilage, joint, tendon NEC (without fracture) (see also Dislocation) 839.8

  with fracture — see Fracture, by site

adrenal gland (congenital) 759.1

alveolus and teeth, vertical 524.75

appendix, retrocecal (congenital) 751.5

auricle (congenital) 744.29

bladder (acquired) 596.8

  congenital 753.8

brachial plexus (congenital) 742.8

brain stem, caudal 742.4

canaliculus lacrimalis 743.65

cardia, through esophageal hiatus 750.6

cerebellum, caudal 742.4

cervix — see Displacement, uterus

colon (congenital) 751.4

device, implant, or graft — see Complications, mechanical

epithelium

  columnar of cervix 622.10

  cuboidal, beyond limits of external os (uterus) 752.49

esophageal mucosa into cardia of stomach, congenital 750.4

esophagus (acquired) 530.89

  congenital 750.4

eyeball (acquired) (old) 376.36

  congenital 743.8

  current injury 871.3

  lateral 376.36

fallopian tube (acquired) 620.4

  congenital 752.19

  opening (congenital) 752.19

gallbladder (congenital) 751.69

gastric mucosa 750.7

  into

    duodenum 750.7

    esophagus 750.7

    Meckel's diverticulum, congenital 750.7

globe (acquired) (lateral) (old) 376.36

  current injury 871.3

graft

  artificial skin graft 996.55

  decellularized allodermis graft 996.55

heart (congenital) 746.87

  acquired 429.89

hymen (congenital) (upward) 752.49

internal prosthesis NEC — see Complications, mechanical

intervertebral disc (with neuritis, radiculitis, sciatica, or other pain) 722.2

  with myelopathy 722.70

  cervical, cervicodorsal, cervicothoracic 722.0

    with myelopathy 722.71

Displacement, displaced — continued

intervertebral disc — continued

  cervical, cervicodorsal, cervicothoracic — continued

    due to major trauma — see Dislocation, vertebra, cervical

    due to trauma — see Dislocation, vertebra

  lumbar, lumbosacral 722.10

    with myelopathy 722.73

    due to major trauma — see Dislocation, vertebra, lumbar

  thoracic, thoracolumbar 722.11

    with myelopathy 722.72

    due to major trauma — see Dislocation, vertebra, thoracic

intrauterine device 996.32

kidney (acquired) 593.0

  congenital 753.3

lacrimal apparatus or duct (congenital) 743.65

macula (congenital) 743.55

Meckel's diverticulum (congenital) 751.0

nail (congenital) 757.5

  acquired 703.8

opening of Wharton's duct in mouth 750.26

organ or site, congenital NEC — see Malposition, congenital

ovary (acquired) 620.4

  congenital 752.0

  free in peritoneal cavity (congenital) 752.0

  into hernial sac 620.4

oviduct (acquired) 620.4

  congenital 752.19

parathyroid (gland) 252.8

parotid gland (congenital) 750.26

punctum lacrimale (congenital) 743.65

sacroiliac (congenital) (joint) 755.69

  current injury — see Dislocation, sacroiliac

  old 724.6

spine (congenital) 756.19

spleen, congenital 759.0

stomach (congenital) 750.7

  acquired 537.89

subglenoid (closed) 831.01

sublingual duct (congenital) 750.26

teeth, tooth 524.30

  horizontal 524.33

  vertical 524.34

tongue (congenital) (downward) 750.19

trachea (congenital) 748.3

ureter or ureteric opening or orifice (congenital) 753.4

uterine opening of oviducts or fallopian tubes 752.19

uterus, uterine (see also Malposition, uterus) 621.6

  congenital 752.3

ventricular septum 746.89

  with rudimentary ventricle 746.89

xyphoid bone (process) 738.3

Disproportion 653.9 ☑

affecting fetus or newborn 763.1

breast, reconstructed 612.1

  between native and reconstructed 612.1

caused by

  conjoined twins 678.1 ☑

  contraction, pelvis (general) 653.1 ☑

    inlet 653.2 ☑

    midpelvic 653.8 ☑

    midplane 653.8 ☑

    outlet 653.3 ☑

  fetal

    ascites 653.7 ☑

    hydrocephalus 653.6 ☑

    hydrops 653.7 ☑

    meningomyelocele 653.7 ☑

    sacral teratoma 653.7 ☑

    tumor 653.7 ☑

  hydrocephalic fetus 653.6 ☑

  pelvis, pelvic, abnormality (bony) NEC 653.0 ☑

  unusually large fetus 653.5 ☑

    causing obstructed labor 660.1 ☑

  cephalopelvic, normally formed fetus 653.4 ☑

    causing obstructed labor 660.1 ☑

  fetal NEC 653.5 ☑

    causing obstructed labor 660.1 ☑

Disproportion — continued

fetopelvic, normally formed fetus 653.4 ☑

  causing obstructed labor 660.1 ☑

mixed maternal and fetal origin, normally formed fetus 653.4 ☑

pelvis, pelvic (bony) NEC 653.1 ☑

  causing obstructed labor 660.1 ☑

specified type NEC 653.8 ☑

Disruption

cesarean wound 674.1 ☑

family V61.09

  due to

    child in

      care of non-parental family member V61.06

      foster care V61.06

      welfare custody V61.05

    death of family member V61.07 ●

    divorce V61.03

    estrangement V61.09

      parent-child V61.04

    extended absence of family member ●

      NEC V61.08 ●

    family member

      on military deployment V61.01

      return from military deployment V61.02

    legal separation V61.03

gastrointestinal anastomosis 997.4

ligament(s) (see also Sprain)

  knee

    current injury — see Dislocation, knee

    old 717.89

      capsular 717.85

      collateral (medial) 717.82

        lateral 717.81

      cruciate (posterior) 717.84

        anterior 717.83

      specified site NEC 717.85

marital V61.10

  involving

    divorce V61.03

    estrangement V61.09

operation wound (external) (see also Dehiscence) 998.32

  internal 998.31

organ transplant, anastomosis site — see Complications, transplant, organ, by site

ossicles, ossicular chain 385.23

  traumatic — see Fracture, skull, base

parenchyma

  liver (hepatic) — see Laceration, liver, major

  spleen — see Laceration, spleen, parenchyma, massive

phase-shift, of 24-hour sleep-wake cycle, unspecified 780.55

  nonorganic origin 307.45

sleep-wake cycle (24-hour), unspecified 780.55

  circadian rhythm 327.33

  nonorganic origin 307.45

suture line (external) (see also Dehiscence) 998.32

  internal 998.31

wound 998.30

  cesarean operation 674.1 ☑

  episiotomy 674.2 ☑

  operation (surgical) 998.32

    cesarean 674.1 ☑

    internal 998.31

  perineal (obstetric) 674.2 ☑

  uterine 674.1 ☑

Disruptio uteri — see also Rupture, uterus

complicating delivery — see Delivery, complicated, rupture, uterus

Dissatisfaction with

employment V62.29

school environment V62.3

Dissecting — see condition

Dissection

aorta 441.00

  abdominal 441.02

  thoracic 441.01

  thoracoabdominal 441.03

Dissection — continued
  artery, arterial
    carotid 443.21
    coronary 414.12
    iliac 443.22
    renal 443.23
    specified NEC 443.29
    vertebral 443.24
  vascular 459.9
  wound — see Wound, open, by site
Disseminated — see condition
Dissociated personality NEC 300.15
Dissociation
  auriculoventricular or atrioventricular (any degree) (AV) 426.89
    with heart block 426.0
  interference 426.89
  isorhythmic 426.89
  rhythm
    atrioventricular (AV) 426.89
    interference 426.89
Dissociative
  identity disorder 300.14
  reaction NEC 300.15
Dissolution, vertebra — see also Osteoporosis 733.00
Distention
  abdomen (gaseous) 787.3
  bladder 596.8
  cecum 569.89
  colon 569.89
  gallbladder 575.8
  gaseous (abdomen) 787.3
  intestine 569.89
  kidney 593.89
  liver 573.9
  seminal vesicle 608.89
  stomach 536.8
    acute 536.1
    psychogenic 306.4
  ureter 593.5
  uterus 621.8
Distichia, distichiasis (eyelid) 743.63
Distoma hepaticum infestation 121.3
Distomiasis 121.9
  bile passages 121.3
    due to Clonorchis sinensis 121.1
  hemic 120.9
  hepatic (liver) 121.3
    due to Clonorchis sinensis (clonorchiasis) 121.1
  intestinal 121.4
  liver 121.3
    due to Clonorchis sinensis 121.1
  lung 121.2
  pulmonary 121.2
Distomolar (fourth molar) 520.1
  causing crowding 524.31
Disto-occlusion (division I) (division II) 524.22
Distortion (congenital)
  adrenal (gland) 759.1
  ankle (joint) 755.69
  anus 751.5
  aorta 747.29
  appendix 751.5
  arm 755.59
  artery (peripheral) NEC (see also Distortion, peripheral vascular system) 747.60
    cerebral 747.81
    coronary 746.85
    pulmonary 747.3
    retinal 743.58
    umbilical 747.5
  auditory canal 744.29
    causing impairment of hearing 744.02
  bile duct or passage 751.69
  bladder 753.8
  brain 742.4
  bronchus 748.3
  cecum 751.5
  cervix (uteri) 752.49
  chest (wall) 756.3
  clavicle 755.51
  clitoris 752.49
  coccyx 756.19
  colon 751.5

Distortion — continued
  common duct 751.69
  cornea 743.41
  cricoid cartilage 748.3
  cystic duct 751.69
  duodenum 751.5
  ear 744.29
    auricle 744.29
      causing impairment of hearing 744.02
    causing impairment of hearing 744.09
    external 744.29
      causing impairment of hearing 744.02
    inner 744.05
    middle, except ossicles 744.03
      ossicles 744.04
    ossicles 744.04
  endocrine (gland) NEC 759.2
  epiglottis 748.3
  Eustachian tube 744.24
  eye 743.8
    adnexa 743.69
  face bone(s) 756.0
  fallopian tube 752.19
  femur 755.69
  fibula 755.69
  finger(s) 755.59
  foot 755.67
  gallbladder 751.69
  genitalia, genital organ(s)
    female 752.89
      external 752.49
      internal NEC 752.89
    male 752.89
      penis 752.69
  glottis 748.3
  gyri 742.4
  hand bone(s) 755.59
  heart (auricle) (ventricle) 746.89
    valve (cusp) 746.89
  hepatic duct 751.69
  humerus 755.59
  hymen 752.49
  ileum 751.5
  intestine (large) (small) 751.5
    with anomalous adhesions, fixation or malrotation 751.4
  jaw NEC 524.89
  jejunum 751.5
  kidney 753.3
  knee (joint) 755.64
  labium (majus) (minus) 752.49
  larynx 748.3
  leg 755.69
  lens 743.36
  liver 751.69
  lumbar spine 756.19
    with disproportion (fetopelvic) 653.0 ☑
      affecting fetus or newborn 763.1
      causing obstructed labor 660.1 ☑
  lumbosacral (joint) (region) 756.19
  lung (fissures) (lobe) 748.69
  nerve 742.8
  nose 748.1
  organ
    of Corti 744.05
    of site not listed — see Anomaly, specified type NEC
  ossicles, ear 744.04
  ovary 752.0
  oviduct 752.19
  pancreas 751.7
  parathyroid (gland) 759.2
  patella 755.64
  peripheral vascular system NEC 747.60
    gastrointestinal 747.61
    lower limb 747.64
    renal 747.62
    spinal 747.82
    upper limb 747.63
  pituitary (gland) 759.2
  radius 755.59
  rectum 751.5
  rib 756.3
  sacroiliac joint 755.69
  sacrum 756.19
  scapula 755.59

Distortion — continued
  shoulder girdle 755.59
  site not listed — see Anomaly, specified type NEC
  skull bone(s) 756.0
    with
      anencephalus 740.0
      encephalocele 742.0
      hydrocephalus 742.3
        with spina bifida (see also Spina bifida) 741.0 ☑
      microcephalus 742.1
  spinal cord 742.59
  spine 756.19
  spleen 759.0
  sternum 756.3
  thorax (wall) 756.3
  thymus (gland) 759.2
  thyroid (gland) 759.2
    cartilage 748.3
  tibia 755.69
  toe(s) 755.66
  tongue 750.19
  trachea (cartilage) 748.3
  ulna 755.59
  ureter 753.4
    causing obstruction 753.20
  urethra 753.8
    causing obstruction 753.6
  uterus 752.3
  vagina 752.49
  vein (peripheral) NEC (see also Distortion, peripheral vascular system) 747.60
    great 747.49
    portal 747.49
    pulmonary 747.49
  vena cava (inferior) (superior) 747.49
  vertebra 756.19
  visual NEC 368.15
    shape or size 368.14
  vulva 752.49
  wrist (bones) (joint) 755.59
Distress
  abdomen 789.0 ☑
  colon 564.9
  emotional V40.9
  epigastric 789.0 ☑
  fetal (syndrome) 768.4
    affecting management of pregnancy or childbirth 656.8 ☑
    liveborn infant 768.4
    first noted
      before onset of labor 768.2
      during labor and delivery 768.3
    stillborn infant (death before onset of labor) 768.0
      death during labor 768.1
  gastrointestinal (functional) 536.9
    psychogenic 306.4
  intestinal (functional) NEC 564.9
    psychogenic 306.4
  intrauterine — see Distress, fetal
  leg 729.5
  maternal 669.0 ☑
  mental V40.9
  respiratory 786.09
    acute (adult) 518.82
    adult syndrome (following shock, surgery, or trauma) 518.5
      specified NEC 518.82
    fetus or newborn 770.89
    syndrome (idiopathic) (newborn) 769
  stomach 536.9
    psychogenic 306.4
Distribution vessel, atypical NEC 747.60
  coronary artery 746.85
  spinal 747.82
Districhiasis 704.2
Disturbance — see also Disease
  absorption NEC 579.9
    calcium 269.3
    carbohydrate 579.8
    fat 579.8
    protein 579.8
    specified type NEC 579.8
    vitamin (see also Deficiency, vitamin) 269.2

Disturbance — see also Disease — continued
  acid-base equilibrium 276.9
  activity and attention, simple, with hyperkinesis 314.01
  amino acid (metabolic) (see also Disorder, amino acid) 270.9
    imidazole 270.5
    maple syrup (urine) disease 270.3
    transport 270.0
  assimilation, food 579.9
  attention, simple 314.00
    with hyperactivity 314.01
  auditory, nerve, except deafness 388.5
  behavior (see also Disturbance, conduct) 312.9
  blood clotting (hypoproteinemia) (mechanism) (see also Defect, coagulation) 286.9
  central nervous system NEC 349.9
  cerebral nerve NEC 352.9
  circulatory 459.9
  conduct 312.9

  Note — Use the following fifth-digit subclassification with categories 312.0–312.2:

  0 unspecified

  1 mild

  2 moderate

  3 severe

    adjustment reaction 309.3
    adolescent onset type 312.82
    childhood onset type 312.81
    compulsive 312.30
      intermittent explosive disorder 312.34
      isolated explosive disorder 312.35
      kleptomania 312.32
      pathological gambling 312.31
      pyromania 312.33
    hyperkinetic 314.2
    intermittent explosive 312.34
    isolated explosive 312.35
    mixed with emotions 312.4
    socialized (type) 312.20
      aggressive 312.23
      unaggressive 312.21
    specified type NEC 312.89
    undersocialized, unsocialized
      aggressive (type) 312.0 ☑
      unaggressive (type) 312.1 ☑
  coordination 781.3
  cranial nerve NEC 352.9
  deep sensibility — see Disturbance, sensation
  digestive 536.9
    psychogenic 306.4
  electrolyte — see Imbalance, electrolyte
  emotions specific to childhood or adolescence 313.9
    with
      academic underachievement 313.83
      anxiety and fearfulness 313.0
      elective mutism 313.23
      identity disorder 313.82
      jealousy 313.3
      misery and unhappiness 313.1
      oppositional defiant disorder 313.81
      overanxiousness 313.0
      sensitivity 313.21
      shyness 313.21
      social withdrawal 313.22
      withdrawal reaction 313.22
    involving relationship problems 313.3
    mixed 313.89
    specified type NEC 313.89
  endocrine (gland) 259.9
    neonatal, transitory 775.9
      specified NEC 775.89
  equilibrium 780.4
  feeding (elderly) (infant) 783.3
    newborn 779.31 ▲
    nonorganic origin NEC 307.59
    psychogenic NEC 307.59
  fructose metabolism 271.2
  gait 781.2
    hysterical 300.11
  gastric (functional) 536.9
    motility 536.8

☑ Additional Digit Required — Refer to the Tabular List for Digit Selection   🔻 Subterms under main terms may continue to next column or page

92 — Volume 2 · October 2009   ▶◀ Revised Text   ● New Line   ▲ Revised Code   2010 ICD-9-CM

Disturbance — *see also* Disease — *continued*
  gastric — *continued*
    psychogenic 306.4
    secretion 536.8
  gastrointestinal (functional) 536.9
    psychogenic 306.4
  habit, child 307.9
  hearing, except deafness 388.40
  heart, functional (conditions classifiable to 426, 427, 428)
    due to presence of (cardiac) prosthesis 429.4
    postoperative (immediate) 997.1
      long-term effect of cardiac surgery 429.4
    psychogenic 306.2
  hormone 259.9
  innervation uterus, sympathetic, parasympathetic 621.8
  keratinization NEC
    gingiva 523.10
    lip 528.5
    oral (mucosa) (soft tissue) 528.79
      residual ridge mucosa
        excessive 528.72
        minimal 528.71
    tongue 528.79
  labyrinth, labyrinthine (vestibule) 386.9
  learning, specific NEC 315.2
  memory (*see also* Amnesia) 780.93
    mild, following organic brain damage 310.8
  mental (*see also* Disorder, mental) 300.9
    associated with diseases classified elsewhere 316
  metabolism (acquired) (congenital) (*see also* Disorder, metabolism) 277.9
    with
      abortion — *see* Abortion, by type, with metabolic disorder
      ectopic pregnancy (*see also* categories 633.0–633.9) 639.4
      molar pregnancy (*see also* categories 630–632) 639.4
    amino acid (*see also* Disorder, amino acid) 270.9
      aromatic NEC 270.2
      branched-chain 270.3
      specified type NEC 270.8
      straight-chain NEC 270.7
      sulfur-bearing 270.4
      transport 270.0
    ammonia 270.6
    arginine 270.6
    argininosuccinic acid 270.6
    carbohydrate NEC 271.9
    cholesterol 272.9
    citrulline 270.6
    cystathionine 270.4
    fat 272.9
    following
      abortion 639.4
      ectopic or molar pregnancy 639.4
    general 277.9
      carbohydrate 271.9
      iron 275.0
      phosphate 275.3
      sodium 276.9
    glutamine 270.7
    glycine 270.7
    histidine 270.5
    homocystine 270.4
    in labor or delivery 669.0 ☑
    iron 275.0
    isoleucine 270.3
    leucine 270.3
    lipoid 272.9
      specified type NEC 272.8
    lysine 270.7
    methionine 270.4
    neonatal, transitory 775.9
      specified type NEC 775.89
    nitrogen 788.99
    ornithine 270.6
    phosphate 275.3
    phosphatides 272.7

Disturbance — *see also* Disease — *continued*
  metabolism (*see also* Disorder, metabolism) — *continued*
    serine 270.7
    sodium NEC 276.9
    threonine 270.7
    tryptophan 270.2
    tyrosine 270.2
    urea cycle 270.6
    valine 270.3
  motor 796.1
  nervous functional 799.21 ▲
  neuromuscular mechanism (eye) due to syphilis 094.84
  nutritional 269.9
    nail 703.8
  ocular motion 378.87
    psychogenic 306.7
  oculogyric 378.87
    psychogenic 306.7
  oculomotor NEC 378.87
    psychogenic 306.7
  olfactory nerve 781.1
  optic nerve NEC 377.49
  oral epithelium, including tongue 528.79
    residual ridge mucosa
      excessive 528.72
      minimal 528.71
  personality (pattern) (trait) (*see also* Disorder, personality) 301.9
    following organic brain damage 310.1
  polyglandular 258.9
  psychomotor 307.9
  pupillary 379.49
  reflex 796.1
  rhythm, heart 427.9
    postoperative (immediate) 997.1
      long-term effect of cardiac surgery 429.4
    psychogenic 306.2
  salivary secretion 527.7
  sensation (cold) (heat) (localization) (tactile discrimination localization) (texture) (vibratory) NEC 782.0
    hysterical 300.11
    skin 782.0
    smell 781.1
    taste 781.1
  sensory (*see also* Disturbance, sensation) 782.0
    innervation 782.0
  situational (transient) (*see also* Reaction, adjustment) 309.9
    acute 308.3
  sleep 780.50
    with apnea — *see* Apnea, sleep
    initiation or maintenance (*see also* Insomnia) 780.52
      nonorganic origin 307.41
    nonorganic origin 307.40
      specified type NEC 307.49
    specified NEC 780.59
      nonorganic origin 307.49
    wakefulness (*see also* Hypersomnia) 780.54
      nonorganic origin 307.43
  sociopathic 301.7
  speech NEC 784.59 ▲
    developmental 315.39
      associated with hyperkinesis 314.1
    secondary to organic lesion 784.59 ▲
  stomach (functional) (*see also* Disturbance, gastric) 536.9
  sympathetic (nerve) (*see also* Neuropathy, peripheral, autonomic) 337.9
  temperature sense 782.0
    hysterical 300.11
  tooth
    eruption 520.6
    formation 520.4
    structure, hereditary NEC 520.5
  touch (*see also* Disturbance, sensation) 782.0
  vascular 459.9
    arteriosclerotic — *see* Arteriosclerosis
  vasomotor 443.9
  vasospastic 443.9
  vestibular labyrinth 386.9
  vision, visual NEC 368.9

Disturbance — *see also* Disease — *continued*
  vision, visual — *continued*
    psychophysical 368.16
    specified NEC 368.8
    subjective 368.10
  voice ▶and resonance◀ 784.40
  wakefulness (initiation or maintenance) (*see also* Hypersomnia) 780.54
    nonorganic origin 307.43
Disulfiduria, beta-mercaptolactate-cysteine 270.0
Disuse atrophy, bone 733.7 ▲
Ditthomska syndrome 307.81
Diuresis 788.42
Divers'
  palsy or paralysis 993.3
  squeeze 993.3
Diverticula, diverticulosis, diverticulum (acute) (multiple) (perforated) (ruptured) 562.10
  with diverticulitis 562.11
  aorta (Kommerell's) 747.21
  appendix (noninflammatory) 543.9
  bladder (acquired) (sphincter) 596.3
    congenital 753.8
  broad ligament 620.8
  bronchus (congenital) 748.3
    acquired 494.0
      with acute exacerbation 494.1
  calyx, calyceal (kidney) 593.89
  cardia (stomach) 537.1
  cecum 562.10
    with
      diverticulitis 562.11
        with hemorrhage 562.13
      hemorrhage 562.12
    congenital 751.5
  colon (acquired) 562.10
    with
      diverticulitis 562.11
        with hemorrhage 562.13
      hemorrhage 562.12
    congenital 751.5
  duodenum 562.00
    with
      diverticulitis 562.01
        with hemorrhage 562.03
      hemorrhage 562.02
    congenital 751.5
  epiphrenic (esophagus) 530.6
  esophagus (congenital) 750.4
    acquired 530.6
    epiphrenic 530.6
    pulsion 530.6
    traction 530.6
    Zenker's 530.6
  Eustachian tube 381.89
  fallopian tube 620.8
  gallbladder (congenital) 751.69
  gastric 537.1
  heart (congenital) 746.89
  ileum 562.00
    with
      diverticulitis 562.01
        with hemorrhage 562.03
      hemorrhage 562.02
  intestine (large) 562.10
    with
      diverticulitis 562.11
        with hemorrhage 562.13
      hemorrhage 562.12
    congenital 751.5
    small 562.00
      with
        diverticulitis 562.01
          with hemorrhage 562.03
        hemorrhage 562.02
      congenital 751.5
  jejunum 562.00
    with
      diverticulitis 562.01
        with hemorrhage 562.03
      hemorrhage 562.02
  kidney (calyx) (pelvis) 593.89
    with calculus 592.0
  Kommerell's 747.21
  laryngeal ventricle (congenital) 748.3

Diverticula, diverticulosis, diverticulum — *continued*
  Meckel's (displaced) (hypertrophic) 751.0
  midthoracic 562.10
  organ or site, congenital NEC — *see* Distortion
  pericardium (congenital) (cyst) 746.89
    acquired (true) 423.8
  pharyngoesophageal (pulsion) 530.6
  pharynx (congenital) 750.27
  pulsion (esophagus) 530.6
  rectosigmoid 562.10
    with
      diverticulitis 562.11
        with hemorrhage 562.13
      hemorrhage 562.12
    congenital 751.5
  rectum 562.10
    with
      diverticulitis 562.11
        with hemorrhage 562.13
      hemorrhage 562.12
  renal (calyces) (pelvis) 593.89
    with calculus 592.0
  Rokitansky's 530.6
  seminal vesicle 608.0
  sigmoid 562.10
    with
      diverticulitis 562.11
        with hemorrhage 562.13
      hemorrhage 562.12
    congenital 751.5
  small intestine 562.00
    with
      diverticulitis 562.01
        with hemorrhage 562.03
      hemorrhage 562.02
  stomach (cardia) (juxtacardia) (juxtapyloric) (acquired) 537.1
    congenital 750.7
  subdiaphragmatic 530.6
  trachea (congenital) 748.3
    acquired 519.19
  traction (esophagus) 530.6
  ureter (acquired) 593.89
    congenital 753.4
  ureterovesical orifice 593.89
  urethra (acquired) 599.2
    congenital 753.8
  ventricle, left (congenital) 746.89
  vesical (urinary) 596.3
    congenital 753.8
  Zenker's (esophagus) 530.6
Diverticulitis (acute) — *see also* Diverticula 562.11
  with hemorrhage 562.13
  bladder (urinary) 596.3
  cecum (perforated) 562.11
    with hemorrhage 562.13
  colon (perforated) 562.11
    with hemorrhage 562.13
  duodenum 562.01
    with hemorrhage 562.03
  esophagus 530.6
  ileum (perforated) 562.01
    with hemorrhage 562.03
  intestine (large) (perforated) 562.11
    with hemorrhage 562.13
    small 562.01
      with hemorrhage 562.03
  jejunum (perforated) 562.01
    with hemorrhage 562.03
  Meckel's (perforated) 751.0
  pharyngoesophageal 530.6
  rectosigmoid (perforated) 562.11
    with hemorrhage 562.13
  rectum 562.11
    with hemorrhage 562.13
  sigmoid (old) (perforated) 562.11
    with hemorrhage 562.13
  small intestine (perforated) 562.01
    with hemorrhage 562.03
  vesical (urinary) 596.3
Diverticulosis — *see* Diverticula
Division
  cervix uteri 622.8

Index

Division — Dupré's disease or syndrome

☑ Additional Digit Required — Refer to the Tabular List for Digit Selection   ▽ Subterms under main terms may continue to next column or page

94 — Volume 2 • October 2009   ▶◀ Revised Text   ● New Line   ▲ Revised Code   2010 ICD-9-CM

Dupuytren's
  contraction 728.6
  disease (muscle contracture) 728.6
  fracture (closed) 824.4
    ankle (closed) 824.4
      open 824.5
    fibula (closed) 824.4
      open 824.5
    open 824.5
    radius (closed) 813.42
      open 813.52
  muscle contracture 728.6
Durand-Nicolas-Favre disease (climatic bubo) 099.1
Durotomy, incidental (inadvertent) — *see also* Tear, dural 349.31
Duroziez's disease (congenital mitral stenosis) 746.5
Dust
  conjunctivitis 372.05
  reticulation (occupational) 504
Dutton's
  disease (trypanosomiasis) 086.9
  relapsing fever (West African) 087.1
Dwarf, dwarfism 259.4
  with infantilism (hypophyseal) 253.3
  achondroplastic 756.4
  Amsterdam 759.89
  bird-headed 759.89
  congenital 259.4
  constitutional 259.4
  hypophyseal 253.3
  infantile 259.4
  Levi type 253.3
  Lorain-Levi (pituitary) 253.3
  Lorain type (pituitary) 253.3
  metatropic 756.4
  nephrotic-glycosuric, with hypophosphatemic rickets 270.0
  nutritional 263.2
  ovarian 758.6
  pancreatic 577.8
  pituitary 253.3
  polydystrophic 277.5
  primordial 253.3
  psychosocial 259.4
  renal 588.0
    with hypertension — *see* Hypertension, kidney
  Russell's (uterine dwarfism and craniofacial dysostosis) 759.89
Dyke-Young anemia or syndrome (acquired macrocytic hemolytic anemia) (secondary) (symptomatic) 283.9
Dynia abnormality — *see also* Defect, coagulation 286.9
Dysacousis 388.40
Dysadrenocortism 255.9
  hyperfunction 255.3
  hypofunction 255.41
Dysarthria 784.51 ▲
  due to late effect of cerebrovascular disease ●
    (*see also* Late effect(s) (of) cerebrovas- ●
    cular disease) 438.13 ●
Dysautonomia — *see also* Neuropathy, peripheral, autonomic 337.9
  familial 742.8
Dysbarism 993.3
Dysbasia 719.7
  angiosclerotica intermittens 443.9
    due to atherosclerosis 440.21
  hysterical 300.11
  lordotica (progressiva) 333.6
  nonorganic origin 307.9
  psychogenic 307.9
Dysbetalipoproteinemia (familial) 272.2
Dyscalculia 315.1
Dyschezia — *see also* Constipation 564.00
Dyschondroplasia (with hemangiomata) 756.4
  Voorhoeve's 756.4
Dyschondrosteosis 756.59
Dyschromia 709.00
Dyscollagenosis 710.9
Dyscoria 743.41
Dyscraniopyophalangy 759.89

Dyscrasia
  blood 289.9
    with antepartum hemorrhage 641.3 ☑
    hemorrhage, subungual 287.8
    puerperal, postpartum 666.3 ☑
  ovary 256.8
  plasma cell 273.9
  pluriglandular 258.9
  polyglandular 258.9
Dysdiadochokinesia 781.3
Dysectasia, vesical neck 596.8
Dysendocrinism 259.9
Dysentery, dysenteric (bilious) (catarrhal) (diarrhea) (epidemic) (gangrenous) (hemorrhagic) (infectious) (sporadic) (tropical) (ulcerative) 009.0
  abscess, liver (*see also* Abscess, amebic) 006.3
  amebic (*see also* Amebiasis) 006.9
    with abscess — *see* Abscess, amebic
    acute 006.0
    carrier (suspected) of V02.2
    chronic 006.1
  arthritis (*see also* Arthritis, due to, dysentery) 009.0 [711.3] ☑
    bacillary 004.9 [711.3] ☑
  asylum 004.9
  bacillary 004.9
    arthritis 004.9 [711.3] ☑
    Boyd 004.2
    Flexner 004.1
    Schmitz (-Stutzer) 004.0
    Shiga 004.0
    Shigella 004.9
      group A 004.0
      group B 004.1
      group C 004.2
      group D 004.3
      specified type NEC 004.8
    Sonne 004.3
    specified type NEC 004.8
  bacterium 004.9
  balantidial 007.0
  Balantidium coli 007.0
  Boyd's 004.2
  Chilomastix 007.8
  Chinese 004.9
  choleriform 001.1
  coccidial 007.2
  Dientamoeba fragilis 007.8
  due to specified organism NEC — *see* Enteritis, due to, by organism
  Embadomonas 007.8
  Endolimax nana — *see* Dysentery, amebic
  Entamoba, entamebic — *see* Dysentery, amebic
  Flexner's 004.1
  Flexner-Boyd 004.2
  giardial 007.1
  Giardia lamblia 007.1
  Hiss-Russell 004.1
  lamblia 007.1
  leishmanial 085.0
  malarial (*see also* Malaria) 084.6
  metazoal 127.9
  Monilia 112.89
  protozoal NEC 007.9
  Russell's 004.8
  salmonella 003.0
  schistosomal 120.1
  Schmitz (-Stutzer) 004.0
  Shiga 004.0
  Shigella NEC (*see also* Dysentery, bacillary) 004.9
    boydii 004.2
    dysenteriae 004.0
      Schmitz 004.0
      Shiga 004.0
    flexneri 004.1
    group A 004.0
    group B 004.1
    group C 004.2
    group D 004.3
    Schmitz 004.0
    Shiga 004.0
    Sonnei 004.3
  Sonne 004.3

Dysentery, dysenteric — *continued*
  strongyloidiasis 127.2
  trichomonal 007.3
  tuberculous (*see also* Tuberculosis) 014.8 ☑
  viral (*see also* Enteritis, viral) 008.8
Dysequilibrium 780.4
Dysesthesia 782.0
  hysterical 300.11
Dysfibrinogenemia (congenital) — *see also* Defect, coagulation 286.3
Dysfunction
  adrenal (cortical) 255.9
    hyperfunction 255.3
    hypofunction 255.41
  associated with sleep stages or arousal from sleep 780.56
    nonorganic origin 307.47
  bladder NEC 596.59
  bleeding, uterus 626.8
  brain, minimal (*see also* Hyperkinesia) 314.9
  cerebral 348.30
  colon 564.9
    psychogenic 306.4
  colostomy or enterostomy 569.62
  cystic duct 575.8
  diastolic 429.9
    with heart failure — *see* Failure, heart
    due to
      cardiomyopathy — *see* Cardiomyopathy
      hypertension — *see* Hypertension, heart
  endocrine NEC 259.9
  endometrium 621.8
  enteric stoma 569.62
  enterostomy 569.62
  erectile 607.84
    nonorganic origin 302.72
  esophagostomy 530.87
  Eustachian tube 381.81
  gallbladder 575.8
  gastrointestinal 536.9
  gland, glandular NEC 259.9
  heart 427.9
    postoperative (immediate) 997.1
      long-term effect of cardiac surgery 429.4
  hemoglobin 289.89
  hepatic 573.9
  hepatocellular NEC 573.9
  hypophysis 253.9
    hyperfunction 253.1
    hypofunction 253.2
    posterior lobe 253.6
      hypofunction 253.5
  kidney (*see also* Disease, renal) 593.9
  labyrinthine 386.50
    specified NEC 386.58
  liver 573.9
    constitutional 277.4
  minimal brain (child) (*see also* Hyperkinesia) 314.9
  ovary, ovarian 256.9
    hyperfunction 256.1
      estrogen 256.0
    hypofunction 256.39
      postablative 256.2
    postablative 256.2
    specified NEC 256.8
  papillary muscle 429.81
    with myocardial infarction 410.8 ☑
  parathyroid 252.8
    hyperfunction 252.00
    hypofunction 252.1
  pineal gland 259.8
  pituitary (gland) 253.9
    hyperfunction 253.1
    hypofunction 253.2
    posterior 253.6
      hypofunction 253.5
  placental — *see* Placenta, insufficiency
  platelets (blood) 287.1
  polyglandular 258.9
    specified NEC 258.8
  psychosexual 302.70

Dysfunction — *continued*
  psychosexual — *continued*
    with
      dyspareunia (functional) (psychogenic) 302.76
      frigidity 302.72
      impotence 302.72
      inhibition
        orgasm
          female 302.73
          male 302.74
        sexual
          desire 302.71
          excitement 302.72
      premature ejaculation 302.75
      sexual aversion 302.79
      specified disorder NEC 302.79
      vaginismus 306.51
  pylorus 537.9
  rectum 564.9
    psychogenic 306.4
  segmental (*see also* Dysfunction, somatic) 739.9
  senile 797
  sexual 302.70
  sinoatrial node 427.81
  somatic 739.9
    abdomen 739.9
    acromioclavicular 739.7
    cervical 739.1
    cervicothoracic 739.1
    costochondral 739.8
    costovertebral 739.8
    extremities
      lower 739.6
      upper 739.7
    head 739.0
    hip 739.5
    lumbar, lumbosacral 739.3
    occipitocervical 739.0
    pelvic 739.5
    pubic 739.5
    rib cage 739.8
    sacral 739.4
    sacrococcygeal 739.4
    sacroiliac 739.4
    specified site NEC 739.9
    sternochondral 739.8
    sternoclavicular 739.7
    temporomandibular 739.0
    thoracic, thoracolumbar 739.2
  stomach 536.9
    psychogenic 306.4
  suprarenal 255.9
    hyperfunction 255.3
    hypofunction 255.41
  symbolic NEC 784.60
    specified type NEC 784.69
  systolic 429.9
    with heart failure — *see* Failure, heart
  temporomandibular (joint) (joint-pain-syndrome) NEC 524.60
    sounds on opening or closing 524.64
    specified NEC 524.69
  testicular 257.9
    hyperfunction 257.0
    hypofunction 257.2
    specified type NEC 257.8
  thymus 254.9
  thyroid 246.9
    complicating pregnancy, childbirth, or puerperium 648.1 ☑
    hyperfunction — *see* Hyperthyroidism
    hypofunction — *see* Hypothyroidism
  uterus, complicating delivery 661.9 ☑
    affecting fetus or newborn 763.7
    hypertonic 661.4 ☑
    hypotonic 661.2 ☑
      primary 661.0 ☑
      secondary 661.1 ☑
  velopharyngeal (acquired) 528.9
    congenital 750.29
  ventricular 429.9
    with congestive heart failure (*see also* Failure, heart) 428.0

☑ Additional Digit Required — Refer to the Tabular List for Digit Selection   ▼ Subterms under main terms may continue to next column or page

2010 ICD-9-CM   ▶◀ Revised Text   ● New Line   ▲ Revised Code   October 2009 • Volume 2 — 95

Index

Dysfunction — Dystrophy, dystrophia

Dysfunction — *continued*
ventricular — *continued*
due to
cardiomyopathy — *see* Cardiomyopathy
hypertension — *see* Hypertension, heart
left, reversible following sudden emotional stress 429.83
vesicourethral NEC 596.59
vestibular 386.50
specified type NEC 386.58
Dysgammaglobulinemia 279.06
Dysgenesis
gonadal (due to chromosomal anomaly) 758.6
pure 752.7
kidney(s) 753.0
ovarian 758.6
renal 753.0
reticular 279.2
seminiferous tubules 758.6
tidal platelet 287.31
Dysgerminoma (M9060/3)
specified site — *see* Neoplasm, by site, malignant
unspecified site
female 183.0
male 186.9
Dysgeusia 781.1
Dysgraphia 781.3
Dyshidrosis 705.81
Dysidrosis 705.81
Dysinsulinism 251.8
Dyskaryotic cervical smear 795.09
Dyskeratosis — *see also* Keratosis 701.1
bullosa hereditaria 757.39
cervix 622.10
congenital 757.39
follicularis 757.39
vitamin A deficiency 264.8
gingiva 523.8
oral soft tissue NEC 528.79
tongue 528.79
uterus NEC 621.8
Dyskinesia 781.3
biliary 575.8
esophagus 530.5
hysterical 300.11
intestinal 564.89
neuroleptic-induced tardive 333.85
nonorganic origin 307.9
orofacial 333.82
due to drugs 333.85
psychogenic 307.9
subacute, due to drugs 333.85
tardive (oral) 333.85
Dyslalia 784.59 ▲
developmental 315.39
Dyslexia 784.61
developmental 315.02
secondary to organic lesion 784.61
Dyslipidemia 272.4
Dysmaturity — *see also* Immaturity 765.1 ☑
lung 770.4
pulmonary 770.4
Dysmenorrhea (essential) (exfoliative) (functional) (intrinsic) (membranous) (primary) (secondary) 625.3
psychogenic 306.52
Dysmetabolic syndrome X 277.7
Dysmetria 781.3
Dysmorodystrophia mesodermalis congenita 759.82
Dysnomia 784.3
Dysorexia 783.0
hysterical 300.11
Dysostosis
cleidocranial, cleidocranialis 755.59
craniofacial 756.0
Fairbank's (idiopathic familial generalized osteophytosis) 756.50
mandibularis 756.0
mandibulofacial, incomplete 756.0
multiplex 277.5
orodigitofacial 759.89
Dyspareunia (female) 625.0

Dyspareunia — *continued*
male 608.89
psychogenic 302.76
Dyspepsia (allergic) (congenital) (fermentative) (flatulent) (functional) (gastric) (gastrointestinal) (neurogenic) (occupational) (reflex) 536.8
acid 536.8
atonic 536.3
psychogenic 306.4
diarrhea 787.91
psychogenic 306.4
intestinal 564.89
psychogenic 306.4
nervous 306.4
neurotic 306.4
psychogenic 306.4
Dysphagia 787.20
cervical 787.29
functional 300.11
hysterical 300.11
nervous 300.11
neurogenic 787.29
oral phase 787.21
oropharyngeal phase 787.22
pharyngeal phase 787.23
pharyngoesophageal phase 787.24
psychogenic 306.4
sideropenic 280.8
spastica 530.5
specified NEC 787.29
Dysphagocytosis, congenital 288.1
Dysphasia 784.59 ▲
Dysphonia 784.42 ▲
clericorum 784.49
functional 300.11
hysterical 300.11
psychogenic 306.1
spastica 478.79
Dyspigmentation — *see also* Pigmentation
eyelid (acquired) 374.52
Dyspituitarism 253.9
hyperfunction 253.1
hypofunction 253.2
posterior lobe 253.6
Dysplasia — *see also* Anomaly
anus 569.44
intraepithelial neoplasia I [AIN I] (histologically confirmed) 569.44
intraepithelial neoplasia II [AIN II] (histologically confirmed) 569.44
intraepithelial neoplasia III [AIN III] 230.6
anal canal 230.5
mild (histologically confirmed) 569.44
moderate (histologically confirmed) 569.44
severe 230.6
anal canal 230.5
artery
fibromuscular NEC 447.8
carotid 447.8
renal 447.3
bladder 596.8
bone (fibrous) NEC 733.29
diaphyseal, progressive 756.59
jaw 526.89
monostotic 733.29
polyostotic 756.54
solitary 733.29
brain 742.9
bronchopulmonary, fetus or newborn 770.7
cervix (uteri) 622.10
cervical intraepithelial neoplasia I [CIN I] 622.11
cervical intraepithelial neoplasia II [CIN II] 622.12
cervical intraepithelial neoplasia III [CIN III] 233.1
CIN I 622.11
CIN II 622.12
CIN III 233.1
mild 622.11
moderate 622.12
severe 233.1
chondroectodermal 756.55
chondromatose 756.4
colon 211.3

Dysplasia — *see also* Anomaly — *continued*
craniocarpotarsal 759.89
craniometaphyseal 756.89
dentinal 520.5
diaphyseal, progressive 756.59
ectodermal (anhidrotic) (Bason) (Clouston's) (congenital) (Feinmesser) (hereditary) (hidrotic) (Marshall) (Robinson's) 757.31
epiphysealis 756.9
multiplex 756.56
punctata 756.59
epiphysis 756.9
multiple 756.56
epithelial
epiglottis 478.79
uterine cervix 622.10
erythroid NEC 289.89
eye (*see also* Microphthalmos) 743.10
familial metaphyseal 756.89
fibromuscular, artery NEC 447.8
carotid 447.8
renal 447.3
fibrous
bone NEC 733.29
diaphyseal, progressive 756.59
jaw 526.89
monostotic 733.29
polyostotic 756.54
solitary 733.29
high-grade, focal — *see* Neoplasm, by site, benign
hip (congenital) 755.63
with dislocation (*see also* Dislocation, hip, congenital) 754.30
hypohidrotic ectodermal 757.31
joint 755.8
kidney 753.15
leg 755.69
linguofacialis 759.89
lung 748.5
macular 743.55
mammary (benign) (gland) 610.9
cystic 610.1
specified type NEC 610.8
metaphyseal 756.9
familial 756.89
monostotic fibrous 733.29
muscle 756.89
myeloid NEC 289.89
nervous system (general) 742.9
neuroectodermal 759.6
oculoauriculovertebral 756.0
oculodentodigital 759.89
olfactogenital 253.4
osteo-onycho-arthro (hereditary) 756.89
periosteum 733.99
polyostotic fibrous 756.54
progressive diaphyseal 756.59
prostate 602.3
intraepithelial neoplasia I [PIN I] 602.3
intraepithelial neoplasia II [PIN II] 602.3
intraepithelial neoplasia III [PIN III] 233.4
renal 753.15
renofacialis 753.0
retinal NEC 743.56
retrolental (*see also* Retinopathy of prematurity) 362.21
skin 709.8
spinal cord 742.9
thymic, with immunodeficiency 279.2
vagina 623.0
mild 623.0
moderate 623.0
severe 233.31
vocal cord 478.5
vulva 624.8
intraepithelial neoplasia I [VIN I] 624.01
intraepithelial neoplasia II [VIN II] 624.02
intraepithelial neoplasia III [VIN III] 233.32
mild 624.01
moderate 624.02
severe 233.32
VIN I 624.01
VIN II 624.02
VIN III 233.32
Dyspnea (nocturnal) (paroxysmal) 786.09

Dyspnea — *continued*
asthmatic (bronchial) (*see also* Asthma) 493.9 ☑
with bronchitis (*see also* Asthma) 493.9 ☑
chronic 493.2 ☑
cardiac (*see also* Failure, ventricular, left) 428.1
cardiac (*see also* Failure, ventricular, left) 428.1
functional 300.11
hyperventilation 786.01
hysterical 300.11
Monday morning 504
newborn 770.89
psychogenic 306.1
uremic — *see* Uremia
Dyspraxia 781.3
syndrome 315.4
Dysproteinemia 273.8
transient with copper deficiency 281.4
Dysprothrombinemia (constitutional) — *see also* Defect, coagulation 286.3
Dysreflexia, autonomic 337.3
Dysrhythmia
cardiac 427.9
postoperative (immediate) 997.1
long-term effect of cardiac surgery 429.4
specified type NEC 427.89
cerebral or cortical 348.30
Dyssecretosis, mucoserous 710.2
Dyssocial reaction, without manifest psychiatric disorder
adolescent V71.02
adult V71.01
child V71.02
Dyssomnia NEC 780.56
nonorganic origin 307.47
Dyssplenism 289.4
Dyssynergia
biliary (*see also* Disease, biliary) 576.8
cerebellaris myoclonica 334.2
detrusor sphincter (bladder) 596.55
ventricular 429.89
Dystasia, hereditary areflexic 334.3
Dysthymia 300.4
Dysthymic disorder 300.4
Dysthyroidism 246.9
Dystocia 660.9 ☑
affecting fetus or newborn 763.1
cervical 661.2 ☑
affecting fetus or newborn 763.7
contraction ring 661.4 ☑
affecting fetus or newborn 763.7
fetal 660.9 ☑
abnormal size 653.5 ☑
affecting fetus or newborn 763.1
deformity 653.7 ☑
maternal 660.9 ☑
affecting fetus or newborn 763.1
positional 660.0 ☑
affecting fetus or newborn 763.1
shoulder (girdle) 660.4 ☑
affecting fetus or newborn 763.1
uterine NEC 661.4 ☑
affecting fetus or newborn 763.7
Dystonia
acute
due to drugs 333.72
neuroleptic-induced acute 333.72
deformans progressiva 333.6
lenticularis 333.6
musculorum deformans 333.6
torsion (idiopathic) 333.6
acquired 333.79
fragments (of) 333.89
genetic 333.6
symptomatic 333.79
Dystonic
movements 781.0
Dystopia kidney 753.3
Dystrophia myotonica 359.2 ☑
Dystrophy, dystrophia 783.9
adiposogenital 253.8
asphyxiating thoracic 756.4
Becker's type 359.22
brevicollis 756.16

Dystrophy, dystrophia — *continued*
  Bruch's membrane 362.77
  cervical (sympathetic) NEC 337.09
  chondro-osseus with punctate epiphyseal
    dysplasia 756.59
  choroid (hereditary) 363.50
    central (areolar) (partial) 363.53
      total (gyrate) 363.54
    circinate 363.53
    circumpapillary (partial) 363.51
      total 363.52
    diffuse
      partial 363.56
      total 363.57
    generalized
      partial 363.56
      total 363.57
    gyrate
      central 363.54
      generalized 363.57
    helicoid 363.52
    peripapillary — *see* Dystrophy, choroid,
      circumpapillary
    serpiginous 363.54
  cornea (hereditary) 371.50
    anterior NEC 371.52
    Cogan's 371.52
    combined 371.57
    crystalline 371.56
    endothelial (Fuchs') 371.57
    epithelial 371.50
      juvenile 371.51
      microscopic cystic 371.52
    granular 371.53
    lattice 371.54
    macular 371.55
    marginal (Terrien's) 371.48
    Meesman's 371.51
    microscopic cystic (epithelial) 371.52
    nodular, Salzmann's 371.46
    polymorphous 371.58
    posterior NEC 371.58
    ring-like 371.52
    Salzmann's nodular 371.46
    stromal NEC 371.56
  dermatochondrocorneal 371.50
  Duchenne's 359.1
  due to malnutrition 263.9
  Erb's 359.1
  familial
    hyperplastic periosteal 756.59
    osseous 277.5
  foveal 362.77
  Fuchs', cornea 371.57
  Gowers' muscular 359.1
  hair 704.2
  hereditary, progressive muscular 359.1
  hypogenital, with diabetic tendency 759.81
  Landouzy-Déjérine 359.1
  Leyden-Möbius 359.1
  mesodermalis congenita 759.82
  muscular 359.1
    congenital (hereditary) 359.0
      myotonic 359.22
    distal 359.1
    Duchenne's 359.1
    Erb's 359.1
    fascioscapulohumeral 359.1
    Gowers' 359.1
    hereditary (progressive) 359.1
    Landouzy-Déjérine 359.1
    limb-girdle 359.1
    myotonic 359.21
    progressive (hereditary) 359.1
      Charcôt-Marie-Tooth 356.1
    pseudohypertrophic (infantile) 359.1
  myocardium, myocardial (*see also* Degenera-
    tion, myocardial) 429.1
  myotonic 359.21
  myotonica 359.21
  nail 703.8
    congenital 757.5
  neurovascular (traumatic) (*see also* Neuropa-
    thy, peripheral, autonomic) 337.9
  nutritional 263.9
  ocular 359.1

Dystrophy, dystrophia — *continued*
  oculocerebrorenal 270.8
  oculopharyngeal 359.1
  ovarian 620.8
  papillary (and pigmentary) 701.1
  pelvicrural atrophic 359.1
  pigmentary (*see also* Acanthosis) 701.2
  pituitary (gland) 253.8
  polyglandular 258.8
  posttraumatic sympathetic — *see* Dystrophy,
    sympathetic
  progressive ophthalmoplegic 359.1
  reflex neuromuscular — *see* Dystrophy, sym-
    pathetic
  retina, retinal (hereditary) 362.70
    albipunctate 362.74
    Bruch's membrane 362.77
    cone, progressive 362.75
    hyaline 362.77
    in
      Bassen-Kornzweig syndrome
        272.5 *[362.72]*
      cerebroretinal lipidosis 330.1 *[362.71]*
      Refsum's disease 356.3 *[362.72]*
      systemic lipidosis 272.7 *[362.71]*
    juvenile (Stargardt's) 362.75
    pigmentary 362.74
    pigment epithelium 362.76
    progressive cone (-rod) 362.75
    pseudoinflammatory foveal 362.77
    rod, progressive 362.75
    sensory 362.75
    vitelliform 362.76
  Salzmann's nodular 371.46
  scapuloperoneal 359.1
  skin NEC 709.9
  sympathetic (posttraumatic) (reflex) 337.20
    lower limb 337.22
    specified site NEC 337.29
    upper limb 337.21
  tapetoretinal 362.74
  thoracic asphyxiating 756.4
  unguium 703.8
    congenital 757.5
  vitreoretinal (primary) 362.73
    secondary 362.66
  vulva 624.09
Dysuria 788.1
  psychogenic 306.53

E

Eagle-Barrett syndrome 756.71
Eales' disease (syndrome) 362.18
Ear — *see also* condition
  ache 388.70
    otogenic 388.71
    referred 388.72
  lop 744.29
  piercing V50.3
  swimmers' acute 380.12
  tank 380.12
  tropical 111.8 *[380.15]*
  wax 380.4
Earache 388.70
  otogenic 388.71
  referred 388.72
Early satiety 780.94
Eaton-Lambert syndrome — *see also* Neoplasm,
  by site, malignant 199.1 *[358.1]*
Eberth's disease (typhoid fever) 002.0
Ebstein's
  anomaly or syndrome (downward displace-
    ment, tricuspid valve into right ventri-
    cle) 746.2
  disease (diabetes) 250.4 ☑ *[581.81]*
    due to secondary diabetes
      249.4 ☑ *[581.81]*
Eccentro-osteochondrodysplasia 277.5
Ecchondroma (M9210/0) — *see* Neoplasm, bone,
  benign
Ecchondrosis (M9210/1) 238.0
Ecchordosis physaliphora 756.0
Ecchymosis (multiple) 459.89
  conjunctiva 372.72
  eye (traumatic) 921.0
  eyelids (traumatic) 921.1

Ecchymosis — *continued*
  newborn 772.6
  spontaneous 782.7
  traumatic — *see* Contusion
ECD (Erdheim-Chester disease) 277.89 ●
Echinococciasis — *see* Echinococcus
Echinococcosis — *see* Echinococcus
Echinococcus (infection) 122.9
  granulosus 122.4
    liver 122.0
    lung 122.1
    orbit 122.3 *[376.13]*
    specified site NEC 122.3
    thyroid 122.2
  liver NEC 122.8
    granulosus 122.0
    multilocularis 122.5
  lung NEC 122.9
    granulosus 122.1
    multilocularis 122.6
  multilocularis 122.7
    liver 122.5
    specified site NEC 122.6
  orbit 122.9 *[376.13]*
    granulosus 122.3 *[376.13]*
    multilocularis 122.6 *[376.13]*
  specified site NEC 122.9
    granulosus 122.3
    multilocularis 122.6 *[376.13]*
  thyroid NEC 122.9
    granulosus 122.2
    multilocularis 122.6
Echinorhynchiasis 127.7
Echinostomiasis 121.8
Echolalia 784.69
ECHO virus infection NEC 079.1
Eclampsia, eclamptic (coma) (convulsions)
  (delirium) 780.39
  female, child-bearing age NEC — *see*
    Eclampsia, pregnancy
  gravidarum — *see* Eclampsia, pregnancy
  male 780.39
  not associated with pregnancy or childbirth
    780.39
  pregnancy, childbirth, or puerperium 642.6 ☑
    with pre-existing hypertension 642.7 ☑
    affecting fetus or newborn 760.0
  uremic 586
Eclipse blindness (total) 363.31
Economic circumstance affecting care V60.9
  specified type NEC V60.89   ▲
Economo's disease (encephalitis lethargica)
  049.8
Ectasia, ectasis
  aorta (*see also* Aneurysm, aorta) 441.9
    ruptured 441.5
  breast 610.4
  capillary 448.9
  cornea (marginal) (postinfectional) 371.71
  duct (mammary) 610.4
  gastric antral vascular (GAVE) 537.82
    with hemorrhage 537.83
    without hemorrhage 537.82
  kidney 593.89
  mammary duct (gland) 610.4
  papillary 448.9
  renal 593.89
  salivary gland (duct) 527.8
  scar, cornea 371.71
  sclera 379.11
Ecthyma 686.8
  contagiosum 051.2
  gangrenosum 686.09
  infectiosum 051.2
Ectocardia 746.87
Ectodermal dysplasia, congenital 757.31
Ectodermosis erosiva pluriorificialis 695.19
Ectopic, ectopia (congenital) 759.89
  abdominal viscera 751.8
    due to defect in anterior abdominal wall
      756.79
  ACTH syndrome 255.0
  adrenal gland 759.1
  anus 751.5
  auricular beats 427.61
  beats 427.60

Ectopic, ectopia — *continued*
  bladder 753.5
  bone and cartilage in lung 748.69
  brain 742.4
  breast tissue 757.6
  cardiac 746.87
  cerebral 742.4
  cordis 746.87
  endometrium 617.9
  gallbladder 751.69
  gastric mucosa 750.7
  gestation — *see* Pregnancy, ectopic
  heart 746.87
  hormone secretion NEC 259.3
  hyperparathyroidism 259.3
  kidney (crossed) (intrathoracic) (pelvis) 753.3
    in pregnancy or childbirth 654.4 ☑
      causing obstructed labor 660.2 ☑
  lens 743.37
  lentis 743.37
  mole — *see* Pregnancy, ectopic
  organ or site NEC — *see* Malposition, congen-
    ital
  ovary 752.0
  pancreas, pancreatic tissue 751.7
  pregnancy — *see* Pregnancy, ectopic
  pupil 364.75
  renal 753.3
  sebaceous glands of mouth 750.26
  secretion
    ACTH 255.0
    adrenal hormone 259.3
    adrenalin 259.3
    adrenocorticotropin 255.0
    antidiuretic hormone (ADH) 259.3
    epinephrine 259.3
    hormone NEC 259.3
    norepinephrine 259.3
    pituitary (posterior) 259.3
  spleen 759.0
  testis 752.51
  thyroid 759.2
  ureter 753.4
  ventricular beats 427.69
  vesicae 753.5
Ectrodactyly 755.4
  finger (*see also* Absence, finger, congenital)
    755.29
  toe (*see also* Absence, toe, congenital) 755.39
Ectromelia 755.4
  lower limb 755.30
  upper limb 755.20
Ectropion 374.10
  anus 569.49
  cervix 622.0
    with mention of cervicitis 616.0
  cicatricial 374.14
  congenital 743.62
  eyelid 374.10
    cicatricial 374.14
    congenital 743.62
    mechanical 374.12
    paralytic 374.12
    senile 374.11
    spastic 374.13
  iris (pigment epithelium) 364.54
  lip (congenital) 750.26
    acquired 528.5
  mechanical 374.12
  paralytic 374.12
  rectum 569.49
  senile 374.11
  spastic 374.13
  urethra 599.84
  uvea 364.54
Eczema (acute) (allergic) (chronic) (erythematous)
  (fissum) (occupational) (rubrum) (squamous) 692.9
  asteatotic 706.8
  atopic 691.8
  contact NEC 692.9
  dermatitis NEC 692.9
  due to specified cause — *see* Dermatitis, due
    to
  dyshidrotic 705.81
  external ear 380.22

☑ Additional Digit Required — Refer to the Tabular List for Digit Selection   ▽ Subterms under main terms may continue to next column or page

2010 ICD-9-CM   ▶◀ Revised Text   ● New Line   ▲ Revised Code   **October 2009 • Volume 2 — 97**

Eczema — *continued*
flexural 691.8
gouty 274.89
herpeticum 054.0
hypertrophicum 701.8
hypostatic — *see* Varicose, vein
impetiginous 684
infantile (acute) (chronic) (due to any substance) (intertriginous) (seborrheic) 690.12
intertriginous NEC 692.9
infantile 690.12
intrinsic 691.8
lichenified NEC 692.9
marginatum 110.3
nummular 692.9
pustular 686.8
seborrheic 690.18
infantile 690.12
solare 692.72
stasis (lower extremity) 454.1
ulcerated 454.2
vaccination, vaccinatum 999.0
varicose (lower extremity) — *see* Varicose, vein
verrucosum callosum 698.3
Eczematoid, exudative 691.8
Eddowes' syndrome (brittle bones and blue sclera) 756.51
Edema, edematous 782.3
with nephritis (*see also* Nephrosis) 581.9
allergic 995.1
angioneurotic (allergic) (any site) (with urticaria) 995.1
hereditary 277.6
angiospastic 443.9
Berlin's (traumatic) 921.3
brain 348.5
due to birth injury 767.8
fetus or newborn 767.8
cardiac (*see also* Failure, heart) 428.0
cardiovascular (*see also* Failure, heart) 428.0
cerebral — *see* Edema, brain
cerebrospinal vessel — *see* Edema, brain
cervix (acute) (uteri) 622.8
puerperal, postpartum 674.8 ☑
chronic hereditary 757.0
circumscribed, acute 995.1
hereditary 277.6
complicating pregnancy (gestational) 646.1 ☑
with hypertension — *see* Toxemia, of pregnancy
conjunctiva 372.73
connective tissue 782.3
cornea 371.20
due to contact lenses 371.24
idiopathic 371.21
secondary 371.22
cystoid macular 362.53
due to
lymphatic obstruction — *see* Edema, lymphatic
salt retention 276.0
epiglottis — *see* Edema, glottis
essential, acute 995.1
hereditary 277.6
extremities, lower — *see* Edema, legs
eyelid NEC 374.82
familial, hereditary (legs) 757.0
famine 262
fetus or newborn 778.5
genital organs
female 629.89
male 608.86
gestational 646.1 ☑
with hypertension — *see* Toxemia, of pregnancy
glottis, glottic, glottides (obstructive) (passive) 478.6
allergic 995.1
hereditary 277.6
due to external agent — *see* Condition, respiratory, acute, due to specified agent
heart (*see also* Failure, heart) 428.0
newborn 779.89
heat 992.7

Edema, edematous — *continued*
hereditary (legs) 757.0
inanition 262
infectious 782.3
intracranial 348.5
due to injury at birth 767.8
iris 364.89
joint (*see also* Effusion, joint) 719.0 ☑
larynx (*see also* Edema, glottis) 478.6
legs 782.3
due to venous obstruction 459.2
hereditary 757.0
localized 782.3
due to venous obstruction 459.2
lower extremity 459.2
lower extremities — *see* Edema, legs
lung 514
acute 518.4
with heart disease or failure (*see also* Failure, ventricular, left) 428.1
congestive 428.0
chemical (due to fumes or vapors) 506.1
due to
external agent(s) NEC 508.9
specified NEC 508.8
fumes and vapors (chemical) (inhalation) 506.1
radiation 508.0
chemical (acute) 506.1
chronic 506.4
chronic 514
chemical (due to fumes or vapors) 506.4
due to
external agent(s) NEC 508.9
specified NEC 508.8
fumes or vapors (chemical) (inhalation) 506.4
radiation 508.1
due to
external agent 508.9
specified NEC 508.8
high altitude 993.2
near drowning 994.1
postoperative 518.4
terminal 514
lymphatic 457.1
due to mastectomy operation 457.0
macula 362.83
cystoid 362.53
diabetic 250.5 ☑ [362.07]
due to secondary diabetes 249.5 ☑ [362.07]
malignant (*see also* Gangrene, gas) 040.0
Milroy's 757.0
nasopharynx 478.25
neonatorum 778.5
nutritional (newborn) 262
with dyspigmentation, skin and hair 260
optic disc or nerve — *see* Papilledema
orbit 376.33
circulatory 459.89
palate (soft) (hard) 528.9
pancreas 577.8
penis 607.83
periodic 995.1
hereditary 277.6
pharynx 478.25
pitting 782.3
pulmonary — *see* Edema, lung
Quincke's 995.1
hereditary 277.6
renal (*see also* Nephrosis) 581.9
retina (localized) (macular) (peripheral) 362.83
cystoid 362.53
diabetic 250.5 ☑ [362.07]
due to secondary diabetes 249.5 ☑ [362.07]
salt 276.0
scrotum 608.86
seminal vesicle 608.86
spermatic cord 608.86
spinal cord 336.1
starvation 262
stasis (*see also* Hypertension, venous) 459.30

Edema, edematous — *continued*
subconjunctival 372.73
subglottic (*see also* Edema, glottis) 478.6
supraglottic (*see also* Edema, glottis) 478.6
testis 608.86
toxic NEC 782.3
traumatic NEC 782.3
tunica vaginalis 608.86
vas deferens 608.86
vocal cord — *see* Edema, glottis
vulva (acute) 624.8
Edentia (complete) (partial) — *see also* Absence, tooth 520.0
acquired (*see also* Edentulism) 525.40
due to
caries 525.13
extraction 525.10
periodontal disease 525.12
specified NEC 525.19
trauma 525.11
causing malocclusion 524.30
congenital (deficiency of tooth buds) 520.0
Edentulism 525.40
complete 525.40
class I 525.41
class II 525.42
class III 525.43
class IV 525.44
partial 525.50
class I 525.51
class II 525.52
class III 525.53
class IV 525.54
Edsall's disease 992.2
Educational handicap V62.3
Edwards' syndrome 758.2
Effect, adverse NEC
abnormal gravitational (G) forces or states 994.9
air pressure — *see* Effect, adverse, atmospheric pressure
altitude (high) — *see* Effect, adverse, high altitude
anesthetic
in labor and delivery NEC 668.9 ☑
affecting fetus or newborn 763.5
antitoxin — *see* Complications, vaccination
atmospheric pressure 993.9
due to explosion 993.4
high 993.3
low — *see* Effect, adverse, high altitude
specified effect NEC 993.8
biological, correct substance properly administered (*see also* Effect, adverse, drug) 995.20
blood (derivatives) (serum) (transfusion) — *see* Complications, transfusion
chemical substance NEC 989.9
specified — *see* Table of Drugs and Chemicals
cobalt, radioactive (*see also* Effect, adverse, radioactive substance) 990
cold (temperature) (weather) 991.9
chilblains 991.5
frostbite — *see* Frostbite
specified effect NEC 991.8
drugs and medicinals 995.20
correct substance properly administered 995.20
overdose or wrong substance given or taken 977.9
specified drug — *see* Table of Drugs and Chemicals
electric current (shock) 994.8
burn — *see* Burn, by site
electricity (electrocution) (shock) 994.8
burn — *see* Burn, by site
exertion (excessive) 994.5
exposure 994.9
exhaustion 994.4
external cause NEC 994.9
fallout (radioactive) NEC 990
fluoroscopy NEC 990
foodstuffs
allergic reaction (*see also* Allergy, food) 693.1

Effect, adverse — *continued*
foodstuffs — *continued*
allergic reaction (*see also* Allergy, food) — *continued*
anaphylactic shock due to food NEC 995.60
noxious 988.9
specified type NEC (*see also* Poisoning, by name of noxious foodstuff) 988.8
gases, fumes, or vapors — *see* Table of Drugs and Chemicals
glue (airplane) sniffing 304.6 ☑
heat — *see* Heat
high altitude NEC 993.2
anoxia 993.2
on
ears 993.0
sinuses 993.1
polycythemia 289.0
hot weather — *see* Heat
hunger 994.2
immersion, foot 991.4
immunization — *see* Complications, vaccination
immunological agents — *see* Complications, vaccination
implantation (removable) of isotope or radium NEC 990
infrared (radiation) (rays) NEC 990
burn — *see* Burn, by site
dermatitis or eczema 692.82
infusion — *see* Complications, infusion
ingestion or injection of isotope (therapeutic) NEC 990
irradiation NEC (*see also* Effect, adverse, radiation) 990
isotope (radioactive) NEC 990
lack of care (child) (infant) (newborn) 995.52
adult 995.84
lightning 994.0
burn — *see* Burn, by site
Lirugin — *see* Complications, vaccination
medicinal substance, correct, properly administered (*see also* Effect, adverse, drugs) 995.20
mesothorium NEC 990
motion 994.6
noise, inner ear 388.10
other drug, medicinal and biological substance 995.29
overheated places — *see* Heat
polonium NEC 990
psychosocial, of work environment V62.1
radiation (diagnostic) (fallout) (infrared) (natural source) (therapeutic) (tracer) (ultraviolet) (x-ray) NEC 990
with pulmonary manifestations
acute 508.0
chronic 508.1
dermatitis or eczema 692.82
due to sun NEC (*see also* Dermatitis, due to, sun) 692.70
fibrosis of lungs 508.1
maternal with suspected damage to fetus affecting management of pregnancy 655.6 ☑
pneumonitis 508.0
radioactive substance NEC 990
dermatitis or eczema 692.82
radioactivity NEC 990
radiotherapy NEC 990
dermatitis or eczema 692.82
radium NEC 990
reduced temperature 991.9
frostbite — *see* Frostbite
immersion, foot (hand) 991.4
specified effect NEC 991.8
roentgenography NEC 990
roentgenoscopy NEC 990
roentgen rays NEC 990
serum (prophylactic) (therapeutic) NEC 999.5
specified NEC 995.89
external cause NEC 994.9
strangulation 994.7
submersion 994.1

Effect, adverse — *continued*
  teletherapy NEC 990
  thirst 994.3
  transfusion — *see* Complications, transfusion
  ultraviolet (radiation) (rays) NEC 990
    burn (*see also* Burn, by site)
      from sun (*see also* Sunburn) 692.71
    dermatitis or eczema 692.82
      due to sun NEC (*see also* Dermatitis, due to, sun) 692.70
  uranium NEC 990
  vaccine (any) — *see* Complications, vaccination
  weightlessness 994.9
  whole blood (*see also* Complications, transfusion)
    overdose or wrong substance given (*see also* Table of Drugs and Chemicals) 964.7
  working environment V62.1
  x-rays NEC 990
    dermatitis or eczema 692.82
Effect, remote
  of cancer — *see* condition
Effects, late — *see* Late, effect (of)
Effluvium, telogen 704.02
Effort
  intolerance 306.2
  syndrome (aviators) (psychogenic) 306.2
Effusion
  amniotic fluid (*see also* Rupture, membranes, premature) 658.1 ☑
  brain (serous) 348.5
  bronchial (*see also* Bronchitis) 490
  cerebral 348.5
  cerebrospinal (*see also* Meningitis) 322.9
    vessel 348.5
  chest — *see* Effusion, pleura
  intracranial 348.5
  joint 719.00
    ankle 719.07
    elbow 719.02
    foot 719.07
    hand 719.04
    hip 719.05
    knee 719.06
    multiple sites 719.09
    pelvic region 719.05
    shoulder (region) 719.01
    specified site NEC 719.08
    wrist 719.03
  meninges (*see also* Meningitis) 322.9
  pericardium, pericardial (*see also* Pericarditis) 423.9
    acute 420.90
  peritoneal (chronic) 568.82
  pleura, pleurisy, pleuritic, pleuropericardial 511.9
    bacterial, nontuberculous 511.1
    fetus or newborn 511.9
    malignant 511.81
    nontuberculous 511.9
      bacterial 511.1
    pneumococcal 511.1
    staphylococcal 511.1
    streptococcal 511.1
    traumatic 862.29
      with open wound 862.39
    tuberculous (*see also* Tuberculosis, pleura) 012.0 ☑
      primary progressive 010.1 ☑
  pulmonary — *see* Effusion, pleura
  spinal (*see also* Meningitis) 322.9
  thorax, thoracic — *see* Effusion, pleura
Egg (oocyte) (ovum)
  donor V59.70
    over age 35 V59.73
      anonymous recipient V59.73
      designated recipient V59.74
    under age 35 V59.71
      anonymous recipient V59.71
      designated recipient V59.72
Eggshell nails 703.8
  congenital 757.5
Ego-dystonic
  homosexuality 302.0

Ego-dystonic — *continued*
  lesbianism 302.0
  sexual orientation 302.0
Egyptian splenomegaly 120.1
Ehlers-Danlos syndrome 756.83
Ehrlichiosis 082.40
  chaffeensis 082.41
  specified type NEC 082.49
Eichstedt's disease (pityriasis versicolor) 111.0
EIN (endometrial intraepithelial neoplasia) 621.35
Eisenmenger's complex or syndrome (ventricular septal defect) 745.4
Ejaculation, semen
  painful 608.89
    psychogenic 306.59
  premature 302.75
  retrograde 608.87
Ekbom syndrome (restless legs) 333.94
Ekman's syndrome (brittle bones and blue sclera) 756.51
Elastic skin 756.83
  acquired 701.8
Elastofibroma (M8820/0) — *see* Neoplasm, connective tissue, benign
Elastoidosis
  cutanea nodularis 701.8
  cutis cystica et comedonica 701.8
Elastoma 757.39
  juvenile 757.39
  Miescher's (elastosis perforans serpiginosa) 701.1
Elastomyofibrosis 425.3
Elastosis 701.8
  atrophicans 701.8
  perforans serpiginosa 701.1
  reactive perforating 701.1
  senilis 701.8
  solar (actinic) 692.74
Elbow — *see* condition
Electric
  current, electricity, effects (concussion) (fatal) (nonfatal) (shock) 994.8
    burn — *see* Burn, by site
  feet (foot) syndrome 266.2
  shock from electroshock gun (taser) 994.8
Electrocution 994.8
Electrolyte imbalance 276.9
  with
    abortion — *see* Abortion, by type, with metabolic disorder
    ectopic pregnancy (*see also* categories 633.0–633.9) 639.4
    hyperemesis gravidarum (before 22 completed weeks gestation) 643.1 ☑
    molar pregnancy (*see also* categories 630–632) 639.4
  following
    abortion 639.4
    ectopic or molar pregnancy 639.4
Elephantiasis (nonfilarial) 457.1
  arabicum (*see also* Infestation, filarial) 125.9
  congenita hereditaria 757.0
  congenital (any site) 757.0
  due to
    Brugia (malayi) 125.1
    mastectomy operation 457.0
    Wuchereria (bancrofti) 125.0
      malayi 125.1
  eyelid 374.83
  filarial (*see also* Infestation, filarial) 125.9
  filariensis (*see also* Infestation, filarial) 125.9
  gingival 523.8
  glandular 457.1
  graecorum 030.9
  lymphangiectatic 457.1
  lymphatic vessel 457.1
    due to mastectomy operation 457.0
  neuromatosa 237.71
  postmastectomy 457.0
  scrotum 457.1
  streptococcal 457.1
  surgical 997.99
    postmastectomy 457.0
  telangiectodes 457.1
  vulva (nonfilarial) 624.8

Elephant man syndrome 237.71
Elevated — *see* Elevation
  findings on laboratory examination — *see* ●
    Findings, abnormal, without diagnosis (examination) (laboratory test) ●
  GFR (glomerular filtration rate) — *see* Find-●
    ings, abnormal, without diagnosis (examination) (laboratory test) ●
Elevation
  17-ketosteroids 791.9
  acid phosphatase 790.5
  alkaline phosphatase 790.5
  amylase 790.5
  antibody titers 795.79
  basal metabolic rate (BMR) 794.7
  blood pressure (*see also* Hypertension) 401.9
    reading (incidental) (isolated) (nonspecific), no diagnosis of hypertension 796.2
  blood sugar 790.29
  body temperature (of unknown origin) (*see also* Pyrexia) 780.60
  cancer antigen 125 [CA 125] 795.82
  carcinoembryonic antigen [CEA] 795.81
  cholesterol 272.0
    with high triglycerides 272.2
  conjugate, eye 378.81
  C-reactive protein (CRP) 790.95
  CRP (C-reactive protein) 790.95
  diaphragm, congenital 756.6
  GFR (glomerular filtration rate) — *see* Find-●
    ings, abnormal, without diagnosis ●
    (examination) (laboratory test) ●
  glucose
    fasting 790.21
    tolerance test 790.22
  immunoglobulin level 795.79
  indolacetic acid 791.9
  lactic acid dehydrogenase (LDH) level 790.4
  leukocytes 288.60
  lipase 790.5
  lipoprotein a level 272.8
  liver function test (LFT) 790.6
    alkaline phosphatase 790.5
    aminotransferase 790.4
    bilirubin 782.4
    hepatic enzyme NEC 790.5
    lactate dehydrogenase 790.4
  lymphocytes 288.61
  prostate specific antigen (PSA) 790.93
  renin 790.99
    in hypertension (*see also* Hypertension, renovascular) 405.91
  Rh titer 999.7
  scapula, congenital 755.52
  sedimentation rate 790.1
  SGOT 790.4
  SGPT 790.4
  transaminase 790.4
  triglycerides 272.1
    with high cholesterol 272.2
  vanillylmandelic acid 791.9
  venous pressure 459.89
  VMA 791.9
  white blood cell count 288.60
    specified NEC 288.69
Elliptocytosis (congenital) (hereditary) 282.1
  Hb-C (disease) 282.7
  hemoglobin disease 282.7
  sickle-cell (disease) 282.60
  trait 282.5
Ellison-Zollinger syndrome (gastric hypersecretion with pancreatic islet cell tumor) 251.5
Ellis-van Creveld disease or syndrome (chondroectodermal dysplasia) 756.55
Elongation, elongated (congenital) — *see also* Distortion
  bone 756.9
  cervix (uteri) 752.49
    acquired 622.6
    hypertrophic 622.6
  colon 751.5
  common bile duct 751.69
  cystic duct 751.69
  frenulum, penis 752.69
  labia minora, acquired 624.8
  ligamentum patellae 756.89

Elongation, elongated — *see also* Distortion — *continued*
  petiolus (epiglottidis) 748.3
  styloid bone (process) 733.99
  tooth, teeth 520.2
  uvula 750.26
    acquired 528.9
Elschnig bodies or pearls 366.51
El Tor cholera 001.1
Emaciation (due to malnutrition) 261
Emancipation disorder 309.22
Embadomoniasis 007.8
Embarrassment heart, cardiac — *see* Disease, heart
Embedded tooth, teeth 520.6
  root only 525.3
Embolic — *see* condition
Embolism 444.9
  with
    abortion — *see* Abortion, by type, with embolism
    ectopic pregnancy (*see also* categories 633.0–633.9) 639.6
    molar pregnancy (*see also* categories 630–632) 639.6
  air (any site) 958.0
    with
      abortion — *see* Abortion, by type, with embolism
      ectopic pregnancy (*see also* categories 633.0–633.9) 639.6
      molar pregnancy (*see also* categories 630–632) 639.6
    due to implanted device — *see* Complications, due to (presence of) any device, implant, or graft classified to 996.0–996.5 NEC
    following
      abortion 639.6
      ectopic or molar pregnancy 639.6
    infusion, perfusion, or transfusion 999.1
    in pregnancy, childbirth, or puerperium 673.0 ☑
    traumatic 958.0
  amniotic fluid (pulmonary) 673.1 ☑
    with
      abortion — *see* Abortion, by type, with embolism
      ectopic pregnancy (*see also* categories 633.0–633.9) 639.6
      molar pregnancy (*see also* categories 630–632) 639.6
    following
      abortion 639.6
      ectopic or molar pregnancy 639.6
  aorta, aortic 444.1
    abdominal 444.0
    bifurcation 444.0
    saddle 444.0
    thoracic 444.1
  artery 444.9
    auditory, internal 433.8 ☑
    basilar (*see also* Occlusion, artery, basilar) 433.0 ☑
    bladder 444.89
    carotid (common) (internal) (*see also* Occlusion, artery, carotid) 433.1 ☑
    cerebellar (anterior inferior) (posterior inferior) (superior) 433.8 ☑
    cerebral (*see also* Embolism, brain) 434.1 ☑
    choroidal (anterior) 433.8 ☑
    communicating posterior 433.8 ☑
    coronary (*see also* Infarct, myocardium) 410.9 ☑
      without myocardial infarction 411.81
    extremity 444.22
      lower 444.22
      upper 444.21
    hypophyseal 433.8 ☑
    mesenteric (with gangrene) 557.0
    ophthalmic (*see also* Occlusion, retina) 362.30
    peripheral 444.22
    pontine 433.8 ☑

Embolism — *continued*
  artery — *continued*
    precerebral NEC — *see* Occlusion, artery, precerebral
    pulmonary — *see* Embolism, pulmonary
    pyemic 449
      pulmonary 415.12
    renal 593.81
    retinal (*see also* Occlusion, retina) 362.30
    septic 449
      pulmonary 415.12
    specified site NEC 444.89
    vertebral (*see also* Occlusion, artery, vertebral) 433.2 ✔
  auditory, internal 433.8 ✔
  basilar (artery) (*see also* Occlusion, artery, basilar) 433.0 ✔
  birth, mother — *see* Embolism, obstetrical
  blood-clot
    with
      abortion — *see* Abortion, by type, with embolism
      ectopic pregnancy (*see also* categories 633.0–633.9) 639.6
      molar pregnancy (*see also* categories 630–632) 639.6
    following
      abortion 639.6
      ectopic or molar pregnancy 639.6
    in pregnancy, childbirth, or puerperium 673.2 ✔
  brain 434.1 ✔
    with
      abortion — *see* Abortion, by type, with embolism
      ectopic pregnancy (*see also* categories 633.0–633.9) 639.6
      molar pregnancy (*see also* categories 630–632) 639.6
    following
      abortion 639.6
      ectopic or molar pregnancy 639.6
    late effect — *see* Late effect(s) (of) cerebrovascular disease
    puerperal, postpartum, childbirth 674.0 ✔
  capillary 448.9
  cardiac (*see also* Infarct, myocardium) 410.9 ✔
  carotid (artery) (common) (internal) (*see also* Occlusion, artery, carotid) 433.1 ✔
  cavernous sinus (venous) — *see* Embolism, intracranial venous sinus
  cerebral (*see also* Embolism, brain) 434.1 ✔
  cholesterol — *see* Atheroembolism
  choroidal (anterior) (artery) 433.8 ✔
  coronary (artery or vein) (systemic) (*see also* Infarct, myocardium) 410.9 ✔
    without myocardial infarction 411.81
  due to (presence of) any device, implant, or graft classifiable to 996.0–996.5 — *see* Complications, due to (presence of) any device, implant, or graft classified to 996.0–996.5 NEC
  encephalomalacia (*see also* Embolism, brain) 434.1 ✔
  extremities 444.22
    lower 444.22
    upper 444.21
  eye 362.30
  fat (cerebral) (pulmonary) (systemic) 958.1
    with
      abortion — *see* Abortion, by type, with embolism
      ectopic pregnancy (*see also* categories 633.0–633.9) 639.6
      molar pregnancy (*see also* categories 630–632) 639.6
    complicating delivery or puerperium 673.8 ✔
    following
      abortion 639.6
      ectopic or molar pregnancy 639.6
    in pregnancy, childbirth, or the puerperium 673.8 ✔
  femoral (artery) 444.22
    vein 453.6 ▲
    deep 453.41

Embolism — *continued*
  following
    abortion 639.6
    ectopic or molar pregnancy 639.6
    infusion, perfusion, or transfusion
      air 999.1
      thrombus 999.2
  heart (fatty) (*see also* Infarct, myocardium) 410.9 ✔
  hepatic (vein) 453.0
  iliac (artery) 444.81
  iliofemoral 444.81
  in pregnancy, childbirth, or puerperium (pulmonary) — *see* Embolism, obstetrical
  intestine (artery) (vein) (with gangrene) 557.0
  intracranial (*see also* Embolism, brain) 434.1 ✔
    venous sinus (any) 325
      late effect — *see* category 326
      nonpyogenic 437.6
        in pregnancy or puerperium 671.5 ✔
  kidney (artery) 593.81
  lateral sinus (venous) — *see* Embolism, intracranial venous sinus
  longitudinal sinus (venous) — *see* Embolism, intracranial venous sinus
  lower extremity 444.22
  lung (massive) — *see* Embolism, pulmonary
  meninges (*see also* Embolism, brain) 434.1 ✔
  mesenteric (artery) (with gangrene) 557.0
  multiple NEC 444.9
  obstetrical (pulmonary) 673.2 ✔
    air 673.0 ✔
    amniotic fluid (pulmonary) 673.1 ✔
    blood-clot 673.2 ✔
    cardiac 674.8 ✔
    fat 673.8 ✔
    heart 674.8 ✔
    pyemic 673.3 ✔
    septic 673.3 ✔
    specified NEC 674.8 ✔
  ophthalmic (*see also* Occlusion, retina) 362.30
  paradoxical NEC 444.9
  penis 607.82
  peripheral arteries NEC 444.22
    lower 444.22
    upper 444.21
  pituitary 253.8
  popliteal (artery) 444.22
  portal (vein) 452
  postoperative NEC 997.2
    cerebral 997.02
    mesenteric artery 997.71
    other vessels 997.79
    peripheral vascular 997.2
    pulmonary 415.11
      septic 415.11
    renal artery 997.72
  precerebral artery (*see also* Occlusion, artery, precerebral) 433.9 ✔
  puerperal — *see* Embolism, obstetrical
  pulmonary ▶(acute)◀ (artery) (vein) 415.19
    with
      abortion — *see* Abortion, by type, with embolism
      ectopic pregnancy (*see also* categories 633.0–633.9) 639.6
      molar pregnancy (*see also* categories 630–632) 639.6
    chronic 416.2 ●
    following
      abortion 639.6
      ectopic or molar pregnancy 639.6
    healed or old V12.51 ●
    iatrogenic 415.11
    in pregnancy, childbirth, or puerperium — *see* Embolism, obstetrical
    personal history of V12.51 ●
    postoperative 415.11
    septic 415.12
  pyemic (multiple) (*see also* Septicemia) 415.12
    with
      abortion — *see* Abortion, by type, with embolism
      ectopic pregnancy (*see also* categories 633.0–633.9) 639.6

Embolism — *continued*
  pyemic (*see also* Septicemia) — *continued*
    with — *continued*
      molar pregnancy (*see also* categories 630–632) 639.6
    Aerobacter aerogenes 415.12
    enteric gram-negative bacilli 415.12
    Enterobacter aerogenes 415.12
    Escherichia coli 415.12
    following
      abortion 639.6
      ectopic or molar pregnancy 639.6
    Hemophilus influenzae 415.12
    pneumococcal 415.12
    Proteus vulgaris 415.12
    Pseudomonas (aeruginosa) 415.12
    puerperal, postpartum, childbirth (any organism) 673.3 ✔
    Serratia 415.12
    specified organism NEC 415.12
    staphylococcal 415.12
      aureus 415.12
      specified organism NEC 415.12
    streptococcal 415.12
  renal (artery) 593.81
    vein 453.3
  retina, retinal (*see also* Occlusion, retina) 362.30
  saddle (aorta) 444.0
  septic 415.12
    arterial 449
  septicemic — *see* Embolism, pyemic
  sinus — *see* Embolism, intracranial venous sinus
  soap
    with
      abortion — *see* Abortion, by type, with embolism
      ectopic pregnancy (*see also* categories 633.0–633.9) 639.6
      molar pregnancy (*see also* categories 630–632) 639.6
    following
      abortion 639.6
      ectopic or molar pregnancy 639.6
  spinal cord (nonpyogenic) 336.1
    in pregnancy or puerperium 671.5 ✔
    pyogenic origin 324.1
      late effect — *see* category 326
  spleen, splenic (artery) 444.89
  thrombus (thromboembolism) following infusion, perfusion, or transfusion 999.2
  upper extremity 444.21
  vein 453.9
    with inflammation or phlebitis — *see* Thrombophlebitis
    antecubital ●
      acute 453.81 ●
      chronic 453.71 ●
    axillary ●
      acute 453.84 ●
      chronic 453.74 ●
    basilic ●
      acute 453.81 ●
      chronic 453.71 ●
    brachial ●
      acute 453.82 ●
      chronic 453.72 ●
    brachiocephalic (innominate) ●
      acute 453.87 ●
      chronic 453.77 ●
    cephalic ●
      acute 453.81 ●
      chronic 453.71 ●
    cerebral (*see also* Embolism, brain) 434.1 ✔
    coronary (*see also* Infarct, myocardium) 410.9 ✔
      without myocardial infarction 411.81
    hepatic 453.0
    internal jugular ●
      acute 453.86 ●
      chronic 453.76 ●
    lower extremity ▶(superficial)◀ 453.6 ▲
      deep 453.40
        acute 453.40 ●

Embolism — *continued*
  vein — *continued*
    lower extremity — *continued*
      deep — *continued*
        acute — *continued*
          calf 453.42 ●
          distal (lower leg) 453.42 ●
          femoral 453.41 ●
          iliac 453.41 ●
          lower leg 453.42 ●
          peroneal 453.42 ●
          popliteal 453.41 ●
          proximal (upper leg) 453.41 ●
          thigh 453.41 ●
          tibial 453.42 ●
        chronic 453.50 ●
          calf 453.52 ●
          disal (lower leg) 453.52 ●
          femoral 453.51 ●
          iliac 453.51 ●
          lower leg 453.52 ●
          peroneal 453.52 ●
          popliteal 453.51 ●
          proximal (upper leg) 453.51 ●
          thigh 453.51 ●
          tibial 453.52 ●
      saphenous (greater) (lesser) 453.6 ●
      superficial 453.6 ●
    mesenteric (with gangrene) 557.0
    portal 452
    pulmonary — *see* Embolism, pulmonary
    radial ●
      acute 453.82 ●
      chronic 453.72 ●
    renal 453.3
    saphenous (greater) (lesser) 453.6 ●
    specified NEC ▶(acute)◀ 453.89 ▲
      with inflammation or phlebitis — *see* Thrombophlebitis
      chronic 453.79 ●
    subclavian ●
      acute 453.85 ●
      chronic 453.75 ●
    superior vena cava ●
      acute 453.87 ●
      chronic 453.77 ●
    thoracic ●
      acute 453.87 ●
      chronic 453.77 ●
    ulnar ●
      acute 453.82 ●
      chronic 453.72 ●
    upper extremity 453.83 ●
      acute 453.83 ●
        deep 453.82 ●
        superficial 453.81 ●
      chronic 453.73 ●
        deep 453.72 ●
        superficial 453.71 ●
    vena cava
      inferior 453.2 ●
      superior ●
        acute 453.87 ●
        chronic 453.77 ●
  vessels of brain (*see also* Embolism, brain) 434.1 ✔
Embolization — *see* **Embolism**
Embolus — *see* Embolism
Embryoma (M9080/1) — *see also* Neoplasm, by site, uncertain behavior
  benign (M9080/0) — *see* Neoplasm, by site, benign
  kidney (M8960/3) 189.0
  liver (M8970/3) 155.0
  malignant (M9080/3) (*see also* Neoplasm, by site, malignant)
    kidney (M8960/3) 189.0
    liver (M8970/3) 155.0
    testis (M9070/3) 186.9
      undescended 186.0
  testis (M9070/3) 186.9
    undescended 186.0
Embryonic
  circulation 747.9
  heart 747.9
  vas deferens 752.89

Embryopathia NEC 759.9
Embryotomy, fetal 763.89
Embryotoxon 743.43
　interfering with vision 743.42
Emesis — *see also* Vomiting
　bilious 787.04 ●
　gravidarum — *see* Hyperemesis, gravidarum
Emissions, nocturnal (semen) 608.89
Emotional
　crisis — *see* Crisis, emotional
　disorder (*see also* Disorder, mental) 300.9
　instability (excessive) 301.3
　lability 799.24 ●
　overlay — *see* Reaction, adjustment
　upset 300.9
Emotionality, pathological 301.3
Emotogenic disease — *see also* Disorder, psychogenic 306.9
Emphysema (atrophic) (centriacinar) (centrilobular) (chronic) (diffuse) (essential) (hypertrophic) (interlobular) (lung) (obstructive) (panlobular) (paracicatricial) (paracinar) (postural) (pulmonary) (senile) (subpleural) (traction) (unilateral) (unilobular) (vesicular) 492.8
　with bronchitis
　　chronic 491.20
　　　with
　　　　acute bronchitis 491.22
　　　　exacerbation (acute) 491.21
　bullous (giant) 492.0
　cellular tissue 958.7
　　surgical 998.81
　compensatory 518.2
　congenital 770.2
　conjunctiva 372.89
　connective tissue 958.7
　　surgical 998.81
　due to fumes or vapors 506.4
　eye 376.89
　eyelid 374.85
　　surgical 998.81
　　traumatic 958.7
　fetus or newborn (interstitial) (mediastinal) (unilobular) 770.2
　heart 416.9
　interstitial 518.1
　　congenital 770.2
　　fetus or newborn 770.2
　laminated tissue 958.7
　　surgical 998.81
　mediastinal 518.1
　　fetus or newborn 770.2
　newborn (interstitial) (mediastinal) (unilobular) 770.2
　obstructive diffuse with fibrosis 492.8
　orbit 376.89
　subcutaneous 958.7
　　due to trauma 958.7
　　nontraumatic 518.1
　　surgical 998.81
　surgical 998.81
　thymus (gland) (congenital) 254.8
　traumatic 958.7
　tuberculous (*see also* Tuberculosis, pulmonary) 011.9 ☑
Employment examination (certification) V70.5
Empty sella (turcica) syndrome 253.8
Empyema (chest) (diaphragmatic) (double) (encapsulated) (general) (interlobar) (lung) (medial) (necessitatis) (perforating chest wall) (pleura) (pneumococcal) (residual) (sacculated) (streptococcal) (supradiaphragmatic) 510.9
　with fistula 510.0
　accessory sinus (chronic) (*see also* Sinusitis) 473.9
　acute 510.9
　　with fistula 510.0
　antrum (chronic) (*see also* Sinusitis, maxillary) 473.0
　brain (any part) (*see also* Abscess, brain) 324.0
　ethmoidal (sinus) (chronic) (*see also* Sinusitis, ethmoidal) 473.2
　extradural (*see also* Abscess, extradural) 324.9

Empyema — *continued*
　frontal (sinus) (chronic) (*see also* Sinusitis, frontal) 473.1
　gallbladder (*see also* Cholecystitis, acute) 575.0
　mastoid (process) (acute) (*see also* Mastoiditis, acute) 383.00
　maxilla, maxillary 526.4
　　sinus (chronic) (*see also* Sinusitis, maxillary) 473.0
　nasal sinus (chronic) (*see also* Sinusitis) 473.9
　sinus (accessory) (nasal) (*see also* Sinusitis) 473.9
　sphenoidal (chronic) (sinus) (*see also* Sinusitis, sphenoidal) 473.3
　subarachnoid (*see also* Abscess, extradural) 324.9
　subdural (*see also* Abscess, extradural) 324.9
　tuberculous (*see also* Tuberculosis, pleura) 012.0 ☑
　ureter (*see also* Ureteritis) 593.89
　ventricular (*see also* Abscess, brain) 324.0
Enameloma 520.2
Encephalitis (bacterial) (chronic) (hemorrhagic) (idiopathic) (nonepidemic) (spurious) (subacute) 323.9
　acute (*see also* Encephalitis, viral)
　　disseminated (postinfectious) NEC 136.9 [323.61]
　　　postimmunization or postvaccination 323.51
　　inclusional 049.8
　　inclusion body 049.8
　　necrotizing 049.8
　arboviral, arbovirus NEC 064
　arthropod-borne (*see also* Encephalitis, viral, arthropod-borne) 064
　Australian X 062.4
　Bwamba fever 066.3
　California (virus) 062.5
　Central European 063.2
　Czechoslovakian 063.2
　Dawson's (inclusion body) 046.2
　diffuse sclerosing 046.2
　due to
　　actinomycosis 039.8 [323.41]
　　cat-scratch disease 078.3 [323.01]
　　human herpesvirus NEC 058.29
　　human herpesvirus 6 058.21
　　human herpesvirus 7 058.29
　　infection classified elsewhere 136.9 [323.41]
　　infectious mononucleosis 075 [323.01]
　　malaria (*see also* Malaria) 084.6 [323.2]
　　Negishi virus 064
　　ornithosis 073.7 [323.01]
　　prophylactic inoculation against smallpox 323.51
　　rickettsiosis (*see also* Rickettsiosis) 083.9 [323.1]
　　rubella 056.01
　　toxoplasmosis (acquired) 130.0
　　　congenital (active) 771.2 [323.41]
　　typhus (fever) (*see also* Typhus) 081.9 [323.1]
　　vaccination (smallpox) 323.51
　Eastern equine 062.2
　endemic 049.8
　epidemic 049.8
　equine (acute) (infectious) (viral) 062.9
　　Eastern 062.2
　　Venezuelan 066.2
　　Western 062.1
　Far Eastern 063.0
　following vaccination or other immunization procedure 323.51
　herpes 054.3
　human herpesvirus NEC 058.29
　human herpesvirus 6 058.21
　human herpesvirus 7 058.29
　Ilheus virus 062.8
　inclusion body 046.2
　infectious (acute) (virus) NEC 049.8
　influenzal 487.8 [323.41]
　　lethargic 049.8
　Japanese (B type) 062.0
　La Crosse 062.5

Encephalitis — *continued*
　Langat 063.8
　late effect — *see* Late, effect, encephalitis
　lead 984.9 [323.71]
　lethargic (acute) (infectious) (influenzal) 049.8
　lethargica 049.8
　louping ill 063.1
　lupus 710.0 [323.81]
　lymphatica 049.0
　Mengo 049.8
　meningococcal 036.1
　mumps 072.2
　Murray Valley 062.4
　myoclonic 049.8
　Negishi virus 064
　otitic NEC 382.4 [323.41]
　parasitic NEC 123.9 [323.41]
　periaxialis (concentrica) (diffusa) 341.1
　postchickenpox 052.0
　postexanthematous NEC 057.9 [323.62]
　postimmunization 323.51
　postinfectious NEC 136.9 [323.62]
　postmeasles 055.0
　posttraumatic 323.81
　postvaccinal (smallpox) 323.51
　postvaricella 052.0
　postviral NEC 079.99 [323.62]
　　postexanthematous 057.9 [323.62]
　　specified NEC 057.8 [323.62]
　Powassan 063.8
　progressive subcortical (Binswanger's) 290.12
　Rasmussen 323.81
　Rio Bravo 049.8
　rubella 056.01
　Russian
　　autumnal 062.0
　　spring-summer type (taiga) 063.0
　saturnine 984.9 [323.71]
　Semliki Forest 062.8
　serous 048
　slow-acting virus NEC 046.8
　specified cause NEC 323.81
　St. Louis type 062.3
　subacute sclerosing 046.2
　subcorticalis chronica 290.12
　summer 062.0
　suppurative 324.0
　syphilitic 094.81
　　congenital 090.41
　tick-borne 063.9
　torula, torular 117.5 [323.41]
　toxic NEC 989.9 [323.71]
　toxoplasmic (acquired) 130.0
　　congenital (active) 771.2 [323.41]
　trichinosis 124 [323.41]
　Trypanosomiasis (*see also* Trypanosomiasis) 086.9 [323.2]
　tuberculous (*see also* Tuberculosis) 013.6 ☑
　type B (Japanese) 062.0
　type C 062.3
　van Bogaert's 046.2
　Venezuelan 066.2
　Vienna type 049.8
　viral, virus 049.9
　　arthropod-borne NEC 064
　　mosquito-borne 062.9
　　　Australian X disease 062.4
　　　California virus 062.5
　　　Eastern equine 062.2
　　　Ilheus virus 062.8
　　　Japanese (B type) 062.0
　　　Murray Valley 062.4
　　　specified type NEC 062.8
　　　St. Louis 062.3
　　　type B 062.0
　　　type C 062.3
　　　Western equine 062.1
　　tick-borne 063.9
　　　biundulant 063.2
　　　Central European 063.2
　　　Czechoslovakian 063.2
　　　diphasic meningoencephalitis 063.2
　　　Far Eastern 063.0
　　　Langat 063.8
　　　louping ill 063.1

Encephalitis — *continued*
　viral, virus — *continued*
　　arthropod-borne — *continued*
　　　tick-borne — *continued*
　　　　Powassan 063.8
　　　　Russian spring-summer (taiga) 063.0
　　　　specified type NEC 063.8
　　　vector unknown 064
　　　Western equine 062.1
　　slow acting NEC 046.8
　　specified type NEC 049.8
　　vaccination, prophylactic (against) V05.0
　von Economo's 049.8
　Western equine 062.1
　West Nile type 066.41
Encephalocele 742.0
　orbit 376.81
Encephalocystocele 742.0
Encephalomalacia (brain) (cerebellar) (cerebral) (cerebrospinal) — *see also* Softening, brain 434.9 ☑
　due to
　　hemorrhage (*see also* Hemorrhage, brain) 431
　　recurrent spasm of artery 435.9
　embolic (cerebral) (*see also* Embolism, brain) 434.1 ☑
　subcorticalis chronicus arteriosclerotica 290.12
　thrombotic (*see also* Thrombosis, brain) 434.0 ☑
Encephalomeningitis — *see* Meningoencephalitis
Encephalomeningocele 742.0
Encephalomeningomyelitis — *see* Meningoencephalitis
Encephalomeningopathy — *see also* Meningoencephalitis 349.9
Encephalomyelitis (chronic) (granulomatous) (myalgic, benign) — *see also* Encephalitis 323.9
　abortive disseminated 049.8
　acute disseminated (ADEM) (postinfectious) 136.9 [323.61]
　　infectious 136.9 [323.61]
　　noninfectious 323.81
　　postimmunization 323.51
　due to
　　cat-scratch disease 078.3 [323.01]
　　infectious mononucleosis 075 [323.01]
　　ornithosis 073.7 [323.01]
　　vaccination (any) 323.51
　equine (acute) (infectious) 062.9
　　Eastern 062.2
　　Venezuelan 066.2
　　Western 062.1
　funicularis infectiosa 049.8
　late effect — *see* Late, effect, encephalitis
　Munch-Peterson's 049.8
　postchickenpox 052.0
　postimmunization 323.51
　postmeasles 055.0
　postvaccinal (smallpox) 323.51
　rubella 056.01
　specified cause NEC 323.81
　syphilitic 094.81
　West Nile 066.41
Encephalomyelocele 742.0
Encephalomyelomeningitis — *see* Meningoencephalitis
Encephalomyeloneuropathy 349.9
Encephalomyelopathy 349.9
　subacute necrotizing (infantile) 330.8
Encephalomyeloradiculitis (acute) 357.0
Encephalomyeloradiculoneuritis (acute) 357.0
Encephalomyeloradiculopathy 349.9
Encephalomyocarditis 074.23
Encephalopathia hyperbilirubinemica, newborn 774.7
　due to isoimmunization (conditions classifiable to 773.0–773.2) 773.4
Encephalopathy (acute) 348.30
　alcoholic 291.2
　anoxic — *see* Damage, brain, anoxic
　arteriosclerotic 437.0

☑ Additional Digit Required — Refer to the Tabular List for Digit Selection　　　　　　　　　　　　　▽ Subterms under main terms may continue to next column or page

2010 ICD-9-CM　　　　　　▶◀ Revised Text　　　　● New Line　　　▲ Revised Code　　　　　　October 2009 • Volume 2 — 101

Encephalopathy — *continued*
  arteriosclerotic — *continued*
    late effect — *see* Late effect(s) (of) cerebrovascular disease
  bilirubin, newborn 774.7
    due to isoimmunization 773.4
  congenital 742.9
  demyelinating (callosal) 341.8
  due to
    birth injury (intracranial) 767.8
    dialysis 294.8
      transient 293.9
    drugs — (*see also* Table of Drugs and Chemicals) 348.39
    hyperinsulinism — *see* Hyperinsulinism
    influenza (virus) 487.8
    lack of vitamin (*see also* Deficiency, vitamin) 269.2
    nicotinic acid deficiency 291.2
    serum (nontherapeutic) (therapeutic) 999.5
    syphilis 094.81
    trauma (postconcussional) 310.2
      current (*see also* Concussion, brain) 850.9
        with skull fracture — *see* Fracture, skull, by site, with intracranial injury
    vaccination 323.51
  hepatic 572.2
  hyperbilirubinemic, newborn 774.7
    due to isoimmunization (conditions classifiable to 773.0–773.2) 773.4
  hypertensive 437.2
  hypoglycemic 251.2
  hypoxic (*see also* Damage, brain, anoxic)
    ischemic (HIE) 768.70   ▲
      mild 768.71   ●
      moderate 768.72   ●
      severe 768.73   ●
  infantile cystic necrotizing (congenital) 341.8
  lead 984.9 [*323.71*]
  leukopolio 330.0
  metabolic (*see also* Delirium) 348.31
    toxic 349.82
  necrotizing
    hemorrhagic (acute) 323.61
    subacute 330.8
  other specified type NEC 348.39
  pellagrous 265.2
  portal-systemic 572.2
  postcontusional 310.2
  posttraumatic 310.2
  saturnine 984.9 [*323.71*]
  septic 348.31
  spongioform, subacute (viral) 046.19
  subacute
    necrotizing 330.8
    spongioform 046.19
    viral, spongioform 046.19
  subcortical progressive (Schilder) 341.1
    chronic (Binswanger's) 290.12
  toxic 349.82
    metabolic 349.82
  traumatic (postconcussional) 310.2
    current (*see also* Concussion, brain) 850.9
      with skull fracture — *see* Fracture, skull, by site, with intracranial injury
  vitamin B deficiency NEC 266.9
  Wernicke's (superior hemorrhagic polioencephalitis) 265.1
Encephalorrhagia — *see also* Hemorrhage, brain 432.9
  healed or old V12.54
  late effect — *see* Late effect(s) (of) cerebrovascular disease
Encephalosis, posttraumatic 310.2
Enchondroma (M9220/0) — *see also* Neoplasm, bone, benign
  multiple, congenital 756.4
Enchondromatosis (cartilaginous) (congenital) (multiple) 756.4
Enchondroses, multiple (cartilaginous) (congenital) 756.4
Encopresis — *see also* Incontinence, feces 787.6
  nonorganic origin 307.7
Encounter for — *see also* Admission for

Encounter for — *see also* Admission for — *continued*
  administrative purpose only V68.9
    referral of patient without examination or treatment V68.81
    specified purpose NEC V68.89
  chemotherapy, ▶(oral) (intravenous),◀ antineoplastic V58.11
  dialysis
    extracorporeal (renal) V56.0
    peritoneal V56.8
  disability examination V68.01
  end-of-life care V66.7
  hospice care V66.7
  immunizations (childhood) appropriate for ●
    age V20.2   ●
  immunotherapy, antineoplastic V58.12
  palliative care V66.7
  paternity testing V70.4
  radiotherapy V58.0
  respirator [ventilator] dependence during
    mechanical failure V46.14
    power failure V46.12
    for weaning V46.13
  routine infant and child vision and hearing ●
    testing V20.2   ●
  school examination V70.3   ●
    following surgery V67.09   ●
  screening mammogram NEC V76.12
    for high-risk patient V76.11
  terminal care V66.7
  weaning from respirator [ventilator] V46.13
Encystment — *see* Cyst
Endamebiasis — *see* Amebiasis
Endamoeba — *see* Amebiasis
Endarteritis (bacterial, subacute) (infective) (septic) 447.6
  brain, cerebral or cerebrospinal 437.4
    late effect — *see* Late effect(s) (of) cerebrovascular disease
  coronary (artery) — *see* Arteriosclerosis, coronary
  deformans — *see* Arteriosclerosis
  embolic (*see also* Embolism) 444.9
  obliterans (*see also* Arteriosclerosis)
    pulmonary 417.8
  pulmonary 417.8
  retina 362.18
  senile — *see* Arteriosclerosis
  syphilitic 093.89
    brain or cerebral 094.89
    congenital 090.5
    spinal 094.89
  tuberculous (*see also* Tuberculosis) 017.9 ☑
Endemic — *see* condition
Endocarditis (chronic) (indeterminate) (interstitial) (marantic) (nonbacterial thrombotic) (residual) (sclerotic) (sclerous) (senile) (valvular) 424.90
  with
    rheumatic fever (conditions classifiable to 390)
      active — *see* Endocarditis, acute, rheumatic
      inactive or quiescent (with chorea) 397.9
  acute or subacute 421.9
    rheumatic (aortic) (mitral) (pulmonary) (tricuspid) 391.1
      with chorea (acute) (rheumatic) (Sydenham's) 392.0
      bacterial 421.0
  aortic (heart) (nonrheumatic) (valve) 424.1
    with
      mitral (valve) disease 396.9
        active or acute 391.1
          with chorea (acute) (rheumatic) (Sydenham's) 392.0
          bacterial 421.0
      rheumatic fever (conditions classifiable to 390)
        active — *see* Endocarditis, acute, rheumatic
        inactive or quiescent (with chorea) 395.9
          with mitral disease 396.9

Endocarditis — *continued*
  aortic — *continued*
    acute or subacute 421.9
    arteriosclerotic 424.1
    congenital 746.89
    hypertensive 424.1
    rheumatic (chronic) (inactive) 395.9
      with mitral (valve) disease 396.9
        active or acute 391.1
          with chorea (acute) (rheumatic) (Sydenham's) 392.0
      active or acute 391.1
        with chorea (acute) (rheumatic) (Sydenham's) 392.0
      specified cause, except rheumatic 424.1
    syphilitic 093.22
  arteriosclerotic or due to arteriosclerosis 424.99
  atypical verrucous (Libman-Sacks) 710.0 [*424.91*]
  bacterial (acute) (any valve) (chronic) (subacute) 421.0
  blastomycotic 116.0 [*421.1*]
  candidal 112.81
  congenital 425.3
  constrictive 421.0
  Coxsackie 074.22
  due to
    blastomycosis 116.0 [*421.1*]
    candidiasis 112.81
    Coxsackie (virus) 074.22
    disseminated lupus erythematosus 710.0 [*424.91*]
    histoplasmosis (*see also* Histoplasmosis) 115.94
    hypertension (benign) 424.99
    moniliasis 112.81
    prosthetic cardiac valve 996.61
    Q fever 083.0 [*421.1*]
    serratia marcescens 421.0
    typhoid (fever) 002.0 [*421.1*]
  fetal 425.3
  gonococcal 098.84
  hypertensive 424.99
  infectious or infective (acute) (any valve) (chronic) (subacute) 421.0
  lenta (acute) (any valve) (chronic) (subacute) 421.0
  Libman-Sacks 710.0 [*424.91*]
  Loeffler's (parietal fibroplastic) 421.0
  malignant (acute) (any valve) (chronic) (subacute) 421.0
  meningococcal 036.42
  mitral (chronic) (double) (fibroid) (heart) (inactive) (valve) (with chorea) 394.9
    with
      aortic (valve) disease 396.9
        active or acute 391.1
          with chorea (acute) (rheumatic) (Sydenham's) 392.0
      rheumatic fever (conditions classifiable to 390)
        active — *see* Endocarditis, acute, rheumatic
        inactive or quiescent (with chorea) 394.9
          with aortic valve disease 396.9
    active or acute 391.1
      with chorea (acute) (rheumatic) (Sydenham's) 392.0
      bacterial 421.0
    arteriosclerotic 424.0
    congenital 746.89
    hypertensive 424.0
    nonrheumatic 424.0
      acute or subacute 421.9
    syphilitic 093.21
  monilial 112.81
  mycotic (acute) (any valve) (chronic) (subacute) 421.0
  pneumococcic (acute) (any valve) (chronic) (subacute) 421.0
  pulmonary (chronic) (heart) (valve) 424.3

Endocarditis — *continued*
  pulmonary — *continued*
    with
      rheumatic fever (conditions classifiable to 390)
        active — *see* Endocarditis, acute, rheumatic
        inactive or quiescent (with chorea) 397.1
    acute or subacute 421.9
      rheumatic 391.1
        with chorea (acute) (rheumatic) (Sydenham's) 392.0
    arteriosclerotic or due to arteriosclerosis 424.3
    congenital 746.09
    hypertensive or due to hypertension (benign) 424.3
    rheumatic (chronic) (inactive) (with chorea) 397.1
      active or acute 391.1
        with chorea (acute) (rheumatic) (Sydenham's) 392.0
    syphilitic 093.24
  purulent (acute) (any valve) (chronic) (subacute) 421.0
  rheumatic (chronic) (inactive) (with chorea) 397.9
    active or acute (aortic) (mitral) (pulmonary) (tricuspid) 391.1
      with chorea (acute) (rheumatic) (Sydenham's) 392.0
  septic (acute) (any valve) (chronic) (subacute) 421.0
  specified cause, except rheumatic 424.99
  streptococcal (acute) (any valve) (chronic) (subacute) 421.0
  subacute — *see* Endocarditis, acute
  suppurative (any valve) (acute) (chronic) (subacute) 421.0
  syphilitic NEC 093.20
  toxic (*see also* Endocarditis, acute) 421.9
  tricuspid (chronic) (heart) (inactive) (rheumatic) (valve) (with chorea) 397.0
    with
      rheumatic fever (conditions classifiable to 390)
        active — *see* Endocarditis, acute, rheumatic
        inactive or quiescent (with chorea) 397.0
    active or acute 391.1
      with chorea (acute) (rheumatic) (Sydenham's) 392.0
    arteriosclerotic 424.2
    congenital 746.89
    hypertensive 424.2
    nonrheumatic 424.2
      acute or subacute 421.9
    specified cause, except rheumatic 424.2
    syphilitic 093.23
  tuberculous (*see also* Tuberculosis) 017.9 ☑ [*424.91*]
  typhoid 002.0 [*421.1*]
  ulcerative (acute) (any valve) (chronic) (subacute) 421.0
  vegetative (acute) (any valve) (chronic) (subacute) 421.0
  verrucous (acute) (any valve) (chronic) (subacute) NEC 710.0 [*424.91*]
    nonbacterial 710.0 [*424.91*]
    nonrheumatic 710.0 [*424.91*]
Endocardium, endocardial — *see also* condition
  cushion defect 745.60
    specified type NEC 745.69
Endocervicitis — *see also* Cervicitis 616.0
  due to
    intrauterine (contraceptive) device 996.65
  gonorrheal (acute) 098.15
    chronic or duration of 2 months or over 098.35
  hyperplastic 616.0
  syphilitic 095.8
  trichomonal 131.09
  tuberculous (*see also* Tuberculosis) 016.7 ☑
Endocrine — *see* condition

☑ Additional Digit Required — Refer to the Tabular List for Digit Selection   ⊽ Subterms under main terms may continue to next column or page

102 — Volume 2 · October 2009   ▶◀ Revised Text   ● New Line   ▲ Revised Code   **2010 ICD-9-CM**

Endocrinopathy, pluriglandular 258.9
Endodontitis 522.0
End-of-life care V66.7
Endomastoiditis — *see also* Mastoiditis 383.9
Endometrioma 617.6
Endometriosis 617.9
  appendix 617.5
  bladder 617.8
  bowel 617.5
  broad ligament 617.3
  cervix 617.0
  colon 617.5
  cul-de-sac (Douglas') 617.3
  exocervix 617.0
  fallopian tube 617.2
  female genital organ NEC 617.8
  gallbladder 617.8
  in scar of skin 617.6
  internal 617.0
  intestine 617.5
  lung 617.8
  myometrium 617.0
  ovary 617.1
  parametrium 617.3
  pelvic peritoneum 617.3
  peritoneal (pelvic) 617.3
  rectovaginal septum 617.4
  rectum 617.5
  round ligament 617.3
  skin 617.6
  specified site NEC 617.8
  stromal (M8931/1) 236.0
  umbilicus 617.8
  uterus 617.0
    internal 617.0
  vagina 617.4
  vulva 617.8
Endometritis (nonspecific) (purulent) (septic) (suppurative) 615.9
  with
    abortion — *see* Abortion, by type, with sepsis
    ectopic pregnancy (*see also* categories 633.0–633.9) 639.0
    molar pregnancy (*see also* categories 630–632) 639.0
  acute 615.0
  blennorrhagic 098.16
    acute 098.16
    chronic or duration of 2 months or over 098.36
  cervix, cervical (*see also* Cervicitis) 616.0
    hyperplastic 616.0
  chronic 615.1
  complicating pregnancy 670.1 ☑   ▲
    affecting fetus or newborn 760.8
    septic 670.2 ☑   ●
  decidual 615.9
  following
    abortion 639.0
    ectopic or molar pregnancy 639.0
  gonorrheal (acute) 098.16
    chronic or duration of 2 months or over 098.36
  hyperplastic (*see also* Hyperplasia, endometrium) 621.30
    cervix 616.0
  polypoid — *see* Endometritis, hyperplastic
  puerperal, postpartum, childbirth 670.1 ☑   ▲
    septic 670.2 ☑   ●
  senile (atrophic) 615.9
  subacute 615.0
  tuberculous (*see also* Tuberculosis) 016.7 ☑
Endometrium — *see* condition
Endomyocardiopathy, South African 425.2
Endomyocarditis — *see* Endocarditis
Endomyofibrosis 425.0
Endomyometritis — *see also* Endometritis 615.9
Endopericarditis — *see* Endocarditis
Endoperineuritis — *see* Disorder, nerve
Endophlebitis — *see also* Phlebitis 451.9
  leg 451.2
    deep (vessels) 451.19
    superficial (vessels) 451.0
  portal (vein) 572.1

Endophlebitis — *see also* Phlebitis — *continued*
  retina 362.18
  specified site NEC 451.89
  syphilitic 093.89
Endophthalmia — *see also* Endophthalmitis 360.00
  gonorrheal 098.42
Endophthalmitis (globe) (infective) (metastatic) (purulent) (subacute) 360.00
  acute 360.01
  bleb associated 379.63
  chronic 360.03
  parasitic 360.13
  phacoanaphylactic 360.19
  specified type NEC 360.19
  sympathetic 360.11
Endosalpingioma (M9111/1) 236.2
Endosalpingiosis 629.89
Endosteitis — *see* Osteomyelitis
Endothelioma, bone (M9260/3) — *see* Neoplasm, bone, malignant
Endotheliosis 287.8
  hemorrhagic infectional 287.8
Endotoxemia — *code to* condition
Endotoxic shock 785.52
Endotrachelitis — *see also* Cervicitis 616.0
Enema rash 692.89
Engelmann's disease (diaphyseal sclerosis) 756.9
Engel-von Recklinghausen disease or syndrome (osteitis fibrosa cystica) 252.01
English disease — *see also* Rickets 268.0
Engman's disease (infectious eczematoid dermatitis) 690.8
Engorgement
  breast 611.79
    newborn 778.7
    puerperal, postpartum 676.2 ☑
  liver 573.9
  lung 514
  pulmonary 514
  retina, venous 362.37
  stomach 536.8
  venous, retina 362.37
Enlargement, enlarged — *see also* Hypertrophy
  abdomen 789.3 ☑
  adenoids 474.12
    and tonsils 474.10
  alveolar process or ridge 525.8
  apertures of diaphragm (congenital) 756.6
  blind spot, visual field 368.42
  gingival 523.8
  heart, cardiac (*see also* Hypertrophy, cardiac) 429.3
  lacrimal gland, chronic 375.03
  liver (*see also* Hypertrophy, liver) 789.1
  lymph gland or node 785.6
  orbit 376.46
  organ or site, congenital NEC — *see* Anomaly, specified type NEC
  parathyroid (gland) 252.01
  pituitary fossa 793.0
  prostate (simple) (soft) 600.00
    with
      other lower urinary tract symptoms (LUTS) 600.01
      urinary
        obstruction 600.01
        retention 600.01
  sella turcica 793.0
  spleen (*see also* Splenomegaly) 789.2
    congenital 759.0
  thymus (congenital) (gland) 254.0
  thyroid (gland) (*see also* Goiter) 240.9
  tongue 529.8
  tonsils 474.11
    and adenoids 474.10
  uterus 621.2
Enophthalmos 376.50
  due to
    atrophy of orbital tissue 376.51
    surgery 376.52
    trauma 376.52
Enostosis 526.89
Entamebiasis — *see* Amebiasis
Entamebic — *see* Amebiasis

Entanglement, umbilical cord(s) 663.3 ☑
  with compression 663.2 ☑
  affecting fetus or newborn 762.5
  around neck with compression 663.1 ☑
  twins in monoamniotic sac 663.2 ☑
Enteralgia 789.0
Enteric — *see* condition
Enteritis (acute) (catarrhal) (choleraic) (chronic) (congestive) (diarrheal) (exudative) (follicular) (hemorrhagic) (infantile) (lienteric) (noninfectious) (perforative) (phlegmonous) (presumed noninfectious) (pseudomembranous) 558.9
  adaptive 564.9
  aertrycke infection 003.0
  allergic 558.3
  amebic (*see also* Amebiasis) 006.9
    with abscess — *see* Abscess, amebic
    acute 006.0
      with abscess — *see* Abscess, amebic
      nondysenteric 006.2
    chronic 006.1
      with abscess — *see* Abscess, amebic
      nondysenteric 006.2
    nondysenteric 006.2
  anaerobic (cocci) (gram-negative) (gram-positive) (mixed) NEC 008.46
  bacillary NEC 004.9
  bacterial NEC 008.5
    specified NEC 008.49
  Bacteroides (fragilis) (melaninogeniscus) (oralis) 008.46
  Butyrivibrio (fibriosolvens) 008.46
  Campylobacter 008.43
  Candida 112.85
  Chilomastix 007.8
  choleriformis 001.1
  chronic 558.9
    ulcerative (*see also* Colitis, ulcerative) 556.9
  cicatrizing (chronic) 555.0
  Clostridium
    botulinum 005.1
    difficile 008.45
    haemolyticum 008.46
    novyi 008.46
    perfringens (C) (F) 008.46
    specified type NEC 008.46
  coccidial 007.2
  dietetic 558.9
  due to
    achylia gastrica 536.8
    adenovirus 008.62
    Aerobacter aerogenes 008.2
    anaerobes (*see also* Enteritis, anaerobic) 008.46
    Arizona (bacillus) 008.1
    astrovirus 008.66
    Bacillus coli — *see* Enteritis, E. coli
    bacteria NEC 008.5
      specified NEC 008.49
    Bacteroides (*see also* Enteritis, Bacteroides) 008.46
    Butyrivibrio (fibriosolvens) 008.46
    calicivirus 008.65
    Camplyobacter 008.43
    Clostridium — *see* Enteritis, Clostridium
    Cockle agent 008.64
    Coxsackie (virus) 008.67
    Ditchling agent 008.64
    ECHO virus 008.67
    Enterobacter aerogenes 008.2
    enterococci 008.49
    enterovirus NEC 008.67
    Escherichia coli — *see* Enteritis, E. coli
    Eubacterium 008.46
    Fusobacterium (nucleatum) 008.46
    gram-negative bacteria NEC 008.47
      anaerobic NEC 008.46
    Hawaii agent 008.63
    irritating foods 558.9
    Klebsiella aerogenes 008.47
    Marin County agent 008.66
    Montgomery County agent 008.63
    norovirus 008.63   ●
    Norwalk-like agent 008.63
    Norwalk virus 008.63

Enteritis — *continued*
  due to — *continued*
    Otofuke agent 008.63
    Paracolobactrum arizonae 008.1
    paracolon bacillus NEC 008.47
      Arizona 008.1
    Paramatta agent 008.64
    Peptococcus 008.46
    Peptostreptococcus 008.46
    Proprionibacterium 008.46
    Proteus (bacillus) (mirabilis) (morganii) 008.3
    Pseudomonas aeruginosa 008.42
    Rotavirus 008.61
    Sapporo agent 008.63
    small round virus (SRV) NEC 008.64
      featureless NEC 008.63
      structured NEC 008.63
    Snow Mountain (SM) agent 008.63
    specified
      bacteria NEC 008.49
      organism, nonbacterial NEC 008.8
      virus NEC 008.69
    Staphylococcus 008.41
    Streptococcus 008.49
      anaerobic 008.46
    Taunton agent 008.63
    Torovirus 008.69
    Treponema 008.46
    Veillonella 008.46
    virus 008.8
      specified type NEC 008.69
    Wollan (W) agent 008.64
    Yersinia enterocolitica 008.44
  dysentery — *see* Dysentery
  E. coli 008.00
    enterohemorrhagic 008.04
    enteroinvasive 008.03
    enteropathogenic 008.01
    enterotoxigenic 008.02
    specified type NEC 008.09
  el tor 001.1
  embadomonial 007.8
  eosinophilic 558.41
  epidemic 009.0
  Eubacterium 008.46
  fermentative 558.9
  fulminant 557.0
  Fusobacterium (nucleatum) 008.46
  gangrenous (*see also* Enteritis, due to, by organism) 009.0
  giardial 007.1
  gram-negative bacteria NEC 008.47
    anaerobic NEC 008.46
  infectious NEC (*see also* Enteritis, due to, by organism) 009.0
    presumed 009.1
  influenzal 487.8
  ischemic 557.9
    acute 557.0
    chronic 557.1
    due to mesenteric artery insufficiency 557.1
  membranous 564.9
  mucous 564.9
  myxomembranous 564.9
  necrotic (*see also* Enteritis, due to, by organism) 009.0
  necroticans 005.2
  necrotizing of fetus or newborn (*see also* Enterocolitis, necrotizing, newborn) 777.50
  neurogenic 564.9
  newborn 777.8
    necrotizing (*see also* Enterocolitis, necrotizing, newborn) 777.50
  parasitic NEC 129
  paratyphoid (fever) (*see also* Fever, paratyphoid) 002.9
  Peptococcus 008.46
  Peptostreptococcus 008.46
  Proprionibacterium 008.46
  protozoal NEC 007.9
  radiation 558.1
  regional (of) 555.9
    intestine
      large (bowel, colon, or rectum) 555.1

☑ Additional Digit Required — Refer to the Tabular List for Digit Selection   ◤ Subterms under main terms may continue to next column or page

2010 ICD-9-CM   ▶◀ Revised Text   ● New Line   ▲ Revised Code   October 2009 · Volume 2 — 103

Enteritis — *continued*
  regional — *continued*
    intestine — *continued*
      large — *continued*
        with small intestine 555.2
        small (duodenum, ileum, or jejunum) 555.0
          with large intestine 555.2
    Salmonella infection 003.0
    salmonellosis 003.0
    segmental (*see also* Enteritis, regional) 555.9
    septic (*see also* Enteritis, due to, by organism) 009.0
    Shigella 004.9
    simple 558.9
    spasmodic 564.9
    spastic 564.9
    staphylococcal 008.41
      due to food 005.0
    streptococcal 008.49
      anaerobic 008.46
    toxic 558.2
    Treponema (denticola) (macrodentium) 008.46
    trichomonal 007.3
    tuberculous (*see also* Tuberculosis) 014.8 ☑
    typhosa 002.0
    ulcerative (chronic) (*see also* Colitis, ulcerative) 556.9
    Veillonella 008.46
    viral 008.8
      adenovirus 008.62
      enterovirus 008.67
      specified virus NEC 008.69
    Yersinia enterocolitica 008.44
    zymotic 009.0
Enteroarticular syndrome 099.3
Enterobiasis 127.4
Enterobius vermicularis 127.4
Enterocele — *see also* Hernia 553.9
  pelvis, pelvic (acquired) (congenital) 618.6
  vagina, vaginal (acquired) (congenital) 618.6
Enterocolitis — *see also* Enteritis
  fetus or newborn (*see also* Enterocolitis, necrotizing, newborn) 777.8
    necrotizing 777.50
  fulminant 557.0
  granulomatous 555.2
  hemorrhagic (acute) 557.0
    chronic 557.1
  necrotizing (acute) (membranous) 557.0
    newborn 777.50
      with
        perforation 777.53
        pneumatosis and perforation 777.53
        pneumatosis without perforation 777.52
        without pneumatosis, without perforation 777.51 ●
      stage I 777.51
      stage II 777.52
      stage III 777.53
  primary necrotizing (*see also* Enterocolitis, necrotizing, newborn) 777.50
  pseudomembranous 008.45
    newborn 008.45 ●
  radiation 558.1
    newborn (*see also* Enterocolitis, necrotizing, newborn) 777.50
  ulcerative 556.0
Enterocystoma 751.5
Enterogastritis — *see* Enteritis
Enterogenous cyanosis 289.7
Enterolith, enterolithiasis (impaction) 560.39
  with hernia (*see also* Hernia, by site, with obstruction)
    gangrenous — *see* Hernia, by site, with gangrene
Enteropathy 569.9
  exudative (of Gordon) 579.8
  gluten 579.0
  hemorrhagic, terminal 557.0
  protein-losing 579.8
Enteroperitonitis — *see also* Peritonitis 567.9
Enteroptosis 569.89
Enterorrhagia 578.9

Enterospasm 564.9
  psychogenic 306.4
Enterostenosis — *see also* Obstruction, intestine 560.9
Enterostomy status V44.4
  with complication 569.60
Enthesopathy 726.90
  ankle and tarsus 726.70
  elbow region 726.30
    specified NEC 726.39
  hip 726.5
  knee 726.60
  peripheral NEC 726.8
  shoulder region 726.10
    adhesive 726.0
  spinal 720.1
  wrist and carpus 726.4
Entrance, air into vein — *see* Embolism, air
Entrapment, nerve — *see* Neuropathy, entrapment
Entropion (eyelid) 374.00
  cicatricial 374.04
  congenital 743.62
  late effect of trachoma (healed) 139.1
  mechanical 374.02
  paralytic 374.02
  senile 374.01
  spastic 374.03
Enucleation of eye (current) (traumatic) 871.3
Enuresis 788.30
  habit disturbance 307.6
  nocturnal 788.36
    psychogenic 307.6
  nonorganic origin 307.6
  psychogenic 307.6
Enzymopathy 277.9
Eosinopenia 288.59
Eosinophilia 288.3
  allergic 288.3
  hereditary 288.3
  idiopathic 288.3
  infiltrative 518.3
  Loeffler's 518.3
  myalgia syndrome 710.5
  pulmonary (tropical) 518.3
  secondary 288.3
  tropical 518.3
Eosinophilic — *see also* condition
  fasciitis 728.89
  granuloma (bone) 277.89
  infiltration lung 518.3
Ependymitis (acute) (cerebral) (chronic) (granular) — *see also* Meningitis 322.9
Ependymoblastoma (M9392/3)
  specified site — *see* Neoplasm, by site, malignant
  unspecified site 191.9
Ependymoma (epithelial) (malignant) (M9391/3)
  anaplastic type (M9392/3)
    specified site — *see* Neoplasm, by site, malignant
    unspecified site 191.9
  benign (M9391/0)
    specified site — *see* Neoplasm, by site, benign
    unspecified site 225.0
  myxopapillary (M9394/1) 237.5
  papillary (M9393/1) 237.5
    specified site — *see* Neoplasm, by site, malignant
    unspecified site 191.9
Ependymopathy 349.2
  spinal cord 349.2
Ephelides, ephelis 709.09
Ephemeral fever — *see also* Pyrexia 780.60
Epiblepharon (congenital) 743.62
Epicanthus, epicanthic fold (congenital) (eyelid) 743.63
Epicondylitis (elbow) (lateral) 726.32
  medial 726.31
Epicystitis — *see also* Cystitis 595.9
Epidemic — *see* condition
Epidermidalization, cervix — *see* condition
Epidermidization, cervix — *see* condition
Epidermis, epidermal — *see* condition
Epidermization, cervix — *see* condition

Epidermodysplasia verruciformis 078.19
Epidermoid
  cholesteatoma — *see* Cholesteatoma
  inclusion (*see also* Cyst, skin) 706.2
Epidermolysis
  acuta (combustiformis) (toxica) 695.15
  bullosa 757.39
  necroticans combustiformis 695.15
    due to drug
      correct substance properly administered 695.15
      overdose or wrong substance given or taken 977.9
        specified drug — *see* Table of Drugs and Chemicals
Epidermophytid — *see* Dermatophytosis
Epidermophytosis (infected) — *see* Dermatophytosis
Epidermosis, ear (middle) — *see also* Cholesteatoma 385.30
Epididymis — *see* condition
Epididymitis (nonvenereal) 604.90
  with abscess 604.0
  acute 604.99
  blennorrhagic (acute) 098.0
    chronic or duration of 2 months or over 098.2
  caseous (*see also* Tuberculosis) 016.4 ☑
  chlamydial 099.54
  diphtheritic 032.89 *[604.91]*
  filarial 125.9 *[604.91]*
  gonococcal (acute) 098.0
    chronic or duration of 2 months or over 098.2
  recurrent 604.99
  residual 604.99
  syphilitic 095.8 *[604.91]*
  tuberculous (*see also* Tuberculosis) 016.4 ☑
Epididymo-orchitis — *see also* Epididymitis 604.90
  with abscess 604.0
  chlamydial 099.54
  gonococcal (acute) 098.13
    chronic or duration of 2 months or over 098.33
Epidural — *see* condition
Epigastritis — *see also* Gastritis 535.5 ☑
Epigastrium, epigastric — *see* condition
Epigastrocele — *see also* Hernia, epigastric 553.29
Epiglottiditis (acute) 464.30
  with obstruction 464.31
  chronic 476.1
  viral 464.30
    with obstruction 464.31
Epiglottis — *see* condition
Epiglottitis (acute) 464.30
  with obstruction 464.31
  chronic 476.1
  viral 464.30
    with obstruction 464.31
Epignathus 759.4
Epilepsia
  partialis continua (*see also* Epilepsy) 345.7 ☑
  procursiva (*see also* Epilepsy) 345.8 ☑
Epilepsy, epileptic (idiopathic) 345.9 ☑

> Note — Use the following fifth-digit subclassification with categories 345.0, 345.1, 345.4–345.9:
>
> 0   without mention of intractable epilepsy
>
> 1   with intractable epilepsy
>
> ▶ pharmacoresistant (pharmacologically resistant)
>
>   poorly controlled
>
>   refractory (medically)
>
>   treatment resistant ◀

  abdominal 345.5 ☑
  absence (attack) 345.0 ☑
  akinetic 345.0 ☑
    psychomotor 345.4 ☑
  automatism 345.4 ☑
  autonomic diencephalic 345.5 ☑

Epilepsy, epileptic — *continued*
  brain 345.9 ☑
  Bravais-Jacksonian 345.5 ☑
  cerebral 345.9 ☑
  climacteric 345.9 ☑
  clonic 345.1 ☑
  clouded state 345.9 ☑
  coma 345.3
  communicating 345.4 ☑
  complicating pregnancy, childbirth, or the puerperium 649.4 ☑
  congenital 345.9 ☑
  convulsions 345.9 ☑
  cortical (focal) (motor) 345.5 ☑
  cursive (running) 345.8 ☑
  cysticercosis 123.1
  deterioration
    with behavioral disturbance 345.9 ☑ *[294.11]*
    without behavioral disturbance 345.9 ☑ *[294.10]*
  due to syphilis 094.89
  equivalent 345.5 ☑
  fit 345.9 ☑
  focal (motor) 345.5 ☑
  gelastic 345.8 ☑
  generalized 345.9 ☑
    convulsive 345.1 ☑
    flexion 345.1 ☑
    nonconvulsive 345.0 ☑
  grand mal (idiopathic) 345.1 ☑
  Jacksonian (motor) (sensory) 345.5 ☑
  Kojevnikoff's, Kojevnikov's, Kojewnikoff's 345.7 ☑
  laryngeal 786.2
  limbic system 345.4 ☑
  localization related (focal) (partial) and epileptic syndromes
    with
      complex partial seizures 345.4 ☑
      simple partial seizures 345.5 ☑
  major (motor) 345.1 ☑
  minor 345.0 ☑
  mixed (type) 345.9 ☑
  motor partial 345.5 ☑
  musicogenic 345.1 ☑
  myoclonus, myoclonic 345.1 ☑
    progressive (familial) 345.1 ☑ ▲
  nonconvulsive, generalized 345.0 ☑
  parasitic NEC 123.9
  partial (focalized) 345.5 ☑
    with
      impairment of consciousness 345.4 ☑
      memory and ideational disturbances 345.4 ☑
    without impairment of consciousness 345.5 ☑
    abdominal type 345.5 ☑
    motor type 345.5 ☑
    psychomotor type 345.4 ☑
    psychosensory type 345.4 ☑
    secondarily generalized 345.4 ☑
    sensory type 345.5 ☑
    somatomotor type 345.5 ☑
    somatosensory type 345.5 ☑
    temporal lobe type 345.4 ☑
    visceral type 345.5 ☑
    visual type 345.5 ☑
  peripheral 345.9 ☑
  petit mal 345.0 ☑
  photokinetic 345.8 ☑
  progressive myoclonic (familial) 345.1 ☑ ▲
  psychic equivalent 345.5 ☑
  psychomotor 345.4 ☑
  psychosensory 345.4 ☑
  reflex 345.1 ☑
  seizure 345.9 ☑
  senile 345.9 ☑
  sensory-induced 345.5 ☑
  sleep (*see also* Narcolepsy) 347.00
  somatomotor type 345.5 ☑
  somatosensory 345.5 ☑
  specified type NEC 345.8 ☑

☑ Additional Digit Required — Refer to the Tabular List for Digit Selection

▽ Subterms under main terms may continue to next column or page

▶◀ Revised Text   ● New Line   ▲ Revised Code

Epilepsy, epileptic — continued
- status (grand mal) 345.3
  - focal motor 345.7 ☑
  - petit mal 345.2
  - psychomotor 345.7 ☑
  - temporal lobe 345.7 ☑
- symptomatic 345.9 ☑
- temporal lobe 345.4 ☑
- tonic (-clonic) 345.1 ☑
- traumatic (injury unspecified) 907.0
  - injury specified — see Late, effect (of) specified injury
- twilight 293.0
- uncinate (gyrus) 345.4 ☑
- ▶Unverricht◀ (-Lundborg) (familial myoclonic) 345.1 ☑ ▲
- visceral 345.5 ☑
- visual 345.5 ☑

Epileptiform
- convulsions 780.39
- seizure 780.39

Epiloia 759.5
Epimenorrhea 626.2
Epipharyngitis — see also Nasopharyngitis 460
Epiphora 375.20
- due to
  - excess lacrimation 375.21
  - insufficient drainage 375.22

Epiphyseal arrest 733.91
- femoral head 732.2

Epiphyseolysis, epiphysiolysis — see also Osteochondrosis 732.9
Epiphysitis — see also Osteochondrosis 732.9
- juvenile 732.6
- marginal (Scheuermann's) 732.0
- os calcis 732.5
- syphilitic (congenital) 090.0
- vertebral (Scheuermann's) 732.0

Epiplocele — see also Hernia 553.9
Epiploitis — see also Peritonitis 567.9
Epiplosarcomphalocele — see also Hernia, umbilicus 553.1
Episcleritis 379.00
- gouty 274.89 [379.09]
- nodular 379.02
- periodica fugax 379.01
  - angioneurotic — see Edema, angioneurotic
- specified NEC 379.09
- staphylococcal 379.00
- suppurative 379.00
- syphilitic 095.0
- tuberculous (see also Tuberculosis) 017.3 ☑ [379.09]

Episode
- brain (see also Disease, cerebrovascular, acute) 436
- cerebral (see also Disease, cerebrovascular, acute) 436
- depersonalization (in neurotic state) 300.6
- hyporesponsive 780.09
- psychotic (see also Psychosis) 298.9
  - organic, transient 293.9
- schizophrenic (acute) NEC (see also Schizophrenia) 295.4 ☑

Epispadias
- female 753.8
- male 752.62

Episplenitis 289.59
Epistaxis (multiple) 784.7
- hereditary 448.0
- vicarious menstruation 625.8

Epithelioma (malignant) (M8011/3) — see also Neoplasm, by site, malignant
- adenoides cysticum (M8100/0) — see Neoplasm, skin, benign
- basal cell (M8090/3) — see Neoplasm, skin, malignant
- benign (M8011/0) — see Neoplasm, by site, benign
- Bowen's (M8081/2) — see Neoplasm, skin, in situ
- calcifying (benign) (Malherbe's) (M8110/0) — see Neoplasm, skin, benign
- external site — see Neoplasm, skin, malignant

Epithelioma — see also Neoplasm, by site, malignant — continued
- intraepidermal, Jadassohn (M8096/0) — see Neoplasm, skin, benign
- squamous cell (M8070/3) — see Neoplasm, by site, malignant

Epitheliopathy
- pigment, retina 363.15
- posterior multifocal placoid (acute) 363.15

Epithelium, epithelial — see condition
Epituberculosis (allergic) (with atelectasis) — see also Tuberculosis 010.8 ☑
Eponychia 757.5
Epstein's
- nephrosis or syndrome (see also Nephrosis) 581.9
- pearl (mouth) 528.4

Epstein-Barr infection (viral) 075
- chronic 780.79 [139.8]

Epulis (giant cell) (gingiva) 523.8
Equinia 024
Equinovarus (congenital) 754.51
- acquired 736.71

Equivalent
- angina 413.9 ●
- convulsive (abdominal) (see also Epilepsy) 345.5 ☑
- epileptic (psychic) (see also Epilepsy) 345.5 ☑

Erb's
- disease 359.1
- palsy, paralysis (birth) (brachial) (newborn) 767.6
  - spinal (spastic) syphilitic 094.89
- pseudohypertrophic muscular dystrophy 359.1

Erb-Goldflam disease or syndrome 358.00
Erb (-Duchenne) paralysis (birth injury) (newborn) 767.6
Erdheim-Chester disease (ECD) 277.89 ●
Erdheim's syndrome (acromegalic macrospondylitis) 253.0
Erection, painful (persistent) 607.3
Ergosterol deficiency (vitamin D) 268.9
- with
  - osteomalacia 268.2
  - rickets (see also Rickets) 268.0

Ergotism (ergotized grain) 988.2
- from ergot used as drug (migraine therapy)
  - correct substance properly administered 349.82
  - overdose or wrong substance given or taken 975.0

Erichsen's disease (railway spine) 300.16
Erlacher-Blount syndrome (tibia vara) 732.4
Erosio interdigitalis blastomycetica 112.3
Erosion
- arteriosclerotic plaque — see Arteriosclerosis, by site
- artery NEC 447.2
  - without rupture 447.8
- bone 733.99
- bronchus 519.19
- cartilage (joint) 733.99
- cervix (uteri) (acquired) (chronic) (congenital) 622.0
  - with mention of cervicitis 616.0
- cornea (recurrent) (see also Keratitis) 371.42
  - traumatic 918.1
- dental (idiopathic) (occupational) 521.30
  - extending into
    - dentine 521.32
    - pulp 521.33
  - generalized 521.35
  - limited to enamel 521.31
  - localized 521.34
- duodenum, postpyloric — see Ulcer, duodenum
- esophagus 530.89
- gastric 535.4 ☑
- intestine 569.89
- lymphatic vessel 457.8
- pylorus, pyloric (ulcer) 535.4 ☑
- sclera 379.16
- spine, aneurysmal 094.89
- spleen 289.59
- stomach 535.4 ☑

Erosion — continued
- teeth (idiopathic) (occupational) (see also Erosion, dental) 521.30
  - due to
    - medicine 521.30
    - persistent vomiting 521.30
- urethra 599.84
- uterus 621.8
- vertebra 733.99

Erotomania 302.89
- Clérambault's 297.8

Error
- in diet 269.9
- refractive 367.9
  - astigmatism (see also Astigmatism) 367.20
  - drug-induced 367.89
  - hypermetropia 367.0
  - hyperopia 367.0
  - myopia 367.1
  - presbyopia 367.4
  - toxic 367.89

Eructation 787.3
- nervous 306.4
- psychogenic 306.4

Eruption
- creeping 126.9
- drug — see Dermatitis, due to, drug
- Hutchinson, summer 692.72
- Kaposi's varicelliform 054.0
- napkin (psoriasiform) 691.0
- polymorphous
  - light (sun) 692.72
  - other source 692.82
- psoriasiform, napkin 691.0
- recalcitrant pustular 694.8
- ringed 695.89
- skin (see also Dermatitis) 782.1
  - creeping (meaning hookworm) 126.9
  - due to
    - chemical(s) NEC 692.4
      - internal use 693.8
    - drug — see Dermatitis, due to, drug
    - prophylactic inoculation or vaccination against disease — see Dermatitis, due to, vaccine
    - smallpox vaccination NEC — see Dermatitis, due to, vaccine
  - erysipeloid 027.1
  - feigned 698.4
  - Hutchinson, summer 692.72
  - Kaposi's, varicelliform 054.0
    - vaccinia 999.0
  - lichenoid, axilla 698.3
  - polymorphous, due to light 692.72
  - toxic NEC 695.0
  - vesicular 709.8
- teeth, tooth
  - accelerated 520.6
  - delayed 520.6
  - difficult 520.6
  - disturbance of 520.6
  - in abnormal sequence 520.6
  - incomplete 520.6
  - late 520.6
  - natal 520.6
  - neonatal 520.6
  - obstructed 520.6
  - partial 520.6
  - persistent primary 520.6
  - premature 520.6
  - prenatal 520.6
- vesicular 709.8

Erysipelas (gangrenous) (infantile) (newborn) (phlegmonous) (suppurative) 035
- external ear 035 [380.13]
- puerperal, postpartum, childbirth 670.8 ☑ ▲

Erysipelatoid (Rosenbach's) 027.1
Erysipeloid (Rosenbach's) 027.1
Erythema, erythematous (generalized) 695.9
- ab igne — see Burn, by site, first degree
- annulare (centrifugum) (rheumaticum) 695.0
- arthriticum epidemicum 026.1
- brucellum (see also Brucellosis) 023.9
- bullosum 695.19
- caloricum — see Burn, by site, first degree

Erythema, erythematous — continued
- chronicum migrans 088.81
- circinatum 695.19
- diaper 691.0
- due to
  - chemical (contact) NEC 692.4
    - internal 693.8
  - drug (internal use) 693.0
    - contact 692.3
- elevatum diutinum 695.89
- endemic 265.2
- epidemic, arthritic 026.1
- figuratum perstans 695.0
- gluteal 691.0
- gyratum (perstans) (repens) 695.19
- heat — see Burn, by site, first degree
- ichthyosiforme congenitum 757.1
- induratum (primary) (scrofulosorum) (see also Tuberculosis) 017.1 ☑
  - nontuberculous 695.2
- infantum febrile 057.8
- infectional NEC 695.9
- infectiosum 057.0
- inflammation NEC 695.9
- intertrigo 695.89
- iris 695.10
- lupus (discoid) (localized) (see also Lupus, erythematosus) 695.4
- marginatum 695.0
  - rheumaticum — see Fever, rheumatic
- medicamentosum — see Dermatitis, due to, drug
- migrans 529.1
  - chronicum 088.81
- multiforme 695.10
  - bullosum 695.19
  - conjunctiva 695.19
  - exudativum (Hebra) 695.19
  - major 695.12
  - minor 695.11
  - pemphigoides 694.5
- napkin 691.0
- neonatorum 778.8
- nodosum 695.2
  - tuberculous (see also Tuberculosis) 017.1 ☑
- nummular, nummulare 695.19
- palmar 695.0
- palmaris hereditarium 695.0
- pernio 991.5
- perstans solare 692.72
- rash, newborn 778.8
- scarlatiniform (exfoliative) (recurrent) 695.0
- simplex marginatum 057.8
- solare (see also Sunburn) 692.71
- streptogenes 696.5
- toxic, toxicum NEC 695.0
  - newborn 778.8
- tuberculous (primary) (see also Tuberculosis) 017.0 ☑
- venenatum 695.0

Erythematosus — see condition
Erythematous — see condition
Erythermalgia (primary) 443.82
Erythralgia 443.82
Erythrasma 039.0
Erythredema 985.0
- polyneuritica 985.0
- polyneuropathy 985.0

Erythremia (acute) (M9841/3) 207.0 ☑
- chronic (M9842/3) 207.1 ☑
- secondary 289.0

Erythroblastopenia (acquired) 284.89
- congenital 284.01

Erythroblastophthisis 284.01
Erythroblastosis (fetalis) (newborn) 773.2
- due to
  - ABO
    - antibodies 773.1
    - incompatibility, maternal/fetal 773.1
    - isoimmunization 773.1
  - Rh
    - antibodies 773.0
    - incompatibility, maternal/fetal 773.0
    - isoimmunization 773.0

Erythrocyanosis (crurum) 443.89

☑ Additional Digit Required — Refer to the Tabular List for Digit Selection   ▽ Subterms under main terms may continue to next column or page

2010 ICD-9-CM   ▶◀ Revised Text   ● New Line   ▲ Revised Code   **October 2009 · Volume 2 — 105**

Erythrocythemia — see Erythremia
Erythrocytopenia 285.9
Erythrocytosis (megalosplenic)
   familial 289.6
   oval, hereditary (see also Elliptocytosis) 282.1
   secondary 289.0
   stress 289.0
Erythroderma — see also Erythema 695.9
   desquamativa (in infants) 695.89
   exfoliative 695.89
   ichthyosiform, congenital 757.1
   infantum 695.89
   maculopapular 696.2
   neonatorum 778.8
   psoriaticum 696.1
   secondary 695.9
Erythrodysesthesia, palmar plantar (PPE)
   693.0
Erythrogenesis imperfecta 284.09
Erythroleukemia (M9840/3) 207.0 ☑
Erythromelalgia 443.82
Erythromelia 701.8
Erythropenia 285.9
Erythrophagocytosis 289.9
Erythrophobia 300.23
Erythroplakia
   oral mucosa 528.79
   tongue 528.79
Erythroplasia (Queyrat) (M8080/2)
   specified site — see Neoplasm, skin, in situ
   unspecified site 233.5
Erythropoiesis, idiopathic ineffective 285.0
Escaped beats, heart 427.60
   postoperative 997.1
Esoenteritis — see Enteritis
Esophagalgia 530.89
Esophagectasis 530.89
   due to cardiospasm 530.0
Esophagismus 530.5
Esophagitis (alkaline) (chemical) (chronic) (infectional) (necrotic) (peptic) (postoperative) (regurgitant) 530.10
   acute 530.12
   candidal 112.84
   eosinophilic 530.13
   reflux 530.11
   specified NEC 530.19
   tuberculous (see also Tuberculosis) 017.8 ☑
   ulcerative 530.19
Esophagocele 530.6
Esophagodynia 530.89
Esophagomalacia 530.89
Esophagoptosis 530.89
Esophagospasm 530.5
Esophagostenosis 530.3
Esophagostomiasis 127.7
Esophagostomy
   complication 530.87
      infection 530.86
      malfunctioning 530.87
      mechanical 530.87
Esophagotracheal — see condition
Esophagus — see condition
Esophoria 378.41
   convergence, excess 378.84
   divergence, insufficiency 378.85
Esotropia (nonaccommodative) 378.00
   accommodative 378.35
   alternating 378.05
      with
         A pattern 378.06
         specified noncomitancy NEC 378.08
         V pattern 378.07
         X pattern 378.08
         Y pattern 378.08
      intermittent 378.22
   intermittent 378.20
      alternating 378.22
      monocular 378.21
   monocular 378.01
      with
         A pattern 378.02
         specified noncomitancy NEC 378.04
         V pattern 378.03
         X pattern 378.04
         Y pattern 378.04

Esotropia — continued
   monocular — continued
      intermittent 378.21
Espundia 085.5
Essential — see condition
Esterapenia 289.89
Esthesioneuroblastoma (M9522/3) 160.0
Esthesioneurocytoma (M9521/3) 160.0
Esthesioneuroepithelioma (M9523/3) 160.0
Esthiomene 099.1
Estivo-autumnal
   fever 084.0
   malaria 084.0
Estrangement V61.09
Estriasis 134.0
Ethanolaminuria 270.8
Ethanolism — see also Alcoholism 303.9 ☑
Ether dependence, dependency — see also
   Dependence 304.6 ☑
Etherism — see also Dependence 304.6 ☑
Ethmoid, ethmoidal — see condition
Ethmoiditis (chronic) (nonpurulent) (purulent)
   — see also Sinusitis, ethmoidal 473.2
   influenzal 487.1
   Woakes' 471.1
Ethylism — see also Alcoholism 303.9 ☑
Eulenburg's disease (congenital paramyotonia)
   359.29
Eunuchism 257.2
Eunuchoidism 257.2
   hypogonadotropic 257.2
European blastomycosis 117.5
Eustachian — see condition
Euthyroidism 244.9
Euthyroid sick syndrome 790.94
Evaluation
   fetal lung maturity 659.8 ☑
   for suspected condition (see also Observation)
      V71.9
      abuse V71.81
      exposure
         anthrax V71.82
         biologic agent NEC V71.83
         SARS V71.83
      neglect V71.81
      newborn — see Observation, suspected, condition, newborn
      specified condition NEC V71.89
   mental health V70.2
      requested by authority V70.1
   nursing care V63.8
   social service V63.8
Evans' syndrome (thrombocytopenic purpura)
   287.32
**Event, apparent life threatening in newborn ●
   and infant** (ALTE) 799.82
Eventration
   colon into chest — see Hernia, diaphragm
   diaphragm (congenital) 756.6
Eversion
   bladder 596.8
   cervix (uteri) 622.0
      with mention of cervicitis 616.0
   foot NEC 736.79
      congenital 755.67
   lacrimal punctum 375.51
   punctum lacrimale (postinfectional) (senile)
      375.51
   ureter (meatus) 593.89
   urethra (meatus) 599.84
   uterus 618.1
      complicating delivery 665.2 ☑
         affecting fetus or newborn 763.89
      puerperal, postpartum 674.8 ☑
Evidence
   of malignancy
      cytologic
         without histologic confirmation
            anus 796.76
            cervix 795.06
            vagina 795.16
Evisceration
   birth injury 767.8
   bowel (congenital) — see Hernia, ventral
   congenital (see also Hernia, ventral) 553.29
   operative wound 998.32

Evisceration — continued
   traumatic NEC 869.1
      eye 871.3
Evulsion — see Avulsion
Ewing's
   angioendothelioma (M9260/3) — see Neoplasm, bone, malignant
   sarcoma (M9260/3) — see Neoplasm, bone, malignant
   tumor (M9260/3) — see Neoplasm, bone, malignant
Exaggerated lumbosacral angle (with impinging spine) 756.12
Examination (general) (routine) (of) (for) V70.9
   allergy V72.7
   annual V70.0
   cardiovascular preoperative V72.81
   cervical Papanicolaou smear V76.2
      as a part of routine gynecological examination V72.31
      to confirm findings of recent normal smear following initial abnormal smear V72.32
   child care (routine) V20.2
   clinical research investigation (normal control patient) (participant) V70.7
   dental V72.2
   developmental testing (child) (infant) V20.2
   donor (potential) V70.8
   ear V72.19
   eye V72.0
   following
      accident (motor vehicle) V71.4
      alleged rape or seduction (victim or culprit) V71.5
      inflicted injury (victim or culprit) NEC V71.6
      rape or seduction, alleged (victim or culprit) V71.5
      treatment (for) V67.9
         combined V67.6
         fracture V67.4
         involving high-risk medication NEC V67.51
         mental disorder V67.3
         specified condition NEC V67.59
   follow-up (routine) (following) V67.9
      cancer chemotherapy V67.2
      chemotherapy V67.2
      disease V67.59
      high-risk medication NEC V67.51
      injury NEC V67.59
      population survey V70.6
      postpartum V24.2
      psychiatric V67.3
      psychotherapy V67.3
      radiotherapy V67.1
      specified surgery NEC V67.09
      surgery V67.00
         vaginal pap smear V67.01
   gynecological V72.31
      for contraceptive maintenance V25.40
         intrauterine device V25.42
         pill V25.41
         specified method NEC V25.49
   health (of)
      armed forces personnel V70.5
      checkup V70.0
      child, routine V20.2
      defined subpopulation NEC V70.5
      inhabitants of institutions V70.5
      occupational V70.5
      pre-employment screening V70.5
      preschool children V70.5
         for admission to school V70.3
      prisoners V70.5
         for entrance into prison V70.3
      prostitutes V70.5
      refugees V70.5
      school children V70.5
      students V70.5
   hearing V72.19
      following failed hearing screening V72.11
   infant
      8 to 28 days old V20.32 ●
      over 28 days old, routine V20.2 ●
      under 8 days old V20.31 ●

Examination — continued
   laboratory V72.60 ▲
      ordered as part of a routine general medical examination V72.62 ●
      pre-operative V72.63 ●
      pre-procedural V72.63 ●
      specified NEC V72.69 ●
   lactating mother V24.1
   medical (for) (of) V70.9
      administrative purpose NEC V70.3
      admission to
         old age home V70.3
         prison V70.3
         school V70.3
      adoption V70.3
      armed forces personnel V70.5
      at health care facility V70.0
      camp V70.3
      child, routine V20.2
      clinical research (control) (normal comparison) (participant) V70.7
      defined subpopulation NEC V70.5
      donor (potential) V70.8
      driving license V70.3
      general V70.9
         routine V70.0
         specified reason NEC V70.8
      immigration V70.3
      inhabitants of institutions V70.5
      insurance certification V70.3
      marriage V70.3
      medicolegal reasons V70.4
      naturalization V70.3
      occupational V70.5
      population survey V70.6
      pre-employment V70.5
      preschool children V70.5
         for admission to school V70.3
      prison V70.3
      prisoners V70.5
         for entrance into prison V70.3
      prostitutes V70.5
      refugees V70.5
      school children V70.5
      specified reason NEC V70.8
      sport competition V70.3
      students V70.5
   medicolegal reason V70.4
   pelvic (annual) (periodic) V72.31
   periodic (annual) (routine) V70.0
   postpartum
      immediately after delivery V24.0
      routine follow-up V24.2
   pregnancy (unconfirmed) (possible) V72.40
      negative result V72.41
      positive result V72.42
   prenatal V22.1
      first pregnancy V22.0
      high-risk pregnancy V23.9
         specified problem NEC V23.89
   preoperative V72.84
      cardiovascular V72.81
      respiratory V72.82
      specified NEC V72.83
   preprocedural V72.84
      cardiovascular V72.81
      general physical V72.83
      respiratory V72.82
      specified NEC V72.83
   prior to chemotherapy V72.83 ●
   psychiatric V70.2
      follow-up not needing further care V67.3
      requested by authority V70.1
   radiological NEC V72.5
   respiratory preoperative V72.82
   screening — see Screening
   sensitization V72.7
   skin V72.7
      hypersensitivity V72.7
   special V72.9
   specified type or reason NEC V72.85
      preoperative V72.83
         specified NEC V72.83
   teeth V72.2
   vaginal Papanicolaou smear V76.47

Extravasation — *continued*
　vesicant — *continued*
　　chemotherapy 999.81 ▲
Extremity — *see* condition
Extrophy — *see* Exstrophy
Extroversion
　bladder 753.5
　uterus 618.1
　　complicating delivery 665.2 ☑
　　　affecting fetus or newborn 763.89
　　postpartal (old) 618.1
Extruded tooth 524.34
Extrusion
　alveolus and teeth 524.75
　breast implant (prosthetic) 996.54
　device, implant, or graft — *see* Complications, mechanical
　eye implant (ball) (globe) 996.59
　intervertebral disc — *see* Displacement, intervertebral disc
　lacrimal gland 375.43
　mesh (reinforcing) 996.59
　ocular lens implant 996.53
　prosthetic device NEC — *see* Complications, mechanical
　vitreous 379.26
Exudate, pleura — *see* Effusion, pleura
Exudates, retina 362.82
Exudative — *see* condition
Eye, eyeball, eyelid — *see* condition
Eyestrain 368.13
Eyeworm disease of Africa 125.2

F

Faber's anemia or syndrome (achlorhydric anemia) 280.9
Fabry's disease (angiokeratoma corporis diffusum) 272.7
Face, facial — *see* condition
Facet of cornea 371.44
Faciocephalalgia, autonomic — *see also* Neuropathy, peripheral, autonomic 337.9
Facioscapulohumeral myopathy 359.1
Factitious disorder, illness — *see* Illness, factitious
Factor
　deficiency — *see* Deficiency, factor
　psychic, associated with diseases classified elsewhere 316
　risk — *see* Problem
Fahr-Volhard disease (malignant nephrosclerosis) 403.00
Failure, failed
　adenohypophyseal 253.2
　attempted abortion (legal) (*see also* Abortion, failed) 638.9
　bone marrow (anemia) 284.9
　　acquired (secondary) 284.89
　　congenital 284.09
　　idiopathic 284.9
　cardiac (*see also* Failure, heart) 428.9
　　newborn 779.89
　cardiorenal (chronic) 428.9
　　hypertensive (*see also* Hypertension, cardiorenal) 404.93
　cardiorespiratory 799.1
　　specified during or due to a procedure 997.1
　　long-term effect of cardiac surgery 429.4
　cardiovascular (chronic) 428.9
　cerebrovascular 437.8
　cervical dilatation in labor 661.0 ☑
　　affecting fetus or newborn 763.7
　circulation, circulatory 799.89
　　fetus or newborn 779.89
　　peripheral 785.50
　compensation — *see* Disease, heart
　congestive (*see also* Failure, heart) 428.0
　conscious sedation, during procedure 995.24 ●
　coronary (*see also* Insufficiency, coronary) 411.89
　dental implant 525.79
　　due to
　　　infection 525.71
　　　lack of attached gingiva 525.72

Failure, failed — *continued*
　dental implant — *continued*
　　due to — *continued*
　　　occlusal trauma (caused by poor prosthetic design) 525.72
　　　parafunctional habits 525.72
　　　periodontal infection (peri-implantitis) 525.72
　　　poor oral hygiene 525.72
　　　unintentional loading 525.71
　　endosseous NEC 525.79
　　mechanical 525.73
　　osseointegration 525.71
　　　due to
　　　　complications of systemic disease 525.71
　　　　poor bone quality 525.71
　　　　premature loading 525.71
　　　iatrogenic 525.71
　　　prior to intentional prosthetic loading 525.71
　　post-osseointegration
　　　biological 525.72
　　　iatrogenic 525.72
　　　due to complications of systemic disease 525.72
　　　mechanical 525.73
　　pre-integration 525.71
　　pre-osseointegration 525.71
　　dental prosthesis causing loss of dental implant 525.73
　dental restoration
　　marginal integrity 525.61
　　periodontal anatomical integrity 525.65
　descent of head (at term) 652.5 ☑
　　affecting fetus or newborn 763.1
　　in labor 660.0 ☑
　　　affecting fetus or newborn 763.1
　device, implant, or graft — *see* Complications, mechanical
　engagement of head NEC 652.5 ☑
　　in labor 660.0 ☑
　extrarenal 788.99
　fetal head to enter pelvic brim 652.5 ☑
　　affecting fetus or newborn 763.1
　　in labor 660.0 ☑
　　　affecting fetus or newborn 763.1
　forceps NEC 660.7 ☑
　　affecting fetus or newborn 763.1
　fusion (joint) (spinal) 996.49
　growth in childhood 783.43
　heart (acute) (sudden) 428.9
　　with
　　　abortion — *see* Abortion, by type, with specified complication NEC
　　　acute pulmonary edema (*see also* Failure, ventricular, left) 428.1
　　　　with congestion (*see also* Failure, heart) 428.0
　　　decompensation (*see also* Failure, heart) 428.0
　　　dilation — *see* Disease, heart
　　　ectopic pregnancy (*see also* categories 633.0–633.9) 639.8
　　　molar pregnancy (*see also* categories 630–632) 639.8
　　arteriosclerotic 440.9
　　combined left-right sided 428.0
　　combined systolic and diastolic 428.40
　　　acute 428.41
　　　acute on chronic 428.43
　　　chronic 428.42
　　compensated (*see also* Failure, heart) 428.0
　　complicating
　　　abortion — *see* Abortion, by type, with specified complication NEC
　　　delivery (cesarean) (instrumental) 669.4 ☑
　　　ectopic pregnancy (*see also* categories 633.0–633.9) 639.8
　　　molar pregnancy (*see also* categories 630–632) 639.8
　　　obstetric anesthesia or sedation 668.1 ☑
　　　surgery 997.1

Failure, failed — *continued*
　heart — *continued*
　　congestive (compensated) (decompensated) (*see also* Failure, heart) 428.0
　　　with rheumatic fever (conditions classifiable to 390)
　　　　active 391.8
　　　　inactive or quiescent (with chorea) 398.91
　　　fetus or newborn 779.89
　　　hypertensive (*see also* Hypertension, heart) 402.91
　　　　with renal disease (*see also* Hypertension, cardiorenal) 404.91
　　　　　with renal failure 404.93
　　　　benign 402.11
　　　　malignant 402.01
　　　rheumatic (chronic) (inactive) (with chorea) 398.91
　　　　active or acute 391.8
　　　　　with chorea (Sydenham's) 392.0
　　decompensated (*see also* Failure, heart) 428.0
　　degenerative (*see also* Degeneration, myocardial) 429.1
　　diastolic 428.30
　　　acute 428.31
　　　acute on chronic 428.33
　　　chronic 428.32
　　due to presence of (cardiac) prosthesis 429.4
　　fetus or newborn 779.89
　　following
　　　abortion 639.8
　　　cardiac surgery 429.4
　　　ectopic or molar pregnancy 639.8
　　high output NEC 428.9
　　hypertensive (*see also* Hypertension, heart) 402.91
　　　with renal disease (*see also* Hypertension, cardiorenal) 404.91
　　　　with renal failure 404.93
　　　benign 402.11
　　　malignant 402.01
　　left (ventricular) (*see also* Failure, ventricular, left) 428.1
　　　with right-sided failure (see also Failure, heart) 428.0
　　low output (syndrome) NEC 428.9
　　organic — *see* Disease, heart
　　postoperative (immediate) 997.1
　　　long term effect of cardiac surgery 429.4
　　rheumatic (chronic) (congestive) (inactive) 398.91
　　right (secondary to left heart failure, conditions classifiable to 428.1) (ventricular) (*see also* Failure, heart) 428.0
　　senile 797
　　specified during or due to a procedure 997.1
　　　long-term effect of cardiac surgery 429.4
　　systolic 428.20
　　　acute 428.21
　　　acute on chronic 428.23
　　　chronic 428.22
　　thyrotoxic (*see also* Thyrotoxicosis) 242.9 ☑ [425.7]
　　valvular — *see* Endocarditis
　hepatic 572.8
　　acute 570
　　due to a procedure 997.4
　hepatorenal 572.4
　hypertensive heart (*see also* Hypertension, heart) 402.91
　　benign 402.11
　　malignant 402.01
　induction (of labor) 659.1 ☑
　　abortion (legal) (*see also* Abortion, failed) 638.9
　　affecting fetus or newborn 763.89
　　by oxytocic drugs 659.1 ☑
　　instrumental 659.0 ☑
　　mechanical 659.0 ☑
　　medical 659.1 ☑

Failure, failed — *continued*
　induction — *continued*
　　surgical 659.0 ☑
　initial alveolar expansion, newborn 770.4
　involution, thymus (gland) 254.8
　kidney — *see* Failure, renal
　lactation 676.4 ☑
　Leydig's cell, adult 257.2
　liver 572.8
　　acute 570
　medullary 799.89
　mitral — *see* Endocarditis, mitral
　moderate sedation, during procedure 995.24 ●
　myocardium, myocardial (*see also* Failure, heart) 428.9
　　chronic (*see also* Failure, heart) 428.0
　　congestive (*see also* Failure, heart) 428.0
　ovarian (primary) 256.39
　　iatrogenic 256.2
　　postablative 256.2
　　postirradiation 256.2
　　postsurgical 256.2
　ovulation 628.0
　prerenal 788.99
　renal ▶(kidney)◄ 586
　　with
　　　abortion — *see* Abortion, by type, with renal failure
　　　ectopic pregnancy (*see also* categories 633.0–633.9) 639.3
　　　edema (*see also* Nephrosis) 581.9
　　　hypertension (*see also* Hypertension, kidney) 403.91
　　　hypertensive heart disease (conditions classifiable to 402) 404.92
　　　　with heart failure 404.93
　　　　benign 404.12
　　　　　with heart failure 404.13
　　　　malignant 404.02
　　　　　with heart failure 404.03
　　　molar pregnancy (*see also* categories 630–632) 639.3
　　　tubular necrosis (acute) 584.5
　　acute 584.9
　　　with lesion of
　　　　necrosis
　　　　　cortical (renal) 584.6
　　　　　medullary (renal) (papillary) 584.7
　　　　　tubular 584.5
　　　　specified pathology NEC 584.8
　　chronic 585.9
　　　hypertensive or with hypertension (*see also* Hypertension, kidney) 403.91
　　due to a procedure 997.5
　　following
　　　abortion 639.3
　　　crushing 958.5
　　　ectopic or molar pregnancy 639.3
　　　labor and delivery (acute) 669.3 ☑
　　hypertensive (*see also* Hypertension, kidney) 403.91
　　puerperal, postpartum 669.3 ☑
　respiration, respiratory 518.81
　　acute 518.81
　　acute and chronic 518.84
　　center 348.89 ▲
　　　newborn 770.84
　　chronic 518.83
　　due to trauma, surgery or shock 518.5
　　newborn 770.84
　rotation
　　cecum 751.4
　　colon 751.4
　　intestine 751.4
　　kidney 753.3
　sedation, during procedure ●
　　conscious 995.24 ●
　　moderate 995.24 ●
　segmentation (*see also* Fusion)
　　fingers (*see also* Syndactylism, fingers) 755.11
　　toes (*see also* Syndactylism, toes) 755.13
　seminiferous tubule, adult 257.2
　senile (general) 797

☑ Additional Digit Required — Refer to the Tabular List for Digit Selection　　　　　▼ Subterms under main terms may continue to next column or page

108 — Volume 2 • October 2009　　▶◄ Revised Text　　● New Line　　▲ Revised Code　　2010 ICD-9-CM

Failure, failed — *continued*
 senile — *continued*
  with psychosis 290.20
 testis, primary (seminal) 257.2
 to progress 661.2 ☑
 to thrive
  adult 783.7
  child 783.41
  newborn 779.34 ●
 transplant 996.80
  bone marrow 996.85
  organ (immune or nonimmune cause)
    996.80
   bone marrow 996.85
   heart 996.83
   intestines 996.87
   kidney 996.81
   liver 996.82
   lung 996.84
   pancreas 996.86
   specified NEC 996.89
  skin 996.52
   artificial 996.55
   decellularized allodermis 996.55
   temporary allograft or pigskin graft —
     omit code
 trial of labor NEC 660.6 ☑
  affecting fetus or newborn 763.1
 tubal ligation 998.89
 urinary 586
 vacuum extraction
  abortion — *see* Abortion, failed
  delivery NEC 660.7 ☑
   affecting fetus or newborn 763.1
 vasectomy 998.89
 ventouse NEC 660.7 ☑
  affecting fetus or newborn 763.1
 ventricular (*see also* Failure, heart) 428.9
  left 428.1
   with rheumatic fever (conditions classi-
     fiable to 390)
    active 391.8
     with chorea 392.0
    inactive or quiescent (with chorea)
      398.91
   hypertensive (*see also* Hypertension,
     heart) 402.91
    benign 402.11
    malignant 402.01
   rheumatic (chronic) (inactive) (with
     chorea) 398.91
    active or acute 391.8
     with chorea 392.0
  right (*see also* Failure, heart) 428.0
 vital centers, fetus or newborn 779.89
 weight gain in childhood 783.41
Fainting (fit) (spell) 780.2
Falciform hymen 752.49
Fallen arches 734
Falling, any organ or part — *see* Prolapse
Fall, maternal, affecting fetus or newborn
   760.5
Fallopian
 insufflation
  fertility testing V26.21
  following sterilization reversal V26.22
 tube — *see* condition
Fallot's
 pentalogy 745.2
 tetrad or tetralogy 745.2
 triad or trilogy 746.09
Fallout, radioactive (adverse effect) NEC 990
False — *see also* condition
 bundle branch block 426.50
 bursa 727.89
 croup 478.75
 joint 733.82
 labor (pains) 644.1 ☑
 opening, urinary, male 752.69
 passage, urethra (prostatic) 599.4
 positive
  serological test for syphilis 795.6
  Wassermann reaction 795.6
 pregnancy 300.11
Family, familial — *see also* condition

Family, familial — *see also* condition —
  continued
 affected by
  family member
   currently on deployment (military)
     V61.01
   returned from deployment (military)
     (current or past conflict) V61.02
 disruption (*see also* Disruption, family) V61.09
 estrangement V61.09
 hemophagocytic
  lymphohistiocytosis 288.4
  reticulosis 288.4
 Li-Fraumeni (syndrome) V84.01
 planning advice V25.09
  natural
   procreative V26.41
   to avoid pregnancy V25.04
 problem V61.9
  specified circumstance NEC V61.8
 retinoblastoma (syndrome) 190.5
Famine 994.2
 edema 262
Fanconi's anemia (congenital pancytopenia)
   284.09
Fanconi (-de Toni) (-Debré) syndrome (cystinosis) 270.0
Farber (-Uzman) syndrome or disease (disseminated lipogranulomatosis) 272.8
Farcin 024
Farcy 024
Farmers'
 lung 495.0
 skin 692.74
Farsightedness 367.0
Fascia — *see* condition
Fasciculation 781.0
Fasciculitis optica 377.32
Fasciitis 729.4
 eosinophilic 728.89
 necrotizing 728.86
 nodular 728.79
 perirenal 593.4
 plantar 728.71
 pseudosarcomatous 728.79
 traumatic (old) NEC 728.79
  current — *see* Sprain, by site
Fasciola hepatica infestation 121.3
Fascioliasis 121.3
Fasciolopsiasis (small intestine) 121.4
Fasciolopsis (small intestine) 121.4
Fast pulse 785.0
Fat
 embolism (cerebral) (pulmonary) (systemic)
   958.1
  with
   abortion — *see* Abortion, by type, with
     embolism
   ectopic pregnancy (*see also* categories
     633.0–633.9) 639.6
   molar pregnancy (*see also* categories
     630–632) 639.6
  complicating delivery or puerperium
    673.8 ☑
  following
   abortion 639.6
   ectopic or molar pregnancy 639.6
  in pregnancy, childbirth, or the puerperium
    673.8 ☑
 excessive 278.02
  in heart (*see also* Degeneration, myocar-
    dial) 429.1
 general 278.02
 hernia, herniation 729.30
  eyelid 374.34
  knee 729.31
  orbit 374.34
  retro-orbital 374.34
  retropatellar 729.31
  specified site NEC 729.39
 indigestion 579.8
 in stool 792.1
 localized (pad) 278.1
  heart (*see also* Degeneration, myocardial)
    429.1
  knee 729.31

Fat — *continued*
 localized — *continued*
  retropatellar 729.31
 necrosis (*see also* Fatty, degeneration)
  breast (aseptic) (segmental) 611.3
  mesentery 567.82
  omentum 567.82
  peritoneum 567.82
 pad 278.1
Fatal familial insomnia (FFI) 046.72
Fatal syncope 798.1
Fatigue 780.79
 auditory deafness (*see also* Deafness) 389.9
 chronic, syndrome 780.71
 combat (*see also* Reaction, stress, acute) 308.9
 during pregnancy 646.8 ☑
 general 780.79
  psychogenic 300.5
 heat (transient) 992.6
 muscle 729.89
 myocardium (*see also* Failure, heart) 428.9
 nervous 300.5
 neurosis 300.5
 operational 300.89
 postural 729.89
 posture 729.89
 psychogenic (general) 300.5
 senile 797
 syndrome NEC 300.5
  chronic 780.71
 undue 780.79
 voice 784.49
Fatness 278.02
Fatty — *see also* condition
 apron 278.1
 degeneration (diffuse) (general) NEC 272.8
  localized — *see* Degeneration, by site, fatty
  placenta — *see* Placenta, abnormal
  heart (enlarged) (*see also* Degeneration, my-
    ocardial) 429.1
 infiltration (diffuse) (general) (*see also* Degeneration, by site, fatty) 272.8
  heart (enlarged) (*see also* Degeneration,
    myocardial) 429.1
 liver 571.8
  alcoholic 571.0
 necrosis — *see* Degeneration, fatty
 phanerosis 272.8
Fauces — *see* condition
Fauchard's disease (periodontitis) 523.40
Faucitis 478.29
Faulty — *see also* condition
 position of teeth 524.30
Favism (anemia) 282.2
Favre-Racouchot disease (elastoidosis cutanea
   nodularis) 701.8
Favus 110.9
 beard 110.0
 capitis 110.0
 corporis 110.5
 eyelid 110.8
 foot 110.4
 hand 110.2
 scalp 110.0
 specified site NEC 110.8
Feared complaint unfounded V65.5
Fear, fearfulness (complex) (reaction) 300.20
 child 313.0
 of
  animals 300.29
  closed spaces 300.29
  crowds 300.29
  eating in public 300.23
  heights 300.29
  open spaces 300.22
   with panic attacks 300.21
  public speaking 300.23
  streets 300.22
   with panic attacks 300.21
  travel 300.22
   with panic attacks 300.21
  washing in public 300.23
 transient 308.0
Febricula (continued) (simple) — *see also* Pyrexia
   780.60
Febrile — *see also* Pyrexia 780.60

Febrile — *see also* Pyrexia — *continued*
 convulsion (simple) 780.31
  complex 780.32
 seizure (simple) 780.31
  atypical 780.32
  complex 780.32
  complicated 780.32
Febris — *see also* Fever 780.60
 aestiva (*see also* Fever, hay) 477.9
 flava (*see also* Fever, yellow) 060.9
 melitensis 023.0
 pestis (*see also* Plague) 020.9
 puerperalis 672.0 ☑
 recurrens (*see also* Fever, relapsing) 087.9
  pediculo vestimenti 087.0
 rubra 034.1
 typhoidea 002.0
 typhosa 002.0
Fecal — *see* condition
Fecalith (impaction) 560.39
 with hernia (*see also* Hernia, by site, with obstruction)
  gangrenous — *see* Hernia, by site, with
    gangrene
 appendix 543.9
 congenital 777.1
Fede's disease 529.0
Feeble-minded 317
**Feeble rapid pulse due to shock following
   injury** 958.4
Feeding
 faulty (elderly) (infant) 783.3
  newborn 779.31 ▲
 formula check V20.2
 improper (elderly) (infant) 783.3
  newborn 779.31 ▲
 problem (elderly) (infant) 783.3
  newborn 779.31 ▲
  nonorganic origin 307.59
Feeling of foreign body in throat 784.99
Feer's disease 985.0
Feet — *see* condition
Feigned illness V65.2
Feil-Klippel syndrome (brevicollis) 756.16
Feinmesser's (hidrotic) **ectodermal dysplasia**
   757.31
Felix's disease (juvenile osteochondrosis, hip)
   732.1
Felon (any digit) (with lymphangitis) 681.01
 herpetic 054.6
Felty's syndrome (rheumatoid arthritis with
   splenomegaly and leukopenia) 714.1
Feminism in boys 302.6
Feminization, testicular 259.51
 with pseudohermaphroditism, male 259.51
Femoral hernia — *see* Hernia, femoral
Femora vara 736.32
Femur, femoral — *see* condition
Fenestrata placenta — *see* Placenta, abnormal
Fenestration, fenestrated — *see also* Imperfect,
   closure
 aorta-pulmonary 745.0
 aorticopulmonary 745.0
 aortopulmonary 745.0
 cusps, heart valve NEC 746.89
  pulmonary 746.09
 hymen 752.49
 pulmonic cusps 746.09
Fenwick's disease 537.89
Fermentation (gastric) (gastrointestinal) (stomach) 536.8
 intestine 564.89
  psychogenic 306.4
 psychogenic 306.4
Fernell's disease (aortic aneurysm) 441.9
Fertile eunuch syndrome 257.2
Fertility, meaning multiparity — *see* Multiparity
Fetal
 alcohol syndrome 760.71
 anemia 678.0 ☑
  thrombocytopenia 678.0 ☑
  twin to twin transfusion 678.0 ☑
Fetalis uterus 752.3
Fetid
 breath 784.99

☑ Additional Digit Required — Refer to the Tabular List for Digit Selection ⬛ Subterms under main terms may continue to next column or page

2010 ICD-9-CM ▶◀ Revised Text ● New Line ▲ Revised Code October 2009 • Volume 2 — 109

Failure, failed — Fetid

Index

Fetid — Fever

Fetid — *continued*
sweat 705.89
Fetishism 302.81
transvestic 302.3
Fetomaternal hemorrhage
affecting management of pregnancy 656.0 ☑
fetus or newborn 772.0
Fetus, fetal — *see also* condition
papyraceous 779.89
type lung tissue 770.4
Fever 780.60
with chills 780.60
in malarial regions (*see also* Malaria) 084.6
abortus NEC 023.9
aden 061
African tick-borne 087.1
American
mountain tick 066.1
spotted 082.0
and ague (*see also* Malaria) 084.6
aphthous 078.4
arbovirus hemorrhagic 065.9
Assam 085.0
Australian A or Q 083.0
Bangkok hemorrhagic 065.4
biliary, Charcôt's intermittent — *see* Choledocholithiasis
bilious, hemoglobinuric 084.8
blackwater 084.8
blister 054.9
Bonvale Dam 780.79
boutonneuse 082.1
brain 323.9
late effect — *see* category 326
breakbone 061
Bullis 082.8
Bunyamwera 066.3
Burdwan 085.0
Bwamba (encephalitis) 066.3
Cameroon (*see also* Malaria) 084.6
Canton 081.9
catarrhal (acute) 460
chronic 472.0
cat-scratch 078.3
cerebral 323.9
late effect — *see* category 326
cerebrospinal (meningococcal) (*see also*
Meningitis, cerebrospinal) 036.0
Chagres 084.0
Chandipura 066.8
changuinola 066.0
Charcôt's (biliary) (hepatic) (intermittent) —
see Choledocholithiasis
Chikungunya (viral) 066.3
hemorrhagic 065.4
childbed 670.8 ☑ ▲
Chitral 066.0
Colombo (*see also* Fever, paratyphoid) 002.9
Colorado tick (virus) 066.1
congestive
malarial (*see also* Malaria) 084.6
remittent (*see also* Malaria) 084.6
Congo virus 065.0
continued 780.60
malarial 084.0
Corsican (*see also* Malaria) 084.6
Crimean hemorrhagic 065.0
Cyprus (*see also* Brucellosis) 023.9
dandy 061
deer fly (*see also* Tularemia) 021.9
dehydration, newborn 778.4
dengue (virus) 061
hemorrhagic 065.4
desert 114.0
due to heat 992.0
Dumdum 085.0
enteric 002.0
ephemeral (of unknown origin) (*see also*
Pyrexia) 780.60
epidemic, hemorrhagic of the Far East 065.0
erysipelatous (*see also* Erysipelas) 035
estivo-autumnal (malarial) 084.0
etiocholanolone 277.31
famine (*see also* Fever, relapsing)
meaning typhus — *see* Typhus
Far Eastern hemorrhagic 065.0

Fever — *continued*
five day 083.1
Fort Bragg 100.89
gastroenteric 002.0
gastromalarial (*see also* Malaria) 084.6
Gibraltar (*see also* Brucellosis) 023.9
glandular 075
Guama (viral) 066.3
Haverhill 026.1
hay (allergic) (with rhinitis) 477.9
with
asthma (bronchial) (*see also* Asthma)
493.0 ☑
due to
dander, animal (cat) (dog) 477.2
dust 477.8
fowl 477.8
hair, animal (cat) (dog) 477.2
pollen, any plant or tree 477.0
specified allergen other than pollen
477.8
heat (effects) 992.0
hematuric, bilious 084.8
hemoglobinuric (malarial) 084.8
bilious 084.8
hemorrhagic (arthropod-borne) NEC 065.9
with renal syndrome 078.6
arenaviral 078.7
Argentine 078.7
Bangkok 065.4
Bolivian 078.7
Central Asian 065.0
chikungunya 065.4
Crimean 065.0
dengue (virus) 065.4
Ebola 065.8
epidemic 078.6
of Far East 065.0
Far Eastern 065.0
Junin virus 078.7
Korean 078.6
Kyasanur forest 065.2
Machupo virus 078.7
mite-borne NEC 065.8
mosquito-borne 065.4
Omsk 065.1
Philippine 065.4
Russian (Yaroslav) 078.6
Singapore 065.4
Southeast Asia 065.4
Thailand 065.4
tick-borne NEC 065.3
hepatic (*see also* Cholecystitis) 575.8
intermittent (Charcôt's) — *see* Choledocholithiasis
herpetic (*see also* Herpes) 054.9
Hyalomma tick 065.0
icterohemorrhagic 100.0
inanition 780.60
newborn 778.4
in conditions classified elsewhere 780.61
infective NEC 136.9
intermittent (bilious) (*see also* Malaria) 084.6
hepatic (Charcôt) — *see* Choledocholithiasis
of unknown origin (*see also* Pyrexia) 780.60
pernicious 084.0
iodide
correct substance properly administered
780.60
overdose or wrong substance given or
taken 975.5
Japanese river 081.2
jungle yellow 060.0
Junin virus, hemorrhagic 078.7
Katayama 120.2
Kedani 081.2
Kenya 082.1
Korean hemorrhagic 078.6
Lassa 078.89
Lone Star 082.8
lung — *see* Pneumonia
Machupo virus, hemorrhagic 078.7
malaria, malarial (*see also* Malaria) 084.6
Malta (*see also* Brucellosis) 023.9
Marseilles 082.1

Fever — *continued*
marsh (*see also* Malaria) 084.6
Mayaro (viral) 066.3
Mediterranean (*see also* Brucellosis) 023.9
familial 277.31
tick 082.1
meningeal — *see* Meningitis
metal fumes NEC 985.8
Meuse 083.1
Mexican — *see* Typhus, Mexican
Mianeh 087.1
miasmatic (*see also* Malaria) 084.6
miliary 078.2
milk, female 672.0 ☑
mill 504
mite-borne hemorrhagic 065.8
Monday 504
mosquito-borne NEC 066.3
hemorrhagic NEC 065.4
mountain 066.1
meaning
Rocky Mountain spotted 082.0
undulant fever (*see also* Brucellosis)
023.9
tick (American) 066.1
Mucambo (viral) 066.3
mud 100.89
Neapolitan (*see also* Brucellosis) 023.9
neutropenic 288.00
newborn (environmentally-induced) 778.4
nine-mile 083.0
nonexanthematous tick 066.1
North Asian tick-borne typhus 082.2
Omsk hemorrhagic 065.1
O'nyong-nyong (viral) 066.3
Oropouche (viral) 066.3
Oroya 088.0
paludal (*see also* Malaria) 084.6
Panama 084.0
pappataci 066.0
paratyphoid 002.9
A 002.1
B (Schottmüller's) 002.2
C (Hirschfeld) 002.3
parrot 073.9
periodic 277.31
pernicious, acute 084.0
persistent (of unknown origin) (*see also*
Pyrexia) 780.60
petechial 036.0
pharyngoconjunctival 077.2
adenoviral type 3 077.2
Philippine hemorrhagic 065.4
phlebotomus 066.0
Piry 066.8
Pixuna (viral) 066.3
Plasmodium ovale 084.3
pleural (*see also* Pleurisy) 511.0
pneumonic — *see* Pneumonia
polymer fume 987.8
postimmunization 780.63
postoperative 780.62
due to infection 998.59
postvaccination 780.63
pretibial 100.89
puerperal, postpartum 672.0 ☑
putrid — *see* Septicemia
pyemic — *see* Septicemia
Q 083.0
with pneumonia 083.0 [484.8]
quadrilateral 083.0
quartan (malaria) 084.2
Queensland (coastal) 083.0
seven-day 100.89
Quintan (A) 083.1
quotidian 084.0
rabbit (*see also* Tularemia) 021.9
rat-bite 026.9
due to
Spirillum minor or minus 026.0
Spirochaeta morsus muris 026.0
Streptobacillus moniliformis 026.1
recurrent — *see* Fever, relapsing
relapsing 087.9
Carter's (Asiatic) 087.0
Dutton's (West African) 087.1

Fever — *continued*
relapsing — *continued*
Koch's 087.9
louse-borne (epidemic) 087.0
Novy's (American) 087.1
Obermeyer's (European) 087.0
spirillum NEC 087.9
tick-borne (endemic) 087.1
remittent (bilious) (congestive) (gastric) (*see
also* Malaria) 084.6
rheumatic (active) (acute) (chronic) (subacute)
390
with heart involvement 391.9
carditis 391.9
endocarditis (aortic) (mitral) (pulmonary) (tricuspid) 391.1
multiple sites 391.8
myocarditis 391.2
pancarditis, acute 391.8
pericarditis 391.0
specified type NEC 391.8
valvulitis 391.1
cardiac hypertrophy 398.99
inactive or quiescent
with cardiac hypertrophy 398.99
carditis 398.90
endocarditis 397.9
aortic (valve) 395.9
with mitral (valve) disease 396.9
mitral (valve) 394.9
with aortic (valve) disease 396.9
pulmonary (valve) 397.1
tricuspid (valve) 397.0
heart conditions (classifiable to 429.3,
429.6, 429.9) 398.99
failure (congestive) (conditions
classifiable to 428.0, 428.9)
398.91
left ventricular failure (conditions classifiable to 428.1) 398.91
myocardial degeneration (conditions
classifiable to 429.1) 398.0
myocarditis (conditions classifiable to
429.0) 398.0
pancarditis 398.99
pericarditis 393
Rift Valley (viral) 066.3
Rocky Mountain spotted 082.0
rose 477.0
Ross river (viral) 066.3
Russian hemorrhagic 078.6
sandfly 066.0
San Joaquin (valley) 114.0
São Paulo 082.0
scarlet 034.1
septic — *see* Septicemia
seven-day 061
Japan 100.89
Queensland 100.89
shin bone 083.1
Singapore hemorrhagic 065.4
solar 061
sore 054.9
South African tick-bite 087.1
Southeast Asia hemorrhagic 065.4
spinal — *see* Meningitis
spirillary 026.0
splenic (*see also* Anthrax) 022.9
spotted (Rocky Mountain) 082.0
American 082.0
Brazilian 082.0
Colombian 082.0
meaning
cerebrospinal meningitis 036.0
typhus 082.9
spring 309.23
steroid
correct substance properly administered
780.60
overdose or wrong substance given or
taken 962.0
streptobacillary 026.1
subtertian 084.0
Sumatran mite 081.2
sun 061
swamp 100.89

☑ Additional Digit Required — Refer to the Tabular List for Digit Selection
▽ Subterms under main terms may continue to next column or page
110 — Volume 2 · October 2009
►◄ Revised Text   ● New Line   ▲ Revised Code
2010 ICD-9-CM

Fever — continued
sweating 078.2
swine 003.8
sylvatic yellow 060.0
Tahyna 062.5
tertian — see Malaria, tertian
Thailand hemorrhagic 065.4
thermic 992.0
three day 066.0
　with Coxsackie exanthem 074.8
tick
　American mountain 066.1
　Colorado 066.1
　Kemerovo 066.1
　Mediterranean 082.1
　mountain 066.1
　nonexanthematous 066.1
　Quaranfil 066.1
tick-bite NEC 066.1
tick-borne NEC 066.1
　hemorrhagic NEC 065.3
transitory of newborn 778.4
trench 083.1
tsutsugamushi 081.2
typhogastric 002.0
typhoid (abortive) (ambulant) (any site) (hemorrhagic) (infection) (intermittent) (malignant) (rheumatic) 002.0
typhomalarial (see also Malaria) 084.6
typhus — see Typhus
undulant (see also Brucellosis) 023.9
unknown origin (see also Pyrexia) 780.60
uremic — see Uremia
uveoparotid 135
valley (Coccidioidomycosis) 114.0
Venezuelan equine 066.2
Volhynian 083.1
Wesselsbron (viral) 066.3
West
　African 084.8
　Nile (viral) 066.40
　　with
　　　cranial nerve disorders 066.42
　　　encephalitis 066.41
　　　optic neuritis 066.42
　　　other complications 066.49
　　　other neurologic manifestations 066.42
　　　polyradiculitis 066.42
　Whitmore's 025
　Wolhynian 083.1
worm 128.9
Yaroslav hemorrhagic 078.6
yellow 060.9
　jungle 060.0
　sylvatic 060.0
　urban 060.1
　vaccination, prophylactic (against) V04.4
Zika (viral) 066.3
Fibrillation
atrial (established) (paroxysmal) 427.31
auricular (atrial) (established) 427.31
cardiac (ventricular) 427.41
coronary (see also Infarct, myocardium) 410.9 ☑
heart (ventricular) 427.41
muscular 728.9
postoperative 997.1
ventricular 427.41
Fibrin
ball or bodies, pleural (sac) 511.0
chamber, anterior (eye) (gelatinous exudate) 364.04
Fibrinogenolysis (hemorrhagic) — see Fibrinolysis
Fibrinogenopenia (congenital) (hereditary) — see also Defect, coagulation 286.3
acquired 286.6
Fibrinolysis (acquired) (hemorrhagic) (pathologic) 286.6
with
　abortion — see Abortion, by type, with hemorrhage, delayed or excessive
　ectopic pregnancy (see also categories 633.0–633.9) 639.1

Fibrinolysis — continued
with — continued
　molar pregnancy (see also categories 630–632) 639.1
antepartum or intrapartum 641.3 ☑
　affecting fetus or newborn 762.1
following
　abortion 639.1
　ectopic or molar pregnancy 639.1
newborn, transient 776.2
postpartum 666.3 ☑
Fibrinopenia (hereditary) — see also Defect, coagulation 286.3
acquired 286.6
Fibrinopurulent — see condition
Fibrinous — see condition
Fibroadenoma (M9010/0)
cellular intracanalicular (M9020/0) 217
giant (intracanalicular) (M9020/0) 217
intracanalicular (M9011/0)
　cellular (M9020/0) 217
　giant (M9020/0) 217
　specified site — see Neoplasm, by site, benign
　unspecified site 217
juvenile (M9030/0) 217
pericanicular (M9012/0)
　specified site — see Neoplasm, by site, benign
　unspecified site 217
phyllodes (M9020/0) 217
prostate 600.20
　with
　　other lower urinary tract symptoms (LUTS) 600.21
　　urinary
　　　obstruction 600.21
　　　retention 600.21
specified site — see Neoplasm, by site, benign
unspecified site 217
Fibroadenosis, breast (chronic) (cystic) (diffuse) (periodic) (segmental) 610.2
Fibroangioma (M9160/0) — see also Neoplasm, by site, benign
juvenile (M9160/0)
　specified site — see Neoplasm, by site, benign
　unspecified site 210.7
Fibrocellulitis progressiva ossificans 728.11
Fibrochondrosarcoma (M9220/3) — see Neoplasm, cartilage, malignant
Fibrocystic
disease 277.00
　bone NEC 733.29
　breast 610.1
　jaw 526.2
　kidney (congenital) 753.19
　liver 751.62
　lung 518.89
　　congenital 748.4
　pancreas 277.00
kidney (congenital) 753.19
Fibrodysplasia ossificans multiplex (progressiva) 728.11
Fibroelastosis (cordis) (endocardial) (endomyocardial) 425.3
Fibroid (tumor) (M8890/0) — see also Neoplasm, connective tissue, benign
disease, lung (chronic) (see also Fibrosis, lung) 515
heart (disease) (see also Myocarditis) 429.0
induration, lung (chronic) (see also Fibrosis, lung) 515
in pregnancy or childbirth 654.1 ☑
　affecting fetus or newborn 763.89
　causing obstructed labor 660.2 ☑
　　affecting fetus or newborn 763.1
liver — see Cirrhosis, liver
lung (see also Fibrosis, lung) 515
pneumonia (chronic) (see also Fibrosis, lung) 515
uterus (M8890/0) (see also Leiomyoma, uterus) 218.9
Fibrolipoma (M8851/0) — see Lipoma, by site 214.9

Fibroliposarcoma (M8850/3) — see Neoplasm, connective tissue, malignant
Fibroma (M8810/0) — see also Neoplasm, connective tissue, benign
ameloblastic (M9330/0) 213.1
　upper jaw (bone) 213.0
bone (nonossifying) 733.99
　ossifying (M9262/0) — see Neoplasm, bone, benign
cementifying (M9274/0) — see Neoplasm, bone, benign
chondromyxoid (M9241/0) — see Neoplasm, bone, benign
desmoplastic (M8823/1) — see Neoplasm, connective tissue, uncertain behavior
facial (M8813/0) — see Neoplasm, connective tissue, benign
invasive (M8821/1) — see Neoplasm, connective tissue, uncertain behavior
molle (M8851/0) (see also Lipoma, by site) 214.9
myxoid (M8811/0) — see Neoplasm, connective tissue, benign
nasopharynx, nasopharyngeal (juvenile) (M9160/0) 210.7
nonosteogenic (nonossifying) — see Dysplasia, fibrous
odontogenic (M9321/0) 213.1
　upper jaw (bone) 213.0
ossifying (M9262/0) — see Neoplasm, bone, benign
periosteal (M8812/0) — see Neoplasm, bone, benign
prostate 600.20
　with
　　other lower urinary tract symptoms (LUTS) 600.21
　　urinary
　　　obstruction 600.21
　　　retention 600.21
soft (M8851/0) (see also Lipoma, by site) 214.9
Fibromatosis 728.79
abdominal (M8822/1) — see Neoplasm, connective tissue, uncertain behavior
aggressive (M8821/1) — see Neoplasm, connective tissue, uncertain behavior
congenital generalized (CGF) 759.89
Dupuytren's 728.6
gingival 523.8
plantar fascia 728.71
proliferative 728.79
pseudosarcomatous (proliferative) (subcutaneous) 728.79
subcutaneous pseudosarcomatous (proliferative) 728.79
Fibromyalgia 729.1
Fibromyoma (M8890/0) — see also Neoplasm, connective tissue, benign
uterus (corpus) (see also Leiomyoma, uterus) 218.9
　in pregnancy or childbirth 654.1 ☑
　　affecting fetus or newborn 763.89
　　causing obstructed labor 660.2 ☑
　　　affecting fetus or newborn 763.1
Fibromyositis — see also Myositis 729.1
scapulohumeral 726.2
Fibromyxolipoma (M8852/0) — see Lipoma, by site 214.9
Fibromyxoma (M8811/0) — see Neoplasm, connective tissue, benign
Fibromyxosarcoma (M8811/3) — see Neoplasm, connective tissue, malignant
Fibro-odontoma, ameloblastic (M9290/0) 213.1
upper jaw (bone) 213.0
Fibro-osteoma (M9262/0) — see Neoplasm, bone, benign
Fibroplasia, retrolental (see also Retinopathy of prematurity) 362.21
Fibropurulent — see condition
Fibrosarcoma (M8810/3) — see also Neoplasm, connective tissue, malignant
ameloblastic (M9330/3) 170.1
　upper jaw (bone) 170.0
congenital (M8814/3) — see Neoplasm, connective tissue, malignant

Fibrosarcoma — see also Neoplasm, connective tissue, malignant — continued
fascial (M8813/3) — see Neoplasm, connective tissue, malignant
infantile (M8814/3) — see Neoplasm, connective tissue, malignant
odontogenic (M9330/3) 170.1
　upper jaw (bone) 170.0
periosteal (M8812/3) — see Neoplasm, bone, malignant
Fibrosclerosis
breast 610.3
corpora cavernosa (penis) 607.89
familial multifocal NEC 710.8
multifocal (idiopathic) NEC 710.8
penis (corpora cavernosa) 607.89
Fibrosis, fibrotic
adrenal (gland) 255.8
alveolar (diffuse) 516.3
amnion 658.8 ☑
anal papillae 569.49
anus 569.49
appendix, appendiceal, noninflammatory 543.9
arteriocapillary — see Arteriosclerosis
bauxite (of lung) 503
biliary 576.8
　due to Clonorchis sinensis 121.1
bladder 596.8
　interstitial 595.1
　localized submucosal 595.1
　panmural 595.1
bone, diffuse 756.59
breast 610.3
capillary (see also Arteriosclerosis)
　lung (chronic) (see also Fibrosis, lung) 515
cardiac (see also Myocarditis) 429.0
cervix 622.8
chorion 658.8 ☑
corpus cavernosum 607.89
cystic (of pancreas) 277.00
　with
　　manifestations
　　　gastrointestinal 277.03
　　　pulmonary 277.02
　　　specified NEC 277.09
　　meconium ileus 277.01
　　pulmonary exacerbation 277.02
due to (presence of) any device, implant, or graft — see Complications, due to (presence of) any device, implant, or graft classified to 996.0–996.5 NEC
ejaculatory duct 608.89
endocardium (see also Endocarditis) 424.90
endomyocardial (African) 425.0
epididymis 608.89
eye muscle 378.62
graphite (of lung) 503
heart (see also Myocarditis) 429.0
hepatic (see also Cirrhosis, liver)
　due to Clonorchis sinensis 121.1
hepatolienal — see Cirrhosis, liver
hepatosplenic — see Cirrhosis, liver
infrapatellar fat pad 729.31
interstitial pulmonary, newborn 770.7
intrascrotal 608.89
kidney (see also Sclerosis, renal) 587
liver — see Cirrhosis, liver
lung (atrophic) (capillary) (chronic) (confluent) (massive) (perialveolar) (peribronchial) 515
　with
　　anthracosilicosis (occupational) 500
　　anthracosis (occupational) 500
　　asbestosis (occupational) 501
　　bagassosis (occupational) 495.1
　　bauxite 503
　　berylliosis (occupational) 503
　　byssinosis (occupational) 504
　　calcicosis (occupational) 502
　　chalicosis (occupational) 502
　　dust reticulation (occupational) 504
　　farmers' lung 495.0
　　gannister disease (occupational) 502
　　graphite 503
　　pneumonoconiosis (occupational) 505

☑ Additional Digit Required — Refer to the Tabular List for Digit Selection
▶◀ Revised Text　　● New Line　　▲ Revised Code
Subterms under main terms may continue to next column or page
2010 ICD-9-CM
Volume 2 — 111

Fibrosis, fibrotic — *continued*
  lung — *continued*
    with — *continued*
      pneumosiderosis (occupational) 503
      siderosis (occupational) 503
      silicosis (occupational) 502
      tuberculosis (*see also* Tuberculosis)
        011.4 ☑
    diffuse (idiopathic) (interstitial) 516.3
    due to
      bauxite 503
      fumes or vapors (chemical) (inhalation)
        506.4
      graphite 503
    following radiation 508.1
    postinflammatory 515
    silicotic (massive) (occupational) 502
    tuberculous (*see also* Tuberculosis)
      011.4 ☑
  lymphatic gland 289.3
  median bar 600.90
    with
      other lower urinary tract symptoms
        (LUTS) 600.91
      urinary
        obstruction 600.91
        retention 600.91
  mediastinum (idiopathic) 519.3
  meninges 349.2
  muscle NEC 728.2
    iatrogenic (from injection) 999.9
  myocardium, myocardial (*see also* Myocarditis)
    429.0
  oral submucous 528.8
  ovary 620.8
  oviduct 620.8
  pancreas 577.8
    cystic 277.00
      with
        manifestations
          gastrointestinal 277.03
          pulmonary 277.02
          specified NEC 277.09
        meconium ileus 277.01
        pulmonary exacerbation 277.02
  penis 607.89
  periappendiceal 543.9
  periarticular (*see also* Ankylosis) 718.5 ☑
  pericardium 423.1
  perineum, in pregnancy or childbirth 654.8 ☑
    affecting fetus or newborn 763.89
    causing obstructed labor 660.2 ☑
      affecting fetus or newborn 763.1
  perineural NEC 355.9
    foot 355.6
  periureteral 593.89
  placenta — *see* Placenta, abnormal
  pleura 511.0
  popliteal fat pad 729.31
  preretinal 362.56
  prostate (chronic) 600.90
    with
      other lower urinary tract symptoms
        (LUTS) 600.91
      urinary
        obstruction 600.91
        retention 600.91
  pulmonary (chronic) (*see also* Fibrosis, lung)
    515
    alveolar capillary block 516.3
    interstitial
      diffuse (idiopathic) 516.3
      newborn 770.7
  radiation — *see* Effect, adverse, radiation
  rectal sphincter 569.49
  retroperitoneal, idiopathic 593.4
  sclerosing mesenteric (idiopathic) 567.82
  scrotum 608.89
  seminal vesicle 608.89
  senile 797
  skin NEC 709.2
  spermatic cord 608.89
  spleen 289.59
    bilharzial (*see also* Schistosomiasis) 120.9
  subepidermal nodular (M8832/0) — *see* Neo-
    plasm, skin, benign

Fibrosis, fibrotic — *continued*
  submucous NEC 709.2
    oral 528.8
    tongue 528.8
  syncytium — *see* Placenta, abnormal
  testis 608.89
    chronic, due to syphilis 095.8
  thymus (gland) 254.8
  tunica vaginalis 608.89
  ureter 593.89
  urethra 599.84
  uterus (nonneoplastic) 621.8
    bilharzial (*see also* Schistosomiasis) 120.9
    neoplastic (*see also* Leiomyoma, uterus)
      218.9
  vagina 623.8
  valve, heart (*see also* Endocarditis) 424.90
  vas deferens 608.89
  vein 459.89
    lower extremities 459.89
  vesical 595.1
Fibrositis (periarticular) (rheumatoid) 729.0
  humeroscapular region 726.2
  nodular, chronic
    Jaccoud's 714.4
    rheumatoid 714.4
  ossificans 728.11
  scapulohumeral 726.2
Fibrothorax 511.0
Fibrotic — *see* Fibrosis
Fibrous — *see* condition
Fibroxanthoma (M8831/0) — *see also* Neoplasm,
  connective tissue, benign
  atypical (M8831/1) — *see* Neoplasm, connec-
    tive tissue, uncertain behavior
  malignant (M8831/3) — *see* Neoplasm, con-
    nective tissue, malignant
Fibroxanthosarcoma (M8831/3) — *see* Neoplasm, connective tissue, malignant
Fiedler's
  disease (leptospiral jaundice) 100.0
  myocarditis or syndrome (acute isolated my-
    ocarditis) 422.91
Fiessinger-Leroy (-Reiter) syndrome 099.3
Fiessinger-Rendu syndrome (erythema muli-
  forme exudativum) 695.19
Fifth disease (eruptive) 057.0
  venereal 099.1
Filaria, filarial — *see* Infestation, filarial
Filariasis — *see also* Infestation, filarial 125.9
  bancroftian 125.0
  Brug's 125.1
  due to
    bancrofti 125.0
    Brugia (Wuchereria) (malayi) 125.1
    Loa loa 125.2
    malayi 125.1
    organism NEC 125.6
    Wuchereria (bancrofti) 125.0
      malayi 125.1
  Malayan 125.1
  ozzardi 125.5
  specified type NEC 125.6
Filatoff's, Filatov's, Filatow's disease (infectious
  mononucleosis) 075
File-cutters' disease 984.9
  specified type of lead — *see* Table of Drugs
    and Chemicals
Filling defect
  biliary tract 793.3
  bladder 793.5
  duodenum 793.4
  gallbladder 793.3
  gastrointestinal tract 793.4
  intestine 793.4
  kidney 793.5
  stomach 793.4
  ureter 793.5
Filtering bleb, eye (postglaucoma) (status)
  V45.69
  with complication or rupture 997.99
  postcataract extraction (complication) 997.99
Fimbrial cyst (congenital) 752.11
Fimbriated hymen 752.49
Financial problem affecting care V60.2

Findings, (abnormal), without diagnosis (examination) (laboratory test) 796.4
  17-ketosteroids, elevated 791.9
  acetonuria 791.6
  acid phosphatase 790.5
  albumin-globulin ratio 790.99
  albuminuria 791.0
  alcohol in blood 790.3
  alkaline phosphatase 790.5
  amniotic fluid 792.3
  amylase 790.5
  anisocytosis 790.09
  antenatal screening 796.5
  anthrax, positive 795.31
  antibody titers, elevated 795.79
  anticardiolipin antibody 795.79
  antigen-antibody reaction 795.79
  antiphospholipid antibody 795.79
  bacteriuria 791.9
  ballistocardiogram 794.39
  bicarbonate 276.9
  bile in urine 791.4
  bilirubin 277.4
  bleeding time (prolonged) 790.92
  blood culture, positive 790.7
  blood gas level (arterial) 790.91
  blood sugar level 790.29
    high 790.29
      fasting glucose 790.21
      glucose tolerance test 790.22
    low 251.2
  calcium 275.40
  cancer antigen 125 [CA 125] 795.82
  carbonate 276.9
  carcinoembryonic antigen [CEA] 795.81
  casts, urine 791.7
  catecholamines 791.9
  cells, urine 791.7
  cerebrospinal fluid (color) (content) (pressure)
    792.0
  cervical
    high risk human papillomavirus (HPV) DNA
      test positive 795.05
    low risk human papillomavirus (HPV) DNA
      test positive 795.09
  chloride 276.9
  cholesterol 272.9
    high 272.0
      with high triglycerides 272.2
  chromosome analysis 795.2
  chyluria 791.1
  circulation time 794.39
  cloudy dialysis effluent 792.5
  cloudy urine 791.9
  coagulation study 790.92
  cobalt, blood 790.6
  color of urine (unusual) NEC 791.9
  copper, blood 790.6
  C-reactive protein (CRP) 790.95
  creatinine clearance 794.4
  crystals, urine 791.9
  culture, positive NEC 795.39
    blood 790.7
    HIV V08
    human immunodeficiency virus V08
    nose 795.39
      Staphylococcus — *see* Carrier (suspect-
      ed) of, Staphylococcus
    skin lesion NEC 795.39
    spinal fluid 792.0
    sputum 795.39
    stool 792.1
    throat 795.39
    urine 791.9
    viral
      human immunodeficiency V08
    wound 795.39
  cytology specified site NEC 796.9 ●
  echocardiogram 793.2
  echoencephalogram 794.01
  echogram NEC — *see* Findings, abnormal,
    structure
  electrocardiogram (ECG) (EKG) 794.31
  electroencephalogram (EEG) 794.02
  electrolyte level, urinary 791.9
  electromyogram (EMG) 794.17

Findings, (abnormal), without diagnosis —
  continued
  electromyogram — *continued*
    ocular 794.14
  electro-oculogram (EOG) 794.12
  electroretinogram (ERG) 794.11
  enzymes, serum NEC 790.5
  fibrinogen titer coagulation study 790.92
  filling defect — *see* Filling defect
  function study NEC 794.9
    auditory 794.15
    bladder 794.9
    brain 794.00
    cardiac 794.30
    endocrine NEC 794.6
      thyroid 794.5
    kidney 794.4
    liver 794.8
    nervous system
      central 794.00
      peripheral 794.19
    oculomotor 794.14
    pancreas 794.9
    placenta 794.9
    pulmonary 794.2
    retina 794.11
    special senses 794.19
    spleen 794.9
    vestibular 794.16
  gallbladder, nonvisualization 793.3
  glucose 790.29
    elevated
      fasting 790.21
      tolerance test 790.22
  glycosuria 791.5
  heart
    shadow 793.2
    sounds 785.3
  hematinuria 791.2
  hematocrit
    drop (precipitous) 790.01
    elevated 282.7
    low 285.9
  hematologic NEC 790.99
  hematuria 599.70
  hemoglobin
    drop 790.01   ●
    elevated 282.7
    low 285.9
  hemoglobinuria 791.2
  histological NEC 795.4
  hormones 259.9
  immunoglobulins, elevated 795.79
  indolacetic acid, elevated 791.9
  iron 790.6
  karyotype 795.2
  ketonuria 791.6
  lactic acid dehydrogenase (LDH) 790.4
  lead 790.6
  lipase 790.5
  lipids NEC 272.9
  lithium, blood 790.6
  liver function test 790.6
  lung field (coin lesion) (shadow) 793.1
  magnesium, blood 790.6
  mammogram 793.80
    calcification 793.89
    calculus 793.89
    dense breasts 793.82   ●
    inconclusive 793.82   ●
      due to dense breasts 793.82 ●
    microcalcification 793.81
  mediastinal shift 793.2
  melanin, urine 791.9
  microbiologic NEC 795.39
  mineral, blood NEC 790.6
  myoglobinuria 791.3
  nasal swab, anthrax 795.31
  neonatal screening 796.6
  nitrogen derivatives, blood 790.6
  nonvisualization of gallbladder 793.3
  nose culture, positive 795.39
  odor of urine (unusual) NEC 791.9
  oxygen saturation 790.91
  Papanicolaou (smear) 796.9
    anus 796.70

Findings, (abnormal), without diagnosis — *continued*
Papanicolaou — *continued*
  anus — *continued*
    with
      atypical squamous cells
        cannot exclude high grade
          squamous intraepithelial
          lesion (ASC-H) 796.72
        of undetermined significance
          (ASC-US) 796.71
      cytologic evidence of malignancy
        796.76
      high grade squamous intraepithe-
        lial lesion (HGSIL) 796.74
      low grade squamous intraepithelial
        lesion (LGSIL) 796.73
    glandular 796.70
    specified finding NEC 796.79
  cervix 795.00
    with
      atypical squamous cells
        cannot exclude high grade
          squamous intraepithelial
          lesion (ASC-H) 795.02
        of undetermined significance
          (ASC-US) 795.01
      cytologic evidence of malignancy
        795.06
      high grade squamous intraepithe-
        lial lesion (HGSIL) 795.04
      low grade squamous intraepithelial
        lesion (LGSIL) 795.03
    dyskaryotic 795.09
    nonspecific finding NEC 795.09
  other site 796.9
  vagina 795.10
    with
      atypical squamous cells
        cannot exclude high grade
          squamous intraepithelial
          lesion (ASC-H) 795.12
        of undetermined significance
          (ASC-US) 795.11
      cytologic evidence of malignancy
        795.16
      high grade squamous intraepithe-
        lial lesion (HGSIL) 795.14
      low grade squamous intraepithelial
        lesion (LGSIL) 795.13
    glandular 795.10
    specified NEC 795.19
peritoneal fluid 792.9
phonocardiogram 794.39
phosphorus 275.3
pleural fluid 792.9
pneumoencephalogram 793.0
PO₂-oxygen ratio 790.91
poikilocytosis 790.09
potassium
  deficiency 276.8
  excess 276.7
PPD 795.5
prostate specific antigen (PSA) 790.93
protein, serum NEC 790.99
proteinuria 791.0
prothrombin time (partial) (prolonged) (PT)
  (PTT) 790.92
pyuria 791.9
radiologic (x-ray) 793.99
  abdomen 793.6
  biliary tract 793.3
  breast 793.89
    abnormal mammogram NOS 793.80
    mammographic
      calcification 793.89
      calculus 793.89
      microcalcification 793.81
  gastrointestinal tract 793.4
  genitourinary organs 793.5
  head 793.0
  image test inconclusive due to excess body
    fat 793.91
  intrathoracic organs NEC 793.2
  lung 793.1
  musculoskeletal 793.7

Findings, (abnormal), without diagnosis — *continued*
  radiologic — *continued*
    placenta 793.99
    retroperitoneum 793.6
    skin 793.99
    skull 793.0
    subcutaneous tissue 793.99
  red blood cell 790.09
    count 790.09
    morphology 790.09
    sickling 790.09
    volume 790.09
  saliva 792.4
  scan NEC 794.9
    bladder 794.9
    bone 794.9
    brain 794.09
    kidney 794.4
    liver 794.8
    lung 794.2
    pancreas 794.9
    placental 794.9
    spleen 794.9
    thyroid 794.5
  sedimentation rate, elevated 790.1
  semen 792.2
  serological (for)
    human immunodeficiency virus (HIV)
      inconclusive 795.71
      positive V08
    syphilis — *see* Findings, serology for
      syphilis
  serology for syphilis
    false positive 795.6
    positive 097.1
      false 795.6
      follow-up of latent syphilis — *see*
        Syphilis, latent
      only finding — *see* Syphilis, latent
  serum 790.99
    blood NEC 790.99
    enzymes NEC 790.5
    proteins 790.99
  SGOT 790.4
  SGPT 790.4
  sickling of red blood cells 790.09
  skin test, positive 795.79
    tuberculin (without active tuberculosis)
      795.5
  sodium 790.6
    deficiency 276.1
    excess 276.0
  specified NEC 796.9   •
  spermatozoa 792.2
  spinal fluid 792.0
    culture, positive 792.0
  sputum culture, positive 795.39
    for acid-fast bacilli 795.39
  stool NEC 792.1
    bloody 578.1
      occult 792.1
    color 792.1
    culture, positive 792.1
    occult blood 792.1
  stress test 794.39
  structure, body (echogram) (thermogram)
    (ultrasound) (x-ray) NEC 793.99
    abdomen 793.6
    breast 793.89
      abnormal mammogram 793.80
      mammographic
        calcification 793.89
        calculus 793.89
        microcalcification 793.81
    gastrointestinal tract 793.4
    genitourinary organs 793.5
    head 793.0
      echogram (ultrasound) 794.01
    intrathoracic organs NEC 793.2
    lung 793.1
    musculoskeletal 793.7
    placenta 793.99
    retroperitoneum 793.6
    skin 793.99
    subcutaneous tissue NEC 793.99

Findings, (abnormal), without diagnosis — *continued*
  synovial fluid 792.9
  thermogram — *see* Findings, abnormal,
    structure
  throat culture, positive 795.39
  thyroid (function) 794.5
    metabolism (rate) 794.5
    scan 794.5
    uptake 794.5
  total proteins 790.99
  toxicology (drugs) (heavy metals) 796.0
  transaminase (level) 790.4
  triglycerides 272.9
    high 272.1
      with high cholesterol 272.2
  tuberculin skin test (without active tuberculo-
    sis) 795.5
  tumor markers NEC 795.89
  ultrasound (*see also* Findings, abnormal,
    structure)
    cardiogram 793.2
  uric acid, blood 790.6
  urine, urinary constituents 791.9
    acetone 791.6
    albumin 791.0
    bacteria 791.9
    bile 791.4
    blood 599.70
    casts or cells 791.7
    chyle 791.1
    culture, positive 791.9
    glucose 791.5
    hemoglobin 791.2
    ketone 791.6
    protein 791.0
    pus 791.9
    sugar 791.5
  vaginal
    fluid 792.9
    high risk human papillomavirus (HPV) DNA
      test positive 795.15
    low risk human papillomavirus (HPV) DNA
      test positive 795.19
  vanillylmandelic acid, elevated 791.9
  vectorcardiogram (VCG) 794.39
  ventriculogram (cerebral) 793.0
  VMA, elevated 791.9
  Wassermann reaction
    false positive 795.6
    positive 097.1
      follow-up of latent syphilis — *see*
        Syphilis, latent
      only finding — *see* Syphilis, latent
  white blood cell 288.9
    count 288.9
      elevated 288.60
      low 288.50
    differential 288.9
    morphology 288.9
  wound culture 795.39
  xerography 793.89
  zinc, blood 790.6
Finger — *see* condition
Finnish type nephrosis (congenital) 759.89
Fire, St. Anthony's — *see also* Erysipelas 035
Fish
  hook stomach 537.89
  meal workers' lung 495.8
Fisher's syndrome 357.0
Fissure, fissured
  abdominal wall (congenital) 756.79
  anus, anal 565.0
    congenital 751.5
  buccal cavity 528.9
  clitoris (congenital) 752.49
  ear, lobule (congenital) 744.29
  epiglottis (congenital) 748.3
  larynx 478.79
    congenital 748.3
  lip 528.5
    congenital (*see also* Cleft, lip) 749.10
  nipple 611.2
    puerperal, postpartum 676.1 ☑
  palate (congenital) (*see also* Cleft, palate)
    749.00

Fissure, fissured — *continued*
  postanal 565.0
  rectum 565.0
  skin 709.8
    streptococcal 686.9
  spine (congenital) (*see also* Spina bifida)
    741.9 ☑
  sternum (congenital) 756.3
  tongue (acquired) 529.5
    congenital 750.13
Fistula (sinus) 686.9
  abdomen (wall) 569.81
    bladder 596.2
    intestine 569.81
    ureter 593.82
    uterus 619.2
  abdominorectal 569.81
  abdominosigmoidal 569.81
  abdominothoracic 510.0
  abdominouterine 619.2
    congenital 752.3
  abdominovesical 596.2
  accessory sinuses (*see also* Sinusitis) 473.9
  actinomycotic — *see* Actinomycosis
  alveolar
    antrum (*see also* Sinusitis, maxillary) 473.0
    process 522.7
  anorectal 565.1
  antrobuccal (*see also* Sinusitis, maxillary) 473.0
  antrum (*see also* Sinusitis, maxillary) 473.0
  anus, anal (infectional) (recurrent) 565.1
    congenital 751.5
    tuberculous (*see also* Tuberculosis)
      014.8 ☑
  aortic sinus 747.29
  aortoduodenal 447.2
  appendix, appendicular 543.9
  arteriovenous (acquired) 447.0
    brain 437.3
      congenital 747.81
        ruptured (*see also* Hemorrhage,
          subarachnoid) 430
      ruptured (*see also* Hemorrhage, sub-
        arachnoid) 430
    cerebral 437.3
      congenital 747.81
    congenital (peripheral) 747.60
      brain — *see* Fistula, arteriovenous,
        brain, congenital
      coronary 746.85
      gastrointestinal 747.61
      lower limb 747.64
      pulmonary 747.3
      renal 747.62
      specified site NEC 747.69
      upper limb 747.63
    coronary 414.19
      congenital 746.85
    heart 414.19
    pulmonary (vessels) 417.0
      congenital 747.3
    surgically created (for dialysis) V45.11
      complication NEC 996.73
        atherosclerosis — *see* Arteriosclero-
          sis, extremities
        embolism 996.74
        infection or inflammation 996.62
        mechanical 996.1
        occlusion NEC 996.74
        thrombus 996.74
      traumatic — *see* Injury, blood vessel, by
        site
  artery 447.2
  aural 383.81
    congenital 744.49
  auricle 383.81
    congenital 744.49
  Bartholin's gland 619.8
  bile duct (*see also* Fistula, biliary) 576.4
  biliary (duct) (tract) 576.4
    congenital 751.69
  bladder (neck) (sphincter) 596.2
    into seminal vesicle 596.2
  bone 733.99
  brain 348.89   ▲

☑ Additional Digit Required — Refer to the Tabular List for Digit Selection   ▽ Subterms under main terms may continue to next column or page

2010 ICD-9-CM   ▶◀ Revised Text   ● New Line   ▲ Revised Code   October 2009 • Volume 2 — 113

Fistula — continued
  uteroenteric 619.1
  uterofecal 619.1
  uterointestinal 619.1
    congenital 752.3
  uterorectal 619.1
    congenital 752.3
  uteroureteric 619.0
  uterovaginal 619.8
  uterovesical 619.0
    congenital 752.3
  uterus 619.8
  vagina (wall) 619.8
    postpartal, old 619.8
  vaginocutaneous (postpartal) 619.2
  vaginoileal (acquired) 619.1
  vaginoperineal 619.2
  vesical NEC 596.2
  vesicoabdominal 596.2
  vesicocervicovaginal 619.0
  vesicocolic 596.1
  vesicocutaneous 596.2
  vesicoenteric 596.1
  vesicointestinal 596.1
  vesicometrorectal 619.1
  vesicoperineal 596.2
  vesicorectal 596.1
    congenital 753.8
  vesicosigmoidal 596.1
  vesicosigmoidovaginal 619.1
  vesicoureteral 596.2
  vesicoureterovaginal 619.0
  vesicourethral 596.2
  vesicourethrorectal 596.1
  vesicouterine 619.0
    congenital 752.3
  vesicovaginal 619.0
  vulvorectal 619.1
    congenital 752.49

Fit 780.39
  apoplectic (see also Disease, cerebrovascular, acute) 436
    late effect — see Late effect(s) (of) cerebrovascular disease
  epileptic (see also Epilepsy) 345.9 ☑
  fainting 780.2
  hysterical 300.11
  newborn 779.0

Fitting (of)
  artificial
    arm (complete) (partial) V52.0
    breast V52.4
      implant exchange (different material) (different size) V52.4
    eye(s) V52.2
    leg(s) (complete) (partial) V52.1
  brain neuropacemaker V53.02
  cardiac pacemaker V53.31
  carotid sinus pacemaker V53.39
  cerebral ventricle (communicating) shunt V53.01
  colostomy belt V53.5 ☑
  contact lenses V53.1
  cystostomy device V53.6
  defibrillator, automatic implantable cardiac V53.32
  dentures V52.3
  device, unspecified type V53.90
    abdominal V53.59 ▲
    cardiac
      defibrillator, automatic implantable V53.32
      pacemaker V53.31
      specified NEC V53.39
    cerebral ventricle (communicating) shunt V53.01
    gastrointestinal NEC V53.59 ●
    insulin pump V53.91
    intestinal V53.50 ●
    intrauterine contraceptive V25.1
    nervous system V53.09
    orthodontic V53.4
    orthoptic V53.1
    other device V53.99
    prosthetic V52.9
      breast V52.4

Fitting — continued
  device, unspecified type — continued
    prosthetic — continued
      dental V52.3
      eye V52.2
      specified type NEC V52.8
    special senses V53.09
    substitution
      auditory V53.09
      nervous system V53.09
      visual V53.09
    urinary V53.6
  diaphragm (contraceptive) V25.02
  gastric lap band V53.51 ●
  gastrointestinal appliance and device NEC ●
    V53.59 ●
  glasses (reading) V53.1
  growth rod V54.02
  hearing aid V53.2
  ileostomy device V53.5 ☑
  intestinal appliance ►and◄ device V53.50 ▲
  intestinal appliance or device NEC V53.5 ☑
  intrauterine contraceptive device V25.1
  neuropacemaker (brain) (peripheral nerve) (spinal cord) V53.02
  orthodontic device V53.4
  orthopedic (device) V53.7
    brace V53.7
    cast V53.7
    corset V53.7
    shoes V53.7
  pacemaker (cardiac) V53.31
    brain V53.02
    carotid sinus V53.39
    peripheral nerve V53.02
    spinal cord V53.02
  prosthesis V52.9
    arm (complete) (partial) V52.0
    breast V52.4
      implant exchange (different material) (different size) V52.4
    dental V52.3
    eye V52.2
    leg (complete) (partial) V52.1
    specified type NEC V52.8
  spectacles V53.1
  wheelchair V53.8

Fitz-Hugh and Curtis syndrome 098.86
  due to
    Chlamydia trachomatis 099.56
    Neisseria gonorrhoeae (gonococcal peritonitis) 098.86

Fitz's syndrome (acute hemorrhagic pancreatitis) 577.0

Fixation
  joint — see Ankylosis
  larynx 478.79
  pupil 364.76
  stapes 385.22
    deafness (see also Deafness, conductive) 389.04
  uterus (acquired) — see Malposition, uterus
  vocal cord 478.5

Flaccid — see also condition
  foot 736.79
  forearm 736.09
  palate, congenital 750.26

Flail
  chest 807.4
    newborn 767.3
  joint (paralytic) 718.80
    ankle 718.87
    elbow 718.82
    foot 718.87
    hand 718.84
    hip 718.85
    knee 718.86
    multiple sites 718.89
    pelvic region 718.85
    shoulder (region) 718.81
    specified site NEC 718.88
    wrist 718.83

Flajani (-Basedow) syndrome or disease (exophthalmic goiter) 242.0 ☑

Flap, liver 572.8

Flare, anterior chamber (aqueous) (eye) 364.04

Flashback phenomena (drug) (hallucinogenic) 292.89

Flat
  chamber (anterior) (eye) 360.34
  chest, congenital 754.89
  electroencephalogram (EEG) 348.89 ▲
  foot (acquired) (fixed type) (painful) (postural) (spastic) 734
    congenital 754.61
      rocker bottom 754.61
      vertical talus 754.61
    rachitic 268.1
    rocker bottom (congenital) 754.61
    vertical talus, congenital 754.61
  organ or site, congenital NEC — see Anomaly, specified type NEC
  pelvis 738.6
    with disproportion (fetopelvic) 653.2 ☑
      affecting fetus or newborn 763.1
      causing obstructed labor 660.1 ☑
        affecting fetus or newborn 763.1
    congenital 755.69

Flatau-Schilder disease 341.1

Flattening
  head, femur 736.39
  hip 736.39
  lip (congenital) 744.89
  nose (congenital) 754.0
    acquired 738.0

Flatulence 787.3

Flatus 787.3
  vaginalis 629.89

Flax dressers' disease 504

Flea bite — see Injury, superficial, by site

Fleischer (-Kayser) ring (corneal pigmentation) 275.1 [371.14]

Fleischner's disease 732.3

Fleshy mole 631

Flexibilitas cerea — see also Catalepsy 300.11

Flexion
  cervix — see Flexion, uterus
  contracture, joint (see also Contraction, joint) 718.4 ☑
  deformity, joint (see also Contraction, joint) 736.9
  hip, congenital (see also Subluxation, congenital, hip) 754.32
  uterus (see also Malposition, uterus) 621.6

Flexner's
  bacillus 004.1
  diarrhea (ulcerative) 004.1
  dysentery 004.1

Flexner-Boyd dysentery 004.2

Flexure — see condition

Floater, vitreous 379.24

Floating
  cartilage (joint) (see also Disorder, cartilage, articular) 718.0 ☑
    knee 717.6
  gallbladder (congenital) 751.69
  kidney 593.0
    congenital 753.3
  liver (congenital) 751.69
  rib 756.3
  spleen 289.59

Flooding 626.2

Floor — see condition

Floppy
  infant NEC 781.99
  iris syndrome 364.81
  valve syndrome (mitral) 424.0

Flu — see also Influenza
  bird 488.0 ●
  gastric NEC 008.8
  swine 488.1 ●

Fluctuating blood pressure 796.4

Fluid
  abdomen 789.59
  chest (see also Pleurisy, with effusion) 511.9
  heart (see also Failure, heart) 428.0
  joint (see also Effusion, joint) 719.0 ☑
  loss (acute) 276.50
    with
      hypernatremia 276.0
      hyponatremia 276.1

Fluid — continued
  lung (see also Edema, lung)
    encysted 511.89
  peritoneal cavity 789.59
    malignant 789.51
  pleural cavity (see also Pleurisy, with effusion) 511.9
  retention 276.6

Flukes NEC — see also Infestation, fluke 121.9
  blood NEC (see also Infestation, Schistosoma) 120.9
  liver 121.3

Fluor (albus) (vaginalis) 623.5
  trichomonal (Trichomonas vaginalis) 131.00

Fluorosis (dental) (chronic) 520.3

Flushing 782.62
  menopausal 627.2

Flush syndrome 259.2

Flutter
  atrial or auricular 427.32
  heart (ventricular) 427.42
    atrial 427.32
  impure 427.32
  postoperative 997.1
  ventricular 427.42

Flux (bloody) (serosanguineous) 009.0

Focal — see condition

Fochier's abscess — see Abscess, by site

Focus, Assmann's — see also Tuberculosis 011.0 ☑

Fogo selvagem 694.4

Foix-Alajouanine syndrome 336.1

Folds, anomalous — see also Anomaly, specified type NEC
  Bowman's membrane 371.31
  Descemet's membrane 371.32
  epicanthic 743.63
  heart 746.89
  posterior segment of eye, congenital 743.54

Folie à deux 297.3

Follicle
  cervix (nabothian) (ruptured) 616.0
  graafian, ruptured, with hemorrhage 620.0
  nabothian 616.0

Folliclis (primary) — see also Tuberculosis 017.0 ☑

Follicular — see also condition
  cyst (atretic) 620.0

Folliculitis 704.8
  abscedens et suffodiens 704.8
  decalvans 704.09
  gonorrheal (acute) 098.0
    chronic or duration of 2 months or more 098.2
  keloid, keloidalis 706.1
  pustular 704.8
  ulerythematosa reticulata 701.8

Folliculosis, conjunctival 372.02

Følling's disease (phenylketonuria) 270.1

Follow-up (examination) (routine) (following) V67.9
  cancer chemotherapy V67.2
  chemotherapy V67.2
  fracture V67.4
  high-risk medication V67.51
  injury NEC V67.59
  postpartum
    immediately after delivery V24.0
    routine V24.2
  psychiatric V67.3
  psychotherapy V67.3
  radiotherapy V67.1
  specified condition NEC V67.59
  specified surgery NEC V67.09
  surgery V67.00
    vaginal pap smear V67.01
  treatment V67.9
    combined NEC V67.6
    fracture V67.4
    involving high-risk medication NEC V67.51
    mental disorder V67.3
    specified NEC V67.59

Fong's syndrome (hereditary osteoonychodysplasia) 756.89

Food
  allergy 693.1

Fistula — Food

☑ Additional Digit Required — Refer to the Tabular List for Digit Selection   ▼ Subterms under main terms may continue to next column or page

2010 ICD-9-CM   ►◄ Revised Text   ● New Line   ▲ Revised Code   October 2009 • Volume 2 — 115

Index

Food — Fracture

Food — continued
  anaphylactic shock — see Anaphylactic shock, due to, food
  asphyxia (from aspiration or inhalation) (see also Asphyxia, food) 933.1
  choked on (see also Asphyxia, food) 933.1
  deprivation 994.2
    specified kind of food NEC 269.8
  intoxication (see also Poisoning, food) 005.9
  lack of 994.2
  poisoning (see also Poisoning, food) 005.9
  refusal or rejection NEC 307.59
  strangulation or suffocation (see also Asphyxia, food) 933.1
  toxemia (see also Poisoning, food) 005.9
Foot — see also condition
  and mouth disease 078.4
  process disease 581.3
Foramen ovale (nonclosure) (patent) (persistent) 745.5
Forbes-Albright syndrome (nonpuerperal amenorrhea and lactation associated with pituitary tumor) 253.1
Forbes'(glycogen storage) disease 271.0
Forced birth or delivery NEC 669.8 ☑
  affecting fetus or newborn NEC 763.89
Forceps
  delivery NEC 669.5 ☑
    affecting fetus or newborn 763.2
Fordyce's disease (ectopic sebaceous glands) (mouth) 750.26
Fordyce-Fox disease (apocrine miliaria) 705.82
Forearm — see condition
Foreign body

  Note — For foreign body with open wound, or other injury, see Wound, open, or the type of injury specified.

  accidentally left during a procedure 998.4
  anterior chamber (eye) 871.6
    magnetic 871.5
      retained or old 360.51
    retained or old 360.61
  ciliary body (eye) 871.6
    magnetic 871.5
      retained or old 360.52
    retained or old 360.62
  entering through orifice (current) (old)
    accessory sinus 932
    air passage (upper) 933.0
      lower 934.8
    alimentary canal 938
    alveolar process 935.0
    antrum (Highmore) 932
    anus 937
    appendix 936
    asphyxia due to (see also Asphyxia, food) 933.1
    auditory canal 931
    auricle 931
    bladder 939.0
    bronchioles 934.8
    bronchus (main) 934.1
    buccal cavity 935.0
    canthus (inner) 930.1
    cecum 936
    cervix (canal) uterine 939.1
    coil, ileocecal 936
    colon 936
    conjunctiva 930.1
    conjunctival sac 930.1
    cornea 930.0
    digestive organ or tract NEC 938
    duodenum 936
    ear (external) 931
    esophagus 935.1
    eye (external) 930.9
      combined sites 930.8
      intraocular — see Foreign body, by site
      specified site NEC 930.8
    eyeball 930.8
      intraocular — see Foreign body, intraocular
    eyelid 930.1
      retained or old 374.86
    frontal sinus 932
    gastrointestinal tract 938

Foreign body — continued
  entering through orifice — continued
    genitourinary tract 939.9
    globe 930.8
      penetrating 871.6
        magnetic 871.5
          retained or old 360.50
        retained or old 360.60
    gum 935.0
    Highmore's antrum 932
    hypopharynx 933.0
    ileocecal coil 936
    ileum 936
    inspiration (of) 933.1
    intestine (large) (small) 936
    lacrimal apparatus, duct, gland, or sac 930.2
    larynx 933.1
    lung 934.8
    maxillary sinus 932
    mouth 935.0
    nasal sinus 932
    nasopharynx 933.0
    nose (passage) 932
    nostril 932
    oral cavity 935.0
    palate 935.0
    penis 939.3
    pharynx 933.0
    pyriform sinus 933.0
    rectosigmoid 937
      junction 937
    rectum 937
    respiratory tract 934.9
      specified part NEC 934.8
    sclera 930.1
    sinus 932
      accessory 932
      frontal 932
      maxillary 932
      nasal 932
      pyriform 933.0
    small intestine 936
    stomach (hairball) 935.2
    suffocation by (see also Asphyxia, food) 933.1
    swallowed 938
      tongue 933.0
    tear ducts or glands 930.2
    throat 933.0
    tongue 935.0
      swallowed 933.0
    tonsil, tonsillar 933.0
      fossa 933.0
    trachea 934.0
    ureter 939.0
    urethra 939.0
    uterus (any part) 939.1
    vagina 939.2
    vulva 939.2
    wind pipe 934.0
  feeling of, in throat 784.99
  granuloma (old) 728.82
    bone 733.99
    in operative wound (inadvertently left) 998.4
      due to surgical material intentionally left — see Complications, due to (presence of) any device, implant, or graft classified to 996.0–996.5 NEC
    muscle 728.82
    skin 709.4
    soft tissue 709.4
    subcutaneous tissue 709.4
  in
    bone (residual) 733.99
    open wound — see Wound, open, by site complicated
    soft tissue (residual) 729.6
  inadvertently left in operation wound (causing adhesions, obstruction, or perforation) 998.4
  ingestion, ingested NEC 938
  inhalation or inspiration (see also Asphyxia, food) 933.1

Foreign body — continued
  internal organ, not entering through an orifice — see Injury, internal, by site, with open wound
  intraocular (nonmagnetic) 871.6
    combined sites 871.6
      magnetic 871.5
        retained or old 360.59
      retained or old 360.69
    magnetic 871.5
      retained or old 360.50
    retained or old 360.60
    specified site NEC 871.6
      magnetic 871.5
        retained or old 360.59
      retained or old 360.69
    iris (nonmagnetic) 871.6
      magnetic 871.5
        retained or old 360.52
      retained or old 360.62
    lens (nonmagnetic) 871.6
      magnetic 871.5
        retained or old 360.53
      retained or old 360.63
    lid, eye 930.1
    ocular muscle 870.4
      retained or old 376.6
    old or residual
      bone 733.99
      eyelid 374.86
      middle ear 385.83
      muscle 729.6
        ocular 376.6
      retrobulbar 376.6
      skin 729.6
        with granuloma 709.4
      soft tissue 729.6
        with granuloma 709.4
      subcutaneous tissue 729.6
        with granuloma 709.4
    operation wound, left accidentally 998.4
    orbit 870.4
      retained or old 376.6
    posterior wall, eye 871.6
      magnetic 871.5
        retained or old 360.55
      retained or old 360.65
    respiratory tree 934.9
      specified site NEC 934.8
    retained (old) (nonmagnetic) (in)
      anterior chamber (eye) 360.61
        magnetic 360.51
      ciliary body 360.62
        magnetic 360.52
      eyelid 374.86
      globe 360.60
        magnetic 360.50
      intraocular 360.60
        magnetic 360.50
        specified site NEC 360.69
          magnetic 360.59
      iris 360.62
        magnetic 360.52
      lens 360.63
        magnetic 360.53
      muscle 729.6
      orbit 376.6
      posterior wall of globe 360.65
        magnetic 360.55
      retina 360.65
        magnetic 360.55
      retrobulbar 376.6
      skin 729.6
        with granuloma 709.4
      soft tissue 729.6
        with granuloma 709.4
      subcutaneous tissue 729.6
        with granuloma 709.4
      vitreous 360.64
        magnetic 360.54
    retina 871.6
      magnetic 871.5
        retained or old 360.55
      retained or old 360.65
    superficial, without major open wound (see also Injury, superficial, by site) 919.6

Foreign body — continued
  swallowed NEC 938
  throat, feeling of 784.99
  vitreous (humor) 871.6
    magnetic 871.5
      retained or old 360.54
    retained or old 360.64
Forking, aqueduct of Sylvius 742.3
  with spina bifida (see also Spina bifida) 741.0 ☑
Formation
  bone in scar tissue (skin) 709.3
  connective tissue in vitreous 379.25
  Elschnig pearls (postcataract extraction) 366.51
  hyaline in cornea 371.49
  sequestrum in bone (due to infection) (see also Osteomyelitis) 730.1 ☑
  valve
    colon, congenital 751.5
    ureter (congenital) 753.29
Formication 782.0
Fort Bragg fever 100.89
Fossa — see also condition
  pyriform — see condition
Foster care (status) V60.81 ●
Foster-Kennedy syndrome 377.04
Fothergill's
  disease, meaning scarlatina anginosa 034.1
  neuralgia (see also Neuralgia, trigeminal) 350.1
Foul breath 784.99
Found dead (cause unknown) 798.9
Foundling V20.0
Fournier's disease (idiopathic gangrene) 608.83
Fourth
  cranial nerve — see condition
  disease 057.8
  molar 520.1
Foville's syndrome 344.89
Fox's
  disease (apocrine miliaria) 705.82
  impetigo (contagiosa) 684
Fox-Fordyce disease (apocrine miliaria) 705.82
Fracture (abduction) (adduction) (avulsion) (compression) (crush) (dislocation) (oblique) (separation) (closed) 829.0

  Note — For fracture of any of the following sites with fracture of other bones — see Fracture, multiple.

  "Closed" includes the following descriptions of fractures, with or without delayed healing, unless they are specified as open or compound:

comminuted	linear
depressed	simple
elevated	slipped epiphysis
fissured	spiral
greenstick	unspecified
impacted	

  "Open" includes the following descriptions of fractures, with or without delayed healing:

compound	puncture
infected	with foreign body
missile	

  For late effect of fracture, see Late, effect, fracture, by site.

  with
    internal injuries in same region (conditions classifiable to 860–869) (see also Injury, internal, by site)
    pelvic region — see Fracture, pelvis
  acetabulum (with visceral injury) (closed) 808.0
    open 808.1
  acromion (process) (closed) 811.01
    open 811.11
  alveolus (closed) 802.8
    open 802.9
  ankle (malleolus) (closed) 824.8
    bimalleolar (Dupuytren's) (Pott's) 824.4
      open 824.5

Fracture — *continued*
ankle — *continued*
  bone 825.21
    open 825.31
  lateral malleolus only (fibular) 824.2
    open 824.3
  medial malleolus only (tibial) 824.0
    open 824.1
  open 824.9
  pathologic 733.16
  talus 825.21
    open 825.31
  trimalleolar 824.6
    open 824.7
antrum — *see* Fracture, skull, base
arm (closed) 818.0
  and leg(s) (any bones) 828.0
    open 828.1
  both (any bones) (with rib(s)) (with sternum) 819.0
    open 819.1
  lower 813.80
    open 813.90
  open 818.1
  upper — *see* Fracture, humerus
astragalus (closed) 825.21
  open 825.31
atlas — *see* Fracture, vertebra, cervical, first
axis — *see* Fracture, vertebra, cervical, second
back — *see* Fracture, vertebra, by site
Barton's — *see* Fracture, radius, lower end
basal (skull) — *see* Fracture, skull, base
Bennett's (closed) 815.01
  open 815.11
bimalleolar (closed) 824.4
  open 824.5
bone (closed) NEC 829.0
  birth injury NEC 767.3
  open 829.1
  pathologic NEC (*see also* Fracture, pathologic) 733.10
  stress NEC (*see also* Fracture, stress) 733.95
boot top — *see* Fracture, fibula
boxers' — *see* Fracture, metacarpal bone(s)
breast bone — *see* Fracture, sternum
bucket handle (semilunar cartilage) — *see* Tear, meniscus
buckle — *see* Fracture, torus ●
burst — *see* Fracture, traumatic, by site
bursting — *see* Fracture, phalanx, hand, distal
calcaneus (closed) 825.0
  open 825.1
capitate (bone) (closed) 814.07
  open 814.17
capitellum (humerus) (closed) 812.49
  open 812.59
carpal bone(s) (wrist NEC) (closed) 814.00
  open 814.10
  specified site NEC 814.09
    open 814.19
cartilage, knee (semilunar) — *see* Tear, meniscus
cervical — *see* Fracture, vertebra, cervical
chauffeur's — *see* Fracture, ulna, lower end
chisel — *see* Fracture, radius, upper end
chronic — *see* Fracture, pathologic ●
clavicle (interligamentous part) (closed) 810.00
  acromial end 810.03
    open 810.13
  due to birth trauma 767.2
  open 810.10
  shaft (middle third) 810.02
    open 810.12
  sternal end 810.01
    open 810.11
clayshovelers' — *see* Fracture, vertebra, cervical
coccyx (*see also* Fracture, vertebra, coccyx)
  complicating delivery 665.6 ☑
collar bone — *see* Fracture, clavicle
Colles' (reversed) (closed) 813.41
  open 813.51
comminuted — *see* Fracture, by site
compression (*see also* Fracture, by site)
  nontraumatic — *see* Fracture, pathologic
congenital 756.9

Fracture — *continued*
  coracoid process (closed) 811.02
    open 811.12
  coronoid process (ulna) (closed) 813.02
    mandible (closed) 802.23
      open 802.33
    open 813.12
  corpus cavernosum penis 959.13
  costochondral junction — *see* Fracture, rib
  costosternal junction — *see* Fracture, rib
  cranium — *see* Fracture, skull, by site
  cricoid cartilage (closed) 807.5
    open 807.6
  cuboid (ankle) (closed) 825.23
    open 825.33
  cuneiform
    foot (closed) 825.24
      open 825.34
    wrist (closed) 814.03
      open 814.13
  dental implant 525.73
  dental restorative material
    with loss of material 525.64
    without loss of material 525.63
  due to
    birth injury — *see* Birth injury, fracture
    gunshot — *see* Fracture, by site, open
    neoplasm — *see* Fracture, pathologic
    osteoporosis — *see* Fracture, pathologic
  Dupuytren's (ankle) (fibula) (closed) 824.4
    open 824.5
    radius 813.42
      open 813.52
  Duverney's — *see* Fracture, ilium
  elbow (*see also* Fracture, humerus, lower end)
    olecranon (process) (closed) 813.01
      open 813.11
    supracondylar (closed) 812.41
      open 812.51
  ethmoid (bone) (sinus) — *see* Fracture, skull, base
  face bone(s) (closed) NEC 802.8
    with
      other bone(s) — *see* Fracture, multiple, skull
      skull (*see also* Fracture, skull)
        involving other bones — *see* Fracture, multiple, skull
    open 802.9
  fatigue — *see* Fracture, march
  femur, femoral (closed) 821.00
    cervicotrochanteric 820.03
      open 820.13
    condyles, epicondyles 821.21
      open 821.31
    distal end — *see* Fracture, femur, lower end
    epiphysis (separation)
      capital 820.01
        open 820.11
      head 820.01
        open 820.11
      lower 821.22
        open 821.32
      trochanteric 820.01
        open 820.11
      upper 820.01
        open 820.11
    head 820.09
      open 820.19
    lower end or extremity (distal end) (closed) 821.20
      condyles, epicondyles 821.21
        open 821.31
      epiphysis (separation) 821.22
        open 821.32
      multiple sites 821.29
        open 821.39
      open 821.30
      specified site NEC 821.29
        open 821.39
      supracondylar 821.23
        open 821.33
      T-shaped 821.21
        open 821.31
    neck (closed) 820.8

Fracture — *continued*
femur, femoral — *continued*
  neck — *continued*
    base (cervicotrochanteric) 820.03
      open 820.13
    extracapsular 820.20
      open 820.30
    intertrochanteric (section) 820.21
      open 820.31
    intracapsular 820.00
      open 820.10
    intratrochanteric 820.21
      open 820.31
    midcervical 820.02
      open 820.12
    open 820.9
    pathologic 733.14
      specified part NEC 733.15
    specified site NEC 820.09
      open 820.19
    transcervical 820.02
      open 820.12
    transtrochanteric 820.20
      open 820.30
  open 821.10
  pathologic 733.14
    specified part NEC 733.15
  peritrochanteric (section) 820.20
    open 820.30
  shaft (lower third) (middle third) (upper third) 821.01
    open 821.11
  subcapital 820.09
    open 820.19
  subtrochanteric (region) (section) 820.22
    open 820.32
  supracondylar 821.23
    open 821.33
  transepiphyseal 820.01
    open 820.11
  trochanter (greater) (lesser) (*see also* Fracture, femur, neck, by site) 820.20
    open 820.30
  T-shaped, into knee joint 821.21
    open 821.31
  upper end 820.8
    open 820.9
fibula (closed) 823.81
  with tibia 823.82
    open 823.92
  distal end 824.8
    open 824.9
  epiphysis
    lower 824.8
      open 824.9
    upper — *see* Fracture, fibula, upper end
  head — *see* Fracture, fibula, upper end
  involving ankle 824.2
    open 824.3
  lower end or extremity 824.8
    open 824.9
  malleolus (external) (lateral) 824.2
    open 824.3
  open NEC 823.91
  pathologic 733.16
  proximal end — *see* Fracture, fibula, upper end
  shaft 823.21
    with tibia 823.22
      open 823.32
    open 823.31
  stress 733.93
  torus 823.41
    with tibia 823.42
  upper end or extremity (epiphysis) (head) (proximal end) (styloid) 823.01
    with tibia 823.02
      open 823.12
    open 823.11
finger(s), of one hand (closed) (*see also* Fracture, phalanx, hand) 816.00
  with
    metacarpal bone(s), of same hand 817.0
      open 817.1

Fracture — *continued*
finger(s), of one hand (*see also* Fracture, phalanx, hand) — *continued*
  with — *continued*
    thumb of same hand 816.03
      open 816.13
    open 816.10
foot, except toe(s) alone (closed) 825.20
  open 825.30
forearm (closed) NEC 813.80
  lower end (distal end) (lower epiphysis) 813.40
    open 813.50
  open 813.90
  shaft 813.20
    open 813.30
  upper end (proximal end) (upper epiphysis) 813.00
    open 813.10
fossa, anterior, middle, or posterior — *see* Fracture, skull, base
Fracture (abduction) (adduction) (avulsion) (compression) (crush) (dislocation) (oblique) (separation) (closed) 829.0
frontal (bone) (*see also* Fracture, skull, vault)
  sinus — *see* Fracture, skull, base
Galeazzi's — *see* Fracture, radius, lower end
glenoid (cavity) (fossa) (scapula) (closed) 811.03
  open 811.13
Gosselin's — *see* Fracture, ankle
greenstick — *see* Fracture, by site
grenade-throwers' — *see* Fracture, humerus, shaft
gutter — *see* Fracture, skull, vault
hamate (closed) 814.08
  open 814.18
hand, one (closed) 815.00
  carpals 814.00
    open 814.10
    specified site NEC 814.09
      open 814.19
  metacarpals 815.00
    open 815.10
  multiple, bones of one hand 817.0
    open 817.1
  open 815.10
  phalanges (*see also* Fracture, phalanx, hand) 816.00
    open 816.10
healing
  aftercare (*see also* Aftercare, fracture) V54.89
  change of cast V54.89
  complications — *see* condition
  convalescence V66.4
  removal of
    cast V54.89
    fixation device
      external V54.89
      internal V54.01
heel bone (closed) 825.0
  open 825.1
Hill-Sachs 812.09
hip (closed) (*see also* Fracture, femur, neck) 820.8
  open 820.9
  pathologic 733.14
humerus (closed) 812.20
  anatomical neck 812.02
    open 812.12
  articular process (*see also* Fracture humerus, condyle(s)) 812.44
    open 812.54
  capitellum 812.49
    open 812.59
  condyle(s) 812.44
    lateral (external) 812.42
      open 812.52
    medial (internal epicondyle) 812.43
      open 812.53
    open 812.54
  distal end — *see* Fracture, humerus, lower end

☑ Additional Digit Required — Refer to the Tabular List for Digit Selection   ▽ Subterms under main terms may continue to next column or page

2010 ICD-9-CM   ►◄ Revised Text   ● New Line   ▲ Revised Code   October 2009 • Volume 2 — 117

Fracture — *continued*
  humerus — *continued*
    epiphysis
      lower (*see also* Fracture, humerus, condyle(s)) 812.44
        open 812.54
        upper 812.09
          open 812.19
      external condyle 812.42
        open 812.52
      great tuberosity 812.03
        open 812.13
      head 812.09
        open 812.19
      internal epicondyle 812.43
        open 812.53
      lesser tuberosity 812.09
        open 812.19
      lower end or extremity (distal end) (*see also* Fracture, humerus, by site) 812.40
      multiple sites NEC 812.49
        open 812.59
        open 812.50
      specified site NEC 812.49
        open 812.59
      neck 812.01
        open 812.11
      open 812.30
      pathologic 733.11
      proximal end — *see* Fracture, humerus, upper end
      shaft 812.21
        open 812.31
      supracondylar 812.41
        open 812.51
      surgical neck 812.01
        open 812.11
      trochlea 812.49
        open 812.59
      T-shaped 812.44
        open 812.54
      tuberosity — *see* Fracture, humerus, upper end
      upper end or extremity (proximal end) (*see also* Fracture, humerus, by site) 812.00
        open 812.10
        specified site NEC 812.09
          open 812.19
  hyoid bone (closed) 807.5
    open 807.6
  hyperextension — *see* Fracture, radius, lower end
  ilium (with visceral injury) (closed) 808.41
    open 808.51
  impaction, impacted — *see* Fracture, by site
  incus — *see* Fracture, skull, base
  innominate bone (with visceral injury) (closed) 808.49
    open 808.59
  instep, of one foot (closed) 825.20
    with toe(s) of same foot 827.0
      open 827.1
    open 825.30
  insufficiency — *see* Fracture, pathologic, by site
  internal
    ear — *see* Fracture, skull, base
    semilunar cartilage, knee — *see* Tear, meniscus, medial
  intertrochanteric — *see* Fracture, femur, neck, intertrochanteric
  ischium (with visceral injury) (closed) 808.42
    open 808.52
  jaw (bone) (lower) (closed) (*see also* Fracture, mandible) 802.20
    angle 802.25
      open 802.35
    open 802.30
    upper — *see* Fracture, maxilla
  knee
    cap (closed) 822.0
      open 822.1
    cartilage (semilunar) — *see* Tear, meniscus
  labyrinth (osseous) — *see* Fracture, skull, base
  larynx (closed) 807.5

Fracture — *continued*
  larynx — *continued*
    open 807.6
  late effect — *see* Late, effects (of), fracture
  Le Fort's — *see* Fracture, maxilla
  leg (closed) 827.0
    with rib(s) or sternum 828.0
      open 828.1
    both (any bones) 828.0
      open 828.1
    lower — *see* Fracture, tibia
      open 827.1
    upper — *see* Fracture, femur
  limb
    lower (multiple) (closed) NEC 827.0
      open 827.1
    upper (multiple) (closed) NEC 818.0
      open 818.1
  long bones, due to birth trauma — *see* Birth injury, fracture
  lower end or extremity (anterior lip) (posterior) 824.8
    open 824.9
  lumbar — *see* Fracture, vertebra, lumbar
  lunate bone (closed) 814.02
    open 814.12
  malar bone (closed) 802.4
    open 802.5
  Malgaigne's (closed) 808.43
    open 808.53
  malleolus (closed) 824.8
    bimalleolar 824.4
      open 824.5
    lateral 824.2
      and medial (*see also* Fracture, malleolus, bimalleolar)
        with lip of tibia — *see* Fracture, malleolus, trimalleolar
        open 824.3
    medial (closed) 824.0
      and lateral (*see also* Fracture, malleolus, bimalleolar)
        with lip of tibia — *see* Fracture, malleolus, trimalleolar
        open 824.1
      open 824.9
    trimalleolar (closed) 824.6
      open 824.7
  malleus — *see* Fracture, skull, base
  malunion 733.81
  mandible (closed) 802.20
    angle 802.25
      open 802.35
    body 802.28
      alveolar border 802.27
        open 802.37
        open 802.38
      symphysis 802.26
        open 802.36
    condylar process 802.21
      open 802.31
    coronoid process 802.23
      open 802.33
    multiple sites 802.29
      open 802.39
    open 802.30
    ramus NEC 802.24
      open 802.34
    subcondylar 802.22
      open 802.32
  manubrium — *see* Fracture, sternum
  march 733.95
    fibula 733.93
    metatarsals 733.94
    tibia 733.93
  maxilla, maxillary (superior) (upper jaw) (closed) 802.4
    inferior — *see* Fracture, mandible
    open 802.5
  meniscus, knee — *see* Tear, meniscus
  metacarpus, metacarpal (bone(s)), of one hand (closed) 815.00
    with phalanx, phalanges, hand (finger(s)) (thumb) of same hand 817.0
      open 817.1
    base 815.02

Fracture — *continued*
  metacarpus, metacarpal(s), of one hand — *continued*
    base — *continued*
      first metacarpal 815.01
        open 815.11
        open 815.12
      thumb 815.01
        open 815.11
    multiple sites 815.09
      open 815.19
    neck 815.04
      open 815.14
    open 815.10
    shaft 815.03
      open 815.13
  metatarsus, metatarsal (bone(s)), of one foot (closed) 825.25
    with tarsal bone(s) 825.29
      open 825.39
    open 825.35
  Montegia's (closed) 813.03
    open 813.13
  Moore's — *see* Fracture, radius, lower end
  multangular bone (closed)
    larger 814.05
      open 814.15
    smaller 814.06
      open 814.16
  multiple (closed) 829.0

Note — Multiple fractures of sites classifiable to the same three- or four-digit category are coded to that category, except for sites classifiable to 810–818 or 820–827 in different limbs.

Multiple fractures of sites classifiable to different fourth-digit subdivisions within the same three-digit category should be dealt with according to coding rules.

Multiple fractures of sites classifiable to different three-digit categories (identifiable from the listing under "Fracture"), and of sites classifiable to 810–818 or 820–827 in different limbs should be coded according to the following list, which should be referred to in the following priority order: skull or face bones, pelvis or vertebral column, legs, arms.

      arm (multiple bones in same arm except in hand alone) (sites classifiable to 810–817 with sites classifiable to a different three-digit category in 810–817 in same arm) (closed) 818.0
        open 818.1
      arms, both or arm(s) with rib(s) or sternum (sites classifiable to 810–818 with sites classifiable to same range of categories in other limb or to 807) (closed) 819.0
        open 819.1
      bones of trunk NEC (closed) 809.0
        open 809.1
      hand, metacarpal bone(s) with phalanx or phalanges of same hand (sites classifiable to 815 with sites classifiable to 816 in same hand) (closed) 817.0
        open 817.1
      leg (multiple bones in same leg) (sites classifiable to 820–826 with sites classifiable to a different three-digit category in that range in same leg) (closed) 827.0
        open 827.1
      legs, both or leg(s) with arm(s), rib(s), or sternum (sites classifiable to 820–827 with sites classifiable to same range of categories in other leg or to 807 or 810–819) (closed) 828.0
        open 828.1
      open 829.1

Fracture — *continued*
  multiple — *continued*
    pelvis with other bones except skull or face bones (sites classifiable to 808 with sites classifiable to 805–807 or 810–829) (closed) 809.0
      open 809.1
    skull, specified or unspecified bones, or face bone(s) with any other bone(s) (sites classifiable to 800–803 with sites classifiable to 805–829) (closed) 804.0 ☑

Note — Use the following fifth-digit subclassification with categories 800, 801, 803, and 804:

0   unspecified state of consciousness

1   with no loss of consciousness

2   with brief [less than one hour] loss of consciousness

3   with moderate [1–24 hours] loss of consciousness

4   with prolonged [more than 24 hours] loss of consciousness and return to pre–existing conscious level

5   with prolonged [more than 24 hours] loss of consciousness, without return to pre–existing conscious level

Use fifth-digit 5 to designate when a patient is unconscious and dies before regaining consciousness, regardless of the duration of the loss of consciousness

6   with loss of consciousness of unspecified duration

9   with concussion, unspecified

    with
      contusion, cerebral 804.1 ☑
      epidural hemorrhage 804.2 ☑
      extradural hemorrhage 804.2 ☑
      hemorrhage (intracranial) NEC 804.3 ☑
      intracranial injury NEC 804.4 ☑
      laceration, cerebral 804.1 ☑
      subarachnoid hemorrhage 804.2 ☑
      subdural hemorrhage 804.2 ☑
    open 804.5 ☑
      with
        contusion, cerebral 804.6 ☑
        epidural hemorrhage 804.7 ☑
        extradural hemorrhage 804.7 ☑
        hemorrhage (intracranial) NEC 804.8 ☑
        intracranial injury NEC 804.9 ☑
        laceration, cerebral 804.6 ☑
        subarachnoid hemorrhage 804.7 ☑
        subdural hemorrhage 804.7 ☑
    vertebral column with other bones, except skull or face bones (sites classifiable to 805 or 806 with sites classifiable to 807–808 or 810–829) (closed) 809.0
      open 809.1
  nasal (bone(s)) (closed) 802.0
    open 802.1
    sinus — *see* Fracture, skull, base
  navicular
    carpal (wrist) (closed) 814.01
      open 814.11
    tarsal (ankle) (closed) 825.22
      open 825.32
  neck — *see* Fracture, vertebra, cervical
  neural arch — *see* Fracture, vertebra, by site
  nonunion 733.82
  nose, nasal, (bone) (septum) (closed) 802.0
    open 802.1
  occiput — *see* Fracture, skull, base
  odontoid process — *see* Fracture, vertebra, cervical
  olecranon (process) (ulna) (closed) 813.01

☑ Additional Digit Required — Refer to the Tabular List for Digit Selection

118 — Volume 2   ►◄ Revised Text   ● New Line   ▲ Revised Code   ᵛᵉᵍ Subterms under main terms may continue to next column or page   2010 ICD-9-CM

Fracture — *continued*
olecranon — *continued*
open 813.11
open 829.1
orbit, orbital (bone) (region) (closed) 802.8
floor (blow-out) 802.6
open 802.7
open 802.9
roof — *see* Fracture, skull, base
specified part NEC 802.8
open 802.9
os
calcis (closed) 825.0
open 825.1
magnum (closed) 814.07
open 814.17
pubis (with visceral injury) (closed) 808.2
open 808.3
triquetrum (closed) 814.03
open 814.13
osseous
auditory meatus — *see* Fracture, skull, base
labyrinth — *see* Fracture, skull, base
ossicles, auditory (incus) (malleus) (stapes) — *see* Fracture, skull, base
osteoporotic — *see* Fracture, pathologic
palate (closed) 802.8
open 802.9
paratrooper — *see* Fracture, tibia, lower end
parietal bone — *see* Fracture, skull, vault
parry — *see* Fracture, Monteggia's
patella (closed) 822.0
open 822.1
pathologic (cause unknown) 733.10
ankle 733.16
femur (neck) 733.14
specified NEC 733.15
fibula 733.16
hip 733.14
humerus 733.11
radius (distal) 733.12
specified site NEC 733.19
tibia 733.16
ulna 733.12
vertebrae (collapse) 733.13
wrist 733.12
pedicle (of vertebral arch) — *see* Fracture, vertebra, by site
pelvis, pelvic (bone(s)) (with visceral injury) (closed) 808.8
multiple (with disruption of pelvic circle) 808.43
open 808.53
open 808.9
rim (closed) 808.49
open 808.59
peritrochanteric (closed) 820.20
open 820.30
phalanx, phalanges, of one
foot (closed) 826.0
with bone(s) of same lower limb 827.0
open 827.1
open 826.1
hand (closed) 816.00
with metacarpal bone(s) of same hand 817.0
open 817.1
distal 816.02
open 816.12
middle 816.01
open 816.11
multiple sites NEC 816.03
open 816.13
open 816.10
proximal 816.01
open 816.11
pisiform (closed) 814.04
open 814.14
pond — *see* Fracture, skull, vault
Pott's (closed) 824.4
open 824.5
prosthetic device, internal — *see* Complications, mechanical
pubis (with visceral injury) (closed) 808.2
open 808.3
Quervain's (closed) 814.01

Fracture — *continued*
Quervain's — *continued*
open 814.11
radius (alone) (closed) 813.81
with ulna NEC 813.83
open 813.93
distal end — *see* Fracture, radius, lower end
epiphysis
lower — *see* Fracture, radius, lower end
upper — *see* Fracture, radius, upper end
head — *see* Fracture, radius, upper end
lower end or extremity (distal end) (lower epiphysis) 813.42
with ulna (lower end) 813.44
open 813.54
open 813.52
torus 813.45
with ulna 813.47   ●
neck — *see* Fracture, radius, upper end
open NEC 813.91
pathologic 733.12
proximal end — *see* Fracture, radius, upper end
shaft (closed) 813.21
with ulna (shaft) 813.23
open 813.33
open 813.31
upper end 813.07
with ulna (upper end) 813.08
open 813.18
epiphysis 813.05
open 813.15
head 813.05
open 813.15
multiple sites 813.07
open 813.17
neck 813.06
open 813.16
open 813.17
specified site NEC 813.07
open 813.17
ramus
inferior or superior (with visceral injury) (closed) 808.2
open 808.3
ischium — *see* Fracture, ischium
mandible 802.24
open 802.34
rib(s) (closed) 807.0 ☑

Note — *Use the following fifth-digit subclassification with categories 807.0–807.1:*
0   *rib(s), unspecified*
1   *one rib*
2   *two ribs*
3   *three ribs*
4   *four ribs*
5   *five ribs*
6   *six ribs*
7   *seven ribs*
8   *eight or more ribs*
9   *multiple ribs, unspecified*

with flail chest (open) 807.4
open 807.1 ☑
root, tooth 873.63
complicated 873.73
sacrum — *see* Fracture, vertebra, sacrum
scaphoid
ankle (closed) 825.22
open 825.32
wrist (closed) 814.01
open 814.11
scapula (closed) 811.00
acromial, acromion (process) 811.01
open 811.11
body 811.09
open 811.19
coracoid process 811.02
open 811.12
glenoid (cavity) (fossa) 811.03

Fracture — *continued*
scapula — *continued*
glenoid — *continued*
open 811.13
neck 811.03
open 811.13
open 811.10
semilunar
bone, wrist (closed) 814.02
open 814.12
cartilage (interior) (knee) — *see* Tear, meniscus
sesamoid bone — *see* Fracture, by site
Shepherd's (closed) 825.21
open 825.31
shoulder (*see also* Fracture, humerus, upper end)
blade — *see* Fracture, scapula
silverfork — *see* Fracture, radius, lower end
sinus (ethmoid) (frontal) (maxillary) (nasal) (sphenoidal) — *see* Fracture, skull, base
Skillern's — *see* Fracture, radius, shaft
skull (multiple NEC) (with face bones) (closed) 803.0 ☑

Note — *Use the following fifth-digit subclassification with categories 800, 801, 803, and 804:*
0   *unspecified state of consciousness*
1   *with no loss of consciousness*
2   *with brief [less than one hour] loss of consciousness*
3   *with moderate [1-24 hours] loss of consciousness*
4   *with prolonged [more than 24 hours] loss of consciousness and return to pre-existing conscious level*
5   *with prolonged [more than 24 hours] loss of consciousness, without return to pre-existing conscious level*

Use fifth-digit 5 to designate when a patient is unconscious and dies before regaining consciousness, regardless of the duration of the loss of consciousness
6   *with loss of consciousness of unspecified duration*
9   *with concussion, unspecified*

with
contusion, cerebral 803.1 ☑
epidural hemorrhage 803.2 ☑
extradural hemorrhage 803.2 ☑
hemorrhage (intracranial) NEC 803.3 ☑
intracranial injury NEC 803.4 ☑
laceration, cerebral 803.1 ☑
other bones — *see* Fracture, multiple, skull
subarachnoid hemorrhage 803.2 ☑
subdural hemorrhage 803.2 ☑
base (antrum) (ethmoid bone) (fossa) (internal ear) (nasal sinus) (occiput) (sphenoid) (temporal bone) (closed) 801.0 ☑
with
contusion, cerebral 801.1 ☑
epidural hemorrhage 801.2 ☑
extradural hemorrhage 801.2 ☑
hemorrhage (intracranial) NEC 801.3 ☑
intracranial injury NEC 801.4 ☑
laceration, cerebral 801.1 ☑
subarachnoid hemorrhage 801.2 ☑
subdural hemorrhage 801.2 ☑
open 801.5 ☑
with
contusion, cerebral 801.6 ☑

Fracture — *continued*
skull — *continued*
base — *continued*
open — *continued*
with — *continued*
epidural hemorrhage 801.7 ☑
extradural hemorrhage 801.7 ☑
hemorrhage (intracranial) NEC 801.8 ☑
intracranial injury NEC 801.9 ☑
laceration, cerebral 801.6 ☑
subarachnoid hemorrhage 801.7 ☑
subdural hemorrhage 801.7 ☑
birth injury 767.3
face bones — *see* Fracture, face bones
open 803.5 ☑
with
contusion, cerebral 803.6 ☑
epidural hemorrhage 803.7 ☑
extradural hemorrhage 803.7 ☑
hemorrhage (intracranial) NEC 803.8 ☑
intracranial injury NEC 803.9 ☑
laceration, cerebral 803.6 ☑
subarachnoid hemorrhage 803.7 ☑
subdural hemorrhage 803.7 ☑
vault (frontal bone) (parietal bone) (vertex) (closed) 800.0 ☑
with
contusion, cerebral 800.1 ☑
epidural hemorrhage 800.2 ☑
extradural hemorrhage 800.2 ☑
hemorrhage (intracranial) NEC 800.3 ☑
intracranial injury NEC 800.4 ☑
laceration, cerebral 800.1 ☑
subarachnoid hemorrhage 800.2 ☑
subdural hemorrhage 800.2 ☑
open 800.5 ☑
with
contusion, cerebral 800.6 ☑
epidural hemorrhage 800.7 ☑
extradural hemorrhage 800.7 ☑
hemorrhage (intracranial) NEC 800.8 ☑
intracranial injury NEC 800.9 ☑
laceration, cerebral 800.6 ☑
subarachnoid hemorrhage 800.7 ☑
subdural hemorrhage 800.7 ☑
Smith's 813.41
open 813.51
sphenoid (bone) (sinus) — *see* Fracture, skull, base
spine (*see also* Fracture, vertebra, by site due to birth trauma) 767.4
spinous process — *see* Fracture, vertebra, by site
spontaneous — *see* Fracture, pathologic
sprinters' — *see* Fracture, ilium
stapes — *see* Fracture, skull, base
stave (*see also* Fracture, metacarpus, metacarpal bone(s))
spine — *see* Fracture, tibia, upper end
sternum (closed) 807.2
with flail chest (open) 807.4
open 807.3
Stieda's — *see* Fracture, femur, lower end
stress 733.95
fibula 733.93
metatarsals 733.94

☑ Additional Digit Required — Refer to the Tabular List for Digit Selection   ▽ Subterms under main terms may continue to next column or page

Index

Fracture — Fremitus, friction, cardiac

Fracture — continued
  stress — continued
    specified site NEC 733.95
    tibia 733.93
  styloid process
    metacarpal (closed) 815.02
      open 815.12
    radius — see Fracture, radius, lower end
    temporal bone — see Fracture, skull, base
    ulna — see Fracture, ulna, lower end
  supracondylar, elbow 812.41
    open 812.51
  symphysis pubis (with visceral injury) (closed) 808.2
    open 808.3
  talus (ankle bone) (closed) 825.21
    open 825.31
  tarsus, tarsal bone(s) (with metatarsus) of one foot (closed) NEC 825.29
    open 825.39
  temporal bone (styloid) — see Fracture, skull, base
  tendon — see Sprain, by site
  thigh — see Fracture, femur, shaft
  thumb (and finger(s)) of one hand (closed) (see also Fracture, phalanx, hand) 816.00
    with metacarpal bone(s) of same hand 817.0
      open 817.1
    metacarpal(s) — see Fracture, metacarpus
    open 816.10
  thyroid cartilage (closed) 807.5
    open 807.6
  tibia (closed) 823.80
    with fibula 823.82
      open 823.92
    condyles — see Fracture, tibia, upper end
    distal end 824.8
      open 824.9
    epiphysis
      lower 824.8
        open 824.9
      upper — see Fracture, tibia, upper end
    head (involving knee joint) — see Fracture, tibia, upper end
    intercondyloid eminence — see Fracture, tibia, upper end
    involving ankle 824.0
      open 824.9
    lower end or extremity (anterior lip) (posterior lip) 824.8
      open 824.9
    malleolus (internal) (medial) 824.0
      open 824.1
    open NEC 823.90
    pathologic 733.16
    proximal end — see Fracture, tibia, upper end
    shaft 823.20
      with fibula 823.22
        open 823.32
      open 823.30
    spine — see Fracture, tibia, upper end
    stress 733.93
    torus 823.40
      with fibula 823.42
    tuberosity — see Fracture, tibia, upper end
    upper end or extremity (condyle) (epiphysis) (head) (spine) (proximal end) (tuberosity) 823.00
      with fibula 823.02
        open 823.12
      open 823.10
  toe(s), of one foot (closed) 826.0
    with bone(s) of same lower limb 827.0
      open 827.1
    open 826.1
  tooth (root) 873.63
    complicated 873.73
  torus
    fibula 823.41
      with tibia 823.42
    humerus 812.49
    radius ▶(alone)◀ 813.45
      with ulna 813.47

Fracture — continued
  torus — continued
    tibia 823.40
      with fibula 823.42
    ulna (alone) 813.46
      with radius 813.47
  trachea (closed) 807.5
    open 807.6
  transverse process — see Fracture, vertebra, by site
  trapezium (closed) 814.05
    open 814.15
  trapezoid bone (closed) 814.06
    open 814.16
  trimalleolar (closed) 824.6
    open 824.7
  triquetral (bone) (closed) 814.03
    open 814.13
  trochanter (greater) (lesser) (closed) (see also Fracture, femur, neck, by site) 820.20
    open 820.30
  trunk (bones) (closed) 809.0
    open 809.1
  tuberosity (external) — see Fracture, by site
  ulna (alone) (closed) 813.82
    with radius NEC 813.83
      open 813.93
    coronoid process (closed) 813.02
      open 813.12
    distal end — see Fracture, ulna, lower end
    epiphysis
      lower — see Fracture, ulna, lower end
      upper — see Fracture, ulna, upper end
    head — see Fracture, ulna, lower end
    lower end (distal end) (head) (lower epiphysis) (styloid process) 813.43
      with radius (lower end) 813.44
        open 813.54
      open 813.53
    olecranon process (closed) 813.01
      open 813.11
    open NEC 813.92
    pathologic 733.12
    proximal end — see Fracture, ulna, upper end
    shaft 813.22
      with radius (shaft) 813.23
        open 813.33
      open 813.32
    styloid process — see Fracture, ulna, lower end
    torus 813.46
      with radius 813.47
    transverse — see Fracture, ulna, by site
    upper end (epiphysis) 813.04
      with radius (upper end) 813.08
        open 813.18
      multiple sites 813.04
        open 813.14
      open 813.14
      specified site NEC 813.04
        open 813.14
  unciform (closed) 814.08
    open 814.18
  vertebra, vertebral (back) (body) (column) (neural arch) (pedicle) (spine) (spinous process) (transverse process) (closed) 805.8
    with
      hematomyelia — see Fracture, vertebra, by site, with spinal cord injury
      injury to
        cauda equina — see Fracture, vertebra, sacrum, with spinal cord injury
        nerve — see Fracture, vertebra, by site, with spinal cord injury
      paralysis — see Fracture, vertebra, by site, with spinal cord injury
      paraplegia — see Fracture, vertebra, by site, with spinal cord injury
      quadriplegia — see Fracture, vertebra, by site, with spinal cord injury

Fracture — continued
  vertebra, vertebral — continued
    with — continued
      spinal concussion — see Fracture, vertebra, by site, with spinal cord injury
      spinal cord injury (closed) NEC 806.8

    Note — Use the following fifth-digit subclassification with categories 806.0–806.3:

    $C_1–C_4$ or unspecified level and $D_1–D_6$ ($T_1–T_6$) or unspecified level with

    0   unspecified spinal cord injury
    1   complete lesion of cord
    2   anterior cord syndrome
    3   central cord syndrome
    4   specified injury NEC

    $C_5–C_7$ level and $D_7–D_{12}$ level with:

    5   unspecified spinal cord injury
    6   complete lesion of cord
    7   anterior cord syndrome
    8   central cord syndrome
    9   specified injury NEC

      cervical 806.0 ☑•
        open 806.1 ☑
      dorsal, dorsolumbar 806.2 ☑
        open 806.9
      thoracic, thoracolumbar 806.2 ☑
        open 806.3 ☑
    atlanto-axial — see Fracture, vertebra, cervical
    cervical (hangman) (teardrop) (closed) 805.00
      with spinal cord injury — see Fracture, vertebra, with spinal cord injury, cervical
      first (atlas) 805.01
        open 805.11
      second (axis) 805.02
        open 805.12
      third 805.03
        open 805.13
      fourth 805.04
        open 805.14
      fifth 805.05
        open 805.15
      sixth 805.06
        open 805.16
      seventh 805.07
        open 805.17
      multiple sites 805.08
        open 805.18
      open 805.10
    chronic 733.13
    coccyx (closed) 805.6
      with spinal cord injury (closed) 806.60
        cauda equina injury 806.62
          complete lesion 806.61
            open 806.71
          open 806.72
        open 806.70
        specified type NEC 806.69
          open 806.79
      open 805.7
    collapsed 733.13
    compression, not due to trauma 733.13
    dorsal (closed) 805.2
      with spinal cord injury — see Fracture, vertebra, with spinal cord injury, dorsal
      open 805.3
    dorsolumbar (closed) 805.2
      with spinal cord injury — see Fracture, vertebra, with spinal cord injury, dorsal
      open 805.3
    due to osteoporosis 733.13
    fetus or newborn 767.4
    lumbar (closed) 805.4

Fracture — continued
  vertebra, vertebral — continued
    lumbar — continued
      with spinal cord injury (closed) 806.4
        open 806.5
      open 805.5
      nontraumatic 733.13
      open NEC 805.9
      pathologic (any site) 733.13
    sacrum (closed) 805.6
      with spinal cord injury 806.60
        cauda equina injury 806.62
          complete lesion 806.61
            open 806.71
          open 806.72
        open 806.70
        specified type NEC 806.69
          open 806.79
      open 805.7
    site unspecified (closed) 805.8
      with spinal cord injury (closed) 806.8
        open 806.9
      open 805.9
    stress (any site) 733.95
    thoracic (closed) 805.2
      with spinal cord injury — see Fracture, vertebra, with spinal cord injury, thoracic
      open 805.3
  vertex — see Fracture, skull, vault
  vomer (bone) 802.0
    open 802.1
  Wagstaffe's — see Fracture, ankle
  wrist (closed) 814.00
    open 814.10
    pathologic 733.12
  xiphoid (process) — see Fracture, sternum
  zygoma (zygomatic arch) (closed) 802.4
    open 802.5

Fragile X syndrome 759.83
Fragilitas
  crinium 704.2
  hair 704.2
  ossium 756.51
    with blue sclera 756.51
  unguium 703.8
    congenital 757.5
Fragility
  bone 756.51
    with deafness and blue sclera 756.51
  capillary (hereditary) 287.8
  hair 704.2
  nails 703.8
Fragmentation — see Fracture, by site
Frailty 797
Frambesia, frambesial (tropica) — see also Yaws 102.9
  initial lesion or ulcer 102.0
  primary 102.0
Frambeside
  gummatous 102.4
  of early yaws 102.2
Frambesioma 102.1
Franceschetti's syndrome (mandibulofacial dysostosis) 756.0
Francis' disease — see also Tularemia 021.9
Franklin's disease (heavy chain) 273.2
Frank's essential thrombocytopenia — see also Purpura, thrombocytopenic 287.39
Fraser's syndrome 759.89
Freckle 709.09
  malignant melanoma in (M8742/3) — see Melanoma
  melanotic (of Hutchinson) (M8742/2) — see Neoplasm, skin, in situ
  retinal 239.81
Freeman-Sheldon syndrome 759.89
Freezing 991.9
  specified effect NEC 991.8
Freiberg's
  disease (osteochondrosis, second metatarsal) 732.5
  infraction of metatarsal head 732.5
  osteochondrosis 732.5
Frei's disease (climatic bubo) 099.1
Fremitus, friction, cardiac 785.3

☑ Additional Digit Required — Refer to the Tabular List for Digit Selection

120 — Volume 2 • October 2009   ▶◀ Revised Text   ● New Line   ▲ Revised Code   👁 Subterms under main terms may continue to next column or page   **2010 ICD-9-CM**

Frenulum linguae 750.0
Frenum
  external os 752.49
  tongue 750.0
Frequency (urinary) NEC 788.41
  micturition 788.41
  nocturnal 788.43
  polyuria 788.42
  psychogenic 306.53
Frey's syndrome (auriculotemporal syndrome) 705.22
Friction
  burn (see also Injury, superficial, by site) 919.0
  fremitus, cardiac 785.3
  precordial 785.3
  sounds, chest 786.7
Friderichsen-Waterhouse syndrome or disease 036.3
Friedländer's
  B (bacillus) NEC (see also condition) 041.3
    sepsis or septicemia 038.49
  disease (endarteritis obliterans) — see Arteriosclerosis
Friedreich's
  ataxia 334.0
  combined systemic disease 334.0
  disease 333.2
    combined systemic 334.0
  myoclonia 333.2
  sclerosis (spinal cord) 334.0
Friedrich-Erb-Arnold syndrome (acropachyderma) 757.39
Frigidity 302.72
  psychic or psychogenic 302.72
Fröhlich's disease or syndrome (adiposogenital dystrophy) 253.8
Froin's syndrome 336.8
Frommel-Chiari syndrome 676.6 ☑
Frommel's disease 676.6 ☑
Frontal — see also condition
  lobe syndrome 310.0
Frostbite 991.3
  face 991.0
  foot 991.2
  hand 991.1
  specified site NEC 991.3
Frotteurism 302.89
Frozen 991.9
  pelvis 620.8
  shoulder 726.0
Fructosemia 271.2
Fructosuria (benign) (essential) 271.2
Fuchs'
  black spot (myopic) 360.21
  corneal dystrophy (endothelial) 371.57
  heterochromic cyclitis 364.21
Fucosidosis 271.8
Fugue 780.99
  dissociative 300.13
  hysterical (dissociative) 300.13
  reaction to exceptional stress (transient) 308.1
Fukuhara syndrome 277.87

Fuller Albright's syndrome (osteitis fibrosa disseminata) 756.59
Fuller's earth disease 502
Fulminant, fulminating — see condition
Functional — see condition
Functioning
  borderline intellectual V62.89
Fundus — see also condition
  flavimaculatus 362.76
Fungemia 117.9
Fungus, fungous
  cerebral 348.89 ▲
  disease NEC 117.9
  infection — see Infection, fungus
  testis (see also Tuberculosis) 016.5 ☑ [608.81]
Funiculitis (acute) 608.4
  chronic 608.4
  endemic 608.4
  gonococcal (acute) 098.14
    chronic or duration of 2 months or over 098.34
  tuberculous (see also Tuberculosis) 016.5 ☑
Funnel
  breast (acquired) 738.3
    congenital 754.81
    late effect of rickets 268.1
  chest (acquired) 738.3
    congenital 754.81
    late effect of rickets 268.1
  pelvis (acquired) 738.6
    with disproportion (fetopelvic) 653.3 ☑
      affecting fetus or newborn 763.1
      causing obstructed labor 660.1 ☑
        affecting fetus or newborn 763.1
    congenital 755.69
    tuberculous (see also Tuberculosis) 016.9 ☑
FUO — see also Pyrexia 780.60
Furfur 690.18
  microsporon 111.0
Furor, paroxysmal (idiopathic) — see also Epilepsy 345.8 ☑
Furriers' lung 495.8
Furrowed tongue 529.5
  congenital 750.13
Furrowing nail(s) (transverse) 703.8
  congenital 757.5
Furuncle 680.9
  abdominal wall 680.2
  ankle 680.6
  anus 680.5
  arm (any part, above wrist) 680.3
  auditory canal, external 680.0
  axilla 680.3
  back (any part) 680.2
  breast 680.2
  buttock 680.5
  chest wall 680.2
  corpus cavernosum 607.2
  ear (any part) 680.0
  eyelid 373.13

Furuncle — continued
  face (any part, except eye) 680.0
  finger (any) 680.4
  flank 680.2
  foot (any part) 680.7
  forearm 680.3
  gluteal (region) 680.5
  groin 680.2
  hand (any part) 680.4
  head (any part, except face) 680.8
  heel 680.7
  hip 680.6
  kidney (see also Abscess, kidney) 590.2
  knee 680.6
  labium (majus) (minus) 616.4
  lacrimal
    gland (see also Dacryoadenitis) 375.00
    passages (duct) (sac) (see also Dacryocystitis) 375.30
  leg, any part except foot 680.6
  malignant 022.0
  multiple sites 680.9
  neck 680.1
  nose (external) (septum) 680.0
  orbit 376.01
  partes posteriores 680.5
  pectoral region 680.2
  penis 607.2
  perineum 680.2
  pinna 680.0
  scalp (any part) 680.8
  scrotum 608.4
  seminal vesicle 608.0
  shoulder 680.3
  skin NEC 680.9
  specified site NEC 680.8
  spermatic cord 608.4
  temple (region) 680.0
  testis 604.90
  thigh 680.6
  thumb 680.4
  toe (any) 680.7
  trunk 680.2
  tunica vaginalis 608.4
  umbilicus 680.2
  upper arm 680.3
  vas deferens 608.4
  vulva 616.4
  wrist 680.4
Furunculosis — see also Furuncle 680.9
  external auditory meatus 680.0 [380.13]
Fusarium (infection) 118
Fusion, fused (congenital)
  anal (with urogenital canal) 751.5
  aorta and pulmonary artery 745.0
  astragaloscaphoid 755.67
  atria 745.5
  atrium and ventricle 745.69
  auditory canal 744.02
  auricles, heart 745.5
  binocular, with defective stereopsis 368.33
  bone 756.9

Fusion, fused — continued
  cervical spine — see Fusion, spine
  choanal 748.0
  commissure, mitral valve 746.5
  cranial sutures, premature 756.0
  cusps, heart valve NEC 746.89
    mitral 746.5
    tricuspid 746.89
  ear ossicles 744.04
  fingers (see also Syndactylism, fingers) 755.11
  hymen 752.42
  hymeno-urethral 599.89
    causing obstructed labor 660.1 ☑
      affecting fetus or newborn 763.1
  joint (acquired) (see also Ankylosis)
    congenital 755.8
  kidneys (incomplete) 753.3
  labium (majus) (minus) 752.49
  larynx and trachea 748.3
  limb 755.8
    lower 755.69
    upper 755.59
  lobe, lung 748.5
  lumbosacral (acquired) 724.6
    congenital 756.15
    surgical V45.4
  nares (anterior) (posterior) 748.0
  nose, nasal 748.0
  nostril(s) 748.0
  organ or site NEC — see Anomaly, specified type NEC
  ossicles 756.9
    auditory 744.04
  pulmonary valve segment 746.02
  pulmonic cusps 746.02
  ribs 756.3
  sacroiliac (acquired) (joint) 724.6
    congenital 755.69
    surgical V45.4
  skull, imperfect 756.0
  spine (acquired) 724.9
    arthrodesis status V45.4
    congenital (vertebra) 756.15
    postoperative status V45.4
  sublingual duct with submaxillary duct at opening in mouth 750.26
  talonavicular (bar) 755.67
  teeth, tooth 520.2
  testes 752.89
  toes (see also Syndactylism, toes) 755.13
  trachea and esophagus 750.3
  twins 759.4
  urethral-hymenal 599.89
  vagina 752.49
  valve cusps — see Fusion, cusps, heart valve
  ventricles, heart 745.4
  vertebra (arch) — see Fusion, spine
  vulva 752.49
Fusospirillosis (mouth) (tongue) (tonsil) 101
Fussy infant (baby) 780.91

G

Gafsa boil 085.1
Gain, weight (abnormal) (excessive) — *see also*
   Weight, gain 783.1
Gaisböck's disease or syndrome (polycythemia
   hypertonica) 289.0
Gait
   abnormality 781.2
      hysterical 300.11
   ataxic 781.2
      hysterical 300.11
   disturbance 781.2
      hysterical 300.11
   paralytic 781.2
   scissor 781.2
   spastic 781.2
   staggering 781.2
      hysterical 300.11
Galactocele (breast) (infected) 611.5
   puerperal, postpartum 676.8 ☑
Galactophoritis 611.0
   puerperal, postpartum 675.2 ☑
Galactorrhea 676.6 ☑
   not associated with childbirth 611.6
Galactosemia (classic) (congenital) 271.1
Galactosuria 271.1
Galacturia 791.1
   bilharziasis 120.0
Galen's vein — *see* condition
Gallbladder — *see also* condition
   acute (*see also* Disease, gallbladder) 575.0
Gall duct — *see* condition
Gallop rhythm 427.89
Gallstone (cholemic) (colic) (impacted) — *see*
   Cholelithiasis
   causing intestinal obstruction 560.31
Gambling, pathological 312.31
Gammaloidosis 277.39
Gammopathy 273.9
   macroglobulinemia 273.3
   monoclonal (benign) (essential) (idiopathic)
      (with lymphoplasmacytic dyscrasia)
      273.1
Gamna's disease (siderotic splenomegaly) 289.51
Gampsodactylia (congenital) 754.71
Gamstorp's disease (adynamia episodica
   hereditaria) 359.3
Gandy-Nanta disease (siderotic splenomegaly)
   289.51
**Gang activity, without manifest psychiatric
   disorder** V71.09
   adolescent V71.02
   adult V71.01
   child V71.02
Gangliocytoma (M9490/0) — *see* Neoplasm,
   connective tissue, benign
Ganglioglioma (M9505/1) — *see* Neoplasm, by
   site, uncertain behavior
Ganglion 727.43
   joint 727.41
   of yaws (early) (late) 102.6
   periosteal (*see also* Periostitis) 730.3 ☑
   tendon sheath (compound) (diffuse) 727.42
   tuberculous (*see also* Tuberculosis) 015.9 ☑
Ganglioneuroblastoma (M9490/3) — *see* Neoplasm, connective tissue, malignant
Ganglioneuroma (M9490/0) — *see also* Neoplasm, connective tissue, benign
   malignant (M9490/3) — *see* Neoplasm, con-
      nective tissue, malignant
Ganglioneuromatosis (M9491/0) — *see* Neoplasm, connective tissue, benign
Ganglionitis
   fifth nerve (*see also* Neuralgia, trigeminal) 350.1
   gasserian 350.1
   geniculate 351.1
      herpetic 053.11
      newborn 767.5
   herpes zoster 053.11
   herpetic geniculate (Hunt's syndrome) 053.11
Gangliosidosis 330.1
Gangosa 102.5

Gangrene, gangrenous (anemia) (artery) (cellulitis) (dermatitis) (dry) (infective) (moist)
   (pemphigus) (septic) (skin) (stasis) (ulcer)
   785.4
   with
      arteriosclerosis (native artery) 440.24
         bypass graft 440.30
            autologous vein 440.31
            nonautologous biological 440.32
      diabetes (mellitus) 250.7 ☑ *[785.4]*
         due to secondary diabetes
            249.7 ☑ *[785.4]*
   abdomen (wall) 785.4
   adenitis 683
   alveolar 526.5
   angina 462
      diphtheritic 032.0
   anus 569.49
   appendices epiploicae — *see* Gangrene,
      mesentery
   appendix — *see* Appendicitis, acute
   arteriosclerotic — *see* Arteriosclerosis, with,
      gangrene
   auricle 785.4
   Bacillus welchii (*see also* Gangrene, gas) 040.0
   bile duct (*see also* Cholangitis) 576.8
   bladder 595.89
   bowel — *see* Gangrene, intestine
   cecum — *see* Gangrene, intestine
   Clostridium perfringens or welchii (*see also*
      Gangrene, gas) 040.0
   colon — *see* Gangrene, intestine
   connective tissue 785.4
   cornea 371.40
   corpora cavernosa (infective) 607.2
      noninfective 607.89
   cutaneous, spreading 785.4
   decubital (*see also* Ulcer, pressure)
      707.00 *[785.4]*
   diabetic (any site) 250.7 ☑ *[785.4]*
      due to secondary diabetes 249.7 ☑ *[785.4]*
   dropsical 785.4
   emphysematous (*see also* Gangrene, gas) 040.0
   epidemic (ergotized grain) 988.2
   epididymis (infectional) (*see also* Epididymitis)
      604.99
   erysipelas (*see also* Erysipelas) 035
   extremity (lower) (upper) 785.4
   gallbladder or duct (*see also* Cholecystitis,
      acute) 575.0
   gas (bacillus) 040.0
      with
         abortion — *see* Abortion, by type, with
            sepsis
         ectopic pregnancy (*see also* categories
            633.0–633.9) 639.0
         molar pregnancy (*see also* categories
            630–632) 639.0
      following
         abortion 639.0
         ectopic or molar pregnancy 639.0
      puerperal, postpartum, childbirth
         670.8 ☑ ▲
   glossitis 529.0
   gum 523.8
   hernia — *see* Hernia, by site, with gangrene
   hospital noma 528.1
   intestine, intestinal (acute) (hemorrhagic)
      (massive) 557.0
      with
         hernia — *see* Hernia, by site, with gan-
            grene
         mesenteric embolism or infarction
            557.0
         obstruction (*see also* Obstruction, intes-
            tine) 560.9
   laryngitis 464.00
      with obstruction 464.01
   liver 573.8
   lung 513.0
      spirochetal 104.8
   lymphangitis 457.2
   Meleney's (cutaneous) 686.09
   mesentery 557.0
      with
         embolism or infarction 557.0

Gangrene, gangrenous — *continued*
   mesentery — *continued*
      with — *continued*
         intestinal obstruction (*see also* Obstruc-
            tion, intestine) 560.9
   mouth 528.1
   noma 528.1
   orchitis 604.90
   ovary (*see also* Salpingo-oophoritis) 614.2
   pancreas 577.0
   penis (infectional) 607.2
      noninfective 607.89
   perineum 785.4
   pharynx 462
   pneumonia 513.0
   Pott's 440.24
   presenile 443.1
   pulmonary 513.0
   pulp, tooth 522.1
   quinsy 475
   Raynaud's (symmetric gangrene) 443.0 *[785.4]*
   rectum 569.49
   retropharyngeal 478.24
   rupture — *see* Hernia, by site, with gangrene
   scrotum 608.4
      noninfective 608.83
   senile 440.24
   septic 034.0
   septic 034.0
   sore throat 462
   spermatic cord 608.4
      noninfective 608.89
   spine 785.4
   spirochetal NEC 104.8
   spreading cutaneous 785.4
   stomach 537.89
   stomatitis 528.1
   symmetrical 443.0 *[785.4]*
   testis (infectional) (*see also* Orchitis) 604.99
      noninfective 608.89
   throat 462
      diphtheritic 032.0
   thyroid (gland) 246.8
   tonsillitis (acute) 463
   tooth (pulp) 522.1
   tuberculous NEC (*see also* Tuberculosis)
      011.9 ☑
   tunica vaginalis 608.4
      noninfective 608.89
   umbilicus 785.4
   uterus (*see also* Endometritis) 615.9
   uvulitis 528.3
   vas deferens 608.4
      noninfective 608.89
   vulva (*see also* Vulvitis) 616.10
Gannister disease (occupational) 502
   with tuberculosis — *see* Tuberculosis, pul-
      monary
Ganser's syndrome, hysterical 300.16
Gardner-Diamond syndrome (autoerythrocyte
   sensitization) 287.2
Gargoylism 277.5
Garré's
   disease (*see also* Osteomyelitis) 730.1 ☑
   osteitis (sclerosing) (*see also* Osteomyelitis)
      730.1 ☑
   osteomyelitis (*see also* Osteomyelitis) 730.1 ☑
Garrod's pads, knuckle 728.79
Gartner's duct
   cyst 752.41
   persistent 752.41
Gas 787.3
   asphyxia, asphyxiation, inhalation, poisoning,
      suffocation NEC 987.9
      specified gas — *see* Table of Drugs and
         Chemicals
   bacillus gangrene or infection — *see* Gas,
      gangrene
   cyst, mesentery 568.89
   excessive 787.3
   gangrene 040.0
      with
         abortion — *see* Abortion, by type, with
            sepsis
         ectopic pregnancy (*see also* categories
            633.0–633.9) 639.0

Gas — *continued*
   gangrene — *continued*
      with — *continued*
         molar pregnancy (*see also* categories
            630–632) 639.0
      following
         abortion 639.0
         ectopic or molar pregnancy 639.0
      puerperal, postpartum, childbirth
         670.8 ☑ ▲
   on stomach 787.3
   pains 787.3
Gastradenitis 535.0 ☑
Gastralgia 536.8
   psychogenic 307.89
Gastrectasis, gastrectasia 536.1
   psychogenic 306.4
Gastric — *see* condition
Gastrinoma (M8153/1)
   malignant (M8153/3)
      pancreas 157.4
      specified site NEC — *see* Neoplasm, by site,
         malignant
      unspecified site 157.4
   specified site — *see* Neoplasm, by site, uncer-
      tain behavior
   unspecified site 235.5
Gastritis 535.5 ☑

> Note — Use the following fifth-digit subclas-
> sification for category 535:
>
> 0   without mention of hemorrhage
>
> 1   with hemorrhage

   acute 535.0 ☑
   alcoholic 535.3 ☑
   allergic 535.4 ☑
   antral 535.4 ☑
   atrophic 535.1 ☑
   atrophic-hyperplastic 535.1 ☑
   bile-induced 535.4 ☑
   catarrhal 535.0 ☑
   chronic (atrophic) 535.1 ☑
   cirrhotic 535.4 ☑
   corrosive (acute) 535.4 ☑
   dietetic 535.4 ☑
   due to diet deficiency 269.9 *[535.4]* ☑
   eosinophilic 535.7 ☑
   erosive 535.4 ☑
   follicular 535.4 ☑
      chronic 535.1 ☑
   giant hypertrophic 535.2 ☑
   glandular 535.4 ☑
      chronic 535.1 ☑
   hypertrophic (mucosa) 535.2 ☑
      chronic giant 211.1
   irritant 535.4 ☑
   nervous 306.4
   phlegmonous 535.0 ☑
   psychogenic 306.4
   sclerotic 535.4 ☑
   spastic 536.8
   subacute 535.0 ☑
   superficial 535.4 ☑
   suppurative 535.0 ☑
   toxic 535.4 ☑
   tuberculous (*see also* Tuberculosis) 017.9 ☑
Gastrocarcinoma (M8010/3) 151.9
Gastrocolic — *see* condition
Gastrocolitis — *see* Enteritis
Gastrodisciasis 121.8
Gastroduodenitis — *see also* Gastritis 535.5 ☑
   catarrhal 535.0 ☑
   infectional 535.0 ☑
   virus, viral 008.8
      specified type NEC 008.69
Gastrodynia 536.8
Gastroenteritis (acute) (catarrhal) (congestive)
   (hemorrhagic) (noninfectious) — *see also*
   Enteritis 558.9
   aertrycke infection 003.0
   allergic 558.3
   chronic 558.9
      ulcerative (*see also* Colitis, ulcerative) 556.9
   dietetic 558.9

☑ Additional Digit Required — Refer to the Tabular List for Digit Selection   ᴺᴱ Subterms under main terms may continue to next column or page

2010 ICD-9-CM   ▶◀ Revised Text   ● New Line   ▲ Revised Code   October 2009 · Volume 2 — 123

Index

Gastroenteritis — Glioblastoma

Gastroenteritis — *see also* Enteritis — *continued*
  due to
    antineoplastic chemotherapy 558.9
    food poisoning (*see also* Poisoning, food) 005.9
    radiation 558.1
  eosinophilic 558.41
  epidemic 009.0
  functional 558.9
  infectious (*see also* Enteritis, due to, by organism) 009.0
    presumed 009.1
  salmonella 003.0
  septic (*see also* Enteritis, due to, by organism) 009.0
  toxic 558.2
  tuberculous (*see also* Tuberculosis) 014.8 ☑
  ulcerative (*see also* Colitis, ulcerative) 556.9
  viral NEC 008.8
    specified type NEC 008.69
  zymotic 009.0
Gastroenterocolitis — *see* Enteritis
Gastroenteropathy, protein-losing 579.8
Gastroenteroptosis 569.89
Gastroesophageal laceration-hemorrhage syndrome 530.7
Gastroesophagitis 530.19
Gastrohepatitis — *see also* Gastritis 535.5 ☑
Gastrointestinal — *see* condition
Gastrojejunal — *see* condition
Gastrojejunitis — *see also* Gastritis 535.5 ☑
Gastrojejunocolic — *see* condition
Gastroliths 537.89
Gastromalacia 537.89
Gastroparalysis 536.3
  diabetic 250.6 ☑ [536.3]
    due to secondary diabetes 249.6 ☑ [536.3]
Gastroparesis 536.3
  diabetic 250.6 ☑ [536.3]
    due to secondary diabetes 249.6 ☑ [536.3]
Gastropathy 537.9
  congestive portal 537.89
  erythematous 535.5 ☑
  exudative 579.8
  portal hypertensive 537.89
Gastroptosis 537.5
Gastrorrhagia 578.0
Gastrorrhea 536.8
  psychogenic 306.4
Gastroschisis (congenital) 756.73 ▲
  acquired 569.89
Gastrospasm (neurogenic) (reflex) 536.8
  neurotic 306.4
  psychogenic 306.4
Gastrostaxis 578.0
Gastrostenosis 537.89
Gastrostomy
  attention to V55.1
  complication 536.40
    specified type 536.49
  infection 536.41
  malfunctioning 536.42
  status V44.1
Gastrosuccorrhea (continuous) (intermittent) 536.8
  neurotic 306.4
  psychogenic 306.4
Gaucher's
  disease (adult) (cerebroside lipidosis) (infantile) 272.7
  hepatomegaly 272.7
  splenomegaly (cerebroside lipidosis) 272.7
GAVE (gastric antral vascular ectasia) 537.82
  with hemorrhage 537.83
  without hemorrhage 537.82
Gayet's disease (superior hemorrhagic polioencephalitis) 265.1
Gayet-Wernicke's syndrome (superior hemorrhagic polioencephalitis) 265.1
Gee (-Herter) (-Heubner) (-Thaysen) disease or syndrome (nontropical sprue) 579.0
Gélineau's syndrome — *see also* Narcolepsy 347.00
Gemination, teeth 520.2

Gemistocytoma (M9411/3)
  specified site — *see* Neoplasm, by site, malignant
  unspecified site 191.9
General, generalized — *see* condtion
Genetic
  susceptibility to
    MEN (multiple endocrine neoplasia) V84.81
    neoplasia
      multiple endocrine [MEN] V84.81
    neoplasm
      malignant, of
        breast V84.01
        endometrium V84.04
        other V84.09
        ovary V84.02
        prostate V84.03
      specified disease NEC V84.89
Genital — *see* condition
  warts 078.11
Genito-anorectal syndrome 099.1
Genitourinary system — *see* condition
Genu
  congenital 755.64
  extrorsum (acquired) 736.42
    congenital 755.64
    late effects of rickets 268.1
  introrsum (acquired) 736.41
    congenital 755.64
    late effects of rickets 268.1
  rachitic (old) 268.1
  recurvatum (acquired) 736.5
    congenital 754.40
      with dislocation of knee 754.41
    late effects of rickets 268.1
  valgum (acquired) (knock-knee) 736.41
    congenital 755.64
    late effects of rickets 268.1
  varum (acquired) (bowleg) 736.42
    congenital 755.64
    late effect of rickets 268.1
Geographic tongue 529.1
Geophagia 307.52
Geotrichosis 117.9
  intestine 117.9
  lung 117.9
  mouth 117.9
Gephyrophobia 300.29
Gerbode defect 745.4
GERD (gastroesophageal reflux disease) 530.81
Gerhardt's
  disease (erythromelalgia) 443.82
  syndrome (vocal cord paralysis) 478.30
Gerlier's disease (epidemic vertigo) 078.81
German measles 056.9
  exposure to V01.4
Germinoblastoma (diffuse) (M9614/3) 202.8 ☑
  follicular (M9692/3) 202.0 ☑
Germinoma (M9064/3) — *see* Neoplasm, by site, malignant
Gerontoxon 371.41
Gerstmann-Sträussler-Scheinker syndrome (GSS) 046.71
Gerstmann's syndrome (finger agnosia) 784.69
Gestation (period) — *see also* Pregnancy
  ectopic NEC (*see also* Pregnancy, ectopic) 633.90
    with intrauterine pregnancy 633.91
Gestational proteinuria 646.2 ☑
  with hypertension — *see* Toxemia, of pregnancy
Ghon tubercle primary infection — *see also* Tuberculosis 010.0 ☑
Ghost
  teeth 520.4
  vessels, cornea 370.64
Ghoul hand 102.3
Gianotti Crosti syndrome 057.8
  due to known virus — *see* Infection, virus
  due to unknown virus 057.8
Giant
  cell
    epulis 523.8
    peripheral (gingiva) 523.8
    tumor, tendon sheath 727.02
  colon (congenital) 751.3

Giant — *continued*
  esophagus (congenital) 750.4
  kidney 753.3
  urticaria 995.1
    hereditary 277.6
Giardia lamblia infestation 007.1
Giardiasis 007.1
Gibert's disease (pityriasis rosea) 696.3
Gibraltar fever — *see* Brucellosis
Giddiness 780.4
  hysterical 300.11
  psychogenic 306.9
Gierke's disease (glycogenosis I) 271.0
Gigantism (cerebral) (hypophyseal) (pituitary) 253.0
Gilbert's disease or cholemia (familial non-hemolytic jaundice) 277.4
Gilchrist's disease (North American blastomycosis) 116.0
Gilford (-Hutchinson) disease or syndrome (progeria) 259.8
Gilles de la Tourette's disease (motor-verbal tic) 307.23
Gillespie's syndrome (dysplasia oculodentodigitalis) 759.89
Gingivitis 523.10
  acute 523.00
    necrotizing 101
    non-plaque induced 523.01
    plaque induced 523.00
  catarrhal 523.00
  chronic 523.10
    non-plaque induced 523.11
  desquamative 523.10
  expulsiva 523.40
  hyperplastic 523.10
  marginal, simple 523.10
  necrotizing, acute 101
  non-plaque induced 523.11
  pellagrous 265.2
  plaque induced 523.10
  ulcerative 523.10
    acute necrotizing 101
  Vincent's 101
Gingivoglossitis 529.0
Gingivopericementitis 523.40
Gingivosis 523.10
Gingivostomatitis 523.10
  herpetic 054.2
Giovannini's disease 117.9
GISA (glycopeptide intermediate staphylococcus aureus) V09.8 ☑
Glanders 024
Gland, glandular — *see* condition
Glanzmann (-Naegeli) disease or thrombasthenia 287.1
Glassblowers' disease 527.1
Glaucoma (capsular) (inflammatory) (noninflammatory) (primary) 365.9
  with increased episcleral venous pressure 365.82
  absolute 360.42
  acute 365.22
    narrow angle 365.22
    secondary 365.60
  angle closure 365.20
    acute 365.22
    chronic 365.23
    intermittent 365.21
    interval 365.21
    residual stage 365.24
    subacute 365.21
  borderline 365.00
  chronic 365.11
    noncongestive 365.11
    open angle 365.11
    simple 365.11
  closed angle — *see* Glaucoma, angle closure
  congenital 743.20
    associated with other eye anomalies 743.22
    simple 743.21
  congestive — *see* Glaucoma, narrow angle
  corticosteroid-induced (glaucomatous stage) 365.31
    residual stage 365.32

Glaucoma — *continued*
  hemorrhagic 365.60
  hypersecretion 365.81
  infantile 365.14
    congenital 743.20
      associated with other eye anomalies 743.22
      simple 743.21
  in or with
    aniridia 365.42
    Axenfeld's anomaly 365.41
    congenital syndromes NEC 759.89 [365.44]
    disorder of lens NEC 365.59
    inflammation, ocular 365.62
    iris
      anomalies NEC 365.42
      atrophy, essential 365.42
      bombé 365.61
    microcornea 365.43
    neurofibromatosis 237.71 [365.44]
    ocular
      cysts NEC 365.64
      disorders NEC 365.60
      trauma 365.65
      tumors NEC 365.64
    pupillary block or seclusion 365.61
    Rieger's anomaly or syndrome 365.41
    seclusion of pupil 365.61
    Sturge-Weber (-Dimitri) syndrome 759.6 [365.44]
    systemic syndrome NEC 365.44
    tumor of globe 365.64
    vascular disorders NEC 365.63
  juvenile 365.14
  low tension 365.12
  malignant 365.83
  narrow angle (primary) 365.20
    acute 365.22
    chronic 365.23
    intermittent 365.21
    interval 365.21
    residual stage 365.24
    subacute 365.21
  newborn 743.20
    associated with other eye anomalies 743.22
    simple 743.21
  noncongestive (chronic) 365.11
  nonobstructive (chronic) 365.11
  obstructive 365.60
    due to lens changes 365.59
  open angle 365.10
    with
      borderline intraocular pressure 365.01
      cupping of optic discs 365.01
    primary 365.11
    residual stage 365.15
  phacolytic 365.51
  pigmentary 365.13
  postinfectious 365.60
  pseudoexfoliation 365.52
  secondary NEC 365.60
  simple (chronic) 365.11
  simplex 365.11
  steroid responders 365.03
  suspect 365.00
  syphilitic 095.8
  traumatic NEC 365.65
    newborn 767.8
  wide angle (*see also* Glaucoma, open angle) 365.10
Glaucomatous flecks (subcapsular) 366.31
Glazed tongue 529.4
Gleet 098.2
Glénard's disease or syndrome (enteroptosis) 569.89
Glinski-Simmonds syndrome (pituitary cachexia) 253.2
Glioblastoma (multiforme) (M9440/3)
  with sarcomatous component (M9442/3)
    specified site — *see* Neoplasm, by site, malignant
    unspecified site 191.9
  giant cell (M9441/3)
    specified site — *see* Neoplasm, by site, malignant

☑ Additional Digit Required — Refer to the Tabular List for Digit Selection

▽ Subterms under main terms may continue to next column or page

Glioblastoma — continued
  giant cell — continued
    unspecified site 191.9
    specified site — see Neoplasm, by site, malignant
  unspecified site 191.9
Glioma (malignant) (M9380/3)
  astrocytic (M9400/3)
    specified site — see Neoplasm, by site, malignant
    unspecified site 191.9
  mixed (M9382/3)
    specified site — see Neoplasm, by site, malignant
    unspecified site 191.9
  nose 748.1
  specified site NEC — see Neoplasm, by site, malignant
  subependymal (M9383/1) 237.5
  unspecified site 191.9
Gliomatosis cerebri (M9381/3) 191.0
Glioneuroma (M9505/1) — see Neoplasm, by site, uncertain behavior
Gliosarcoma (M9380/3)
  specified site — see Neoplasm, by site, malignant
  unspecified site 191.9
Gliosis (cerebral) 349.89
  spinal 336.0
Glisson's
  cirrhosis — see Cirrhosis, portal
  disease (see also Rickets) 268.0
Glissonitis 573.3
Globinuria 791.2
Globus 306.4
  hystericus 300.11
Glomangioma (M8712/0) — see also Hemangioma 228.00
Glomangiosarcoma (M8710/3) — see Neoplasm, connective tissue, malignant
Glomerular nephritis — see also Nephritis 583.9
Glomerulitis — see also Nephritis 583.9
Glomerulonephritis — see also Nephritis 583.9
  with
    edema (see also Nephrosis) 581.9
    lesion of
      exudative nephritis 583.89
      interstitial nephritis (diffuse) (focal) 583.89
      necrotizing glomerulitis 583.4
        acute 580.4
        chronic 582.4
      renal necrosis 583.9
        cortical 583.6
        medullary 583.7
      specified pathology NEC 583.89
        acute 580.89
        chronic 582.89
    necrosis, renal 583.9
      cortical 583.6
      medullary (papillary) 583.7
    specified pathology or lesion NEC 583.89
  acute 580.9
    with
      exudative nephritis 580.89
      interstitial nephritis (diffuse) (focal) 580.89
      necrotizing glomerulitis 580.4
      extracapillary with epithelial crescents 580.4
      poststreptococcal 580.0
      proliferative (diffuse) 580.0
      rapidly progressive 580.4
      specified pathology NEC 580.89
  arteriolar (see also Hypertension, kidney) 403.90
  arteriosclerotic (see also Hypertension, kidney) 403.90
  ascending (see also Pyelitis) 590.80
  basement membrane NEC 583.89
    with
      pulmonary hemorrhage (Goodpasture's syndrome) 446.21 [583.81]
  chronic 582.9

Glomerulonephritis — see also Nephritis — continued
  chronic — continued
    with
      exudative nephritis 582.89
      interstitial nephritis (diffuse) (focal) 582.89
      necrotizing glomerulitis 582.4
      specified pathology or lesion NEC 582.89
    endothelial 582.2
    extracapillary with epithelial crescents 582.4
    hypocomplementemic persistent 582.2
    lobular 582.2
    membranoproliferative 582.2
    membranous 582.1
      and proliferative (mixed) 582.2
      sclerosing 582.1
    mesangiocapillary 582.2
    mixed membranous and proliferative 582.2
    proliferative (diffuse) 582.0
    rapidly progressive 582.4
    sclerosing 582.1
  cirrhotic — see Sclerosis, renal
  desquamative — see Nephrosis
  due to or associated with
    amyloidosis 277.39 [583.81]
      with nephrotic syndrome 277.39 [581.81]
      chronic 277.39 [582.81]
    diabetes mellitus 250.4 ☑ [583.81]
      with nephrotic syndrome 250.4 ☑ [581.81]
      due to secondary diabetes 249.4 ☑ [581.81]
      due to secondary diabetes 249.4 ☑ [581.81]
    diphtheria 032.89 [580.81]
    gonococcal infection (acute) 098.19 [583.81]
      chronic or duration of 2 months or over 098.39 [583.81]
    infectious hepatitis 070.9 [580.81]
    malaria (with nephrotic syndrome) 084.9 [581.81]
    mumps 072.79 [580.81]
    polyarteritis (nodosa) (with nephrotic syndrome) 446.0 [581.81]
    specified pathology NEC 583.89
      acute 580.89
      chronic 582.89
    streptotrichosis 039.8 [583.81]
    subacute bacterial endocarditis 421.0 [580.81]
    syphilis (late) 095.4
      congenital 090.5 [583.81]
      early 091.69 [583.81]
    systemic lupus erythematosus 710.0 [583.81]
      with nephrotic syndrome 710.0 [581.81]
      chronic 710.0 [582.81]
    tuberculosis (see also Tuberculosis) 016.0 ☑ [583.81]
    typhoid fever 002.0 [580.81]
  extracapillary with epithelial crescents 583.4
    acute 580.4
    chronic 582.4
  exudative 583.89
    acute 580.89
    chronic 582.89
  focal (see also Nephritis) 583.9
    embolic 580.4
  granular 582.89
  granulomatous 582.89
  hydremic (see also Nephrosis) 581.9
  hypocomplementemic persistent 583.2
    with nephrotic syndrome 581.2
    chronic 582.2
  immune complex NEC 583.89
  infective (see also Pyelitis) 590.80
  interstitial (diffuse) (focal) 583.89
    with nephrotic syndrome 581.89
    acute 580.89
    chronic 582.89

Glomerulonephritis — see also Nephritis — continued
  latent or quiescent 582.9
  lobular 583.2
    with nephrotic syndrome 581.2
    chronic 582.2
  membranoproliferative 583.2
    with nephrotic syndrome 581.2
    chronic 582.2
  membranous 583.1
    with nephrotic syndrome 581.1
    and proliferative (mixed) 583.2
      with nephrotic syndrome 581.2
      chronic 582.2
    chronic 582.1
    sclerosing 582.1
      with nephrotic syndrome 581.1
  mesangiocapillary 583.2
    with nephrotic syndrome 581.2
    chronic 582.2
  minimal change 581.3
  mixed membranous and proliferative 583.2
    with nephrotic syndrome 581.2
    chronic 582.2
  necrotizing 583.4
    acute 580.4
    chronic 582.4
  nephrotic (see also Nephrosis) 581.9
  old — see Glomerulonephritis, chronic
  parenchymatous 581.89
  poststreptococcal 580.0
  proliferative (diffuse) 583.0
    with nephrotic syndrome 581.0
    acute 580.0
    chronic 582.0
  purulent (see also Pyelitis) 590.80
  quiescent — see Nephritis, chronic
  rapidly progressive 583.4
    acute 580.4
    chronic 582.4
  sclerosing membranous (chronic) 582.1
    with nephrotic syndrome 581.1
  septic (see also Pyelitis) 590.80
  specified pathology or lesion NEC 583.89
    with nephrotic syndrome 581.89
    acute 580.89
    chronic 582.89
  suppurative (acute) (disseminated) (see also Pyelitis) 590.80
  toxic — see Nephritis, acute
  tubal, tubular — see Nephrosis, tubular
  type II (Ellis) — see Nephrosis
  vascular — see Hypertension, kidney
Glomerulosclerosis — see also Sclerosis, renal 587
  focal 582.1
    with nephrotic syndrome 581.1
  intercapillary (nodular) (with diabetes) 250.4 ☑ [581.81]
    due to secondary diabetes 249.4 ☑ [581.81]
Glossagra 529.6
Glossalgia 529.6
Glossitis 529.0
  areata exfoliativa 529.1
  atrophic 529.4
  benign migratory 529.1
  gangrenous 529.0
  Hunter's 529.4
  median rhomboid 529.2
  Moeller's 529.4
  pellagrous 265.2
Glossocele 529.8
Glossodynia 529.6
  exfoliativa 529.4
Glossoncus 529.8
Glossophytia 529.3
Glossoplegia 529.8
Glossoptosis 529.8
Glossopyrosis 529.6
Glossotrichia 529.3
Glossy skin 701.9
Glottis — see condition
Glottitis — see Glossitis

Glucagonoma (M8152/0)
  malignant (M8152/3)
    pancreas 157.4
    specified site NEC — see Neoplasm, by site, malignant
  pancreas 211.7
  specified site NEC — see Neoplasm, by site, benign
  unspecified site 211.7
Glucoglycinuria 270.7
Glue ear syndrome 381.20
Glue sniffing (airplane glue) — see also Dependence 304.6 ☑
Glycinemia (with methylmalonic acidemia) 270.7
Glycinuria (renal) (with ketosis) 270.0
Glycogen
  infiltration (see also Disease, glycogen storage) 271.0
  storage disease (see also Disease, glycogen storage) 271.0
Glycogenosis — see also Disease, glycogen storage 271.0
  cardiac 271.0 [425.7]
  Cori, types I-VII 271.0
  diabetic, secondary 250.8 ☑ [259.8]
    due to secondary diabetes 249.8 ☑ [259.8]
  diffuse (with hepatic cirrhosis) 271.0
  generalized 271.0
  glucose-6-phosphatase deficiency 271.0
  hepatophosphorylase deficiency 271.0
  hepatorenal 271.0
  myophosphorylase deficiency 271.0
Glycopenia 251.2
Glycopeptide
  intermediate staphylococcus aureus (GISA) V09.8 ☑
  resistant
    enterococcus V09.8 ☑
    staphylococcus aureus (GRSA) V09.8 ☑
Glycoprolinuria 270.8
Glycosuria 791.5
  renal 271.4
Gnathostoma (spinigerum) (infection) (infestation) 128.1
  wandering swellings from 128.1
Gnathostomiasis 128.1
Goiter (adolescent) (colloid) (diffuse) (dipping) (due to iodine deficiency) (endemic) (euthyroid) (heart) (hyperplastic) (internal) (intrathoracic) (juvenile) (mixed type) (nonendemic) (parenchymatous) (plunging) (sporadic) (subclavicular) (substernal) 240.9
  with
    hyperthyroidism (recurrent) (see also Goiter, toxic) 242.0 ☑
    thyrotoxicosis (see also Goiter, toxic) 242.0 ☑
  adenomatous (see also Goiter, nodular) 241.9
  cancerous (M8000/3) 193
  complicating pregnancy, childbirth, or puerperium 648.1 ☑
  congenital 246.1
  cystic (see also Goiter, nodular) 241.9
  due to enzyme defect in synthesis of thyroid hormone (butane-insoluble iodine) (coupling) (deiodinase) (iodide trapping or organification) (iodotyrosine dehalogenase) (peroxidase) 246.1
  dyshormonogenic 246.1
  exophthalmic (see also Goiter, toxic) 242.0 ☑
  familial (with deaf-mutism) 243
  fibrous 245.3
  lingual 759.2
  lymphadenoid 245.2
  malignant (M8000/3) 193
  multinodular (nontoxic) 241.1
    toxic or with hyperthyroidism (see also Goiter, toxic) 242.2 ☑
  nodular (nontoxic) 241.9
    with
      hyperthyroidism (see also Goiter, toxic) 242.3 ☑
      thyrotoxicosis (see also Goiter, toxic) 242.3 ☑

☑ Additional Digit Required — Refer to the Tabular List for Digit Selection   ▽ Subterms under main terms may continue to next column or page

Goiter — continued
  nodular — continued
    endemic 241.9
    exophthalmic (diffuse) (see also Goiter, toxic) 242.0 ☑
    multinodular (nontoxic) 241.1
    sporadic 241.9
    toxic (see also Goiter, toxic) 242.3 ☑
    uninodular (nontoxic) 241.0
  nontoxic (nodular) 241.9
    multinodular 241.1
    uninodular 241.0
  pulsating (see also Goiter, toxic) 242.0 ☑
  simple 240.0
  toxic 242.0 ☑

Note — Use the following fifth-digit subclassification with category 242:

0   without mention of thyrotoxic crisis or storm

1   with mention of thyrotoxic crisis or storm

  adenomatous 242.3 ☑
    multinodular 242.2 ☑
    uninodular 242.1 ☑
  multinodular 242.2 ☑
  nodular 242.3 ☑
    multinodular 242.2 ☑
    uninodular 242.1 ☑
  uninodular 242.1 ☑
  uninodular (nontoxic) 241.0
  toxic or with hyperthyroidism (see also Goiter, toxic) 242.1 ☑
Goldberg (-Maxwell) (-Morris) syndrome (testicular feminization) 259.51
Goldblatt's
  hypertension 440.1
  kidney 440.1
Goldenhar's syndrome (oculoauriculovertebral dysplasia) 756.0
Goldflam-Erb disease or syndrome 358.00
Goldscheider's disease (epidermolysis bullosa) 757.39
Goldstein's disease (familial hemorrhagic telangiectasia) 448.0
Golfer's elbow 726.32
Goltz-Gorlin syndrome (dermal hypoplasia) 757.39
Gonadoblastoma (M9073/1)
  specified site — see Neoplasm, by site uncertain behavior
  unspecified site
    female 236.2
    male 236.4
Gonecystitis — see also Vesiculitis 608.0
Gongylonemiasis 125.6
  mouth 125.6
Goniosynechiae 364.73
Gonococcemia 098.89
Gonococcus, gonococcal (disease) (infection) — see also condition 098.0
  anus 098.7
  bursa 098.52
  chronic NEC 098.2
  complicating pregnancy, childbirth, or puerperium 647.1 ☑
    affecting fetus or newborn 760.2
  conjunctiva, conjunctivitis (neonatorum) 098.40
  dermatosis 098.89
  endocardium 098.84
  epididymo-orchitis 098.13
    chronic or duration of 2 months or over 098.33
  eye (newborn) 098.40
  fallopian tube (chronic) 098.37
    acute 098.17
  genitourinary (acute) (organ) (system) (tract) (see also Gonorrhea) 098.0
    lower 098.0
      chronic 098.2
    upper 098.10
      chronic 098.30
  heart NEC 098.85
  joint 098.50

Gonococcus, gonococcal — see also condition — continued
  keratoderma 098.81
  keratosis (blennorrhagica) 098.81
  lymphatic (gland) (node) 098.89
  meninges 098.82
  orchitis (acute) 098.13
    chronic or duration of 2 months or over 098.33
  pelvis (acute) 098.19
    chronic or duration of 2 months or over 098.39
  pericarditis 098.83
  peritonitis 098.86
  pharyngitis 098.6
  pharynx 098.6
  proctitis 098.7
  pyosalpinx (chronic) 098.37
    acute 098.17
  rectum 098.7
  septicemia 098.89
  skin 098.89
  specified site NEC 098.89
  synovitis 098.51
  tendon sheath 098.51
  throat 098.6
  urethra (acute) 098.0
    chronic or duration of 2 months or over 098.2
  vulva (acute) 098.0
    chronic or duration of 2 months or over 098.2
Gonocytoma (M9073/1)
  specified site — see Neoplasm, by site, uncertain behavior
  unspecified site
    female 236.2
    male 236.4
Gonorrhea 098.0
  acute 098.0
  Bartholin's gland (acute) 098.0
    chronic or duration of 2 months or over 098.2
  bladder (acute) 098.11
    chronic or duration of 2 months or over 098.31
  carrier (suspected of) V02.7
  cervix (acute) 098.15
    chronic or duration of 2 months or over 098.35
  chronic 098.2
  complicating pregnancy, childbirth, or puerperium 647.1 ☑
    affecting fetus or newborn 760.2
  conjunctiva, conjunctivitis (neonatorum) 098.40
  contact V01.6
  Cowper's gland (acute) 098.0
    chronic or duration of 2 months or over 098.2
  duration of two months or over 098.2
  exposure to V01.6
  fallopian tube (chronic) 098.37
    acute 098.17
  genitourinary (acute) (organ) (system) (tract) 098.0
    chronic 098.2
    duration of two months or over 098.2
  kidney (acute) 098.19
    chronic or duration of 2 months or over 098.39
  ovary (acute) 098.19
    chronic or duration of 2 months or over 098.39
  pelvis (acute) 098.19
    chronic or duration of 2 months or over 098.39
  penis (acute) 098.0
    chronic or duration of 2 months or over 098.2
  prostate (acute) 098.12
    chronic or duration of 2 months or over 098.32
  seminal vesicle (acute) 098.14
    chronic or duration of 2 months or over 098.34

Gonorrhea — continued
  specified site NEC — see Gonococcus
  spermatic cord (acute) 098.14
    chronic or duration of 2 months or over 098.34
  urethra (acute) 098.0
    chronic or duration of 2 months or over 098.2
  vagina (acute) 098.0
    chronic or duration of 2 months or over 098.2
  vas deferens (acute) 098.14
    chronic or duration of 2 months or over 098.34
  vulva (acute) 098.0
    chronic or duration of 2 months or over 098.2
Goodpasture's syndrome (pneumorenal) 446.21
Good's syndrome 279.06
Gopalan's syndrome (burning feet) 266.2
Gordon's disease (exudative enteropathy) 579.8
Gorlin-Chaudhry-Moss syndrome 759.89
Gougerot-Blum syndrome (pigmented purpuric lichenoid dermatitis) 709.1
Gougerot-Carteaud disease or syndrome (confluent reticulate papillomatosis) 701.8
Gougerot-Hailey-Hailey disease (benign familial chronic pemphigus) 757.39
Gougerot (-Houwer) -Sjögren syndrome (keratoconjunctivitis sicca) 710.2
Gougerot's syndrome (trisymptomatic) 709.1
Gouley's syndrome (constrictive pericarditis) 423.2
Goundou 102.6
Gout, gouty 274.9
  with
    specified manifestations NEC 274.89 ●
    tophi (tophus) 274.03 ●
  acute 274.01 ●
  arthritis 274.00 ▲
    acute 274.01 ●
  arthropathy 274.00 ▲
    acute 274.01 ●
    chronic (without mention of tophus (tophi)) 274.02 ●
      with tophus (tophi) 274.03 ●
  attack 274.01 ●
  chronic 274.02 ●
    tophaceous 274.03 ●
  degeneration, heart 274.82
  diathesis 274.9
  eczema 274.89
  episcleritis 274.89 [379.09]
  external ear (tophus) 274.81
  flare 274.01 ●
  glomerulonephritis 274.10
  iritis 274.89 [364.11]
  joint 274.00 ▲
  kidney 274.10
  lead 984.9
    specified type of lead — see Table of Drugs and Chemicals
  nephritis 274.10
  neuritis 274.89 [357.4]
  phlebitis 274.89 [451.9]
  rheumatic 714.0
  saturnine 984.9
    specified type of lead — see Table of Drugs and Chemicals
  spondylitis 274.00 ▲
  synovitis 274.00 ▲
  syphilitic 095.8
  tophi 274.03 ▲
    ear 274.81
    heart 274.82
    specified site NEC 274.82
Gowers'
  muscular dystrophy 359.1
  syndrome (vasovagal attack) 780.2
Gowers-Paton-Kennedy syndrome 377.04
Gradenigo's syndrome 383.02
Graft-versus-host disease 279.50
  due to organ transplant NEC — see Complications, transplant, organ

Graham Steell's murmur (pulmonic regurgitation) — see also Endocarditis, pulmonary 424.3
Grain-handlers' disease or lung 495.8
Grain mite (itch) 133.8
Grand
  mal (idiopathic) (see also Epilepsy) 345.1 ☑
    hysteria of Charcôt 300.11
    nonrecurrent or isolated 780.39
  multipara
    affecting management of labor and delivery 659.4 ☑
    status only (not pregnant) V61.5
Granite workers' lung 502
Granular — see also condition
  inflammation, pharynx 472.1
  kidney (contracting) (see also Sclerosis, renal) 587
  liver — see Cirrhosis, liver
  nephritis — see Nephritis
Granulation tissue, abnormal — see also Granuloma
  abnormal or excessive 701.5
  postmastoidectomy cavity 383.33
  postoperative 701.5
  skin 701.5
Granulocytopenia, granulocytopenic (primary) 288.00
  malignant 288.09
Granuloma NEC 686.1
  abdomen (wall) 568.89
    skin (pyogenicum) 686.1
      from residual foreign body 709.4
  annulare 695.89
  anus 569.49
  apical 522.6
  appendix 543.9
  aural 380.23
  beryllium (skin) 709.4
    lung 503
  bone (see also Osteomyelitis) 730.1 ☑
    eosinophilic 277.89
    from residual foreign body 733.99
  canaliculus lacrimalis 375.81
  cerebral 348.89   ▲
  cholesterin, middle ear 385.82
  coccidioidal (progressive) 114.3
    lung 114.4
    meninges 114.2
    primary (lung) 114.0
  colon 569.89
  conjunctiva 372.61
  dental 522.6
  ear, middle (cholesterin) 385.82
    with otitis media — see Otitis media
  eosinophilic 277.89
    bone 277.89
    lung 277.89
    oral mucosa 528.9
  exuberant 701.5
  eyelid 374.89
  facial
    lethal midline 446.3
    malignant 446.3
  faciale 701.8
  fissuratum (gum) 523.8
  foot NEC 686.1
  foreign body (in soft tissue) NEC 728.82
    bone 733.99
    in operative wound 998.4
    muscle 728.82
    skin 709.4
    subcutaneous tissue 709.4
  fungoides 202.1 ☑
  gangraenescens 446.3
  giant cell (central) (jaw) (reparative) 526.3
    gingiva 523.8
    peripheral (gingiva) 523.8
  gland (lymph) 289.3
  Hodgkin's (M9661/3) 201.1 ☑
  ileum 569.89
  infectious NEC 136.9
  inguinale (Donovan) 099.2
    venereal 099.2
  intestine 569.89
  iridocyclitis 364.10

Granuloma — *continued*
  jaw (bone) 526.3
    reparative giant cell 526.3
  kidney (*see also* Infection, kidney) 590.9
  lacrimal sac 375.81
  larynx 478.79
  lethal midline 446.3
  lipid 277.89
  lipoid 277.89
  liver 572.8
  lung (infectious) (*see also* Fibrosis, lung) 515
    coccidioidal 114.4
    eosinophilic 277.89
  lymph gland 289.3
  Majocchi's 110.6
  malignant, face 446.3
  mandible 526.3
  mediastinum 519.3
  midline 446.3
  monilial 112.3
  muscle 728.82
    from residual foreign body 728.82
  nasal sinus (*see also* Sinusitis) 473.9
  operation wound 998.59
    foreign body 998.4
    stitch (external) 998.89
      internal wound 998.89
    talc 998.7
  oral mucosa, eosinophilic or pyogenic 528.9
  orbit, orbital 376.11
  paracoccidioidal 116.1
  penis, venereal 099.2
  periapical 522.6
  peritoneum 568.89
    due to ova of helminths NEC (*see also*
      Helminthiasis) 128.9
  postmastoidectomy cavity 383.33
  postoperative — *see* Granuloma, operation
    wound
  prostate 601.8
  pudendi (ulcerating) 099.2
  pudendorum (ulcerative) 099.2
  pulp, internal (tooth) 521.49
  pyogenic, pyogenicum (skin) 686.1
    maxillary alveolar ridge 522.6
    oral mucosa 528.9
  rectum 569.49
  reticulohistiocytic 277.89
  rubrum nasi 705.89
  sarcoid 135
  Schistosoma 120.9
  septic (skin) 686.1
  silica (skin) 709.4
  sinus (accessory) (infectional) (nasal) (*see also*
    Sinusitis) 473.9
  skin (pyogenicum) 686.1
    from foreign body or material 709.4
  sperm 608.89
  spine
    syphilitic (epidural) 094.89
    tuberculous (*see also* Tuberculosis)
      015.0 ☑ *[730.88]*
  stitch (postoperative) 998.89
    internal wound 998.89
  suppurative (skin) 686.1
  suture (postoperative) 998.89
    internal wound 998.89
  swimming pool 031.1
  talc 728.82
    in operation wound 998.7
  telangiectaticum (skin) 686.1
  tracheostomy 519.09
  trichophyticum 110.6
  tropicum 102.4
  umbilicus 686.1
    newborn 771.4
  urethra 599.84
  uveitis 364.10
  vagina 099.2
  venereum 099.2
  vocal cords 478.5
  Wegener's (necrotizing respiratory granulo-
    matosis) 446.4
Granulomatosis NEC 686.1
  disciformis chronica et progressiva 709.3
  infantiseptica 771.2

Granulomatosis — *continued*
  lipoid 277.89
  lipophagic, intestinal 040.2
  miliary 027.0
  necrotizing, respiratory 446.4
  progressive, septic 288.1
  Wegener's (necrotizing respiratory) 446.4
Granulomatous tissue — *see* Granuloma
Granulosis rubra nasi 705.89
Graphite fibrosis (of lung) 503
Graphospasm 300.89
  organic 333.84
Grating scapula 733.99
Gravel (urinary) — *see also* Calculus 592.9
Graves' disease (exophthalmic goiter) — *see also*
  Goiter, toxic 242.0 ☑
Gravis — *see* condition
Grawitz's tumor (hypernephroma) (M8312/3)
  189.0
Grayness, hair (premature) 704.3
  congenital 757.4
Gray or grey syndrome (chloramphenicol)
  (newborn) 779.4
Greenfield's disease 330.0
Green sickness 280.9
Greenstick fracture — *see* Fracture, by site
Greig's syndrome (hypertelorism) 756.0
Grief 309.0
Griesinger's disease — *see also* Ancylostomiasis
  126.9
Grinders'
  asthma 502
  lung 502
  phthisis (*see also* Tuberculosis) 011.4 ☑
Grinding, teeth 306.8
Grip
  Dabney's 074.1
  devil's 074.1
Grippe, grippal — *see also* Influenza
  Balkan 083.0
  intestinal 487.8
  summer 074.8
Grippy cold 487.1
Grisel's disease 723.5
Groin — *see* condition
Grooved
  nails (transverse) 703.8
  tongue 529.5
    congenital 750.13
Ground itch 126.9
Growing pains, children 781.99
Growth (fungoid) (neoplastic) (new) (M8000/1)
  — *see also* Neoplasm, by site, unspecified
  nature
  adenoid (vegetative) 474.12
  benign (M8000/0) — *see* Neoplasm, by site,
    benign
  fetal, poor 764.9 ☑
    affecting management of pregnancy
      656.5 ☑
  malignant (M8000/3) — *see* Neoplasm, by
    site, malignant
  rapid, childhood V21.0
  secondary (M8000/6) — *see* Neoplasm, by
    site, malignant, secondary
GRSA (glycopeptide resistant staphylococcus
  aureus) V09.8 ☑
Gruber's hernia — *see* Hernia, Gruber's
Gruby's disease (tinea tonsurans) 110.0
GSS (Gerstmann-Sträussler-Scheinker syndrome)
  046.71
G-trisomy 758.0
Guama fever 066.3
Gubler (-Millard) paralysis or syndrome 344.89
Guérin-Stern syndrome (arthrogryposis multi-
  plex congenita) 754.89
Guertin's disease (electric chorea) 049.8
Guillain-Barré disease or syndrome 357.0
Guinea worms (infection) (infestation) 125.7
Guinon's disease (motor-verbal tic) 307.23
Gull and Sutton's disease — *see* Hypertension,
  kidney
Gull's disease (thyroid atrophy with myxedema)
  244.8
Gum — *see* condition
Gumboil 522.7

Gumma (syphilitic) 095.9
  artery 093.89
    cerebral or spinal 094.89
  bone 095.5
    of yaws (late) 102.6
  brain 094.89
  cauda equina 094.89
  central nervous system NEC 094.9
  ciliary body 095.8 *[364.11]*
  congenital 090.5
    testis 090.5
  eyelid 095.8 *[373.5]*
  heart 093.89
  intracranial 094.89
  iris 095.8 *[364.11]*
  kidney 095.4
  larynx 095.8
  leptomeninges 094.2
  liver 095.3
  meninges 094.2
  myocardium 093.82
  nasopharynx 095.8
  neurosyphilitic 094.9
  nose 095.8
  orbit 095.8
  palate (soft) 095.8
  penis 095.8
  pericardium 093.81
  pharynx 095.8
  pituitary 095.8
  scrofulous (*see also* Tuberculosis) 017.0 ☑
  skin 095.8
  specified site NEC 095.8
  spinal cord 094.89
  tongue 095.8
  tonsil 095.8
  trachea 095.8
  tuberculous (*see also* Tuberculosis) 017.0 ☑
  ulcerative due to yaws 102.4
  ureter 095.8
  yaws 102.4
    bone 102.6
Gunn's syndrome (jaw-winking syndrome) 742.8
Gunshot wound — *see also* Wound, open, by
  site
  fracture — *see* Fracture, by site, open
  internal organs (abdomen, chest, or pelvis) —
    see Injury, internal, by site, with open
    wound
  intracranial — *see* Laceration, brain, with open
    intracranial wound
Günther's disease or syndrome (congenital
  erythropoietic porphyria) 277.1
Gustatory hallucination 780.1
Gynandrism 752.7
Gynandroblastoma (M8632/1)
  specified site — *see* Neoplasm, by site, uncer-
    tain behavior
  unspecified site
    female 236.2
    male 236.4
Gynandromorphism 752.7
Gynatresia (congenital) 752.49
Gynecoid pelvis, male 738.6
Gynecological examination V72.31
  for contraceptive maintenance V25.40
Gynecomastia 611.1
Gynephobia 300.29
Gyrate scalp 757.39

H

Haas' disease (osteochondrosis head of humerus)
  732.3
Habermann's disease (acute parapsoriasis varioliformis) 696.2
Habit, habituation
  chorea 307.22
  disturbance, child 307.9
  drug (*see also* Dependence) 304.9 ☑
  laxative (*see also* Abuse, drugs, nondependent)
    305.9 ☑
  spasm 307.20
    chronic 307.22
    transient (of childhood) 307.21
  tic 307.20
    chronic 307.22

Habit, habituation — *continued*
  tic — *continued*
    transient (of childhood) 307.21
  use of
    nonprescribed drugs (*see also* Abuse,
      drugs, nondependent) 305.9 ☑
    patent medicines (*see also* Abuse, drugs,
      nondependent) 305.9 ☑
  vomiting 536.2
Hadfield-Clarke syndrome (pancreatic infantil-
  ism) 577.8
Haff disease 985.1
Hageman factor defect, deficiency, or disease
  — *see also* Defect, coagulation 286.3
Haglund's disease (osteochondrosis os tibiale
  externum) 732.5
Haglund-Läwen-Fründ syndrome 717.89
Hagner's disease (hypertrophic pulmonary os-
  teoarthropathy) 731.2
Hag teeth, tooth 524.39
Hailey-Hailey disease (benign familial chronic
  pemphigus) 757.39
Hair — *see also* condition
  plucking 307.9
Hairball in stomach 935.2
Hairy black tongue 529.3
Half vertebra 756.14
Halitosis 784.99
Hallermann-Streiff syndrome 756.0
Hallervorden-Spatz disease or syndrome 333.0
Hallopeau's
  acrodermatitis (continua) 696.1
  disease (lichen sclerosis et atrophicus) 701.0
Hallucination (auditory) (gustatory) (olfactory)
  (tactile) 780.1
  alcohol-induced 291.3
  drug-induced 292.12
  visual 368.16
Hallucinosis 298.9
  alcohol-induced (acute) 291.3
  drug-induced 292.12
Hallus — *see* Hallux
Hallux 735.9
  limitus 735.8
  malleus (acquired) 735.3
  rigidus (acquired) 735.2
    congenital 755.66
    late effects of rickets 268.1
  valgus (acquired) 735.0
    congenital 755.66
  varus (acquired) 735.1
    congenital 755.66
Halo, visual 368.15
Hamartoblastoma 759.6
Hamartoma 759.6
  epithelial (gingival), odontogenic, central, or
    peripheral (M9321/0) 213.1
    upper jaw (bone) 213.0
  vascular 757.32
Hamartosis, hamartoses NEC 759.6
Hamman's disease or syndrome (spontaneous
  mediastinal emphysema) 518.1
Hamman-Rich syndrome (diffuse interstitial
  pulmonary fibrosis) 516.3
Hammer toe (acquired) 735.4
  congenital 755.66
  late effects of rickets 268.1
Hand — *see* condition
Hand-foot syndrome 693.0
Hand-Schüller-Christian disease or syndrome
  (chronic histiocytosis x) 277.89
Hanging (asphyxia) (strangulation) (suffocation)
  994.7
Hangnail (finger) (with lymphangitis) 681.02
Hangover (alcohol) — *see also* Abuse, drugs,
  nondependent 305.0 ☑
Hanot-Chauffard (-Troisier) syndrome (bronze
  diabetes) 275.0
Hanot's cirrhosis or disease — *see* Cirrhosis,
  biliary
Hansen's disease (leprosy) 030.9
  benign form 030.1
  malignant form 030.0
Harada's disease or syndrome 363.22
Hard chancre 091.0

Hardening
artery — *see* Arteriosclerosis
brain 348.89 ▲
liver 571.8
Hard firm prostate 600.10
with
urinary
obstruction 600.11
retention 600.11
Harelip — *see also* Cleft, lip 749.10
Hare's syndrome (M8010/3) (carcinoma, pulmonary apex) 162.3
Harkavy's syndrome 446.0
Harlequin (fetus) 757.1
color change syndrome 779.89
Harley's disease (intermittent hemoglobinuria) 283.2
Harris'
lines 733.91
syndrome (organic hyperinsulinism) 251.1
Hart's disease or syndrome (pellagra-cerebellar ataxia-renal aminoaciduria) 270.0
Hartmann's pouch (abnormal sacculation of gallbladder neck) 575.8
of intestine V44.3
attention to V55.3
Hartnup disease (pellagra-cerebellar ataxia-renal aminoaciduria) 270.0
Harvester lung 495.0
Hashimoto's disease or struma (struma lymphomatosa) 245.2
Hassall-Henle bodies (corneal warts) 371.41
Haut mal — *see also* Epilepsy 345.1 ☑
Haverhill fever 026.1
Hawaiian wood rose dependence 304.5 ☑
Hawkins' keloid 701.4
Hay
asthma (*see also* Asthma) 493.0 ☑
fever (allergic) (with rhinitis) 477.9
with asthma (bronchial) (*see also* Asthma) 493.0 ☑
allergic, due to grass, pollen, ragweed, or tree 477.0
conjunctivitis 372.05
due to
dander, animal (cat) (dog) 477.2
dust 477.8
fowl 477.8
hair, animal (cat) (dog) 477.2
pollen 477.0
specified allergen other than pollen 477.8
Hayem-Faber syndrome (achlorhydric anemia) 280.9
Hayem-Widal syndrome (acquired hemolytic jaundice) 283.9
Haygarth's nodosities 715.04
Hazard-Crile tumor (M8350/3) 193
Hb (abnormal)
disease — *see* Disease, hemoglobin
trait — *see* Trait
H disease 270.0
Head — *see also* condition
banging 307.3
Headache 784.0
allergic 339.00
associated with sexual activity 339.82
cluster 339.00
chronic 339.02
episodic 339.01
daily
chronic 784.0
new persistent (NPDH) 339.42
drug induced 339.3
due to
loss, spinal fluid 349.0
lumbar puncture 349.0
saddle block 349.0
emotional 307.81
histamine 339.00
hypnic 339.81
lumbar puncture 349.0
medication overuse 339.3
menopausal 627.2
menstrual 346.4 ☑
migraine 346.9 ☑

Headache — *continued*
nasal septum 784.0
nonorganic origin 307.81
orgasmic 339.82
postspinal 349.0
post-traumatic 339.20
acute 339.21
chronic 339.22
premenstrual 346.4 ☑
preorgasmic 339.82
primary
cough 339.83
exertional 339.84
stabbing 339.85
thunderclap 339.43
psychogenic 307.81
psychophysiologic 307.81
rebound 339.3
short lasting unilateral neuralgiform with conjunctival injection and tearing (SUNCT) 339.05
sick 346.9 ☑
spinal 349.0
complicating labor and delivery 668.8 ☑
postpartum 668.8 ☑
spinal fluid loss 349.0
syndrome
cluster 339.00
complicated NEC 339.44
periodic in child or adolescent 346.2 ☑
specified NEC 339.89
tension 307.81
type 339.10
chronic 339.12
episodic 339.11
vascular 784.0
migraine type 346.9 ☑
vasomotor 346.9 ☑
Health
advice V65.4 ☑
audit V70.0
checkup V70.0
education V65.4 ☑
hazard (*see also* History of) V15.9
falling V15.88
specified cause NEC V15.89
instruction V65.4 ☑
services provided because (of)
boarding school residence V60.6
holiday relief for person providing home care V60.5
inadequate
housing V60.1
resources V60.2
lack of housing V60.0
no care available in home V60.4
person living alone V60.3
poverty V60.3
residence in institution V60.6
specified cause NEC V60.89 ▲
vacation relief for person providing home care V60.5
Healthy
donor (*see also* Donor) V59.9
infant or child
accompanying sick mother V65.0
receiving care V20.1
person
accompanying sick relative V65.0
admitted for sterilization V25.2
receiving prophylactic inoculation or vaccination (*see also* Vaccination, prophylactic) V05.9
Hearing
conservation and treatment V72.12
examination V72.19
following failed hearing screening V72.11
Heart — *see* condition
Heartburn 787.1
psychogenic 306.4
Heat (effects) 992.9
apoplexy 992.0
burn (*see also* Burn, by site)
from sun (*see also* Sunburn) 692.71
collapse 992.1
cramps 992.2

Heat — *continued*
dermatitis or eczema 692.89
edema 992.7
erythema — *see* Burn, by site
excessive 992.9
specified effect NEC 992.8
exhaustion 992.5
anhydrotic 992.3
due to
salt (and water) depletion 992.4
water depletion 992.3
fatigue (transient) 992.6
fever 992.0
hyperpyrexia 992.0
prickly 705.1
prostration — *see* Heat, exhaustion
pyrexia 992.0
rash 705.1
specified effect NEC 992.8
stroke 992.0
sunburn (*see also* Sunburn) 692.71
syncope 992.1
Heavy-chain disease 273.2
Heavy-for-dates (fetus or infant) 766.1
4500 grams or more 766.0
exceptionally 766.0
Hebephrenia, hebephrenic (acute) — *see also* Schizophrenia 295.1 ☑
dementia (praecox) (*see also* Schizophrenia) 295.1 ☑
schizophrenia (*see also* Schizophrenia) 295.1 ☑
Heberden's
disease or nodes 715.04
syndrome (angina pectoris) 413.9
Hebra's disease
dermatitis exfoliativa 695.89
erythema multiforme exudativum 695.19
pityriasis 695.89
maculata et circinata 696.3
rubra 695.89
pilaris 696.4
prurigo 698.2
Hebra, nose 040.1
Hedinger's syndrome (malignant carcinoid) 259.2
Heel — *see* condition
Heerfordt's disease or syndrome (uveoparotitis) 135
Hegglin's anomaly or syndrome 288.2
Heidenhain's disease 290.10
with dementia 290.10
Heilmeyer-Schöner disease (M9842/3) 207.1 ☑
Heine-Medin disease — *see also* Poliomyelitis 045.9 ☑
Heinz-body anemia, congenital 282.7
Heller's disease or syndrome (infantile psychosis) — *see also* Psychosis, childhood 299.1 ☑
H.E.L.L.P 642.5 ☑
Helminthiasis — *see also* Infestation, by specific parasite 128.9
Ancylostoma (*see also* Ancylostoma) 126.9
intestinal 127.9
mixed types (types classifiable to more than one of the categories 120.0–127.7) 127.8
specified type 127.7
mixed types (intestinal) (types classifiable to more than one of the categories 120.0–127.7) 127.8
Necator americanus 126.1
specified type NEC 128.8
Trichinella 124
Heloma 700
Hemangioblastoma (M9161/1) — *see also* Neoplasm, connective tissue, uncertain behavior
malignant (M9161/3) — *see* Neoplasm, connective tissue, malignant
Hemangioblastomatosis, cerebelloretinal 759.6
Hemangioendothelioma (M9130/1) — *see also* Neoplasm, by site, uncertain behavior
benign (M9130/0) 228.00

Hemangioendothelioma — *see also* Neoplasm, by site, uncertain behavior — *continued*
bone (diffuse) (M9130/3) — *see* Neoplasm, bone, malignant
malignant (M9130/3) — *see* Neoplasm, connective tissue, malignant
nervous system (M9130/0) 228.09
Hemangioendotheliosarcoma (M9130/3) — *see* Neoplasm, connective tissue, malignant
Hemangiofibroma (M9160/0) — *see* Neoplasm, by site, benign
Hemangiolipoma (M8861/0) — *see* Lipoma
Hemangioma (M9120/0) 228.00
arteriovenous (M9123/0) — *see* Hemangioma, by site
brain 228.02
capillary (M9131/0) — *see* Hemangioma, by site
cavernous (M9121/0) — *see* Hemangioma, by site
central nervous system NEC 228.09
choroid 228.09
heart 228.09
infantile (M9131/0) — *see* Hemangioma, by site
intra-abdominal structures 228.04
intracranial structures 228.02
intramuscular (M9132/0) — *see* Hemangioma, by site
iris 228.09
juvenile (M9131/0) — *see* Hemangioma, by site
malignant (M9120/3) — *see* Neoplasm, connective tissue, malignant
meninges 228.09
brain 228.02
spinal cord 228.09
peritoneum 228.04
placenta — *see* Placenta, abnormal
plexiform (M9131/0) — *see* Hemangioma, by site
racemose (M9123/0) — *see* Hemangioma, by site
retina 228.03
retroperitoneal tissue 228.04
sclerosing (M8832/0) — *see* Neoplasm, skin, benign
simplex (M9131/0) — *see* Hemangioma, by site
skin and subcutaneous tissue 228.01
specified site NEC 228.09
spinal cord 228.09
venous (M9122/0) — *see* Hemangioma, by site
verrucous keratotic (M9142/0) — *see* Hemangioma, by site
Hemangiomatosis (systemic) 757.32
involving single site — *see* Hemangioma
Hemangiopericytoma (M9150/1) — *see also* Neoplasm, connective tissue, uncertain behavior
benign (M9150/0) — *see* Neoplasm, connective tissue, benign
malignant (M9150/3) — *see* Neoplasm, connective tissue, malignant
Hemangiosarcoma (M9120/3) — *see* Neoplasm, connective tissue, malignant
Hemarthrosis (nontraumatic) 719.10
ankle 719.17
elbow 719.12
foot 719.17
hand 719.14
hip 719.15
knee 719.16
multiple sites 719.19
pelvic region 719.15
shoulder (region) 719.11
specified site NEC 719.18
traumatic — *see* Sprain, by site
wrist 719.13
Hematemesis 578.0
with ulcer — *see* Ulcer, by site, with hemorrhage
due to S. japonicum 120.2

Hematemesis — *continued*
Goldstein's (familial hemorrhagic telangiectasia) 448.0
newborn 772.4
due to swallowed maternal blood 777.3
Hematidrosis 705.89
Hematinuria — *see also* Hemoglobinuria 791.2
malarial 084.8
paroxysmal 283.2
Hematite miners' lung 503
Hematobilia 576.8
Hematocele (congenital) (diffuse) (idiopathic) 608.83
broad ligament 620.7
canal of Nuck 629.0
cord, male 608.83
fallopian tube 620.8
female NEC 629.0
ischiorectal 569.89
male NEC 608.83
ovary 629.0
pelvis, pelvic
female 629.0
with ectopic pregnancy (*see also* Pregnancy, ectopic) 633.90
with intrauterine pregnancy 633.91
male 608.83
periuterine 629.0
retrouterine 629.0
scrotum 608.83
spermatic cord (diffuse) 608.83
testis 608.84
traumatic — *see* Injury, internal, pelvis
tunica vaginalis 608.83
uterine ligament 629.0
uterus 621.4
vagina 623.6
vulva 624.5
Hematocephalus 742.4
Hematochezia — *see also* Melena 578.1
Hematochyluria — *see also* Infestation, filarial 125.9
Hematocolpos 626.8
Hematocornea 371.12
Hematogenous — *see* condition
Hematoma (skin surface intact) (traumatic) — *see also* Contusion

Note — Hematomas are coded according to origin and the nature and site of the hematoma or the accompanying injury. Hematomas of unspecified origin are coded as injuries of the sites involved, except:

(a) hematomas of genital organs which are coded as diseases of the organ involved unless they complicate pregnancy or delivery

(b) hematomas of the eye which are coded as diseases of the eye.

For late effect of hematoma classifiable to 920–924 see Late, effect, contusion

with
crush injury — *see* Crush
fracture — *see* Fracture, by site
injury of internal organs (*see also* Injury, internal, by site)
kidney — *see* Hematoma, kidney traumatic
liver — *see* Hematoma, liver, traumatic
spleen — *see* Hematoma, spleen
nerve injury — *see* Injury, nerve
open wound — *see* Wound, open, by site
skin surface intact — *see* Contusion
abdomen (wall) — *see* Contusion, abdomen
amnion 658.8 ☑
aorta, dissecting 441.00
abdominal 441.02
thoracic 441.01
thoracoabdominal 441.03
arterial (complicating trauma) 904.9
specified site — *see* Injury, blood vessel, by site
auricle (ear) 380.31
birth injury 767.8
skull 767.19

Hematoma — *see also* Contusion — *continued*
brain (traumatic) 853.0 ☑

Note — Use the following fifth-digit subclassification with categories 851–854:

0   unspecified state of consciousness

1   with no loss of consciousness

2   with brief [less than one hour] loss of consciousness

3   with moderate [1–24 hours] loss of consciousness

4   with prolonged [more than 24 hours] loss of consciousness and return to pre-existing conscious level

5   with prolonged [more than 24 hours] loss of consciousness, without return to pre-existing conscious level

Use fifth-digit 5 to designate when a patient is unconscious and dies before regaining consciousness, regardless of the duration of the loss of consciousness

6   with loss of consciousness of unspecified duration

9   with concussion, unspecified

with
cerebral
contusion — *see* Contusion, brain
laceration — *see* Laceration, brain
open intracranial wound 853.1 ☑
skull fracture — *see* Fracture, skull, by site
extradural or epidural 852.4 ☑
with open intracranial wound 852.5 ☑
fetus or newborn 767.0
nontraumatic 432.0
fetus or newborn NEC 767.0
nontraumatic (*see also* Hemorrhage, brain) 431
epidural or extradural 432.0
newborn NEC 772.8
subarachnoid, arachnoid, or meningeal (*see also* Hemorrhage, subarachnoid) 430
subdural (*see also* Hemorrhage, subdural) 432.1
subarachnoid, arachnoid, or meningeal 852.0 ☑
with open intracranial wound 852.1 ☑
fetus or newborn 772.2
nontraumatic (*see also* Hemorrhage, subarachnoid) 430
subdural 852.2 ☑
with open intracranial wound 852.3 ☑
fetus or newborn (localized) 767.0
nontraumatic (*see also* Hemorrhage, subdural) 432.1
breast (nontraumatic) 611.89
broad ligament (nontraumatic) 620.7
complicating delivery 665.7 ☑
traumatic — *see* Injury, internal, broad ligament
calcified NEC 959.9
capitis 920
due to birth injury 767.19
newborn 767.19
cerebral — *see* Hematoma, brain
cesarean section wound 674.3 ☑
chorion — *see* Placenta, abnormal
complicating delivery (perineum) (vulva) 664.5 ☑
pelvic 665.7 ☑
vagina 665.7 ☑
corpus
cavernosum (nontraumatic) 607.82
luteum (nontraumatic) (ruptured) 620.1
dura (mater) — *see* Hematoma, brain, subdural
epididymis (nontraumatic) 608.83
epidural (traumatic) (*see also* Hematoma, brain, extradural)
spinal — *see* Injury, spinal, by site

Hematoma — *see also* Contusion — *continued*
episiotomy 674.3 ☑
external ear 380.31
extradural (*see also* Hematoma, brain, extradural)
fetus or newborn 767.0
nontraumatic 432.0
fetus or newborn 767.0
fallopian tube 620.8
genital organ (nontraumatic)
female NEC 629.89
male NEC 608.83
traumatic (external site) 922.4
internal — *see* Injury, internal, genital organ
graafian follicle (ruptured) 620.0
internal organs (abdomen, chest, or pelvis) (*see also* Injury, internal, by site)
kidney — *see* Hematoma, kidney, traumatic
liver — *see* Hematoma, liver, traumatic
spleen — *see* Hematoma, spleen
intracranial — *see* Hematoma, brain
kidney, cystic 593.81
traumatic 866.01
with open wound into cavity 866.11
labia (nontraumatic) 624.5
lingual (and other parts of neck, scalp, or face, except eye) 920
liver (subcapsular) 573.8
birth injury 767.8
fetus or newborn 767.8
traumatic NEC 864.01
with
laceration — *see* Laceration, liver
open wound into cavity 864.11
mediastinum — *see* Injury, internal, mediastinum
meninges, meningeal (brain) (*see also* Hematoma, brain, subarachnoid)
spinal — *see* Injury, spinal, by site
mesosalpinx (nontraumatic) 620.8
traumatic — *see* Injury, internal, pelvis
muscle (traumatic) — *see* Contusion, by site
nontraumatic 729.92
nasal (septum) (and other part(s) of neck, scalp, or face, except eye) 920
obstetrical surgical wound 674.3 ☑
orbit, orbital (nontraumatic) 376.32
traumatic 921.2
ovary (corpus luteum) (nontraumatic) 620.1
traumatic — *see* Injury, internal, ovary
pelvis (female) (nontraumatic) 629.89
complicating delivery 665.7 ☑
male 608.83
traumatic (*see also* Injury, internal, pelvis)
specified organ NEC (*see also* Injury, internal, pelvis) 867.6
penis (nontraumatic) 607.82
pericranial (and neck, or face any part, except eye) 920
due to injury at birth 767.19
perineal wound (obstetrical) 674.3 ☑
complicating delivery 664.5 ☑
perirenal, cystic 593.81
pinna 380.31
placenta — *see* Placenta, abnormal
postoperative 998.12
retroperitoneal (nontraumatic) 568.81
traumatic — *see* Injury, internal, retroperitoneum
retropubic, male 568.81
scalp (and neck, or face any part, except eye) 920
fetus or newborn 767.19
scrotum (nontraumatic) 608.83
traumatic 922.4
seminal vesicle (nontraumatic) 608.83
traumatic — *see* Injury, internal, seminal, vesicle
soft tissue 729.92
spermatic cord (*see also* Injury, internal, spermatic cord)
nontraumatic 608.83

Hematoma — *see also* Contusion — *continued*
spinal (cord) (meninges) (*see also* Injury, spinal, by site)
fetus or newborn 767.4
nontraumatic 336.1
spleen 865.01
with
laceration — *see* Laceration, spleen
open wound into cavity 865.11
sternocleidomastoid, birth injury 767.8
sternomastoid, birth injury 767.8
subarachnoid (*see also* Hematoma, brain, subarachnoid)
fetus or newborn 772.2
nontraumatic (*see also* Hemorrhage, subarachnoid) 430
newborn 772.2
subdural (*see also* Hematoma, brain, subdural)
fetus or newborn (localized) 767.0
nontraumatic (*see also* Hemorrhage, subdural) 432.1
subperiosteal (syndrome) 267
traumatic — *see* Hematoma, by site
superficial, fetus or newborn 772.6
syncytium — *see* Placenta, abnormal
testis (nontraumatic) 608.83
birth injury 767.8
traumatic 922.4
tunica vaginalis (nontraumatic) 608.83
umbilical cord 663.6 ☑
affecting fetus or newborn 762.6
uterine ligament (nontraumatic) 620.7
traumatic — *see* Injury, internal, pelvis
uterus 621.4
traumatic — *see* Injury, internal, pelvis
vagina (nontraumatic) (ruptured) 623.6
complicating delivery 665.7 ☑
traumatic 922.4
vas deferens (nontraumatic) 608.83
traumatic — *see* Injury, internal, vas deferens
vitreous 379.23
vocal cord 920
vulva (nontraumatic) 624.5
complicating delivery 664.5 ☑
fetus or newborn 767.8
traumatic 922.4
Hematometra 621.4
Hematomyelia 336.1
with fracture of vertebra (*see also* Fracture, vertebra, by site, with spinal cord injury) 806.8
fetus or newborn 767.4
Hematomyelitis 323.9
late effect — *see* category 326
Hematoperitoneum — *see also* Hemoperitoneum 568.81
Hematopneumothorax — *see also* Hemothorax 511.89
Hematopoiesis, cyclic 288.02
Hematoporphyria (acquired) (congenital) 277.1
Hematoporphyrinuria (acquired) (congenital) 277.1
Hematorachis, hematorrhachis 336.1
fetus or newborn 767.4
Hematosalpinx 620.8
with
ectopic pregnancy (*see also* categories 633.0–633.9) 639.2
infectional (*see also* Salpingo-oophoritis) 614.2
molar pregnancy (*see also* categories 630–632) 639.2
Hematospermia 608.82
Hematothorax — *see also* Hemothorax 511.89
Hematotympanum 381.03
Hematuria (benign) (essential) (idiopathic) 599.70
due to S. hematobium 120.0
endemic 120.0
gross 599.71
intermittent 599.70
malarial 084.8
microscopic 599.72
paroxysmal 599.70

☑ Additional Digit Required — Refer to the Tabular List for Digit Selection   ▽ Subterms under main terms may continue to next column or page

2010 ICD-9-CM   ▶◀ Revised Text   ● New Line   ▲ Revised Code   Volume 2 — 129

Index

Hematuria — Hemorrhage, hemorrhagic

Hematuria — *continued*
  sulfonamide
    correct substance properly administered
      599.70
    overdose or wrong substance given or
      taken 961.0
  tropical (bilharziasis) 120.0
  tuberculous (*see also* Tuberculosis) 016.9 ☑
Hematuric bilious fever 084.8
Hemeralopia 368.10
Hemiabiotrophy 799.89
Hemi-akinesia 781.8
Hemianalgesia — *see also* Disturbance, sensation
  782.0
Hemianencephaly 740.0
Hemianesthesia — *see also* Disturbance, sensa-
  tion 782.0
Hemianopia, hemianopsia (altitudinal)
  (homonymous) 368.46
  binasal 368.47
  bitemporal 368.47
  heteronymous 368.47
  syphilitic 095.8
Hemiasomatognosia 307.9
Hemiathetosis 781.0
Hemiatrophy 799.89
  cerebellar 334.8
  face 349.89
    progressive 349.89
  fascia 728.9
  leg 728.2
  tongue 529.8
Hemiballism (us) 333.5
Hemiblock (cardiac) (heart) (left) 426.2
Hemicardia 746.89
Hemicephalus, hemicephaly 740.0
Hemichorea 333.5
Hemicrania 346.9 ☑
  congenital malformation 740.0
  continua 339.41
  paroxysmal 339.03
    chronic 339.04
    episodic 339.03
Hemidystrophy — *see* Hemiatrophy
Hemiectromelia 755.4
Hemihypalgesia — *see also* Disturbance, sensation 782.0
Hemihypertrophy (congenital) 759.89
  cranial 756.0
Hemihypesthesia — *see also* Disturbance, sen-
  sation 782.0
Hemi-inattention 781.8
Hemimelia 755.4
  lower limb 755.30
    paraxial (complete) (incomplete) (inter-
      calary) (terminal) 755.32
      fibula 755.37
      tibia 755.36
    transverse (complete) (partial) 755.31
  upper limb 755.20
    paraxial (complete) (incomplete) (inter-
      calary) (terminal) 755.22
      radial 755.26
      ulnar 755.27
    transverse (complete) (partial) 755.21
Hemiparalysis — *see also* Hemiplegia 342.9 ☑
Hemiparesis — *see also* Hemiplegia 342.9 ☑
Hemiparesthesia — *see also* Disturbance, sensation 782.0
Hemiplegia 342.9 ☑
  acute (*see also* Disease, cerebrovascular, acute)
    436
  alternans facialis 344.89
  apoplectic (*see also* Disease, cerebrovascular,
    acute) 436
    late effect or residual
      affecting
        dominant side 438.21
        nondominant side 438.22
        unspecified side 438.20
  arteriosclerotic 437.0
    late effect or residual
      affecting
        dominant side 438.21
        nondominant side 438.22
        unspecified side 438.20

Hemiplegia — *continued*
  ascending (spinal) NEC 344.89
  attack (*see also* Disease, cerebrovascular, acute)
    436
  brain, cerebral (current episode) 437.8
    congenital 343.1
  cerebral — *see* Hemiplegia, brain
  congenital (cerebral) (spastic) (spinal) 343.1
  conversion neurosis (hysterical) 300.11
  cortical — *see* Hemiplegia, brain
  due to
    arteriosclerosis 437.0
      late effect or residual
        affecting
          dominant side 438.21
          nondominant side 438.22
          unspecified side 438.20
    cerebrovascular lesion (*see also* Disease,
      cerebrovascular, acute) 436
      late effect
        affecting
          dominant side 438.21
          nondominant side 438.22
          unspecified side 438.20
  embolic (current) (*see also* Embolism, brain)
    434.1 ☑
    late effect
      affecting
        dominant side 438.21
        nondominant side 438.22
        unspecified side 438.20
  flaccid 342.0 ☑
  hypertensive (current episode) 437.8
  infantile (postnatal) 343.4
  late effect
    birth injury, intracranial or spinal 343.4
    cerebrovascular lesion — *see* Late effect(s)
      (of) cerebrovascular disease
    viral encephalitis 139.0
  middle alternating NEC 344.89
  newborn NEC 767.0
  seizure (current episode) (*see also* Disease,
    cerebrovascular, acute) 436
  spastic 342.1 ☑
    congenital or infantile 343.1
  specified NEC 342.8 ☑
  thrombotic (current) (*see also* Thrombosis,
    brain) 434.0 ☑
    late effect — *see* Late effect(s) (of) cere-
      brovascular disease
Hemisection, spinal cord — *see* Fracture, vertebra, by site, with spinal cord injury
Hemispasm 781.0
  facial 781.0
Hemispatial neglect 781.8
Hemisporosis 117.9
Hemitremor 781.0
Hemivertebra 756.14
Hemobilia 576.8
Hemocholecyst 575.8
Hemochromatosis (acquired) (diabetic) (heredi-
  tary) (liver) (myocardium) (primary idiopath-
  ic) (secondary) 275.0
  with refractory anemia 238.72
Hemodialysis V56.0
Hemoglobin — *see also* condition
  abnormal (disease) — *see* Disease,
    hemoglobin
  AS genotype 282.5
  fetal, hereditary persistence 282.7
  high-oxygen-affinity 289.0
  low NEC 285.9
  S (Hb-S), heterozygous 282.5
Hemoglobinemia 283.2
  due to blood transfusion NEC 999.89
    bone marrow 996.85
  paroxysmal 283.2
Hemoglobinopathy (mixed) — *see also* Disease,
  hemoglobin 282.7
  with thalassemia 282.49
  sickle-cell 282.60
    with thalassemia (without crisis) 282.41
      with
        crisis 282.42
        vaso-occlusive pain 282.42
Hemoglobinuria, hemoglobinuric 791.2

Hemoglobinuria, hemoglobinuric —
  continued
  with anemia, hemolytic, acquired (chronic)
    NEC 283.2
  cold (agglutinin) (paroxysmal) (with Raynaud's
    syndrome) 283.2
  due to
    exertion 283.2
    hemolysis (from external causes) NEC 283.2
  exercise 283.2
  fever (malaria) 084.8
  infantile 791.2
  intermittent 283.2
  malarial 084.8
  march 283.2
  nocturnal (paroxysmal) 283.2
  paroxysmal (cold) (nocturnal) 283.2
Hemolymphangioma (M9175/0) 228.1
Hemolysis
  fetal — *see* Jaundice, fetus or newborn
  intravascular (disseminated) NEC 286.6
    with
      abortion — *see* Abortion, by type, with
        hemorrhage, delayed or exces-
        sive
      ectopic pregnancy (*see also* categories
        633.0–633.9) 639.1
      hemorrhage of pregnancy 641.3 ☑
        affecting fetus or newborn 762.1
      molar pregnancy (*see also* categories
        630–632) 639.1
    acute 283.2
    following
      abortion 639.1
      ectopic or molar pregnancy 639.1
  neonatal — *see* Jaundice, fetus or newborn
  transfusion NEC 999.89
    bone marrow 996.85
Hemolytic — *see also* condition
  anemia — *see* Anemia, hemolytic
  uremic syndrome 283.11
Hemometra 621.4
Hemopericardium (with effusion) 423.0
  newborn 772.8
  traumatic (*see also* Hemothorax, traumatic)
    860.2
    with open wound into thorax 860.3
Hemoperitoneum 568.81
  infectional (*see also* Peritonitis) 567.29
  traumatic — *see* Injury, internal, peritoneum
Hemophagocytic syndrome 288.4
  infection-associated 288.4
Hemophilia (familial) (hereditary) 286.0
  A 286.0
    carrier (asymptomatic) V83.01
      symptomatic V83.02
    acquired 286.5
  B (Leyden) 286.1
  C 286.2
  calcipriva (*see also* Fibrinolysis) 286.7
  classical 286.0
  nonfamilial 286.7
  secondary 286.5
  vascular 286.4
Hemophilus influenzae NEC 041.5
  arachnoiditis (basic) (brain) (spinal) 320.0
    late effect — *see* category 326
  bronchopneumonia 482.2
  cerebral verttriculitis 320.0
    late effect — *see* category 326
  cerebrospinal inflammation 320.0
    late effect — *see* category 326
  infection NEC 041.5
  leptomeningitis 320.0
    late effect — *see* category 326
  meningitis (cerebral) (cerebrospinal) (spinal)
    320.0
    late effect — *see* category 326
  meningomyelitis 320.0
    late effect — *see* category 326
  pachymeningitis (adhesive) (fibrous) (hemor-
    rhagic) (hypertrophic) (spinal) 320.0
    late effect — *see* category 326
  pneumonia (broncho-) 482.2
Hemophthalmos 360.43

Hemopneumothorax — *see also* Hemothorax
  511.89
  traumatic 860.4
    with open wound into thorax 860.5
Hemoptysis 786.3
  due to Paragonimus (westermani) 121.2
  newborn 770.3
  tuberculous (*see also* Tuberculosis, pulmonary)
    011.9 ☑
Hemorrhage, hemorrhagic (nontraumatic)
  459.0
  abdomen 459.0
  accidental (antepartum) 641.2 ☑
    affecting fetus or newborn 762.1
  adenoid 474.8
  adrenal (capsule) (gland) (medulla) 255.41
    newborn 772.5
  after labor — *see* Hemorrhage, postpartum
  alveolar
    lung, newborn 770.3
    process 525.8
  alveolus 525.8
  amputation stump (surgical) 998.11
    secondary, delayed 997.69
  anemia (chronic) 280.0
    acute 285.1
  antepartum — *see* Hemorrhage, pregnancy
  anus (sphincter) 569.3
  apoplexy (stroke) 432.9
  arachnoid — *see* Hemorrhage, subarachnoid
  artery NEC 459.0
    brain (*see also* Hemorrhage, brain) 431
    middle meningeal — *see* Hemorrhage,
      subarachnoid
  basilar (ganglion) (*see also* Hemorrhage, brain)
    431
  bladder 596.8
  blood dyscrasia 289.9
  bowel 578.9
    newborn 772.4
  brain (miliary) (nontraumatic) 431
    with
      birth injury 767.0
      arachnoid — *see* Hemorrhage, subarach-
        noid
    due to
      birth injury 767.0
      rupture of aneurysm (congenital) (*see
        also* Hemorrhage, subarach-
        noid) 430
      mycotic 431
      syphilis 094.89
    epidural or extradural — *see* Hemorrhage,
      extradural
    fetus or newborn (anoxic) (hypoxic) (due
      to birth trauma) (nontraumatic)
      767.0
      intraventricular 772.10
        grade I 772.11
        grade II 772.12
        grade III 772.13
        grade IV 772.14
    iatrogenic 997.02
    postoperative 997.02
    puerperal, postpartum, childbirth 674.0 ☑
    stem 431
    subarachnoid, arachnoid, or meningeal —
      see Hemorrhage, subarachnoid
    subdural — *see* Hemorrhage, subdural

☑ Additional Digit Required — Refer to the Tabular List for Digit Selection   ▼ Subterms under main terms may continue to next column or page

130 — Volume 2   ▶◀ Revised Text   ● New Line   ▲ Revised Code   2010 ICD-9-CM

Hemorrhage, hemorrhagic — *continued*
  brain — *continued*
    traumatic NEC 853.0 ☑

> *Note* — Use the following fifth-digit sub-classification with categories 851–854:
>
> 0   *unspecified state of consciousness*
>
> 1   *with no loss of consciousness*
>
> 2   *with brief [less than one hour] loss of consciousness*
>
> 3   *with moderate [1–24 hours] loss of consciousness*
>
> 4   *with prolonged [more than 24 hours] loss of consciousness and return to pre–existing conscious level*
>
> 5   *with prolonged [more than 24 hours] loss of consciousness, without return to pre–existing conscious level*
>
> *Use fifth-digit 5 to designate when a patient is unconscious and dies before regaining consciousness, regardless of the duration of the loss of consciousness*
>
> 6   *with loss of consciousness of unspecified duration*
>
> 9   *with concussion, unspecified*

    with
      cerebral
        contusion — *see* Contusion, brain
        laceration — *see* Laceration, brain
        open intracranial wound 853.1 ☑
        skull fracture — *see* Fracture, skull, by site
      extradural or epidural 852.4 ☑
        with open intracranial wound 852.5 ☑
      subarachnoid 852.0 ☑
        with open intracranial wound 852.1 ☑
      subdural 852.2 ☑
        with open intracranial wound 852.3 ☑
  breast 611.79
  bronchial tube — *see* Hemorrhage, lung
  bronchopulmonary — *see* Hemorrhage, lung
  bronchus (cause unknown) (*see also* Hemorrhage, lung) 786.3
  bulbar (*see also* Hemorrhage, brain) 431
  bursa 727.89
  capillary 448.9
    primary 287.8
  capsular — *see* Hemorrhage, brain
  cardiovascular 429.89
  cecum 578.9
  cephalic (*see also* Hemorrhage, brain) 431
  cerebellar (*see also* Hemorrhage, brain) 431
  cerebellum (*see also* Hemorrhage, brain) 431
  cerebral (*see also* Hemorrhage, brain) 431
    fetus or newborn (anoxic) (traumatic) 767.0
  cerebromeningeal (*see also* Hemorrhage, brain) 431
  cerebrospinal (*see also* Hemorrhage, brain) 431
  cerebrovascular accident — *see* Hemorrhage, brain
  cerebrum (*see also* Hemorrhage, brain) 431
  cervix (stump) (uteri) 622.8
  cesarean section wound 674.3 ☑
  chamber, anterior (eye) 364.41
  childbirth — *see* Hemorrhage, complicating, delivery
  choroid 363.61
    expulsive 363.62
  ciliary body 364.41
  cochlea 386.8
  colon — *see* Hemorrhage, intestine
  complicating
    delivery 641.9 ☑
      affecting fetus or newborn 762.1
      associated with
        afibrinogenemia 641.3 ☑

Hemorrhage, hemorrhagic — *continued*
  complicating — *continued*
    delivery — *continued*
      associated with — *continued*
        afibrinogenemia — *continued*
          affecting fetus or newborn 763.89
        coagulation defect 641.3 ☑
          affecting fetus or newborn 763.89
        hyperfibrinolysis 641.3 ☑
          affecting fetus or newborn 763.89
        hypofibrinogenemia 641.3 ☑
          affecting fetus or newborn 763.89
      due to
        low-lying placenta 641.1 ☑
          affecting fetus or newborn 762.0
        placenta previa 641.1 ☑
          affecting fetus or newborn 762.0
        premature separation of placenta 641.2 ☑
          affecting fetus or newborn 762.1
        retained
          placenta 666.0 ☑
          secundines 666.2 ☑
        trauma 641.8 ☑
          affecting fetus or newborn 763.89
        uterine leiomyoma 641.8 ☑
          affecting fetus or newborn 763.89
    surgical procedure 998.11
  complication(s)
    of dental implant placement 525.71
  concealed NEC 459.0
  congenital 772.9
  conjunctiva 372.72
    newborn 772.8
  cord, newborn 772.0
    slipped ligature 772.3
    stump 772.3
  corpus luteum (ruptured) 620.1
  cortical (*see also* Hemorrhage, brain) 431
  cranial 432.9
  cutaneous 782.7
    newborn 772.6
  cystitis — *see* Cystitis
  cyst, pancreas 577.2
  delayed
    with
      abortion — *see* Abortion, by type, with hemorrhage, delayed or excessive
      ectopic pregnancy (*see also* categories 633.0–633.9) 639.1
      molar pregnancy (*see also* categories 630–632) 639.1
    following
      abortion 639.1
      ectopic or molar pregnancy 639.1
    postpartum 666.2 ☑
  diathesis (familial) 287.9
    newborn 776.0
  disease 287.9
    newborn 776.0
    specified type NEC 287.8
  disorder 287.9
    due to intrinsic circulating anticoagulants 286.5
    specified type NEC 287.8
  due to
    any device, implant or graft (presence of) classifiable to 996.0–996.5 — *see* Complications, due to (presence of) any device, implant, or graft classified to 996.0–996.5NEC
    intrinsic circulating anticoagulant 286.5
  duodenum, duodenal 537.89
    ulcer — *see* Ulcer, duodenum, with hemorrhage
  dura mater — *see* Hemorrhage, subdural

Hemorrhage, hemorrhagic — *continued*
  endotracheal — *see* Hemorrhage, lung
  epicranial subaponeurotic (massive) 767.11
  epidural — *see* Hemorrhage, extradural
  episiotomy 674.3 ☑
  esophagus 530.82
    varix (*see also* Varix, esophagus, bleeding) 456.0
  excessive
    with
      abortion — *see* Abortion, by type, with hemorrhage, delayed or excessive
      ectopic pregnancy (*see also* categories 633.0–633.9) 639.1
      molar pregnancy (*see also* categories 630–632) 639.1
    following
      abortion 639.1
      ectopic or molar pregnancy 639.1
  external 459.0
  extradural (traumatic) (*see also* Hemorrhage, brain, traumatic, extradural)
    birth injury 767.0
    fetus or newborn (anoxic) (traumatic) 767.0
    nontraumatic 432.0
  eye 360.43
    chamber (anterior) (aqueous) 364.41
    fundus 362.81
  eyelid 374.81
  fallopian tube 620.8
  fetomaternal 772.0
    affecting management of pregnancy or puerperium 656.0 ☑
  fetus, fetal, ▶affecting newborn◀ 772.0
    from
      cut end of co-twin's cord 772.0
      placenta 772.0
      ruptured cord 772.0
      vasa previa 772.0
    into
      co-twin 772.0
      mother's circulation 772.0
        affecting management of pregnancy or puerperium 656.0 ☑
  fever (*see also* Fever, hemorrhagic) 065.9
    with renal syndrome 078.6
    arthropod-borne NEC 065.9
    Bangkok 065.4
    Crimean 065.0
    dengue virus 065.4
    epidemic 078.6
    Junin virus 078.7
    Korean 078.6
    Machupo virus 078.7
    mite-borne 065.8
    mosquito-borne 065.4
    Philippine 065.4
    Russian (Yaroslav) 078.6
    Singapore 065.4
    southeast Asia 065.4
    Thailand 065.4
    tick-borne NEC 065.3
  fibrinogenolysis (*see also* Fibrinolysis) 286.6
  fibrinolytic (acquired) (*see also* Fibrinolysis) 286.6
  fontanel 767.19
  from tracheostomy stoma 519.09
  fundus, eye 362.81
  funis
    affecting fetus or newborn 772.0
    complicating delivery 663.8 ☑
  gastric (*see also* Hemorrhage, stomach) 578.9
  gastroenteric 578.9
    newborn 772.4
  gastrointestinal (tract) 578.9
    newborn 772.4
  genitourinary (tract) NEC 599.89
  gingiva 523.8
  globe 360.43
  gravidarum — *see* Hemorrhage, pregnancy
  gum 523.8
  heart 429.89
  hypopharyngeal (throat) 784.8
  intermenstrual 626.6
    irregular 626.6

Hemorrhage, hemorrhagic — *continued*
  intermenstrual — *continued*
    regular 626.5
  internal (organs) 459.0
    capsule (*see also* Hemorrhage, brain) 431
    ear 386.8
    newborn 772.8
  intestine 578.9
    congenital 772.4
    newborn 772.4
  into
    bladder wall 596.7
    bursa 727.89
    corpus luysii (*see also* Hemorrhage, brain) 431
  intra-abdominal 459.0
    during or following surgery 998.11
  intra-alveolar, newborn (lung) 770.3
  intracerebral (*see also* Hemorrhage, brain) 431
  intracranial NEC 432.9
    puerperal, postpartum, childbirth 674.0 ☑
    traumatic — *see* Hemorrhage, brain, traumatic
  intramedullary NEC 336.1
  intraocular 360.43
  intraoperative 998.11
  intrapartum — *see* Hemorrhage, complicating, delivery
  intrapelvic
    female 629.89
    male 459.0
  intraperitoneal 459.0
  intrapontine (*see also* Hemorrhage, brain) 431
  intrauterine 621.4
    complicating delivery — *see* Hemorrhage, complicating, delivery
    in pregnancy or childbirth — *see* Hemorrhage, pregnancy
    postpartum (*see also* Hemorrhage, postpartum) 666.1 ☑
  intraventricular (*see also* Hemorrhage, brain) 431
    fetus or newborn (anoxic) (traumatic) 772.10
      grade I 772.11
      grade II 772.12
      grade III 772.13
      grade IV 772.14
  intravesical 596.7
  iris (postinfectional) (postinflammatory) (toxic) 364.41
  joint (nontraumatic) 719.10
    ankle 719.17
    elbow 719.12
    foot 719.17
    forearm 719.13
    hand 719.14
    hip 719.15
    knee 719.16
    lower leg 719.16
    multiple sites 719.19
    pelvic region 719.15
    shoulder (region) 719.11
    specified site NEC 719.18
    thigh 719.15
    upper arm 719.12
    wrist 719.13
  kidney 593.81
  knee (joint) 719.16
  labyrinth 386.8
  leg NEC 459.0
  lenticular striate artery (*see also* Hemorrhage, brain) 431
  ligature, vessel 998.11
  liver 573.8
  lower extremity NEC 459.0
  lung 786.3
    newborn 770.3
    tuberculous (*see also* Tuberculosis, pulmonary) 011.9 ☑
  malaria 084.8
  marginal sinus 641.2 ☑
  massive subaponeurotic, birth injury 767.11
  maternal, affecting fetus or newborn 762.1
  mediastinum 786.3
  medulla (*see also* Hemorrhage, brain) 431

☑ Additional Digit Required — Refer to the Tabular List for Digit Selection

▽ Subterms under main terms may continue to next column or page

Hemorrhage, hemorrhagic — *continued*
membrane (brain) (*see also* Hemorrhage, sub-arachnoid) 430
spinal cord — *see* Hemorrhage, spinal cord
meninges, meningeal (brain) (middle) (*see also* Hemorrhage, subarachnoid) 430
spinal cord — *see* Hemorrhage, spinal cord
mesentery 568.81
metritis 626.8
midbrain (*see also* Hemorrhage, brain) 431
mole 631
mouth 528.9
mucous membrane NEC 459.0
newborn 772.8
muscle 728.89
nail (subungual) 703.8
nasal turbinate 784.7
newborn 772.8
nasopharynx 478.29
navel, newborn 772.3
newborn 772.9
adrenal 772.5
alveolar (lung) 770.3
brain (anoxic) (hypoxic) (due to birth trauma) 767.0
cerebral (anoxic) (hypoxic) (due to birth trauma) 767.0
conjunctiva 772.8
cutaneous 772.6
diathesis 776.0
due to vitamin K deficiency 776.0
epicranial subaponeurotic (massive) 767.11
gastrointestinal 772.4
internal (organs) 772.8
intestines 772.4
intra-alveolar (lung) 770.3
intracranial (from any perinatal cause) 767.0
intraventricular (from any perinatal cause) 772.10
grade I 772.11
grade II 772.12
grade III 772.13
grade IV 772.14
lung 770.3
pulmonary (massive) 770.3
spinal cord, traumatic 767.4
stomach 772.4
subaponeurotic (massive) 767.11
subarachnoid (from any perinatal cause) 772.2
subconjunctival 772.8
subgaleal 767.11
umbilicus 772.0
slipped ligature 772.3
vasa previa 772.0
nipple 611.79
nose 784.7
newborn 772.8
obstetrical surgical wound 674.3 ☑
omentum 568.89
newborn 772.4
optic nerve (sheath) 377.42
orbit 376.32
ovary 620.1
oviduct 620.8
pancreas 577.8
parathyroid (gland) (spontaneous) 252.8
parturition — *see* Hemorrhage, complicating, delivery
penis 607.82
pericardium, pericarditis 423.0
perineal wound (obstetrical) 674.3 ☑
peritoneum, peritoneal 459.0
peritonsillar tissue 474.8
after operation on tonsils 998.11
due to infection 475
petechial 782.7
pituitary (gland) 253.8
placenta NEC 641.9 ☑
affecting fetus or newborn 762.1
from surgical or instrumental damage 641.8 ☑
affecting fetus or newborn 762.1
previa 641.1 ☑
affecting fetus or newborn 762.0

Hemorrhage, hemorrhagic — *continued*
pleura — *see* Hemorrhage, lung
polioencephalitis, superior 265.1
polymyositis — *see* Polymyositis
pons (*see also* Hemorrhage, brain) 431
pontine (*see also* Hemorrhage, brain) 431
popliteal 459.0
postcoital 626.7
postextraction (dental) 998.11
postmenopausal 627.1
postnasal 784.7
postoperative 998.11
postpartum (atonic) (following delivery of placenta) 666.1 ☑
delayed or secondary (after 24 hours) 666.2 ☑
retained placenta 666.0 ☑
third stage 666.0 ☑
pregnancy (concealed) 641.9 ☑
accidental 641.2 ☑
affecting fetus or newborn 762.1
affecting fetus or newborn 762.1
before 22 completed weeks gestation 640.9 ☑
affecting fetus or newborn 762.1
due to
abruptio placenta 641.2 ☑
affecting fetus or newborn 762.1
afibrinogenemia or other coagulation defect (conditions classifiable to 286.0–286.9) 641.3 ☑
affecting fetus or newborn 762.1
coagulation defect 641.3 ☑
affecting fetus or newborn 762.1
hyperfibrinolysis 641.3 ☑
affecting fetus or newborn 762.1
hypofibrinogenemia 641.3 ☑
affecting fetus or newborn 762.1
leiomyoma, uterus 641.8 ☑
affecting fetus or newborn 762.1
low-lying placenta 641.1 ☑
affecting fetus or newborn 762.1
marginal sinus (rupture) 641.2 ☑
affecting fetus or newborn 762.1
placenta previa 641.1 ☑
affecting fetus or newborn 762.0
premature separation of placenta (normally implanted) 641.2 ☑
affecting fetus or newborn 762.1
threatened abortion 640.0 ☑
affecting fetus or newborn 762.1
trauma 641.8 ☑
affecting fetus or newborn 762.1
early (before 22 completed weeks gestation) 640.9 ☑
affecting fetus or newborn 762.1
previous, affecting management of pregnancy or childbirth V23.49
unavoidable — *see* Hemorrhage, pregnancy, due to placenta previa
prepartum (mother) — *see* Hemorrhage, pregnancy
preretinal, cause unspecified 362.81
prostate 602.1
puerperal (*see also* Hemorrhage, postpartum) 666.1 ☑
pulmonary (*see also* Hemorrhage, lung)
newborn (massive) 770.3
renal syndrome 446.21
purpura (primary) (*see also* Purpura, thrombocytopenic) 287.39
rectum (sphincter) 569.3
recurring, following initial hemorrhage at time of injury 958.2
renal 593.81
pulmonary syndrome 446.21
respiratory tract (*see also* Hemorrhage, lung) 786.3
retina, retinal (deep) (superficial) (vessels) 362.81
diabetic 250.5 ☑ [362.01]
due to secondary diabetes 249.5 ☑ [362.01]
due to birth injury 772.8
retrobulbar 376.89

Hemorrhage, hemorrhagic — *continued*
retroperitoneal 459.0
retroplacental (*see also* Placenta, separation) 641.2 ☑
scalp 459.0
due to injury at birth 767.19
scrotum 608.83
secondary (nontraumatic) 459.0
following initial hemorrhage at time of injury 958.2
seminal vesicle 608.83
skin 782.7
newborn 772.6
spermatic cord 608.83
spinal (cord) 336.1
aneurysm (ruptured) 336.1
syphilitic 094.89
due to birth injury 767.4
fetus or newborn 767.4
spleen 289.59
spontaneous NEC 459.0
petechial 782.7
stomach 578.9
newborn 772.4
ulcer — *see* Ulcer, stomach, with hemorrhage
subaponeurotic, newborn 767.11
massive (birth injury) 767.11
subarachnoid (nontraumatic) 430
fetus or newborn (anoxic) (traumatic) 772.2
puerperal, postpartum, childbirth 674.0 ☑
traumatic — *see* Hemorrhage, brain, traumatic, subarachnoid
subconjunctival 372.72
due to birth injury 772.8
newborn 772.8
subcortical (*see also* Hemorrhage, brain) 431
subcutaneous 782.7
subdiaphragmatic 459.0
subdural (nontraumatic) 432.1
due to birth injury 767.0
fetus or newborn (anoxic) (hypoxic) (due to birth trauma) 767.0
puerperal, postpartum, childbirth 674.0 ☑
spinal 336.1
traumatic — *see* Hemorrhage, brain, traumatic, subdural
subgaleal 767.11
subhyaloid 362.81
subperiosteal 733.99
subretinal 362.81
subtentorial (*see also* Hemorrhage, subdural) 432.1
subungual 703.8
due to blood dyscrasia 287.8
suprarenal (capsule) (gland) 255.41
fetus or newborn 772.5
tentorium (traumatic) (*see also* Hemorrhage, brain, traumatic)
fetus or newborn 767.0
nontraumatic — *see* Hemorrhage, subdural
testis 608.83
thigh 459.0
third stage 666.0 ☑
thorax — *see* Hemorrhage, lung
throat 784.8
thrombocythemia 238.71
thymus (gland) 254.8
thyroid (gland) 246.3
cyst 246.3
tongue 529.8
tonsil 474.8
postoperative 998.11
tooth socket (postextraction) 998.11
trachea — *see* Hemorrhage, lung
traumatic (*see also* nature of injury)
brain — *see* Hemorrhage, brain, traumatic
recurring or secondary (following initial hemorrhage at time of injury) 958.2
tuberculous NEC (*see also* Tuberculosis, pulmonary) 011.9 ☑
tunica vaginalis 608.83
ulcer — *see* Ulcer, by site, with hemorrhage
umbilicus, umbilical cord 772.0
after birth, newborn 772.3

Hemorrhage, hemorrhagic — *continued*
umbilicus, umbilical cord — *continued*
complicating delivery 663.8 ☑
affecting fetus or newborn 772.0
slipped ligature 772.3
stump 772.3
unavoidable (due to placenta previa) 641.1 ☑
affecting fetus or newborn 762.0
upper extremity 459.0
urethra (idiopathic) 599.84
uterus, uterine (abnormal) 626.9
climacteric 627.0
complicating delivery — *see* Hemorrhage, complicating, delivery
due to
intrauterine contraceptive device 996.76
perforating uterus 996.32
functional or dysfunctional 626.8
in pregnancy — *see* Hemorrhage, pregnancy
intermenstrual 626.6
irregular 626.6
regular 626.5
postmenopausal 627.1
postpartum (*see also* Hemorrhage, postpartum) 666.1 ☑
prepubertal 626.8
pubertal 626.3
puerperal (immediate) 666.1 ☑
vagina 623.8
vasa previa 663.5 ☑
affecting fetus or newborn 772.0
vas deferens 608.83
ventricular (*see also* Hemorrhage, brain) 431
vesical 596.8
viscera 459.0
newborn 772.8
vitreous (humor) (intraocular) 379.23
vocal cord 478.5
vulva 624.8
Hemorrhoids (anus) (rectum) (without complication) 455.6
bleeding, prolapsed, strangulated, or ulcerated NEC 455.8
external 455.5
internal 455.2
complicated NEC 455.8
complicating pregnancy and puerperium 671.8 ☑
external 455.3
with complication NEC 455.5
bleeding, prolapsed, strangulated, or ulcerated 455.5
thrombosed 455.4
internal 455.0
with complication NEC 455.2
bleeding, prolapsed, strangulated, or ulcerated 455.2
thrombosed 455.1
residual skin tag 455.9
sentinel pile 455.9
thrombosed NEC 455.7
external 455.4
internal 455.1
Hemosalpinx 620.8
Hemosiderosis 275.0
dietary 275.0
pulmonary (idiopathic) 275.0 [516.1]
transfusion NEC 999.89
bone marrow 996.85
Hemospermia 608.82
Hemothorax 511.89
bacterial, nontuberculous 511.1
newborn 772.8
nontuberculous 511.89
bacterial 511.1
pneumococcal 511.1
postoperative 998.11
staphylococcal 511.1
streptococcal 511.1
traumatic 860.2
with
open wound into thorax 860.3
pneumothorax 860.4
with open wound into thorax 860.5

☑ Additional Digit Required — Refer to the Tabular List for Digit Selection

☷ Subterms under main terms may continue to next column or page

Hemothorax — *continued*
 tuberculous (*see also* Tuberculosis, pleura) 012.0 ☑
Hemotympanum 385.89
Hench-Rosenberg syndrome (palindromic arthritis) — *see also* Rheumatism, palindromic 719.3 ☑
Henle's warts 371.41
Henoch (-Schönlein)
 disease or syndrome (allergic purpura) 287.0
 purpura (allergic) 287.0
Henpue, henpuye 102.6
Heparin-induced thrombocytopenia (HIT) 289.84
Heparitinuria 277.5
Hepar lobatum 095.3
Hepatalgia 573.8
Hepatic — *see also* condition
 flexure syndrome 569.89
Hepatitis 573.3
 acute (*see also* Necrosis, liver) 570
  alcoholic 571.1
  infective 070.1
   with hepatic coma 070.0
 alcoholic 571.1
 amebic — *see* Abscess, liver, amebic
 anicteric (acute) — *see* Hepatitis, viral
 antigen-associated (HAA) — *see* Hepatitis, viral, type B
 Australian antigen (positive) — *see* Hepatitis, viral, type B
 autoimmune 571.42
 catarrhal (acute) 070.1
  with hepatic coma 070.0
  chronic 571.40
  newborn 070.1
   with hepatic coma 070.0
 chemical 573.3
 cholangiolitic 573.8
 cholestatic 573.8
 chronic 571.40
  active 571.49
   viral — *see* Hepatitis, viral
  aggressive 571.49
  persistent 571.49
  viral — *see* Hepatitis, viral
 cytomegalic inclusion virus 078.5 *[573.1]*
 diffuse 573.3
 "dirty needle" — *see* Hepatitis, viral
 drug-induced 573.3
 due to
  Coxsackie 074.8 *[573.1]*
  cytomegalic inclusion virus 078.5 *[573.1]*
  infectious mononucleosis 075 *[573.1]*
  malaria 084.9 *[573.2]*
  mumps 072.71
  secondary syphilis 091.62
  toxoplasmosis (acquired) 130.5
   congenital (active) 771.2
 epidemic — *see* Hepatitis, viral, type A
 fetus or newborn 774.4
 fibrous (chronic) 571.49
  acute 570
 from injection, inoculation, or transfusion (blood) (other substance) (plasma) (serum) (onset within 8 months after administration) — *see* Hepatitis, viral
 fulminant (viral) (*see also* Hepatitis, viral) 070.9
  with hepatic coma 070.6
  type A 070.1
   with hepatic coma 070.0
  type B — *see* Hepatitis, viral, type B
 giant cell (neonatal) 774.4
 hemorrhagic 573.8
 history of
  B V12.09
  C V12.09
 homologous serum — *see* Hepatitis, viral
 hypertrophic (chronic) 571.49
  acute 570
 infectious, infective (acute) (chronic) (subacute) 070.1
  with hepatic coma 070.0
 inoculation — *see* Hepatitis, viral
 interstitial (chronic) 571.49
  acute 570

Hepatitis — *continued*
 lupoid 571.49
 malarial 084.9 *[573.2]*
 malignant (*see also* Necrosis, liver) 570
 neonatal (toxic) 774.4
 newborn 774.4
 parenchymatous (acute) (*see also* Necrosis, liver) 570
 peliosis 573.3
 persistent, chronic 571.41
 plasma cell 571.49
 postimmunization — *see* Hepatitis, viral
 postnecrotic 571.49
 posttransfusion — *see* Hepatitis, viral
 recurrent 571.49
 septic 573.3
 serum — *see* Hepatitis, viral
  carrier (suspected of) V02.61
 subacute (*see also* Necrosis, liver) 570
 suppurative (diffuse) 572.0
 syphilitic (late) 095.3
  congenital (early) 090.0 *[573.2]*
   late 090.5 *[573.2]*
  secondary 091.62
 toxic (noninfectious) 573.3
  fetus or newborn 774.4
 tuberculous (*see also* Tuberculosis) 017.9 ☑
 viral (acute) (anicteric) (cholangiolitic) (cholestatic) (chronic) (subacute) 070.9
  with hepatic coma 070.6
  AU-SH type virus — *see* Hepatitis, viral, type B
  Australian antigen — *see* Hepatitis, viral, type B
  B-antigen — *see* Hepatitis, viral, type B
  Coxsackie 074.8 *[573.1]*
  cytomegalic inclusion 078.5 *[573.1]*
  IH (virus) — *see* Hepatitis, viral, type A
  infectious hepatitis virus — *see* Hepatitis, viral, type A
  serum hepatitis virus — *see* Hepatitis, viral, type B
  SH — *see* Hepatitis, viral, type B
  specified type NEC 070.59
   with hepatic coma 070.49
  type A 070.1
   with hepatic coma 070.0
  type B (acute) 070.30
   with
    hepatic coma 070.20
     with hepatitis delta 070.21
    hepatitis delta 070.31
     with hepatic coma 070.21
   carrier status V02.61
   chronic 070.32
    with
     hepatic coma 070.22
      with hepatitis delta 070.23
     hepatitis delta 070.33
      with hepatic coma 070.23
  type C
   acute 070.51
    with hepatic coma 070.41
   carrier status V02.62
   chronic 070.54
    with hepatic coma 070.44
   in remission 070.54
   unspecified 070.70
    with hepatic coma 070.71
  type delta (with hepatitis B carrier state) 070.52
   with
    active hepatitis B disease — *see* Hepatitis, viral, type B
    hepatic coma 070.42
  type E 070.53
   with hepatic coma 070.43
  vaccination and inoculation (prophylactic) V05.3
  Waldenström's (lupoid hepatitis) 571.49
Hepatization, lung (acute) — *see also* Pneumonia, lobar
 chronic (*see also* Fibrosis, lung) 515
Hepatoblastoma (M8970/3) 155.0
Hepatocarcinoma (M8170/3) 155.0
Hepatocholangiocarcinoma (M8180/3) 155.0

Hepatocholangioma, benign (M8180/0) 211.5
Hepatocholangitis 573.8
Hepatocystitis — *see also* Cholecystitis 575.10
Hepatodystrophy 570
Hepatolenticular degeneration 275.1
Hepatolithiasis — *see* Choledocholithiasis
Hepatoma (malignant) (M8170/3) 155.0
 benign (M8170/0) 211.5
 congenital (M8970/3) 155.0
 embryonal (M8970/3) 155.0
Hepatomegalia glycogenica diffusa 271.0
Hepatomegaly — *see also* Hypertrophy, liver 789.1
 congenital 751.69
  syphilitic 090.0
 due to Clonorchis sinensis 121.1
 Gaucher's 272.7
 syphilitic (congenital) 090.0
Hepatoptosis 573.8
Hepatorrhexis 573.8
Hepatosis, toxic 573.8
Hepatosplenomegaly 571.8
 due to S. japonicum 120.2
 hyperlipemic (Bürger-Grutz type) 272.3
Herald patch 696.3
Hereditary — *see* condition
Heredodegeneration 330.9
 macular 362.70
Heredopathia atactica polyneuritiformis 356.3
Heredosyphilis — *see also* Syphilis, congenital 090.9
Hermaphroditism (true) 752.7
 with specified chromosomal anomaly — *see* Anomaly, chromosomes, sex
Hernia, hernial (acquired) (recurrent) 553.9
 with
  gangrene (obstructed) NEC 551.9
  obstruction NEC 552.9
   and gangrene 551.9
 abdomen (wall) — *see* Hernia, ventral
 abdominal, specified site NEC 553.8
  with
   gangrene (obstructed) 551.8
   obstruction 552.8
    and gangrene 551.8
 appendix 553.8
  with
   gangrene (obstructed) 551.8
   obstruction 552.8
    and gangrene 551.8
 bilateral (inguinal) — *see* Hernia, inguinal
 bladder (sphincter)
  congenital (female) (male) 756.71
  female (*see also* Cystocele, female) 618.01
  male 596.8
 brain 348.4
  congenital 742.0
 broad ligament 553.8
 cartilage, vertebral — *see* Displacement, intervertebral disc
 cerebral 348.4
  congenital 742.0
  endaural 742.0
 ciliary body 364.89
  traumatic 871.1
 colic 553.9
  with
   gangrene (obstructed) 551.9
   obstruction 552.9
    and gangrene 551.9
 colon 553.9
  with
   gangrene (obstructed) 551.9
   obstruction 552.9
    and gangrene 551.9
 colostomy (stoma) 569.69
 Cooper's (retroperitoneal) 553.8
  with
   gangrene (obstructed) 551.8
   obstruction 552.8
    and gangrene 551.8
 crural — *see* Hernia, femoral
 diaphragm, diaphragmatic 553.3
  with
   gangrene (obstructed) 551.3
   obstruction 552.3

Hernia, hernial — *continued*
 diaphragm, diaphragmatic — *continued*
  with — *continued*
   obstruction — *continued*
    and gangrene 551.3
   congenital 756.6
   due to gross defect of diaphragm 756.6
   traumatic 862.0
    with open wound into cavity 862.1
 direct (inguinal) — *see* Hernia, inguinal
 disc, intervertebral — *see* Displacement, intervertebral disc
 diverticulum, intestine 553.9
  with
   gangrene (obstructed) 551.9
   obstruction 552.9
    and gangrene 551.9
 double (inguinal) — *see* Hernia, inguinal
 due to adhesion with obstruction 560.81
 duodenojejunal 553.8
  with
   gangrene (obstructed) 551.8
   obstruction 552.8
    and gangrene 551.8
 en glissade — *see* Hernia, inguinal
 enterostomy (stoma) 569.69
 epigastric 553.29
  with
   gangrene (obstruction) 551.29
   obstruction 552.29
    and gangrene 551.29
  recurrent 553.21
   with
    gangrene (obstructed) 551.21
    obstruction 552.21
     and gangrene 551.21
 esophageal hiatus (sliding) 553.3
  with
   gangrene (obstructed) 551.3
   obstruction 552.3
    and gangrene 551.3
  congenital 750.6
 external (inguinal) — *see* Hernia, inguinal
 fallopian tube 620.4
 fascia 728.89
 fat 729.30
  eyelid 374.34
  orbital 374.34
  pad 729.30
   eye, eyelid 374.34
   knee 729.31
   orbit 374.34
   popliteal (space) 729.31
   specified site NEC 729.39
 femoral (unilateral) 553.00
  with
   gangrene (obstructed) 551.00
   obstruction 552.00
    with gangrene 551.00
  bilateral 553.02
   gangrenous (obstructed) 551.02
   obstructed 552.02
    with gangrene 551.02
   recurrent 553.03
    gangrenous (obstructed) 551.03
    obstructed 552.03
     with gangrene 551.03
  recurrent (unilateral) 553.01
   bilateral 553.03
    gangrenous (obstructed) 551.03
    obstructed 552.03
     with gangrene 551.01
   gangrenous (obstructed) 551.01
   obstructed 552.01
    with gangrene 551.01
 foramen
  Bochdalek 553.3
   with
    gangrene (obstructed) 551.3
    obstruction 552.3
     and gangrene 551.3
   congenital 756.6
  magnum 348.4
  Morgagni, Morgagnian 553.3
   with
    gangrene 551.3

☑ Additional Digit Required — Refer to the Tabular List for Digit Selection ▷◁ Revised Text ● New Line ▲ Revised Code ▽ Subterms under main terms may continue to next column or page

2010 ICD-9-CM **Volume 2 — 133**

Hemothorax — Hernia, hernial

Hernia, hernial — *continued*
  foramen — *continued*
    Morgagni, Morgagnian — *continued*
      with — *continued*
        obstruction 552.3
        and gangrene 551.3
      congenital 756.6
    funicular (umbilical) 553.1
      with
        gangrene (obstructed) 551.1
        obstruction 552.1
          and gangrene 551.1
      spermatic cord — *see* Hernia, inguinal
    gangrenous — *see* Hernia, by site, with gangrene
    gastrointestinal tract 553.9
      with
        gangrene (obstructed) 551.9
        obstruction 552.9
          and gangrene 551.9
    gluteal — *see* Hernia, femoral
    Gruber's (internal mesogastric) 553.8
      with
        gangrene (obstructed) 551.8
        obstruction 552.8
          and gangrene 551.8
    Hesselbach's 553.8
      with
        gangrene (obstructed) 551.8
        obstruction 552.8
          and gangrene 551.8
    hiatal (esophageal) (sliding) 553.3
      with
        gangrene (obstructed) 551.3
        obstruction 552.3
          and gangrene 551.3
      congenital 750.6
    incarcerated (*see also* Hernia, by site, with obstruction) 552.9
      gangrenous (*see also* Hernia, by site, with gangrene) 551.9
    incisional 553.21
      with
        gangrene (obstructed) 551.21
        obstruction 552.21
          and gangrene 551.21
      lumbar — *see* Hernia, lumbar
      recurrent 553.21
        with
          gangrene (obstructed) 551.21
          obstruction 552.21
            and gangrene 551.21
    indirect (inguinal) — *see* Hernia, inguinal
    infantile — *see* Hernia, inguinal
    infrapatellar fat pad 729.31
    inguinal (direct) (double) (encysted) (external) (funicular) (indirect) (infantile) (internal) (interstitial) (oblique) (scrotal) (sliding) 550.9 ☑

Note — *Use the following fifth-digit subclassification with category 550:*

0	*unilateral or unspecified (not specified as recurrent)*
1	*unilateral or unspecified, recurrent*
2	*bilateral (not specified as recurrent)*
3	*bilateral, recurrent*

      with
        gangrene (obstructed) 550.0 ☑
        obstruction 550.1 ☑
          and gangrene 550.0 ☑
    internal 553.8
      with
        gangrene (obstructed) 551.8
        obstruction 552.8
          and gangrene 551.8
      inguinal — *see* Hernia, inguinal
    interstitial 553.9
      with
        gangrene (obstructed) 551.9
        obstruction 552.9
          and gangrene 551.9
      inguinal — *see* Hernia, inguinal
    intervertebral cartilage or disc — *see* Displacement, intervertebral disc

Hernia, hernial — *continued*
  intestine, intestinal 553.9
    with
      gangrene (obstructed) 551.9
      obstruction 552.9
        and gangrene 551.9
  intra-abdominal 553.9
    with
      gangrene (obstructed) 551.9
      obstruction 552.9
        and gangrene 551.9
  intraparietal 553.9
    with
      gangrene (obstructed) 551.9
      obstruction 552.9
        and gangrene 551.9
  iris 364.89
    traumatic 871.1
  irreducible (*see also* Hernia, by site, with obstruction) 552.9
    gangrenous (with obstruction) (*see also* Hernia, by site, with gangrene) 551.9
  ischiatic 553.8
    with
      gangrene (obstructed) 551.8
      obstruction 552.8
        and gangrene 551.8
  ischiorectal 553.8
    with
      gangrene (obstructed) 551.8
      obstruction 552.8
        and gangrene 551.8
  lens 379.32
    traumatic 871.1
  linea
    alba — *see* Hernia, epigastric
    semilunaris — *see* Hernia, spigelian
  Littre's (diverticular) 553.9
    with
      gangrene (obstructed) 551.9
      obstruction 552.9
        and gangrene 551.9
  lumbar 553.8
    with
      gangrene (obstructed) 551.8
      obstruction 552.8
        and gangrene 551.8
    intervertebral disc 722.10
  lung (subcutaneous) 518.89
    congenital 748.69
  mediastinum 519.3
  mesenteric (internal) 553.8
    with
      gangrene (obstructed) 551.8
      obstruction 552.8
        and gangrene 551.8
  mesocolon 553.8
    with
      gangrene (obstructed) 551.8
      obstruction 552.8
        and gangrene 551.8
  muscle (sheath) 728.89
  nucleus pulposus — *see* Displacement, intervertebral disc
  oblique (inguinal) — *see* Hernia, inguinal
  obstructive (*see also* Hernia, by site, with obstruction) 552.9
    gangrenous (with obstruction) (*see also* Hernia, by site, with gangrene) 551.9
  obturator 553.8
    with
      gangrene (obstructed) 551.8
      obstruction 552.8
        and gangrene 551.8
  omental 553.8
    with
      gangrene (obstructed) 551.8
      obstruction 552.8
        and gangrene 551.8
  orbital fat (pad) 374.34
  ovary 620.4
  oviduct 620.4
  paracolostomy (stoma) 569.69
  paraduodenal 553.8

Hernia, hernial — *continued*
  paraduodenal — *continued*
    with
      gangrene (obstructed) 551.8
      obstruction 552.8
        and gangrene 551.8
  paraesophageal 553.3
    with
      gangrene (obstructed) 551.3
      obstruction 552.3
        and gangrene 551.3
    congenital 750.6
  parahiatal 553.3
    with
      gangrene (obstructed) 551.3
      obstruction 552.3
        and gangrene 551.3
  paraumbilical 553.1
    with
      gangrene (obstructed) 551.1
      obstruction 552.1
        and gangrene 551.1
  parietal 553.9
    with
      gangrene (obstructed) 551.9
      obstruction 552.9
        and gangrene 551.9
  perineal 553.8
    with
      gangrene (obstructed) 551.8
      obstruction 552.8
        and gangrene 551.8
  peritoneal sac, lesser 553.8
    with
      gangrene (obstructed) 551.8
      obstruction 552.8
        and gangrene 551.8
  popliteal fat pad 729.31
  postoperative 553.21
    with
      gangrene (obstructed) 551.21
      obstruction 552.21
        and gangrene 551.21
  pregnant uterus 654.4 ☑
  prevesical 596.8
  properitoneal 553.8
    with
      gangrene (obstructed) 551.8
      obstruction 552.8
        and gangrene 551.8
  pudendal 553.8
    with
      gangrene (obstructed) 551.8
      obstruction 552.8
        and gangrene 551.8
  rectovaginal 618.6
  retroperitoneal 553.8
    with
      gangrene (obstructed) 551.8
      obstruction 552.8
        and gangrene 551.8
  Richter's (parietal) 553.9
    with
      gangrene (obstructed) 551.9
      obstruction 552.9
        and gangrene 551.9
  Rieux's, Riex's (retrocecal) 553.8
    with
      gangrene (obstructed) 551.8
      obstruction 552.8
        and gangrene 551.8
  sciatic 553.8
    with
      gangrene (obstructed) 551.8
      obstruction 552.8
        and gangrene 551.8
  scrotum, scrotal — *see* Hernia, inguinal
  sliding (inguinal) (*see also* Hernia, inguinal)
    hiatus — *see* Hernia, hiatal
  spigelian 553.29
    with
      gangrene (obstructed) 551.29
      obstruction 552.29
        and gangrene 551.29
  spinal (*see also* Spina bifida) 741.9 ☑
    with hydrocephalus 741.0 ☑

Hernia, hernial — *continued*
  strangulated (*see also* Hernia, by site, with obstruction) 552.9
    gangrenous (with obstruction) (*see also* Hernia, by site, with gangrene) 551.9
  supraumbilicus (linea alba) — *see* Hernia, epigastric
  tendon 727.9
  testis (nontraumatic) 550.9 ☑
    meaning
      scrotal hernia 550.9 ☑
      symptomatic late syphilis 095.8
  Treitz's (fossa) 553.8
    with
      gangrene (obstructed) 551.8
      obstruction 552.8
        and gangrene 551.8
  tunica
    albuginea 608.89
    vaginalis 752.89
  umbilicus, umbilical 553.1
    with
      gangrene (obstructed) 551.1
      obstruction 552.1
        and gangrene 551.1
  ureter 593.89
    with obstruction 593.4
  uterus 621.8
    pregnant 654.4 ☑
  vaginal (posterior) 618.6
  Velpeau's (femoral) (*see also* Hernia, femoral) 553.00
  ventral 553.20
    with
      gangrene (obstructed) 551.20
      obstruction 552.20
        and gangrene 551.20
    incisional 553.21
    recurrent 553.21
      with
        gangrene (obstructed) 551.21
        obstruction 552.21
          and gangrene 551.21
  vesical
    congenital (female) (male) 756.71
    female (*see also* Cystocele, female) 618.01
    male 596.8
  vitreous (into anterior chamber) 379.21
    traumatic 871.1
Herniation — *see also* Hernia
  brain (stem) 348.4
  cerebral 348.4
  gastric mucosa (into duodenal bulb) 537.89
  mediastinum 519.3
  nucleus pulposus — *see* Displacement, intervertebral disc
Herpangina 074.0
Herpes, herpetic 054.9
  auricularis (zoster) 053.71
    simplex 054.73
  blepharitis (zoster) 053.20
    simplex 054.41
  circinate 110.5
  circinatus 110.5
    bullous 694.5
  conjunctiva (simplex) 054.43
    zoster 053.21
  cornea (simplex) 054.43
    disciform (simplex) 054.43
    zoster 053.21
  encephalitis 054.3
  eye (zoster) 053.29
    simplex 054.40
  eyelid (zoster) 053.20
    simplex 054.41
  febrilis 054.9
  fever 054.9
  geniculate ganglionitis 053.11
  genital, genitalis 054.10
    specified site NEC 054.19
  gestationis 646.8 ☑
  gingivostomatitis 054.2
  iridocyclitis (simplex) 054.44
    zoster 053.22
  iris (any site) 695.10

☑ Additional Digit Required — Refer to the Tabular List for Digit Selection

◤ Subterms under main terms may continue to next column or page

▶◀ Revised Text   ● New Line   ▲ Revised Code

Herpes, herpetic — *continued*
  iritis (simplex) 054.44
  keratitis (simplex) 054.43
    dendritic 054.42
    disciform 054.43
    interstitial 054.43
      zoster 053.21
  keratoconjunctivitis (simplex) 054.43
    zoster 053.21
  labialis 054.9
    meningococcal 036.89
  lip 054.9
  meningitis (simplex) 054.72
    zoster 053.0
  ophthalmicus (zoster) 053.20
    simplex 054.40
  otitis externa (zoster) 053.71
    simplex 054.73
  penis 054.13
  perianal 054.10
  pharyngitis 054.79
  progenitalis 054.10
  scrotum 054.19
  septicemia 054.5
  simplex 054.9
    complicated 054.8
      ophthalmic 054.40
        specified NEC 054.49
      specified NEC 054.79
    congenital 771.2
    external ear 054.73
    keratitis 054.43
      dendritic 054.42
    meningitis 054.72
    myelitis 054.74
    neuritis 054.79
    specified complication NEC 054.79
      ophthalmic 054.49
    visceral 054.71
  stomatitis 054.2
  tonsurans 110.0
    maculosus (of Hebra) 696.3
  visceral 054.71
  vulva 054.12
  vulvovaginitis 054.11
  whitlow 054.6
  zoster 053.9
    auricularis 053.71
    complicated 053.8
      specified NEC 053.79
    conjunctiva 053.21
    cornea 053.21
    ear 053.71
    eye 053.29
    geniculate 053.11
    keratitis 053.21
      interstitial 053.21
    myelitis 053.14
    neuritis 053.10
    ophthalmicus(a) 053.20
    oticus 053.71
    otitis externa 053.71
    specified complication NEC 053.79
    specified site NEC 053.9
  zosteriform, intermediate type 053.9

Herrick's
  anemia (hemoglobin S disease) 282.61
  syndrome (hemoglobin S disease) 282.61
Hers' disease (glycogenosis VI) 271.0
Herter (-Gee) disease or syndrome (nontropical sprue) 579.0
Herter's infantilism (nontropical sprue) 579.0
Herxheimer's disease (diffuse idiopathic cutaneous atrophy) 701.8
Herxheimer's reaction 995.0
Hesitancy, urinary 788.64
Hesselbach's hernia — *see* Hernia, Hesselbach's
Heterochromia (congenital) 743.46
  acquired 364.53
  cataract 366.33
  cyclitis 364.21
  hair 704.3
  iritis 364.21
  retained metallic foreign body 360.62
    magnetic 360.52
  uveitis 364.21

Heterophoria 378.40
  alternating 378.45
  vertical 378.43
Heterophyes, small intestine 121.6
Heterophyiasis 121.6
Heteropsia 368.8
Heterotopia, heterotopic — *see also* Malposition, congenital
  cerebralis 742.4
  pancreas, pancreatic 751.7
  spinalis 742.59
Heterotropia 378.30
  intermittent 378.20
    vertical 378.31
  vertical (constant) (intermittent) 378.31
Heubner's disease 094.89
Heubner-Herter disease or syndrome (nontropical sprue) 579.0
Hexadactylism 755.0
Heyd's syndrome (hepatorenal) 572.4
HGSIL (high grade squamous intraepithelial lesion) (cytologic finding) (Pap smear finding)
  anus 796.74
  cervix 795.04
    biopsy finding — code to CIN II or CIN III
  vagina 795.14
Hibernoma (M8880/0) — *see* Lipoma
Hiccough 786.8
  epidemic 078.89
  psychogenic 306.1
Hiccup — *see also* Hiccough 786.8
Hicks (-Braxton) contractures 644.1
Hidden penis 752.65
Hidradenitis (axillaris) (suppurative) 705.83
Hidradenoma (nodular) (M8400/0) — *see also* Neoplasm, skin, benign
  clear cell (M8402/0) — *see* Neoplasm, skin, benign
  papillary (M8405/0) — *see* Neoplasm, skin, benign
Hidrocystoma (M8404/0) — *see* Neoplasm, skin, benign
HIE (hypoxic-ischemic encephalopathy) 768.70 ▲
  mild 768.71 ●
  moderate 768.72 ●
  severe 768.73 ●
High
  A₂ anemia 282.49
  altitude effects 993.2
    anoxia 993.2
    on
      ears 993.0
      sinuses 993.1
    polycythemia 289.0
  arch
    foot 755.67
    palate 750.26
  artery (arterial) tension (*see also* Hypertension) 401.9
    without diagnosis of hypertension 796.2
  basal metabolic rate (BMR) 794.7
  blood pressure (*see also* Hypertension) 401.9
    incidental reading (isolated) (nonspecific), no diagnosis of hypertension 796.2
  cholesterol 272.0
    with high triglycerides 272.2
  compliance bladder 596.4
  diaphragm (congenital) 756.6
  frequency deafness (congenital) (regional) 389.8
  head at term 652.5
    affecting fetus or newborn 763.1
  output failure (cardiac) (*see also* Failure, heart) 428.9
  oxygen-affinity hemoglobin 289.0
  palate 750.26
  risk
    behavior — *see* Problem
    family situation V61.9
      specified circumstance NEC V61.8
    human papillomavirus (HPV) DNA test positive
      anal 796.75
      cervical 795.05

High — *continued*
  risk — *continued*
    human papillomavirus DNA test positive — *continued*
      vaginal 795.15
    individual V62.89
    infant NEC V20.1
    patient taking drugs (prescribed) V67.51
      nonprescribed (*see also* Abuse, drugs, nondependent) 305.9
    pregnancy V23.9
      inadequate prenatal care V23.7
      specified problem NEC V23.89
  temperature (of unknown origin) (*see also* Pyrexia) 780.60
  thoracic rib 756.3
  triglycerides 272.1
    with high cholesterol 272.2
Hildenbrand's disease (typhus) 081.9
Hilger's syndrome 337.09
Hill diarrhea 579.1
Hilliard's lupus — *see also* Tuberculosis 017.0
Hilum — *see* condition
Hip — *see* condition
Hippel's disease (retinocerebral angiomatosis) 759.6
Hippus 379.49
Hirschfeld's disease (acute diabetes mellitus) — *see also* Diabetes 250.0
  due to secondary diabetes 249.0
Hirschsprung's disease or megacolon (congenital) 751.3
Hirsuties — *see also* Hypertrichosis 704.1
Hirsutism — *see also* Hypertrichosis 704.1
Hirudiniasis (external) (internal) 134.2
Hiss-Russell dysentery 004.1
Histamine cephalgia 339.00
Histidinemia 270.5
Histidinuria 270.5
Histiocytic syndromes 288.4
Histiocytoma (M8832/0) — *see also* Neoplasm, skin, benign
  fibrous (M8830/0) (*see also* Neoplasm, skin, benign)
    atypical (M8830/1) — *see* Neoplasm, connective tissue, uncertain behavior
    malignant (M8830/3) — *see* Neoplasm, connective tissue, malignant
Histiocytosis (acute) (chronic) (subacute) 277.89
  acute differentiated progressive (M9722/3) 202.5
  cholesterol 277.89
  essential 277.89
  lipid, lipoid (essential) 272.7
  lipochrome (familial) 288.1
  malignant (M9720/3) 202.3
  non-Langerhans cell 277.89 ●
  polyostotic sclerosing 277.89 ●
  X (chronic) 277.89
    acute (progressive) (M9722/3) 202.5
Histoplasmosis 115.90
  with
    endocarditis 115.94
    meningitis 115.91
    pericarditis 115.93
    pneumonia 115.95
    retinitis 115.92
    specified manifestation NEC 115.99
  African (due to Histoplasma duboisii) 115.10
    with
      endocarditis 115.14
      meningitis 115.11
      pericarditis 115.13
      pneumonia 115.15
      retinitis 115.12
      specified manifestation NEC 115.19
  American (due to Histoplasma capsulatum) 115.00
    with
      endocarditis 115.04
      meningitis 115.01
      pericarditis 115.03
      pneumonia 115.05
      retinitis 115.02
      specified manifestation NEC 115.09
  Darling's — *see* Histoplasmosis, American

Histoplasmosis — *continued*
  large form (*see also* Histoplasmosis, African) 115.10
  lung 115.05
  small form (*see also* Histoplasmosis, American) 115.00
History (personal) of
  abuse
    emotional V15.42
    neglect V15.42
    physical V15.41
    sexual V15.41
  affective psychosis V11.1
  alcoholism V11.3
    specified as drinking problem (*see also* Abuse, drugs, nondependent) 305.0
  allergy to
    analgesic agent NEC V14.6
    anesthetic NEC V14.4
    antibiotic agent NEC V14.1
      penicillin V14.0
    anti-infective agent NEC V14.3
    arachnid bite V15.06 ●
    diathesis V15.09
    drug V14.9
      specified type NEC V14.8
    eggs V15.03
    food additives V15.05
    insect bite V15.06
    latex V15.07
    medicinal agents V14.9
      specified type NEC V14.8
    milk products V15.02
    narcotic agent NEC V14.5
    nuts V15.05
      peanuts V15.01
    penicillin V14.0
    radiographic dye V15.08
    seafood V15.04
    serum V14.7
    specified food NEC V15.05
    specified nonmedicinal agents NEC V15.09
    spider bite V15.06
    sulfa V14.2
    sulfonamides V14.2
    therapeutic agent NEC V15.09
    vaccine V14.7
  anemia V12.3
  arrest, sudden cardiac V12.53
  arthritis V13.4
  attack, transient ischemic (TIA) V12.54
  benign neoplasm of brain V12.41
  blood disease V12.3
  calculi, urinary V13.01
  cardiovascular disease V12.50
    myocardial infarction 412
  chemotherapy, antineoplastic V87.41
  child abuse V15.41
  cigarette smoking V15.82
  circulatory system disease V12.50
    myocardial infarction 412
  congenital malformation V13.69
  contraception V15.7
  death, sudden, successfully resuscitated V12.53
  deficit
    prolonged reversible ischemic neurologic (PRIND) V12.54
    reversible ischemic neurologic (RIND) V12.54
  diathesis, allergic V15.09
  digestive system disease V12.70
    peptic ulcer V12.71
    polyps, colonic V12.72
    specified NEC V12.79
  disease (of) V13.9
    blood V12.3
    blood-forming organs V12.3
    cardiovascular system V12.50
    circulatory system V12.50
      specified NEC V12.59
    digestive system V12.70
      peptic ulcer V12.71
      polyps, colonic V12.72
      specified NEC V12.79
    infectious V12.00

☑ Additional Digit Required — Refer to the Tabular List for Digit Selection   ▽ Subterms under main terms may continue to next column or page

2010 ICD-9-CM   ▶◀ Revised Text   ● New Line   ▲ Revised Code   **October 2009 · Volume 2 — 135**

History of — *continued*
  disease — *continued*
    infectious — *continued*
      malaria V12.03
      methicillin resistant Staphylococcus aureus (MRSA) V12.04
      MRSA (methicillin resistant Staphylococcus aureus) V12.04
      poliomyelitis V12.02
      specified NEC V12.09
      tuberculosis V12.01
    parasitic V12.00
      specified NEC V12.09
    respiratory system V12.60
      pneumonia V12.61
      specified NEC V12.69
    skin V13.3
    specified site NEC V13.8
    subcutaneous tissue V13.3
    trophoblastic V13.1
      affecting management of pregnancy V23.1
  disorder (of) V13.9
    endocrine V12.2
    genital system V13.29
    hematological V12.3
    immunity V12.2
    mental V11.9
      affective type V11.1
      manic-depressive V11.1
      neurosis V11.2
      schizophrenia V11.0
      specified type NEC V11.8
    metabolic V12.2
    musculoskeletal NEC V13.59
    nervous system V12.40
      specified type NEC V12.49
    obstetric V13.29
      affecting management of current pregnancy V23.49
      pre-term labor V23.41
      pre-term labor V13.21
    sense organs V12.40
      specified type NEC V12.49
    specified site NEC V13.8
    urinary system V13.00
      calculi V13.01
      infection V13.02
      nephrotic syndrome V13.03
      specified NEC V13.09
  drug use
    nonprescribed (*see also* Abuse, drugs, nondependent) 305.9 ☑
    patent (*see also* Abuse, drugs, non-dependent) 305.9 ☑
  dysplasia
    cervical (conditions classifiable to 622.10-622.12) V13.22
  effect NEC of external cause V15.89
  embolism (pulmonary) V12.51
  emotional abuse V15.42
  encephalitis V12.42
  endocrine disorder V12.2
  estrogen therapy V87.43 ●
  extracorporeal membrane oxygenation (EC-MO) V15.87
  failed ●
    conscious sedation V15.80 ●
    moderate sedation V15.80 ●
  falling V15.88
  family
    allergy V19.6
    anemia V18.2
    arteriosclerosis V17.49
    arthritis V17.7
    asthma V17.5
    blindness V19.0
    blood disorder NEC V18.3
    cardiovascular disease V17.49
    carrier, genetic disease V18.9
    cerebrovascular disease V17.1
    chronic respiratory condition NEC V17.6
    colonic polyps V18.51
    congenital anomalies V19.5
    consanguinity V19.7
    coronary artery disease V17.3

History of — *continued*
  family — *continued*
    cystic fibrosis V18.19
    deafness V19.2
    diabetes mellitus V18.0
    digestive disorders V18.59
    disease or disorder (of)
      allergic V19.6
      blood NEC V18.3
      cardiovascular NEC V17.49
      cerebrovascular V17.1
      colonic polyps V18.51
      coronary artery V17.3
      death, sudden cardiac (SCD) V17.41
      digestive V18.59
      ear NEC V19.3
      endocrine V18.19
        multiple neoplasia [MEN] syndrome V18.11
      eye NEC V19.1
      genitourinary NEC V18.7
      hypertensive V17.49
      infectious V18.8
      ischemic heart V17.3
      kidney V18.69
        polycystic V18.61
      mental V17.0
      metabolic V18.19
      musculoskeletal NEC V17.89
        osteoporosis V17.81
      neurological NEC V17.2
      parasitic V18.8
      psychiatric condition V17.0
      skin condition V19.4
    ear disorder NEC V19.3
    endocrine disease V18.19
      multiple neoplasia [MEN] syndrome V18.11
    epilepsy V17.2
    eye disorder NEC V19.1
    genetic disease carrier V18.9
    genitourinary disease NEC V18.7
    glomerulonephritis V18.69
    gout V18.19
    hay fever V17.6
    hearing loss V19.2
    hematopoietic neoplasia V16.7
    Hodgkin's disease V16.7
    Huntington's chorea V17.2
    hydrocephalus V19.5
    hypertension V17.49
    infarction, myocardial V17.3
    infectious disease V18.8
    ischemic heart disease V17.3
    kidney disease V18.69
      polycystic V18.61
    leukemia V16.6
    lymphatic malignant neoplasia NEC V16.7
    malignant neoplasm (of) NEC V16.9
      anorectal V16.0
      anus V16.0
      appendix V16.0
      bladder V16.52
      bone V16.8
      brain V16.8
      breast V16.3
        male V16.8
      bronchus V16.1
      cecum V16.0
      cervix V16.49
      colon V16.0
      duodenum V16.0
      esophagus V16.0
      eye V16.8
      gallbladder V16.0
      gastrointestinal tract V16.0
      genital organs V16.40
      hemopoietic NEC V16.7
      ileum V16.0
      ilium V16.8
      intestine V16.0
      intrathoracic organs NEC V16.2
      kidney V16.51
      larynx V16.2
      liver V16.0
      lung V16.1

History of — *continued*
  family — *continued*
    malignant neoplasm — *continued*
      lymphatic NEC V16.7
      ovary V16.41
      oviduct V16.41
      pancreas V16.0
      penis V16.49
      prostate V16.42
      rectum V16.0
      respiratory organs NEC V16.2
      skin V16.8
      specified site NEC V16.8
      stomach V16.0
      testis V16.43
      trachea V16.1
      ureter V16.59
      urethra V16.59
      urinary organs V16.59
      uterus V16.49
      vagina V16.49
      vulva V16.49
    MEN (multiple endocrine neoplasia syndrome) V18.11
    mental retardation V18.4
    metabolic disease NEC V18.19
    mongolism V19.5
    multiple
      endocrine neoplasia [MEN] syndrome V18.11
      myeloma V16.7
    musculoskeletal disease NEC V17.89
      osteoporosis V17.81
    myocardial infarction V17.3
    nephritis V18.69
    nephrosis V18.69
    osteoporosis V17.81
    parasitic disease V18.8
    polycystic kidney disease V18.61
    psychiatric disorder V17.0
    psychosis V17.0
    retardation, mental V18.4
    retinitis pigmentosa V19.1
    schizophrenia V17.0
    skin conditions V19.4
    specified condition NEC V19.8
    stroke (cerebrovascular) V17.1
    sudden cardiac death (SCD) V17.41
    visual loss V19.0
  fracture, healed
    pathologic V13.51
    stress V13.52
    traumatic V15.51
  genital system disorder V13.29
    pre-term labor V13.21
  health hazard V15.9
    falling V15.88
    specified cause NEC V15.89
  hepatitis
    B V12.09
    C V12.09
  Hodgkin's disease V10.72
  hypospadias V13.61
  immunity disorder V12.2
  immunosuppression therapy V87.46 ●
  infarction, cerebral, without residual deficits V12.54
  infection
    central nervous system V12.42
    urinary (tract) V13.02
  infectious disease V12.00
    malaria V12.03
    methicillin resistant Staphylococcus aureus (MRSA) V12.04
    MRSA (methicillin resistant Staphylococcus aureus) V12.04
    poliomyelitis V12.02
    specified NEC V12.09
    tuberculosis V12.01
  injury NEC V15.59
    traumatic brain V15.52 ●
  insufficient prenatal care V23.7
  in utero procedure
    during pregnancy V15.21
    while a fetus V15.22
  irradiation V15.3

History of — *continued*
  leukemia V10.60
    lymphoid V10.61
    monocytic V10.63
    myeloid V10.62
    specified type NEC V10.69
  little or no prenatal care V23.7
  low birth weight (*see also* Status, low birth weight) V21.30
  lymphosarcoma V10.71
  malaria V12.03
  malignant carcinoid tumor V10.91 ●
  malignant neoplasm (of) V10.90 ▲
    accessory sinus V10.22
    adrenal V10.88
    anus V10.06
    bile duct V10.09
    bladder V10.51
    bone V10.81
    brain V10.85
    breast V10.3
    bronchus V10.11
    cervix uteri V10.41
    colon V10.05
    connective tissue NEC V10.89
    corpus uteri V10.42
    digestive system V10.00
      specified part NEC V10.09
    duodenum V10.09
    endocrine gland NEC V10.88
    epididymis V10.48
    esophagus V10.03
    eye V10.84
    fallopian tube V10.44
    female genital organ V10.40
      specified site NEC V10.44
    gallbladder V10.09
    gastrointestinal tract V10.00
    gum V10.02
    hematopoietic NEC V10.79
    hypopharynx V10.02
    ileum V10.09
    intrathoracic organs NEC V10.20
    jejunum V10.09
    kidney V10.52
    large intestine V10.05
    larynx V10.21
    lip V10.02
    liver V10.07
    lung V10.11
    lymphatic NEC V10.79
    lymph glands or nodes NEC V10.79
    male genital organ V10.45
      specified site NEC V10.49
    mediastinum V10.29
    melanoma (of skin) V10.82
    middle ear V10.22
    mouth V10.02
      specified part NEC V10.02
    nasal cavities V10.22
    nasopharynx V10.02
    nervous system NEC V10.86
    nose V10.22
    oropharynx V10.02
    ovary V10.43
    pancreas V10.09
    parathyroid V10.88
    penis V10.49
    pharynx V10.02
    pineal V10.88
    pituitary V10.88
    placenta V10.44
    pleura V10.29
    prostate V10.46
    rectosigmoid junction V10.06
    rectum V10.06
    renal pelvis V10.53
    respiratory organs NEC V10.20
    salivary gland V10.02
    skin V10.83
      melanoma V10.82
    small intestine NEC V10.09
    soft tissue NEC V10.89
    specified site NEC V10.89
    stomach V10.04
    testis V10.47

History of — *continued*
  malignant neoplasm — *continued*
    thymus V10.29
    thyroid V10.87
    tongue V10.01
    trachea V10.12
    ureter V10.59
    urethra V10.59
    urinary organ V10.50
    uterine adnexa V10.44
    uterus V10.42
    vagina V10.44
    vulva V10.44
  malignant neuroendocrine tumor V10.91 ●
  manic-depressive psychosis V11.1
  meningitis V12.42
  mental disorder V11.9
    affective type V11.1
    manic-depressive V11.1
    neurosis V11.2
    schizophrenia V11.0
    specified type NEC V11.8
  Merkel cell carcinoma V10.91 ●
  metabolic disorder V12.2
  methicillin resistant Staphylococcus aureus
    (MRSA) V12.04
  MRSA (methicillin resistant Staphylococcus
    aureus) V12.04
  musculoskeletal disorder NEC V13.59
  myocardial infarction 412
  neglect (emotional) V15.42
  nephrotic syndrome V13.03
  nervous system disorder V12.40
    specified type NEC V12.49
  neurosis V11.2
  noncompliance with medical treatment
    V15.81
  nutritional deficiency V12.1
  obstetric disorder V13.29
    affecting management of current pregnan-
      cy V23.49
      pre-term labor V23.41
    pre-term labor V13.21
  parasitic disease V12.00
    specified NEC V12.09
  perinatal problems V13.7
    low birth weight (*see also* Status, low birth
      weight) V21.30
  physical abuse V15.41
  poisoning V15.6
  poliomyelitis V12.02
  polyps, colonic V12.72
  poor obstetric V13.29
    affecting management of current pregnan-
      cy V23.49
      pre-term labor V23.41
    pre-term labor V13.21
  prolonged reversible ischemic neurologic
    deficit (PRIND) V12.54
  psychiatric disorder V11.9
    affective type V11.1
    manic-depressive V11.1
    neurosis V11.2
    schizophrenia V11.0
    specified type NEC V11.8
  psychological trauma V15.49
    emotional abuse V15.42
    neglect V15.42
    physical abuse V15.41
    rape V15.41
  psychoneurosis V11.2
  radiation therapy V15.3
  rape V15.41
  respiratory system disease V12.60
    pneumonia V12.61
    specified NEC V12.69
  reticulosarcoma V10.71
  return from military deployment V62.22
  reversible ischemic neurologic deficit (RIND)
    V12.54
  schizophrenia V11.0
  skin disease V13.3
  smoking (tobacco) V15.82
  steroid therapy V87.45 ●
    inhaled V87.44 ●
    systemic V87.45 ●

History of — *continued*
  stroke without residual deficits V12.54
  subcutaneous tissue disease V13.3
  sudden
    cardiac
      arrest V12.53
      death (successfully resuscitated) V12.53
  surgery to
    great vessels V15.1
    heart V15.1
    in utero
      during pregnancy V15.21
      while a fetus V15.22
    organs NEC V15.29
  syndrome, nephrotic V13.03
  therapy
    antineoplastic drug V87.41
    drug NEC V87.49
    estrogen V87.43 ●
    immunosuppression V87.46 ●
    monoclonal drug V87.42
    steroid V87.45 ●
      inhaled V87.44 ●
      systemic V87.45 ●
  thrombophlebitis V12.52
  thrombosis V12.51
  tobacco use V15.82
  trophoblastic disease V13.1
    affecting management of pregnancy V23.1
  tuberculosis V12.01
  ulcer, peptic V12.71
  urinary system disorder V13.00
    calculi V13.01
    infection V13.02
    nephrotic syndrome V13.03
    specified NEC V13.09
His-Werner disease (trench fever) 083.1
HIT (heparin-induced thrombocytopenia) 289.84
Hives (bold) — *see also* Urticaria 708.9
HIV infection (disease) (illness) — *see* Human
  immunodeficiency virus (disease) (illness)
  (infection)
Hoarseness 784.42 ▲
Hobnail liver — *see* Cirrhosis, portal
Hobo, hoboism V60.0
Hodgkin's
  disease (M9650/3) 201.9 ☑
    lymphocytic
      depletion (M9653/3) 201.7 ☑
        diffuse fibrosis (M9654/3) 201.7 ☑
        reticular type (M9655/3) 201.7 ☑
      predominance (M9651/3) 201.4 ☑
    lymphocytic-histiocytic predominance
      (M9651/3) 201.4 ☑
    mixed cellularity (M9652/3) 201.6 ☑
    nodular sclerosis (M9656/3) 201.5 ☑
      cellular phase (M9657/3) 201.5 ☑
  granuloma (M9661/3) 201.1 ☑
  lymphogranulomatosis (M9650/3) 201.9 ☑
  lymphoma (M9650/3) 201.9 ☑
  lymphosarcoma (M9650/3) 201.9 ☑
  paragranuloma (M9660/3) 201.0 ☑
  sarcoma (M9662/3) 201.2 ☑
Hodgson's disease (aneurysmal dilatation of
  aorta) 441.9
  ruptured 441.5
Hodi-potsy 111.0
Hoffa (-Kastert) disease or syndrome (liposynovitis prepatellaris) 272.8
Hoffmann-Bouveret syndrome (paroxysmal
  tachycardia) 427.2
Hoffman's syndrome 244.9 *[359.5]*
Hole
  macula 362.54
  optic disc, crater-like 377.22
  retina (macula) 362.54
    round 361.31
      with detachment 361.01
Holla disease — *see also* Spherocytosis 282.0
Holländer-Simons syndrome (progressive
  lipodystrophy) 272.6
Hollow foot (congenital) 754.71
  acquired 736.73
Holmes' syndrome (visual disorientation) 368.16
Holoprosencephaly 742.2

Holoprosencephaly — *continued*
  due to
    trisomy 13 758.1
    trisomy 18 758.2
Holthouse's hernia — *see* Hernia, inguinal
Homesickness 309.89
Homocystinemia 270.4
Homocystinuria 270.4
Homologous serum jaundice (prophylactic)
  (therapeutic) — *see* Hepatitis, viral
Homosexuality — omit code
  ego-dystonic 302.0
  pedophilic 302.2
  problems with 302.0
Homozygous Hb-S disease 282.61
Honeycomb lung 518.89
  congenital 748.4
Hong Kong ear 117.3
HOOD (hereditary osteo-onychodysplasia) 756.89
Hooded
  clitoris 752.49
  penis 752.69
Hookworm (anemia) (disease) (infestation) —
  see Ancylostomiasis
Hoppe-Goldflam syndrome 358.00
Hordeolum (external) (eyelid) 373.11
  internal 373.12
Horn
  cutaneous 702.8
    cheek 702.8
    eyelid 702.8
    penis 702.8
  iliac 756.89
  nail 703.8
    congenital 757.5
  papillary 700
Horner's
  syndrome (*see also* Neuropathy, peripheral,
    autonomic) 337.9
    traumatic 954.0
  teeth 520.4
Horseshoe kidney (congenital) 753.3
Horton's
  disease (temporal arteritis) 446.5
  headache or neuralgia 339.00
Hospice care V66.7
Hospitalism (in children) NEC 309.83
Hourglass contraction, contracture
  bladder 596.8
  gallbladder 575.2
    congenital 751.69
  stomach 536.8
    congenital 750.7
    psychogenic 306.4
  uterus 661.4 ☑
    affecting fetus or newborn 763.7
Household circumstance affecting care V60.9
  specified type NEC V60.89 ▲
Housemaid's knee 727.2
Housing circumstance affecting care V60.9
  specified type NEC V60.89 ▲
HTLV-I infection 079.51
HTLV-II infection 079.52
HTLV-III/LAV (disease) (illness) (infection) — *see*
  Human immunodeficiency virus (disease)
  (illness) (infection)
HTLV-III (disease) (illness) (infection) — *see* Hu-
  man immunodeficiency virus (disease) (ill-
  ness) (infection)
Huchard's disease (continued arterial hyperten-
  sion) 401.9
Hudson-Ståhli lines 371.11
Huguier's disease (uterine fibroma) 218.9
Human bite (open wound) — *see also* Wound,
  open, by site
  intact skin surface — *see* Contusion
Human immunodeficiency virus (disease) (illness) 042
  infection V08
    with symptoms, symptomatic 042
Human immunodeficiency virus-2 infection
  079.53
Human immunovirus (disease) (illness) (infection) — *see* Human immunodeficiency
  virus (disease) (illness) (infection)
Human papillomavirus 079.4

Human papillomavirus — *continued*
  high risk, DNA test positive
    anal 796.75
    cervical 795.05
    vaginal 795.15
  low risk, DNA test positive
    anal 796.79
    cervical 795.09
    vaginal 795.19
Human parvovirus 079.83
Human T-cell lymphotrophic virus-I infection
  079.51
Human T-cell lymphotrophic virus-II infection
  079.52
Human T-cell lymphotrophic virus-III (disease)
  (illness) (infection) — *see* Human immunodeficiency virus (disease) (illness) (infec-
  tion)
Humpback (acquired) 737.9
  congenital 756.19
Hum, venous — omit code
Hunchback (acquired) 737.9
  congenital 756.19
Hunger 994.2
  air, psychogenic 306.1
  disease 251.1
Hungry bone syndrome 275.5
Hunner's ulcer — *see also* Cystitis 595.1
Hunt's
  neuralgia 053.11
  syndrome (herpetic geniculate ganglionitis)
    053.11
    dyssynergia cerebellaris myoclonica 334.2
Hunter's glossitis 529.4
Hunterian chancre 091.0
Hunter (-Hurler) syndrome (mucopolysaccharidosis II) 277.5
Huntington's
  chorea 333.4
  disease 333.4
Huppert's disease (multiple myeloma)
  (M9730/3) 203.0 ☑
Hurler (-Hunter) disease or syndrome (mucopolysaccharidosis II) 277.5
Hürthle cell
  adenocarcinoma (M8290/3) 193
  adenoma (M8290/0) 226
  carcinoma (M8290/3) 193
  tumor (M8290/0) 226
Hutchinson's
  disease meaning
    angioma serpiginosum 709.1
    cheiropompholyx 705.81
    prurigo estivalis 692.72
    summer eruption, or summer prurigo
      692.72
  incisors 090.5
  melanotic freckle (M8742/2) (*see also* Neo-
    plasm, skin, in situ)
    malignant melanoma in (M8742/3) — *see*
      Melanoma
  teeth or incisors (congenital syphilis) 090.5
Hutchinson-Boeck disease or syndrome (sarcoidosis) 135
Hutchinson-Gilford disease or syndrome
  (progeria) 259.8
Hyaline
  degeneration (diffuse) (generalized) 728.9
    localized — *see* Degeneration, by site
  membrane (disease) (lung) (newborn) 769
Hyalinosis cutis et mucosae 272.8
Hyalin plaque, sclera, senile 379.16
Hyalitis (asteroid) 379.22
  syphilitic 095.8
Hydatid
  cyst or tumor (*see also* Echinococcus)
    fallopian tube 752.11
  mole — *see* Hydatidiform mole
  Morgagni (congenital) 752.89
    fallopian tube 752.11
Hydatidiform mole (benign) (complicating
  pregnancy) (delivered) (undelivered) 630
  invasive (M9100/1) 236.1
  malignant (M9100/1) 236.1
  previous, affecting management of pregnancy
    V23.1

☑ Additional Digit Required — Refer to the Tabular List for Digit Selection   Subterms under main terms may continue to next column or page

2010 ICD-9-CM   ▶◀ Revised Text   ● New Line   ▲ Revised Code   **October 2009 · Volume 2 — 137**

Hydatidosis — *see* Echinococcus
Hyde's disease (prurigo nodularis) 698.3
Hydradenitis 705.83
Hydradenoma (M8400/0) — *see* Hidradenoma
Hydralazine lupus or syndrome
  correct substance properly administered 695.4
  overdose or wrong substance given or taken 972.6
Hydramnios 657.0 ☑
  affecting fetus or newborn 761.3
Hydrancephaly 742.3
  with spina bifida (*see also* Spina bifida) 741.0 ☑
Hydranencephaly 742.3
  with spina bifida (*see also* Spina bifida) 741.0 ☑
Hydrargyrism NEC 985.0
Hydrarthrosis — *see also* Effusion, joint 719.0 ☑
  gonococcal 098.50
  intermittent (*see also* Rheumatism, palindromic) 719.3 ☑
  of yaws (early) (late) 102.6
  syphilitic 095.8
    congenital 090.5
Hydremia 285.9
Hydrencephalocele (congenital) 742.0
Hydrencephalomeningocele (congenital) 742.0
Hydroa 694.0
  aestivale 692.72
  gestationis 646.8 ☑
  herpetiformis 694.0
  pruriginosa 694.0
  vacciniforme 692.72
Hydroadenitis 705.83
Hydrocalycosis — *see also* Hydronephrosis 591
  congenital 753.29
Hydrocalyx — *see also* Hydronephrosis 591
Hydrocele (calcified) (chylous) (idiopathic) (infantile) (inguinal canal) (recurrent) (senile) (spermatic cord) (testis) (tunica vaginalis) 603.9
  canal of Nuck (female) 629.1
    male 603.9
  congenital 778.6
  encysted 603.0
    congenital 778.6
  female NEC 629.89
  infected 603.1
  round ligament 629.89
  specified type NEC 603.8
    congenital 778.6
  spinalis (*see also* Spina bifida) 741.9 ☑
  vulva 624.8
Hydrocephalic fetus
  affecting management or pregnancy 655.0 ☑
  causing disproportion 653.6 ☑
    with obstructed labor 660.1 ☑
      affecting fetus or newborn 763.1
Hydrocephalus (acquired) (external) (internal) (malignant) (noncommunicating) (obstructive) (recurrent) 331.4
  aqueduct of Sylvius stricture 742.3
    with spina bifida (*see also* Spina bifida) 741.0 ☑
  chronic 742.3
    with spina bifida (*see also* Spina bifida) 741.0 ☑
  communicating 331.3
  congenital (external) (internal) 742.3
    with spina bifida (*see also* Spina bifida) 741.0 ☑
  due to
    stricture of aqueduct of Sylvius 742.3
      with spina bifida (*see also* Spina bifida) 741.0 ☑
    toxoplasmosis (congenital) 771.2
  fetal affecting management of pregnancy 655.0 ☑
  foramen Magendie block (acquired) 331.3
    congenital 742.3
      with spina bifida (*see also* Spina bifida) 741.0 ☑
  newborn 742.3
    with spina bifida (*see also* Spina bifida) 741.0 ☑
  normal pressure 331.5

Hydrocephalus — *continued*
  normal pressure — *continued*
    idiopathic (INPH) 331.5
    secondary 331.3
  otitic 348.2
  syphilitic, congenital 090.49
  tuberculous (*see also* Tuberculosis) 013.8 ☑
Hydrocolpos (congenital) 623.8
Hydrocystoma (M8404/0) — *see* Neoplasm, skin, benign
Hydroencephalocele (congenital) 742.0
Hydroencephalomeningocele (congenital) 742.0
Hydrohematopneumothorax — *see also* Hemothorax 511.89
Hydromeningitis — *see* Meningitis
Hydromeningocele (spinal) — *see also* Spina bifida 741.9 ☑
  cranial 742.0
Hydrometra 621.8
Hydrometrocolpos 623.8
Hydromicrocephaly 742.1
Hydromphalus (congenital) (since birth) 757.39
Hydromyelia 742.53
Hydromyelocele — *see also* Spina bifida 741.9 ☑
Hydronephrosis 591
  atrophic 591
  congenital 753.29
  due to S. hematobium 120.0
  early 591
  functionless (infected) 591
  infected 591
  intermittent 591
  primary 591
  secondary 591
  tuberculous (*see also* Tuberculosis) 016.0 ☑
Hydropericarditis — *see also* Pericarditis 423.9
Hydropericardium — *see also* Pericarditis 423.9
Hydroperitoneum 789.59
Hydrophobia 071
Hydrophthalmos — *see also* Buphthalmia 743.20
Hydropneumohemothorax — *see also* Hemothorax 511.89
Hydropneumopericarditis — *see also* Pericarditis 423.9
Hydropneumopericardium — *see also* Pericarditis 423.9
Hydropneumothorax 511.89
  nontuberculous 511.89
    bacterial 511.1
    pneumococcal 511.1
    staphylococcal 511.1
    streptococcal 511.1
  traumatic 860.0
    with open wound into thorax 860.1
  tuberculous (*see also* Tuberculosis, pleura) 012.0 ☑
Hydrops 782.3
  abdominis 789.59
  amnii (complicating pregnancy) (*see also* Hydramnios) 657.0 ☑
  articulorum intermittens (*see also* Rheumatism, palindromic) 719.3 ☑
  cardiac (*see also* Failure, heart) 428.0
  congenital — *see* Hydrops, fetalis
  endolymphatic (*see also* Disease, Ménière's) 386.00
  fetal(is) or newborn 778.0
    due to isoimmunization 773.3
    not due to isoimmunization 778.0
  gallbladder 575.3
  idiopathic (fetus or newborn) 778.0
  joint (see also Effusion, joint) 719.0 ☑
  labyrinth (*see also* Disease, Ménière's) 386.00
  meningeal NEC 331.4
  nutritional 262
  pericardium — *see* Pericarditis
  pleura (*see also* Hydrothorax) 511.89
  renal (*see also* Nephrosis) 581.9
  spermatic cord (*see also* Hydrocele) 603.9
Hydropyonephrosis — *see also* Pyelitis 590.80
  chronic 590.00
Hydrorachis 742.53
Hydrorrhea (nasal) 478.19
  gravidarum 658.1 ☑

Hydrorrhea — *continued*
  pregnancy 658.1 ☑
Hydrosadenitis 705.83
Hydrosalpinx (fallopian tube) (follicularis) 614.1
Hydrothorax (double) (pleural) 511.89
  chylous (nonfilarial) 457.8
    filaria (*see also* Infestation, filarial) 125.9
  nontuberculous 511.89
    bacterial 511.1
    pneumococcal 511.1
    staphylococcal 511.1
    streptococcal 511.1
  traumatic 862.29
    with open wound into thorax 862.39
  tuberculous (*see also* Tuberculosis, pleura) 012.0 ☑
Hydroureter 593.5
  congenital 753.22
Hydroureteronephrosis — *see also* Hydronephrosis 591
Hydrourethra 599.84
Hydroxykynureninuria 270.2
Hydroxyprolinemia 270.8
Hydroxyprolinuria 270.8
Hygroma (congenital) (cystic) (M9173/0) 228.1
  prepatellar 727.3
  subdural — *see* Hematoma, subdural
Hymen — *see* condition
Hymenolepiasis (diminuta) (infection) (infestation) (nana) 123.6
Hymenolepis (diminuta) (infection) (infestation) (nana) 123.6
Hypalgesia — *see also* Disturbance, sensation 782.0
Hyperabduction syndrome 447.8
Hyperacidity, gastric 536.8
  psychogenic 306.4
Hyperactive, hyperactivity 314.01
  basal cell, uterine cervix 622.10
  bladder 596.51
  bowel (syndrome) 564.9
    sounds 787.5
  cervix epithelial (basal) 622.10
  child 314.01
  colon 564.9
  gastrointestinal 536.8
    psychogenic 306.4
  intestine 564.9
  labyrinth (unilateral) 386.51
    with loss of labyrinthine reactivity 386.58
    bilateral 386.52
  nasal mucous membrane 478.19
  stomach 536.8
  thyroid (gland) (*see also* Thyrotoxicosis) 242.9 ☑
Hyperacusis 388.42
Hyperadrenalism (cortical) 255.3
  medullary 255.6
Hyperadrenocorticism 255.3
  congenital 255.2
  iatrogenic
    correct substance properly administered 255.3
    overdose or wrong substance given or taken 962.0
Hyperaffectivity 301.11
Hyperaldosteronism (atypical) (hyperplastic) (normoaldosteronal) (normotensive) (primary) 255.10
  secondary 255.14
Hyperalgesia — *see also* Disturbance, sensation 782.0
Hyperalimentation 783.6
  carotene 278.3
  specified NEC 278.8
  vitamin A 278.2
  vitamin D 278.4
Hyperaminoaciduria 270.9
  arginine 270.6
  citrulline 270.6
  cystine 270.0
  glycine 270.0
  lysine 270.7
  ornithine 270.6
  renal (types I, II, III) 270.0
Hyperammonemia (congenital) 270.6

Hyperamnesia 780.99
Hyperamylasemia 790.5
Hyperaphia 782.0
Hyperazotemia 791.9
Hyperbetalipoproteinemia (acquired) (essential) (familial) (hereditary) (primary) (secondary) 272.0
  with prebetalipoproteinemia 272.2
Hyperbilirubinemia 782.4
  congenital 277.4
  constitutional 277.4
  neonatal (transient) (*see also* Jaundice, fetus or newborn) 774.6
  of prematurity 774.2
Hyperbilirubinemica encephalopathia, new-born 774.7
  due to isoimmunization 773.4
Hypercalcemia, hypercalcemic (idiopathic) 275.42
  nephropathy 588.89
Hypercalcinuria 275.40
Hypercapnia 786.09
  with mixed acid-based disorder 276.4
  fetal, affecting newborn 770.89
Hypercarotinemia 278.3
Hypercementosis 521.5
Hyperchloremia 276.9
Hyperchlorhydria 536.8
  neurotic 306.4
  psychogenic 306.4
Hypercholesterinemia — *see* Hypercholesterolemia
Hypercholesterolemia 272.0
  with hyperglyceridemia, endogenous 272.2
  essential 272.0
  familial 272.0
  hereditary 272.0
  primary 272.0
  pure 272.0
Hypercholesterolosis 272.0
Hyperchylia gastrica 536.8
  psychogenic 306.4
Hyperchylomicronemia (familial) (with hyperbetalipoproteinemia) 272.3
Hypercoagulation syndrome (primary) 289.81
  secondary 289.82
Hypercorticosteronism
  correct substance properly administered 255.3
  overdose or wrong substance given or taken 962.0
Hypercortisonism
  correct substance properly administered 255.3
  overdose or wrong substance given or taken 962.0
Hyperdynamic beta-adrenergic state or syndrome (circulatory) 429.82
Hyperekplexia 759.89
Hyperelectrolytemia 276.9
Hyperemesis 536.2
  arising during pregnancy — *see* Hyperemesis, gravidarum
  gravidarum (mild) (before 22 completed weeks gestation) 643.0 ☑
    with
      carbohydrate depletion 643.1 ☑
      dehydration 643.1 ☑
      electrolyte imbalance 643.1 ☑
      metabolic disturbance 643.1 ☑
      affecting fetus or newborn 761.8
    severe (with metabolic disturbance) 643.1 ☑
  psychogenic 306.4
Hyperemia (acute) 780.99
  anal mucosa 569.49
  bladder 596.7
  cerebral 437.8
  conjunctiva 372.71
  ear, internal, acute 386.30
  enteric 564.89
  eye 372.71
  eyelid (active) (passive) 374.82
  intestine 564.89
  iris 364.41
  kidney 593.81
  labyrinth 386.30
  liver (active) (passive) 573.8

Hyperemia — *continued*
  lung 514
  ovary 620.8
  passive 780.99
  pulmonary 514
  renal 593.81
  retina 362.89
  spleen 289.59
  stomach 537.89
Hyperesthesia (body surface) — *see also* Disturbance, sensation 782.0
  larynx (reflex) 478.79
    hysterical 300.11
  pharynx (reflex) 478.29
Hyperestrinism 256.0
Hyperestrogenism 256.0
Hyperestrogenosis 256.0
Hyperexplexia 759.89
Hyperextension, joint 718.80
  ankle 718.87
  elbow 718.82
  foot 718.87
  hand 718.84
  hip 718.85
  knee 718.86
  multiple sites 718.89
  pelvic region 718.85
  shoulder (region) 718.81
  specified site NEC 718.88
  wrist 718.83
Hyperfibrinolysis — *see* Fibrinolysis
Hyperfolliculinism 256.0
Hyperfructosemia 271.2
Hyperfunction
  adrenal (cortex) 255.3
    androgenic, acquired benign 255.3
    medulla 255.6
    virilism 255.2
  corticoadrenal NEC 255.3
  labyrinth — *see* Hyperactive, labyrinth
  medulloadrenal 255.6
  ovary 256.1
    estrogen 256.0
  pancreas 577.8
  parathyroid (gland) 252.00
  pituitary (anterior) (gland) (lobe) 253.1
  testicular 257.0
Hypergammaglobulinemia 289.89
  monoclonal, benign (BMH) 273.1
  polyclonal 273.0
  Waldenström's 273.0
Hyperglobulinemia 273.8
Hyperglycemia 790.29
  maternal
    affecting fetus or newborn 775.0
      manifest diabetes in infant 775.1
  postpancreatectomy (complete) (partial) 251.3
Hyperglyceridemia 272.1
  endogenous 272.1
  essential 272.1
  familial 272.1
  hereditary 272.1
  mixed 272.3
  pure 272.1
Hyperglycinemia 270.7
Hypergonadism
  ovarian 256.1
  testicular (infantile) (primary) 257.0
Hyperheparinemia — *see also* Circulating anticoagulants 286.5
Hyperhidrosis, hyperidrosis 705.21
  axilla 705.21
  face 705.21
  focal (localized) 705.21
    primary 705.21
      axilla 705.21
      face 705.21
      palms 705.21
      soles 705.21
    secondary 705.22
      axilla 705.22
      face 705.22
      palms 705.22
      soles 705.22
  generalized 780.8
  palms 705.21

Hyperhidrosis, hyperidrosis — *continued*
  psychogenic 306.3
  secondary 780.8
  soles 705.21
Hyperhistidinemia 270.5
Hyperinsulinism (ectopic) (functional) (organic) NEC 251.1
  iatrogenic 251.0
  reactive 251.2
  spontaneous 251.2
  therapeutic misadventure (from administration of insulin) 962.3
Hyperiodemia 276.9
Hyperirritability (cerebral), in newborn 779.1
Hyperkalemia 276.7
Hyperkeratosis — *see also* Keratosis 701.1
  cervix 622.2
  congenital 757.39
  cornea 371.89
  due to yaws (early) (late) (palmar or plantar) 102.3
  eccentrica 757.39
  figurata centrifuga atrophica 757.39
  follicularis 757.39
    in cutem penetrans 701.1
  limbic (cornea) 371.89
  palmoplantaris climacterica 701.1
  pinta (carate) 103.1
  senile (with pruritus) 702.0
  tongue 528.79
  universalis congenita 757.1
  vagina 623.1
  vocal cord 478.5
  vulva 624.09
Hyperkinesia, hyperkinetic (disease) (reaction) (syndrome) 314.9
  with
    attention deficit — *see* Disorder, attention deficit
    conduct disorder 314.2
    developmental delay 314.1
    simple disturbance of activity and attention 314.01
    specified manifestation NEC 314.8
  heart (disease) 429.82
  of childhood or adolescence NEC 314.9
Hyperlacrimation — *see also* Epiphora 375.20
Hyperlipemia — *see also* Hyperlipidemia 272.4
Hyperlipidemia 272.4
  carbohydrate-induced 272.1
  combined 272.2 ▲
  endogenous 272.1
  exogenous 272.3
  fat-induced 272.3
  group
    A 272.0
    B 272.1
    C 272.2
    D 272.3
  mixed 272.2
  specified type NEC 272.4
Hyperlipidosis 272.7
  hereditary 272.7
Hyperlipoproteinemia (acquired) (essential) (familial) (hereditary) (primary) (secondary) 272.4
  Fredrickson type
    I 272.3
    IIa 272.0
    IIb 272.2
    III 272.2
    IV 272.1
    V 272.3
  low-density-lipoid-type (LDL) 272.0
  very-low-density-lipoid-type (VLDL) 272.1
Hyperlucent lung, unilateral 492.8
Hyperluteinization 256.1
Hyperlysinemia 270.7
Hypermagnesemia 275.2
  neonatal 775.5
Hypermaturity (fetus or newborn)
  post-term infant 766.21
  prolonged gestation infant 766.22
Hypermenorrhea 626.2
Hypermetabolism 794.7
Hypermethioninemia 270.4

Hypermetropia (congenital) 367.0
Hypermobility
  cecum 564.9
  coccyx 724.71
  colon 564.9
    psychogenic 306.4
  ileum 564.89
  joint (acquired) 718.80
    ankle 718.87
    elbow 718.82
    foot 718.87
    hand 718.84
    hip 718.85
    knee 718.86
    multiple sites 718.89
    pelvic region 718.85
    shoulder (region) 718.81
    specified site NEC 718.88
    wrist 718.83
  kidney, congenital 753.3
  meniscus (knee) 717.5
  scapula 718.81
  stomach 536.8
    psychogenic 306.4
  syndrome 728.5
  testis, congenital 752.52
  urethral 599.81
Hypermotility
  gastrointestinal 536.8
  intestine 564.9
    psychogenic 306.4
  stomach 536.8
Hypernasality 784.43 ▲
Hypernatremia 276.0 – Elevated level of Sodium in the blood
  with water depletion 276.0
Hypernephroma (M8312/3) 189.0
Hyperopia 367.0
Hyperorexia 783.6
Hyperornithinemia 270.6
Hyperosmia — *see also* Disturbance, sensation 781.1
Hyperosmolality 276.0
Hyperosmolality 276.0
Hyperosteogenesis 733.99
Hyperostosis 733.99
  calvarial 733.3
  cortical 733.3
    infantile 756.59
  frontal, internal of skull 733.3
  interna frontalis 733.3
  monomelic 733.99
  skull 733.3
    congenital 756.0
  vertebral 721.8
    with spondylosis — *see* Spondylosis
    ankylosing 721.6
Hyperovarianism 256.1
Hyperovarism, hyperovaria 256.1
Hyperoxaluria (primary) 271.8
Hyperoxia 987.8
Hyperparathyroidism 252.00
  ectopic 259.3
  other 252.08
  primary 252.01
  secondary (of renal origin) 588.81
    non-renal 252.02
  tertiary 252.08
Hyperpathia — *see also* Disturbance, sensation 782.0
  psychogenic 307.80
Hyperperistalsis 787.4
  psychogenic 306.4
Hyperpermeability, capillary 448.9
Hyperphagia 783.6
Hyperphenylalaninemia 270.1
Hyperphoria 378.40
  alternating 378.45
Hyperphosphatemia 275.3
Hyperpiesia — *see also* Hypertension 401.9
Hyperpiesis — *see also* Hypertension 401.9
Hyperpigmentation — *see* Pigmentation
Hyperpinealism 259.8
Hyperpipecolatemia 270.7
Hyperpituitarism 253.1
Hyperplasia, hyperplastic
  adenoids (lymphoid tissue) 474.12
    and tonsils 474.10

Hyperplasia, hyperplastic — *continued*
  adrenal (capsule) (cortex) (gland) 255.8
    with
      sexual precocity (male) 255.2
      virilism, adrenal 255.2
      virilization (female) 255.2
    congenital 255.2
    due to excess ACTH (ectopic) (pituitary) 255.0
    medulla 255.8
  alpha cells (pancreatic)
    with
      gastrin excess 251.5
      glucagon excess 251.4
  appendix (lymphoid) 543.0
  artery, fibromuscular NEC 447.8
    carotid 447.8
    renal 447.3
  bone 733.99
    marrow 289.9
  breast (*see also* Hypertrophy, breast) 611.1
    ductal 610.8 ●
      atypical 610.8 ●
  carotid artery 447.8
  cementation, cementum (teeth) (tooth) 521.5
  cervical gland 785.6
  cervix (uteri) 622.10
    basal cell 622.10
    congenital 752.49
    endometrium 622.10
    polypoid 622.10
  chin 524.05
  clitoris, congenital 752.49
  dentin 521.5
  endocervicitis 616.0
  endometrium, endometrial (adenomatous) (atypical) (cystic) (glandular) (polypoid) (uterus) 621.30
    with atypia 621.33
    without atypia
      complex 621.32
      simple 621.31
    benign 621.34 ●
  cervix 622.10
  epithelial 709.8
    focal, oral, including tongue 528.79
    mouth (focal) 528.79
    nipple 611.89
    skin 709.8
    tongue (focal) 528.79
    vaginal wall 623.0
  erythroid 289.9
  fascialis ossificans (progressiva) 728.11
  fibromuscular, artery NEC 447.8
    carotid 447.8
    renal 447.3
  genital
    female 629.89
    male 608.89
  gingiva 523.8
  glandularis
    cystica uteri 621.30
    endometrium (uterus) 621.30
    interstitialis uteri 621.30
  granulocytic 288.69
  gum 523.8
  hymen, congenital 752.49
  islands of Langerhans 251.1
  islet cell (pancreatic) 251.9
    alpha cells
      with excess
        gastrin 251.5
        glucagon 251.4
    beta cells 251.1
  juxtaglomerular (complex) (kidney) 593.89
  kidney (congenital) 753.3
  liver (congenital) 751.69
  lymph node (gland) 785.6
  lymphoid (diffuse) (nodular) 785.6
    appendix 543.0
    intestine 569.89
  mandibular 524.02
    alveolar 524.72
      unilateral condylar 526.89
  Marchand multiple nodular (liver) — *see* Cirrhosis, postnecrotic

Hyperplasia, hyperplastic — *continued*
- maxillary 524.01
  - alveolar 524.71
- medulla, adrenal 255.8
- myometrium, myometrial 621.2
- nose (lymphoid) (polypoid) 478.19
- oral soft tissue (inflammatory) (irritative) (mucosa) NEC 528.9
  - gingiva 523.8
  - tongue 529.8
- organ or site, congenital NEC — *see* Anomaly, specified type NEC
- ovary 620.8
- palate, papillary 528.9
- pancreatic islet cells 251.9
  - alpha
    - with excess
      - gastrin 251.5
      - glucagon 251.4
    - beta 251.1
- parathyroid (gland) 252.01
- persistent, vitreous (primary) 743.51
- pharynx (lymphoid) 478.29
- prostate 600.90
  - with
    - other lower urinary tract symptoms (LUTS) 600.91
    - urinary
      - obstruction 600.91
      - retention 600.91
  - adenofibromatous 600.20
    - with
      - other lower urinary tract symptoms (LUTS) 600.21
      - urinary
        - obstruction 600.21
        - retention 600.21
  - nodular 600.10
    - with
      - urinary
        - obstruction 600.11
        - retention 600.11

Hyperplasia, hyperplastic — *continued*
- renal artery (fibromuscular) 447.3
- reticuloendothelial (cell) 289.9
- salivary gland (any) 527.1
- Schimmelbusch's 610.1
- suprarenal (capsule) (gland) 255.8
- thymus (gland) (persistent) 254.0
- thyroid (*see also* Goiter) 240.9
  - primary 242.0 ☑
  - secondary 242.2 ☑
- tonsil (lymphoid tissue) 474.11
  - and adenoids 474.10
- urethrovaginal 599.89
- uterus, uterine (myometrium) 621.2
  - endometrium (*see also* Hyperplasia, endometrium) 621.30
- vitreous (humor), primary persistent 743.51
- vulva 624.3
- zygoma 738.11

Hyperpnea — *see also* Hyperventilation 786.01
Hyperpotassemia 276.7
Hyperprebetalipoproteinemia 272.1
- with chylomicronemia 272.3
- familial 272.1

Hyperprolactinemia 253.1
Hyperprolinemia 270.8
Hyperproteinemia 273.8
Hyperprothrombinemia 289.89
Hyperpselaphesia 782.0
Hyperpyrexia 780.60
- heat (effects of) 992.0
- malarial (*see also* Malaria) 084.6
- malignant, due to anesthetic 995.86
- rheumatic — *see* Fever, rheumatic
- unknown origin (*see also* Pyrexia) 780.60
Hyperreactor, vascular 780.2
Hyperreflexia 796.1
- bladder, autonomic 596.54
  - with cauda equina 344.61
- detrusor 344.61
Hypersalivation — *see also* Ptyalism 527.7
Hypersarcosinemia 270.8

Hypersecretion
- ACTH 255.3
- androgens (ovarian) 256.1
- calcitonin 246.0
- corticoadrenal 255.3
- cortisol 255.0
- estrogen 256.0
- gastric 536.8
  - psychogenic 306.4
- gastrin 251.5
- glucagon 251.4
- hormone
  - ACTH 255.3
  - anterior pituitary 253.1
  - growth NEC 253.0
  - ovarian androgen 256.1
  - testicular 257.0
  - thyroid stimulating 242.8 ☑
- insulin — *see* Hyperinsulinism
- lacrimal glands (*see also* Epiphora) 375.20
- medulloadrenal 255.6
- milk 676.6 ☑
- ovarian androgens 256.1
- pituitary (anterior) 253.1
- salivary gland (any) 527.7
- testicular hormones 257.0
- thyrocalcitonin 246.0
- upper respiratory 478.9
Hypersegmentation, hereditary 288.2
- eosinophils 288.2
- neutrophil nuclei 288.2
Hypersensitive, hypersensitiveness, hypersensitivity — *see also* Allergy
- angiitis 446.20
  - specified NEC 446.29
- carotid sinus 337.01
- colon 564.9
  - psychogenic 306.4
- DNA (deoxyribonucleic acid) NEC 287.2
- drug (*see also* Allergy, drug) 995.27
- esophagus 530.89
- insect bites — *see* Injury, superficial, by site

Hypersensitive, hypersensitiveness, hypersensitivity — *see also* Allergy — *continued*
- labyrinth 386.58
- pain (*see also* Disturbance, sensation) 782.0
- pneumonitis NEC 495.9
- reaction (*see also* Allergy) 995.3
  - upper respiratory tract NEC 478.8
- stomach (allergic) (nonallergic) 536.8
  - psychogenic 306.4
Hypersomatotropism (classic) 253.0
Hypersomnia, unspecified 780.54
- with sleep apnea, unspecified 780.53
- alcohol induced 291.82
- drug induced 292.85
- due to
  - medical condition classified elsewhere 327.14
  - mental disorder 327.15
- idiopathic
  - with long sleep time 327.11
  - without long sleep time 327.12
- menstrual related 327.13
- nonorganic origin 307.43
  - persistent (primary) 307.44
  - transient 307.43
- organic 327.10
  - other 327.19
- primary 307.44
- recurrent 327.13
Hypersplenia 289.4
Hypersplenism 289.4
Hypersteatosis 706.3
Hyperstimulation, ovarian 256.1
Hypersuprarenalism 255.3
Hypersusceptibility — *see* Allergy
Hyper-TBG-nemia 246.8
Hypertelorism 756.0
- orbit, orbital 376.41

☑ Additional Digit Required — Refer to the Tabular List for Digit Selection   ▽ Subterms under main terms may continue to next column or page

140 — Volume 2   ▶◀ Revised Text   ● New Line   ▲ Revised Code   **2010 ICD-9-CM**

A diagnosis of elevated blood pressure reading — without a diagnosis of hypertension — is assigned to code 796.2

	Malignant	Benign	Unspecified
Hypertension, hypertensive (arterial) (arteriolar) (crisis) (degeneration) (disease) (essential) (fluctuating) (idiopathic) (intermittent) (labile) (low renin) (orthostatic) (paroxysmal) (primary) (systemic) (uncontrolled) (vascular)	401.0	401.1	401.9
with			
chronic kidney disease			
stage I through stage IV, or unspecified	403.00	403.10	403.90
stage V or end stage renal disese	403.01	403.11	403.91
heart involvement (conditions classifiable to 429.0–429.3, 429.8, 429.9 due to hypertension) (see also Hypertension, heart)	402.00	402.10	402.90
with kidney involvement — see Hypertension, cardiorenal			
renal ►(kidney)◄ involvement (only conditions classifiable to 585) (excludes conditions classifiable to 584) (see also Hypertension, kidney)	403.00	403.10	403.90
with heart involvement — see Hypertension, cardiorenal			
failure (and sclerosis) (see also Hypertension, kidney)	403.01	403.11	403.91
sclerosis without failure (see also Hypertension, kidney)	403.00	403.10	403.90
accelerated (see also Hypertension, by type, malignant))	401.0	—	—
antepartum — see Hypertension, complicating pregnancy, childbirth, or the puerperium			
cardiorenal (disease)	404.00	404.10	404.90
with			
chronic kidney disease			
stage I through stage IV, or unspecified	404.00	404.10	404.90
and heart failure	404.01	404.11	404.91
stage V or end stage renal disease	404.02	404.12	404.92
and heart failure	404.03	404.13	404.93
heart failure	404.01	404.11	404.91
and chronic kidney disease	404.01	404.11	404.91
stage I through stage IV or unspecified	404.01	404.11	404.91
stave V or end stage renal disease	404.03	404.13	404.93
cardiovascular disease (arteriosclerotic) (sclerotic)	402.00	402.10	402.90
with			
heart failure	402.01	402.11	402.91
renal involvement (conditions classifiable to 403) (see also Hypertension, cardiorenal)	404.00	404.10	404.90
cardiovascular renal (disease) (sclerosis) (see also Hypertension, cardiorenal)	404.00	404.10	404.90
cerebrovascular disease NEC	437.2	437.2	437.2
complicating pregnancy, childbirth, or the puerperium	642.2 ☑	642.0 ☑	642.9 ☑
with			
albuminuria (and edema) (mild)	—	—	642.4 ☑
severe	—	—	642.5 ☑
chronic kidney disesae	642.2 ☑	642.2 ☑	642.2 ☑
and heart disease	642.2 ☑	642.2 ☑	642.2 ☑
edema (mild)	—	—	642.4 ☑
severe	—	—	642.5 ☑
heart disease	642.2 ☑	642.2 ☑	642.2 ☑
and chronic kidney disease	642.2 ☑	642.2 ☑	642.2 ☑
renal disease	642.2 ☑	642.2 ☑	642.2 ☑
and heart disease	642.2 ☑	642.2 ☑	642.2 ☑
chronic	642.2 ☑	642.0 ☑	642.0 ☑
with pre-eclampsia or eclampsia	642.7 ☑	642.7 ☑	642.7 ☑
fetus or newborn	760.0	760.0	760.0
essential	—	642.0 ☑	642.0 ☑
with pre-eclampsia or eclampsia	—	642.7 ☑	642.7 ☑
fetus or newborn	760.0	760.0	760.0
fetus or newborn	760.0	760.0	760.0
gestational	—	—	642.3 ☑
pre-existing	642.2 ☑	642.0 ☑	642.0 ☑
with pre-eclampsia or eclampsia	642.7 ☑	642.7 ☑	642.7 ☑
fetus or newborn	760.0	760.0	760.0
secondary to renal disease	642.1 ☑	642.1 ☑	642.1 ☑
with pre-eclampsia or eclampsia	642.7 ☑	642.7 ☑	642.7 ☑
fetus or newborn	760.0	760.0	760.0
transient	—	—	642.3 ☑
due to			
aldosteronism, primary	405.09	405.19	405.99
brain tumor	405.09	405.19	405.99
bulbar poliomyelitis	405.09	405.19	405.99
calculus			
kidney	405.09	405.19	405.99
ureter	405.09	405.19	405.99

	Malignant	Benign	Unspecified
Hypertension, hypertensive — continued			
due to — continued			
coarctation, aorta	405.09	405.19	405.99
Cushing's disease	405.09	405.19	405.99
glomerulosclerosis (see also Hypertension, kidney)	403.00	403.10	403.90
periarteritis nodosa	405.09	405.19	405.99
pheochromocytoma	405.09	405.19	405.99
polycystic kidney(s)	405.09	405.19	405.99
polycythemia	405.09	405.19	405.99
porphyria	405.09	405.19	405.99
pyelonephritis	405.09	405.19	405.99
renal (artery)			
aneurysm	405.01	405.11	405.91
anomaly	405.01	405.11	405.91
embolism	405.01	405.11	405.91
fibromuscular hyperplasia	405.01	405.11	405.91
occlusion	405.01	405.11	405.91
stenosis	405.01	405.11	405.91
thrombosis	405.01	405.11	405.91
encephalopathy	437.2	437.2	437.2
gestational (transient) NEC	—	—	642.3 ☑
Goldblatt's	440.1	440.1	440.1
heart (disease) (conditions classifiable to 429.0–429.3, 429.8, 429.9 due to hypertension)	402.00	402.10	402.90
with heart failure	402.01	402.11	402.91
hypertensive kidney disease (conditions classifiable to 403) (see also Hypertension, cardiorenal)	404.00	404.10	404.90
renal sclerosis (see also Hypertension, cardiorenal)	404.00	404.10	404.90
intracranial, benign	—	348.2	
intraocular	—	—	365.04
kidney	403.00	403.10	403.90
with			
chronic kidney disease			
stage I through stage IV, or unspecified	403.00	403.10	403.90
stage V or end stage renal disese	403.01	403.11	403.91
heart involvement (conditions classifiable to 429.0–429.3, 429.8, 429.9 due to hypertension) (see also Hypertension, cardiorenal)	404.00	404.10	404.90
hypertensive heart (disease) (conditions classifiable to 402) (see also Hypertension, cardiorenal)	404.00	404.10	404.90
lesser circulation	—	—	416.0
necrotizing	401.0	—	—
ocular	—	—	365.04
pancreatic duct — code to underlying condition			
with			
chronic pancreatitis	—	—	577.1
portal (due to chronic liver disease)	—	—	572.3
postoperative	—	—	997.91
psychogenic	—	—	306.2
puerperal, postpartum — see Hypertension, complicating pregnancy, childbirth, or the puerperium			
pulmonary (artery)	—	—	416.8
with cor pulmonale (chronic)	—	—	416.8
acute	—	—	415.0
idiopathic	—	—	416.0
primary	—	—	416.0
of newborn	—	—	747.83
secondary	—	—	416.8
renal (disease) (see also Hypertension, kidney)	403.00	403.10	403.90
renovascular NEC	405.01	405.11	405.91
secondary NEC	405.09	405.19	405.99
due to			
aldosteronism, primary	405.09	405.19	405.99
brain tumor	405.09	405.19	405.99
bulbar poliomyelitis	405.09	405.19	405.99
calculus			
kidney	405.09	405.19	405.99
ureter	405.09	405.19	405.99
coarctation, aorta	405.09	405.19	405.99
Cushing's disease	405.09	405.19	405.99
glomerulosclerosis (see also Hypertension, kidney)	403.00	403.10	403.90
periarteritis nodosa	405.09	405.19	405.99
pheochromocytoma	405.09	405.19	405.99
polycystic kidney(s)	405.09	405.19	405.99
polycythemia	405.09	405.19	405.99
porphyria	405.09	405.19	405.99
pyelonephritis	405.09	405.19	405.99
renal (artery)			
aneurysm	405.01	405.11	405.91

☑ Additional Digit Required — Refer to the Tabular List for Digit Selection

⚕ Subterms under main terms may continue to next column or page

	Malignant	Benign	Unspecified
Hypertension, hypertensive — *continued*			
secondary — *continued*			
due to — *continued*			
renal — *continued*			
anomaly	405.01	405.11	405.91
embolism	405.01	405.11	405.91
fibromuscular hyperplasia	405.01	405.11	405.91
occlusion	405.01	405.11	405.91
stenosis	405.01	405.11	405.91
thrombosis	405.01	405.11	405.91
transient	—	—	796.2
of pregnancy	—	—	642.3 ☑
vascular degeneration	401.0	401.1	401.9
venous, chronic (asymptomatic) (idiopathic)	—	—	459.30
with			
complication, NEC	—	—	459.39
inflammation	—	—	459.32
with ulcer	—	—	459.33
ulcer	—	—	459.31
with inflammation	—	—	459.33
due to			
deep vein thrombosis (*see also* Syndrome, postphlebetic)	—	—	459.10

☑ Additional Digit Required — Refer to the Tabular List for Digit Selection

142 — **Volume 2**   ▶◀ Revised Text   ● New Line   ▲ Revised Code   ▽ Subterms under main terms may continue to next column or page   **2010 ICD-9-CM**

Hyperthecosis, ovary 256.8
Hyperthermia (of unknown origin) — see also
Pyrexia 780.60
malignant (due to anesthesia) 995.86
newborn 778.4
Hyperthymergasia — see also Psychosis, affective 296.0 ☑
reactive (from emotional stress, psychological
trauma) 298.1
recurrent episode 296.1 ☑
single episode 296.0 ☑
Hyperthymism 254.8
Hyperthyroid (recurrent) — see Hyperthyroidism
Hyperthyroidism (latent) (preadult) (recurrent)
(without goiter) 242.9 ☑

Note—Use the following fifth-digit
subclassification with category 242:

0   without mention of thyrotoxic crisis
     or storm

1   with mention of thyrotoxic crisis or
     storm

with
goiter (diffuse) 242.0 ☑
adenomatous 242.3 ☑
multinodular 242.2 ☑
uninodular 242.1 ☑
nodular 242.3 ☑
multinodular 242.2 ☑
uninodular 242.1 ☑
thyroid nodule 242.1 ☑
complicating pregnancy, childbirth, or puerperium 648.1 ☑
neonatal (transient) 775.3
Hypertonia — see Hypertonicity
Hypertonicity
bladder 596.51
fetus or newborn 779.89
gastrointestinal (tract) 536.8
infancy 779.89
due to electrolyte imbalance 779.89
muscle 728.85
stomach 536.8
psychogenic 306.4
uterus, uterine (contractions) 661.4 ☑
affecting fetus or newborn 763.7
Hypertony — see Hypertonicity
Hypertransaminemia 790.4
Hypertrichosis 704.1
congenital 757.4
eyelid 374.54
lanuginosa 757.4
acquired 704.1
Hypertriglyceridemia, essential 272.1
Hypertrophy, hypertrophic
adenoids (infectional) 474.12
and tonsils (faucial) (infective) (lingual)
(lymphoid) 474.10
adrenal 255.8
alveolar process or ridge 525.8
anal papillae 569.49
apocrine gland 705.82
artery NEC 447.8
carotid 447.8
congenital (peripheral) NEC 747.60
gastrointestinal 747.61
lower limb 747.64
renal 747.62
specified NEC 747.69
spinal 747.82
upper limb 747.63
renal 447.3
arthritis (chronic) (see also Osteoarthrosis)
715.9 ☑
spine (see also Spondylosis) 721.90
arytenoid 478.79
asymmetrical (heart) 429.9
auricular — see Hypertrophy, cardiac
Bartholin's gland 624.8
bile duct 576.8
bladder (sphincter) (trigone) 596.8
blind spot, visual field 368.42
bone 733.99
brain 348.89
breast 611.1

Hypertrophy, hypertrophic — continued
breast — continued
cystic 610.1
fetus or newborn 778.7
fibrocystic 610.1
massive pubertal 611.1
puerperal, postpartum 676.3 ☑
senile (parenchymatous) 611.1
cardiac (chronic) (idiopathic) 429.3
with
rheumatic fever (conditions classifiable
to 390)
active 391.8
with chorea 392.0
inactive or quiescent (with chorea)
398.99
congenital NEC 746.89
fatty (see also Degeneration, myocardial)
429.1
hypertensive (see also Hypertension, heart)
402.90
rheumatic (with chorea) 398.99
active or acute 391.8
with chorea 392.0
valve (see also Endocarditis) 424.90
congenital NEC 746.89
cartilage 733.99
cecum 569.89
cervix (uteri) 622.6
congenital 752.49
elongation 622.6
clitoris (cirrhotic) 624.2
congenital 752.49
colon 569.89
congenital 751.3
conjunctiva, lymphoid 372.73
cornea 371.89
corpora cavernosa 607.89
duodenum 537.89
endometrium (uterus) (see also Hyperplasia,
endometrium) 621.30
cervix 622.6
epididymis 608.89
esophageal hiatus (congenital) 756.6
with hernia — see Hernia, diaphragm
eyelid 374.30
falx, skull 733.99
fat pad 729.30
infrapatellar 729.31
knee 729.31
orbital 374.34
popliteal 729.31
prepatellar 729.31
retropatellar 729.31
specified site NEC 729.39
foot (congenital) 755.67
frenum, frenulum (tongue) 529.8
linguae 529.8
lip 528.5
gallbladder or cystic duct 575.8
gastric mucosa 535.2 ☑
gingiva 523.8
gland, glandular (general) NEC 785.6
gum (mucous membrane) 523.8
heart (idiopathic) (see also Hypertrophy, cardiac)
valve (see also Endocarditis)
congenital NEC 746.89
hemifacial 754.0
hepatic — see Hypertrophy, liver
hiatus (esophageal) 756.6
hilus gland 785.6
hymen, congenital 752.49
ileum 569.89
infrapatellar fat pad 729.31
intestine 569.89
jejunum 569.89
kidney (compensatory) 593.1
congenital 753.3
labial frenulum 528.5
labium (majus) (minus) 624.3
lacrimal gland, chronic 375.03
ligament 728.9
spinal 724.8
linguae frenulum 529.8
lingual tonsil (infectional) 474.11

Hypertrophy, hypertrophic — continued
lip (frenum) 528.5
congenital 744.81
liver 789.1
acute 573.8
cirrhotic — see Cirrhosis, liver
congenital 751.69
fatty — see Fatty, liver
lymph gland 785.6
tuberculous — see Tuberculosis, lymph
gland
mammary gland — see Hypertrophy, breast
maxillary frenulum 528.5
Meckel's diverticulum (congenital) 751.0
medial meniscus, acquired 717.3
median bar 600.90
with
other lower urinary tract symptoms
(LUTS) 600.91
urinary
obstruction 600.91
retention 600.91
mediastinum 519.3
meibomian gland 373.2
meniscus, knee, congenital 755.64
metatarsal head 733.99
metatarsus 733.99
mouth 528.9
mucous membrane
alveolar process 523.8
nose 478.19
turbinate (nasal) 478.0
muscle 728.9
muscular coat, artery NEC 447.8
carotid 447.8
renal 447.3
myocardium (see also Hypertrophy, cardiac)
429.3
idiopathic 425.4
myometrium 621.2
nail 703.8
congenital 757.5
nasal 478.19
alae 478.19
bone 738.0
cartilage 478.19
mucous membrane (septum) 478.19
sinus (see also Sinusitis) 473.9
turbinate 478.0
nasopharynx, lymphoid (infectional) (tissue)
(wall) 478.29
neck, uterus 622.6
nipple 611.1
normal aperture diaphragm (congenital) 756.6
nose (see also Hypertrophy, nasal) 478.19
orbit 376.46
organ or site, congenital NEC — see Anomaly,
specified type NEC
osteoarthropathy (pulmonary) 731.2
ovary 620.8
palate (hard) 526.89
soft 528.9
pancreas (congenital) 751.7
papillae
anal 569.49
tongue 529.3
parathyroid (gland) 252.01
parotid gland 527.1
penis 607.89
phallus 607.89
female (clitoris) 624.2
pharyngeal tonsil 474.12
pharyngitis 472.1
pharynx 478.29
lymphoid (infectional) (tissue) (wall) 478.29
pituitary (fossa) (gland) 253.8
popliteal fat pad 729.31
preauricular (lymph) gland (Hampstead) 785.6
prepuce (congenital) 605
female 624.2
prostate (asymptomatic) (early) (recurrent)
600.90
with
other lower urinary tract symptlms
(LUTS) 600.91

Hypertrophy, hypertrophic — continued
prostate — continued
with — continued
urinary
obstruction 600.91
retention 600.91
adenofibromatous 600.20
with
other lower urinary tract symptoms
(LUTS) 600.21
urinary
obstruction 600.21
retention 600.21
benign 600.00
with
other lower urinary tract symptoms
(LUTS) 600.01
urinary
obstruction 600.01
retention 600.01
congenital 752.89
pseudoedematous hypodermal 757.0
pseudomuscular 359.1
pylorus (muscle) (sphincter) 537.0
congenital 750.5
infantile 750.5
rectal sphincter 569.49
rectum 569.49
renal 593.1
rhinitis (turbinate) 472.0
salivary duct or gland 527.1
congenital 750.26
scaphoid (tarsal) 733.99
scar 701.4
scrotum 608.89
sella turcica 253.8
seminal vesicle 608.89
sigmoid 569.89
skin condition NEC 701.9
spermatic cord 608.89
spinal ligament 724.8
spleen — see Splenomegaly
spondylitis (spine) (see also Spondylosis)
721.90
stomach 537.89
subaortic stenosis (idiopathic) 425.1
sublingual gland 527.1
congenital 750.26
submaxillary gland 527.1
suprarenal (gland) 255.8
tendon 727.9
testis 608.89
congenital 752.89
thymic, thymus (congenital) (gland) 254.0
thyroid (gland) (see also Goiter) 240.9
primary 242.0 ☑
secondary 242.2 ☑
toe (congenital) 755.65
acquired 735.8
tongue 529.8
congenital 750.15
frenum 529.8
papillae (foliate) 529.3
tonsil (faucial) (infective) (lingual) (lymphoid)
474.11
with
adenoiditis 474.01
tonsillitis 474.00
and adenoiditis 474.02
and adenoids 474.10
tunica vaginalis 608.89
turbinate (mucous membrane) 478.0
ureter 593.89
urethra 599.84
uterus 621.2
puerperal, postpartum 674.8 ☑
uvula 528.9
vagina 623.8
vas deferens 608.89
vein 459.89
ventricle, ventricular (heart) (left) (right) (see
also Hypertrophy, cardiac)
congenital 746.89
due to hypertension (left) (right) (see also
Hypertension, heart) 402.90
benign 402.10

▲ (Revised Code marker near brain 348.89)

☑ Additional Digit Required — Refer to the Tabular List for Digit Selection
☑ Subterms under main terms may continue to next column or page
2010 ICD-9-CM
►◄ Revised Text
● New Line
▲ Revised Code
October 2009 • Volume 2 — 143

Hypoplasia, hypoplasis — *continued*
- intestine (small) 751.1
  - large 751.2
- iris 743.46
- jaw 524.09
- kidney(s) 753.0
- labium (majus) (minus) 752.49
- labyrinth, membranous 744.05
- lacrimal duct (apparatus) 743.65
- larynx 748.3
- leg (*see also* Absence, limb, congenital, lower) 755.30
- limb 755.4
  - lower (*see also* Absence, limb, congenital, lower) 755.30
  - upper (*see also* Absence, limb, congenital, upper) 755.20
- liver 751.69
- lung (lobe) 748.5
- mammary (areolar) 611.82
- mandibular 524.04
  - alveolar 524.74
  - unilateral condylar 526.89
- maxillary 524.03
  - alveolar 524.73
- medullary 284.9
- megakaryocytic 287.30
- metacarpus (*see also* Absence, metacarpal, congenital) 755.28
- metatarsus (*see also* Absence, metatarsal, congenital) 755.38
- muscle 756.89
  - eye 743.69
- myocardium (congenital) (Uhl's anomaly) 746.84
- nail(s) 757.5
- nasolacrimal duct 743.65
- nervous system NEC 742.8
- neural 742.8
- nose, nasal 748.1
- ophthalmic (*see also* Microphthalmos) 743.10
- optic nerve 377.43
- organ
  - of Corti 744.05
  - or site NEC — *see* Anomaly, by site
- osseous meatus (ear) 744.03
- ovary 752.0
- oviduct 752.19
- pancreas 751.7
- parathyroid (gland) 759.2
- parotid gland 750.26
- patella 755.64
- pelvis, pelvic girdle 755.69
- penis 752.69
- peripheral vascular system (congenital) NEC 747.60
  - gastrointestinal 747.61
  - lower limb 747.64
  - renal 747.62
  - specified NEC 747.69
  - spinal 747.82
  - upper limb 747.63
- pituitary (gland) 759.2
- pulmonary 748.5
  - arteriovenous 747.3
  - artery 747.3
  - valve 746.01
- punctum lacrimale 743.65
- radioulnar (*see also* Absence, radius, congenital, with ulna) 755.25
- radius (*see also* Absence, radius, congenital) 755.26
- rectum 751.2

Hypoplasia, hypoplasis — *continued*
- respiratory system NEC 748.9
- rib 756.3
- sacrum 756.19
- scapula 755.59
- shoulder girdle 755.59
- skin 757.39
- skull (bone) 756.0
  - with
    - anencephalus 740.0
    - encephalocele 742.0
    - hydrocephalus 742.3
      - with spina bifida (*see also* Spina bifida) 741.0 ☑
    - microcephalus 742.1
- spinal (cord) (ventral horn cell) 742.59
  - vessel 747.82
- spine 756.19
- spleen 759.0
- sternum 756.3
- tarsus (*see also* Absence, tarsal, congenital) 755.38
- testis, testicle 752.89
- thymus (gland) 279.11
- thyroid (gland) 243
  - cartilage 748.3
- tibiofibular (*see also* Absence, tibia, congenital, with fibula) 755.35
- toe (*see also* Absence, toe, congenital) 755.39
- tongue 750.16
- trachea (cartilage) (rings) 748.3
- Turner's (tooth) 520.4
- ulna (*see also* Absence, ulna, congenital) 755.27
- umbilical artery 747.5
- ureter 753.29
- uterus 752.3
- vagina 752.49
- vascular (peripheral) NEC (*see also* Hypoplasia, peripheral vascular system) 747.60
  - brain 747.81
- vein(s) (peripheral) NEC (*see also* Hypoplasia, peripheral vascular system) 747.60
  - brain 747.81
  - cardiac 746.89
  - great 747.49
  - portal 747.49
  - pulmonary 747.49
  - vena cava (inferior) (superior) 747.49
- vertebra 756.19
- vulva 752.49
- zonule (ciliary) 743.39
- zygoma 738.12

Hypopotassemia 276.8

Hypoproaccelerinemia — *see also* Defect, coagulation 286.3

Hypoproconvertinemia (congenital) — *see also* Defect, coagulation 286.3

Hypoproteinemia (essential) (hypermetabolic) (idiopathic) 273.8

Hypoproteinosis 260

Hypoprothrombinemia (congenital) (hereditary) (idiopathic) — *see also* Defect, coagulation 286.3
- acquired 286.7
- newborn 776.3

Hypopselaphesia 782.0

Hypopyon (anterior chamber) (eye) 364.05
- iritis 364.05
- ulcer (cornea) 370.04

Hypopyrexia 780.99

Hyporeflex 796.1

Hyporeninemia, extreme 790.99

Hyporeninemia, extreme — *continued*
- in primary aldosteronism 255.10

Hyporesponsive episode 780.09

Hyposecretion
- ACTH 253.4
- ovary 256.39
  - postablative 256.2
- salivary gland (any) 527.7

Hyposegmentation of neutrophils, hereditary 288.2

Hyposiderinemia 280.9

Hyposmolality 276.1
- syndrome 276.1

Hyposomatotropism 253.3

Hyposomnia, unspecified — *see also* Insomnia 780.52
- with sleep apnea, unspecified 780.51

Hypospadias (male) 752.61
- female 753.8

Hypospermatogenesis 606.1

Hyposphagma 372.72

Hyposplenism 289.59

Hypostasis, pulmonary 514

Hypostatic — *see* condition

Hyposthenuria 593.89

Hyposuprarenalism 255.41

Hypo-TBG-nemia 246.8

Hypotension (arterial) (constitutional) 458.9
- chronic 458.1
- iatrogenic 458.29
- maternal, syndrome (following labor and delivery) 669.2 ☑
- of hemodialysis 458.21
- orthostatic (chronic) 458.0
  - dysautonomic-dyskinetic syndrome 333.0
- permanent idiopathic 458.1
- postoperative 458.29
- postural 458.0
- specified type NEC 458.8
- transient 796.3

Hypothermia (accidental) 991.6
- anesthetic 995.89
- associated with low environmental temperature 991.6
- newborn NEC 778.3
- not associated with low environmental temperature 780.65

Hypothymergasia — *see also* Psychosis, affective 296.2 ☑
- recurrent episode 296.3 ☑
- single episode 296.2 ☑

Hypothyroidism (acquired) 244.9
- complicating pregnancy, childbirth, or puerperium 648.1 ☑
- congenital 243
- due to
  - ablation 244.1
    - radioactive iodine 244.1
    - surgical 244.0
  - iodine (administration) (ingestion) 244.2
    - radioactive 244.1
  - irradiation therapy 244.1
  - p-aminosalicylic acid (PAS) 244.3
  - phenylbutazone 244.3
  - resorcinol 244.3
  - specified cause NEC 244.8
  - surgery 244.0
- goitrous (sporadic) 246.1
- iatrogenic NEC 244.3
- iodine 244.2
- pituitary 244.8
- postablative NEC 244.1

Hypothyroidism — *continued*
- postsurgical 244.0
- primary 244.9
- secondary NEC 244.8
- specified cause NEC 244.8
- sporadic goitrous 246.1

Hypotonia, hypotonicity, hypotony 781.3
- benign congenital 358.8
- bladder 596.4
- congenital 779.89
  - benign 358.8
- eye 360.30
  - due to
    - fistula 360.32
    - ocular disorder NEC 360.33
  - following loss of aqueous or vitreous 360.33
  - primary 360.31
- infantile muscular (benign) 359.0
- muscle 728.9
- uterus, uterine (contractions) — *see* Inertia, uterus

Hypotrichosis 704.09
- congenital 757.4
- lid (congenital) 757.4
  - acquired 374.55
- postinfectional NEC 704.09

Hypotropia 378.32

Hypoventilation 786.09
- congenital central alveolar syndrome 327.25
- idiopathic sleep related nonobstructive alveolar 327.24
- sleep related, in conditions classifiable elsewhere 327.26

Hypovitaminosis — *see also* Deficiency, vitamin 269.2

Hypovolemia 276.52
- surgical shock 998.0
- traumatic (shock) 958.4

Hypoxemia — *see also* Anoxia 799.02
- sleep related, in conditions classifiable elsewhere 327.26

Hypoxia — *see also* Anoxia 799.02
- cerebral 348.1
  - during or resulting from a procedure 997.01
  - newborn 770.88
    - mild or moderate 768.6
    - severe 768.5
- fetal, affecting newborn 770.88
- intrauterine — *see* Distress, fetal
- myocardial (*see also* Insufficiency, coronary) 411.89
  - arteriosclerotic — *see* Arteriosclerosis, coronary
- newborn 770.88
- sleep related 327.24

Hypoxic-ischemic encephalopathy (HIE) 768.70 ▲
- mild 768.71 ●
- moderate 768.72 ●
- severe 768.73 ●

Hypsarrhythmia — *see also* Epilepsy 345.6 ☑

Hysteralgia, pregnant uterus 646.8 ☑

Hysteria, hysterical 300.10
- anxiety 300.20
- Charcôt's gland 300.11
- conversion (any manifestation) 300.11
- dissociative type NEC 300.15
- psychosis, acute 298.1

Hysteroepilepsy 300.11

Hysterotomy, affecting fetus or newborn 763.89

☑ Additional Digit Required — Refer to the Tabular List for Digit Selection   ▽ Subterms under main terms may continue to next column or page

2010 ICD-9-CM   ▶◀ Revised Text   ● New Line   ▲ Revised Code   **October 2009 • Volume 2 — 145**

I

Iatrogenic syndrome of excess cortisol 255.0
IBM (inclusion body myositis) 359.71 ●
Iceland disease (epidemic neuromyasthenia) 049.8
Ichthyosis (congenita) 757.1
    acquired 701.1
    fetalis gravior 757.1
    follicularis 757.1
    hystrix 757.39
    lamellar 757.1
    lingual 528.6
    palmaris and plantaris 757.39
    simplex 757.1
    vera 757.1
    vulgaris 757.1
Ichthyotoxism 988.0
    bacterial (see also Poisoning, food) 005.9
Icteroanemia, hemolytic (acquired) 283.9
    congenital (see also Spherocytosis) 282.0
Icterus — see also Jaundice 782.4
    catarrhal — see Icterus, infectious
    conjunctiva 782.4
        newborn 774.6
    epidemic — see Icterus, infectious
    febrilis — see Icterus, infectious
    fetus or newborn — see Jaundice, fetus or newborn
    gravis (see also Necrosis, liver) 570
        complicating pregnancy 646.7 ☑
            affecting fetus or newborn 760.8
        fetus or newborn NEC 773.0
        obstetrical 646.7 ☑
            affecting fetus or newborn 760.8
    hematogenous (acquired) 283.9
    hemolytic (acquired) 283.9
        congenital (see also Spherocytosis) 282.0
    hemorrhagic (acute) 100.0
        leptospiral 100.0
        newborn 776.0
        spirochetal 100.0
    infectious 070.1
        with hepatic coma 070.0
        leptospiral 100.0
        spirochetal 100.0
    intermittens juvenilis 277.4
    malignant (see also Necrosis, liver) 570
    neonatorum (see also Jaundice, fetus or newborn) 774.6
    pernicious (see also Necrosis, liver) 570
    spirochetal 100.0
Ictus solaris, solis 992.0
Ideation
    suicidal V62.84
Identity disorder 313.82
    dissociative 300.14
    gender role (child) 302.6
        adult 302.85
    psychosexual (child) 302.6
        adult 302.85
Idioglossia 307.9
Idiopathic — see condition
Idiosyncrasy — see also Allergy 995.3
    drug, medicinal substance, and biological — see Allergy, drug
Idiot, idiocy (congenital) 318.2
    amaurotic (Bielschowsky) (-Jansky) (family) (infantile) (late) (juvenile) (late) (Vogt-Spielmeyer) 330.1
    microcephalic 742.1
    Mongolian 758.0
    oxycephalic 756.0
Id reaction (due to bacteria) 692.89
IEED (involuntary emotional expression disorder) 310.8
IFIS (intraoperative floppy iris syndrome) 364.81
IgE asthma 493.0 ☑
Ileitis (chronic) — see also Enteritis 558.9
    infectious 009.0
    noninfectious 558.9
    regional (ulcerative) 555.0
        with large intestine 555.2
    segmental 555.0
        with large intestine 555.2
    terminal (ulcerative) 555.0

Ileitis — see also Enteritis — continued
    terminal — continued
        with large intestine 555.2
Ileocolitis — see also Enteritis 558.9
    infectious 009.0
    regional 555.2
    ulcerative 556.1
Ileostomy status V44.2
    with complication 569.60
Ileotyphus 002.0
Ileum — see condition
Ileus (adynamic) (bowel) (colon) (inhibitory) (intestine) (neurogenic) (paralytic) 560.1
    arteriomesenteric duodenal 537.2
    due to gallstone (in intestine) 560.31
    duodenal, chronic 537.2
    following gastrointestinal surgery 997.4
    gallstone 560.31
    mechanical (see also Obstruction, intestine) 560.9
    meconium 777.1
        due to cystic fibrosis 277.01
    myxedema 564.89
    postoperative 997.4
    transitory, newborn 777.4
Iliac — see condition
Iliotibial band friction syndrome 728.89
Illegitimacy V61.6
Ill, louping 063.1
Illness — see also Disease
    factitious 300.19
        with
            combined psychological and physical signs and symptoms 300.19
            predominantly
                physical signs and symptoms 300.19
                psychological symptoms 300.16
        chronic (with physical symptoms) 301.51
    heart — see Disease, heart
    manic-depressive (see also Psychosis, affective) 296.80
    mental (see also Disorder, mental) 300.9
Imbalance 781.2
    autonomic (see also Neuropathy, peripheral, autonomic) 337.9
    electrolyte 276.9
        with
            abortion — see Abortion, by type, with metabolic disorder
            ectopic pregnancy (see also categories 633.0–633.9) 639.4
            hyperemesis gravidarum (before 22 completed weeks gestation) 643.1 ☑
            molar pregnancy (see also categories 630–632) 639.4
        following
            abortion 639.4
            ectopic or molar pregnancy 639.4
        neonatal, transitory NEC 775.5
    endocrine 259.9
    eye muscle NEC 378.9
        heterophoria — see Heterophoria
    glomerulotubular NEC 593.89
    hormone 259.9
    hysterical (see also Hysteria) 300.10
    labyrinth NEC 386.50
    posture 729.90
    sympathetic (see also Neuropathy, peripheral, autonomic) 337.9
Imbecile, imbecility 318.0
    moral 301.7
    old age 290.9
    senile 290.9
    specified IQ — see IQ
    unspecified IQ 318.0
Imbedding, intrauterine device 996.32
Imbibition, cholesterol (gallbladder) 575.6
Imerslund (-Gräsbeck) syndrome (anemia due to familial selective vitamin B_{12} malabsorption) 281.1
Iminoacidopathy 270.8
Iminoglycinuria, familial 270.8
Immature — see also Immaturity
    personality 301.89

Immaturity 765.1 ☑
    extreme 765.0 ☑
    fetus or infant light-for-dates — see Light-for-dates
    lung, fetus or newborn 770.4
    organ or site NEC — see Hypoplasia
    pulmonary, fetus or newborn 770.4
    reaction 301.89
    sexual (female) (male) 259.0
Immersion 994.1
    foot 991.4
    hand 991.4
Immobile, immobility
    complete
        due to severe physical disability or frailty 780.72
    intestine 564.89
    joint — see Ankylosis
    syndrome (paraplegic) 728.3
Immunization
    ABO
        affecting management of pregnancy 656.2 ☑
        fetus or newborn 773.1
    complication — see Complications, vaccination
    Rh factor
        affecting management of pregnancy 656.1 ☑
        fetus or newborn 773.0
        from transfusion 999.7
Immunodeficiency 279.3
    with
        adenosine-deaminase deficiency 279.2
        defect, predominant
            B-cell 279.00
            T-cell 279.10
        hyperimmunoglobulinemia 279.2
        lymphopenia, hereditary 279.2
        thrombocytopenia and eczema 279.12
        thymic
            aplasia 279.2
            dysplasia 279.2
    autosomal recessive, Swiss-type 279.2
    common variable 279.06
    severe combined (SCID) 279.2
    to Rh factor
        affecting management of pregnancy 656.1 ☑
        fetus or newborn 773.0
    X-linked, with increased IgM 279.05
Immunotherapy, prophylactic V07.2
    antineoplastic V58.12
Impaction, impacted
    bowel, colon, rectum 560.30
        with hernia (see also Hernia, by site, with obstruction)
            gangrenous — see Hernia, by site, with gangrene
        by
            calculus 560.39
            gallstone 560.31
        fecal 560.39
        specified type NEC 560.39
    calculus — see Calculus
    cerumen (ear) (external) 380.4
    cuspid 520.6
    dental 520.6
    fecal, feces 560.39
        with hernia (see also Hernia, by site, with obstruction)
            gangrenous — see Hernia, by site, with gangrene
    fracture — see Fracture, by site
    gallbladder — see Cholelithiasis
    gallstone(s) — see Cholelithiasis
        in intestine (any part) 560.31
    intestine(s) 560.30
        with hernia (see also Hernia, by site, with obstruction)
            gangrenous — see Hernia, by site, with gangrene
        by
            calculus 560.39
            gallstone 560.31
        fecal 560.39

Impaction, impacted — continued
    intestine(s) — continued
        specified type NEC 560.39
    intrauterine device (IUD) 996.32
    molar 520.6
    shoulder 660.4 ☑
        affecting fetus or newborn 763.1
    tooth, teeth 520.6
    turbinate 733.99
Impaired, impairment (function)
    arm V49.1
        movement, involving
            musculoskeletal system V49.1
            nervous system V49.2
    auditory discrimination 388.43
    back V48.3
    body (entire) V49.89
    cognitive, mild, so stated 331.83
    combined visual hearing V49.85
    dual sensory V49.85
    glucose
        fasting 790.21
        tolerance test (oral) 790.22
    hearing (see also Deafness) 389.9
        combined with visual impairment V49.85
    heart — see Disease, heart
    kidney (see also Disease, renal) 593.9
        disorder resulting from 588.9
            specified NEC 588.89
    leg V49.1
        movement, involving
            musculoskeletal system V49.1
            nervous system V49.2
    limb V49.1
        movement, involving
            musculoskeletal system V49.1
            nervous system V49.2
    liver 573.8
    mastication 524.9
    mild cognitive, so stated 331.83
    mobility
        ear ossicles NEC 385.22
            incostapedial joint 385.22
            malleus 385.21
    myocardium, myocardial (see also Insufficiency, myocardial) 428.0
    neuromusculoskeletal NEC V49.89
        back V48.3
        head V48.2
        limb V49.2
        neck V48.3
        spine V48.3
        trunk V48.3
    rectal sphincter 787.99
    renal (see also Disease, renal) 593.9
        disorder resulting from 588.9
            specified NEC 588.89
    spine V48.3
    vision NEC 369.9
        both eyes NEC 369.3
        combined with hearing impairment V49.85
        moderate 369.74
            both eyes 369.25
                with impairment of lesser eye (specified as)
                    blind, not further specified 369.15
                    low vision, not further specified 369.23
                near-total 369.17
                profound 369.18
                severe 369.24
                total 369.16
            one eye 369.74
                with vision of other eye (specified as)
                    near-normal 369.75
                    normal 369.76
        near-total 369.64
            both eyes 369.04
                with impairment of lesser eye (specified as)
                    blind, not further specified 369.02
                total 369.03
            one eye 369.64

Impaired, impairment — *continued*
vision — *continued*
near-total — *continued*
one eye — *continued*
with vision of other eye (specified as)
near normal 369.65
normal 369.66
one eye 369.60
with low vision of other eye 369.10
profound 369.67
both eyes 369.08
with impairment of lesser eye (specified as)
blind, not further specified 369.05
near-total 369.07
total 369.06
one eye 369.67
with vision of other eye (specified as)
near-normal 369.68
normal 369.69
severe 369.71
both eyes 369.22
with impairment of lesser eye (specified as)
blind, not further specified 369.11
low vision, not further specified 369.21
near-total 369.13
profound 369.14
total 369.12
one eye 369.71
with vision of other eye (specified as)
near-normal 369.72
normal 369.73
total
both eyes 369.01
one eye 369.61
with vision of other eye (specified as)
near-normal 369.62
normal 369.63
Impaludism — *see* Malaria
Impediment, speech NEC 784.59 ▲
psychogenic 307.9
secondary to organic lesion 784.59 ▲
Impending
cerebrovascular accident or attack 435.9
coronary syndrome 411.1
delirium tremens 291.0
myocardial infarction 411.1
Imperception, auditory (acquired) (congenital) 389.9
Imperfect
aeration, lung (newborn) 770.5
closure (congenital)
alimentary tract NEC 751.8
lower 751.5
upper 750.8
atrioventricular ostium 745.69
atrium (secundum) 745.5
primum 745.61
branchial cleft or sinus 744.41
choroid 743.59
cricoid cartilage 748.3
cusps, heart valve NEC 746.89
pulmonary 746.09
ductus
arteriosus 747.0
Botalli 747.0
ear drum 744.29
causing impairment of hearing 744.03
endocardial cushion 745.60
epiglottis 748.3
esophagus with communication to bronchus or trachea 750.3
Eustachian valve 746.89
eyelid 743.62
face, facial (*see also* Cleft, lip) 749.10
foramen
Botalli 745.5
ovale 745.5

Imperfect — *continued*
closure — *continued*
genitalia, genital organ(s) or system
female 752.89
external 752.49
internal NEC 752.89
uterus 752.3
male 752.89
penis 752.69
glottis 748.3
heart valve (cusps) NEC 746.89
interatrial ostium or septum 745.5
interauricular ostium or septum 745.5
interventricular ostium or septum 745.4
iris 743.46
kidney 753.3
larynx 748.3
lens 743.36
lip (*see also* Cleft, lip) 749.10
nasal septum or sinus 748.1
nose 748.1
omphalomesenteric duct 751.0
optic nerve entry 743.57
organ or site NEC — *see* Anomaly, specified type, by site
ostium
interatrial 745.5
interauricular 745.5
interventricular 745.4
palate (*see also* Cleft, palate) 749.00
preauricular sinus 744.46
retina 743.56
roof of orbit 742.0
sclera 743.47
septum
aortic 745.0
aorticopulmonary 745.0
atrial (secundum) 745.5
primum 745.61
between aorta and pulmonary artery 745.0
heart 745.9
interatrial (secundum) 745.5
primum 745.61
interauricular (secundum) 745.5
primum 745.61
interventricular 745.4
with pulmonary stenosis or atresia, dextraposition of aorta, and hypertrophy of right ventricle 745.2
in tetralogy of Fallot 745.2
nasal 748.1
ventricular 745.4
with pulmonary stenosis or atresia, dextraposition of aorta, and hypertrophy of right ventricle 745.2
in tetralogy of Fallot 745.2
skull 756.0
with
anencephalus 740.0
encephalocele 742.0
hydrocephalus 742.3
with spina bifida (*see also* Spina bifida) 741.0 ☑
microcephalus 742.1
spine (with meningocele) (*see also* Spina bifida) 741.90
thyroid cartilage 748.3
trachea 748.3
tympanic membrane 744.29
causing impairment of hearing 744.03
uterus (with communication to bladder, intestine, or rectum) 752.3
uvula 749.02
with cleft lip (*see also* Cleft, palate, with cleft lip) 749.20
vitelline duct 751.0
development — *see* Anomaly, by site
erection 607.84
fusion — *see* Imperfect, closure
inflation lung (newborn) 770.5
intestinal canal 751.5
poise 729.90
rotation — *see* Malrotation

Imperfect — *continued*
septum, ventricular 745.4
Imperfectly descended testis 752.51
Imperforate (congenital) — *see also* Atresia
anus 751.2
bile duct 751.61
cervix (uteri) 752.49
esophagus 750.3
hymen 752.42
intestine (small) 751.1
large 751.2
jejunum 751.1
pharynx 750.29
rectum 751.2
salivary duct 750.23
urethra 753.6
urinary meatus 753.6
vagina 752.49
Impervious (congenital) — *see also* Atresia
anus 751.2
bile duct 751.61
esophagus 750.3
intestine (small) 751.1
large 751.5
rectum 751.2
urethra 753.6
Impetiginization of other dermatoses 684
Impetigo (any organism) (any site) (bullous) (circinate) (contagiosa) (neonatorum) (simplex) 684
Bockhart's (superficial folliculitis) 704.8
external ear 684 [380.13]
eyelid 684 [373.5]
Fox's (contagiosa) 684
furfuracea 696.5
herpetiformis 694.3
nonobstetrical 694.3
staphylococcal infection 684
ulcerative 686.8
vulgaris 684
Impingement, soft tissue between teeth 524.89
anterior 524.81
posterior 524.82
Implantation
anomalous (*see also* Anomaly, specified type, by site)
ureter 753.4
cyst
external area or site (skin) NEC 709.8
iris 364.61
vagina 623.8
vulva 624.8
dermoid (cyst)
external area or site (skin) NEC 709.8
iris 364.61
vagina 623.8
vulva 624.8
placenta, low or marginal — *see* Placenta previa
Implant, endometrial 617.9
Impotence (sexual) 607.84
organic origin NEC 607.84
psychogenic 302.72
Impoverished blood 285.9
Impression, basilar 756.0
Imprisonment V62.5
Improper
development, infant 764.9 ☑
Improperly tied umbilical cord (causing hemorrhage) 772.3
Impulses, obsessional 300.3
Impulsive 799.23 ▲
neurosis 300.3 ●
Impulsiveness 799.23 ●
Inaction, kidney — *see also* Disease, renal 593.9
Inactive — *see* condition
Inadequate, inadequacy
aesthetics of dental restoration 525.67
biologic 301.6
cardiac and renal — *see* Hypertension, cardiorenal
constitutional 301.6
development
child 783.40
fetus 764.9 ☑

Inadequate, inadequacy — *continued*
development — *continued*
fetus — *continued*
affecting management of pregnancy 656.5 ☑
genitalia
after puberty NEC 259.0
congenital — *see* Hypoplasia, genitalia
lungs 748.5
organ or site NEC — *see* Hypoplasia, by site
dietary 269.9
distance, interarch 524.28
education V62.3
environment
economic problem V60.2
household condition NEC V60.1
poverty V60.2
unemployment V62.0
functional 301.6
household care, due to
family member
handicapped or ill V60.4
temporarily away from home V60.4
on vacation V60.5
technical defects in home V60.1
temporary absence from home of person rendering care V60.4
housing (heating) (space) V60.1
interarch distance 524.28
material resources V60.2
mental (*see also* Retardation, mental) 319
nervous system 799.29 ▲
personality 301.6
prenatal care in current pregnancy V23.7
pulmonary
function 786.09
newborn 770.89
ventilation, newborn 770.89
respiration 786.09
newborn 770.89
sample
cytology
anal 796.78
cervical 795.08
vaginal 795.18
social 301.6
Inanition 263.9
with edema 262
due to
deprivation of food 994.2
malnutrition 263.9
fever 780.60
Inappropriate secretion
ACTH 255.0
antidiuretic hormone (ADH) (excessive) 253.6
deficiency 253.5
ectopic hormone NEC 259.3
pituitary (posterior) 253.6
Inattention after or at birth 995.52
Inborn errors of metabolism — *see* Disorder, metabolism
Incarceration, incarcerated
bubonocele (*see also* Hernia, inguinal, with obstruction)
gangrenous — *see* Hernia, inguinal, with gangrene
colon (by hernia) (*see also* Hernia, by site with obstruction)
gangrenous — *see* Hernia, by site, with gangrene
enterocele 552.9
gangrenous 551.9
epigastrocele 552.29
gangrenous 551.29
epiplocele 552.9
gangrenous 551.9
exomphalos 552.1
gangrenous 551.1
fallopian tube 620.8
hernia (*see also* Hernia, by site, with obstruction)
gangrenous — *see* Hernia, by site, with gangrene
iris, in wound 871.1
lens, in wound 871.1

☑ Additional Digit Required — Refer to the Tabular List for Digit Selection

2010 ICD-9-CM

►◄ Revised Text

● New Line

▲ Revised Code

⟱ Subterms under main terms may continue to next column or page

October 2009 • Volume 2 — 147

Index

Incarceration, incarcerated — Infarct, infarction

Incarceration, incarcerated — continued
  merocele (see also Hernia, femoral, with obstruction) 552.00
  omentum (by hernia) (see also Hernia, by site, with obstruction)
    gangrenous — see Hernia, by site, with gangrene
  omphalocele 756.72 ▲
  rupture (meaning hernia) (see also Hernia, by site, with obstruction) 552.9
    gangrenous (see also Hernia, by site, with gangrene) 551.9
  sarcoepiplocele 552.9
    gangrenous 551.9
  sarcoepiplomphalocele 552.1
    with gangrene 551.1
  uterus 621.8
    gravid 654.3 ☑
      causing obstructed labor 660.2 ☑
      affecting fetus or newborn 763.1
Incident, cerebrovascular — see also Disease, cerebrovascular, acute 436
Incineration (entire body) (from fire, conflagration, electricity, or lightning) — see Burn, multiple, specified sites
Incised wound
  external — see Wound, open, by site
  internal organs (abdomen, chest, or pelvis) — see Injury, internal, by site, with open wound
Incision, incisional
  hernia — see Hernia, incisional
  surgical, complication — see Complications, surgical procedures
  traumatic
    external — see Wound, open, by site
    internal organs (abdomen, chest, or pelvis) — see Injury, internal, by site, with open wound
Inclusion
  azurophilic leukocytic 288.2
  blennorrhea (neonatal) (newborn) 771.6
  cyst — see Cyst, skin
  gallbladder in liver (congenital) 751.69
Incompatibility
  ABO
    affecting management of pregnancy 656.2 ☑
    fetus or newborn 773.1
    infusion or transfusion reaction 999.6
  blood (group) (Duffy) (E) (K(ell)) (Kidd) (Lewis) (M) (N) (P) (S) NEC
    affecting management of pregnancy 656.2 ☑
    fetus or newborn 773.2
    infusion or transfusion reaction 999.8 ▲
  contour of existing restoration of tooth with oral health 525.65
  marital V61.10
    involving
      divorce V61.03
      estrangement V61.09
  Rh (blood group) (factor)
    affecting management of pregnancy 656.1 ☑
    fetus or newborn 773.0
    infusion or transfusion reaction 999.7
  Rhesus — see Incompatibility, Rh
Incompetency, incompetence, incompetent
  annular
    aortic (valve) (see also Insufficiency, aortic) 424.1
    mitral (valve) (see also Insufficiency, mitral) 424.0
    pulmonary valve (heart) (see also Endocarditis, pulmonary) 424.3
  aortic (valve) (see also Insufficiency, aortic) 424.1
    syphilitic 093.22
  cardiac (orifice) 530.0
    valve — see Endocarditis
  cervix, cervical (os) 622.5
    in pregnancy 654.5 ☑
      affecting fetus or newborn 761.0
  chronotropic 426.89

Incompetency, incompetence, incompetent — continued
  chronotropic — continued
    with
      autonomic dysfunction 337.9
      ischemic heart disease 414.9
      left ventricular dysfunction 429.89 ▲
      sinus node dysfunction 427.81
  esophagogastric (junction) (sphincter) 530.0
  heart valve, congenital 746.89
  mitral (valve) — see Insufficiency, mitral
  papillary muscle (heart) 429.81
  pelvic fundus
    pubocervical tissue 618.81
    rectovaginal tissue 618.82
  pulmonary valve (heart) (see also Endocarditis, pulmonary) 424.3
    congenital 746.09
  tricuspid (annular) (rheumatic) (valve) (see also Endocarditis, tricuspid) 397.0
  valvular — see Endocarditis
  vein, venous (saphenous) (varicose) (see also Varicose, vein) 454.9
  velopharyngeal (closure)
    acquired 528.9
    congenital 750.29
Incomplete — see also condition
  bladder emptying 788.21
  expansion lungs (newborn) 770.5
  gestation (liveborn) — see Immaturity
  rotation — see Malrotation
Inconclusive   ●
  image test due to excess body fat 793.91 ●
  mammogram, mammography 793.82 ●
    due to dense breasts 793.82 ●
Incontinence 788.30
  without sensory awareness 788.34
  anal sphincter 787.6
  continuous leakage 788.37
  feces 787.6
    due to hysteria 300.11
    nonorganic origin 307.7
  hysterical 300.11
  mixed (male) (female) (urge and stress) 788.33
  overflow 788.38
  paradoxical 788.39
  rectal 787.6
  specified NEC 788.39
  stress (female) 625.6
    male NEC 788.32
  urethral sphincter 599.84
  urge 788.31
    and stress (male) (female) 788.33
  urine 788.30
    active 788.30
    due to
      cognitive impairment 788.91
      immobility 788.91
      severe physical disability 788.91
    functional 788.91
    male 788.30
      stress 788.32
        and urge 788.33
    neurogenic 788.39
    nonorganic origin 307.6
    stress (female) 625.6
      male NEC 788.32
    urge 788.31
      and stress 788.33
Incontinentia pigmenti 757.33
Incoordinate
  uterus (action) (contractions) 661.4 ☑
    affecting fetus or newborn 763.7
Incoordination
  esophageal-pharyngeal (newborn) 787.24
  muscular 781.3
  papillary muscle 429.81
Increase, increased
  abnormal, in development 783.9
  androgens (ovarian) 256.1
  anticoagulants (antithrombin) (anti-VIIIa) (anti-IXa) (anti-Xa) (anti-XIa) 286.5
    postpartum 666.3 ☑
  cold sense (see also Disturbance, sensation) 782.0

Increase, increased — continued
  estrogen 256.0
  function
    adrenal (cortex) 255.3
      medulla 255.6
    pituitary (anterior) (gland) (lobe) 253.1
      posterior 253.6
  heat sense (see also Disturbance, sensation) 782.0
  intracranial pressure 781.99
    injury at birth 767.8
  light reflex of retina 362.13
  permeability, capillary 448.9
  pressure
    intracranial 781.99
      injury at birth 767.8
    intraocular 365.00
  pulsations 785.9
  pulse pressure 785.9
  sphericity, lens 743.36
  splenic activity 289.4
  venous pressure 459.89
    portal 572.3
Incrustation, cornea, lead or zinc 930.0
Incyclophoria 378.44
Incyclotropia 378.33
Indeterminate sex 752.7
India rubber skin 756.83
Indicanuria 270.2
Indigestion (bilious) (functional) 536.8
  acid 536.8
  catarrhal 536.8
  due to decomposed food NEC 005.9
  fat 579.8
  nervous 306.4
  psychogenic 306.4
Indirect — see condition
Indolent bubo NEC 099.8
Induced
  abortion — see Abortion, induced
  birth, affecting fetus or newborn 763.89
  delivery — see Delivery
  labor — see Delivery
Induration, indurated
  brain 348.89   ▲
  breast (fibrous) 611.79
    puerperal, postpartum 676.3 ☑
  broad ligament 620.8
  chancre 091.0
    anus 091.1
    congenital 090.0
    extragenital NEC 091.2
  corpora cavernosa (penis) (plastic) 607.89
  liver (chronic) 573.8
    acute 573.8
  lung (black) (brown) (chronic) (fibroid) (see also Fibrosis, lung) 515
    essential brown 275.0 [516.1]
  penile 607.89
  phlebitic — see Phlebitis
  skin 782.8
  stomach 537.89
Induratio penis plastica 607.89
Industrial — see condition
Inebriety — see also Abuse, drugs, nondependent 305.0 ☑
Inefficiency
  kidney (see also Disease, renal) 593.9
  thyroid (acquired) (gland) 244.9
Inelasticity, skin 782.8
Inequality, leg (acquired) (length) 736.81
  congenital 755.30
Inertia
  bladder 596.4
    neurogenic 596.54
      with cauda equina syndrome 344.61
  stomach 536.8
    psychogenic 306.4
  uterus, uterine 661.2 ☑
    affecting fetus or newborn 763.7
    primary 661.0 ☑
    secondary 661.1 ☑
  vesical 596.4
    neurogenic 596.54
      with cauda equina 344.61
Infant — see also condition

Infant — see also condition — continued
  excessive crying of 780.92
  fussy (baby) 780.91
  held for adoption V68.89
  newborn — see Newborn
  post-term (gestation period over 40 completed weeks to 42 completed weeks) 766.21
  prolonged gestation of (period over 42 completed weeks) 766.22
  syndrome of diabetic mother 775.0
"Infant Hercules" syndrome 255.2
Infantile — see also condition
  genitalia, genitals 259.0
    in pregnancy or childbirth NEC 654.4 ☑
      affecting fetus or newborn 763.89
      causing obstructed labor 660.2 ☑
        affecting fetus or newborn 763.1
  heart 746.9
  kidney 753.3
  lack of care 995.52
  macula degeneration 362.75
  melanodontia 521.05
  os, uterus (see also Infantile, genitalia) 259.0
  pelvis 738.6
    with disproportion (fetopelvic) 653.1 ☑
      affecting fetus or newborn 763.1
      causing obstructed labor 660.1 ☑
        affecting fetus or newborn 763.1
  penis 259.0
  testis 257.2
  uterus (see also Infantile, genitalia) 259.0
  vulva 752.49
Infantilism 259.9
  with dwarfism (hypophyseal) 253.3
  Brissaud's (infantile myxedema) 244.9
  celiac 579.0
  Herter's (nontropical sprue) 579.0
  hypophyseal 253.3
  hypothalamic (with obesity) 253.8
  idiopathic 259.9
  intestinal 579.0
  pancreatic 577.8
  pituitary 253.3
  renal 588.0
  sexual (with obesity) 259.0
Infants, healthy liveborn — see Newborn
Infarct, infarction
  adrenal (capsule) (gland) 255.41
  amnion 658.8 ☑
  anterior (with contiguous portion of intraventricular septum) NEC (see also Infarct, myocardium) 410.1 ☑
  appendices epiploicae 557.0
  bowel 557.0
  brain (stem) 434.91
    embolic (see also Embolism, brain) 434.11
    healed or old without residuals V12.54
    iatrogenic 997.02
    lacunar 434.91
    late effect — see Late effect(s) (of) cerebrovascular disease
    postoperative 997.02
    puerperal, postpartum, childbirth 674.0 ☑
    thrombotic (see also Thrombosis, brain) 434.01
  breast 611.89
  Brewer's (kidney) 593.81
  cardiac (see also Infarct, myocardium) 410.9 ☑
  cerebellar (see also Infarct, brain) 434.91
    embolic (see also Embolism, brain) 434.11
  cerebral (see also Infarct, brain) 434.91
    aborted 434.91
    embolic (see also Embolism, brain) 434.11
    thrombotic (see also Infarct, brain) 434.01
  chorion 658.8 ☑
  colon (acute) (agnogenic) (embolic) (hemorrhagic) (nonocclusive) (nonthrombotic) (occlusive) (segmental) (thrombotic) (with gangrene) 557.0
  coronary artery (see also Infarct, myocardium) 410.9 ☑
  cortical 434.91
  embolic (see also Embolism) 444.9
  fallopian tube 620.8
  gallbladder 575.8

☑ Additional Digit Required — Refer to the Tabular List for Digit Selection   ▽ Subterms under main terms may continue to next column or page

148 — Volume 2 • October 2009   ►◄ Revised Text   ● New Line   ▲ Revised Code   2010 ICD-9-CM

Infarct, infarction — *continued*

  heart (*see also* Infarct, myocardium) 410.9 ☑

  hepatic 573.4

  hypophysis (anterior lobe) 253.8

  impending (myocardium) 411.1

  intestine (acute) (agnogenic) (embolic) (hemorrhagic) (nonocclusive) (nonthrombotic) (occlusive) (thrombotic) (with gangrene) 557.0

  kidney 593.81

  lacunar 434.91

  liver 573.4

  lung (embolic) (thrombotic) 415.19

    with

      abortion — *see* Abortion, by type, with, embolism

      ectopic pregnancy (*see also* categories 633.0–633.9) 639.6

      molar pregnancy (*see also* categories 630–632) 639.6

    following

      abortion 639.6

      ectopic or molar pregnancy 639.6

    iatrogenic 415.11

    in pregnancy, childbirth, or puerperium — *see* Embolism, obstetrical

    postoperative 415.11

    septic 415.12

  lymph node or vessel 457.8

  medullary (brain) — *see* Infarct, brain

  meibomian gland (eyelid) 374.85

  mesentery, mesenteric (embolic) (thrombotic) (with gangrene) 557.0

  midbrain — *see* Infarct, brain

  myocardium, myocardial (acute or with a stated duration of 8 weeks or less) (with hypertension) 410.9 ☑

> *Note* — *Use the following fifth-digit subclassification with category 410:*
>
> 0   *episode unspecified*
>
> 1   *initial episode*
>
> 2   *subsequent episode without recurrence*

    with symptoms after 8 weeks from date of infarction 414.8

    anterior (wall) (with contiguous portion of intraventricular septum) NEC 410.1 ☑

    anteroapical (with contiguous portion of intraventricular septum) 410.1 ☑

    anterolateral (wall) 410.0 ☑

    anteroseptal (with contiguous portion of intraventricular septum) 410.1 ☑

    apical-lateral 410.5 ☑

    atrial 410.8 ☑

    basal-lateral 410.5 ☑

    chronic (with symptoms after 8 weeks from date of infarction) 414.8

    diagnosed on ECG, but presenting no symptoms 412

    diaphragmatic wall (with contiguous portion of intraventricular septum) 410.4 ☑

    healed or old, currently presenting no symptoms 412

    high lateral 410.5 ☑

    impending 411.1

    inferior (wall) (with contiguous portion of intraventricular septum) 410.4 ☑

    inferolateral (wall) 410.2 ☑

    inferoposterior wall 410.3 ☑

    intraoperative 997.1

    lateral wall 410.5 ☑

    non-Q wave 410.7 ☑

    non-ST elevation (NSTEMI)

    nontransmural 410.7 ☑

    papillary muscle 410.8 ☑

    past (diagnosed on ECG or other special investigation, but currently presenting no symptoms) 412

      with symptoms NEC 414.8

    posterior (strictly) (true) (wall) 410.6 ☑

    posterobasal 410.6 ☑

Infarct, infarction — *continued*

  myocardium, myocardial — *continued*

    posteroinferior 410.3 ☑

    posterolateral 410.5 ☑

    postprocedural 997.1

    previous, currently presenting no symptoms 412

    Q wave (*see also* Infarct, myo-cardium, by site) 410.9 ☑

    septal 410.8 ☑

    specified site NEC 410.8 ☑

    ST elevation (STEMI) 410.9 ☑

      anterior (wall) 410.1 ☑

      anterolateral (wall) 410.0 ☑

      inferior (wall) 410.4 ☑

      inferolateral (wall) 410.2 ☑

      inferoposterior wall 410.3 ☑

      lateral wall 410.5 ☑

      posterior (strictly) (true) (wall) 410.6 ☑

      specified site NEC 410.8 ☑

    subendocardial 410.7 ☑

    syphilitic 093.82

    non-ST elevation myocardial infarction (NSTEMI) 410.7 ☑

  nontransmural 410.7 ☑

  omentum 557.0

  ovary 620.8

  pancreas 577.8

  papillary muscle (*see also* Infarct, myocardium) 410.8 ☑

  parathyroid gland 252.8

  pituitary (gland) 253.8

  placenta (complicating pregnancy) 656.7 ☑

    affecting fetus or newborn 762.2

  pontine — *see* Infarct, brain

  posterior NEC (*see also* Infarct, myocardium) 410.6 ☑

  prostate 602.8

  pulmonary (artery) (hemorrhagic) (vein) 415.19

    with

      abortion — *see* Abortion, by type, with embolism

      ectopic pregnancy (*see also* categories 633.0–633.9) 639.6

      molar pregnancy (*see also* categories 630–632) 639.6

    following

      abortion 639.6

      ectopic or molar pregnancy 639.6

    iatrogenic 415.11

    in pregnancy, childbirth, or puerperium — *see* Embolism, obstetrical

    postoperative 415.11

    septic 415.12

  renal 593.81

    embolic or thrombotic 593.81

  retina, retinal 362.84

    with occlusion — *see* Occlusion, retina

  spinal (acute) (cord) (embolic) (nonembolic) 336.1

  spleen 289.59

    embolic or thrombotic 444.89

  subchorionic — *see* Infarct, placenta

  subendocardial (*see also* Infarct, myocardium) 410.7 ☑

  suprarenal (capsule) (gland) 255.41

  syncytium — *see* Infarct, placenta

  testis 608.83

  thrombotic (*see also* Thrombosis) 453.9

    artery, arterial — *see* Embolism

  thyroid (gland) 246.3

  ventricle (heart) (*see also* Infarct, myocardium) 410.9 ☑

Infecting — *see* condition

Infection, infected, infective (opportunistic) 136.9

  with lymphangitis — *see* Lymphangitis

  abortion — *see* Abortion, by type, with, sepsis

  abscess (skin) — *see* Abscess, by site

  Absidia 117.7

  acanthamoeba 136.21

  Acanthocheilonema (perstans) 125.4

    streptocerca 125.6

  accessory sinus (chronic) (*see also* Sinusitis) 473.9

  Achorion — *see* Dermatophytosis

Infection, infected, infective — *continued*

  Acremonium falciforme 117.4

  acromioclavicular (joint) 711.91

  actinobacillus

    lignieresii 027.8

    mallei 024

    muris 026.1

  actinomadura — *see* Actinomycosis

  Actinomyces (israelii) (*see also* Actinomycosis)

    muris-ratti 026.1

  Actinomycetales (actinomadura) (Actinomyces) (Nocardia) (Streptomyces) — *see* Actinomycosis

  actinomycotic NEC (*see also* Actinomycosis) 039.9

  adenoid (chronic) 474.01

    acute 463

    and tonsil (chronic) 474.02

      acute or subacute 463

  adenovirus NEC 079.0

    in diseases classified elsewhere — *see* category 079 ☑

    unspecified nature or site 079.0

  Aerobacter aerogenes NEC 041.85

    enteritis 008.2

  aerogenes capsulatus (*see also* Gangrene, gas) 040.0

  aertrycke (*see also* Infection, Salmonella) 003.9

  ajellomyces dermatitidis 116.0

  alimentary canal NEC (*see also* Enteritis, due to, by organism) 009.0

  Allescheria boydii 117.6

  Alternaria 118

  alveolus, alveolar (process) (pulpal origin) 522.4

  ameba, amebic (histolytica) (*see also* Amebiasis) 006.9

    acute 006.0

    chronic 006.1

    free-living 136.29

    hartmanni 007.8

    specified

      site NEC 006.8

      type NEC 007.8

  amniotic fluid or cavity 658.4 ☑

    affecting fetus or newborn 762.7

  anaerobes (cocci) (gram-negative) (gram-positive) (mixed) NEC 041.84

  anal canal 569.49

  Ancylostoma braziliense 126.2

  Angiostrongylus cantonensis 128.8

  anisakiasis 127.1

  Anisakis larva 127.1

  anthrax (*see also* Anthrax) 022.9

  antrum (chronic) (*see also* Sinusitis, maxillary) 473.0

  anus (papillae) (sphincter) 569.49

  arbor virus NEC 066.9

  arbovirus NEC 066.9

  argentophil-rod 027.0

  Ascaris lumbricoides 127.0

  ascomycetes 117.4

  Aspergillus (flavus) (fumigatus) (terreus) 117.3

  atypical

    acid-fast (bacilli) (*see also* Mycobacterium, atypical) 031.9

    mycobacteria (*see also* Mycobacterium, atypical) 031.9

  auditory meatus (circumscribed) (diffuse) (external) (*see also* Otitis, externa) 380.10

  auricle (ear) (*see also* Otitis, externa) 380.10

  axillary gland 683

  Babesiasis 088.82

  Babesiosis 088.82

  Bacillus NEC 041.89

    abortus 023.1

    anthracis (*see also* Anthrax) 022.9

    cereus (food poisoning) 005.89

    coli — *see* Infection, Escherichia coli

    coliform NEC 041.85

    Ducrey's (any location) 099.0

    Flexner's 004.1

    Friedländer's NEC 041.3

    fusiformis 101

    gas (gangrene) (*see also* Gangrene, gas) 040.0

Infection, infected, infective — *continued*

  Bacillus — *continued*

    mallei 024

    melitensis 023.0

    paratyphoid, paratyphosus 002.9

      A 002.1

      B 002.2

      C 002.3

    Schmorl's 040.3

    Shiga 004.0

    suipestifer (*see also* Infection, Salmonella) 003.9

    swimming pool 031.1

    typhosa 002.0

    welchii (*see also* Gangrene, gas) 040.0

    Whitmore's 025

  bacterial NEC 041.9

    specified NEC 041.89

      anaerobic NEC 041.84

      gram-negative NEC 041.85

        anaerobic NEC 041.84

  Bacterium

    paratyphosum 002.9

      A 002.1

      B 002.2

      C 002.3

    typhosum 002.0

  Bacteroides (fragilis) (melaninogenicus) (oralis) NEC 041.82

  balantidium coli 007.0

  Bartholin's gland 616.89

  Basidiobolus 117.7

  Bedsonia 079.98

    specified NEC 079.88

  bile duct 576.1

  bladder (*see also* Cystitis) 595.9

  Blastomyces, blastomycotic 116.0

    brasiliensis 116.1

    dermatitidis 116.0

    European 117.5

    loboi 116.2

    North American 116.0

    South American 116.1

  bleb

    postprocedural 379.60

      stage 1 379.61

      stage 2 379.62

      stage 3 379.63

  blood stream — *see also* Septicemia

    catheter-related (CRBSI) 999.31

  bone 730.9 ☑

    specified — *see* Osteomyelitis

  Bordetella 033.9

    bronchiseptica 033.8

    parapertussis 033.1

    pertussis 033.0

  Borrelia

    bergdorfi 088.81

    vincentii (mouth) (pharynx) (tonsil) 101

  bovine stomatitis 059.11

  brain (*see also* Encephalitis) 323.9

    late effect — *see* category 326

    membranes (*see also* Meningitis) 322.9

    septic 324.0

      late effect — *see* category 326

      meninges (*see also* Meningitis) 320.9

  branchial cyst 744.42

  breast 611.0

    puerperal, postpartum 675.2 ☑

      with nipple 675.9 ☑

        specified type NEC 675.8 ☑

      nonpurulent 675.2 ☑

      purulent 675.1 ☑

  bronchus (*see also* Bronchitis) 490

    fungus NEC 117.9

  Brucella 023.9

    abortus 023.1

    canis 023.3

    melitensis 023.0

    mixed 023.8

    suis 023.2

  Brugia (Wuchereria) malayi 125.1

  bursa — *see* Bursitis

  buttocks (skin) 686.9

  Candida (albicans) (tropicalis) (*see also* Candidiasis) 112.9

☑ Additional Digit Required — Refer to the Tabular List for Digit Selection   ▽ Subterms under main terms may continue to next column or page

2010 ICD-9-CM   ▶◀ Revised Text   ● New Line   ▲ Revised Code   **Volume 2 — 149**

✱ Gram-negative infections are ordinarily more severe and require more intensive care than gram-positive infections. (handwritten)

Infection, infected, infective — *continued*
Candida (*see also* Candidiasis) — *continued*
  congenital 771.7
Candiru 136.8
Capillaria
  hepatica 128.8
  philippinensis 127.5
cartilage 733.99
catheter-related bloodstream (CRBSI) 999.31
cat liver fluke 121.0
cellulitis — *see* Cellulitis, by site
Cephalosporum falciforme 117.4
Cercomonas hominis (intestinal) 007.3
cerebrospinal (*see also* Meningitis) 322.9
  late effect — *see* category 326
cervical gland 683
cervix (*see also* Cervicitis) 616.0
cesarean section wound 674.3 ☑
Chilomastix (intestinal) 007.8
Chlamydia 079.98
  specified NEC 079.88
cholera (*see also* Cholera) 001.9
chorionic plate 658.8 ☑
Cladosporium
  bantianum 117.8
  carrionii 117.2
  mansoni 111.1
  trichoides 117.8
  wernecki 111.1
Clonorchis (sinensis) (liver) 121.1
Clostridium (haemolyticum) (novyi) NEC 041.84
  botulinum 005.1
  histolyticum (*see also* Gangrene, gas) 040.0
  oedematiens (*see also* Gangrene, gas) 040.0
  perfringens 041.83
    due to food 005.2
  septicum (*see also* Gangrene, gas) 040.0
  sordellii (*see also* Gangrene, gas) 040.0
  welchii (*see also* Gangrene, gas) 040.0
    due to food 005.2
Coccidioides (immitis) (*see also* Coccidioidomycosis) 114.9
coccus NEC 041.89
colon (*see also* Enteritis, due to, by organism) 009.0
  bacillus — *see* Infection, Escherichia coli
colostomy or enterostomy 569.61
common duct 576.1
complicating pregnancy, childbirth, or puerperium NEC 647.9 ☑
  affecting fetus or newborn 760.2
Condiobolus 117.7
congenital NEC 771.89
  Candida albicans 771.7
  chronic 771.2
  cytomegalovirus 771.1
  hepatitis, viral 771.2
  herpes simplex 771.2
  listeriosis 771.2
  malaria 771.2
  poliomyelitis 771.2
  rubella 771.0
  toxoplasmosis 771.2
  tuberculosis 771.2
  urinary (tract) 771.82
  vaccinia 771.2
coronavirus 079.89
  SARS-associated 079.82
corpus luteum (*see also* Salpingo-oophoritis) 614.2
Corynebacterium diphtheriae — *see* Diphtheria
cotia virus 059.8
Coxsackie (*see also* Coxsackie) 079.2
  endocardium 074.22
  heart NEC 074.20
  in diseases classified elsewhere — *see* category 079 ☑
  meninges 047.0
  myocardium 074.23
  pericardium 074.21
  pharynx 074.0
  specified disease NEC 074.8
  unspecified nature or site 079.2

Infection, infected, infective — *continued*
Cryptococcus neoformans 117.5
Cryptosporidia 007.4
Cunninghamella 117.7
cyst — *see* Cyst
Cysticercus cellulosae 123.1
cytomegalovirus 078.5
  congenital 771.1
dental (pulpal origin) 522.4
deuteromycetes 117.4
Dicrocoelium dendriticum 121.8
Dipetalonema (perstans) 125.4
  streptocerca 125.6
diphtherial — *see* Diphtheria
Diphyllobothrium (adult) (latum) (pacificum) 123.4
  larval 123.5
Diplogonoporus (grandis) 123.8
Dipylidium (caninum) 123.8
Dirofilaria 125.6
dog tapeworm 123.8
Dracunculus medinensis 125.7
Dreschlera 118
  hawaiiensis 117.8
Ducrey's bacillus (any site) 099.0
due to or resulting from
  central venous catheter 999.31
  device, implant, or graft (any) (presence of) — *see* Complications, infection and inflammation, due to (presence of) any device, implant, or graft classified to 996.0–996.5 NEC
  injection, inoculation, infusion, transfusion, or vaccination (prophylactic) (therapeutic) 999.39
  injury NEC — *see* Wound, open, by site, complicated
  surgery 998.59
duodenum 535.6 ☑
ear (*see also* Otitis)
  external (*see also* Otitis, externa) 380.10
  inner (*see also* Labyrinthitis) 386.30
  middle — *see* Otitis, media
Eaton's agent NEC 041.81
Eberthella typhosa 002.0
Ebola 078.89
echinococcosis 122.9
Echinococcus (*see also* Echinococcus) 122.9
Echinostoma 121.8
ECHO virus 079.1
  in diseases classified elsewhere — *see* category 079 ☑
  unspecified nature or site 079.1
Ehrlichiosis 082.40
  chaffeensis 082.41
  specified type NEC 082.49
Endamoeba — *see* Infection, ameba
endocardium (*see also* Endocarditis) 421.0
endocervix (*see also* Cervicitis) 616.0
Entamoeba — *see* Infection, ameba
enteric (*see also* Enteritis, due to, by organism) 009.0
Enterobacter aerogenes NEC 041.85
Enterobacter sakazakii 041.85
Enterobius vermicularis 127.4
enterococcus NEC 041.04
enterovirus NEC 079.89
  central nervous system NEC 048
  enteritis 008.67
  meningitis 047.9
Entomophthora 117.7
Epidermophyton — *see* Dermatophytosis
epidermophytosis — *see* Dermatophytosis
episiotomy 674.3 ☑
Epstein-Barr virus 075
  chronic 780.79 [139.8]
erysipeloid 027.1
Erysipelothrix (insidiosa) (rhusiopathiae) 027.1
erythema infectiosum 057.0
Escherichia coli NEC 041.4
  enteritis — *see* Enteritis, E. coli
  generalized 038.42
  intestinal — *see* Enteritis, E. coli
esophagostomy 530.86
ethmoidal (chronic) (sinus) (*see also* Sinusitis, ethmoidal) 473.2

Infection, infected, infective — *continued*
Eubacterium 041.84
Eustachian tube (ear) 381.50
  acute 381.51
  chronic 381.52
exanthema subitum (*see also* Exanthem subitum) 058.10
external auditory canal (meatus) (*see also* Otitis, externa) 380.10
eye NEC 360.00
eyelid 373.9
  specified NEC 373.8
fallopian tube (*see also* Salpingo-oophoritis) 614.2
fascia 728.89
Fasciola
  gigantica 121.3
  hepatica 121.3
Fasciolopsis (buski) 121.4
fetus (intra-amniotic) — *see* Infection, congenital
filarial — *see* Infestation, filarial
finger (skin) 686.9
  abscess (with lymphangitis) 681.00
    pulp 681.01
  cellulitis (with lymphangitis) 681.00
  distal closed space (with lymphangitis) 681.00
  nail 681.02
    fungus 110.1
fish tapeworm 123.4
  larval 123.5
flagellate, intestinal 007.9
fluke — *see* Infestation, fluke
focal
  teeth (pulpal origin) 522.4
  tonsils 474.00
    and adenoids 474.02
Fonsecaea
  compactum 117.2
  pedrosoi 117.2
food (*see also* Poisoning, food) 005.9
foot (skin) 686.9
  fungus 110.4
Francisella tularensis (*see also* Tularemia) 021.9
frontal sinus (chronic) (*see also* Sinusitis, frontal) 473.1
fungus NEC 117.9
  beard 110.0
  body 110.5
  dermatiacious NEC 117.8
  foot 110.4
  groin 110.3
  hand 110.2
  nail 110.1
  pathogenic to compromised host only 118
  perianal (area) 110.3
  scalp 110.0
  scrotum 110.8
  skin 111.9
    foot 110.4
    hand 110.2
  toenails 110.1
  trachea 117.9
Fusarium 118
Fusobacterium 041.84
gallbladder (*see also* Cholecystitis, acute) 575.0
Gardnerella vaginalis 041.89
gas bacillus (*see also* Gas, gangrene) 040.0
gastric (*see also* Gastritis) 535.5 ☑
Gastrodiscoides hominis 121.8
gastroenteric (*see also* Enteritis, due to, by organism) 009.0
gastrointestinal (*see also* Enteritis, due to, by organism) 009.0
gastrostomy 536.41
generalized NEC (*see also* Septicemia) 038.9
genital organ or tract NEC
  female 614.9
    with
      abortion — *see* Abortion, by type, with sepsis
      ectopic pregnancy (*see also* categories 633.0–633.9) 639.0
      molar pregnancy (*see also* categories 630–632) 639.0

Infection, infected, infective — *continued*
genital organ or tract — *continued*
  female — *continued*
    complicating pregnancy 646.6 ☑
      affecting fetus or newborn 760.8
    following
      abortion 639.0
      ectopic or molar pregnancy 639.0
    puerperal, postpartum, childbirth 670.8 ☑ ▲
    minor or localized 646.6 ☑
      affecting fetus or newborn 760.8
  male 608.4
genitourinary tract NEC 599.0
Ghon tubercle, primary (*see also* Tuberculosis) 010.0 ☑
Giardia lamblia 007.1
gingival (chronic) 523.10
  acute 523.00
  Vincent's 101
glanders 024
Glenosporopsis amazonica 116.2
Gnathostoma spinigerum 128.1
Gongylonema 125.6
gonococcal NEC (*see also* Gonococcus) 098.0
✱ gram-negative bacilli NEC 041.85
  anaerobic 041.84
guinea worm 125.7
gum (*see also* Infection, gingival) 523.10
Hantavirus 079.81
heart 429.89
Helicobacter pylori [H. pylori] 041.86
helminths NEC 128.9
  intestinal 127.9
    mixed (types classifiable to more than one category in 120.0–127.7) 127.8
    specified type NEC 127.7
  specified type NEC 128.8
Hemophilus influenzae NEC 041.5
  generalized 038.41
herpes (simplex) (*see also* Herpes, simplex) 054.9
  congenital 771.2
  zoster (*see also* Herpes, zoster) 053.9
    eye NEC 053.29
Heterophyes heterophyes 121.6
Histoplasma (*see also* Histoplasmosis) 115.90
  capsulatum (*see also* Histoplasmosis, American) 115.00
  duboisii (*see also* Histoplasmosis, African) 115.10
HIV V08
  with symptoms, symptomatic 042
hookworm (*see also* Ancylostomiasis) 126.9
human herpesvirus NEC 058.89
human herpesvirus 6 058.81
human herpesvirus 7 058.82
human herpesvirus 8 058.89
human immunodeficiency virus V08
  with symptoms, symptomatic 042
human papillomavirus 079.4
hydrocele 603.1
hydronephrosis 591
Hymenolepis 123.6
hypopharynx 478.29
inguinal glands 683
  due to soft chancre 099.0
intestine, intestinal (*see also* Enteritis, due to, by organism) 009.0
intrauterine (*see also* Endometritis) 615.9
  complicating delivery 646.6 ☑
isospora belli or hominis 007.2
Japanese B encephalitis 062.0
jaw (bone) (acute) (chronic) (lower) (subacute) (upper) 526.4
joint — *see* Arthritis, infectious or infective
Kaposi's sarcoma-associated herpesvirus 058.89
kidney (cortex) (hematogenous) 590.9
  with
    abortion — *see* Abortion, by type, with urinary tract infection
    calculus 592.0

Infection, infected, infective — continued
kidney — continued
  with — continued
    ectopic pregnancy (see also categories
      633.0–633.9) 639.8
    molar pregnancy (see also categories
      630–632) 639.8
  complicating pregnancy or puerperium
    646.6 ☑
    affecting fetus or newborn 760.1
  following
    abortion 639.8
    ectopic or molar pregnancy 639.8
  pelvis and ureter 590.3
Klebsiella pneumoniae NEC 041.3
knee (skin) NEC 686.9
  joint — see Arthritis, infectious
Koch's (see also Tuberculosis, pulmonary)
  011.9 ☑
labia (majora) (minora) (see also Vulvitis)
  616.10
lacrimal
  gland (see also Dacryoadenitis) 375.00
  passages (duct) (sac) (see also Dacryocysti-
    tis) 375.30
larynx NEC 478.79
leg (skin) NEC 686.9
Leishmania (see also Leishmaniasis) 085.9
  braziliensis 085.5
  donovani 085.0
  ethiopica 085.3
  furunculosa 085.1
  infantum 085.0
  mexicana 085.4
  tropica (minor) 085.1
    major 085.2
Leptosphaeria senegalensis 117.4
leptospira (see also Leptospirosis) 100.9
  Australis 100.89
  Bataviae 100.89
  pyrogenes 100.89
  specified type NEC 100.89
leptospirochetal NEC (see also Leptospirosis)
  100.9
Leptothrix — see Actinomycosis
Listeria monocytogenes (listeriosis) 027.0
  congenital 771.2
liver fluke — see Infestation, fluke, liver
Loa loa 125.2
  eyelid 125.2 [373.6]
Loboa loboi 116.2
local, skin (staphylococcal) (streptococcal) NEC
  686.9
  abscess — see Abscess, by site
  cellulitis — see Cellulitis, by site
  ulcer (see also Ulcer, skin) 707.9
Loefflerella
  mallei 024
  whitmori 025
lung 518.89
  atypical Mycobacterium 031.0
    tuberculous (see also Tuberculosis,
      pulmonary) 011.9 ☑
  basilar 518.89
  chronic 518.89
  fungus NEC 117.9
  spirochetal 104.8
  virus — see Pneumonia, virus
lymph gland (axillary) (cervical) (inguinal) 683
  mesenteric 289.2
lymphoid tissue, base of tongue or posterior
  pharynx, NEC 474.00
madurella
  grisea 117.4
  mycetomii 117.4
major
  with
    abortion — see Abortion, by type, with
      sepsis
    ectopic pregnancy (see also categories
      633.0–633.9) 639.0
    molar pregnancy (see also categories
      630–632) 639.0
  following
    abortion 639.0
    ectopic or molar pregnancy 639.0

Infection, infected, infective — continued
major — continued
  puerperal, postpartum, childbirth 670.0 ☑
Malassezia furfur 111.0
Malleomyces
  mallei 024
  pseudomallei 025
mammary gland 611.0
  puerperal, postpartum 675.2 ☑
Mansonella (ozzardi) 125.5
mastoid (suppurative) — see Mastoiditis
maxilla, maxillary 526.4
  sinus (chronic) (see also Sinusitis, maxillary)
    473.0
mediastinum 519.2
medina 125.7
meibomian
  cyst 373.12
  gland 373.12
melioidosis 025
meninges (see also Meningitis) 320.9
meningococcal (see also condition) 036.9
  brain 036.1
  cerebrospinal 036.0
  endocardium 036.42
  generalized 036.2
  meninges 036.0
  meningococcemia 036.2
  specified site NEC 036.89
mesenteric lymph nodes or glands NEC 289.2
Metagonimus 121.5
metatarsophalangeal 711.97
methicillin
  resistant Staphylococcus aureus (MRSA)
    041.12
  susceptible Staphylococcus aureus (MSSA)
    041.11
microorganism resistant to drugs — see Resistance (to), drugs by microorganisms
Microsporidia 136.8
microsporum, microsporic — see Dermatophytosis
Mima polymorpha NEC 041.85
mixed flora NEC 041.89
Monilia (see also Candidiasis) 112.9
  neonatal 771.7
monkeypox 059.01
Monosporium apiospermum 117.6
mouth (focus) NEC 528.9
  parasitic 136.9
MRSA (methicillin resistant Staphylococcus
  aureus) 041.12
MSSA (methicillin susceptible Staphylococcus
  aureus) 041.11
Mucor 117.7
muscle NEC 728.89
mycelium NEC 117.9
mycetoma
  actinomycotic NEC (see also Actinomyco-
    sis) 039.9
  mycotic NEC 117.4
Mycobacterium, mycobacterial (see also Mycobacterium) 031.9
Mycoplasma NEC 041.81
mycotic NEC 117.9
  pathogenic to compromised host only 118
  skin NEC 111.9
  systemic 117.9
myocardium NEC 422.90
nail (chronic) (with lymphangitis) 681.9
  finger 681.02
    fungus 110.1
    ingrowing 703.0
  toe 681.11
    fungus 110.1
nasal sinus (chronic) (see also Sinusitis) 473.9
nasopharynx (chronic) 478.29
  acute 460
navel 686.9
  newborn 771.4
Neisserian — see Gonococcus
Neotestudina rosatii 117.4
newborn, generalized 771.89
nipple 611.0
  puerperal, postpartum 675.0 ☑
    with breast 675.9 ☑

Infection, infected, infective — continued
nipple — continued
  puerperal, postpartum — continued
    with breast — continued
      specified type NEC 675.8 ☑
Nocardia — see Actinomycosis
nose 478.19
nostril 478.19
obstetrical surgical wound 674.3 ☑
Oesophagostomum (apiostomum) 127.7
Oestrus ovis 134.0
Oidium albicans (see also Candidiasis) 112.9
Onchocerca (volvulus) 125.3
  eye 125.3 [360.13]
  eyelid 125.3 [373.6]
  operation wound 998.59
Opisthorchis (felineus) (tenuicollis) (viverrini)
  121.0
orbit 376.00
  chronic 376.10
orthopoxvirus 059.00
  specified NEC 059.09
ovary (see also Salpingo-oophoritis) 614.2
Oxyuris vermicularis 127.4
pancreas 577.0
Paracoccidioides brasiliensis 116.1
Paragonimus (westermani) 121.2
parainfluenza virus 079.89
parameningococcus NEC 036.9
  with meningitis 036.0
parapoxvirus 059.10
  specified NEC 059.19
parasitic NEC 136.9
paratyphoid 002.9
  type A 002.1
  type B 002.2
  type C 002.3
paraurethral ducts 597.89
parotid gland 527.2
Pasteurella NEC 027.2
  multocida (cat-bite) (dog-bite) 027.2
  pestis (see also Plague) 020.9
  pseudotuberculosis 027.2
  septica (cat-bite) (dog-bite) 027.2
  tularensis (see also Tularemia) 021.9
pelvic, female (see also Disease, pelvis, inflammatory) 614.9
penis (glans) (retention) NEC 607.2
  herpetic 054.13
Peptococcus 041.84
Peptostreptococcus 041.84
periapical (pulpal origin) 522.4
peridental 523.30
perineal wound (obstetrical) 674.3 ☑
periodontal 523.31
periorbital 376.00
  chronic 376.10
perirectal 569.49
perirenal (see also Infection, kidney) 590.9
peritoneal (see also Peritonitis) 567.9
periureteral 593.89
periurethral 597.89
Petriellidium boydii 117.6
pharynx 478.29
  Coxsackie virus 074.0
  phlegmonous 462
  posterior, lymphoid 474.00
Phialophora
  gougerotii 117.8
  jeanselmei 117.8
  verrucosa 117.2
Piedraia hortai 111.3
pinna, acute 380.11
pinta 103.9
  intermediate 103.1
  late 103.2
  mixed 103.3
  primary 103.0
pinworm 127.4
pityrosporum furfur 111.0
pleuropneumonia-like organisms NEC (PPLO)
  041.81
pneumococcal NEC 041.2
  generalized (purulent) 038.2
Pneumococcus NEC 041.2
postoperative wound 998.59

Infection, infected, infective — continued
posttraumatic NEC 958.3
postvaccinal 999.39
poxvirus 059.9
  specified NEC 059.8
prepuce NEC 607.1
Proprionibacterium 041.84
prostate (capsule) (see also Prostatitis) 601.9
Proteus (mirabilis) (morganii) (vulgaris) NEC
  041.6
  enteritis 008.3
protozoal NEC 136.8
  intestinal NEC 007.9
Pseudomonas NEC 041.7
  mallei 024
  pneumonia 482.1
  pseudomallei 025
psittacosis 073.9
puerperal, postpartum (major) 670.0 ☑
  minor 646.6 ☑
pulmonary — see Infection, lung
purulent — see Abscess
putrid, generalized — see Septicemia
pyemic — see Septicemia
Pyrenochaeta romeroi 117.4
Q fever 083.0
rabies 071
rectum (sphincter) 569.49
renal (see also Infection, kidney) 590.9
  pelvis and ureter 590.3
resistant to drugs — see Resistance (to), drugs
  by microorganisms
respiratory 519.8
  chronic 519.8
  influenzal (acute) (upper) 487.1
  lung 518.89
  rhinovirus 460
  syncytial virus 079.6
  upper (acute) (infectious) NEC 465.9
    with flu, grippe, or influenza 487.1
    influenzal 487.1
    multiple sites NEC 465.8
    streptococcal 034.0
    viral NEC 465.9
respiratory syncytial virus (RSV) 079.6
resulting from presence of shunt or other internal prosthetic device — see Complications, infection and inflammation,
  due to (presence of) any device, implant, or graft classified to 996.0–996.5
  NEC
retroperitoneal 567.39
retrovirus 079.50
  human immunodeficiency virus type 2
    [HIV2] 079.53
  human T-cell lymphotrophic virus type I
    [HTLV-I] 079.51
  human T-cell lymphotrophic virus type II
    [HTLV-II] 079.52
  specified NEC 079.59
Rhinocladium 117.1
Rhinosporidium — see beri 117.0
rhinovirus
  in diseases classified elsewhere — see
    category 079 ☑
  unspecified nature or site 079.3
Rhizopus 117.7
rickettsial 083.9
rickettsialpox 083.2
rubella (see also Rubella) 056.9
  congenital 771.0
Saccharomyces (see also Candidiasis) 112.9
Saksenaea 117.7
salivary duct or gland (any) 527.2
Salmonella (aertrycke) (callinarum) (choleraesuis) (enteritidis) (suipestifer) (typhimurium) 003.9
  with
    arthritis 003.23
    gastroenteritis 003.0
    localized infection 003.20
      specified type NEC 003.29
    meningitis 003.21
    osteomyelitis 003.24
    pneumonia 003.22
    septicemia 003.1

Infection, infected, infective — *continued*
- Salmonella — *continued*
  - with — *continued*
    - specified manifestation NEC 003.8
  - due to food (poisoning) (any serotype) (*see also* Poisoning, food, due to, Salmonella)
  - hirschfeldii 002.3
  - localized 003.20
    - specified type NEC 003.29
  - paratyphi 002.9
    - A 002.1
    - B 002.2
    - C 002.3
  - schottmuelleri 002.2
  - specified type NEC 003.8
  - typhi 002.0
  - typhosa 002.0
- saprophytic 136.8
- Sarcocystis, lindemanni 136.5
- SARS-associated coronavirus 079.82
- scabies 133.0
- Schistosoma — *see* Infestation, Schistosoma
- Schmorl's bacillus 040.3
- scratch or other superficial injury — *see* Injury, superficial, by site
- scrotum (acute) NEC 608.4
- sealpox 059.12
- secondary, burn or open wound (dislocation) (fracture) 958.3
- seminal vesicle (*see also* Vesiculitis) 608.0
- septic
  - generalized — *see* Septicemia
  - localized, skin (*see also* Abscess) 682.9
- septicemic — *see* Septicemia
- seroma 998.51
- Serratia (marcescens) 041.85
  - generalized 038.44
- sheep liver fluke 121.3
- Shigella 004.9
  - boydii 004.2
  - dysenteriae 004.0
  - flexneri 004.1
  - group
    - A 004.0
    - B 004.1
    - C 004.2
    - D 004.3
  - Schmitz (-Stutzer) 004.0
  - schmitzii 004.0
  - Shiga 004.0
  - sonnei 004.3
  - specified type NEC 004.8
- Sin Nombre virus 079.81
- sinus (*see also* Sinusitis) 473.9
  - pilonidal 685.1
    - with abscess 685.0
  - skin NEC 686.9
- Skene's duct or gland (*see also* Urethritis) 597.89
- skin (local) (staphylococcal) (streptococcal) NEC 686.9
  - abscess — *see* Abscess, by site
  - cellulitis — *see* Cellulitis, by site
  - due to fungus 111.9
    - specified type NEC 111.8
  - mycotic 111.9
    - specified type NEC 111.8
  - ulcer (*see also* Ulcer, skin) 707.9
- slow virus 046.9
  - specified condition NEC 046.8
- Sparganum (mansoni) (proliferum) 123.5
- spermatic cord NEC 608.4
- sphenoidal (chronic) (sinus) (*see also* Sinusitis, sphenoidal) 473.3
- Spherophorus necrophorus 040.3
- spinal cord NEC (*see also* Encephalitis) 323.9
  - abscess 324.1
    - late effect — *see* category 326
  - late effect — *see* category 326
  - meninges — *see* Meningitis
  - streptococcal 320.2
- Spirillum
  - minus or minor 026.0
  - morsus muris 026.0
  - obermeieri 087.0

Infection, infected, infective — *continued*
- spirochetal NEC 104.9
  - lung 104.8
  - specified nature or site NEC 104.8
- spleen 289.59
- Sporothrix schenckii 117.1
- Sporotrichum (schenckii) 117.1
- Sporozoa 136.8
- staphylococcal NEC 041.10
  - aureus 041.11
    - methicillin
      - resistant (MRSA) 041.12
      - susceptible (MSSA) 041.11
  - food poisoning 005.0
  - generalized (purulent) 038.10
    - aureus 038.11
      - methicillin
        - resistant 038.12
        - susceptible 038.11
    - specified organism NEC 038.19
  - pneumonia 482.40
    - aureus 482.41
      - methicillin
        - resistant (MRSA) 482.42
        - susceptible (MSSA) 482.41
    - MRSA (methicillin resistant Staphylococcus aureus) 482.42
    - MSSA (methicillin susceptible Staphylococcus aureus) 482.41
    - specified type NEC 482.49
  - septicemia 038.10
    - aureus 038.11
      - methicillin
        - resistant (MRSA) 038.12
        - susceptible (MSSA) 038.11
    - MRSA (methicillin resistant Staphylococcus aureus) 038.12
    - MSSA (methicillin susceptible Staphylococcus aureus) 038.11
    - specified organism NEC 038.19
  - specified NEC 041.19
- steatoma 706.2
- Stellantchasmus falcatus 121.6
- Streptobacillus moniliformis 026.1
- streptococcal NEC 041.00
  - generalized (purulent) 038.0
  - Group
    - A 041.01
    - B 041.02
    - C 041.03
    - D [enterococcus] 041.04
    - G 041.05
  - pneumonia — *see* Pneumonia, streptococcal
  - septicemia 038.0
  - sore throat 034.0
  - specified NEC 041.09
- Streptomyces — *see* Actinomycosis
- streptotrichosis — *see* Actinomycosis
- Strongyloides (stercoralis) 127.2
- stump (amputation) (posttraumatic) (surgical) 997.62
  - traumatic — *see* Amputation, traumatic, by site, complicated
- subcutaneous tissue, local NEC 686.9
- submaxillary region 528.9
- suipestifer (*see also* Infection, Salmonella) 003.9
- swimming pool bacillus 031.1
- syphilitic — *see* Syphilis
- systemic — *see* Septicemia
- Taenia — *see* Infestation, Taenia
- Taeniarhynchus saginatus 123.2
- tanapox 059.21
- tapeworm — *see* Infestation, tapeworm
- tendon (sheath) 727.89
- Ternidens diminutus 127.7
- testis (*see also* Orchitis) 604.90
- thigh (skin) 686.9
- threadworm 127.4
- throat 478.29
  - pneumococcal 462
  - staphylococcal 462
  - streptococcal 034.0
  - viral NEC (*see also* Pharyngitis) 462
- thumb (skin) 686.9
  - abscess (with lymphangitis) 681.00

Infection, infected, infective — *continued*
- thumb — *continued*
  - abscess — *continued*
    - pulp 681.01
  - cellulitis (with lymphangitis) 681.00
  - nail 681.02
- thyroglossal duct 529.8
- toe (skin) 686.9
  - abscess (with lymphangitis) 681.10
  - cellulitis (with lymphangitis) 681.10
  - nail 681.11
    - fungus 110.1
- tongue NEC 529.0
  - parasitic 112.0
- tonsil (faucial) (lingual) (pharyngeal) 474.00
  - acute or subacute 463
  - and adenoid 474.02
  - tag 474.00
- tooth, teeth 522.4
  - periapical (pulpal origin) 522.4
  - peridental 523.30
  - periodontal 523.31
  - pulp 522.0
  - socket 526.5
- TORCH — *see* Infection, congenital NEC
  - without active infection 760.2
- Torula histolytica 117.5
- Toxocara (cani) (cati) (felis) 128.0
- Toxoplasma gondii (*see also* Toxoplasmosis) 130.9
- trachea, chronic 491.8
  - fungus 117.9
- traumatic NEC 958.3
- trematode NEC 121.9
- trench fever 083.1
- Treponema
  - denticola 041.84
  - macrodenticum 041.84
  - pallidum (*see also* Syphilis) 097.9
- Trichinella (spiralis) 124
- Trichomonas 131.9
  - bladder 131.9
  - cervix 131.09
  - hominis 007.3
  - intestine 007.3
  - prostate 131.03
  - specified site NEC 131.8
  - urethra 131.02
  - urogenitalis 131.00
  - vagina 131.01
  - vulva 131.01
- Trichophyton, trichophytid — *see* Dermatophytosis
- Trichosporon (beigelii) cutaneum 111.2
- Trichostrongylus 127.6
- Trichuris (trichiuria) 127.3
- Trombicula (irritans) 133.8
- Trypanosoma (*see also* Trypanosomiasis) 086.9
  - cruzi 086.2
- tubal (*see also* Salpingo-oophoritis) 614.2
- tuberculous NEC (*see also* Tuberculosis) 011.9 ☑
- tubo-ovarian (*see also* Salpingo-oophoritis) 614.2
- tunica vaginalis 608.4
- tympanic membrane — *see* Myringitis
- typhoid (abortive) (ambulant) (bacillus) 002.0
- typhus 081.9
  - flea-borne (endemic) 081.0
  - louse-borne (epidemic) 080
  - mite-borne 081.2
  - recrudescent 081.1
  - tick-borne 082.9
    - African 082.1
    - North Asian 082.2
- umbilicus (septic) 686.9
  - newborn NEC 771.4
- ureter 593.89
- urethra (*see also* Urethritis) 597.80
- urinary (tract) NEC 599.0
  - with
    - abortion — *see* Abortion, by type, with urinary tract infection
    - ectopic pregnancy (*see also* categories 633.0–633.9) 639.8

Infection, infected, infective — *continued*
- urinary — *continued*
  - with — *continued*
    - molar pregnancy (*see also* categories 630–632) 639.8
  - candidal 112.2
  - complicating pregnancy, childbirth, or puerperium 646.6 ☑
    - affecting fetus or newborn 760.1
    - asymptomatic 646.5 ☑
      - affecting fetus or newborn 760.1
  - diplococcal (acute) 098.0
    - chronic 098.2
  - due to Trichomonas (vaginalis) 131.00
  - following
    - abortion 639.8
    - ectopic or molar pregnancy 639.8
  - gonococcal (acute) 098.0
    - chronic or duration of 2 months or over 098.2
  - newborn 771.82
  - trichomonal 131.00
  - tuberculous (*see also* Tuberculosis) 016.3 ☑
  - uterus, uterine (*see also* Endometritis) 615.9
  - utriculus masculinus NEC 597.89
  - vaccination 999.39
  - vagina (granulation tissue) (wall) (*see also* Vaginitis) 616.10
  - varicella 052.9
  - varicose veins — *see* Varicose, veins
  - variola 050.9
    - major 050.0
    - minor 050.1
  - vas deferens NEC 608.4
  - Veillonella 041.84
  - verumontanum 597.89
  - vesical (*see also* Cystitis) 595.9
  - Vibrio
    - cholerae 001.0
      - El Tor 001.1
    - parahaemolyticus (food poisoning) 005.4
    - vulnificus 041.85
  - Vincent's (gums) (mouth) (tonsil) 101
- vaccination 999.39
- virus, viral 079.99
  - adenovirus
    - in diseases classified elsewhere — *see* category 079 ☑
    - unspecified nature or site 079.0
  - central nervous system NEC 049.9
    - enterovirus 048
      - meningitis 047.9
        - specified type NEC 047.8
    - slow virus 046.9
    - specified condition NEC 046.8
  - chest 519.8
  - conjunctivitis 077.99
    - specified type NEC 077.8
  - coronavirus 079.89
    - SARS-associated 079.82
  - Coxsackie (*see also* Infection, Coxsackie) 079.2
  - Ebola 065.8
  - ECHO
    - in diseases classified elsewhere — *see* category 079 ☑
    - unspecified nature or site 079.1
  - encephalitis 049.9
    - arthropod-borne NEC 064
    - tick-borne 063.9
      - specified type NEC 063.8
  - enteritis NEC (*see also* Enteritis, viral) 008.8
  - exanthem NEC 057.9
  - Hantavirus 079.81
  - human papilloma 079.4
  - in diseases classified elsewhere — *see* category 079 ☑
  - intestine (*see also* Enteritis, viral) 008.8
  - lung — *see* Pneumonia, viral
  - respiratory syncytial (RSV) 079.6
  - retrovirus 079.50
  - rhinovirus
    - in diseases classified elsewhere — *see* category 079 ☑

Infection, infected, infective — continued
  virus, viral — continued
    rhinovirus — continued
      unspecified nature or site 079.3
    salivary gland disease 078.5
    slow 046.9
      specified condition NEC 046.8
    specified type NEC 079.89
      in diseases classified elsewhere — see
        category 079 ☑
    unspecified nature or site 079.99
    warts 078.10
      specified NEC 078.19
    yaba monkey tumor 059.22
  vulva (see also Vulvitis) 616.10
  whipworm 127.3
  Whitmore's bacillus 025
  wound (local) (posttraumatic) NEC 958.3
    with
      dislocation — see Dislocation, by site,
        open
      fracture — see Fracture, by site, open
      open wound — see Wound, open, by
        site, complicated
    postoperative 998.59
    surgical 998.59
  Wuchereria 125.0
    bancrofti 125.0
    malayi 125.1
  yaba monkey tumor virus 059.22
  yatapoxvirus 059.20
  yaws — see Yaws
  yeast (see also Candidiasis) 112.9
  yellow fever (see also Fever, yellow) 060.9
  Yersinia pestis (see also Plague) 020.9
  Zeis' gland 373.12
  zoonotic bacterial NEC 027.9
  Zopfia senegalensis 117.4
Infective, infectious — see condition
Inferiority complex 301.9
  constitutional psychopathic 301.9
Infertility
  female 628.9
    age related 628.8
    associated with
      adhesions, peritubal 614.6 [628.2]
      anomaly
        cervical mucus 628.4
        congenital
          cervix 628.4
          fallopian tube 628.2
          uterus 628.3
          vagina 628.4
      anovulation 628.0
      dysmucorrhea 628.4
      endometritis, tuberculous (see also Tu-
        berculosis) 016.7 ☑ [628.3]
      Stein-Leventhal syndrome 256.4 [628.0]
    due to
      adiposogenital dystrophy 253.8 [628.1]
      anterior pituitary disorder NEC
        253.4 [628.1]
        hyperfunction 253.1 [628.1]
      cervical anomaly 628.4
      fallopian tube anomaly 628.2
      ovarian failure 256.39 [628.0]
      Stein-Leventhal syndrome 256.4 [628.0]
      uterine anomaly 628.3
      vaginal anomaly 628.4
    nonimplantation 628.3
    origin
      cervical 628.4
      pituitary-hypothalamus NEC
        253.8 [628.1]
        anterior pituitary NEC 253.4 [628.1]
          hyperfunction NEC 253.1 [628.1]
        dwarfism 253.3 [628.1]
        panhypopituitarism 253.2 [628.1]
      specified NEC 628.8
      tubal (block) (occlusion) (stenosis)
        628.2
        adhesions 614.6 [628.2]
      uterine 628.3
      vaginal 628.4
    previous, requiring supervision of pregnan-
      cy V23.0

Infertility — continued
  male 606.9
    absolute 606.0
    due to
      azoospermia 606.0
      drug therapy 606.8
      extratesticular cause NEC 606.8
      germinal cell
        aplasia 606.0
        desquamation 606.1
      hypospermatogenesis 606.1
      infection 606.8
      obstruction, afferent ducts 606.8
      oligospermia 606.1
      radiation 606.8
      spermatogenic arrest (complete) 606.0
        incomplete 606.1
      systemic disease 606.8
Infestation 134.9
  Acanthocheilonema (perstans) 125.4
    streptocerca 125.6
  Acariasis 133.9
    demodex folliculorum 133.8
    Sarcoptes scabiei 133.0
    trombiculae 133.8
  Agamofilaria streptocerca 125.6
  Ancylostoma, Ankylostoma 126.9
    americanum 126.1
    braziliense 126.2
    canium 126.8
    ceylanicum 126.3
    duodenale 126.0
    new world 126.1
    old world 126.0
  Angiostrongylus cantonensis 128.8
  anisakiasis 127.1
  Anisakis larva 127.1
  arthropod NEC 134.1
  Ascaris lumbricoides 127.0
  Bacillus fusiformis 101
  Balantidium coli 007.0
  beef tapeworm 123.2
  Bothriocephalus (latus) 123.4
    larval 123.5
  broad tapeworm 123.4
    larval 123.5
  Brugia malayi 125.1
  Candiru 136.8
  Capillaria
    hepatica 128.8
    philippinensis 127.5
  cat liver fluke 121.0
  Cercomonas hominis (intestinal) 007.3
  cestodes 123.9
    specified type NEC 123.8
  chigger 133.8
  chigoe 134.1
  Chilomastix 007.8
  Clonorchis (sinensis) (liver) 121.1
  coccidia 007.2
  complicating pregnancy, childbirth, or puer-
    perium 647.9 ☑
    affecting fetus or newborn 760.8
  Cysticercus cellulosae 123.1
  Demodex folliculorum 133.8
  Dermatobia (hominis) 134.0
  Dibothriocephalus (latus) 123.4
    larval 123.5
  Dicrocoelium dendriticum 121.8
  Diphyllobothrium (adult) (intestinal) (latum)
    (pacificum) 123.4
    larval 123.5
  Diplogonoporus (grandis) 123.8
  Dipylidium (caninum) 123.8
  Distoma hepaticum 121.3
  dog tapeworm 123.8
  Dracunculus medinensis 125.7
  dragon worm 125.7
  dwarf tapeworm 123.6
  Echinococcus (see also Echinococcus) 122.9
  Echinostoma ilocanum 121.8
  Embadomonas 007.8
  Endamoeba (histolytica) — see Infection,
    ameba
  Entamoeba (histolytica) — see Infection,
    ameba

Infestation — continued
  Enterobius vermicularis 127.4
  Epidermophyton — see Dermatophytosis
  eyeworm 125.2
  Fasciola
    gigantica 121.3
    hepatica 121.3
  Fasciolopsis (buski) (small intestine) 121.4
    blood NEC (see also Schistosomiasis) 120.9
    cat liver 121.0
    filarial 125.9
      due to
        Acanthocheilonema (perstans)
          125.4
          streptocerca 125.6
        Brugia (Wuchereria) malayi 125.1
        Dracunculus medinensis 125.7
        guinea worms 125.7
        Mansonella (ozzardi) 125.5
        Onchocerca volvulus 125.3
          eye 125.3 [360.13]
          eyelid 125.3 [373.6]
        Wuchereria (bancrofti) 125.0
          malayi 125.1
      specified type NEC 125.6
    fish tapeworm 123.4
      larval 123.5
    fluke 121.9
    intestinal (giant) 121.4
    liver (sheep) 121.3
      cat 121.0
      Chinese 121.1
      clonorchiasis 121.1
      fasciolasis 121.3
      Oriental 121.1
    lung (oriental) 121.2
    sheep liver 121.3
  fly larva 134.0
  Gasterophilus (intestinalis) 134.0
  Gastrodiscoides hominis 121.8
  Giardia lamblia 007.1
  Gnathostoma (spinigerum) 128.1
  Gongylonema 125.6
  guinea worm 125.7
  helminth NEC 128.9
    intestinal 127.9
      mixed (types classifiable to more than
        one category in 120.0–127.7)
        127.8
      specified type NEC 127.7
    specified type NEC 128.8
  Heterophyes heterophyes (small intestine)
    121.6
  hookworm (see also Infestation, ancylostoma)
    126.9
  Hymenolepis (diminuta) (nana) 123.6
  intestinal NEC 129
  leeches (aquatic) (land) 134.2
  Leishmania — see Leishmaniasis
  lice (see also Infestation, pediculus) 132.9
  Linguatulidae, linguatula (pentastoma) (serra-
    ta) 134.1
  Loa loa 125.2
    eyelid 125.2 [373.6]
  louse (see also Infestation, pediculus) 132.9
    body 132.1
    head 132.0
    pubic 132.2
  maggots 134.0
  Mansonella (ozzardi) 125.5
  medina 125.7
  Metagonimus yokogawai (small intestine)
    121.5
  Microfilaria streptocerca 125.3
    eye 125.3 [360.13]
    eyelid 125.3 [373.6]
  Microsporon furfur 111.0
  microsporum — see Dermatophytosis
  mites 133.9
    scabic 133.0
    specified type NEC 133.8
  monilia (albicans) (see also Candidiasis) 112.9
    vagina 112.1
    vulva 112.1
  mouth 112.0
  Necator americanus 126.1

Infestation — continued
  nematode (intestinal) 127.9
    Ancylostoma (see also Ancylostoma) 126.9
    Ascaris lumbricoides 127.0
    conjunctiva NEC 128.9
    Dioctophyma 128.8
    Enterobius vermicularis 127.4
    Gnathostoma spinigerum 128.1
    Oesophagostomum (apiostomum) 127.7
    Physaloptera 127.4
    specified type NEC 127.7
    Strongyloides stercoralis 127.2
    Ternidens diminutus 127.7
    Trichinella spiralis 124
    Trichostrongylus 127.6
    Trichuris (trichiuria) 127.3
  Oesophagostomum (apiostomum) 127.7
  Oestrus ovis 134.0
  Onchocerca (volvulus) 125.3
    eye 125.3 [360.13]
    eyelid 125.3 [373.6]
  Opisthorchis (felineus) (tenuicollis) (viverrini)
    121.0
  Oxyuris vermicularis 127.4
  Paragonimus (westermani) 121.2
  parasite, parasitic NEC 136.9
    eyelid 134.9 [373.6]
    intestinal 129
    mouth 112.0
    orbit 376.13
    skin 134.9
    tongue 112.0
  pediculus 132.9
    capitis (humanus) (any site) 132.0
    corporis (humanus) (any site) 132.1
    eyelid 132.0 [373.6]
    mixed (classifiable to more than one cate-
      gory in 132.0–132.2) 132.3
    pubis (any site) 132.2
  phthirus (pubis) (any site) 132.2
    with any infestation classifiable to 132.0,
      132.1 and 132.3
  pinworm 127.4
  pork tapeworm (adult) 123.0
  protozoal NEC 136.8
  pubic louse 132.2
  rat tapeworm 123.6
  red bug 133.8
  roundworm (large) NEC 127.0
  sand flea 134.1
  saprophytic NEC 136.8
  Sarcoptes scabiei 133.0
  scabies 133.0
  Schistosoma 120.9
    bovis 120.8
    cercariae 120.3
    hematobium 120.0
    intercalatum 120.8
    japonicum 120.2
    mansoni 120.1
    mattheii 120.8
    specified
      site — see Schistosomiasis
      type NEC 120.8
    spindale 120.8
  screw worms 134.0
  skin NEC 134.9
  Sparganum (mansoni) (proliferum) 123.5
    larval 123.5
  specified type NEC 134.8
  Spirometra larvae 123.5
  Sporozoa NEC 136.8
  Stellantchasmus falcatus 121.6
  Strongyloides 127.2
  Strongylus (gibsoni) 127.7
  Taenia 123.3
    diminuta 123.6
    Echinococcus (see also Echinococcus) 122.9
    mediocanellata 123.2
    nana 123.6
    saginata (mediocanellata) 123.2
    solium (intestinal form) 123.0
      larval form 123.1
  Taeniarhynchus saginatus 123.2
  tapeworm 123.9
    beef 123.2

☑ Additional Digit Required — Refer to the Tabular List for Digit Selection   ▽ Subterms under main terms may continue to next column or page

2010 ICD-9-CM   ▶◀ Revised Text   ● New Line   ▲ Revised Code   Volume 2 — 153

Infestation — continued
- tapeworm — continued
  - broad 123.4
    - larval 123.5
  - dog 123.8
  - dwarf 123.6
  - fish 123.4
    - larval 123.5
  - pork 123.0
  - rat 123.6
- Ternidens diminutus 127.7
- Tetranychus molestissimus 133.8
- threadworm 127.4
- tongue 112.0
- Toxocara (cani) (cati) (felis) 128.0
- trematode(s) NEC 121.9
- Trichina spiralis 124
- Trichinella spiralis 124
- Trichocephalus 127.3
- Trichomonas 131.9
  - bladder 131.09
  - cervix 131.09
  - intestine 007.3
  - prostate 131.03
  - specified site NEC 131.8
  - urethra (female) (male) 131.02
  - urogenital 131.00
  - vagina 131.01
  - vulva 131.01
- Trichophyton — see Dermatophytosis
- Trichostrongylus instabilis 127.6
- Trichuris (trichiuria) 127.3
- Trombicula (irritans) 133.8
- Trypanosoma — see Trypanosomiasis
- Tunga penetrans 134.1
- Uncinaria americana 126.1
- whipworm 127.3
- worms NEC 128.9
  - intestinal 127.9
- Wuchereria 125.0
  - bancrofti 125.0
  - malayi 125.1

Infiltrate, infiltration
- with an iron compound 275.0
- amyloid (any site) (generalized) 277.39
- calcareous (muscle) NEC 275.49
  - localized — see Degeneration, by site
- calcium salt (muscle) 275.49
- chemotherapy, vesicant 999.81 ▲
- corneal (see also Edema, cornea) 371.20
- eyelid 373.9
- fatty (diffuse) (generalized) 272.8
  - localized — see Degeneration, by site, fatty
- glycogen, glycogenic (see also Disease, glycogen storage) 271.0
- heart, cardiac
  - fatty (see also Degeneration, myocardial) 429.1
  - glycogenic 271.0 [425.7]
- inflammatory in vitreous 379.29
- kidney (see also Disease, renal) 593.9
- leukemic (M9800/3) — see Leukemia
- liver 573.8
  - fatty — see Fatty, liver
  - glycogen (see also Disease, glycogen storage) 271.0
- lung (see also Infiltrate, pulmonary) 518.3
  - eosinophilic 518.3
  - x-ray finding only 793.1
- lymphatic (see also Leukemia, lymphatic) 204.9 ☑
  - gland, pigmentary 289.3
- muscle, fatty 728.9
- myelogenous (see also Leukemia, myeloid) 205.9 ☑
- myocardium, myocardial
  - fatty (see also Degeneration, myocardial) 429.1
  - glycogenic 271.0 [425.7]
- pulmonary 518.3
  - with
    - eosinophilia 518.3
    - pneumonia — see Pneumonia, by type
    - x-ray finding only 793.1
- Ranke's primary (see also Tuberculosis) 010.0 ☑

Infiltrate, infiltration — continued
- skin, lymphocytic (benign) 709.8
- thymus (gland) (fatty) 254.8
- urine 788.8
- vesicant
  - agent NEC 999.82 ▲
  - chemotherapy 999.81 ▲
- vitreous humor 379.29

Infirmity 799.89
- senile 797

Inflammation, inflamed, inflammatory (with exudation)
- abducens (nerve) 378.54
- accessory sinus (chronic) (see also Sinusitis) 473.9
- adrenal (gland) 255.8
- alimentary canal — see Enteritis
- alveoli (teeth) 526.5
  - scorbutic 267
- amnion — see Amnionitis
- anal canal 569.49
- antrum (chronic) (see also Sinusitis, maxillary) 473.0
- anus 569.49
- appendix (see also Appendicitis) 541
- arachnoid — see Meningitis
- areola 611.0
  - puerperal, postpartum 675.0 ☑
- areolar tissue NEC 686.9
- artery — see Arteritis
- auditory meatus (external) (see also Otitis, externa) 380.10
- Bartholin's gland 616.89
- bile duct or passage 576.1
- bladder (see also Cystitis) 595.9
- bleb
  - postprocedural 379.60
    - stage 1 379.61
    - stage 2 379.62
    - stage 3 379.63
- bone — see Osteomyelitis
- bowel (see also Enteritis) 558.9
- brain (see also Encephalitis) 323.9
  - late effect — see category 326
  - membrane — see Meningitis
- breast 611.0
  - puerperal, postpartum 675.2 ☑
- broad ligament (see also Disease, pelvis, inflammatory) 614.4
  - acute 614.3
- bronchus — see Bronchitis
- bursa — see Bursitis
- capsule
  - liver 573.3
  - spleen 289.59
- catarrhal (see also Catarrh) 460
  - vagina 616.10
- cecum (see also Appendicitis) 541
- cerebral (see also Encephalitis) 323.9
  - late effect — see category 326
  - membrane — see Meningitis
- cerebrospinal (see also Meningitis) 322.9
  - late effect — see category 326
  - meningococcal 036.0
  - tuberculous (see also Tuberculosis) 013.6 ☑
- cervix (uteri) (see also Cervicitis) 616.0
- chest 519.9
- choroid NEC (see also Choroiditis) 363.20
- cicatrix (tissue) — see Cicatrix
- colon (see also Enteritis) 558.9
  - granulomatous 555.1
  - newborn 558.9
- connective tissue (diffuse) NEC 728.9
- cornea (see also Keratitis) 370.9
  - with ulcer (see also Ulcer, cornea) 370.00
- corpora cavernosa (penis) 607.2
- cranial nerve — see Disorder, nerve, cranial
- diarrhea — see Diarrhea
- disc (intervertebral) (space) 722.90
  - cervical, cervicothoracic 722.91
  - lumbar, lumbosacral 722.93
  - thoracic, thoracolumbar 722.92
- Douglas' cul-de-sac or pouch (chronic) (see also Disease, pelvis, inflammatory) 614.4

Inflammation, inflamed, inflammatory — continued
- Douglas' cul-de-sac or pouch (see also Disease, pelvis, inflammatory) — continued
  - acute 614.3
- due to (presence of) any device, implant, or graft classifiable to 996.0–996.5 — see Complications, infection and inflammation, due to (presence of) any device, implant, or graft classified to 996.0–996.5 NEC
- duodenum 535.6 ☑
- dura mater — see Meningitis
- ear (see also Otitis)
  - external (see also Otitis, externa) 380.10
  - inner (see also Labyrinthitis) 386.30
  - middle — see Otitis media
- esophagus 530.10
- ethmoidal (chronic) (sinus) (see also Sinusitis, ethmoidal) 473.2
- Eustachian tube (catarrhal) 381.50
  - acute 381.51
  - chronic 381.52
- extrarectal 569.49
- eye 379.99
- eyelid 373.9
  - specified NEC 373.8
- fallopian tube (see also Salpingo-oophoritis) 614.2
- fascia 728.9
- fetal membranes (acute) 658.4 ☑
  - affecting fetus or newborn 762.7
- follicular, pharynx 472.1
- frontal (chronic) (sinus) (see also Sinusitis, frontal) 473.1
- gallbladder (see also Cholecystitis, acute) 575.0
- gall duct (see also Cholecystitis) 575.10
- gastrointestinal (see also Enteritis) 558.9
- genital organ (diffuse) (internal)
  - female 614.9
    - with
      - abortion — see Abortion, by type, with sepsis
      - ectopic pregnancy (see also categories 633.0–633.9) 639.0
      - molar pregnancy (see also categories 630–632) 639.0
    - complicating pregnancy, childbirth, or puerperium 646.6 ☑
      - affecting fetus or newborn 760.8
    - following
      - abortion 639.0
      - ectopic or molar pregnancy 639.0
  - male 608.4
- gland (lymph) (see also Lymphadenitis) 289.3
- glottis (see also Laryngitis) 464.00
  - with obstruction 464.01
- granular, pharynx 472.1
- gum 523.10
- heart (see also Carditis) 429.89
- hepatic duct 576.8
- hernial sac — see Hernia, by site
- ileum (see also Enteritis) 558.9
  - terminal or regional 555.0
    - with large intestine 555.2
- intervertebral disc 722.90
  - cervical, cervicothoracic 722.91
  - lumbar, lumbosacral 722.93
  - thoracic, thoracolumbar 722.92
- intestine (see also Enteritis) 558.9
- jaw (acute) (bone) (chronic) (lower) (suppurative) (upper) 526.4
- jejunum — see Enteritis
- joint NEC (see also Arthritis) 716.9 ☑
  - sacroiliac 720.2
- kidney (see also Nephritis) 583.9
- knee (joint) 716.66
  - tuberculous (active) (see also Tuberculosis) 015.2 ☑
- labium (majus) (minus) (see also Vulvitis) 616.10
- lacrimal
  - gland (see also Dacryoadenitis) 375.00
  - passages (duct) (sac) (see also Dacryocystitis) 375.30
- larynx (see also Laryngitis) 464.00

Inflammation, inflamed, inflammatory — continued
- larynx (see also Laryngitis) — continued
  - with obstruction 464.01
  - diphtheritic 032.3
- leg NEC 686.9
- lip 528.5
- liver (capsule) (see also Hepatitis) 573.3
  - acute 570
  - chronic 571.40
  - suppurative 572.0
- lung (acute) (see also Pneumonia) 486
  - chronic (interstitial) 518.89
- lymphatic vessel (see also Lymphangitis) 457.2
- lymph node or gland (see also Lymphadenitis) 289.3
- mammary gland 611.0
  - puerperal, postpartum 675.2 ☑
- maxilla, maxillary 526.4
  - sinus (chronic) (see also Sinusitis, maxillary) 473.0
- membranes of brain or spinal cord — see Meningitis
- meninges — see Meningitis
- mouth 528.00
- muscle 728.9
- myocardium (see also Myocarditis) 429.0
- nasal sinus (chronic) (see also Sinusitis) 473.9
- nasopharynx — see Nasopharyngitis
- navel 686.9
  - newborn NEC 771.4
- nerve NEC 729.2
- nipple 611.0
  - puerperal, postpartum 675.0 ☑
- nose 478.19
  - suppurative 472.0
- oculomotor nerve 378.51
- optic nerve 377.30
- orbit (chronic) 376.10
  - acute 376.00
  - chronic 376.10
- ovary (see also Salpingo-oophoritis) 614.2
- oviduct (see also Salpingo-oophoritis) 614.2
- pancreas — see Pancreatitis
- parametrium (chronic) (see also Disease, pelvis, inflammatory) 614.4
  - acute 614.3
- parotid region 686.9
  - gland 527.2
- pelvis, female (see also Disease, pelvis, inflammatory) 614.9
- penis (corpora cavernosa) 607.2
- perianal 569.49
- pericardium (see also Pericarditis) 423.9
- perineum (female) (male) 686.9
- perirectal 569.49
- peritoneum (see also Peritonitis) 567.9
- periuterine (see also Disease, pelvis, inflammatory) 614.9
- perivesical (see also Cystitis) 595.9
- petrous bone (see also Petrositis) 383.20
- pharynx (see also Pharyngitis) 462
  - follicular 472.1
  - granular 472.1
- pia mater — see Meningitis
- pleura — see Pleurisy
- postmastoidectomy cavity 383.30
  - chronic 383.33
- pouch, internal ileoanal 569.71 ●
- prostate (see also Prostatitis) 601.9
- rectosigmoid — see Rectosigmoiditis
- rectum (see also Proctitis) 569.49
- respiratory, upper (see also Infection, respiratory, upper) 465.9
  - chronic, due to external agent — see Condition, respiratory, chronic, due to, external agent
  - due to
    - fumes or vapors (chemical) (inhalation) 506.2
    - radiation 508.1
- retina (see also Retinitis) 363.20
- retrocecal (see also Appendicitis) 541
- retroperitoneal (see also Peritonitis) 567.9
- salivary duct or gland (any) (suppurative) 527.2
- scorbutic, alveoli, teeth 267

Inflammation, inflamed, inflammatory — *continued*
- scrotum 608.4
- sigmoid — *see* Enteritis
- sinus (*see also* Sinusitis) 473.9
- Skene's duct or gland (*see also* Urethritis) 597.89
- skin 686.9
- spermatic cord 608.4
- sphenoidal (sinus) (*see also* Sinusitis, sphenoidal) 473.3
- spinal
  - cord (*see also* Encephalitis) 323.9
    - late effect — *see* category 326
  - membrane — *see* Meningitis
  - nerve — *see* Disorder, nerve
- spine (*see also* Spondylitis) 720.9
- spleen (capsule) 289.59
- stomach — *see* Gastritis
- stricture, rectum 569.49
- subcutaneous tissue NEC 686.9
- suprarenal (gland) 255.8
- synovial (fringe) (membrane) — *see* Bursitis
- tendon (sheath) NEC 726.90
- testis (*see also* Orchitis) 604.90
- thigh 686.9
- throat (*see also* Sore throat) 462
- thymus (gland) 254.8
- thyroid (gland) (*see also* Thyroiditis) 245.9
- tongue 529.0
- tonsil — *see* Tonsillitis
- trachea — *see* Tracheitis
- trochlear nerve 378.53
- tubal (*see also* Salpingo-oophoritis) 614.2
- tuberculous NEC (*see also* Tuberculosis) 011.9 ✓
- tubo-ovarian (*see also* Salpingo-oophoritis) 614.2
- tunica vaginalis 608.4
- tympanic membrane — *see* Myringitis
- umbilicus, umbilical 686.9
  - newborn NEC 771.4
- uterine ligament (*see also* Disease, pelvis, inflammatory) 614.4
  - acute 614.3
- uterus (catarrhal) (*see also* Endometritis) 615.9
- uveal tract (anterior) (*see also* Iridocyclitis) 364.3
  - posterior — *see* Chorioretinitis
  - sympathetic 360.11
- vagina (*see also* Vaginitis) 616.10
- vas deferens 608.4
- vein (*see also* Phlebitis) 451.9
  - thrombotic 451.9
    - cerebral (*see also* Thrombosis, brain) 434.0 ✓
    - leg 451.2
      - deep (vessels) NEC 451.19
      - superficial (vessels) 451.0
    - lower extremity 451.2
      - deep (vessels) NEC 451.19
      - superficial (vessels) 451.0
- vocal cord 478.5
- vulva (*see also* Vulvitis) 616.10

Inflation, lung imperfect (newborn) 770.5
Influenza, influenzal 487.1
- with
  - bronchitis 487.1
  - bronchopneumonia 487.0
  - cold (any type) 487.1
  - digestive manifestations 487.8
  - hemoptysis 487.1
  - involvement of
    - gastrointestinal tract 487.8
    - nervous system 487.8
  - laryngitis 487.1
  - manifestations NEC 487.8
    - respiratory 487.1
      - pneumonia 487.0
  - pharyngitis 487.1
  - pneumonia (any form classifiable to 480–483, 485–486) 487.0
  - respiratory manifestations NEC 487.1
  - sinusitis 487.1
  - sore throat 487.1
  - tonsillitis 487.1

Influenza, influenzal — *continued*
- with — *continued*
  - tracheitis 487.1
  - upper respiratory infection (acute) 487.1
  - abdominal 487.8
  - A/H5N1 488.0 ●
  - Asian 487.1
  - avian 488.0 ●
  - bronchial 487.1
  - bronchopneumonia 487.0
  - catarrhal 487.1
  - due to identified
    - avian influenza virus 488.0 ●
    - novel H1N1 influenza virus 488.1 ●
  - epidemic 487.1
  - gastric 487.8
  - intestinal 487.8
  - laryngitis 487.1
  - maternal affecting fetus or newborn 760.2
    - manifest influenza in infant 771.2
  - novel A/H1N1 488.1 ●
  - novel (2009) H1N1 488.1 ●
  - pharyngitis 487.1
  - pneumonia (any form) 487.0
  - respiratory (upper) 487.1
  - specified NEC 487.1 ●
  - stomach 487.8
  - vaccination, prophylactic (against) V04.81
Influenza-like disease 487.1
Infraction, Freiberg's (metatarsal head) 732.5
Infraeruption, teeth 524.34
Infusion complication, misadventure, or reaction — *see* Complication, infusion
Ingestion
- chemical — *see* Table of Drugs and Chemicals
- drug or medicinal substance
  - overdose or wrong substance given or taken 977.9
    - specified drug — *see* Table of Drugs and Chemicals
- foreign body NEC (*see also* Foreign body) 938
Ingrowing
- hair 704.8
- nail (finger) (toe) (infected) 703.0
Inguinal — *see also* condition
- testis 752.51
Inhalation
- carbon monoxide 986
- flame
  - lung 947.1
  - mouth 947.0
- food or foreign body (*see also* Asphyxia, food or foreign body) 933.1
- gas, fumes, or vapor (noxious) 987.9
  - specified agent — *see* Table of Drugs and Chemicals
- liquid or vomitus (*see also* Asphyxia, food or foreign body) 933.1
- lower respiratory tract NEC 934.9
- meconium (fetus or newborn) 770.11
  - with respiratory symptoms 770.12
- mucus (*see also* Asphyxia, mucus) 933.1
- oil (causing suffocation) (*see also* Asphyxia, food or foreign body) 933.1
- pneumonia — *see* Pneumonia, aspiration
- smoke 987.9
- steam 987.9
- stomach contents or secretions (*see also* Asphyxia, food or foreign body) 933.1
  - in labor and delivery 668.0 ✓
Inhibition, inhibited
- academic as adjustment reaction 309.23
- orgasm
  - female 302.73
  - male 302.74
- sexual
  - desire 302.71
  - excitement 302.72
- work as adjustment reaction 309.23
Inhibitor, systemic lupus erythematosus (presence of) 286.5
Iniencephalus, iniencephaly 740.2
Injected eye 372.74

Injury 959.9

> *Note* — For abrasion, insect bite (nonvenomous), blister, or scratch, see Injury, superficial.
>
> For laceration, traumatic rupture, tear, or penetrating wound of internal organs, such as heart, lung, liver, kidney, pelvic organs, whether or not accompanied by open wound in the same region, see Injury, internal.
>
> For nerve injury, see Injury, nerve.
>
> For late effect of injuries classifiable to 850–854, 860–869, 900–919, 950–959, see Late, effect, injury, by type.

- abdomen, abdominal (viscera) (*see also* Injury, internal, abdomen)
  - muscle or wall 959.12
- acoustic, resulting in deafness 951.5
- adenoid 959.09
- adrenal (gland) — *see* Injury, internal, adrenal
- alveolar (process) 959.09
- ankle (and foot) (and knee) (and leg, except thigh) 959.7
- anterior chamber, eye 921.3
- anus 959.19
- aorta (thoracic) 901.0
  - abdominal 902.0
- appendix — *see* Injury, internal, appendix
- arm, upper (and shoulder) 959.2
- artery (complicating trauma) (*see also* Injury, blood vessel, by site) 904.9
  - cerebral or meningeal (*see also* Hemorrhage, brain, traumatic, subarachnoid) 852.0 ✓
- auditory canal (external) (meatus) 959.09
- auricle, auris, ear 959.09
- axilla 959.2
- back 959.19
- bile duct — *see* Injury, internal, bile duct
- birth (*see also* Birth, injury)
  - canal NEC, complicating delivery 665.9 ✓
- bladder (sphincter) — *see* Injury, internal, bladder
- blast (air) (hydraulic) (immersion) (underwater) NEC 869.0
  - with open wound into cavity NEC 869.1
  - abdomen or thorax — *see* Injury, internal, by site
  - brain — *see* Concussion, brain
  - ear (acoustic nerve trauma) 951.5
    - with perforation of tympanic membrane — *see* Wound, open, ear, drum
- blood vessel NEC 904.9
  - abdomen 902.9
    - multiple 902.87
    - specified NEC 902.89
  - aorta (thoracic) 901.0
    - abdominal 902.0
  - arm NEC 903.9
  - axillary 903.00
    - artery 903.01
    - vein 903.02
  - azygos vein 901.89
  - basilic vein 903.1
  - brachial (artery) (vein) 903.1
  - bronchial 901.89
  - carotid artery 900.00
    - common 900.01
    - external 900.02
    - internal 900.03
  - celiac artery 902.20
    - specified branch NEC 902.24
  - cephalic vein (arm) 903.1
  - colica dextra 902.26
  - cystic
    - artery 902.24
    - vein 902.39
  - deep plantar 904.6
  - digital (artery) (vein) 903.5
  - due to accidental puncture or laceration during procedure 998.2
  - extremity
    - lower 904.8
      - multiple 904.7

Injury — *continued*
- blood vessel — *continued*
  - extremity — *continued*
    - lower — *continued*
      - specified NEC 904.7
    - upper 903.9
      - multiple 903.8
      - specified NEC 903.8
  - femoral
    - artery (superficial) 904.1
      - above profunda origin 904.0
      - common 904.0
    - vein 904.2
  - gastric
    - artery 902.21
    - vein 902.39
  - head 900.9
    - intracranial — *see* Injury, intracranial
    - multiple 900.82
    - specified NEC 900.89
  - hemiazygos vein 901.89
  - hepatic
    - artery 902.22
    - vein 902.11
  - hypogastric 902.59
    - artery 902.51
    - vein 902.52
  - ileocolic
    - artery 902.26
    - vein 902.31
  - iliac 902.50
    - artery 902.53
    - specified branch NEC 902.59
    - vein 902.54
  - innominate
    - artery 901.1
    - vein 901.3
  - intercostal (artery) (vein) 901.81
  - jugular vein (external) 900.81
    - internal 900.1
  - leg NEC 904.8
  - mammary (artery) (vein) 901.82
  - mesenteric
    - artery 902.20
      - inferior 902.27
        - specified branch NEC 902.29
      - superior (trunk) 902.25
        - branches, primary 902.26
    - vein 902.39
      - inferior 902.32
      - superior (and primary subdivisions) 902.31
  - neck 900.9
    - multiple 900.82
    - specified NEC 900.89
  - ovarian 902.89
    - artery 902.81
    - vein 902.82
  - palmar artery 903.4
  - pelvis 902.9
    - multiple 902.87
    - specified NEC 902.89
  - plantar (deep) (artery) (vein) 904.6
  - popliteal 904.40
    - artery 904.41
    - vein 904.42
  - portal 902.33
  - pulmonary 901.40
    - artery 901.41
    - vein 901.42
  - radial (artery) (vein) 903.2
  - renal 902.40
    - artery 902.41
    - specified NEC 902.49
    - vein 902.42
  - saphenous
    - artery 904.7
    - vein (greater) (lesser) 904.3
  - splenic
    - artery 902.23
    - vein 902.34
  - subclavian
    - artery 901.1
    - vein 901.3
  - suprarenal 902.49
  - thoracic 901.9

✓ Additional Digit Required — Refer to the Tabular List for Digit Selection   ▼ Subterms under main terms may continue to next column or page

2010 ICD-9-CM   ▶◀ Revised Text   ● New Line   ▲ Revised Code   October 2009 • Volume 2 — 155

Injury — continued
　blood vessel — continued
　　thoracic — continued
　　　multiple 901.83
　　　specified NEC 901.89
　　tibial 904.50
　　　artery 904.50
　　　　anterior 904.51
　　　　posterior 904.53
　　　vein 904.50
　　　　anterior 904.52
　　　　posterior 904.54
　　ulnar (artery) (vein) 903.3
　　uterine 902.59
　　　artery 902.55
　　　vein 902.56
　　vena cava
　　　inferior 902.10
　　　　specified branches NEC 902.19
　　　superior 901.2
　brachial plexus 953.4
　　newborn 767.6
　brain ▶(traumatic)◀ NEC (see also Injury, intracranial) 854.0 ●
　　due to fracture of skull — see Fracture, ●
　　　skull, by site ●
　breast 959.19
　broad ligament — see Injury, internal, broad ligament
　bronchus, bronchi — see Injury, internal, bronchus
　brow 959.09
　buttock 959.19
　canthus, eye 921.1
　cathode ray 990
　cauda equina 952.4
　　with fracture, vertebra — see Fracture, vertebra, sacrum
　cavernous sinus (see also Injury, intracranial) 854.0 ☑
　cecum — see Injury, internal, cecum
　celiac ganglion or plexus 954.1
　cerebellum (see also Injury, intracranial) 854.0 ☑
　cervix (uteri) — see Injury, internal, cervix
　cheek 959.09
　chest (see also Injury, internal, chest) 959.11
　　wall 959.11
　childbirth (see also Birth, injury) 959.11
　　maternal NEC 665.9 ☑
　chin 959.09
　choroid (eye) 921.3
　clitoris 959.14
　coccyx 959.14
　　complicating delivery 665.6 ☑
　colon — see Injury, internal, colon
　common duct — see Injury, internal, common duct
　conjunctiva 921.1
　　superficial 918.2
　cord
　　spermatic — see Injury, internal, spermatic cord
　　spinal — see Injury, spinal, by site
　cornea 921.3
　　abrasion 918.1
　　due to contact lens 371.82
　　penetrating — see Injury, eyeball, penetrating
　　superficial 918.1
　　due to contact lens 371.82
　cortex (cerebral) (see also Injury, intracranial) 854.0 ☑
　　visual 950.3
　costal region 959.11
　costochondral 959.11
　cranial
　　bones — see Fracture, skull, by site
　　cavity (see also Injury, intracranial) 854.0 ☑
　　nerve — see Injury, nerve, cranial
　crushing — see Crush
　cutaneous sensory nerve
　　lower limb 956.4
　　upper limb 955.5
　deep tissue — see Contusion, by site
　　meaning pressure ulcer 707.25

Injury — continued
　delivery (see also Birth, injury)
　　maternal NEC 665.9 ☑
　Descemet's membrane — see Injury, eyeball, penetrating
　diaphragm — see Injury, internal, diaphragm
　diffuse axonal — see Injury, intracranial
　duodenum — see Injury, internal, duodenum
　ear (auricle) (canal) (drum) (external) 959.09
　elbow (and forearm) (and wrist) 959.3
　epididymis 959.14
　epigastric region 959.12
　epiglottis 959.09
　epiphyseal, current — see Fracture, by site
　esophagus — see Injury, internal, esophagus
　Eustachian tube 959.09
　extremity (lower) (upper) NEC 959.8
　eye 921.9
　　penetrating eyeball — see Injury, eyeball, penetrating
　　superficial 918.9
　eyeball 921.3
　　penetrating 871.7
　　　with
　　　　partial loss (of intraocular tissue) 871.2
　　　　prolapse or exposure (of intraocular tissue) 871.1
　　　without prolapse 871.0
　　　foreign body (nonmagnetic) 871.6
　　　　magnetic 871.5
　　superficial 918.9
　eyebrow 959.09
　eyelid(s) 921.1
　　laceration — see Laceration, eyelid
　　superficial 918.0
　face (and neck) 959.09
　fallopian tube — see Injury, internal, fallopian tube
　finger(s) (nail) 959.5
　flank 959.19
　foot (and ankle) (and knee) (and leg, except thigh) 959.7
　forceps NEC 767.9
　　scalp 767.19
　forearm (and elbow) (and wrist) 959.3
　forehead 959.09
　gallbladder — see Injury, internal, gallbladder
　gasserian ganglion 951.2
　gastrointestinal tract — see Injury, internal, gastrointestinal tract
　genital organ(s)
　　with
　　　abortion — see Abortion, by type, with, damage to pelvic organs
　　　ectopic pregnancy (see also categories 633.0–633.9) 639.2
　　　molar pregnancy (see also categories 630–632) 639.2
　　external 959.14
　　　fracture of corpus cavernosum penis 959.13
　　following
　　　abortion 639.2
　　　ectopic or molar pregnancy 639.2
　　internal — see Injury, internal, genital organs
　　obstetrical trauma NEC 665.9 ☑
　　　affecting fetus or newborn 763.89
　gland
　　lacrimal 921.1
　　　laceration 870.8
　　parathyroid 959.09
　　salivary 959.09
　　thyroid 959.09
　globe (eye) (see also Injury, eyeball) 921.3
　grease gun — see Wound, open, by site, complicated
　groin 959.19
　gum 959.09
　hand(s) (except fingers) 959.4
　head NEC 959.01
　　with
　　　loss of consciousness 850.5
　　　skull fracture — see Fracture, skull, by site

Injury — continued
　heart — see Injury, internal, heart
　heel 959.7
　hip (and thigh) 959.6
　hymen 959.14
　hyperextension (cervical) (vertebra) 847.0
　ileum — see Injury, internal, ileum
　iliac region 959.19
　infrared rays NEC 990
　instrumental (during surgery) 998.2
　　birth injury — see Birth, injury
　　nonsurgical (see also Injury, by site) 959.9
　　obstetrical 665.9 ☑
　　　affecting fetus or newborn 763.89
　　　bladder 665.5 ☑
　　　cervix 665.3 ☑
　　　high vaginal 665.4 ☑
　　　perineal NEC 664.9 ☑
　　　urethra 665.5 ☑
　　　uterus 665.5 ☑
　internal 869.0

> Note — For injury of internal organ(s) by foreign body entering through a natural orifice (e.g., inhaled, ingested, or swallowed) — see Foreign body, entering through orifice.
>
> For internal injury of any of the following sites with internal injury of any other of the sites — see Injury, internal, multiple.

　　with
　　　fracture
　　　　pelvis — see Fracture, pelvis
　　　　specified site, except pelvis — see Injury, internal, by site
　　　open wound into cavity 869.1
　　abdomen, abdominal (viscera) NEC 868.00
　　　with
　　　　fracture, pelvis — see Fracture, pelvis
　　　　open wound into cavity 868.10
　　　specified site NEC 868.09
　　　　with open wound into cavity 868.19
　　adrenal (gland) 868.01
　　　with open wound into cavity 868.11
　　aorta (thoracic) 901.0
　　　abdominal 902.0
　　appendix 863.85
　　　with open wound into cavity 863.95
　　bile duct 868.02
　　　with open wound into cavity 868.12
　　bladder (sphincter) 867.0
　　　with
　　　　abortion — see Abortion, by type, with damage to pelvic organs
　　　　ectopic pregnancy (see also categories 633.0–633.9) 639.2
　　　　molar pregnancy (see also categories 630–632) 639.2
　　　　open wound into cavity 867.1
　　　following
　　　　abortion 639.2
　　　　ectopic or molar pregnancy 639.2
　　　obstetrical trauma 665.5 ☑
　　　　affecting fetus or newborn 763.89
　　blood vessel — see Injury, blood vessel, by site
　　broad ligament 867.6
　　　with open wound into cavity 867.7
　　bronchus, bronchi 862.21
　　　with open wound into cavity 862.31
　　cecum 863.89
　　　with open wound into cavity 863.99
　　cervix (uteri) 867.4
　　　with
　　　　abortion — see Abortion, by type, with damage to pelvic organs
　　　　ectopic pregnancy (see also categories 633.0–633.9) 639.2
　　　　molar pregnancy (see also categories 630–632) 639.2
　　　　open wound into cavity 867.5

Injury — continued
　internal — continued
　　cervix — continued
　　　following
　　　　abortion 639.2
　　　　ectopic or molar pregnancy 639.2
　　　obstetrical trauma 665.3 ☑
　　　　affecting fetus or newborn 763.89
　　chest (see also Injury, internal, intrathoracic organs) 862.8
　　　with open wound into cavity 862.9
　　colon 863.40
　　　with
　　　　open wound into cavity 863.50
　　　　rectum 863.46
　　　　　with open wound into cavity 863.56
　　　ascending (right) 863.41
　　　　with open wound into cavity 863.51
　　　descending (left) 863.43
　　　　with open wound into cavity 863.53
　　　multiple sites 863.46
　　　　with open wound into cavity 863.56
　　　sigmoid 863.44
　　　　with open wound into cavity 863.54
　　　specified site NEC 863.49
　　　　with open wound into cavity 863.59
　　　transverse 863.42
　　　　with open wound into cavity 863.52
　　common duct 868.02
　　　with open wound into cavity 868.12
　　complicating delivery 665.9 ☑
　　　affecting fetus or newborn 763.89
　　diaphragm 862.0
　　　with open wound into cavity 862.1
　　duodenum 863.21
　　　with open wound into cavity 863.31
　　esophagus (intrathoracic) 862.22
　　　with open wound into cavity 862.32
　　　cervical region 874.4
　　　　complicated 874.5
　　fallopian tube 867.6
　　　with open wound into cavity 867.7
　　gallbladder 868.02
　　　with open wound into cavity 868.12
　　gastrointestinal tract NEC 863.80
　　　with open wound into cavity 863.90
　　genital organ NEC 867.6
　　　with open wound into cavity 867.7
　　heart 861.00
　　　with open wound into thorax 861.10
　　ileum 863.29
　　　with open wound into cavity 863.39
　　intestine NEC 863.89
　　　with open wound into cavity 863.99
　　　large NEC 863.40
　　　　with open wound into cavity 863.50
　　　small NEC 863.20
　　　　with open wound into cavity 863.30
　　intra-abdominal (organ) 868.00
　　　with open wound into cavity 868.10
　　　multiple sites 868.09
　　　　with open wound into cavity 868.19
　　　specified site NEC 868.09
　　　　with open wound into cavity 868.19
　　intrathoracic organs (multiple) 862.8
　　　with open wound into cavity 862.9
　　　diaphragm (only) — see Injury, internal, diaphragm
　　　heart (only) — see Injury, internal, heart
　　　lung (only) — see Injury, internal, lung
　　　specified site NEC 862.29
　　　　with open wound into cavity 862.39
　　intrauterine (see also Injury, internal, uterus) 867.4

☑ Additional Digit Required — Refer to the Tabular List for Digit Selection　　　　　　　　　　　　　　　　　　　　Subterms under main terms may continue to next column or page

156 — Volume 2 · October 2009　　　　▶◀ Revised Text　　　● New Line　　　▲ Revised Code　　　2010 ICD-9-CM

Injury — *continued*
  internal — *continued*
    intrauterine (*see also* Injury, internal, uterus)
      — *continued*
      with open wound into cavity 867.5
    jejunum 863.29
      with open wound into cavity 863.39
    kidney (subcapsular) 866.00
      with
        disruption of parenchyma (complete) 866.03
          with open wound into cavity 866.13
        hematoma (without rupture of capsule) 866.01
          with open wound into cavity 866.11
        laceration 866.02
          with open wound into cavity 866.12
        open wound into cavity 866.10
    liver 864.00
      with
        contusion 864.01
          with open wound into cavity 864.11
        hematoma 864.01
          with open wound into cavity 864.11
        laceration 864.05
          with open wound into cavity 864.15
          major (disruption of hepatic parenchyma) 864.04
            with open wound into cavity 864.14
          minor (capsule only) 864.02
            with open wound into cavity 864.12
          moderate (involving parenchyma) 864.03
            with open wound into cavity 864.13
          multiple 864.04
          stellate 864.04
            with open wound into cavity 864.14
        open wound into cavity 864.10
    lung 861.20
      with open wound into thorax 861.30
      hemopneumothorax — *see* Hemopneumothorax, traumatic
      hemothorax — *see* Hemothorax, traumatic
      pneumohemothorax — *see* Pneumohemothorax, traumatic
      pneumothorax — *see* Pneumothorax, traumatic
      transfusion related, acute (TRALI) 518.7
    mediastinum 862.29
      with open wound into cavity 862.39
    mesentery 863.89
      with open wound into cavity 863.99
    mesosalpinx 867.6
      with open wound into cavity 867.7
    multiple 869.0

Note — *Multiple internal injuries of sites classifiable to the same three- or four-digit category should be classified to that category.*

Multiple injuries classifiable to different fourth-digit subdivisions of 861 (heart and lung injuries) should be dealt with according to coding rules.

      internal
        with open wound into cavity 869.1
      intra–abdominal organ (sites classifiable to 863–868)
        with
          intrathoracic organ(s) (sites classifiable to 861–862) 869.0
            with open wound into cavity 869.1

Injury — *continued*
  internal — *continued*
    multiple — *continued*
      intra–abdominal organ — *continued*
        with — *continued*
          other intra–abdominal organ(s) (sites classifiable to 863–868, except where classifiable to the same three–digit category) 868.09
            with open wound into cavity 868.19
      intrathoracic organ (sites classifiable to 861–862)
        with
          intra–abdominal organ(s) (sites classifiable to 863–868) 869.0
            with open wound into cavity 869.1
          other intrathoracic organ(s) (sites classifiable to 861–862, except where classifiable to the same three–digit category) 862.8
            with open wound into cavity 862.9
    myocardium — *see* Injury, internal, heart
    ovary 867.6
      with open wound into cavity 867.7
    pancreas (multiple sites) 863.84
      with open wound into cavity 863.94
      body 863.82
        with open wound into cavity 863.92
      head 863.81
        with open wound into cavity 863.91
      tail 863.83
        with open wound into cavity 863.93
    pelvis, pelvic (organs) (viscera) 867.8
      with
        fracture, pelvis — *see* Fracture, pelvis
        open wound into cavity 867.9
      specified site NEC 867.6
        with open wound into cavity 867.7
    peritoneum 868.03
      with open wound into cavity 868.13
    pleura 862.29
      with open wound into cavity 862.39
    prostate 867.6
      with open wound into cavity 867.7
    rectum 863.45
      with
        colon 863.46
          with open wound into cavity 863.56
        open wound into cavity 863.55
    retroperitoneum 868.04
      with open wound into cavity 868.14
    round ligament 867.6
      with open wound into cavity 867.7
    seminal vesicle 867.6
      with open wound into cavity 867.7
    spermatic cord 867.6
      with open wound into cavity 867.7
      scrotal — *see* Wound, open, spermatic cord
    spleen 865.00
      with
        disruption of parenchyma (massive) 865.04
          with open wound into cavity 865.14
        hematoma (without rupture of capsule) 865.01
          with open wound into cavity 865.11
        open wound into cavity 865.10
        tear, capsular 865.02

Injury — *continued*
  internal — *continued*
    spleen — *continued*
      with — *continued*
        tear, capsular — *continued*
          with open wound into cavity 865.12
          extending into parenchyma 865.03
            with open wound into cavity 865.13
    stomach 863.0
      with open wound into cavity 863.1
    suprarenal gland (multiple) 868.01
      with open wound into cavity 868.11
    thorax, thoracic (cavity) (organs) (multiple) (*see also* Injury, internal, intrathoracic organs) 862.8
      with open wound into cavity 862.9
    thymus (gland) 862.29
      with open wound into cavity 862.39
    trachea (intrathoracic) 862.29
      with open wound into cavity 862.39
      cervical region (*see also* Wound, open, trachea) 874.02
    ureter 867.2
      with open wound into cavity 867.3
    urethra (sphincter) 867.0
      with
        abortion — *see* Abortion, by type, with damage to pelvic organs
        ectopic pregnancy (*see also* categories 633.0–633.9) 639.2
        molar pregnancy (*see also* categories 630–632) 639.2
        open wound into cavity 867.1
      following
        abortion 639.2
        ectopic or molar pregnancy 639.2
      obstetrical trauma 665.5 ☑
        affecting fetus or newborn 763.89
    uterus 867.4
      with
        abortion — *see* Abortion, by type, with damage to pelvic organs
        ectopic pregnancy (*see also* categories 633.0–633.9) 639.2
        molar pregnancy (*see also* categories 630–632) 639.2
        open wound into cavity 867.5
      following
        abortion 639.2
        ectopic or molar pregnancy 639.2
      obstetrical trauma NEC 665.5 ☑
        affecting fetus or newborn 763.89
    vas deferens 867.6
      with open wound into cavity 867.7
    vesical (sphincter) 867.0
      with open wound into cavity 867.1
    viscera (abdominal) (*see also* Injury, internal, multiple) 868.00
      with
        fracture, pelvis — *see* Fracture, pelvis
        open wound into cavity 868.10
    thoracic NEC (*see also* Injury, internal, intrathoracic organs) 862.8
      with open wound into cavity 862.9
  interscapular region 959.19
  intervertebral disc 959.19
  intestine — *see* Injury, internal, intestine
  intra-abdominal (organs) NEC — *see* Injury, internal, intra-abdominal

Injury — *continued*
  intracranial ▶(traumatic)◀ 854.0 ☑

Note — *Use the following fifth-digit subclassification with categories 851–854:*

  0   *unspecified state of consciousness*
  1   *with no loss of consciousness*
  2   *with brief [less than one hour] loss of consciousness*
  3   *with moderate [1–24 hours] loss of consciousness*
  4   *with prolonged [more than 24 hours] loss of consciousness and return to pre–existing conscious level*
  5   *with prolonged [more than 24 hours] loss of consciousness, without return to pre–existing conscious level*

Use fifth-digit 5 to designate when a patient is unconscious and dies before regaining consciousness, regardless of the duration of the loss of consciousness

  6   *with loss of consciousness of unspecified duration*
  9   *with concussion, unspecified*

    with
      open intracranial wound 854.1 ☑
      skull fracture — *see* Fracture, skull, by site
    contusion 851.8 ☑
      with open intracranial wound 851.9 ☑
      brain stem 851.4 ☑
        with open intracranial wound 851.5 ☑
      cerebellum 851.4 ☑
        with open intracranial wound 851.5 ☑
      cortex (cerebral) 851.0 ☑
        with open intracranial wound 851.2 ☑
    hematoma — *see* Injury, intracranial, hemorrhage
    hemorrhage 853.0 ☑
      with
        laceration — *see* Injury, intracranial, laceration
        open intracranial wound 853.1 ☑
      extradural 852.4 ☑
        with open intracranial wound 852.5 ☑
      subarachnoid 852.0 ☑
        with open intracranial wound 852.1 ☑
      subdural 852.2 ☑
        with open intracranial wound 852.3 ☑
    laceration 851.8 ☑
      with open intracranial wound 851.9 ☑
      brain stem 851.6 ☑
        with open intracranial wound 851.7 ☑
      cerebellum 851.6 ☑
        with open intracranial wound 851.7 ☑
      cortex (cerebral) 851.2 ☑
        with open intracranial wound 851.3 ☑
  intraocular — *see* Injury, eyeball, penetrating
  intrathoracic organs (multiple) — *see* Injury, internal, intrathoracic organs
  intrauterine — *see* Injury, internal, intrauterine
  iris 921.3
    penetrating — *see* Injury, eyeball, penetrating
  jaw 959.09
  jejunum — *see* Injury, internal, jejunum
  joint NEC 959.9
    old or residual 718.80
      ankle 718.87
      elbow 718.82
      foot 718.87
      hand 718.84

☑ Additional Digit Required — Refer to the Tabular List for Digit Selection   ᵂ Subterms under main terms may continue to next column or page

Injury — *continued*
joint — *continued*
old or residual — *continued*
hip 718.85
knee 718.86
multiple sites 718.89
pelvic region 718.85
shoulder (region) 718.81
specified site NEC 718.88
wrist 718.83
kidney — *see* Injury, internal, kidney
acute (nontraumatic) 584.9
knee (and ankle) (and foot) (and leg, except thigh) 959.7
labium (majus) (minus) 959.14
labyrinth, ear 959.09
lacrimal apparatus, gland, or sac 921.1
laceration 870.8
larynx 959.09
late effect — *see* Late, effects (of), injury
leg, except thigh (and ankle) (and foot) (and knee) 959.7
upper or thigh 959.6
lens, eye 921.3
penetrating — *see* Injury, eyeball, penetrating
lid, eye — *see* Injury, eyelid
lip 959.09
liver — *see* Injury, internal, liver
lobe, parietal — *see* Injury, intracranial
lumbar (region) 959.19
plexus 953.5
lumbosacral (region) 959.19
plexus 953.5
lung — *see* Injury, internal, lung
malar region 959.09
mastoid region 959.09
maternal, during pregnancy, affecting fetus or newborn 760.5
maxilla 959.09
mediastinum — *see* Injury, internal, mediastinum
membrane
brain (*see also* Injury, intracranial) 854.0 ☑
tympanic 959.09
meningeal artery — *see* Hemorrhage, brain, traumatic, subarachnoid
meninges (cerebral) — *see* Injury, intracranial
mesenteric
artery — *see* Injury, blood vessel, mesenteric, artery
plexus, inferior 954.1
vein — *see* Injury, blood vessel, mesenteric, vein
mesentery — *see* Injury, internal, mesentery
mesosalpinx — *see* Injury, internal, mesosalpinx
middle ear 959.09
midthoracic region 959.11
mouth 959.09
multiple (sites not classifiable to the same four–digit category in 959.0–959.7) 959.8
internal 869.0
with open wound into cavity 869.1
musculocutaneous nerve 955.4
nail
finger 959.5
toe 959.7
nasal (septum) (sinus) 959.09
nasopharynx 959.09
neck (and face) 959.09
nerve 957.9
abducens 951.3
abducent 951.3
accessory 951.6
acoustic 951.5
ankle and foot 956.9
anterior crural, femoral 956.1
arm (*see also* Injury, nerve, upper limb) 955.9
auditory 951.5
axillary 955.0
brachial plexus 953.4
cervical sympathetic 954.0
cranial 951.9

Injury — *continued*
nerve — *continued*
cranial — *continued*
first or olfactory 951.8
second or optic 950.0
third or oculomotor 951.0
fourth or trochlear 951.1
fifth or trigeminal 951.2
sixth or abducens 951.3
seventh or facial 951.4
eighth, acoustic, or auditory 951.5
ninth or glossopharyngeal 951.8
tenth, pneumogastric, or vagus 951.8
eleventh or accessory 951.6
twelfth or hypoglossal 951.7
newborn 767.7
cutaneous sensory
lower limb 956.4
upper limb 955.5
digital (finger) 955.6
toe 956.5
facial 951.4
newborn 767.5
femoral 956.1
finger 955.9
foot and ankle 956.9
forearm 955.9
glossopharyngeal 951.8
hand and wrist 955.9
head and neck, superficial 957.0
hypoglossal 951.7
involving several parts of body 957.8
leg (*see also* Injury, nerve, lower limb) 956.9
lower limb 956.9
multiple 956.8
specified site NEC 956.5
lumbar plexus 953.5
lumbosacral plexus 953.5
median 955.1
forearm 955.1
wrist and hand 955.1
multiple (in several parts of body) (sites not classifiable to the same three-digit category) 957.8
musculocutaneous 955.4
musculospiral 955.3
upper arm 955.3
oculomotor 951.0
olfactory 951.8
optic 950.0
pelvic girdle 956.9
multiple sites 956.8
specified site NEC 956.5
peripheral 957.9
multiple (in several regions) (sites not classifiable to the same three-digit category) 957.8
specified site NEC 957.1
peroneal 956.3
ankle and foot 956.3
lower leg 956.3
plantar 956.5
plexus 957.9
celiac 954.1
mesenteric, inferior 954.1
spinal 953.9
brachial 953.4
lumbosacral 953.5
multiple sites 953.8
sympathetic NEC 954.1
pneumogastric 951.8
radial 955.3
wrist and hand 955.3
sacral plexus 953.5
sciatic 956.0
thigh 956.0
shoulder girdle 955.9
multiple 955.8
specified site NEC 955.7
specified site NEC 957.1
spinal 953.9
plexus — *see* Injury, nerve, plexus, spinal
root 953.9
cervical 953.0
dorsal 953.1

Injury — *continued*
nerve — *continued*
spinal — *continued*
root — *continued*
lumbar 953.2
multiple sites 953.8
sacral 953.3
splanchnic 954.1
sympathetic NEC 954.1
cervical 954.0
thigh 956.9
tibial 956.5
ankle and foot 956.2
lower leg 956.5
posterior 956.2
toe 956.9
trigeminal 951.2
trochlear 951.1
trunk, excluding shoulder and pelvic girdles 954.9
specified site NEC 954.8
sympathetic NEC 954.1
ulnar 955.2
forearm 955.2
wrist (and hand) 955.2
upper limb 955.9
multiple 955.8
specified site NEC 955.7
vagus 951.8
wrist and hand 955.9
nervous system, diffuse 957.8
nose (septum) 959.09
obstetrical NEC 665.9 ☑
affecting fetus or newborn 763.89
occipital (region) (scalp) 959.09
lobe (*see also* Injury, intracranial) 854.0 ☑
optic 950.9
chiasm 950.1
cortex 950.3
nerve 950.0
pathways 950.2
orbit, orbital (region) 921.2
penetrating 870.3
with foreign body 870.4
ovary — *see* Injury, internal, ovary
paint-gun — *see* Wound, open, by site, complicated
palate (soft) 959.09
pancreas — *see* Injury, internal, pancreas
parathyroid (gland) 959.09
parietal (region) (scalp) 959.09
lobe — *see* Injury, intracranial
pelvic
floor 959.19
complicating delivery 664.1 ☑
affecting fetus or newborn 763.89
joint or ligament, complicating delivery 665.6 ☑
affecting fetus or newborn 763.89
organs (*see also* Injury, internal, pelvis)
with
abortion — *see* Abortion, by type, with damage to pelvic organs
ectopic pregnancy (*see also* categories 633.0–633.9) 639.2
molar pregnancy (*see also* categories 633.0–633.9) 639.2
following
abortion 639.2
ectopic or molar pregnancy 639.2
obstetrical trauma 665.5 ☑
affecting fetus or newborn 763.89
pelvis 959.19
penis 959.14
fracture of corpus cavernosum 959.13
perineum 959.14
peritoneum — *see* Injury, internal, peritoneum
periurethral tissue
with
abortion — *see* Abortion, by type, with damage to pelvic organs
ectopic pregnancy (*see also* categories 633.0–633.9) 639.2
molar pregnancy (*see also* categories 630–632) 639.2

Injury — *continued*
periurethral tissue — *continued*
complicating delivery 665.5 ☑
affecting fetus or newborn 763.89
following
abortion 639.2
ectopic or molar pregnancy 639.2
phalanges
foot 959.7
hand 959.5
pharynx 959.09
pleura — *see* Injury, internal, pleura
popliteal space 959.7
post-cardiac surgery (syndrome) 429.4
prepuce 959.14
prostate — *see* Injury, internal, prostate
pubic region 959.19
pudenda 959.14
radiation NEC 990
radioactive substance or radium NEC 990
rectovaginal septum 959.14
rectum — *see* Injury, internal, rectum
retina 921.3
penetrating — *see* Injury, eyeball, penetrating
retroperitoneal — *see* Injury, internal, retroperitoneum
roentgen rays NEC 990
round ligament — *see* Injury, internal, round ligament
sacral (region) 959.19
plexus 953.5
sacroiliac ligament NEC 959.19
sacrum 959.19
salivary ducts or glands 959.09
scalp 959.09
due to birth trauma 767.19
fetus or newborn 767.19
scapular region 959.2
sclera 921.3
penetrating — *see* Injury, eyeball, penetrating
superficial 918.2
scrotum 959.14
seminal vesicle — *see* Injury, internal, seminal vesicle
shoulder (and upper arm) 959.2
sinus
cavernous (*see also* Injury, intracranial) 854.0 ☑
nasal 959.09
skeleton NEC, birth injury 767.3
skin NEC 959.9
skull — *see* Fracture, skull, by site
soft tissue (of external sites) (severe) — *see* Wound, open, by site
specified site NEC 959.8
spermatic cord — *see* Injury, internal, spermatic cord
spinal (cord) 952.9
with fracture, vertebra — *see* Fracture, vertebra, by site, with spinal cord injury
cervical (C₁-C₄) 952.00
with
anterior cord syndrome 952.02
central cord syndrome 952.03
complete lesion of cord 952.01
incomplete lesion NEC 952.04
posterior cord syndrome 952.04
C₅-C₇ level 952.05
with
anterior cord syndrome 952.07
central cord syndrome 952.08
complete lesion of cord 952.06
incomplete lesion NEC 952.09
posterior cord syndrome 952.09
specified type NEC 952.09
specified type NEC 952.04
dorsal (D₁-D₆) (T₁-T₆) (thoracic) 952.10
with
anterior cord syndrome 952.12
central cord syndrome 952.13
complete lesion of cord 952.11
incomplete lesion NEC 952.14
posterior cord syndrome 952.14

☑ Additional Digit Required — Refer to the Tabular List for Digit Selection

ᴹᴱᴸ Subterms under main terms may continue to next column or page

Injury — *continued*
  spinal — *continued*
    dorsal — *continued*
      D_7-D_{12} level (T_7-T_{12}) 952.15
        with
          anterior cord syndrome 952.17
          central cord syndrome 952.18
          complete lesion of cord 952.16
          incomplete lesion NEC 952.19
          posterior cord syndrome 952.19
          specified type NEC 952.19
      specified type NEC 952.14
    lumbar 952.2
    multiple sites 952.8
    nerve (root) NEC — *see* Injury, nerve, spinal, root
    plexus 953.9
      brachial 953.4
      lumbosacral 953.5
      multiple sites 953.8
    sacral 952.3
    thoracic (*see also* Injury, spinal, dorsal) 952.10
  spleen — *see* Injury, internal, spleen
  stellate ganglion 954.1
  sternal region 959.11
  stomach — *see* Injury, internal, stomach
  subconjunctival 921.1
  subcutaneous 959.9
  subdural — *see* Injury, intracranial
  submaxillary region 959.09
  submental region 959.09
  subungual
    fingers 959.5
    toes 959.7
  superficial 919 ☑

Note — Use the following fourth-digit subdivisions with categories 910–919:

0 *Abrasion or friction burn without mention of infection*

1 *Abrasion or friction burn, infected*

2 *Blister without mention of infection*

3 *Blister, infected*

4 *Insect bite, nonvenomous, without mention of infection*

5 *Insect bite, nonvenomous, infected*

6 *Superficial foreign body (splinter) without major open wound and without mention of infection*

7 *Superficial foreign body (splinter) without major open wound, infected*

8 *Other and unspecified superficial injury without mention of infection*

9 *Other and unspecified superficial injury, infected*

For late effects of superficial injury, see category 906.2.

---

    abdomen, abdominal (muscle) (wall) (and other part(s) of trunk) 911 ☑
    ankle (and hip, knee, leg, or thigh) 916 ☑
    anus (and other part(s) of trunk) 911 ☑
    arm 913 ☑
      upper (and shoulder) 912 ☑
    auditory canal (external) (meatus) (and other part(s) of face, neck, or scalp, except eye) 910 ☑
    axilla (and upper arm) 912 ☑
    back (and other part(s) of trunk) 911 ☑
    breast (and other part(s) of trunk) 911 ☑
    brow (and other part(s) of face, neck, or scalp, except eye) 910 ☑
    buttock (and other part(s) of trunk) 911 ☑
    canthus, eye 918.0
    cheek(s) (and other part(s) of face, neck, or scalp, except eye) 910 ☑
    chest wall (and other part(s) of trunk) 911 ☑
    chin (and other part(s) of face, neck, or scalp, except eye) 910 ☑
    clitoris (and other part(s) of trunk) 911 ☑

Injury — *continued*
  superficial — *continued*
    conjunctiva 918.2
    cornea 918.1
      due to contact lens 371.82
    costal region (and other part(s) of trunk) 911 ☑
    ear(s) (auricle) (canal) (drum) (external) (and other part(s) of face, neck, or scalp, except eye) 910 ☑
    elbow (and forearm) (and wrist) 913 ☑
    epididymis (and other part(s) of trunk) 911 ☑
    epigastric region (and other part(s) of trunk) 911 ☑
    epiglottis (and other part(s) of face, neck, or scalp, except eye) 910 ☑
    eye(s) (and adnexa) NEC 918.9
    eyelid(s) (and periocular area) 918.0
    face (any part, except eye) (and neck or scalp) 910 ☑
    finger(s) (nail) (any) 915 ☑
    flank (and other part(s) of trunk) 911 ☑
    foot (phalanges) (and toe(s)) 917 ☑
    forearm (and elbow) (and wrist) 913 ☑
    forehead (and other part(s) of face, neck, or scalp, except eye) 910 ☑
    globe (eye) 918.9
    groin (and other part(s) of trunk) 911 ☑
    gum(s) (and other part(s) of face, neck, or scalp, except eye) 910 ☑
    hand(s) (except fingers alone) 914 ☑
    head (and other part(s) of face, neck, or scalp, except eye) 910 ☑
    heel (and foot or toe) 917 ☑
    hip (and ankle, knee, leg, or thigh) 916 ☑
    iliac region (and other part(s) of trunk) 911 ☑
    interscapular region (and other part(s) of trunk) 911 ☑
    iris 918.9
    knee (and ankle, hip, leg, or thigh) 916 ☑
    labium (majus) (minus) (and other part(s) of trunk) 911 ☑
    lacrimal (apparatus) (gland) (sac) 918.0
    leg (lower) (upper) (and ankle, hip, knee, or thigh) 916 ☑
    lip(s) (and other part(s) of face, neck, or scalp, except eye) 910 ☑
    lower extremity (except foot) 916 ☑
    lumbar region (and other part(s) of trunk) 911 ☑
    malar region (and other part(s) of face, neck, or scalp, except eye) 910 ☑
    mastoid region (and other part(s) of face, neck, or scalp, except eye) 910 ☑
    midthoracic region (and other part(s) of trunk) 911 ☑
    mouth (and other part(s) of face, neck, or scalp, except eye) 910 ☑
    multiple sites (not classifiable to the same three-digit category) 919 ☑
    nasal (septum) (and other part(s) of face, neck, or scalp, except eye) 910 ☑
    neck (and face or scalp, any part(s), except eye) 910 ☑
    nose (septum) (and other part(s) of face, neck, or scalp, except eye) 910 ☑
    occipital region (and other part(s) of face, neck, or scalp, except eye) 910 ☑
    orbital region 918.0
    palate (soft) (and other part(s) of face, neck, or scalp, except eye) 910 ☑
    parietal region (and other part(s) of face, neck, or scalp, except eye) 910 ☑
    penis (and other part(s) of trunk) 911 ☑
    perineum (and other part(s) of trunk) 911 ☑
    periocular area 918.0
    pharynx (and other part(s) of face, neck, or scalp, except eye) 910 ☑
    popliteal space (and ankle, hip, leg, or thigh) 916 ☑
    prepuce (and other part(s) of trunk) 911 ☑

Injury — *continued*
  superficial — *continued*
    pubic region (and other part(s) of trunk) 911 ☑
    pudenda (and other part(s) of trunk) 911 ☑
    sacral region (and other part(s) of trunk) 911 ☑
    salivary (ducts) (glands) (and other part(s) of face, neck, or scalp, except eye) 910 ☑
    scalp (and other part(s) of face or neck, except eye) 910 ☑
    scapular region (and upper arm) 912 ☑
    sclera 918.2
    scrotum (and other part(s) of trunk) 911 ☑
    shoulder (and upper arm) 912 ☑
    skin NEC 919 ☑
    specified site(s) NEC 919 ☑
    sternal region (and other part(s) of trunk) 911 ☑
    subconjunctival 918.2
    subcutaneous NEC 919 ☑
    submaxillary region (and other part(s) of face, neck, or scalp, except eye) 910 ☑
    submental region (and other part(s) of face, neck, or scalp, except eye) 910 ☑
    supraclavicular fossa (and other part(s) of face, neck, or scalp, except eye) 910 ☑
    supraorbital 918.0
    temple (and other part(s) of face, neck, or scalp, except eye) 910 ☑
    temporal region (and other part(s) of face, neck, or scalp, except eye) 910 ☑
    testis (and other part(s) of trunk) 911 ☑
    thigh (and ankle, hip, knee, or leg) 916 ☑
    thorax, thoracic (external) (and other part(s) of trunk) 911 ☑
    throat (and other part(s) of face, neck, or scalp, except eye) 910 ☑
    thumb(s) (nail) 915 ☑
    toe(s) (nail) (subungual) (and foot) 917 ☑
    tongue (and other part(s) of face, neck, or scalp, except eye) 910 ☑
    tooth, teeth (*see also* Abrasion, dental) 521.20
    trunk (any part(s)) 911 ☑
    tunica vaginalis 959.14
    tympanum, tympanic membrane (and other part(s) of face, neck, or scalp, except eye) 910 ☑
    upper extremity NEC 913 ☑
    uvula (and other part(s) of face, neck, or scalp, except eye) 910 ☑
    vagina (and other part(s) of trunk) 911 ☑
    vulva (and other part(s) of trunk) 911 ☑
    wrist (and elbow) (and forearm) 913 ☑
  supraclavicular fossa 959.19
  supraorbital 959.09
  surgical complication (external or internal site) 998.2
  symphysis pubis 959.19
    complicating delivery 665.6 ☑
      affecting fetus or newborn 763.89
  temple 959.09
  temporal region 959.09
  testis 959.14
  thigh (and hip) 959.6
  thorax, thoracic (external) 959.11
    cavity — *see* Injury, internal, thorax
    internal — *see* Injury, internal, intrathoracic organs
  throat 959.09
  thumb(s) (nail) 959.5
  thymus — *see* Injury, internal, thymus
  thyroid (gland) 959.09
  toe (nail) (any) 959.7
  tongue 959.09
  tonsil 959.09
  tooth NEC 873.63
    complicated 873.73
  trachea — *see* Injury, internal, trachea

Injury — *continued*
  trunk 959.19
  tunica vaginalis 959.14
  tympanum, tympanic membrane 959.09
  ultraviolet rays NEC 990
  ureter — *see* Injury, internal, ureter
  urethra (sphincter) — *see* Injury, internal, urethra
  uterus — *see* Injury, internal, uterus
  uvula 959.09
  vagina 959.14
  vascular — *see* Injury, blood vessel
  vas deferens — *see* Injury, internal, vas deferens
  vein (*see also* Injury, blood vessel, by site) 904.9
  vena cava
    inferior 902.10
    superior 901.2
  vesical (sphincter) — *see* Injury, internal, vesical
  viscera (abdominal) — *see* Injury, internal, viscera
    with fracture, pelvis — *see* Fracture, pelvis
  visual 950.9
    cortex 950.3
  vitreous (humor) 871.2
  vulva 959.14
  whiplash (cervical spine) 847.0
  wringer — *see* Crush, by site
  wrist (and elbow) (and forearm) 959.3
  x-ray NEC 990
Inoculation — *see also* Vaccination
  complication or reaction — *see* Complication, vaccination
INPH (idiopathic normal pressure hydrocephalus) 331.5
Insanity, insane — *see also* Psychosis 298.9
  adolescent (*see also* Schizophrenia) 295.9 ☑
  alternating (*see also* Psychosis, affective, circular) 296.7
  confusional 298.9
    acute 293.0
    subacute 293.1
  delusional 298.9
  paralysis, general 094.1
    progressive 094.1
  paresis, general 094.1
  senile 290.20
Insect
  bite — *see* Injury, superficial, by site
  venomous, poisoning by 989.5
Insemination, artificial V26.1
Insensitivity
  adrenocorticotropin hormone (ACTH) 255.41
  androgen 259.50
    complete 259.51
    partial 259.52
Insertion
  cord (umbilical) lateral or velamentous 663.8 ☑
    affecting fetus or newborn 762.6
  intrauterine contraceptive device V25.1
  placenta, vicious — *see* Placenta, previa
  subdermal implantable contraceptive V25.5
  velamentous, umbilical cord 663.8 ☑
    affecting fetus or newborn 762.6
Insolation 992.0
  meaning sunstroke 992.0
Insomnia, unspecified 780.52
  with sleep apnea, unspecified 780.51
  adjustment 307.41
  alcohol induced 291.82
  behavioral, of childhood V69.5
  drug induced 292.85
  due to
    medical condition classified elsewhere 327.01
    mental disorder 327.02
  fatal familial (FFI) 046.72
  idiopathic 307.42
  nonorganic origin 307.41
    persistent (primary) 307.42
    transient 307.41
  organic 327.00
    other 327.09
  paradoxical 307.42

☑ Additional Digit Required — Refer to the Tabular List for Digit Selection   ▽ Subterms under main terms may continue to next column or page

2010 ICD-9-CM   ▶◀ Revised Text   ● New Line   ▲ Revised Code   **Volume 2 — 159**

Insomnia, unspecified — *continued*
  primary 307.42
  psychophysiological 307.42
  subjective complaint 307.49
Inspiration
  food or foreign body (*see also* Asphyxia, food or foreign body) 933.1
  mucus (*see also* Asphyxia, mucus) 933.1
Inspissated bile syndrome, newborn 774.4
Instability
  detrusor 596.59
  emotional (excessive) 301.3
  joint (posttraumatic) 718.80
    ankle 718.87
    elbow 718.82
    foot 718.87
    hand 718.84
    hip 718.85
    knee 718.86
    lumbosacral 724.6
    multiple sites 718.89
    pelvic region 718.85
    sacroiliac 724.6
    shoulder (region) 718.81
    specified site NEC 718.88
    wrist 718.83
  lumbosacral 724.6
  nervous 301.89
  personality (emotional) 301.59
  thyroid, paroxysmal 242.9 ☑
  urethral 599.83
  vasomotor 780.2
Insufficiency, insufficient
  accommodation 367.4
  adrenal (gland) (acute) (chronic) 255.41
    medulla 255.5
    primary 255.41
    specified site NEC 255.5
  adrenocortical 255.41
  anterior (occlusal) guidance 524.54
  anus 569.49
  aortic (valve) 424.1
    with
      mitral (valve) disease 396.1
        insufficiency, incompetence, or regurgitation 396.3
        stenosis or obstruction 396.1
      stenosis or obstruction 424.1
        with mitral (valve) disease 396.8
    congenital 746.4
    rheumatic 395.1
      with
        mitral (valve) disease 396.1
          insufficiency, incompetence, or regurgitation 396.3
          stenosis or obstruction 396.1
        stenosis or obstruction 395.2
          with mitral (valve) disease 396.8
    specified cause NEC 424.1
    syphilitic 093.22
  arterial 447.1
    basilar artery 435.0
    carotid artery 435.8
    cerebral 437.1
    coronary (acute or subacute) 411.89
    mesenteric 557.1
    peripheral 443.9
    precerebral 435.9
    vertebral artery 435.1
    vertebrobasilar 435.3
  arteriovenous 459.9
  basilar artery 435.0
  biliary 575.8
  cardiac (*see also* Insufficiency, myocardial) 428.0
    complicating surgery 997.1
    due to presence of (cardiac) prosthesis 429.4
    postoperative 997.1
      long-term effect of cardiac surgery 429.4
    specified during or due to a procedure 997.1
      long-term effect of cardiac surgery 429.4

Insufficiency, insufficient — *continued*
  cardiorenal (*see also* Hypertension, cardiorenal) 404.90
  cardiovascular (*see also* Disease, cardiovascular) 429.2
    renal (*see also* Hypertension, cardiorenal) 404.90
  carotid artery 435.8
  cerebral (vascular) 437.9
  cerebrovascular 437.9
    with transient focal neurological signs and symptoms 435.9
    acute 437.1
      with transient focal neurological signs and symptoms 435.9
  circulatory NEC 459.9
    fetus or newborn 779.89
  convergence 378.83
  coronary (acute or subacute) 411.89
    chronic or with a stated duration of over 8 weeks 414.8
  corticoadrenal 255.41
  dietary 269.9
  divergence 378.85
  food 994.2
  gastroesophageal 530.89
  gonadal
    ovary 256.39
    testis 257.2
  gonadotropic hormone secretion 253.4
  heart (*see also* Insufficiency, myocardial)
    fetus or newborn 779.89
    valve (*see also* Endocarditis) 424.90
      congenital NEC 746.89
  hepatic 573.8
  idiopathic autonomic 333.0
  interocclusal distance of teeth (ridge) 524.36
  kidney
    acute 593.9
    chronic 585.9
  labyrinth, labyrinthine (function) 386.53
    bilateral 386.54
    unilateral 386.53
  lacrimal 375.15
  liver 573.8
  lung (acute) (*see also* Insufficiency, pulmonary) 518.82
    following trauma, surgery, or shock 518.5
    newborn 770.89
  mental (congenital) (*see also* Retardation, mental) 319
  mesenteric 557.1
  mitral (valve) 424.0
    with
      aortic (valve) disease 396.3
        insufficiency, incompetence, or regurgitation 396.3
        stenosis or obstruction 396.2
      obstruction or stenosis 394.2
        with aortic valve disease 396.8
    congenital 746.6
    rheumatic 394.1
      with
        aortic (valve) disease 396.3
          insufficiency, incompetence, or regurgitation 396.3
          stenosis or obstruction 396.2
        obstruction or stenosis 394.2
          with aortic valve disease 396.8
    active or acute 391.1
      with chorea, rheumatic (Sydenham's) 392.0
    specified cause, except rheumatic 424.0
  muscle
    heart — *see* Insufficiency, myocardial
    ocular (*see also* Strabismus) 378.9
  myocardial, myocardium (with arteriosclerosis) 428.0
    with rheumatic fever (conditions classifiable to 390)
      active, acute, or subacute 391.2
        with chorea 392.0
      inactive or quiescent (with chorea) 398.0
    congenital 746.89

Insufficiency, insufficient — *continued*
  myocardial, myocardium — *continued*
    due to presence of (cardiac) prosthesis 429.4
    fetus or newborn 779.89
    following cardiac surgery 429.4
    hypertensive (*see also* Hypertension, heart) 402.91
      benign 402.11
      malignant 402.01
    postoperative 997.1
      long-term effect of cardiac surgery 429.4
    rheumatic 398.0
      active, acute, or subacute 391.2
        with chorea (Sydenham's) 392.0
    syphilitic 093.82
  nourishment 994.2
  organic 799.89
  ovary 256.39
    postablative 256.2
  pancreatic 577.8
  parathyroid (gland) 252.1
  peripheral vascular (arterial) 443.9
  pituitary (anterior) 253.2
    posterior 253.5
  placental — *see* Placenta, insufficiency
  platelets 287.5
  prenatal care in current pregnancy V23.7
  progressive pluriglandular 258.9
  pseudocholinesterase 289.89
  pulmonary (acute) 518.82
    following
      shock 518.5
      surgery 518.5
      trauma 518.5
    newborn 770.89
    valve (*see also* Endocarditis, pulmonary) 424.3
      congenital 746.09
  pyloric 537.0
  renal 593.9
    acute 593.9
    chronic 585.9
    due to a procedure 997.5
  respiratory 786.09
    acute 518.82
      following shock, surgery, or trauma 518.5
    newborn 770.89
  rotation — *see* Malrotation
  suprarenal 255.41
    medulla 255.5
  tarso-orbital fascia, congenital 743.66
  tear film 375.15
  testis 257.2
  thyroid (gland) (acquired) (*see also* Hypothyroidism)
    congenital 243
  tricuspid (*see also* Endocarditis, tricuspid) 397.0
    congenital 746.89
    syphilitic 093.23
  urethral sphincter 599.84
  valve, valvular (heart) (*see also* Endocarditis) 424.90
  vascular 459.9
    intestine NEC 557.9
    mesenteric 557.1
    peripheral 443.9
    renal (*see also* Hypertension, kidney) 403.90
  velopharyngeal
    acquired 528.9
    congenital 750.29
  venous (peripheral) 459.81
  ventricular — *see* Insufficiency, myocardial
  vertebral artery 435.1
  vertebrobasilar artery 435.3
  weight gain during pregnancy 646.8 ☑
  zinc 269.3
Insufflation
  fallopian
    fertility testing V26.21
    following sterilization reversal V26.22
  meconium 770.11
    with respiratory symptoms 770.12
Insular — *see* condition

Insulinoma (M8151/0)
  malignant (M8151/3)
    pancreas 157.4
    specified site — *see* Neoplasm, by site, malignant
    unspecified site 157.4
  pancreas 211.7
  specified site — *see* Neoplasm, by site, benign
  unspecified site 211.7
Insuloma — *see* Insulinoma
Insult
  brain 437.9
    acute 436
  cerebral 437.9
    acute 436
  cerebrovascular 437.9
    acute 436
  vascular NEC 437.9
    acute 436
Insurance examination (certification) V70.3
Intemperance — *see also* Alcoholism 303.9 ☑
Interception of pregnancy (menstrual extraction) V25.3
Interference
  balancing side 524.56
  non-working side 524.56
Intermenstrual
  bleeding 626.6
    irregular 626.6
    regular 626.5
  hemorrhage 626.6
    irregular 626.6
    regular 626.5
  pain(s) 625.2
Intermittent — *see* condition
Internal — *see* condition
Interproximal wear 521.10
Interruption
  aortic arch 747.11
  bundle of His 426.50
  fallopian tube (for sterilization) V25.2
  phase-shift, sleep cycle 307.45
  repeated REM-sleep 307.48
  sleep
    due to perceived environmental disturbances 307.48
    phase-shift, of 24-hour sleep-wake cycle 307.45
    repeated REM-sleep type 307.48
  vas deferens (for sterilization) V25.2
Intersexuality 752.7
Interstitial — *see* condition
Intertrigo 695.89
  labialis 528.5
Intervertebral disc — *see* condition
Intestine, intestinal — *see also* condition
  flu 487.8
Intolerance
  carbohydrate NEC 579.8
  cardiovascular exercise, with pain (at rest) (with less than ordinary activity) (with ordinary activity) V47.2
  cold 780.99
  dissacharide (hereditary) 271.3
  drug
    correct substance properly administered 995.27
    wrong substance given or taken in error 977.9
      specified drug — *see* Table of Drugs and Chemicals
  effort 306.2
  fat NEC 579.8
  foods NEC 579.8
  fructose (hereditary) 271.2
  glucose (-galactose) (congenital) 271.3
  gluten 579.0
  lactose (hereditary) (infantile) 271.3
  lysine (congenital) 270.7
  milk NEC 579.8
  protein (familial) 270.7
  starch NEC 579.8
  sucrose (-isomaltose) (congenital) 271.3
Intoxicated NEC — *see also* Alcoholism 305.0 ☑
Intoxication
  acid 276.2

☑ Additional Digit Required — Refer to the Tabular List for Digit Selection
▼ Subterms under main terms may continue to next column or page
160 — Volume 2
►◄ Revised Text   ● New Line   ▲ Revised Code
2010 ICD-9-CM

Intoxication — *continued*
- acute
  - alcoholic 305.0 ☑
    - with alcoholism 303.0 ☑
    - hangover effects 305.0 ☑
  - caffeine 305.9 ☑
  - hallucinogenic (*see also* Abuse, drugs, nondependent) 305.3 ☑
- alcohol (acute) 305.0 ☑
  - with alcoholism 303.0 ☑
  - hangover effects 305.0 ☑
  - idiosyncratic 291.4
  - pathological 291.4
- alimentary canal 558.2
- ammonia (hepatic) 572.2
- caffeine 305.9 ☑
- chemical (*see also* Table of Drugs and Chemicals)
  - via placenta or breast milk 760.70
    - alcohol 760.71
    - anticonvulsants
    - antifungals
    - anti-infective agents 760.74
    - antimetabolics
    - cocaine 760.75
    - "crack" 760.75
    - hallucinogenic agents NEC 760.73
    - medicinal agents NEC 760.79
    - narcotics 760.72
    - obstetric anesthetic or analgesic drug 763.5
    - specified agent NEC 760.79
    - suspected, affecting management of pregnancy 655.5 ☑
- cocaine, through placenta or breast milk 760.75
- delirium
  - alcohol 291.0
  - drug 292.81
- drug 292.89
  - with delirium 292.81
  - correct substance properly administered (*see also* Allergy, drug) 995.27
  - newborn 779.4
  - obstetric anesthetic or sedation 668.9 ☑
    - affecting fetus or newborn 763.5
  - overdose or wrong substance given or taken — *see* Table of Drugs and Chemicals
  - pathologic 292.2
  - specific to newborn 779.4
  - via placenta or breast milk 760.70
    - alcohol 760.71
    - anticonvulsants 760.77
    - antifungals 760.74
    - anti-infective agents 760.74
    - antimetabolics 760.78
    - cocaine 760.75
    - "crack" 760.75
    - hallucinogenic agents 760.73
    - medicinal agents NEC 760.79
    - narcotics 760.72
    - obstetric anesthetic or analgesic drug 763.5
    - specified agent NEC 760.79
    - suspected, affecting management of pregnancy 655.5 ☑
- enteric — *see* Intoxication, intestinal
- fetus or newborn, via placenta or breast milk 760.70
  - alcohol 760.71
  - anticonvulsants 760.77
  - antifungals 760.74
  - anti-infective agents 760.74
  - antimetabolics 760.78
  - cocaine 760.75
  - "crack" 760.75
  - hallucinogenic agents 760.73
  - medicinal agents NEC 760.79
  - narcotics 760.72
  - obstetric anesthetic or analgesic drug 763.5
  - specified agent NEC 760.79
  - suspected, affecting management of pregnancy 655.5 ☑
- food — *see* Poisoning, food

Intoxication — *continued*
- gastrointestinal 558.2
- hallucinogenic (acute) 305.3 ☑
- hepatocerebral 572.2
- idiosyncratic alcohol 291.4
- intestinal 569.89
  - due to putrefaction of food 005.9
- methyl alcohol (*see also* Alcoholism) 305.0 ☑
  - with alcoholism 303.0 ☑
- non-foodborne due to toxins of Clostridium botulinum [C. botulinum] — *see* Botulism
- pathologic 291.4
  - drug 292.2
- potassium (K) 276.7
- septic
  - with
    - abortion — *see* Abortion, by type, with sepsis
    - ectopic pregnancy (*see also* categories 633.0–633.9) 639.0
    - molar pregnancy (*see also* categories 630–632) 639.0
  - during labor 659.3 ☑
  - following
    - abortion 639.0
    - ectopic or molar pregnancy 639.0
  - generalized — *see* Septicemia
  - puerperal, postpartum, childbirth 670.2 ☑ ▲
- serum (prophylactic) (therapeutic) 999.5
- uremic — *see* Uremia
- water 276.6
Intracranial — *see* condition
Intrahepatic gallbladder 751.69
Intraligamentous — *see also* condition
- pregnancy — *see* Pregnancy, cornual
Intraocular — *see also* condition
- sepsis 360.00
Intrathoracic — *see also* condition
- kidney 753.3
- stomach — *see* Hernia, diaphragm
Intrauterine contraceptive device
- checking V25.42
- insertion V25.1
- in situ V45.51
- management V25.42
- prescription V25.02
  - repeat V25.42
- reinsertion V25.42
- removal V25.42
Intraventricular — *see* condition
Intrinsic deformity — *see* Deformity
Intruded tooth 524.34
Intrusion, repetitive, of sleep (due to environmental disturbances) (with atypical polysomnographic features) 307.48
Intumescent, lens (eye) NEC 366.9
- senile 366.12
Intussusception (colon) (enteric) (intestine) (rectum) 560.0
- appendix 543.9
- congenital 751.5
- fallopian tube 620.8
- ileocecal 560.0
- ileocolic 560.0
- ureter (with obstruction) 593.4
Invagination
- basilar 756.0
- colon or intestine 560.0
Invalid (since birth) 799.89
Invalidism (chronic) 799.89
Inversion
- albumin-globulin (A-G) ratio 273.8
- bladder 596.8
- cecum (*see also* Intussusception) 560.0
- cervix 622.8
- nipple 611.79
  - congenital 757.6
  - puerperal, postpartum 676.3 ☑
- optic papilla 743.57
- organ or site, congenital NEC — *see* Anomaly, specified type NEC
- sleep rhythm 327.39
  - nonorganic origin 307.45
- testis (congenital) 752.51

Inversion — *continued*
- uterus (postinfectional) (postpartal, old) 621.7
  - chronic 621.7
  - complicating delivery 665.2 ☑
    - affecting fetus or newborn 763.89
- vagina — *see* Prolapse, vagina
Investigation
- allergens V72.7
- clinical research (control) (normal comparison) (participant) V70.7
Inviability — *see* Immaturity
Involuntary movement, abnormal 781.0
Involution, involutional — *see also* condition
- breast, cystic or fibrocystic 610.1
- depression (*see also* Psychosis, affective) 296.2 ☑
  - recurrent episode 296.3 ☑
  - single episode 296.2 ☑
- melancholia (*see also* Psychosis, affective) 296.2 ☑
  - recurrent episode 296.3 ☑
  - single episode 296.2 ☑
- ovary, senile 620.3
- paranoid state (reaction) 297.2
- paraphrenia (climacteric) (menopause) 297.2
- psychosis 298.8
- thymus failure 254.8
IQ
- under 20 318.2
- 20-34 318.1
- 35-49 318.0
- 50-70 317
IRDS 769
Irideremia 743.45
Iridis rubeosis 364.42
- diabetic 250.5 ☑ [364.42]
  - due to secondary diabetes 249.5 ☑ [364.42]
Iridochoroiditis (panuveitis) 360.12
Iridocyclitis NEC 364.3
- acute 364.00
  - primary 364.01
  - recurrent 364.02
- chronic 364.10
  - in
    - lepromatous leprosy 030.0 [364.11]
    - sarcoidosis 135 [364.11]
    - tuberculosis (*see also* Tuberculosis) 017.3 ☑ [364.11]
- due to allergy 364.04
- endogenous 364.01
- gonococcal 098.41
- granulomatous 364.10
- herpetic (simplex) 054.44
  - zoster 053.22
- hypopyon 364.05
- lens induced 364.23
- nongranulomatous 364.00
- primary 364.01
- recurrent 364.02
- rheumatic 364.10
- secondary 364.04
  - infectious 364.03
  - noninfectious 364.04
- subacute 364.00
  - primary 364.01
  - recurrent 364.02
- sympathetic 360.11
- syphilitic (secondary) 091.52
- tuberculous (chronic) (*see also* Tuberculosis) 017.3 ☑ [364.11]
Iridocyclochoroiditis (panuveitis) 360.12
Iridodialysis 364.76
Iridodonesis 364.89
Iridoplegia (complete) (partial) (reflex) 379.49
Iridoschisis 364.52
Iris — *see* condition
Iritis 364.3
- acute 364.00
  - primary 364.01
  - recurrent 364.02
- chronic 364.10
  - in
    - sarcoidosis 135 [364.11]
    - tuberculosis (*see also* Tuberculosis) 017.3 ☑ [364.11]

Iritis — *continued*
- diabetic 250.5 ☑ [364.42]
  - due to secondary diabetes 249.5 ☑ [364.42]
- due to
  - allergy 364.04
  - herpes simplex 054.44
  - leprosy 030.0 [364.11]
- endogenous 364.01
- gonococcal 098.41
- gouty 274.89 [364.11]
- granulomatous 364.10
- hypopyon 364.05
- lens induced 364.23
- nongranulomatous 364.00
- papulosa 095.8 [364.11]
- primary 364.01
- recurrent 364.02
- rheumatic 364.10
- secondary 364.04
  - infectious 364.03
  - noninfectious 364.04
- subacute 364.00
  - primary 364.01
  - recurrent 364.02
- sympathetic 360.11
- syphilitic (secondary) 091.52
  - congenital 090.0 [364.11]
  - late 095.8 [364.11]
- tuberculous (*see also* Tuberculosis) 017.3 ☑ [364.11]
- uratic 274.89 [364.11]
Iron
- deficiency anemia 280.9
- metabolism disease 275.0
- storage disease 275.0
Iron-miners' lung 503
Irradiated enamel (tooth, teeth) 521.89
Irradiation
- burn — *see* Burn, by site
- effects, adverse 990
Irreducible, irreducibility — *see* condition
Irregular, irregularity
- action, heart 427.9
- alveolar process 525.8
- bleeding NEC 626.4
- breathing 786.09
- colon 569.89
- contour
  - acquired 371.70
  - of cornea 743.41
    - acquired 371.70
  - reconstructed breast 612.0
- dentin in pulp 522.3
- eye movements NEC 379.59
- menstruation (cause unknown) 626.4
- periods 626.4
- prostate 602.9
- pupil 364.75
- respiratory 786.09
- septum (nasal) 470
- shape, organ or site, congenital NEC — *see* Distortion
- sleep-wake rhythm (non-24-hour) 327.39
  - nonorganic origin 307.45
- vertebra 733.99
Irritability 799.22 ▲
- bladder 596.8
  - neurogenic 596.54
    - with cauda equina syndrome 344.61
- bowel (syndrome) 564.1
- bronchial (*see also* Bronchitis) 490
- cerebral, newborn 779.1
- colon 564.1
  - psychogenic 306.4
- duodenum 564.89
- heart (psychogenic) 306.2
- ileum 564.89
- jejunum 564.89
- myocardium 306.2
- nervousness 799.21 ●
- rectum 564.89
- stomach 536.9
  - psychogenic 306.4
- sympathetic (nervous system) (*see also* Neuropathy, peripheral, autonomic) 337.9

☑ Additional Digit Required — Refer to the Tabular List for Digit Selection   ▼ Subterms under main terms may continue to next column or page

2010 ICD-9-CM   ▶◀ Revised Text   ● New Line   ▲ Revised Code   **October 2009 • Volume 2 — 161**

Intoxication — Irritability

Index

Irritability — Ixodiasis

Irritability — *continued*
  urethra 599.84
  ventricular (heart) (psychogenic) 306.2
Irritable — ▶*see also* Irritability◀ 799.22
Irritation
  anus 569.49
  axillary nerve 353.0
  bladder 596.8
  brachial plexus 353.0
  brain (traumatic) (*see also* Injury, intracranial) 854.0 ☑
    nontraumatic — *see* Encephalitis
  bronchial (*see also* Bronchitis) 490
  cerebral (traumatic) (*see also* Injury, intracranial) 854.0 ☑
    nontraumatic — *see* Encephalitis
  cervical plexus 353.2
  cervix (*see also* Cervicitis) 616.0
  choroid, sympathetic 360.11
  cranial nerve — *see* Disorder, nerve, cranial
  digestive tract 536.9
    psychogenic 306.4
  gastric 536.9
    psychogenic 306.4
  gastrointestinal (tract) 536.9
    functional 536.9
    psychogenic 306.4
  globe, sympathetic 360.11
  intestinal (bowel) 564.9
  labyrinth 386.50
  lumbosacral plexus 353.1
  meninges (traumatic) (*see also* Injury, intracranial) 854.0 ☑
    nontraumatic — *see* Meningitis
  myocardium 306.2
  nerve — *see* Disorder, nerve
  nervous 799.21 ▲
  nose 478.19
  penis 607.89
  perineum 709.9
  peripheral
    autonomic nervous system (*see also* Neuropathy, peripheral, autonomic) 337.9
    nerve — *see* Disorder, nerve
  peritoneum (*see also* Peritonitis) 567.9
  pharynx 478.29
  plantar nerve 355.6
  spinal (cord) (traumatic) (*see also* Injury, spinal, by site)
    nerve (*see also* Disorder, nerve)
      root NEC 724.9
        traumatic — *see* Injury, nerve, spinal
    nontraumatic — *see* Myelitis

Irritation — *continued*
  stomach 536.9
    psychogenic 306.4
  sympathetic nerve NEC (*see also* Neuropathy, peripheral, autonomic) 337.9
  ulnar nerve 354.2
  vagina 623.9
Isambert's disease 012.3 ☑
Ischemia, ischemic 459.9
  basilar artery (with transient neurologic deficit) 435.0
  bone NEC 733.40
  bowel (transient) 557.9
    acute 557.0
    chronic 557.1
    due to mesenteric artery insufficiency 557.1
  brain (*see also* Ischemia, cerebral)
    recurrent focal 435.9
  cardiac (*see also* Ischemia, heart) 414.9
  cardiomyopathy 414.8
  carotid artery (with transient neurologic deficit) 435.8
  cerebral (chronic) (generalized) 437.1
    arteriosclerotic 437.0
    intermittent (with transient neurologic deficit) 435.9
    newborn 779.2
    puerperal, postpartum, childbirth 674.0 ☑
    recurrent focal (with transient neurologic deficit) 435.9
    transient (with transient neurologic deficit) 435.9
  colon 557.9
    acute 557.0
    chronic 557.1
    due to mesenteric artery insufficiency 557.1
  coronary (chronic) (*see also* Ischemia, heart) 414.9
  heart (chronic or with a stated duration of over 8 weeks) 414.9
    acute or with a stated duration of 8 weeks or less (*see also* Infarct, myocardium) 410.9 ☑
      without myocardial infarction 411.89
        with coronary (artery) occlusion 411.81
    subacute 411.89
  intestine (transient) 557.9
    acute 557.0
    chronic 557.1
    due to mesenteric artery insufficiency 557.1

Ischemia, ischemic — *continued*
  kidney 593.81
  labyrinth 386.50
  muscles, leg 728.89
  myocardium, myocardial (chronic or with a stated duration of over 8 weeks) 414.8
    acute (*see also* Infarct, myocardium) 410.9 ☑
      without myocardial infarction 411.89
        with coronary (artery) occlusion 411.81
  renal 593.81
  retina, retinal 362.84
  small bowel 557.9
    acute 557.0
    chronic 557.1
    due to mesenteric artery insufficiency 557.1
  spinal cord 336.1
  subendocardial (*see also* Insufficiency, coronary) 411.89
  vertebral artery (with transient neurologic deficit) 435.1
Ischialgia — *see also* Sciatica 724.3
Ischiopagus 759.4
Ischium, ischial — *see* condition
Ischomenia 626.8
Ischuria 788.5
Iselin's disease or osteochondrosis 732.5
Islands of
  parotid tissue in
    lymph nodes 750.26
    neck structures 750.26
  submaxillary glands in
    fascia 750.26
    lymph nodes 750.26
    neck muscles 750.26
Islet cell tumor, pancreas (M8150/0) 211.7
Isoimmunization NEC — *see also* Incompatibility 656.2 ☑
  anti-E 656.2 ☑
  fetus or newborn 773.2
    ABO blood groups 773.1
    Rhesus (Rh) factor 773.0
Isolation V07.0
  social V62.4
Isosporosis 007.2
Issue
  medical certificate NEC V68.09
    cause of death V68.09
    disability examination V68.01
    fitness V68.09
    incapacity V68.09
  repeat prescription NEC V68.1

Issue — *continued*
  repeat prescription — *continued*
    appliance V68.1
    contraceptive V25.40
      device NEC V25.49
        intrauterine V25.42
        specified type NEC V25.49
      pill V25.41
    glasses V68.1
    medicinal substance V68.1
Itch — *see also* Pruritus 698.9
  bakers' 692.89
  barbers' 110.0
  bricklayers' 692.89
  cheese 133.8
  clam diggers' 120.3
  coolie 126.9
  copra 133.8
  Cuban 050.1
  dew 126.9
  dhobie 110.3
  eye 379.99
  filarial (*see also* Infestation, filarial) 125.9
  grain 133.8
  grocers' 133.8
  ground 126.9
  harvest 133.8
  jock 110.3
  Malabar 110.9
    beard 110.0
    foot 110.4
    scalp 110.0
  meaning scabies 133.0
  Norwegian 133.0
  perianal 698.0
  poultrymen's 133.8
  sarcoptic 133.0
  scrub 134.1
  seven year V61.10
    meaning scabies 133.0
  straw 133.8
  swimmers' 120.3
  washerwoman's 692.4
  water 120.3
  winter 698.8
Itsenko-Cushing syndrome (pituitary basophilism) 255.0
Ivemark's syndrome (asplenia with congenital heart disease) 759.0
Ivory bones 756.52
Ixodes 134.8
Ixodiasis 134.8

J

Jaccoud's nodular fibrositis, chronic (Jaccoud's syndrome) 714.4
Jackson's
  membrane 751.4
  paralysis or syndrome 344.89
  veil 751.4
Jacksonian
  epilepsy (see also Epilepsy) 345.5 ☑
  seizures (focal) (see also Epilepsy) 345.5 ☑
Jacob's ulcer (M8090/3) — see Neoplasm, skin, malignant, by site
Jacquet's dermatitis (diaper dermatitis) 691.0
Jadassohn's
  blue nevus (M8780/0) — see Neoplasm, skin, benign
  disease (maculopapular erythroderma) 696.2
  intraepidermal epithelioma (M8096/0) — see Neoplasm, skin, benign
Jadassohn-Lewandowski syndrome (pachyonychia congenita) 757.5
Jadassohn-Pellizari's disease (anetoderma) 701.3
Jadassohn-Tièche nevus (M8780/0) — see Neoplasm, skin, benign
Jaffe-Lichtenstein (-Uehlinger) syndrome 252.01
Jahnke's syndrome (encephalocutaneous angiomatosis) 759.6
Jakob-Creutzfeldt disease (CJD) (syndrome) 046.19
  with dementia
    with behavioral disturbance 046.19 [294.11]
    without behavioral disturbance 046.19 [294.10]
  familial 046.19
  iatrogenic 046.19
  specified NEC 046.19
  sporadic 046.19
  variant (vCJD) 046.11
    with dementia
      with behavioral disturbance 046.11 [294.11]
      without behavioral disturbance 046.11 [294.10]
Jaksch (-Luzet) disease or syndrome (pseudoleukemia infantum) 285.8
Jamaican
  neuropathy 349.82
  paraplegic tropical ataxic-spastic syndrome 349.82
Janet's disease (psychasthenia) 300.89
Janiceps 759.4
Jansky-Bielschowsky amaurotic familial idiocy 330.1
Japanese
  B type encephalitis 062.0
  river fever 081.2
  seven-day fever 100.89
Jaundice (yellow) 782.4
  acholuric (familial) (splenomegalic) (see also Spherocytosis) 282.0
    acquired 283.9
  breast milk 774.39
  catarrhal (acute) 070.1
    with hepatic coma 070.0
    chronic 571.9
    epidemic — see Jaundice, epidemic
  cholestatic (benign) 782.4
  chronic idiopathic 277.4
  epidemic (catarrhal) 070.1
    with hepatic coma 070.0
    leptospiral 100.0
    spirochetal 100.0
  febrile (acute) 070.1
    with hepatic coma 070.0
    leptospiral 100.0
    spirochetal 100.0
  fetus or newborn 774.6
    due to or associated with
      ABO
        absence or deficiency of enzyme system for bilirubin conjugation (congenital) 774.39
        antibodies 773.1

Jaundice — continued
  fetus or newborn — continued
    due to or associated with — continued
      blood group incompatibility NEC 773.2
      breast milk inhibitors to conjugation 774.39
        associated with preterm delivery 774.2
      bruising 774.1
      Crigler-Najjar syndrome 277.4 [774.31]
      delayed conjugation 774.30
        associated with preterm delivery 774.2
        development 774.39
      drugs or toxins transmitted from mother 774.1
      G-6-PD deficiency 282.2 [774.0]
      galactosemia 271.1 [774.5]
      Gilbert's syndrome 277.4 [774.31]
      hepatocellular damage 774.4
      hereditary hemolytic anemia (see also Anemia, hemolytic) 282.9 [774.0]
      hypothyroidism, congenital 243 [774.31]
      incompatibility, maternal/fetal NEC 773.2
      incompatibility, maternal/fetal 773.1
      infection 774.1
      inspissated bile syndrome 774.4
      isoimmunization NEC 773.2
      isoimmunization 773.1
      mucoviscidosis 277.01 [774.5]
      obliteration of bile duct, congenital 751.61 [774.5]
      polycythemia 774.1
      preterm delivery 774.2
      red cell defect 282.9 [774.0]
      Rh
        antibodies 773.0
        incompatibility, maternal/fetal 773.0
        isoimmunization 773.0
      spherocytosis (congenital) 282.0 [774.0]
      swallowed maternal blood 774.1
    physiological NEC 774.6
  from injection, inoculation, infusion, or transfusion (blood) (plasma) (serum) (other substance) (onset within 8 months after administration) — see Hepatitis, viral
  Gilbert's (familial nonhemolytic) 277.4
  hematogenous 283.9
  hemolytic (acquired) 283.9
    congenital (see also Spherocytosis) 282.0
  hemorrhagic (acute) 100.0
    leptospiral 100.0
    newborn 776.0
    spirochetal 100.0
  hepatocellular 573.8
  homologous (serum) — see Hepatitis, viral
  idiopathic, chronic 277.4
  infectious (acute) (subacute) 070.1
    with hepatic coma 070.0
    leptospiral 100.0
    spirochetal 100.0
  leptospiral 100.0
  malignant (see also Necrosis, liver) 570
  newborn (physiological) (see also Jaundice, fetus or newborn) 774.6
  nonhemolytic, congenital familial (Gilbert's) 277.4
  nuclear, newborn (see also Kernicterus of newborn) 774.7
  obstructive NEC (see also Obstruction, biliary) 576.8
  postimmunization — see Hepatitis, viral
  posttransfusion — see Hepatitis, viral
  regurgitation (see also Obstruction, biliary) 576.8
  serum (homologous) (prophylactic) (therapeutic) — see Hepatitis, viral
  spirochetal (hemorrhagic) 100.0
  symptomatic 782.4
    newborn 774.6
Jaw — see condition

Jaw-blinking 374.43
  congenital 742.8
Jaw-winking phenomenon or syndrome 742.8
Jealousy
  alcoholic 291.5
  childhood 313.3
  sibling 313.3
Jejunitis — see also Enteritis 558.9
Jejunostomy status V44.4
Jejunum, jejunal — see condition
Jensen's disease 363.05
Jericho boil 085.1
Jerks, myoclonic 333.2
Jervell-Lange-Nielsen syndrome 426.82
Jeune's disease or syndrome (asphyxiating thoracic dystrophy) 756.4
Jigger disease 134.1
Job's syndrome (chronic granulomatous disease) 288.1
Jod-Basedow phenomenon 242.8 ☑
Johnson-Stevens disease (erythema multiforme exudativum) 695.13
Joint — see also condition
  Charcôt's 094.0 [713.5]
  false 733.82
  flail — see Flail, joint
  mice — see Loose, body, joint, by site
  sinus to bone 730.9 ☑
  von Gies' 095.8
Jordan's anomaly or syndrome 288.2
Josephs-Diamond-Blackfan anemia (congenital hypoplastic) 284.01
Joubert syndrome 759.89
Jumpers' knee 727.2
Jungle yellow fever 060.0
Jüngling's disease (sarcoidosis) 135
Junin virus hemorrhagic fever 078.7
Juvenile — see also condition
  delinquent 312.9
    group (see also Disturbance, conduct) 312.2 ☑
    neurotic 312.4

K

Kabuki syndrome 759.89
Kahler (-Bozzolo) disease (multiple myeloma) (M9730/3) 203.0 ☑
Kakergasia 300.9
Kakke 265.0
Kala-azar (Indian) (infantile) (Mediterranean) (Sudanese) 085.0
Kalischer's syndrome (encephalocutaneous angiomatosis) 759.6
Kallmann's syndrome (hypogonadotropic hypogonadism with anosmia) 253.4
Kanner's syndrome (autism) — see also Psychosis, childhood 299.0 ☑
Kaolinosis 502
Kaposi's
  disease 757.33
    lichen ruber 696.4
      acuminatus 696.4
      moniliformis 697.8
    xeroderma pigmentosum 757.33
  sarcoma (M9140/3) 176.9
    adipose tissue 176.1
    aponeurosis 176.1
    artery 176.1
    associated herpesvirus infection 058.89
    blood vessel 176.1
    bursa 176.1
    connective tissue 176.1
    external genitalia 176.8
    fascia 176.1
    fatty tissue 176.1
    fibrous tissue 176.1
    gastrointestinal tract NEC 176.3
    ligament 176.1
    lung 176.4
    lymph
      gland(s) 176.5
      node(s) 176.5
    lymphatic(s) NEC 176.1
    muscle (skeletal) 176.1
    oral cavity NEC 176.8
    palate 176.2

Kaposi's — continued
  sarcoma — continued
    scrotum 176.8
    skin 176.0
    soft tissue 176.1
    specified site NEC 176.8
    subcutaneous tissue 176.1
    synovia 176.1
    tendon (sheath) 176.1
    vein 176.1
    vessel 176.1
    viscera NEC 176.9
    vulva 176.8
  varicelliform eruption 054.0
    vaccinia 999.0
Kartagener's syndrome or triad (sinusitis, bronchiectasis, situs inversus) 759.3
Kasabach-Merritt syndrome (capillary hemangioma associated with thrombocytopenic purpura) 287.39
Kaschin-Beck disease (endemic polyarthritis) — see Disease, Kaschin-Beck
Kast's syndrome (dyschondroplasia with hemangiomas) 756.4
Katatonia — see Catatonia
Katayama disease or fever 120.2
Kathisophobia 781.0
Kawasaki disease 446.1
Kayser-Fleischer ring (cornea) (pseudosclerosis) 275.1 [371.14]
Kaznelson's syndrome (congenital hypoplastic anemia) 284.01
Kearns-Sayre syndrome 277.87
Kedani fever 081.2
Kelis 701.4
Kelly (-Patterson) syndrome (sideropenic dysphagia) 280.8
Keloid, cheloid 701.4
  Addison's (morphea) 701.0
  cornea 371.00
  Hawkins' 701.4
  scar 701.4
Keloma 701.4
Kenya fever 082.1
Keratectasia 371.71
  congenital 743.41
Keratinization NEC
  alveolar ridge mucosa
    excessive 528.72
    minimal 528.71
Keratitis (nodular) (nonulcerative) (simple) (zonular) NEC 370.9
  with ulceration (see also Ulcer, cornea) 370.00
  actinic 370.24
  arborescens 054.42
  areolar 370.22
  bullosa 370.8
  deep — see Keratitis, interstitial
  dendritic(a) 054.42
  desiccation 370.34
  diffuse interstitial 370.52
  disciform(is) 054.43
    varicella 052.7 [370.44]
  epithelialis vernalis 372.13 [370.32]
  exposure 370.34
  filamentary 370.23
  gonococcal (congenital) (prenatal) 098.43
  herpes, herpetic (simplex) NEC 054.43
    zoster 053.21
  hypopyon 370.04
  in
    chickenpox 052.7 [370.44]
    exanthema (see also Exanthem) 057.9 [370.44]
    paravaccinia (see also Paravaccinia) 051.9 [370.44]
    smallpox (see also Smallpox) 050.9 [370.44]
    vernal conjunctivitis 372.13 [370.32]
  interstitial (nonsyphilitic) 370.50
    with ulcer (see also Ulcer, cornea) 370.00
    diffuse 370.52
    herpes, herpetic (simplex) 054.43
      zoster 053.21
    syphilitic (congenital) (hereditary) 090.3
    tuberculous (see also Tuberculosis) 017.3 ☑ [370.59]

☑ Additional Digit Required — Refer to the Tabular List for Digit Selection   ᵛᵉᵇ Subterms under main terms may continue to next column or page

2010 ICD-9-CM   ▶◀ Revised Text   ● New Line   ▲ Revised Code   **Volume 2 — 163**

Keratitis — continued
  lagophthalmic 370.34
  macular 370.22
  neuroparalytic 370.35
  neurotrophic 370.35
  nummular 370.22
  oyster-shuckers' 370.8
  parenchymatous — see Keratitis, interstitial
  petrificans 370.8
  phlyctenular 370.31
  postmeasles 055.71
  punctata, punctate 370.21
    leprosa 030.0 [370.21]
    profunda 090.3
    superficial (Thygeson's) 370.21
  purulent 370.8
  pustuliformis profunda 090.3
  rosacea 695.3 [370.49]
  sclerosing 370.54
  specified type NEC 370.8
  stellate 370.22
  striate 370.22
  superficial 370.20
    with conjunctivitis (see also Keratoconjunc-
      tivitis) 370.40
    punctate (Thygeson's) 370.21
  suppurative 370.8
  syphilitic (congenital) (prenatal) 090.3
  trachomatous 076.1
    late effect 139.1
  tuberculous (phlyctenular) (see also Tubercu-
    losis) 017.3 ☑ [370.31]
  ulcerated (see also Ulcer, cornea) 370.00
  vesicular 370.8
  welders' 370.24
  xerotic (see also Keratomalacia) 371.45
    vitamin A deficiency 264.4
Keratoacanthoma 238.2
Keratocele 371.72
Keratoconjunctivitis — see also Keratitis 370.40
  adenovirus type 8 077.1
  epidemic 077.1
  exposure 370.34
  gonococcal 098.43
  herpetic (simplex) 054.43
    zoster 053.21
  in
    chickenpox 052.7 [370.44]
    exanthema (see also Exanthem)
      057.9 [370.44]
    paravaccinia (see also Paravaccinia)
      051.9 [370.44]
    smallpox (see also Smallpox) 050.9 [370.44]
  infectious 077.1
  neurotrophic 370.35
  phlyctenular 370.31
  postmeasles 055.71
  shipyard 077.1
  sicca (Sjögren's syndrome) 710.2
    not in Sjögren's syndrome 370.33
  specified type NEC 370.49
  tuberculous (phlyctenular) (see also Tubercu-
    losis) 017.3 ☑ [370.31]
Keratoconus 371.60
  acute hydrops 371.62
  congenital 743.41
  stable 371.61
Keratocyst (dental) 526.0
Keratoderma, keratodermia (congenital) (pal-
    maris et plantaris) (symmetrical) 757.39
  acquired 701.1
  blennorrhagica 701.1
    gonococcal 098.81
  climacterium 701.1
  eccentrica 757.39
  gonorrheal 098.81
  punctata 701.1
  tylodes, progressive 701.1
Keratodermatocele 371.72
Keratoglobus 371.70
  congenital 743.41
    associated with buphthalmos 743.22
Keratohemia 371.12
Keratoiritis — see also Iridocyclitis 364.3
  syphilitic 090.3

Keratoiritis — see also Iridocyclitis —
    continued
  tuberculous (see also Tuberculosis)
    017.3 ☑ [364.11]
Keratolysis exfoliativa (congenital) 757.39
  acquired 695.89
  neonatorum 757.39
Keratoma 701.1
  congenital 757.39
  malignum congenitale 757.1
  palmaris et plantaris hereditarium 757.39
  senile 702.0
Keratomalacia 371.45
  vitamin A deficiency 264.4
Keratomegaly 743.41
Keratomycosis 111.1
  nigricans (palmaris) 111.1
Keratopathy 371.40
  band (see also Keratitis) 371.43
  bullous (see also Keratitis) 371.23
  degenerative (see also Degeneration, cornea)
    371.40
    hereditary (see also Dystrophy, cornea)
    371.50
  discrete colliquative 371.49
Keratoscleritis, tuberculous — see also Tuber-
    culosis 017.3 ☑ [370.31]
Keratosis 701.1
  actinic 702.0
  arsenical 692.4
  blennorrhagica 701.1
    gonococcal 098.81
  congenital (any type) 757.39
  ear (middle) (see also Cholesteatoma) 385.30
  female genital (external) 629.89
  follicularis 757.39
    acquired 701.1
    congenital (acneiformis) (Siemens') 757.39
    spinulosa (decalvans) 757.39
    vitamin A deficiency 264.8
  follicular, vitamin A deficiency 264.8
  gonococcal 098.81
  larynx, laryngeal 478.79
  male genital (external) 608.89
  middle ear (see also Cholesteatoma) 385.30
  nigricans 701.2
    congenital 757.39
  obturans 380.21
  oral epithelium
    residual ridge mucosa
      excessive 528.72
      minimal 528.71
  palmaris et plantaris (symmetrical) 757.39
  penile 607.89
  pharyngeus 478.29
  pilaris 757.39
    acquired 701.1
  punctata (palmaris et plantaris) 701.1
  scrotal 608.89
  seborrheic 702.19
    inflamed 702.11
  senilis 702.0
  solar 702.0
  suprafollicularis 757.39
  tonsillaris 478.29
  vagina 623.1
  vegetans 757.39
  vitamin A deficiency 264.8
Kerato-uveitis — see also Iridocyclitis 364.3
Keraunoparalysis 994.0
Kerion (celsi) 110.0
Kernicterus of newborn (not due to isoimmu-
    nization) 774.7
  due to isoimmunization (conditions classifiable
    to 773.0–773.2) 773.4
Ketoacidosis 276.2
  diabetic 250.1 ☑
    due to secondary diabetes 249.1 ☑
Ketonuria 791.6
  branched-chain, intermittent 270.3
Ketosis 276.2
  diabetic 250.1 ☑
    due to secondary diabetes 249.1 ☑
Kidney — see condition
Kienböck's
  disease 732.3

Kienböck's — continued
  disease — continued
    adult 732.8
    osteochondrosis 732.3
Kimmelstiel (-Wilson) disease or syndrome
    (intercapillary glomerulosclerosis)
    250.4 ☑ [581.81]
  due to secondary diabetes 249.4 ☑ [581.81]
Kink, kinking
  appendix 543.9
  artery 447.1
  cystic duct, congenital 751.61
  hair (acquired) 704.2
  ileum or intestine (see also Obstruction, intes-
    tine) 560.9
  Lane's (see also Obstruction, intestine) 560.9
  organ or site, congenital NEC — see Anomaly,
    specified type NEC, by site
  ureter (pelvic junction) 593.3
    congenital 753.20
  vein(s) 459.2
    caval 459.2
    peripheral 459.2
Kinnier Wilson's disease (hepatolenticular de-
    generation) 275.1
Kissing
  osteophytes 721.5
  spine 721.5
  vertebra 721.5
Klauder's syndrome (erythema multiforme, ex-
    udativum) 695.19
Klebs' disease — see also Nephritis 583.9
Kleine-Levin syndrome 327.13
Klein-Waardenburg syndrome (ptosisepican-
    thus) 270.2
Kleptomania 312.32
Klinefelter's syndrome 758.7
Klinger's disease 446.4
Klippel's disease 723.8
Klippel-Feil disease or syndrome (brevicollis)
    756.16
Klippel-Trenaunay syndrome 759.89
Klumpke (-Déjérine) palsy, paralysis (birth)
    (newborn) 767.6
Klüver-Bucy (-Terzian) syndrome 310.0
Knee — see condition
Knifegrinders' rot — see also Tuberculosis
    011.4 ☑
Knock-knee (acquired) 736.41
  congenital 755.64
Knot
  intestinal, syndrome (volvulus) 560.2
  umbilical cord (true) 663.2 ☑
    affecting fetus or newborn 762.5
Knots, surfer 919.8
  infected 919.9
Knotting (of)
  hair 704.2
  intestine 560.2
Knuckle pads (Garrod's) 728.79
Köbner's disease (epidermolysis bullosa) 757.39
Koch's
  infection (see also Tuberculosis, pulmonary)
    011.9 ☑
  relapsing fever 087.9
Koch-Weeks conjunctivitis 372.03
Koenig-Wichman disease (pemphigus) 694.4
Köhler's disease (osteochondrosis) 732.5
  first (osteochondrosis juvenilis) 732.5
  second (Freiburg's infarction, metatarsal head)
    732.5
  patellar 732.4
  tarsal navicular (bone) (osteoarthrosis juvenilis)
    732.5
Köhler-Mouchet disease (osteoarthrosis juve-
    nilis) 732.5
Köhler-Pellegrini-Stieda disease or syndrome
    (calcification, knee joint) 726.62
Koilonychia 703.8
  congenital 757.5
Kojevnikov's, Kojewnikoff's epilepsy — see
    also Epilepsy 345.7 ☑
König's
  disease (osteochondritis dissecans) 732.7
  syndrome 564.89
Koniophthisis — see also Tuberculosis 011.4 ☑

Koplik's spots 055.9
Kopp's asthma 254.8
Korean hemorrhagic fever 078.6
Korsakoff (-Wernicke) disease, psychosis, or
    syndrome (nonalcoholic) 294.0
  alcoholic 291.1
Korsakov's disease — see Korsakoff's disease
Korsakow's disease — see Korsakoff's disease
Kostmann's disease or syndrome (infantile
    genetic agranulocytosis) 288.01
Krabbe's
  disease (leukodystrophy) 330.0
  syndrome
    congenital muscle hypoplasia 756.89
    cutaneocerebral angioma 759.6
Kraepelin-Morel disease — see also
    Schizophrenia 295.9 ☑
Kraft-Weber-Dimitri disease 759.6
Kraurosis
  ani 569.49
  penis 607.0
  vagina 623.8
  vulva 624.09
Kreotoxism 005.9
Krukenberg's
  spindle 371.13
  tumor (M8490/6) 198.6
Kufs' disease 330.1
Kugelberg-Welander disease 335.11
Kuhnt-Junius degeneration or disease 362.52
Kulchitsky's cell carcinoma (carcinoid tumor of
    intestine) 259.2
Kümmell's disease or spondylitis 721.7
Kundrat's disease (lymphosarcoma) 200.1 ☑
Kunekune — see Dermatophytosis
Kunkel syndrome (lupoid hepatitis) 571.49
Kupffer cell sarcoma (M9124/3) 155.0
Kuru 046.0
Kussmaul's
  coma (diabetic) 250.3 ☑
    due to secondary diabetes 249.3 ☑
  disease (polyarteritis nodosa) 446.0
  respiration (air hunger) 786.09
Kwashiorkor (marasmus type) 260
Kyasanur Forest disease 065.2
Kyphoscoliosis, kyphoscoliotic (acquired) —
    see also Scoliosis 737.30
  congenital 756.19
  due to radiation 737.33
  heart (disease) 416.1
  idiopathic 737.30
  infantile
    progressive 737.32
    resolving 737.31
  late effect of rickets 268.1 [737.43]
  specified NEC 737.39
  thoracogenic 737.34
  tuberculous (see also Tuberculosis)
    015.0 ☑ [737.43]
Kyphosis, kyphotic (acquired) (postural) 737.10
  adolescent postural 737.0
  congenital 756.19
  dorsalis juvenilis 732.0
  due to or associated with
    Charcôt-Marie-Tooth disease 356.1 [737.41]
    mucopolysaccharidosis 277.5 [737.41]
    neurofibromatosis 237.71 [737.41]
    osteitis
      deformans 731.0 [737.41]
      fibrosa cystica 252.01 [737.41]
    osteoporosis (see also Osteoporosis)
      733.0 ☑ [737.41]
    poliomyelitis (see also Poliomyelitis)
      138 [737.41]
    radiation 737.11
    tuberculosis (see also Tuberculosis)
      015.0 ☑ [737.41]
  Kümmell's 721.7
  late effect of rickets 268.1 [737.41]
  Morquio-Brailsford type (spinal) 277.5 [737.41]
  pelvis 738.6
  postlaminectomy 737.12
  specified cause NEC 737.19
  syphilitic, congenital 090.5 [737.41]
  tuberculous (see also Tuberculosis)
    015.0 ☑ [737.41]

Kyrle's disease (hyperkeratosis follicularis in cutem penetrans) 701.1

L

Labia, labium — *see* condition
Labiated hymen 752.49
Labile
  blood pressure 796.2
  emotions, emotionality 301.3
  vasomotor system 443.9
Lability, emotional 799.24 ●
Labioglossal paralysis 335.22
Labium leporinum — *see also* Cleft, lip 749.10
Labor — *see also* Delivery
  with complications — *see* Delivery, complicated
  abnormal NEC 661.9 ☑
    affecting fetus or newborn 763.7
  arrested active phase 661.1 ☑
    affecting fetus or newborn 763.7
  desultory 661.2 ☑
    affecting fetus or newborn 763.7
  dyscoordinate 661.4 ☑
    affecting fetus or newborn 763.7
  early onset (22-36 weeks gestation) 644.2 ☑
  failed
    induction 659.1 ☑
      mechanical 659.0 ☑
      medical 659.1 ☑
      surgical 659.0 ☑
    trial (vaginal delivery) 660.6 ☑
  false 644.1 ☑
  forced or induced, affecting fetus or newborn 763.89
  hypertonic 661.4 ☑
    affecting fetus or newborn 763.7
  hypotonic 661.2 ☑
    affecting fetus or newborn 763.7
    primary 661.0 ☑
      affecting fetus or newborn 763.7
    secondary 661.1 ☑
      affecting fetus or newborn 763.7
  incoordinate 661.4 ☑
    affecting fetus or newborn 763.7
  irregular 661.2 ☑
    affecting fetus or newborn 763.7
  long — *see* Labor, prolonged
  missed (at or near term) 656.4 ☑
  obstructed NEC 660.9 ☑
    affecting fetus or newborn 763.1
    due to female genital mutilation 660.8 ☑
    specified cause NEC 660.8 ☑
      affecting fetus or newborn 763.1
  pains, spurious 644.1 ☑
  precipitate 661.3 ☑
    affecting fetus or newborn 763.6
  premature 644.2 ☑
    threatened 644.0 ☑
  prolonged or protracted 662.1 ☑
    first stage 662.0 ☑
      affecting fetus or newborn 763.89
    second stage 662.2 ☑
      affecting fetus or newborn 763.89
    affecting fetus or newborn 763.89
  threatened NEC 644.1 ☑
  undelivered 644.1 ☑
Labored breathing — *see also* Hyperventilation 786.09
Labyrinthitis (inner ear) (destructive) (latent) 386.30
  circumscribed 386.32
  diffuse 386.31
  focal 386.32
  purulent 386.33
  serous 386.31
  suppurative 386.33
  syphilitic 095.8
  toxic 386.34
  viral 386.35
Laceration — *see also* Wound, open, by site
  accidental, complicating surgery 998.2
  Achilles tendon 845.09
    with open wound 892.2
  anus (sphincter) 879.6

Laceration — *see also* Wound, open, by site — *continued*
  anus — *continued*
    with
      abortion — *see* Abortion, by type, with damage to pelvic organs
      ectopic pregnancy (*see also* categories 633.0–633.9) 639.2
      molar pregnancy (*see also* categories 630–632) 639.2
    complicated 879.7
    complicating delivery (healed) (old) 654.8 ☑
      with laceration of anal or rectal mucosa 664.3 ☑
      not associated with third-degree perineal laceration 664.6 ☑
    following
      abortion 639.2
      ectopic or molar pregnancy 639.2
    nontraumatic, nonpuerperal (healed) (old) 569.43
  bladder (urinary)
    with
      abortion — *see* Abortion, by type, with damage to pelvic organs
      ectopic pregnancy (*see also* categories 633.0–633.9) 639.2
      molar pregnancy (*see also* categories 630–632) 639.2
    following
      abortion 639.2
      ectopic or molar pregnancy 639.2
    obstetrical trauma 665.5 ☑
  blood vessel — *see* Injury, blood vessel, by site
  bowel
    with
      abortion — *see* Abortion, by type, with damage to pelvic organs
      ectopic pregnancy (*see also* categories 633.0–633.9) 639.2
      molar pregnancy (*see also* categories 630–632) 639.2
    following
      abortion 639.2
      ectopic or molar pregnancy 639.2
    obstetrical trauma 665.5 ☑
  brain (cerebral) (membrane) (with hemorrhage) 851.8 ☑

Note — *Use the following fifth-digit subclassification with categories 851–854:*

0   *unspecified state of consciousness*

1   *with no loss of consciousness*

2   *with brief [less than one hour] loss of consciousness*

3   *with moderate [1–24 hours] loss of consciousness*

4   *with prolonged [more than 24 hours] loss of consciousness and return to pre–existing conscious level*

5   *with prolonged [more than 24 hours] loss of consciousness, without return to pre–existing conscious level*

Use fifth-digit 5 to designate when a patient is unconscious and dies before regaining consciousness, regardless of the duration of the loss of consciousness

6   *with loss of consciousness of unspecified duration*

9   *with concussion, unspecified*

---

    with
      open intracranial wound 851.9 ☑
      skull fracture — *see* Fracture, skull, by site
    cerebellum 851.6 ☑
      with open intracranial wound 851.7 ☑
    cortex 851.2 ☑
      with open intracranial wound 851.3 ☑
    during birth 767.0
    stem 851.6 ☑
      with open intracranial wound 851.7 ☑

Laceration — *see also* Wound, open, by site — *continued*
  broad ligament
    with
      abortion — *see* Abortion, by type, with damage to pelvic organs
      ectopic pregnancy (*see also* categories 633.0–633.9) 639.2
      molar pregnancy (*see also* categories 630–632) 639.2
    following
      abortion 639.2
      ectopic or molar pregnancy 639.2
    nontraumatic 620.6
    obstetrical trauma 665.6 ☑
    syndrome (nontraumatic) 620.6
  capsule, joint — *see* Sprain, by site
  cardiac — *see* Laceration, heart
  causing eversion of cervix uteri (old) 622.0
  central, complicating delivery 664.4 ☑
  cerebellum — *see* Laceration, brain, cerebellum
  cerebral (*see also* Laceration, brain)
    during birth 767.0
  cervix (uteri)
    with
      abortion — *see* Abortion, by type, with damage to pelvic organs
      ectopic pregnancy (*see also* categories 633.0–633.9) 639.2
      molar pregnancy (*see also* categories 630–632) 639.2
    following
      abortion 639.2
      ectopic or molar pregnancy 639.2
    nonpuerperal, nontraumatic 622.3
    obstetrical trauma (current) 665.3 ☑
    old (postpartal) 622.3
    traumatic — *see* Injury, internal, cervix
  chordae heart 429.5
  complicated 879.9
  cornea — *see* Laceration, eyeball
    superficial 918.1
  cortex (cerebral) — *see* Laceration, brain, cortex
  esophagus 530.89
  eye(s) — *see* Laceration, ocular
  eyeball NEC 871.4
    with prolapse or exposure of intraocular tissue 871.1
    penetrating — *see* Penetrating wound, eyeball
    specified as without prolapse of intraocular tissue 871.0
  eyelid NEC 870.8
    full thickness 870.1
      involving lacrimal passages 870.2
    skin (and periocular area) 870.0
      penetrating — *see* Penetrating wound, orbit
  fourchette
    with
      abortion — *see* Abortion, by type, with damage to pelvic organs
      ectopic pregnancy (*see also* categories 633.0–633.9) 639.2
      molar pregnancy (*see also* categories 630–632) 639.2
    complicating delivery 664.0 ☑
    following
      abortion 639.2
      ectopic or molar pregnancy 639.2
  heart (without penetration of heart chambers) 861.02
    with
      open wound into thorax 861.12
      penetration of heart chambers 861.03
        with open wound into thorax 861.13
  hernial sac — *see* Hernia, by site
  internal organ (abdomen) (chest) (pelvis) NEC — *see* Injury, internal, by site
    NEC — *see* Injury, internal, by site
  kidney (parenchyma) 866.02

Laceration — *see also* Wound, open, by site — *continued*
  kidney — *continued*
    with
      complete disruption of parenchyma (rupture) 866.03
        with open wound into cavity 866.13
      open wound into cavity 866.12
  labia
    complicating delivery 664.0 ☑
  ligament (*see also* Sprain, by site)
    with open wound — *see* Wound, open, by site
  liver 864.05
    with open wound into cavity 864.15
    major (disruption of hepatic parenchyma) 864.04
      with open wound into cavity 864.14
    minor (capsule only) 864.02
      with open wound into cavity 864.12
    moderate (involving parenchyma without major disruption) 864.03
      with open wound into cavity 864.13
    multiple 864.04
      with open wound into cavity 864.14
    stellate 864.04
      with open wound into cavity 864.14
  lung 861.22
    with open wound into thorax 861.32
  meninges — *see* Laceration, brain
  meniscus (knee) (*see also* Tear, meniscus) 836.2
    old 717.5
    site other than knee (*see also* Sprain, by site)
      old NEC (*see also* Disorder, cartilage, articular) 718.0
  muscle (*see also* Sprain, by site)
    with open wound — *see* Wound, open, by site
  myocardium — *see* Laceration, heart
  nerve — *see* Injury, nerve, by site
  ocular NEC (*see also* Laceration, eyeball) 871.4
    adnexa NEC 870.8
      penetrating 870.3
        with foreign body 870.4
  orbit (eye) 870.8
    penetrating 870.3
      with foreign body 870.4
  pelvic
    floor (muscles)
      with
        abortion — *see* Abortion, by type, with damage to pelvic organs
        ectopic pregnancy (*see also* categories 633.0–633.9) 639.2
        molar pregnancy (*see also* categories 630–632) 639.2
      complicating delivery 664.1 ☑
      following
        abortion 639.2
        ectopic or molar pregnancy 639.2
      nonpuerperal 618.7
      old (postpartal) 618.7
    organ NEC
      with
        abortion — *see* Abortion, by type, with damage to pelvic organs
        ectopic pregnancy (*see also* categories 633.0–633.9) 639.2
        molar pregnancy (*see also* categories 630–632) 639.2
      complicating delivery 665.5 ☑
        affecting fetus or newborn 763.89
      following
        abortion 639.2
        ectopic or molar pregnancy 639.2
      obstetrical trauma 665.5 ☑
    perineum, perineal (old) (postpartal) 618.7
      with
        abortion — *see* Abortion, by type, with damage to pelvic floor

Index
Kyrle's disease — Laceration

Laceration — see also Wound, open, by site — continued
  perineum, perineal — continued
    with — continued
      ectopic pregnancy (see also categories 633.0–633.9) 639.2
      molar pregnancy (see also categories 630–632) 639.2
    complicating delivery 664.4 ☑
      first degree 664.0 ☑
      second degree 664.1 ☑
      third degree 664.2 ☑
      fourth degree 664.3 ☑
      anal sphincter (healed) (old) 654.8 ☑
        not associated with third-degree perineal laceration 664.6 ☑
      sphincter (anal) (healed) (old) 654.8 ☑
        not associated with third-degree perineal laceration 664.6 ☑
    central 664.4 ☑
    involving
      anal sphincter 664.2 ☑
      fourchette 664.0 ☑
      hymen 664.0 ☑
      labia 664.0 ☑
      pelvic floor 664.1 ☑
      perineal muscles 664.1 ☑
      rectovaginal septum 664.2 ☑
        with anal mucosa 664.3 ☑
      skin 664.0 ☑
      sphincter (anal) 664.2 ☑
        with anal mucosa 664.3 ☑
      vagina 664.0 ☑
      vaginal muscles 664.1 ☑
      vulva 664.0 ☑
    secondary 674.2 ☑
    following
      abortion 639.2
      ectopic or molar pregnancy 639.2
    male 879.6
      complicated 879.7
    muscles, complicating delivery 664.1 ☑
    nonpuerperal, current injury 879.6
      complicated 879.7
    secondary (postpartal) 674.2 ☑
  peritoneum
    with
      abortion — see Abortion, by type, with damage to pelvic organs
      ectopic pregnancy (see also categories 633.0–633.9) 639.2
      molar pregnancy (see also categories 630–632) 639.2
    following
      abortion 639.2
      ectopic or molar pregnancy 639.2
    obstetrical trauma 665.5 ☑
  periurethral tissue
    with
      abortion — see Abortion, by type, with damage to pelvic organs
      ectopic pregnancy (see also categories 633.0–633.9) 639.2
      molar pregnancy (see also categories 630–632) 639.2
    following
      abortion 639.2
      ectopic or molar pregnancy 639.2
    obstetrical trauma 665.5 ☑
  rectovaginal (septum)
    with
      abortion — see Abortion, by type, with damage to pelvic organs
      ectopic pregnancy (see also categories 633.0–633.9) 639.2
      molar pregnancy (see also categories 630–632) 639.2
    complicating delivery 665.4 ☑
      with perineum 664.2 ☑
        involving anal or rectal mucosa 664.3 ☑
    following
      abortion 639.2

Laceration — see also Wound, open, by site — continued
  rectovaginal — continued
    following — continued
      ectopic or molar pregnancy 639.2
    nonpuerperal 623.4
    old (postpartal) 623.4
  spinal cord (meninges) (see also Injury, spinal, by site)
    due to injury at birth 767.4
    fetus or newborn 767.4
  spleen 865.09
    with
      disruption of parenchyma (massive) 865.04
        with open wound into cavity 865.14
      open wound into cavity 865.19
    capsule (without disruption of parenchyma) 865.02
      with open wound into cavity 865.12
    parenchyma 865.03
      with open wound into cavity 865.13
      massive disruption (rupture) 865.04
        with open wound into cavity 865.14
  tendon 848.9
    with open wound — see Wound, open, by site
    Achilles 845.09
      with open wound 892.2
    lower limb NEC 844.9
      with open wound NEC 894.2
    upper limb NEC 840.9
      with open wound NEC 884.2
  tentorium cerebelli — see Laceration, brain, cerebellum
  tongue 873.64
    complicated 873.74
  urethra
    with
      abortion — see Abortion, by type, with damage to pelvic organs
      ectopic pregnancy (see also categories 633.0–633.9) 639.2
      molar pregnancy (see also categories 630–632) 639.2
    following
      abortion 639.2
      ectopic or molar pregnancy 639.2
    nonpuerperal, nontraumatic 599.84
    obstetrical trauma 665.5 ☑
  uterus
    with
      abortion — see Abortion, by type, with damage to pelvic organs
      ectopic pregnancy (see also categories 633.0–633.9) 639.2
      molar pregnancy (see also categories 630–632) 639.2
    following
      abortion 639.2
      ectopic or molar pregnancy 639.2
    nonpuerperal, nontraumatic 621.8
    obstetrical trauma NEC 665.5 ☑
    old (postpartal) 621.8
  vagina
    with
      abortion — see Abortion, by type, with damage to pelvic organs
      ectopic pregnancy (see also categories 633.0–633.9) 639.2
      molar pregnancy (see also categories 630–632) 639.2
      perineal involvement, complicating delivery 664.0 ☑
    complicating delivery 665.4 ☑
      first degree 664.0 ☑
      second degree 664.1 ☑
      third degree 664.2 ☑
      fourth degree 664.3 ☑
      high 665.4 ☑
      muscles 664.1 ☑
      sulcus 665.4 ☑
      wall 665.4 ☑

Laceration — see also Wound, open, by site — continued
  vagina — continued
    following
      abortion 639.2
      ectopic or molar pregnancy 639.2
    nonpuerperal, nontraumatic 623.4
    old (postpartal) 623.4
  valve, heart — see Endocarditis
  vulva
    with
      abortion — see Abortion, by type, with damage to pelvic organs
      ectopic pregnancy (see also categories 633.0–633.9) 639.2
      molar pregnancy (see also categories 630–632) 639.2
    complicating delivery 664.0 ☑
    following
      abortion 639.2
      ectopic or molar pregnancy 639.2
    nonpuerperal, nontraumatic 624.4
    old (postpartal) 624.4
Lachrymal — see condition
Lachrymonasal duct — see condition
Lack of
  adequate intermaxillary vertical dimension 524.36
  appetite (see also Anorexia) 783.0
  care
    in home V60.4
    of adult 995.84
    of infant (at or after birth) 995.52
  coordination 781.3
  development (see also Hypoplasia)
    physiological in childhood 783.40
  education V62.3
  energy 780.79
  financial resources V60.2
  food 994.2
    in environment V60.89   ▲
  growth in childhood 783.43
  heating V60.1
  housing (permanent) (temporary) V60.0
    adequate V60.1
  material resources V60.2
  medical attention 799.89
  memory (see also Amnesia) 780.93
    mild, following organic brain damage 310.8   ▲
  ovulation 628.0
  person able to render necessary care V60.4
  physical exercise V69.0
  physiologic development in childhood 783.40
  posterior occlusal support 524.57
  prenatal care in current pregnancy V23.7
  shelter V60.0
  sleep V69.4
  water 994.3
Lacrimal — see condition
Lacrimation, abnormal — see also Epiphora 375.20
Lacrimonasal duct — see condition
Lactation, lactating (breast) (puerperal) (postpartum)
  defective 676.4 ☑
  disorder 676.9 ☑
    specified type NEC 676.8 ☑
  excessive 676.6 ☑
  failed 676.4 ☑
  mastitis NEC 675.2 ☑
  mother (care and/or examination) V24.1
  nonpuerperal 611.6
  suppressed 676.5 ☑
Lacticemia 271.3
  excessive 276.2
Lactosuria 271.3
Lacunar skull 756.0
Laennec's cirrhosis (alcoholic) 571.2
  nonalcoholic 571.5
Lafora's disease 333.2
Lagleyze-von Hippel disease (retinocerebral angiomatosis) 759.6
Lag, lid (nervous) 374.41
Lagophthalmos (eyelid) (nervous) 374.20
  cicatricial 374.23

Lagophthalmos — continued
  keratitis (see also Keratitis) 370.34
  mechanical 374.22
  paralytic 374.21
La grippe — see Influenza
Lahore sore 085.1
Lakes, venous (cerebral) 437.8
Laki-Lorand factor deficiency — see also Defect, coagulation 286.3
Lalling 307.9
Lambliasis 007.1
Lame back 724.5
Lancereaux's diabetes (diabetes mellitus with marked emaciation) 250.8 ☑ [261]
  due to secondary diabetes 249.8 ☑ [261]
Landau-Kleffner syndrome 345.8 ☑
Landouzy-Déjérine dystrophy (fascioscapulo-humeral atrophy) 359.1
Landry's disease or paralysis 357.0
Landry-Guillain-Barré syndrome 357.0
Lane's
  band 751.4
  disease 569.89
  kink (see also Obstruction, intestine) 560.9
Langdon Down's syndrome (mongolism) 758.0
Language abolition 784.69
Lanugo (persistent) 757.4
Laparoscopic surgical procedure converted to open procedure V64.41
Lardaceous
  degeneration (any site) 277.39
  disease 277.39
  kidney 277.39 [583.81]
  liver 277.39
Large
  baby (regardless of gestational age) 766.1
    exceptionally (weight of 4500 grams or more) 766.0
    of diabetic mother 775.0
  ear 744.22
  fetus (see also Oversize, fetus)
    causing disproportion 653.5 ☑
      with obstructed labor 660.1 ☑
  for dates
    fetus or newborn (regardless of gestational age) 766.1
      affecting management of pregnancy 656.6 ☑
      exceptionally (weight of 4500 grams or more) 766.0
  physiological cup 743.57
  stature 783.9
  waxy liver 277.39
  white kidney — see Nephrosis
Larsen-Johansson disease (juvenile osteopathia patellae) 732.4
Larsen's syndrome (flattened facies and multiple congenital dislocations) 755.8
Larva migrans
  cutaneous NEC 126.9
    ancylostoma 126.9
  of Diptera in vitreous 128.0
  visceral NEC 128.0
Laryngeal — see also condition 786.2
  syncope 786.2
Laryngismus (acute) (infectious) (stridulous) 478.75
  congenital 748.3
  diphtheritic 032.3
Laryngitis (acute) (edematous) (fibrinous) (gangrenous) (infective) (infiltrative) (malignant) (membranous) (phlegmonous) (pneumococcal) (pseudomembranous) (septic) (subglottic) (suppurative) (ulcerative) (viral) 464.00
  with
    influenza, flu, or grippe 487.1
    obstruction 464.01
    tracheitis (see also Laryngotracheitis) 464.20
      with obstruction 464.21
      acute 464.20
        with obstruction 464.21
      chronic 476.1
  atrophic 476.0
  Borrelia vincentii 101

☑ Additional Digit Required — Refer to the Tabular List for Digit Selection   ⱽᴮˢ Subterms under main terms may continue to next column or page

166 — Volume 2 • October 2009   ▶◀ Revised Text   ● New Line   ▲ Revised Code   2010 ICD-9-CM

ryngitis — *continued*
catarrhal 476.0
chronic 476.0
with tracheitis (chronic) 476.1
due to external agent — *see* Condition, respiratory, chronic, due to
diphtheritic (membranous) 032.3
due to external agent — *see* Inflammation, respiratory, upper, due to
Hemophilus influenzae 464.00
with obstruction 464.01
H. influenzae 464.00
with obstruction 464.01
hypertrophic 476.0
influenzal 487.1
pachydermic 478.79
sicca 476.0
spasmodic 478.75
acute 464.00
with obstruction 464.01
streptococcal 034.0
stridulous 478.75
syphilitic 095.8
congenital 090.5
tuberculous (*see also* Tuberculosis, larynx) 012.3 ☑
Vincent's 101
ryngocele (congenital) (ventricular) 748.3
ryngofissure 478.79
congenital 748.3
ryngomalacia (congenital) 748.3
ryngopharyngitis (acute) 465.0
chronic 478.9
due to external agent — *see* Condition, respiratory, chronic, due to
due to external agent — *see* Inflammation, respiratory, upper, due to
septic 034.0
ryngoplegia — *see also* Paralysis, vocal cord 478.30
ryngoptosis 478.79
ryngospasm 478.75
due to external agent — *see* Condition, respiratory, acute, due to
ryngostenosis 478.74
congenital 748.3
ryngotracheitis (acute) (infectional) (viral) — *see also* Laryngitis 464.20
with obstruction 464.21
atrophic 476.1
Borrelia vincenti 101
catarrhal 476.1
chronic 476.1
due to external agent — *see* Condition, respiratory, chronic, due to
diphtheritic (membranous) 032.3
due to external agent — *see* Inflammation, respiratory, upper, due to
H. influenzae 464.20
with obstruction 464.21
hypertrophic 476.1
influenzal 487.1
pachydermic 478.75
sicca 476.1
spasmodic 478.75
acute 464.20
with obstruction 464.21
streptococcal 034.0
stridulous 478.75
syphilitic 095.8
congenital 090.5
tuberculous (*see also* Tuberculosis, larynx) 012.3 ☑
Vincent's 101
ryngotracheobronchitis — *see also* Bronchitis 490
acute 466.0
chronic 491.8
viral 466.0
ryngotracheobronchopneumonitis — *see* Pneumonia, broncho-
arynx, laryngeal — *see* condition
asègue's disease (persecution mania) 297.9
assa fever 078.89
assitude — *see also* Weakness 780.79
ate — *see also* condition

Late — *see also* condition — *continued*
effect(s) (of) (*see also* condition)
abscess
intracranial or intraspinal (conditions classifiable to 324) — *see* category 326
adverse effect of drug, medicinal or biological substance 909.5
allergic reaction 909.9
amputation
postoperative (late) 997.60
traumatic (injury classifiable to 885–887 and 895–897) 905.9
burn (injury classifiable to 948–949) 906.9
extremities NEC (injury classifiable to 943 or 945) 906.7
hand or wrist (injury classifiable to 944) 906.6
eye (injury classifiable to 940) 906.5
face, head, and neck (injury classifiable to 941) 906.5
specified site NEC (injury classifiable to 942 and 946–947) 906.8
cerebrovascular disease (conditions classifiable to 430–437) 438.9
with
alterations of sensations 438.6
aphasia 438.11
apraxia 438.81
ataxia 438.84
cognitive deficits 438.0
disturbances of vision 438.7
dysarthria 438.13 ●
dysphagia 438.82
dysphasia 438.12
facial droop 438.83
facial weakness 438.83
fluency disorder 438.14 ●
hemiplegia/hemiparesis
affecting
dominant side 438.21
nondominant side 438.22
unspecified side 438.20
monoplegia of lower limb
affecting
dominant side 438.41
nondominant side 438.42
unspecified side 438.40
monoplegia of upper limb
affecting
dominant side 438.31
nondominant side 438.32
unspecified side 438.30
paralytic syndrome NEC
affecting
bilateral 438.53
dominant side 438.51
nondominant side 438.52
unspecified side 438.50
speech and language deficit 438.10
specified type NEC 438.19
stuttering 438.14 ●
vertigo 438.85
specified type NEC 438.89
childbirth complication(s) 677
complication(s) of
childbirth 677
delivery 677
pregnancy 677
puerperium 677
surgical and medical care (conditions classifiable to 996–999) 909.3
trauma (conditions classifiable to 958) 908.6
contusion (injury classifiable to 920–924) 906.3
crushing (injury classifiable to 925–929) 906.4
delivery complication(s) 677
dislocation (injury classifiable to 830–839) 905.6
encephalitis or encephalomyelitis (conditions classifiable to 323) — *see* category 326
in infectious diseases 139.8

Late — *see also* condition — *continued*
effect(s) (*see also* condition) — *continued*
encephalitis or encephalomyelitis — *see* category — *continued*
in infectious diseases — *continued*
viral (conditions classifiable to 049.8, 049.9, 062–064) 139.0
external cause NEC (conditions classifiable to 995) 909.9
certain conditions classifiable to categories 991-994 909.4
foreign body in orifice (injury classifiable to 930–939) 908.5
fracture (multiple) (injury classifiable to 828–829) 905.5
extremity
lower (injury classifiable to 821–827) 905.4
neck of femur (injury classifiable to 820) 905.3
upper (injury classifiable to 810–819) 905.2
face and skull (injury classifiable to 800–804) 905.0
skull and face (injury classifiable to 800–804) 905.0
spine and trunk (injury classifiable to 805 and 807–809) 905.1
with spinal cord lesion (injury classifiable to 806) 907.2
infection
pyogenic, intracranial — *see* category 326
infectious diseases (conditions classifiable to 001–136) NEC 139.8
injury (injury classifiable to 959) 908.9
blood vessel 908.3
abdomen and pelvis (injury classifiable to 902) 908.4
extremity (injury classifiable to 903–904) 908.3
head and neck (injury classifiable to 900) 908.3
intracranial (injury classifiable to 850–854) 907.0
with skull fracture 905.0
thorax (injury classifiable to 901) 908.4
internal organ NEC (injury classifiable to 867 and 869) 908.2
abdomen (injury classifiable to 863–866 and 868) 908.1
thorax (injury classifiable to 860–862) 908.0
intracranial (injury classifiable to 850–854) 907.0
with skull fracture (injury classifiable to 800–801 and 803–804) 905.0
nerve NEC (injury classifiable to 957) 907.9
cranial (injury classifiable to 950–951) 907.1
peripheral NEC (injury classifiable to 957) 907.9
lower limb and pelvic girdle (injury classifiable to 956) 907.5
upper limb and shoulder girdle (injury classifiable to 955) 907.4
roots and plexus(es), spinal (injury classifiable to 953) 907.3
trunk (injury classifiable to 954) 907.3
spinal
cord (injury classifiable to 806 and 952) 907.2
nerve root(s) and plexus(es) (injury classifiable to 953) 907.3
superficial (injury classifiable to 910–919) 906.2
tendon (tendon injury classifiable to 840–848, 880–884 with .2, and 890–894 with .2) 905.8

Late — *see also* condition — *continued*
effect(s) (*see also* condition) — *continued*
meningitis
bacterial (conditions classifiable to 320) — *see* category 326
unspecified cause (conditions classifiable to 322) — *see* category 326
myelitis (*see also* Late, effect(s) (of), encephalitis) — *see* category 326
parasitic diseases (conditions classifiable to 001–136 NEC) 139.8
phlebitis or thrombophlebitis of intracranial venous sinuses (conditions classifiable to 325) — *see* category 326
poisoning due to drug, medicinal or biological substance (conditions classifiable to 960–979) 909.0
poliomyelitis, acute (conditions classifiable to 045) 138
pregnancy complication(s) 677
puerperal complication(s) 677
radiation (conditions classifiable to 990) 909.2
rickets 268.1
sprain and strain without mention of tendon injury (injury classifiable to 840–848, except tendon injury) 905.7
tendon involvement 905.8
toxic effect of
drug, medicinal or biological substance (conditions classifiable to 960–979) 909.0
nonmedical substance (conditions classifiable to 980–989) 909.1
trachoma (conditions classifiable to 076) 139.1
tuberculosis 137.0
bones and joints (conditions classifiable to 015) 137.3
central nervous system (conditions classifiable to 013) 137.1
genitourinary (conditions classifiable to 016) 137.2
pulmonary (conditions classifiable to 010–012) 137.0
specified organs NEC (conditions classifiable to 014, 017–018) 137.4
viral encephalitis (conditions classifiable to 049.8, 049.9, 062–064) 139.0
wound, open
extremity (injury classifiable to 880–884 and 890–894, except .2) 906.1
tendon (injury classifiable to 880–884 with .2 and 890–894 with .2) 905.8
head, neck, and trunk (injury classifiable to 870–879) 906.0
infant
post-term (gestation period over 40 completed weeks to 42 completed weeks) 766.21
prolonged gestation (period over 42 completed weeks) 766.22
Latent — *see* condition
Lateral — *see* condition
Laterocession — *see* Lateroversion
Lateroflexion — *see* Lateroversion
Lateroversion
cervix — *see* Lateroversion, uterus
uterus, uterine (cervix) (postinfectional) (postpartal, old) 621.6
congenital 752.3
in pregnancy or childbirth 654.4 ☑
affecting fetus or newborn 763.89
Lathyrism 988.2
Launois-Bensaude's lipomatosis 272.8
Launois-Cléret syndrome (adiposogenital dystrophy) 253.8
Launois' syndrome (pituitary gigantism) 253.0
Laurence-Moon-Biedl syndrome (obesity, polydactyly, and mental retardation) 759.89

☑ Additional Digit Required — Refer to the Tabular List for Digit Selection   ▽ Subterms under main terms may continue to next column or page

010 ICD-9-CM   ►◄ Revised Text   ● New Line   ▲ Revised Code   October 2009 • Volume 2 — 167

Index

LAV — Lesion(s)

LAV (disease) (illness) (infection) — *see* Human immunodeficiency virus (disease) (illness) (infection)

LAV/HTLV-III (disease) (illness) (infection) — *see* Human immunodeficiency virus (disease) (illness) (infection)

Lawford's syndrome (encephalocutaneous angiomatosis) 759.6

Laxative habit — *see also* Abuse, drugs, nondependent 305.9 ☑

Lax, laxity — *see also* Relaxation
 ligament 728.4
 skin (acquired) 701.8
  congenital 756.83

Lazy leukocyte syndrome 288.09

LCAD (long chain/very long chain acyl CoA dehydrogenase deficiency, VLCAD) 277.85

LCHAD (long chain 3-hydroxyacyl CoA dehydrogenase deficiency) 277.85

Lead — *see also* condition
 exposure ▶(suspected)◀ to V15.86
 incrustation of cornea 371.15
 poisoning 984.9
  specified type of lead — *see* Table of Drugs and Chemicals

Lead miners' lung 503

Leakage
 amniotic fluid 658.1 ☑
  with delayed delivery 658.2 ☑
  affecting fetus or newborn 761.1
 bile from drainage tube (T tube) 997.4
 blood (microscopic), fetal, into maternal circulation 656.0 ☑
  affecting management of pregnancy or puerperium 656.0 ☑
 device, implant, or graft — *see* Complications, mechanical
 spinal fluid at lumbar puncture site 997.09
 urine, continuous 788.37

Leaky heart — *see* Endocarditis

Learning defect, specific NEC (strephosymbolia) 315.2

Leather bottle stomach (M8142/3) 151.9

Leber's
 congenital amaurosis 362.76
 optic atrophy (hereditary) 377.16

Lederer's anemia or disease (acquired infectious hemolytic anemia) 283.19

Lederer-Brill syndrome (acquired infectious hemolytic anemia) 283.19

Leeches (aquatic) (land) 134.2

Left-sided neglect 781.8

Leg — *see* condition

Legal investigation V62.5

Legg (-Calvé) -Perthes disease or syndrome (osteochondrosis, femoral capital) 732.1

Legionnaires' disease 482.84

Leigh's disease 330.8

Leiner's disease (exfoliative dermatitis) 695.89

Leiofibromyoma (M8890/0) — *see also* Leiomyoma
 uterus (cervix) (corpus) (*see also* Leiomyoma, uterus) 218.9

Leiomyoblastoma (M8891/1) — *see* Neoplasm, connective tissue, uncertain behavior

Leiomyofibroma (M8890/0) — *see also* Neoplasm, connective tissue, benign
 uterus (cervix) (corpus) (*see also* Leiomyoma, uterus) 218.9

Leiomyoma (M8890/0) — *see also* Neoplasm, connective tissue, benign
 bizarre (M8893/0) — *see* Neoplasm, connective tissue, benign
 cellular (M8892/1) — *see* Neoplasm, connective tissue, uncertain behavior
 epithelioid (M8891/1) — *see* Neoplasm, connective tissue, uncertain behavior
 prostate (polypoid) 600.20
  with
   other lower urinary tract symptoms (LUTS) 600.21
   urinary
    obstruction 600.21
    retention 600.21
 uterus (cervix) (corpus) 218.9
  interstitial 218.1

Leiomyoma — *see also* Neoplasm, connective tissue, benign — *continued*
 uterus — *continued*
  intramural 218.1
  submucous 218.0
  subperitoneal 218.2
  subserous 218.2
 vascular (M8894/0) — *see* Neoplasm, connective tissue, benign

Leiomyomatosis (intravascular) (M8890/1) — *see* Neoplasm, connective tissue, uncertain behavior

Leiomyosarcoma (M8890/3) — *see also* Neoplasm, connective tissue, malignant
 epithelioid (M8891/3) — *see* Neoplasm, connective tissue, malignant

Leishmaniasis 085.9
 American 085.5
  cutaneous 085.4
  mucocutaneous 085.5
 Asian desert 085.2
 Brazilian 085.5
 cutaneous 085.9
  acute necrotizing 085.2
  American 085.4
  Asian desert 085.2
  diffuse 085.3
  dry form 085.1
  Ethiopian 085.3
  eyelid 085.5 [373.6]
  late 085.1
  lepromatous 085.3
  recurrent 085.1
  rural 085.1
  ulcerating 085.1
  urban 085.1
  wet form 085.2
  zoonotic form 085.2
 dermal (*see also* Leishmaniasis, cutaneous)
  post kala-azar 085.0
 eyelid 085.5 [373.6]
 infantile 085.0
 Mediterranean 085.0
 mucocutaneous (American) 085.5
 naso-oral 085.5
 nasopharyngeal 085.5
 Old World 085.1
 tegumentaria diffusa 085.4
 vaccination, prophylactic (against) V05.2
 visceral (Indian) 085.0

Leishmanoid, dermal — *see also* Leishmaniasis, cutaneous
 post kala-azar 085.0

Leloir's disease 695.4

Lemiere syndrome 451.89

Lenegre's disease 426.0

Lengthening, leg 736.81

Lennox-Gastaut syndrome 345.0 ☑
 with tonic seizures 345.1 ☑

Lennox's syndrome — *see also* Epilepsy 345.0 ☑

Lens — *see* condition

Lenticonus (anterior) (posterior) (congenital) 743.36

Lenticular degeneration, progressive 275.1

Lentiglobus (posterior) (congenital) 743.36

Lentigo (congenital) 709.09
 juvenile 709.09
 Maligna (M8742/2) (*see also* Neoplasm, skin, in situ)
  melanoma (M8742/3) — *see* Melanoma
 senile 709.09

Leonine leprosy 030.0

Leontiasis
 ossium 733.3
 syphilitic 095.8
  congenital 090.5

Léopold-Lévi's syndrome (paroxysmal thyroid instability) 242.9 ☑

Lepore hemoglobin syndrome 282.49

Lepothrix 039.0

Lepra 030.9
 Willan's 696.1

Leprechaunism 259.8

Lepromatous leprosy 030.0

Leprosy 030.9

Leprosy — *continued*
 anesthetic 030.1
 beriberi 030.1
 borderline (group B) (infiltrated) (neuritic) 030.3
 cornea (*see also* Leprosy, by type) 030.9 [371.89]
 dimorphous (group B) (infiltrated) (lepromatous) (neuritic) (tuberculoid) 030.3
 eyelid 030.0 [373.4]
 indeterminate (group I) (macular) (neuritic) (uncharacteristic) 030.2
 leonine 030.0
 lepromatous (diffuse) (infiltrated) (macular) (neuritic) (nodular) (type L) 030.0
 macular (early) (neuritic) (simple) 030.2
 maculoanesthetic 030.1
 mixed 030.0
 neuro 030.1
 nodular 030.0
 primary neuritic 030.3
 specified type or group NEC 030.8
 tubercular 030.1
 tuberculoid (macular) (maculoanesthetic) (major) (minor) (neuritic) (type T) 030.1

Leptocytosis, hereditary 282.49

Leptomeningitis (chronic) (circumscribed) (hemorrhagic) (nonsuppurative) — *see also* Meningitis 322.9
 aseptic 047.9
  adenovirus 049.1
  Coxsackie virus 047.0
  ECHO virus 047.1
  enterovirus 047.9
  lymphocytic choriomeningitis 049.0
 epidemic 036.0
 late effect — *see* category 326
 meningococcal 036.0
 pneumococcal 320.1
 syphilitic 094.2
 tuberculous (*see also* Tuberculosis, meninges) 013.0 ☑

Leptomeningopathy — *see also* Meningitis 322.9

Leptospiral — *see* condition

Leptospirochetal — *see* condition

Leptospirosis 100.9
 autumnalis 100.89
 canicula 100.89
 grippotyphosa 100.89
 hebdomidis 100.89
 icterohemorrhagica 100.0
 nanukayami 100.89
 pomona 100.89
 Weil's disease 100.0

Leptothricosis — *see* Actinomycosis

Leptothrix infestation — *see* Actinomycosis

Leptotricosis — *see* Actinomycosis

Leptus dermatitis 133.8

Leriche's syndrome (aortic bifurcation occlusion) 444.0

Léris pleonosteosis 756.89

Léri-Weill syndrome 756.59

Lermoyez's syndrome — *see also* Disease, Ménière's 386.00

Lesbianism — omit code
 ego-dystonic 302.0
 problems with 302.0

Lesch-Nyhan syndrome (hypoxanthineguanine-phosphoribosyltransferase deficiency) 277.2

Lesion(s)
 abducens nerve 378.54
 alveolar process 525.8
 anorectal 569.49
 aortic (valve) — *see* Endocarditis, aortic
 auditory nerve 388.5
 basal ganglion 333.90
 bile duct (*see also* Disease, biliary) 576.8
 bladder 596.9
 bone 733.90
 brachial plexus 353.0
 brain 348.89 ▲
  congenital 742.9
  vascular (*see also* Lesion, cerebrovascular) 437.9

Lesion(s) — *continued*
 brain — *continued*
  vascular (*see also* Lesion, cerebrovascular) — *continued*
   degenerative 437.1
   healed or old without residuals V12.
   hypertensive 437.2
   late effect — *see* Late effect(s) (of) cerebrovascular disease
 buccal 528.9
 calcified — *see* Calcification
 canthus 373.9
 carate — *see* Pinta, lesions
 cardia 537.89
 cardiac — *see also* Disease, heart
  congenital 746.9
  valvular — *see* Endocarditis
 cauda equina 344.60
  with neurogenic bladder 344.61
 cecum 569.89
 cerebral — *see* Lesion, brain
 cerebrovascular (*see also* Disease, cerebrovascular NEC) 437.9
  degenerative 437.1
   healed or old without residuals V12.
  hypertensive 437.2
  specified type NEC 437.8
 cervical root (nerve) NEC 353.2
 chiasmal 377.54
  associated with
   inflammatory disorders 377.54
   neoplasm NEC 377.52
    pituitary 377.51
   pituitary disorders 377.51
   vascular disorders 377.53
 chorda tympani 351.8
 coin, lung 793.1
 colon 569.89
 congenital — *see* Anomaly
 conjunctiva 372.9
 coronary artery (*see also* Ischemia, heart) 414
 cranial nerve 352.9
  first 352.0
  second 377.49
  third
   partial 378.51
   total 378.52
  fourth 378.53
  fifth 350.9
  sixth 378.54
  seventh 351.9
  eighth 388.5
  ninth 352.2
  tenth 352.3
  eleventh 352.4
  twelfth 352.5
 cystic — *see* Cyst
 degenerative — *see* Degeneration
 dermal (skin) 709.9
 Dieulafoy (hemorrhagic)
  of
   duodenum 537.84
   intestine 569.86
   stomach 537.84
 duodenum 537.89
  with obstruction 537.3
 eyelid 373.9
 gasserian ganglion 350.8
 gastric 537.89
 gastroduodenal 537.89
 gastrointestinal 569.89
 glossopharyngeal nerve 352.2
 heart (organic) (*see also* Disease, heart)
  vascular — *see* Disease, cardiovascular
 helix (ear) 709.9
 high grade myelodysplastic syndrome 238.73
 hyperchromic, due to pinta (carate) 103.1
 hyperkeratotic (*see also* Hyperkeratosis) 701.1
 hypoglossal nerve 352.5
 hypopharynx 478.29
 hypothalamic 253.9
 ileocecal coil 569.89
 ileum 569.89
 iliohypogastric nerve 355.79
 ilioinguinal nerve 355.79
 in continuity — *see* Injury, nerve, by site

Lesion(s) — continued
- inflammatory — see Inflammation
- intestine 569.89
- intracerebral — see Lesion, brain
- intrachiasmal (optic) (see also Lesion, chiasmal) 377.54
- intracranial, space-occupying NEC 784.2
- joint 719.90
  - ankle 719.97
  - elbow 719.92
  - foot 719.97
  - hand 719.94
  - hip 719.95
  - knee 719.96
  - multiple sites 719.99
  - pelvic region 719.95
  - sacroiliac (old) 724.6
  - shoulder (region) 719.91
  - specified site NEC 719.98
  - wrist 719.93
- keratotic (see also Keratosis) 701.1
- kidney (see also Disease, renal) 593.9
- laryngeal nerve (recurrent) 352.3
- leonine 030.0
- lip 528.5
- liver 573.8
- low grade myelodysplastic syndrome 238.72
- lumbosacral
  - plexus 353.1
  - root (nerve) NEC 353.4
- lung 518.89
  - coin 793.1
- maxillary sinus 473.0
- mitral — see Endocarditis, mitral
- Morel Lavallée — see Hematoma, by site ●
- motor cortex 348.89 ▲
- nerve (see also Disorder, nerve) 355.9
- nervous system 349.9
  - congenital 742.9
- nonallopathic NEC 739.9
  - in region (of)
    - abdomen 739.9
    - acromioclavicular 739.7
    - cervical, cervicothoracic 739.1
    - costochondral 739.8
    - costovertebral 739.8
    - extremity
      - lower 739.6
      - upper 739.7
    - head 739.0
    - hip 739.5
    - lower extremity 739.6
    - lumbar, lumbosacral 739.3
    - occipitocervical 739.0
    - pelvic 739.5
    - pubic 739.5
    - rib cage 739.8
    - sacral, sacrococcygeal, sacroiliac 739.4
    - sternochondral 739.8
    - sternoclavicular 739.7
    - thoracic, thoracolumbar 739.2
    - upper extremity 739.7
- nose (internal) 478.19
- obstructive — see Obstruction
- obturator nerve 355.79
- occlusive
  - artery — see Embolism, artery
- organ or site NEC — see Disease, by site
- osteolytic 733.90
- paramacular, of retina 363.32
- peptic 537.89
- periodontal, due to traumatic occlusion 523.8
- perirectal 569.49
- peritoneum (granulomatous) 568.89
- pigmented (skin) 709.00
- pinta — see Pinta, lesions
- polypoid — see Polyp
- prechiasmal (optic) (see also Lesion, chiasmal) 377.54
- primary (see also Syphilis, primary)
  - carate 103.0
  - pinta 103.0
  - yaws 102.0
- pulmonary 518.89
  - valve (see also Endocarditis, pulmonary) 424.3

Lesion(s) — continued
- pylorus 537.89
- radiation NEC 990
- radium NEC 990
- rectosigmoid 569.89
- retina, retinal (see also Retinopathy)
  - vascular 362.17
- retroperitoneal 568.89
- romanus 720.1
- sacroiliac (joint) 724.6
- salivary gland 527.8
  - benign lymphoepithelial 527.8
- saphenous nerve 355.79
- secondary — see Syphilis, secondary
- sigmoid 569.89
- sinus (accessory) (nasal) (see also Sinusitis) 473.9
- skin 709.9
  - suppurative 686.00
- SLAP (superior glenoid labrum) 840.7
- space-occupying, intracranial NEC 784.2
- spinal cord 336.9
  - congenital 742.9
  - traumatic (complete) (incomplete) (transverse) (see also Injury, spinal, by site)
    - with
      - broken
        - back — see Fracture, vertebra, by site, with spinal cord injury
        - neck — see Fracture, vertebra, cervical, with spinal cord injury
      - fracture, vertebra — see Fracture, vertebra, by site, with spinal cord injury
- spleen 289.50
- stomach 537.89
- superior glenoid labrum (SLAP) 840.7
- syphilitic — see Syphilis
  - tertiary — see Syphilis, tertiary
- thoracic root (nerve) 353.3
- tonsillar fossa 474.9
- tooth, teeth 525.8
  - white spot 521.01
- traumatic NEC (see also nature and site of injury) 959.9
- tricuspid (valve) — see Endocarditis, tricuspid
- trigeminal nerve 350.9
- ulcerated or ulcerative — see Ulcer
- uterus NEC 621.9
- vagina 623.8
- vagus nerve 352.3
- valvular — see Endocarditis
- vascular 459.9
  - affecting central nervous system (see also Lesion, cerebrovascular) 437.9
  - following trauma (see also Injury, blood vessel, by site) 904.9
  - retina 362.17
  - traumatic — see Injury, blood vessel, by site
  - umbilical cord 663.6 ☑
    - affecting fetus or newborn 762.6
- visual
  - cortex NEC (see also Disorder, visual, cortex) 377.73
  - pathway NEC (see also Disorder, visual, pathway) 377.63
- warty — see Verruca
- white spot, on teeth 521.01
- x-ray NEC 990

Lethargic — see condition
Lethargy 780.79
Letterer-Siwe disease (acute histiocytosis X) (M9722/3) 202.5 ☑
Leucinosis 270.3
Leucocoria 360.44
Leucosarcoma (M9850/3) 207.8 ☑
Leukasmus 270.2

Leukemia, leukemic (congenital) (M9800/3) 208.9 ☑

Note – Use the following fifth-digit subclassification for categories 203–208:
- 0 without mention of having achieved remission
  failed remission
- 1 with remission
- 2 in relapse

- acute NEC (M9801/3) 208.0 ☑
- aleukemic NEC (M9804/3) 208.8 ☑
  - granulocytic (M9864/3) 205.8 ☑
- basophilic (M9870/3) 205.1 ☑
- blast (cell) (M9801/3) 208.0 ☑
- blastic (M9801/3) 208.0 ☑
  - granulocytic (M9861/3) 205.0 ☑
- chronic NEC (M9803/3) 208.1 ☑
- compound (M9810/3) 207.8 ☑
- eosinophilic (M9880/3) 205.1 ☑
- giant cell (M9910/3) 207.2 ☑
- granulocytic (M9860/3) 205.9 ☑
  - acute (M9861/3) 205.0 ☑
  - aleukemic (M9864/3) 205.8 ☑
  - blastic (M9861/3) 205.0 ☑
  - chronic (M9863/3) 205.1 ☑
  - subacute (M9862/3) 205.2 ☑
  - subleukemic (M9864/3) 205.8 ☑
- hairy cell (M9940/3) 202.4 ☑
- hemoblastic (M9801/3) 208.0 ☑
- histiocytic (M9890/3) 206.9 ☑
- lymphatic (M9820/3) 204.9 ☑
  - acute (M9821/3) 204.0 ☑
  - aleukemic (M9824/3) 204.8 ☑
  - chronic (M9823/3) 204.1 ☑
  - subacute (M9822/3) 204.2 ☑
  - subleukemic (M9824/3) 204.8 ☑
- lymphoblastic (M9821/3) 204.0 ☑
- lymphocytic (M9820/3) 204.9 ☑
  - acute (M9821/3) 204.0 ☑
  - aleukemic (M9824/3) 204.8 ☑
  - chronic (M9823/3) 204.1 ☑
  - granular
    - large T-cell 204.8 ☑ ●
  - subacute (M9822/3) 204.2 ☑
  - subleukemic (M9824/3) 204.8 ☑
- lymphogenous (M9820/3) — see Leukemia, lymphoid
- lymphoid (M9820/3) 204.9 ☑
  - acute (M9821/3) 204.0 ☑
  - aleukemic (M9824/3) 204.8 ☑
  - blastic (M9821/3) 204.0 ☑
  - chronic (M9823/3) 204.1 ☑
  - subacute (M9822/3) 204.2 ☑
  - subleukemic (M9824/3) 204.8 ☑
- lymphosarcoma cell (M9850/3) 207.8 ☑
- mast cell (M9900/3) 207.8 ☑
- megakaryocytic (M9910/3) 207.2 ☑
- megakaryocytoid (M9910/3) 207.2 ☑
- mixed (cell) (M9810/3) 207.8 ☑
- monoblastic (M9891/3) 206.0 ☑
- monocytic (Schilling-type) (M9890/3) 206.9 ☑
  - acute (M9891/3) 206.0 ☑
  - aleukemic (M9894/3) 206.8 ☑
  - chronic (M9893/3) 206.1 ☑
  - Naegeli-type (M9863/3) 205.1 ☑
  - subacute (M9892/3) 206.2 ☑
  - subleukemic (M9894/3) 206.8 ☑
- monocytoid (M9890/3) 206.9 ☑
  - acute (M9891/3) 206.0 ☑
  - aleukemic (M9894/3) 206.8 ☑
  - chronic (M9893/3) 206.1 ☑
  - myelogenous (M9863/3) 205.1 ☑
  - subacute (M9892/3) 206.2 ☑
  - subleukemic (M9894/3) 206.8 ☑
- monomyocytic (M9860/3) — see Leukemia, myelomonocytic
- myeloblastic (M9861/3) 205.0 ☑
- myelocytic (M9863/3) 205.1 ☑
  - acute (M9861/3) 205.0 ☑
- myelogenous (M9860/3) 205.9 ☑
  - acute (M9861/3) 205.0 ☑

Leukemia, leukemic — continued
- myelogenous — continued
  - aleukemic (M9864/3) 205.8 ☑
  - chronic (M9863/3) 205.1 ☑
  - monocytoid (M9863/3) 205.1 ☑
  - subacute (M9862/3) 205.2 ☑
  - subleukemic (M9864) 205.8 ☑
- myeloid (M9860/3) 205.9 ☑
  - acute (M9861/3) 205.0 ☑
  - aleukemic (M9864/3) 205.8 ☑
  - chronic (M9863/3) 205.1 ☑
  - subacute (M9862/3) 205.2 ☑
  - subleukemic (M9864/3) 205.8 ☑
- myelomonocytic (M9860/3) 205.9 ☑
  - acute (M9861/3) 205.0 ☑
  - chronic (M9863/3) 205.1 ☑
- Naegeli-type monocytic (M9863/3) 205.1 ☑
- neutrophilic (M9865/3) 205.1 ☑
- plasma cell (M9830/3) 203.1 ☑
- plasmacytic (M9830/3) 203.1 ☑
- prolymphocytic (M9825/3) — see Leukemia, lymphoid
- promyelocytic, acute (M9866/3) 205.0 ☑
- Schilling-type monocytic (M9890/3) — see Leukemia, monocytic
- stem cell (M9801/3) 208.0 ☑
- subacute NEC (M9802/3) 208.2 ☑
- subleukemic NEC (M9804/3) 208.8 ☑
- thrombocytic (M9910/3) 207.2 ☑
- undifferentiated (M9801/3) 208.0 ☑

Leukemoid reaction (basophilic) (lymphocytic) (monocytic) (myelocytic) (neutrophilic) 288.62
Leukoaraiosis (hypertensive) 437.1 ●
Leukoariosis — see Leukoaraiosis ●
Leukoclastic vasculitis 446.29
Leukocoria 360.44
Leukocythemia — see Leukemia
Leukocytopenia 288.50
Leukocytosis 288.60
- basophilic 288.8
- eosinophilic 288.3
- lymphocytic 288.8
- monocytic 288.8
- neutrophilic 288.8
Leukoderma 709.09
- syphilitic 091.3
  - late 095.8
Leukodermia — see also Leukoderma 709.09
Leukodystrophy (cerebral) (globoid cell) (metachromatic) (progressive) (sudanophilic) 330.0
Leukoedema, mouth or tongue 528.79
Leukoencephalitis
- acute hemorrhagic (postinfectious) NEC 136.9 [323.61]
  - postimmunization or postvaccinal 323.51
- subacute sclerosing 046.2
  - van Bogaert's 046.2
  - van Bogaert's (sclerosing) 046.2
Leukoencephalopathy — see also Encephalitis 323.9
- acute necrotizing hemorrhagic (postinfectious) 136.9 [323.61]
  - postimmunization or postvaccinal 323.51
- Binswanger's 290.12 ●
- metachromatic 330.0
- multifocal (progressive) 046.3
- progressive multifocal 046.3
- reversible, posterior 348.5
Leukoerythroblastosis 289.9
Leukoerythrosis 289.0
Leukokeratosis — see also Leukoplakia 702.8
- mouth 528.6
- nicotina palati 528.79
- tongue 528.6
Leukokoria 360.44
Leukokraurosis vulva, vulvae 624.09
Leukolymphosarcoma (M9850/3) 207.8 ☑
Leukoma (cornea) (interfering with central vision) 371.03
- adherent 371.04
Leukomalacia, periventricular 779.7
Leukomelanopathy, hereditary 288.2
Leukonychia (punctata) (striata) 703.8

☑ Additional Digit Required — Refer to the Tabular List for Digit Selection
Subterms under main terms may continue to next column or page

2010 ICD-9-CM   ▶◀ Revised Text   ● New Line   ▲ Revised Code   October 2009 • Volume 2 — 169

Lesion(s) — Leukonychia

Index

Leukonychia — Littre's

Leukonychia — *continued*
congenital 757.5
Leukopathia
unguium 703.8
congenital 757.5
Leukopenia 288.50
basophilic 288.59
cyclic 288.02
eosinophilic 288.59
familial 288.59
malignant (*see also* Agranulocytosis) 288.09
periodic 288.02
transitory neonatal 776.7
Leukopenic — *see* condition
Leukoplakia 702.8
anus 569.49
bladder (postinfectional) 596.8
buccal 528.6
cervix (uteri) 622.2
esophagus 530.83
gingiva 528.6
kidney (pelvis) 593.89
larynx 478.79
lip 528.6
mouth 528.6
oral soft tissue (including tongue) (mucosa) 528.6
palate 528.6
pelvis (kidney) 593.89
penis (infectional) 607.0
rectum 569.49
syphilitic 095.8
tongue 528.6
tonsil 478.29
ureter (postinfectional) 593.89
urethra (postinfectional) 599.84
uterus 621.8
vagina 623.1
vesical 596.8
vocal cords 478.5
vulva 624.09
Leukopolioencephalopathy 330.0
Leukorrhea (vagina) 623.5
due to trichomonas (vaginalis) 131.00
trichomonal (Trichomonas vaginalis) 131.00
Leukosarcoma (M9850/3) 207.8 ☑
Leukosis (M9800/3) — *see* Leukemia
Lev's disease or syndrome (acquired complete heart block) 426.0
Levi's syndrome (pituitary dwarfism) 253.3
Levocardia (isolated) 746.87
with situs inversus 759.3
Levulosuria 271.2
Lewandowski's disease (primary) — *see also* Tuberculosis 017.0 ☑
Lewandowski-Lutz disease (epidermodysplasia verruciformis) 078.19
Lewy body dementia 331.82
Lewy body disease 331.82
Leyden's disease (periodic vomiting) 536.2
Leyden-Möbius dystrophy 359.1
Leydig cell
carcinoma (M8650/3)
specified site — *see* Neoplasm, by site, malignant
unspecified site
female 183.0
male 186.9
tumor (M8650/1)
benign (M8650/0)
specified site — *see* Neoplasm, by site, benign
unspecified site
female 220
male 222.0
malignant (M8650/3)
specified site — *see* Neoplasm, by site, malignant
unspecified site
female 183.0
male 186.9
specified site — *see* Neoplasm, by site, uncertain behavior
unspecified site
female 236.2
male 236.4

Leydig-Sertoli cell tumor (M8631/0)
specified site — *see* Neoplasm, by site, benign
unspecified site
female 220
male 222.0
LGSIL (low grade squamous intraepithelial lesion)
anus 796.73
cervix 795.03
vagina 795.13
Liar, pathologic 301.7
Libman-Sacks disease or syndrome 710.0 *[424.91]*
Lice (infestation) 132.9
body (pediculus corporis) 132.1
crab 132.2
head (pediculus capitis) 132.0
mixed (classifiable to more than one of the categories 132.0–132.2) 132.3
pubic (pediculus pubis) 132.2
Lichen 697.9
albus 701.0
annularis 695.89
atrophicus 701.0
corneus obtusus 698.3
myxedematous 701.8
nitidus 697.1
pilaris 757.39
acquired 701.1
planopilaris 697.0
planus (acute) (chronicus) (hypertrophic) (verrucous) 697.0
morphoeicus 701.0
sclerosus (et atrophicus) 701.0
ruber 696.4
acuminatus 696.4
moniliformis 697.8
obtusus corneus 698.3
of Wilson 697.0
planus 697.0
sclerosus (et atrophicus) 701.0
scrofulosus (primary) (*see also* Tuberculosis) 017.0 ☑
simplex (Vidal's) 698.3
chronicus 698.3
circumscriptus 698.3
spinulosus 757.39
mycotic 117.9
striata 697.8
urticatus 698.2
Lichenification 698.3
nodular 698.3
Lichenoides tuberculosis (primary) — *see also* Tuberculosis 017.0 ☑
Lichtheim's disease or syndrome (subacute combined sclerosis with pernicious anemia) 281.0 *[336.2]*
Lien migrans 289.59
Lientery — *see also* Diarrhea 787.91
infectious 009.2
Life circumstance problem NEC V62.89
Li-Fraumeni cancer syndrome V84.01
Ligament — *see* condition
Light-for-dates (infant) 764.0 ☑
with signs of fetal malnutrition 764.1 ☑
affecting management of pregnancy 656.5 ☑
Light-headedness 780.4
Lightning (effects) (shock) (stroke) (struck by) 994.0
burn — *see* Burn, by site
foot 266.2
Lightwood's disease or syndrome (renal tubular acidosis) 588.89
Lignac's disease (cystinosis) 270.0
Lignac (-Fanconi) syndrome (cystinosis) 270.0
Lignac (-de Toni) (-Fanconi) (-Debré) syndrome (cystinosis) 270.0
Ligneous thyroiditis 245.3
Likoff's syndrome (angina in menopausal women) 413.9
Limb — *see* condition
Limitation of joint motion — *see also* Stiffness, joint 719.5 ☑
sacroiliac 724.6
Limit dextrinosis 271.0
Limited
cardiac reserve — *see* Disease, heart

Limited — *continued*
duction, eye NEC 378.63
mandibular range of motion 524.52
Lindau (-von Hippel) disease (angiomatosis retinocerebellosa) 759.6
Lindau's disease (retinocerebral angiomatosis) 759.6
Linea corneae senilis 371.41
Lines
Beau's (transverse furrows on fingernails) 703.8
Harris' 733.91
Hudson-Stähli 371.11
Stähli's 371.11
Lingua
geographical 529.1
nigra (villosa) 529.3
plicata 529.5
congenital 750.13
tylosis 528.6
Lingual (tongue) — *see also* condition
thyroid 759.2
Linitis (gastric) 535.4 ☑
plastica (M8142/3) 151.9
Lioderma essentialis (cum melanosis et telangiectasia) 757.33
Lip — *see also* condition
biting 528.9
Lipalgia 272.8
Lipedema — *see* Edema
Lipemia — *see also* Hyperlipidemia 272.4
retina, retinalis 272.3
Lipidosis 272.7
cephalin 272.7
cerebral (infantile) (juvenile) (late) 330.1
cerebroretinal 330.1 *[362.71]*
cerebroside 272.7
cerebrospinal 272.7
chemically-induced 272.7
cholesterol 272.7
diabetic 250.8 ☑ *[272.7]*
due to secondary diabetes 249.8 ☑ *[272.7]*
dystopic (hereditary) 272.7
glycolipid 272.7
hepatosplenomegalic 272.3
hereditary, dystopic 272.7
sulfatide 330.0
Lipoadenoma (M8324/0) — *see* Neoplasm, by site, benign
Lipoblastoma (M8881/0) — *see* Lipoma, by site
Lipoblastomatosis (M8881/0) — *see* Lipoma, by site
Lipochondrodystrophy 277.5
Lipochrome histiocytosis (familial) 288.1
Lipodystrophia progressiva 272.6
Lipodystrophy (progressive) 272.6
insulin 272.6
intestinal 040.2
mesenteric 567.82
Lipofibroma (M8851/0) — *see* Lipoma, by site
Lipoglycoproteinosis 272.8
Lipogranuloma, sclerosing 709.8
Lipogranulomatosis (disseminated) 272.8
kidney 272.8
Lipoid — *see also* condition
histiocytosis 272.7
essential 272.7
nephrosis (*see also* Nephrosis) 581.3
proteinosis of Urbach 272.8
Lipoidemia — *see also* Hyperlipidemia 272.4
Lipoidosis — *see also* Lipidosis 272.7
Lipoma (M8850/0) 214.9
breast (skin) 214.1
face 214.0
fetal (M8881/0) (*see also* Lipoma, by site)
fat cell (M8880/0) — *see* Lipoma, by site
infiltrating (M8856/0) — *see* Lipoma, by site
intra-abdominal 214.3
intramuscular (M8856/0) — *see* Lipoma, by site
intrathoracic 214.2
kidney 214.3
mediastinum 214.2
muscle 214.8
peritoneum 214.3
retroperitoneum 214.3
skin 214.1

Lipoma — *continued*
skin — *continued*
face 214.0
spermatic cord 214.4
spindle cell (M8857/0) — *see* Lipoma, by site
stomach 214.3
subcutaneous tissue 214.1
face 214.0
thymus 214.2
thyroid gland 214.2
Lipomatosis (dolorosa) 272.8
epidural 214.8
fetal (M8881/0) — *see* Lipoma, by site
Launois-Bensaude's 272.8
Lipomyohemangioma (M8860/0)
specified site — *see* Neoplasm, connective tissue, benign
unspecified site 223.0
Lipomyoma (M8860/0)
specified site — *see* Neoplasm, connective tissue, benign
unspecified site 223.0
Lipomyxoma (M8852/0) — *see* Lipoma, by site
Lipomyxosarcoma (M8852/3) — *see* Neoplasm, connective tissue, malignant
Lipophagocytosis 289.89
Lipoproteinemia (alpha) 272.4
broad-beta 272.2
floating-beta 272.2
hyper-pre-beta 272.1
Lipoproteinosis (Rössle-Urbach-Wiethe) 272.8
Liposarcoma (M8850/3) — *see also* Neoplasm, connective tissue, malignant
differentiated type (M8851/3) — *see* Neoplasm, connective tissue, malignant
embryonal (M8852/3) — *see* Neoplasm, connective tissue, malignant
mixed type (M8855/3) — *see* Neoplasm, connective tissue, malignant
myxoid (M8852/3) — *see* Neoplasm, connective tissue, malignant
pleomorphic (M8854/3) — *see* Neoplasm, connective tissue, malignant
round cell (M8853/3) — *see* Neoplasm, connective tissue, malignant
well differentiated type (M8851/3) — *see* Neoplasm, connective tissue, malignant
Liposynovitis prepatellaris 272.8
Lipping
cervix 622.0
spine (*see also* Spondylosis) 721.90
vertebra (*see also* Spondylosis) 721.90
Lip pits (mucus), congenital 750.25
Lipschütz disease or ulcer 616.50
Lipuria 791.1
bilharziasis 120.0
Liquefaction, vitreous humor 379.21
Lisping 307.9
Lissauer's paralysis 094.1
Lissencephalia, lissencephaly 742.2
Listerellose 027.0
Listeriose 027.0
Listeriosis 027.0
congenital 771.2
fetal 771.2
suspected fetal damage affecting management of pregnancy 655.4 ☑
Listlessness 780.79
Lithemia 790.6
Lithiasis — *see also* Calculus
hepatic (duct) — *see* Choledocholithiasis
urinary 592.9
Lithopedion 779.9
affecting management of pregnancy 656.8 ☑
Lithosis (occupational) 502
with tuberculosis — *see* Tuberculosis, pulmonary
Lithuria 791.9
Litigation V62.5
Little
league elbow 718.82
stroke syndrome 435.9
Little's disease — *see* Palsy, cerebral
Littre's
gland — *see* condition

Littre's — *continued*
  hernia — *see* Hernia, Littre's
Littritis — *see also* Urethritis 597.89
Livedo 782.61
  annularis 782.61
  racemose 782.61
  reticularis 782.61
Live flesh 781.0
Liver — *see also* condition
  donor V59.6
Livida, asphyxia
  newborn 768.6
Living
  alone V60.3
    with handicapped person V60.4
Lloyd's syndrome 258.1
Loa loa 125.2
Loasis 125.2
Lobe, lobar — *see* condition
Lobo's disease or blastomycosis 116.2
Lobomycosis 116.2
Lobotomy syndrome 310.0
Lobstein's disease (brittle bones and blue sclera) 756.51
Lobster-claw hand 755.58
Lobulation (congenital) — *see also* Anomaly, specified type NEC, by site
  kidney, fetal 753.3
  liver, abnormal 751.69
  spleen 759.0
Lobule, lobular — *see* condition
Local, localized — *see* condition
Locked bowel or intestine — *see also* Obstruction, intestine 560.9
Locked-in state 344.81
Locked twins 660.5 ☑
  affecting fetus or newborn 763.1
Locking
  joint (*see also* Derangement, joint) 718.90
  knee 717.9
Lockjaw — *see also* Tetanus 037
Locomotor ataxia (progressive) 094.0
Löffler's
  endocarditis 421.0
  eosinophilia or syndrome 518.3
  pneumonia 518.3
  syndrome (eosinophilic pneumonitis) 518.3
Löfgren's syndrome (sarcoidosis) 135
Loiasis 125.2
  eyelid 125.2 [373.6]
Loneliness V62.89
Lone star fever 082.8
Longitudinal stripes or grooves, nails 703.8
  congenital 757.5
Long labor 662.1 ☑
  affecting fetus or newborn 763.89
  first stage 662.0 ☑
  second stage 662.2 ☑
Long-term (current) **drug use** V58.69
  antibiotics V58.62
  anticoagulants V58.61
  anti-inflammatories, non-steroidal (NSAID) V58.64
  antiplatelets/antithrombotics V58.63
  aspirin V58.66
  high-risk medications NEC V58.69
  insulin V58.67
  methadone V58.69
  opiate analgesic V58.69
  pain killers V58.69
    anti-inflammatories, non-steroidal (NSAID) V58.64
    aspirin V58.66
  steroids V58.65
  tamoxifen V07.51 ▲
Loop
  intestine (*see also* Volvulus) 560.2
  intrascleral nerve 379.29
  vascular on papilla (optic) 743.57
Loose — *see also* condition
  body
    in tendon sheath 727.82
    joint 718.10
      ankle 718.17
      elbow 718.12
      foot 718.17

Loose — *see also* condition — *continued*
  body — *continued*
    joint — *continued*
      hand 718.14
      hip 718.15
      knee 717.6
      multiple sites 718.19
      pelvic region 718.15
      prosthetic implant — *see* Complications, mechanical
      shoulder (region) 718.11
      specified site NEC 718.18
      wrist 718.13
    cartilage (joint) (*see also* Loose, body, joint) 718.1 ☑
      knee 717.6
    facet (vertebral) 724.9
    prosthetic implant — *see* Complications, mechanical
    sesamoid, joint (*see also* Loose, body, joint) 718.1 ☑
    tooth, teeth 525.8
Loosening epiphysis 732.9
Looser (-Debray) -Milkman syndrome (osteomalacia with pseudofractures) 268.2
Lop ear (deformity) 744.29
Lorain's disease or syndrome (pituitary dwarfism) 253.3
Lorain-Levi syndrome (pituitary dwarfism) 253.3
Lordosis (acquired) (postural) 737.20
  congenital 754.2
  due to or associated with
    Charcôt-Marie-Tooth disease 356.1 [737.42]
    mucopolysaccharidosis 277.5 [737.42]
    neurofibromatosis 237.71 [737.42]
    osteitis
      deformans 731.0 [737.42]
      fibrosa cystica 252.01 [737.42]
    osteoporosis (*see also* Osteoporosis) 733.00 [737.42]
    poliomyelitis (*see also* Poliomyelitis) 138 [737.42]
    tuberculosis (*see also* Tuberculosis) 015.0 ☑ [737.42]
  late effect of rickets 268.1 [737.42]
  postlaminectomy 737.21
  postsurgical NEC 737.22
  rachitic 268.1 [737.42]
  specified NEC 737.29
  tuberculous (*see also* Tuberculosis) 015.0 ☑ [737.42]
Loss
  appetite 783.0
    hysterical 300.11
    nonorganic origin 307.59
    psychogenic 307.59
  blood — *see* Hemorrhage
  central vision 368.41
  consciousness 780.09
    transient 780.2
  control, sphincter, rectum 787.6
    nonorganic origin 307.7
  ear ossicle, partial 385.24
  elasticity, skin 782.8
  extremity or member, traumatic, current — *see* Amputation, traumatic
  fluid (acute) 276.50
    with
      hypernatremia 276.0
      hyponatremia 276.1
    fetus or newborn 775.5
  hair 704.00
  hearing (*see also* Deafness)
    central 389.14
    conductive (air) 389.00
      with sensorineural hearing loss 389.20
        bilateral 389.22
        unilateral 389.21
      bilateral 389.06
      combined types 389.08
      external ear 389.01
      inner ear 389.04
      middle ear 389.03
      multiple types 389.08
      tympanic membrane 389.02
      unilateral 389.05

Loss — *continued*
  hearing (*see also* Deafness) — *continued*
    mixed conductive and sensorineural 389.20
      bilateral 389.22
      unilateral 389.21
    mixed type 389.20
      bilateral 389.22
      unilateral 389.21
    nerve
      bilateral 389.12
      unilateral 389.13
    neural
      bilateral 389.12
      unilateral 389.13
    noise-induced 388.12
    perceptive NEC (*see also* Loss, hearing, sensorineural) 389.10
    sensorineural 389.10
      with conductive hearing loss 389.20
        bilateral 389.22
        unilateral 389.21
      asymmetrical 389.16
        bilateral 389.18
      central 389.14
      neural 389.12
        bilateral 389.12
        unilateral 389.13
      sensory
        bilateral 389.11
        unilateral 389.17
      unilateral 389.15
    sensory
      bilateral 389.11
      unilateral 389.17
    specified type NEC 389.8
    sudden NEC 388.2
  height 781.91
  labyrinthine reactivity (unilateral) 386.55
    bilateral 386.56
  memory (*see also* Amnesia) 780.93
    mild, following organic brain damage 310.8 ▲
  mind (*see also* Psychosis) 298.9
  occlusal vertical dimension 524.37
  organ or part — *see* Absence, by site, acquired
  sensation 782.0
  sense of
    smell (*see also* Disturbance, sensation) 781.1
    taste (*see also* Disturbance, sensation) 781.1
    touch (*see also* Disturbance, sensation) 781.1
  sight (acquired) (complete) (congenital) — *see* Blindness
  spinal fluid
    headache 349.0
  substance of
    bone (*see also* Osteoporosis) 733.00
    cartilage 733.99
      ear 380.32
    vitreous (humor) 379.26
  tooth, teeth
    acquired 525.10
    due to
      caries 525.13
      extraction 525.10
      periodontal disease 525.12
      specified NEC 525.19
      trauma 525.11
  vision, visual (*see also* Blindness) 369.9
    both eyes (*see also* Blindness, both eyes) 369.3
    complete (*see also* Blindness, both eyes) 369.00
    one eye 369.8
    sudden 368.11
    transient 368.12
  vitreous 379.26
  voice (*see also* Aphonia) 784.41
  weight (cause unknown) 783.21
Lou Gehrig's disease 335.20
Louis-Bar syndrome (ataxia-telangiectasia) 334.8
Louping ill 063.1
Lousiness — *see* Lice

Low
  back syndrome 724.2
  basal metabolic rate (BMR) 794.7
  birthweight 765.1 ☑
    extreme (less than 1000 grams) 765.0 ☑
    for gestational age 764.0 ☑
    status (*see also* Status, low birth weight) V21.30
  bladder compliance 596.52
  blood pressure (*see also* Hypotension) 458.9
    reading (incidental) (isolated) (nonspecific) 796.3
  cardiac reserve — *see* Disease, heart
  compliance bladder 596.52
  frequency deafness — *see* Disorder, hearing
  function (*see also* Hypofunction)
    kidney (*see also* Disease, renal) 593.9
    liver 573.9
  hemoglobin 285.9
  implantation, placenta — *see* Placenta, previa
  insertion, placenta — *see* Placenta, previa
  lying
    kidney 593.0
    organ or site, congenital — *see* Malposition, congenital
    placenta — *see* Placenta, previa
  output syndrome (cardiac) (*see also* Failure, heart) 428.9
  platelets (blood) (*see also* Thrombocytopenia) 287.5
  reserve, kidney (*see also* Disease, renal) 593.9
  risk
    human papillomavirus (HPA) DNA test positive
      anal 796.79
      cervical 795.09
      vaginal 795.19
  salt syndrome 593.9
  tension glaucoma 365.12
  vision 369.9
    both eyes 369.20
    one eye 369.70
Lower extremity — *see* condition
Lowe (-Terrey-MacLachlan) syndrome (oculocerebrorenal dystrophy) 270.8
Lown (-Ganong) -Levine syndrome (short P-R interval, normal QRS complex, and paroxysmal supraventricular tachycardia) 426.81
LSD reaction — *see also* Abuse, drugs, nondependent 305.3 ☑
L-shaped kidney 753.3
Lucas-Championnière disease (fibrinous bronchitis) 466.0
Lucey-Driscoll syndrome (jaundice due to delayed conjugation) 774.30
Ludwig's
  angina 528.3
  disease (submaxillary cellulitis) 528.3
Lues (venerea), **luetic** — *see* Syphilis
Luetscher's syndrome (dehydration) 276.51
Lumbago 724.2
  due to displacement, intervertebral disc 722.10
Lumbalgia 724.2
  due to displacement, intervertebral disc 722.10
Lumbar — *see* condition
Lumbarization, vertebra 756.15
Lumbermen's itch 133.8
Lump — *see also* Mass
  abdominal 789.3 ☑
  breast 611.72
  chest 786.6
  epigastric 789.3 ☑
  head 784.2
  kidney 753.3
  liver 789.1
  lung 786.6
  mediastinal 786.6
  neck 784.2
  nose or sinus 784.2
  pelvic 789.3 ☑
  skin 782.2
  substernal 786.6
  throat 784.2
  umbilicus 789.3 ☑
Lunacy — *see also* Psychosis 298.9
Lunatomalacia 732.3

☑ Additional Digit Required — Refer to the Tabular List for Digit Selection   ▽ Subterms under main terms may continue to next column or page

2010 ICD-9-CM   ▶◀ Revised Text   ● New Line   ▲ Revised Code   October 2009 • Volume 2 — 171

Index

Lung — Lymphoma

Lung — see also condition
- donor V59.8
- drug addict's 417.8
- mainliners' 417.8
- vanishing 492.0

Lupoid (miliary) **of Boeck** 135

Lupus 710.0
- anticoagulant 289.81
- Cazenave's (erythematosus) 695.4
- discoid (local) 695.4
- disseminated 710.0
- erythematodes (discoid) (local) 695.4
- erythematosus (discoid) (local) 695.4
  - disseminated 710.0
  - eyelid 373.34
  - systemic 710.0
    - with
      - encephalitis 710.0 [323.81]
      - lung involvement 710.0 [517.8]
    - inhibitor (presence of) 286.5
- exedens 017.0 ☑
- eyelid (see also Tuberculosis) 017.0 ☑ [373.4]
- Hilliard's 017.0 ☑
- hydralazine
  - correct substance properly administered 695.4
  - overdose or wrong substance given or taken 972.6
- miliaris disseminatus faciei 017.0 ☑
- nephritis 710.0 [583.81]
  - acute 710.0 [580.81]
  - chronic 710.0 [582.81]
- nontuberculous, not disseminated 695.4
- pernio (Besnier) 135
- tuberculous (see also Tuberculosis) 017.0 ☑
  - eyelid (see also Tuberculosis) 017.0 ☑ [373.4]
- vulgaris 017.0 ☑

Luschka's joint disease 721.90

Luteinoma (M8610/0) 220

Lutembacher's disease or syndrome (atrial septal defect with mitral stenosis) 745.5

Luteoma (M8610/0) 220

Lutz-Miescher disease (elastosis perforans serpiginosa) 701.1

Lutz-Splendore-de Almeida disease (Brazilian blastomycosis) 116.1

Luxatio
- bulbi due to birth injury 767.8
- coxae congenita (see also Dislocation, hip, congenital) 754.30
- erecta — see Dislocation, shoulder
- imperfecta — see Sprain, by site
- perinealis — see Dislocation, hip

Luxation — see also Dislocation, by site
- eyeball 360.81
  - due to birth injury 767.8
  - lateral 376.36
- genital organs (external) NEC — see Wound, open, genital organs
- globe (eye) 360.81
  - lateral 376.36
- lacrimal gland (postinfectional) 375.16
- lens (old) (partial) 379.32
  - congenital 743.37
    - syphilitic 090.49 [379.32]
  - Marfan's disease 090.49
  - spontaneous 379.32
- penis — see Wound, open, penis
- scrotum — see Wound, open, scrotum
- testis — see Wound, open, testis

L-xyloketosuria 271.8

Lycanthropy — see also Psychosis 298.9

Lyell's disease or syndrome (toxic epidermal necrolysis) 695.15
- due to drug
  - correct substance properly administered 695.15
  - overdose or wrong substance given or taken 977.9
    - specified drug — see Table of Drugs and Chemicals

Lyme disease 088.81

Lymph
- gland or node — see condition
- scrotum (see also Infestation, filarial) 125.9

Lymphadenitis 289.3
- with
  - abortion — see Abortion, by type, with sepsis
  - ectopic pregnancy (see also categories 633.0–633.9) 639.0
  - molar pregnancy (see also categories 630–632) 639.0
- acute 683
  - mesenteric 289.2
- any site, except mesenteric 289.3
  - acute 683
  - chronic 289.1
  - mesenteric (acute) (chronic) (nonspecific) (subacute) 289.2
  - subacute 289.1
    - mesenteric 289.2
- breast, puerperal, postpartum 675.2 ☑
- chancroidal (congenital) 099.0
- chronic 289.1
  - mesenteric 289.2
- dermatopathic 695.89
- due to
  - anthracosis (occupational) 500
  - Brugia (Wuchereria) malayi 125.1
  - diphtheria (toxin) 032.89
  - lymphogranuloma venereum 099.1
  - Wuchereria bancrofti 125.0
- following
  - abortion 639.0
  - ectopic or molar pregnancy 639.0
- generalized 289.3
- gonorrheal 098.89
- granulomatous 289.1
- infectional 683
- mesenteric (acute) (chronic) (nonspecific) (subacute) 289.2
  - due to Bacillus typhi 002.0
  - tuberculous (see also Tuberculosis) 014.8 ☑
- mycobacterial 031.8
- purulent 683
- pyogenic 683
- regional 078.3
- septic 683
- streptococcal 683
- subacute, unspecified site 289.1
- suppurative 683
- syphilitic (early) (secondary) 091.4
  - late 095.8
- tuberculous — see Tuberculosis, lymph gland
- venereal 099.1

Lymphadenoid goiter 245.2

Lymphadenopathy (general) 785.6
- due to toxoplasmosis (acquired) 130.7
  - congenital (active) 771.2

Lymphadenopathy-associated virus (disease) (illness) (infection) — see Human immunodeficiency virus (disease) (illness) (infection)

Lymphadenosis 785.6
- acute 075

Lymphangiectasis 457.1
- conjunctiva 372.89
- postinfectional 457.1
- scrotum 457.1

Lymphangiectatic elephantiasis, nonfilarial 457.1

Lymphangioendothelioma (M9170/0) 228.1
- malignant (M9170/3) — see Neoplasm, connective tissue, malignant

Lymphangioma (M9170/0) 228.1
- capillary (M9171/0) 228.1
- cavernous (M9172/0) 228.1
- cystic (M9173/0) 228.1
- malignant (M9170/3) — see Neoplasm, connective tissue, malignant

Lymphangiomyoma (M9174/0) 228.1

Lymphangiomyomatosis (M9174/1) — see Neoplasm, connective tissue, uncertain behavior

Lymphangiosarcoma (M9170/3) — see Neoplasm, connective tissue, malignant

Lymphangitis 457.2

Lymphangitis — continued
- with
  - abortion — see Abortion, by type, with sepsis
  - abscess — see Abscess, by site
  - cellulitis — see Abscess, by site
  - ectopic pregnancy (see also categories 633.0–633.9) 639.0
  - molar pregnancy (see also categories 630–632) 639.0
- acute (with abscess or cellulitis) 682.9
  - specified site — see Abscess, by site
- breast, puerperal, postpartum 675.2 ☑
- chancroidal 099.0
- chronic (any site) 457.2
- due to
  - Brugia (Wuchereria) malayi 125.1
  - Wuchereria bancrofti 125.0
- following
  - abortion 639.0
  - ectopic or molar pregnancy 639.0
- gangrenous 457.2
- penis
  - acute 607.2
  - gonococcal (acute) 098.0
    - chronic or duration of 2 months or more 098.2
- puerperal, postpartum, childbirth 670.8 ▲
- strumous, tuberculous (see also Tuberculosis) 017.2 ☑
- subacute (any site) 457.2
- tuberculous — see Tuberculosis, lymph gland

Lymphatic (vessel) — see condition

Lymphatism 254.8
- scrofulous (see also Tuberculosis) 017.2 ☑

Lymphectasia 457.1

Lymphedema — see also Elephantiasis 457.1
- acquired (chronic) 457.1
- chronic hereditary 757.0
- congenital 757.0
- idiopathic hereditary 757.0
- praecox 457.1
- secondary 457.1
- surgical NEC 997.99
  - postmastectomy (syndrome) 457.0

Lymph-hemangioma (M9120/0) — see Hemangioma, by site

Lymphoblastic — see condition

Lymphoblastoma (diffuse) (M9630/3) 200.1 ☑
- giant follicular (M9690/3) 202.0 ☑
- macrofollicular (M9690/3) 202.0 ☑

Lymphoblastosis, acute benign 075

Lymphocele 457.8

Lymphocythemia 288.51

Lymphocytic — see also condition
- chorioencephalitis (acute) (serous) 049.0
- choriomeningitis (acute) (serous) 049.0

Lymphocytoma (diffuse) (malignant) (M9620/3) 200.1 ☑

Lymphocytomatosis (M9620/3) 200.1 ☑

Lymphocytopenia 288.51

Lymphocytosis (symptomatic) 288.61
- infectious (acute) 078.89

Lymphoepithelioma (M8082/3) — see Neoplasm, by site, malignant

Lymphogranuloma (malignant) (M9650/3) 201.9 ☑
- inguinale 099.1
- venereal (any site) 099.1
  - with stricture of rectum 099.1
- venereum 099.1

Lymphogranulomatosis (malignant) (M9650/3) 201.9 ☑
- benign (Boeck's sarcoid) (Schaumann's) 135
- Hodgkin's (M9650/3) 201.9 ☑

Lymphohistiocytosis, familial hemophagocytic 288.4

Lymphoid — see condition

Lympholeukoblastoma (M9850/3) 207.8 ☑

Lympholeukosarcoma (M9850/3) 207.8 ☑

Lymphoma (malignant) (M9590/3) 202.8 ☑

> Note — Use the following fifth-digit subclassification with categories 200–202:
>
> 0   unspecified site, extranodal and solid organ sites
>
> 1   lymph nodes of head, face, and neck
>
> 2   intrathoracic lymph nodes
>
> 3   intra–abdominal lymph nodes
>
> 4   lymph nodes of axilla and upper limb
>
> 5   lymph nodes of inguinal region and lower limb
>
> 6   intrapelvic lymph nodes
>
> 7   spleen
>
> 8   lymph nodes of multiple sites

- benign (M9590/0) — see Neoplasm, by site, benign
- Burkitt's type (lymphoblastic) (undifferentiated) (M9750/3) 200.2 ☑
- Castleman's (mediastinal lymph node hyperplasia) 785.6
- centroblastic-centrocytic
  - diffuse (M9614/3) 202.8 ☑
  - follicular (M9692/3) 202.0 ☑
- centroblastic type (diffuse) (M9632/3) 202.8 ☑
  - follicular (M9697/3) 202.0 ☑
- centrocytic (M9622/3) 202.8 ☑
- compound (M9613/3) 200.8 ☑
- convoluted cell type (lymphoblastic) (M9602/3) 202.8 ☑
- diffuse NEC (M9590/3) 202.8 ☑
  - large B cell 202.8 ☑
- follicular (giant) (M9690/3) 202.0 ☑
  - center cell (diffuse) (M9615/3) 202.8 ☑
    - cleaved (diffuse) (M9623/3) 202.8 ☑
      - follicular (M9695/3) 202.0 ☑
    - non-cleaved (diffuse) (M9633/3) 202.8 ☑
      - follicular (M9698/3) 202.0 ☑
  - centroblastic-centrocytic (M9692/3) 202.0 ☑
  - centroblastic type (M9697/3) 202.0 ☑
  - large cell 202.0 ☑ ●
  - lymphocytic
    - intermediate differentiation (M9694/3) 202.0 ☑
    - poorly differentiated (M9696/3) 202.0 ☑
  - mixed (cell type) (lymphocytic-histiocytic) (small cell and large cell) (M9691/3) 202.0 ☑
- germinocytic (M9622/3) 202.8 ☑
- giant, follicular or follicle (M9690/3) 202.0 ☑
- histiocytic (M9640/3) 200.0 ☑
  - nodular (M9642/3) 200.0 ☑
  - pleomorphic cell type (M9641/3) 200.0 ☑
- Hodgkin's (M9650/3) (see also Disease, Hodgkin's) 201.9 ☑
- immunoblastic (type) (M9612/3) 200.8 ☑
- large cell (M9640/3) 200.7 ☑
  - anaplastic 200.6 ☑
  - nodular (M9642/3) 202.0 ☑ ▲
  - pleomorphic cell type (M9641/3) 200.0 ☑
- lymphoblastic (diffuse) (M9630/3) 200.1 ☑
  - Burkitt's type (M9750/3) 200.2 ☑
  - convoluted cell type (M9602/3) 202.8 ☑
- lymphocytic (cell type) (diffuse) (M9620/3) 200.1 ☑
  - with plasmacytoid differentiation, diffuse (M9611/3) 200.8 ☑
  - intermediate differentiation (diffuse) (M9621/3) 200.1 ☑
    - follicular (M9694/3) 202.0 ☑
    - nodular (M9694/3) 202.0 ☑
  - nodular (M9690/3) 202.0 ☑
  - poorly differentiated (diffuse) (M9630/3) 200.1 ☑
    - follicular (M9696/3) 202.0 ☑
    - nodular (M9696/3) 202.0 ☑

☑ Additional Digit Required — Refer to the Tabular List for Digit Selection   🐦 Subterms under main terms may continue to next column or page

172 — Volume 2 • October 2009   ▶◀ Revised Text   ● New Line   ▲ Revised Code   **2010 ICD-9-CM**

Index to Diseases
Male type pelvis
Index
Lymphoma — Male type pelvis

Lymphoma — *continued*
  lymphocytic — *continued*
    well differentiated (diffuse) (M9620/3) 200.1 ☑
      follicular (M9693/3) 202.0 ☑
      nodular (M9693/3) 202.0 ☑
    lymphocytic-histiocytic, mixed (diffuse) (M9613/3) 200.8 ☑
      follicular (M9691/3) 202.0 ☑
      nodular (M9691/3) 202.0 ☑
    lymphoplasmacytoid type (M9611/3) 200.8 ☑
    lymphosarcoma type (M9610/3) 200.1 ☑
    macrofollicular (M9690/3) 202.0 ☑
    mantle cell 200.4 ☑
    marginal zone 200.3 ☑
      extranodal B-cell 200.3 ☑
      nodal B-cell 200.3 ☑
      splenic B-cell 200.3 ☑
    mixed cell type (diffuse) (M9613/3) 200.8 ☑
      follicular (M9691/3) 202.0 ☑
      nodular (M9691/3) 202.0 ☑
    nodular (M9690/3) 202.0 ☑
      histiocytic (M9642/3) 200.0 ☑
      lymphocytic (M9690/3) 202.0 ☑
        intermediate differentiation (M9694/3) 202.0 ☑
        poorly differentiated (M9696/3) 202.0 ☑
      mixed (cell type) (lymphocytic-histiocytic) (small cell and large cell) (M9691/3) 202.0 ☑
    non-Hodgkin's type NEC (M9591/3) 202.8 ☑
    peripheral T-cell 202.7 ☑
    primary central nervous system 200.5 ☑
    reticulum cell (type) (M9640/3) 200.0 ☑
    small cell and large cell, mixed (diffuse) (M9613/3) 200.8 ☑
      follicular (M9691/3) 202.0 ☑
      nodular (9691/3) 202.0 ☑
    stem cell (type) (M9601/3) 202.8 ☑
    T-cell 202.1 ☑
      peripheral 202.7 ☑
    undifferentiated (cell type) (non-Burkitt's) (M9600/3) 202.8 ☑
      Burkitt's type (M9750/3) 200.2 ☑
Lymphomatosis (M9590/3) — *see also* Lymphoma
  granulomatous 099.1
Lymphopathia
  venereum 099.1
  veneris 099.1
Lymphopenia 288.51
  familial 279.2
Lymphoreticulosis, benign (of inoculation) 078.3
Lymphorrhea 457.8
Lymphosarcoma (M9610/3) 200.1 ☑
  diffuse (M9610/3) 200.1 ☑
    with plasmacytoid differentiation (M9611/3) 200.8 ☑
    lymphoplasmacytic (M9611/3) 200.8 ☑
  follicular (giant) (M9690/3) 202.0 ☑
    lymphoblastic (M9696/3) 202.0 ☑
    lymphocytic, intermediate differentiation (M9694/3) 202.0 ☑
    mixed cell type (M9691/3) 202.0 ☑
  giant follicular (M9690/3) 202.0 ☑
  Hodgkin's (M9650/3) 201.9 ☑
  immunoblastic (M9612/3) 200.8 ☑
  lymphoblastic (diffuse) (M9630/3) 200.1 ☑
    follicular (M9696/3) 202.0 ☑
    nodular (M9696/3) 202.0 ☑
  lymphocytic (diffuse) (M9620/3) 200.1 ☑
    intermediate differentiation (diffuse) (M9621/3) 200.1 ☑
    follicular (M9694/3) 202.0 ☑
    nodular (M9694/3) 202.0 ☑
  mixed cell type (diffuse) (M9613/3) 200.8 ☑
    follicular (M9691/3) 202.0 ☑
    nodular (M9691/3) 202.0 ☑
  nodular (M9690/3) 202.0 ☑
    lymphoblastic (M9696/3) 202.0 ☑
    lymphocytic, intermediate differentiation (M9694/3) 202.0 ☑

Lymphosarcoma — *continued*
  nodular — *continued*
    mixed cell type (M9691/3) 202.0 ☑
    prolymphocytic (M9631/3) 200.1 ☑
    reticulum cell (M9640/3) 200.0 ☑
Lymphostasis 457.8
Lypemania — *see also* Melancholia 296.2 ☑
Lyssa 071

M

Macacus ear 744.29
Maceration
  fetus (cause not stated) 779.9
  wet feet, tropical (syndrome) 991.4
Machado-Joseph disease 334.8
Machupo virus hemorrhagic fever 078.7
Macleod's syndrome (abnormal transradiancy, one lung) 492.8
Macrocephalia, macrocephaly 756.0
Macrocheilia (congenital) 744.81
Macrochilia (congenital) 744.81
Macrocolon (congenital) 751.3
Macrocornea 743.41
  associated with buphthalmos 743.22
Macrocytic — *see* condition
Macrocytosis 289.89
Macrodactylia, macrodactylism (fingers) (thumbs) 755.57
  toes 755.65
Macrodontia 520.2
Macroencephaly 742.4
Macrogenia 524.05
Macrogenitosomia (female) (male) (praecox) 255.2
Macrogingivae 523.8
Macroglobulinemia (essential) (idiopathic) (monoclonal) (primary) (syndrome) (Waldenström's) 273.3
  acquired 529.8
Macroglossia (congenital) 750.15
Macrognathia, macrognathism (congenital) 524.00
  mandibular 524.02
    alveolar 524.72
  maxillary 524.01
    alveolar 524.71
Macrogyria (congenital) 742.4
Macrohydrocephalus — *see also* Hydrocephalus 331.4
Macromastia — *see also* Hypertrophy, breast 611.1
Macrophage activation syndrome 288.4
Macropsia 368.14
Macrosigmoid 564.7
  congenital 751.3
Macrospondylitis, acromegalic 253.0
Macrostomia (congenital) 744.83
Macrotia (external ear) (congenital) 744.22
Macula
  cornea, corneal
    congenital 743.43
      interfering with vision 743.42
    interfering with central vision 371.03
    not interfering with central vision 371.02
  degeneration (*see also* Degeneration, macula) 362.50
    hereditary (*see also* Dystrophy, retina) 362.70
  edema, cystoid 362.53
Maculae ceruleae 132.1
Macules and papules 709.8
Maculopathy, toxic 362.55
Madarosis 374.55
Madelung's
  deformity (radius) 755.54
  disease (lipomatosis) 272.8
  lipomatosis 272.8
Madness — *see also* Psychosis 298.9
  myxedema (acute) 293.0
    subacute 293.1
Madura
  disease (actinomycotic) 039.9
    mycotic 117.4
  foot (actinomycotic) 039.4
    mycotic 117.4
Maduromycosis (actinomycotic) 039.9

Maduromycosis — *continued*
  mycotic 117.4
Maffucci's syndrome (dyschondroplasia with hemangiomas) 756.4
Magenblase syndrome 306.4
Main en griffe (acquired) 736.06
  congenital 755.59
Maintenance
  chemotherapy regimen or treatment V58.11
  dialysis regimen or treatment
    extracorporeal (renal) V56.0
    peritoneal V56.8
    renal V56.0
  drug therapy or regimen
    chemotherapy, antineoplastic V58.11
    immunotherapy, antineoplastic V58.12
  external fixation NEC V54.89
  radiotherapy V58.0
  traction NEC V54.89
Majocchi's
  disease (purpura annularis telangiectodes) 709.1
  granuloma 110.6
Major — *see* condition
Mal
  cerebral (idiopathic) (*see also* Epilepsy) 345.9 ☑
  comital (*see also* Epilepsy) 345.9 ☑
  de los pintos (*see also* Pinta) 103.9
  de Meleda 757.39
  de mer 994.6
  lie — *see* Presentation, fetal
  perforant (*see also* Ulcer, lower extremity) 707.15
Malabar itch 110.9
  beard 110.0
  foot 110.4
  scalp 110.0
Malabsorption 579.9
  calcium 579.8
  carbohydrate 579.8
  disaccharide 271.3
  drug-induced 579.8
  due to bacterial overgrowth 579.8
  fat 579.8
  folate, congenital 281.2
  galactose 271.1
  glucose-galactose (congenital) 271.3
  intestinal 579.9
  isomaltose 271.3
  lactose (hereditary) 271.3
  methionine 270.4
  monosaccharide 271.8
  postgastrectomy 579.3
  postsurgical 579.3
  protein 579.8
  sucrose (-isomaltose) (congenital) 271.3
  syndrome 579.9
    postgastrectomy 579.3
    postsurgical 579.3
Malacia, bone 268.2
  juvenile (*see also* Rickets) 268.0
  Kienböck's (juvenile) (lunate) (wrist) 732.3
    adult 732.8
Malacoplakia
  bladder 596.8
  colon 569.89
  pelvis (kidney) 593.89
  ureter 593.89
  urethra 599.84
Malacosteon 268.2
  juvenile (*see also* Rickets) 268.0
Maladaptation — *see* Maladjustment
Maladie de Roger 745.4
Maladjustment
  conjugal V61.10
    involving
      divorce V61.03
      estrangement V61.09
  educational V62.3
  family V61.9
    specified circumstance NEC V61.8
  marital V61.10
    involving
      divorce V61.03
      estrangement V61.09

Maladjustment — *continued*
  occupational V62.29
    current military deployment status V62.21
  simple, adult (*see also* Reaction, adjustment) 309.9
  situational acute (*see also* Reaction, adjustment) 309.9
  social V62.4
Malaise 780.79
Malakoplakia — *see* Malacoplakia
Malaria, malarial (fever) 084.6
  algid 084.9
  any type, with
    algid malaria 084.9
    blackwater fever 084.8
    fever
      blackwater 084.8
      hemoglobinuric (bilious) 084.8
    hemoglobinuria, malarial 084.8
    hepatitis 084.9 *[573.2]*
    nephrosis 084.9 *[581.81]*
    pernicious complication NEC 084.9
      cardiac 084.9
      cerebral 084.9
  cardiac 084.9
  carrier (suspected) of V02.9
  cerebral 084.9
  complicating pregnancy, childbirth, or puerperium 647.4 ☑
  congenital 771.2
  congestion, congestive 084.6
    brain 084.9
  continued 084.0
  estivo-autumnal 084.0
  falciparum (malignant tertian) 084.0
  hematinuria 084.8
  hematuria 084.8
  hemoglobinuria 084.8
  hemorrhagic 084.6
  induced (therapeutically) 084.7
    accidental — *see* Malaria, by type
  liver 084.9 *[573.2]*
  malariae (quartan) 084.2
  malignant (tertian) 084.0
  mixed infections 084.5
  monkey 084.4
  ovale 084.3
  pernicious, acute 084.0
  Plasmodium, P.
    falciparum 084.0
    malariae 084.2
    ovale 084.3
    vivax 084.1
  quartan 084.2
  quotidian 084.0
  recurrent 084.6
    induced (therapeutically) 084.7
      accidental — *see* Malaria, by type
  remittent 084.6
  specified types NEC 084.4
  spleen 084.6
  subtertian 084.0
  tertian (benign) 084.1
    malignant 084.0
  tropical 084.0
  typhoid 084.6
  vivax (benign tertian) 084.1
Malassez's disease (testicular cyst) 608.89
Malassimilation 579.9
Maldescent, testis 752.51
Maldevelopment — *see also* Anomaly, by site
  brain 742.9
  colon 751.5
  hip (joint) 755.63
    congenital dislocation (*see also* Dislocation, hip, congenital) 754.30
  mastoid process 756.0
  middle ear, except ossicles 744.03
    ossicles 744.04
  newborn (not malformation) 764.9 ☑
  ossicles, ear 744.04
  spine 756.10
  toe 755.66
Male type pelvis 755.69
  with disproportion (fetopelvic) 653.2 ☑
    affecting fetus or newborn 763.1

☑ Additional Digit Required — Refer to the Tabular List for Digit Selection
☷ Subterms under main terms may continue to next column or page
2010 ICD-9-CM
►◄ Revised Text
● New Line
▲ Revised Code
Volume 2 — 173

Index

Male type pelvis — Maltreatment

Male type pelvis — *continued*
with disproportion — *continued*
causing obstructed labor 660.1 ☑
affecting fetus or newborn 763.1
Malformation (congenital) — *see also* Anomaly
bone 756.9
bursa 756.9
Chiari
type I 348.4
type II (*see also* Spina bifida) 741.0 ☑
type III 742.0
type IV 742.2
circulatory system NEC 747.9
specified type NEC 747.89
cochlea 744.05
digestive system NEC 751.9
lower 751.5
specified type NEC 751.8
upper 750.9
eye 743.9
gum 750.9
heart NEC 746.9
specified type NEC 746.89
valve 746.9
internal ear 744.05
joint NEC 755.9
specified type NEC 755.8
Mondini's (congenital) (malformation, cochlea) 744.05
muscle 756.9
nervous system (central) 742.9
pelvic organs or tissues
in pregnancy or childbirth 654.9 ☑
affecting fetus or newborn 763.89
causing obstructed labor 660.2 ☑
affecting fetus or newborn 763.1
placenta (*see also* Placenta, abnormal) 656.7 ☑
respiratory organs 748.9
specified type NEC 748.8
Rieger's 743.44
sense organs NEC 742.9
specified type NEC 742.8
skin 757.9
specified type NEC 757.8
spinal cord 742.9
teeth, tooth NEC 520.9
tendon 756.9
throat 750.9
umbilical cord (complicating delivery) 663.9 ☑
affecting fetus or newborn 762.6
umbilicus 759.9
urinary system NEC 753.9
specified type NEC 753.8
venous — *see* Anomaly, vein
Malfunction — *see also* Dysfunction
arterial graft 996.1
cardiac pacemaker 996.01
catheter device — *see* Complications, mechanical, catheter
colostomy 569.62
valve 569.62
cystostomy 997.5
device, implant, or graft NEC — *see* Complications, mechanical
enteric stoma 569.62
enterostomy 569.62
esophagostomy 530.87
gastroenteric 536.8
gastrostomy 536.42
ileostomy
valve 569.62
nephrostomy 997.5
pacemaker — *see* Complications, mechanical, pacemaker
prosthetic device, internal — *see* Complications, mechanical
tracheostomy 519.02
valve
colostomy 569.62
ileostomy 569.62
vascular graft or shunt 996.1
Malgaigne's fracture (closed) 808.43
open 808.53

Malherbe's
calcifying epithelioma (M8110/0) — *see* Neoplasm, skin, benign
tumor (M8110/0) — *see* Neoplasm, skin, benign
Malibu disease 919.8
infected 919.9
Malignancy (M8000/3) — *see* Neoplasm, by site, malignant
Malignant — *see* condition
Malingerer, malingering V65.2
Mallet, finger (acquired) 736.1
congenital 755.59
late effect of rickets 268.1
Malleus 024
Mallory's bodies 034.1
Mallory-Weiss syndrome 530.7
Malnutrition (calorie) 263.9
complicating pregnancy 648.9 ☑
degree
first 263.1
second 263.0
third 262
mild 263.1
moderate 263.0
severe 261
protein-calorie 262
fetus 764.2 ☑
"light-for-dates" 764.1 ☑
following gastrointestinal surgery 579.3
intrauterine or fetal 764.2 ☑
fetus or infant "light-for-dates" 764.1 ☑
lack of care, or neglect (child) (infant) 995.52
adult 995.84
malignant 260
mild 263.1
moderate 263.0
protein 260
protein-calorie 263.9
severe 262
specified type NEC 263.8
severe 261
protein-calorie NEC 262
Malocclusion (teeth) 524.4
angle's class I 524.21
angle's class II 524.22
angle's class III 524.23
due to
abnormal swallowing 524.59
accessory teeth (causing crowding) 524.31
dentofacial abnormality NEC 524.89
impacted teeth (causing crowding) 520.6
missing teeth 524.30
mouth breathing 524.59
sleep postures 524.59
supernumerary teeth (causing crowding) 524.31
thumb sucking 524.59
tongue, lip, or finger habits 524.59
temporomandibular (joint) 524.69
Malposition
cardiac apex (congenital) 746.87
cervix — *see* Malposition, uterus
congenital
adrenal (gland) 759.1
alimentary tract 751.8
lower 751.5
upper 750.8
aorta 747.21
appendix 751.5
arterial trunk 747.29
artery (peripheral) NEC (*see also* Malposition, congenital, peripheral vascular system) 747.60
coronary 746.85
pulmonary 747.3
auditory canal 744.29
causing impairment of hearing 744.02
auricle (ear) 744.29
causing impairment of hearing 744.02
cervical 744.43
biliary duct or passage 751.69
bladder (mucosa) 753.8
exteriorized or extroverted 753.5
brachial plexus 742.8
brain tissue 742.4

Malposition — *continued*
congenital — *continued*
breast 757.6
bronchus 748.3
cardiac apex 746.87
cecum 751.5
clavicle 755.51
colon 751.5
digestive organ or tract NEC 751.8
lower 751.5
upper 750.8
ear (auricle) (external) 744.29
ossicles 744.04
endocrine (gland) NEC 759.2
epiglottis 748.3
Eustachian tube 744.24
eye 743.8
facial features 744.89
fallopian tube 752.19
finger(s) 755.59
supernumerary 755.01
foot 755.67
gallbladder 751.69
gastrointestinal tract 751.8
genitalia, genital organ(s) or tract
female 752.89
external 752.49
internal NEC 752.89
male 752.89
penis 752.69
scrotal transposition 752.81
glottis 748.3
hand 755.59
heart 746.87
dextrocardia 746.87
with complete transposition of viscera 759.3
hepatic duct 751.69
hip (joint) (*see also* Dislocation, hip, congenital) 754.30
intestine (large) (small) 751.5
with anomalous adhesions, fixation, or malrotation 751.4
joint NEC 755.8
kidney 753.3
larynx 748.3
limb 755.8
lower 755.69
upper 755.59
liver 751.69
lung (lobe) 748.69
nail(s) 757.5
nerve 742.8
nervous system NEC 742.8
nose, nasal (septum) 748.1
organ or site NEC — *see* Anomaly, specified type NEC, by site
ovary 752.0
pancreas 751.7
parathyroid (gland) 759.2
patella 755.64
peripheral vascular system 747.60
gastrointestinal 747.61
lower limb 747.64
renal 747.62
specified NEC 747.69
spinal 747.82
upper limb 747.63
pituitary (gland) 759.2
respiratory organ or system NEC 748.9
rib (cage) 756.3
supernumerary in cervical region 756.2
scapula 755.59
shoulder 755.59
spinal cord 742.59
spine 756.19
spleen 759.0
sternum 756.3
stomach 750.7
symphysis pubis 755.69
testis (undescended) 752.51
thymus (gland) 759.2
thyroid (gland) (tissue) 759.2
cartilage 748.3
toe(s) 755.66
supernumerary 755.02

Malposition — *continued*
congenital — *continued*
tongue 750.19
trachea 748.3
uterus 752.3
vein(s) (peripheral) NEC (*see also* Malposition, congenital, peripheral vascular system) 747.60
great 747.49
portal 747.49
pulmonary 747.49
vena cava (inferior) (superior) 747.49
device, implant, or graft — *see* Complications, mechanical
fetus NEC (*see also* Presentation, fetal) 652.9 ☑
with successful version 652.1 ☑
affecting fetus or newborn 763.1
before labor, affecting fetus or newborn 761.7
causing obstructed labor 660.0 ☑
in multiple gestation (one fetus or more) 652.6 ☑
with locking 660.5 ☑
causing obstructed labor 660.0 ☑
gallbladder (*see also* Disease, gallbladder) 575.8
gastrointestinal tract 569.89
congenital 751.8
heart (*see also* Malposition, congenital, heart) 746.87
intestine 569.89
congenital 751.5
pelvic organs or tissues
in pregnancy or childbirth 654.4 ☑
affecting fetus or newborn 763.89
causing obstructed labor 660.2 ☑
affecting fetus or newborn 763.1
placenta — *see* Placenta, previa
stomach 537.89
congenital 750.7
tooth, teeth 524.30
with impaction 520.6
uterus (acquired) (acute) (adherent) (any degree) (asymptomatic) (postinfectional) (postpartal, old) 621.6
anteflexion or anteversion (*see also* Anteversion, uterus) 621.6
congenital 752.3
flexion 621.6
lateral (*see also* Lateroversion, uterus) 621.6
in pregnancy or childbirth 654.4 ☑
affecting fetus or newborn 763.89
causing obstructed labor 660.2 ☑
affecting fetus or newborn 763.1
inversion 621.6
lateral (flexion) (version) (*see also* Lateroversion, uterus) 621.6
lateroflexion (*see also* Lateroversion, uterus) 621.6
lateroversion (*see also* Lateroversion, uterus) 621.6
retroflexion or retroversion (*see also* Retroversion, uterus) 621.6
Malposture 729.90
Malpresentation, fetus — *see also* Presentation, fetal 652.9 ☑
Malrotation
cecum 751.4
colon 751.4
intestine 751.4
kidney 753.3
MALT (mucosa associated lymphoid tissue) 200.3 ☑
Malta fever — *see also* Brucellosis 023.9
Maltosuria 271.3
Maltreatment (of)
adult 995.80
emotional 995.82
multiple forms 995.85
neglect (nutritional) 995.84
physical 995.81
psychological 995.82
sexual 995.83
child 995.50
emotional 995.51

☑ Additional Digit Required — Refer to the Tabular List for Digit Selection
▶◀ Revised Text ● New Line ▲ Revised Code
Subterms under main terms may continue to next column or page
174 — Volume 2
2010 ICD-9-CM

Maltreatment — continued
  child — continued
    multiple forms 995.59
    neglect (nutritional) 995.52
    physical 995.54
      shaken infant syndrome 995.55
    psychological 995.51
    sexual 995.53
  spouse (see also Maltreatment, adult) 995.80
Malt workers' lung 495.4
Malum coxae senilis 715.25
Malunion, fracture 733.81
Mammillitis — see also Mastitis 611.0
  puerperal, postpartum 675.2 ☑
Mammitis — see also Mastitis 611.0
  puerperal, postpartum 675.2 ☑
Mammographic
  calcification 793.89
  calculus 793.89
  microcalcification 793.81
Mammoplasia 611.1
Management
  contraceptive V25.9
    specified type NEC V25.8
  procreative V26.9
    specified type NEC V26.89
Mangled NEC — see also nature and site of injury 959.9
Mania (monopolar) — see also Psychosis, affective 296.0 ☑
  alcoholic (acute) (chronic) 291.9
  Bell's — see Mania, chronic
  chronic 296.0 ☑
    recurrent episode 296.1 ☑
    single episode 296.0 ☑
  compulsive 300.3
  delirious (acute) 296.0 ☑
    recurrent episode 296.1 ☑
    single episode 296.0 ☑
  epileptic (see also Epilepsy) 345.4 ☑
  hysterical 300.10
  inhibited 296.89
  puerperal (after delivery) 296.0 ☑
    recurrent episode 296.1 ☑
    single episode 296.0 ☑
  recurrent episode 296.1 ☑
  senile 290.8
  single episode 296.0 ☑
  stupor 296.89
  stuporous 296.89
  unproductive 296.89
Manic-depressive insanity, psychosis, reaction, or syndrome — see also Psychosis, affective 296.80
  circular (alternating) 296.7
    currently
      depressed 296.5 ☑
      episode unspecified 296.7
      hypomanic, previously depressed 296.4 ☑
      manic 296.4 ☑
      mixed 296.6 ☑
  depressed (type), depressive 296.2 ☑
    atypical 296.82
    recurrent episode 296.3 ☑
    single episode 296.2 ☑
  hypomanic 296.0 ☑
    recurrent episode 296.1 ☑
    single episode 296.0 ☑
  manic 296.0 ☑
    atypical 296.81
    recurrent episode 296.1 ☑
    single episode 296.0 ☑
  mixed NEC 296.89
  perplexed 296.89
  stuporous 296.89
Manifestations, rheumatoid
  lungs 714.81
  pannus — see Arthritis, rheumatoid
  subcutaneous nodules — see Arthritis, rheumatoid
Mankowsky's syndrome (familial dysplastic osteopathy) 731.2
Mannoheptulosuria 271.8
Mannosidosis 271.8

Manson's
  disease (schistosomiasis) 120.1
  pyosis (pemphigus contagiosus) 684
  schistosomiasis 120.1
Mansonellosis 125.5
Manual — see condition
Maple bark disease 495.6
Maple bark-strippers' lung 495.6
Maple syrup (urine) disease or syndrome 270.3
Marable's syndrome (celiac artery compression) 447.4
Marasmus 261
  brain 331.9
  due to malnutrition 261
  intestinal 569.89
  nutritional 261
  senile 797
  tuberculous NEC (see also Tuberculosis) 011.9 ☑
Marble
  bones 756.52
  skin 782.61
Marburg disease (virus) 078.89
March
  foot 733.94
  hemoglobinuria 283.2
Marchand multiple nodular hyperplasia (liver) 571.5
Marchesani (-Weill) syndrome (brachymorphism and ectopia lentis) 759.89
Marchiafava (-Bignami) disease or syndrome 341.8
Marchiafava-Micheli syndrome (paroxysmal nocturnal hemoglobinuria) 283.2
Marcus Gunn's syndrome (jaw-winking syndrome) 742.8
Marfan's
  congenital syphilis 090.49
  disease 090.49
  syndrome (arachnodactyly) 759.82
    meaning congenital syphilis 090.49
    with luxation of lens 090.49 [379.32]
Marginal
  implantation, placenta — see Placenta, previa
  placenta — see Placenta, previa
  sinus (hemorrhage) (rupture) 641.2 ☑
    affecting fetus or newborn 762.1
Marie's
  cerebellar ataxia 334.2
  syndrome (acromegaly) 253.0
Marie-Bamberger disease or syndrome (hypertrophic) (pulmonary) (secondary) 731.2
  idiopathic (acropachyderma) 757.39
  primary (acropachyderma) 757.39
Marie-Charcôt-Tooth neuropathic atrophy, muscle 356.1
Marie-Strümpell arthritis or disease (ankylosing spondylitis) 720.0
Marihuana, marijuana
  abuse (see also Abuse, drugs, nondependent) 305.2 ☑
  dependence (see also Dependence) 304.3 ☑
Marion's disease (bladder neck obstruction) 596.0
Marital conflict V61.10
Mark
  port wine 757.32
  raspberry 757.32
  strawberry 757.32
  stretch 701.3
  tattoo 709.09
Maroteaux-Lamy syndrome (mucopolysaccharidosis VI) 277.5
Marriage license examination V70.3
Marrow (bone)
  arrest 284.9
  megakaryocytic 287.30
  poor function 289.9
Marseilles fever 082.1
Marshall's (hidrotic) **ectodermal dysplasia** 757.31
Marsh's disease (exophthalmic goiter) 242.0 ☑
Marsh fever — see also Malaria 084.6
Martin-Albright syndrome (pseudohypoparathyroidism) 275.49
Martin's disease 715.27

Martorell-Fabre syndrome (pulseless disease) 446.7
Masculinization, female, with adrenal hyperplasia 255.2
Masculinovoblastoma (M8670/0) 220
Masochism 302.83
Masons' lung 502
Mass
  abdominal 789.3 ☑
  anus 787.99
  bone 733.90
  breast 611.72
  cheek 784.2
  chest 786.6
  cystic — see Cyst
  ear 388.8
  epigastric 789.3 ☑
  eye 379.92
  female genital organ 625.8
  gum 784.2
  head 784.2
  intracranial 784.2
  joint 719.60
    ankle 719.67
    elbow 719.62
    foot 719.67
    hand 719.64
    hip 719.65
    knee 719.66
    multiple sites 719.69
    pelvic region 719.65
    shoulder (region) 719.61
    specified site NEC 719.68
    wrist 719.63
  kidney (see also Disease, kidney) 593.9
  lung 786.6
  lymph node 785.6
  malignant (M8000/3) — see Neoplasm, by site, malignant
  mediastinal 786.6
  mouth 784.2
  muscle (limb) 729.89
  neck 784.2
  nose or sinus 784.2
  palate 784.2
  pelvis, pelvic 789.3 ☑
  penis 607.89
  perineum 625.8
  rectum 787.99
  scrotum 608.89
  skin 782.2
  specified organ NEC — see Disease of specified organ or site
  splenic 789.2
  substernal 786.6
    thyroid (see also Goiter) 240.9
  superficial (localized) 782.2
  testes 608.89
  throat 784.2
  tongue 784.2
  umbilicus 789.3 ☑
  uterus 625.8
  vagina 625.8
  vulva 625.8
Massive — see condition
Mastalgia 611.71
  psychogenic 307.89
Mast cell
  disease 757.33
    systemic (M9741/3) 202.6 ☑
  leukemia (M9900/3) 207.8 ☑
  sarcoma (M9742/3) 202.6 ☑
  tumor (M9740/1) 238.5
    malignant (M9740/3) 202.6 ☑
Masters-Allen syndrome 620.6
Mastitis (acute) (adolescent) (diffuse) (interstitial) (lobular) (nonpuerperal) (nonsuppurative) (parenchymatous) (phlegmonous) (simple) (subacute) (suppurative) 611.0
  chronic (cystic) (fibrocystic) 610.1
  cystic 610.1
    Schimmelbusch's type 610.1
  fibrocystic 610.1
  infective 611.0
  lactational 675.2 ☑
  lymphangitis 611.0

Mastitis — continued
  neonatal (noninfective) 778.7
    infective 771.5
  periductal 610.4
  plasma cell 610.4
  puerperalis 675.2 ☑
  puerperal, postpartum, (interstitial) (nonpurulent) (parenchymatous) 675.2 ☑
    purulent 675.1 ☑
    stagnation 676.2 ☑
  retromammary 611.0
    puerperal, postpartum 675.1 ☑
  submammary 611.0
    puerperal, postpartum 675.1 ☑
Mastocytoma (M9740/1) 238.5
  malignant (M9740/3) 202.6 ☑
Mastocytosis 757.33
  malignant (M9741/3) 202.6 ☑
  systemic (M9741/3) 202.6 ☑
Mastodynia 611.71
  psychogenic 307.89
Mastoid — see condition
Mastoidalgia — see also Otalgia 388.70
Mastoiditis (coalescent) (hemorrhagic) (pneumococcal) (streptococcal) (suppurative) 383.9
  acute or subacute 383.00
    with
      Gradenigo's syndrome 383.02
      petrositis 383.02
      specified complication NEC 383.02
      subperiosteal abscess 383.01
  chronic (necrotic) (recurrent) 383.1
  tuberculous (see also Tuberculosis) 015.6 ☑
Mastopathy, mastopathia 611.9
  chronica cystica 610.1
  diffuse cystic 610.1
  estrogenic 611.89
  ovarian origin 611.89
Mastoplasia 611.1
Masturbation 307.9
Maternal condition, affecting fetus or newborn
  acute yellow atrophy of liver 760.8
  albuminuria 760.1
  anesthesia or analgesia 763.5
  blood loss 762.1
  chorioamnionitis 762.7
  circulatory disease, chronic (conditions classifiable to 390–459, 745–747) 760.3
  congenital heart disease (conditions classifiable to 745–746) 760.3
  cortical necrosis of kidney 760.1
  death 761.6
  diabetes mellitus 775.0
    manifest diabetes in the infant 775.1
  disease NEC 760.9
    circulatory system, chronic (conditions classifiable to 390–459, 745–747) 760.3
    genitourinary system (conditions classifiable to 580–599) 760.1
    respiratory (conditions classifiable to 490–519, 748) 760.3
  eclampsia 760.0
  hemorrhage NEC 762.1
  hepatitis acute, malignant, or subacute 760.8
  hyperemesis (gravidarum) 761.8
  hypertension (arising during pregnancy) (conditions classifiable to 642) 760.0
  infection
    disease classifiable to 001-136 ☑, 760.2
    genital tract NEC 760.8
    urinary tract 760.1
  influenza 760.2
    manifest influenza in the infant 771.2
  injury (conditions classifiable to 800–996) 760.5
  malaria 760.2
    manifest malaria in infant or fetus 771.2
  malnutrition 760.4
  necrosis of liver 760.8
  nephritis (conditions classifiable to 580–583) 760.1
  nephrosis (conditions classifiable to 581) 760.1
  noxious substance transmitted via breast milk or placenta 760.70

☑ Additional Digit Required — Refer to the Tabular List for Digit Selection   ▽ Subterms under main terms may continue to next column or page

2010 ICD-9-CM   ▶◀ Revised Text   ● New Line   ▲ Revised Code   **Volume 2 — 175**

Maternal condition, affecting fetus or newborn — *continued*
noxious substance transmitted via breast milk or placenta — *continued*
alcohol 760.71
anticonvulsants 760.77
antifungals 760.74
anti-infective agents 760.74
antimetabolics 760.78
cocaine 760.75
"crack" 760.75
diethylstilbestrol [DES] 760.76
hallucinogenic agents 760.73
medicinal agents NEC 760.79
narcotics 760.72
obstetric anesthetic or analgesic drug 760.72
specified agent NEC 760.79
nutritional disorder (conditions classifiable to 260–269) 760.4
operation unrelated to current delivery (*see also* Newborn, affected by) 760.64
pre-eclampsia 760.0
pyelitis or pyelonephritis, arising during pregnancy (conditions classifiable to 590) 760.1
renal disease or failure 760.1
respiratory disease, chronic (conditions classifiable to 490–519, 748) 760.3
rheumatic heart disease (chronic) (conditions classifiable to 393–398) 760.3
rubella (conditions classifiable to 056) 760.2
manifest rubella in the infant or fetus 771.0
surgery unrelated to current delivery (*see also* Newborn, affected by) 760.64
to uterus or pelvic organs 760.64
syphilis (conditions classifiable to 090–097) 760.2
manifest syphilis in the infant or fetus 090.0
thrombophlebitis 760.3
toxemia (of pregnancy) 760.0
pre-eclamptic 760.0
toxoplasmosis (conditions classifiable to 130) 760.2
manifest toxoplasmosis in the infant or fetus 771.2
transmission of chemical substance through the placenta 760.70
alcohol 760.71
anticonvulsants 760.77
antifungals 760.74
anti-infective 760.74
antimetabolics 760.78
cocaine 760.75
"crack" 760.75
diethylstilbestrol [DES] 760.76
hallucinogenic agents 760.73
narcotics 760.72
specified substance NEC 760.79
uremia 760.1
urinary tract conditions (conditions classifiable to 580–599) 760.1
vomiting (pernicious) (persistent) (vicious) 761.8
Maternity — *see* Delivery
Matheiu's disease (leptospiral jaundice) 100.0
Mauclaire's disease or osteochondrosis 732.3
Maxcy's disease 081.0
Maxilla, maxillary — *see* condition
May (-Hegglin) anomaly or syndrome 288.2
Mayaro fever 066.3
Mazoplasia 610.8
MBD (minimal brain dysfunction), child — *see also* Hyperkinesia 314.9
MCAD (medium chain acyl CoA dehydrogenase deficiency) 277.85
McArdle (-Schmid-Pearson) disease or syndrome (glycogenosis V) 271.0
McCune-Albright syndrome (osteitis fibrosa disseminata) 756.59
MCLS (mucocutaneous lymph node syndrome) 446.1
McQuarrie's syndrome (idiopathic familial hypoglycemia) 251.2
Measles (black) (hemorrhagic) (suppressed) 055.9

Measles — *continued*
with
encephalitis 055.0
keratitis 055.71
keratoconjunctivitis 055.71
otitis media 055.2
pneumonia 055.1
complication 055.8
specified type NEC 055.79
encephalitis 055.0
French 056.9
German 056.9
keratitis 055.71
keratoconjunctivitis 055.71
liberty 056.9
otitis media 055.2
pneumonia 055.1
specified complications NEC 055.79
vaccination, prophylactic (against) V04.2
Meatitis, urethral — *see also* Urethritis 597.89
Meat poisoning — *see* Poisoning, food
Meatus, meatal — *see* condition
Meat-wrappers' asthma 506.9
Meckel's
diverticulitis 751.0
diverticulum (displaced) (hypertrophic) 751.0
Meconium
aspiration 770.11
with
pneumonia 770.12
pneumonitis 770.12
respiratory symptoms 770.12
below vocal cords 770.11
with respiratory symptoms 770.12
syndrome 770.12
delayed passage in newborn 777.1
ileus 777.1
due to cystic fibrosis 277.01
in liquor 792.3
noted during delivery 656.8 ☑
insufflation 770.11
with respiratory symptoms 770.12
obstruction
fetus or newborn 777.1
in mucoviscidosis 277.01
passage of 792.3
noted during delivery 763.84
peritonitis 777.6
plug syndrome (newborn) NEC 777.1
staining 779.84
Median — *see also* condition
arcuate ligament syndrome 447.4
bar (prostate) 600.90
with
other lower urinary tract symptoms (LUTS) 600.91
urinary
obstruction 600.91
retention 600.91
rhomboid glossitis 529.2
vesical orifice 600.90
with
other lower urinary tract symptoms (LUTS) 600.91
urinary
obstruction 600.91
retention 600.91
Mediastinal shift 793.2
Mediastinitis (acute) (chronic) 519.2
actinomycotic 039.8
syphilitic 095.8
tuberculous (*see also* Tuberculosis) 012.8 ☑
Mediastinopericarditis — *see also* Pericarditis 423.9
acute 420.90
chronic 423.8
rheumatic 393
rheumatic, chronic 393
Mediastinum, mediastinal — *see* condition
Medical services provided for — *see* Health, services provided because (of)
Medicine poisoning (by overdose) (wrong substance given or taken in error) 977.9
specified drug or substance — *see* Table of Drugs and Chemicals
Medin's disease (poliomyelitis) 045.9 ☑

Mediterranean
anemia (with other hemoglobinopathy) 282.49
disease or syndrome (hemipathic) 282.49
fever (*see also* Brucellosis) 023.9
familial 277.31
kala-azar 085.0
leishmaniasis 085.0
tick fever 082.1
Medulla — *see* condition
Medullary
cystic kidney 753.16
sponge kidney 753.17
Medullated fibers
optic (nerve) 743.57
retina 362.85
Medulloblastoma (M9470/3) 191.6
desmoplastic (M9471/3) 191.6
specified site — *see* Neoplasm, by site, malignant
unspecified site 191.6
Medulloepithelioma (M9501/3) — *see also* Neoplasm, by site, malignant
teratoid (M9502/3) — *see* Neoplasm, by site, malignant
Medullomyoblastoma (M9472/3)
specified site — *see* Neoplasm, by site, malignant
unspecified site 191.6
Meekeren-Ehlers-Danlos syndrome 756.83
Megacaryocytic — *see* condition
Megacolon (acquired) (functional) (not Hirschsprung's disease) 564.7
aganglionic 751.3
congenital, congenitum 751.3
Hirschsprung's (disease) 751.3
psychogenic 306.4
toxic (*see also* Colitis, ulcerative) 556.9
Megaduodenum 537.3
Megaesophagus (functional) 530.0
congenital 750.4
Megakaryocytic — *see* condition
Megalencephaly 742.4
Megalerythema (epidermicum) (infectiosum) 057.0
Megalia, cutis et ossium 757.39
Megaloappendix 751.5
Megalocephalus, megalocephaly NEC 756.0
Megalocornea 743.41
associated with buphthalmos 743.22
Megalocytic anemia 281.9
Megalodactylia (fingers) (thumbs) 755.57
toes 755.65
Megaloduodenum 751.5
Megaloesophagus (functional) 530.0
congenital 750.4
Megalogastria (congenital) 750.7
Megalomania 307.9
Megalophthalmos 743.8
Megalopsia 368.14
Megalosplenia — *see also* Splenomegaly 789.2
Megaloureter 593.89
congenital 753.22
Megarectum 569.49
Megasigmoid 564.7
congenital 751.3
Megaureter 593.89
congenital 753.22
Megrim 346.9 ☑
Meibomian
cyst 373.2
infected 373.12
gland — *see* condition
infarct (eyelid) 374.85
stye 373.11
Meibomitis 373.12
Meige
-Milroy disease (chronic hereditary edema) 757.0
syndrome (blepharospasm-oromandibular dystonia) 333.82
Melalgia, nutritional 266.2
Melancholia — *see also* Psychosis, affective 296.90
climacteric 296.2 ☑
recurrent episode 296.3 ☑
single episode 296.2 ☑

Melancholia — *see also* Psychosis, affective — *continued*
hypochondriac 300.7
intermittent 296.2 ☑
recurrent episode 296.3 ☑
single episode 296.2 ☑
involutional 296.2 ☑
recurrent episode 296.3 ☑
single episode 296.2 ☑
menopausal 296.2 ☑
recurrent episode 296.3 ☑
single episode 296.2 ☑
puerperal 296.2 ☑
reactive (from emotional stress, psychological trauma) 298.0
recurrent 296.3 ☑
senile 290.21
stuporous 296.2 ☑
recurrent episode 296.3 ☑
single episode 296.2 ☑
Melanemia 275.0
Melanoameloblastoma (M9363/0) — *see* Neoplasm, bone, benign
Melanoblastoma (M8720/3) — *see* Melanoma
Melanoblastosis
Block-Sulzberger 757.33
cutis linearis sive systematisata 757.33
Melanocarcinoma (M8720/3) — *see* Melanoma
Melanocytoma, eyeball (M8726/0) 224.0
Melanoderma, melanodermia 709.09
Addison's (primary adrenal insufficiency) 255.41
Melanodontia, infantile 521.05
Melanodontoclasia 521.05
Melanoepithelioma (M8720/3) — *see* Melanoma
Melanoma (malignant) (M8720/3) 172.9

> *Note* — Except where otherwise indicated, the morphological varieties of melanoma in the list below should be coded by site as for "Melanoma (malignant)". Internal sites should be coded to malignant neoplasm of those sites.

abdominal wall 172.5
ala nasi 172.3
amelanotic (M8730/3) — *see* Melanoma, by site
ankle 172.7
anus, anal 154.3
canal 154.2
arm 172.6
auditory canal (external) 172.2
auricle (ear) 172.2
auricular canal (external) 172.2
axilla 172.5
axillary fold 172.5
back 172.5
balloon cell (M8722/3) — *see* Melanoma, by site
benign (M8720/0) — *see* Neoplasm, skin, benign
breast (female) (male) 172.5
brow 172.3
buttock 172.5
canthus (eye) 172.1
cheek (external) 172.3
chest wall 172.5
chin 172.3
choroid 190.6
conjunctiva 190.3
ear (external) 172.2
epithelioid cell (M8771/3) (*see also* Melanoma, by site)
and spindle cell, mixed (M8775/3) — *see* Melanoma, by site
external meatus (ear) 172.2
eye 190.9
eyebrow 172.3
eyelid (lower) (upper) 172.1
face NEC 172.3
female genital organ (external) NEC 184.4
finger 172.6
flank 172.5
foot 172.7
forearm 172.6

Melanoma — *continued*
  forehead 172.3
  foreskin 187.1
  gluteal region 172.5
  groin 172.5
  hand 172.6
  heel 172.7
  helix 172.2
  hip 172.7
  in
    giant pigmented nevus (M8761/3) — *see* Melanoma, by site
    Hutchinson's melanotic freckle (M8742/3) — *see* Melanoma, by site
    junctional nevus (M8740/3) — *see* Melanoma, by site
    precancerous melanosis (M8741/3) — *see* Melanoma, by site
  in situ — *see* Melanoma, by site
    skin 172.9
  interscapular region 172.5
  iris 190.0
  jaw 172.3
  juvenile (M8770/0) — *see* Neoplasm, skin, benign
  knee 172.7
  labium
    majus 184.1
    minus 184.2
  lacrimal gland 190.2
  leg 172.7
  lip (lower) (upper) 172.0
  liver 197.7
  lower limb NEC 172.7
  male genital organ (external) NEC 187.9
  meatus, acoustic (external) 172.2
  meibomian gland 172.1
  metastatic
    of or from specified site — *see* Melanoma, by site
    site not of skin — *see* Neoplasm, by site, malignant, secondary
    to specified site — *see* Neoplasm, by site, malignant, secondary
    unspecified site 172.9
  nail 172.9
    finger 172.6
    toe 172.7
  neck 172.4
  nodular (M8721/3) — *see* Melanoma, by site
  nose, external 172.3
  orbit 190.1
  penis 187.4
  perianal skin 172.5
  perineum 172.5
  pinna 172.2
  popliteal (fossa) (space) 172.7
  prepuce 187.1
  pubes 172.5
  pudendum 184.4
  retina 190.5
  scalp 172.4
  scrotum 187.7
  septum nasal (skin) 172.3
  shoulder 172.6
  skin NEC 172.8
    in situ 172.9
  spindle cell (M8772/3) (*see also* Melanoma, by site)
    type A (M8773/3) 190.0
    type B (M8774/3) 190.0
  submammary fold 172.5
  superficial spreading (M8743/3) — *see* Melanoma, by site
  temple 172.3
  thigh 172.7
  toe 172.7
  trunk NEC 172.5
  umbilicus 172.5
  upper limb NEC 172.6
  vagina vault 184.0
  vulva 184.4
Melanoplakia 528.9
Melanosarcoma (M8720/3) — *see also* Melanoma
  epithelioid cell (M8771/3) — *see* Melanoma

Melanosis 709.09
  addisonian (primary adrenal insufficiency) 255.41
    tuberculous (*see also* Tuberculosis) 017.6 ☑
  adrenal 255.41
  colon 569.89
  conjunctiva 372.55
    congenital 743.49
  corii degenerativa 757.33
  cornea (presenile) (senile) 371.12
    congenital 743.43
      interfering with vision 743.42
  eye 372.55
    congenital 743.49
  jute spinners' 709.09
  lenticularis progressiva 757.33
  liver 573.8
  precancerous (M8741/2) (*see also* Neoplasm, skin, in situ)
    malignant melanoma in (M8741/3) — *see* Melanoma
  prenatal 743.43
    interfering with vision 743.42
  Riehl's 709.09
  sclera 379.19
    congenital 743.47
  suprarenal 255.41
  tar 709.09
  toxic 709.09
Melanuria 791.9
Melasma 709.09
  adrenal (gland) 255.41
  suprarenal (gland) 255.41
MELAS syndrome (mitochondrial encephalopathy, lactic acidosis and stroke-like episodes) 277.87
Melena 578.1
  due to
    swallowed maternal blood 777.3
    ulcer — *see* Ulcer, by site, with hemorrhage
  newborn 772.4
    due to swallowed maternal blood 777.3
Meleney's
  gangrene (cutaneous) 686.09
  ulcer (chronic undermining) 686.09
Melioidosis 025
Melitensis, febris 023.0
Melitococcosis 023.0
Melkersson (-Rosenthal) syndrome 351.8
Mellitus, diabetes — *see* Diabetes
Melorheostosis (bone) (leri) 733.99
Meloschisis 744.83
Melotia 744.29
Membrana
  capsularis lentis posterior 743.39
  epipapillaris 743.57
Membranacea placenta — *see* Placenta, abnormal
Membranaceous uterus 621.8
Membrane, membranous — *see also* condition
  folds, congenital — *see* Web
  Jackson's 751.4
  over face (causing asphyxia), fetus or newborn 768.9
  premature rupture — *see* Rupture, membranes, premature
  pupillary 364.74
    persistent 743.46
  retained (complicating delivery) (with hemorrhage) 666.2 ☑
    without hemorrhage 667.1 ☑
  secondary (eye) 366.50
  unruptured (causing asphyxia) 768.9
  vitreous humor 379.25
Membranitis, fetal 658.4 ☑
  affecting fetus or newborn 762.7
Memory disturbance, loss or lack — *see also* Amnesia 780.93
  mild, following organic brain damage 310.8 ▲
MEN (multiple endocrine neoplasia) (syndromes)
  type I 258.01
  type IIA 258.02
  type IIB 258.03

Menadione (vitamin K) **deficiency** 269.0
Menarche, precocious 259.1
Mendacity, pathologic 301.7
Mendelson's syndrome (resulting from a procedure) 997.39
  obstetric 668.0 ☑
Mende's syndrome (ptosis-epicanthus) 270.2
Ménétrier's disease or syndrome (hypertrophic gastritis) 535.2 ☑
Ménière's disease, syndrome, or vertigo 386.00
  cochlear 386.02
  cochleovestibular 386.01
  inactive 386.04
  in remission 386.04
  vestibular 386.03
Meninges, meningeal — *see* condition
Meningioma (M9530/0) — *see also* Neoplasm, meninges, benign
  angioblastic (M9535/0) — *see* Neoplasm, meninges, benign
  angiomatous (M9534/0) — *see* Neoplasm, meninges, benign
  endotheliomatous (M9531/0) — *see* Neoplasm, meninges, benign
  fibroblastic (M9532/0) — *see* Neoplasm, meninges, benign
  fibrous (M9532/0) — *see* Neoplasm, meninges, benign
  hemangioblastic (M9535/0) — *see* Neoplasm, meninges, benign
  hemangiopericytic (M9536/0) — *see* Neoplasm, meninges, benign
  malignant (M9530/3) — *see* Neoplasm, meninges, malignant
  meningiothelial (M9531/0) — *see* Neoplasm, meninges, benign
  meningotheliomatous (M9531/0) — *see* Neoplasm, meninges, benign
  mixed (M9537/0) — *see* Neoplasm, meninges, benign
  multiple (M9530/1) 237.6
  papillary (M9538/1) 237.6
  psammomatous (M9533/0) — *see* Neoplasm, meninges, benign
  syncytial (M9531/0) — *see* Neoplasm, meninges, benign
  transitional (M9537/0) — *see* Neoplasm, meninges, benign
Meningiomatosis (diffuse) (M9530/1) 237.6
Meningism — *see also* Meningismus 781.6
Meningismus (infectional) (pneumococcal) 781.6
  due to serum or vaccine 997.09 [321.8]
  influenzal NEC 487.8
Meningitis (basal) (basic) (basilar) (brain) (cerebral) (cerebral) (congestive) (diffuse) (hemorrhagic) (infantile) (membranous) (metastatic) (nonspecific) (pontine) (progressive) (simple) (spinal) (subacute) (sympathetica) (toxic) 322.9
  abacterial NEC (*see also* Meningitis, aseptic) 047.9
  actinomycotic 039.8 [320.7]
  adenoviral 049.1
  Aerobacter aerogenes 320.82
  anaerobes (cocci) (gram-negative) (gram-positive) (mixed) (NEC) 320.81
  arbovirus NEC 066.9 [321.2]
    specified type NEC 066.8 [321.2]
  aseptic (acute) NEC 047.9
    adenovirus 049.1
    Coxsackie virus 047.0
    due to
      adenovirus 049.1
      Coxsackie virus 047.0
      ECHO virus 047.1
      enterovirus 047.9
      mumps 072.1
      poliovirus (*see also* Poliomyelitis) 045.2 ☑ [321.2]
    ECHO virus 047.1
    herpes (simplex) virus 054.72
      zoster 053.0
    leptospiral 100.81
    lymphocytic choriomeningitis 049.0
    noninfective 322.0

Meningitis — *continued*
  Bacillus pyocyaneus 320.89
  bacterial NEC 320.9
    anaerobic 320.81
    gram-negative 320.82
      anaerobic 320.81
  Bacteroides (fragilis) (oralis) (melaninogenicus) 320.81
  cancerous (M8000/6) 198.4
  candidal 112.83
  carcinomatous (M8010/6) 198.4
  caseous (*see also* Tuberculosis, meninges) 013.0 ☑
  cerebrospinal (acute) (chronic) (diplococcal) (endemic) (epidemic) (fulminant) (infectious) (malignant) (meningococcal) (sporadic) 036.0
    carrier (suspected) of V02.59
  chronic NEC 322.2
  clear cerebrospinal fluid NEC 322.0
  Clostridium (haemolyticum) (novyi) NEC 320.81
  coccidioidomycosis 114.2
  Coxsackie virus 047.0
  cryptococcal 117.5 [321.0]
  diplococcal 036.0
    gram-negative 036.0
    gram-positive 320.1
  Diplococcus pneumoniae 320.1
  due to
    actinomycosis 039.8 [320.7]
    adenovirus 049.1
    coccidiomycosis 114.2
    enterovirus 047.9
      specified NEC 047.8
    histoplasmosis (*see also* Histoplasmosis) 115.91
    Listerosis 027.0 [320.7]
    Lyme disease 088.81 [320.7]
    moniliasis 112.83
    mumps 072.1
    neurosyphilis 094.2
    nonbacterial organisms NEC 321.8
    oidiomycosis 112.83
    poliovirus (*see also* Poliomyelitis) 045.2 ☑ [321.2]
    preventive immunization, inoculation, or vaccination 997.09 [321.8]
    sarcoidosis 135 [321.4]
    sporotrichosis 117.1 [321.1]
    syphilis 094.2
      acute 091.81
      congenital 090.42
      secondary 091.81
    trypanosomiasis (*see also* Trypanosomiasis) 086.9 [321.3]
    whooping cough 033.9 [320.7]
  ECHO virus 047.1
  E. coli 320.82
  endothelial-leukocytic, benign, recurrent 047.9
  Enterobacter aerogenes 320.82
  enteroviral 047.9
    specified type NEC 047.8
  enterovirus 047.9
    specified NEC 047.8
  eosinophilic 322.1
  epidemic NEC 036.0
  Escherichia coli (E. coli) 320.82
  Eubacterium 320.81
  fibrinopurulent NEC 320.9
    specified type NEC 320.89
  Friedländer (bacillus) 320.82
  fungal NEC 117.9 [321.1]
  Fusobacterium 320.81
  gonococcal 098.82
  gram-negative bacteria NEC 320.82
    anaerobic 320.81
    cocci 036.0
      specified NEC 320.82
  gram-negative cocci NEC 036.0
    specified NEC 320.82
  gram-positive cocci NEC 320.9
  herpes (simplex) virus 054.72
    zoster 053.0
  H. influenzae 320.0
  infectious NEC 320.9

Melanoma — Meningitis

☑ Additional Digit Required — Refer to the Tabular List for Digit Selection   ▽ Subterms under main terms may continue to next column or page

2010 ICD-9-CM   ▶◀ Revised Text   ● New Line   ▲ Revised Code   October 2009 • Volume 2 — 177

Meningitis — Meryicism

Meningitis — continued
influenzal 320.0
Klebsiella pneumoniae 320.82
late effect — *see* Late, effect, meningitis
leptospiral (aseptic) 100.81
Listerella (monocytogenes) 027.0 [320.7]
Listeria monocytogenes 027.0 [320.7]
lymphocytic (acute) (benign) (serous) 049.0
choriomeningitis virus 049.0
meningococcal (chronic) 036.0
Mima polymorpha 320.82
Mollaret's 047.9
monilial 112.83
mumps (virus) 072.1
mycotic NEC 117.9 [321.1]
Neisseria 036.0
neurosyphilis 094.2
nonbacterial NEC (*see also* Meningitis, aseptic)
047.9
nonpyogenic NEC 322.0
oidiomycosis 112.83
ossificans 349.2
Peptococcus 320.81
Peptostreptococcus 320.81
pneumococcal 320.1
poliovirus (*see also* Poliomyelitis)
045.2 ☑ [321.2]
Proprionibacterium 320.81
Proteus morganii 320.82
Pseudomonas (aeruginosa) (pyocyaneus)
320.82
purulent NEC 320.9
specified organism NEC 320.89
pyogenic NEC 320.9
specified organism NEC 320.89
Salmonella 003.21
septic NEC 320.9
specified organism NEC 320.89
serosa circumscripta NEC 322.0
serous NEC (*see also* Meningitis, aseptic) 047.9
lymphocytic 049.0
syndrome 348.2
Serratia (marcescens) 320.82
specified organism NEC 320.89
sporadic cerebrospinal 036.0
sporotrichosis 117.1 [321.1]
staphylococcal 320.3
sterile 997.09
streptococcal (acute) 320.2
suppurative 320.9
specified organism NEC 320.89
syphilitic 094.2
acute 091.81
congenital 090.42
secondary 091.81
torula 117.5 [321.0]
traumatic (complication of injury) 958.8
Treponema (denticola) (macrodenticum)
320.81
trypanosomiasis 086.1 [321.3]
tuberculous (*see also* Tuberculosis, meninges)
013.0 ☑
typhoid 002.0 [320.7]
Veillonella 320.81
Vibrio vulnificus 320.82
viral, virus NEC (*see also* Meningitis, aseptic)
047.9
Wallgren's (*see also* Meningitis, aseptic) 047.9
Meningocele (congenital) (spinal) — *see also*
Spina bifida 741.9 ☑
acquired (traumatic) 349.2
cerebral 742.0
cranial 742.0
Meningocerebritis — *see* Meningoencephalitis
Meningococcemia (acute) (chronic) 036.2
Meningococcus, meningococcal — *see also*
condition 036.9
adrenalitis, hemorrhagic 036.3
carditis 036.40
carrier (suspected) of V02.59
cerebrospinal fever 036.0
encephalitis 036.1
endocarditis 036.42
exposure to V01.84
infection NEC 036.9
meningitis (cerebrospinal) 036.0

Meningococcus, meningococcal — *see also*
condition — *continued*
myocarditis 036.43
optic neuritis 036.81
pericarditis 036.41
septicemia (chronic) 036.2
Meningoencephalitis — *see also* Encephalitis
323.9
acute NEC 048
bacterial, purulent, pyogenic, or septic — *see*
Meningitis
chronic NEC 094.1
diffuse NEC 094.1
diphasic 063.2
due to
actinomycosis 039.8 [320.7]
blastomycosis NEC (*see also* Blastomycosis)
116.0 [323.41]
free-living amebae 136.29
Listeria monocytogenes 027.0 [320.7]
Lyme disease 088.81 [320.7]
mumps 072.3
Naegleria (amebae) (gruberi) (organisms)
136.29
rubella 056.01
sporotrichosis 117.1 [321.1]
toxoplasmosis (acquired) 130.0
congenital (active) 771.2 [323.41]
Trypanosoma 086.1 [323.2]
epidemic 036.0
herpes 054.3
herpetic 054.3
H. influenzae 320.0
infectious (acute) 048
influenzal 320.0
late effect — *see* category 326
Listeria monocytogenes 027.0 [320.7]
lymphocytic (serous) 049.0
mumps 072.2
parasitic NEC 123.9 [323.41]
pneumococcal 320.1
primary amebic 136.29
rubella 056.01
serous 048
lymphocytic 049.0
specific 094.2
staphylococcal 320.3
streptococcal 320.2
syphilitic 094.2
toxic NEC 989.9 [323.71]
due to
carbon tetrachloride (vapor)
987.8 [323.71]
hydroxyquinoline derivatives poisoning
961.3 [323.71]
lead 984.9 [323.71]
mercury 985.0 [323.71]
thallium 985.8 [323.71]
toxoplasmosis (acquired) 130.0
trypanosomic 086.1 [323.2]
tuberculous (*see also* Tuberculosis, meninges)
013.0 ☑
virus NEC 048
Meningoencephalocele 742.0
syphilitic 094.89
congenital 090.49
Meningoencephalomyelitis — *see also* Meningoencephalitis 323.9
acute NEC 048
disseminated (postinfectious)
136.9 [323.61]
postimmunization or postvaccination
323.51
due to
actinomycosis 039.8 [320.7]
torula 117.5 [323.41]
toxoplasma or toxoplasmosis (acquired)
130.0
congenital (active) 771.2 [323.41]
late effect — *see* category 326
Meningoencephalomyelopathy — *see also*
Meningoencephalomyelitis 349.9
Meningoencephalopathy — *see also* Meningoencephalitis 348.39
Meningoencephalopoliomyelitis — *see also*
Poliomyelitis, bulbar 045.0 ☑

Meningoencephalopoliomyelitis — *see also*
Poliomyelitis, bulbar — *continued*
late effect 138
Meningomyelitis — *see also* Meningoencephalitis 323.9
blastomycotic NEC (*see also* Blastomycosis)
116.0 [323.41]
due to
actinomycosis 039.8 [320.7]
blastomycosis (*see also* Blastomycosis)
116.0 [323.41]
Meningococcus 036.0
sporotrichosis 117.1 [323.41]
torula 117.5 [323.41]
late effect — *see* category 326
lethargic 049.8
meningococcal 036.0
syphilitic 094.2
tuberculous (*see also* Tuberculosis, meninges)
013.0 ☑
Meningomyelocele — *see also* Spina bifida
741.9 ☑
syphilitic 094.89
Meningomyeloneuritis — *see* Meningoencephalitis
Meningoradiculitis — *see* Meningitis
Meningovascular — *see* condition
Meniscocytosis 282.60
Menkes' syndrome — *see* Syndrome, Menkes'
Menolipsis 626.0
Menometrorrhagia 626.2
Menopause, menopausal (symptoms) (syndrome) 627.2
arthritis (any site) NEC 716.3 ☑
artificial 627.4
bleeding 627.0
crisis 627.2
depression (*see also* Psychosis, affective)
296.2 ☑
agitated 296.2 ☑
recurrent episode 296.3 ☑
single episode 296.2 ☑
psychotic 296.2 ☑
recurrent episode 296.3 ☑
single episode 296.2 ☑
recurrent episode 296.3 ☑
single episode 296.2 ☑
melancholia (*see also* Psychosis, affective)
296.2 ☑
recurrent episode 296.3 ☑
single episode 296.2 ☑
paranoid state 297.2
paraphrenia 297.2
postsurgical 627.4
premature 256.31
postirradiation 256.2
postsurgical 256.2
psychoneurosis 627.2
psychosis NEC 298.8
surgical 627.4
toxic polyarthritis NEC 716.39
Menorrhagia (primary) 626.2
climacteric 627.0
menopausal 627.0
postclimacteric 627.1
postmenopausal 627.1
preclimacteric 627.0
premenopausal 627.0
puberty (menses retained) 626.3
Menorrhalgia 625.3
Menoschesis 626.8
Menostaxis 626.2
Menses, retention 626.8
Menstrual — *see also* Menstruation
cycle, irregular 626.4
disorders NEC 626.9
extraction V25.3
fluid, retained 626.8
molimen 625.4
period, normal V65.5
regulation V25.3
Menstruation
absent 626.0
anovulatory 628.0
delayed 626.8
difficult 625.3

Menstruation — *continued*
disorder 626.9
psychogenic 306.52
specified NEC 626.8
during pregnancy 640.8 ☑
excessive 626.2
frequent 626.2
infrequent 626.1
irregular 626.4
latent 626.8
membranous 626.8
painful (primary) (secondary) 625.3
psychogenic 306.52
passage of clots 626.2
precocious 626.8
protracted 626.8
retained 626.8
retrograde 626.8
scanty 626.1
suppression 626.8
vicarious (nasal) 625.8
Mentagra — *see also* Sycosis 704.8
Mental — *see also* condition
deficiency (*see also* Retardation, mental) 319
deterioration (*see also* Psychosis) 298.9
disorder (*see also* Disorder, mental) 300.9
exhaustion 300.5
insufficiency (congenital) (*see also* Retardation,
mental) 319
observation without need for further medical
care NEC V71.09
retardation (*see also* Retardation, mental) 319
subnormality (*see also* Retardation, mental)
319
mild 317
moderate 318.0
profound 318.2
severe 318.1
upset (*see also* Disorder, mental) 300.9
Meralgia paresthetica 355.1
Mercurial — *see* condition
Mercurialism NEC 985.0
Merergasia 300.9
Merkel cell tumor — *see* ►Carcinoma, Merkel
cell◄
Merocele — *see also* Hernia, femoral 553.00
Meromelia 755.4
lower limb 755.30
intercalary 755.32
femur 755.34
tibiofibular (complete) (incomplete)
755.33
fibula 755.37
metatarsal(s) 755.38
tarsal(s) 755.38
tibia 755.36
tibiofibular 755.35
terminal (complete) (partial) (transverse)
755.31
longitudinal 755.32
metatarsal(s) 755.38
phalange(s) 755.39
tarsal(s) 755.38
transverse 755.31
upper limb 755.20
intercalary 755.22
carpal(s) 755.28
humeral 755.24
radioulnar (complete) (incomplete)
755.23
metacarpal(s) 755.28
phalange(s) 755.29
radial 755.26
radioulnar 755.25
ulnar 755.27
terminal (complete) (partial) (transverse)
755.21
longitudinal 755.22
carpal(s) 755.28
metacarpal(s) 755.28
phalange(s) 755.29
transverse 755.21
Merosmia 781.1
MERRF syndrome (myoclonus with epilepsy and
with ragged red fibers) 277.87
Merycism — *see also* Vomiting

Merycism — see also Vomiting — continued
  psychogenic 307.53
Merzbacher-Pelizaeus disease 330.0
Mesaortitis — see Aortitis
Mesarteritis — see Arteritis
Mesencephalitis — see also Encephalitis 323.9
  late effect — see category 326
Mesenchymoma (M8990/1) — see also Neo-
  plasm, connective tissue, uncertain behav-
  ior
  benign (M8990/0) — see Neoplasm, connec-
    tive tissue, benign
  malignant (M8990/3) — see Neoplasm, con-
    nective tissue, malignant
Mesenteritis
  retractile 567.82
  sclerosing 567.82
Mesentery, mesenteric — see condition
Mesiodens, mesiodentes 520.1
  causing crowding 524.31
Mesio-occlusion 524.23
Mesocardia (with asplenia) 746.87
Mesocolon — see condition
Mesonephroma (malignant) (M9110/3) — see
  also Neoplasm, by site, malignant
  benign (M9110/0) — see Neoplasm, by site,
    benign
Mesophlebitis — see Phlebitis
Mesostromal dysgenesis 743.51
Mesothelioma (malignant) (M9050/3) — see also
  Neoplasm, by site, malignant
  benign (M9050/0) — see Neoplasm, by site,
    benign
  biphasic type (M9053/3) (see also Neoplasm,
    by site, malignant)
    benign (M9053/0) — see Neoplasm, by
      site, benign
  epithelioid (M9052/3) (see also Neoplasm, by
    site, malignant)
    benign (M9052/0) — see Neoplasm, by
      site, benign
  fibrous (M9051/3) (see also Neoplasm, by site,
    malignant)
    benign (M9051/0) — see Neoplasm, by
      site, benign
Metabolic syndrome 277.7
Metabolism disorder 277.9
  specified type NEC 277.89
Metagonimiasis 121.5
Metagonimus infestation (small intestine) 121.5
Metal
  pigmentation (skin) 709.00
  polishers' disease 502
Metalliferous miners' lung 503
Metamorphopsia 368.14
Metaplasia
  bone, in skin 709.3
  breast 611.89
  cervix — omit code
  endometrium (squamous) 621.8
  esophagus 530.85
  intestinal, of gastric mucosa 537.89
  kidney (pelvis) (squamous) (see also Disease,
    renal) 593.89
  myelogenous 289.89
  myeloid 289.89
    agnogenic 238.76
    megakaryocytic 238.76
  spleen 289.59
  squamous cell
    amnion 658.8 ☑
    bladder 596.8
    cervix — see condition
    trachea 519.19
    tracheobronchial tree 519.19
    uterus 621.8
      cervix — see condition
Metastasis, metastatic
  abscess — see Abscess
  calcification 275.40
  cancer, neoplasm, or disease
    from specified site (M8000/3) — see Neo-
      plasm, by site, malignant
    to specified site (M8000/6) — see Neo-
      plasm, by site, secondary

Metastasis, metastatic — continued
  deposits (in) (M8000/6) — see Neoplasm, by
    site, secondary
  mesentery, of neuroendocrine tumor 209.71 ●
  pneumonia 038.8 [484.8]
  spread (to) (M8000/6) — see Neoplasm, by
    site, secondary
Metatarsalgia 726.70
  anterior 355.6
  due to Freiberg's disease 732.5
  Morton's 355.6
Metatarsus, metatarsal — see also condition
  abductus valgus (congenital) 754.60
  adductus varus (congenital) 754.53
  primus varus 754.52
  valgus (adductus) (congenital) 754.60
  varus (abductus) (congenital) 754.53
    primus 754.52
Methadone use 304.00
Methemoglobinemia 289.7
  acquired (with sulfhemoglobinemia) 289.7
  congenital 289.7
  enzymatic 289.7
  Hb-M disease 289.7
  hereditary 289.7
  toxic 289.7
Methemoglobinuria — see also Hemoglobinuria
  791.2
Methicillin
  resistant staphyloccocus aureus (MRSA) 041.12
    colonization V02.54
      personal history of V12.04
  susceptible staphylococcus aureus (MSSA)
    041.11
    colonization V02.53
Methioninemia 270.4
Metritis (catarrhal) (septic) (suppurative) — see
  also Endometritis 615.9
  blennorrhagic 098.16
    chronic or duration of 2 months or over
      098.36
  cervical (see also Cervicitis) 616.0
  gonococcal 098.16
    chronic or duration of 2 months or over
      098.36
  hemorrhagic 626.8
  puerperal, postpartum, childbirth
    670.1 ☑ ▲
    septic 670.2 ☑ ●
  tuberculous (see also Tuberculosis) 016.7 ☑
Metropathia hemorrhagica 626.8
Metroperitonitis — see also Peritonitis, pelvic,
  female 614.5
Metrorrhagia 626.6
  arising during pregnancy — see Hemorrhage,
    pregnancy
  postpartum NEC 666.2 ☑
  primary 626.6
  psychogenic 306.59
  puerperal 666.2 ☑
Metrorrhexis — see Rupture, uterus
Metrosalpingitis — see also Salpingo-oophoritis
  614.2
Metrostaxis 626.6
Metrovaginitis — see also Endometritis 615.9
  gonococcal (acute) 098.16
    chronic or duration of 2 months or over
      098.36
Mexican fever — see Typhus, Mexican
Meyenburg-Altherr-Uehlinger syndrome
  733.99
Meyer-Schwickerath and Weyers syndrome
  (dysplasia oculodentodigitalis) 759.89
Meynert's amentia (nonalcoholic) 294.0
  alcoholic 291.1
Mibelli's disease 757.39
Mice, joint — see also Loose, body, joint 718.1 ☑
  knee 717.6
Micheli-Rietti syndrome (thalassemia minor)
  282.49
Michotte's syndrome 721.5
Micrencephalon, micrencephaly 742.1
Microalbuminuria 791.0
Microaneurysm, retina 362.14
  diabetic 250.5 ☑ [362.01]

Microaneurysm, retina — continued
  diabetic — continued
    due to secondary diabetes
      249.5 ☑ [362.01]
Microangiopathy 443.9
  diabetic (peripheral) 250.7 ☑ [443.81]
    due to secondary diabetes
      249.7 ☑ [443.81]
    retinal 250.5 ☑ [362.01]
      due to secondary diabetes
        249.5 ☑ [362.01]
  peripheral 443.9
    diabetic 250.7 ☑ [443.81]
      due to secondary diabetes
        249.7 ☑ [443.81]
  retinal 362.18
    diabetic 250.5 ☑ [362.01]
      due to secondary diabetes
        249.5 ☑ [362.01]
  thrombotic 446.6
    Moschcowitz's (thrombotic thrombocy-
      topenic purpura) 446.6
Microcalcification, mammographic 793.81
Microcephalus, microcephalic, microcephaly
  742.1
  due to toxoplasmosis (congenital) 771.2
Microcheilia 744.82
Microcolon (congenital) 751.5
Microcornea (congenital) 743.41
Microcytic — see condition
Microdeletions NEC 758.33
Microdontia 520.2
Microdrepanocytosis (thalassemia-Hb-S disease)
  282.49
Microembolism
  atherothrombotic — see Atheroembolism
  retina 362.33
Microencephalon 742.1
Microfilaria streptocerca infestation 125.3
Microgastria (congenital) 750.7
Microgenia 524.06
Microgenitalia (congenital) 752.89
  penis 752.64
Microglioma (M9710/3)
  specified site — see Neoplasm, by site, malig-
    nant
  unspecified site 191.9
Microglossia (congenital) 750.16
Micrognathia, micrognathism (congenital)
  524.00
  mandibular 524.04
    alveolar 524.74
  maxillary 524.03
    alveolar 524.73
Microgyria (congenital) 742.2
Microinfarct, heart — see also Insufficiency,
  coronary 411.89
Microlithiasis, alveolar, pulmonary 516.2
Micromastia 611.82
Micromyelia (congenital) 742.59
Micropenis 752.64
Microphakia (congenital) 743.36
Microphthalmia (congenital) — see also Microph-
  thalmos 743.10
Microphthalmos (congenital) 743.10
  associated with eye and adnexal anomalies
    NEC 743.12
  due to toxoplasmosis (congenital) 771.2
  isolated 743.11
  simple 743.11
  syndrome 759.89
Micropsia 368.14
Microsporidiosis 136.8
Microsporon furfur infestation 111.0
Microsporosis — see also Dermatophytosis 110.9
  nigra 111.1
Microstomia (congenital) 744.84
Microthelia 757.6
Microthromboembolism — see Embolism
Microtia (congenital) (external ear) 744.23
Microtropia 378.34
Micturition
  disorder NEC 788.69
    psychogenic 306.53
  frequency 788.41
    psychogenic 306.53

Micturition — continued
  nocturnal 788.43
  painful 788.1
    psychogenic 306.53
Middle
  ear — see condition
  lobe (right) syndrome 518.0
Midplane — see condition
Miescher's disease 709.3
  cheilitis 351.8
  granulomatosis disciformis 709.3
Miescher-Leder syndrome or granulomatosis
  709.3
Mieten's syndrome 759.89
Migraine (idiopathic) 346.9 ☑

> *Note* — *The following fifth digit subclassifi-*
> *cation is for use with category 346:*
>
> 0 *without mention of intractable mi-*
>   *graine without mention of status mi-*
>   *grainosus*
>
> 1 *with intractable migraine, so stated,*
>   *without mention of status migrain-*
>   *osus*
>
> 2 *without mention of intractable mi-*
>   *graine with status migrainosus*
>
> 3 *with intractable migraine, so stated,*
>   *with status migrainosus*

  with aura (acute-onset) (without headache)
    (prolonged) (typical) 346.0 ☑
  without aura 346.1 ☑
    chronic 346.7 ☑
    transformed 346.7 ☑
  abdominal (syndrome) 346.2 ☑
  allergic (histamine) 346.2 ☑
  atypical 346.8 ☑
  basilar 346.0 ☑
  chronic without aura 346.7 ☑
  classic(al) 346.0 ☑
  common 346.1 ☑
  hemiplegic 346.3 ☑
    familial 346.3 ☑
    sporadic 346.3 ☑
  lower-half 339.00
  menstrual 346.4 ☑
  menstrually related 346.4 ☑
  ophthalmic 346.8 ☑
  ophthalmoplegic 346.2 ☑
  premenstrual 346.4 ☑
  pure menstrual 346.4 ☑
  retinal 346.0 ☑
  specified form NEC 346.8 ☑
  transformed without aura 346.7 ☑
  variant 346.2 ☑
Migrant, social V60.0
Migratory, migrating — see also condition
  person V60.0
  testis, congenital 752.52
Mikulicz's disease or syndrome (dryness of
  mouth, absent or decreased lacrimation)
  527.1
Milian atrophia blanche 701.3
Miliaria (crystallina) (rubra) (tropicalis) 705.1
  apocrine 705.82
Miliary — see condition
Milium — see also Cyst, sebaceous 706.2
  colloid 709.3
  eyelid 374.84
Milk
  crust 690.11
  excess secretion 676.6 ☑
  fever, female 672.0 ☑
  poisoning 988.8
  retention 676.2 ☑
  sickness 988.8
  spots 423.1
Milkers' nodes 051.1
Milk-leg (deep vessels) 671.4 ☑
  complicating pregnancy 671.3 ☑
  nonpuerperal 451.19
  puerperal, postpartum, childbirth 671.4 ☑
Milkman (-Looser) disease or syndrome (osteomalacia with pseudofractures) 268.2

☑ Additional Digit Required — Refer to the Tabular List for Digit Selection   ▽ Subterms under main terms may continue to next column or page

2010 ICD-9-CM   ▶◀ Revised Text   ● New Line   ▲ Revised Code   October 2009 • Volume 2 — 179

Milky urine — see also Chyluria 791.1
Millar's asthma (laryngismus stridulus) 478.75
Millard-Gubler-Foville paralysis 344.89
Millard-Gubler paralysis or syndrome 344.89
Miller-Dieker syndrome 758.33
Miller's disease (osteomalacia) 268.2
Miller Fisher's syndrome 357.0
Milles' syndrome (encephalocutaneous angiomatosis) 759.6
Mills' disease 335.29
Millstone makers' asthma or lung 502
Milroy's disease (chronic hereditary edema) 757.0
Miners' — see also condition
    asthma 500
    elbow 727.2
    knee 727.2
    lung 500
    nystagmus 300.89
    phthisis (see also Tuberculosis) 011.4 ☑
    tuberculosis (see also Tuberculosis) 011.4 ☑
Minkowski-Chauffard syndrome — see also Spherocytosis 282.0
Minor — see condition
Minor's disease 336.1
Minot's disease (hemorrhagic disease, newborn) 776.0
Minot-von Willebrand (-Jürgens) disease or syndrome (angiohemophilia) 286.4
Minus (and plus) hand (intrinsic) 736.09
Miosis (persistent) (pupil) 379.42
Mirizzi's syndrome (hepatic duct stenosis) — see also Obstruction, biliary 576.2
    with calculus, cholelithiasis, or stones — see Choledocholithiasis
Mirror writing 315.09
    secondary to organic lesion 784.69
Misadventure (prophylactic) (therapeutic) — see also Complications 999.9
    administration of insulin 962.3
    infusion — see Complications, infusion
    local applications (of fomentations, plasters, etc.) 999.9
        burn or scald — see Burn, by site
    medical care (early) (late) NEC 999.9
        adverse effect of drugs or chemicals — see Table of Drugs and Chemicals
        burn or scald — see Burn, by site
        radiation NEC 990
        radiotherapy NEC 990
    surgical procedure (early) (late) — see Complications, surgical procedure
    transfusion — see Complications, transfusion
    vaccination or other immunological procedure — see Complications, vaccination
Misanthropy 301.7
Miscarriage — see Abortion, spontaneous
Mischief, malicious, child — see also Disturbance, conduct 312.0 ☑
Misdirection
    aqueous 365.83
Mismanagement, feeding 783.3
Misplaced, misplacement
    kidney (see also Disease, renal) 593.0
        congenital 753.3
    organ or site, congenital NEC — see Malposition, congenital
Missed
    abortion 632
    delivery (at or near term) 656.4 ☑
    labor (at or near term) 656.4 ☑
Misshapen reconstructed breast 612.0
Missing — see also Absence
    teeth (acquired) 525.10
        congenital (see also Anodontia) 520.0
        due to
            caries 525.13
            extraction 525.10
            periodontal disease 525.12
            specified NEC 525.19
            trauma 525.11
    vertebrae (congenital) 756.13
Misuse of drugs NEC — see also Abuse, drug, nondependent 305.9 ☑
Mitchell's disease (erythromelalgia) 443.82

Mite(s)
    diarrhea 133.8
    grain (itch) 133.8
    hair follicle (itch) 133.8
    in sputum 133.8
Mitochondrial encephalopathy, lactic acidosis and stroke-like episodes (MELAS syndrome) 277.87
Mitochondrial neurogastrointestinal encephalopathy syndrome (MNGIE) 277.87
Mitral — see condition
Mittelschmerz 625.2
Mixed — see condition
Mljet disease (mal de Meleda) 757.39
Mobile, mobility
    cecum 751.4
    coccyx 733.99
    excessive — see Hypermobility
    gallbladder 751.69
    kidney 593.0
        congenital 753.3
    organ or site, congenital NEC — see Malposition, congenital
    spleen 289.59
Mobitz heart block (atrioventricular) 426.10
    type I (Wenckebach's) 426.13
    type II 426.12
Möbius'
    disease 346.2 ☑
    syndrome
        congenital oculofacial paralysis 352.6
        ophthalmoplegic migraine 346.2 ☑
Moeller(-Barlow) disease (infantile scurvy) 267
    glossitis 529.4
Mohr's syndrome (types I and II) 759.89
Mola destruens (M9100/1) 236.1
Molarization, premolars 520.2
Molar pregnancy 631
    hydatidiform (delivered) (undelivered) 630
Molding, head (during birth) — omit code
Mold(s) in vitreous 117.9
Mole (pigmented) (M8720/0) — see also Neoplasm, skin, benign
    blood 631
    Breus' 631
    cancerous (M8720/3) — see Melanoma
    carneous 631
    destructive (M9100/1) 236.1
    ectopic — see Pregnancy, ectopic
    fleshy 631
    hemorrhagic 631
    hydatid, hydatidiform (benign) (complicating pregnancy) (delivered) (undelivered) (see also Hydatidiform mole) 630
        invasive (M9100/1) 236.1
        malignant (M9100/1) 236.1
        previous, affecting management of pregnancy V23.1
    invasive (hydatidiform) (M9100/1) 236.1
    malignant
        meaning
            malignant hydatidiform mole (9100/1) 236.1
            melanoma (M8720/3) — see Melanoma
    nonpigmented (M8730/0) — see Neoplasm, skin, benign
    pregnancy NEC 631
    skin (M8720/0) — see Neoplasm, skin, benign
    tubal — see Pregnancy, tubal
    vesicular (see also Hydatidiform mole) 630
Molimen, molimina (menstrual) 625.4
Mollaret's meningitis 047.9
Mollities (cerebellar) (cerebral) 437.8
    ossium 268.2
Molluscum
    contagiosum 078.0
    epitheliale 078.0
    fibrosum (M8851/0) — see Lipoma, by site
    pendulum (M8851/0) — see Lipoma, by site
Mönckeberg's arteriosclerosis, degeneration, disease, or sclerosis — see also Arteriosclerosis, extremities 440.20
Monday fever 504
Monday morning dyspnea or asthma 504
Mondini's malformation (cochlea) 744.05

Mondor's disease (thrombophlebitis of breast) 451.89
Mongolian, mongolianism, mongolism, mongoloid 758.0
    spot 757.33
Monilethrix (congenital) 757.4
Monilia infestation — see Candidiasis
Moniliasis — see also Candidiasis
    neonatal 771.7
    vulvovaginitis 112.1
Monkeypox 059.01
Monoarthritis 716.60
    ankle 716.67
    arm 716.62
        lower (and wrist) 716.63
        upper (and elbow) 716.62
    foot (and ankle) 716.67
    forearm (and wrist) 716.63
    hand 716.64
    leg 716.66
        lower 716.66
        upper 716.65
    pelvic region (hip) (thigh) 716.65
    shoulder (region) 716.61
    specified site NEC 716.68
Monoblastic — see condition
Monochromatism (cone) (rod) 368.54
Monocytic — see condition
Monocytopenia 288.59
Monocytosis (symptomatic) 288.63
Monofixation syndrome 378.34
Monomania — see also Psychosis 298.9
Mononeuritis 355.9
    cranial nerve — see Disorder, nerve, cranial
    femoral nerve 355.2
    lateral
        cutaneous nerve of thigh 355.1
        popliteal nerve 355.3
    lower limb 355.8
        specified nerve NEC 355.79
    medial popliteal nerve 355.4
    median nerve 354.1
    multiplex 354.5
    plantar nerve 355.6
    posterior tibial nerve 355.5
    radial nerve 354.3
    sciatic nerve 355.0
    ulnar nerve 354.2
    upper limb 354.9
        specified nerve NEC 354.8
    vestibular 388.5
Mononeuropathy — see also Mononeuritis 355.9
    diabetic NEC 250.6 ☑ [355.9]
        due to secondary diabetes 249.6 ☑ [355.9]
        lower limb 250.6 ☑ [355.8]
            due to secondary diabetes 249.6 ☑ [355.8]
        upper limb 250.6 ☑ [354.9]
            due to secondary diabetes 249.6 ☑ [354.9]
    iliohypogastric nerve 355.79
    ilioinguinal nerve 355.79
    obturator nerve 355.79
    saphenous nerve 355.79
Mononucleosis, infectious 075
    with hepatitis 075 [573.1]
Monoplegia 344.5
    brain (current episode) (see also Paralysis, brain) 437.8
        fetus or newborn 767.8
    cerebral (current episode) (see also Paralysis, brain) 437.8
    congenital or infantile (cerebral) (spastic) (spinal) 343.3
    embolic (current) (see also Embolism, brain) 434.1 ☑
        late effect — see Late effect(s) (of) cerebrovascular disease
    infantile (cerebral) (spastic) (spinal) 343.3
    lower limb 344.30
        affecting
            dominant side 344.31
            nondominant side 344.32
        due to late effect of cerebrovascular accident — see Late effect(s) (of) cerebrovascular accident

Monoplegia — continued
    newborn 767.8
    psychogenic 306.0
        specified as conversion reaction 300.11
    thrombotic (current) (see also Thrombosis, brain) 434.0 ☑
        late effect — see Late effect(s) (of) cerebrovascular disease
    transient 781.4
    upper limb 344.40
        affecting
            dominant side 344.41
            nondominant side 344.42
        due to late effect of cerebrovascular accident — see Late effect(s) (of) cerebrovascular accident
Monorchism, monorchidism 752.89
Monteggia's fracture (closed) 813.03
    open 813.13
Mood swings
    brief compensatory 296.99
    rebound 296.99
Mooren's ulcer (cornea) 370.07
Moore's syndrome — see also Epilepsy 345.5 ☑
Mooser bodies 081.0
Mooser-Neill reaction 081.0
Moral
    deficiency 301.7
    imbecility 301.7
Morax-Axenfeld conjunctivitis 372.03
Morbilli — see also Measles 055.9
Morbus
    anglicus, anglorum 268.0
    Beigel 111.2
    caducus (see also Epilepsy) 345.9 ☑
    caeruleus 746.89
    celiacus 579.0
    comitialis (see also Epilepsy) 345.9 ☑
    cordis (see also Disease, heart)
        valvulorum — see Endocarditis
    coxae 719.95
        tuberculous (see also Tuberculosis) 015.1 ☑
    hemorrhagicus neonatorum 776.0
    maculosus neonatorum 772.6
    renum 593.0
    senilis (see also Osteoarthrosis) 715.9 ☑
Morel-Kraepelin disease — see also Schizophrenia 295.9 ☑
Morel-Moore syndrome (hyperostosis frontalis interna) 733.3
Morel-Morgagni syndrome (hyperostosis frontalis interna) 733.3
Morgagni
    cyst, organ, hydatid, or appendage 752.89
        fallopian tube 752.11
    disease or syndrome (hyperostosis frontalis interna) 733.3
Morgagni-Adams-Stokes syndrome (syncope with heart block) 426.9
Morgagni-Stewart-Morel syndrome (hyperostosis frontalis interna) 733.3
Moria — see also Psychosis 298.9
Morning sickness 643.0 ☑
Moron 317
Morphea (guttate) (linear) 701.0
Morphine dependence — see also Dependence 304.0 ☑
Morphinism — see also Dependence 304.0 ☑
Morphinomania — see also Dependence 304.0 ☑
Morphoea 701.0
Morquio (-Brailsford) (-Ullrich) disease or syndrome (mucopolysaccharidosis IV) 277.5
    kyphosis 277.5
Morris syndrome (testicular feminization) 259.51
Morsus humanus (open wound) — see also Wound, open, by site
    skin surface intact — see Contusion
Mortification (dry) (moist) — see also Gangrene 785.4
Morton's
    disease 355.6
    foot 355.6
    metatarsalgia (syndrome) 355.6

Morton's — *continued*
neuralgia 355.6
neuroma 355.6
syndrome (metatarsalgia) (neuralgia) 355.6
toe 355.6
Morvan's disease 336.0
Mosaicism, mosaic (chromosomal) 758.9
autosomal 758.5
sex 758.81
Moschcowitz's syndrome (thrombotic thrombocytopenic purpura) 446.6
Mother yaw 102.0
Motion sickness (from travel, any vehicle) (from roundabouts or swings) 994.6
Mottled teeth (enamel) (endemic) (nonendemic) 520.3
Mottling enamel (endemic) (nonendemic) (teeth) 520.3
Mouchet's disease 732.5
Mould(s) (in vitreous) 117.9
Moulders'
bronchitis 502
tuberculosis (*see also* Tuberculosis) 011.4 ☑
Mounier-Kuhn syndrome 748.3
with
acute exacerbation 494.1
bronchiectasis 494.0
with (acute) exacerbation 494.1
acquired 519.19
with bronchiectasis 494.0
with (acute) exacerbation 494.1
Mountain
fever — *see* Fever, mountain
sickness 993.2
with polycythemia, acquired 289.0
acute 289.0
tick fever 066.1
Mouse, joint — *see also* Loose, body, joint 718.1 ☑
knee 717.6
Mouth — *see* condition
Movable
coccyx 724.71
kidney (*see also* Disease, renal) 593.0
congenital 753.3
organ or site, congenital NEC — *see* Malposition, congenital
spleen 289.59
Movement
abnormal (dystonic) (involuntary) 781.0
decreased fetal 655.7 ☑
paradoxical facial 374.43
Moya Moya disease 437.5
Mozart's ear 744.29
MRSA (methicillin-resistant staphylococcus aureus) 041.12
colonization V02.54
personal history of V12.04
MSSA (methicillin susceptible staphylococcus aureus) 041.11
colonization V02.53
Mucha's disease (acute parapsoriasis varioliformis) 696.2
Mucha-Haberman syndrome (acute parapsoriasis varioliformis) 696.2
Mu-chain disease 273.2
Mucinosis (cutaneous) (papular) 701.8
Mucocele
appendix 543.9
buccal cavity 528.9
gallbladder (*see also* Disease, gallbladder) 575.3
lacrimal sac 375.43
orbit (eye) 376.81
salivary gland (any) 527.6
sinus (accessory) (nasal) 478.19
turbinate (bone) (middle) (nasal) 478.19
uterus 621.8
Mucocutaneous lymph node syndrome (acute) (febrile) (infantile) 446.1
Mucoenteritis 564.9
Mucolipidosis I, II, III 272.7
Mucopolysaccharidosis (types 1-6) 277.5
cardiopathy 277.5 *[425.7]*
Mucormycosis (lung) 117.7

Mucosa associated lymphoid tissue (MALT) 200.3 ☑
Mucositis — *see also* Inflammation, by site 528.00
cervix (ulcerative) 616.81
due to
antineoplastic therapy (ulcerative) 528.01
other drugs (ulcerative) 528.02
specified NEC 528.09
gastrointestinal (ulcerative) 538
nasal (ulcerative) 478.11
necroticans agranulocytica (*see also* Agranulocytosis) 288.09
ulcerative 528.00
vagina (ulcerative) 616.81
vulva (ulcerative) 616.81
Mucous — *see also* condition
patches (syphilitic) 091.3
congenital 090.0
Mucoviscidosis 277.00
with meconium obstruction 277.01
Mucus
asphyxia or suffocation (*see also* Asphyxia, mucus) 933.1
newborn 770.18
in stool 792.1
plug (*see also* Asphyxia, mucus) 933.1
aspiration, of newborn 770.17
tracheobronchial 519.19
newborn 770.18
Muguet 112.0
Mulberry molars 090.5
Müllerian mixed tumor (M8950/3) — *see* Neoplasm, by site, malignant
Multicystic kidney 753.19
Multilobed placenta — *see* Placenta, abnormal
Multinodular prostate 600.10
with
urinary
obstruction 600.11
retention 600.11
Multiparity V61.5
affecting
fetus or newborn 763.89
management of
labor and delivery 659.4 ☑
pregnancy V23.3
requiring contraceptive management (*see also* Contraception) V25.9
Multipartita placenta — *see* Placenta, abnormal
Multiple, multiplex — *see also* condition
birth
affecting fetus or newborn 761.5
healthy liveborn — *see* Newborn, multiple
digits (congenital) 755.00
fingers 755.01
toes 755.02
organ or site NEC — *see* Accessory
personality 300.14
renal arteries 747.62
Mumps 072.9
with complication 072.8
specified type NEC 072.79
encephalitis 072.2
hepatitis 072.71
meningitis (aseptic) 072.1
meningoencephalitis 072.2
oophoritis 072.79
orchitis 072.0
pancreatitis 072.3
polyneuropathy 072.72
vaccination, prophylactic (against) V04.6
Mumu — *see also* Infestation, filarial 125.9
Münchausen syndrome 301.51
Münchmeyer's disease or syndrome (exostosis luxurians) 728.11
Mural — *see also* condition
Murmur (cardiac) (heart) (nonorganic) (organic) 785.2
abdominal 787.5
aortic (valve) (*see also* Endocarditis, aortic) 424.1
benign — *omit code*
cardiorespiratory 785.2
diastolic — *see* condition
Flint (*see also* Endocarditis, aortic) 424.1

Murmur — *continued*
functional — *omit code*
Graham Steell (pulmonic regurgitation) (*see also* Endocarditis, pulmonary) 424.3
innocent — *omit code*
insignificant — *omit code*
midsystolic 785.2
mitral (valve) — *see* Stenosis, mitral
physiologic — *see* condition
presystolic, mitral — *see* Insufficiency, mitral
pulmonic (valve) (*see also* Endocarditis, pulmonary) 424.3
Still's (vibratory) — *omit code*
systolic (valvular) — *see* condition
tricuspid (valve) — *see* Endocarditis, tricuspid
undiagnosed 785.2
valvular — *see* condition
vibratory — *omit code*
Murri's disease (intermittent hemoglobinuria) 283.2
Muscae volitantes 379.24
Muscle, muscular — *see* condition
Musculoneuralgia 729.1
Mushrooming hip 718.95
Mushroom workers' (pickers') lung 495.5
Mutation
factor V leiden 289.81
prothrombin gene 289.81
Mutism — *see also* Aphasia 784.3
akinetic 784.3
deaf (acquired) (congenital) 389.7
hysterical 300.11
selective (elective) 313.23
adjustment reaction 309.83
Myà's disease (congenital dilation, colon) 751.3
Myalgia (intercostal) 729.1
eosinophilia syndrome 710.5
epidemic 074.1
cervical 078.89
psychogenic 307.89
traumatic NEC 959.9
Myasthenia 358.00
cordis — *see* Failure, heart
gravis 358.00
with exacerbation (acute) 358.01
in crisis 358.01
neonatal 775.2
pseudoparalytica 358.00
stomach 536.8
psychogenic 306.4
syndrome
in
botulism 005.1 *[358.1]*
diabetes mellitus 250.6 ☑ *[358.1]*
due to secondary diabetes 249.6 ☑ *[358.1]*
hypothyroidism (*see also* Hypothyroidism) 244.9 *[358.1]*
malignant neoplasm NEC 199.1 *[358.1]*
pernicious anemia 281.0 *[358.1]*
thyrotoxicosis (*see also* Thyrotoxicosis) 242.9 ☑ *[358.1]*
Myasthenic 728.87
Mycelium infection NEC 117.9
Mycetismus 988.1
Mycetoma (actinomycotic) 039.9
bone 039.8
mycotic 117.4
foot 039.4
mycotic 117.4
madurae 039.9
mycotic 117.4
maduromycotic 039.9
mycotic 117.4
mycotic 117.4
nocardial 039.9
Mycobacteriosis — *see* Mycobacterium
Mycobacterium, mycobacterial (infection) 031.9
acid-fast (bacilli) 031.9
anonymous (*see also* Mycobacterium, atypical) 031.9
atypical (acid-fast bacilli) 031.9
cutaneous 031.1
pulmonary 031.0

Mycobacterium, mycobacterial — *continued*
atypical — *continued*
pulmonary — *continued*
tuberculous (*see also* Tuberculosis, pulmonary) 011.9 ☑
specified site NEC 031.8
avium 031.0
intracellulare complex bacteremia (MAC) 031.2
balnei 031.1
Battey 031.0
cutaneous 031.1
disseminated 031.2
avium-intracellulare complex (DMAC) 031.2
fortuitum 031.0
intracellulare (battey bacillus) 031.0
kakerifu 031.8
kansasii 031.0
kasongo 031.8
leprae — *see* Leprosy
luciflavum 031.0
marinum 031.1
pulmonary 031.0
tuberculous (*see also* Tuberculosis, pulmonary) 011.9 ☑
scrofulaceum 031.1
tuberculosis (human, bovine) (*see also* Tuberculosis)
avian type 031.0
ulcerans 031.1
xenopi 031.0
Mycosis, mycotic 117.9
cutaneous NEC 111.9
ear 111.8 *[380.15]*
fungoides (M9700/3) 202.1 ☑
mouth 112.0
pharynx 117.9
skin NEC 111.9
stomatitis 112.0
systemic NEC 117.9
tonsil 117.9
vagina, vaginitis 112.1
Mydriasis (persistent) (pupil) 379.43
Myelatelia 742.59
Myelinoclasis, perivascular, acute (postinfectious) NEC 136.9 *[323.61]*
postimmunization or postvaccinal 323.51
Myelinosis, central pontine 341.8
Myelitis (ascending) (cerebellar) (childhood) (chronic) (descending) (diffuse) (disseminated) (pressure) (progressive) (spinal cord) (subacute) — *see also* Encephalitis 323.9
acute (transverse) 341.20
idiopathic 341.22
in conditions classified elsewhere 341.21
due to
infection classified elsewhere 136.9 *[323.42]*
specified cause NEC 323.82
vaccination (any) 323.52
viral diseases classified elsewhere 323.02
herpes simplex 054.74
herpes zoster 053.14
late effect — *see* category 326
optic neuritis in 341.0
postchickenpox 052.2
postimmunization 323.52
postinfectious 136.9 *[323.63]*
postvaccinal 323.52
postvaricella 052.2
syphilitic (transverse) 094.89
toxic 989.9 *[323.72]*
transverse 323.82
acute 341.20
idiopathic 341.22
in conditions classified elsewhere 341.21
idiopathic 341.22
tuberculous (*see also* Tuberculosis) 013.6 ☑
virus 049.9
Myeloblastic — *see* condition
Myelocele — *see also* Spina bifida 741.9 ☑
with hydrocephalus 741.0 ☑
Myelocystocele — *see also* Spina bifida 741.9 ☑

☑ Additional Digit Required — Refer to the Tabular List for Digit Selection   ⬇ Subterms under main terms may continue to next column or page

2010 ICD-9-CM   ▶◀ Revised Text   ● New Line   ▲ Revised Code   Volume 2 — 181

Myelocytic — see condition
Myelocytoma 205.1 ☑
Myelodysplasia (spinal cord) 742.59
  meaning myelodysplastic syndrome — see
    Syndrome, myelodysplastic
Myeloencephalitis — see Encephalitis
Myelofibrosis 289.83
  with myeloid metaplasia 238.76
  idiopathic (chronic) 238.76
  megakaryocytic 238.79
  primary 238.76
  secondary 289.83
Myelogenous — see condition
Myeloid — see condition
Myelokathexis 288.09
Myeloleukodystrophy 330.0
Myelolipoma (M8870/0) — see Neoplasm, by
  site, benign
Myeloma (multiple) (plasma cell) (plasmacytic)
  (M9730/3) 203.0 ☑
  monostotic (M9731/1) 238.6
  solitary (M9731/1) 238.6
Myelomalacia 336.8
Myelomata, multiple (M9730/3) 203.0 ☑
Myelomatosis (M9730/3) 203.0 ☑
Myelomeningitis — see Meningoencephalitis
Myelomeningocele (spinal cord) — see also
  Spina bifida 741.9 ☑
  fetal, causing fetopelvic disproportion
    653.7 ☑
Myelo-osteo-musculodysplasia hereditaria
  756.89
Myelopathic — see condition
Myelopathy (spinal cord) 336.9
  cervical 721.1
  diabetic 250.6 ☑ [336.3]
    due to secondary diabetes 249.6 ☑ [336.3]
  drug-induced 336.8
  due to or with
    carbon tetrachloride 987.8 [323.72]
    degeneration or displacement, interverte-
      bral disc 722.70
      cervical, cervicothoracic 722.71
      lumbar, lumbosacral 722.73
      thoracic, thoracolumbar 722.72
    hydroxyquinoline derivatives 961.3 [323.72]
    infection — see Encephalitis
    intervertebral disc disorder 722.70
      cervical, cervicothoracic 722.71
      lumbar, lumbosacral 722.73
      thoracic, thoracolumbar 722.72
    lead 984.9 [323.72]
    mercury 985.0 [323.72]
    neoplastic disease (see also Neoplasm, by
      site) 239.9 [336.3]
    pernicious anemia 281.0 [336.3]
    spondylosis 721.91
      cervical 721.1
      lumbar, lumbosacral 721.42
      thoracic 721.41
    thallium 985.8 [323.72]
  lumbar, lumbosacral 721.42
  necrotic (subacute) 336.1
  radiation-induced 336.8
  spondylogenic NEC 721.91
    cervical 721.1
    lumbar, lumbosacral 721.42
    thoracic 721.41
  thoracic 721.41
  toxic NEC 989.9 [323.72]
  transverse (see also Myelitis) 323.82
  vascular 336.1
Myelophthisis 284.2
Myeloproliferative disease (M9960/1) 238.79
Myeloradiculitis — see also Polyneuropathy
  357.0
Myeloradiculodysplasia (spinal) 742.59
Myelosarcoma (M9930/3) 205.3 ☑
Myelosclerosis 289.89
  with myeloid metaplasia (M9961/1) 238.76
  disseminated, of nervous system 340
  megakaryocytic (M9961/1) 238.79
Myelosis (M9860/3) — see also Leukemia,
  myeloid 205.9 ☑
  acute (M9861/3) 205.0 ☑
  aleukemic (M9864/3) 205.8 ☑

Myelosis — see also Leukemia, myeloid —
  continued
  chronic (M9863/3) 205.1 ☑
  erythremic (M9840/3) 207.0 ☑
    acute (M9841/3) 207.0 ☑
  megakaryocytic (M9920/3) 207.2 ☑
  nonleukemic (chronic) 288.8
  subacute (M9862/3) 205.2 ☑
Myesthenia — see Myasthenia
Myiasis (cavernous) 134.0
  orbit 134.0 [376.13]
Myoadenoma, prostate 600.20
  with
    other lower urinary tract symptoms (LUTS)
      600.21
    urinary
      obstruction 600.21
      retention 600.21
Myoblastoma
  granular cell (M9580/0) (see also Neoplasm,
    connective tissue, benign)
    malignant (M9580/3) — see Neoplasm,
      connective tissue, malignant
  tongue (M9580/0) 210.1
Myocardial — see condition
Myocardiopathy (congestive) (constrictive) (familial) (hypertrophic nonobstructive) (idiopathic) (infiltrative) (obstructive) (primary)
  (restrictive) (sporadic) 425.4
  alcoholic 425.5
  amyloid 277.39 [425.7]
  beriberi 265.0 [425.7]
  cobalt-beer 425.5
  due to
    amyloidosis 277.39 [425.7]
    beriberi 265.0 [425.7]
    cardiac glycogenosis 271.0 [425.7]
    Chagas' disease 086.0
    Friedreich's ataxia 334.0 [425.8]
    influenza 487.8 [425.8]
    mucopolysaccharidosis 277.5 [425.7]
    myotonia atrophica 359.21 [425.8]
    progressive muscular dystrophy
      359.1 [425.8]
    sarcoidosis 135 [425.8]
  glycogen storage 271.0 [425.7]
  hypertrophic obstructive 425.1
  metabolic NEC 277.9 [425.7]
  nutritional 269.9 [425.7]
  obscure (African) 425.2
  peripartum 674.5 ☑
  postpartum 674.5 ☑
  secondary 425.9
  thyrotoxic (see also Thyrotoxicosis)
    242.9 ☑ [425.7]
  toxic NEC 425.9
Myocarditis (fibroid) (interstitial) (old) (progressive) (senile) (with arteriosclerosis) 429.0
  with
    rheumatic fever (conditions classifiable to
      390) 398.0
      active (see also Myocarditis, acute,
        rheumatic) 391.2
      inactive or quiescent (with chorea)
        398.0
  active (nonrheumatic) 422.90
    rheumatic 391.2
      with chorea (acute) (rheumatic)
        (Sydenham's) 392.0
  acute or subacute (interstitial) 422.90
    due to Streptococcus (beta-hemolytic)
      391.2
    idiopathic 422.91
    rheumatic 391.2
      with chorea (acute) (rheumatic)
        (Sydenham's) 392.0
    specified type NEC 422.99
  aseptic of newborn 074.23
  bacterial (acute) 422.92
  chagasic 086.0
  chronic (interstitial) 429.0
  congenital 746.89
  constrictive 425.4
  Coxsackie (virus) 074.23
  diphtheritic 032.82

Myocarditis — continued
  due to or in
    Coxsackie (virus) 074.23
    diphtheria 032.82
    epidemic louse-borne typhus 080 [422.0]
    influenza 487.8 [422.0]
    Lyme disease 088.81 [422.0]
    scarlet fever 034.1 [422.0]
    toxoplasmosis (acquired) 130.3
    tuberculosis (see also Tuberculosis)
      017.9 ☑ [422.0]
    typhoid 002.0 [422.0]
    typhus NEC 081.9 [422.0]
  eosinophilic 422.91
  epidemic of newborn 074.23
  Fiedler's (acute) (isolated) (subacute) 422.91
  giant cell (acute) (subacute) 422.91
  gonococcal 098.85
  granulomatous (idiopathic) (isolated) (nonspe-
    cific) 422.91
  hypertensive (see also Hypertension, heart)
    402.90
  idiopathic 422.91
    granulomatous 422.91
  infective 422.92
  influenzal 487.8 [422.0]
  isolated (diffuse) (granulomatous) 422.91
  malignant 422.99
  meningococcal 036.43
  nonrheumatic, active 422.90
  parenchymatous 422.90
  pneumococcal (acute) (subacute) 422.92
  rheumatic (chronic) (inactive) (with chorea)
    398.0
    active or acute 391.2
      with chorea (acute) (rheumatic)
        (Sydenham's) 392.0
  septic 422.92
  specific (giant cell) (productive) 422.91
  staphylococcal (acute) (subacute) 422.92
  suppurative 422.92
  syphilitic (chronic) 093.82
  toxic 422.93
    rheumatic (see also Myocarditis, acute
      rheumatic) 391.2
  tuberculous (see also Tuberculosis)
    017.9 ☑ [422.0]
  typhoid 002.0 [422.0]
  valvular — see Endocarditis
  viral, except Coxsackie 422.91
    Coxsackie 074.23
    of newborn (Coxsackie) 074.23
Myocardium, myocardial — see condition
Myocardosis — see also Cardiomyopathy 425.4
Myoclonia (essential) 333.2
  epileptica 345.1 ☑ ▲
  Friedrich's 333.2
  massive 333.2
Myoclonic
  epilepsy, familial (progressive) 345.1 ☑ ▲
  jerks 333.2
Myoclonus (familial essential) (multifocal) (simplex) 333.2
  with epilepsy and with ragged red fibers
    (MERRF syndrome) 277.87
  facial 351.8
  massive (infantile) 333.2
  palatal 333.2 ●
  pharyngeal 333.2 ▲
Myocytolysis 429.1 ●
Myodiastasis 728.84
Myoendocarditis — see also Endocarditis
  acute or subacute 421.9
Myoepithelioma (M8982/0) — see Neoplasm,
  by site, benign
Myofascitis (acute) 729.1
  low back 724.2
Myofibroma (M8890/0) — see also Neoplasm,
  connective tissue, benign
  uterus (cervix) (corpus) (see also Leiomyoma)
    218.9
Myofibromatosis
  infantile 759.89
Myofibrosis 728.2
  heart (see also Myocarditis) 429.0
  humeroscapular region 726.2

Myofibrosis — continued
  scapulohumeral 726.2
Myofibrositis — see also Myositis 729.1
  scapulohumeral 726.2
Myogelosis (occupational) 728.89
Myoglobinuria 791.3
Myoglobulinuria, primary 791.3
Myokymia — see also Myoclonus
  facial 351.8
Myolipoma (M8860/0)
  specified site — see Neoplasm, connective
    tissue, benign
  unspecified site 223.0
Myoma (M8895/0) — see also Neoplasm, connective tissue, benign
  cervix (stump) (uterus) (see also Leiomyoma)
    218.9
  malignant (M8895/3) — see Neoplasm, con-
    nective tissue, malignant
  prostate 600.20
    with
      other lower urinary tract symptoms
        (LUTS) 600.21
      urinary
        obstruction 600.21
        retention 600.21
  uterus (cervix) (corpus) (see also Leiomyoma)
    218.9
    in pregnancy or childbirth 654.1 ☑
      affecting fetus or newborn 763.89
      causing obstructed labor 660.2 ☑
        affecting fetus or newborn 763.1
Myomalacia 728.9
  cordis, heart (see also Degeneration, myocar-
    dial) 429.1
Myometritis — see also Endometritis 615.9
Myometrium — see condition
Myonecrosis, clostridial 040.0
Myopathy 359.9
  alcoholic 359.4
  amyloid 277.39 [359.6]
  benign, congenital 359.0
  central core 359.0
  centronuclear 359.0
  congenital (benign) 359.0
  critical illness 359.81
  distal 359.1
  due to drugs 359.4
  endocrine 259.9 [359.5]
    specified type NEC 259.8 [359.5]
  extraocular muscles 376.82
  facioscapulohumeral 359.1
  in
    Addison's disease 255.41 [359.5]
    amyloidosis 277.39 [359.6]
    cretinism 243 [359.5]
    Cushing's syndrome 255.0 [359.5]
    disseminated lupus erythematosus
      710.0 [359.6]
    giant cell arteritis 446.5 [359.6]
    hyperadrenocorticism NEC 255.3 [359.5]
    hyperparathyroidism 252.01 [359.5]
    hypopituitarism 253.2 [359.5]
    hypothyroidism (see also Hypothyroidism)
      244.9 [359.5]
    malignant neoplasm NEC (M8000/3) 199.1
      [359.6]
    myxedema (see also Myxedema)
      244.9 [359.5]
    polyarteritis nodosa 446.0 [359.6]
    rheumatoid arthritis 714.0 [359.6]
    sarcoidosis 135 [359.6]
    scleroderma 710.1 [359.6]
    Sjögren's disease 710.2 [359.6]
    thyrotoxicosis (see also Thyrotoxicosis)
      242.9 ☑ [359.5]
  inflammatory 359.79 ▲
    immune NEC 359.79 ●
    specified NEC 359.79 ●
  intensive care (ICU) 359.81
  limb-girdle 359.1
  myotubular 359.0
  necrotizing, acute 359.81
  nemaline 359.0
  ocular 359.1
  oculopharyngeal 359.1

Myopathy — *continued*
of critical illness 359.81
primary 359.89
progressive NEC 359.89
proximal myotonic (PROMM) 359.21
quadriplegic, acute 359.81
rod body 359.0
scapulohumeral 359.1
specified type NEC 359.89
toxic 359.4
Myopericarditis — *see also* Pericarditis 423.9
Myopia (axial) (congenital) (increased curvature or refraction, nucleus of lens) 367.1
degenerative, malignant 360.21
malignant 360.21
progressive high (degenerative) 360.21
Myosarcoma (M8895/3) — *see* Neoplasm, connective tissue, malignant
Myosis (persistent) 379.42
stromal (endolymphatic) (M8931/1) 236.0
Myositis 729.1
clostridial 040.0
due to posture 729.1
epidemic 074.1
fibrosa or fibrous (chronic) 728.2
Volkmann's (complicating trauma) 958.6
inclusion body (IBM) 359.71   ●
infective 728.0
interstitial 728.81
multiple — *see* Polymyositis
occupational 729.1
orbital, chronic 376.12
ossificans 728.12
circumscribed 728.12
progressive 728.11
traumatic 728.12
progressive fibrosing 728.11
purulent 728.0
rheumatic 729.1
rheumatoid 729.1
suppurative 728.0
syphilitic 095.6
traumatic (old) 729.1
Myospasia impulsiva 307.23
Myotonia (acquisita) (intermittens) 728.85
atrophica 359.21
congenita 359.22
acetazolamide responsive 359.22
dominant form 359.22
recessive form 359.22
drug-induced 359.24
dystrophica 359.21
fluctuans 359.29
levior 359.22   ▲
permanens 359.29
Myotonic pupil 379.46
Myriapodiasis 134.1
Myringitis
with otitis media — *see* Otitis media
acute 384.00
specified type NEC 384.09
bullosa hemorrhagica 384.01
bullous 384.01
chronic 384.1
Mysophobia 300.29
Mytilotoxism 988.0
Myxadenitis labialis 528.5
Myxedema (adult) (idiocy) (infantile) (juvenile) (thyroid gland) — *see also* Hypothyroidism 244.9
circumscribed 242.9 ☑
congenital 243
cutis 701.8
localized (pretibial) 242.9 ☑
madness (acute) 293.0
subacute 293.1
papular 701.8
pituitary 244.8
postpartum 674.8 ☑
pretibial 242.9 ☑
primary 244.9
Myxochondrosarcoma (M9220/3) — *see* Neoplasm, cartilage, malignant
Myxofibroma (M8811/0) — *see also* Neoplasm, connective tissue, benign
odontogenic (M9320/0) 213.1

Myxofibroma — *see also* Neoplasm, connective tissue, benign — *continued*
odontogenic — *continued*
upper jaw (bone) 213.0
Myxofibrosarcoma (M8811/3) — *see* Neoplasm, connective tissue, malignant
Myxolipoma (M8852/0) — *see also* Lipoma, by site 214.9
Myxoliposarcoma (M8852/3) — *see* Neoplasm, connective tissue, malignant
Myxoma (M8840/0) — *see also* Neoplasm, connective tissue, benign
odontogenic (M9320/0) 213.1
upper jaw (bone) 213.0
Myxosarcoma (M8840/3) — *see* Neoplasm, connective tissue, malignant

N

Naegeli's
disease (hereditary hemorrhagic thrombasthenia) 287.1
leukemia, monocytic (M9863/3) 205.1 ☑
syndrome (incontinentia pigmenti) 757.33
Naffziger's syndrome 353.0
Naga sore — *see also* Ulcer, skin 707.9
Nägele's pelvis 738.6
with disproportion (fetopelvic) 653.0 ☑
affecting fetus or newborn 763.1
causing obstructed labor 660.1 ☑
affecting fetus or newborn 763.1
Nager-de Reynier syndrome (dysostosis mandibularis) 756.0
Nail — *see also* condition
biting 307.9
patella syndrome (hereditary osteoonychodysplasia) 756.89
Nanism, nanosomia — *see also* Dwarfism 259.4
hypophyseal 253.3
pituitary 253.3
renis, renalis 588.0
Nanukayami 100.89
Napkin rash 691.0
Narcissism 301.81
Narcolepsy 347.00
with cataplexy 347.01
in conditions classified elsewhere 347.10
with cataplexy 347.11
Narcosis
carbon dioxide (respiratory) 786.09
due to drug
correct substance properly administered 780.09
overdose or wrong substance given or taken 977.9
specified drug — *see* Table of Drugs and Chemicals
Narcotism (chronic) — *see also* Dependence 304.9 ☑
acute
correct substance properly administered 349.82
overdose or wrong substance given or taken 967.8
specified drug — *see* Table of Drugs and Chemicals
NARP (ataxia and retinitis pigmentosa) 277.87
Narrow
anterior chamber angle 365.02
pelvis (inlet) (outlet) — *see* Contraction, pelvis
Narrowing
artery NEC 447.1
auditory, internal 433.8 ☑
basilar 433.0 ☑
with other precerebral artery 433.3 ☑
bilateral 433.3 ☑
carotid 433.1 ☑
with other precerebral artery 433.3 ☑
bilateral 433.3 ☑
cerebellar 433.8 ☑
choroidal 433.8 ☑
communicating posterior 433.8 ☑
coronary (*see also* Arteriosclerosis, coronary)
congenital 746.85
due to syphilis 090.5

Narrowing — *continued*
artery — *continued*
hypophyseal 433.8 ☑
pontine 433.8 ☑
precerebral NEC 433.9 ☑
multiple or bilateral 433.3 ☑
specified NEC 433.8 ☑
vertebral 433.2 ☑
with other precerebral artery 433.3 ☑
bilateral 433.3 ☑
auditory canal (external) (*see also* Stricture, ear canal, acquired) 380.50
cerebral arteries 437.0
cicatricial — *see* Cicatrix
congenital — *see* Anomaly, congenital
coronary artery — *see* Narrowing, artery, coronary
ear, middle 385.22
Eustachian tube (*see also* Obstruction, Eustachian tube) 381.60
eyelid 374.46
congenital 743.62
intervertebral disc or space NEC — *see* Degeneration, intervertebral disc
joint space, hip 719.85
larynx 478.74
lids 374.46
congenital 743.62
mesenteric artery (with gangrene) 557.0
palate 524.89
palpebral fissure 374.46
retinal artery 362.13
ureter 593.3
urethra (*see also* Stricture, urethra) 598.9
Narrowness, abnormal, eyelid 743.62
Nasal — *see* condition
Nasolacrimal — *see* condition
Nasopharyngeal — *see also* condition
bursa 478.29
pituitary gland 759.2
torticollis 723.5
Nasopharyngitis (acute) (infective) (subacute) 460
chronic 472.2
due to external agent — *see* Condition, respiratory, chronic, due to
due to external agent — *see* Condition, respiratory, due to
septic 034.0
streptococcal 034.0
suppurative (chronic) 472.2
ulcerative (chronic) 472.2
Nasopharynx, nasopharyngeal — *see* condition
Natal tooth, teeth 520.6
Nausea — *see also* Vomiting 787.02
with vomiting 787.01
epidemic 078.82
gravidarum — *see* Hyperemesis, gravidarum
marina 994.6
Navel — *see* condition
Neapolitan fever — *see also* Brucellosis 023.9
Near drowning 994.1
Nearsightedness 367.1
Near-syncope 780.2
Nebécourt's syndrome 253.3
Nebula, cornea (eye) 371.01
congenital 743.43
interfering with vision 743.42
Necator americanus infestation 126.1
Necatoriasis 126.1
Neck — *see* condition
Necrencephalus — *see also* Softening, brain 437.8
Necrobacillosis 040.3
Necrobiosis 799.89
brain or cerebral (*see also* Softening, brain) 437.8
lipoidica 709.3
diabeticorum 250.8 ☑ [709.3]
due to secondary diabetes 249.8 ☑ [709.3]
Necrodermolysis 695.15
Necrolysis, toxic epidermal 695.15
due to drug
correct substance properly administered 695.15

Necrolysis, toxic epidermal — *continued*
due to drug — *continued*
overdose or wrong substance given or taken 977.9
specified drug — *see* Table of Drugs and Chemicals
Stevens-Johnson syndrome overlap (SJS-TEN overlap syndrome) 695.14
Necrophilia 302.89
Necrosis, necrotic
adrenal (capsule) (gland) 255.8
antrum, nasal sinus 478.19
aorta (hyaline) (*see also* Aneurysm, aorta) 441.9
cystic medial 441.00
abdominal 441.02
thoracic 441.01
thoracoabdominal 441.03
ruptured 441.5
arteritis 446.0
artery 447.5
aseptic, bone 733.40
femur (head) (neck) 733.42
medial condyle 733.43
humoral head 733.41
jaw 733.45
medial femoral condyle 733.43
specific site NEC 733.49
talus 733.44
avascular, bone NEC (*see also* Necrosis, aseptic, bone) 733.40
bladder (aseptic) (sphincter) 596.8
bone (*see also* Osteomyelitis) 730.1 ☑
acute 730.0 ☑
aseptic or avascular 733.40
femur (head) (neck) 733.42
medial condyle 733.43
humoral head 733.41
jaw 733.45
medial femoral condyle 733.43
specified site NEC 733.49
talus 733.44
ethmoid 478.19
ischemic 733.40
jaw 526.4
aseptic 733.45
marrow 289.89
Paget's (osteitis deformans) 731.0
tuberculous — *see* Tuberculosis, bone
brain (softening) (*see also* Softening, brain) 437.8
breast (aseptic) (fat) (segmental) 611.3
bronchus, bronchi 519.19
central nervous system NEC (*see also* Softening, brain) 437.8
cerebellar (*see also* Softening, brain) 437.8
cerebral (softening) (*see also* Softening, brain) 437.8
cerebrospinal (softening) (*see also* Softening, brain) 437.8
colon 557.0
cornea (*see also* Keratitis) 371.40
cortical, kidney 583.6
cystic medial (aorta) 441.00
abdominal 441.02
thoracic 441.01
thoracoabdominal 441.03
dental 521.09
pulp 522.1
due to swallowing corrosive substance — *see* Burn, by site
ear (ossicle) 385.24
esophagus 530.89
ethmoid (bone) 478.19
eyelid 374.50
fat, fatty (generalized) (*see also* Degeneration, fatty) 272.8
abdominal wall 567.82
breast (aseptic) (segmental) 611.3
intestine 569.89
localized — *see* Degeneration, by site, fatty
mesentery 567.82
omentum 567.82
pancreas 577.8
peritoneum 567.82
skin (subcutaneous) 709.3
newborn 778.1

Index

Necrosis, necrotic — Neoplasia

Necrosis, necrotic — *continued*
femur (aseptic) (avascular) 733.42
head 733.42
medial condyle 733.43
neck 733.42
gallbladder (*see also* Cholecystitis, acute) 575.0
gangrenous 785.4
gastric 537.89
glottis 478.79
heart (myocardium) — *see* Infarct, myocardium
hepatic (*see also* Necrosis, liver) 570
hip (aseptic) (avascular) 733.42
intestine (acute) (hemorrhagic) (massive) 557.0
ischemic 785.4
jaw 526.4
aseptic 733.45
kidney (bilateral) 583.9
acute 584.9
cortical 583.6
acute 584.6
with
abortion — *see* Abortion, by type, with renal failure
ectopic pregnancy (*see also* categories 633.0–633.9) 639.3
molar pregnancy (*see also* categories 630–632) 639.3
complicating pregnancy 646.2 ☑
affecting fetus or newborn 760.1
following labor and delivery 669.3 ☑
medullary (papillary) (*see also* Pyelitis) 590.80
in
acute renal failure 584.7
nephritis, nephropathy 583.7
papillary (*see also* Pyelitis) 590.80
in
acute renal failure 584.7
nephritis, nephropathy 583.7
tubular 584.5
with
abortion — *see* Abortion, by type, with renal failure
ectopic pregnancy (*see also* categories 633.0–633.9) 639.3

Necrosis, necrotic — *continued*
kidney — *continued*
tubular — *continued*
with — *continued*
molar pregnancy (*see also* categories 630–632) 639.3
complicating
abortion 639.3
ectopic or molar pregnancy 639.3
pregnancy 646.2 ☑
affecting fetus or newborn 760.1
following labor and delivery 669.3 ☑
traumatic 958.5
larynx 478.79
liver (acute) (congenital) (diffuse) (massive) (subacute) 570
with
abortion — *see* Abortion, by type, with specified complication NEC
ectopic pregnancy (*see also* categories 633.0–633.9) 639.8
molar pregnancy (*see also* categories 630–632) 639.8
complicating pregnancy 646.7 ☑
affecting fetus or newborn 760.8
following
abortion 639.8
ectopic or molar pregnancy 639.8
obstetrical 646.7 ☑
postabortal 639.8
puerperal, postpartum 674.8 ☑
toxic 573.3
lung 513.0
lymphatic gland 683
mammary gland 611.3
mastoid (chronic) 383.1
mesentery 557.0
fat 567.82
mitral valve — *see* Insufficiency, mitral
myocardium, myocardial — *see* Infarct, myocardium
nose (septum) 478.19
omentum 557.0
with mesenteric infarction 557.0
fat 567.82
orbit, orbital 376.10
ossicles, ear (aseptic) 385.24
ovary (*see also* Salpingo-oophoritis) 614.2

Necrosis, necrotic — *continued*
pancreas (aseptic) (duct) (fat) 577.8
acute 577.0
infective 577.0
papillary, kidney (*see also* Pyelitis) 590.80
perineum 624.8
peritoneum 557.0
with mesenteric infarction 557.0
fat 567.82
pharynx 462
in granulocytopenia 288.09
phosphorus 983.9
pituitary (gland) (postpartum) (Sheehan) 253.2
placenta (*see also* Placenta, abnormal) 656.7 ☑
pneumonia 513.0
pulmonary 513.0
pulp (dental) 522.1
pylorus 537.89
radiation — *see* Necrosis, by site
radium — *see* Necrosis, by site
renal — *see* Necrosis, kidney
sclera 379.19
scrotum 608.89
skin or subcutaneous tissue 709.8
due to burn — *see* Burn, by site
gangrenous 785.4
spine, spinal (column) 730.18
acute 730.18
cord 336.1
spleen 289.59
stomach 537.89
stomatitis 528.1
subcutaneous fat 709.3
fetus or newborn 778.1
subendocardial — *see* Infarct, myocardium
suprarenal (capsule) (gland) 255.8
teeth, tooth 521.09
testis 608.89
thymus (gland) 254.8
tonsil 474.8
trachea 519.19
tuberculous NEC — *see* Tuberculosis
tubular (acute) (anoxic) (toxic) 584.5
due to a procedure 997.5
umbilical cord, affecting fetus or newborn 762.6
vagina 623.8
vertebra (lumbar) 730.18

Necrosis, necrotic — *continued*
vertebra — *continued*
acute 730.18
tuberculous (*see also* Tuberculosis) 015.0 ☑ *[730.8]* ☑
vesical (aseptic) (bladder) 596.8
vulva 624.8
x-ray — *see* Necrosis, by site
Necrospermia 606.0
Necrotizing angiitis 446.0
Negativism 301.7
Neglect (child) (newborn) NEC 995.52
adult 995.84
after or at birth 995.52
hemispatial 781.8
left-sided 781.8
sensory 781.8
visuospatial 781.8
Negri bodies 071
Neill-Dingwall syndrome (microcephaly and dwarfism) 759.89
Neisserian infection NEC — *see* Gonococcus
Nematodiasis NEC — *see also* Infestation, Nematode 127.9
ancylostoma (*see also* Ancylostomiasis) 126.9
Neoformans cryptococcus infection 117.5
Neonatal — *see also* condition
abstinence syndrome 779.5 ●
adrenoleukodystrophy 277.86
teeth, tooth 520.6
Neonatorum — *see* condition
Neoplasia
anal intraepithelial I (AIN I) (histologically confirmed) 569.44
anal intraepithelial II (AIN II) (histologically confirmed) 569.44
anal intraepithelial III (AIN III) 230.6
anal canal 230.5
endometrial intraepithelial (EIN) 621.35 ●
multiple endocrine (MEN)
type I 258.01
type IIA 258.02
type IIB 258.03
vaginal intraepithelial I (VAIN I) 623.0
vaginal intraepithelial II (VAIN II) 623.0
vaginal intraepithelial III (VAIN III) 233.31
vulvular intraepithelial I (VIN I) 624.01
vulvular intraepithelial II (VIN II) 624.02
vulvular intraepithelial III (VIN III) 233.32

Handwritten annotations: *undergoes malignant changes but still confined* · *non-invasive – do not spread* · *cannot be determined without further study*

	Malignant					
	Primary	Secondary	Ca in situ	Benign	Uncertain Behavior	Unspecified
Neoplasm, neoplastic	199.1	199.1	234.9	229.9	238.9	239.9

Notes — 1. The list below gives the code numbers for neoplasms by anatomical site. For each site there are six possible code numbers according to whether the neoplasm in question is malignant, benign, in situ, of uncertain behavior, or of unspecified nature. The description of the neoplasm will often indicate which of the six columns is appropriate; e.g., malignant melanoma of skin, benign fibroadenoma of breast, carcinoma in situ of cervix uteri.

Where such descriptors are not present, the remainder of the Index should be consulted where guidance is given to the appropriate column for each morphological (histological) variety listed; e.g., Mesonephroma — see Neoplasm, malignant; Embryoma — see also Neoplasm, uncertain behavior; Disease, Bowen's — see Neoplasm, skin, in situ. However, the guidance in the Index can be overridden if one of the descriptors mentioned above is present; e.g., malignant adenoma of colon is coded to 153.9 and not to 211.3 as the adjective "malignant" overrides the Index entry "Adenoma — see also Neoplasm, benign."

2. Sites marked with the sign * (e.g., face NEC*) should be classified to malignant neoplasm of skin of these sites if the variety of neoplasm is a squamous cell carcinoma or an epidermoid carcinoma, and to benign neoplasm of skin of these sites if the variety of neoplasm is a papilloma (any type).

	Primary	Secondary	Ca in situ	Benign	Uncertain Behavior	Unspecified
abdomen, abdominal	195.2	198.89	234.8	229.8	238.8	239.89 ▲
cavity	195.2	198.89	234.8	229.8	238.8	239.89 ▲
organ	195.2	198.89	234.8	229.8	238.8	239.89 ▲
viscera	195.2	198.89	234.8	229.8	238.8	239.89 ▲
wall	173.5	198.2	232.5	216.5	238.2	239.2
connective tissue	171.5	198.89	—	215.5	238.1	239.2
abdominopelvic	195.8	198.89	234.8	229.8	238.8	239.89 ▲
accessory sinus — see Neoplasm, sinus						
acoustic nerve	192.0	198.4	—	225.1	237.9	239.7
acromion (process)	170.4	198.5	—	213.4	238.0	239.2
adenoid (pharynx) (tissue)	147.1	198.89	230.0	210.7	235.1	239.0
adipose tissue (see also Neoplasm, connective tissue)	171.9	198.89	—	215.9	238.1	239.2
adnexa (uterine)	183.9	198.82	233.39	221.8	236.3	239.5
adrenal (cortex) (gland) (medulla)	194.0	198.7	234.8	227.0	237.2	239.7
ala nasi (external)	173.3	198.2	232.3	216.3	238.2	239.2
alimentary canal or tract NEC	159.9	197.8	230.9	211.9	235.5	239.0
alveolar	143.9	198.89	230.0	210.4	235.1	239.0
mucosa	143.9	198.89	230.0	210.4	235.1	239.0
lower	143.1	198.89	230.0	210.4	235.1	239.0
upper	143.0	198.89	230.0	210.4	235.1	239.0
ridge or process	170.1	198.5	—	213.1	238.0	239.2
carcinoma	143.9	—	—	—	—	—
lower	143.1	—	—	—	—	—
upper	143.0	—	—	—	—	—
lower	170.1	198.5	—	213.1	238.0	239.2
mucosa	143.9	198.89	230.0	210.4	235.1	239.0
lower	143.1	198.89	230.0	210.4	235.1	239.0
upper	143.0	198.89	230.0	210.4	235.1	239.0
upper	170.0	198.5	—	213.0	238.0	239.2
sulcus	145.1	198.89	230.0	210.4	235.1	239.0
alveolus	143.9	198.89	230.0	210.4	235.1	239.0
lower	143.1	198.89	230.0	210.4	235.1	239.0
upper	143.0	198.89	230.0	210.4	235.1	239.0
ampulla of Vater	156.2	197.8	230.8	211.5	235.3	239.0
ankle NEC*	195.5	198.89	232.7	229.8	238.8	239.89 ▲
anorectum, anorectal (junction)	154.8	197.5	230.7	211.4	235.2	239.0
antecubital fossa or space*	195.4	198.89	232.6	229.8	238.8	239.89 ▲
antrum (Highmore) (maxillary)	160.2	197.3	231.8	212.0	235.9	239.1
pyloric	151.2	197.8	230.2	211.1	235.2	239.0
tympanicum	160.1	197.3	231.8	212.0	235.9	239.1
anus, anal	154.3	197.5	230.6	211.4	235.5	239.0
canal	154.2	197.5	230.5	211.4	235.5	239.0
contiguous sites with rectosigmoid	154.8	—	—	—	—	—

	Primary	Secondary	Ca in situ	Benign	Uncertain Behavior	Unspecified
Neoplasm, neoplastic — *continued*						
anus, anal — *continued*						
contiguous sites with rectosigmoid junction or rectum — *continued* junction or rectum						
margin	173.5	198.2	232.5	216.5	238.2	239.2
skin	173.5	198.2	232.5	216.5	238.2	239.2
sphincter	154.2	197.5	230.5	211.4	235.5	239.0
aorta (thoracic)	171.4	198.89	—	215.4	238.1	239.2
abdominal	171.5	198.89	—	215.5	238.1	239.2
aortic body	194.6	198.89	—	227.6	237.3	239.7
aponeurosis	171.9	198.89	—	215.9	238.1	239.2
palmar	171.2	198.89	—	215.2	238.1	239.2
plantar	171.3	198.89	—	215.3	238.1	239.2
appendix	153.5	197.5	230.3	211.3	235.2	239.0
arachnoid (cerebral)	192.1	198.4	—	225.2	237.6	239.7
spinal	192.3	198.4	—	225.4	237.6	239.7
areola (female)	174.0	198.81	233.0	217	238.3	239.3
male	175.0	198.81	233.0	217	238.3	239.3
arm NEC*	195.4	198.89	232.6	229.8	238.8	239.89 ▲
artery — see Neoplasm, connective tissue						
aryepiglottic fold	148.2	198.89	230.0	210.8	235.1	239.0
hypopharyngeal aspect	148.2	198.89	230.0	210.8	235.1	239.0
laryngeal aspect	161.1	197.3	231.0	212.1	235.6	239.1
marginal zone	148.2	198.89	230.0	210.8	235.1	239.0
arytenoid (cartilage)	161.3	197.3	231.0	212.1	235.6	239.1
fold — see Neoplasm, aryepiglottic						
associated with transplanted organ	199.2	—	—	—	—	—
atlas	170.2	198.5	—	213.2	238.0	239.2
atrium, cardiac	164.1	198.89	—	212.7	238.8	239.89 ▲
auditory canal (external) (skin)	173.2	198.2	232.2	216.2	238.2	239.2
internal	160.1	197.3	231.8	212.0	235.9	239.1
nerve	192.0	198.4	—	225.1	237.9	239.7
tube	160.1	197.3	231.8	212.0	235.9	239.1
Eustachian	160.1	197.3	231.8	212.0	235.9	239.1
opening	147.2	198.89	230.0	210.7	235.1	239.0
auricle, ear	173.2	198.2	232.2	216.2	238.2	239.2
cartilage	171.0	198.89	—	215.0	238.1	239.2
auricular canal (external)	173.2	198.2	232.2	216.2	238.2	239.2
internal	160.1	197.3	231.8	212.0	235.9	239.1
autonomic nerve or nervous system NEC	171.9	198.89		215.9	238.1	239.2
axilla, axillary	195.1	198.89	234.8	229.8	238.8	239.89 ▲
fold	173.5	198.2	232.5	216.5	238.2	239.2
back NEC*	195.8	198.89	232.5	229.8	238.8	239.89 ▲
Bartholin's gland	184.1	198.82	233.32	221.2	236.3	239.5
basal ganglia	191.0	198.3	—	225.0	237.5	239.6
basis pedunculi	191.7	198.3	—	225.0	237.5	239.6
bile or biliary (tract)	156.9	197.8	230.8	211.5	235.3	239.0
canaliculi (biliferi) (intrahepatic)	155.1	197.8	230.8	211.5	235.3	239.0
canals, interlobular	155.1	197.8	230.8	211.5	235.3	239.0
contiguous sites	156.8	—	—	—	—	—
duct or passage (common) (cystic) (extrahepatic)	156.1	197.8	230.8	211.5	235.3	239.0
contiguous sites with gallbladder	156.8	—	—	—	—	—
interlobular	155.1	197.8	230.8	211.5	235.3	239.0
intrahepatic	155.1	197.8	230.8	211.5	235.3	239.0

☑ Additional Digit Required — Refer to the Tabular List for Digit Selection · Subterms under main terms may continue to next column or page

	Malignant					
Neoplasm, neoplastic —	Primary	Secondary	Ca in situ	Benign	Uncertain Behavior	Unspecified
continued						
bile or biliary —						
continued						
duct or passage —						
continued						
intrahepatic —						
continued						
and						
extrahepatic ...	156.9	197.8	230.8	211.5	235.3	239.0
bladder (urinary)	188.9	198.1	233.7	223.3	236.7	239.4
contiguous sites	188.8	—	—	—	—	—
dome	188.1	198.1	233.7	223.3	236.7	239.4
neck	188.5	198.1	233.7	223.3	236.7	239.4
orifice	188.9	198.1	233.7	223.3	236.7	239.4
ureteric	188.6	198.1	233.7	223.3	236.7	239.4
urethral	188.5	198.1	233.7	223.3	236.7	239.4
sphincter	188.8	198.1	233.7	223.3	236.7	239.4
trigone	188.0	198.1	233.7	223.3	236.7	239.4
urachus	188.7	—	233.7	223.3	236.7	239.4
wall	188.9	198.1	233.7	223.3	236.7	239.4
anterior	188.3	198.1	233.7	223.3	236.7	239.4
lateral	188.2	198.1	233.7	223.3	236.7	239.4
posterior	188.4	198.1	233.7	223.3	236.7	239.4
blood vessel — *see*						
Neoplasm,						
connective tissue						
bone (periosteum)	170.9	198.5		213.9	238.0	239.2

Note — Carcinomas and adenocarcinomas, of any type other than intraosseous or odontogenic, of the sites listed under "Neoplasm, bone" should be considered as constituting metastatic spread from an unspecified primary site and coded to 198.5 for morbidity coding.

	Malignant					
	Primary	Secondary	Ca in situ	Benign	Uncertain Behavior	Unspecified
acetabulum	170.6	198.5	—	213.6	238.0	239.2
acromion						
(process)	170.4	198.5	—	213.4	238.0	239.2
ankle	170.8	198.5	—	213.8	238.0	239.2
arm NEC	170.4	198.5	—	213.4	238.0	239.2
astragalus	170.8	198.5	—	213.8	238.0	239.2
atlas	170.2	198.5	—	213.2	238.0	239.2
axis	170.2	198.5	—	213.2	238.0	239.2
back NEC	170.2	198.5	—	213.2	238.0	239.2
calcaneus	170.8	198.5	—	213.8	238.0	239.2
calvarium	170.0	198.5	—	213.0	238.0	239.2
carpus (any)	170.5	198.5	—	213.5	238.0	239.2
cartilage NEC	170.9	198.5	—	213.9	238.0	239.2
clavicle	170.3	198.5	—	213.3	238.0	239.2
clivus	170.0	198.5	—	213.0	238.0	239.2
coccygeal						
vertebra	170.6	198.5	—	213.6	238.0	239.2
coccyx	170.6	198.5	—	213.6	238.0	239.2
costal cartilage	170.3	198.5	—	213.3	238.0	239.2
costovertebral						
joint	170.3	198.5	—	213.3	238.0	239.2
cranial	170.0	198.5	—	213.0	238.0	239.2
cuboid	170.8	198.5	—	213.8	238.0	239.2
cuneiform	170.9	198.5	—	213.9	238.0	239.2
ankle	170.8	198.5	—	213.8	238.0	239.2
wrist	170.5	198.5	—	213.5	238.0	239.2
digital	170.9	198.5	—	213.9	238.0	239.2
finger	170.5	198.5	—	213.5	238.0	239.2
toe	170.8	198.5	—	213.8	238.0	239.2
elbow	170.4	198.5	—	213.4	238.0	239.2
ethmoid						
(labyrinth)	170.0	198.5	—	213.0	238.0	239.2
face	170.0	198.5	—	213.0	238.0	239.2
lower jaw	170.1	198.5	—	213.1	238.0	239.2
femur (any part)	170.7	198.5	—	213.7	238.0	239.2
fibula (any part)	170.7	198.5	—	213.7	238.0	239.2
finger (any)	170.5	198.5	—	213.5	238.0	239.2
foot	170.8	198.5	—	213.8	238.0	239.2
forearm	170.4	198.5	—	213.4	238.0	239.2
frontal	170.0	198.5	—	213.0	238.0	239.2
hand	170.5	198.5	—	213.5	238.0	239.2
heel	170.8	198.5	—	213.8	238.0	239.2
hip	170.6	198.5	—	213.6	238.0	239.2

	Malignant					
Neoplasm, neoplastic —	Primary	Secondary	Ca in situ	Benign	Uncertain Behavior	Unspecified
continued						
bone — *continued*						
humerus (any						
part)	170.4	198.5	—	213.4	238.0	239.2
hyoid	170.0	198.5	—	213.0	238.0	239.2
ilium	170.6	198.5	—	213.6	238.0	239.2
innominate	170.6	198.5	—	213.6	238.0	239.2
intervertebral cartilage						
or disc	170.2	198.5	—	213.2	238.0	239.2
ischium	170.6	198.5	—	213.6	238.0	239.2
jaw (lower)	170.1	198.5	—	213.1	238.0	239.2
upper	170.0	198.5	—	213.0	238.0	239.2
knee	170.7	198.5	—	213.7	238.0	239.2
leg NEC	170.7	198.5	—	213.7	238.0	239.2
limb NEC	170.9	198.5	—	213.9	238.0	239.2
lower (long						
bones)	170.7	198.5	—	213.7	238.0	239.2
short bones	170.8	198.5	—	213.8	238.0	239.2
upper (long						
bones)	170.4	198.5	—	213.4	238.0	239.2
short bones	170.5	198.5	—	213.5	238.0	239.2
long	170.9	198.5	—	213.9	238.0	239.2
lower limbs						
NEC	170.7	198.5	—	213.7	238.0	239.2
upper limbs						
NEC	170.4	198.5	—	213.4	238.0	239.2
malar	170.0	198.5	—	213.0	238.0	239.2
mandible	170.1	198.5	—	213.1	238.0	239.2
marrow NEC	202.9 ☑	198.5	—	—	—	238.79
mastoid	170.0	198.5	—	213.0	238.0	239.2
maxilla, maxillary						
(superior)	170.0	198.5	—	213.0	238.0	239.2
inferior	170.1	198.5	—	213.1	238.0	239.2
metacarpus (any)	170.5	198.5	—	213.5	238.0	239.2
metatarsus (any)	170.8	198.5	—	213.8	238.0	239.2
navicular (ankle)	170.8	198.5	—	213.8	238.0	239.2
hand	170.5	198.5	—	213.5	238.0	239.2
nose, nasal	170.0	198.5	—	213.0	238.0	239.2
occipital	170.0	198.5	—	213.0	238.0	239.2
orbit	170.0	198.5	—	213.0	238.0	239.2
parietal	170.0	198.5	—	213.0	238.0	239.2
patella	170.8	198.5	—	213.8	238.0	239.2
pelvic	170.6	198.5	—	213.6	238.0	239.2
phalanges	170.9	198.5	—	213.9	238.0	239.2
foot	170.8	198.5	—	213.8	238.0	239.2
hand	170.5	198.5	—	213.5	238.0	239.2
pubic	170.6	198.5	—	213.6	238.0	239.2
radius (any part)	170.4	198.5	—	213.4	238.0	239.2
rib	170.3	198.5	—	213.3	238.0	239.2
sacral vertebra	170.6	198.5	—	213.6	238.0	239.2
sacrum	170.6	198.5	—	213.6	238.0	239.2
scaphoid (of						
hand)	170.5	198.5	—	213.5	238.0	239.2
of ankle	170.8	198.5	—	213.8	238.0	239.2
scapula (any part)	170.4	198.5	—	213.4	238.0	239.2
sella turcica	170.0	198.5	—	213.0	238.0	239.2
short	170.9	198.5	—	213.9	238.0	239.2
lower limb	170.8	198.5	—	213.8	238.0	239.2
upper limb	170.5	198.5	—	213.5	238.0	239.2
shoulder	170.4	198.5	—	213.4	238.0	239.2
skeleton, skeletal						
NEC	170.9	198.5	—	213.9	238.0	239.2
skull	170.0	198.5	—	213.0	238.0	239.2
sphenoid	170.0	198.5	—	213.0		239.2
spine, spinal						
(column)	170.2	198.5	—	213.2	238.0	239.2
coccyx	170.6	198.5	—	213.6	238.0	239.2
sacrum	170.6	198.5	—	213.6	238.0	239.2
sternum	170.3	198.5	—	213.3	238.0	239.2
tarsus (any)	170.8	198.5	—	213.8	238.0	239.2
temporal	170.0	198.5	—	213.0	238.0	239.2
thumb	170.5	198.5	—	213.5	238.0	239.2
tibia (any part)	170.7	198.5	—	213.7	238.0	239.2
toe (any)	170.8	198.5	—	213.8	238.0	239.2
trapezium	170.5	198.5	—	213.5	238.0	239.2

☑ Additional Digit Required — Refer to the Tabular List for Digit Selection   ▽ Subterms under main terms may continue to next column or page

	Malignant					
	Primary	Secondary	Ca in situ	Benign	Uncertain Behavior	Unspecified
Neoplasm, neoplastic — *continued*						
bone — *continued*						
trapezoid	170.5	198.5	—	213.5	238.0	239.2
turbinate	170.0	198.5	—	213.0	238.0	239.2
ulna (any part)	170.4	198.5	—	213.4	238.0	239.2
unciform	170.5	198.5	—	213.5	238.0	239.2
vertebra (column)	170.2	198.5	—	213.2	238.0	239.2
coccyx	170.6	198.5	—	213.6	238.0	239.2
sacrum	170.6	198.5	—	213.6	238.0	239.2
vomer	170.0	198.5	—	213.0	238.0	239.2
wrist	170.5	198.5	—	213.5	238.0	239.2
xiphoid process	170.3	198.5	—	213.3	238.0	239.2
zygomatic	170.0	198.5	—	213.0	238.0	239.2
book-leaf (mouth)	145.8	198.89	230.0	210.4	235.1	239.0
bowel — *see* Neoplasm, intestine						
brachial plexus	171.2	198.89	—	215.2	238.1	239.2
brain NEC	191.9	198.3	—	225.0	237.5	239.6
basal ganglia	191.0	198.3	—	225.0	237.5	239.6
cerebellopontine angle	191.6	198.3	—	225.0	237.5	239.6
cerebellum NOS	191.6	198.3	—	225.0	237.5	239.6
cerebrum	191.0	198.3	—	225.0	237.5	239.6
choroid plexus	191.5	198.3	—	225.0	237.5	239.6
contiguous sites	191.8	—	—	—	—	—
corpus callosum	191.8	198.3	—	225.0	237.5	239.6
corpus striatum	191.0	198.3	—	225.0	237.5	239.6
cortex (cerebral)	191.0	198.3	—	225.0	237.5	239.6
frontal lobe	191.1	198.3	—	225.0	237.5	239.6
globus pallidus	191.0	198.3	—	225.0	237.5	239.6
hippocampus	191.2	198.3	—	225.0	237.5	239.6
hypothalamus	191.0	198.3	—	225.0	237.5	239.6
internal capsule	191.0	198.3	—	225.0	237.5	239.6
medulla oblongata	191.7	198.3	—	225.0	237.5	239.6
meninges	192.1	198.4	—	225.2	237.6	239.7
midbrain	191.7	198.3	—	225.0	237.5	239.6
occipital lobe	191.4	198.3	—	225.0	237.5	239.6
parietal lobe	191.3	198.3	—	225.0	237.5	239.6
peduncle	191.7	198.3	—	225.0	237.5	239.6
pons	191.7	198.3	—	225.0	237.5	239.6
stem	191.7	198.3	—	225.0	237.5	239.6
tapetum	191.8	198.3	—	225.0	237.5	239.6
temporal lobe	191.2	198.3	—	225.0	237.5	239.6
thalamus	191.0	198.3	—	225.0	237.5	239.6
uncus	191.2	198.3	—	225.0	237.5	239.6
ventricle (floor)	191.5	198.3	—	225.0	237.5	239.6
branchial (cleft) (vestiges)	146.8	198.89	230.0	210.6	235.1	239.0
breast (connective tissue) (female) (glandular tissue) (soft parts)	174.9	198.81	233.0	217	238.3	239.3
areola	174.0	198.81	233.0	217	238.3	239.3
male	175.0	198.81	233.0	217	238.3	239.3
axillary tail	174.6	198.81	233.0	217	238.3	239.3
central portion	174.1	198.81	233.0	217	238.3	239.3
contiguous sites	174.8	—	—	—	—	—
ectopic sites	174.8	198.81	233.0	217	238.3	239.3
inner	174.8	198.81	233.0	217	238.3	239.3
lower	174.8	198.81	233.0	217	238.3	239.3
lower-inner quadrant	174.3	198.81	233.0	217	238.3	239.3
lower-outer quadrant	174.5	198.81	233.0	217	238.3	239.3
male	175.9	198.81	233.0	217	238.3	239.3
areola	175.0	198.81	233.0	217	238.3	239.3
ectopic tissue	175.9	198.81	233.0	217	238.3	239.3
nipple	175.0	198.81	233.0	217	238.3	239.3
mastectomy site (skin)	173.5	198.2	—	—	—	—
specified as breast tissue	174.8	198.81	—	—	—	—
midline	174.8	198.81	233.0	217	238.3	239.3

	Malignant					
	Primary	Secondary	Ca in situ	Benign	Uncertain Behavior	Unspecified
Neoplasm, neoplastic — *continued*						
breast — *continued*						
nipple	174.0	198.81	233.0	217	238.3	239.3
male	175.0	198.81	233.0	217	238.3	239.3
outer	174.8	198.81	233.0	217	238.3	239.3
skin	173.5	198.2	232.5	216.5	238.2	239.2
tail (axillary)	174.6	198.81	233.0	217	238.3	239.3
upper	174.8	198.81	233.0	217	238.3	239.3
upper-inner quadrant	174.2	198.81	233.0	217	238.3	239.3
upper-outer quadrant	174.4	198.81	233.0	217	238.3	239.3
broad ligament	183.3	198.82	233.39	221.0	236.3	239.5
bronchiogenic, bronchogenic (lung)	162.9	197.0	231.2	212.3	235.7	239.1
bronchiole	162.9	197.0	231.2	212.3	235.7	239.1
bronchus	162.9	197.0	231.2	212.3	235.7	239.1
carina	162.2	197.0	231.2	212.3	235.7	239.1
contiguous sites with lung or trachea	162.8	—	—	—	—	—
lower lobe of lung	162.5	197.0	231.2	212.3	235.7	239.1
main	162.2	197.0	231.2	212.3	235.7	239.1
middle lobe of lung	162.4	197.0	231.2	212.3	235.7	239.1
upper lobe of lung	162.3	197.0	231.2	212.3	235.7	239.1
brow	173.3	198.2	232.3	216.3	238.2	239.2
buccal (cavity)	145.9	198.89	230.0	210.4	235.1	239.0
commissure	145.0	198.89	230.0	210.4	235.1	239.0
groove (lower) (upper)	145.1	198.89	230.0	210.4	235.1	239.0
mucosa	145.0	198.89	230.0	210.4	235.1	239.0
sulcus (lower) (upper)	145.1	198.89	230.0	210.4	235.1	239.0
bulbourethral gland	189.3	198.1	233.9	223.81	236.99	239.5
bursa — *see* Neoplasm, connective tissue						
buttock NEC*	195.3	198.89	232.5	229.8	238.8	239.89 ▲
calf*	195.5	198.89	232.7	229.8	238.8	239.89 ▲
calvarium	170.0	198.5	—	213.0	238.0	239.2
calyx, renal	189.1	198.0	233.9	223.1	236.91	239.5
canal						
anal	154.2	197.5	230.5	211.4	235.5	239.0
auditory (external)	173.2	198.2	232.2	216.2	238.2	239.2
auricular (external)	173.2	198.2	232.2	216.2	238.2	239.2
canaliculi, biliary (biliferi) (intrahepatic)	155.1	197.8	230.8	211.5	235.3	239.0
canthus (eye) (inner) (outer)	173.1	198.2	232.1	216.1	238.2	239.2
capillary — *see* Neoplasm, connective tissue						
caput coli	153.4	197.5	230.3	211.3	235.2	239.0
cardia (gastric)	151.0	197.8	230.2	211.1	235.2	239.0
cardiac orifice (stomach)	151.0	197.8	230.2	211.1	235.2	239.0
cardio-esophageal junction	151.0	197.8	230.2	211.1	235.2	239.0
cardio-esophagus	151.0	197.8	230.2	211.1	235.2	239.0
carina (bronchus)	162.2	197.0	231.2	212.3	235.7	239.1
carotid (artery)	171.0	198.89	—	215.0	238.1	239.2
body	194.5	198.89	—	227.5	237.3	239.7
carpus (any bone)	170.5	198.5	—	213.5	238.0	239.2
cartilage (articular) (joint) NEC (*see also* Neoplasm, bone)	170.9	198.5	—	213.9	238.0	239.2
arytenoid	161.3	197.3	231.0	212.1	235.6	239.1
auricular	171.0	198.89	—	215.0	238.1	239.2
bronchi	162.2	197.3	—	212.3	235.7	239.1

☑ Additional Digit Required — Refer to the Tabular List for Digit Selection　　　▽ Subterms under main terms may continue to next column or page

2010 ICD-9-CM　　▶◀ Revised Text　　● New Line　　▲ Revised Code　　October 2009 • Volume 2 — 187

Index

Neoplasm, cartilage — Neoplasm, connective tissue

	Malignant					
	Primary	Secondary	Ca in situ	Benign	Uncertain Behavior	Unspecified
Neoplasm, neoplastic — *continued*						
cartilage (*see also* Neoplasm, bone) — *continued*						
connective tissue — *see* Neoplasm, connective tissue						
costal	170.3	198.5	—	213.3	238.0	239.2
cricoid	161.3	197.3	231.0	212.1	235.6	239.1
cuneiform	161.3	197.3	231.0	212.1	235.6	239.1
ear (external)	171.0	198.89	—	215.0	238.1	239.2
ensiform	170.3	198.5	—	213.3	238.0	239.2
epiglottis	161.1	197.3	231.0	212.1	235.6	239.1
anterior surface	146.4	198.89	230.0	210.6	235.1	239.0
eyelid	171.0	198.89	—	215.0	238.1	239.2
intervertebral	170.2	198.5	—	213.2	238.0	239.2
larynx, laryngeal	161.3	197.3	231.0	212.1	235.6	239.1
nose, nasal	160.0	197.3	231.8	212.0	235.9	239.1
pinna	171.0	198.89	—	215.0	238.1	239.2
rib	170.3	198.5	—	213.3	238.0	239.2
semilunar (knee)	170.7	198.5	—	213.7	238.0	239.2
thyroid	161.3	197.3	231.0	212.1	235.6	239.1
trachea	162.0	197.3	231.1	212.2	235.7	239.1
cauda equina	192.2	198.3	—	225.3	237.5	239.7
cavity						
buccal	145.9	198.89	230.0	210.4	235.1	239.0
nasal	160.0	197.3	231.8	212.0	235.9	239.1
oral	145.9	198.89	230.0	210.4	235.1	239.0
peritoneal	158.9	197.6	—	211.8	235.4	239.0
tympanic	160.1	197.3	231.8	212.0	235.9	239.1
cecum	153.4	197.5	230.3	211.3	235.2	239.0
central						
nervous system — *see* Neoplasm, nervous system						
white matter	191.0	198.3	—	225.0	237.5	239.6
cerebellopontine (angle)	191.6	198.3	—	225.0	237.5	239.6
cerebellum, cerebellar	191.6	198.3	—	225.0	237.5	239.6
cerebrum, cerebral (cortex) (hemisphere) (white matter)	191.0	198.3	—	225.0	237.5	239.6
meninges	192.1	198.4	—	225.2	237.6	239.7
peduncle	191.7	198.3	—	225.0	237.5	239.6
ventricle (any)	191.5	198.3	—	225.0	237.5	239.6
cervical region	195.0	198.89	234.8	229.8	238.8	239.89 ▲
cervix (cervical) (uteri) (uterus)	180.9	198.82	233.1	219.0	236.0	239.5
canal	180.0	198.82	233.1	219.0	236.0	239.5
contiguous sites	180.8	—	—	—	—	—
endocervix (canal) (gland)	180.0	198.82	233.1	219.0	236.0	239.5
exocervix	180.1	198.82	233.1	219.0	236.0	239.5
external os	180.1	198.82	233.1	219.0	236.0	239.5
internal os	180.0	198.82	233.1	219.0	236.0	239.5
nabothian gland	180.0	198.82	233.1	219.0	236.0	239.5
squamocolumnar junction	180.8	198.82	233.1	219.0	236.0	239.5
stump	180.8	198.82	233.1	219.0	236.0	239.5
cheek	195.0	198.89	234.8	229.8	238.8	239.89 ▲
external	173.3	198.2	232.3	216.3	238.2	239.2
inner aspect	145.0	198.89	230.0	210.4	235.1	239.0
internal	145.0	198.89	230.0	210.4	235.1	239.0
mucosa	145.0	198.89	230.0	210.4	235.1	239.0
chest (wall) NEC	195.1	198.89	234.8	229.8	238.8	239.89 ▲
chiasma opticum	192.0	198.4	—	225.1	237.9	239.7
chin	173.3	198.2	232.3	216.3	238.2	239.2
choana	147.3	198.89	230.0	210.7	235.1	239.0
cholangiole	155.1	197.8	230.8	211.5	235.3	239.0
choledochal duct	156.1	197.8	230.8	211.5	235.3	239.0
choroid	190.6	198.4	234.0	224.6	238.8	239.81 ▲
plexus	191.5	198.3	—	225.0	237.5	239.6
ciliary body	190.0	198.4	234.0	224.0	238.8	239.89 ▲
clavicle	170.3	198.5	—	213.3	238.0	239.2
Neoplasm, neoplastic — *continued*						
clitoris	184.3	198.82	233.32	221.2	236.3	239.5
clivus	170.0	198.5	—	213.0	238.0	239.2
cloacogenic zone	154.8	197.5	230.7	211.4	235.5	239.0
coccygeal						
body or glomus	194.6	198.89	—	227.6	237.3	239.7
vertebra	170.6	198.5	—	213.6	238.0	239.2
coccyx	170.6	198.5	—	213.6	238.0	239.2
colon (*see also* Neoplasm, intestine, large)						
and rectum	154.0	197.5	230.4	211.4	235.2	239.0
columnella	173.3	198.2	232.3	216.3	238.2	239.2
column, spinal — *see* Neoplasm, spine						
commissure						
labial, lip	140.6	198.89	230.0	210.4	235.1	239.0
laryngeal	161.0	197.3	231.0	212.1	235.6	239.1
common (bile) duct	156.1	197.8	230.8	211.5	235.3	239.0
concha	173.2	198.2	232.2	216.2	238.2	239.2
nose	160.0	197.3	231.8	212.0	235.9	239.1
conjunctiva	190.3	198.4	234.0	224.3	238.8	239.89 ▲
connective tissue NEC	171.9	198.89	—	215.9	238.1	239.2

Note — For neoplasms of connective tissue (blood vessel, bursa, fascia, ligament, muscle, peripheral nerves, sympathetic and parasympathetic nerves and ganglia, synovia, tendon, etc.) or of morphological types that indicate connective tissue, code according to the list under "Neoplasm, connective tissue"; for sites that do not appear in this list, code to neoplasm of that site; e.g.,

liposarcoma, shoulder 171.2

leiomyosarcoma, stomach 151.9

neurofibroma, chest wall 215.4

Morphological types that indicate connective tissue appear in the proper place in the alphabetical index with the instruction "see Neoplasm, connective tissue…"

	Primary	Secondary	Ca in situ	Benign	Uncertain Behavior	Unspecified
abdomen	171.5	198.89	—	215.5	238.1	239.2
abdominal wall	171.5	198.89	—	215.5	238.1	239.2
ankle	171.3	198.89	—	215.3	238.1	239.2
antecubital fossa or space	171.2	198.89	—	215.2	238.1	239.2
arm	171.2	198.89	—	215.2	238.1	239.2
auricle (ear)	171.0	198.89	—	215.0	238.1	239.2
axilla	171.4	198.89	—	215.4	238.1	239.2
back	171.7	198.89	—	215.7	238.1	239.2
breast (female) (*see also* Neoplasm, breast)	174.9	198.81	233.0	217	238.3	239.3
male	175.9	198.81	233.0	217	238.3	239.3
buttock	171.6	198.89	—	215.6	238.1	239.2
calf	171.3	198.89	—	215.3	238.1	239.2
cervical region	171.0	198.89	—	215.0	238.1	239.2
cheek	171.0	198.89	—	215.0	238.1	239.2
chest (wall)	171.4	198.89	—	215.4	238.1	239.2
chin	171.0	198.89	—	215.0	238.1	239.2
contiguous sites	171.8	—	—	—	—	—
diaphragm	171.4	198.89	—	215.4	238.1	239.2
ear (external)	171.0	198.89	—	215.0	238.1	239.2
elbow	171.2	198.89	—	215.2	238.1	239.2
extrarectal	171.6	198.89	—	215.6	238.1	239.2
extremity	171.8	198.89	—	215.8	238.1	239.2
lower	171.3	198.89	—	215.3	238.1	239.2
upper	171.2	198.89	—	215.2	238.1	239.2
eyelid	171.0	198.89	—	215.0	238.1	239.2
face	171.0	198.89	—	215.0	238.1	239.2
finger	171.2	198.89	—	215.2	238.1	239.2
flank	171.7	198.89	—	215.7	238.1	239.2
foot	171.3	198.89	—	215.3	238.1	239.2
forearm	171.2	198.89	—	215.2	238.1	239.2
forehead	171.0	198.89	—	215.0	238.1	239.2
gastric	171.5	198.89	—	215.5	238.1	—
gastrointestinal	171.5	198.89	—	215.5	238.1	—
gluteal region	171.6	198.89	—	215.6	238.1	239.2
great vessels NEC	171.4	198.89	—	215.4	238.1	239.2
groin	171.6	198.89	—	215.6	238.1	239.2

Neoplasm, neoplastic — continued	Primary (Malignant)	Secondary (Malignant)	Ca in situ (Malignant)	Benign	Uncertain Behavior	Unspecified
connective tissue — continued						
hand	171.2	198.89	—	215.2	238.1	239.2
head	171.0	198.89	—	215.0	238.1	239.2
heel	171.3	198.89	—	215.3	238.1	239.2
hip	171.3	198.89	—	215.3	238.1	239.2
hypochondrium	171.5	198.89	—	215.5	238.1	239.2
iliopsoas muscle	171.6	198.89	—	215.5	238.1	239.2
infraclavicular region	171.4	198.89	—	215.4	238.1	239.2
inguinal (canal) (region)	171.6	198.89	—	215.6	238.1	239.2
intestine	171.5	198.89	—	215.5	238.1	—
intrathoracic	171.4	198.89	—	215.4	238.1	239.2
ischiorectal fossa	171.6	198.89	—	215.6	238.1	239.2
jaw	143.9	198.89	230.0	210.4	235.1	239.0
knee	171.3	198.89	—	215.3	238.1	239.2
leg	171.3	198.89	—	215.3	238.1	239.2
limb NEC	171.9	198.89	—	215.8	238.1	239.2
lower	171.3	198.89	—	215.3	238.1	239.2
upper	171.2	198.89	—	215.2	238.1	239.2
nates	171.6	198.89	—	215.6	238.1	239.2
neck	171.0	198.89	—	215.0	238.1	239.2
orbit	190.1	198.4	234.0	224.1	238.8	239.89 ▲
pararectal	171.6	198.89	—	215.6	238.1	239.2
para-urethral	171.6	198.89	—	215.6	238.1	239.2
paravaginal	171.6	198.89	—	215.6	238.1	239.2
pelvis (floor)	171.6	198.89	—	215.6	238.1	239.2
pelvo-abdominal	171.8	198.89	—	215.8	238.1	239.2
perineum	171.6	198.89	—	215.6	238.1	239.2
perirectal (tissue)	171.6	198.89	—	215.6	238.1	239.2
periurethral (tissue)	171.6	198.89	—	215.6	238.1	239.2
popliteal fossa or space	171.3	198.89	—	215.3	238.1	239.2
presacral	171.6	198.89	—	215.6	238.1	239.2
psoas muscle	171.5	198.89	—	215.5	238.1	239.2
pterygoid fossa	171.0	198.89	—	215.0	238.1	239.2
rectovaginal septum or wall	171.6	198.89	—	215.6	238.1	239.2
rectovesical	171.6	198.89	—	215.6	238.1	239.2
retroperitoneum	158.0	197.6	—	211.8	235.4	239.0
sacrococcygeal region	171.6	198.89	—	215.6	238.1	239.2
scalp	171.0	198.89	—	215.0	238.1	239.2
scapular region	171.4	198.89	—	215.4	238.1	239.2
shoulder	171.2	198.89	—	215.2	238.1	239.2
skin (dermis) NEC	173.9	198.2	232.9	216.9	238.2	239.2
stomach	171.5	198.89	—	215.5	238.1	—
submental	171.0	198.89	—	215.0	238.1	239.2
supraclavicular region	171.0	198.89	—	215.0	238.1	239.2
temple	171.0	198.89	—	215.0	238.1	239.2
temporal region	171.0	198.89	—	215.0	238.1	239.2
thigh	171.3	198.89	—	215.3	238.1	239.2
thoracic (duct) (wall)	171.4	198.89	—	215.4	238.1	239.2
thorax	171.4	198.89	—	215.4	238.1	239.2
thumb	171.2	198.89	—	215.2	238.1	239.2
toe	171.3	198.89	—	215.3	238.1	239.2
trunk	171.7	198.89	—	215.7	238.1	239.2
umbilicus	171.5	198.89	—	215.5	238.1	239.2
vesicorectal	171.6	198.89	—	215.6	238.1	239.2
wrist	171.2	198.89	—	215.2	238.1	239.2
conus medullaris	192.2	198.3		225.3	237.5	239.7
cord (true) (vocal)	161.0	197.3	231.0	212.1	235.6	239.1
false	161.1	197.3	231.0	212.1	235.6	239.1
spermatic	187.6	198.82	233.6	222.8	236.6	239.5
spinal (cervical) (lumbar) (thoracic)	192.2	198.3	—	225.3	237.5	239.7
cornea (limbus)	190.4	198.4	234.0	224.4	238.8	239.89 ▲
corpus						
albicans	183.0	198.6	233.39	220	236.2	239.5

Neoplasm, neoplastic — continued	Primary (Malignant)	Secondary (Malignant)	Ca in situ (Malignant)	Benign	Uncertain Behavior	Unspecified
corpus — continued						
callosum, brain	191.8	198.3	—	225.0	237.5	239.6
cavernosum	187.3	198.82	233.5	222.1	236.6	239.5
gastric	151.4	197.8	230.2	211.1	235.2	239.0
penis	187.3	198.82	233.5	222.1	236.6	239.5
striatum, cerebrum	191.0	198.3	—	225.0	237.5	239.6
uteri	182.0	198.82	233.2	219.1	236.0	239.5
isthmus	182.1	198.82	233.2	219.1	236.0	239.5
cortex						
adrenal	194.0	198.7	234.8	227.0	237.2	239.7
cerebral	191.0	198.3	—	225.0	237.5	239.6
costal cartilage	170.3	198.5	—	213.3	238.0	239.2
costovertebral joint	170.3	198.5	—	213.3	238.0	239.2
Cowper's gland	189.3	198.1	233.9	223.81	236.99	239.5
cranial (fossa, any)	191.9	198.3	—	225.0	237.5	239.6
meninges	192.1	198.4	—	225.2	237.6	239.7
nerve (any)	192.0	198.4	—	225.1	237.9	239.7
craniobuccal pouch	194.3	198.89	234.8	227.3	237.0	239.7
craniopharyngeal (duct) (pouch)	194.3	198.89	234.8	227.3	237.0	239.7
cricoid	148.0	198.89	230.0	210.8	235.1	239.0
cartilage	161.3	197.3	231.0	212.1	235.6	239.1
cricopharynx	148.0	198.89	230.0	210.8	235.1	239.0
crypt of Morgagni	154.8	197.5	230.7	211.4	235.2	239.0
crystalline lens	190.0	198.4	234.0	224.0	238.8	239.89 ▲
cul-de-sac (Douglas')	158.8	197.6	—	211.8	235.4	239.0
cuneiform cartilage	161.3	197.3	231.0	212.1	235.6	239.1
cutaneous — see Neoplasm, skin						
cutis — see Neoplasm, skin						
cystic (bile) duct (common)	156.1	197.8	230.8	211.5	235.3	239.0
dermis — see Neoplasm, skin						
diaphragm	171.4	198.89	—	215.4	238.1	239.2
digestive organs, system, tube, or tract NEC	159.9	197.8	230.9	211.9	235.5	239.0
contiguous sites with peritoneum	159.8	—	—	—	—	—
disc, intervertebral	170.2	198.5	—	213.2	238.0	239.2
disease, generalized	199.0	199.0	234.9	229.9	238.9	199.0
disseminated	199.0	199.0	234.9	229.9	238.9	199.0
Douglas' cul-de-sac or pouch	158.8	197.6	—	211.8	235.4	239.0
duodenojejunal junction	152.8	197.4	230.7	211.2	235.2	239.0
duodenum	152.0	197.4	230.7	211.2	235.2	239.0
dura (cranial) (mater)	192.1	198.4	—	225.2	237.6	239.7
cerebral	192.1	198.4	—	225.2	237.6	239.7
spinal	192.3	198.4	—	225.4	237.6	239.7
ear (external)	173.2	198.2	232.2	216.2	238.2	239.2
auricle or auris	173.2	198.2	232.2	216.2	238.2	239.2
canal, external	173.2	198.2	232.2	216.2	238.2	239.2
cartilage	171.0	198.89	—	215.0	238.1	239.2
external meatus	173.2	198.2	232.2	216.2	238.2	239.2
inner	160.1	197.3	231.8	212.0	235.9	239.89 ▲
lobule	173.2	198.2	232.2	216.2	238.2	239.2
middle	160.1	197.3	231.8	212.0	235.9	239.89 ▲
contiguous sites with accessory sinuses or nasal cavities	160.8	—	—	—	—	—
skin	173.2	198.2	232.2	216.2	238.2	239.2
earlobe	173.2	198.2	232.2	216.2	238.2	239.2
ejaculatory duct	187.8	198.82	233.6	222.8	236.6	239.5
elbow NEC*	195.4	198.89	232.6	229.8	238.8	239.89 ▲
endocardium	164.1	198.89	—	212.7	238.8	239.89 ▲
endocervix (canal) (gland)	180.0	198.82	233.1	219.0	236.0	239.5

Neoplasm, neoplastic — continued	Malignant			Benign	Uncertain Behavior	Unspecified
	Primary	Secondary	Ca in situ			
endocrine gland NEC	194.9	198.89	—	227.9	237.4	239.7
pluriglandular NEC	194.8	198.89	234.8	227.8	237.4	239.7
endometrium (gland) (stroma)	182.0	198.82	233.2	219.1	236.0	239.5
ensiform cartilage	170.3	198.5	—	213.3	238.0	239.2
enteric — see Neoplasm, intestine						
ependyma (brain)	191.5	198.3	—	225.0	237.5	239.6
epicardium	164.1	198.89	—	212.7	238.8	239.89 ▲
epididymis	187.5	198.82	233.6	222.3	236.6	239.5
epidural	192.9	198.4	—	225.9	237.9	239.7
epiglottis	161.1	197.3	231.0	212.1	235.6	239.1
anterior aspect or surface	146.4	198.89	230.0	210.6	235.1	239.0
cartilage	161.3	197.3	231.0	212.1	235.6	239.1
free border (margin)	146.4	198.89	230.0	210.6	235.1	239.0
junctional region	146.5	198.89	230.0	210.6	235.1	239.0
posterior (laryngeal) surface	161.1	197.3	231.0	212.1	235.6	239.1
suprahyoid portion	161.1	197.3	231.0	212.1	235.6	239.1
esophagogastric junction	151.0	197.8	230.2	211.1	235.2	239.0
esophagus	150.9	197.8	230.1	211.0	235.5	239.0
abdominal	150.2	197.8	230.1	211.0	235.5	239.0
cervical	150.0	197.8	230.1	211.0	235.5	239.0
contiguous sites	150.8	—	—	—	—	—
distal (third)	150.5	197.8	230.1	211.0	235.5	239.0
lower (third)	150.5	197.8	230.1	211.0	235.5	239.0
middle (third)	150.4	197.8	230.1	211.0	235.5	239.0
proximal (third)	150.3	197.8	230.1	211.0	235.5	239.0
specified part NEC	150.8	197.8	230.1	211.0	235.5	239.0
thoracic	150.1	197.8	230.1	211.0	235.5	239.0
upper (third)	150.3	197.8	230.1	211.0	235.5	239.0
ethmoid (sinus)	160.3	197.3	231.8	212.0	235.9	239.1
bone or labyrinth	170.0	198.5	—	213.0	238.0	239.2
Eustachian tube	160.1	197.3	231.8	212.0	235.9	239.1
exocervix	180.1	198.82	233.1	219.0	236.0	239.5
external						
meatus (ear)	173.2	198.2	232.2	216.2	238.2	239.2
os, cervix uteri	180.1	198.82	233.1	219.0	236.0	239.5
extradural	192.9	198.4	—	225.9	237.9	239.7
extrahepatic (bile) duct	156.1	197.8	230.8	211.5	235.3	239.0
contiguous sites with gallbladder	156.8	—	—	—	—	—
extraocular muscle	190.1	198.4	234.0	224.1	238.8	239.89 ▲
extrarectal	195.3	198.89	234.8	229.8	238.8	239.89 ▲
extremity*	195.8	198.89	232.8	229.8	238.8	239.89 ▲
lower*	195.5	198.89	232.7	229.8	238.8	239.89 ▲
upper*	195.4	198.89	232.6	229.8	238.8	239.89 ▲
eye NEC	190.9	198.4	234.0	224.9	238.8	239.89 ▲
contiguous sites	190.8	—	—	—	—	—
specified sites NEC	190.8	198.4	234.0	224.8	238.8	239.89 ▲
eyeball	190.0	198.4	234.0	224.0	238.8	239.89 ▲
eyebrow	173.3	198.2	232.3	216.3	238.2	239.2
eyelid (lower) (skin) (upper)	173.1	198.2	232.1	216.1	238.2	239.2
cartilage	171.0	198.89	—	215.0	238.1	239.2
face NEC*	195.0	198.89	232.3	229.8	238.8	239.89 ▲
fallopian tube (accessory)	183.2	198.82	233.39	221.0	236.3	239.5
falx (cerebelli) (cerebri)	192.1	198.4	—	225.2	237.6	239.7
fascia (see also Neoplasm, connective tissue)						
palmar	171.2	198.89	—	215.2	238.1	239.2
plantar	171.3	198.89	—	215.3	238.1	239.2

Neoplasm, neoplastic — continued	Malignant			Benign	Uncertain Behavior	Unspecified
	Primary	Secondary	Ca in situ			
fatty tissue — see Neoplasm, connective tissue						
fauces, faucial NEC	146.9	198.89	230.0	210.6	235.1	239.0
pillars	146.2	198.89	230.0	210.6	235.1	239.0
tonsil	146.0	198.89	230.0	210.5	235.1	239.0
femur (any part)	170.7	198.5	—	213.7	238.0	239.2
fetal membrane	181	198.82	233.2	219.8	236.1	239.5
fibrous tissue — see Neoplasm, connective tissue						
fibula (any part)	170.7	198.5	—	213.7	238.0	239.2
filum terminale	192.2	198.3	—	225.3	237.5	239.7
finger NEC*	195.4	198.89	232.6	229.8	238.8	239.89 ▲
flank NEC*	195.8	198.89	232.5	229.8	238.8	239.89 ▲
follicle, nabothian	180.0	198.82	233.1	219.0	236.0	239.5
foot NEC*	195.5	198.89	232.7	229.8	238.8	239.89 ▲
forearm NEC*	195.4	198.89	232.6	229.8	238.8	239.89 ▲
forehead (skin)	173.3	198.2	232.3	216.3	238.2	239.2
foreskin	187.1	198.82	233.5	222.1	236.6	239.5
fornix						
pharyngeal	147.3	198.89	230.0	210.7	235.1	239.0
vagina	184.0	198.82	233.31	221.1	236.3	239.5
fossa (of)						
anterior (cranial)	191.9	198.3	—	225.0	237.5	239.6
cranial	191.9	198.3	—	225.0	237.5	239.6
ischiorectal	195.3	198.89	234.8	229.8	238.8	239.89 ▲
middle (cranial)	191.9	198.3	—	225.0	237.5	239.6
pituitary	194.3	198.89	234.8	227.3	237.0	239.7
posterior (cranial)	191.9	198.3	—	225.0	237.5	239.6
pterygoid	171.0	198.89	—	215.0	238.1	239.2
pyriform	148.1	198.89	230.0	210.8	235.1	239.0
Rosenmüller	147.2	198.89	230.0	210.7	235.1	239.0
tonsillar	146.1	198.89	230.0	210.6	235.1	239.0
fourchette	184.4	198.82	233.32	221.2	236.3	239.5
frenulum						
labii — see Neoplasm, lip, internal						
linguae	141.3	198.89	230.0	210.1	235.1	239.0
frontal						
bone	170.0	198.5	—	213.0	238.0	239.2
lobe, brain	191.1	198.3	—	225.0	237.5	239.6
meninges	192.1	198.4	—	225.2	237.6	239.7
pole	191.1	198.3	—	225.0	237.5	239.6
sinus	160.4	197.3	231.8	212.0	235.9	239.1
fundus						
stomach	151.3	197.8	230.2	211.1	235.2	239.0
uterus	182.0	198.82	233.2	219.1	236.0	239.5
gallbladder	156.0	197.8	230.8	211.5	235.3	239.0
contiguous sites with extrahepatic bile ducts	156.8	—	—	—	—	—
gall duct (extrahepatic)	156.1	197.8	230.8	211.5	235.3	239.0
intrahepatic	155.1	197.8	230.8	211.5	235.3	239.0
ganglia (see also Neoplasm, connective tissue)	171.9	198.89	—	215.9	238.1	239.2
basal	191.0	198.3	—	225.0	237.5	239.6
ganglion (see also Neoplasm, connective tissue)	171.9	198.89	—	215.9	238.1	239.2
cranial nerve	192.0	198.4	—	225.1	237.9	239.7
Gartner's duct	184.0	198.82	233.31	221.1	236.3	239.5
gastric — see Neoplasm, stomach						
gastrocolic	159.8	197.8	230.9	211.9	235.5	239.0
gastroesophageal junction	151.0	197.8	230.2	211.1	235.2	239.0
gastrointestinal (tract) NEC	159.9	197.8	230.9	211.9	235.5	239.0
generalized	199.0	199.0	234.9	229.9	238.9	199.0
genital organ or tract						

Neoplasm, neoplastic —	Malignant			Benign	Uncertain Behavior	Unspecified
	Primary	Secondary	Ca in situ			
continued						
genital organ or tract — *continued*						
female NEC	184.9	198.82	233.39	221.9	236.3	239.5
contiguous sites	184.8	—	—	—	—	—
specified site NEC	184.8	198.82	233.39	221.8	236.3	239.5
male NEC	187.9	198.82	233.6	222.9	236.6	239.5
contiguous sites	187.8	—	—	—	—	—
specified site NEC	187.8	198.82	233.6	222.8	236.6	239.5
genitourinary tract						
female	184.9	198.82	233.39	221.9	236.3	239.5
male	187.9	198.82	233.6	222.9	236.6	239.5
gingiva (alveolar) (marginal)	143.9	198.89	230.0	210.4	235.1	239.0
lower	143.1	198.89	230.0	210.4	235.1	239.0
mandibular	143.1	198.89	230.0	210.4	235.1	239.0
maxillary	143.0	198.89	230.0	210.4	235.1	239.0
upper	143.0	198.89	230.0	210.4	235.1	239.0
gland, glandular (lymphatic) (system) (see also Neoplasm, lymph gland)						
endocrine NEC	194.9	198.89	—	227.9	237.4	239.7
salivary — see Neoplasm, salivary, gland						
glans penis	187.2	198.82	233.5	222.1	236.6	239.5
globus pallidus	191.0	198.3	—	225.0	237.5	239.6
glomus						
coccygeal	194.6	198.89	—	227.6	237.3	239.7
jugularis	194.6	198.89	—	227.6	237.3	239.7
glosso-epiglottic fold(s)	146.4	198.89	230.0	210.6	235.1	239.0
glossopalatine fold	146.2	198.89	230.0	210.6	235.1	239.0
glossopharyngeal sulcus	146.1	198.89	230.0	210.6	235.1	239.0
glottis	161.0	197.3	231.0	212.1	235.6	239.1
gluteal region*	195.3	198.89	232.5	229.8	238.8	239.89 ▲
great vessels NEC	171.4	198.89	—	215.4	238.1	239.2
groin NEC	195.3	198.89	232.5	229.8	238.8	239.89 ▲
gum	143.9	198.89	230.0	210.4	235.1	239.0
contiguous sites	143.8	—	—	—	—	—
lower	143.1	198.89	230.0	210.4	235.1	239.0
upper	143.0	198.89	230.0	210.4	235.1	239.0
hand NEC*	195.4	198.89	232.6	229.8	238.8	239.89 ▲
head NEC*	195.0	198.89	232.4	229.8	238.8	239.89 ▲
heart	164.1	198.89	—	212.7	238.8	239.89 ▲
contiguous sites with mediastinum or thymus	164.8	—	—	—	—	—
heel NEC*	195.5	198.89	232.7	229.8	238.8	239.89 ▲
helix	173.2	198.2	232.2	216.2	238.2	239.2
hematopoietic, hemopoietic tissue NEC	202.8 ☑	198.89	—	—	—	238.79
hemisphere, cerebral	191.0	198.3	—	225.0	237.5	239.6
hemorrhoidal zone	154.2	197.5	230.5	211.4	235.5	239.0
hepatic	155.2	197.7	230.8	211.5	235.3	239.0
duct (bile)	156.1	197.8	230.8	211.5	235.3	239.0
flexure (colon)	153.0	197.5	230.3	211.3	235.2	239.0
primary	155.0	—	—	—	—	—
hilus of lung	162.2	197.0	231.2	212.3	235.7	239.1
hip NEC*	195.5	198.89	232.7	229.8	238.8	239.89 ▲
hippocampus, brain	191.2	198.3	—	225.0	237.5	239.6
humerus (any part)	170.4	198.5	—	213.4	238.0	239.2
hymen	184.0	198.82	233.31	221.1	236.3	239.5
hypopharynx, hypopharyngeal NEC	148.9	198.89	230.0	210.8	235.1	239.0
contiguous sites	148.8	—	—	—	—	—

Neoplasm, neoplastic —	Malignant			Benign	Uncertain Behavior	Unspecified
	Primary	Secondary	Ca in situ			
continued						
hypopharynx, hypopharyngeal — *continued*						
postcricoid region	148.0	198.89	230.0	210.8	235.1	239.0
posterior wall	148.3	198.89	230.0	210.8	235.1	239.0
pyriform fossa (sinus)	148.1	198.89	230.0	210.8	235.1	239.0
specified site NEC	148.8	198.89	230.0	210.8	235.1	239.0
wall	148.9	198.89	230.0	210.8	235.1	239.0
posterior	148.3	198.89	230.0	210.8	235.1	239.0
hypophysis	194.3	198.89	234.8	227.3	237.0	239.7
hypothalamus	191.0	198.3	—	225.0	237.5	239.6
ileocecum, ileocecal (coil) (junction) (valve)	153.4	197.5	230.3	211.3	235.2	239.0
ileum	152.2	197.4	230.7	211.2	235.2	239.0
ilium	170.6	198.5	—	213.6	238.0	239.2
immunoproliferative NEC	203.8 ☑	—	—	—	—	—
infraclavicular (region)*	195.1	198.89	232.5	229.8	238.8	239.89 ▲
inguinal (region)*	195.3	198.89	232.5	229.8	238.8	239.89 ▲
insula	191.0	198.3	—	225.0	237.5	239.6
insular tissue (pancreas)	157.4	197.8	230.9	211.7	235.5	239.0
brain	191.0	198.3	—	225.0	237.5	239.6
interarytenoid fold	148.2	198.89	230.0	210.8	235.1	239.0
hypopharyngeal aspect	148.2	198.89	230.0	210.8	235.1	239.0
laryngeal aspect	161.1	197.3	231.0	212.1	235.6	239.1
marginal zone	148.2	198.89	230.0	210.8	235.1	239.0
interdental papillae	143.9	198.89	230.0	210.4	235.1	239.0
lower	143.1	198.89	230.0	210.4	235.1	239.0
upper	143.0	198.89	230.0	210.4	235.1	239.0
internal						
capsule	191.0	198.3	—	225.0	237.5	239.6
os (cervix)	180.0	198.82	233.1	219.0	236.0	239.5
intervertebral cartilage or disc	170.2	198.5	—	213.2	238.0	239.2
intestine, intestinal	159.0	197.8	230.7	211.9	235.2	239.0
large	153.9	197.5	230.3	211.3	235.2	239.0
appendix	153.5	197.5	230.3	211.3	235.2	239.0
caput coli	153.4	197.5	230.3	211.3	235.2	239.0
cecum	153.4	197.5	230.3	211.3	235.2	239.0
colon	153.9	197.5	230.3	211.3	235.2	239.0
and rectum	154.0	197.5	230.4	211.4	235.2	239.0
ascending	153.6	197.5	230.3	211.3	235.2	239.0
caput	153.4	197.5	230.3	211.3	235.2	239.0
contiguous sites	153.8	—	—	—	—	—
descending	153.2	197.5	230.3	211.3	235.2	239.0
distal	153.2	197.5	230.3	211.3	235.2	239.0
left	153.2	197.5	230.3	211.3	235.2	239.0
pelvic	153.3	197.5	230.3	211.3	235.2	239.0
right	153.6	197.5	230.3	211.3	235.2	239.0
sigmoid (flexure)	153.3	197.5	230.3	211.3	235.2	239.0
transverse	153.1	197.5	230.3	211.3	235.2	239.0
contiguous sites	153.8	—	—	—	—	—
hepatic flexure	153.0	197.5	230.3	211.3	235.2	239.0
ileocecum, ileocecal (coil) (valve)	153.4	197.5	230.3	211.3	235.2	239.0
sigmoid flexure (lower) (upper)	153.3	197.5	230.3	211.3	235.2	239.0
splenic flexure	153.7	197.5	230.3	211.3	235.2	239.0
small	152.9	197.4	230.7	211.2	235.2	239.0
contiguous sites	152.8	—	—	—	—	—
duodenum	152.0	197.4	230.7	211.2	235.2	239.0
ileum	152.2	197.4	230.7	211.2	235.2	239.0
jejunum	152.1	197.4	230.7	211.2	235.2	239.0

Index

Neoplasm, intestine, intestinal — Neoplasm, lip

	Malignant			Benign	Uncertain Behavior	Unspecified
	Primary	Secondary	Ca in situ			
Neoplasm, neoplastic—						
continued						
intestine, intestinal —						
continued						
tract NEC	159.0	197.8	230.7	211.9	235.2	239.0
intra-abdominal	195.2	198.89	234.8	229.8	238.8	239.89 ▲
intracranial NEC	191.9	198.3	—	225.0	237.5	239.6
intrahepatic (bile)						
duct	155.1	197.8	230.8	211.5	235.3	239.0
intraocular	190.0	198.4	234.0	224.0	238.8	239.89 ▲
intraorbital	190.1	198.4	234.0	224.1	238.8	239.89 ▲
intrasellar	194.3	198.89	234.8	227.3	237.0	239.7
intrathoracic (cavity) (organs NEC)	195.1	198.89	234.8	229.8	238.8	239.89 ▲
contiguous sites with respiratory organs	165.8	—	—	—	—	—
iris	190.0	198.4	234.0	224.0	238.8	239.89 ▲
ischiorectal (fossa)	195.3	198.89	234.8	229.8	238.8	239.89 ▲
ischium	170.6	198.5	—	213.6	238.0	239.2
island of Reil	191.0	198.3	—	225.0	237.5	239.6
islands or islets of Langerhans	157.4	197.8	230.9	211.7	235.5	239.0
isthmus uteri	182.1	198.82	233.2	219.1	236.0	239.5
jaw	195.0	198.89	234.8	229.8	238.8	239.89 ▲
bone	170.1	198.5	—	213.1	238.0	239.2
carcinoma	143.9	—	—	—	—	—
lower	143.1	—	—	—	—	—
upper	143.0	—	—	—	—	—
lower	170.1	198.5	—	213.1	238.0	239.2
upper	170.0	198.5	—	213.0	238.0	239.2
carcinoma (any type) (lower) (upper)	195.0	—	—	—	—	—
skin	173.3	198.2	232.3	216.3	238.2	239.2
soft tissues	143.9	198.89	230.0	210.4	235.1	239.0
lower	143.1	198.89	230.0	210.4	235.1	239.0
upper	143.0	198.89	230.0	210.4	235.1	239.0
jejunum	152.1	197.4	230.7	211.2	235.2	239.0
joint NEC (see also Neoplasm, bone)	170.9	198.5	—	213.9	238.0	239.2
acromioclavicular	170.4	198.5	—	213.4	238.0	239.2
bursa or synovial membrane — see Neoplasm, connective tissue						
costovertebral	170.3	198.5	—	213.3	238.0	239.2
sternocostal	170.3	198.5	—	213.3	238.0	239.2
temporomandibular	170.1	198.5	—	213.1	238.0	239.2
junction						
anorectal	154.8	197.5	230.7	211.4	235.5	239.0
cardioesophageal	151.0	197.8	230.2	211.1	235.2	239.0
esophagogastric	151.0	197.8	230.2	211.1	235.2	239.0
gastroesophageal	151.0	197.8	230.2	211.1	235.2	239.0
hard and soft palate	145.5	198.89	230.0	210.4	235.1	239.0
ileocecal	153.4	197.5	230.3	211.3	235.2	239.0
pelvirectal	154.0	197.5	230.4	211.4	235.2	239.0
pelviureteric	189.1	198.0	233.9	223.1	236.91	239.5
rectosigmoid	154.0	197.5	230.4	211.4	235.2	239.0
squamocolumnar, of cervix	180.8	198.82	233.1	219.0	236.0	239.5
kidney (parenchyma)	189.0	198.0	233.9	223.0	236.91	239.5
calyx	189.1	198.0	233.9	223.1	236.91	239.5
hilus	189.1	198.0	233.9	223.1	236.91	239.5
pelvis	189.1	198.0	233.9	223.1	236.91	239.5
knee NEC*	195.5	198.89	232.7	229.8	238.8	239.89 ▲
labia (skin)	184.4	198.82	233.32	221.2	236.3	239.5
majora	184.1	198.82	233.32	221.2	236.3	239.5
minora	184.2	198.82	233.32	221.2	236.3	239.5
labial (see also Neoplasm, lip)						
sulcus (lower) (upper)	145.1	198.89	230.0	210.4	235.1	239.0
labium (skin)	184.4	198.82	233.32	221.2	236.3	239.5
Neoplasm, neoplastic—						
continued						
labium — *continued*						
majus	184.1	198.82	233.32	221.2	236.3	239.5
minus	184.2	198.82	233.32	221.2	236.3	239.5
lacrimal						
canaliculi	190.7	198.4	234.0	224.7	238.8	239.89 ▲
duct (nasal)	190.7	198.4	234.0	224.7	238.8	239.89 ▲
gland	190.2	198.4	234.0	224.2	238.8	239.89 ▲
punctum	190.7	198.4	234.0	224.7	238.8	239.89 ▲
sac	190.7	198.4	234.0	224.7	238.8	239.89 ▲
Langerhans, islands or islets	157.4	197.8	230.9	211.7	235.5	239.0
laryngopharynx	148.9	198.89	230.0	210.8	235.1	239.0
larynx, laryngeal NEC	161.9	197.3	231.0	212.1	235.6	239.1
aryepiglottic fold	161.1	197.3	231.0	212.1	235.6	239.1
cartilage (arytenoid) (cricoid) (cuneiform) (thyroid)	161.3	197.3	231.0	212.1	235.6	239.1
commissure (anterior) (posterior)	161.0	197.3	231.0	212.1	235.6	239.1
contiguous sites	161.8	—	—	—	—	—
extrinsic NEC	161.1	197.3	231.0	212.1	235.6	239.1
meaning hypopharynx	148.9	198.89	230.0	210.8	235.1	239.0
interarytenoid fold	161.1	197.3	231.0	212.1	235.6	239.1
intrinsic	161.0	197.3	231.0	212.1	235.6	239.1
ventricular band	161.1	197.3	231.0	212.1	235.6	239.1
leg NEC*	195.5	198.89	232.7	229.8	238.8	239.89 ▲
lens, crystalline	190.0	198.4	234.0	224.0	238.8	239.89 ▲
lid (lower) (upper)	173.1	198.2	232.1	216.1	238.2	239.2
ligament (see also Neoplasm, connective tissue)						
broad	183.3	198.82	233.39	221.0	236.3	239.5
Mackenrodt's	183.8	198.82	233.39	221.8	236.3	239.5
non-uterine — see Neoplasm, connective tissue						
round	183.5	198.82	—	221.0	236.3	239.5
sacro-uterine	183.4	198.82	—	221.0	236.3	239.5
uterine	183.4	198.82	—	221.0	236.3	239.5
utero-ovarian	183.8	198.82	233.39	221.8	236.3	239.5
uterosacral	183.4	198.82	—	221.0	236.3	239.5
limb*	195.8	198.89	232.8	229.8	238.8	239.89 ▲
lower*	195.5	198.89	232.7	229.8	238.8	239.89 ▲
upper*	195.4	198.89	232.6	229.8	238.8	239.89 ▲
limbus of cornea	190.4	198.4	234.0	224.4	238.8	239.89 ▲
lingual NEC (see also Neoplasm, tongue)	141.9	198.89	230.0	210.1	235.1	239.0
lingula, lung	162.3	197.0	231.2	212.3	235.7	239.1
lip (external) (lipstick area) (vermillion border)	140.9	198.89	230.0	210.0	235.1	239.0
buccal aspect — see Neoplasm, lip, internal						
commissure	140.6	198.89	230.0	210.4	235.1	239.0
contiguous sites	140.8	—	—	—	—	—
with oral cavity or pharynx	149.8	—	—	—	—	—
frenulum — see Neoplasm, lip, internal						
inner aspect — see Neoplasm, lip, internal						
internal (buccal) (frenulum) (mucosa) (oral)	140.5	198.89	230.0	210.0	235.1	239.0
lower	140.4	198.89	230.0	210.0	235.1	239.0
upper	140.3	198.89	230.0	210.0	235.1	239.0

☑ Additional Digit Required — Refer to the Tabular List for Digit Selection   ▽ Subterms under main terms may continue to next column or page

Neoplasm, neoplastic — continued

	Malignant					
	Primary	Secondary	Ca in situ	Benign	Uncertain Behavior	Unspecified
lip — continued						
lower	140.1	198.89	230.0	210.0	235.1	239.0
internal (buccal) (frenulum) (mucosa) (oral)	140.4	198.89	230.0	210.0	235.1	239.0
mucosa — *see* Neoplasm, lip, internal						
oral aspect — *see* Neoplasm, lip, internal						
skin (commissure) (lower) (upper)	173.0	198.2	232.0	216.0	238.2	239.2
upper	140.0	198.89	230.0	210.0	235.1	239.0
internal (buccal) (frenulum) (mucosa) (oral)	140.3	198.89	230.0	210.0	235.1	239.0
liver	155.2	197.7	230.8	211.5	235.3	239.0
primary	155.0	—	—	—	—	—
lobe						
azygos	162.3	197.0	231.2	212.3	235.7	239.1
frontal	191.1	198.3	—	225.0	237.5	239.6
lower	162.5	197.0	231.2	212.3	235.7	239.1
middle	162.4	197.0	231.2	212.3	235.7	239.1
occipital	191.4	198.3	—	225.0	237.5	239.6
parietal	191.3	198.3	—	225.0	237.5	239.6
temporal	191.2	198.3	—	225.0	237.5	239.6
upper	162.3	197.0	231.2	212.3	235.7	239.1
lumbosacral plexus	171.6	198.4	—	215.6	238.1	239.2
lung	162.9	197.0	231.2	212.3	235.7	239.1
azygos lobe	162.3	197.0	231.2	212.3	235.7	239.1
carina	162.2	197.0	231.2	212.3	235.7	239.1
contiguous sites with bronchus or trachea	162.8	—	—	—	—	—
hilus	162.2	197.0	231.2	212.3	235.7	239.1
lingula	162.3	197.0	231.2	212.3	235.7	239.1
lobe NEC	162.9	197.0	231.2	212.3	235.7	239.1
lower lobe	162.5	197.0	231.2	212.3	235.7	239.1
main bronchus	162.2	197.0	231.2	212.3	235.7	239.1
middle lobe	162.4	197.0	231.2	212.3	235.7	239.1
upper lobe	162.3	197.0	231.2	212.3	235.7	239.1
lymph, lymphatic						
channel NEC (*see also* Neoplasm, connective tissue)	171.9	198.89	—	215.9	238.1	239.2
gland (secondary)	—	196.9	—	229.0	238.8	239.89 ▲
abdominal	—	196.2	—	229.0	238.8	239.89 ▲
aortic	—	196.2	—	229.0	238.8	239.89 ▲
arm	—	196.3	—	229.0	238.8	239.89 ▲
auricular (anterior) (posterior)	—	196.0	—	229.0	238.8	239.89 ▲
axilla, axillary	—	196.3	—	229.0	238.8	239.89 ▲
brachial	—	196.3	—	229.0	238.8	239.89 ▲
bronchial	—	196.1	—	229.0	238.8	239.89 ▲
bronchopulmonary	—	196.1	—	229.0	238.8	239.89 ▲
celiac	—	196.2	—	229.0	238.8	239.89 ▲
cervical	—	196.0	—	229.0	238.8	239.89 ▲
cervicofacial	—	196.0	—	229.0	238.8	239.89 ▲
Cloquet	—	196.5	—	229.0	238.8	239.89 ▲
colic	—	196.2	—	229.0	238.8	239.89 ▲
common duct	—	196.2	—	229.0	238.8	239.89 ▲
cubital	—	196.3	—	229.0	238.8	239.89 ▲
diaphragmatic	—	196.1	—	229.0	238.8	239.89 ▲
epigastric, inferior	—	196.6	—	229.0	238.8	239.89 ▲
epitrochlear	—	196.3	—	229.0	238.8	239.89 ▲
esophageal	—	196.1	—	229.0	238.8	239.89 ▲
face	—	196.0	—	229.0	238.8	239.89 ▲
femoral	—	196.5	—	229.0	238.8	239.89 ▲
gastric	—	196.2	—	229.0	238.8	239.89 ▲

Neoplasm, neoplastic — continued

	Malignant					
	Primary	Secondary	Ca in situ	Benign	Uncertain Behavior	Unspecified
lymph, lymphatic — continued						
gland — continued						
groin	—	196.5	—	229.0	238.8	239.89 ▲
head	—	196.0	—	229.0	238.8	239.89 ▲
hepatic	—	196.2	—	229.0	238.8	239.89 ▲
hilar (pulmonary)	—	196.1	—	229.0	238.8	239.89 ▲
splenic	—	196.2	—	229.0	238.8	239.89 ▲
hypogastric	—	196.6	—	229.0	238.8	239.89 ▲
ileocolic	—	196.2	—	229.0	238.8	239.89 ▲
iliac	—	196.6	—	229.0	238.8	239.89 ▲
infraclavicular	—	196.3	—	229.0	238.8	239.89 ▲
inguina, inguinal	—	196.5	—	229.0	238.8	239.89 ▲
innominate	—	196.1	—	229.0	238.8	239.89 ▲
intercostal	—	196.1	—	229.0	238.8	239.89 ▲
intestinal	—	196.2	—	229.0	238.8	239.89 ▲
intra-abdominal	—	196.2	—	229.0	238.8	239.89 ▲
intrapelvic	—	196.6	—	229.0	238.8	239.89 ▲
intrathoracic	—	196.1	—	229.0	238.8	239.9
jugular	—	196.0	—	229.0	238.8	239.89 ▲
leg	—	196.5	—	229.0	238.8	239.89 ▲
limb						
lower	—	196.5	—	229.0	238.8	239.89 ▲
upper	—	196.3	—	229.0	238.8	239.89 ▲
lower limb	—	196.5	—	229.0	238.8	239.89 ▲
lumbar	—	196.2	—	229.0	238.8	239.89 ▲
mandibular	—	196.0	—	229.0	238.8	239.89 ▲
mediastinal	—	196.1	—	229.0	238.8	239.89 ▲
mesenteric (inferior) (superior)	—	196.2	—	229.0	238.8	239.89 ▲
midcolic	—	196.2	—	229.0	238.8	239.89 ▲
multiple sites in categories 196.0–196.6	—	196.8	—	229.0	238.8	239.89 ▲
neck	—	196.0	—	229.0	238.8	239.89 ▲
obturator	—	196.6	—	229.0	238.8	239.89 ▲
occipital	—	196.0	—	229.0	238.8	239.89 ▲
pancreatic	—	196.2	—	229.0	238.8	239.89 ▲
para-aortic	—	196.2	—	229.0	238.8	239.89 ▲
paracervical	—	196.6	—	229.0	238.8	239.89 ▲
parametrial	—	196.6	—	229.0	238.8	239.89 ▲
parasternal	—	196.1	—	229.0	238.8	239.89 ▲
parotid	—	196.0	—	229.0	238.8	239.89 ▲
pectoral	—	196.3	—	229.0	238.8	239.89 ▲
pelvic	—	196.6	—	229.0	238.8	239.89 ▲
peri-aortic	—	196.2	—	229.0	238.8	239.89 ▲
peripancreatic	—	196.2	—	229.0	238.8	239.89 ▲
popliteal	—	196.5	—	229.0	238.8	239.89 ▲
porta hepatis	—	196.2	—	229.0	238.8	239.89 ▲
portal	—	196.2	—	229.0	238.8	239.89 ▲
preauricular	—	196.0	—	229.0	238.8	239.89 ▲
prelaryngeal	—	196.0	—	229.0	238.8	239.89 ▲
presymphysial	—	196.6	—	229.0	238.8	239.89 ▲
pretracheal	—	196.0	—	229.0	238.8	239.89 ▲
primary (any site) NEC	202.9 ☑	—	—	—	—	—
pulmonary (hiler)	—	196.1	—	229.0	238.8	239.89 ▲
pyloric	—	196.2	—	229.0	238.8	239.89 ▲
retroperitoneal	—	196.2	—	229.0	238.8	239.89 ▲
retropharyngeal	—	196.0	—	229.0	238.8	239.89 ▲
Rosenmüller's	—	196.5	—	229.0	238.8	239.89 ▲
sacral	—	196.6	—	229.0	238.8	239.89 ▲
scalene	—	196.0	—	229.0	238.8	239.89 ▲
site NEC	—	196.9	—	229.0	238.8	239.89 ▲
splenic (hilar)	—	196.2	—	229.0	238.8	239.89 ▲
subclavicular	—	196.3	—	229.0	238.8	239.89 ▲
subinguinal	—	196.5	—	229.0	238.8	239.89 ▲
sublingual	—	196.0	—	229.0	238.8	239.89 ▲
submandibular	—	196.0	—	229.0	238.8	239.89 ▲
submaxillary	—	196.0	—	229.0	238.8	239.89 ▲
submental	—	196.0	—	229.0	238.8	239.89 ▲

☑ Additional Digit Required — Refer to the Tabular List for Digit Selection

▽ Subterms under main terms may continue to next column or page

Index

Neoplasm, lymph, lymphatic — Neoplasm, nasopharynx, nasopharyngeal

Left table

	Malignant					
Neoplasm, neoplastic —	Primary	Secondary	Ca in situ	Benign	Uncertain Behavior	Unspecified
continued						
lymph, lymphatic — *continued*						
gland — *continued*						
subscapular	—	196.3	—	229.0	238.8	239.89 ▲
supraclavicular	—	196.0	—	229.0	238.8	239.89 ▲
thoracic	—	196.1	—	229.0	238.8	239.89 ▲
tibial	—	196.5	—	229.0	238.8	239.89 ▲
tracheal	—	196.1	—	229.0	238.8	239.89 ▲
tracheobronchial	—	196.1	—	229.0	238.8	239.89 ▲
upper limb	—	196.3	—	229.0	238.8	239.89 ▲
Virchow's	—	196.0	—	229.0	238.8	239.89 ▲
node (*see also* Neoplasm, lymph gland)						
primary NEC	202.9 ☑	—	—	—	—	—
vessel (*see also* Neoplasm, connective tissue)	171.9	198.89	—	215.9	238.1	239.2
Mackenrodt's ligament	183.8	198.82	233.39	221.8	236.3	239.5
malar	170.0	198.5	—	213.0	238.0	239.2
region — *see* Neoplasm, cheek						
mammary gland — *see* Neoplasm, breast						
mandible	170.1	198.5	—	213.1	238.0	239.2
alveolar						
mucosa	143.1	198.89	230.0	210.4	235.1	239.0
mucose	143.1	198.89	230.0	210.4	235.1	239.0
ridge or process	170.1	198.5	—	213.1	238.0	239.2
carcinoma	143.1	—	—	—	—	—
carcinoma	143.1	—	—	—	—	—
marrow (bone) NEC	202.9 ☑	198.5	—	—	☑	238.79
mastectomy site (skin)	173.5	198.2	—	—	—	—
specified as breast tissue	174.8	198.81	—	—	—	—
mastoid (air cells) (antrum) (cavity)	160.1	197.3	231.8	212.0	235.9	239.1
bone or process	170.0	198.5	—	213.0	238.0	239.2
maxilla, maxillary (superior)	170.0	198.5	—	213.0	238.0	239.2
alveolar						
mucosa	143.0	198.89	230.0	210.4	235.1	239.0
ridge or process	170.0	198.5	—	213.0	238.0	239.2
carcinoma	143.0	—	—	—	—	—
antrum	160.2	197.3	231.8	212.0	235.9	239.1
carcinoma	143.0	—	—	—	—	—
inferior — *see* Neoplasm, mandible						
sinus	160.2	197.3	231.8	212.0	235.9	239.1
meatus						
external (ear)	173.2	198.2	232.2	216.2	238.2	239.2
Meckel's diverticulum	152.3	197.4	230.7	211.2	235.2	239.0
mediastinum, mediastinal	164.9	197.1	—	212.5	235.8	239.89 ▲
anterior	164.2	197.1	—	212.5	235.8	239.89 ▲
contiguous sites with heart and thymus	164.8	—	—	—	—	—
posterior	164.3	197.1	—	212.5	235.8	239.89 ▲
medulla						
adrenal	194.0	198.7	234.8	227.0	237.2	239.7
oblongata	191.7	198.3	—	225.0	237.5	239.6
meibomian gland	173.1	198.2	232.1	216.1	238.2	239.2
meninges (brain) (cerebral) (cranial) (intracranial)	192.1	198.4	—	225.2	237.6	239.7
spinal (cord)	192.3	198.4	—	225.4	237.6	239.7

Right table

	Malignant					
Neoplasm, neoplastic —	Primary	Secondary	Ca in situ	Benign	Uncertain Behavior	Unspecified
continued						
meniscus, knee joint (lateral) (medial)	170.7	198.5	—	213.7	238.0	239.2
mesentery, mesenteric	158.8	197.6	—	211.8	235.4	239.0
mesoappendix	158.8	197.6	—	211.8	235.4	239.0
mesocolon	158.8	197.6	—	211.8	235.4	239.0
mesopharynx — *see* Neoplasm, oropharynx						
mesosalpinx	183.3	198.82	233.39	221.0	236.3	239.5
mesovarium	183.3	198.82	233.39	221.0	236.3	239.5
metacarpus (any bone)	170.5	198.5	—	213.5	238.0	239.2
metastatic NEC (*see also* Neoplasm, by site, secondary)	—	199.1	—	—	—	—
metatarsus (any bone)	170.8	198.5	—	213.8	238.0	239.2
midbrain	191.7	198.3	—	225.0	237.5	239.6
milk duct — *see* Neoplasm, breast						
mons						
pubis	184.4	198.82	233.32	221.2	236.3	239.5
veneris	184.4	198.82	233.32	221.2	236.3	239.5
motor tract	192.9	198.4	—	225.9	237.9	239.7
brain	191.9	198.3	—	225.0	237.5	239.6
spinal	192.2	198.3	—	225.3	237.5	239.7
mouth	145.9	198.89	230.0	210.4	235.1	239.0
contiguous sites	145.8	—	—	—	—	—
floor	144.9	198.89	230.0	210.3	235.1	239.0
anterior portion	144.0	198.89	230.0	210.3	235.1	239.0
contiguous sites	144.8	—	—	—	—	—
lateral portion	144.1	198.89	230.0	210.3	235.1	239.0
roof	145.5	198.89	230.0	210.4	235.1	239.0
specified part NEC	145.8	198.89	230.0	210.4	235.1	239.0
vestibule	145.1	198.89	230.0	210.4	235.1	239.0
mucosa						
alveolar (ridge or process)	143.9	198.89	230.0	210.4	235.1	239.0
lower	143.1	198.89	230.0	210.4	235.1	239.0
upper	143.0	198.89	230.0	210.4	235.1	239.0
buccal	145.0	198.89	230.0	210.4	235.1	239.0
cheek	145.0	198.89	230.0	210.4	235.1	239.0
lip — *see* Neoplasm, lip, internal						
nasal	160.0	197.3	231.8	212.0	235.9	239.1
oral	145.0	198.89	230.0	210.4	235.1	239.0
Müllerian duct						
female	184.8	198.82	233.39	221.8	236.3	239.5
male	187.8	198.82	233.6	222.8	236.6	239.5
multiple sites NEC	199.0	199.0	234.9	229.9	238.9	199.0
muscle (*see also* Neoplasm, connective tissue)						
extraocular	190.1	198.4	234.0	224.1	238.8	239.89 ▲
myocardium	164.1	198.89	—	212.7	238.8	239.89 ▲
myometrium	182.0	198.82	233.2	219.1	236.0	239.5
myopericardium	164.1	198.89	—	212.7	238.8	239.89 ▲
nabothian gland (follicle)	180.0	198.82	233.1	219.0	236.0	239.5
nail	173.9	198.2	232.9	216.9	238.2	239.2
finger	173.6	198.2	232.6	216.6	238.2	239.2
toe	173.7	198.2	232.7	216.7	238.2	239.2
nares, naris (anterior) (posterior)	160.0	197.3	231.8	212.0	235.9	239.1
nasal — *see* Neoplasm, nose						
nasolabial groove	173.3	198.2	232.3	216.3	238.2	239.2
nasolacrimal duct	190.7	198.4	234.0	224.7	238.8	239.89 ▲
nasopharynx, nasopharyngeal	147.9	198.89	230.0	210.7	235.1	239.0
contiguous sites	147.8	—	—	—	—	—

☑ Additional Digit Required — Refer to the Tabular List for Digit Selection

Subterms under main terms may continue to next column or page

▶◀ Revised Text   ● New Line   ▲ Revised Code

2010 ICD-9-CM

	Malignant					
	Primary	Secondary	Ca in situ	Benign	Uncertain Behavior	Unspecified
Neoplasm, neoplastic — *continued*						
nasopharynx, nasopharyngeal — *continued*						
floor	147.3	198.89	230.0	210.7	235.1	239.0
roof	147.0	198.89	230.0	210.7	235.1	239.0
specified site NEC	147.8	198.89	230.0	210.7	235.1	239.0
wall	147.9	198.89	230.0	210.7	235.1	239.0
anterior	147.3	198.89	230.0	210.7	235.1	239.0
lateral	147.2	198.89	230.0	210.7	235.1	239.0
posterior	147.1	198.89	230.0	210.7	235.1	239.0
superior	147.0	198.89	230.0	210.7	235.1	239.0
nates	173.5	198.2	232.5	216.5	238.2	239.2
neck NEC*	195.0	198.89	234.8	229.8	238.8	239.89 ▲
nerve (autonomic) (ganglion) (parasympathetic) (peripheral) (sympathetic) (*see also* Neoplasm, connective tissue)						
abducens	192.0	198.4	—	225.1	237.9	239.7
accessory (spinal)	192.0	198.4	—	225.1	237.9	239.7
acoustic	192.0	198.4	—	225.1	237.9	239.7
auditory	192.0	198.4	—	225.1	237.9	239.7
brachial	171.2	198.89	—	215.2	238.1	239.2
cranial (any)	192.0	198.4	—	225.1	237.9	239.7
facial	192.0	198.4	—	225.1	237.9	239.7
femoral	171.3	198.89	—	215.3	238.1	239.2
glossopharyngeal	192.0	198.4	—	225.1	237.9	239.7
hypoglossal	192.0	198.4	—	225.1	237.9	239.7
intercostal	171.4	198.89	—	215.4	238.1	239.2
lumbar	171.7	198.89	—	215.7	238.1	239.2
median	171.2	198.89	—	215.2	238.1	239.2
obturator	171.3	198.89	—	215.3	238.1	239.2
oculomotor	192.0	198.4	—	225.1	237.9	239.7
olfactory	192.0	198.4	—	225.1	237.9	239.7
optic	192.0	198.4	—	225.1	237.9	239.7
peripheral NEC	171.9	198.89	—	215.9	238.1	239.2
radial	171.2	198.89	—	215.2	238.1	239.2
sacral	171.6	198.89	—	215.6	238.1	239.2
sciatic	171.3	198.89	—	215.3	238.1	239.2
spinal NEC	171.9	198.89	—	215.9	238.1	239.2
trigeminal	192.0	198.4	—	225.1	237.9	239.7
trochlear	192.0	198.4	—	225.1	237.9	239.7
ulnar	171.2	198.89	—	215.2	238.1	239.2
vagus	192.0	198.4	—	225.1	237.9	239.7
nervous system (central)						
NEC	192.9	198.4	—	225.9	237.9	239.7
autonomic NEC	171.9	198.89	—	215.9	238.1	239.2
brain (*see also* Neoplasm, brain)						
membrane or meninges	192.1	198.4	—	225.2	237.6	239.7
contiguous sites	192.8	—	—	—	—	—
parasympathetic NEC	171.9	198.89	—	215.9	238.1	239.2
sympathetic NEC	171.9	198.89	—	215.9	238.1	239.2
nipple (female)	174.0	198.81	233.0	217	238.3	239.3
male	175.0	198.81	233.0	217	238.3	239.3
nose, nasal	195.0	198.89	234.8	229.8	238.8	239.89 ▲
ala (external)	173.3	198.2	232.3	216.3	238.2	239.2
bone	170.0	198.5	—	213.0	238.0	239.2
cartilage	160.0	197.3	231.8	212.0	235.9	239.1
cavity	160.0	197.3	231.8	212.0	235.9	239.1
contiguous sites with accessory sinuses or middle ear	160.8	—	—	—	—	—
choana	147.3	198.89	230.0	210.7	235.1	239.0
external (skin)	173.3	198.2	232.3	216.3	238.2	239.2
fossa	160.0	197.3	231.8	212.0	235.9	239.1
internal	160.0	197.3	231.8	212.0	235.9	239.1
mucosa	160.0	197.3	231.8	212.0	235.9	239.1
septum	160.0	197.3	231.8	212.0	235.9	239.1
Neoplasm, neoplastic — *continued*						
nose, nasal — *continued*						
septum — *continued*						
posterior margin	147.3	198.89	230.0	210.7	235.1	239.0
sinus — *see* Neoplasm, sinus						
skin	173.3	198.2	232.3	216.3	238.2	239.2
turbinate (mucosa)	160.0	197.3	231.8	212.0	235.9	239.1
bone	170.0	198.5	—	213.0	238.0	239.2
vestibule	160.0	197.3	231.8	212.0	235.9	239.1
nostril	160.0	197.3	231.8	212.0	235.9	239.1
nucleus pulposus	170.2	198.5	—	213.2	238.0	239.2
occipital bone	170.0	198.5	—	213.0	238.0	239.2
lobe or pole, brain	191.4	198.3	—	225.0	237.5	239.6
odontogenic — *see* Neoplasm, jaw bone						
oesophagus — *see* Neoplasm, esophagus						
olfactory nerve or bulb	192.0	198.4	—	225.1	237.9	239.7
olive (brain)	191.7	198.3	—	225.0	237.5	239.6
omentum	158.8	197.6	—	211.8	235.4	239.0
operculum (brain)	191.0	198.3	—	225.0	237.5	239.6
optic nerve, chiasm, or tract	192.0	198.4	—	225.1	237.9	239.7
oral (cavity)	145.9	198.89	230.0	210.4	235.1	239.0
contiguous sites with lip or pharynx	149.8	—	—	—	—	—
ill-defined	149.9	198.89	230.0	210.4	235.1	239.0
mucosa	145.9	198.89	230.0	210.4	235.1	239.0
orbit	190.1	198.4	234.0	224.1	238.8	239.89 ▲
bone	170.0	198.5	—	213.0	238.0	239.2
eye	190.1	198.4	234.0	224.1	238.8	239.89 ▲
soft parts	190.1	198.4	234.0	224.1	238.8	239.89 ▲
organ of Zuckerkandl	194.6	198.89	—	227.6	237.3	239.7
oropharynx	146.9	198.89	230.0	210.6	235.1	239.0
branchial cleft (vestige)	146.8	198.89	230.0	210.6	235.1	239.0
contiguous sites	146.8	—	—	—	—	—
junctional region	146.5	198.89	230.0	210.6	235.1	239.0
lateral wall	146.6	198.89	230.0	210.6	235.1	239.0
pillars of fauces	146.2	198.89	230.0	210.6	235.1	239.0
posterior wall	146.7	198.89	230.0	210.6	235.1	239.0
specified part NEC	146.8	198.89	230.0	210.6	235.1	239.0
vallecula	146.3	198.89	230.0	210.6	235.1	239.0
os						
external	180.1	198.82	233.1	219.0	236.0	239.5
internal	180.0	198.82	233.1	219.0	236.0	239.5
ovary	183.0	198.6	233.39	220	236.2	239.5
oviduct	183.2	198.82	233.39	221.0	236.3	239.5
palate	145.5	198.89	230.0	210.4	235.1	239.0
hard	145.2	198.89	230.0	210.4	235.1	239.0
junction of hard and soft palate	145.5	198.89	230.0	210.4	235.1	239.0
soft	145.3	198.89	230.0	210.4	235.1	239.0
nasopharyngeal surface	147.3	198.89	230.0	210.7	235.1	239.0
posterior surface	147.3	198.89	230.0	210.7	235.1	239.0
superior surface	147.3	198.89	230.0	210.7	235.1	239.0
palatoglossal arch	146.2	198.89	230.0	210.6	235.1	239.0
palatopharyngeal arch	146.2	198.89	230.0	210.6	235.1	239.0
pallium	191.0	198.3	—	225.0	237.5	239.6
palpebra	173.1	198.2	232.1	216.1	238.2	239.2
pancreas	157.9	197.8	230.9	211.6	235.5	239.0
body	157.1	197.8	230.9	211.6	235.5	239.0
contiguous sites	157.8	—	—	—	—	—

☑ Additional Digit Required — Refer to the Tabular List for Digit Selection   ▽ Subterms under main terms may continue to next column or page

2010 ICD-9-CM   ▶◀ Revised Text   ● New Line   ▲ Revised Code   October 2009 • Volume 2 — 195

Neoplasm, neoplastic — continued	Malignant			Benign	Uncertain Behavior	Unspecified
	Primary	Secondary	Ca in situ			
pancreas — continued						
duct (of Santorini) (of Wirsung)	157.3	197.8	230.9	211.6	235.5	239.0
ectopic tissue	157.8	197.8	230.9	211.6	235.5	239.0
head	157.0	197.8	230.9	211.6	235.5	239.0
islet cells	157.4	197.8	230.9	211.7	235.5	239.0
neck	157.8	197.8	230.9	211.6	235.5	239.0
tail	157.2	197.8	230.9	211.6	235.5	239.0
para-aortic body	194.6	198.89	—	227.6	237.3	239.7
paraganglion NEC	194.6	198.89	—	227.6	237.3	239.7
parametrium	183.4	198.82	—	221.0	236.3	239.5
paranephric	158.0	197.6	—	211.8	235.4	239.0
pararectal	195.3	198.89	—	229.8	238.8	239.89 ▲
parasagittal (region)	195.0	198.89	234.8	229.8	238.8	239.89 ▲
parasellar	192.9	198.4	—	225.9	237.9	239.7
parathyroid (gland)	194.1	198.89	234.8	227.1	237.4	239.7
paraurethral	195.3	198.89	—	229.8	238.8	239.89 ▲
gland	189.4	198.1	233.9	223.89	236.99	239.5
paravaginal	195.3	198.89	—	229.8	238.8	239.89 ▲
parenchyma, kidney	189.0	198.0	233.9	223.0	236.91	239.5
parietal						
bone	170.0	198.5	—	213.0	238.0	239.2
lobe, brain	191.3	198.3	—	225.0	237.5	239.6
paroophoron	183.3	198.82	233.39	221.0	236.3	239.5
parotid (duct) (gland)	142.0	198.89	230.0	210.2	235.0	239.0
parovarium	183.3	198.82	233.39	221.0	236.3	239.5
patella	170.8	198.5	—	213.8	238.0	239.2
peduncle, cerebral	191.7	198.3	—	225.0	237.5	239.6
pelvirectal junction	154.0	197.5	230.4	211.4	235.2	239.0
pelvis, pelvic	195.3	198.89	234.8	229.8	238.8	239.89 ▲
bone	170.6	198.5	—	213.6	238.0	239.2
floor	195.3	198.89	234.8	229.8	238.8	239.89 ▲
renal	189.1	198.0	233.9	223.1	236.91	239.5
viscera	195.3	198.89	234.8	229.8	238.8	239.89 ▲
wall	195.3	198.89	234.8	229.8	238.8	239.89 ▲
pelvo-abdominal	195.8	198.89	234.8	229.8	238.8	239.89 ▲
penis	187.4	198.82	233.5	222.1	236.6	239.5
body	187.3	198.82	233.5	222.1	236.6	239.5
corpus (cavernosum)	187.3	198.82	233.5	222.1	236.6	239.5
glans	187.2	198.82	233.5	222.1	236.6	239.5
skin NEC	187.4	198.82	233.5	222.1	236.6	239.5
periadrenal (tissue)	158.0	197.6	—	211.8	235.4	239.0
perianal (skin)	173.5	198.2	232.5	216.5	238.2	239.2
pericardium	164.1	198.89	—	212.7	238.8	239.89 ▲
perinephric	158.0	197.6	—	211.8	235.4	239.0
perineum	195.3	198.89	234.8	229.8	238.8	239.89 ▲
periodontal tissue NEC	143.9	198.89	230.0	210.4	235.1	239.0
periosteum — see Neoplasm, bone						
peripancreatic	158.0	197.6	—	211.8	235.4	239.0
peripheral nerve NEC	171.9	198.89	—	215.9	238.1	239.2
perirectal (tissue)	195.3	198.89	—	229.8	238.8	239.89 ▲
perirenal (tissue)	158.0	197.6	—	211.8	235.4	239.0
peritoneum, peritoneal (cavity)	158.9	197.6	—	211.8	235.4	239.0
contiguous sites	158.8	—	—	—	—	—
with digestive organs	159.8	—	—	—	—	—
parietal	158.8	197.6	—	211.8	235.4	239.0
pelvic	158.8	197.6	—	211.8	235.4	239.0
specified part NEC	158.8	197.6	—	211.8	235.4	239.0
peritonsillar (tissue)	195.0	198.89	234.8	229.8	238.8	239.89 ▲
periurethral tissue	195.3	198.89	—	229.8	238.8	239.89 ▲
phalanges	170.9	198.5	—	213.9	238.0	239.2
foot	170.8	198.5	—	213.8	238.0	239.2
hand	170.5	198.5	—	213.5	238.0	239.2

Neoplasm, neoplastic — continued	Malignant			Benign	Uncertain Behavior	Unspecified
	Primary	Secondary	Ca in situ			
pharynx, pharyngeal	149.0	198.89	230.0	210.9	235.1	239.0
bursa	147.1	198.89	230.0	210.7	235.1	239.0
fornix	147.3	198.89	230.0	210.7	235.1	239.0
recess	147.2	198.89	230.0	210.7	235.1	239.0
region	149.0	198.89	230.0	210.9	235.1	239.0
tonsil	147.1	198.89	230.0	210.7	235.1	239.0
wall (lateral) (posterior)	149.0	198.89	230.0	210.9	235.1	239.0
pia mater (cerebral) (cranial)	192.1	198.4	—	225.2	237.6	239.7
spinal	192.3	198.4	—	225.4	237.6	239.7
pillars of fauces	146.2	198.89	230.0	210.6	235.1	239.0
pineal (body) (gland)	194.4	198.89	234.8	227.4	237.1	239.7
pinna (ear) NEC	173.2	198.2	232.2	216.2	238.2	239.2
cartilage	171.0	198.89	—	215.0	238.1	239.2
piriform fossa or sinus	148.1	198.89	230.0	210.8	235.1	239.0
pituitary (body) (fossa) (gland) (lobe)	194.3	198.89	234.8	227.3	237.0	239.7
placenta	181	198.82	233.2	219.8	236.1	239.5
pleura, pleural (cavity)	163.9	197.2	—	212.4	235.8	239.1
contiguous sites	163.8	—	—	—	—	—
parietal	163.0	197.2	—	212.4	235.8	239.1
visceral	163.1	197.2	—	212.4	235.8	239.1
plexus						
brachial	171.2	198.89	—	215.2	238.1	239.2
cervical	171.0	198.89	—	215.0	238.1	239.2
choroid	191.5	198.3	—	225.0	237.5	239.6
lumbosacral	171.6	198.89	—	215.6	238.1	239.2
sacral	171.6	198.89	—	215.6	238.1	239.2
pluri-endocrine	194.8	198.89	234.8	227.8	237.4	239.7
pole						
frontal	191.1	198.3	—	225.0	237.5	239.6
occipital	191.4	198.3	—	225.0	237.5	239.6
pons (varolii)	191.7	198.3	—	225.0	237.5	239.6
popliteal fossa or space*	195.5	198.89	234.8	229.8	238.8	239.89 ▲
postcricoid (region)	148.0	198.89	230.0	210.8	235.1	239.0
posterior fossa (cranial)	191.9	198.3	—	225.0	237.5	239.6
postnasal space	147.9	198.89	230.0	210.7	235.1	239.0
prepuce	187.1	198.82	233.5	222.1	236.6	239.5
prepylorus	151.1	197.8	230.2	211.1	235.2	239.0
presacral (region)	195.3	198.89	—	229.8	238.8	239.89 ▲
prostate (gland)	185	198.82	233.4	222.2	236.5	239.5
utricle	189.3	198.1	233.9	223.81	236.99	239.5
pterygoid fossa	171.0	198.89	—	215.0	238.1	239.2
pubic bone	170.6	198.5	—	213.6	238.0	239.2
pudenda, pudendum (female)	184.4	198.82	233.32	221.2	236.3	239.5
pulmonary	162.9	197.0	231.2	212.3	235.7	239.1
putamen	191.0	198.3	—	225.0	237.5	239.6
pyloric						
antrum	151.2	197.8	230.2	211.1	235.2	239.0
canal	151.1	197.8	230.2	211.1	235.2	239.0
pylorus	151.1	197.8	230.2	211.1	235.2	239.0
pyramid (brain)	191.7	198.3	—	225.0	237.5	239.6
pyriform fossa or sinus	148.1	198.89	230.0	210.8	235.1	239.0
radius (any part)	170.4	198.5	—	213.4	238.0	239.2
Rathke's pouch	194.3	198.89	234.8	227.3	237.0	239.7
rectosigmoid (colon) (junction)	154.0	197.5	230.4	211.4	235.2	239.0
contiguous sites with anus or rectum	154.8	—	—	—	—	—
rectouterine pouch	158.8	197.6	—	211.8	235.4	239.0
rectovaginal septum or wall	195.3	198.89	234.8	229.8	238.8	239.89 ▲
rectovesical septum	195.3	198.89	234.8	229.8	238.8	239.89 ▲
rectum (ampulla)	154.1	197.5	230.4	211.4	235.2	239.0
and colon	154.0	197.5	230.4	211.4	235.2	239.0

☑ Additional Digit Required — Refer to the Tabular List for Digit Selection

▽ Subterms under main terms may continue to next column or page

	Malignant					
	Primary	Secondary	Ca in situ	Benign	Uncertain Behavior	Unspecified
Neoplasm, neoplastic — *continued*						
rectum — *continued*						
contiguous sites with anus or rectosigmoid junction	154.8	—	—	—	—	—
renal	189.0	198.0	233.9	223.0	236.91	239.5
calyx	189.1	198.0	233.9	223.1	236.91	239.5
hilus	189.1	198.0	233.9	223.1	236.91	239.5
parenchyma	189.0	198.0	233.9	223.0	236.91	239.5
pelvis	189.1	198.0	233.9	223.1	236.91	239.5
respiratory						
organs or system NEC	165.9	197.3	231.9	212.9	235.9	239.1
contiguous sites with intrathoracic organs	165.8	—	—	—	—	—
specified sites NEC	165.8	197.3	231.8	212.8	235.9	239.1
tract NEC	165.9	197.3	231.9	212.9	235.9	239.1
upper	165.0	197.3	231.9	212.9	235.9	239.1
retina	190.5	198.4	234.0	224.5	238.8	239.81 ▲
retrobulbar	190.1	198.4	—	224.1	238.8	239.89 ▲
retrocecal	158.0	197.6	—	211.8	235.4	239.0
retromolar (area) (triangle) (trigone)	145.6	198.89	230.0	210.4	235.1	239.0
retro-orbital	195.0	198.89	234.8	229.8	238.8	239.89 ▲
retroperitoneal (space) (tissue)	158.0	197.6	—	211.8	235.4	239.0
contiguous sites	158.8	—	—	—	—	—
retroperitoneum	158.0	197.6	—	211.8	235.4	239.0
contiguous sites	158.8	—	—	—	—	—
retropharyngeal	149.0	198.89	230.0	210.9	235.1	239.0
retrovesical (septum)	195.3	198.89	234.8	229.8	238.8	239.89 ▲
rhinencephalon	191.0	198.3	—	225.0	237.5	239.6
rib	170.3	198.5	—	213.3	238.0	239.2
Rosenmüller's fossa	147.2	198.89	230.0	210.7	235.1	239.0
round ligament	183.5	198.82	—	221.0	236.3	239.5
sacrococcyx, sacrococcygeal	170.6	198.5	—	213.6	238.0	239.2
region	195.3	198.89	234.8	229.8	238.8	239.89 ▲
sacrouterine ligament	183.4	198.82	—	221.0	236.3	239.5
sacrum, sacral (vertebra)	170.6	198.5	—	213.6	238.0	239.2
salivary gland or duct (major)	142.9	198.89	230.0	210.2	235.0	239.0
contiguous sites	142.8	—	—	—	—	—
minor NEC	145.9	198.89	230.0	210.4	235.1	239.0
parotid	142.0	198.89	230.0	210.2	235.0	239.0
pluriglandular	142.8	198.89	—	210.2	235.0	239.0
sublingual	142.2	198.89	230.0	210.2	235.0	239.0
submandibular	142.1	198.89	230.0	210.2	235.0	239.0
submaxillary	142.1	198.89	230.0	210.2	235.0	239.0
salpinx (uterine)	183.2	198.82	233.39	221.0	236.3	239.5
Santorini's duct	157.3	197.8	230.9	211.6	235.5	239.0
scalp	173.4	198.2	232.4	216.4	238.2	239.2
scapula (any part)	170.4	198.5	—	213.4	238.0	239.2
scapular region	195.1	198.89	234.8	229.8	238.8	239.89 ▲
scar NEC (*see also* Neoplasm, skin)	173.9	198.2	232.9	216.9	238.2	239.2
sciatic nerve	171.3	198.89	—	215.3	238.1	239.2
sclera	190.0	198.4	234.0	224.0	238.8	239.89 ▲
scrotum (skin)	187.7	198.82	—	222.4	236.6	239.5
sebaceous gland — *see* Neoplasm, skin						
sella turcica	194.3	198.89	234.8	227.3	237.0	239.7
bone	170.0	198.5	—	213.0	238.0	239.2
semilunar cartilage (knee)	170.7	198.5	—	213.7	238.0	239.2
seminal vesicle	187.8	198.82	233.6	222.8	236.6	239.5
septum						
nasal	160.0	197.3	231.8	212.0	235.9	239.1
Neoplasm, neoplastic — *continued*						
septum — *continued*						
nasal — *continued*						
posterior margin	147.3	198.89	230.0	210.7	235.1	239.0
rectovaginal	195.3	198.89	234.8	229.8	238.8	239.89 ▲
rectovesical	195.3	198.89	234.8	229.8	238.8	239.89 ▲
urethrovaginal	184.9	198.82	233.39	221.9	236.3	239.5
vesicovaginal	184.9	198.82	233.39	221.9	236.3	239.5
shoulder NEC*	195.4	198.89	232.6	229.8	238.8	239.89 ▲
sigmoid flexure (lower) (upper)	153.3	197.5	230.3	211.3	235.2	239.0
sinus (accessory)	160.9	197.3	231.8	212.0	235.9	239.1
bone (any)	170.0	198.5	—	213.0	238.0	239.2
contiguous sites with middle ear or nasal cavities	160.8	—	—	—	—	—
ethmoidal	160.3	197.3	231.8	212.0	235.9	239.1
frontal	160.4	197.3	231.8	212.0	235.9	239.1
maxillary	160.2	197.3	231.8	212.0	235.9	239.1
nasal, paranasal NEC	160.9	197.3	231.8	212.0	235.9	239.1
pyriform	148.1	198.89	230.0	210.8	235.1	239.0
sphenoidal	160.5	197.3	231.8	212.0	235.9	239.1
skeleton, skeletal NEC	170.9	198.5	—	213.9	238.0	239.2
Skene's gland	189.4	198.1	233.9	223.89	236.99	239.5
skin NEC	173.9	198.2	232.9	216.9	238.2	239.2
abdominal wall	173.5	198.2	232.5	216.5	238.2	239.2
ala nasi	173.3	198.2	232.3	216.3	238.2	239.2
ankle	173.7	198.2	232.7	216.7	238.2	239.2
antecubital space	173.6	198.2	232.6	216.6	238.2	239.2
anus	173.5	198.2	232.5	216.5	238.2	239.2
arm	173.6	198.2	232.6	216.6	238.2	239.2
auditory canal (external)	173.2	198.2	232.2	216.2	238.2	239.2
auricle (ear)	173.2	198.2	232.2	216.2	238.2	239.2
auricular canal (external)	173.2	198.2	232.2	216.2	238.2	239.2
axilla, axillary fold	173.5	198.2	232.5	216.5	238.2	239.2
back	173.5	198.2	232.5	216.5	238.2	239.2
breast	173.5	198.2	232.5	216.5	238.2	239.2
brow	173.3	198.2	232.3	216.3	238.2	239.2
buttock	173.5	198.2	232.5	216.5	238.2	239.2
calf	173.7	198.2	232.7	216.7	238.2	239.2
canthus (eye) (inner) (outer)	173.1	198.2	232.1	216.1	238.2	239.2
cervical region	173.4	198.2	232.4	216.4	238.2	239.2
cheek (external)	173.3	198.2	232.3	216.3	238.2	239.2
chest (wall)	173.5	198.2	232.5	216.5	238.2	239.2
chin	173.3	198.2	232.3	216.3	238.2	239.2
clavicular area	173.5	198.2	232.5	216.5	238.2	239.2
clitoris	184.3	198.82	233.32	221.2	236.3	239.5
columnella	173.3	198.2	232.3	216.3	238.2	239.2
concha	173.2	198.2	232.2	216.2	238.2	239.2
contiguous sites	173.8	—	—	—	—	—
ear (external)	173.2	198.2	232.2	216.2	238.2	239.2
elbow	173.6	198.2	232.6	216.6	238.2	239.2
eyebrow	173.3	198.2	232.3	216.3	238.2	239.2
eyelid	173.1	198.2	232.1	—	238.2	239.2
face NEC	173.3	198.2	232.3	216.3	238.2	239.2
female genital organs (external)	184.4	198.82	233.30	221.2	236.3	239.5
clitoris	184.3	198.82	233.32	221.2	236.3	239.5
labium NEC	184.4	198.82	233.32	221.2	236.3	239.5
majus	184.1	198.82	233.32	221.2	236.3	239.5
minus	184.2	198.82	233.32	221.2	236.3	239.5
pudendum	184.4	198.82	233.32	221.2	236.3	239.5
vulva	184.4	198.82	233.32	221.2	236.3	239.5
finger	173.6	198.2	232.6	216.6	238.2	239.2
flank	173.5	198.2	232.5	216.5	238.2	239.2
foot	173.7	198.2	232.7	216.7	238.2	239.2
forearm	173.6	198.2	232.6	216.6	238.2	239.2
forehead	173.3	198.2	232.3	216.3	238.2	239.2
glabella	173.3	198.2	232.3	216.3	238.2	239.2

✔ Additional Digit Required — Refer to the Tabular List for Digit Selection
▼ Subterms under main terms may continue to next column or page
2010 ICD-9-CM ▶◀ Revised Text ● New Line ▲ Revised Code **October 2009 · Volume 2 — 197**

Index

Neoplasm, skin — Neoplasm, sudoriferous, sudoriparous gland, site unspecified

Neoplasm, neoplastic — continued skin — continued	Malignant			Benign	Uncertain Behavior	Unspecified
	Primary	Secondary	Ca in situ			
gluteal region	173.5	198.2	232.5	216.5	238.2	239.2
groin	173.5	198.2	232.5	216.5	238.2	239.2
hand	173.6	198.2	232.6	216.6	238.2	239.2
head NEC	173.4	198.2	232.4	216.4	238.2	239.2
heel	173.7	198.2	232.7	216.7	238.2	239.2
helix	173.2	198.2	—	216.2	238.2	239.2
hip	173.7	198.2	232.7	216.7	238.2	239.2
infraclavicular region	173.5	198.2	232.5	216.5	238.2	239.2
inguinal region	173.5	198.2	232.5	216.5	238.2	239.2
jaw	173.3	198.2	232.3	216.3	238.2	239.2
knee	173.7	198.2	232.7	216.7	238.2	239.2
labia						
majora	184.1	198.82	233.32	221.2	236.3	239.5
minora	184.2	198.82	233.32	221.2	236.3	239.5
leg	173.7	198.2	232.7	216.7	238.2	239.2
lid (lower) (upper)	—	198.2	232.1	216.1	238.2	239.2
limb NEC	173.9	198.2	232.9	216.9	238.2	239.5
lower	173.7	198.2	232.7	216.7	238.2	239.2
upper	173.6	198.2	232.6	216.6	238.2	239.2
lip (lower) (upper)	173.0	198.2	232.0	216.0	238.2	239.2
male genital						
organs	187.9	198.82	233.6	222.9	236.6	239.5
penis	187.4	198.82	233.5	222.1	236.6	239.5
prepuce	187.1	198.82	233.5	222.1	236.6	239.5
scrotum	187.7	198.82	233.6	222.4	236.6	239.5
mastectomy site	173.5	198.2	—	—	—	—
specified as breast tissue	174.8	198.81	—	—	—	—
meatus, acoustic (external)	173.2	198.2	232.2	216.2	238.2	239.2
nates	173.5	198.2	232.5	216.5	238.2	239.0
neck	173.4	198.2	232.4	216.4	238.2	239.2
nose (external)	173.3	198.2	232.3	216.3	238.2	239.2
palm	173.6	198.2	232.6	216.6	238.2	239.2
palpebra	173.1	198.2	232.1	216.1	238.2	239.2
penis NEC	187.4	198.82	233.5	222.1	236.6	239.5
perianal	173.5	198.2	232.5	216.5	238.2	239.2
perineum	173.5	198.2	232.5	216.5	238.2	239.2
pinna	173.2	198.2	232.2	216.2	238.2	239.2
plantar	173.7	198.2	232.7	216.7	238.2	239.2
popliteal fossa or space	173.7	198.2	232.7	216.7	238.2	239.2
prepuce	187.1	198.82	233.5	222.1	236.6	239.5
pubes	173.5	198.2	232.5	216.5	238.2	239.2
sacrococcygeal region	173.5	198.2	232.5	216.5	238.2	239.2
scalp	173.4	198.2	232.4	216.4	238.2	239.2
scapular region	173.5	198.2	232.5	216.5	238.2	239.2
scrotum	187.7	198.82	233.6	222.4	236.6	239.5
shoulder	173.6	198.2	232.6	216.6	238.2	239.2
sole (foot)	173.7	198.2	232.7	216.7	238.2	239.2
specified sites NEC	173.8	198.2	232.8	216.8	232.8	239.2
submammary fold	173.5	198.2	232.5	216.5	238.2	239.2
supraclavicular region	173.4	198.2	232.4	216.4	238.2	239.2
temple	173.3	198.2	232.3	216.3	238.2	239.2
thigh	173.7	198.2	232.7	216.7	238.2	239.2
thoracic wall	173.5	198.2	232.5	216.5	238.2	239.2
thumb	173.6	198.2	232.6	216.6	238.2	239.2
toe	173.7	198.2	232.7	216.7	238.2	239.2
tragus	173.2	198.2	232.2	216.2	238.2	239.2
trunk	173.5	198.2	232.5	216.5	238.2	239.2
umbilicus	173.5	198.2	232.5	216.5	238.2	239.2
vulva	184.4	198.82	233.32	221.2	236.3	239.5
wrist	173.6	198.2	232.6	216.6	238.2	239.2
skull	170.0	198.5	—	213.0	238.0	239.2

Neoplasm, neoplastic — continued	Malignant			Benign	Uncertain Behavior	Unspecified
	Primary	Secondary	Ca in situ			
soft parts or tissues — see Neoplasm, connective tissue						
specified site NEC	195.8	198.89	234.8	229.8	238.8	239.89 ▲
specified site — see Neoplasm, skin						
spermatic cord	187.6	198.82	233.6	222.8	236.6	239.5
sphenoid	160.5	197.3	231.8	212.0	235.9	239.1
bone	170.0	198.5	—	213.0	238.0	239.2
sinus	160.5	197.3	231.8	212.0	235.9	239.1
sphincter						
anal	154.2	197.5	230.5	211.4	235.5	239.0
of Oddi	156.1	197.8	230.8	211.5	235.3	239.0
spine, spinal (column)	170.2	198.5	—	213.2	238.0	239.2
bulb	191.7	198.3	—	225.0	237.5	239.6
coccyx	170.6	198.5	—	213.6	238.0	239.2
cord (cervical) (lumbar) (sacral) (thoracic)	192.2	198.3	—	225.3	237.5	239.7
dura mater	192.3	198.4	—	225.4	237.6	239.7
lumbosacral	170.2	198.5	—	213.2	238.0	239.2
membrane	192.3	198.4	—	225.4	237.6	239.7
meninges	192.3	198.4	—	225.4	237.6	239.7
nerve (root)	171.9	198.89	—	215.9	238.1	239.2
pia mater	192.3	198.4	—	225.4	237.6	239.7
root	171.9	198.89	—	215.9	238.1	239.2
sacrum	170.6	198.5	—	213.6	238.0	239.2
spleen, splenic NEC	159.1	197.8	230.9	211.9	235.5	239.0
flexure (colon)	153.7	197.5	230.3	211.3	235.2	239.0
stem, brain	191.7	198.3	—	225.0	237.5	239.6
Stensen's duct	142.0	198.89	230.0	210.2	235.0	239.0
sternum	170.3	198.5	—	213.3	238.0	239.2
stomach	151.9	197.8	230.2	211.1	235.2	239.0
antrum (pyloric)	151.2	197.8	230.2	211.1	235.2	239.0
body	151.4	197.8	230.2	211.1	235.2	239.0
cardia	151.0	197.8	230.2	211.1	235.2	239.0
cardiac orifice	151.0	197.8	230.2	211.1	235.2	239.0
contiguous sites	151.8	—	—	—	—	—
corpus	151.4	197.8	230.2	211.1	235.2	239.0
fundus	151.3	197.8	230.2	211.1	235.2	239.0
greater curvature NEC	151.6	197.8	230.2	211.1	235.2	239.0
lesser curvature NEC	151.5	197.8	230.2	211.1	235.2	239.0
prepylorus	151.1	197.8	230.2	211.1	235.2	239.0
pylorus	151.1	197.8	230.2	211.1	235.2	239.0
wall NEC	151.9	197.8	230.2	211.1	235.2	239.0
anterior NEC	151.8	197.8	230.2	211.1	235.2	239.0
posterior NEC	151.8	197.8	230.2	211.1	235.2	239.0
stroma, endometrial	182.0	198.82	233.2	219.1	236.0	239.5
stump, cervical	180.8	198.82	233.1	219.0	236.0	239.5
subcutaneous (nodule) (tissue) NEC — see Neoplasm, connective tissue						
subdural	192.1	198.4	—	225.2	237.6	239.7
subglottis, subglottic	161.2	197.3	231.0	212.1	235.6	239.1
sublingual	144.9	198.89	230.0	210.3	235.1	239.0
gland or duct	142.2	198.89	230.0	210.2	235.0	239.0
submandibular gland	142.1	198.89	230.0	210.2	235.0	239.0
submaxillary gland or duct	142.1	198.89	230.0	210.2	235.0	239.0
submental	195.0	198.89	234.8	229.8	238.8	239.89 ▲
subpleural	162.9	197.0	—	212.3	235.7	239.1
substernal	164.2	197.1	—	212.5	235.8	239.89 ▲
sudoriferous, sudoriparous gland, site unspecified	173.9	198.2	232.9	216.9	238.2	239.2
specified site — see Neoplasm, skin						

☑ Additional Digit Required — Refer to the Tabular List for Digit Selection　　　　　　▽ Subterms under main terms may continue to next column or page

198 — Volume 2 • October 2009　　　►◄ Revised Text　　　● New Line　　　▲ Revised Code　　　2010 ICD-9-CM

	Malignant					
	Primary	Secondary	Ca in situ	Benign	Uncertain Behavior	Unspecified
Neoplasm, neoplastic —						
continued						
supraclavicular						
region	195.0	198.89	234.8	229.8	238.8	239.89 ▲
supraglottis	161.1	197.3	231.0	212.1	235.6	239.1
suprarenal (capsule)						
(cortex) (gland)						
(medulla)	194.0	198.7	234.8	227.0	237.2	239.7
suprasellar (region)	191.9	198.3	—	225.0	237.5	239.6
sweat gland (apocrine)						
(eccrine), site						
unspecified	173.9	198.2	232.9	216.9	238.2	239.2
sympathetic nerve or						
nervous system						
NEC	171.9	198.89	—	215.9	238.1	239.2
symphysis pubis	170.6	198.5	—	213.6	238.0	239.2
synovial membrane —						
see Neoplasm,						
connective tissue						
tapetum, brain	191.8	198.3	—	225.0	237.5	239.6
tarsus (any bone)	170.8	198.5	—	213.8	238.0	239.2
temple (skin)	173.3	198.2	232.3	216.3	238.2	239.2
temporal						
bone	170.0	198.5	—	213.0	238.0	239.2
lobe or pole	191.2	198.3	—	225.0	237.5	239.6
region	195.0	198.89	234.8	229.8	238.8	239.89 ▲
skin	173.3	198.2	232.3	216.3	238.2	239.2
tendon (sheath) — *see*						
Neoplasm,						
connective tissue						
tentorium						
(cerebelli)	192.1	198.4	—	225.2	237.6	239.7
testis, testes (descended)						
(scrotal)	186.9	198.82	233.6	222.0	236.4	239.5
ectopic	186.0	198.82	233.6	222.0	236.4	239.5
retained	186.0	198.82	233.6	222.0	236.4	239.5
undescended	186.0	198.82	233.6	222.0	236.4	239.5
thalamus	191.0	198.3	—	225.0	237.5	239.6
thigh NEC*	195.5	198.89	234.8	229.8	238.8	239.89 ▲
thorax, thoracic (cavity)						
(organs NEC)	195.1	198.89	234.8	229.8	238.8	239.89 ▲
duct	171.4	198.89	—	215.4	238.1	239.2
wall NEC	195.1	198.89	234.8	229.8	238.8	239.89 ▲
throat	149.0	198.89	230.0	210.9	235.1	239.0
thumb NEC*	195.4	198.89	232.6	229.8	238.8	239.89 ▲
thymus (gland)	164.0	198.89	—	212.6	235.8	239.89 ▲
contiguous sites with						
heart and						
mediastinum	164.8	—	—	—	—	—
thyroglossal duct	193	198.89	234.8	226	237.4	239.7
thyroid (gland)	193	198.89	234.8	226	237.4	239.7
cartilage	161.3	197.3	231.0	212.1	235.6	239.1
tibia (any part)	170.7	198.5	—	213.7	238.0	239.2
toe NEC*	195.5	198.89	232.7	229.8	238.8	239.89 ▲
tongue	141.9	198.89	230.0	210.1	235.1	239.0
anterior (two-thirds)						
NEC	141.4	198.89	230.0	210.1	235.1	239.0
dorsal surface	141.1	198.89	230.0	210.1	235.1	239.0
ventral surface	141.3	198.89	230.0	210.1	235.1	239.0
base (dorsal						
surface)	141.0	198.89	230.0	210.1	235.1	239.0
border (lateral)	141.2	198.89	230.0	210.1	235.1	239.0
contiguous sites	141.8	—	—	—	—	—
dorsal surface						
NEC	141.1	198.89	230.0	210.1	235.1	239.0
fixed part NEC	141.0	198.89	230.0	210.1	235.1	239.0
foreamen cecum	141.1	198.89	230.0	210.1	235.1	239.0
frenulum linguae	141.3	198.89	230.0	210.1	235.1	239.0
junctional zone	141.5	198.89	230.0	210.1	235.1	239.0
margin (lateral)	141.2	198.89	230.0	210.1	235.1	239.0
midline NEC	141.1	198.89	230.0	210.1	235.1	239.0
mobile part NEC	141.4	198.89	230.0	210.1	235.1	239.0
posterior (third)	141.0	198.89	230.0	210.1	235.1	239.0
root	141.0	198.89	230.0	210.1	235.1	239.0
surface (dorsal)	141.1	198.89	230.0	210.1	235.1	239.0
base	141.0	198.89	230.0	210.1	235.1	239.0
ventral	141.3	198.89	230.0	210.1	235.1	239.0

	Malignant					
	Primary	Secondary	Ca in situ	Benign	Uncertain Behavior	Unspecified
Neoplasm, neoplastic —						
continued						
tongue — *continued*						
tip	141.2	198.89	230.0	210.1	235.1	239.0
tonsil	141.6	198.89	230.0	210.1	235.1	239.0
tonsil	146.0	198.89	230.0	210.5	235.1	239.0
fauces, faucial	146.0	198.89	230.0	210.5	235.1	239.0
lingual	141.6	198.89	230.0	210.1	235.1	239.0
palatine	146.0	198.89	230.0	210.5	235.1	239.0
pharyngeal	147.1	198.89	230.0	210.7	235.1	239.0
pillar (anterior)						
(posterior)	146.2	198.89	230.0	210.6	235.1	239.0
tonsillar fossa	146.1	198.89	230.0	210.6	235.1	239.0
tooth socket NEC	143.9	198.89	230.0	210.4	235.1	239.0
trachea (cartilage)						
(mucosa)	162.0	197.3	231.1	212.2	235.7	239.1
contiguous sites with						
bronchus or						
lung	162.8	—	—	—	—	—
tracheobronchial	162.8	197.3	231.1	212.2	235.7	239.1
contiguous sites with						
lung	162.8	—	—	—	—	—
tragus	173.2	198.2	232.2	216.2	238.2	239.2
trunk NEC*	195.8	198.89	232.5	229.8	238.8	239.89 ▲
tubo-ovarian	183.8	198.82	233.39	221.8	236.3	239.5
tunica vaginalis	187.8	198.82	233.6	222.8	236.6	239.5
turbinate (bone)	170.0	198.5	—	213.0	238.0	239.2
nasal	160.0	197.3	231.8	212.0	235.9	239.1
tympanic cavity	160.1	197.3	231.8	212.0	235.9	239.1
ulna (any part)	170.4	198.5	—	213.4	238.0	239.2
umbilicus, umbilical	173.5	198.2	232.5	216.5	238.2	239.2
uncus, brain	191.2	198.3	—	225.0	237.5	239.6
unknown site or						
unspecified	199.1	199.1	234.9	229.9	238.9	239.9
urachus	188.7	198.1	233.7	223.3	236.7	239.4
ureter-bladder						
junction)	188.6	198.1	233.7	223.3	236.7	239.4
ureter, ureteral	189.2	198.1	233.9	223.2	236.91	239.5
orifice (bladder)	188.6	198.1	233.7	223.3	236.7	239.4
urethra, urethral						
(gland)	189.3	198.1	233.9	223.81	236.99	239.5
orifice, internal	188.5	198.1	233.7	223.3	236.7	239.4
urethrovaginal						
(septum)	184.9	198.82	233.39	221.9	236.3	239.5
urinary organ or system						
NEC	189.9	198.1	233.9	223.9	236.99	239.5
bladder — *see*						
Neoplasm,						
bladder						
contiguous sites	189.8	—	—	—	—	—
specified sites						
NEC	189.8	198.1	233.9	223.89	236.99	239.5
utero-ovarian	183.8	198.82	233.39	221.8	236.3	239.5
ligament	183.3	198.82	—	221.0	236.3	239.5
uterosacral						
ligament	183.4	198.82	—	221.0	236.3	239.5
uterus, uteri,						
uterine	179	198.82	233.2	219.9	236.0	239.5
adnexa NEC	183.9	198.82	233.39	221.8	236.3	239.5
contiguous						
sites	183.8	—	—	—	—	—
body	182.0	198.82	233.2	219.1	236.0	239.5
contiguous						
sites	182.8	—	—	—	—	—
cervix	180.9	198.82	233.1	219.0	236.0	239.5
cornu	182.0	198.82	233.2	219.1	236.0	239.5
corpus	182.0	198.82	233.2	219.1	236.0	239.5
endocervix (canal)						
(gland)	180.0	198.82	233.1	219.0	236.0	239.5
endometrium	182.0	198.82	233.2	219.1	236.0	239.5
exocervix	180.1	198.82	233.1	219.0	236.0	239.5
external os	180.1	198.82	233.2	219.0	236.0	239.5
fundus	182.0	198.82	233.2	219.1	236.0	239.5
internal os	180.0	198.82	233.1	219.0	236.0	239.5
isthmus	182.1	198.82	233.2	219.1	236.0	239.5
ligament	183.4	198.82	—	221.0	236.3	239.5
broad	183.3	198.82	233.39	221.0	236.3	239.5

☑ Additional Digit Required — Refer to the Tabular List for Digit Selection   🖢 Subterms under main terms may continue to next column or page

2010 ICD-9-CM   ►◄ Revised Text   ● New Line   ▲ Revised Code   October 2009 • Volume 2 — 199

	Malignant					
	Primary	Secondary	Ca in situ	Benign	Uncertain Behavior	Unspecified
Neoplasm, neoplastic — *continued*						
uterus, uteri, uterine — *continued*						
ligament — *continued*						
round	183.5	198.82	—	221.0	236.3	239.5
lower segment	182.1	198.82	233.2	219.1	236.0	239.5
myometrium	182.0	198.82	233.2	219.1	236.0	239.5
squamocolumnar junction	180.8	198.82	233.1	219.0	236.0	239.5
tube	183.2	198.82	233.39	221.0	236.3	239.5
utricle, prostatic	189.3	198.1	233.9	223.81	236.99	239.5
uveal tract	190.0	198.4	234.0	224.0	238.8	239.89 ▲
uvula	145.4	198.89	230.0	210.4	235.1	239.0
vagina, vaginal (fornix) (vault) (wall)	184.0	198.82	233.31	221.1	236.3	239.5
vaginovesical	184.9	198.82	233.39	221.9	236.3	239.5
septum	184.9	198.82	233.39	221.9	236.3	239.5
vallecula (epiglottis)	146.3	198.89	230.0	210.6	235.1	239.0
vascular — *see* Neoplasm, connective tissue						
vas deferens	187.6	198.82	233.6	222.8	236.6	239.5
Vater's ampulla	156.2	197.8	230.8	211.5	235.3	239.0
vein, venous — *see* Neoplasm, connective tissue						
vena cava (abdominal) (inferior)	171.5	198.89	—	215.5	238.1	239.2
superior	171.4	198.89	—	215.4	238.1	239.2
ventricle (cerebral) (floor) (fourth) (lateral) (third)	191.5	198.3	—	225.0	237.5	239.6
cardiac (left) (right)	164.1	198.89	—	212.7	238.8	239.89 ▲
ventricular band of larynx	161.1	197.3	231.0	212.1	235.6	239.1
ventriculus — *see* Neoplasm, stomach						
vermillion border — *see* Neoplasm, lip						
vermis, cerebellum	191.6	198.3	—	225.0	237.5	239.6
vertebra (column)	170.2	198.5	—	213.2	238.0	239.2
coccyx	170.6	198.5	—	213.6	238.0	239.2
sacrum	170.6	198.5	—	213.6	238.0	239.2
vesical — *see* Neoplasm, bladder						
vesicle, seminal	187.8	198.82	233.6	222.8	236.6	239.5
vesicocervical tissue	184.9	198.82	233.39	221.9	236.3	239.5
vesicorectal	195.3	198.89	234.8	229.8	238.8	239.89 ▲
vesicovaginal	184.9	198.82	233.39	221.9	236.3	239.5
septum	184.9	198.82	233.39	221.9	236.3	239.5
vessel (blood) — *see* Neoplasm, connective tissue						
vestibular gland, greater	184.1	198.82	233.32	221.2	236.3	239.5
vestibule						
mouth	145.1	198.89	230.0	210.4	235.1	239.0
nose	160.0	197.3	231.8	212.0	235.9	239.1
Virchow's gland	—	196.0	—	229.0	238.8	239.89 ▲
viscera NEC	195.8	198.89	234.8	229.8	238.8	239.89 ▲
vocal cords (true)	161.0	197.3	231.0	212.1	235.6	239.1
false	161.1	197.3	231.0	212.1	235.6	239.1
vomer	170.0	198.5	—	213.0	238.0	239.2
vulva	184.4	198.82	233.32	221.2	236.3	239.5
vulvovaginal gland	184.4	198.82	233.32	221.2	236.3	239.5
Waldeyer's ring	149.1	198.89	230.0	210.9	235.1	239.0
Wharton's duct	142.1	198.89	230.0	210.2	235.0	239.0
white matter (central) (cerebral)	191.0	198.3	—	225.0	237.5	239.6
windpipe	162.0	197.3	231.1	212.2	235.7	239.1
Wirsung's duct	157.3	197.8	230.9	211.6	235.5	239.0
wolffian (body) (duct)						
female	184.8	198.82	233.39	221.8	236.3	239.5
male	187.8	198.82	233.6	222.8	236.6	239.5

	Malignant					
	Primary	Secondary	Ca in situ	Benign	Uncertain Behavior	Unspecified
Neoplasm, neoplastic — *continued*						
womb — *see* Neoplasm, uterus						
wrist NEC*	195.4	198.89	232.6	229.8	238.8	239.89 ▲
xiphoid process	170.3	198.5	—	213.3	238.0	239.2
Zuckerkandl's organ	194.6	198.89	—	227.6	237.3	239.7

☑ Additional Digit Required — Refer to the Tabular List for Digit Selection　　　　　　🖝 Subterms under main terms may continue to next column or page

Neovascularization
  choroid 362.16
  ciliary body 364.42
  cornea 370.60
    deep 370.63
    localized 370.61
  iris 364.42
  retina 362.16
  subretinal 362.16
Nephralgia 788.0
Nephritis, nephritic (albuminuric) (azotemic) (congenital) (degenerative) (diffuse) (disseminated) (epithelial) (familial) (focal) (granulomatous) (hemorrhagic) (infantile) (nonsuppurative, excretory) (uremic) 583.9
  with
    edema — see Nephrosis
    lesion of
      glomerulonephritis
        hypocomplementemic persistent 583.2
          with nephrotic syndrome 581.2
            chronic 582.2
        lobular 583.2
          with nephrotic syndrome 581.2
            chronic 582.2
        membranoproliferative 583.2
          with nephrotic syndrome 581.2
            chronic 582.2
        membranous 583.1
          with nephrotic syndrome 581.1
            chronic 582.1
        mesangiocapillary 583.2
          with nephrotic syndrome 581.2
            chronic 582.2
        mixed membranous and proliferative 583.2
          with nephrotic syndrome 581.2
            chronic 582.2
        proliferative (diffuse) 583.0
          with nephrotic syndrome 581.0
            acute 580.0
            chronic 582.0
        rapidly progressive 583.4
          acute 580.4
          chronic 582.4
      interstitial nephritis (diffuse) (focal) 583.89
        with nephrotic syndrome 581.89
          acute 580.89
          chronic 582.89
      necrotizing glomerulitis 583.4
        acute 580.4
        chronic 582.4
      renal necrosis 583.9
        cortical 583.6
        medullary 583.7
      specified pathology NEC 583.89
        with nephrotic syndrome 581.89
          acute 580.89
          chronic 582.89
  necrosis, renal 583.9
    cortical 583.6
    medullary (papillary) 583.7
  nephrotic syndrome (see also Nephrosis) 581.9
  papillary necrosis 583.7
  specified pathology NEC 583.89
  acute 580.9
    extracapillary with epithelial crescents 580.4
    hypertensive (see also Hypertension, kidney) 403.90
    necrotizing 580.4
    poststreptococcal 580.0
    proliferative (diffuse) 580.0
    rapidly progressive 580.4
    specified pathology NEC 580.89
  amyloid 277.39 [583.81]
    chronic 277.39 [582.81]
  arteriolar (see also Hypertension, kidney) 403.90
  arteriosclerotic (see also Hypertension, kidney) 403.90
  ascending (see also Pyelitis) 590.80
  atrophic 582.9

Nephritis, nephritic — continued
  basement membrane NEC 583.89
    with
      pulmonary hemorrhage (Goodpasture's syndrome) 446.21 [583.81]
  calculous, calculus 592.0
  cardiac (see also Hypertension, kidney) 403.90
  cardiovascular (see also Hypertension, kidney) 403.90
  chronic 582.9
    arteriosclerotic (see also Hypertension, kidney) 403.90
    hypertensive (see also Hypertension, kidney) 403.90
  cirrhotic (see also Sclerosis, renal) 587
  complicating pregnancy, childbirth, or puerperium 646.2 ☑
    with hypertension 642.1 ☑
      affecting fetus or newborn 760.0
    affecting fetus or newborn 760.1
  croupous 580.9
  desquamative — see Nephrosis
  due to
    amyloidosis 277.39 [583.81]
      chronic 277.39 [582.81]
    arteriosclerosis (see also Hypertension, kidney) 403.90
    diabetes mellitus 250.4 ☑ [583.81]
      with nephrotic syndrome 250.4 ☑ [581.81]
        due to secondary diabetes 249.4 ☑ [583.81]   ▲
      due to secondary diabetes 249.4 ☑ [583.81]   ▲
    diphtheria 032.89 [580.81]
    gonococcal infection (acute) 098.19 [583.81]
      chronic or duration of 2 months or over 098.39 [583.81]
    gout 274.10
    infectious hepatitis 070.9 [580.81]
    mumps 072.79 [580.81]
    specified kidney pathology NEC 583.89
      acute 580.89
      chronic 582.89
    streptotrichosis 039.8 [583.81]
    subacute bacterial endocarditis 421.0 [580.81]
    systemic lupus erythematosus 710.0 [583.81]
      chronic 710.0 [582.81]
    typhoid fever 002.0 [580.81]
  endothelial 582.2
  end stage (chronic) (terminal) NEC 585.6
  epimembranous 581.1
  exudative 583.89
    with nephrotic syndrome 581.89
      acute 580.89
      chronic 582.89
  gonococcal (acute) 098.19 [583.81]
    chronic or duration of 2 months or over 098.39 [583.81]
  gouty 274.10
  hereditary (Alport's syndrome) 759.89
  hydremic — see Nephrosis
  hypertensive (see also Hypertension, kidney) 403.90
  hypocomplementemic persistent 583.2
    with nephrotic syndrome 581.2
      chronic 582.2
  immune complex NEC 583.89
  infective (see also Pyelitis) 590.80
  interstitial (diffuse) (focal) 583.89
    with nephrotic syndrome 581.89
      acute 580.89
      chronic 582.89
  latent or quiescent — see Nephritis, chronic
  lead 984.9
    specified type of lead — see Table of Drugs and Chemicals
  lobular 583.2
    with nephrotic syndrome 581.2
      chronic 582.2
  lupus 710.0 [583.81]
    acute 710.0 [580.81]

Nephritis, nephritic — continued
  lupus — continued
    chronic 710.0 [582.81]
  membranoproliferative 583.2
    with nephrotic syndrome 581.2
      chronic 582.2
  membranous 583.1
    with nephrotic syndrome 581.1
      chronic 582.1
  mesangiocapillary 583.2
    with nephrotic syndrome 581.2
      chronic 582.2
  minimal change 581.3
  mixed membranous and proliferative 583.2
    with nephrotic syndrome 581.2
      chronic 582.2
  necrotic, necrotizing 583.4
    acute 580.4
    chronic 582.4
  nephrotic — see Nephrosis
  old — see Nephritis, chronic
  parenchymatous 581.89
  polycystic 753.12
    adult type (APKD) 753.13
    autosomal dominant 753.13
    autosomal recessive 753.14
    childhood type (CPKD) 753.14
    infantile type 753.14
  poststreptococcal 580.0
  pregnancy — see Nephritis, complicating pregnancy
  proliferative 583.0
    with nephrotic syndrome 581.0
    acute 580.0
    chronic 582.0
  purulent (see also Pyelitis) 590.80
  rapidly progressive 583.4
    acute 580.4
    chronic 582.4
  salt-losing or salt-wasting (see also Disease, renal) 593.9
  saturnine 984.9
    specified type of lead — see Table of Drugs and Chemicals
  septic (see also Pyelitis) 590.80
  specified pathology NEC 583.89
    acute 580.89
    chronic 582.89
  staphylococcal (see also Pyelitis) 590.80
  streptotrichosis 039.8 [583.81]
  subacute (see also Nephrosis) 581.9
  suppurative (see also Pyelitis) 590.80
  syphilitic (late) 095.4
    congenital 090.5 [583.81]
    early 091.69 [583.81]
  terminal (chronic) (end-stage) NEC 585.6
  toxic — see Nephritis, acute
  tubal, tubular — see Nephrosis, tubular
  tuberculous (see also Tuberculosis) 016.0 ☑ [583.81]
  type II (Ellis) — see Nephrosis
  vascular — see Hypertension, kidney
  war 580.9
Nephroblastoma (M8960/3) 189.0
  epithelial (M8961/3) 189.0
  mesenchymal (M8962/3) 189.0
Nephrocalcinosis 275.49
Nephrocystitis, pustular — see also Pyelitis 590.80
Nephrolithiasis (congenital) (pelvis) (recurrent) 592.0
  uric acid 274.11
Nephroma (M8960/3) 189.0
  mesoblastic (M8960/1) 236.9 ☑
Nephronephritis — see also Nephrosis 581.9
Nephronopthisis 753.16
Nephropathy — see also Nephritis 583.9
  with
    exudative nephritis 583.89
    interstitial nephritis (diffuse) (focal) 583.89
    medullary necrosis 583.7
    necrosis 583.9
      cortical 583.6
      medullary or papillary 583.7
    papillary necrosis 583.7
    specified lesion or cause NEC 583.89

Nephropathy — see also Nephritis — continued
  analgesic 583.89
    with medullary necrosis, acute 584.7
  arteriolar (see also Hypertension, kidney) 403.90
  arteriosclerotic (see also Hypertension, kidney) 403.90
  complicating pregnancy 646.2 ☑
  diabetic 250.4 ☑ [583.81]
    due to secondary diabetes 249.4 ☑ [583.81]
  gouty 274.10
    specified type NEC 274.19
  hereditary amyloid 277.31
  hypercalcemic 588.89
  hypertensive (see also Hypertension, kidney) 403.90
  hypokalemic (vacuolar) 588.89
  IgA 583.9
  obstructive 593.89
    congenital 753.20
  phenacetin 584.7
  phosphate-losing 588.0
  potassium depletion 588.89
  proliferative (see also Nephritis, proliferative) 583.0
  protein-losing 588.89
  salt-losing or salt-wasting (see also Disease, renal) 593.9
  sickle-cell (see also Disease, sickle-cell) 282.60 [583.81]
  toxic 584.5
  vasomotor 584.5
  water-losing 588.89
Nephroptosis — see also Disease, renal 593.0
  congenital (displaced) 753.3
Nephropyosis — see also Abscess, kidney 590.2
Nephrorrhagia 593.81
Nephrosclerosis (arteriolar) (arteriosclerotic) (chronic) (hyaline) — see also Hypertension, kidney 403.90
  gouty 274.10
  hyperplastic (arteriolar) (see also Hypertension, kidney) 403.90
  senile (see also Sclerosis, renal) 587
Nephrosis, nephrotic (Epstein's) (syndrome) 581.9
  with
    lesion of
      focal glomerulosclerosis 581.1
      glomerulonephritis
        endothelial 581.2
        hypocomplementemic persistent 581.2
        lobular 581.2
        membranoproliferative 581.2
        membranous 581.1
        mesangiocapillary 581.2
        minimal change 581.3
        mixed membranous and proliferative 581.2
        proliferative 581.0
      segmental hyalinosis 581.1
    specified pathology NEC 581.89
  acute — see Nephrosis, tubular
  anoxic — see Nephrosis, tubular
  arteriosclerotic (see also Hypertension, kidney) 403.90
  chemical — see Nephrosis, tubular
  cholemic 572.4
  complicating pregnancy, childbirth, or puerperium — see Nephritis, complicating pregnancy
  diabetic 250.4 ☑ [581.81]
    due to secondary diabetes 249.4 ☑ [581.81]
  Finnish type (congenital) 759.89
  hemoglobinuric — see Nephrosis, tubular
  in
    amyloidosis 277.39 [581.81]
    diabetes mellitus 250.4 ☑ [581.81]
      due to secondary diabetes 249.4 ☑ [581.81]
    epidemic hemorrhagic fever 078.6
    malaria 084.9 [581.81]

Nephrosis, nephrotic — continued
  in — continued
    polyarteritis 446.0 [581.81]
    systemic lupus erythematosus
      710.0 [581.81]
  ischemic — see Nephrosis, tubular
  lipoid 581.3
  lower nephron — see Nephrosis, tubular
  lupoid 710.0 [581.81]
  lupus 710.0 [581.81]
  malarial 084.9 [581.81]
  minimal change 581.3
  necrotizing — see Nephrosis, tubular
  osmotic (sucrose) 588.89
  polyarteritic 446.0 [581.81]
  radiation 581.9
  specified lesion or cause NEC 581.89
  syphilitic 095.4
  toxic — see Nephrosis, tubular
  tubular (acute) 584.5
    due to a procedure 997.5
    radiation 581.9
Nephrosonephritis hemorrhagic (endemic)
  078.6
Nephrostomy status V44.6
  with complication 997.5
Nerve — see condition
Nerves 799.21 ▲
Nervous — see also condition 799.21 ▲
  breakdown 300.9
  heart 306.2
  stomach 306.4
  tension 799.21 ▲
Nervousness 799.21 ▲
Nesidioblastoma (M8150/0)
  pancreas 211.7
  specified site NEC — see Neoplasm, by site,
    benign
  unspecified site 211.7
Netherton's syndrome (ichthyosiform erythroderma) 757.1
Nettle rash 708.8
Nettleship's disease (urticaria pigmentosa)
  757.33
Neumann's disease (pemphigus vegetans) 694.4
Neuralgia, neuralgic (acute) — see also Neuritis
  729.2
  accessory (nerve) 352.4
  acoustic (nerve) 388.5
  ankle 355.8
  anterior crural 355.8
  anus 787.99
  arm 723.4
  auditory (nerve) 388.5
  axilla 353.0
  bladder 788.1
  brachial 723.4
  brain — see Disorder, nerve, cranial
  broad ligament 625.9
  cerebral — see Disorder, nerve, cranial
  ciliary 339.00
  cranial nerve (see also Disorder, nerve, cranial)
    fifth or trigeminal (see also Neuralgia,
      trigeminal) 350.1
  ear 388.71
    middle 352.1
  facial 351.8
  finger 354.9
  flank 355.8
  foot 355.8
  forearm 354.9
  Fothergill's (see also Neuralgia, trigeminal)
    350.1
    postherpetic 053.12
  glossopharyngeal (nerve) 352.1
  groin 355.8
  hand 354.9
  heel 355.8
  Horton's 339.00
  Hunt's 053.11
  hypoglossal (nerve) 352.5
  iliac region 355.8
  infraorbital (see also Neuralgia, trigeminal)
    350.1
  inguinal 355.8
  intercostal (nerve) 353.8

Neuralgia, neuralgic — see also Neuritis —
  continued
  intercostal — continued
    postherpetic 053.19
  jaw 352.1
  kidney 788.0
  knee 355.8
  loin 355.8
  malarial (see also Malaria) 084.6
  mastoid 385.89
  maxilla 352.1
  median thenar 354.1
  metatarsal 355.6
  middle ear 352.1
  migrainous 339.00
  Morton's 355.6
  nerve, cranial — see Disorder, nerve, cranial
  nose 352.0
  occipital 723.8
  olfactory (nerve) 352.0
  ophthalmic 377.30
    postherpetic 053.19
  optic (nerve) 377.30
  penis 607.9
  perineum 355.8
  pleura 511.0
  postherpetic NEC 053.19
    geniculate ganglion 053.11
    ophthalmic 053.19
    trifacial 053.12
    trigeminal 053.12
  pubic region 355.8
  radial (nerve) 723.4
  rectum 787.99
  sacroiliac joint 724.3
  sciatic (nerve) 724.3
  scrotum 608.9
  seminal vesicle 608.9
  shoulder 354.9
  Sluder's 337.09
  specified nerve NEC — see Disorder, nerve
  spermatic cord 608.9
  sphenopalatine (ganglion) 337.09
  subscapular (nerve) 723.4
  suprascapular (nerve) 723.4
  testis 608.89
  thenar (median) 354.1
  thigh 355.8
  tongue 352.5
  trifacial (nerve) (see also Neuralgia, trigeminal)
    350.1
  trigeminal (nerve) 350.1
    postherpetic 053.12
  tympanic plexus 388.71
  ulnar (nerve) 723.4
  vagus (nerve) 352.3
  wrist 354.9
  writers' 300.89
    organic 333.84
Neurapraxia — see Injury, nerve, by site
Neurasthenia 300.5
  cardiac 306.2
  gastric 306.4
  heart 306.2
  postfebrile 780.79
  postviral 780.79
Neurilemmoma (M9560/0) — see also Neoplasm,
  connective tissue, benign
  acoustic (nerve) 225.1
  malignant (M9560/3) (see also Neoplasm,
    connective tissue, malignant)
    acoustic (nerve) 192.0
Neurilemmosarcoma (M9560/3) — see Neoplasm, connective tissue, malignant
Neurilemoma — see Neurilemmoma
Neurinoma (M9560/0) — see Neurilemmoma
Neurinomatosis (M9560/1) — see also Neoplasm, connective tissue, uncertain behavior
  centralis 759.5
Neuritis — see also Neuralgia 729.2
  abducens (nerve) 378.54
  accessory (nerve) 352.4
  acoustic (nerve) 388.5
    syphilitic 094.86
  alcoholic 357.5

Neuritis — see also Neuralgia — continued
  alcoholic — continued
    with psychosis 291.1
  amyloid, any site 277.39 [357.4]
  anterior crural 355.8
  arising during pregnancy 646.4 ☑
  arm 723.4
  ascending 355.2
  auditory (nerve) 388.5
  brachial (nerve) NEC 723.4
    due to displacement, intervertebral disc
      722.0
  cervical 723.4
  chest (wall) 353.8
  costal region 353.8
  cranial nerve (see also Disorder, nerve, cranial)
    first or olfactory 352.0
    second or optic 377.30
    third or oculomotor 378.52
    fourth or trochlear 378.53
    fifth or trigeminal (see also Neuralgia,
      trigeminal) 350.1
    sixth or abducens 378.54
    seventh or facial 351.8
      newborn 767.5
    eighth or acoustic 388.5
    ninth or glossopharyngeal 352.1
    tenth or vagus 352.3
    eleventh or accessory 352.4
    twelfth or hypoglossal 352.5
  Déjérine-Sottas 356.0
  diabetic 250.6 ☑ [357.2]
    due to secondary diabetes 249.6 ☑ [357.2]
  diphtheritic 032.89 [357.4]
  due to
    beriberi 265.0 [357.4]
    displacement, prolapse, protrusion, or
      rupture of intervertebral disc 722.2
      cervical 722.0
      lumbar, lumbosacral 722.10
      thoracic, thoracolumbar 722.11
    herniation, nucleus pulposus 722.2
      cervical 722.0
      lumbar, lumbosacral 722.10
      thoracic, thoracolumbar 722.11
  endemic 265.0 [357.4]
  facial (nerve) 351.8
    newborn 767.5
  general — see Polyneuropathy
  geniculate ganglion 351.1
    due to herpes 053.11
  glossopharyngeal (nerve) 352.1
  gouty 274.89 [357.4]
  hypoglossal (nerve) 352.5
  ilioinguinal (nerve) 355.8
  in diseases classified elsewhere — see
    Polyneuropathy, in
  infectious (multiple) 357.0
  intercostal (nerve) 353.8
  interstitial hypertrophic progressive NEC 356.9
  leg 355.8
  lumbosacral NEC 724.4
  median (nerve) 354.1
    thenar 354.1
  multiple (acute) (infective) 356.9
    endemic 265.0 [357.4]
  multiplex endemica 265.0 [357.4]
  nerve root (see also Radiculitis) 729.2
  oculomotor (nerve) 378.52
  olfactory (nerve) 352.0
  optic (nerve) 377.30
    in myelitis 341.0
    meningococcal 036.81
  pelvic 355.8
  peripheral (nerve) (see also Neuropathy, periph-
    eral)
    complicating pregnancy or puerperium
      646.4 ☑
    specified nerve NEC — see Mononeuritis
  pneumogastric (nerve) 352.3
  postchickenpox 052.7
  postherpetic 053.19
  progressive hypertrophic interstitial NEC 356.9
  puerperal, postpartum 646.4 ☑
  radial (nerve) 723.4
  retrobulbar 377.32

Neuritis — see also Neuralgia — continued
  retrobulbar — continued
    syphilitic 094.85
  rheumatic (chronic) 729.2
  sacral region 355.8
  sciatic (nerve) 724.3
    due to displacement of intervertebral disc
      722.10
  serum 999.5
  specified nerve NEC — see Disorder, nerve
  spinal (nerve) 355.9
    root (see also Radiculitis) 729.2
  subscapular (nerve) 723.4
  suprascapular (nerve) 723.4
  syphilitic 095.8
  thenar (median) 354.1
  thoracic NEC 724.4
  toxic NEC 357.7
  trochlear (nerve) 378.53
  ulnar (nerve) 723.4
  vagus (nerve) 352.3
Neuroangiomatosis, encephalofacial 759.6
Neuroastrocytoma (M9505/1) — see Neoplasm,
  by site, uncertain behavior
Neuro-avitaminosis 269.2
Neuroblastoma (M9500/3)
  olfactory (M9522/3) 160.0
  specified site — see Neoplasm, by site, malig-
    nant
  unspecified site 194.0
Neurochorioretinitis — see also Chorioretinitis
  363.20
Neurocirculatory asthenia 306.2
Neurocytoma (M9506/0) — see Neoplasm, by
  site, benign
Neurodermatitis (circumscribed) (circumscripta)
  (local) 698.3
  atopic 691.8
  diffuse (Brocq) 691.8
  disseminated 691.8
  nodulosa 698.3
Neuroencephalomyelopathy, optic 341.0
Neuroendocrine tumor — see Tumor, neuroendocrine
Neuroepithelioma (M9503/3) — see also Neoplasm, by site, malignant
  olfactory (M9521/3) 160.0
Neurofibroma (M9540/0) — see also Neoplasm,
  connective tissue, benign
  melanotic (M9541/0) — see Neoplasm, con-
    nective tissue, benign
  multiple (M9540/1) 237.70
    type 1 237.71
    type 2 237.72
  plexiform (M9550/0) — see Neoplasm, connec-
    tive tissue, benign
Neurofibromatosis (multiple) (M9540/1) 237.70
  acoustic 237.72
  malignant (M9540/3) — see Neoplasm, con-
    nective tissue, malignant
  type 1 237.71
  type 2 237.72
  von Recklinghausen's 237.71
Neurofibrosarcoma (M9540/3) — see Neoplasm,
  connective tissue, malignant
Neurogenic — see also condition
  bladder (atonic) (automatic) (autonomic)
    (flaccid) (hypertonic) (hypotonic) (iner-
    tia) (infranuclear) (irritable) (motor)
    (nonreflex) (nuclear) (paralysis) (reflex)
    (sensory) (spastic) (supranuclear) (unin-
    hibited) 596.54
    with cauda equina syndrome 344.61
  bowel 564.81
  heart 306.2
Neuroglioma (M9505/1) — see Neoplasm, by
  site, uncertain behavior
Neurolabyrinthitis (of Dix and Hallpike) 386.12
Neurolathyrism 988.2
Neuroleprosy 030.1
Neuroleptic malignant syndrome 333.92
Neurolipomatosis 272.8
Neuroma (M9570/0) — see also Neoplasm, con-
  nective tissue, benign
  acoustic (nerve) (M9560/0) 225.1

Neuroma — *see also* Neoplasm, connective tissue, benign — *continued*
  amputation (traumatic) (*see also* Injury, nerve, by site)
    surgical complication (late) 997.61
  appendix 211.3
  auditory nerve 225.1
  digital 355.6
    toe 355.6
  interdigital (toe) 355.6
  intermetatarsal 355.6
  Morton's 355.6
  multiple 237.70
    type 1 237.71
    type 2 237.72
  nonneoplastic 355.9
    arm NEC 354.9
    leg NEC 355.8
    lower extremity NEC 355.8
    specified site NEC — *see* Mononeuritis, by site
    upper extremity NEC 354.9
  optic (nerve) 225.1
  plantar 355.6
  plexiform (M9550/0) — *see* Neoplasm, connective tissue, benign
  surgical (nonneoplastic) 355.9
    arm NEC 354.9
    leg NEC 355.8
    lower extremity NEC 355.8
    upper extremity NEC 354.9
  traumatic (*see also* Injury, nerve, by site)
    old — *see* Neuroma, nonneoplastic
Neuromyalgia 729.1
Neuromyasthenia (epidemic) 049.8
Neuromyelitis 341.8
  ascending 357.0
  optica 341.0
Neuromyopathy NEC 358.9
Neuromyositis 729.1
Neuronevus (M8725/0) — *see* Neoplasm, skin, benign
Neuronitis 357.0
  ascending (acute) 355.2
  vestibular 386.12
Neuroparalytic — *see* condition
Neuropathy, neuropathic — *see also* Disorder, nerve 355.9
  acute motor 357.82
  alcoholic 357.5
    with psychosis 291.1
  arm NEC 354.9
  ataxia and retinitis pigmentosa (NARP syndrome) 277.87
  autonomic (peripheral) — *see* Neuropathy, peripheral, autonomic
  axillary nerve 353.0
  brachial plexus 353.0
  cervical plexus 353.2
  chronic
    progressive segmentally demyelinating 357.89
    relapsing demyelinating 357.89
  congenital sensory 356.2
  Déjérine-Sottas 356.0
  diabetic 250.6 ☑ *[357.2]*
    autonomic (peripheral) 250.6 ☑ *[337.1]* ●
    due to secondary diabetes 249.6 ☑ *[357.2]*
      autonomic (peripheral) 249.6 ☑ *[337.1]* ●
  entrapment 355.9
    iliohypogastric nerve 355.79
    ilioinguinal nerve 355.79
    lateral cutaneous nerve of thigh 355.1
    median nerve 354.0
    obturator nerve 355.79
    peroneal nerve 355.3
    posterior tibial nerve 355.5
    saphenous nerve 355.79
    ulnar nerve 354.2
  facial nerve 351.9
  hereditary 356.9
    peripheral 356.0
    sensory (radicular) 356.2
  hypertrophic
    Charcôt-Marie-Tooth 356.1

Neuropathy, neuropathic — *see also* Disorder, nerve — *continued*
  hypertrophic — *continued*
    Déjérine-Sottas 356.0
    interstitial 356.9
    Refsum 356.3
  intercostal nerve 354.8
  ischemic — *see* Disorder, nerve
  Jamaican (ginger) 357.7
  leg NEC 355.8
  lower extremity NEC 355.8
  lumbar plexus 353.1
  median nerve 354.1
  motor
    acute 357.82
  multiple (acute) (chronic) (*see also* Polyneuropathy) 356.9
  optic 377.39
    ischemic 377.41
    nutritional 377.33
    toxic 377.34
  peripheral (nerve) (*see also* Polyneuropathy) 356.9
    arm NEC 354.9
    autonomic 337.9
      amyloid 277.39 *[337.1]*
      idiopathic 337.00
      in
        amyloidosis 277.39 *[337.1]*
        diabetes (mellitus) 250.6 ☑ *[337.1]*
          due to secondary diabetes 249.6 ☑ *[337.1]*
        diseases classified elsewhere 337.1
        gout 274.89 *[337.1]*
        hyperthyroidism 242.9 ☑ *[337.1]*
    due to
      antitetanus serum 357.6
      arsenic 357.7
      drugs 357.6
      lead 357.7
      organophosphate compounds 357.7
      toxic agent NEC 357.7
    hereditary 356.0
    idiopathic 356.9
      progressive 356.4
      specified type NEC 356.8
    in diseases classified elsewhere — *see* Polyneuropathy, in
    leg NEC 355.8
    lower extremity NEC 355.8
    upper extremity NEC 354.9
  plantar nerves 355.6
  progressive
    hypertrophic interstitial 356.9 ●
    inflammatory 357.89 ●
  radicular NEC 729.2
    brachial 723.4
    cervical NEC 723.4
    hereditary sensory 356.2
    lumbar 724.4
    lumbosacral 724.4
    thoracic NEC 724.4
  sacral plexus 353.1
  sciatic 355.0
  spinal nerve NEC 355.9
    root (*see also* Radiculitis) 729.2
  toxic 357.7
  trigeminal sensory 350.8
  ulnar nerve 354.2
  upper extremity NEC 354.9
  uremic 585.9 *[357.4]*
  vitamin B$_{12}$ 266.2 *[357.4]*
    with anemia (pernicious) 281.0 *[357.4]*
      due to dietary deficiency 281.1 *[357.4]*
Neurophthisis — *see also* Disorder, nerve
  diabetic 250.6 ☑ *[357.2]*
    due to secondary diabetes 249.6 ☑ *[357.2]*
  peripheral 356.9
Neuropraxia — *see* Injury, nerve
Neuroretinitis 363.05
  syphilitic 094.85
Neurosarcoma (M9540/3) — *see* Neoplasm, connective tissue, malignant
Neurosclerosis — *see* Disorder, nerve
Neurosis, neurotic 300.9
  accident 300.16

Neurosis, neurotic — *continued*
  anancastic, anankastic 300.3
  anxiety (state) 300.00
    generalized 300.02
    panic type 300.01
  asthenic 300.5
  bladder 306.53
  cardiac (reflex) 306.2
  cardiovascular 306.2
  climacteric, unspecified type 627.2
  colon 306.4
  compensation 300.16
  compulsive, compulsion 300.3
  conversion 300.11
  craft 300.89
  cutaneous 306.3
  depersonalization 300.6
  depressive (reaction) (type) 300.4
  endocrine 306.6
  environmental 300.89
  fatigue 300.5
  functional (*see also* Disorder, psychosomatic) 306.9
  gastric 306.4
  gastrointestinal 306.4
  genitourinary 306.50
  heart 306.2
  hypochondriacal 300.7
  hysterical 300.10
    conversion type 300.11
    dissociative type 300.15
  impulsive 300.3
  incoordination 306.0
    larynx 306.1
    vocal cord 306.1
  intestine 306.4
  larynx 306.1
    hysterical 300.11
    sensory 306.1
  menopause, unspecified type 627.2
  mixed NEC 300.89
  musculoskeletal 306.0
  obsessional 300.3
    phobia 300.3
  obsessive-compulsive 300.3
  occupational 300.89
  ocular 306.7
  oral 307.0
  organ (*see also* Disorder, psychosomatic) 306.9
  pharynx 306.1
  phobic 300.20
  posttraumatic (acute) (situational) 309.81
    chronic 309.81
  psychasthenic (type) 300.89
  railroad 300.16
  rectum 306.4
  respiratory 306.1
  rumination 306.4
  senile 300.89
  sexual 302.70
  situational 300.89
  specified type NEC 300.89
  state 300.9
    with depersonalization episode 300.6
  stomach 306.4
  vasomotor 306.2
  visceral 306.4
  war 300.16
Neurospongioblastosis diffusa 759.5
Neurosyphilis (arrested) (early) (inactive) (late) (latent) (recurrent) 094.9
  with ataxia (cerebellar) (locomotor) (spastic) (spinal) 094.0
  acute meningitis 094.2
  aneurysm 094.89
  arachnoid (adhesive) 094.2
  arteritis (any artery) 094.89
  asymptomatic 094.3
  congenital 090.40
  dura (mater) 094.89
  general paresis 094.1
  gumma 094.9
  hemorrhagic 094.9
  juvenile (asymptomatic) (meningeal) 090.40
  leptomeninges (aseptic) 094.2
  meningeal 094.2

Neurosyphilis — *continued*
  meninges (adhesive) 094.2
  meningovascular (diffuse) 094.2
  optic atrophy 094.84
  parenchymatous (degenerative) 094.1
  paresis (*see also* Paresis, general) 094.1
  paretic (*see also* Paresis, general) 094.1
  relapse 094.9
  remission in (sustained) 094.9
  serological 094.3
  specified nature or site NEC 094.89
  tabes (dorsalis) 094.0
    juvenile 090.40
  tabetic 094.0
    juvenile 090.40
  taboparesis 094.1
    juvenile 090.40
  thrombosis 094.89
  vascular 094.89
Neurotic — *see also* Neurosis 300.9
  excoriation 698.4
    psychogenic 306.3
Neurotmesis — *see* Injury, nerve, by site
Neurotoxemia — *see* Toxemia
Neutro-occlusion 524.21
Neutropenia, neutropenic (idiopathic) (pernicious) (primary) 288.00
  chronic 288.09
    hypoplastic 288.09
  congenital (nontransient) 288.01
  cyclic 288.02
  drug induced 288.03
  due to infection 288.04
  fever 288.00
  genetic 288.01
  immune 288.09
  infantile 288.01
  malignant 288.09
  neonatal, transitory (isoimmune) (maternal transfer) 776.7
  periodic 288.02
  splenic 289.53
  splenomegaly 289.53
  toxic 288.09
Neutrophilia, hereditary giant 288.2
Nevocarcinoma (M8720/3) — *see* Melanoma
Nevus (M8720/0) — *see also* Neoplasm, skin, benign

> *Note* — Except where otherwise indicated, varieties of nevus in the list below that are followed by a morphology code number (M-‑‑‑/0) should be coded by site as for "Neoplasm, skin, benign."

  acanthotic 702.8
  achromic (M8730/0)
  amelanotic (M8730/0)
  anemic, anemicus 709.09
  angiomatous (M9120/0) (*see also* Hemangioma) 228.00
  araneus 448.1
  avasculosus 709.09
  balloon cell (M8722/0)
  bathing trunk (M8761/1) 238.2
  blue (M8780/0)
    cellular (M8790/0)
    giant (M8790/0)
    Jadassohn's (M8780/0)
    malignant (M8780/3) — *see* Melanoma
  capillary (M9131/0) (*see also* Hemangioma) 228.00
  cavernous (M9121/0) (*see also* Hemangioma) 228.00
  cellular (M8720/0)
    blue (M8790/0)
  comedonicus 757.33
  compound (M8760/0)
  conjunctiva (M8720/0) 224.3
  dermal (M8750/0)
    and epidermal (M8760/0)
  epithelioid cell (and spindle cell) (M8770/0)
  flammeus 757.32
    osteohypertrophic 759.89
  hairy (M8720/0)
  halo (M8723/0)
  hemangiomatous (M9120/0) (*see also* Hemangioma) 228.00

☑ Additional Digit Required — Refer to the Tabular List for Digit Selection   Subterms under main terms may continue to next column or page

2010 ICD-9-CM   ▶◀ Revised Text   ● New Line   ▲ Revised Code   October 2009 • Volume 2 — 203

Nevus — see also Neoplasm, skin, benign — continued
  intradermal (M8750/0)
  intraepidermal (M8740/0)
  involuting (M8724/0)
  Jadassohn's (blue) (M8780/0)
  junction, junctional (M8740/0)
    malignant melanoma in (M8740/3) — see Melanoma
  juvenile (M8770/0)
  lymphatic (M9170/0) 228.1
  magnocellular (M8726/0)
    specified site — see Neoplasm, by site, benign
    unspecified site 224.0
  malignant (M8720/3) — see Melanoma
  meaning hemangioma (M9120/0) (see also Hemangioma) 228.00
  melanotic (pigmented) (M8720/0)
  multiplex 759.5
  nonneoplastic 448.1
  nonpigmented (M8730/0)
  nonvascular (M8720/0)
  oral mucosa, white sponge 750.26
  osteohypertrophic, flammeus 759.89
  papillaris (M8720/0)
  papillomatosus (M8720/0)
  pigmented (M8720/0)
    giant (M8761/1) (see also Neoplasm, skin, uncertain behavior)
      malignant melanoma in (M8761/3) — see Melanoma
    systematicus 757.33
  pilosus (M8720/0)
  port wine 757.32
  sanguineous 757.32
  sebaceous (senile) 702.8
  senile 448.1
  spider 448.1
  spindle cell (and epithelioid cell) (M8770/0)
  stellar 448.1
  strawberry 757.32
  syringocystadenomatous papilliferous (M8406/0)
  unius lateris 757.33
  Unna's 757.32
  vascular 757.32
  verrucous 757.33
  white sponge (oral mucosa) 750.26
Newborn (infant) (liveborn)
  abstinence syndrome 779.5 ●
  affected by
    amniocentesis 760.61
    maternal abuse of drugs (gestational) (via placenta) (via breast milk) (see also Noxious, substances transmitted through placenta or breast milk (affecting fetus or newborn)) 760.70
      methamphetamine(s) 760.72
    procedure
      amniocentesis 760.61
      in utero NEC 760.62
      surgical on mother
        during pregnancy NEC 760.63
        previous not associated with pregnancy 760.64
  apnea 770.81
    obstructive 770.82
    specified NEC 770.82
  breast buds 779.89
  cardiomyopathy 425.4
    congenital 425.3
  convulsion 779.0
  electrolyte imbalance NEC (transitory) 775.5
  fever (environmentally-induced) 778.4
  gestation
    24 completed weeks 765.22
    25-26 completed weeks 765.23
    27-28 completed weeks 765.24
    29-30 completed weeks 765.25
    31-32 completed weeks 765.26
    33-34 completed weeks 765.27
    35-36 completed weeks 765.28
    37 or more completed weeks 765.29
    less than 24 completed weeks 765.21
    unspecified completed weeks 765.20

Newborn — continued
  infection 771.89
    candida 771.7
    mastitis 771.5
    specified NEC 771.89
    urinary tract 771.82
  mastitis 771.5
  multiple NEC
    born in hospital (without mention of cesarean delivery or section) V37.00
      with cesarean delivery or section V37.01
    born outside hospital
      hospitalized V37.1
      not hospitalized V37.2
    mates all liveborn
      born in hospital (without mention of cesarean delivery or section) V34.00
        with cesarean delivery or section V34.01
      born outside hospital
        hospitalized V34.1
        not hospitalized V34.2
    mates all stillborn
      born in hospital (without mention of cesarean delivery or section) V35.00
        with cesarean delivery or section V35.01
      born outside hospital
        hospitalized V35.1
        not hospitalized V35.2
    mates liveborn and stillborn
      born in hospital (without mention of cesarean delivery or section) V36.00
        with cesarean delivery or section V36.01
      born outside hospital
        hospitalized V36.1
        not hospitalized V36.2
  omphalitis 771.4
  seizure 779.0
  sepsis 771.81
  single
    born in hospital (without mention of cesarean delivery or section) V30.00
      with cesarean delivery or section V30.01
    born outside hospital
      hospitalized V30.1
      not hospitalized V30.2
  specified condition NEC 779.89
  twin NEC
    born in hospital (without mention of cesarean delivery or section) V33.00
      with cesarean delivery or section V33.01
    born outside hospital
      hospitalized V33.1
      not hospitalized V33.2
    mate liveborn
      born in hospital V31.0 ☑
      born outside hospital
        hospitalized V31.1
        not hospitalized V31.2
    mate stillborn
      born in hospital V32.0 ☑
      born outside hospital
        hospitalized V32.1
        not hospitalized V32.2
  unspecified as to single or multiple birth
    born in hospital (without mention of cesarean delivery or section) V39.00
      with cesarean delivery or section V39.01
    born outside hospital
      hospitalized V39.1
      not hospitalized V39.2
  weight check V20.32 ●
Newcastle's conjunctivitis or disease 077.8
Nezelof's syndrome (pure alymphocytosis) 279.13
Niacin (amide) **deficiency** 265.2

Nicolas-Durand-Favre disease (climatic bubo) 099.1
Nicolas-Favre disease (climatic bubo) 099.1
Nicotinic acid (amide) **deficiency** 265.2
Niemann-Pick disease (lipid histiocytosis) (splenomegaly) 272.7
Night
  blindness (see also Blindness, night) 368.60
    congenital 368.61
      vitamin A deficiency 264.5
  cramps 729.82
  sweats 780.8
  terrors, child 307.46
Nightmare 307.47
  REM-sleep type 307.47
Nipple — see condition
Nisbet's chancre 099.0
Nishimoto (-Takeuchi) disease 437.5
Nitritoid crisis or reaction — see Crisis, nitritoid
Nitrogen retention, extrarenal 788.99
Nitrosohemoglobinemia 289.89
Njovera 104.0
No
  diagnosis 799.9
  disease (found) V71.9
  room at the inn V65.0
Nocardiasis — see Nocardiosis
Nocardiosis 039.9
  with pneumonia 039.1
  lung 039.1
  specified type NEC 039.8
Nocturia 788.43
  psychogenic 306.53
Nocturnal — see condition
  dyspnea (paroxysmal) 786.09
  emissions 608.89
  enuresis 788.36
    psychogenic 307.6
  frequency (micturition) 788.43
    psychogenic 306.53
Nodal rhythm disorder 427.89
Nodding of head 781.0
Node(s) — see also Nodule(s)
  Heberden's 715.04
  larynx 478.79
  lymph — see condition
  milkers' 051.1
  Osler's 421.0
  rheumatic 729.89
  Schmorl's 722.30
    lumbar, lumbosacral 722.32
    specified region NEC 722.39
    thoracic, thoracolumbar 722.31
  singers' 478.5
  skin NEC 782.2
  tuberculous — see Tuberculosis, lymph gland
  vocal cords 478.5
Nodosities, Haygarth's 715.04
Nodule(s), nodular
  actinomycotic (see also Actinomycosis) 039.9
  arthritic — see Arthritis, nodosa
  breast 793.89
  cutaneous 782.2
  Haygarth's 715.04
  inflammatory — see Inflammation
  juxta-articular 102.7
    syphilitic 095.7
    yaws 102.7
  larynx 478.79
  lung, solitary 518.89
    emphysematous 492.8
  milkers' 051.1
  prostate 600.10
    with
      urinary
        obstruction 600.11
        retention 600.11
  retrocardiac 785.9
  rheumatic 729.89
  rheumatoid — see Arthritis, rheumatoid
  scrotum (inflammatory) 608.4
  singers' 478.5
  skin NEC 782.2
  solitary, lung 518.89
    emphysematous 492.8
  subcutaneous 782.2

Nodule(s), nodular — continued
  thyroid (gland) (nontoxic) (uninodular) 241.0
    with
      hyperthyroidism 242.1 ☑
      thyrotoxicosis 242.1 ☑
    toxic or with hyperthyroidism 242.1 ☑
  vocal cords 478.5
Noma (gangrenous) (hospital) (infective) 528.1
  auricle (see also Gangrene) 785.4
  mouth 528.1
  pudendi (see also Vulvitis) 616.10
  vulvae (see also Vulvitis) 616.10
Nomadism V60.0
Non-adherence
  artificial skin graft 996.55
  decellularized allodermis graft 996.55
Non-autoimmune hemolytic anemia NEC 283.10
Nonclosure — see also Imperfect, closure
  ductus
    arteriosus 747.0
    Botalli 747.0
  Eustachian valve 746.89
  foramen
    Botalli 745.5
    ovale 745.5
Noncompliance with medical treatment V15.81
  renal dialysis V45.12
Nondescent (congenital) — see also Malposition, congenital
  cecum 751.4
  colon 751.4
  testis 752.51
Nondevelopment
  brain 742.1
    specified part 742.2
  heart 746.89
  organ or site, congenital NEC — see Hypoplasia
Nonengagement
  head NEC 652.5 ☑
    in labor 660.1 ☑
      affecting fetus or newborn 763.1
Nonexanthematous tick fever 066.1
Nonexpansion, lung (newborn) NEC 770.4
Nonfunctioning
  cystic duct (see also Disease, gallbladder) 575.8
  gallbladder (see also Disease, gallbladder) 575.8
  kidney (see also Disease, renal) 593.9
  labyrinth 386.58
Nonhealing
  stump (surgical) 997.69
  wound, surgical 998.83
Nonimplantation of ovum, causing infertility 628.3
Noninsufflation, fallopian tube 628.2
Nonne-Milroy-Meige syndrome (chronic hereditary edema) 757.0
Nonovulation 628.0
Nonpatent fallopian tube 628.2
Nonpneumatization, lung NEC 770.4
Nonreflex bladder 596.54
  with cauda equina 344.61
Nonretention of food — see Vomiting
Nonrotation — see Malrotation
Nonsecretion, urine — see also Anuria 788.5
  newborn 753.3
Nonunion
  fracture 733.82
  organ or site, congenital NEC — see Imperfect, closure
  symphysis pubis, congenital 755.69
  top sacrum, congenital 756.19
Nonviability 765.0 ☑
Nonvisualization, gallbladder 793.3
Nonvitalized tooth 522.9
Non-working side interference 524.56
Normal
  delivery — see category 650
  menses V65.5
  state (feared complaint unfounded) V65.5
Normoblastosis 289.89
Normocytic anemia (infectional) 285.9
  due to blood loss (chronic) 280.0

☑ Additional Digit Required — Refer to the Tabular List for Digit Selection

▽ Subterms under main terms may continue to next column or page

Normocytic anemia — *continued*
  due to blood loss — *continued*
    acute 285.1
Norrie's disease (congenital) (progressive ocu-
  loacousticocerebral degeneration) 743.8
North American blastomycosis 116.0
Norwegian itch 133.0
Nosebleed 784.7
Nose, nasal — *see* condition
Nosomania 298.9
Nosophobia 300.29
Nostalgia 309.89
Notched lip, congenital — *see also* Cleft, lip
  749.10
Notching nose, congenital (tip) 748.1
Notch of iris 743.46
Nothnagel's
  syndrome 378.52
  vasomotor acroparesthesia 443.89
Novy's relapsing fever (American) 087.1
Noxious
  foodstuffs, poisoning by
    fish 988.0
    fungi 988.1
    mushrooms 988.1
    plants (food) 988.2
    shellfish 988.0
    specified type NEC 988.8
    toadstool 988.1
  substances transmitted through placenta or
    breast milk (affecting fetus or newborn)
    760.70

Noxious — *continued*
  substances transmitted through placenta or
    breast milk — *continued*
    acetretin 760.78
    alcohol 760.71
    aminopterin 760.78
    antiandrogens 760.79
    anticonvulsant 760.77
    antifungal 760.74
    anti-infective agents 760.74
    antimetabolic 760.78
    atorvastatin 760.78
    carbamazepine 760.77
    cocaine 760.75
    "crack" 760.75
    diethylstilbestrol (DES) 760.76
    divalproex sodium 760.77
    endocrine disrupting chemicals 760.79
    estrogens 760.79
    etretinate 760.78
    fluconazole 760.74
    fluvastatin 760.78
    hallucinogenic agents NEC 760.73
    hormones 760.79
    lithium 760.79
    lovastatin 760.78
    medicinal agents NEC 760.79
    methotrexate 760.78
    misoprostil 760.79
    narcotics 760.72
    obstetric anesthetic or analgesic 763.5
    phenobarbital 760.77

Noxious — *continued*
  substances transmitted through placenta or
    breast milk — *continued*
    phenytoin 760.77
    pravastatin 760.78
    progestins 760.79
    retinoic acid 760.78
    simvastatin 760.78
    solvents 760.79
    specified agent NEC 760.79
    statins 760.78
    suspected, affecting management of
     pregnancy 655.5 ☑
    tetracycline 760.74
    thalidomide 760.79
    trimethadione 760.77
    valproate 760.77
    valproic acid 760.77
    vitamin A 760.78
NPDH (new persistent daily headache) 339.42
Nuchal hitch (arm) 652.8 ☑
Nucleus pulposus — *see* condition
Numbness 782.0
Nuns' knee 727.2
Nursemaid's
  elbow 832.2   ▲
  shoulder 831.0 ☑

Nutmeg liver 573.8
Nutrition, deficient or insufficient (particular
  kind of food) 269.9
  due to
    insufficient food 994.2
    lack of
     care (child) (infant) 995.52
      adult 995.84
     food 994.2
Nyctalopia — *see also* Blindness, night 368.60
  vitamin A deficiency 264.5
Nycturia 788.43
  psychogenic 306.53
Nymphomania 302.89
Nystagmus 379.50
  associated with vestibular system disorders
    379.54
  benign paroxysmal positional 386.11
  central positional 386.2
  congenital 379.51
  deprivation 379.53
  dissociated 379.55
  latent 379.52
  miners' 300.89
  positional
    benign paroxysmal 386.11
    central 386.2
  specified NEC 379.56
  vestibular 379.54
  visual deprivation 379.53

O

Oasthouse urine disease 270.2
Obermeyer's relapsing fever (European) 087.0
Obesity (constitutional) (exogenous) (familial) (nutritional) (simple) 278.00
  adrenal 255.8
  complicating pregnancy, childbirth, or puerperium 649.1 ☑
  due to hyperalimentation 278.00
  endocrine NEC 259.9
  endogenous 259.9
  Fröhlich's (adiposogenital dystrophy) 253.8
  glandular NEC 259.9
  hypothyroid (see also Hypothyroidism) 244.9
  morbid 278.01
  of pregnancy 649.1 ☑
  pituitary 253.8
  severe 278.01
  thyroid (see also Hypothyroidism) 244.9
Oblique — see also condition
  lie before labor, affecting fetus or newborn 761.7
Obliquity, pelvis 738.6
Obliteration
  abdominal aorta 446.7
  appendix (lumen) 543.9
  artery 447.1
  ascending aorta 446.7
  bile ducts 576.8
    with calculus, choledocholithiasis, or stones — see Choledocholithiasis
    congenital 751.61
      jaundice from 751.61 [774.5]
  common duct 576.8
    with calculus, choledocholithiasis, or stones — see Choledocholithiasis
    congenital 751.61
  cystic duct 575.8
    with calculus, choledocholithiasis, or stones — see Choledocholithiasis
  disease, arteriolar 447.1
  endometrium 621.8
  eye, anterior chamber 360.34
  fallopian tube 628.2
  lymphatic vessel 457.1
    postmastectomy 457.0
  organ or site, congenital NEC — see Atresia
  placental blood vessels — see Placenta, abnormal
  supra-aortic branches 446.7
  ureter 593.89
  urethra 599.84
  vein 459.9
  vestibule (oral) 525.8
Observation (for) V71.9
  without need for further medical care V71.9
  accident NEC V71.4
    at work V71.3
  criminal assault V71.6
  deleterious agent ingestion V71.89
  disease V71.9
    cardiovascular V71.7
    heart V71.7
    mental V71.09
    specified condition NEC V71.89
  foreign body ingestion V71.89
  growth and development variations V21.8
  injuries (accidental) V71.4
    inflicted NEC V71.6
      during alleged rape or seduction V71.5
  malignant neoplasm, suspected V71.1
  postpartum
    immediately after delivery V24.0
    routine follow-up V24.2
  pregnancy
    high-risk V23.9
      specified problem NEC V23.89
    normal (without complication) V22.1
      with nonobstetric complication V22.2
      first V22.0
  rape or seduction, alleged V71.5
    injury during V71.5
  suicide attempt, alleged V71.89
  suspected (undiagnosed) (unproven)
    abuse V71.81
    cardiovascular disease V71.7

Observation — continued
  suspected — continued
    child or wife battering victim V71.6
    concussion (cerebral) V71.6
    condition NEC V71.89
      infant — see Observation, suspected, condition, newborn
      maternal and fetal
        amniotic cavity and membrane problem V89.01
        cervical shortening V89.05
        fetal anomaly V89.03
        fetal growth problem V89.04
        oligohydramnios V89.01
        other specified problem NEC V89.09
        placental problem V89.02
        polyhydramnios V89.01
      newborn V29.9
        cardiovascular disease V29.8
        congenital anomaly V29.8
        genetic V29.3
        infectious V29.0
        ingestion foreign object V29.8
        injury V29.8
        metabolic V29.3
        neoplasm V29.8
        neurological V29.1
        poison, poisoning V29.8
        respiratory V29.2
        specified NEC V29.8
    exposure
      anthrax V71.82
      biologic agent NEC V71.83
      SARS V71.83
    infectious disease not requiring isolation V71.89
    malignant neoplasm V71.1
    mental disorder V71.09
    neglect V71.81
    neoplasm
      benign V71.89
      malignant V71.1
    specified condition NEC V71.89
    tuberculosis V71.2
    tuberculosis, suspected V71.2
Obsession, obsessional 300.3
  ideas and mental images 300.3
  impulses 300.3
  neurosis 300.3
  phobia 300.3
  psychasthenia 300.3
  ruminations 300.3
  state 300.3
  syndrome 300.3
Obsessive-compulsive 300.3
  neurosis 300.3
  personality 301.4
  reaction 300.3
Obstetrical trauma NEC (complicating delivery) 665.9 ☑
  with
    abortion — see Abortion, by type, with damage to pelvic organs
    ectopic pregnancy (see also categories 633.0–633.9) 639.2
    molar pregnancy (see also categories 630–632) 639.2
  affecting fetus or newborn 763.89
  following
    abortion 639.2
    ectopic or molar pregnancy 639.2
Obstipation — see also Constipation 564.00
  psychogenic 306.4
Obstruction, obstructed, obstructive
  airway NEC 519.8
    with
      allergic alveolitis NEC 495.9
      asthma NEC (see also Asthma) 493.9 ☑
      bronchiectasis 494.0
        with acute exacerbation 494.1
      bronchitis (chronic) (see also Bronchitis, with, obstruction) 491.20
      emphysema NEC 492.8
      chronic 496

Obstruction, obstructed, obstructive — continued
  airway — continued
    chronic — continued
      with
        allergic alveolitis NEC 495.5
        asthma NEC (see also Asthma) 493.2 ☑
        bronchiectasis 494.0
          with acute exacerbation 494.1
        bronchitis (chronic) (see also Bronchitis, with, obstruction) 491.20
        emphysema NEC 492.8
    due to
      bronchospasm 519.11
      foreign body 934.9
      inhalation of fumes or vapors 506.9
      laryngospasm 478.75
  alimentary canal (see also Obstruction, intestine) 560.9
  ampulla of Vater 576.2
    with calculus, cholelithiasis, or stones — see Choledocholithiasis
  aortic (heart) (valve) (see also Stenosis, aortic) 424.1
    rheumatic (see also Stenosis, aortic, rheumatic) 395.0
  aortoiliac 444.0
  aqueduct of Sylvius 331.4
    congenital 742.3
      with spina bifida (see also Spina bifida) 741.0 ☑
  Arnold-Chiari (see also Spina bifida) 741.0 ☑
  artery (see also Embolism, artery) 444.9
    basilar (complete) (partial) (see also Occlusion, artery, basilar) 433.0 ☑
    carotid (complete) (partial) (see also Occlusion, artery, carotid) 433.1 ☑
    precerebral — see Occlusion, artery, precerebral NEC
    retinal (central) (see also Occlusion, retina) 362.30
    vertebral (complete) (partial) (see also Occlusion, artery, vertebral) 433.2 ☑
  asthma (chronic) (with obstructive pulmonary disease) 493.2 ☑
  band (intestinal) 560.81
  bile duct or passage (see also Obstruction, biliary) 576.2
    congenital 751.61
      jaundice from 751.61 [774.5]
  biliary (duct) (tract) 576.2
    with calculus 574.51
      with cholecystitis (chronic) 574.41
        acute 574.31
    congenital 751.61
      jaundice from 751.61 [774.5]
    gallbladder 575.2
      with calculus 574.21
        with cholecystitis (chronic) 574.11
        acute 574.01
  bladder neck (acquired) 596.0
    congenital 753.6
  bowel (see also Obstruction, intestine) 560.9
  bronchus 519.19
  canal, ear (see also Stricture, ear canal, acquired) 380.50
  cardia 537.89
  caval veins (inferior) (superior) 459.2
  cecum (see also Obstruction, intestine) 560.9
  circulatory 459.9
  colon (see also Obstruction, intestine) 560.9
    sympathicotonic 560.89
  common duct (see also Obstruction, biliary) 576.2
    congenital 751.61
  coronary (artery) (heart) (see also Arteriosclerosis, coronary)
    acute (see also Infarct, myocardium) 410.9 ☑
      without myocardial infarction 411.81
  cystic duct (see also Obstruction, gallbladder) 575.2
    congenital 751.61

Obstruction, obstructed, obstructive — continued
  device, implant, or graft — see Complications, due to (presence of) any device, implant, or graft classified to 996.0–996.5 NEC
  due to foreign body accidentally left in operation wound 998.4
  duodenum 537.3
    congenital 751.1
    due to
      compression NEC 537.3
      cyst 537.3
      intrinsic lesion or disease NEC 537.3
      scarring 537.3
      torsion 537.3
      ulcer 532.91
      volvulus 537.3
  ejaculatory duct 608.89
  endocardium 424.90
    arteriosclerotic 424.99
    specified cause, except rheumatic 424.99
  esophagus 530.3
  eustachian tube (complete) (partial) 381.60
    cartilaginous
      extrinsic 381.63
      intrinsic 381.62
    due to
      cholesteatoma 381.61
      osseous lesion NEC 381.61
      polyp 381.61
    osseous 381.61
  fallopian tube (bilateral) 628.2
  fecal 560.39
    with hernia (see also Hernia, by site, with obstruction)
      gangrenous — see Hernia, by site, with gangrene
  foramen of Monro (congenital) 742.3
    with spina bifida (see also Spina bifida) 741.0 ☑
  foreign body — see Foreign body
  gallbladder 575.2
    with calculus, cholelithiasis, or stones 574.21
      with cholecystitis (chronic) 574.11
        acute 574.01
    congenital 751.69
      jaundice from 751.69 [774.5]
  gastric outlet 537.0
  gastrointestinal (see also Obstruction, intestine) 560.9
  glottis 478.79
  hepatic 573.8
    duct (see also Obstruction, biliary) 576.2
      congenital 751.61
  icterus (see also Obstruction, biliary) 576.8
    congenital 751.61
  ileocecal coil (see also Obstruction, intestine) 560.9
  ileum (see also Obstruction, intestine) 560.9
  iliofemoral (artery) 444.81
  internal anastomosis — see Complications, mechanical, graft
  intestine (mechanical) (neurogenic) (paroxysmal) (postinfectional) (reflex) 560.9
    with
      adhesions (intestinal) (peritoneal) 560.81
      hernia (see also Hernia, by site, with obstruction)
        gangrenous — see Hernia, by site, with gangrene
    adynamic (see also Ileus) 560.1
    by gallstone 560.31
    congenital or infantile (small) 751.1
      large 751.2
    due to
      Ascaris lumbricoides 127.0
      mural thickening 560.89
      procedure 997.4
        involving urinary tract 997.5
    impaction 560.39
    infantile — see Obstruction, intestine, congenital

☑ Additional Digit Required — Refer to the Tabular List for Digit Selection   ▽ Subterms under main terms may continue to next column or page

2010 ICD-9-CM   ▶◀ Revised Text   ● New Line   ▲ Revised Code   Volume 2 — 207

☑ Additional Digit Required — Refer to the Tabular List for Digit Selection   ▽ Subterms under main terms may continue to next column or page

Occlusion — *continued*
  ureter — *continued*
    congenital 753.29
  urethra (*see also* Stricture, urethra) 598.9
    congenital 753.6
  uterus 621.8
  vagina 623.2
  vascular NEC 459.9
  vein — *see* Thrombosis
  vena cava
    inferior 453.2   ●
    superior   ●
      acute 453.87   ●
      chronic 453.77   ●
  ventricle (brain) NEC 331.4
  vertebral (artery) — *see* Occlusion, artery, vertebral
  vessel (blood) NEC 459.9
  vulva 624.8
Occlusio pupillae 364.74
Occupational
  problems NEC V62.29
  therapy V57.21
Ochlophobia 300.29
Ochronosis (alkaptonuric) (congenital) (endogenous) 270.2
  with chloasma of eyelid 270.2
Ocular muscle — *see also* condition
  myopathy 359.1
  torticollis 781.93
Oculoauriculovertebral dysplasia 756.0
Oculogyric
  crisis or disturbance 378.87
    psychogenic 306.7
Oculomotor syndrome 378.81
Oddi's sphincter spasm 576.5
Odelberg's disease (juvenile osteochondrosis) 732.1
Odontalgia 525.9
Odontoameloblastoma (M9311/0) 213.1
  upper jaw (bone) 213.0
Odontoclasia 521.05
Odontoclasis 873.63
  complicated 873.73
Odontodysplasia, regional 520.4
Odontogenesis imperfecta 520.5
Odontoma (M9280/0) 213.1
  ameloblastic (M9311/0) 213.1
    upper jaw (bone) 213.0
  calcified (M9280/0) 213.1
    upper jaw (bone) 213.0
  complex (M9282/0) 213.1
    upper jaw (bone) 213.0
  compound (M9281/0) 213.1
    upper jaw (bone) 213.0
  fibroameloblastic (M9290/0) 213.1
    upper jaw (bone) 213.0
  follicular 526.0
    upper jaw (bone) 213.0
Odontomyelitis (closed) (open) 522.0
Odontonecrosis 521.09
Odontorrhagia 525.8
Odontosarcoma, ameloblastic (M9290/3) 170.1
  upper jaw (bone) 170.0
Odynophagia 787.20
Oesophagostomiasis 127.7
Oesophagostomum infestation 127.7
Oestriasis 134.0
Ogilvie's syndrome (sympathicotonic colon obstruction) 560.89
Oguchi's disease (retina) 368.61
Ohara's disease — *see also* Tularemia 021.9
Oidiomycosis — *see also* Candidiasis 112.9
Oidiomycotic meningitis 112.83
Oidium albicans infection — *see also* Candidiasis 112.9
Old age 797
  dementia (of) 290.0
Olfactory — *see* condition
Oligemia 285.9
Oligergasia — *see also* Retardation, mental 319
Oligoamnios 658.0 ☑
  affecting fetus or newborn 761.2
Oligoastrocytoma, mixed (M9382/3)
  specified site — *see* Neoplasm, by site, malignant

Oligoastrocytoma, mixed — *continued*
  unspecified site 191.9
Oligocythemia 285.9
Oligodendroblastoma (M9460/3)
  specified site — *see* Neoplasm, by site, malignant
  unspecified site 191.9
Oligodendroglioma (M9450/3)
  anaplastic type (M9451/3)
    specified site — *see* Neoplasm, by site, malignant
    unspecified site 191.9
  specified site — *see* Neoplasm, by site, malignant
  unspecified site 191.9
Oligodendroma — *see* Oligodendroglioma
Oligodontia — *see also* Anodontia 520.0
Oligoencephalon 742.1
Oligohydramnios 658.0 ☑
  affecting fetus or newborn 761.2
  due to premature rupture of membranes 658.1 ☑
    affecting fetus or newborn 761.2
Oligohydrosis 705.0
Oligomenorrhea 626.1
Oligophrenia — *see also* Retardation, mental 319
  phenylpyruvic 270.1
Oligospermia 606.1
Oligotrichia 704.09
  congenita 757.4
Oliguria 788.5
  with
    abortion — *see* Abortion, by type, with renal failure
    ectopic pregnancy (*see also* categories 633.0–633.9) 639.3
    molar pregnancy (*see also* categories 630–632) 639.3
  complicating
    abortion 639.3
    ectopic or molar pregnancy 639.3
    pregnancy 646.2 ☑
      with hypertension — *see* Toxemia, of pregnancy
  due to a procedure 997.5
  following labor and delivery 669.3 ☑
  heart or cardiac — *see* Failure, heart
  puerperal, postpartum 669.3 ☑
  specified due to a procedure 997.5
Ollier's disease (chondrodysplasia) 756.4
Omentitis — *see also* Peritonitis 567.9
Omentocele — *see also* Hernia, omental 553.8
Omentum, omental — *see* condition
Omphalitis (congenital) (newborn) 771.4
  not of newborn 686.9
  tetanus 771.3
Omphalocele 756.72   ▲
Omphalomesenteric duct, persistent 751.0
Omphalorrhagia, newborn 772.3
Omsk hemorrhagic fever 065.1
Onanism 307.9
Onchocerciasis 125.3
  eye 125.3 *[360.13]*
Onchocercosis 125.3
Oncocytoma (M8290/0) — *see* Neoplasm, by site, benign
Ondine's curse 348.89   ▲
Oneirophrenia — *see also* Schizophrenia 295.4 ☑
Onychauxis 703.8
  congenital 757.5
Onychia (with lymphangitis) 681.9
  dermatophytic 110.1
  finger 681.02
  toe 681.11
Onychitis (with lymphangitis) 681.9
  finger 681.02
  toe 681.11
Onychocryptosis 703.0
Onychodystrophy 703.8
  congenital 757.5
Onychogryphosis 703.8
Onychogryposis 703.8
Onycholysis 703.8
Onychomadesis 703.8
Onychomalacia 703.8

Onychomycosis 110.1
  finger 110.1
  toe 110.1
Onycho-osteodysplasia 756.89
Onychophagy 307.9
Onychoptosis 703.8
Onychorrhexis 703.8
  congenital 757.5
Onychoschizia 703.8
Onychotrophia — *see also* Atrophy, nail 703.8
O'nyong-nyong fever 066.3
Onyxis (finger) (toe) 703.0
Onyxitis (with lymphangitis) 681.9
  finger 681.02
  toe 681.11
Oocyte (egg) (ovum)
  donor V59.70
    over age 35 V59.73
      anonymous recipient V59.73
      designated recipient V59.74
    under age 35 V59.71
      anonymous recipient V59.71
      designated recipient V59.72
Oophoritis (cystic) (infectional) (interstitial) — *see also* Salpingo-oophoritis 614.2
  complicating pregnancy 646.6 ☑
  fetal (acute) 752.0
  gonococcal (acute) 098.19
    chronic or duration of 2 months or over 098.39
  tuberculous (*see also* Tuberculosis) 016.6 ☑
Opacity, opacities
  cornea 371.00
    central 371.03
      congenital 743.43
        interfering with vision 743.42
    degenerative (*see also* Degeneration, cornea) 371.40
    hereditary (*see also* Dystrophy, cornea) 371.50
    inflammatory (*see also* Keratitis) 370.9
    late effect of trachoma (healed) 139.1
    minor 371.01
    peripheral 371.02
  enamel (fluoride) (nonfluoride) (teeth) 520.3
  lens (*see also* Cataract) 366.9
  snowball 379.22
  vitreous (humor) 379.24
    congenital 743.51
Opalescent dentin (hereditary) 520.5
Open, opening
  abnormal, organ or site, congenital — *see* Imperfect, closure
  angle
    with
      borderline intraocular pressure 365.01
      cupping of discs 365.01
    bite
      anterior 524.24
      posterior 524.25
    false — *see* Imperfect, closure
  margin on tooth restoration 525.61
  restoration margins 525.61
  wound — *see* Wound, open, by site
Operation
  causing mutilation of fetus 763.89
  destructive, on live fetus, to facilitate birth 763.89
  for delivery, fetus or newborn 763.89
  maternal, unrelated to current delivery, affecting fetus or newborn (*see also* Newborn, affected by) 760.64
Operational fatigue 300.89
Operative — *see* condition
Operculitis (chronic) 523.40
  acute 523.30
Operculum, retina 361.32
  with detachment 361.01
Ophiasis 704.01
Ophthalmia — *see also* Conjunctivitis 372.30
  actinic rays 370.24
  allergic (acute) 372.05
    chronic 372.14
  blennorrhagic (neonatorum) 098.40
  catarrhal 372.03
  diphtheritic 032.81
  Egyptian 076.1

Ophthalmia — *see also* Conjunctivitis — *continued*
  electric, electrica 370.24
  gonococcal (neonatorum) 098.40
  metastatic 360.11
  migraine 346.8 ☑
  neonatorum, newborn 771.6
    gonococcal 098.40
  nodosa 360.14
  phlyctenular 370.31
    with ulcer (*see also* Ulcer, cornea) 370.00
  sympathetic 360.11
Ophthalmitis — *see* Ophthalmia
Ophthalmocele (congenital) 743.66
Ophthalmoneuromyelitis 341.0
Ophthalmopathy, infiltrative with thyrotoxicosis 242.0 ☑
Ophthalmoplegia — *see also* Strabismus 378.9
  anterior internuclear 378.86
  ataxia-areflexia syndrome 357.0
  bilateral 378.9
  diabetic 250.5 ☑ *[378.86]*
    due to secondary diabetes 249.5 ☑ *[378.86]*
  exophthalmic 242.0 ☑ *[376.22]*
  external 378.55
    progressive 378.72
    total 378.56
  internal (complete) (total) 367.52
  internuclear 378.86
  migraine 346.2 ☑
  painful 378.55
  Parinaud's 378.81
  progressive external 378.72
  supranuclear, progressive 333.0
  total (external) 378.56
    internal 367.52
  unilateral 378.9
Opisthognathism 524.00
Opisthorchiasis (felineus) (tenuicollis) (viverrini) 121.0
Opisthotonos, opisthotonus 781.0
Opitz's disease (congestive splenomegaly) 289.51
Opiumism — *see also* Dependence 304.0 ☑
Oppenheim's disease 358.8
Oppenheim-Urbach disease or syndrome (necrobiosis lipoidica diabeticorum) 250.8 ☑ *[709.3]*
  due to secondary diabetes 249.8 ☑ *[709.3]*
Opsoclonia 379.59
Optic nerve — *see* condition
Orbit — *see* condition
Orchioblastoma (M9071/3) 186.9
Orchitis (nonspecific) (septic) 604.90
  with abscess 604.0
  blennorrhagic (acute) 098.13
    chronic or duration of 2 months or over 098.33
  diphtheritic 032.89 *[604.91]*
  filarial 125.9 *[604.91]*
  gangrenous 604.99
  gonococcal (acute) 098.13
    chronic or duration of 2 months or over 098.33
  mumps 072.0
  parotidea 072.0
  suppurative 604.99
  syphilitic 095.8 *[604.91]*
  tuberculous (*see also* Tuberculosis) 016.5 ☑ *[608.81]*
Orf 051.2
Organic — *see also* condition
  heart — *see* Disease, heart
  insufficiency 799.89
Oriental
  bilharziasis 120.2
  schistosomiasis 120.2
  sore 085.1
Orientation
  ego-dystonic sexual 302.0
Orifice — *see* condition
Origin, both great vessels from right ventricle 745.11
Ormond's disease or syndrome 593.4
Ornithosis 073.9

Index

Ornithosis — Osteomyelitis

Ornithosis — *continued*
  with
    complication 073.8
      specified NEC 073.7
    pneumonia 073.0
    pneumonitis (lobular) 073.0
Orodigitofacial dysostosis 759.89
Oropouche fever 066.3
Orotacidwhile, oroticaciduria (congenital)
  (hereditary) (pyrimidine deficiency) 281.4
Oroya fever 088.0
Orthodontics V58.5
  adjustment V53.4
  aftercare V58.5
  fitting V53.4
Orthopnea 786.02
Orthoptic training V57.4
Osgood-Schlatter
  disease 732.4
  osteochondrosis 732.4
Osler's
  disease (M9950/1) (polycythemia vera) 238.4
  nodes 421.0
Osler-Rendu disease (familial hemorrhagic
  telangiectasia) 448.0
Osler-Vaquez disease (M9950/1) (polycythemia
  vera) 238.4
Osler-Weber-Rendu syndrome (familial hemorrhagic telangiectasia) 448.0
Osmidrosis 705.89
Osseous — *see* condition
Ossification
  artery — *see* Arteriosclerosis
  auricle (ear) 380.39
  bronchus 519.19
  cardiac (*see also* Degeneration, myocardial)
    429.1
  cartilage (senile) 733.99
  coronary (artery) — *see* Arteriosclerosis, coro-
    nary
  diaphragm 728.10
  ear 380.39
    middle (*see also* Otosclerosis) 387.9
  falx cerebri 349.2
  fascia 728.10
  fontanel
    defective or delayed 756.0
    premature 756.0
  heart (*see also* Degeneration, myocardial) 429.1
    valve — *see* Endocarditis
  larynx 478.79
  ligament
    posterior longitudinal 724.8
      cervical 723.7
  meninges (cerebral) 349.2
    spinal 336.8
  multiple, eccentric centers 733.99
  muscle 728.10
    heterotopic, postoperative 728.13
  myocardium, myocardial (*see also* Degenera-
    tion, myocardial) 429.1
  penis 607.81
  periarticular 728.89
  sclera 379.16
  tendon 727.82
  trachea 519.19
  tympanic membrane (*see also* Tympanosclero-
    sis) 385.00
  vitreous (humor) 360.44
Osteitis — *see also* Osteomyelitis 730.2 ☑
  acute 730.0 ☑
  alveolar 526.5
  chronic 730.1 ☑
  condensans (ilii) 733.5
  deformans (Paget's) 731.0
    due to or associated with malignant neo-
      plasm (*see also* Neoplasm, bone,
      malignant) 170.9 *[731.1]*
  due to yaws 102.6
  fibrosa NEC 733.29
    cystica (generalisata) 252.01
    disseminata 756.59
    osteoplastica 252.01
  fragilitans 756.51
  Garré's (sclerosing) 730.1 ☑
  infectious (acute) (subacute) 730.0 ☑

Osteitis — *see also* Osteomyelitis —
  continued
  infectious — *continued*
    chronic or old 730.1 ☑
  jaw (acute) (chronic) (lower) (neonatal) (sup-
    purative) (upper) 526.4
  parathyroid 252.01
  petrous bone (*see also* Petrositis) 383.20
  pubis 733.5
  sclerotic, nonsuppurative 730.1 ☑
  syphilitic 095.5
  tuberculosa
    cystica (of Jüngling) 135
    multiplex cystoides 135
Osteoarthritica spondylitis (spine) — *see also*
  Spondylosis 721.90
Osteoarthritis — *see also* Osteoarthrosis 715.9 ☑
  distal interphalangeal 715.9 ☑
  hyperplastic 731.2
  interspinalis (*see also* Spondylosis) 721.90
  spine, spinal NEC (*see also* Spondylosis) 721.90
Osteoarthropathy — *see also* Osteoarthrosis
  715.9 ☑
  chronic idiopathic hypertrophic 757.39
  familial idiopathic 757.39
  hypertrophic pulmonary 731.2
    secondary 731.2
  idiopathic hypertrophic 757.39
  primary hypertrophic 731.2
  pulmonary hypertrophic 731.2
  secondary hypertrophic 731.2
Osteoarthrosis (degenerative) (hypertrophic)
  (rheumatoid) 715.9 ☑

> *Note* — Use the following fifth-digit
> subclassification with category 715:
>
> 0   site unspecified
> 1   shoulder region
> 2   upper arm
> 3   forearm
> 4   hand
> 5   pelvic region and thigh
> 6   lower leg
> 7   ankle and foot
> 8   other specified sites except spine
> 9   multiple sites

  Deformans alkaptonurica 270.2
  generalized 715.09
  juvenilis (Köhler's) 732.5
  localized 715.3 ☑
    idiopathic 715.1 ☑
    primary 715.1 ☑
    secondary 715.2 ☑
  multiple sites, not specified as generalized
    715.89
  polyarticular 715.09
  spine (*see also* Spondylosis) 721.90
  temporomandibular joint 524.69
Osteoblastoma (M9200/0) — *see* Neoplasm,
  bone, benign
Osteochondritis — *see also* Osteochondrosis
  732.9
  dissecans 732.7
    hip 732.7
  ischiopubica 732.1
  multiple 756.59
  syphilitic (congenital) 090.0
Osteochondrodermodysplasia 756.59
Osteochondrodystrophy 277.5
  deformans 277.5
  familial 277.5
  fetalis 756.4
Osteochondrolysis 732.7
Osteochondroma (M9210/0) — *see also* Neoplasm, bone, benign
  multiple, congenital 756.4
Osteochondromatosis (M9210/1) 238.0
  synovial 727.82
Osteochondromyxosarcoma (M9180/3) — *see*
  Neoplasm, bone, malignant
Osteochondropathy NEC 732.9

Osteochondrosarcoma (M9180/3) — *see* Neoplasm, bone, malignant
Osteochondrosis 732.9
  acetabulum 732.1
  adult spine 732.8
  astragalus 732.5
  Blount's 732.4
  Buchanan's (juvenile osteochondrosis of iliac
    crest) 732.1
  Buchman's (juvenile osteochondrosis) 732.1
  Burns' 732.3
  calcaneus 732.5
  capitular epiphysis (femur) 732.1
  carpal
    lunate (wrist) 732.3
    scaphoid 732.3
  coxae juvenilis 732.1
  deformans juvenilis (coxae) (hip) 732.1
    Scheuermann's 732.0
    spine 732.0
    tibia 732.4
    vertebra 732.0
  Diaz's (astragalus) 732.5
  dissecans (knee) (shoulder) 732.7
  femoral capital epiphysis 732.1
  femur (head) (juvenile) 732.1
  foot (juvenile) 732.5
  Freiberg's (disease) (second metatarsal) 732.5
  Haas' 732.3
  Haglund's (os tibiale externum) 732.5
  hand (juvenile) 732.3
  head of
    femur 732.1
    humerus (juvenile) 732.3
  hip (juvenile) 732.1
  humerus (juvenile) 732.3
  iliac crest (juvenile) 732.1
  ilium (juvenile) 732.1
  ischiopubic synchondrosis 732.1
  Iselin's (osteochondrosis fifth metatarsal) 732.5
  juvenile, juvenilis 732.6
    arm 732.3
    capital femoral epiphysis 732.1
    capitellum humeri 732.3
    capitular epiphysis 732.1
    carpal scaphoid 732.3
    clavicle, sternal epiphysis 732.6
    coxae 732.1
    deformans 732.1
    foot 732.5
    hand 732.3
    hip and pelvis 732.1
    lower extremity, except foot 732.4
    lunate, wrist 732.3
    medial cuneiform bone 732.5
    metatarsal (head) 732.5
    metatarsophalangeal 732.5
    navicular, ankle 732.5
    patella 732.4
    primary patellar center (of Köhler) 732.4
    specified site NEC 732.6
    spine 732.0
    tarsal scaphoid 732.5
    tibia (epiphysis) (tuberosity) 732.4
    upper extremity 732.3
    vertebra (body) (Calvé) 732.0
      epiphyseal plates (of Scheuermann)
      732.0
  Kienböck's (disease) 732.3
  Köhler's (disease) (navicular, ankle) 732.5
    patellar 732.4
    tarsal navicular 732.5
  Legg-Calvé-Perthes (disease) 732.1
  lower extremity (juvenile) 732.4
  lunate bone 732.3
  Mauclaire's 732.3
  metacarpal heads (of Mauclaire) 732.3
  metatarsal (fifth) (head) (second) 732.5
  navicular, ankle 732.5
  os calcis 732.5
  Osgood-Schlatter 732.4
  os tibiale externum 732.5
  Panner's 732.3
  patella (juvenile) 732.4
  patellar center
    primary (of Köhler) 732.4

Osteochondrosis — *continued*
  patellar center — *continued*
    secondary (of Sinding-Larsen) 732.4
  pelvis (juvenile) 732.1
  Pierson's 732.1
  radial head (juvenile) 732.3
  Scheuermann's 732.0
  Sever's (calcaneum) 732.5
  Sinding-Larsen (secondary patellar center)
    732.4
  spine (juvenile) 732.0
    adult 732.8
  symphysis pubis (of Pierson) (juvenile) 732.1
  syphilitic (congenital) 090.0
  tarsal (navicular) (scaphoid) 732.5
  tibia (proximal) (tubercle) 732.4
  tuberculous — *see* Tuberculosis, bone
  ulna 732.3
  upper extremity (juvenile) 732.3
  van Neck's (juvenile osteochondrosis) 732.1
  vertebral (juvenile) 732.0
    adult 732.8
Osteoclastoma (M9250/1) 238.0
  malignant (M9250/3) — *see* Neoplasm, bone,
    malignant
Osteocopic pain 733.90
Osteodynia 733.90
Osteodystrophy
  azotemic 588.0
  chronica deformans hypertrophica 731.0
  congenital 756.50
    specified type NEC 756.59
  deformans 731.0
  fibrosa localisata 731.0
  parathyroid 252.01
  renal 588.0
Osteofibroma (M9262/0) — *see* Neoplasm, bone,
  benign
Osteofibrosarcoma (M9182/3) — *see* Neoplasm,
  bone, malignant
Osteogenesis imperfecta 756.51
Osteogenic — *see* condition
Osteoma (M9180/0) — *see also* Neoplasm, bone,
  benign
  osteoid (M9191/0) (*see also* Neoplasm, bone,
    benign)
    giant (M9200/0) — *see* Neoplasm, bone,
      benign
Osteomalacia 268.2
  chronica deformans hypertrophica 731.0
  due to vitamin D deficiency 268.2
  infantile (*see also* Rickets) 268.0
  juvenile (*see also* Rickets) 268.0
  pelvis 268.2
  vitamin D-resistant 275.3
Osteomalacic bone 268.2
Osteomalacosis 268.2
Osteomyelitis (general) (infective) (localized)
  (neonatal) (purulent) (pyogenic) (septic)
  (staphylococcal) (streptococcal) (suppurative) (with periostitis) 730.2 ☑

> *Note* — Use the following fifth-digit
> subclassification with category 730:
>
> 0   site unspecified
> 1   shoulder region
> 2   upper arm
> 3   forearm
> 4   hand
> 5   pelvic region and thigh
> 6   lower leg
> 7   ankle and foot
> 8   other specified sites
> 9   multiple sites

  acute or subacute 730.0 ☑
  chronic or old 730.1 ☑
  due to or associated with
    diabetes mellitus 250.8 ☑ *[731.8]*
      due to secondary diabetes
      249.8 ☑ *[731.8]*
    tuberculosis (*see also* Tuberculosis, bone)
      015.9 ☑ *[730.8]* ☑

☑ Additional Digit Required — Refer to the Tabular List for Digit Selection   ▽ Subterms under main terms may continue to next column or page

Osteomyelitis — *continued*
  due to or associated with — *continued*
    tuberculosis (*see also* Tuberculosis, bone)
      — *continued*
      limb bones 015.5 ☑ *[730.8]* ☑
      specified bones NEC
        015.7 ☑ *[730.8]* ☑
      spine 015.0 ☑ *[730.8]* ☑
      typhoid 002.0 *[730.8]* ☑
    Garré's 730.1 ☑
  jaw (acute) (chronic) (lower) (neonatal) (suppurative) (upper) 526.4
  nonsuppurating 730.1 ☑
  orbital 376.03
  petrous bone (*see also* Petrositis) 383.20
  Salmonella 003.24
  sclerosing, nonsuppurative 730.1 ☑
  sicca 730.1 ☑
  syphilitic 095.5
    congenital 090.0 *[730.8]* ☑
  tuberculous — *see* Tuberculosis, bone
  typhoid 002.0 *[730.8]* ☑
Osteomyelofibrosis 289.89
Osteomyelosclerosis 289.89
Osteonecrosis 733.40
  meaning osteomyelitis 730.1 ☑
Osteo-onycho-arthro dysplasia 756.89
Osteo-onychodysplasia, hereditary 756.89
Osteopathia
  condensans disseminata 756.53
  hyperostotica multiplex infantilis 756.59
  hypertrophica toxica 731.2
  striata 756.4
Osteopathy resulting from poliomyelitis —
  see also Poliomyelitis 045.9 ☑ *[730.7]* ☑
  familial dysplastic 731.2
Osteopecilia 756.53
Osteopenia 733.90
  borderline 733.90
Osteoperiostitis — *see also* Osteomyelitis
  730.2 ☑
  ossificans toxica 731.2
  toxica ossificans 731.2
Osteopetrosis (familial) 756.52
Osteophyte — *see* Exostosis
Osteophytosis — *see* Exostosis
Osteopoikilosis 756.53
Osteoporosis (generalized) 733.00
  circumscripta 731.0
  disuse 733.03
  drug-induced 733.09
  idiopathic 733.02
  postmenopausal 733.01
  posttraumatic 733.7
  screening V82.81
  senile 733.01
  specified type NEC 733.09
Osteoporosis-osteomalacia syndrome 268.2
Osteopsathyrosis 756.51
Osteoradionecrosis, jaw 526.89
Osteosarcoma (M9180/3) — *see also* Neoplasm, bone, malignant
  chondroblastic (M9181/3) — *see* Neoplasm, bone, malignant
  fibroblastic (M9182/3) — *see* Neoplasm, bone, malignant
  in Paget's disease of bone (M9184/3) — *see* Neoplasm, bone, malignant
  juxtacortical (M9190/3) — *see* Neoplasm, bone, malignant
  parosteal (M9190/3) — *see* Neoplasm, bone, malignant
  telangiectatic (M9183/3) — *see* Neoplasm, bone, malignant
Osteosclerosis 756.52
  fragilis (generalisata) 756.52
Osteosclerotic anemia 289.89
Osteosis
  acromegaloid 757.39
  cutis 709.3
  parathyroid 252.01
  renal fibrocystic 588.0
Österreicher-Turner syndrome 756.89
Ostium
  atrioventriculare commune 745.69

Ostium — *continued*
  primum (arteriosum) (defect) (persistent) 745.61
  secundum (arteriosum) (defect) (patent) (persistent) 745.5
Ostrum-Furst syndrome 756.59
Os, uterus — *see* condition
Otalgia 388.70
  otogenic 388.71
  referred 388.72
Othematoma 380.31
Otitic hydrocephalus 348.2
Otitis 382.9
  with effusion 381.4
    purulent 382.4
    secretory 381.4
    serous 381.4
    suppurative 382.4
  acute 382.9
  adhesive (*see also* Adhesions, middle ear) 385.10
  chronic 382.9
    with effusion 381.3
    mucoid, mucous (simple) 381.20
    purulent 382.3
    secretory 381.3
    serous 381.10
    suppurative 382.3
  diffuse parasitic 136.8
  externa (acute) (diffuse) (hemorrhagica) 380.10
    actinic 380.22
    candidal 112.82
    chemical 380.22
    chronic 380.23
      mycotic — *see* Otitis, externa, mycotic
      specified type NEC 380.23
    circumscribed 380.10
    contact 380.22
    due to
      erysipelas 035 *[380.13]*
      impetigo 684 *[380.13]*
      seborrheic dermatitis 690.10 *[380.13]*
    eczematoid 380.22
    furuncular 680.0 *[380.13]*
    infective 380.10
      chronic 380.16
    malignant 380.14
    mycotic (chronic) 380.15
      due to
        aspergillosis 117.3 *[380.15]*
        moniliasis 112.82
        otomycosis 111.8 *[380.15]*
    reactive 380.22
    specified type NEC 380.22
    tropical 111.8 *[380.15]*
  insidiosa (*see also* Otosclerosis) 387.9
  interna (*see also* Labyrinthitis) 386.30
  media (hemorrhagic) (staphylococcal) (streptococcal) 382.9
    acute 382.9
      with effusion 381.00
      allergic 381.04
        mucoid 381.05
        sanguineous 381.06
        serous 381.04
      catarrhal 381.00
      exudative 381.00
      mucoid 381.02
        allergic 381.05
      necrotizing 382.00
        with spontaneous rupture of ear drum 382.01
      in
        influenza 487.8 *[382.02]*
        measles 055.2
        scarlet fever 034.1 *[382.02]*
      nonsuppurative 381.00
      purulent 382.00
        with spontaneous rupture of ear drum 382.01
      sanguineous 381.03
        allergic 381.06
      secretory 381.01
      seromucinous 381.02
      serous 381.01
        allergic 381.04

Otitis — *continued*
  media — *continued*
    acute — *continued*
      suppurative 382.00
        with spontaneous rupture of ear drum 382.01
        due to
          influenza 487.8 *[382.02]*
          scarlet fever 034.1 *[382.02]*
      transudative 381.00
    adhesive (*see also* Adhesions, middle ear) 385.10
    allergic 381.4
      acute 381.04
        mucoid 381.05
        sanguineous 381.06
        serous 381.04
      chronic 381.3
    catarrhal 381.4
      acute 381.00
      chronic (simple) 381.10
    chronic 382.9
      with effusion 381.3
      adhesive (*see also* Adhesions, middle ear) 385.10
      allergic 381.3
      atticoantral, suppurative (with posterior or superior marginal perforation of ear drum) 382.2
      benign suppurative (with anterior perforation of ear drum) 382.1
      catarrhal 381.10
      exudative 381.3
      mucinous 381.20
      mucoid, mucous (simple) 381.20
      mucosanguineous 381.29
      nonsuppurative 381.3
      purulent 382.3
      secretory 381.3
      seromucinous 381.3
      serosanguineous 381.19
      serous (simple) 381.10
      suppurative 382.3
        atticoantral (with posterior or superior marginal perforation of ear drum) 382.2
        benign (with anterior perforation of ear drum) 382.1
        tuberculous (*see also* Tuberculosis) 017.4 ☑
        tubotympanic 382.1
      transudative 381.3
    exudative 381.4
      acute 381.00
      chronic 381.3
    fibrotic (*see also* Adhesions, middle ear) 385.10
    mucoid, mucous 381.4
      acute 381.02
      chronic (simple) 381.20
    mucosanguineous, chronic 381.29
    nonsuppurative 381.4
      acute 381.00
      chronic 381.3
    postmeasles 055.2
    purulent 382.4
      acute 382.00
        with spontaneous rupture of ear drum 382.01
      chronic 382.3
    sanguineous, acute 381.03
      allergic 381.06
    secretory 381.4
      acute or subacute 381.01
      chronic 381.3
    seromucinous 381.4
      acute or subacute 381.02
      chronic 381.3
    serosanguineous, chronic 381.19
    serous 381.4
      acute or subacute 381.01
      chronic (simple) 381.10
    subacute — *see* Otitis, media, acute
    suppurative 382.4
      acute 382.00

Otitis — *continued*
  media — *continued*
    suppurative — *continued*
      acute — *continued*
        with spontaneous rupture of ear drum 382.01
      chronic 382.3
        atticoantral 382.2
        benign 382.1
        tuberculous (*see also* Tuberculosis) 017.4 ☑
        tubotympanic 382.1
    transudative 381.4
      acute 381.00
      chronic 381.3
    tuberculous (*see also* Tuberculosis) 017.4 ☑
    postmeasles 055.2
Otoconia 386.8
Otolith syndrome 386.19
Otomycosis 111.8 *[380.15]*
  in
    aspergillosis 117.3 *[380.15]*
    moniliasis 112.82
Otopathy 388.9
Otoporosis — *see also* Otosclerosis 387.9
Otorrhagia 388.69
  traumatic — *see* nature of injury
Otorrhea 388.60
  blood 388.69
  cerebrospinal (fluid) 388.61
Otosclerosis (general) 387.9
  cochlear (endosteal) 387.2
  involving
    otic capsule 387.2
    oval window
      nonobliterative 387.0
      obliterative 387.1
    round window 387.2
  nonobliterative 387.0
  obliterative 387.1
  specified type NEC 387.8
Otospongiosis — *see also* Otosclerosis 387.9
Otto's disease or pelvis 715.35
Outburst, aggressive — *see also* Disturbance, conduct 312.0 ☑
  in children or adolescents 313.9
Outcome of delivery
  multiple birth NEC V27.9
    all liveborn V27.5
    all stillborn V27.7
    some liveborn V27.6
    unspecified V27.9
  single V27.9
    liveborn V27.0
    stillborn V27.1
  twins V27.9
    both liveborn V27.2
    both stillborn V27.4
    one liveborn, one stillborn V27.3
Outlet — *see also* condition
  syndrome (thoracic) 353.0
Outstanding ears (bilateral) 744.29
Ovalocytosis (congenital) (hereditary) — *see also* Elliptocytosis 282.1
Ovarian — *see also* condition
  pregnancy — *see* Pregnancy, ovarian
  remnant syndrome 620.8
  vein syndrome 593.4
Ovaritis (cystic) — *see also* Salpingo-oophoritis 614.2
Ovary, ovarian — *see* condition
Overactive — *see also* Hyperfunction
  bladder 596.51
  eye muscle (*see also* Strabismus) 378.9
  hypothalamus 253.8
  thyroid (*see also* Thyrotoxicosis) 242.9 ☑
Overactivity, child 314.01
Overbite (deep) (excessive) (horizontal) (vertical) 524.29
Overbreathing — *see also* Hyperventilation 786.01
Overconscientious personality 301.4
Overdevelopment — *see also* Hypertrophy
  breast (female) (male) 611.1
  nasal bones 738.0

☑ Additional Digit Required — Refer to the Tabular List for Digit Selection   ▽ Subterms under main terms may continue to next column or page

2010 ICD-9-CM   ▶◀ Revised Text   ● New Line   ▲ Revised Code   Volume 2 — 211

Index

Overdevelopment — Pain(s)

Overdevelopment — *see also* Hypertrophy — *continued*
   prostate, congenital 752.89
Overdistention — *see* Distention
Overdose overdosage (drug) 977.9
   specified drug or substance — *see* Table of Drugs and Chemicals
Overeating 783.6
   nonorganic origin 307.51
Overexertion (effects) (exhaustion) 994.5
Overexposure (effects) 994.9
   exhaustion 994.4
Overfeeding — *see also* Overeating 783.6
Overfill, endodontic 526.62
Overgrowth, bone NEC 733.99
Overhanging
   tooth restoration 525.62
   unrepairable, dental restorative materials 525.62
Overheated (effects) (places) — *see* Heat
Overinhibited child 313.0
Overjet 524.29
   excessive horizontal 524.26
Overlaid, overlying (suffocation) 994.7
Overlap
   excessive horizontal 524.26
Overlapping toe (acquired) 735.8
   congenital (fifth toe) 755.66
Overload
   fluid 276.6
   potassium (K) 276.7
   sodium (Na) 276.0
Overnutrition — *see also* Hyperalimentation 783.6
Overproduction — *see also* Hypersecretion
   ACTH 255.3
   cortisol 255.0
   growth hormone 253.0
   thyroid-stimulating hormone (TSH) 242.8 ✓
Overriding
   aorta 747.21
   finger (acquired) 736.29
      congenital 755.59
   toe (acquired) 735.8
      congenital 755.66
Oversize
   fetus (weight of 4500 grams or more) 766.0
      affecting management of pregnancy 656.6 ✓
      causing disproportion 653.5 ✓
         with obstructed labor 660.1 ✓
            affecting fetus or newborn 763.1
Overstimulation, ovarian 256.1
Overstrained 780.79
   heart — *see* Hypertrophy, cardiac
Overweight — *see also* Obesity 278.02
Overwork 780.79
Oviduct — *see* condition
Ovotestis 752.7
Ovulation (cycle)
   failure or lack of 628.0
   pain 625.2
Ovum
   blighted 631
   donor V59.70
      over age 35 V59.73
         anonymous recipient V59.73
         designated recipient V59.74
      under age 35 V59.71
         anonymous recipient V59.71
         designated recipient V59.72
   dropsical 631
   pathologic 631
Owren's disease or syndrome (parahemophilia) — *see also* Defect, coagulation 286.3
Oxalosis 271.8
Oxaluria 271.8
Ox heart — *see* Hypertrophy, cardiac
OX syndrome 758.6
Oxycephaly, oxycephalic 756.0
   syphilitic, congenital 090.0
Oxyuriasis 127.4
Oxyuris vermicularis (infestation) 127.4
Ozena 472.0

P

Pacemaker syndrome 429.4
Pachyderma, pachydermia 701.8
   laryngis 478.5
   laryngitis 478.79
   larynx (verrucosa) 478.79
Pachydermatitis 701.8
Pachydermatocele (congenital) 757.39
   acquired 701.8
Pachydermatosis 701.8
Pachydermoperiostitis
   secondary 731.2
Pachydermoperiostosis
   primary idiopathic 757.39
   secondary 731.2
Pachymeningitis (adhesive) (basal) (brain) (cerebral) (cervical) (chronic) (circumscribed) (external) (fibrous) (hemorrhagic) (hypertrophic) (internal) (purulent) (spinal) (suppurative) — *see also* Meningitis 322.9
   gonococcal 098.82
Pachyonychia (congenital) 757.5
   acquired 703.8
Pachyperiosteodermia
   primary or idiopathic 757.39
   secondary 731.2
Pachyperiostosis
   primary or idiopathic 757.39
   secondary 731.2
Pacinian tumor (M9507/0) — *see* Neoplasm, skin, benign
Pads, knuckle or Garrod's 728.79
Paget's disease (osteitis deformans) 731.0
   with infiltrating duct carcinoma of the breast (M8541/3) — *see* Neoplasm, breast, malignant
   bone 731.0
      osteosarcoma in (M9184/3) — *see* Neoplasm, bone, malignant
   breast (M8540/3) 174.0
   extramammary (M8542/3) (*see also* Neoplasm, skin, malignant)
      anus 154.3
      skin 173.5
   malignant (M8540/3)
      breast 174.0
      specified site NEC (M8542/3) — *see* Neoplasm, skin, malignant
      unspecified site 174.0
   mammary (M8540/3) 174.0
   necrosis of bone 731.0
   nipple (M8540/3) 174.0
   osteitis deformans 731.0
Paget-Schroetter syndrome (intermittent venous claudication) 453.89 ▲
Pain(s) (*see also* Painful) 780.96
   abdominal 789.0 ✓
   acute 338.19
      due to trauma 338.11
      postoperative 338.18
         post-thoracotomy 338.12
   adnexa (uteri) 625.9
   alimentary, due to vascular insufficiency 557.9
   anginoid (*see also* Pain, precordial) 786.51
   anus 569.42
   arch 729.5
   arm 729.5
   axillary 729.5
   back (postural) 724.5
      low 724.2
         psychogenic 307.89
   bile duct 576.9
   bladder 788.99
   bone 733.90
   breast 611.71
      psychogenic 307.89
   broad ligament 625.9
   cancer associated 338.3
   cartilage NEC 733.90
   cecum 789.0 ✓
   cervicobrachial 723.3
   chest (central) 786.50
      atypical 786.59
      midsternal 786.51
      musculoskeletal 786.59
      noncardiac 786.59

Pain(s) (*see also* Painful) — *continued*
   chest — *continued*
      substernal 786.51
      wall (anterior) 786.52
   chronic 338.29
      associated with significant psychosocial dysfunction 338.4
      due to trauma 338.21
      postoperative 338.28
         post-thoracotomy 338.22
      syndrome 338.4
   coccyx 724.79
   colon 789.0 ✓
   common duct 576.9
   coronary — *see* Angina
   costochondral 786.52
   diaphragm 786.52
   due to (presence of) any device, implant, or graft classifiable to 996.0–996.5 — *see* Complications, due to (presence of) any device, implant, or graft classified to 996.0–996.5 NEC
      malignancy (primary) (secondary) 338.3
   ear (*see also* Otalgia) 388.70
   epigastric, epigastrium 789.06
   extremity (lower) (upper) 729.5
   eye 379.91
   face, facial 784.0
      atypical 350.2
      nerve 351.8
   false (labor) 644.1 ✓
   female genital organ NEC 625.9
      psychogenic 307.89
   finger 729.5
   flank 789.0 ✓
   foot 729.5
   gallbladder 575.9
   gas (intestinal) 787.3
   gastric 536.8
   generalized 780.96
   genital organ
      female 625.9
      male 608.9
      psychogenic 307.89
   groin 789.0 ✓
   growing 781.99
   hand 729.5
   head (*see also* Headache) 784.0
   heart (see also Pain, precordial) 786.51
   infraorbital (*see also* Neuralgia, trigeminal) 350.1
   intermenstrual 625.2
   jaw 526.9
   joint 719.40
      ankle 719.47
      elbow 719.42
      foot 719.47
      hand 719.44
      hip 719.45
      knee 719.46
      multiple sites 719.49
      pelvic region 719.45
      psychogenic 307.89
      shoulder (region) 719.41
      specified site NEC 719.48
      wrist 719.43
   kidney 788.0
   labor, false or spurious 644.1 ✓
   laryngeal 784.1
   leg 729.5
   limb 729.5
   low back 724.2
   lumbar region 724.2
   mastoid (*see also* Otalgia) 388.70
   maxilla 526.9
   menstrual 625.3
   metacarpophalangeal (joint) 719.44
   metatarsophalangeal (joint) 719.47
   mouth 528.9
   muscle 729.1
      intercostal 786.59
   musculoskeletal (see also Pain, by site) 729.1
   nasal 478.19
   nasopharynx 478.29
   neck NEC 723.1
      psychogenic 307.89

Pain(s) (*see also* Painful) — *continued*
   neoplasm related (acute) (chronic) 338.3
   nerve NEC 729.2
   neuromuscular 729.1
   nose 478.19
   ocular 379.91
   ophthalmic 379.91
   orbital region 379.91
   osteocopic 733.90
   ovary 625.9
      psychogenic 307.89
   over heart (*see also* Pain, precordial) 786.51
   ovulation 625.2
   pelvic (female) 625.9
      male NEC 789.0 ✓
         psychogenic 307.89
      psychogenic 307.89
   penis 607.9
      psychogenic 307.89
   pericardial (*see also* Pain, precordial) 786.51
   perineum
      female 625.9
      male 608.9
   pharynx 478.29
   pleura, pleural, pleuritic 786.52
   postoperative 338.18
      acute 338.18
      chronic 338.28
   post-thoracotomy 338.12
      acute 338.12
      chronic 338.22
   preauricular 388.70
   precordial (region) 786.51
      psychogenic 307.89
   premenstrual 625.4
   psychogenic 307.80
      cardiovascular system 307.89
      gastrointestinal system 307.89
      genitourinary system 307.89
      heart 307.89
      musculoskeletal system 307.89
      respiratory system 307.89
      skin 306.3
   radicular (spinal) (*see also* Radiculitis) 729.2
   rectum 569.42
   respiration 786.52
   retrosternal 786.51
   rheumatic NEC 729.0
      muscular 729.1
   rib 786.50
   root (spinal) (*see also* Radiculitis) 729.2
   round ligament (stretch) 625.9
   sacroiliac 724.6
   sciatic 724.3
   scrotum 608.9
      psychogenic 307.89
   seminal vesicle 608.9
   sinus 478.19
   skin 782.0
   spermatic cord 608.9
   spinal root (*see also* Radiculitis) 729.2
   stomach 536.8
      psychogenic 307.89
   substernal 786.51
   temporomandibular (joint) 524.62
   temporomaxillary joint 524.62
   testis 608.9
      psychogenic 307.89
   thoracic spine 724.1
      with radicular and visceral pain 724.4
   throat 784.1
   tibia 733.90
   toe 729.5
   tongue 529.6
   tooth 525.9
   total hip replacement 996.77
   total knee replacement 996.77
   trigeminal (*see also* Neuralgia, trigeminal) 350.1
   tumor associated 338.3
   umbilicus 789.05
   ureter 788.0
   urinary (organ) (system) 788.0
   uterus 625.9
      psychogenic 307.89
   vagina 625.9
   vertebrogenic (syndrome) 724.5

✓ Additional Digit Required — Refer to the Tabular List for Digit Selection
212 — Volume 2 • October 2009   ►◄ Revised Text   ● New Line   ▲ Revised Code
Subterms under main terms may continue to next column or page
2010 ICD-9-CM

Pain(s) (see also Painful) — continued
  vesical 788.99
  vulva 625.9
  xiphoid 733.90
Painful — see also Pain
  arc syndrome 726.19
  coitus
    female 625.0
    male 608.89
      psychogenic 302.76
  ejaculation (semen) 608.89
    psychogenic 302.79
  erection 607.3
  feet syndrome 266.2
  menstruation 625.3
    psychogenic 306.52
  micturition 788.1
  ophthalmoplegia 378.55
  respiration 786.52
  scar NEC 709.2
  urination 788.1
  wire sutures 998.89
Painters' colic 984.9
  specified type of lead — see Table of Drugs
    and Chemicals
Palate — see condition
Palatoplegia 528.9
Palatoschisis — see also Cleft, palate 749.00
Palilalia 784.69
Palindromic arthritis — see also Rheumatism,
    palindromic 719.3 ☑
Palliative care V66.7
Pallor 782.61
  temporal, optic disc 377.15
Palmar — see also condition
  fascia — see condition
Palpable
  cecum 569.89
  kidney 593.89
  liver 573.9
  lymph nodes 785.6
  ovary 620.8
  prostate 602.9
  spleen (see also Splenomegaly) 789.2
  uterus 625.8
Palpitation (heart) 785.1
  psychogenic 306.2
Palsy — see also Paralysis 344.9
  atrophic diffuse 335.20
  Bell's 351.0
    newborn 767.5
  birth 767.7
  brachial plexus 353.0
    fetus or newborn 767.6
  brain (see also Palsy, cerebral)
    noncongenital or noninfantile 344.89
      late effect — see Late effect(s) (of)
        cerebrovascular disease
    syphilitic 094.89
      congenital 090.49
  bulbar (chronic) (progressive) 335.22
    pseudo NEC 335.23
    supranuclear NEC 344.8 ☑
  cerebral (congenital) (infantile) (spastic) 343.9
    athetoid 333.71
    diplegic 343.0
      late effect — see Late effect(s) (of)
        cerebrovascular disease
    hemiplegic 343.1
    monoplegic 343.3
    noncongenital or noninfantile 437.8
      late effect — see Late effect(s) (of)
        cerebrovascular disease
    paraplegic 343.0
    quadriplegic 343.2
    spastic, not congenital or infantile 344.89
    syphilitic 094.89
      congenital 090.49
    tetraplegic 343.2
  cranial nerve (see also Disorder, nerve, cranial)
    multiple 352.6
  creeping 335.21
  divers' 993.3
  Erb's (birth injury) 767.6
  facial 351.0
    newborn 767.5

Palsy — see also Paralysis — continued
  glossopharyngeal 352.2
  Klumpke (-Déjérine) 767.6
  lead 984.9
    specified type of lead — see Table of Drugs
      and Chemicals
  median nerve (tardy) 354.0
  peroneal nerve (acute) (tardy) 355.3
  progressive supranuclear 333.0
  pseudobulbar NEC 335.23
  radial nerve (acute) 354.3
  seventh nerve 351.0
    newborn 767.5
  shaking (see also Parkinsonism) 332.0
  spastic (cerebral) (spinal) 343.9
    hemiplegic 343.1
  specified nerve NEC — see Disorder, nerve
  supranuclear NEC 356.8
    progressive 333.0
  ulnar nerve (tardy) 354.2
  wasting 335.21
Paltauf-Sternberg disease 201.9 ☑
Paludism — see Malaria
Panama fever 084.0
Panaris (with lymphangitis) 681.9
  finger 681.02
  toe 681.11
Panaritium (with lymphangitis) 681.9
  finger 681.02
  toe 681.11
Panarteritis (nodosa) 446.0
  brain or cerebral 437.4
Pancake heart 793.2
  with cor pulmonale (chronic) 416.9
Pancarditis (acute) (chronic) 429.89
  with
    rheumatic
      fever (active) (acute) (chronic) (suba-
        cute) 391.8
        inactive or quiescent 398.99
    rheumatic, acute 391.8
    chronic or inactive 398.99
Pancoast's syndrome or tumor (carcinoma,
    pulmonary apex) (M8010/3) 162.3
Pancoast-Tobias syndrome (M8010/3) (carcino-
    ma, pulmonary apex) 162.3
Pancolitis 556.6
Pancreas, pancreatic — see condition
Pancreatitis 577.0
  acute (edematous) (hemorrhagic) (recurrent)
    577.0
  annular 577.0
  apoplectic 577.0
  calcerceous 577.0
  chronic (infectious) 577.1
    recurrent 577.1
  cystic 577.2
  fibrous 577.8
  gangrenous 577.0
  hemorrhagic (acute) 577.0
  interstitial (chronic) 577.1
    acute 577.0
  malignant 577.0
  mumps 072.3
  painless 577.1
  recurrent 577.1
  relapsing 577.1
  subacute 577.0
  suppurative 577.0
  syphilitic 095.8
Pancreatolithiasis 577.8
Pancytolysis 289.9
Pancytopenia (acquired) 284.1
  with malformations 284.09
  congenital 284.09
Panencephalitis — see also Encephalitis
  subacute, sclerosing 046.2
Panhematopenia 284.81
  congenital 284.09
  constitutional 284.09
  splenic, primary 289.4
Panhemocytopenia 284.81
  congenital 284.09
  constitutional 284.09
Panhypogonadism 257.2
Panhypopituitarism 253.2

Panhypopituitarism — continued
  prepubertal 253.3
Panic (attack) (state) 300.01
  reaction to exceptional stress (transient) 308.0
Panmyelopathy, familial constitutional 284.09
Panmyelophthisis 284.2
  acquired (secondary) 284.81
  congenital 284.2
  idiopathic 284.9
Panmyelosis (acute) (M9951/1) 238.79
Panner's disease 732.3
  capitellum humeri 732.3
  head of humerus 732.3
  tarsal navicular (bone) (osteochondrosis) 732.5
Panneuritis endemica 265.0 [357.4]
Panniculitis 729.30
  back 724.8
  knee 729.31
  mesenteric 567.82
  neck 723.6
  nodular, nonsuppurative 729.30
  sacral 724.8
  specified site NEC 729.39
Panniculus adiposus (abdominal) 278.1
Pannus (corneal) 370.62
  abdominal (symptomatic) 278.1
  allergic eczematous 370.62
  degenerativus 370.62
  keratic 370.62
  rheumatoid — see Arthritis, rheumatoid
  trachomatosus, trachomatous (active)
    076.1 [370.62]
    late effect 139.1
Panophthalmitis 360.02
Panotitis — see Otitis media
Pansinusitis (chronic) (hyperplastic) (nonpuru-
    lent) (purulent) 473.8
  acute 461.8
  due to fungus NEC 117.9
  tuberculous (see also Tuberculosis) 012.8 ☑
Panuveitis 360.12
  sympathetic 360.11
Panvalvular disease — see Endocarditis, mitral
Papageienkrankheit 073.9
Papanicolaou smear
  anus 796.70
    with
      atypical squamous cells
        cannot exclude high grade squa-
          mous intraepithelial lesion
          (ASC-H) 796.72
        of undetermined significance (ASC-
          US) 796.71
      cytologic evidence of malignancy
        796.76
      high grade squamous intraepithelial
        lesion (HGSIL) 796.74
      low grade squamous intraepithelial le-
        sion (LGSIL) 796.73
    glandular 796.70
    specified finding NEC 796.79
    unsatisfactory cytology 796.78
  cervix (screening test) V76.2
    as part of gynecological examination
      V72.31
    for suspected malignant neoplasm V76.2
      no disease found V71.1
    inadequate cytology sample 795.08
    nonspecific abnormal finding 795.00
      with
        atypical squamous cells
          cannot exclude high grade
            squamous intraepithelial
            lesion (ASC-H) 795.02
          of undetermined significance
            (ASC-US) 795.01
        cytologic evidence of malignancy
          795.06
        high grade squamous intraepithe-
          lial lesion (HGSIL) 795.04
        low grade squamous intraepithelial
          lesion (LGSIL) 795.03
      nonspecific finding NEC 795.09
      to confirm findings of recent normal
        smear following initial abnor-
        mal smear V72.32

Papanicolaou smear — continued
  cervix — continued
    satisfactory smear but lacking transforma-
      tion zone 795.07
    unsatisfactory cervical cytology 795.08
  other specified site (see also Screening, malig-
    nant neoplasm)
    for suspected malignant neoplasm (see al-
      so Screening, malignant neoplasm)
    no disease found V71.1
    nonspecific abnormal finding 796.9
  vagina V76.47
    with
      atypical squamous cells
        cannot exclude high grade squa-
          mous intraepithelial lesion
          (ASC-H) 795.12
        of undetermined significance (ASC-
          US) 795.11
      cytologic evidence of malignancy
        795.16
      high grade squamous intraepithelial
        lesion (HGSIL) 795.14
      low grade squamous intraepithelial le-
        sion (LGSIL) 795.13
    abnormal NEC 795.19
    following hysterectomy for malignant
      condition V67.01
    inadequate cytology sample 795.18
    unsatisfactory cytology 795.18
Papilledema 377.00
  associated with
    decreased ocular pressure 377.02
    increased intracranial pressure 377.01
    retinal disorder 377.03
  choked disc 377.00
  infectional 377.00
Papillitis 377.31
  anus 569.49
  chronic lingual 529.4
  necrotizing, kidney 584.7
  optic 377.31
  rectum 569.49
  renal, necrotizing 584.7
  tongue 529.0
Papilloma (M8050/0) — see also Neoplasm, by
    site, benign

  Note — Except where otherwise indicated,
  the morphological varieties of papilloma in
  the list below should be coded by site as for
  "Neoplasm, benign."

  acuminatum (female) (male) 078.11
  bladder (urinary) (transitional cell) (M8120/1)
    236.7
    benign (M8120/0) 223.3
  choroid plexus (M9390/0) 225.0
    anaplastic type (M9390/3) 191.5
    malignant (M9390/3) 191.5
  ductal (M8503/0)
  dyskeratotic (M8052/0)
  epidermoid (M8052/0)
  hyperkeratotic (M8052/0)
  intracystic (M8504/0)
  intraductal (M8503/0)
  inverted (M8053/0)
  keratotic (M8052/0)
  parakeratotic (M8052/0)
  pinta (primary) 103.0
  renal pelvis (transitional cell) (M8120/1) 236.99
    benign (M8120/0) 223.1
  Schneiderian (M8121/0)
    specified site — see Neoplasm, by site,
      benign
    unspecified site 212.0
  serous surface (M8461/0)
    borderline malignancy (M8461/1)
      specified site — see Neoplasm, by site,
        uncertain behavior
      unspecified site 236.2
    specified site — see Neoplasm, by site,
      benign
    unspecified site 220
  squamous (cell) (M8052/0)
  transitional (cell) (M8120/0)
    bladder (urinary) (M8120/1) 236.7

Pain(s) — Papilloma

☑ Additional Digit Required — Refer to the Tabular List for Digit Selection | ▽ Subterms under main terms may continue to next column or page

2010 ICD-9-CM | ▶◀ Revised Text | ● New Line | ▲ Revised Code | Volume 2 — 213

Papilloma — see also Neoplasm, by site, benign
— continued
transitional — continued
inverted type (M8121/1) — see Neoplasm, by site, uncertain behavior
renal pelvis (M8120/1) 236.91
ureter (M8120/1) 236.91
ureter (transitional cell) (M8120/1) 236.91
benign (M8120/0) 223.2
urothelial (M8120/1) — see Neoplasm, by site, uncertain behavior
verrucous (M8051/0)
villous (M8261/1) — see Neoplasm, by site, uncertain behavior
yaws, plantar or palmar 102.1
Papillomata, multiple, of yaws 102.1
Papillomatosis (M8060/0) — see also Neoplasm, by site, benign
confluent and reticulate 701.8
cutaneous 701.8
ductal, breast 610.1
Gougerot-Carteaud (confluent reticulate) 701.8
intraductal (diffuse) (M8505/0) — see Neoplasm, by site, benign
subareolar duct (M8506/0) 217
Papillon-Léage and Psaume syndrome (orodigitofacial dysostosis) 759.89
Papule 709.8
carate (primary) 103.0
fibrous, of nose (M8724/0) 216.3
pinta (primary) 103.0
Papulosis, malignant 447.8
Papyraceous fetus 779.89
complicating pregnancy 646.0 ☑
Paracephalus 759.7
Parachute mitral valve 746.5
Paracoccidioidomycosis 116.1
mucocutaneous-lymphangitic 116.1
pulmonary 116.1
visceral 116.1
Paracoccidiomycosis — see Paracoccidioidomycosis
Paracusis 388.40
Paradentosis 523.5
Paradoxical facial movements 374.43
Paraffinoma 999.9
Paraganglioma (M8680/1)
adrenal (M8700/0) 227.0
malignant (M8700/3) 194.0
aortic body (M8691/1) 237.3
malignant (M8691/3) 194.6
carotid body (M8692/1) 237.3
malignant (M8692/3) 194.5
chromaffin (M8700/0) (see also Neoplasm, by site, benign)
malignant (M8700/3) — see Neoplasm, by site, malignant
extra-adrenal (M8693/1)
malignant (M8693/3)
specified site — see Neoplasm, by site, malignant
unspecified site 194.6
specified site — see Neoplasm, by site, uncertain behavior
unspecified site 237.3
glomus jugulare (M8690/1) 237.3
malignant (M8690/3) 194.6
jugular (M8690/1) 237.3
malignant (M8680/3)
specified site — see Neoplasm, by site, malignant
unspecified site 194.6
nonchromaffin (M8693/1)
malignant (M8693/3)
specified site — see Neoplasm, by site, malignant
unspecified site 194.6
specified site — see Neoplasm, by site, uncertain behavior
unspecified site 237.3
parasympathetic (M8682/1)
specified site — see Neoplasm, by site, uncertain behavior
unspecified site 237.3
specified site — see Neoplasm, by site, uncertain behavior

Paraganglioma — continued
sympathetic (M8681/1)
specified site — see Neoplasm, by site, uncertain behavior
unspecified site 237.3
unspecified site 237.3
Parageusia 781.1
psychogenic 306.7
Paragonimiasis 121.2
Paragranuloma, Hodgkin's (M9660/3) 201.0 ☑
Parahemophilia — see also Defect, coagulation
286.3
Parakeratosis 690.8
psoriasiformis 696.2
variegata 696.2
Paralysis, paralytic (complete) (incomplete)
344.9
with
broken
back — see Fracture, vertebra, by site, with spinal cord injury
neck — see Fracture, vertebra, cervical, with spinal cord injury
fracture, vertebra — see Fracture, vertebra, by site, with spinal cord injury
syphilis 094.89
abdomen and back muscles 355.9
abdominal muscles 355.9
abducens (nerve) 378.54
abductor 355.9
lower extremity 355.8
upper extremity 354.9
accessory nerve 352.4
accommodation 367.51
hysterical 300.11
acoustic nerve 388.5
agitans 332.0
arteriosclerotic 332.0
alternating 344.89
oculomotor 344.89
amyotrophic 335.20
ankle 355.8
anterior serratus 355.9
anus (sphincter) 569.49
apoplectic (current episode) (see also Disease, cerebrovascular, acute)
late effect — see Late effect(s) (of) cerebrovascular disease
arm 344.40
affecting
dominant side 344.41
nondominant side 344.42
both 344.2
hysterical 300.11
late effect — see Late effect(s) (of) cerebrovascular disease
psychogenic 306.0
transient 781.4
traumatic NEC (see also Injury, nerve, upper limb) 955.9
arteriosclerotic (current episode) 437.0
late effect — see Late effect(s) (of) cerebrovascular disease
ascending (spinal), acute 357.0
associated, nuclear 344.89
asthenic bulbar 358.00
ataxic NEC 334.9
general 094.1
athetoid 333.71
atrophic 356.9
infantile, acute (see also Poliomyelitis, with paralysis) 045.1 ☑
muscle NEC 355.9
progressive 335.21
spinal (acute) (see also Poliomyelitis, with paralysis) 045.1 ☑
attack (see also Disease, cerebrovascular, acute) 436
axillary 353.0
Babinski-Nageotte's 344.89
Bell's 351.0
newborn 767.5
Benedikt's 344.89
birth (injury) 767.7
brain 767.0
intracranial 767.0

Paralysis, paralytic — continued
birth — continued
spinal cord 767.4
bladder (sphincter) 596.53
neurogenic 596.54
with cauda equina syndrome 344.61
puerperal, postpartum, childbirth 665.5 ☑
sensory 596.54
with cauda equina 344.61
spastic 596.54
with cauda equina 344.61
bowel, colon, or intestine (see also Ileus) 560.1
brachial plexus 353.0
due to birth injury 767.6
newborn 767.6
brain
congenital — see Palsy, cerebral
current episode 437.8
diplegia 344.2
hemiplegia 342.9 ☑
late effect — see Late effect(s) (of) cerebrovascular disease
infantile — see Palsy, cerebral
late effect — see Late effect(s) (of) cerebrovascular disease
monoplegia (see also Monoplegia)
late effect — see Late effect(s) (of) cerebrovascular disease
paraplegia 344.1
quadriplegia — see Quadriplegia
syphilitic, congenital 090.49
triplegia 344.89
bronchi 519.19
Brown-Séquard's 344.89
bulbar (chronic) (progressive) 335.22
infantile (see also Poliomyelitis, bulbar) 045.0 ☑
poliomyelitic (see also Poliomyelitis, bulbar) 045.0 ☑
pseudo 335.23
supranuclear 344.89
bulbospinal 358.00
cardiac (see also Failure, heart) 428.9
cerebral
current episode 437.8
spastic, infantile — see Palsy, cerebral
cerebrocerebellar 437.8
diplegic infantile 343.0
cervical
plexus 353.2
sympathetic NEC 337.09
Céstan-Chenais 344.89
Charcôt-Marie-Tooth type 356.1
childhood — see Palsy, cerebral
Clark's 343.9
colon (see also Ileus) 560.1
compressed air 993.3
compression
arm NEC 354.9
cerebral — see Paralysis, brain
leg NEC 355.8
lower extremity NEC 355.8
upper extremity NEC 354.9
congenital (cerebral) (spastic) (spinal) — see Palsy, cerebral
conjugate movement (of eye) 378.81
cortical (nuclear) (supranuclear) 378.81
convergence 378.83
cordis (see also Failure, heart) 428.9
cortical (see also Paralysis, brain) 437.8
cranial or cerebral nerve (see also Disorder, nerve, cranial) 352.9
creeping 335.21
crossed leg 344.89
crutch 953.4
deglutition 784.99
hysterical 300.11
dementia 094.1
descending (spinal) NEC 335.9
diaphragm (flaccid) 519.4
due to accidental section of phrenic nerve during procedure 998.2
digestive organs NEC 564.89
diplegic — see Diplegia
divergence (nuclear) 378.85
divers' 993.3

Paralysis, paralytic — continued
Duchenne's 335.22
due to intracranial or spinal birth injury — see Palsy, cerebral
embolic (current episode) (see also Embolism, brain) 434.1 ☑
late effect — see Late effect(s) (of) cerebrovascular disease
enteric (see also Ileus) 560.1
with hernia — see Hernia, by site, with obstruction
Erb (-Duchenne) (birth) (newborn) 767.6
Erb's syphilitic spastic spinal 094.89
esophagus 530.89
essential, infancy (see also Poliomyelitis) 045.9 ☑
extremity
lower — see Paralysis, leg
spastic (hereditary) 343.3
noncongenital or noninfantile 344.1
transient (cause unknown) 781.4
upper — see Paralysis, arm
eye muscle (extrinsic) 378.55
intrinsic 367.51
facial (nerve) 351.0
birth injury 767.5
congenital 767.5
following operation NEC 998.2
newborn 767.5
familial 359.3
periodic 359.3
spastic 334.1
fauces 478.29
finger NEC 354.9
foot NEC 355.8
gait 781.2
gastric nerve 352.3
gaze 378.81
general 094.1
ataxic 094.1
insane 094.1
juvenile 090.40
progressive 094.1
tabetic 094.1
glossopharyngeal (nerve) 352.2
glottis (see also Paralysis, vocal cord) 478.30
gluteal 353.4
Gubler (-Millard) 344.89
hand 354.9
hysterical 300.11
psychogenic 306.0
heart (see also Failure, heart) 428.9
hemifacial, progressive 349.89
hemiplegic — see Hemiplegia
hyperkalemic periodic (familial) 359.3
hypertensive (current episode) 437.8
hypoglossal (nerve) 352.5
hypokalemic periodic 359.3
Hyrtl's sphincter (rectum) 569.49
hysterical 300.11
ileus (see also Ileus) 560.1
infantile (see also Poliomyelitis) 045.9 ☑
atrophic acute 045.1 ☑
bulbar 045.0 ☑
cerebral — see Palsy, cerebral
paralytic 045.1 ☑
progressive acute 045.9 ☑
spastic — see Palsy, cerebral
spinal 045.9 ☑
infective (see also Poliomyelitis) 045.9 ☑
inferior nuclear 344.9
insane, general or progressive 094.1
internuclear 378.86
interosseous 355.9
intestine (see also Ileus) 560.1
intracranial (current episode) (see also Paralysis, brain) 437.8
due to birth injury 767.0
iris 379.49
due to diphtheria (toxin) 032.81 [379.49]
ischemic, Volkmann's (complicating trauma) 958.6
isolated sleep, recurrent
Jackson's 344.89
jake 357.7
Jamaica ginger (jake) 357.7

Paralysis, paralytic — *continued*
  juvenile general 090.40
  Klumpke (-Déjérine) (birth) (newborn) 767.6
  labioglossal (laryngeal) (pharyngeal) 335.22
  Landry's 357.0
  laryngeal nerve (recurrent) (superior) (*see also* Paralysis, vocal cord) 478.30
  larynx (*see also* Paralysis, vocal cord) 478.30
    due to diphtheria (toxin) 032.3
  late effect
    due to
      birth injury, brain or spinal (cord) — *see* Palsy, cerebral
      edema, brain or cerebral — *see* Paralysis, brain
      lesion
        late effect — *see* Late effect(s) (of) cerebrovascular disease
        spinal (cord) — *see* Paralysis, spinal
  lateral 335.24
  lead 984.9
    specified type of lead — *see* Table of Drugs and Chemicals
  left side — *see* Hemiplegia
  leg 344.30
    affecting
      dominant side 344.31
      nondominant side 344.32
    both (*see also* Paraplegia) 344.1
    crossed 344.89
    hysterical 300.11
    psychogenic 306.0
    transient or transitory 781.4
      traumatic NEC (*see also* Injury, nerve, lower limb) 956.9
  levator palpebrae superioris 374.31
  limb NEC 344.5
    all four — *see* Quadriplegia
    quadriplegia — *see* Quadriplegia
  lip 528.5
  Lissauer's 094.1
  local 355.9
  lower limb (*see also* Paralysis, leg)
    both (*see also* Paraplegia) 344.1
  lung 518.89
    newborn 770.89
  median nerve 354.1
  medullary (tegmental) 344.89
  mesencephalic NEC 344.89
    tegmental 344.89
  middle alternating 344.89
  Millard-Gubler-Foville 344.89
  monoplegic — *see* Monoplegia
  motor NEC 344.9
    cerebral — *see* Paralysis, brain
    spinal — *see* Paralysis, spinal
  multiple
    cerebral — *see* Paralysis, brain
    spinal — *see* Paralysis, spinal
  muscle (flaccid) 359.9
    due to nerve lesion NEC 355.9
    eye (extrinsic) 378.55
      intrinsic 367.51
      oblique 378.51
    iris sphincter 364.89
    ischemic (complicating trauma) (Volkmann's) 958.6
    pseudohypertrophic 359.1
  muscular (atrophic) 359.9
    progressive 335.21
  musculocutaneous nerve 354.9
  musculospiral 354.9
  nerve (*see also* Disorder, nerve)
    third or oculomotor (partial) 378.51
      total 378.52
    fourth or trochlear 378.53
    sixth or abducens 378.54
    seventh or facial 351.0
      birth injury 767.5
      due to
        injection NEC 999.9
        operation NEC 997.09
      newborn 767.5
    accessory 352.4
    auditory 388.5
    birth injury 767.7

Paralysis, paralytic — *continued*
  nerve (*see also* Disorder, nerve) — *continued*
    cranial or cerebral (*see also* Disorder, nerve, cranial) 352.9
    facial 351.0
      birth injury 767.5
      newborn 767.5
    laryngeal (*see also* Paralysis, vocal cord) 478.30
    newborn 767.7
    phrenic 354.8
      newborn 767.7
    radial 354.3
      birth injury 767.6
      newborn 767.6
    syphilitic 094.89
    traumatic NEC (*see also* Injury, nerve, by site) 957.9
    trigeminal 350.9
    ulnar 354.2
  newborn NEC 767.0
  normokalemic periodic 359.3
  obstetrical, newborn 767.7
  ocular 378.9
  oculofacial, congenital 352.6
  oculomotor (nerve) (partial) 378.51
    alternating 344.89
    external bilateral 378.55
    total 378.52
  olfactory nerve 352.0
  palate 528.9
  palatopharyngolaryngeal 352.6
  paratrigeminal 350.9
  periodic (familial) (hyperkalemic) (hypokalemic) (normokalemic) (potassium sensitive) (secondary) 359.3
  peripheral
    autonomic nervous system — *see* Neuropathy, peripheral, autonomic
    nerve NEC 355.9
  peroneal (nerve) 355.3
  pharynx 478.29
  phrenic nerve 354.8
  plantar nerves 355.6
  pneumogastric nerve 352.3
  poliomyelitis (current) (*see also* Poliomyelitis, with paralysis) 045.1 ☑
    bulbar 045.0 ☑
  popliteal nerve 355.3
  pressure (*see also* Neuropathy, entrapment) 355.9
  progressive 335.21
    atrophic 335.21
    bulbar 335.22
    general 094.1
    hemifacial 349.89
    infantile, acute (*see also* Poliomyelitis) 045.9 ☑
    multiple 335.20
  pseudobulbar 335.23
  pseudohypertrophic 359.1
    muscle 359.1
  psychogenic 306.0
  pupil, pupillary 379.49
  quadriceps 355.8
  quadriplegic (*see also* Quadriplegia) 344.0 ☑
  radial nerve 354.3
    birth injury 767.6
  rectum (sphincter) 569.49
  rectus muscle (eye) 378.55
  recurrent
    isolated sleep 327.43
    laryngeal nerve (*see also* Paralysis, vocal cord) 478.30
  respiratory (muscle) (system) (tract) 786.09
    center NEC 344.89
      fetus or newborn 770.87
    congenital 768.9
    newborn 768.9
  right side — *see* Hemiplegia
  Saturday night 354.3
  saturnine 984.9
    specified type of lead — *see* Table of Drugs and Chemicals
  sciatic nerve 355.0

Paralysis, paralytic — *continued*
  secondary — *see* Paralysis, late effect
  seizure (cerebral) (current episode) (*see also* Disease, cerebrovascular, acute) 436
    late effect — *see* Late effect(s) (of) cerebrovascular disease
  senile NEC 344.9
  serratus magnus 355.9
  shaking (*see also* Parkinsonism) 332.0
  shock (*see also* Disease, cerebrovascular, acute) 436
    late effect — *see* Late effect(s) (of) cerebrovascular disease
  shoulder 354.9
  soft palate 528.9
  spasmodic — *see* Paralysis, spastic
  spastic 344.9
    cerebral infantile — *see* Palsy, cerebral
    congenital (cerebral) — *see* Palsy, cerebral
    familial 334.1
    hereditary 334.1
    infantile 343.9
    noncongenital or noninfantile, cerebral 344.9
    syphilitic 094.0
      spinal 094.89
  sphincter, bladder (*see also* Paralysis, bladder) 596.53
  spinal (cord) NEC 344.1
    accessory nerve 352.4
    acute (*see also* Poliomyelitis) 045.9 ☑
    ascending acute 357.0
    atrophic (acute) (*see also* Poliomyelitis, with paralysis) 045.1 ☑
      spastic, syphilitic 094.89
    congenital NEC 343.9
    hemiplegic — *see* Hemiplegia
    hereditary 336.8
    infantile (*see also* Poliomyelitis) 045.9 ☑
    late effect NEC 344.89
    monoplegic — *see* Monoplegia
    nerve 355.9
    progressive 335.10
    quadriplegic — *see* Quadriplegia
    spastic NEC 343.9
    traumatic — *see* Injury, spinal, by site
  sternomastoid 352.4
  stomach 536.3
    diabetic 250.6 ☑ *[536.3]*
      due to secondary diabetes 249.6 ☑ *[536.3]*
    nerve (nondiabetic) 352.3
  stroke (current episode) — *see* Infarct, brain
    late effect — *see* Late effect(s) (of) cerebrovascular disease
  subscapularis 354.8
  superior nuclear NEC 334.9
  supranuclear 356.8
  sympathetic
    cervical NEC 337.09
    nerve NEC (*see also* Neuropathy, peripheral, autonomic) 337.9
    nervous system — *see* Neuropathy, peripheral, autonomic
  syndrome 344.9
    specified NEC 344.89
  syphilitic spastic spinal (Erb's) 094.89
  tabetic general 094.1
  thigh 355.8
  throat 478.29
    diphtheritic 032.0
    muscle 478.29
  thrombotic (current episode) (*see also* Thrombosis, brain) 434.0 ☑
    late effect — *see* Late effect(s) (of) cerebrovascular disease
  thumb NEC 354.9
  tick (-bite) 989.5
  Todd's (postepileptic transitory paralysis) 344.89
  toe 355.6
  tongue 529.8
  transient
    arm or leg NEC 781.4
    traumatic NEC (*see also* Injury, nerve, by site) 957.9

Paralysis, paralytic — *continued*
  trapezius 352.4
  traumatic, transient NEC (*see also* Injury, nerve, by site) 957.9
  trembling (*see also* Parkinsonism) 332.0
  triceps brachii 354.9
  trigeminal nerve 350.9
  trochlear nerve 378.53
  ulnar nerve 354.2
  upper limb (*see also* Paralysis, arm)
    both (*see also* Diplegia) 344.2
  uremic — *see* Uremia
  uveoparotitic 135
  uvula 528.9
    hysterical 300.11
    postdiphtheritic 032.0
  vagus nerve 352.3
  vasomotor NEC 337.9
  velum palati 528.9
  vesical (*see also* Paralysis, bladder) 596.53
  vestibular nerve 388.5
  visual field, psychic 368.16
  vocal cord 478.30
    bilateral (partial) 478.33
      complete 478.34
    complete (bilateral) 478.34
    unilateral (partial) 478.31
      complete 478.32
  Volkmann's (complicating trauma) 958.6
  wasting 335.21
  Weber's 344.89
  wrist NEC 354.9

Paramedial orifice, urethrovesical 753.8
Paramenia 626.9
Parametritis (chronic) — *see also* Disease, pelvis, inflammatory 614.4
  acute 614.3
  puerperal, postpartum, childbirth 670.8 ☑   ▲
Parametrium, parametric — *see* condition
Paramnesia — *see also* Amnesia 780.93
Paramolar 520.1
  causing crowding 524.31
Paramyloidosis 277.30
Paramyoclonus multiplex 333.2
Paramyotonia 359.29
  congenita (of von Eulenburg) 359.29
Paraneoplastic syndrome — *see* condition
Parangi — *see also* Yaws 102.9
Paranoia 297.1
  alcoholic 291.5
  querulans 297.8
  senile 290.20
Paranoid
  dementia (*see also* Schizophrenia) 295.3 ☑
    praecox (acute) 295.3 ☑
    senile 290.20
  personality 301.0
  psychosis 297.9
    alcoholic 291.5
    climacteric 297.2
    drug-induced 292.11
    involutional 297.2
    menopausal 297.2
    protracted reactive 298.4
    psychogenic 298.4
      acute 298.3
    senile 290.20
  reaction (chronic) 297.9
    acute 298.3
  schizophrenia (acute) (*see also* Schizophrenia) 295.3 ☑
  state 297.9
    alcohol-induced 291.5
    climacteric 297.2
    drug-induced 292.11
    due to or associated with
      arteriosclerosis (cerebrovascular) 290.42
      presenile brain disease 290.12
      senile brain disease 290.20
    involutional 297.2
    menopausal 297.2
    senile 290.20
    simple 297.0
    specified type NEC 297.8

☑ Additional Digit Required — Refer to the Tabular List for Digit Selection   ▽ Subterms under main terms may continue to next column or page

2010 ICD-9-CM   ▶◀ Revised Text   ● New Line   ▲ Revised Code   **October 2009 · Volume 2 — 215**

Index

Paranoid — Pelviperitonitis

Paranoid — *continued*
  tendencies 301.0
  traits 301.0
  trends 301.0
  type, psychopathic personality 301.0
Paraparesis — *see also* Paraplegia 344.1
Paraphasia 784.3
Paraphilia — *see also* Deviation, sexual 302.9
Paraphimosis (congenital) 605
  chancroidal 099.0
Paraphrenia, paraphrenic (late) 297.2
  climacteric 297.2
  dementia (*see also* Schizophrenia) 295.3 ☑
  involutional 297.2
  menopausal 297.2
  schizophrenia (acute) (*see also* Schizophrenia)
    295.3 ☑
Paraplegia 344.1
  with
    broken back — *see* Fracture, vertebra, by
      site, with spinal cord injury
    fracture, vertebra — *see* Fracture, vertebra,
      by site, with spinal cord injury
  ataxic — *see* Degeneration, combined, spinal
    cord
  brain (current episode) (*see also* Paralysis,
    brain) 437.8
  cerebral (current episode) (*see also* Paralysis,
    brain) 437.8
  congenital or infantile (cerebral) (spastic)
    (spinal) 343.0
  cortical — *see* Paralysis, brain
  familial spastic 334.1
  functional (hysterical) 300.11
  hysterical 300.11
  infantile 343.0
  late effect 344.1
  Pott's (*see also* Tuberculosis) 015.0 ☑ *[730.88]*
  psychogenic 306.0
  spastic
    Erb's spinal 094.89
    hereditary 334.1
    not infantile or congenital 344.1
  spinal (cord)
    traumatic NEC — *see* Injury, spinal, by site
  syphilitic (spastic) 094.89
  traumatic NEC — *see* Injury, spinal, by site
Paraproteinemia 273.2
  benign (familial) 273.1
  monoclonal 273.1
  secondary to malignant or inflammatory dis-
    ease 273.1
Parapsoriasis 696.2
  en plaques 696.2
  guttata 696.2
  lichenoides chronica 696.2
  retiformis 696.2
  varioliformis (acuta) 696.2
Parascarlatina 057.8
Parasitic — *see also* condition
  disease NEC (*see also* Infestation, parasitic)
    136.9
    contact V01.89
    exposure to V01.89
    intestinal NEC 129
    skin NEC 134.9
  stomatitis 112.0
  sycosis 110.0
    beard 110.0
    scalp 110.0
  twin 759.4
Parasitism NEC 136.9
  intestinal NEC 129
  skin NEC 134.9
  specified — *see* Infestation
Parasitophobia 300.29
Parasomnia 307.47
  alcohol induced 291.82
  drug induced 292.85
  nonorganic origin 307.47
  organic 327.40
    in conditions classified elsewhere 327.44
    other 327.49
Paraspadias 752.69
Paraspasm facialis 351.8
Parathyroid gland — *see* condition

Parathyroiditis (autoimmune) 252.1
Parathyroprival tetany 252.1
Paratrachoma 077.0
Paratyphilitis — *see also* Appendicitis 541
Paratyphoid (fever) — *see* Fever, paratyphoid
Paratyphus — *see* Fever, paratyphoid
Paraurethral duct 753.8
Para-urethritis 597.89
  gonococcal (acute) 098.0
    chronic or duration of 2 months or over
      098.2
Paravaccinia NEC 051.9
  milkers' node 051.1
Paravaginitis — *see also* Vaginitis 616.10
Parencephalitis — *see also* Encephalitis 323.9
  late effect — *see* category 326
Parergasia 298.9
Paresis — *see also* Paralysis 344.9
  accommodation 367.51
  bladder (spastic) (sphincter) (*see also* Paralysis,
    bladder) 596.53
    tabetic 094.0
  bowel, colon, or intestine (*see also* Ileus) 560.1
  brain or cerebral — *see* Paralysis, brain
  extrinsic muscle, eye 378.55
  general 094.1
    arrested 094.1
    brain 094.1
    cerebral 094.1
    insane 094.1
    juvenile 090.40
      remission 090.49
    progressive 094.1
    remission (sustained) 094.1
    tabetic 094.1
  heart (*see also* Failure, heart) 428.9
  infantile (*see also* Poliomyelitis) 045.9 ☑
  insane 094.1
  juvenile 090.40
  late effect — *see* Paralysis, late effect
  luetic (general) 094.1
  peripheral progressive 356.9
  pseudohypertrophic 359.1
  senile NEC 344.9
  stomach 536.3
    diabetic 250.6 ☑ *[536.3]*
      due to secondary diabetes
        249.6 ☑ *[536.3]*
  syphilitic (general) 094.1
    congenital 090.40
  transient, limb 781.4
  vesical (sphincter) NEC 596.53
Paresthesia — *see also* Disturbance, sensation
  782.0
  Berger's (paresthesia of lower limb) 782.0
  Bernhardt 355.1
  Magnan's 782.0
Paretic — *see* condition
Parinaud's
  conjunctivitis 372.02
  oculoglandular syndrome 372.02
  ophthalmoplegia 378.81
  syndrome (paralysis of conjugate upward
    gaze) 378.81
Parkes Weber and Dimitri syndrome (encephalocutaneous angiomatosis) 759.6
Parkinson's disease, syndrome, or tremor —
  see Parkinsonism
Parkinsonism (arteriosclerotic) (idiopathic) (primary) 332.0
  associated with orthostatic hypotension (idio-
    pathic) (symptomatic) 333.0
  due to drugs 332.1
  neuroleptic-induced 332.1
  secondary 332.1
  syphilitic 094.82
Parodontitis 523.40
Parodontosis 523.5
Paronychia (with lymphangitis) 681.9
  candidal (chronic) 112.3
  chronic 681.9
    candidal 112.3
    finger 681.02
    toe 681.11
  finger 681.02
  toe 681.11

Paronychia — *continued*
  tuberculous (primary) (*see also* Tuberculosis)
    017.0 ☑
Parorexia NEC 307.52
  hysterical 300.11
Parosmia 781.1
  psychogenic 306.7
Parotid gland — *see* condition
Parotiditis — *see also* Parotitis 527.2
  epidemic 072.9
  infectious 072.9
Parotitis 527.2
  allergic 527.2
  chronic 527.2
  epidemic (*see also* Mumps) 072.9
  infectious (*see also* Mumps) 072.9
  noninfectious 527.2
  nonspecific toxic 527.2
  not mumps 527.2
  postoperative 527.2
  purulent 527.2
  septic 527.2
  suppurative (acute) 527.2
  surgical 527.2
  toxic 527.2
Paroxysmal — *see also* condition
  dyspnea (nocturnal) 786.09
Parrot's disease (syphilitic osteochondritis) 090.0
Parrot fever 073.9
Parry's disease or syndrome (exophthalmic
  goiter) 242.0 ☑
Parry-Romberg syndrome 349.89
Parsonage-Aldren-Turner syndrome 353.5
Parsonage-Turner syndrome 353.5
Parson's disease (exophthalmic goiter) 242.0 ☑
Pars planitis 363.21
Particolored infant 757.39
Parturition — *see* Delivery
Parvovirus 079.83
  B19 079.83
  human 079.83
Passage
  false, urethra 599.4
  meconium noted during delivery 763.84
  of sounds or bougies (*see also* Attention to ar-
    tificial opening) V55.9
Passive — *see* condition
Pasteurella septica 027.2
Pasteurellosis — *see also* Infection, Pasteurella
  027.2
PAT (paroxysmal atrial tachycardia) 427.0
Patau's syndrome (trisomy D1) 758.1
Patch
  herald 696.3
Patches
  mucous (syphilitic) 091.3
    congenital 090.0
  smokers' (mouth) 528.6
Patellar — *see* condition
Patellofemoral syndrome 719.46
Patent — *see also* Imperfect closure
  atrioventricular ostium 745.69
  canal of Nuck 752.41
  cervix 622.5
    complicating pregnancy 654.5 ☑
      affecting fetus or newborn 761.0
  ductus arteriosus or Botalli 747.0
  Eustachian
    tube 381.7
    valve 746.89
  foramen
    Botalli 745.5
    ovale 745.5
  interauricular septum 745.5
  interventricular septum 745.4
  omphalomesenteric duct 751.0
  os (uteri) — *see* Patent, cervix
  ostium secundum 745.5
  urachus 753.7
  vitelline duct 751.0
Paternity testing V70.4
Paterson-Kelly syndrome or web (sideropenic
  dysphagia) 280.8
Paterson (-Brown) (-Kelly) syndrome
  (sideropenic dysphagia) 280.8

Paterson's syndrome (sideropenic dysphagia)
  280.8
Pathologic, pathological — *see also* condition
  asphyxia 799.01
  drunkenness 291.4
  emotionality 301.3
  fracture — *see* Fracture, pathologic
  liar 301.7
  personality 301.9
  resorption, tooth 521.40
    external 521.42
    internal 521.41
    specified NEC 521.49
  sexuality (*see also* Deviation, sexual) 302.9
Pathology (of) — *see also* Disease
  periradicular, associated with previous en-
    dodontic treatment 526.69
Patterned motor discharge, idiopathic — *see
  also* Epilepsy 345.5 ☑
Patulous — *see also* Patent
  anus 569.49
  Eustachian tube 381.7
Pause, sinoatrial 427.81
Pavor nocturnus 307.46
Pavy's disease 593.6
Paxton's disease (white piedra) 111.2
Payr's disease or syndrome (splenic flexure
  syndrome) 569.89
PBA (pseudobulbar affect) 310.8
Pearls
  Elschnig 366.51
  enamel 520.2
Pearl-workers' disease (chronic osteomyelitis)
  — *see also* Osteomyelitis 730.1 ☑
Pectenitis 569.49
Pectenosis 569.49
Pectoral — *see* condition
Pectus
  carinatum (congenital) 754.82
    acquired 738.3
    rachitic (*see also* Rickets) 268.0
  excavatum (congenital) 754.81
    acquired 738.3
    rachitic (*see also* Rickets) 268.0
  recurvatum (congenital) 754.81
    acquired 738.3
Pedatrophia 261
Pederosis 302.2
Pediculosis (infestation) 132.9
  capitis (head louse) (any site) 132.0
  corporis (body louse) (any site) 132.1
  eyelid 132.0 *[373.6]*
  mixed (classifiable to more than one category
    in 132.0–132.2) 132.3
  pubis (pubic louse) (any site) 132.2
  vestimenti 132.1
  vulvae 132.2
Pediculus (infestation) — *see* Pediculosis
Pedophilia 302.2
Peg-shaped teeth 520.2
Pelade 704.01
Pel's crisis 094.0
Pel-Ebstein disease — *see* Disease, Hodgkin's
Pelger-Huët anomaly or syndrome (hereditary
  hyposegmentation) 288.2
Peliosis (rheumatica) 287.0
Pelizaeus-Merzbacher
  disease 330.0
  sclerosis, diffuse cerebral 330.0
Pellagra (alcoholic or with alcoholism) 265.2
  with polyneuropathy 265.2 *[357.4]*
**Pellagra-cerebellar-ataxia-renal
  aminoaciduria syndrome** 270.0
Pellegrini's disease (calcification, knee joint)
  726.62
Pellegrini (-Stieda) disease or syndrome (cal-
  cification, knee joint) 726.62
Pellizzi's syndrome (pineal) 259.8
Pelvic — *see also* condition
  congestion-fibrosis syndrome 625.5
  kidney 753.3
Pelvioectasis 591
Pelviolithiasis 592.0
Pelviperitonitis
  female (*see also* Peritonitis, pelvic, female)
    614.5

Pelviperitonitis — continued
  male (see also Peritonitis) 567.21
Pelvis, pelvic — see also condition or type
  infantile 738.6
  Nägele's 738.6
  obliquity 738.6
  Robert's 755.69
Pemphigoid 694.5
  benign, mucous membrane 694.60
    with ocular involvement 694.61
  bullous 694.5
  cicatricial 694.60
    with ocular involvement 694.61
  juvenile 694.2
Pemphigus 694.4
  benign 694.5
    chronic familial 757.39
  Brazilian 694.4
  circinatus 694.0
  congenital, traumatic 757.39
  conjunctiva 694.61
  contagiosus 684
  erythematodes 694.4
  erythematosus 694.4
  foliaceus 694.4
  frambesiodes 694.4
  gangrenous (see also Gangrene) 785.4
  malignant 694.4
  neonatorum, newborn 684
  ocular 694.61
  papillaris 694.4
  seborrheic 694.4
  South American 694.4
  syphilitic (congenital) 090.0
  vegetans 694.4
  vulgaris 694.4
  wildfire 694.4
Pendred's syndrome (familial goiter with deaf-mutism) 243
Pendulous
  abdomen 701.9
    in pregnancy or childbirth 654.4 ☑
      affecting fetus or newborn 763.89
  breast 611.89
Penetrating wound — see also Wound, open, by site
  with internal injury — see Injury, internal, by site, with open wound
  eyeball 871.7
    with foreign body (nonmagnetic) 871.6
      magnetic 871.5
  ocular (see also Penetrating wound, eyeball) 871.7
    adnexa 870.3
      with foreign body 870.4
    orbit 870.3
      with foreign body 870.4
Penetration, pregnant uterus by instrument
  with
    abortion — see Abortion, by type, with damage to pelvic organs
    ectopic pregnancy (see also categories 633.0–633.9) 639.2
    molar pregnancy (see also categories 630–632) 639.2
  complication of delivery 665.1 ☑
    affecting fetus or newborn 763.89
  following
    abortion 639.2
    ectopic or molar pregnancy 639.2
Penfield's syndrome — see also Epilepsy 345.5 ☑
Penicilliosis of lung 117.3
Penis — see condition
Penitis 607.2
Pentalogy (of Fallot) 745.2
Penta X syndrome 758.81
Pentosuria (benign) (essential) 271.8
Peptic acid disease 536.8
Peregrinating patient V65.2
Perforated — see Perforation
Perforation, perforative (nontraumatic)
  antrum (see also Sinusitis, maxillary) 473.0
  appendix 540.0
    with peritoneal abscess 540.1
  atrial septum, multiple 745.5

Perforation, perforative — continued
  attic, ear 384.22
    healed 384.81
  bile duct, except cystic (see also Disease, biliary) 576.3
    cystic 575.4
  bladder (urinary) 596.6
    with
      abortion — see Abortion, by type, with damage to pelvic organs
      ectopic pregnancy (see also categories 633.0–633.9) 639.2
      molar pregnancy (see also categories 630–632) 639.2
    following
      abortion 639.2
      ectopic or molar pregnancy 639.2
    obstetrical trauma 665.5 ☑
  bowel 569.83
    with
      abortion — see Abortion, by type, with damage to pelvic organs
      ectopic pregnancy (see also categories 633.0–633.9) 639.2
      molar pregnancy (see also categories 630–632) 639.2
    fetus or newborn 777.6
    following
      abortion 639.2
      ectopic or molar pregnancy 639.2
    obstetrical trauma 665.5 ☑
  broad ligament
    with
      abortion — see Abortion, by type, with damage to pelvic organs
      ectopic pregnancy (see also categories 633.0–633.9) 639.2
      molar pregnancy (see also categories 630–632) 639.2
    following
      abortion 639.2
      ectopic or molar pregnancy 639.2
    obstetrical trauma 665.6 ☑
  by
    device, implant, or graft — see Complications, mechanical
    foreign body left accidentally in operation wound 998.4
    instrument (any) during a procedure, accidental 998.2
  cecum 540.0
    with peritoneal abscess 540.1
  cervix (uteri) (see also Injury, internal, cervix)
    with
      abortion — see Abortion, by type, with damage to pelvic organs
      ectopic pregnancy (see also categories 633.0–633.9) 639.2
      molar pregnancy (see also categories 630–632) 639.2
    following
      abortion 639.2
      ectopic or molar pregnancy 639.2
    obstetrical trauma 665.3 ☑
  colon 569.83
  common duct (bile) 576.3
  cornea (see also Ulcer, cornea) 370.00
    due to ulceration 370.06
  cystic duct 575.4
  diverticulum (see also Diverticula) 562.10
    small intestine 562.00
  duodenum, duodenal (ulcer) — see Ulcer, duodenum, with perforation
  ear drum — see Perforation, tympanum
  enteritis — see Enteritis
  esophagus 530.4
  ethmoidal sinus (see also Sinusitis, ethmoidal) 473.2
  foreign body (external site) (see also Wound, open, by site, complicated)
    internal site, by ingested object — see Foreign body
  frontal sinus (see also Sinusitis, frontal) 473.1
  gallbladder or duct (see also Disease, gallbladder) 575.4

Perforation, perforative — continued
  gastric (ulcer) — see Ulcer, stomach, with perforation
  heart valve — see Endocarditis
  ileum (see also Perforation, intestine) 569.83
  instrumental
    external — see Wound, open, by site
    pregnant uterus, complicating delivery 665.9 ☑
    surgical (accidental) (blood vessel) (nerve) (organ) 998.2
  intestine 569.83
    with
      abortion — see Abortion, by type, with damage to pelvic organs
      ectopic pregnancy (see also categories 633.0–633.9) 639.2
      molar pregnancy (see also categories 630–632) 639.2
    fetus or newborn 777.6
    obstetrical trauma 665.5 ☑
    ulcerative NEC 569.83
  jejunum, jejunal 569.83
    ulcer — see Ulcer, gastrojejunal, with perforation
  mastoid (antrum) (cell) 383.89
  maxillary sinus (see also Sinusitis, maxillary) 473.0
  membrana tympani — see Perforation, tympanum
  nasal
    septum 478.19
      congenital 748.1
      syphilitic 095.8
    sinus (see also Sinusitis) 473.9
      congenital 748.1
  palate (hard) 526.89
    soft 528.9
      syphilitic 095.8
  palatine vault 526.89
    syphilitic 095.8
      congenital 090.5
  pelvic
    floor
      with
        abortion — see Abortion, by type, with damage to pelvic organs
        ectopic pregnancy (see also categories 633.0–633.9) 639.2
        molar pregnancy (see also categories 630–632) 639.2
      obstetrical trauma 664.1 ☑
    organ
      with
        abortion — see Abortion, by type, with damage to pelvic organs
        ectopic pregnancy (see also categories 633.0–633.9) 639.2
        molar pregnancy (see also categories 630–632) 639.2
      following
        abortion 639.2
        ectopic or molar pregnancy 639.2
      obstetrical trauma 665.5 ☑
  perineum — see Laceration, perineum
  periurethral tissue
    with
      abortion — see Abortion, by type, with damage to pelvic organs
      ectopic pregnancy (see also categories 633.0–633.9) 639.2
      molar pregnancy (see also categories 630–632) 639.2
  pharynx 478.29
  pylorus, pyloric (ulcer) — see Ulcer, stomach, with perforation
  rectum 569.49
  root canal space 526.61
  sigmoid 569.83
  sinus (accessory) (chronic) (nasal) (see also Sinusitis) 473.9
  sphenoidal sinus (see also Sinusitis, sphenoidal) 473.3

Perforation, perforative — continued
  stomach (due to ulcer) — see Ulcer, stomach, with perforation
  surgical (accidental) (by instrument) (blood vessel) (nerve) (organ) 998.2
  traumatic
    external — see Wound, open, by site
    eye (see also Penetrating wound, ocular) 871.7
    internal organ — see Injury, internal, by site
  tympanum (membrane) (persistent posttraumatic) (postinflammatory) 384.20
    with
      otitis media — see Otitis media
    attic 384.22
    central 384.21
    healed 384.81
    marginal NEC 384.23
    multiple 384.24
    pars flaccida 384.22
    total 384.25
    traumatic — see Wound, open, ear, drum
  typhoid, gastrointestinal 002.0
  ulcer — see Ulcer, by site, with perforation
  ureter 593.89
  urethra
    with
      abortion — see Abortion, by type, with damage to pelvic organs
      ectopic pregnancy (see also categories 633.0–633.9) 639.2
      molar pregnancy (see also categories 630–632) 639.2
    following
      abortion 639.2
      ectopic or molar pregnancy 639.2
    obstetrical trauma 665.5 ☑
  uterus (see also Injury, internal, uterus)
    with
      abortion — see Abortion, by type, with damage to pelvic organs
      ectopic pregnancy (see also categories 633.0–633.9) 639.2
      molar pregnancy (see also categories 630–632) 639.2
    by intrauterine contraceptive device 996.32
    following
      abortion 639.2
      ectopic or molar pregnancy 639.2
    obstetrical trauma — see Injury, internal, uterus, obstetrical trauma
  uvula 528.9
    syphilitic 095.8
  vagina — see Laceration, vagina
  viscus NEC 799.89
    traumatic 868.00
      with open wound into cavity 868.10
Periadenitis mucosa necrotica recurrens 528.2
Periangiitis 446.0
Periantritis 535.4 ☑
Periappendicitis (acute) — see also Appendicitis 541
Periarteritis (disseminated) (infectious) (necrotizing) (nodosa) 446.0
Periarthritis (joint) 726.90
  Duplay's 726.2
  gonococcal 098.50
  humeroscapularis 726.2
  scapulohumeral 726.2
  shoulder 726.2
  wrist 726.4
Periarthrosis (angioneural) — see Periarthritis
Peribronchitis 491.9
  tuberculous (see also Tuberculosis) 011.3 ☑
Pericapsulitis, adhesive (shoulder) 726.0
Pericarditis (granular) (with decompensation) (with effusion) 423.9
  with
    rheumatic fever (conditions classifiable to 390)
      active (see also Pericarditis, rheumatic) 391.0
      inactive or quiescent 393
  actinomycotic 039.8 [420.0]
  acute (nonrheumatic) 420.90

☑ Additional Digit Required — Refer to the Tabular List for Digit Selection   ▽ Subterms under main terms may continue to next column or page

2010 ICD-9-CM   ▶◀ Revised Text   ● New Line   ▲ Revised Code   Volume 2 — 217

Pericarditis — *continued*
 acute — *continued*
  with chorea (acute) (rheumatic) (Sydenham's) 392.0
  bacterial 420.99
  benign 420.91
  hemorrhagic 420.90
  idiopathic 420.91
  infective 420.90
  nonspecific 420.91
  rheumatic 391.0
   with chorea (acute) (rheumatic) (Sydenham's) 392.0
  sicca 420.90
  viral 420.91
 adhesive or adherent (external) (internal) 423.1
  acute — *see* Pericarditis, acute
  rheumatic (external) (internal) 393
 amebic 006.8 *[420.0]*
 bacterial (acute) (subacute) (with serous or seropurulent effusion) 420.99
 calcareous 423.2
 cholesterol (chronic) 423.8
  acute 420.90
 chronic (nonrheumatic) 423.8
  rheumatic 393
 constrictive 423.2
 Coxsackie 074.21
 due to
  actinomycosis 039.8 *[420.0]*
  amebiasis 006.8 *[420.0]*
  Coxsackie (virus) 074.21
  histoplasmosis (*see also* Histoplasmosis) 115.93
  nocardiosis 039.8 *[420.0]*
  tuberculosis (*see also* Tuberculosis) 017.9 ☑ *[420.0]*
 fibrinocaseous (*see also* Tuberculosis) 017.9 ☑ *[420.0]*
 fibrinopurulent 420.99
 fibrinous — *see* Pericarditis, rheumatic
 fibropurulent 420.99
 fibrous 423.1
 gonococcal 098.83
 hemorrhagic 423.0
 idiopathic (acute) 420.91
 infective (acute) 420.90
 meningococcal 036.41
 neoplastic (chronic) 423.8
  acute 420.90
 nonspecific 420.91
 obliterans, obliterating 423.1
 plastic 423.1
 pneumococcal (acute) 420.99
 postinfarction 411.0
 purulent (acute) 420.99
 rheumatic (active) (acute) (with effusion) (with pneumonia) 391.0
  with chorea (acute) (rheumatic) (Sydenham's) 392.0
  chronic or inactive (with chorea) 393
 septic (acute) 420.99
 serofibrinous — *see* Pericarditis, rheumatic
 staphylococcal (acute) 420.99
 streptococcal (acute) 420.99
 suppurative (acute) 420.99
 syphilitic 093.81
 tuberculous (acute) (chronic) (*see also* Tuberculosis) 017.9 ☑ *[420.0]*
 uremic 585.9 *[420.0]*
 viral (acute) 420.91
Pericardium, pericardial — *see* condition
Pericellulitis — *see also* Cellulitis 682.9
Pericementitis 523.40
 acute 523.30
 chronic (suppurative) 523.40
Pericholecystitis — *see also* Cholecystitis 575.10
Perichondritis
 auricle 380.00
  acute 380.01
  chronic 380.02
 bronchus 491.9
 ear (external) 380.00
  acute 380.01
  chronic 380.02
 larynx 478.71

Perichondritis — *continued*
 larynx — *continued*
  syphilitic 095.8
  typhoid 002.0 *[478.71]*
 nose 478.19
 pinna 380.00
  acute 380.01
  chronic 380.02
 trachea 478.9
Periclasia 523.5
Pericolitis 569.89
Pericoronitis (chronic) 523.40
 acute 523.33
Pericystitis — *see also* Cystitis 595.9
Pericytoma (M9150/1) — *see also* Neoplasm, connective tissue, uncertain behavior
 benign (M9150/0) — *see* Neoplasm, connective tissue, benign
 malignant (M9150/3) — *see* Neoplasm, connective tissue, malignant
Peridacryocystitis, acute 375.32
Peridiverticulitis — *see also* Diverticulitis 562.11
Periduodenitis 535.6 ☑
Periendocarditis — *see also* Endocarditis 424.90
 acute or subacute 421.9
Periepididymitis — *see also* Epididymitis 604.90
Perifolliculitis (abscedens) 704.8
 capitis, abscedens et suffodiens 704.8
 dissecting, scalp 704.8
 scalp 704.8
 superficial pustular 704.8
Perigastritis (acute) 535.0 ☑
Perigastrojejunitis (acute) 535.0 ☑
Perihepatitis (acute) 573.3
 chlamydial 099.56
 gonococcal 098.86
Peri-ileitis 569.89
Perilabyrinthitis (acute) — *see* Labyrinthitis
Perimeningitis — *see* Meningitis
Perimetritis — *see also* Endometritis 615.9
Perimetrosalpingitis — *see also* Salpingo-oophoritis 614.2
Perineocele 618.05
Perinephric — *see* condition
Perinephritic — *see* condition
Perinephritis — *see also* Infection, kidney 590.9
 purulent (*see also* Abscess, kidney) 590.2
Perineum, perineal — *see* condition
Perineuritis NEC 729.2
Periodic — *see also* condition
 disease (familial) 277.31
 edema 995.1
  hereditary 277.6
 fever 277.31
 headache syndromes in child or adolescent 346.2 ☑
 limb movement disorder 327.51
 paralysis (familial) 359.3
 peritonitis 277.31
 polyserositis 277.31
 somnolence (*see also* Narcolepsy) 347.00
Periodontal
 cyst 522.8
 pocket 523.8
Periodontitis (chronic) (complex) (compound) (simplex) 523.40
 acute 523.33
 aggressive 523.30
  generalized 523.32
  localized 523.31
 apical 522.6
  acute (pulpal origin) 522.4
 generalized 523.42
 localized 523.41
Periodontoclasia 523.5
Periodontosis 523.5
Periods — *see also* Menstruation
 heavy 626.2
 irregular 626.4
Perionychia (with lymphangitis) 681.9
 finger 681.02
 toe 681.11
Perioophoritis — *see also* Salpingo-oophoritis 614.2
Periorchitis — *see also* Orchitis 604.90
Periosteum, periosteal — *see* condition

Periostitis (circumscribed) (diffuse) (infective) 730.3 ☑

Note — Use the following fifth-digit subclassification with category 730:

0	site unspecified
1	shoulder region
2	upper arm
3	forearm
4	hand
5	pelvic region and thigh
6	lower leg
7	ankle and foot
8	other specified sites
9	multiple sites

 with osteomyelitis (*see also* Osteomyelitis) 730.2 ☑
  acute or subacute 730.0 ☑
  chronic or old 730.1 ☑
 albuminosa, albuminosus 730.3 ☑
 alveolar 526.5
 alveolodental 526.5
 dental 526.5
 gonorrheal 098.89
 hyperplastica, generalized 731.2
 jaw (lower) (upper) 526.4
 monomelic 733.99
 orbital 376.02
 syphilitic 095.5
  congenital 090.0 *[730.8]* ☑
  secondary 091.61
 tuberculous (*see also* Tuberculosis, bone) 015.9 ☑ *[730.8]* ☑
 yaws (early) (hypertrophic) (late) 102.6
Periostosis — *see also* Periostitis 730.3 ☑
 with osteomyelitis (*see also* Osteomyelitis) 730.2 ☑
  acute or subacute 730.0 ☑
  chronic or old 730.1 ☑
 hyperplastic 756.59
Peripartum cardiomyopathy 674.5 ☑
Periphlebitis — *see also* Phlebitis 451.9
 lower extremity 451.2
  deep (vessels) 451.19
  superficial (vessels) 451.0
 portal 572.1
 retina 362.18
 superficial (vessels) 451.0
 tuberculous (*see also* Tuberculosis) 017.9 ☑
  retina 017.3 ☑ *[362.18]*
Peripneumonia — *see* Pneumonia
Periproctitis 569.49
Periprostatitis — *see also* Prostatitis 601.9
Perirectal — *see* condition
Perirenal — *see* condition
Perisalpingitis — *see also* Salpingo-oophoritis 614.2
Perisigmoiditis 569.89
Perisplenitis (infectional) 289.59
Perispondylitis — *see* Spondylitis
Peristalsis reversed or visible 787.4
Peritendinitis — *see also* Tenosynovitis 726.90
 adhesive (shoulder) 726.0
Perithelioma (M9150/1) — *see* Pericytoma
Peritoneum, peritoneal — *see also* condition
 equilibration test V56.32
Peritonitis (acute) (adhesive) (fibrinous) (hemorrhagic) (idiopathic) (localized) (perforative) (primary) (with adhesions) (with effusion) 567.9
 with or following
  abortion — *see* Abortion, by type, with sepsis
  abscess 567.21
  appendicitis 540.0
   with peritoneal abscess 540.1
  ectopic pregnancy (*see also* categories 633.0–633.9) 639.0
  molar pregnancy (*see also* categories 630–632) 639.0
 aseptic 998.7

Peritonitis — *continued*
 bacterial 567.29
  spontaneous 567.23
 bile, biliary 567.81
 chemical 998.7
 chlamydial 099.56
 chronic proliferative 567.89
 congenital NEC 777.6
 diaphragmatic 567.22
 diffuse NEC 567.29
 diphtheritic 032.83
 disseminated NEC 567.29
 due to
  bile 567.81
  foreign
   body or object accidentally left during a procedure (instrument) (sponge) (swab) 998.4
   substance accidentally left during a procedure (chemical) (powder) (talc) 998.7
  talc 998.7
  urine 567.89
 fibrinopurulent 567.29
 fibrinous 567.29
 fibrocaseous (*see also* Tuberculosis) 014.0 ☑
 fibropurulent 567.29
 general, generalized (acute) 567.21
 gonococcal 098.86
 in infective disease NEC 136.9 *[567.0]*
 meconium (newborn) 777.6
 pancreatic 577.8
 paroxysmal, benign 277.31
 pelvic
  female (acute) 614.5
   chronic NEC 614.7
    with adhesions 614.6
   puerperal, postpartum, childbirth 670.8 ☑ ▲
  male (acute) 567.21
 periodic (familial) 277.31
 phlegmonous 567.29
 pneumococcal 567.1
 postabortal 639.0
 proliferative, chronic 567.89
 puerperal, postpartum, childbirth 670.8 ☑ ▲
 purulent 567.29
 septic 567.29
 spontaneous bacterial 567.23
 staphylococcal 567.29
 streptococcal 567.29
 subdiaphragmatic 567.29
 subphrenic 567.29
 suppurative 567.29
 syphilitic 095.2
  congenital 090.0 *[567.0]*
 talc 998.7
 tuberculous (*see also* Tuberculosis) 014.0 ☑
 urine 567.89
Peritonsillar — *see* condition
Peritonsillitis 475
Perityphlitis — *see also* Appendicitis 541
Periureteritis 593.89
Periurethral — *see* condition
Periurethritis (gangrenous) 597.89
Periuterine — *see* condition
Perivaginitis — *see also* Vaginitis 616.10
Perivasculitis, retinal 362.18
Perivasitis (chronic) 608.4
Periventricular leukomalacia 779.7
Perivesiculitis (seminal) — *see also* Vesiculitis 608.0
Perlèche 686.8
 due to
  moniliasis 112.0
  riboflavin deficiency 266.0
Pernicious — *see* condition
Pernio, perniosis 991.5
Persecution
 delusion 297.9
 social V62.4
Perseveration (tonic) 784.69
Persistence, persistent (congenital) 759.89
 anal membrane 751.2
 arteria stapedia 744.04

Persistence, persistent — *continued*
 atrioventricular canal 745.69
 bloody ejaculate 792.2
 branchial cleft 744.41
 bulbus cordis in left ventricle 745.8
 canal of Cloquet 743.51
 capsule (opaque) 743.51
 cilioretinal artery or vein 743.51
 cloaca 751.5
 communication — *see* Fistula, congenital
 convolutions
  aortic arch 747.21
  fallopian tube 752.19
  oviduct 752.19
  uterine tube 752.19
 double aortic arch 747.21
 ductus
  arteriosus 747.0
  Botalli 747.0
 fetal
  circulation 747.83
  form of cervix (uteri) 752.49
  hemoglobin (hereditary) ("Swiss variety")
   282.7
  pulmonary hypertension 747.83
 foramen
  Botalli 745.5
  ovale 745.5
 Gartner's duct 752.41
 hemoglobin, fetal (hereditary) (HPFH) 282.7
 hyaloid
  artery (generally incomplete) 743.51
  system 743.51
 hymen (tag)
  in pregnancy or childbirth 654.8 ☑
   causing obstructed labor 660.2 ☑
 lanugo 757.4
 left
  posterior cardinal vein 747.49
  root with right arch of aorta 747.21
  superior vena cava 747.49
 Meckel's diverticulum 751.0
 mesonephric duct 752.89
  fallopian tube 752.11
 mucosal disease (middle ear) (with posterior
  or superior marginal perforation of ear
  drum) 382.2
 nail(s), anomalous 757.5
 occiput, anterior or posterior 660.3 ☑
  fetus or newborn 763.1
 omphalomesenteric duct 751.0
 organ or site NEC — *see* Anomaly, specified
  type NEC
 ostium
  atrioventriculare commune 745.69
  primum 745.61
  secundum 745.5
 ovarian rests in fallopian tube 752.19
 pancreatic tissue in intestinal tract 751.5
 primary (deciduous)
  teeth 520.6
  vitreous hyperplasia 743.51
 pulmonary hypertension 747.83
 pupillary membrane 743.46
  iris 743.46
 Rhesus (Rh) titer 999.7
 right aortic arch 747.21
 sinus
  urogenitalis 752.89
  venosus with imperfect incorporation in
   right auricle 747.49
 thymus (gland) 254.8
  hyperplasia 254.0
 thyroglossal duct 759.2
 thyrolingual duct 759.2
 truncus arteriosus or communis 745.0
 tunica vasculosa lentis 743.39
 umbilical sinus 753.7
 urachus 753.7
 vegetative state 780.03
 vitelline duct 751.0
 wolffian duct 752.89
Person (with)
 admitted for clinical research, as participant
  or control subject V70.7

Person — *continued*
 affected by
  family member
   currently on deployment (military)
    V61.01
   returned from deployment (military)
    (current or past conflict) V61.02
 awaiting admission to adequate facility elsewhere V63.2
 undergoing social agency investigation
  V63.8
 concern (normal) about sick person in family
  V61.49
 consulting on behalf of another V65.19
  pediatric
   pre-adoption visit for adoptive par- ●
    ents V65.11 ●
   pre-birth visit for expectant parents ●
    V65.11 ●
 currently deployed in theater or in support of
  military war, peacekeeping and humanitarian operations V62.21
 feared
  complaint in whom no diagnosis was
   made V65.5
  condition not demonstrated V65.5
 feigning illness V65.2
 healthy, accompanying sick person V65.0
 history of military war, peacekeeping and humanitarian deployment (current or past
  conflict) V62.22
 living (in)
  without
   adequate
    financial resources V60.2
    housing (heating) (space) V60.1
   housing (permanent) (temporary)
    V60.0
   material resources V60.2
   person able to render necessary care
    V60.4
   shelter V60.0
  alone V60.3
  boarding school V60.6
  residence remote from hospital or medical
   care facility V63.0
  residential institution V60.6
 medical services in home not available V63.1
 on waiting list V63.2
  undergoing social agency investigation
   V63.8
 sick or handicapped in family V61.49
 "worried well" V65.5
Personality
 affective 301.10
 aggressive 301.3
 amoral 301.7
 anancastic, anankastic 301.4
 antisocial 301.7
 asocial 301.7
 asthenic 301.6
 avoidant 301.82
 borderline 301.83
 change 310.1
 compulsive 301.4
 cycloid 301.13
 cyclothymic 301.13
 dependent 301.6
 depressive (chronic) 301.12
 disorder, disturbance NEC 301.9
  with
   antisocial disturbance 301.7
   pattern disturbance NEC 301.9
   sociopathic disturbance 301.7
   trait disturbance 301.9
 dual 300.14
 dyssocial 301.7
 eccentric 301.89
  "haltlose" type 301.89
 emotionally unstable 301.59
 epileptoid 301.3
 explosive 301.3
 fanatic 301.0
 histrionic 301.50
 hyperthymic 301.11
 hypomanic 301.11

Personality — *continued*
 hypothymic 301.12
 hysterical 301.50
 immature 301.89
 inadequate 301.6
 labile 301.59
 masochistic 301.89
 morally defective 301.7
 multiple 300.14
 narcissistic 301.81
 obsessional 301.4
 obsessive-compulsive 301.4
 overconscientious 301.4
 paranoid 301.0
 passive (-dependent) 301.6
 passive-aggressive 301.84
 pathologic NEC 301.9
 pattern defect or disturbance 301.9
 pseudosocial 301.7
 psychoinfantile 301.59
 psychoneurotic NEC 301.89
 psychopathic 301.9
  with
   amoral trend 301.7
   antisocial trend 301.7
   asocial trend 301.7
   pathologic sexuality (*see also* Deviation,
    sexual) 302.9
  mixed types 301.9
 schizoid 301.20
 type A 301.4
 unstable (emotional) 301.59
Perthes' disease (capital femoral osteochondrosis) 732.1
Pertussis — *see also* Whooping cough 033.9
 vaccination, prophylactic (against) V03.6
Peruvian wart 088.0
Perversion, perverted
 appetite 307.52
  hysterical 300.11
 function
  pineal gland 259.8
  pituitary gland 253.9
   anterior lobe
    deficient 253.2
    excessive 253.1
   posterior lobe 253.6
  placenta — *see* Placenta, abnormal
 sense of smell or taste 781.1
  psychogenic 306.7
 sexual (*see also* Deviation, sexual) 302.9
Pervious, congenital — *see also* Imperfect, closure
 ductus arteriosus 747.0
Pes (congenital) — *see also* Talipes 754.70
 abductus (congenital) 754.60
  acquired 736.79
 acquired NEC 736.79
  planus 734
 adductus (congenital) 754.79
  acquired 736.79
 cavus 754.71
  acquired 736.73
 planovalgus (congenital) 754.69
  acquired 736.79
 planus (acquired) (any degree) 734
  congenital 754.61
  rachitic 268.1
 valgus (congenital) 754.61
  acquired 736.79
 varus (congenital) 754.50
  acquired 736.79
Pest — *see also* Plague 020.9
Pestis — *see also* Plague 020.9
 bubonica 020.0
 fulminans 020.0
 minor 020.8
 pneumonica — *see* Plague, pneumonic
Petechial
 fever 036.0
 typhus 081.9
Petechia, petechiae 782.7
 fetus or newborn 772.6
Petges-Cléjat or Petges-Clégat syndrome
 (poikilodermatomyositis) 710.3

Petit's
 disease (*see also* Hernia, lumbar) 553.8
Petit mal (idiopathic) — *see also* Epilepsy
 345.0 ☑
 status 345.2
Petrellidosis 117.6
Petrositis 383.20
 acute 383.21
 chronic 383.22
Peutz-Jeghers disease or syndrome 759.6
Peyronie's disease 607.85
Pfeiffer's disease 075
Phacentocele 379.32
 traumatic 921.3
Phacoanaphylaxis 360.19
Phacocele (old) 379.32
 traumatic 921.3
Phaehyphomycosis 117.8
Phagedena (dry) (moist) — *see also* Gangrene
 785.4
 arteriosclerotic 440.24
 geometric 686.09
 penis 607.89
 senile 440.2 ☑ *[785.4]*
 sloughing 785.4
 tropical (*see also* Ulcer, skin) 707.9
 vulva 616.50
Phagedenic — *see also* condition
 abscess (*see also* Abscess)
  chancroid 099.0
 bubo NEC 099.8
 chancre 099.0
 ulcer (tropical) (*see also* Ulcer, skin) 707.9
Phagomania 307.52
Phakoma 362.89
Phantom limb (syndrome) 353.6
Pharyngeal — *see also* condition
 arch remnant 744.41
 pouch syndrome 279.11
Pharyngitis (acute) (catarrhal) (gangrenous) (infective) (malignant) (membranous)
 (phlegmonous) (pneumococcal) (pseudomembranous) (simple) (staphylococcal)
 (subacute) (suppurative) (ulcerative) (viral)
 462
 with influenza, flu, or grippe 487.1
 aphthous 074.0
 atrophic 472.1
 chlamydial 099.51
 chronic 472.1
 Coxsackie virus 074.0
 diphtheritic (membranous) 032.0
 follicular 472.1
 fusospirochetal 101
 gonococcal 098.6
 granular (chronic) 472.1
 herpetic 054.79
 hypertrophic 472.1
 infectional, chronic 472.1
 influenzal 487.1
 lymphonodular, acute 074.8
 septic 034.0
 streptococcal 034.0
 tuberculous (*see also* Tuberculosis) 012.8 ☑
 vesicular 074.0
Pharyngoconjunctival fever 077.2
Pharyngoconjunctivitis, viral 077.2
Pharyngolaryngitis (acute) 465.0
 chronic 478.9
 septic 034.0
Pharyngoplegia 478.29
Pharyngotonsillitis 465.8
 tuberculous 012.8 ☑
Pharyngotracheitis (acute) 465.8
 chronic 478.9
Pharynx, pharyngeal — *see* condition
Phase of life problem NEC V62.89
Phenomenon
 Arthus' 995.21
 flashback (drug) 292.89
 jaw-winking 742.8
 Jod-Basedow 242.8 ☑
 L. E. cell 710.0
 lupus erythematosus cell 710.0
 Pelger-Huët (hereditary hyposegmentation)
  288.2

☑ Additional Digit Required — Refer to the Tabular List for Digit Selection   ▽ Subterms under main terms may continue to next column or page

2010 ICD-9-CM   ▶◀ Revised Text   ● New Line   ▲ Revised Code   October 2009 · Volume 2 — 219

Phenomenon — *continued*
- Raynaud's (paroxysmal digital cyanosis) (secondary) 443.0
- Reilly's (*see also* Neuropathy, peripheral, autonomic) 337.9
- vasomotor 780.2
- vasospastic 443.9
- vasovagal 780.2
- Wenckebach's, heart block (second degree) 426.13

Phenylketonuria (PKU) 270.1
Phenylpyruvicaciduria 270.1
Pheochromoblastoma (M8700/3)
- specified site — *see* Neoplasm, by site, malignant
- unspecified site 194.0

Pheochromocytoma (M8700/0)
- malignant (M8700/3)
  - specified site — *see* Neoplasm, by site, malignant
  - unspecified site 194.0
- specified site — *see* Neoplasm, by site, benign
- unspecified site 227.0

Phimosis (congenital) 605
- chancroidal 099.0
- due to infection 605

Phlebectasia — *see also* Varicose, vein 454.9
- congenital NEC 747.60
- esophagus (*see also* Varix, esophagus) 456.1
  - with hemorrhage (*see also* Varix, esophagus, bleeding) 456.0

Phlebitis (infective) (pyemic) (septic) (suppurative) 451.9
- antecubital vein 451.82
- arm NEC 451.84
  - axillary vein 451.89
  - basilic vein 451.82
  - deep 451.83
  - superficial 451.82
- axillary vein 451.89
- basilic vein 451.82
- blue 451.9
- brachial vein 451.83
- breast, superficial 451.89
- cavernous (venous) sinus — *see* Phlebitis, intracranial sinus
- cephalic vein 451.82
- cerebral (venous) sinus — *see* Phlebitis, intracranial sinus
- chest wall, superficial 451.89
- complicating pregnancy or puerperium 671.2 ☑ ▲
  - affecting fetus or newborn 760.3
- cranial (venous) sinus — *see* Phlebitis, intracranial sinus
- deep (vessels) 451.19
  - femoral vein 451.11
  - specified vessel NEC 451.19
- due to implanted device — *see* Complications, due to (presence of) any device, implant, or graft classified to 996.0–996.5 NEC
- during or resulting from a procedure 997.2
- femoral vein (deep) (superficial) 451.11
- femoropopliteal 451.19
- following infusion, perfusion, or transfusion 999.2
- gouty 274.89 *[451.9]*
- hepatic veins 451.89
- iliac vein 451.81
- iliofemoral 451.11
- intracranial sinus (any) (venous) 325
  - late effect — *see* category 326
  - nonpyogenic 437.6
    - in pregnancy or puerperium 671.5 ☑
- jugular vein 451.89
- lateral (venous) sinus — *see* Phlebitis, intracranial sinus
- leg 451.2
  - deep (vessels) 451.19
    - femoral vein 451.11
    - specified vessel NEC 451.19
  - superficial (vessels) 451.0
    - femoral vein 451.11
- longitudinal sinus — *see* Phlebitis, intracranial sinus

Phlebitis — *continued*
- lower extremity 451.2
  - deep (vessels) 451.19
    - femoral vein 451.11
    - specified vessel NEC 451.19
  - migrans, migrating (superficial) 453.1
  - superficial (vessels) 451.0
    - femoral vein 451.11
- pelvic
  - with
    - abortion — *see* Abortion, by type, with sepsis
    - ectopic pregnancy (*see also* categories 633.0–633.9) 639.0
    - molar pregnancy (*see also* categories 630–632) 639.0
  - following
    - abortion 639.0
    - ectopic or molar pregnancy 639.0
  - puerperal, postpartum 671.4 ☑
- popliteal vein 451.19
- portal (vein) 572.1
- postoperative 997.2
- pregnancy 671.2 ☑ ▲
  - deep 671.3 ☑
  - specified type NEC 671.5 ☑
  - superficial 671.2 ☑
- puerperal, postpartum, childbirth 671.2 ☑ ▲
  - deep 671.4 ☑
  - lower extremities 671.2 ☑
  - pelvis 671.4 ☑
  - specified site NEC 671.5 ☑
  - superficial 671.2 ☑
- radial vein 451.83
- retina 362.18
- saphenous (great) (long) 451.0
  - accessory or small 451.0
- sinus (meninges) — *see* Phlebitis, intracranial sinus
- specified site NEC 451.89
- subclavian vein 451.89
- syphilitic 093.89
- tibial vein 451.19
- ulcer, ulcerative 451.9
  - leg 451.2
    - deep (vessels) 451.19
      - femoral vein 451.11
      - specified vessel NEC 451.19
    - superficial (vessels) 451.0
      - femoral vein 451.11
  - lower extremity 451.2
    - deep (vessels) 451.19
      - femoral vein 451.11
      - specified vessel NEC 451.19
    - superficial (vessels) 451.0
- ulnar vein 451.83
- umbilicus 451.89
- upper extremity (*see also* Phlebitis, arm)
  - deep (veins) 451.83
    - brachial vein 451.83
    - radial vein 451.83
    - ulnar vein 451.83
  - superficial (veins) 451.82
    - antecubital vein 451.82
    - basilic vein 451.82
    - cephalic vein 451.82
- uterus (septic) (*see also* Endometritis) 615.9
- varicose (leg) (lower extremity) (*see also* Varicose, vein) 454.1

Phlebofibrosis 459.89
Phleboliths 459.89
Phlebosclerosis 459.89
Phlebothrombosis — *see* Thrombosis
Phlebotomus fever 066.0
Phlegmasia
- alba dolens (deep vessels) 451.19
  - complicating pregnancy 671.3 ☑
  - nonpuerperal 451.19
  - puerperal, postpartum, childbirth 671.4 ☑
- cerulea dolens 451.19
Phlegm, choked on 933.1
Phlegmon — *see also* Abscess 682.9
- erysipelatous (*see also* Erysipelas) 035
- iliac 682.2
  - fossa 540.1

Phlegmon — *see also* Abscess — *continued*
- throat 478.29
Phlegmonous — *see* condition
Phlyctenulosis (allergic) (keratoconjunctivitis) (nontuberculous) 370.31
- cornea 370.31
  - with ulcer (*see also* Ulcer, cornea) 370.00
- tuberculous (*see also* Tuberculosis) 017.3 ☑ *[370.31]*
Phobia, phobic (reaction) 300.20
- animal 300.29
- isolated NEC 300.29
- obsessional 300.3
- simple NEC 300.29
- social 300.23
- specified NEC 300.29
- state 300.20
Phocas' disease 610.1
Phocomelia 755.4
- lower limb 755.32
  - complete 755.33
  - distal 755.35
  - proximal 755.34
- upper limb 755.22
  - complete 755.23
  - distal 755.25
  - proximal 755.24
Phoria — *see also* Heterophoria 378.40
Phosphate-losing tubular disorder 588.0
Phosphatemia 275.3
Phosphaturia 275.3
Photoallergic response 692.72
Photocoproporphyria 277.1
Photodermatitis (sun) 692.72
- light other than sun 692.82
Photokeratitis 370.24
Photo-ophthalmia 370.24
Photophobia 368.13
Photopsia 368.15
Photoretinitis 363.31
Photoretinopathy 363.31
Photosensitiveness (sun) 692.72
- light other than sun 692.82
Photosensitization (skin) (sun) 692.72
- light other than sun 692.82
Phototoxic response 692.72
Phrenitis 323.9
Phrynoderma 264.8
Phthiriasis (pubis) (any site) 132.2
- with any infestation classifiable to 132.0, 132.1, 132.3
Phthirus infestation — *see* Phthiriasis
Phthisis — *see also* Tuberculosis 011.9 ☑
- bulbi (infectional) 360.41
- colliers' 011.4 ☑
- cornea 371.05
- eyeball (due to infection) 360.41
- millstone makers' 011.4 ☑
- miners' 011.4 ☑
- potters' 011.4 ☑
- sandblasters' 011.4 ☑
- stonemasons' 011.4 ☑
Phycomycosis 117.7
Physalopteriasis 127.7
Physical therapy NEC V57.1
- breathing exercises V57.0
Physiological cup, optic papilla
- borderline, glaucoma suspect 365.00
- enlarged 377.14
- glaucomatous 377.14
Phytobezoar 938
- intestine 936
- stomach 935.2
Pian — *see also* Yaws 102.9
Pianoma 102.1
Piarhemia, piarrhemia — *see also* Hyperlipemia 272.4
- bilharziasis 120.9
Pica 307.52
- hysterical 300.11
Pick's
- cerebral atrophy 331.11
  - with dementia
    - with behavioral disturbance 331.11 *[294.11]*

Pick's — *continued*
- cerebral atrophy — *continued*
  - with dementia — *continued*
    - without behavioral disturbance 331.11 *[294.10]*
- disease
  - brain 331.11
    - dementia in
      - with behavioral disturbance 331.11 *[294.11]*
      - without behavioral disturbance 331.11 *[294.10]*
  - lipid histiocytosis 272.7
  - liver (pericardial pseudocirrhosis of liver) 423.2
  - pericardium (pericardial pseudocirrhosis of liver) 423.2
  - polyserositis (pericardial pseudocirrhosis of liver) 423.2
  - syndrome
    - heart (pericardial pseudocirrhosis of liver) 423.2
    - liver (pericardial pseudocirrhosis of liver) 423.2
  - tubular adenoma (M8640/0)
    - specified site — *see* Neoplasm, by site, benign
    - unspecified site
      - female 220
      - male 222.0
Pick-Herxheimer syndrome (diffuse idiopathic cutaneous atrophy) 701.8
Pick-Niemann disease (lipid histiocytosis) 272.7
Pickwickian syndrome (cardiopulmonary obesity) 278.8
Piebaldism, classic 709.09
Piedra 111.2
- beard 111.2
  - black 111.3
  - white 111.2
- black 111.3
- scalp 111.3
  - black 111.3
  - white 111.2
- white 111.2
Pierre Marie-Bamberger syndrome (hypertrophic pulmonary osteoarthropathy) 731.2
Pierre Marie's syndrome (pulmonary hypertrophic osteoarthropathy) 731.2
Pierre Mauriac's syndrome (diabetes-dwarfism-obesity) 258.1
Pierre Robin deformity or syndrome (congenital) 756.0
Pierson's disease or osteochondrosis 732.1
Pigeon
- breast or chest (acquired) 738.3
  - congenital 754.82
  - rachitic (*see also* Rickets) 268.0
- breeders' disease or lung 495.2
- fanciers' disease or lung 495.2
- toe 735.8
Pigmentation (abnormal) 709.00
- anomaly 709.00
  - congenital 757.33
  - specified NEC 709.09
- conjunctiva 372.55
- cornea 371.10
  - anterior 371.11
  - posterior 371.13
  - stromal 371.12
- lids (congenital) 757.33
  - acquired 374.52
- limbus corneae 371.10
- metals 709.00
- optic papilla, congenital 743.57
- retina (congenital) (grouped) (nevoid) 743.53
  - acquired 362.74
- scrotum, congenital 757.33
Piles — *see* Hemorrhoids
Pili
- annulati or torti (congenital) 757.4
- incarnati 704.8
Pill roller hand (intrinsic) 736.09
Pilomatrixoma (M8110/0) — *see* Neoplasm, skin, benign
Pilonidal — *see* condition

☑ Additional Digit Required — Refer to the Tabular List for Digit Selection   ⬛ Subterms under main terms may continue to next column or page

220 — Volume 2 • October 2009   ▶◀ Revised Text   ● New Line   ▲ Revised Code   2010 ICD-9-CM

Pimple 709.8
PIN I (prostatic intraepithelial neoplasia I) 602.3
PIN II (prostatic intraepithelial neoplasia II) 602.3
PIN III (prostatic intraepithelial neoplasia III) 233.4
Pinched nerve — see Neuropathy, entrapment
Pineal body or gland — see condition
Pinealoblastoma (M9362/3) 194.4
Pinealoma (M9360/1) 237.1
    malignant (M9360/3) 194.4
Pineoblastoma (M9362/3) 194.4
Pineocytoma (M9361/1) 237.1
Pinguecula 372.51
Pingueculitis 372.34
Pinhole meatus — see also Stricture, urethra
    598.9
Pink
    disease 985.0
    eye 372.03
    puffer 492.8
Pinkus' disease (lichen nitidus) 697.1
Pinpoint
    meatus (see also Stricture, urethra) 598.9
    os uteri (see also Stricture, cervix) 622.4
Pinselhaare (congenital) 757.4
Pinta 103.9
    cardiovascular lesions 103.2
    chancre (primary) 103.0
    erythematous plaques 103.1
    hyperchromic lesions 103.1
    hyperkeratosis 103.1
    lesions 103.9
        cardiovascular 103.2
        hyperchromic 103.1
        intermediate 103.1
        late 103.2
        mixed 103.3
        primary 103.0
        skin (achromic) (cicatricial) (dyschromic)
            103.2
            hyperchromic 103.1
            mixed (achromic and hyperchromic)
                103.3
    papule (primary) 103.0
    skin lesions (achromic) (cicatricial)
        (dyschromic) 103.2
        hyperchromic 103.1
        mixed (achromic and hyperchromic) 103.3
    vitiligo 103.2
Pintid 103.0
Pinworms (disease) (infection) (infestation) 127.4
Piry fever 066.8
Pistol wound — see Gunshot wound
Pitchers' elbow 718.82
Pithecoid pelvis 755.69
    with disproportion (fetopelvic) 653.2 ☑
        affecting fetus or newborn 763.1
        causing obstructed labor 660.1 ☑
Pithiatism 300.11
Pit, lip (mucus), congenital 750.25
Pitted — see also Pitting
    teeth 520.4
Pitting (edema) — see also Edema 782.3
    lip 782.3
    nail 703.8
        congenital 757.5
Pituitary gland — see condition
Pituitary snuff-takers' disease 495.8
Pityriasis 696.5
    alba 696.5
    capitis 690.11
    circinata (et maculata) 696.3
    Hebra's (exfoliative dermatitis) 695.89
    lichenoides et varioliformis 696.2
    maculata (et circinata) 696.3
    nigra 111.1
    pilaris 757.39
        acquired 701.1
        Hebra's 696.4
    rosea 696.3
    rotunda 696.3
    rubra (Hebra) 695.89
        pilaris 696.4
    sicca 690.18
    simplex 690.18
    specified type NEC 696.5
    streptogenes 696.5

Pityriasis — continued
    versicolor 111.0
    scrotal 111.0
Placenta, placental
    ablatio 641.2 ☑
        affecting fetus or newborn 762.1
    abnormal, abnormality 656.7 ☑
        with hemorrhage 641.8 ☑
            affecting fetus or newborn 762.1
        affecting fetus or newborn 762.2
    abruptio 641.2 ☑
        affecting fetus or newborn 762.1
    accessory lobe — see Placenta, abnormal
    accreta (without hemorrhage) 667.0 ☑
        with hemorrhage 666.0 ☑
    adherent (without hemorrhage) 667.0 ☑
        with hemorrhage 666.0 ☑
    apoplexy — see Placenta, separation
    battledore — see Placenta, abnormal
    bilobate — see Placenta, abnormal
    bipartita — see Placenta, abnormal
    carneous mole 631
    centralis — see Placenta, previa
    circumvallata — see Placenta, abnormal
    cyst (amniotic) — see Placenta, abnormal
    deficiency — see Placenta, insufficiency
    degeneration — see Placenta, insufficiency
    detachment (partial) (premature) (with hem-
        orrhage) 641.2 ☑
        affecting fetus or newborn 762.1
    dimidiata — see Placenta, abnormal
    disease 656.7 ☑
        affecting fetus or newborn 762.2
    duplex — see Placenta, abnormal
    dysfunction — see Placenta, insufficiency
    fenestrata — see Placenta, abnormal
    fibrosis — see Placenta, abnormal
    fleshy mole 631
    hematoma — see Placenta, abnormal
    hemorrhage NEC — see Placenta, separation
    hormone disturbance or malfunction — see
        Placenta, abnormal
    hyperplasia — see Placenta, abnormal
    increta (without hemorrhage) 667.0 ☑
        with hemorrhage 666.0 ☑
    infarction 656.7 ☑
        affecting fetus or newborn 762.2
    insertion, vicious — see Placenta, previa
    insufficiency
        affecting
            fetus or newborn 762.2
            management of pregnancy 656.5 ☑
    lateral — see Placenta, previa
    low implantation or insertion — see Placenta,
        previa
    low-lying — see Placenta, previa
    malformation — see Placenta, abnormal
    malposition — see Placenta, previa
    marginalis, marginata — see Placenta, previa
    marginal sinus (hemorrhage) (rupture)
        641.2 ☑
        affecting fetus or newborn 762.1
    membranacea — see Placenta, abnormal
    multilobed — see Placenta, abnormal
    multipartita — see Placenta, abnormal
    necrosis — see Placenta, abnormal
    percreta (without hemorrhage) 667.0 ☑
        with hemorrhage 666.0 ☑
    polyp 674.4 ☑
    previa (central) (centralis) (complete) (lateral)
        (marginal) (marginalis) (partial) (par-
        tialis) (total) (with hemorrhage)
        641.1 ☑
        without hemorrhage (before labor and
            delivery) (during pregnancy)
            641.0 ☑
        affecting fetus or newborn 762.0
        noted
            before labor, without hemorrhage
                (with cesarean delivery)
                641.0 ☑
            during pregnancy (without hemor-
                rhage) 641.0 ☑
    retention (with hemorrhage) 666.0 ☑
        without hemorrhage 667.0 ☑

Placenta, placental — continued
    retention — continued
        fragments, complicating puerperium (de-
            layed hemorrhage) 666.2 ☑
            without hemorrhage 667.1 ☑
        postpartum, puerperal 666.2 ☑
    separation (normally implanted) (partial)
        (premature) (with hemorrhage)
        641.2 ☑
        affecting fetus or newborn 762.1
    septuplex — see Placenta, abnormal
    small — see Placenta, insufficiency
    softening (premature) — see Placenta, abnor-
        mal
    spuria — see Placenta, abnormal
    succenturiata — see Placenta, abnormal
    syphilitic 095.8
    transfusion syndromes 762.3
    transmission of chemical substance — see
        Absorption, chemical, through placen-
        ta
    trapped (with hemorrhage) 666.0 ☑
        without hemorrhage 667.0 ☑
    trilobate — see Placenta, abnormal
    tripartita — see Placenta, abnormal
    triplex — see Placenta, abnormal
    varicose vessel — see Placenta, abnormal
    vicious insertion — see Placenta, previa
Placentitis
    affecting fetus or newborn 762.7
    complicating pregnancy 658.4 ☑
Plagiocephaly (skull) 754.0
Plague 020.9
    abortive 020.8
    ambulatory 020.8
    bubonic 020.0
    cellulocutaneous 020.1
    lymphatic gland 020.0
    pneumonic 020.5
        primary 020.3
        secondary 020.4
    pulmonary — see Plague, pneumonic
    pulmonic — see Plague, pneumonic
    septicemic 020.2
    tonsillar 020.9
        septicemic 020.2
    vaccination, prophylactic (against) V03.3
Planning, family V25.09
    contraception V25.9
    natural
        procreative V26.41
        to avoid pregnancy V25.04
    procreation V26.49
        natural V26.41
Plaque
    artery, arterial — see Arteriosclerosis
    calcareous — see Calcification
    Hollenhorst's (retinal) 362.33
    tongue 528.6
Plasma cell myeloma 203.0 ☑
Plasmacytoma, plasmacytoma (solitary)
    (M9731/1) 238.6
    benign (M9731/0) — see Neoplasm, by site,
        benign
    malignant (M9731/3) 203.8 ☑
Plasmacytopenia 288.59
Plasmacytosis 288.64
Plaster ulcer — see also Ulcer, pressure 707.00
Plateau iris syndrome 364.82
Platybasia 756.0
Platyonychia (congenital) 757.5
    acquired 703.8
Platypelloid pelvis 738.6
    with disproportion (fetopelvic) 653.2 ☑
        affecting fetus or newborn 763.1
        causing obstructed labor 660.1 ☑
            affecting fetus or newborn 763.1
    congenital 755.69
Platyspondylia 756.19
Plethora 782.62
    newborn 776.4
Pleuralgia 786.52
Pleura, pleural — see condition

Pleurisy (acute) (adhesive) (chronic) (costal) (di-
    aphragmatic) (double) (dry) (fetid) (fibri-
    nous) (fibrous) (interlobar) (latent) (lung)
    (old) (plastic) (primary) (residual) (sicca)
    (sterile) (subacute) (unresolved) (with ad-
    herent pleura) 511.0
    with
        effusion (without mention of cause) 511.9
            bacterial, nontuberculous 511.1
            nontuberculous NEC 511.9
                bacterial 511.1
            pneumococcal 511.1
            specified type NEC 511.89
            staphylococcal 511.1
            streptococcal 511.1
            tuberculous (see also Tuberculosis,
                pleura) 012.0 ☑
                primary, progressive 010.1 ☑
    influenza, flu, or grippe 487.1
    tuberculosis — see Pleurisy, tuberculous
    encysted 511.89
    exudative (see also Pleurisy, with effusion)
        511.9
        bacterial, nontuberculous 511.1
    fibrinopurulent 510.9
        with fistula 510.0
    fibropurulent 510.9
        with fistula 510.0
    hemorrhagic 511.89
    influenzal 487.1
    pneumococcal 511.0
        with effusion 511.1
    purulent 510.9
        with fistula 510.0
    septic 510.9
        with fistula 510.0
    serofibrinous (see also Pleurisy, with effusion)
        511.9
        bacterial, nontuberculous 511.1
    seropurulent 510.9
        with fistula 510.0
    serous (see also Pleurisy, with effusion) 511.9
        bacterial, nontuberculous 511.1
    staphylococcal 511.0
        with effusion 511.1
    streptococcal 511.0
        with effusion 511.1
    suppurative 510.9
        with fistula 510.0
    traumatic (post) (current) 862.29
        with open wound into cavity 862.39
    tuberculous (with effusion) (see also Tubercu-
        losis, pleura) 012.0 ☑
        primary, progressive 010.1 ☑
Pleuritis sicca — see Pleurisy
Pleurobronchopneumonia — see also Pneumo-
    nia, broncho- 485
Pleurodynia 786.52
    epidemic 074.1
    viral 074.1
Pleurohepatitis 573.8
Pleuropericarditis — see also Pericarditis 423.9
    acute 420.90
Pleuropneumonia (acute) (bilateral) (double)
    (septic) — see also Pneumonia 486
    chronic (see also Fibrosis, lung) 515
Pleurorrhea — see also Hydrothorax 511.89
Plexitis, brachial 353.0
Plica
    knee 727.83
    polonica 132.0
    syndrome 727.83
    tonsil 474.8
Plicae dysphonia ventricularis 784.49
Plicated tongue 529.5
    congenital 750.13
Plug
    bronchus NEC 519.19
    meconium (newborn) NEC 777.1
    mucus — see Mucus, plug
Plumbism 984.9
    specified type of lead — see Table of Drugs
        and Chemicals
Plummer's disease (toxic nodular goiter)
    242.3 ☑

☑ Additional Digit Required — Refer to the Tabular List for Digit Selection   ▽ Subterms under main terms may continue to next column or page

2010 ICD-9-CM   ▶◀ Revised Text   ● New Line   ▲ Revised Code   Volume 2 — 221

Pneumonia — continued
  lobar — continued
    Hemophilus influenzae (H. influenzae) 482.2
    hypostatic 514
    influenzal 487.0
    Klebsiella 482.0
    ornithosis 073.0
    Proteus 482.83
    Pseudomonas 482.1
    psittacosis 073.0
    specified organism NEC 483.8
      bacterial NEC 482.89
    staphylococcal 482.40
      aureus 482.41
        methicillin
          resistant (MRSA) 482.42
          susceptible (MSSA) 482.41
      specified type NEC 482.49
    streptococcal — see Pneumonia, strepto-
      coccal
    viral, virus (see also Pneumonia, viral) 480.9
  lobular (confluent) — see Pneumonia, broncho-
  Löffler's 518.3
  massive — see Pneumonia, lobar
  meconium aspiration 770.12
  metastatic NEC 038.8 [484.8]
  methicillin resistant Staphylococcus aureus (MRSA) 482.42
  methicillin susceptible Staphylococcus aureus (MSSA) 482.41
  MRSA (methicillin resistant Staphylococcus aureus) 482.42
  MSSA (methicillin susceptible Staphylococcus aureus) 482.41
  Mycoplasma (pneumoniae) 483.0
  necrotic 513.0
  nitrogen dioxide 506.9
  orthostatic 514
  parainfluenza virus 480.2
  parenchymatous (see also Fibrosis, lung) 515
  passive 514
  patchy — see Pneumonia, broncho-
  Peptococcus 482.81
  Peptostreptococcus 482.81
  plasma cell 136.3
  pleurolobar — see Pneumonia, lobar
  pleuropneumonia-like organism (PPLO) 483.0
  pneumococcal (broncho) (lobar) 481
  Pneumocystis (carinii) (jiroveci) 136.3
  postinfectional NEC 136.9 [484.8]
  postmeasles 055.1
  postoperative 997.39
  primary atypical 486
  Proprionibacterium 482.81
  Proteus 482.83
  Pseudomonas 482.1
  psittacosis 073.0
  radiation 508.0
  respiratory syncytial virus 480.1
  resulting from a procedure 997.39
  rheumatic 390 [517.1]
  Salmonella 003.22
  SARS-associated coronavirus 480.3
  segmented, segmental — see Pneumonia, broncho-
  Serratia (marcescens) 482.83
  specified
    bacteria NEC 482.89
    organism NEC 483.8
    virus NEC 480.8
  spirochetal 104.8 [484.8]
  staphylococcal (broncho) (lobar) 482.40
    aureus 482.41
      methicillin
        resistant 482.42
        susceptible (MSSA) 482.41
    specified type NEC 482.49
  static, stasis 514
  streptococcal (broncho) (lobar) NEC 482.30
    Group
      A 482.31
      B 482.32
      specified NEC 482.39
    pneumoniae 481

Pneumonia — continued
  streptococcal — continued
    specified type NEC 482.39
  Streptococcus pneumoniae 481
  traumatic (complication) (early) (secondary) 958.8
  tuberculous (any) (see also Tuberculosis) 011.6 ☑
  tularemic 021.2
  TWAR agent 483.1
  varicella 052.1
  Veillonella 482.81
  ventilator associated 997.31
  viral, virus (broncho) (interstitial) (lobar) 480.9
    with influenza, flu, or grippe 487.0
    adenoviral 480.0
    parainfluenza 480.2
    respiratory syncytial 480.1
    SARS-associated coronavirus 480.3
    specified type NEC 480.8
  white (congenital) 090.0
Pneumonic — see condition
Pneumonitis (acute) (primary) — see also Pneumonia 486
  allergic 495.9
    specified type NEC 495.8
  aspiration 507.0
    due to fumes or gases 506.0
    fetal 770.18
      due to
        blood 770.16
        clear amniotic fluid 770.14
        meconium 770.12
        postnatal stomach contents 770.86
    newborn 770.18
      due to
        blood 770.16
        clear amniotic fluid 770.14
        meconium 770.12
        postnatal stomach contents 770.86
    obstetric 668.0 ☑
  chemical 506.0
    due to fumes or gases 506.0
  cholesterol 516.8
  chronic (see also Fibrosis, lung) 515
  congenital rubella 771.0
  crack 506.0
  due to
    crack (cocaine) 506.0
    fumes or vapors 506.0
    inhalation
      food (regurgitated), milk, vomitus 507.0
      oils, essences 507.1
      saliva 507.0
      solids, liquids NEC 507.8
    toxoplasmosis (acquired) 130.4
      congenital (active) 771.2 [484.8]
  eosinophilic 518.3
  fetal aspiration 770.18
    due to
      blood 770.16
      clear amniotic fluid 770.14
      meconium 770.12
      postnatal stomach contents 770.86
  hypersensitivity 495.9
  interstitial (chronic) (see also Fibrosis, lung) 515
    lymphoid 516.8
  lymphoid, interstitial 516.8
  meconium aspiration 770.12
  postanesthetic
    correct substance properly administered 507.0
    obstetric 668.0 ☑
    overdose or wrong substance given 968.4
      specified anesthetic — see Table of Drugs and Chemicals
  postoperative 997.3 ☑
    obstetric 668.0 ☑
  radiation 508.0
  rubella, congenital 771.0
  "ventilation" 495.7
  ventilator associated 997.31 ●
  wood-dust 495.8
Pneumonoconiosis — see Pneumoconiosis
Pneumoparotid 527.8
Pneumopathy NEC 518.89

Pneumopathy — continued
  alveolar 516.9
    specified NEC 516.8
  due to dust NEC 504
  parietoalveolar 516.9
    specified condition NEC 516.8
Pneumopericarditis — see also Pericarditis 423.9
  acute 420.90
Pneumopericardium — see also Pericarditis
  congenital 770.2
  fetus or newborn 770.2
  traumatic (post) (see also Pneumothorax, traumatic) 860.0
    with open wound into thorax 860.1
Pneumoperitoneum 568.89
  fetus or newborn 770.2
Pneumophagia (psychogenic) 306.4
Pneumopleurisy, pneumopleuritis — see also Pneumonia 486
Pneumopyopericardium 420.99
Pneumopyothorax — see also Pyopneumothorax 510.9
  with fistula 510.0
Pneumorrhagia 786.3
  newborn 770.3
  tuberculous (see also Tuberculosis, pulmonary) 011.9 ☑
Pneumosiderosis (occupational) 503
Pneumothorax (acute) (chronic) 512.8
  congenital 770.2
  due to operative injury of chest wall or lung 512.1
    accidental puncture or laceration 512.1
  fetus or newborn 770.2
  iatrogenic 512.1
  postoperative 512.1
  spontaneous 512.8
    fetus or newborn 770.2
    tension 512.0
  sucking 512.8
    iatrogenic 512.1
    postoperative 512.1
  tense valvular, infectional 512.0
  tension 512.0
    iatrogenic 512.1
    postoperative 512.1
    spontaneous 512.0
  traumatic 860.0
    with
      hemothorax 860.4
        with open wound into thorax 860.5
      open wound into thorax 860.1
  tuberculous (see also Tuberculosis) 011.7 ☑
Pocket(s)
  endocardial (see also Endocarditis) 424.90
  periodontal 523.8
Podagra 274.01 ▲
Podencephalus 759.89
Poikilocytosis 790.09
Poikiloderma 709.09
  Civatte's 709.09
  congenital 757.33
  vasculare atrophicans 696.2
Poikilodermatomyositis 710.3
Pointed ear 744.29
Poise imperfect 729.90
Poisoned — see Poisoning
Poisoning (acute) — see also Table of Drugs and Chemicals
  Bacillus, B.
    aertrycke (see also Infection, Salmonella) 003.9
    botulinus 005.1
    cholerae (suis) (see also Infection, Salmonella) 003.9
    paratyphosus (see also Infection, Salmonella) 003.9
    suipestifer (see also Infection, Salmonella) 003.9
  bacterial toxins NEC 005.9
  berries, noxious 988.2
  blood (general) — see Septicemia
  botulism 005.1
  bread, moldy, mouldy — see Poisoning, food
  Ciguatera 988.0
  damaged meat — see Poisoning, food

Poisoning — see also Table of Drugs and Chemicals — continued
  death-cap (Amanita phalloides) (Amanita verna) 988.1
  decomposed food — see Poisoning, food
  diseased food — see Poisoning, food
  drug — see Table of Drugs and Chemicals
  epidemic, fish, meat, or other food — see Poisoning, food
  fava bean 282.2
  fish (bacterial) (see also Poisoning, food)
    noxious 988.0
  food (acute) (bacterial) (diseased) (infected) NEC 005.9
    due to
      bacillus
        aertrycke (see also Poisoning, food, due to Salmonella) 003.9
        botulinus 005.1
        cereus 005.89
        choleraesuis (see also Poisoning, food, due to Salmonella) 003.9
        paratyphosus (see also Poisoning, food, due to Salmonella) 003.9
        suipestifer (see also Poisoning, food, due to Salmonella) 003.9
      Clostridium 005.3
        botulinum 005.1
        perfringens 005.2
        welchii 005.2
      Salmonella (aertrycke) (callinarum) (choleraesuis) (enteritidis) (paratyphi) (suipestifer) 003.9
        with
          gastroenteritis 003.0
          localized infection(s) (see also Infection, Salmonella) 003.20
          septicemia 003.1
          specified manifestation NEC 003.8
      specified bacterium NEC 005.89
      Staphylococcus 005.0
      Streptococcus 005.89
      Vibrio parahaemolyticus 005.4
      Vibrio vulnificus 005.81
    noxious or naturally toxic 988.0
      berries 988.2
      fish 988.0
      mushroom 988.1
      plants NEC 988.2
  ice cream — see Poisoning, food
  ichthyotoxism (bacterial) 005.9
  kreotoxism, food 005.9
  malarial — see Malaria
  meat — see Poisoning, food
  mushroom (noxious) 988.1
  mussel (see also Poisoning, food)
    noxious 988.0
  noxious foodstuffs (see also Poisoning, food, noxious) 988.9
    specified type NEC 988.8
  plants, noxious 988.2
  pork (see also Poisoning, food)
    specified NEC 988.8
    Trichinosis 124
  ptomaine — see Poisoning, food
  putrefaction, food — see Poisoning, food
  radiation 508.0
  Salmonella (see also Infection, Salmonella) 003.9
  sausage (see also Poisoning, food)
    Trichinosis 124
  saxitoxin 988.0
  shellfish (see also Poisoning, food)
    noxious (amnesic) (azaspiracid) (diarrheic) (neurotoxic) (paralytic) 988.0
  Staphylococcus, food 005.0
  toxic, from disease NEC 799.89
  truffles — see Poisoning, food
  uremic — see Uremia
  uric acid 274.9
  water 276.6

☑ Additional Digit Required — Refer to the Tabular List for Digit Selection   ▼ Subterms under main terms may continue to next column or page

2010 ICD-9-CM   ▶◀ Revised Text   ● New Line   ▲ Revised Code   October 2009 • Volume 2 — 223

✓ Additional Digit Required — Refer to the Tabular List for Digit Selection   ▽ Subterms under main terms may continue to next column or page

224 — Volume 2 • October 2009   ▶◀ Revised Text   ● New Line   ▲ Revised Code   2010 ICD-9-CM

Polyp, polypus — *continued*
urethra 599.3
uterine
ligament 620.8
tube 620.8
uterus (body) (corpus) (mucous) 621.0
in pregnancy or childbirth 654.1 ☑
affecting fetus or newborn 763.89
causing obstructed labor 660.2 ☑
vagina 623.7
vocal cord (mucous) 478.4
vulva 624.6
Polyradiculitis (acute) 357.0
Polyradiculoneuropathy (acute) (segmentally demyelinating) 357.0
Polysarcia 278.00
Polyserositis (peritoneal) 568.82
due to pericarditis 423.2
paroxysmal (familial) 277.31
pericardial 423.2
periodic (familial) 277.31
pleural — *see* Pleurisy
recurrent 277.31
tuberculous (*see also* Tuberculosis, polyserositis) 018.9 ☑
Polysialia 527.7
Polysplenia syndrome 759.0
Polythelia 757.6
Polytrichia — *see also* Hypertrichosis 704.1
Polyunguia (congenital) 757.5
acquired 703.8
Polyuria 788.42
Pompe's disease (glycogenosis II) 271.0
Pompholyx 705.81
Poncet's disease (tuberculous rheumatism) — *see also* Tuberculosis 015.9 ☑
Pond fracture — *see* Fracture, skull, vault
Ponos 085.0
Pons, pontine — *see* condition
Poor
aesthetics of existing restoration of tooth 525.67
contractions, labor 661.2 ☑
affecting fetus or newborn 763.7
fetal growth NEC 764.9 ☑
affecting management of pregnancy 656.5 ☑
incorporation
artificial skin graft 996.55
decellularized allodermis graft 996.55
obstetric history V13.29
affecting management of current pregnancy V23.49
pre-term labor V23.41
pre-term labor V13.21
sucking reflex (newborn) 796.1
vision NEC 369.9
Poradenitis, nostras 099.1
Porencephaly (congenital) (developmental) (true) 742.4
acquired 348.0
nondevelopmental 348.0
traumatic (post) 310.2
Porocephaliasis 134.1
Porokeratosis 757.39
disseminated superficial actinic (DSAP) 692.75
Poroma, eccrine (M8402/0) — *see* Neoplasm, skin, benign
Porphyria (acute) (congenital) (constitutional) (erythropoietic) (familial) (hepatica) (idiopathic) (idiosyncratic) (intermittent) (latent) (mixed hepatic) (photosensitive) (South African genetic) (Swedish) 277.1
acquired 277.1
cutaneatarda
hereditaria 277.1
symptomatica 277.1
due to drugs
correct substance properly administered 277.1
overdose or wrong substance given or taken 977.9
specified drug — *see* Table of Drugs and Chemicals
secondary 277.1
toxic NEC 277.1

Porphyria — *continued*
variegata 277.1
Porphyrinuria (acquired) (congenital) (secondary) 277.1
Porphyruria (acquired) (congenital) 277.1
Portal — *see* condition
Port wine nevus or mark 757.32
Posadas-Wernicke disease 114.9
Position
fetus, abnormal (*see also* Presentation, fetal) 652.9 ☑
teeth, faulty (*see also* Anomaly, position tooth) 524.30
Positive
culture (nonspecific) 795.39
AIDS virus V08
blood 790.7
HIV V08
human immunodeficiency virus V08
nose 795.39
Staphylococcus — *see* Carrier (suspected) of, Staphylococcus
skin lesion NEC 795.39
spinal fluid 792.0
sputum 795.39
stool 792.1
throat 795.39
urine 791.9
wound 795.39
findings, anthrax 795.31
HIV V08
human immunodeficiency virus (HIV) V08
PPD 795.5
serology
AIDS virus V08
inconclusive 795.71
HIV V08
inconclusive 795.71
human immunodeficiency virus (HIV) V08
inconclusive 795.71
syphilis 097.1
with signs or symptoms — *see* Syphilis, by site and stage
false 795.6
skin test 795.7 ☑
tuberculin (without active tuberculosis) 795.5
VDRL 097.1
with signs or symptoms — *see* Syphilis, by site and stage
false 795.6
Wassermann reaction 097.1
false 795.6
Postcardiotomy syndrome 429.4
Postcaval ureter 753.4
Postcholecystectomy syndrome 576.0
Postclimacteric bleeding 627.1
Postcommissurotomy syndrome 429.4
Postconcussional syndrome 310.2
Postcontusional syndrome 310.2
Postcricoid region — *see* condition
Post-dates (pregnancy) — *see* Pregnancy
Postencephalitic — *see also* condition
syndrome 310.8
Posterior — *see* condition
Posterolateral sclerosis (spinal cord) — *see* Degeneration, combined
Postexanthematous — *see* condition
Postfebrile — *see* condition
Postgastrectomy dumping syndrome 564.2
Posthemiplegic chorea 344.89
Posthemorrhagic anemia (chronic) 280.0
acute 285.1
newborn 776.5
Posthepatitis syndrome 780.79
Postherpetic neuralgia (intercostal) (syndrome) (zoster) 053.19
geniculate ganglion 053.11
ophthalmica 053.19
trigeminal 053.12
Posthitis 607.1
Postimmunization complication or reaction — *see* Complications, vaccination
Postinfectious — *see* condition
Postinfluenzal syndrome 780.79
Postlaminectomy syndrome 722.80

Postlaminectomy syndrome — *continued*
cervical, cervicothoracic 722.81
kyphosis 737.12
lumbar, lumbosacral 722.83
thoracic, thoracolumbar 722.82
Postleukotomy syndrome 310.0
Postlobectomy syndrome 310.0
Postmastectomy lymphedema (syndrome) 457.0
Postmaturity, postmature (fetus or newborn) (gestation period over 42 completed weeks) 766.22
affecting management of pregnancy
post-term pregnancy 645.1 ☑
prolonged pregnancy 645.2 ☑
syndrome 766.22
Postmeasles — *see also* condition
complication 055.8
specified NEC 055.79
Postmenopausal
endometrium (atrophic) 627.8
suppurative (see also Endometritis) 615.9
hormone replacement therapy V07.4
status (age related) (natural) V49.81
Postnasal drip 784.91
Postnatal — *see* condition
Postoperative — *see also* condition
confusion state 293.9
psychosis 293.9
status NEC (*see also* Status (post)) V45.89
Postpancreatectomy hyperglycemia 251.3
Postpartum — *see also* condition
anemia 648.2 ☑
cardiomyopathy 674.5 ☑
observation
immediately after delivery V24.0
routine follow-up V24.2
Postperfusion syndrome NEC 999.89
bone marrow 996.85
Postpoliomyelitic — *see* condition
Postsurgery status NEC — *see also* Status (post) V45.89
Post-term (pregnancy) 645.1 ☑
infant (gestation period over 40 completed weeks to 42 completed weeks) 766.21
Post-transplant lymphoproliferative disorder (PTLD) 238.77
Posttraumatic — *see* condition
Posttraumatic brain syndrome, nonpsychotic 310.2
Post-traumatic stress disorder (PTSD) 309.81
Post-typhoid abscess 002.0
Postures, hysterical 300.11
Postvaccinal reaction or complication — *see* Complications, vaccination
Postvagotomy syndrome 564.2
Postvalvulotomy syndrome 429.4
Postvasectomy sperm count V25.8
Potain's disease (pulmonary edema) 514
Potain's syndrome (gastrectasis with dyspepsia) 536.1
Pott's
curvature (spinal) (*See also* Tuberculosis) 015.0 ☑ *[737.43]*
disease or paraplegia (*see also* Tuberculosis) 015.0 ☑ *[730.88]*
fracture (closed) 824.4
open 824.5
gangrene 440.24
osteomyelitis (*see also* Tuberculosis) 015.0 ☑ *[730.88]*
spinal curvature (*see also* Tuberculosis) 015.0 ☑ *[737.43]*
tumor, puffy (*see also* Osteomyelitis) 730.2 ☑
Potter's
asthma 502
disease 753.0
facies 754.0
lung 502
syndrome (with renal agenesis) 753.0
Pouch
bronchus 748.3
Douglas — *see* condition
esophagus, esophageal (congenital) 750.4
acquired 530.6
gastric 537.1

Pouch — *continued*
Hartmann's (abnormal sacculation of gallbladder neck) 575.8
of intestine V44.3
attention to V55.3
pharynx, pharyngeal (congenital) 750.27
Pouchitis 569.71 ●
Poulet's disease 714.2
Poultrymen's itch 133.8
Poverty V60.2
PPE (palmar plantar erythrodysesthesia) 693.0
Prader-Labhart-Willi-Fanconi syndrome (hypogenital dystrophy with diabetic tendency) 759.81
Prader-Willi syndrome (hypogenital dystrophy with diabetic tendency) 759.81
Preachers' voice 784.49
Pre-AIDS — *see* Human immunodeficiency virus (disease) (illness) (infection)
Preauricular appendage 744.1
Prebetalipoproteinemia (acquired) (essential) (familial) (hereditary) (primary) (secondary) 272.1
with chylomicronemia 272.3
Precipitate labor 661.3 ☑
affecting fetus or newborn 763.6
Preclimacteric bleeding 627.0
menorrhagia 627.0
Precocious
adrenarche 259.1
menarche 259.1
menstruation 626.8
pubarche 259.1
puberty NEC 259.1
sexual development NEC 259.1
thelarche 259.1
Precocity, sexual (constitutional) (cryptogenic) (female) (idiopathic) (male) NEC 259.1
with adrenal hyperplasia 255.2
Precordial pain 786.51
psychogenic 307.89
Predeciduous teeth 520.2
Prediabetes, prediabetic 790.29
complicating pregnancy, childbirth, or puerperium 648.8 ☑
fetus or newborn 775.89
Predislocation status of hip, at birth — *see also* Subluxation, congenital, hip 754.32
Preeclampsia (mild) 642.4 ☑
with pre-existing hypertension 642.7 ☑
affecting fetus or newborn 760.0
severe 642.5 ☑
superimposed on pre-existing hypertensive disease 642.7 ☑
Preeruptive color change, teeth, tooth 520.8
Preexcitation 426.7
atrioventricular conduction 426.7
ventricular 426.7
Preglaucoma 365.00
Pregnancy (single) (uterine) (without sickness) V22.2

Note — Use the following fifth-digit subclassification with categories 640–649, 651–▶679◀:

0   *unspecified as to episode of care*

1   *delivered, with or without mention of antepartum condition*

2   *delivered, with mention of postpartum complication*

3   *antepartum condition or complication*

4   *postpartum condition or complication*

abdominal (ectopic) 633.00
with intrauterine pregnancy 633.01
affecting fetus or newborn 761.4
abnormal NEC 646.9 ☑
ampular — *see* Pregnancy, tubal
broad ligament — *see* Pregnancy, cornual
cervical — *see* Pregnancy, cornual
chemical 631 ●
combined (extrauterine and intrauterine) — *see* Pregnancy, cornual

☑ Additional Digit Required — Refer to the Tabular List for Digit Selection

Subterms under main terms may continue to next column or page

Index

Pregnancy — Pregnancy

Pregnancy — *continued*
complicated (by)
abnormal, abnormality NEC 646.9 ☑
cervix 654.6 ☑
cord (umbilical) 663.9 ☑
glucose tolerance (conditions classifiable to 790.21–790.29) 648.8 ☑
pelvic organs or tissues NEC 654.9 ☑
pelvis (bony) 653.0 ☑
perineum or vulva 654.8 ☑
placenta, placental (vessel) 656.7 ☑
position
cervix 654.4 ☑
placenta 641.1 ☑
without hemorrhage 641.0 ☑
uterus 654.4 ☑
size, fetus 653.5 ☑
uterus (congenital) 654.0 ☑
abscess or cellulitis
bladder 646.6 ☑
genitourinary tract (conditions classifiable to 590, 595, 597, 599.0, 614.0–614.5, 614.7–614.9, 615) 646.6 ☑
kidney 646.6 ☑
urinary tract NEC 646.6 ☑
adhesion, pelvic peritoneal 648.9 ☑
air embolism 673.0 ☑
albuminuria 646.2 ☑
with hypertension — *see* Toxemia, of pregnancy
amnionitis 658.4 ☑
amniotic fluid embolism 673.1 ☑
anemia (conditions classifiable to 280–285) 648.2 ☑
appendicitis 648.9 ☑
atrophy, yellow (acute) (liver) (subacute) 646.7 ☑
bacilluria, asymptomatic 646.5 ☑
bacteriuria, asymptomatic 646.5 ☑
bariatric surgery status 649.2 ☑
bicornis or bicornuate uterus 654.0 ☑
biliary problems 646.8 ☑
bone and joint disorders (conditions classifiable to 720–724 or conditions affecting lower limbs classifiable to 711–719, 725–738) 648.7 ☑
breech presentation (buttocks) (complete) (frank) 652.2 ☑
with successful version 652.1 ☑
cardiovascular disease (conditions classifiable to 390–398, 410–429) 648.6 ☑
congenital (conditions classifiable to 745–747) 648.5 ☑
cerebrovascular disorders (conditions classifiable to 430–434, 436–437) 674.0 ☑
cervicitis (conditions classifiable to 616.0) 646.6 ☑
chloasma (gravidarum) 646.8 ☑
cholelithiasis 646.8 ☑
chorea (gravidarum) — *see* Eclampsia, pregnancy
coagulation defect 649.3 ☑
conjoined twins 678.1 ☑
contraction, pelvis (general) 653.1 ☑
inlet 653.2 ☑
outlet 653.3 ☑
convulsions (eclamptic) (uremic) 642.6 ☑
with pre-existing hypertension 642.7 ☑
current disease or condition (nonobstetric)
abnormal glucose tolerance 648.8 ☑
anemia 648.2 ☑
bone and joint (lower limb) 648.7 ☑
cardiovascular 648.6 ☑
congenital 648.5 ☑
cerebrovascular 674.0 ☑
diabetes (conditions classifiable to 249 and 250) 648.0 ☑
drug dependence 648.3 ☑
female genital mutilation 648.9 ☑

Pregnancy — *continued*
complicated — *continued*
current disease or condition — *continued*
genital organ or tract 646.6 ☑
gonorrheal 647.1 ☑
hypertensive 642.2 ☑
chronic kidney 642.2 ☑
renal 642.1 ☑
infectious 647.9 ☑
specified type NEC 647.8 ☑
liver 646.7 ☑
malarial 647.4 ☑
nutritional deficiency 648.9 ☑
parasitic NEC 647.8 ☑
periodontal disease 648.9 ☑
renal 646.2 ☑
hypertensive 642.1 ☑
rubella 647.5 ☑
specified condition NEC 648.9 ☑
syphilitic 647.0 ☑
thyroid 648.1 ☑
tuberculous 647.3 ☑
urinary 646.6 ☑
venereal 647.2 ☑
viral NEC 647.6 ☑
cystitis 646.6 ☑
cystocele 654.4 ☑
death of fetus (near term) 656.4 ☑
early pregnancy (before 22 completed weeks gestation) 632
deciduitis 646.6 ☑
decreased fetal movements 655.7 ☑
diabetes (mellitus) (conditions classifiable to 249 and 250) 648.0 ☑
disorders of liver 646.7 ☑
displacement, uterus NEC 654.4 ☑
disproportion — *see* Disproportion
double uterus 654.0 ☑
drug dependence (conditions classifiable to 304) 648.3 ☑
dysplasia, cervix 654.6 ☑
early onset of delivery (spontaneous) 644.2 ☑
eclampsia, eclamptic (coma) (convulsions) (delirium) (nephritis) (uremia) 642.6 ☑
with pre-existing hypertension 642.7 ☑
edema 646.1 ☑
with hypertension — *see* Toxemia, of pregnancy
effusion, amniotic fluid 658.1 ☑
delayed delivery following 658.2 ☑
embolism
air 673.0 ☑
amniotic fluid 673.1 ☑
blood-clot 673.2 ☑
cerebral 674.0 ☑
pulmonary NEC 673.2 ☑
pyemic 673.3 ☑
septic 673.3 ☑
emesis (gravidarum) — *see* Pregnancy, complicated, vomiting
endometritis (conditions classifiable to 615.0–615.9) 670.1 ☑ ▲
decidual 646.6 ☑
epilepsy 649.4 ☑
excessive weight gain NEC 646.1 ☑
face presentation 652.4 ☑
failure, fetal head to enter pelvic brim 652.5 ☑
false labor (pains) 644.1 ☑
fatigue 646.8 ☑
fatty metamorphosis of liver 646.7 ☑
female genital mutilation 648.9 ☑
fetal
anemia 678.0 ☑ ●
complications from in utero procedure 679.1 ☑ ●
conjoined twins 678.1 ☑
death (near term) 656.4 ☑
early (before 22 completed weeks gestation) 632

Pregnancy — *continued*
complicated — *continued*
fetal — *continued*
deformity 653.7 ☑
distress 656.8 ☑
hematologic conditions 678.0 ☑ ●
reduction of multiple fetuses reduced to single fetus 651.7 ☑
thrombocytopenia 678.0 ☑ ●
twin to twin transfusion 678.0 ☑ ●
fibroid (tumor) (uterus) 654.1 ☑
footling presentation 652.8 ☑
with successful version 652.1 ☑
gallbladder disease 646.8 ☑
gastric banding status 649.2 ☑
gastric bypass status for obesity
goiter 648.1 ☑
gonococcal infection (conditions classifiable to 098) 647.1 ☑
gonorrhea (conditions classifiable to 098) 647.1 ☑
hemorrhage 641.9 ☑
accidental 641.2 ☑
before 22 completed weeks gestation NEC 640.9 ☑
cerebrovascular 674.0 ☑
due to
afibrinogenemia or other coagulation defect (conditions classifiable to 286.0–286.9) 641.3 ☑
leiomyoma, uterine 641.8 ☑
marginal sinus (rupture) 641.2 ☑
premature separation, placenta 641.2 ☑
trauma 641.8 ☑
early (before 22 completed weeks gestation) 640.9 ☑
threatened abortion 640.0 ☑
unavoidable 641.1 ☑
hepatitis (acute) (malignant) (subacute) 646.7 ☑
viral 647.6 ☑
herniation of uterus 654.4 ☑
high head at term 652.5 ☑
hydatidiform mole (delivered) (undelivered) 630
hydramnios 657.0 ☑
hydrocephalic fetus 653.6 ☑
hydrops amnii 657.0 ☑
hydrorrhea 658.1 ☑
hyperemesis (gravidarum) — *see* Hyperemesis, gravidarum
hypertension — *see* Hypertension, complicating pregnancy
hypertensive
chronic kidney disease 642.2 ☑
heart and chronic kidney disease 642.2 ☑
heart and renal disease 642.2 ☑
heart disease 642.2 ☑
renal disease 642.2 ☑
hypertensive heart and chronic kidney disease 642.2 ☑
hyperthyroidism 648.1 ☑
hypothyroidism 648.1 ☑
hysteralgia 646.8 ☑
icterus gravis 646.7 ☑
incarceration, uterus 654.3 ☑
incompetent cervix (os) 654.5 ☑
infection 647.9 ☑
amniotic fluid 658.4 ☑
bladder 646.6 ☑
genital organ (conditions classifiable to 614.0–614.5, 614.7–614.9, 615) 646.6 ☑
kidney (conditions classifiable to 590.0–590.9) 646.6 ☑
urinary (tract) 646.6 ☑
asymptomatic 646.5 ☑
infective and parasitic diseases NEC 647.8 ☑
inflammation
bladder 646.6 ☑

Pregnancy — *continued*
complicated — *continued*
inflammation — *continued*
genital organ (conditions classifiable to 614.0–614.5, 614.7–614.9, 615) 646.6 ☑
urinary tract NEC 646.6 ☑
insufficient weight gain 646.8 ☑
intrauterine fetal death (near term) NEC 656.4 ☑
early (before 22 completed weeks' gestation) 632
malaria (conditions classifiable to 084) 647.4 ☑
malformation, uterus (congenital) 654.0 ☑
malnutrition (conditions classifiable to 260–269) 648.9 ☑
malposition
fetus — *see* Pregnancy, complicated, malpresentation
uterus or cervix 654.4 ☑
malpresentation 652.9 ☑
with successful version 652.1 ☑
in multiple gestation 652.6 ☑
specified type NEC 652.8 ☑
marginal sinus hemorrhage or rupture 641.2 ☑
maternal complications from in utero procedure 679.0 ☑
maternal drug abuse 648.4 ☑
maternal obesity syndrome 646.1 ☑
menstruation 640.8 ☑
mental disorders (conditions classifiable to 290–303, 305.0, 305.2–305.9, 306–316, 317–319) 648.4 ☑
mentum presentation 652.4 ☑
missed
abortion 632
delivery (at or near term) 656.4 ☑
labor (at or near term) 656.4 ☑
necrosis
genital organ or tract (conditions classifiable to 614.0–614.5, 614.7–614.9, 615) 646.6 ☑
liver (conditions classifiable to 570) 646.7 ☑
renal, cortical 646.2 ☑
nephritis or nephrosis (conditions classifiable to 580–589) 646.2 ☑
with hypertension 642.1 ☑
nephropathy NEC 646.2 ☑
neuritis (peripheral) 646.4 ☑
nutritional deficiency (conditions classifiable to 260–269) 648.9 ☑
obesity 649.1 ☑
surgery status 649.2 ☑
oblique lie or presentation 652.3 ☑
with successful version 652.1 ☑
obstetrical trauma NEC 665.9 ☑
oligohydramnios NEC 658.0 ☑
onset of contractions before 37 weeks 644.0 ☑
oversize fetus 653.5 ☑
papyraceous fetus 646.0 ☑
patent cervix 654.5 ☑
pelvic inflammatory disease (conditions classifiable to 614.0–614.5, 614.7–614.9, 615) 646.6 ☑
pelvic peritoneal adhesion 648.9 ☑
placenta, placental
abnormality 656.7 ☑
abruptio or ablatio 641.2 ☑
detachment 641.2 ☑
disease 656.7 ☑
infarct 656.7 ☑
low implantation 641.1 ☑
without hemorrhage 641.0 ☑
malformation 656.7 ☑
malposition 641.1 ☑
without hemorrhage 641.0 ☑
marginal sinus hemorrhage 641.2 ☑
previa 641.1 ☑
without hemorrhage 641.0 ☑

☑ Additional Digit Required — Refer to the Tabular List for Digit Selection

▼ Subterms under main terms may continue to next column or page

Pregnancy — *continued*
  complicated — *continued*
    placenta, placental — *continued*
      separation (premature) (undelivered) 641.2 ☑
    placentitis 658.4 ☑
    polyhydramnios 657.0 ☑
    postmaturity
      post-term 645.1 ☑
      prolonged 645.2 ☑
    prediabetes 648.8 ☑
    pre-eclampsia (mild) 642.4 ☑
      severe 642.5 ☑
      superimposed on pre-existing hypertensive disease 642.7 ☑
    premature rupture of membranes 658.1 ☑
      with delayed delivery 658.2 ☑
    previous
      infertility V23.0
      in utero procedure during previous pregnancy V23.86
      nonobstetric condition V23.89
      poor obstetrical history V23.49
      premature delivery V23.41
      trophoblastic disease (conditions classifiable to 630) V23.1
    prolapse, uterus 654.4 ☑
    proteinuria (gestational) 646.2 ☑
      with hypertension — *see* Toxemia, of pregnancy
    pruritus (neurogenic) 646.8 ☑
    psychosis or psychoneurosis 648.4 ☑
    ptyalism 646.8 ☑
    pyelitis (conditions classifiable to 590.0–590.9) 646.6 ☑
    renal disease or failure NEC 646.2 ☑
      with secondary hypertension 642.1 ☑
      hypertensive 642.2 ☑
    retention, retained dead ovum 631
    retroversion, uterus 654.3 ☑
    Rh immunization, incompatibility, or sensitization 656.1 ☑
    rubella (conditions classifiable to 056) 647.5 ☑
    rupture
      amnion (premature) 658.1 ☑
        with delayed delivery 658.2 ☑
      marginal sinus (hemorrhage) 641.2 ☑
      membranes (premature) 658.1 ☑
        with delayed delivery 658.2 ☑
      uterus (before onset of labor) 665.0 ☑
    salivation (excessive) 646.8 ☑
    salpingo–oophoritis (conditions classifiable to 614.0–614.2) 646.6 ☑
    septicemia (conditions classifiable to 038.0–038.9) 647.8 ☑
      postpartum 670.2 ☑ ▲
      puerperal 670.2 ☑ ▲
    smoking 649.0 ☑
    spasms, uterus (abnormal) 646.8 ☑
    specified condition NEC 646.8 ☑
    spotting 649.5 ☑
    spurious labor pains 644.1 ☑
    status post
      bariatric surgery 649.2 ☑
      gastric banding 649.2 ☑
      gastric bypass for obesity 649.2 ☑
      obesity surgery 649.2 ☑
    superfecundation 651.9 ☑
    superfetation 651.9 ☑
    syphilis (conditions classifiable to 090–097) 647.0 ☑
    threatened
      abortion 640.0 ☑
      premature delivery 644.2 ☑
      premature labor 644.0 ☑
    thrombophlebitis (superficial) 671.2 ☑
      deep 671.3 ☑
      septic 670.3 ☑ ●
    thrombosis 671.2 ☑ ▲
      venous (superficial) 671.2 ☑
        deep 671.3 ☑
    thyroid dysfunction (conditions classifiable to 240–246) 648.1 ☑

Pregnancy — *continued*
  complicated — *continued*
    thyroiditis 648.1 ☑
    thyrotoxicosis 648.1 ☑
    tobacco use disorder 649.0 ☑
    torsion of uterus 654.4 ☑
    toxemia — *see* Toxemia, of pregnancy
    transverse lie or presentation 652.3 ☑
      with successful version 652.1 ☑
    trauma 648.9 ☑
      obstetrical 665.9 ☑
    tuberculosis (conditions classifiable to 010–018) 647.3 ☑
    tumor
      cervix 654.6 ☑
      ovary 654.4 ☑
      pelvic organs or tissue NEC 654.4 ☑
      uterus (body) 654.1 ☑
        cervix 654.6 ☑
      vagina 654.7 ☑
      vulva 654.8 ☑
    unstable lie 652.0 ☑
    uremia — *see* Pregnancy, complicated, renal disease
    urethritis 646.6 ☑
    vaginitis or vulvitis (conditions classifiable to 616.1) 646.6 ☑
    varicose
      placental vessels 656.7 ☑
      veins (legs) 671.0 ☑
        perineum 671.1 ☑
        vulva 671.1 ☑
    varicosity, labia or vulva 671.1 ☑
    venereal disease NEC (conditions classifiable to 099) 647.2 ☑
    venous complication 671.9 ☑ ●
    viral disease NEC (conditions classifiable to 042, 050–055, 057–079, 795.05, 795.15, 796.75) 647.6 ☑
    vomiting (incoercible) (pernicious) (persistent) (uncontrollable) (vicious) 643.9 ☑
      due to organic disease or other cause 643.8 ☑
      early — *see* Hyperemesis, gravidarum
      late (after 22 completed weeks gestation) 643.2 ☑
    young maternal age 659.8 ☑
  complications NEC 646.9 ☑
  cornual 633.80
    with intrauterine pregnancy 633.81
    affecting fetus or newborn 761.4
  death, maternal NEC 646.9 ☑
  delivered — *see* Delivery
  ectopic (ruptured) NEC 633.90
    with intrauterine pregnancy 633.91
    abdominal — *see* Pregnancy, abdominal
    affecting fetus or newborn 761.4
    combined (extrauterine and intrauterine) — *see* Pregnancy, cornual
    ovarian — *see* Pregnancy, ovarian
    specified type NEC 633.80
      with intrauterine pregnancy 633.81
      affecting fetus or newborn 761.4
    tubal — *see* Pregnancy, tubal
  examination, pregnancy
    negative result V72.41
    not confirmed V72.40
    positive result V72.42
  extrauterine — *see* Pregnancy, ectopic
  fallopian — *see* Pregnancy, tubal
  false 300.11
    labor (pains) 644.1 ☑
  fatigue 646.8 ☑
  illegitimate V61.6
  incidental finding V22.2
  in double uterus 654.0 ☑
  interstitial — *see* Pregnancy, cornual
  intraligamentous — *see* Pregnancy, cornual
  intramural — *see* Pregnancy, cornual
  intraperitoneal — *see* Pregnancy, abdominal
  isthmian — *see* Pregnancy, tubal
  management affected by
    abnormal, abnormality
      fetus (suspected) 655.9 ☑

Pregnancy — *continued*
  management affected by — *continued*
    abnormal, abnormality — *continued*
      fetus — *continued*
        specified NEC 655.8 ☑
      placenta 656.7 ☑
    advanced maternal age NEC 659.6 ☑
      multigravida 659.6 ☑
      primigravida 659.5 ☑
    antibodies (maternal)
      anti-c 656.1 ☑
      anti-d 656.1 ☑
      anti-e 656.1 ☑
      blood group (ABO) 656.2 ☑
        Rh(esus) 656.1 ☑
    appendicitis 648.9 ☑
    bariatric surgery status 649.2 ☑
    coagulation defect 649.3 ☑
    elderly multigravida 659.6 ☑
    elderly primigravida 659.5 ☑
    epilepsy 649.4 ☑
    fetal (suspected)
      abnormality 655.9 ☑
        abdominal 655.8 ☑
        acid-base balance 656.8 ☑
        cardiovascular 655.8 ☑
        facial 655.8 ☑
        gastrointestinal 655.8 ☑
        gentourinary 655.8 ☑
        heart rate or rhythm 659.7 ☑
        limb 655.8 ☑
        specified NEC 655.8 ☑
      acidemia 656.3 ☑
      anencephaly 655.0 ☑
      aneuploidy 655.1 ☑
      bradycardia 659.7 ☑
      central nervous system malformation 655.0 ☑
      chromosomal abnormalities (conditions classifiable to 758.0–758.9) 655.1 ☑
      damage from
        drugs 655.5 ☑
          obstetric, anesthetic, or sedative 655.5 ☑
        environmental toxins 655.8 ☑
        intrauterine contraceptive device 655.8 ☑
        maternal
          alcohol addiction 655.4 ☑
          disease NEC 655.4 ☑
          drug use 655.5 ☑
          listeriosis 655.4 ☑
          rubella 655.3 ☑
          toxoplasmosis 655.4 ☑
          viral infection 655.3 ☑
        radiation 655.6 ☑
      death (near term) 656.4 ☑
        early (before 22 completed weeks' gestation) 632
      distress 656.8 ☑
      excessive growth 656.6 ☑
      fetal-maternal hemorrhage 656.0 ☑
      growth retardation 656.5 ☑
      hereditary disease 655.2 ☑
      hereditary disease in family (possibly) affecting fetus 655.2 ☑
      hydrocephalus 655.0 ☑
      incompatibility, blood groups (ABO) 656.2 ☑
      intrauterine death 656.4 ☑
      poor growth 656.5 ☑
      Rh(esus) 656.1 ☑
      spina bifida (with myelomeningocele) 655.0 ☑
    gastric banding status 649.2 ☑
    gastric bypass status for obesity 649.2 ☑
    insufficient prenatal care V23.7
    intrauterine death 656.4 ☑
    isoimmunization (ABO) 656.2 ☑
      Rh(esus) 656.1 ☑
    large-for-dates fetus 656.6 ☑
    light-for-dates fetus 656.5 ☑
    meconium in liquor 656.8 ☑

Pregnancy — *continued*
  management affected by — *continued*
    mental disorder (conditions classifiable to 290–303, 305.0, 305.2–305.9, 306–316, 317–319) 648.4 ☑
    multiparity (grand) 659.4 ☑
    obesity 649.1 ☑
      surgery status 649.2 ☑
    poor obstetric history V23.49
    pre-term labor V23.41
    postmaturity
      post-term 645.1 ☑
      prolonged 645.2 ☑
    post-term pregnancy 645.1 ☑
    previous
      abortion V23.2
        habitual 646.3 ☑
      cesarean delivery 654.2 ☑
      difficult delivery V23.49
      forceps delivery V23.49
      habitual abortions 646.3 ☑
      hemorrhage, antepartum or postpartum V23.49
      hydatidiform mole V23.1
      infertility V23.0
      in utero procedure during previous pregnancy V23.86
      malignancy NEC V23.89
      nonobstetrical conditions V23.8 ☑
      premature delivery V23.41
      trophoblastic disease (conditions in 630) V23.1
      vesicular mole V23.1
    prolonged pregnancy 645.2 ☑
    small-for-dates fetus 656.5 ☑
    smoking 649.0 ☑
    spotting 649.5 ☑
    suspected conditions not found
      amniotic cavity and membrane problem V89.01
      cervical shortening V89.05
      fetal anomaly V89.03
      fetal growth problem V89.04
      oligohydramnios V89.01
      other specified problem NEC V89.09
      placental problem V89.02
      polyhydramnios V89.01
    tobacco use disorder 649.0 ☑
    venous complication 671.9 ☑ ●
    young maternal age 659.8 ☑
  maternal death NEC 646.9 ☑
  mesometric (mural) — *see* Pregnancy, cornual
  molar 631
    hydatidiform (*see also* Hydatidiform mole) 630
      previous, affecting management of pregnancy V23.1
    previous, affecting management of pregnancy V23.49
  multiple NEC 651.9 ☑
    with fetal loss and retention of one or more fetus(es) 651.6 ☑
    affecting fetus or newborn 761.5
    following (elective) fetal reduction 651.7 ☑
    specified type NEC 651.8 ☑
      with fetal loss and retention of one or more fetus(es) 651.6 ☑
      following (elective) fetal reduction 651.7 ☑
  mural — *see* Pregnancy, cornual
  observation NEC V22.1
    first pregnancy V22.0
    high-risk V23.9
      specified problem NEC V23.89
  ovarian 633.20
    with intrauterine pregnancy 633.21
    affecting fetus or newborn 761.4
  possible, not (yet) confirmed V72.40
  postmature
    post-term 645.1 ☑
    prolonged 645.2 ☑
  post-term 645.1 ☑
  prenatal care only V22.1
    first pregnancy V22.0

☑ Additional Digit Required — Refer to the Tabular List for Digit Selection   ᵂᴱᴵ Subterms under main terms may continue to next column or page

2010 ICD-9-CM   ▶◀ Revised Text   ● New Line   ▲ Revised Code   October 2009 • Volume 2 — 227

Index

Pregnancy — Problem

Pregnancy — continued
prenatal care only — continued
high-risk V23.9
specified problem NEC V23.89
prolonged 645.2 ☑
quadruplet NEC 651.2 ☑
with fetal loss and retention of one or more
fetus(es) 651.5 ☑
affecting fetus or newborn 761.5
following (elective) fetal reduction
651.7 ☑
quintuplet NEC 651.8 ☑
with fetal loss and retention of one or more
fetus(es) 651.6 ☑
affecting fetus or newborn 761.5
following (elective) fetal reduction
651.7 ☑
resulting from
assisted reproductive technology V23.85
in vitro fertilization V23.85
sextuplet NEC 651.8 ☑
with fetal loss and retention of one or more
fetus(es) 651.6 ☑
affecting fetus or newborn 761.5
following (elective) fetal reduction
651.7 ☑
spurious 300.11
superfecundation NEC 651.9 ☑
with fetal loss and retention of one or more
fetus(es) 651.6 ☑
following (elective) fetal reduction
651.7 ☑
superfetation NEC 651.9 ☑
with fetal loss and retention of one or more
fetus(es) 651.6 ☑
following (elective) fetal reduction
651.7 ☑
supervision (of) (for) (see also Pregnancy,
management affected by)
elderly
multigravida V23.82
primigravida V23.81
high-risk V23.9
insufficient prenatal care V23.7
specified problem NEC V23.89
multiparity V23.3
normal NEC V22.1
first V22.0
poor
obstetric history V23.49
pre-term labor V23.41
reproductive history V23.5
previous
abortion V23.2
hydatidiform mole V23.1
infertility V23.0
neonatal death V23.5
stillbirth V23.5
trophoblastic disease V23.1
vesicular mole V23.1
specified problem NEC V23.89
young
multigravida V23.84
primigravida V23.83
triplet NEC 651.1 ☑
with fetal loss and retention of one or more
fetus(es) 651.4 ☑
affecting fetus or newborn 761.5
following (elective) fetal reduction
651.7 ☑
tubal (with rupture) 633.10
with intrauterine pregnancy 633.11
affecting fetus or newborn 761.4
twin NEC 651.0 ☑
with fetal loss and retention of one fetus
651.3 ☑
affecting fetus or newborn 761.5
conjoined 678.1 ☑
following (elective) fetal reduction
651.7 ☑
unconfirmed V72.40
undelivered (no other diagnosis) V22.2
with false labor 644.1 ☑
high-risk V23.9
specified problem NEC V23.89

Pregnancy — continued
unwanted NEC V61.7
Pregnant uterus — see condition
Preiser's disease (osteoporosis) 733.09
Prekwashiorkor 260
Preleukemia 238.75
Preluxation of hip, congenital — see also Subluxation, congenital, hip 754.32
Premature — see also condition
beats (nodal) 427.60
atrial 427.61
auricular 427.61
postoperative 997.1
specified type NEC 427.69
supraventricular 427.61
ventricular 427.69
birth NEC 765.1 ☑
closure
cranial suture 756.0
fontanel 756.0
foramen ovale 745.8
contractions 427.60
atrial 427.61
auricular 427.61
auriculoventricular 427.61
heart (extrasystole) 427.60
junctional 427.60
nodal 427.60
postoperative 997.1
ventricular 427.69
ejaculation 302.75
infant NEC 765.1 ☑
excessive 765.0 ☑
light-for-dates — see Light-for-dates
labor 644.2 ☑
threatened 644.0 ☑
lungs 770.4
menopause 256.31
puberty 259.1
rupture of membranes or amnion 658.1 ☑
affecting fetus or newborn 761.1
delayed delivery following 658.2 ☑
senility (syndrome) 259.8
separation, placenta (partial) — see Placenta,
separation
ventricular systole 427.69
Prematurity NEC 765.1 ☑
extreme 765.0 ☑
Premenstrual syndrome 625.4
Premenstrual tension 625.4
Premolarization, cuspids 520.2
Premyeloma 273.1
Prenatal
care, normal pregnancy V22.1
first V22.0
death, cause unknown — see Death, fetus
screening — see Antenatal, screening
teeth 520.6
Prepartum — see condition
Preponderance, left or right ventricular 429.3
Prepuce — see condition
PRES (posterior reversible encephalopathy syndrome) 348.39
Presbycardia 797
hypertensive (see also Hypertension, heart)
402.90
Presbycusis 388.01
Presbyesophagus 530.89
Presbyophrenia 310.1
Presbyopia 367.4
Prescription of contraceptives NEC V25.02
diaphragm V25.02
oral (pill) V25.01
emergency V25.03
postcoital V25.03
repeat V25.41
repeat V25.40
oral (pill) V25.41
Presenile — see also condition
aging 259.8
dementia (see also Dementia, presenile) 290.10
Presenility 259.8
Presentation, fetal
abnormal 652.9 ☑
with successful version 652.1 ☑

Presentation, fetal — continued
abnormal — continued
before labor, affecting fetus or newborn
761.7
causing obstructed labor 660.0 ☑
affecting fetus or newborn, any, except
breech 763.1
in multiple gestation (one or more)
652.6 ☑
specified NEC 652.8 ☑
arm 652.7 ☑
causing obstructed labor 660.0 ☑
breech (buttocks) (complete) (frank) 652.2 ☑
with successful version 652.1 ☑
before labor, affecting fetus or newborn 761.7
before labor, affecting fetus or newborn
761.7
brow 652.4 ☑
causing obstructed labor 660.0 ☑
buttocks 652.2 ☑
chin 652.4 ☑
complete 652.2 ☑
compound 652.8 ☑
cord 663.0 ☑
extended head 652.4 ☑
face 652.4 ☑
to pubes 652.8 ☑
footling 652.8 ☑
frank 652.2 ☑
hand, leg, or foot NEC 652.8 ☑
incomplete 652.8 ☑
mentum 652.4 ☑
multiple gestation (one fetus or more)
652.6 ☑
oblique 652.3 ☑
with successful version 652.1 ☑
shoulder 652.8 ☑
affecting fetus or newborn 763.1
transverse 652.3 ☑
with successful version 652.1 ☑
umbilical cord 663.0 ☑
unstable 652.0 ☑
Prespondylolisthesis (congenital) (lumbosacral)
756.11
Pressure
area, skin ulcer (see also Ulcer, pressure) 707.00
atrophy, spine 733.99
birth, fetus or newborn NEC 767.9
brachial plexus 353.0
brain 348.4
injury at birth 767.0
cerebral — see Pressure, brain
chest 786.59
cone, tentorial 348.4
injury at birth 767.0
funis — see Compression, umbilical cord
hyposystolic (see also Hypotension) 458.9
increased
intracranial 781.99
due to
benign intracranial hypertension
348.2
hydrocephalus — see hydrocephalus
injury at birth 767.8
intraocular 365.00
lumbosacral plexus 353.1
mediastinum 519.3
necrosis (chronic) (skin) (see also Decubitus)
707.00
nerve — see Compression, nerve
paralysis (see also Neuropathy, entrapment)
355.9
pre-ulcer skin changes limited to persistent
focal erythema (see also Ulcer, pressure)
707.21
sore (chronic) (see also Ulcer, pressure) 707.00
spinal cord 336.9
ulcer (chronic) (see also Ulcer, pressure) 707.00
umbilical cord — see Compression, umbilical
cord
venous, increased 459.89
Pre-syncope 780.2
Preterm infant NEC 765.1 ☑

Preterm infant — continued
extreme 765.0 ☑
Priapism (penis) 607.3
Prickling sensation — see also Disturbance,
sensation 782.0
Prickly heat 705.1
Primary — see condition
Primigravida, elderly
affecting
fetus or newborn 763.89
management of pregnancy, labor, and
delivery 659.5 ☑
Primipara, old
affecting
fetus or newborn 763.89
management of pregnancy, labor, and
delivery 659.5 ☑
Primula dermatitis 692.6
Primus varus (bilateral) (metatarsus) 754.52
PRIND (prolonged reversible ischemic neurolog
deficit) 434.91
history of (personal) V12.54
Pringle's disease (tuberous sclerosis) 759.5
Prinzmetal's angina 413.1
Prinzmetal-Massumi syndrome (anterior che
wall) 786.52
Prizefighter ear 738.7
Problem (with) V49.9
academic V62.3
acculturation V62.4
adopted child V61.24
aged
in-law V61.3
parent V61.3
person NEC V61.8
alcoholism in family V61.41
anger reaction (see also Disturbance, conduct
312.0 ☑
behavioral V40.9
specified NEC V40.3
behavior, child 312.9
betting V69.3
biological child V61.23
cardiorespiratory NEC V47.2
career choice V62.29
care of sick or handicapped person in family
or household V61.49
communication V40.1
conscience regarding medical care V62.6
delinquency (juvenile) 312.9
diet, inappropriate V69.1
digestive NEC V47.3
ear NEC V41.3
eating habits, inappropriate V69.1
economic V60.2
affecting care V60.9
specified type NEC V60.89 ◄
educational V62.3
enuresis, child 307.6
exercise, lack of V69.0
eye NEC V41.1
family V61.9
specified circumstance NEC V61.8
fear reaction, child 313.0
feeding (elderly) (infant) 783.3
newborn 779.31 ◄
nonorganic 307.59
fetal, affecting management of pregnancy
656.9 ☑
specified type NEC 656.8 ☑
financial V60.2
foster child V61.25 ◄
functional V41.9
specified type NEC V41.8
gambling V69.3
genital NEC V47.5
head V48.9
deficiency V48.0
disfigurement V48.6
mechanical V48.2
motor V48.2
movement of V48.2
sensory V48.4
specified condition NEC V48.8
hearing V41.2
high-risk sexual behavior V69.2

☑ Additional Digit Required — Refer to the Tabular List for Digit Selection   ⬚ Subterms under main terms may continue to next column or page

228 — Volume 2 • October 2009   ►◄ Revised Text   ● New Line   ▲ Revised Code   2010 ICD-9-CM

Problem — continued
identity 313.82
influencing health status NEC V49.89
internal organ NEC V47.9
  deficiency V47.0
  mechanical or motor V47.1
interpersonal NEC V62.81
jealousy, child 313.3
learning V40.0
legal V62.5
life circumstance NEC V62.89
lifestyle V69.9
  specified NEC V69.8
limb V49.9
  deficiency V49.0
  disfigurement V49.4
  mechanical V49.1
  motor V49.2
  movement, involving
    musculoskeletal system V49.1
    nervous system V49.2
  sensory V49.3
  specified condition NEC V49.5
litigation V62.5
living alone V60.3
loneliness NEC V62.89
marital V61.10
  involving
    divorce V61.03
    estrangement V61.09
    psychosexual disorder 302.9
    sexual function V41.7
  relationship V61.10
mastication V41.6
medical care, within family V61.49
mental V40.9
  specified NEC V40.2
mental hygiene, adult V40.9
multiparity V61.5
nail biting, child 307.9
neck V48.9
  deficiency V48.1
  disfigurement V48.7
  mechanical V48.3
  motor V48.3
  movement V48.3
  sensory V48.5
  specified condition NEC V48.8
neurological NEC 781.99
none (feared complaint unfounded) V65.5
occupational V62.29
parent-child V61.20
  adopted child V61.24 ●
  biological child V61.23 ●
  foster child V61.25 ●
  relationship V61.20
partner V61.10
  relationship V61.10
personal NEC V62.89
  interpersonal conflict NEC V62.81
personality (see also Disorder, personality) 301.9
phase of life V62.89
placenta, affecting management of pregnancy 656.9 ☑
  specified type NEC 656.8 ☑
poverty V60.2
presence of sick or handicapped person in family or household V61.49
psychiatric 300.9
psychosocial V62.9
  specified type NEC V62.89
relational NEC V62.81
relationship, childhood 313.3
religious or spiritual belief
  other than medical care V62.89
  regarding medical care V62.6
self-damaging behavior V69.8
sexual
  behavior, high-risk V69.2
  function NEC V41.7
sibling
  relational V61.8
  relationship V61.8
sight V41.0
sleep disorder, child 307.40

Problem — continued
sleep, lack of V69.4
smell V41.5
speech V40.1
spite reaction, child (see also Disturbance, conduct) 312.0 ☑
spoiled child reaction (see also Disturbance, conduct) 312.1 ☑
substance abuse in family V61.42 ●
swallowing V41.6
tantrum, child (see also Disturbance, conduct) 312.1 ☑
taste V41.5
thumb sucking, child 307.9
tic (child) 307.21
trunk V48.9
  deficiency V48.1
  disfigurement V48.7
  mechanical V48.3
  motor V48.3
  movement V48.3
  sensory V48.5
  specified condition NEC V48.8
unemployment V62.0
urinary NEC V47.4
voice production V41.4
Procedure (surgical) **not done** NEC V64.3
because of
  contraindication V64.1
  patient's decision V64.2
    for reasons of conscience or religion V62.6
  specified reason NEC V64.3
Procidentia
anus (sphincter) 569.1
rectum (sphincter) 569.1
stomach 537.89
uteri 618.1
Proctalgia 569.42
fugax 564.6
spasmodic 564.6
  psychogenic 307.89
Proctitis 569.49
amebic 006.8
chlamydial 099.52
gonococcal 098.7
granulomatous 555.1
idiopathic 556.2
  with ulcerative sigmoiditis 556.3
tuberculous (see also Tuberculosis) 014.8 ☑
ulcerative (chronic) (nonspecific) 556.2
  with ulcerative sigmoiditis 556.3
Proctocele
female (without uterine prolapse) 618.04
  with uterine prolapse 618.4
    complete 618.3
    incomplete 618.2
male 569.49
Proctocolitis, idiopathic 556.2
with ulcerative sigmoiditis 556.3
Proctoptosis 569.1
Proctosigmoiditis 569.89
ulcerative (chronic) 556.3
Proctospasm 564.6
psychogenic 306.4
Prodromal-AIDS — see Human immunodeficiency virus (disease) (illness) (infection)
Profichet's disease or syndrome 729.90
Progeria (adultorum) (syndrome) 259.8
Prognathism (mandibular) (maxillary) 524.00
Progonoma (melanotic) (M9363/0) — see Neoplasm, by site, benign
Progressive — see condition
Prolapse, prolapsed
anus, anal (canal) (sphincter) 569.1
arm or hand, complicating delivery 652.7 ☑
  causing obstructed labor 660.0 ☑
    affecting fetus or newborn 763.1
  fetus or newborn 763.1
bladder (acquired) (mucosa) (sphincter)
  congenital (female) (male) 756.71
  female (see also Cystocele, female) 618.01
  male 596.8
breast implant (prosthetic) 996.54
cecostomy 569.69
cecum 569.89

Prolapse, prolapsed — continued
cervix, cervical (hypertrophied) 618.1
  anterior lip, obstructing labor 660.2 ☑
    affecting fetus or newborn 763.1
  congenital 752.49
  postpartal (old) 618.1
  stump 618.84
ciliary body 871.1
colon (pedunculated) 569.89
colostomy 569.69
conjunctiva 372.73
cord — see Prolapse, umbilical cord
disc (intervertebral) — see Displacement, intervertebral disc
duodenum 537.89
eye implant (orbital) 996.59
  lens (ocular) 996.53
fallopian tube 620.4
fetal extremity, complicating delivery 652.8 ☑
  causing obstructed labor 660.0 ☑
  fetus or newborn 763.1
funis — see Prolapse, umbilical cord
gastric (mucosa) 537.89
genital, female 618.9
  specified NEC 618.89
globe 360.81
ileostomy bud 569.69
intervertebral disc — see Displacement, intervertebral disc
intestine (small) 569.89
iris 364.89
  traumatic 871.1
kidney (see also Disease, renal) 593.0
  congenital 753.3
laryngeal muscles or ventricle 478.79
leg, complicating delivery 652.8 ☑
  causing obstructed labor 660.0 ☑
  fetus or newborn 763.1
liver 573.8
meatus urinarius 599.5
mitral valve 424.0
ocular lens implant 996.53
organ or site, congenital NEC — see Malposition, congenital
ovary 620.4
pelvic (floor), female 618.89
perineum, female 618.89
pregnant uterus 654.4 ☑
rectum (mucosa) (sphincter) 569.1
  due to Trichuris trichiuria 127.3
spleen 289.59
stomach 537.89
umbilical cord
  affecting fetus or newborn 762.4
  complicating delivery 663.0 ☑
ureter 593.89
  with obstruction 593.4
ureterovesical orifice 593.89
urethra (acquired) (infected) (mucosa) 599.5
  congenital 753.8
uterovaginal 618.4
  complete 618.3
  incomplete 618.2
  specified NEC 618.89
uterus (first degree) (second degree) (third degree) (complete) (without vaginal wall prolapse) 618.1
  with mention of vaginal wall prolapse — see Prolapse, uterovaginal
  congenital 752.3
  in pregnancy or childbirth 654.4 ☑
    affecting fetus or newborn 763.1
    causing obstructed labor 660.2 ☑
      affecting fetus or newborn 763.1
  postpartal (old) 618.1
uveal 871.1
vagina (anterior) (posterior) (vault) (wall) (without uterine prolapse) 618.00
  with uterine prolapse 618.4
    complete 618.3
    incomplete 618.2
  paravaginal 618.02
  posthysterectomy 618.5
  specified NEC 618.09
vitreous (humor) 379.26
  traumatic 871.1

Prolapse, prolapsed — continued
womb — see Prolapse, uterus
Prolapsus, female 618.9
Proliferative — see condition
Prolinemia 270.8
Prolinuria 270.8
Prolonged, prolongation
bleeding time (see also Defect, coagulation) 790.92
  "idiopathic" (in von Willebrand's disease) 286.4
coagulation time (see also Defect, coagulation) 790.92
gestation syndrome 766.22
labor 662.1 ☑
  affecting fetus or newborn 763.89
  first stage 662.0 ☑
  second stage 662.2 ☑
pregnancy 645.2 ☑
PR interval 426.11
prothrombin time (see also Defect, coagulation) 790.92
QT interval 794.31
  syndrome 426.82
rupture of membranes (24 hours or more prior to onset of labor) 658.2 ☑
uterine contractions in labor 661.4 ☑
  affecting fetus or newborn 763.7
Prominauris 744.29
Prominence
auricle (ear) (congenital) 744.29
  acquired 380.32
ischial spine or sacral promontory
  with disproportion (fetopelvic) 653.3 ☑
    affecting fetus or newborn 763.1
    causing obstructed labor 660.1 ☑
      affecting fetus or newborn 763.1
nose (congenital) 748.1
  acquired 738.0
PROMM (proximal myotonic myotonia) 359.21
Pronation
ankle 736.79
foot 736.79
  congenital 755.67
Prophylactic — *[handwritten: Organ Removal V50.XX]*
administration of
  agents affecting estrogen receptors and estrogen levels NEC V07.59
  anastrozole (Arimidex) V07.52
  antibiotics V58.62
  antitoxin, any V07.2
  antivenin V07.2
  aromatase inhibitors V07.52
  chemotherapeutic agent NEC V07.39
    fluoride V07.31
  diphtheria antitoxin V07.2
  drug V07.39
  estrogen receptor downregulators V07.59
  exemestane (Aromasin) V07.52 ●
  exemestar (Aromasin) V07.52
  fulvestrant (Faslodex) V07.59
  gamma globulin V07.2
  gonadotropin-releasing hormone (GnRH) agonist V07.59
  goserelin acetate (Zoladex) V07.59
  immune sera (gamma globulin) V07.2
  letrozole (Femara) V07.52
  leuprolide acetate (leuprorelin) (Lupron) V07.59
  megestrol acetate (Megace) V07.59
  raloxifene (Evista) V07.51
  RhoGAM V07.2
  selective estrogen receptor modulators (SERMs) V07.51
  tamoxifen (Nolvadex) V07.51
  tetanus antitoxin V07.2
  toremifene (Fareston) V07.51
chemotherapy NEC V07.39
  fluoride V07.31
hormone replacement (postmenopausal) V07.4
immunotherapy V07.2
measure V07.9
  specified type NEC V07.8
medication V07.39
postmenopausal hormone replacement V07.4

☑ Additional Digit Required — Refer to the Tabular List for Digit Selection
▶◀ Revised Text   ● New Line   ▲ Revised Code
▽ Subterms under main terms may continue to next column or page
2010 ICD-9-CM   October 2009 · Volume 2 — 229

[handwritten notes at bottom: Code Also: Genetic Suceptibility V84.XX; Family History V16.XX]

Index

Prophylactic — Psychosis

Prophylactic — *continued*
  sterilization V25.2
Proptosis (ocular) — *see also* Exophthalmos 376.30
  thyroid 242.0 ☑
Propulsion
  eyeball 360.81
Prosecution, anxiety concerning V62.5
Prosopagnosia 368.16
Prostate, prostatic — *see* condition
Prostatism 600.90
  with
    other lower urinary tract symptoms (LUTS) 600.91
    urinary
      obstruction 600.91
      retention 600.91
Prostatitis (congestive) (suppurative) 601.9
  acute 601.0
  cavitary 601.8
  chlamydial 099.54
  chronic 601.1
  diverticular 601.8
  due to Trichomonas (vaginalis) 131.03
  fibrous 600.90
    with
      other lower urinary tract symptoms (LUTS) 600.91
      urinary
        obstruction 600.91
        retention 600.91
  gonococcal (acute) 098.12
    chronic or duration of 2 months or over 098.32
  granulomatous 601.8
  hypertrophic 600.00
    with
      other lower urinary tract symptoms (LUTS) 600.01
      urinary
        obstruction 600.01
        retention 600.01
  specified type NEC 601.8
  subacute 601.1
  trichomonal 131.03
  tuberculous (see also Tuberculosis) 016.5 ☑ [601.4]
Prostatocystitis 601.3
Prostatorrhea 602.8
Prostatoseminovesiculitis, trichomonal 131.03
Prostration 780.79
  heat 992.5
    anhydrotic 992.3
    due to
      salt (and water) depletion 992.4
      water depletion 992.3
  nervous 300.5
  newborn 779.89
  senile 797
Protanomaly 368.51
Protanopia (anomalous trichromat) (complete) (incomplete) 368.51
Protection (against) (from) — *see* Prophylactic
Protein
  deficiency 260
  malnutrition 260
  sickness (prophylactic) (therapeutic) 999.5
Proteinemia 790.99
Proteinosis
  alveolar, lung or pulmonary 516.0
  lipid 272.8
  lipoid (of Urbach) 272.8
Proteinuria — *see also* Albuminuria 791.0
  Bence-Jones NEC 791.0
  gestational 646.2 ☑
    with hypertension — *see* Toxemia, of pregnancy
  orthostatic 593.6
  postural 593.6
Proteolysis, pathologic 286.6
Protocoproporphyria 277.1
Protoporphyria (erythrohepatic) (erythropoietic) 277.1
Protrusio acetabuli 718.65
Protrusion
  acetabulum (into pelvis) 718.65

Protrusion — *continued*
  device, implant, or graft — *see* Complications, mechanical
  ear, congenital 744.29
  intervertebral disc — *see* Displacement, intervertebral disc
  nucleus pulposus — *see* Displacement, intervertebral disc
Proud flesh 701.5
Prune belly (syndrome) 756.71
Prurigo (ferox) (gravis) (Hebra's) (hebrae) (mitis) (simplex) 698.2
  agria 698.3
  asthma syndrome 691.8
  Besnier's (atopic dermatitis) (infantile eczema) 691.8
  eczematodes allergicum 691.8
  estivalis (Hutchinson's) 692.72
  Hutchinson's 692.72
  nodularis 698.3
  psychogenic 306.3
Pruritus, pruritic 698.9
  ani 698.0
    psychogenic 306.3
  conditions NEC 698.9
    psychogenic 306.3
  due to Onchocerca volvulus 125.3
  ear 698.9
  essential 698.9
  genital organ(s) 698.1
    psychogenic 306.3
  gravidarum 646.8 ☑
  hiemalis 698.8
  neurogenic (any site) 306.3
  perianal 698.0
  psychogenic (any site) 306.3
  scrotum 698.1
    psychogenic 306.3
  senile, senilis 698.8
  Trichomonas 131.9
  vulva, vulvae 698.1
    psychogenic 306.3
Psammocarcinoma (M8140/3) — *see* Neoplasm, by site, malignant
Pseudarthrosis, pseudoarthrosis (bone) 733.82
  joint following fusion V45.4
Pseudoacanthosis
  nigricans 701.8
Pseudoaneurysm — *see* Aneurysm
Pseudoangina (pectoris) — *see* Angina
Pseudoangioma 452
Pseudo-Argyll-Robertson pupil 379.45
Pseudoarteriosus 747.89
Pseudoarthrosis — *see* Pseudarthrosis
Pseudoataxia 799.89
Pseudobulbar affect (PBA) 310.8
Pseudobursa 727.89
Pseudocholera 025
Pseudochromidrosis 705.89
Pseudocirrhosis, liver, pericardial 423.2
Pseudocoarctation 747.21
Pseudocowpox 051.1
Pseudocoxalgia 732.1
Pseudocroup 478.75
Pseudocyesis 300.11
Pseudocyst
  lung 518.89
  pancreas 577.2
  retina 361.19
Pseudodementia 300.16
Pseudoelephantiasis neuroarthritica 757.0
Pseudoemphysema 518.89
Pseudoencephalitis
  superior (acute) hemorrhagic 265.1
Pseudoerosion cervix, congenital 752.49
Pseudoexfoliation, lens capsule 366.11
Pseudofracture (idiopathic) (multiple) (spontaneous) (symmetrical) 268.2
Pseudoglanders 025
Pseudoglioma 360.44
Pseudogout — *see* Chondrocalcinosis
Pseudohallucination 780.1
Pseudohemianesthesia 782.0
Pseudohemophilia (Bernuth's) (hereditary) (typeB) 286.4
  type A 287.8

Pseudohemophilia — *continued*
  vascular 287.8
Pseudohermaphroditism 752.7
  with chromosomal anomaly — *see* Anomaly, chromosomal
  adrenal 255.2
  female (without adrenocortical disorder) 752.7
    with adrenocortical disorder 255.2
    adrenal 255.2
  male (without gonadal disorder) 752.7
    with
      adrenocortical disorder 255.2
      cleft scrotum 752.7
      feminizing testis 259.51
      gonadal disorder 257.9
    adrenal 255.2
Pseudohole, macula 362.54
Pseudo-Hurler's disease (mucolipidosis III) 272.7
Pseudohydrocephalus 348.2
Pseudohypertrophic muscular dystrophy (Erb's) 359.1
Pseudohypertrophy, muscle 359.1
Pseudohypoparathyroidism 275.49
Pseudoinfluenza 487.1
Pseudoinsomnia 307.49
Pseudoleukemia 288.8
  infantile 285.8
Pseudomembranous — *see* condition
Pseudomeningocele (cerebral) (infective) 349.2
  postprocedural 997.01
  spinal 349.2
Pseudomenstruation 626.8
Pseudomucinous
  cyst (ovary) (M8470/0) 220
  peritoneum 568.89
Pseudomyeloma 273.1
Pseudomyxoma peritonei (M8480/6) 197.6
Pseudoneuritis optic (nerve) 377.24
  papilla 377.24
    congenital 743.57
Pseudoneuroma — *see* Injury, nerve, by site
Pseudo-obstruction
  intestine (chronic) (idiopathic) (intermittent secondary) (primary) 564.89
  acute 560.89
Pseudopapilledema 377.24
Pseudoparalysis
  arm or leg 781.4
  atonic, congenital 358.8
Pseudopelade 704.09
Pseudophakia V43.1
Pseudopolycythemia 289.0
Pseudopolyposis, colon 556.4
Pseudoporencephaly 348.0
Pseudopseudohypoparathyroidism 275.49
Pseudopsychosis 300.16
Pseudopterygium 372.52
Pseudoptosis (eyelid) 374.34
Pseudorabies 078.89
Pseudoretinitis, pigmentosa 362.65
Pseudorickets 588.0
  senile (Pozzi's) 731.0
Pseudorubella 057.8
Pseudoscarlatina 057.8
Pseudosclerema 778.1
Pseudosclerosis (brain)
  Jakob's 046.19
  of Westphal (-Strümpell) (hepatolenticular degeneration) 275.1
  spastic 046.19
    with dementia
      with behavioral disturbance 046.19 [294.11]
      without behavioral disturbance 046.19 [294.10]
Pseudoseizure 780.39
  non-psychiatric 780.39
  psychiatric 300.11
Pseudotabes 799.89
  diabetic 250.6 ☑ [337.1]
    due to secondary diabetes 249.6 ☑ [337.1]
Pseudotetanus — *see also* Convulsions 780.39
Pseudotetany 781.7
  hysterical 300.11
Pseudothalassemia 285.0
Pseudotrichinosis 710.3

Pseudotruncus arteriosus 747.29
Pseudotuberculosis, pasteurella (infection) 027.2
Pseudotumor
  cerebri 348.2
  orbit (inflammatory) 376.11
Pseudo-Turner's syndrome 759.89
Pseudoxanthoma elasticum 757.39
Psilosis (sprue) (tropical) 579.1
  Monilia 112.89
  nontropical 579.0
  not sprue 704.00
Psittacosis 073.9
Psoitis 728.89
Psora NEC 696.1
Psoriasis 696.1
  any type, except arthropathic 696.1
  arthritic, arthropathic 696.0
  buccal 528.6
  flexural 696.1
  follicularis 696.1
  guttate 696.1
  inverse 696.1
  mouth 528.6
  nummularis 696.1
  psychogenic 316 [696.1]
  punctata 696.1
  pustular 696.1
  rupioides 696.1
  vulgaris 696.1
Psorospermiasis 136.4
Psorospermosis 136.4
  follicularis (vegetans) 757.39
Psychalgia 307.80
Psychasthenia 300.89
  compulsive 300.3
  mixed compulsive states 300.3
  obsession 300.3
Psychiatric disorder or problem NEC 300.9
Psychogenic — *see also* condition
  factors associated with physical conditions 316
Psychoneurosis, psychoneurotic — *see also* Neurosis 300.9
  anxiety (state) 300.00
  climacteric 627.2
  compensation 300.16
  compulsion 300.3
  conversion hysteria 300.11
  depersonalization 300.6
  depressive type 300.4
  dissociative hysteria 300.15
  hypochondriacal 300.7
  hysteria 300.10
    conversion type 300.11
    dissociative type 300.15
  mixed NEC 300.89
  neurasthenic 300.5
  obsessional 300.3
  obsessive-compulsive 300.3
  occupational 300.89
  personality NEC 301.89
  phobia 300.20
  senile NEC 300.89
Psychopathic — *see also* condition
  constitution, posttraumatic 310.2
    with psychosis 293.9
  personality 301.9
    amoral trends 301.7
    antisocial trends 301.7
    asocial trends 301.7
    mixed types 301.7
  state 301.9
Psychopathy, sexual — *see also* Deviation, sexual 302.9
Psychophysiologic, psychophysiological condition — *see* Reaction, psychophysiologic
Psychose passionelle 297.8
Psychosexual identity disorder 302.6
  adult-life 302.85
  childhood 302.6
Psychosis 298.9
  acute hysterical 298.1
  affecting management of pregnancy, childbirth, or puerperium 648.4 ☑

☑ Additional Digit Required — Refer to the Tabular List for Digit Selection   ᵂ Subterms under main terms may continue to next column or page

Psychosis — *continued*
affective (*see also* Disorder, mood) 296.90

ote — Use the following fifth-digit subclassification with categories 296.0–296.6:

   unspecified

   mild

   moderate

   severe, without mention of psychotic
   behavior

   severe, specified as with psychotic
   behavior

5   in partial or unspecified remission

6   in full remission

drug-induced 292.84
due to or associated with physical condition 293.83
involutional 293.83
  recurrent episode 296.3 ☑
  single episode 296.2 ☑
manic-depressive 296.80
  circular (alternating) 296.7
    currently depressed 296.5 ☑
    currently manic 296.4 ☑
  depressed type 296.2 ☑
    atypical 296.82
    recurrent episode 296.3 ☑
    single episode 296.2 ☑
  manic 296.0 ☑
    atypical 296.81
    recurrent episode 296.1 ☑
    single episode 296.0 ☑
  mixed type NEC 296.89
  specified type NEC 296.89
senile 290.21
specified type NEC 296.99
alcoholic 291.9
  with
    anxiety 291.89
    delirium tremens 291.0
    delusions 291.5
    dementia 291.2
    hallucinosis 291.3
    jealousy 291.5
    mood disturbance 291.89
    paranoia 291.5
    persisting amnesia 291.1
    sexual dysfunction 291.89
    sleep disturbance 291.89
  amnestic confabulatory 291.1
  delirium tremens 291.0
  hallucinosis 291.3
  Korsakoff's, Korsakov's, Korsakow's 291.1
  paranoid type 291.5
  pathological intoxication 291.4
  polyneuritic 291.1
  specified type NEC 291.89
alternating (*see also* Psychosis, manic-depressive, circular) 296.7
anergastic (*see also* Psychosis, organic) 294.9
arteriosclerotic 290.40
  with
    acute confusional state 290.41
    delirium 290.41
    delusions 290.42
    depressed mood 290.43
  depressed type 290.43
  paranoid type 290.42
  simple type 290.40
  uncomplicated 290.40
atypical 298.9
  depressive 296.82
  manic 296.81
borderline (schizophrenia) (*see also*
  Schizophrenia) 295.5 ☑
  of childhood (*see also* Psychosis, child-
    hood) 299.8 ☑
  prepubertal 299.8 ☑
brief reactive 298.8

Psychosis — *continued*
childhood, with origin specific to 299.9 ☑

Note — Use the following fifth-digit subclassification with category 299:

0   current or active state

1   residual state

atypical 299.8 ☑
  specified type NEC 299.8 ☑
circular (*see also* Psychosis, manic-depressive,
  circular) 296.7
climacteric (*see also* Psychosis, involutional)
  298.8
confusional 298.9
  acute 293.0
  reactive 298.2
  subacute 293.1
depressive (*see also* Psychosis, affective)
  296.2 ☑
  atypical 296.82
  involutional 296.2 ☑
    with hypomania (bipolar II) 296.89
    recurrent episode 296.3 ☑
    single episode 296.2 ☑
  psychogenic 298.0
  reactive (emotional stress) (psychological
    trauma) 298.0
  recurrent episode 296.3 ☑
    with hypomania (bipolar II) 296.89
  single episode 296.2 ☑
disintegrative, childhood (*see also* Psychosis,
  childhood) 299.1 ☑
drug 292.9
  with
    affective syndrome 292.84
    amnestic syndrome 292.83
    anxiety 292.89
    delirium 292.81
      withdrawal 292.0
    delusions 292.11
    dementia 292.82
    depressive state 292.84
    hallucinations 292.12
    hallucinosis 292.12
    mood disorder 292.84
    mood disturbance 292.84
    organic personality syndrome NEC
      292.89
    sexual dysfunction 292.89
    sleep disturbance 292.89
    withdrawal syndrome (and delirium)
      292.0
  affective syndrome 292.84
  delusions 292.11
  hallucinatory state 292.12
  hallucinosis 292.12
  paranoid state 292.11
  specified type NEC 292.89
  withdrawal syndrome (and delirium) 292.0
due to or associated with physical condition
  (*see also* Psychosis, organic) 293.9
epileptic NEC 294.8
excitation (psychogenic) (reactive) 298.1
exhaustive (*see also* Reaction, stress, acute)
  308.9
hypomanic (*see also* Psychosis, affective)
  296.0 ☑
  recurrent episode 296.1 ☑
  single episode 296.0 ☑
hysterical 298.8
  acute 298.1
in
  conditions classified elsewhere
    with
      delusions 293.81
      hallucinations 293.82
  pregnancy, childbirth, or puerperium
    648.4 ☑
incipient 298.8
  schizophrenic (*see also* Schizophrenia)
    295.5 ☑
induced 297.3
infantile (*see also* Psychosis, childhood)
  299.0 ☑
infective 293.9

Psychosis — *continued*
infective — *continued*
  acute 293.0
  subacute 293.1
interactional (childhood) (*see also* Psychosis,
  childhood) 299.1 ☑
involutional 298.8
  depressive (*see also* Psychosis, affective)
    296.2 ☑
    recurrent episode 296.3 ☑
    single episode 296.2 ☑
  melancholic 296.2 ☑
    recurrent episode 296.3 ☑
    single episode 296.2 ☑
  paranoid state 297.2
  paraphrenia 297.2
Korsakoff's, Korakov's, Korsakow's (nonalcoholic) 294.0
  alcoholic 291.1
mania (phase) (*see also* Psychosis, affective)
  296.0 ☑
  recurrent episode 296.1 ☑
  single episode 296.0 ☑
manic (*see also* Psychosis, affective) 296.0 ☑
  atypical 296.81
  recurrent episode 296.1 ☑
  single episode 296.0 ☑
manic-depressive 296.80
  circular 296.7
    currently
      depressed 296.5 ☑
      manic 296.4 ☑
      mixed 296.6 ☑
  depressive 296.2 ☑
    recurrent episode 296.3 ☑
      with hypomania (bipolar II) 296.89
    single episode 296.2 ☑
  hypomanic 296.0 ☑
    recurrent episode 296.1 ☑
    single episode 296.0 ☑
  manic 296.0 ☑
    atypical 296.81
    recurrent episode 296.1 ☑
    single episode 296.0 ☑
  mixed NEC 296.89
  perplexed 296.89
  stuporous 296.89
menopausal (*see also* Psychosis, involutional)
  298.8
mixed schizophrenic and affective (*see also*
  Schizophrenia) 295.7 ☑
multi-infarct (cerebrovascular) (*see also* Psychosis, arteriosclerotic) 290.40
organic NEC 294.9
  due to or associated with
    addiction
      alcohol (*see also* Psychosis, alco-
        holic) 291.9
      drug (*see also* Psychosis, drug)
        292.9
    alcohol intoxication, acute (*see also*
      Psychosis, alcoholic) 291.9
    alcoholism (*see also* Psychosis, alco-
      holic) 291.9
    arteriosclerosis (cerebral) (*see also* Psy-
      chosis, arteriosclerotic) 290.40
    cerebrovascular disease
      acute (psychosis) 293.0
      arteriosclerotic (*see also* Psychosis,
        arteriosclerotic) 290.40
    childbirth — *see* Psychosis, puerperal
    dependence
      alcohol (*see also* Psychosis, alco-
        holic) 291.9
      drug 292.9
    disease
      alcoholic liver (*see also* Psychosis,
        alcoholic) 291.9
      brain
        arteriosclerotic (*see also* Psy-
          chosis, arteriosclerotic)
          290.40
      cerebrovascular
        acute (psychosis) 293.0

Psychosis — *continued*
organic — *continued*
  due to or associated with — *continued*
    disease — *continued*
      cerebrovascular — *continued*
        arteriosclerotic (*see also* Psy-
          chosis, arteriosclerotic)
          290.40
      endocrine or metabolic 293.9
        acute (psychosis) 293.0
        subacute (psychosis) 293.1
      Jakob-Creutzfeldt 046.19
        with behavioral disturbance
          046.19 [294.11]
        without behavioral disturbance
          046.19 [294.10]
        familial 046.19
        iatrogenic 046.19
        specified NEC 046.19
        sporadic 046.19
        variant 046.11
          with dementia
            with behavioral distur-
              bance
              046.11 [294.11]
            without behavioral dis-
              turbance
              046.11 [294.10]
      liver, alcoholic (*see also* Psychosis,
        alcoholic) 291.9
    disorder
      cerebrovascular
        acute (psychosis) 293.0
      endocrine or metabolic 293.9
        acute (psychosis) 293.0
        subacute (psychosis) 293.1
    epilepsy
      with behavioral disturbance
        345.9 ☑ [294.11]
      without behavioral disturbance
        345.9 ☑ [294.10]
      transient (acute) 293.0
    Huntington's chorea
      with behavioral disturbance
        333.4 [294.11]
      without behavioral disturbance
        333.4 [294.10]
    infection
      brain 293.9
        acute (psychosis) 293.0
        chronic 294.8
        subacute (psychosis) 293.1
      intracranial NEC 293.9
        acute (psychosis) 293.0
        chronic 294.8
        subacute (psychosis) 293.1
    intoxication
      alcoholic (acute) (*see also* Psychosis,
        alcoholic) 291.9
        pathological 291.4
      drug (*see also* Psychosis, drug)
        292.2
    ischemia
      cerebrovascular (generalized) (*see*
        also Psychosis, arteriosclerot-
        ic) 290.40
    Jakob-Creutzfeldt disease (syndrome)
      046.19
      with behavioral disturbance
        046.19 [294.11]
      without behavioral disturbance
        046.19 [294.10]
      variant 046.11
        with dementia
          with behavioral disturbance
            046.11 [294.11]
          without behavioral distur-
            bance
            046.11 [294.10]
    multiple sclerosis
      with behavioral disturbance
        340 [294.11]
      without behavioral disturbance
        340 [294.10]
    physical condition NEC 293.9

Psychosis — *continued*
organic — *continued*
due to or associated with — *continued*
physical condition — *continued*
with
delusions 293.81
hallucinations 293.82
presenility 290.10
puerperium — *see* Psychosis, puerperal
sclerosis, multiple
with behavioral disturbance
340 *[294.11]*
without behavioral disturbance
340 *[294.10]*
senility 290.20
status epilepticus
with behavioral disturbance
345.3 *[294.11]*
without behavioral disturbance
345.3 *[294.10]*
trauma
brain (birth) (from electrical current)
(surgical) 293.9
acute (psychosis) 293.0
chronic 294.8
subacute (psychosis) 293.1
unspecified physical condition
293.9
with
delusion 293.81
hallucinations 293.82
infective 293.9
acute (psychosis) 293.0
subacute 293.1
posttraumatic 293.9
acute 293.0
subacute 293.1
specified type NEC 294.8
transient 293.9
with
anxiety 293.84
delusions 293.81
depression 293.83
hallucinations 293.82
depressive type 293.83
hallucinatory type 293.82
paranoid type 293.81
specified type NEC 293.89
paranoic 297.1
paranoid (chronic) 297.9
alcoholic 291.5
chronic 297.1
climacteric 297.2
involutional 297.2
menopausal 297.2
protracted reactive 298.4
psychogenic 298.4
acute 298.3
schizophrenic (*see also* Schizophrenia)
295.3 ✓
senile 290.20
paroxysmal 298.9
senile 290.20
polyneuritic, alcoholic 291.1
postoperative 293.9
postpartum — *see* Psychosis, puerperal
prepsychotic (*see also* Schizophrenia) 295.5 ✓
presbyophrenic (type) 290.8
presenile (*see also* Dementia, presenile) 290.10
prison 300.16
psychogenic 298.8
depressive 298.0
paranoid 298.4
acute 298.3
puerperal
specified type — *see* categories
295-298 ✓
unspecified type 293.89
acute 293.0
chronic 293.89
subacute 293.1
reactive (emotional stress) (psychological
trauma) 298.8
brief 298.8
confusion 298.2
depressive 298.0

Psychosis — *continued*
reactive — *continued*
excitation 298.1
schizo-affective (depressed) (excited) (*see also*
Schizophrenia) 295.7 ✓
schizophrenia, schizophrenic (*see also*
Schizophrenia) 295.9 ✓
borderline type 295.5 ✓
of childhood (*see also* Psychosis, childhood) 299.8 ✓
catatonic (excited) (withdrawn) 295.2 ✓
childhood type (*see also* Psychosis, childhood) 299.9 ✓
hebephrenic 295.1 ✓
incipient 295.5 ✓
latent 295.5 ✓
paranoid 295.3 ✓
prepsychotic 295.5 ✓
prodromal 295.5 ✓
pseudoneurotic 295.5 ✓
pseudopsychopathic 295.5 ✓
schizophreniform 295.4 ✓
simple 295.0 ✓
undifferentiated type 295.9 ✓
schizophreniform 295.4 ✓
senile NEC 290.20
with
delusional features 290.20
depressive features 290.21
depressed type 290.21
paranoid type 290.20
simple deterioration 290.20
specified type — *see* categories
295-298 ✓
shared 297.3
situational (reactive) 298.8
symbiotic (childhood) (*see also* Psychosis,
childhood) 299.1 ✓
toxic (acute) 293.9
Psychotic — *see also* condition 298.9
episode 298.9
due to or associated with physical conditions (*see also* Psychosis, organic)
293.9
Pterygium (eye) 372.40
central 372.43
colli 744.5
double 372.44
peripheral (stationary) 372.41
progressive 372.42
recurrent 372.45
Ptilosis 374.55
PTLD (post-transplant lymphoproliferative disorder) 238.77
Ptomaine (poisoning) — *see also* Poisoning, food
005.9
Ptosis (adiposa) 374.30
breast 611.81
cecum 569.89
colon 569.89
congenital (eyelid) 743.61
specified site NEC — *see* Anomaly, specified type NEC
epicanthus syndrome 270.2
eyelid 374.30
congenital 743.61
mechanical 374.33
myogenic 374.32
paralytic 374.31
gastric 537.5
intestine 569.89
kidney (*see also* Disease, renal) 593.0
congenital 753.3
liver 573.8
renal (*see also* Disease, renal) 593.0
congenital 753.3
splanchnic 569.89
spleen 289.59
stomach 537.5
viscera 569.89
PTSD (Post-traumatic stress disorder) 309.81
Ptyalism 527.7
hysterical 300.11
periodic 527.2
pregnancy 646.8 ✓
psychogenic 306.4

Ptyalolithiasis 527.5
Pubalgia 848.8
Pubarche, precocious 259.1
Pubertas praecox 259.1
Puberty V21.1
abnormal 259.9
bleeding 626.3
delayed 259.0
precocious (constitutional) (cryptogenic) (idiopathic) NEC 259.1
due to
adrenal
cortical hyperfunction 255.2
hyperplasia 255.2
cortical hyperfunction 255.2
ovarian hyperfunction 256.1
estrogen 256.0
pineal tumor 259.8
testicular hyperfunction 257.0
premature 259.1
due to
adrenal cortical hyperfunction 255.2
pineal tumor 259.8
pituitary (anterior) hyperfunction 253.1
Puckering, macula 362.56
Pudenda, pudendum — *see* condition
Puente's disease (simple glandular cheilitis)
528.5
Puerperal
abscess
areola 675.1 ✓
Bartholin's gland 646.6 ✓
breast 675.1 ✓
cervix (uteri) 670.8 ✓ ▲
fallopian tube 670.8 ✓ ▲
genital organ 670.8 ✓ ▲
kidney 646.6 ✓
mammary 675.1 ✓
mesosalpinx 670.8 ✓ ▲
nabothian 646.6 ✓
nipple 675.0 ✓
ovary, ovarian 670.8 ✓ ▲
oviduct 670.8 ✓ ▲
parametric 670.8 ✓ ▲
para-uterine 670.8 ✓ ▲
pelvic 670.8 ✓ ▲
perimetric 670.8 ✓ ▲
periuterine 670.8 ✓ ▲
retro-uterine 670.8 ✓ ▲
subareolar 675.1 ✓
suprapelvic 670.8 ✓ ▲
tubal (ruptured) 670.8 ✓ ▲
tubo-ovarian 670.8 ✓ ▲
urinary tract NEC 646.6 ✓
uterine, uterus 670.8 ✓ ▲
vagina (wall) 646.6 ✓
vaginorectal 646.6 ✓
vulvovaginal gland 646.6 ✓
accident 674.9 ✓
adnexitis 670.8 ✓ ▲
afibrinogenemia, or other coagulation defect
666.3 ✓
albuminuria (acute) (subacute) 646.2 ✓
pre-eclamptic 642.4 ✓
anemia (conditions classifiable to 280–285)
648.2 ✓
anuria 669.3 ✓
apoplexy 674.0 ✓
asymptomatic bacteriuria 646.5 ✓
atrophy, breast 676.3 ✓
blood dyscrasia 666.3 ✓
caked breast 676.2 ✓
cardiomyopathy 674.5 ✓
cellulitis — *see* Puerperal, abscess
cerebrovascular disorder (conditions classifiable to 430–434, 436–437) 674.0 ✓
cervicitis (conditions classifiable to 616.0)
646.6 ✓
coagulopathy (any) 666.3 ✓
complications 674.9 ✓
specified type NEC 674.8 ✓
convulsions (eclamptic) (uremic) 642.6 ✓
with pre-existing hypertension 642.7 ✓
cracked nipple 676.1 ✓

Puerperal — *continued*
cystitis 646.6 ✓
cystopyelitis 646.6 ✓
deciduitis (acute) 670.8 ✓
delirium NEC 293.9
diabetes (mellitus) (conditions classifiabl
249 and 250) 648.0 ✓
disease 674.9 ✓
breast NEC 676.3 ✓
cerebrovascular (acute) 674.0 ✓
nonobstetric NEC (*see also* Pregnancy,
complicated, current disease o
condition) 648.9 ✓
pelvis inflammatory 670.8 ✓
renal NEC 646.2 ✓
tubo-ovarian 670.8 ✓
Valsuani's (progressive pernicious aner
648.2 ✓
disorder
lactation 676.9 ✓
specified type NEC 676.8 ✓
nonobstetric NEC (*see also* Pregnancy,
complicated, current disease o
condition) 648.9 ✓
disruption
cesarean wound 674.1 ✓
episiotomy wound 674.2 ✓
perineal laceration wound 674.2 ✓
drug dependence (conditions classifiable
304) 648.3 ✓
eclampsia 642.6 ✓
with pre-existing hypertension 642.7
embolism (pulmonary) 673.2 ✓
air 673.0 ✓
amniotic fluid 673.1 ✓
blood-clot 673.2 ✓
brain or cerebral 674.0 ✓
cardiac 674.8 ✓
fat 673.8 ✓
intracranial sinus (venous) 671.5 ✓
pyemic 673.3 ✓
septic 673.3 ✓
spinal cord 671.5 ✓
endometritis (conditions classifiable to
615.0–615.9) 670.1 ✓
endophlebitis — *see* Puerperal, phlebitis
endotrachelitis 646.6 ✓
engorgement, breasts 676.2 ✓
erysipelas 670.8 ✓
failure
lactation 676.4 ✓
renal, acute 669.3 ✓
fever 670.8 ✓
meaning pyrexia (of unknown origin)
672.0 ✓
meaning sepsis 670.2 ✓
fissure, nipple 676.1 ✓
fistula
breast 675.1 ✓
mammary gland 675.1 ✓
nipple 675.0 ✓
galactophoritis 675.2 ✓
galactorrhea 676.6 ✓
gangrene
gas 670.8 ✓
with sepsis 670.2 ✓
uterus 670.8 ✓
gonorrhea (conditions classifiable to 098)
647.1 ✓
hematoma, subdural 674.0 ✓
hematosalpinx, infectional 670.8 ✓
hemiplegia, cerebral 674.0 ✓
hemorrhage 666.1 ✓
brain 674.0 ✓
bulbar 674.0 ✓
cerebellar 674.0 ✓
cerebral 674.0 ✓
cortical 674.0 ✓
delayed (after 24 hours) (uterine) 666.2 ✓
extradural 674.0 ✓
internal capsule 674.0 ✓
intracranial 674.0 ✓
intrapontine 674.0 ✓
meningeal 674.0 ✓

rperal — *continued*
hemorrhage — *continued*
  pontine 674.0 ☑
  subarachnoid 674.0 ☑
  subcortical 674.0 ☑
  subdural 674.0 ☑
  uterine, delayed 666.2 ☑
  ventricular 674.0 ☑
hemorrhoids 671.8 ☑
hepatorenal syndrome 674.8 ☑
hypertrophy
  breast 676.3 ☑
  mammary gland 676.3 ☑
induration breast (fibrous) 676.3 ☑
infarction
  lung — *see* Puerperal, embolism
  pulmonary — *see* Puerperal, embolism
infection
  Bartholin's gland 646.6 ☑
  breast 675.2 ☑
    with nipple 675.9 ☑
      specified type NEC 675.8 ☑
  cervix 646.6 ☑
  endocervix 646.6 ☑
  fallopian tube 670.8 ☑ ▲
  generalized 670.0 ☑
  genital tract (major) 670.0 ☑
    minor or localized 646.6 ☑
  kidney (bacillus coli) 646.6 ☑
  mammary gland 675.2 ☑
    with nipple 675.9 ☑
      specified type NEC 675.8 ☑
  nipple 675.0 ☑
    with breast 675.9 ☑
      specified type NEC 675.8 ☑
  ovary 670.8 ☑ ▲
  pelvic 670.8 ☑ ▲
  peritoneum 670.8 ☑ ▲
  renal 646.6 ☑
  tubo-ovarian 670.8 ☑ ▲
  urinary (tract) NEC 646.6 ☑
    asymptomatic 646.5 ☑
  uterus, uterine 670.8 ☑
  vagina 646.6 ☑
inflammation (*see also* Puerperal, infection)
  areola 675.1 ☑
  Bartholin's gland 646.6 ☑
  breast 675.2 ☑
  broad ligament 670.8 ☑ ▲
  cervix (uteri) 646.6 ☑
  fallopian tube 670.8 ☑ ▲
  genital organs 670.8 ☑ ▲
    localized 646.6 ☑
  mammary gland 675.2 ☑
  nipple 675.0 ☑
  ovary 670.8 ☑ ▲
  oviduct 670.8 ☑ ▲
  pelvis 670.8 ☑ ▲
  periuterine 670.8 ☑ ▲
  tubal 670.8 ☑ ▲
  vagina 646.6 ☑
  vein — *see* Puerperal, phlebitis
inversion, nipple 676.3 ☑
ischemia, cerebral 674.0 ☑
lymphangitis 670.8 ☑ ▲
  breast 675.2 ☑
malaria (conditions classifiable to 084)
    647.4 ☑
malnutrition 648.9 ☑
mammillitis 675.0 ☑
mammitis 675.2 ☑
mania 296.0 ☑
  recurrent episode 296.1 ☑
  single episode 296.0 ☑
mastitis 675.2 ☑
  purulent 675.1 ☑
  retromammary 675.1 ☑
  submammary 675.1 ☑
melancholia 296.2 ☑
  recurrent episode 296.3 ☑
  single episode 296.2 ☑

Puerperal — *continued*
mental disorder (conditions classifiable to 290–303, 305.0, 305.2–305.9, 306–316, 317–319) 648.4 ☑
metritis (suppurative) 670.1 ☑ ▲
  septic 670.2 ☑ ●
metroperitonitis 670.8 ☑ ▲
metrorrhagia 666.2 ☑
metrosalpingitis 670.8 ☑ ▲
metrovaginitis 670.8 ☑ ▲
milk leg 671.4 ☑
monoplegia, cerebral 674.0 ☑
necrosis
  kidney, tubular 669.3 ☑
  liver (acute) (subacute) (conditions classifiable to 570) 674.8 ☑
  ovary 670.8 ☑ ▲
  renal cortex 669.3 ☑
nephritis or nephrosis (conditions classifiable to 580–589) 646.2 ☑
  with hypertension 642.1 ☑
nutritional deficiency (conditions classifiable to 260–269) 648.9 ☑
occlusion, precerebral artery 674.0 ☑
oliguria 669.3 ☑
oophoritis 670.8 ☑ ▲
ovaritis 670.8 ☑ ▲
paralysis
  bladder (sphincter) 665.5 ☑
  cerebral 674.0 ☑
paralytic stroke 674.0 ☑
parametritis 670.8 ☑ ▲
paravaginitis 670.8 ☑
pelviperitonitis 670.8 ☑ ▲
perimetritis 670.8 ☑ ▲
perimetrosalpingitis 670.8 ☑ ▲
perinephritis 646.6 ☑
perioophoritis 670.8 ☑ ▲
periphlebitis — *see* Puerperal, phlebitis
perisalpingitis 670.8 ☑ ▲
peritoneal infection 670.8 ☑ ▲
peritonitis (pelvic) 670.8 ☑ ▲
perivaginitis 646.6 ☑
phlebitis 671.2 ☑ ▲
  deep 671.4 ☑
  intracranial sinus (venous) 671.5 ☑
  pelvic 671.4 ☑
  specified site NEC 671.5 ☑
  superficial 671.2 ☑
phlegmasia alba dolens 671.4 ☑
placental polyp 674.4 ☑
pneumonia, embolic — *see* Puerperal, embolism
prediabetes 648.8 ☑
pre-eclampsia (mild) 642.4 ☑
  with pre-existing hypertension 642.7 ☑
  severe 642.5 ☑
psychosis, unspecified (*see also* Psychosis, puerperal) 293.89
pyelitis 646.6 ☑
pyelocystitis 646.6 ☑
pyelohydronephrosis 646.6 ☑
pyelonephritis 646.6 ☑
pyelonephrosis 646.6 ☑
pyemia 670.2 ☑ ▲
pyocystitis 646.6 ☑
pyohemia 670.2 ☑ ▲
pyometra 670.8 ☑ ▲
pyonephritis 646.6 ☑
pyonephrosis 646.6 ☑
pyo-oophoritis 670.8 ☑ ▲
pyosalpingitis 670.8 ☑ ▲
pyosalpinx 670.8 ☑ ▲
pyrexia (of unknown origin) 672.0 ☑
renal
  disease NEC 646.2 ☑
  failure, acute 669.3 ☑
retention
  decidua (fragments) (with delayed hemorrhage) 666.2 ☑
    without hemorrhage 667.1 ☑
  placenta (fragments) (with delayed hemorrhage) 666.2 ☑
    without hemorrhage 667.1 ☑

Puerperal — *continued*
retention — *continued*
  secundines (fragments) (with delayed hemorrhage) 666.2 ☑
    without hemorrhage 667.1 ☑
retracted nipple 676.0 ☑
rubella (conditions classifiable to 056) 647.5 ☑
salpingitis 670.8 ☑ ▲
salpingo-oophoritis 670.8 ☑ ▲
salpingo-ovaritis 670.8 ☑ ▲
salpingoperitonitis 670.8 ☑ ▲
sapremia 670.2 ☑ ▲
secondary perineal tear 674.2 ☑
sepsis (pelvic) 670.2 ☑ ▲
septicemia 670.2 ☑ ▲
subinvolution (uterus) 674.8 ☑
sudden death (cause unknown) 674.9 ☑
suppuration — *see* Puerperal, abscess
syphilis (conditions classifiable to 090–097) 647.0 ☑
tetanus 670.8 ☑
thelitis 675.0 ☑
thrombocytopenia 666.3 ☑
thrombophlebitis (superficial) 671.2 ☑
  deep 671.4 ☑
  pelvic 671.4 ☑
  septic 670.3 ☑ ●
  specified site NEC 671.5 ☑
thrombosis (venous) — *see* Thrombosis, puerperal
thyroid dysfunction (conditions classifiable to 240–246) 648.1 ☑
toxemia (*see also* Toxemia, of pregnancy) 642.4 ☑
  eclamptic 642.6 ☑
    with pre-existing hypertension 642.7 ☑
  pre-eclamptic (mild) 642.4 ☑
    with
      convulsions 642.6 ☑
      pre-existing hypertension 642.7 ☑
    severe 642.5 ☑
tuberculosis (conditions classifiable to 010–018) 647.3 ☑
uremia 669.3 ☑
vaginitis (conditions classifiable to 616.1) 646.6 ☑
varicose veins (legs) 671.0 ☑
  vulva or perineum 671.1 ☑
venous complication 671.9 ☑ ●
vulvitis (conditions classifiable to 616.1) 646.6 ☑
vulvovaginitis (conditions classifiable to 616.1) 646.6 ☑
white leg 671.4 ☑
Pulled muscle — *see* Sprain, by site
Pulmolithiasis 518.89
Pulmonary — *see* condition
Pulmonitis (unknown etiology) 486
Pulpitis (acute) (anachoretic) (chronic) (hyperplastic) (putrescent) (suppurative) (ulcerative) 522.0
Pulpless tooth 522.9
Pulse
  alternating 427.89
    psychogenic 306.2
  bigeminal 427.89
  fast 785.0
  feeble, rapid, due to shock following injury 958.4
  rapid 785.0
  slow 427.89
  strong 785.9
  trigeminal 427.89
  water-hammer (*see also* Insufficiency, aortic) 424.1
  weak 785.9
Pulseless disease 446.7
Pulsus
  alternans or trigeminy 427.89
    psychogenic 306.2
Punch drunk 310.2
Puncta lacrimalia occlusion 375.52
Punctiform hymen 752.49

Puncture (traumatic) — *see also* Wound, open, by site
accidental, complicating surgery 998.2
bladder, nontraumatic 596.6
by
  device, implant, or graft — *see* Complications, mechanical
  foreign body
    internal organs (*see also* Injury, internal, by site)
      by ingested object — *see* Foreign body
    left accidentally in operation wound 998.4
  instrument (any) during a procedure, accidental 998.2
internal organs, abdomen, chest, or pelvis — *see* Injury, internal, by site
kidney, nontraumatic 593.89
Pupil — *see* condition
Pupillary membrane 364.74
  persistent 743.46
Pupillotonia 379.46
  pseudotabetic 379.46
Purpura 287.2
abdominal 287.0
allergic 287.0
anaphylactoid 287.0
annularis telangiectodes 709.1
arthritic 287.0
autoerythrocyte sensitization 287.2
autoimmune 287.0
bacterial 287.0
Bateman's (senile) 287.2
capillary fragility (hereditary) (idiopathic) 287.8
cryoglobulinemic 273.2
devil's pinches 287.2
fibrinolytic (*see also* Fibrinolysis) 286.6
fulminans, fulminous 286.6
gangrenous 287.0
hemorrhagic (*see also* Purpura, thrombocytopenic) 287.39
  nodular 272.7
  nonthrombocytopenic 287.0
  thrombocytopenic 287.39
Henoch's (purpura nervosa) 287.0
Henoch-Schönlein (allergic) 287.0
hypergammaglobulinemic (benign primary) (Waldenström's) 273.0
idiopathic 287.31
  nonthrombocytopenic 287.0
  thrombocytopenic 287.31
immune thrombocytopenic 287.31
infectious 287.0
malignant 287.0
neonatorum 772.6
nervosa 287.0
newborn NEC 772.6
nonthrombocytopenic 287.2
  hemorrhagic 287.0
  idiopathic 287.0
nonthrombopenic 287.2
peliosis rheumatica 287.0
pigmentaria, progressiva 709.09
posttransfusion 287.4
primary 287.0
primitive 287.0
red cell membrane sensitivity 287.2
rheumatica 287.0
Schönlein (-Henoch) (allergic) 287.0
scorbutic 267
senile 287.2
simplex 287.2
symptomatica 287.0
telangiectasia annularis 709.1
thrombocytopenic (*see also* Thrombocytopenia) 287.30
  congenital 287.33
  essential 287.30
  hereditary 287.31
  idiopathic 287.31
  immune 287.31
  neonatal, transitory (*see also* Thrombocytopenia, neonatal transitory) 776.1
  primary 287.30
  puerperal, postpartum 666.3 ☑

☑ Additional Digit Required — Refer to the Tabular List for Digit Selection   Subterms under main terms may continue to next column or page

Purpura — continued
  thrombocytopenic (see also Thrombocytope-
    nia) — continued
    thrombotic 446.6
  thrombohemolytic (see also Fibrinolysis) 286.6
  thrombopenic (see also Thrombocytopenia)
    287.30
    congenital 287.33
    essential 287.30
    thrombotic 446.6
      thrombocytic 446.6
      thrombocytopenic 446.6
  toxic 287.0
  variolosa 050.0
  vascular 287.0
  visceral symptoms 287.0
  Werlhof's (see also Purpura, thrombocytopenic)
    287.39
Purpuric spots 782.7
Purulent — see condition
Pus
  absorption, general — see Septicemia
  in
    stool 792.1
    urine 791.9
  tube (rupture) (see also Salpingo-oophoritis)
    614.2
Pustular rash 782.1
Pustule 686.9
  malignant 022.0
  nonmalignant 686.9
Putnam-Dana syndrome (subacute combined
  sclerosis with pernicious anemia)
  281.0 [336.2]
Putnam's disease (subacute combined sclerosis
  with pernicious anemia) 281.0 [336.2]
Putrefaction, intestinal 569.89
Putrescent pulp (dental) 522.1
Pyarthritis — see Pyarthrosis
Pyarthrosis — see also Arthritis, pyogenic
  711.0 ☑
  tuberculous — see Tuberculosis, joint
Pycnoepilepsy, pycnolepsy (idiopathic) — see
  also Epilepsy 345.0 ☑
Pyelectasia 593.89
Pyelectasis 593.89
Pyelitis (congenital) (uremic) 590.80
  with
    abortion — see Abortion, by type, with
      specified complication NEC
    contracted kidney 590.00
    ectopic pregnancy (see also categories
      633.0–633.9) 639.8
    molar pregnancy (see also categories
      630–632) 639.8
  acute 590.10
    with renal medullary necrosis 590.11
  chronic 590.00
    with
      renal medullary necrosis 590.01
  complicating pregnancy, childbirth, or puer-
    perium 646.6 ☑
    affecting fetus or newborn 760.1
  cystica 590.3
  following
    abortion 639.8
    ectopic or molar pregnancy 639.8
  gonococcal 098.19
    chronic or duration of 2 months or over
      098.39
  tuberculous (see also Tuberculosis)
    016.0 ☑ [590.81]
Pyelocaliectasis 593.89
Pyelocystitis — see also Pyelitis 590.80
Pyelohydronephrosis 591
Pyelonephritis — see also Pyelitis 590.80
  acute 590.10
    with renal medullary necrosis 590.11
  chronic 590.00
  syphilitic (late) 095.4
  tuberculous (see also Tuberculosis)
    016.0 ☑ [590.81]
Pyelonephrosis — see also Pyelitis 590.80
  chronic 590.00
Pyelophlebitis 451.89
Pyelo-ureteritis cystica 590.3

(handwritten margin note:) Infection of the upper urinary tract (physicians may use the term "UTI")

Pyemia, pyemic (purulent) — see also Septicemia 038.9
  abscess — see Abscess
  arthritis (see also Arthritis, pyogenic) 711.0 ☑
  Bacillus coli 038.42
  embolism (see also Septicemia) 415.12
  fever 038.9
  infection 038.9
  joint (see also Arthritis, pyogenic) 711.0 ☑
  liver 572.1
  meningococcal 036.2
  newborn 771.81
  phlebitis — see Phlebitis
  pneumococcal 038.2
  portal 572.1
  postvaccinal 999.39
  puerperal 670.2 ☑ ●
  specified organism NEC 038.8
  staphylococcal 038.10
    aureus 038.11
      methicillin
        resistant 038.12
        susceptible 038.11
    specified organism NEC 038.19
  streptococcal 038.0
  tuberculous — see Tuberculosis, miliary
Pygopagus 759.4
Pykno-epilepsy, pyknolepsy (idiopathic) — see
  also Epilepsy 345.0 ☑
Pyle (-Cohn) disease (craniometaphyseal dysplasia) 756.89
Pylephlebitis (suppurative) 572.1
Pylethrombophlebitis 572.1
Pylethrombosis 572.1
Pyloritis — see also Gastritis 535.5 ☑
Pylorospasm (reflex) 537.81
  congenital or infantile 750.5
  neurotic 306.4
  newborn 750.5
  psychogenic 306.4
Pylorus, pyloric — see condition
Pyoarthrosis — see Pyarthrosis
Pyocele
  mastoid 383.00
  sinus (accessory) (nasal) (see also Sinusitis)
    473.9
  turbinate (bone) 473.9
  urethra (see also Urethritis) 597.0
Pyococcal dermatitis 686.00
Pyococcide, skin 686.00
Pyocolpos — see also Vaginitis 616.10
Pyocyaneus dermatitis 686.09
Pyocystitis — see also Cystitis 595.9
Pyoderma, pyodermia 686.00
  gangrenosum 686.01
  specified type NEC 686.09
  vegetans 686.8
Pyodermatitis 686.00
  vegetans 686.8
Pyogenic — see condition
Pyohemia — see Septicemia
Pyohydronephrosis — see Pyelitis 590.80
Pyometra 615.9
Pyometritis — see also Endometritis 615.9
Pyometrium — see Endometritis 615.9
Pyomyositis 728.0
  ossificans 728.19
  tropical (bungpagga) 040.81
Pyonephritis — see also Pyelitis 590.80
  chronic 590.00
Pyonephrosis (congenital) — see also Pyelitis
  590.80
  acute 590.10
Pyo-oophoritis — see also Salpingo-oophoritis
  614.2
Pyo-ovarium — see also Salpingo-oophoritis
  614.2
Pyopericarditis 420.99
Pyopericardium 420.99
Pyophlebitis — see Phlebitis
Pyopneumopericardium 420.99
Pyopneumothorax (infectional) 510.9
  with fistula 510.0
  subdiaphragmatic (see also Peritonitis) 567.29
  subphrenic (see also Peritonitis) 567.29

Pyopneumothorax — continued
  tuberculous (see also Tuberculosis, pleura)
    012.0 ☑
Pyorrhea (alveolar) (alveolaris) 523.40
  degenerative 523.5
Pyosalpingitis — see also Salpingo-oophoritis
  614.2
Pyosalpinx — see also Salpingo-oophoritis 614.2
Pyosepticemia — see Septicemia
Pyosis
  Corlett's (impetigo) 684
  Manson's (pemphigus contagiosus) 684
Pyothorax 510.9
  with fistula 510.0
  tuberculous (see also Tuberculosis, pleura)
    012.0 ☑
Pyoureter 593.89
  tuberculous (see also Tuberculosis) 016.2 ☑
Pyramidopallidonigral syndrome 332.0
Pyrexia (of unknown origin) (P.U.O.) 780.60
  atmospheric 992.0
  during labor 659.2 ☑
  environmentally-induced newborn 778.4
  heat 992.0
  newborn, environmentally-induced 778.4
  puerperal 672.0 ☑
Pyroglobulinemia 273.8
Pyromania 312.33
Pyrosis 787.1
Pyrroloporphyria 277.1
Pyuria (bacterial) 791.9

Q

Q fever 083.0
  with pneumonia 083.0 [484.8]
Quadricuspid aortic valve 746.89
Quadrilateral fever 083.0
Quadriparesis — see Quadriplegia
  meaning muscle weakness 728.87
Quadriplegia 344.00
  with fracture, vertebra (process) — see Frac-
    ture, vertebra, cervical, with spinal cord
    injury
  brain (current episode) 437.8
  C1-C4
    complete 344.01
    incomplete 344.02
  C5-C7
    complete 344.03
    incomplete 344.04
  cerebral (current episode) 437.8
  congenital or infantile (cerebral) (spastic)
    (spinal) 343.2
  cortical 437.8
  embolic (current episode) (see also Embolism,
    brain) 434.1 ☑
  functional 780.72
  infantile (cerebral) (spastic) (spinal) 343.2
  newborn NEC 767.0
  specified NEC 344.09
  thrombotic (current episode) (see also
    Thrombosis, brain) 434.0 ☑
  traumatic — see Injury, spinal, cervical
Quadruplet
  affected by maternal complications of preg-
    nancy 761.5
  healthy liveborn — see Newborn, multiple
  pregnancy (complicating delivery) NEC
    651.8 ☑
    with fetal loss and retention of one or more
      fetus(es) 651.5 ☑
    following (elective) fetal reduction
      651.7 ☑
Quarrelsomeness 301.3
Quartan
  fever 084.2
  malaria (fever) 084.2
Queensland fever 083.0
  coastal 083.0
  seven-day 100.89
Quervain's disease 727.04
  thyroid (subacute granulomatous thyroiditis)
    245.1
Queyrat's erythroplasia (M8080/2)
  specified site — see Neoplasm, skin, in situ

Queyrat's erythroplasia — continued
  unspecified site 233.5
Quincke's disease or edema — see Edema
  gioneurotic
Quinquaud's disease (acne decalvans) 704
Quinsy (gangrenous) 475
Quintan fever 083.1
Quintuplet
  affected by maternal complications of pr
    nancy 761.5
  healthy liveborn — see Newborn, multip
  pregnancy (complicating delivery) NEC
    651.2 ☑
    with fetal loss and retention of one or n
      fetus(es) 651.6 ☑
    following (elective) fetal reduction
      651.7 ☑
Quotidian
  fever 084.0
  malaria (fever) 084.0

R

Rabbia 071
Rabbit fever — see also Tularemia 021.9
Rabies 071
  contact V01.5
  exposure to V01.5
  inoculation V04.5
    reaction — see Complications, vaccinat
  vaccination, prophylactic (against) V04.5
Rachischisis — see also Spina bifida 741.9 ☑
Rachitic — see condition
  deformities of spine 268.1
  pelvis 268.1
    with disproportion (fetopelvic) 653.2 ☑
      affecting fetus or newborn 763.1
      causing obstructed labor 660.1 ☑
        affecting fetus or newborn 763.
Rachitis, rachitism — see also Rickets
  acute 268.0
  fetalis 756.4
  renalis 588.0
  tarda 268.0
Racket nail 757.5
Radial nerve — see condition
Radiation effects or sickness — see also Effe
  adverse, radiation
  cataract 366.46
  dermatitis 692.82
    sunburn (see also Sunburn) 692.71
Radiculitis (pressure) (vertebrogenic) 729.2
  accessory nerve 723.4
  anterior crural 724.4
  arm 723.4
  brachial 723.4
  cervical NEC 723.4
  due to displacement of intervertebral disc –
    see Neuritis, due to, displacement inte
    vertebral disc
  leg 724.4
  lumbar NEC 724.4
  lumbosacral 724.4
  rheumatic 729.2
  syphilitic 094.89
  thoracic (with visceral pain) 724.4
Radiculomyelitis 357.0
  toxic, due to
    Clostridium tetani 037
    Corynebacterium diphtheriae 032.89
Radiculopathy — see also Radiculitis 729.2
Radioactive substances, adverse effect — s
  Effect, adverse, radioactive substance
Radiodermal burns (acute) (chronic) (occupa
  tional) — see Burn, by site
Radiodermatitis 692.82
Radionecrosis — see Effect, adverse, radiation
Radiotherapy session V58.0
Radium, adverse effect — see Effect, adverse
  radioactive substance
Raeder-Harbitz syndrome (pulseless disease)
  446.7
Rage — see also Disturbance, conduct 312.0 ☑
  meaning rabies 071
Rag sorters' disease 022.1
Raillietiniasis 123.8
Railroad neurosis 300.16

Railway spine 300.16
Raised — *see* Elevation
Raiva 071
Rake teeth, tooth 524.39
Rales 786.7
Ramifying renal pelvis 753.3
Ramsay Hunt syndrome (herpetic geniculate ganglionitis) 053.11
  meaning dyssynergia cerebellaris myoclonica 334.2
Ranke's primary infiltration — *see also* Tuberculosis 010.0 ☑
Ranula 527.6
  congenital 750.26
Rape
  adult 995.83
  alleged, observation or examination V71.5
  child 995.53
Rapid
  feeble pulse, due to shock, following injury 958.4
  heart (beat) 785.0
    psychogenic 306.2
  respiration 786.06
    psychogenic 306.1
  second stage (delivery) 661.3 ☑
    affecting fetus or newborn 763.6
  time-zone change syndrome 327.35
Rarefaction, bone 733.99
Rash 782.1
  canker 034.1
  diaper 691.0
  drug (internal use) 693.0
    contact 692.3
  ECHO 9 virus 078.89
  enema 692.89
  food (*see also* Allergy, food) 693.1
  heat 705.1
  napkin 691.0
  nettle 708.8
  pustular 782.1
  rose 782.1
    epidemic 056.9
    of infants 057.8
  scarlet 034.1
  serum (prophylactic) (therapeutic) 999.5
  toxic 782.1
  wandering tongue 529.1
Rasmussen's aneurysm — *see also* Tuberculosis 011.2 ☑
Rat-bite fever 026.9
  due to Streptobacillus moniliformis 026.1
  spirochetal (morsus muris) 026.0
Rathke's pouch tumor (M9350/1) 237.0
Raymond (-Céstan) syndrome 433.8 ☑
Raynaud's
  disease or syndrome (paroxysmal digital cyanosis) 443.0
  gangrene (symmetric) 443.0 [785.4]
  phenomenon (paroxysmal digital cyanosis) (secondary) 443.0
RDS 769
Reaction
  acute situational maladjustment (*see also* Reaction, adjustment) 309.9
  adaptation (*see also* Reaction, adjustment) 309.9
  adjustment 309.9
    with
      anxious mood 309.24
        with depressed mood 309.28
      conduct disturbance 309.3
        combined with disturbance of emotions 309.4
      depressed mood 309.0
        brief 309.0
          with anxious mood 309.28
        prolonged 309.1
      elective mutism 309.83
      mixed emotions and conduct 309.4
      mutism, elective 309.83
      physical symptoms 309.82
      predominant disturbance (of)
        conduct 309.3
        emotions NEC 309.29
          mixed 309.28

Reaction — *continued*
  adjustment — *continued*
    with — *continued*
      predominant disturbance — *continued*
        mixed, emotions and conduct 309.4
        specified type NEC 309.89
        specific academic or work inhibition 309.23
      withdrawal 309.83
    depressive 309.0
      with conduct disturbance 309.4
      brief 309.0
      prolonged 309.1
    specified type NEC 309.89
  adverse food NEC 995.7
  affective (*see also* Psychosis, affective) 296.90
    specified type NEC 296.99
  aggressive 301.3
    unsocialized (*see also* Disturbance, conduct) 312.0 ☑
  allergic (*see also* Allergy) 995.3
    drug, medicinal substance, and biological — *see* Allergy, drug
    food — *see* Allergy, food
    serum 999.5
  anaphylactic — *see* Shock, anaphylactic
  anesthesia — *see* Anesthesia, complication
  anger 312.0 ☑
  antisocial 301.7
  antitoxin (prophylactic) (therapeutic) — *see* Complications, vaccination
  anxiety 300.00
  Arthus 995.21
  asthenic 300.5
  compulsive 300.3
  conversion (anesthetic) (autonomic) (hyperkinetic) (mixed paralytic) (paresthetic) 300.11
  deoxyribonuclease (DNA) (DNase) hypersensitivity NEC 287.2
  depressive 300.4
    acute 309.0
    affective (*see also* Psychosis, affective) 296.2 ☑
      recurrent episode 296.3 ☑
      single episode 296.2 ☑
    brief 309.0
    manic (*see also* Psychosis, affective) 296.80
    neurotic 300.4
    psychoneurotic 300.4
    psychotic 298.0
  dissociative 300.15
  drug NEC (*see also* Table of Drugs and Chemicals) 995.20
    allergic (*see also* Allergy, drug) 995.27
    correct substance properly administered 995.20
    obstetric anesthetic or analgesic NEC 668.9 ☑
      affecting fetus or newborn 763.5
    specified drug — *see* Table of Drugs and Chemicals
    overdose or poisoning 977.9
      specified drug — *see* Table of Drugs and Chemicals
    specific to newborn 779.4
    transmitted via placenta or breast milk — *see* Absorption, drug, through placenta
    withdrawal NEC 292.0
      infant of dependent mother 779.5
    wrong substance given or taken in error 977.9
      specified drug — *see* Table of Drugs and Chemicals
  dyssocial 301.7
  dystonic, acute, due to drugs 333.72
  erysipeloid 027.1
  fear 300.20
    child 313.0
  fluid loss, cerebrospinal 349.0
  food (*see also* Allergy, food)
    adverse NEC 995.7

Reaction — *continued*
  food (*see also* Allergy, food) — *continued*
    anaphylactic shock — *see* Anaphylactic shock, due to, food
  foreign
    body NEC 728.82
      in operative wound (inadvertently left) 998.4
      due to surgical material intentionally left — *see* Complications, due to (presence of) any device, implant, or graft classified to 996.0–996.5 NEC
    substance accidentally left during a procedure (chemical) (powder) (talc) 998.7
    body or object (instrument) (sponge) (swab) 998.4
  graft-versus-host (GVH) 279.50
  grief (acute) (brief) 309.0
    prolonged 309.1
  gross stress (*see also* Reaction, stress, acute) 308.9
  group delinquent (*see also* Disturbance, conduct) 312.2 ☑
  Herxheimer's 995.0
  hyperkinetic (*see also* Hyperkinesia) 314.9
  hypochondriacal 300.7
  hypoglycemic, due to insulin 251.0
    therapeutic misadventure 962.3
  hypomanic (*see also* Psychosis, affective) 296.0 ☑
    recurrent episode 296.1 ☑
    single episode 296.0 ☑
  hysterical 300.10
    conversion type 300.11
    dissociative 300.15
  id (bacterial cause) 692.89
  immaturity NEC 301.89
    aggressive 301.3
    emotional instability 301.59
  immunization — *see* Complications, vaccination
  incompatibility
    blood group
      ABO 999.6 ●
      minor blood group 999.89 ●
      Rh (factor) (infusion) (transfusion) 999.7
  inflammatory — *see* Infection
  infusion — *see* Complications, infusion
  inoculation (immune serum) — *see* Complications, vaccination
  insulin 995.23
  involutional
    paranoid 297.2
    psychotic (*see also* Psychosis, affective, depressive) 296.2 ☑
  leukemoid (basophilic) (lymphocytic) (monocytic) (myelocytic) (neutrophilic) 288.62
  LSD (*see also* Abuse, drugs, nondependent) 305.3 ☑
  lumbar puncture 349.0
  manic-depressive (*see also* Psychosis, affective) 296.80
    depressed 296.2 ☑
      recurrent episode 296.3 ☑
      single episode 296.2 ☑
    hypomanic 296.0 ☑
  neurasthenic 300.5
  neurogenic (*see also* Neurosis) 300.9
  neurotic NEC 300.9
  neurotic-depressive 300.4
  nitritoid — *see* Crisis, nitritoid
  obsessive compulsive 300.3
  organic 293.9
    acute 293.0
    subacute 293.1
  overanxious, child or adolescent 313.0
  paranoid (chronic) 297.9
    acute 298.3
    climacteric 297.2
    involutional 297.2
    menopausal 297.2
    senile 290.20
    simple 297.0

Reaction — *continued*
  passive
    aggressive 301.84
    dependency 301.6
  personality (*see also* Disorder, personality) 301.9
  phobic 300.20
  postradiation — *see* Effect, adverse, radiation
  psychogenic NEC 300.9
  psychoneurotic (*see also* Neurosis) 300.9
    anxiety 300.00
    compulsive 300.3
    conversion 300.11
    depersonalization 300.6
    depressive 300.4
    dissociative 300.15
    hypochondriacal 300.7
    hysterical 300.10
      conversion type 300.11
      dissociative type 300.15
    neurasthenic 300.5
    obsessive 300.3
    obsessive-compulsive 300.3
    phobic 300.20
    tension state 300.9
  psychophysiologic NEC (*see also* Disorder, psychosomatic) 306.9
    cardiovascular 306.2
    digestive 306.4
    endocrine 306.6
    gastrointestinal 306.4
    genitourinary 306.50
    heart 306.2
    hemic 306.8
    intestinal (large) (small) 306.4
    laryngeal 306.1
    lymphatic 306.8
    musculoskeletal 306.0
    pharyngeal 306.1
    respiratory 306.1
    skin 306.3
    special sense organs 306.7
  psychosomatic (*see also* Disorder, psychosomatic) 306.9
  psychotic (*see also* Psychosis) 298.9
    depressive 298.0
    due to or associated with physical condition (*see also* Psychosis, organic) 293.9
    involutional (*see also* Psychosis, affective) 296.2 ☑
      recurrent episode 296.3 ☑
      single episode 296.2 ☑
  pupillary (myotonic) (tonic) 379.46
  radiation — *see* Effect, adverse, radiation
  runaway (*see also* Disturbance, conduct)
    socialized 312.2 ☑
    undersocialized, unsocialized 312.1 ☑
  scarlet fever toxin — *see* Complications, vaccination
  schizophrenic (*see also* Schizophrenia) 295.9 ☑
    latent 295.5 ☑
  serological for syphilis — *see* Serology for syphilis
  serum (prophylactic) (therapeutic) 999.5
    immediate 999.4
  situational (*see also* Reaction, adjustment) 309.9
    acute, to stress 308.3
    adjustment (*see also* Reaction, adjustment) 309.9
  somatization (*see also* Disorder, psychosomatic) 306.9
  spinal puncture 349.0
  spite, child (*see also* Disturbance, conduct) 312.0 ☑
  stress, acute 308.9
    with predominant disturbance (of)
      consciousness 308.1
      emotions 308.0
      mixed 308.4
      psychomotor 308.2
      specified type NEC 308.3
    bone or cartilage — *see* Fracture, stress

☑ Additional Digit Required — Refer to the Tabular List for Digit Selection   Subterms under main terms may continue to next column or page

2010 ICD-9-CM   ▶◀ Revised Text   ● New Line   ▲ Revised Code   October 2009 • Volume 2 — 235

Railway spine — Reaction

Reaction — *continued*
  surgical procedure — *see* Complications, surgical procedure
  tetanus antitoxin — *see* Complications, vaccination
  toxin-antitoxin — *see* Complications, vaccination
  transfusion (blood) (bone marrow) (lymphocytes) (allergic) — *see* Complications, transfusion
  tuberculin skin test, nonspecific (without active tuberculosis) 795.5
    positive (without active tuberculosis) 795.5
  ultraviolet — *see* Effect, adverse, ultraviolet
  undersocialized, unsocialized (*see also* Disturbance, conduct)
    aggressive (type) 312.0 ☑
    unaggressive (type) 312.1 ☑
  vaccination (any) — *see* Complications, vaccination
  white graft (skin) 996.52
  withdrawing, child or adolescent 313.22
  x-ray — *see* Effect, adverse, x-rays
Reactive depression — *see also* Reaction, depressive 300.4
  neurotic 300.4
  psychoneurotic 300.4
  psychotic 298.0
Rebound tenderness 789.6 ☑
Recalcitrant patient V15.81
Recanalization, thrombus — *see* Thrombosis
Recession, receding
  chamber angle (eye) 364.77
  chin 524.06
  gingival (postinfective) (postoperative) 523.20
    generalized 523.25
    localized 523.24
    minimal 523.21
    moderate 523.22
    severe 523.23
Recklinghausen-Applebaum disease (hemochromatosis) 275.0
Recklinghausen's disease (M9540/1) 237.71
  bones (osteitis fibrosa cystica) 252.01
Reclus' disease (cystic) 610.1
Recrudescent typhus (fever) 081.1
Recruitment, auditory 388.44
Rectalgia 569.42
Rectitis 569.49
Rectocele
  female (without uterine prolapse) 618.04
    with uterine prolapse 618.4
      complete 618.3
      incomplete 618.2
    in pregnancy or childbirth 654.4 ☑
      causing obstructed labor 660.2 ☑
        affecting fetus or newborn 763.1
  male 569.49
  vagina, vaginal (outlet) 618.04
Rectosigmoiditis 569.89
  ulcerative (chronic) 556.3
Rectosigmoid junction — *see* condition
Rectourethral — *see* condition
Rectovaginal — *see* condition
Rectovesical — *see* condition
Rectum, rectal — *see* condition
Recurrent — *see* condition
Red bugs 133.8
Red cedar asthma 495.8
Redness
  conjunctiva 379.93
  eye 379.93
  nose 478.19
Reduced ventilatory or vital capacity 794.2
Reduction
  function
    kidney (*see also* Disease, renal) 593.9
    liver 573.8
  ventilatory capacity 794.2
  vital capacity 794.2
Redundant, redundancy
  abdomen 701.9
  anus 751.5
  cardia 537.89
  clitoris 624.2
  colon (congenital) 751.5

Redundant, redundancy — *continued*
  foreskin (congenital) 605
  intestine 751.5
  labia 624.3
  organ or site, congenital NEC — *see* Accessory
  panniculus (abdominal) 278.1
  prepuce (congenital) 605
  pylorus 537.89
  rectum 751.5
  scrotum 608.89
  sigmoid 751.5
  skin (of face) 701.9
    eyelids 374.30
  stomach 537.89
  uvula 528.9
  vagina 623.8
Reduplication — *see* Duplication
Referral
  adoption (agency) V68.89
  nursing care V63.8
  patient without examination or treatment V68.81
  social services V63.8
Reflex — *see also* condition
  blink, deficient 374.45
  hyperactive gag 478.29
  neurogenic bladder NEC 596.54
    atonic 596.54
      with cauda equina syndrome 344.61
  vasoconstriction 443.9
  vasovagal 780.2
Reflux 530.81
  acid 530.81
  esophageal 530.81
    with esophagitis 530.11
  esophagitis 530.11
  gastroesophageal 530.81
  mitral — *see* Insufficiency, mitral
  ureteral — *see* Reflux, vesicoureteral
  vesicoureteral 593.70
    with
      reflux nephropathy 593.73
        bilateral 593.72
        unilateral 593.71
Reformed gallbladder 576.0
Reforming, artificial openings — *see also* Attention to, artificial, opening V55.9
Refractive error — *see also* Error, refractive 367.9
Refsum's disease or syndrome (heredopathia atactica polyneuritiformis) 356.3
Refusal of
  food 307.59
    hysterical 300.11
  treatment because of, due to
    patient's decision NEC V64.2
    reason of conscience or religion V62.6
Regaud
  tumor (M8082/3) — *see* Neoplasm, nasopharynx, malignant
  type carcinoma (M8082/3) — *see* Neoplasm, nasopharynx, malignant
Regional — *see* condition
Regulation feeding (elderly) (infant) 783.3
  newborn 779.31 ▲
Regurgitated
  food, choked on 933.1
  stomach contents, choked on 933.1
Regurgitation 787.03
  aortic (valve) (*see also* Insufficiency, aortic) 424.1
    congenital 746.4
    syphilitic 093.22
  food (*see also* Vomiting)
    with reswallowing — *see* Rumination
    newborn 779.33 ▲
  gastric contents — *see* Vomiting
  heart — *see* Endocarditis
  mitral (valve) (*see also* Insufficiency, mitral)
    congenital 746.6
  myocardial — *see* Endocarditis
  pulmonary (heart) (valve) (*see also* Endocarditis, pulmonary) 424.3
  stomach — *see* Vomiting
  tricuspid — *see* Endocarditis, tricuspid
  valve, valvular — *see* Endocarditis
  vesicoureteral — *see* Reflux, vesicoureteral

Rehabilitation V57.9
  multiple types V57.89
  occupational V57.21
  specified type NEC V57.89
  speech ▶(-language)◀ V57.3
  vocational V57.22
Reichmann's disease or syndrome (gastrosuccorrhea) 536.8
Reifenstein's syndrome (hereditary familial hypogonadism, male) 259.52
Reilly's syndrome or phenomenon — *see also* Neuropathy, peripheral, autonomic 337.9
Reimann's periodic disease 277.31
Reinsertion, contraceptive device V25.42
Reiter's disease, syndrome, or urethritis 099.3 [711.1] ☑
Rejection
  food, hysterical 300.11
  transplant 996.80
    bone marrow 996.85
    corneal 996.51
    organ (immune or nonimmune cause) 996.80
      bone marrow 996.85
      heart 996.83
      intestines 996.87
      kidney 996.81
      liver 996.82
      lung 996.84
      pancreas 996.86
      specified NEC 996.89
    skin 996.52
      artificial 996.55
      decellularized allodermis 996.55
Relapsing fever 087.9
  Carter's (Asiatic) 087.0
  Dutton's (West African) 087.1
  Koch's 087.9
  louse-borne (epidemic) 087.0
  Novy's (American) 087.1
  Obermeyer's (European) 087.0
  Spirillum 087.9
  tick-borne (endemic) 087.1
Relaxation
  anus (sphincter) 569.49
    due to hysteria 300.11
  arch (foot) 734
    congenital 754.61
  back ligaments 728.4
  bladder (sphincter) 596.59
  cardio-esophageal 530.89
  cervix (*see also* Incompetency, cervix) 622.5
  diaphragm 519.4
  inguinal rings — *see* Hernia, inguinal
  joint (capsule) (ligament) (paralytic) (*see also* Derangement, joint) 718.90
    congenital 755.8
  lumbosacral joint 724.6
  pelvic floor 618.89
  pelvis 618.89
  perineum 618.89
  posture 729.90
  rectum (sphincter) 569.49
  sacroiliac (joint) 724.6
  scrotum 608.89
  urethra (sphincter) 599.84
  uterus (outlet) 618.89
  vagina (outlet) 618.89
  vesical 596.59
Remains
  canal of Cloquet 743.51
  capsule (opaque) 743.51
Remittent fever (malarial) 084.6
Remnant
  canal of Cloquet 743.51
  capsule (opaque) 743.51
  cervix, cervical stump (acquired) (postoperative) 622.8
  cystic duct, postcholecystectomy 576.0
  fingernail 703.8
    congenital 757.5
  meniscus, knee 717.5
  thyroglossal duct 759.2
  tonsil 474.8
    infected 474.00
  urachus 753.7

Remote effect of cancer — *see* condition
Removal (of)
  catheter (urinary) (indwelling) V53.6
    from artificial opening — *see* Attention to artificial, opening
    non-vascular V58.82
    vascular V58.81
  cerebral ventricle (communicating) shunt V53.01
  device (*see also* Fitting (of))
    contraceptive V25.42
    fixation
      external V54.89
      internal V54.01
    traction V54.89
  drains V58.49
  dressing
    wound V58.30
      nonsurgical V58.30
      surgical V58.31
  ileostomy V55.2
  Kirschner wire V54.89
  nonvascular catheter V58.82
  pin V54.01
  plaster cast V54.89
  plate (fracture) V54.01
  rod V54.01
  screw V54.01
  splint, external V54.89
  staples V58.32
  subdermal implantable contraceptive V25.43
  sutures V58.32
  traction device, external V54.89
  vascular catheter V58.81
  wound packing V58.30
    nonsurgical V58.30
    surgical V58.31
Ren
  arcuatus 753.3
  mobile, mobilis (*see also* Disease, renal) 593.0
    congenital 753.3
  unguliformis 753.3
Renal — *see also* condition
  glomerulohyalinosis-diabetic syndrome 250.4 ☑ [581.81]
    due to secondary diabetes 249.4 ☑ [581.81]
Rendu-Osler-Weber disease or syndrome (familial hemorrhagic telangiectasia) 448.0
Reninoma (M8361/1) 236.91
Rénon-Delille syndrome 253.8
Repair
  pelvic floor, previous, in pregnancy or childbirth 654.4 ☑
    affecting fetus or newborn 763.89
  scarred tissue V51.8
Replacement by artificial or mechanical device or prosthesis of — *see also* Fitting (of
  artificial skin V43.83
  bladder V43.5
  blood vessel V43.4
  breast V43.82
  eye globe V43.0
  heart
    with
      assist device V43.21
      fully implantable artificial heart V43.22
    valve V43.3
  intestine V43.89
  joint V43.60
    ankle V43.66
    elbow V43.62
    finger V43.69
    hip (partial) (total) V43.64
    knee V43.65
    shoulder V43.61
    specified NEC V43.69
    wrist V43.63
  kidney V43.89
  larynx V43.81
  lens V43.1
  limb(s) V43.7
  liver V43.89
  lung V43.89
  organ NEC V43.89

Replacement by artificial or mechanical device or prosthesis of — *see also* Fitting (of — *continued*
    continued
    pancreas V43.89
    skin (artificial) V43.83
    tissue NEC V43.89
Reprogramming
    cardiac pacemaker V53.31
Request for expert evidence V68.2
Reserve, decreased or low
    cardiac — *see* Disease, heart
    kidney (*see also* Disease, renal) 593.9
Residual — *see also* condition
    bladder 596.8
    foreign body — *see* Retention, foreign body
    state, schizophrenic (*see also* Schizophrenia) 295.6 ☑
    urine 788.69
Resistance, resistant (to)
    activated protein C 289.81

> *Note* — use the following subclassification for categories V09.5, V09.7, V09.8, V09.9:
>
> 0   *without mention of resistance to multiple drugs*
>
> 1   *with resistance to multiple drugs*
>
>   V09.5 *quinolones and fluoro-quinolones*
>
>   V09.7 *antimycobacterial agents*
>
>   V09.8 *specified drugs NEC*
>
>   V09.9 *unspecified drugs*

    drugs by microorganisms V09.9 ☑
        Amikacin V09.4
        aminoglycosides V09.4 ☑
        Amodiaquine V09.5 ☑
        Amoxicillin V09.0
        Ampicillin V09.0
        antimycobacterial agents V09.7 ☑
        Azithromycin V09.2
        Azlocillin V09.0
        Aztreonam V09.1
        Bacampicillin V09.0
        Bacitracin V09.8 ☑
        Benznidazole V09.8 ☑
        B-lactam antibiotics V09.1
        Capreomycin V09.7 ☑
        Carbenicillin V09.0
        Cefaclor V09.1
        Cefadroxil V09.1
        Cefamandole V09.1
        Cefatetan V09.1
        Cefazolin V09.1
        Cefixime V09.1
        Cefonicid V09.1
        Cefoperazone V09.1
        Ceforanide V09.1
        Cefotaxime V09.1
        Cefoxitin V09.1
        Ceftazidime V09.1
        Ceftizoxime V09.1
        Ceftriaxone V09.1
        Cefuroxime V09.1
        Cephalexin V09.1
        Cephaloglycin V09.1
        Cephaloridine V09.1
        Cephalosporins V09.1
        Cephalothin V09.1
        Cephapirin V09.1
        Cephradine V09.1
        Chloramphenicol V09.8 ☑
        Chloraquine V09.5 ☑
        Chlorguanide V09.8 ☑
        Chlorproguanil V09.8 ☑
        Chlortetracycline V09.3
        Cinoxacin V09.5 ☑
        Ciprofloxacin V09.5 ☑
        Clarithromycin V09.2
        Clindamycin V09.8 ☑
        Clioquinol V09.5 ☑
        Clofazimine V09.7 ☑
        Cloxacillin V09.0
        Cyclacillin V09.0
        Cycloserine V09.7 ☑

Resistance, resistant — *continued*
    drugs by microorganisms — *continued*
        Dapsone [DZ] V09.7 ☑
        Demeclocycline V09.3
        Dicloxacillin V09.0
        Doxycycline V09.3
        Enoxacin V09.5 ☑
        Erythromycin V09.2
        Ethambutol [EMB] V09.7 ☑
        Ethionamide [ETA] V09.7 ☑
        fluoroquinolones V09.5 ☑
        Gentamicin V09.4
        Halofantrine V09.8 ☑
        Imipenem V09.1
        Iodoquinol V09.5 ☑
        Isoniazid [INH] V09.7 ☑
        Kanamycin V09.4
        macrolides V09.2
        Mafenide V09.6
        MDRO (multiple drug resistant organisms) NOS V09.91
        Mefloquine V09.8 ☑
        Melasoprol V09.8 ☑
        Methacycline V09.3
        Methenamine V09.8 ☑
        Methicillin — *see* Infection, Methicillin V09.0
        Metronidazole V09.8 ☑
        Mezlocillin V09.0
        Minocycline V09.3
        multiple drug resistant organisms NOS V09.91
        Nafcillin V09.0
        Nalidixic acid V09.5 ☑
        Natamycin V09.2
        Neomycin V09.4
        Netilmicin V09.4
        Nimorazole V09.8 ☑
        Nitrofurantoin V09.8 ☑
        Nitrofurtimox V09.8 ☑
        Norfloxacin V09.5 ☑
        Nystatin V09.2
        Ofloxacin V09.5 ☑
        Oleandomycin V09.2
        Oxacillin V09.0
        Oxytetracycline V09.3
        Para-amino salicylic acid [PAS] V09.7 ☑
        Paromomycin V09.4
        Penicillin (G) (V) (VK) V09.0
        penicillins V09.0
        Pentamidine V09.8 ☑
        Piperacillin V09.0
        Primaquine V09.5 ☑
        Proguanil V09.8 ☑
        Pyrazinamide [PZA] V09.7 ☑
        Pyrimethamine/Sulfalene V09.8 ☑
        Pyrimethamine/Sulfodoxine V09.8 ☑
        Quinacrine V09.5 ☑
        Quinidine V09.8 ☑
        Quinine V09.8 ☑
        quinolones V09.5 ☑
        Rifabutin V09.7 ☑
        Rifampin [RIF] V09.7 ☑
        Rifamycin V09.7 ☑
        Roliettracycline V09.3
        specified drugs NEC V09.8 ☑
        Spectinomycin V09.8 ☑
        Spiramycin V09.2
        Streptomycin [SM] V09.4
        Sulfacetamide V09.6
        Sulfacytine V09.6
        Sulfadiazine V09.6
        Sulfadoxine V09.6
        Sulfamethoxazole V09.6
        Sulfapyridine V09.6
        Sulfasalizine V09.6
        Sulfasoxazole V09.6
        sulfonamides V09.6
        Sulfoxone V09.7 ☑
        tetracycline V09.3
        tetracyclines V09.3
        Thiamphenicol V09.8 ☑
        Ticarcillin V09.0
        Tinidazole V09.8 ☑
        Tobramycin V09.4

Resistance, resistant — *continued*
    drugs by microorganisms — *continued*
        Triamphenicol V09.8 ☑
        Trimethoprim V09.8 ☑
        Vancomycin V09.8 ☑
    insulin 277.7
    thyroid hormone 246.8
Resorption
    biliary 576.8
        purulent or putrid (*see also* Cholecystitis) 576.8
    dental (roots) 521.40
        alveoli 525.8
        pathological
            external 521.42
            internal 521.41
            specified NEC 521.49
    septic — *see* Septicemia
    teeth (roots) 521.40
        pathological
            external 521.42
            internal 521.41
            specified NEC 521.49
Respiration
    asymmetrical 786.09
    bronchial 786.09
    Cheyne-Stokes (periodic respiration) 786.04
    decreased, due to shock following injury 958.4
    disorder of 786.00
        psychogenic 306.1
        specified NEC 786.09
    failure 518.81
        acute 518.81
        acute and chronic 518.84
        chronic 518.83
        newborn 770.84
    insufficiency 786.09
        acute 518.82
        newborn NEC 770.89
    Kussmaul (air hunger) 786.09
    painful 786.52
    periodic 786.09
        high altitude 327.22
    poor 786.09
        newborn NEC 770.89
    sighing 786.7
        psychogenic 306.1
    wheezing 786.07
Respiratory — *see also* condition
    distress 786.09
        acute 518.82
        fetus or newborn NEC 770.89
        syndrome (newborn) 769
            adult (following shock, surgery, or trauma) 518.5
            specified NEC 518.82
    failure 518.81
        acute 518.81
        acute and chronic 518.84
        chronic 518.83
Respiratory syncytial virus (RSV) 079.6
    bronchiolitis 466.11
    pneumonia 480.1
    vaccination, prophylactic (against) V04.82
Response
    photoallergic 692.72
    phototoxic 692.72
Restless legs syndrome (RLS) 333.94
Restlessness 799.29 ▲
Restoration of organ continuity from previous sterilization (tuboplasty) (vasoplasty) V26.0
Rest, rests
    mesonephric duct 752.89
        fallopian tube 752.11
    ovarian, in fallopian tubes 752.19
    wolffian duct 752.89
Restriction of housing space V60.1
Restzustand, schizophrenic — *see also* Schizophrenia 295.6 ☑
Retained — *see* Retention
Retardation
    development, developmental, specific (*see also* Disorder, development, specific) 315.9
        learning, specific 315.2
            arithmetical 315.1

Retardation — *continued*
    development, developmental, specific (*see also* Disorder, development, specific) — *continued*
        learning, specific — *continued*
            language (skills) 315.31
                expressive 315.31
                mixed receptive-expressive 315.32
            mathematics 315.1
            reading 315.00
                phonological 315.39
            written expression 315.2
        motor 315.4
    endochondral bone growth 733.91
    growth (physical) in childhood 783.43
        due to malnutrition 263.2
        fetal (intrauterine) 764.9 ☑
            affecting management of pregnancy 656.5 ☑
    intrauterine growth 764.9 ☑
        affecting management of pregnancy 656.5 ☑
    mental 319
        borderline V62.89
        mild, IQ 50-70 317
        moderate, IQ 35-49 318.0
        profound, IQ under 20 318.2
        severe, IQ 20-34 318.1
    motor, specific 315.4
    physical 783.43
        child 783.43
        due to malnutrition 263.2
        fetus (intrauterine) 764.9 ☑
            affecting management of pregnancy 656.5 ☑
    psychomotor NEC 307.9
    reading 315.00
Retching — *see* Vomiting
Retention, retained
    bladder (*see also* Retention, urine) 788.20
        psychogenic 306.53
    carbon dioxide 276.2
    cholelithiasis 997.4
    cyst — *see* Cyst
    dead
        fetus (after 22 completed weeks gestation) 656.4 ☑
            early fetal death (before 22 completed weeks gestation) 632
        ovum 631
    decidua (following delivery) (fragments) (with hemorrhage) 666.2 ☑
        without hemorrhage 667.1 ☑
    deciduous tooth 520.6
    dental root 525.3
    fecal (*see also* Constipation) 564.00
    fluid 276.6
    foreign body (*see also* Foreign body, retained)
        bone 733.99
        current trauma — *see* Foreign body, by site or type
        middle ear 385.83
        muscle 729.6
        soft tissue NEC 729.6
    gallstones 997.4
    gastric 536.8
    membranes (following delivery) (with hemorrhage) 666.2 ☑
        with abortion — *see* Abortion, by type
        without hemorrhage 667.1 ☑
    menses 626.8
    milk (puerperal) 676.2 ☑
    nitrogen, extrarenal 788.99
    placenta (total) (with hemorrhage) 666.0 ☑
        with abortion — *see* Abortion, by type
        without hemorrhage 667.0 ☑
        portions or fragments 666.2 ☑
            without hemorrhage 667.1 ☑
    products of conception
        early pregnancy (fetal death before 22 completed weeks gestation) 632
        following
            abortion — *see* Abortion, by type
            delivery 666.2 ☑
                with hemorrhage 666.2 ☑
                without hemorrhage 667.1 ☑

☑ Additional Digit Required — Refer to the Tabular List for Digit Selection   ▽ Subterms under main terms may continue to next column or page

2010 ICD-9-CM   ►◄ Revised Text   ● New Line   ▲ Revised Code   October 2009 • Volume 2 — 237

Retention, retained — *continued*
secundines (following delivery) (with hemorrhage) 666.2 ☑
with abortion — *see* Abortion, by type
without hemorrhage 667.1 ☑
complicating puerperium (delayed hemorrhage) 666.2 ☑
smegma, clitoris 624.8
urine NEC 788.20
bladder, incomplete emptying 788.21
due to
benign prostatic hypertrophy (BPH) — *see* category 600
due to
benign prostatic hypertrophy (BPH) — see category 600
psychogenic 306.53
specified NEC 788.29
water (in tissue) (*see also* Edema) 782.3
Reticulation, dust (occupational) 504
Reticulocytosis NEC 790.99
Reticuloendotheliosis
acute infantile (M9722/3) 202.5 ☑
leukemic (M9940/3) 202.4 ☑
malignant (M9720/3) 202.3 ☑
nonlipid (M9722/3) 202.5 ☑
Reticulohistiocytoma (giant cell) 277.89
Reticulohistiocytosis, multicentric 272.8
Reticulolymphosarcoma (diffuse) (M9613/3) 200.8 ☑
follicular (M9691/3) 202.0 ☑
nodular (M9691/3) 202.0 ☑
Reticulosarcoma (M9640/3) 200.0 ☑
nodular (M9642/3) 200.0 ☑
pleomorphic cell type (M9641/3) 200.0 ☑
Reticulosis (skin)
acute of infancy (M9722/3) 202.5 ☑
familial hemophagocytic 288.4
histiocytic medullary (M9721/3) 202.3 ☑
lipomelanotic 695.89
malignant (M9720/3) 202.3 ☑
Sézary's (M9701/3) 202.2 ☑
Retina, retinal — *see* condition
Retinitis — *see also* Chorioretinitis 363.20
albuminurica 585.9 *[363.10]*
arteriosclerotic 440.8 *[362.13]*
central angiospastic 362.41
Coat's 362.12
diabetic 250.5 ☑ *[362.01]*
due to secondary diabetes 249.5 ☑ *[362.01]*
disciformis 362.52
disseminated 363.10
metastatic 363.14
neurosyphilitic 094.83
pigment epitheliopathy 363.15
exudative 362.12
focal 363.00
in histoplasmosis 115.92
capsulatum 115.02
duboisii 115.12
juxtapapillary 363.05
macular 363.06
paramacular 363.06
peripheral 363.08
posterior pole NEC 363.07
gravidarum 646.8 ☑
hemorrhagica externa 362.12
juxtapapillary (Jensen's) 363.05
luetic — *see* Retinitis, syphilitic
metastatic 363.14
pigmentosa 362.74
proliferans 362.29
proliferating 362.29
punctata albescens 362.76
renal 585.9 *[363.13]*
syphilitic (secondary) 091.51
congenital 090.0 *[363.13]*
early 091.51
late 095.8 *[363.13]*
syphilitica, central, recurrent 095.8 *[363.13]*
tuberculous (*see also* Tuberculous) 017.3 ☑ *[363.13]*
Retinoblastoma (M9510/3) 190.5
differentiated type (M9511/3) 190.5
undifferentiated type (M9512/3) 190.5

Retinochoroiditis — *see also* Chorioretinitis 363.20
central angiospastic 362.41
disseminated 363.10
metastatic 363.14
neurosyphilitic 094.83
pigment epitheliopathy 363.15
syphilitic 094.83
due to toxoplasmosis (acquired) (focal) 130.2
focal 363.00
in histoplasmosis 115.92
capsulatum 115.02
duboisii 115.12
juxtapapillary (Jensen's) 363.05
macular 363.06
paramacular 363.06
peripheral 363.08
posterior pole NEC 363.07
juxtapapillaris 363.05
syphilitic (disseminated) 094.83
Retinopathy (background) 362.10
arteriosclerotic 440.8 *[362.13]*
atherosclerotic 440.8 *[362.13]*
central serous 362.41
circinate 362.10
Coat's 362.12
diabetic 250.5 ☑ *[362.01]*
due to secondary diabetes 249.5 ☑ *[362.01]*
nonproliferative 250.5 ☑ *[362.03]*
due to secondary diabetes 249.5 ☑ *[362.03]*
mild 250.5 ☑ *[362.04]*
due to secondary diabetes 249.5 ☑ *[362.04]*
moderate 250.5 ☑ *[362.05]*
due to secondary diabetes 249.5 ☑ *[362.05]*
severe 250.5 ☑ *[362.06]*
due to secondary diabetes 249.5 ☑ *[362.06]*
proliferative 250.5 ☑ *[362.02]*
due to secondary diabetes 249.5 ☑ *[362.02]*
exudative 362.12
hypertensive 362.11
nonproliferative
diabetic 250.5 ☑ *[362.03]*
due to secondary diabetes 249.5 ☑ *[362.03]*
mild 250.5 ☑ *[362.04]*
due to secondary diabetes 249.5 ☑ *[362.04]*
moderate 250.5 ☑ *[362.05]*
due to secondary diabetes 249.5 ☑ *[362.05]*
severe 250.5 ☑ *[362.06]*
due to secondary diabetes 249.5 ☑ *[362.06]*
of prematurity 362.20
cicatricial 362.21
stage
0 362.22
1 362.23
2 362.24
3 362.25
4 362.26
5 362.27
pigmentary, congenital 362.74
proliferative 362.29
diabetic 250.5 ☑ *[362.02]*
due to secondary diabetes 249.5 ☑ *[362.02]*
sickle-cell 282.60 *[362.29]*
solar 363.31
Retinoschisis 361.10
bullous 361.12
congenital 743.56
flat 361.11
juvenile 362.73
Retractile testis 752.52
Retraction
cervix — *see* Retraction, uterus
drum (membrane) 384.82
eyelid 374.41
finger 736.29

Retraction — *continued*
head 781.0
lid 374.41
lung 518.89
mediastinum 519.3
nipple 611.79
congenital 757.6
puerperal, postpartum 676.0 ☑
palmar fascia 728.6
pleura (*see also* Pleurisy) 511.0
ring, uterus (Bandl's) (pathological) 661.4 ☑
affecting fetus or newborn 763.7
sternum (congenital) 756.3
acquired 738.3
during respiration 786.9
substernal 738.3
supraclavicular 738.8
syndrome (Duane's) 378.71
uterus 621.6
valve (heart) — *see* Endocarditis
Retrobulbar — *see* condition
Retrocaval ureter 753.4
Retrocecal — *see also* condition
appendix (congenital) 751.5
Retrocession — *see* Retroversion
Retrodisplacement — *see* Retroversion
Retroflection, retroflexion — *see* Retroversion
Retrognathia, retrognathism (mandibular) (maxillary) 524.10
Retrograde
ejaculation 608.87
menstruation 626.8
Retroiliac ureter 753.4
Retroperineal — *see* condition
Retroperitoneal — *see* condition
Retroperitonitis 567.39
Retropharyngeal — *see* condition
Retroplacental — *see* condition
Retroposition — *see* Retroversion
Retrosternal thyroid (congenital) 759.2
Retroversion, retroverted
cervix — *see* Retroversion, uterus
female NEC (*see also* Retroversion, uterus) 621.6
iris 364.70
testis (congenital) 752.51
uterus, uterine (acquired) (acute) (adherent) (any degree) (asymptomatic) (cervix) (postinfectional) (postpartal, old) 621.6
congenital 752.3
in pregnancy or childbirth 654.3 ☑
affecting fetus or newborn 763.89
causing obstructed labor 660.2 ☑
affecting fetus or newborn 763.1
Retrusion, premaxilla (developmental) 524.04
Rett's syndrome 330.8
Reverse, reversed
peristalsis 787.4
Reye-Sheehan syndrome (postpartum pituitary necrosis) 253.2
Reye's syndrome 331.81
Rh (factor)
hemolytic disease 773.0
incompatibility, immunization, or sensitization
affecting management of pregnancy 656.1 ☑
fetus or newborn 773.0
transfusion reaction 999.7
negative mother, affecting fetus or newborn 773.0
titer elevated 999.7
transfusion reaction 999.7
Rhabdomyolysis (idiopathic) 728.88
Rhabdomyoma (M8900/0) — *see also* Neoplasm, connective tissue, benign
adult (M8904/0) — *see* Neoplasm, connective tissue, benign
fetal (M8903/0) — *see* Neoplasm, connective tissue, benign
glycogenic (M8904/0) — *see* Neoplasm, connective tissue, benign
Rhabdomyosarcoma (M8900/3) — *see also* Neoplasm, connective tissue, malignant
alveolar (M8920/3) — *see* Neoplasm, connective tissue, malignant

Rhabdomyosarcoma — *see also* Neoplasm, connective tissue, malignant — *continued*
embryonal (M8910/3) — *see* Neoplasm, connective tissue, malignant
mixed type (M8902/3) — *see* Neoplasm, connective tissue, malignant
pleomorphic (M8901/3) — *see* Neoplasm, connective tissue, malignant
Rhabdosarcoma (M8900/3) — *see* Rhabdomyosarcoma
Rhesus (factor) (Rh) incompatibility — *see* Rh, incompatibility
Rheumaticosis — *see* Rheumatism
Rheumatism, rheumatic (acute NEC) 729.0
adherent pericardium 393
arthritis
acute or subacute — *see* Fever, rheumatic
chronic 714.0
spine 720.0
articular (chronic) NEC (*see also* Arthritis) 716.9 ☑
acute or subacute — *see* Fever, rheumatic
back 724.9
blennorrhagic 098.59
carditis — *see* Disease, heart, rheumatic
cerebral — *see* Fever, rheumatic
chorea (acute) — *see* Chorea, rheumatic
chronic NEC 729.0
coronary arteritis 391.9
chronic 398.99
degeneration, myocardium (*see also* Degeneration, myocardium, with rheumatic fever) 398.0
desert 114.0
febrile — *see* Fever, rheumatic
fever — *see* Fever, rheumatic
gonococcal 098.59
gout 274.00 ▲
heart
disease (*see also* Disease, heart, rheumatic) 398.90
failure (chronic) (congestive) (inactive) 398.91
hemopericardium — *see* Rheumatic, pericarditis
hydropericardium — *see* Rheumatic, pericarditis
inflammatory (acute) (chronic) (subacute) — *see* Fever, rheumatic
intercostal 729.0
meaning Tietze's disease 733.6
joint (chronic) NEC (*see also* Arthritis) 716.9 ☑
acute — *see* Fever, rheumatic
mediastinopericarditis — *see* Rheumatic, pericarditis
muscular 729.0
myocardial degeneration (*see also* Degeneration, myocardium, with rheumatic fever) 398.0
myocarditis (chronic) (inactive) (with chorea) 398.0
active or acute 391.2
with chorea (acute) (rheumatic) (Sydenham's) 392.0
myositis 729.1
neck 724.9
neuralgic 729.0
neuritis (acute) (chronic) 729.2
neuromuscular 729.0
nodose — *see* Arthritis, nodosa
nonarticular 729.0
palindromic 719.30
ankle 719.37
elbow 719.32
foot 719.37
hand 719.34
hip 719.35
knee 719.36
multiple sites 719.39
pelvic region 719.35
shoulder (region) 719.31
specified site NEC 719.38
wrist 719.33
pancarditis, acute 391.8

☑ Additional Digit Required — Refer to the Tabular List for Digit Selection

� Subterms under main terms may continue to next column or page

▶◀ Revised Text   ● New Line   ▲ Revised Code

Rheumatism, rheumatic — *continued*
  pancarditis, acute — *continued*
    with chorea (acute) (rheumatic) (Sydenham's) 392.0
    chronic or inactive 398.99
  pericarditis (active) (acute) (with effusion) (with pneumonia) 391.0
    with chorea (acute) (rheumatic) (Sydenham's) 392.0
    chronic or inactive 393
  pericardium — *see* Rheumatic, pericarditis
  pleuropericarditis — *see* Rheumatic, pericarditis
  pneumonia 390 *[517.1]*
  pneumonitis 390 *[517.1]*
  pneumopericarditis — *see* Rheumatic, pericarditis
  polyarthritis
    acute or subacute — *see* Fever, rheumatic
    chronic 714.0
  polyarticular NEC (*see also* Arthritis) 716.9 ☑
  psychogenic 306.0
  radiculitis 729.2
  sciatic 724.3
  septic — *see* Fever, rheumatic
  spine 724.9
  subacute NEC 729.0
  torticollis 723.5
  tuberculous NEC (*see also* Tuberculosis) 015.9 ☑
  typhoid fever 002.0
Rheumatoid — *see also* condition
  lungs 714.81
Rhinitis (atrophic) (catarrhal) (chronic) (croupous) (fibrinous) (hyperplastic) (hypertrophic) (membranous) (purulent) (suppurative) (ulcerative) 472.0
  with
    hay fever (*see also* Fever, hay) 477.9
      with asthma (bronchial) 493.0 ☑
    sore throat — *see* Nasopharyngitis
  acute 460
  allergic (nonseasonal) (seasonal) (*see also* Fever, hay) 477.9
    with asthma (*see also* Asthma) 493.0 ☑
    due to food 477.1
  granulomatous 472.0
  infective 460
  obstructive 472.0
  pneumococcal 460
  syphilitic 095.8
    congenital 090.0
  tuberculous (*see also* Tuberculosis) 012.8 ☑
  vasomotor (*see also* Fever, hay) 477.9
Rhinoantritis (chronic) 473.0
  acute 461.0
Rhinodacryolith 375.57
Rhinolalia (aperta) (clausa) (open) 784.43 ▲
Rhinolith 478.19
  nasal sinus (*see also* Sinusitis) 473.9
Rhinomegaly 478.19
Rhinopharyngitis (acute) (subacute) — *see also* Nasopharyngitis 460
  chronic 472.2
  destructive ulcerating 102.5
  mutilans 102.5
Rhinophyma 695.3
Rhinorrhea 478.19
  cerebrospinal (fluid) 349.81
  paroxysmal (*see also* Fever, hay) 477.9
  spasmodic (*see also* Fever, hay) 477.9
Rhinosalpingitis 381.50
  acute 381.51
  chronic 381.52
Rhinoscleroma 040.1
Rhinosporidiosis 117.0
Rhinovirus infection 079.3
Rhizomelic chrondrodysplasia punctata 277.86
Rhizomelique, pseudopolyarthritic 446.5
Rhoads and Bomford anemia (refractory) 238.72
Rhus
  diversiloba dermatitis 692.6
  radicans dermatitis 692.6
  toxicodendron dermatitis 692.6
  venenata dermatitis 692.6
  verniciflua dermatitis 692.6

Rhythm
  atrioventricular nodal 427.89
  disorder 427.9
    coronary sinus 427.89
    ectopic 427.89
    nodal 427.89
  escape 427.89
  heart, abnormal 427.9
    fetus or newborn — *see* Abnormal, heart rate
  idioventricular 426.89
    accelerated 427.89
    nodal 427.89
  sleep, inversion 327.39
    nonorganic origin 307.45
Rhytidosis facialis 701.8
Rib — *see also* condition
  cervical 756.2
Riboflavin deficiency 266.0
Rice bodies — *see also* Loose, body, joint 718.1
  knee 717.6
Richter's hernia — *see* Hernia, Richter's
Ricinism 988.2
Rickets (active) (acute) (adolescent) (adult) (chest wall) (congenital) (current) (infantile) (intestinal) 268.0
  celiac 579.0
  fetal 756.4
  hemorrhagic 267
  hypophosphatemic with nephrotic-glycosuric dwarfism 270.0
  kidney 588.0
  late effect 268.1
  renal 588.0
  scurvy 267
  vitamin D-resistant 275.3
Rickettsial disease 083.9
  specified type NEC 083.8
Rickettsialpox 083.2
Rickettsiosis NEC 083.9
  specified type NEC 083.8
  tick-borne 082.9
    specified type NEC 082.8
  vesicular 083.2
Ricord's chancre 091.0
Riddoch's syndrome (visual disorientation) 368.16
Rider's
  bone 733.99
  chancre 091.0
Ridge, alveolus — *see also* condition
  edentulous
    atrophy 525.20
      mandible 525.20
        minimal 525.21
        moderate 525.22
        severe 525.23
      maxilla 525.20
        minimal 525.24
        moderate 525.25
        severe 525.26
    flabby 525.20
Ridged ear 744.29
Riedel's
  disease (ligneous thyroiditis) 245.3
  lobe, liver 751.69
  struma (ligneous thyroiditis) 245.3
  thyroiditis (ligneous) 245.3
Rieger's anomaly or syndrome (mesodermal dysgenesis, anterior ocular segment) 743.44
Riehl's melanosis 709.09
Rietti-Greppi-Micheli anemia or syndrome 282.49
Rieux's hernia — *see* Hernia, Rieux's
Rift Valley fever 066.3
Riga's disease (cachectic aphthae) 529.0
Riga-Fede disease (cachectic aphthae) 529.0
Riggs' disease (compound periodontitis) 523.40
Rigid, rigidity — *see also* condition
  abdominal 789.4 ☑
  articular, multiple congenital 754.89
  back 724.8

Rigid, rigidity — *see also* condition — *continued*
  cervix uteri
    in pregnancy or childbirth 654.6 ☑
      affecting fetus or newborn 763.89
      causing obstructed labor 660.2 ☑
        affecting fetus or newborn 763.1
  hymen (acquired) (congenital) 623.3
  nuchal 781.6
  pelvic floor
    in pregnancy or childbirth 654.4 ☑
      affecting fetus or newborn 763.89
      causing obstructed labor 660.2 ☑
        affecting fetus or newborn 763.1
  perineum or vulva
    in pregnancy or childbirth 654.8 ☑
      affecting fetus or newborn 763.89
      causing obstructed labor 660.2 ☑
        affecting fetus or newborn 763.1
  spine 724.8
  vagina
    in pregnancy or childbirth 654.7 ☑
      affecting fetus or newborn 763.89
      causing obstructed labor 660.2 ☑
        affecting fetus or newborn 763.1
Rigors 780.99
Riley-Day syndrome (familial dysautonomia) 742.8
RIND (reversible ischemic neurological deficit) 434.91
  history of (personal) V12.54
Ring(s)
  aorta 747.21
  Bandl's, complicating delivery 661.4 ☑
    affecting fetus or newborn 763.7
  contraction, complicating delivery 661.4 ☑
    affecting fetus or newborn 763.7
  esophageal (congenital) 750.3
  Fleischer (-Kayser) (cornea) 275.1 *[371.14]*
  hymenal, tight (acquired) (congenital) 623.3
  Kayser-Fleischer (cornea) 275.1 *[371.14]*
  retraction, uterus, pathological 661.4 ☑
    affecting fetus or newborn 763.7
  Schatzki's (esophagus) (congenital) (lower) 750.3
    acquired 530.3
  Soemmering's 366.51
  trachea, abnormal 748.3
  vascular (congenital) 747.21
  Vossius' 921.3
    late effect 366.21
Ringed hair (congenital) 757.4
Ringing in the ear — *see also* Tinnitus 388.30
Ringworm 110.9
  beard 110.0
  body 110.5
  Burmese 110.9
  corporeal 110.5
  foot 110.4
  groin 110.3
  hand 110.2
  honeycomb 110.0
  nails 110.1
  perianal (area) 110.3
  scalp 110.0
  specified site NEC 110.8
  Tokelau 110.5
Rise, venous pressure 459.89
Risk
  factor — *see* Problem
  falling
    suicidal 300.9
Rivalry, sibling 313.3
Rivalta's disease (cervicofacial actinomycosis) 039.3
River blindness 125.3 *[360.13]*
Robert's pelvis 755.69
  with disproportion (fetopelvic) 653.0 ☑
    affecting fetus or newborn 763.1
    causing obstructed labor 660.1 ☑
      affecting fetus or newborn 763.1
Robinson's (hidrotic) **ectodermal dysplasia** 757.31
Robin's syndrome 756.0

Robles' disease (onchocerciasis) 125.3 *[360.13]*
Rochalimea — *see* Rickettsial disease
Rocky Mountain fever (spotted) 082.0
Rodent ulcer (M8090/3) — *see also* Neoplasm, skin, malignant
  cornea 370.07
Roentgen ray, adverse effect — *see* Effect, adverse, x-ray
Roetheln 056.9
Roger's disease (congenital interventricular septal defect) 745.4
Rokitansky's
  disease (*see also* Necrosis, liver) 570
  tumor 620.2
Rokitansky-Aschoff sinuses (mucosal outpouching of gallbladder) — *see also* Disease, gallbladder 575.8
Rokitansky-Kuster-Hauser syndrome (congenital absence vagina) 752.49
Rollet's chancre (syphilitic) 091.0
Rolling of head 781.0
Romano-Ward syndrome (prolonged QT interval syndrome) 426.82
Romanus lesion 720.1
Romberg's disease or syndrome 349.89
Roof, mouth — *see* condition
Rosacea 695.3
  acne 695.3
  keratitis 695.3 *[370.49]*
Rosary, rachitic 268.0
Rose
  cold 477.0
  fever 477.0
  rash 782.1
    epidemic 056.9
    of infants 057.8
Rosenbach's erysipelatoid or erysipeloid 027.1
Rosen-Castleman-Liebow syndrome (pulmonary proteinosis) 516.0
Rosenthal's disease (factor XI deficiency) 286.2
Roseola 057.8
  infantum, infantilis (*see also* Exanthem subitum) 058.10
Rossbach's disease (hyperchlorhydria) 536.8
  psychogenic 306.4
Rössle-Urbach-Wiethe lipoproteinosis 272.8
Ross river fever 066.3
Rostan's asthma (cardiac) — *see also* Failure, ventricular, left 428.1
Rot
  Barcoo (*see also* Ulcer, skin) 707.9
  knife-grinders' (*see also* Tuberculosis) 011.4 ☑
Rotation
  anomalous, incomplete or insufficient — *see* Malrotation
  cecum (congenital) 751.4
  colon (congenital) 751.4
  manual, affecting fetus or newborn 763.89
  spine, incomplete or insufficient 737.8
  tooth, teeth 524.35
  vertebra, incomplete or insufficient 737.8
Rot-Bernhardt disease 355.1
Röteln 056.9
Roth-Bernhardt disease or syndrome 355.1
Roth's disease or meralgia 355.1
Rothmund (-Thomson) syndrome 757.33
Rotor's disease or syndrome (idiopathic hyperbilirubinemia) 277.4
Rotundum ulcus — *see* Ulcer, stomach
Round
  back (with wedging of vertebrae) 737.10
    late effect of rickets 268.1
  hole, retina 361.31
    with detachment 361.01
  ulcer (stomach) — *see* Ulcer, stomach
  worms (infestation) (large) NEC 127.0
Roussy-Lévy syndrome 334.3
Routine postpartum follow-up V24.2
Roy (-Jutras) syndrome (acropachyderma) 757.39
Rubella (German measles) 056.9
  complicating pregnancy, childbirth, or puerperium 647.5 ☑
  complication 056.8
    neurological 056.00
      encephalomyelitis 056.01

☑ Additional Digit Required — Refer to the Tabular List for Digit Selection

▼ Subterms under main terms may continue to next column or page

Rubella — *continued*
  complication — *continued*
    neurological — *continued*
      specified type NEC 056.09
      specified type NEC 056.79
    congenital 771.0
    contact V01.4
    exposure to V01.4
    maternal
      with suspected fetal damage affecting management of pregnancy 655.3 ☑
      affecting fetus or newborn 760.2
        manifest rubella in infant 771.0
    specified complications NEC 056.79
    vaccination, prophylactic (against) V04.3
Rubeola (measles) — *see also* Measles 055.9
  complicated 055.8
  meaning rubella (*see also* Rubella) 056.9
  scarlatinosis 057.8
Rubeosis iridis 364.42
  diabetica 250.5 ☑ *[364.42]*
    due to secondary diabetes 249.5 ☑ *[364.42]*
Rubinstein-Taybi's syndrome (brachydactylia, short stature and mental retardation) 759.89
Rudimentary (congenital) — *see also* Agenesis
  arm 755.22
  bone 756.9
  cervix uteri 752.49
  eye (*see also* Microphthalmos) 743.10
  fallopian tube 752.19
  leg 755.32
  lobule of ear 744.21
  patella 755.64
  respiratory organs in thoracopagus 759.4
  tracheal bronchus 748.3
  uterine horn 752.3
  uterus 752.3
    in male 752.7
    solid or with cavity 752.3
  vagina 752.49
Rud's syndrome (mental deficiency, epilepsy, and infantilism) 759.89
Ruiter-Pompen (-Wyers) syndrome (angiokeratoma corporis diffusum) 272.7
Ruled out condition — *see also* Observation, suspected V71.9
Rumination — *see also* Vomiting
  disorder 307.53
  neurotic 300.3
  obsessional 300.3
  psychogenic 307.53
Runaway reaction — *see also* Disturbance, conduct
  socialized 312.2 ☑
  undersocialized, unsocialized 312.1 ☑
Runeberg's disease (progressive pernicious anemia) 281.0
Runge's syndrome (postmaturity) 766.22
Runny nose 784.99
Rupia 091.3
  congenital 090.0
  tertiary 095.9
Rupture, ruptured 553.9
  abdominal viscera NEC 799.89
    obstetrical trauma 665.5 ☑
  abscess (spontaneous) — *see* Abscess, by site
  amnion — *see* Rupture, membranes
  aneurysm — *see* Aneurysm
  anus (sphincter) — *see* Laceration, anus
  aorta, aortic 441.5
    abdominal 441.3
    arch 441.1
    ascending 441.1
    descending 441.5
      abdominal 441.3
      thoracic 441.1
    syphilitic 093.0
    thoracoabdominal 441.6
    thorax, thoracic 441.1
    transverse 441.1
    traumatic (thoracic) 901.0
      abdominal 902.0

Rupture, ruptured — *continued*
  aorta, aortic — *continued*
    valve or cusp (*see also* Endocarditis, aortic) 424.1
  appendix (with peritonitis) 540.0
    with peritoneal abscess 540.1
    traumatic — *see* Injury, internal, gastrointestinal tract
  arteriovenous fistula, brain (congenital) 430
  artery 447.2
    brain (*see also* Hemorrhage, brain) 431
    coronary (*see also* Infarct, myocardium) 410.9 ☑
    heart (*see also* Infarct, myocardium) 410.9 ☑
    pulmonary 417.8
    traumatic (complication) (*see also* Injury, blood vessel, by site) 904.9
  bile duct, except cystic (*see also* Disease, biliary) 576.3
    cystic 575.4
    traumatic — *see* Injury, internal, intra-abdominal
  bladder (sphincter) 596.6
    with
      abortion — *see* Abortion, by type, with damage to pelvic organs
      ectopic pregnancy (*see also* categories 633.0–633.9) 639.2
      molar pregnancy (*see also* categories 630–632) 639.2
    following
      abortion 639.2
      ectopic or molar pregnancy 639.2
    nontraumatic 596.6
    obstetrical trauma 665.5 ☑
    spontaneous 596.6
    traumatic — *see* Injury, internal, bladder
  blood vessel (*see also* Hemorrhage) 459.0
    brain (*see also* Hemorrhage, brain) 431
    heart (*see also* Infarct, myocardium) 410.9 ☑
    traumatic (complication) (*see also* Injury, blood vessel, by site) 904.9
  bone — *see* Fracture, by site
  bowel 569.89
    traumatic — *see* Injury, internal, intestine
  Bowman's membrane 371.31
  brain
    aneurysm (congenital) (*see also* Hemorrhage, subarachnoid) 430
      late effect — *see* Late effect(s) (of) cerebrovascular disease
      syphilitic 094.87
    hemorrhagic (*see also* Hemorrhage, brain) 431
    injury at birth 767.0
    syphilitic 094.89
  capillaries 448.9
  cardiac (*see also* Infarct, myocardium) 410.9 ☑
  cartilage (articular) (current) (*see also* Sprain, by site)
    knee — *see* Tear, meniscus
    semilunar — *see* Tear, meniscus
  cecum (with peritonitis) 540.0
    with peritoneal abscess 540.1
    traumatic 863.89
      with open wound into cavity 863.99
  cerebral aneurysm (congenital) (*see also* Hemorrhage, subarachnoid) 430
    late effect — *see* Late effect(s) (of) cerebrovascular disease
  cervix (uteri)
    with
      abortion — *see* Abortion, by type, with damage to pelvic organs
      ectopic pregnancy (*see also* categories 633.0–633.9) 639.2
      molar pregnancy (*see also* categories 630–632) 639.2
    following
      abortion 639.2
      ectopic or molar pregnancy 639.2
    obstetrical trauma 665.3 ☑
    traumatic — *see* Injury, internal, cervix
  chordae tendineae 429.5

Rupture, ruptured — *continued*
  choroid (direct) (indirect) (traumatic) 363.63
  circle of Willis (*see also* Hemorrhage, subarachnoid) 430
    late effect — *see* Late effect(s) (of) cerebrovascular disease
  colon 569.89
    traumatic — *see* Injury, internal, colon
  cornea (traumatic) (*see also* Rupture, eye)
    due to ulcer 370.00
  coronary (artery) (thrombotic) (*see also* Infarct, myocardium) 410.9 ☑
  corpus luteum (infected) (ovary) 620.1
  cyst — *see* Cyst
  cystic duct (*see also* Disease, gallbladder) 575.4
  Descemet's membrane 371.33
    traumatic — *see* Rupture, eye
  diaphragm (*see also* Hernia, diaphragm)
    traumatic — *see* Injury, internal, diaphragm
  diverticulum
    bladder 596.3
    intestine (large) (*see also* Diverticula) 562.10
      small 562.00
  duodenal stump 537.89
  duodenum (ulcer) — *see* Ulcer, duodenum, with perforation
  ear drum (*see also* Perforation, tympanum) 384.20
    with otitis media — *see* Otitis media
    traumatic — *see* Wound, open, ear
  esophagus 530.4
    traumatic 862.22
      with open wound into cavity 862.32
      cervical region — *see* Wound, open, esophagus
  eye (without prolapse of intraocular tissue) 871.0
    with
      exposure of intraocular tissue 871.1
      partial loss of intraocular tissue 871.2
      prolapse of intraocular tissue 871.1
    due to burn 940.5
  fallopian tube 620.8
    due to pregnancy — *see* Pregnancy, tubal
    traumatic — *see* Injury, internal, fallopian tube
  fontanel 767.3
  free wall (ventricle) (*see also* Infarct, myocardium) 410.9 ☑
  gallbladder or duct (*see also* Disease, gallbladder) 575.4
    traumatic — *see* Injury, internal, gallbladder
  gastric (*see also* Rupture, stomach) 537.89
    vessel 459.0
  globe (eye) (traumatic) — *see* Rupture, eye
  graafian follicle (hematoma) 620.0
  heart (auricle) (ventricle) (*see also* Infarct, myocardium) 410.9 ☑
    infectional 422.90
    traumatic — *see* Rupture, myocardium, traumatic
  hymen 623.8
  internal
    organ, traumatic (*see also* Injury, internal, by site)
      heart — *see* Rupture, myocardium, traumatic
      kidney — *see* Rupture, kidney
      liver — *see* Rupture, liver
      spleen — *see* Rupture, spleen, traumatic
    semilunar cartilage — *see* Tear, meniscus
  intervertebral disc — *see* Displacement, intervertebral disc
    traumatic (current) — *see* Dislocation, vertebra
  intestine 569.89
    traumatic — *see* Injury, internal, intestine
  intracranial, birth injury 767.0
  iris 364.76
    traumatic — *see* Rupture, eye
  joint capsule — *see* Sprain, by site
  kidney (traumatic) 866.03

Rupture, ruptured — *continued*
  kidney — *continued*
    with open wound into cavity 866.13
    due to birth injury 767.8
    nontraumatic 593.89
  lacrimal apparatus (traumatic) 870.2
  lens (traumatic) 366.20
  ligament (*see also* Sprain, by site)
    with open wound — *see* Wound, open, by site
    old (*see also* Disorder, cartilage, articular) 718.0 ☑
  liver (traumatic) 864.04
    with open wound into cavity 864.14
    due to birth injury 767.8
    nontraumatic 573.8
  lymphatic (node) (vessel) 457.8
  marginal sinus (placental) (with hemorrhage) 641.2 ☑
    affecting fetus or newborn 762.1
  meaning hernia — *see* Hernia
  membrana tympani (*see also* Perforation, tympanum) 384.20
    with otitis media — *see* Otitis media
    traumatic — *see* Wound, open, ear
  membranes (spontaneous)
    artificial
      delayed delivery following 658.3 ☑
        affecting fetus or newborn 761.1
      fetus or newborn 761.1
    delayed delivery following 658.2 ☑
      affecting fetus or newborn 761.1
    premature (less than 24 hours prior to onset of labor) 658.1 ☑
      affecting fetus or newborn 761.1
      delayed delivery following 658.2 ☑
        affecting fetus or newborn 761.1
  meningeal artery (*see also* Hemorrhage, subarachnoid) 430
    late effect — *see* Late effect(s) (of) cerebrovascular disease
  meniscus (knee) (*see also* Tear, meniscus)
    old (*see also* Derangement, meniscus) 717.5
      site other than knee — *see* Disorder, cartilage, articular
    site other than knee — *see* Sprain, by site
  mesentery 568.89
    traumatic — *see* Injury, internal, mesentery
  mitral — *see* Insufficiency, mitral
  muscle (traumatic) NEC (*see also* Sprain, by site)
    with open wound — *see* Wound, open, by site
    nontraumatic 728.83
  musculotendinous cuff (nontraumatic) (shoulder) 840.4
  mycotic aneurysm, causing cerebral hemorrhage (*see also* Hemorrhage, subarachnoid) 430
    late effect — *see* Late effect(s) (of) cerebrovascular disease
  myocardium, myocardial (*see also* Infarct, myocardium) 410.9 ☑
    traumatic 861.03
      with open wound into thorax 861.13
  nontraumatic (meaning hernia) (*see also* Hernia, by site) 553.9
  obstructed (*see also* Hernia, by site, with obstruction) 552.9
    gangrenous (*see also* Hernia, by site, with gangrene) 551.9
  operation wound (*see also* Dehiscence) 998.32
    internal 998.31
  ovary, ovarian 620.8
    corpus luteum 620.1
    follicle (graafian) 620.0
  oviduct 620.8
    due to pregnancy — *see* Pregnancy, tubal
  pancreas 577.8
    traumatic — *see* Injury, internal, pancreas
  papillary muscle (ventricular) 429.6
  pelvic
    floor, complicating delivery 664.1 ☑
    organ NEC — *see* Injury, pelvic, organs
  penis (traumatic) — *see* Wound, open, penis

☑ Additional Digit Required — Refer to the Tabular List for Digit Selection
🐾 Subterms under main terms may continue to next column or page
240 — Volume 2   ►◄ Revised Text   ● New Line   ▲ Revised Code   2010 ICD-9-CM

Rupture, ruptured — *continued*
  perineum 624.8
    during delivery (*see also* Laceration, perineum, complicating delivery)
      664.4 ☑
  pharynx (*nontraumatic*) (*spontaneous*) 478.29
  pregnant uterus (before onset of labor)
    665.0 ☑
  prostate (*traumatic*) — *see* Injury, internal, prostate
  pulmonary
    artery 417.8
    valve (heart) (*see also* Endocarditis, pulmonary) 424.3
    vein 417.8
    vessel 417.8
  pupil, sphincter 364.75
  pus tube (*see also* Salpingo-oophoritis) 614.2
  pyosalpinx (*see also* Salpingo-oophoritis) 614.2
  rectum 569.49
    traumatic — *see* Injury, internal, rectum
  retina, retinal (*traumatic*) (*without detachment*) 361.30
    with detachment (*see also* Detachment, retina, with retinal defect) 361.00
  rotator cuff (capsule) (*traumatic*) 840.4
    nontraumatic, complete 727.61
  sclera 871.0
  semilunar cartilage, knee (*see also* Tear, meniscus) 836.2
    old (*see also* Derangement, meniscus) 717.5
  septum (cardiac) 410.8 ☑
  sigmoid 569.89
    traumatic — *see* Injury, internal, colon, sigmoid
  sinus of Valsalva 747.29
  spinal cord (*see also* Injury, spinal, by site)
    due to injury at birth 767.4
    fetus or newborn 767.4
    syphilitic 094.89
    traumatic (*see also* Injury, spinal, by site)
      with fracture — *see* Fracture, vertebra, by site, with spinal cord injury
  spleen 289.59
    congenital 767.8
    due to injury at birth 767.8
    malarial 084.9
    nontraumatic 289.59
    spontaneous 289.59
    traumatic 865.04

Rupture, ruptured — *continued*
  spleen — *continued*
    traumatic — *continued*
      with open wound into cavity 865.14
  splenic vein 459.0
  stomach 537.89
    due to injury at birth 767.8
    traumatic — *see* Injury, internal, stomach
    ulcer — *see* Ulcer, stomach, with perforation
  synovium 727.50
    specified site NEC 727.59
  tendon (traumatic) (*see also* Sprain, by site)
    with open wound — *see* Wound, open, by site
    Achilles 845.09
      nontraumatic 727.67
    ankle 845.09
      nontraumatic 727.68
    biceps (long bead) 840.8
      nontraumatic 727.62
    foot 845.10
      interphalangeal (joint) 845.13
      metatarsophalangeal (joint) 845.12
      nontraumatic 727.68
      specified site NEC 845.19
      tarsometatarsal (joint) 845.11
    hand 842.10
      carpometacarpal (joint) 842.11
      interphalangeal (joint) 842.13
      metacarpophalangeal (joint) 842.12
      nontraumatic 727.63
        extensors 727.63
        flexors 727.64
      specified site NEC 842.19
    nontraumatic 727.60
      specified site NEC 727.69
    patellar 844.8
      nontraumatic 727.66
    quadriceps 844.8
      nontraumatic 727.65
    rotator cuff (capsule) 840.4
      nontraumatic, complete 727.61
    wrist 842.00
      carpal (joint) 842.01
      nontraumatic 727.63
        extensors 727.63
        flexors 727.64
      radiocarpal (joint) (ligament) 842.02
      radioulnar (joint), distal 842.09
      specified site NEC 842.09

Rupture, ruptured — *continued*
  testis (traumatic) 878.2
    complicated 878.3
    due to syphilis 095.8
  thoracic duct 457.8
  tonsil 474.8
  traumatic
    with open wound — *see* Wound, open, by site
    aorta — *see* Rupture, aorta, traumatic
    ear drum — *see* Wound, open, ear, drum
    external site — *see* Wound, open, by site
    eye 871.2
    globe (eye) — *see* Wound, open, eyeball
    internal organ (abdomen, chest, or pelvis) (*see also* Injury, internal, by site)
      heart — *see* Rupture, myocardium, traumatic
      kidney — *see* Rupture, kidney
      liver — *see* Rupture, liver
      spleen — *see* Rupture, spleen, traumatic
    ligament, muscle, or tendon (*see also* Sprain, by site)
      with open wound — *see* Wound, open, by site
    meaning hernia — *see* Hernia
  tricuspid (heart) (valve) — *see* Endocarditis, tricuspid
  tube, tubal 620.8
    abscess (*see also* Salpingo-oophoritis) 614.2
    due to pregnancy — *see* Pregnancy, tubal
  tympanum, tympanic (membrane) (*see also* Perforation, tympanum) 384.20
    with otitis media — *see* Otitis media
    traumatic — *see* Wound, open, ear, drum
  umbilical cord 663.8 ☑
    fetus or newborn 772.0
  ureter (traumatic) (*see also* Injury, internal, ureter) 867.2
    nontraumatic 593.89
  urethra 599.84
    with
      abortion — *see* Abortion, by type, with damage to pelvic organs
      ectopic pregnancy (*see also* categories 633.0–633.9) 639.2
      molar pregnancy (*see also* categories 630–632) 639.2
    following
      abortion 639.2

Rupture, ruptured — *continued*
  urethra — *continued*
    following — *continued*
      ectopic or molar pregnancy 639.2
    obstetrical trauma 665.5 ☑
    traumatic — *see* Injury, internal urethra
  uterosacral ligament 620.8
  uterus (traumatic) (*see also* Injury, internal, uterus)
    affecting fetus or newborn 763.89
    during labor 665.1 ☑
    nonpuerperal, nontraumatic 621.8
    nontraumatic 621.8
    pregnant (during labor) 665.1 ☑
      before labor 665.0 ☑
  vagina 878.6
    complicated 878.7
    complicating delivery — *see* Laceration, vagina, complicating delivery
  valve, valvular (heart) — *see* Endocarditis
  varicose vein — *see* Varicose, vein
  varix — *see* Varix
  vena cava 459.0
  varix — *see* Varix
  ventricle (free wall) (left) (*see also* Infarct, myocardium) 410.9 ☑
  vesical (urinary) 596.6
    traumatic — *see* Injury, internal, bladder
  vessel (blood) 459.0
    pulmonary 417.8
  viscus 799.89
  vulva 878.4
    complicated 878.5
    complicating delivery 664.0 ☑
Russell's dwarf (uterine dwarfism and craniofacial dysostosis) 759.89
Russell's dysentery 004.8
Russell (-Silver) syndrome (congenital hemihypertrophy and short stature) 759.89
Russian spring-summer type encephalitis 063.0
Rust's disease (tuberculous spondylitis) 015.0 ☑ [720.81]
Rustitskii's disease (multiple myeloma) (M9730/3) 203.0 ☑
Ruysch's disease (Hirschsprung's disease) 751.3
Rytand-Lipsitch syndrome (complete atrioventricular block) 426.0

S

Saber
 shin 090.5
 tibia 090.5
Saccharomyces infection — *see also* Candidiasis
 112.9
Saccharopinuria 270.7
Saccular — *see* condition
Sacculation
 aorta (nonsyphilitic) (*see also* Aneurysm, aorta)
 441.9
 ruptured 441.5
 syphilitic 093.0
 bladder 596.3
 colon 569.89
 intralaryngeal (congenital) (ventricular) 748.3
 larynx (congenital) (ventricular) 748.3
 organ or site, congenital — *see* Distortion
 pregnant uterus, complicating delivery
 654.4 ☑
 affecting fetus or newborn 763.1
 causing obstructed labor 660.2 ☑
 affecting fetus or newborn 763.1
 rectosigmoid 569.89
 sigmoid 569.89
 ureter 593.89
 urethra 599.2
 vesical 596.3
Sachs (-Tay) disease (amaurotic familial idiocy)
 330.1
Sacks-Libman disease 710.0 *[424.91]*
Sac, lacrimal — *see* condition
Sacralgia 724.6
Sacralization
 fifth lumbar vertebra 756.15
 incomplete (vertebra) 756.15
Sacrodynia 724.6
Sacroiliac joint — *see* condition
Sacroiliitis NEC 720.2
Sacrum — *see* condition
Saddle
 back 737.8
 embolus, aorta 444.0
 nose 738.0
 congenital 754.0
 due to syphilis 090.5
Sadism (sexual) 302.84
Saemisch's ulcer 370.04
Saenger's syndrome 379.46
Sago spleen 277.39
Sailors' skin 692.74
Saint
 Anthony's fire (*see also* Erysipelas) 035
 Guy's dance — *see* Chorea
 Louis-type encephalitis 062.3
 triad (*see also* Hernia, diaphragm) 553.3
 Vitus' dance — *see* Chorea
Salicylism
 correct substance properly administered
 535.4 ☑
 overdose or wrong substance given or taken
 965.1
Salivary duct or gland — *see also* condition
 virus disease 078.5
Salivation (excessive) — *see also* Ptyalism 527.7
Salmonella (aertrycke) (choleraesuis) (enteritidis)
 (gallinarum) (suipestifer) (typhimurium)
 — *see also* Infection, Salmonella 003.9
 arthritis 003.23
 carrier (suspected) of V02.3
 meningitis 003.21
 osteomyelitis 003.24
 pneumonia 003.22
 septicemia 003.1
 typhosa 002.0
 carrier (suspected) of V02.1
Salmonellosis 003.0
 with pneumonia 003.22
Salpingitis (catarrhal) (fallopian tube) (nodular)
 (pseudofollicular) (purulent) (septic) — *see
 also* Salpingo-oophoritis 614.2
 ear 381.50
 acute 381.51
 chronic 381.52
 Eustachian (tube) 381.50

Salpingitis — *see also* Salpingo-oophoritis —
 continued
 Eustachian — *continued*
 acute 381.51
 chronic 381.52
 follicularis 614.1
 gonococcal (chronic) 098.37
 acute 098.17
 interstitial, chronic 614.1
 isthmica nodosa 614.1
 old — *see* Salpingo-oophoritis, chronic
 puerperal, postpartum, childbirth
 670.8 ☑ ▲
 specific (chronic) 098.37
 acute 098.17
 tuberculous (acute) (chronic) (*see also* Tuberculosis) 016.6 ☑
 venereal (chronic) 098.37
 acute 098.17
Salpingocele 620.4
Salpingo-oophoritis (catarrhal) (purulent) (ruptured) (septic) (suppurative) 614.2
 acute 614.0
 with
 abortion — *see* Abortion, by type, with
 sepsis
 ectopic pregnancy (*see also* categories
 633.0–633.9) 639.0
 molar pregnancy (*see also* categories
 630–632) 639.0
 following
 abortion 639.0
 ectopic or molar pregnancy 639.0
 gonococcal 098.17
 puerperal, postpartum, childbirth
 670.8 ☑ ▲
 tuberculous (*see also* Tuberculosis)
 016.6 ☑
 chronic 614.1
 gonococcal 098.37
 tuberculous (see also Tuberculosis)
 016.6 ☑
 complicating pregnancy 646.6 ☑
 affecting fetus or newborn 760.8
 gonococcal (chronic) 098.37
 acute 098.17
 old — *see* Salpingo-oophoritis, chronic
 puerperal 670.8 ☑ ▲
 specific — *see* Salpingo-oophoritis, gonococcal
 subacute (*see also* Salpingo-oophoritis, acute)
 614.0
 tuberculous (acute) (chronic) (*see also* Tuberculosis) 016.6 ☑
 venereal — *see* Salpingo-oophoritis, gonococcal
Salpingo-ovaritis — *see also* Salpingo-oophoritis
 614.2
Salpingoperitonitis — *see also* Salpingo-
 oophoritis 614.2
Salt-losing
 nephritis (*see also* Disease, renal) 593.9
 syndrome (*see also* Disease, renal) 593.9
Salt-rheum — *see also* Eczema 692.9
Salzmann's nodular dystrophy 371.46
Sampling
 chorionic villus V28.89
Sampson's cyst or tumor 617.1
Sandblasters'
 asthma 502
 lung 502
Sander's disease (paranoia) 297.1
Sandfly fever 066.0
Sandhoff's disease 330.1
Sanfilippo's syndrome (mucopolysaccharidosis
 III) 277.5
Sanger-Brown's ataxia 334.2
San Joaquin Valley fever 114.0
Sao Paulo fever or typhus 082.0
Saponification, mesenteric 567.89
Sapremia — *see* Septicemia
Sarcocele (benign)
 syphilitic 095.8
 congenital 090.5
Sarcoepiplocele — *see also* Hernia 553.9

Sarcoepiplomphalocele — *see also* Hernia,
 umbilicus 553.1
Sarcoid (any site) 135
 with lung involvement 135 *[517.8]*
 Boeck's 135
 Darier-Roussy 135
 Spiegler-Fendt 686.8
Sarcoidosis 135
 cardiac 135 *[425.8]*
 lung 135 *[517.8]*
Sarcoma (M8800/3) — *see also* Neoplasm, connective tissue, malignant
 alveolar soft part (M9581/3) — *see* Neoplasm,
 connective tissue, malignant
 ameloblastic (M9330/3) 170.1
 upper jaw (bone) 170.0
 botryoid (M8910/3) — *see* Neoplasm, connective tissue, malignant
 botryoides (M8910/3) — *see* Neoplasm, connective tissue, malignant
 cerebellar (M9480/3) 191.6
 circumscribed (arachnoidal) (M9471/3)
 191.6
 circumscribed (arachnoidal) cerebellar
 (M9471/3) 191.6
 clear cell, of tendons and aponeuroses
 (M9044/3) — *see* Neoplasm, connective tissue, malignant
 embryonal (M8991/3) — *see* Neoplasm, connective tissue, malignant
 endometrial (stromal) (M8930/3) 182.0
 isthmus 182.1
 endothelial (M9130/3) (*see also* Neoplasm,
 connective tissue, malignant)
 bone (M9260/3) — *see* Neoplasm, bone,
 malignant
 epithelioid cell (M8804/3) — *see* Neoplasm,
 connective tissue, malignant
 Ewing's (M9260/3) — *see* Neoplasm, bone,
 malignant
 follicular dendritic cell 202.9 ☑
 germinoblastic (diffuse) (M9632/3) 202.8 ☑
 follicular (M9697/3) 202.0 ☑
 giant cell (M8802/3) (*see also* Neoplasm, connective tissue, malignant)
 bone (M9250/3) — *see* Neoplasm, bone,
 malignant
 glomoid (M8710/3) — *see* Neoplasm, connective tissue, malignant
 granulocytic (M9930/3) 205.3 ☑
 hemangioendothelial (M9130/3) — *see* Neoplasm, connective tissue, malignant
 hemorrhagic, multiple (M9140/3) — *see* Kaposi's, sarcoma
 Hodgkin's (M9662/3) 201.2 ☑
 immunoblastic (M9612/3) 200.8 ☑
 interdigitating dendritic cell 202.9 ☑
 Kaposi's (M9140/3) — *see* Kaposi's, sarcoma
 Kupffer cell (M9124/3) 155.0
 Langerhans cell 202.9 ☑
 leptomeningeal (M9530/3) — *see* Neoplasm,
 meninges, malignant
 lymphangioendothelial (M9170/3) — *see*
 Neoplasm, connective tissue, malignant
 lymphoblastic (M9630/3) 200.1 ☑
 lymphocytic (M9620/3) 200.1 ☑
 mast cell (M9740/3) 202.6 ☑
 melanotic (M8720/3) — *see* Melanoma
 meningeal (M9530/3) — *see* Neoplasm,
 meninges, malignant
 meningothelial (M9530/3) — *see* Neoplasm,
 meninges, malignant
 mesenchymal (M8800/3) (*see also* Neoplasm,
 connective tissue, malignant)
 mixed (M8990/3) — *see* Neoplasm, connective tissue, malignant
 mesothelial (M9050/3) — *see* Neoplasm, by
 site, malignant
 monstrocellular (M9481/3)
 specified site — *see* Neoplasm, by site,
 malignant
 unspecified site 191.9
 myeloid (M9930/3) 205.3 ☑
 neurogenic (M9540/3) — *see* Neoplasm,
 connective tissue, malignant

Sarcoma — *see also* Neoplasm, connective tissue,
 malignant — *continued*
 odontogenic (M9270/3) 170.1
 upper jaw (bone) 170.0
 osteoblastic (M9180/3) — *see* Neoplasm,
 bone, malignant
 osteogenic (M9180/3) (*see also* Neoplasm,
 bone, malignant)
 juxtacortical (M9190/3) — *see* Neoplasm,
 bone, malignant
 periosteal (M9190/3) — *see* Neoplasm,
 bone, malignant
 periosteal (M8812/3) (*see also* Neoplasm, bone,
 malignant)
 osteogenic (M9190/3) — *see* Neoplasm,
 bone, malignant
 plasma cell (M9731/3) 203.8 ☑
 pleomorphic cell (M8802/3) — *see* Neoplasm,
 connective tissue, malignant
 reticuloendothelial (M9720/3) 202.3 ☑
 reticulum cell (M9640/3) 200.0 ☑
 nodular (M9642/3) 200.0 ☑
 pleomorphic cell type (M9641/3) 200.0 ☑
 round cell (M8803/3) — *see* Neoplasm, connective tissue, malignant
 small cell (M8803/3) — *see* Neoplasm, connective tissue, malignant
 spindle cell (M8801/3) — *see* Neoplasm, connective tissue, malignant
 stromal (endometrial) (M8930/3) 182.0
 isthmus 182.1
 synovial (M9040/3) (*see also* Neoplasm, connective tissue, malignant)
 biphasic type (M9043/3) — *see* Neoplasm,
 connective tissue, malignant
 epithelioid cell type (M9042/3) — *see*
 Neoplasm, connective tissue, malignant
 spindle cell type (M9041/3) — *see* Neoplasm, connective tissue, malignant
Sarcomatosis
 meningeal (M9539/3) — *see* Neoplasm,
 meninges, malignant
 specified site NEC (M8800/3) — *see* Neoplasm,
 connective tissue, malignant
 unspecified site (M8800/6) 171.9
Sarcosinemia 270.8
Sarcosporidiosis 136.5
Satiety, early 780.94
**Satisfactory smear but lacking transformation
 zone**
 anal 796.77
 cervical 795.07
Saturnine — *see* condition
Saturnism 984.9
 specified type of lead — *see* Table of Drugs
 and Chemicals
Satyriasis 302.89
Sauriasis — *see* Ichthyosis
Sauriderma 757.39
Sauriosis — *see* Ichthyosis
Savill's disease (epidemic exfoliative dermatitis)
 695.89
SBE (subacute bacterial endocarditis) 421.0
Scabies (any site) 133.0
Scabs 782.8
Scaglietti-Dagnini syndrome (acromegalic
 macrospondylitis) 253.0
Scald, scalded — *see also* Burn, by site
 skin syndrome 695.81
Scalenus anticus (anterior) syndrome 353.0
Scales 782.8
Scalp — *see* condition
Scaphocephaly 756.0
Scaphoiditis, tarsal 732.5
Scapulalgia 733.90
Scapulohumeral myopathy 359.1
Scarabiasis 134.1
Scarlatina 034.1
 anginosa 034.1
 maligna 034.1
 myocarditis, acute 034.1 *[422.0]*
 old (*see also* Myocarditis) 429.0
 otitis media 034.1 *[382.02]*
 ulcerosa 034.1
Scarlatinella 057.8

☑ Additional Digit Required — Refer to the Tabular List for Digit Selection

Ⓦ Subterms under main terms may continue to next column or page

Scarlet fever (albuminuria) (angina) (convulsions) (lesions of lid) (rash) 034.1
Scar, scarring — *see also* Cicatrix 709.2
  adherent 709.2
  atrophic 709.2
  cervix
    in pregnancy or childbirth 654.6 ☑
      affecting fetus or newborn 763.89
        causing obstructed labor 660.2 ☑
          affecting fetus or newborn 763.1
  cheloid 701.4
  chorioretinal 363.30
    disseminated 363.35
    macular 363.32
    peripheral 363.34
    posterior pole NEC 363.33
  choroid (*see also* Scar, chorioretinal) 363.30
  compression, pericardial 423.9
  congenital 757.39
  conjunctiva 372.64
  cornea 371.00
    xerophthalmic 264.6
  due to previous cesarean delivery, complicating pregnancy or childbirth 654.2 ☑
    affecting fetus or newborn 763.89
  duodenal (bulb) (cap) 537.3
  hypertrophic 701.4
  keloid 701.4
  labia 624.4
  lung (base) 518.89
  macula 363.32
    disseminated 363.35
    peripheral 363.34
  muscle 728.89
  myocardium, myocardial 412
  painful 709.2
  papillary muscle 429.81
  posterior pole NEC 363.33
    macular — *see* Scar, macula
  postnecrotic (hepatic) (liver) 571.9
  psychic V15.49
  retina (*see also* Scar, chorioretinal) 363.30
  trachea 478.9
  uterus 621.8
    in pregnancy or childbirth NEC 654.9 ☑
      affecting fetus or newborn 763.89
      due to previous cesarean delivery 654.2 ☑
  vulva 624.4
Schamberg's disease, dermatitis, or dermatosis (progressive pigmentary dermatosis) 709.09
Schatzki's ring (esophagus) (lower) (congenital) 750.3
  acquired 530.3
Schaufenster krankheit 413.9
Schaumann's
  benign lymphogranulomatosis 135
  disease (sarcoidosis) 135
  syndrome (sarcoidosis) 135
Scheie's syndrome (mucopolysaccharidosis IS) 277.5
Schenck's disease (sporotrichosis) 117.1
Scheuermann's disease or osteochondrosis 732.0
Scheuthauer-Marie-Sainton syndrome (cleidocranialis dysostosis) 755.59
Schilder (-Flatau) disease 341.1
Schilling-type monocytic leukemia (M9890/3) 206.9 ☑
Schimmelbusch's disease, cystic mastitis, or hyperplasia 610.1
Schirmer's syndrome (encephalocutaneous angiomatosis) 759.6
Schistocelia 756.79
Schistoglossia 750.13
Schistosoma infestation — *see* Infestation, Schistosoma
Schistosomiasis 120.9
  Asiatic 120.2
  bladder 120.0
  chestermani 120.8
  colon 120.1
  cutaneous 120.3
  due to
    S. hematobium 120.0

Schistosomiasis — *continued*
  due to — *continued*
    S. japonicum 120.2
    S. mansoni 120.1
    S. mattheii 120.8
  eastern 120.2
  genitourinary tract 120.0
  intestinal 120.1
  lung 120.2
  Manson's (intestinal) 120.1
  Oriental 120.2
  pulmonary 120.2
  specified type NEC 120.8
  vesical 120.0
Schizencephaly 742.4
Schizo-affective psychosis — *see also* Schizophrenia 295.7 ☑
Schizodontia 520.2
Schizoid personality 301.20
  introverted 301.21
  schizotypal 301.22
Schizophrenia, schizophrenic (reaction) 295.9 ☑

Note — Use the following fifth-digit subclassification with category 295:

  0 unspecified
  1 subchronic
  2 chronic
  3 subchronic with acute exacerbation
  4 chronic with acute exacerbation
  5 in remission

  acute (attack) NEC 295.8 ☑
    episode 295.4 ☑
  atypical form 295.8 ☑
  borderline 295.5 ☑
  catalepsy 295.2 ☑
  catatonic (type) (acute) (excited) (withdrawn) 295.2 ☑
  childhood (type) (*see also* Psychosis, childhood) 299.9 ☑
  chronic NEC 295.6 ☑
  coenesthesiopathic 295.8 ☑
  cyclic (type) 295.7 ☑
  disorganized (type) 295.1 ☑
  flexibilitas cerea 295.2 ☑
  hebephrenic (type) (acute) 295.1 ☑
  incipient 295.5 ☑
  latent 295.5 ☑
  paranoid (type) (acute) 295.3 ☑
  paraphrenic (acute) 295.3 ☑
  prepsychotic 295.5 ☑
  primary (acute) 295.0 ☑
  prodromal 295.5 ☑
  pseudoneurotic 295.5 ☑
  pseudopsychopathic 295.5 ☑
  reaction 295.9 ☑
  residual type (state) 295.6 ☑
  restzustand 295.6 ☑
  schizo-affective (type) (depressed) (excited) 295.7 ☑
  schizophreniform type 295.4 ☑
  simple (type) (acute) 295.0 ☑
  simplex (acute) 295.0 ☑
  specified type NEC 295.8 ☑
  syndrome of childhood NEC (*see also* Psychosis, childhood) 299.9 ☑
  undifferentiated type 295.9 ☑
    acute 295.8 ☑
    chronic 295.6 ☑
Schizothymia 301.20
  introverted 301.21
  schizotypal 301.22
Schlafkrankheit 086.5
Schlatter-Osgood disease (osteochondrosis, tibial tubercle) 732.4
Schlatter's tibia (osteochondrosis) 732.4
Schloffer's tumor — *see also* Peritonitis 567.29
Schmidt's syndrome
  sphallo-pharyngo-laryngeal hemiplegia 352.6
  thyroid-adrenocortical insufficiency 258.1
  vagoaccessory 352.6

Schmincke
  carcinoma (M8082/3) — *see* Neoplasm, nasopharynx, malignant
  tumor (M8082/3) — *see* Neoplasm, nasopharynx, malignant
Schmitz (-Stutzer) dysentery 004.0
Schmorl's disease or nodes 722.30
  lumbar, lumbosacral 722.32
  specified region NEC 722.39
  thoracic, thoracolumbar 722.31
Schneiderian
  carcinoma (M8121/3)
    specified site — *see* Neoplasm, by site, malignant
    unspecified site 160.0
  papilloma (M8121/0)
    specified site — *see* Neoplasm, by site, benign
    unspecified site 212.0
Schneider's syndrome 047.9
Schnitzler syndrome 273.1
Schoffer's tumor — *see also* Peritonitis 567.29
Scholte's syndrome (malignant carcinoid) 259.2
Scholz's disease 330.0
Scholz (-Bielschowsky-Henneberg) syndrome 330.0
Schönlein (-Henoch) disease (primary) (purpura) (rheumatic) 287.0
School examination V70.3
  following surgery V67.09   ●
Schottmüller's disease — *see also* Fever, paratyphoid 002.9
Schroeder's syndrome (endocrine-hypertensive) 255.3
Schüller-Christian disease or syndrome (chronic histiocytosis X) 277.89
Schultz's disease or syndrome (agranulocytosis) 288.09
Schultze's acroparesthesia, simple 443.89
Schwalbe-Ziehen-Oppenheimer disease 333.6
Schwannoma (M9560/0) — *see also* Neoplasm, connective tissue, benign
  malignant (M9560/3) — *see* Neoplasm, connective tissue, malignant
Schwartz-Bartter syndrome (inappropriate secretion of antidiuretic hormone) 253.6
Schwartz (-Jampel) syndrome 359.23
Schweninger-Buzzi disease (macular atrophy) 701.3
Sciatic — *see* condition
Sciatica (infectional) 724.3
  due to
    displacement of intervertebral disc 722.10
    herniation, nucleus pulposus 722.10
  wallet 724.3
Scimitar syndrome (anomalous venous drainage, right lung to inferior vena cava) 747.49
Sclera — *see* condition
Sclerectasia 379.11
Scleredema
  adultorum 710.1
  Buschke's 710.1
  newborn 778.1
Sclerema
  adiposum (newborn) 778.1
  adultorum 710.1
  edematosum (newborn) 778.1
  neonatorum 778.1
  newborn 778.1
Scleriasis — *see* Scleroderma
Scleritis 379.00
  with corneal involvement 379.05
  anterior (annular) (localized) 379.03
  brawny 379.06
  granulomatous 379.09
  posterior 379.07
  specified NEC 379.09
  suppurative 379.09
  syphilitic 095.0
  tuberculous (nodular) (*see also* Tuberculosis) 017.3 ☑ [379.09]
Sclerochoroiditis — *see also* Scleritis 379.00
Scleroconjunctivitis — *see also* Scleritis 379.00
Sclerocystic ovary (syndrome) 256.4
Sclerodactylia 701.0

Scleroderma, sclerodermia (acrosclerotic) (diffuse) (generalized) (progressive) (pulmonary) 710.1
  circumscribed 701.0
  linear 701.0
  localized (linear) 701.0
  newborn 778.1
Sclerokeratitis 379.05
  meaning sclerosing keratitis 370.54
  tuberculous (*see also* Tuberculosis) 017.3 ☑ [379.09]
Scleromalacia
  multiple 731.0
  perforans 379.04
Scleroma, trachea 040.1
Scleromyxedema 701.8
Scleroperikeratitis 379.05
Sclerose en plaques 340
Sclerosis, sclerotic
  adrenal (gland) 255.8
  Alzheimer's 331.0
    with dementia — *see* Alzheimer's, dementia
  amyotrophic (lateral) 335.20
  annularis fibrosi
    aortic 424.1
    mitral 424.0
  aorta, aortic 440.0
    valve (*see also* Endocarditis, aortic) 424.1
  artery, arterial, arteriolar, arteriovascular — *see* Arteriosclerosis
  ascending multiple 340
  Baló's (concentric) 341.1
  basilar — *see* Sclerosis, brain
  bone (localized) NEC 733.99
  brain (general) (lobular) 348.89   ▲
    Alzheimer's — *see* Alzheimer's, dementia
    artery, arterial 437.0
    atrophic lobar 331.0
      with dementia
        with behavioral disturbance 331.0 [294.11]
        without behavioral disturbance 331.0 [294.10]
    diffuse 341.1
      familial (chronic) (infantile) 330.0
      infantile (chronic) (familial) 330.0
      Pelizaeus-Merzbacher type 330.0
    disseminated 340
    hereditary 334.2
    hippocampal 348.81   ●
    infantile (degenerative) (diffuse) 330.0
    insular 340
    Krabbe's 330.0
    mesial temporal 348.81   ●
    miliary 340
    multiple 340
    Pelizaeus-Merzbacher 330.0
    progressive familial 330.0
    senile 437.0
    temporal 348.81   ●
      mesial 348.81
    tuberous 759.5
  bulbar, progressive 340
  bundle of His 426.50
    left 426.3
    right 426.4
  cardiac — *see* Arteriosclerosis, coronary
  cardiorenal (*see also* Hypertension, cardiorenal) 404.90
  cardiovascular (*see also* Disease, cardiovascular) 429.2
    renal (*see also* Hypertension, cardiorenal) 404.90
  centrolobar, familial 330.0
  cerebellar — *see* Sclerosis, brain
  cerebral — *see* Sclerosis, brain
  cerebrospinal 340
    disseminated 340
    multiple 340
  cerebrovascular 437.0
  choroid 363.40
    diffuse 363.56
  combined (spinal cord) (*see also* Degeneration, combined)
    multiple 340

☑ Additional Digit Required — Refer to the Tabular List for Digit Selection   ▽ Subterms under main terms may continue to next column or page

Sclerosis, sclerotic — *continued*
  concentric, Baló's 341.1
  cornea 370.54
  coronary (artery) — *see* Arteriosclerosis, coronary
  corpus cavernosum
    female 624.8
    male 607.89
  Dewitzky's
    aortic 424.1
    mitral 424.0
  diffuse NEC 341.1
  disease, heart — *see* Arteriosclerosis, coronary
  disseminated 340
  dorsal 340
  dorsolateral (spinal cord) — *see* Degeneration, combined
  endometrium 621.8
  extrapyramidal 333.90
  eye, nuclear (senile) 366.16
  Friedreich's (spinal cord) 334.0
  funicular (spermatic cord) 608.89
  gastritis 535.4 ☑
  general (vascular) — *see* Arteriosclerosis
  gland (lymphatic) 457.8
  hepatic 571.9
  hereditary
    cerebellar 334.2
    spinal 334.0
  hippocampal 348.81   ●
  idiopathic cortical (Garré's) (*see also* Osteomyelitis) 730.1 ☑
  ilium, piriform 733.5
  insular 340
    pancreas 251.8
  Islands of Langerhans 251.8
  kidney — *see* Sclerosis, renal
  larynx 478.79
  lateral 335.24
    amyotrophic 335.20
    descending 335.24
    primary 335.24
    spinal 335.24
  liver 571.9
  lobar, atrophic (of brain) 331.0
    with dementia
      with behavioral disturbance 331.0 *[294.11]*
      without behavioral disturbance 331.0 *[294.10]*
  lung (*see also* Fibrosis, lung) 515
  mastoid 383.1
  mesial temporal 348.81   ●
  mitral — *see* Endocarditis, mitral
  Mönckeberg's (medial) (*see also* Arteriosclerosis, extremities) 440.20
  multiple (brain stem) (cerebral) (generalized) (spinal cord) 340
  myocardium, myocardial — *see* Arteriosclerosis, coronary
  nuclear (senile), eye 366.16
  ovary 620.8
  pancreas 577.8
  penis 607.89
  peripheral arteries (*see also* Arteriosclerosis, extremities) 440.20
  plaques 340
  pluriglandular 258.8
  polyglandular 258.8
  posterior (spinal cord) (syphilitic) 094.0
  posterolateral (spinal cord) — *see* Degeneration, combined
  prepuce 607.89
  primary lateral 335.24
  progressive systemic 710.1
  pulmonary (*see also* Fibrosis, lung) 515
    artery 416.0
    valve (heart) (*see also* Endocarditis, pulmonary) 424.3
  renal 587
    with
      cystine storage disease 270.0
      hypertension (*see also* Hypertension, kidney) 403.90

Sclerosis, sclerotic — *continued*
  renal — *continued*
    with — *continued*
      hypertensive heart disease (conditions classifiable to 402) (*see also* Hypertension, cardiorenal) 404.90
    arteriolar (hyaline) (*see also* Hypertension, kidney) 403.90
    hyperplastic (*see also* Hypertension, kidney) 403.90
  retina (senile) (vascular) 362.17
  rheumatic
    aortic valve 395.9
    mitral valve 394.9
  Schilder's 341.1
  senile — *see* Arteriosclerosis
  spinal (cord) (general) (progressive) (transverse) 336.8
    ascending 357.0
    combined (*see also* Degeneration, combined)
      multiple 340
      syphilitic 094.89
    disseminated 340
    dorsolateral — *see* Degeneration, combined
    hereditary (Friedreich's) (mixed form) 334.0
    lateral (amyotrophic) 335.24
    multiple 340
    posterior (syphilitic) 094.0
  stomach 537.89
  subendocardial, congenital 425.3
  systemic (progressive) 710.1
    with lung involvement 710.1 *[517.2]*
  temporal 348.81   ●
    mesial 348.81   ●
  tricuspid (heart) (valve) — *see* Endocarditis, tricuspid
  tuberous (brain) 759.5
  tympanic membrane (*see also* Tympanosclerosis) 385.00
  valve, valvular (heart) — *see* Endocarditis
  vascular — *see* Arteriosclerosis
  vein 459.89

Sclerotenonitis 379.07
Sclerotitis — *see also* Scleritis 379.00
  syphilitic 095.0
  tuberculous (*see also* Tuberculosis) 017.3 ☑ *[379.09]*
Scoliosis (acquired) (postural) 737.30
  congenital 754.2
  due to or associated with
    Charcôt-Marie-Tooth disease 356.1 *[737.43]*
    mucopolysaccharidosis 277.5 *[737.43]*
    neurofibromatosis 237.71 *[737.43]*
    osteitis
      deformans 731.0 *[737.43]*
      fibrosa cystica 252.01 *[737.43]*
    osteoporosis (*see also* Osteoporosis) 733.00 *[737.43]*
    poliomyelitis 138 *[737.43]*
    radiation 737.33
    tuberculosis (*see also* Tuberculosis) 015.0 ☑ *[737.43]*
  idiopathic 737.30
    infantile
      progressive 737.32
      resolving 737.31
  paralytic 737.39
  rachitic 268.1
  sciatic 724.3
  specified NEC 737.39
  thoracogenic 737.34
  tuberculous (*see also* Tuberculosis) 015.0 ☑ *[737.43]*
Scoliotic pelvis 738.6
  with disproportion (fetopelvic) 653.0 ☑
    affecting fetus or newborn 763.1
    causing obstructed labor 660.1 ☑
      affecting fetus or newborn 763.1
Scorbutus, scorbutic 267
  anemia 281.8
Scotoma (ring) 368.44
  arcuate 368.43
  Bjerrum 368.43
  blind spot area 368.42

Scotoma — *continued*
  central 368.41
  centrocecal 368.41
  paracecal 368.42
  paracentral 368.41
  scintillating 368.12
  Seidel 368.43
Scratch — *see* Injury, superficial, by site
Scratchy throat 784.99
Screening (for) V82.9
  alcoholism V79.1
  anemia, deficiency NEC V78.1
    iron V78.0
  anomaly, congenital V82.89
  antenatal, of mother V28.9
    alphafetoprotein levels, raised V28.1
    based on amniocentesis V28.2
      chromosomal anomalies V28.0
      raised alphafetoprotein levels V28.1
    fetal growth retardation using ultrasonics V28.4
      ultrasonics V28.4
    genomic V28.89
    isoimmunization V28.5
    malformations using ultrasonics V28.3
    proteomic V28.89
    raised alphafetoprotein levels V28.1
    risk
      pre-term labor V28.82
    specified condition NEC V28.89
    Streptococcus B V28.6
  arterial hypertension V81.1
  arthropod-borne viral disease NEC V73.5
  asymptomatic bacteriuria V81.5
  bacterial
    and spirochetal sexually transmitted diseases V74.5
    conjunctivitis V74.4
    disease V74.9
      sexually transmitted V74.5
      specified condition NEC V74.8
  bacteriuria, asymptomatic V81.5
  blood disorder NEC V78.9
    specified type NEC V78.8
  bronchitis, chronic V81.3
  brucellosis V74.8
  cancer — *see* Screening, malignant neoplasm
  cardiovascular disease NEC V81.2
  cataract V80.2
  Chagas' disease V75.3
  chemical poisoning V82.5
  cholera V74.0
  cholesterol level V77.91
  chromosomal
    anomalies
      by amniocentesis, antenatal V28.0
      maternal postnatal V82.4
    athletes V70.3
  condition
    cardiovascular NEC V81.2
    eye NEC V80.2
    genitourinary NEC V81.6
    neurological ▶NEC◀ V80.09   ▲
    respiratory NEC V81.4
    skin V82.0
    specified NEC V82.89
  congenital
    anomaly V82.89
      eye V80.2
    dislocation of hip V82.3
    eye condition or disease V80.2
  conjunctivitis, bacterial V74.4
  contamination NEC (*see also* Poisoning) V82.5
  coronary artery disease V81.0
  cystic fibrosis V77.6
  deficiency anemia NEC V78.1
    iron V78.0
  dengue fever V73.5
  depression V79.0
  developmental handicap V79.9
    in early childhood V79.3
    specified type NEC V79.8
  diabetes mellitus V77.1
  diphtheria V74.3
  disease or disorder V82.9
    bacterial V74.9

Screening — *continued*
  disease or disorder — *continued*
    bacterial — *continued*
      specified NEC V74.8
    blood V78.9
      specified type NEC V78.8
    blood-forming organ V78.9
      specified type NEC V78.8
    cardiovascular NEC V81.2
      hypertensive V81.1
      ischemic V81.0
    Chagas' V75.3
    chlamydial V73.98
      specified NEC V73.88
    ear NEC V80.3
    endocrine NEC V77.99
    eye NEC V80.2
    genitourinary NEC V81.6
    heart NEC V81.2
      hypertensive V81.1
      ischemic V81.0
    HPV (human papillomavirus) V73.81
    human papillomavirus V73.81
    immunity NEC V77.99
    infectious NEC V75.9
    lipoid NEC V77.91
    mental V79.9
      specified type NEC V79.8
    metabolic NEC V77.99
      inborn NEC V77.7
    neurological ▶NEC◀ V80.09   ▲
    nutritional NEC V77.99
    rheumatic NEC V82.2
    rickettsial V75.0
    sexually transmitted V74.5
      bacterial V74.5
      spirochetal V74.5
    sickle-cell V78.2
      trait V78.2
    specified type NEC V82.89
    thyroid V77.0
    vascular NEC V81.2
      ischemic V81.0
    venereal V74.5
    viral V73.99
      arthropod-borne NEC V73.5
      specified type NEC V73.89
  dislocation of hip, congenital V82.3
  drugs in athletes V70.3
  elevated titer V82.9
  emphysema (chronic) V81.3
  encephalitis, viral (mosquito or tick borne) V73.5
  endocrine disorder NEC V77.99
  eye disorder NEC V80.2
    congenital V80.2
  fever
    dengue V73.5
    hemorrhagic V73.5
    yellow V73.4
  filariasis V75.6
  galactosemia V77.4
  genetic V82.79
    disease carrier status V82.71
  genitourinary condition NEC V81.6
  glaucoma V80.1
  gonorrhea V74.5
  gout V77.5
  Hansen's disease V74.2
  heart disease NEC V81.2
    hypertensive V81.1
    ischemic V81.0
  heavy metal poisoning V82.5
  helminthiasis, intestinal V75.7
  hematopoietic malignancy V76.89
  hemoglobinopathies NEC V78.3
  hemorrhagic fever V73.5
  Hodgkin's disease V76.89
  hormones in athletes V70.3
  HPV (human papillomavirus) V73.81
  human papillomavirus (HPV) V73.81
  hypercholesterolemia V77.91
  hyperlipidemia V77.91
  hypertension V81.1
  immunity disorder NEC V77.99
  inborn errors of metabolism NEC V77.7

☑ Additional Digit Required — Refer to the Tabular List for Digit Selection   ⏍ Subterms under main terms may continue to next column or page

2010 ICD-9-CM   ▶◀ Revised Text   ● New Line   ▲ Revised Code   October 2009 • Volume 2 — 245

Screening — *continued*
infection
    bacterial V74.9
        specified type NEC V74.8
    mycotic V75.4
    parasitic NEC V75.8
infectious disease V75.9
    specified type NEC V75.8
ingestion of radioactive substance V82.5
intestinal helminthiasis V75.7
iron deficiency anemia V78.0
ischemic heart disease V81.0
lead poisoning V82.5
leishmaniasis V75.2
leprosy V74.2
leptospirosis V74.8
leukemia V76.89
lipoid disorder NEC V77.91
lymphoma V76.89
malaria V75.1
malignant neoplasm (of) V76.9
    bladder V76.3
    blood V76.89
    breast V76.10
        mammogram NEC V76.12
            for high-risk patient V76.11
        specified type NEC V76.19
    cervix V76.2
    colon V76.51
    colorectal V76.51
    hematopoietic system V76.89
    intestine V76.50
        colon V76.51
        small V76.52
    lung V76.0
    lymph (glands) V76.89
    nervous system V76.81
    oral cavity V76.42
    other specified neoplasm NEC V76.89
    ovary V76.46
    prostate V76.44
    rectum V76.41
    respiratory organs V76.0
    skin V76.43
    specified sites NEC V76.49
    testis V76.45
    vagina V76.47
        following hysterectomy for malignant condition V67.01
malnutrition V77.2
mammogram NEC V76.12
    for high-risk patient V76.11
maternal postnatal chromosomal anomalies V82.4
measles V73.2
mental
    disorder V79.9
        specified type NEC V79.8
    retardation V79.2
metabolic disorder NEC V77.99
metabolic errors, inborn V77.7
mucoviscidosis V77.6
multiphasic V82.6
mycosis V75.4
mycotic infection V75.4
nephropathy V81.5
neurological condition ▶NEC◀ V80.09 ▲
nutritional disorder V77.99
obesity V77.8
osteoporosis V82.81
parasitic infection NEC V75.8
phenylketonuria V77.3
plague V74.8
poisoning
    chemical NEC V82.5
        contaminated water supply V82.5
            heavy metal V82.5
poliomyelitis V73.0
postnatal chromosomal anomalies, maternal V82.4
prenatal — *see* Screening, antenatal
pulmonary tuberculosis V74.1
radiation exposure V82.5
renal disease V81.5
respiratory condition NEC V81.4
rheumatic disorder NEC V82.2

Screening — *continued*
rheumatoid arthritis V82.1
rickettsial disease V75.0
rubella V73.3
schistosomiasis V75.5
senile macular lesions of eye V80.2
sexually transmitted diseases V74.5
    bacterial V74.5
    spirochetal V74.5
sickle-cell anemia, disease, or trait V78.2
skin condition V82.0
sleeping sickness V75.3
smallpox V73.1
special V82.9
    specified condition NEC V82.89
specified type NEC V82.89
spirochetal disease V74.9
    sexually transmitted V74.5
    specified type NEC V74.8
stimulants in athletes V70.3
syphilis V74.5
tetanus V74.8
thyroid disorder V77.0
trachoma V73.6
traumatic brain injury V80.01   ●
trypanosomiasis V75.3
tuberculosis, pulmonary V74.1
venereal disease V74.5
viral encephalitis
    mosquito-borne V73.5
    tick-borne V73.5
whooping cough V74.8
worms, intestinal V75.7
yaws V74.6
yellow fever V73.4
Scrofula — *see also* Tuberculosis 017.2 ☑
Scrofulide (primary) — *see also* Tuberculosis 017.0 ☑
Scrofuloderma, scrofulodermia (any site) (primary) — *see also* Tuberculosis 017.0 ☑
Scrofulosis (universal) — *see also* Tuberculosis 017.2 ☑
Scrofulosis lichen (primary) — *see also* Tuberculosis 017.0 ☑
Scrofulous — *see* condition
Scrotal tongue 529.5
    congenital 750.13
Scrotum — *see* condition
Scurvy (gum) (infantile) (rickets) (scorbutic) 267
Sea-blue histiocyte syndrome 272.7
Seabright-Bantam syndrome (pseudohypoparathyroidism) 275.49
Sealpox 059.12
Seasickness 994.6
Seatworm 127.4
Sebaceous
    cyst (*see also* Cyst, sebaceous) 706.2
    gland disease NEC 706.9
Sebocystomatosis 706.2
Seborrhea, seborrheic 706.3
    adiposa 706.3
    capitis 690.11
    congestiva 695.4
    corporis 706.3
    dermatitis 690.10
        infantile 690.12
    diathesis in infants 695.89
    eczema 690.18
        infantile 690.12
    keratosis 702.19
        inflamed 702.11
    nigricans 705.89
    sicca 690.18
    wart 702.19
        inflamed 702.11
Seckel's syndrome 759.89
Seclusion pupil 364.74
Seclusiveness, child 313.22
Secondary — *see also* condition
    neoplasm — *see* Neoplasm, by site, malignant, secondary
Secretan's disease or syndrome (posttraumatic edema) 782.3
Secretion
    antidiuretic hormone, inappropriate (syndrome) 253.6

Secretion — *continued*
    catecholamine, by pheochromocytoma 255.6
    hormone
        antidiuretic, inappropriate (syndrome) 253.6
        by
            carcinoid tumor 259.2
            pheochromocytoma 255.6
        ectopic NEC 259.3
    urinary
        excessive 788.42
        suppression 788.5
Section
    cesarean
        affecting fetus or newborn 763.4
        post mortem, affecting fetus or newborn 761.6
        previous, in pregnancy or childbirth 654.2 ☑
            affecting fetus or newborn 763.89
    nerve, traumatic — *see* Injury, nerve, by site
Seeligmann's syndrome (ichthyosis congenita) 757.1
Segmentation, incomplete (congenital) — *see also* Fusion
    bone NEC 756.9
    lumbosacral (joint) 756.15
    vertebra 756.15
        lumbosacral 756.15
Seizure(s) 780.39
    akinetic (idiopathic) (*see also* Epilepsy) 345.0 ☑
        psychomotor 345.4 ☑
    apoplexy, apoplectic (*see also* Disease, cerebrovascular, acute) 436
    atonic (*see also* Epilepsy) 345.0 ☑
    autonomic 300.11
    brain or cerebral (*see also* Disease, cerebrovascular, acute) 436
    convulsive (*see also* Convulsions) 780.39
    cortical (focal) (motor) (*see also* Epilepsy) 345.5 ☑
    disorder (*see also* Epilepsy) 345.9 ☑   ●
    due to stroke 438.89
    epilepsy, epileptic (cryptogenic) (*see also* Epilepsy) 345.9 ☑
    epileptiform, epileptoid 780.39
        focal (*see also* Epilepsy) 345.5 ☑
    febrile (simple) 780.31
        with status epilepticus 345.3
        atypical 780.32
        complex 780.32
        complicated 780.32
    heart — *see* Disease, heart
    hysterical 300.11
    Jacksonian (focal) (*see also* Epilepsy) 345.5 ☑
        motor type 345.5 ☑
        sensory type 345.5 ☑
    migraine triggered 346.0 ☑
    newborn 779.0
    paralysis (*see also* Disease, cerebrovascular, acute) 436
    recurrent 345.9 ☑
        epileptic — *see* Epilepsy
    repetitive 780.39
        epileptic — *see* Epilepsy
    salaam (*see also* Epilepsy) 345.6 ☑
    uncinate (*see also* Epilepsy) 345.4 ☑
Self-mutilation 300.9
Semicoma 780.09
Semiconsciousness 780.09
Seminal
    vesicle — *see* condition
    vesiculitis (*see also* Vesiculitis) 608.0
Seminoma (M9061/3)
    anaplastic type (M9062/3)
        specified site — *see* Neoplasm, by site, malignant
        unspecified site 186.9
    specified site — *see* Neoplasm, by site, malignant
    spermatocytic (M9063/3)
        specified site — *see* Neoplasm, by site, malignant
        unspecified site 186.9
    unspecified site 186.9

Semliki Forest encephalitis 062.8
Senear-Usher disease or syndrome (pemphigus erythematosus) 694.4
Senecio jacobae dermatitis 692.6
Senectus 797
Senescence 797
Senile — *see also* condition 797
    cervix (atrophic) 622.8
    degenerative atrophy, skin 701.3
    endometrium (atrophic) 621.8
    fallopian tube (atrophic) 620.3
    heart (failure) 797
    lung 492.8
    ovary (atrophic) 620.3
    syndrome 259.8
    vagina, vaginitis (atrophic) 627.3
    wart 702.0
Senility 797
    with
        acute confusional state 290.3
        delirium 290.3
        mental changes 290.9
        psychosis NEC (*see also* Psychosis, senile) 290.20
    premature (syndrome) 259.8
Sensation
    burning (*see also* Disturbance, sensation) 782.0
        tongue 529.6
    choking 784.99
    loss of (*see also* Disturbance, sensation) 782.0
    prickling (*see also* Disturbance, sensation) 782.0
    tingling (*see also* Disturbance, sensation) 782.0
Sense loss (touch) — *see also* Disturbance, sensation 782.0
    smell 781.1
    taste 781.1
Sensibility disturbance NEC (cortical) (deep) (vibratory) — *see also* Disturbance, sensation 782.0
Sensitive dentine 521.89
Sensitiver Beziehungswahn 297.8
Sensitivity, sensitization — *see also* Allergy
    autoerythrocyte 287.2
    carotid sinus 337.01
    child (excessive) 313.21
    cold, autoimmune 283.0
    methemoglobin 289.7
    suxamethonium 289.89
    tuberculin, without clinical or radiological symptoms 795.5
Sensory
    extinction 781.8
    neglect 781.8
Separation
    acromioclavicular — *see* Dislocation, acromioclavicular
    anxiety, abnormal 309.21
    apophysis, traumatic — *see* Fracture, by site
    choroid 363.70
        hemorrhagic 363.72
        serous 363.71
    costochondral (simple) (traumatic) — *see* Dislocation, costochondral
    delayed
        umbilical cord 779.83
    epiphysis, epiphyseal
        nontraumatic 732.9
            upper femoral 732.2
        traumatic — *see* Fracture, by site
    fracture — *see* Fracture, by site
    infundibulum cardiac from right ventricle by a partition 746.83
    joint (current) (traumatic) — *see* Dislocation, by site
    placenta (normally implanted) — *see* Placenta, separation
    pubic bone, obstetrical trauma 665.6 ☑
    retina, retinal (*see also* Detachment, retina) 361.9
        layers 362.40
            sensory (*see also* Retinoschisis) 361.10
        pigment epithelium (exudative) 362.42
            hemorrhagic 362.43
    sternoclavicular (traumatic) — *see* Dislocation, sternoclavicular

☑ Additional Digit Required — Refer to the Tabular List for Digit Selection   ▽ Subterms under main terms may continue to next column or page

246 — Volume 2 • October 2009   ▶◀ Revised Text   ● New Line   ▲ Revised Code   2010 ICD-9-CM

eparation — continued
  symphysis pubis, obstetrical trauma 665.6 ☑
  tracheal ring, incomplete (congenital) 748.3
epsis (generalized) 995.91
  with
    abortion — see Abortion, by type, with
      sepsis
    acute organ dysfunction 995.92
    ectopic pregnancy (see also categories
      633.0–633.9) 639.0
    molar pregnancy (see also categories
      630–632) 639.0
    multiple organ dysfunction (MOD) 995.92
  buccal 528.3
  complicating labor 659.3 ☑
  dental (pulpal origin) 522.4
  female genital organ NEC 614.9
  fetus (intrauterine) 771.81
  following
    abortion 639.0
    ectopic or molar pregnancy 639.0
    infusion, perfusion, or transfusion 999.39
  Friedländer's 038.49
  intraocular 360.00
  localized
    in operation wound 998.59
    skin (see also Abscess) 682.9
  malleus 024
  nadir 038.9
  newborn (organism unspecified) NEC 771.81
  oral 528.3
  puerperal, postpartum, childbirth (pelvic)
    670.2 ▲
  resulting from infusion, injection, transfusion,
    or vaccination 999.39
  severe 995.92
  skin, localized (see also Abscess) 682.9
  umbilical (newborn) (organism unspecified)
    771.89
    tetanus 771.3
  urinary 599.0
    meaning sepsis 995.91
    meaning urinary tract infection 599.0
Septate — see also Septum
Septic — see also condition
  adenoids 474.01
    and tonsils 474.02
  arm (with lymphangitis) 682.3
  embolus — see Embolism
  finger (with lymphangitis) 681.00
  foot (with lymphangitis) 682.7
  gallbladder (see also Cholecystitis) 575.8
  hand (with lymphangitis) 682.4
  joint (see also Arthritis, septic) 711.0 ☑
  kidney (see also Infection, kidney) 590.9
  leg (with lymphangitis) 682.6
  mouth 528.3
  nail 681.9
    finger 681.02
    toe 681.11
  shock (endotoxic) 785.52
  sore (see also Abscess) 682.9
    throat 034.0
      milk-borne 034.0
      streptococcal 034.0
  spleen (acute) 289.59
  teeth (pulpal origin) 522.4
  throat 034.0
  thrombus — see Thrombosis
  toe (with lymphangitis) 681.10
  tonsils 474.00
    and adenoids 474.02
  umbilical cord (newborn) (organism unspeci-
    fied) 771.89
  uterus (see also Endometritis) 615.9
Septicemia, septicemic (generalized) (suppurative) 038.9
  with
    abortion — see Abortion, by type, with
      sepsis
    ectopic pregnancy (see also categories
      633.0–633.9) 639.0
    molar pregnancy (see also categories
      630–632) 639.0
  Aerobacter aerogenes 038.49
  anaerobic 038.3

Septicemia, septicemic — continued
  anthrax 022.3
  Bacillus coli 038.42
  Bacteroides 038.3
  Clostridium 038.3
  complicating labor 659.3 ☑
  cryptogenic 038.9
  enteric gram-negative bacilli 038.40
  Enterobacter aerogenes 038.49
  Erysipelothrix (insidiosa) (rhusiopathiae) 027.1
  Escherichia coli 038.42
  following
    abortion 639.0
    ectopic or molar pregnancy 639.0
    infusion, injection, transfusion, or vaccina-
      tion 999.39
  Friedländer's (bacillus) 038.49
  gangrenous 038.9
  gonococcal 098.89
  gram-negative (organism) 038.40
    anaerobic 038.3
  Hemophilus influenzae 038.41
  herpes (simplex) 054.5
  herpetic 054.5
  Listeria monocytogenes 027.0
  meningeal — see Meningitis
  meningococcal (chronic) (fulminating) 036.2
  methicillin
    resistant Staphylococcus aureus (MRSA)
      038.12
    susceptible Staphylococcus aureus (MSSA)
      038.11
  MRSA (methicillin resistant Staphylococcus
    aureus) 038.12
  MSSA (methicillin susceptible Staphylococcus
    aureus) 038.11
  navel, newborn (organism unspecified) 771.89
  newborn (organism unspecified) 771.81
  plague 020.2
  pneumococcal 038.2
  postabortal 639.0
  postoperative 998.59
  Proteus vulgaris 038.49
  Pseudomonas (aeruginosa) 038.43
  puerperal, postpartum 670.2 ☑ ▲
  Salmonella (aertrycke) (callinarum) (cholerac-
    suis) (enteritidis) (suipestifer) 003.1
  Serratia 038.44
  Shigella (see also Dysentery, bacillary) 004.9
  specified organism NEC 038.8
  staphylococcal 038.10
    aureus 038.11
      methicillin
        resistant (MRSA) 038.12
        susceptible (MSSA) 038.11
    specified organism NEC 038.19
  streptococcal (anaerobic) 038.0
  Streptococcus pneumoniae 038.2
  suipestifer 003.1
  umbilicus, newborn (organism unspecified)
    771.89
  viral 079.99
  Yersinia enterocolitica 038.49
Septum, septate (congenital) — see also
  Anomaly, specified type NEC
  anal 751.2
  aqueduct of Sylvius 742.3
    with spina bifida (see also Spina bifida)
      741.0 ☑
  hymen 752.49
  uterus (see also Double, uterus) 752.2
  vagina 752.49
    in pregnancy or childbirth 654.7 ☑
      affecting fetus or newborn 763.89
      causing obstructed labor 660.2 ☑
        affecting fetus or newborn 763.1
Sequestration
  lung (congenital) (extralobar) (intralobar) 748.5
  orbit 376.10
  pulmonary artery (congenital) 747.3
  splenic 289.52
Sequestrum
  bone (see also Osteomyelitis) 730.1 ●
    jaw 526.4
  dental 525.8
  jaw bone 526.4

Sequestrum — continued
  sinus (accessory) (nasal) (see also Sinusitis)
    473.9
    maxillary 473.0
Sequoiosis asthma 495.8
Serology for syphilis
  doubtful
    with signs or symptoms — see Syphilis, by
      site and stage
    follow-up of latent syphilis — see Syphilis,
      latent
  false positive 795.6
  negative, with signs or symptoms — see
    Syphilis, by site and stage
  positive 097.1
    with signs or symptoms — see Syphilis, by
      site and stage
    false 795.6
    follow-up of latent syphilis — see Syphilis,
      latent
    only finding — see Syphilis, latent
  reactivated 097.1
Seroma (postoperative) (non-infected) 998.13
  infected 998.51
  post-traumatic 729.91
Seropurulent — see condition
Serositis, multiple 569.89
  pericardial 423.2
  peritoneal 568.82
  pleural — see Pleurisy
Serotonin syndrome 333.99
Serous — see condition
Sertoli cell
  adenoma (M8640/0)
    specified site — see Neoplasm, by site,
      benign
    unspecified site
      female 220
      male 222.0
  carcinoma (M8640/3)
    specified site — see Neoplasm, by site,
      malignant
    unspecified site 186.9
  syndrome (germinal aplasia) 606.0
  tumor (M8640/0)
    with lipid storage (M8641/0)
      specified site — see Neoplasm, by site,
        benign
      unspecified site
        female 220
        male 222.0
    specified site — see Neoplasm, by site,
      benign
    unspecified site
      female 220
      male 222.0
Sertoli-Leydig cell tumor (M8631/0)
  specified site — see Neoplasm, by site, benign
  unspecified site
    female 220
    male 222.0
Serum
  allergy, allergic reaction 999.5
    shock 999.4
  arthritis 999.5 [713.6]
  complication or reaction NEC 999.5
  disease NEC 999.5
  hepatitis 070.3 ☑
  intoxication 999.5
  jaundice (homologous) — see Hepatitis, viral,
    type B
  neuritis 999.5
  poisoning NEC 999.5
  rash NEC 999.5
  reaction NEC 999.5
  sickness NEC 999.5
Sesamoiditis 733.99
Seven-day fever 061
  of
    Japan 100.89
    Queensland 100.89
Sever's disease or osteochondrosis (calcaneum) 732.5
Sex chromosome mosaics 758.81
Sex reassignment surgery status (see also
  Trans-sexualism) 302.50

Sextuplet
  affected by maternal complications of preg-
    nancy 761.5
  healthy liveborn — see Newborn, multiple
  pregnancy (complicating delivery) NEC
    651.8 ☑
    with fetal loss and retention of one or more
      fetus(es) 651.6 ☑
    following (elective) fetal reduction
      651.7 ☑
Sexual
  anesthesia 302.72
  deviation (see also Deviation, sexual) 302.9
  disorder (see also Deviation, sexual) 302.9
  frigidity (female) 302.72
  function, disorder of (psychogenic) 302.70
    specified type NEC 302.79
  immaturity (female) (male) 259.0
  impotence 607.84
    organic origin NEC 607.84
    psychogenic 302.72
  precocity (constitutional) (cryptogenic) (fe-
    male) (idiopathic) (male) NEC 259.1
    with adrenal hyperplasia 255.2
  sadism 302.84
Sexuality, pathological — see also Deviation,
  sexual 302.9
Sézary's disease, reticulosis, or syndrome
  (M9701/3) 202.2 ☑
Shadow, lung 793.1
Shaken infant syndrome 995.55
Shaking
  head (tremor) 781.0
  palsy or paralysis (see also Parkinsonism) 332.0
Shallowness, acetabulum 736.39
Shaver's disease or syndrome (bauxite pneu-
  moconiosis) 503
Shearing
  artificial skin graft 996.55
  decellularized allodermis graft 996.55
Sheath (tendon) — see condition
Shedding
  nail 703.8
  teeth, premature, primary (deciduous) 520.6
Sheehan's disease or syndrome (postpartum
  pituitary necrosis) 253.2
Shelf, rectal 569.49
Shell
  shock (current) (see also Reaction, stress, acute)
    308.9
    lasting state 300.16
  teeth 520.5
Shield kidney 753.3
Shifting
  pacemaker 427.89
  sleep-work schedule (affecting sleep) 327.36
Shift, mediastinal 793.2
Shiga's
  bacillus 004.0
  dysentery 004.0
Shigella (dysentery) — see also Dysentery, bacil-
  lary 004.9
  carrier (suspected) of V02.3
Shigellosis — see also Dysentery, bacillary 004.9
Shingles — see also Herpes, zoster 053.9
  eye NEC 053.29
Shin splints 844.9
Shipyard eye or disease 077.1
Shirodkar suture, in pregnancy 654.5 ☑
Shock 785.50
  with
    abortion — see Abortion, by type, with
      shock
    ectopic pregnancy (see also categories
      633.0–633.9) 639.5
    molar pregnancy (see also categories
      630–632) 639.5
  allergic — see Shock, anaphylactic
  anaclitic 309.21
  anaphylactic 995.0
    chemical — see Table of Drugs and
      Chemicals
    correct medicinal substance properly ad-
      ministered 995.0

☑ Additional Digit Required — Refer to the Tabular List for Digit Selection   ⧖ Subterms under main terms may continue to next column or page

Index

Shock — Sinding-Larsen disease

Shock — *continued*
anaphylactic — *continued*
drug or medicinal substance
correct substance properly administered 995.0
overdose or wrong substance given or taken 977.9
specified drug — *see* Table of Drugs and Chemicals
following sting(s) 989.5
food — *see* Anaphylactic shock, due to, food
immunization 999.4
serum 999.4
anaphylactoid — *see* Shock, anaphylactic
anesthetic
correct substance properly administered 995.4
overdose or wrong substance given 968.4
specified anesthetic — *see* Table of Drugs and Chemicals
birth, fetus or newborn NEC 779.89
cardiogenic 785.51
chemical substance — *see* Table of Drugs and Chemicals
circulatory 785.59
complicating
abortion — *see* Abortion, by type, with shock
ectopic pregnancy (*see also* categories 633.0–633.9) 639.5
labor and delivery 669.1 ☑
molar pregnancy (*see also* categories 630–632) 639.5
culture 309.29
due to
drug 995.0
correct substance properly administered 995.0
overdose or wrong substance given or taken 977.9
specified drug — *see* Table of Drugs and Chemicals
food — *see* Anaphylactic shock, due to, food
during labor and delivery 669.1 ☑
electric 994.8
from electroshock gun (taser) 994.8
endotoxic 785.52
due to surgical procedure 998.0
following
abortion 639.5
ectopic or molar pregnancy 639.5
injury (immediate) (delayed) 958.4
labor and delivery 669.1 ☑
gram-negative 785.52
hematogenic 785.59
hemorrhagic
due to
disease 785.59
surgery (intraoperative) (postoperative) 998.0
trauma 958.4
hypovolemic NEC 785.59
surgical 998.0
traumatic 958.4
insulin 251.0
therapeutic misadventure 962.3
kidney 584.5
traumatic (following crushing) 958.5
lightning 994.0
lung 518.5
nervous (*see also* Reaction, stress, acute) 308.9
obstetric 669.1 ☑
with
abortion — *see* Abortion, by type, with shock
ectopic pregnancy (*see also* categories 633.0–633.9) 639.5
molar pregnancy (*see also* categories 630–632) 639.5
following
abortion 639.5
ectopic or molar pregnancy 639.5
paralysis, paralytic (*see also* Disease, cerebrovascular, acute) 436

Shock — *continued*
paralysis, paralytic (*see also* Disease, cerebrovascular, acute) — *continued*
late effect — *see* Late effect(s) (of) cerebrovascular disease
pleural (surgical) 998.0
due to trauma 958.4
postoperative 998.0
with
abortion — *see* Abortion, by type, with shock
ectopic pregnancy (*see also* categories 633.0–633.9) 639.5
molar pregnancy (*see also* categories 630–632) 639.5
following
abortion 639.5
ectopic or molar pregnancy 639.5
psychic (*see also* Reaction, stress, acute) 308.9
past history (of) V15.49
psychogenic (*see also* Reaction, stress, acute) 308.9
septic 785.52
with
abortion — *see* Abortion, by type, with shock
ectopic pregnancy (*see also* categories 633.0–633.9) 639.5
molar pregnancy (*see also* categories 630–632) 639.5
due to
surgical procedure 998.0
transfusion NEC 999.89 ▲
bone marrow 996.85
following
abortion 639.5
ectopic or molar pregnancy 639.5
surgical procedure 998.0
transfusion NEC 999.89 ▲
bone marrow 996.85
spinal (*see also* Injury, spinal, by site)
with spinal bone injury — *see* Fracture, vertebra, by site, with spinal cord injury
surgical 998.0
therapeutic misadventure NEC (*see also* Complications) 998.89
thyroxin 962.7
toxic 040.82
transfusion — *see* Complications, transfusion
traumatic (immediate) (delayed) 958.4
Shoemakers' chest 738.3
Short, shortening, shortness
Achilles tendon (acquired) 727.81
arm 736.89
congenital 755.20
back 737.9
bowel syndrome 579.3
breath 786.05
cervical, cervix 649.7 ☑
gravid uterus 649.7 ☑
non-gravid uterus 622.5
acquired 622.5
congenital 752.49
chain acyl CoA dehydrogenase deficiency (SCAD) 277.85
common bile duct, congenital 751.69
cord (umbilical) 663.4 ☑
affecting fetus or newborn 762.6
cystic duct, congenital 751.69
esophagus (congenital) 750.4
femur (acquired) 736.81
congenital 755.34
frenulum linguae 750.0
frenum, lingual 750.0
hamstrings 727.81
hip (acquired) 736.39
congenital 755.63
leg (acquired) 736.81
congenital 755.30
metatarsus (congenital) 754.79
acquired 736.79
organ or site, congenital NEC — *see* Distortion
palate (congenital) 750.26
P-R interval syndrome 426.81
radius (acquired) 736.09

Short, shortening, shortness — *continued*
radius — *continued*
congenital 755.26
round ligament 629.89
sleeper 307.49
stature, constitutional (hereditary) (idiopathic) 783.43
tendon 727.81
Achilles (acquired) 727.81
congenital 754.79
congenital 756.89
thigh (acquired) 736.81
congenital 755.34
tibialis anticus 727.81
umbilical cord 663.4 ☑
affecting fetus or newborn 762.6
urethra 599.84
uvula (congenital) 750.26
vagina 623.8
Shortsightedness 367.1
Shoshin (acute fulminating beriberi) 265.0
Shoulder — *see* condition
Shovel-shaped incisors 520.2
Shower, thromboembolic — *see* Embolism
Shunt (status)
aortocoronary bypass V45.81
arterial-venous (dialysis) V45.11
arteriovenous, pulmonary (acquired) 417.0
congenital 747.3
traumatic (complication) 901.40
cerebral ventricle (communicating) in situ V45.2
coronary artery bypass V45.81
surgical, prosthetic, with complications — *see* Complications, shunt
vascular NEC V45.89
Shutdown
renal 586
with
abortion — *see* Abortion, by type, with renal failure
ectopic pregnancy (*see also* categories 633.0–633.9) 639.3
molar pregnancy (*see also* categories 630–632) 639.3
complicating
abortion 639.3
ectopic or molar pregnancy 639.3
following labor and delivery 669.3 ☑
Shwachman's syndrome 288.02
Shy-Drager syndrome (orthostatic hypotension with multisystem degeneration) 333.0
Sialadenitis (any gland) (chronic) (suppurative) 527.2
epidemic — *see* Mumps
Sialadenosis, periodic 527.2
Sialaporia 527.7
Sialectasia 527.8
Sialitis 527.2
Sialoadenitis — *see also* Sialadenitis 527.2
Sialoangitis 527.2
Sialodochitis (fibrinosa) 527.2
Sialodocholithiasis 527.5
Sialolithiasis 527.5
Sialorrhea — *see also* Ptyalism 527.7
periodic 527.2
Sialosis 527.8
rheumatic 710.2
Siamese twin 759.4
complicating pregnancy 678.1 ☑
Sicard's syndrome 352.6
Sicca syndrome (keratoconjunctivitis) 710.2
Sick 799.9
cilia syndrome 759.89
or handicapped person in family V61.49
Sickle-cell
anemia (see also Disease, sickle-cell) 282.60
disease (see also Disease, sickle-cell) 282.60
hemoglobin
C disease (without crisis) 282.63
with
crisis 282.64
vaso-occlusive pain 282.64
D disease (without crisis) 282.68
with crisis 282.69
E disease (without crisis) 282.68

Sickle-cell — *continued*
hemoglobin — *continued*
E disease — *continued*
with crisis 282.69
thalassemia (without crisis) 282.41
with
crisis 282.42
vaso-occlusive pain 282.42
trait 282.5
Sicklemia — *see also* Disease, sickle-cell 282.60
trait 282.5
Sickness
air (travel) 994.6
airplane 994.6
alpine 993.2
altitude 993.2
Andes 993.2
aviators' 993.2
balloon 993.2
car 994.6
compressed air 993.3
decompression 993.3
green 280.9
harvest 100.89
milk 988.8
morning 643.0 ☑
motion 994.6
mountain 993.2
acute 289.0
protein (*see also* Complications, vaccination) 999.5
radiation NEC 990
roundabout (motion) 994.6
sea 994.6
serum NEC 999.5
sleeping (African) 086.5
by Trypanosoma 086.5
gambiense 086.3
rhodesiense 086.4
Gambian 086.3
late effect 139.8
Rhodesian 086.4
sweating 078.2
swing (motion) 994.6
train (railway) (travel) 994.6
travel (any vehicle) 994.6
Sick sinus syndrome 427.81
Sideropenia — *see also* Anemia, iron deficiency 280.9
Siderosis (lung) (occupational) 503
cornea 371.15
eye (bulbi) (vitreous) 360.23
lens 360.23
Siegal-Cattan-Mamou disease (periodic) 277.31
Siemens' syndrome
ectodermal dysplasia 757.31
keratosis follicularis spinulosa (decalvans) 757.39
Sighing respiration 786.7
Sigmoid
flexure — *see* condition
kidney 753.3
Sigmoiditis — *see* Enteritis
Silfverskiöld's syndrome 756.50
Silicosis, silicotic (complicated) (occupational) (simple) 502
fibrosis, lung (confluent) (massive) (occupational) 502
non-nodular 503
pulmonum 502
Silicotuberculosis — *see also* Tuberculosis 011.4 ☑
Silo fillers' disease 506.9
Silver's syndrome (congenital hemihypertrophy and short stature) 759.89
Silver wire arteries, retina 362.13
Silvestroni-Bianco syndrome (thalassemia minima) 282.49
Simian crease 757.2
Simmonds' cachexia or disease (pituitary cachexia) 253.2
Simons' disease or syndrome (progressive lipodystrophy) 272.6
Simple, simplex — *see* condition
Sinding-Larsen disease (juvenile osteopathia patellae) 732.4

☑ Additional Digit Required — Refer to the Tabular List for Digit Selection

▽ Subterms under main terms may continue to next column or page

►◄ Revised Text   ● New Line   ▲ Revised Code

☑ Additional Digit Required — Refer to the Tabular List for Digit Selection   ⸋ Subterms under main terms may continue to next column or page

2010 ICD-9-CM   ▶◀ Revised Text   ● New Line   ▲ Revised Code   October 2009 · Volume 2 — 249

Sore — *continued*
  throat — *continued*
    with influenza, flu, or grippe 487.1
    acute 462
    chronic 472.1
    clergyman's 784.49
    coxsackie (virus) 074.0
    diphtheritic 032.0
    epidemic 034.0
    gangrenous 462
    herpetic 054.79
    influenzal 487.1
    malignant 462
    purulent 462
    putrid 462
    septic 034.0
    streptococcal (ulcerative) 034.0
    ulcerated 462
    viral NEC 462
      Coxsackie 074.0
  tropical (*see also* Ulcer, skin) 707.9
  veldt (*see also* Ulcer, skin) 707.9
Sotos' syndrome (cerebral gigantism) 253.0
Sounds
  friction, pleural 786.7
  succussion, chest 786.7
  temporomandibular joint
    on opening or closing 524.64
South African cardiomyopathy syndrome 425.2
South American
  blastomycosis 116.1
  trypanosomiasis — *see* Trypanosomiasis
Southeast Asian hemorrhagic fever 065.4
Spacing, teeth, abnormal 524.30
  excessive 524.32
Spade-like hand (congenital) 754.89
Spading nail 703.8
  congenital 757.5
Spanemia 285.9
Spanish collar 605
Sparganosis 123.5
Spasmodic — *see* condition
Spasmophilia — *see also* Tetany 781.7
Spasm, spastic, spasticity — *see also* condition 781.0
  accommodation 367.53
  ampulla of Vater (*see also* Disease, gallbladder) 576.8
  anus, ani (sphincter) (reflex) 564.6
    psychogenic 306.4
  artery NEC 443.9
    basilar 435.0
    carotid 435.8
    cerebral 435.9
      specified artery NEC 435.8
    retinal (*see also* Occlusion, retinal, artery) 362.30
    vertebral 435.1
    vertebrobasilar 435.3
  Bell's 351.0
  bladder (sphincter, external or internal) 596.8
  bowel 564.9
    psychogenic 306.4
  bronchus, bronchiole 519.11
  cardia 530.0
  cardiac — *see* Angina
  carpopedal (*see also* Tetany) 781.7
  cecum 564.9
    psychogenic 306.4
  cerebral (arteries) (vascular) 435.9
    specified artery NEC 435.8
  cerebrovascular 435.9
  cervix, complicating delivery 661.4 ☑
    affecting fetus or newborn 763.7
  ciliary body (of accommodation) 367.53
  colon 564.1
    psychogenic 306.4
  common duct (*see also* Disease, biliary) 576.8
  compulsive 307.22
  conjugate 378.82
  convergence 378.84
  coronary (artery) — *see* Angina
  diaphragm (reflex) 786.8
    psychogenic 306.1
  duodenum, duodenal (bulb) 564.89

Spasm, spastic, spasticity — *see also* condition — *continued*
  esophagus (diffuse) 530.5
    psychogenic 306.4
  facial 351.8
  fallopian tube 620.8
  gait 781.2
  gastrointestinal (tract) 536.8
    psychogenic 306.4
  glottis 478.75
    hysterical 300.11
    psychogenic 306.1
      specified as conversion reaction 300.11
    reflex through recurrent laryngeal nerve 478.75
  habit 307.20
    chronic 307.22
    transient (of childhood) 307.21
  heart — *see* Angina
  hourglass — *see* Contraction, hourglass
  hysterical 300.11
  infantile (*see also* Epilepsy) 345.6 ☑
  internal oblique, eye 378.51
  intestinal 564.9
    psychogenic 306.4
  larynx, laryngeal 478.75
    hysterical 300.11
    psychogenic 306.1
      specified as conversion reaction 300.11
  levator palpebrae superioris 333.81
  lightning (*see also* Epilepsy) 345.6 ☑
  mobile 781.0
  muscle 728.85
    back 724.8
    psychogenic 306.0
  nerve, trigeminal 350.1
  nervous 306.0
  nodding 307.3
    infantile (*see also* Epilepsy) 345.6 ☑
  occupational 300.89
  oculogyric 378.87
  ophthalmic artery 362.30
  orbicularis 781.0
  perineal 625.8
  peroneo-extensor (*see also* Flat, foot) 734
  pharynx (reflex) 478.29
    hysterical 300.11
    psychogenic 306.1
      specified as conversion reaction 300.11
  pregnant uterus, complicating delivery 661.4 ☑
  psychogenic 306.0
  pylorus 537.81
    adult hypertrophic 537.0
    congenital or infantile 750.5
    psychogenic 306.4
  rectum (sphincter) 564.6
    psychogenic 306.4
  retinal artery NEC (*see also* Occlusion, retina, artery) 362.30
  sacroiliac 724.6
  salaam (infantile) (*see also* Epilepsy) 345.6 ☑
  saltatory 781.0
  sigmoid 564.9
    psychogenic 306.4
  sphincter of Oddi (*see also* Disease, gallbladder) 576.5
  stomach 536.8
    neurotic 306.4
  throat 478.29
    hysterical 300.11
    psychogenic 306.1
      specified as conversion reaction 300.11
  tic 307.20
    chronic 307.22
    transient (of childhood) 307.21
  tongue 529.8
  torsion 333.6
  trigeminal nerve 350.1
    postherpetic 053.12
  ureter 593.89
  urethra (sphincter) 599.84
  uterus 625.8
    complicating labor 661.4 ☑
      affecting fetus or newborn 763.7
  vagina 625.1

Spasm, spastic, spasticity — *see also* condition — *continued*
  vagina — *continued*
    psychogenic 306.51
  vascular NEC 443.9
  vasomotor NEC 443.9
  vein NEC 459.89
  vesical (sphincter, external or internal) 596.8
  viscera 789.0 ☑
Spasmus nutans 307.3
Spastic — *see also* Spasm
  child 343.9
Spasticity — *see also* Spasm
  cerebral, child 343.9
Speakers' throat 784.49
Specific, specified — *see* condition
Speech
  defect, disorder, disturbance, impediment NEC 784.59 ▲
    psychogenic 307.9
  ▶(language)◀ therapy V57.3
Spells 780.39
  breath-holding 786.9
Spencer's disease (epidemic vomiting) 078.82
Spens' syndrome (syncope with heart block) 426.9
Spermatic cord — *see* condition
Spermatocele 608.1
  congenital 752.89
Spermatocystitis 608.4
Spermatocytoma (M9063/3)
  specified site — *see* Neoplasm, by site, malignant
  unspecified site 186.9
Spermatorrhea 608.89
Sperm counts
  fertility testing V26.21
  following sterilization reversal V26.22
  postvasectomy V25.8
Sphacelus — *see also* Gangrene 785.4
Sphenoidal — *see* condition
Sphenoiditis (chronic) — *see also* Sinusitis, sphenoidal 473.3
Sphenopalatine ganglion neuralgia 337.09
Sphericity, increased, lens 743.36
Spherocytosis (congenital) (familial) (hereditary) 282.0
  hemoglobin disease 282.7
  sickle-cell (disease) 282.60
Spherophakia 743.36
Sphincter — *see* condition
Sphincteritis, sphincter of Oddi — *see also* Cholecystitis 576.8
Sphingolipidosis 272.7
Sphingolipodystrophy 272.7
Sphingomyelinosis 272.7
Spicule tooth 520.2
Spider
  finger 755.59
  nevus 448.1
  vascular 448.1
Spiegler-Fendt sarcoid 686.8
Spielmeyer-Stock disease 330.1
Spielmeyer-Vogt disease 330.1
Spina bifida (aperta) 741.9 ☑

> *Note* — Use the following fifth-digit subclassification with category 741:
>
> *0*   *unspecified region*
>
> *1*   *cervical region*
>
> *2*   *dorsal [thoracic] region*
>
> *3*   *lumbar region*

  with hydrocephalus 741.0 ☑
  fetal (suspected), affecting management of pregnancy 655.0 ☑
  occulta 756.17
Spindle, Krukenberg's 371.13
Spine, spinal — *see* condition
Spiradenoma (eccrine) (M8403/0) — *see* Neoplasm, skin, benign
Spirillosis NEC — *see also* Fever, relapsing 087.9
Spirillum minus 026.0
Spirillum obermeieri infection 087.0
Spirochetal — *see* condition
Spirochetosis 104.9

Spirochetosis — *continued*
  arthritic, arthritica 104.9 *[711.8]* ☑
  bronchopulmonary 104.8
  icterohemorrhagica 100.0
  lung 104.8
Spitting blood — *see also* Hemoptysis 786.3
Splanchnomegaly 569.89
Splanchnoptosis 569.89
Spleen, splenic — *see also* condition
  agenesis 759.0
  flexure syndrome 569.89
  neutropenia syndrome 289.53
  sequestration syndrome 289.52
Splenectasis — *see also* Splenomegaly 789.2
Splenitis (interstitial) (malignant) (nonspecific) 289.59
  malarial (*see also* Malaria) 084.6
  tuberculous (*see also* Tuberculosis) 017.7 ☑
Splenocele 289.59
Splenomegalia — *see* Splenomegaly
Splenomegalic — *see* condition
Splenomegaly 789.2
  Bengal 789.2
  cirrhotic 289.51
  congenital 759.0
  congestive, chronic 289.51
  cryptogenic 789.2
  Egyptian 120.1
  Gaucher's (cerebroside lipidosis) 272.7
  idiopathic 789.2
  malarial (*see also* Malaria) 084.6
  neutropenic 289.53
  Niemann-Pick (lipid histiocytosis) 272.7
  siderotic 289.51
  syphilitic 095.8
    congenital 090.0
  tropical (Bengal) (idiopathic) 789.2
Splenopathy 289.50
Splenopneumonia — *see* Pneumonia
Splenoptosis 289.59
Splinter — *see* Injury, superficial, by site
Split, splitting
  heart sounds 427.89
  lip, congenital (*see also* Cleft, lip) 749.10
  nails 703.8
  urinary stream 788.61
Spoiled child reaction — *see also* Disturbance, conduct 312.1 ☑
Spondylarthritis — *see also* Spondylosis 721.90
Spondylarthrosis — *see also* Spondylosis 721.90
Spondylitis 720.9
  ankylopoietica 720.0
  ankylosing (chronic) 720.0
  atrophic 720.9
    ligamentous 720.9
  chronic (traumatic) (*see also* Spondylosis) 721.90
  deformans (chronic) (*see also* Spondylosis) 721.90
  gonococcal 098.53
  gouty 274.00 ▲
  hypertrophic (*see also* Spondylosis) 721.90
  infectious NEC 720.9
  juvenile (adolescent) 720.0
  Kümmell's 721.7
  Marie-Strümpell (ankylosing) 720.0
  muscularis 720.9
  ossificans ligamentosa 721.6
  osteoarthritica (*see also* Spondylosis) 721.90
  posttraumatic 721.7
  proliferative 720.0
  rheumatoid 720.0
  rhizomelica 720.0
  sacroiliac NEC 720.2
  senescent (*see also* Spondylosis) 721.90
  senile (*see also* Spondylosis) 721.90
  static (*see also* Spondylosis) 721.90
  traumatic (chronic) (*see also* Spondylosis) 721.90
  tuberculous (*see also* Tuberculosis) 015.0 ☑ *[720.81]*
  typhosa 002.0 *[720.81]*
Spondyloarthrosis — *see also* Spondylosis 721.90
Spondylolisthesis (congenital) (lumbosacral) 756.12

☑ Additional Digit Required — Refer to the Tabular List for Digit Selection

� Subterms under main terms may continue to next column or page

▶◀ Revised Text   ● New Line   ▲ Revised Code

Spondylolisthesis — Sprain, strain

☑ Additional Digit Required — Refer to the Tabular List for Digit Selection   ▽ Subterms under main terms may continue to next column or page

2010 ICD-9-CM   ▶◀ Revised Text   ● New Line   ▲ Revised Code   **Volume 2 — 251**

Sprain, strain — *continued*
   tibiofibular — *continued*
      superior 844.3
   toe(s) 845.10
   trachea 848.8
   trapezoid 840.8
   ulna, ulnar (proximal end) 841.9
      collateral 841.1
      distal end 842.00
   ulnohumeral 841.3
   vertebrae (*see also* Sprain, spine) 847.9
      cervical, cervicodorsal, cervicothoracic 847.0
   wrist (cuneiform) (scaphoid) (semilunar) 842.00
   xiphoid cartilage 848.49
Sprengel's deformity (congenital) 755.52
Spring fever 309.23
Sprue 579.1
   celiac 579.0
   idiopathic 579.0
   meaning thrush 112.0
   nontropical 579.0
   tropical 579.1
Spur — *see also* Exostosis
   bone 726.91
      calcaneal 726.73
   calcaneal 726.73
   iliac crest 726.5
   nose (septum) 478.19
      bone 726.91
   septal 478.19
Spuria placenta — *see* Placenta, abnormal
Spurway's syndrome (brittle bones and blue sclera) 756.51
Sputum, abnormal (amount) (color) (excessive) (odor) (purulent) 786.4
   bloody 786.3
Squamous — *see also* condition
   cell metaplasia
      bladder 596.8
      cervix — *see* condition
   epithelium in
      cervical canal (congenital) 752.49
      uterine mucosa (congenital) 752.3
   metaplasia
      bladder 596.8
      cervix — *see* condition
Squashed nose 738.0
   congenital 754.0
Squeeze, divers' 993.3
Squint — *see also* Strabismus 378.9
   accommodative (*see also* Esotropia) 378.00
   concomitant (*see also* Heterotropia) 378.30
Stab — *see also* Wound, open, by site
   internal organs — *see* Injury, internal, by site, with open wound
Staggering gait 781.2
   hysterical 300.11
Staghorn calculus 592.0
Stain, staining
   meconium 779.84
   port wine 757.32
   tooth, teeth (hard tissues) 521.7
      due to
         accretions 523.6
         deposits (betel) (black) (green) (materia alba) (orange) (tobacco) 523.6
         metals (copper) (silver) 521.7
         nicotine 523.6
         pulpal bleeding 521.7
         tobacco 523.6
Stälh's
   ear 744.29
   pigment line (cornea) 371.11
Stälhi's pigment lines (cornea) 371.11
Stammering 307.0
Standstill
   atrial 426.6
   auricular 426.6
   cardiac (*see also* Arrest, cardiac) 427.5
   sinoatrial 426.6
   sinus 426.6
   ventricular (*see also* Arrest, cardiac) 427.5
Stannosis 503
Stanton's disease (melioidosis) 025

Staphylitis (acute) (catarrhal) (chronic) (gangrenous) (membranous) (suppurative) (ulcerative) 528.3
Staphylococcemia 038.10
   aureus 038.11
   specified organism NEC 038.19
Staphylococcus, staphylococcal — *see* condition
Staphyloderma (skin) 686.00
Staphyloma 379.11
   anterior, localized 379.14
   ciliary 379.11
   cornea 371.73
   equatorial 379.13
   posterior 379.12
   posticum 379.12
   ring 379.15
   sclera NEC 379.11
Starch eating 307.52
Stargardt's disease 362.75
Starvation (inanition) (due to lack of food) 994.2
   edema 262
   voluntary NEC 307.1
Stasis
   bile (duct) (*see also* Disease, biliary) 576.8
   bronchus (*see also* Bronchitis) 490
   cardiac (*see also* Failure, heart) 428.0
   cecum 564.89
   colon 564.89
   dermatitis (*see also* Varix, with stasis dermatitis) 454.1
   duodenal 536.8
   eczema (*see also* Varix, with stasis dermatitis) 454.1
   edema (*see also* Hypertension, venous) 459.30
   foot 991.4
   gastric 536.3
   ileocecal coil 564.89
   ileum 564.89
   intestinal 564.89
   jejunum 564.89
   kidney 586
   liver 571.9
      cirrhotic — *see* Cirrhosis, liver
   lymphatic 457.8
   pneumonia 514
   portal 571.9
   pulmonary 514
   rectal 564.89
   renal 586
      tubular 584.5
   stomach 536.3
   ulcer
      with varicose veins 454.0
      without varicose veins 459.81
   urine NEC (*see also* Retention, urine) 788.20
   venous 459.81
State
   affective and paranoid, mixed, organic psychotic 294.8
   agitated 307.9
      acute reaction to stress 308.2
   anxiety (neurotic) (*see also* Anxiety) 300.00
      specified type NEC 300.09
   apprehension (*see also* Anxiety) 300.00
      specified type NEC 300.09
   climacteric, female 627.2
      following induced menopause 627.4
   clouded
      epileptic (*see also* Epilepsy) 345.9 ☑
      paroxysmal (idiopathic) (*see also* Epilepsy) 345.9 ☑
   compulsive (mixed) (with obsession) 300.3
   confusional 298.9
      acute 293.0
         with
            arteriosclerotic dementia 290.41
            presenile brain disease 290.11
            senility 290.3
         alcoholic 291.0
         drug-induced 292.81
      epileptic 293.0
      postoperative 293.9
      reactive (emotional stress) (psychological trauma) 298.2
      subacute 293.1

State — *continued*
   constitutional psychopathic 301.9
   convulsive (*see also* Convulsions) 780.39
   depressive NEC 311
      induced by drug 292.84
      neurotic 300.4
   dissociative 300.15
   hallucinatory 780.1
      induced by drug 292.12
   hypercoagulable (primary) 289.81
      secondary 289.82
   hyperdynamic beta-adrenergic circulatory 429.82
   locked-in 344.81
   menopausal 627.2
      artificial 627.4
      following induced menopause 627.4
   neurotic NEC 300.9
      with depersonalization episode 300.6
   obsessional 300.3
   oneiroid (*see also* Schizophrenia) 295.4 ☑
   panic 300.01
   paranoid 297.9
      alcohol-induced 291.5
      arteriosclerotic 290.42
      climacteric 297.2
      drug-induced 292.11
      in
         presenile brain disease 290.12
         senile brain disease 290.20
      involutional 297.2
      menopausal 297.2
      senile 290.20
      simple 297.0
   postleukotomy 310.0
   pregnant (*see also* Pregnancy) V22.2
   psychogenic, twilight 298.2
   psychotic, organic (*see also* Psychosis, organic) 294.9
      mixed paranoid and affective 294.8
      senile or presenile NEC 290.9
      transient NEC 293.9
         with
            anxiety 293.84
            delusions 293.81
            depression 293.83
            hallucinations 293.82
   residual schizophrenic (*see also* Schizophrenia) 295.6 ☑
   tension (*see also* Anxiety) 300.9
   transient organic psychotic 293.9
      anxiety type 293.84
      depressive type 293.83
      hallucinatory type 293.83
      paranoid type 293.81
      specified type NEC 293.89
   twilight
      epileptic 293.0
      psychogenic 298.2
   vegetative (persistent) 780.03
Status (post)
   absence
      epileptic (*see also* Epilepsy) 345.2
      of organ, acquired (postsurgical) — *see* Absence, by site, acquired
   administration of tPA(rtPA) in a different institution within the last 24 hours prior to admission to facility V45.88
   anastomosis of intestine (for bypass) V45.3
   anginosus 413.9
   angioplasty, percutaneous transluminal coronary V45.82
   ankle prosthesis V43.66
   aortocoronary bypass or shunt V45.81
   arthrodesis V45.4
   artificially induced condition NEC V45.89
   artificial opening (of) V44.9
      gastrointestinal tract NEC V44.4
      specified site NEC V44.8
      urinary tract NEC V44.6
      vagina V44.7
   aspirator V46.0
   asthmaticus (*see also* Asthma) 493.9 ☑
   awaiting organ transplant V49.83
   bariatric surgery V45.86

Status — *continued*
   bariatric surgery — *continued*
      complicating pregnancy, childbirth, or the puerperium 649.2 ☑
   bed confinement V49.84
   breast
      correction V43.82
      implant removal V45.83
      reconstruction V43.82
   cardiac
      device (in situ) V45.00
         carotid sinus V45.09
            fitting or adjustment V53.39
         defibrillator, automatic implantable V45.02
         pacemaker V45.01
            fitting or adjustment V53.31
   carotid sinus stimulator V45.09
   cataract extraction V45.61
   chemotherapy V66.2
      current V58.69
   circumcision, female 629.20
   clitorectomy (female genital mutilation type I) 629.21
      with excision of labia minora (female genital mutilation type II) 629.22
   colonization — *see* Carrier (suspected) of
   colostomy V44.3
   contraceptive device V45.59
      intrauterine V45.51
      subdermal V45.52
   convulsivus idiopathicus (*see also* Epilepsy) 345.3
   coronary artery bypass or shunt V45.81
   cutting
      female genital 629.20
         specified NEC 629.29
         type I 629.21
         type II 629.22
         type III 629.23
         type IV 629.29
   cystostomy V44.50
      appendico-vesicostomy V44.52
      cutaneous-vesicostomy V44.51
      specified type NEC V44.59
   defibrillator, automatic implantable cardiac V45.02
   delinquent immunization V15.83
   dental crowns V45.84
   dental fillings V45.84
   dental restoration V45.84
   dental sealant V49.82
   dialysis (hemo) (peritoneal) V45.11
   donor V59.9
   drug therapy or regimen V67.59
      high-risk medication NEC V67.51
   elbow prosthesis V43.62
   enterostomy V44.4
   epileptic, epilepticus (absence) (grand mal) (*see also* Epilepsy) 345.3
      focal motor 345.7 ☑
      partial 345.7 ☑
      petit mal 345.2
      psychomotor 345.7 ☑
      temporal lobe 345.7 ☑
   estrogen receptor
      negative [ER-] V86.1
      positive [ER+] V86.0
   eye (adnexa) surgery V45.69
   female genital
      cutting 629.20
         specified NEC 629.29
         type I 629.21
         type II 629.22
         type III 629.23
         type IV 629.29
      mutilation 629.20
         type I 629.21
         type II 629.22
         type III 629.23
         type IV 629.29
   filtering bleb (eye) (postglaucoma) V45.69
      with rupture or complication 997.99
      postcataract extraction (complication) 997.99
   finger joint prosthesis V43.69

☑ Additional Digit Required — Refer to the Tabular List for Digit Selection   ▽ Subterms under main terms may continue to next column or page

252 — Volume 2 • October 2009   ▶◀ Revised Text   ● New Line   ▲ Revised Code   **2010 ICD-9-CM**

Status — *continued*
  foster care V60.81 •
  gastric
    banding V45.86
      complicating pregnancy, childbirth, or
        the puerperium 649.2 ☑
    bypass for obesity V45.86
      complicating pregnancy, childbirth, or
        the puerperium 649.2 ☑
  gastrostomy V44.1
  grand mal 345.3
  heart valve prosthesis V43.3
  hemodialysis V45.11
  hip prosthesis (joint) (partial) (total) V43.64
  hysterectomy V88.01
    partial with remaining cervical stump
      V88.02
    total V88.01
  ileostomy V44.2
  infibulation (female genital mutilation type III)
    629.23
  insulin pump V45.85
  intestinal bypass V45.3
  intrauterine contraceptive device V45.51
  jejunostomy V44.4
  knee joint prosthesis V43.65
  lacunaris 437.8
  lacunosis 437.8
  lapsed immunization schedule V15.83 •
  low birth weight V21.30
    less than 500 grams V21.31
    1000–1499 grams V21.33
    1500–1999 grams V21.34
    2000–2500 grams V21.35
    500–999 grams V21.32
  lymphaticus 254.8
  malignant neoplasm, ablated or excised —
    see History, malignant neoplasm
  marmoratus 333.79
  military deployment V62.22 •
  mutilation, female 629.20
    type I 629.21
    type II 629.22
    type III 629.23
    type IV 629.29
  nephrostomy V44.6
  neuropacemaker NEC V45.89
    brain V45.89
    carotid sinus V45.09
    neurologic NEC V45.89
  obesity surgery V45.86
    compliating pregnancy, childbirth, or the
      puerperium 649.2 ☑
  organ replacement
    by artificial or mechanical device or pros-
      thesis of
      artery V43.4
      artificial skin V43.83
      bladder V43.5
      blood vessel V43.4
      breast V43.82
      eye globe V43.0
      heart
        assist device V43.21
        fully implantable artificial heart
          V43.22
        valve V43.3
      intestine V43.89
      joint V43.60
        ankle V43.66
        elbow V43.62
        finger V43.69
        hip (partial) (total) V43.64
        knee V43.65
        shoulder V43.61
        specified NEC V43.69
        wrist V43.63
      kidney V43.89
      larynx V43.81
      lens V43.1
      limb(s) V43.7
      liver V43.89
      lung V43.89
      organ NEC V43.89
      pancreas V43.89
      skin (artificial) V43.83

Status — *continued*
  organ replacement — *continued*
    by artificial or mechanical device or pros-
      thesis of — *continued*
      tissue NEC V43.89
      vein V43.4
    by organ transplant (heterologous) (homol-
      ogous) — *see* Status, transplant
  pacemaker
    brain V45.89
    cardiac V45.01
    carotid sinus V45.09
    neurologic NEC V45.89
    specified site NEC V45.89
  percutaneous transluminal coronary angioplas-
    ty V45.82
  peritoneal dialysis V45.11
  petit mal 345.2
  postcommotio cerebri 310.2
  postmenopausal (age related) (natural) V49.81
  postoperative NEC V45.89
  postpartum NEC V24.2
    care immediately following delivery V24.0
    routine follow-up V24.2
  postsurgical NEC V45.89
  renal dialysis V45.11
    noncompliance V45.12
  respirator [ventilator] V46.11
    encounter
      during
        mechanical failure V46.14
        power failure V46.12
      for weaning V46.13
  reversed jejunal transposition (for bypass)
    V45.3
  sex reassignment surgery (*see also* Trans-sexu-
    alism) 302.50
  shoulder prosthesis V43.61
  shunt
    aortocoronary bypass V45.81
    arteriovenous (for dialysis) V45.11
    cerebrospinal fluid V45.2
    vascular NEC V45.89
      aortocoronary (bypass) V45.81
    ventricular (communicating) (for drainage)
      V45.2
  sterilization
    tubal ligation V26.51
    vasectomy V26.52
  subdermal contraceptive device V45.52
  thymicolymphaticus 254.8
  thymicus 254.8
  thymolymphaticus 254.8
  tooth extraction 525.10
  tracheostomy V44.0
  transplant
    blood vessel V42.89
    bone V42.4
      marrow V42.81
    cornea V42.5
    heart V42.1
      valve V42.2
    intestine V42.84
    kidney V42.0
    liver V42.7
    lung V42.6
    organ V42.9
      removal (due to complication, failure,
        rejection or infection) V45.87
      specified site NEC V42.89
    pancreas V42.83
    peripheral stem cells V42.82
    skin V42.3
    stem cells, peripheral V42.82
    tissue V42.9
      specified type NEC V42.89
    vessel, blood V42.89
  tubal ligation V26.51
  underimmunization V15.83 •
  ureterostomy V44.6
  urethrostomy V44.6
  vagina, artificial V44.7
  vascular shunt NEC V45.89
    aortocoronary (bypass) V45.81
  vasectomy V26.52
  ventilator [respirator] V46.11

Status — *continued*
  ventilator [respirator] — *continued*
    encounter
      during
        mechanical failure V46.14
        power failure V46.12
      for weaning V46.13
    wheelchair confinement V46.3
    wrist prosthesis V43.63
Stave fracture — *see* Fracture, metacarpus,
    metacarpal bone(s)
Steal
  subclavian artery 435.2
  vertebral artery 435.1
Stealing, solitary, child problem — *see also*
    Disturbance, conduct 312.1 ☑
Steam burn — *see* Burn, by site
Steatocystoma multiplex 706.2
Steatoma (infected) 706.2
  eyelid (cystic) 374.84
    infected 373.13
Steatorrhea (chronic) 579.8
  with lacteal obstruction 579.2
  idiopathic 579.0
    adult 579.0
    infantile 579.0
  pancreatic 579.4
  primary 579.0
  secondary 579.8
  specified cause NEC 579.8
  tropical 579.1
Steatosis 272.8
  heart (*see also* Degeneration, myocardial) 429.1
  kidney 593.89
  liver 571.8
Steele-Richardson (-Olszewski) Syndrome
    333.0
Steinbrocker's syndrome — *see also* Neuropa-
    thy, peripheral, autonomic 337.9
Steinert's disease 359.21
Stein-Leventhal syndrome (polycystic ovary)
    256.4
Stein's syndrome (polycystic ovary) 256.4
STEMI (ST elevation myocardial infarction — *see
    also* — Infarct, myocardium, ST elevation
    410.9 ☑
Stenocardia — *see also* Angina 413.9
Stenocephaly 756.0
Stenosis (cicatricial) — *see also* Stricture
  ampulla of Vater 576.2
    with calculus, cholelithiasis, or stones —
      see Choledocholithiasis
  anus, anal (canal) (sphincter) 569.2
    congenital 751.2
  aorta (ascending) 747.22
    arch 747.10
    arteriosclerotic 440.0
      calcified 440.0
  aortic (valve) 424.1
    with
      mitral (valve)
        insufficiency or incompetence
          396.2
        stenosis or obstruction 396.0
    atypical 396.0
    congenital 746.3
    rheumatic 395.0
      with
        insufficiency, incompetency or re-
          gurgitation 395.2
          with mitral (valve) disease 396.8
        mitral (valve)
          disease (stenosis) 396.0
          insufficiency or incompetence
            396.2
          stenosis or obstruction 396.0
    specified cause, except rheumatic 424.1
    syphilitic 093.22
  aqueduct of Sylvius (congenital) 742.3
    with spina bifida (*see also* Spina bifida)
      741.0 ☑
    acquired 331.4
  artery NEC (*see also* Arteriosclerosis) 447.1
    basilar — *see* Narrowing, artery, basilar
    carotid (common) (internal) — *see* Narrow-
      ing, artery, carotid

Stenosis — *see also* Stricture — *continued*
  artery (*see also* Arteriosclerosis) — *contin-
    ued*
    celiac 447.4
    cerebral 437.0
      due to
        embolism (*see also* Embolism,
          brain) 434.1 ☑
        thrombus (*see also* Thrombosis,
          brain) 434.0 ☑
    extremities 440.20
    precerebral — *see* Narrowing, artery, pre-
      cerebral
    pulmonary (congenital) 747.3
      acquired 417.8
    renal 440.1
    vertebral — *see* Narrowing, artery, verte-
      bral
  bile duct or biliary passage (*see also* Obstruc-
    tion, biliary) 576.2
    congenital 751.61
  bladder neck (acquired) 596.0
    congenital 753.6
  brain 348.89   ▲
  bronchus 519.19
    syphilitic 095.8
  cardia (stomach) 537.89
    congenital 750.7
  cardiovascular (*see also* Disease, cardiovascu-
    lar) 429.2
  carotid artery — *see* Narrowing, artery, carotid
  cervix, cervical (canal) 622.4
    congenital 752.49
    in pregnancy or childbirth 654.6 ☑
      affecting fetus or newborn 763.89
      causing obstructed labor 660.2 ☑
        affecting fetus or newborn 763.1
  colon (*see also* Obstruction, intestine) 560.9
    congenital 751.2
  colostomy 569.62
  common bile duct (*see also* Obstruction, bil-
    iary) 576.2
    congenital 751.61
  coronary (artery) — *see* Arteriosclerosis, coro-
    nary
  cystic duct (*see also* Obstruction, gallbladder)
    575.2
    congenital 751.61
  due to (presence of) any device, implant, or
    graft classifiable to 996.0–996.5 — *see*
    Complications, due to (presence of)
    any device, implant, or graft classified
    to 996.0–996.5 NEC
  duodenum 537.3
    congenital 751.1
  ejaculatory duct NEC 608.89
  endocervical os — *see* Stenosis, cervix
  enterostomy 569.62
  esophagostomy 530.87
  esophagus 530.3
    congenital 750.3
    syphilitic 095.8
      congenital 090.5
  external ear canal 380.50
    secondary to
      inflammation 380.53
      surgery 380.52
      trauma 380.51
  gallbladder (*see also* Obstruction, gallbladder)
    575.2
  glottis 478.74
  heart valve (acquired) (*see also* Endocarditis)
    congenital NEC 746.89
      aortic 746.3
      mitral 746.5
      pulmonary 746.02
      tricuspid 746.1
  hepatic duct (*see also* Obstruction, biliary)
    576.2
  hymen 623.3
  hypertrophic subaortic (idiopathic) 425.1
  infundibulum cardiac 746.83
  intestine (*see also* Obstruction, intestine) 560.9
    congenital (small) 751.1
      large 751.2

☑ Additional Digit Required — Refer to the Tabular List for Digit Selection   ⬚ Subterms under main terms may continue to next column or page

2010 ICD-9-CM   ▶◀ Revised Text   • New Line   ▲ Revised Code   October 2009 • Volume 2 — 253

Stenosis — *see also* Stricture — *continued*
lacrimal
canaliculi 375.53
duct 375.56
congenital 743.65
punctum 375.52
congenital 743.65
sac 375.54
congenital 743.65
lacrimonasal duct 375.56
congenital 743.65
neonatal 375.55
larynx 478.74
congenital 748.3
syphilitic 095.8
congenital 090.5
mitral (valve) (chronic) (inactive) 394.0
with
aortic (valve)
disease (insufficiency) 396.1
insufficiency or incompetence 396.1
stenosis or obstruction 396.0
incompetency, insufficiency or regurgitation 394.2
with aortic valve disease 396.8
active or acute 391.1
with chorea (acute) (rheumatic) (Sydenham's) 392.0
congenital 746.5
specified cause, except rheumatic 424.0
syphilitic 093.21
myocardium, myocardial (*see also* Degeneration, myocardial) 429.1
hypertrophic subaortic (idiopathic) 425.1
nares (anterior) (posterior) 478.19
congenital 748.0
nasal duct 375.56
congenital 743.65
nasolacrimal duct 375.56
congenital 743.65
neonatal 375.55
organ or site, congenital NEC — *see* Atresia
papilla of Vater 576.2
with calculus, cholelithiasis, or stones — *see* Choledocholithiasis
pulmonary (artery) (congenital) 747.3
with ventricular septal defect, dextraposition of aorta and hypertrophy of right ventricle 745.2
acquired 417.8
infundibular 746.83
in tetralogy of Fallot 745.2
subvalvular 746.83
valve (*see also* Endocarditis, pulmonary) 424.3
congenital 746.02
vein 747.49
acquired 417.8
vessel NEC 417.8
pulmonic (congenital) 746.02
infundibular 746.83
subvalvular 746.83
pylorus (hypertrophic) 537.0
adult 537.0
congenital 750.5
infantile 750.5
rectum (sphincter) (*see also* Stricture, rectum) 569.2
renal artery 440.1
salivary duct (any) 527.8
sphincter of Oddi (*see also* Obstruction, biliary) 576.2
spinal 724.00
cervical 723.0
lumbar, lumbosacral 724.02
nerve (root) NEC 724.9
specified region NEC 724.09
thoracic, thoracolumbar 724.01
stomach, hourglass 537.6
subaortic 746.81
hypertrophic (idiopathic) 425.1
supra (valvular)-aortic 747.22
trachea 519.19
congenital 748.3
syphilitic 095.8

Stenosis — *see also* Stricture — *continued*
trachea — *continued*
tuberculous (*see also* Tuberculosis) 012.8 ☑
tracheostomy 519.02
tricuspid (valve) (*see also* Endocarditis, tricuspid) 397.0
congenital 746.1
nonrheumatic 424.2
tubal 628.2
ureter (*see also* Stricture, ureter) 593.3
congenital 753.29
urethra (*see also* Stricture, urethra) 598.9
vagina 623.2
congenital 752.49
in pregnancy or childbirth 654.7 ☑
affecting fetus or newborn 763.89
causing obstructed labor 660.2 ☑
affecting fetus or newborn 763.1
valve (cardiac) (heart) (*see also* Endocarditis) 424.90
congenital NEC 746.89
aortic 746.3
mitral 746.5
pulmonary 746.02
tricuspid 746.1
urethra 753.6
valvular (*see also* Endocarditis) 424.90
congenital NEC 746.89
urethra 753.6
vascular graft or shunt 996.1
atherosclerosis — *see* Arteriosclerosis, extremities
embolism 996.74
occlusion NEC 996.74
thrombus 996.74
vena cava (inferior) (superior) 459.2
congenital 747.49
ventricular shunt 996.2
vulva 624.8
Stercolith — *see also* Fecalith 560.39
appendix 543.9
Stercoraceous, stercoral ulcer 569.82
anus or rectum 569.41
Stereopsis, defective
with fusion 368.33
without fusion 368.32
Stereotypes NEC 307.3
Sterility
female — *see* Infertility, female
male (*see also* Infertility, male) 606.9
Sterilization, admission for V25.2
status
tubal ligation V26.51
vasectomy V26.52
Sternalgia — *see also* Angina 413.9
Sternopagus 759.4
Sternum bifidum 756.3
Sternutation 784.99
Steroid
effects (adverse) (iatrogenic)
cushingoid
correct substance properly administered 255.0
overdose or wrong substance given or taken 962.0
diabetes — *see* Diabetes, secondary
correct substance properly administered 251.8
overdose or wrong substance given or taken 962.0
due to
correct substance properly administered 255.8
overdose or wrong substance given or taken 962.0
fever
correct substance properly administered 780.60
overdose or wrong substance given or taken 962.0
withdrawal
correct substance properly administered 255.41
overdose or wrong substance given or taken 962.0

Steroid — *continued*
responder 365.03
Stevens-Johnson disease or syndrome (erythema multiforme exudativum) 695.13
toxic epidermal necrolysis overlap (SJS-TEN overlap syndrome) 695.14
Stewart-Morel syndrome (hyperostosis frontalis interna) 733.3
Sticker's disease (erythema infectiosum) 057.0
Stickler syndrome 759.89
Sticky eye 372.03
Stieda's disease (calcification, knee joint) 726.62
Stiff
back 724.8
neck (*see also* Torticollis) 723.5
Stiff-baby 759.89
Stiff-man syndrome 333.91
Stiffness, joint NEC 719.50
ankle 719.57
back 724.8
elbow 719.52
finger 719.54
hip 719.55
knee 719.56
multiple sites 719.59
sacroiliac 724.6
shoulder 719.51
specified site NEC 719.58
spine 724.9
surgical fusion V45.4
wrist 719.53
Stigmata, congenital syphilis 090.5
Stillbirth, stillborn NEC 779.9
Still's disease or syndrome 714.30
adult onset 714.2
Stiller's disease (asthenia) 780.79
Still-Felty syndrome (rheumatoid arthritis with splenomegaly and leukopenia) 714.1
Stilling-Türk-Duane syndrome (ocular retraction syndrome) 378.71
Stimulation, ovary 256.1
Sting (animal) (bee) (fish) (insect) (jellyfish) (Portuguese man-o-war) (wasp) (venomous) 989.5
anaphylactic shock or reaction 989.5
plant 692.6
Stippled epiphyses 756.59
Stitch
abscess 998.59
burst (in external operation wound) (*see also* Dehiscence) 998.32
internal 998.31
in back 724.5
Stojano's (subcostal) **syndrome** 098.86
Stokes-Adams syndrome (syncope with heart block) 426.9
Stokes' disease (exophthalmic goiter) 242.0 ☑
Stokvis' (-Talma) disease (enterogenous cyanosis) 289.7
Stomach — *see* condition
Stoma malfunction
colostomy 569.62
cystostomy 997.5
enterostomy 569.62
esophagostomy 530.87
gastrostomy 536.42
ileostomy 569.62
nephrostomy 997.5
tracheostomy 519.02
ureterostomy 997.5
Stomatitis 528.00
angular 528.5
due to dietary or vitamin deficiency 266.0
aphthous 528.2
bovine 059.11
candidal 112.0
catarrhal 528.00
denture 528.9
diphtheritic (membranous) 032.0
due to
dietary deficiency 266.0
thrush 112.0
vitamin deficiency 266.0
epidemic 078.4
epizootic 078.4
follicular 528.00

Stomatitis — *continued*
gangrenous 528.1
herpetic 054.2
herpetiformis 528.2
malignant 528.00
membranous acute 528.00
monilial 112.0
mycotic 112.0
necrotic 528.1
ulcerative 101
necrotizing ulcerative 101
parasitic 112.0
septic 528.00
specified NEC 528.09
spirochetal 101
suppurative (acute) 528.00
ulcerative 528.00
necrotizing 101
ulceromembranous 101
vesicular 528.00
with exanthem 074.3
Vincent's 101
Stomatocytosis 282.8
Stomatomycosis 112.0
Stomatorrhagia 528.9
Stone(s) — *see also* Calculus
bladder 594.1
diverticulum 594.0
cystine 270.0
heart syndrome (*see also* Failure, ventricular, left) 428.1
kidney 592.0
prostate 602.0
pulp (dental) 522.2
renal 592.0
salivary duct or gland (any) 527.5
ureter 592.1
urethra (impacted) 594.2
urinary (duct) (impacted) (passage) 592.9
bladder 594.1
diverticulum 594.0
lower tract NEC 594.9
specified site 594.8
xanthine 277.2
Stonecutters' lung 502
tuberculous (*see also* Tuberculosis) 011.4 ☑
Stonemasons'
asthma, disease, or lung 502
tuberculous (*see also* Tuberculosis) 011.4 ☑
phthisis (*see also* Tuberculosis) 011.4 ☑
Stoppage
bowel (*see also* Obstruction, intestine) 560.9
heart (*see also* Arrest, cardiac) 427.5
intestine (*see also* Obstruction, intestine) 560.9
urine NEC (*see also* Retention, urine) 788.20
Storm, thyroid (apathetic) — *see also* Thyrotoxicosis 242.9 ☑
Strabismus (alternating) (congenital) (nonparalytic) 378.9
concomitant (*see also* Heterotropia) 378.30
convergent (*see also* Esotropia) 378.00
divergent (*see also* Exotropia) 378.10
convergent (*see also* Esotropia) 378.00
divergent (*see also* Exotropia) 378.10
due to adhesions, scars — *see* Strabismus, mechanical
in neuromuscular disorder NEC 378.73
intermittent 378.20
vertical 378.31
latent 378.40
convergent (esophoria) 378.41
divergent (exophoria) 378.42
vertical 378.43
mechanical 378.60
due to
Brown's tendon sheath syndrome 378.61
specified musculofascial disorder NEC 378.62
paralytic 378.50
third or oculomotor nerve (partial) 378.51
total 378.52
fourth or trochlear nerve 378.53
sixth or abducens nerve 378.54
specified type NEC 378.73

Strabismus — *continued*
  vertical (hypertropia) 378.31
Strain — *see also* Sprain, by site
  eye NEC 368.13
  heart — *see* Disease, heart
  meaning gonorrhea — *see* Gonorrhea
  on urination 788.65
  physical NEC V62.89
  postural 729.90
  psychological NEC V62.89
Strands
  conjunctiva 372.62
  vitreous humor 379.25
Strangulation, strangulated 994.7
  appendix 543.9
  asphyxiation or suffocation by 994.7
  bladder neck 596.0
  bowel — *see* Strangulation, intestine
  colon — *see* Strangulation, intestine
  cord (umbilical) — *see* Compression, umbilical cord
  due to birth injury 767.8
  food or foreign body (*see also* Asphyxia, food) 933.1
  hemorrhoids 455.8
    external 455.5
    internal 455.2
  hernia (*see also* Hernia, by site, with obstruction)
    gangrenous — *see* Hernia, by site, with gangrene
  intestine (large) (small) 560.2
    with hernia (*see also* Hernia, by site, with obstruction)
      gangrenous — *see* Hernia, by site, with gangrene
    congenital (small) 751.1
      large 751.2
  mesentery 560.2
  mucus (*see also* Asphyxia, mucus) 933.1
    newborn 770.18
  omentum 560.2
  organ or site, congenital NEC — *see* Atresia
  ovary 620.8
    due to hernia 620.4
  penis 607.89
    foreign body 939.3
  rupture (*see also* Hernia, by site, with obstruction) 552.9
    gangrenous (*see also* Hernia, by site, with gangrene) 551.9
  stomach, due to hernia (*see also* Hernia, by site, with obstruction) 552.9
    with gangrene (*see also* Hernia, by site, with gangrene) 551.9
  umbilical cord — *see* Compression, umbilical cord
  vesicourethral orifice 596.0
Strangury 788.1
Strawberry
  gallbladder (*see also* Disease, gallbladder) 575.6
  mark 757.32
  tongue (red) (white) 529.3
Straw itch 133.8
Streak, ovarian 752.0
Strephosymbolia 315.01
  secondary to organic lesion 784.69
Streptobacillary fever 026.1
Streptobacillus moniliformis 026.1
Streptococcemia 038.0
Streptococcicosis — *see* Infection, streptococcal
Streptococcus, streptococcal — *see* condition
Streptoderma 686.00
Streptomycosis — *see* Actinomycosis
Streptothricosis — *see* Actinomycosis
Streptothrix — *see* Actinomycosis
Streptotrichosis — *see* Actinomycosis
Stress 308.9
  fracture — *see* Fracture, stress
  polycythemia 289.0
  reaction (gross) (*see also* Reaction, stress, acute) 308.9
Stretching, nerve — *see* Injury, nerve, by site
Striae (albicantes) (atrophicae) (cutis distensae) (distensae) 701.3

Striations of nails 703.8
Stricture — *see also* Stenosis 799.89
  ampulla of Vater 576.2
    with calculus, cholelithiasis, or stones — *see* Choledocholithiasis
  anus (sphincter) 569.2
    congenital 751.2
    infantile 751.2
  aorta (ascending) 747.22
    arch 747.10
    arteriosclerotic 440.0
    calcified 440.0
  aortic (valve) (*see also* Stenosis, aortic) 424.1
    congenital 746.3
  aqueduct of Sylvius (congenital) 742.3
    with spina bifida (*see also* Spina bifida) 741.0 ☑
    acquired 331.4
  artery 447.1
    basilar — *see* Narrowing, artery, basilar
    carotid (common) (internal) — *see* Narrowing, artery, carotid
    celiac 447.4
    cerebral 437.0
      congenital 747.81
      due to
        embolism (*see also* Embolism, brain) 434.1 ☑
        thrombus (*see also* Thrombosis, brain) 434.0 ☑
    congenital (peripheral) 747.60
      cerebral 747.81
      coronary 746.85
      gastrointestinal 747.61
      lower limb 747.64
      renal 747.62
      retinal 743.58
      specified NEC 747.69
      spinal 747.82
      umbilical 747.5
      upper limb 747.63
    coronary — *see* Arteriosclerosis, coronary
      congenital 746.85
    precerebral — *see* Narrowing, artery, precerebral NEC
    pulmonary (congenital) 747.3
      acquired 417.8
    renal 440.1
    vertebral — *see* Narrowing, artery, vertebral
  auditory canal (congenital) (external) 744.02
    acquired (*see also* Stricture, ear canal, acquired) 380.50
  bile duct or passage (any) (postoperative) (*see also* Obstruction, biliary) 576.2
    congenital 751.61
  bladder 596.8
    congenital 753.6
    neck 596.0
      congenital 753.6
  bowel (*see also* Obstruction, intestine) 560.9
  brain 348.89 ▲
  bronchus 519.19
    syphilitic 095.8
  cardia (stomach) 537.89
    congenital 750.7
  cardiac (*see also* Disease, heart)
    orifice (stomach) 537.89
  cardiovascular (*see also* Disease, cardiovascular) 429.2
  carotid artery — *see* Narrowing, artery, carotid
  cecum (*see also* Obstruction, intestine) 560.9
  cervix, cervical (canal) 622.4
    congenital 752.49
    in pregnancy or childbirth 654.6 ☑
      affecting fetus or newborn 763.89
      causing obstructed labor 660.2 ☑
        affecting fetus or newborn 763.1
  colon (*see also* Obstruction, intestine) 560.9
    congenital 751.2
  colostomy 569.62
  common bile duct (*see also* Obstruction, biliary) 576.2
    congenital 751.61
  coronary (artery) — *see* Arteriosclerosis, coronary

Stricture — *see also* Stenosis — *continued*
  coronary — *see* Arteriosclerosis, coronary — *continued*
    congenital 746.85
  cystic duct (*see also* Obstruction, gallbladder) 575.2
    congenital 751.61
  cystostomy 997.5
  digestive organs NEC, congenital 751.8
  duodenum 537.3
    congenital 751.1
  ear canal (external) (congenital) 744.02
    acquired 380.50
      secondary to
        inflammation 380.53
        surgery 380.52
        trauma 380.51
  ejaculatory duct 608.85
  enterostomy 569.62
  esophagostomy 530.87
  esophagus (corrosive) (peptic) 530.3
    congenital 750.3
    syphilitic 095.8
      congenital 090.5
  eustachian tube (*see also* Obstruction, Eustachian tube) 381.60
    congenital 744.24
  fallopian tube 628.2
    gonococcal (chronic) 098.37
      acute 098.17
    tuberculous (*see also* Tuberculosis) 016.6 ☑
  gallbladder (*see also* Obstruction, gallbladder) 575.2
    congenital 751.69
  glottis 478.74
  heart (*see also* Disease, heart)
    congenital NEC 746.89
    valve (*see also* Endocarditis)
      congenital NEC 746.89
        aortic 746.3
        mitral 746.5
        pulmonary 746.02
        tricuspid 746.1
  hepatic duct (*see also* Obstruction, biliary) 576.2
  hourglass, of stomach 537.6
  hymen 623.3
  hypopharynx 478.29
  intestine (*see also* Obstruction, intestine) 560.9
    congenital (small) 751.1
      large 751.2
    ischemic 557.1
  lacrimal
    canaliculi 375.53
      congenital 743.65
    punctum 375.52
      congenital 743.65
    sac 375.54
      congenital 743.65
  lacrimonasal duct 375.56
    congenital 743.65
    neonatal 375.55
  larynx 478.79
    congenital 748.3
    syphilitic 095.8
      congenital 090.5
  lung 518.89
  meatus
    ear (congenital) 744.02
      acquired (*see also* Stricture, ear canal, acquired) 380.50
    osseous (congenital) (ear) 744.03
      acquired (*see also* Stricture, ear canal, acquired) 380.50
    urinarius (*see also* Stricture, urethra) 598.9
      congenital 753.6
  mitral (valve) (*see also* Stenosis, mitral) 394.0
    congenital 746.5
    specified cause, except rheumatic 424.0
  myocardium, myocardial (*see also* Degeneration, myocardial) 429.1
    hypertrophic subaortic (idiopathic) 425.1
  nares (anterior) (posterior) 478.19
    congenital 748.0
  nasal duct 375.56

Stricture — *see also* Stenosis — *continued*
  nasal duct — *continued*
    congenital 743.65
    neonatal 375.55
  nasolacrimal duct 375.56
    congenital 743.65
    neonatal 375.55
  nasopharynx 478.29
    syphilitic 095.8
  nephrostomy 997.5
  nose 478.19
    congenital 748.0
  nostril (anterior) (posterior) 478.19
    congenital 748.0
  organ or site, congenital NEC — *see* Atresia
  osseous meatus (congenital) (ear) 744.03
    acquired (*see also* Stricture, ear canal, acquired) 380.50
  os uteri (*see also* Stricture, cervix) 622.4
  oviduct — *see* Stricture, fallopian tube
  pelviureteric junction 593.3
  pharynx (dilation) 478.29
  prostate 602.8
  pulmonary, pulmonic
    artery (congenital) 747.3
      acquired 417.8
      noncongenital 417.8
    infundibulum (congenital) 746.83
    valve (*see also* Endocarditis, pulmonary) 424.3
      congenital 746.02
    vein (congenital) 747.49
      acquired 417.8
    vessel NEC 417.8
  punctum lacrimale 375.52
    congenital 743.65
  pylorus (hypertrophic) 537.0
    adult 537.0
    congenital 750.5
    infantile 750.5
  rectosigmoid 569.89
  rectum (sphincter) 569.2
    congenital 751.2
    due to
      chemical burn 947.3
      irradiation 569.2
      lymphogranuloma venereum 099.1
    gonococcal 098.7
    inflammatory 099.1
    syphilitic 095.8
    tuberculous (*see also* Tuberculosis) 014.8 ☑
  renal artery 440.1
  salivary duct or gland (any) 527.8
  sigmoid (flexure) (*see also* Obstruction, intestine) 560.9
  spermatic cord 608.85
  stoma (following) (of)
    colostomy 569.62
    cystostomy 997.5
    enterostomy 569.62
    esophagostomy 530.87
    gastrostomy 536.42
    ileostomy 569.62
    nephrostomy 997.5
    tracheostomy 519.02
    ureterostomy 997.5
  stomach 537.89
    congenital 750.7
    hourglass 537.6
  subaortic 746.81
    hypertrophic (acquired) (idiopathic) 425.1
  subglottic 478.74
  syphilitic NEC 095.8
  tendon (sheath) 727.81
  trachea 519.19
    congenital 748.3
    syphilitic 095.8
    tuberculous (*see also* Tuberculosis) 012.8 ☑
  tracheostomy 519.02
  tricuspid (valve) (*see also* Endocarditis, tricuspid) 397.0
    congenital 746.1
    nonrheumatic 424.2
  tunica vaginalis 608.85

Strabismus — Stricture

☑ Additional Digit Required — Refer to the Tabular List for Digit Selection   ▼ Subterms under main terms may continue to next column or page

2010 ICD-9-CM   ▶◀ Revised Text   ● New Line   ▲ Revised Code   October 2009 · Volume 2 — 255

Stricture — *see also* Stenosis — *continued*
ureter (postoperative) 593.3
congenital 753.29
tuberculous (*see also* Tuberculosis) 016.2 ☑
ureteropelvic junction 593.3
congenital 753.21
ureterovesical orifice 593.3
congenital 753.22
urethra (anterior) (meatal) (organic) (posterior) (spasmodic) 598.9
associated with schistosomiasis (*see also* Schistosomiasis) 120.9 *[598.01]*
congenital (valvular) 753.6
due to
infection 598.00
syphilis 095.8 *[598.01]*
trauma 598.1
gonococcal 098.2 *[598.01]*
gonorrheal 098.2 *[598.01]*
infective 598.00
late effect of injury 598.1
postcatheterization 598.2
postobstetric 598.1
postoperative 598.2
specified cause NEC 598.8
syphilitic 095.8 *[598.01]*
traumatic 598.1
valvular, congenital 753.6
urinary meatus (*see also* Stricture, urethra) 598.9
congenital 753.6
uterus, uterine 621.5
os (external) (internal) — *see* Stricture, cervix
vagina (outlet) 623.2
congenital 752.49
valve (cardiac) (heart) (*see also* Endocarditis) 424.90
congenital (cardiac) (heart) NEC 746.89
aortic 746.3
mitral 746.5
pulmonary 746.02
tricuspid 746.1
urethra 753.6
valvular (*see also* Endocarditis) 424.90
vascular graft or shunt 996.1
atherosclerosis — *see* Arteriosclerosis, extremities
embolism 996.74
occlusion NEC 996.74
thrombus 996.74
vas deferens 608.85
congenital 752.89
vein 459.2
vena cava (inferior) (superior) NEC 459.2
congenital 747.49
ventricular shunt 996.2
vesicourethral orifice 596.0
congenital 753.6
vulva (acquired) 624.8
Stridor 786.1
congenital (larynx) 748.3
Stridulous — *see* condition
Strippling of nails 703.8
Stroke 434.91
apoplectic (*see also* Disease, cerebrovascular, acute) 436
brain — *see* Infarct, brain
embolic 434.11
epileptic — *see* Epilepsy
healed or old V12.54
heart — *see* Disease, heart
heat 992.0
hemorrhagic — *see* Hemorrhage, brain
iatrogenic 997.02
in evolution 434.91
ischemic 434.91
late effect — *see* Late effect(s) (of) cerebrovascular disease
lightning 994.0
paralytic — *see* Infarct, brain
postoperative 997.02
progressive 435.9
thrombotic 434.01
Stromatosis, endometrial (M8931/1) 236.0

Strong pulse 785.9
Strongyloides stercoralis infestation 127.2
Strongyloidiasis 127.2
Strongyloidosis 127.2
Strongylus (gibsoni) infestation 127.7
Strophulus (newborn) 779.89
pruriginosus 698.2
Struck by lightning 994.0
Struma — *see also* Goiter 240.9
fibrosa 245.3
Hashimoto (struma lymphomatosa) 245.2
lymphomatosa 245.2
nodosa (simplex) 241.9
endemic 241.9
multinodular 241.1
sporadic 241.9
toxic or with hyperthyroidism 242.3 ☑
multinodular 242.2 ☑
uninodular 242.1 ☑
toxicosa 242.3 ☑
multinodular 242.2 ☑
uninodular 242.1 ☑
uninodular 241.0
ovarii (M9090/0) 220
and carcinoid (M9091/1) 236.2
malignant (M9090/3) 183.0
Riedel's (ligneous thyroiditis) 245.3
scrofulous (*see also* Tuberculosis) 017.2 ☑
tuberculous (*see also* Tuberculosis) 017.2 ☑
abscess 017.2 ☑
adenitis 017.2 ☑
lymphangitis 017.2 ☑
ulcer 017.2 ☑
Strumipriva cachexia — *see also* Hypothyroidism 244.9
Strümpell-Marie disease or spine (ankylosing spondylitis) 720.0
Strümpell-Westphal pseudosclerosis (hepatolenticular degeneration) 275.1
Stuart's disease (congenital factor X deficiency) — *see also* Defect, coagulation 286.3
Stuart-Prower factor deficiency (congenital factor X deficiency) — *see also* Defect, coagulation 286.3
Students' elbow 727.2
Stuffy nose 478.19
Stump — *see also* Amputation
cervix, cervical (healed) 622.8
Stupor 780.09
catatonic (*see also* Schizophrenia) 295.2 ☑
circular (*see also* Psychosis, manic-depressive, circular) 296.7
manic 296.89
manic-depressive (*see also* Psychosis, affective) 296.89
mental (anergic) (delusional) 298.9
psychogenic 298.8
reaction to exceptional stress (transient) 308.2
traumatic NEC (*see also* Injury, intracranial)
with spinal (cord)
lesion — *see* Injury, spinal, by site
shock — *see* Injury, spinal, by site
Sturge (-Weber) (-Dimitri) disease or syndrome (encephalocutaneous angiomatosis) 759.6
Sturge-Kalischer-Weber syndrome (encephalocutaneous angiomatosis) 759.6
Stuttering 307.0
due to late effect of cerebrovascular disease ● 798.1 (*see also* Late effect(s) (of) cerebrovascular disease) 438.14 ●
Sty, stye 373.11
external 373.11
internal 373.12
meibomian 373.12
Subacidity, gastric 536.8
psychogenic 306.4
Subacute — *see* condition
Subarachnoid — *see* condition
Subclavian steal syndrome 435.2
Subcortical — *see* condition
Subcostal syndrome 098.86
nerve compression 354.8
Subcutaneous, subcuticular — *see* condition
Subdelirium 293.1
Subdural — *see* condition

Subendocardium — *see* condition
Subependymoma (M9383/1) 237.5
Suberosis 495.3
Subglossitis — *see* Glossitis
Subhemophilia 286.0
Subinvolution (uterus) 621.1
breast (postlactational) (postpartum) 611.89
chronic 621.1
puerperal, postpartum 674.8 ☑
Sublingual — *see* condition
Sublinguitis 527.2
Subluxation — *see also* Dislocation, by site
congenital NEC (*see also* Malposition, congenital)
hip (unilateral) 754.32
with dislocation of other hip 754.35
bilateral 754.33
joint
lower limb 755.69
shoulder 755.59
upper limb 755.59
lower limb (joint) 755.69
shoulder (joint) 755.59
upper limb (joint) 755.59
lens 379.32
anterior 379.33
posterior 379.34
radial head 832.2 ●
rotary, cervical region of spine — *see* Fracture, vertebra, cervical
Submaxillary — *see* condition
Submersion (fatal) (nonfatal) 994.1
Submissiveness (undue), in child 313.0
Submucous — *see* condition
Subnormal, subnormality
accommodation (*see also* Disorder, accommodation) 367.9
mental (*see also* Retardation, mental) 319
mild 317
moderate 318.0
profound 318.2
severe 318.1
temperature (accidental) 991.6
not associated with low environmental temperature 780.99
Subphrenic — *see* condition
Subscapular nerve — *see* condition
Subseptus uterus 752.3
Subsiding appendicitis 542
Substance abuse in family V61.42 ●
Substernal thyroid — *see also* Goiter 240.9
congenital 759.2
Substitution disorder 300.11
Subtentorial — *see* condition
Subtertian
fever 084.0
malaria (fever) 084.0
Subthyroidism (acquired) — *see also* Hypothyroidism 244.9
congenital 243
Succenturiata placenta — *see* Placenta, abnormal
Succussion sounds, chest 786.7
Sucking thumb, child 307.9
Sudamen 705.1
Sudamina 705.1
Sudanese kala-azar 085.0
Sudden
death, cause unknown (less than 24 hours) 798.1
cardiac (SCD)
family history of V17.41
personal history of, successfully resuscitated V12.53
during childbirth 669.9 ☑
infant 798.0
puerperal, postpartum 674.9 ☑
hearing loss NEC 388.2
heart failure (*see also* Failure, heart) 428.9
infant death syndrome 798.0
Sudeck's atrophy, disease, or syndrome 733.7
SUDS (sudden unexplained death) 798.2
Suffocation — *see also* Asphyxia 799.01
by
bed clothes 994.7
bunny bag 994.7

Suffocation — *see also* Asphyxia — *continued*
by — *continued*
cave-in 994.7
constriction 994.7
drowning 994.1
inhalation
food or foreign body (*see also* Asphyxia, food or foreign body) 933.1
oil or gasoline (*see also* Asphyxia, food or foreign body) 933.1
overlying 994.7
plastic bag 994.7
pressure 994.7
strangulation 994.7
during birth 768.1
mechanical 994.7
Sugar
blood
high 790.29
low 251.2
in urine 791.5
Suicide, suicidal (attempted)
by poisoning — *see* Table of Drugs and Chemicals
ideation V62.84
risk 300.9
tendencies 300.9
trauma NEC (*see also* nature and site of injury) 959.9
Suipestifer infection — *see also* Infection, Salmonella 003.9
Sulfatidosis 330.0
Sulfhemoglobinemia, sulphemoglobinemia (acquired) (congenital) 289.7
Sumatran mite fever 081.2
Summer — *see* condition
Sunburn 692.71
first degree 692.71
second degree 692.76
third degree 692.77
dermatitis 692.71
due to
other ultraviolet radiation 692.82
tanning bed 692.82
SUNCT (short lasting unilateral neuralgiform headache with conjunctival injection and tearing) 339.05
Sunken
acetabulum 718.85
fontanels 756.0
Sunstroke 992.0
Superfecundation 651.9 ☑
with fetal loss and retention of one or more fetus(es) 651.6 ☑
following (elective) fetal reduction 651.7 ☑
Superfetation 651.9 ☑
with fetal loss and retention of one or more fetus(es) 651.6 ☑
following (elective) fetal reduction 651.7 ☑
Superinvolution uterus 621.8
Supernumerary (congenital)
aortic cusps 746.89
auditory ossicles 744.04
bone 756.9
breast 757.6
carpal bones 755.56
cusps, heart valve NEC 746.89
mitral 746.5
pulmonary 746.09
digit(s) 755.00
finger 755.01
toe 755.02
ear (lobule) 744.1
fallopian tube 752.19
finger 755.01
hymen 752.49
kidney 753.3
lacrimal glands 743.64
lacrimonasal duct 743.65
lobule (ear) 744.1
mitral cusps 746.5
muscle 756.82
nipples 757.6
organ or site NEC — *see* Accessory
ossicles, auditory 744.04

Supernumerary — continued
- ovary 752.0
- oviduct 752.19
- pulmonic cusps 746.09
- rib 756.3
  - cervical or first 756.2
    - syndrome 756.2
- roots (of teeth) 520.2
- spinal vertebra 756.19
- spleen 759.0
- tarsal bones 755.67
- teeth 520.1
  - causing crowding 524.31
- testis 752.89
- thumb 755.01
- toe 755.02
- uterus 752.2
- vagina 752.49
- vertebra 756.19

Supervision (of)
- contraceptive method previously prescribed V25.40
  - intrauterine device V25.42
  - oral contraceptive (pill) V25.41
  - specified type NEC V25.49
  - subdermal implantable contraceptive V25.43
- dietary (for) V65.3
  - allergy (food) V65.3
  - colitis V65.3
  - diabetes mellitus V65.3
  - food allergy intolerance V65.3
  - gastritis V65.3
  - hypercholesterolemia V65.3
  - hypoglycemia V65.3
  - intolerance (food) V65.3
  - obesity V65.3
  - specified NEC V65.3
- lactation V24.1
- newborn health ●
  - 8 to 28 days old V20.32 ●
  - under 8 days old V20.31 ●
- pregnancy — see Pregnancy, supervision of

Supplemental teeth 520.1
- causing crowding 524.31

Suppression
- binocular vision 368.31
- lactation 676.5 ☑
- menstruation 626.8
- ovarian secretion 256.39
- renal 586
- urinary secretion 788.5
- urine 788.5

Suppuration, suppurative — see also condition
- accessory sinus (chronic) (see also Sinusitis) 473.9
- adrenal gland 255.8
- antrum (chronic) (see also Sinusitis, maxillary) 473.0
- bladder (see also Cystitis) 595.89
- bowel 569.89
- brain 324.0
  - late effect 326
- breast 611.0
  - puerperal, postpartum 675.1 ☑
- dental periosteum 526.5
- diffuse (skin) 686.00
- ear (middle) (see also Otitis media) 382.4
  - external (see also Otitis, externa) 380.10
  - internal 386.33
- ethmoidal (sinus) (chronic) (see also Sinusitis, ethmoidal) 473.2
- fallopian tube (see also Salpingo-oophoritis) 614.2
- frontal (sinus) (chronic) (see also Sinusitis, frontal) 473.1
- gallbladder (see also Cholecystitis, acute) 575.0
- gum 523.30
- hernial sac — see Hernia, by site
- intestine 569.89
- joint (see also Arthritis, suppurative) 711.0 ☑
- labyrinthine 386.33
- lung 513.0
- mammary gland 611.0
  - puerperal, postpartum 675.1 ☑
- maxilla, maxillary 526.4

Suppuration, suppurative — see also condition — continued
- maxilla, maxillary — continued
  - sinus (chronic) (see also Sinusitis, maxillary) 473.0
- muscle 728.0
- nasal sinus (chronic) (see also Sinusitis) 473.9
- pancreas 577.0
- parotid gland 527.2
- pelvis, pelvic
  - female (see also Disease, pelvis, inflammatory) 614.4
    - acute 614.3
  - male (see also Peritonitis) 567.21
- pericranial (see also Osteomyelitis) 730.2 ☑
- salivary duct or gland (any) 527.2
- sinus (nasal) (see also Sinusitis) 473.9
- sphenoidal (sinus) (chronic) (see also Sinusitis, sphenoidal) 473.3
- thymus (gland) 254.1
- thyroid (gland) 245.0
- tonsil 474.8
- uterus (see also Endometritis) 615.9
- vagina 616.10
- wound (see also Wound, open, by site, complicated)
  - dislocation — see Dislocation, by site, compound
  - fracture — see Fracture, by site, open
  - scratch or other superficial injury — see Injury, superficial, by site

Supraeruption, teeth 524.34
Supraglottitis 464.50
- with obstruction 464.51
Suprapubic drainage 596.8
Suprarenal (gland) — see condition
Suprascapular nerve — see condition
Suprasellar — see condition
Supraspinatus syndrome 726.10
Surfer knots 919.8
- infected 919.9
Surgery
- cosmetic NEC V50.1
  - breast reconstruction following mastectomy V51.0
  - following healed injury or operation V51.8
  - hair transplant V50.0
- elective V50.9
  - breast
    - augmentation or reduction V50.1
    - reconstruction following mastectomy V51.0
  - circumcision, ritual or routine (in absence of medical indication) V50.2
  - cosmetic NEC V50.1
  - ear piercing V50.3
  - face-lift V50.1
  - following healed injury or operation V51.8
  - hair transplant V50.0
- not done because of
  - contraindication V64.1
  - patient's decision V64.2
  - specified reason NEC V64.3
- plastic
  - breast
    - augmentation or reduction V50.1
    - reconstruction following mastectomy V51.0
  - cosmetic V50.1
  - face-lift V50.1
  - following healed injury or operation V51.8
  - repair of scarred tissue (following healed injury or operation) V51.8
  - specified type NEC V50.8
- previous, in pregnancy or childbirth
  - cervix 654.6 ☑
    - affecting fetus or newborn (see also Newborn, affected by) 760.63
    - causing obstructed labor 660.2 ☑
      - affecting fetus or newborn 763.1
  - pelvic soft tissues NEC 654.9 ☑
    - affecting fetus or newborn (see also Newborn, affected by) 760.63
    - causing obstructed labor 660.2 ☑
      - affecting fetus or newborn 763.1
  - perineum or vulva 654.8 ☑

Surgery — continued
- previous, in pregnancy or childbirth — continued
  - uterus NEC 654.9 ☑
    - affecting fetus or newborn (see also Newborn, affected by) 760.63
    - causing obstructed labor 660.2 ☑
      - affecting fetus or newborn 763.1
      - due to previous cesarean delivery 654.2 ☑
  - vagina 654.7 ☑
Surgical
- abortion — see Abortion, legal
- emphysema 998.81
- kidney (see also Pyelitis) 590.80
- operation NEC 799.9
- procedures, complication or misadventure — see Complications, surgical procedure
- shock 998.0
Survey
- fetal anatomic V28.81
Susceptibility
- genetic
  - to
    - MEN (multiple endocrine neoplasia) V84.81
    - neoplasia
      - multiple endocrine [MEN] V84.81
    - neoplasm
      - malignant, of
        - breast V84.01
        - endometrium V84.04
        - other V84.09
        - ovary V84.02
        - prostate V84.03
      - specified disease V84.89
Suspected condition, ruled out — see also Observation, suspected V71.9
- specified condition NEC V71.89
Suspended uterus, in pregnancy or childbirth 654.4 ☑
- affecting fetus or newborn 763.89
- causing obstructed labor 660.2 ☑
  - affecting fetus or newborn 763.1
Sutton and Gull's disease (arteriolar nephrosclerosis) — see also Hypertension, kidney 403.90
Sutton's disease 709.09
Suture
- burst (in external operation wound) (see also Dehiscence) 998.32
  - internal 998.31
- inadvertently left in operation wound 998.4
- removal V58.32
- Shirodkar, in pregnancy (with or without cervical incompetence) 654.5 ☑
Swab inadvertently left in operation wound 998.4
Swallowed, swallowing
- difficulty (see also Dysphagia) 787.20
- foreign body NEC (see also Foreign body) 938
Swamp fever 100.89
Swan neck hand (intrinsic) 736.09
Sweat(s), sweating
- disease or sickness 078.2
- excessive (see also Hyperhidrosis) 780.8
- fetid 705.89
- fever 078.2
- gland disease 705.9
  - specified type NEC 705.89
- miliary 078.2
- night 780.8
Sweeley-Klionsky disease (angiokeratoma corporis diffusum) 272.7
Sweet's syndrome (acute febrile neutrophilic dermatosis) 695.89
Swelling 782.3
- abdominal (not referable to specific organ) 789.3 ☑
- adrenal gland, cloudy 255.8
- ankle 719.07
- anus 787.99
- arm 729.81
- breast 611.72
- Calabar 125.2
- cervical gland 785.6

Swelling — continued
- cheek 784.2
- chest 786.6
- ear 388.8
- epigastric 789.3 ☑
- extremity (lower) (upper) 729.81
- eye 379.92
- female genital organ 625.8
- finger 729.81
- foot 729.81
- glands 785.6
- gum 784.2
- hand 729.81
- head 784.2
- inflammatory — see Inflammation
- joint (see also Effusion, joint) 719.0 ☑
  - tuberculous — see Tuberculosis, joint
- kidney, cloudy 593.89
- leg 729.81
- limb 729.81
- liver 573.8
- lung 786.6
- lymph nodes 785.6
- mediastinal 786.6
- mouth 784.2
- muscle (limb) 729.81
- neck 784.2
- nose or sinus 784.2
- palate 784.2
- pelvis 789.3 ☑
- penis 607.83
- perineum 625.8
- rectum 787.99
- scrotum 608.86
- skin 782.2
- splenic (see also Splenomegaly) 789.2
- substernal 786.6
- superficial, localized (skin) 782.2
- testicle 608.86
- throat 784.2
- toe 729.81
- tongue 784.2
- tubular (see also Disease, renal) 593.9
- umbilicus 789.3 ☑
- uterus 625.8
- vagina 625.8
- vulva 625.8
- wandering, due to Gnathostoma (spinigerum) 128.1
- white — see Tuberculosis, arthritis
Swift's disease 985.0
Swimmers'
- ear (acute) 380.12
- itch 120.3
Swimming in the head 780.4
Swollen — see also Swelling
- glands 785.6
Swyer-James syndrome (unilateral hyperlucent lung) 492.8
Swyer's syndrome (XY pure gonadal dysgenesis) 752.7
Sycosis 704.8
- barbae (not parasitic) 704.8
- contagiosa 110.0
- lupoid 704.8
- mycotic 110.0
- parasitic 110.0
- vulgaris 704.8
Sydenham's chorea — see Chorea, Sydenham's
Sylvatic yellow fever 060.0
Sylvest's disease (epidemic pleurodynia) 074.1
Symblepharon 372.63
- congenital 743.62
Symonds' syndrome 348.2
Sympathetic — see condition
Sympatheticotonia — see also Neuropathy, peripheral, autonomic 337.9
Sympathicoblastoma (M9500/3)
- specified site — see Neoplasm, by site, malignant
- unspecified site 194.0
Sympathicogonioma (M9500/3) — see Sympathicoblastoma
Sympathoblastoma (M9500/3) — see Sympathicoblastoma

Index

Sympathogonioma — Syndrome

☑ Additional Digit Required — Refer to the Tabular List for Digit Selection   ▽ Subterms under main terms may continue to next column or page

Syndrome — *see also* Disease — *continued*
blue
bloater 491.20
with
acute bronchitis 491.22
exacerbation (acute) 491.21
diaper 270.0
drum 381.02
sclera 756.51
toe 445.02
Boder-Sedgwick (ataxia-telangiectasia) 334.8
Boerhaave's (spontaneous esophageal rupture) 530.4
Bonnevie-Ullrich 758.6
Bonnier's 386.19
Borjeson-Forssman-Lehmann 759.89
Bouillaud's (rheumatic heart disease) 391.9
Bourneville (-Pringle) (tuberous sclerosis) 759.5
Bouveret (-Hoffmann) (paroxysmal tachycardia) 427.2
brachial plexus 353.0
Brachman-de Lange (Amsterdam dwarf, mental retardation, and brachycephaly) 759.89
bradycardia-tachycardia 427.81
Brailsford-Morquio (dystrophy) (mucopolysaccharidosis IV) 277.5
brain (acute) (chronic) (nonpsychotic) (organic) (with behavioral reaction) (with neurotic reaction) 310.9
with
presenile brain disease (*see also* Dementia, presenile) 290.10
psychosis, psychotic reaction (*see also* Psychosis, organic) 294.9
chronic alcoholic 291.2
congenital (*see also* Retardation, mental) 319
postcontusional 310.2
posttraumatic
nonpsychotic 310.2
psychotic 293.9
acute 293.0
chronic (*see also* Psychosis, organic) 294.8
subacute 293.1
psycho-organic (*see also* Syndrome, psycho-organic) 310.9
psychotic (*see also* Psychosis, organic) 294.9
senile (*see also* Dementia, senile) 290.0
branchial arch 744.41
Brandt's (acrodermatitis enteropathica) 686.8
Brennemann's 289.2
Briquet's 300.81
Brissaud-Meige (infantile myxedema) 244.9
broad ligament laceration 620.6
Brock's (atelectasis due to enlarged lymph nodes) 518.0
broken heart 429.83
Brown-Séquard 344.89
brown spot 756.59
Brown's tendon sheath 378.61
Brugada 746.89
Brugsch's (acropachyderma) 757.39
bubbly lung 770.7
Buchem's (hyperostosis corticalis) 733.3
Budd-Chiari (hepatic vein thrombosis) 453.0
Büdinger-Ludloff-Läwen 717.89
bulbar 335.22
lateral (*see also* Disease, cerebrovascular, acute) 436
Bullis fever 082.8
bundle of Kent (anomalous atrioventricular excitation) 426.7
Bürger-Grütz (essential familial hyperlipemia) 272.3
Burke's (pancreatic insufficiency and chronic neutropenia) 577.8
Burnett's (milk-alkali) 275.42
Burnier's (hypophyseal dwarfism) 253.3
burning feet 266.2
Bywaters' 958.5
Caffey's (infantile cortical hyperostosis) 756.59
Calvé-Legg-Perthes (osteochrondrosis, femoral capital) 732.1

Syndrome — *see also* Disease — *continued*
Caplan (-Colinet) syndrome 714.81
capsular thrombosis (*see also* Thrombosis, brain) 434.0 ☑
carbohydrate-deficient glycoprotein (CDGS) 271.8
carcinogenic thrombophlebitis 453.1
carcinoid 259.2
cardiac asthma (*see also* Failure, ventricular, left) 428.1
cardiacos negros 416.0
cardiofaciocutaneous 759.89   ●
cardiopulmonary obesity 278.8
cardiorenal (*see also* Hypertension, cardiorenal) 404.90
cardiorespiratory distress (idiopathic), newborn 769
cardiovascular renal (*see also* Hypertension, cardiorenal) 404.90
cardiovasorenal 272.7
Carini's (ichthyosis congenita) 757.1
carotid
artery (internal) 435.8
body or sinus 337.01
carpal tunnel 354.0
Carpenter's 759.89
Cassidy (-Scholte) (malignant carcinoid) 259.2
cat-cry 758.31
cauda equina 344.60
causalgia 355.9
lower limb 355.71
upper limb 354.4
cavernous sinus 437.6
celiac 579.0
artery compression 447.4
axis 447.4
central pain 338.0
cerebellomedullary malformation (*see also* Spina bifida) 741.0 ☑
cerebral gigantism 253.0
cerebrohepatorenal 759.89
cervical (root) (spine) NEC 723.8
disc 722.71
posterior, sympathetic 723.2
rib 353.0
sympathetic paralysis 337.09
traumatic (acute) NEC 847.0
cervicobrachial (diffuse) 723.3
cervicocranial 723.2
cervicodorsal outlet 353.2
Céstan (-Raymond) 433.8 ☑
Céstan's 344.89
Céstan-Chenais 344.89
chancriform 114.1
Charcôt's (intermittent claudication) 443.9
angina cruris 443.9
due to atherosclerosis 440.21
Charcôt-Marie-Tooth 356.1
Charcôt-Weiss-Baker 337.01
CHARGE association 759.89
Cheadle (-Möller) (-Barlow) (infantile scurvy) 267
Chédiak-Higashi (-Steinbrinck) (congenital gigantism of peroxidase granules) 288.2
chest wall 786.52
Chiari's (hepatic vein thrombosis) 453.0
Chiari-Frommel 676.6 ☑
chiasmatic 368.41
Chilaiditi's (subphrenic displacement, colon) 751.4
chondroectodermal dysplasia 756.55
chorea-athetosis-agitans 275.1
Christian's (chronic histiocytosis X) 277.89
chromosome 4 short arm deletion 758.39
chronic pain 338.4
Churg-Strauss 446.4
Clarke-Hadfield (pancreatic infantilism) 577.8
Claude's 352.6
Claude Bernard-Horner (*see also* Neuropathy, peripheral, autonomic) 337.9
Clérambault's
automatism 348.89
erotomania 297.8   ▲
Clifford's (postmaturity) 766.22
climacteric 627.2

Syndrome — *see also* Disease — *continued*
Clouston's (hidrotic ectodermal dysplasia) 757.31
clumsiness 315.4
Cockayne's (microencephaly and dwarfism) 759.89
Cockayne-Weber (epidermolysis bullosa) 757.39
Coffin-Lowry 759.89
Cogan's (nonsyphilitic interstitial keratitis) 370.52
cold injury (newborn) 778.2
Collet (-Sicard) 352.6
combined immunity deficiency 279.2
compartment(al) (anterior) (deep) (posterior) 958.8
nontraumatic
abdomen 729.73
arm 729.71
buttock 729.72
fingers 729.71
foot 729.72
forearm 729.71
hand 729.71
hip 729.72
leg 729.72
lower extremity 729.72
shoulder 729.71
specified site NEC 729.79
thigh 729.72
toes 729.72
upper extremity 729.71
wrist 729.71
post-surgical (*see also* Syndrome, compartment, non-traumatic) 998.89
traumatic 958.90
abdomen 958.93
arm 958.91
buttock 958.92
fingers 958.91
foot 958.92
forearm 958.91
hand 958.91
hip 958.92
leg 958.92
lower extremity 958.92
shoulder 958.91
specified site NEC 958.99
thigh 958.92
tibial 958.92
toes 958.92
upper extremity 958.91
wrist 958.91
complex regional pain — *see also* Dystrophy, sympathetic
type I — *see* Dystrophy, sympathetic (posttraumatic) (reflex)
type II — *see* Causalgia
compression 958.5
cauda equina 344.60
with neurogenic bladder 344.61
concussion 310.2
congenital
affecting more than one system 759.7
specified type NEC 759.89
congenital central alveolar hypoventilation 327.25
facial diplegia 352.6
muscular hypertrophy-cerebral 759.89
congestion-fibrosis (pelvic) 625.5
conjunctivourethrosynovial 099.3
Conn (-Louis) (primary aldosteronism) 255.12
Conradi (-Hünermann) (chondrodysplasia calcificans congenita) 756.59
conus medullaris 336.8
Cooke-Apert-Gallais (adrenogenital) 255.2
Cornelia de Lange's (Amsterdam dwarf, mental retardation, and brachycephaly) 759.8 ☑
coronary insufficiency or intermediate 411.1
cor pulmonale 416.9
corticosexual 255.2
Costen's (complex) 524.60
costochondral junction 733.6
costoclavicular 353.0
costovertebral 253.0

Syndrome — *see also* Disease — *continued*
Cotard's (paranoia) 297.1
Cowden 759.6
craniovertebral 723.2
Creutzfeldt-Jakob 046.19
with dementia
with behavioral disturbance 046.19 [294.11]
without behavioral disturbance 046.19 [294.10]
variant 046.11
with dementia
with behavioral disturbance 046.11 [294.11]
without behavioral disturbance 046.11 [294.10]
crib death 798.0
cricopharyngeal 787.20
cri-du-chat 758.31
Crigler-Najjar (congenital hyperbilirubinemia) 277.4
crocodile tears 351.8
Cronkhite-Canada 211.3
croup 464.4
CRST (cutaneous systemic sclerosis) 710.1
crush 958.5
crushed lung (*see also* Injury, internal, lung) 861.20
Cruveilhier-Baumgarten (cirrhosis of liver) 571.5
cubital tunnel 354.2
Cuiffini-Pancoast (M8010/3) (carcinoma, pulmonary apex) 162.3
Curschmann (-Batten) (-Steinert) 359.21
Cushing's (iatrogenic) (idiopathic) (pituitary basophilism) (pituitary-dependent) 255.0
overdose or wrong substance given or taken 962.0
Cyriax's (slipping rib) 733.99
cystic duct stump 576.0
Da Costa's (neurocirculatory asthenia) 306.2
Dameshek's (erythroblastic anemia) 282.49
Dana-Putnam (subacute combined sclerosis with pernicious anemia) 281.0 [336.2]
Danbolt (-Closs) (acrodermatitis enteropathica) 686.8
Dandy-Walker (atresia, foramen of Magendie) 742.3
with spina bifida (*see also* Spina bifida) 741.0 ☑
Danlos' 756.83
Davies-Colley (slipping rib) 733.99
dead fetus 641.3 ☑
defeminization 255.2
defibrination (*see also* Fibrinolysis) 286.6
Degos' 447.8
Deiters' nucleus 386.19
Déjérine-Roussy 338.0
Déjérine-Thomas 333.0
de Lange's (Amsterdam dwarf, mental retardation, and brachycephaly) (Cornelia) 759.89
Del Castillo's (germinal aplasia) 606.0
deletion chromosomes 758.39
delusional
induced by drug 292.11
dementia-aphonia, of childhood (*see also* Psychosis, childhood) 299.1 ☑
demyelinating NEC 341.9
denial visual hallucination 307.9
depersonalization 300.6
de Quervain's 259.51
Dercum's (adiposis dolorosa) 272.8
de Toni-Fanconi (-Debré) (cystinosis) 270.0
diabetes-dwarfism-obesity (juvenile) 258.1
diabetes mellitus-hypertension-nephrosis 250.4 ☑ [581.81]
due to secondary diabetes 249.4 ☑ [581.81]
diabetes mellitus in newborn infant 775.1
diabetes-nephrosis 250.4 ☑ [581.81]
due to secondary diabetes 249.4 ☑ [581.81]
diabetic amyotrophy 250.6 ☑ [353.5]
due to secondary diabetes 249.6 ☑ [353.5]

☑ Additional Digit Required — Refer to the Tabular List for Digit Selection   ▽ Subterms under main terms may continue to next column or page

2010 ICD-9-CM   ▶◀ Revised Text   ● New Line   ▲ Revised Code   October 2009 · Volume 2 — 259

Syndrome — *see also* Disease — *continued*
Diamond-Blackfan (congenital hypoplastic anemia) 284.01
Diamond-Gardener (autoerythrocyte sensitization) 287.2
DIC (diffuse or disseminated intravascular coagulopathy) (*see also* Fibrinolysis) 286.6
diencephalohypophyseal NEC 253.8
diffuse cervicobrachial 723.3
diffuse obstructive pulmonary 496
DiGeorge's (thymic hypoplasia) 279.11
Dighton's 756.51
Di Guglielmo's (erythremic myelosis) (M9841/3) 207.0 ✓
disequilibrium 276.9
disseminated platelet thrombosis 446.6
Ditthomska 307.81
Doan-Wisemann (primary splenic neutropenia) 289.53
Döhle body-panmyelopathic 288.2
Donohue's (leprechaunism) 259.8
dorsolateral medullary (*see also* Disease, cerebrovascular, acute) 436
double athetosis 333.71
double whammy 360.81
Down's (mongolism) 758.0
Dresbach's (elliptocytosis) 282.1
Dressler's (postmyocardial infarction) 411.0
hemoglobinuria 283.2
postcardiotomy 429.4
drug withdrawal, infant, of dependent mother 779.5
dry skin 701.1
eye 375.15
DSAP (disseminated superficial actinic porokeratosis) 692.75
Duane's (retraction) 378.71
Duane-Stilling-Türk (ocular retraction syndrome) 378.71
Dubin-Johnson (constitutional hyperbilirubinemia) 277.4
Dubin-Sprinz (constitutional hyperbilirubinemia) 277.4
Duchenne's 335.22
due to abnormality
autosomal NEC (*see also* Abnormal, autosomes NEC) 758.5
13 758.1
18 758.2
21 or 22 758.0
D1 758.1
E3 758.2
G 758.0
chromosomal 758.89
sex 758.81
dumping 564.2
nonsurgical 536.8
Duplay's 726.2
Dupré's (meningism) 781.6
Dyke-Young (acquired macrocytic hemolytic anemia) 283.9
dyspraxia 315.4
dystocia, dystrophia 654.9 ✓
Eagle-Barret 756.71
Eales' 362.18
Eaton-Lambert (*see also* Neoplasm, by site, malignant) 199.1 *[358.1]*
Ebstein's (downward displacement, tricuspid valve into right ventricle) 746.2
ectopic ACTH secretion 255.0
eczema-thrombocytopenia 279.12
Eddowes' (brittle bones and blue sclera) 756.51
Edwards' 758.2
efferent loop 537.89
effort (aviators') (psychogenic) 306.2
Ehlers-Danlos 756.83
Eisenmenger's (ventricular septal defect) 745.4
Ekbom's (restless legs) 333.94
Ekman's (brittle bones and blue sclera) 756.51
electric feet 266.2
Elephant man 237.71
Ellison-Zollinger (gastric hypersecretion with pancreatic islet cell tumor) 251.5
Ellis-van Creveld (chondroectodermal dysplasia) 756.55

Syndrome — *see also* Disease — *continued*
embryonic fixation 270.2
empty sella (turcica) 253.8
endocrine-hypertensive 255.3
Engel-von Recklinghausen (osteitis fibrosa cystica) 252.01
enteroarticular 099.3
entrapment — *see* Neuropathy, entrapment
eosinophilia myalgia 710.5
epidemic vomiting 078.82
Epstein's — *see* Nephrosis
Erb (-Oppenheim)-Goldflam 358.00
Erdheim's (acromegalic macrospondylitis) 253.0
Erdheim-Chester 277.89
Erlacher-Blount (tibia vara) 732.4
erythrocyte fragmentation 283.19
euthyroid sick 790.94
Evans' (thrombocytopenic purpura) 287.32
excess cortisol, iatrogenic 255.0
exhaustion 300.5
extrapyramidal 333.90
eyelid-malar-mandible 756.0
eye retraction 378.71
Faber's (achlorhydric anemia) 280.9
Fabry (-Anderson) (angiokeratoma corporis diffusum) 272.7
facet 724.8
Fallot's 745.2
falx (*see also* Hemorrhage, brain) 431
familial eczema-thrombocytopenia 279.12
Fanconi (-de Toni) (-Debré) (cystinosis) 270.0
Fanconi's (anemia) (congenital pancytopenia) 284.09
Farber (-Uzman) (disseminated lipogranulomatosis) 272.8
fatigue NEC 300.5
chronic 780.71
faulty bowel habit (idiopathic megacolon) 564.7
FDH (focal dermal hypoplasia) 757.39
fecal reservoir 560.39
Feil-Klippel (brevicollis) 756.16
Felty's (rheumatoid arthritis with splenomegaly and leukopenia) 714.1
fertile eunuch 257.2
fetal alcohol 760.71
late effect 760.71
fibrillation-flutter 427.32
fibrositis (periarticular) 729.0
Fiedler's (acute isolated myocarditis) 422.91
Fiessinger-Leroy (-Reiter) 099.3
Fiessinger-Rendu (erythema multiforme exudativum) 695.19
first arch 756.0
Fisher's 357.0
fish odor 270.8
Fitz's (acute hemorrhagic pancreatitis) 577.0
Fitz-Hugh and Curtis 098.86
due to
Chlamydia trachomatis 099.56
Neisseria gonorrhoeae (gonococcal peritonitis) 098.86
Flajani (-Basedow) (exophthalmic goiter) 242.0 ✓
flat back
acquired 737.29
postprocedural 738.5
floppy
infant 781.99
iris 364.81
valve (mitral) 424.0
flush 259.2
Foix-Alajouanine 336.1
Fong's (hereditary osteo-onychodysplasia) 756.89
foramen magnum 348.4
Forbes-Albright (nonpuerperal amenorrhea and lactation associated with pituitary tumor) 253.1
Foster-Kennedy 377.04
Foville's (peduncular) 344.89
fragile X 759.83
Franceschetti's (mandibulofacial dysostosis) 756.0
Fraser's 759.89

Syndrome — *see also* Disease — *continued*
Freeman-Sheldon 759.89
Frey's (auriculotemporal) 705.22
Friderichsen-Waterhouse 036.3
Friedrich-Erb-Arnold (acropachyderma) 757.39
Fröhlich's (adiposogenital dystrophy) 253.8
Froin's 336.8
Frommel-Chiari 676.6 ✓
frontal lobe 310.0
Fukuhara 277.87
Fuller Albright's (osteitis fibrosa disseminata) 756.59
functional
bowel 564.9
prepubertal castrate 752.89
Gaisböck's (polycythemia hypertonica) 289.0
ganglion (basal, brain) 333.90
geniculi 351.1
Ganser's, hysterical 300.16
Gardner-Diamond (autoerythrocyte sensitization) 287.2
gastroesophageal junction 530.0
gastroesophageal laceration-hemorrhage 530.7
gastrojejunal loop obstruction 537.89
Gayet-Wernicke's (superior hemorrhagic polioencephalitis) 265.1
Gee-Herter-Heubner (nontropical sprue) 579.0
Gélineau's (*see also* Narcolepsy) 347.00
genito-anorectal 099.1
Gerhardt's (vocal cord paralysis) 478.30
Gerstmann's (finger agnosia) 784.69
Gerstmann-Sträussler-Scheinker (GSS) 046.71
Gianotti Crosti 057.8
due to known virus — *see* Infection, virus
due to unknown virus 057.8
Gilbert's 277.4
Gilford (-Hutchinson) (progeria) 259.8
Gilles de la Tourette's 307.23
Gillespie's (dysplasia oculodentodigitalis) 759.89
Glénard's (enteroptosis) 569.89
Glinski-Simmonds (pituitary cachexia) 253.2
glucuronyl transferase 277.4
glue ear 381.20
Goldberg (-Maxwell) (-Morris) (testicular feminization) 259.51
Goldenhar's (oculoauriculovertebral dysplasia) 756.0
Goldflam-Erb 358.00
Goltz-Gorlin (dermal hypoplasia) 757.39
Good's 279.06
Goodpasture's (pneumorenal) 446.21
Gopalan's (burning feet) 266.2
Gorlin's 759.89 ●
Gorlin-Chaudhry-Moss 759.89
Gougerot-Blum (pigmented purpuric lichenoid dermatitis) 709.1
Gougerot-Carteaud (confluent reticulate papillomatosis) 701.8
Gougerot (-Houwer)-Sjögren (keratoconjunctivitis sicca) 710.2
Gouley's (constrictive pericarditis) 423.2
Gowers' (vasovagal attack) 780.2
Gowers-Paton-Kennedy 377.04
Gradenigo's 383.02
gray or grey (chloramphenicol) (newborn) 779.4
Greig's (hypertelorism) 756.0
GSS (Gerstmann-Sträussler-Scheinker) 046.71
Gubler-Millard 344.89
Guérin-Stern (arthrogryposis multiplex congenita) 754.89
Guillain-Barré (-Strohl) 357.0
Gunn's (jaw-winking syndrome) 742.8
Günther's (congenital erythropoietic porphyria) 277.1
gustatory sweating 350.8
H3O 759.81
Hadfield-Clarke (pancreatic infantilism) 577.8
Haglund-Läwen-Fründ 717.89
hairless women 257.8
hair tourniquet (*see also* Injury, superficial, by site)
finger 915.8
infected 915.9

Syndrome — *see also* Disease — *continued*
hair tourniquet (*see also* Injury, superficial, by site) — *continued*
penis 911.8
infected 911.9
toe 917.8
infected 917.9
Hallermann-Streiff 756.0
Hallervorden-Spatz 333.0
Hamman's (spontaneous mediastinal emphysema) 518.1
Hamman-Rich (diffuse interstitial pulmonary fibrosis) 516.3
hand-foot 693.0
Hand-Schüller-Christian (chronic histiocytosis X) 277.89
Hanot-Chauffard (-Troisier) (bronze diabetes) 275.0
Harada's 363.22
Hare's (M8010/3) (carcinoma, pulmonary apex) 162.3
Harkavy's 446.0
harlequin color change 779.89
Harris' (organic hyperinsulinism) 251.1
Hart's (pellagra-cerebellar ataxia-renal aminoaciduria) 270.0
Hayem-Faber (achlorhydric anemia) 280.9
Hayem-Widal (acquired hemolytic jaundice) 283.9
headache — *see* Headache, syndrome
Heberden's (angina pectoris) 413.9
Hedinger's (malignant carcinoid) 259.2
Hegglin's 288.2
Heller's (infantile psychosis) (*see also* Psychosis, childhood) 299.1 ✓
H.E.L.L.P 642.5 ✓
hemolytic-uremic (adult) (child) 283.11
hemophagocytic 288.4
infection-associated 288.4
Hench-Rosenberg (palindromic arthritis) (*see also* Rheumatism, palindromic) 719.3
Henoch-Schönlein (allergic purpura) 287.0
hepatic flexure 569.89
hepatorenal 572.4
due to a procedure 997.4
following delivery 674.8 ✓
hepatourologic 572.4
Herrick's (hemoglobin S disease) 282.61
Herter (-Gee) (nontropical sprue) 579.0
Heubner-Herter (nontropical sprue) 579.0
Heyd's (hepatorenal) 572.4
HHHO 759.81
high grade myelodysplastic 238.73
with 5q deletion 238.73
Hilger's 337.09
histocytic 288.4
Hoffa (-Kastert) (liposynovitis prepatellaris) 272.8
Hoffmann's 244.9 *[359.5]*
Hoffmann-Bouveret (paroxysmal tachycardia) 427.2
Hoffmann-Werdnig 335.0
Holländer-Simons (progressive lipodystrophy) 272.6
Holmes' (visual disorientation) 368.16
Holmes-Adie 379.46
Hoppe-Goldflam 358.00
Horner's (*see also* Neuropathy, peripheral, autonomic) 337.9
traumatic — *see* Injury, nerve, cervical sympathetic
hospital addiction 301.51
hungry bone 275.5
Hunt's (herpetic geniculate ganglionitis) 053.11
dyssynergia cerebellaris myoclonica 334.2
Hunter (-Hurler) (mucopolysaccharidosis II) 277.5
hunterian glossitis 529.4
Hurler (-Hunter) (mucopolysaccharidosis II) 277.5
Hutchinson-Boeck (sarcoidosis) 135
Hutchinson-Gilford (progeria) 259.8
Hutchinson's incisors or teeth 090.5

Syndrome — see also Disease — continued

hydralazine

    correct substance properly administered 695.4

    overdose or wrong substance given or taken 972.6

hydraulic concussion (abdomen) (see also Injury, internal, abdomen) 868.00

hyperabduction 447.8

hyperactive bowel 564.9

hyperaldosteronism with hypokalemic alkalosis (Bartter's) 255.13

hypercalcemic 275.42

hypercoagulation NEC 289.89

hypereosinophilic (idiopathic) 288.3

hyperkalemic 276.7

hyperkinetic (see also Hyperkinesia)

    heart 429.82

hyperlipemia-hemolytic anemia-icterus 571.1

hypermobility 728.5

hypernatremia 276.0

hyperosmolarity 276.0

hyperperfusion 997.01

hypersomnia-bulimia 349.89

hypersplenic 289.4

hypersympathetic (see also Neuropathy, peripheral, autonomic) 337.9

hypertransfusion, newborn 776.4

hyperventilation, psychogenic 306.1

hyperviscosity (of serum) NEC 273.3

    polycythemic 289.0

    sclerothymic 282.8

hypoglycemic (familial) (neonatal) 251.2

    functional 251.1

hypokalemic 276.8

hypophyseal 253.8

hypophyseothalamic 253.8

hypopituitarism 253.2

hypoplastic left heart 746.7

hypopotassemia 276.8

hyposmolality 276.1

hypotension, maternal 669.2 ☑

hypothenar hammer 443.89

hypotonia-hypomentia-hypogonadism-obesity 759.81

ICF (intravascular coagulation-fibrinolysis) (see also Fibrinolysis) 286.6

idiopathic cardiorespiratory distress, newborn 769

idiopathic nephrotic (infantile) 581.9

iliotibial band 728.89

Imerslund (-Gräsbeck) (anemia due to familial selective vitamin B₁₂ malabsorption) 281.1

immobility (paraplegic) 728.3

immunity deficiency, combined 279.2

impending coronary 411.1

impingement

    shoulder 726.2

    vertebral bodies 724.4

inappropriate secretion of antidiuretic hormone (ADH) 253.6

incomplete

    mandibulofacial 756.0

infant

    death, sudden (SIDS) 798.0

    Hercules 255.2

    of diabetic mother 775.0

    shaken 995.55

infantilism 253.3

inferior vena cava 459.2

influenza-like 487.1

inspissated bile, newborn 774.4

insufficient sleep 307.44

intermediate coronary (artery) 411.1

internal carotid artery (see also Occlusion, artery, carotid) 433.1 ☑

interspinous ligament 724.8

intestinal

    carcinoid 259.2

    gas 787.3

    knot 560.2

intraoperative floppy iris (IFIS) 364.81

intravascular

    coagulation-fibrinolysis (ICF) (see also Fibrinolysis) 286.6

Syndrome — see also Disease — continued

intravascular — continued

    coagulopathy (see also Fibrinolysis) 286.6

inverted Marfan's 759.89

IRDS (idiopathic respiratory distress, newborn) 769

irritable

    bowel 564.1

    heart 306.2

    weakness 300.5

ischemic bowel (transient) 557.9

    chronic 557.1

    due to mesenteric artery insufficiency 557.1

Itsenko-Cushing (pituitary basophilism) 255.0

IVC (intravascular coagulopathy) (see also Fibrinolysis) 286.6

Ivemark's (asplenia with congenital heart disease) 759.0

Jaccoud's 714.4

Jackson's 344.89

Jadassohn-Lewandowski (pachyonchia congenita) 757.5

Jaffe-Lichtenstein (-Uehlinger) 252.01

Jahnke's (encephalocutaneous angiomatosis) 759.6

Jakob-Creutzfeldt 046.19

    with dementia

        with behavioral disturbance 046.19 [294.11]

        without behavioral disturbance 046.19 [294.10]

    variant 046.11

        with dementia

            with behavioral disturbance 046.11 [294.11]

            without behavioral disturbance 046.11 [294.10]

Jaksch's (pseudoleukemia infantum) 285.8

Jaksch-Hayem (-Luzet) (pseudoleukemia infantum) 285.8

jaw-winking 742.8

jejunal 564.2

Jervell-Lange-Nielsen 426.82

jet lag 327.35

Jeune's (asphyxiating thoracic dystrophy of newborn) 756.4

Job's (chronic granulomatous disease) 288.1

Jordan's 288.2

Joseph-Diamond-Blackfan (congenital hypoplastic anemia) 284.01

Joubert 759.89

jugular foramen 352.6

Kabuki 759.89

Kahler's (multiple myeloma) (M9730/3) 203.0 ☑

Kalischer's (encephalocutaneous angiomatosis) 759.6

Kallmann's (hypogonadotropic hypogonadism with anosmia) 253.4

Kanner's (autism) (see also Psychosis, childhood) 299.0 ☑

Kartagener's (sinusitis, bronchiectasis, situs inversus) 759.3

Kasabach-Merritt (capillary hemangioma associated with thrombocytopenic purpura) 287.39

Kast's (dyschondroplasia with hemangiomas) 756.4

Kaznelson's (congenital hypoplastic anemia) 284.01

Kearns-Sayre 277.87

Kelly's (sideropenic dysphagia) 280.8

Kimmelstiel-Wilson (intercapillary glomerulosclerosis) 250.4 ☑ [581.81]

    due to secondary diabetes 249.4 ☑ [581.81]

Klauder's (erythema multiforme exudativum) 695.19

Kleine-Levin 327.13

Klein-Waardenburg (ptosis-epicanthus) 270.2

Klinefelter's 758.7

Klippel-Feil (brevicollis) 756.16

Klippel-Trenaunay 759.89

Klumpke (-Déjérine) (injury to brachial plexus at birth) 767.6

Syndrome — see also Disease — continued

Klüver-Bucy (-Terzian) 310.0

Köhler-Pellegrini-Stieda (calcification, knee joint) 726.62

König's 564.89

Korsakoff (-Wernicke) (nonalcoholic) 294.0

Korsakoff's (nonalcoholic) 294.0

    alcoholic 291.1

    alcoholic 291.1

Kostmann's (infantile genetic agranulocytosis) 288.01

Krabbe's

    congenital muscle hypoplasia 756.89

    cutaneocerebral angioma 759.6

Kunkel (lupoid hepatitis) 571.49

labyrinthine 386.50

laceration, broad ligament 620.6

Landau-Kleffner 345.8 ☑

Langdon Down (mongolism) 758.0

Larsen's (flattened facies and multiple congenital dislocations) 755.8

lateral

    cutaneous nerve of thigh 355.1

    medullary (see also Disease, cerebrovascular acute) 436

Launois' (pituitary gigantism) 253.0

Launois-Cléret (adiposogenital dystrophy) 253.8

Laurence-Moon (-Bardet)-Biedl (obesity, polydactyly, and mental retardation) 759.89

Lawford's (encephalocutaneous angiomatosis) 759.6

lazy

    leukocyte 288.09

    posture 728.3

Lederer-Brill (acquired infectious hemolytic anemia) 283.19

Legg-Calvé-Perthes (osteochondrosis capital femoral) 732.1

Lemiere 451.89

Lennox's (see also Epilepsy) 345.0 ☑

Lennox-Gastaut syndrome 345.0 ☑

    with tonic seizures 345.1 ☑

lenticular 275.1

Léopold-Lévi's (paroxysmal thyroid instability) 242.9 ☑

Lepore hemoglobin 282.49

Leriche's (aortic bifurcation occlusion) 444.0

Léri-Weill 756.59

Lermoyez's (see also Disease, Ménière's) 386.00

Lesch-Nyhan (hypoxanthine-guanine-phosphoribosyltransferase deficiency) 277.2

leukoencephalopathy, reversible, posterior 348.5

Lev's (acquired complete heart block) 426.0

Levi's (pituitary dwarfism) 253.3

Lévy-Roussy 334.3

Lichtheim's (subacute combined sclerosis with pernicious anemia) 281.0 [336.2]

Li-Fraumeni V84.01

Lightwood's (renal tubular acidosis) 588.89

Lignac (-de Toni) (-Fanconi) (-Debré) (cystinosis) 270.0

Likoff's (angina in menopausal women) 413.9

liver-kidney 572.4

Lloyd's 258.1

lobotomy 310.0

Löffler's (eosinophilic pneumonitis) 518.3

Löfgren's (sarcoidosis) 135

long arm 18 or 21 deletion 758.39

Looser (-Debray)-Milkman (osteomalacia with pseudofractures) 268.2

Lorain-Levi (pituitary dwarfism) 253.3

Louis-Bar (ataxia-telangiectasia) 334.8

low

    atmospheric pressure 993.2

    back 724.2

        psychogenic 306.0

    output (cardiac) (see also Failure, heart) 428.9

Lowe's (oculocerebrorenal dystrophy) 270.8

lower radicular, newborn 767.4

Lowe-Terrey-MacLachlan (oculocerebrorenal dystrophy) 270.8

Syndrome — see also Disease — continued

Lown (-Ganong)-Levine (short P-R interval, normal QRS complex, and supraventricular tachycardia) 426.81

Lucey-Driscoll (jaundice due to delayed conjugation) 774.30

Luetscher's (dehydration) 276.51

lumbar vertebral 724.4

Lutembacher's (atrial septal defect with mitral stenosis) 745.5

Lyell's (toxic epidermal necrolysis) 695.15

    due to drug

        correct substance properly administered 695.15

        overdose or wrong substance given or taken 977.9

        specified drug — see Table of Drugs and Chemicals

MacLeod's 492.8

macrogenitosomia praecox 259.8

macroglobulinemia 273.3

macrophage activation 288.4

Maffucci's (dyschondroplasia with hemangiomas) 756.4

Magenblase 306.4

magnesium-deficiency 781.7

malabsorption 579.9

    postsurgical 579.3

    spinal fluid 331.3

Mal de Debarquement 780.4

malignant carcinoid 259.2

Mallory-Weiss 530.7

mandibulofacial dysostosis 756.0

manic-depressive (see also Psychosis, affective) 296.80

Mankowsky's (familial dysplastic osteopathy) 731.2

maple syrup (urine) 270.3

Marable's (celiac artery compression) 447.4

Marchesani (-Weill) (brachymorphism and ectopia lentis) 759.89

Marchiafava-Bignami 341.8

Marchiafava-Micheli (paroxysmal nocturnal hemoglobinuria) 283.2

Marcus Gunn (jaw-winking syndrome) 742.8

Marfan's (arachnodactyly) 759.82

    meaning congenital syphilis 090.49

    with luxation of lens 090.49 [379.32]

Marie's (acromegaly) 253.0

    primary or idiopathic (acropachyderma) 757.39

    secondary (hypertrophic pulmonary osteoarthropathy) 731.2

Markus-Adie 379.46

Maroteaux-Lamy (mucopolysaccharidosis VI) 277.5

Martin's 715.27

Martin-Albright (pseudohypoparathyroidism) 275.49

Martorell-Fabré (pulseless disease) 446.7

massive aspiration of newborn 770.18

Masters-Allen 620.6

mastocytosis 757.33

maternal hypotension 669.2 ☑

maternal obesity 646.1 ☑

May (-Hegglin) 288.2

McArdle (-Schmid) (-Pearson) (glycogenosis V) 271.0

McCune-Albright (osteitis fibrosa disseminata) 756.59

McQuarrie's (idiopathic familial hypoglycemia) 251.2

meconium

    aspiration 770.12

    plug (newborn) NEC 777.1

median arcuate ligament 447.4

mediastinal fibrosis 519.3

Meekeren-Ehlers-Danlos 756.83

Meige (blepharospasm-oromandibular dystonia) 333.82

    -Milroy (chronic hereditary edema) 757.0

MELAS (mitochondrial encephalopathy, lactic acidosis and stroke-like episodes) 277.87

Melkersson (-Rosenthal) 351.8

☑ Additional Digit Required — Refer to the Tabular List for Digit Selection   ⬇ Subterms under main terms may continue to next column or page

Index

Syndrome — Syndrome

Syndrome — *see also* Disease — *continued*
postirradiation 990
postlaminectomy 722.80
   cervical, cervicothoracic 722.81
   lumbar, lumbosacral 722.83
   thoracic, thoracolumbar 722.82
postleukotomy 310.0
postlobotomy 310.0
postmastectomy lymphedema 457.0
postmature (of newborn) 766.22
postmyocardial infarction 411.0
postoperative NEC 998.9
   blind loop 579.2
postpartum panhypopituitary 253.2
postperfusion NEC 999.89
   bone marrow 996.85
postpericardiotomy 429.4
postphlebitic (asymptomatic) 459.10
   with
      complications NEC 459.19
         inflammation 459.12
            and ulcer 459.13
         stasis dermatitis 459.12
            with ulcer 459.13
         ulcer 459.11
            with inflammation 459.13
postpolio (myelitis) 138
postvagotomy 564.2
postvalvulotomy 429.4
postviral (asthenia) NEC 780.79
Potain's (gastrectasis with dyspepsia) 536.1
potassium intoxication 276.7
Potter's 753.0
Prader (-Labhart) -Willi (-Fanconi) 759.81
preinfarction 411.1
preleukemic 238.75
premature senility 259.8
premenstrual 625.4
premenstrual tension 625.4
pre ulcer 536.9
Prinzmetal-Massumi (anterior chest wall syndrome) 786.52
Profichet's 729.90
progeria 259.8
progressive pallidal degeneration 333.0
prolonged gestation 766.22
Proteus (dermal hypoplasia) 757.39
prune belly 756.71
prurigo-asthma 691.8
pseudocarpal tunnel (sublimis) 354.0
pseudohermaphroditism-virilism-hirsutism
   255.2
pseudoparalytica 358.00
pseudo-Turner's 759.89
psycho-organic 293.9
   acute 293.0
   anxiety type 293.84
   depressive type 293.83
   hallucinatory type 293.82
   nonpsychotic severity 310.1
      specified focal (partial) NEC 310.8
   paranoid type 293.81
   specified type NEC 293.89
   subacute 293.1
pterygolymphangiectasia 758.6
ptosis-epicanthus 270.2
pulmonary
   arteriosclerosis 416.0
   hypoperfusion (idiopathic) 769
   renal (hemorrhagic) 446.21
pulseless 446.7
Putnam-Dana (subacute combined sclerosis
   with pernicious anemia) 281.0 *[336.2]*
pyloroduodenal 537.89
pyramidopallidonigral 332.0
pyriformis 355.0
QT interval prolongation 426.82
radicular NEC 729.2
   lower limbs 724.4
   upper limbs 723.4
      newborn 767.4
Raeder-Harbitz (pulseless disease) 446.7
Ramsay Hunt's
   dyssynergia cerebellaris myoclonica 334.2
   herpetic geniculate ganglionitis 053.11
rapid time-zone change 327.35

Syndrome — *see also* Disease — *continued*
Raymond (-Céstan) 433.8 ☑
Raynaud's (paroxysmal digital cyanosis) 443.0
RDS (respiratory distress syndrome, newborn)
   769
Refsum's (heredopathia atactica polyneuritiformis) 356.3
Reichmann's (gastrosuccorrhea) 536.8
Reifenstein's (hereditary familial hypogonadism, male) 259.52
Reilly's (*see also* Neuropathy, peripheral, autonomic) 337.9
Reiter's 099.3
renal glomerulohyalinosis-diabetic
   250.4 ☑ *[581.81]*
   due to secondary diabetes
      249.4 ☑ *[581.81]*
Rendu-Osler-Weber (familial hemorrhagic
   telangiectasia) 448.0
renofacial (congenital biliary fibroangiomato-
   sis) 753.0
Rénon-Delille 253.8
respiratory distress (idiopathic) (newborn) 769
   adult (following shock, surgery, or trauma)
      518.5
   specified NEC 518.82
   type II 770.6
restless legs (RLS) 333.94
retinoblastoma (familial) 190.5
retraction (Duane's) 378.71
retroperitoneal fibrosis 593.4
retroviral seroconversion (acute) V08
Rett's 330.8
Reye's 331.81
Reye-Sheehan (postpartum pituitary necrosis)
   253.2
Riddoch's (visual disorientation) 368.16
Ridley's (*see also* Failure, ventricular, left) 428.1
Rieger's (mesodermal dysgenesis, anterior
   ocular segment) 743.44
Rietti-Greppi-Micheli (thalassemia minor)
   282.49
right ventricular obstruction — *see* Failure,
   heart
Riley-Day (familial dysautonomia) 742.8
Robin's 756.0
Rokitansky-Kuster-Hauser (congenital absence,
   vagina) 752.49
Romano-Ward (prolonged QT interval syn-
   drome) 426.82
Romberg's 349.89
Rosen-Castleman-Liebow (pulmonary pro-
   teinosis) 516.0
rotator cuff, shoulder 726.10
Roth's 355.1
Rothmund's (congenital poikiloderma) 757.33
Rotor's (idiopathic hyperbilirubinemia) 277.4
Roussy-Lévy 334.3
Roy (-Jutras) (acropachyderma) 757.39
rubella (congenital) 771.0
Rubinstein-Taybi's (brachydactylia, short
   stature, and mental retardation) 759.89
Rud's (mental deficiency, epilepsy, and infantilism) 759.89
Ruiter-Pompen (-Wyers) (angiokeratoma cor-
   poris diffusum) 272.7
Runge's (postmaturity) 766.22
Russell (-Silver) (congenital hemihypertrophy
   and short stature) 759.89
Rytand-Lipsitch (complete atrioventricular
   block) 426.0
sacralization-scoliosis-sciatica 756.15
sacroiliac 724.6
Saenger's 379.46
salt
   depletion (*see also* Disease, renal) 593.9
      due to heat NEC 992.8
         causing heat exhaustion or prostra-
            tion 992.4
   low (*see also* Disease, renal) 593.9
   salt-losing (*see also* Disease, renal) 593.9
Sanfilippo's (mucopolysaccharidosis III) 277.5
Scaglietti-Dagnini (acromegalic
   macrospondylitis) 253.0
scalded skin 695.81
scalenus anticus (anterior) 353.0

Syndrome — *see also* Disease — *continued*
scapulocostal 354.8
scapuloperoneal 359.1
scapulovertebral 723.4
Schaumann's (sarcoidosis) 135
Scheie's (mucopolysaccharidosis IS) 277.5
Scheuthauer-Marie-Sainton (cleidocranialis
   dysostosis) 755.59
Schirmer's (encephalocutaneous angiomato-
   sis) 759.6
schizophrenic, of childhood NEC (*see also*
   Psychosis, childhood) 299.9 ☑
Schmidt's
   sphallo-pharyngo-laryngeal hemiplegia
      352.6
   thyroid-adrenocortical insufficiency 258.1
   vagoaccessory 352.6
Schneider's 047.9
Schnitzler 273.1
Scholte's (malignant carcinoid) 259.2
Scholz (-Bielschowsky-Henneberg) 330.0
Schroeder's (endocrine-hypertensive) 255.3
Schüller-Christian (chronic histiocytosis X)
   277.89
Schultz's (agranulocytosis) 288.09
Schwartz (-Jampel) 359.23
Schwartz-Bartter (inappropriate secretion of
   antidiuretic hormone) 253.6
Scimitar (anomalous venous drainage, right
   lung to inferior vena cava) 747.49
sclerocystic ovary 256.4
sea-blue histiocyte 272.7
Seabright-Bantam (pseudohypoparathy-
   roidism) 275.49
Seckel's 759.89
Secretan's (posttraumatic edema) 782.3
secretoinhibitor (keratoconjunctivitis sicca)
   710.2
Seeligmann's (ichthyosis congenita) 757.1
Senear-Usher (pemphigus erythematosus)
   694.4
senilism 259.8
seroconversion, retroviral (acute) V08
serotonin 333.99
serous meningitis 348.2
Sertoli cell (germinal aplasia) 606.0
sex chromosome mosaic 758.81
Sézary's (reticulosis) (M9701/3) 202.2 ☑
shaken infant 995.55
Shaver's (bauxite pneumoconiosis) 503
Sheehan's (postpartum pituitary necrosis)
   253.2
shock (traumatic) 958.4
   kidney 584.5
      following crush injury 958.5
   lung 518.5
   neurogenic 308.9
   psychic 308.9
Shone's 746.84
short
   bowel 579.3
   P-R interval 426.81
shoulder-arm (*see also* Neuropathy, peripheral,
   autonomic) 337.9
shoulder-girdle 723.4
shoulder-hand (*see also* Neuropathy, peripheral, autonomic) 337.9
Shwachman's 288.02
Shy-Drager (orthostatic hypotension with
   multisystem degeneration) 333.0
Sicard's 352.6
sicca (keratoconjunctivitis) 710.2
sick
   cell 276.1
   cilia 759.89
   sinus 427.81
sideropenic 280.8
Siemens'
   ectodermal dysplasia 757.31
   keratosis follicularis spinulosa (decalvans)
      757.39
Silfverskiöld's (osteochondrodystrophy, extremities) 756.50
Silver's (congenital hemihypertrophy and short
   stature) 759.89
Silvestroni-Bianco (thalassemia minima) 282.49

Syndrome — *see also* Disease — *continued*
Simons' (progressive lipodystrophy) 272.6
sinusitis-bronchiectasis-situs inversus 759.3
sinus tarsi 726.79
Sipple's (medullary thyroid carcinoma-
   pheochromocytoma) 258.02
Sjögren (-Gougerot) (keratoconjunctivitis sicca)
   710.2
   with lung involvement 710.2 *[517.8]*
Sjögren-Larsson (ichthyosis congenita) 757.1
SJS-TEN (Stevens-Johnson syndrome - toxic
   epidermal necrolysis overlap) 695.14
Slocumb's 255.3
Sluder's 337.09
Smith-Lemli-Opitz (cerebrohepatorenal syndrome) 759.89
Smith-Magenis 758.33
smokers' 305.1
Sneddon-Wilkinson (subcorneal pustular dermatosis) 694.1
Sotos' (cerebral gigantism) 253.0
South African cardiomyopathy 425.2
spasmodic
   upward movement, eye(s) 378.82
   winking 307.20
Spens' (syncope with heart block) 426.9
spherophakia-brachymorphia 759.89
spinal cord injury (*see also* Injury, spinal, by
   site)
   with fracture, vertebra — *see* Fracture,
      vertebra, by site, with spinal cord
      injury
   cervical — *see* Injury, spinal, cervical
   fluid malabsorption (acquired) 331.3
splenic
   agenesis 759.0
   flexure 569.89
   neutropenia 289.53
   sequestration 289.52
Spurway's (brittle bones and blue sclera)
   756.51
staphylococcal scalded skin 695.81
Stein's (polycystic ovary) 256.4
Steinbrocker's (*see also* Neuropathy, peripheral,
   autonomic) 337.9
Stein-Leventhal (polycystic ovary) 256.4
Stevens-Johnson (erythema multiforme exudativum) 695.13
   toxic epidermal necrolysis overlap (SJS-TEN
      overlap syndrome) 695.14
Stewart-Morel (hyperostosis frontalis interna)
   733.3
Stickler 759.89
stiff-baby 759.89
stiff-man 333.91
Still's (juvenile rheumatoid arthritis) 714.30
Still-Felty (rheumatoid arthritis with
   splenomegaly and leukopenia) 714.1
Stilling-Türk-Duane (ocular retraction syndrome) 378.71
Stojano's (subcostal) 098.86
Stokes (-Adams) (syncope with heart block)
   426.9
Stokvis-Talma (enterogenous cyanosis) 289.7
stone heart (*see also* Failure, ventricular, left)
   428.1
straight-back 756.19
stroke (*see also* Disease, cerebrovascular, acute)
   436
   little 435.9
Sturge-Kalischer-Weber (encephalotrigeminal
   angiomatosis) 759.6
Sturge-Weber (-Dimitri) (encephalocutaneous
   angiomatosis) 759.6
subclavian-carotid obstruction (chronic) 446.7
subclavian steal 435.2
subcoracoid-pectoralis minor 447.8
subcostal 098.86
   nerve compression 354.8
subperiosteal hematoma 267
subphrenic interposition 751.4
sudden infant death (SIDS) 798.0
Sudeck's 733.7
Sudeck-Leriche 733.7

☑ Additional Digit Required — Refer to the Tabular List for Digit Selection   ▽ Subterms under main terms may continue to next column or page

2010 ICD-9-CM   ▶◀ Revised Text   ● New Line   ▲ Revised Code   **Volume 2 — 263**

Index

Syndrome—Syphilis, syphilitic

Syndrome — *see also* Disease — *continued*
superior
cerebellar artery (*see also* Disease, cerebrovascular, acute) 436
mesenteric artery 557.1
pulmonary sulcus (tumor) (M8010/3) 162.3
vena cava 459.2
suprarenal cortical 255.3
supraspinatus 726.10
Susac 348.39
swallowed blood 777.3
sweat retention 705.1
Sweet's (acute febrile neutrophilic dermatosis) 695.89
Swyer's (XY pure gonadal dysgenesis) 752.7
Swyer-James (unilateral hyperlucent lung) 492.8
Symonds' 348.2
sympathetic
cervical paralysis 337.09
pelvic 625.5
syndactylic oxycephaly 755.55
syphilitic-cardiovascular 093.89
systemic
fibrosclerosing 710.8
inflammatory response (SIRS) 995.90
due to
infectious process 995.91
with acute organ dysfunction 995.92
non-infectious process 995.93
with acute organ dysfunction 995.94
systolic click (-murmur) 785.2
Tabagism 305.1
tachycardia-bradycardia 427.81
Takayasu (-Onishi) (pulseless disease) 446.7
Takotsubo 429.83
Tapia's 352.6
tarsal tunnel 355.5
Taussig-Bing (transposition, aorta and overriding pulmonary artery) 745.11
Taybi's (otopalatodigital) 759.89
Taylor's 625.5
teething 520.7
tegmental 344.89
telangiectasis-pigmentation-cataract 757.33
temporal 383.02
lobectomy behavior 310.0
temporomandibular joint-pain-dysfunction [TMJ] NEC 524.60
specified NEC 524.69
Terry's (*see also* Retinopathy of prematurity) 362.21
testicular feminization 259.51
testis, nonvirilizing 257.8
tethered (spinal) cord 742.59
thalamic 338.0
Thibierge-Weissenbach (cutaneous systemic sclerosis) 710.1
Thiele 724.6
thoracic outlet (compression) 353.0
thoracogenous rheumatic (hypertrophic pulmonary osteoarthropathy) 731.2
Thorn's (*see also* Disease, renal) 593.9
Thorson-Biörck (malignant carcinoid) 259.2
thrombopenia-hemangioma 287.39
thyroid-adrenocortical insufficiency 258.1
Tietze's 733.6
time-zone (rapid) 327.35
Tobias' (carcinoma, pulmonary apex) (M8010/3) 162.3
toilet seat 926.0
Tolosa-Hunt 378.55
Toni-Fanconi (cystinosis) 270.0
Touraine's (hereditary osteo-onychodysplasia) 756.89
Touraine-Solente-Golé (acropachyderma) 757.39
toxic
oil 710.5
shock 040.82
transfusion
fetal-maternal 772.0
twin
donor (infant) 772.0

Syndrome — *see also* Disease — *continued*
transfusion — *continued*
twin — *continued*
recipient (infant) 776.4
transient left ventricular apical ballooning 429.83
Treacher Collins' (incomplete mandibulofacial dysostosis) 756.0
trigeminal plate 259.8
triple X female 758.81
trisomy NEC 758.5
13 or D₁ 758.1
16-18 or E 758.2
18 or E₃ 758.2
20 758.5
21 or G (mongolism) 758.0
22 or G (mongolism) 758.0
G 758.0
Troisier-Hanot-Chauffard (bronze diabetes) 275.0
tropical wet feet 991.4
Trousseau's (thrombophlebitis migrans visceral cancer) 453.1
tumor lysis (following antineoplastic drug therapy) (spontaneous) 277.88
Türk's (ocular retraction syndrome) 378.71
Turner's 758.6
Turner-Varny 758.6
Twiddler's (due to)
automatic implantable defibrillator 996.04
pacemaker 996.01
twin-to-twin transfusion 762.3
recipient twin 776.4
Uehlinger's (acropachyderma) 757.39
Ullrich (-Bonnevie) (-Turner) 758.6
Ullrich-Feichtiger 759.89
underwater blast injury (abdominal) (*see also* Injury, internal, abdomen) 868.00
universal joint, cervix 620.6
Unverricht (-Lundborg) 345.1 ☑ ▲
Unverricht-Wagner (dermatomyositis) 710.3
upward gaze 378.81
Urbach-Oppenheim (necrobiosis lipoidica diabeticorum) 250.8 ☑ [709.3]
due to secondary diabetes 249.8 ☑ [709.3]
Urbach-Wiethe (lipoid proteinosis) 272.8
uremia, chronic 585.9
urethral 597.81
urethro-oculoarticular 099.3
urethro-oculosynovial 099.3
urohepatic 572.4
uveocutaneous 364.24
uveomeningeal, uveomeningitis 363.22
vagohypoglossal 352.6
vagovagal 780.2
van Buchem's (hyperostosis corticalis) 733.3
van der Hoeve's (brittle bones and blue sclera, deafness) 756.51
van der Hoeve-Halbertsma-Waardenburg (ptosis-epicanthus) 270.2
van der Hoeve-Waardenburg-Gualdi (ptosis-epicanthus) 270.2
vanishing twin 651.33
van Neck-Odelberg (juvenile osteochondrosis) 732.1
vascular splanchnic 557.0
vasomotor 443.9
vasovagal 780.2
VATER 759.89
Velo-cardio-facial 758.32
vena cava (inferior) (superior) (obstruction) 459.2
Verbiest's (claudicatio intermittens spinalis) 435.1
Vernet's 352.6
vertebral
artery 435.1
compression 721.1
lumbar 724.4
steal 435.1
vertebrogenic (pain) 724.5
vertiginous NEC 386.9
video display tube 723.8
Villaret's 352.6
Vinson-Plummer (sideropenic dysphagia) 280.8

Syndrome — *see also* Disease — *continued*
virilizing adrenocortical hyperplasia, congenital 255.2
virus, viral 079.99
visceral larval migrans 128.0
visual disorientation 368.16
vitamin B₆ deficiency 266.1
vitreous touch 997.99
Vogt's (corpus striatum) 333.71
Vogt-Koyanagi 364.24
Volkmann's 958.6
von Bechterew-Strümpell (ankylosing spondylitis) 720.0
von Graefe's 378.72
von Hippel-Lindau (angiomatosis retinocerebellosa) 759.6
von Schroetter's (intermittent venous claudication) 453.89 ▲
von Willebrand (-Jürgens) (angiohemophilia) 286.4
Waardenburg-Klein (ptosis epicanthus) 270.2
Wagner (-Unverricht) (dermatomyositis) 710.3
Waldenström's (macroglobulinemia) 273.3
Waldenström-Kjellberg (sideropenic dysphagia) 280.8
Wallenberg's (posterior inferior cerebellar artery) (*see also* Disease, cerebrovascular, acute) 436
Waterhouse (-Friderichsen) 036.3
water retention 276.6
Weber's 344.89
Weber-Christian (nodular nonsuppurative panniculitis) 729.30
Weber-Cockayne (epidermolysis bullosa) 757.39
Weber-Dimitri (encephalocutaneous angiomatosis) 759.6
Weber-Gubler 344.89
Weber-Leyden 344.89
Weber-Osler (familial hemorrhagic telangiectasia) 448.0
Wegener's (necrotizing respiratory granulomatosis) 446.4
Weill-Marchesani (brachymorphism and ectopia lentis) 759.89
Weingarten's (tropical eosinophilia) 518.3
Weiss-Baker (carotid sinus syncope) 337.01
Weissenbach-Thibierge (cutaneous systemic sclerosis) 710.1
Werdnig-Hoffmann 335.0
Werlhof-Wichmann (*see also* Purpura, thrombocytopenic) 287.39
Wermer's (polyendocrine adenomatosis) 258.01
Werner's (progeria adultorum) 259.8
Wernicke's (nonalcoholic) (superior hemorrhagic polioencephalitis) 265.1
Wernicke-Korsakoff (nonalcoholic) 294.0
alcoholic 291.1
Westphal-Strümpell (hepatolenticular degeneration) 275.1
wet
brain (alcoholic) 303.9 ☑
feet (maceration) (tropical) 991.4
lung
adult 518.5
newborn 770.6
whiplash 847.0
Whipple's (intestinal lipodystrophy) 040.2
"whistling face" (craniocarpotarsal dystrophy) 759.89
Widal (-Abrami) (acquired hemolytic jaundice) 283.9
Wilkie's 557.1
Wilkinson-Sneddon (subcorneal pustular dermatosis) 694.1
Willan-Plumbe (psoriasis) 696.1
Willebrand (-Jürgens) (angiohemophilia) 286.4
Willi-Prader (hypogenital dystrophy with diabetic tendency) 759.81
Wilson's (hepatolenticular degeneration) 275.1
Wilson-Mikity 770.7
Wiskott-Aldrich (eczema-thrombocytopenia) 279.12
withdrawal
alcohol 291.81

Syndrome — *see also* Disease — *continued*
withdrawal — *continued*
drug 292.0
infant of dependent mother 779.5
Woakes' (ethmoiditis) 471.1
Wolff-Parkinson-White (anomalous atrioventricular excitation) 426.7
Wright's (hyperabduction) 447.8
X
cardiac 413.9
dysmetabolic 277.7
xiphoidalgia 733.99
XO 758.6
XXX 758.81
XXXXY 758.81
XXY 758.7
yellow vernix (placental dysfunction) 762.2
Zahorsky's 074.0
Zellweger 277.86
Zieve's (jaundice, hyperlipemia and hemolytic anemia) 571.1
Zollinger-Ellison (gastric hypersecretion with pancreatic islet cell tumor) 251.5
Zuelzer-Ogden (nutritional megaloblastic anemia) 281.2
Synechia (iris) (pupil) 364.70
anterior 364.72
peripheral 364.73
intrauterine (traumatic) 621.5
posterior 364.71
vulvae, congenital 752.49
Synesthesia — *see also* Disturbance, sensation 782.0
Synodontia 520.2
Synophthalmus 759.89
Synorchidism 752.89
Synorchism 752.89
Synostosis (congenital) 756.59
astragaloscaphoid 755.67
radioulnar 755.53
talonavicular (bar) 755.67
tarsal 755.67
Synovial — *see* condition
Synovioma (M9040/3) — *see also* Neoplasm, connective tissue, malignant
benign (M9040/0) — *see* Neoplasm, connective tissue, benign
Synoviosarcoma (M9040/3) — *see* Neoplasm, connective tissue, malignant
Synovitis (*see also* Tenosynovitis) 727.00
chronic crepitant, wrist 727.2
due to crystals — *see* Arthritis, due to crystals
gonococcal 098.51
gouty 274.00 ▲
specified NEC 727.09
syphilitic 095.7
congenital 090.0
traumatic, current — *see* Sprain, by site
tuberculous — *see* Tuberculosis, synovitis
villonodular 719.20
ankle 719.27
elbow 719.22
foot 719.27
hand 719.24
hip 719.25
knee 719.26
multiple sites 719.29
pelvic region 719.25
shoulder (region) 719.21
specified site NEC 719.28
wrist 719.23
Syphilide 091.3
congenital 090.0
newborn 090.0
tubercular 095.8
congenital 090.0
Syphilis, syphilitic (acquired) 097.9
with lung involvement 095.1
abdomen (late) 095.2
acoustic nerve 094.86
adenopathy (secondary) 091.4
adrenal (gland) 095.8
with cortical hypofunction 095.8
age under 2 years NEC (*see also* Syphilis, congenital) 090.9
acquired 097.9

☑ Additional Digit Required — Refer to the Tabular List for Digit Selection ▼ Subterms under main terms may continue to next column or page

264 — Volume 2 • October 2009 ▶◀ Revised Text ● New Line ▲ Revised Code 2010 ICD-9-CM

Syphilis, syphilitic — *continued*
- alopecia (secondary) 091.82
- anemia 095.8
- aneurysm (artery) (ruptured) 093.89
  - aorta 093.0
  - central nervous system 094.89
  - congenital 090.5
- anus 095.8
  - primary 091.1
  - secondary 091.3
- aorta, aortic (arch) (abdominal) (insufficiency) (pulmonary) (regurgitation) (stenosis) (thoracic) 093.89
  - aneurysm 093.0
- arachnoid (adhesive) 094.2
- artery 093.89
  - cerebral 094.89
  - spinal 094.89
- arthropathy (neurogenic) (tabetic) 094.0 *[713.5]*
- asymptomatic — *see* Syphilis, latent
- ataxia, locomotor (progressive) 094.0
- atrophoderma maculatum 091.3
- auricular fibrillation 093.89
- Bell's palsy 094.89
- bladder 095.8
- bone 095.5
  - secondary 091.61
- brain 094.89
- breast 095.8
- bronchus 095.8
- bubo 091.0
- bulbar palsy 094.89
- bursa (late) 095.7
- cardiac decompensation 093.89
- cardiovascular (early) (late) (primary) (secondary) (tertiary) 093.9
  - specified type and site NEC 093.89
- causing death under 2 years of age (*see also* Syphilis, congenital) 090.9
  - stated to be acquired NEC 097.9
- central nervous system (any site) (early) (late) (latent) (primary) (recurrent) (relapse) (secondary) (tertiary) 094.9
  - with
    - ataxia 094.0
    - paralysis, general 094.1
      - juvenile 090.40
    - paresis (general) 094.1
      - juvenile 090.40
    - tabes (dorsalis) 094.0
      - juvenile 090.40
    - taboparesis 094.1
      - juvenile 090.40
  - aneurysm (ruptured) 094.87
  - congenital 090.40
    - juvenile 090.40
  - remission in (sustained) 094.9
  - serology doubtful, negative, or positive 094.9
  - specified nature or site NEC 094.89
  - vascular 094.89
- cerebral 094.89
  - meningovascular 094.2
  - nerves 094.89
  - sclerosis 094.89
  - thrombosis 094.89
- cerebrospinal 094.89
  - tabetic 094.0
- cerebrovascular 094.89
- cervix 095.8
- chancre (multiple) 091.0
  - extragenital 091.2
  - Rollet's 091.2
- Charcôt's joint 094.0 *[713.5]*
- choked disc 094.89 *[377.00]*
- chorioretinitis 091.51
  - congenital 090.0 *[363.13]*
  - late 094.83
- choroiditis 091.51
  - congenital 090.0 *[363.13]*
  - late 094.83
  - prenatal 090.0 *[363.13]*
- choroidoretinitis (secondary) 091.51
  - congenital 090.0 *[363.13]*
  - late 094.83

Syphilis, syphilitic — *continued*
- ciliary body (secondary) 091.52
  - late 095.8 *[364.11]*
- colon (late) 095.8
- combined sclerosis 094.89
- complicating pregnancy, childbirth or puerperium 647.0 ☑
  - affecting fetus or newborn 760.2
- condyloma (latum) 091.3
- congenital 090.9
  - with
    - encephalitis 090.41
    - paresis (general) 090.40
    - tabes (dorsalis) 090.40
    - taboparesis 090.40
  - chorioretinitis, choroiditis 090.0 *[363.13]*
  - early or less than 2 years after birth NEC 090.2
    - with manifestations 090.0
    - latent (without manifestations) 090.1
      - negative spinal fluid test 090.1
      - serology, positive 090.1
    - symptomatic 090.0
  - interstitial keratitis 090.3
  - juvenile neurosyphilis 090.40
  - late or 2 years or more after birth NEC 090.7
    - chorioretinitis, choroiditis 090.5 *[363.13]*
    - interstitial keratitis 090.3
    - juvenile neurosyphilis NEC 090.40
    - latent (without manifestations) 090.6
      - negative spinal fluid test 090.6
      - serology, positive 090.6
    - symptomatic or with manifestations NEC 090.5
      - interstitial keratitis 090.3
- conjugal 097.9
  - tabes 094.0
- conjunctiva 095.8 *[372.10]*
- contact V01.6
- cord, bladder 094.0
- cornea, late 095.8 *[370.59]*
- coronary (artery) 093.89
  - sclerosis 093.89
- coryza 095.8
  - congenital 090.0
- cranial nerve 094.89
- cutaneous — *see* Syphilis, skin
- dacryocystitis 095.8
- degeneration, spinal cord 094.89
- d'emblée 095.8
- dementia 094.1
  - paralytica 094.1
    - juvenilis 090.40
- destruction of bone 095.5
- dilatation, aorta 093.0
- due to blood transfusion 097.9
- dura mater 094.89
- ear 095.8
  - inner 095.8
    - nerve (eighth) 094.86
    - neurorecurrence 094.86
- early NEC 091.0
  - cardiovascular 093.9
  - central nervous system 094.9
    - paresis 094.1
    - tabes 094.0
  - latent (without manifestations) (less than 2 years after infection) 092.9
    - negative spinal fluid test 092.9
    - serological relapse following treatment 092.0
    - serology positive 092.9
  - paresis 094.1
  - relapse (treated, untreated) 091.7
  - skin 091.3
  - symptomatic NEC 091.89
    - extragenital chancre 091.2
    - primary, except extragenital chancre 091.0
    - secondary (*see also* Syphilis, secondary) 091.3
      - relapse (treated, untreated) 091.7
  - tabes 094.0
  - ulcer 091.3
- eighth nerve 094.86

Syphilis, syphilitic — *continued*
- endemic, nonvenereal 104.0
- endocarditis 093.20
  - aortic 093.22
  - mitral 093.21
  - pulmonary 093.24
  - tricuspid 093.23
- epididymis (late) 095.8
- epiglottis 095.8
- epiphysitis (congenital) 090.0
- esophagus 095.8
- Eustachian tube 095.8
- exposure to V01.6
- eye 095.8 *[363.13]*
  - neuromuscular mechanism 094.85
- eyelid 095.8 *[373.5]*
  - with gumma 095.8 *[373.5]*
  - ptosis 094.89
- fallopian tube 095.8
- fracture 095.5
- gallbladder (late) 095.8
- gastric 095.8
  - crisis 094.0
  - polyposis 095.8
- general 097.9
  - paralysis 094.1
    - juvenile 090.40
- genital (primary) 091.0
- glaucoma 095.8
- gumma (late) NEC 095.9
  - cardiovascular system 093.9
  - central nervous system 094.9
  - congenital 090.5
  - heart or artery 093.89
- heart 093.89
  - block 093.89
  - decompensation 093.89
  - disease 093.89
  - failure 093.89
  - valve (*see also* Syphilis, endocarditis) 093.20
- hemianesthesia 094.89
- hemianopsia 095.8
- hemiparesis 094.89
- hemiplegia 094.89
- hepatic artery 093.89
- hepatitis 095.3
- hepatomegaly 095.3
  - congenital 090.0
- hereditaria tarda (*see also* Syphilis, congenital, late) 090.7
- hereditary (*see also* Syphilis, congenital) 090.9
  - interstitial keratitis 090.3
- Hutchinson's teeth 090.5
- hyalitis 095.8
- inactive — *see* Syphilis, latent
- infantum NEC (*see also* Syphilis, congenital) 090.9
- inherited — *see* Syphilis, congenital
- internal ear 095.8
- intestine (late) 095.8
- iris, iritis (secondary) 091.52
  - late 095.8 *[364.11]*
- joint (late) 095.8
- keratitis (congenital) (early) (interstitial) (late) (parenchymatous) (punctata profunda) 090.3
- kidney 095.4
- lacrimal apparatus 095.8
- laryngeal paralysis 095.8
- larynx 095.8
- late 097.0
  - cardiovascular 093.9
  - central nervous system 094.9
    - latent or 2 years or more after infection (without manifestations) 096
      - negative spinal fluid test 096
      - serology positive 096
    - paresis 094.1
  - specified site NEC 095.8
  - symptomatic or with symptoms 095.9
  - tabes 094.0
  - latent 097.1
    - central nervous system 094.9
    - date of infection unspecified 097.1
    - early or less than 2 years after infection 092.9

Syphilis, syphilitic — *continued*
- latent — *continued*
  - late or 2 years or more after infection 096
  - serology
    - doubtful
      - follow-up of latent syphilis 097.1
        - central nervous system 094.9
      - date of infection unspecified 097.1
      - early or less than 2 years after infection 092.9
      - late or 2 years or more after infection 096
    - positive, only finding 097.1
      - date of infection unspecified 097.1
      - early or less than 2 years after infection 097.1
      - late or 2 years or more after infection 097.1
- lens 095.8
- leukoderma 091.3
  - late 095.8
- lienis 095.8
- lip 091.3
  - chancre 091.2
  - late 095.8
  - primary 091.2
- Lissauer's paralysis 094.1
- liver 095.3
  - secondary 091.62
- locomotor ataxia 094.0
- lung 095.1
- lymphadenitis (secondary) 091.4
- lymph gland (early) (secondary) 091.4
  - late 095.8
- macular atrophy of skin 091.3
  - striated 095.8
- maternal, affecting fetus or newborn 760.2
  - manifest syphilis in newborn — *see* Syphilis, congenital
- mediastinum (late) 095.8
- meninges (adhesive) (basilar) (brain) (spinal cord) 094.2
- meningitis 094.2
  - acute 091.81
  - congenital 090.42
- meningoencephalitis 094.2
- meningovascular 094.2
  - congenital 090.49
- mesarteritis 093.89
  - brain 094.89
  - spine 094.89
- middle ear 095.8
- mitral stenosis 093.21
- monoplegia 094.89
- mouth (secondary) 091.3
  - late 095.8
- mucocutaneous 091.3
  - late 095.8
- mucous
  - membrane 091.3
    - late 095.8
  - patches 091.3
    - congenital 090.0
- mulberry molars 090.5
- muscle 095.6
- myocardium 093.82
- myositis 095.6
- nasal sinus 095.8
- neonatorum NEC (*see also* Syphilis, congenital) 090.9
- nerve palsy (any cranial nerve) 094.89
- nervous system, central 094.9
- neuritis 095.8
  - acoustic nerve 094.86
- neurorecidive of retina 094.83
- neuroretinitis 094.85
- newborn (*see also* Syphilis, congenital) 090.9
- nodular superficial 095.8
- nonvenereal, endemic 104.0
- nose 095.8
  - saddle back deformity 090.5
  - septum 095.8
    - perforated 095.8
- occlusive arterial disease 093.89
- ophthalmic 095.8 *[363.13]*

Taenia — *see also* Infestation, taenia — *continued*
  saginata infestation 123.2
  solium (intestinal form) 123.0
    larval form 123.1
Taeniasis (intestine) — *see also* Infestation, taenia 123.3
  saginata 123.2
  solium 123.0
Taenzer's disease 757.4
Tag (hypertrophied skin) (infected) 701.9
  adenoid 474.8
  anus 455.9
  endocardial (*see also* Endocarditis) 424.90
  hemorrhoidal 455.9
  hymen 623.8
  perineal 624.8
  preauricular 744.1
  rectum 455.9
  sentinel 455.9
  skin 701.9
    accessory 757.39
    anus 455.9
    congenital 757.39
    preauricular 744.1
    rectum 455.9
  tonsil 474.8
  urethra, urethral 599.84
  vulva 624.8
Tahyna fever 062.5
Takayasu (-Onishi) disease or syndrome (pulseless disease) 446.7
Takotsubo syndrome 429.83
Talc granuloma 728.82
  in operation wound 998.7
Talcosis 502
Talipes (congenital) 754.70
  acquired NEC 736.79
    planus 734
  asymmetric 754.79
    acquired 736.79
  calcaneovalgus 754.62
    acquired 736.76
  calcaneovarus 754.59
    acquired 736.76
  calcaneus 754.79
    acquired 736.76
  cavovarus 754.59
    acquired 736.75
  cavus 754.71
    acquired 736.73
  equinovalgus 754.69
    acquired 736.72
  equinovarus 754.51
    acquired 736.71
  equinus 754.79
    acquired, NEC 736.72
  percavus 754.71
    acquired 736.73
  planovalgus 754.69
    acquired 736.79
  planus (acquired) (any degree) 734
    congenital 754.61
    due to rickets 268.1
  valgus 754.60
    acquired 736.79
  varus 754.50
    acquired 736.79
Talma's disease 728.85
Talon noir 924.20
  hand 923.20
  heel 924.20
  toe 924.3
Tamponade heart (Rose's) — *see also* Pericarditis 423.3
Tanapox 059.21
Tangier disease (familial high-density lipoprotein deficiency) 272.5
Tank ear 380.12
Tantrum (childhood) — *see also* Disturbance, conduct 312.1 ✓
Tapeworm (infection) (infestation) — *see also* Infestation, tapeworm 123.9
Tapia's syndrome 352.6
Tarantism 297.8
Target-oval cell anemia 282.49

Tarlov's cyst 355.9
Tarral-Besnier disease (pityriasis rubra pilaris) 696.4
Tarsalgia 729.2
Tarsal tunnel syndrome 355.5
Tarsitis (eyelid) 373.00
  syphilitic 095.8 *[373.00]*
  tuberculous (*see also* Tuberculosis) 017.0 ✓ *[373.4]*
Tartar (teeth) 523.6
Tattoo (mark) 709.09
Taurodontism 520.2
Taussig-Bing defect, heart, or syndrome (transposition, aorta and overriding pulmonary artery) 745.11
Taybi's syndrome (otopalatodigital) 759.89
Tay's choroiditis 363.41
Taylor's
  disease (diffuse idiopathic cutaneous atrophy) 701.8
  syndrome 625.5
Tay-Sachs
  amaurotic familial idiocy 330.1
  disease 330.1
TBI (traumatic brain injury) (*see also* Injury, intracranial) 854.0 ✓ ●
  with skull fracture — *see* Fracture, skull, by site ●
Tear stone 375.57
Tear, torn (traumatic) — *see also* Wound, open, by site
  anus, anal (sphincter) 863.89
    with open wound in cavity 863.99
    complicating delivery (healed) (old) 654.8 ✓
      with mucosa 664.3 ✓
      not associated with third-degree perineal laceration 664.6 ✓
    nontraumatic, nonpuerperal (healed) (old) 569.43
  articular cartilage, old (*see also* Disorder, cartilage, articular) 718.0 ✓
  bladder
    with
      abortion — *see* Abortion, by type, with damage to pelvic organs
      ectopic pregnancy (*see also* categories 633.0–633.9) 639.2
      molar pregnancy (*see also* categories 630–632) 639.2
    following
      abortion 639.2
      ectopic or molar pregnancy 639.2
    obstetrical trauma 665.5 ✓
  bowel
    with
      abortion — *see* Abortion, by type, with damage to pelvic organs
      ectopic pregnancy (*see also* categories 633.0–633.9) 639.2
      molar pregnancy (*see also* categories 630–632) 639.2
    following
      abortion 639.2
      ectopic or molar pregnancy 639.2
    obstetrical trauma 665.5 ✓
  broad ligament
    with
      abortion — *see* Abortion, by type, with damage to pelvic organs
      ectopic pregnancy (*see also* categories 633.0–633.9) 639.2
      molar pregnancy (*see also* categories 630–632) 639.2
    following
      abortion 639.2
      ectopic or molar pregnancy 639.2
    obstetrical trauma 665.6 ✓
  bucket handle (knee) (meniscus) — *see* Tear, meniscus
  capsule
    joint — *see* Sprain, by site
    spleen — *see* Laceration, spleen, capsule
  cartilage (*see also* Sprain, by site)
    articular, old (*see also* Disorder, cartilage, articular) 718.0 ✓

Tear, torn — *see also* Wound, open, by site — *continued*
  cartilage (*see also* Sprain, by site) — *continued*
    knee — *see* Tear, meniscus
    semilunar (knee) (current injury) — *see* Tear, meniscus
  cervix
    with
      abortion — *see* Abortion, by type, with damage to pelvic organs
      ectopic pregnancy (*see also* categories 633.0–633.9) 639.2
      molar pregnancy (*see also* categories 630–632) 639.2
    following
      abortion 639.2
      ectopic or molar pregnancy 639.2
    obstetrical trauma (current) 665.3 ✓
    old 622.3
  dural 349.31
    accidental puncture or laceration during a procedure 349.31
    incidental (inadvertent) 349.31
    nontraumatic NEC 349.39
  internal organ (abdomen, chest, or pelvis) — *see* Injury, internal, by site
  ligament (*see also* Sprain, by site)
    with open wound — *see* Wound, open, by site
  meniscus (knee) (current injury) 836.2
    bucket handle 836.0
      old 717.0
    lateral 836.1
      anterior horn 836.1
        old 717.42
      bucket handle 836.1
        old 717.41
      old 717.40
      posterior horn 836.1
        old 717.43
      specified site NEC 836.1
        old 717.49
    medial 836.0
      anterior horn 836.0
        old 717.1
      bucket handle 836.0
        old 717.0
      old 717.3
      posterior horn 836.0
        old 717.2
    old NEC 717.5
    site other than knee — *see* Sprain, by site
  muscle (*see also* Sprain, by site)
    with open wound — *see* Wound, open, by site
  pelvic
    floor, complicating delivery 664.1 ✓
    organ NEC
      with
        abortion — *see* Abortion, by type, with damage to pelvic organs
        ectopic pregnancy (*see also* categories 633.0–633.9) 639.2
        molar pregnancy (*see also* categories 630–632) 639.2
      following
        abortion 639.2
        ectopic or molar pregnancy 639.2
      obstetrical trauma 665.5 ✓
  perineum (*see also* Laceration, perineum)
    obstetrical trauma 665.5 ✓
  periurethral tissue
    with
      abortion — *see* Abortion, by type, with damage to pelvic organs
      ectopic pregnancy (*see also* categories 633.0–633.9) 639.2
      molar pregnancy (*see also* categories 630–632) 639.2
    following
      abortion 639.2
      ectopic or molar pregnancy 639.2
    obstetrical trauma 665.5 ✓

Tear, torn — *see also* Wound, open, by site — *continued*
  rectovaginal septum — *see* Laceration, rectovaginal septum
  retina, retinal (recent) (with detachment) 361.00
    without detachment 361.30
    dialysis (juvenile) (with detachment) 361.04
    giant (with detachment) 361.03
    horseshoe (without detachment) 361.32
    multiple (with detachment) 361.02
      without detachment 361.33
    old
      delimited (partial) 361.06
      partial 361.06
      total or subtotal 361.07
    partial (without detachment)
      giant 361.03
      multiple defects 361.02
      old (delimited) 361.06
      single defect 361.01
    round hole (without detachment) 361.31
    single defect (with detachment) 361.01
    total or subtotal (recent) 361.05
      old 361.07
  rotator cuff (traumatic) 840.4
    current injury 840.4
    degenerative 726.10
    nontraumatic 727.61
  semilunar cartilage, knee (*see also* Tear, meniscus) 836.2
    old 717.5
  tendon (*see also* Sprain, by site)
    with open wound — *see* Wound, open, by site
  tentorial, at birth 767.0
  umbilical cord
    affecting fetus or newborn 772.0
    complicating delivery 663.8 ✓
  urethra
    with
      abortion — *see* Abortion, by type, with damage to pelvic organs
      ectopic pregnancy (*see also* categories 633.0–633.9) 639.2
      molar pregnancy (*see also* categories 630–632) 639.2
    following
      abortion 639.2
      ectopic or molar pregnancy 639.2
    obstetrical trauma 665.5 ✓
  uterus — *see* Injury, internal, uterus
  vagina — *see* Laceration, vagina
  vessel, from catheter 998.2
  vulva, complicating delivery 664.0 ✓
Teething 520.7
  syndrome 520.7
Teeth, tooth — *see also* condition
  grinding 306.8
  prenatal 520.6
Tegmental syndrome 344.89
Telangiectasia, telangiectasis (verrucous) 448.9
  ataxic (cerebellar) 334.8
  familial 448.0
  hemorrhagic, hereditary (congenital) (senile) 448.0
  hereditary hemorrhagic 448.0
  retina 362.15
  spider 448.1
Telecanthus (congenital) 743.63
Telescoped bowel or intestine — *see also* Intussusception 560.0
Teletherapy, adverse effect NEC 990
Telogen effluvium 704.02
Temperature
  body, high (of unknown origin) (*see also* Pyrexia) 780.60
  cold, trauma from 991.9
    newborn 778.2
    specified effect NEC 991.8
  high
    body (of unknown origin) (*see also* Pyrexia) 780.60
    trauma from — *see* Heat

✓ Additional Digit Required — Refer to the Tabular List for Digit Selection   ▽ Subterms under main terms may continue to next column or page

2010 ICD-9-CM   ►◄ Revised Text   ● New Line   ▲ Revised Code   October 2009 • Volume 2 — 267

Temper tantrum (childhood) — *see also* Disturbance, conduct 312.1 ☑
Temple — *see* condition
Temporal — *see also* condition
  lobe syndrome 310.0
Temporomandibular joint-pain-dysfunction syndrome 524.60
Temporosphenoidal — *see* condition
Tendency
  bleeding (*see also* Defect, coagulation) 286.9
  homosexual, ego-dystonic 302.0
  paranoid 301.0
  suicide 300.9
Tenderness
  abdominal (generalized) (localized) 789.6 ☑
  rebound 789.6 ☑
  skin 782.0
Tendinitis, tendonitis — *see also* Tenosynovitis 726.90
  Achilles 726.71
  adhesive 726.90
    shoulder 726.0
  calcific 727.82
    shoulder 726.11
  gluteal 726.5
  patellar 726.64
  peroneal 726.79
  pes anserinus 726.61
  psoas 726.5
  tibialis (anterior) (posterior) 726.72
  trochanteric 726.5
Tendon — *see* condition
Tendosynovitis — *see* Tenosynovitis
Tendovaginitis — *see* Tenosynovitis
Tenesmus 787.99
  rectal 787.99
  vesical 788.99
Tenia — *see* Taenia
Teniasis — *see* Taeniasis
Tennis elbow 726.32
Tenonitis — *see also* Tenosynovitis
  eye (capsule) 376.04
Tenontosynovitis — *see* Tenosynovitis
Tenontothecitis — *see* Tenosynovitis
Tenophyte 727.9
Tenosynovitis (*see also* Synovitis) 727.00
  adhesive 726.90
    shoulder 726.0
  ankle 727.06
  bicipital (calcifying) 726.12
  buttock 727.09
  due to crystals — *see* Arthritis, due to crystals
  elbow 727.09
  finger 727.05
  foot 727.06
  gonococcal 098.51
  hand 727.05
  hip 727.09
  knee 727.09
  radial styloid 727.04
  shoulder 726.10
    adhesive 726.0
  specified NEC 727.09
  spine 720.1
  supraspinatus 726.10
  toe 727.06
  tuberculous — *see* Tuberculosis, tenosynovitis
  wrist 727.05
Tenovaginitis — *see* Tenosynovitis
Tension
  arterial, high (*see also* Hypertension) 401.9
    without diagnosis of hypertension 796.2
  headache 307.81
  intraocular (elevated) 365.00
  nervous 799.21 ▲
  ocular (elevated) 365.00
  pneumothorax 512.0
    iatrogenic 512.1
    postoperative 512.1
    spontaneous 512.0
  premenstrual 625.4
  state 300.9
Tentorium — *see* condition
Teratencephalus 759.89
Teratism 759.7

Teratoblastoma (malignant) (M9080/3) — *see* Neoplasm, by site, malignant
Teratocarcinoma (M9081/3) — *see also* Neoplasm, by site, malignant
  liver 155.0
Teratoma (solid) (M9080/1) — *see also* Neoplasm, by site, uncertain behavior
  adult (cystic) (M9080/0) — *see* Neoplasm, by site, benign
  and embryonal carcinoma, mixed (M9081/3) — *see* Neoplasm, by site, malignant
  benign (M9080/0) — *see* Neoplasm, by site, benign
  combined with choriocarcinoma (M9101/3) — *see* Neoplasm, by site, malignant
  cystic (adult) (M9080/0) — *see* Neoplasm, by site, benign
  differentiated type (M9080/0) — *see* Neoplasm, by site, benign
  embryonal (M9080/3) (*see also* Neoplasm, by site, malignant)
    liver 155.0
  fetal
    sacral, causing fetopelvic disproportion 653.7 ☑
  immature (M9080/3) — *see* Neoplasm, by site, malignant
  liver (M9080/3) 155.0
    adult, benign, cystic, differentiated type or mature (M9080/0) 211.5
  malignant (M9080/3) (*see also* Neoplasm, by site, malignant)
    anaplastic type (M9082/3) — *see* Neoplasm, by site, malignant
    intermediate type (M9083/3) — *see* Neoplasm, by site, malignant
    liver (M9080/3) 155.0
    trophoblastic (M9102/3)
      specified site — *see* Neoplasm, by site, malignant
      unspecified site 186.9
    undifferentiated type (M9082/3) — *see* Neoplasm, by site, malignant
  mature (M9080/0) — *see* Neoplasm, by site, benign
  malignant (M9080/3) — *see* Neoplasm, by site, malignant
  ovary (M9080/0) 220
    embryonal, immature, or malignant (M9080/3) 183.0
  suprasellar (M9080/3) — *see* Neoplasm, by site, malignant
  testis (M9080/3) 186.9
    adult, benign, cystic, differentiated type or mature (M9080/0) 222.0
    undescended 186.0
Terminal care V66.7
Termination
  anomalous (*see also* Malposition, congenital)
    portal vein 747.49
    right pulmonary vein 747.42
  pregnancy (legal) (therapeutic) — *see* Abortion, legal 635.9 ☑
    fetus NEC 779.6
    illegal (*see also* Abortion, illegal) 636.9 ☑
Ternidens diminutus infestation 127.7
Terrors, night (child) 307.46
Terry's syndrome (*see also* Retinopathy of prematurity) 362.21
Tertiary — *see* condition
Tessellated fundus, retina (tigroid) 362.89
Test(s)
  adequacy
    hemodialysis V56.31
    peritoneal dialysis V56.32
  AIDS virus V72.69 ▲
  allergen V72.7
  bacterial disease NEC (*see also* Screening, by name of disease) V74.9
  basal metabolic rate V72.69
  blood
    alcohol V70.4 ●
    drug V70.4 ●
    for therapeutic drug monitoring V58.83 ●

Test(s) — *continued*
  blood — *continued*
    for routine general physical examination ● V72.62
    prior to treatment or procedure V72.63 ●
    typing V72.86 ●
      Rh typing V72.86 ●
  developmental, infant or child V20.2
  Dick V74.8
  fertility V26.21
  genetic
    female V26.32
    for genetic disease carrier status
      female V26.31
      male V26.34
    male V26.39
  hearing V72.19
    following failed hearing screening V72.11
    routine, for infant and child V20.2 ●
  HIV V72.69 ▲
  human immunodeficiency virus V72.69 ▲
  immunity status V72.61 ●
  Kveim V82.89
  laboratory V72.60 ▲
    for medicolegal reason V70.4
    ordered as part of a routine general ● medical examination V72.62 ●
    pre-operative V72.63 ●
    pre-procedural V72.63 ●
    specified NEC V72.69 ●
  male partner of habitual aborter V26.35
  Mantoux (for tuberculosis) V74.1
  mycotic organism V75.4
  nuchal translucency V28.89
  parasitic agent NEC V75.8
  paternity V70.4
  peritoneal equilibration V56.32
  pregnancy
    negative result V72.41
    positive result V72.42
      first pregnancy V72.42
    unconfirmed V72.40
  preoperative V72.84
    cardiovascular V72.81
    respiratory V72.82
    specified NEC V72.83
  procreative management NEC V26.29
    genetic disease carrier status
      female V26.31
      male V26.34
  Rh typing V72.86
  sarcoidosis V82.89
  Schick V74.3
  Schultz-Charlton V74.8
  skin, diagnostic
    allergy V72.7
    bacterial agent NEC (*see also* Screening, by name of disease) V74.9
    Dick V74.8
    hypersensitivity V72.7
    Kveim V82.89
    Mantoux V74.1
    mycotic organism V75.4
    parasitic agent NEC V75.8
    sarcoidosis V82.89
    Schick V74.3
    Schultz-Charlton V74.8
    tuberculin V74.1
  specified type NEC V72.85
  tuberculin V74.1
  vision V72.0
    routine, for infant and child V20.2 ●
  Wassermann
    positive (*see also* Serology for syphilis, positive) 097.1
    false 795.6
Testicle, testicular, testis — *see also* condition
  feminization (syndrome) 259.51
Tetanus, tetanic (cephalic) (convulsions) 037
  with
    abortion — *see* Abortion, by type, with sepsis
    ectopic pregnancy (*see also* categories 633.0–633.9) 639.0
    molar pregnancy — *see* categories 630–632 639.0

Tetanus, tetanic — *continued*
  following
    abortion 639.0
    ectopic or molar pregnancy 639.0
  inoculation V03.7
    reaction (due to serum) — *see* Complications, vaccination
  neonatorum 771.3
  puerperal, postpartum, childbirth 670.8 ☑ ▲
Tetany, tetanic 781.7
  alkalosis 276.3
  associated with rickets 268.0
  convulsions 781.7
    hysterical 300.11
  functional (hysterical) 300.11
  hyperkinetic 781.7
    hysterical 300.11
    psychogenic 306.1
  hyperpnea 786.01
    hysterical 300.11
    psychogenic 306.1
  hyperventilation 786.01
    hysterical 300.11
    psychogenic 306.1
  hypocalcemic, neonatal 775.4
  hysterical 300.11
  neonatal 775.4
  parathyroid (gland) 252.1
  parathyroprival 252.1
  postoperative 252.1
  postthyroidectomy 252.1
  pseudotetany 781.7
    hysterical 300.11
  psychogenic 306.1
    specified as conversion reaction 300.11
Tetralogy of Fallot 745.2
Tetraplegia — *see* Quadriplegia
Thailand hemorrhagic fever 065.4
Thalassanemia 282.49
Thalassemia (alpha) (beta) (disease) (Hb-C) (Hb-D) (Hb-E) (Hb-H) (Hb-I) (high fetal gene) (high fetal hemoglobin) (intermedia) (major) (minima) (minor) (mixed) (trait) (with other hemoglobinopathy) 282.49
  Hb-S (without crisis) 282.41
    with
      crisis 282.42
      vaso-occlusive pain 282.42
  sickle-cell (without crisis) 282.41
    with
      crisis 282.42
      vaso-occlusive pain 282.42
Thalassemic variants 282.49
Thaysen-Gee disease (nontropical sprue) 579.0 ●
Thecoma (M8600/0) 220
  malignant (M8600/3) 183.0
Thelarche, precocious 259.1
Thelitis 611.0
  puerperal, postpartum 675.0 ☑
Therapeutic — *see* condition
Therapy V57.9
  blood transfusion, without reported diagnosis V58.2
  breathing V57.0
  chemotherapy, antineoplastic V58.11
    fluoride V07.31
    prophylactic NEC V07.39
  dialysis (intermittent) (treatment)
    extracorporeal V56.0
    peritoneal V56.8
    renal V56.0
    specified type NEC V56.8
  exercise NEC V57.1
    breathing V57.0
  extracorporeal dialysis (renal) V56.0
  fluoride prophylaxis V07.31
  hemodialysis V56.0
  hormone replacement (postmenopausal) V07.4
  immunotherapy antineoplastic V58.12
  long term oxygen therapy V46.2
  occupational V57.21
  orthoptic V57.4
  orthotic V57.81
  peritoneal dialysis V56.8
  physical NEC V57.1

☑ Additional Digit Required — Refer to the Tabular List for Digit Selection

▽ Subterms under main terms may continue to next column or page

Therapy — *continued*
  postmenopausal hormone replacement V07.4
  radiation V58.0
  speech ►(-language)◄ V57.3
  vocational V57.22
Thermalgesia 782.0
Thermalgia 782.0
Thermanalgesia 782.0
Thermanesthesia 782.0
Thermic — *see* condition
Thermography (abnormal) 793.99
  breast 793.89
Thermoplegia 992.0
Thesaurismosis
  amyloid 277.39
  bilirubin 277.4
  calcium 275.40
  cystine 270.0
  glycogen (*see also* Disease, glycogen storage) 271.0
  kerasin 272.7
  lipoid 272.7
  melanin 255.41
  phosphatide 272.7
  urate 274.9
Thiaminic deficiency 265.1
  with beriberi 265.0
Thibierge-Weissenbach syndrome (cutaneous systemic sclerosis) 710.1
Thickened endometrium 793.5
Thickening
  bone 733.99
    extremity 733.99
  breast 611.79
  hymen 623.3
  larynx 478.79
  nail 703.8
    congenital 757.5
  periosteal 733.99
  pleura (*see also* Pleurisy) 511.0
  skin 782.8
  subepiglottic 478.79
  tongue 529.8
  valve, heart — *see* Endocarditis
Thiele syndrome 724.6
Thigh — *see* condition
Thinning vertebra — *see also* Osteoporosis 733.00
Thirst, excessive 783.5
  due to deprivation of water 994.3
Thomsen's disease 359.22
Thomson's disease (congenital poikiloderma) 757.33
Thoracic — *see also* condition
  kidney 753.3
  outlet syndrome 353.0
  stomach — *see* Hernia, diaphragm
Thoracogastroschisis (congenital) 759.89
Thoracopagus 759.4
Thoracoschisis 756.3
Thoracoscopic surgical procedure converted to open procedure V64.42
Thorax — *see* condition
Thorn's syndrome — *see also* Disease, renal 593.9
Thornwaldt's, Tornwaldt's
  bursitis (pharyngeal) 478.29
  cyst 478.26
  disease (pharyngeal bursitis) 478.29
Thorson-Biörck syndrome (malignant carcinoid) 259.2
Threadworm (infection) (infestation) 127.4
Threatened
  abortion or miscarriage 640.0 ☑
    with subsequent abortion (*see also* Abortion, spontaneous) 634.9 ☑
      affecting fetus 762.1
    labor 644.1 ☑
      affecting fetus or newborn 761.8
      premature 644.0 ☑
    miscarriage 640.0 ☑
      affecting fetus 762.1
    premature
      delivery 644.2 ☑
        affecting fetus or newborn 761.8
      labor 644.0 ☑

Threatened — *continued*
  premature — *continued*
    labor — *continued*
      before 22 completed weeks gestation 640.0 ☑
Three-day fever 066.0
Threshers' lung 495.0
Thrix annulata (congenital) 757.4
Throat — *see* condition
Thrombasthenia (Glanzmann's) (hemorrhagic) (hereditary) 287.1
Thromboangiitis 443.1
  obliterans (general) 443.1
    cerebral 437.1
    vessels
      brain 437.1
      spinal cord 437.1
Thromboarteritis — *see* Arteritis
Thromboasthenia (Glanzmann's) (hemorrhagic) (hereditary) 287.1
Thrombocytasthenia (Glanzmann's) 287.1
Thrombocythemia (primary) (M9962/1) 238.71
  essential 238.71
  hemorrhagic 238.71
  idiopathic (hemorrhagic) (M9962/1) 238.71
Thrombocytopathy (dystrophic) (granulopenic) 287.1
Thrombocytopenia, thrombocytopenic 287.5
  with
    absent radii (TAR) syndrome
    giant hemangioma
  amegakaryocytic, congenital 287.33
  congenital 287.33
  cyclic 287.39
  dilutional 287.4
  due to
    drugs 287.4
    extracorporeal circulation of blood 287.4
    massive blood transfusion 287.4
    platelet alloimmunization 287.4
  essential 287.30
  fetal 678.0 ☑
  heparin-induced (HIT) 289.84
  hereditary 287.33
  Kasabach-Merritt 287.39
  neonatal, transitory 776.1
    due to
      exchange transfusion 776.1
      idiopathic maternal thrombocytopenia 776.1
      isoimmunization 776.1
  primary 287.30
  puerperal, postpartum 666.3 ☑
  purpura (*see also* Purpura, thrombocytopenic) 287.30
    thrombotic 446.6
  secondary 287.4
  sex-linked 287.39
Thrombocytosis 238.71
  essential 238.71
  primary 238.71
Thromboembolism — *see* Embolism
Thrombopathy (Bernard-Soulier) 287.1
  constitutional 286.4
  Willebrand-Jürgens (angiohemophilia) 286.4
Thrombopenia — *see also* Thrombocytopenia 287.5
Thrombophlebitis 451.9
  antecubital vein 451.82
  antepartum (superficial) 671.2 ☑
    affecting fetus or newborn 760.3
    deep 671.3 ☑
  arm 451.89
    deep 451.83
    superficial 451.82
  breast, superficial 451.89
  cavernous (venous) sinus — *see* Thrombophlebitis, intracranial venous sinus
  cephalic vein 451.82
  cerebral (sinus) (vein) 325
    late effect — *see* category 326
    nonpyogenic 437.6
      in pregnancy or puerperium 671.5 ☑
      late effect — *see* Late effect(s) (of) cerebrovascular disease

Thrombophlebitis — *continued*
  due to implanted device — *see* Complications, due to (presence of) any device, implant or graft classified to 996.0–996.5 NEC
  during or resulting from a procedure NEC 997.2
  femoral 451.11
  femoropopliteal 451.19
  following infusion, perfusion, or transfusion 999.2
  hepatic (vein) 451.89
  idiopathic, recurrent 453.1
  iliac vein 451.81
  iliofemoral 451.11
  intracranial venous sinus (any) 325
    late effect — *see* category 326
    nonpyogenic 437.6
      in pregnancy or puerperium 671.5 ☑
      late effect — *see* Late effect(s) (of) cerebrovascular disease
  jugular vein 451.89
  lateral (venous) sinus — *see* Thrombophlebitis, intracranial venous sinus
  leg 451.2
    deep (vessels) 451.19
      femoral vein 451.11
      specified vessel NEC 451.19
    superficial (vessels) 451.0
      femoral vein 451.11
  longitudinal (venous) sinus — *see* Thrombophlebitis, intracranial venous sinus
  lower extremity 451.2
    deep (vessels) 451.19
      femoral vein 451.11
      specified vessel NEC 451.19
    superficial (vessels) 451.0
  migrans, migrating 453.1
  pelvic
    with
      abortion — *see* Abortion, by type, with sepsis
      ectopic pregnancy (*see also* categories 633.0–633.9) 639.0
      molar pregnancy (*see also* categories 630–632) 639.0
    following
      abortion 639.0
      ectopic or molar pregnancy 639.0
    puerperal 671.4 ☑
  popliteal vein 451.19
  portal (vein) 572.1
  postoperative 997.2
  pregnancy (superficial) 671.2 ☑
    affecting fetus or newborn 760.3
    deep 671.3 ☑
  puerperal, postpartum, childbirth (extremities) (superficial) 671.2 ☑
    deep 671.4 ☑
    pelvic 671.4 ☑
    septic 670.3 ☑ ●
    specified site NEC 671.5 ☑
  radial vein 451.83
  saphenous (greater) (lesser) 451.0
  sinus (intracranial) — *see* Thrombophlebitis, intracranial venous sinus
  specified site NEC 451.89
  tibial vein 451.19
Thrombosis, thrombotic (marantic) (multiple) (progressive) (vein) (vessel) 453.9
  with childbirth or during the puerperium — *see* Thrombosis, puerperal, postpartum
  antepartum — *see* Thrombosis, pregnancy
  aorta, aortic 444.1
    abdominal 444.0
    bifurcation 444.0
    saddle 444.0
    terminal 444.0
    thoracic 444.1
    valve — *see* Endocarditis, aortic
  apoplexy (*see also* Thrombosis, brain) 434.0 ☑
    late effect — *see* Late effect(s) (of) cerebrovascular disease
  appendix, septic — *see* Appendicitis, acute
  arteriolar-capillary platelet, disseminated 446.6
  artery, arteries (postinfectional) 444.9

Thrombosis, thrombotic — *continued*
  artery, arteries — *continued*
    auditory, internal 433.8 ☑
    basilar (*see also* Occlusion, artery, basilar) 433.0 ☑
    carotid (common) (internal) (*see also* Occlusion, artery, carotid) 433.1 ☑
      with other precerebral artery 433.3 ☑
    cerebellar (anterior inferior) (posterior inferior) (superior) 433.8 ☑
    cerebral (*see also* Thrombosis, brain) 434.0 ☑
    choroidal (anterior) 433.8 ☑
    communicating posterior 433.8 ☑
    coronary (*see also* Infarct, myocardium) 410.9 ☑
      without myocardial infarction 411.81
      due to syphilis 093.89
      healed or specified as old 412
    extremities 444.22
      lower 444.22
      upper 444.21
    femoral 444.22
    hepatic 444.89
    hypophyseal 433.8 ☑
    meningeal, anterior or posterior 433.8 ☑
    mesenteric (with gangrene) 557.0
    ophthalmic (*see also* Occlusion, retina) 362.30
    pontine 433.8 ☑
    popliteal 444.22
    precerebral — *see* Occlusion, artery, precerebral NEC
    pulmonary 415.19
      iatrogenic 415.11
      personal history of V12.51 ●
      postoperative 415.11
      septic 415.12
    renal 593.81
    retinal (*see also* Occlusion, retina) 362.30
    specified site NEC 444.89
    spinal, anterior or posterior 433.8 ☑
    traumatic (complication) (early) (*see also* Injury, blood vessel, by site) 904.9
    vertebral (*see also* Occlusion, artery, vertebral) 433.2 ☑
      with other precerebral artery 433.3 ☑
  atrial (endocardial) 424.90
    without endocarditis 429.89
    due to syphilis 093.89
  auricular (*see also* Infarct, myocardium) 410.9 ☑
  axillary ►(acute)◄ (vein) 453.84 ▲
    chronic 453.74 ●
    personal history of V12.51 ●
  basilar (artery) (*see also* Occlusion, artery, basilar) 433.0 ☑
  bland NEC 453.9
  brain (artery) (stem) 434.0 ☑
    due to syphilis 094.89
    iatrogenic 997.02
    late effect — *see* Late effect(s) (of) cerebrovascular disease
    postoperative 997.02
    puerperal, postpartum, childbirth 674.0 ☑
    sinus (*see also* Thrombosis, intracranial venous sinus) 325
  capillary 448.9
    arteriolar, generalized 446.6
  cardiac (*see also* Infarct, myocardium) 410.9 ☑
    due to syphilis 093.89
    healed or specified as old 412
    valve — *see* Endocarditis
  carotid (artery) (common) (internal) (*see also* Occlusion, artery, carotid) 433.1 ☑
    with other precerebral artery 433.3 ☑
  cavernous sinus (venous) — *see* Thrombosis, intracranial venous sinus
  cerebellar artery (anterior inferior) (posterior inferior) (superior) 433.8 ☑
    late effect — *see* Late effect(s) (of) cerebrovascular disease
  cerebral (arteries) (*see also* Thrombosis, brain) 434.0 ☑

☑ Additional Digit Required — Refer to the Tabular List for Digit Selection

▼ Subterms under main terms may continue to next column or page

2010 ICD-9-CM

►◄ Revised Text   ● New Line   ▲ Revised Code

October 2009 • Volume 2 — 269

Therapy — Thrombosis, thrombotic

Thrombosis, thrombotic — *continued*
  cerebral (*see also* Thrombosis, brain) — *continued*
    late effect — *see* Late effect(s) (of) cerebrovascular disese
  coronary (artery) (*see also* Infarct, myocardium) 410.9 ☑
    without myocardial infarction 411.81
    due to syphilis 093.89
    healed or specified as old 412
  corpus cavernosum 607.82
  cortical (*see also* Thrombosis, brain) 434.0 ☑
  due to (presence of) any device, implant, or graft classifiable to 996.0–996.5 — *see* Complications, due to (presence of) any device, implant, or graft classified to 996.0–996.5 NEC
  effort 453.89 ▲
  endocardial — *see* Infarct, myocardium
  eye (*see also* Occlusion, retina) 362.30
  femoral (vein) 453.6 ▲
    with inflammation or phlebitis 451.11
    artery 444.22
    deep 453.41
    personal history of V12.51 ●
  genital organ, male 608.83
  heart (chamber) (*see also* Infarct, myocardium) 410.9 ☑
  hepatic (vein) 453.0
    artery 444.89
    infectional or septic 572.1
  iliac (vein) 453.89 ▲
    with inflammation or phlebitis 451.81
    artery (common) (external) (internal) 444.81
    personal history of V12.51 ●
  inflammation, vein — *see* Thrombophlebitis
  internal carotid artery (*see also* Occlusion, artery, carotid) 433.1 ☑
    with other precerebral artery 433.3 ☑
  intestine (with gangrene) 557.0
  intracranial (*see also* Thrombosis, brain) 434.0 ☑
    venous sinus (any) 325
      nonpyogenic origin 437.6
        in pregnancy or puerperium 671.5 ☑
  intramural (*see also* Infarct, myocardium) 410.9 ☑
    without
      cardiac condition 429.89
      coronary artery disease 429.89
      myocardial infarction 429.89
    healed or specified as old 412
  jugular (bulb)
    external
      acute 453.89 ●
      chronic 453.79 ●
    internal
      acute 453.86 ●
      chronic 453.76 ●
  kidney 593.81
    artery 593.81
  lateral sinus (venous) — *see* Thrombosis, intracranial venous sinus
  leg ▶(*see also* Thrombosis, lower extremity)◀ 453.6 ▲
    with inflammation or phlebitis — *see* Thrombophlebitis
    deep (vessels) 453.40
      acute 453.40 ●
        lower distal 453.42 ●
        upper (proximal) 453.41 ●
      chronic 453.50 ●
        lower (distal) 453.52 ●
        upper (proximal) 453.51 ●
      lower (distal) 453.42
      upper (proximal) 453.41
    personal history of V12.51 ●
    superficial (vessels) 453.6 ▲
  liver (venous) 453.0
    artery 444.89
    infectional or septic 572.1
    portal vein 452
  longitudinal sinus (venous) — *see* Thrombosis, intracranial venous sinus

Thrombosis, thrombotic — *continued*
  lower extremity ▶(superficial)◀ 453.6 ▲
    deep vessels 453.40
      acute 453.40 ●
        calf 453.42 ●
        distal (lower leg) 453.42 ●
        femoral 453.41 ●
        iliac 453.41 ●
        lower leg 453.42 ●
        peroneal 453.42 ●
        popliteal 453.41 ●
        proximal (upper leg) 453.41 ●
        thigh 453.41 ●
        tibial 453.42 ●
      chronic 453.50 ●
        calf 453.52 ●
        distal (lower leg) 453.52 ●
        femoral 453.51 ●
        iliac 453.51 ●
        lower leg 453.52 ●
        peroneal 453.52 ●
        popliteal 453.51 ●
        proximal (upper leg) 453.51 ●
        thigh 453.51 ●
        tibial 453.52 ●
    personal history of V12.51 ●
    saphenous (greater) (lesser) 453.6 ●
    superficial 453.6 ●
  lung 415.19
    iatrogenic 415.11
    personal history of V12.51 ●
    postoperative 415.11
    septic 415.12
  marantic, dural sinus 437.6
  meninges (brain) (*see also* Thrombosis, brain) 434.0 ☑
  mesenteric (artery) (with gangrene) 557.0
    vein (inferior) (superior) 557.0
  mitral — *see* Insufficiency, mitral
  mural (heart chamber) (*see also* Infarct, myocardium) 410.9 ☑
    without
      cardiac condition 429.89
      coronary artery disease 429.89
      myocardial infarction 429.89
    due to syphilis 093.89
    following myocardial infarction 429.79
    healed or specified as old 412
  omentum (with gangrene) 557.0
  ophthalmic (artery) (*see also* Occlusion, retina) 362.30
  pampiniform plexus (male) 608.83
    female 620.8
  parietal (*see also* Infarct, myocardium) 410.9 ☑
  penis, penile 607.82
  peripheral arteries 444.22
    lower 444.22
    upper 444.21
  platelet 446.6
  portal 452
    due to syphilis 093.89
    infectional or septic 572.1
  precerebral artery (*see also* Occlusion, artery, precerebral NEC)
  pregnancy 671.2 ☑ ▲
    deep (vein) 671.3 ☑
    superficial (vein) 671.2 ☑
  puerperal, postpartum, childbirth 671.2 ☑ ▲
    brain (artery) 674.0 ☑
      venous 671.5 ☑
    cardiac 674.8 ☑
    cerebral (artery) 674.0 ☑
      venous 671.5 ☑
    deep (vein) 671.4 ☑
    intracranial sinus (nonpyogenic) (venous) 671.5 ☑
    pelvic 671.4 ☑
    pulmonary (artery) 673.2 ☑
    specified site NEC 671.5 ☑
    superficial 671.2 ☑
  pulmonary (artery) (vein) 415.19
    iatrogenic 415.11
    personal history of V12.51 ●
    postoperative 415.11
    septic 415.12

Thrombosis, thrombotic — *continued*
  renal (artery) 593.81
    vein 453.3
  resulting from presence of shunt or other internal prosthetic device — *see* Complications, due to (presence of) any device, implant, or graft classified to 996.0–996.5 NEC
  retina, retinal (artery) 362.30
    arterial branch 362.32
    central 362.31
    partial 362.33
    vein
      central 362.35
      tributary (branch) 362.36
  saphenous vein (greater) (lesser) 453.6 ●
  scrotum 608.83
  seminal vesicle 608.83
  sigmoid (venous) sinus — *see* Thrombosis, intracranial venous sinus 325
  silent NEC 453.9
  sinus, intracranial (venous) (any) (*see also* Thrombosis, intracranial venous sinus) 325
  softening, brain (*see also* Thrombosis, brain) 434.0 ☑
  specified site NEC ▶(acute)◀ 453.89 ▲
    chronic 453.79 ●
  spermatic cord 608.83
  spinal cord 336.1
    due to syphilis 094.89
    in pregnancy or puerperium 671.5 ☑
    pyogenic origin 324.1
      late effect — *see* category 326
  spleen, splenic 289.59
    artery 444.89
  testis 608.83
  traumatic (complication) (early) (*see also* Injury, blood vessel, by site) 904.9
  tricuspid — *see* Endocarditis, tricuspid
  tumor — *see* Neoplasm, by site
  tunica vaginalis 608.83
  umbilical cord (vessels) 663.6 ☑
    affecting fetus or newborn 762.6
  upper extremity 453.83 ●
    acute 453.83 ●
      deep 453.82 ●
      superficial 453.81 ●
    chronic 453.73 ●
      deep 453.72 ●
      superficial 453.71 ●
  vas deferens 608.83
  vein
    antecubital
      acute 453.81 ●
      chronic 453.71 ●
    axillary
      acute 453.84 ●
      chronic 453.74 ●
    basilic
      acute 453.81 ●
      chronic 453.71 ●
    brachial
      acute 453.82 ●
      chronic 453.72 ●
    brachiocephalic (innominate)
      acute 453.87 ●
      chronic 453.77 ●
    cephalic
      acute 453.81 ●
      chronic 453.71 ●
    deep 453.40
      personal history of V12.51 ●
    internal jugular
      acute 453.86 ●
      chronic 453.76 ●
    lower extremity — *see* Thrombosis, lower extremity
    personal history of V12.51 ●
    radial
      acute 453.82 ●
      chronic 453.72 ●
    saphenous (greater) (lesser) 453.6 ●
    specified site NEC
      acute 453.89 ●
      chronic 453.79 ●

Thrombosis, thrombotic — *continued*
  vein — *continued*
    subclavian
      acute 453.85 ●
      chronic 453.75 ●
    superior vena cava
      acute 453.87 ●
      chronic 453.77 ●
    thoracic
      acute 453.87 ●
      chronic 453.77 ●
    ulnar
      acute 453.82 ●
      chronic 453.72 ●
    upper extremity — *see* Thrombosis, upper extremity ●
  vena cava
    inferior 453.2
    personal history of V12.51 ●
    superior
      acute 453.87 ●
      chronic 453.77 ●
Thrombus — *see* Thrombosis
Thrush 112.0
  newborn 771.7
Thumb — *see also* condition
  gamekeeper's 842.12
  sucking (child problem) 307.9
Thygeson's superficial punctate keratitis 370.21
Thymergasia — *see also* Psychosis, affective 296.80
Thymitis 254.8
Thymoma (benign) (M8580/0) 212.6
  malignant (M8580/3) 164.0
Thymus, thymic (gland) — *see* condition
Thyrocele — *see also* Goiter 240.9
Thyroglossal — *see also* condition
  cyst 759.2
  duct, persistent 759.2
Thyroid (body) (gland) — *see also* condition
  hormone resistance 246.8
  lingual 759.2
Thyroiditis 245.9
  acute (pyogenic) (suppurative) 245.0
    nonsuppurative 245.0
  autoimmune 245.2
  chronic (nonspecific) (sclerosing) 245.8
    fibrous 245.3
    lymphadenoid 245.2
    lymphocytic 245.2
    lymphoid 245.2
  complicating pregnancy, childbirth, or puerperium 648.1 ☑
  de Quervain's (subacute granulomatous) 245.1
  fibrous (chronic) 245.3
  giant (cell) (follicular) 245.1
  granulomatous (de Quervain's) (subacute) 245.1
  Hashimoto's (struma lymphomatosa) 245.2
  iatrogenic 245.4
  invasive (fibrous) 245.3
  ligneous 245.3
  lymphocytic (chronic) 245.2
  lymphoid 245.2
  lymphomatous 245.2
  pseudotuberculous 245.1
  pyogenic 245.0
  radiation 245.4
  Riedel's (ligneous) 245.3
  subacute 245.1
  suppurative 245.0
  tuberculous (*see also* Tuberculosis) 017.5 ☑
  viral 245.1
  woody 245.3
Thyrolingual duct, persistent 759.2
Thyromegaly 240.9
Thyrotoxic
  crisis or storm (*see also* Thyrotoxicosis) 242.9 ☑
  heart failure (*see also* Thyrotoxicosis) 242.9 ☑ [425.7]

hyrotoxicosis 242.9 ✓

Note — Use the following fifth-digit subclassification with category 242:

0   *without mention of thyrotoxic crisis or storm*

1   *with mention of thyrotoxic crisis or storm*

with
   goiter (diffuse) 242.0 ✓
      adenomatous 242.3 ✓
         multinodular 242.2 ✓
         uninodular 242.1 ✓
      nodular 242.3 ✓
         multinodular 242.2 ✓
         uninodular 242.1 ✓
   infiltrative
      dermopathy 242.0 ✓
      ophthalmopathy 242.0 ✓
   thyroid acropachy 242.0 ✓
   complicating pregnancy, childbirth, or puerperium 648.1 ✓
   due to
      ectopic thyroid nodule 242.4 ✓
      ingestion of (excessive) thyroid material 242.8 ✓
      specified cause NEC 242.8 ✓
   factitia 242.8 ✓
   heart 242.9 ✓ [425.7]
   neonatal (transient) 775.3
TIA (transient ischemic attack) 435.9
   with transient neurologic deficit 435.9
   late effect — *see* Late effect(s) (of) cerebrovascular disease
Tibia vara 732.4
Tic 307.20
   breathing 307.20
   child problem 307.21
   compulsive 307.22
   convulsive 307.20
   degenerative (generalized) (localized) 333.3
      facial 351.8
   douloureux (*see also* Neuralgia, trigeminal) 350.1
      atypical 350.2
   habit 307.20
      chronic (motor or vocal) 307.22
      transient (of childhood) 307.21
   lid 307.20
      transient (of childhood) 307.21
   motor-verbal 307.23
   occupational 300.89
   orbicularis 307.20
      transient (of childhood) 307.21
   organic origin 333.3
   postchoreic — *see* Chorea
   psychogenic 307.20
      compulsive 307.22
   salaam 781.0
   spasm 307.20
      chronic (motor or vocal) 307.22
      transient (of childhood) 307.21
Tick-bite fever NEC 066.1
   African 087.1
   Colorado (virus) 066.1
   Rocky Mountain 082.0
Tick (-borne) fever NEC 066.1
   American mountain 066.1
   Colorado 066.1
   hemorrhagic NEC 065.3
      Crimean 065.0
      Kyasanur Forest 065.2
      Omsk 065.1
   mountain 066.1
   nonxanthematous 066.1
Tick paralysis 989.5
Tics and spasms, compulsive 307.22
Tietze's disease or syndrome 733.6
Tight, tightness
   anus 564.89
   chest 786.59
   fascia (lata) 728.9
   foreskin (congenital) 605
   hymen 623.3
   introitus (acquired) (congenital) 623.3

Tight, tightness — *continued*
   rectal sphincter 564.89
   tendon 727.81
      Achilles (heel) 727.81
   urethral sphincter 598.9
Tilting vertebra 737.9
Timidity, child 313.21
Tinea (intersecta) (tarsi) 110.9
   amiantacea 110.0
   asbestina 110.0
   barbae 110.0
   beard 110.0
   black dot 110.0
   blanca 111.2
   capitis 110.0
   corporis 110.5
   cruris 110.3
   decalvans 704.09
   flava 111.0
   foot 110.4
   furfuracea 111.0
   imbricata (Tokelau) 110.5
   lepothrix 039.0
   manuum 110.2
   microsporic (*see also* Dermatophytosis) 110.9
   nigra 111.1
   nodosa 111.2
   pedis 110.4
   scalp 110.0
   specified site NEC 110.8
   sycosis 110.0
   tonsurans 110.0
   trichophytic (*see also* Dermatophytosis) 110.9
   unguium 110.1
   versicolor 111.0
Tingling sensation — *see also* Disturbance, sensation 782.0
Tin-miners' lung 503
Tinnitus (aurium) 388.30
   audible 388.32
   objective 388.32
   subjective 388.31
Tipped, teeth 524.33
Tipping
   pelvis 738.6
      with disproportion (fetopelvic) 653.0 ✓
         affecting fetus or newborn 763.1
         causing obstructed labor 660.1 ✓
            affecting fetus or newborn 763.1
   teeth 524.33
Tiredness 780.79
Tissue — *see* condition
Tobacco
   abuse (affecting health) NEC (*see also* Abuse, drugs, nondependent) 305.1
   heart 989.84
   use disorder complicating pregnancy, childbirth, or the puerperium 649.0 ✓
Tobias' syndrome (carcinoma, pulmonary apex) (M8010/3) 162.3
Tocopherol deficiency 269.1
Todd's
   cirrhosis — *see* Cirrhosis, biliary
   paralysis (postepileptic transitory paralysis) 344.89
Toe — *see* condition
Toilet, artificial opening — *see also* Attention to, artificial, opening V55.9
Tokelau ringworm 110.5
Tollwut 071
Tolosa-Hunt syndrome 378.55
Tommaselli's disease
   correct substance properly administered 599.70
   overdose or wrong substance given or taken 961.4
Tongue — *see also* condition
   worms 134.1
Tongue tie 750.0
Tonic pupil 379.46
Toni-Fanconi syndrome (cystinosis) 270.0
Tonsil — *see* condition

Tonsillitis (acute) (catarrhal) (croupous) (follicular) (gangrenous) (infective) (lacunar) (lingual) (malignant) (membranous) (phlegmonous) (pneumococcal) (pseudomembranous) (purulent) (septic) (staphylococcal) (subacute) (suppurative) (toxic) (ulcerative) (vesicular) (viral) 463
   with influenza, flu, or grippe 487.1
   chronic 474.00
   diphtheritic (membranous) 032.0
   hypertrophic 474.00
   influenzal 487.1
   parenchymatous 475
   streptococcal 034.0
   tuberculous (*see also* Tuberculosis) 012.8 ✓
   Vincent's 101
Tonsillopharyngitis 465.8
Toothache 525.9
Tooth, teeth — *see* condition
Topagnosis 782.0
Tophi (gouty) 274.03 ▲
   ear 274.81
   heart 274.82
   specified site NEC 274.82
TORCH infection — *see also* Infection, congenital 760.2
Torn — *see* Tear, torn
Tornwaldt's bursitis (disease) (pharyngeal bursitis) 478.29
   cyst 478.26
Torpid liver 573.9
Torsion
   accessory tube 620.5
   adnexa (female) 620.5
   aorta (congenital) 747.29
      acquired 447.1
   appendix
      epididymis 608.24
      testis 608.23
   bile duct 576.8
      with calculus, choledocholithiasis or stones — *see* Choledocholithiasis
      congenital 751.69
   bowel, colon, or intestine 560.2
   cervix — *see* Malposition, uterus
   duodenum 537.3
   dystonia — *see* Dystonia, torsion
   epididymis 608.24
      appendix 608.24
   fallopian tube 620.5
   gallbladder (*see also* Disease, gallbladder) 575.8
      congenital 751.69
   gastric 537.89
   hydatid of Morgagni (female) 620.5
   kidney (pedicle) 593.89
   Meckel's diverticulum (congenital) 751.0
   mesentery 560.2
   omentum 560.2
   organ or site, congenital NEC — *see* Anomaly, specified type NEC
   ovary (pedicle) 620.5
      congenital 752.0
   oviduct 620.5
   penis 607.89
      congenital 752.69
   renal 593.89
   spasm — *see* Dystonia, torsion
   spermatic cord 608.22
      extravaginal 608.21
      intravaginal 608.22
   spleen 289.59
   testicle, testis 608.20
      appendix 608.23
   tibia 736.89
   umbilical cord — *see* Compression, umbilical cord
   uterus (*see also* Malposition, uterus) 621.6
Torticollis (intermittent) (spastic) 723.5
   congenital 754.1
      sternomastoid 754.1
   due to birth injury 767.8
   hysterical 300.11
   ocular 781.93
   psychogenic 306.0
      specified as conversion reaction 300.11

Torticollis — *continued*
   rheumatic 723.5
   rheumatoid 714.0
   spasmodic 333.83
   traumatic, current NEC 847.0
Tortuous
   artery 447.1
   fallopian tube 752.19
   organ or site, congenital NEC — *see* Distortion
   renal vessel (congenital) 747.62
   retina vessel (congenital) 743.58
      acquired 362.17
   ureter 593.4
   urethra 599.84
   vein — *see* Varicose, vein
Torula, torular (infection) 117.5
   histolytica 117.5
   lung 117.5
Torulosis 117.5
Torus
   fracture
      fibula 823.41
         with tibia 823.42
      humerus 812.49 ●
      radius ▶(alone)◀ 813.45 ●
         with ulna 813.47 ●
      tibia 823.40
         with fibula 823.42
      ulna (alone) 813.46 ●
         with radius 813.47 ●
   mandibularis 526.81
   palatinus 526.81
Touch, vitreous 997.99
Touraine-Solente-Golé syndrome (acropachyderma) 757.39
Touraine's syndrome (hereditary osteo-onychodysplasia) 756.89
Tourette's disease (motor-verbal tic) 307.23
Tower skull 756.0
   with exophthalmos 756.0
Toxemia 799.89
   with
      abortion — *see* Abortion, by type, with toxemia
   bacterial — *see* Septicemia
   biliary (*see also* Disease, biliary) 576.8
   burn — *see* Burn, by site
   congenital NEC 779.89
   eclamptic 642.6 ✓
      with pre-existing hypertension 642.7 ✓
   erysipelatous (*see also* Erysipelas) 035
   fatigue 799.89
   fetus or newborn NEC 779.89
   food (*see also* Poisoning, food) 005.9
   gastric 537.89
   gastrointestinal 558.2
   intestinal 558.2
   kidney (*see also* Disease, renal) 593.9
   lung 518.89
   malarial NEC (*see also* Malaria) 084.6
   maternal (of pregnancy), affecting fetus or newborn 760.0
   myocardial — *see* Myocarditis, toxic
   of pregnancy (mild) (pre-eclamptic) 642.4 ✓
      with
         convulsions 642.6 ✓
         pre-existing hypertension 642.7 ✓
      affecting fetus or newborn 760.0
      severe 642.5 ✓
   pre-eclamptic — *see* Toxemia, of pregnancy
   puerperal, postpartum — *see* Toxemia, of pregnancy
   pulmonary 518.89
   renal (*see also* Disease, renal) 593.9
   septic (*see also* Septicemia) 038.9
   small intestine 558.2
   staphylococcal 038.10
      aureus 038.11
      due to food 005.0
      specified organism NEC 038.19
   stasis 799.89
   stomach 537.89
   uremic (*see also* Uremia) 586
   urinary 586
Toxemica cerebropathia psychica (nonalcoholic) 294.0

Toxemica cerebropathia psychica — continued
alcoholic 291.1
Toxic (poisoning) — see also condition
from drug or poison — see Table of Drugs and Chemicals
oil syndrome 710.5
shock syndrome 040.82
thyroid (gland) (see also Thyrotoxicosis) 242.9 ☑
Toxicemia — see Toxemia
Toxicity
dilantin
asymptomatic 796.0
symptomatic — see Table of Drugs and Chemicals
drug
asymptomatic 796.0
symptomatic — see Table of Drugs and Chemicals
fava bean 282.2
from drug or poison
asymptomatic 796.0
symptomatic — see Table of Drugs and Chemicals
Toxicosis — see also Toxemia 799.89
capillary, hemorrhagic 287.0
Toxinfection 799.89
gastrointestinal 558.2
Toxocariasis 128.0
Toxoplasma infection, generalized 130.9
Toxoplasmosis (acquired) 130.9
with pneumonia 130.4
congenital, active 771.2
disseminated (multisystemic) 130.8
maternal
with suspected damage to fetus affecting management of pregnancy 655.4 ☑
affecting fetus or newborn 760.2
manifest toxoplasmosis in fetus or newborn 771.2
multiple sites 130.8
multisystemic disseminated 130.8
specified site NEC 130.7
Trabeculation, bladder 596.8
Trachea — see condition
Tracheitis (acute) (catarrhal) (infantile) (membranous) (plastic) (pneumococcal) (septic) (suppurative) (viral) 464.10
with
bronchitis 490
acute or subacute 466.0
chronic 491.8
tuberculosis — see Tuberculosis, pulmonary
laryngitis (acute) 464.20
with obstruction 464.21
chronic 476.1
tuberculous (see also Tuberculosis, larynx) 012.3 ☑
obstruction 464.11
chronic 491.8
with
bronchitis (chronic) 491.8
laryngitis (chronic) 476.1
due to external agent — see Condition, respiratory, chronic, due to
diphtheritic (membranous) 032.3
due to external agent — see Inflammation, respiratory, upper, due to
edematous 464.11
influenzal 487.1
streptococcal 034.0
syphilitic 095.8
tuberculous (see also Tuberculosis) 012.8 ☑
Trachelitis (nonvenereal) — see also Cervicitis 616.0
trichomonal 131.09
Tracheobronchial — see condition
Tracheobronchitis — see also Bronchitis 490
acute or subacute 466.0
with bronchospasm or obstruction 466.0
chronic 491.8
influenzal 487.1
senile 491.8

Tracheobronchomegaly (congenital) 748.3
with bronchiectasis 494.0
with (acute) exacerbation 494.1
acquired 519.19
with bronchiectasis 494.0
with (acute) exacerbation 494.1
Tracheobronchopneumonitis — see Pneumonia, broncho
Tracheocele (external) (internal) 519.19
congenital 748.3
Tracheomalacia 519.19
congenital 748.3
Tracheopharyngitis (acute) 465.8
chronic 478.9
due to external agent — see Condition, respiratory, chronic, due to
due to external agent — see Inflammation, respiratory, upper, due to
Tracheostenosis 519.19
congenital 748.3
Tracheostomy
attention to V55.0
complication 519.00
granuloma 519.09
hemorrhage 519.09
infection 519.01
malfunctioning 519.02
obstruction 519.09
sepsis 519.01
status V44.0
stenosis 519.02
Trachoma, trachomatous 076.9
active (stage) 076.1
contraction of conjunctiva 076.1
dubium 076.0
healed or late effect 139.1
initial (stage) 076.0
Türck's (chronic catarrhal laryngitis) 476.0
Trachyphonia 784.49
Training
insulin pump V65.46
orthoptic V57.4
orthotic V57.81
Train sickness 994.6
Trait
hemoglobin
abnormal NEC 282.7
with thalassemia 282.49
C (see also Disease, hemoglobin, C) 282.7
with elliptocytosis 282.7
S (Hb-S) 282.5
Lepore 282.49
with other abnormal hemoglobin NEC 282.49
paranoid 301.0
sickle-cell 282.5
with
elliptocytosis 282.5
spherocytosis 282.5
Traits, paranoid 301.0
Tramp V60.0
Trance 780.09
hysterical 300.13
Transaminasemia 790.4
Transfusion, blood
without reported diagnosis V58.2
donor V59.01
stem cells V59.02
fetal twin to twin 678.0 ☑
incompatible
ABO 999.6 ●
minor blood group 999.89 ●
reaction or complication — see Complications, transfusion
related acute lung injury (TRALI) 518.7
syndrome
fetomaternal 772.0
twin-to-twin
blood loss (donor twin) 772.0
recipient twin 776.4
twin to twin fetal 678.0 ☑
Transient — see also condition
alteration of awareness 780.02
blindness 368.12
deafness (ischemic) 388.02
global amnesia 437.7

Transient — see also condition — continued
hyperglycemia (post-procedural) 790.29 ●
hypoglycemia (post-procedural) 251.2 ●
person (homeless) NEC V60.0
Transitional, lumbosacral joint of vertebra 756.19
Translocation
autosomes NEC 758.5
13-15 758.1
16-18 758.2
21 or 22 758.0
balanced in normal individual 758.4
D_1 758.1
E_3 758.2
G 758.0
balanced autosomal in normal individual 758.4
chromosomes NEC 758.89
Down's syndrome 758.0
Translucency, iris 364.53
Transmission of chemical substances through the placenta (affecting fetus or newborn) 760.70
alcohol 760.71
anticonvulsants 760.77
antifungals 760.74
anti-infective agents 760.74
antimetabolics 760.78
cocaine 760.75
"crack" 760.75
diethylstilbestrol [DES] 760.76
hallucinogenic agents 760.73
medicinal agents NEC 760.79
narcotics 760.72
obstetric anesthetic or analgesic drug 763.5
specified agent NEC 760.79
suspected, affecting management of pregnancy 655.5 ☑
Transplant(ed)
bone V42.4
marrow V42.81
complication (see also Complications, due to (presence of) any device, implant, or graft classified to 996.0–996.5 NEC)
bone marrow 996.85
corneal graft NEC 996.79
infection or inflammation 996.69
reaction 996.51
rejection 996.51
organ (failure) (immune or nonimmune cause) (infection) (rejection) 996.80
bone marrow 996.85
heart 996.83
intestines 996.87
kidney 996.81
liver 996.82
lung 996.84
pancreas 996.86
specified NEC 996.89
previously removed due to complication, failure, rejection or infection V45.87
removal status V45.87
skin NEC 996.79
infection or inflammation 996.69
rejection 996.52
artificial 996.55
decellularized allodermis 996.55
cornea V42.5
hair V50.0
heart V42.1
valve V42.2
intestine V42.84
kidney V42.0
liver V42.7
lung V42.6
organ V42.9
specified NEC V42.89
pancreas V42.83
peripheral stem cells V42.82
skin V42.3
stem cells, peripheral V42.82
tissue V42.9
specified NEC V42.89
Transplants, ovarian, endometrial 617.1
Transposed — see Transposition
Transposition (congenital) — see also Malposition, congenital

Transposition — see also Malposition, congenital — continued
abdominal viscera 759.3
aorta (dextra) 745.11
appendix 751.5
arterial trunk 745.10
colon 751.5
great vessels (complete) 745.10
both originating from right ventricle 745.11
corrected 745.12
double outlet right ventricle 745.11
incomplete 745.11
partial 745.11
specified type NEC 745.19
heart 746.87
with complete transposition of viscera 759.3
intestine (large) (small) 751.5
pulmonary veins 747.49
reversed jejunal (for bypass) (status) V45.3
scrotal 752.81
stomach 750.7
with general transposition of viscera 759.
teeth, tooth 524.30
vessels (complete) 745.10
partial 745.11
viscera (abdominal) (thoracic) 759.3
Trans-sexualism 302.50
with
asexual history 302.51
heterosexual history 302.53
homosexual history 302.52
Transverse — see also condition
arrest (deep), in labor 660.3 ☑
affecting fetus or newborn 763.1
lie 652.3 ☑
before labor, affecting fetus or newborn 761.7
causing obstructed labor 660.0 ☑
affecting fetus or newborn 763.1
during labor, affecting fetus or newborn 763.1
Transvestism, transvestitism (transvestic fetishism) 302.3
Trapped placenta (with hemorrhage) 666.0 ☑
without hemorrhage 667.0 ☑
Traumatic — see ▶also◀ condition
brain injury (TBI) (see also Injury, intracranial) ●
854.0 ☑ ●
with skull fracture — see Fracture, skull, ●
by site ●
Trauma, traumatism — see also Injury, by site 959.9
birth — see Birth, injury NEC
causing hemorrhage of pregnancy or delivery 641.8 ☑
complicating
abortion — see Abortion, by type, with damage to pelvic organs
ectopic pregnancy (see also categories 633.0–633.9) 639.2
molar pregnancy (see also categories 630–632) 639.2
during delivery NEC 665.9 ☑
following
abortion 639.2
ectopic or molar pregnancy 639.2
maternal, during pregnancy, affecting fetus or newborn 760.5
neuroma — see Injury, nerve, by site
previous major, affecting management of pregnancy, childbirth, or puerperium V23.89
psychic (current) (see also Reaction, adjustment)
previous (history) V15.49
psychologic, previous (affecting health) V15.49
transient paralysis — see Injury, nerve, by site
Treacher Collins' syndrome (incomplete facial dysostosis) 756.0
Treitz's hernia — see Hernia, Treitz's
Trematode infestation NEC 121.9
Trematodiasis NEC 121.9
Trembles 988.8
Trembling paralysis — see also Parkinsonism 332.0

Tremor 781.0
  essential (benign) 333.1
  familial 333.1
  flapping (liver) 572.8
  hereditary 333.1
  hysterical 300.11
  intention 333.1
  medication-induced postural 333.1
  mercurial 985.0
  muscle 728.85
  Parkinson's (see also Parkinsonism) 332.0
  psychogenic 306.0
    specified as conversion reaction 300.11
  senilis 797
  specified type NEC 333.1
Trench
  fever 083.1
  foot 991.4
  mouth 101
  nephritis — see Nephritis, acute
Treponema pallidum infection — see also
    Syphilis 097.9
Treponematosis 102.9
  due to
    T. pallidum — see Syphilis
    T. pertenue (yaws) (see also Yaws) 102.9
Triad
  Kartagener's 759.3
  Reiter's (complete) (incomplete) 099.3
  Saint's (see also Hernia, diaphragm) 553.3
Trichiasis 704.2
  cicatricial 704.2
  eyelid 374.05
    with entropion (see also Entropion) 374.00
Trichinella spiralis (infection) (infestation) 124
Trichinelliasis 124
Trichinellosis 124
Trichiniasis 124
Trichinosis 124
Trichobezoar 938
  intestine 936
  stomach 935.2
Trichocephaliasis 127.3
Trichocephalosis 127.3
Trichocephalus infestation 127.3
Trichoclasis 704.2
Trichoepithelioma (M8100/0) — see also Neo-
    plasm, skin, benign
  breast 217
  genital organ NEC — see Neoplasm, by site,
    benign
  malignant (M8100/3) — see Neoplasm, skin,
    malignant
Trichofolliculoma (M8101/0) — see Neoplasm,
    skin, benign
Tricholemmoma (M8102/0) — see Neoplasm,
    skin, benign
Trichomatosis 704.2
Trichomoniasis 131.9
  bladder 131.09
  cervix 131.09
  intestinal 007.3
  prostate 131.03
  seminal vesicle 131.09
  specified site NEC 131.8
  urethra 131.02
  urogenitalis 131.00
  vagina 131.01
  vulva 131.01
  vulvovaginal 131.01
Trichomycosis 039.0
  axillaris 039.0
  nodosa 111.2
  nodularis 111.2
  rubra 039.0
Trichonocardiosis (axillaris) (palmellina) 039.0
Trichonodosis 704.2
Trichophytide — see Dermatophytosis
Trichophytid, trichophyton infection — see
    also Dermatophytosis 110.9
Trichophytobezoar 938
  intestine 936
  stomach 935.2
Trichophytosis — see Dermatophytosis
Trichoptilosis 704.2
Trichorrhexis (nodosa) 704.2

Trichosporosis nodosa 111.2
Trichostasis spinulosa (congenital) 757.4
Trichostrongyliasis (small intestine) 127.6
Trichostrongylosis 127.6
Trichostrongylus (instabilis) infection 127.6
Trichotillomania 312.39
Trichromat, anomalous (congenital) 368.59
Trichromatopsia, anomalous (congenital)
    368.59
Trichuriasis 127.3
Trichuris trichiuria (any site) (infection) (infesta-
    tion) 127.3
Tricuspid (valve) — see condition
Trifid — see also Accessory
  kidney (pelvis) 753.3
  tongue 750.13
Trigeminal neuralgia — see also Neuralgia,
    trigeminal 350.1
Trigeminoencephaloangiomatosis 759.6
Trigeminy 427.89
  postoperative 997.1
Trigger finger (acquired) 727.03
  congenital 756.89
Trigonitis (bladder) (chronic) (pseudomembra-
    nous) 595.3
  tuberculous (see also Tuberculosis) 016.1 ☑
Trigonocephaly 756.0
Trihexosidosis 272.7
Trilobate placenta — see Placenta, abnormal
Trilocular heart 745.8
Trimethylaminuria 270.8
Tripartita placenta — see Placenta, abnormal
Triple — see also Accessory
  kidneys 753.3
  uteri 752.2
  X female 758.81
Triplegia 344.89
  congenital or infantile 343.8
Triplet
  affected by maternal complications of preg-
    nancy 761.5
  healthy liveborn — see Newborn, multiple
  pregnancy (complicating delivery) NEC
    651.1 ☑
    with fetal loss and retention of one or more
      fetus(es) 651.4 ☑
    following (elective) fetal reduction
      651.7 ☑
Triplex placenta — see Placenta, abnormal
Triplication — see Accessory
Trismus 781.0
  neonatorum 771.3
  newborn 771.3
Trisomy (syndrome) NEC 758.5
  13 (partial) 758.1
  16-18 758.2
  18 (partial) 758.2
  21 (partial) 758.0
  22 758.0
  autosomes NEC 758.5
  D₁ 758.1
  E₃ 758.2
  G (group) 758.0
  group D₁ 758.1
  group E 758.2
  group G 758.0
Tritanomaly 368.53
Tritanopia 368.53
Troisier-Hanot-Chauffard syndrome (bronze
    diabetes) 275.0
Trombidiosis 133.8
Trophedema (hereditary) 757.0
  congenital 757.0
Trophoblastic disease — see also Hydatidiform
    mole 630
  previous, affecting management of pregnancy
    V23.1
Tropholymphedema 757.0
Trophoneurosis NEC 356.9
  arm NEC 354.9
  disseminated 710.1
  facial 349.89
  leg NEC 355.8
  lower extremity NEC 355.8
  upper extremity NEC 354.9
Tropical — see also condition

Tropical — see also condition — continued
  maceration feet (syndrome) 991.4
  wet foot (syndrome) 991.4
Trouble — see also Disease
  bowel 569.9
  heart — see Disease, heart
  intestine 569.9
  kidney (see also Disease, renal) 593.9
  nervous 799.21 ▲
  sinus (see also Sinusitis) 473.9
Trousseau's syndrome (thrombophlebitis mi-
    grans) 453.1
Truancy, childhood — see also Disturbance,
    conduct
  socialized 312.2 ☑
  undersocialized, unsocialized 312.1 ☑
Truncus
  arteriosus (persistent) 745.0
  common 745.0
  communis 745.0
Trunk — see condition
Trychophytide — see Dermatophytosis
Trypanosoma infestation — see Trypanosomi-
    asis
Trypanosomiasis 086.9
  with meningoencephalitis 086.9 [323.2]
  African 086.5
    due to Trypanosoma 086.5
      gambiense 086.3
      rhodesiense 086.4
  American 086.2
    with
      heart involvement 086.0
      other organ involvement 086.1
    without mention of organ involvement
      086.2
  Brazilian — see Trypanosomiasis, American
  Chagas' — see Trypanosomiasis, American
  due to Trypanosoma
    cruzi — see Trypanosomiasis, American
    gambiense 086.3
    rhodesiense 086.4
  gambiensis, Gambian 086.3
  North American — see Trypanosomiasis,
    American
  rhodesiensis, Rhodesian 086.4
  South American — see Trypanosomiasis,
    American
T-shaped incisors 520.2
Tsutsugamushi fever 081.2
Tubercle — see also Tuberculosis
  brain, solitary 013.2 ☑
  Darwin's 744.29
  epithelioid noncaseating 135
  Ghon, primary infection 010.0 ☑
Tuberculid, tuberculide (indurating) (lichenoid)
    (miliary) (papulonecrotic) (primary) (skin)
    (subcutaneous) — see also Tuberculosis
    017.0 ☑
Tuberculoma — see also Tuberculosis
  brain (any part) 013.2 ☑
  meninges (cerebral) (spinal) 013.1 ☑
  spinal cord 013.4 ☑

Tuberculosis, tubercular, tuberculous (calcifi-
    cation) (calcified) (caseous) (chromogenic
    acid-fast bacilli) (congenital) (degenera-
    tion) (disease) (fibrocaseous) (fistula)
    (gangrene) (interstitial) (isolated circum-
    scribed lesions) (necrosis) (parenchyma-
    tous) (ulcerative) 011.9 ☑

> Note — Use the following fifth-digit subclas-
> sification with categories 010–018:
>
> 0   unspecified
>
> 1   bacteriological or histological exami-
> nation not done
>
> 2   bacteriological or histological exami-
> nation unknown (at present)
>
> 3   tubercle bacilli found (in sputum) by
> microscopy
>
> 4   tubercle bacilli not found (in sputum)
> by microscopy, but found by bacterial
> culture
>
> 5   tubercle bacilli not found by bacteri-
> ological exam–ination, but tubercu-
> losis confirmed histologically
>
> 6   tubercle bacilli not found by bacteri-
> ological or histological examination,
> but tuberculosis confirmed by other
> methods [inoculation of animals]
>
> For tuberculous conditions specified as late
> effects or sequelae, see category 137.

  abdomen 014.8 ☑
    lymph gland 014.8 ☑
  abscess 011.9 ☑
    arm 017.9 ☑
    bone (see also Osteomyelitis, due to, tuber-
      culosis) 015.9 ☑ [730.8] ☑
      hip 015.1 ☑ [730.85]
      knee 015.2 ☑ [730.86]
      sacrum 015.0 ☑ [730.88]
      specified site NEC 015.7 ☑ [730.88]
      spinal 015.0 ☑ [730.88]
      vertebra 015.0 ☑ [730.88]
    brain 013.3 ☑
    breast 017.9 ☑
    Cowper's gland 016.5 ☑
    dura (mater) 013.8 ☑
      brain 013.3 ☑
      spinal cord 013.5 ☑
    epidural 013.8 ☑
      brain 013.3 ☑
      spinal cord 013.5 ☑
    frontal sinus — see Tuberculosis, sinus
    genital organs NEC 016.9 ☑
      female 016.7 ☑
      male 016.5 ☑
    genitourinary NEC 016.9 ☑
    gland (lymphatic) — see Tuberculosis,
      lymph gland
    hip 015.1 ☑
    iliopsoas 015.0 ☑ [730.88]
    intestine 014.8 ☑
    ischiorectal 014.8 ☑
    joint 015.9 ☑
      hip 015.1 ☑
      knee 015.2 ☑
      specified joint NEC 015.8 ☑
      vertebral 015.0 ☑ [730.88]
    kidney 016.0 ☑ [590.81]
    knee 015.2 ☑
    lumbar 015.0 ☑ [730.88]
    lung 011.2 ☑
      primary, progressive 010.8 ☑
    meninges (cerebral) (spinal) 013.0 ☑
    pelvic 016.9 ☑
      female 016.7 ☑
      male 016.5 ☑
    perianal 014.8 ☑
      fistula 014.8 ☑
    perinephritic 016.0 ☑ [590.81]
    perineum 017.9 ☑
    perirectal 014.8 ☑
    psoas 015.0 ☑ [730.88]

☑ Additional Digit Required — Refer to the Tabular List for Digit Selection   ▽ Subterms under main terms may continue to next column or page

2010 ICD-9-CM   ►◄ Revised Text   ● New Line   ▲ Revised Code   October 2009 • Volume 2 — 273

Tuberculosis, tubercular, tuberculous — *continued*
- abscess — *continued*
  - rectum 014.8 ☑
  - retropharyngeal 012.8 ☑
  - sacrum 015.0 ☑ *[730.88]*
  - scrofulous 017.2 ☑
  - scrotum 016.5 ☑
  - skin 017.0 ☑
    - primary 017.0 ☑
  - spinal cord 013.5 ☑
  - spine or vertebra (column) 015.0 ☑ *[730.88]*
  - strumous 017.2 ☑
  - subdiaphragmatic 014.8 ☑
  - testis 016.5 ☑
  - thigh 017.9 ☑
  - urinary 016.3 ☑
    - kidney 016.0 ☑ *[590.81]*
  - uterus 016.7 ☑
- accessory sinus — *see* Tuberculosis, sinus
- Addison's disease 017.6 ☑
- adenitis (*see also* Tuberculosis, lymph gland) 017.2 ☑
- adenoids 012.8 ☑
- adenopathy (*see also* Tuberculosis, lymph gland) 017.2 ☑
  - tracheobronchial 012.1 ☑
    - primary progressive 010.8 ☑
- adherent pericardium 017.9 ☑ *[420.0]*
- adnexa (uteri) 016.7 ☑
- adrenal (capsule) (gland) 017.6 ☑
- air passage NEC 012.8 ☑
- alimentary canal 014.8 ☑
- anemia 017.9 ☑
- ankle (joint) 015.8 ☑
  - bone 015.5 ☑ *[730.87]*
- anus 014.8 ☑
- apex (*see also* Tuberculosis, pulmonary) 011.9 ☑
- apical (*see also* Tuberculosis, pulmonary) 011.9 ☑
- appendicitis 014.8 ☑
- appendix 014.8 ☑
- arachnoid 013.0 ☑
- artery 017.9 ☑
- arthritis (chronic) (synovial) 015.9 ☑ *[711.40]*
  - ankle 015.8 ☑ *[730.87]*
  - hip 015.1 ☑ *[711.45]*
  - knee 015.2 ☑ *[711.46]*
  - specified site NEC 015.8 ☑ *[711.48]*
  - spine or vertebra (column) 015.0 ☑ *[720.81]*
  - wrist 015.8 ☑ *[730.83]*
- articular — *see* Tuberculosis, joint
- ascites 014.0 ☑
- asthma (*see also* Tuberculosis, pulmonary) 011.9 ☑
- axilla, axillary 017.2 ☑
  - gland 017.2 ☑
- bilateral (*see also* Tuberculosis, pulmonary) 011.9 ☑
- bladder 016.1 ☑
- bone (*see also* Osteomyelitis, due to, tuberculosis) 015.9 ☑ *[730.8]* ☑
  - hip 015.1 ☑ *[730.85]*
  - knee 015.2 ☑ *[730.86]*
  - limb NEC 015.5 ☑ *[730.88]*
  - sacrum 015.0 ☑ *[730.88]*
  - specified site NEC 015.7 ☑ *[730.88]*
  - spinal or vertebral column 015.0 ☑ *[730.88]*
- bowel 014.8 ☑
  - miliary 018.9 ☑
- brain 013.2 ☑
- breast 017.9 ☑
- broad ligament 016.7 ☑
- bronchi, bronchial, bronchus 011.3 ☑
  - ectasia, ectasis 011.5 ☑
  - fistula 011.3 ☑
    - primary, progressive 010.8 ☑
  - gland 012.1 ☑
    - primary, progressive 010.8 ☑

Tuberculosis, tubercular, tuberculous — *continued*
- bronchi, bronchial, bronchus — *continued*
  - isolated 012.2 ☑
  - lymph gland or node 012.1 ☑
    - primary, progressive 010.8 ☑
- bronchiectasis 011.5 ☑
- bronchitis 011.3 ☑
- bronchopleural 012.0 ☑
- bronchopneumonia, bronchopneumonic 011.6 ☑
- bronchorrhagia 011.3 ☑
- bronchotracheal 011.3 ☑
  - isolated 012.2 ☑
- bronchus — *see* Tuberculosis, bronchi
- bronze disease (Addison's) 017.6 ☑
- buccal cavity 017.9 ☑
- bulbourethral gland 016.5 ☑
- bursa (*see also* Tuberculosis, joint) 015.9 ☑
- cachexia NEC (*see also* Tuberculosis, pulmonary) 011.9 ☑
- cardiomyopathy 017.9 ☑ *[425.8]*
- caries (*see also* Tuberculosis, bone) 015.9 ☑ *[730.8]*
- cartilage (*see also* Tuberculosis, bone) 015.9 ☑ *[730.8]* ☑
  - intervertebral 015.0 ☑ *[730.88]*
- catarrhal (*see also* Tuberculosis, pulmonary) 011.9 ☑
- cecum 014.8 ☑
- cellular tissue (primary) 017.0 ☑
- cellulitis (primary) 017.0 ☑
- central nervous system 013.9 ☑
  - specified site NEC 013.8 ☑
- cerebellum (current) 013.2 ☑
- cerebral (current) 013.2 ☑
  - meninges 013.0 ☑
- cerebrospinal 013.6 ☑
  - meninges 013.0 ☑
- cerebrum (current) 013.2 ☑
- cervical 017.2 ☑
  - gland 017.2 ☑
  - lymph nodes 017.2 ☑
- cervicitis (uteri) 016.7 ☑
- cervix 016.7 ☑
- chest (*see also* Tuberculosis, pulmonary) 011.9 ☑
- childhood type or first infection 010.0 ☑
- choroid 017.3 ☑ *[363.13]*
- choroiditis 017.3 ☑ *[363.13]*
- ciliary body 017.3 ☑ *[364.11]*
- colitis 014.8 ☑
- colliers' 011.4 ☑
- colliquativa (primary) 017.0 ☑
- colon 014.8 ☑
  - ulceration 014.8 ☑
- complex, primary 010.0 ☑
- complicating pregnancy, childbirth, or puerperium 647.3 ☑
  - affecting fetus or newborn 760.2
- congenital 771.2
- conjunctiva 017.3 ☑ *[370.31]*
- connective tissue 017.9 ☑
  - bone — *see* Tuberculosis, bone
- contact V01.1
- converter (tuberculin skin test) (without disease) 795.5
- cornea (ulcer) 017.3 ☑ *[370.31]*
- Cowper's gland 016.5 ☑
- coxae 015.1 ☑ *[730.85]*
- coxalgia 015.1 ☑ *[730.85]*
- cul-de-sac of Douglas 014.8 ☑
- curvature, spine 015.0 ☑ *[737.40]*
- cutis (colliquativa) (primary) 017.0 ☑
- cystitis 016.1 ☑
- cyst, ovary 016.6 ☑
- dacryocystitis 017.3 ☑ *[375.32]*
- dactylitis 015.5 ☑
- diarrhea 014.8 ☑
- diffuse (*see also* Tuberculosis, miliary) 018.9 ☑
  - lung — *see* Tuberculosis, pulmonary
  - meninges 013.0 ☑
- digestive tract 014.8 ☑

Tuberculosis, tubercular, tuberculous — *continued*
- disseminated (*see also* Tuberculosis, miliary) 018.9 ☑
  - meninges 013.0 ☑
- duodenum 014.8 ☑
- dura (mater) 013.9 ☑
  - abscess 013.8 ☑
    - cerebral 013.3 ☑
    - spinal 013.5 ☑
- dysentery 014.8 ☑
- ear (inner) (middle) 017.4 ☑
  - bone 015.6 ☑
  - external (primary) 017.0 ☑
  - skin (primary) 017.0 ☑
- elbow 015.8 ☑
- emphysema — *see* Tuberculosis, pulmonary
- empyema 012.0 ☑
- encephalitis 013.6 ☑
- endarteritis 017.9 ☑
- endocarditis (any valve) 017.9 ☑ *[424.91]*
- endocardium (any valve) 017.9 ☑ *[424.91]*
- endocrine glands NEC 017.9 ☑
- endometrium 016.7 ☑
- enteric, enterica 014.8 ☑
- enteritis 014.8 ☑
- enterocolitis 014.8 ☑
- epididymis 016.4 ☑
- epididymitis 016.4 ☑
- epidural abscess 013.8 ☑
  - brain 013.3 ☑
  - spinal cord 013.5 ☑
- epiglottis 012.3 ☑
- episcleritis 017.3 ☑ *[379.00]*
- erythema (induratum) (nodosum) (primary) 017.1 ☑
- esophagus 017.8 ☑
- Eustachian tube 017.4 ☑
- exposure to V01.1
- exudative 012.0 ☑
  - primary, progressive 010.1 ☑
- eye 017.3 ☑
- eyelid (primary) 017.0 ☑
  - lupus 017.0 ☑ *[373.4]*
- fallopian tube 016.6 ☑
- fascia 017.9 ☑
- fauces 012.8 ☑
- finger 017.9 ☑
- first infection 010.0 ☑
- fistula, perirectal 014.8 ☑
- Florida 011.6 ☑
- foot 017.9 ☑
- funnel pelvis 137.3
- gallbladder 017.9 ☑
- galloping (*see also* Tuberculosis, pulmonary) 011.9 ☑
- ganglionic 015.9 ☑
- gastritis 017.9 ☑
- gastrocolic fistula 014.8 ☑
- gastroenteritis 014.8 ☑
- gastrointestinal tract 014.8 ☑
- general, generalized 018.9 ☑
  - acute 018.0 ☑
  - chronic 018.8 ☑
- genital organs NEC 016.9 ☑
  - female 016.7 ☑
  - male 016.5 ☑
- genitourinary NEC 016.9 ☑
- genu 015.2 ☑
- glandulae suprarenalis 017.6 ☑
- glandular, general 017.2 ☑
- glottis 012.3 ☑
- grinders' 011.4 ☑
- groin 017.2 ☑
- gum 017.9 ☑
- hand 017.9 ☑
- heart 017.9 ☑ *[425.8]*
- hematogenous — *see* Tuberculosis, miliary
- hemoptysis (*see also* Tuberculosis, pulmonary) 011.9 ☑
- hemorrhage NEC (*see also* Tuberculosis, pulmonary) 011.9 ☑
- hemothorax 012.0 ☑

Tuberculosis, tubercular, tuberculous — *continued*
- hepatitis 017.9 ☑
- hilar lymph nodes 012.1 ☑
  - primary, progressive 010.8 ☑
- hip (disease) (joint) 015.1 ☑
  - bone 015.1 ☑ *[730.85]*
- hydrocephalus 013.8 ☑
- hydropneumothorax 012.0 ☑
- hydrothorax 012.0 ☑
- hypoadrenalism 017.6 ☑
- hypopharynx 012.8 ☑
- ileocecal (hyperplastic) 014.8 ☑
- ileocolitis 014.8 ☑
- ileum 014.8 ☑
- iliac spine (superior) 015.0 ☑ *[730.88]*
- incipient NEC (*see also* Tuberculosis, pulmonary) 011.9 ☑
- indurativa (primary) 017.1 ☑
- infantile 010.0 ☑
- infection NEC 011.9 ☑
  - without clinical manifestation 010.0 ☑
- infraclavicular gland 017.2 ☑
- inguinal gland 017.2 ☑
- inguinalis 017.2 ☑
- intestine (any part) 014.8 ☑
- iris 017.3 ☑ *[364.11]*
- iritis 017.3 ☑ *[364.11]*
- ischiorectal 014.8 ☑
- jaw 015.7 ☑ *[730.88]*
- jejunum 014.8 ☑
- joint 015.9 ☑
  - hip 015.1 ☑
  - knee 015.2 ☑
  - specified site NEC 015.8 ☑
  - vertebral 015.0 ☑ *[730.88]*
- keratitis 017.3 ☑ *[370.31]*
  - interstitial 017.3 ☑ *[370.59]*
- keratoconjunctivitis 017.3 ☑ *[370.31]*
- kidney 016.0 ☑
- knee (joint) 015.2 ☑
- kyphoscoliosis 015.0 ☑ *[737.43]*
- kyphosis 015.0 ☑ *[737.41]*
- lacrimal apparatus, gland 017.3 ☑
- laryngitis 012.3 ☑
- larynx 012.3 ☑
- leptomeninges, leptomeningitis (cerebral) (spinal) 013.0 ☑
- lichenoides (primary) 017.0 ☑
- linguae 017.9 ☑
- lip 017.9 ☑
- liver 017.9 ☑
- lordosis 015.0 ☑ *[737.42]*
- lung — *see* Tuberculosis, pulmonary
- luposa 017.0 ☑
  - eyelid 017.0 ☑ *[373.4]*
- lymphadenitis — *see* Tuberculosis, lymph gland
- lymphangitis — *see* Tuberculosis, lymph gland
- lymphatic (gland) (vessel) — *see* Tuberculosis, lymph gland
- lymph gland or node (peripheral) 017.2 ☑
  - abdomen 014.8 ☑
  - bronchial 012.1 ☑
    - primary, progressive 010.8 ☑
  - cervical 017.2 ☑
  - hilar 012.1 ☑
    - primary, progressive 010.8 ☑
  - intrathoracic 012.1 ☑
    - primary, progressive 010.8 ☑
  - mediastinal 012.1 ☑
    - primary, progressive 010.8 ☑
  - mesenteric 014.8 ☑
  - peripheral 017.2 ☑
  - retroperitoneal 014.8 ☑
  - tracheobronchial 012.1 ☑
    - primary, progressive 010.8 ☑
- malignant NEC (*see also* Tuberculosis, pulmonary) 011.9 ☑
- mammary gland 017.9 ☑
- marasmus NEC (*see also* Tuberculosis, pulmonary) 011.9 ☑
- mastoiditis 015.6 ☑

Tuberculosis, tubercular, tuberculous — *continued*
- maternal, affecting fetus or newborn 760.2
- mediastinal (lymph) gland or node 012.1 ☑
  - primary, progressive 010.8 ☑
- mediastinitis 012.8 ☑
  - primary, progressive 010.8 ☑
- mediastinopericarditis 017.9 ☑ *[420.0]*
- mediastinum 012.8 ☑
  - primary, progressive 010.8 ☑
- medulla 013.9 ☑
  - brain 013.2 ☑
  - spinal cord 013.4 ☑
- melanosis, Addisonian 017.6 ☑
- membrane, brain 013.0 ☑
- meninges (cerebral) (spinal) 013.0 ☑
- meningitis (basilar) (brain) (cerebral) (cerebrospinal) (spinal) 013.0 ☑
- meningoencephalitis 013.0 ☑
- mesentery, mesenteric 014.8 ☑
  - lymph gland or node 014.8 ☑
- miliary (any site) 018.9 ☑
  - acute 018.0 ☑
  - chronic 018.8 ☑
  - specified type NEC 018.8 ☑
- millstone makers' 011.4 ☑
- miners' 011.4 ☑
- moulders' 011.4 ☑
- mouth 017.9 ☑
- multiple 018.9 ☑
  - acute 018.0 ☑
  - chronic 018.8 ☑
- muscle 017.9 ☑
- myelitis 013.6 ☑
- myocarditis 017.9 ☑ *[422.0]*
- myocardium 017.9 ☑ *[422.0]*
- nasal (passage) (sinus) 012.8 ☑
- nasopharynx 012.8 ☑
- neck gland 017.2 ☑
- nephritis 016.0 ☑ *[583.81]*
- nerve 017.9 ☑
- nose (septum) 012.8 ☑
- ocular 017.3 ☑
- old NEC 137.0
  - without residuals V12.01
- omentum 014.8 ☑
- oophoritis (acute) (chronic) 016.6 ☑
- optic 017.3 ☑ *[377.39]*
  - nerve trunk 017.3 ☑ *[377.39]*
  - papilla, papillae 017.3 ☑ *[377.39]*
- orbit 017.3 ☑ *[608.81]*
- orchitis 016.5 ☑ *[608.81]*
- organ, specified NEC 017.9 ☑
- orificialis (primary) 017.0 ☑
- osseous (*see also* Tuberculosis, bone) 015.9 ☑ *[730.8]*
- osteitis (*see also* Tuberculosis, bone) 015.9 ☑ *[730.8]*
- osteomyelitis (*see also* Tuberculosis, bone) 015.9 ☑ *[730.8]*
- otitis (media) 017.4 ☑
- ovaritis (acute) (chronic) 016.6 ☑
- ovary (acute) (chronic) 016.6 ☑
- oviducts (acute) (chronic) 016.6 ☑
- pachymeningitis 013.0 ☑
- palate (soft) 017.9 ☑
- pancreas 017.9 ☑
- papulonecrotic (primary) 017.0 ☑
- parathyroid glands 017.9 ☑
- paronychia (primary) 017.0 ☑
- parotid gland or region 017.9 ☑
- pelvic organ NEC 016.9 ☑
  - female 016.7 ☑
  - male 016.5 ☑
- pelvis (bony) 015.7 ☑ *[730.85]*
- penis 016.5 ☑
- peribronchitis 011.3 ☑
- pericarditis 017.9 ☑ *[420.0]*
- pericardium 017.9 ☑ *[420.0]*
- perichondritis, larynx 012.3 ☑
- perineum 017.9 ☑
- periostitis (*see also* Tuberculosis, bone) 015.9 ☑ *[730.8]*

Tuberculosis, tubercular, tuberculous — *continued*
- periphlebitis 017.9 ☑
  - eye vessel 017.3 ☑ *[362.18]*
  - retina 017.3 ☑ *[362.18]*
- perirectal fistula 014.8 ☑
- peritoneal gland 014.8 ☑
- peritoneum 014.0 ☑
- peritonitis 014.0 ☑
- pernicious NEC (*see also* Tuberculosis, pulmonary) 011.9 ☑
- pharyngitis 012.8 ☑
- pharynx 012.8 ☑
- phlyctenulosis (conjunctiva) 017.3 ☑ *[370.31]*
- phthisis NEC (*see also* Tuberculosis, pulmonary) 011.9 ☑
- pituitary gland 017.9 ☑
- placenta 016.7 ☑
- pleura, pleural, pleurisy, pleuritis (fibrinous) (obliterative) (purulent) (simple plastic) (with effusion) 012.0 ☑
  - primary, progressive 010.1 ☑
- pneumonia, pneumonic 011.6 ☑
- pneumothorax 011.7 ☑
- polyserositis 018.9 ☑
  - acute 018.0 ☑
  - chronic 018.8 ☑
- potters' 011.4 ☑
- prepuce 016.5 ☑
- primary 010.9 ☑
  - complex 010.0 ☑
  - complicated 010.8 ☑
    - with pleurisy or effusion 010.1 ☑
  - progressive 010.8 ☑
    - with pleurisy or effusion 010.1 ☑
  - skin 017.0 ☑
- proctitis 014.8 ☑
- prostate 016.5 ☑ *[601.4]*
- prostatitis 016.5 ☑ *[601.4]*
- pulmonaris (*see also* Tuberculosis, pulmonary) 011.9 ☑
- pulmonary (artery) (incipient) (malignant) (multiple round foci) (pernicious) (reinfection stage) 011.9 ☑
  - cavitated or with cavitation 011.2 ☑
    - primary, progressive 010.8 ☑
  - childhood type or first infection 010.0 ☑
  - chromogenic acid-fast bacilli 795.39
  - fibrosis or fibrotic 011.4 ☑
  - infiltrative 011.0 ☑
    - primary, progressive 010.9 ☑
  - nodular 011.1 ☑
  - specified NEC 011.8 ☑
  - sputum positive only 795.39
  - status following surgical collapse of lung NEC 011.9 ☑
- pyelitis 016.0 ☑ *[590.81]*
- pyelonephritis 016.0 ☑ *[590.81]*
- pyemia — *see* Tuberculosis, miliary
- pyonephrosis 016.0 ☑
- pyopneumothorax 012.0 ☑
- pyothorax 012.0 ☑
- rectum (with abscess) 014.8 ☑
  - fistula 014.8 ☑
- reinfection stage (*see also* Tuberculosis, pulmonary) 011.9 ☑
- renal 016.0 ☑
- renis 016.0 ☑
- reproductive organ 016.7 ☑
- respiratory NEC (*see also* Tuberculosis, pulmonary) 011.9 ☑
  - specified site NEC 012.8 ☑
- retina 017.3 ☑ *[363.13]*
- retroperitoneal (lymph gland or node) 014.8 ☑
  - gland 014.8 ☑
- retropharyngeal abscess 012.8 ☑
- rheumatism 015.9 ☑
- rhinitis 012.8 ☑
- sacroiliac (joint) 015.8 ☑
- sacrum 015.0 ☑ *[730.88]*
- salivary gland 017.9 ☑
- salpingitis (acute) (chronic) 016.6 ☑
- sandblasters' 011.4 ☑

Tuberculosis, tubercular, tuberculous — *continued*
- sclera 017.3 ☑ *[379.09]*
- scoliosis 015.0 ☑ *[737.43]*
- scrofulous 017.2 ☑
- scrotum 016.5 ☑
- seminal tract or vesicle 016.5 ☑ *[608.81]*
- senile NEC (*see also* Tuberculosis, pulmonary) 011.9 ☑
- septic NEC (*see also* Tuberculosis, miliary) 018.9 ☑
- shoulder 015.8 ☑
  - blade 015.7 ☑ *[730.8]*
- sigmoid 014.8 ☑
- sinus (accessory) (nasal) 012.8 ☑
  - bone 015.7 ☑ *[730.88]*
  - epididymis 016.4 ☑
- skeletal NEC (*see also* Osteomyelitis, due to tuberculosis) 015.9 ☑ *[730.8]*
- skin (any site) (primary) 017.0 ☑
- small intestine 014.8 ☑
- soft palate 017.9 ☑
- spermatic cord 016.5 ☑
- spinal
  - column 015.0 ☑ *[730.88]*
  - cord 013.4 ☑
  - disease 015.0 ☑ *[730.88]*
  - medulla 013.4 ☑
  - membrane 013.0 ☑
  - meninges 013.0 ☑
- spine 015.0 ☑ *[730.88]*
- spleen 017.7 ☑
- splenitis 017.7 ☑
- spondylitis 015.0 ☑ *[720.81]*
- spontaneous pneumothorax — *see* Tuberculosis, pulmonary
- sternoclavicular joint 015.8 ☑
- stomach 017.9 ☑
- stonemasons' 011.4 ☑
- struma 017.2 ☑
- subcutaneous tissue (cellular) (primary) 017.0 ☑
- subcutis (primary) 017.0 ☑
- subdeltoid bursa 017.9 ☑
- submaxillary 017.9 ☑
  - region 017.9 ☑
- supraclavicular gland 017.2 ☑
- suprarenal (capsule) (gland) 017.6 ☑
- swelling, joint (*see also* Tuberculosis, joint) 015.9 ☑
- symphysis pubis 015.7 ☑ *[730.88]*
- synovitis 015.9 ☑ *[727.01]*
  - hip 015.1 ☑ *[727.01]*
  - knee 015.2 ☑ *[727.01]*
  - specified site NEC 015.8 ☑ *[727.01]*
  - spine or vertebra 015.0 ☑ *[727.01]*
- systemic — *see* Tuberculosis, miliary
- tarsitis (eyelid) 017.0 ☑ *[373.4]*
  - ankle (bone) 015.5 ☑ *[730.87]*
- tendon (sheath) — *see* Tuberculosis, tenosynovitis
- tenosynovitis 015.9 ☑ *[727.01]*
  - hip 015.1 ☑ *[727.01]*
  - knee 015.2 ☑ *[727.01]*
  - specified site NEC 015.8 ☑ *[727.01]*
  - spine or vertebra 015.0 ☑ *[727.01]*
- testis 016.5 ☑ *[608.81]*
- throat 012.8 ☑
- thymus gland 017.9 ☑
- thyroid gland 017.5 ☑
- toe 017.9 ☑
- tongue 017.9 ☑
- tonsil (lingual) 012.8 ☑
- tonsillitis 012.8 ☑
- trachea, tracheal 012.8 ☑
  - gland 012.1 ☑
    - primary, progressive 010.8 ☑
  - isolated 012.2 ☑
- tracheobronchial 011.3 ☑
  - glandular 012.1 ☑
    - primary, progressive 010.8 ☑
  - isolated 012.2 ☑
  - lymph gland or node 012.1 ☑

Tuberculosis, tubercular, tuberculous — *continued*
- tracheobronchial — *continued*
  - lymph gland or node — *continued*
    - primary, progressive 010.8 ☑
- tubal 016.6 ☑
- tunica vaginalis 016.5 ☑
- typhlitis 014.8 ☑
- ulcer (primary) (skin) 017.0 ☑
  - bowel or intestine 014.8 ☑
  - specified site NEC — *see* Tuberculosis, by site
  - unspecified site — *see* Tuberculosis, pulmonary
- ureter 016.2 ☑
- urethra, urethral 016.3 ☑
- urinary organ or tract 016.3 ☑
  - kidney 016.0 ☑
- uterus 016.7 ☑
- uveal tract 017.3 ☑ *[363.13]*
- uvula 017.9 ☑
- vaccination, prophylactic (against) V03.2
- vagina 016.7 ☑
- vas deferens 016.5 ☑
- vein 017.9 ☑
- verruca (primary) 017.0 ☑
- verrucosa (cutis) (primary) 017.0 ☑
- vertebra (column) 015.0 ☑ *[730.88]*
- vesiculitis 016.5 ☑ *[608.81]*
- viscera NEC 014.8 ☑
- vulva 016.7 ☑ *[616.51]*
- wrist (joint) 015.8 ☑
  - bone 015.5 ☑ *[730.83]*

Tuberculum
- auriculae 744.29
- occlusal 520.2
- paramolare 520.2

Tuberosity
- jaw, excessive 524.07
- maxillary, entire 524.07

Tuberous sclerosis (brain) 759.5

Tube, tubal, tubular — *see also* condition
- ligation, admission for V25.2

Tubo-ovarian — *see* condition

Tuboplasty, after previous sterilization V26.0

Tubotympanitis 381.10

Tularemia 021.9
- with
  - conjunctivitis 021.3
  - pneumonia 021.2
- bronchopneumonic 021.2
- conjunctivitis 021.3
- cryptogenic 021.1
- disseminated 021.8
- enteric 021.1
- generalized 021.8
- glandular 021.8
- intestinal 021.1
- oculoglandular 021.3
- ophthalmic 021.3
- pneumonia 021.2
- pulmonary 021.2
- specified NEC 021.8
- typhoidal 021.1
- ulceroglandular 021.0
- vaccination, prophylactic (against) V03.4

Tularensis conjunctivitis 021.3

Tumefaction — *see also* Swelling
- liver (*see also* Hypertrophy, liver) 789.1

Tumor (M8000/1) — *see also* Neoplasm, by site, unspecified nature
- Abrikossov's (M9580/0) (*see also* Neoplasm, connective tissue, benign)
  - malignant (M9580/3) — *see* Neoplasm, connective tissue, malignant
- acinar cell (M8550/1) — *see* Neoplasm, by site, uncertain behavior
- acinic cell (M8550/1) — *see* Neoplasm, by site, uncertain behavior
- adenomatoid (M9054/0) (*see also* Neoplasm, by site, benign)
  - odontogenic (M9300/0) 213.1
    - upper jaw (bone) 213.0
- adnexal (skin) (M8390/0) — *see* Neoplasm, skin, benign

Index

Tumor — Tumor

Tumor — see also Neoplasm, by site, unspecified
nature — continued
- adrenal
  - cortical (benign) (M8370/0) 227.0
    - malignant (M8370/3) 194.0
  - rest (M8671/0) — see Neoplasm, by site, benign
- alpha cell (M8152/0)
  - malignant (M8152/3)
    - pancreas 157.4
    - specified site NEC — see Neoplasm, by site, malignant
    - unspecified site 157.4
  - pancreas 211.7
  - specified site NEC — see Neoplasm, by site, benign
  - unspecified site 211.7
- aneurysmal (see also Aneurysm) 442.9
- aortic body (M8691/1) 237.3
  - malignant (M8691/3) 194.6
- argentaffin (M8241/1) — see Neoplasm, by site, uncertain behavior
- basal cell (M8090/1) (see also Neoplasm, skin, uncertain behavior)
- benign (M8000/0) — see Neoplasm, by site, benign
- beta cell (M8151/0)
  - malignant (M8151/3)
    - pancreas 157.4
    - specified site — see Neoplasm, by site, malignant
    - unspecified site 157.4
  - pancreas 211.7
  - specified site NEC — see Neoplasm, by site, benign
  - unspecified site 211.7
- blood — see Hematoma
- Brenner (M9000/0) 220
  - borderline malignancy (M9000/1) 236.2
  - malignant (M9000/3) 183.0
  - proliferating (M9000/1) 236.2
- Brooke's (M8100/0) — see Neoplasm, skin, benign
- brown fat (M8880/0) — see Lipoma, by site
- Burkitt's (M9750/3) 200.2 ✓
- calcifying epithelial odontogenic (M9340/0) 213.1
  - upper jaw (bone) 213.0
- carcinoid (M8240/1) 209.60
  - benign 209.60
    - appendix 209.51
    - ascending colon 209.53
    - bronchus 209.61
    - cecum 209.52
    - colon 209.50
    - descending colon 209.55
    - duodenum 209.41
    - foregut 209.65
    - hindgut 209.67
    - ileum 209.43
    - jejunum 209.42
    - kidney 209.64
    - large intestine 209.50
    - lung 209.61
    - midgut 209.66
    - rectum 209.57
    - sigmoid colon 209.56
    - small intestine 209.40
    - specified NEC 209.69
    - stomach 209.63
    - thymus 209.62
    - transverse colon 209.54
  - malignant (of) 209.20
    - appendix 209.11
    - ascending colon 209.13
    - bronchus 209.21
    - cecum 209.12
    - colon 209.10
    - descending colon 209.15
    - duodenum 209.01
    - foregut 209.25
    - hindgut 209.27
    - ileum 209.03
    - jejunum 209.02
    - kidney 209.24
    - large intestine 209.10

Tumor — see also Neoplasm, by site, unspecified
nature — continued
- carcinoid — continued
  - malignant — continued
    - lung 209.21
    - midgut 209.26
    - rectum 209.17
    - sigmoid colon 209.16
    - small intestine 209.00
    - specified NEC 209.29
    - stomach 209.23
    - thymus 209.22
    - transverse colon 209.14
  - secondary — see Tumor, neuroendocrine, secondary ●
- carotid body (M8692/1) 237.3
  - malignant (M8692/3) 194.5
- Castleman's (mediastinal lymph node hyperplasia) 785.6
- cells (M8001/1) (see also Neoplasm, by site, unspecified nature)
  - benign (M8001/0) — see Neoplasm, by site, benign
  - malignant (M8001/3) — see Neoplasm, by site, malignant
  - uncertain whether benign or malignant (M8001/1) — see Neoplasm, by site, uncertain nature
- cervix
  - in pregnancy or childbirth 654.6 ✓
    - affecting fetus or newborn 763.89
    - causing obstructed labor 660.2 ✓
      - affecting fetus or newborn 763.1
- chondromatous giant cell (M9230/0) — see Neoplasm, bone, benign
- chromaffin (M8700/0) (see also Neoplasm, by site, benign)
  - malignant (M8700/3) — see Neoplasm, by site, malignant
- Cock's peculiar 706.2
- Codman's (benign chondroblastoma) (M9230/0) — see Neoplasm, bone, benign
- dentigerous, mixed (M9282/0) 213.1
  - upper jaw (bone) 213.0
- dermoid (M9084/0) — see Neoplasm, by site, benign
  - with malignant transformation (M9084/3) 183.0
- desmoid (extra-abdominal) (M8821/1) (see also Neoplasm, connective tissue, uncertain behavior)
  - abdominal (M8822/1) — see Neoplasm, connective tissue, uncertain behavior
- embryonal (mixed) (M9080/1) (see also Neoplasm, by site, uncertain behavior)
  - liver (M9080/3) 155.0
- endodermal sinus (M9071/3)
  - specified site — see Neoplasm, by site, malignant
  - unspecified site
    - female 183.0
    - male 186.9
- epithelial
  - benign (M8010/0) — see Neoplasm, by site, benign
  - malignant (M8010/3) — see Neoplasm, by site, malignant
- Ewing's (M9260/3) — see Neoplasm, bone, malignant
- fatty — see Lipoma
- fetal, causing disproportion 653.7 ✓
  - causing obstructed labor 660.1 ✓
- fibroid (M8890/0) — see Leiomyoma
- G cell (M8153/1)
  - malignant (M8153/3)
    - pancreas 157.4
    - specified site NEC — see Neoplasm, by site, malignant
    - unspecified site 157.4
  - specified site — see Neoplasm, by site, uncertain behavior
  - unspecified site 235.5
- giant cell (type) (M8003/1) (see also Neoplasm, by site, unspecified nature)

Tumor — see also Neoplasm, by site, unspecified
nature — continued
- giant cell (see also Neoplasm, by site, unspecified nature) — continued
  - bone (M9250/1) 238.0
    - malignant (M9250/3) — see Neoplasm, bone, malignant
  - chondromatous (M9230/0) — see Neoplasm, bone, benign
  - malignant (M8003/3) — see Neoplasm, by site, malignant
  - peripheral (gingiva) 523.8
  - soft parts (M9251/1) (see also Neoplasm, connective tissue, uncertain behavior)
    - malignant (M9251/3) — see Neoplasm, connective tissue, malignant
  - tendon sheath 727.02
- glomus (M8711/0) (see also Hemangioma, by site)
  - jugulare (M8690/1) 237.3
    - malignant (M8690/3) 194.6
- gonadal stromal (M8590/1) — see Neoplasm, by site, uncertain behavior
- granular cell (M9580/0) (see also Neoplasm, connective tissue, benign)
  - malignant (M9580/3) — see Neoplasm, connective tissue, malignant
- granulosa cell (M8620/1) 236.2
  - malignant (M8620/3) 183.0
- granulosa cell-theca cell (M8621/1) 236.2
  - malignant (M8621/3) 183.0
- Grawitz's (hypernephroma) (M8312/3) 189.0
- hazard-crile (M8350/3) 193
- hemorrhoidal — see Hemorrhoids
- hilar cell (M8660/0) 220
- Hürthle cell (benign) (M8290/0) 226
  - malignant (M8290/3) 193
- hydatid (see also Echinococcus) 122.9
- hypernephroid (M8311/1) (see also Neoplasm, by site, uncertain behavior)
- interstitial cell (M8650/1) (see also Neoplasm, by site, uncertain behavior)
  - benign (M8650/0) — see Neoplasm, by site, benign
  - malignant (M8650/3) — see Neoplasm, by site, malignant
- islet cell (M8150/0)
  - malignant (M8150/3)
    - pancreas 157.4
    - specified site — see Neoplasm, by site, malignant
    - unspecified site 157.4
  - pancreas 211.7
  - specified site NEC — see Neoplasm, by site, benign
  - unspecified site 211.7
- juxtaglomerular (M8361/1) 236.91
- Krukenberg's (M8490/6) 198.6
- Leydig cell (M8650/1)
  - benign (M8650/0)
    - specified site — see Neoplasm, by site, benign
    - unspecified site
      - female 220
      - male 222.0
  - malignant (M8650/3)
    - specified site — see Neoplasm, by site, malignant
    - unspecified site
      - female 183.0
      - male 186.9
  - specified site — see Neoplasm, by site, uncertain behavior
  - unspecified site
    - female 236.2
    - male 236.4
- lipid cell, ovary (M8670/0) 220
- lipoid cell, ovary (M8670/0) 220
- lymphomatous, benign (M9590/0) (see also Neoplasm, by site, benign)
- lysis syndrome (following antineoplastic drug therapy) (spontaneous) 277.88 ●
- Malherbe's (M8110/0) — see Neoplasm, skin, benign

Tumor — see also Neoplasm, by site, unspecified
nature — continued
- malignant (M8000/3) (see also Neoplasm, by site, malignant)
  - fusiform cell (type) (M8004/3) — see Neoplasm, by site, malignant
  - giant cell (type) (M8003/3) — see Neoplasm, by site, malignant
  - mixed NEC (M8940/3) — see Neoplasm, by site, malignant
  - small cell (type) (M8002/3) — see Neoplasm, by site, malignant
  - spindle cell (type) (M8004/3) — see Neoplasm, by site, malignant
- mast cell (M9740/1) 238.5
  - malignant (M9740/3) 202.6 ✓
- melanotic, neuroectodermal (M9363/0) — see Neoplasm, by site, benign
- Merkel cell — see ▶Carcinoma, Merkel cell◀
- mesenchymal
  - malignant (M8800/3) — see Neoplasm, connective tissue, malignant
  - mixed (M8990/1) — see Neoplasm, connective tissue, uncertain behavior
- mesodermal, mixed (M8951/3) (see also Neoplasm, by site, malignant)
  - liver 155.0
- mesonephric (M9110/1) (see also Neoplasm, by site, uncertain behavior)
  - malignant (M9110/3) — see Neoplasm, by site, malignant
- metastatic
  - from specified site (M8000/3) — see Neoplasm, by site, malignant
  - to specified site (M8000/6) — see Neoplasm, by site, malignant, secondary
- mixed NEC (M8940/0) (see also Neoplasm, by site, benign)
  - malignant (M8940/3) — see Neoplasm, by site, malignant
- mucocarcinoid, malignant (M8243/3) — see Neoplasm, by site, malignant
- mucoepidermoid (M8430/1) — see Neoplasm, by site, uncertain behavior
- Müllerian, mixed (M8950/3) — see Neoplasm, by site, malignant
- myoepithelial (M8982/0) — see Neoplasm, by site, benign
- neuroendocrine 209.60
  - malignant poorly differentiated 209.30 ●
  - secondary 209.70 ●
    - bone 209.73 ●
    - distant lymph nodes 209.71 ●
    - liver 209.72 ●
    - peritoneum 209.74 ●
    - site specified NEC 209.79 ●
- neurogenic olfactory (M9520/3) 160.0
- nonencapsulated sclerosing (M8350/3) 193
- odontogenic (M9270/1) 238.0
  - adenomatoid (M9300/0) 213.1
    - upper jaw (bone) 213.0
  - benign (M9270/0) 213.1
    - upper jaw (bone) 213.0
  - calcifying epithelial (M9340/0) 213.1
    - upper jaw (bone) 213.0
  - malignant (M9270/3) 170.1
    - upper jaw (bone) 170.0
  - squamous (M9312/0) 213.1
    - upper jaw (bone) 213.0
- ovarian stromal (M8590/1) 236.2
- ovary
  - in pregnancy or childbirth 654.4 ✓
    - affecting fetus or newborn 763.89
    - causing obstructed labor 660.2 ✓
      - affecting fetus or newborn 763.1
- pacinian (M9507/0) — see Neoplasm, skin, benign
- Pancoast's (M8010/3) 162.3
- papillary — see Papilloma
- pelvic, in pregnancy or childbirth 654.9 ✓
  - affecting fetus or newborn 763.89
  - causing obstructed labor 660.2 ✓
    - affecting fetus or newborn 763.1
- phantom 300.11
- plasma cell (M9731/1) 238.6

mor — *see also* Neoplasm, by site, unspecified nature — *continued*
- plasma cell — *continued*
  - benign (M9731/0) — *see* Neoplasm, by site, benign
  - malignant (M9731/3) 203.8 ☑
- polyvesicular vitelline (M9071/3)
  - specified site — *see* Neoplasm, by site, malignant
  - unspecified site
    - female 183.0
    - male 186.9
- Pott's puffy (*see also* Osteomyelitis) 730.2 ☑
- Rathke's pouch (M9350/1) 237.0
- regaud's (M8082/3) — *see* Neoplasm, nasopharynx, malignant
- rete cell (M8140/0) 222.0
- retinal anlage (M9363/0) — *see* Neoplasm, by site, benign
- Rokitansky's 620.2
- salivary gland type, mixed (M8940/0) (*see also* Neoplasm, by site, benign)
  - malignant (M8940/3) — *see* Neoplasm, by site, malignant
- Sampson's 617.1
- Schloffer's (*see also* Peritonitis) 567.29
- Schmincke (M8082/3) — *see* Neoplasm, nasopharynx, malignant
- sebaceous (*see also* Cyst, sebaceous) 706.2
- secondary (M8000/6) — *see* Neoplasm, by site, secondary
  - carcinoid — *see* Tumor, neuroendocrine, ●
    - secondary ●
  - neuroendocrine — *see* Tumor, neuroendocrine, secondary ●
- Sertoli cell (M8640/0)
  - with lipid storage (M8641/0)
    - specified site — *see* Neoplasm, by site, benign
    - unspecified site
      - female 220
      - male 222.0
  - specified site — *see* Neoplasm, by site, benign
  - unspecified site
    - female 220
    - male 222.0
- Sertoli-Leydig cell (M8631/0)
  - specified site, — *see* Neoplasm, by site, benign
  - unspecified site
    - female 220
    - male 222.0
- sex cord (-stromal) (M8590/1) — *see* Neoplasm, by site, uncertain behavior
- skin appendage (M8390/0) — *see* Neoplasm, skin, benign
- soft tissue
  - benign (M8800/0) — *see* Neoplasm, connective tissue, benign
  - malignant (M8800/3) — *see* Neoplasm, connective tissue, malignant
- sternomastoid 754.1
- stromal
  - abdomen
    - benign 215.5
    - malignant NEC 171.5
    - uncertain behavior 238.1
  - digestive system 238.1
    - benign 215.5
    - malignant NEC 171.5
    - uncertain behavior 238.1
  - gastric 238.1
    - benign 215.5
    - malignant 151.9
    - uncertain behavior 238.1
  - gastrointestinal 238.1
    - benign 215.5
    - malignant NEC 171.5
    - uncertain behavior 238.1
  - intestine (small) 238.1
    - benign 215.5
    - malignant 152.9
    - uncertain behavior 238.1
  - stomach 238.1
    - benign 215.5

Tumor — *see also* Neoplasm, by site, unspecified nature — *continued*
- stromal — *continued*
  - stomach — *continued*
    - malignant 151.9
    - uncertain behavior 238.1
- superior sulcus (lung) (pulmonary) (syndrome) (M8010/3) 162.3
- suprasulcus (M8010/3) 162.3
- sweat gland (M8400/1) (*see also* Neoplasm, skin, uncertain behavior)
  - benign (M8400/0) — *see* Neoplasm, skin, benign
  - malignant (M8400/3) — *see* Neoplasm, skin, malignant
- syphilitic brain 094.89
  - congenital 090.49
- testicular stromal (M8590/1) 236.4
- theca cell (M8600/0) 220
- theca cell-granulosa cell (M8621/1) 236.2
- theca-lutein (M8610/0) 220
- turban (M8200/0) 216.4
- uterus
  - in pregnancy or childbirth 654.1 ☑
    - affecting fetus or newborn 763.89
    - causing obstructed labor 660.2 ☑
      - affecting fetus or newborn 763.1
- vagina
  - in pregnancy or childbirth 654.7 ☑
    - affecting fetus or newborn 763.89
    - causing obstructed labor 660.2 ☑
      - affecting fetus or newborn 763.1
- varicose (*see also* Varicose, vein) 454.9
- von Recklinghausen's (M9540/1) 237.71
- vulva
  - in pregnancy or childbirth 654.8 ☑
    - affecting fetus or newborn 763.89
    - causing obstructed labor 660.2 ☑
      - affecting fetus or newborn 763.1
- Warthin's (salivary gland) (M8561/0) 210.2
- white (*see also* Tuberculosis, arthritis)
- White-Darier 757.39
- Wilms' (nephroblastoma) (M8960/3) 189.0
- yolk sac (M9071/3)
  - specified site — *see* Neoplasm, by site, malignant
  - unspecified site
    - female 183.0
    - male 186.9

Tumorlet (M8040/1) — *see* Neoplasm, by site, uncertain behavior
Tungiasis 134.1
Tunica vasculosa lentis 743.39
Tunnel vision 368.45
Turban tumor (M8200/0) 216.4
Türck's trachoma (chronic catarrhal laryngitis) 476.0
Türk's syndrome (ocular retraction syndrome) 378.71
Turner's
- hypoplasia (tooth) 520.4
- syndrome 758.6
- tooth 520.4

Turner-Kieser syndrome (hereditary osteo-onychodysplasia) 756.89
Turner-Varny syndrome 758.6
Turricephaly 756.0
Tussis convulsiva — *see also* Whooping cough 033.9
Twiddler's syndrome (due to)
- automatic implantable defibrillator 996.04
- pacemaker 996.01

Twin
- affected by maternal complications of pregnancy 761.5
- conjoined 759.4
  - fetal 678.1 ☑
- healthy liveborn — *see* Newborn, twin
- pregnancy (complicating delivery) NEC 651.0 ☑
  - with fetal loss and retention of one fetus 651.3 ☑
  - conjoined 678.1 ☑
  - following (elective) fetal reduction

Twinning, teeth 520.2

Twist, twisted
- bowel, colon, or intestine 560.2
- hair (congenital) 757.4
- mesentery 560.2
- omentum 560.2
- organ or site, congenital NEC — *see* Anomaly, specified type NEC
- ovarian pedicle 620.5
  - congenital 752.0
- umbilical cord — *see* Compression, umbilical cord

Twitch 781.0
Tylosis 700
- buccalis 528.6
- gingiva 523.8
- linguae 528.6
- palmaris et plantaris 757.39

Tympanism 787.3
Tympanites (abdominal) (intestine) 787.3
Tympanitis — *see* Myringitis
Tympanosclerosis 385.00
- involving
  - combined sites NEC 385.09
    - with tympanic membrane 385.03
  - tympanic membrane 385.01
    - with ossicles 385.02
      - and middle ear 385.03

Tympanum — *see* condition
Tympany
- abdomen 787.3
- chest 786.7

Typhlitis — *see also* Appendicitis 541
Typhoenteritis 002.0
Typhogastric fever 002.0
Typhoid (abortive) (ambulant) (any site) (fever) (hemorrhagic) (infection) (intermittent) (malignant) (rheumatic) 002.0
- with pneumonia 002.0 [484.8]
- abdominal 002.0
- carrier (suspected) of V02.1
- cholecystitis (current) 002.0
- clinical (Widal and blood test negative) 002.0
- endocarditis 002.0 [421.1]
- inoculation reaction — *see* Complications, vaccination
- meningitis 002.0 [320.7]
- mesenteric lymph nodes 002.0
- myocarditis 002.0 [422.0]
- osteomyelitis (*see also* Osteomyelitis, due to, typhoid) 002.0 [730.8] ☑
- perichondritis, larynx 002.0 [478.71]
- pneumonia 002.0 [484.8]
- spine 002.0 [720.81]
- ulcer (perforating) 002.0
- vaccination, prophylactic (against) V03.1
- Widal negative 002.0

Typhomalaria (fever) — *see also* Malaria 084.6
Typhomania 002.0
Typhoperitonitis 002.0
Typhus (fever) 081.9
- abdominal, abdominalis 002.0
- African tick 082.1
- amarillic (*see also* Fever, Yellow) 060.9
- brain 081.9
- cerebral 081.9
- classical 080
- endemic (flea-borne) 081.0
- epidemic (louse-borne) 080
- exanthematic NEC 080
- exanthematicus SAI 080
  - brillii SAI 081.1
  - Mexicanus SAI 081.0
  - pediculo vestimenti causa 080
  - typhus murinus 081.0
- flea-borne 081.0
- Indian tick 082.1
- Kenya tick 082.1
- louse-borne 080
- Mexican 081.0
  - flea-borne 081.0
  - louse-borne 080
  - tabardillo 080
- mite-borne 081.2
- murine 081.0
- North Asian tick-borne 082.2
- petechial 081.9

Typhus — *continued*
- Queensland tick 082.3
- rat 081.0
- recrudescent 081.1
- recurrent (*see also* Fever, relapsing) 087.9
- São Paulo 082.0
- scrub (China) (India) (Malaya) (New Guinea) 081.2
- shop (of Malaya) 081.0
- Siberian tick 082.2
- tick-borne NEC 082.9
- tropical 081.2
- vaccination, prophylactic (against) V05.8

Tyrosinemia 270.2
- neonatal 775.89
Tyrosinosis (Medes) (Sakai) 270.2
Tyrosinuria 270.2
Tyrosyluria 270.2

U

Uehlinger's syndrome (acropachyderma) 757.39
Uhl's anomaly or disease (hypoplasia of myocardium, right ventricle) 746.84
Ulcerosa scarlatina 034.1
Ulcer, ulcerated, ulcerating, ulceration, ulcerative 707.9
- with gangrene 707.9 [785.4]
- abdomen (wall) (*see also* Ulcer, skin) 707.8
- ala, nose 478.19
- alveolar process 526.5
- amebic (intestine) 006.9
  - skin 006.6
- anastomotic — *see* Ulcer, gastrojejunal
- anorectal 569.41
- antral — *see* Ulcer, stomach
- anus (sphincter) (solitary) 569.41
  - varicose — *see* Varicose, ulcer, anus
- aorta — *see* Aneuysm
- aphthous (oral) (recurrent) 528.2
  - genital organ(s)
    - female 616.50
    - male 608.89
  - mouth 528.2
- arm (*see also* Ulcer, skin) 707.8
- arteriosclerotic plaque — *see* Arteriosclerosis, by site
- artery NEC 447.2
  - without rupture 447.8
- atrophic NEC — *see* Ulcer, skin
- Barrett's (chronic peptic ulcer of esophagus) 530.85
- bile duct 576.8
- bladder (solitary) (sphincter) 596.8
  - bilharzial (*see also* Schistosomiasis) 120.9 [595.4]
  - submucosal (*see also* Cystitis) 595.1
  - tuberculous (*see also* Tuberculosis) 016.1 ☑
- bleeding NEC — *see* Ulcer, peptic, with hemorrhage
- bone 730.9 ☑
- bowel (*see also* Ulcer, intestine) 569.82
- breast 611.0
- bronchitis 491.8
- bronchus 519.19
- buccal (cavity) (traumatic) 528.9
- burn (acute) — *see* Ulcer, duodenum
- Buruli 031.1
- buttock (*see also* Ulcer, skin) 707.8
  - decubitus (*see also* Ulcer, pressure) 707.00
- cancerous (M8000/3) — *see* Neoplasm, by site, malignant
- cardia — *see* Ulcer, stomach
- cardio-esophageal (peptic) 530.20
  - with bleeding 530.21
- cecum (*see also* Ulcer, intestine) 569.82
- cervix (uteri) (trophic) 622.0
  - with mention of cervicitis 616.0
- chancroidal 099.0
- chest (wall) (*see also* Ulcer, skin) 707.8
- Chiclero 085.4
- chin (pyogenic) (*see also* Ulcer, skin) 707.8
- chronic (cause unknown) (*see also* Ulcer, skin)
  - penis 607.89
- Cochin-China 085.1
- colitis — *see* Colitis, ulcerative

Ulcer, ulcerated, ulcerating, ulceration, ulcerative — continued

colon (see also Ulcer, intestine) 569.82
conjunctiva (acute) (postinfectional) 372.00
cornea (infectional) 370.00
  with perforation 370.06
  annular 370.02
  catarrhal 370.01
  central 370.03
  dendritic 054.42
  marginal 370.01
  mycotic 370.05
  phlyctenular, tuberculous (see also Tuberculosis) 017.3 ☑ [370.31]
  ring 370.02
  rodent 370.07
  serpent, serpiginous 370.04
  superficial marginal 370.01
  tuberculous (see also Tuberculosis) 017.3 ☑ [370.31]
corpus cavernosum (chronic) 607.89
crural — see Ulcer, lower extremity
Curling's — see Ulcer, duodenum
Cushing's — see Ulcer, peptic
cystitis (interstitial) 595.1
decubitus (unspecified site) (see also Ulcer, pressure) 707.00
  with gangrene 707.00 [785.4]
  ankle 707.06
  back
    lower 707.03
    upper 707.02
  buttock 707.05
  coccyx 707.03
  elbow 707.01
  head 707.09
  heel 707.07
  hip 707.04
  other site 707.09
  sacrum 707.03
  shoulder blades 707.02
dendritic 054.42
diabetes, diabetic (mellitus) 250.8 ☑ [707.9]
  due to secondary diabetes 249.8 ☑ [707.9]
  lower limb 250.8 ☑ [707.10]
    ankle 250.8 ☑ [707.13]
      due to secondary diabetes 249.8 ☑ [707.13]
    calf 250.8 ☑ [707.12]
      due to secondary diabetes 249.8 ☑ [707.12]
      due to secondary diabetes 249.8 ☑ [707.10]
    foot 250.8 ☑ [707.15]
      due to secondary diabetes 249.8 ☑ [707.15]
    heel 250.8 ☑ [707.14]
      due to secondary diabetes 249.8 ☑ [707.14]
    knee 250.8 ☑ [707.19]
      due to secondary diabetes 249.8 ☑ [707.19]
    specified site NEC 250.8 ☑ [707.19]
      due to secondary diabetes 249.8 ☑ [707.19]
    thigh 250.8 ☑ [707.11]
      due to secondary diabetes 249.8 ☑ [707.11]
    toes 250.8 ☑ [707.15]
      due to secondary diabetes 249.8 ☑ [707.15]
  specified site NEC 250.8 ☑ [707.8]
    due to secondary diabetes 249.8 ☑ [707.8]
Dieulafoy — see Lesion, Dieulafoy
due to
  infection NEC — see Ulcer, skin
  radiation, radium — see Ulcer, by site
  trophic disturbance (any region) — see Ulcer, skin
  x-ray — see Ulcer, by site

Ulcer, ulcerated, ulcerating, ulceration, ulcerative — continued

duodenum, duodenal (eroded) (peptic) 532.9 ☑

Note — Use the following fifth-digit subclassification with categories 531–534:

0   without mention of obstruction

1   with obstruction

  with
    hemorrhage (chronic) 532.4 ☑
      and perforation 532.6 ☑
    perforation (chronic) 532.5 ☑
      and hemorrhage 532.6 ☑
  acute 532.3 ☑
    with
      hemorrhage 532.0 ☑
        and perforation 532.2 ☑
      perforation 532.1 ☑
        and hemorrhage 532.2 ☑
  bleeding (recurrent) — see Ulcer, duodenum, with hemorrhage
  chronic 532.7 ☑
    with
      hemorrhage 532.4 ☑
        and perforation 532.6 ☑
      perforation 532.5 ☑
        and hemorrhage 532.6 ☑
  penetrating — see Ulcer, duodenum, with perforation
  perforating — see Ulcer, duodenum, with perforation
dysenteric NEC 009.0
elusive 595.1
endocarditis (any valve) (acute) (chronic) (subacute) 421.0
enteritis — see Colitis, ulcerative
enterocolitis 556.0
epiglottis 478.79
esophagus (peptic) 530.20
  with bleeding 530.21
  due to ingestion
    aspirin 530.20
    chemicals 530.20
    medicinal agents 530.20
  fungal 530.20
  infectional 530.20
  varicose (see also Varix, esophagus) 456.1
    bleeding (see also Varix, esophagus, bleeding) 456.0
eye NEC 360.00
  dendritic 054.42
eyelid (region) 373.01
face (see also Ulcer, skin) 707.8
fauces 478.29
Fenwick (-Hunner) (solitary) (see also Cystitis) 595.1
fistulous NEC — see Ulcer, skin
foot (indolent) (see also Ulcer, lower extremity) 707.15
  perforating 707.15
    leprous 030.1
    syphilitic 094.0
  trophic 707.15
  varicose 454.0
    inflamed or infected 454.2
frambesial, initial or primary 102.0
gallbladder or duct 575.8
gall duct 576.8
gangrenous (see also Gangrene) 785.4
gastric — see Ulcer, stomach
gastrocolic — see Ulcer, gastrojejunal
gastroduodenal — see Ulcer, peptic
gastroesophageal — see Ulcer, stomach
gastrohepatic — see Ulcer, stomach
gastrointestinal — see Ulcer, gastrojejunal
gastrojejunal (eroded) (peptic) 534.9 ☑

Note — Use the following fifth-digit subclassification with categories 531–534:

0   without mention of obstruction

1   with obstruction

  with
    hemorrhage (chronic) 534.4 ☑

Ulcer, ulcerated, ulcerating, ulceration, ulcerative — continued

gastrojejunal — continued
  with — continued
    hemorrhage — continued
      and perforation 534.6 ☑
    perforation 534.5 ☑
      and hemorrhage 534.6 ☑
  acute 534.3 ☑
    with
      hemorrhage 534.0 ☑
        and perforation 534.2 ☑
      perforation 534.1 ☑
        and hemorrhage 534.2 ☑
  bleeding (recurrent) — see Ulcer, gastrojejunal, with hemorrhage
  chronic 534.7 ☑
    with
      hemorrhage 534.4 ☑
        and perforation 534.6 ☑
      perforation 534.5 ☑
        and hemorrhage 534.6 ☑
  penetrating — see Ulcer, gastrojejunal, with perforation
  perforating — see Ulcer, gastrojejunal, with perforation
gastrojejunocolic — see Ulcer, gastrojejunal
genital organ
  female 629.89
  male 608.89
gingiva 523.8
gingivitis 523.10
glottis 478.79
granuloma of pudenda 099.2
groin (see also Ulcer, skin) 707.8
gum 523.8
gumma, due to yaws 102.4
hand (see also Ulcer, skin) 707.8
hard palate 528.9
heel (see also Ulcer, lower extremity) 707.14
  decubitus (see also Ulcer, pressure) 707.07
hemorrhoids 455.8
  external 455.5
  internal 455.2
hip (see also Ulcer, skin) 707.8
  decubitus (see also Ulcer, pressure) 707.04
Hunner's 595.1
hypopharynx 478.29
hypopyon (chronic) (subacute) 370.04
hypostaticum — see Ulcer, varicose
ileocolitis 556.1
ileum (see also Ulcer, intestine) 569.82
intestine, intestinal 569.82
  with perforation 569.83
  amebic 006.9
  duodenal — see Ulcer, duodenum
  granulocytopenic (with hemorrhage) 288.09
  marginal 569.82
  perforating 569.83
  small, primary 569.82
  stercoraceous 569.82
  stercoral 569.82
  tuberculous (see also Tuberculosis) 014.8 ☑
  typhoid (fever) 002.0
  varicose 456.8
ischemic 707.9
  lower extremity (see also Ulcer, lower extremity) 707.10
    ankle 707.13
    calf 707.12
    foot 707.15
    heel 707.14
    knee 707.19
    specified site NEC 707.19
    thigh 707.11
    toes 707.15
jejunum, jejunal — see Ulcer, gastrojejunal
keratitis (see also Ulcer, cornea) 370.00
knee — see Ulcer, lower extremity
labium (majus) (minus) 616.50
laryngitis (see also Laryngitis) 464.00
  with obstruction 464.01
larynx (aphthous) (contact) 478.79
  diphtheritic 032.3

Ulcer, ulcerated, ulcerating, ulceration, ulcerative — continued

leg — see Ulcer, lower extremity
lip 528.5
Lipschütz's 616.50
lower extremity (atrophic) (chronic) (neurogenic) (perforating) (pyogenic) (trophic) (tropical) 707.10
  with gangrene (see also Ulcer, lower extremity) 707.10 [785.4]
    arteriosclerotic 440.24
  ankle 707.13
    arteriosclerotic 440.23
      with gangrene 440.24
  calf 707.12
  decubitus (see also Ulcer, pressure) 707
    with gangrene 707.00 [785.4]
    ankle 707.06
    buttock 707.05
    heel 707.07
    hip 707.04
  foot 707.15
  heel 707.14
  knee 707.19
  specified site NEC 707.19
  thigh 707.11
  toes 707.15
  varicose 454.0
    inflamed or infected 454.2
luetic — see Ulcer, syphilitic
lung 518.89
  tuberculous (see also Tuberculosis) 011.2 ☑
malignant (M8000/3) — see Neoplasm, by site, malignant
marginal NEC — see Ulcer, gastrojejunal
meatus (urinarius) 597.89
Meckel's diverticulum 751.0
Meleney's (chronic undermining) 686.09
Mooren's (cornea) 370.07
mouth (traumatic) 528.9
mycobacterial (skin) 031.1
nasopharynx 478.29
navel cord (newborn) 771.4
neck (see also Ulcer, skin) 707.8
  uterus 622.0
neurogenic NEC — see Ulcer, skin
nose, nasal (infectional) (passage) 478.19
  septum 478.19
  varicose 456.8
  skin — see Ulcer, skin
  spirochetal NEC 104.8
oral mucosa (traumatic) 528.9
palate (soft) 528.9
penetrating NEC — see Ulcer, peptic, with perforation
penis (chronic) 607.89
peptic (site unspecified) 533.9 ☑

Note — Use the following fifth-digit subclassification with categories 531–534:

0   without mention of obstruction

1   with obstruction

  with
    hemorrhage 533.4 ☑
      and perforation 533.6 ☑
    perforation (chronic) 533.5 ☑
      and hemorrhage 533.6 ☑
  acute 533.3 ☑
    with
      hemorrhage 533.0 ☑
        and perforation 533.2 ☑
      perforation 533.1 ☑
        and hemorrhage 533.2 ☑
  bleeding (recurrent) — see Ulcer, peptic, with hemorrhage
  chronic 533.7 ☑
    with
      hemorrhage 533.4 ☑
        and perforation 533.6 ☑
      perforation 533.5 ☑
        and hemorrhage 533.6 ☑
  penetrating — see Ulcer, peptic, with perforation

Ulcer, ulcerated, ulcerating, ulceration, ulcerative — Upper respiratory

Ulcer, ulcerated, ulcerating, ulceration, ulcerative — *continued*
perforating NEC (*see also* Ulcer, peptic, with perforation) 533.5 ☑
skin 707.9
perineum (*see also* Ulcer, skin) 707.8
peritonsillar 474.8
phagedenic (tropical) NEC — *see* Ulcer, skin
pharynx 478.29
phlebitis — *see* Phlebitis
plaster (*see also* Ulcer, pressure) 707.00
popliteal space — *see* Ulcer, lower extremity
postpyloric — *see* Ulcer, duodenum
prepuce 607.89
prepyloric — *see* Ulcer, stomach
pressure 707.00
with
abrasion, blister, partial thickness skin loss involving epidermis and/or dermis 707.22
full thickness skin loss involving damage or necrosis of subcutaneous tissue 707.23
gangrene 707.00 [785.4]
necrosis of soft tissue through to underlying muscle, tendon, or bone 707.24
ankle 707.06
back
lower 707.03
upper 707.02
buttock 707.05
coccyx 707.03
elbow 707.01
head 707.09
healed — omit code
healing — code to Ulcer, pressure, by stage
heel 707.07
hip 707.04
other site 707.09
sacrum 707.03
shoulder blades 707.02
stage
I (healing) 707.21
II (healing) 707.22
III (healing) 707.23
IV (healing) 707.24
unspecified (healing) 707.20
unstageable 707.25
primary of intestine 569.82
with perforation 569.83
proctitis 556.2
with ulcerative sigmoiditis 556.3
prostate 601.8
pseudopeptic — *see* Ulcer, peptic
pyloric — *see* Ulcer, stomach
rectosigmoid 569.82
with perforation 569.83
rectum (sphincter) (solitary) 569.41
stercoraceous, stercoral 569.41
varicose — *see* Varicose, ulcer, anus
retina (*see also* Chorioretinitis) 363.20
rodent (M8090/3) (*see also* Neoplasm, skin, malignant)
cornea 370.07
round — *see* Ulcer, stomach
sacrum (region) (*see also* Ulcer, skin) 707.8
Saemisch's 370.04
scalp (*see also* Ulcer, skin) 707.8
sclera 379.09
scrofulous (*see also* Tuberculosis) 017.2 ☑
scrotum 608.89
tuberculous (*see also* Tuberculosis) 016.5 ☑
varicose 456.4
seminal vesicle 608.89
sigmoid 569.82
with perforation 569.83
skin (atrophic) (chronic) (neurogenic) (non-healing) (perforating) (pyogenic) (trophic) 707.9
with gangrene 707.9 [785.4]
amebic 006.6
decubitus (*see also* Ulcer, pressure) 707.00
with gangrene 707.00 [785.4]

Ulcer, ulcerated, ulcerating, ulceration, ulcerative — *continued*
skin — *continued*
in granulocytopenia 288.09
lower extremity (*see also* Ulcer, lower extremity) 707.10
with gangrene 707.10 [785.4]
arteriosclerotic 440.24
ankle 707.13
arteriosclerotic 440.23
with gangrene 440.24
calf 707.12
foot 707.15
heel 707.14
knee 707.19
specified site NEC 707.19
thigh 707.11
toes 707.15
mycobacterial 031.1
syphilitic (early) (secondary) 091.3
tuberculous (primary) (*see also* Tuberculosis) 017.0 ☑
varicose — *see* Ulcer, varicose
sloughing NEC — *see* Ulcer, skin
soft palate 528.9
solitary, anus or rectum (sphincter) 569.41
sore throat 462
streptococcal 034.0
spermatic cord 608.89
spine (tuberculous) 015.0 ☑ [730.88]
stasis (leg) (venous) 454.0
with varicose veins 454.0
without varicose veins 459.81
inflamed or infected 454.2
stercoral, stercoraceous 569.82
with perforation 569.83
anus or rectum 569.41
stomach (eroded) (peptic) (round) 531.9 ☑

Note — Use the following fifth-digit subclassification with categories 531–534:

0   *without mention of obstruction*

1   *with obstruction*

with
hemorrhage 531.4 ☑
and perforation 531.6 ☑
perforation (chronic) 531.5 ☑
and hemorrhage 531.6 ☑
acute 531.3 ☑
with
hemorrhage 531.0 ☑
and perforation 531.2 ☑
perforation 531.1 ☑
and hemorrhage 531.2 ☑
bleeding (recurrent) — *see* Ulcer, stomach, with hemorrhage
chronic 531.7 ☑
with
hemorrhage 531.4 ☑
and perforation 531.6 ☑
perforation 531.5 ☑
and hemorrhage 531.6 ☑
penetrating — *see* Ulcer, stomach, with perforation
perforating — *see* Ulcer, stomach, with perforation
stoma, stomal — *see* Ulcer, gastrojejunal
stomatitis 528.00
stress — *see* Ulcer, peptic
strumous (tuberculous) (*see also* Tuberculosis) 017.2 ☑
submental (*see also* Ulcer, skin) 707.8
submucosal, bladder 595.1
syphilitic (any site) (early) (secondary) 091.3
late 095.9
perforating 095.9
foot 094.0
testis 608.89
thigh — *see* Ulcer, lower extremity
throat 478.29
diphtheritic 032.0
toe — *see* Ulcer, lower extremity
tongue (traumatic) 529.0
tonsil 474.8
diphtheritic 032.0

Ulcer, ulcerated, ulcerating, ulceration, ulcerative — *continued*
trachea 519.19
trophic — *see* Ulcer, skin
tropical NEC (*see also* Ulcer, skin) 707.9
tuberculous — *see* Tuberculosis, ulcer
tunica vaginalis 608.89
turbinate 730.9 ☑
typhoid (fever) 002.0
perforating 002.0
umbilicus (newborn) 771.4
unspecified site NEC — *see* Ulcer, skin
urethra (meatus) (*see also* Urethritis) 597.89
uterus 621.8
cervix 622.0
with mention of cervicitis 616.0
neck 622.0
with mention of cervicitis 616.0
vagina 616.89
valve, heart 421.0
varicose (lower extremity, any part) 454.0
anus — *see* Varicose, ulcer, anus
broad ligament 456.5
esophagus (*see also* Varix, esophagus) 456.1
bleeding (*see also* Varix, esophagus, bleeding) 456.0
inflamed or infected 454.2
nasal septum 456.8
perineum 456.6
rectum — *see* Varicose, ulcer, anus
scrotum 456.4
specified site NEC 456.8
sublingual 456.3
vulva 456.6
vas deferens 608.89
vesical (*see also* Ulcer, bladder) 596.8
vulva (acute) (infectional) 616.50
Behçet's syndrome 136.1 [616.51]
herpetic 054.12
tuberculous 016.7 ☑ [616.51]
vulvobuccal, recurring 616.50
x-ray — *see* Ulcer, by site
yaws 102.4
Ulcus — *see also* Ulcer
cutis tuberculosum (*see also* Tuberculosis) 017.0 ☑
duodeni — *see* Ulcer, duodenum
durum 091.0
extragenital 091.2
gastrojejunale — *see* Ulcer, gastrojejunal
hypostaticum — *see* Ulcer, varicose
molle (cutis) (skin) 099.0
serpens corneae (pneumococcal) 370.04
ventriculi — *see* Ulcer, stomach
Ulegyria 742.4
Ulerythema
acneiforma 701.8
centrifugum 695.4
ophryogenes 757.4
Ullrich-Feichtiger syndrome 759.89
Ullrich (-Bonnevie) (-Turner) syndrome 758.6
Ulnar — *see* condition
Ulorrhagia 523.8
Ulorrhea 523.8
Umbilicus, umbilical — *see also* condition
cord necrosis, affecting fetus or newborn 762.6
Unacceptable
existing dental restoration
contours 525.65
morphology 525.65
Unavailability of medical facilities (at) V63.9
due to
investigation by social service agency V63.8
lack of services at home V63.1
remoteness from facility V63.0
waiting list V63.2
home V63.1
outpatient clinic V63.0
specified reason NEC V63.8
Uncinaria americana infestation 126.1
Uncinariasis — *see also* Ancylostomiasis 126.9
Unconscious, unconsciousness 780.09
Underdevelopment — *see also* Undeveloped
sexual 259.0

Underfill, endodontic 526.63
Undernourishment 269.9
Undernutrition 269.9
Under observation — *see* Observation
Underweight 783.22
for gestational age — *see* Light-for-dates
Underwood's disease (sclerema neonatorum) 778.1
Undescended — *see also* Malposition, congenital
cecum 751.4
colon 751.4
testis 752.51
Undetermined diagnosis or cause 799.9
Undeveloped, undevelopment — *see also* Hypoplasia
brain (congenital) 742.1
cerebral (congenital) 742.1
fetus or newborn 764.9 ☑
heart 746.89
lung 748.5
testis 257.2
uterus 259.0
Undiagnosed (disease) 799.9
Undulant fever — *see also* Brucellosis 023.9
Unemployment, anxiety concerning V62.0
Unequal leg (acquired) (length) 736.81
congenital 755.30
Unerupted teeth, tooth 520.6
Unextracted dental root 525.3
Unguis incarnatus 703.0
Unicornis uterus 752.3
Unicorporeus uterus 752.3
Uniformis uterus 752.3
Unilateral — *see also* condition
development, breast 611.89
organ or site, congenital NEC — *see* Agenesis
vagina 752.49
Unilateralis uterus 752.3
Unilocular heart 745.8
Uninhibited bladder 596.54
with cauda equina syndrome 344.61
neurogenic — *see* Neurogenic, bladder 596.54
Union, abnormal — *see also* Fusion
divided tendon 727.89
larynx and trachea 748.3
Universal
joint, cervix 620.6
mesentery 751.4
Unknown
cause of death 799.9
diagnosis 799.9
Unna's disease (seborrheic dermatitis) 690.10
Unresponsiveness, adrenocorticotropin (ACTH) 255.41
Unsatisfactory
cytology smear
anal 796.78
cervical 795.08
vaginal 795.18
restoration, tooth (existing) 525.60
specified NEC 525.69
Unsoundness of mind — *see* Psychosis 298.9
Unspecified cause of death 799.9
Unstable
back NEC 724.9
colon 569.89
joint — *see* Instability, joint
lie 652.0 ☑
affecting fetus or newborn (before labor) 761.7
causing obstructed labor 660.0 ☑
affecting fetus or newborn 763.1
lumbosacral joint (congenital) 756.19
acquired 724.6
sacroiliac 724.6
spine NEC 724.9
Untruthfulness, child problem — *see also* Disturbance, conduct 312.0 ☑
Unverricht (-Lundborg) disease, syndrome, or epilepsy 345.1 ☑   ▲
Unverricht-Wagner syndrome (dermatomyositis) 710.3
Upper respiratory — *see* condition

Infection of the lower urinary tract (physicians sometimes use the term "UTI")

Upset
- gastric 536.8
  - psychogenic 306.4
- gastrointestinal 536.8
  - psychogenic 306.4
  - virus (see also Enteritis, viral) 008.8
- intestinal (large) (small) 564.9
  - psychogenic 306.4
- menstruation 626.9
- mental 300.9
- stomach 536.8
  - psychogenic 306.4

Urachus — see also condition
- patent 753.7
- persistent 753.7

Uratic arthritis 274.00 ▲

Urbach's lipoid proteinosis 272.8

Urbach-Oppenheim disease or syndrome (necrobiosis lipoidica diabeticorum) 250.8 ☑ [709.3]
- due to secondary diabetes 249.8 ☑ [709.3]

Urbach-Wiethe disease or syndrome (lipoid proteinosis) 272.8

Urban yellow fever 060.1

Urea, blood, high — see Uremia

Uremia, uremic (absorption) (amaurosis) (amblyopia) (aphasia) (apoplexy) (coma) (delirium) (dementia) (dropsy) (dyspnea) (fever) (intoxication) (mania) (paralysis) (poisoning) (toxemia) (vomiting) 586
- with
  - abortion — see Abortion, by type, with renal failure
  - ectopic pregnancy (see also categories 633.0–633.9) 639.3
  - hypertension (see also Hypertension, kidney) 403.91
  - molar pregnancy (see also categories 630–632) 639.3
- chronic 585.9
- complicating
  - abortion 639.3
  - ectopic or molar pregnancy 639.3
  - hypertension (see also Hypertension, kidney) 403.91
  - labor and delivery 669.3 ☑
- congenital 779.89
- extrarenal 788.99
- hypertensive (chronic) (see also Hypertension, kidney) 403.91
- maternal NEC, affecting fetus or newborn 760.1
- neuropathy 585.9 [357.4]
- pericarditis 585.9 [420.0]
- prerenal 788.99
- pyelitic (see also Pyelitis) 590.80

Ureteralgia 788.0

Ureterectasis 593.89

Ureteritis 593.89
- cystica 590.3
- due to calculus 592.1
- gonococcal (acute) 098.19
  - chronic or duration of 2 months or over 098.39
- nonspecific 593.89

Ureterocele (acquired) 593.89
- congenital 753.23

Ureterolith 592.1

Ureterolithiasis 592.1

Ureterostomy status V44.6
- with complication 997.5

Ureter, ureteral — see condition

Urethralgia 788.99

Urethra, urethral — see condition

Urethritis (abacterial) (acute) (allergic) (anterior) (chronic) (nonvenereal) (posterior) (recurrent) (simple) (subacute) (ulcerative) (undifferentiated) 597.80
- diplococcal (acute) 098.0
  - chronic or duration of 2 months or over 098.2
- due to Trichomonas (vaginalis) 131.02
- gonococcal (acute) 098.0
  - chronic or duration of 2 months or over 098.2
- nongonococcal (sexually transmitted) 099.40
  - Chlamydia trachomatis 099.41
  - Reiter's 099.3
  - specified organism NEC 099.49
- nonspecific (sexually transmitted) (see also Urethritis, nongonococcal) 099.40
- not sexually transmitted 597.80
- Reiter's 099.3
- trichomonal or due to Trichomonas (vaginalis) 131.02
- tuberculous (see also Tuberculosis) 016.3 ☑
- venereal NEC (see also Urethritis, nongonococcal) 099.40

Urethrocele
- female 618.03
  - with uterine prolapse 618.4
    - complete 618.3
    - incomplete 618.2
- male 599.5

Urethrolithiasis 594.2

Urethro-oculoarticular syndrome 099.3

Urethro-oculosynovial syndrome 099.3

Urethrorectal — see condition

Urethrorrhagia 599.84

Urethrorrhea 788.7

Urethrostomy status V44.6
- with complication 997.5

Urethrotrigonitis 595.3

Urethrovaginal — see condition

Urhidrosis, uridrosis 705.89

Uric acid
- diathesis 274.9
- in blood 790.6

Uricacidemia 790.6

Uricemia 790.6

Uricosuria 791.9

Urination
- frequent 788.41
- painful 788.1
- urgency 788.63

Urinemia — see Uremia

Urine, urinary — see also condition
- abnormality NEC 788.69
- blood in (see also Hematuria) 599.70
- discharge, excessive 788.42
- enuresis 788.30
  - nonorganic origin 307.6
- extravasation 788.8
- frequency 788.41
- hesitancy 788.64
- incontinence 788.30
  - active 788.30
  - female 788.30
    - stress 625.6
    - and urge 788.33
  - male 788.30
    - stress 788.32

Urine, urinary — see also condition — continued
- incontinence — continued
  - male — continued
    - stress — continued
      - and urge 788.33
    - mixed (stress and urge) 788.33
    - neurogenic 788.39
    - nonorganic origin 307.6
    - overflow 788.38
    - stress (female) 625.6
      - male NEC 788.32
  - intermittent stream 788.61
  - pus in 791.9
  - retention or stasis NEC 788.20
    - bladder, incomplete emptying 788.21
    - psychogenic 306.53
    - specified NEC 788.29
  - secretion
    - deficient 788.5
    - excessive 788.42
    - frequency 788.41
  - strain 788.65
  - stream
    - intermittent 788.61
    - slowing 788.62
    - splitting 788.61
    - weak 788.62
  - urgency 788.63

Urinoma NEC 599.9
- bladder 596.8
- kidney 593.89
- renal 593.89
- ureter 593.89
- urethra 599.84

Uroarthritis, infectious 099.3

Urodialysis 788.5

Urolithiasis 592.9

Uronephrosis 593.89

Uropathy 599.9
- obstructive 599.60

Urosepsis 599.0
- meaning sepsis 995.91
- meaning urinary tract infection 599.0

Urticaria 708.9
- with angioneurotic edema 995.1
  - hereditary 277.6
- allergic 708.0
- cholinergic 708.5
- chronic 708.8
- cold, familial 708.2
- dermatographic 708.3
- due to
  - cold or heat 708.2
  - drugs 708.0
  - food 708.0
  - inhalants 708.0
  - plants 708.8
  - serum 999.5
- factitial 708.3
- giant 995.1
  - hereditary 277.6
- gigantea 995.1
  - hereditary 277.6
- idiopathic 708.1
- larynx 995.1
  - hereditary 277.6
- neonatorum 778.8
- nonallergic 708.1
- papulosa (Hebra) 698.2
- perstans hemorrhagica 757.39

Urticaria — continued
- pigmentosa 757.33
- recurrent periodic 708.8
- serum 999.5
- solare 692.72
- specified type NEC 708.8
- thermal (cold) (heat) 708.2
- vibratory 708.4

Urticarioides acarodermatitis 133.9

Use of
- methadone 304.00
- nonprescribed drugs (see also Abuse, drugs, nondependent) 305.9 ☑
- patent medicines (see also Abuse, drugs, nondependent) 305.9 ☑

Usher-Senear disease (pemphigus erythematosus) 694.4

Uta 085.5

Uterine size-date discrepancy 649.6 ☑

Uteromegaly 621.2

Uterovaginal — see condition

Uterovesical — see condition

Uterus — see condition

Utriculitis (utriculus prostaticus) 597.89

Uveal — see condition

Uveitis (anterior) — see also Iridocyclitis 364.3
- acute or subacute 364.00
  - due to or associated with
    - gonococcal infection 098.41
    - herpes (simplex) 054.44
      - zoster 053.22
  - primary 364.01
  - recurrent 364.02
  - secondary (noninfectious) 364.04
    - infectious 364.03
- allergic 360.11
- chronic 364.10
  - due to or associated with
    - sarcoidosis 135 [364.11]
    - tuberculosis (see also Tuberculosis) 017.3 ☑ [364.11]
- due to
  - operation 360.11
  - toxoplasmosis (acquired) 130.2
    - congenital (active) 771.2
- granulomatous 364.10
- heterochromic 364.21
- lens-induced 364.23
- nongranulomatous 364.00
- posterior 363.20
  - disseminated — see Chorioretinitis, disseminated
  - focal — see Chorioretinitis, focal
- recurrent 364.02
- sympathetic 360.11
- syphilitic (secondary) 091.50
  - congenital 090.0 [363.13]
  - late 095.8 [363.13]
- tuberculous (see also Tuberculosis) 017.3 ☑ [364.11]

Uveoencephalitis 363.22

Uveokeratitis — see also Iridocyclitis 364.3

Uveoparotid fever 135

Uveoparotitis 135

Uvula — see condition

Uvulitis (acute) (catarrhal) (chronic) (gangrenous) (membranous) (suppurative) (ulcerative) 528.3

V

accination
complication or reaction — *see* Complications, vaccination
delayed V64.00
not carried out V64.00
because of
acute illness V64.01
allergy to vaccine or component V64.04
caregiver refusal V64.05
chronic illness V64.02
guardian refusal V64.05
immune compromised state V64.03
parent refusal V64.05
patient had disease being vaccinated against V64.08
patient refusal V64.06
reason NEC V64.09
religious reasons V64.07
prophylactic (against) V05.9
arthropod-borne viral
disease NEC V05.1
encephalitis V05.0
chickenpox V05.4
cholera (alone) V03.0
with typhoid-paratyphoid (cholera + TAB) V06.0
common cold V04.7
diphtheria (alone) V03.5
with
poliomyelitis (DTP+ polio) V06.3
tetanus V06.5
pertussis combined (DTP) (DTaP) V06.1
typhoid-paratyphoid (DTP + TAB) V06.2
disease (single) NEC V05.9
bacterial NEC V03.9
specified type NEC V03.89
combination NEC V06.9
specified type NEC V06.8
specified type NEC V05.8
encephalitis, viral, arthropod-borne V05.0
Hemophilus influenzae, type B [Hib] V03.81
hepatitis, viral V05.3
influenza V04.81
with
Streptococcus pneumoniae [pneumococcus] V06.6
leishmaniasis V05.2
measles (alone) V04.2
with mumps-rubella (MMR) V06.4
mumps (alone) V04.6
with measles and rubella (MMR) V06.4
pertussis alone V03.6
plague V03.3
poliomyelitis V04.0
with diphtheria-tetanus-pertussis (DTP + polio) V06.3
rabies V04.5
respiratory syncytial virus (RSV) V04.82
rubella (alone) V04.3
with measles and mumps (MMR) V06.4
smallpox V04.1
Streptococcus pneumoniae [pneumococcus] V03.82
with
influenza V06.6
tetanus toxoid (alone) V03.7
with diphtheria [Td] [DT] V06.5
with
pertussis (DTP) (DTaP) V06.1
with poliomyelitis (DTP+polio) V06.3
tuberculosis (BCG) V03.2
tularemia V03.4
typhoid-paratyphoid (TAB) (alone) V03.1
with diphtheria-tetanus-pertussis (TAB + DTP) V06.2
varicella V05.4
viral
disease NEC V04.89
encephalitis, arthropod-borne V05.0
hepatitis V05.3
yellow fever V04.4

Vaccinia (generalized) 999.0
without vaccination 051.02
congenital 771.2
conjunctiva 999.39
eyelids 999.0 [373.5]
localized 999.39
nose 999.39
not from vaccination 051.02
eyelid 051.02 [373.5]
sine vaccinatione 051.02
Vacuum
extraction of fetus or newborn 763.3
in sinus (accessory) (nasal) (*see also* Sinusitis) 473.9
Vagabond V60.0
Vagabondage V60.0
Vagabonds' disease 132.1
Vaginalitis (tunica) 608.4
Vagina, vaginal — *see also* condition
high risk human papillomavirus (HPV) DNA test positive 795.15
low risk human papillomavirus (HPV) DNA test positive 795.19
Vaginismus (reflex) 625.1
functional 306.51
hysterical 300.11
psychogenic 306.51
Vaginitis (acute) (chronic) (circumscribed) (diffuse) (emphysematous) (Hemophilus vaginalis) (nonspecific) (nonvenereal) (ulcerative) 616.10
with
abortion — *see* Abortion, by type, with sepsis
ectopic pregnancy (*see also* categories 633.0–633.9) 639.0
molar pregnancy (*see also* categories 630–632) 639.0
adhesive, congenital 752.49
atrophic, postmenopausal 627.3
bacterial 616.10
blennorrhagic (acute) 098.0
chronic or duration of 2 months or over 098.2
candidal 112.1
chlamydial 099.53
complicating pregnancy or puerperium 646.6 ☑
affecting fetus or newborn 760.8
congenital (adhesive) 752.49
due to
C. albicans 112.1
Trichomonas (vaginalis) 131.01
following
abortion 639.0
ectopic or molar pregnancy 639.0
gonococcal (acute) 098.0
chronic or duration of 2 months or over 098.2
granuloma 099.2
Monilia 112.1
mycotic 112.1
pinworm 127.4 [616.11]
postirradiation 616.10
postmenopausal atrophic 627.3
senile (atrophic) 627.3
syphilitic (early) 091.0
late 095.8
trichomonal 131.01
tuberculous (*see also* Tuberculosis) 016.7 ☑
venereal NEC 099.8
Vaginosis — *see* Vaginitis
Vagotonia 352.3
Vagrancy V60.0
VAIN I (vaginal intraepithelial neoplasia I) 623.0
VAIN II (vaginal intraepithelial neoplasia II) 623.0
VAIN III (vaginal intraepithelial neoplasia III) 233.31
Vallecula — *see* condition
Valley fever 114.0
Valsuani's disease (progressive pernicious anemia, puerperal) 648.2 ☑
Valve, valvular (formation) — *see also* condition
cerebral ventricle (communicating) in situ V45.2
cervix, internal os 752.49

Valve, valvular — *see also* condition — *continued*
colon 751.5
congenital NEC — *see* Atresia
formation, congenital NEC — *see* Atresia
heart defect — *see* Anomaly, heart, valve
ureter 753.29
pelvic junction 753.21
vesical orifice 753.22
urethra 753.6
Valvulitis (chronic) — *see also* Endocarditis 424.90
rheumatic (chronic) (inactive) (with chorea) 397.9
active or acute (aortic) (mitral) (pulmonary) (tricuspid) 391.1
syphilitic NEC 093.20
aortic 093.22
mitral 093.21
pulmonary 093.24
tricuspid 093.23
Valvulopathy — *see* Endocarditis
van Bogaert-Nijssen (-Peiffer) disease 330.0
van Bogaert's leukoencephalitis (sclerosing) (subacute) 046.2
van Buchem's syndrome (hyperostosis corticalis) 733.3
Vancomycin (glycopeptide)
intermediate staphylococcus aureus (VISA/GISA) V09.8 ☑
resistant
enterococcus (VRE) V09.8 ☑
staphylococcus aureus (VRSA/GRSA) V09.8 ☑
van Creveld-von Gierke disease (glycogenosis I) 271.0
van den Bergh's disease (enterogenous cyanosis) 289.7
van der Hoeve-Halbertsma-Waardenburg syndrome (ptosis-epicanthus) 270.2
van der Hoeve-Waardenburg-Gualdi syndrome (ptosis epicanthus) 270.2
van der Hoeve's syndrome (brittle bones and blue sclera, deafness) 756.51
Vanillism 692.89
Vanishing lung 492.0
Vanishing twin 651.33
van Neck (-Odelberg) disease or syndrome (juvenile osteochondrosis) 732.1
Vapor asphyxia or suffocation NEC 987.9
specified agent — *see* Table of Drugs and Chemicals
Vaquez's disease (M9950/1) 238.4
Vaquez-Osler disease (polycythemia vera) (M9950/1) 238.4
Variance, lethal ball, prosthetic heart valve 996.02
Variants, thalassemic 282.49
Variations in hair color 704.3
Varicella 052.9
with
complication 052.8
specified NEC 052.7
pneumonia 052.1
vaccination and inoculation (prophylactic) V05.4
exposure to V01.71
vaccination and inoculation (against) (prophylactic) V05.4
Varices — *see* Varix
Varicocele (scrotum) (thrombosed) 456.4
ovary 456.5
perineum 456.6
spermatic cord (ulcerated) 456.4
Varicose
aneurysm (ruptured) (*see also* Aneurysm) 442.9
dermatitis (lower extremity) — *see* Varicose, vein, inflamed or infected
eczema — *see* Varicose, vein
phlebitis — *see* Varicose, vein, inflamed or infected
placental vessel — *see* Placenta, abnormal
tumor — *see* Varicose, vein
ulcer (lower extremity, any part) 454.0
anus 455.8
external 455.5

Varicose — *continued*
ulcer — *continued*
anus — *continued*
internal 455.2
esophagus (*see also* Varix, esophagus) 456.1
bleeding (*see also* Varix, esophagus, bleeding) 456.0
inflamed or infected 454.2
nasal septum 456.8
perineum 456.6
rectum — *see* Varicose, ulcer, anus
scrotum 456.4
specified site NEC 456.8
vein (lower extremity) (ruptured) (*see also* Varix) 454.9
with
complications NEC 454.8
edema 454.8
inflammation or infection 454.1
ulcerated 454.2
pain 454.8
stasis dermatitis 454.1
with ulcer 454.2
swelling 454.8
ulcer 454.0
inflamed or infected 454.2
anus — *see* Hemorrhoids
broad ligament 456.5
congenital (peripheral) 747.60
gastrointestinal 747.61
lower limb 747.64
renal 747.62
specified NEC 747.69
upper limb 747.63
esophagus (ulcerated) (*see also* Varix, esophagus) 456.1
bleeding (*see also* Varix, esophagus, bleeding) 456.0
inflamed or infected 454.1
with ulcer 454.2
in pregnancy or puerperium 671.0 ☑
vulva or perineum 671.1 ☑
nasal septum (with ulcer) 456.8
pelvis 456.5
perineum 456.6
in pregnancy, childbirth, or puerperium 671.1 ☑
rectum — *see* Hemorrhoids
scrotum (ulcerated) 456.4
specified site NEC 456.8
sublingual 456.3
ulcerated 454.0
inflamed or infected 454.2
umbilical cord, affecting fetus or newborn 762.6
urethra 456.8
vulva 456.6
in pregnancy, childbirth, or puerperium 671.1 ☑
vessel (*see also* Varix)
placenta — *see* Placenta, abnormal
Varicosis, varicosities, varicosity — *see also* Varix 454.9
Variola 050.9
hemorrhagic (pustular) 050.0
major 050.0
minor 050.1
modified 050.2
Varioloid 050.2
Variolosa, purpura 050.0
Varix (lower extremity) (ruptured) 454.9
with
complications NEC 454.8
edema 454.8
inflammation or infection 454.1
with ulcer 454.2
pain 454.8
stasis dermatitis 454.1
with ulcer 454.2
swelling 454.8
ulcer 454.0
with inflammation or infection 454.2
aneurysmal (*see also* Aneurysm) 442.9
anus — *see* Hemorrhoids

Vaccination — Varix

Varix — continued
arteriovenous (congenital) (peripheral) NEC
747.60
gastrointestinal 747.61
lower limb 747.64
renal 747.62
specified NEC 747.69
spinal 747.82
upper limb 747.63
bladder 456.5
broad ligament 456.5
congenital (peripheral) 747.60
esophagus (ulcerated) 456.1
bleeding 456.0
in
cirrhosis of liver 571.5 [456.20]
portal hypertension 572.3 [456.20]
congenital 747.69
in
cirrhosis of liver 571.5 [456.21]
with bleeding 571.5 [456.20]
portal hypertension 572.3 [456.21]
with bleeding 572.3 [456.20]
gastric 456.8
inflamed or infected 454.1
ulcerated 454.2
in pregnancy or puerperium 671.0 ☑
perineum 671.1 ☑
vulva 671.1 ☑
labia (majora) 456.6
orbit 456.8
congenital 747.69
ovary 456.5
papillary 448.1
pelvis 456.5
perineum 456.6
in pregnancy or puerperium 671.1 ☑
pharynx 456.8
placenta — see Placenta, abnormal
prostate 456.8
rectum — see Hemorrhoids
renal papilla 456.8
retina 362.17
scrotum (ulcerated) 456.4
sigmoid colon 456.8
specified site NEC 456.8
spinal (cord) (vessels) 456.8
spleen, splenic (vein) (with phlebolith) 456.8
sublingual 456.3
ulcerated 454.0
inflamed or infected 454.2
umbilical cord, affecting fetus or newborn
762.6
uterine ligament 456.5
vocal cord 456.8
vulva 456.6
in pregnancy, childbirth, or puerperium
671.1 ☑
Vasa previa 663.5 ☑
affecting fetus or newborn 762.6
hemorrhage from, affecting fetus or newborn
772.0
Vascular — see also condition
loop on papilla (optic) 743.57
sheathing, retina 362.13
spasm 443.9
spider 448.1
Vascularity, pulmonary, congenital 747.3
Vascularization
choroid 362.16
cornea 370.60
deep 370.63
localized 370.61
retina 362.16
subretinal 362.16
Vasculitis 447.6
allergic 287.0
cryoglobulinemic 273.2
disseminated 447.6
kidney 447.8
leukocytoclastic 446.29
nodular 695.2
retinal 362.18
rheumatic — see Fever, rheumatic
Vasculopathy
cardiac allograft 996.83

Vas deferens — see condition
Vas deferentitis 608.4
Vasectomy, admission for V25.2
Vasitis 608.4
nodosa 608.4
scrotum 608.4
spermatic cord 608.4
testis 608.4
tuberculous (see also Tuberculosis) 016.5 ☑
tunica vaginalis 608.4
vas deferens 608.4
Vasodilation 443.9
Vasomotor — see condition
Vasoplasty, after previous sterilization V26.0
Vasoplegia, splanchnic — see also Neuropathy,
peripheral, autonomic 337.9
Vasospasm 443.9
cerebral (artery) 435.9
with transient neurologic deficit 435.9
coronary 413.1
nerve
arm NEC 354.9
autonomic 337.9
brachial plexus 353.0
cervical plexus 353.2
leg NEC 355.8
lower extremity NEC 355.8
peripheral NEC 355.9
spinal NEC 355.9
sympathetic 337.9
upper extremity NEC 354.9
peripheral NEC 443.9
retina (artery) (see also Occlusion, retinal,
artery) 362.30
Vasospastic — see condition
Vasovagal attack (paroxysmal) 780.2
psychogenic 306.2
Vater's ampulla — see condition
VATER syndrome 759.89
vCJD (variant Creutzfeldt-Jakob disease) 046.11
Vegetation, vegetative
adenoid (nasal fossa) 474.2
consciousness (persistent) 780.03
endocarditis (acute) (any valve) (chronic)
(subacute) 421.0
heart (mycotic) (valve) 421.0
state (persistent) 780.03
Veil
Jackson's 751.4
over face (causing asphyxia) 768.9
Vein, venous — see condition
Veldt sore — see also Ulcer, skin 707.9
Velo-cardio-facial syndrome 758.32
Velpeau's hernia — see Hernia, femoral
Venereal
balanitis NEC 099.8
bubo 099.1
disease 099.9
specified nature or type NEC 099.8
granuloma inguinale 099.2
lymphogranuloma (Durand-Nicolas-Favre),
any site 099.1
salpingitis 098.37
urethritis (see also Urethritis, nongonococcal)
099.40
vaginitis NEC 099.8
warts 078.11
Vengefulness, in child — see also Disturbance,
conduct 312.0 ☑
Venofibrosis 459.89
Venom, venomous
bite or sting (animal or insect) 989.5
poisoning 989.5
Venous — see condition
Ventouse delivery NEC 669.5 ☑
affecting fetus or newborn 763.3
Ventral — see condition
Ventricle, ventricular — see also condition
escape 427.69
standstill (see also Arrest, cardiac) 427.5
Ventriculitis, cerebral — see also Meningitis
322.9
Ventriculostomy status V45.2
Verbiest's syndrome (claudicatio intermittens
spinalis) 435.1
Vernet's syndrome 352.6

Verneuil's disease (syphilitic bursitis) 095.7
Verruca (filiformis) 078.10
acuminata (any site) 078.11
necrogenica (primary) (see also Tuberculosis)
017.0 ☑
peruana 088.0
peruviana 088.0
plana (juvenilis) 078.19
plantaris 078.12
seborrheica 702.19
inflamed 702.11
senilis 702.0
tuberculosa (primary) (see also Tuberculosis)
017.0 ☑
venereal 078.11
viral 078.10
specified NEC 078.19
vulgaris 078.10
Verrucosities — see also Verruca 078.10
Verrucous endocarditis (acute) (any valve)
(chronic) (subacute) 710.0 [424.91]
nonbacterial 710.0 [424.91]
Verruga
peruana 088.0
peruviana 088.0
Verse's disease (calcinosis intervertebralis)
275.49 [722.90]
Version
before labor, affecting fetus or newborn 761.7
cephalic (correcting previous malposition)
652.1 ☑
affecting fetus or newborn 763.1
cervix — see Version, uterus
uterus (postinfectional) (postpartal, old) (see
also Malposition, uterus) 621.6
forward — see Anteversion, uterus
lateral — see Lateroversion, uterus
Vertebra, vertebral — see condition
Vertigo 780.4
auditory 386.19
aural 386.19
benign paroxysmal positional 386.11
central origin 386.2
cerebral 386.2
Dix and Hallpike (epidemic) 386.12
endemic paralytic 078.81
epidemic 078.81
Dix and Hallpike 386.12
Gerlier's 078.81
Pedersen's 386.12
vestibular neuronitis 386.12
epileptic — see Epilepsy
Gerlier's (epidemic) 078.81
hysterical 300.11
labyrinthine 386.10
laryngeal 786.2
malignant positional 386.2
Ménière's (see also Disease, Ménière's) 386.00
menopausal 627.2
otogenic 386.19
paralytic 078.81
paroxysmal positional, benign 386.11
Pedersen's (epidemic) 386.12
peripheral 386.10
specified type NEC 386.19
positional
benign paroxysmal 386.11
malignant 386.2
Verumontanitis (chronic) — see also Urethritis
597.89
Vesania — see also Psychosis 298.9
Vesical — see condition
Vesicle
cutaneous 709.8
seminal — see condition
skin 709.8
Vesicocolic — see condition
Vesicoperineal — see condition
Vesicorectal — see condition
Vesicourethrorectal — see condition
Vesicovaginal — see condition
Vesicular — see condition
Vesiculitis (seminal) 608.0
amebic 006.8
gonorrheal (acute) 098.14

Vesiculitis — continued
gonorrheal — continued
chronic or duration of 2 months or over
098.34
trichomonal 131.09
tuberculous (see also Tuberculosis)
016.5 ☑ [608.81]
Vestibulitis (ear) — see also Labyrinthitis 386.30
nose (external) 478.19
vulvar 625.71
Vestibulopathy, acute peripheral (recurrent)
386.12
Vestige, vestigial — see also Persistence
branchial 744.41
structures in vitreous 743.51
Vibriosis NEC 027.9
Vidal's disease (lichen simplex chronicus) 698.3
Video display tube syndrome 723.8
Vienna-type encephalitis 049.8
Villaret's syndrome 352.6
Villous — see condition
VIN I (vulvar intraepithelial neoplasia I) 624.01
VIN II (vulvar intraepithelial neoplasia II) 624.02
VIN III (vulvar intraepithelial neoplasia III) 233.32
Vincent's
angina 101
bronchitis 101
disease 101
gingivitis 101
infection (any site) 101
laryngitis 101
stomatitis 101
tonsillitis 101
Vinson-Plummer syndrome (sideropenic dysphagia) 280.8
Viosterol deficiency — see also Deficiency, calciferol 268.9
Virchow's disease 733.99
Viremia 790.8
Virilism (adrenal) (female) NEC 255.2
with
3-beta-hydroxysteroid dehydrogenase
defect 255.2
11-hydroxylase defect 255.2
21-hydroxylase defect 255.2
adrenal
hyperplasia 255.2
insufficiency (congenital) 255.2
cortical hyperfunction 255.2
Virilization (female) (suprarenal) — see also Virilism 255.2
isosexual 256.4
Virulent bubo 099.0
Virus, viral — see also condition
infection NEC (see also Infection, viral) 079.99
septicemia 079.99
yaba monkey tumor 059.22
VISA (vancomycin intermediate staphylococcus
aureus) V09.8 ☑
Viscera, visceral — see condition
Visceroptosis 569.89
Visible peristalsis 787.4
Vision, visual
binocular, suppression 368.31
blurred, blurring 368.8
hysterical 300.11
defect, defective (see also Impaired, vision)
369.9
disorientation (syndrome) 368.16
disturbance NEC (see also Disturbance, vision)
368.9
hysterical 300.11
examination V72.0
field, limitation 368.40
fusion, with defective steropsis 368.33
hallucinations 368.16
halos 368.16
loss 369.9
both eyes (see also Blindness, both eyes)
369.3
complete (see also Blindness, both eyes)
369.00
one eye 369.8
sudden 368.16
low (both eyes) 369.20

...on, visual — *continued*
  ow — *continued*
    one eye (other eye normal) (*see also* Impaired, vision) 369.70
      blindness, other eye 369.10
  perception, simultaneous without fusion 368.32
  tunnel 368.45
...ality, lack or want of 780.79
  newborn 779.89
...amin deficiency NEC — *see also* Deficiency, vitamin 269.2
...elline duct, persistent 751.0
...ligo 709.01
  due to pinta (carate) 103.2
  eyelid 374.53
  vulva 624.8
...ium cordis — *see* Disease, heart
...reous — *see also* condition
  touch syndrome 997.99
...CAD (long chain/very long chain acyl CoA dehydrogenase deficiency, LCAD) 277.85
...cal cord — *see* condition
...cational rehabilitation V57.22
...gt's (Cecile) disease or syndrome 333.7 ☑
...gt-Koyanagi syndrome 364.24
...gt-Spielmeyer disease (amaurotic familial idiocy) 330.1
...ice
  change (*see also* Dysphonia) 784.49 ▲
  loss (*see also* Aphonia) 784.41
...lhard-Fahr disease (malignant nephrosclerosis) 403.00
...lhynian fever 083.1
...lkmann's ischemic contracture or paralysis (complicating trauma) 958.6
...luntary starvation 307.1
...lvulus (bowel) (colon) (intestine) 560.2
  with
    hernia (*see also* Hernia, by site, with obstruction)
      gangrenous — *see* Hernia, by site, with gangrene
    perforation 560.2
  congenital 751.5
  duodenum 537.3
  fallopian tube 620.5
  oviduct 620.5
  stomach (due to absence of gastrocolic ligament) 537.89
...omiting 787.03
  with nausea 787.01
  allergic 535.4 ☑
  asphyxia 933.1
  bilious (cause unknown) 787.04 ▲
    following gastrointestinal surgery 564.3
    newborn 779.32 ●
  blood (*see also* Hematemesis) 578.0
  causing asphyxia, choking, or suffocation (*see also* Asphyxia, food) 933.1
  cyclical 536.2
    associated with migraine 346.2 ☑
    psychogenic 306.4
  epidemic 078.82
  fecal matter 569.87 ▲
  following gastrointestinal surgery 564.3
  functional 536.8
    psychogenic 306.4
  habit 536.2
  hysterical 300.11
  nervous 306.4
  neurotic 306.4
  newborn 779.33 ▲
    bilious 779.32 ●
  of or complicating pregnancy 643.9 ☑
    due to
      organic disease 643.8 ☑
      specific cause NEC 643.8 ☑
    early — *see* Hyperemesis, gravidarum
    late (after 22 completed weeks of gestation) 643.2 ☑
  pernicious or persistent 536.2
    complicating pregnancy — *see* Hyperemesis, gravidarum
    psychogenic 306.4
  physiological 787.03 ▲

Vomiting — *continued*
  physiological — *continued*
    bilious 787.04 ●
  psychic 306.4
  psychogenic 307.54
  stercoral 569.89
  uncontrollable 536.2
    psychogenic 306.4
  uremic — *see* Uremia
  winter 078.82
von Bechterew (-Strumpell) disease or syndrome (ankylosing spondylitis) 720.0
von Bezold's abscess 383.01
von Economo's disease (encephalitis lethargica) 049.8
von Eulenburg's disease (congenital paramyotonia) 359.29
von Gierke's disease (glycogenosis I) 271.0
von Gies' joint 095.8
von Graefe's disease or syndrome 378.72
von Hippel (-Lindau) disease or syndrome (retinocerebral angiomatosis) 759.6
von Jaksch's anemia or disease (pseudoleukemia infantum) 285.8
von Recklinghausen-Applebaum disease (hemochromatosis) 275.0
von Recklinghausen's
  disease or syndrome (nerves) (skin) (M9540/1) 237.71
  bones (osteitis fibrosa cystica) 252.01
  tumor (M9540/1) 237.71
von Schroetter's syndrome (intermittent venous claudication) 453.89 ▲
von Willebrand (-Jürgens) (-Minot) disease or syndrome (angiohemophilia) 286.4
von Zambusch's disease (lichen sclerosus et atrophicus) 701.0
Voorhoeve's disease or dyschondroplasia 756.4
Vossius' ring 921.3
  late effect 366.21
Voyeurism 302.82
VRE (vancomycin resistant enterococcus) V09.8 ☑
Vrolik's disease (osteogenesis imperfecta) 756.51
VRSA (vancomycin resistant staphylococcus aureus) V09.8 ☑
Vulva — *see* condition
Vulvismus 625.1
Vulvitis (acute) (allergic) (chronic) (gangrenous) (hypertrophic) (intertriginous) 616.10
  with
    abortion — *see* Abortion, by type, with sepsis
    ectopic pregnancy (*see also* categories 633.0–633.9) 639.0
    molar pregnancy (*see also* categories 630–632) 639.0
  adhesive, congenital 752.49
  blennorrhagic (acute) 098.0
    chronic or duration of 2 months or over 098.2
  chlamydial 099.53
  complicating pregnancy or puerperium 646.6 ☑
  due to Ducrey's bacillus 099.0
  following
    abortion 639.0
    ectopic or molar pregnancy 639.0
  gonococcal (acute) 098.0
    chronic or duration of 2 months or over 098.2
  herpetic 054.11
  leukoplakic 624.09
  monilial 112.1
  puerperal, postpartum, childbirth 646.6 ☑
  syphilitic (early) 091.0
    late 095.8
  trichomonal 131.01
Vulvodynia 625.70
  specified NEC 625.79
Vulvorectal — *see* condition
Vulvovaginitis — *see also* Vulvitis 616.10
  amebic 006.8
  chlamydial 099.53
  gonococcal (acute) 098.0

Vulvovaginitis — *see also* Vulvitis — *continued*
  gonococcal — *continued*
    chronic or duration of 2 months or over 098.2
  herpetic 054.11
  monilial 112.1
  trichomonal (Trichomonas vaginalis) 131.01

W

Waardenburg-Klein syndrome (ptosis-epicanthus) 270.2
Waardenburg's syndrome 756.89
  meaning ptosis-epicanthus 270.2
Wagner's disease (colloid milium) 709.3
Wagner (-Unverricht) syndrome (dermatomyositis) 710.3
Waiting list, person on V63.2
  undergoing social agency investigation V63.8
Wakefulness disorder — *see also* Hypersomnia 780.54
  nonorganic origin 307.43
Waldenström's
  disease (osteochondrosis, capital femoral) 732.1
  hepatitis (lupoid hepatitis) 571.49
  hypergammaglobulinemia 273.0
  macroglobulinemia 273.3
  purpura, hypergammaglobulinemic 273.0
  syndrome (macroglobulinemia) 273.3
Waldenström-Kjellberg syndrome (sideropenic dysphagia) 280.8
Walking
  difficulty 719.7
    psychogenic 307.9
  sleep 307.46
    hysterical 300.13
Wall, abdominal — *see* condition
Wallenberg's syndrome (posterior inferior cerebellar artery) — *see also* Disease, cerebrovascular, acute 436
Wallgren's
  disease (obstruction of splenic vein with collateral circulation) 459.89
  meningitis (*see also* Meningitis, aseptic) 047.9
Wandering
  acetabulum 736.39
  gallbladder 751.69
  kidney, congenital 753.3
  organ or site, congenital NEC — *see* Malposition, congenital
  pacemaker (atrial) (heart) 427.89
  spleen 289.59
Wardrop's disease (with lymphangitis) 681.9
  finger 681.02
  toe 681.11
War neurosis 300.16
Wart (digitate) (filiform) (infectious) (viral) 078.10
  common 078.19
  external genital organs (venereal) 078.11
  fig 078.19
  flat 078.19
  genital 078.11
  Hassall-Henle's (of cornea) 371.41
  Henle's (of cornea) 371.41
  juvenile 078.19
  moist 078.10
  Peruvian 088.0
  plantar 078.12
  prosector (*see also* Tuberculosis) 017.0 ☑
  seborrheic 702.19
    inflamed 702.11
  senile 702.0
  specified NEC 078.19
  syphilitic 091.3
  tuberculous (*see also* Tuberculosis) 017.0 ☑
  venereal (female) (male) 078.11
Warthin's tumor (salivary gland) (M8561/0) 210.2
Washerwoman's itch 692.4
Wassilieff's disease (leptospiral jaundice) 100.0
Wasting
  disease 799.4
    due to malnutrition 261
  extreme (due to malnutrition) 261
  muscular NEC 728.2
  palsy, paralysis 335.21

Wasting — *continued*
  pelvic muscle 618.83
Water
  clefts 366.12
  deprivation of 994.3
  in joint (*see also* Effusion, joint) 719.0 ☑
  intoxication 276.6
  itch 120.3
  lack of 994.3
  loading 276.6
  on
    brain — *see* Hydrocephalus
    chest 511.89
  poisoning 276.6
Waterbrash 787.1
Water-hammer pulse — *see also* Insufficiency, aortic 424.1
Waterhouse (-Friderichsen) disease or syndrome 036.3
Water-losing nephritis 588.89
Watermelon stomach 537.82
  with hemorrhage 537.83
  without hemorrhage 537.82
Wax in ear 380.4
Waxy
  degeneration, any site 277.39
  disease 277.39
  kidney 277.39 *[583.81]*
  liver (large) 277.39
  spleen 277.39
Weak, weakness (generalized) 780.79
  arches (acquired) 734
    congenital 754.61
  bladder sphincter 596.59
  congenital 779.89
  eye muscle — *see* Strabismus
  facial 781.94
  foot (double) — *see* Weak, arches
  heart, cardiac (*see also* Failure, heart) 428.9
    congenital 746.9
  mind 317
  muscle (generalized) 728.87
  myocardium (*see also* Failure, heart) 428.9
  newborn 779.89
  pelvic fundus
    pubocervical tissue 618.81
    rectovaginal tissue 618.82
  pulse 785.9
  senile 797
  urinary stream 788.62
  valvular — *see* Endocarditis
Wear, worn, tooth, teeth (approximal) (hard tissues) (interproximal) (occlusal) — *see* Attrition, teeth 521.10
Weather, weathered
  effects of
    cold NEC 991.9
      specified effect NEC 991.8
    hot (*see also* Heat) 992.9
  skin 692.74
Weber-Christian disease or syndrome (nodular nonsuppurative panniculitis) 729.30
Weber-Cockayne syndrome (epidermolysis bullosa) 757.39
Weber-Dimitri syndrome 759.6
Weber-Gubler syndrome 344.89
Weber-Leyden syndrome 344.89
Weber-Osler syndrome (familial hemorrhagic telangiectasia) 448.0
Weber's paralysis or syndrome 344.89
Web, webbed (congenital) — *see also* Anomaly, specified type NEC
  canthus 743.63
  digits (*see also* Syndactylism) 755.10
  duodenal 751.5
  esophagus 750.3
  fingers (*see also* Syndactylism, fingers) 755.11
  larynx (glottic) (subglottic) 748.2
  neck (pterygium colli) 744.5
  Paterson-Kelly (sideropenic dysphagia) 280.8
  popliteal syndrome 756.89
  toes (*see also* Syndactylism, toes) 755.13
Wedge-shaped or wedging vertebra — *see also* Osteoporosis 733.00
Wegener's granulomatosis or syndrome 446.4

☑ Additional Digit Required — Refer to the Tabular List for Digit Selection   ▽ Subterms under main terms may continue to next column or page

Wegner's disease (syphilitic osteochondritis) 090.0
Weight
  gain (abnormal) (excessive) 783.1
    during pregnancy 646.1 ✓
      insufficient 646.8 ✓
    less than 1000 grams at birth 765.0 ✓
  loss (cause unknown) 783.21
Weightlessness 994.9
Weil's disease (leptospiral jaundice) 100.0
Weill-Marchesani syndrome (brachymorphism and ectopia lentis) 759.89
Weingarten's syndrome (tropical eosinophilia) 518.3
Weir Mitchell's disease (erythromelalgia) 443.82
Weiss-Baker syndrome (carotid sinus syncope) 337.01
Weissenbach-Thibierge syndrome (cutaneous systemic sclerosis) 710.1
Wen — see also Cyst, sebaceous 706.2
Wenckebach's phenomenon, heart block (second degree) 426.13
Werdnig-Hoffmann syndrome (muscular atrophy) 335.0
Werlhof-Wichmann syndrome — see also Purpura, thrombocytopenic 287.39
Werlhof's disease — see also Purpura, thrombocytopenic 287.39
Wermer's syndrome or disease (polyendocrine adenomatosis) 258.01
Werner's disease or syndrome (progeria adultorum) 259.8
Werner-His disease (trench fever) 083.1
Werner-Schultz disease (agranulocytosis) 288.09
Wernicke's encephalopathy, disease, or syndrome (superior hemorrhagic polioencephalitis) 265.1
Wernicke-Korsakoff syndrome or psychosis (nonalcoholic) 294.0
  alcoholic 291.1
Wernicke-Posadas disease — see also Coccidioidomycosis 114.9
Wesselsbron fever 066.3
West African fever 084.8
West Nile
  encephalitis 066.41
  encephalomyelitis 066.41
  fever 066.40
    with
      cranial nerve disorders 066.42
      encephalitis 066.41
      optic neuritis 066.42
      other complications 066.49
      other neurologic manifestations 066.42
      polyradiculitis 066.42
  virus 066.40
Westphal-Strümpell syndrome (hepatolenticular degeneration) 275.1
Wet
  brain (alcoholic) (see also Alcoholism) 303.9 ✓
  feet, tropical (syndrome) (maceration) 991.4
  lung (syndrome)
    adult 518.5
    newborn 770.6
Wharton's duct — see condition
Wheal 709.8
Wheelchair confinement status V46.3
Wheezing 786.07
Whiplash injury or syndrome 847.0
Whipple's disease or syndrome (intestinal lipodystrophy) 040.2
Whipworm 127.3
"Whistling face" syndrome (craniocarpotarsal dystrophy) 759.89
White — see also condition
  kidney
    large — see Nephrosis
    small 582.9
  leg, puerperal, postpartum, childbirth 671.4 ✓
    nonpuerperal 451.19
  mouth 112.0
  patches of mouth 528.6
  sponge nevus of oral mucosa 750.26
  spot lesions, teeth 521.01
White's disease (congenital) (keratosis follicularis) 757.39

Whitehead 706.2
Whitlow (with lymphangitis) 681.01
  herpetic 054.6
Whitmore's disease or fever (melioidosis) 025
Whooping cough 033.9
  with pneumonia 033.9 [484.3]
  due to
    Bordetella
      bronchoseptica 033.8
        with pneumonia 033.8 [484.3]
      parapertussis 033.1
        with pneumonia 033.1 [484.3]
      pertussis 033.0
        with pneumonia 033.0 [484.3]
    specified organism NEC 033.8
      with pneumonia 033.8 [484.3]
  vaccination, prophylactic (against) V03.6
Wichmann's asthma (laryngismus stridulus) 478.75
Widal (-Abrami) syndrome (acquired hemolytic jaundice) 283.9
Widening aorta — see also Aneurysm, aorta 441.9
  ruptured 441.5
Wilkie's disease or syndrome 557.1
Wilkinson-Sneddon disease or syndrome (subcorneal pustular dermatosis) 694.1
Willan's lepra 696.1
Willan-Plumbe syndrome (psoriasis) 696.1
Willebrand (-Jürgens) syndrome or thrombopathy (angiohemophilia) 286.4
Willi-Prader syndrome (hypogenital dystrophy with diabetic tendency) 759.81
Willis' disease (diabetes mellitus) — see also Diabetes 250.0 ✓
  due to secondary diabetes 249.0 ✓
Wilms' tumor or neoplasm (nephroblastoma) (M8960/3) 189.0
Wilson's
  disease or syndrome (hepatolenticular degeneration) 275.1
  hepatolenticular degeneration 275.1
  lichen ruber 697.0
Wilson-Brocq disease (dermatitis exfoliativa) 695.89
Wilson-Mikity syndrome 770.7
Window — see also Imperfect, closure aorticopulmonary 745.0
Winged scapula 736.89
Winter — see also condition
  vomiting disease 078.82
Wise's disease 696.2
Wiskott-Aldrich syndrome (eczema-thrombocytopenia) 279.12
Withdrawal symptoms, syndrome
  alcohol 291.81
    delirium (acute) 291.0
      chronic 291.1
    newborn 760.71
  drug or narcotic 292.0
    newborn, infant of dependent mother 779.5
    steroid NEC
      correct substance properly administered 255.41
      overdose or wrong substance given or taken 962.0
Withdrawing reaction, child or adolescent 313.22
Witts' anemia (achlorhydric anemia) 280.9
Witzelsucht 301.9
Woakes' syndrome (ethmoiditis) 471.1
Wohlfart-Kugelberg-Welander disease 335.11
Woillez's disease (acute idiopathic pulmonary congestion) 518.5
Wolff-Parkinson-White syndrome (anomalous atrioventricular excitation) 426.7
Wolhynian fever 083.1
Wolman's disease (primary familial xanthomatosis) 272.7
Wood asthma 495.8
Woolly, wooly hair (congenital) (nevus) 757.4
Wool-sorters' disease 022.1
Word
  blindness (congenital) (developmental) 315.01
    secondary to organic lesion 784.61
  deafness (secondary to organic lesion) 784.69

Word — continued
  deafness — continued
    developmental 315.31
Worm(s) (colic) (fever) (infection) (infestation) — see also Infestation 128.9
  guinea 125.7
  in intestine NEC 127.9
Worm-eaten soles 102.3
Worn out — see also Exhaustion 780.79
  artificial heart valve 996.02 ●
  cardiac defibrillator V53.32 ●
  cardiac pacemaker lead or battery V53.31 ●
  joint prosthesis (see also Complications, mechanical, device NEC, prosthetic NEC, joint) 996.46
"Worried well" V65.5
Wound, open (by cutting or piercing instrument) (by firearms) (cut) (dissection) (incised) (laceration) (penetration) (perforating) (puncture) with initial hemorrhage, not internal) 879.8

Note — For fracture with open wound, see Fracture.

For laceration, traumatic rupture, tear or penetrating wound of internal organs, such as heart, lung, liver, kidney, pelvic organs, etc., whether or not accompanied by open wound or fracture in the same region, see Injury, internal.

For contused wound, see Contusion. For crush injury, see Crush. For abrasion, insect bite (nonvenomous), blister, or scratch, see Injury, superficial.

Complicated includes wounds with:
  delayed healing
  delayed treatment
  foreign body
  primary infection

For late effect of open wound, see Late, effect, wound, open, by site.

  abdomen, abdominal (external) (muscle) 879.2
    complicated 879.3
    wall (anterior) 879.2
      complicated 879.3
      lateral 879.4
        complicated 879.5
  alveolar (process) 873.62
    complicated 873.72
  ankle 891.0
    with tendon involvement 891.2
    complicated 891.1
  anterior chamber, eye (see also Wound, open, intraocular) 871.9
  anus 879.6
    complicated 879.7
  arm 884.0
    with tendon involvement 884.2
    complicated 884.1
    forearm 881.00
      with tendon involvement 881.20
      complicated 881.10
    multiple sites — see Wound, open, multiple, upper limb
    upper 880.03
      with tendon involvement 880.23
      complicated 880.13
      multiple sites (with axillary or shoulder regions) 880.09
        with tendon involvement 880.29
        complicated 880.19
  artery — see Injury, blood vessel, by site
  auditory
    canal (external) (meatus) 872.02
      complicated 872.12
    ossicles (incus) (malleus) (stapes) 872.62
      complicated 872.72
  auricle, ear 872.01
    complicated 872.11
  axilla 880.02
    with tendon involvement 880.22
    complicated 880.12
      with tendon involvement 880.29

Wound, open — continued
  axilla — continued
    involving other sites of upper arm 88
      complicated 880.19
  back 876.0
    complicated 876.1
  bladder — see Injury, internal, bladder
  blood vessel — see Injury, blood vessel, by
  brain — see Injury, intracranial, with ope tracranial wound
  breast 879.0
    complicated 879.1
  brow 873.42
    complicated 873.52
  buccal mucosa 873.61
    complicated 873.71
  buttock 877.0
    complicated 877.1
  calf 891.0
    with tendon involvement 891.2
    complicated 891.1
  canaliculus lacrimalis 870.8
    with laceration of eyelid 870.2
  canthus, eye 870.8
    laceration — see Laceration, eyelid
  cavernous sinus — see Injury, intracranial
  cerebellum — see Injury, intracranial
  cervical esophagus 874.4
    complicated 874.5
  cervix — see Injury, internal, cervix
  cheek(s) (external) 873.41
    complicated 873.51
    internal 873.61
      complicated 873.71
  chest (wall) (external) 875.0
    complicated 875.1
  chin 873.44
    complicated 873.54
  choroid 363.63
  ciliary body (eye) (see also Wound, open, i traocular) 871.9
  clitoris 878.8
    complicated 878.9
  cochlea 872.64
    complicated 872.74
  complicated 879.9
  conjunctiva — see Wound, open, intraocu
  cornea (nonpenetrating) (see also Wound, open, intraocular) 871.9
  costal region 875.0
    complicated 875.1
  Descemet's membrane (see also Wound, op intraocular) 871.9
  digit(s)
    foot 893.0
      with tendon involvement 893.2
      complicated 893.1
    hand 883.0
      with tendon involvement 883.2
      complicated 883.1
  drumhead, ear 872.61
    complicated 872.71
  ear 872.8
    canal 872.02
      complicated 872.12
      complicated 872.9
    drum 872.61
      complicated 872.71
    external 872.00
      complicated 872.10
    multiple sites 872.69
      complicated 872.79
    ossicles (incus) (malleus) (stapes) 872.6
      complicated 872.72
    specified part NEC 872.69
      complicated 872.79
  elbow 881.01
    with tendon involvement 881.21
    complicated 881.11
  epididymis 878.2
    complicated 878.3
  epigastric region 879.2
    complicated 879.3
  epiglottis 874.01
    complicated 874.11
  esophagus (cervical) 874.4

☑ Additional Digit Required — Refer to the Tabular List for Digit Selection   ▽ Subterms under main terms may continue to next column or page

Wound, open — *continued*
thigh 890.0
with tendon involvement 890.2
complicated 890.1
thorax, thoracic (external) 875.0
complicated 875.1
throat 874.8
complicated 874.9
thumb (nail) (subungual) 883.0
with tendon involvement 883.2
complicated 883.1
thyroid (gland) 874.2
complicated 874.3
toe(s) (nail) (subungual) 893.0
with tendon involvement 893.2
complicated 893.1
tongue 873.64
complicated 873.74
tonsil — *see* Wound, open, neck
trachea (cervical region) 874.02
with larynx 874.00
complicated 874.10
complicated 874.12
intrathoracic — *see* Injury, internal, trachea
trunk (multiple) NEC 879.6
complicated 879.7
specified site NEC 879.6
complicated 879.7
tunica vaginalis 878.2
complicated 878.3
tympanic membrane 872.61
complicated 872.71
tympanum 872.61
complicated 872.71
umbilical region 879.2
complicated 879.3
ureter — *see* Injury, internal, ureter
urethra — *see* Injury, internal, urethra
uterus — *see* Injury, internal, uterus
uvula 873.69
complicated 873.79
vagina 878.6
complicated 878.7
vas deferens — *see* Injury, internal, vas deferens
vitreous (humor) 871.2
vulva 878.4
complicated 878.5
wrist 881.02
with tendon involvement 881.22
complicated 881.12
Wright's syndrome (hyperabduction) 447.8
pneumonia 390 *[517.1]*
Wringer injury — *see* Crush injury, by site
Wrinkling of skin 701.8
Wrist — *see also* condition
drop (acquired) 736.05
Wrong drug (given in error) NEC 977.9
specified drug or substance — *see* Table of Drugs and Chemicals

Wry neck — *see also* Torticollis
congenital 754.1
Wuchereria infestation 125.0
bancrofti 125.0
Brugia malayi 125.1
malayi 125.1
Wuchereriasis 125.0
Wuchereriosis 125.0
Wuchernde struma langhans (M8332/3) 193

X

Xanthelasma 272.2
eyelid 272.2 *[374.51]*
palpebrarum 272.2 *[374.51]*
Xanthelasmatosis (essential) 272.2
Xanthelasmoidea 757.33
Xanthine stones 277.2
Xanthinuria 277.2
Xanthofibroma (M8831/0) — *see* Neoplasm, connective tissue, benign
Xanthoma(s), xanthomatosis 272.2
with
hyperlipoproteinemia
type I 272.3
type III 272.2
type IV 272.1
type V 272.3
bone 272.7
craniohypophyseal 277.89
cutaneotendinous 272.7
diabeticorum 250.8 ☑ *[272.2]*
due to secondary diabetes 249.8 ☑ *[272.2]*
disseminatum 272.7
eruptive 272.2
eyelid 272.2 *[374.51]*
familial 272.7
hereditary 272.7
hypercholesterinemic 272.0
hypercholesterolemic 272.0
hyperlipemic 272.4
hyperlipidemic 272.4
infantile 272.7
joint 272.7
juvenile 272.7
multiple 272.7
multiplex 272.7
primary familial 272.7
tendon (sheath) 272.7
tuberosum 272.2
tuberous 272.2
tubo-eruptive 272.2
Xanthosis 709.09
surgical 998.81
Xenophobia 300.29
Xeroderma (congenital) 757.39
acquired 701.1
eyelid 373.33
eyelid 373.33

Xeroderma — *continued*
pigmentosum 757.33
vitamin A deficiency 264.8
Xerophthalmia 372.53
vitamin A deficiency 264.7
Xerosis
conjunctiva 372.53
with Bitôt's spot 372.53
vitamin A deficiency 264.1
vitamin A deficiency 264.0
cornea 371.40
with corneal ulceration 370.00
vitamin A deficiency 264.3
vitamin A deficiency 264.2
cutis 706.8
skin 706.8
Xerostomia 527.7
Xiphodynia 733.90
Xiphoidalgia 733.90
Xiphoiditis 733.99
Xiphopagus 759.4
XO syndrome 758.6
X-ray
effects, adverse, NEC 990
of chest
for suspected tuberculosis V71.2
routine V72.5
XXX syndrome 758.81
XXXXY syndrome 758.81
XXY syndrome 758.7
Xyloketosuria 271.8
Xylosuria 271.8
Xylulosuria 271.8
XYY syndrome 758.81

Y

Yaba monkey tumor virus 059.22
Yawning 786.09
psychogenic 306.1
Yaws 102.9
bone or joint lesions 102.6
butter 102.1
chancre 102.0
cutaneous, less than five years after infection 102.2
early (cutaneous) (macular) (maculopapular) (micropapular) (papular) 102.2
frambeside 102.2
skin lesions NEC 102.2
eyelid 102.9 *[373.4]*
ganglion 102.6
gangosis, gangosa 102.5
gumma, gummata 102.4
bone 102.6
gummatous
frambeside 102.4
osteitis 102.6
periostitis 102.6
hydrarthrosis 102.6

Yaws — *continued*
hyperkeratosis (early) (late) (palmar) (plant 102.3
initial lesions 102.0
joint lesions 102.6
juxta-articular nodules 102.7
late nodular (ulcerated) 102.4
latent (without clinical manifestations) (wi positive serology) 102.8
mother 102.0
mucosal 102.7
multiple papillomata 102.1
nodular, late (ulcerated) 102.4
osteitis 102.6
papilloma, papillomata (palmar) (plantar) 10
periostitis (hypertrophic) 102.6
ulcers 102.4
wet crab 102.1
Yeast infection — *see also* Candidiasis 112.9
Yellow
atrophy (liver) 570
chronic 571.8
resulting from administration of blood, plasma, serum, or other biologic substance (within 8 months of a ministration) — *see* Hepatitis, vi
fever — *see* Fever, yellow
jack (*see also* Fever, yellow) 060.9
jaundice (*see also* Jaundice) 782.4
vernix syndrome 762.2
Yersinia septica 027.8

Z

Zagari's disease (xerostomia) 527.7
Zahorsky's disease (exanthema subitum) (se *also* Exanthem subitum) 058.10
syndrome (herpangina) 074.0
Zellweger syndrome 277.86
Zenker's diverticulum (esophagus) 530.6
Ziehen-Oppenheim disease 333.6
Zieve's syndrome (jaundice, hyperlipemia, an hemolytic anemia) 571.1
Zika fever 066.3
Zollinger-Ellison syndrome (gastric hypersecr tion with pancreatic islet cell tumor) 251
Zona — *see also* Herpes, zoster 053.9
Zoophilia (erotica) 302.1
Zoophobia 300.29
Zoster (herpes) — *see also* Herpes, zoster 053.
Zuelzer (-Ogden) anemia or syndrome (nut tional megaloblastic anemia) 281.2
Zygodactyly — *see also* Syndactylism 755.10
Zygomycosis 117.7
Zymotic — *see* condition

SECTION 2

Alphabetic Index to Poisoning and External Causes of Adverse Effects of Drugs and Other Chemical Substances

TABLE OF DRUGS AND CHEMICALS

This table contains a classification of drugs and other chemical substances to identify poisoning states and external causes of adverse effects.

Each of the listed substances in the table is assigned a code according to the poisoning classification (960-989). These codes are used when there is a statement of poisoning, overdose, wrong substance given or taken, or intoxication.

The table also contains a listing of external causes of adverse effects. An adverse effect is a pathologic manifestation due to ingestion or exposure to drugs or other chemical substances (e.g., dermatitis, hypersensitivity reaction, aspirin gastritis). The adverse effect is to be identified by the appropriate code found in Section 1, Index to Diseases and Injuries. An external cause code can then be used to identify the circumstances involved. The table headings pertaining to external causes are defined below:

Accidental poisoning (E850-E869) — accidental overdose of drug, wrong substance given or taken, drug taken inadvertently, accidents in the usage of drugs and biologicals in medical and surgical procedures, and to show external causes of poisonings classifiable to 980-989.

Therapeutic use (E930-E949) — a correct substance properly administered in therapeutic or prophylactic dosage as the external cause of adverse effects.

Suicide attempt (E950-E952) — instances in which self-inflicted injuries or poisonings are involved.

Assault (E96I-E962) — injury or poisoning inflicted by another person with the intent to injure or kill.

Undetermined (E980-E982) — to be used when the intent of the poisoning or injury cannot be determined whether it was intentional or accidental.

The American Hospital Formulary Service list numbers are included in the table to help classify new drugs not identified in the table by name. The AHFS list numbers are keyed to the continually revised American Hospital Formulary Service (AHFS).* These listings are found in the table under the main term **Drug**.

Excluded from the table are radium and other radioactive substances. The classification of adverse effects and complications pertaining to these substances will be found in Section 1, Index to Diseases and Injuries, and Section 3, Index to External Causes of Injuries.

Although certain substances are indexed with one or more subentries, the majority are listed according to one use or state. It is recognized that many substances may be used in various ways, in medicine and in industry, and may cause adverse effects whatever the state of the agent (solid, liquid, or fumes arising from a liquid). In cases in which the reported data indicates a use or state not in the table, or which is clearly different from the one listed, an attempt should be made to classify the substance in the form which most nearly expresses the reported facts.

*American Hospital Formulary Service, 2 vol. (Washington, D.C.: American Society of Hospital Pharmacists, 1959-)

☑ Additional Digit Required — Refer to the Tabular List for Digit Selection   ▽ Subterms under main terms may continue to next column or page

2010 ICD-9-CM   ▶◀ Revised Text   ● New Line   ▲ Revised Code   Volume 2 — 287

	Poisoning	Accident	Therapeutic Use	Suicide Attempt	Assault	Undetermined
1-propanol	980.3	E860.4	—	E950.9	E962.1	E980.9
2-propanol	980.2	E860.3	—	E950.9	E962.1	E980.9
2, 4-D (dichlorophenoxyacetic acid)	989.4	E863.5	—	E950.6	E962.1	E980.7
2, 4-toluene diisocyanate	983.0	E864.0	—	E950.7	E962.1	E980.6
2, 4, 5-T (trichlorophenoxyacetic acid)	989.2	E863.5	—	E950.6	E962.1	E980.7
14-hydroxydihydromorphinone	965.09	E850.2	E935.2	E950.0	E962.0	E980.0
ABOB	961.7	E857	E931.7	E950.4	E962.0	E980.4
Abrus (seed)	988.2	E865.3	—	E950.9	E962.1	E980.9
Absinthe	980.0	E860.1	—	E950.9	E962.1	E980.9
beverage	980.0	E860.0	—	E950.9	E962.1	E980.9
Acenocoumarin, acenocoumarol	964.2	E858.2	E934.2	E950.4	E962.0	E980.4
Acepromazine	969.1	E853.0	E939.1	E950.3	E962.0	E980.3
Acetal	982.8	E862.4	—	E950.9	E962.1	E980.9
Acetaldehyde (vapor)	987.8	E869.8	—	E952.8	E962.2	E982.8
liquid	989.89	E866.8	—	E950.9	E962.1	E980.9
Acetaminophen	965.4	E850.4	E935.4	E950.0	E962.0	E980.0
Acetaminosalol	965.1	E850.3	E935.3	E950.0	E962.0	E980.0
Acetanilid(e)	965.4	E850.4	E935.4	E950.0	E962.0	E980.0
Acetarsol, acetarsone	961.1	E857	E931.1	E950.4	E962.0	E980.4
Acetazolamide	974.2	E858.5	E944.2	E950.4	E962.0	E980.4
Acetic						
acid	983.1	E864.1	—	E950.7	E962.1	E980.6
with sodium acetate (ointment)	976.3	E858.7	E946.3	E950.4	E962.0	E980.4
irrigating solution	974.5	E858.5	E944.5	E950.4	E962.0	E980.4
lotion	976.2	E858.7	E946.2	E950.4	E962.0	E980.4
anhydride	983.1	E864.1	—	E950.7	E962.1	E980.6
ether (vapor)	982.8	E862.4	—	E950.9	E962.1	E980.9
Acetohexamide	962.3	E858.0	E932.3	E950.4	E962.0	E980.4
Acetomenaphthone	964.3	E858.2	E934.3	E950.4	E962.0	E980.4
Acetomorphine	965.01	E850.0	E935.0	E950.0	E962.0	E980.0
Acetone (oils) (vapor)	982.8	E862.4	—	E950.9	E962.1	E980.9
Acetophenazine						
(maleate)	969.1	E853.0	E939.1	E950.3	E962.0	E980.3
Acetophenetidin	965.4	E850.4	E935.4	E950.0	E962.0	E980.0
Acetophenone	982.0	E862.4	—	E950.9	E962.1	E980.9
Acetorphine	965.09	E850.2	E935.2	E950.0	E962.0	E980.0
Acetosulfone (sodium)	961.8	E857	E931.8	E950.4	E962.0	E980.4
Acetrizoate (sodium)	977.8	E858.8	E947.8	E950.4	E962.0	E980.4
Acetylcarbromal	967.3	E852.2	E937.3	E950.2	E962.0	E980.2
Acetylcholine (chloride)	971.0	E855.3	E941.0	E950.4	E962.0	E980.4
Acetylcysteine	975.5	E858.6	E945.5	E950.4	E962.0	E980.4
Acetyldigitoxin	972.1	E858.3	E942.1	E950.4	E962.0	E980.4
Acetyldihydrocodeine	965.09	E850.2	E935.2	E950.0	E962.0	E980.0
Acetyldihydrocodeinone	965.09	E850.2	E935.2	E950.0	E962.0	E980.0
Acetylene (gas) (industrial)	987.1	E868.1	—	E951.8	E962.2	E981.8
incomplete combustion of — see Carbon monoxide, fuel, utility						
tetrachloride (vapor)	982.3	E862.4	—	E950.9	E962.1	E980.9
Acetyliodosalicylic acid	965.1	E850.3	E935.3	E950.0	E962.0	E980.0
Acetylphenylhydrazine	965.8	E850.8	E935.8	E950.0	E962.0	E980.0
Acetylsalicylic acid	965.1	E850.3	E935.3	E950.0	E962.0	E980.0
Achromycin	960.4	E856	E930.4	E950.4	E962.0	E980.4
ophthalmic preparation	976.5	E858.7	E946.5	E950.4	E962.0	E980.4
topical NEC	976.0	E858.7	E946.0	E950.4	E962.0	E980.4
Acidifying agents	963.2	E858.1	E933.2	E950.4	E962.0	E980.4
Acids (corrosive) NEC	983.1	E864.1	—	E950.7	E962.1	E980.6
Aconite (wild)	988.2	E865.4	—	E950.9	E962.1	E980.9
Aconitine (liniment)	976.8	E858.7	E946.8	E950.4	E962.0	E980.4
Aconitum ferox	988.2	E865.4	—	E950.9	E962.1	E980.9
Acridine	983.0	E864.0	—	E950.7	E962.1	E980.6
vapor	987.8	E869.8	—	E952.8	E962.2	E982.8
Acriflavine	961.9	E857	E931.9	E950.4	E962.0	E980.4
Acrisorcin	976.0	E858.7	E946.0	E950.4	E962.0	E980.4
Acrolein (gas)	987.8	E869.8	—	E952.8	E962.2	E982.8
liquid	989.89	E866.8	—	E950.9	E962.1	E980.9
Actaea spicata	988.2	E865.4	—	E950.9	E962.1	E980.9
Acterol	961.5	E857	E931.5	E950.4	E962.0	E980.4
ACTH	962.4	E858.0	E932.4	E950.4	E962.0	E980.4
Acthar	962.4	E858.0	E932.4	E950.4	E962.0	E980.4
Actinomycin (C) (D)	960.7	E856	E930.7	E950.4	E962.0	E980.4
Adalin (acetyl)	967.3	E852.2	E937.3	E950.2	E962.0	E980.2
Adenosine (phosphate)	977.8	E858.8	E947.8	E950.4	E962.0	E980.4
ADH	962.5	E858.0	E932.5	E950.4	E962.0	E980.4
Adhesives	989.89	E866.6	—	E950.9	E962.1	E980.9
Adicillin	960.0	E856	E930.0	E950.4	E962.0	E980.4
Adiphenine	975.1	E855.6	E945.1	E950.4	E962.0	E980.4
Adjunct, pharmaceutical	977.4	E858.8	E947.4	E950.4	E962.0	E980.4

	Poisoning	Accident	Therapeutic Use	Suicide Attempt	Assault	Undetermined
Adrenal (extract, cortex or medulla) (glucocorticoids) (hormones)						
(mineralocorticoids)	962.0	E858.0	E932.0	E950.4	E962.0	E980.4
ENT agent	976.6	E858.7	E946.6	E950.4	E962.0	E980.4
ophthalmic preparation	976.5	E858.7	E946.5	E950.4	E962.0	E980.4
topical NEC	976.0	E858.7	E946.0	E950.4	E962.0	E980.4
Adrenalin	971.2	E855.5	E941.2	E950.4	E962.0	E980.4
Adrenergic blocking agents	971.3	E855.6	E941.3	E950.4	E962.0	E980.4
Adrenergics	971.2	E855.5	E941.2	E950.4	E962.0	E980.4
Adrenochrome (derivatives)	972.8	E858.3	E942.8	E950.4	E962.0	E980.4
Adrenocorticotropic hormone	962.4	E858.0	E932.4	E950.4	E962.0	E980.4
Adrenocorticotropin	962.4	E858.0	E932.4	E950.4	E962.0	E980.4
Adriamycin	960.7	E856	E930.7	E950.4	E962.0	E980.4
Aerosol spray — see Sprays						
Aerosporin	960.8	E856	E930.8	E950.4	E962.0	E980.4
ENT agent	976.6	E858.7	E946.6	E950.4	E962.0	E980.4
ophthalmic preparation	976.5	E858.7	E946.5	E950.4	E962.0	E980.4
topical NEC	976.0	E858.7	E946.0	E950.4	E962.0	E980.4
Aethusa cynapium	988.2	E865.4	—	E950.9	E962.1	E980.9
Afghanistan black	969.6	E854.1	E939.6	E950.3	E962.0	E980.3
Aflatoxin	989.7	E865.9	—	E950.9	E962.1	E980.9
African boxwood	988.2	E865.4	—	E950.9	E962.1	E980.9
Agar (-agar)	973.3	E858.4	E943.3	E950.4	E962.0	E980.4
Agricultural agent NEC	989.89	E863.9	—	E950.6	E962.1	E980.7
Agrypnal	967.0	E851	E937.0	E950.1	E962.0	—
Air contaminant(s), source or type not specified	987.9	E869.9	—	E952.9	E962.2	E982.9
specified type — see specific substance						
Akee	988.2	E865.4	—	E950.9	E962.1	E980.9
Akrinol	976.0	E858.7	E946.0	E950.4	E962.0	E980.4
Alantolactone	961.6	E857	E931.6	E950.4	E962.0	E980.4
Albamycin	960.8	E856	E930.8	E950.4	E962.0	E980.4
Albumin (normal human serum)	964.7	E858.2	E934.7	E950.4	E962.0	E980.4
Albuterol	975.7	E858.6	E945.7	E950.4	E962.0	E980.4
Alcohol	980.9	E860.9	—	E950.9	E962.1	E980.9
absolute	980.0	E860.1	—	E950.9	E962.1	E980.9
beverage	980.0	E860.0	E947.8	E950.9	E962.1	E980.9
amyl	980.3	E860.4	—	E950.9	E962.1	E980.9
antifreeze	980.1	E860.2	—	E950.9	E962.1	E980.9
butyl	980.3	E860.4	—	E950.9	E962.1	E980.9
dehydrated	980.0	E860.1	—	E950.9	E962.1	E980.9
beverage	980.0	E860.0	E947.8	E950.9	E962.1	E980.9
denatured	980.0	E860.1	—	E950.9	E962.1	E980.9
deterrents	977.3	E858.8	E947.3	E950.4	E962.0	E980.4
diagnostic (gastric function)	977.8	E858.8	E947.8	E950.4	E962.0	E980.4
ethyl	980.0	E860.1	—	E950.9	E962.1	E980.9
beverage	980.0	E860.0	E947.8	E950.9	E962.1	E980.9
grain	980.0	E860.1	—	E950.9	E962.1	E980.9
beverage	980.0	E860.0	E947.8	E950.9	E962.1	E980.9
industrial	980.9	E860.9	—	E950.9	E962.1	E980.9
isopropyl	980.2	E860.3	—	E950.9	E962.1	E980.9
methyl	980.1	E860.2	—	E950.9	E962.1	E980.9
preparation for consumption	980.0	E860.0	E947.8	E950.9	E962.1	E980.9
propyl	980.3	E860.4	—	E950.9	E962.1	E980.9
secondary	980.2	E860.3	—	E950.9	E962.1	E980.9
radiator	980.1	E860.2	—	E950.9	E962.1	E980.9
rubbing	980.2	E860.3	—	E950.9	E962.1	E980.9
specified type NEC	980.8	E860.8	—	E950.9	E962.1	E980.9
surgical	980.9	E860.9	—	E950.9	E962.1	E980.9
vapor (from any type of alcohol)	987.8	E869.8	—	E952.8	E962.2	E982.8
wood	980.1	E860.2	—	E950.9	E962.1	E980.9
Alcuronium chloride	975.2	E858.6	E945.2	E950.4	E962.0	E980.4
Aldactone	974.4	E858.5	E944.4	E950.4	E962.0	E980.4
Aldicarb	989.3	E863.2	—	E950.6	E962.1	E980.7
Aldomet	972.6	E858.3	E942.6	E950.4	E962.0	E980.4
Aldosterone	962.0	E858.0	E932.0	E950.4	E962.0	E980.4
Aldrin (dust)	989.2	E863.0	—	E950.6	E962.1	E980.7
Algeldrate	973.0	E858.4	E943.0	E950.4	E962.0	E980.4
Alidase	963.4	E858.1	E933.4	E950.4	E962.0	E980.4
Aliphatic thiocyanates	989.0	E866.8	—	E950.9	E962.1	E980.9
Alkaline antiseptic solution (aromatic)	976.6	E858.7	E946.6	E950.4	E962.0	E980.4

		External Cause (E-Code)				
	Poisoning	Accident	Therapeutic Use	Suicide Attempt	Assault	Undetermined
Alkalinizing agents						
(medicinal)	963.3	E858.1	E933.3	E950.4	E962.0	E980.4
Alkalis, caustic	983.2	E864.2	—	E950.7	E962.1	E980.6
Alkalizing agents						
(medicinal)	963.3	E858.1	E933.3	E950.4	E962.0	E980.4
Alka-seltzer	965.1	E850.3	E935.3	E950.0	E962.0	E980.0
Alkavervir	972.6	E858.3	E942.6	E950.4	E962.0	E980.4
Allegron	969.05 ▲	E854.0	E939.0	E950.3	E962.0	E980.3
Alleve — Naproxen						
Allobarbital,						
allobarbitone	967.0	E851	E937.0	E950.1	E962.0	E980.1
Allopurinol	974.7	E858.5	E944.7	E950.4	E962.0	E980.4
Allylestrenol	962.2	E858.0	E932.2	E950.4	E962.0	E980.4
Allylisopropylacetylurea	967.8	E852.8	E937.8	E950.2	E962.0	E980.2
Allylisopropylmalonylurea	967.0	E851	E937.0	E950.1	E962.0	E980.1
Allyltribromide	967.3	E852.2	E937.3	E950.2	E962.0	E980.2
Aloe, aloes, aloin	973.1	E858.4	E943.1	E950.4	E962.0	E980.4
Alosetron	973.8	E858.4	E943.8	E950.4	E962.0	E980.4
Aloxidone	966.0	E855.0	E936.0	E950.4	E962.0	E980.4
Aloxiprin	965.1	E850.3	E935.3	E950.0	E962.0	E980.0
Alpha-1 blockers	971.3	E855.6	E941.3	E950.4	E962.0	E980.4
Alpha amylase	963.4	E858.1	E933.4	E950.4	E962.0	E980.4
Alphaprodine						
(hydrochloride)	965.09	E850.2	E935.2	E950.0	E962.0	E980.0
Alpha tocopherol	963.5	E858.1	E933.5	E950.4	E962.0	E980.4
Alseroxylon	972.6	E858.3	E942.6	E950.4	E962.0	E980.4
Alum (ammonium)						
(potassium)	983.2	E864.2	—	E950.7	E962.1	E980.6
medicinal (astringent)						
NEC	976.2	E858.7	E946.2	E950.4	E962.0	E980.4
Aluminium, aluminum (gel)	973.0	E858.4	E943.0	E950.4	E962.0	E980.4
(hydroxide)	973.0	E858.4	E943.0	E950.4	E962.0	E980.4
acetate solution	976.2	E858.7	E946.2	E950.4	E962.0	E980.4
aspirin	965.1	E850.3	E935.3	E950.0	E962.0	E980.0
carbonate	973.0	E858.4	E943.0	E950.4	E962.0	E980.4
glycinate	973.0	E858.4	E943.0	E950.4	E962.0	E980.4
nicotinate	972.2	E858.3	E942.2	E950.4	E962.0	E980.4
ointment (surgical)						
(topical)	976.3	E858.7	E946.3	E950.4	E962.0	E980.4
phosphate	973.0	E858.4	E943.0	E950.4	E962.0	E980.4
subacetate	976.2	E858.7	E946.2	E950.4	E962.0	E980.4
topical NEC	976.3	E858.7	E946.3	E950.4	E962.0	E980.4
Alurate	967.0	E851	E937.0	E950.1	E962.0	E980.1
Alverine (citrate)	975.1	E858.6	E945.1	E950.4	E962.0	E980.4
Alvodine	965.09	E850.2	E935.2	E950.0	E962.0	E980.0
Amanita phalloides	988.1	E865.5	—	E950.9	E962.1	E980.9
Amantadine						
(hydrochloride)	966.4	E855.0	E936.4	E950.4	E962.0	E980.4
Ambazone	961.9	E857	E931.9	E950.4	E962.0	E980.4
Ambenonium	971.0	E855.3	E941.0	E950.4	E962.0	E980.4
Ambutonium bromide	971.1	E855.4	E941.1	E950.4	E962.0	E980.4
Ametazole	977.8	E858.8	E947.8	E950.4	E962.0	E980.4
Amethocaine (infiltration)						
(topical)	968.5	E855.2	E938.5	E950.4	E962.0	E980.4
nerve block (peripheral)						
(plexus)	968.6	E855.2	E938.6	E950.4	E962.0	E980.4
spinal	968.7	E855.2	E938.7	E950.4	E962.0	E980.4
Amethopterin	963.1	E858.1	E933.1	E950.4	E962.0	E980.4
Amfepramone	977.0	E858.8	E947.0	E950.4	E962.0	E980.4
Amidon	965.02	E850.1	E935.1	E950.0	E962.0	E980.0
Amidopyrine	965.5	E850.5	E935.5	E950.0	E962.0	E980.0
Aminacrine	976.0	E858.7	E946.0	E950.4	E962.0	E980.4
Aminitrozole	961.5	E857	E931.5	E950.4	E962.0	E980.4
Aminoacetic acid	974.5	E858.5	E944.5	E950.4	E962.0	E980.4
Amino acids	974.5	E858.5	E944.5	E950.4	E962.0	E980.4
Aminocaproic acid	964.4	E858.2	E934.4	E950.4	E962.0	E980.4
Aminoethylisothiourium	963.8	E858.1	E933.8	E950.4	E962.0	E980.4
Aminoglutethimide	966.3	E855.0	E936.3	E950.4	E962.0	E980.4
Aminometradine	974.3	E858.5	E944.3	E950.4	E962.0	E980.4
Aminopentamide	971.1	E855.4	E941.1	E950.4	E962.0	E980.4
Aminophenazone	965.5	E850.5	E935.5	E950.0	E962.0	E980.0
Aminophenol	983.0	E864.0	—	E950.7	E962.1	E980.6
Aminophenylpyridone	969.5	E853.8	E939.5	E950.3	E962.0	E980.3
Aminophyllin	975.7	E858.6	E945.7	E950.4	E962.0	E980.4
Aminopterin	963.1	E858.1	E933.1	E950.4	E962.0	E980.4
Aminopyrine	965.5	E850.5	E935.5	E950.0	E962.0	E980.0
Aminosalicylic acid	961.8	E857	E931.8	E950.4	E962.0	E980.4
Amiphenazole	970.1	E854.3	E940.1	E950.4	E962.0	E980.4
Amiquinsin	972.6	E858.3	E942.6	E950.4	E962.0	E980.4
Amisometradine	974.3	E858.5	E944.3	E950.4	E962.0	E980.4
Amitriptyline	969.05 ▲	E854.0	E939.0	E950.3	E962.0	E980.3

		External Cause (E-Code)				
	Poisoning	Accident	Therapeutic Use	Suicide Attempt	Assault	Undetermined
Ammonia (fumes) (gas)						
(vapor)	987.8	E869.8	—	E952.8	E962.2	E982.8
liquid (household) NEC	983.2	E861.4	—	E950.7	E962.1	E980.6
spirit, aromatic	970.8	E854.3	E940.8	E950.4	E962.0	E980.4
Ammoniated mercury	976.0	E858.7	E946.0	E950.4	E962.0	E980.4
Ammonium						
carbonate	983.2	E864.2	—	E950.7	E962.1	E980.6
chloride (acidifying agent)	963.2	E858.1	E933.2	E950.4	E962.0	E980.4
expectorant	975.5	E858.6	E945.5	E950.4	E962.0	E980.4
compounds (household)						
NEC	983.2	E861.4	—	E950.7	E962.1	E980.6
fumes (any usage)	987.8	E869.8	—	E952.8	E962.2	E982.8
industrial	983.2	E864.2	—	E950.7	E962.1	E980.6
ichthyosulfonate	976.4	E858.7	E946.4	E950.4	E962.0	E980.4
mandelate	961.9	E857	E931.9	E950.4	E962.0	E980.4
Amobarbital	967.0	E851	E937.0	E950.1	E962.0	E980.1
Amodiaquin(e)	961.4	E857	E931.4	E950.4	E962.0	E980.4
Amopyroquin(e)	961.4	E857	E931.4	E950.4	E962.0	E980.4
Amphenidone	969.5	E853.8	E939.5	E950.3	E962.0	E980.3
Amphetamine	969.72 ▲	E854.2	E939.7	E950.3	E962.0	E980.3
Amphomycin	960.8	E856	E930.8	E950.4	E962.0	E980.4
Amphotericin B	960.1	E856	E930.1	E950.4	E962.0	E980.4
topical	976.0	E858.7	E946.0	E950.4	E962.0	E980.4
Ampicillin	960.0	E856	E930.0	E950.4	E962.0	E980.4
Amprotropine	971.1	E855.4	E941.1	E950.4	E962.0	E980.4
Amygdalin	977.8	E858.8	E947.8	E950.4	E962.0	E980.4
Amyl						
acetate (vapor)	982.8	E862.4	—	E950.9	E962.1	E980.9
alcohol	980.3	E860.4	—	E950.9	E962.1	E980.9
nitrite (medicinal)	972.4	E858.3	E942.4	E950.4	E962.0	E980.4
Amylase (alpha)	963.4	E858.1	E933.4	E950.4	E962.0	E980.4
Amylene hydrate	980.8	E860.8	—	E950.9	E962.1	E980.9
Amylobarbitone	967.0	E851	E937.0	E950.1	E962.0	E980.1
Amylocaine	968.9	E855.2	E938.9	E950.4	E962.0	E980.4
infiltration (subcutaneous)	968.5	E855.2	E938.5	E950.4	E962.0	E980.4
nerve block (peripheral)						
(plexus)	968.6	E855.2	E938.6	E950.4	E962.0	E980.4
spinal	968.7	E855.2	E938.7	E950.4	E962.0	E980.4
topical (surface)	968.5	E855.2	E938.5	E950.4	E962.0	E980.4
Amytal (sodium)	967.0	E851	E937.0	E950.1	E962.0	E980.1
Analeptics	970.0	E854.3	E940.0	E950.4	E962.0	E980.4
Analgesics	965.9	E850.9	E935.9	E950.0	E962.0	E980.0
aromatic NEC	965.4	E850.4	E935.4	E950.0	E962.0	E980.0
non-narcotic NEC	965.7	E850.7	E935.7	E950.0	E962.0	E980.0
specified NEC	965.8	E850.8	E935.8	E950.0	E962.0	E980.0
Anamirta cocculus	988.2	E865.3	—	E950.9	E962.1	E980.9
Ancillin	960.0	E856	E930.0	E950.4	E962.0	E980.4
Androgens (anabolic						
congeners)	962.1	E858.0	E932.1	E950.4	E962.0	E980.4
Androstalone	962.1	E858.0	E932.1	E950.4	E962.0	E980.4
Androsterone	962.1	E858.0	E932.1	E950.4	E962.0	E980.4
Anemone pulsatilla	988.2	E865.4	—	E950.9	E962.1	E980.9
Anesthesia, anesthetic						
(general) NEC	968.4	E855.1	E938.4	E950.4	E962.0	E980.4
block (nerve) (plexus)	968.6	E855.2	E938.6	E950.4	E962.0	E980.4
gaseous NEC	968.2	E855.1	E938.2	E950.4	E962.0	E980.4
halogenated hydrocarbon						
derivatives NEC	968.2	E855.1	E938.2	E950.4	E962.0	E980.4
infiltration (intradermal)						
(subcutaneous)						
(submucosal)	968.5	E855.2	E938.5	E950.4	E962.0	E980.4
intravenous	968.3	E855.1	E938.3	E950.4	E962.0	E980.4
local NEC	968.9	E855.2	E938.9	E950.4	E962.0	E980.4
nerve blocking (peripheral)						
(plexus)	968.6	E855.2	E938.6	E950.4	E962.0	E980.4
rectal NEC	968.3	E855.1	E938.3	E950.4	E962.0	E980.4
spinal	968.7	E855.2	E938.7	E950.4	E962.0	E980.4
surface	968.5	E855.2	E938.5	E950.4	E962.0	E980.4
topical	968.5	E855.2	E938.5	E950.4	E962.0	E980.4
Aneurine	963.5	E858.1	E933.5	E950.4	E962.0	E980.4
Anginine — see Glyceryl						
trinitrate						
Angio-Conray	977.8	E858.8	E947.8	E950.4	E962.0	E980.4
Angiotensin	971.2	E855.5	E941.2	E950.4	E962.0	E980.4
Anhydrohydroxyprogesterone	962.2	E858.0	E932.2	E950.4	E962.0	E980.4
Anhydron	974.3	E858.5	E944.3	E950.4	E962.0	E980.4
Anileridine	965.09	E850.2	E935.2	E950.0	E962.0	E980.0
Aniline (dye) (liquid)	983.0	E864.0	—	E950.7	E962.1	E980.6
analgesic	965.4	E850.4	E935.4	E950.0	E962.0	E980.0
derivatives, therapeutic						
NEC	965.4	E850.4	E935.4	E950.0	E962.0	E980.0
vapor	987.8	E869.8	—	E952.8	E962.2	E982.8

Nontherapeutic use substance

▽ Subterms under main terms may continue to next column or page

▶◀ Revised Text   ● New Line   ▲ Revised Code

Alkalinizing agents — Aniline

	Poisoning	Accident	Therapeutic Use	Suicide Attempt	Assault	Undetermined
External Cause (E-Code)						
Aniscoropine	971.1	E855.4	E941.1	E950.4	E962.0	E980.4
Anisindione	964.2	E858.2	E934.2	E950.4	E962.0	E980.4
Anorexic agents	977.0	E858.8	E947.0	E950.4	E962.0	E980.4
Ant (bite) (sting)	—	E905.5	—	E950.9	E962.1	E980.9
Antabuse	977.3	E858.8	E947.3	E950.4	E962.0	E980.4
Antacids	973.0	E858.4	E943.0	E950.4	E962.0	E980.4
Antazoline	963.0	E858.1	E933.0	E950.4	E962.0	E980.4
Antiallergic agents	976.4	E858.7	E946.4	E950.4	E962.0	E980.4
Anthramycin	960.7	E856	E930.7	E950.4	E962.0	E980.4
Antiadrenergics	971.3	E855.6	E941.3	E950.4	E962.0	E980.4
Antiallergic agents	963.0	E858.1	E933.0	E950.4	E962.0	E980.4
Antianemic agents NEC	964.1	E858.2	E934.1	E950.4	E962.0	E980.4
Antiaris toxicaria	988.2	E865.4	—	E950.9	E962.1	E980.9
Antiarteriosclerotic agents	972.2	E858.3	E942.2	E950.4	E962.0	E980.4
Antiasthmatics	975.7	E858.6	E945.7	E950.4	E962.0	E980.4
Antibiotics	960.9	E856	E930.9	E950.4	E962.0	E980.4
antifungal	960.1	E856	E930.1	E950.4	E962.0	E980.4
antimycobacterial	960.6	E856	E930.6	E950.4	E962.0	E980.4
antineoplastic	960.7	E856	E930.7	E950.4	E962.0	E980.4
cephalosporin (group)	960.5	E856	E930.5	E950.4	E962.0	E980.4
chloramphenicol (group)	960.2	E856	E930.2	E950.4	E962.0	E980.4
macrolides	960.3	E856	E930.3	E950.4	E962.0	E980.4
specified NEC	960.8	E856	E930.8	E950.4	E962.0	E980.4
tetracycline (group)	960.4	E856	E930.4	E950.4	E962.0	E980.4
Anticancer agents NEC	963.1	E858.1	E933.1	E950.4	E962.0	E980.4
antibiotics	960.7	E856	E930.7	E950.4	E962.0	E980.4
Anticholinergics	971.1	E855.4	E941.1	E950.4	E962.0	E980.4
Anticholinesterase (organophosphorus) (reversible)	971.0	E855.3	E941.0	E950.4	E962.0	E980.4
Anticoagulants	964.2	E858.2	E934.2	E950.4	E962.0	E980.4
antagonists	964.5	E858.2	E934.5	E950.4	E962.0	E980.4
Anti-common cold agents NEC	975.6	E858.6	E945.6	E950.4	E962.0	E980.4
Anticonvulsants NEC	966.3	E855.0	E936.3	E950.4	E962.0	E980.4
Antidepressants	969.00 ▲	E854.0	E939.0	E950.3	E962.0	E980.3
monoamine oxidase inhibitors (MAOI) ●	969.01	E854.0	E939.0	E950.3	E962.0	E980.3
specified type NEC ●	969.09	E854.0	E939.0	E950.3	E962.0	E980.3
SSNRI (selective serotonin and norepinephrine reuptake inhibitors) ●	969.02	E854.0	E939.0	E950.3	E962.0	E980.3
SSRI (selective serotonin reuptake inhibitors) ●	969.03	E854.0	E939.0	E950.3	E962.0	E980.3
tetracyclic ●	969.04	E854.0	E939.0	E950.3	E962.0	E980.3
tricyclic ●	969.05	E854.0	E939.0	E950.3	E962.0	E980.3
Antidiabetic agents	962.3	E858.0	E932.3	E950.4	E962.0	E980.4
Antidiarrheal agents	973.5	E858.4	E943.5	E950.4	E962.0	E980.4
Antidiuretic hormone	962.5	E858.0	E932.5	E950.4	E962.0	E980.4
Antidotes NEC	977.2	E858.8	E947.2	E950.4	E962.0	E980.4
Antiemetic agents	963.0	E858.1	E933.0	E950.4	E962.0	E980.4
Antiepilepsy agent NEC	966.3	E855.0	E936.3	E950.4	E962.0	E980.4
Antifertility pills	962.2	E858.0	E932.2	E950.4	E962.0	E980.4
Antiflatulents	973.8	E858.4	E943.8	E950.4	E962.0	E980.4
Antifreeze	989.89	E866.8	—	E950.9	E962.1	E980.9
alcohol	980.1	E860.2	—	E950.9	E962.1	E980.9
ethylene glycol	982.8	E862.4	—	E950.9	E962.1	E980.9
Antifungals (nonmedicinal) (sprays)	989.4	E863.6	—	E950.6	E962.1	E980.7
medicinal NEC	961.9	E857	E931.9	E950.4	E962.0	E980.4
antibiotic	960.1	E856	E930.1	E950.4	E962.0	E980.4
topical	976.0	E858.7	E946.0	E950.4	E962.0	E980.4
Antigastric secretion agents	973.0	E858.4	E943.0	E950.4	E962.0	E980.4
Antihelmintics	961.6	E857	E931.6	E950.4	E962.0	E980.4
Antihemophilic factor (human)	964.7	E858.2	E934.7	E950.4	E962.0	E980.4
Antihistamine	963.0	E858.1	E933.0	E950.4	E962.0	E980.4
Antihypertensive agents NEC	972.6	E858.3	E942.6	E950.4	E962.0	E980.4
Anti-infectives NEC	961.9	E857	E931.9	E950.4	E962.0	E980.4
antibiotics	960.9	E856	E930.9	E950.4	E962.0	E980.4
specified NEC	960.8	E856	E930.8	E950.4	E962.0	E980.4
antihelmintic	961.6	E857	E931.6	E950.4	E962.0	E980.4
antimalarial	961.4	E857	E931.4	E950.4	E962.0	E980.4
antimycobacterial NEC	961.8	E857	E931.8	E950.4	E962.0	E980.4
antibiotics	960.6	E856	E930.6	E950.4	E962.0	E980.4
antiprotozoal NEC	961.5	E857	E931.5	E950.4	E962.0	—
blood	961.4	E857	E931.4	E950.4	E962.0	E980.4
antiviral	961.7	E857	E931.7	E950.4	E962.0	E980.4
arsenical	961.1	E857	E931.1	E950.4	E962.0	E980.4
Anti-infectives — *continued*						
ENT agents	976.6	E858.7	E946.6	E950.4	E962.0	E980.4
heavy metals NEC	961.2	E857	E931.2	E950.4	E962.0	E980.4
local	976.0	E858.7	E946.0	E950.4	E962.0	E980.4
ophthalmic preparation	976.5	E858.7	E946.5	E950.4	E962.0	E980.4
topical NEC	976.0	E858.7	E946.0	E950.4	E962.0	E980.4
Anti-inflammatory agents (topical)	976.0	E858.7	E946.0	E950.4	E962.0	E980.4
Antiknock (tetraethyl lead)	984.1	E862.1	—	E950.9	—	E980.9
Antilipemics	972.2	E858.3	E942.2	E950.4	E962.0	E980.4
Antimalarials	961.4	E857	E931.4	E950.4	E962.0	E980.4
Antimony (compounds) (vapor) NEC	985.4	E866.2	—	E950.9	E962.1	E980.9
anti-infectives	961.2	E857	E931.2	E950.4	E962.0	E980.4
pesticides (vapor)	985.4	E863.4	—	E950.6	E962.2	E980.7
potassium tartrate	961.2	E857	E931.2	E950.4	E962.0	E980.4
tartrated	961.2	E857	E931.2	E950.4	E962.0	E980.4
Antimuscarinic agents	971.1	E855.4	E941.1	E950.4	E962.0	E980.4
Antimycobacterials NEC	961.8	E857	E931.8	E950.4	E962.0	E980.4
antibiotics	960.6	E856	E930.6	E950.4	E962.0	E980.4
Antineoplastic agents	963.1	E858.1	E933.1	E950.4	E962.0	E980.4
antibiotics	960.7	E856	E930.7	E950.4	E962.0	E980.4
Anti-Parkinsonism agents	966.4	E855.0	E936.4	E950.4	E962.0	E980.4
Antiphlogistics	965.69	E850.6	E935.6	E950.0	E962.0	E980.0
Antiprotozoals NEC	961.5	E857	E931.5	E950.4	E962.0	E980.4
blood	961.4	E857	E931.4	E950.4	E962.0	E980.4
Antipruritics (local)	976.1	E858.7	E946.1	E950.4	E962.0	E980.4
Antipsychotic agents NEC	969.3	E853.8	E939.3	E950.3	E962.0	E980.3
Antipyretics	965.9	E850.9	E935.9	E950.0	E962.0	E980.0
specified NEC	965.8	E850.8	E935.8	E950.0	E962.0	E980.0
Antipyrine	965.5	E850.5	E935.5	E950.0	E962.0	E980.0
Antirabies serum (equine)	979.9	E858.8	E949.9	E950.4	E962.0	E980.4
Antirheumatics	965.69	E850.6	E935.6	E950.0	E962.0	E980.0
Antiseborrheics	976.4	E858.7	E946.4	E950.4	E962.0	E980.4
Antiseptics (external) (medicinal)	976.0	E858.7	E946.0	E950.4	E962.0	E980.4
Antistine	963.0	E858.1	E933.0	E950.4	E962.0	E980.4
Antithyroid agents	962.8	E858.0	E932.8	E950.4	E962.0	E980.4
Antitoxin, any	979.9	E858.8	E949.9	E950.4	E962.0	E980.4
Antituberculars	961.8	E857	E931.8	E950.4	E962.0	E980.4
antibiotics	960.6	E856	E930.6	E950.4	E962.0	E980.4
Antitussives	975.4	E858.6	E945.4	E950.4	E962.0	E980.4
Antivaricose agents (sclerosing)	972.7	E858.3	E942.7	E950.4	E962.0	E980.4
Antivenin (crotaline) (spider-bite)	979.9	E858.8	E949.9	E950.4	E962.0	E980.4
Antivert	963.0	E858.1	E933.0	E950.4	E962.0	E980.4
Antivirals NEC	961.7	E857	E931.7	E950.4	E962.0	E980.4
Ant poisons — *see* Pesticides						
Antrol	989.4	E863.4	—	E950.6	E962.1	E980.7
fungicide	989.4	E863.6	—	E950.6	E962.1	E980.7
Apomorphine hydrochloride (emetic)	973.6	E858.4	E943.6	E950.4	E962.0	E980.4
Appetite depressants, central	977.0	E858.8	E947.0	E950.4	E962.0	E980.4
Apresoline	972.6	E858.3	E942.6	E950.4	E962.0	E980.4
Aprobarbital, aprobarbitone	967.0	E851	E937.0	E950.1	E962.0	E980.1
Apronalide	967.8	E852.8	E937.8	E950.2	E962.0	E980.2
Aqua fortis	983.1	E864.1	—	E950.7	E962.1	E980.6
Arachis oil (topical)	976.3	E858.7	E946.3	E950.4	E962.0	E980.4
cathartic	973.2	E858.4	E943.2	E950.4	E962.0	E980.4
Aralen	961.4	E857	E931.4	E950.4	E962.0	E980.4
Arginine salts	974.5	E858.5	E944.5	E950.4	E962.0	E980.4
Argyrol	976.0	E858.7	E946.0	E950.4	E962.0	E980.4
ENT agent	976.6	E858.7	E946.6	E950.4	E962.0	E980.4
ophthalmic preparation	976.5	E858.7	E946.5	E950.4	E962.0	E980.4
Aristocort	962.0	E858.0	E932.0	E950.4	E962.0	E980.4
ENT agent	976.6	E858.7	E946.6	E950.4	E962.0	E980.4
ophthalmic preparation	976.5	E858.7	E946.5	E950.4	E962.0	E980.4
topical NEC	976.0	E858.7	E946.0	E950.4	E962.0	E980.4
Aromatics, corrosive	983.0	E864.0	—	E950.7	E962.1	E980.6
disinfectants	983.0	E861.4	—	E950.7	E962.1	E980.6
Arsenate of lead (insecticide)	985.1	E863.4	—	E950.8	E962.1	E980.8
herbicide	985.1	E863.5	—	E950.8	E962.1	E980.8
Arsenic, arsenicals (compounds) (dust) (fumes) (vapor) NEC	985.1	E866.3	—	E950.8	E962.1	E980.8
anti-infectives	961.1	E857	E931.1	E950.4	E962.0	E980.4
pesticide (dust) (fumes)	985.1	E863.4	—	E950.8	E962.1	E980.8

	Poisoning	Accident	Therapeutic Use	Suicide Attempt	Assault	Undeter-mined
Arsine (gas)	985.1	E866.3	—	E950.8	E962.1	E980.8
Arsphenamine (silver)	961.1	E857	E931.1	E950.4	E962.0	E980.4
Arsthinol	961.1	E857	E931.1	E950.4	E962.0	E980.4
Artane	971.1	E855.4	E941.1	E950.4	E962.0	E980.4
Arthropod (venomous) NEC	989.5	E905.5	—	E950.9	E962.1	E980.9
Asbestos	989.81	E866.8	—	E950.9	E962.1	E980.9
Ascaridole	961.6	E857	E931.6	E950.4	E962.0	E980.4
Ascorbic acid	963.5	E858.1	E933.5	E950.4	E962.0	E980.4
Asiaticoside	976.0	E858.7	E946.0	E950.4	E962.0	E980.4
Aspidium (oleoresin)	961.6	E857	E931.6	E950.4	E962.0	E980.4
Aspirin	965.1	E850.3	E935.3	E950.0	E962.0	E980.0
Astringents (local)	976.2	E858.7	E946.2	E950.4	E962.0	E980.4
Atabrine	961.3	E857	E931.3	E950.4	E962.0	E980.4
Ataractics	969.5	E853.8	E939.5	E950.3	E962.0	E980.3
Atonia drug, intestinal	973.3	E858.4	E943.3	E950.4	E962.0	E980.4
Atophan	974.7	E858.5	E944.7	E950.4	E962.0	E980.4
Atropine	971.1	E855.4	E941.1	E950.4	E962.0	E980.4
Attapulgite	973.5	E858.4	E943.5	E950.4	E962.0	E980.4
Attenuvax	979.4	E858.8	E949.4	E950.4	E962.0	E980.4
Aureomycin	960.4	E856	E930.4	E950.4	E962.0	E980.4
ophthalmic preparation	976.5	E858.7	E946.5	E950.4	E962.0	E980.4
topical NEC	976.0	E858.7	E946.0	E950.4	E962.0	E980.4
Aurothioglucose	965.69	E850.6	E935.6	E950.0	E962.0	E980.0
Aurothioglycanide	965.69	E850.6	E935.6	E950.0	E962.0	E980.0
Aurothiomalate	965.69	E850.6	E935.6	E950.0	E962.0	E980.0
Automobile fuel	981	E862.1	—	E950.9	E962.1	E980.9
Autonomic nervous system agents NEC	971.9	E855.9	E941.9	E950.4	E962.0	E980.4
Avlosulfon	961.8	E857	E931.8	E950.4	E962.0	E980.4
Avomine	967.8	E852.8	E937.8	E950.2	E962.0	E980.2
Azacyclonol	969.5	E853.8	E939.5	E950.3	E962.0	E980.3
Azapetine	971.3	E855.6	E941.3	E950.4	E962.0	E980.4
Azaribine	963.1	E858.1	E933.1	E950.4	E962.0	E980.4
Azaserine	960.7	E856	E930.7	E950.4	E962.0	E980.4
Azathioprine	963.1	E858.1	E933.1	E950.4	E962.0	E980.4
Azosulfamide	961.0	E857	E931.0	E950.4	E962.0	E980.4
Azulfidine	961.0	E857	E931.0	E950.4	E962.0	E980.4
Azuresin	977.8	E858.8	E947.8	E950.4	E962.0	E980.4
Bacimycin	976.0	E858.7	E946.0	E950.4	E962.0	E980.4
ophthalmic preparation	976.5	E858.7	E946.5	E950.4	E962.0	E980.4
Bacitracin	960.8	E856	E930.8	E950.4	E962.0	E980.4
ENT agent	976.6	E858.7	E946.6	E950.4	E962.0	E980.4
ophthalmic preparation	976.5	E858.7	E946.5	E950.4	E962.0	E980.4
topical NEC	976.0	E858.7	E946.0	E950.4	E962.0	E980.4
Baking soda	963.3	E858.1	E933.3	E950.4	E962.0	E980.4
BAL	963.8	E858.1	E933.8	E950.4	E962.0	E980.4
Bamethan (sulfate)	972.5	E858.3	E942.5	E950.4	E962.0	E980.4
Bamipine	963.0	E858.1	E933.0	E950.4	E962.0	E980.4
Baneberry	988.2	E865.4	—	E950.9	E962.1	E980.9
Banewort	988.2	E865.4	—	E950.9	E962.1	E980.9
Barbenyl	967.0	E851	E937.0	E950.1	E962.0	E980.1
Barbital, barbitone	967.0	E851	E937.0	E950.1	E962.0	E980.1
Barbiturates, barbituric acid	967.0	E851	E937.0	E950.1	E962.0	E980.1
anesthetic (intravenous)	968.3	E855.1	E938.3	E950.4	E962.0	E980.4
Barium (carbonate) (chloride) (sulfate)	985.8	E866.4	—	E950.9	E962.1	E980.9
diagnostic agent	977.8	E858.8	E947.8	E950.4	E962.0	E980.4
pesticide	985.8	E863.4	—	E950.6	E962.1	E980.7
rodenticide	985.8	E863.7	—	E950.6	E962.1	E980.7
Barrier cream	976.3	E858.7	E946.3	E950.4	E962.0	E980.4
Battery acid or fluid	983.1	E864.1	—	E950.7	E962.1	E980.6
Bay rum	980.8	E860.8	—	E950.9	E962.1	E980.9
BCG vaccine	978.0	E858.8	E948.0	E950.4	E962.0	E980.4
Bearsfoot	988.2	E865.4	—	E950.9	E962.1	E980.9
Beclamide	966.3	E855.0	E936.3	E950.4	E962.0	E980.4
Bee (sting) (venom)	989.5	E905.3	—	E950.9	E962.1	E980.9
Belladonna (alkaloids)	971.1	E855.4	E941.1	E950.4	E962.0	E980.4
Bemegride	970.0	E854.3	E940.0	E950.4	E962.0	E980.4
Benactyzine	969.8	E855.8	E939.8	E950.3	E962.0	E980.3
Benadryl	963.0	E858.1	E933.0	E950.4	E962.0	E980.4
Bendrofluazide	974.3	E858.5	E944.3	E950.4	E962.0	E980.4
Bendroflumethiazide	974.3	E858.5	E944.3	E950.4	E962.0	E980.4
Benemid	974.7	E858.5	E944.7	E950.4	E962.0	E980.4
Benethamine penicillin G	960.0	E856	E930.0	E950.4	E962.0	E980.4
Benisone	976.0	E858.7	E946.0	E950.4	E962.0	E980.4
Benoquin	976.8	E858.7	E946.8	E950.4	E962.0	E980.4
Benoxinate	968.5	E855.2	E938.5	E950.4	E962.0	E980.4
Bentonite	976.3	E858.7	E946.3	E950.4	E962.0	E980.4
Benzalkonium (chloride)	976.0	E858.7	E946.0	E950.4	E962.0	E980.4
ophthalmic preparation	976.5	E858.7	E946.5	E950.4	E962.0	E980.4

	Poisoning	Accident	Therapeutic Use	Suicide Attempt	Assault	Undeter-mined
Benzamidosalicylate (calcium)	961.8	E857	E931.8	E950.4	E962.0	E980.4
Benzathine penicillin	960.0	E856	E930.0	E950.4	E962.0	E980.4
Benzcarbimine	963.1	E858.1	E933.1	E950.4	E962.0	E980.4
Benzedrex	971.2	E855.5	E941.2	E950.4	E962.0	E980.4
Benzedrine (amphetamine)	969.72 ▲	E854.2	E939.7	E950.3	E962.0	E980.3
Benzene (acetyl) (dimethyl) (methyl) (solvent) (vapor)	982.0	E862.4	—	E950.9	E962.1	E980.9
hexachloride (gamma) (insecticide) (vapor)	989.2	E863.0	—	E950.6	E962.1	E980.7
Benzethonium	976.0	E858.7	E946.0	E950.4	E962.0	E980.4
Benzhexol (chloride)	966.4	E855.0	E936.4	E950.4	E962.0	E980.4
Benzilonium	971.1	E855.4	E941.1	E950.4	E962.0	E980.4
Benzin(e) — see Ligroin						
Benziodarone	972.4	E858.3	E942.4	E950.4	E962.0	E980.4
Benzocaine	968.5	E855.2	E938.5	E950.4	E962.0	E980.4
Benzodiapin	969.4	E853.2	E939.4	E950.3	E962.0	E980.3
Benzodiazepines (tranquilizers) NEC	969.4	E853.2	E939.4	E950.3	E962.0	E980.3
Benzoic acid (with salicylic acid) (anti-infective)	976.0	E858.7	E946.0	E950.4	E962.0	E980.4
Benzoin	976.3	E858.7	E946.3	E950.4	E962.0	E980.4
Benzol (vapor)	982.0	E862.4	—	E950.9	E962.1	E980.9
Benzomorphan	965.09	E850.2	E935.2	E950.0	E962.0	E980.0
Benzonatate	975.4	E858.6	E945.4	E950.4	E962.0	E980.4
Benzothiadiazides	974.3	E858.5	E944.3	E950.4	E962.0	E980.4
Benzoylpas	961.8	E857	E931.8	E950.4	E962.0	E980.4
Benzperidol	969.5	E853.8	E939.5	E950.3	E962.0	E980.3
Benzphetamine	977.0	E858.8	E947.0	E950.4	E962.0	E980.4
Benzpyrinium	971.0	E855.3	E941.0	E950.4	E962.0	E980.4
Benzquinamide	963.0	E858.1	E933.0	E950.4	E962.0	E980.4
Benzthiazide	974.3	E858.5	E944.3	E950.4	E962.0	E980.4
Benztropine	971.1	E855.4	E941.1	E950.4	E962.0	E980.4
Benzyl acetate	982.8	E862.4	—	E950.9	E962.1	E980.9
benzoate (anti-infective)	976.0	E858.7	E946.0	E950.4	E962.0	E980.4
morphine	965.09	E850.2	E935.2	E950.0	E962.0	E980.0
penicillin	960.0	E856	E930.0	E950.4	E962.0	E980.4
Bephenium hydroxynapthoate	961.6	E857	E931.6	E950.4	E962.0	E980.4
Bergamot oil	989.89	E866.8	—	E950.9	E962.1	E980.9
Berries, poisonous	988.2	E865.3	—	E950.9	E962.1	E980.9
Beryllium (compounds) (fumes)	985.3	E866.4	—	E950.9	E962.1	E980.9
Beta-carotene	976.3	E858.7	E946.3	E950.4	E962.0	E980.4
Beta-Chlor	967.1	E852.0	E937.1	E950.2	E962.0	E980.2
Betamethasone	962.0	E858.0	E932.0	E950.4	E962.0	E980.4
topical	976.0	E858.7	E946.0	E950.4	E962.0	E980.4
Betazole	977.8	E858.8	E947.8	E950.4	E962.0	E980.4
Bethanechol	971.0	E855.3	E941.0	E950.4	E962.0	E980.4
Bethanidine	972.6	E858.3	E942.6	E950.4	E962.0	E980.4
Betula oil	976.3	E858.7	E946.3	E950.4	E962.0	E980.4
Bhang	969.6	E854.1	E939.6	E950.3	E962.0	E980.3
Bialamicol	961.5	E857	E931.5	E950.4	E962.0	E980.4
Bichloride of mercury — see Mercury, chloride						
Bichromates (calcium) (crystals) (potassium) (sodium)	983.9	E864.3	—	E950.7	E962.1	E980.6
fumes	987.8	E869.8	—	E952.8	E962.2	E982.8
Biguanide derivatives, oral	962.3	E858.0	E932.3	E950.4	E962.0	E980.4
Biligrafin	977.8	E858.8	E947.8	E950.4	E962.0	E980.4
Bilopaque	977.8	E858.8	E947.8	E950.4	E962.0	E980.4
Bioflavonoids	972.8	E858.3	E942.8	E950.4	E962.0	E980.4
Biological substance NEC	979.9	E858.8	E949.9	E950.4	E962.0	E980.4
Biperiden	966.4	E855.0	E936.4	E950.4	E962.0	E980.4
Bisacodyl	973.1	E858.4	E943.1	E950.4	E962.0	E980.4
Bishydroxycoumarin	964.2	E858.2	E934.2	E950.4	E962.0	E980.4
Bismarsen	961.1	E857	E931.1	E950.4	E962.0	E980.4
Bismuth (compounds) NEC	985.8	E866.4	—	E950.9	E962.1	E980.9
anti-infectives	961.2	E857	E931.2	E950.4	E962.0	E980.4
subcarbonate	973.5	E858.4	E943.5	E950.4	E962.0	E980.4
sulfarsphenamine	961.1	E857	E931.1	E950.4	E962.0	E980.4
Bisphosphonates intravenous	963.1	E858.1	E933.7	E950.4	E962.0	E980.4
oral	963.1	E858.1	E933.6	E950.4	E962.0	E980.4
Bithionol	961.6	E857	E931.6	E950.4	E962.0	E980.4
Bitter almond oil	989.0	E866.8	—	E950.9	E962.1	E980.9
Bittersweet	988.2	E865.4	—	E950.9	E962.1	E930.9
Black						

		External Cause (E-Code)				
	Poisoning	Accident	Therapeutic Use	Suicide Attempt	Assault	Undetermined
Black — *continued*						
flag	989.4	E863.4	—	E950.6	E962.1	E980.7
henbane	988.2	E865.4	—	E950.9	E962.1	E980.9
leaf (40)	989.4	E863.4	—	E950.6	E962.1	E980.7
widow spider (bite)	989.5	E905.1	—	E950.9	E962.1	E980.9
antivenin	979.9	E858.8	E949.9	E950.4	E962.0	E980.4
Blast furnace gas (carbon monoxide from)	986	E868.8	—	E952.1	E962.2	E982.1
Bleach NEC	983.9	E864.3	—	E950.7	E962.1	E980.6
Bleaching solutions	983.9	E864.3	—	E950.7	E962.1	E980.6
Bleomycin (sulfate)	960.7	E856	E930.7	E950.4	E962.0	E980.4
Blockain	968.9	E855.2	E938.9	E950.4	E962.0	E980.4
infiltration (subcutaneous)	968.5	E855.2	E938.5	E950.4	E962.0	E980.4
nerve block (peripheral) (plexus)	968.6	E855.2	E938.6	E950.4	E962.0	E980.4
topical (surface)	968.5	E855.2	E938.5	E950.4	E962.0	E980.4
Blood (derivatives) (natural) (plasma) (whole)	964.7	E858.2	E934.7	E950.4	E962.0	E980.4
affecting agent	964.9	E858.2	E934.9	E950.4	E962.0	E980.4
specified NEC	964.8	E858.2	E934.8	E950.4	E962.0	E980.4
substitute (macromolecular)	964.8	E858.2	E934.8	E950.4	E962.0	E980.4
Blue velvet	965.09	E850.2	E935.2	E950.0	E962.0	E980.0
Bone meal	989.89	E866.5	—	E950.9	E962.1	E980.9
Bonine	963.0	E858.1	E933.0	E950.4	E962.0	E980.4
Boracic acid	976.0	E858.7	E946.0	E950.4	E962.0	E980.4
ENT agent	976.6	E858.7	E946.6	E950.4	E962.0	E980.4
ophthalmic preparation	976.5	E858.7	E946.5	E950.4	E962.0	E980.4
Borate (cleanser) (sodium)	989.6	E861.3	—	E950.9	E962.1	E980.9
Borax (cleanser)	989.6	E861.3	—	E950.9	E962.1	E980.9
Boric acid	976.0	E858.7	E946.0	E950.4	E962.0	E980.4
ENT agent	976.6	E858.7	E946.6	E950.4	E962.0	E980.4
ophthalmic preparation	976.5	E858.7	E946.5	E950.4	E962.0	E980.4
Boron hydride NEC	989.89	E866.8	—	E950.9	E962.1	E980.9
fumes or gas	987.8	E869.8	—	E952.8	E962.2	E982.8
Botox	975.3	E858.6	E945.3	E950.4	E962.0	E980.4
Brake fluid vapor	987.8	E869.8	—	E952.8	E962.2	E982.8
Brass (compounds) (fumes)	985.8	E866.4	—	E950.9	E962.1	E980.9
Brasso	981	E861.3	—	E950.9	E962.1	E980.9
Bretylium (tosylate)	972.6	E858.3	E942.6	E950.4	E962.0	E980.4
Brevital (sodium)	968.3	E855.1	E938.3	E950.4	E962.0	E980.4
British antilewisite	963.8	E858.1	E933.8	E950.4	E962.0	E980.4
Bromal (hydrate)	967.3	E852.2	E937.3	E950.2	E962.0	E980.2
Bromelains	963.4	E858.1	E933.4	E950.4	E962.0	E980.4
Bromides NEC	967.3	E852.2	E937.3	E950.2	E962.0	E980.2
Bromine (vapor)	987.8	E869.8	—	E952.8	E962.2	E982.8
compounds (medicinal)	967.3	E852.2	E937.3	E950.2	E962.0	E980.2
Bromisovalum	967.3	E852.2	E937.3	E950.2	E962.0	E980.2
Bromobenzyl cyanide	987.5	E869.3	—	E952.8	E962.2	E982.8
Bromodiphenhydramine	963.0	E858.1	E933.0	E950.4	E962.0	E980.4
Bromoform	967.3	E852.2	E937.3	E950.2	E962.0	E980.2
Bromophenol blue reagent	977.8	E858.8	E947.8	E950.4	E962.0	E980.4
Bromosalicylhydroxamic acid	961.8	E857	E931.8	E950.4	E962.0	E980.4
Bromo-seltzer	965.4	E850.4	E935.4	E950.0	E962.0	E980.0
Brompheniramine	963.0	E858.1	E933.0	E950.4	E962.0	E980.4
Bromural	967.3	E852.2	E937.3	E950.2	E962.0	E980.2
Brown spider (bite) (venom)	989.5	E905.1	—	E950.9	E962.1	E980.9
Brucia	988.2	E865.3	—	E950.9	E962.1	E980.9
Brucine	989.1	E863.7	—	E950.6	E962.1	E980.7
Brunswick green — *see* Copper						
Bruten — *see* Ibuprofen						
Bryonia (alba) (dioica)	988.2	E865.4	—	E950.9	E962.1	E980.9
Buclizine	969.5	E853.8	E939.5	E950.3	E962.0	E980.3
Bufferin	965.1	E850.3	E935.3	E950.0	E962.0	E980.0
Bufotenine	969.6	E854.1	E939.6	E950.3	E962.0	E980.3
Buphenine	971.2	E855.5	E941.2	E950.4	E962.0	E980.4
Bupivacaine	968.9	E855.2	E938.9	E950.4	E962.0	E980.4
infiltration (subcutaneous)	968.5	E855.2	E938.5	E950.4	E962.0	E980.4
nerve block (peripheral) (plexus)	968.6	E855.2	E938.6	E950.4	E962.0	E980.4
Busulfan	963.1	E858.1	E933.1	E950.4	E962.0	E980.4
Butabarbital (sodium)	967.0	E851	E937.0	E950.1	E962.0	E980.1
Butabarbitone	967.0	E851	E937.0	E950.1	E962.0	E980.1
Butabarpal	967.0	E851	E937.0	E950.1	E962.0	E980.1
Butacaine	968.5	E855.2	E938.5	E950.4	E962.0	E980.4
Butallylonal	967.0	E851	E937.0	E950.1	E962.0	E980.1
Butane (distributed in mobile container)	987.0	E868.0	—	E951.1	E962.2	E981.1

		External Cause (E-Code)				
	Poisoning	Accident	Therapeutic Use	Suicide Attempt	Assault	Undetermined
Butane — *continued*						
distributed through pipes	987.0	E867	—	E951.0	E962.2	E981.0
incomplete combustion of — *see* Carbon monoxide, butane						
Butanol	980.3	E860.4	—	E950.9	E962.1	E980.9
Butanone	982.8	E862.4	—	E950.9	E962.1	E980.9
Butaperazine	969.1	E853.0	E939.1	E950.3	E962.0	E980.3
Butazolidin	965.5	E850.5	E935.5	E950.0	E962.0	E980.0
Butethal	967.0	E851	E937.0	E950.1	E962.0	E980.1
Butethamate	971.1	E855.4	E941.1	E950.4	E962.0	E980.4
Buthalitone (sodium)	968.3	E855.1	E938.3	E950.4	E962.0	E980.4
Butisol (sodium)	967.0	E851	E937.0	E950.1	E962.0	E980.1
Butobarbital, butobarbitone	967.0	E851	E937.0	E950.1	E962.0	E980.1
Butriptyline	969.05 ▲	E854.0	E939.0	E950.3	E962.0	E980.3
Buttercups	988.2	E865.4	—	E950.9	E962.1	E980.9
Butter of antimony — *see* Antimony						
Butyl						
acetate (secondary)	982.8	E862.4	—	E950.9	E962.1	E980.9
alcohol	980.3	E860.4	—	E950.9	E962.1	E980.9
carbinol	980.8	E860.8	—	E950.9	E962.1	E980.9
carbitol	982.8	E862.4	—	E950.9	E962.1	E980.9
cellosolve	982.8	E862.4	—	E950.9	E962.1	E980.9
chloral (hydrate)	967.1	E852.0	E937.1	E950.2	E962.0	E980.2
formate	982.8	E862.4	—	E950.9	E962.1	E980.9
scopolammonium bromide	971.1	E855.4	E941.1	E950.4	E962.0	E980.4
Butyn	968.5	E855.2	E938.5	E950.4	E962.0	E980.4
Butyrophenone (-based tranquilizers)	969.2	E853.1	E939.2	E950.3	E962.0	E980.3
Cacodyl, cacodylic acid — *see* Arsenic						
Cactinomycin	960.7	E856	E930.7	E950.4	E962.0	E980.4
Cade oil	976.4	E858.7	E946.4	E950.4	E962.0	E980.4
Cadmium (chloride) (compounds) (dust) (fumes) (oxide)	985.5	E866.4	—	E950.9	E962.1	E980.9
sulfide (medicinal) NEC	976.4	E858.7	E946.4	E950.4	E962.0	E980.4
Caffeine	969.71 ▲	E854.2	E939.7	E950.3	E962.0	E980.3
Calabar bean	988.2	E865.4	—	E950.9	E962.1	E980.9
Caladium seguinium	988.2	E865.4	—	E950.9	E962.1	E980.9
Calamine (liniment) (lotion)	976.3	E858.7	E946.3	E950.4	E962.0	E980.4
Calciferol	963.5	E858.1	E933.5	E950.4	E962.0	E980.4
Calcium (salts) NEC	974.5	E858.5	E944.5	E950.4	E962.0	E980.4
acetylsalicylate	965.1	E850.3	E935.3	E950.0	E962.0	E980.0
benzamidosalicylate	961.8	E857	E931.8	E950.4	E962.0	E980.4
carbaspirin	965.1	E850.3	E935.3	E950.0	E962.0	E980.0
carbimide (citrated)	977.3	E858.8	E947.3	E950.4	E962.0	E980.4
carbonate (antacid)	973.0	E858.4	E943.0	E950.4	E962.0	E980.4
cyanide (citrated)	977.3	E858.8	E947.3	E950.4	E962.0	E980.4
dioctyl sulfosuccinate	973.2	E858.4	E943.2	E950.4	E962.0	E980.4
disodium edathamil	963.8	E858.1	E933.8	E950.4	E962.0	E980.4
disodium edetate	963.8	E858.1	E933.8	E950.4	E962.0	E980.4
EDTA	963.8	E858.1	E933.8	E950.4	E962.0	E980.4
hydrate, hydroxide	983.2	E864.2	—	E950.7	E962.1	E980.6
mandelate	961.9	E857	E931.9	E950.4	E962.0	E980.4
oxide	983.2	E864.2	—	E950.7	E962.1	E980.6
Calomel — *see* Mercury, chloride						
Caloric agents NEC	974.5	E858.5	E944.5	E950.4	E962.0	E980.4
Calusterone	963.1	E858.1	E933.1	E950.4	E962.0	E980.4
Camoquin	961.4	E857	E931.4	E950.4	E962.0	E980.4
Camphor (oil)	976.1	E858.7	E946.1	E950.4	E962.0	E980.4
Candeptin	976.0	E858.7	E946.0	E950.4	E962.0	E980.4
Candicidin	976.0	E858.7	E946.0	E950.4	E962.0	E980.4
Cannabinols	969.6	E854.1	E939.6	E950.3	E962.0	E980.3
Cannabis (derivatives) (indica) (sativa)	969.6	E854.1	E939.6	E950.3	E962.0	E980.3
Canned heat	980.1	E860.2	—	E950.9	E962.1	E980.9
Cantharides, cantharidin, cantharis	976.8	E858.7	E946.8	E950.4	E962.0	E980.4
Capillary agents	972.8	E858.3	E942.8	E950.4	E962.0	E980.4
Capreomycin	960.6	E856	E930.6	E950.4	E962.0	E980.4
Captodiame, captodiamine	969.5	E853.8	E939.5	E950.3	E962.0	E980.3
Caramiphen (hydrochloride)	971.1	E855.4	E941.1	E950.4	E962.0	E980.4
Carbachol	971.0	E855.3	E941.0	E950.4	E962.0	E980.4
Carbacrylamine resins	974.5	E858.5	E944.5	E950.4	E962.0	E980.4

Nontherapeutic use substance

292 — Volume 2 • October 2009   ▶◀ Revised Text   ● New Line   ▲ Revised Code   ▽ Subterms under main terms may continue to next column or page

2010 ICD-9-CM

	Poisoning	Accident	Therapeutic Use	Suicide Attempt	Assault	Undeter-mined
Carbamate (sedative)	967.8	E852.8	E937.8	E950.2	E962.0	E980.2
herbicide	989.3	E863.5	—	E950.6	E962.1	E980.7
insecticide	989.3	E863.2	—	E950.6	E962.1	E980.7
Carbamazepine	966.3	E855.0	E936.3	E950.4	E962.0	E980.4
Carbamic esters	967.8	E852.8	E937.8	E950.2	E962.0	E980.2
Carbamide	974.4	E858.5	E944.4	E950.4	E962.0	E980.4
topical	976.8	E858.7	E946.8	E950.4	E962.0	E980.4
Carbamylcholine chloride	971.0	E855.3	E941.0	E950.4	E962.0	E980.4
Carbarsone	961.1	E857	E931.1	E950.4	E962.0	E980.4
Carbaryl	989.3	E863.2	—	E950.6	E962.1	E980.7
Carbaspirin	965.1	E850.3	E935.3	E950.0	E962.0	E980.0
Carbazochrome	972.8	E858.3	E942.8	E950.4	E962.0	E980.4
Carbenicillin	960.0	E856	E930.0	E950.4	E962.0	E980.4
Carbenoxolone	973.8	E858.4	E943.8	E950.4	E962.0	E980.4
Carbetapentane	975.4	E858.6	E945.4	E950.4	E962.0	E980.4
Carbimazole	962.8	E858.0	E932.8	E950.4	E962.0	E980.4
Carbinol	980.1	E860.2	—	E950.9	E962.1	E980.9
Carbinoxamine	963.0	E858.1	E933.0	E950.4	E962.0	E980.4
Carbitol	982.8	E862.4	—	E950.9	E962.1	E980.9
Carbocaine	968.9	E855.2	E938.9	E950.4	E962.0	E980.4
infiltration (subcutaneous)	968.5	E855.2	E938.5	E950.4	E962.0	E980.4
nerve block (peripheral) (plexus)	968.6	E855.2	E938.6	E950.4	E962.0	E980.4
topical (surface)	968.5	E855.2	E938.5	E950.4	E962.0	E980.4
Carbol-fuchsin solution	976.0	E858.7	E946.0	E950.4	E962.0	E980.4
Carbolic acid — *see also* Phenol	983.0	E864.0	—	E950.7	E962.1	E980.6
Carbomycin	960.8	E856	E930.8	E950.4	E962.0	E980.4
Carbon						
bisulfide (liquid) (vapor)	982.2	E862.4	—	E950.9	E962.1	E980.9
dioxide (gas)	987.8	E869.8	—	E952.8	E962.2	E982.8
disulfide (liquid) (vapor)	982.2	E862.4	—	E950.9	E962.1	E980.9
monoxide (from incomplete combustion of) (in) NEC	986	E868.9	—	E952.1	E962.2	E982.1
blast furnace gas	986	E868.8	—	E952.1	E962.2	E982.1
butane (distributed in mobile container)	986	E868.0	—	E951.1	E962.2	E981.1
distributed through pipes	986	E867	—	E951.0	E962.2	E981.0
charcoal fumes	986	E868.3	—	E952.1	E962.2	E982.1
coal						
gas (piped)	986	E867	—	E951.0	E962.2	E981.0
solid (in domestic stoves, fireplaces)	986	E868.3	—	E952.1	E962.2	E982.1
coke (in domestic stoves, fireplaces)	986	E868.3	—	E952.1	E962.2	E982.1
exhaust gas (motor) not in transit	986	E868.2	—	E952.0	E962.2	E982.0
combustion engine, any not in watercraft	986	E868.2	—	E952.0	E962.2	E982.0
farm tractor, not in transit	986	E868.2	—	E952.0	E962.2	E982.0
gas engine	986	E868.2	—	E952.0	E962.2	E982.0
motor pump	986	E868.2	—	E952.0	E962.2	E982.0
motor vehicle, not in transit	986	E868.2	—	E952.0	E962.2	E982.0
fuel (in domestic use)	986	E868.3	—	E952.1	E962.2	E982.1
gas (piped)	986	E867	—	E951.0	E962.2	E981.0
in mobile container	986	E868.0	—	E951.1	E962.2	E981.1
utility	986	E868.1	—	E951.8	E962.2	E981.1
in mobile container	986	E868.0	—	E951.1	E962.2	E981.1
piped (natural)	986	E867	—	E951.0	E962.2	E981.0
illuminating gas	986	E868.1	—	E951.8	E962.2	E981.8
industrial fuels or gases, any	986	E868.8	—	E952.1	E962.2	E982.1
kerosene (in domestic stoves, fireplaces)	986	E868.3	—	E952.1	E962.2	E982.1
kiln gas or vapor	986	E868.8	—	E952.1	E962.2	E982.1
motor exhaust gas, not in transit	986	E868.2	—	E952.0	E962.2	E982.0
piped gas (manufactured) (natural)	986	E867	—	E951.0	E962.2	E981.0
producer gas	986	E868.8	—	E952.1	E962.2	E982.1
propane (distributed in mobile container)	986	E868.0	—	E951.1	E962.2	E981.1
distributed through pipes	986	E867	—	E951.0	E962.2	E981.0
specified source NEC	986	E868.8	—	E952.1	E962.2	E982.1
stove gas	986	E868.1	—	E951.8	E962.2	E981.8
piped	986	E867	—	E951.0	E962.2	E981.0
utility gas	986	E868.1	—	E951.8	E962.2	E981.8
piped	986	E867	—	E951.0	E962.2	E981.0

	Poisoning	Accident	Therapeutic Use	Suicide Attempt	Assault	Undeter-mined
Carbon — *continued*						
monoxide — *continued*						
water gas	986	E868.1	—	E951.8	E962.2	E981.8
wood (in domestic stoves, fireplaces)	986	E868.3	—	E952.1	E962.2	E982.1
tetrachloride (vapor) NEC	987.8	E869.8	—	E952.8	E962.2	E982.8
liquid (cleansing agent) NEC	982.1	E861.3	—	E950.9	E962.1	E980.9
solvent	982.1	E862.4	—	E950.9	E962.1	E980.9
Carbonic acid (gas)	987.8	E869.8	—	E952.8	E962.2	E982.8
anhydrase inhibitors	974.2	E858.5	E944.2	E950.4	E962.0	E980.4
Carbowax	976.3	E858.7	E946.3	E950.4	E962.0	E980.4
Carbrital	967.0	E851	E937.0	E950.1	E962.0	E980.1
Carbromal (derivatives)	967.3	E852.2	E937.3	E950.2	E962.0	E980.2
Cardiac						
depressants	972.0	E858.3	E942.0	E950.4	E962.0	E980.4
rhythm regulators	972.0	E858.3	E942.0	E950.4	E962.0	E980.4
Cardiografin	977.8	E858.8	E947.8	E950.4	E962.0	E980.4
Cardio-green	977.8	E858.8	E947.8	E950.4	E962.0	E980.4
Cardiotonic glycosides	972.1	E858.3	E942.1	E950.4	E962.0	E980.4
Cardiovascular agents NEC	972.9	E858.3	E942.9	E950.4	E962.0	E980.4
Cardrase	974.2	E858.5	E944.2	E950.4	E962.0	E980.4
Carfusin	976.0	E858.7	E946.0	E950.4	E962.0	E980.4
Carisoprodol	968.0	E855.1	E938.0	E950.4	E962.0	E980.4
Carmustine	963.1	E858.1	E933.1	E950.4	E962.0	E980.4
Carotene	963.5	E858.1	E933.5	E950.4	E962.0	E980.4
Carphenazine (maleate)	969.1	E853.0	E939.1	E950.3	E962.0	E980.3
Carter's Little Pills	973.1	E858.4	E943.1	E950.4	E962.0	E980.4
Cascara (sagrada)	973.1	E858.4	E943.1	E950.4	E962.0	E980.4
Cassava	988.2	E865.4	—	E950.9	E962.1	E980.9
Castellani's paint	976.0	E858.7	E946.0	E950.4	E962.0	E980.4
Castor						
bean	988.2	E865.3	—	E950.9	E962.1	E980.9
oil	973.1	E858.4	E943.1	E950.4	E962.0	E980.4
Caterpillar (sting)	989.5	E905.5	—	E950.9	E962.1	E980.9
Catha (edulis)	970.8	E854.3	E940.8	E950.4	E962.0	E980.4
Cathartics NEC	973.3	E858.4	E943.3	E950.4	E962.0	E980.4
contact	973.1	E858.4	E943.1	E950.4	E962.0	E980.4
emollient	973.2	E858.4	E943.2	E950.4	E962.0	E980.4
intestinal irritants	973.1	E858.4	E943.1	E950.4	E962.0	E980.4
saline	973.3	E858.4	E943.3	E950.4	E962.0	E980.4
Cathomycin	960.8	E856	E930.8	E950.4	E962.0	E980.4
Caustic(s)	983.9	E864.4	—	E950.7	E962.1	E980.6
alkali	983.2	E864.2	—	E950.7	E962.1	E980.6
hydroxide	983.2	E864.2	—	E950.7	E962.1	E980.6
potash	983.2	E864.2	—	E950.7	E962.1	E980.6
soda	983.2	E864.2	—	E950.7	E962.1	E980.6
specified NEC	983.9	E864.3	—	E950.7	E962.1	E980.6
Ceepryn	976.0	E858.7	E946.0	E950.4	E962.0	E980.4
ENT agent	976.6	E858.7	E946.6	E950.4	E962.0	E980.4
lozenges	976.6	E858.7	E946.6	E950.4	E962.0	E980.4
Celestone	962.0	E858.0	E932.0	E950.4	E962.0	E980.4
topical	976.0	E858.7	E946.0	E950.4	E962.0	E980.4
Cellosolve	982.8	E862.4	—	E950.9	E962.1	E980.9
Cell stimulants and proliferants	976.8	E858.7	E946.8	E950.4	E962.0	E980.4
Cellulose derivatives, cathartic	973.3	E858.4	E943.3	E950.4	E962.0	E980.4
nitrates (topical)	976.3	E858.7	E946.3	E950.4	E962.0	E980.4
Centipede (bite)	989.5	E905.4	—	E950.9	E962.1	E980.9
Central nervous system						
depressants	968.4	E855.1	E938.4	E950.4	E962.0	E980.4
anesthetic (general) NEC	968.4	E855.1	E938.4	E950.4	E962.0	E980.4
gases NEC	968.2	E855.1	E938.2	E950.4	E962.0	E980.4
intravenous	968.3	E855.1	E938.3	E950.4	E962.0	E980.4
barbiturates	967.0	E851	E937.0	E950.1	E962.0	E980.1
bromides	967.3	E852.2	E937.3	E950.2	E962.0	E980.2
cannabis sativa	969.6	E854.1	E939.6	E950.3	E962.0	E980.3
chloral hydrate	967.1	E852.0	E937.1	E950.2	E962.0	E980.2
hallucinogenics	969.6	E854.1	E939.6	E950.3	E962.0	E980.3
hypnotics	967.9	E852.9	E937.9	E950.2	E962.0	E980.2
specified NEC	967.8	E852.8	E937.8	E950.2	E962.0	E980.2
muscle relaxants	968.0	E855.1	E938.0	E950.4	E962.0	E980.4
paraldehyde	967.2	E852.1	E937.2	E950.2	E962.0	E980.2
sedatives	967.9	E852.9	E937.9	E950.2	E962.0	E980.2
mixed NEC	967.6	E852.8	E937.6	E950.2	E962.0	E980.2
specified NEC	967.8	E852.8	E937.8	E950.2	E962.0	E980.2
muscle-tone depressants	—	—	—	—	—	E980.4
stimulants	970.9	E854.3	E940.9	E950.4	E962.0	E980.4
amphetamines	969.72 ▲	E854.2	E939.7	E950.3	E962.0	E980.3
analeptics	970.0	E854.3	E940.0	E950.4	E962.0	E980.4

Carbamate — Central nervous system

Nontherapeutic use substance

2010 ICD-9-CM

▶◀ Revised Text   ● New Line   ▲ Revised Code

▽ Subterms under main terms may continue to next column or page

October 2009 • Volume 2 — 293

	External Cause (E-Code)					
	Poisoning	Accident	Therapeutic Use	Suicide Attempt	Assault	Undetermined
Central nervous system — *continued* stimulants — *continued*						
antidepressants	969.00 ▲	E854.0	E939.0	E950.3	E962.0	E980.3
opiate antagonists	970.1	E854.1	E940.0	E950.4	E962.0	E980.4
specified NEC	970.8	E854.3	E940.8	E950.4	E962.0	E980.4
Cephalexin	960.5	E856	E930.5	E950.4	E962.0	E980.4
Cephaloglycin	960.5	E856	E930.5	E950.4	E962.0	E980.4
Cephaloridine	960.5	E856	E930.5	E950.4	E962.0	E980.4
Cephalosporins NEC	960.5	E856	E930.5	E950.4	E962.0	E980.4
N (adicillin)	960.0	E856	E930.0	E950.4	E962.0	E980.4
Cephalothin (sodium)	960.5	E856	E930.5	E950.4	E962.0	E980.4
Cerbera (odallam)	988.2	E865.4	—	E950.9	E962.1	E980.9
Cerberin	972.1	E858.3	E942.1	E950.4	E962.0	E980.4
Cerebral stimulants	970.9	E854.3	E940.9	E950.4	E962.0	E980.4
psychotherapeutic	969.79 ▲	E854.2	E939.7	E950.3	E962.0	E980.3
specified NEC	970.8	E854.3	E940.8	E950.4	E962.0	E980.4
Cetalkonium (chloride)	976.0	E858.7	E946.0	E950.4	E962.0	E980.4
Cetoxime	963.0	E858.1	E933.0	E950.4	E962.0	E980.4
Cetrimide	976.2	E858.7	E946.2	E950.4	E962.0	E980.4
Cetylpyridinium	976.0	E858.7	E946.0	E950.4	E962.0	E980.4
ENT agent	976.6	E858.7	E946.6	E950.4	E962.0	E980.4
lozenges	976.6	E858.7	E946.6	E950.4	E962.0	E980.4
Cevadilla — see Sabadilla						
Cevitamic acid	963.5	E858.1	E933.5	E950.4	E962.0	E980.4
Chalk, precipitated	973.0	E858.4	E943.0	E950.4	E962.0	E980.4
Charcoal						
fumes (carbon monoxide)	986	E868.3	—	E952.1	E962.2	E982.1
industrial	986	E868.8	—	E952.1	E962.2	E982.1
medicinal (activated)	973.0	E858.4	E943.0	E950.4	E962.0	E980.4
Chelating agents NEC	977.2	E858.8	E947.2	E950.4	E962.0	E980.4
Chelidonium majus	988.2	E865.4	—	E950.9	E962.1	E980.9
Chemical substance	989.9	E866.9	—	E950.9	E962.1	E980.9
specified NEC	989.89	E866.8	—	E950.9	E962.1	E980.9
Chemotherapy, antineoplastic	963.1	E858.1	E933.1	E950.4	E962.0	E980.4
Chenopodium (oil)	961.6	E857	E931.6	E950.4	E962.0	E980.4
Cherry laurel	988.2	E865.4	—	E950.9	E962.1	E980.9
Chiniofon	961.3	E857	E931.3	E950.4	E962.0	E980.4
Chlophedianol	975.4	E858.6	E945.4	E950.4	E962.0	E980.4
Chloral (betaine) (formamide) (hydrate)	967.1	E852.0	E937.1	E950.2	E962.0	E980.2
Chloralamide	967.1	E852.0	E937.1	E950.2	E962.0	E980.2
Chlorambucil	963.1	E858.1	E933.1	E950.4	E962.0	E980.4
Chloramphenicol	960.2	E856	E930.2	E950.4	E962.0	E980.4
ENT agent	976.6	E858.7	E946.6	E950.4	E962.0	E980.4
ophthalmic preparation	976.5	E858.7	E946.5	E950.4	E962.0	E980.4
topical NEC	976.0	E858.7	E946.0	E950.4	E962.0	E980.4
Chlorate(s) (potassium) (sodium) NEC	983.9	E864.3	—	E950.7	E962.1	E980.6
herbicides	989.4	E863.5	—	E950.6	E962.1	E980.7
Chlorcyclizine	963.0	E858.1	E933.0	E950.4	E962.0	E980.4
Chlordan(e) (dust)	989.2	E863.0	—	E950.6	E962.1	E980.7
Chlordantoin	976.0	E858.7	E946.0	E950.4	E962.0	E980.4
Chlordiazepoxide	969.4	E853.2	E939.4	E950.3	E962.0	E980.3
Chloresium	976.8	E858.7	E946.8	E950.4	E962.0	E980.4
Chlorethiazol	967.1	E852.0	E937.1	E950.2	E962.0	E980.2
Chlorethyl — see Ethyl, chloride						
Chloretone	967.1	E852.0	E937.1	E950.2	E962.0	E980.2
Chlorex	982.3	E862.4	—	E950.9	E962.1	E980.9
Chlorhexadol	967.1	E852.0	E937.1	E950.2	E962.0	E980.2
Chlorhexidine (hydrochloride)	976.0	E858.7	E946.0	E950.4	E962.0	E980.4
Chlorhydroxyquinolin	976.0	E858.7	E946.0	E950.4	E962.0	E980.4
Chloride of lime (bleach)	983.9	E864.3	—	E950.7	E962.1	E980.6
Chlorinated						
camphene	989.2	E863.0	—	E950.6	E962.1	E980.7
diphenyl	989.89	E866.8	—	E950.9	E962.1	E980.9
hydrocarbons NEC	989.2	E863.0	—	E950.6	E962.1	E980.7
solvent	982.3	E862.4	—	E950.9	E962.1	E980.9
lime (bleach)	983.9	E864.3	—	E950.7	E962.1	E980.6
naphthalene — see Naphthalene						
pesticides NEC	989.2	E863.0	—	E950.6	E962.1	E980.7
soda — see Sodium, hypochlorite						
Chlorine (fumes) (gas)	987.6	E869.8	—	E952.8	E962.2	E982.8
bleach	983.9	E864.3	—	E950.7	E962.1	E980.6
compounds NEC	983.9	E864.3	—	E950.7	E962.1	E980.6
disinfectant	983.9	E861.4	—	E950.7	E962.1	E980.6
releasing agents NEC	983.9	E864.3	—	E950.7	E962.1	E980.6
Chlorisondamine	972.3	E858.3	E942.3	E950.4	E962.0	E980.4
Chlormadinone	962.2	E858.0	E932.2	E950.4	E962.0	E980.4
Chlormerodrin	974.0	E858.5	E944.0	E950.4	E962.0	E980.4
Chlormethiazole	967.1	E852.0	E937.1	E950.2	E962.0	E980.2
Chlormethylenecycline	960.4	E856	E930.4	E950.4	E962.0	E980.4
Chlormezanone	969.5	E853.8	E939.5	E950.3	E962.0	E980.3
Chloroacetophenone	987.5	E869.3	—	E952.8	E962.2	E982.8
Chloroaniline	983.0	E864.0	—	E950.7	E962.1	E980.6
Chlorobenzene, chlorobenzol	982.0	E862.4	—	E950.9	E962.1	E980.9
Chlorobutanol	967.1	E852.0	E937.1	E950.2	E962.0	E980.2
Chlorodinitrobenzene	983.0	E864.0	—	E950.7	E962.1	E980.6
dust or vapor	987.8	E869.8	—	E952.8	E962.2	E982.8
Chloroethane — see Ethyl, chloride						
Chloroform (fumes) (vapor)	987.8	E869.8	—	E952.8	E962.2	E982.8
anesthetic (gas)	968.2	E855.1	E938.2	E950.4	E962.0	E980.4
liquid NEC	968.4	E855.1	E938.4	E950.4	E962.0	E980.4
solvent	982.3	E862.4	—	E950.9	E962.1	E980.9
Chloroguanide	961.4	E857	E931.4	E950.4	E962.0	E980.4
Chloromycetin	960.2	E856	E930.2	E950.4	E962.0	E980.4
ENT agent	976.6	E858.7	E946.6	E950.4	E962.0	E980.4
ophthalmic preparation	976.5	E858.7	E946.5	E950.4	E962.0	E980.4
otic solution	976.6	E858.7	E946.6	E950.4	E962.0	E980.4
topical NEC	976.0	E858.7	E946.0	E950.4	E962.0	E980.4
Chloronitrobenzene	983.0	E864.0	—	E950.7	E962.1	E980.6
dust or vapor	987.8	E869.8	—	E952.8	E962.2	E982.8
Chlorophenol	983.0	E864.0	—	E950.7	E962.1	E980.6
Chlorophenothane	989.2	E863.0	—	E950.6	E962.1	E980.7
Chlorophyll (derivatives)	976.8	E858.7	E946.8	E950.4	E962.0	E980.4
Chloropicrin (fumes)	987.8	E869.8	—	E952.8	E962.2	E982.8
fumigant	989.4	E863.8	—	E950.6	E962.1	E980.7
fungicide	989.4	E863.6	—	E950.6	E962.1	E980.7
pesticide (fumes)	989.4	E863.4	—	E950.6	E962.1	E980.7
Chloroprocaine	968.9	E855.2	E938.9	E950.4	E962.0	E980.4
infiltration (subcutaneous)	968.5	E855.2	E938.5	E950.4	E962.0	E980.4
nerve block (peripheral) (plexus)	968.6	E855.2	E938.6	E950.4	E962.0	E980.4
Chloroptic	976.5	E858.7	E946.5	E950.4	E962.0	E980.4
Chloropurine	963.1	E858.1	E933.1	E950.4	E962.0	E980.4
Chloroquine (hydrochloride) (phosphate)	961.4	E857	E931.4	E950.4	E962.0	E980.4
Chlorothen	963.0	E858.1	E933.0	E950.4	E962.0	E980.4
Chlorothiazide	974.3	E858.5	E944.3	E950.4	E962.0	E980.4
Chlorotrianisene	962.2	E858.0	E932.2	E950.4	E962.0	E980.4
Chlorovinyldichloroarsine	985.1	E866.3	—	E950.8	E962.1	E980.8
Chloroxylenol	976.0	E858.7	E946.0	E950.4	E962.0	E980.4
Chlorphenesin (carbamate)	968.0	E855.1	E938.0	E950.4	E962.0	E980.4
topical (antifungal)	976.0	E858.7	E946.0	E950.4	E962.0	E980.4
Chlorpheniramine	963.0	E858.1	E933.0	E950.4	E962.0	E980.4
Chlorphenoxamine	966.4	E855.0	E936.4	E950.4	E962.0	E980.4
Chlorphentermine	977.0	E858.8	E947.0	E950.4	E962.0	E980.4
Chlorproguanil	961.4	E857	E931.4	E950.4	E962.0	E980.4
Chlorpromazine	969.1	E853.0	E939.1	E950.3	E962.0	E980.3
Chlorpropamide	962.3	E858.0	E932.3	E950.4	E962.0	E980.4
Chlorprothixene	969.3	E853.8	E939.3	E950.3	E962.0	E980.3
Chlorquinaldol	976.0	E858.7	E946.0	E950.4	E962.0	E980.4
Chlortetracycline	960.4	E856	E930.4	E950.4	E962.0	E980.4
Chlorthalidone	974.4	E858.5	E944.4	E950.4	E962.0	E980.4
Chlortrianisene	962.2	E858.0	E932.2	E950.4	E962.0	E980.4
Chlor-Trimeton	963.0	E858.1	E933.0	E950.4	E962.0	E980.4
Chlorzoxazone	968.0	E855.1	E938.0	E950.4	E962.0	E980.4
Choke damp	987.8	E869.8	—	E952.8	E962.2	E982.8
Cholebrine	977.8	E858.8	E947.8	E950.4	E962.0	E980.4
Cholera vaccine	978.2	E858.8	E948.2	E950.4	E962.0	E980.4
Cholesterol-lowering agents	972.2	E858.3	E942.2	E950.4	E962.0	E980.4
Cholestyramine (resin)	972.2	E858.3	E942.2	E950.4	E962.0	E980.4
Cholic acid	973.4	E858.4	E943.4	E950.4	E962.0	E980.4
Choline						
dihydrogen citrate	977.1	E858.8	E947.1	E950.4	E962.0	E980.4
salicylate	965.1	E850.3	E935.3	E950.0	E962.0	E980.0
theophyllinate	974.1	E858.5	E944.1	E950.4	E962.0	E980.4
Cholinergics	971.0	E855.3	E941.0	E950.4	E962.0	E980.4
Cholografin	977.8	E858.8	E947.8	E950.4	E962.0	E980.4
Chorionic gonadotropin	962.4	E858.0	E932.4	E950.4	E962.0	E980.4
Chromates	983.9	E864.3	—	E950.7	E962.1	E980.6
dust or mist	987.8	E869.8	—	E952.8	E962.2	E982.8
lead	984.0	E866.0	—	E950.9	E962.1	E980.9
paint	984.0	E861.5	—	E950.9	E962.1	E980.9

Nontherapeutic use substance

Subterms under main terms may continue to next column or page

		External Cause (E-Code)				
	Poisoning	Accident	Therapeutic Use	Suicide Attempt	Assault	Undetermined
Chromic acid	983.9	E864.3	—	E950.7	E962.1	E980.6
dust or mist	987.8	E869.8	—	E952.8	E962.2	E982.8
Chromium	985.6	E866.4	—	E950.9	E962.1	E980.9
compounds — see Chromates						
Chromonar	972.4	E858.3	E942.4	E950.4	E962.0	E980.4
Chromyl chloride	983.9	E864.3	—	E950.7	E962.1	E980.6
Chrysarobin (ointment)	976.4	E858.7	E946.4	E950.4	E962.0	E980.4
Chrysazin	973.1	E858.4	E943.1	E950.4	E962.0	E980.4
Chymar	963.4	E858.1	E933.4	E950.4	E962.0	E980.4
ophthalmic preparation	976.5	E858.7	E946.5	E950.4	E962.0	E980.4
Chymotrypsin	963.4	E858.1	E933.4	E950.4	E962.0	E980.4
ophthalmic preparation	976.5	E858.7	E946.5	E950.4	E962.0	E980.4
Cicuta maculata or virosa	988.2	E865.4	—	E950.9	E962.1	E980.9
Cigarette lighter fluid	981	E862.1	—	E950.9	E962.1	E980.9
Cinchocaine (spinal)	968.7	E855.2	E938.7	E950.4	E962.0	E980.4
topical (surface)	968.5	E855.2	E938.5	E950.4	E962.0	E980.4
Cinchona	961.4	E857	E931.4	E950.4	E962.0	E980.4
Cinchonine alkaloids	961.4	E857	E931.4	E950.4	E962.0	E980.4
Cinchophen	974.7	E858.5	E944.7	E950.4	E962.0	E980.4
Cinnarizine	963.0	E858.1	E933.0	E950.4	E962.0	E980.4
Citanest	968.9	E855.2	E938.9	E950.4	E962.0	E980.4
infiltration (subcutaneous)	968.5	E855.2	E938.5	E950.4	E962.0	E980.4
nerve block (peripheral)						
(plexus)	968.6	E855.2	E938.6	E950.4	E962.0	E980.4
Citric acid	989.89	E866.8	—	E950.9	E962.1	E980.9
Citrovorum factor	964.1	E858.2	E934.1	E950.4	E962.0	E980.4
Claviceps purpurea	988.2	E865.4	—	E950.9	E962.1	E980.9
Cleaner, cleansing agent						
NEC	989.89	E861.3	—	E950.9	E962.1	E980.9
of paint or varnish	982.8	E862.9	—	E950.9	E962.1	E980.9
Clematis vitalba	988.2	E865.4	—	E950.9	E962.1	E980.9
Clemizole	963.0	E858.1	E933.0	E950.4	E962.0	E980.4
penicillin	960.0	E856	E930.0	E950.4	E962.0	E980.4
Clidinium	971.1	E855.4	E941.1	E950.4	E962.0	E980.4
Clindamycin	960.8	E856	E930.8	E950.4	E962.0	E980.4
Cliradon	965.09	E850.2	E935.2	E950.0	E962.0	E980.0
Clocortolone	962.0	E858.0	E932.0	E950.4	E962.0	E980.4
Clofedanol	975.4	E858.6	E945.4	E950.4	E962.0	E980.4
Clofibrate	972.2	E858.3	E942.2	E950.4	E962.0	E980.4
Clomethiazole	967.1	E852.0	E937.1	E950.2	E962.0	E980.2
Clomiphene	977.8	E858.8	E947.8	E950.4	E962.0	E980.4
Clonazepam	969.4	E853.2	E939.4	E950.3	E962.0	E980.3
Clonidine	972.6	E858.3	E942.6	E950.4	E962.0	E980.4
Clopamide	974.3	E858.5	E944.3	E950.4	E962.0	E980.4
Clorazepate	969.4	E853.2	E939.4	E950.3	E962.0	E980.3
Clorexolone	974.4	E858.5	E944.4	E950.4	E962.0	E980.4
Clorox (bleach)	983.9	E864.3	—	E950.7	E962.1	E980.6
Clortermine	977.0	E858.8	E947.0	E950.4	E962.0	E980.4
Clotrimazole	976.0	E858.7	E946.0	E950.4	E962.0	E980.4
Cloxacillin	960.0	E856	E930.0	E950.4	E962.0	E980.4
Coagulants NEC	964.5	E858.2	E934.5	E950.4	E962.0	E980.4
Coal (carbon monoxide from) —						
see also Carbon, monoxide,						
coal						
oil — see Kerosene						
tar NEC	983.0	E864.0	—	E950.7	E962.1	E980.6
fumes	987.8	E869.8	—	E952.8	E962.2	E982.8
medicinal (ointment)	976.4	E858.7	E946.4	E950.4	E962.0	E980.4
analgesics NEC	965.5	E850.5	E935.5	E950.0	E962.0	E980.0
naphtha (solvent)	981	E862.0	—	E950.9	E962.1	E980.9
Cobalt (fumes) (industrial)	985.8	E866.4	—	E950.9	E962.1	E980.9
Cobra (venom)	989.5	E905.0	—	E950.9	E962.1	E980.9
Coca (leaf)	970.8	E854.3	E940.8	E950.4	E962.0	E980.4
Cocaine (hydrochloride)						
(salt)	970.8	E854.3	E940.8	E950.4	E962.0	E980.4
topical anesthetic	968.5	E855.2	E938.5	E950.4	E962.0	E980.4
Coccidioidin	977.8	E858.8	E947.8	E950.4	E962.0	E980.4
Cocculus indicus	988.2	E865.3	—	E950.9	E962.1	E980.9
Cochineal	989.89	E866.8	—	E950.9	E962.1	E980.9
medicinal products	977.4	E858.8	E947.4	E950.4	E962.0	E980.4
Codeine	965.09	E850.2	E935.2	E950.0	E962.0	E980.0
Coffee	989.89	E866.8	—	E950.9	E962.1	E980.9
Cogentin	971.1	E855.4	E941.1	E950.4	E962.0	E980.4
Coke fumes or gas (carbon						
monoxide)	986	E868.3	—	E952.1	E962.2	E982.1
industrial use	986	E868.8	—	E952.1	E962.2	E982.1
Colace	973.2	E858.4	E943.2	E950.4	E962.0	E980.4
Colchicine	974.7	E858.5	E944.7	E950.4	E962.0	E980.4
Colchicum	988.2	E865.3	—	E950.9	E962.1	E980.9
Cold cream	976.3	E858.7	E946.3	E950.4	E962.0	E980.4
Colestipol	972.2	E858.3	E942.2	E950.4	E962.0	E980.4
Colistimethate	960.8	E856	E930.8	E950.4	E962.0	E980.4
Colistin	960.8	E856	E930.8	E950.4	E962.0	E980.4
Collagen	977.8	E866.8	E947.8	E950.9	E962.1	E980.9
Collagenase	976.8	E858.7	E946.8	E950.4	E962.0	E980.4
Collodion (flexible)	976.3	E858.7	E946.3	E950.4	E962.0	E980.4
Colocynth	973.1	E858.4	E943.1	E950.4	E962.0	E980.4
Coloring matter — see Dye(s)						
Combustion gas — see Carbon,						
monoxide						
Compazine	969.1	E853.0	E939.1	E950.3	E962.0	E980.3
Compound						
42 (warfarin)	989.4	E863.7	—	E950.6	E962.1	E980.7
269 (endrin)	989.2	E863.0	—	E950.6	E962.1	E980.7
497 (dieldrin)	989.2	E863.0	—	E950.6	E962.1	E980.7
1080 (sodium						
fluoroacetate)	989.4	E863.7	—	E950.6	E962.1	E980.7
3422 (parathion)	989.3	E863.1	—	E950.6	E962.1	E980.7
3911 (phorate)	989.3	E863.1	—	E950.6	E962.1	E980.7
3956 (toxaphene)	989.2	E863.0	—	E950.6	E962.1	E980.7
4049 (malathion)	989.3	E863.1	—	E950.6	E962.1	E980.7
4124 (dicapthon)	989.4	E863.4	—	E950.6	E962.1	E980.7
E (cortisone)	962.0	E858.0	E932.0	E950.4	E962.0	E980.4
F (hydrocortisone)	962.0	E858.0	E932.0	E950.4	E962.0	E980.4
Congo red	977.8	E858.8	E947.8	E950.4	E962.0	E980.4
Coniine, conine	965.7	E850.7	E935.7	E950.0	E962.0	E980.0
Conium (maculatum)	988.2	E865.4	—	E950.9	E962.1	E980.9
Conjugated estrogens						
(equine)	962.2	E858.0	E932.2	E950.4	E962.0	E980.4
Contac	975.6	E858.6	E945.6	E950.4	E962.0	E980.4
Contact lens solution	976.5	E858.7	E946.5	E950.4	E962.0	E980.4
Contraceptives (oral)	962.2	E858.0	E932.2	E950.4	E962.0	E980.4
vaginal	976.8	E858.7	E946.8	E950.4	E962.0	E980.4
Contrast media						
(roentgenographic)	977.8	E858.8	E947.8	E950.4	E962.0	E980.4
Convallaria majalis	988.2	E865.4	—	E950.9	E962.1	E980.9
Copper (dust) (fumes) (salts)						
NEC	985.8	E866.4	—	E950.9	E962.1	E980.9
arsenate, arsenite	985.1	E866.3	—	E950.8	E962.1	E980.8
insecticide	985.1	E863.4	—	E950.8	E962.1	E980.8
emetic	973.6	E858.4	E943.6	E950.4	E962.0	E980.4
fungicide	985.8	E863.6	—	E950.6	E962.1	E980.7
insecticide	985.8	E863.4	—	E950.6	E962.1	E980.7
oleate	976.0	E858.7	E946.0	E950.4	E962.0	E980.4
sulfate	983.9	E864.3	—	E950.7	E962.1	E980.6
cupric	973.6	E858.4	E943.6	E950.4	E962.0	E980.4
cuprous	983.9	E864.3	—	E950.7	E962.1	E980.6
fungicide	983.9	E863.6	—	E950.7	E962.1	E980.6
Copperhead snake (bite)						
(venom)	989.5	E905.0	—	E950.9	E962.1	E980.9
Coral (sting)	989.5	E905.6	—	E950.9	E962.1	E980.9
snake (bite) (venom)	989.5	E905.0	—	E950.9	E962.1	E980.9
Cordran	976.0	E858.7	E946.0	E950.4	E962.0	E980.4
Corn cures	976.4	E858.7	E946.4	E950.4	E962.0	E980.4
Cornhusker's lotion	976.3	E858.7	E946.3	E950.4	E962.0	E980.4
Corn starch	976.3	E858.7	E946.3	E950.4	E962.0	E980.4
Corrosive	983.9	E864.4	—	E950.7	E962.1	E980.6
acids NEC	983.1	E864.1	—	E950.7	E962.1	E980.6
aromatics	983.0	E864.0	—	E950.7	E962.1	E980.6
disinfectant	983.0	E861.4	—	E950.7	E962.1	E980.6
fumes NEC	987.9	E869.9	—	E952.9	E962.2	E982.9
specified NEC	983.9	E864.3	—	E950.7	E962.1	E980.6
sublimate — see Mercury,						
chloride						
Cortate	962.0	E858.0	E932.0	E950.4	E962.0	E980.4
Cort-Dome	962.0	E858.0	E932.0	E950.4	E962.0	E980.4
ENT agent	976.6	E858.7	E946.6	E950.4	E962.0	E980.4
ophthalmic preparation	976.5	E858.7	E946.5	E950.4	E962.0	E980.4
topical NEC	976.0	E858.7	E946.0	E950.4	E962.0	E980.4
Cortef	962.0	E858.0	E932.0	E950.4	E962.0	E980.4
ENT agent	976.6	E858.7	E946.6	E950.4	E962.0	E980.4
ophthalmic preparation	976.5	E858.7	E946.5	E950.4	E962.0	E980.4
topical NEC	976.0	E858.7	E946.0	E950.4	E962.0	E980.4
Corticosteroids						
(fluorinated)	962.0	E858.0	E932.0	E950.4	E962.0	E980.4
ENT agent	976.6	E858.7	E946.6	E950.4	E962.0	E980.4
ophthalmic preparation	976.5	E858.7	E946.5	E950.4	E962.0	E980.4
topical NEC	976.0	E858.7	E946.0	E950.4	E962.0	E980.4
Corticotropin	962.4	E858.0	E932.4	E950.4	E962.0	E980.4
Cortisol	962.0	E858.0	E932.0	E950.4	E962.0	E980.4
ENT agent	976.6	E858.7	E946.6	E950.4	E962.0	E980.4
ophthalmic preparation	976.5	E858.7	E946.5	E950.4	E962.0	E980.4
topical NEC	976.0	E858.7	E946.0	E950.4	E962.0	E980.4

Nontherapeutic use substance

▽ Subterms under main terms may continue to next column or page

	Poisoning	Accident	Therapeutic Use	Suicide Attempt	Assault	Undetermined
Cortisone derivatives	962.0	E858.0	E932.0	E950.4	E962.0	E980.4
(acetate)	962.0	E858.0	E932.0	E950.4	E962.0	E980.4
ENT agent	976.6	E858.7	E946.6	E950.4	E962.0	E980.4
ophthalmic preparation	976.5	E858.7	E946.5	E950.4	E962.0	E980.4
topical NEC	976.0	E858.7	E946.0	E950.4	E962.0	E980.4
Cortogen	962.0	E858.0	E932.0	E950.4	E962.0	E980.4
ENT agent	976.6	E858.7	E946.6	E950.4	E962.0	E980.4
ophthalmic preparation	976.5	E858.7	E946.5	E950.4	E962.0	E980.4
Cortone	962.0	E858.0	E932.0	E950.4	E962.0	E980.4
ENT agent	976.6	E858.7	E946.6	E950.4	E962.0	E980.4
ophthalmic preparation	976.5	E858.7	E946.5	E950.4	E962.0	E980.4
Cortril	962.0	E858.0	E932.0	E950.4	E962.0	E980.4
ENT agent	976.6	E858.7	E946.6	E950.4	E962.0	E980.4
ophthalmic preparation	976.5	E858.7	E946.5	E950.4	E962.0	E980.4
topical NEC	976.0	E858.7	E946.0	E950.4	E962.0	E980.4
Cosmetics	989.89	E866.7	—	E950.9	E962.1	E980.9
Cosyntropin	977.8	E858.8	E947.8	E950.4	E962.0	E980.4
Cotarnine	964.5	E858.2	E934.5	E950.4	E962.0	E980.4
Cottonseed oil	976.3	E858.7	E946.3	E950.4	E962.0	E980.4
Cough mixtures						
(antitussives)	975.4	E858.6	E945.4	E950.4	E962.0	E980.4
containing opiates	965.09	E850.2	E935.2	E950.0	E962.0	E980.0
expectorants	975.5	E858.6	E945.5	E950.4	E962.0	E980.4
Coumadin	964.2	E858.2	E934.2	E950.4	E962.0	E980.4
rodenticide	989.4	E863.7	—	E950.6	E962.1	E980.7
Coumarin	964.2	E858.2	E934.2	E950.4	E962.0	E980.4
Coumetarol	964.2	E858.2	E934.2	E950.4	E962.0	E980.4
Cowbane	988.2	E865.4	—	E950.9	E962.1	E980.9
Cozyme	963.5	E858.1	E933.5	E950.4	E962.0	E980.4
Crack	970.8	E854.3	E940.8	E950.4	E962.0	E980.4
Creolin	983.0	E864.0	—	E950.7	E962.1	E980.6
disinfectant	983.0	E861.4	—	E950.7	E962.1	E980.6
Creosol (compound)	983.0	E864.0	—	E950.7	E962.1	E980.6
Creosote (beechwood) (coal tar)	983.0	E864.0	—	E950.7	E962.1	E980.6
medicinal (expectorant)	975.5	E858.6	E945.5	E950.4	E962.0	E980.4
syrup	975.5	E858.6	E945.5	E950.4	E962.0	E980.4
Cresol	983.0	E864.0	—	E950.7	E962.1	E980.6
disinfectant	983.0	E861.4	—	E950.7	E962.1	E980.6
Cresylic acid	983.0	E864.0	—	E950.7	E962.1	E980.6
Cropropamide	965.7	E850.7	E935.7	E950.0	E962.0	E980.0
with crotethamide	970.0	E854.3	E940.0	E950.4	E962.0	E980.4
Crotamiton	976.0	E858.7	E946.0	E950.4	E962.0	E980.4
Crotethamide	965.7	E850.7	E935.7	E950.0	E962.0	E980.0
with cropropamide	970.0	E854.3	E940.0	E950.4	E962.0	E980.4
Croton (oil)	973.1	E858.4	E943.1	E950.4	E962.0	E980.4
chloral	967.1	E852.0	E937.1	E950.2	E962.0	E980.2
Crude oil	981	E862.1	—	E950.9	E962.1	E980.9
Cryogenine	965.8	E850.8	E935.8	E950.0	E962.0	E980.0
Cryolite (pesticide)	989.4	E863.4	—	E950.6	E962.1	E980.7
Cryptenamine	972.6	E858.3	E942.6	E950.4	E962.0	E980.4
Crystal violet	976.0	E858.7	E946.0	E950.4	E962.0	E980.4
Cuckoopint	988.2	E865.4	—	E950.9	E962.1	E980.9
Cumetharol	964.2	E858.2	E934.2	E950.4	E962.0	E980.4
Cupric sulfate	973.6	E858.4	E943.6	E950.4	E962.0	E980.4
Cuprous sulfate	983.9	E864.3	—	E950.7	E962.1	E980.6
Curare, curarine	975.2	E858.6	E945.2	E950.4	E962.0	E980.4
Cyanic acid — see Cyanide(s)						
Cyanide(s) (compounds) (hydrogen) (potassium) (sodium) NEC	989.0	E866.8	—	E950.9	E962.1	E980.9
dust or gas (inhalation) NEC	987.7	E869.8	—	E952.8	E962.2	E982.8
fumigant	989.0	E863.8	—	E950.6	E962.1	E980.7
mercuric — see Mercury						
pesticide (dust) (fumes)	989.0	E863.4	—	E950.6	E962.1	E980.7
Cyanocobalamin	964.1	E858.2	E934.1	E950.4	E962.0	E980.4
Cyanogen (chloride) (gas) NEC	987.8	E869.8	—	E952.8	E962.2	E982.8
Cyclaine	968.5	E855.2	E938.5	E950.4	E962.0	E980.4
Cyclamen europaeum	988.2	E865.4	—	E950.9	E962.1	E980.9
Cyclandelate	972.5	E858.3	E942.5	E950.4	E962.0	E980.4
Cyclazocine	965.09	E850.2	E935.2	E950.0	E962.0	E980.0
Cyclizine	963.0	E858.1	E933.0	E950.4	E962.0	E980.4
Cyclobarbital, cyclobarbitone	967.0	E851	E937.0	E950.1	E962.0	E980.1
Cycloguanil	961.4	E857	E931.4	E950.4	E962.0	E980.4
Cyclohexane	982.0	E862.4	—	E950.9	E962.1	E980.9
Cyclohexanol	980.8	E860.8	—	E950.9	E962.1	E980.9
Cyclohexanone	982.8	E862.4	—	E950.9	E962.1	E980.9
Cyclomethycaine	968.5	E855.2	E938.5	E950.4	E962.0	E980.4
Cyclopentamine	971.2	E855.5	E941.2	E950.4	E962.0	E980.4
Cyclopenthiazide	974.3	E858.5	E944.3	E950.4	E962.0	E980.4
Cyclopentolate	971.1	E855.4	E941.1	E950.4	E962.0	E980.4
Cyclophosphamide	963.1	E858.1	E933.1	E950.4	E962.0	E980.4
Cyclopropane	968.2	E855.1	E938.2	E950.4	E962.0	E980.4
Cycloserine	960.6	E856	E930.6	E950.4	E962.0	E980.4
Cyclothiazide	974.3	E858.5	E944.3	E950.4	E962.0	E980.4
Cycrimine	966.4	E855.0	E936.4	E950.4	E962.0	E980.4
Cymarin	972.1	E858.3	E942.1	E950.4	E962.0	E980.4
Cyproheptadine	963.0	E858.1	E933.0	E950.4	E962.0	E980.4
Cyprolidol	969.09 ▲	E854.0	E939.0	E950.3	E962.0	E980.3
Cytarabine	963.1	E858.1	E933.1	E950.4	E962.0	E980.4
Cytisus						
laburnum	988.2	E865.4	—	E950.9	E962.1	E980.9
scoparius	988.2	E865.4	—	E950.9	E962.1	E980.9
Cytomel	962.7	E858.0	E932.7	E950.4	E962.0	E980.4
Cytosine (antineoplastic)	963.1	E858.1	E933.1	E950.4	E962.0	E980.4
Cytoxan	963.1	E858.1	E933.1	E950.4	E962.0	E980.4
Dacarbazine	963.1	E858.1	E933.1	E950.4	E962.0	E980.4
Dactinomycin	960.7	E856	E930.7	E950.4	E962.0	E980.4
DADPS	961.8	E857	E931.8	E950.4	E962.0	E980.4
Dakin's solution (external)	976.0	E858.7	E946.0	E950.4	E962.0	E980.4
Dalmane	969.4	E853.2	E939.4	E950.3	E962.0	E980.3
DAM	977.2	E858.8	E947.2	E950.4	E962.0	E980.4
Danilone	964.2	E858.2	E934.2	E950.4	E962.0	E980.4
Danthron	973.1	E858.4	E943.1	E950.4	E962.0	E980.4
Dantrolene	975.2	E858.6	E945.2	E950.4	E962.0	E980.4
Daphne (gnidium) (mezereum)	988.2	E865.4	—	E950.9	E962.1	E980.9
berry	988.2	E865.3	—	E950.9	E962.1	E980.9
Dapsone	961.8	E857	E931.8	E950.4	E962.0	E980.4
Daraprim	961.4	E857	E931.4	E950.4	E962.0	E980.4
Darnel	988.2	E865.3	—	E950.9	E962.1	E980.9
Darvon	965.8	E850.8	E935.8	E950.0	E962.0	E980.0
Daunorubicin	960.7	E856	E930.7	E950.4	E962.0	E980.4
DBI	962.3	E858.0	E932.3	E950.4	E962.0	E980.4
D-Con (rodenticide)	989.4	E863.7	—	E950.6	E962.1	E980.7
DDS	961.8	E857	E931.8	E950.4	E962.0	E980.4
DDT	989.2	E863.0	—	E950.6	E962.1	E980.7
Deadly nightshade	988.2	E865.4	—	E950.9	E962.1	E980.9
berry	988.2	E865.3	—	E950.9	E962.1	E980.9
Deanol	969.79 ▲	E854.2	E939.7	E950.3	E962.0	E980.3
Debrisoquine	972.6	E858.3	E942.6	E950.4	E962.0	E980.4
Decaborane	989.89	E866.8	—	E950.9	E962.1	E980.9
fumes	987.8	E869.8	—	E952.8	E962.2	E982.8
Decadron	962.0	E858.0	E932.0	E950.4	E962.0	E980.4
ENT agent	976.6	E858.7	E946.6	E950.4	E962.0	E980.4
ophthalmic preparation	976.5	E858.7	E946.5	E950.4	E962.0	E980.4
topical NEC	976.0	E858.7	E946.0	E950.4	E962.0	E980.4
Decahydronaphthalene	982.0	E862.4	—	E950.9	E962.1	E980.9
Decalin	982.0	E862.4	—	E950.9	E962.1	E980.9
Decamethonium	975.2	E858.6	E945.2	E950.4	E962.0	E980.4
Decholin	973.4	E858.4	E943.4	E950.4	E962.0	E980.4
sodium (diagnostic)	977.8	E858.8	E947.8	E950.4	E962.0	E980.4
Declomycin	960.4	E856	E930.4	E950.4	E962.0	E980.4
Deferoxamine	963.8	E858.1	E933.8	E950.4	E962.0	E980.4
Dehydrocholic acid	973.4	E858.4	E943.4	E950.4	E962.0	E980.4
DeKalin	982.0	E862.4	—	E950.9	E962.1	E980.9
Delalutin	962.2	E858.0	E932.2	E950.4	E962.0	E980.4
Delphinium	988.2	E865.3	—	E950.9	E962.1	E980.9
Deltasone	962.0	E858.0	E932.0	E950.4	E962.0	E980.4
Deltra	962.0	E858.0	E932.0	E950.4	E962.0	E980.4
Delvinal	967.0	E851	E937.0	E950.1	E962.0	E980.1
Demecarium (bromide)	971.0	E855.3	E941.0	E950.4	E962.0	E980.4
Demeclocycline	960.4	E856	E930.4	E950.4	E962.0	E980.4
Demecolcine	963.1	E858.1	E933.1	E950.4	E962.0	E980.4
Demelanizing agents	976.8	E858.7	E946.8	E950.4	E962.0	E980.4
Demerol	965.09	E850.2	E935.2	E950.0	E962.0	E980.0
Demethylchlortetracycline	960.4	E856	E930.4	E950.4	E962.0	E980.4
Demethyltetracycline	960.4	E856	E930.4	E950.4	E962.0	E980.4
Demeton	989.3	E863.1	—	E950.6	E962.1	E980.7
Demulcents	976.3	E858.7	E946.3	E950.4	E962.0	E980.4
Demulen	962.2	E858.0	E932.2	E950.4	E962.0	E980.4
Denatured alcohol	980.0	E860.1	—	E950.9	E962.1	E980.9
Dendrid	976.5	E858.7	E946.5	E950.4	E962.0	E980.4
Dental agents, topical	976.7	E858.7	E946.7	E950.4	E962.0	E980.4
Deodorant spray (feminine hygiene)	976.8	E858.7	E946.8	E950.4	E962.0	E980.4
Deoxyribonuclease	963.4	E858.1	E933.4	E950.4	E962.0	E980.4
Depressants						
appetite, central	977.0	E858.8	E947.0	E950.4	E962.0	E980.4
cardiac	972.0	E858.3	E942.0	E950.4	E962.0	E980.4

Index

Cortisone derivatives — Depressants

Nontherapeutic use substance

▽ Subterms under main terms may continue to next column or page

	Poisoning	Accident	Therapeutic Use	Suicide Attempt	Assault	Undetermined
Depressants — *continued*						
central nervous system						
(anesthetic)	968.4	E855.1	E938.4	E950.4	E962.0	E980.4
psychotherapeutic	969.5	E853.9	E939.5	E950.3	E962.0	E980.3
Dequalinium	976.0	E858.7	E946.0	E950.4	E962.0	E980.4
Dermolate	976.2	E858.7	E946.2	E950.4	E962.0	E980.4
DES	962.2	E858.0	E932.2	E950.4	E962.0	E980.4
Desenex	976.0	E858.7	E946.0	E950.4	E962.0	E980.4
Deserpidine	972.6	E858.3	E942.6	E950.4	E962.0	E980.4
Desipramine	969.05 ▲	E854.0	E939.0	E950.3	E962.0	E980.3
Deslanoside	972.1	E858.3	E942.1	E950.4	E962.0	E980.4
Desocodeine	965.09	E850.2	E935.2	E950.0	E962.0	E980.0
Desomorphine	965.09	E850.2	E935.2	E950.0	E962.0	E980.0
Desonide	976.0	E858.7	E946.0	E950.4	E962.0	E980.4
Desoxycorticosterone						
derivatives	962.0	E858.0	E932.0	E950.4	E962.0	E980.4
Desoxyephedrine	969.72 ▲	E854.2	E939.7	E950.3	E962.0	E980.3
DET	969.6	E854.1	E939.6	E950.3	E962.0	E980.3
Detergents (ingested)	989.6	E861.0	—	E950.9	E962.1	E980.9
(synthetic)	989.6	E861.0	—	E950.9	E962.1	E980.9
ENT agent	976.6	E858.7	E946.6	E950.4	E962.0	E980.4
external medication	976.2	E858.7	E946.2	E950.4	E962.0	E980.4
ophthalmic preparation	976.5	E858.7	E946.5	E950.4	E962.0	E980.4
topical NEC	976.0	E858.7	E946.0	E950.4	E962.0	E980.4
Deterrent, alcohol	977.3	E858.8	E947.3	E950.4	E962.0	E980.4
Detrothyronine	962.7	E858.0	E932.7	E950.4	E962.0	E980.4
Dettol (external						
medication)	976.0	E858.7	E946.0	E950.4	E962.0	E980.4
Dexamethasone	962.0	E858.0	E932.0	E950.4	E962.0	E980.4
Dexamphetamine	969.72 ▲	E854.2	E939.7	E950.3	E962.0	E980.3
Dexedrine	969.72 ▲	E854.2	E939.7	E950.3	E962.0	E980.3
Dexpanthenol	963.5	E858.1	E933.5	E950.4	E962.0	E980.4
Dextran	964.8	E858.2	E934.8	E950.4	E962.0	E980.4
Dextriferron	964.0	E858.2	E934.0	E950.4	E962.0	E980.4
Dextroamphetamine	969.72 ▲	E854.2	E939.7	E950.3	E962.0	E980.3
Dextro calcium						
pantothenate	963.5	E858.1	E933.5	E950.4	E962.0	E980.4
Dextromethorphan	975.4	E858.6	E945.4	E950.4	E962.0	E980.4
Dextromoramide	965.09	E850.2	E935.2	E950.0	E962.0	E980.0
Dextro pantothenyl						
alcohol	963.5	E858.1	E933.5	E950.4	E962.0	E980.4
topical	976.8	E858.7	E946.8	E950.4	E962.0	E980.4
Dextropropoxyphene						
(hydrochloride)	965.8	E850.8	E935.8	E950.0	E962.0	E980.0
Dextrorphan	965.09	E850.2	E935.2	E950.0	E962.0	E980.0
Dextrose NEC	974.5	E858.5	E944.5	E950.4	E962.0	E980.4
Dextrothyroxin	962.7	E858.0	E932.7	E950.4	E962.0	E980.4
DFP	971.0	E855.3	E941.0	E950.4	E962.0	E980.4
DHE-45	972.9	E858.3	E942.9	E950.4	E962.0	E980.4
Diabinese	962.3	E858.0	E932.3	E950.4	E962.0	E980.4
Diacetyl monoxime	977.2	E858.8	E947.2	E950.4	E962.0	E980.4
Diacetylmorphine	965.01	E850.0	E935.0	E950.0	E962.0	E980.0
Diagnostic agents	977.8	E858.8	E947.8	E950.4	E962.0	E980.4
Dial (soap)	976.2	E858.7	E946.2	E950.4	E962.0	E980.4
sedative	967.0	E851	E937.0	E950.1	E962.0	E980.1
Diallylbarbituric acid	967.0	E851	E937.0	E950.1	E962.0	E980.1
Diaminodiphenylsulfone	961.8	E857	E931.8	E950.4	E962.0	E980.4
Diamorphine	965.01	E850.0	E935.0	E950.0	E962.0	E980.0
Diamox	974.2	E858.5	E944.2	E950.4	E962.0	E980.4
Diamthazole	976.0	E858.7	E946.0	E950.4	E962.0	E980.4
Diaphenylsulfone	961.8	E857	E931.8	E950.4	E962.0	E980.4
Diasone (sodium)	961.8	E857	E931.8	E950.4	E962.0	E980.4
Diazepam	969.4	E853.2	E939.4	E950.3	E962.0	E980.3
Diazinon	989.3	E863.1	—	E950.6	E962.1	E980.7
Diazomethane (gas)	987.8	E869.8	—	E952.8	E962.2	E982.8
Diazoxide	972.5	E858.3	E942.5	E950.4	E962.0	E980.4
Dibenamine	971.3	E855.6	E941.3	E950.4	E962.0	E980.4
Dibenzheptropine	963.0	E858.1	E933.0	E950.4	E962.0	E980.4
Dibenzyline	971.3	E855.6	E941.3	E950.4	E962.0	E980.4
Diborane (gas)	987.8	E869.8	—	E952.8	E962.2	E982.8
Dibromomannitol	963.1	E858.1	E933.1	E950.4	E962.0	E980.4
Dibucaine (spinal)	968.7	E855.2	E938.7	E950.4	E962.0	E980.4
topical (surface)	968.5	E855.2	E938.5	E950.4	E962.0	E980.4
Dibunate sodium	975.4	E858.6	E945.4	E950.4	E962.0	E980.4
Dibutoline	971.1	E855.4	E941.1	E950.4	E962.0	E980.4
Dicapthon	989.4	E863.4	—	E950.6	E962.1	E980.7
Dichloralphenazone	967.1	E852.0	E937.1	E950.2	E962.0	E980.2
Dichlorodifluoromethane	987.4	E869.2	—	E952.8	E962.2	E982.8
Dichloroethane	982.3	E862.4	—	E950.9	E962.1	E980.9
Dichloroethylene	982.3	E862.4	—	E950.9	E962.1	E980.9
Dichloroethyl sulfide	987.8	E869.8	—	E952.8	E962.2	E982.8
Dichlorohydrin	982.3	E862.4	—	E950.9	E962.1	E980.9

	Poisoning	Accident	Therapeutic Use	Suicide Attempt	Assault	Undetermined
Dichloromethane (solvent)						
(vapor)	982.3	E862.4	—	E950.9	E962.1	E980.9
Dichlorophen(e)	961.6	E857	E931.6	E950.4	E962.0	E980.4
Dichlorphenamide	974.2	E858.5	E944.2	E950.4	E962.0	E980.4
Dichlorvos	989.3	E863.1	—	E950.6	E962.1	E980.7
Diclofenac sodium	965.69	E850.6	E935.6	E950.0	E962.0	E980.0
Dicoumarin, dicumarol	964.2	E858.2	E934.2	E950.4	E962.0	E980.4
Dicyanogen (gas)	987.8	E869.8	—	E952.8	E962.2	E982.8
Dicyclomine	971.1	E855.4	E941.1	E950.4	E962.0	E980.4
Dieldrin (vapor)	989.2	E863.0	—	E950.6	E962.1	E980.7
Dienestrol	962.2	E858.0	E932.2	E950.4	E962.0	E980.4
Dietetics	977.0	E858.8	E947.0	E950.4	E962.0	E980.4
Diethazine	966.4	E855.0	E936.4	E950.4	E962.0	E980.4
Diethyl						
barbituric acid	967.0	E851	E937.0	E950.1	E962.0	E980.1
carbamazine	961.6	E857	E931.6	E950.4	E962.0	E980.4
carbinol	980.8	E860.8	—	E950.9	E962.1	E980.9
carbonate	982.8	E862.4	—	E950.9	E962.1	E980.9
dioxide	982.8	E862.4	—	E950.9	E962.1	E980.9
ether (vapor) — see ther(s)						
glycol (monoacetate)						
(monoethyl ether)	982.8	E862.4	—	E950.9	E962.1	E980.9
propion	977.0	E858.8	E947.0	E950.4	E962.0	E980.4
stilbestrol	962.2	E858.0	E932.2	E950.4	E962.0	E980.4
Diethylene						
Diethylsulfone-diethylmethane	967.8	E852.8	E937.8	E950.2	E962.0	E980.2
Difencloxazine	965.09	E850.2	E935.2	E950.0	E962.0	E980.0
Diffusin	963.4	E858.1	E933.4	E950.4	E962.0	E980.4
Diflos	971.0	E855.3	E941.0	E950.4	E962.0	E980.4
Digestants	973.4	E858.4	E943.4	E950.4	E962.0	E980.4
Digitalin(e)	972.1	E858.3	E942.1	E950.4	E962.0	E980.4
Digitalis glycosides	972.1	E858.3	E942.1	E950.4	E962.0	E980.4
Digitoxin	972.1	E858.3	E942.1	E950.4	E962.0	E980.4
Digoxin	972.1	E858.3	E942.1	E950.4	E962.0	E980.4
Dihydrocodeine	965.09	E850.2	E935.2	E950.0	E962.0	E980.0
Dihydrocodeinone	965.09	E850.2	E935.2	E950.0	E962.0	E980.0
Dihydroergocristine	972.9	E858.3	E942.9	E950.4	E962.0	E980.4
Dihydroergotamine	972.9	E858.3	E942.9	E950.4	E962.0	E980.4
Dihydroergotoxine	972.9	E858.3	E942.9	E950.4	E962.0	E980.4
Dihydrohydroxycodeinone	965.09	E850.2	E935.2	E950.0	E962.0	E980.0
Dihydrohydroxymorphinone	965.09	E850.2	E935.2	E950.0	E962.0	E980.0
Dihydroisocodeine	965.09	E850.2	E935.2	E950.0	E962.0	E980.0
Dihydromorphine	965.09	E850.2	E935.2	E950.0	E962.0	E980.0
Dihydromorphinone	965.09	E850.2	E935.2	E950.0	E962.0	E980.0
Dihydrostreptomycin	960.6	E856	E930.6	E950.4	E962.0	E980.4
Dihydrotachysterol	962.6	E858.0	E932.6	E950.4	E962.0	E980.4
Dihydroxyanthraquinone	973.1	E858.4	E943.1	E950.4	E962.0	E980.4
Dihydroxycodeinone	965.09	E850.2	E935.2	E950.0	E962.0	E980.0
Diiodohydroxyquin	961.3	E857	E931.3	E950.4	E962.0	E980.4
topical	976.0	E858.7	E946.0	E950.4	E962.0	E980.4
Diiodohydroxyquinoline	961.3	E857	E931.3	E950.4	E962.0	E980.4
Dilantin	966.1	E855.0	E936.1	E950.4	E962.0	E980.4
Dilaudid	965.09	E850.2	E935.2	E950.0	E962.0	E980.0
Diloxanide	961.5	E857	E931.5	E950.4	E962.0	E980.4
Dimefline	970.0	E854.3	E940.0	E950.4	E962.0	E980.4
Dimenhydrinate	963.0	E858.1	E933.0	E950.4	E962.0	E980.4
Dimercaprol	963.8	E858.1	E933.8	E950.4	E962.0	E980.4
Dimercaptopropanol	963.8	E858.1	E933.8	E950.4	E962.0	E980.4
Dimetane	963.0	E858.1	E933.0	E950.4	E962.0	E980.4
Dimethicone	976.3	E858.7	E946.3	E950.4	E962.0	E980.4
Dimethindene	963.0	E858.1	E933.0	E950.4	E962.0	E980.4
Dimethisoquin	968.5	E855.2	E938.5	E950.4	E962.0	E980.4
Dimethisterone	962.2	E858.0	E932.2	E950.4	E962.0	E980.4
Dimethoxanate	975.4	E858.6	E945.4	E950.4	E962.0	E980.4
Dimethyl						
arsine, arsinic acid — see Arsenic						
carbinol	980.2	E860.3	—	E950.9	E962.1	E980.9
diguanide	962.3	E858.0	E932.3	E950.4	E962.0	E980.4
ketone	982.8	E862.4	—	E950.9	E962.1	E980.9
vapor	987.8	E869.8	—	E952.8	E962.2	E982.8
meperidine	965.09	E850.2	E935.2	E950.0	E962.0	E980.0
parathion	989.3	E863.1	—	E950.6	E962.1	E980.7
polysiloxane	973.8	E858.4	E943.8	E950.4	E962.0	E980.4
sulfate (fumes)	987.8	E869.8	—	E952.8	E962.2	E982.8
liquid	983.9	E864.3	—	E950.7	E962.1	E980.6
sulfoxide NEC	982.8	E862.4	—	E950.9	E962.1	E980.9
medicinal	976.4	E858.7	E946.4	E950.4	E962.0	E980.4
triptamine	969.6	E854.1	E939.6	E950.3	E962.0	E980.3
tubocurarine	975.2	E858.6	E945.2	E950.4	E962.0	E980.4
Dindevan	964.2	E858.2	E934.2	E950.4	E962.0	E980.4
Dinitrobenzene	983.0	E864.0	—	E950.7	E962.1	E980.6

Nontherapeutic use substance

▽ Subterms under main terms may continue to next column or page

	Poisoning	Accident	Therapeutic Use	Suicide Attempt	Assault	Undeter-mined
Dinitrobenzene — *continued*						
vapor	987.8	E869.8	—	E952.8	E962.2	E982.8
Dinitro (-ortho-) cresol						
(herbicide) (spray)	989.4	E863.5	—	E950.6	E962.1	E980.7
insecticide	989.4	E863.4	—	E950.6	E962.1	E980.7
Dinitro-orthocresol						
(herbicide)	989.4	E863.5	—	E950.6	E962.1	E980.7
insecticide	989.4	E863.4	—	E950.6	E962.1	E980.7
Dinitrophenol (herbicide)						
(spray)	989.4	E863.5	—	E950.6	E962.1	E980.7
insecticide	989.4	E863.4	—	E950.6	E962.1	E980.7
Dinoprost	975.0	E858.6	E945.0	E950.4	E962.0	E980.4
Dioctyl sulfosuccinate (calcium)						
(sodium)	973.2	E858.4	E943.2	E950.4	E962.0	E980.4
Diodoquin	961.3	E857	E931.3	E950.4	E962.0	E980.4
Dione derivatives NEC	966.3	E855.0	E936.3	E950.4	E962.0	E980.4
Dionin	965.09	E850.2	E935.2	E950.0	E962.0	E980.0
Dioxane	982.8	E862.4	—	E950.9	E962.1	E980.9
Dioxin — *see* Herbicide						
Dioxyline	972.5	E858.3	E942.5	E950.4	E962.0	E980.4
Dipentene	982.8	E862.4	—	E950.9	E962.1	E980.9
Diphemanil	971.1	E855.4	E941.1	E950.4	E962.0	E980.4
Diphenadione	964.2	E858.2	E934.2	E950.4	E962.0	E980.4
Diphenhydramine	963.0	E858.1	E933.0	E950.4	E962.0	E980.4
Diphenidol	963.0	E858.1	E933.0	E950.4	E962.0	E980.4
Diphenoxylate	973.5	E858.4	E943.5	E950.4	E962.0	E980.4
Diphenylchloroarsine	985.1	E866.3	—	E950.8	E962.1	E980.8
Diphenylhydantoin						
(sodium)	966.1	E855.0	E936.1	E950.4	E962.0	E980.4
Diphenylpyraline	963.0	E858.1	E933.0	E950.4	E962.0	E980.4
Diphtheria						
antitoxin	979.9	E858.8	E949.9	E950.4	E962.0	E980.4
toxoid	978.5	E858.8	E948.5	E950.4	E962.0	E980.4
with tetanus toxoid	978.9	E858.8	E948.9	E950.4	E962.0	E980.4
with pertussis						
component	978.6	E858.8	E948.6	E950.4	E962.0	E980.4
vaccine	978.5	E858.8	E948.5	E950.4	E962.0	E980.4
Dipipanone	965.09	E850.2	E935.2	E950.0	E962.0	E980.0
Diplovax	979.5	E858.8	E949.5	E950.4	E962.0	E980.4
Diprophylline	975.1	E858.6	E945.1	E950.4	E962.0	E980.4
Dipyridamole	972.4	E858.3	E942.4	E950.4	E962.0	E980.4
Dipyrone	965.5	E850.5	E935.5	E950.0	E962.0	E980.0
Diquat	989.4	E863.5	—	E950.6	E962.1	E980.7
Disinfectant NEC	983.9	E861.4	—	E950.7	E962.1	E980.6
alkaline	983.2	E861.4	—	E950.7	E962.1	E980.6
aromatic	983.0	E861.4	—	E950.7	E962.1	E980.6
Disipal	966.4	E855.0	E936.4	E950.4	E962.0	E980.4
Disodium edetate	963.8	E858.1	E933.8	E950.4	E962.0	E980.4
Disulfamide	974.4	E858.5	E944.4	E950.4	E962.0	E980.4
Disulfanilamide	961.0	E857	E931.0	E950.4	E962.0	E980.4
Disulfiram	977.3	E858.8	E947.3	E950.4	E962.0	E980.4
Dithiazanine	961.6	E857	E931.6	E950.4	E962.0	E980.4
Dithioglycerol	963.8	E858.1	E933.8	E950.4	E962.0	E980.4
Dithranol	976.4	E858.7	E946.4	E950.4	E962.0	E980.4
Diucardin	974.3	E858.5	E944.3	E950.4	E962.0	E980.4
Diupres	974.3	E858.5	E944.3	E950.4	E962.0	E980.4
Diuretics NEC	974.4	E858.5	E944.4	E950.4	E962.0	E980.4
carbonic acid anhydrase inhibitors	974.2	E858.5	E944.2	E950.4	E962.0	E980.4
mercurial	974.0	E858.5	E944.0	E950.4	E962.0	E980.4
osmotic	974.4	E858.5	E944.4	E950.4	E962.0	E980.4
purine derivatives	974.1	E858.5	E944.1	E950.4	E962.0	E980.4
saluretic	974.3	E858.5	E944.3	E950.4	E962.0	E980.4
Diuril	974.3	E858.5	E944.3	E950.4	E962.0	E980.4
Divinyl ether	968.2	E855.1	E938.2	E950.4	E962.0	E980.4
D-lysergic acid						
diethylamide	969.6	E854.1	E939.6	E950.3	E962.0	E980.3
DMCT	960.4	E856	E930.4	E950.4	E962.0	E980.4
DMSO	982.8	E862.4	—	E950.9	E962.1	E980.9
DMT	969.6	E854.1	E939.6	E950.3	E962.0	E980.3
DNOC	989.4	E863.5	—	E950.6	E962.1	E980.7
DOCA	962.0	E858.0	E932.0	E950.4	E962.0	E980.4
Dolophine	965.02	E850.1	E935.1	E950.0	E962.0	E980.0
Doloxene	965.8	E850.8	E935.8	E950.0	E962.0	E980.0
DOM	969.6	E854.1	E939.6	E950.3	E962.0	E980.3
Domestic gas — *see* Gas, utility						
Domiphen (bromide)						
(lozenges)	976.6	E858.7	E946.6	E950.4	E962.0	E980.4
Dopa (levo)	966.4	E855.0	E936.4	E950.4	E962.0	E980.4
Dopamine	971.2	E855.5	E941.2	E950.4	E962.0	E980.4
Doriden	967.5	E852.4	E937.5	E950.2	E962.0	E980.2
Dormiral	967.0	E851	E937.0	E950.1	E962.0	E980.1

	Poisoning	Accident	Therapeutic Use	Suicide Attempt	Assault	Undeter-mined
Dormison	967.8	E852.8	E937.8	E950.2	E962.0	E980.2
Dornase	963.4	E858.1	E933.4	E950.4	E962.0	E980.4
Dorsacaine	968.5	E855.2	E938.5	E950.4	E962.0	E980.4
Dothiepin hydrochloride ▲	969.05 ▲	E854.0	E939.0	E950.3	E962.0	E980.3
Doxapram	970.0	E854.3	E940.0	E950.4	E962.0	E980.4
Doxepin	969.05 ▲	E854.0	E939.0	E950.3	E962.0	E980.3
Doxorubicin	960.7	E856	E930.7	E950.4	E962.0	E980.4
Doxycycline	960.4	E856	E930.4	E950.4	E962.0	E980.4
Doxylamine	963.0	E858.1	E933.0	E950.4	E962.0	E980.4
Dramamine	963.0	E858.1	E933.0	E950.4	E962.0	E980.4
Drano (drain cleaner)	983.2	E864.2	—	E950.7	E962.1	E980.6
Dromoran	965.09	E850.2	E935.2	E950.0	E962.0	E980.0
Dromostanolone	962.1	E858.0	E932.1	E950.4	E962.0	E980.4
Droperidol	969.2	E853.1	E939.2	E950.3	E962.0	E980.3
Drotrecogin alfa	964.2	E858.2	E934.2	E950.4	E962.0	E980.4
Drug	977.9	E858.9	E947.9	E950.5	E962.0	E980.5
AHFS List						
4:00 antihistamine drugs	963.0	E858.1	E933.0	E950.4	E962.0	E980.4
8:04 amebacides	961.5	E857	E931.5	E950.4	E962.0	E980.4
arsenical anti-infectives	961.1	E857	E931.1	E950.4	E962.0	E980.4
quinoline derivatives	961.3	E857	E931.3	E950.4	E962.0	E980.4
8:08 anthelmintics	961.6	E857	E931.6	E950.4	E962.0	E980.4
quinoline derivatives	961.3	E857	E931.3	E950.4	E962.0	E980.4
8:12.04 antifungal antibiotics	960.1	E856	E930.1	E950.4	E962.0	E980.4
8:12.06 cephalosporins	960.5	E856	E930.5	E950.4	E962.0	E980.4
8:12.08 chloramphenicol	960.2	E856	E930.2	E950.4	E962.0	E980.4
8:12.12 erythromycins	960.3	E856	E930.3	E950.4	E962.0	E980.4
8:12.16 penicillins	960.0	E856	E930.0	E950.4	E962.0	E980.4
8:12.20 streptomycins	960.6	E856	E930.6	E950.4	E962.0	E980.4
8:12.24 tetracyclines	960.4	E856	E930.4	E950.4	E962.0	E980.4
8:12.28 other antibiotics	960.8	E856	E930.8	E950.4	E962.0	E980.4
antimycobacterial	960.6	E856	E930.6	E950.4	E962.0	E980.4
macrolides	960.3	E856	E930.3	E950.4	E962.0	E980.4
8:16 antituberculars	961.8	E857	E931.8	E950.4	E962.0	E980.4
antibiotics	960.6	E856	E930.6	E950.4	E962.0	E980.4
8:18 antivirals	961.7	E857	E931.7	E950.4	E962.0	E980.4
8:20 plasmodicides (antimalarials)	961.4	E857	E931.4	E950.4	E962.0	E980.4
8:24 sulfonamides	961.0	E857	E931.0	E950.4	E962.0	E980.4
8:26 sulfones	961.8	E857	E931.8	E950.4	E962.0	E980.4
8:28 treponemicides	961.2	E857	E931.2	E950.4	E962.0	E980.4
8:32 trichomonacides	961.5	E857	E931.5	E950.4	E962.0	E980.4
nitrofuran derivatives	961.9	E857	E931.9	E950.4	E962.0	E980.4
quinoline derivatives	961.3	E857	E931.3	E950.4	E962.0	E980.4
8:36 urinary germicides	961.9	E857	E931.9	E950.4	E962.0	E980.4
quinoline derivatives	961.3	E857	E931.3	E950.4	E962.0	E980.4
8:40 other anti-infectives	961.9	E857	E931.9	E950.4	E962.0	E980.4
10:00 antineoplastic agents	963.1	E858.1	E933.1	E950.4	E962.0	E980.4
antibiotics	960.7	E856	E930.7	E950.4	E962.0	E980.4
progestogens	962.2	E858.0	E932.2	E950.4	E962.0	E980.4
12:04 parasympathomimetic (cholinergic) agents	971.0	E855.3	E941.0	E950.4	E962.0	E980.4
12:08 parasympatholytic (cholinergic-blocking) agents	971.1	E855.4	E941.1	E950.4	E962.0	E980.4
12:12 Sympathomimetic (adrenergic) agents	971.2	E855.5	E941.2	E950.4	E962.0	E980.4
12:16 sympatholytic (adrenergic-blocking) agents	971.3	E855.6	E941.3	E950.4	E962.0	E980.4
12:20 skeletal muscle relaxants central nervous system muscle-tone depressants	968.0	E855.1	E938.0	E950.4	E962.0	E980.4
myoneural blocking agents	975.2	E858.6	E945.2	E950.4	E962.0	E980.4
16:00 blood derivatives	964.7	E858.2	E934.7	E950.4	E962.0	E980.4
20:04.04 iron preparations	964.0	E858.2	E934.0	E950.4	E962.0	E980.4
20:04.08 liver and stomach preparations	964.1	E858.2	E934.1	E950.4	E962.0	E980.4
20:04 antianemia drugs	964.1	E858.2	E934.1	E950.4	E962.0	E980.4
20:12.04 anticoagulants	964.2	E858.2	E934.2	E950.4	E962.0	E980.4
20:12.08 antiheparin agents	964.5	E858.2	E934.5	E950.4	E962.0	E980.4
20:12.12 coagulants	964.5	E858.2	E934.5	E950.4	E962.0	E980.4
20:12.16 hemostatics NEC	964.5	E858.2	E934.5	E950.4	E962.0	E980.4
capillary active drugs	972.8	E858.3	E942.8	E950.4	E962.0	E980.4
24:04 cardiac drugs	972.9	E858.3	E942.9	E950.4	E962.0	E980.4
cardiotonic agents	972.1	E858.3	E942.1	E950.4	E962.0	E980.4
rhythm regulators	972.0	E858.3	E942.0	E950.4	E962.0	E980.4

Drug — continued	Poisoning	Accident	Therapeutic Use	Suicide Attempt	Assault	Undeter-mined
24:06 antilipemic agents	972.2	E858.3	E942.2	E950.4	E962.0	E980.4
thyroid derivatives	962.7	E858.0	E932.7	E950.4	E962.0	E980.4
24:08 hypotensive agents	972.6	E858.3	E942.6	E950.4	E962.0	E980.4
adrenergic blocking agents	971.3	E855.6	E941.3	E950.4	E962.0	E980.4
ganglion blocking agents	972.3	E858.3	E942.3	E950.4	E962.0	E980.4
vasodilators	972.5	E858.3	E942.5	E950.4	E962.0	E980.4
24:12 vasodilating agents NEC	972.5	E858.3	E942.5	E950.4	E962.0	E980.4
coronary	972.4	E858.3	E942.4	E950.4	E962.0	E980.4
nicotinic acid derivatives	972.2	E858.3	E942.2	E950.4	E962.0	E980.4
24:16 sclerosing agents	972.7	E858.3	E942.7	E950.4	E962.0	E980.4
28:04 general anesthetics	968.4	E855.1	E938.4	E950.4	E962.0	E980.4
gaseous anesthetics	968.2	E855.1	E938.2	E950.4	E962.0	E980.4
halothane	968.1	E855.1	E938.1	E950.4	E962.0	E980.4
intravenous anesthetics	968.3	E855.1	E938.3	E950.4	E962.0	E980.4
28:08 analgesics and antipyretics	965.9	E850.9	E935.9	E950.0	E962.0	E980.0
antirheumatics	965.69	E850.6	E935.6	E950.0	E962.0	E980.0
aromatic analgesics	965.4	E850.4	E935.4	E950.0	E962.0	E980.0
non-narcotic NEC	965.7	E850.7	E935.7	E950.0	E962.0	E980.0
opium alkaloids	965.00	E850.2	E935.2	E950.0	E962.0	E980.0
heroin	965.01	E850.0	E935.0	E950.0	E962.0	E980.0
methadone	965.02	E850.1	E935.1	E950.0	E962.0	E980.0
specified type NEC	965.09	E850.2	E935.2	E950.0	E962.0	E980.0
pyrazole derivatives	965.5	E850.5	E935.5	E950.0	E962.0	E980.0
salicylates	965.1	E850.3	E935.3	E950.0	E962.0	E980.0
specified NEC	965.8	E850.8	E935.8	E950.0	E962.0	E980.0
28:10 narcotic antagonists	970.1	E854.3	E940.1	E950.4	E962.0	E980.4
28:12 anticonvulsants	966.3	E855.0	E936.3	E950.4	E962.0	E980.4
barbiturates	967.0	E851	E937.0	E950.1	E962.0	E980.1
benzodiazepine-based tranquilizers	969.4	E853.2	E939.4	E950.3	E962.0	E980.3
bromides	967.3	E852.2	E937.3	E950.2	E962.0	E980.2
hydantoin derivatives	966.1	E855.0	E936.1	E950.4	E962.0	E980.4
oxazolidine (derivatives)	966.0	E855.0	E936.0	E950.4	E962.0	E980.4
succinimides	966.2	E855.0	E936.2	E950.4	E962.0	E980.4
28:16.04 antidepressants	969.00 ▲	E854.0	E939.0	E950.3	E962.0	E980.3
28:16.08 tranquilizers	969.5	E853.9	E939.5	E950.3	E962.0	E980.3
benzodiazepine-based	969.4	E853.2	E939.4	E950.3	E962.0	E980.3
butyrophenone-based	969.2	E853.1	E939.2	E950.3	E962.0	E980.3
major NEC	969.3	E853.8	E939.3	E950.3	E962.0	E980.3
phenothiazine-based	969.1	E853.0	E939.1	E950.3	E962.0	E980.3
28:16.12 other psychotherapeutic agents	969.8	E855.8	E939.8	E950.3	E962.0	E980.3
28:20 respiratory and cerebral stimulants	970.9	E854.3	E940.9	E950.4	E962.0	E980.4
analeptics	970.0	E854.3	E940.0	E950.4	E962.0	E980.4
anorexigenic agents	977.0	E858.8	E947.0	E950.4	E962.0	E980.4
psychostimulants	969.70 ▲	E854.2	E939.7	E950.3	E962.0	E980.3
specified NEC	970.8	E854.3	E940.8	E950.4	E962.0	E980.4
28:24 sedatives and hypnotics	967.9	E852.9	E937.9	E950.2	E962.0	E980.2
barbiturates	967.0	E851	E937.0	E950.1	E962.0	E980.1
benzodiazepine-based tranquilizers	969.4	E853.2	E939.4	E950.3	E962.0	E980.3
chloral hydrate (group)	967.1	E852.0	E937.1	E950.2	E962.0	E980.2
glutethamide group	967.5	E852.4	E937.5	E950.2	E962.0	E980.2
intravenous anesthetics	968.3	E855.1	E938.3	E950.4	E962.0	E980.4
methaqualone (compounds)	967.4	E852.3	E937.4	E950.2	E962.0	E980.2
paraldehyde	967.2	E852.1	E937.2	E950.2	E962.0	E980.2
phenothiazine-based tranquilizers	969.1	E853.0	E939.1	E950.3	E962.0	E980.3
specified NEC	967.8	E852.8	E937.8	E950.2	E962.0	E980.2
thiobarbiturates	968.3	E855.1	E938.3	E950.4	E962.0	E980.4
tranquilizer NEC	969.5	E853.9	E939.5	E950.3	E962.0	E980.3
36:04 to 36:88 diagnostic agents	977.8	E858.8	E947.8	E950.4	E962.0	E980.4
40:00 electrolyte, caloric, and water balance agents NEC	974.5	E858.5	E944.5	E950.4	E962.0	E980.4
40:04 acidifying agents	963.2	E858.1	E933.2	E950.4	E962.0	E980.4
40:08 alkalinizing agents	963.3	E858.1	E933.3	E950.4	E962.0	E980.4
40:10 ammonia detoxicants	974.5	E858.5	E944.5	E950.4	E962.0	E980.4
40:12 replacement solutions	974.5	E858.5	E944.5	E950.4	E962.0	E980.4
plasma expanders	964.8	E858.2	E934.8	E950.4	E962.0	E980.4

Drug — continued	Poisoning	Accident	Therapeutic Use	Suicide Attempt	Assault	Undeter-mined
40:16 sodium-removing resins	974.5	E858.5	E944.5	E950.4	E962.0	E980.4
40:18 potassium-removing resins	974.5	E858.5	E944.5	E950.4	E962.0	E980.4
40:20 caloric agents	974.5	E858.5	E944.5	E950.4	E962.0	E980.4
40:24 salt and sugar substitutes	974.5	E858.5	E944.5	E950.4	E962.0	E980.4
40:28 diuretics NEC	974.4	E858.5	E944.4	E950.4	E962.0	E980.4
carbonic acid anhydrase inhibitors	974.2	E858.5	E944.2	E950.4	E962.0	E980.4
mercurials	974.0	E858.5	E944.0	E950.4	E962.0	E980.4
purine derivatives	974.1	E858.5	E944.1	E950.4	E962.0	E980.4
saluretics	974.3	E858.5	E944.3	E950.4	E962.0	E980.4
thiazides	974.3	E858.5	E944.3	E950.4	E962.0	E980.4
40:36 irrigating solutions	974.5	E858.5	E944.5	E950.4	E962.0	E980.4
40:40 uricosuric agents	974.7	E858.5	E944.7	E950.4	E962.0	E980.4
44:00 enzymes	963.4	E858.1	E933.4	E950.4	E962.0	E980.4
fibrinolysis-affecting agents	964.4	E858.2	E934.4	E950.4	E962.0	E980.4
gastric agents	973.4	E858.4	E943.4	E950.4	E962.0	E980.4
48:00 expectorants and cough preparations antihistamine agents	963.0	E858.1	E933.0	E950.4	E962.0	E980.4
antitussives	975.4	E858.6	E945.4	E950.4	E962.0	E980.4
codeine derivatives	965.09	E850.2	E935.2	E950.0	E962.0	E980.0
expectorants	975.5	E858.6	E945.5	E950.4	E962.0	E980.4
narcotic agents NEC	965.09	E850.2	E935.2	E950.0	E962.0	E980.0
52:04.04 antibiotics (EENT) ENT agent	976.6	E858.7	E946.6	E950.4	E962.0	E980.4
ophthalmic preparation	976.5	E858.7	E946.5	E950.4	E962.0	E980.4
52:04.06 antivirals (EENT) ENT agent	976.6	E858.7	E946.6	E950.4	E962.0	E980.4
ophthalmic preparation	976.5	E858.7	E946.5	E950.4	E962.0	E980.4
52:04.08 sulfonamides (EENT) ENT agent	976.6	E858.7	E946.6	E950.4	E962.0	E980.4
ophthalmic preparation	976.5	E858.7	E946.5	E950.4	E962.0	E980.4
52:04.12 miscellaneous anti-infectives (EENT) ENT agent	976.6	E858.7	E946.6	E950.4	E962.0	E980.4
ophthalmic preparation	976.5	E858.7	E946.5	E950.4	E962.0	E980.4
52:04 anti-infectives (EENT) ENT agent	976.6	E858.7	E946.6	E950.4	E962.0	E980.4
ophthalmic preparation	976.5	E858.7	E946.5	E950.4	E962.0	E980.4
52:08 anti-inflammatory agents (EENT) ENT agent	976.6	E858.7	E946.6	E950.4	E962.0	E980.4
ophthalmic preparation	976.5	E858.7	E946.5	E950.4	E962.0	E980.4
52:10 carbonic anhydrase inhibitors	974.2	E858.5	E944.2	E950.4	E962.0	E980.4
52:12 contact lens solutions	976.5	E858.7	E946.5	E950.4	E962.0	E980.4
52:16 local anesthetics (EENT)	968.5	E855.2	E938.5	E950.4	E962.0	E980.4
52:20 miotics	971.0	E855.3	E941.0	E950.4	E962.0	E980.4
52:24 mydriatics adrenergics	971.2	E855.5	E941.2	E950.4	E962.0	E980.4
anticholinergics	971.1	E855.4	E941.1	E950.4	E962.0	E980.4
antimuscarinics	971.1	E855.4	E941.1	E950.4	E962.0	E980.4
parasympatholytics	971.1	E855.4	E941.1	E950.4	E962.0	E980.4
spasmolytics	971.1	E855.4	E941.1	E950.4	E962.0	E980.4
sympathomimetics	971.2	E855.5	E941.2	E950.4	E962.0	E980.4
52:28 mouth washes and gargles	976.6	E858.7	E946.6	E950.4	E962.0	E980.4
52:32 vasoconstrictors (EENT)	971.2	E855.5	E941.2	E950.4	E962.0	E980.4
52:36 unclassified agents (EENT) ENT agent	976.6	E858.7	E946.6	E950.4	E962.0	E980.4
ophthalmic preparation	976.5	E858.7	E946.5	E950.4	E962.0	E980.4
56:04 antacids and adsorbents	973.0	E858.4	E943.0	E950.4	E962.0	E980.4
56:08 antidiarrhea agents	973.5	E858.4	E943.5	E950.4	E962.0	E980.4
56:10 antiflatulents	973.8	E858.4	E943.8	E950.4	E962.0	E980.4
56:12 cathartics NEC	973.3	E858.4	E943.3	E950.4	E962.0	E980.4
emollients	973.2	E858.4	E943.2	E950.4	E962.0	E980.4
irritants	973.1	E858.4	E943.1	E950.4	E962.0	E980.4
56:16 digestants	973.4	E858.4	E943.4	E950.4	E962.0	E980.4
56:20 emetics and antiemetics antiemetics	963.0	E858.1	E933.0	E950.4	E962.0	E980.4
emetics	973.6	E858.4	E943.6	E950.4	E962.0	E980.4
56:24 lipotropic agents	977.1	E858.8	E947.1	E950.4	E962.0	E980.4

Nontherapeutic use substance   ▶◀ Revised Text   ● New Line   ▲ Revised Code   ▽ Subterms under main terms may continue to next column or page

2010 ICD-9-CM   October 2009 • Volume 2 — 299

Drug — continued	Poisoning	Accident	Therapeutic Use	Suicide Attempt	Assault	Undetermined
56:40 miscellaneous G.I. drugs	973.8	E858.4	E943.8	E950.4	E962.0	E980.4
60:00 gold compounds	965.69	E850.6	E935.6	E950.0	E962.0	E980.0
64:00 heavy metal antagonists	963.8	E858.1	E933.8	E950.4	E962.0	E980.4
68:04 adrenals	962.0	E858.0	E932.0	E950.4	E962.0	E980.4
68:08 androgens	962.1	E858.0	E932.1	E950.4	E962.0	E980.4
68:12 contraceptives, oral	962.2	E858.0	E932.2	E950.4	E962.0	E980.4
68:16 estrogens	962.2	E858.0	E932.2	E950.4	E962.0	E980.4
68:18 gonadotropins	962.4	E858.0	E932.4	E950.4	E962.0	E980.4
68:20.08 insulins	962.3	E858.0	E932.3	E950.4	E962.0	E980.4
68:20 insulins and antidiabetic agents	962.3	E858.0	E932.3	E950.4	E962.0	E980.4
68:24 parathyroid	962.6	E858.0	E932.6	E950.4	E962.0	E980.4
68:28 pituitary (posterior)	962.5	E858.0	E932.5	E950.4	E962.0	E980.4
anterior	962.4	E858.0	E932.4	E950.4	E962.0	E980.4
68:32 progestogens	962.2	E858.0	E932.2	E950.4	E962.0	E980.4
68:34 other corpus luteum hormones NEC	962.2	E858.0	E932.2	E950.4	E962.0	E980.4
68:36 thyroid and antithyroid antithyroid	962.8	E858.0	E932.8	E950.4	E962.0	E980.4
thyroid (derivatives)	962.7	E858.0	E932.7	E950.4	E962.0	E980.4
72:00 local anesthetics NEC	968.9	E855.2	E938.9	E950.4	E962.0	E980.4
infiltration (intradermal) (subcutaneous) (submucosal)	968.5	E855.2	E938.5	E950.4	E962.0	E980.4
nerve blocking (peripheral) (plexus) (regional)	968.6	E855.2	E938.6	E950.4	E962.0	E980.4
spinal	968.7	E855.2	E938.7	E950.4	E962.0	E980.4
topical (surface)	968.5	E855.2	E938.5	E950.4	E962.0	E980.4
76:00 oxytocics	975.0	E858.6	E945.0	E950.4	E962.0	E980.4
78:00 radioactive agents	990	—	—	—	—	—
80:04 serums NEC	979.9	E858.8	E949.9	E950.4	E962.0	E980.4
immune gamma globulin (human)	964.6	E858.2	E934.6	E950.4	E962.0	E980.4
80:08 toxoids NEC	978.8	E858.8	E948.8	E950.4	E962.0	E980.4
diphtheria	978.5	E858.8	E948.5	E950.4	E962.0	E980.4
and diphtheria with pertussis	978.9	E858.8	E948.9	E950.4	E962.0	E980.4
component	978.6	E858.8	E948.6	E950.4	E962.0	E980.4
and tetanus	978.9	E858.8	E948.9	E950.4	E962.0	E980.4
with pertussis component	978.6	E858.8	E948.6	E950.4	E962.0	E980.4
tetanus	978.4	E858.8	E948.4	E950.4	E962.0	E980.4
80:12 vaccines	979.9	E858.8	E949.9	E950.4	E962.0	E980.4
bacterial NEC	978.8	E858.8	E948.8	E950.4	E962.0	E980.4
with other bacterial components	978.9	E858.8	E948.9	E950.4	E962.0	E980.4
pertussis component	978.6	E858.8	E948.6	E950.4	E962.0	E980.4
viral and rickettsial components	979.7	E858.8	E949.7	E950.4	E962.0	E980.4
rickettsial NEC	979.6	E858.8	E949.6	E950.4	E962.0	E980.4
with bacterial component	979.7	E858.8	E949.7	E950.4	E962.0	E980.4
pertussis component	978.6	E858.8	E948.6	E950.4	E962.0	E980.4
viral component	979.7	E858.8	E949.7	E950.4	E962.0	E980.4
viral NEC	979.6	E858.8	E949.6	E950.4	E962.0	E980.4
with bacterial component	979.7	E858.8	E949.7	E950.4	E962.0	E980.4
pertussis component	978.6	E858.8	E948.6	E950.4	E962.0	E980.4
rickettsial component	979.7	E858.8	E949.7	E950.4	E962.0	E980.4
84:04.04 antibiotics (skin and mucous membrane)	976.0	E858.7	E946.0	E950.4	E962.0	E980.4
84:04.08 fungicides (skin and mucous membrane)	976.0	E858.7	E946.0	E950.4	E962.0	E980.4
84:04.12 scabicides and pediculicides (skin and mucous membrane)	976.0	E858.7	E946.0	E950.4	E962.0	E980.4
84:04.16 miscellaneous local anti-infectives (skin and mucous membrane)	976.0	E858.7	E946.0	E950.4	E962.0	E980.4
84:06 anti-inflammatory agents (skin and mucous membrane)	976.0	E858.7	E946.0	E950.4	E962.0	E980.4
84:08 antipruritics and local anesthetics antipruritics	976.1	E858.7	E946.1	E950.4	E962.0	E980.4
local anesthetics	968.5	E855.2	E938.5	E950.4	E962.0	E980.4

Drug — continued	Poisoning	Accident	Therapeutic Use	Suicide Attempt	Assault	Undetermined
84:12 astringents	976.2	E858.7	E946.2	E950.4	E962.0	E980.4
84:16 cell stimulants and proliferants	976.8	E858.7	E946.8	E950.4	E962.0	E980.4
84:20 detergents	976.2	E858.7	E946.2	E950.4	E962.0	E980.4
84:24 emollients, demulcents, and protectants	976.3	E858.7	E946.3	E950.4	E962.0	E980.4
84:28 keratolytic agents	976.4	E858.7	E946.4	E950.4	E962.0	E980.4
84:32 keratoplastic agents	976.4	E858.7	E946.4	E950.4	E962.0	E980.4
84:36 miscellaneous agents (skin and mucous membrane)	976.8	E858.7	E946.8	E950.4	E962.0	E980.4
86:00 spasmolytic agents	975.1	E858.6	E945.1	E950.4	E962.0	E980.4
antiasthmatics	975.7	E858.6	E945.7	E950.4	E962.0	E980.4
papaverine	972.5	E858.3	E942.5	E950.4	E962.0	E980.4
theophylline	974.1	E858.5	E944.1	E950.4	E962.0	E980.4
88:04 vitamin A	963.5	E858.1	E933.5	E950.4	E962.0	E980.4
88:08 vitamin B complex	963.5	E858.1	E933.5	E950.4	E962.0	E980.4
hematopoietic vitamin	964.1	E858.2	E934.1	E950.4	E962.0	E980.4
nicotinic acid derivatives	972.2	E858.3	E942.2	E950.4	E962.0	E980.4
88:12 vitamin C	963.5	E858.1	E933.5	E950.4	E962.0	E980.4
88:16 vitamin D	963.5	E858.1	E933.5	E950.4	E962.0	E980.4
88:20 vitamin E	963.5	E858.1	E933.5	E950.4	E962.0	E980.4
88:24 vitamin K activity	964.3	E858.2	E934.3	E950.4	E962.0	E980.4
88:28 multivitamin preparations	963.5	E858.1	E933.5	E950.4	E962.0	E980.4
92:00 unclassified therapeutic agents	977.8	E858.8	E947.8	E950.4	E962.0	E980.4
specified NEC	977.8	E858.8	E947.8	E950.4	E962.0	E980.4
Duboisine	971.1	E855.4	E941.1	E950.4	E962.0	E980.4
Dulcolax	973.1	E858.4	E943.1	E950.4	E962.0	E980.4
Duponol (C) (EP)	976.2	E858.7	E946.2	E950.4	E962.0	E980.4
Durabolin	962.1	E858.0	E932.1	E950.4	E962.0	E980.4
Dyclone	968.5	E855.2	E938.5	E950.4	E962.0	E980.4
Dyclonine	968.5	E855.2	E938.5	E950.4	E962.0	E980.4
Dydrogesterone	962.2	E858.0	E932.2	E950.4	E962.0	E980.4
Dyes NEC	989.89	E866.8	—	E950.9	E962.1	E980.9
diagnostic agents	977.8	E858.8	E947.8	E950.4	E962.0	E980.4
pharmaceutical NEC	977.4	E858.8	E947.4	E950.4	E962.0	E980.4
Dyfols	971.0	E855.3	E941.0	E950.4	E962.0	E980.4
Dymelor	962.3	E858.0	E932.3	E950.4	E962.0	E980.4
Dynamite	989.89	E866.8	—	E950.9	E962.1	E980.9
fumes	987.8	E869.8	—	E952.8	E962.2	E982.8
Dyphylline	975.1	E858.6	E945.1	E950.4	E962.0	E980.4
Ear preparations	976.6	E858.7	E946.6	E950.4	E962.0	E980.4
Echothiopate, ecothiopate	971.0	E855.3	E941.0	E950.4	E962.0	E980.4
Ecstasy	969.72 ▲	E854.2	E939.7	E950.3	E962.0	E980.3
Ectylurea	967.8	E852.8	E937.8	E950.2	E962.0	E980.2
Edathamil disodium	963.8	E858.1	E933.8	E950.4	E962.0	E980.4
Edecrin	974.4	E858.5	E944.4	E950.4	E962.0	E980.4
Edetate, disodium (calcium)	963.8	E858.1	E933.8	E950.4	E962.0	E980.4
Edrophonium	971.0	E855.3	E941.0	E950.4	E962.0	E980.4
Elase	976.8	E858.7	E946.8	E950.4	E962.0	E980.4
Elaterium	973.1	E858.4	E943.1	E950.4	E962.0	E980.4
Elder	988.2	E865.4	—	E950.9	E962.1	E980.9
berry (unripe)	988.2	E865.3	—	E950.9	E962.1	E980.9
Electrolytes NEC	974.5	E858.5	E944.5	E950.4	E962.0	E980.4
Electrolytic agent NEC	974.5	E858.5	E944.5	E950.4	E962.0	E980.4
Embramine	963.0	E858.1	E933.0	E950.4	E962.0	E980.4
Emetics	973.6	E858.4	E943.6	E950.4	E962.0	E980.4
Emetine (hydrochloride)	961.5	E857	E931.5	E950.4	E962.0	E980.4
Emollients	976.3	E858.7	E946.3	E950.4	E962.0	E980.4
Emylcamate	969.5	E853.8	E939.5	E950.3	E962.0	E980.3
Encyprate	969.09 ▲	E854.0	E939.0	E950.3	E962.0	E980.3
Endocaine	968.5	E855.2	E938.5	E950.4	E962.0	E980.4
Endrin	989.2	E863.0	—	E950.6	E962.1	E980.7
Enflurane	968.2	E855.1	E938.2	E950.4	E962.0	E980.4
Enovid	962.2	E858.0	E932.2	E950.4	E962.0	E980.4
ENT preparations (anti-infectives)	976.6	E858.7	E946.6	E950.4	E962.0	E980.4
Enzodase	963.4	E858.1	E933.4	E950.4	E962.0	E980.4
Enzymes NEC	963.4	E858.1	E933.4	E950.4	E962.0	E980.4
Epanutin	966.1	E855.0	E936.1	E950.4	E962.0	E980.4
Ephedra (tincture)	971.2	E855.5	E941.2	E950.4	E962.0	E980.4
Ephedrine	971.2	E855.5	E941.2	E950.4	E962.0	E980.4
Epiestriol	962.2	E858.0	E932.2	E950.4	E962.0	E980.4
Epilim — see Sodium valproate						
Epinephrine	971.2	E855.5	E941.2	E950.4	E962.0	E980.4
Epsom salt	973.3	E858.4	E943.3	E950.4	E962.0	E980.4
Equanil	969.5	E853.8	E939.5	E950.3	E962.0	E980.3

	Poisoning	Accident	Therapeutic Use	Suicide Attempt	Assault	Undetermined
			External Cause (E-Code)			
Equisetum (diuretic)	974.4	E858.5	E944.4	E950.4	E962.0	E980.4
Ergometrine	975.0	E858.6	E945.0	E950.4	E962.0	E980.4
Ergonovine	975.0	E858.6	E945.0	E950.4	E962.0	E980.4
Ergot NEC	988.2	E865.4	—	E950.9	E962.1	E980.9
medicinal (alkaloids)	975.0	E858.6	E945.0	E950.4	E962.0	E980.4
Ergotamine (tartrate) (for migraine) NEC	972.9	E858.3	E942.9	E950.4	E962.0	E980.4
Ergotrate	975.0	E858.6	E945.0	E950.4	E962.0	E980.4
Erythrityl tetranitrate	972.4	E858.3	E942.4	E950.4	E962.0	E980.4
Erythrol tetranitrate	972.4	E858.3	E942.4	E950.4	E962.0	E980.4
Erythromycin	960.3	E856	E930.3	E950.4	E962.0	E980.4
ophthalmic preparation	976.5	E858.7	E946.5	E950.4	E962.0	E980.4
topical NEC	976.0	E858.7	E946.0	E950.4	E962.0	E980.4
Eserine	971.0	E855.3	E941.0	E950.4	E962.0	E980.4
Eskabarb	967.0	E851	E937.0	E950.1	E962.0	E980.1
Eskalith	969.8	E855.8	E939.8	E950.3	E962.0	E980.3
Estradiol (cypionate) (dipropionate) (valerate)	962.2	E858.0	E932.2	E950.4	E962.0	E980.4
Estriol	962.2	E858.0	E932.2	E950.4	E962.0	E980.4
Estrogens (with progestogens)	962.2	E858.0	E932.2	E950.4	E962.0	E980.4
Estrone	962.2	E858.0	E932.2	E950.4	E962.0	E980.4
Etafedrine	971.2	E855.5	E941.2	E950.4	E962.0	E980.4
Ethacrynate sodium	974.4	E858.5	E944.4	E950.4	E962.0	E980.4
Ethacrynic acid	974.4	E858.5	E944.4	E950.4	E962.0	E980.4
Ethambutol	961.8	E857	E931.8	E950.4	E962.0	E980.4
Ethamide	974.2	E858.5	E944.2	E950.4	E962.0	E980.4
Ethamivan	970.0	E854.3	E940.0	E950.4	E962.0	E980.4
Ethamsylate	964.5	E858.2	E934.5	E950.4	E962.0	E980.4
Ethanol	980.0	E860.1	—	E950.9	E962.1	E980.9
beverage	980.0	E860.0	—	E950.9	E962.1	E980.9
Ethchlorvynol	967.8	E852.8	E937.8	E950.2	E962.0	E980.2
Ethebenecid	974.7	E858.5	E944.7	E950.4	E962.0	E980.4
Ether(s) (diethyl) (ethyl) (vapor)	987.8	E869.8	—	E952.8	E962.2	E982.8
anesthetic	968.2	E855.1	E938.2	E950.4	E962.0	E980.4
petroleum — see Ligroin						
solvent	982.8	E862.4	—	E950.9	E962.1	E980.9
Ethidine chloride (vapor)	987.8	E869.8	—	E952.8	E962.2	E982.8
liquid (solvent)	982.3	E862.4	—	E950.9	E962.1	E980.9
Ethinamate	967.8	E852.8	E937.8	E950.2	E962.0	E980.2
Ethinylestradiol	962.2	E858.0	E932.2	E950.4	E962.0	E980.4
Ethionamide	961.8	E857	E931.8	E950.4	E962.0	E980.4
Ethisterone	962.2	E858.0	E932.2	E950.4	E962.0	E980.4
Ethobral	967.0	E851	E937.0	E950.1	E962.0	E980.1
Ethocaine (infiltration) (topical)	968.5	E855.2	E938.5	E950.4	E962.0	E980.4
nerve block (peripheral) (plexus)	968.6	E855.2	E938.6	E950.4	E962.0	E980.4
spinal	968.7	E855.2	E938.7	E950.4	E962.0	E980.4
Ethoheptazine (citrate)	965.7	E850.7	E935.7	E950.0	E962.0	E980.0
Ethopropazine	966.4	E855.0	E936.4	E950.4	E962.0	E980.4
Ethosuximide	966.2	E855.0	E936.2	E950.4	E962.0	E980.4
Ethotoin	966.1	E855.0	E936.1	E950.4	E962.0	E980.4
Ethoxazene	961.9	E857	E931.9	E950.4	E962.0	E980.4
Ethoxzolamide	974.2	E858.5	E944.2	E950.4	E962.0	E980.4
Ethyl						
acetate (vapor)	982.8	E862.4	—	E950.9	E962.1	E980.9
alcohol	980.0	E860.1	—	E950.9	E962.1	E980.9
beverage	980.0	E860.0	—	E950.9	E962.1	E980.9
aldehyde (vapor)	987.8	E869.8	—	E952.8	E962.2	E982.8
liquid	989.89	E866.8	—	E950.9	E962.1	E980.9
aminobenzoate	968.5	E855.2	E938.5	E950.4	E962.0	E980.4
biscoumacetate	964.2	E858.2	E934.2	E950.4	E962.0	E980.4
bromide (anesthetic)	968.2	E855.1	E938.2	E950.4	E962.0	E980.4
carbamate (antineoplastic)	963.1	E858.1	E933.1	E950.4	E962.0	E980.4
carbinol	980.3	E860.4	—	E950.9	E962.1	E980.9
chaulmoograte	961.8	E857	E931.8	E950.4	E962.0	E980.4
chloride (vapor)	987.8	E869.8	—	E952.8	E962.2	E982.8
anesthetic (local)	968.5	E855.2	E938.5	E950.4	E962.0	E980.4
inhaled	968.2	E855.1	E938.2	E950.4	E962.0	E980.4
solvent	982.3	E862.4	—	E950.9	E962.1	E980.9
estranol	962.1	E858.0	E932.1	E950.4	E962.0	E980.4
ether — see Ether(s)						
formate (solvent) NEC	982.8	E862.4	—	E950.9	E962.1	E980.9
iodoacetate	987.5	E869.3	—	E952.8	E962.2	E982.8
lactate (solvent) NEC	982.8	E862.4	—	E950.9	E962.1	E980.9
methylcarbinol	980.8	E860.8	—	E950.9	E962.1	E980.9
morphine	965.09	E850.2	E935.2	E950.0	E962.0	E980.0
Ethylene (gas)	987.1	E869.8	—	E952.8	E962.2	E982.8
anesthetic (general)	968.2	E855.1	E938.2	E950.4	E962.0	E980.4

	Poisoning	Accident	Therapeutic Use	Suicide Attempt	Assault	Undetermined
			External Cause (E-Code)			
Ethylene — continued						
chlorohydrin (vapor)	982.3	E862.4	—	E950.9	E962.1	E980.9
dichloride (vapor)	982.3	E862.4	—	E950.9	E962.1	E980.9
glycol(s) (any) (vapor)	982.8	E862.4	—	E950.9	E962.1	E980.9
Ethylidene						
chloride NEC	982.3	E862.4	—	E950.9	E962.1	E980.9
diethyl ether	982.8	E862.4	—	E950.9	E962.1	E980.9
Ethynodiol	962.2	E858.0	E932.2	E950.4	E962.0	E980.4
Etidocaine	968.9	E855.2	E938.9	E950.4	E962.0	E980.4
infiltration (subcutaneous)	968.5	E855.2	E938.5	E950.4	E962.0	E980.4
nerve (peripheral) (plexus)	968.6	E855.2	E938.6	E950.4	E962.0	E980.4
Etilfen	967.0	E851	E937.0	E950.1	E962.0	E980.1
Etomide	965.7	E850.7	E935.7	E950.0	E962.0	E980.0
Etorphine	965.09	E850.2	E935.2	E950.0	E962.0	E980.0
Etoval	967.0	E851	E937.0	E950.1	E962.0	E980.1
Etryptamine	969.01 ▲	E854.0	E939.0	E950.3	E962.0	E980.3
Eucaine	968.5	E855.2	E938.5	E950.4	E962.0	E980.4
Eucalyptus (oil) NEC	975.5	E858.6	E945.5	E950.4	E962.0	E980.4
Eucatropine	971.1	E855.4	E941.1	E950.4	E962.0	E980.4
Eucodal	965.09	E850.2	E935.2	E950.0	E962.0	E980.0
Euneryl	967.0	E851	E937.0	E950.1	E962.0	E980.1
Euphthalmine	971.1	E855.4	E941.1	E950.4	E962.0	E980.4
Eurax	976.0	E858.7	E946.0	E950.4	E962.0	E980.4
Euresol	976.4	E858.7	E946.4	E950.4	E962.0	E980.4
Euthroid	962.7	E858.0	E932.7	E950.4	E962.0	E980.4
Evans blue	977.8	E858.8	E947.8	E950.4	E962.0	E980.4
Evipal	967.0	E851	E937.0	E950.1	E962.0	E980.1
sodium	968.3	E855.1	E938.3	E950.4	E962.0	E980.4
Evipan	967.0	E851	E937.0	E950.1	E962.0	E980.1
sodium	968.3	E855.1	E938.3	E950.4	E962.0	E980.4
Exalgin	965.4	E850.4	E935.4	E950.0	E962.0	E980.0
Excipients, pharmaceutical	977.4	E858.8	E947.4	E950.4	E962.0	E980.4
Exhaust gas — see Carbon, monoxide						
Ex-Lax (phenolphthalein)	973.1	E858.4	E943.1	E950.4	E962.0	E980.4
Expectorants	975.5	E858.6	E945.5	E950.4	E962.0	E980.4
External medications (skin) (mucous membrane)	976.9	E858.7	E946.9	E950.4	E962.0	E980.4
dental agent	976.7	E858.7	E946.7	E950.4	E962.0	E980.4
ENT agent	976.6	E858.7	E946.6	E950.4	E962.0	E980.4
ophthalmic preparation	976.5	E858.7	E946.5	E950.4	E962.0	E980.4
specified NEC	976.8	E858.7	E946.8	E950.4	E962.0	E980.4
Eye agents (anti-infective)	976.5	E858.7	E946.5	E950.4	E962.0	E980.4
Factor IX complex (human)	964.5	E858.2	E934.5	E950.4	E962.0	E980.4
Fecal softeners	973.2	E858.4	E943.2	E950.4	E962.0	E980.4
Fenbutrazate	977.0	E858.8	E947.0	E950.4	E962.0	E980.4
Fencamfamin	970.8	E854.3	E940.8	E950.4	E962.0	E980.4
Fenfluramine	977.0	E858.8	E947.0	E950.4	E962.0	E980.4
Fenoprofen	965.61	E850.6	E935.6	E950.0	E962.0	E980.0
Fentanyl	965.09	E850.2	E935.2	E950.0	E962.0	E980.0
Fentazin	969.1	E853.0	E939.1	E950.3	E962.0	E980.3
Fenticlor, fentichlor	976.0	E858.7	E946.0	E950.4	E962.0	E980.4
Fer de lance (bite) (venom)	989.5	E905.0	—	E950.9	E962.1	E980.9
Ferric — see Iron						
Ferrocholinate	964.0	E858.2	E934.0	E950.4	E962.0	E980.4
Ferrous fumerate, gluconate, lactate, salt NEC, sulfate (medicinal)	964.0	E858.2	E934.0	E950.4	E962.0	E980.4
Ferrum — see Iron						
Fertilizers NEC	989.89	E866.5	—	E950.9	E962.1	E980.4
with herbicide mixture	989.4	E863.5	—	E950.6	E962.1	E980.7
Fibrinogen (human)	964.7	E858.2	E934.7	E950.4	E962.0	E980.4
Fibrinolysin	964.4	E858.2	E934.4	E950.4	E962.0	E980.4
Fibrinolysis-affecting agents	964.4	E858.2	E934.4	E950.4	E962.0	E980.4
Filix mas	961.6	E857	E931.6	E950.4	E962.0	E980.4
Fiorinal	965.1	E850.3	E935.3	E950.0	E962.0	E980.0
Fire damp	987.1	E869.8	—	E952.8	E962.2	E982.8
Fish, nonbacterial or noxious	988.0	E865.2	—	E950.9	E962.1	E980.9
shell	988.0	E865.1	—	E950.9	E962.1	E980.9
Flagyl	961.5	E857	E931.5	E950.4	E962.0	E980.4
Flavoxate	975.1	E858.6	E945.1	E950.4	E962.0	E980.4
Flaxedil	975.2	E858.6	E945.2	E950.4	E962.0	E980.4
Flaxseed (medicinal)	976.3	E858.7	E946.3	E950.4	E962.0	E980.4
Flomax	971.3	E855.6	E941.3	E950.4	E962.0	E980.4
Florantyrone	973.4	E858.4	E943.4	E950.4	E962.0	E980.4
Floraquin	961.3	E857	E931.3	E950.4	E962.0	E980.4
Florinef	962.0	E858.0	E932.0	E950.4	E962.0	E980.4
ENT agent	976.6	E858.7	E946.6	E950.4	E962.0	E980.4

Equisetum — Florinef

Index

Florinef — Gamma globulin

	Poisoning	Accident	Therapeutic Use	Suicide Attempt	Assault	Undetermined
Florinef — continued						
ophthalmic preparation	976.5	E858.7	E946.5	E950.4	E962.0	E980.4
topical NEC	976.0	E858.7	E946.0	E950.4	E962.0	E980.4
Flowers of sulfur	976.4	E858.7	E946.4	E950.4	E962.0	E980.4
Floxuridine	963.1	E858.1	E933.1	E950.4	E962.0	E980.4
Flucytosine	961.9	E857	E931.9	E950.4	E962.0	E980.4
Fludrocortisone	962.0	E858.0	E932.0	E950.4	E962.0	E980.4
ENT agent	976.6	E858.7	E946.6	E950.4	E962.0	E980.4
ophthalmic preparation	976.5	E858.7	E946.5	E950.4	E962.0	E980.4
topical NEC	976.0	E858.7	E946.0	E950.4	E962.0	E980.4
Flumethasone	976.0	E858.7	E946.0	E950.4	E962.0	E980.4
Flumethiazide	974.3	E858.5	E944.3	E950.4	E962.0	E980.4
Flumidin	961.7	E857	E931.7	E950.4	E962.0	E980.4
Flunitrazepam	969.4	E853.2	E939.4	E950.3	E962.0	E980.3
Fluocinolone	976.0	E858.7	E946.0	E950.4	E962.0	E980.4
Fluocortolone	962.0	E858.0	E932.0	E950.4	E962.0	E980.4
Fluohydrocortisone	962.0	E858.0	E932.0	E950.4	E962.0	E980.4
ENT agent	976.6	E858.7	E946.6	E950.4	E962.0	E980.4
ophthalmic preparation	976.5	E858.7	E946.5	E950.4	E962.0	E980.4
topical NEC	976.0	E858.7	E946.0	E950.4	E962.0	E980.4
Fluonid	976.0	E858.7	E946.0	E950.4	E962.0	E980.4
Fluopromazine	969.1	E853.0	E939.1	E950.3	E962.0	E980.3
Fluoracetate	989.4	E863.7	—	E950.6	E962.1	E980.7
Fluorescein (sodium)	977.8	E858.8	E947.8	E950.4	E962.0	E980.4
Fluoride(s) (pesticides) (sodium) NEC	989.4	E863.4		E950.6	E962.1	E980.7
hydrogen — see Hydrofluoric acid						
medicinal	976.7	E858.7	E946.7	E950.4	E962.0	E980.4
not pesticide NEC	983.9	E864.4	—	E950.7	E962.1	E980.6
stannous	976.7	E858.7	E946.7	E950.4	E962.0	E980.4
Fluorinated corticosteroids	962.0	E858.0	E932.0	E950.4	E962.0	E980.4
Fluorine (compounds)						
(gas)	987.8	E869.8	—	E952.8	E962.2	E982.8
salt — see Fluoride(s)						
Fluoristan	976.7	E858.7	E946.7	E950.4	E962.0	E980.4
Fluoroacetate	989.4	E863.7	—	E950.6	E962.1	E980.7
Fluorodeoxyuridine	963.1	E858.1	E933.1	E950.4	E962.0	E980.4
Fluorometholone (topical) NEC	976.0	E858.7	E946.0	E950.4	E962.0	E980.4
ophthalmic preparation	976.5	E858.7	E946.5	E950.4	E962.0	E980.4
Fluorouracil	963.1	E858.1	E933.1	E950.4	E962.0	E980.4
Fluothane	968.1	E855.1	E938.1	E950.4	E962.0	E980.4
Fluoxetine hydrochloride ▲	969.03 ▲	E854.0	E939.0	E950.3	E962.0	E980.3
Fluoxymesterone	962.1	E858.0	E932.1	E950.4	E962.0	E980.4
Fluphenazine	969.1	E853.0	E939.1	E950.3	E962.0	E980.3
Fluprednisolone	962.0	E858.0	E932.0	E950.4	E962.0	E980.4
Flurandrenolide	976.0	E858.7	E946.0	E950.4	E962.0	E980.4
Flurazepam						
(hydrochloride)	969.4	E853.2	E939.4	E950.3	E962.0	E980.3
Flurbiprofen	965.61	E850.6	E935.6	E950.0	E962.0	E980.0
Flurobate	976.0	E858.7	E946.0	E950.4	E962.0	E980.4
Flurothyl	969.8	E855.8	E939.8	E950.3	E962.0	E980.3
Fluroxene	968.2	E855.1	E938.2	E950.4	E962.0	E980.4
Folacin	964.1	E858.2	E934.1	E950.4	E962.0	E980.4
Folic acid	964.1	E858.2	E934.1	E950.4	E962.0	E980.4
Follicle stimulating hormone	962.4	E858.0	E932.4	E950.4	E962.0	E980.4
Food, foodstuffs, nonbacterial or noxious	988.9	E865.9		E950.9	E962.1	E980.9
berries, seeds	988.2	E865.3	—	E950.9	E962.1	E980.9
fish	988.0	E865.2	—	E950.9	E962.1	E980.9
mushrooms	988.1	E865.5	—	E950.9	E962.1	E980.9
plants	988.2	E865.9	—	E950.9	E962.1	E980.9
specified type NEC	988.2	E865.4	—	E950.9	E962.1	E980.9
shellfish	988.0	E865.1	—	E950.9	E962.1	E980.9
specified NEC	988.8	E865.8	—	E950.9	E962.1	E980.9
Fool's parsley	988.2	E865.4	—	E950.9	E962.1	E980.9
Formaldehyde (solution)	989.89	E861.4	—	E950.9	E962.1	E980.9
fungicide	989.4	E863.6	—	E950.6	E962.1	E980.7
gas or vapor	987.8	E869.8	—	E952.8	E962.2	E982.8
Formalin	989.89	E861.4	—	E950.9	E962.1	E980.9
fungicide	989.4	E863.6	—	E950.6	E962.1	E980.7
vapor	987.8	E869.8	—	E952.8	E962.2	E982.8
Formic acid	983.1	E864.1	—	E950.7	E962.1	E980.6
automobile	981	E862.1	—	E950.9	E962.1	E980.9
exhaust gas, not in transit	986	E868.2	—	E952.0	E962.2	E982.0
vapor NEC	987.1	E869.8	—	E952.8	E962.2	E982.8
gas (domestic use) (see also Carbon, monoxide, fuel)						

	Poisoning	Accident	Therapeutic Use	Suicide Attempt	Assault	Undetermined
Formic acid — continued						
gas (see also Carbon, monoxide, fuel) — continued						
utility	987.1	E868.1	—	E951.8	E962.2	E981.8
incomplete combustion of — see Carbon, monoxide, fuel, utility						
in mobile container	987.0	E868.0	—	E951.1	E962.2	E981.1
piped (natural)	987.1	E867	—	E951.0	E962.2	E981.0
industrial, incomplete combustion	986	E868.3	—	E952.1	E962.2	E982.1
vapor	987.8	E869.8	—	E952.8	E962.2	E982.8
Fowler's solution	985.1	E866.3	—	E950.8	E962.1	E980.8
Foxglove	988.2	E865.4	—	E950.9	E962.1	E980.9
Fox green	977.8	E858.8	E947.8	E950.4	E962.0	E980.4
Framycetin	960.8	E856	E930.8	E950.4	E962.0	E980.4
Frangula (extract)	973.1	E858.4	E943.1	E950.4	E962.0	E980.4
Frei antigen	977.8	E858.8	E947.8	E950.4	E962.0	E980.4
Freons	987.4	E869.2	—	E952.8	E962.2	E982.8
Fructose	974.5	E858.5	E944.5	E950.4	E962.0	E980.4
Frusemide	974.4	E858.5	E944.4	E950.4	E962.0	E980.4
FSH	962.4	E858.0	E932.4	E950.4	E962.0	E980.4
Fuel						
Fugillin	960.8	E856	E930.8	E950.4	E962.0	E980.4
Fulminate of mercury	985.0	E866.1	—	E950.9	E962.1	E980.9
Fulvicin	960.1	E856	E930.1	E950.4	E962.0	E980.4
Fumadil	960.8	E856	E930.8	E950.4	E962.0	E980.4
Fumagillin	960.8	E856	E930.8	E950.4	E962.0	E980.4
Fumes (from)	987.9	E869.9	—	E952.9	E962.2	E982.9
carbon monoxide — see Carbon, monoxide						
charcoal (domestic use)	986	E868.3	—	E952.1	E962.2	E982.1
chloroform — see Chloroform						
coke (in domestic stoves, fireplaces)	986	E868.3	—	E952.1	E962.2	E982.1
corrosive NEC	987.8	E869.8	—	E952.8	E962.2	E982.8
ether — see Ether(s)						
freons	987.4	E869.2	—	E952.8	E962.2	E982.8
hydrocarbons	987.1	E869.8	—	E952.8	E962.2	E982.8
petroleum (liquefied)	987.0	E868.0	—	E951.1	E962.2	E981.1
distributed through pipes (pure or mixed with air)	987.0	E867	—	E951.0	E962.2	E981.0
lead — see Lead						
metals — see specified metal						
nitrogen dioxide	987.2	E869.0	—	E952.8	E962.2	E982.8
pesticides — see Pesticides						
petroleum (liquefied)	987.0	E868.0	—	E951.1	E962.2	E981.1
distributed through pipes (pure or mixed with air)	987.0	E867	—	E951.0	E962.2	E981.0
polyester	987.8	E869.8	—	E952.8	E962.2	E982.8
specified, source other (see also substance specified)	987.8	E869.8	—	E952.8	E962.2	E982.8
sulfur dioxide	987.3	E869.1	—	E952.8	E962.2	E982.8
Fumigants	989.4	E863.8	—	E950.6	E962.1	E980.7
Fungicides — see also Antifungals	989.4	E863.6	—	E950.6	E962.1	E980.7
Fungi, noxious, used as food	988.1	E865.5	—	E950.9	E962.1	E980.9
Fungizone	960.1	E856	E930.1	E950.4	E962.0	E980.4
topical	976.0	E858.7	E946.0	E950.4	E962.0	E980.4
Furacin	976.0	E858.7	E946.0	E950.4	E962.0	E980.4
Furadantin	961.9	E857	E931.9	E950.4	E962.0	E980.4
Furazolidone	961.9	E857	E931.9	E950.4	E962.0	E980.4
Furnace (coal burning)						
(domestic), gas from	986	E868.3	—	E952.1	E962.2	E982.1
industrial	986	E868.8	—	E952.1	E962.2	E982.1
Furniture polish	989.89	E861.2	—	E950.9	E962.1	E980.9
Furosemide	974.4	E858.5	E944.4	E950.4	E962.0	E980.4
Furoxone	961.9	E857	E931.9	E950.4	E962.0	E980.4
Fusel oil (amyl) (butyl) (propyl)	980.3	E860.4	—	E950.9	E962.1	E980.9
Fusidic acid	960.8	E856	E930.8	E950.4	E962.0	E980.4
Gallamine	975.2	E858.6	E945.2	E950.4	E962.0	E980.4
Gallotannic acid	976.2	E858.7	E946.2	E950.4	E962.0	E980.4
Gamboge	973.1	E858.4	E943.1	E950.4	E962.0	E980.4
Gamimune	964.6	E858.2	E934.6	E950.4	E962.0	E980.4
Gamma-benzene hexachloride (vapor)	989.2	E863.0	—	E950.6	E962.1	E980.7
Gamma globulin	964.6	E858.2	E934.6	E950.4	E962.0	E980.4

Nontherapeutic use substance

⊽ Subterms under main terms may continue to next column or page

▶◀ Revised Text   ● New Line   ▲ Revised Code

2010 ICD-9-CM

	Poisoning	Accident	Therapeutic Use	Suicide Attempt	Assault	Undetermined
Gamma hydroxy butyrate						
(GHB)	968.4	E855.1	E938.4	E950.4	E962.0	E980.4
Gamulin	964.6	E858.2	E934.6	E950.4	E962.0	E980.4
Ganglionic blocking						
agents	972.3	E858.3	E942.3	E950.4	E962.0	E980.4
Ganja	969.6	E854.1	E939.6	E950.3	E962.0	E980.3
Garamycin	960.8	E856	E930.8	E950.4	E962.0	E980.4
ophthalmic preparation	976.5	E858.7	E946.5	E950.4	E962.0	E980.4
topical NEC	976.0	E858.7	E946.0	E950.4	E962.0	E980.4
Gardenal	967.0	E851	E937.0	E950.1	E962.0	E980.1
Gardepanyl	967.0	E851	E937.0	E950.1	E962.0	E980.1
Gas	987.9	E869.9	—	E952.9	E962.2	E982.9
acetylene	987.1	E868.1	—	E951.8	E962.2	E981.8
incomplete combustion of — see Carbon, monoxide, fuel, utility						
air contaminants, source or type not specified	987.9	E869.9	—	E952.9	E962.2	E982.9
anesthetic (general) NEC	968.2	E855.1	E938.2	E950.4	E962.0	E980.4
blast furnace	986	E868.8	—	E952.1	E962.2	E982.1
butane — see Butane						
carbon monoxide — see Carbon, monoxide						
chlorine	987.6	E869.8	—	E952.8	E962.2	E982.8
coal — see Carbon, monoxide, coal						
cyanide	987.7	E869.8	—	E952.8	E962.2	E982.8
dicyanogen	987.8	E869.8	—	E952.8	E962.2	E982.8
domestic — see Gas, utility						
exhaust — see Carbon, monoxide, exhaust gas						
from wood- or coal-burning stove or fireplace	986	E868.3	—	E952.1	E962.2	E982.1
fuel (domestic use) (see also Carbon, monoxide, fuel)						
industrial use	986	E868.8	—	E952.1	E962.2	E982.1
utility	987.1	E868.1	—	E951.8	E962.2	E981.8
incomplete combustion of — see Carbon, monoxide, fuel, utility						
in mobile container	987.0	E868.0	—	E951.1	E962.2	E981.1
piped (natural)	987.1	E867	—	E951.0	E962.2	E981.0
garage	986	E868.2	—	E952.0	E962.2	E982.0
hydrocarbon NEC	987.1	E869.9	—	E952.8	E962.2	E982.8
incomplete combustion of — see Carbon, monoxide, fuel, utility						
liquefied (mobile container)	987.0	E868.0	—	E951.1	E962.2	E981.1
piped	987.0	E867	—	E951.0	E962.2	E981.0
hydrocyanic acid	987.7	E869.8	—	E952.8	E962.2	E982.8
illuminating — see Gas, utility						
incomplete combustion, any — see Carbon, monoxide						
kiln	986	E868.8	—	E952.1	E962.2	E982.1
lacrimogenic	987.5	E869.3	—	E952.8	E962.2	E982.8
marsh	987.1	E869.8	—	E952.8	E962.2	E982.8
motor exhaust, not in transit	986	E868.8	—	E952.1	E962.2	E982.1
mustard — see Mustard, gas						
natural	987.1	E867	—	E951.0	E962.2	E981.0
nerve (war)	987.9	E869.9	—	E952.9	E962.2	E982.9
oils	981	E862.1	—	E950.9	E962.1	E980.9
petroleum (liquefied) (distributed in mobile containers)	987.0	E868.0	—	E951.1	E962.2	E981.1
piped (pure or mixed with air)	987.0	E867	—	E951.1	E962.2	E981.1
piped (manufactured) (natural) NEC	987.1	E867	—	E951.0	E962.2	E981.0
producer	986	E868.8	—	E952.1	E962.2	E982.1
propane — see Propane						
refrigerant (freon)	987.4	E869.2	—	E952.8	E962.2	E982.8
not freon	987.9	E869.9	—	E952.9	E962.2	E982.9
sewer	987.8	E869.8	—	E952.8	E962.2	E982.8
specified source NEC (see also substance specified)	987.8	E869.8	—	E952.8	E962.2	E982.8
stove — see Gas, utility						
tear	987.5	E869.3	—	E952.8	E962.2	E982.8
utility (for cooking, heating, or lighting) (piped) NEC	987.1	E868.1	—	E951.8	E962.2	E981.8

	Poisoning	Accident	Therapeutic Use	Suicide Attempt	Assault	Undetermined
Gas — continued						
utility — continued						
incomplete combustion of — see Carbon, monoxide, fuel, utilty						
in mobile container	987.0	E868.0	—	E951.1	E962.2	E981.1
piped (natural)	987.1	E867	—	E951.0	E962.2	E981.0
water	987.1	E868.1	—	E951.8	E962.2	E981.8
incomplete combustion of — see Carbon, monoxide, fuel, utility						
Gaseous substance — see Gas						
Gasoline, gasolene	981	E862.1	—	E950.9	E962.1	E980.9
vapor	987.1	E869.8	—	E952.8	E962.2	E982.8
Gastric enzymes	973.4	E858.4	E943.4	E950.4	E962.0	E980.4
Gastrografin	977.8	E858.8	E947.8	E950.4	E962.0	E980.4
Gastrointestinal agents	973.9	E858.4	E943.9	E950.4	E962.0	E980.4
specified NEC	973.8	E858.4	E943.8	E950.4	E962.0	E980.4
Gaultheria procumbens	988.2	E865.4	—	E950.9	E962.1	E980.9
Gelatin (intravenous)	964.8	E858.2	E934.8	E950.4	E962.0	E980.4
absorbable (sponge)	964.5	E858.2	E934.5	E950.4	E962.0	E980.4
Gelfilm	976.8	E858.7	E946.8	E950.4	E962.0	E980.4
Gelfoam	964.5	E858.2	E934.5	E950.4	E962.0	E980.4
Gelsemine	970.8	E854.3	E940.8	E950.4	E962.0	E980.4
Gelsemium (sempervirens)	988.2	E865.4	—	E950.9	E962.1	E980.9
Gemonil	967.0	E851	E937.0	E950.1	E962.0	E980.1
Gentamicin	960.8	E856	E930.8	E950.4	E962.0	E980.4
ophthalmic preparation	976.5	E858.7	E946.5	E950.4	E962.0	E980.4
topical NEC	976.0	E858.7	E946.0	E950.4	E962.0	E980.4
Gentian violet	976.0	E858.7	E946.0	E950.4	E962.0	E980.4
Gexane	976.0	E858.7	E946.0	E950.4	E962.0	E980.4
Gila monster (venom)	989.5	E905.0	—	E950.9	E962.1	E980.9
Ginger, Jamaica	989.89	E866.8	—	E950.9	E962.1	E980.9
Gitalin	972.1	E858.3	E942.1	E950.4	E962.0	E980.4
Gitoxin	972.1	E858.3	E942.1	E950.4	E962.0	E980.4
Glandular extract (medicinal)						
NEC	977.9	E858.9	E947.9	E950.5	E962.0	E980.5
Glaucarubin	961.5	E857	E931.5	E950.4	E962.0	E980.4
Globin zinc insulin	962.3	E858.0	E932.3	E950.4	E962.0	E980.4
Glucagon	962.3	E858.0	E932.3	E950.4	E962.0	E980.4
Glucochloral	967.1	E852.0	E937.1	E950.2	E962.0	E980.2
Glucocorticoids	962.0	E858.0	E932.0	E950.4	E962.0	E980.4
Glucose	974.5	E858.5	E944.5	E950.4	E962.0	E980.4
oxidase reagent	977.8	E858.8	E947.8	E950.4	E962.0	E980.4
Glucosulfone sodium	961.8	E857	E931.8	E950.4	E962.0	E980.4
Glue(s)	989.89	E866.6	—	E950.9	E962.1	E980.9
Glutamic acid						
(hydrochloride)	973.4	E858.4	E943.4	E950.4	E962.0	E980.4
Glutaraldehyde	989.89	E861.4	—	E950.9	E962.1	E980.9
Glutathione	963.8	E858.1	E933.8	E950.4	E962.0	E980.4
Glutethimide (group)	967.5	E852.4	E937.5	E950.2	E962.0	E980.2
Glycerin (lotion)	976.3	E858.7	E946.3	E950.4	E962.0	E980.4
Glycerol (topical)	976.3	E858.7	E946.3	E950.4	E962.0	E980.4
Glyceryl						
guaiacolate	975.5	E858.6	E945.5	E950.4	E962.0	E980.4
triacetate (topical)	976.0	E858.7	E946.0	E950.4	E962.0	E980.4
trinitrate	972.4	E858.3	E942.4	E950.4	E962.0	E980.4
Glycine	974.5	E858.5	E944.5	E950.4	E962.0	E980.4
Glycobiarsol	961.1	E857	E931.1	E950.4	E962.0	E980.4
Glycols (ether)	982.8	E862.4	—	E950.9	E962.1	E980.9
Glycopyrrolate	971.1	E855.4	E941.1	E950.4	E962.0	E980.4
Glymidine	962.3	E858.0	E932.3	E950.4	E962.0	E980.4
Gold (compounds) (salts)	965.69	E850.6	E935.6	E950.0	E962.0	E980.0
Golden sulfide of						
antimony	985.4	E866.2	—	E950.9	E962.1	E980.9
Goldylocks	988.2	E865.4	—	E950.9	E962.1	E980.9
Gonadal tissue extract	962.9	E858.0	E932.9	E950.4	E962.0	E980.4
beverage	980.0	E860.0	—	E950.9	E962.1	E980.9
female	962.2	E858.0	E932.2	E950.4	E962.0	E980.4
male	962.1	E858.0	E932.1	E950.4	E962.0	E980.4
Gonadotropin	962.4	E858.0	E932.4	E950.4	E962.0	E980.4
Grain alcohol	980.0	E860.1	—	E950.9	E962.1	E980.9
Gramicidin	960.8	E856	E930.8	E950.4	E962.0	E980.4
Gratiola officinalis	988.2	E865.4	—	E950.9	E962.1	E980.9
Grease	989.89	E866.8	—	E950.9	E962.1	E980.9
Green hellebore	988.2	E865.4	—	E950.9	E962.1	E980.9
Green soap	976.2	E858.7	E946.2	E950.4	E962.0	E980.4
Grifulvin	960.1	E856	E930.1	E950.4	E962.0	E980.4
Griseofulvin	960.1	E856	E930.1	E950.4	E962.0	E980.4
Growth hormone	962.4	E858.0	E932.4	E950.4	E962.0	E980.4
Guaiacol	975.5	E858.6	E945.5	E950.4	E962.0	E980.4
Guaiac reagent	977.8	E858.8	E947.8	E950.4	E962.0	E980.4

		External Cause (E-Code)			
	Poisoning	Accident	Therapeutic Use	Suicide Attempt	Assault	Undetermined

Substance	Poisoning	Accident	Therapeutic Use	Suicide Attempt	Assault	Undetermined
Guaifenesin	975.5	E858.6	E945.5	E950.4	E962.0	E980.4
Guaiphenesin	975.5	E858.6	E945.5	E950.4	E962.0	E980.4
Guanatol	961.4	E857	E931.4	E950.4	E962.0	E980.4
Guanethidine	972.6	E858.3	E942.6	E950.4	E962.0	E980.4
Guano	989.89	E866.5	—	E950.9	E962.1	E980.9
Guanochlor	972.6	E858.3	E942.6	E950.4	E962.0	E980.4
Guanoctine	972.6	E858.3	E942.6	E950.4	E962.0	E980.4
Guanoxan	972.6	E858.3	E942.6	E950.4	E962.0	E980.4
Hair treatment agent NEC	976.4	E858.7	E946.4	E950.4	E962.0	E980.4
Halcinonide	976.0	E858.7	E946.0	E950.4	E962.0	E980.4
Halethazole	976.0	E858.7	E946.0	E950.4	E962.0	E980.4
Hallucinogens	969.6	E854.1	E939.6	E950.3	E962.0	E980.3
Haloperidol	969.2	E853.1	E939.2	E950.3	E962.0	E980.3
Haloprogin	976.0	E858.7	E946.0	E950.4	E962.0	E980.4
Halotex	976.0	E858.7	E946.0	E950.4	E962.0	E980.4
Halothane	968.1	E855.1	E938.1	E950.4	E962.0	E980.4
Halquinols	976.0	E858.7	E946.0	E950.4	E962.0	E980.4
Hand sanitizer	976.0	E858.7	E946.0	E950.4	E962.0	E980.4
Harmonyl	972.6	E858.3	E942.6	E950.4	E962.0	E980.4
Hartmann's solution	974.5	E858.5	E944.5	E950.4	E962.0	E980.4
Hashish	969.6	E854.1	E939.6	E950.3	E962.0	E980.3
Hawaiian wood rose seeds	969.6	E854.1	E939.6	E950.3	E962.0	E980.3
Headache cures, drugs, powders NEC	977.9	E858.9	E947.9	E950.5	E962.0	E980.9
Heavenly Blue (morning glory)	969.6	E854.1	E939.6	E950.3	E962.0	E980.3
Heavy metal antagonists	963.8	E858.1	E933.8	E950.4	E962.0	E980.4
anti-infectives	961.2	E857	E931.2	E950.4	E962.0	E980.4
Hedaquinium	976.0	E858.7	E946.0	E950.4	E962.0	E980.4
Hedge hyssop	988.2	E865.4	—	E950.9	E962.1	E980.9
Heet	976.8	E858.7	E946.8	E950.4	E962.0	E980.4
Helenin	961.6	E857	E931.6	E950.4	E962.0	E980.4
Hellebore (black) (green) (white)	988.2	E865.4	—	E950.9	E962.1	E980.9
Hemlock	988.2	E865.4	—	E950.9	E962.1	E980.9
Hemostatics	964.5	E858.2	E934.5	E950.4	E962.0	E980.4
capillary active drugs	972.8	E858.3	E942.8	E950.4	E962.0	E980.4
Henbane	988.2	E865.4	—	E950.9	E962.1	E980.9
Heparin (sodium)	964.2	E858.2	E934.2	E950.4	E962.0	E980.4
Heptabarbital, heptabarbitone	967.0	E851	E937.0	E950.1	E962.0	E980.1
Heptachlor	989.2	E863.0	—	E950.6	E962.1	E980.7
Heptalgin	965.09	E850.2	E935.2	E950.0	E962.0	E980.0
Herbicides	989.4	E863.5	—	E950.6	E962.1	E980.7
Heroin	965.01	E850.0	E935.0	E950.0	E962.0	E980.0
Herplex	976.5	E858.7	E946.5	E950.4	E962.0	E980.4
HES	964.8	E858.2	E934.8	E950.4	E962.0	E980.4
Hetastarch	964.8	E858.2	E934.8	E950.4	E962.0	E980.4
Hexachlorocyclohexane	989.2	E863.0	—	E950.6	E962.1	E980.7
Hexachlorophene	976.2	E858.7	E946.2	E950.4	E962.0	E980.4
Hexadimethrine (bromide)	964.5	E858.2	E934.5	E950.4	E962.0	E980.4
Hexafluorenium	975.2	E858.6	E945.2	E950.4	E962.0	E980.4
Hexa-germ	976.2	E858.7	E946.2	E950.4	E962.0	E980.4
Hexahydrophenol	980.8	E860.8	—	E950.9	E962.1	E980.9
Hexalin	980.8	E860.8	—	E950.9	E962.1	E980.9
Hexamethonium	972.3	E858.3	E942.3	E950.4	E962.0	E980.4
Hexamethyleneamine	961.9	E857	E931.9	E950.4	E962.0	E980.4
Hexamine	961.9	E857	E931.9	E950.4	E962.0	E980.4
Hexanone	982.8	E862.4	—	E950.9	E962.1	E980.9
Hexapropymate	967.8	E852.8	E937.8	E950.2	E962.0	E980.2
Hexestrol	962.2	E858.0	E932.2	E950.4	E962.0	E980.4
Hexethal (sodium)	967.0	E851	E937.0	E950.1	E962.0	E980.1
Hexetidine	976.0	E858.7	E946.0	E950.4	E962.0	E980.4
Hexobarbital, hexobarbitone	967.0	E851	E937.0	E950.1	E962.0	E980.1
sodium (anesthetic)	968.3	E855.1	E938.3	E950.4	E962.0	E980.4
soluble	968.3	E855.1	E938.3	E950.4	E962.0	E980.4
Hexocyclium	971.1	E855.4	E941.1	E950.4	E962.0	E980.4
Hexoestrol	962.2	E858.0	E932.2	E950.4	E962.0	E980.4
Hexone	982.8	E862.4	—	E950.9	E962.1	E980.9
Hexylcaine	968.5	E855.2	E938.5	E950.4	E962.0	E980.4
Hexylresorcinol	961.6	E857	E931.6	E950.4	E962.0	E980.4
Hinkle's pills	973.1	E858.4	E943.1	E950.4	E962.0	E980.4
Histalog	977.8	E858.8	E947.8	E950.4	E962.0	E980.4
Histamine (phosphate)	972.5	E858.3	E942.5	E950.4	E962.0	E980.4
Histoplasmin	977.8	E858.8	E947.8	E950.4	E962.0	E980.4
Holly berries	988.2	E865.3	—	E950.9	E962.1	E980.9
Homatropine	971.1	E855.4	E941.1	E950.4	E962.0	E980.4
Homo-tet	964.6	E858.2	E934.6	E950.4	E962.0	E980.4
Hormones (synthetic substitute)						
NEC	962.9	E858.0	E932.9	E950.4	E962.0	E980.4
adrenal cortical steroids	962.0	E858.0	E932.0	E950.4	E962.0	E980.4
antidiabetic agents	962.3	E858.0	E932.3	E950.4	E962.0	E980.4
follicle stimulating	962.4	E858.0	E932.4	E950.4	E962.0	E980.4
gonadotropic	962.4	E858.0	E932.4	E950.4	E962.0	E980.4
growth	962.4	E858.0	E932.4	E950.4	E962.0	E980.4
ovarian (substitutes)	962.2	E858.0	E932.2	E950.4	E962.0	E980.4
parathyroid (derivatives)	962.6	E858.0	E932.6	E950.4	E962.0	E980.4
pituitary (posterior)	962.5	E858.0	E932.5	E950.4	E962.0	E980.4
anterior	962.4	E858.0	E932.4	E950.4	E962.0	E980.4
thyroid (derivative)	962.7	E858.0	E932.7	E950.4	E962.0	E980.4
Hornet (sting)	989.5	E905.3	—	E950.9	E962.1	E980.9
Horticulture agent NEC	989.4	E863.9	—	E950.6	E962.1	E980.7
Hyaluronidase	963.4	E858.1	E933.4	E950.4	E962.0	E980.4
Hyazyme	963.4	E858.1	E933.4	E950.4	E962.0	E980.4
Hycodan	965.09	E850.2	E935.2	E950.0	E962.0	E980.0
Hydantoin derivatives	966.1	E855.0	E936.1	E950.4	E962.0	E980.4
Hydeltra	962.0	E858.0	E932.0	E950.4	E962.0	E980.4
Hydergine	971.3	E855.6	E941.3	E950.4	E962.0	E980.4
Hydrabamine penicillin	960.0	E856	E930.0	E950.4	E962.0	E980.4
Hydralazine, hydrallazine	972.6	E858.3	E942.6	E950.4	E962.0	E980.4
Hydrargaphen	976.0	E858.7	E946.0	E950.4	E962.0	E980.4
Hydrazine	983.9	E864.3	—	E950.7	E962.1	E980.6
Hydriodic acid	975.5	E858.6	E945.5	E950.4	E962.0	E980.4
Hydrocarbon gas	987.1	E869.8	—	E952.8	E962.2	E982.8
incomplete combustion of — see Carbon, monoxide, fuel, utility						
liquefied (mobile container)	987.0	E868.0	—	E951.1	E962.2	E981.1
piped (natural)	987.0	E867	—	E951.0	E962.2	E981.0
Hydrochloric acid (liquid)	983.1	E864.1	—	E950.7	E962.1	E980.6
medicinal	973.4	E858.4	E943.4	E950.4	E962.0	E980.4
vapor	987.8	E869.8	—	E952.8	E962.2	E982.8
Hydrochlorothiazide	974.3	E858.5	E944.3	E950.4	E962.0	E980.4
Hydrocodone	965.09	E850.2	E935.2	E950.0	E962.0	E980.0
Hydrocortisone	962.0	E858.0	E932.0	E950.4	E962.0	E980.4
ENT agent	976.6	E858.7	E946.6	E950.4	E962.0	E980.4
ophthalmic preparation	976.5	E858.7	E946.5	E950.4	E962.0	E980.4
topical NEC	976.0	E858.7	E946.0	E950.4	E962.0	E980.4
Hydrocortone	962.0	E858.0	E932.0	E950.4	E962.0	E980.4
ENT agent	976.6	E858.7	E946.6	E950.4	E962.0	E980.4
ophthalmic preparation	976.5	E858.7	E946.5	E950.4	E962.0	E980.4
topical NEC	976.0	E858.7	E946.0	E950.4	E962.0	E980.4
Hydrocyanic acid — see Cyanide(s)						
Hydroflumethiazide	974.3	E858.5	E944.3	E950.4	E962.0	E980.4
Hydrofluoric acid (liquid)	983.1	E864.1	—	E950.7	E962.1	E980.6
vapor	987.8	E869.8	—	E952.8	E962.2	E982.8
Hydrogen	987.8	E869.8	—	E952.8	E962.2	E982.8
arsenide	985.1	E866.3	—	E950.8	E962.1	E980.8
arseniureted	985.1	E866.3	—	E950.8	E962.1	E980.8
cyanide (salts)	989.0	E866.8	—	E950.9	E962.1	E980.9
gas	987.7	E869.8	—	E952.8	E962.2	E982.8
fluoride (liquid)	983.1	E864.1	—	E950.7	E962.1	E980.6
vapor	987.8	E869.8	—	E952.8	E962.2	E982.8
peroxide (solution)	976.6	E858.7	E946.6	E950.4	E962.0	E980.4
phosphureted	987.8	E869.8	—	E952.8	E962.2	E982.8
sulfide (gas)	987.8	E869.8	—	E952.8	E962.2	E982.8
arseniureted	985.1	E866.3	—	E950.8	E962.1	E980.8
sulfureted	987.8	E869.8	—	E952.8	E962.2	E982.8
Hydromorphinol	965.09	E850.2	E935.2	E950.0	E962.0	E980.0
Hydromorphinone	965.09	E850.2	E935.2	E950.0	E962.0	E980.0
Hydromorphone	965.09	E850.2	E935.2	E950.0	E962.0	E980.0
Hydromox	974.3	E858.5	E944.3	E950.4	E962.0	E980.4
Hydrophilic lotion	976.3	E858.7	E946.3	E950.4	E962.0	E980.4
Hydroquinone	983.0	E864.0	—	E950.7	E962.1	E980.6
vapor	987.8	E869.8	—	E952.8	E962.2	E982.8
Hydrosulfuric acid (gas)	987.8	E869.8	—	E952.8	E962.2	E982.8
Hydrous wool fat (lotion)	976.3	E858.7	E946.3	E950.4	E962.0	E980.4
Hydroxide, caustic	983.2	E864.2	—	E950.7	E962.1	E980.6
Hydroxocobalamin	964.1	E858.2	E934.1	E950.4	E962.0	E980.4
Hydroxyamphetamine	971.2	E855.5	E941.2	E950.4	E962.0	E980.4
Hydroxychloroquine	961.4	E857	E931.4	E950.4	E962.0	E980.4
Hydroxydihydrocodeinone	965.09	E850.2	E935.2	E950.0	E962.0	E980.0
Hydroxyethyl starch	964.8	E858.2	E934.8	E950.4	E962.0	E980.4
Hydroxyphenamate	969.5	E853.8	E939.5	E950.3	E962.0	E980.3
Hydroxyphenylbutazone	965.5	E850.5	E935.5	E950.0	E962.0	E980.0
Hydroxyprogesterone	962.2	E858.0	E932.2	E950.4	E962.0	E980.4
Hydroxyquinoline derivatives	961.3	E857	E931.3	E950.4	E962.0	E980.4

Nontherapeutic use substance

Subterms under main terms may continue to next column or page

►◄ Revised Text   ● New Line   ▲ Revised Code

	Poisoning	Accident	Therapeutic Use	Suicide Attempt	Assault	Undetermined
Hydroxystilbamidine	961.5	E857	E931.5	E950.4	E962.0	E980.4
Hydroxyurea	963.1	E858.1	E933.1	E950.4	E962.0	E980.4
Hydroxyzine	969.5	E853.8	E939.5	E950.3	E962.0	E980.3
Hyoscine (hydrobromide)	971.1	E855.4	E941.1	E950.4	E962.0	E980.4
Hyoscyamine	971.1	E855.4	E941.1	E950.4	E962.0	E980.4
Hyoscyamus (albus)						
(niger)	988.2	E865.4	—	E950.9	E962.1	E980.9
Hypaque	977.8	E858.8	E947.8	E950.4	E962.0	E980.4
Hypertussis	964.6	E858.2	E934.6	E950.4	E962.0	E980.4
Hypnotics NEC	967.9	E852.9	E937.9	E950.2	E962.0	E980.2
Hypochlorites — see Sodium, hypochlorite						
Hypotensive agents NEC	972.6	E858.3	E942.6	E950.4	E962.0	E980.4
Ibufenac	965.69	E850.6	E935.6	E950.0	E962.0	E980.0
Ibuprofen	965.61	E850.6	E935.6	E950.0	E962.0	E980.0
ICG	977.8	E858.8	E947.8	E950.4	E962.0	E980.4
Ichthammol	976.4	E858.7	E946.4	E950.4	E962.0	E980.4
Ichthyol	976.4	E858.7	E946.4	E950.4	E962.0	E980.4
Idoxuridine	976.5	E858.7	E946.5	E950.4	E962.0	E980.4
IDU	976.5	E858.7	E946.5	E950.4	E962.0	E980.4
Iletin	962.3	E858.0	E932.3	E950.4	E962.0	E980.4
Ilex	988.2	E865.4	—	E950.9	E962.1	E980.9
Illuminating gas — see Gas, utility						
Ilopan	963.5	E858.1	E933.5	E950.4	E962.0	E980.4
Ilotycin	960.3	E856	E930.3	E950.4	E962.0	E980.4
ophthalmic preparation	976.5	E858.7	E946.5	E950.4	E962.0	E980.4
topical NEC	976.0	E858.7	E946.0	E950.4	E962.0	E980.4
Imipramine	969.05 ▲	E854.0	E939.0	E950.3	E962.0	E980.3
Immu-G	964.6	E858.2	E934.6	E950.4	E962.0	E980.4
Immuglobin	964.6	E858.2	E934.6	E950.4	E962.0	E980.4
Immune serum globulin	964.6	E858.2	E934.6	E950.4	E962.0	E980.4
Immunosuppressive agents	963.1	E858.1	E933.1	E950.4	E962.0	E980.4
Immu-tetanus	964.6	E858.2	E934.6	E950.4	E962.0	E980.4
Indandione (derivatives)	964.2	E858.2	E934.2	E950.4	E962.0	E980.4
Inderal	972.0	E858.3	E942.0	E950.4	E962.0	E980.4
Indian						
hemp	969.6	E854.1	E939.6	E950.3	E962.0	E980.3
tobacco	988.2	E865.4	—	E950.9	E962.1	E980.9
Indigo carmine	977.8	E858.8	E947.8	E950.4	E962.0	E980.4
Indocin	965.69	E850.6	E935.6	E950.0	E962.0	E980.0
Indocyanine green	977.8	E858.8	E947.8	E950.4	E962.0	E980.4
Indomethacin	965.69	E850.6	E935.6	E950.0	E962.0	E980.0
Industrial						
alcohol	980.9	E860.9	—	E950.9	E962.1	E980.9
fumes	987.8	E869.8	—	E952.8	E962.2	E982.8
solvents (fumes) (vapors)	982.8	E862.9	—	E950.9	E962.1	E980.9
Influenza vaccine	979.6	E858.8	E949.6	E950.4	E962.0	E982.8
Ingested substances NEC	989.9	E866.9	—	E950.9	E962.1	E980.9
INH (isoniazid)	961.8	E857	E931.8	E950.4	E962.0	E980.4
Inhalation, gas (noxious) — see Gas						
Ink	989.89	E866.8	—	E950.9	E962.1	E980.9
Innovar	967.6	E852.5	E937.6	E950.2	E962.0	E980.2
Inositol niacinate	972.2	E858.3	E942.2	E950.4	E962.0	E980.4
Inproquone	963.1	E858.1	E933.1	E950.4	E962.0	E980.4
Insecticides — see also						
Pesticides	989.4	E863.4	—	E950.6	E962.1	E980.7
chlorinated	989.2	E863.0	—	E950.6	E962.1	E980.7
mixtures	989.4	E863.3	—	E950.6	E962.1	E980.7
organochlorine (compounds)	989.2	E863.0	—	E950.6	E962.1	E980.7
organophosphorus (compounds)	989.3	E863.1	—	E950.6	E962.1	E980.7
Insect (sting), venomous	989.5	E905.5	—	E950.9	E962.1	E980.9
Insular tissue extract	962.3	E858.0	E932.3	E950.4	E962.0	E980.4
Insulin (amorphous) (globin) (isophane) (Lente) (NPH) (protamine) (Semilente) (Ultralente) (zinc)	962.3	E858.0	E932.3	E950.4	E962.0	E980.4
Intranarcon	968.3	E855.1	E938.3	E950.4	E962.0	E980.4
Inulin	977.8	E858.8	E947.8	E950.4	E962.0	E980.4
Invert sugar	974.5	E858.5	E944.5	E950.4	E962.0	E980.4
Inza — see Naproxen						
Iodide NEC — see also						
iodine	976.0	E858.7	E946.0	E950.4	E962.0	E980.4
mercury (ointment)	976.0	E858.7	E946.0	E950.4	E962.0	E980.4
methylate	976.0	E858.7	E946.0	E950.4	E962.0	E980.4
potassium (expectorant) NEC	975.5	E858.6	E945.5	E950.4	E962.0	E980.4
Iodinated glycerol	975.5	E858.6	E945.5	E950.4	E962.0	E980.4

	Poisoning	Accident	Therapeutic Use	Suicide Attempt	Assault	Undetermined
Iodine (antiseptic, external) (tincture) NEC	976.0	E858.7	E946.0	E950.4	E962.0	E980.4
diagnostic	977.8	E858.8	E947.8	E950.4	E962.0	E980.4
for thyroid conditions (antithyroid)	962.8	E858.0	E932.8	E950.4	E962.0	E980.4
vapor	987.8	E869.8	—	E952.8	E962.2	E982.8
Iodized oil	977.8	E858.8	E947.8	E950.4	E962.0	E980.4
Iodobismitol	961.2	E857	E931.2	E950.4	E962.0	E980.4
Iodochlorhydroxyquin	961.3	E857	E931.3	E950.4	E962.0	E980.4
topical	976.0	E858.7	E946.0	E950.4	E962.0	E980.4
Iodoform	976.0	E858.7	E946.0	E950.4	E962.0	E980.4
Iodopanoic acid	977.8	E858.8	E947.8	E950.4	E962.0	E980.4
Iodophthalein	977.8	E858.8	E947.8	E950.4	E962.0	E980.4
Ion exchange resins	974.5	E858.5	E944.5	E950.4	E962.0	E980.4
Iopanoic acid	977.8	E858.8	E947.8	E950.4	E962.0	E980.4
Iophendylate	977.8	E858.8	E947.8	E950.4	E962.0	E980.4
Iothiouracil	962.8	E858.0	E932.8	E950.4	E962.0	E980.4
Ipecac	973.6	E858.4	E943.6	E950.4	E962.0	E980.4
Ipecacuanha	973.6	E858.4	E943.6	E950.4	E962.0	E980.4
Ipodate	977.8	E858.8	E947.8	E950.4	E962.0	E980.4
Ipral	967.0	E851	E937.0	E950.1	E962.0	E980.1
Ipratropium	975.1	E858.6	E945.1	E950.4	E962.0	E980.4
Iproniazid	969.01 ▲	E854.0	E939.0	E950.3	E962.0	E980.3
Iron (compounds) (medicinal) (preparations)	964.0	E858.2	E934.0	E950.4	E962.0	E980.4
dextran	964.0	E858.2	E934.0	E950.4	E962.0	E980.4
nonmedicinal (dust) (fumes) NEC	985.8	E866.4	—	E950.9	E962.1	E980.9
Irritant drug	977.9	E858.9	E947.9	E950.5	E962.0	E980.5
Ismelin	972.6	E858.3	E942.6	E950.4	E962.0	E980.4
Isoamyl nitrite	972.4	E858.3	E942.4	E950.4	E962.0	E980.4
Isobutyl acetate	982.8	E862.4	—	E950.9	E962.1	E980.9
Isocarboxazid	969.01 ▲	E854.0	E939.0	E950.3	E962.0	E980.3
Isoephedrine	971.2	E855.5	E941.2	E950.4	E962.0	E980.4
Isoetharine	971.2	E855.5	E941.2	E950.4	E962.0	E980.4
Isofluorophate	971.0	E855.3	E941.0	E950.4	E962.0	E980.4
Isoniazid (INH)	961.8	E857	E931.8	E950.4	E962.0	E980.4
Isopentaquine	961.4	E857	E931.4	E950.4	E962.0	E980.4
Isophane insulin	962.3	E858.0	E932.3	E950.4	E962.0	E980.4
Isopregnenone	962.2	E858.0	E932.2	E950.4	E962.0	E980.4
Isoprenaline	971.2	E855.5	E941.2	E950.4	E962.0	E980.4
Isopropamide	971.1	E855.4	E941.1	E950.4	E962.0	E980.4
Isopropanol	980.2	E860.3	—	E950.9	E962.1	E980.9
topical (germicide)	976.0	E858.7	E946.0	E950.4	E962.0	E980.4
Isopropyl						
acetate	982.8	E862.4	—	E950.9	E962.1	E980.9
alcohol	980.2	E860.3	—	E950.9	E962.1	E980.9
topical (germicide)	976.0	E858.7	E946.0	E950.4	E962.0	E980.4
ether	982.8	E862.4	—	E950.9	E962.1	E980.9
Isoproterenol	971.2	E855.5	E941.2	E950.4	E962.0	E980.4
Isosorbide dinitrate	972.4	E858.3	E942.4	E950.4	E962.0	E980.4
Isothipendyl	963.0	E858.1	E933.0	E950.4	E962.0	E980.4
Isoxazolyl penicillin	960.0	E856	E930.0	E950.4	E962.0	E980.4
Isoxsuprine hydrochloride	972.5	E858.3	E942.5	E950.4	E962.0	E980.4
I-thyroxine sodium	962.7	E858.0	E932.7	E950.4	E962.0	E980.4
Jaborandi (pilocarpus) (extract)	971.0	E855.3	E941.0	E950.4	E962.0	E980.4
Jalap	973.1	E858.4	E943.1	E950.4	E962.0	E980.4
Jamaica						
dogwood (bark)	965.7	E850.7	E935.7	E950.0	E962.0	E980.0
ginger	989.89	E866.8	—	E950.9	E962.1	E980.9
Jatropha	988.2	E865.4	—	E950.9	E962.1	E980.9
curcas	988.2	E865.3	—	E950.9	E962.1	E980.9
Jectofer	964.0	E858.2	E934.0	E950.4	E962.0	E980.4
Jellyfish (sting)	989.5	E905.6	—	E950.9	E962.1	E980.9
Jequirity (bean)	988.2	E865.3	—	E950.9	E962.1	E980.9
Jimson weed	988.2	E865.4	—	E950.9	E962.1	E980.9
seeds	988.2	E865.3	—	E950.9	E962.1	E980.9
Juniper tar (oil) (ointment)	976.4	E858.7	E946.4	E950.4	E962.0	E980.4
Kallikrein	972.5	E858.3	E942.5	E950.4	E962.0	E980.4
Kanamycin	960.6	E856	E930.6	E950.4	E962.0	E980.4
Kantrex	960.6	E856	E930.6	E950.4	E962.0	E980.4
Kaolin	973.5	E858.4	E943.5	E950.4	E962.0	E980.4
Karaya (gum)	973.3	E858.4	E943.3	E950.4	E962.0	E980.4
Kemithal	968.3	E855.1	E938.3	E950.4	E962.0	E980.4
Kenacort	962.0	E858.0	E932.0	E950.4	E962.0	E980.4
Keratolytics	976.4	E858.7	E946.4	E950.4	E962.0	E980.4
Keratoplastics	976.4	E858.7	E946.4	E950.4	E962.0	E980.4
Kerosene, kerosine (fuel) (solvent) NEC	981	E862.1	—	E950.9	E962.1	E980.9
insecticide	981	E863.4	—	E950.6	E962.1	E980.7

	Poisoning	Accident	Therapeutic Use	Suicide Attempt	Assault	Undetermined
Kerosene, kerosine (fuel) (solvent) — *continued*						
vapor	987.1	E869.8	—	E952.8	E962.2	E982.8
Ketamine	968.3	E855.1	E938.3	E950.4	E962.0	E980.4
Ketobemidone	965.09	E850.2	E935.2	E950.0	E962.0	E980.0
Ketols	982.8	E862.4	—	E950.9	E962.1	E980.9
Ketone oils	982.8	E862.4	—	E950.9	E962.1	E980.9
Ketoprofen	965.61	E850.6	E935.6	E950.0	E962.0	E980.0
Kiln gas or vapor (carbon monoxide)	986	E868.8	—	E952.1	E962.2	E982.1
Konsyl	973.3	E858.4	E943.3	E950.4	E962.0	E980.4
Kosam seed	988.2	E865.3		E950.9	E962.1	E980.9
Krait (venom)	989.5	E905.0	—	E950.9	E962.1	E980.9
Kwell (insecticide)	989.2	E863.0	—	E950.6	E962.1	E980.7
anti-infective (topical)	976.0	E858.7	E946.0	E950.4	E962.0	E980.4
Laburnum (flowers)						
(seeds)	988.2	E865.3		E950.9	E962.1	E980.9
leaves	988.2	E865.4	—	E950.9	E962.1	E980.9
Lacquers	989.89	E861.6		E950.9	E962.1	E980.9
Lacrimogenic gas	987.5	E869.3		E952.8	E962.2	E982.8
Lactic acid	983.1	E864.1		E950.7	E962.1	E980.6
Lactobacillus acidophilus	973.5	E858.4	E943.5	E950.4	E962.0	E980.4
Lactoflavin	963.5	E858.1	E933.5	E950.4	E962.0	E980.4
Lactuca (virosa) (extract)	967.8	E852.8	E937.8	E950.2	E962.0	E980.2
Lactucarium	967.8	E852.8	E937.8	E950.2	E962.0	E980.2
Laevulose	974.5	E858.5	E944.5	E950.4	E962.0	E980.4
Lanatoside (C)	972.1	E858.3	E942.1	E950.4	E962.0	E980.4
Lanolin (lotion)	976.3	E858.7	E946.3	E950.4	E962.0	E980.4
Largactil	969.1	E853.0	E939.1	E950.3	E962.0	E980.3
Larkspur	988.2	E865.3		E950.9	E962.1	E980.9
Laroxyl	969.05 ▲	E854.0	E939.0	E950.3	E962.0	E980.3
Lasix	974.4	E858.5	E944.4	E950.4	E962.0	E980.4
Latex	989.82	E866.8	—	E950.9	E962.1	E980.9
Lathyrus (seed)	988.2	E865.3		E950.9	E962.1	E980.9
Laudanum	965.09	E850.2	E935.2	E950.0	E962.0	E980.0
Laudexium	975.2	E858.6	E945.2	E950.4	E962.0	E980.4
Laurel, black or cherry	988.2	E865.4	—	E950.9	E962.1	E980.9
Laurolinium	976.0	E858.7	E946.0	E950.4	E962.0	E980.4
Lauryl sulfoacetate	976.2	E858.7	E946.2	E950.4	E962.0	E980.4
Laxatives NEC	973.3	E858.4	E943.3	E950.4	E962.0	E980.4
emollient	973.2	E858.4	E943.2	E950.4	E962.0	E980.4
L-dopa	966.4	E855.0	E936.4	E950.4	E962.0	E980.4
Lead (dust) (fumes) (vapor)						
NEC	984.9	E866.0	—	E950.9	E962.1	E980.9
acetate (dust)	984.1	E866.0	—	E950.9	E962.1	E980.9
anti-infectives	961.2	E857	E931.2	E950.4	E962.0	E980.4
antiknock compound (tetraethyl)	984.1	E862.1	—	E950.9	E962.1	E980.9
arsenate, arsenite (dust) (insecticide) (vapor)	985.1	E863.4		E950.8	E962.1	E980.8
herbicide	985.1	E863.5		E950.8	E962.1	E980.8
carbonate	984.0	E866.0	—	E950.9	E962.1	E980.9
paint	984.0	E861.5	—	E950.9	E962.1	E980.9
chromate	984.0	E866.0	—	E950.9	E962.1	E980.9
paint	984.0	E861.5	—	E950.9	E962.1	E980.9
dioxide	984.0	E866.0	—	E950.9	E962.1	E980.9
inorganic (compound)	984.0	E866.0	—	E950.9	E962.1	E980.9
paint	984.0	E861.5	—	E950.9	E962.1	E980.9
iodide	984.0	E866.0	—	E950.9	E962.1	E980.9
pigment (paint)	984.0	E861.5	—	E950.9	E962.1	E980.9
monoxide (dust)	984.0	E866.0	—	E950.9	E962.1	E980.9
paint	984.0	E861.5	—	E950.9	E962.1	E980.9
organic	984.1	E866.0	—	E950.9	E962.1	E980.9
oxide	984.0	E866.0	—	E950.9	E962.1	E980.9
paint	984.0	E861.5	—	E950.9	E962.1	E980.9
paint	984.0	E861.5	—	E950.9	E962.1	E980.9
salts	984.0	E866.0	—	E950.9	E962.1	E980.9
specified compound NEC	984.8	E866.0	—	E950.9	E962.1	E980.9
tetra-ethyl	984.1	E862.1	—	E950.9	E962.1	E980.9
Lebanese red	969.6	E854.1	E939.6	E950.3	E962.0	E980.3
Lente Iletin (insulin)	962.3	E858.0	E932.3	E950.4	E962.0	E980.4
Leptazol	970.0	E854.3	E940.0	E950.4	E962.0	E980.4
Leritine	965.09	E850.2	E935.2	E950.0	E962.0	E980.0
Letter	962.7	E858.0	E932.7	E950.4	E962.0	E980.4
Lettuce opium	967.8	E852.8	E937.8	E950.2	E962.0	E980.2
Leucovorin (factor)	964.1	E858.2	E934.1	E950.4	E962.0	E980.4
Leukeran	963.1	E858.1	E933.1	E950.4	E962.0	E980.4
Levalbuterol	975.7	E858.6	E945.7	E950.4	E962.0	E980.4
Levallorphan	970.1	E854.3	E940.1	E950.4	E962.0	E980.4
Levanil	967.8	E852.8	E937.8	E950.2	E962.0	E980.2
Levarterenol	971.2	E855.5	E941.2	E950.4	E962.0	E980.4
Levodopa	966.4	E855.0	E936.4	E950.4	E962.0	E980.4

	Poisoning	Accident	Therapeutic Use	Suicide Attempt	Assault	Undetermined
Levo-dromoran	965.09	E850.2	E935.2	E950.0	E962.0	E980.0
Levoid	962.7	E858.0	E932.7	E950.4	E962.0	E980.4
Levo-iso-methadone	965.02	E850.1	E935.1	E950.0	E962.0	E980.0
Levomepromazine	967.8	E852.8	E937.8	E950.2	E962.0	E980.2
Levoprome	967.8	E852.8	E937.8	E950.2	E962.0	E980.2
Levopropoxyphene	975.4	E858.6	E945.4	E950.4	E962.0	E980.4
Levorphan, levophanol	965.09	E850.2	E935.2	E950.0	E962.0	E980.0
Levothyroxine (sodium)	962.7	E858.0	E932.7	E950.4	E962.0	E980.4
Levsin	971.1	E855.4	E941.1	E950.4	E962.0	E980.4
Levulose	974.5	E858.5	E944.5	E950.4	E962.0	E980.4
Lewisite (gas)	985.1	E866.3	—	E950.8	E962.1	E980.8
Librium	969.4	E853.2	E939.4	E950.3	E962.0	E980.3
Lidex	976.0	E858.7	E946.0	E950.4	E962.0	E980.4
Lidocaine (infiltration) (topical)	968.5	E855.2	E938.5	E950.4	E962.0	E980.4
nerve block (peripheral) (plexus)	968.6	E855.2	E938.6	E950.4	E962.0	E980.4
spinal	968.7	E855.2	E938.7	E950.4	E962.0	E980.4
Lighter fluid	981	E862.1	—	E950.9	E962.1	E980.9
Lignocaine (infiltration) (topical)	968.5	E855.2	E938.5	E950.4	E962.0	E980.4
nerve block (peripheral) (plexus)	968.6	E855.2	E938.6	E950.4	E962.0	E980.4
spinal	968.7	E855.2	E938.7	E950.4	E962.0	E980.4
Ligroin(e) (solvent)	981	E862.0	—	E950.9	E962.1	E980.9
vapor	987.1	E869.8	—	E952.8	E962.2	E982.8
Ligustrum vulgare	988.2	E865.3		E950.9	E962.1	E980.9
Lily of the valley	988.2	E865.4		E950.9	E962.1	E980.9
Lime (chloride)	983.2	E864.2	—	E950.7	E962.1	E980.6
solution, sulferated	976.4	E858.7	E946.4	E950.4	E962.0	E980.4
Limonene	982.8	E862.4	—	E950.9	E962.1	E980.9
Lincomycin	960.8	E856	E930.8	E950.4	E962.0	E980.4
Lindane (insecticide) (vapor)	989.2	E863.0	—	E950.6	E962.1	E980.7
anti-infective (topical)	976.0	E858.7	E946.0	E950.4	E962.0	E980.4
Liniments NEC	976.9	E858.7	E946.9	E950.4	E962.0	E980.4
Linoleic acid	972.2	E858.3	E942.2	E950.4	E962.0	E980.4
Liothyronine	962.7	E858.0	E932.7	E950.4	E962.0	E980.4
Liotrix	962.7	E858.0	E932.7	E950.4	E962.0	E980.4
Lipancreatin	973.4	E858.4	E943.4	E950.4	E962.0	E980.4
Lipo-Lutin	962.2	E858.0	E932.2	E950.4	E962.0	E980.4
Lipotropic agents	977.1	E858.8	E947.1	E950.4	E962.0	E980.4
Liquefied petroleum gases	987.0	E868.0	—	E951.1	E962.2	E981.1
piped (pure or mixed with air)	987.0	E867	—	E951.0	E962.2	E981.0
Liquid petrolatum	973.2	E858.4	E943.2	E950.4	E962.0	E980.4
substance	989.9	E866.9	—	E950.9	E962.1	E980.9
specified NEC	989.89	E866.8	—	E950.9	E962.1	E980.9
Lirugen	979.4	E858.8	E949.4	E950.4	E962.0	E980.4
Lithane	969.8	E855.8	E939.8	E950.3	E962.0	E980.3
Lithium	985.8	E866.4	—	E950.9	E962.1	E980.9
carbonate	969.8	E855.8	E939.8	E950.3	E962.0	E980.3
Lithonate	969.8	E855.8	E939.8	E950.3	E962.0	E980.3
Liver (extract) (injection) (preparations)	964.1	E858.2	E934.1	E950.4	E962.0	E980.4
Lizard (bite) (venom)	989.5	E905.0	—	E950.9	E962.1	E980.9
LMD	964.8	E858.2	E934.8	E950.4	E962.0	E980.4
Lobelia	988.2	E865.4	—	E950.9	E962.1	E980.9
Lobeline	970.0	E854.3	E940.0	E950.4	E962.0	E980.4
Locorten	976.0	E858.7	E946.0	E950.4	E962.0	E980.4
Lolium temulentum	988.2	E865.3	—	E950.9	E962.1	E980.9
Lomotil	973.5	E858.4	E943.5	E950.4	E962.0	E980.4
Lomustine	963.1	E858.1	E933.1	E950.4	E962.0	E980.4
Lophophora williamsii	969.6	E854.1	E939.6	E950.3	E962.0	E980.3
Lorazepam	969.4	E853.2	E939.4	E950.3	E962.0	E980.3
Lotions NEC	976.9	E858.7	E946.9	E950.4	E962.0	E980.4
Lotronex	973.8	E858.4	E943.8	E950.4	E962.0	E980.4
Lotusate	967.0	E851	E937.0	E950.1	E962.0	E980.1
Lowila	976.2	E858.7	E946.2	E950.4	E962.0	E980.4
Loxapine	969.3	E853.8	E939.3	E950.3	E962.0	E980.3
Lozenges (throat)	976.6	E858.7	E946.6	E950.4	E962.0	E980.4
LSD (25)	969.6	E854.1	E939.6	E950.3	E962.0	E980.3
L-Tryptophan — *see* amino acid						
Lubricating oil NEC	981	E862.2	—	E950.9	E962.1	E980.9
Lucanthone	961.6	E857	E931.6	E950.4	E962.0	E980.4
Luminal	967.0	E851	E937.0	E950.1	E962.0	E980.1
Lung irritant (gas) NEC	987.9	E869.9	—	E952.9	E962.2	E982.9
Lutocylol	962.2	E858.0	E932.2	E950.4	E962.0	E980.4
Lutromone	962.2	E858.0	E932.2	E950.4	E962.0	E980.4
Lututrin	975.0	E858.6	E945.0	E950.4	E962.0	E980.4

▽ Subterms under main terms may continue to next column or page

▶◀ Revised Text   ● New Line   ▲ Revised Code

		External Cause (E-Code)				
	Poisoning	Accident	Therapeutic Use	Suicide Attempt	Assault	Undetermined
Lye (concentrated)	983.2	E864.2	—	E950.7	E962.1	E980.6
Lygranum (skin test)	977.8	E858.8	E947.8	E950.4	E962.0	E980.4
Lymecycline	960.4	E856	E930.4	E950.4	E962.0	E980.4
Lymphogranuloma venereum antigen	977.8	E858.8	E947.8	E950.4	E962.0	E980.4
Lynestrenol	962.2	E858.0	E932.2	E950.4	E962.0	E980.4
Lyovac Sodium Edecrin	974.4	E858.5	E944.4	E950.4	E962.0	E980.4
Lypressin	962.5	E858.0	E932.5	E950.4	E962.0	E980.4
Lysergic acid (amide) (diethylamide)	969.6	E854.1	E939.6	E950.3	E962.0	E980.3
Lysergide	969.6	E854.1	E939.6	E950.3	E962.0	E980.3
Lysine vasopressin	962.5	E858.0	E932.5	E950.4	E962.0	E980.4
Lysol	983.0	E864.0	—	E950.7	E962.1	E980.6
Lytta (vitatta)	976.8	E858.7	E946.8	E950.4	E962.0	E980.4
Mace	987.5	E869.3	—	E952.8	E962.2	E982.8
Macrolides (antibiotics)	960.3	E856	E930.3	E950.4	E962.0	E980.4
Mafenide	976.0	E858.7	E946.0	E950.4	E962.0	E980.4
Magaldrate	973.0	E858.4	E943.0	E950.4	E962.0	E980.4
Magic mushroom	969.6	E854.1	E939.6	E950.3	E962.0	E980.3
Magnamycin	960.8	E856	E930.8	E950.4	E962.0	E980.4
Magnesia magma	973.0	E858.4	E943.0	E950.4	E962.0	E980.4
Magnesium (compounds) (fumes) NEC	985.8	E866.4	—	E950.9	E962.1	E980.9
antacid	973.0	E858.4	E943.0	E950.4	E962.0	E980.4
carbonate	973.0	E858.4	E943.0	E950.4	E962.0	E980.4
cathartic	973.3	E858.4	E943.3	E950.4	E962.0	E980.4
citrate	973.3	E858.4	E943.3	E950.4	E962.0	E980.4
hydroxide	973.0	E858.4	E943.0	E950.4	E962.0	E980.4
oxide	973.0	E858.4	E943.0	E950.4	E962.0	E980.4
sulfate (oral)	973.3	E858.4	E943.3	E950.4	E962.0	E980.4
intravenous	966.3	E855.0	E936.3	E950.4	E962.0	E980.4
trisilicate	973.0	E858.4	E943.0	E950.4	E962.0	E980.4
Malathion (insecticide)	989.3	E863.1	—	E950.6	E962.1	E980.7
Male fern (oleoresin)	961.6	E857	E931.6	E950.4	E962.0	E980.4
Mandelic acid	961.9	E857	E931.9	E950.4	E962.0	E980.4
Manganese compounds (fumes) NEC	985.2	E866.4	—	E950.9	E962.1	E980.9
Mannitol (diuretic) (medicinal) NEC	974.4	E858.5	E944.4	E950.4	E962.0	E980.4
hexanitrate	972.4	E858.3	E942.4	E950.4	E962.0	E980.4
mustard	963.1	E858.1	E933.1	E950.4	E962.0	E980.4
Mannomustine	963.1	E858.1	E933.1	E950.4	E962.0	E980.4
MAO inhibitors ▲	969.01	E854.0	E939.0	E950.3	E962.0	E980.3
Mapharsen	961.1	E857	E931.1	E950.4	E962.0	E980.4
Marcaine	968.9	E855.2	E938.9	E950.4	E962.0	E980.4
infiltration (subcutaneous)	968.5	E855.2	E938.5	E950.4	E962.0	E980.4
nerve block (peripheral) (plexus)	968.6	E855.2	E938.6	E950.4	E962.0	E980.4
Marezine	963.0	E858.1	E933.0	E950.4	E962.0	E980.4
Marihuana, marijuana (derivatives)	969.6	E854.1	E939.6	E950.3	E962.0	E980.3
Marine animals or plants (sting)	989.5	E905.6	—	E950.9	E962.1	E980.9
Marplan ▲	969.01	E854.0	E939.0	E950.3	E962.0	E980.3
Marsh gas	987.1	E869.8	—	E952.8	E962.2	E982.8
Marsilid ▲	969.01	E854.0	E939.0	E950.3	E962.0	E980.3
Matulane	963.1	E858.1	E933.1	E950.4	E962.0	E980.4
Mazindol	977.0	E858.8	E947.0	E950.4	E962.0	E980.4
MDMA ▲	969.72	E854.2	E939.7	E950.3	E962.0	E980.3
Meadow saffron	988.2	E865.3	—	E950.9	E962.1	E980.9
Measles vaccine	979.4	E858.8	E949.4	E950.4	E962.0	E980.4
Meat, noxious or nonbacterial	988.8	E865.0	—	E950.9	E962.1	E980.9
Mebanazine ▲	969.01	E854.0	E939.0	E950.3	E962.0	E980.3
Mebaral	967.0	E851	E937.0	E950.1	E962.0	E980.1
Mebendazole	961.6	E857	E931.6	E950.4	E962.0	E980.4
Mebeverine	975.1	E858.6	E945.1	E950.4	E962.0	E980.4
Mebhydroline	963.0	E858.1	E933.0	E950.4	E962.0	E980.4
Mebrophenhydramine	963.0	E858.1	E933.0	E950.4	E962.0	E980.4
Mebutamate	969.5	E853.8	E939.5	E950.3	E962.0	E980.3
Mecamylamine (chloride)	972.3	E858.3	E942.3	E950.4	E962.0	E980.4
Mechlorethamine hydrochloride	963.1	E858.1	E933.1	E950.4	E962.0	E980.4
Meclizine (hydrochloride)	963.0	E858.1	E933.0	E950.4	E962.0	E980.4
Meclofenoxate	970.0	E854.3	E940.0	E950.4	E962.0	E980.4
Meclozine (hydrochloride)	963.0	E858.1	E933.0	E950.4	E962.0	E980.4
Medazepam	969.4	E853.2	E939.4	E950.3	E962.0	E980.3
Medicine, medicinal substance	977.9	E858.9	E947.9	E950.5	E962.0	E980.5
specified NEC	977.8	E858.8	E947.8	E950.4	E962.0	E980.4
Medinal	967.0	E851	E937.0	E950.1	E962.0	E980.1
Medomin	967.0	E851	E937.0	E950.1	E962.0	E980.1

		External Cause (E-Code)				
	Poisoning	Accident	Therapeutic Use	Suicide Attempt	Assault	Undetermined
Medroxyprogesterone	962.2	E858.0	E932.2	E950.4	E962.0	E980.4
Medrysone	976.5	E858.7	E946.5	E950.4	E962.0	E980.4
Mefenamic acid	965.7	E850.7	E935.7	E950.0	E962.0	E980.0
Megahallucinogen	969.6	E854.1	E939.6	E950.3	E962.0	E980.3
Megestrol	962.2	E858.0	E932.2	E950.4	E962.0	E980.4
Meglumine	977.8	E858.8	E947.8	E950.4	E962.0	E980.4
Meladinin	976.3	E858.7	E946.3	E950.4	E962.0	E980.4
Melanizing agents	976.3	E858.7	E946.3	E950.4	E962.0	E980.4
Melarsoprol	961.1	E857	E931.1	E950.4	E962.0	E980.4
Melia azedarach	988.2	E865.3	—	E950.9	E962.1	E980.9
Mellaril	969.1	E853.0	E939.1	E950.3	E962.0	E980.3
Meloxine	976.3	E858.7	E946.3	E950.4	E962.0	E980.4
Melphalan	963.1	E858.1	E933.1	E950.4	E962.0	E980.4
Menadiol sodium diphosphate	964.3	E858.2	E934.3	E950.4	E962.0	E980.4
Menadione (sodium bisulfite)	964.3	E858.2	E934.3	E950.4	E962.0	E980.4
Menaphthone	964.3	E858.2	E934.3	E950.4	E962.0	E980.4
Meningococcal vaccine	978.8	E858.8	E948.8	E950.4	E962.0	E980.4
Menningovax-C	978.8	E858.8	E948.8	E950.4	E962.0	E980.4
Menotropins	962.4	E858.0	E932.4	E950.4	E962.0	E980.4
Menthol NEC	976.1	E858.7	E946.1	E950.4	E962.0	E980.4
Mepacrine	961.3	E857	E931.3	E950.4	E962.0	E980.4
Meparfynol	967.8	E852.8	E937.8	E950.2	E962.0	E980.2
Mepazine	969.1	E853.0	E939.1	E950.3	E962.0	E980.3
Mepenzolate	971.1	E855.4	E941.1	E950.4	E962.0	E980.4
Meperidine	965.09	E850.2	E935.2	E950.0	E962.0	E980.0
Mephenamin(e)	966.4	E855.0	E936.4	E950.4	E962.0	E980.4
Mephenesin (carbamate)	968.0	E855.1	E938.0	E950.4	E962.0	E980.4
Mephenoxalone	969.5	E853.8	E939.5	E950.3	E962.0	E980.3
Mephentermine	971.2	E855.5	E941.2	E950.4	E962.0	E980.4
Mephenytoin	966.1	E855.0	E936.1	E950.4	E962.0	E980.4
Mephobarbital	967.0	E851	E937.0	E950.1	E962.0	E980.1
Mepiperphenidol	971.1	E855.4	E941.1	E950.4	E962.0	E980.4
Mepivacaine	968.9	E855.2	E938.9	E950.4	E962.0	E980.4
infiltration (subcutaneous)	968.5	E855.2	E938.5	E950.4	E962.0	E980.4
nerve block (peripheral) (plexus)	968.6	E855.2	E938.6	E950.4	E962.0	E980.4
topical (surface)	968.5	E855.2	E938.5	E950.4	E962.0	E980.4
Meprednisone	962.0	E858.0	E932.0	E950.4	E962.0	E980.4
Meprobam	969.5	E853.8	E939.5	E950.3	E962.0	E980.3
Meprobamate	969.5	E853.8	E939.5	E950.3	E962.0	E980.3
Mepyramine (maleate)	963.0	E858.1	E933.0	E950.4	E962.0	E980.4
Meralluride	974.0	E858.5	E944.0	E950.4	E962.0	E980.4
Merbaphen	974.0	E858.5	E944.0	E950.4	E962.0	E980.4
Merbromin	976.0	E858.7	E946.0	E950.4	E962.0	E980.4
Mercaptomerin	974.0	E858.5	E944.0	E950.4	E962.0	E980.4
Mercaptopurine	963.1	E858.1	E933.1	E950.4	E962.0	E980.4
Mercumatilin	974.0	E858.5	E944.0	E950.4	E962.0	E980.4
Mercuramide	974.0	E858.5	E944.0	E950.4	E962.0	E980.4
Mercuranin	976.0	E858.7	E946.0	E950.4	E962.0	E980.4
Mercurochrome	976.0	E858.7	E946.0	E950.4	E962.0	E980.4
Mercury, mercuric, mercurous (compounds) (cyanide) (fumes) (nonmedicinal) (vapor) NEC	985.0	E866.1	—	E950.9	E962.1	E980.9
ammoniated	976.0	E858.7	E946.0	E950.4	E962.0	E980.4
anti-infective	961.2	E857	E931.2	E950.4	E962.0	E980.4
topical	976.0	E858.7	E946.0	E950.4	E962.0	E980.4
chloride (antiseptic) NEC	976.0	E858.7	E946.0	E950.4	E962.0	E980.4
fungicide	985.0	E863.6	—	E950.6	E962.1	E980.7
diuretic compounds	974.0	E858.5	E944.0	E950.4	E962.0	E980.4
fungicide	985.0	E863.6	—	E950.6	E962.1	E980.7
organic (fungicide)	985.0	E863.6	—	E950.6	E962.1	E980.7
Merethoxylline	974.0	E858.5	E944.0	E950.4	E962.0	E980.4
Mersalyl	974.0	E858.5	E944.0	E950.4	E962.0	E980.4
Merthiolate (topical)	976.0	E858.7	E946.0	E950.4	E962.0	E980.4
ophthalmic preparation	976.5	E858.7	E946.5	E950.4	E962.0	E980.4
Meruvax	979.4	E858.8	E949.4	E950.4	E962.0	E980.4
Mescal buttons	969.6	E854.1	E939.6	E950.3	E962.0	E980.3
Mescaline (salts)	969.6	E854.1	E939.6	E950.3	E962.0	E980.3
Mesoridazine besylate	969.1	E853.0	E939.1	E950.3	E962.0	E980.3
Mestanolone	962.1	E858.0	E932.1	E950.4	E962.0	E980.4
Mestranol	962.2	E858.0	E932.2	E950.4	E962.0	E980.4
Metacresylacetate	976.0	E858.7	E946.0	E950.4	E962.0	E980.4
Metaldehyde (snail killer) NEC	989.4	E863.4	—	E950.6	E962.1	E980.7
Metals (heavy) (nonmedicinal) NEC	985.9	E866.4	—	E950.9	E962.1	E980.9
dust, fumes, or vapor NEC	985.9	E866.4	—	E950.9	E962.1	E980.9
light NEC	985.9	E866.4	—	E950.9	E962.1	E980.9

Nontherapeutic use substance

🔲 Subterms under main terms may continue to next column or page

Index

Metals (heavy) (nonmedicinal) NEC — Morning glory seeds

		External Cause (E-Code)				
	Poisoning	Accident	Therapeutic Use	Suicide Attempt	Assault	Undeter-mined
Metals (heavy) (nonmedicinal)						
— *continued*						
light — *continued*						
dust, fumes, or vapor						
NEC	985.9	E866.4	—	E950.9	E962.1	E980.9
pesticides (dust) (vapor)	985.9	E863.4	—	E950.6	E962.1	E980.7
Metamucil	973.3	E858.4	E943.3	E950.4	E962.0	E980.4
Metaphen	976.0	E858.7	E946.0	E950.4	E962.0	E980.4
Metaproterenol	975.1	E858.6	E945.1	E950.4	E962.0	E980.4
Metaraminol	972.8	E858.3	E942.8	E950.4	E962.0	E980.4
Metaxalone	968.0	E855.1	E938.0	E950.4	E962.0	E980.4
Metformin	962.3	E858.0	E932.3	E950.4	E962.0	E980.4
Methacycline	960.4	E856	E930.4	E950.4	E962.0	E980.4
Methadone	965.02	E850.1	E935.1	E950.0	E962.0	E980.0
Methallenestril	962.2	E858.0	E932.2	E950.4	E962.0	E980.4
Methamphetamine	969.72 ▲	E854.2	E939.7	E950.3	E962.0	E980.3
Methandienone	962.1	E858.0	E932.1	E950.4	E962.0	E980.4
Methandriol	962.1	E858.0	E932.1	E950.4	E962.0	E980.4
Methandrostenolone	962.1	E858.0	E932.1	E950.4	E962.0	E980.4
Methane gas	987.1	E869.8	—	E952.8	E962.2	E982.8
Methanol	980.1	E860.2	—	E950.9	E962.1	E980.9
vapor	987.8	E869.8	—	E952.8	E962.2	E982.8
Methantheline	971.1	E855.4	E941.1	E950.4	E962.0	E980.4
Methaphenilene	963.0	E858.1	E933.0	E950.4	E962.0	E980.4
Methapyrilene	963.0	E858.1	E933.0	E950.4	E962.0	E980.4
Methaqualone						
(compounds)	967.4	E852.3	E937.4	E950.2	E962.0	E980.2
Metharbital,						
metharbitone	967.0	E851	E937.0	E950.1	E962.0	E980.1
Methazolamide	974.2	E858.5	E944.2	E950.4	E962.0	E980.4
Methdilazine	963.0	E858.1	E933.0	E950.4	E962.0	E980.4
Methedrine	969.72 ▲	E854.2	E939.7	E950.3	E962.0	E980.3
Methenamine (mandelate)	961.9	E857	E931.9	E950.4	E962.0	E980.4
Methenolone	962.1	E858.0	E932.1	E950.4	E962.0	E980.4
Methergine	975.0	E858.6	E945.0	E950.4	E962.0	E980.4
Methiacil	962.8	E858.0	E932.8	E950.4	E962.0	E980.4
Methicillin (sodium)	960.0	E856	E930.0	E950.4	E962.0	E980.4
Methimazole	962.8	E858.0	E932.8	E950.4	E962.0	E980.4
Methionine	977.1	E858.8	E947.1	E950.4	E962.0	E980.4
Methisazone	961.7	E857	E931.7	E950.4	E962.0	E980.4
Methitural	967.0	E851	E937.0	E950.1	E962.0	E980.1
Methixene	971.1	E855.4	E941.1	E950.4	E962.0	E980.4
Methobarbital,						
methobarbitone	967.0	E851	E937.0	E950.1	E962.0	E980.1
Methocarbamol	968.0	E855.1	E938.0	E950.4	E962.0	E980.4
Methohexital, methohexitone						
(sodium)	968.3	E855.1	E938.3	E950.4	E962.0	E980.4
Methoin	966.1	E855.0	E936.1	E950.4	E962.0	E980.4
Methopholine	965.7	E850.7	E935.7	E950.0	E962.0	E980.0
Methorate	975.4	E858.6	E945.4	E950.4	E962.0	E980.4
Methoserpidine	972.6	E858.3	E942.6	E950.4	E962.0	E980.4
Methotrexate	963.1	E858.1	E933.1	E950.4	E962.0	E980.4
Methotrimeprazine	967.8	E852.8	E937.8	E950.2	E962.0	E980.2
Methoxa-Dome	976.3	E858.7	E946.3	E950.4	E962.0	E980.4
Methoxamine	971.2	E855.5	E941.2	E950.4	E962.0	E980.4
Methoxsalen	976.3	E858.7	E946.3	E950.4	E962.0	E980.4
Methoxybenzyl penicillin	960.0	E856	E930.0	E950.4	E962.0	E980.4
Methoxychlor	989.2	E863.0	—	E950.6	E962.1	E980.7
Methoxyflurane	968.2	E855.1	E938.2	E950.4	E962.0	E980.4
Methoxyphenamine	971.2	E855.5	E941.2	E950.4	E962.0	E980.4
Methoxypromazine	969.1	E853.0	E939.1	E950.3	E962.0	E980.3
Methoxypsoralen	976.3	E858.7	E946.3	E950.4	E962.0	E980.4
Methscopolamine						
(bromide)	971.1	E855.4	E941.1	E950.4	E962.0	E980.4
Methsuximide	966.2	E855.0	E936.2	E950.4	E962.0	E980.4
Methyclothiazide	974.3	E858.5	E944.3	E950.4	E962.0	E980.4
Methyl						
acetate	982.8	E862.4	—	E950.9	E962.1	E980.9
acetone	982.8	E862.4	—	E950.9	E962.1	E980.9
alcohol	980.1	E860.2	—	E950.9	E962.1	E980.9
amphetamine	969.72 ▲	E854.2	E939.7	E950.3	E962.0	E980.3
androstanolone	962.1	E858.0	E932.1	E950.4	E962.0	E980.4
atropine	971.1	E855.4	E941.1	E950.4	E962.0	E980.4
benzene	982.0	E862.4	—	E950.9	E962.1	E980.9
bromide (gas)	987.8	E869.8	—	E952.8	E962.2	E982.8
fumigant	987.8	E863.8	—	E950.6	E962.1	E980.7
butanol	980.8	E860.8	—	E950.9	E962.1	E980.9
carbinol	980.1	E860.2	—	E950.9	E962.1	E980.9
cellosolve	982.8	E862.4	—	E950.9	E962.1	E980.9
cellulose	973.3	E858.4	E943.3	E950.4	E962.0	E980.4
chloride (gas)	987.8	E869.8	—	E952.8	E962.2	E982.8
cyclohexane	982.8	E862.4	—	E950.9	E962.1	

		External Cause (E-Code)				
	Poisoning	Accident	Therapeutic Use	Suicide Attempt	Assault	Undeter-mined
Methyl — *continued*						
cyclohexanone	982.8	E862.4	—	E950.9	E962.1	E980.9
dihydromorphinone	965.09	E850.2	E935.2	E950.0	E962.0	E980.0
ergometrine	975.0	E858.6	E945.0	E950.4	E962.0	E980.4
ergonovine	975.0	E858.6	E945.0	E950.4	E962.0	E980.4
ethyl ketone	982.8	E862.4	—	E950.9	E962.1	E980.9
hydrazine	983.9	E864.3	—	E950.7	E962.1	E980.6
isobutyl ketone	982.8	E862.4	—	E950.9	E962.1	E980.9
morphine NEC	965.09	E850.2	E935.2	E950.0	E962.0	E980.0
parafynol	967.8	E852.8	E937.8	E950.2	E962.0	E980.2
parathion	989.3	E863.1	—	E950.6	E962.1	E980.7
pentynol NEC	967.8	E852.8	E937.8	E950.2	E962.0	E980.2
peridol	969.2	E853.1	E939.2	E950.3	E962.0	E980.3
phenidate	969.73 ▲	E854.2	E939.7	E950.3	E962.0	E980.3
prednisolone	962.0	E858.0	E932.0	E950.4	E962.0	E980.4
ENT agent	976.6	E858.7	E946.6	E950.4	E962.0	E980.4
ophthalmic preparation	976.5	E858.7	E946.5	E950.4	E962.0	E980.4
topical NEC	976.0	E858.7	E946.0	E950.4	E962.0	E980.4
propylcarbinol	980.8	E860.8	—	E950.9	E962.1	E980.9
rosaniline NEC	976.0	E858.7	E946.0	E950.4	E962.0	E980.4
salicylate NEC	976.3	E858.7	E946.3	E950.4	E962.0	E980.4
sulfate (fumes)	987.8	E869.8	—	E952.8	E962.2	E982.8
liquid	983.9	E864.3	—	E950.7	E962.1	E980.6
sulfonal	967.8	E852.8	E937.8	E950.2	E962.0	E980.2
testosterone	962.1	E858.0	E932.1	E950.4	E962.0	E980.4
thiouracil	962.8	E858.0	E932.8	E950.4	E962.0	E980.4
Methylated spirit	980.0	E860.1	—	E950.9	E962.1	E980.9
Methyldopa	972.6	E858.3	E942.6	E950.4	E962.0	E980.4
Methylene						
blue	961.9	E857	E931.9	E950.4	E962.0	E980.4
chloride or dichloride (solvent)						
NEC	982.3	E862.4	—	E950.9	E962.1	E980.9
Methylhexabital	967.0	E851	E937.0	E950.1	E962.0	E980.1
Methylparaben						
(ophthalmic)	976.5	E858.7	E946.5	E950.4	E962.0	E980.4
Methyprylon	967.5	E852.4	E937.5	E950.2	E962.0	E980.2
Methysergide	971.3	E855.6	E941.3	E950.4	E962.0	E980.4
Metoclopramide	963.0	E858.1	E933.0	E950.4	E962.0	E980.4
Metofoline	965.7	E850.7	E935.7	E950.0	E962.0	E980.0
Metopon	965.09	E850.2	E935.2	E950.0	E962.0	E980.0
Metronidazole	961.5	E857	E931.5	E950.4	E962.0	E980.4
Metycaine	968.9	E855.2	E938.9	E950.4	E962.0	E980.4
infiltration (subcutaneous)	968.5	E855.2	E938.5	E950.4	E962.0	E980.4
nerve block (peripheral)						
(plexus)	968.6	E855.2	E938.6	E950.4	E962.0	E980.4
topical (surface)	968.5	E855.2	E938.5	E950.4	E962.0	E980.4
Metyrapone	977.8	E858.8	E947.8	E950.4	E962.0	E980.4
Mevinphos	989.3	E863.1	—	E950.6	E962.1	E980.7
Mezereon (berries)	988.2	E865.3	—	E950.9	E962.1	E980.9
Micatin	976.0	E858.7	E946.0	E950.4	E962.0	E980.4
Miconazole	976.0	E858.7	E946.0	E950.4	E962.0	E980.4
Midol	965.1	E850.3	E935.3	E950.0	E962.0	E980.0
Mifepristone	962.9	E858.0	E932.9	E950.4	E962.0	E980.4
Milk of magnesia	973.0	E858.4	E943.0	E950.4	E962.0	E980.4
Millipede (tropical)						
(venomous)	989.5	E905.4	—	E950.9	E962.1	E980.9
Miltown	969.5	E853.8	E939.5	E950.3	E962.0	E980.3
Mineral						
oil (medicinal)	973.2	E858.4	E943.2	E950.4	E962.0	E980.4
nonmedicinal	981	E862.1	—	E950.9	E962.1	E980.9
topical	976.3	E858.7	E946.3	E950.4	E962.0	E980.4
salts NEC	974.6	E858.5	E944.6	E950.4	E962.0	E980.4
spirits	981	E862.0	—	E950.9	E962.1	E980.9
Minocycline	960.4	E856	E930.4	E950.4	E962.0	E980.4
Mithramycin						
(antineoplastic)	960.7	E856	E930.7	E950.4	E962.0	E980.4
Mitobronitol	963.1	E858.1	E933.1	E950.4	E962.0	E980.4
Mitomycin (antineoplastic)	960.7	E856	E930.7	E950.4	E962.0	E980.4
Mitotane	963.1	E858.1	E933.1	E950.4	E962.0	E980.4
Moderil	972.6	E858.3	E942.6	E950.4	E962.0	E980.4
Mogadon — *see* Nitrazepam						
Molindone	969.3	E853.8	E939.3	E950.3	E962.0	E980.3
Monistat	976.0	E858.7	E946.0	E950.4	E962.0	E980.4
Monkshood	988.2	E865.4	—	E950.9	E962.1	E980.9
Monoamine oxidase						
inhibitors	969.01 ▲	E854.0	E939.0	E950.3	E962.0	E980.3
Monochlorobenzene	982.0	E862.4	—	E950.9	E962.1	E980.9
Monosodium glutamate	989.89	E866.8	—	E950.9	E962.1	E980.9
Monoxide, carbon — *see*						
Carbon, monoxide						
Moperone	969.2	E853.1	E939.2	E950.3	E962.0	E980.3
Morning glory seeds	969.6	E854.1	E939.6	E950.3	E962.0	E980.3

Nontherapeutic use substance

▽ Subterms under main terms may continue to next column or page

	Poisoning	Accident	Therapeutic Use	Suicide Attempt	Assault	Undetermined
Moroxydine						
(hydrochloride)	961.7	E857	E931.7	E950.4	E962.0	E980.4
Morphazinamide	961.8	E857	E931.8	E950.4	E962.0	E980.4
Morphinans	965.09	E850.2	E935.2	E950.0	E962.0	E980.0
Morphine NEC	965.09	E850.2	E935.2	E950.0	E962.0	E980.0
antagonists	970.1	E854.3	E940.1	E950.4	E962.0	E980.4
Morpholinylethylmorphine	965.09	E850.2	E935.2	E950.0	E962.0	E980.0
Morrhuate sodium	972.7	E858.3	E942.7	E950.4	E962.0	E980.4
Moth balls — *see also*						
Pesticides	989.4	E863.4	—	E950.6	E962.1	E980.7
naphthalene	983.0	E863.4	—	E950.7	E962.1	E980.6
Motor exhaust gas — *see* Carbon, monoxide, exhaust gas						
Mouth wash	976.6	E858.7	E946.6	E950.4	E962.0	E980.4
Mucolytic agent	975.5	E858.6	E945.5	E950.4	E962.0	E980.4
Mucomyst	975.5	E858.6	E945.5	E950.4	E962.0	E980.4
Mucous membrane agents						
(external)	976.9	E858.7	E946.9	E950.4	E962.0	E980.4
specified NEC	976.8	E858.7	E946.8	E950.4	E962.0	E980.4
Mumps						
immune globulin (human)	964.6	E858.2	E934.6	E950.4	E962.0	E980.4
skin test antigen	977.8	E858.8	E947.8	E950.4	E962.0	E980.4
vaccine	979.6	E858.8	E949.6	E950.4	E962.0	E980.4
Mumpsvax	979.6	E858.8	E949.6	E950.4	E962.0	E980.4
Muriatic acid — *see* Hydrochloric acid						
Muscarine	971.0	E855.3	E941.0	E950.4	E962.0	E980.4
Muscle affecting agents						
NEC	975.3	E858.6	E945.3	E950.4	E962.0	E980.4
oxytocic	975.0	E858.6	E945.0	E950.4	E962.0	E980.4
relaxants	975.3	E858.6	E945.3	E950.4	E962.0	E980.4
central nervous system	968.0	E855.1	E938.0	E950.4	E962.0	E980.4
skeletal	975.2	E858.6	E945.2	E950.4	E962.0	E980.4
smooth	975.1	E858.6	E945.1	E950.4	E962.0	E980.4
Mushrooms, noxious	988.1	E865.5	—	E950.9	E962.1	E980.9
Mussel, noxious	988.0	E865.1	—	E950.9	E962.1	E980.9
Mustard (emetic)	973.6	E858.4	E943.6	E950.4	E962.0	E980.4
gas	987.8	E869.8	—	E952.8	E962.2	E982.8
nitrogen	963.1	E858.1	E933.1	E950.4	E962.0	E980.4
Mustine	963.1	E858.1	E933.1	E950.4	E962.0	E980.4
M-vac	979.4	E858.8	E949.4	E950.4	E962.0	E980.4
Mycifradin	960.8	E856	E930.8	E950.4	E962.0	E980.4
topical	976.0	E858.7	E946.0	E950.4	E962.0	E980.4
Mycitracin	960.8	E856	E930.8	E950.4	E962.0	E980.4
ophthalmic preparation	976.5	E858.7	E946.5	E950.4	E962.0	E980.4
Mycostatin	960.1	E856	E930.1	E950.4	E962.0	E980.4
topical	976.0	E858.7	E946.0	E950.4	E962.0	E980.4
Mydriacyl	971.1	E855.4	E941.1	E950.4	E962.0	E980.4
Myelobromal	963.1	E858.1	E933.1	E950.4	E962.0	E980.4
Myleran	963.1	E858.1	E933.1	E950.4	E962.0	E980.4
Myochrysin(e)	965.69	E850.6	E935.6	E950.0	E962.0	E980.0
Myoneural blocking agents	975.2	E858.6	E945.2	E950.4	E962.0	E980.4
Myristica fragrans	988.2	E865.3	—	E950.9	E962.1	E980.9
Myristicin	988.2	E865.3	—	E950.9	E962.1	E980.9
Mysoline	966.3	E855.0	E936.3	E950.4	E962.0	E980.4
Nafcillin (sodium)	960.0	E856	E930.0	E950.4	E962.0	E980.4
Nail polish remover	982.8	E862.4	—	E950.9	E962.1	E908.9
Nalidixic acid	961.9	E857	E931.9	E950.4	E962.0	E980.4
Nalorphine	970.1	E854.3	E940.1	E950.4	E962.0	E980.4
Naloxone	970.1	E854.3	E940.1	E950.4	E962.0	E980.4
Nandrolone (decanoate)						
(phenproprioate)	962.1	E858.0	E932.1	E950.4	E962.0	E980.4
Naphazoline	971.2	E855.5	E941.2	E950.4	E962.0	E980.4
Naphtha (painter's)						
(petroleum)	981	E862.0	—	E950.9	E962.1	E980.9
solvent	981	E862.0	—	E950.9	E962.1	E980.9
vapor	987.1	E869.8	—	E952.8	E962.2	E982.8
Naphthalene (chlorinated)	983.0	E864.0	—	E950.7	E962.1	E980.6
insecticide or moth repellent	983.0	E863.4	—	E950.7	E962.1	E980.6
vapor	987.8	E869.8	—	E952.8	E962.2	E982.8
Naphthol	983.0	E864.0	—	E950.7	E962.1	E980.6
Naphthylamine	983.0	E864.0	—	E950.7	E962.1	E980.6
Naprosyn — see Naproxen						
Naproxen	965.61	E850.6	E935.6	E950.0	E962.0	E980.0
Narcotic (drug)	967.9	E852.9	E937.9	E950.2	E962.0	E980.2
analgesic NEC	965.8	E850.8	E935.8	E950.0	E962.0	E980.0
antagonist	970.1	E854.3	E940.1	E950.4	E962.0	E980.4
specified NEC	967.8	E852.8	E937.8	E950.2	E962.0	E980.2
Narcotine	975.4	E858.6	E945.4	E950.4	E962.0	E980.4
Nardil	969.01 ▲	E854.0	E939.0	E950.3	E962.0	E980.3

	Poisoning	Accident	Therapeutic Use	Suicide Attempt	Assault	Undetermined
Natrium cyanide — see Cyanide(s)						
Natural						
blood (product)	964.7	E858.2	E934.7	E950.4	E962.0	E980.4
gas (piped)	987.1	E867	—	E951.0	E962.2	E981.0
incomplete combustion	986	E867	—	E951.0	E962.2	E981.0
Nealbarbital, nealbarbitone	967.0	E851	E937.0	E950.1	E962.0	E980.1
Nectadon	975.4	E858.6	E945.4	E950.4	E962.0	E980.4
Nematocyst (sting)	989.5	E905.6	—	E950.9	E962.1	E980.9
Nembutal	967.0	E851	E937.0	E950.1	E962.0	E980.1
Neoarsphenamine	961.1	E857	E931.1	E950.4	E962.0	E980.4
Neocinchophen	974.7	E858.5	E944.7	E950.4	E962.0	E980.4
Neomycin	960.8	E856	E930.8	E950.4	E962.0	E980.4
ENT agent	976.6	E858.7	E946.6	E950.4	E962.0	E980.4
ophthalmic preparation	976.5	E858.7	E946.5	E950.4	E962.0	E980.4
topical NEC	976.0	E858.7	E946.0	E950.4	E962.0	E980.4
Neonal	967.0	E851	E937.0	E950.1	E962.0	E980.1
Neoprontosil	961.0	E857	E931.0	E950.4	E962.0	E980.4
Neosalvarsan	961.1	E857	E931.1	E950.4	E962.0	E980.4
Neosilversalvarsan	961.1	E857	E931.1	E950.4	E962.0	E980.4
Neosporin	960.8	E856	E930.8	E950.4	E962.0	E980.4
ENT agent	976.6	E858.7	E946.6	E950.4	E962.0	E980.4
opthalmic preparation	976.5	E858.7	E946.5	E950.4	E962.0	E980.4
topical NEC	976.0	E858.7	E946.0	E950.4	E962.0	E980.4
Neostigmine	971.0	E855.3	E941.0	E950.4	E962.0	E980.4
Neraval	967.0	E851	E937.0	E950.1	E962.0	E980.1
Neravan	967.0	E851	E937.0	E950.1	E962.0	E980.1
Nerium oleander	988.2	E865.4	—	E950.9	E962.1	E980.9
Nerve gases (war)	987.9	E869.9	—	E952.9	E962.2	E982.9
Nesacaine	968.9	E855.2	E938.9	E950.4	E962.0	E980.4
infiltration (subcutaneous)	968.5	E855.2	E938.5	E950.4	E962.0	E980.4
nerve block (peripheral) (plexus)	968.6	E855.2	E938.6	E950.4	E962.0	E980.4
Neurobarb	967.0	E851	E937.0	E950.1	E962.0	E980.1
Neuroleptics NEC	969.3	E853.8	E939.3	E950.3	E962.0	E980.3
Neuroprotective agent	977.8	E858.8	E947.8	E950.4	E962.0	E980.4
Neutral spirits	980.0	E860.1	—	E950.9	E962.1	E980.9
beverage	980.0	E860.0	—	E950.9	E962.1	E980.9
Niacin, niacinamide	972.2	E858.3	E942.2	E950.4	E962.0	E980.4
Nialamide	969.01 ▲	E854.0	E939.0	E950.3	E962.0	E980.3
Nickle (carbonyl) (compounds) (fumes) (tetracarbonyl)						
(vapor)	985.8	E866.4	—	E950.9	E962.1	E980.9
Niclosamide	961.6	E857	E931.6	E950.4	E962.0	E980.4
Nicomorphine	965.09	E850.2	E935.2	E950.0	E962.0	E980.0
Nicotinamide	972.2	E858.3	E942.2	E950.4	E962.0	E980.4
Nicotine (insecticide) (spray) (sulfate) NEC	989.4	E863.4	—	E950.6	E962.1	E980.7
not insecticide	989.89	E866.8	—	E950.9	E962.1	E980.9
Nicotinic acid (derivatives)	972.2	E858.3	E942.2	E950.4	E962.0	E980.4
Nicotinyl alcohol	972.2	E858.3	E942.2	E950.4	E962.0	E980.4
Nicoumalone	964.2	E858.2	E934.2	E950.4	E962.0	E980.4
Nifenazone	965.5	E850.5	E935.5	E950.0	E962.0	E980.0
Nifuraldezone	961.9	E857	E931.9	E950.4	E962.0	E980.4
Nightshade (deadly)	988.2	E865.4	—	E950.9	E962.1	E980.9
Nikethamide	970.0	E854.3	E940.0	E950.4	E962.0	E980.4
Nilstat	960.1	E856	E930.1	E950.4	E962.0	E980.4
topical	976.0	E858.7	E946.0	E950.4	E962.0	E980.4
Nimodipine	977.8	E858.8	E947.8	E950.4	E962.0	E980.4
Niridazole	961.6	E857	E931.6	E950.4	E962.0	E980.4
Nisentil	965.09	E850.2	E935.2	E950.0	E962.0	E980.0
Nitrates	972.4	E858.3	E942.4	E950.4	E962.0	E980.4
Nitrazepam	969.4	E853.2	E939.4	E950.3	E962.0	E980.3
Nitric						
acid (liquid)	983.1	E864.1	—	E950.7	E962.1	E980.6
vapor	987.8	E869.8	—	E952.8	E962.2	E982.8
oxide (gas)	987.2	E869.0	—	E952.8	E962.2	E982.8
Nitrite, amyl (medicinal)						
(vapor)	972.4	E858.3	E942.4	E950.4	E962.0	E980.4
Nitroaniline	983.0	E864.0	—	E950.7	E962.1	E980.6
vapor	987.8	E869.8	—	E952.8	E962.2	E982.8
Nitrobenzene, nitrobenzol	983.0	E864.0	—	E950.7	E962.1	E980.6
vapor	987.8	E869.8	—	E952.8	E962.2	E982.8
Nitrocellulose	976.3	E858.7	E946.3	E950.4	E962.0	E980.4
Nitrofuran derivatives	961.9	E857	E931.9	E950.4	E962.0	E980.4
Nitrofurantoin	961.9	E857	E931.9	E950.4	E962.0	E980.4
Nitrofurazone	976.0	E858.7	E946.0	E950.4	E962.0	E980.4
Nitrogen (dioxide) (gas) (oxide)	987.2	E869.0	—	E952.8	E962.2	E982.8
mustard (antineoplastic)	963.1	E858.1	E933.1	E950.4	E962.0	E980.4

Nontherapeutic use substance

▽ Subterms under main terms may continue to next column or page

Nitrogen — continued	Poisoning	Accident	Therapeutic Use	Suicide Attempt	Assault	Undetermined
nonmedicinal	989.89	E866.8	—	E950.9	E962.1	E980.9
fumes	987.8	E869.8	—	E952.8	E962.2	E982.8
Nitroglycerin, nitroglycerol						
(medicinal)	972.4	E858.3	E942.4	E950.4	E962.0	E980.4
Nitrohydrochloric acid	983.1	E864.1	—	E950.7	E962.1	E980.6
Nitromersol	976.0	E858.7	E946.0	E950.4	E962.0	E980.4
Nitronaphthalene	983.0	E864.0	—	E950.7	E962.2	E980.6
Nitrophenol	983.0	E864.0	—	E950.7	E962.2	E980.6
Nitrothiazol	961.6	E857	E931.6	E950.4	E962.0	E980.4
Nitrotoluene, nitrotoluol	983.0	E864.0	—	E950.7	E962.1	E980.6
vapor	987.8	E869.8	—	E952.8	E962.2	E982.8
Nitrous	968.2	E855.1	E938.2	E950.4	E962.0	E980.4
acid (liquid)	983.1	E864.1	—	E950.7	E962.1	E980.6
fumes	987.2	E869.0	—	E952.8	E962.2	E982.8
oxide (anesthetic) NEC	968.2	E855.1	E938.2	E950.4	E962.0	E980.4
Nitrozone	976.0	E858.7	E946.0	E950.4	E962.0	E980.4
Noctec	967.1	E852.0	E937.1	E950.2	E962.0	E980.2
Noludar	967.5	E852.4	E937.5	E950.2	E962.0	E980.2
Noptil	967.0	E851	E937.0	E950.1	E962.0	E980.1
Noradrenalin	971.2	E855.5	E941.2	E950.4	E962.0	E980.4
Noramidopyrine	965.5	E850.5	E935.5	E950.0	E962.0	E980.0
Norepinephrine	971.2	E855.5	E941.2	E950.4	E962.0	E980.4
Norethandrolone	962.1	E858.0	E932.1	E950.4	E962.0	E980.4
Norethindrone	962.2	E858.0	E932.2	E950.4	E962.0	E980.4
Norethisterone	962.2	E858.0	E932.2	E950.4	E962.0	E980.4
Norethynodrel	962.2	E858.0	E932.2	E950.4	E962.0	E980.4
Norlestrin	962.2	E858.0	E932.2	E950.4	E962.0	E980.4
Norlutin	962.2	E858.0	E932.2	E950.4	E962.0	E980.4
Normison — see Benzodiazepines						
Normorphine	965.09	E850.2	E935.2	E950.0	E962.0	E980.0
Nortriptyline	969.05 ▲	E854.0	E939.0	E950.3	E962.0	E980.3
Noscapine	975.4	E858.6	E945.4	E950.4	E962.0	E980.4
Nose preparations	976.6	E858.7	E946.6	E950.4	E962.0	E980.4
Novobiocin	960.8	E856	E930.8	E950.4	E962.0	E980.4
Novocain (infiltration)						
(topical)	968.5	E855.2	E938.5	E950.4	E962.0	E980.4
nerve block (peripheral)						
(plexus)	968.6	E855.2	E938.6	E950.4	E962.0	E980.4
spinal	968.7	E855.2	E938.7	E950.4	E962.0	E980.4
Noxythiolin	961.9	E857	E931.9	E950.4	E962.0	E980.4
NPH Iletin (insulin)	962.3	E858.0	E932.3	E950.4	E962.0	E980.4
Numorphan	965.09	E850.2	E935.2	E950.0	E962.0	E980.0
Nunol	967.0	E851	E937.0	E950.1	E962.0	E980.1
Nupercaine (spinal						
anesthetic)	968.7	E855.2	E938.7	E950.4	E962.0	E980.4
topical (surface)	968.5	E855.2	E938.5	E950.4	E962.0	E980.4
Nutmeg oil (liniment)	976.3	E858.7	E946.3	E950.4	E962.0	E980.4
Nux vomica	989.1	E863.7	—	E950.6	E962.1	E980.7
Nydrazid	961.8	E857	E931.8	E950.4	E962.0	E980.4
Nylidrin	971.2	E855.5	E941.2	E950.4	E962.0	E980.4
Nystatin	960.1	E856	E930.1	E950.4	E962.0	E980.4
topical	976.0	E858.7	E946.0	E950.4	E962.0	E980.4
Nytol	963.0	E858.1	E933.0	E950.4	E962.0	E980.4
Oblivion	967.8	E852.8	E937.8	E950.2	E962.0	E980.2
Octyl nitrite	972.4	E858.3	E942.4	E950.4	E962.0	E980.4
Oestradiol (cypionate)						
(dipropionate) (valerate)	962.2	E858.0	E932.2	E950.4	E962.0	E980.4
Oestriol	962.2	E858.0	E932.2	E950.4	E962.0	E980.4
Oestrone	962.2	E858.0	E932.2	E950.4	E962.0	E980.4
Oil (of) NEC	989.89	E866.8	—	E950.9	E962.1	E980.9
bitter almond	989.0	E866.8	—	E950.9	E962.1	E980.9
camphor	976.1	E858.7	E946.1	E950.4	E962.0	E980.4
colors	989.89	E861.6	—	E950.9	E962.1	E980.9
fumes	987.8	E869.8	—	E952.8	E962.2	E982.8
lubricating	981	E862.2	—	E950.9	E962.1	E980.9
specified source, other — see substance specified						
vitriol (liquid)	983.1	E864.1	—	E950.7	E962.1	E980.6
fumes	987.8	E869.8	—	E952.8	E962.2	E982.8
wintergreen (bitter) NEC	976.3	E858.7	E946.3	E950.4	E962.0	E980.4
Ointments NEC	976.9	E858.7	E946.9	E950.4	E962.0	E980.4
Oleander	988.2	E865.4	—	E950.9	E962.1	E980.9
Oleandomycin	960.3	E856	E930.3	E950.4	E962.0	E980.4
Oleovitamin A	963.5	E858.1	E933.5	E950.4	E962.0	E980.4
Oleum ricini	973.1	E858.4	E943.1	E950.4	E962.0	E980.4
Olive oil (medicinal) NEC	973.2	E858.4	E943.2	E950.4	E962.0	E980.4
OMPA	989.3	E863.1	—	E950.6	E962.1	E980.7
Oncovin	963.1	E858.1	E933.1	E950.4	E962.0	E980.4
Ophthaine	968.5	E855.2	E938.5	E950.4	E962.0	E980.4
Ophthetic	968.5	E855.2	E938.5	E950.4	E962.0	E980.4

Opiates, opioids, opium	Poisoning	Accident	Therapeutic Use	Suicide Attempt	Assault	Undetermined
NEC	965.00	E850.2	E935.2	E950.0	E962.0	E980.0
antagonists	970.1	E854.3	E940.1	E950.4	E962.0	E980.4
Oracon	962.2	E858.0	E932.2	E950.4	E962.0	E980.4
Oragrafin	977.8	E858.8	E947.8	E950.4	E962.0	E980.4
Oral contraceptives	962.2	E858.0	E932.2	E950.4	E962.0	E980.4
Orciprenaline	975.1	E858.6	E945.1	E950.4	E962.0	E980.4
Organidin	975.5	E858.6	E945.5	E950.4	E962.0	E980.4
Organophosphates	989.3	E863.1	—	E950.6	E962.1	E980.7
Orimune	979.5	E858.8	E949.5	E950.4	E962.0	E980.4
Orinase	962.3	E858.0	E932.3	E950.4	E962.0	E980.4
Orphenadrine	966.4	E855.0	E936.4	E950.4	E962.0	E980.4
Ortal (sodium)	967.0	E851	E937.0	E950.1	E962.0	E980.1
Orthoboric acid	976.0	E858.7	E946.0	E950.4	E962.0	E980.4
ENT agent	976.6	E858.7	E946.6	E950.4	E962.0	E980.4
ophthalmic preparation	976.5	E858.7	E946.5	E950.4	E962.0	E980.4
Orthocaine	968.5	E855.2	E938.5	E950.4	E962.0	E980.4
Ortho-Novum	962.2	E858.0	E932.2	E950.4	E962.0	E980.4
Orthotolidine (reagent)	977.8	E858.8	E947.8	E950.4	E962.0	E980.4
Osmic acid (liquid)	983.1	E864.1	—	E950.7	E962.1	E980.6
fumes	987.8	E869.8	—	E952.8	E962.2	E982.8
Osmotic diuretics	974.4	E858.5	E944.4	E950.4	E962.0	E980.4
Ouabain	972.1	E858.3	E942.1	E950.4	E962.0	E980.4
Ovarian hormones (synthetic						
substitutes)	962.2	E858.0	E932.2	E950.4	E962.0	E980.4
Ovral	962.2	E858.0	E932.2	E950.4	E962.0	E980.4
Ovulation suppressants	962.2	E858.0	E932.2	E950.4	E962.0	E980.4
Ovulen	962.2	E858.0	E932.2	E950.4	E962.0	E980.4
Oxacillin (sodium)	960.0	E856	E930.0	E950.4	E962.0	E980.4
Oxalic acid	983.1	E864.1	—	E950.7	E962.1	E980.6
Oxanamide	969.5	E853.8	E939.5	E950.3	E962.0	E980.3
Oxandrolone	962.1	E858.0	E932.1	E950.4	E962.0	E980.4
Oxaprozin	965.61	E850.6	E935.6	E950.0	E962.0	E980.0
Oxazepam	969.4	E853.2	E939.4	E950.3	E962.0	E980.3
Oxazolidine derivatives	966.0	E855.0	E936.0	E950.4	E962.0	E980.4
Ox bile extract	973.4	E858.4	E943.4	E950.4	E962.0	E980.4
Oxedrine	971.2	E855.5	E941.2	E950.4	E962.0	E980.4
Oxeladin	975.4	E858.6	E945.4	E950.4	E962.0	E980.4
Oxethazaine NEC	968.5	E855.2	E938.5	E950.4	E962.0	E980.4
Oxidizing agents NEC	983.9	E864.3	—	E950.7	E962.1	E980.6
Oxolinic acid	961.3	E857	E931.3	E950.4	E962.0	E980.4
Oxophenarsine	961.1	E857	E931.1	E950.4	E962.0	E980.4
Oxsoralen	976.3	E858.7	E946.3	E950.4	E962.0	E980.4
Oxtriphylline	975.7	E858.6	E945.7	E950.4	E962.0	E980.4
Oxybuprocaine	968.5	E855.2	E938.5	E950.4	E962.0	E980.4
Oxybutynin	975.1	E858.6	E945.1	E950.4	E962.0	E980.4
Oxycodone	965.09	E850.2	E935.2	E950.0	E962.0	E980.0
Oxygen	987.8	E869.8	—	E952.8	E962.2	E982.8
Oxylone	976.0	E858.7	E946.0	E950.4	E962.0	E980.4
ophthalmic preparation	976.5	E858.7	E946.5	E950.4	E962.0	E980.4
Oxymesterone	962.1	E858.0	E932.1	E950.4	E962.0	E980.4
Oxymetazoline	971.2	E855.5	E941.2	E950.4	E962.0	E980.4
Oxymetholone	962.1	E858.0	E932.1	E950.4	E962.0	E980.4
Oxymorphone	965.09	E850.2	E935.2	E950.0	E962.0	E980.0
Oxypertine	969.09 ▲	E854.0	E939.0	E950.3	E962.0	E980.3
Oxyphenbutazone	965.5	E850.5	E935.5	E950.0	E962.0	E980.0
Oxyphencyclimine	971.1	E855.4	E941.1	E950.4	E962.0	E980.4
Oxyphenisatin	973.1	E858.4	E943.1	E950.4	E962.0	E980.4
Oxyphenonium	971.1	E855.4	E941.1	E950.4	E962.0	E980.4
Oxyquinoline	961.3	E857	E931.3	E950.4	E962.0	E980.4
Oxytetracycline	960.4	E856	E930.4	E950.4	E962.0	E980.4
Oxytocics	975.0	E858.6	E945.0	E950.4	E962.0	E980.4
Oxytocin	975.0	E858.6	E945.0	E950.4	E962.0	E980.4
Ozone	987.8	E869.8	—	E952.8	E962.2	E982.8
PABA	976.3	E858.7	E946.3	E950.4	E962.0	E980.4
Packed red cells	964.7	E858.2	E934.7	E950.4	E962.0	E980.4
Paint NEC	989.89	E861.6	—	E950.9	E962.1	E980.9
cleaner	982.8	E862.9	—	E950.9	E962.1	E980.9
fumes NEC	987.8	E869.8	—	E952.8	E962.1	E982.8
lead (fumes)	984.0	E861.5	—	E950.9	E962.1	E980.9
solvent NEC	982.8	E862.9	—	E950.9	E962.1	E980.9
stripper	982.8	E862.9	—	E950.9	E962.1	E980.9
Palfium	965.09	E850.2	E935.2	E950.0	E962.0	E980.0
Palivizumab	979.9	E858.8	E949.6	E950.4	E962.0	E980.4
Paludrine	961.4	E857	E931.4	E950.4	E962.0	E980.4
PAM	977.2	E855.8	E947.2	E950.4	E962.0	E980.4
Pamaquine (naphthoate)	961.4	E857	E931.4	E950.4	E962.0	E980.4
Pamprin	965.1	E850.3	E935.3	E950.0	E962.0	E980.0
Panadol	965.4	E850.4	E935.4	E950.0	E962.0	E980.0
Pancreatic dornase						
(mucolytic)	963.4	E858.1	E933.4	E950.4	E962.0	E980.4
Pancreatin	973.4	E858.4	E943.4	E950.4	E962.0	E980.4

Nontherapeutic use substance

Subterms under main terms may continue to next column or page

Substance	Poisoning	Accident	Therapeutic Use	Suicide Attempt	Assault	Undetermined
Pancrelipase	973.4	E858.4	E943.4	E950.4	E962.0	E980.4
Pangamic acid	963.5	E858.1	E933.5	E950.4	E962.0	E980.4
Panthenol	963.5	E858.1	E933.5	E950.4	E962.0	E980.4
topical	976.8	E858.7	E946.8	E950.4	E962.0	E980.4
Pantopaque	977.8	E858.8	E947.8	E950.4	E962.0	E980.4
Pantopon	965.00	E850.2	E935.2	E950.0	E962.0	E980.0
Pantothenic acid	963.5	E858.1	E933.5	E950.4	E962.0	E980.4
Panwarfin	964.2	E858.2	E934.2	E950.4	E962.0	E980.4
Papain	973.4	E858.4	E943.4	E950.4	E962.0	E980.4
Papaverine	972.5	E858.3	E942.5	E950.4	E962.0	E980.4
Para-aminobenzoic acid	976.3	E858.7	E946.3	E950.4	E962.0	E980.4
Para-aminophenol derivatives	965.4	E850.4	E935.4	E950.0	E962.0	E980.0
Para-aminosalicylic acid (derivatives)	961.8	E857	E931.8	E950.4	E962.0	E980.4
Paracetaldehyde (medicinal)	967.2	E852.1	E937.2	E950.2	E962.0	E980.2
Paracetamol	965.4	E850.4	E935.4	E950.0	E962.0	E980.0
Paracodin	965.09	E850.2	E935.2	E950.0	E962.0	E980.0
Paradione	966.0	E855.0	E936.0	E950.4	E962.0	E980.4
Paraffin(s) (wax)	981	E862.3	—	E950.9	E962.1	E980.9
liquid (medicinal)	973.2	E858.4	E943.2	E950.4	E962.0	E980.4
nonmedicinal (oil)	981	E962.1		E950.9	E962.1	E980.9
Paraldehyde (medicinal)	967.2	E852.1	E937.2	E950.2	E962.0	E980.2
Paramethadione	966.0	E855.0	E936.0	E950.4	E962.0	E980.4
Paramethasone	962.0	E858.0	E932.0	E950.4	E962.0	E980.4
Paraquat	989.4	E863.5	—	E950.6	E962.1	E980.7
Parasympatholytics	971.1	E855.4	E941.1	E950.4	E962.0	E980.4
Parasympathomimetics	971.0	E855.3	E941.0	E950.4	E962.0	E980.4
Parathion	989.3	E863.1	—	E950.6	E962.1	E980.7
Parathormone	962.6	E858.0	E932.6	E950.4	E962.0	E980.4
Parathyroid (derivatives)	962.6	E858.0	E932.6	E950.4	E962.0	E980.4
Paratyphoid vaccine	978.1	E858.8	E948.1	E950.4	E962.0	E980.4
Paredrine	971.2	E855.5	E941.2	E950.4	E962.0	E980.4
Paregoric	965.00	E850.2	E935.2	E950.0	E962.0	E980.0
Pargyline	972.3	E858.3	E942.3	E950.4	E962.0	E980.4
Paris green	985.1	E866.3	—	E950.8	E962.1	E980.8
insecticide	985.1	E863.4	—	E950.8	E962.1	E980.8
Parnate ▲	969.01	E854.0	E939.0	E950.3	E962.0	E980.3
Paromomycin	960.8	E856	E930.8	E950.4	E962.0	E980.4
Paroxypropione	963.1	E858.1	E933.1	E950.4	E962.0	E980.4
Parzone	965.09	E850.2	E935.2	E950.0	E962.0	E980.0
PAS	961.8	E857	E931.8	E950.4	E962.0	E980.4
PCBs	981	E862.3		E950.9	E962.1	E980.9
PCP (pentachlorophenol)	989.4	E863.6	—	E950.6	E962.1	E980.7
herbicide	989.4	E863.5	—	E950.6	E962.1	E980.7
insecticide	989.4	E863.4	—	E950.6	E962.1	E980.7
phencyclidine	968.3	E855.1	E938.3	E950.4	E962.0	E980.4
Peach kernel oil (emulsion)	973.2	E858.4	E943.2	E950.4	E962.0	E980.4
Peanut oil (emulsion) NEC	973.2	E858.4	E943.2	E950.4	E962.0	E980.4
topical	976.3	E858.7	E946.3	E950.4	E962.0	E980.4
Pearly Gates (morning glory seeds)	969.6	E854.1	E939.6	E950.3	E962.0	E980.3
Pecazine	969.1	E853.0	E939.1	E950.3	E962.0	E980.3
Pecilocin	960.1	E856	E930.1	E950.4	E962.0	E980.4
Pectin (with kaolin) NEC	973.5	E858.4	E943.5	E950.4	E962.0	E980.4
Pelletierine tannate	961.6	E857	E931.6	E950.4	E962.0	E980.4
Pemoline ▲	969.79	E854.2	E939.7	E950.3	E962.0	E980.3
Pempidine	972.3	E858.3	E942.3	E950.4	E962.0	E980.4
Penamecillin	960.0	E856	E930.0	E950.4	E962.0	E980.4
Penethamate hydriodide	960.0	E856	E930.0	E950.4	E962.0	E980.4
Penicillamine	963.8	E858.1	E933.8	E950.4	E962.0	E980.4
Penicillin (any type)	960.0	E856	E930.0	E950.4	E962.0	E980.4
Penicillinase	963.4	E858.1	E933.4	E950.4	E962.0	E980.4
Pentachlorophenol (fungicide)	989.4	E863.6	—	E950.6	E962.1	E980.7
herbicide	989.4	E863.5	—	E950.6	E962.1	E980.7
insecticide	989.4	E863.4	—	E950.6	E962.1	E980.7
Pentaerythritol	972.4	E858.3	E942.4	E950.4	E962.0	E980.4
chloral	967.1	E852.0	E937.1	E950.2	E962.0	E980.2
tetranitrate NEC	972.4	E858.3	E942.4	E950.4	E962.0	E980.4
Pentagastrin	977.8	E858.8	E947.8	E950.4	E962.0	E980.4
Pentalin	982.3	E862.4	—	E950.9	E962.1	E980.9
Pentamethonium (bromide)	972.3	E858.3	E942.3	E950.4	E962.0	E980.4
Pentamidine	961.5	E857	E931.5	E950.4	E962.0	E980.4
Pentanol	980.8	E860.8	—	E950.9	E962.1	E980.9
Pentaquine	961.4	E857	E931.4	E950.4	E962.0	E980.4
Pentazocine	965.8	E850.8	E935.8	E950.0	E962.0	E980.0
Penthienate	971.1	E855.4	E941.1	E950.4	E962.0	E980.4
Pentobarbital, pentobarbitone (sodium)	967.0	E851	E937.0	E950.1	E962.0	E980.1
Pentolinium (tartrate)	972.3	E858.3	E942.3	E950.4	E962.0	E980.4
Pentothal	968.3	E855.1	E938.3	E950.4	E962.0	E980.4
Pentylenetetrazol	970.0	E854.3	E940.0	E950.4	E962.0	E980.4
Pentylsalicylamide	961.8	E857	E931.8	E950.4	E962.0	E980.4
Pepsin	973.4	E858.4	E943.4	E950.4	E962.0	E980.4
Peptavlon	977.8	E858.8	E947.8	E950.4	E962.0	E980.4
Percaine (spinal)	968.7	E855.2	E938.7	E950.4	E962.0	E980.4
topical (surface)	968.5	E855.2	E938.5	E950.4	E962.0	E980.4
Perchloroethylene (vapor)	982.3	E862.4	—	E950.9	E962.1	E980.9
medicinal	961.6	E857	E931.6	E950.4	E962.0	E980.4
Percodan	965.09	E850.2	E935.2	E950.0	E962.0	E980.0
Percogesic	965.09	E850.2	E935.2	E950.0	E962.0	E980.0
Percorten	962.0	E858.0	E932.0	E950.4	E962.0	E980.4
Pergonal	962.4	E858.0	E932.4	E950.4	E962.0	E980.4
Perhexiline	972.4	E858.3	E942.4	E950.4	E962.0	E980.4
Periactin	963.0	E858.1	E933.0	E950.4	E962.0	E980.4
Periclor	967.1	E852.0	E937.1	E950.2	E962.0	E980.2
Pericyazine	969.1	E853.0	E939.1	E950.3	E962.0	E980.3
Peritrate	972.4	E858.3	E942.4	E950.4	E962.0	E980.4
Permanganates NEC	983.9	E864.3	—	E950.7	E962.1	E980.6
potassium (topical)	976.0	E858.7	E946.0	E950.4	E962.0	E980.4
Pernocton	967.0	E851	E937.0	E950.1	E962.0	E980.1
Pernoston	967.0	E851	E937.0	E950.1	E962.0	E980.1
Peronin(e)	965.09	E850.2	E935.2	E950.0	E962.0	E980.0
Perphenazine	969.1	E853.0	E939.1	E950.3	E962.0	E980.3
Pertofrane ▲	969.05	E854.0	E939.0	E950.3	E962.0	E980.3
Pertussis immune serum (human)	964.6	E858.2	E934.6	E950.4	E962.0	E980.4
vaccine (with diphtheria toxoid) (with tetanus toxoid)	978.6	E858.8	E948.6	E950.4	E962.0	E980.4
Peruvian balsam	976.8	E858.7	E946.8	E950.4	E962.0	E980.4
Pesticides (dust) (fumes) (vapor)	989.4	E863.4	—	E950.6	E962.1	E980.7
arsenic	985.1	E863.4	—	E950.8	E962.1	E980.8
chlorinated	989.2	E863.0	—	E950.6	E962.1	E980.7
cyanide	989.0	E863.4	—	E950.6	E962.1	E980.7
kerosene	981	E863.4	—	E950.6	E962.1	E980.7
mixture (of compounds)	989.4	E863.3	—	E950.6	E962.1	E980.7
naphthalene	983.0	E863.4	—	E950.7	E962.1	E980.6
organochlorine (compounds)	989.2	E863.0	—	E950.6	E962.1	E980.7
petroleum (distillate) (products) NEC	981	E863.4	—	E950.6	E962.1	E980.7
specified ingredient NEC	989.4	E863.4	—	E950.6	E962.1	E980.7
strychnine	989.1	E863.4	—	E950.6	E962.1	E980.7
thallium	985.8	E863.7	—	E950.6	E962.1	E980.7
Pethidine (hydrochloride)	965.09	E850.2	E935.2	E950.0	E962.0	E980.0
Petrichloral	967.1	E852.0	E937.1	E950.2	E962.0	E980.2
Petrol	981	E862.1	—	E950.9	E962.1	E980.9
vapor	987.1	E869.8	—	E952.8	E962.2	E982.8
Petrolatum (jelly) (ointment)	976.3	E858.7	E946.3	E950.4	E962.0	E980.4
hydrophilic	976.3	E858.7	E946.3	E950.4	E962.0	E980.4
liquid	973.2	E858.4	E943.2	E950.4	E962.0	E980.4
topical	976.3	E858.7	E946.3	E950.4	E962.0	E980.4
nonmedicinal	981	E862.1	—	E950.9	E962.1	E980.9
Petroleum (cleaners) (fuels) (products) NEC	981	E862.1	—	E950.9	E962.1	E980.9
benzin(e) — see Ligroin						
ether — see Ligroin						
jelly — see Petrolatum						
naphtha — see Ligroin						
pesticide	981	E863.4	—	E950.6	E962.1	E980.7
solids	981	E862.3	—	E950.9	E962.1	E980.9
solvents	981	E862.0	—	E950.9	E962.1	E980.9
vapor	987.1	E869.8	—	E952.8	E962.2	E982.8
Peyote	969.6	E854.1	E939.6	E950.3	E962.0	E980.3
Phanodorm, phanodorn	967.0	E851	E937.0	E950.1	E962.0	E980.1
Phanquinone, phanquone	961.5	E857	E931.5	E950.4	E962.0	E980.4
Pharmaceutical excipient or adjunct	977.4	E858.8	E947.4	E950.4	E962.0	E980.4
Phenacemide	966.3	E855.0	E936.3	E950.4	E962.0	E980.4
Phenacetin	965.4	E850.4	E935.4	E950.0	E962.0	E980.0
Phenadoxone	965.09	E850.2	E935.2	E950.0	E962.0	E980.0
Phenaglycodol	969.5	E853.8	E939.5	E950.3	E962.0	E980.3
Phenantoin	966.1	E855.0	E936.1	E950.4	E962.0	E980.4
Phenaphthazine reagent	977.8	E858.8	E947.8	E950.4	E962.0	E980.4
Phenazocine	965.09	E850.2	E935.2	E950.0	E962.0	E980.0
Phenazone	965.5	E850.5	E935.5	E950.0	E962.0	E980.0

Nontherapeutic use substance

▶◀ Revised Text   ● New Line   ▲ Revised Code

Subterms under main terms may continue to next column or page

2010 ICD-9-CM

October 2009 • Volume 2 — 311

Pancrelipase — Phenazone

	Poisoning	Accident	Therapeutic Use	Suicide Attempt	Assault	Undetermined
External Cause (E-Code)						
Phenazopyridine	976.1	E858.7	E946.1	E950.4	E962.0	E980.4
Phenbenicillin	960.0	E856	E930.0	E950.4	E962.0	E980.4
Phenbutrazate	977.0	E858.8	E947.0	E950.4	E962.0	E980.4
Phencyclidine	968.3	E855.1	E938.3	E950.4	E962.0	E980.4
Phendimetrazine	977.0	E858.8	E947.0	E950.4	E962.0	E980.4
Phenelzine	969.01 ▲	E854.0	E939.0	E950.3	E962.0	E980.3
Phenergan	967.8	E852.8	E937.8	E950.2	E962.0	E980.2
Phenethicillin (potassium)	960.0	E856	E930.0	E950.4	E962.0	E980.4
Phenetsal	965.1	E850.3	E935.3	E950.0	E962.0	E980.0
Pheneturide	966.3	E855.0	E936.3	E950.4	E962.0	E980.4
Phenformin	962.3	E858.0	E932.3	E950.4	E962.0	E980.4
Phenglutarimide	971.1	E855.4	E941.1	E950.4	E962.0	E980.4
Phenicarbazide	965.8	E850.8	E935.8	E950.0	E962.0	E980.0
Phenindamine (tartrate)	963.0	E858.1	E933.0	E950.4	E962.0	E980.4
Phenindione	964.2	E858.2	E934.2	E950.4	E962.0	E980.4
Pheniprazine	969.01 ▲	E854.0	E939.0	E950.3	E962.0	E980.3
Pheniramine (maleate)	963.0	E858.1	E933.0	E950.4	E962.0	E980.4
Phenmetrazine	977.0	E858.8	E947.0	E950.4	E962.0	E980.4
Phenobal	967.0	E851	E937.0	E950.1	E962.0	E980.1
Phenobarbital	967.0	E851	E937.0	E950.1	E962.0	E980.1
Phenobarbitone	967.0	E851	E937.0	E950.1	E962.0	E980.1
Phenoctide	976.0	E858.7	E946.0	E950.4	E962.0	E980.4
Phenol (derivatives) NEC	983.0	E864.0	—	E950.7	E962.1	E980.6
disinfectant	983.0	E864.0	—	E950.7	E962.1	E980.6
pesticide	989.4	E863.4	—	E950.6	E962.1	E980.7
red	977.8	E858.8	E947.8	E950.4	E962.0	E980.4
Phenolphthalein	973.1	E858.4	E943.1	E950.4	E962.0	E980.4
Phenolsulfonphthalein	977.8	E858.8	E947.8	E950.4	E962.0	E980.4
Phenomorphan	965.09	E850.2	E935.2	E950.0	E962.0	E980.0
Phenonyl	967.0	E851	E937.0	E950.1	E962.0	E980.1
Phenoperidine	965.09	E850.2	E935.2	E950.0	E962.0	E980.0
Phenoquin	974.7	E858.5	E944.7	E950.4	E962.0	E980.4
Phenothiazines (tranquilizers) NEC	969.1	E853.0	E939.1	E950.3	E962.0	E980.3
insecticide	989.3	E863.4	—	E950.6	E962.1	E980.7
Phenoxybenzamine	971.3	E855.6	E941.3	E950.4	E962.0	E980.4
Phenoxymethyl penicillin	960.0	E856	E930.0	E950.4	E962.0	E980.4
Phenprocoumon	964.2	E858.2	E934.2	E950.4	E962.0	E980.4
Phensuximide	966.2	E855.0	E936.2	E950.4	E962.0	E980.4
Phentermine	977.0	E858.8	E947.0	E950.4	E962.0	E980.4
Phentolamine	971.3	E855.6	E941.3	E950.4	E962.0	E980.4
Phenyl						
butazone	965.5	E850.5	E935.5	E950.0	E962.0	E980.0
enediamine	983.0	E864.0	—	E950.7	E962.1	E980.6
hydrazine	983.0	E864.0	—	E950.7	E962.1	E980.6
antineoplastic	963.1	E858.1	E933.1	E950.4	E962.0	E980.4
mercuric compounds — see Mercury						
salicylate	976.3	E858.7	E946.3	E950.4	E962.0	E980.4
Phenylephrin	971.2	E855.5	E941.2	E950.4	E962.0	E980.4
Phenylethylbiguanide	962.3	E858.0	E932.3	E950.4	E962.0	E980.4
Phenylpropanolamine	971.2	E855.5	E941.2	E950.4	E962.0	E980.4
Phenylsulfthion	989.3	E863.1	—	E950.6	E962.1	E980.7
Phenyramidol, phenyramidon	965.7	E850.7	E935.7	E950.0	E962.0	E980.0
Phenytoin	966.1	E855.0	E936.1	E950.4	E962.0	E980.4
pHisoHex	976.2	E858.7	E946.2	E950.4	E962.0	E980.4
Pholcodine	965.09	E850.2	E935.2	E950.0	E962.0	E980.0
Phorate	989.3	E863.1	—	E950.6	E962.1	E980.7
Phosdrin	989.3	E863.1	—	E950.6	E962.1	E980.7
Phosgene (gas)	987.8	E869.8	—	E952.8	E962.2	E982.8
Phosphate (tricresyl)	989.89	E866.8	—	E950.9	E962.1	E980.9
organic	989.3	E863.1	—	E950.6	E962.1	E980.7
solvent	982.8	E862.4	—	E950.9	E926.1	E980.9
Phosphine	987.8	E869.8	—	E952.8	E962.2	E982.8
fumigant	987.8	E863.8	—	E950.6	E962.2	E980.7
Phospholine	971.0	E855.3	E941.0	E950.4	E962.0	E980.4
Phosphoric acid	983.1	E864.1	—	E950.7	E962.1	E980.6
Phosphorus (compounds) NEC	983.9	E864.3	—	E950.7	E962.1	E980.6
rodenticide	983.9	E863.7	—	E950.7	E962.1	E980.6
Phthalimidoglutarimide	967.8	E852.8	E937.8	E950.2	E962.0	E980.2
Phthalylsulfathiazole	961.0	E857	E931.0	E950.4	E962.0	E980.4
Phylloquinone	964.3	E858.2	E934.3	E950.4	E962.0	E980.4
Physeptone	965.02	E850.1	E935.1	E950.0	E962.0	E980.0
Physostigma venenosum	988.2	E865.4	—	E950.9	E962.1	E980.9
Physostigmine	971.0	E855.3	E941.0	E950.4	E962.0	E980.4
Phytolacca decandra	988.2	E865.4	—	E950.9	E962.1	E980.9
Phytomenadione	964.3	E858.2	E934.3	E950.4	E962.0	E980.4
Phytonadione	964.3	E858.2	E934.3	E950.4	E962.0	E980.4
Picric (acid)	983.0	E864.0	—	E950.7	E962.1	E980.6
Picrotoxin	970.0	E854.3	E940.0	E950.4	E962.0	E980.4

	Poisoning	Accident	Therapeutic Use	Suicide Attempt	Assault	Undetermined
External Cause (E-Code)						
Pilocarpine	971.0	E855.3	E941.0	E950.4	E962.0	E980.4
Pilocarpus (jaborandi) extract	971.0	E855.3	E941.0	E950.4	E962.0	E980.4
Pimaricin	960.1	E856	E930.1	E950.4	E962.0	E980.4
Piminodine	965.09	E850.2	E935.2	E950.0	E962.0	E980.0
Pine oil, pinesol (disinfectant)	983.9	E861.4	—	E950.7	E962.1	E980.6
Pinkroot	961.6	E857	E931.6	E950.4	E962.0	E980.4
Pipadone	965.09	E850.2	E935.2	E950.0	E962.0	E980.0
Pipamazine	963.0	E858.1	E933.0	E950.4	E962.0	E980.4
Pipazethate	975.4	E858.6	E945.4	E950.4	E962.0	E980.4
Pipenzolate	971.1	E855.4	E941.1	E950.4	E962.0	E980.4
Piperacetazine	969.1	E853.0	E939.1	E950.3	E962.0	E980.3
Piperazine NEC	961.6	E857	E931.6	E950.4	E962.0	E980.4
estrone sulfate	962.2	E858.0	E932.2	E950.4	E962.0	E980.4
Piper cubeba	988.2	E865.4	—	E950.9	E962.1	E980.9
Piperidione	975.4	E858.6	E945.4	E950.4	E962.0	E980.4
Piperidolate	971.1	E855.4	E941.1	E950.4	E962.0	E980.4
Piperocaine	968.9	E855.2	E938.9	E950.4	E962.0	E980.4
infiltration (subcutaneous)	968.5	E855.2	E938.5	E950.4	E962.0	E980.4
nerve block (peripheral) (plexus)	968.6	E855.2	E938.6	E950.4	E962.0	E980.4
topical (surface)	968.5	E855.2	E938.5	E950.4	E962.0	E980.4
Pipobroman	963.1	E858.1	E933.1	E950.4	E962.0	E980.4
Pipradrol	970.8	E854.3	E940.8	E950.4	E962.0	E980.4
Piscidia (bark) (erythrina)	965.7	E850.7	E935.7	E950.0	E962.0	E980.0
Pitch	983.0	E864.0	—	E950.7	E962.1	E980.6
Pitkin's solution	968.7	E855.2	E938.7	E950.4	E962.0	E980.4
Pitocin	975.0	E858.6	E945.0	E950.4	E962.0	E980.4
Pitressin (tannate)	962.5	E858.0	E932.5	E950.4	E962.0	E980.4
Pituitary extracts (posterior)	962.5	E858.0	E932.5	E950.4	E962.0	E980.4
anterior	962.4	E858.0	E932.4	E950.4	E962.0	E980.4
Pituitrin	962.5	E858.0	E932.5	E950.4	E962.0	E980.4
Placental extract	962.9	E858.0	E932.9	E950.4	E962.0	E980.4
Placidyl	967.8	E852.8	E937.8	E950.2	E962.0	E980.2
Plague vaccine	978.3	E858.8	E948.3	E950.4	E962.0	E980.4
Plant foods or fertilizers NEC	989.89	E866.5	—	E950.9	E962.1	E980.9
mixed with herbicides	989.4	E863.5	—	E950.6	E962.1	E980.7
Plants, noxious, used as food	988.2	E865.9	—	E950.9	E962.1	E980.9
berries and seeds	988.2	E865.3	—	E950.9	E962.1	E980.9
specified type NEC	988.2	E865.4	—	E950.9	E962.1	E980.9
Plasma (blood)	964.7	E858.2	E934.7	E950.4	E962.0	E980.4
expanders	964.8	E858.2	E934.8	E950.4	E962.0	E980.4
Plasmanate	964.7	E858.2	E934.7	E950.4	E962.0	E980.4
Plegicil	969.1	E853.0	E939.1	E950.3	E962.0	E980.3
Podophyllin	976.4	E858.7	E946.4	E950.4	E962.0	E980.4
Podophyllum resin	976.4	E858.7	E946.4	E950.4	E962.0	E980.4
Poison NEC	989.9	E866.9	—	E950.9	E962.1	E980.9
Poisonous berries	988.2	E865.3	—	E950.9	E962.1	E980.9
Pokeweed (any part)	988.2	E865.4	—	E950.9	E962.1	E980.9
Poldine	971.1	E855.4	E941.1	E950.4	E962.0	E980.4
Poliomyelitis vaccine	979.5	E858.8	E949.5	E950.4	E962.0	E980.4
Poliovirus vaccine	979.5	E858.8	E949.5	E950.4	E962.0	E980.4
Polish (car) (floor) (furniture) (metal) (silver)	989.89	E861.2	—	E950.9	E962.1	E980.9
abrasive	989.89	E861.3	—	E950.9	E962.1	E980.9
porcelain	989.89	E861.3	—	E950.9	E962.1	E980.9
Poloxalkol	973.2	E858.4	E943.2	E950.4	E962.0	E980.4
Polyaminostyrene resins	974.5	E858.5	E944.5	E950.4	E962.0	E980.4
Polychlorinated biphenyl — see PCBs						
Polycycline	960.4	E856	E930.4	E950.4	E962.0	E980.4
Polyester resin hardener	982.8	E862.4	—	E950.9	E962.1	E980.9
fumes	987.8	E869.8	—	E952.8	E962.2	E982.8
Polyestradiol (phosphate)	962.2	E858.0	E932.2	E950.4	E962.0	E980.4
Polyethanolamine alkyl sulfate	976.2	E858.7	E946.2	E950.4	E962.0	E980.4
Polyethylene glycol	976.3	E858.7	E946.3	E950.4	E962.0	E980.4
Polyferose	964.0	E858.2	E934.0	E950.4	E962.0	E980.4
Polymyxin B	960.8	E856	E930.8	E950.4	E962.0	E980.4
ENT agent	976.6	E858.7	E946.6	E950.4	E962.0	E980.4
ophthalmic preparation	976.5	E858.7	E946.5	E950.4	E962.0	E980.4
topical NEC	976.0	E858.7	E946.0	E950.4	E962.0	E980.4
Polynoxylin(e)	976.0	E858.7	E946.0	E950.4	E962.0	E980.4
Polyoxymethyleneurea	976.0	E858.7	E946.0	E950.4	E962.0	E980.4
Polytetrafluoroethylene (inhaled)	987.8	E869.8	—	E952.8	E962.2	E982.8
Polythiazide	974.3	E858.5	E944.3	E950.4	E962.0	E980.4
Polyvinylpyrrolidone	964.8	E858.2	E934.8	E950.4	E962.0	E980.4

Index

Phenazopyridine — Polyvinylpyrrolidone

	Poisoning	External Cause (E-Code)				
		Accident	Therapeutic Use	Suicide Attempt	Assault	Undetermined
Pontocaine (hydrochloride) (infiltration) (topical)	968.5	E855.2	E938.5	E950.4	E962.0	E980.4
nerve block (peripheral) (plexus)	968.6	E855.2	E938.6	E950.4	E962.0	E980.4
spinal	968.7	E855.2	E938.7	E950.4	E962.0	E980.4
Pot	969.6	E854.1	E939.6	E950.3	E962.0	E980.3
Potash (caustic)	983.2	E864.2	—	E950.7	E962.1	E980.6
Potassic saline injection (lactated)	974.5	E858.5	E944.5	E950.4	E962.0	E980.4
Potassium (salts) NEC	974.5	E858.5	E944.5	E950.4	E962.0	E980.4
aminosalicylate	961.8	E857	E931.8	E950.4	E962.0	E980.4
arsenite (solution)	985.1	E866.3	—	E950.8	E962.1	E980.8
bichromate	983.9	E864.3	—	E950.7	E962.1	E980.6
bisulfate	983.9	E864.3	—	E950.7	E962.1	E980.6
bromide (medicinal) NEC	967.3	E852.2	E937.3	E950.2	E962.0	E980.2
carbonate	983.2	E864.2	—	E950.7	E962.1	E980.6
chlorate NEC	983.9	E864.3	—	E950.7	E962.1	E980.6
cyanide — see Cyanide						
hydroxide	983.2	E864.2	—	E950.7	E962.1	E980.6
iodide (expectorant) NEC	975.5	E858.6	E945.5	E950.4	E962.0	E980.4
nitrate	989.89	E866.8	—	E950.9	E962.1	E980.9
oxalate	983.9	E864.3	—	E950.7	E962.1	E980.6
perchlorate NEC	977.8	E858.8	E947.8	E950.4	E962.0	E980.4
antithyroid	962.8	E858.0	E932.8	E950.4	E962.0	E980.4
permanganate	976.0	E858.7	E946.0	E950.4	E962.0	E980.4
nonmedicinal	983.9	E864.3	—	E950.7	E962.1	E980.6
Povidone-iodine (anti-infective) NEC	976.0	E858.7	E946.0	E950.4	E962.0	E980.4
Practolol	972.0	E858.3	E942.0	E950.4	E962.0	E980.4
Pralidoxime (chloride)	977.2	E858.8	E947.2	E950.4	E962.0	E980.4
Pramoxine	968.5	E855.2	E938.5	E950.4	E962.0	E980.4
Prazosin	972.6	E858.3	E942.6	E950.4	E962.0	E980.4
Prednisolone	962.0	E858.0	E932.0	E950.4	E962.0	E980.4
ENT agent	976.6	E858.7	E946.6	E950.4	E962.0	E980.4
ophthalmic preparation	976.5	E858.7	E946.5	E950.4	E962.0	E980.4
topical NEC	976.0	E858.7	E946.0	E950.4	E962.0	E980.4
Prednisone	962.0	E858.0	E932.0	E950.4	E962.0	E980.4
Pregnanediol	962.2	E858.0	E932.2	E950.4	E962.0	E980.4
Pregneninolone	962.2	E858.0	E932.2	E950.4	E962.0	E980.4
Preludin	977.0	E858.8	E947.0	E950.4	E962.0	E980.4
Premarin	962.2	E858.0	E932.2	E950.4	E962.0	E980.4
Prenylamine	972.4	E858.3	E942.4	E950.4	E962.0	E980.4
Preparation H	976.8	E858.7	E946.8	E950.4	E962.0	E980.4
Preservatives	989.89	E866.8	—	E950.9	E962.1	E980.9
Pride of China	988.2	E865.3	—	E950.9	E962.1	E980.9
Prilocaine	968.9	E855.2	E938.9	E950.4	E962.0	E980.4
infiltration (subcutaneous)	968.5	E855.2	E938.5	E950.4	E962.0	E980.4
nerve block (peripheral) (plexus)	968.6	E855.2	E938.6	E950.4	E962.0	E980.4
Primaquine	961.4	E857	E931.4	E950.4	E962.0	E980.4
Primidone	966.3	E855.0	E936.3	E950.4	E962.0	E980.4
Primula (veris)	988.2	E865.4	—	E950.9	E962.1	E980.9
Prinadol	965.09	E850.2	E935.2	E950.0	E962.0	E980.0
Priscol, Priscoline	971.3	E855.6	E941.3	E950.4	E962.0	E980.4
Privet	988.2	E865.4	—	E950.9	E962.1	E980.9
Privine	971.2	E855.5	E941.2	E950.4	E962.0	E980.4
Pro-Banthine	971.1	E855.4	E941.1	E950.4	E962.0	E980.4
Probarbital	967.0	E851	E937.0	E950.1	E962.0	E980.1
Probenecid	974.7	E858.5	E944.7	E950.4	E962.0	E980.4
Procainamide (hydrochloride)	972.0	E858.3	E942.0	E950.4	E962.0	E980.4
Procaine (hydrochloride) (infiltration) (topical)	968.5	E855.2	E938.5	E950.4	E962.0	E980.4
nerve block (peripheral) (plexus)	968.6	E855.2	E938.6	E950.4	E962.0	E980.4
penicillin G	960.0	E856	E930.0	E950.4	E962.0	E980.4
spinal	968.7	E855.2	E938.7	E950.4	E962.0	E980.4
Procalmidol	969.5	E853.8	E939.5	E950.3	E962.0	E980.3
Procarbazine	963.1	E858.1	E933.1	E950.4	E962.0	E980.4
Prochlorperazine	969.1	E853.0	E939.1	E950.3	E962.0	E980.3
Procyclidine	966.4	E855.0	E936.4	E950.4	E962.0	E980.4
Producer gas	986	E868.8	—	E952.1	E962.2	E982.1
Profenamine	966.4	E855.0	E936.4	E950.4	E962.0	E980.4
Profenil	975.1	E858.6	E945.1	E950.4	E962.0	E980.4
Progesterones	962.2	E858.0	E932.2	E950.4	E962.0	E980.4
Progestin	962.2	E858.0	E932.2	E950.4	E962.0	E980.4
Progestogens (with estrogens)	962.2	E858.0	E932.2	E950.4	E962.0	E980.4
Progestone	962.2	E858.0	E932.2	E950.4	E962.0	E980.4
Proguanil	961.4	E857	E931.4	E950.4	E962.0	E980.4
Prolactin	962.4	E858.0	E932.4	E950.4	E962.0	E980.4
Proloid	962.7	E858.0	E932.7	E950.4	E962.0	E980.4
Proluton	962.2	E858.0	E932.2	E950.4	E962.0	E980.4
Promacetin	961.8	E857	E931.8	E950.4	E962.0	E980.4
Promazine	969.1	E853.0	E939.1	E950.3	E962.0	E980.3
Promedol	965.09	E850.2	E935.2	E950.0	E962.0	E980.0
Promethazine	967.8	E852.8	E937.8	E950.2	E962.0	E980.2
Promin	961.8	E857	E931.8	E950.4	E962.0	E980.4
Pronestyl (hydrochloride)	972.0	E858.3	E942.0	E950.4	E962.0	E980.4
Pronetalol, pronethalol	972.0	E858.3	E942.0	E950.4	E962.0	E980.4
Prontosil	961.0	E857	E931.0	E950.4	E962.0	E980.4
Propamidine isethionate	961.5	E857	E931.5	E950.4	E962.0	E980.4
Propanal (medicinal)	967.8	E852.8	E937.8	E950.2	E962.0	E980.2
Propane (gas) (distributed in mobile container)	987.0	E868.0	—	E951.1	E962.2	E981.1
distributed through pipes	987.0	E867	—	E951.0	E962.2	E981.0
incomplete combustion of — see Carbon monoxide, Propane						
Propanidid	968.3	E855.1	E938.3	E950.4	E962.0	E980.4
Propanol	980.3	E860.4	—	E950.9	E962.1	E980.9
Propantheline	971.1	E855.4	E941.1	E950.4	E962.0	E980.4
Proparacaine	968.5	E855.2	E938.5	E950.4	E962.0	E980.4
Propatyl nitrate	972.4	E858.3	E942.4	E950.4	E962.0	E980.4
Propicillin	960.0	E856	E930.0	E950.4	E962.0	E980.4
Propiolactone (vapor)	987.8	E869.8	—	E952.8	E962.2	E982.8
Propiomazine	967.8	E852.8	E937.8	E950.2	E962.0	E980.2
Propionaldehyde (medicinal)	967.8	E852.8	E937.8	E950.2	E962.0	E980.2
Propionate compound	976.0	E858.7	E946.0	E950.4	E962.0	E980.4
Propion gel	976.0	E858.7	E946.0	E950.4	E962.0	E980.4
Propitocaine	968.9	E855.2	E938.9	E950.4	E962.0	E980.4
infiltration (subcutaneous)	968.5	E855.2	E938.5	E950.4	E962.0	E980.4
nerve block (peripheral) (plexus)	968.6	E855.2	E938.6	E950.4	E962.0	E980.4
Propoxur	989.3	E863.2	—	E950.6	E962.1	E980.7
Propoxycaine	968.9	E855.2	E938.9	E950.4	E962.0	E980.4
infiltration (subcutaneous)	968.5	E855.2	E938.5	E950.4	E962.0	E980.4
nerve block (peripheral) (plexus)	968.6	E855.2	E938.6	E950.4	E962.0	E980.4
topical (surface)	968.5	E855.2	E938.5	E950.4	E962.0	E980.4
Propoxyphene (hydrochloride)	965.8	E850.8	E935.8	E950.0	E962.0	E980.0
Propranolol	972.0	E858.3	E942.0	E950.4	E962.0	E980.4
Propyl alcohol	980.3	E860.4	—	E950.9	E962.1	E980.9
carbinol	980.3	E860.4	—	E950.9	E962.1	E980.9
hexadrine	971.2	E855.5	E941.2	E950.4	E962.0	E980.4
iodone	977.8	E858.8	E947.8	E950.4	E962.0	E980.4
thiouracil	962.8	E858.0	E932.8	E950.4	E962.0	E980.4
Propylene	987.1	E869.8	—	E952.8	E962.2	E982.8
Propylparaben (ophthalmic)	976.5	E858.7	E946.5	E950.4	E962.0	E980.4
Proscillaridin	972.1	E858.3	E942.1	E950.4	E962.0	E980.4
Prostaglandins	975.0	E858.6	E945.0	E950.4	E962.0	E980.4
Prostigmin	971.0	E855.3	E941.0	E950.4	E962.0	E980.4
Protamine (sulfate)	964.5	E858.2	E934.5	E950.4	E962.0	E980.4
zinc insulin	962.3	E858.0	E932.3	E950.4	E962.0	E980.4
Protectants (topical)	976.3	E858.7	E946.3	E950.4	E962.0	E980.4
Protein hydrolysate	974.5	E858.5	E944.5	E950.4	E962.0	E980.4
Prothiaden — see Dothiepin hydrochloride						
Prothionamide	961.8	E857	E931.8	E950.4	E962.0	E980.4
Prothipendyl	969.5	E853.8	E939.5	E950.3	E962.0	E980.3
Protokylol	971.2	E855.5	E941.2	E950.4	E962.0	E980.4
Protopam	977.2	E858.8	E947.2	E950.4	E962.0	E980.4
Protoveratrine(s) (A) (B)	972.6	E858.3	E942.6	E950.4	E962.0	E980.4
Protriptyline	969.05 ▲	E854.0	E939.0	E950.3	E962.0	E980.3
Provera	962.2	E858.0	E932.2	E950.4	E962.0	E980.4
Provitamin A	963.5	E858.1	E933.5	E950.4	E962.0	E980.4
Proxymetacaine	968.5	E855.2	E938.5	E950.4	E962.0	E980.4
Proxyphylline	975.1	E858.6	E945.1	E950.4	E962.0	E980.4
Prozac — see Fluoxetine hydrochloride						
Prunus laurocerasus	988.2	E865.4	—	E950.9	E962.1	E980.9
virginiana	988.2	E865.4	—	E950.9	E962.1	E980.9
Prussic acid	989.0	E866.8	—	E950.9	E962.1	E980.9
vapor	987.7	E869.8	—	E952.8	E962.2	E982.8
Pseudoephedrine	971.2	E855.5	E941.2	E950.4	E962.0	E980.4
Psilocin	969.6	E854.1	E939.6	E950.3	E962.0	E980.3
Psilocybin	969.6	E854.1	E939.6	E950.3	E962.0	E980.3
PSP	977.8	E858.8	E947.8	E950.4	E962.0	E980.4
Psychedelic agents	969.6	E854.1	E939.6	E950.3	E962.0	E980.3

Nontherapeutic use substance

▶◀ Revised Text   ● New Line   ▲ Revised Code

▽ Subterms under main terms may continue to next column or page

	Poisoning	Accident	Therapeutic Use	Suicide Attempt	Assault	Undeter- mined
Psychodysleptics	969.6	E854.1	E939.6	E950.3	E962.0	E980.3
Psychostimulants	969.70 ▲	E854.2	E939.7	E950.3	E962.0	E980.3
Psychotherapeutic						
agents	969.9	E855.9	E939.9	E950.3	E962.0	E980.3
antidepressants	969.00 ▲	E854.0	E939.0	E950.3	E962.0	E980.3
specified NEC	969.8	E855.8	E939.8	E950.3	E962.0	E980.3
tranquilizers NEC	969.5	E853.9	E939.5	E950.3	E962.0	E980.3
Psychotomimetic agents	969.6	E854.1	E939.6	E950.3	E962.0	E980.3
Psychotropic agents	969.9	E854.8	E939.9	E950.3	E962.0	E980.3
specified NEC	969.8	E854.8	E939.8	E950.3	E962.0	E980.3
Psyllium	973.3	E858.4	E943.3	E950.4	E962.0	E980.4
Pteroylglutamic acid	964.1	E858.2	E934.1	E950.4	E962.0	E980.4
Pteroyltriglutamate	963.1	E858.1	E933.1	E950.4	E962.0	E980.4
PTFE	987.8	E869.8	—	E952.8	E962.2	E982.8
Pulsatilla	988.2	E865.4	—	E950.9	E962.1	E980.9
Purex (bleach)	983.9	E864.3	—	E950.7	E962.1	E980.6
Purine diuretics	974.1	E858.5	E944.1	E950.4	E962.0	E980.4
Purinethol	963.1	E858.1	E933.1	E950.4	E962.0	E980.4
PVP	964.8	E858.2	E934.8	E950.4	E962.0	E980.4
Pyrabital	965.7	E850.7	E935.7	E950.0	E962.0	E980.0
Pyramidon	965.5	E850.5	E935.5	E950.0	E962.0	E980.0
Pyrantel (pamoate)	961.6	E857	E931.6	E950.4	E962.0	E980.4
Pyrathiazine	963.0	E858.1	E933.0	E950.4	E962.0	E980.4
Pyrazinamide	961.8	E857	E931.8	E950.4	E962.0	E980.4
Pyrazinoic acid (amide)	961.8	E857	E931.8	E950.4	E962.0	E980.4
Pyrazole (derivatives)	965.5	E850.5	E935.5	E950.0	E962.0	E980.0
Pyrazolone (analgesics)	965.5	E850.5	E935.5	E950.0	E962.0	E980.0
Pyrethrins, pyrethrum	989.4	E863.4	—	E950.6	E962.1	E980.7
Pyribenzamine	963.0	E858.1	E933.0	E950.4	E962.0	E980.4
Pyridine (liquid) (vapor)	982.0	E862.4	—	E950.9	E962.1	E980.9
aldoxime chloride	977.2	E858.8	E947.2	E950.4	E962.0	E980.4
Pyridium	976.1	E858.7	E946.1	E950.4	E962.0	E980.4
Pyridostigmine	971.0	E855.3	E941.0	E950.4	E962.0	E980.4
Pyridoxine	963.5	E858.1	E933.5	E950.4	E962.0	E980.4
Pyrilamine	963.0	E858.1	E933.0	E950.4	E962.0	E980.4
Pyrimethamine	961.4	E857	E931.4	E950.4	E962.0	E980.4
Pyrogallic acid	983.0	E864.0	—	E950.7	E962.1	E980.6
Pyroxylin	976.3	E858.7	E946.3	E950.4	E962.0	E980.4
Pyrrobutamine	963.0	E858.1	E933.0	E950.4	E962.0	E980.4
Pyrrocitine	968.5	E855.2	E938.5	E950.4	E962.0	E980.4
Pyrvinium (pamoate)	961.6	E857	E931.6	E950.4	E962.0	E980.4
PZI	962.3	E858.0	E932.3	E950.4	E962.0	E980.4
Quaalude	967.4	E852.3	E937.4	E950.2	E962.0	E980.2
Quaternary ammonium						
derivatives	971.1	E855.4	E941.1	E950.4	E962.0	E980.4
Quicklime	983.2	E864.2	—	E950.7	E962.1	E980.6
Quinacrine	961.3	E857	E931.3	E950.4	E962.0	E980.4
Quinaglute	972.0	E858.3	E942.0	E950.4	E962.0	E980.4
Quinalbarbitone	967.0	E851	E937.0	E950.1	E962.0	E980.1
Quinestradiol	962.2	E858.0	E932.2	E950.4	E962.0	E980.4
Quinethazone	974.3	E858.5	E944.3	E950.4	E962.0	E980.4
Quinidine (gluconate)						
(polygalacturonate) (salts)						
(sulfate)	972.0	E858.3	E942.0	E950.4	E962.0	E980.4
Quinine	961.4	E857	E931.4	E950.4	E962.0	E980.4
Quiniobine	961.3	E857	E931.3	E950.4	E962.0	E980.4
Quinolines	961.3	E857	E931.3	E950.4	E962.0	E980.4
Quotane	968.5	E855.2	E938.5	E950.4	E962.0	E980.4
Rabies						
immune globulin (human)	964.6	E858.2	E934.6	E950.4	E962.0	E980.4
vaccine	979.1	E858.8	E949.1	E950.4	E962.0	E980.4
Racemoramide	965.09	E850.2	E935.2	E950.0	E962.0	E980.0
Racemorphan	965.09	E850.2	E935.2	E950.0	E962.0	E980.0
Radiator alcohol	980.1	E860.2	—	E950.9	E962.1	E980.9
Radio-opaque (drugs)						
(materials)	977.8	E858.8	E947.8	E950.4	E962.0	E980.4
Ranunculus	988.2	E865.4	—	E950.9	E962.1	E980.9
Rat poison	989.4	E863.7	—	E950.6	E962.1	E980.7
Rattlesnake (venom)	989.5	E905.0	—	E950.9	E962.1	E980.9
Raudixin	972.6	E858.3	E942.6	E950.4	E962.0	E980.4
Rautensin	972.6	E858.3	E942.6	E950.4	E962.0	E980.4
Rautina	972.6	E858.3	E942.6	E950.4	E962.0	E980.4
Rautotal	972.6	E858.3	E942.6	E950.4	E962.0	E980.4
Rauwiloid	972.6	E858.3	E942.6	E950.4	E962.0	E980.4
Rauwoldin	972.6	E858.3	E942.6	E950.4	E962.0	E980.4
Rauwolfia (alkaloids)	972.6	E858.3	E942.6	E950.4	E962.0	E980.4
Realgar	985.1	E866.3	—	E950.8	E962.1	E980.8
Red cells, packed	964.7	E858.2	E934.7	E950.4	E962.0	E980.4
Reducing agents, industrial						
NEC	983.9	E864.3	—	E950.7	E962.1	E980.6
Refrigerant gas (freon)	987.4	E869.2	—	E952.8	E962.2	E982.8
central nervous system	968.0	E855.1	E938.0	E950.4	E962.0	E980.4

	Poisoning	Accident	Therapeutic Use	Suicide Attempt	Assault	Undeter- mined
Refrigerant gas — *continued*						
not freon	987.9	E869.9	—	E952.9	E962.2	E982.9
Regroton	974.4	E858.5	E944.4	E950.4	E962.0	E980.4
Rela	968.0	E855.1	E938.0	E950.4	E962.0	E980.4
Relaxants, skeletal muscle						
(autonomic)	975.2	E858.6	E945.2	E950.4	E962.0	E980.4
Renese	974.3	E858.5	E944.3	E950.4	E962.0	E980.4
Renografin	977.8	E858.8	E947.8	E950.4	E962.0	E980.4
Replacement solutions	974.5	E858.5	E944.5	E950.4	E962.0	E980.4
Rescinnamine	972.6	E858.3	E942.6	E950.4	E962.0	E980.4
Reserpine	972.6	E858.3	E942.6	E950.4	E962.0	E980.4
Resorcin, resorcinol	976.4	E858.7	E946.4	E950.4	E962.0	E980.4
Respaire	975.5	E858.6	E945.5	E950.4	E962.0	E980.4
Respiratory agents NEC	975.8	E858.6	E945.8	E950.4	E962.0	E980.4
Retinoic acid	976.8	E858.7	E946.8	E950.4	E962.0	E980.4
Retinol	963.5	E858.1	E933.5	E950.4	E962.0	E980.4
Rh (D) immune globulin						
(human)	964.6	E858.2	E934.6	E950.4	E962.0	E980.4
Rhodine	965.1	E850.3	E935.3	E950.0	E962.0	E980.0
RhoGAM	964.6	E858.2	E934.6	E950.4	E962.0	E980.4
Riboflavin	963.5	E858.1	E933.5	E950.4	E962.0	E980.4
Ricin	989.89	E866.8	—	E950.9	E962.1	E980.9
Ricinus communis	988.2	E865.3	—	E950.9	E962.1	E980.9
Rickettsial vaccine NEC	979.6	E858.8	E949.6	E950.4	E962.0	E980.4
with viral and bacterial						
vaccine	979.7	E858.8	E949.7	E950.4	E962.0	E980.4
Rifampin	960.6	E856	E930.6	E950.4	E962.0	E980.4
Rimifon	961.8	E857	E931.8	E950.4	E962.0	E980.4
Ringer's injection						
(lactated)	974.5	E858.5	E944.5	E950.4	E962.0	E980.4
Ristocetin	960.8	E856	E930.8	E950.4	E962.0	E980.4
Ritalin	969.73 ▲	E854.2	E939.7	E950.3	E962.0	E980.3
Roach killers — *see* Pesticides						
Rocky Mountain spotted fever						
vaccine	979.6	E858.8	E949.6	E950.4	E962.0	E980.4
Rodenticides	989.4	E863.7	—	E950.6	E962.1	E980.7
Rohypnol	969.4	E853.2	E939.4	E950.3	E962.0	E980.3
Rolaids	973.0	E858.4	E943.0	E950.4	E962.0	E980.4
Rolitetracycline	960.4	E856	E930.4	E950.4	E962.0	E980.4
Romilar	975.4	E858.6	E945.4	E950.4	E962.0	E980.4
Rose water ointment	976.3	E858.7	E946.3	E950.4	E962.0	E980.4
Rosuvastatin calcium	972.1	E858.3	E942.2	E950.4	E962.0	E980.4
Rotenone	989.4	E863.7	—	E950.6	E962.1	E980.7
Rotoxamine	963.0	E858.1	E933.0	E950.4	E962.0	E980.4
Rough-on-rats	989.4	E863.7	—	E950.6	E962.1	E980.7
RU486	962.9	E858.0	E932.9	E950.4	E962.0	E980.4
Rubbing alcohol	980.2	E860.3	—	E950.9	E962.1	E980.9
Rubella virus vaccine	979.4	E858.8	E949.4	E950.4	E962.0	E980.4
Rubelogen	979.4	E858.8	E949.4	E950.4	E962.0	E980.4
Rubeovax	979.4	E858.8	E949.4	E950.4	E962.0	E980.4
Rubidomycin	960.7	E856	E930.7	E950.4	E962.0	E980.4
Rue	988.2	E865.4	—	E950.9	E962.1	E980.9
Ruta	988.2	E865.4	—	E950.9	E962.1	E980.9
Sabadilla (medicinal)	976.0	E858.7	E946.0	E950.4	E962.0	E980.4
pesticide	989.4	E863.4	—	E950.6	E962.1	E980.7
Sabin oral vaccine	979.5	E858.8	E949.5	E950.4	E962.0	E980.4
Saccharated iron oxide	964.0	E858.2	E934.0	E950.4	E962.0	E980.4
Saccharin	974.5	E858.5	E944.5	E950.4	E962.0	E980.4
Safflower oil	972.2	E858.3	E942.2	E950.4	E962.0	E980.4
Salbutamol sulfate	975.7	E858.6	E945.7	E950.4	E962.0	E980.4
Salicylamide	965.1	E850.3	E935.3	E950.0	E962.0	E980.0
Salicylate(s)	965.1	E850.3	E935.3	E950.0	E962.0	E980.0
methyl	976.3	E858.7	E946.3	E950.4	E962.0	E980.4
theobromine calcium	974.1	E858.5	E944.1	E950.4	E962.0	E980.4
Salicylazosulfapyridine	961.0	E857	E931.0	E950.4	E962.0	E980.4
Salicylhydroxamic acid	976.0	E858.7	E946.0	E950.4	E962.0	E980.4
Salicylic acid (keratolytic)						
NEC	976.4	E858.7	E946.4	E950.4	E962.0	E980.4
congeners	965.1	E850.3	E935.3	E950.0	E962.0	E980.0
salts	965.1	E850.3	E935.3	E950.0	E962.0	E980.0
Saliniazid	961.8	E857	E931.8	E950.4	E962.0	E980.4
Salol	976.3	E858.7	E946.3	E950.4	E962.0	E980.4
Salt (substitute) NEC	974.5	E858.5	E944.5	E950.4	E962.0	E980.4
Saluretics	974.3	E858.5	E944.3	E950.4	E962.0	E980.4
Saluron	974.3	E858.5	E944.3	E950.4	E962.0	E980.4
Salvarsan 606 (neosilver)						
(silver)	961.1	E857	E931.1	E950.4	E962.0	E980.4
Sambucus canadensis	988.2	E865.4	—	E950.9	E962.1	E980.9
berry	988.2	E865.3	—	E950.9	E962.1	E980.9
Sandril	972.6	E858.3	E942.6	E950.4	E962.0	E980.4
Sanguinaria canadensis	988.2	E865.4	—	E950.9	E962.1	E980.9
Saniflush (cleaner)	983.9	E861.3	—	E950.7	E962.1	E980.6

Nontherapeutic use substance

▶◀ Revised Text   ● New Line   ▲ Revised Code

▽ Subterms under main terms may continue to next column or page

	Poisoning	Accident	Therapeutic Use	Suicide Attempt	Assault	Undetermined
antonin	961.6	E857	E931.6	E950.4	E962.0	E980.4
antyl	976.8	E858.7	E946.8	E950.4	E962.0	E980.4
arkomycin	960.7	E856	E930.7	E950.4	E962.0	E980.4
aroten	969.05 ▲	E854.0	E939.0	E950.3	E962.0	E980.3
aturnine — see Lead						
avin (oil)	976.4	E858.7	E946.4	E950.4	E962.0	E980.4
cammony	973.1	E858.4	E943.1	E950.4	E962.0	E980.4
carlet red	976.8	E858.7	E946.8	E950.4	E962.0	E980.4
cheele's green	985.1	E866.3	—	E950.8	E962.1	E980.8
insecticide	985.1	E863.4	—	E950.8	E962.1	E980.8
chradan	989.3	E863.1	—	E950.6	E962.1	E980.7
chweinfurt(h) green	985.1	E866.3	—	E950.8	E962.1	E980.8
insecticide	985.1	E863.4	—	E950.8	E962.1	E980.8
cilla — see Squill						
clerosing agents	972.7	E858.3	E942.7	E950.4	E962.0	E980.4
copolamine	971.1	E855.4	E941.1	E950.4	E962.0	E980.4
couring powder	989.89	E861.3	—	E950.9	E962.1	E980.9
ea						
anemone (sting)	989.5	E905.6	—	E950.9	E962.1	E980.9
cucumber (sting)	989.5	E905.6	—	E950.9	E962.1	E980.9
snake (bite) (venom)	989.5	E905.0	—	E950.9	E962.1	E980.9
urchin spine (puncture)	989.5	E905.6	—	E950.9	E962.1	E980.9
ecbutabarbital	967.0	E851	E937.0	E950.1	E962.0	E980.1
ecbutabarbitone	967.0	E851	E937.0	E950.1	E962.0	E980.1
ecobarbital	967.0	E851	E937.0	E950.1	E962.0	E980.1
econal	967.0	E851	E937.0	E950.1	E962.0	E980.1
ecretin	977.8	E858.8	E947.8	E950.4	E962.0	E980.4
edatives,						
nonbarbiturate	967.9	E852.9	E937.9	E950.2	E962.0	E980.2
specified NEC	967.8	E852.8	E937.8	E950.2	E962.0	E980.2
edormid	967.8	E852.8	E937.8	E950.2	E962.0	E980.2
eed (plant)	988.2	E865.3	—	E950.9	E962.1	E980.9
disinfectant or dressing	989.89	E866.5	—	E950.9	E962.1	E980.9
elective serotonin and norepinephrine reuptake inhibitors (SSNRI) ●	969.02	E854.0	E939.0	E950.3	E962.0	E980.3
elective serotonin reuptake inhibitors (SSRI) ●	969.03	E854.0	E939.0	E950.3	E962.0	E980.3
elenium (fumes) NEC	985.8	E866.4	—	E950.9	E962.1	E980.9
disulfide or sulfide	976.4	E858.7	E946.4	E950.4	E962.0	E980.4
elsun	976.4	E858.7	E946.4	E950.4	E962.0	E980.4
enna	973.1	E858.4	E943.1	E950.4	E962.0	E980.4
eptisol	976.2	E858.7	E946.2	E950.4	E962.0	E980.4
erax	969.4	E853.2	E939.4	E950.3	E962.0	E980.3
erenesil	967.8	E852.8	E937.8	E950.2	E962.0	E980.2
erenium (hydrochloride)	961.9	E857	E931.9	E950.4	E962.0	E980.4
erepax — see Oxazepam						
ernyl	968.3	E855.1	E938.3	E950.4	E962.0	E980.4
erotonin	977.8	E858.8	E947.8	E950.4	E962.0	E980.4
erpasil	972.6	E858.3	E942.6	E950.4	E962.0	E980.4
ewer gas	987.8	E869.8	—	E952.8	E962.2	E982.8
hampoo	989.6	E861.0	—	E950.9	E962.1	E980.9
hellfish, nonbacterial or noxious	988.0	E865.1	—	E950.9	E962.1	E980.9
ilicones NEC	989.83	E866.8	E947.8	E950.9	E962.1	E980.9
ilvadene	976.0	E858.7	E946.0	E950.4	E962.0	E980.4
ilver (compound) (medicinal)						
NEC	976.0	E858.7	E946.0	E950.4	E962.0	E980.4
anti-infectives	976.0	E858.7	E946.0	E950.4	E962.0	E980.4
arsphenamine	961.1	E857	E931.1	E950.4	E962.0	E980.4
nitrate	976.0	E858.7	E946.0	E950.4	E962.0	E980.4
ophthalmic preparation	976.5	E858.7	E946.5	E950.4	E962.0	E980.4
toughened (keratolytic)	976.4	E858.7	E946.4	E950.4	E962.0	E980.4
nonmedicinal (dust)	985.8	E866.4	—	E950.9	E962.1	E980.9
protein (mild) (strong)	976.0	E858.7	E946.0	E950.4	E962.0	E980.4
salvarsan	961.1	E857	E931.1	E950.4	E962.0	E980.4
imethicone	973.8	E858.4	E943.8	E950.4	E962.0	E980.4
inequan	969.05 ▲	E854.0	E939.0	E950.3	E962.0	E980.3
ingoserp	972.6	E858.3	E942.6	E950.4	E962.0	E980.4
introm	964.2	E858.2	E934.2	E950.4	E962.0	E980.4
itosterols	972.2	E858.3	E942.2	E950.4	E962.0	E980.4
keletal muscle relaxants	975.2	E858.6	E945.2	E950.4	E962.0	E980.4
kin						
agents (external)	976.9	E858.7	E946.9	E950.4	E962.0	E980.4
specified NEC	976.8	E858.7	E946.8	E950.4	E962.0	E980.4
test antigen	977.8	E858.8	E947.8	E950.4	E962.0	E980.4
leep-eze	963.0	E858.1	E933.0	E950.4	E962.0	E980.4
leeping draught (drug) (pill) (tablet)	967.9	E852.9	E937.9	E950.2	E962.0	E980.2
mallpox vaccine	979.0	E858.8	E949.0	E950.4	E962.0	E980.4
melter fumes NEC	985.9	E866.4	—	E950.9	E962.1	E980.9
mog	987.3	E869.1	—	E952.8	E962.2	E982.8

	Poisoning	Accident	Therapeutic Use	Suicide Attempt	Assault	Undetermined
Smoke NEC	987.9	E869.9	—	E952.9	E962.2	E982.9
Smooth muscle relaxant	975.1	E858.6	E945.1	E950.4	E962.0	E980.4
Snail killer	989.4	E863.4	—	E950.6	E962.1	E980.7
Snake (bite) (venom)	989.5	E905.0	—	E950.9	E962.1	E980.9
Snuff	989.89	E866.8	—	E950.9	E962.1	E980.9
Soap (powder) (product)	989.6	E861.1	—	E950.9	E962.1	E980.9
bicarb	963.3	E858.1	E933.3	E950.4	E962.0	E980.4
chlorinated — see Sodium, hypochlorite						
medicinal, soft	976.2	E858.7	E946.2	E950.4	E962.0	E980.4
Soda (caustic)	983.2	E864.2	—	E950.7	E962.1	E980.6
Sodium						
acetosulfone	961.8	E857	E931.8	E950.4	E962.0	E980.4
acetrizoate	977.8	E858.8	E947.8	E950.4	E962.0	E980.4
amytal	967.0	E851	E937.0	E950.1	E962.0	E980.1
arsenate — see Arsenic						
bicarbonate	963.3	E858.1	E933.3	E950.4	E962.0	E980.4
bichromate	983.9	E864.3	—	E950.7	E962.1	E980.6
biphosphate	963.2	E858.1	E933.2	E950.4	E962.0	E980.4
bisulfate	983.9	E864.3	—	E950.7	E962.1	E980.6
borate (cleanser)	989.6	E861.3	—	E950.9	E962.1	E980.9
bromide NEC	967.3	E852.2	E937.3	E950.2	E962.0	E980.2
cacodylate (nonmedicinal)						
NEC	978.8	E858.8	E948.8	E950.4	E962.0	E980.4
anti-infective	961.1	E857	E931.1	E950.4	E962.0	E980.4
herbicide	989.4	E863.5	—	E950.6	E962.1	E980.7
calcium edetate	963.8	E858.1	E933.8	E950.4	E962.0	E980.4
carbonate NEC	983.2	E864.2	—	E950.7	E962.1	E980.6
chlorate NEC	983.9	E864.3	—	E950.7	E962.1	E980.6
herbicide	983.9	E863.5	—	E950.7	E962.1	E980.6
chloride NEC	974.5	E858.5	E944.5	E950.4	E962.0	E980.4
chromate	983.9	E864.3	—	E950.7	E962.1	E980.6
citrate	963.3	E858.1	E933.3	E950.4	E962.0	E980.4
cyanide — see Cyanide(s)						
cyclamate	974.5	E858.5	E944.5	E950.4	E962.0	E980.4
diatrizoate	977.8	E858.8	E947.8	E950.4	E962.0	E980.4
dibunate	975.4	E858.6	E945.4	E950.4	E962.0	E980.4
dioctyl sulfosuccinate	973.2	E858.4	E943.2	E950.4	E962.0	E980.4
edetate	963.8	E858.1	E933.8	E950.4	E962.0	E980.4
ethacrynate	974.4	E858.5	E944.4	E950.4	E962.0	E980.4
fluoracetate (dust) (rodenticide)	989.4	E863.7	—	E950.6	E962.1	E980.7
fluoride — see Fluoride(s)						
free salt	974.5	E858.5	E944.5	E950.4	E962.0	E980.4
glucosulfone	961.8	E857	E931.8	E950.4	E962.0	E980.4
hydroxide	983.2	E864.2	—	E950.7	E962.1	E980.6
hypochlorite (bleach) NEC	983.9	E864.3	—	E950.7	E962.1	E980.6
disinfectant	983.9	E861.4	—	E950.7	E962.1	E980.6
medicinal (anti-infective) (external)	976.0	E858.7	E946.0	E950.4	E962.0	E980.4
vapor	987.8	E869.8	—	E952.8	E962.2	E982.8
hyposulfite	976.0	E858.7	E946.0	E950.4	E962.0	E980.4
indigotindisulfonate	977.8	E858.8	E947.8	E950.4	E962.0	E980.4
iodide	977.8	E858.8	E947.8	E950.4	E962.0	E980.4
iothalamate	977.8	E858.8	E947.8	E950.4	E962.0	E980.4
iron edetate	964.0	E858.2	E934.0	E950.4	E962.0	E980.4
lactate	963.3	E858.1	E933.3	E950.4	E962.0	E980.4
lauryl sulfate	976.2	E858.7	E946.2	E950.4	E962.0	E980.4
L-triiodothyronine	962.7	E858.0	E932.7	E950.4	E962.0	E980.4
metrizoate	977.8	E858.8	E947.8	E950.4	E962.0	E980.4
monofluoracetate (dust) (rodenticide)	989.4	E863.7	—	E950.6	E962.1	E980.7
morrhuate	972.7	E858.3	E942.7	E950.4	E962.0	E980.4
nafcillin	960.0	E856	E930.0	E950.4	E962.0	E980.4
nitrate (oxidizing agent)	983.9	E864.3	—	E950.7	E962.1	E980.6
nitrite (medicinal)	972.4	E858.3	E942.4	E950.4	E962.0	E980.4
nitroferricyanide	972.6	E858.3	E942.6	E950.4	E962.0	E980.4
nitroprusside	972.6	E858.3	E942.6	E950.4	E962.0	E980.4
para-aminohippurate	977.8	E858.8	E947.8	E950.4	E962.0	E980.4
perborate (nonmedicinal)						
NEC	989.89	E866.8	—	E950.9	E962.1	E980.9
medicinal	976.6	E858.7	E946.6	E950.4	E962.0	E980.4
soap	989.6	E861.1	—	E950.9	E962.1	E980.9
percarbonate — see Sodium, perborate						
phosphate	973.3	E858.4	E943.3	E950.4	E962.0	E980.4
polystyrene sulfonate	974.5	E858.5	E944.5	E950.4	E962.0	E980.4
propionate	976.0	E858.7	E946.0	E950.4	E962.0	E980.4
psylliate	972.7	E858.3	E942.7	E950.4	E962.0	E980.4
removing resins	974.5	E858.5	E944.5	E950.4	E962.0	E980.4
salicylate	965.1	E850.3	E935.3	E950.0	E962.0	E980.0
sulfate	973.3	E858.4	E943.3	E950.4	E962.0	E980.4

Nontherapeutic use substance

▽ Subterms under main terms may continue to next column or page

		External Cause (E-Code)				
	Poisoning	Accident	Therapeutic Use	Suicide Attempt	Assault	Undeter-mined
Sodium — *continued*						
sulfoxone	961.8	E857	E931.8	E950.4	E962.0	E980.4
tetradecyl sulfate	972.7	E858.3	E942.7	E950.4	E962.0	E980.4
thiopental	968.3	E855.1	E938.3	E950.4	E962.0	E980.4
thiosalicylate	965.1	E850.3	E935.3	E950.0	E962.0	E980.0
thiosulfate	976.0	E858.7	E946.0	E950.4	E962.0	E980.4
tolbutamide	977.8	E858.8	E947.8	E950.4	E962.0	E980.4
tyropanoate	977.8	E858.8	E947.8	E950.4	E962.0	E980.4
valproate	966.3	E855.0	E936.3	E950.4	E962.0	E980.4
Solanine	977.8	E858.8	E947.8	E950.4	E962.0	E980.4
Solanum dulcamara	988.2	E865.4	—	E950.9	E962.1	E980.9
Solapsone	961.8	E857	E931.8	E950.4	E962.0	E980.4
Solasulfone	961.8	E857	E931.8	E950.4	E962.0	E980.4
Soldering fluid	983.1	E864.1	—	E950.7	E962.1	E980.6
Solid substance	989.9	E866.9	—	E950.9	E962.1	E980.9
specified NEC	989.9	E866.8	—	E950.9	E962.1	E980.9
Solvents, industrial	982.8	E862.9	—	E950.9	E962.1	E980.9
naphtha	981	E862.0	—	E950.9	E962.1	E980.9
petroleum	981	E862.0	—	E950.9	E962.1	E980.9
specified NEC	982.8	E862.4	—	E950.9	E962.1	E980.9
Soma	968.0	E855.1	E938.0	E950.4	E962.0	E980.4
Somatotropin	962.4	E858.0	E932.4	E950.4	E962.0	E980.4
Sominex	963.0	E858.1	E933.0	E950.4	E962.0	E980.4
Somnos	967.1	E852.0	E937.1	E950.2	E962.0	E980.2
Somonal	967.0	E851	E937.0	E950.1	E962.0	E980.1
Soneryl	967.0	E851	E937.0	E950.1	E962.0	E980.1
Soothing syrup	977.9	E858.9	E947.9	E950.5	E962.0	E980.5
Sopor	967.4	E852.3	E937.4	E950.2	E962.0	E980.2
Soporific drug	967.9	E852.9	E937.9	E950.2	E962.0	E980.2
specified type NEC	967.8	E852.8	E937.8	E950.2	E962.0	E980.2
Sorbitol NEC	977.4	E858.8	E947.4	E950.4	E962.0	E980.4
Sotradecol	972.7	E858.3	E942.7	E950.4	E962.0	E980.4
Spacoline	975.1	E858.6	E945.1	E950.4	E962.0	E980.4
Spanish fly	976.8	E858.7	E946.8	E950.4	E962.0	E980.4
Sparine	969.1	E853.0	E939.1	E950.3	E962.0	E980.3
Sparteine	975.0	E858.6	E945.0	E950.4	E962.0	E980.4
Spasmolytics	975.1	E858.6	E945.1	E950.4	E962.0	E980.4
anticholinergics	971.1	E855.4	E941.1	E950.4	E962.0	E980.4
Spectinomycin	960.8	E856	E930.8	E950.4	E962.0	E980.4
Speed	969.72 ▲	E854.2	E939.7	E950.3	E962.0	E980.3
Spermicides	976.8	E858.7	E946.8	E950.4	E962.0	E980.4
Spider (bite) (venom)	989.5	E905.1	—	E950.9	E962.1	E980.9
antivenin	979.9	E858.8	E949.9	E950.4	E962.0	E980.4
Spigelia (root)	961.6	E857	E931.6	E950.4	E962.0	E980.4
Spiperone	969.2	E853.1	E939.2	E950.3	E962.0	E980.3
Spiramycin	960.3	E856	E930.3	E950.4	E962.0	E980.4
Spirilene	969.5	E853.8	E939.5	E950.3	E962.0	E980.3
Spirit(s) (neutral) NEC	980.0	E860.1	—	E950.9	E962.1	E980.9
beverage	980.0	E860.0	—	E950.9	E962.1	E980.9
industrial	980.9	E860.9	—	E950.9	E962.1	E980.9
mineral	981	E862.0	—	E950.9	E962.1	E980.9
of salt — *see* Hydrochloric acid						
surgical	980.9	E860.9	—	E950.9	E962.1	E980.9
Spironolactone	974.4	E858.5	E944.4	E950.4	E962.0	E980.4
Sponge, absorbable						
(gelatin)	964.5	E858.2	E934.5	E950.4	E962.0	E980.4
Sporostacin	976.0	E858.7	E946.0	E950.4	E962.0	E980.4
Sprays (aerosol)	989.89	E866.8	—	E950.9	E962.1	E980.9
cosmetic	989.89	E866.7	—	E950.9	E962.1	E980.9
medicinal NEC	977.9	E858.9	E947.9	E950.5	E962.0	E980.5
pesticides — *see* Pesticides						
specified content — *see* substance specified						
Spurge flax	988.2	E865.4	—	E950.9	E962.1	E980.9
Spurges	988.2	E865.4	—	E950.9	E962.1	E980.9
Squill (expectorant) NEC	975.5	E858.6	E945.5	E950.4	E962.0	E980.4
rat poison	989.4	E863.7	—	E950.6	E962.1	E980.7
Squirting cucumber						
(cathartic)	973.1	E858.4	E943.1	E950.4	E962.0	E980.4
SSNRI (selective serotonin and norepinephrine reuptake inhibitors) ●	969.02	E854.0	E939.0	E950.3	E962.0	E980.3
SSRI (selective serotonin reuptake inhibitors) ●	969.03	E854.0	E939.0	E950.3	E962.0	E980.3
Stains	989.89	E866.8	—	E950.9	E962.1	E980.9
Stannous — *see also* Tin						
fluoride	976.7	E858.7	E946.7	E950.4	E962.0	E980.4
Stanolone	962.1	E858.0	E932.1	E950.4	E962.0	E980.4
Stanozolol	962.1	E858.0	E932.1	E950.4	E962.0	E980.4
Staphisagria or stavesacre						
(pediculicide)	976.0	E858.7	E946.0	E950.4	E962.0	E980.4
Stelazine	969.1	E853.0	E939.1	E950.3	E962.0	E980.3

		External Cause (E-Code)				
	Poisoning	Accident	Therapeutic Use	Suicide Attempt	Assault	Undeter-mined
Stemetil	969.1	E853.0	E939.1	E950.3	E962.0	E980.3
Sterculia (cathartic) (gum)	973.3	E858.4	E943.3	E950.4	E962.0	E980.4
Sternutator gas	987.8	E869.8	—	E952.8	E962.2	E982.8
Steroids NEC	962.0	E858.0	E932.0	E950.4	E962.0	E980.4
ENT agent	976.6	E858.7	E946.6	E950.4	E962.0	E980.4
ophthalmic preparation	976.5	E858.7	E946.5	E950.4	E962.0	E980.4
topical NEC	976.0	E858.7	E946.0	E950.4	E962.0	E980.4
Stibine	985.8	E866.4	—	E950.9	E962.1	E980.9
Stibophen	961.2	E857	E931.2	E950.4	E962.0	E980.4
Stilbamide, stilbamidine	961.5	E857	E931.5	E950.4	E962.0	E980.4
Stilbestrol	962.2	E858.0	E932.2	E950.4	E962.0	E980.4
Stimulants (central nervous system)	970.9	E854.3	E940.9	E950.4	E962.0	E980.4
analeptics	970.0	E854.3	E940.0	E950.4	E962.0	E980.4
opiate antagonist	970.1	E854.3	E940.1	E950.4	E962.0	E980.4
psychotherapeutic NEC	969.09 ▲	E854.0	E939.0	E950.3	E962.0	E980.3
specified NEC	970.8	E854.3	E940.8	E950.4	E962.0	E980.4
Storage batteries (acid) (cells)	983.1	E864.1	—	E950.7	E962.1	E980.6
Stovaine	968.9	E855.2	E938.9	E950.4	E962.0	E980.4
infiltration (subcutaneous)	968.5	E855.2	E938.5	E950.4	E962.0	E980.4
nerve block (peripheral) (plexus)	968.6	E855.2	E938.6	E950.4	E962.0	E980.4
spinal	968.7	E855.2	E938.7	E950.4	E962.0	E980.4
topical (surface)	968.5	E855.2	E938.5	E950.4	E962.0	E980.4
Stovarsal	961.1	E857	E931.1	E950.4	E962.0	E980.4
Stove gas — *see* Gas, utility						
Stoxil	976.5	E858.7	E946.5	E950.4	E962.0	E980.4
STP	969.6	E854.1	E939.6	E950.3	E962.0	E980.3
Stramonium (medicinal)						
NEC	971.1	E855.4	E941.1	E950.4	E962.0	E980.4
natural state	988.2	E865.4	—	E950.9	E962.1	E980.9
Streptodornase	964.4	E858.2	E934.4	E950.4	E962.0	E980.4
Streptoduocin	960.6	E856	E930.6	E950.4	E962.0	E980.4
Streptokinase	964.4	E858.2	E934.4	E950.4	E962.0	E980.4
Streptomycin	960.6	E856	E930.6	E950.4	E962.0	E980.4
Streptozocin	960.7	E856	E930.7	E950.4	E962.0	E980.4
Stripper (paint) (solvent)	982.8	E862.9	—	E950.9	E962.1	E980.9
Strobane	989.2	E863.0	—	E950.6	E962.1	E980.7
Strophanthin	972.1	E858.3	E942.1	E950.4	E962.0	E980.4
Strophanthus hispidus or kombe	988.2	E865.4	—	E950.9	E962.1	E980.9
Strychnine (rodenticide) (salts)	989.1	E863.7	—	E950.6	E962.1	E980.7
medicinal NEC	970.8	E854.3	E940.8	E950.4	E962.0	E980.4
Strychnos (ignatii) — *see* Strychnine						
Styramate	968.0	E855.1	E938.0	E950.4	E962.0	E980.4
Styrene	983.0	E864.0	—	E950.7	E962.1	E980.6
Succinimide (anticonvulsant)	966.2	E855.0	E936.2	E950.4	E962.0	E980.4
mercuric — *see* Mercury						
Succinylcholine	975.2	E858.6	E945.2	E950.4	E962.0	E980.4
Succinylsulfathiazole	961.0	E857	E931.0	E950.4	E962.0	E980.4
Sucrose	974.5	E858.5	E944.5	E950.4	E962.0	E980.4
Sulfacetamide	961.0	E857	E931.0	E950.4	E962.0	E980.4
ophthalmic preparation	976.5	E858.7	E946.5	E950.4	E962.0	E980.4
Sulfachlorpyridazine	961.0	E857	E931.0	E950.4	E962.0	E980.4
Sulfacytine	961.0	E857	E931.0	E950.4	E962.0	E980.4
Sulfadiazine	961.0	E857	E931.0	E950.4	E962.0	E980.4
silver (topical)	976.0	E858.7	E946.0	E950.4	E962.0	E980.4
Sulfadimethoxine	961.0	E857	E931.0	E950.4	E962.0	E980.4
Sulfadimidine	961.0	E857	E931.0	E950.4	E962.0	E980.4
Sulfaethidole	961.0	E857	E931.0	E950.4	E962.0	E980.4
Sulfafurazole	961.0	E857	E931.0	E950.4	E962.0	E980.4
Sulfaguanidine	961.0	E857	E931.0	E950.4	E962.0	E980.4
Sulfamerazine	961.0	E857	E931.0	E950.4	E962.0	E980.4
Sulfameter	961.0	E857	E931.0	E950.4	E962.0	E980.4
Sulfamethizole	961.0	E857	E931.0	E950.4	E962.0	E980.4
Sulfamethoxazole	961.0	E857	E931.0	E950.4	E962.0	E980.4
Sulfamethoxydiazine	961.0	E857	E931.0	E950.4	E962.0	E980.4
Sulfamethoxypyridazine	961.0	E857	E931.0	E950.4	E962.0	E980.4
Sulfamethylthiazole	961.0	E857	E931.0	E950.4	E962.0	E980.4
Sulfamylon	976.0	E858.7	E946.0	E950.4	E962.0	E980.4
Sulfan blue (diagnostic dye)	977.8	E858.8	E947.8	E950.4	E962.0	E980.4
Sulfanilamide	961.0	E857	E931.0	E950.4	E962.0	E980.4
Sulfanilylguanidine	961.0	E857	E931.0	E950.4	E962.0	E980.4
Sulfaphenazole	961.0	E857	E931.0	E950.4	E962.0	E980.4
Sulfaphenylthiazole	961.0	E857	E931.0	E950.4	E962.0	E980.4
Sulfaproxyline	961.0	E857	E931.0	E950.4	E962.0	E980.4
Sulfapyridine	961.0	E857	E931.0	E950.4	E962.0	E980.4

	Poisoning	Accident	Therapeutic Use	Suicide Attempt	Assault	Undetermined
			External Cause (E-Code)			
Sulfapyrimidine	961.0	E857	E931.0	E950.4	E962.0	E980.4
Sulfarsphenamine	961.1	E857	E931.1	E950.4	E962.0	E980.4
Sulfasalazine	961.0	E857	E931.0	E950.4	E962.0	E980.4
Sulfasomizole	961.0	E857	E931.0	E950.4	E962.0	E980.4
Sulfasuxidine	961.0	E857	E931.0	E950.4	E962.0	E980.4
Sulfinpyrazone	974.7	E858.5	E944.7	E950.4	E962.0	E980.4
Sulfisoxazole	961.0	E857	E931.0	E950.4	E962.0	E980.4
ophthalmic preparation	976.5	E858.7	E946.5	E950.4	E962.0	E980.4
Sulfomyxin	960.8	E856	E930.8	E950.4	E962.0	E980.4
Sulfonal	967.8	E852.8	E937.8	E950.2	E962.0	E980.2
Sulfonamides (mixtures)	961.0	E857	E931.0	E950.4	E962.0	E980.4
Sulfones	961.8	E857	E931.8	E950.4	E962.0	E980.4
Sulfonethylmethane	967.8	E852.8	E937.8	E950.2	E962.0	E980.2
Sulfonmethane	967.8	E852.8	E937.8	E950.2	E962.0	E980.2
Sulfonphthal, sulfonphthol	977.8	E858.8	E947.8	E950.4	E962.0	E980.4
Sulfonylurea derivatives, oral	962.3	E858.0	E932.3	E950.4	E962.0	E980.4
Sulfoxone	961.8	E857	E931.8	E950.4	E962.0	E980.4
Sulfur, sulfureted, sulfuric, sulfurous, sulfuryl (compounds) NEC	989.89	E866.8	—	E950.9	E962.1	E980.9
acid	983.1	E864.1	—	E950.7	E962.1	E980.6
dioxide	987.3	E869.1	—	E952.8	E962.2	E982.8
ether — see Ether(s)						
hydrogen	987.8	E869.8	—	E952.8	E962.2	E982.8
medicinal (keratolytic) (ointment) NEC	976.4	E858.7	E946.4	E950.4	E962.0	E980.4
pesticide (vapor)	989.4	E863.4	—	E950.6	E962.1	E980.7
vapor NEC	987.8	E869.8	—	E952.8	E962.2	E982.8
Sulkowitch's reagent	977.8	E858.8	E947.8	E950.4	E962.0	E980.4
Sulphadione	961.8	E857	E931.8	E950.4	E962.0	E980.4
Sulph — see also Sulf-						
Sulthiame, sultiame	966.3	E855.0	E936.3	E950.4	E962.0	E980.4
Superinone	975.5	E858.6	E945.5	E950.4	E962.0	E980.4
Suramin	961.5	E857	E931.5	E950.4	E962.0	E980.4
Surfacaine	968.5	E855.2	E938.5	E950.4	E962.0	E980.4
Surital	968.3	E855.1	E938.3	E950.4	E962.0	E980.4
Sutilains	976.8	E858.7	E946.8	E950.4	E962.0	E980.4
Suxamethonium (bromide) (chloride) (iodide)	975.2	E858.6	E945.2	E950.4	E962.0	E980.4
Suxethonium (bromide)	975.2	E858.6	E945.2	E950.4	E962.0	E980.4
Sweet oil (birch)	976.3	E858.7	E946.3	E950.4	E962.0	E980.4
Sym-dichloroethyl ether	982.3	E862.4	—	E950.9	E962.1	E980.9
Sympatholytics	971.3	E855.6	E941.3	E950.4	E962.0	E980.4
Sympathomimetics	971.2	E855.5	E941.2	E950.4	E962.0	E980.4
Synagis	979.6	E858.8	E949.6	E950.4	E962.0	E980.4
Synalar	976.0	E858.7	E946.0	E950.4	E962.0	E980.4
Synthroid	962.7	E858.0	E932.7	E950.4	E962.0	E980.4
Syntocinon	975.0	E858.6	E945.0	E950.4	E962.0	E980.4
Syrosingopine	972.6	E858.3	E942.6	E950.4	E962.0	E980.4
Systemic agents (primarily)	963.9	E858.1	E933.9	E950.4	E962.0	E980.4
specified NEC	963.8	E858.1	E933.8	E950.4	E962.0	E980.4
Tablets — see also specified substance	977.9	E858.9	E947.9	E950.5	E962.0	E980.5
Tace	962.2	E858.0	E932.2	E950.4	E962.0	E980.4
Tacrine	971.0	E855.3	E941.0	E950.4	E962.0	E980.4
Talbutal	967.0	E851	E937.0	E950.1	E962.0	E980.1
Talc	976.3	E858.7	E946.3	E950.4	E962.0	E980.4
Talcum	976.3	E858.7	E946.3	E950.4	E962.0	E980.4
Tamsulosin	971.3	E855.6	E941.3	E950.4	E962.0	E980.4
Tandearil, tanderil	965.5	E850.5	E935.5	E950.0	E962.0	E980.0
Tannic acid	983.1	E864.1	—	E950.7	E962.1	E980.6
medicinal (astringent)	976.2	E858.7	E946.2	E950.4	E962.0	E980.4
Tannin — see Tannic acid						
Tansy	988.2	E865.4	—	E950.9	E962.1	E980.9
TAO	960.3	E856	E930.3	E950.4	E962.0	E980.4
Tapazole	962.8	E858.0	E932.8	E950.4	E962.0	E980.4
Tar NEC	983.0	E864.0	—	E950.7	E962.1	E980.6
camphor — see Naphthalene						
fumes	987.8	E869.8	—	E952.8	E962.2	E982.8
Taractan	969.3	E853.8	E939.3	E950.3	E962.0	E980.3
Tarantula (venomous)	989.5	E905.1	—	E950.9	E962.1	E980.9
Tartar emetic (anti-infective)	961.2	E857	E931.2	E950.4	E962.0	E980.4
Tartaric acid	983.1	E864.1	—	E950.7	E962.1	E980.6
Tartrated antimony (anti-infective)	961.2	E857	E931.2	E950.4	E962.0	E980.4
TCA — see Trichloroacetic acid						
TDI	983.0	E864.0	—	E950.7	E962.1	E980.6
vapor	987.8	E869.8	—	E952.8	E962.2	E982.8
Tear gas	987.5	E869.3	—	E952.8	E962.2	E982.8
Teclothiazide	974.3	E858.5	E944.3	E950.4	E962.0	E980.4
Tegretol	966.3	E855.0	E936.3	E950.4	E962.0	E980.4
Telepaque	977.8	E858.8	E947.8	E950.4	E962.0	E980.4
Tellurium	985.8	E866.4	—	E950.9	E962.1	E980.9
fumes	985.8	E866.4	—	E950.9	E962.1	E980.9
TEM	963.1	E858.1	E933.1	E950.4	E962.0	E980.4
Temazepan — see Benzodiazepines						
TEPA	963.1	E858.1	E933.1	E950.4	E962.0	E980.4
TEPP	989.3	E863.1	—	E950.6	E962.1	E980.7
Terbutaline	971.2	E855.5	E941.2	E950.4	E962.0	E980.4
Teroxalene	961.6	E857	E931.6	E950.4	E962.0	E980.4
Terpin hydrate	975.5	E858.6	E945.5	E950.4	E962.0	E980.4
Terramycin	960.4	E856	E930.4	E950.4	E962.0	E980.4
Tessalon	975.4	E858.6	E945.4	E950.4	E962.0	E980.4
Testosterone	962.1	E858.0	E932.1	E950.4	E962.0	E980.4
Tetanus (vaccine)	978.4	E858.8	E948.4	E950.4	E962.0	E980.4
antitoxin	979.9	E858.8	E949.9	E950.4	E962.0	E980.4
immune globulin (human)	964.6	E858.2	E934.6	E950.4	E962.0	E980.4
toxoid	978.4	E858.8	E948.4	E950.4	E962.0	E980.4
with diphtheria toxoid	978.9	E858.8	E948.9	E950.4	E962.0	E980.4
with pertussis	978.6	E858.8	E948.6	E950.4	E962.0	E980.4
Tetrabenazine	969.5	E853.8	E939.5	E950.3	E962.0	E980.3
Tetracaine (infiltration) (topical)	968.5	E855.2	E938.5	E950.4	E962.0	E980.4
nerve block (peripheral) (plexus)	968.6	E855.2	E938.6	E950.4	E962.0	E980.4
spinal	968.7	E855.2	E938.7	E950.4	E962.0	E980.4
Tetrachlorethylene — see Tetrachloroethylene						
Tetrachlormethiazide	974.3	E858.5	E944.3	E950.4	E962.0	E980.4
Tetrachloroethane (liquid) (vapor)	982.3	E862.4	—	E950.9	E962.1	E980.9
paint or varnish	982.3	E861.6	—	E950.9	E962.1	E980.9
Tetrachloroethylene (liquid) (vapor)	982.3	E862.4	—	E950.9	E962.1	E980.9
medicinal	961.6	E857	E931.6	E950.4	E962.0	E980.4
Tetrachloromethane — see Carbon, tetrachloride						
Tetracycline	960.4	E856	E930.4	E950.4	E962.0	E980.4
ophthalmic preparation	976.5	E858.7	E946.5	E950.4	E962.0	E980.4
topical NEC	976.0	E858.7	E946.0	E950.4	E962.0	E980.4
Tetraethylammonium chloride	972.3	E858.3	E942.3	E950.4	E962.0	E980.4
Tetraethyl lead (antiknock compound)	984.1	E862.1	—	E950.9	E962.1	E980.9
Tetraethyl pyrophosphate	989.3	E863.1	—	E950.6	E962.1	E980.7
Tetraethylthiuram disulfide	977.3	E858.8	E947.3	E950.4	E962.0	E980.4
Tetrahydroaminoacridine	971.0	E855.3	E941.0	E950.4	E962.0	E980.4
Tetrahydrocannabinol	969.6	E854.1	E939.6	E950.3	E962.0	E980.3
Tetrahydronaphthalene	982.0	E862.4	—	E950.9	E962.1	E980.9
Tetrahydrozoline	971.2	E855.5	E941.2	E950.4	E962.0	E980.4
Tetralin	982.0	E862.4	—	E950.9	E962.1	E980.9
Tetramethylthiuram (disulfide) NEC	989.4	E863.6	—	E950.6	E962.1	E980.7
medicinal	976.2	E858.7	E946.2	E950.4	E962.0	E980.4
Tetronal	967.8	E852.8	E937.8	E950.2	E962.0	E980.2
Tetryl	983.0	E864.0	—	E950.7	E962.1	E980.6
Thalidomide	967.8	E852.8	E937.8	E950.2	E962.0	E980.2
Thallium (compounds) (dust) NEC	985.8	E866.4	—	E950.9	E962.1	E980.9
pesticide (rodenticide)	985.8	E863.7	—	E950.6	E962.1	E980.7
THC	969.6	E854.1	E939.6	E950.3	E962.0	E980.3
Thebacon	965.09	E850.2	E935.2	E950.0	E962.0	E980.0
Thebaine	965.09	E850.2	E935.2	E950.0	E962.0	E980.0
Theobromine (calcium salicylate)	974.1	E858.5	E944.1	E950.4	E962.0	E980.4
Theophylline (diuretic)	974.1	E858.5	E944.1	E950.4	E962.0	E980.4
ethylenediamine	975.7	E858.6	E945.7	E950.4	E962.0	E980.4
Thiabendazole	961.6	E857	E931.6	E950.4	E962.0	E980.4
Thialbarbital, thialbarbitone	968.3	E855.1	E938.3	E950.4	E962.0	E980.4
Thiamine	963.5	E858.1	E933.5	E950.4	E962.0	E980.4
Thiamylal (sodium)	968.3	E855.1	E938.3	E950.4	E962.0	E980.4
Thiazesim	969.09 ▲	E854.0	E939.0	E950.3	E962.0	E980.3
Thiazides (diuretics)	974.3	E858.5	E944.3	E950.4	E962.0	E980.4
Thiethylperazine	963.0	E858.1	E933.0	E950.4	E962.0	E980.4
Thimerosal (topical)	976.0	E858.7	E946.0	E950.4	E962.0	E980.4
ophthalmic preparation	976.5	E858.7	E946.5	E950.4	E962.0	E980.4

	Poisoning	Accident	Therapeutic Use	Suicide Attempt	Assault	Undetermined
External Cause (E-Code)						
Thioacetazone	961.8	E857	E931.8	E950.4	E962.0	E980.4
Thiobarbiturates	968.3	E855.1	E938.3	E950.4	E962.0	E980.4
Thiobismol	961.2	E857	E931.2	E950.4	E962.0	E980.4
Thiocarbamide	962.8	E858.0	E932.8	E950.4	E962.0	E980.4
Thiocarbarsone	961.1	E857	E931.1	E950.4	E962.0	E980.4
Thiocarlide	961.8	E857	E931.8	E950.4	E962.0	E980.4
Thioguanine	963.1	E858.1	E933.1	E950.4	E962.0	E980.4
Thiomercaptomerin	974.0	E858.5	E944.0	E950.4	E962.0	E980.4
Thiomerin	974.0	E858.5	E944.0	E950.4	E962.0	E980.4
Thiopental, thiopentone (sodium)	968.3	E855.1	E938.3	E950.4	E962.0	E980.4
Thiopropazate	969.1	E853.0	E939.1	E950.3	E962.0	E980.3
Thioproperazine	969.1	E853.0	E939.1	E950.3	E962.0	E980.3
Thioridazine	969.1	E853.0	E939.1	E950.3	E962.0	E980.3
Thio-TEPA, thiotepa	963.1	E858.1	E933.1	E950.4	E962.0	E980.4
Thiothixene	969.3	E853.8	E939.3	E950.3	E962.0	E980.3
Thiouracil	962.8	E858.0	E932.8	E950.4	E962.0	E980.4
Thiourea	962.8	E858.0	E932.8	E950.4	E962.0	E980.4
Thiphenamil	971.1	E855.4	E941.1	E950.4	E962.0	E980.4
Thiram NEC	989.4	E863.6	—	E950.6	E962.1	E980.7
medicinal	976.2	E858.7	E946.2	E950.4	E962.0	E980.4
Thonzylamine	963.0	E858.1	E933.0	E950.4	E962.0	E980.4
Thorazine	969.1	E853.0	E939.1	E950.3	E962.0	E980.3
Thornapple	988.2	E865.4	—	E950.9	E962.1	E980.9
Throat preparation (lozenges) NEC	976.6	E858.7	E946.6	E950.4	E962.0	E980.4
Thrombin	964.5	E858.2	E934.5	E950.4	E962.0	E980.4
Thrombolysin	964.4	E858.2	E934.4	E950.4	E962.0	E980.4
Thymol	983.0	E864.0	—	E950.7	E962.1	E980.6
Thymus extract	962.9	E858.0	E932.9	E950.4	E962.0	E980.4
Thyroglobulin	962.7	E858.0	E932.7	E950.4	E962.0	E980.4
Thyroid (derivatives) (extract)	962.7	E858.0	E932.7	E950.4	E962.0	E980.4
Thyrolar	962.7	E858.0	E932.7	E950.4	E962.0	E980.4
Thyrothrophin, thyrotropin	977.8	E858.8	E947.8	E950.4	E962.0	E980.4
Thyroxin(e)	962.7	E858.0	E932.7	E950.4	E962.0	E980.4
Tigan	963.0	E858.1	E933.0	E950.4	E962.0	E980.4
Tigloidine	968.0	E855.1	E938.0	E950.4	E962.0	E980.4
Tin (chloride) (dust) (oxide) NEC	985.8	E866.4	—	E950.9	E962.1	E980.9
anti-infectives	961.2	E857	E931.2	E950.4	E962.0	E980.4
Tinactin	976.0	E858.7	E946.0	E950.4	E962.0	E980.4
Tincture, iodine — see Iodine						
Tindal	969.1	E853.0	E939.1	E950.3	E962.0	E980.3
Titanium (compounds) (vapor)	985.8	E866.4	—	E950.9	E962.1	E980.9
ointment	976.3	E858.7	E946.3	E950.4	E962.0	E980.4
Titroid	962.7	E858.0	E932.7	E950.4	E962.0	E980.4
TMTD — see Tetramethylthiuram disulfide						
TNT	989.89	E866.8	—	E950.9	E962.1	E980.9
fumes	987.8	E869.8	—	E952.8	E962.2	E982.8
Toadstool	988.1	E865.5	—	E950.9	E962.1	E980.9
Tobacco NEC	989.84	E866.8	—	E950.9	E962.1	E980.9
Indian	988.2	E865.4	—	E950.9	E962.1	E980.9
smoke, second-hand	987.8	E869.4	—	—	—	—
Tocopherol	963.5	E858.1	E933.5	E950.4	E962.0	E980.4
Tocosamine	975.0	E858.6	E945.0	E950.4	E962.0	E980.4
Tofranil	969.05 ▲	E854.0	E939.0	E950.3	E962.0	E980.3
Toilet deodorizer	989.89	E866.8	—	E950.9	E962.1	E980.9
Tolazamide	962.3	E858.0	E932.3	E950.4	E962.0	E980.4
Tolazoline	971.3	E855.6	E941.3	E950.4	E962.0	E980.4
Tolbutamide	962.3	E858.0	E932.3	E950.4	E962.0	E980.4
sodium	977.8	E858.8	E947.8	E950.4	E962.0	E980.4
Tolmetin	965.69	E850.6	E935.6	E950.0	E962.0	E980.0
Tolnaftate	976.0	E858.7	E946.0	E950.4	E962.0	E980.4
Tolpropamine	976.1	E858.7	E946.1	E950.4	E962.0	E980.4
Tolserol	968.0	E855.1	E938.0	E950.4	E962.0	E980.4
Toluene (liquid) (vapor)	982.0	E862.4	—	E950.9	E962.1	E980.9
diisocyanate	983.0	E864.0	—	E950.7	E962.1	E980.6
Toluidine	983.0	E864.0	—	E950.7	E962.1	E980.6
vapor	987.8	E869.8	—	E952.8	E962.2	E982.8
Toluol (liquid) (vapor)	982.0	E862.4	—	E950.9	E962.1	E980.9
Tolylene-2, 4-diisocyanate	983.0	E864.0	—	E950.7	E962.1	E980.6
Tonics, cardiac	972.1	E858.3	E942.1	E950.4	E962.0	E980.4
Toxaphene (dust) (spray)	989.2	E863.0	—	E950.6	E962.1	E980.7
Toxoids NEC	978.8	E858.8	E948.8	E950.4	E962.0	E980.4
Tractor fuel NEC	981	E862.1	—	E950.9	E962.1	E980.9
Tragacanth	973.3	E858.4	E943.3	E950.4	E962.0	E980.4
Tramazoline	971.2	E855.5	E941.2	E950.4	E962.0	E980.4

	Poisoning	Accident	Therapeutic Use	Suicide Attempt	Assault	Undetermined
External Cause (E-Code)						
Tranquilizers	969.5	E853.9	E939.5	E950.3	E962.0	E980.3
benzodiazepine-based	969.4	E853.2	E939.4	E950.3	E962.0	E980.3
butyrophenone-based	969.2	E853.1	E939.2	E950.3	E962.0	E980.3
major NEC	969.3	E853.8	E939.3	E950.3	E962.0	E980.3
phenothiazine-based	969.1	E853.0	E939.1	E950.3	E962.0	E980.3
specified NEC	969.5	E853.8	E939.5	E950.3	E962.0	E980.3
Trantoin	961.9	E857	E931.9	E950.4	E962.0	E980.4
Tranxene	969.4	E853.2	E939.4	E950.3	E962.0	E980.3
Tranylcypromine (sulfate)	969.01 ▲	E854.0	E939.0	E950.3	E962.0	E980.3
Trasentine	975.1	E858.6	E945.1	E950.4	E962.0	E980.4
Travert	974.5	E858.5	E944.5	E950.4	E962.0	E980.4
Trecator	961.8	E857	E931.8	E950.4	E962.0	E980.4
Tretinoin	976.8	E858.7	E946.8	E950.4	E962.0	E980.4
Triacetin	976.0	E858.7	E946.0	E950.4	E962.0	E980.4
Triacetyloleandomycin	960.3	E856	E930.3	E950.4	E962.0	E980.4
Triamcinolone	962.0	E858.0	E932.0	E950.4	E962.0	E980.4
ENT agent	976.6	E858.7	E946.6	E950.4	E962.0	E980.4
medicinal (keratolytic)	976.4	E858.7	E946.4	E950.4	E962.0	E980.4
ophthalmic preparation	976.5	E858.7	E946.5	E950.4	E962.0	E980.4
topical NEC	976.0	E858.7	E946.0	E950.4	E962.0	E980.4
Triamterene	974.4	E858.5	E944.4	E950.4	E962.0	E980.4
Triaziquone	963.1	E858.1	E933.1	E950.4	E962.0	E980.4
Tribromacetaldehyde	967.3	E852.2	E937.3	E950.2	E962.0	E980.2
Tribromoethanol	968.2	E855.1	E938.2	E950.4	E962.0	E980.4
Tribromomethane	967.3	E852.2	E937.3	E950.2	E962.0	E980.2
Trichlorethane	982.3	E862.4	—	E950.9	E962.1	E980.9
Trichlormethiazide	974.3	E858.5	E944.3	E950.4	E962.0	E980.4
Trichloroacetic acid	983.1	E864.1	—	E950.7	E962.1	E980.6
Trichloroethanol	967.1	E852.0	E937.1	E950.2	E962.0	E980.2
Trichloroethylene (liquid) (vapor)	982.3	E862.4	—	E950.9	E962.1	E980.9
anesthetic (gas)	968.2	E855.1	E938.2	E950.4	E962.0	E980.4
Trichloroethyl phosphate	967.1	E852.0	E937.1	E950.2	E962.0	E980.2
Trichlorofluoromethane NEC	987.4	E869.2	—	E952.8	E962.2	E982.8
Trichlorotriethylamine	963.1	E858.1	E933.1	E950.4	E962.0	E980.4
Trichomonacides NEC	961.5	E857	E931.5	E950.4	E962.0	E980.4
Trichomycin	960.1	E856	E930.1	E950.4	E962.0	E980.4
Triclofos	967.1	E852.0	E937.1	E950.2	E962.0	E980.2
Tricresyl phosphate	989.89	E866.8	—	E950.9	E962.1	E980.9
solvent	982.8	E862.4	—	E950.9	E962.1	E980.9
Tricyclamol	966.4	E855.0	E936.4	E950.4	E962.0	E980.4
Tridesilon	976.0	E858.7	E946.0	E950.4	E962.0	E980.4
Tridihexethyl	971.1	E855.4	E941.1	E950.4	E962.0	E980.4
Tridione	966.0	E855.0	E936.0	E950.4	E962.0	E980.4
Triethanolamine NEC	983.2	E864.2	—	E950.7	E962.1	E980.6
detergent	983.2	E861.0	—	E950.7	E962.1	E980.6
trinitrate	972.4	E858.3	E942.4	E950.4	E962.0	E980.4
Triethanomelamine	963.1	E858.1	E933.1	E950.4	E962.0	E980.4
Triethylene melamine	963.1	E858.1	E933.1	E950.4	E962.0	E980.4
Triethylenephosphoramide	963.1	E858.1	E933.1	E950.4	E962.0	E980.4
Triethylenethiophosphoramide	963.1	E858.1	E933.1	E950.4	E962.0	E980.4
Trifluoperazine	969.1	E853.0	E939.1	E950.3	E962.0	E980.3
Trifluperidol	969.2	E853.1	E939.2	E950.3	E962.0	E980.3
Triflupromazine	969.1	E853.0	E939.1	E950.3	E962.0	E980.3
Trihexyphenidyl	971.1	E855.4	E941.1	E950.4	E962.0	E980.4
Triiodothyronine	962.7	E858.0	E932.7	E950.4	E962.0	E980.4
Trilene	968.2	E855.1	E938.2	E950.4	E962.0	E980.4
Trimeprazine	963.0	E858.1	E933.0	E950.4	E962.0	E980.4
Trimetazidine	972.4	E858.3	E942.4	E950.4	E962.0	E980.4
Trimethadione	966.0	E855.0	E936.0	E950.4	E962.0	E980.4
Trimethaphan	972.3	E858.3	E942.3	E950.4	E962.0	E980.4
Trimethidinium	972.3	E858.3	E942.3	E950.4	E962.0	E980.4
Trimethobenzamide	963.0	E858.1	E933.0	E950.4	E962.0	E980.4
Trimethylcarbinol	980.8	E860.8	—	E950.9	E962.1	E980.9
Trimethylpsoralen	976.3	E858.7	E946.3	E950.4	E962.0	E980.4
Trimeton	963.0	E858.1	E933.0	E950.4	E962.0	E980.4
Trimipramine	969.05 ▲	E854.0	E939.0	E950.3	E962.0	E980.3
Trimustine	963.1	E858.1	E933.1	E950.4	E962.0	E980.4
Trinitrin	972.4	E858.3	E942.4	E950.4	E962.0	E980.4
Trinitrophenol	983.0	E864.0	—	E950.7	E962.1	E980.6
Trinitrotoluene	989.89	E866.8	—	E950.9	E962.1	E980.9
fumes	987.8	E869.8	—	E952.8	E962.2	E982.8
Trional	967.8	E852.8	E937.8	E950.2	E962.0	E980.2
Trioxide of arsenic — see Arsenic						
Trioxsalen	976.3	E858.7	E946.3	E950.4	E962.0	E980.4
Tripelennamine	963.0	E858.1	E933.0	E950.4	E962.0	E980.4
Triperidol	969.2	E853.1	E939.2	E950.3	E962.0	E980.3
Triprolidine	963.0	E858.1	E933.0	E950.4	E962.0	E980.4
Trisoralen	976.3	E858.7	E946.3	E950.4	E962.0	E980.4
Troleandomycin	960.3	E856	E930.3	E950.4	E962.0	E980.4

Nontherapeutic use substance

▽ Subterms under main terms may continue to next column or page

▶◀ Revised Text   ● New Line   ▲ Revised Code

2010 ICD-9-CM

Index

Thioacetazone — Troleandomycin

	Poisoning	Accident	Therapeutic Use	Suicide Attempt	Assault	Undetermined
External Cause (E-Code)						
Trolnitrate (phosphate)	972.4	E858.3	E942.4	E950.4	E962.0	E980.4
Trometamol	963.3	E858.1	E933.3	E950.4	E962.0	E980.4
Tromethamine	963.3	E858.1	E933.3	E950.4	E962.0	E980.4
Tronothane	968.5	E855.2	E938.5	E950.4	E962.0	E980.4
Tropicamide	971.1	E855.4	E941.1	E950.4	E962.0	E980.4
Troxidone	966.0	E855.0	E936.0	E950.4	E962.0	E980.4
Tryparsamide	961.1	E857	E931.1	E950.4	E962.0	E980.4
Trypsin	963.4	E858.1	E933.4	E950.4	E962.0	E980.4
Tryptizol	969.05 ▲	E854.0	E939.0	E950.3	E962.0	E980.3
Tuaminoheptane	971.2	E855.5	E941.2	E950.4	E962.0	E980.4
Tuberculin (old)	977.8	E858.8	E947.8	E950.4	E962.0	E980.4
Tubocurare	975.2	E858.6	E945.2	E950.4	E962.0	E980.4
Tubocurarine	975.2	E858.6	E945.2	E950.4	E962.0	E980.4
Turkish green	969.6	E854.1	E939.6	E950.3	E962.0	E980.3
Turpentine (spirits of) (liquid)						
(vapor)	982.8	E862.4	—	E950.9	E962.1	E980.9
Tybamate	969.5	E853.8	E939.5	E950.3	E962.0	E980.3
Tyloxapol	975.5	E858.6	E945.5	E950.4	E962.0	E980.4
Tymazoline	971.2	E855.5	E941.2	E950.4	E962.0	E980.4
Typhoid vaccine	978.1	E858.8	E948.1	E950.4	E962.0	E980.4
Typhus vaccine	979.2	E858.8	E949.2	E950.4	E962.0	E980.4
Tyrothricin	976.0	E858.7	E946.0	E950.4	E962.0	E980.4
ENT agent	976.6	E858.7	E946.6	E950.4	E962.0	E980.4
ophthalmic preparation	976.5	E858.7	E946.5	E950.4	E962.0	E980.4
Undecenoic acid	976.0	E858.7	E946.0	E950.4	E962.0	E980.4
Undecylenic acid	976.0	E858.7	E946.0	E950.4	E962.0	E980.4
Unna's boot	976.3	E858.7	E946.3	E950.4	E962.0	E980.4
Uracil mustard	963.1	E858.1	E933.1	E950.4	E962.0	E980.4
Uramustine	963.1	E858.1	E933.1	E950.4	E962.0	E980.4
Urari	975.2	E858.6	E945.2	E950.4	E962.0	E980.4
Urea	974.4	E858.5	E944.4	E950.4	E962.0	E980.4
topical	976.8	E858.7	E946.8	E950.4	E962.0	E980.4
Urethan(e)						
(antineoplastic)	963.1	E858.1	E933.1	E950.4	E962.0	E980.4
Urginea (maritima) (scilla) — see Squill						
Uric acid metabolism agents						
NEC	974.7	E858.5	E944.7	E950.4	E962.0	E980.4
Urokinase	964.4	E858.2	E934.4	E950.4	E962.0	E980.4
Urokon	977.8	E858.8	E947.8	E950.4	E962.0	E980.4
Urotropin	961.9	E857	E931.9	E950.4	E962.0	E980.4
Urtica	988.2	E865.4	—	E950.9	E962.1	E980.9
Utility gas — see Gas, utility						
Vaccine NEC	979.9	E858.8	E949.9	E950.4	E962.0	E980.4
bacterial NEC	978.8	E858.8	E948.8	E950.4	E962.0	E980.4
with						
other bacterial component	978.9	E858.8	E948.9	E950.4	E962.0	E980.4
pertussis component	978.6	E858.8	E948.6	E950.4	E962.0	E980.4
viral-rickettsial component	979.7	E858.8	E949.7	E950.4	E962.0	E980.4
mixed NEC	978.9	E858.8	E948.9	E950.4	E962.0	E980.4
BCG	978.0	E858.8	E948.0	E950.4	E962.0	E980.4
cholera	978.2	E858.8	E948.2	E950.4	E962.0	E980.4
diphtheria	978.5	E858.8	E948.5	E950.4	E962.0	E980.4
influenza	979.6	E858.8	E949.6	E950.4	E962.0	E980.4
measles	979.4	E858.8	E949.4	E950.4	E962.0	E980.4
meningococcal	978.8	E858.8	E948.8	E950.4	E962.0	E980.4
mumps	979.6	E858.8	E949.6	E950.4	E962.0	E980.4
paratyphoid	978.1	E858.8	E948.1	E950.4	E962.0	E980.4
pertussis (with diphtheria toxoid) (with tetanus toxoid)	978.6	E858.8	E948.6	E950.4	E962.0	E980.4
plague	978.3	E858.8	E948.3	E950.4	E962.0	E980.4
poliomyelitis	979.5	E858.8	E949.5	E950.4	E962.0	E980.4
poliovirus	979.5	E858.8	E949.5	E950.4	E962.0	E980.4
rabies	979.1	E858.8	E949.1	E950.4	E962.0	E980.4
respiratory syncytial virus	979.6	E858.8	E949.6	E950.4	E962.0	E980.4
rickettsial NEC	979.6	E858.8	E949.6	E950.4	E962.0	E980.4
with						
bacterial component	979.7	E858.8	E949.7	E950.4	E962.0	E980.4
pertussis component	978.6	E858.8	E948.6	E950.4	E962.0	E980.4
viral component	979.7	E858.8	E949.7	E950.4	E962.0	E980.4
Rocky mountain spotted fever	979.6	E858.8	E949.6	E950.4	E962.0	E980.4
rotavirus	979.6	E858.8	E949.6	E950.4	E962.0	E980.4
rubella virus	979.4	E858.8	E949.4	E950.4	E962.0	E980.4
sabin oral	979.5	E858.8	E949.5	E950.4	E962.0	E980.4
smallpox	979.0	E858.8	E949.0	E950.4	E962.0	E980.4
tetanus	978.4	E858.8	E948.4	E950.4	E962.0	E980.4
typhoid	978.1	E858.8	E948.1	E950.4	E962.0	E980.4
typhus	979.2	E858.8	E949.2	E950.4	E962.0	E980.4

	Poisoning	Accident	Therapeutic Use	Suicide Attempt	Assault	Undetermined
External Cause (E-Code)						
Vaccine — continued						
viral NEC	979.6	E858.8	E949.6	E950.4	E962.0	E980.4
with						
bacterial component	979.7	E858.8	E949.7	E950.4	E962.0	E980.4
pertussis component	978.6	E858.8	E948.6	E950.4	E962.0	E980.4
rickettsial component	979.7	E858.8	E949.7	E950.4	E962.0	E980.4
yellow fever	979.3	E858.8	E949.3	E950.4	E962.0	E980.4
Vaccinia immune globulin						
(human)	964.6	E858.2	E934.6	E950.4	E962.0	E980.4
Vaginal contraceptives	976.8	E858.7	E946.8	E950.4	E962.0	E980.4
Valethamate	971.1	E855.4	E941.1	E950.4	E962.0	E980.4
Valisone	976.0	E858.7	E946.0	E950.4	E962.0	E980.4
Valium	969.4	E853.2	E939.4	E950.3	E962.0	E980.3
Valmid	967.8	E852.8	E937.8	E950.2	E962.0	E980.2
Vanadium	985.8	E866.4	—	E950.9	E962.1	E980.9
Vancomycin	960.8	E856	E930.8	E950.4	E962.0	E980.4
Vapor — see also Gas	987.9	E869.9	—	E952.9	E962.2	E982.9
kiln (carbon monoxide)	986	E868.8	—	E952.1	E962.2	E982.1
lead — see Lead						
specified source NEC (see also specific substance)	987.8	E869.8	—	E952.8	E962.2	E982.8
Varidase	964.4	E858.2	E934.4	E950.4	E962.0	E980.4
Varnish	989.89	E861.6	—	E950.9	E962.1	E980.9
cleaner	982.8	E862.9	—	E950.9	E962.1	E980.9
Vaseline	976.3	E858.7	E946.3	E950.4	E962.0	E980.4
Vasodilan	972.5	E858.3	E942.5	E950.4	E962.0	E980.4
Vasodilators NEC	972.5	E858.3	E942.5	E950.4	E962.0	E980.4
coronary	972.4	E858.3	E942.4	E950.4	E962.0	E980.4
Vasopressin	962.5	E858.0	E932.5	E950.4	E962.0	E980.4
Vasopressor drugs	962.5	E858.0	E932.5	E950.4	E962.0	E980.4
Venom, venomous (bite)						
(sting)	989.5	E905.9	—	E950.9	E962.1	E980.9
arthropod NEC	989.5	E905.5	—	E950.9	E962.1	E980.9
bee	989.5	E905.3	—	E950.9	E962.1	E980.9
centipede	989.5	E905.4	—	E950.9	E962.1	E980.9
hornet	989.5	E905.3	—	E950.9	E962.1	E980.9
lizard	989.5	E905.0	—	E950.9	E962.1	E980.9
marine animals or plants	989.5	E905.6	—	E950.9	E962.1	E980.9
millipede (tropical)	989.5	E905.4	—	E950.9	E962.1	E980.9
plant NEC	989.5	E905.7	—	E950.9	E962.1	E980.9
marine	989.5	E905.6	—	E950.9	E962.1	E980.9
scorpion	989.5	E905.2	—	E950.9	E962.1	E980.9
snake	989.5	E905.0	—	E950.9	E962.1	E980.9
specified NEC	989.5	E905.8	—	E950.9	E962.1	E980.9
spider	989.5	E905.1	—	E950.9	E962.1	E980.9
wasp	989.5	E905.3	—	E950.9	E962.1	E980.9
Ventolin — see Salbutamol sulfate						
Veramon	967.0	E851	E937.0	E950.1	E962.0	E980.1
Veratrum						
album	988.2	E865.4	—	E950.9	E962.1	E980.9
alkaloids	972.6	E858.3	E942.6	E950.4	E962.0	E980.4
viride	988.2	E865.4	—	E950.9	E962.1	E980.9
Verdigris — see also Copper	985.8	E866.4	—	E950.9	E962.1	E980.9
Veronal	967.0	E851	E937.0	E950.1	E962.0	E980.1
Veroxil	961.6	E857	E931.6	E950.4	E962.0	E980.4
Versidyne	965.7	E850.7	E935.7	E950.0	E962.0	E980.0
Viagra	972.5	E858.3	E942.5	E950.4	E962.0	E980.4
Vienna						
green	985.1	E866.3	—	E950.8	E962.1	E980.8
insecticide	985.1	E863.4	—	E950.6	E962.1	E980.7
red	989.89	E866.8	—	E950.9	E962.1	E980.9
pharmaceutical dye	977.4	E858.8	E947.4	E950.4	E962.0	E980.4
Vinbarbital, vinbarbitone	967.0	E851	E937.0	E950.1	E962.0	E980.1
Vinblastine	963.1	E858.1	E933.1	E950.4	E962.0	E980.4
Vincristine	963.1	E858.1	E933.1	E950.4	E962.0	E980.4
Vinesthene, vinethene	968.2	E855.1	E938.2	E950.4	E962.0	E980.4
Vinyl						
bital	967.0	E851	E937.0	E950.1	E962.0	E980.1
ether	968.2	E855.1	E938.2	E950.4	E962.0	E980.4
Vioform	961.3	E857	E931.3	E950.4	E962.0	E980.4
topical	976.0	E858.7	E946.0	E950.4	E962.0	E980.4
Viomycin	960.6	E856	E930.6	E950.4	E962.0	E980.4
Viosterol	963.5	E858.1	E933.5	E950.4	E962.0	E980.4
Viper (venom)	989.5	E905.0	—	E950.9	E962.1	E980.9
Viprynium (embonate)	961.6	E857	E931.6	E950.4	E962.0	E980.4
Virugon	961.7	E857	E931.7	E950.4	E962.0	E980.4
Visine	976.5	E858.7	E946.5	E950.4	E962.0	E980.4
Vitamins NEC	963.5	E858.1	E933.5	E950.4	E962.0	E980.4
B_{12}	964.1	E858.2	E934.1	E950.4	E962.0	E980.4
hematopoietic	964.1	E858.2	E934.1	E950.4	E962.0	E980.4

Nontherapeutic use substance

▽ Subterms under main terms may continue to next column or page

Index

Trolnitrate — Vitamins NEC

		External Cause (E-Code)				
	Poisoning	Accident	Therapeutic Use	Suicide Attempt	Assault	Undeter- mined
Vitamins — *continued*						
K	964.3	E858.2	E934.3	E950.4	E962.0	E980.4
Vleminckx's solution	976.4	E858.7	E946.4	E950.4	E962.0	E980.4
Voltaren — *see* Diclofenac sodium						
Warfarin (potassium)						
(sodium)	964.2	E858.2	E934.2	E950.4	E962.0	E980.4
rodenticide	989.4	E863.7	—	E950.6	E962.1	E980.7
Wasp (sting)	989.5	E905.3	—	E950.9	E962.1	E980.9
Water						
balance agents NEC	974.5	E858.5	E944.5	E950.4	E962.0	E980.4
gas	987.1	E868.1	—	E951.8	E962.2	E981.8
incomplete combustion of — see Carbon, monoxide, fuel, utility						
hemlock	988.2	E865.4	—	E950.9	E962.1	E980.9
moccasin (venom)	989.5	E905.0	—	E950.9	E962.1	E980.9
Wax (paraffin) (petroleum)	981	E862.3	—	E950.9	E962.1	E980.9
automobile	989.89	E861.2	—	E950.9	E962.1	E980.9
floor	981	E862.0	—	E950.9	E962.1	E980.9
Weed killers NEC	989.4	E863.5	—	E950.6	E962.1	E980.7
Welldorm	967.1	E852.0	E937.1	E950.2	E962.0	E980.2
White						
arsenic — see Arsenic						
hellebore	988.2	E865.4	—	E950.9	E962.1	E980.9
lotion (keratolytic)	976.4	E858.7	E946.4	E950.4	E962.0	E980.4
spirit	981	E862.0	—	E950.9	E962.1	E980.9
Whitewashes	989.89	E861.6	—	E950.9	E962.1	E980.9
Whole blood	964.7	E858.2	E934.7	E950.4	E962.0	E980.4
Wild						
black cherry	988.2	E865.4	—	E950.9	E962.1	E980.9
poisonous plants NEC	988.2	E865.4	—	E950.9	E962.1	E980.9
Window cleaning fluid	989.89	E861.3	—	E950.9	E962.1	E980.9
Wintergreen (oil)	976.3	E858.7	E946.3	E950.4	E962.0	E980.4
Witch hazel	976.2	E858.7	E946.2	E950.4	E962.0	E980.4
Wood						
alcohol	980.1	E860.2	—	E950.9	E962.1	E980.9
spirit	980.1	E860.2	—	E950.9	E962.1	E980.9
Woorali	975.2	E858.6	E945.2	E950.4	E962.0	E980.4
Wormseed, American	961.6	E857	E931.6	E950.4	E962.0	E980.4
Xanthine diuretics	974.1	E858.5	E944.1	E950.4	E962.0	E980.4
Xanthocillin	960.0	E856	E930.0	E950.4	E962.0	E980.4
Xanthotoxin	976.3	E858.7	E946.3	E950.4	E962.0	E980.4
Xigris	964.2	E858.2	E934.2	E950.4	E962.0	E980.4
Xylene (liquid) (vapor)	982.0	E862.4	—	E950.9	E962.1	E980.9
Xylocaine (infiltration)						
(topical)	968.5	E855.2	E938.5	E950.4	E962.0	E980.4
nerve block (peripheral)						
(plexus)	968.6	E855.2	E938.6	E950.4	E962.0	E980.4
spinal	968.7	E855.2	E938.7	E950.4	E962.0	E980.4
Xylol (liquid) (vapor)	982.0	E862.4	—	E950.9	E962.1	E980.9
Xylometazoline	971.2	E855.5	E941.2	E950.4	E962.0	E980.4
Yellow						
fever vaccine	979.3	E858.8	E949.3	E950.4	E962.0	E980.4
jasmine	988.2	E865.4	—	E950.9	E962.1	E980.9
Yew	988.2	E865.4	—	E950.9	E962.1	E980.9
Zactane	965.7	E850.7	E935.7	E950.0	E962.0	E980.0
Zaroxolyn	974.3	E858.5	E944.3	E950.4	E962.0	E980.4
Zephiran (topical)	976.0	E858.7	E946.0	E950.4	E962.0	E980.4
ophthalmic preparation	976.5	E858.7	E946.5	E950.4	E962.0	E980.4
Zerone	980.1	E860.2	—	E950.9	E962.1	E980.9
Zinc (compounds) (fumes) (salts)						
(vapor) NEC	985.8	E866.4	—	E950.9	E962.1	E980.9
anti-infectives	976.0	E858.7	E946.0	E950.4	E962.0	E980.4
antivaricose	972.7	E858.3	E942.7	E950.4	E962.0	E980.4
bacitracin	976.0	E858.7	E946.0	E950.4	E962.0	E980.4
chloride	976.2	E858.7	E946.2	E950.4	E962.0	E980.4
gelatin	976.3	E858.7	E946.3	E950.4	E962.0	E980.4
oxide	976.3	E858.7	E946.3	E950.4	E962.0	E980.4
peroxide	976.0	E858.7	E946.0	E950.4	E962.0	E980.4
pesticides	985.8	E863.4	—	E950.6	E962.1	E980.7
phosphide (rodenticide)	985.8	E863.7	—	E950.6	E962.1	E980.7
stearate	976.3	E858.7	E946.3	E950.4	E962.0	E980.4
sulfate (antivaricose)	972.7	E858.3	E942.7	E950.4	E962.0	E980.4
ENT agent	976.6	E858.7	E946.6	E950.4	E962.0	E980.4
ophthalmic solution	976.5	E858.7	E946.5	E950.4	E962.0	E980.4
topical NEC	976.0	E858.7	E946.0	E950.4	E962.0	E980.4
undecylenate	976.0	E858.7	E946.0	E950.4	E962.0	E980.4
Zovant	964.2	E858.2	E934.2	E950.4	E962.0	E980.4
Zoxazolamine	968.0	E855.1	E938.0	E950.4	E962.0	E980.4
Zygadenus (venenosus)	988.2	E865.4	—	E950.9	E962.1	E980.9

Nontherapeutic use substance

△ Subterms under main terms may continue to next column or page

►◄ Revised Text   ● New Line   ▲ Revised Code

SECTION 3

Alphabetic Index to External Causes of Injury and Poisoning (E Code)

This section contains the index to the codes which classify environmental events, circumstances, and other conditions as the cause of injury and other adverse effects. Where a code from the section Supplementary Classification of External Causes of Injury and Poisoning (E800-E999) is applicable, it is intended that the E code shall be used in addition to a code from the main body of the classification, chapters 1 to 17.

The alphabetic index to the E codes is organized by main terms which describe the accident, circumstance, event, or specific agent which caused the injury or other adverse effect.

Note — Transport accidents (E800-E848) include accidents involving:

aircraft and spacecraft (E840-E845)

watercraft (E830-E838)

motor vehicle (E810-E825)

railway (E800-E807)

other road vehicles (E826-E829)

For definitions and examples related to transport accidents — see Volume 1 code categories E800-E848.

The fourth-digit subdivisions for use with categories E800-E848 to identify the injured person are found at the end of this section.

For identifying the place in which an accident or poisoning occurred (circumstances classifiable to categories E850-E869 and E880-E928) — see the listing in this section under "Accident, occurring."

See the Table of Drugs and Chemicals (Section 2 of this volume) for identifying the specific agent involved in drug overdose or a wrong substance given or taken in error, and for intoxication or poisoning by a drug or other chemical substance.

The specific adverse effect, reaction, or localized toxic effect to a correct drug or substance properly administered in therapeutic or prophylactic dosage should be classified according to the nature of the adverse effect (e.g., allergy, dermatitis, tachycardia) listed in Section 1 of this volume.

Reporting E codes provides data for injury research and evaluation of injury-prevention strategies.

Reporting of E codes is optional unless mandated by state or carrier regulation... health care providers are strongly encouraged to report E codes for all initial treatments of injuries.

Sequencing heirarchy:

- Child/adult abuse
  - Terrorism activities
    - Cataclysmic events (floods, tornadoes, earthquakes, etc)
      - Transport accidents
        - Activity/external causes following causal (intent) E codes

☑ Additional Digit Required — Refer to the Tabular List for Digit Selection ▽ Subterms under main terms may continue to next column or page

2010 ICD-9-CM   ▶◀ Revised Text   ● New Line   ▲ Revised Code   Volume 2 — 321

A

Abandonment
- causing exposure to weather conditions — *see* Exposure
- child, with intent to injure or kill E968.4
- helpless person, infant, newborn E904.0
  - with intent to injure or kill E968.4

Abortion, criminal, injury to child E968.8

Abuse (alleged) (suspected)
- adult
  - by
    - child E967.4
    - ex-partner E967.3
    - ex-spouse E967.3
    - father E967.0
    - grandchild E967.7
    - grandparent E967.6
    - mother E967.2
    - non-related caregiver E967.8
    - other relative E967.7
    - other specified person E967.1
    - partner E967.3
    - sibling E967.5
    - spouse E967.3
    - stepfather E967.0
    - stepmother E967.2
    - unspecified person E967.9
- child
  - by
    - boyfriend of parent or guardian E967.0
    - child E967.4
    - father E967.0
    - female partner of parent or guardian E967.2
    - girlfriend of parent or guardian E967.2
    - grandchild E967.7
    - grandparent E967.6
    - male partner of parent or guardian E967.0
    - mother E967.2
    - non-related caregiver E967.8
    - other relative E967.7
    - other specified person(s) E967.1
    - sibling E967.5
    - stepfather E967.0
    - stepmother E967.2
    - unspecified person E967.9

Accident (to) E928.9
- aircraft (in transit) (powered) E841 ☑
  - at landing, take-off E840 ☑
  - due to, caused by cataclysm — *see* categories E908 ☑, E909 ☑
  - late effect of E929.1
  - unpowered (*see also* Collision, aircraft, unpowered) E842 ☑
  - while alighting, boarding E843 ☑
- amphibious vehicle
  - on
    - land — *see* Accident, motor vehicle
    - water — *see* Accident, watercraft
- animal-drawn vehicle NEC E827 ☑
- animal, ridden NEC E828 ☑
- balloon (*see also* Collision, aircraft, unpowered) E842 ☑
- caused by, due to
  - abrasive wheel (metalworking) E919.3
  - animal NEC E906.9
    - being ridden (in sport or transport) E828 ☑
  - avalanche NEC E909.2
  - band saw E919.4
  - bench saw E919.4
  - bore, earth-drilling or mining (land) (seabed) E919.1
  - bulldozer E919.7
  - cataclysmic
    - earth surface movement or eruption E909.9
    - storm E908.9
  - chain
    - hoist E919.2
      - agricultural operations E919.0
      - mining operations E919.1
    - saw E920.1
    - circular saw E919.4

Accident (to) — *continued*
- caused by, due to — *continued*
  - cold (excessive) (*see also* Cold, exposure to) E901.9
  - combine E919.0
  - conflagration — *see* Conflagration
  - corrosive liquid, substance NEC E924.1
  - cotton gin E919.8
  - crane E919.2
    - agricultural operations E919.0
    - mining operations E919.1
  - cutting or piercing instrument (*see also* Cut) E920.9
  - dairy equipment E919.8
  - derrick E919.2
    - agricultural operations E919.0
    - mining operations E919.1
  - drill E920.1
    - earth (land) (seabed) E919.1
    - hand (powered) E920.1
      - not powered E920.4
    - metalworking E919.3
    - woodworking E919.4
  - earth(-)
    - drilling machine E919.1
    - moving machine E919.7
    - scraping machine E919.7
  - electric
    - current (*see also* Electric shock) E925.9
    - motor (*see also* Accident, machine, by type of machine)
      - current (of) — *see* Electric shock
  - elevator (building) (grain) E919.2
    - agricultural operations E919.0
    - mining operations E919.1
  - environmental factors NEC E928.9
  - excavating machine E919.7
  - explosive material (*see also* Explosion) E923.9
  - farm machine E919.0
  - firearm missile — *see* Shooting
  - fire, flames (*see also* Fire)
    - conflagration — *see* Conflagration
  - forging (metalworking) machine E919.3
  - forklift (truck) E919.2
    - agricultural operations E919.0
    - mining operations E919.1
  - gas turbine E919.5
  - harvester E919.0
  - hay derrick, mower, or rake E919.0
  - heat (excessive) (*see also* Heat) E900.9
  - hoist (*see also* Accident, caused by, due to, lift) E919.2
    - chain — *see* Accident, caused by, due to, chain
    - shaft E919.1
  - hot
    - liquid E924.0
      - caustic or corrosive E924.1
    - object (not producing fire or flames) E924.8
    - substance E924.9
      - caustic or corrosive E924.1
      - liquid (metal) NEC E924.0
      - specified type NEC E924.8
  - human bite E928.3
  - ignition — *see* Ignition
  - internal combustion engine E919.5
  - landslide NEC E909.2
  - lathe (metalworking) E919.3
    - turnings E920.8
    - woodworking E919.4
  - lift, lifting (appliances) E919.2
    - agricultural operations E919.0
    - mining operations E919.1
    - shaft E919.1
  - lightning NEC E907
  - machine, machinery (*see also* Accident, machine)
    - drilling, metal E919.3
    - manufacturing, for manufacture of
      - beverages E919.8
      - clothing E919.8
      - foodstuffs E919.8
      - paper E919.8
      - textiles E919.8

Accident (to) — *continued*
- caused by, due to — *continued*
  - machine, machinery (*see also* Accident, machine) — *continued*
    - milling, metal E919.3
    - moulding E919.4
    - power press, metal E919.3
    - printing E919.8
    - rolling mill, metal E919.3
    - sawing, metal E919.3
    - specified type NEC E919.8
    - spinning E919.8
    - weaving E919.8
  - natural factor NEC E928.9
  - overhead plane E919.4
  - plane E920.4
    - overhead E919.4
  - powered
    - hand tool NEC E920.1
    - saw E919.4
      - hand E920.1
  - printing machine E919.8
  - pulley (block) E919.2
    - agricultural operations E919.0
    - mining operations E919.1
    - transmission E919.6
  - radial saw E919.4
  - radiation — *see* Radiation
  - reaper E919.0
  - road scraper E919.7
    - when in transport under its own power — *see* categories E810-E825 ☑
  - roller coaster E919.8
  - sander E919.4
  - saw E920.4
    - band E919.4
    - bench E919.4
    - chain E920.1
    - circular E919.4
    - hand E920.4
      - powered E920.1
    - powered, except hand E919.4
    - radial E919.4
  - sawing machine, metal E919.3
  - shaft
    - hoist E919.1
    - lift E919.1
    - transmission E919.6
  - shears E920.4
    - hand E920.4
      - powered E920.1
    - mechanical E919.3
  - shovel E920.4
    - steam E919.7
  - spinning machine E919.8
  - steam (*see also* Burning, steam)
    - engine E919.5
    - shovel E919.7
  - thresher E919.0
  - thunderbolt NEC E907
  - tractor E919.0
    - when in transport under its own power — *see* categories E810-E825 ☑
  - transmission belt, cable, chain, gear, pinion, pulley, shaft E919.6
  - turbine (gas) (water driven) E919.5
  - under-cutter E919.1
  - weaving machine E919.8
  - winch E919.2
    - agricultural operations E919.0
    - mining operations E919.1
- diving E883.0
  - with insufficient air supply E913.2
- glider (hang) (*see also* Collision, aircraft, unpowered) E842 ☑
- hovercraft
  - on
    - land — *see* Accident, motor vehicle
    - water — *see* Accident, watercraft
- ice yacht (*see also* Accident, vehicle NEC) E848
- in
  - medical, surgical procedure
    - as, or due to misadventure — *see* Misadventure

Accident (to) — *continued*
- in — *continued*
  - medical, surgical procedure — *continued*
    - causing an abnormal reaction or later complication without mention of misadventure — *see* Reaction, abnormal
- kite carrying a person (*see also* Collision, involving aircraft, unpowered) E842 ☑
- land yacht (*see also* Accident, vehicle NEC) E848
- late effect of — *see* Late effect
- launching pad E845 ☑
- machine, machinery (*see also* Accident, caused by, due to, by specific type of machine) E919.9
  - agricultural including animal-powered E919.0
  - earth-drilling E919.1
  - earth moving or scraping E919.7
  - excavating E919.7
  - involving transport under own power on highway or transport vehicle — *see* categories E810-E825 ☑, E840-E845 ☑
  - lifting (appliances) E919.2
  - metalworking E919.3
  - mining E919.1
  - prime movers, except electric motors E919.5
    - electric motors — *see* Accident, machine, by specific type of machine
  - recreational E919.8
  - specified type NEC E919.8
  - transmission E919.6
  - watercraft (deck) (engine room) (galley) (laundry) (loading) E836 ☑
  - woodworking or forming E919.4
- motor vehicle (on public highway) (traffic) E819 ☑
  - due to cataclysm — *see* categories E908 ☑, E909 ☑
  - involving
    - collision (*see also* Collision, motor vehicle) E812 ☑
    - nontraffic, not on public highway — *see* categories E820-E825 ☑
    - not involving collision — *see* categories E816-E819 ☑
- nonmotor vehicle NEC E829 ☑
  - nonroad — *see* Accident, vehicle NEC
  - road, except pedal cycle, animal-drawn vehicle, or animal being ridden E829 ☑
- nonroad vehicle NEC — *see* Accident, vehicle NEC
- not elsewhere classifiable involving
  - cable car (not on rails) E847
    - on rails E829 ☑
  - coal car in mine E846
  - hand truck — *see* Accident, vehicle NEC
  - logging car E846
  - sled(ge), meaning snow or ice vehicle E848
  - tram, mine or quarry E846
  - truck
    - mine or quarry E846
    - self-propelled, industrial E846
    - station baggage E846
  - tub, mine or quarry E846
  - vehicle NEC E848
    - snow and ice E848
    - used only on industrial premises E846
  - wheelbarrow E848
- occurring (at) (in)
  - apartment E849.0
  - baseball field, diamond E849.4
  - construction site, any E849.3
  - dock E849.8
    - yard E849.3
  - dormitory E849.7
  - factory (building) (premises) E849.3
  - farm E849.1
    - buildings E849.1
    - house E849.0

☑ Additional Digit Required — Refer to the Tabular List for Digit Selection

⊽ Subterms under main terms may continue to next column or page

Index to External Causes

Accident (to) — continued
occurring — continued
football field E849.4
forest E849.8
garage (place of work) E849.3
private (home) E849.0
gravel pit E849.2
gymnasium E849.4
highway E849.5
home (private) (residential) E849.0
institutional E849.7
hospital E849.7
hotel E849.6
house (private) (residential) E849.0
movie E849.6
public E849.6
institution, residential E849.7
jail E849.7
mine E849.2
motel E849.6
movie house E849.6
office (building) E849.6
orphanage E849.7
park (public) E849.4
mobile home E849.8
trailer E849.8
parking lot or place E849.8
place
industrial NEC E849.3
parking E849.8
public E849.8
specified place NEC E849.5
recreational NEC E849.4
sport NEC E849.4
playground (park) (school) E849.4
prison E849.6
public building NEC E849.6
quarry E849.2
railway
line NEC E849.8
yard E849.3
residence
home (private) E849.0
resort (beach) (lake) (mountain) (seashore) (vacation) E849.4
restaurant E849.6
sand pit E849.2
school (building) (private) (public) (state) E849.6
reform E849.7
riding E849.4
seashore E849.8
resort E849.4
shop (place of work) E849.3
commercial E849.6
skating rink E849.4
sports palace E849.4
stadium E849.4
store E849.6
street E849.5
swimming pool (public) E849.4
private home or garden E849.0
tennis court, public E849.4
theatre, theater E849.6
trailer court E849.8
tunnel E849.8
under construction E849.2
warehouse E849.3
yard
dock E849.3
industrial E849.3
private (home) E849.0
railway E849.3
off-road type motor vehicle (not on public highway) NEC E821 ☑
on public highway — see categories E810-E819 ☑
pedal cycle E826 ☑
railway E807 ☑
due to cataclysm — see categories E908 ☑, E909 ☑
involving
avalanche E909.2
burning by engine, locomotive, train (see also Explosion, railway engine) E803 ☑

Accident (to) — continued
railway — continued
involving — continued
collision (see also Collision, railway) E800 ☑
derailment (see also Derailment, railway) E802 ☑
explosion (see also Explosion, railway engine) E803 ☑
fall (see also Fall, from, railway rolling stock) E804 ☑
fire (see also Explosion, railway engine) E803 ☑
hitting by, being struck by
object falling in, on, from, rolling stock, train, vehicle E806 ☑
rolling stock, train, vehicle E805 ☑
overturning, railway rolling stock, train, vehicle (see also Derailment, railway) E802 ☑
running off rails, railway (see also Derailment, railway) E802 ☑
specified circumstances NEC E806 ☑
train or vehicle hit by
avalanche E909.2
falling object (earth, rock, tree) E806 ☑
due to cataclysm — see categories E908 ☑, E909 ☑
landslide E909.2
roller skate E885.1
scooter (nonmotorized) E885.0
skateboard E885.2
ski(ing) E885.3
jump E884.9
lift or tow (with chair or gondola) E847
snowboard E885.4
snow vehicle, motor driven (not on public highway) E820 ☑
on public highway — see categories E810-E819 ☑
spacecraft E845 ☑
specified cause NEC E928.8
street car E829 ☑
traffic NEC E819 ☑
vehicle NEC (with pedestrian) E848
battery powered
airport passenger vehicle E846
truck (baggage) (mail) E846
powered commercial or industrial (with other vehicle or object within commercial or industrial premises) E846
watercraft E838 ☑
with
drowning or submersion resulting from
accident other than to watercraft E832 ☑
accident to watercraft E830 ☑
injury, except drowning or submersion, resulting from
accident other than to watercraft — see categories E833-E838 ☑
accident to watercraft E831 ☑
due to, caused by cataclysm — see categories E908 ☑, E909 ☑
machinery E836 ☑
Acid throwing E961
Acosta syndrome E902.0
Activity (involving) E030 ●
aerobic and step exercise (class) E009.2 ●
alpine skiing E003.2 ●
animal care NEC E019.9 ●
arts and handcrafts NEC E012.9 ●
athletics NEC E008.9 ●
played
as a team or group NEC E007.9 ●
individually NEC E006.9 ●
baking E015.2 ●
ballet E005.0 ●
barbells E010.2 ●
baseball E007.3 ●
BASE (Building, Antenna, Span, Earth) jumping E004.2 ●

Activity — continued
basketball E007.6 ●
bathing (personal) E013.0 ●
beach volleyball E007.7 ●
bike riding E006.4 ●
boogie boarding E002.7 ●
bowling E006.3 ●
boxing E008.0 ●
brass instrument playing E018.3 ●
building and construction E016.2 ●
bungee jumping E004.3 ●
calisthenics E009.1 ●
canoeing (in calm and turbulent water) E002.5 ●
capture the flag E007.8 ●
cardiorespiratory exercise NEC E009.9 ●
caregiving (providing) NEC E014.9 ●
bathing E014.0 ●
lifting E014.1 ●
cellular
communication device E011.1 ●
telephone E011.1 ●
challenge course E009.4 ●
cheerleading E005.4 ●
circuit training E009.3 ●
cleaning
floor E013.4 ●
climbing NEC E004.9 ●
mountain E004.0 ●
rock E004.0 ●
wall climbing E004.0 ●
combatives E008.4 ●
computer
keyboarding E011.0 ●
technology NEC E011.9 ●
confidence course E009.4 ●
construction (building) E016.2 ●
cooking and baking E015.2 ●
cooking and grilling NEC E015.9 ●
cool down exercises E009.1 ●
cricket E007.9 ●
crocheting E012.0 ●
cross country skiing E003.3 ●
dancing (all types) E005.0 ●
digging
dirt E016.0 ●
dirt digging E016.0 ●
dishwashing E015.0 ●
diving (platform) (springboard) E002.1 ●
underwater E002.4 ●
dodge ball E007.8 ●
downhill skiing E003.2 ●
drum playing E018.1 ●
dumbbells E010.2 ●
electronic
devices NEC E011.9 ●
hand held interactive E011.1 ●
game playing (using) (with) E011.1 ●
interactive device E011.1 ●
keyboard or other stationary device E011.0 ●
elliptical machine E009.0 ●
exercise(s)
machines (primarily for)
cardiorespiratory conditioning E009.0 ●
muscle strengthening E010.0 ●
muscle strengthening (non-machine) NEC E010.9 ●
external motion NEC E017.9 ●
rollercoaster E017.0 ●
field hockey E007.4 ●
figure skating (pairs) (singles) E003.0 ●
flag football E007.1 ●
floor mopping and cleaning E013.4 ●
food preparation and clean up E015.0 ●
football (American) NOS E007.0 ●
flag E007.1 ●
tackle E007.0 ●
touch E007.1 ●
four square E007.8 ●
free weights E010.2 ●
frisbee (ultimate) E008.3 ●
furniture
building E012.2 ●
finishing E012.2 ●
repair E012.2 ●

Activity — continued
game playing (electronic) ●
using
interactive device E011.1 ●
keyboard or other stationary device E011.0 ●
gardening E016.1 ●
golf E006.2 ●
grass drills E009.5 ●
grilling and smoking food E015.1 ●
grooming and shearing an animal E019.2 ●
guerilla drills E009.5 ●
gymnastics (rhythmic) E005.2 ●
handball E008.2 ●
handcrafts NEC E012.9 ●
hand held interactive electronic device E011.1 ●
hang gliding E004.4 ●
hiking (on level or elevated terrain) E001.0 ●
hockey (ice) E003.1 ●
field E007.4 ●
horseback riding E006.1 ●
household maintenance NEC E013.9 ●
ice NEC E003.9 ●
dancing E003.0 ●
hockey E003.1 ●
skating E003.0 ●
inline roller skating E006.0 ●
ironing E013.3 ●
judo E008.4 ●
jumping (off) NEC E004.9 ●
BASE (Building, Antenna, Span, Earth) E004.2 ●
bungee E004.3 ●
jacks E009.1 ●
rope E006.5 ●
jumping jacks E009.1 ●
jumping rope E006.5 ●
karate E008.4 ●
kayaking (in calm and turbulent water) E002.5 ●
keyboarding (computer) E011.0 ●
kickball E007.8 ●
knitting E012.0 ●
lacrosse E007.4 ●
land maintenance NEC E016.9 ●
landscaping E016.1 ●
laundry E013.1 ●
machines (exercise) primarily for cardiorespiratory conditioning E009.0 ●
maintenance
building E016.9 ●
household NEC E013.9 ●
land E016.9 ●
property E016.9 ●
marching (on level or elevated terrain) E001.0 ●
martial arts E008.4 ●
microwave oven E015.2 ●
milking an animal E019.1 ●
mopping (floor) E013.4 ●
mountain climbing E004.0 ●
muscle strengthening
exercises (non-machine) NEC E010.9 ●
machines E010.0 ●
musical keyboard (electronic) playing E018.0 ●
nordic skiing E003.3 ●
obstacle course E009.4 ●
oven (microwave) E015.2 ●
packing up and unpacking in moving to a new residence E013.5 ●
parasailing E002.9 ●
percussion instrument playing NEC E018.1 ●
personal
bathing and showering E013.0 ●
hygiene NEC E013.8 ●
showering E013.0 ●
physical
games generally associated with school recess, summer camp and children E007.8 ●
training NEC E009.9 ●
piano playing E018.0 ●
pilates E010.3 ●
platform diving E002.1 ●

☑ Additional Digit Required — Refer to the Tabular List for Digit Selection
▶◀ Revised Text ● New Line ▲ Revised Code
🔲 Subterms under main terms may continue to next column or page
2010 ICD-9-CM
October 2009 • Volume 2 — 323

Activity — continued

playing musical instrument ●
   brass instrument E018.3 ●
   drum E018.1 ●
   musical keyboard (electronic) E018.0 ●
   percussion instrument NEC E018.1 ●
   piano E018.0 ●
   string instrument E018.2 ●
   wind instrument E018.3 ●
property maintenance NEC E016.9 ●
pruning (garden and lawn) E016.1 ●
pull-ups E010.1 ●
push-ups E010.1 ●
racquetball E008.2 ●
rafting (in calm and turbulent water) E002.5 ●
raking (leaves) E016.0 ●
rappelling E004.1 ●
refereeing a sports activity E029.0 ●
residential relocation E013.5 ●
rhythmic
   gymnastics E005.2 ●
   movement NEC E005.9 ●
riding
   horseback E006.1 ●
   rollercoaster E017.0 ●
rock climbing E004.0 ●
rollercoaster riding E017.0 ●
roller skating (inline) E006.0 ●
rough housing and horseplay E029.2 ●
rowing (in calm and turbulent water) E002.5 ●
rugby E007.2 ●
running E001.1 ●
SCUBA diving E002.4 ●
sewing E012.1 ●
shoveling E016.0 ●
   dirt E016.0 ●
   snow E016.0 ●
showering (personal) E013.0 ●
sit-ups E010.1 ●
skateboarding E006.0 ●
skating (ice) E003.0 ●
   roller E006.0 ●
skiing (alpine) (downhill) E003.2 ●
   cross country E003.3 ●
   nordic E003.3 ●
sledding (snow) E003.2 ●
smoking and grilling food E015.1 ●
snorkeling E002.4 ●
snow NEC E003.9 ●
   boarding E003.2 ●
   shoveling E016.0 ●
   sledding E003.2 ●
   tubing E003.2 ●
soccer E007.5 ●
softball E007.3 ●
specified NEC E029.9 ●
spectator at an event E029.1 ●
sports NEC E008.9 ●
sports played as a team or group NEC E007.9 ●
sports played individually NEC E006.9 ●
springboard diving E002.1 ●
squash E008.2 ●
stationary bike E009.0 ●
step (stepping) exercise (class) E009.2 ●
stepper machine E009.0 ●
stove E015.2 ●
string instrument playing E018.2 ●
surfing E002.7 ●
swimming E002.0 ●
tackle football E007.0 ●
tap dancing E005.0 ●
tennis E008.2 ●
tobogganing E003.2 ●
touch football E007.1 ●
track and field events (non-running) E006.6 ●
   running E001.1 ●
trampoline E005.3 ●
treadmill E009.0 ●
trimming shrubs E016.1 ●
tubing (in calm and turbulent water) E002.5 ●
   snow E003.2 ●
ultimate frisbee E008.3 ●
underwater diving E002.4 ●
unpacking in moving to a new residence E013.5 ●

Activity — continued

use of stove, oven and microwave oven E015.2 ●
vacuuming E013.2 ●
volleyball (beach) (court) E007.7 ●
wake boarding E002.6 ●
walking (on level or elevated terrain) E001.0 ●
   an animal E019.0 ●
walking an animal E019.0 ●
wall climbing E004.0 ●
warm up and cool down exercises E009.1 ●
water NEC E002.9 ●
   aerobics E002.3 ●
   craft NEC E002.9 ●
   exercise E002.3 ●
   polo E002.2 ●
   skiing E002.6 ●
   sliding E002.8 ●
   survival training and testing E002.9 ●
weeding (garden and lawn) E016.1 ●
wind instrument playing E018.3 ●
windsurfing E002.7 ●
wrestling E008.1 ●
yoga E005.1 ●
Activity status E000.9 ●
civilian ●
   done for ●
      financial or other compensation E000.0 ●
      pay or income E000.0 ●
   for income E000.0 ●
   hobby or leisure E000.8 ●
   military E000.1 ●
      off duty E000.8 ●
   off duty military E000.8 ●
   recreation E000.8 ●
   specified NEC E000.8 ●
   sport not for income E000.8 ●
   student E000.8 ●
   volunteer E000.8 ●
Aeroneurosis E902.1 ●
Aero-otitis media — see Effects of, air pressure ●
Aerosinusitis — see Effects of, air pressure ●
After-effect, late — see Late effect ●
Air ●
   blast ●
      in ●
         terrorism E979.2 ●
         war operations E993.9 ▲
   embolism (traumatic) NEC E928.9 ●
      in ●
         infusion or transfusion E874.1 ●
         perfusion E874.2 ●
   sickness E903 ●
Alpine sickness E902.0 ●
Altitude sickness — see Effects of, air pressure ●
Anaphylactic shock, anaphylaxis — see also Table of Drugs and Chemicals E947.9 ●
   due to bite or sting (venomous) — see Bite, venomous
Andes disease E902.0 ●
Apoplexy ●
   heat — see Heat ●
Arachnidism E905.1 ●
Arson E968.0 ●
Asphyxia, asphyxiation ●
   by ●
      chemical ●
         in ●
            terrorism E979.7 ●
            war operations E997.2 ●
      explosion — see Explosion ●
      food (bone) (regurgitated food) (seed) E911 ●
      foreign object, except food E912 ●
      fumes ●
         in ●
            terrorism (chemical weapons) E979.7 ●
            war operations E997.2 ●
      gas (see also Table of Drugs and Chemicals) ●
         in ●
            terrorism E979.7 ●
            war operations E997.2 ●
         legal ●
            execution E978 ●

Asphyxia, asphyxiation — continued

by — continued
   gas (see also Table of Drugs and Chemicals) — continued
      legal — continued
         intervention (tear) E972
         tear E972
   mechanical means (see also Suffocation) E913.9
from
   conflagration — see Conflagration
   fire (see also Fire) E899
      in
         terrorism E979.3
         war operations E990.9
   ignition — see Ignition
Aspiration
   foreign body — see Foreign body, aspiration
   mucus, not of newborn (with asphyxia, obstruction respiratory passage, suffocation) E912
   phlegm (with asphyxia, obstruction respiratory passage, suffocation) E912
   vomitus (with asphyxia, obstruction respiratory passage, suffocation) (see also Foreign body, aspiration, food) E911
Assassination (attempt) — see also Assault E968.9
Assault (homicidal) (by) (in) E968.9
   acid E961
      swallowed E962.1
   air gun E968.6
   BB gun E968.6
   bite NEC E968.8
      of human being E968.7
   bomb ((placed in) car or house) E965.8
      antipersonnel E965.5
      letter E965.7
      petrol E965.6
   brawl (hand) (fists) (foot) E960.0
   burning, burns (by fire) E968.0
      acid E961
         swallowed E962.1
      caustic, corrosive substance E961
         swallowed E962.1
      chemical from swallowing caustic, corrosive substance NEC E962.1
      hot liquid E968.3
      scalding E968.3
      vitriol E961
         swallowed E962.1
   caustic, corrosive substance E961
      swallowed E962.1
   cut, any part of body E966
   dagger E966
   drowning E964
   explosive(s) E965.9
      bomb (see also Assault, bomb) E965.8
      dynamite E965.8
   fight (hand) (fists) (foot) E960.0
      with weapon E968.9
         blunt or thrown E968.2
         cutting or piercing E966
         firearm — see Shooting, homicide
   fire E968.0
   firearm(s) — see Shooting, homicide
   garrotting E963
   gunshot (wound) — see Shooting, homicide
   hanging E963
   injury NEC E968.9
   knife E966
   late effect of E969
   ligature E963
   poisoning E962.9
      drugs or medicinals E962.0
      gas(es) or vapors, except drugs and medicinals E962.2
      solid or liquid substances, except drugs and medicinals E962.1
   puncture, any part of body E966
   pushing
      before moving object, train, vehicle E968.5
      from high place E968.1
   rape E960.1
   scalding E968.3
   shooting — see Shooting, homicide

Assault — continued

sodomy E960.1
stab, any part of body E966
strangulation E963
submersion E964
suffocation E963
transport vehicle E968.5
violence NEC E968.9
vitriol E961
   swallowed E962.1
weapon E968.9
   blunt or thrown E968.2
   cutting or piercing E966
   firearm — see Shooting, homicide
wound E968.9
   cutting E966
   gunshot — see Shooting, homicide
   knife E966
   piercing E966
   puncture E966
   stab E966
Attack by animal NEC E906.9
Avalanche E909.2
   falling on or hitting
      motor vehicle (in motion) (on public highway) E909.2
      railway train E909.2
Aviators' disease E902.1

B

Barotitis, barodontalgia, barosinusitis, barotrauma (otitic) (sinus) — see Effects of, air pressure
Battered
   baby or child (syndrome) see Abuse, child; category E967 ☑
   person other than baby or child — see Assault
Bayonet wound — see also Cut, by bayonet E920.3
   in
      legal intervention E974
      terrorism E979.8
      war operations E995.2 ▲
Bean in nose E912
Bed set on fire NEC E898.0
Beheading (by guillotine)
   homicide E966
   legal execution E978
Bending, injury in E927.8
Bends E902.0
Bite
   animal NEC E906.5
      other specified (except arthropod) E906.3
      venomous NEC E905.9
   arthropod (nonvenomous) NEC E906.4
      venomous — see Sting
   black widow spider E905.1
   cat E906.3
   centipede E905.4
   cobra E905.0
   copperhead snake E905.0
   coral snake E905.0
   dog E906.0
   fer de lance E905.0
   gila monster E905.0
   human being
      accidental E928.3
      assault E968.7
   insect (nonvenomous) E906.4
      venomous — see Sting
   krait E905.0
   late effect of — see Late effect
   lizard E906.2
      venomous E905.0
   mamba E905.0
   marine animal
      nonvenomous E906.3
         snake E906.2
      venomous E905.6
         snake E905.0
   millipede E906.4
      venomous E905.4
   moray eel E906.3
   rat E906.1
   rattlesnake E905.0
   rodent, except rat E906.3

Activity — Bite

☑ Additional Digit Required — Refer to the Tabular List for Digit Selection   ▽ Subterms under main terms may continue to next column or page

324 — Volume 2 • October 2009   ▶◀ Revised Text   ● New Line   ▲ Revised Code   2010 ICD-9-CM

Bite — continued
serpent — see Bite, snake
shark E906.3
snake (venomous) E905.0
nonvenomous E906.2
sea E905.0
spider E905.1
nonvenomous E906.4
tarantula (venomous) E905.1
venomous NEC E905.9
by specific animal — see category E905 ☑
viper E905.0
water moccasin E905.0
Blast (air)
from nuclear explosion E996 ☑
in
terrorism E979.2
from nuclear explosion E979.5
underwater E979.0
war operations E993.9 ▲
from nuclear explosion ►(see also War
operations, injury due to, nuclear weapons)◄ E996.0 ▲
underwater E992.9 ▲
Blizzard E908.3
Blow E928.9
by law-enforcing agent, police (on duty) E975
with blunt object (baton) (nightstick)
(stave) (truncheon) E973
Blowing up — see also Explosion E923.9
Brawl (hand) (fists) (foot) E960.0
Breakage (accidental)
cable of cable car not on rails E847
ladder (causing fall) E881.0
part (any) of
animal-drawn vehicle E827 ☑
ladder (causing fall) E881.0
motor vehicle
in motion (on public highway) E818 ☑
not on public highway E825 ☑
nonmotor road vehicle, except animal-
drawn vehicle or pedal cycle
E829 ☑
off-road type motor vehicle (not on public
highway) NEC E821 ☑
on public highway E818 ☑
pedal cycle E826 ☑
scaffolding (causing fall) E881.1
snow vehicle, motor-driven (not on public
highway) E820 ☑
on public highway E818 ☑
vehicle NEC — see Accident, vehicle
Broken
glass
fall on E888.0
injury by E920.8
power line (causing electric shock) E925.1
Bumping against, into (accidentally)
object (moving) E917.9
caused by crowd E917.1
with subsequent fall E917.6
furniture E917.3
with subsequent fall E917.7
in
running water E917.2
sports E917.0
with subsequent fall E917.5
stationary E917.4
with subsequent fall E917.8
person(s) E917.9
with fall E886.9
in sports E886.0
as, or caused by, a crowd E917.1
with subsequent fall E917.6
in sports E917.0
with fall E886.0
Burning, burns (accidental) (by) (from) (on) E899
acid (any kind) E924.1
swallowed — see Table of Drugs and
Chemicals
airgun E928.7 ●
bedclothes (see also Fire, specified NEC) E898.0
blowlamp (see also Fire, specified NEC) E898.1
blowtorch (see also Fire, specified NEC) E898.1
boat, ship, watercraft — see categories
E830 ☑, E831 ☑, E837 ☑

Burning, burns — continued
bonfire (controlled) E897
uncontrolled E892
candle (see also Fire, specified NEC) E898.1
caustic liquid, substance E924.1
swallowed — see Table of Drugs and
Chemicals
chemical E924.1
from swallowing caustic, corrosive substance — see Table of Drugs and
Chemicals
in
terrorism E979.7
war operations E997.2
cigar(s) or cigarette(s) (see also Fire, specified
NEC) E898.1
clothes, clothing, nightdress — see Ignition,
clothes
with conflagration — see Conflagration
conflagration — see Conflagration
corrosive liquid, substance E924.1
swallowed — see Table of Drugs and
Chemicals
electric current (see also Electric shock) E925.9
firearm E928.7 ●
fire, flames (see also Fire) E899
flare, Verey pistol E922.8
heat
from appliance (electrical) E924.8
in local application, or packing during
medical or surgical procedure
E873.5
homicide (attempt) (see also Assault, burning)
E968.0
hot
liquid E924.0
caustic or corrosive E924.1
object (not producing fire or flames) E924.8
substance E924.9
caustic or corrosive E924.1
liquid (metal) NEC E924.0
specified type NEC E924.8
tap water E924.2
ignition (see also Ignition)
clothes, clothing, nightdress (see also Ignition, clothes)
with conflagration — see Conflagration
highly inflammable material (benzine) (fat)
(gasoline) (kerosene) (paraffin)
(petrol) E894
in
terrorism E979.3
from nuclear explosion E979.5
petrol bomb E979.3
war operations (from fire-producing device
or conventional weapon) E990.9
from nuclear explosion ►(see also War
operations, injury due to, nuclear weapons)◄ E996.2 ▲
incendiary bomb E990.0 ●
petrol bomb E990.0
inflicted by other person
stated as
homicidal, intentional (see also Assault,
burning) E968.0
undetermined whether accidental or
intentional (see also Burn, stated
as undetermined whether accidental or intentional) E988.1
internal, from swallowed caustic, corrosive
liquid, substance — see Table of Drugs
and Chemicals
lamp (see also Fire, specified NEC) E898.1
late effect of NEC E929.4
lighter (cigar) (cigarette) (see also Fire, specified
NEC) E898.1
lightning E907
liquid (boiling) (hot) (molten) E924.0
caustic, corrosive (external) E924.1
swallowed — see Table of Drugs and
Chemicals
local application of externally applied substance in medical or surgical care
E873.5
machinery — see Accident, machine
matches (see also Fire, specified NEC) E898.1

Burning, burns — continued
medicament, externally applied E873.5
metal, molten E924.0
object (hot) E924.8
producing fire or flames — see Fire
oven (electric) (gas) E924.8
pipe (smoking) (see also Fire, specified NEC)
E898.1
radiation — see Radiation
railway engine, locomotive, train (see also Explosion, railway engine) E803 ☑
self-inflicted (unspecified whether accidental
or intentional) E988.1
caustic or corrosive substance NEC E988.7
stated as intentional, purposeful E958.1
caustic or corrosive substance NEC
E958.7
stated as undetermined whether accidental
or intentional E988.1
caustic or corrosive substance NEC E988.7
steam E924.0
pipe E924.8
substance (hot) E924.9
boiling or molten E924.0
caustic, corrosive (external) E924.1
swallowed — see Table of Drugs and
Chemicals
suicidal (attempt) NEC E958.1
caustic substance E958.7
late effect of E959
tanning bed E926.2
therapeutic misadventure
overdose of radiation E873.2
torch, welding (see also Fire, specified NEC)
E898.1
trash fire (see also Burning, bonfire) E897
vapor E924.0
vitriol E924.1
x-rays E926.3
in medical, surgical procedure — see Misadventure, failure, in dosage, radiation
Butted by animal E906.8

C

Cachexia, lead or saturnine E866.0
from pesticide NEC (see also Table of Drugs
and Chemicals) E863.4
Caisson disease E902.2
Capital punishment (any means) E978
Car sickness E903
Casualty (not due to war) NEC E928.9
terrorism E979.8
war (see also War operations) E995.9 ▲
Cat
bite E906.3
scratch E906.8
Cataclysmic (any injury)
earth surface movement or eruption E909.9
specified type NEC E909.8
storm or flood resulting from storm E908.9
specified type NEC E909.8
Catching fire — see Ignition
Caught
between
objects (moving) (stationary and moving)
E918
and machinery — see Accident, machine
by cable car, not on rails E847
in
machinery (moving parts of) — see, Accident, machine
object E918
Cave-in (causing asphyxia, suffocation (by pressure)) — see also Suffocation, due to, cave-
in E913.3
with injury other than asphyxia or suffocation
E916
with asphyxia or suffocation (see also Suffocation, due to, cave-in) E913.3
struck or crushed by E916
with asphyxia or suffocation (see also Suffocation, due to, cave-in) E913.3
Change(s) in air pressure — see also Effects of,
air pressure

Change(s) in air pressure — see also Effects of,
air pressure — continued
sudden, in aircraft (ascent) (descent) (causing
aeroneurosis or aviators' disease)
E902.1
Chilblains E901.0
due to manmade conditions E901.1
Choking (on) (any object except food or vomitus)
E912
apple E911
bone E911
food, any type (regurgitated) E911
mucus or phlegm E912
seed E911
Civil insurrection — see War operations
Cloudburst E908.8
Cold, exposure to (accidental) (excessive) (extreme) (place) E901.9
causing chilblains or immersion foot E901.0
due to
manmade conditions E901.1
specified cause NEC E901.8
weather (conditions) E901.0
late effect of NEC E929.5
self-inflicted (undetermined whether accidental or intentional) E988.3
suicidal E958.3
suicide E958.3
Colic, lead, painter's, or saturnine — see category E866 ☑
Collapse
building E916
burning (uncontrolled fire) E891.8
in terrorism E979.3
private E890.8
dam E909.3
due to heat — see Heat
machinery — see Accident, machine or vehicle
man-made structure E909.3
postoperative NEC E878.9
structure
burning (uncontrolled fire) NEC E891.8
in terrorism E979.3
Collision (accidental)

Note — In the case of collisions between
different types of vehicles, persons and objects, priority in classification is in the following order:

Aircraft

Watercraft

Motor vehicle

Railway vehicle

Pedal cycle

Animal-drawn vehicle

Animal being ridden

Streetcar or other nonmotor road vehicle

Other vehicle

Pedestrian or person using pedestrian
conveyance

Object (except where falling from or
set in motion by vehicle etc. listed
above)

In the listing below, the combinations are
listed only under the vehicle etc. having priority. For definitions, see Supplementary
Classification of External Causes of Injury
and Poisoning (E800-E999).

aircraft (with object or vehicle) (fixed) (movable) (moving) E841 ☑
with
person (while landing, taking off)
(without accident to aircraft)
E844 ☑
powered (in transit) (with unpowered aircraft) E841 ☑
while landing, taking off E840 ☑
unpowered E842 ☑
while landing, taking off E840 ☑

☑ Additional Digit Required — Refer to the Tabular List for Digit Selection   ▽ Subterms under main terms may continue to next column or page

☑ Additional Digit Required — Refer to the Tabular List for Digit Selection   Subterms under main terms may continue to next column or page

326 — Volume 2   ▶◀ Revised Text   ● New Line   ▲ Revised Code   2010 ICD-9-CM

Index

Collision — Conflagration

Conflagration — *continued*
  building or structure, except private dwelling
    — *continued*
    with or causing (injury due to)
      accident or injury NEC E891.9
        specified circumstance NEC E891.8
      burns, burning E891.3
      carbon monoxide E891.2
      fumes E891.2
        polyvinylchloride (PVC) or similar
          material E891.1
      smoke E891.2
      causing explosion E891.0
    in terrorism E979.3
  not in building or structure E892
  private dwelling (apartment) (boarding house)
    (camping place) (caravan) (farmhouse)
    (home (private)) (house) (lodging
    house) (private garage) (rooming
    house) (tenement) E890.9
    with or causing (injury due to)
      accident or injury NEC E890.9
        specified circumstance NEC E890.8
      burns, burning E890.3
      carbon monoxide E890.2
      fumes E890.2
        polyvinylchloride (PVC) or similar
          material E890.1
      smoke E890.2
      causing explosion E890.0

Constriction, external
  caused by
    hair E928.4
    other object E928.5
Contact with
  dry ice E901.1
  liquid air, hydrogen, nitrogen E901.1
Cramp(s)
  Heat — *see* Heat
  swimmers (*see also* category E910) E910.2
    not in recreation or sport E910.3
Cranking (car) (truck) (bus) (engine), injury by
  E917.9
Crash
  aircraft (in transit) (powered) E841 ☑
    at landing, take-off E840 ☑
    in
      terrorism E979.1
      war operations E994.9 ▲
    on runway NEC E840 ☑
    stated as
      homicidal E968.8
      suicidal E958.6
      undetermined whether accidental or
        intentional E988.6
    unpowered E842 ☑
  glider E842 ☑
  motor vehicle (*see also* Accident, motor vehi-
    cle)
    homicidal E968.5
    suicidal E958.5
    undetermined whether accidental or inten-
      tional E988.5
Crushed (accidentally) E928.9
  between
    boat(s), ship(s), watercraft (and dock or
      pier) (without accident to water-
      craft) E838 ☑
      after accident to, or collision, watercraft
        E831 ☑
    objects (moving) (stationary and moving)
      E918
  by
    avalanche NEC E909.2
    boat, ship, watercraft after accident to,
      collision, watercraft E831 ☑
    cave-in E916
      with asphyxiation or suffocation (*see
        also* Suffocation, due to, cave-
        in) E913.3
    crowd, human stampede E917.1
    falling
      aircraft (*see also* Accident, aircraft)
        E841 ☑
      in
        terrorism E979.1

Crushed — *continued*
  by — *continued*
    falling — *continued*
      aircraft (*see also* Accident, aircraft) —
        continued
        in — *continued*
          war operations E994.8 ▲
      earth, material E916
        with asphyxiation or suffocation
          (*see also* Suffocation, due to,
          cave-in) E913.3
      object E916
        on ship, watercraft E838 ☑
        while loading, unloading watercraft
          E838 ☑
    firearm E928.7 ●
    landslide NEC E909.2
    lifeboat after abandoning ship E831 ☑
    machinery — *see* Accident, machine
    railway rolling stock, train, vehicle (part of)
      E805 ☑
    slide trigger mechanism, scope or other ●
      part of gun E928.7 ●
    street car E829 ☑
    vehicle NEC — *see* Accident, vehicle NEC
  in
    machinery — *see* Accident, machine
    object E918
    transport accident — *see* categories
      E800-E848 ☑
  late effect of NEC E929.9
Cut, cutting (any part of body) (accidental) E920.9
  by
    arrow E920.8
    axe E920.4
    bayonet (*see also* Bayonet wound) E920.3
      in war operations E995.2 ●
    blender E920.2
    broken glass E920.8
      following fall E888.0
    can opener E920.4
      powered E920.2
    chisel E920.4
    circular saw E919.4
    cutting or piercing instrument (*see also*
      category) E920 ☑
      following fall E888.0
      late effect of E929.8
    dagger E920.3
    dart E920.8
    drill — *see* Accident, caused by drill
    edge of stiff paper E920.8
    electric
      beater E920.2
      fan E920.2
      knife E920.2
      mixer E920.2
    firearm component E928.7 ●
    fork E920.4
    garden fork E920.4
    hand saw or tool (not powered) E920.4
      powered E920.1
    hedge clipper E920.4
      powered E920.1
    hoe E920.4
    ice pick E920.4
    knife E920.3
      electric E920.2
      in war operations E995.2 ●
    lathe turnings E920.8
    lawn mower E920.4
      powered E920.0
      riding E919.8
    machine — *see* Accident, machine
    meat
      grinder E919.8
      slicer E919.8
    nails E920.8
    needle E920.4
      hypodermic E920.5
    object, edged, pointed, sharp — *see* cate-
      gory E920 ☑
      following fall E888.0
    paper cutter E920.4
    piercing instrument (*see also* category)
      E920 ☑

Cut, cutting — *continued*
  by — *continued*
    piercing instrument (*see also* category) —
      continued
      late effect of E929.8
    pitchfork E920.4
    powered
      can opener E920.2
      garden cultivator E920.1
        riding E919.8
      hand saw E920.1
      hand tool NEC E920.1
      hedge clipper E920.1
      household appliance or implement
        E920.2
      lawn mower (hand) E920.0
        riding E919.8
      rivet gun E920.1
      staple gun E920.1
    rake E920.4
    saw
      circular E919.4
      hand E920.4
    scissors E920.4
    screwdriver E920.4
    sewing machine (electric) (powered)
      E920.2
      not powered E920.4
    shears E920.4
    shovel E920.4
    slide trigger mechanism, scope or other ●
      part of gun E928.7 ●
    spade E920.4
    splinters E920.8
    sword E920.3
      in war operations E995.2 ●
    tin can lid E920.8
    wood slivers E920.8
  homicide (attempt) E966
  inflicted by other person
    stated as
      intentional, homicidal E966
      undetermined whether accidental or
        intentional E986
  late effect of NEC E929.8
  legal
    execution E978
    intervention E974
  self-inflicted (unspecified whether accidental
    or intentional) E986
    stated as intentional, purposeful E956
  stated as undetermined whether accidental
    or intentional E986
  suicidal (attempt) E956
  terrorism E979.8
  war operations E995.2 ▲
Cyclone E908.1

D

**Death due to injury occurring one year or
  more previous** — *see* Late effect
Decapitation (accidental circumstances) NEC
  E928.9
  homicidal E966
  legal execution (by guillotine) E978
Deprivation — *see also* Privation
  homicidal intent E968.4
Derailment (accidental)
  railway (rolling stock) (train) (vehicle) (with
    subsequent collision) E802 ☑
    with
      collision (antecedent) (*see also* Colli-
        sion, railway) E800 ☑
      explosion (subsequent) (without an-
        tecedent collision) E802 ☑
      antecedent collision E803 ☑
      fall (without collision (antecedent))
        E802 ☑
      fire (without collision (antecedent))
        E802 ☑
  street car E829 ☑
Descent
  parachute (voluntary) (without accident to
    aircraft) E844 ☑

Descent — *continued*
  parachute — *continued*
    due to accident to aircraft — *see* cate-
      gories E840-E842 ☑
Desertion
  child, with intent to injure or kill E968.4
  helpless person, infant, newborn E904.0
    with intent to injure or kill E968.4
Destitution — *see* Privation
Dirty bomb (*see also* War operations, injury due ●
  to, nuclear weapons) E996.9 ●
Disability, late effect or sequela of injury —
  see Late effect
Disease
  Andes E902.0
  aviators' E902.1
  caisson E902.2
  range E902.0
Divers' disease, palsy, paralysis, squeeze
  E902.0
Dog bite E906.0
Dragged by
  cable car (not on rails) E847
    on rails E829 ☑
  motor vehicle (on highway) E814 ☑
    not on highway, nontraffic accident
      E825 ☑
  street car E829 ☑
Drinking poison (accidental) — *see* Table of
  Drugs and Chemicals
Drowning — *see* Submersion
Dust in eye E914

E

Earth falling (on) (with asphyxia or suffocation
  (by pressure)) (*see also* Suffocation, due
  to, cave-in E913.3
  as, or due to, a cataclysm (involving any
    transport vehicle) — *see* categories
    E908 ☑, E909 ☑
  not due to cataclysmic action E913.3
    motor vehicle (in motion) (on public
      highway) E813 ☑
      not on public highway E825 ☑
    nonmotor road vehicle NEC E829 ☑
    pedal cycle E826 ☑
    railway rolling stock, train, vehicle E806 ☑
    street car E829 ☑
    struck or crushed by E916
      with asphyxiation or suffocation E913.3
      with injury other than asphyxia, suffo-
        cation E916
Earthquake (any injury) E909.0
Effect(s) (adverse) of
  air pressure E902.9
    at high altitude E902.9
      in aircraft E902.1
      residence or prolonged visit (causing
        conditions classifiable to
        E902.0) E902.0
    due to
      diving E902.2
      specified cause NEC E902.8
    in aircraft E902.1
  cold, excessive (exposure to) (*see also* Cold,
    exposure to) E901.9
  heat (excessive) (*see also* Heat) E900.9
  hot
    place — *see* Heat
    weather E900.0
  insulation — *see* Heat
  late — *see* Late effect of
  motion E903
  nuclear explosion or weapon
    in
      terrorism E979.5
      war operations ▶(*see also* War opera-
        tions, injury due to, nuclear
        weapons)◀ E996.9 ▲
  radiation — *see* Radiation
  terrorism, secondary E979.9
  travel E903

☑ Additional Digit Required — Refer to the Tabular List for Digit Selection   Subterms under main terms may continue to next column or page

2010 ICD-9-CM   ▶◀ Revised Text   ● New Line   ▲ Revised Code   October 2009 • Volume 2 — 327

Electric shock, electrocution (accidental) (from exposed wire, faulty appliance, high voltage cable, live rail, open socket) (by) (in) E925.9
- appliance or wiring
  - domestic E925.0
  - factory E925.2
  - farm (building) E925.8
    - house E925.0
  - home E925.0
  - industrial (conductor) (control apparatus) (transformer) E925.2
  - outdoors E925.8
  - public building E925.8
  - residential institution E925.8
  - school E925.8
  - specified place NEC E925.8
- caused by other person
  - stated as
    - intentional, homicidal E968.8
    - undetermined whether accidental or intentional E988.4
- electric power generating plant, distribution station E925.1
- electroshock gun (taser) (stun gun) E925.8
  - caused by other person E968.8
    - legal intervention E975
    - stated as accidental E925.8
    - stated as intentional E968.8
  - due to legal intervention E975
  - stated as intentional self-harm (suicidal attempt) E958.4
  - stated as undetermined whether accidental or intentional E988.4
  - suicide (attempt) E958.4
- homicidal (attempt) E968.8
- legal execution E978
- lightning E907
- machinery E925.9
  - domestic E925.0
  - factory E925.2
  - farm E925.8
  - home E925.0
- misadventure in medical or surgical procedure in electroshock therapy E873.4
- self-inflicted (undetermined whether accidental or intentional) E988.4
- stated as intentional E958.4
- stated as undetermined whether accidental or intentional E988.4
- suicidal (attempt) E958.4
- transmission line E925.1

Electrocution — *see* Electric shock
Embolism
- air (traumatic) NEC — *see* Air, embolism
Encephalitis
- lead or saturnine E866.0
  - from pesticide NEC E863.4
Entanglement
- in
  - bedclothes, causing suffocation E913.0
  - wheel of pedal cycle E826 ☑
Entry of foreign body, material, any — *see* Foreign body
Execution, legal (any method) E978
Exertion, excessive physical, from prolonged activity E927.2
Exhaustion
- cold — *see* Cold, exposure to
- due to excessive exertion E927.8
- heat — *see* Heat
Explosion (accidental) (in) (of) (on) E923.9
- acetylene E923.2
- aerosol can E921.8
- aircraft (in transit) (powered) E841 ☑
  - at landing, take-off E840 ☑
  - in
    - terrorism E979.1
    - war operations
      - from
        - enemy fire or explosive(s) ●
          - (device placed on air-●
            - craft) E994.0
        - own onboard explosives ●
          - E994.1
  - unpowered E842 ☑

Explosion — *continued*
- air tank (compressed) (in machinery) E921.1
- anesthetic gas in operating theatre E923.2
- automobile tire NEC E921.8
  - causing transport accident — *see* categories E810-E825 ☑
- blasting (cap) (materials) E923.1
- boiler (machinery), not on transport vehicle E921.0
  - steamship — *see* Explosion, watercraft
- bomb E923.8
  - in
    - terrorism E979.2
    - war operations E993.8 ▲
      - after cessation of hostilities E998.1 ▲
      - atom, hydrogen or nuclear ▶(*see also* War operations, injury due to, nuclear weapons)◀ E996.9
      - injury by fragments from E991.9
        - antipersonnel bomb E991.3
- butane E923.2
- caused by
  - other person
    - stated as
      - intentional, homicidal — *see* Assault, explosive
      - undetermined whether accidental or homicidal E985.5
- coal gas E923.2
- detonator E923.1
- dynamite E923.1
- explosive (material) NEC E923.9
  - gas(es) E923.2
  - missile E923.8
    - in
      - terrorism E979.2
      - war operations E993.1 ▲
        - injury by fragments from E991.9
          - antipersonnel bomb E991.3
  - used in blasting operations E923.1
- fire-damp E923.2
- fireworks E923.0
- gas E923.2
  - cylinder (in machinery) E921.1
  - pressure tank (in machinery) E921.1
- gasoline (fumes) (tank) not in moving motor vehicle E923.2
- grain store (military) (munitions) E923.8
- grenade E923.8
  - in
    - terrorism E979.2
    - war operations E993.8 ▲
      - injury by fragments from E991.4 ▲
- homicide (attempt) — *see* Assault, explosive
- hot water heater, tank (in machinery) E921.0
- in mine (of explosive gases) NEC E923.2
- late effect of NEC E929.8
- machinery (*see also* Accident, machine)
  - pressure vessel — *see* Explosion, pressure vessel
- methane E923.2
- missile E923.8
  - in
    - terrorism E979.2
    - war operations E993.1 ▲
      - injury by fragments from E991.4
- motor vehicle (part of)
  - in motion (on public highway) E818 ☑
  - not on public highway E825 ☑
- munitions (dump) (factory) E923.8
  - in
    - terrorism E979.2
    - war operations E993.9 ▲
- of mine E923.8
  - in
    - terrorism
      - at sea or in harbor E979.0
      - land E979.2
      - marine E979.0
    - war operations
      - after cessation of hostilities E998.0 ▲
      - at sea or in harbor E992.2 ▲

Explosion — *continued*
- of mine — *continued*
  - in — *continued*
    - war operations — *continued*
      - land E993.8 ▲
        - after cessation of hostilities E998.0 ▲
      - injury by fragments from E991.4 ▲
      - marine E992.2 ▲
- own weapons
  - in
    - terrorism (*see also* Suicide) E979.2
    - war operations E993.7 ▲
      - injury by fragments from E991.9
        - antipersonnel bomb E991.3
- pressure
  - cooker E921.8
  - gas tank (in machinery) E921.1
  - vessel (in machinery) E921.9
    - on transport vehicle — *see* categories E800-E848 ☑
    - specified type NEC E921.8
- propane E923.2
- railway engine, locomotive, train (boiler) (with subsequent collision, derailment, fall) E803 ☑
  - with
    - collision (antecedent) (*see also* Collision, railway) E800 ☑
    - derailment (antecedent) E802 ☑
    - fire (without antecedent collision or derailment) E803 ☑
- secondary fire resulting from — *see* Fire
- self-inflicted (unspecified whether accidental or intentional) E985.5
  - stated as intentional, purposeful E955.5
- shell (artillery) E923.8
  - in
    - terrorism E979.2
    - war operations E993.2 ▲
      - injury by fragments from E991.4 ▲
- stated as undetermined whether caused accidentally or purposely inflicted E985.5
- steam or water lines (in machinery) E921.0
- suicide (attempted) E955.5
- terrorism — *see* Terrorism, explosion
- torpedo E923.8
  - in
    - terrorism E979.0
    - war operations E992.0 ▲
- transport accident — *see* categories E800-E848 ☑
- war operations — *see* War operations, explosion
- watercraft (boiler) E837 ☑
  - causing drowning, submersion (after jumping from watercraft) E830 ☑
Exposure (weather) (conditions) (rain) (wind) E904.3
- with homicidal intent E968.4
- environmental
  - to
    - algae bloom E928.6
    - blue-green algae bloom E928.6
    - brown tide E928.6
    - cyanobacteria bloom E928.6
    - Florida red tide E928.6
    - harmful alage
      - and toxins E928.6
      - bloom E928.6
    - pfiesteria piscicida E928.6
    - red tide E928.6
- excessive E904.3
  - cold (*see also* Cold, exposure to) E901.9
    - self-inflicted — *see* Cold, exposure to, self-inflicted
  - heat (*see also* Heat) E900.9
- helpless person, infant, newborn due to abandonment or neglect E904.0
- noise E928.1
- prolonged in deep-freeze unit or refrigerator E901.1
- radiation — *see* Radiation

Exposure — *continued*
- resulting from transport accident — *see* categories E800-E848 ☑
- smoke from, due to
  - fire — *see* Fire
- tobacco, second-hand E869.4
- vibration E928.2
External cause status E000.9 ●
- civilian ●
  - done for ●
    - financial or other compensation ●
      - E000.0 ●
    - pay or income E000.0 ●
- for income E000.0 ●
- hobby or leisure E000.8 ●
- military E000.1 ●
  - off duty E000.8 ●
- off duty military E000.8 ●
- recreation E000.8 ●
- specified NEC E000.8 ●
- sport not for income E000.8 ●
- student E000.8 ●
- volunteer E000.8 ●

F

Fallen on by
- animal (horse) (not being ridden) E906.8
  - being ridden (in sport or transport) E828 ☑
Fall, falling (accidental) E888.9
- building E916
  - burning E891.8
    - private E890.8
- down
  - escalator E880.0
  - ladder E881.0
    - in boat, ship, watercraft E833 ☑
  - staircase E880.9
  - stairs, steps — *see* Fall, from, stairs
- earth (with asphyxia or suffocation (by pressure)) (*see also* Earth, falling) E913.3
- from, off
  - aircraft (at landing, take-off) (in-transit) (while alighting, boarding) E843 ☑
    - resulting from accident to aircraft — *see* categories E840-E842 ☑
  - animal (in sport or transport) E828 ☑
  - animal-drawn vehicle E827 ☑
  - balcony E882
  - bed E884.4
  - bicycle E826 ☑
  - boat, ship, watercraft (into water) E832 ☑
    - after accident to, collision, fire on E830 ☑
      - and subsequently struck by (part of) boat E831 ☑
    - and subsequently struck by (part of) while alighting, boat E831 ☑
    - burning, crushed, sinking E830 ☑
      - and subsequently struck by (part of) boat E831 ☑
  - bridge E882
  - building E882
    - burning (uncontrolled fire) E891.8
      - in terrorism E979.3
    - private E890.8
  - bunk in boat, ship, watercraft E834 ☑
    - due to accident to watercraft E831 ☑
  - cable car (not on rails) E847
    - on rails E829 ☑
  - car — *see* Fall from motor vehicle
  - chair E884.2
  - cliff E884.1
  - commode E884.6
  - curb (sidewalk) E880.1
  - elevation aboard ship E834 ☑
    - due to accident to ship E831 ☑
  - embankment E884.9
  - escalator E880.0
  - fire escape E882
  - flagpole E882
  - furniture NEC E884.5
  - gangplank (into water) (*see also* Fall, from, boat) E832 ☑
    - to deck, dock E834 ☑

☑ Additional Digit Required — Refer to the Tabular List for Digit Selection   ▽ Subterms under main terms may continue to next column or page

328 — Volume 2 • October 2009   ▶◀ Revised Text   ● New Line   ▲ Revised Code   2010 ICD-9-CM

Fall, falling — *continued*
  from, off — *continued*
    hammock on ship E834 ☑
      due to accident to watercraft E831 ☑
    haystack E884.9
    heelies E885.1
    high place NEC E884.9
      stated as undetermined whether accidental or intentional — *see* Jumping, from, high place
    horse (in sport or transport) E828 ☑
    in-line skates E885.1
    ladder E881.0
      in boat, ship, watercraft E833 ☑
        due to accident to watercraft E831 ☑
    machinery (*see also* Accident, machine)
      not in operation E884.9
    motor vehicle (in motion) (on public highway) E818 ☑
      not on public highway E825 ☑
        stationary, except while alighting, boarding, entering, leaving E884.9
        while alighting, boarding, entering, leaving E824 ☑
      stationary, except while alighting, boarding, entering, leaving E884.9
      while alighting, boarding, entering, leaving, except off-road type motor vehicle E817 ☑
      off-road type — *see* Fall, from, off-road type motor vehicle
    nonmotor road vehicle (while alighting, boarding) NEC E829 ☑
      stationary, except while alighting, boarding, entering, leaving E884.9
    off road type motor vehicle (not on public highway) NEC E821 ☑
      on public highway E818 ☑
        while alighting, boarding, entering, leaving E817 ☑
      snow vehicle — *see* Fall from snow vehicle, motor-driven
    one
      deck to another on ship E834 ☑
        due to accident to ship E831 ☑
      level to another NEC E884.9
        boat, ship, or watercraft E834 ☑
          due to accident to watercraft E831 ☑
    pedal cycle E826 ☑
    playground equipment E884.0
    railway rolling stock, train, vehicle (while alighting, boarding) E804 ☑
      with
        collision (*see also* Collision, railway) E800 ☑
        derailment (*see also* Derailment, railway) E802 ☑
        explosion (*see also* Explosion, railway engine) E803 ☑
    rigging (aboard ship) E834 ☑
      due to accident to watercraft E831 ☑
    roller skates E885.1
    scaffolding E881.1
    scooter (nonmotorized) E885.0
    sidewalk (curb) E880.1
      moving E885.9
    skateboard E885.2
    skis E885.3
    snowboard E885.4
    snow vehicle, motor-driven (not on public highway) E820 ☑
      on public highway E818 ☑
        while alighting, boarding, entering, leaving E817 ☑
    stairs, steps E880.9
      boat, ship, watercraft E833 ☑
        due to accident to watercraft E831 ☑

Fall, falling — *continued*
  from, off — *continued*
    stairs, steps — *continued*
      motor bus, motor vehicle — *see* Fall, from, motor vehicle, while alighting, boarding
      street car E829 ☑
    stationary vehicle NEC E884.9
    stepladder E881.0
    street car (while boarding, alighting) E829 ☑
      stationary, except while boarding or alighting E884.9
    structure NEC E882
      burning (uncontrolled fire) E891.8
        in terrorism E979.3
    table E884.9
    toilet E884.6
    tower E882
    tree E884.9
    turret E882
    vehicle NEC (*see also* Accident, vehicle NEC)
      stationary E884.9
    viaduct E882
    wall E882
    wheelchair E884.3
    wheelies E885.1
    window E882
  in, on
    aircraft (at landing, take-off) (in-transit) E843 ☑
      resulting from accident to aircraft — *see* categories E840-E842 ☑
    boat, ship, watercraft E835 ☑
      due to accident to watercraft E831 ☑
      one level to another NEC E834 ☑
      on ladder, stairs E833 ☑
    cutting or piercing instrument or machine E888.0
    deck (of boat, ship, watercraft) E835 ☑
      due to accident to watercraft E831 ☑
    escalator E880.0
    gangplank E835 ☑
    glass, broken E888.0
    knife E888.0
    ladder E881.0
      in boat, ship, watercraft E833 ☑
        due to accident to watercraft E831 ☑
    object
      edged, pointed or sharp E888.0
      other E888.1
    pitchfork E888.0
    railway rolling stock, train, vehicle (while alighting, boarding) E804 ☑
      with
        collision (*see also* Collision, railway) E800 ☑
        derailment (*see also* Derailment, railway) E802 ☑
        explosion (see also Explosion, railway engine) E803 ☑
    scaffolding E881.1
    scissors E888.0
    staircase, stairs, steps (*see also* Fall, from, stairs) E880.9
    street car E829 ☑
    water transport (*see also* Fall, in, boat) E835 ☑
  into
    cavity E883.9
    dock E883.9
      from boat, ship, watercraft (*see also* Fall, from, boat) E832 ☑
    hold (of ship) E834 ☑
      due to accident to watercraft E831 ☑
    hole E883.9
    manhole E883.2
    moving part of machinery — *see* Accident, machine
    opening in surface NEC E883.9
    pit E883.9
    quarry E883.9
    shaft E883.9
    storm drain E883.2

Fall, falling — *continued*
  into — *continued*
    tank E883.9
    water (with drowning or submersion) E910.9
    well E883.1
    late effect of NEC E929.3
  object (*see also* Hit by, object, falling) E916
  other E888.8
  over
    animal E885.9
    cliff E884.1
    embankment E884.9
    small object E885.9
  overboard (*see also* Fall, from, boat) E832 ☑
  resulting in striking against object E888.1
    sharp E888.0
  rock E916
  same level NEC E888.9
    aircraft (any kind) E843 ☑
      resulting from accident to aircraft — *see* categories E840-E842 ☑
    boat, ship, watercraft E835 ☑
      due to accident to, collision, watercraft E831 ☑
    from
      collision, pushing, shoving, by or with other person(s) E886.9
        as, or caused by, a crowd E917.6
        in sports E886.0
      in-line skates E885.1
      roller skates E885.1
      scooter (nonmotorized) E885.0
      skateboard E885.2
      slipping stumbling, tripping E885
      snowboard E885.4
  snowslide E916
    as avalanche E909.2
  stone E916
  through
    hatch (on ship) E834 ☑
      due to accident to watercraft E831 ☑
    roof E882
    window E882
  timber E916
  while alighting from, boarding, entering, leaving
    aircraft (any kind) E843 ☑
    motor bus, motor vehicle — *see* Fall, from, motor vehicle, while alighting, boarding
    nonmotor road vehicle NEC E829 ☑
    railway train E804 ☑
    street car E829 ☑

Fell or jumped from high place, so stated — *see* Jumping, from, high place

Felo-de-se — *see also* Suicide E958.9

Fever
  heat — *see* Heat
  thermic — *see* Heat

Fight (hand) (fist) (foot) — *see also* Assault, fight E960.0

Fire (accidental) (caused by great heat from appliance (electrical), hot object or hot substance) (secondary, resulting from explosion) E899
  conflagration — *see* Conflagration
  controlled, normal (in brazier, fireplace, furnace, or stove) (charcoal) (coal) (coke) (electric) (gas) (wood)
    bonfire E897
    brazier, not in building or structure E897
    in building or structure, except private dwelling (barn) (church) (convalescent or residential home) (factory) (farm outbuilding) (hospital) (institution (educational) (dormitory) (residential)) (private garage) (school) (shop) (store) (theatre) E896
    in private dwelling (apartment) (boarding house) (camping place) (caravan) (farmhouse) (home (private)) (house) (lodging house) (rooming house) (tenement) E895
    not in building or structure E897

Fire, hot object or hot substance — *continued*
  controlled, normal — *continued*
    trash E897
  forest (uncontrolled) E892
  grass (uncontrolled) E892
  hay (uncontrolled) E892
  homicide (attempt) E968.0
    late effect of E969
  in, of, on, starting in E892
    aircraft (in transit) (powered) E841 ☑
      at landing, take-off E840 ☑
      stationary E892
      unpowered (balloon) (glider) E842 ☑
    balloon E842 ☑
    boat, ship, watercraft — *see* categories E830 ☑, E831 ☑, E837 ☑
    building or structure, except private dwelling (barn) (church) (convalescent or residential home) (factory) (farm outbuilding) (hospital) (hotel) (institution (educational) (dormitory) (residential)) (school) (shop) (store) (theatre) (*see also* Conflagration, building or structure, except private dwelling) E891.9
    forest (uncontrolled) E892
    glider E842 ☑
    grass (uncontrolled) E892
    hay (uncontrolled) E892
    lumber (uncontrolled) E892
    machinery — *see* Accident, machine
    mine (uncontrolled) E892
    motor vehicle (in motion) (on public highway) E818 ☑
      not on public highway E825 ☑
      stationary E892
    prairie (uncontrolled) E892
    private dwelling (apartment) (boarding house) (camping place) (caravan) (farmhouse) (home (private)) (house) (lodging house) (private garage) (rooming house) (tenement) (*see also* Conflagration, private dwelling) E890.9
    railway rolling stock, train, vehicle (*see also* Explosion, railway engine) E803 ☑
      stationary E892
    room NEC E898.1
    street car (in motion) E829 ☑
      stationary E892
    terrorism (by fire-producing device) E979.3
      fittings or furniture (burning building) (uncontrolled fire) E979.3
      from nuclear explosion E979.5
    transport vehicle, stationary NEC E892
    tunnel (uncontrolled) E892
    war operations (by fire-producing device or conventional weapon) E990.9
      from nuclear explosion ►(*see also* War operations, injury due to, nuclear weapons)◄ E996.2 ▲
      incendiary bomb E990.0 ●
      petrol bomb E990.0
  late effect of NEC E929.4
  lumber (uncontrolled) E892
  mine (uncontrolled) E892
  prairie (uncontrolled) E892
  self-inflicted (unspecified whether accidental or intentional) E988.1
    stated as intentional, purposeful E958.1
  specified NEC E898.1
    with
      conflagration — *see* Conflagration
      ignition (of)
        clothing — *see* Ignition, clothes
        highly inflammable material (benzine) (fat) (gasoline) (kerosene) (paraffin) (petrol) E894
  started by other person
    stated as
      with intent to injure or kill E968.0
      undetermined whether or not with intent to injure or kill E988.1
  suicide (attempted) E958.1
    late effect of E959

☑ Additional Digit Required — Refer to the Tabular List for Digit Selection

▼ Subterms under main terms may continue to next column or page

2010 ICD-9-CM

►◄ Revised Text   ● New Line   ▲ Revised Code

October 2009 • Volume 2 — 329

Fall, falling — Fire

Fire, hot object or hot substance — *continued*
tunnel (uncontrolled) E892
Fireball effects from nuclear explosion
in
terrorism E979.5
war operations ▶(*see also* War operations,
injury due to, nuclear weapons)◀
E996.2 ▲
Fireworks (explosion) E923.0
Flash burns from explosion — *see also* Explosion E923.9
Flood (any injury) (resulting from storm) E908.2
caused by collapse of dam or manmade
structure E909.3
Forced landing (aircraft) E840 ☑
Foreign body, object or material (entrance into)
(accidental)
air passage (causing injury) E915
with asphyxia, obstruction, suffocation
E912
food or vomitus E911
nose (with asphyxia, obstruction, suffocation) E912
causing injury without asphyxia, obstruction, suffocation E915
alimentary canal (causing injury) (with obstruction) E915
with asphyxia, obstruction respiratory
passage, suffocation E912
food E911
mouth E915
with asphyxia, obstruction, suffocation
E912
food E911
pharynx E915
with asphyxia, obstruction, suffocation
E912
food E911
aspiration (with asphyxia, obstruction respiratory passage, suffocation) E912
causing injury without asphyxia, obstruction respiratory passage, suffocation E915
food (regurgitated) (vomited) E911
causing injury without asphyxia, obstruction respiratory passage,
suffocation E915
mucus (not of newborn) E912
phlegm E912
bladder (causing injury or obstruction) E915
bronchus, bronchi — *see* Foreign body, air
passages
conjunctival sac E914
digestive system — *see* Foreign body, alimentary canal
ear (causing injury or obstruction) E915
esophagus (causing injury or obstruction) (*see
also* Foreign body, alimentary canal)
E915
eye (any part) E914
eyelid E914
hairball (stomach) (with obstruction) E915
ingestion — *see* Foreign body, alimentary
canal
inhalation — *see* Foreign body, aspiration
intestine (causing injury or obstruction) E915
iris E914
lacrimal apparatus E914
larynx — *see* Foreign body, air passage
late effect of NEC E929.8
lung — *see* Foreign body, air passage
mouth — *see* Foreign body, alimentary canal,
mouth
nasal passage — *see* Foreign body, air passage, nose
nose — *see* Foreign body, air passage, nose
ocular muscle E914
operation wound (left in) — *see* Misadventure,
foreign object
orbit E914
pharynx — *see* Foreign body, alimentary canal,
pharynx
rectum (causing injury or obstruction) E915
stomach (hairball) (causing injury or obstruction) E915
tear ducts or glands E914

Foreign body, object or material —
continued
trachea — *see* Foreign body, air passage
urethra (causing injury or obstruction) E915
vagina (causing injury or obstruction) E915
Found dead, injured
from exposure (to) — *see* Exposure
on
public highway E819 ☑
railway right of way E807 ☑
Fracture (circumstances unknown or unspecified)
E887
due to specified external means — *see* manner of accident
late effect of NEC E929.3
occurring in water transport NEC E835 ☑
Freezing — *see* Cold, exposure to
Frostbite E901.0
due to manmade conditions E901.1
Frozen — *see* Cold, exposure to

G

Garrotting, homicidal (attempted) E963
Gored E906.8
Gunshot wound — *see also* Shooting E922.9

H

Hailstones, injury by E904.3
Hairball (stomach) (with obstruction) E915
Hanged himself — *see also* Hanging, self-inflicted E983.0
Hang gliding E842 ☑
Hanging (accidental) E913.8
caused by other person
in accidental circumstances E913.8
stated as
intentional, homicidal E963
undetermined whether accidental or
intentional E983.0
homicide (attempt) E963
in bed or cradle E913.0
legal execution E978
self-inflicted (unspecified whether accidental
or intentional) E983.0
in accidental circumstances E913.8
stated as intentional, purposeful E953.0
stated as undetermined whether accidental
or intentional E983.0
suicidal (attempt) E953.0
Heat (apoplexy) (collapse) (cramps) (effects of)
(excessive) (exhaustion) (fever) (prostration) (stroke) E900.9
due to
manmade conditions (as listed in E900.1,
except boat, ship, watercraft)
E900.1
weather (conditions) E900.0
from
electric heating appartus causing burning
E924.8
nuclear explosion
in
terrorism E979.5
war operations ▶(*see also* War operations, injury due to, nuclear weapons)◀ E996.2 ▲
generated in, boiler, engine, evaporator, fire
room of boat, ship, watercraft E838 ☑
inappropriate in local application or packing
in medical or surgical procedure E873.5
late effect of NEC E989
Hemorrhage
delayed following medical or surgical treatment without mention of misadventure — *see* Reaction, abnormal
during medical or surgical treatment as misadventure — *see* Misadventure, cut
High
altitude, effects E902.9
level of radioactivity, effects — *see* Radiation
pressure effects (*see also* Effects of, air pressure)
from rapid descent in water (causing caisson or divers' disease, palsy, or
paralysis) E902.2
temperature, effects — *see* Heat

Hit, hitting (accidental) by
aircraft (propeller) (without accident to aircraft)
E844 ☑
unpowered E842 ☑
avalanche E909.2
being thrown against object in or part of
motor vehicle (in motion) (on public
highway) E818 ☑
not on public highway E825 ☑
nonmotor road vehicle NEC E829 ☑
street car E829 ☑
boat, ship, watercraft
after fall from watercraft E838 ☑
damaged, involved in accident E831 ☑
while swimming, water skiing E838 ☑
bullet (*see also* Shooting) E922.9
from air gun E922.4
in
terrorism E979.4
war operations E991.2
rubber E991.0
flare, Verey pistol (*see also* Shooting) E922.8
hailstones E904.3
landslide E909.2
law-enforcing agent (on duty) E975
with blunt object (baton) (night stick)
(stave) (truncheon) E973
machine — *see* Accident, machine
missile
firearm (*see also* Shooting) E922.9
in
terrorism — *see* Terrorism, missile
war operations — *see* War operations,
missile
motor vehicle (on public highway) (traffic accident) E814 ☑
not on public highway, nontraffic accident
E822 ☑
nonmotor road vehicle NEC E829 ☑
object
falling E916
from, in, on
aircraft E844 ☑
due to accident to aircraft —
see categories
E840-E842 ☑
unpowered E842 ☑
boat, ship, watercraft E838 ☑
due to accident to watercraft
E831 ☑
building E916
burning (uncontrolled fire)
E891.8
in terrorism E979.3
private E890.8
cataclysmic
earth surface movement or
eruption E909.9
storm E908.9
cave-in E916
with asphyxiation or suffocation
(*see also* Suffocation,
due to, cave-in) E913.3
earthquake E909.0
motor vehicle (in motion) (on public highway) E818 ☑
not on public highway E825 ☑
stationary E916
nonmotor road vehicle NEC
E829 ☑
pedal cycle E826 ☑
railway rolling stock, train, vehicle
E806 ☑
street car E829 ☑
structure, burning NEC E891.8
vehicle, stationary E916
moving NEC — *see* Striking against, object
projected NEC — *see* Striking against, object
set in motion by
compressed air or gas, spring, striking,
throwing — *see* Striking
against, object
explosion — *see* Explosion

Hit, hitting by — *continued*
object — *continued*
thrown into, on, or towards
motor vehicle (in motion) (on public
highway) E818 ☑
not on public highway E825 ☑
nonmotor road vehicle NEC E829 ☑
pedal cycle E826 ☑
street car E829 ☑
off-road type motor vehicle (not on public
highway) E821 ☑
on public highway E814 ☑
other person(s) E917.9
with blunt or thrown object E917.9
in sports E917.0
with subsequent fall E917.5
intentionally, homicidal E968.2
as, or caused by, a crowd E917.1
with subsequent fall E917.6
in sports E917.0
pedal cycle E826 ☑
police (on duty) E975
with blunt object (baton) (nightstick)
(stave) (truncheon) E973
railway, rolling stock, train, vehicle (part of)
E805 ☑
shot — *see* Shooting
snow vehicle, motor-driven (not on public
highway) E820 ☑
on public highway E814 ☑
street car E829 ☑
vehicle NEC — *see* Accident, vehicle NEC
Homicide, homicidal (attempt) (justifiable) —
see also Assault E968.9
Hot
liquid, object, substance, accident caused by
(*see also* Accident, caused by, hot, by
type of substance)
late effect of E929.8
place, effects — *see* Heat
weather, effects E900.0
Humidity, causing problem E904.3
Hunger E904.1
resulting from
abandonment or neglect E904.0
transport accident — *see* categories
E800-E848 ☑
Hurricane (any injury) E908.0
Hypobarism, hypobaropathy — *see* Effects of,
air pressure
Hypothermia — *see* Cold, exposure to

I

Ictus
caloris — *see* Heat
solaris E900.0
Ignition (accidental)
anesthetic gas in operating theatre E923.2
bedclothes
with
conflagration — *see* Conflagration
ignition (of)
clothing — *see* Ignition, clothes
highly inflammable material (benzine) (fat) (gasoline)
(kerosene) (paraffin) (petrol)
E894
benzine E894
clothes, clothing (from controlled fire) (in
building) E893.9
with conflagration — *see* Conflagration
from
bonfire E893.2
highly inflammable material E894
sources or material as listed in E893.8
trash fire E893.2
uncontrolled fire — *see* Conflagration
in
private dwelling E893.0
specified building or structure, except
private dwelling E893.1
not in building or structure E893.2
explosive material — *see* Explosion
fat E894
gasoline E894

Ignition — *continued*
  kerosene E894
  material
    explosive — *see* Explosion
    highly inflammable E894
      with conflagration — *see* Conflagration
      with explosion E923.2
  nightdress — *see* Ignition, clothes
  paraffin E894
  petrol E894
Immersion — *see* Submersion
Implantation of quills of porcupine E906.8
Inanition (from) E904.9
  hunger — *see* Lack of, food
  resulting from homicidal intent E968.4
  thirst — *see* Lack of, water
Inattention after, at birth E904.0
  homicidal, infanticidal intent E968.4
Infanticide — *see also* Assault
Ingestion
  foreign body (causing injury) (with obstruction) — *see* Foreign body, alimentary canal
  poisonous substance NEC — *see* Table of Drugs and Chemicals
Inhalation
  excessively cold substance, manmade E901.1
  foreign body — *see* Foreign body, aspiration
  liquid air, hydrogen, nitrogen E901.1
  mucus, not of newborn (with asphyxia, obstruction respiratory passage, suffocation) E912
  phlegm (with asphyxia, obstruction respiratory passage, suffocation) E912
  poisonous gas — *see* Table of Drugs and Chemicals
  smoke from, due to
    fire — *see* Fire
    tobacco, second-hand E869.4
  vomitus (with asphyxia, obstruction respiratory passage, suffocation) E911
Injury, injured (accidental(ly)) NEC E928.9
  by, caused by, from
    air rifle (BB gun) E922.4
    animal (not being ridden) NEC E906.9
      being ridden (in sport or transport) E828 ☑
    assault (*see also* Assault) E968.9
    avalanche E909.2
    bayonet (*see also* Bayonet wound) E920.3
    being thrown against some part of, or object in
      motor vehicle (in motion) (on public highway) E818 ☑
        not on public highway E825 ☑
      nonmotor road vehicle NEC E829 ☑
      off-road motor vehicle NEC E821 ☑
      railway train E806 ☑
      snow vehicle, motor-driven E820 ☑
      street car E829 ☑
    bending E927.8
    bite, human E928.3
    broken glass E920.8
    bullet — *see* Shooting
    cave-in (*see also* Suffocation, due to, cave-in) E913.3
      without asphyxiation or suffocation E916
      earth surface movement or eruption E909.9
      storm E908.9
    cloudburst E908.8
    component of firearm or air gun E928.7 ●
    cutting or piercing instrument (*see also* Cut) E920.9
    cyclone E908.1
    earthquake E909.0
    earth surface movement or eruption E909.9
    electric current (*see also* Electric shock) E925.9
    explosion (*see also* Explosion) E923.9
      of gun part E928.7 ●
    fire — *see* Fire
    flare, Verey pistol E922.8
    flood E908.2

Injury, injured — *continued*
  by, caused by, from — *continued*
    foreign body — *see* Foreign body
    gun recoil E928.7 ●
    hailstones E904.3
    hurricane E908.0
    landslide E909.2
    law-enforcing agent, police, in course of legal intervention — *see* Legal intervention
    lightning E907
    live rail or live wire — *see* Electric shock
    machinery (*see also* Accident, machine)
      aircraft, without accident to aircraft E844 ☑
      boat, ship, watercraft (deck) (engine room) (galley) (laundry) (loading) E836 ☑
    mechanism of firearm or air gun E928.7 ●
    missile
      explosive E923.8
      firearm — *see* Shooting
      in
        terrorism — *see* Terrorism, missile
        war operations — *see* War operations, missile
    moving part of motor vehicle (in motion) (on public highway) E818 ☑
      not on public highway, nontraffic accident E825 ☑
      while alighting, boarding, entering, leaving — *see* Fall, from, motor vehicle, while alighting, boarding
    nail E920.8
    needle (sewing) E920.4
      hypodermic E920.5
    noise E928.1
    object
      fallen on
        motor vehicle (in motion) (on public highway) E818 ☑
          not on public highway E825 ☑
      falling — *see* Hit by, object, falling
    paintball gun E922.5
    radiation — *see* Radiation
    railway rolling stock, train, vehicle (part of) E805 ☑
      door or window E806 ☑
    recoil of firearm E928.7 ●
    rotating propeller, aircraft E844 ☑
    rough landing of off-road type motor vehicle (after leaving ground or rough terrain) E821 ☑
    snow vehicle E820 ☑
    saber (*see also* Wound, saber) E920.3
    shot — *see* Shooting
    sound waves E928.1
    splinter or sliver, wood E920.8
    straining E927.8
    street car (door) E829 ☑
    suicide (attempt) E958.9
    sword E920.3
    terrorism — *see* Terrorism
    third rail — *see* Electric shock
    thunderbolt E907
    tidal wave E909.4
      caused by storm E908.0
    tornado E908.1
    torrential rain E908.2
    twisting E927.8
    vehicle NEC — *see* Accident, vehicle NEC
    vibration E928.2
    volcanic eruption E909.1
    weapon burst, in war operations E993.9 ▲
    weightlessness (in spacecraft, real or simulated) E928.0
    wood splinter or sliver E920.8
  due to
    civil insurrection — *see* War operations
      occurring after cessation of hostilities E998.9 ▲
    terrorism — *see* Terrorism
    war operations — *see* War operations

Injury, injured — *continued*
  due to — *continued*
    war operations — *see* War operations — *continued*
      occurring after cessation of hostilities E998.9 ▲
      weapon of mass destruction [WMD] E997.3
  homicidal (*see also* Assault) E968.9
  inflicted (by)
    in course of arrest (attempted), suppression of disturbance, maintenance of order, by law enforcing agents — *see* Legal intervention
    law-enforcing agent (on duty) — *see* Legal intervention
    other person
      stated as
        accidental E928.9
        homicidal, intentional — *see* Assault
        undetermined whether accidental or intentional — *see* Injury, stated as undetermined
    police (on duty) — *see* Legal intervention
  in, on
    civil insurrection — *see* War operations
    fight E960.0
    parachute descent (voluntary) (without accident to aircraft) E844 ☑
      with accident to aircraft — *see* categories E840–E842 ☑
    public highway E819 ☑
    railway right of way E807 ☑
    terrorism — *see* Terrorism
    war operations — *see* War operations
  late effect of E929.9
  purposely (inflicted) by other person(s) — *see* Assault
  self-inflicted (unspecified whether accidental or intentional) E988.9
    stated as
      accidental E928.9
      intentionally, purposely E958.9
  specified cause NEC E928.8
  stated as
    hanging E983.0
    knife E986
    late effect of E989
    puncture (any part of body) E986
    shooting — *see* Shooting, stated as undetermined whether accidental or intentional
    specified means NEC E988.8
    stab (any part of body) E986
    strangulation — *see* Suffocation, stated as undetermined whether accidental or intentional
    submersion E984
    suffocation — *see* Suffocation, stated as undetermined whether accidental or intentional
    undetermined whether accidentally or purposely inflicted (by) E988.9
      cut (any part of body) E986
      cutting or piercing instrument (classifiable to E920) E986
      drowning E984
      explosive(s) (missile) E985.5
      falling from high place E987.9
        manmade structure, except residential E987.1
        natural site E987.2
        residential premises E987.0
  to child due to criminal abortion E968.8
Insufficient nourishment — *see also* Lack of, food
  homicidal intent E968.4
Insulation, effects — *see* Heat
Interruption of respiration by
  food lodged in esophagus E911
  foreign body, except food, in esophagus E912
Intervention, legal — *see* Legal intervention
Intoxication, drug or poison — *see* Table of Drugs and Chemicals
Irradiation — *see* Radiation

Jammed (accidentally)
  between objects (moving) (stationary and moving) E918
  in object E918
Jumped or fell from high place, so stated — *see* Jumping, from, high place, stated as in undetermined circumstances
Jumping
  before train, vehicle or other moving object (unspecified whether accidental or intentional) E988.0
    stated as
      intentional, purposeful E958.0
      suicidal (attempt) E958.0
  from
    aircraft
      by parachute (voluntarily) (without accident to aircraft) E844 ☑
      due to accident to aircraft — *see* categories E840–E842
    boat, ship, watercraft (into water)
      after accident to, fire on, watercraft E830 ☑
        and subsequently struck by (part of) boat E831 ☑
      burning, crushed, sinking E830 ☑
        and subsequently struck by (part of) boat E831 ☑
      voluntarily, without accident (to boat)
        with injury other than drowning or submersion E883.0
    building (*see also* Jumping, from, high place)
      burning (uncontrolled fire) E891.8
        in terrorism E979.3
        private E890.8
    cable car (not on rails) E847
      on rails E829 ☑
    high place
      in accidental circumstances or in sport — *see* categories E880–E884
      stated as
        with intent to injure self E957.9
          man-made structures NEC E957.1
          natural sites E957.2
          residential premises E957.0
        in undetermined circumstances E987.9
          man-made structures NEC E987.1
          natural sites E987.2
          residential premises E987.0
        suicidal (attempt) E957.9
          man-made structures NEC E957.1
          natural sites E957.1
          residential premises E957.0
    motor vehicle (in motion) (on public highway) — *see* Fall, from, motor vehicle
    nonmotor road vehicle NEC E829 ☑
    street car E829 ☑
    structure (*see also* Jumping, from, high place)
      burning NEC (uncontrolled fire) E891.8
        in terrorism E979.3
  into water
    with injury other than drowning or submersion E883.0
    drowning or submersion — *see* Submersion
  from, off, watercraft — *see* Jumping, from, boat
Justifiable homicide — *see* Assault

Kicked by
  animal E906.8
  person(s) (accidentally) E917.9
    with intent to injure or kill E960.0
    as, or caused by a crowd E917.1
      with subsequent fall E917.6
    in fight E960.0

☑ Additional Digit Required — Refer to the Tabular List for Digit Selection   ▽ Subterms under main terms may continue to next column or page

Kicked by — *continued*
person(s) — *continued*
  in sports E917.0
    with subsequent fall E917.5
Kicking against
  object (moving) E917.9
    in sports E917.0
      with subsequent fall E917.5
    stationary E917.4
      with subsequent fall E917.8
  person — *see* Striking against, person
Killed, killing (accidentally) NEC — *see also* Injury E928.9
  in
    action — *see* War operations
    brawl, fight (hand) (fists) (foot) E960.0
      by weapon (*see also* Assault)
        cutting, piercing E966
        firearm — *see* Shooting, homicide
  self
    stated as
      accident E928.9
      suicide — *see* Suicide
    unspecified whether accidental or suicidal E988.9
Knocked down (accidentally) (by) NEC E928.9
  animal (not being ridden) E906.8
    being ridden (in sport or transport) E828 ☑
  blast from explosion (*see also* Explosion) E923.9
  crowd, human stampede E917.6
  late effect of — *see* Late effect
  person (accidentally) E917.9
    in brawl, fight E960.0
    in sports E917.5
  transport vehicle — *see* vehicle involved under Hit by
  while boxing E917.5

L

Laceration NEC E928.9
Lack of
  air (refrigerator or closed place), suffocation by E913.2
  care (helpless person) (infant) (newborn) E904.0
    homicidal intent E968.4
  food except as result of transport accident E904.1
    helpless person, infant, newborn due to abandonment or neglect E904.0
  water except as result of transport accident E904.2
    helpless person, infant, newborn due to abandonment or neglect E904.0
Landslide E909.2
  falling on, hitting
    motor vehicle (any) (in motion) (on or off public highway) E909.2
    railway rolling stock, train, vehicle E909.2
Late effect of
  accident NEC (accident classifiable to E928.9) E929.9
    specified NEC (accident classifiable to E9l0–E928.8) E929.8
  assault E969
  fall, accidental (accident classifiable to E880–E888) E929.3
  fire, accident caused by (accident classifiable to E890–E899) E929.4
  homicide, attempt (any means) E969
  injury due to terrorism E999.1
  injury undetermined whether accidentally or purposely inflicted (injury classifiable to E980–E988) E989
  legal intervention (injury classifiable to E970–E976) E977
  medical or surgical procedure, test or therapy
    as, or resulting in, or from
      abnormal or delayed reaction or complication — *see* Reaction, abnormal
      misadventure — *see* Misadventure
  motor vehicle accident (accident classifiable to E810–E825) E929.0

Late effect of — *continued*
  natural or environmental factor, accident due to (accident classifiable to E900–E909) E929.5
  poisoning, accidental (accident classifiable to E850–E858, E860–E869) E929.2
  suicide, attempt (any means) E959
  transport accident NEC (accident classifiable to E800–E807, E826–E838, E840–E848) E929.1
  war operations, injury due to (injury classifiable to E990–E998) E999.0
Launching pad accident E845 ☑
Legal
  execution, any method E978
  intervention (by) (injury from) E976
    baton E973
    bayonet E974
    blow E975
    blunt object (baton) (nightstick) (stave) (truncheon) E973
    cutting or piercing instrument E974
    dynamite E971
    execution, any method E973
    explosive(s) (shell) E971
    firearm(s) E970
    gas (asphyxiation) (poisoning) (tear) E972
    grenade E971
    late effect of E977
    machine gun E970
    manhandling E975
    mortar bomb E971
    nightstick E973
    revolver E970
    rifle E970
    specified means NEC E975
    stabbing E974
    stave E973
    truncheon E973
Lifting, injury in E927.8
Lightning (shock) (stroke) (struck by) E907
Liquid (noncorrosive) in eye E914
  corrosive E924.1
Loss of control
  motor vehicle (on public highway) (without antecedent collision) E816 ☑
    with
      antecedent collision on public highway — *see* Collision, motor vehicle
      involving any object, person or vehicle not on public highway E816 ☑
      not on public highway, nontraffic accident E825 ☑
        with antecedent collision — *see* Collision, motor vehicle, not on public highway
    on public highway — *see* Collision, motor vehicle
    off-road type motor vehicle (not on public highway) E821 ☑
      on public highway — *see* Loss of control, motor vehicle
    snow vehicle, motor-driven (not on public highway) E820 ☑
      on public highway — *see* Loss of control, motor vehicle
Lost at sea E832 ☑
  with accident to watercraft E830 ☑
  in war operations E995.8 ▲
Low
  pressure, effects — *see* Effects of, air pressure
  temperature, effects — *see* Cold, exposure to
Lying before train, vehicle or other moving object (unspecified whether accidental or intentional) E988.0
  stated as intentional, purposeful, suicidal (attempt) E958.0
Lynching — *see also* Assault E968.9

M

Malfunction, atomic power plant in water transport E838 ☑
Mangled (accidentally) NEC E928.9
Manhandling (in brawl, fight) E960.0

Manhandling — *continued*
  legal intervention E975
Manslaughter (nonaccidental) — *see* Assault
Marble in nose E912
Mauled by animal E906.8
Medical procedure, complication of
  delayed or as an abnormal reaction
    without mention of misadventure — *see* Reaction, abnormal
  due to or as a result of misadventure — *see* Misadventure
Melting of fittings and furniture in burning
  in terrorism E979.3
Minamata disease E865.2
Misadventure(s) to patient(s) during surgical or medical care E876.9
  contaminated blood, fluid, drug or biological substance (presence of agents and toxins as listed in E875) E875.9
    administered (by) NEC E875.9
      infusion E875.0
      injection E875.1
      specified means NEC E875.2
      transfusion E875.0
      vaccination E875.1
  cut, cutting, puncture, perforation or hemorrhage (accidental) (inadvertent) (inappropriate) (during) E870.9
    aspiration of fluid or tissue (by puncture or catheterization, except heart) E870.5
    biopsy E870.8
      needle (aspirating) E870.5
    blood sampling E870.5
    catheterization E870.5
      heart E870.6
    dialysis (kidney) E870.2
    endoscopic examination E870.4
    enema E870.7
    infusion E870.1
    injection E870.3
    lumbar puncture E870.5
    needle biopsy E870.5
    paracentesis, abdominal E870.5
    perfusion E870.2
    specified procedure NEC E870.8
    surgical operation E870.0
    thoracentesis E870.5
    transfusion E870.1
    vaccination E870.3
  excessive amount of blood or other fluid during transfusion or infusion E873.0
  failure
    in dosage E873.9
      electroshock therapy E873.4
      inappropriate temperature (too hot or too cold) in local application and packing E873.5
      infusion
        excessive amount of fluid E873.0
        incorrect dilution of fluid E873.1
      insulin-shock therapy E873.4
      nonadministration of necessary drug or medicinal E873.6
      overdose (*see also* Overdose)
        radiation, in therapy E873.2
      radiation
        inadvertent exposure of patient (receiving radiation for test or therapy) E873.3
        not receiving radiation for test or therapy — *see* Radiation
      overdose E873.2
      specified procedure NEC E873.8
      transfusion
        excessive amount of blood E873.0
    mechanical, of instrument or apparatus (during procedure) E874.9
      aspiration of fluid or tissue (by puncture or catheterization, except of heart) E874.4
      biopsy E874.8
        needle (aspirating) E874.4
      blood sampling E874.4
      catheterization E874.4

Misadventure(s) to patient(s) during surgical or medical care — *continued*
  failure — *continued*
    mechanical, of instrument or apparatus — *continued*
      catheterization — *continued*
        heart E874.5
      dialysis (kidney) E874.2
      endoscopic examination E874.3
      enema E874.8
      infusion E874.1
      injection E874.8
      lumbar puncture E874.4
      needle biopsy E874.4
      paracentesis, abdominal E874.4
      perfusion E874.2
      specified procedure NEC E874.8
      surgical operation E874.0
      thoracentesis E874.4
      transfusion E874.1
      vaccination E874.8
    sterile precautions (during procedure) E872.9
      aspiration of fluid or tissue (by puncture or catheterization, except heart) E872.5
      biopsy E872.8
        needle (aspirating) E872.5
      blood sampling E872.5
      catheterization E872.5
        heart E872.6
      dialysis (kidney) E872.2
      endoscopic examination E872.4
      enema E872.8
      infusion E872.1
      injection E872.3
      lumbar puncture E872.5
      needle biopsy E872.5
      paracentesis, abdominal E872.5
      perfusion E872.2
      removal of catheter or packing E872.8
      specified procedure NEC E872.8
      surgical operation E872.0
      thoracentesis E872.5
      transfusion E872.1
      vaccination E872.3
    suture or ligature during surgical procedure E876.2
    to introduce or to remove tube or instrument E876.4
      foreign object left in body — *see* Misadventure, foreign object
  foreign object left in body (during procedure) E871.9
    aspiration of fluid or tissue (by puncture or catheterization, except heart) E871.5
    biopsy E871.8
      needle (aspirating) E871.5
    blood sampling E871.5
    catheterization E871.5
      heart E871.6
    dialysis (kidney) E871.2
    endoscopic examination E871.4
    enema E871.8
    infusion E871.1
    injection E871.3
    lumbar puncture E871.5
    needle biopsy E871.5
    paracentesis, abdominal E871.5
    perfusion E871.2
    removal of catheter or packing E871.7
    specified procedure NEC E871.8
    surgical operation E871.0
    thoracentesis E871.5
    transfusion E871.1
    vaccination E871.3
  hemorrhage — *see* Misadventure, cut
  inadvertent exposure of patient to radiation (being received for test or therapy) E873.3
  inappropriate
    temperature (too hot or too cold) in local application or packing E873.5
  infusion (*see also* Misadventure, by specific type, infusion)

☑ Additional Digit Required — Refer to the Tabular List for Digit Selection   ▽ Subterms under main terms may continue to next column or page

332 — Volume 2 • October 2009   ▶◀ Revised Text   ● New Line   ▲ Revised Code   2010 ICD-9-CM

Misadventure(s) to patient(s) during surgical or medical care — *continued*
  infusion (*see also* Misadventure, by specific type, infusion) — *continued*
    excessive amount of fluid E873.0
    incorrect dilution of fluid E873.1
    wrong fluid E876.1
  mismatched blood in transfusion E876.0
  nonadministration of necessary drug or medicinal E873.6
  overdose (*see also* Overdose)
    radiation, in therapy E873.2
  perforation — *see* Misadventure, cut
  performance of correct operation (procedure) on wrong ●
    body part E876.7 ●
    side E876.7 ●
    site E876.7 ●
  performance of operation (procedure)
    intended for another patient E876.6 ●
    on patient not scheduled for surgery E876.6 ●
    on wrong patient E876.6 ●
  performance of ►wrong◄ operation ►on correct patient◄ E876.5 ●
  puncture — *see* Misadventure, cut
  specified type NEC E876.8
    failure
      suture or ligature during surgical operation E876.2
      to introduce or to remove tube or instrument E876.4
        foreign object left in body E871.9
    infusion of wrong fluid E876.1
    performance of inappropriate operation E876.5
    transfusion of mismatched blood E876.0
    wrong
      fluid in infusion E876.1
      placement of endotracheal tube during anesthetic procedure E876.3
  transfusion (*see also* Misadventure, by specific type, transfusion)
    excessive amount of blood E873.0
    mismatched blood E876.0
  wrong
    device implanted into correct surgical ● site E876.5 ●
    drug given in error — *see* Table of Drugs and Chemicals
    fluid in infusion E876.1
    placement of endotracheal tube during anesthetic procedure E876.3
    procedure (operation) performed on the ● correct patient E876.5 ●
Motion (effects) E903
  sickness E903
Mountain sickness E902.0
Mucus aspiration or inhalation, not of newborn (with asphyxia, obstruction respiratory passage, suffocation) E912
Mudslide of cataclysmic nature E909.2
Murder (attempt) — *see also* Assault E968.9

N

Nail, injury by E920.8
Needlestick (sewing needle) E920.4
  hypodermic E920.5
Neglect — *see also* Privation
  criminal E968.4
  homicidal intent E968.4
Noise (causing injury) (pollution) E928.1
Nuclear weapon — *see also* War operations, ●
  injury due to, nuclear weapons E996.9 ●

O

Object
  falling
    from, in, on, hitting
      aircraft E844 ☑
        due to accident to aircraft — *see* categories E840-E842 ☑
      machinery (*see also* Accident, machine)
        not in operation E916

Object — *continued*
  falling — *continued*
    from, in, on, hitting — *continued*
      motor vehicle (in motion) (on public highway) E818 ☑
        not on public highway E825 ☑
        stationary E916
      nonmotor road vehicle NEC E829 ☑
      pedal cycle E826 ☑
      person E916
      railway rolling stock, train, vehicle E806 ☑
      street car E829 ☑
      watercraft E838 ☑
        due to accident to watercraft E831 ☑
    set in motion by
      accidental explosion of pressure vessel — *see* category E921 ☑
      firearm — *see* category E922 ☑
      machine(ry) — *see* Accident, machine
      transport vehicle — *see* categories E800-E848 ☑
    thrown from, in, on, towards
      aircraft E844 ☑
      cable car (not on rails) E847
        on rails E829 ☑
      motor vehicle (in motion) (on public highway) E818 ☑
        not on public highway E825 ☑
      nonmotor road vehicle NEC E829 ☑
      pedal cycle E826 ☑
      street car E829 ☑
      vehicle NEC — *see* Accident, vehicle NEC
Obstruction
  air passages, larynx, respiratory passages
    by
      external means NEC — *see* Suffocation
      food, any type (regurgitated) (vomited) E911
      material or object, except food E912
      mucus E912
      phlegm E912
      vomitus E911
  digestive tract, except mouth or pharynx
    by
      food, any type E915
      foreign body (any) E915
  esophagus
    without asphyxia or obstruction of respiratory passage E915
    food E911
    foreign body, except food E912
  mouth or pharynx
    by
      food, any type E911
      material or object, except food E912
  respiration — *see* Obstruction, air passages
Oil in eye E914
Overdose
  anesthetic (drug) — *see* Table of Drugs and Chemicals
  drug — *see* Table of Drugs and Chemicals
Overexertion E927.9
  from
    lifting E927.8
    maintaining prolonged positions E927.1
      holding E927.1
      sitting E927.1
      standing E927.1
    prolonged static position E927.1
    pulling E927.8
    pushing E927.8
    sudden strenuous movement E927.0
Overexposure (accidental) (to)
  cold (*see also* Cold, exposure to) E901.9
    due to manmade conditions E901.1
  heat (*see also* Heat) E900.9
  radiation — *see* Radiation
  radioactivity — *see* Radiation
  sun, except sunburn E900.0
  weather — *see* Exposure
  wind — *see* Exposure
Overheated — *see also* Heat E900.9
Overlaid E913.0

Overturning (accidental)
  animal-drawn vehicle E827 ☑
  boat, ship, watercraft
    causing
      drowning, submersion E830 ☑
      injury except drowning, submersion E831 ☑
  machinery — *see* Accident, machine
  motor vehicle (*see also* Loss of control, motor vehicle) E816 ☑
    with antecedent collision on public highway — *see* Collision, motor vehicle
    not on public highway, nontraffic accident E825 ☑
      with antecedent collision — *see* Collision, motor vehicle, not on public highway
  nonmotor road vehicle NEC E829 ☑
  off-road type motor vehicle — *see* Loss of control, off-road type motor vehicle
  pedal cycle E826 ☑
  railway rolling stock, train, vehicle (*see also* Derailment, railway) E802 ☑
  street car E829 ☑
  vehicle NEC — *see* Accident, vehicle NEC

P

Palsy, divers' E902.2
Parachuting (voluntary) (without accident to aircraft) E844 ☑
  due to accident to aircraft — *see* categories E840-E842 ☑
Paralysis
  divers' E902.2
  lead or saturnine E866.0
    from pesticide NEC E863.4
Pecked by bird E906.8
Performance of correct operation (procedure) **on wrong** ●
  body part E876.7 ●
  side E876.7 ●
  site E876.7 ●
Performance of operation (procedure)
  intended for another patient E876.6 ●
  on patient not scheduled for surgery E876.6 ●
  on wrong patient E876.6 ●
Performance of wrong operation on correct ●
  patient E876.5 ●
Phlegm aspiration or inhalation (with asphyxia, obstruction respiratory passage, suffocation) E912
Piercing — *see also* Cut E920.9
  by slide trigger mechanism, scope or other ● part of gun E928.7 ●
Pinched
  between objects (moving) (stationary and moving) E918
  by slide trigger mechanism, scope or other ● part of gun E928.7 ●
  in object E918
Pinned under
  machine(ry) — *see* Accident, machine
Place of occurrence of accident — *see* Accident (to), occurring (at) (in)
Plumbism E866.0
  from insecticide NEC E863.4
Poisoning (accidental) (by) — *see also* Table of Drugs and Chemicals
  carbon monoxide
    generated by
      aircraft in transit E844 ☑
      motor vehicle
        in motion (on public highway) E818 ☑
          not on public highway E825 ☑
      watercraft (in transit) (not in transit) E838 ☑
  caused by injection of poisons or toxins into or through skin by plant thorns, spines, or other mechanism E905.7
    marine or sea plants E905.6
  fumes or smoke due to
    conflagration — *see* Conflagration
    explosion or fire — *see* Fire
    ignition — *see* Ignition

Poisoning — *see also* Table of Drugs and Chemicals — *continued*
  gas
    in legal intervention E972
    legal execution, by E978
    on watercraft E838 ☑
    used as anesthetic — *see* Table of Drugs and Chemicals
    in
      terrorism (chemical weapons) E979.7
      war operations E997.2
        execution E978
        intervention
          by gas E972
  late effect of — *see* Late effect
  legal
Pressure, external, causing asphyxia, suffocation — *see also* Suffocation E913.9
Privation E904.9
  food (*see also* Lack of, food) E904.1
  helpless person, infant, newborn due to abandonment or neglect E904.0
  late effect of NEC E929.5
  resulting from transport accident — *see* categories E800-E848 ☑
  water (*see also* Lack of, water) E904.2
Projected objects, striking against or struck by — *see* Striking against, object
Prolonged stay in
  high altitude (causing conditions as listed in E902.0) E902.0
  weightless environment E928.0
Prostration
  heat — *see* Heat
Pulling, injury in E927.8
Puncture, puncturing — *see also* Cut E920.9
  by
    plant thorns or spines E920.8
      toxic reaction E905.7
        marine or sea plants E905.6
    sea-urchin spine E905.6
Pushing (injury in) (overexertion) E927.8
  by other person(s) (accidental) E917.9
    with fall E886.9
      in sports E886.0
    as, or caused by, a crowd, human stampede E917.1
      with subsequent fall E917.6
    before moving vehicle or object
      stated as
        intentional, homicidal E968.5
        undetemined whether accidental or intentional E988.8
    from
      high place
        in accidental circum-stances — *see* categories E880-E884 ☑
        stated as
          intentional, homicidal E968.1
          undetermined whether accidental or intentional E987.9
          man-made structure, except residential E987.1
          natural site E987.2
          residential E987.0
      motor vehicle (*see also* Fall, from, motor vehicle) E818 ☑
        stated as
          intentional, homicidal E968.5
          undetermined whether accidental or intentional E988.8
    in sports E917.0
      with fall E886.0

R

Radiation (exposure to) E926.9
  abnormal reaction to medical test or therapy E879.2
  arc lamps E926.2
  atomic power plant (malfunction) NEC E926.9
    in water transport E838 ☑
  electromagnetic, ionizing E926.3
  gamma rays E926.3
  in
    terrorism (from or following nuclear explosion) (direct) (secondary) E979.5

☑ Additional Digit Required — Refer to the Tabular List for Digit Selection   ▼ Subterms under main terms may continue to next column or page

2010 ICD-9-CM   ►◄ Revised Text   ● New Line   ▲ Revised Code   October 2009 • Volume 2 — 333

Misadventure(s) to patient(s) — Radiation

Radiation — continued
in — continued
terrorism — continued
laser E979.8
war operations ►(see also War operations, injury due to, nuclear weapons)◄ E996.3 ▲
laser(s) E997.0
water transport E838 ☑
inadvertent exposure of patient (receiving test or therapy) E873.3
infrared (heaters and lamps) E926.1
excessive heat E900.1
ionized, ionizing (particles, artificially accelerated) E926.8
electromagnetic E926.3
isotopes, radioactive — see Radiation, radioactive isotopes
laser(s) E926.4
in
terrorism E979.8
war operations E997.0
misadventure in medical care — see Misadventure, failure, in dosage, radiation
late effect of NEC E929.8
excessive heat from — see Heat
light sources (visible) (ultraviolet) E926.2
misadventure in medical or surgical procedure — see Misadventure, failure, in dosage, radiation
overdose (in medical or surgical procedure) E873.2
radar E926.0
radioactive isotopes E926.5
atomic power plant malfunction E926.5
in water transport E838 ☑
misadventure in medical or surgical treatment — see Misadventure, failure, in dosage, radiation
radiobiologicals — see Radiation, radioactive isotopes
radiofrequency E926.0
radiopharmaceuticals — see Radiation, radioactive isotopes
radium NEC E926.9
sun E926.2
excessive heat from E900.0
tanning bed E926.2
welding arc or torch E926.2
excessive heat from E900.1
x-rays (hard) (soft) E926.3
misadventure in medical or surgical treatment — see Misadventure, failure, in dosage, radiation
Rape E960.1
Reaction, abnormal to or following (medical or surgical procedure) E879.9
amputation (of limbs) E878.5
anastomosis (arteriovenous) (blood vessel) (gastrojejunal) (skin) (tendon) (natural, artificial material, tissue) E878.2
external stoma, creation of E878.3
aspiration (of fluid) E879.4
tissue E878.8
biopsy E879.8
blood
sampling E879.7
transfusion
procedure E879.8
bypass — see Reaction, abnormal, anastomosis
catheterization
cardiac E879.0
urinary E879.6
colostomy E878.3
cystostomy E878.3
dialysis (kidney) E879.1
drugs or biologicals — see Table of Drugs and Chemicals
duodenostomy E878.3
electroshock therapy E879.3
formation of external stoma E878.3
gastrostomy E878.3
graft — see Reaction, abnormal, anastomosis
hypothermia E879.8

Reaction, abnormal to or following — continued
implant, implantation (of)
artificial
internal device (cardiac pacemaker) (electrodes in brain) (heart valve prosthesis) (orthopedic) E878.1
material or tissue (for anastomosis or bypass) E878.2
with creation of external stoma E878.3
natural tissues (for anastomosis or bypass) E878.2
with creation of external stoma E878.3
as transplantion — see Reaction, abnormal, transplant
infusion
procedure E879.8
injection
procedure E879.8
specific type of procedure) E879.9
insertion of gastric or duodenal sound E879.5
insulin-shock therapy E879.3
lumbar puncture E879.4
perfusion E879.1
procedures other than surgical operation (see also Reaction, abnormal, by specified procedure NEC E879.8
radiological procedure or therapy E879.2
removal of organ (partial) (total) NEC E878.6
with
anastomosis, bypass or graft E878.2
formation of external stoma E878.3
implant of artificial internal device E878.1
transplant(ation)
partial organ E878.4
whole organ E878.0
sampling
blood E879.7
fluid NEC E879.4
tissue E879.8
shock therapy E879.3
surgical operation (see also Reaction, abnormal, by specified type of operation) E878.9
restorative NEC E878.4
with
anastomosis, bypass or graft E878.2
fomation of external stoma E878.3
implant(ation) — see Reaction, abnormal, implant
transplant(ation) — see Reaction, abnormal, transplant
specified operation NEC E878.8
thoracentesis E879.4
transfusion
procedure E879.8
transplant, transplantation (heart) (kidney) (liver) E878.0
partial organ E878.4
ureterostomy E878.3
vaccination E879.8
Reduction in
atmospheric pressure (see also Effects of, air pressure)
while surfacing from
deep water diving causing caisson or divers' disease, palsy or paralysis E902.2
underground E902.8
Residual (effect) — see Late effect
Rock falling on or hitting (accidentally)
motor vehicle (in motion) (on public highway) E818 ☑
not on public highway E825 ☑
nonmotor road vehicle NEC E829 ☑
pedal cycle E826 ☑
person E916
railway rolling stock, train, vehicle E806 ☑
Running off, away
animal (being ridden) (in sport or transport) E828 ☑
not being ridden E906.8
animal-drawn vehicle E827 ☑
rails, railway (see also Derailment) E802 ☑

Running off, away — continued
roadway
motor vehicle (without antecedent collision) E816 ☑
with
antecedent collision — see Collision motor vehicle
subsequent collision
involving any object, person or vehicle not on public highway E816 ☑
on public highway E811 ☑
nontraffic accident E825 ☑
with antecedent collision — see Collision, motor vehicle, not on public highway
nonmotor road vehicle NEC E829 ☑
pedal cycle E826 ☑
Run over (accidentally) (by)
animal (not being ridden) E906.8
being ridden (in sport or transport) E828 ☑
animal-drawn vehicle E827 ☑
machinery — see Accident, machine
motor vehicle (on public highway) — see Hit by, motor vehicle
nonmotor road vehicle NEC E829 ☑
railway train E805 ☑
street car E829 ☑
vehicle NEC E848

S

Saturnism E866.0
from insecticide NEC E863.4
Scald, scalding (accidental) (by) (from) (in) E924.0
acid — see Scald, caustic
boiling tap water E924.2
caustic or corrosive liquid, substance E924.1
swallowed — see Table of Drugs and Chemicals
homicide (attempt) — see Assault, burning
inflicted by other person
stated as
intentional or homicidal E968.3
undetermined whether accidental or intentional E988.2
late effect of NEC E929.8
liquid (boiling) (hot) E924.0
local application of externally applied substance in medical or surgical care E873.5
molten metal E924.0
self-inflicted (unspecified whether accidental or intentional) E988.2
stated as intentional, purposeful E958.2
stated as undetermined whether accidental or intentional E988.2
steam E924.0
tap water (boiling) E924.2
transport accident — see categories E800-E848 ☑
vapor E924.0
Scratch, cat E906.8
Sea
sickness E903
Self-mutilation — see Suicide
Sequelae (of)
in
terrorism E999.1
war operations E999.0
Shock
anaphylactic (see also Table of Drugs and Chemicals) E947.9
due to
bite (venomous) — see Bite, venomous NEC
sting — see Sting
electric (see also Electric shock) E925.9
from electric appliance or current (see also Electric shock) E925.9
Shooting, shot (accidental(ly)) E922.9
air gun E922.4
BB gun E922.4
hand gun (pistol) (revolver) E922.0
himself (see also Shooting, self-inflicted) E985.4

Shooting, shot — continued
himself (see also Shooting, self-inflicted) — continued
hand gun (pistol) (revolver) E985.0
military firearm, except hand gun E985.3
hand gun (pistol) (revolver) E985.0
rifle (hunting) E985.2
military E985.3
shotgun (automatic) E985.1
specified firearm NEC E985.4
Verey pistol E985.4
homicide (attempt) E965.4
air gun E968.6
BB gun E968.6
hand gun (pistol) (revolver) E965.0
military firearm, except hand gun E965.3
hand gun (pistol) (revolver) E965.0
paintball gun E965.4
rifle (hunting) E965.2
military E965.3
shotgun (automatic) E965.1
specified firearm NEC E965.4
Verey pistol E965.4
in
terrorism — see Terrorism, shooting
war operations — see War operations, shooting
inflicted by other person
in accidental circumstances E922.9
hand gun (pistol) (revolver) E922.0
military firearm, except hand gun E922.3
hand gun (pistol) (revolver) E922.0
rifle (hunting) E922.2
military E922.3
shotgun (automatic) E922.1
specified firearm NEC E922.8
Verey pistol E922.8
stated as
intentional, homicidal E965.4
hand gun (pistol) (revolver) E965.0
military firearm, except hand gun E965.3
hand gun (pistol) (revolver) E965.0
paintball gun E965.4
rifle (hunting) E965.2
military E965.3
shotgun (automatic) E965.1
specified firearm E965.4
Verey pistol E965.4
undetermined whether accidental or intentional E985.4
air gun E985.6
BB gun E985.6
hand gun (pistol) (revolver) E985.0
military firearm, except hand gun E985.3
hand gun (pistol) (revolver) E985.0
paintball gun E985.7
rifle (hunting) E985.2
shotgun (automatic) E985.1
specified firearm NEC E985.4
Verey pistol E985.4
legal
execution E978
intervention E970
military firearm, except hand gun E922.3
hand gun (pistol) (revolver) E922.0
paintball gun E922.5
rifle (hunting) E922.2
military E922.3
self-inflicted (unspecified whether accidental or intentional) E985.4
air gun E985.6
BB gun E985.6
hand gun (pistol) (revolver) E985.0
military firearm, except hand gun E985.3
hand gun (pistol) (revolver) E985.0
paintball gun E985.7
rifle (hunting) E985.2
military E985.3
shotgun (automatic) E985.1
specified firearm NEC E985.4

Shooting, shot — *continued*
  self-inflicted — *continued*
    stated as
      accidental E922.9
        hand gun (pistol) (revolver) E922.0
        military firearm, except hand gun
          E922.3
          hand gun (pistol) (revolver)
            E922.0
        paintball gun E922.5
        rifle (hunting) E922.2
          military E922.3
        shotgun (automatic) E922.1
        specified firearm NEC E922.8
        Verey pistol E922.8
      intentional, purposeful E955.4
        hand gun (pistol) (revolver) E955.0
        military firearm, except hand gun
          E955.3
          hand gun (pistol) (revolver)
            E955.0
        paintball gun E955.7
        rifle (hunting) E955.2
          military E955.3
        shotgun (automatic) E955.1
        specified firearm NEC E955.4
        Verey pistol E955.4
      shotgun (automatic) E922.1
      specified firearm NEC E922.8
      stated as undetermined whether accidental
        or intentional E985.4
      hand gun (pistol) (revolver) E985.0
      military firearm, except hand gun E985.3
        hand gun (pistol) (revolver) E985.0
      paintball gun E985.7
      rifle (hunting) E985.2
        military E985.3
      shotgun (automatic) E985.1
      specified firearm NEC E985.4
      Verey pistol E985.4
    suicidal (attempt) E955.4
      air gun E955.6
      BB gun E955.6
      hand gun (pistol) (revolver) E955.0
      military firearm, except hand gun E955.3
        hand gun (pistol) (revolver) E955.0
      paintball gun E955.7
      rifle (hunting) E955.2
        military E955.3
      shotgun (automatic) E955.1
      specified firearm NEC E955.4
      Verey pistol E955.4
      Verey pistol E922.8
Shoving (accidentally) by other person — *see
  also* Pushing by other person E917.9
Sickness
  air E903
  alpine E902.0
  car E903
  motion E903
  mountain E902.0
  sea E903
  travel E903
Sinking (accidental)
  boat, ship, watercraft (causing drowning,
    submersion) E830 ☑
    causing injury except drowning, submer-
      sion E831 ☑
Siriasis E900.0
Skydiving E844 ☑
Slashed wrists — *see also* Cut, self-inflicted E986
Slipping (accidental)
  on
    deck (of boat, ship, watercraft) (icy) (oily)
      (wet) E835 ☑
    ice E885.9
    ladder of ship E833 ☑
      due to accident to watercraft E831 ☑
    mud E885.9
    oil E885.9
    snow E885.9
    stairs of ship E833 ☑
      due to accident to watercraft E831 ☑
    surface
      slippery E885 ☑
      wet E885 ☑

Sliver, wood, injury by E920.8
Smothering, smothered — *see also* Suffocation
  E913.9
**Smouldering building or structure in terror-
  ism** E979.3
Sodomy (assault) E960.1
Solid substance in eye (any part) or adnexa
  E914
Sound waves (causing injury) E928.1
Splinter, injury by E920.8
Stab, stabbing E966
  accidental — *see* Cut
Starvation E904.1
  helpless person, infant, newborn — *see* Lack
    of food
  homicidal intent E968.4
  late effect of NEC E929.5
  resulting from accident connected with
    transport — *see* categories
      E800-E848 ☑
Stepped on
  by
    animal (not being ridden) E906.8
      being ridden (in sport or transport)
        E828 ☑
    crowd E917.1
    person E917.9
      in sports E917.0
  in sports E917.0
Stepping on
  object (moving) E917.9
    in sports E917.0
      with subsequent fall E917.5
    stationary E917.4
      with subsequent fall E917.8
  person E917.9
    as, or caused by a crowd E917.1
      with subsequent fall E917.6
    in sports E917.0
Sting E905.9
  ant E905.5
  bee E905.3
  caterpillar E905.5
  coral E905.6
  hornet E905.3
  insect NEC E905.5
  jellyfish E905.6
  marine animal or plant E905.6
  nematocysts E905.6
  scorpion E905.2
  sea anemone E905.6
  sea cucumber E905.6
  wasp E905.3
  yellow jacket E905.3
Storm E908.9
  specified type NEC E908.8
Straining, injury in E927.8
Strangling — *see* Suffocation
Strangulation — *see* Suffocation
Strenuous movements (in recreational or other
  activities) E927.8
Striking against
  bottom (when jumping or diving into water)
    E883.0
  object (moving) E917.9
    caused by crowd E917.1
      with subsequent fall E917.6
    furniture E917.3
      with subsequent fall E917.7
    in
      running water E917.2
        with drowning or submersion —
          see Submersion
    sports E917.0
      with subsequent fall E917.5
    stationary E917.4
      with subsequent fall E917.8
  person(s) E917.9
    with fall E886.9
      in sports E886.0
    as, or caused by, a crowd E917.1
      with subsequent fall E917.6
      in sports E917.0
        with fall E886.0
Stroke
  heat — *see* Heat

Stroke — *continued*
  lightning E907
Struck by — *see also* Hit by
  bullet
    in
      terrorism E979.4
      war operations E991.2
        rubber E991.0
  lightning E907
  missile
    in terrorism — *see* Terrorism, missile
  object
    falling
      from, in, on
        building
          burning (uncontrolled fire)
            in terrorism E979.3
  thunderbolt E907
**Stumbling over animal, carpet, curb, rug or
  (small) object (with fall)** E885.9
  without fall — *see* Striking against, object
Submersion (accidental) E910.8
  boat, ship, watercraft (causing drowning,
    submersion) E830 ☑
    causing injury except drowning, submer-
      sion E831 ☑
  by other person
    in accidental circumstances — *see* catego-
      ry E910 ☑
    intentional, homicidal E964
    stated as undetermined whether acciden-
      tal or intentional E984
  due to
    accident
      machinery — *see* Accident, machine
      to boat, ship, watercraft E830 ☑
      transport — *see* categories
        E800-E848 ☑
    avalanche E909.2
    cataclysmic
      earth surface movement or eruption
        E909.9
      storm E908.9
    cloudburst E908.8
    cyclone E908.1
    fall
      from
        boat, ship, watercraft (not involved
          in accident) E832 ☑
          burning, crushed E830 ☑
          involved in accident, collision
            E830 ☑
        gangplank (into water) E832 ☑
        overboard NEC E832 ☑
    flood E908.2
    hurricane E908.0
    jumping into water E910.8
      from boat, ship, watercraft
        burning, crushed, sinking E830 ☑
        involved in accident, collision
          E830 ☑
        not involved in accident, for swim
          E910.2
      in recreational activity (without diving
        equipment) E910.2
        with or using diving equipment
          E910.1
      to rescue another person E910.3
    homicide (attempt) E964
    in
      bathtub E910.4
      specified activity, not sport, transport or
        recreational E910.3
      sport or recreational activity (without div-
        ing equipment) E910.2
        with or using diving equipment E910.1
        water skiing E910.0
      swimming pool NEC E910.8
      terrorism E979.8
      war operations E995.4 ▲
        intentional E995.3 ●
      water transport E832 ☑
        due to accident to boat, ship, water-
          craft E830 ☑
    landslide E909.2
      overturning boat, ship, watercraft E909.2

Submersion (accidental) — *continued*
  landslide — *continued*
    sinking boat, ship, watercraft E909.2
    submersion boat, ship, watercraft E909.2
    tidal wave E909.4
      caused by storm E908.0
    torrential rain E908.2
  late effect of NEC E929.8
  quenching tank E910.8
  self-inflicted (unspecified whether accidental
    or intentional) E984
    in accidental circumstances — *see* catego-
      ry E910 ☑
    stated as intentional, purposeful E954
    stated as undetermined whether accidental
      or intentional E984
  suicidal (attempted) E954
  while
    attempting rescue of another person
      E910.3
    engaged in
      marine salvage E910.3
      underwater construction or repairs
        E910.3
    fishing, not from boat E910.2
    hunting, not from boat E910.2
    ice skating E910.2
    pearl diving E910.3
    placing fishing nets E910.3
    playing in water E910.2
    scuba diving E910.1
      nonrecreational E910.3
    skin diving E910.1
    snorkel diving E910.2
    spear fishing underwater E910.1
    surfboarding E910.2
    swimming (swimming pool) E910.2
    wading (in water) E910.2
    water skiing E910.0
Sucked
  into
    jet (aircraft) E844 ☑
Suffocation (accidental) (by external means) (by
  pressure) (mechanical) E913.9
  caused by other person
    in accidental circumstances — *see category*
      E913 ☑
    stated as
      intentional, homicidal E963
      undetermined whether accidental or
        intentional E983.9
      by, in
        hanging E983.0
        plastic bag E983.1
        specified means NEC E983.8
  due to, by
    avalanche E909.2
    bedclothes E913.0
    bib E913.0
    blanket E913.0
    cave-in E913.3
      caused by cataclysmic earth surface
        movement or eruption E909.9
    conflagration — *see* Conflagration
    explosion — *see* Explosion
    falling earth, other substance E913.3
    fire — *see* Fire
    food, any type (ingestion) (inhalation) (re-
      gurgitated) (vomited) E911
    foreign body, except food (ingestion) (in-
      halation) E912
    ignition — *see* Ignition
    landslide E909.2
    machine(ry) — *see* Accident, machine
    material, object except food entering by
      nose or mouth, ingested, inhaled
      E912
    mucus (aspiration) (inhalation), not of
      newborn E912
    phlegm (aspiration) (inhalation) E912
    pillow E913.0
    plastic bag — *see* Suffocation, in, plastic
      bag
    sheet (plastic) E913.0
    specified means NEC E913.8
    vomitus (aspiration) (inhalation) E911

☑ Additional Digit Required — Refer to the Tabular List for Digit Selection   ▽ Subterms under main terms may continue to next column or page

2010 ICD-9-CM   ►◄ Revised Text   ● New Line   ▲ Revised Code   **October 2009 • Volume 2 — 335**

Shooting, shot — Suffocation

Suffocation — continued
homicidal (attempt) E963
   in war operations E995.3 ●
in
   airtight enclosed place E913.2
   baby carriage E913.0
   bed E913.0
   closed place E913.2
   cot, cradle E913.0
   perambulator E913.0
   plastic bag (in accidental circumstances) E913.1
      homicidal, purposely inflicted by other person E963
      self-inflicted (unspecified whether accidental or intentional) E983.1
         in accidental circumstances E913.1
         intentional, suicidal E953.1
      stated as undetermined whether accidentally or purposely inflicted E983.1
      suicidal, purposely self-inflicted E953.1
   refrigerator E913.2
   war operations E995.3 ●
self-inflicted (see also Suffocation, stated as undetermined whether accidental or intentional) E953.9
   in accidental circumstances — see category E913 ☑
   stated as intentional, purposeful — see Suicide, suffocation
   stated as undetermined whether accidental or intentional E983.9
      by, in
         hanging E983.0
         plastic bag E983.1
         specified means NEC E983.8
suicidal — see Suicide, suffocation
Suicide, suicidal (attempted) (by) E958.9
burning, burns E958.1
caustic substance E958.7
   poisoning E950.7
   swallowed E950.7
cold, extreme E958.3
cut (any part of body) E956
cutting or piercing instrument (classifiable to E920) E956
drowning E954
electrocution E958.4
explosive(s) (classifiable to E923) E955.5
fire E958.1
firearm (classifiable to E922) — see Shooting, suicidal
hanging E953.0
jumping
   before moving object, train, vehicle E958.0
   from high place — see Jumping, from, high place, stated as, suicidal
knife E956
late effect of E959
motor vehicle, crashing of E958.5
poisoning — see Table of Drugs and Chemicals
puncture (any part of body) E956
scald E958.2
shooting — see Shooting, suicidal
specified means NEC E958.8
stab (any part of body) E956
strangulation — see Suicide, suffocation
submersion E954
suffocation E953.9
   by, in
      hanging E953.0
      plastic bag E953.1
      specified means NEC E953.8
wound NEC E958.9
Sunburn E926.2
Sunstroke E900.0
Supersonic waves (causing injury) E928.1
Surgical procedure, complication of
delayed or as an abnormal reaction without mention of misadventure — see Reaction, abnormal
due to or as a result of misadventure — see Misadventure

Swallowed, swallowing
foreign body — see Foreign body, alimentary canal
poison — see Table of Drugs and Chemicals
substance
   caustic — see Table of Drugs and Chemicals
   corrosive — see Table of Drugs and Chemicals
   poisonous — see Table of Drugs and Chemicals
Swimmers cramp — see also category E910 E910.2
not in recreation or sport E910.3
Syndrome, battered
baby or child — see Abuse, child
wife — see Assault

T

Tackle in sport E886.0
Terrorism (injury) (by) (in) E979.8
air blast E979.2
aircraft burned, destroyed, exploded, shot down E979.1
   used as a weapon E979.1
anthrax E979.6
asphyxia from
   chemical (weapons) E979.7
   fire, conflagration (caused by fire-producing device) E979.3
   from nuclear explosion E979.5
   gas or fumes E979.7
bayonet E979.8
biological agents E979.6
blast (air) (effects) E979.2
   from nuclear explosion E979.5
   underwater E979.0
bomb (antipersonnel) (mortar) (explosion) (fragments) E979.2
bullet(s) (from carbine, machine gun, pistol, rifle, shotgun) E979.4
burn from
   chemical E979.7
   fire, conflagration (caused by fire-producing device) E979.3
   from nuclear explosion E979.5
   gas E979.7
burning aircraft E979.1
chemical E979.7
cholera E979.6
conflagration E979.3
crushed by falling aircraft E979.1
depth-charge E979.0
destruction of aircraft E979.1
disability, as sequelae one year or more after injury E999.1
drowning E979.8
effect
   of nuclear weapon (direct) (secondary) E979.5
   secondary NEC E979.9
   sequelae E999.1
explosion (artillery shell) (breech-block) (cannon block) E979.2
   aircraft E979.1
   bomb (antipersonnel) (mortar) E979.2
      nuclear (atom) (hydrogen) E979.5
   depth-charge E979.0
   grenade E979.2
   injury by fragments from E979.2
   land-mine E979.2
   marine weapon E979.0
   mine (land) E979.2
      at sea or in harbor E979.0
      marine E979.0
   missile (explosive) NEC E979.2
   munitions (dump) (factory) E979.2
   nuclear (weapon) E979.5
      other direct and secondary effects of E979.5
   sea-based artillery shell E979.0
   torpedo E979.0
exposure to ionizing radiation from nuclear explosion E979.5
falling aircraft E979.1
firearms E979.4

Terrorism — continued
fireball effects from nuclear explosion E979.5
fire or fire-producing device E979.3
fragments from artillery shell, bomb NEC, grenade, guided missile, land-mine, rocket, shell, shrapnel E979.2
gas or fumes E979.7
grenade (explosion) (fragments) E979.2
guided missile (explosion) (fragments) E979.2
   nuclear E979.5
heat from nuclear explosion E979.5
hot substances E979.3
hydrogen cyanide E979.7
land-mine (explosion) (fragments) E979.2
laser(s) E979.8
late effect of E999.1
lewisite E979.7
lung irritant (chemical) (fumes) (gas) E979.7
marine mine E979.0
mine E979.2
   at sea E979.0
   in harbor E979.0
   land (explosion) (fragments) E979.2
   marine E979.0
missile (explosion) (fragments) (guided) E979.2
   marine E979.0
   nuclear weapons E979.5
mortar bomb (explosion) (fragments) E979.2
mustard gas E979.7
nerve gas E979.7
nuclear weapons E979.5
pellets (shotgun) E979.4
petrol bomb E979.3
phosgene E979.7
piercing object E979.8
poisoning (chemical) (fumes) (gas) E979.7
radiation, ionizing from nuclear explosion E979.5
rocket (explosion) (fragments) E979.2
saber, sabre E979.8
sarin E979.7
screening smoke E979.7
sequelae effect (of) E999.1
shell (aircraft) (artillery) (cannon) (land-based) (explosion) (fragments) E979.2
   sea-based E979.0
shooting E979.4
   bullet(s) E979.4
   pellet(s) (rifle) (shotgun) E979.4
shrapnel E979.2
smallpox E979.7
stabbing object(s) E979.8
submersion E979.8
torpedo E979.0
underwater blast E979.0
vesicant (chemical) (fumes) (gas) E979.7
weapon burst E979.2
Thermic fever E900.9
Thermoplegia E900.9
Thirst — see also Lack of water
resulting from accident connected with transport — see categories E800-E848 ☑
Thrown (accidently)
against object in or part of vehicle
   by motion of vehicle
      aircraft E844 ☑
      boat, ship, watercraft E838 ☑
      motor vehicle (on public highway) E818 ☑
         not on public highway E825 ☑
         off-road type (not on public highway) E821 ☑
            on public highway E818 ☑
         snow vehicle E820 ☑
            on public highway E818 ☑
      nonmotor road vehicle NEC E829 ☑
      railway rolling stock, train, vehicle E806 ☑
      street car E829 ☑
from
   animal (being ridden) (in sport or transport) E828 ☑
   high place, homicide (attempt) E968.1
   machinery — see Accident, machine
   vehicle NEC — see Accident, vehicle NEC
off — see Thrown, from

Thrown — continued
overboard (by motion of boat, ship, watercraft) E832 ☑
   by accident to boat, ship, watercraft E830 ☑
Thunderbolt NEC E907
Tidal wave (any injury) E909.4
caused by storm E908.0
Took
overdose of drug — see Table of Drugs and Chemicals
poison — see Table of Drugs and Chemicals
Tornado (any injury) E908.1
Torrential rain (any injury) E908.2
Traffic accident NEC E819
Trampled by animal E906.8
being ridden (in sport or transport) E828 ☑
Trapped (accidentally)
between
   objects (moving) (stationary and moving) E918
by
   door of
      elevator E918
      motor vehicle (on public highway) (while alighting, boarding) — see Fall, from, motor vehicle, while alighting
      railway train (underground) E806 ☑
      street car E829 ☑
      subway train E806 ☑
in object E918
Trauma
cumulative
   from
      repetitive
         impact E927.4
         motion or movements E927.3
   sudden from strenuous movement E927.0
Travel (effects) E903
sickness E903
Tree
falling on or hitting E916
   motor vehicle (in motion) (on public highway) E818 ☑
      not on public highway E825 ☑
   nonmotor road vehicle NEC E829 ☑
   pedal cycle E826 ☑
   person E916
   railway rolling stock, train, vehicle E806 ☑
   street car E829 ☑
Trench foot E901.0
Tripping over animal, carpet, curb, rug, or small object (with fall) E885 ☑
without fall — see Striking against, object
Tsunami E909.4
Twisting, injury in E927.8

V

Violence, nonaccidental — see also Assault E968.9
Volcanic eruption (any injury) E909.1
Vomitus in air passages (with asphyxia, obstruction or suffocation) E911

W

War operations (during hostilities) (injury) (by) (in) E995.9 ▲
after cessation of hostilities, injury due to E998.9 ▲
air blast E993.9 ▲
aircraft burned, destroyed, exploded, shot down E994 ☑
asphyxia from
   chemical E997.2
   fire, conflagration (caused by fire producing device or conventional weapon) E990.9
      from nuclear explosion ▶(see also War operations, injury due to, nuclear weapons)◀ E996.8
   incendiary bomb E990.0 ●
   petrol bomb E990.0
fumes E997.2
gas E997.2

War operations — *continued*
- baton (nightstick) E995.1 ●
- battle wound NEC E995.8 ▲
- bayonet E995.2 ▲
- biological warfare agents E997.1
- blast (air) (effects) E993.9
  - from nuclear explosion ▶(*see also* War operations, injury due to, nuclear weapons)◀ E996.1
  - underwater E992.9 ▲
- bomb (mortar) (explosion) E993.2
  - after cessation of hostilities E998.1 ▲
  - fragments, injury by E991.4 ▲
    - antipersonnel E991.3
- bullet(s) (from carbine, machine gun, pistol, rifle, shotgun) E991.2
  - rubber E991.0
- burn from
  - chemical E997.2
  - fire, conflagration (caused by fire-producing device or conventional weapon) E990.9
    - from
      - conventional weapon E990.3 ●
      - flamethrower E990.1 ●
      - incendiary bomb E990.0 ●
      - incendiary bullet E990.2 ●
      - nuclear explosion E996.2 ●
      - petrol bomb E990.0 ●
  - gas E997.2
- burning aircraft E994.3 ▲
- chemical E997.2
- chlorine E997.2
- conventional warfare, specified form NEC E995.8 ▲
- crushing by falling aircraft E994.8 ▲
- depth charge E992.1 ▲
- destruction of aircraft E994.9 ▲
- detonation of own munitions (ammunition) (artillery) (mortars), unintentional E993.6 ●
- disability as sequela one year or more after injury E999.0
- discharge of own munitions launch device (autocannons) (automatic grenade launchers) (missile launchers) (small arms), unintentional E993.7 ●
- drowning E995.4 ▲
- effect nuclear weapon ▶(*see also* War operations, injury due to, nuclear weapons)◀ E996.9
- explosion (breech block) (cannon shell) E993.9 ▲
  - after cessation of hostilities
    - bomb placed in war E998.1 ●
    - mine placed in war E998.0 ●
  - aircraft E994.1 ▲
    - due to
      - enemy fire or explosives E994.0 ▲
      - own onboard explosives E994.1 ▲
  - artillery shell E993.2 ▲
  - bomb (mortar) E993.2 ▲
    - aerial E993.0 ●
    - atom ▶(*see also* War operations, injury due to, nuclear weapons)◀ E996.9 ▲
    - hydrogen ▶(*see also* War operations, injury due to, nuclear weapons)◀ E996.9 ▲
    - injury by fragments from E991.4 ▲
      - antipersonnel E991.3
    - nuclear ▶(*see also* War operations, injury due to, nuclear weapons)◀ E996.9 ▲
  - depth charge E992.1 ▲
  - injury by fragments from E991.4 ▲
    - antipersonnel E991.3
  - marine weapon ▶NEC◀ E992.8 ●
  - mine
    - at sea or in harbor E992.2 ▲
    - land E993.8 ▲
      - injury by fragments from E991.4 ▲
    - marine E992.2 ▲
  - missile, guided E993.1 ●
  - mortar E993.2 ●

War operations — *continued*
- explosion — *continued*
  - munitions (accidental) (being used in war) (dump) (factory) E993.9 ●
    - own E993.7 ●
      - ammunition (artillery) (mortars) E993.6 ●
      - launch device (autocannons) (automatic grenade launchers) (missile launchers) (small arms) E993.7 ●
  - nuclear (weapon) ▶(*see also* War operations, injury due to, nuclear weapons)◀ E996.9
  - own weapons (accidental) E993.7 ●
    - injury by fragments from E991.9 ●
      - antipersonnel E991.3
  - sea-based artillery shell E992.3 ▲
  - specified NEC E993.8 ●
  - torpedo E992.0 ▲
- exposure to ionizing radiation from nuclear explosion ▶(*see also* War operations, injury due to, nuclear weapons)◀ E996.3
- falling aircraft E994.8 ▲
- fireball effects from nuclear explosion E996.2 ▲
- fire or fire-producing device E990.9
  - flamethrower E990.1 ●
  - incendiary bomb E990.0 ●
  - incendiary bullet E990.2 ●
  - indirectly caused from conventional weapon E990.3 ●
  - petrol bomb E990.0 ●
- fragments from
  - antipersonnel bomb E991.3 ●
  - artillery shell E991.4 ▲
  - bomb NEC E991.4 ●
  - grenade E991.4 ●
  - guided missile E991.4 ●
  - land mine E991.4 ●
  - rocket E991.4 ●
  - shell E991.4 ●
  - shrapnel E991.9 ●
- fumes E997.2
- gas E997.2
- grenade (explosion) E993.8 ▲
  - fragments, injury by E991.4 ▲
- guided missile (explosion) E993.1 ▲
  - fragments, injury by E991.4 ▲
  - nuclear ▶(*see also* War operations, injury due to, nuclear weapons)◀ E996.9
- heat from nuclear explosion E996.2 ▲
- injury due to
  - aerial bomb E993.0 ●
  - air blast E993.9 ●
  - aircraft shot down E994.0 ●
  - artillery shell E993.2 ●
  - blast E993.9 ●
    - wave E993.9 ●
    - wind E993.9 ●
  - bomb E993.8 ●
  - but occurring after cessation of hostilities ●
    - explosion of bombs E998.1 ●
    - explosion of mines E998.0 ●
    - specified NEC E998.8 ●
  - conventional warfare E995.9 ●
    - specified form NEC E995.8 ●
  - depth charge E992.1 ●
  - destruction of aircraft E994.9 ●
    - due to
      - air to air missile E994.0 ●
      - collision with other aircraft E994.2 ●
      - enemy fire or explosives E994.0 ●
      - on board explosion (explosives) E994.1 ●
      - on board fire E994.3 ●
      - rocket propelled grenade [RPG] E994.0 ●
      - small arms fire E994.0 ●
      - surface to air missile E994.0 ●
    - specified NEC E994.8 ●

War operations — *continued*
- injury due to — *continued*
  - dirty bomb (*see also* War operations, injury due to, nuclear weapons) E996.9 ●
  - drowning E995.4 ●
  - explosion (direct pressure) (indirect pressure) (due to) E993.9 ●
    - depth charge E992.1 ●
    - improvised explosive device [IED]
      - person borne E993.3 ●
      - roadside E993.5 ●
      - specified NEC E993.5 ●
      - transport vehicle (air) (land) (water) borne E993.4 ●
      - vehicle (air) (land) (water) borne E993.4 ●
    - marine mines (in harbor) (at sea) E992.2 ●
    - marine weapons E992.9 ●
      - specified NEC E992.8 ●
    - sea based artillery shell E992.3 ●
    - specified NEC E993.8 ●
    - torpedo E992.0 ●
    - unintentional (of own)
      - autocannons E993.7 ●
      - automatic grenade launchers E993.7 ●
      - launch device discharge E993.7 ●
      - missile launchers E993.7 ●
      - munitions detonation (ammunition) (artillery) (mortars) E993.6 ●
      - small arms E993.7 ●
  - fragments (from) E991.9 ●
    - artillery E991.8 ●
    - artillery shells E991.4 ●
    - autocannons E991.8 ●
    - automatic grenade launchers [AGL] E991.8 ●
    - bombs E991.4 ●
      - antipersonnel E991.3 ●
    - detonation of unexploded ordnance [UXO] E991.4 ●
    - grenade E991.4 ●
    - guided missile E991.4 ●
    - improvised explosive device [IED]
      - person borne E991.5 ●
      - roadside E991.7 ●
      - specified NEC E991.7 ●
      - transport vehicle (air) (land) (water) borne E991.6 ●
      - vehicle (air) (land) (water) borne E991.6 ●
    - land mine E991.4 ●
    - missile launchers E991.8 ●
    - mortars E991.8 ●
    - munitions (artillery shells) (bombs) (grenades) (rockets) (shells) E991.4 ●
    - rockets E991.4 ●
    - shells E991.4 ●
    - small arms E991.8 ●
    - specified NEC E991.9 ●
    - weapons (artillery) (autocannons) (mortars) (small arms) E991.8 ●
  - grenade E993.8 ●
  - guided missile E993.1 ●
  - hand to hand combat, unarmed E995.0 ●
  - improvised explosive device [IED]
    - person borne E993.3 ●
    - roadside E993.5 ●
    - specified NEC E993.5 ●
    - transport vehicle (air) (land) (water) borne E993.4 ●
    - vehicle (air) (land) (water) borne E993.4 ●
  - inability to surface or obtain air E995.4 ●
  - land mine E993.8 ●
  - marine mines (in harbor) (at sea) E992.2 ●
  - marine weapons E992.9 ●
    - specified NEC E992.8 ●
  - mortar E993.2 ●
  - nuclear weapons E996.9 ●
    - beta burns E996.3 ●
    - blast debris E996.1 ●

War operations — *continued*
- injury due to — *continued*
  - nuclear weapons (*see also* War operations, injury due to, nuclear weapons) E996.9 ● — *continued*
    - blast pressure E996.0 ●
    - burns due to thermal radiation E996.2 ●
    - direct blast effect E996.0 ●
    - fallout exposure E996.3 ●
    - fireball effect E996.2 ●
    - flash burns E996.2 ●
    - heat effect E996.2 ●
    - indirect blast effect E996.1 ●
    - nuclear radiation effects E996.3 ●
    - radiation exposure (acute) E996.3 ●
    - radiation sickness E996.3 ●
    - secondary effects E996.3 ●
    - specified effects NEC E996.8 ●
    - thermal radiation effect E996.2 ●
  - piercing object E995.2 ●
  - restriction of airway, intentional E995.3 ●
  - sea based artillery shell E992.3 ●
  - shrapnel E991.9 ●
  - stave E995.1 ●
  - strangulation E995.3 ●
  - strike by blunt object (baton) (nightstick) (stave) E995.1 ●
  - submersion (accidental) (unintentional) E995.4 ●
    - intentional E995.3 ●
  - suffocation E995.3 ●
    - accidental E995.4 ●
  - torpedo E992.0 ●
  - underwater blast E992.9 ●
  - weapon of mass destruction [WMD] E997.3 ●
- knife E995.2 ●
- lacrimator (gas) (chemical) E997.2
- land mine (explosion) E993.8 ▲
  - after cessation of hostilities E998.0 ▲
  - fragments, injury by E991.4 ▲
- laser(s) E997.0
- late effect of E999.0
- lewisite E997.2
- lung irritant (chemical) (fumes) (gas) E997.2
- marine mine E992.2 ▲
- mine
  - after cessation of hostilities E998.0 ▲
  - at sea E992.2 ▲
  - in harbor E992.2 ▲
  - land (explosion) E993.8 ▲
    - fragments, injury by E991.4 ▲
  - marine E992.2 ▲
- missile (guided) (explosion) E993.1 ▲
  - fragments, injury by E991.4 ▲
  - marine E992.8 ▲
  - nuclear ▶(*see also* War operations, injury due to, nuclear weapons)◀ E996.9 ▲
- mortar bomb (explosion) E993.2 ▲
  - fragments, injury by E991.4 ▲
- mustard gas E997.2
- nerve gas E997.2
- phosgene E997.2
- piercing object E995.2 ●
- poisoning (chemical) (fumes) (gas) E997.2
- radiation, ionizing from nuclear explosion ▶(*see also* War operations, injury due to, nuclear weapons)◀ E996.3 ▲
- rocket (explosion) E993.8 ▲
  - fragments, injury by E991.4 ▲
- saber, sabre E995.2 ▲
- screening smoke E997.8
- shell (aircraft) (artillery) (cannon) (land based) (explosion) E993.2 ▲
  - fragments, injury by E991.4 ▲
  - sea-based E992.3 ▲
- shooting E991.2
  - after cessation of hostilities E998.8 ▲
  - bullet(s) E991.2
    - rubber E991.0
  - pellet(s) (rifle) E991.1
  - shrapnel E991.9
  - submersion E995 ☑
  - torpedo E992 ☑
- stave E995.2 ●

☑ Additional Digit Required — Refer to the Tabular List for Digit Selection   ▽ Subterms under main terms may continue to next column or page

2010 ICD-9-CM   ▶◀ Revised Text   ● New Line   ▲ Revised Code   October 2009 • Volume 2 — 337

War operations — *continued*
　strike by blunt object (baton) (nightstick)　●
　　(stave) E995.1　　　　　　　　　　　　　　●
　submersion E995.4　　　　　　　　　　　　　▲
　　intentional E995.3　　　　　　　　　　　　●
　sword E995.2　　　　　　　　　　　　　　　●
　torpedo E992.0　　　　　　　　　　　　　　▲
　unconventional warfare, except by nuclear
　　weapon E997.9
　　biological (warfare) E997.1
　　gas, fumes, chemicals E997.2
　　laser(s) E997.0
　　specified type NEC E997.8

War operations — *continued*
　underwater blast E992.9　　　　　　　　　　▲
　vesicant (chemical) (fumes) (gas) E997.2
　weapon burst E993.9　　　　　　　　　　　　▲
Washed
　away by flood — *see* Flood
　away by tidal wave — *see* Tidal wave
　off road by storm (transport vehicle) E908.9
　overboard E832　☑
Weapon of mass destruction [WMD] E997.3　●
Weather exposure — *see also* Exposure
　cold E901.0
　hot E900.0

Weightlessness (causing injury) (effects of) (in
　spacecraft, real or simulated) E928.0
Wound (accidental) NEC — *see also* Injury E928.9
　battle (*see also* War operations) E995.9　　▲
　bayonet E920.3
　　in
　　　legal intervention E974
　　　war operations E995.2　　　　　　　　　▲
　gunshot — *see* Shooting
　incised — *see* Cut
　saber, sabre E920.3
　　in war operations E995.2　　　　　　　　　▲

Wrong　　　　　　　　　　　　　　　　　　●
　body part, performance of correct operation　●
　　(procedure) on E876.7
　device implanted into correct surgical site　●
　　E876.5
　patient, performance of operation (proce-　　●
　　dure) on E876.6
　procedure (operation) performed on correct ●
　　patient E876.5
　side, performance of correct operation　　　●
　　(procedure) on E876.7
　site, performance of correct operation (pro-　●
　　cedure) on E876.7

☑ Additional Digit Required — Refer to the Tabular List for Digit Selection　　　　　　　　　　　　　　　　　▽ Subterms under main terms may continue to next column or page

338 — Volume 2 • October 2009　　　　　　　▶◀ Revised Text　　　　　● New Line　　▲ Revised Code　　　　　　　2010 ICD-9-CM

Railway Accidents (E800-E807)

The following fourth-digit subdivisions are for use with categories E800-E807 to identify the injured person:

.0 **Railway employee**
Any person who by virtue of his employment in connection with a railway, whether by the railway company or not, is at increased risk of involvement in a railway accident, such as:
catering staff on train
postal staff on train
driver
railway fireman
guard
shunter
porter
sleeping car attendant

.1 **Passenger on railway**
Any authorized person traveling on a train, except a railway employee
EXCLUDES   intending passenger waiting at station (.8)
unauthorized rider on railway vehicle (.8)

.2 **Pedestrian** See definition (r), E-Codes-2

.3 **Pedal cyclist** See definition (p), E-Codes-2

.8 **Other specified person** Intending passenger waiting at station
Unauthorized rider on railway vehicle

.9 **Unspecified person**

Motor Vehicle Traffic and Nontraffic Accidents (E810-E825)

The following fourth-digit subdivisions are for use with categories E810-E819 and E820-E825 to identify the injured person:

.0 **Driver of motor vehicle other than motorcycle** See definition (1), E-Codes-2

.1 **Passenger in motor vehicle other than motorcycle** See definition (1), E-Codes-2

.2 **Motorcyclist** See definition (1), E-Codes-2

.3 **Passenger on motorcycle** See definition (1), E-Codes-2

.4 **Occupant of streetcar**

.5 **Rider of animal; occupant of animal-drawn vehicle**

.6 **Pedal cyclist** See definition (p), E-Codes-2

.7 **Pedestrian** See definition (r), E-Codes-2

.8 **Other specified person**
Occupant of vehicle other than above
Person in railway train involved in accident
Unauthorized rider of motor vehicle

.9 **Unspecified person**

Other Road Vehicle Accidents (E826-E829)

(animal-drawn vehicle, streetcar, pedal cycle, and other nonmotor road vehicle accidents)

The following fourth-digit subdivisions are for use with categories E826-E829 to identify the injured person:

.0 **Pedestrian** See definition (r), E-Codes-2

.1 **Pedal cyclist** (does not apply to codes E827, E828, E829) See definition (p), E-Codes-2

.2 **Rider of animal** (does not apply to code E829)

.3 **Occupant of animal-drawn vehicle** (does not apply to codes E828, E829)

.4 **Occupant of streetcar**

.8 **Other specified person**

.9 **Unspecified person**

Water Transport Accidents (E830-E838)

The following fourth-digit subdivisions are for use with categories E830-E838 to identify the injured person:

.0 **Occupant of small boat, unpowered**

.1 **Occupant of small boat, powered** See definition (t), E-Codes-2
EXCLUDES   water skier (.4)

.2 **Occupant of other watercraft — crew**
Persons:
engaged in operation of watercraft
providing passenger services [cabin attendants, ship's physician, catering personnel]
working on ship during voyage in other capacity [musician in band, operators of shops and beauty parlors]

.3 **Occupant of other watercraft — other than crew**
Passenger
Occupant of lifeboat, other than crew, after abandoning ship

.4 **Water skier**

.5 **Swimmer**

.6 **Dockers, stevedores**
Longshoreman employed on the dock in loading and unloading ships

.8 **Other specified person**
Immigration and custom officials on board ship
Persons:
accompanying passenger or member of crew visiting boat
Pilot (guiding ship into port)

.9 **Unspecified person**

Air and Space Transport Accidents (E840-E845)

The following fourth-digit subdivisions are for use with categories E840-E845 to identify the injured person:

.0 **Occupant of spacecraft**
Crew
Passenger (civilian)
(military)   } in military aircraft [air force]
Troops   [army] [national guard] [navy]

.1 **Occupant of military aircraft, any**
EXCLUDES   occupants of aircraft operated under jurisdiction of police departments (.5) parachutist (.7)

.2 **Crew of commercial aircraft (powered) in surface to surface transport**

.3 **Other occupant of commercial aircraft (powered) in surface to surface transport**
Flight personnel:
not part of crew
on familiarization flight Passenger on aircraft

.4 **Occupant of commercial aircraft (powered) in surface to air transport**
Occupant [crew] [passenger] of aircraft (powered) engaged in activities, such as:
air drops of emergency supplies
air drops of parachutists, except from military craft
crop dusting
lowering of construction material [bridge or telephone pole]
sky writing

.5 **Occupant of other powered aircraft**
Occupant [crew] [passenger] of aircraft (powered) engaged in activities, such as:
aerial spraying (crops)(fire retardants)
aerobatic flying
aircraft racing
rescue operation
storm surveillance
traffic suveillance
Occupant of private plane NOS

.6 **Occupant of unpowered aircraft, except parachutist**
Occupant of aircraft classifiable to E842

.7 **Parachutist (military)(other)**
Person making voluntary descent
person making descent after accident to aircraft (.1-.6)

.8 **Ground crew, airline employee**
Persons employed at airfields (civil)(military) or launching pads, not occupants of aircraft

.9 **Other person**

☑ Additional Digit Required — Refer to the Tabular List for Digit Selection

▽ Subterms under main terms may continue to next column or page

795.71 Inconclusive HIV test result

1. INFECTIOUS AND PARASITIC DISEASES (001-139)

Note: Categories for "late effects" of infectious and parasitic diseases are to be found at 137-139.

INCLUDES diseases generally recognized as communicable or transmissible as well as a few diseases of unknown but possibly infectious origin

EXCLUDES acute respiratory infections (460-466)
carrier or suspected carrier of infectious organism (V02.0-V02.9)
certain localized infections
influenza ►(487.0-487.8, 488.0-488.1)◄

INTESTINAL INFECTIOUS DISEASES (001-009)

EXCLUDES helminthiases (120.0-129)

✓4ᵗʰ 001 Cholera

DEF: An acute infectious enteritis caused by a potent enterotoxin produced by *Vibrio cholerae*; changes the permeability of the mucosa of the intestines and leads to diarrhea and dehydration.

001.0 Due to Vibrio cholerae CC
CC Excl: 001.0-001.9

001.1 Due to Vibrio cholerae el tor CC
CC Excl: See code: 001.0

001.9 Cholera, unspecified CC
CC Excl: See code: 001.0

✓4ᵗʰ 002 Typhoid and paratyphoid fevers

DEF: Typhoid fever: an acute generalized illness caused by *Salmonella typhi*; clinical features are fever, headache, abdominal pain, cough, toxemia, leukopenia, abnormal pulse, rose spots on the skin, bacteremia, hyperplasia of intestinal lymph nodes, mesenteric lymphadenopathy, and Peyer's patches in the intestines.
DEF: Paratyphoid fever: a prolonged febrile illness, caused by salmonella serotypes other than *S. typhi*, especially *S. enteritidis* serotypes paratyphi A and B and *S. choleraesuis*.

002.0 Typhoid fever CC
Typhoid (fever) (infection) [any site]
CC Excl: 002.0-002.9

002.1 Paratyphoid fever A CC
CC Excl: See code: 002.0

002.2 Paratyphoid fever B CC
CC Excl: See code: 002.0

002.3 Paratyphoid fever C CC
CC Excl: See code: 002.0

002.9 Paratyphoid fever, unspecified CC
CC Excl: See code: 002.0

✓4ᵗʰ 003 Other salmonella infections

INCLUDES infection or food poisoning by Salmonella [any serotype]

DEF: Infections caused by a genus of gram-negative, anaerobic bacteria of the family *Enterobacteriaceae*; major symptoms are enteric fevers, acute gastroenteritis and septicemia.

003.0 Salmonella gastroenteritis CC
Salmonellosis
CC Excl: 002.0, 002.9-003.0, 004.9-005.2, 007.5, 008.00-009.0, 040.41-040.42, 536.8, 558.2-558.3, 558.9, 564.1, 567.21, 567.23, 567.31-567.39, 567.89,777.50-777.53, 777.8

003.1 Salmonella septicemia MCC HIV
CC Excl: 003.1, 020.2, 022.3, 036.2, 038.0-038.9, 040.89-041.85, 041.89-041.9, 054.5, 139.8, 771.81, 771.83-771.89, 995.90-995.94, V09.0-V09.91

✓5ᵗʰ 003.2 Localized salmonella infections

003.20 Localized salmonella infection, unspecified HIV

003.21 Salmonella meningitis MCC HIV
CC Excl: 003.21, 013.00-013.16, 036.0, 047.0-047.9, 049.0-049.1, 072.1, 078.88-078.89, 079.81, 079.88-079.99, 090.42, 091.81, 094.2, 098.89, 100.81, 112.83, 114.2, 115.01, 115.11, 115.91, 130.0, 139.8, 320.0-322.9, 349.89-349.9

003.22 Salmonella pneumonia MCC HIV
CC Excl: 003.22, 011.00-012.16, 012.80-012.86, 017.90-017.96, 020.3-020.5, 021.3, 022.1, 031.0, 039.1, 073.0, 115.05, 115.15, 115.95, 122.1, 130.4, 136.3, 480.0-480.2, 480.8-482.41, 482.49-487.1, 488, 495.0-495.7, 500, 502-508.9, 517.1, 517.8, 518.89, 519.8-519.9

003.23 Salmonella arthritis CC HIV
CC Excl: 003.23, 015.80-015.96, 036.82, 056.71, 098.50-098.51, 098.59, 098.89, 711.00-714.0, 715.00, 715.09-715.10, 715.18-716.99, 718.00-718.08, 719.00-719.10, 719.18-719.69, 719.80-719.99

003.24 Salmonella osteomyelitis CC HIV
CC Excl: 003.24, 015.50-015.56, 015.70-015.76, 015.90-015.96, 730.00-730.39, 730.80-730.99

003.29 Other CC HIV
CC Excl: 003.29

003.8 Other specified salmonella infections CC HIV
CC Excl: 003.8

003.9 Salmonella infection, unspecified CC HIV
CC Excl: 003.9

✓4ᵗʰ 004 Shigellosis

INCLUDES bacillary dysentery

DEF: Acute infectious dysentery caused by the genus *Shigella*, of the family *Enterobacteriaceae*; affecting the colon causing blood-stained stools, tenesmus, abdominal cramps and fever.

004.0 Shigella dysenteriae CC
Infection by group A Shigella (Schmitz) (Shiga)
CC Excl: 001.1, 002.0, 002.9-003.0, 004.0, 004.9-005.2, 006.0-006.2, 006.9, 007.1-007.9, 008.1-008.3, 008.5, 008.8-009.0, 014.80-014.86, 040.41-040.42, 112.85, 129, 487.8, 536.3, 536.8, 555.0-557.9, 558.2-558.3, 558.9, 564.1, 775.0-775.7, 775.9, 777.50-777.53, 777.8

004.1 Shigella flexneri
Infection by group B Shigella

004.2 Shigella boydii
Infection by group C Shigella

004.3 Shigella sonnei
Infection by group D Shigella

004.8 Other specified Shigella infections

004.9 Shigellosis, unspecified

✓4ᵗʰ 005 Other food poisoning (bacterial)

EXCLUDES salmonella infections (003.0-003.9)
toxic effect of:
food contaminants (989.7)
noxious foodstuffs (988.0-988.9)

DEF: Enteritis caused by ingesting contaminated foods and characterized by diarrhea, abdominal pain, vomiting; symptoms may be mild or life threatening.

005.0 Staphylococcal food poisoning CC
Staphylococcal toxemia specified as due to food
CC Excl: 001.0-009.3, 040.41-040.42

005.1 Botulism food poisoning CC
Botulism NOS
Food poisoning due to Clostridium botulinum
EXCLUDES infant botulism (040.41)
wound botulism (040.42)
CC Excl: 005.0-005.2, 008.45-008.46, 040.41-040.42

005.2 Food poisoning due to Clostridium perfringens [C. welchii] CC
Enteritis necroticans
CC Excl: 003.0, 004.9-005.2, 007.5, 008.00-009.0, 040.41-040.42, 487.8, 536.3, 536.8, 558.2-558.9, 564.1, 567.21, 567.23, 567.31-567.39, 567.89, 777.50-777.53, 777.8

005.3 Food poisoning due to other Clostridia CC
CC Excl: See code: 005.0

005.4 Food poisoning due to Vibrio parahaemolyticus CC
CC Excl: See code: 005.0

Infectious and Parasitic Diseases

005.8–008.3

√5ᵗʰ **005.8**   **Other bacterial food poisoning**

> **EXCLUDES**   *salmonella food poisoning (003.0-003.9)*

005.81   **Food poisoning due to Vibrio vulnificus**   `CC`
> **CC Excl:** See code: 005.0

005.89   **Other bacterial food poisoning**   `CC`
> Food poisoning due to Bacillus cereus
> **CC Excl:** See code: 005.0

005.9   **Food poisoning, unspecified**

√4ᵗʰ **006**   **Amebiasis**

> **INCLUDES**   infection due to Entamoeba histolytica
>
> **EXCLUDES**   *amebiasis due to organisms other than Entamoeba histolytica (007.8)*

DEF: Infection of the large intestine caused by *Entamoeba histolytica*; usually asymptomatic but symptoms may range from mild diarrhea to profound life-threatening dysentery. Extraintestinal complications include hepatic abscess, which may rupture, causing life-threatening infections.

006.0   **Acute amebic dysentery without mention of abscess**   `CC`
> Acute amebiasis
> **DEF:** Sudden, severe *Entamoeba histolytica* infection causing bloody stools.
> **CC Excl:** 006.0-006.1, 007.5

006.1   **Chronic intestinal amebiasis without mention of abscess**   `CC`
> Chronic:
>   amebiasis
>   amebic dysentery
> **CC Excl:** See code: 006.0

006.2   **Amebic nondysenteric colitis**   `CC`
> **DEF:** *Entamoeba histolytica* infection with inflamed colon but no dysentery.
> **CC Excl:** 003.0, 004.9-005.0, 005.2, 006.0-006.2, 006.9, 007.1-009.0, 129, 487.8, 536.3, 536.8, 555.0-557.9, 558.2-558.9, 564.1, 777.50-777.53, 777.8

006.3   **Amebic liver abscess**   `MCC`
> Hepatic amebiasis
> **CC Excl:** 006.3, 572.0

006.4   **Amebic lung abscess**   `MCC`
> Amebic abscess of lung (and liver)
> **CC Excl:** 006.4, 513.0

006.5   **Amebic brain abscess**   `MCC`
> Amebic abscess of brain (and liver) (and lung)
> **CC Excl:** 006.5, 324.0

006.6   **Amebic skin ulceration**
> Cutaneous amebiasis

006.8   **Amebic infection of other sites**   `CC`
> Amebic: Ameboma
>   appendicitis
>   balanitis
> **EXCLUDES**   *specific infections by free-living amebae (136.21-136.29)*
> **CC Excl:** 006.0-006.5, 006.8

006.9   **Amebiasis, unspecified**
> Amebiasis NOS

√4ᵗʰ **007**   **Other protozoal intestinal diseases**

> **INCLUDES**   protozoal:
>   colitis
>   diarrhea
>   dysentery

007.0   **Balantidiasis**
> Infection by Balantidium coli

007.1   **Giardiasis**   `CC`
> Infection by Giardia lamblia
> Lambliasis
> **CC Excl:** 003.0, 004.9-005.0, 005.2, 006.0-006.2, 006.9, 007.1-009.0, 129, 487.8, 536.3, 536.8, 558.2-558.9, 564.1

007.2   **Coccidiosis**   `CC` `HIV`
> Infection by Isospora belli and Isospora hominis
> Isosporiasis
> **CC Excl:** See code: 007.1

007.3   **Intestinal trichomoniasis**
> **DEF:** Colitis, diarrhea, or dysentery caused by the protozoa *Trichomonas.*

007.4   **Cryptosporidiosis**   `CC`
> **DEF:** An intestinal infection by protozoan parasites causing intractable diarrhea in patients with AIDS and other immunosuppressed individuals.
> **CC Excl:** See code: 007.1
> **AHA:** 4Q, '97, 30

007.5   **Cyclosporiasis**   `CC`
> **DEF:** An infection of the small intestine by the protozoal organism, *Cyclospora caytenanesis,* spread to humans though ingestion of contaminated water or food. Symptoms include watery diarrhea, loss of appetite, increased gas, stomach cramps, nausea, vomiting, muscle aches, low grade fever, and fatigue.
> **CC Excl:** 003.0, 004.9-005.0, 005.2, 006.0-006.2, 006.9, 007.1-009.0, 129, 487.8, 536.3, 536.8, 558.2-558.9, 564.1, 567.21, 567.23, 567.31-567.39, 567.89
> **AHA:** 4Q, '00, 38

007.8   **Other specified protozoal intestinal diseases**   `CC`
> Amebiasis due to organisms other than Entamoeba histolytica
> **CC Excl:** See code: 007.1

007.9   **Unspecified protozoal intestinal disease**   `CC`
> Flagellate diarrhea
> Protozoal dysentery NOS
> **CC Excl:** See code: 007.1

√4ᵗʰ **008**   **Intestinal infections due to other organisms**

> **INCLUDES**   any condition classifiable to 009.0-009.3 with mention of the responsible organisms
>
> **EXCLUDES**   *food poisoning by these organisms (005.0-005.9)*

√5ᵗʰ **008.0**   **Escherichia coli [E. coli]**
> **AHA:** 4Q, '92, 17

008.00   **E. coli, unspecified**   `CC`
> E. coli enteritis NOS
> **CC Excl:** 003.0, 004.9-005.0, 005.2, 007.5, 008.00-009.0, 487.8, 536.3, 536.8, 558.2-558.9, 564.1, 567.21, 567.23, 567.31-567.39, 567.89, 777.50-777.53, 777.8

008.01   **Enteropathogenic E. coli**   `CC`
> **DEF:** *E. coli* causing inflammation of intestines.
> **CC Excl:** See code: 008.00

008.02   **Enterotoxigenic E. coli**   `CC`
> **DEF:** A toxic reaction to *E. coli* of the intestinal mucosa, causing voluminous watery secretions.
> **CC Excl:** See code: 008.00

008.03   **Enteroinvasive E. coli**   `CC`
> **DEF:** *E. coli* infection penetrating intestinal mucosa.
> **CC Excl:** See code: 008.00

008.04   **Enterohemorrhagic E. coli**   `CC`
> **DEF:** *E. coli* infection penetrating the intestinal mucosa, producing microscopic ulceration and bleeding.
> **CC Excl:** See code: 008.00

008.09   **Other intestinal E. coli infections**   `CC`
> **CC Excl:** See code: 008.00

008.1   **Arizona group of paracolon bacilli**   `CC`
> **CC Excl:** See code: 008.00

008.2   **Aerobacter aerogenes**   `CC`
> Enterobacter aeogenes
> **CC Excl:** See code: 008.00

008.3   **Proteus (mirabilis) (morganii)**   `CC`
> **CC Excl:** See code: 008.00

`N` Newborn Age: 0   `P` Pediatric Age: 0-17   `M` Maternity Age: 12-55   `A` Adult Age: 15-124   `MCC` Major CC Condition   `CC` CC Condition   `HIV` HIV Related Dx

✓5th 008.4 **Other specified bacteria**
AHA: 4Q, '92, 18

008.41 **Staphylococcus** `CC`
Staphylococcal enterocolitis
CC Excl: 001.1, 002.0, 002.9-003.0, 004.9-005.2,
006.0-006.2, 006.9, 007.1-009.0, 014.80-014.86,
040.41-040.42, 112.85, 129, 487.8, 536.3, 536.8,
555.0-557.9, 558.2-558.9, 564.1, 775.0-775.7, 775.9,
777.50-777.53, 777.8

008.42 **Pseudomonas** `CC`
CC Excl: See code: 008.41
AHA: 2Q, '89, 10

008.43 **Campylobacter** `CC`
CC Excl: See code 008.41

008.44 **Yersinia enterocolitica** `CC`
CC Excl: See code 008.41

008.45 **Clostridium difficile** `CC`
Pseudomembranous colitis
DEF: An overgrowth of a species of bacterium that is
a part of the normal colon flora in human infants
and sometimes in adults; produces a toxin that
causes pseudomembranous enterocolitis.; typically
is seen in patients undergoing antibiotic therapy.
CC Excl: See code: 008.41
A04.7 Enterocolitis due to clostridium difficile `I-10`

008.46 **Other anaerobes** `CC`
Anaerobic enteritis NOS
Bacteroides (fragilis)
Gram-negative anaerobes
CC Excl: See code: 008.41

008.47 **Other gram-negative bacteria** `CC`
Gram-negative enteritis NOS
EXCLUDES gram-negative anaerobes (008.46)
CC Excl: See code 008.41

008.49 **Other** `CC`
CC Excl: See code: 008.41
AHA: 2Q, '89, 10; 1Q, '88, 6

008.5 **Bacterial enteritis, unspecified** `CC`
CC Excl: 001.1, 002.0, 002.9-003.0, 004.9-005.0, 005.2,
006.0-006.2, 006.9, 007.1-009.0, 014.80-014.86, 112.85, 129,
487.8, 536.3, 536.8, 558.2-558.9, 564.1, 567.21, 567.23,
567.31-567.39, 567.89, 777.50-777.53, 777.8

✓5th 008.6 **Enteritis due to specified virus**
AHA: 4Q, '92, 18

008.61 **Rotavirus** `CC`
CC Excl: 003.0, 004.9-005.0, 005.2, 006.0-006.2, 006.9,
007.1-009.0, 014.80-014.86, 112.85, 129, 487.8,
536.3, 536.8, 558.2-558.9, 564.1, 567.21, 567.23,
567.31-567.39, 567.89, 777.50-777.53, 777.8

008.62 **Adenovirus** `CC`
CC Excl: See code: 008.61

008.63 **Norwalk virus** `CC`
▶Norovirus◀
Norwalk-like agent
CC Excl: See code: 008.61

008.64 **Other small round viruses [SRVs]** `CC`
Small round virus NOS
CC Excl: See code: 008.61

008.65 **Calicivirus** `CC`
DEF: Enteritis due to a subgroup of *Picornaviruses*.
CC Excl: See code: 008.61

008.66 **Astrovirus** `CC`
CC Excl: See code: 008.61

008.67 **Enterovirus NEC** `CC`
Coxsackie virus
Echovirus
EXCLUDES poliovirus (045.0-045.9)
CC Excl: See code: 008.61

008.69 **Other viral enteritis** `CC`
Torovirus
CC Excl: See code: 008.61
AHA: 1Q, '03, 10

008.8 **Other organism, not elsewhere classified**
Viral:
enteritis NOS
gastroenteritis
EXCLUDES influenza with involvement of gastrointestinal
tract (487.8)
A08.4 Viral intestinal infection unspecified `I-10`

✓4th 009 **Ill-defined intestinal infections**
EXCLUDES diarrheal disease or intestinal infection due to specified
organism (001.0-008.8)
diarrhea following gastrointestinal surgery (564.4)
intestinal malabsorption (579.0-579.9)
ischemic enteritis (557.0-557.9)
other noninfectious gastroenteritis and colitis
(558.1-558.9)
regional enteritis (555.0-555.9)
ulcerative colitis (556)

009.0 **Infectious colitis, enteritis, and gastroenteritis** `CC`
Colitis ⎫
Enteritis ⎬ septic
Gastroenteritis ⎭
Dysentery:
NOS
catarrhal
hemorrhagic
DEF: Colitis: An inflammation of mucous membranes of the
colon.
DEF: Enteritis: An inflammation of mucous membranes of the
small intestine.
DEF: Gastroenteritis: An inflammation of mucous membranes
of stomach and intestines.
CC Excl: 001.0-009.3, 040.41-040.42
AHA: 3Q, '99, 4
A09 Infectious gastroenteritis and colitis unspec `I-10`

009.1 **Colitis, enteritis, and gastroenteritis of presumed** `CC`
infectious origin
EXCLUDES colitis NOS (558.9)
enteritis NOS (558.9)
gastroenteritis NOS (558.9)
CC Excl: 009.1
AHA: 3Q, '99, 6

009.2 **Infectious diarrhea** `CC`
Diarrhea:
dysenteric
epidemic
Infectious diarrheal disease NOS
CC Excl: See code: 009.0

009.3 **Diarrhea of presumed infectious origin** `CC`
EXCLUDES diarrhea NOS (787.91)
CC Excl: 009.3
AHA: N-D, '87, 7

✓4th ✓5th Additional Digit Required   Unacceptable PDx   Manifestation Code   Hospital Acquired Condition   ▶◀ Revised Text   ● New Code   ▲ Revised Code Title

2010 ICD-9-CM   **October 2009 · Volume 1 – 3**

008.4–009.3

Infectious and Parasitic Diseases

010–013.5

TUBERCULOSIS (010-018)

INCLUDES infection by Mycobacterium tuberculosis (human) (bovine)

EXCLUDES *congenital tuberculosis (771.2)*
late effects of tuberculosis (137.0-137.4)

The following fifth digit subclassification is for use with categories 010-018:
0 unspecified
1 bacteriological or histological examination not done
2 bacteriological or histological examination unknown (at present)
3 tubercle bacilli found (in sputum) by microscopy
4 tubercle bacilli not found (in sputum) by microscopy, but found by bacterial culture
5 tubercle bacilli not found by bacteriological examination, but tuberculosis confirmed histologically
6 tubercle bacilli not found by bacteriological or histological examination but tuberculosis confirmed by other methods [inoculation of animals]

DEF: An infection by *Mycobacterium tuberculosis* causing the formation of small, rounded nodules, called tubercles, that can disseminate throughout the body via lymph and blood vessels. Localized tuberculosis is most often seen in the lungs.

√4th **010 Primary tuberculous infection**

DEF: Tuberculosis of the lungs occurring when the patient is first infected.

§ √5th **010.0 Primary tuberculous infection** CC HIV
[0-6] **EXCLUDES** *nonspecific reaction to tuberculin skin test without active tuberculosis (795.5)*
positive PPD (795.5)
positive tuberculin skin test without active tuberculosis (795.5)
CC Excl: 010.00-018.96
DEF: Hilar or paratracheal lymph node enlargement in pulmonary tuberculosis.

§ √5th **010.1 Tuberculous pleurisy in primary progressive tuberculosis** CC HIV
[0-6] **CC Excl:** See code: 010.0
DEF: Inflammation and exudation in the lining of the tubercular lung.

§ √5th **010.8 Other primary progressive tuberculosis** CC HIV
[0-6] **EXCLUDES** *tuberculous erythema nodosum (017.1)*
CC Excl: See code: 010.0

§ √5th **010.9 Primary tuberculous infection, unspecified** CC HIV
[0-6] **CC Excl:** See code: 010.0

√4th **011 Pulmonary tuberculosis**
Use additional code to identify any associated silicosis (502)

§ √5th **011.0 Tuberculosis of lung, infiltrative** CC HIV
[0-6] **CC Excl:** 011.00-012.86, 017.90-018.96, 031.0, 031.2-031.9, 041.81-041.9, 137.0, 139.8, 480.0-480.2, 480.8-487.1, 488, 494.0-508.9, 517.1, 518.89

§ √5th **011.1 Tuberculosis of lung, nodular** CC HIV
[0-6] **CC Excl:** See code: 011.0

§ √5th **011.2 Tuberculosis of lung with cavitation** CC HIV
[0-6] **CC Excl:** See code: 011.0

§ √5th **011.3 Tuberculosis of bronchus** CC HIV
[0-6] **EXCLUDES** *isolated bronchial tuberculosis (012.2)*
CC Excl: See code: 011.0

§ √5th **011.4 Tuberculous fibrosis of lung** CC HIV
[0-6] **CC Excl:** See code: 011.0

§ √5th **011.5 Tuberculous bronchiectasis** CC HIV
[0-6] **CC Excl:** See code: 011.0

§ √5th **011.6 Tuberculous pneumonia [any form]** MCC HIV
[0-6] **DEF:** Inflammatory pulmonary reaction to tuberculous cells.
CC Excl: For codes 011.60-011.65: See code 011.0; **For code 011.66:** 011.66, 139.8, 480.0-480.2, 480.8-487.1, 488, 494.0-508.9, 517.1, 518.89

§ √5th **011.7 Tuberculous pneumothorax** CC HIV
[0-6] **DEF:** Spontaneous rupture of damaged tuberculous pulmonary tissue.
CC Excl: See code: 011.0

§ √5th **011.8 Other specified pulmonary tuberculosis** CC HIV
[0-6] **CC Excl:** See code: 011.0

§ √5th **011.9 Pulmonary tuberculosis, unspecified** CC HIV
[0-6] Respiratory tuberculosis NOS
Tuberculosis of lung NOS
CC Excl: See code: 011.0

√4th **012 Other respiratory tuberculosis**
EXCLUDES *respiratory tuberculosis, unspecified (011.9)*

§ √5th **012.0 Tuberculous pleurisy** CC HIV
[0-6] Tuberculosis of pleura
Tuberculous empyema
Tuberculous hydrothorax
EXCLUDES *pleurisy with effusion without mention of cause (511.9)*
tuberculous pleurisy in primary progressive tuberculosis (010.1)
DEF: Inflammation and exudation in the lining of the tubercular lung.
CC Excl: 011.00-012.86, 017.90-018.96, 031.0, 031.2-031.9, 041.81-041.9, 137.0, 139.8, 480.0-480.2, 480.8-487.1, 488, 494.0-508.9, 517.1, 518.89

§ √5th **012.1 Tuberculosis of intrathoracic lymph nodes** CC HIV
[0-6] Tuberculosis of lymph nodes:
hilar
mediastinal
tracheobronchial
Tuberculous tracheobronchial adenopathy
EXCLUDES *that specified as primary (010.0-010.9)*
CC Excl: See code: 012.0

§ √5th **012.2 Isolated tracheal or bronchial tuberculosis** CC HIV
[0-6] **CC Excl:** 010.00-014.86, 018.00-018.96

§ √5th **012.3 Tuberculous laryngitis** CC HIV
[0-6] Tuberculosis of glottis
CC Excl: See code: 012.2

§ √5th **012.8 Other specified respiratory tuberculosis** CC HIV
[0-6] Tuberculosis of:
mediastinum
nasopharynx
nose (septum)
sinus [any nasal]
CC Excl: See code: 012.2

√4th **013 Tuberculosis of meninges and central nervous system**

§ √5th **013.0 Tuberculous meningitis** MCC HIV
[0-6] Tuberculosis of meninges (cerebral) (spinal)
Tuberculous:
leptomeningitis
meningoencephalitis
EXCLUDES *tuberculoma of meninges (013.1)*
CC Excl: 003.21, 013.00-013.16, 013.40-013.56, 013.80-013.96, 017.90-017.96, 031.2-031.9, 036.0, 041.81-041.9, 047.0-047.9, 049.0-049.1, 053.0, 054.72, 072.1, 090.42, 091.81, 094.2, 098.89, 100.81, 112.83, 114.2, 115.01, 115.11, 115.91, 130.0, 137.1, 139.8, 320.0-322.9, 349.89-349.9, 357.0

§ √5th **013.1 Tuberculoma of meninges** MCC HIV
[0-6] **CC Excl:** See code: 013.0

§ √5th **013.2 Tuberculoma of brain** MCC HIV
[0-6] Tuberculosis of brain (current disease)
CC Excl: 013.20-013.36, 013.60-013.96, 017.90-017.96, 031.2-031.9, 041.81-041.9, 137.1, 139.8

§ √5th **013.3 Tuberculous abscess of brain** MCC HIV
[0-6] **CC Excl:** See code: 013.2

§ √5th **013.4 Tuberculoma of spinal cord** MCC HIV
[0-6] **CC Excl:** 013.00-013.16, 013.40-013.56, 013.80-013.96, 017.90-017.96, 031.2-031.9, 041.81-041.9, 137.1, 139.8

§ √5th **013.5 Tuberculous abscess of spinal cord** MCC HIV
[0-6] **CC Excl:** See code: 013.4

§ Requires fifth digit. Valid digits are in [brackets] under each code. See beginning of section 010-018 for codes and definitions.

N Newborn Age: 0   P Pediatric Age: 0-17   M Maternity Age: 12-55   A Adult Age: 15-124   MCC Major CC Condition   CC CC Condition   HIV HIV Related Dx

§ ✓5th **013.6 Tuberculous encephalitis or myelitis** `MCC` `HIV`
[0-6]   CC Excl: See code: 013.2

§ ✓5th **013.8 Other specified tuberculosis of central** `MCC` `HIV`
[0-6]   **nervous system**
           CC Excl: 013.80-013.96, 017.90-017.96, 031.2-031.9,
           041.81-041.9, 137.1, 139.8

§ ✓5th **013.9 Unspecified tuberculosis of central** `MCC` `HIV`
[0-6]   **nervous system**
           Tuberculosis of central nervous system NOS
           CC Excl: See code: 013.8

✓4th **014 Tuberculosis of intestines, peritoneum, and mesenteric glands**

§ ✓5th **014.0 Tuberculous peritonitis** `MCC` `HIV`
[0-6]   Tuberculous ascites
           DEF: Tuberculous inflammation of the membrane lining the
           abdomen.
           CC Excl: 014.00-014.86, 017.90-017.96, 031.2-031.9,
           041.81-041.9, 139.8

§ ✓5th **014.8 Other** `CC` `HIV`
[0-6]   Tuberculosis (of):
                anus
                intestine (large) (small)
                mesenteric glands
                rectum
                retroperitoneal (lymph nodes)
           Tuberculous enteritis
           CC Excl: For codes **014.80, 014.82-014.86:** 014.00-014.86,
           017.90-017.96, 031.2-031.9, 041.81-041.9, 139.8; **For code
           014.81:** 014.81, 139.8

✓4th **015 Tuberculosis of bones and joints**
           Use additional code to identify manifestation, as:
                tuberculous:
                     arthropathy (711.4)
                     necrosis of bone (730.8)
                     osteitis (730.8)
                     osteomyelitis (730.8)
                     synovitis (727.01)
                     tenosynovitis (727.01)

§ ✓5th **015.0 Vertebral column** `CC` `HIV`
[0-6]   Pott's disease
           Use additional code to identify manifestation, as:
                curvature of spine [Pott's] (737.4)
                kyphosis (737.4)
                spondylitis (720.81)
           CC Excl: 015.00-015.06

§ ✓5th **015.1 Hip** `CC` `HIV`
[0-6]   CC Excl: 015.10-015.16

§ ✓5th **015.2 Knee** `CC` `HIV`
[0-6]   CC Excl: 015.20-015.26

§ ✓5th **015.5 Limb bones** `CC` `HIV`
[0-6]   Tuberculous dactylitis
           CC Excl: 015.10-015.56

§ ✓5th **015.6 Mastoid** `CC` `HIV`
[0-6]   Tuberculous mastoiditis
           CC Excl: 015.60-015.66

§ ✓5th **015.7 Other specified bone** `CC` `HIV`
[0-6]   CC Excl: For code **015.70:** 015.00-015.70; **For code 015.71:**
           015.00-015.66, 015.71; **For code 015.72:** 015.00-015.66, 015.72;
           For code 015.73: 015.00-015.66, 015.73; **For code 015.74:**
           015.00-015.66, 015.74; **For code 015.75:** 015.00-015.66, 015.75;
           For code 015.76: 015.00-015.66, 015.76

§ ✓5th **015.8 Other specified joint** `CC` `HIV`
[0-6]   CC Excl: 015.80-015.86

§ ✓5th **015.9 Tuberculosis of unspecified bones and joints** `CC` `HIV`
[0-6]   CC Excl: For codes **015.90, 015.92-015.96:** 015.00-015.66,
           015.80-015.96; **For codes 015.91:** 015.00-015.66, 015.80-015.93,
           015.95-015.96

✓4th **016 Tuberculosis of genitourinary system**

§ ✓5th **016.0 Kidney** `CC` `HIV`
[0-6]   Renal tuberculosis
           Use additional code to identify manifestation, as:
                tuberculous:
                     nephropathy (583.81)
                     pyelitis (590.81)
                     pyelonephritis (590.81)
           CC Excl: 016.00-016.36, 016.90-016.96, 017.90-017.96,
           031.2-031.9, 041.81-041.9, 137.2, 139.8

§ ✓5th **016.1 Bladder** `CC` `HIV`
[0-6]   CC Excl: See code: 016.0

§ ✓5th **016.2 Ureter** `CC` `HIV`
[0-6]   CC Excl: See code: 016.0

§ ✓5th **016.3 Other urinary organs** `CC` `HIV`
[0-6]   CC Excl: See code: 016.0

§ ✓5th **016.4 Epididymis** `CC` `HIV` ♂
[0-6]   CC Excl: 016.40-016.56, 016.90-016.96, 017.90-017.96,
           031.2-031.9, 041.81-041.9, 137.2, 139.8

§ ✓5th **016.5 Other male genital organs** `CC` `HIV` ♂
[0-6]   Use additional code to identify manifestation, as:
                tuberculosis of:
                     prostate (601.4)
                     seminal vesicle (608.81)
                     testis (608.81)
           CC Excl: See code: 016.4

§ ✓5th **016.6 Tuberculous oophoritis and salpingitis** `CC` `HIV` ♀
[0-6]   CC Excl: 016.60-016.96, 017.90-017.96, 031.2-031.9,
           041.81-041.9, 137.2, 139.8

§ ✓5th **016.7 Other female genital organs** `CC` `HIV` ♀
[0-6]   Tuberculous:
                cervicitis
                endometritis
           CC Excl: See code: 016.6

§ ✓5th **016.9 Genitourinary tuberculosis, unspecified** `CC` `HIV`
[0-6]   CC Excl: 016.90-016.96, 017.90-017.96, 031.2-031.9,
           041.81-041.9, 137.2, 139.8

✓4th **017 Tuberculosis of other organs**

§ ✓5th **017.0 Skin and subcutaneous cellular tissue** `CC` `HIV`
[0-6]   Lupus: Tuberculosis:
                exedens   colliquativa
                vulgaris   cutis
           Scrofuloderma   lichenoides
                                            papulonecrotica
                                            verrucosa cutis
           EXCLUDES lupus erythematosus (695.4)
                            disseminated (710.0)
                        lupus NOS (710.0)
                        nonspecific reaction to tuberculin skin test
                            without active tuberculosis (795.5)
                        positive PPD (795.5)
                        positive tuberculin skin test without active
                            tuberculosis (795.5)
           CC Excl: 010.00-018.96

§ ✓5th **017.1 Erythema nodosum with hypersensitivity** `HIV`
[0-6]   **reaction in tuberculosis**
           Bazin's disease
           Erythema:
                induratum
                nodosum, tuberculous
           Tuberculosis indurativa
           EXCLUDES erythema nodosum NOS (695.2)
           DEF: Tender, inflammatory, bilateral nodules appearing on the
           shins and thought to be an allergic reaction to tuberculotoxin.

§   Requires fifth digit. Valid digits are in [brackets] under each code. See beginning of section 010-018 for codes and definitions.

Additional Digit Required   Unacceptable PDx   Manifestation Code   Hospital Acquired Condition   ►◄ Revised Text   ● New Code   ▲ Revised Code Title

2010 ICD-9-CM   Volume 1 – 5

Infectious and Parasitic Diseases

017.2–021.9

§ ✓5th **017.2 Peripheral lymph nodes** [CC] [HIV]
[0-6]
Scrofula
Scrofulous abscess
Tuberculous adenitis

> **EXCLUDES**   *tuberculosis of lymph nodes:*
> *bronchial and mediastinal (012.1)*
> *mesenteric and retroperitoneal (014.8)*
> *tuberculous tracheobronchial adenopathy*
> *(012.1)*

DEF: Scrofula: Old name for tuberculous cervical lymphadenitis.
CC Excl: 017.20-017.26, 017.90-017.96, 031.2-031.9, 041.81-041.9, 139.8

§ ✓5th **017.3 Eye** [CC] [HIV]
[0-6]
Use additional code to identify manifestation, as:
tuberculous:
chorioretinitis, disseminated (363.13)
episcleritis (379.09)
interstitial keratitis (370.59)
iridocyclitis, chronic (364.11)
keratoconjunctivitis (phlyctenular) (370.31)
CC Excl: 017.30-017.36, 017.90-017.96, 031.2-031.9, 041.81-041.9, 139.8

§ ✓5th **017.4 Ear** [CC] [HIV]
[0-6]
Tuberculosis of ear
Tuberculous otitis media

> **EXCLUDES**   *tuberculous mastoiditis (015.6)*

CC Excl: 017.40-017.46, 017.90-017.96, 031.2-031.9, 041.81-041.9, 139.8

§ ✓5th **017.5 Thyroid gland** [CC] [HIV]
[0-6]
CC Excl: 017.50-017.56, 017.90 017.96, 031.2-031.9, 041.81-041.9, 139.8

§ ✓5th **017.6 Adrenal glands** [CC] [HIV]
[0-6]
Addison's disease, tuberculous
CC Excl: 017.60-017.66, 017.90-017.96, 031.2-031.9, 041.81-041.9, 139.8

§ ✓5th **017.7 Spleen** [CC] [HIV]
[0-6]
CC Excl: 017.70-017.76, 017.90-017.96, 031.2-031.9, 041.81-041.9, 139.8

§ ✓5th **017.8 Esophagus** [CC] [HIV]
[0-6]
CC Excl: 017.80-017.96, 031.2-031.9, 041.81-041.9, 139.8

§ ✓5th **017.9 Other specified organs** [CC] [HIV]
[0-6]
Use additional code to identify manifestation, as:
tuberculosis of:
endocardium [any valve] (424.91)
myocardium (422.0)
pericardium (420.0)
CC Excl: 017.90-017.96, 031.2-031.9, 041.81-041.9, 139.8

✓4th **018 Miliary tuberculosis**

> **INCLUDES**   tuberculosis:
> disseminated
> generalized
> miliary, whether of a single specified site, multiple
> sites, or unspecified site
> polyserositis

DEF: A form of tuberculosis caused by caseous material carried through the bloodstream planting seedlike tubercles in various body organs.

§ ✓5th **018.0 Acute miliary tuberculosis** [MCC] [HIV]
[0-6]
CC Excl: 017.90-018.96, 031.2-031.9, 041.81-041.9, 139.8

§ ✓5th **018.8 Other specified miliary tuberculosis** [MCC] [HIV]
[0-6]
CC Excl: See code: 018.0

§ ✓5th **018.9 Miliary tuberculosis, unspecified** [MCC] [HIV]
[0-6]
CC Excl: See code: 018.0

ZOONOTIC BACTERIAL DISEASES (020-027)

✓4th **020 Plague**

> **INCLUDES**   infection by Yersinia [Pasteurella] pestis

020.0 Bubonic [MCC]
DEF: Most common acute and severe form of plague characterized by lymphadenopathy (buboes), chills, fever and headache.
CC Excl: 020.0-020.9

020.1 Cellulocutaneous [MCC]
DEF: Plague characterized by inflammation and necrosis of skin.
CC Excl: See code: 020.0

020.2 Septicemic [MCC]
DEF: Plague characterized by massive infection in the bloodstream.
CC Excl: 020.0-020.9, 771.81, 771.83-771.89, 995.90-995.94

020.3 Primary pneumonic [MCC]
DEF: Plague characterized by massive pulmonary infection.
CC Excl: 011.00-012.16, 012.80-012.86, 017.90-017.96, 020.0-020.9, 021.3, 022.1, 031.0, 039.1, 073.0, 115.05, 115.15, 115.95, 122.1, 130.4, 136.3, 480.0-487.1, 488, 495.0-495.9, 500-502

020.4 Secondary pneumonic [MCC]
DEF: Lung infection as a secondary complication of plague.
CC Excl: 011.73-011.93, 480.3

020.5 Pneumonic, unspecified [MCC]
CC Excl: 020.5, 480.3

020.8 Other specified types of plague [MCC]
Abortive plague   Pestis minor
Ambulatory plague
CC Excl: 020.8

020.9 Plague, unspecified [MCC]
CC Excl: 020.9

✓4th **021 Tularemia**

> **INCLUDES**   deerfly fever
> infection by Francisella [Pasteurella] tularensis
> rabbit fever

DEF: A febrile disease transmitted by the bites of deer flies, fleas and ticks, by inhalations of aerosolized *F. tularensis* or by ingestion of contaminated food or water; patients quickly develop fever, chills, weakness, headache, backache and malaise.

021.0 Ulceroglandular tularemia [CC]
DEF: Lesions occur at the site *Francisella tularensis* organism enters body, usually the fingers or hands.
CC Excl: 021.0

021.1 Enteric tularemia [CC]
Tularemia:
cryptogenic
intestinal
typhoidal
CC Excl: 021.1

021.2 Pulmonary tularemia [CC]
Bronchopneumonic tularemia
CC Excl: 482.49-487.1, 488, 495.0-495.9, 500-508.9, 517.1, 517.8, 518.89, 519.8-519.9

021.3 Oculoglandular tularemia [CC]
DEF: Painful conjunctival infection by *Francisella tularensis* organism with possible corneal, preauricular lymph, or lacrimal involvement.
CC Excl: 021.3, 480.3

021.8 Other specified tularemia [CC]
Tularemia:
generalized or disseminated
glandular
CC Excl: 021.0-021.9

021.9 Unspecified tularemia [CC]
CC Excl: See code: 021.8

---

§   Requires fifth digit. Valid digits are in [brackets] under each code. See beginning of section 010-018 for codes and definitions.

[N] Newborn Age: 0   [P] Pediatric Age: 0-17   [M] Maternity Age: 12-55   [A] Adult Age: 15-124   [MCC] Major CC Condition   [CC] CC Condition   [HIV] HIV Related Dx

6 – Volume 1   2010 ICD-9-CM

√4th **022 Anthrax**

> **DEF:** A bacterial disease usually transmitted by contact with infected animals or their discharges; primary routes of inoculation are cutaneous, gastrointestinal and inhalation.
> **AHA:** 4Q '02, 70

022.0 Cutaneous anthrax `CC`
> Malignant pustule
> **CC Excl:** 022.0

022.1 Pulmonary anthrax `MCC`
> Respiratory anthrax
> Wool-sorters' disease
> **CC Excl:** 011.00-012.16, 012.80-012.86, 017.90-017.96, 020.3-020.5, 021.3, 022.1, 031.0, 039.1, 073.0, 115.05, 115.15, 115.95, 122.1, 130.4, 136.3, 480.0-487.1, 488, 494.0-495.9, 500-508.9, 517.1, 517.8, 518.89, 519.8-519.9

022.2 Gastrointestinal anthrax `CC`
> **CC Excl:** 022.2

022.3 Anthrax septicemia `MCC`
> **CC Excl:** 003.1, 020.2, 022.3, 036.2, 038.0-038.9, 040.89-041.9, 054.5, 139.8, 771.81, 771.83-771.89, 995.90-995.94, V09.0-V09.91

022.8 Other specified manifestations of anthrax `CC`
> **CC Excl:** 022.8

022.9 Anthrax, unspecified `CC`
> **CC Excl:** 022.0-022.9

√4th **023 Brucellosis**

> `INCLUDES` fever:
> > Malta
> > Mediterranean
> > undulant

> **DEF:** An infectious disease caused by gram-negative, aerobic coccobacilli organisms transmitted to humans through contact with infected tissue or dairy products; fever, sweating, weakness and aching are symptoms.

023.0 Brucella melitensis
> **DEF:** Infection from direct or indirect contact with infected sheep or goats.

023.1 Brucella abortus
> **DEF:** Infection from direct or indirect contact with infected cattle.

023.2 Brucella suis
> **DEF:** Infection from direct or indirect contact with infected swine.

023.3 Brucella canis
> **DEF:** Infection from direct or indirect contact with infected dogs.

023.8 Other brucellosis `CC`
> Infection by more than one organism
> **CC Excl:** 023.0-023.9

023.9 Brucellosis, unspecified `CC`
> **CC Excl:** See code: 023.8

024 Glanders `CC`
> Infection by:
> > actinobacillus mallei
> > malleomyces mallei
> > pseudomonas mallei
> Farcy
> Malleus
> **DEF:** Equine infection causing mucosal inflammation and skin ulcers in humans.
> **CC Excl:** 024

025 Melioidosis `CC`
> Infection by:
> > malleomyces pseudomallei
> > pseudomonas pseudomallei
> > whitmore's bacillus
> Pseudoglanders
> **DEF:** Rare infection caused by *Pseudomonas pseudomallei;* clinical symptoms range from localized infection to fatal septicemia.
> **CC Excl:** 025

√4th **026 Rat-bite fever**

026.0 Spirillary fever `CC`
> Rat-bite fever due to Spirillum minor [S. minus]
> Sodoku
> **CC Excl:** 026.0-026.9

026.1 Streptobacillary fever `CC`
> Epidemic arthritic erythema
> Haverhill fever
> Rat-bite fever due to Streptobacillus moniliformis
> **CC Excl:** See code: 026.0

026.9 Unspecified rat-bite fever `CC`
> **CC Excl:** See code: 026.0

√4th **027 Other zoonotic bacterial diseases**

027.0 Listeriosis `CC`
> Infection ⎫
> Septicemia ⎬ by Listeria monocytogenes
> Use additional code to identify manifestation, as meningitis (320.7)
> `EXCLUDES` congenital listeriosis (771.2)
> **CC Excl:** 027.0-027.9

027.1 Erysipelothrix infection
> Erysipeloid (of Rosenbach)
> Infection ⎫ by Erysipelothrix insidiosa [E.
> Septicemia ⎬ rhusiopathiae]
> **DEF:** Usually associated with handling of fish, meat, or poultry; symptoms range from localized inflammation to septicemia.

027.2 Pasteurellosis `CC`
> Pasteurella pseudotuberculosis infection
> Mesenteric adenitis ⎫
> Septic infection (cat ⎬ by Pasteurella multocida
> bite) (dog bite) ⎭ [P. septica]
> `EXCLUDES` infection by:
> > Francisella [Pasteurella] tularensis (021.0-021.9)
> > Yersinia [Pasteurella] pestis (020.0-020.9)
> **DEF:** Swelling, abscesses, or septicemia from *Pasteurella multocida,* commonly transmitted to humans by a dog or cat scratch.
> **CC Excl:** See code: 027.0

027.8 Other specified zoonotic bacterial diseases `CC`
> **CC Excl:** See code: 027.0

027.9 Unspecified zoonotic bacterial disease `CC`
> **CC Excl:** See code: 027.0

OTHER BACTERIAL DISEASES (030-041)

> `EXCLUDES` bacterial venereal diseases (098.0-099.9)
> bartonellosis (088.0)

√4th **030 Leprosy**

> `INCLUDES` Hansen's disease
> infection by Mycobacterium leprae

030.0 Lepromatous [type L] `CC`
> Lepromatous leprosy (macular) (diffuse) (infiltrated) (nodular) (neuritic)
> **DEF:** Infectious, disseminated leprosy bacilli with lesions and deformities.
> **CC Excl:** 030.0

030.1 Tuberculoid [type T] `CC`
> Tuberculoid leprosy (macular) (maculoanesthetic) (major) (minor) (neuritic)
> **DEF:** Relatively benign, self-limiting leprosy with neuralgia and scales.
> **CC Excl:** 030.1

030.2 Indeterminate [group I] `CC`
> Indeterminate [uncharacteristic] leprosy (macular) (neuritic)
> **DEF:** Uncharacteristic leprosy, frequently an early manifestation.
> **CC Excl:** 030.2

√4th √5th Additional Digit Required   Unacceptable PDx   Manifestation Code   Hospital Acquired Condition   ►◄ Revised Text   ● New Code   ▲ Revised Code Title

2010 ICD-9-CM   **Volume 1 – 7**

Infectious and Parasitic Diseases

030.3–036.3

030.3 Borderline [group B] `CC`
Borderline or dimorphous leprosy (infiltrated) (neuritic)
DEF: Transitional form of leprosy, neither lepromatous nor tuberculoid.
CC Excl: 030.3

030.8 Other specified leprosy `CC`
CC Excl: 030.8

030.9 Leprosy, unspecified `CC`
CC Excl: 030.9

✓4th **031 Diseases due to other mycobacteria**

031.0 Pulmonary `CC`
Battey disease
Infection by Mycobacterium:
avium
intracellulare [Battey bacillus]
kansasii
CC Excl: 011.00-012.86, 017.90-017.96, 031.0, 031.2-031.9, 041.81-041.9, 137.0, 139.8, 480.0-480.2, 480.8-487.1, 488, 494.0-508.9, 517.1, 518.89

031.1 Cutaneous `CC`
Buruli ulcer
Infection by Mycobacterium:
marinum [M. balnei]
ulcerans
CC Excl: 031.0-031.9

031.2 Disseminated `CC` `HIV`
Disseminated mycobacterium avium-intracellulare complex (DMAC)
Mycobacterium avium-intracellulare complex (MAC) bacteremia
DEF: Disseminated mycobacterium avium-intracellulare complex (DMAC): A serious systemic form of MAC commonly observed in patients in the late course of AIDS.
DEF: Mycobacterium avium-intracellulare complex (MAC) bacterium: Human pulmonary disease, lymphadenitis in children and systemic disease in immunocompromised individuals caused by a slow growing, gram-positive, aerobic organism.
CC Excl: See code: 031.1
AHA: 4Q, '97, 31

031.8 Other specified mycobacterial diseases `CC` `HIV`
CC Excl: See code: 031.1

031.9 Unspecified diseases due to mycobacteria `CC` `HIV`
Atypical mycobacterium infection NOS
CC Excl: See code: 031.1

✓4th **032 Diphtheria**
`INCLUDES` infection by Corynebacterium diphtheriae

032.0 Faucial diphtheria `CC`
Membranous angina, diphtheritic
DEF: Diphtheria of the throat.
CC Excl: 032.0-032.9

032.1 Nasopharyngeal diphtheria `CC`
CC Excl: See code: 032.0

032.2 Anterior nasal diphtheria `CC`
CC Excl: See code: 032.0

032.3 Laryngeal diphtheria `CC`
Laryngotracheitis, diphtheritic
CC Excl: See code: 032.0

✓5th **032.8 Other specified diphtheria**

032.81 Conjunctival diphtheria `CC`
Pseudomembranous diphtheritic conjunctivitis
CC Excl: See code: 032.0

032.82 Diphtheritic myocarditis `CC`
CC Excl: 032.82, 074.20, 074.22-074.23, 093.82, 390, 391.2-391.9, 398.0-398.90, 398.99, 422.0-422.99, 429.0, 429.71-429.79, 459.89-459.9

032.83 Diphtheritic peritonitis `CC`
CC Excl: 014.00-014.06, 032.83, 090.0, 095.2, 098.86, 099.56, 540.0-540.1, 567.0-567.1, 567.22, 567.29, 567.81, 567.9, 569.87-569.9, 577.8, 614.5-614.7, 639.0, 670.00-670.84, 777.6, 998.7

032.84 Diphtheritic cystitis `CC`
CC Excl: See code: 032.0

032.85 Cutaneous diphtheria `CC`
CC Excl: See code: 032.0

032.89 Other `CC`
CC Excl: See code: 032.0

032.9 Diphtheria, unspecified `CC`
CC Excl: See code: 032.0

✓4th **033 Whooping cough**
`INCLUDES` pertussis
Use additional code to identify any associated pneumonia (484.3)
DEF: An acute, highly contagious respiratory tract infection caused by *Bordetella pertussis* and *B. bronchiseptica;* characteristic paroxysmal cough.

033.0 Bordetella pertussis [B. pertussis] `CC`
CC Excl: 033.0-033.9

033.1 Bordetella parapertussis [B. parapertussis] `CC`
CC Excl: See code: 033.0

033.8 Whooping cough due to other specified organism `CC`
Bordetella bronchiseptica [B. bronchiseptica]
CC Excl: See code: 033.0

033.9 Whooping cough, unspecified organism `CC`
CC Excl: See code: 033.0

✓4th **034 Streptococcal sore throat and scarlet fever**

034.0 Streptococcal sore throat
Septic: Streptococcal:
angina   angina
sore throat   laryngitis
               pharyngitis
               tonsillitis
J02.0 Streptococcal pharyngitis `I-10`

034.1 Scarlet fever `CC`
Scarlatina
`EXCLUDES` parascarlatina (057.8)
DEF: Streptococcal infection and fever with red rash spreading from trunk.
CC Excl: 034.0-035

035 Erysipelas
`EXCLUDES` postpartum or puerperal erysipelas ▶(670.8)◄
DEF: An acute superficial cellulitis involving the dermal lymphatics; it is often caused by group A streptococci.

✓4th **036 Meningococcal infection**

036.0 Meningococcal meningitis `MCC`
Cerebrospinal fever (meningococcal)
Meningitis:
cerebrospinal
epidemic
CC Excl: 003.21, 013.00-013.16, 036.0, 036.89-036.9, 041.81-041.9, 047.0-047.9, 049.0-049.1, 053.0, 054.72, 072.1, 090.42, 091.81, 094.2, 098.89, 100.81, 112.83, 114.2, 115.01, 115.11, 115.91, 130.0, 139.8, 320.0-322.9, 349.89-349.9, 357.0

036.1 Meningococcal encephalitis `MCC`
CC Excl: 036.1, 036.89-036.9, 041.81-041.9, 139.8

036.2 Meningococcemia `MCC`
Meningococcal septicemia
CC Excl: 003.1, 020.2, 036.2, 036.89-036.9, 038.0-038.9, 041.81-041.9, 054.5, 139.8, 995.90-995.94

036.3 Waterhouse-Friderichsen syndrome, meningococcal `MCC`
Meningococcal hemorrhagic adrenalitis
Meningococcic adrenal syndrome
Waterhouse-Friderichsen syndrome NOS
CC Excl: 036.3, 036.89-036.9, 041.81-041.9, 139.8

`N` Newborn Age: 0   `P` Pediatric Age: 0-17   `M` Maternity Age: 12-55   `A` Adult Age: 15-124   `MCC` Major CC Condition   `CC` CC Condition   `HIV` HIV Related Dx

√5ᵗʰ **036.4 Meningococcal carditis**

036.40 Meningococcal carditis, unspecified `MCC`
CC Excl: 036.40, 036.89-036.9, 041.81-041.9, 139.8

036.41 Meningococcal pericarditis `MCC`
DEF: Meningococcal infection of the outer membrane of the heart.
CC Excl: 036.41, 036.89-036.9, 041.81-041.9, 139.8

036.42 Meningococcal endocarditis `MCC`
DEF: Meningococcal infection of the membranes lining the cavities of the heart.
CC Excl: 036.42, 036.89-036.9, 041.81-041.9, 139.8

036.43 Meningococcal myocarditis `MCC`
DEF: Meningococcal infection of the muscle of the heart.
CC Excl: 036.43, 041.81-041.9, 139.8

√5ᵗʰ **036.8 Other specified meningococcal infections**

036.81 Meningococcal optic neuritis `CC`
CC Excl: 036.81, 036.89-036.9, 041.81-041.9, 139.8

036.82 Meningococcal arthropathy `CC`
CC Excl: 036.82-036.9, 041.81-041.9, 139.8

036.89 Other `CC`
CC Excl: 036.89-036.9, 041.81-041.9, 139.8

036.9 Meningococcal infection, unspecified `CC`
Meningococcal infection NOS
CC Excl: See code: 036.89

037 Tetanus `MCC`
EXCLUDES tetanus:
complicating:
abortion (634-638 with .0, 639.0)
ectopic or molar pregnancy (639.0)
neonatorum (771.3)
puerperal ▶(670.8)◀
DEF: An acute, often fatal, infectious disease caused by the anaerobic, spore-forming bacillus *Clostridium tetani*; the bacillus enters the body through a contaminated wound, burns, surgical wounds, or cutaneous ulcers. Symptoms: lockjaw, spasms, seizures, and paralysis.
CC Excl: 037, 139.8

√4ᵗʰ **038 Septicemia**
Use additional code for systemic inflammatory response syndrome (SIRS) (995.91-995.92)
EXCLUDES bacteremia (790.7)
during labor (659.3)
following ectopic or molar pregnancy (639.0)
following infusion, injection, transfusion, or vaccination (999.3)
postpartum, puerperal (670)
septicemia (sepsis) of newborn (771.81)
that complicating abortion (634-638 with .0, 639.0)
DEF: A systemic disease associated with the presence and persistence of pathogenic microorganisms or their toxins in the blood.
AHA: 2Q, '04, 16; 4Q, '88, 10; 3Q, '88, 12
TIP: Sequence any underlying cause (e.g., due to device or injury) first, before septicemia code.

038.0 Streptococcal septicemia `MCC` `HIV`
CC Excl: 003.1, 020.2, 036.2, 038.0-038.11, 038.19-038.9, 040.82-041.11, 041.19-041.9, 054.5, 139.8, 995.90-995.94, V09.0-V09.91
AHA: 4Q, '03, 79; 2Q, '96, 5

√5ᵗʰ **038.1 Staphylococcal septicemia**
AHA: 4Q, '97, 32

038.10 Staphylococcal septicemia, unspecified `MCC` `HIV`
CC Excl: See code: 038.0

038.11 Methicillin susceptible Staphylococcus aureus septicemia `MCC` `HIV`
MSSA septicemia
Staphylococcus aureus septicemia NOS
CC Excl: See code: 038.0
AHA: 4Q, '08, 69-70;1Q, '05, 7; 2Q, '00, 5; 4Q, '98, 42
A41.0 Sepsis due to Staphylococcus aureus `I-10`

038.12 Methicillin resistant Staphylococcus aureus septicemia `MCC` `HIV`
CC Excl: See code: 038.0
AHA: 4Q, '08, 69-73

038.19 Other staphylococcal septicemia `MCC` `HIV`
CC Excl: See code: 038.0
AHA: 2Q, '00, 5
A41.1 Sepsis due to other specified Staphylococcus `I-10`

038.2 Pneumococcal septicemia [Streptococcus pneumoniae septicemia] `MCC` `HIV`
CC Excl: See code 038.0
AHA: 2Q, '96, 5; 1Q, '91, 13

038.3 Septicemia due to anaerobes `MCC` `HIV`
Septicemia due to bacteroides
EXCLUDES gas gangrene (040.0)
that due to anaerobic streptococci (038.0)
CC Excl: See code 038.0

√5ᵗʰ **038.4 Septicemia due to other gram-negative organisms**
DEF: Infection of blood by microorganisms categorized as gram-negative by Gram's method of staining for identification of bacteria.

038.40 Gram-negative organism, unspecified `MCC` `HIV`
Gram-negative septicemia NOS
CC Excl: See code 038.0

038.41 Hemophilus influenzae [H. influenzae] `MCC` `HIV`
CC Excl: See code 038.0

038.42 Escherichia coli [E. coli] `MCC` `HIV`
CC Excl: See code 038.0
AHA: 4Q, '03, 73
A41.51 Sepsis due to Escherichia coli [E coli] `I-10`

038.43 Pseudomonas `MCC` `HIV`
CC Excl: See code 038.0

038.44 Serratia `MCC` `HIV`
CC Excl: See code 038.0

038.49 Other `MCC` `HIV`
CC Excl: See code 038.0
A41.59 Other Gram-negative sepsis `I-10`

038.8 Other specified septicemias `MCC` `HIV`
EXCLUDES septicemia (due to):
anthrax (022.3)
gonococcal (098.89)
herpetic (054.5)
meningococcal (036.2)
septicemic plague (020.2)
CC Excl: See code 038.0

038.9 Unspecified septicemia `MCC` `HIV`
Septicemia NOS
EXCLUDES bacteremia NOS (790.7)
CC Excl: See code 038.0
AHA: 4Q, '07, 97; 2Q, '05, 18-19; 2Q, '04, 16; 4Q, '03, 79; 2Q, '00, 3; 3Q, '99, 5, 9; 1Q, '98, 5; 3Q, '96, 16; 2Q, '96, 6
TIP: Ensure that documentation includes clinical evidence of systemic infection; do not code if documentation indicates "urosepsis" only.
A41.9 Sepsis unspecified `I-10`

√4ᵗʰ **039 Actinomycotic infections**
`INCLUDES` actinomycotic mycetoma
infection by Actinomycetales, such as species of Actinomyces, Actinomadura, Nocardia, Streptomyces
maduromycosis (actinomycotic)
schizomycetoma (actinomycotic)
DEF: Inflammatory lesions and abscesses at site of infection by *Actinomyces israelii*.

039.0 Cutaneous `CC` `HIV`
Erythrasma   Trichomycosis axillaris
CC Excl: 039.0, 039.8-039.9

√4ᵗʰ √5ᵗʰ Additional Digit Required   Unacceptable PDx   Manifestation Code   Hospital Acquired Condition   ▶◀ Revised Text   ● New Code   ▲ Revised Code Title

2010 ICD-9-CM   **October 2009 • Volume 1 – 9**

Infectious and Parasitic Diseases

039.1–041.7

039.1 Pulmonary `CC` `HIV`
Thoracic actinomycosis
CC Excl: 039.1, 039.8-039.9, 480.3

039.2 Abdominal `CC` `HIV`
CC Excl: 039.2, 039.8-039.9

039.3 Cervicofacial `CC`
CC Excl: 039.3, 039.8-039.9

039.4 Madura foot `CC` `HIV`
> *EXCLUDES*   *madura foot due to mycotic infection (117.4)*

CC Excl: 039.4-039.9

039.8 Of other specified sites `CC` `HIV`
CC Excl: 039.0-039.9

039.9 Of unspecified site `CC` `HIV`
Actinomycosis NOS
Maduromycosis NOS
Nocardiosis NOS
CC Excl: See code: 039.8

✓4th **040 Other bacterial diseases**
> *EXCLUDES*   *bacteremia NOS (790.7)*
> *bacterial infection NOS (041.9)*

040.0 Gas gangrene `MCC`
Gas bacillus infection or gangrene
Infection by Clostridium:
   histolyticum
   oedematiens
   perfringens [welchii]
   septicum
   sordellii
Malignant edema
Myonecrosis, clostridial
Myositis, clostridial
CC Excl: 040.0, 139.8
AHA: 1Q, '95, 11

040.1 Rhinoscleroma
DEF: Growths on the nose and nasopharynx caused by *Klebsiella rhinoscleromatis.*

040.2 Whipple's disease `CC`
Intestinal lipodystrophy
CC Excl: 040.2

040.3 Necrobacillosis `CC`
DEF: Infection with *Fusobacterium necrophorum* causing abscess or necrosis.
CC Excl: 040.3
AHA: 4Q, '07, 85

✓5th **040.4 Other specified botulism**
Non-foodborne intoxication due to toxins of Clostridium botulinum [C. botulinum]
> *EXCLUDES*   *botulism NOS (005.1)*
> *food poisoning due to toxins of Clostridium botulinum (005.1)*

040.41 Infant botulism `P` `CC`
DEF: Colonization of Clostridium botulinum spores in the large intestine; release of neurotoxins results in constipation; may progress to neuromuscular paralysis; affects infants of less than six months.
CC Excl: 005.0-005.2, 008.45-008.46, 040.41-040.42
AHA: 4Q, '07, 60

040.42 Wound botulism `CC`
Non-foodborne botulism NOS
Use additional code to identify complicated open wound
CC Excl: See code 040.41
AHA: 4Q, '07, 60

✓5th **040.8 Other specified bacterial diseases**

040.81 Tropical pyomyositis `CC`
CC Excl: 040.81, 040.89

040.82 Toxic shock syndrome `MCC`
Use additional code to identify the organism
DEF: Syndrome caused by staphylococcal exotoxin that may rapidly progress to severe and intractable shock; symptoms include sunburn-like rash with peeling of skin on palms and soles, sudden onset high fever, vomiting, diarrhea, myalgia, and hypotension.
CC Excl: 040.82, 338.0-338.4, 780.91-780.99, 785.50-785.59, 785.9, 799.81-799.89
AHA: 4Q, '02, 44

040.89 Other
AHA: N-D, '86, 7

✓4th **041 Bacterial infection in conditions classified elsewhere and of unspecified site**
Note: This category is provided to be used as an additional code to identify the bacterial agent in diseases classified elsewhere. This category will also be used to classify bacterial infections of unspecified nature or site.
> *EXCLUDES*   *septicemia (038.0-038.9)*

AHA: 2Q, '01, 12; J-A, '84, 19

✓5th **041.0 Streptococcus**

041.00 Streptococcus, unspecified

041.01 Group A
AHA: 1Q, '02, 3

041.02 Group B
B95.1 Streptococcus group B cause of dz class elsewhere `I-10`

041.03 Group C

041.04 Group D [Enterococcus]
B95.2 Enterococcus as the cause of dz class elsewhere `I-10`

041.05 Group G

041.09 Other Streptococcus
B95.4 Oth streptococcus cause of dz class elsewhere `I-10`

✓5th **041.1 Staphylococcus**

041.10 Staphylococcus, unspecified
AHA: 2Q, '06, 15

041.11 Methicillin susceptible Staphylococcus aureus
MSSA
Staphylococcus aureus NOS
AHA: 4Q, '08, 69-70; 2Q, '06, 16; 4Q, '03, 104, 106; 2Q, '01, 11; 4Q, '98, 42, 54; 4Q, '97, 32
B95.6 Staphylococcus aureus cause dz class elsewhere `I-10`

041.12 Methicillin resistant Staphylococcus aureus
Methicillin-resistant staphylococcus aureus (MRSA)
AHA: 4Q, '08, 69-70, 73
TIP: Do not assign if combination code (with localized infection) available, or if only colonization or carrier status documented.

041.19 Other Staphylococcus
AHA: 2Q, '08, 3
B95.7 Other staphylococcus cause of dz class elsewhere `I-10`

041.2 Pneumococcus

▲ **041.3 Klebsiella pneumoniae**
AHA: 4Q, '08, 149

041.4 Escherichia coli [E. coli]
B96.2 Escherichia coli cause of dz class elsewhere `I-10`

041.5 Hemophilus influenzae [H. influenzae]

041.6 Proteus (mirabilis) (morganii)

041.7 Pseudomonas
AHA: 4Q, '02, 45
B96.5 Pseudomonas as the cause of dz class elsewhere `I-10`

`N` Newborn Age: 0   `P` Pediatric Age: 0-17   `M` Maternity Age: 12-55   `A` Adult Age: 15-124   `MCC` Major CC Condition   `CC` CC Condition   `HIV` HIV Related Dx

√5ᵗʰ **041.8 Other specified bacterial infections**

041.81 Mycoplasma
Eaton's agent
Pleuropneumonia-like organisms [PPLO]

041.82 Bacteroides fragilis
DEF: Anaerobic gram-negative bacilli of the gastrointestinal tract; frequently implicated in intra-abdominal infection; commonly resistant to antibiotics.

041.83 Clostridium perfringens

041.84 Other anaerobes
Gram-negative anaerobes
EXCLUDES   *Helicobacter pylori (041.86)*

041.85 Other gram-negative organisms
Aerobacter aerogenes
Gram-negative bacteria NOS
Mima polymorpha
Serratia
EXCLUDES   *gram-negative anaerobes (041.84)*
AHA: 1Q, '95, 18

▲   **041.86 Helicobacter pylori [H. pylori]**
AHA: 4Q, '95, 60
B96.81 Helicobacter pylori cause of dz class   `I-10`
elsewhere

041.89 Other specified bacteria
AHA: 2Q, '06, 7; 2Q, '03, 7
A49.8 Other bacterial infections of   `I-10`
unspecified site

041.9 Bacterial infection, unspecified
AHA: 2Q, '91, 9

HUMAN IMMUNODEFICIENCY VIRUS (HIV) INFECTION (042)

042 Human immunodeficiency virus [HIV] disease   `MCC`
Acquired immune deficiency syndrome
Acquired immunodeficiency syndrome
AIDS
AIDS-like syndrome
AIDS-related complex
ARC
HIV infection, symptomatic
Use additional code(s) to identify all manifestations of HIV
Use additional code to identify HIV-2 infection (079.53)
EXCLUDES   *asymptomatic HIV infection status (V08)*
exposure to HIV virus (V01.79)
nonspecific serologic evidence of HIV (795.71)
CC Excl: 042, 139.8
AHA: 4Q, '07, 63; 3Q, '06, 15; 1Q, '05, 7; 2Q, '04, 11; 1Q, '04, 5; 1Q, '03, 15; 1Q, '99, 14; 4Q, '97, 30, 31; 1Q, '93, 21; 2Q, '92, 11; 3Q, '90, 17; J-A, '87, 8
TIP: Code only confirmed cases of HIV infection/illness; may be coded from provider's diagnostic statement.
B20 Human immunodeficiency virus [HIV] disease   `I-10`

POLIOMYELITIS AND OTHER NON-ARTHROPOD-BORNE VIRAL DISEASES AND PRION DISEASES OF CENTRAL NERVOUS SYSTEM (045-049)

√4ᵗʰ **045 Acute poliomyelitis**
EXCLUDES   *late effects of acute poliomyelitis (138)*

The following fifth-digit subclassification is for use with category 045:
   0 poliovirus, unspecified type
   1 poliovirus type I
   2 poliovirus type II
   3 poliovirus type III

§ √5ᵗʰ **045.0 Acute paralytic poliomyelitis specified as bulbar**   `MCC`
[0-3]
Infantile paralysis (acute) ⎫
Poliomyelitis (acute) (anterior) ⎬ specified as bulbar
Polioencephalitis (acute) (bulbar)
Polioencephalomyelitis (acute) (anterior) (bulbar)
DEF: Acute paralytic infection occurring where the brain merges with the spinal cord; affecting breathing, swallowing, and heart rate.
CC Excl: 045.00-045.13

§ √5ᵗʰ **045.1 Acute poliomyelitis with other paralysis**   `MCC`
[0-3]
Paralysis:
   acute atrophic, spinal
   infantile, paralytic
Poliomyelitis (acute) ⎫
   anterior ⎬ with paralysis except bulbar
   epidemic ⎭
DEF: Paralytic infection affecting peripheral or spinal nerves.
CC Excl: See code: 045.0

§ √5ᵗʰ **045.2 Acute nonparalytic poliomyelitis**
[0-3]
Poliomyelitis (acute) ⎫
   anterior ⎬ specified as nonparalytic
   epidemic ⎭
DEF: Nonparalytic infection causing pain, stiffness, and paresthesias.

§ √5ᵗʰ **045.9 Acute poliomyelitis, unspecified**
[0-3]
Infantile paralysis ⎫
Poliomyelitis (acute) ⎬ unspecified whether paralytic
   anterior ⎬ or nonparalytic
   epidemic ⎭

√4ᵗʰ **046 Slow virus infections and prion diseases of central nervous system**

046.0 Kuru   `CC`
DEF: A chronic, progressive, fatal nervous system disorder; clinical symptoms include cerebellar ataxia, trembling, spasticity and progressive dementia.
CC Excl: 046.0-046.9

√5ᵗʰ **046.1 Jakob-Creutzfeldt disease**
▶Use additional code to identify dementia:
   with behavioral disturbance (294.11)
   without behavioral disturbance (294.10)◀

046.11 Variant Creutzfeldt-Jakob disease   `CC`
vCJD
AHA: 4Q, '08, 73-75
CC Excl: 013.60-013.66, 046.0-046.9, 048-049.0, 049.8, 052.0, 052.2, 054.3, 054.74, 056.01, 057.8-058.29, 059.00-059.9, 062.0-064, 066.2-066.3, 072.2, 073.7, 079.99, 081.9, 083.9, 090.41, 094.81, 117.5, 124, 130.0, 290.12, 323.01-323.9, 341.1, 487.8, 771.2, 984.9

---

§ Requires fifth digit. Valid digits are in [brackets] under each code. See category 045 for codes and definitions.

√4ᵗʰ Additional Digit Required   √5ᵗʰ   Unacceptable PDx   Manifestation Code   Hospital Acquired Condition   ▶◀ Revised Text   ● New Code   ▲ Revised Code Title

2010 ICD-9-CM   **October 2009 · Volume 1 – 11**

Infectious and Parasitic Diseases

046.19–049.8

046.19 Other and unspecified Creutzfeldt-Jakob disease `CC`
CJD
Familial Creutzfeldt-Jakob disease
Iatrogenic Creutzfeldt-Jakob disease
Jakob-Creutzfeldt disease, unspecified
Sporadic Creutzfeldt-Jakob disease
Subacute spongiform encephalopathy

> **EXCLUDES**   *variant Creutzfeldt-Jakob disease (vCJD) (046.11)*

DEF: Communicable, progressive spongiform encephalopathy thought to be caused by an infectious particle known as a "prion" (proteinaceous infection particle); a progressive, fatal disease manifested principally by mental deterioration.
CC Excl: See code: 046.11
AHA: ▶4Q, '08, 73-75◀

046.2 Subacute sclerosing panencephalitis `CC`
Dawson's inclusion body encephalitis
Van Bogaert's sclerosing leukoencephalitis
CC Excl: 046.2, 139.8
DEF: Progressive viral infection causing cerebral dysfunction, blindness, dementia, and death (SSPE).

046.3 Progressive multifocal leukoencephalopathy `CC` `HIV`
Multifocal leukoencephalopathy NOS
DEF: Infection affecting cerebral cortex in patients with weakened immune systems.
CC Excl: 013.60-013.66, 046.0-046.9, 048-049.0, 049.8, 052.0, 052.2, 054.3, 054.74, 056.01, 057.8-058.29, 059.00-059.19, 059.21-059.9, 062.0-064, 066.2-066.3, 072.2, 073.7, 075, 081.9, 083.9, 090.41, 094.81, 117.5, 124, 130.0, 290.12, 323.01-323.9, 341.1, 487.8, 771.2, 984.9

√5ᵗʰ 046.7 Other specified prion diseases of central nervous system
> **EXCLUDES**   *Creutzfeldt-Jakob disease (046.11-046.19)*
> *Jakob-Creutzfeldt disease (046.11-046.19)*
> *kuru (046.0)*
> *variant Creutzfeldt-Jakob disease (vCJD) (046.11)*

046.71 Gerstmann-Sträussler-Scheinker syndrome `CC` `HIV`
GSS syndrome
AHA: ▶4Q, '08, 73-75◀
CC Excl: 046.0-046.9, 066.40-066.49, 079.82

046.72 Fatal familial insomnia `CC` `HIV`
FFI
AHA: ▶4Q, '08, 73-75◀
CC Excl: See code: 046.71

046.79 Other and unspecified prion disease of central nervous system `CC` `HIV`
CC Excl: See code: 046.71

046.8 Other specified slow virus infection of central nervous system `CC` `HIV`
CC Excl: 046.0-046.9, 066.40-066.49, 079.82

046.9 Unspecified slow virus infection of central nervous system `CC` `HIV`
CC Excl: 046.0-046.9

√4ᵗʰ 047 Meningitis due to enterovirus
> **INCLUDES**   meningitis:
> abacterial
> aseptic
> viral

> **EXCLUDES**   *meningitis due to:*
> *adenovirus (049.1)*
> *arthropod-borne virus (060.0-066.9)*
> *leptospira (100.81)*
> *virus of:*
> *herpes simplex (054.72)*
> *herpes zoster (053.0)*
> *lymphocytic choriomeningitis (049.0)*
> *mumps (072.1)*
> *poliomyelitis (045.0-045.9)*
> *any other infection specifically classified elsewhere*

AHA: J-F, '87, 6

047.0 Coxsackie virus `CC`
CC Excl: 003.21, 013.00-013.16, 036.0, 047.0-047.9, 049.0-049.1, 072.1, 078.88-078.89, 079.81, 079.88-079.99, 090.42, 091.81, 094.2, 098.89, 100.81, 112.83, 114.2, 115.01, 115.11, 115.91, 130.0, 139.8, 320.0-322.9, 349.89-349.9, 357.0

047.1 ECHO virus `CC`
Meningo-eruptive syndrome
CC Excl: See code: 047.0

047.8 Other specified viral meningitis `CC`
CC Excl: See code: 047.0

047.9 Unspecified viral meningitis `CC`
Viral meningitis NOS
CC Excl: See code: 047.0
A87.9 Viral meningitis unspecified `I-10`

048 Other enterovirus diseases of central nervous system `CC`
Boston exanthem
CC Excl: 013.60-013.66, 046.2, 046.71-046.8, 048-049.0, 049.8, 052.0, 052.2, 054.3, 054.74, 056.01, 057.8-058.29, 059.00-059.19, 059.21-059.9, 062.0-064, 066.2-066.49, 072.2, 073.7, 075, 079.82, 079.99, 081.9, 083.9, 090.41, 094.81, 117.5, 124, 130.0, 290.12, 323.01-323.9, 341.1, 487.8, 771.2, 984.9

√4ᵗʰ 049 Other non-arthropod-borne viral diseases of central nervous system
> **EXCLUDES**   *late effects of viral encephalitis (139.0)*

049.0 Lymphocytic choriomeningitis `CC`
Lymphocytic:
meningitis (serous) (benign)
meningoencephalitis (serous) (benign)
CC Excl: 003.21, 013.00-013.16, 036.0, 047.0-047.9, 049.0-049.1, 066.40-066.49, 072.1, 078.88-078.89, 079.81-079.82, 079.88-079.99, 090.42, 091.81, 094.2, 098.89, 100.81, 112.83, 114.2, 115.01, 115.11, 115.91, 130.0, 139.8, 320.0-322.9, 349.89-349.9, 357.0

049.1 Meningitis due to adenovirus `CC`
DEF: Inflammation of lining of brain caused by Arenaviruses and usually occurring in adults in fall and winter months.
CC Excl: 003.21, 013.00-013.16, 036.0, 047.0-047.9, 049.0-049.1, 072.1, 078.88-078.89, 079.81, 079.88-079.99, 090.42, 091.81, 094.2, 098.89, 100.81, 112.83, 114.2, 115.01, 115.11, 115.91, 130.0, 139.8, 320.0-322.9, 349.89-349.9, 357.0

049.8 Other specified non-arthropod-borne viral diseases of central nervous system `CC` `HIV`
Encephalitis: Encephalitis:
acute: lethargica
inclusion body   Rio Bravo
necrotizing   von Economo's disease
epidemic

> **EXCLUDES**   *human herpesvirus 6 encephalitis (058.21)*
> *other human herpesvirus encephalitis (058.29)*

CC Excl: 013.60-013.66, 046.2, 046.71-046.8, 048-049.0, 049.8, 052.0, 052.2, 054.3, 054.74, 056.01, 057.8-058.29, 059.00-059.9, 062.0-064, 066.2-066.49, 072.2, 073.7, 075, 079.82, 079.99, 081.9, 083.9, 090.41, 094.81, 117.5, 124, 130.0, 290.12, 323.01-323.9, 341.1, 382.4, 487.8, 710.0, 771.2, 984.9

`N` Newborn Age: 0   `P` Pediatric Age: 0-17   `M` Maternity Age: 12-55   `A` Adult Age: 15-124   `MCC` Major CC Condition   `CC` CC Condition   `HIV` HIV Related Dx

049.9 Unspecified non-arthropod-borne viral diseases of central nervous system `CC` `HIV`
Viral encephalitis NOS
CC Excl: 013.60-013.66, 046.2, 046.71-046.8, 048-049.0, 049.8-049.9, 052.0, 052.2, 054.3, 054.74, 056.01, 057.8-058.29, 059.00-059.9, 062.0-064, 066.2-066.3, 072.2, 073.7, 075, 079.99, 081.9, 083.9, 090.41, 094.81, 117.5, 124, 130.0, 290.12, 323.01-323.9, 341.1, 382.4, 487.8, 710.0, 771.2, 984.9

VIRAL DISEASES ►GENERALLY◄ ACCOMPANIED BY EXANTHEM (050-059)

EXCLUDES arthropod-borne viral diseases (060.0-066.9)
Boston exanthem (048)

√4ᵗʰ **050 Smallpox**

050.0 Variola major `CC`
Hemorrhagic (pustular)   Malignant smallpox
smallpox   Purpura variolosa
DEF: Form of smallpox known for its high mortality; exists only in laboratories.
CC Excl: 050.0-052.9

050.1 Alastrim `CC`
Variola minor
DEF: Mild form of smallpox known for its low mortality rate.
CC Excl: See code: 050.0

050.2 Modified smallpox `CC`
Varioloid
DEF: Mild form occurring in patients with history of infection or vaccination.
CC Excl: See code: 050.0

050.9 Smallpox, unspecified `CC`
CC Excl: See code: 050.0

√4ᵗʰ **051 Cowpox and paravaccinia**

√5ᵗʰ **051.0 Cowpox and vaccinia not from vaccination**

051.01 Cowpox
DEF: A disease contracted by milking infected cows; vesicles usually appear on the fingers, hands and adjacent areas and usually disappear without scarring; other symptoms: local edema, lymphangitis and regional lymphadenitis with or without fever.
AHA: 4Q, '08, 76-77

051.02 Vaccinia not from vaccination
EXCLUDES vaccinia (generalized) (from vaccination) (999.0)
AHA: 4Q, '08, 76-77

051.1 Pseudocowpox
Milkers' node
DEF: Hand lesions and mild fever in dairy workers caused by exposure to paravaccinia.

051.2 Contagious pustular dermatitis
Ecthyma contagiosum
Orf
DEF: Skin eruptions caused by exposure to poxvirus-infected sheep or goats.

051.9 Paravaccinia, unspecified

√4ᵗʰ **052 Chickenpox**
DEF: Contagious infection by *Varicella-zoster* virus causing rash with pustules and fever.

052.0 Postvaricella encephalitis `MCC`
Postchickenpox encephalitis
CC Excl: 051.9-052.0, 052.2-052.9, 078.88-078.89, 079.81, 079.88-079.99, 139.8

052.1 Varicella (hemorrhagic) pneumonitis `MCC`
CC Excl: 051.9, 052.1-052.9, 078.88-078.89, 079.81, 079.88-079.99, 139.8

052.2 Postvaricella myelitis `MCC`
Postchickenpox myelitis
CC Excl: 051.9, 052.2-052.9, 053.14, 054.74, 078.88-078.89, 079.81, 079.88-079.99, 139.8, 323.01-323.02, 323.41-323.82, 341.20-341.22
AHA: 4Q, '06, 58-63

052.7 With other specified complications `CC`
CC Excl: 051.9, 052.2-052.9, 078.88-078.89, 079.81, 079.88-079.99, 139.8
AHA: 1Q, '02, 3

052.8 With unspecified complication `CC`
CC Excl: See code: 052.7

052.9 Varicella without mention of complication `CC`
Chickenpox NOS   Varicella NOS
CC Excl: See code: 052.7

√4ᵗʰ **053 Herpes zoster**

INCLUDES shingles
zona

DEF: Self-limiting infection by *varicella-zoster* virus causing unilateral eruptions and neuralgia along affected nerves.

053.0 With meningitis `MCC` `HIV`
DEF: *Varicella-zoster* virus infection causing inflammation of the lining of the brain and/or spinal cord.
CC Excl: 003.21, 013.00-013.16, 036.0, 047.0-047.9, 049.0-049.1, 053.0-053.19, 053.79-053.9, 054.72, 054.74-054.9, 058.81-058.89, 072.1, 078.88-078.89, 079.81, 079.88-079.99, 090.42, 091.81, 094.2, 098.89, 100.81, 112.83, 114.2, 115.01, 115.11, 115.91, 130.0, 139.8, 320.0-322.9, 349.89-349.9, 357.0

√5ᵗʰ **053.1 With other nervous system complications**

053.10 With unspecified nervous system complication `CC` `HIV`
CC Excl: 053.0-053.19, 053.79-053.9, 054.72, 054.74-054.9, 058.81-058.89, 078.88-078.89, 079.81, 079.88-079.99, 139.8

053.11 Geniculate herpes zoster `CC` `HIV`
Herpetic geniculate ganglionitis
DEF: Unilateral eruptions and neuralgia along the facial nerve geniculum affecting face and outer and middle ear.
CC Excl: See code: 053.10

053.12 Postherpetic trigeminal neuralgia `CC` `HIV`
DEF: Severe oral or nasal pain following a herpes zoster infection.
CC Excl: See code: 053.10

053.13 Postherpetic polyneuropathy `CC` `HIV`
DEF: Multiple areas of pain following a herpes zoster infection.
CC Excl: See code: 053.10

053.14 Herpes zoster myelitis `MCC`
CC Excl: 052.2, 053.0-053.19, 053.79-053.9, 054.72, 054.74-054.9, 058.81-058.89, 078.88-078.89, 079.81, 079.88-079.99, 139.8, 323.01-323.02, 323.41-323.82, 341.20-341.22
AHA: 4Q, '06, 58-63

053.19 Other `CC` `HIV`
CC Excl: See code: 053.10

√5ᵗʰ **053.2 With ophthalmic complications**

053.20 Herpes zoster dermatitis of eyelid `CC` `HIV`
Herpes zoster ophthalmicus
CC Excl: 053.20-053.29

053.21 Herpes zoster keratoconjunctivitis `CC` `HIV`
CC Excl: See code: 053.20

053.22 Herpes zoster iridocyclitis `CC` `HIV`
CC Excl: See code: 053.20

053.29 Other `CC` `HIV`
CC Excl: See code: 053.20

√4ᵗʰ √5ᵗʰ Additional Digit Required   Unacceptable PDx   Manifestation Code   Hospital Acquired Condition   ►◄ Revised Text   ● New Code   ▲ Revised Code Title

2010 ICD-9-CM   **October 2009 · Volume 1 – 13**

Infectious and Parasitic Diseases

053.7–056.9

√5ᵗʰ **053.7 With other specified complications**

053.71 Otitis externa due to herpes zoster CC HIV
CC Excl: 053.71

053.79 Other CC HIV
CC Excl: 053.0-054.71, 054.73-054.9, 058.21-058.89, 078.88-078.89, 079.81, 079.88-079.99, 139.8

053.8 With unspecified complication CC HIV
CC Excl: See code: 053.79

053.9 Herpes zoster without mention of complication HIV
Herpes zoster NOS

B02.9 Zoster without complications I-10

√4ᵗʰ **054 Herpes simplex**
EXCLUDES congenital herpes simplex (771.2)

054.0 Eczema herpeticum HIV
Kaposi's varicelliform eruption
DEF: Herpes simplex virus invading site of preexisting skin inflammation.

√5ᵗʰ **054.1 Genital herpes**
AHA: J-F, '87, 15, 16

054.10 Genital herpes, unspecified HIV
Herpes progenitalis
A60.00 Herpesviral infection urogenital system unspec I-10

054.11 Herpetic vulvovaginitis HIV ♀

054.12 Herpetic ulceration of vulva HIV ♀

054.13 Herpetic infection of penis HIV ♂

054.19 Other HIV

054.2 Herpetic gingivostomatitis CC HIV
CC Excl: 054.2

054.3 Herpetic meningoencephalitis MCC HIV
Herpes encephalitis
Simian B disease
EXCLUDES human herpesvirus 6 encephalitis (058.21)
other human herpesvirus encephalitis (058.29)
DEF: Inflammation of the brain and its lining, caused by infection of herpes simplex 1 in adults and simplex 2 in newborns.
CC Excl: 054.3, 054.74-054.9, 058.21-058.89, 139.8

√5ᵗʰ **054.4 With ophthalmic complications**

054.40 With unspecified ophthalmic complication CC HIV
CC Excl: 054.40-054.49, 054.79-054.9, 058.81-058.89

054.41 Herpes simplex dermatitis of eyelid CC HIV
CC Excl: See code: 054.40

054.42 Dendritic keratitis CC HIV
CC Excl: See code: 054.40

054.43 Herpes simplex disciform keratitis CC HIV
CC Excl: See code: 054.40

054.44 Herpes simplex iridocyclitis CC HIV
CC Excl: See code: 054.40

054.49 Other CC HIV
CC Excl: See code: 054.40

054.5 Herpetic septicemia MCC HIV
CC Excl: 003.1, 020.2, 036.2, 038.0-038.9, 054.5, 054.74-054.9, 058.81-058.89, 139.8, 995.90-995.94
AHA: 2Q, '00, 5

054.6 Herpetic whitlow HIV
Herpetic felon
DEF: A primary infection of the terminal segment of a finger by herpes simplex; intense itching and pain start the disease, vesicles form, and tissue ultimately is destroyed.

√5ᵗʰ **054.7 With other specified complications**

054.71 Visceral herpes simplex CC HIV
CC Excl: 054.71-054.72, 054.74-054.9, 058.81-058.89, 139.8

054.72 Herpes simplex meningitis MCC HIV
CC Excl: 003.21, 013.00-013.16, 036.0, 047.0-047.9, 049.0-049.1, 053.0, 054.72, 054.74-054.9, 058.81-058.89, 072.1, 090.42, 091.81, 094.2, 098.89, 100.81, 112.83, 114.2, 115.01, 115.11, 115.91, 130.0, 139.8, 320.0-322.9, 349.89-349.9, 357.0

054.73 Herpes simplex otitis externa HIV

054.74 Herpes simplex myelitis MCC
CC Excl: 052.2, 053.14, 054.74-054.9, 058.81-058.89, 078.88-078.89, 079.81, 079.88-079.99, 139.8, 323.01-323.02, 323.41-323.82, 341.20-341.22
AHA: 4Q, '06, 58-63

054.79 Other CC HIV
CC Excl: 054.74-054.9, 058.81-058.89, 078.88-078.89, 079.81, 079.88-079.99, 139.8

054.8 With unspecified complication HIV

054.9 Herpes simplex without mention of complication HIV
B00.9 Herpesviral infection unspecified I-10

√4ᵗʰ **055 Measles**
INCLUDES morbilli
rubeola

055.0 Postmeasles encephalitis MCC
CC Excl: 055.0, 055.79-055.9, 078.88-078.89, 079.81, 079.88-079.99, 139.8

055.1 Postmeasles pneumonia MCC
CC Excl: 055.1, 055.79-055.9, 078.88-078.89, 079.81, 079.88-079.99, 139.8

055.2 Postmeasles otitis media

√5ᵗʰ **055.7 With other specified complications**

055.71 Measles keratoconjunctivitis CC
Measles keratitis
CC Excl: 055.71-055.9, 078.88-078.89, 079.81, 079.88-079.99, 139.8

055.79 Other CC
CC Excl: 055.79-055.9, 078.88-078.89, 079.81, 079.88-079.99, 139.8

055.8 With unspecified complication

055.9 Measles without mention of complication

√4ᵗʰ **056 Rubella**
INCLUDES German measles
EXCLUDES congenital rubella (771.0)
DEF: Acute but usually benign togavirus infection causing fever, sore throat, and rash; associated with complications to fetus as a result of maternal infection.

√5ᵗʰ **056.0 With neurological complications**

056.00 With unspecified neurological complication CC
CC Excl: 056.00-056.09, 056.79-056.9, 078.88-078.89, 079.81, 079.88-079.99, 139.8

056.01 Encephalomyelitis due to rubella MCC
Encephalitis } due to rubella
Meningoencephalitis
CC Excl: See code: 056.00

056.09 Other CC
CC Excl: See code: 056.00

√5ᵗʰ **056.7 With other specified complications**

056.71 Arthritis due to rubella CC
CC Excl: 056.71-056.9, 078.88-078.89, 079.81, 079.88-079.99, 139.8

056.79 Other CC
CC Excl: 056.00-056.09, 056.79-056.9, 078.88-078.89, 079.81, 079.88-079.99, 139.8

056.8 With unspecified complications

056.9 Rubella without mention of complication

N Newborn Age: 0   P Pediatric Age: 0-17   M Maternity Age: 12-55   A Adult Age: 15-124   MCC Major CC Condition   CC CC Condition   HIV HIV Related Dx

14 – Volume 1   2010 ICD-9-CM

√4th **057 Other viral exanthemata**

> **DEF:** Skin eruptions or rashes and fever caused by viruses, including poxviruses.

057.0 Erythema infectiosum [fifth disease] `CC`

> **DEF:** A moderately contagious, benign, epidemic disease, usually seen in children, of probable viral etiology; a red macular rash appears on face and may spread to the limbs and trunk.
> **CC Excl:** 057.0, 079.83

057.8 Other specified viral exanthemata

> Dukes (-Filatow) disease   Parascarlatina
> Fourth disease   Pseudoscarlatina
>
> **EXCLUDES**   *exanthema subitum [sixth disease]*
>   *(058.10-058.12)*
>   *roseola infantum (058.10-058.12)*

057.9 Viral exanthem, unspecified

√4th **058 Other human herpesvirus**

> **EXCLUDES**   *congenital herpes (771.2)*
>   *cytomegalovirus (078.5)*
>   *Epstein-Barr virus (075)*
>   *herpes NOS (054.0-054.9)*
>   *herpes simplex (054.0-054.9)*
>   *herpes zoster (053.0-053.9)*
>   *human herpesvirus NOS (054.0-054.9)*
>   *human herpesvirus 1 (054.0-054.9)*
>   *human herpesvirus 2 (054.0-054.9)*
>   *human herpesvirus 3 (052.0-053.9)*
>   *human herpesvirus 4 (075)*
>   *human herpesvirus 5 (078.5)*
>   *varicella (052.0-052.9)*
>   *varicella-zoster virus (052.0-053.9)*
>
> **AHA:** 4Q, '07, 61

√5th **058.1 Roseola infantum**

> Exanthema subitum [sixth disease]

058.10 Roseola infantum, unspecified `P`

> Exanthema subitum [sixth disease], unspecified
> **AHA:** 4Q, '07, 63

058.11 Roseola infantum due to human herpesvirus 6 `P`

> Exanthema subitum [sixth disease] due to human herpesvirus 6

058.12 Roseola infantum due to human herpesvirus 7 `P`

> Exanthema subitum [sixth disease] due to human herpesvirus 7

√5th **058.2 Other human herpesvirus encephalitis**

> **EXCLUDES**   *herpes encephalitis NOS (054.3)*
>   *herpes simplex encephalitis (054.3)*
>   *human herpesvirus encephalitis NOS (054.3)*
>   *simian B herpesvirus encephalitis (054.3)*

058.21 Human herpesvirus 6 encephalitis `MCC` `HIV`

> **CC Excl:** 054.3, 054.74-054.9, 058.21-058.89, 139.8

058.29 Other human herpesvirus encephalitis `MCC` `HIV`

> Human herpesvirus 7 encephalitis
> **CC Excl:** See code: 058.21

√5th **058.8 Other human herpesvirus infections**

058.81 Human herpesvirus 6 infection

058.82 Human herpesvirus 7 infection

058.89 Other human herpesvirus infection

> Human herpesvirus 8 infection
> Kaposi's sarcoma-associated herpesvirus infection
> **AHA:** 4Q, '07, 63

√4th **059 Other poxvirus infections**

> **EXCLUDES**   *contagious pustular dermatitis (051.2)*
>   *cowpox (051.01)*
>   *ecthyma contagiosum (051.2)*
>   *milker's nodule (051.1)*
>   *orf (051.2)*
>   *paravaccinia NOS (051.9)*
>   *pseudocowpox (051.1)*
>   *smallpox (050.0-050.9)*
>   *vaccinia (generalized) (from vaccination) (999.0)*
>   *vaccinia not from vaccination (051.02)*
>
> **AHA:** ▶4Q, '08, 76-78◀

√5th **059.0 Other orthopoxvirus infections**

059.00 Orthopoxvirus infection, unspecified

059.01 Monkeypox `CC`

> **CC Excl:** 051.01-051.02, 057.0-057.9, 059.00-059.9

059.09 Other orthopoxvirus infection

√5th **059.1 Other parapoxvirus infections**

059.10 Parapoxvirus infection, unspecified

059.11 Bovine stomatitis

059.12 Sealpox

059.19 Other parapoxvirus infections

√5th **059.2 Yatapoxvirus infections**

059.20 Yatapoxvirus infection, unspecified

059.21 Tanapox `CC`

> **CC Excl:** See code: 059.01

059.22 Yaba monkey tumor virus

059.8 Other poxvirus infections

059.9 Poxvirus infections, unspecified

ARTHROPOD-BORNE VIRAL DISEASES (060-066)

> Use additional code to identify any associated meningitis (321.2)
> **EXCLUDES**   *late effects of viral encephalitis (139.0)*

√4th **060 Yellow fever**

> **DEF:** Fever and jaundice from infection by mosquito-borne virus of genus *Flavivirus*.

060.0 Sylvatic `CC`

> Yellow fever: Yellow fever:
>   jungle   sylvan
> **DEF:** Yellow fever transmitted from animal to man, via mosquito.
> **CC Excl:** 060.0-060.9

060.1 Urban `CC`

> **DEF:** Yellow fever transmitted from man to man, via mosquito.
> **CC Excl:** See code: 060.0

060.9 Yellow fever, unspecified `CC`

> **CC Excl:** See code: 060.0

061 Dengue `CC`

> Breakbone fever
> **EXCLUDES**   *hemorrhagic fever caused by dengue virus (065.4)*
> **DEF:** Acute, self-limiting infection by mosquito-borne virus characterized by fever and generalized aches.
> **CC Excl:** 061

√4th **062 Mosquito-borne viral encephalitis**

062.0 Japanese encephalitis `MCC`

> Japanese B encephalitis
> **DEF:** Flavivirus causing inflammation of the brain, with a wide range of clinical manifestations.
> **CC Excl:** 013.60-013.66, 046.2, 046.71-046.8, 048-049.0, 049.8, 052.0, 052.2, 054.3, 054.74, 056.01, 057.8-058.29, 059.00-059.9, 062.0-064, 066.2-066.49, 072.2, 073.7, 075, 079.82, 079.99, 081.9, 083.9, 090.41, 094.81, 117.5, 124, 130.0, 290.12, 323.01-323.9, 341.1, 487.8, 771.2, 984.9

Infectious and Parasitic Diseases

062.1–066.41

062.1 Western equine encephalitis `MCC`
DEF: Alphavirus WEE infection causing inflammation of the brain, found in areas west of the Mississippi; transmitted horse to mosquito to man.
CC Excl: See code: 062.0

062.2 Eastern equine encephalitis `MCC`
EXCLUDES *Venezuelan equine encephalitis (066.2)*
DEF: Alphavirus EEE causing inflammation of the brain and spinal cord, found from Canada to South America and Mexico; transmitted horse to mosquito to man.
CC Excl: See code: 062.0

062.3 St. Louis encephalitis `MCC`
DEF: Epidemic form caused by Flavivirus and transmitted by mosquito, and characterized by fever, difficulty in speech, and headache.
CC Excl: See code: 062.0

062.4 Australian encephalitis `MCC`
Australian arboencephalitis
Australian X disease
Murray Valley encephalitis
DEF: Flavivirus causing inflammation of the brain, occurring in Australia and New Guinea.
CC Excl: See code: 062.0

062.5 California virus encephalitis `MCC`
Encephalitis: Tahyna fever
    California
    La Crosse
DEF: Bunyamwere virus causing inflammation of the brain.
CC Excl: See code: 062.0

062.8 Other specified mosquito-borne viral encephalitis `MCC`
Encephalitis by Ilheus virus
EXCLUDES *West Nile virus (066.40-066.49)*
CC Excl: See code: 062.0

062.9 Mosquito-borne viral encephalitis, unspecified `MCC`
CC Excl: See code: 062.0

√4ᵗʰ 063 Tick-borne viral encephalitis
INCLUDES diphasic meningoencephalitis

063.0 Russian spring-summer [taiga] encephalitis `MCC`
CC Excl: See code: 062.0

063.1 Louping ill `MCC`
DEF: Inflammation of brain caused by virus transmitted sheep to tick to man; incidence usually limited to British Isles.
CC Excl: See code: 062.0

063.2 Central European encephalitis `MCC`
DEF: Inflammation of brain caused by virus transmitted by tick; limited to central Europe and presenting with two distinct phases.
CC Excl: See code: 062.0

063.8 Other specified tick-borne viral encephalitis `MCC`
Langat encephalitis   Powassan encephalitis
CC Excl: See code: 062.0

063.9 Tick-borne viral encephalitis, unspecified `MCC`
CC Excl: See code: 062.0

064 Viral encephalitis transmitted by other and unspecified arthropods `MCC`
Arthropod-borne viral encephalitis, vector unknown
Negishi virus encephalitis
EXCLUDES *viral encephalitis NOS (049.9)*
CC Excl: See code: 062.0

√4ᵗʰ 065 Arthropod-borne hemorrhagic fever

065.0 Crimean hemorrhagic fever [CHF Congo virus] `CC`
Central Asian hemorrhagic fever
CC Excl: 065.0-066.9

065.1 Omsk hemorrhagic fever `CC`
CC Excl: See code: 065.0

065.2 Kyasanur Forest disease `CC`
CC Excl: See code: 065.0

065.3 Other tick-borne hemorrhagic fever `CC`
CC Excl: See code: 065.0

065.4 Mosquito-borne hemorrhagic fever `CC`
Chikungunya hemorrhagic fever
Dengue hemorrhagic fever
EXCLUDES *Chikungunya fever (066.3)*
dengue (061)
yellow fever (060.0-060.9)
CC Excl: See code: 065.0

065.8 Other specified arthropod-borne hemorrhagic fever `CC`
Mite-borne hemorrhagic fever
CC Excl: See code: 065.0

065.9 Arthropod-borne hemorrhagic fever, unspecified `CC`
Arbovirus hemorrhagic fever NOS
CC Excl: See code: 065.0

√4ᵗʰ 066 Other arthropod-borne viral diseases

066.0 Phlebotomus fever `CC`
Changuinola fever
Sandfly fever
DEF: Sandfly-borne viral infection occurring in Asia, Mideast and South America.
CC Excl: See code: 065.0

066.1 Tick-borne fever `CC`
Nairobi sheep disease
Tick fever:
    American mountain
    Colorado
    Kemerovo
    Quaranfil
CC Excl: See code: 065.0

066.2 Venezuelan equine fever `CC`
Venezuelan equine encephalitis
DEF: Alphavirus VEE infection causing inflammation of the brain, usually limited to South America, Mexico, and Florida; transmitted horse to mosquito to man.
CC Excl: 013.60-013.66, 046.2, 046.71-046.8, 048-049.0, 049.8, 052.0, 052.2, 054.3, 054.74, 056.01, 057.8-058.29, 059.00-059.9, 062.0-066.9, 072.2, 073.7, 075, 079.82, 079.99, 081.9, 083.9, 090.41, 094.81, 117.5, 124, 130.0, 290.12, 323.01-323.9, 341.1, 487.8, 771.2, 984.9

066.3 Other mosquito-borne fever `CC`
Fever (viral):   Fever (viral):
   Bunyamwera   Oropouche
   Bwamba   Pixuna
   Chikungunya   Rift valley
   Guama   Ross river
   Mayaro   Wesselsbron
   Mucambo   Zika
   O'Nyong-Nyong
EXCLUDES *dengue (061)*
yellow fever (060.0-060.9)
CC Excl: See code: 066.2

√5ᵗʰ 066.4 West Nile fever
DEF: Mosquito-borne fever causing fatal inflammation of the brain, the lining of the brain, or of the lining of the brain and spinal cord.
AHA: 4Q, '02, 44

066.40 West Nile fever, unspecified `MCC`
West Nile fever NOS
West Nile fever without complications
West Nile virus NOS
CC Excl: 013.60-013.66, 046.2, 046.71-046.8, 048-049.0, 049.8, 052.0, 052.2, 054.3, 054.74, 056.01, 057.8-058.29, 059.00-059.9, 062.0-066.3, 066.8-066.9, 072.2, 073.7, 075, 079.99, 081.9, 083.9, 090.41, 094.81, 117.5, 124, 130.0, 323.01-323.9, 341.1, 487.8, 771.2

066.41 West Nile fever with encephalitis `MCC`
West Nile encephalitis
West Nile encephalomyelitis
CC Excl: See code: 066.40
AHA: 4Q, '04, 51

`N` Newborn Age: 0   `P` Pediatric Age: 0-17   `M` Maternity Age: 12-55   `A` Adult Age: 15-124   `MCC` Major CC Condition   `CC` CC Condition   `HIV` HIV Related Dx

16 – Volume 1   2010 ICD-9-CM

066.42 West Nile fever with other neurologic manifestation `MCC`
Use additional code to specify the neurologic manifestation
CC Excl: See code: 066.40
AHA: 4Q, '04, 51

066.49 West Nile fever with other complications `MCC`
Use additional code to specify the other conditions
CC Excl: See code: 066.40

066.8 Other specified arthropod-borne viral diseases `CC`
Chandipura fever
Piry fever
CC Excl: 065.0-066.9

066.9 Arthropod-borne viral disease, unspecified `CC`
Arbovirus infection NOS
CC Excl: 065.0-066.9

OTHER DISEASES DUE TO VIRUSES AND CHLAMYDIAE (070-079)

✓4ᵗʰ **070 Viral hepatitis**

`INCLUDES`   viral hepatitis (acute) (chronic)
`EXCLUDES`   *cytomegalic inclusion virus hepatitis (078.5)*

The following fifth-digit subclassification is for use with categories 070.2 and 070.3:
    0 acute or unspecified, without mention of hepatitis delta
    1 acute or unspecified, with hepatitis delta
    2 chronic, without mention of hepatitis delta
    3 chronic, with hepatitis delta

DEF: Hepatitis A : HAV infection is self-limiting with flulike symptoms; transmission, fecal-oral.
DEF: Hepatitis B: HBV infection can be chronic and systemic; transmission, bodily fluids.
DEF: Hepatitis C: HCV infection can be chronic and systemic; transmission, blood transfusion and unidentified agents.
DEF: Hepatitis D (delta): HDV occurs only in the presence of hepatitis B virus.
DEF: Hepatitis E: HEV is epidemic form; transmission and nature under investigation.
AHA: 2Q,'07, 5

070.0 Viral hepatitis A with hepatic coma `MCC`
CC Excl: 070.0-070.9, 078.88-078.89, 079.81, 079.88-079.99, 139.8

070.1 Viral hepatitis A without mention of hepatic coma `CC`
Infectious hepatitis
CC Excl: See code: 070.0

§ ✓5ᵗʰ **070.2 Viral hepatitis B with hepatic coma** `MCC`
[0-3]   **CC Excl:** See code: 070.0
AHA: 4Q, '91, 28; **For code 070.20:** 2Q, '07, 6

§ ✓5ᵗʰ **070.3 Viral hepatitis B without mention of hepatic coma** `CC`
[0-3]   Serum hepatitis
CC Excl: See code: 070.0
AHA: 1Q, '93, 28; 4Q, '91, 28
B16.9 Acute hep B w/o delta-agent & w/o hepatic coma `I-10`

✓5ᵗʰ **070.4 Other specified viral hepatitis with hepatic coma**
AHA: 4Q, '91, 28

070.41 Acute hepatitis C with hepatic coma `MCC`
CC Excl: See code: 070.0

070.42 Hepatitis delta without mention of active `MCC` **hepatitis B disease with hepatic coma**
Hepatitis delta with hepatitis B carrier state
CC Excl: See code: 070.0

070.43 Hepatitis E with hepatic coma `MCC`
CC Excl: See code: 070.0

070.44 Chronic hepatitis C with hepatic coma `MCC`
CC Excl: See code: 070.0
AHA: 2Q,'07, 5

070.49 Other specified viral hepatitis `MCC` **with hepatic coma**
CC Excl: See code: 070.0

✓5ᵗʰ **070.5 Other specified viral hepatitis without mention of hepatic coma**
AHA: 4Q, '91, 28

070.51 Acute hepatitis C without mention of hepatic coma `CC`
CC Excl: See code: 070.0

070.52 Hepatitis delta without mention of active hepatititis B disease or hepatic coma `CC`
CC Excl: See code: 070.0

070.53 Hepatitis E without mention of hepatic coma `CC`
CC Excl: See code: 070.0

070.54 Chronic hepatitis C without mention of hepatic coma
AHA: ▶4Q, '08, 120;◀ 3Q, '07, 7; 2Q, '06, 13
B18.2 Chronic viral hepatitis C `I-10`

070.59 Other specified viral hepatitis without mention of hepatic coma `CC`
CC Excl: See code: 070.0

070.6 Unspecified viral hepatitis with hepatic coma `MCC`
`EXCLUDES`   *unspecified viral hepatitis C with hepatic coma (070.71)*
CC Excl: See code: 070.0

✓5ᵗʰ **070.7 Unspecified viral hepatitis C**

070.70 Unspecified viral hepatitis C without hepatic coma
Unspecified viral hepatitis C NOS
AHA: 4Q, '04, 52
B19.20 Unspecified viral hepatits C w/o hepatic coma `I-10`

070.71 Unspecified viral hepatitis C with hepatic coma `MCC`
CC Excl: See code: 070.0
AHA: 4Q, '04, 52

070.9 Unspecified viral hepatitis without mention of hepatic coma `CC`
Viral hepatitis NOS
`EXCLUDES`   *unspecified viral hepatitis C without hepatic coma (070.70)*
CC Excl: See code: 070.0

071 Rabies `CC`
Hydrophobia
Lyssa
DEF: Acute infectious disease of the CNS caused by a rhabdovirus; usually spread by bites by infected animals; progresses from fever, restlessness, and extreme excitability, to hydrophobia, seizures, confusion and death.
CC Excl: 071

✓4ᵗʰ **072 Mumps**
DEF: Acute infectious disease caused by paramyxovirus; usually seen in children less than 15 years of age; salivary glands are typically enlarged, involves other organs, such as testes, pancreas and meninges.

072.0 Mumps orchitis `CC` ♂
CC Excl: 072.0, 072.79-072.9, 078.88-078.89, 079.81, 079.88-079.99, 139.8

072.1 Mumps meningitis `MCC`
CC Excl: 003.21, 013.00-013.16, 036.0, 047.0-047.9, 049.0-049.1, 053.0, 054.72, 072.1, 072.79-072.9, 078.88-078.89, 079.81, 079.88-079.99, 090.42, 091.81, 094.2, 098.89, 100.81, 112.83, 114.2, 115.01, 115.11, 115.91, 130.0, 139.8, 320.0-322.9, 349.89-349.9, 357.0

072.2 Mumps encephalitis `MCC`
Mumps meningoencephalitis
CC Excl: 072.2, 072.79-072.9, 078.88-078.89, 079.81, 079.88-079.99, 139.8

072.3 Mumps pancreatitis `CC`
CC Excl: 072.3, 072.79-072.9, 078.88-078.89, 079.81, 079.88-079.99, 139.8

§   Requires fifth digit. Valid digits are in [brackets] under each code. See category 070 for codes and definitions.

Infectious and Parasitic Diseases

072.7–078.0

√5ᵗʰ **072.7 Mumps with other specified complications**

    072.71 Mumps hepatitis `CC`
        CC Excl: 072.71, 072.79-072.9, 078.88-078.89, 079.81, 079.88-079.99, 139.8

    072.72 Mumps polyneuropathy `CC`
        CC Excl: 072.72-072.9, 078.88-078.89, 079.81, 079.88-079.99, 139.8

    072.79 Other `CC`
        CC Excl: 072.79-072.9, 078.88-078.89, 079.81, 079.88-079.99, 139.8

072.8 Mumps with unspecified complication `CC`
    CC Excl: 072.79-072.9, 078.88-078.89, 079.81, 079.88-079.99

072.9 Mumps without mention of complication
    Epidemic parotitis
    Infectious parotitis

√4ᵗʰ **073 Ornithosis**

    INCLUDES   parrot fever
                 psittacosis

    DEF: *Chlamydia psittaci* infection often transmitted from birds to humans.

073.0 With pneumonia `MCC`
    Lobular pneumonitis due to ornithosis
    CC Excl: 011.00-012.16, 012.80-012.86, 017.90-017.96, 020.3-020.5, 021.3, 022.1, 031.0, 039.1, 073.0, 073.8-073.9, 115.05, 115.15, 115.95, 122.1, 130.4, 136.3, 480.0-482.41, 482.49-487.1, 488, 495.0-495.9, 500-508.9, 517.1, 517.8, 518.89, 519.8-519.9

073.7 With other specified complications `CC`
    CC Excl: 013.60-013.66, 046.2, 046.71-046.8, 048-049.0, 049.8, 052.0, 052.2, 054.3, 054.74, 056.01, 057.8-058.29, 059.00-059.9, 062.0-064, 066.2-066.49, 072.2, 073.0-073.9, 079.82, 079.99, 081.9, 083.9, 090.41, 094.81, 117.5, 124, 130.0, 290.12, 323.01-323.9, 341.1, 487.8, 771.2, 984.9

073.8 With unspecified complication `CC`
    CC Excl: 073.0, 073.8-073.9

073.9 Ornithosis, unspecified `CC`
    CC Excl: See code: 073.8

√4ᵗʰ **074 Specific diseases due to Coxsackie virus**

    EXCLUDES   *Coxsackie virus:*
              infection NOS (079.2)
              meningitis (047.0)

074.0 Herpangina
    Vesicular pharyngitis
    DEF: Acute infectious coxsackie virus infection causing throat lesions, fever, and vomiting; generally affects children in summer.

074.1 Epidemic pleurodynia
    Bornholm disease   Epidemic:
    Devil's grip   myalgia
                     myositis
    DEF: Paroxysmal pain in chest, accompanied by fever and usually limited to children and young adults; caused by coxsackie virus.

√5ᵗʰ **074.2 Coxsackie carditis**

    074.20 Coxsackie carditis, unspecified `CC`
        CC Excl: 074.20, 074.22-074.23, 093.82, 390, 391.2-391.9, 398.0-398.90, 398.99, 422.0-422.99, 429.0, 429.71-429.79, 459.89-459.9

    074.21 Coxsackie pericarditis `CC`
        DEF: Coxsackie infection of the outer lining of the heart.
        CC Excl: 074.21, 093.81, 391.0, 393, 420.0-420.99, 423.3-423.9, 459.89-459.9

    074.22 Coxsackie endocarditis `CC`
        DEF: Coxsackie infection within the heart's cavities.
        CC Excl: 002.0, 036.42, 074.22, 083.0, 093.20-093.24, 098.84, 112.81, 115.94, 116.0, 390, 391.1, 391.8-392.0, 394.0-395.9, 396.9-397.9, 398.90, 398.99, 421.0-421.9, 424.0-424.99, 425.3, 459.89-459.9, 746.09, 746.89, 996.61

074.23 Coxsackie myocarditis `CC`
    Aseptic myocarditis of newborn
    DEF: Coxsackie infection of the muscle of the heart.
    CC Excl: See code: 074.20

074.3 Hand, foot, and mouth disease
    Vesicular stomatitis and exanthem
    DEF: Mild coxsackie infection causing lesions on hands, feet and oral mucosa, most commonly seen in preschool children.

074.8 Other specified diseases due to Coxsackie virus
    Acute lymphonodular pharyngitis

075 Infectious mononucleosis
    Glandular fever   Pfeiffer's disease
    Monocytic angina
    DEF: Acute infection by Epstein-Barr virus causing fever, sore throat, enlarged lymph glands and spleen, and fatigue; usually seen in teens and young adults.
    AHA: 3Q, '01, 13; M-A, '87, 8

√4ᵗʰ **076 Trachoma**

    EXCLUDES   *late effect of trachoma (139.1)*

    DEF: A chronic infectious disease of the cornea and conjunctiva caused by a strain of the bacteria *Chlamydia trachomatis;* the infection can cause photophobia, pain, excessive tearing and sometimes blindness.

076.0 Initial stage
    Trachoma dubium

076.1 Active stage
    Granular conjunctivitis (trachomatous)
    Trachomatous:
        follicular conjunctivitis
        pannus

076.9 Trachoma, unspecified
    Trachoma NOS

√4ᵗʰ **077 Other diseases of conjunctiva due to viruses and Chlamydiae**

    EXCLUDES   *ophthalmic complications of viral diseases classified elsewhere*

077.0 Inclusion conjunctivitis
    Paratrachoma   Swimming pool conjunctivitis
    EXCLUDES   *inclusion blennorrhea (neonatal) (771.6)*
    DEF: Pus in conjunctiva caused by *Chlamydiae trachomatis.*

077.1 Epidemic keratoconjunctivitis
    Shipyard eye
    DEF: Highly contagious corneal or conjunctival infection caused by adenovirus type 8; symptoms include inflammation and corneal infiltrates.

077.2 Pharyngoconjunctival fever
    Viral pharyngoconjunctivitis

077.3 Other adenoviral conjunctivitis
    Acute adenoviral follicular conjunctivitis

077.4 Epidemic hemorrhagic conjunctivitis
    Apollo:
        conjunctivitis
        disease
    Conjunctivitis due to enterovirus type 70
    Hemorrhagic conjunctivitis (acute) (epidemic)

077.8 Other viral conjunctivitis
    Newcastle conjunctivitis

√5ᵗʰ **077.9 Unspecified diseases of conjunctiva due to viruses and Chlamydiae**

    077.98 Due to Chlamydiae

    077.99 Due to viruses
        Viral conjunctivitis NOS

        B97.8 Other viral agents cause of dz class `I-10`
        elsewhere

√4ᵗʰ **078 Other diseases due to viruses and Chlamydiae**

    EXCLUDES   *viral infection NOS (079.0-079.9)*
              viremia NOS (790.8)

078.0 Molluscum contagiosum
    DEF: Benign poxvirus infection causing small bumps on the skin or conjunctiva; transmitted by close contact.

N Newborn Age: 0   P Pediatric Age: 0-17   M Maternity Age: 12-55   A Adult Age: 15-124   MCC Major CC Condition   CC CC Condition   HIV HIV Related Dx

√5th **078.1** **Viral warts**
Viral warts due to human papilloma virus

DEF: A keratotic papilloma of the epidermis caused by the human papilloma virus; the superficial vegetative lesions last for varying durations and eventually regress spontaneously.
AHA: 2Q, '97, 9; 4Q, '93, 22

078.10 **Viral warts, unspecified**
Verruca:
Vulgaris
Warts (infectious)

078.11 **Condyloma acuminatum**
Condyloma NOS
Genital warts NOS

DEF: Clusters of mucosa or epidermal lesions on external genitalia; viral infection is sexually transmitted.

078.12 **Plantar wart**
Verruca plantaris
AHA: ▶4Q. '08, 78-79◀

078.19 **Other specified viral warts**
Common wartx   Veruca planna
Flat wart

078.2 **Sweating fever**
Miliary fever
Sweating disease

DEF: A viral infection characterized by profuse sweating; various papular, vesicular and other eruptions cause the blockage of sweat glands.

078.3 **Cat-scratch disease**   `CC`
Benign lymphoreticulosis (of inoculation)
Cat-scratch fever
CC Excl: 078.3, 079.82

078.4 **Foot and mouth disease**
Aphthous fever   Epizootic:
Epizootic: stomatitis
aphthae

DEF: Ulcers on oral mucosa, legs, and feet after exposure to infected animal.

078.5 **Cytomegaloviral disease**   `CC` `HIV`
Cytomegalic inclusion disease
Salivary gland virus disease

Use additional code to identify manifestation, as:
cytomegalic inclusion virus:
hepatitis (573.1)
pneumonia (484.1)

EXCLUDES congenital cytomegalovirus infection (771.1)

DEF: A herpesvirus associated with serious disease morbidity including fever, leukopenia, pneumonia, retinitis, hepatitis and organ transplant; often leads to hepatomegaly, splenomegaly and thrombocytopenia; a common post-transplant complication.
CC Excl: 078.5-078.7, 078.89-079.50, 079.59, 079.81-079.82, 079.89, 079.99
AHA: 1Q, '03, 10; 3Q, '98, 4; 2Q, '93, 11; 1Q, '89, 9

078.6 **Hemorrhagic nephrosonephritis**   `CC`
Hemorrhagic fever: Hemorrhagic fever:
epidemic   Russian
Korean   with renal syndrome

DEF: Viral infection causing kidney dysfunction and bleeding disorders.
CC Excl: 016.00-016.06, 016.30-016.36, 016.90-016.96, 017.90-017.96, 078.6, 079.82, 098.10, 098.19, 098.30-098.31, 098.89, 112.2, 131.00, 131.8-131.9, 249.40-249.41, 249.80-249.91, 250.40-250.43, 250.80-250.93, 274.10, 274.19, 580.0-584.9, 586-591, 593.0-593.2, 593.89-593.9, 599.70-599.9

078.7 **Arenaviral hemorrhagic fever**   `CC`
Hemorrhagic fever: Hemorrhagic fever:
Argentine   Junin virus
Bolivian   Machupo virus
CC Excl: 078.5-079.82, 079.88-079.99

√5th **078.8** **Other specified diseases due to viruses and Chlamydiae**
EXCLUDES epidemic diarrhea (009.2)
lymphogranuloma venereum (099.1)

078.81 **Epidemic vertigo**

078.82 **Epidemic vomiting syndrome**
Winter vomiting disease

078.88 **Other specified diseases due to Chlamydiae**
AHA: 4Q, '96, 22

078.89 **Other specified diseases due to viruses**
Epidemic cervical myalgia
Marburg disease

√4th **079** **Viral and chlamydial infection in conditions classified elsewhere and of unspecified site**
Note: This category is provided to be used as an additional code to identify the viral agent in diseases classifiable elsewhere. This category will also be used to classify virus infection of unspecified nature or site.

079.0 **Adenovirus**

079.1 **ECHO virus**
DEF: An "orphan" enteric RNA virus, certain serotypes of which are associated with human disease, especially aseptic meningitis.

079.2 **Coxsackie virus**
DEF: A heterogenous group of viruses associated with aseptic meningitis, myocarditis, pericarditis, and acute onset juvenile diabetes.

079.3 **Rhinovirus**
DEF: Rhinoviruses affect primarily the upper respiratory tract. Over 100 distinct types infect humans.

079.4 **Human papillomavirus**
DEF: Viral infection caused by the genus *Papillomavirus* causing cutaneous and genital warts, including verruca vulgaris and condyloma acuminatum; certain types are associated with cervical dysplasia, cancer and other genital malignancies.
AHA: 2Q, '97, 9; 4Q, '93, 22
TIP: Do not assign for viral warts; see instead subcategory 078.1.

√5th **079.5** **Retrovirus**
EXCLUDES human immunodeficiency virus, type 1 [HIV-1] (042)
human T-cell lymphotrophic virus, type III [HTLV-III] (042)
lymphadenopathy-associated virus [LAV] (042)

DEF: A large group of RNA viruses that carry reverse transcriptase and include the leukoviruses and lentiviruses.
AHA: 4Q, '93, 22, 23

079.50 **Retrovirus, unspecified**

079.51 **Human T-cell lymphotrophic virus, type I [HTLV-I]**   `CC`
CC Excl: 079.51-079.59, 079.81-079.82, 079.88-079.99

079.52 **Human T-cell lymphotrophic virus, type II [HTLV-II]**   `CC`
CC Excl: 079.50-079.59, 079.81-079.82, 079.88-079.99

079.53 **Human immunodeficiency virus, type 2 [HIV-2]**   `CC`
CC Excl: 042, 079.50-079.59, 079.81-079.82, 079.88-079.99

079.59 **Other specified retrovirus**

079.6 **Respiratory syncytial virus [RSV]**
DEF: The major respiratory pathogen of young children, causing severe bronchitis and bronchopneumonia, and minor infection in adults.
AHA: 4Q, '96, 27, 28

√5th **079.8** **Other specified viral and chlamydial infections**
AHA: 1Q, '88, 12

079.81 **Hantavirus**   `CC`
DEF: An infection caused by the Muerto Canyon virus whose primary rodent reservoir is the deer mouse Peromyscus maniculatus; commonly characterized by fever, myalgias, headache, cough.
CC Excl: 070.70-070.71, 078.5-079.82, 079.88-079.99
AHA: 4Q, '95, 60

AKA Sin Nombre Virus (handwritten annotation)

Infectious and Parasitic Diseases

079.82–084.1

079.82 SARS-associated coronavirus `CC`

DEF: A life-threatening respiratory disease, severe acute respiratory syndrome (SARS); etiology coronavirus; presenting symptoms may range from mild to severe forms of flu-like conditions; fever, chills, cough, headache, myalgia; diagnosis of SARS is based upon clinical, laboratory, and epidemiological criteria.

CC Excl: 011.00-012.16, 012.80-012.86, 017.90-017.96, 021.2, 031.0, 039.1, 079.82, 079.89, 115.05, 115.15, 115.95, 122.1, 130.4, 136.3, 480.0-480.2, 480.8-487.1, 488, 494.0-508.9, 517.1, 517.8, 518.89, 519.8-519.9, 748.61

AHA: 4Q, '03, 46

079.83 Parvovirus B19 `CC`

Human parvovirus   Parvovirus NOS

EXCLUDES   erythema infectiosum [fifth disease] (057.0)

DEF: The only known parvovirus to cause disease in humans; manifestation is erythema infectiosum; also associated with polyarthropathy, chronic anemia, red cell aplasia, and fetal hydrops.

CC Excl: 057.0, 079.83

AHA: 4Q, '07, 64

079.88 Other specified chlamydial infection

079.89 Other specified viral infection

√5th **079.9 Unspecified viral and chlamydial infections**

EXCLUDES   viremia NOS (790.8)

AHA: 2Q, '91, 8

079.98 Unspecified chlamydial infection

Chlamydial infections NOS

079.99 Unspecified viral infection

Viral infections NOS

B97.8 Other viral agents cause of dz class elsewhere `I-10`

RICKETTSIOSES AND OTHER ARTHROPOD-BORNE DISEASES (080-088)

EXCLUDES   arthropod-borne viral diseases (060.0-066.9)

080 Louse-borne [epidemic] typhus `CC`

Typhus (fever):   Typhus (fever):
  classical   exanthematic NOS
  epidemic   louse-borne

DEF: *Rickettsia prowazekii*; causes severe headache, rash, high fever.

CC Excl: 080-083.9, 085.0-088.9

√4th **081 Other typhus**

081.0 Murine [endemic] typhus `CC`

Typhus (fever):   Typhus (fever):
  endemic   flea-borne

DEF: Milder typhus caused by *Rickettsia typhi (mooseri)*; transmitted by rat flea.

CC Excl: See code: 080

081.1 Brill's disease `CC`

Brill-Zinsser disease   Recrudescent typhus (fever)

CC Excl: See code: 080

081.2 Scrub typhus `CC`

Japanese river fever   Mite-borne typhus
Kedani fever   Tsutsugamushi

CC Excl: See code: 080

081.9 Typhus, unspecified `CC`

Typhus (fever) NOS

CC Excl: 013.60-013.66, 046.2, 046.71-046.8, 048-049.0, 049.8, 052.0, 052.2, 054.3, 054.74, 056.01, 057.8-058.29, 059.00-059.9, 062.0-064, 066.2-066.49, 072.2, 073.7, 079.82, 079.99-084.0, 085.0-088.9, 090.41, 094.81, 117.5, 124, 130.0, 290.12, 323.01-323.9, 341.1, 487.8, 771.2, 984.9

√4th **082 Tick-borne rickettsioses**

082.0 Spotted fevers `CC`

Rocky mountain spotted fever
Sao Paulo fever

CC Excl: See code: 080

082.1 Boutonneuse fever `CC`

African tick typhus   Marseilles fever
India tick typhus   Mediterranean tick fever
Kenya tick typhus

CC Excl: See code: 080

082.2 North Asian tick fever `CC`

Siberian tick typhus

CC Excl: See code: 080

082.3 Queensland tick typhus `CC`

CC Excl: See code: 080

√5th **082.4 Ehrlichiosis**

AHA: 3Q, '06, 11; 4Q, '00, 38

082.40 Ehrlichiosis, unspecified `CC`

CC Excl: See code: 080

082.41 Ehrlichiosis chaffeensis [E. chaffeensis] `CC`

DEF: A febrile illness caused by bacterial infection, also called human monocytic ehrlichiosis (HME). Causal organism is *Ehrlichia chaffeensis*, transmitted by the Lone Star tick. Symptoms include fever, chills, myalgia, nausea, vomiting, diarrhea, confusion, and severe headache occurring one week after a tick bite. Clinical findings are lymphadenopathy, rash, thrombocytopenia, leukopenia, and abnormal liver function tests.

CC Excl: See code: 080

082.49 Other ehrlichiosis `CC`

CC Excl: See code: 080

082.8 Other specified tick-borne rickettsioses `CC`

Lone star fever

CC Excl: See code: 080

AHA: 4Q, '99, 19

082.9 Tick-borne rickettsiosis, unspecified `CC`

Tick-borne typhus NOS

CC Excl: See code: 080

√4th **083 Other rickettsioses**

083.0 Q fever `CC`

DEF: Infection of *Coxiella burnettii* usually acquired through airborne organisms.

CC Excl: See code: 080

083.1 Trench fever `CC`

Quintan fever
Wolhynian fever

CC Excl: See code: 080

083.2 Rickettsialpox `CC`

Vesicular rickettsiosis

DEF: Infection of *Rickettsia akari* usually acquired through a mite bite.

CC Excl: 082.0-083.9

083.8 Other specified rickettsioses `CC`

CC Excl: See code: 083.2

083.9 Rickettsiosis, unspecified `CC`

CC Excl: See code: 083.2

√4th **084 Malaria**

Note: Subcategories 084.0-084.6 exclude the listed conditions with mention of pernicious complications (084.8-084.9).

EXCLUDES   congenital malaria (771.2)

DEF: Mosquito-borne disease causing high fever and prostration and cataloged by species of *Plasmodium: P. falciparum, P. malariae, P. ovale,* and *P. vivax.*

084.0 Falciparum malaria [malignant tertian] `MCC`

Malaria (fever):
    by Plasmodium falciparum
    subtertian

CC Excl: 084.0-086.9

084.1 Vivax malaria [benign tertian] `CC`

Malaria (fever) by Plasmodium vivax

CC Excl: 084.0-088.9

`N` Newborn Age: 0   `P` Pediatric Age: 0-17   `M` Maternity Age: 12-55   `A` Adult Age: 15-124   `MCC` Major CC Condition   `CC` CC Condition   `HIV` HIV Related Dx

20 – Volume 1

2010 ICD-9-CM

084.2 Quartan malaria   `CC`
    Malaria (fever) by Plasmodium malariae
    Malariae malaria
    CC Excl: See code: 084.0

084.3 Ovale malaria   `CC`
    Malaria (fever) by Plasmodium ovale
    CC Excl: See code: 084.0

084.4 Other malaria   `CC`
    Monkey malaria
    CC Excl: See code: 084.0

084.5 Mixed malaria   `CC`
    Malaria (fever) by more than one parasite
    CC Excl: See code: 084.0

084.6 Malaria, unspecified   `CC`
    Malaria (fever) NOS
    CC Excl: 079.82, 084.0-086.9

084.7 Induced malaria   `CC`
    Therapeutically induced malaria
    EXCLUDES *accidental infection from syringe, blood*
               transfusion, etc. (084.0-084.6, above,
               according to parasite species)
               transmission from mother to child during
               delivery (771.2)
    CC Excl: 084.1-086.9

084.8 Blackwater fever   `CC`
    Hemoglobinuric:
        fever (bilious)
        malaria
    Malarial hemoglobinuria
    DEF: Severe hemic and renal complication of *Plasmodium falciparum* infection.
    CC Excl: See code: 084.0

084.9 Other pernicious complications of malaria   `CC`
    Algid malaria
    Cerebral malaria
    Use additional code to identify complication, as:
        malarial:
            hepatitis (573.2)
            nephrosis (581.81)
    CC Excl: See code: 084.0

√4ᵗʰ **085 Leishmaniasis**

085.0 Visceral [kala-azar]   `CC`
    Dumdum fever
    Infection by Leishmania:
        donovani
        infantum
    Leishmaniasis:
        dermal, post-kala-azar
        Mediterranean
        visceral (Indian)
    CC Excl: 080-088.9

085.1 Cutaneous, urban   `CC`
    Aleppo boil
    Baghdad boil
    Delhi boil
    Infection by Leishmania tropica (minor)
    Leishmaniasis, cutaneous:
        dry form
        late
        recurrent
        ulcerating
    Oriental sore
    CC Excl: See code: 085.0

085.2 Cutaneous, Asian desert   `CC`
    Infection by Leishmania tropica major
    Leishmaniasis, cutaneous:
        acute necrotizing
        rural
        wet form
        zoonotic form
    CC Excl: See code: 085.0

085.3 Cutaneous, Ethiopian   `CC`
    Infection by Leishmania ethiopica
    Leishmaniasis, cutaneous:
        diffuse
        lepromatous
    CC Excl: See code: 085.0

085.4 Cutaneous, American   `CC`
    Chiclero ulcer
    Infection by Leishmania mexicana
    Leishmaniasis tegumentaria diffusa
    CC Excl: See code: 085.0

085.5 Mucocutaneous (American)   `CC`
    Espundia
    Infection by Leishmania braziliensis
    Uta
    CC Excl: See code: 085.0

085.9 Leishmaniasis, unspecified   `CC`
    CC Excl: See code: 085.0

√4ᵗʰ **086 Trypanosomiasis**
    Use additional code to identify manifestations, as:
        trypanosomiasis:
            encephalitis (323.2)
            meningitis (321.3)

086.0 Chagas' disease with heart involvement   `CC`
    American trypanosomiasis
    Infection by Trypanosoma } with heart involvement
        cruzi
    Any condition classifiable to 086.2 with heart
        involvement
    CC Excl: 086.0, 139.8

086.1 Chagas' disease with other organ involvement   `CC`
    American trypanosomiasis } with involvement of
    Infection by Trypanosoma } organ other than
        cruzi } heart
    Any condition classifiable to 086.2 with involvement of
        organ other than heart
    CC Excl: 080-088.9

086.2 Chagas' disease without mention of organ involvement   `CC`
    American trypanosomiasis
    Infection by Trypanosoma cruzi
    CC Excl: See code: 086.1

086.3 Gambian trypanosomiasis   `CC`
    Gambian sleeping sickness
    Infection by Trypanosoma gambiense
    CC Excl: See code: 086.1

086.4 Rhodesian trypanosomiasis   `CC`
    Infection by Trypanosoma rhodesiense
    Rhodesian sleeping sickness
    CC Excl: See code: 086.1

086.5 African trypanosomiasis, unspecified   `CC`
    Sleeping sickness NOS
    CC Excl: See code: 086.1

086.9 Trypanosomiasis, unspecified   `CC`
    CC Excl: 013.60-013.66, 046.2, 046.71-046.8, 048-049.0, 049.8, 052.0, 052.2, 054.3, 054.74, 056.01, 057.8-058.29, 059.00-059.9, 062.0-064, 066.2-066.3, 072.2, 073.7, 075, 078.3, 079.99-088.9, 090.41, 094.81, 117.5, 124, 130.0, 290.12, 323.01-323.9, 341.1, 382.4, 487.8, 771.2, 984.9

√4ᵗʰ **087 Relapsing fever**
    INCLUDES recurrent fever
    DEF: Infection of *Borrelia;* symptoms are episodic and include fever and arthralgia.

087.0 Louse-borne   `CC`
    CC Excl: 080-083.9, 085.0-088.9

087.1 Tick-borne   `CC`
    CC Excl: See code: 087.0

087.9 Relapsing fever, unspecified   `CC`
    CC Excl: See code: 087.0

√4ᵗʰ √5ᵗʰ Additional Digit Required   Unacceptable PDx   Manifestation Code   Hospital Acquired Condition   ►◄ Revised Text   ● New Code   ▲ Revised Code Title

2010 ICD-9-CM   **Volume 1 – 21**

✓4ᵗʰ **088 Other arthropod-borne diseases**

088.0 Bartonellosis `CC`

Carrión's disease   Verruga peruana

Oroya fever

CC Excl: See code: 087.0

✓5ᵗʰ **088.8 Other specified arthropod-borne diseases**

088.81 Lyme disease `CC`

Erythema chronicum migrans

DEF: A recurrent multisystem disorder caused by the spirochete *Borrelia burgdorferi* with the carrier being the tick; begins with lesions of erythema chronicum migrans; followed by arthritis of the large joints, myalgia, malaise, and neurological and cardiac manifestations.

CC Excl: See code: 087.0

AHA: 4Q, '91, 15; 3Q, '90, 14; 2Q, '89, 10

TIP: Do not assign if patient has been cured of Lyme disease but has residual chronic condition; refer instead to late-effect code 139.8.

088.82 Babesiosis `CC`

Babesiasis

DEF: A tick-borne disease caused by infection of *Babesia*, characterized by fever, malaise, listlessness, severe anemia and hemoglobinuria.

CC Excl: 080-088.9

AHA: 4Q, '93, 23

088.89 Other

088.9 Arthropod-borne disease, unspecified

SYPHILIS AND OTHER VENEREAL DISEASES (090-099)

EXCLUDES nonvenereal endemic syphilis (104.0)

urogenital trichomoniasis (131.0)

✓4ᵗʰ **090 Congenital syphilis**

DEF: Infection by spirochete*Treponema pallidum* acquired in utero from the infected mother.

090.0 Early congenital syphilis, symptomatic `CC`

Congenital syphilitic: Congenital syphilitic:
   choroiditis   splenomegaly
   coryza (chronic)   Syphilitic (congenital):
   hepatomegaly   epiphysitis
   mucous patches   osteochondritis
   periostitis   pemphigus

Any congenital syphilitic condition specified as early or manifest less than two years after birth

CC Excl: 090.0-097.9

090.1 Early congenital syphilis, latent

Congenital syphilis without clinical manifestations, with positive serological reaction and negative spinal fluid test, less than two years after birth

090.2 Early congenital syphilis, unspecified `CC`

Congenital syphilis NOS, less than two years after birth

CC Excl: 090.0-099.9, 139.8

090.3 Syphilitic interstitial keratitis `CC`

Syphilitic keratitis:
   parenchymatous
   punctata profunda

EXCLUDES interstitial keratitis NOS (370.50)

CC Excl: See code: 090.0

✓5ᵗʰ **090.4 Juvenile neurosyphilis**

Use additional code to identify any associated mental disorder

DEF: *Treponema pallidum* infection involving the nervous system.

090.40 Juvenile neurosyphilis, unspecified `CC`

Congenital neurosyphilis

Dementia paralytica juvenilis

Juvenile:
   general paresis
   tabes
   taboparesis

CC Excl: 090.0-097.9, 099.40-099.9, 139.8

090.41 Congenital syphilitic encephalitis `MCC`

DEF: Congenital *Treponema pallidum* infection involving the brain.

CC Excl: See code: 090.40

090.42 Congenital syphilitic meningitis `MCC`

DEF: Congenital *Treponema pallidum* infection involving the lining of the brain and/or spinal cord.

CC Excl: 003.21, 013.00-013.16, 036.0, 047.0-047.9, 049.0-049.1, 053.0, 054.72, 072.1, 090.0-097.9, 098.89, 099.40-099.9, 100.81, 112.83, 114.2, 115.01, 115.11, 115.91, 130.0, 139.8, 320.0-322.9, 349.89-349.9, 357.0

090.49 Other `CC`

CC Excl: See code: 090.40

090.5 Other late congenital syphilis, symptomatic `CC`

Gumma due to congenital syphilis

Hutchinson's teeth

Syphilitic saddle nose

Any congenital syphilitic condition specified as late or manifest two years or more after birth

CC Excl: 090.0-097.9

090.6 Late congenital syphilis, latent

Congenital syphilis without clinical manifestations, with positive serological reaction and negative spinal fluid test, two years or more after birth

090.7 Late congenital syphilis, unspecified

Congenital syphilis NOS, two years or more after birth

090.9 Congenital syphilis, unspecified

✓4ᵗʰ **091 Early syphilis, symptomatic**

EXCLUDES early cardiovascular syphilis (093.0-093.9)

early neurosyphilis (094.0-094.9)

091.0 Genital syphilis (primary)

Genital chancre

DEF: Genital lesion at the site of initial infection by *Treponema pallidum*.

091.1 Primary anal syphilis

DEF: Anal lesion at the site of initial infection by *Treponema pallidum*.

091.2 Other primary syphilis

Primary syphilis of:
   breast
   fingers
   lip
   tonsils

DEF: Lesion at the site of initial infection by *Treponema pallidum*.

091.3 Secondary syphilis of skin or mucous membranes `CC`

Condyloma latum

Secondary syphilis of:
   anus
   mouth
   pharynx
   skin
   tonsils
   vulva

DEF: Transitory or chronic lesions following initial syphilis infection.

CC Excl: 090.0-097.9

091.4 Adenopathy due to secondary syphilis `CC`

Syphilitic adenopathy (secondary)

Syphilitic lymphadenitis (secondary)

CC Excl: 090.0-097.9

✓5ᵗʰ **091.5 Uveitis due to secondary syphilis**

091.50 Syphilitic uveitis, unspecified `CC`

CC Excl: 090.0-097.9

091.51 Syphilitic chorioretinitis (secondary) `CC`

DEF: Inflammation of choroid and retina as a secondary infection.

CC Excl: 090.0-097.9

`N` Newborn Age: 0   `P` Pediatric Age: 0-17   `M` Maternity Age: 12-55   `A` Adult Age: 15-124   `MCC` Major CC Condition   `CC` CC Condition   `HIV` HIV Related Dx

091.52 Syphilitic iridocyclitis (secondary) `CC`
DEF: Inflammation of iris and ciliary body as a secondary infection.
CC Excl: 090.0-097.9

√5ᵗʰ **091.6 Secondary syphilis of viscera and bone**

091.61 Secondary syphilitic periostitis `CC`
DEF: Inflammation of outer layers of bone as a secondary infection.
CC Excl: 015.90-015.96, 090.0-099.9, 102.6, 730.10-730.19, 730.30-730.39, 733.99

091.62 Secondary syphilitic hepatitis `CC`
Secondary syphilis of liver
CC Excl: 090.0-099.9, 571.42-571.9, 573.1-573.3, 573.8-573.9

091.69 Other viscera `CC`
CC Excl: 090.0-099.9, 139.8

091.7 Secondary syphilis, relapse `CC`
Secondary syphilis, relapse (treated) (untreated)
DEF: Return of symptoms of syphilis following asymptomatic period.
CC Excl: 090.0-099.9, 139.8

√5ᵗʰ **091.8 Other forms of secondary syphilis**

091.81 Acute syphilitic meningitis (secondary) `MCC`
DEF: Sudden, severe inflammation of the lining of the brain and/or spinal cord as a secondary infection.
CC Excl: 003.21, 013.00-013.16, 036.0, 047.0-047.9, 049.0-049.1, 072.1, 078.88-078.89, 079.81, 079.88-079.99, 090.0-099.9, 100.81, 112.83, 114.2, 115.01, 115.11, 115.91, 130.0, 139.8, 320.0-322.9, 349.89-349.9, 357.0

091.82 Syphilitic alopecia `CC`
DEF: Hair loss following initial syphillis infection.
CC Excl: 090.0-099.9

091.89 Other `CC`
CC Excl: 090.0-099.9, 139.8

091.9 Unspecified secondary syphilis `CC`
CC Excl: 090.0-099.9, 139.8

√4ᵗʰ **092 Early syphilis, latent**
INCLUDES syphilis (acquired) without clinical manifestations, with positive serological reaction and negative spinal fluid test, less than two years after infection

092.0 Early syphilis, latent, serological relapse after treatment

092.9 Early syphilis, latent, unspecified

√4ᵗʰ **093 Cardiovascular syphilis**

093.0 Aneurysm of aorta, specified as syphilitic `CC`
Dilatation of aorta, specified as syphilitic
CC Excl: 090.0-097.9, 099.40-099.9, 139.8

093.1 Syphilitic aortitis `CC`
DEF: Inflammation of the aorta – the main artery leading from the heart.
CC Excl: See code: 093.0

√5ᵗʰ **093.2 Syphilitic endocarditis**
DEF: Inflammation of the tissues lining the cavities of the heart.

093.20 Valve, unspecified `CC`
Syphilitic ostial coronary disease
CC Excl: See code: 093.0

093.21 Mitral valve `CC`
CC Excl: See code: 093.0

093.22 Aortic valve `CC`
Syphilitic aortic incompetence or stenosis
CC Excl: See code: 093.0

093.23 Tricuspid valve `CC`
CC Excl: See code: 093.0

093.24 Pulmonary valve `CC`
CC Excl: See code: 093.0

√5ᵗʰ **093.8 Other specified cardiovascular syphilis**

093.81 Syphilitic pericarditis `CC`
DEF: Inflammation of the outer lining of the heart.
CC Excl: See code: 093.0

093.82 Syphilitic myocarditis `CC`
DEF: Inflammation of the muscle of the heart.
CC Excl: See code: 093.0

093.89 Other `CC`
CC Excl: See code: 093.0

093.9 Cardiovascular syphilis, unspecified `CC`
CC Excl: See code: 093.0

√4ᵗʰ **094 Neurosyphilis**
Use additional code to identify any associated mental disorder

094.0 Tabes dorsalis `CC`
Locomotor ataxia (progressive)
Posterior spinal sclerosis (syphilitic)
Tabetic neurosyphilis
Use additional code to identify manifestation, as: neurogenic arthropathy [Charcot's joint disease] (713.5)
DEF: Progressive degeneration of nerves associated with long-term syphilis; causing pain, wasting away, incontinence, and ataxia.
CC Excl: 090.0-097.9, 099.40-099.9, 139.8

094.1 General paresis `CC`
Dementia paralytica
General paralysis (of the insane) (progressive)
Paretic neurosyphilis
Taboparesis
DEF: Degeneration of brain associated with long-term syphilis, causing loss of brain function, progressive dementia, and paralysis.
CC Excl: 090.0-097.9, 099.40-099.9, 139.8

094.2 Syphilitic meningitis `MCC`
Meningovascular syphilis
EXCLUDES acute syphilitic meningitis (secondary) (091.81)
DEF: Inflammation of the lining of the brain and/or spinal cord.
CC Excl: 003.21, 013.00-013.16, 036.0, 047.0-047.9, 049.0-049.1, 053.0, 054.72, 072.1, 090.0-097.9, 098.89, 099.40-099.9, 100.81, 112.83, 114.2, 115.01, 115.11, 115.91, 130.0, 139.8, 320.0-322.9, 349.89-349.9, 357.0

094.3 Asymptomatic neurosyphilis `CC`
CC Excl: 090.0-097.9, 099.40-099.9, 139.8

√5ᵗʰ **094.8 Other specified neurosyphilis**

094.81 Syphilitic encephalitis `MCC`
CC Excl: 090.0-097.9, 099.40-099.9, 139.8

094.82 Syphilitic Parkinsonism `CC`
DEF: Decreased motor function, tremors, and muscular rigidity.
CC Excl: 090.0-099.9, 332.0-333.0

094.83 Syphilitic disseminated retinochoroiditis `CC`
DEF: Inflammation of retina and choroid due to neurosyphilis.
CC Excl: 017.30-017.36, 090.0-099.9, 115.02, 115.12, 362.01, 362.12-362.13, 362.29, 362.41, 362.52, 362.76, 363.00, 363.05-363.10, 363.13-363.15, 646.80-646.84, 679.12, 679.14

094.84 Syphilitic optic atrophy `CC`
DEF: Degeneration of the eye and its nerves due to neurosyphilis.
CC Excl: 003.21, 013.00-013.16, 036.0, 047.0-047.9, 049.0-049.1, 072.1, 078.88-078.89, 079.81, 079.88-079.99, 090.0-099.9, 100.81, 112.83, 114.2, 115.01, 115.11, 115.91, 130.0, 139.8, 320.0-322.9, 349.89-349.9, 357.0

094.85 Syphilitic retrobulbar neuritis `CC`
DEF: Inflammation of the posterior optic nerve to neurosyphilis.
CC Excl: 090.0-099.9, 377.32

Infectious and Parasitic Diseases

094.86–098.36

094.86 Syphilitic acoustic neuritis `CC`
DEF: Inflammation of acoustic nerve due to neurosyphilis.
CC Excl: 090.0-099.9, 388.5

094.87 Syphilitic ruptured cerebral aneurysm `MCC`
CC Excl: 090.0-097.9, 099.40-099.9, 139.8

094.89 Other `CC`
CC Excl: 090.0-097.9, 099.40-099.9, 139.8

094.9 Neurosyphilis, unspecified `CC`
Gumma (syphilitic)
Syphilis (early) (late) } of central nervous system
Syphiloma   NOS
CC Excl: 090.0-097.9, 099.40-099.9, 139.8

✓4ᵗʰ 095 Other forms of late syphilis, with symptoms
INCLUDES   gumma (syphilitic)
syphilis, late, tertiary, or unspecified stage

095.0 Syphilitic episcleritis `CC`
CC Excl: 017.30-017.36, 090.0-099.9, 379.00-379.02, 379.09

095.1 Syphilis of lung `CC`
CC Excl: 090.0-099.9

095.2 Syphilitic peritonitis `CC`
CC Excl: 014.00-014.06, 032.83, 090.0-099.9, 540.0-540.1, 567.0-567.1, 567.22, 567.29, 567.81, 567.9, 569.87-569.9, 577.8, 614.5-614.7, 639.0, 670.00-670.84, 777.6, 998.7

095.3 Syphilis of liver `CC`
CC Excl: 090.0-099.9

095.4 Syphilis of kidney `CC`
CC Excl: 090.0-099.9

095.5 Syphilis of bone `CC`
CC Excl: 090.0-099.9

095.6 Syphilis of muscle `CC`
Syphilitic myositis
CC Excl: 090.0-099.9

095.7 Syphilis of synovium, tendon, and bursa `CC`
Syphilitic:
bursitis
synovitis
CC Excl: 090.0-099.9

095.8 Other specified forms of late symptomatic syphilis `CC`
EXCLUDES   cardiovascular syphilis (093.0-093.9)
neurosyphilis (094.0-094.9)
CC Excl: 090.0-099.9

095.9 Late symptomatic syphilis, unspecified `CC`
CC Excl: 090.0-099.9

096 Late syphilis, latent
Syphilis (acquired) without clinical manifestations, with positive serological reaction and negative spinal fluid test, two years or more after infection

✓4ᵗʰ 097 Other and unspecified syphilis

097.0 Late syphilis, unspecified

097.1 Latent syphilis, unspecified
Positive serological reaction for syphilis

097.9 Syphilis, unspecified
Syphilis (acquired) NOS
EXCLUDES   syphilis NOS causing death under two years of age (090.9)

✓4ᵗʰ 098 Gonococcal infections
DEF: Neisseria gonorrhoeae infection generally acquired in utero or in sexual congress.

098.0 Acute, of lower genitourinary tract `CC`
Gonococcal: Gonorrhea (acute):
Bartholinitis (acute)   NOS
urethritis (acute)   genitourinary (tract) NOS
vulvovaginitis (acute)
CC Excl: 098.0-098.39, 098.89, 099.40-099.9, 139.8

✓5ᵗʰ 098.1 Acute, of upper genitourinary tract

098.10 Gonococcal infection (acute) of upper genitourinary tract, site unspecified `CC`
CC Excl: See code: 098.0

098.11 Gonococcal cystitis (acute) upper `CC`
Gonorrhea (acute) of bladder
CC Excl: See code: 098.0

098.12 Gonococcal prostatitis (acute) `CC`♂
CC Excl: See code: 098.0

098.13 Gonococcal epididymo-orchitis (acute) `CC`♂
Gonococcal orchitis (acute)
DEF: Acute inflammation of the testes.
CC Excl: See code: 098.0

098.14 Gonococcal seminal vesiculitis (acute) `CC`♂
Gonorrhea (acute) of seminal vesicle
CC Excl: See code: 098.0

098.15 Gonococcal cervicitis (acute) `CC`♀
Gonorrhea (acute) of cervix
CC Excl: See code: 098.0

098.16 Gonococcal endometritis (acute) `CC`♀
Gonorrhea (acute) of uterus
CC Excl: See code: 098.0

098.17 Gonococcal salpingitis, specified as acute `CC`♀
DEF: Acute inflammation of the fallopian tubes.
CC Excl: See code: 098.0

098.19 Other `CC`
CC Excl: See code: 098.0

098.2 Chronic, of lower genitourinary tract
Gonoccocal:
Bartholinitis
urethritis } specified as chronic or with
vulvovaginitis   duration of two
Gonorrhea: months or more
NOS
genitourinary (tract)
Any condition classifiable to 098.0 specified as chronic or with duration of two months or more

✓5ᵗʰ 098.3 Chronic, of upper genitourinary tract
INCLUDES   any condition classifiable to 098.1 stated as chronic or with a duration of two months or more

098.30 Chronic gonococcal infection of upper genitourinary tract, site unspecified

098.31 Gonococcal cystitis, chronic
Gonorrhea of bladder, chronic
Any condition classifiable to 098.11, specified as chronic

098.32 Gonococcal prostatitis, chronic ♂
Any condition classifiable to 098.12, specified as chronic

098.33 Gonococcal epididymo-orchitis, chronic ♂
Chronic gonococcal orchitis
Any condition classifiable to 098.13, specified as chronic
DEF: Chronic inflammation of the testes.

098.34 Gonococcal seminal vesiculitis, chronic ♂
Gonorrhea of seminal vesicle, chronic
Any condition classifiable to 098.14, specified as chronic

098.35 Gonococcal cervicitis, chronic ♀
Gonorrhea of cervix, chronic
Any condition classifiable to 098.15, specified as chronic

098.36 Gonococcal endometritis, chronic ♀
Any condition classifiable to 098.16, specified as chronic
DEF: Chronic inflammation of the uterus.

`N` Newborn Age: 0   `P` Pediatric Age: 0-17   `M` Maternity Age: 12-55   `A` Adult Age: 15-124   `MCC` Major CC Condition   `CC` CC Condition   `HIV` HIV Related Dx

24 – Volume 1   2010 ICD-9-CM

098.37 **Gonococcal salpingitis (chronic)** ♀
DEF: Chronic inflammation of the fallopian tubes.

098.39 **Other**

√5th 098.4 **Gonococcal infection of eye**

098.40 **Gonococcal conjunctivitis (neonatorum)** `CC`
Gonococcal ophthalmia (neonatorum)
DEF: Infection of conjunctiva present at birth.
CC Excl: 090.0-099.9

098.41 **Gonococcal iridocyclitis** `CC`
DEF: Inflammation and infection of iris and ciliary body.
CC Excl: 090.0-099.9

098.42 **Gonococcal endophthalmia** `CC`
DEF: Inflammation and infection of contents of eyeball.
CC Excl: 090.0-099.9

098.43 **Gonococcal keratitis** `CC`
DEF: Inflammation and infection of the cornea.
CC Excl: 090.0-099.9

098.49 **Other** `CC`
CC Excl: 090.0-099.9

√5th 098.5 **Gonococcal infection of joint**

098.50 **Gonococcal arthritis** `CC`
Gonococcal infection of joint NOS
CC Excl: 003.23, 015.80-015.96, 017.90-017.96, 036.82, 056.71, 090.0-099.9, 711.00-714.0, 715.00, 715.09-715.10, 715.18-716.99, 718.00-718.08, 719.00-719.10, 719.18-719.69, 719.80-719.99

098.51 **Gonococcal synovitis and tenosynovitis** `CC`
CC Excl: See code: 098.50

098.52 **Gonococcal bursitis** `CC`
DEF: Inflammation of the sac-like cavities in a joint.
CC Excl: See code: 098.50

098.53 **Gonococcal spondylitis** `CC`
CC Excl: See code: 098.50

098.59 **Other** `CC`
Gonococcal rheumatism
CC Excl: See code: 098.50

098.6 **Gonococcal infection of pharynx**

098.7 **Gonococcal infection of anus and rectum**
Gonococcal proctitis

√5th 098.8 **Gonococcal infection of other specified sites**

098.81 **Gonococcal keratosis (blennorrhagica)** `CC`
DEF: Pustular skin lesions caused by *Neisseria gonorrhoeae*.
CC Excl: 098.40-098.49, 098.81

098.82 **Gonococcal meningitis** `MCC`
DEF: Inflammation of lining of brain and/or spinal cord.
CC Excl: 003.21, 013.00-013.16, 036.0, 047.0-047.9, 049.0-049.1, 072.1, 078.88-078.89, 079.81, 079.88-079.99, 090.0-099.9, 100.81, 112.83, 114.2, 115.01, 115.11, 115.91, 130.0, 139.8, 320.0-322.9, 349.89-349.9, 357.0

098.83 **Gonococcal pericarditis** `MCC`
DEF: Inflammation of the outer lining of the heart.
CC Excl: 074.21, 090.0-099.9, 391.0, 393, 420.0-420.99, 423.3-423.9, 459.89-459.9

098.84 **Gonococcal endocarditis** `MCC`
DEF: Inflammation of tissues lining the cavities of heart.
CC Excl: 002.0, 036.42, 074.22, 083.0, 090.0-099.9, 112.81, 115.94, 116.0, 390, 391.1, 391.8-392.0, 394.0-395.9, 396.9-397.9, 398.90, 398.99, 421.0-421.9, 424.0-424.99, 425.3, 459.89-459.9, 711.00, 711.08-711.09, 746.09, 746.89, 996.61

098.85 **Other gonococcal heart disease** `CC`
CC Excl: 002.0, 036.42, 074.20, 074.22-074.23, 083.0, 090.0-099.9, 112.81, 115.94, 116.0, 390, 391.1-392.0, 394.0-395.9, 396.9-398.90, 398.99, 421.0-422.99, 424.0-424.99, 425.3, 429.0, 429.71-429.79, 459.89-459.9, 711.00, 711.08-711.09, 746.09, 746.89, 996.61

098.86 **Gonococcal peritonitis** `CC`
DEF: Inflammation of the membrane lining the abdomen.
CC Excl: 014.00-014.06, 032.83, 090.0-099.9, 540.0-540.1, 567.0-567.1, 567.22, 567.29, 567.81, 567.9, 569.89-569.9, 577.8, 614.5-614.7, 639.0, 670.00-670.04, 777.6, 998.7

098.89 **Other** `CC`
Gonococcemia
CC Excl: 090.0-099.9, 588.81-588.89

√4th 099 **Other venereal diseases**

099.0 **Chancroid**
Bubo (inguinal):
    chancroidal
    due to Hemophilus ducreyi
Chancre:
    Ducrey's
    simple
    soft
Ulcus molle (cutis)(skin)
DEF: A sexually transmitted disease caused by *Haemophilus ducreyi*; identified by a painful primary ulcer at the site of inoculation (usually external genitalia) with related lymphadenitis.

099.1 **Lymphogranuloma venereum**
Climatic or tropical bubo
(Durand-) Nicolas-Favre disease
Esthiomene
Lymphogranuloma inguinale
DEF: Sexually transmitted infection of *Chlamydia trachomatis* causing skin lesions.

099.2 **Granuloma inguinale**
Donovanosis
Granuloma pudendi (ulcerating)
Granuloma venereum
Pudendal ulcer
DEF: Chronic, sexually transmitted infection of *Calymmatobac-terium granulomatis* causing progressive, anogenital skin ulcers.

099.3 **Reiter's disease**
Reiter's syndrome
Use additional code for associated:
    arthropathy (711.1)
    conjunctivitis (372.33)
DEF: A symptom complex of unknown etiology consisting of urethritis, conjunctivitis, arthritis and myocutaneous lesions; occurs most commonly in young men and patients with HIV. Also a form of reactive arthritis.

√5th 099.4 **Other nongonococcal urethritis [NGU]**

099.40 **Unspecified**
Nonspecific urethritis

099.41 **Chlamydia trachomatis**

099.49 **Other specified organism**

√5th 099.5 **Other venereal diseases due to Chlamydia trachomatis**
EXCLUDES *Chlamydia trachomatis* infection of conjunctiva (076.0-076.9, 077.0, 077.9)
Lymphogranuloma venereum (099.1)
DEF: Venereal diseases caused by *Chlamydia trachomatis* at other sites besides the urethra (e.g., pharynx, anus and rectum, conjunctiva and peritoneum).

099.50 **Unspecified site**

099.51 **Pharynx**

099.52 **Anus and rectum**

Infectious and Parasitic Diseases

099.53–104.0

099.53 Lower genitourinary sites
Use additional code to specify site of infection, such as:
bladder (595.4)
cervix (616.0)
vagina and vulva (616.11)
EXCLUDES   urethra (099.41)

099.54 Other genitourinary sites
Use additional code to specify site of infection, such as:
pelvic inflammatory disease NOS (614.9)
testis and epididymis (604.91)

099.55 Unspecified genitourinary site

099.56 Peritoneum   CC
Perihepatitis
CC Excl: 014.00-014.06, 032.83, 090.0-099.9, 540.0-540.1, 567.0-567.1, 567.22, 567.29, 567.81, 567.9, 569.89-569.9, 577.8, 614.5-614.7, 639.0, 670.00-670.04, 777.6, 998.7

099.59 Other specified site

099.8 Other specified venereal diseases

099.9 Venereal disease, unspecified

OTHER SPIROCHETAL DISEASES (100-104)

√4ᵗʰ **100 Leptospirosis**
DEF: A blood infection of any spirochete of the genus Leptospire; transmitted to humans by exposure to contaminated animal tissues or water. Patients present with flulike symptoms, characteristic muscle aches involving the thighs and low back.

100.0 Leptospirosis icterohemorrhagica   CC
Leptospiral or spirochetal jaundice (hemorrhagic)
Weil's disease
CC Excl: 100.0-100.9

√5ᵗʰ **100.8 Other specified leptospiral infections**

100.81 Leptospiral meningitis (aseptic)   MCC
CC Excl: 003.21, 013.00-013.16, 036.0, 047.0-047.9, 049.0-049.1, 072.1, 078.88-078.89, 079.81, 079.88-079.99, 090.42, 091.81, 094.2, 098.89, 100.0-100.9, 112.83, 114.2, 115.01, 115.11, 115.91, 130.0, 139.8, 320.0-322.9, 349.89-349.9, 357.0

100.89 Other   CC
Fever: Infection by Leptospira:
Fort Bragg   australis
pretibial   bataviae
swamp   pyrogenes
CC Excl: See code: 100.0

100.9 Leptospirosis, unspecified   CC
CC Excl: See code: 100.0

101 Vincent's angina   CC
Acute necrotizing ulcerative:
gingivitis
stomatitis
Fusospirochetal pharyngitis
Spirochetal stomatitis
Trench mouth
Vincent's:
gingivitis
infection [any site]
DEF: Painful ulceration with edema and hypermic patches of the oropharyngeal and throat membranes; it is caused by spreading of acute ulcerative gingivitis.
CC Excl: 101

√4ᵗʰ **102 Yaws**
INCLUDES   frambesia
pian
DEF: An infectious, endemic, tropical disease caused by *Treponema pertenue;* usually affects persons 15 years old or younger; a primary cutaneous lesion develops, then a granulomatous skin eruption, and occasionally lesions that destroy skin and bone.

102.0 Initial lesions
Chancre of yaws   Initial frambesial ulcer
Frambesia, initial or primary   Mother yaw

102.1 Multiple papillomata and wet crab yaws
Butter yaws
Frambesioma
Pianoma
Plantar or palmar papilloma of yaws

102.2 Other early skin lesions
Cutaneous yaws, less than five years after infection
Early yaws (cutaneous) (macular) (papular) (maculopapular) (micropapular)
Frambeside of early yaws

102.3 Hyperkeratosis
Ghoul hand
Hyperkeratosis, palmar or plantar (early) (late) due to yaws
Worm-eaten soles
DEF: Overgrowth of skin of palm of bottoms of feet, due to yaws.

102.4 Gummata and ulcers
Gummatous frambeside
Nodular late yaws (ulcerated)
DEF: Rubbery lesions and areas of dead skin caused by yaws.

102.5 Gangosa
Rhinopharyngitis mutilans
DEF: Massive, mutilating lesions of the nose and oral cavity caused by yaws.

102.6 Bone and joint lesions
Goundou
Gumma, bone   } of yaws (late)
Gummatous osteitis or periostitis

Hydrarthrosis
Osteitis   } of yaws (early) (late)
Periostitis (hypertrophic)

102.7 Other manifestations
Juxta-articular nodules of yaws
Mucosal yaws

102.8 Latent yaws
Yaws without clinical manifestations, with positive serology

102.9 Yaws, unspecified

√4ᵗʰ **103 Pinta**
DEF: A chronic form of treponematosis, endemic in areas of tropical America; it is identified by the presence of red, violet, blue, coffee-colored or white spots on the skin.

103.0 Primary lesions
Chancre (primary)
Papule (primary)   } of pinta [carate]
Pintid

103.1 Intermediate lesions
Erythematous plaques
Hyperchronic lesions   } of pinta [carate]
Hyperkeratosis

103.2 Late lesions
Cardiovascular lesions
Skin lesions:
achromic
cicatricial   } of pinta [carate]
dyschromic
Vitiligo

103.3 Mixed lesions
Achromic and hyperchromic skin lesions of pinta [carate]

103.9 Pinta, unspecified

√4ᵗʰ **104 Other spirochetal infection**

104.0 Nonvenereal endemic syphilis
Bejel
Njovera
DEF: *Treponema pallidum, T. pertenue,* or *T. caroteum* infection transmitted non-sexually, causing lesions on mucosa and skin.

N Newborn Age: 0   P Pediatric Age: 0-17   M Maternity Age: 12-55   A Adult Age: 15-124   MCC Major CC Condition   CC CC Condition   HIV HIV Related Dx

104.8   **Other specified spirochetal infections**
      EXCLUDES *relapsing fever (087.0-087.9)*
           syphilis (090.0-097.9)

104.9   **Spirochetal infection, unspecified**

MYCOSES (110-118)

Use additional code to identify manifestation as:
  arthropathy (711.6)
  meningitis (321.0-321.1)
  otitis externa (380.15)
    EXCLUDES *infection by Actinomycetales, such as species of*
          Actinomyces, Actinomadura, Nocardia,
          Streptomyces (039.0-039.9)

√4th **110 Dermatophytosis**
    INCLUDES infection by species of Epidermophyton,
          Microsporum, and Trichophyton
          tinea, any type except those in 111
    DEF: Superficial infection of the skin caused by a parasitic fungus.

110.0   **Of scalp and beard**
    Kerion
    Sycosis, mycotic
    Trichophytic tinea [black dot tinea], scalp

110.1   **Of nail**
    Dermatophytic onychia
    Onychomycosis
    Tinea unguium
    B35.1 Tinea unguium   I-10

110.2   **Of hand**
    Tinea manuum

110.3   **Of groin and perianal area**
    Dhobie itch
    Eczema marginatum
    Tinea cruris

110.4   **Of foot**
    Athlete's foot
    Tinea pedis

110.5   **Of the body**
    Herpes circinatus
    Tinea imbricata [Tokelau]

110.6   **Deep seated dermatophytosis**
    Granuloma trichophyticum
    Majocchi's granuloma

110.8   **Of other specified sites**

110.9   **Of unspecified site**
    Favus NOS
    Microsporic tinea NOS
    Ringworm NOS

√4th **111 Dermatomycosis, other and unspecified**

111.0   **Pityriasis versicolor**
    Infection by Malassezia [Pityrosporum] furfur
    Tinea flava
    Tinea versicolor

111.1   **Tinea nigra**
    Infection by Cladosporium species
    Keratomycosis nigricans
    Microsporosis nigra
    Pityriasis nigra
    Tinea palmaris nigra

111.2   **Tinea blanca**
    Infection by Trichosporon (beigelii) cutaneum
    White piedra

111.3   **Black piedra**
    Infection by Piedraia hortai

111.8   **Other specified dermatomycoses**

111.9   **Dermatomycosis, unspecified**

√4th **112 Candidiasis**
    INCLUDES infection by Candida species
          moniliasis
    EXCLUDES *neonatal monilial infection (771.7)*
    DEF: Fungal infection caused by Candida; usually seen in mucous
    membranes or skin.

112.0   **Of mouth**   CC HIV
    Thrush (oral)
    CC Excl: 112.0-112.9, 117.9, 139.8
    B37.0 Candidal stomatitis   I-10

112.1   **Of vulva and vagina**   ♀
    Candidal vulvovaginitis
    Monilial vulvovaginitis
    B37.3 Candidiasis of vulva and vagina   I-10

8 112.2   **Of other urogenital sites**   CC
    Candidal balanitis
    CC Excl: 112.2, 112.4-112.9, 588.81-588.89
    AHA: 4Q, '03, 105; 4Q, '96, 33

112.3   **Of skin and nails**   HIV
    Candidal intertrigo
    Candidal onychia
    Candidal perionyxis [paronychia]
    B37.2 Candidiasis of skin and nail   I-10

112.4   **Of lung**   MCC HIV
    Candidal pneumonia
    CC Excl: See code: 112.0
    AHA: 2Q, '98, 7

112.5   **Disseminated**   MCC HIV
    Systemic candidiasis
    CC Excl: See code: 112.0
    AHA: 2Q, '00, 5; 2Q, '89, 10

√5th **112.8 Of other specified sites**

112.81   **Candidal endocarditis**   MCC HIV
    CC Excl: See code: 112.0

112.82   **Candidal otitis externa**   CC HIV
    Otomycosis in moniliasis
    CC Excl: See code: 112.0

112.83   **Candidal meningitis**   MCC HIV
    CC Excl: 003.21, 013.00-013.16, 036.0, 047.0-047.9,
    049.0-049.1, 053.0, 054.72, 072.1, 090.42, 091.81,
    094.2, 098.89, 100.81, 112.0-112.9, 114.2, 115.01,
    115.11, 115.91, 117.9, 130.0, 139.8, 320.0-322.9,
    349.89-349.9, 357.0

112.84   **Candidal esophagitis**   CC HIV
    CC Excl: See code: 112.0
    AHA: 4Q, '92, 19
    B37.81 Candidal esophagitis   I-10

112.85   **Candidal enteritis**   CC HIV
    CC Excl: See code: 112.0
    AHA: 4Q, '92, 19

112.89   **Other**   CC
    CC Excl: 112.4-112.9
    AHA: 1Q, '92, 17; 3Q, '91, 20

112.9   **Of unspecified site**   HIV

---

8   CC/MCC except when in combination with 996.64 and POA = N

Infectious and Parasitic Diseases

114–117.3

✓4th **114 Coccidioidomycosis**

INCLUDES infection by Coccidioides (immitis)
Posada-Wernicke disease

DEF: A fungal disease caused by inhalation of dust particles containing arthrospores of *Coccidioides immitis;* a self-limited respiratory infection; the primary form is known as San Joaquin fever, desert fever or valley fever.

AHA: 4Q, '93, 23

114.0 Primary coccidioidomycosis (pulmonary) CC HIV
Acute pulmonary coccidioidomycosis
Coccidioidomycotic pneumonitis
Desert rheumatism
Pulmonary coccidioidomycosis
San Joaquin Valley fever

DEF: Acute, self-limiting *Coccidioides immitis* infection of the lung.

CC Excl: 114.0, 114.3-114.9, 117.9, 139.8

B38.0 Acute pulmonary coccidioidomycosis I-10

114.1 Primary extrapulmonary coccidioidomycosis CC HIV
Chancriform syndrome
Primary cutaneous coccidioidomycosis

DEF: Acute, self-limiting *Coccidioides immitis* infection in nonpulmonary site.

CC Excl: 114.0-114.9

114.2 Coccidioidal meningitis MCC HIV

DEF: *Coccidioides immitis* infection of the lining of the brain and/or spinal cord.

CC Excl: 003.21, 013.00-013.16, 036.0, 047.0-047.9, 049.0-049.1, 053.0, 054.72, 072.1, 090.42, 091.81, 094.2, 098.89, 100.81, 112.83, 114.2-114.3, 114.9, 115.01, 115.11, 115.91, 117.9, 130.0, 139.8, 320.0-322.9, 349.89-349.9, 357.0

114.3 Other forms of progressive coccidioidomycosis CC HIV
Coccidioidal granuloma
Disseminated coccidioidomycosis

CC Excl: 114.3, 114.9, 117.9, 139.8

114.4 Chronic pulmonary coccidioidomycosis CC HIV
CC Excl: 114.0-115.99

114.5 Pulmonary coccidioidomycosis, unspecified CC HIV
CC Excl: See code: 114.4

114.9 Coccidioidomycosis, unspecified CC HIV
CC Excl: See code: 114.3

✓4th **115 Histoplasmosis**

The following fifth-digit subclassification is for use with category 115:
0 **without mention of manifestation**
1 **meningitis**
2 **retinitis**
3 **pericarditis**
4 **endocarditis**
5 **pneumonia**
9 **other**

§ ✓5th **115.0 Infection by Histoplasma capsulatum** MCC 1, 3-5
[0-5, 9] American histoplasmosis CC 2,9 HIV
Darling's disease
Reticuloendothelial cytomycosis
Small form histoplasmosis

CC Excl: For code 115.01: 003.21, 013.00-013.16, 036.0, 047.0-047.9, 049.0-049.1, 053.0, 054.72, 072.1, 090.42, 091.81, 094.2, 098.89, 100.81, 112.83, 114.2, 115.00-115.01, 115.09, 115.11, 115.90-115.91, 115.99, 117.9, 130.0, 139.8, 320.0-322.9, 349.89-349.9, 357.0; **For code 115.02:** 115.00, 115.02, 115.09, 115.90, 115.92, 115.99, 117.9, 139.8; **For code 115.03:** 115.00, 115.03, 115.09, 115.90, 115.93, 115.99, 117.9, 139.8; **For code 115.04:** 115.00, 115.04, 115.09, 115.90, 115.94, 115.99, 117.9, 139.8; **For code 115.05:** 115.00, 115.05-115.09, 115.90, 115.95-115.99, 117.9, 139.8, 480.0-480.2, 480.8-487.1, 488, 494.0-508.9, 517.1, 518.89; **For code 115.09:** 114.0-115.09

§ ✓5th **115.1 Infection by Histoplasma duboisii** MCC 1, 3-5
[0-5, 9] African histoplasmosis CC 2,9 HIV
Large form histoplasmosis

CC Excl: For code 115.11: 003.21, 013.00-013.16, 036.0, 047.0-047.9, 049.0-049.1, 053.0, 054.72, 072.1, 090.42, 091.81, 094.2, 098.89, 100.81, 112.83, 114.2, 115.00-115.01, 115.09, 115.11, 115.90-115.91, 115.99, 117.9, 130.0, 139.8, 320.0-322.9, 349.89-349.9, 357.0; **For code 115.12:** 115.10, 115.12, 115.19-115.90, 115.92, 115.99, 117.9, 139.8; **For code 115.13:** 115.10, 115.13, 115.19-115.90, 115.93, 115.99, 117.9, 139.8; **For code 115.14:** 115.10, 115.14, 115.19-115.90, 115.94, 115.99, 117.9, 139.8; **For code 115.15:** 115.05, 115.10, 115.15-115.90, 115.95-115.99, 117.9, 139.8, 480.0-480.2, 480.8-487.1, 488, 494.0-508.9, 517.1, 518.89; **For code 115.19:** 115.10, 115.19-115.90, 115.99, 117.9, 139.8

§ ✓5th **115.9 Histoplasmosis, unspecified** MCC 1, 3-5
[0-5, 9] Histoplasmosis NOS CC 2 HIV

CC Excl: For code 115.91: 003.21, 013.00-013.16, 036.0, 047.0-047.9, 049.0-049.1, 053.0, 054.72, 072.1, 090.42, 091.81, 094.2, 098.89, 100.81, 112.83, 114.2, 115.01, 115.11, 115.91, 115.99, 117.9, 130.0, 139.8, 320.0-322.9, 349.89-349.9, 357.0; **For code 115.92:** 115.92, 115.99, 117.9, 139.8; **For code 115.93:** 115.93, 115.99, 117.9, 139.8; **For code 115.94:** 115.94, 115.99, 117.9, 139.8; **For code 115.95:** 115.05, 115.15, 115.95-115.99, 117.9, 139.8

✓4th **116 Blastomycotic infection**

116.0 Blastomycosis CC
Blastomycotic dermatitis
Chicago disease
Cutaneous blastomycosis
Disseminated blastomycosis
Gilchrist's disease
Infection by Blastomyces [Ajellomyces] dermatitidis
North American blastomycosis
Primary pulmonary blastomycosis

CC Excl: 116.0, 117.9, 139.8

116.1 Paracoccidioidomycosis CC
Brazilian blastomycosis
Infection by Paracoccidioides [Blastomyces] brasiliensis
Lutz-Splendore-Almeida disease
Mucocutaneous-lymphangitic paracoccidioidomycosis
Pulmonary paracoccidioidomycosis
South American blastomycosis
Visceral paracoccidioidomycosis

CC Excl: 116.1, 117.9, 139.8

116.2 Lobomycosis
Infections by Loboa [Blastomyces] loboi
Keloidal blastomycosis
Lobo's disease

✓4th **117 Other mycoses**

117.0 Rhinosporidiosis
Infection by Rhinosporidium seeberi

117.1 Sporotrichosis
Cutaneous sporotrichosis
Disseminated sporotrichosis
Infection by Sporothrix [Sporotrichum] schenckii
Lymphocutaneous sporotrichosis
Pulmonary sporotrichosis
Sporotrichosis of the bones

117.2 Chromoblastomycosis
Chromomycosis
Infection by Cladosporium carrionii, Fonsecaea compactum, Fonsecaea pedrosoi, Phialophora verrucosa

117.3 Aspergillosis CC
Infection by Aspergillus species, mainly A. fumigatus, A. flavus group, A. terreus group

CC Excl: 117.3, 117.9, 139.8

AHA: 4Q, '97, 40

[handwritten: Pneumonia due to Aspergillosis should have an additional code 484.6]

§ Requires fifth digit. Valid digits are in [brackets] under each code. See category 115 for codes and definitions.

| N Newborn Age: 0 | P Pediatric Age: 0-17 | M Maternity Age: 12-55 | A Adult Age: 15-124 | MCC Major CC Condition | CC CC Condition | HIV HIV Related Dx |

117.4 Mycotic mycetomas `CC`
Infection by various genera and species of Ascomycetes and Deuteromycetes, such as Acremonium [Cephalosporium] falciforme, Neotestudina rosatii, Madurella grisea, Madurella mycetomii, Pyrenochaeta romeroi, Zopfia [Leptosphaeria] senegalensis
Madura foot, mycotic
Maduromycosis, mycotic
> **EXCLUDES** *actinomycotic mycetomas (039.0-039.9)*

CC Excl: 117.4, 117.9, 139.8

117.5 Cryptococcosis `CC` `HIV`
Busse-Buschke's disease
European cryptococcosis
Infection by Cryptococcus neoformans
Pulmonary cryptococcosis
Systemic cryptococcosis
Torula
CC Excl: 117.5, 117.9, 139.8

117.6 Allescheriosis [Petriellidosis] `CC`
Infections by Allescheria [Petriellidium] boydii [Monosporium apiospermum]
> **EXCLUDES** *mycotic mycetoma (117.4)*

CC Excl: 117.6, 117.9, 139.8

117.7 Zygomycosis [Phycomycosis or Mucormycosis] `MCC`
Infection by species of Absidia, Basidiobolus, Conidiobolus, Cunninghamella, Entomophthora, Mucor, Rhizopus, Saksenaea
CC Excl: 117.7, 117.9, 139.8

117.8 Infection by dematiacious fungi, [Phaehyphomycosis] `CC`
Infection by dematiacious fungi, such as Cladosporium trichoides [bantianum], Dreschlera hawaiiensis, Phialophora gougerotii, Phialophora jeanselmi
CC Excl: 117.8-117.9

117.9 Other and unspecified mycoses `CC`
CC Excl: See code: 117.8

118 Opportunistic mycoses `CC` `HIV`
Infection of skin, subcutaneous tissues, and/or organs by a wide variety of fungi generally considered to be pathogenic to compromised hosts only (e.g., infection by species of Alternaria, Dreschlera, Fusarium)
Use additional code to identify manifestation, such as:
keratitis (370.8)
CC Excl: 117.9-118, 139.8

HELMINTHIASES (120-129)

√4ᵗʰ 120 Schistosomiasis [bilharziasis]
DEF: Infection caused by *Schistosoma*, a genus of flukes or trematode parasites.

120.0 Schistosoma haematobium `CC`
Vesical schistosomiasis NOS
CC Excl: 120.0-120.9

120.1 Schistosoma mansoni `CC`
Intestinal schistosomiasis NOS
CC Excl: See code: 120.0

120.2 Schistosoma japonicum `CC`
Asiatic schistosomiasis NOS
Katayama disease or fever
CC Excl: See code: 120.0

120.3 Cutaneous `CC`
Cercarial dermatitis
Infection by cercariae of Schistosoma
Schistosome dermatitis
Swimmers' itch
CC Excl: See code: 120.0

120.8 Other specified schistosomiasis `CC`
Infection by Schistosoma:
bovis
intercalatum
mattheii
spindale
Schistosomiasis chestermani
CC Excl: See code: 120.0

120.9 Schistosomiasis, unspecified `CC`
Blood flukes NOS
Hemic distomiasis
CC Excl: See code: 120.0

√4ᵗʰ 121 Other trematode infections

121.0 Opisthorchiasis `CC`
Infection by:
cat liver fluke
Opisthorchis (felineus) (tenuicollis) (viverrini)
CC Excl: 121.0-121.9

121.1 Clonorchiasis `CC`
Biliary cirrhosis due to clonorchiasis
Chinese liver fluke disease
Hepatic distomiasis due to Clonorchis sinensis
Oriental liver fluke disease
CC Excl: See code: 121.0

121.2 Paragonimiasis `CC`
Infection by Paragonimus
Lung fluke disease (oriental)
Pulmonary distomiasis
CC Excl: See code: 121.0

121.3 Fascioliasis `CC`
Infection by Fasciola:
gigantica
hepatica
Liver flukes NOS
Sheep liver fluke infection
CC Excl: See code: 121.0

121.4 Fasciolopsiasis `CC`
Infection by Fasciolopsis (buski)
Intestinal distomiasis
CC Excl: See code: 121.0

121.5 Metagonimiasis `CC`
Infection by Metagonimus yokogawai
CC Excl: See code: 121.0

121.6 Heterophyiasis `CC`
Infection by:
Heterophyes heterophyes
Stellantchasmus falcatus
CC Excl: See code: 121.0

121.8 Other specified trematode infections `CC`
Infection by:
Dicrocoelium dendriticum
Echinostoma ilocanum
Gastrodiscoides hominis
CC Excl: See code: 121.0

121.9 Trematode infection, unspecified
Distomiasis NOS
Fluke disease NOS

√4ᵗʰ 122 Echinococcosis
> **INCLUDES** echinococciasis
> hydatid disease
> hydatidosis

DEF: Infection caused by larval forms of tapeworms of the genus *Echinococcus*.

122.0 Echinococcus granulosus infection of liver `CC`
CC Excl: 122.0, 122.8-122.9

122.1 Echinococcus granulosus infection of lung `CC`
CC Excl: 122.1, 122.8-122.9, 480.3

122.2 Echinococcus granulosus infection of thyroid `CC`
CC Excl: 122.2, 122.8-122.9

122.3 Echinococcus granulosus infection, other `CC`
CC Excl: 122.3, 122.8-122.9

Infectious and Parasitic Diseases

122.4–126.9

122.4   Echinococcus granulosus infection, unspecified `CC`
     CC Excl: 122.4, 122.8-122.9

122.5   Echinococcus multilocularis infection of liver `CC`
     CC Excl: 122.5, 122.8-122.9

122.6   Echinococcus multilocularis infection, other `CC`
     CC Excl: 122.6, 122.8-122.9

122.7   Echinococcus multilocularis infection, unspecified `CC`
     CC Excl: 122.7-122.9

122.8   Echinococcosis, unspecified, of liver `CC`
     CC Excl: 122.8-122.9

122.9   Echinococcosis, other and unspecified `CC`
     CC Excl: See code: 122.8

√4th **123   Other cestode infection**

123.0   Taenia solium infection, intestinal form `CC`
     Pork tapeworm (adult) (infection)
     CC Excl: 001.1, 002.0, 002.9-003.0, 004.9-005.2, 006.0-006.2, 006.9, 007.1-009.0, 014.80-014.86, 040.41-040.42, 112.85, 123.0-123.9, 129, 487.8, 536.3, 536.8, 558.2-558.3, 558.9, 564.1, 777.50-777.53, 777.8

123.1   Cysticercosis `CC`
     Cysticerciasis
     Infection by Cysticercus cellulosae [larval form of Taenia solium]
     CC Excl: 123.0-123.9
     AHA: 2Q, '97, 8

123.2   Taenia saginata infection `CC`
     Beef tapeworm (infection)
     Infection by Taeniarhynchus saginatus
     CC Excl: See code: 123.1

123.3   Taeniasis, unspecified `CC`
     CC Excl: See code: 123.1

123.4   Diphyllobothriasis, intestinal `CC`
     Diphyllobothrium (adult) (latum) (pacificum) infection
     Fish tapeworm (infection)
     CC Excl: See code: 123.1

123.5   Sparganosis [larval diphyllobothriasis] `CC`
     Infection by:
        Diphyllobothrium larvae
        Sparganum (mansoni) (proliferum)
        Spirometra larvae
     CC Excl: See code: 123.1

123.6   Hymenolepiasis `CC`
     Dwarf tapeworm (infection)
     Hymenolepis (diminuta) (nana) infection
     Rat tapeworm (infection)
     CC Excl: See code: 123.1

123.8   Other specified cestode infection `CC`
     Diplogonoporus (grandis) ⎤
     Dipylidium (caninum)   ⎬ infection
     Dog tapeworm (infection)
     CC Excl: See code: 123.1

123.9   Cestode infection, unspecified
     Tapeworm (infection) NOS

124   Trichinosis `CC`
     Trichinella spiralis infection
     Trichinellosis
     Trichiniasis
     DEF: Infection by *Trichinella spiralis*, the smallest of the parasitic nematodes.
     CC Excl: 013.60-013.66, 046.2, 046.71-046.8, 048-049.0, 049.8, 052.0, 052.2, 054.3, 054.74, 056.01, 057.8-058.29, 059.00-059.9, 062.0-064, 066.2-066.49, 072.2, 073.7, 079.82, 079.99, 081.9, 083.9, 090.41, 094.81, 117.5, 124, 130.0, 290.12, 323.01-323.9, 341.1, 487.8, 771.2, 984.9

√4th **125   Filarial infection and dracontiasis**

125.0   Bancroftian filariasis `CC`
     Chyluria ⎤
     Elephantiasis
     Infection   ⎬ due to Wuchereria bancrofti
     Lymphadenitis
     Lymphangitis ⎦
     Wuchereriasis
     CC Excl: 125.0-125.9

125.1   Malayan filariasis `CC`
     Brugia filariasis ⎤
     Chyluria
     Elephantiasis
     Infection   ⎬ due to Wuchereria bancrofti
     Lymphadenitis
     Lymphangitis ⎦
     CC Excl: See code: 125.0

125.2   Loiasis `CC`
     Eyeworm disease of Africa
     Loa loa infection
     CC Excl: See code: 125.0

125.3   Onchocerciasis `CC`
     Onchocerca volvulus infection
     Onchocercosis
     CC Excl: See code: 125.0

125.4   Dipetalonemiasis `CC`
     Infection by:
        Acanthocheilonema perstans
        Dipetalonema perstans
     CC Excl: See code: 125.0

125.5   Mansonella ozzardi infection `CC`
     Filariasis ozzardi
     CC Excl: See code: 125.0

125.6   Other specified filariasis `CC`
     Dirofilaria infection
     Infection by:
        Acanthocheilonema streptocerca
        Dipetalonema streptocerca
     CC Excl: See code: 125.0

125.7   Dracontiasis `CC`
     Guinea-worm infection
     Infection by Dracunculus medinensis
     CC Excl: See code: 125.0

125.9   Unspecified filariasis `CC`
     CC Excl: See code: 125.0

√4th **126   Ancylostomiasis and necatoriasis**

     INCLUDES   cutaneous larva migrans due to Ancylostoma
                  hookworm (disease) (infection)
                  uncinariasis

126.0   Ancylostoma duodenale `CC`
     CC Excl: 126.0-126.9

126.1   Necator americanus `CC`
     CC Excl: See code: 126.0

126.2   Ancylostoma braziliense `CC`
     CC Excl: See code: 126.0

126.3   Ancylostoma ceylanicum `CC`
     CC Excl: See code: 126.0

126.8   Other specified Ancylostoma `CC`
     CC Excl: See code: 126.0

126.9   Ancylostomiasis and necatoriasis, unspecified `CC`
     Creeping eruption NOS
     Cutaneous larva migrans NOS
     CC Excl: See code: 126.0

N Newborn Age: 0   P Pediatric Age: 0-17   M Maternity Age: 12-55   A Adult Age: 15-124   MCC Major CC Condition   CC CC Condition   HIV HIV Related Dx

30 – Volume 1   **2010 ICD-9-CM**

✓4th **127 Other intestinal helminthiases**

127.0 Ascariasis   `CC`
Ascaridiasis
Infection by Ascaris lumbricoides
Roundworm infection
CC Excl: 127.0-127.9

127.1 Anisakiasis   `CC`
Infection by Anisakis larva
CC Excl: See code: 127.0

127.2 Strongyloidiasis   `CC` `HIV`
Infection by Strongyloides stercoralis
EXCLUDES   trichostrongyliasis (127.6)
CC Excl: See code: 127.0

127.3 Trichuriasis   `CC`
Infection by Trichuris trichiuria
Trichocephaliasis
Whipworm (disease) (infection)
CC Excl: See code: 127.0

127.4 Enterobiasis   `CC`
Infection by Enterobius vermicularis
Oxyuriasis
Oxyuris vermicularis infection
Pinworm (disease) (infection)
Threadworm infection
CC Excl: See code: 127.0

127.5 Capillariasis   `CC`
Infection by Capillaria philippinensis
EXCLUDES   infection by Capillaria hepatica (128.8)
CC Excl: See code: 127.0

127.6 Trichostrongyliasis   `CC`
Infection by Trichostrongylus species
CC Excl: See code: 127.0

127.7 Other specified intestinal helminthiasis   `CC`
Infection by:
    Oesophagostomum apiostomum and related species
    Ternidens diminutus
    other specified intestinal helminth
Physalopteriasis
CC Excl: 127.0-129

127.8 Mixed intestinal helminthiasis   `CC`
Infection by intestinal helminths classified to more than
    one of the categories 120.0-127.7
Mixed helminthiasis NOS
CC Excl: See code: 127.7

127.9 Intestinal helminthiasis, unspecified   `CC`
CC Excl: See code: 127.7

✓4th **128 Other and unspecified helminthiases**

128.0 Toxocariasis
Larva migrans visceralis
Toxocara (canis) (cati) infection
Visceral larva migrans syndrome

128.1 Gnathostomiasis
Infection by Gnathostoma spinigerum and related species

128.8 Other specified helminthiasis
Infection by:
    Angiostrongylus cantonensis
    Capillaria hepatica
    other specified helminth

128.9 Helminth infection, unspecified
Helminthiasis NOS
Worms NOS

129 Intestinal parasitism, unspecified

OTHER INFECTIOUS AND PARASITIC DISEASES (130–136)

✓4th **130 Toxoplasmosis**
INCLUDES   infection by toxoplasma gondii
               toxoplasmosis (acquired)
EXCLUDES   congenital toxoplasmosis (771.2)

130.0 Meningoencephalitis due to toxoplasmosis   `MCC` `HIV`
Encephalitis due to acquired toxoplasmosis
CC Excl: 130.0, 130.7-130.9, 139.8

130.1 Conjunctivitis due to toxoplasmosis   `CC` `HIV`
CC Excl: 130.1, 130.7-130.9, 139.8

130.2 Chorioretinitis due to toxoplasmosis   `CC` `HIV`
Focal retinochoroiditis due to acquired toxoplasmosis
CC Excl: 130.2, 130.7-130.9, 139.8

130.3 Myocarditis due to toxoplasmosis   `MCC` `HIV`
CC Excl: 130.3, 130.7-130.9, 139.8

130.4 Pneumonitis due to toxoplasmosis   `MCC` `HIV`
CC Excl: 130.4, 130.7-130.9, 139.8, 480.0-480.2, 480.8-487.1,
488, 494.0-508.9, 517.1, 518.89

130.5 Hepatitis due to toxoplasmosis   `CC` `HIV`
CC Excl: 130.5-130.9, 139.8

130.7 Toxoplasmosis of other specified sites   `CC` `HIV`
CC Excl: 130.7-130.9, 139.8

130.8 Multisystemic disseminated   `MCC` `HIV`
toxoplasmosis
Toxoplasmosis of multiple sites
CC Excl: See code: 130.7

130.9 Toxoplasmosis, unspecified   `CC` `HIV`
CC Excl: 130.9

131 Trichomoniasis
INCLUDES   infection due to Trichomonas (vaginalis)

✓5th **131.0 Urogenital trichomoniasis**

131.00 Urogenital trichomoniasis, unspecified
Fluor (vaginalis)   ⎫ trichomonal or due to
Leukorrhea   ⎬   Trichomonas
    (vaginalis)   ⎭   (vaginalis)
DEF: *Trichomonas vaginalis* infection of reproductive
and urinary organs, transmitted through coitus.

131.01 Trichomonal vulvovaginitis   ♀
Vaginitis, trichomonal or due to Trichomonas
    (vaginalis)
DEF: *Trichomonas vaginalis* infection of vulva and
vagina; often asymptomatic, transmitted through
coitus.

131.02 Trichomonal urethritis
DEF: *Trichomonas vaginalis* infection of the urethra.

131.03 Trichomonal prostatitis   ♂
DEF: *Trichomonas vaginalis* infection of the prostate.

131.09 Other

131.8 Other specified sites
EXCLUDES   intestinal (007.3)

131.9 Trichomoniasis, unspecified

✓4th **132 Pediculosis and phthirus infestation**

132.0 Pediculus capitis [head louse]

132.1 Pediculus corporis [body louse]

132.2 Phthirus pubis [pubic louse]
Pediculus pubis

132.3 Mixed infestation
Infestation classifiable to more than one of the categories
    132.0-132.2

132.9 Pediculosis, unspecified

✓4th **133 Acariasis**

133.0 Scabies
Infestation by Sarcoptes scabiei
Norwegian scabies
Sarcoptic itch

Infectious and Parasitic Diseases

133.8–139.8

133.8 Other acariasis
Chiggers
Infestation by:
    Demodex folliculorum
    Trombicula

133.9 Acariasis, unspecified
Infestation by mites NOS

✓4th **134 Other infestation**

134.0 Myiasis
Infestation by:
    Dermatobia (hominis)
    fly larvae
    Gasterophilus (intestinalis)
    maggots
    Oestrus ovis

134.1 Other arthropod infestation
Infestation by:
    chigoe
    sand flea
    Tunga penetrans
Jigger disease
Scarabiasis
Tungiasis

134.2 Hirudiniasis
Hirudiniasis (external) (internal)
Leeches (aquatic) (land)

134.8 Other specified infestations

134.9 Infestation, unspecified
Infestation (skin) NOS
Skin parasites NOS

135 Sarcoidosis
Besnier-Boeck-Schaumann disease
Lupoid (miliary) of Boeck
Lupus pernio (Besnier)
Lymphogranulomatosis, benign (Schaumann's)
Sarcoid (any site):
    NOS
    Boeck
    Darier-Roussy
Uveoparotid fever
DEF: A chronic, granulomatous reticulosis (abnormal increase in cells), affecting any organ or tissue; acute form has high rate of remission; chronic form is progressive.
D86.9 Sarcoidosis unspecified   [I-10]

✓4th **136 Other and unspecified infectious and parasitic diseases**

136.0 Ainhum
Dactylolysis spontanea
DEF: A disease affecting the toes, especially the fifth digit, the fingers, mostly seen in black adult males; it is characterized by a linear constriction around the affected digit leading to spontaneous amputation of the distal part of the digit.

136.1 Behçet's syndrome
DEF: A chronic inflammatory disorder of unknown etiology involving the small blood vessels; characterized by recurrent aphthous ulceration of the oral and pharyngeal mucous membranes and the genitalia; skin lesions, severe uvetis, retinal vascularitis and optic atrophy.

✓5th **136.2 Specific infections by free-living amebae**
AHA: ▶4Q, '08, 79-81◀

  136.21 Specific infection due to acanthamoeba
Use additional code to identify manifestation, such as:
    keratitis (370.8)
AHA: ▶4Q, '08, 81◀

  136.29 Other specific infections by   [CC]
free-living amebae
Meningoencephalitis due to Naegleria
CC Excl: 136.0-136.9

136.3 Pneumocystosis   [MCC] [HIV]
Pneumonia due to Pneumocystis carinii
Pneumonia due to Pneumocystis jiroveci
DEF: *Pneumocystis carinii* fungus causing pneumonia in immunocompromised patients; a leading cause of death among AIDS patients.
CC Excl: 136.3, 139.8, 480.0-480.2, 480.8-487.1, 488, 494.0-508.9, 517.1, 518.89
AHA: 1Q, '05, 7; 1Q, '03, 15; N-D, '87, 5-6

136.4 Psorospermiasis   [CC]
CC Excl: See code: 136.2

136.5 Sarcosporidiosis   [CC]
Infection by Sarcocystis lindemanni
DEF: *Sarcocystis* infection causing muscle cysts of intestinal inflammation.
CC Excl: See code: 136.2

136.8 Other specified infectious and parasitic diseases   [HIV]
Candiru infestation

136.9 Unspecified infectious and parasitic diseases
Infectious disease NOS
Parasitic disease NOS
AHA: 2Q, '91, 8

LATE EFFECTS OF INFECTIOUS AND PARASITIC DISEASES (137-139)

✓4th **137 Late effects of tuberculosis**
Note: This category is to be used to indicate conditions classifiable to 010-018 as the cause of late effects, which are themselves classified elsewhere. The "late effects" include those specified as such, as sequelae, or as due to old or inactive tuberculosis, without evidence of active disease.

137.0 Late effects of respiratory or unspecified tuberculosis

137.1 Late effects of central nervous system tuberculosis

137.2 Late effects of genitourinary tuberculosis

137.3 Late effects of tuberculosis of bones and joints

137.4 Late effects of tuberculosis of other specified organs

138 Late effects of acute poliomyelitis
Note: This category is to be used to indicate conditions classifiable to 045 as the cause of late effects, which are themselves classified elsewhere. The "late effects" include conditions specified as such, or as sequelae, or as due to old or inactive poliomyelitis, without evidence of active disease.
B91 Sequelae of poliomyelitis   [I-10]

✓4th **139 Late effects of other infectious and parasitic diseases**
Note: This category is to be used to indicate conditions classifiable to categories 001-009, 020-041, 046-136 as the cause of late effects, which are themselves classified elsewhere. The "late effects" include conditions specified as such; they also include sequela of diseases classifiable to the above categories if there is evidence that the disease itself is no longer present.

139.0 Late effects of viral encephalitis
Late effects of conditions classifiable to 049.8-049.9, 062-064

139.1 Late effects of trachoma
Late effects of conditions classifiable to 076

139.8 Late effects of other and unspecified infectious and parasitic diseases
AHA: 2Q, '06, 17; 4Q, '91, 15; 3Q, '90, 14; M-A, '87, 8

[N] Newborn Age: 0   [P] Pediatric Age: 0-17   [M] Maternity Age: 12-55   [A] Adult Age: 15-124   [MCC] Major CC Condition   [CC] CC Condition   [HIV] HIV Related Dx

32 – Volume 1 · February 2009   2010 ICD-9-CM

"metastasis"- the extension of tumor cells to adjacent sites.

"In Situ" - tumor cells in carcinoma undergoing malignant changes but still confined to the point of origin without invasion of the surrounding normal tissue.

2. NEOPLASMS (140-239)

→ New or abnormal growth

Notes:

1. Content

   This chapter contains the following broad groups: *(behavior groups)*

   140-195 Malignant neoplasms, stated or presumed to be primary, of specified sites, except of lymphatic and hematopoietic tissue

   196-198 Malignant neoplasms, stated or presumed to be secondary, of specified sites

   199 Malignant neoplasms, without specification of site

   200-208 Malignant neoplasms, stated or presumed to be primary, of lymphatic and hematopoietic tissue

   209 Neuroendocrine tumors

   210-229 Benign neoplasms   *aka intraepithelial, non-infiltrating,*

   230-234 Carcinoma in situ   *→ non-invasive, and pre-invasive*

   235-238 Neoplasms of uncertain behavior [see Note, above category 235]

   239 Neoplasms of unspecified nature

2. Functional activity

   All neoplasms are classified in this chapter, whether or not functionally active. An additional code from Chapter 3 may be used to identify such functional activity associated with any neoplasm, e.g.:

   catecholamine-producing malignant pheochromocytoma of adrenal:

   code 194.0, additional code 255.6

   basophil adenoma of pituitary with Cushing's syndrome:

   code 227.3, additional code 255.0

3. Morphology [Histology] - *refers to the form and structure of tumor cells.*

   For those wishing to identify the histological type of neoplasms, a comprehensive coded nomenclature, which comprises the morphology rubrics of the ICD-Oncology, is given in Appendix A.

4. Malignant neoplasms overlapping site boundaries

   Categories 140-195 are for the classification of primary malignant neoplasms according to their point of origin. A malignant neoplasm that overlaps two or more subcategories within a three-digit rubric and whose point of origin cannot be determined should be classified to the subcategory .8 "Other."

   For example, "carcinoma involving tip and ventral surface of tongue" should be assigned to 141.8. On the other hand, "carcinoma of tip of tongue, extending to involve the ventral surface" should be coded to 141.2, as the point of origin, the tip, is known. Three subcategories (149.8, 159.8, 165.8) have been provided for malignant neoplasms that overlap the boundaries of three-digit rubrics within certain systems.

   Overlapping malignant neoplasms that cannot be classified as indicated above should be assigned to the appropriate subdivision of category 195 (Malignant neoplasm of other and ill-defined sites).

   > **DEF:** An abnormal growth; morphology determines behavior, i.e., whether it will remain intact (benign) or spread to adjacent tissue (malignant). The term mass is not synonymous with neoplasm, as it is often used to describe cysts and thickenings such as those occurring with hematoma or infection.
   > **AHA:** 2Q, '90, 7

(left margin handwriting):
that identify histological type, with a slash mark and 5th digit indicating its behavior.

0 - Benign behavior,
1 - uncertain behavior, borderline malignancy
2 - Carcinoma in situ

primary site 6 - Malignant, secondary site

MALIGNANT NEOPLASM OF LIP, ORAL CAVITY, AND PHARYNX (140-149)

EXCLUDES carcinoma in situ (230.0)

√4th **140 Malignant neoplasm of lip**
   EXCLUDES skin of lip (173.0)

   140.0 Upper lip, vermilion border
   Upper lip:
   NOS
   external
   lipstick area

   140.1 Lower lip, vermilion border
   Lower lip:
   NOS
   external
   lipstick area

(left margin handwriting):
solid tumors - single localized point of origin and considered to be primary neoplasms of that site.

(handwriting center):
Codes 140 - 199... solid malignant neoplasms

Codes 200 - 208... Hematopoietic and lymphatic

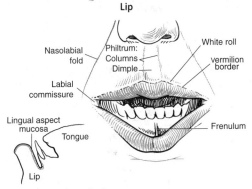

Lip

Labels: Nasolabial fold, Philtrum: Columns, Dimple, Labial commissure, White roll, vermilion border, Frenulum, Lingual aspect mucosa, Tongue, Lip, Lip

140.3 Upper lip, inner aspect
   Upper lip:
   buccal aspect
   frenulum
   mucosa
   oral aspect

140.4 Lower lip, inner aspect
   Lower lip:
   buccal aspect
   frenulum
   mucosa
   oral aspect

140.5 Lip, unspecified, inner aspect
   Lip, not specified whether upper or lower:
   buccal aspect
   frenulum
   mucosa
   oral aspect

140.6 Commissure of lip
   Labial commissure

140.8 Other sites of lip
   Malignant neoplasm of contiguous or overlapping sites of lip whose point of origin cannot be determined

140.9 Lip, unspecified, vermilion border
   Lip, not specified as upper or lower:
   NOS
   external
   lipstick area

√4th **141 Malignant neoplasm of tongue**

   141.0 Base of tongue
   Dorsal surface of base of tongue
   Fixed part of tongue NOS
   AHA: 4Q, '06, 90

   141.1 Dorsal surface of tongue
   Anterior two-thirds of tongue, dorsal surface
   Dorsal tongue NOS
   Midline of tongue
   EXCLUDES dorsal surface of base of tongue (141.0)

   141.2 Tip and lateral border of tongue

Tongue

Labels: Glosso-epiglottic folds, Base (root) of tongue, Lateral border, Tip (apex), Ventral surface, Pharyngeal constrictors, Epiglottis, Vallecula, Palatopharyngeal muscle and fold, Palatine tonsil, Palatoglossal arch and muscle, Lingual tonsil, Dorsal surface, Anterior two-thirds of tongue, Frenulum of tongue

√4th Additional Digit Required | Unacceptable PDx | Manifestation Code | Hospital Acquired Condition | ►◄ Revised Text | ● New Code | ▲ Revised Code Title

2010 ICD-9-CM   **Volume 1 – 33**

(bottom handwriting):
Neoplasms identified during microscopic focus (pathology of excised organ/tissue) are included as additional codes - reason for admission still identified as principal diagnosis,

A code for the primary malignancy is listed as an additional code if admission is exclusively for treatment of neoplasm of a secondary site.

Neoplasms

141.3–146.1

Main Salivary Glands

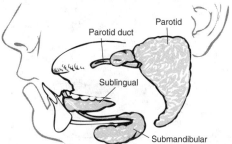

141.3   **Ventral surface of tongue**
Anterior two-thirds of tongue, ventral surface
Frenulum linguae

141.4   **Anterior two-thirds of tongue, part unspecified**
Mobile part of tongue NOS

141.5   **Junctional zone**
Border of tongue at junction of fixed and mobile parts at insertion of anterior tonsillar pillar

141.6   **Lingual tonsil**

141.8   **Other sites of tongue**
Malignant neoplasm of contiguous or overlapping sites of tongue whose point of origin cannot be determined

141.9   **Tongue, unspecified**
Tongue NOS

✓4ᵗʰ   **142**   **Malignant neoplasm of major salivary glands**
    INCLUDES   salivary ducts
    EXCLUDES   *malignant neoplasm of minor salivary glands:*
                NOS (145.9)
                buccal mucosa (145.0)
                soft palate (145.3)
                tongue (141.0-141.9)
                tonsil, palatine (146.0)

142.0   **Parotid gland**

142.1   **Submandibular gland**
Submaxillary gland

142.2   **Sublingual gland**

142.8   **Other major salivary glands**
Malignant neoplasm of contiguous or overlapping sites of salivary glands and ducts whose point of origin cannot be determined

142.9   **Salivary gland, unspecified**
Salivary gland (major) NOS

✓4ᵗʰ   **143**   **Malignant neoplasm of gum**
    INCLUDES   alveolar (ridge) mucosa
                gingiva (alveolar) (marginal)
                interdental papillae
    EXCLUDES   *malignant odontogenic neoplasms (170.0-170.1)*

143.0   **Upper gum**

143.1   **Lower gum**

143.8   **Other sites of gum**
Malignant neoplasm of contiguous or overlapping sites of gum whose point of origin cannot be determined

143.9   **Gum, unspecified**

✓4ᵗʰ   **144**   **Malignant neoplasm of floor of mouth**

144.0   **Anterior portion**
Anterior to the premolar-canine junction

144.1   **Lateral portion**

144.8   **Other sites of floor of mouth**
Malignant neoplasm of contiguous or overlapping sites of floor of mouth whose point of origin cannot be determined

144.9   **Floor of mouth, part unspecified**

Mouth

✓4ᵗʰ   **145**   **Malignant neoplasm of other and unspecified parts of mouth**
    EXCLUDES   *mucosa of lips (140.0-140.9)*

145.0   **Cheek mucosa**
Buccal mucosa
Cheek, inner aspect

145.1   **Vestibule of mouth**
Buccal sulcus (upper) (lower)
Labial sulcus (upper) (lower)

145.2   **Hard palate**

145.3   **Soft palate**
    EXCLUDES   *nasopharyngeal [posterior] [superior] surface of soft palate (147.3)*

145.4   **Uvula**

145.5   **Palate, unspecified**
Junction of hard and soft palate
Roof of mouth

145.6   **Retromolar area**

145.8   **Other specified parts of mouth**
Malignant neoplasm of contiguous or overlapping sites of mouth whose point of origin cannot be determined

145.9   **Mouth, unspecified**
Buccal cavity NOS
Minor salivary gland, unspecified site
Oral cavity NOS

✓4ᵗʰ   **146**   **Malignant neoplasm of oropharynx**

146.0   **Tonsil**
Tonsil:
    NOS
    faucial
    palatine
    EXCLUDES   *lingual tonsil (141.6)*
                pharyngeal tonsil (147.1)
    AHA: S-O, '87, 8

146.1   **Tonsillar fossa**

Oropharynx

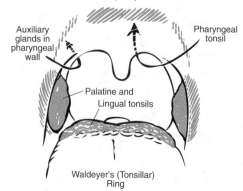

Waldeyer's (Tonsillar) Ring

| N | Newborn Age: 0 | P | Pediatric Age: 0-17 | M | Maternity Age: 12-55 | A | Adult Age: 15-124 | MCC | Major CC Condition | CC | CC Condition | HIV | HIV Related Dx |

34 – Volume 1

2010 ICD-9-CM

V58.0, V58.11 and V58.12... admission solely for administration of chemotherapy, immunotherapy, or radiation therapy. Listed as principal diagnosis with neoplasm listed as additional codes. Complications such as nausea/vomiting are included as additional codes.

Nasopharynx

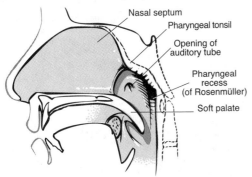

Nasal septum
Pharyngeal tonsil
Opening of auditory tube
Pharyngeal recess (of Rosenmüller)
Soft palate

146.2 Tonsillar pillars (anterior) (posterior)
Faucial pillar
Glossopalatine fold
Palatoglossal arch
Palatopharyngeal arch

146.3 Vallecula
Anterior and medial surface of the pharyngoepiglottic fold

146.4 Anterior aspect of epiglottis
Epiglottis, free border [margin]
Glossoepiglottic fold(s)
EXCLUDES epiglottis:
NOS (161.1)
suprahyoid portion (161.1)

146.5 Junctional region
Junction of the free margin of the epiglottis, the aryepiglottic fold, and the pharyngoepiglottic fold

146.6 Lateral wall of oropharynx

146.7 Posterior wall of oropharynx

146.8 Other specified sites of oropharynx
Branchial cleft
Malignant neoplasm of contiguous or overlapping sites of oropharynx whose point of origin cannot be determined

146.9 Oropharynx, unspecified
AHA: 2Q, '02, 6

✓4th **147 Malignant neoplasm of nasopharynx**

147.0 Superior wall
Roof of nasopharynx

147.1 Posterior wall
Adenoid
Pharyngeal tonsil

147.2 Lateral wall
Fossa of Rosenmüller
Opening of auditory tube
Pharyngeal recess

147.3 Anterior wall
Floor of nasopharynx
Nasopharyngeal [posterior] [superior] surface of soft palate
Posterior margin of nasal septum and choanae

147.8 Other specified sites of nasopharynx
Malignant neoplasm of contiguous or overlapping sites of nasopharynx whose point of origin cannot be determined

147.9 Nasopharynx, unspecified
Nasopharyngeal wall NOS

✓4th **148 Malignant neoplasm of hypopharynx**

148.0 Postcricoid region

148.1 Pyriform sinus
Pyriform fossa

Hypopharynx
Skull base from behind

Nasopharynx
Oropharynx
Hypopharynx
To trachea
Esophagus

Choanae
Soft palate
Uvula
Tongue
Epiglottis junctional zone
Ariepiglottic fold
Piriform sinus (fossa)
Posterior cricoid region

148.2 Aryepiglottic fold, hypopharyngeal aspect
Aryepiglottic fold or interarytenoid fold:
NOS
marginal zone
EXCLUDES aryepiglottic fold or interarytenoid fold, laryngeal aspect (161.1)

148.3 Posterior hypopharyngeal wall

148.8 Other specified sites of hypopharynx
Malignant neoplasm of contiguous or overlapping sites of hypopharynx whose point of origin cannot be determined

148.9 Hypopharynx, unspecified
Hypopharyngeal wall NOS
Hypopharynx NOS

✓4th **149 Malignant neoplasm of other and ill-defined sites within the lip, oral cavity, and pharynx**

149.0 Pharynx, unspecified

149.1 Waldeyer's ring

149.8 Other
Malignant neoplasms of lip, oral cavity, and pharynx whose point of origin cannot be assigned to any one of the categories 140-148
EXCLUDES "book leaf" neoplasm [ventral surface of tongue and floor of mouth] (145.8)

149.9 Ill-defined

MALIGNANT NEOPLASM OF DIGESTIVE ORGANS AND PERITONEUM (150-159)
EXCLUDES carcinoma in situ (230.1-230.9)

✓4th **150 Malignant neoplasm of esophagus**

150.0 Cervical esophagus `CC`
CC Excl: 150.0-150.9, 159.0, 159.8-159.9, 176.3, 195.8, 199.0-199.2, 209.20, 209.29-209.30, 209.70, 239.0, 239.81-239.9

150.1 Thoracic esophagus `CC`
CC Excl: See code: 150.0

150.2 Abdominal esophagus `CC`
EXCLUDES adenocarcinoma (151.0)
cardio-esophageal junction (151.0)
CC Excl: See code 150.0

150.3 Upper third of esophagus `CC`
Proximal third of esophagus
CC Excl: See code 150.0

150.4 Middle third of esophagus `CC`
CC Excl: See code 150.0

150.5 Lower third of esophagus `CC`
Distal third of esophagus
EXCLUDES adenocarcinoma (151.0)
cardio-esophageal junction (151.0)
CC Excl: See code 150.0

150.8 Other specified part `CC`
Malignant neoplasm of contiguous or overlapping sites of esophagus whose point of origin cannot be determined
CC Excl: See code 150.0

150.9 Esophagus, unspecified `CC`
CC Excl: See code 150.0

✓4th **151 Malignant neoplasm of stomach**
> *EXCLUDES*   *benign carcinoid tumor of stomach (209.63)*
> *malignant carcinoid tumor of stomach (209.23)*

151.0 Cardia `CC`
Cardiac orifice
Cardio-esophageal junction
> *EXCLUDES*   *squamous cell carcinoma (150.2, 150.5)*
CC Excl: 151.0-151.9, 159.0, 159.8-159.9, 176.3, 195.8, 199.0-199.2, 209.20, 209.23, 209.25-209.30, 209.70, 239.0, 239.81-239.9

151.1 Pylorus `CC`
Prepylorus
Pyloric canal
CC Excl: See code 151.0

151.2 Pyloric antrum `CC`
Antrum of stomach NOS
CC Excl: See code 151.0

151.3 Fundus of stomach `CC`
CC Excl: See code 151.0

151.4 Body of stomach `CC`
CC Excl: See code 151.0

151.5 Lesser curvature, unspecified `CC`
Lesser curvature, not classifiable to 151.1-151.4
CC Excl: See code 151.0

151.6 Greater curvature, unspecified `CC`
Greater curvature, not classifiable to 151.0-151.4
CC Excl: See code 151.0

151.8 Other specified sites of stomach `CC`
Anterior wall, not classifiable to 151.0-151.4
Posterior wall, not classifiable to 151.0-151.4
Malignant neoplasm of contiguous or overlapping sites of stomach whose point of origin cannot be determined
CC Excl: See code 151.0

151.9 Stomach, unspecified `CC`
Carcinoma ventriculi
Gastric cancer
CC Excl: See code 151.0
AHA: 2Q, '01, 17

✓4th **152 Malignant neoplasm of small intestine, including duodenum**
> *EXCLUDES*   *benign carcinoid tumor of small intestine and duodenum (209.40-209.43)*
> *malignant carcinoid tumor of small intestine and duodenum (209.00-209.03)*

152.0 Duodenum `CC`
CC Excl: 152.0, 152.8-152.9, 159.0, 159.8-159.9, 176.3, 195.8, 199.0-199.2, 209.00-209.01, 209.20, 209.29-209.30, 209.70, 239.0, 239.81-239.9

152.1 Jejunum `CC`
CC Excl: 152.1, 152.8-152.9, 159.0, 159.8-159.9, 176.3, 195.8, 199.0-199.2, 209.00, 209.02, 209.20, 209.29-209.30, 209.70, 239.0, 239.81-239.9

152.2 Ileum `CC`
> *EXCLUDES*   *ileocecal valve (153.4)*
CC Excl: 152.2, 152.8-152.9, 159.0, 159.8-159.9, 176.3, 195.8, 199.0-199.2, 209.00, 209.03, 209.20, 209.29-209.30, 209.70, 239.0, 239.81-239.9

152.3 Meckel's diverticulum `CC`
CC Excl: 152.3-152.9, 159.0, 159.8-159.9, 176.3, 195.8, 199.0-199.2, 209.00, 209.20, 209.29-209.30, 209.70, 239.0, 239.81-239.9

152.8 Other specified sites of small intestine `CC`
Duodenojejunal junction
Malignant neoplasm of contiguous or overlapping sites of small intestine whose point of origin cannot be determined
CC Excl: 152.8-152.9, 159.0, 159.8-159.9, 176.3, 195.8, 199.0-199.2, 209.00, 209.20, 209.29-209.30, 209.70, 239.0, 239.81-239.9

152.9 Small intestine, unspecified `CC`
CC Excl: See code 152.8

✓4th **153 Malignant neoplasm of colon**
> *EXCLUDES*   *benign carcinoid tumor of colon (209.50-209.56)*
> *malignant carcinoid tumor of colon (209.10-209.16)*

153.0 Hepatic flexure `CC`
CC Excl: 153.0, 153.8-153.9, 159.0, 159.8-159.9, 176.3, 195.8, 199.0-199.2, 209.10, 209.20, 209.29-209.30, 209.70, 239.0, 239.81-239.9

153.1 Transverse colon `CC`
CC Excl: 153.1, 153.8-153.9, 159.0, 159.8-159.9, 176.3, 195.8, 199.0-199.2, 209.10, 209.14, 209.20, 209.29-209.30, 209.70, 239.0, 239.81-239.9

153.2 Descending colon `CC`
Left colon
CC Excl: 153.2, 153.8-153.9, 159.0, 159.8-159.9, 176.3, 195.8, 199.0-199.2, 209.10, 209.15, 209.20, 209.29-209.30, 209.70, 239.0, 239.81-239.9

153.3 Sigmoid colon `CC`
Sigmoid (flexure)
> *EXCLUDES*   *rectosigmoid junction (154.0)*
CC Excl: 153.3, 153.8-153.9, 159.0, 159.8-159.9, 176.3, 195.8, 199.0-199.2, 209.10, 209.16, 209.20, 209.29-209.30, 209.70, 239.0, 239.81-239.9

153.4 Cecum `CC`
Ileocecal valve
CC Excl: 153.4, 153.8-153.9, 159.0, 159.8-159.9, 176.3, 195.8, 199.0-199.2, 209.10, 209.12, 209.20, 209.29-209.30, 209.70, 239.0, 239.81-239.9
C18.0 Malignant neoplasm of cecum `I-10`

153.5 Appendix `CC`
CC Excl: 153.5, 153.8-153.9, 159.0, 159.8-159.9, 176.3, 195.8, 199.0-199.2, 209.10-209.11, 209.20, 209.29-209.30, 209.70, 239.0, 239.81-239.9

153.6 Ascending colon `CC`
Right colon
CC Excl: 153.6, 153.8-153.9, 159.0, 159.8-159.9, 176.3, 195.8, 199.0-199.2, 209.10, 209.13, 209.20, 209.29-209.30, 209.70, 239.0, 239.81-239.9
C18.2 Malignant neoplasm of ascending colon `I-10`

153.7 Splenic flexure `CC`
CC Excl: 153.7-153.9, 159.0, 159.8-159.9, 176.3, 195.8, 199.0-199.2, 209.10, 209.20, 209.29-209.30, 209.70, 239.0, 239.81-239.9

Colon

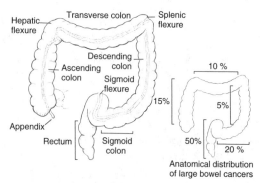

Anatomical distribution of large bowel cancers

| N Newborn Age: 0 | P Pediatric Age: 0-17 | M Maternity Age: 12-55 | A Adult Age: 15-124 | MCC Major CC Condition | CC CC Condition | HIV HIV Related Dx |

36 – Volume 1

2010 ICD-9-CM

153.8 Other specified sites of large intestine
Malignant neoplasm of contiguous or overlapping sites of colon whose point of origin cannot be determined
EXCLUDES *ileocecal valve (153.4)*
rectosigmoid junction (154.0)
CC Excl: 153.8-153.9, 159.0, 159.8-159.9, 176.3, 195.8, 199.0-199.2, 209.10, 209.20, 209.29-209.30, 209.70, 239.0, 239.81-239.9

153.9 Colon, unspecified
Large intestine NOS
CC Excl: See code: 153.8
C18.9 Malignant neoplasm of colon unspecified [I-10]

✓4th 154 Malignant neoplasm of rectum, rectosigmoid junction, and anus
EXCLUDES *benign carcinoid tumor of rectum (209.57)*
malignant carcinoid tumor of rectum (209.17)

154.0 Rectosigmoid junction
Colon with rectum
Rectosigmoid (colon)
CC Excl: 154.0, 154.8, 159.0, 159.8-159.9, 176.3, 195.8, 199.0-199.2, 209.20, 209.29-209.30, 209.70, 239.0, 239.81-239.9

154.1 Rectum
Rectal ampulla
CC Excl: 154.1, 154.8, 159.0, 159.8-159.9, 176.3, 195.8, 199.0-199.2, 209.17-209.20, 209.29-209.30, 209.70, 239.0, 239.81-239.9
C20 Malignant neoplasm of rectum [I-10]

154.2 Anal canal
Anal sphincter
EXCLUDES *skin of anus (172.5, 173.5)*
CC Excl: 154.2-154.8, 159.0, 159.8-159.9, 176.3, 195.8, 199.0-199.2, 209.20, 209.29-209.30, 209.70, 239.0, 239.81-239.9
AHA: 1Q, '01, 8

154.3 Anus, unspecified
EXCLUDES *anus:*
margin (172.5, 173.5)
skin (172.5, 173.5)
perianal skin (172.5, 173.5)
CC Excl: See code: 154.2

154.8 Other
Anorectum
Cloacogenic zone
Malignant neoplasm of contiguous or overlapping sites of rectum, rectosigmoid junction, and anus whose point of origin cannot be determined
CC Excl: 154.8, 159.0, 159.8-159.9, 176.3, 195.8, 199.0-199.2, 209.20, 209.29-209.30, 209.70, 239.0, 239.81-239.9

✓4th 155 Malignant neoplasm of liver and intrahepatic bile ducts

155.0 Liver, primary
Carcinoma:
liver, specified as primary
hepatocellular
liver cell
Hepatoblastoma
CC Excl: 155.0-155.2, 159.0, 159.8-159.9, 176.3, 195.8, 199.0-199.2, 209.20, 209.29-209.30, 209.70, 239.0, 239.81-239.9
AHA: ▶4Q, '08, 82◀
C22.0 Liver cell carcinoma [I-10]

155.1 Intrahepatic bile ducts
Canaliculi biliferi   Intrahepatic:
Interlobular: biliary passages
bile ducts   canaliculi
biliary canals   gall duct
EXCLUDES *hepatic duct (156.1)*
CC Excl: See code 155.0

155.2 Liver, not specified as primary or secondary
CC Excl: See code 155.0

✓4th 156 Malignant neoplasm of gallbladder and extrahepatic bile ducts

156.0 Gallbladder
CC Excl: 156.0, 156.8-156.9, 159.0, 159.8-159.9, 176.3, 195.8, 199.0-199.2, 209.20, 209.29-209.30, 209.70, 239.0, 239.81-239.9

156.1 Extrahepatic bile ducts
Biliary duct or passage NOS
Common bile duct
Cystic duct
Hepatic duct
Sphincter of Oddi
CC Excl: 156.1, 156.8-156.9, 159.0, 159.8-159.9, 176.3, 195.8, 199.0-199.2, 209.20, 209.29-209.30, 209.70, 239.0, 239.81-239.9

156.2 Ampulla of Vater
DEF: Malignant neoplasm in the area of dilation at the juncture of the common bile and pancreatic ducts near the opening into the lumen of the duodenum.
CC Excl: 156.2-156.9, 159.0, 159.8-159.9, 176.3, 195.8, 199.0-199.2, 209.20, 209.29-209.30, 209.70, 239.0, 239.81-239.9

156.8 Other specified sites of gallbladder and extrahepatic bile ducts
Malignant neoplasm of contiguous or overlapping sites of gallbladder and extrahepatic bile ducts whose point of origin cannot be determined
CC Excl: 156.8-156.9, 159.0, 159.8-159.9, 176.3, 195.8, 199.0-199.2, 209.20, 209.29-209.30, 209.70, 239.0, 239.81-239.9

156.9 Biliary tract, part unspecified
Malignant neoplasm involving both intrahepatic and extrahepatic bile ducts
CC Excl: See code: 156.8

✓4th 157 Malignant neoplasm of pancreas
AHA: 4Q, '07, 72

157.0 Head of pancreas
CC Excl: 157.0-157.9, 159.0, 159.8-159.9, 176.3, 195.8, 199.0-199.2, 209.20, 209.29-209.30, 209.70, 239.0, 239.81-239.9
AHA: 2Q, '05, 9; 4Q, '00, 40

157.1 Body of pancreas
CC Excl: See code 157.0

157.2 Tail of pancreas
CC Excl: See code 157.0

157.3 Pancreatic duct
Duct of:
Santorini
Wirsung
CC Excl: See code 157.0

157.4 Islets of Langerhans
Islets of Langerhans, any part of pancreas
Use additional code to identify any functional activity
DEF: Malignant neoplasm within the structures of the pancreas that produce insulin, somatostatin and glucagon.
CC Excl: See code 157.0

157.8 Other specified sites of pancreas
Ectopic pancreatic tissue
Malignant neoplasm of contiguous or overlapping sites of pancreas whose point of origin cannot be determined
CC Excl: See code 157.0

157.9 Pancreas, part unspecified
CC Excl: See code 157.0
AHA: 4Q, '89, 11
C25.9 Malignant neoplasm of pancreas unspecified [I-10]

✓4th 158 Malignant neoplasm of retroperitoneum and peritoneum

158.0 Retroperitoneum
Periadrenal tissue   Perirenal tissue
Perinephric tissue   Retrocecal tissue
CC Excl: 158.0, V58.0

Neoplasms

158.8–162.3

Retroperitoneum and Peritoneum

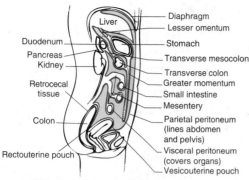

Diaphragm
Liver
Lesser omentum
Duodenum
Stomach
Pancreas
Transverse mesocolon
Kidney
Transverse colon
Retrocecal tissue
Greater momentum
Small intestine
Mesentery
Colon
Parietal peritoneum (lines abdomen and pelvis)
Rectouterine pouch
Visceral peritoneum (covers organs)
Vesicouterine pouch

158.8 Specified parts of peritoneum `CC`
　Cul-de-sac (of Douglas)
　Malignant neoplasm of contiguous or overlapping sites of retroperitoneum and peritoneum whose point of origin cannot be determined
　Mesentery
　Mesocolon
　Omentum
　Peritoneum:
　　parietal
　　pelvic
　Rectouterine pouch
　CC Excl: 158.0-158.9, V58.0

158.9 Peritoneum, unspecified `CC`
　CC Excl: See code: 158.8

✓4th **159 Malignant neoplasm of other and ill-defined sites within the digestive organs and peritoneum**

159.0 Intestinal tract, part unspecified
　Intestine NOS

159.1 Spleen, not elsewhere classified
　Angiosarcoma ⎫ of spleen
　Fibrosarcoma ⎭
　EXCLUDES *Hodgkin's disease (201.0-201.9)*
　　lymphosarcoma (200.1)
　　reticulosarcoma (200.0)

159.8 Other sites of digestive system and intra-abdominal organs
　Malignant neoplasm of digestive organs and peritoneum whose point of origin cannot be assigned to any one of the categories 150-158
　EXCLUDES *anus and rectum (154.8)*
　　cardio-esophageal junction (151.0)
　　colon and rectum (154.0)

159.9 Ill-defined
　Alimentary canal or tract NOS
　Gastrointestinal tract NOS
　EXCLUDES *abdominal NOS (195.2)*
　　intra-abdominal NOS (195.2)

NEOPLASM OF RESPIRATORY AND INTRATHORACIC ORGANS (160-165)

　EXCLUDES *carcinoma in situ (231.0-231.9)*

✓4th **160 Malignant neoplasm of nasal cavities, middle ear, and accessory sinuses**

160.0 Nasal cavities
　Cartilage of nose　　Septum of nose
　Conchae, nasal　　Vestibule of nose
　Internal nose
　EXCLUDES *nasal bone (170.0)*
　　nose NOS (195.0)
　　olfactory bulb (192.0)
　　posterior margin of septum and choanae (147.3)
　　skin of nose (172.3, 173.3)
　　turbinates (170.0)

160.1 Auditory tube, middle ear, and mastoid air cells
　Antrum tympanicum
　Eustachian tube
　Tympanic cavity
　EXCLUDES *auditory canal (external) (172.2, 173.2)*
　　bone of ear (meatus) (170.0)
　　cartilage of ear (171.0)
　　ear (external) (skin) (172.2, 173.2)

160.2 Maxillary sinus
　Antrum (Highmore) (maxillary)

160.3 Ethmoidal sinus

160.4 Frontal sinus

160.5 Sphenoidal sinus

160.8 Other
　Malignant neoplasm of contiguous or overlapping sites of nasal cavities, middle ear, and accessory sinuses whose point of origin cannot be determined

160.9 Accessory sinus, unspecified

✓4th **161 Malignant neoplasm of larynx**

161.0 Glottis
　Intrinsic larynx
　Laryngeal commissure (anterior) (posterior)
　True vocal cord
　Vocal cord NOS

161.1 Supraglottis
　Aryepiglottic fold or interarytenoid fold, laryngeal aspect
　Epiglottis (suprahyoid portion) NOS
　Extrinsic larynx
　False vocal cords
　Posterior (laryngeal) surface of epiglottis
　Ventricular bands
　EXCLUDES *anterior aspect of epiglottis (146.4)*
　　aryepiglottic fold or interarytenoid fold:
　　　NOS (148.2)
　　　hypopharyngeal aspect (148.2)
　　　marginal zone (148.2)

161.2 Subglottis

161.3 Laryngeal cartilages
　Cartilage:
　　arytenoid
　　cricoid
　　cuneiform
　　thyroid

161.8 Other specified sites of larynx
　Malignant neoplasm of contiguous or overlapping sites of larynx whose point of origin cannot be determined
　AHA: 3Q, '07, 7

161.9 Larynx, unspecified

✓4th **162 Malignant neoplasm of trachea, bronchus, and lung**
　EXCLUDES *benign carcinoid tumor of bronchus (209.61)*
　　malignant carcinoid tumor of bronchus (209.21)

162.0 Trachea `CC`
　Cartilage ⎫ of trachea
　Mucosa ⎭
　CC Excl: 162.0-162.9, 165.8-165.9, 176.4, 195.1, 195.8, 197.0-197.1, 197.3, 199.0-199.2, 209.20-209.21, 209.29-209.30, 209.70, 239.1, 239.81-239.9

162.2 Main bronchus `CC`
　Carina
　Hilus of lung
　CC Excl: 162.2, 162.8-162.9, 165.8-165.9, 176.4, 195.8, 199.0-199.2, 209.20-209.21, 209.29-209.30, 209.70, 239.1, 239.81-239.9

162.3 Upper lobe, bronchus or lung `CC`
　CC Excl: 162.3, 162.8-162.9, 165.8-165.9, 176.4, 195.8, 199.0-199.2, 209.20-209.21, 209.29-209.30, 209.70, 239.1, 239.81-239.9
　AHA: 1Q, '04, 4
　C34.10 Malig neoplasm upper lobe bronchus/lung uns side `I-10`

| `N` Newborn Age: 0 | `P` Pediatric Age: 0-17 | `M` Maternity Age: 12-55 | `A` Adult Age: 15-124 | `MCC` Major CC Condition | `CC` CC Condition | `HIV` HIV Related Dx |

38 – Volume 1

2010 ICD-9-CM

162.4 Middle lobe, bronchus or lung `CC`
    CC Excl: 162.4, 162.8-162.9, 165.8-165.9, 176.4, 195.8, 199.0-199.2, 209.20-209.21, 209.29-209.30, 209.70, 239.1, 239.81-239.9

162.5 Lower lobe, bronchus or lung `CC`
    CC Excl: 162.5-162.9, 165.8-165.9, 176.4, 195.8, 199.0-199.2, 209.20-209.21, 209.29-209.30, 209.70, 239.1, 239.81-239.9

162.8 Other parts of bronchus or lung `CC`
    Malignant neoplasm of contiguous or overlapping sites of bronchus or lung whose point of origin cannot be determined
    CC Excl: 162.8-162.9, 165.8-165.9, 176.4, 195.8, 199.0-199.2, 209.20-209.21, 209.29-209.30, 209.70, 239.1, 239.81-239.9
    AHA: 3Q, '06, 7
    TIP: Assign when two separate tumors classifiable to category 162 are present, overlapping and no point of origin is determined.

162.9 Bronchus and lung, unspecified `CC`
    CC Excl: See code: 162.8
    AHA: 3Q, '06, 14-15; 2Q, '97, 3; 4Q, '96, 48
    C34.90 Malig neoplas bronchus/lung unspec, unspec side `I-10`

✓4ᵗʰ **163 Malignant neoplasm of pleura**

163.0 Parietal pleura `CC`
    CC Excl: 163.0-163.9, 165.8-165.9, 195.8, 199.0-199.2, 209.20, 209.29-209.30, 209.70, 239.1, 239.81-239.9

163.1 Visceral pleura `CC`
    CC Excl: See code 163.0

163.8 Other specified sites of pleura `CC`
    Malignant neoplasm of contiguous or overlapping sites of pleura whose point of origin cannot be determined
    CC Excl: See code 163.0

163.9 Pleura, unspecified `CC`
    CC Excl: See code 163.0

✓4ᵗʰ **164 Malignant neoplasm of thymus, heart, and mediastinum**

164.0 Thymus `CC`
    EXCLUDES benign carcinoid tumor of the thymus (209.62)
               malignant carcinoid tumor of the thymus (209.22)
    CC Excl: 164.0, 209.22

164.1 Heart `CC`
    Endocardium
    Epicardium
    Myocardium
    Pericardium
    EXCLUDES great vessels (171.4)
    CC Excl: 164.1

164.2 Anterior mediastinum `CC`
    CC Excl: 164.2-164.9, 165.8-165.9, 195.8, 199.0-199.2, 209.20, 209.29-209.30, 209.70, 239.1, 239.81-239.9

164.3 Posterior mediastinum `CC`
    CC Excl: See code 164.2

164.8 Other `CC`
    Malignant neoplasm of contiguous or overlapping sites of thymus, heart, and mediastinum whose point of origin cannot be determined
    CC Excl: See code 164.2

164.9 Mediastinum, part unspecified `CC`
    CC Excl: See code 164.2

✓4ᵗʰ **165 Malignant neoplasm of other and ill-defined sites within the respiratory system and intrathoracic organs**

165.0 Upper respiratory tract, part unspecified

165.8 Other
    Malignant neoplasm of respiratory and intrathoracic organs whose point of origin cannot be assigned to any one of the categories 160-164

165.9 Ill-defined sites within the respiratory system
    Respiratory tract NOS
    EXCLUDES intrathoracic NOS (195.1)
               thoracic NOS (195.1)

Skull

MALIGNANT NEOPLASM OF BONE, CONNECTIVE TISSUE, SKIN, AND BREAST (170-176)

    EXCLUDES carcinoma in situ:
               breast (233.0)
               skin (232.0-232.9)

✓4ᵗʰ **170 Malignant neoplasm of bone and articular cartilage**

    INCLUDES cartilage (articular) (joint)
              periosteum
    EXCLUDES bone marrow NOS (202.9)
              cartilage:
                 ear (171.0)
                 eyelid (171.0)
                 larynx (161.3)
                 nose (160.0)
              synovia (171.0-171.9)
    AHA: 4Q, '06, 103
    TIP: Do not assign for bone metastasis; see instead code 198.5.

170.0 Bones of skull and face, except mandible `CC`
    Bone: Bone:
      ethmoid   sphenoid
      frontal   temporal
      malar   zygomatic
      nasal   Maxilla (superior)
      occipital   Turbinate
      orbital   Upper jaw bone
      parietal   Vomer
    EXCLUDES carcinoma, any type except intraosseous or odontogenic:
               maxilla, maxillary (sinus) (160.2)
               upper jaw bone (143.0)
            jaw bone (lower) (170.1)
    CC Excl: 170.0, 170.9, V58.0

170.1 Mandible `CC`
    Inferior maxilla
    Jaw bone NOS
    Lower jaw bone
    EXCLUDES carcinoma, any type except intraosseous or odontogenic:
               jaw bone NOS (143.9)
               lower (143.1)
               upper jaw bone (170.0)
    CC Excl: 170.1, 170.9, V58.0

170.2 Vertebral column, excluding sacrum and coccyx `CC`
    Spinal column
    Spine
    Vertebra
    EXCLUDES sacrum and coccyx (170.6)
    CC Excl: 170.2, 170.9, V58.0

170.3 Ribs, sternum, and clavicle `CC`
    Costal cartilage
    Costovertebral joint
    Xiphoid process
    CC Excl: 170.3, 170.9, V58.0

✓4ᵗʰ / ✓5ᵗʰ Additional Digit Required   Unacceptable PDx   Manifestation Code   Hospital Acquired Condition   ►◄ Revised Text   ● New Code   ▲ Revised Code Title

2010 ICD-9-CM   **Volume 1 – 39**

Neoplasms

170.4 Scapula and long bones of upper limb `CC`
Acromion
Bones NOS of upper limb
Humerus
Radius
Ulna
CC Excl: 170.4, 170.9, V58.0
AHA: 2Q, '99, 9

170.5 Short bones of upper limb `CC`
Carpal
Cuneiform, wrist
Metacarpal
Navicular, of hand
Phalanges of hand
Pisiform
Scaphoid (of hand)
Semilunar or lunate
Trapezium
Trapezoid
Unciform
CC Excl: 170.5, 170.9, V58.0

170.6 Pelvic bones, sacrum, and coccyx `CC`
Coccygeal vertebra
Ilium
Ischium
Pubic bone
Sacral vertebra
CC Excl: 170.6, 170.9, V58.0

170.7 Long bones of lower limb `CC`
Bones NOS of lower limb
Femur
Fibula
Tibia
CC Excl: 170.7, 170.9, V58.0

170.8 Short bones of lower limb `CC`
Astragalus [talus]
Calcaneus
Cuboid
Cuneiform, ankle
Metatarsal
Navicular (of ankle)
Patella
Phalanges of foot
Tarsal
CC Excl: 170.8-170.9, V58.0

170.9 Bone and articular cartilage, site unspecified `CC`
CC Excl: 170.0-170.9, V58.0

√4ᵗʰ 171 Malignant neoplasm of connective and other soft tissue
`INCLUDES` blood vessel
bursa
fascia
fat
ligament, except uterine
muscle
peripheral, sympathetic, and parasympathetic nerves
and ganglia
synovia
tendon (sheath)
`EXCLUDES` *cartilage (of):*
articular (170.0-170.9)
larynx (161.3)
nose (160.0)
connective tissue:
breast (174.0-175.9)
internal organs–code to malignant neoplasm of the site [e.g., leiomyosarcoma of stomach, 151.9]
heart (164.1)
uterine ligament (183.4)

171.0 Head, face, and neck `CC`
Cartilage of:
ear
eyelid
CC Excl: V58.0
AHA: 2Q, '99, 6

171.2 Upper limb, including shoulder `CC`
Arm
Finger
Forearm
Hand
CC Excl: See code: 171.0

171.3 Lower limb, including hip `CC`
Foot
Leg
Popliteal space
Thigh
Toe
CC Excl: See code: 171.0

171.4 Thorax `CC`
Axilla
Diaphragm
Great vessels
`EXCLUDES` *heart (164.1)*
mediastinum (164.2-164.9)
thymus (164.0)
CC Excl: See code: 171.0

171.5 Abdomen `CC`
Abdominal wall
Hypochondrium
`EXCLUDES` *peritoneum (158.8)*
retroperitoneum (158.0)
CC Excl: See code: 171.0

171.6 Pelvis `CC`
Buttock
Groin
Inguinal region
Perineum
`EXCLUDES` *pelvic peritoneum (158.8)*
retroperitoneum (158.0)
uterine ligament, any (183.3-183.5)
CC Excl: See code: 171.0

171.7 Trunk, unspecified `CC`
Back NOS
Flank NOS
CC Excl: See code: 171.0

171.8 Other specified sites of connective and other soft tissue `CC`
Malignant neoplasm of contiguous or overlapping sites of connective tissue whose point of origin cannot be determined
CC Excl: See code: 171.0

171.9 Connective and other soft tissue, site unspecified `CC`
CC Excl: See code: 171.0

√4ᵗʰ 172 Malignant melanoma of skin
`INCLUDES` melanocarcinoma
melanoma (skin) NOS
melanoma in situ of skin
`EXCLUDES` *skin of genital organs (184.0-184.9, 187.1-187.9)*
sites other than skin–code to malignant neoplasm of the site
DEF: Malignant neoplasm of melanocytes; most common in skin, may involve oral cavity, esophagus, anal canal, vagina, leptomeninges, or conjunctiva.

172.0 Lip
`EXCLUDES` *vermilion border of lip (140.0-140.1, 140.9)*

172.1 Eyelid, including canthus

172.2 Ear and external auditory canal
Auricle (ear)
Auricular canal, external
External [acoustic] meatus
Pinna

172.3 Other and unspecified parts of face
Cheek (external)
Chin
Eyebrow
Forehead
Nose, external
Temple

172.4 Scalp and neck

`N` Newborn Age: 0   `P` Pediatric Age: 0-17   `M` Maternity Age: 12-55   `A` Adult Age: 15-124   `MCC` Major CC Condition   `CC` CC Condition   `HIV` HIV Related Dx

40 – Volume 1

2010 ICD-9-CM

172.5 Trunk, except scrotum

Axilla	Perianal skin
Breast	Perineum
Buttock	Umbilicus
Groin	

> **EXCLUDES** anal canal (154.2)
> anus NOS (154.3)
> scrotum (187.7)

172.6 Upper limb, including shoulder

Arm	Forearm
Finger	Hand

172.7 Lower limb, including hip

Ankle	Leg
Foot	Popliteal area
Heel	Thigh
Knee	Toe

172.8 Other specified sites of skin
   Malignant melanoma of contiguous or overlapping sites
      of skin whose point of origin cannot be determined

172.9 Melanoma of skin, site unspecified

✓4th **173 Other malignant neoplasm of skin**

> **INCLUDES** malignant neoplasm of:
>   sebaceous glands
>   sudoriferous, sudoriparous glands
>   sweat glands

> **EXCLUDES** Kaposi's sarcoma (176.0-176.9)
>   malignant melanoma of skin (172.0-172.9)
>   skin of genital organs (184.0-184.9, 187.1-187.9)

AHA: 1Q, '00, 18; 2Q, '96, 12

TIP: Do not assign for malignant neoplasm of skin documented as melanoma; see instead category 172.

173.0 Skin of lip
> **EXCLUDES** vermilion border of lip (140.0-140.1, 140.9)

173.1 Eyelid, including canthus
> **EXCLUDES** cartilage of eyelid (171.0)

173.2 Skin of ear and external auditory canal
   Auricle (ear)
   Auricular canal, external
   External meatus
   Pinna
> **EXCLUDES** cartilage of ear (171.0)

173.3 Skin of other and unspecified parts of face

Cheek, external	Forehead
Chin	Nose, external
Eyebrow	Temple

AHA: 1Q, '00, 3

173.4 Scalp and skin of neck

173.5 Skin of trunk, except scrotum

Axillary fold	Skin of:
Perianal skin	buttock
Skin of:	chest wall
abdominal wall	groin
anus	perineum
back	Umbilicus
breast	

> **EXCLUDES** anal canal (154.2)
>   anus NOS (154.3)
>   skin of scrotum (187.7)

AHA: 1Q, '01, 8

173.6 Skin of upper limb, including shoulder

Arm	Forearm
Finger	Hand

173.7 Skin of lower limb, including hip

Ankle	Leg
Foot	Popliteal area
Heel	Thigh
Knee	Toe

173.8 Other specified sites of skin
   Malignant neoplasm of contiguous or overlapping sites of
      skin whose point of origin cannot be determined

173.9 Skin, site unspecified

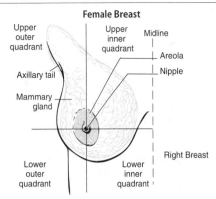

Female Breast

✓4th **174 Malignant neoplasm of female breast**
   Use additional code to identify estrogen receptor status (V86.0,
   V86.1)

> **INCLUDES** breast (female)
>   connective tissue
>   soft parts
>   Paget's disease of:
>   breast
>   nipple

> **EXCLUDES** skin of breast (172.5, 173.5)

AHA: 3Q, '97, 8; 4Q, '89, 11

TIP: For bilateral breast malignancy, do not assign two codes unless documentation indicates separate sites (i.e., different fourth digits).

174.0 Nipple and areola   ♀

174.1 Central portion   ♀

174.2 Upper-inner quadrant   ♀

174.3 Lower-inner quadrant

174.4 Upper-outer quadrant   ♀
   AHA: ▶4Q, '08, 155;◀ 1Q, '04, 3; '3Q, '97, 8

174.5 Lower-outer quadrant   ♀

174.6 Axillary tail   ♀

174.8 Other specified sites of female breast   ♀
   Ectopic sites
   Inner breast
   Lower breast
   Midline of breast
   Outer breast
   Upper breast
   Malignant neoplasm of contiguous or overlapping sites of
      breast whose point of origin cannot be determined

174.9 Breast (female), unspecified   ♀
   AHA: 3Q, '05, 11; 2Q, '94, 10; 4Q, '89, 11
   C50.911 Malig neoplasm of uns site of rt female breast **I-10**

✓4th **175 Malignant neoplasm of male breast**
   Use additional code to identify estrogen receptor status (V86.0,
   V86.1)

> **EXCLUDES** skin of breast (172.5, 173.5)

175.0 Nipple and areola   ♂

175.9 Other and unspecified sites of male breast   ♂
   Ectopic breast tissue, male

✓4th **176 Kaposi's sarcoma**
   AHA: 4Q, '91, 24

176.0 Skin   **CC** **HIV**
   CC Excl: 176.0, 176.8-176.9, V58.0
   AHA: 4Q, '07, 63; 4Q, '94, 29; 4Q, '91, 24

176.1 Soft tissue   **CC** **HIV**
   Blood vessel
   Connective tissue
   Fascia
   Ligament
   Lymphatic(s) NEC
   Muscle
> **EXCLUDES** lymph glands and nodes (176.5)
   CC Excl: 176.1, 176.8-176.9, V58.0

✓4th ✓5th Additional Digit Required   Unacceptable PDx   Manifestation Code   Hospital Acquired Condition   ▶◀ Revised Text   ● New Code   ▲ Revised Code Title

2010 ICD-9-CM   **February 2009 • Volume 1 – 41**

176.2 Palate   `CC` `HIV`
　　CC Excl: 176.2, 176.8-176.9, V58.0

176.3 Gastrointestinal sites   `CC` `HIV`
　　CC Excl: 176.3, 176.8-176.9, V58.0

176.4 Lung   `CC` `HIV`
　　CC Excl: 162.8-162.9, 165.8-165.9, 176.4, 195.8, 199.0-199.2,
　　209.20-209.21, 209.29-209.30, 209.70, 239.1, 239.81-239.9

176.5 Lymph nodes   `CC` `HIV`
　　CC Excl: 176.5, 195.8-196.9, 199.0-199.2, 209.20, 209.29-209.30,
　　209.70-209.71, 239.81-239.9

176.8 Other specified sites   `CC` `HIV`
　　Oral cavity NEC
　　CC Excl: 176.0-176.9, V58.0

176.9 Unspecified   `CC` `HIV`
　　Viscera NOS
　　CC Excl: 176.0-192.9, 195.0-199.2, 209.20, 209.24,
　　209.29-209.30, 209.70-209.74, 209.79, 230.0-237.6,
　　237.9-238.3, 238.8-239.7, 239.81-239.9, V58.0

MALIGNANT NEOPLASM OF GENITOURINARY ORGANS (179-189)

　　EXCLUDES   carcinoma in situ (233.1-233.9)

179 Malignant neoplasm of uterus, part unspecified   ♀

✓4ᵗʰ 180 Malignant neoplasm of cervix uteri
　　INCLUDES   invasive malignancy [carcinoma]
　　EXCLUDES   carcinoma in situ (233.1)

180.0 Endocervix   ♀
　　Cervical canal NOS
　　Endocervical canal
　　Endocervical gland

180.1 Exocervix   ♀

180.8 Other specified sites of cervix   ♀
　　Cervical stump
　　Squamocolumnar junction of cervix
　　Malignant neoplasm of contiguous or overlapping sites of
　　　cervix uteri whose point of origin cannot be
　　　determined

180.9 Cervix uteri, unspecified   ♀

181 Malignant neoplasm of placenta   ♀
　　Choriocarcinoma NOS
　　Chorioepithelioma NOS
　　EXCLUDES   chorioadenoma (destruens) (236.1)
　　　　hydatidiform mole (630)
　　　　　malignant–(236.1)
　　　　invasive mole (236.1)
　　　　male choriocarcinoma NOS (186.0-186.9)

✓4ᵗʰ 182 Malignant neoplasm of body of uterus
　　EXCLUDES   carcinoma in situ (233.2)

182.0 Corpus uteri, except isthmus   ♀
　　Cornu
　　Endometrium
　　Fundus
　　Myometrium
　　C54.9 Malignant neoplasm of corpus uteri unspecified   `I-10`

182.1 Isthmus   ♀
　　Lower uterine segment

182.8 Other specified sites of body of uterus   ♀
　　Malignant neoplasm of contiguous or overlapping sites of
　　　body of uterus whose point of origin cannot be
　　　determined
　　　EXCLUDES   uterus NOS (179)

✓4ᵗʰ 183 Malignant neoplasm of ovary and other uterine adnexa
　　EXCLUDES   Douglas' cul-de-sac (158.8)

183.0 Ovary   `CC` ♀
　　Use additional code to identify any functional activity
　　CC Excl: 183.0-183.9, 195.3, 198.6, 199.0-199.2, 209.20,
　　209.29-209.30, 209.70
　　AHA: 4Q, '07, 96
　　C56.9 Malignant neoplasm of ovary unspecified side   `I-10`

183.2 Fallopian tube   ♀
　　Oviduct   Uterine tube

183.3 Broad ligament   ♀
　　Mesovarium   Parovarian region

183.4 Parametrium   ♀
　　Uterine ligament NOS
　　Uterosacral ligament

183.5 Round ligament   ♀
　　AHA: 3Q, '99, 5

183.8 Other specified sites of uterine adnexa   ♀
　　Tubo-ovarian
　　Utero-ovarian
　　Malignant neoplasm of contiguous or overlapping sites of
　　　ovary and other uterine adnexa whose point of
　　　origin cannot be determined

183.9 Uterine adnexa, unspecified   ♀

✓4ᵗʰ 184 Malignant neoplasm of other and unspecified female genital organs
　　EXCLUDES   carcinoma in situ (233.30-233.39)

184.0 Vagina   ♀
　　Gartner's duct
　　Vaginal vault

184.1 Labia majora   ♀
　　Greater vestibular [Bartholin's] gland

184.2 Labia minora   ♀

184.3 Clitoris   ♀

184.4 Vulva, unspecified   ♀
　　External female genitalia NOS
　　Pudendum

184.8 Other specified sites of female genital organs ♀
　　Malignant neoplasm of contiguous or overlapping sites of
　　　female genital organs whose point of origin cannot
　　　be determined

184.9 Female genital organ, site unspecified   ♀
　　Female genitourinary tract NOS

185 Malignant neoplasm of prostate   ♂
　　EXCLUDES   seminal vesicles (187.8)
　　AHA: 3Q, '03, 13; 3Q, '99, 5; 3Q, '92, 7
　　TIP: Assign as a secondary diagnosis if patient treated for BPH and inci-
　　dental finding of carcinoma of the prostate is made.
　　C61 Malignant neoplasm of prostate   `I-10`

✓4ᵗʰ 186 Malignant neoplasm of testis
　　Use additional code to identify any functional activity

186.0 Undescended testis   ♂
　　Ectopic testis
　　Retained testis

186.9 Other and unspecified testis   ♂
　　Testis:
　　　NOS
　　　descended
　　　scrotal

✓4ᵗʰ 187 Malignant neoplasm of penis and other male genital organs

187.1 Prepuce   ♂
　　Foreskin

187.2 Glans penis   ♂

187.3 Body of penis   ♂
　　Corpus cavernosum

187.4 Penis, part unspecified   ♂
　　Skin of penis NOS

187.5 Epididymis   ♂

187.6 Spermatic cord   ♂
　　Vas deferens

187.7 Scrotum   ♂
　　Skin of scrotum

`N` Newborn Age: 0   `P` Pediatric Age: 0-17   `M` Maternity Age: 12-55   `A` Adult Age: 15-124   `MCC` Major CC Condition   `CC` CC Condition   `HIV` HIV Related Dx

187.8 Other specified sites of male genital organs ♂
Seminal vesicle
Tunica vaginalis
Malignant neoplasm of contiguous or overlapping sites of penis and other male genital organs whose point of origin cannot be determined

187.9 Male genital organ, site unspecified ♂
Male genital organ or tract NOS

√4th **188 Malignant neoplasm of bladder**
EXCLUDES carcinoma in situ (233.7)

188.0 Trigone of urinary bladder

188.1 Dome of urinary bladder

188.2 Lateral wall of urinary bladder

188.3 Anterior wall of urinary bladder

188.4 Posterior wall of urinary bladder

188.5 Bladder neck
Internal urethral orifice

188.6 Ureteric orifice

188.7 Urachus

188.8 Other specified sites of bladder
Malignant neoplasm of contiguous or overlapping sites of bladder whose point of origin cannot be determined

188.9 Bladder, part unspecified
Bladder wall NOS
AHA: 1Q, '00, 5
C67.9 Malignant neoplasm of bladder unspecified   I-10

√4th **189 Malignant neoplasm of kidney and other and unspecified urinary organs**
EXCLUDES benign carcinoid tumor of kidney (209.64)
malignant carcinoid tumor of kidney (209.24)

189.0 Kidney, except pelvis CC
Kidney NOS
Kidney parenchyma
CC Excl: 189.0-189.1, 189.8-189.9, 195.8, 199.0-199.2, 209.20, 209.24, 209.29-209.30, 209.70, 239.5, 239.81-239.9
AHA: 2Q, '05, 4; 2Q, '04, 4
C64.9 Malig neoplasm kidney no renal pelvis uns side   I-10

189.1 Renal pelvis CC
Renal calyces
Ureteropelvic junction
CC Excl: See code: 189.0

189.2 Ureter CC
EXCLUDES ureteric orifice of bladder (188.6)
CC Excl: 189.2, 189.8-189.9, 195.8, 199.0-199.2, 209.20, 209.29-209.30, 209.70, 239.5, 239.81-239.9

189.3 Urethra CC
EXCLUDES urethral orifice of bladder (188.5)
CC Excl: 189.3-189.9, 198.82

189.4 Paraurethral glands CC
CC Excl: See code: 189.3

189.8 Other specified sites of urinary organs CC
Malignant neoplasm of contiguous or overlapping sites of kidney and other urinary organs whose point of origin cannot be determined
CC Excl: 189.0-189.9, 195.3, 198.0-198.1, 209.24

189.9 Urinary organ, site unspecified CC
Urinary system NOS
CC Excl: See code: 189.8

MALIGNANT NEOPLASM OF OTHER AND UNSPECIFIED SITES (190-199)
EXCLUDES carcinoma in situ (234.0-234.9)

√4th **190 Malignant neoplasm of eye**
EXCLUDES carcinoma in situ (234.0)
►dark area on retina and choroid (239.81)◄
eyelid (skin) (172.1, 173.1)
cartilage (171.0)
optic nerve (192.0)
orbital bone (170.0)
►retinal freckle (239.81)◄

190.0 Eyeball, except conjunctiva, cornea, retina, and choroid
Ciliary body   Sclera
Crystalline lens   Uveal tract
Iris

190.1 Orbit
Connective tissue of orbit
Extraocular muscle
Retrobulbar
EXCLUDES bone of orbit (170.0)

190.2 Lacrimal gland

190.3 Conjunctiva

190.4 Cornea

190.5 Retina

190.6 Choroid

190.7 Lacrimal duct
Lacrimal sac
Nasolacrimal duct

190.8 Other specified sites of eye
Malignant neoplasm of contiguous or overlapping sites of eye whose point of origin cannot be determined

190.9 Eye, part unspecified

√4th **191 Malignant neoplasm of brain**
EXCLUDES cranial nerves (192.0)
retrobulbar area (190.1)
AHA: 4Q, '07, 104

191.0 Cerebrum, except lobes and ventricles CC
Basal ganglia   Globus pallidus
Cerebral cortex   Hypothalamus
Corpus striatum   Thalamus
CC Excl: 191.0-192.1, 192.8-192.9, 195.8, 199.0-199.2, 209.20, 209.29-209.30, 209.70, 239.6-239.7, 239.81-239.9

191.1 Frontal lobe CC
CC Excl: See code 191.0
AHA: 4Q, '05, 118

191.2 Temporal lobe CC
Hippocampus
Uncus
CC Excl: See code 191.0
AHA: 4Q, '06, 123

191.3 Parietal lobe CC
CC Excl: See code 191.0

191.4 Occipital lobe CC
CC Excl: See code 191.0

Brain and Meninges

Fourth ventricle
Cerebrum
Corpus callosum
Thalamus
Hypothalamus
Hypophysis
Pons
Cerebellum
Medulla oblongata
Midsagittal Section (between hemispheres)

"metastatic from" indicates the site mentioned is the primary site.

Neoplasms

191.5–195.8

191.5 Ventricles `CC`
Choroid plexus   Floor of ventricle
CC Excl: See code 191.0

191.6 Cerebellum NOS `CC`
Cerebellopontine angle
CC Excl: See code 191.0

191.7 Brain stem `CC`
Cerebral peduncle
Medulla oblongata
Midbrain
Pons
CC Excl: See code 191.0

191.8 Other parts of brain `CC`
Corpus callosum
Tapetum
Malignant neoplasm of contiguous or overlapping sites of brain whose point of origin cannot be determined
CC Excl: See code 191.0

191.9 Brain, unspecified `CC`
Cranial fossa NOS
CC Excl: See code 191.0

✓4ᵗʰ **192 Malignant neoplasm of other and unspecified parts of nervous system**
EXCLUDES *peripheral, sympathetic, and parasympathetic nerves and ganglia (171.0-171.9)*

192.0 Cranial nerves `CC`
Olfactory bulb
CC Excl: 192.0, 192.8-192.9, 195.8, 199.0-199.2, 209.20, 209.29-209.30, 209.70, 239.6-239.7, 239.81-239.9

192.1 Cerebral meninges `CC`
Dura (mater)   Meninges NOS
Falx (cerebelli) (cerebri)   Tentorium
CC Excl: 192.1, 192.8-192.9, 195.8, 199.0-199.2, 209.20, 209.29-209.30, 209.70, 239.6-239.7, 239.81-239.9

192.2 Spinal cord `CC`
Cauda equina
CC Excl: 192.2, 192.8-192.9, 195.8, 199.0-199.2, 209.20, 209.29-209.30, 209.70, 239.6-239.7, 239.81-239.9

192.3 Spinal meninges `CC`
CC Excl: 192.3-192.9, 195.8, 199.0-199.2, 209.20, 209.29-209.30, 209.70, 239.6-239.7, 239.81-239.9

192.8 Other specified sites of nervous system `CC`
Malignant neoplasm of contiguous or overlapping sites of other parts of nervous system whose point of origin cannot be determined
CC Excl: 191.0-192.9, 195.8, 199.0-199.2, 209.20, 209.29-209.30, 209.70, 239.6-239.7, 239.81-239.9

192.9 Nervous system, part unspecified `CC`
Nervous system (central) NOS
EXCLUDES *meninges NOS (192.1)*
CC Excl: 191.0-192.9, 195.8, 198.3-198.4, 199.0-199.2, 209.20, 209.29-209.30, 209.70, 239.6-239.7, 239.81-239.9

193 Malignant neoplasm of thyroid gland
Thyroglossal duct
Use additional code to identify any functional activity
C73 Malignant neoplasm of thyroid gland `I-10`

✓4ᵗʰ **194 Malignant neoplasm of other endocrine glands and related structures**
EXCLUDES *islets of Langerhans (157.4)*
neuroendocrine tumors (209.00-209.69)
ovary (183.0)
testis (186.0-186.9)
thymus (164.0)

194.0 Adrenal gland `CC`
Adrenal cortex   Suprarenal gland
Adrenal medulla
CC Excl: 194.0, 194.9, 195.2, 195.8, 198.7, 199.0-199.2, 209.20, 209.29-209.30, 209.70

194.1 Parathyroid gland `CC`
CC Excl: 194.1, 194.8-194.9

194.3 Pituitary gland and craniopharyngeal duct `CC`
Craniobuccal pouch   Rathke's pouch
Hypophysis   Sella turcica
CC Excl: 194.3, V58.0
AHA: J-A, '85, 9

194.4 Pineal gland `CC`
CC Excl: 194.4, V58.0

194.5 Carotid body `CC`
CC Excl: 194.5, 194.8-194.9

194.6 Aortic body and other paraganglia `CC`
Coccygeal body
Glomus jugulare
Para-aortic body
CC Excl: 194.5-194.9

194.8 Other `CC`
Pluriglandular involvement NOS
Note: If the sites of multiple involvements are known, they should be coded separately.
CC Excl: 194.0-194.9

194.9 Endocrine gland, site unspecified `CC`
CC Excl: See code: 194.8

✓4ᵗʰ **195 Malignant neoplasm of other and ill-defined sites**
INCLUDES malignant neoplasms of contiguous sites, not elsewhere classified, whose point of origin cannot be determined
EXCLUDES *malignant neoplasm:*
lymphatic and hematopoietic tissue (200.0-208.9)
secondary sites (196.0-198.8)
unspecified site (199.0-199.1)

195.0 Head, face, and neck
Cheek NOS   Nose NOS
Jaw NOS   Supraclavicular region NOS
AHA: 4Q, '03, 107

195.1 Thorax
Axilla
Chest (wall) NOS
Intrathoracic NOS

195.2 Abdomen
Intra-abdominal NOS
AHA: 2Q, '97, 3

195.3 Pelvis
Groin
Inguinal region NOS
Presacral region
Sacrococcygeal region
Sites overlapping systems within pelvis, as:
rectovaginal (septum)
rectovesical (septum)

195.4 Upper limb

195.5 Lower limb

195.8 Other specified sites
Back NOS
Flank NOS
Trunk NOS

Lymph Nodes

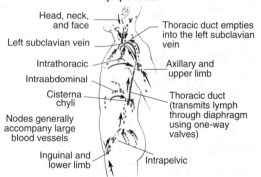

Head, neck, and face
Left subclavian vein
Intrathoracic
Intraabdominal
Cisterna chyli
Nodes generally accompany large blood vessels
Inguinal and lower limb
Thoracic duct empties into the left subclavian vein
Axillary and upper limb
Thoracic duct (transmits lymph through diaphragm using one-way valves)
Intrapelvic

N Newborn Age: 0   P Pediatric Age: 0-17   M Maternity Age: 12-55   A Adult Age: 15-124   MCC Major CC Condition   CC CC Condition   HIV HIV Related Dx

44 – Volume 1   2010 ICD-9-CM

Handwritten note: "Secondary"... also referred to as "metastatic to"

Handwritten note: When a solid tumor spreads to the lymph nodes/glands a code from 196 is assigned

✓4ᵗʰ 196 Secondary and unspecified malignant neoplasm of lymph nodes

> EXCLUDES   any malignant neoplasm of lymph nodes, specified as primary (200.0-202.9)
> Hodgkin's disease (201.0-201.9)
> lymphosarcoma (200.1)
> other forms of lymphoma (202.0-202.9)
> reticulosarcoma (200.0)
> ►secondary neuroendocrine tumor of (distant) lymph nodes (209.71)◄

196.0 Lymph nodes of head, face, and neck `CC`
Cervical   Scalene
Cervicofacial   Supraclavicular
CC Excl: 176.5, 195.8-196.9, 199.0-199.2, 209.20, 209.29-209.30, 209.70-209.71, 239.81-239.9
AHA: 3Q, '07, 7
C77.0 Sec & uns malig neo lymph nodes head face & neck `I-10`

196.1 Intrathoracic lymph nodes `CC`
Bronchopulmonary   Mediastinal
Intercostal   Tracheobronchial
CC Excl: See code 196.0
AHA: 3Q, '06, 7

196.2 Intra-abdominal lymph nodes `CC`
Intestinal
Mesenteric
Retroperitoneal
CC Excl: See code 196.0
AHA: 4Q, '03, 111
C77.2 Sec & uns malig neoplasm intra-abd lymph nodes `I-10`

196.3 Lymph nodes of axilla and upper limb `CC`
Brachial   Infraclavicular
Epitrochlear   Pectoral
CC Excl: See code 196.0

196.5 Lymph nodes of inguinal region and lower limb `CC`
Femoral   Popliteal
Groin   Tibial
CC Excl: See code 196.0

196.6 Intrapelvic lymph nodes `CC`
Hypogastric   Obturator
Iliac   Parametrial
CC Excl: See code 196.0

196.8 Lymph nodes of multiple sites `CC`
CC Excl: See code 196.0

196.9 Site unspecified `CC`
Lymph nodes NOS
CC Excl: See code 196.0

✓4ᵗʰ 197 Secondary malignant neoplasm of respiratory and digestive systems

> EXCLUDES   lymph node metastasis (196.0-196.9)
> ►secondary neuroendocrine tumor of liver (209.72)
> secondary neuroendocrine tumor of respiratory organs (209.79)◄

AHA: M-J, '85, 3

197.0 Lung `CC`
Bronchus
CC Excl: 195.8, 197.0, 197.3, 198.89-199.2, 209.20, 209.29-209.30, 209.70, 209.79, 239.81-239.9
AHA: 1Q, '06, 4; 2Q, '99, 9
C78.00 Secondary malignant neoplasm of lung unspec side `I-10`

197.1 Mediastinum `CC`
CC Excl: 195.8, 197.1, 197.3, 198.89-199.2, 209.20, 209.29-209.30, 209.70, 209.79, 239.81-239.9
AHA: 3Q, '06, 7

197.2 Pleura `CC`
CC Excl: 195.8, 197.2-197.3, 198.89-199.2, 209.20, 209.29-209.30, 209.70, 209.79, 239.81-239.9, 511.81
AHA: 1Q, '08, 16; 3Q, '07, 3; 4Q, '03, 110; 4Q, '89, 11
TIP: Do not assign for malignant pleural effusion; see instead code 511.81.
C78.2 Secondary malignant neoplasm of pleura `I-10`

197.3 Other respiratory organs `CC`
Trachea
CC Excl: 195.8, 197.0-197.3, 198.89-199.2, 209.20, 209.29-209.30, 209.70, 209.79, 239.81-239.9

197.4 Small intestine, including duodenum `CC`
CC Excl: 195.8, 197.4, 197.8, 198.89-199.2, 209.20, 209.29-209.30, 209.70, 209.79, 239.81-239.9

197.5 Large intestine and rectum `CC`
CC Excl: 195.8, 197.5, 197.8, 198.89-199.2, 209.20, 209.29-209.30, 209.70, 209.79, 239.81-239.9

197.6 Retroperitoneum and peritoneum `CC`
CC Excl: 195.8, 197.6, 197.8, 198.89-199.2, 209.20, 209.29-209.30, 209.70, 209.74, 209.79, 239.81-239.9
AHA: 2Q, '04, 4; 4Q, '89, 11
C78.6 Sec malignant neoplasm of retroperiton & periton `I-10`

197.7 Liver, specified as secondary `CC`
CC Excl: 195.8, 197.7-197.8, 198.89-199.2, 209.20, 209.29-209.30, 209.70, 209.72, 209.79, 239.81-239.9
AHA: 1Q, '06, 4; 2Q, '05, 9
C78.7 Secondary malignant neoplasm of liver `I-10`

197.8 Other digestive organs and spleen `CC`
CC Excl: 195.8, 197.4-197.8, 198.89-199.2, 209.20, 209.29-209.30, 209.70, 209.72, 209.74, 209.79, 239.81-239.9
AHA: 2Q, '97, 3; 2Q, '92, 3

✓4ᵗʰ 198 Secondary malignant neoplasm of other specified sites

> EXCLUDES   lymph node metastasis (196.0-196.9)
> ►secondary neuroendocrine tumor of other specified sites (209.79)◄

AHA: M-J, '85, 3

198.0 Kidney `CC`
CC Excl: 195.8, 198.0-198.1, 198.89-199.2, 209.20, 209.29-209.30, 209.70, 209.79, 239.81-239.9

198.1 Other urinary organs `CC`
CC Excl: See code: 198.0

198.2 Skin `CC`
Skin of breast
CC Excl: 195.8, 198.2, 198.89-199.2, 209.20, 209.29-209.30, 209.70, 209.79, 239.81-239.9

198.3 Brain and spinal cord `CC`
CC Excl: 195.8, 198.3, 198.89-199.2, 209.20, 209.29-209.30, 209.70, 209.79, 239.81-239.9
AHA: 3Q, '07, 4; 3Q, '99, 7
C79.31 Secondary malignant neoplasm of brain `I-10`

198.4 Other parts of nervous system `CC`
Meninges (cerebral) (spinal)
CC Excl: 195.8, 198.4, 198.89-199.2, 209.20, 209.29-209.30, 209.70, 209.79, 239.81-239.9
AHA: J-F, '87, 7

198.5 Bone and bone marrow `CC`
CC Excl: 195.8, 198.5, 198.89-199.2, 209.20, 209.29-209.30, 209.70, 209.73, 209.79, 239.81-239.9
AHA: 1Q, '07, 6; 4Q, '03, 110; 3Q, '99, 5; 2Q, '92, 3; 1Q, '91, 16; 4Q, '89, 10
C79.51 Secondary malignant neoplasm of bone `I-10`

198.6 Ovary `CC ♀`
CC Excl: 195.8, 198.6, 198.89-199.2, 209.20, 209.29-209.30, 209.70, 209.79, 239.81-239.9

198.7 Adrenal gland `CC`
Suprarenal gland
CC Excl: 195.8, 198.7, 198.89-199.2, 209.20, 209.29-209.30, 209.70, 209.79, 239.81-239.9
C79.70 Sec malignant neoplasm of adrenal gland uns side `I-10`

✓5ᵗʰ 198.8 Other specified sites

198.81 Breast `CC`
> EXCLUDES   skin of breast (198.2)
CC Excl: 195.8, 198.81, 198.89-199.2, 209.20, 209.29-209.30, 209.70, 209.79, 239.81-239.9

198.82 Genital organs `CC`
CC Excl: 195.8, 198.82-199.2, 209.20, 209.29-209.30, 209.70, 209.79, 239.81-239.9

✓4ᵗʰ Additional Digit Required   **✓5ᵗʰ**
Unacceptable PDx   Manifestation Code   Hospital Acquired Condition   ►◄ Revised Text   ● New Code   ▲ Revised Code Title
2010 ICD-9-CM   **October 2009 · Volume 1 – 45**

When the morphology type is not stated or the only code that can be obtained is 199.0 or 199.1, code as primary malignant neoplasm, unless the site is bone, brain, diaphragm, heart, liver, lymph nodes, mediastinum, meninges, peritoneum, pleura, retroperitoneum, spinal cord or sites classifiable to 195.

Neoplasms (side tab)

198.89   **Other**   CC

Malignant neoplasms of these sites are classified as secondary when not otherwise specified, except for neoplasm of the liver (which is coded to 155.2).

> **EXCLUDES**   retroperitoneal lymph nodes (196.2)
>
> **CC Excl:** 195.8, 198.89-199.2, 209.20, 209.29-209.30, 209.70, 209.79, 239.81-239.9
>
> **AHA:** 2Q, '05, 4; 2Q, '97, 4
>
> **TIP:** Assign for intra-abdominal metastasis when no further specificity of site is documented.
>
> **C79.89** Secondary malignant neoplasm of other spec sites   I-10

✓4th 199   **Malignant neoplasm without specification of site**

> **EXCLUDES**   malignant carcinoid tumor of unknown primary site (209.20)
> ▶malignant (poorly differentiated) neuroendocrine carcinoma, any site (209.30)◀
> malignant ▶(poorly differentiated)◀ neuroendocrine tumor, any site (209.30)
> neuroendocrine carcinoma ▶(high grade),◀ any site (209.30)

✳ **199.0**   **Disseminated**   CC

Carcinomatosis
Generalized:
  cancer
  malignancy
Multiple cancer
       } unspecified site (primary) (secondary)

> **CC Excl:** 195.8, 198.89-199.2, 209.20, 209.29-209.30, 209.70, 209.79, 239.81-239.9
>
> **AHA:** 4Q, '89, 10

✳ **199.1**   **Other**

Cancer
Carcinoma
Malignancy
       } unspecified site (primary) (secondary)

> **AHA:** 3Q, '06, 14-15; 1Q, '06, 4
>
> **TIP:** Assign if patient is assessed for a metastatic tumor but primary site is unknown.
>
> **C80.1** Malignant neoplasm unspecified   I-10

199.2   **Malignant neoplasm associated with transplanted organ**   CC

Code first complication of transplanted organ (996.80-996.89)
▶Use additional code for specific malignancy◀

> **CC Excl:** 195.8, 198.89-199.2, 209.20, 209.29-209.30, 209.70, 209.79, 239.81-239.9
>
> **AHA:** 4Q, '08, 82-83
>
> **TIP:** Assign first the appropriate code from subcategory 996.8, Complications of transplanted organ; use additional code for the specific malignancy.

MALIGNANT NEOPLASM OF LYMPHATIC AND HEMATOPOIETIC TISSUE (200-208)

> **EXCLUDES**   ▶autoimmune lymphoproliferative syndrome (279.41)◀
> secondary neoplasm of:
>   bone marrow (198.5)
>   spleen (197.8)
> secondary and unspecified neoplasm of lymph nodes (196.0-196.9)

neoplasms that arise in the reticuloendothelial and lymphatic systems and the blood-forming tissues. they may (a) arise in a single site or several sites simultaneously (b) circulate in large numbers in the bloodstream (c) spreading to other sites is not considered secondary but also classified as primary neoplasm.

The following fifth-digit subclassification is for use with categories 200-202:

0   unspecified site, extranodal and solid organ sites
1   lymph nodes of head, face, and neck
2   intrathoracic lymph nodes
3   intra-abdominal lymph nodes
4   lymph nodes of axilla and upper limb
5   lymph nodes of inguinal region and lower limb
6   intrapelvic lymph nodes
7   spleen
8   lymph nodes of multiple sites

✓4th 200   **Lymphosarcoma and reticulosarcoma and other specified malignant tumors of lymphatic tissue**

> **AHA:** 4Q, '07, 65; 2Q, '92, 3; N-D, '86, 5

§ **✓5th 200.0**   **Reticulosarcoma**   CC HIV
[0-8]

Lymphoma (malignant):   Reticulum cell sarcoma:
  histiocytic (diffuse):   NOS
    nodular   pleomorphic cell type
    pleomorphic cell type
    reticulum cell type

> **DEF:** Malignant lymphoma of primarily histolytic cells; commonly originates in reticuloendothelium of lymph nodes.
>
> **CC Excl: For code 200.00:** 200.00-200.08, 239.81-239.9; **For code 200.01:** 200.00-200.01, 200.08, 239.81-239.9; **For code 200.02:** 200.00, 200.02, 200.08, 239.81-239.9; **For code 200.03:** 200.00, 200.03, 200.08, 239.81-239.9; **For code 200.04:** 200.00, 200.04, 200.08, 239.81-239.9; **For code 200.05:** 200.00, 200.05, 200.08, 239.81-239.9; **For code 200.06:** 200.00, 200.06, 200.08, 239.81-239.9; **For code 200.07:** 200.00, 200.07-200.08, 239.81-239.9; **For code 200.08:** 200.00-200.08, 239.81-239.9
>
> **AHA: For Code 200.03:** 3Q, '01, 12

§ **✓5th 200.1**   **Lymphosarcoma**   CC
[0-8]

Lymphoblastoma (diffuse)
Lymphoma (malignant):
  lymphoblastic (diffuse)
  lymphocytic (cell type) (diffuse)
  lymphosarcoma type
  prolymphocytic
Lymphosarcoma:
  NOS
  diffuse NOS
  lymphoblastic (diffuse)
  lymphocytic (diffuse)
  prolymphocytic

> **EXCLUDES**   lymphosarcoma:
>   follicular or nodular (202.0)
>   mixed cell type (200.8)
>   lymphosarcoma cell leukemia (207.8)
>
> **DEF:** Malignant lymphoma created from anaplastic lymphoid cells resembling lymphocytes or lymphoblasts.
>
> **CC Excl: For code 200.10:** 200.10-200.18, 239.81-239.9; **For code 200.11:** 200.10-200.11, 200.18, 239.81-239.9; **For code 200.12:** 200.10, 200.12, 200.18, 239.81-239.9; **For code 200.13:** 200.10, 200.13, 200.18, 239.81-239.9; **For code 200.14:** 200.10, 200.14, 200.18, 239.81-239.9; **For code 200.15:** 200.10, 200.15, 200.18, 239.81-239.9; **For code 200.16:** 200.10, 200.16, 200.18, 239.81-239.9; **For code 200.17:** 200.10, 200.17-200.18, 239.81-239.9; **For code 200.18:** 200.10-200.18, 239.81-239.9

§ **✓5th 200.2**   **Burkitt's tumor or lymphoma**   CC HIV
[0-8]

Malignant lymphoma, Burkitt's type

> **DEF:** Large osteolytic lesion most common in jaw or as abdominal mass; usually found in central Africa but reported elsewhere.
>
> **CC Excl: For code 200.20:** 200.20-200.28, 239.81-239.9; **For code 200.21:** 200.20-200.21, 200.28, 239.81-239.9; **For code 200.22:** 200.20, 200.22, 200.28, 239.81-239.9; **For code 200.23:** 200.20, 200.23, 200.28, 239.81-239.9; **For code 200.24:** 200.20, 200.24, 200.28, 239.81-239.9; **For code 200.25:** 200.20, 200.25, 200.28, 239.81-239.9; **For code 200.26:** 200.20, 200.26, 200.28, 239.81-239.9; **For code 200.27:** 200.20, 200.27-200.28, 239.81-239.9; **For code 200.28:** 200.20-200.28, 239.81-239.9

---

§   Requires fifth digit. Valid digits are in [brackets] under each code. See beginning of section 200-208 for codes and definitions.

N Newborn Age: 0   P Pediatric Age: 0-17   M Maternity Age: 12-55   A Adult Age: 15-124   MCC Major CC Condition   CC CC Condition   HIV HIV Related Dx

§ √5th **200.3 Marginal zone lymphoma** CC HIV
[0-8]
Extranodal marginal zone B-cell lymphoma
Mucosa associated lymphoid tissue [MALT]
Nodal marginal zone B-cell lymphoma
Splenic marginal zone B-cell lymphoma

CC Excl: For code 200.30: 200.30-200.78, 202.70-202.90, 239.81-239.9; **For code 200.31:** 200.30-200.31, 200.38-200.41, 200.48-200.51, 200.58-200.61, 200.68-200.71, 200.78, 202.70-202.71, 202.78-202.81, 202.88, 202.91, 239.81-239.9; **For code 200.32:** 200.30, 200.32, 200.38-200.40, 200.42, 200.48-200.50, 200.52, 200.58-200.60, 200.62, 200.68-200.70, 200.72, 200.78, 202.70, 202.72, 202.78-202.80, 202.82, 202.88, 202.92, 239.81-239.9; **For code 200.33:** 200.30, 200.33, 200.38-200.40, 200.43, 200.48-200.50, 200.53, 200.58-200.60, 200.63, 200.68-200.70, 200.73, 200.78, 202.70, 202.73, 202.78-202.80, 202.83, 202.88, 202.93, 239.81-239.9; **For code 200.34:** 200.30, 200.34, 200.38-200.40, 200.44, 200.48-200.50, 200.54, 200.58-200.60, 200.64, 200.68-200.70, 200.74, 200.78, 202.70, 202.74, 202.78-202.80, 202.84, 202.88, 202.94, 239.81-239.9; **For code 200.35:** 200.30, 200.35, 200.38-200.40, 200.45, 200.48-200.50, 200.55, 200.58-200.60, 200.65, 200.68-200.70, 200.75, 200.78, 202.70, 202.75, 202.78-202.80, 202.85, 202.88, 202.95, 239.81-239.9; **For code 200.36:** 200.30, 200.36, 200.38-200.40, 200.46, 200.48-200.50, 200.56, 200.58-200.60, 200.66, 200.68-200.70, 200.76, 200.78, 202.70, 202.76, 202.78-202.80, 202.86, 202.88, 202.96, 239.81-239.9; **For code 200.37:** 200.30, 200.37-200.40, 200.47-200.50, 200.57-200.60, 200.67-200.70, 200.77-200.78, 202.70, 202.77-202.80, 202.87-202.88, 202.97, 239.81-239.9; **For code 200.38:** 200.30-200.78, 202.70-202.88, 202.98, 239.81-239.9

AHA: 4Q, '07, 65

§ √5th **200.4 Mantle cell lymphoma** CC HIV
[0-8]
CC Excl: For code 200.40: 200.30-200.78, 202.70-202.90, 239.81-239.9; **For code 200.41:** 200.30-200.31, 200.38-200.41, 200.48-200.51, 200.58-200.61, 200.68-200.71, 200.78, 202.70-202.71, 202.78-202.81, 202.88, 202.91, 239.81-239.9; **For code 200.42:** 200.30, 200.32, 200.38-200.40, 200.42, 200.48-200.50, 200.52, 200.58-200.60, 200.62, 200.68-200.70, 200.72, 200.78, 202.70, 202.72, 202.78-202.80, 202.82, 202.88, 202.92, 239.81-239.9; **For code 200.43:** 200.30, 200.33, 200.38-200.40, 200.43, 200.48-200.50, 200.53, 200.58-200.60, 200.63, 200.68-200.70, 200.73, 200.78, 202.70, 202.73, 202.78-202.80, 202.83, 202.88, 202.93, 239.81-239.9; **For code 200.44:** 200.30, 200.34, 200.38-200.40, 200.44, 200.48-200.50, 200.54, 200.58-200.60, 200.64, 200.68-200.70, 200.74, 200.78, 202.70, 202.74, 202.78-202.80, 202.84, 202.88, 202.94, 239.81-239.9; **For code 200.45:** 200.30, 200.35, 200.38-200.40, 200.45, 200.48-200.50, 200.55, 200.58-200.60, 200.65, 200.68-200.70, 200.75, 200.78, 202.70, 202.75, 202.78-202.80, 202.85, 202.88, 202.95, 239.81-239.9; **For code 200.46:** 200.30, 200.36, 200.38-200.40, 200.46, 200.48-200.50, 200.56, 200.58-200.60, 200.66, 200.68-200.70, 200.76, 200.78, 202.70, 202.76, 202.78-202.80, 202.86, 202.88, 202.96, 239.81-239.9; **For code 200.47:** 200.30, 200.37-200.40, 200.47-200.50, 200.57-200.60, 200.67-200.70, 200.77-200.78, 202.70, 202.77-202.80, 202.87-202.88, 202.97, 239.81-239.9; **For code 200.48:** 200.30-200.78, 202.70-202.88, 202.98, 239.81-239.9

AHA: 4Q, '07, 65

§ √5th **200.5 Primary central nervous system lymphoma** CC HIV
[0-8]
CC Excl: For code 200.50: 200.30-200.78, 202.70-202.90, 239.81-239.9; **For code 200.51:** 200.30-200.31, 200.38-200.41, 200.48-200.51, 200.58-200.61, 200.68-200.71, 200.78, 202.70-202.71, 202.78-202.81, 202.88, 202.91, 239.81-239.9; **For code 200.52:** 200.30, 200.32, 200.38-200.40, 200.42, 200.48-200.50, 200.52, 200.58-200.60, 200.62, 200.68-200.70, 200.72, 200.78, 202.70, 202.72, 202.78-202.80, 202.82, 202.88, 202.92, 239.81-239.9; **For code 200.53:** 200.30, 200.33, 200.38-200.40, 200.43, 200.48-200.50, 200.53, 200.58-200.60, 200.63, 200.68-200.70, 200.73, 200.78, 202.70, 202.73, 202.78-202.80, 202.83, 202.88, 202.93, 239.81-239.9; **For code 200.54:** 200.30, 200.34, 200.38-200.40, 200.44, 200.48-200.50, 200.54, 200.58-200.60, 200.64, 200.68-200.70, 200.74, 200.78, 202.70, 202.74, 202.78-202.80, 202.84, 202.88, 202.94, 239.81-239.9; **For code 200.55:** 200.30, 200.35, 200.38-200.40, 200.45, 200.48-200.50, 200.55, 200.58-200.60, 200.65, 200.68-200.70, 200.75, 200.78, 202.70, 202.75, 202.78-202.80, 202.85, 202.88, 202.95, 239.81-239.9; **For code 200.56:** 200.30, 200.36, 200.38-200.40, 200.46, 200.48-200.50, 200.56, 200.58-200.60, 200.66, 200.68-200.70, 200.76, 200.78, 202.70, 202.76, 202.78-202.80, 202.86, 202.88, 202.96, 239.81-239.9; **For code 200.57:** 200.30, 200.37-200.40, 200.47-200.50, 200.57-200.60, 200.67-200.70, 200.77-200.78, 202.70, 202.77-202.80, 202.87-202.88, 202.97, 239.81-239.9; **For code 200.58:** 200.30-200.78, 202.70-202.88, 202.98, 239.81-239.9

AHA: 4Q, '07, 66

§ √5th **200.6 Anaplastic large cell lymphoma** CC HIV
[0-8]
CC Excl: For code 200.60: 200.30-200.78, 202.70-202.90, 239.81-239.9; **For code 200.61:** 200.30-200.31, 200.38-200.41, 200.48-200.51, 200.58-200.61, 200.68-200.71, 200.78, 202.70-202.71, 202.78-202.81, 202.88, 202.91, 239.81-239.9; **For code 200.62:** 200.30, 200.32, 200.38-200.40, 200.42, 200.48-200.50, 200.52, 200.58-200.60, 200.62, 200.68-200.70, 200.72, 200.78, 202.70, 202.72, 202.78-202.80, 202.82, 202.88, 202.92, 239.81-239.9; **For code 200.63:** 200.30, 200.33, 200.38-200.40, 200.43, 200.48-200.50, 200.53, 200.58-200.60, 200.63, 200.68-200.70, 200.73, 200.78, 202.70, 202.73, 202.78-202.80, 202.83, 202.88, 202.93, 239.81-239.9; **For code 200.64:** 200.30, 200.34, 200.38-200.40, 200.44, 200.48-200.50, 200.54, 200.58-200.60, 200.64, 200.68-200.70, 200.74, 200.78, 202.70, 202.74, 202.78-202.80, 202.84, 202.88, 202.94, 239.81-239.9; **For code 200.65:** 200.30, 200.35, 200.38-200.40, 200.45, 200.48-200.50, 200.55, 200.58-200.60, 200.65, 200.68-200.70, 200.75, 200.78, 202.70, 202.75, 202.78-202.80, 202.85, 202.88, 202.95, 239.81-239.9; **For code 200.66:** 200.30, 200.36, 200.38-200.40, 200.46, 200.48-200.50, 200.56, 200.58-200.60, 200.66, 200.68-200.70, 200.76, 200.78, 202.70, 202.76, 202.78-202.80, 202.86, 202.88, 202.96, 239.81-239.9; **For code 200.67:** 200.30, 200.37-200.40, 200.47-200.50, 200.57-200.60, 200.67-200.70, 200.77-200.78, 202.70, 202.77-202.80, 202.87-202.88, 202.97, 239.81-239.9; **For code 200.68:** 200.30-200.78, 202.70-202.88, 202.98, 239.81-239.9

AHA: 4Q, '07, 66

§ √5th **200.7 Large cell lymphoma** CC HIV
[0-8]
CC Excl: For code 200.70: 200.30-200.78, 202.70-202.90, 239.81-239.9; **For code 200.71:** 200.30-200.31, 200.38-200.41, 200.48-200.51, 200.58-200.61, 200.68-200.71, 200.78, 202.70-202.71, 202.78-202.81, 202.88, 202.91, 239.81-239.9; **For code 200.72:** 200.30, 200.32, 200.38-200.40, 200.42, 200.48-200.50, 200.52, 200.58-200.60, 200.62, 200.68-200.70, 200.72, 200.78, 202.70, 202.72, 202.78-202.80, 202.82, 202.88, 202.92, 239.81-239.9; **For code 200.73:** 200.30, 200.33, 200.38-200.40, 200.43, 200.48-200.50, 200.53, 200.58-200.60, 200.63, 200.68-200.70, 200.73, 200.78, 202.70, 202.73, 202.78-202.80, 202.83, 202.88, 202.93, 239.81-239.9; **For code 200.74:** 200.30, 200.34, 200.38-200.40, 200.44, 200.48-200.50, 200.54, 200.58-200.60, 200.64, 200.68-200.70, 200.74, 200.78, 202.70, 202.74, 202.78-202.80, 202.84, 202.88, 202.94, 239.81-239.9; **For code 200.75:** 200.30, 200.35, 200.38-200.40, 200.45, 200.48-200.50, 200.55, 200.58-200.60, 200.65, 200.68-200.70, 200.75, 200.78, 202.70, 202.75, 202.78-202.80, 202.85, 202.88, 202.95, 239.81-239.9; **For code 200.76:** 200.30, 200.36, 200.38-200.40, 200.46, 200.48-200.50, 200.56, 200.58-200.60, 200.66, 200.68-200.70, 200.76, 200.78, 202.70, 202.76, 202.78-202.80, 202.86, 202.88, 202.96, 239.81-239.9; **For code 200.77:** 200.30, 200.37-200.40, 200.47-200.50, 200.57-200.60, 200.67-200.70, 200.77-200.78, 202.70, 202.77-202.80, 202.87-202.88, 202.97, 239.81-239.9; **For code 200.78:** 200.30-200.78, 202.70-202.88, 202.98, 239.81-239.9

AHA: 4Q, '07, 66

Handwritten margin notes (200.3): Slow-growing B cell tumors categorized on whether they occur outside the lymph nodes or within the lymph nodes.

MALT lymphomas occur in the intestinal tract, eyes, thyroid, salivary glands, lungs and skin.

Splenic marginal lymphomas affect the spleen, bone marrow, and blood.

Handwritten margin notes (200.4): Aggressive non-Hodgkins lymphoma...frequently diagnosed as stage I disease...found in gastrointestinal tract, bone marrow, and in lymph nodes above and below the diaphragm. Treatment includes antineoplastic drugs such as R-CHOP; rituximab, cyclophosphamide, doxorubicin, vincristine, prednisone, chemotherapy, biological therapies, and other regimens.

Handwritten margin notes (200.5): CNS lymphoma...found in the brain, and spinal cord. Tumors are typically limited to the cranial-spinal axis and eye w/o systemic involvement. Because of the diffuse nature of CNS lymphoma, radiotherapy is the standard treatment.

Handwritten margin notes (200.6): Can present in two forms: systemic or cutaneous of the skin. Cutaneous type manifests itself as a solitary nodule or ulcerating tumor in patients w/o a history of concurrent mycosis fungoides (mF) or lymphatoid papulosis (LyP) with no evidence of disease outside the skin.

Handwritten margin notes (200.7): Most prevalent type on non-Hodgkins lymphoma...disease is aggressive and occurs in the lymph nodes and extranodal sites, such as the gastrointestinal tract, testes, thyroid, skin, breast, CNS, and bone. Treatment includes high-dose chemotherapy and stem cell/bone marrow transplantation

§ Requires fifth digit. Valid digits are in [brackets] under each code. See beginning of section 200-208 for codes and definitions.

√4th √5th Additional Digit Required   Unacceptable PDx   Manifestation Code   Hospital Acquired Condition   ►◄ Revised Text   ● New Code   ▲ Revised Code Title

2010 ICD-9-CM   Volume 1 – 47

200.3–200.7

§ ✓5ᵗʰ **200.8 Other named variants** CC HIV
[0-8] Lymphoma (malignant):
lymphoplasmacytoid type
mixed lymphocytic-histiocytic (diffuse)
Lymphosarcoma, mixed cell type (diffuse)
Reticulolymphosarcoma (diffuse)

CC Excl: For code 200.80: 200.80-200.88, 239.81-239.9; **For code 200.81**: 200.80-200.81, 200.88, 239.81-239.9; **For code 200.82**: 200.80, 200.82, 200.88, 239.81-239.9; **For code 200.83**: 200.80, 200.83, 200.88, 239.81-239.9; **For code 200.84**: 200.80, 200.84, 200.88, 239.81-239.9; **For code 200.85**: 200.80, 200.85, 200.88, 239.81-239.9; **For code 200.86**: 200.80, 200.86, 200.88, 239.81-239.9; **For code 200.87**: 200.80, 200.87-200.88, 239.81-239.9; **For code 200.88**: 200.80-200.88, 239.81-239.9

✓4ᵗʰ **201 Hodgkin's disease**

DEF: Painless, progressive enlargement of lymph nodes, spleen and general lymph tissue; symptoms include anorexia, lassitude, weight loss, fever, pruritis, night sweats, anemia.
AHA: 2Q, '92, 3; N-D, '86, 5

§ ✓5ᵗʰ **201.0 Hodgkin's paragranuloma** CC
[0-8] **CC Excl: For code 201.00**: 201.00-201.08, 201.90, 239.81-239.9; **For code 201.01**: 201.00-201.01, 201.08, 201.90-201.91, 239.81-239.9; **For code 201.02**: 201.00, 201.02, 201.08, 201.90, 201.92, 239.81-239.9; **For code 201.03**: 201.00, 201.03, 201.08, 201.90, 201.93, 239.81-239.9; **For code 201.04**: 201.00, 201.04, 201.08, 201.90, 201.94, 239.81-239.9; **For code 201.05**: 201.00, 201.05, 201.08, 201.90, 201.95, 239.81-239.9; **For code 201.06**: 201.00, 201.06, 201.08, 201.90, 201.96, 239.81-239.9; **For code 201.07**: 201.00, 201.07-201.08, 201.90, 201.97, 239.81-239.9; **For code 201.08**: 201.00-201.08, 201.90, 201.98, 239.81-239.9

§ ✓5ᵗʰ **201.1 Hodgkin's granuloma** CC
[0-8] **CC Excl: For code 201.10**: 201.10-201.18, 201.90, 201.98, 239.81-239.9; **For code 201.11**: 201.10-201.11, 201.18, 201.90-201.91, 201.98, 239.81-239.9; **For code 201.12**: 201.10-201.11, 201.18, 201.90-201.91, 201.98, 239.81-239.9; **For code 201.13**: 201.10, 201.13, 201.18, 201.90, 201.93, 201.98, 239.81-239.9; **For code 201.14**: 201.10, 201.14, 201.18, 201.90, 201.94, 201.98, 239.81-239.9; **For code 201.15**: 201.10, 201.15, 201.18, 201.90, 201.95, 201.98, 239.81-239.9; **For code 201.16**: 201.10, 201.16, 201.18, 201.90, 201.96, 201.98, 239.81-239.9; **For code 201.17**: 201.10, 201.17-201.18, 201.90, 201.97-201.98, 239.81-239.9; **For code 201.18**: 201.10-201.18, 201.90, 201.98, 239.81-239.9

AHA: 2Q, '99, 7

§ ✓5ᵗʰ **201.2 Hodgkin's sarcoma** CC
[0-8] **CC Excl: For code 201.20**: 201.20-201.28, 201.90, 201.98, 239.81-239.9; **For code 201.21**: 201.20-201.21, 201.28, 201.90-201.91, 201.98, 239.81-239.9; **For code 201.22**: 201.20, 201.22, 201.28, 201.90, 201.92, 201.98, 239.81-239.9; **For code 201.23**: 201.20, 201.23, 201.28, 201.90, 201.93, 201.98, 239.81-239.9; **For code 201.24**: 201.20, 201.24, 201.28, 201.90, 201.94, 201.98, 239.81-239.9; **For code 201.25**: 201.20, 201.25, 201.28, 201.90, 201.95, 201.98, 239.81-239.9; **For code 201.26**: 201.20, 201.26, 201.28, 201.90, 201.96, 201.98, 239.81-239.9; **For code 201.27**: 201.20, 201.27-201.28, 201.90, 201.97-201.98, 239.81-239.9; **For code 201.28**: 201.20-201.28, 201.90, 201.98, 239.81-239.9

§ ✓5ᵗʰ **201.4 Lymphocytic-histiocytic predominance** CC
[0-8] **CC Excl: For code 201.40**: 201.40-201.48, 201.90, 201.98, 239.81-239.9; **For code 201.41**: 201.40-201.41, 201.48, 201.90-201.91, 201.98, 239.81-239.9; **For code 201.42**: 201.40, 201.42, 201.48, 201.90, 201.92, 201.98, 239.81-239.9; **For code 201.43**: 201.40, 201.43, 201.48, 201.90, 201.93, 201.98, 239.81-239.9; **For code 201.44**: 201.40, 201.44, 201.48, 201.90, 201.94, 201.98, 239.81-239.9; **For code 201.45**: 201.40, 201.45, 201.48, 201.90, 201.95, 201.98, 239.81-239.9; **For code 201.46**: 201.40, 201.46, 201.48, 201.90, 201.96, 201.98, 239.81-239.9; **For code 201.47**: 201.40, 201.47-201.48, 201.90, 201.97-201.98, 239.81-239.9; **For code 201.48**: 201.40-201.48, 201.90, 201.98, 239.81-239.9

§ ✓5ᵗʰ **201.5 Nodular sclerosis** CC
[0-8] Hodgkin's disease, nodular sclerosis:
NOS
cellular phase

CC Excl: For code 201.50: 201.50-201.58, 201.90, 201.98, 239.81-239.9; **For code 201.51**: 201.50-201.51, 201.58, 201.90-201.91, 201.98, 239.81-239.9; **For code 201.52**: 201.50, 201.52, 201.58, 201.90, 201.92, 201.98, 239.81-239.9; **For code 201.53**: 201.50, 201.53, 201.58, 201.90, 201.93, 201.98, 239.81-239.9; **For code 201.54**: 201.50, 201.54, 201.58, 201.90, 201.94, 201.98, 239.81-239.9; **For code 201.55**: 201.50, 201.55, 201.58, 201.90, 201.95, 201.98, 239.81-239.9; **For code 201.56**: 201.50, 201.56, 201.58, 201.90, 201.96, 201.98, 239.81-239.9; **For code 201.57**: 201.50, 201.57-201.58, 201.90, 201.97-201.98, 239.81-239.9; **For code 201.58**: 201.50-201.58, 201.90, 201.98, 239.81-239.9

§ ✓5ᵗʰ **201.6 Mixed cellularity** CC
[0-8] **CC Excl: For code 201.60**: 201.60-201.68, 201.90, 201.98, 239.81-239.9; **For code 201.61**: 201.60-201.61, 201.68, 201.90-201.91, 201.98, 239.81-239.9; **For code 201.62**: 201.60, 201.62, 201.68, 201.90, 201.92, 201.98, 239.81-239.9; **For code 201.63**: 201.60, 201.63, 201.68, 201.90, 201.93, 201.98, 239.81-239.9; **For code 201.64**: 201.60, 201.64, 201.68, 201.90, 201.94, 201.98, 239.81-239.9; **For code 201.65**: 201.60, 201.65, 201.68, 201.90, 201.95, 201.98, 239.81-239.9; **For code 201.66**: 201.60, 201.66, 201.68, 201.90, 201.96, 201.98, 239.81-239.9; **For code 201.67**: 201.60, 201.67-201.68, 201.90, 201.97-201.98, 239.81-239.9; **For code 201.68**: 201.60-201.68, 201.90, 201.98, 239.81-239.9

§ ✓5ᵗʰ **201.7 Lymphocytic depletion** CC
[0-8] Hodgkin's disease, lymphocytic depletion:
NOS
diffuse fibrosis
reticular type

CC Excl: For code 201.70: 201.70-201.90, 201.98, 239.81-239.9; **For code 201.71**: 201.70-201.71, 201.78, 201.91, 201.98, 239.81-239.9; **For code 201.72**: 201.70, 201.72, 201.78, 201.92, 201.98, 239.81-239.9; **For code 201.73**: 201.70, 201.73, 201.78, 201.93, 201.98, 239.81-239.9; **For code 201.74**: 201.70, 201.74, 201.78, 201.94, 201.98, 239.81-239.9; **For code 201.75**: 201.70, 201.75, 201.78, 201.95, 201.98, 239.81-239.9; **For code 201.76**: 201.70, 201.76, 201.78, 201.96, 201.98, 239.81-239.9; **For code 201.77**: 201.70, 201.77-201.78, 201.97-201.98, 239.81-239.9; **For code 201.78**: 201.70-201.78, 201.98, 239.81-239.9

§ ✓5ᵗʰ **201.9 Hodgkin's disease, unspecified** CC
[0-8] Hodgkin's: Malignant:
disease NOS   lymphogranuloma
lymphoma NOS   lymphogranulomatosis

CC Excl: For code 201.90: 201.90-201.98, 239.81-239.9; **For code 201.91**: 201.90-201.91, 201.98, 239.81-239.9; **For code 201.92**: 201.90, 201.92, 201.98, 239.81-239.9; **For code 201.93**: 201.90, 201.93, 201.98, 239.81-239.9; **For code 201.94**: 201.90, 201.94, 201.98, 239.81-239.9; **For code 201.95**: 201.90, 201.95, 201.98, 239.81-239.9; **For code 201.96**: 201.90, 201.96, 201.98, 239.81-239.9; **For code 201.97**: 201.90, 201.97-201.98, 239.81-239.9; **For code 201.98**: 201.90-201.98, 239.81-239.9

§ Requires fifth digit. Valid digits are in [brackets] under each code. See beginning of section 200-208 for codes and definitions.

N Newborn Age: 0   P Pediatric Age: 0-17   M Maternity Age: 12-55   A Adult Age: 15-124   MCC Major CC Condition   CC CC Condition   HIV HIV Related Dx

48 – Volume 1   **2010 ICD-9-CM**

✓4ᵗʰ 202 Other malignant neoplasms of lymphoid and histiocytic tissue

AHA: 2Q, '92, 3; N-D, '86, 5

§ ✓5ᵗʰ **202.0 Nodular lymphoma**   [CC]
[0-8]
Brill-Symmers disease
Lymphoma:
　follicular (giant) ▶(large cell)◀
　lymphocytic, nodular
Lymphosarcoma:
　follicular (giant)
　nodular

DEF: Lymphomatous cells clustered into nodules within the lymph node; usually occurs in older adults and may involve all nodes and possibly extranodal sites.

CC Excl: For code 202.20: 200.30, 200.40, 200.50, 200.60, 200.70, 202.20-202.28, 202.70, 202.80, 202.90, 239.81-239.9; **For code 202.21:** 200.31, 200.41, 200.51, 200.61, 200.71, 202.20-202.21, 202.28, 202.71, 202.81, 202.91, 239.81-239.9; **For code 202.22:** 200.32, 200.42, 200.52, 200.62, 200.72, 202.20, 202.22, 202.28, 202.72, 202.82, 202.92, 239.81-239.9; **For code 202.23:** 200.33, 200.43, 200.53, 200.63, 200.73, 202.20, 202.23, 202.28, 202.73, 202.83, 202.93, 239.81-239.9; **For code 202.24:** 200.34, 200.44, 200.54, 200.64, 200.74, 202.20, 202.24, 202.28, 202.74, 202.84, 202.94, 239.81-239.9; **For code 202.25:** 200.35, 200.45, 200.55, 200.65, 200.75, 202.20, 202.25, 202.28, 202.75, 202.85, 202.95, 239.81-239.9; **For code 202.26:** 200.36, 200.46, 200.56, 200.66, 200.76, 202.20, 202.26, 202.28, 202.76, 202.86, 202.96, 239.81-239.9; **For code 202.27:** 200.37, 200.47, 200.57, 200.67, 200.77, 202.20, 202.27-202.28, 202.77, 202.87, 202.97, 239.81-239.9; **For code 202.28:** 200.38, 200.48, 200.58, 200.68, 200.78, 202.20-202.28, 202.78, 202.88, 202.98, 239.81-239.9

§ ✓5ᵗʰ **202.1 Mycosis fungoides**   [CC]
[0-8]
EXCLUDES ▶peripheral T-cell lymphoma (202.7)◀

DEF: Type of cutaneous T-cell lymphoma; may evolve into generalized lymphoma; formerly thought to be of fungoid origin.

CC Excl: For code 202.10: 200.30, 200.40, 200.50, 200.60, 200.70, 202.10-202.18, 202.70, 202.80, 202.90, 239.81-239.9; **For code 202.11:** 200.31, 200.41, 200.51, 200.61, 200.71, 202.10-202.11, 202.18, 202.71, 202.81, 202.91, 239.81-239.9; **For code 202.12:** 200.32, 200.42, 200.52, 200.62, 200.72, 202.10, 202.12, 202.18, 202.72, 202.82, 202.92, 239.81-239.9; **For code 202.13:** 200.33, 200.43, 200.53, 200.63, 200.73, 202.10, 202.13, 202.18, 202.73, 202.83, 202.93, 239.81-239.9; **For code 202.14:** 200.34, 200.44, 200.54, 200.64, 200.74, 202.10, 202.14, 202.18, 202.74, 202.84, 202.94, 239.81-239.9; **For code 202.15:** 200.35, 200.45, 200.55, 200.65, 200.75, 202.10, 202.15, 202.18, 202.75, 202.85, 202.95, 239.81-239.9; **For code 202.16:** 200.36, 200.46, 200.56, 200.66, 200.76, 202.10, 202.16, 202.18, 202.76, 202.86, 202.96, 239.81-239.9; **For code 202.17:** 200.37, 200.47, 200.57, 200.67, 200.77, 202.10, 202.17-202.18, 202.77, 202.87, 202.97, 239.81-239.9; **For code 202.18:** 200.38, 200.48, 200.58, 200.68, 200.78, 202.10-202.18, 202.78, 202.88, 202.98, 239.81-239.9

AHA: 2Q, '92, 4

§ ✓5ᵗʰ **202.2 Sézary's disease**   [CC]
[0-8]
DEF: Type of cutaneous T-cell lymphoma with erythroderma, intense pruritus, peripheral lymphadenopathy, abnormal hyperchromatic mononuclear cells in skin, lymph nodes and peripheral blood.

CC Excl: For code 202.20: 200.30, 200.40, 200.50, 200.60, 200.70, 202.20-202.28, 202.70, 202.80, 202.90, 239.81-239.9; **For code 202.21:** 200.31, 200.41, 200.51, 200.61, 200.71, 202.20-202.21, 202.28, 202.71, 202.81, 202.91, 239.81-239.9; **For code 202.22:** 200.32, 200.42, 200.52, 200.62, 200.72, 202.20, 202.22, 202.28, 202.72, 202.82, 202.92, 239.81-239.9; **For code 202.23:** 200.33, 200.43, 200.53, 200.63, 200.73, 202.20, 202.23, 202.28, 202.73, 202.83, 202.93, 239.81-239.9; **For code 202.24:** 200.34, 200.44, 200.54, 200.64, 200.74, 202.20, 202.24, 202.28, 202.74, 202.84, 202.94, 239.81-239.9; **For code 202.25:** 200.35, 200.45, 200.55, 200.65, 200.75, 202.20, 202.25, 202.28, 202.75, 202.85, 202.95, 239.81-239.9; **For code 202.26:** 200.36, 200.46, 200.56, 200.66, 200.76, 202.20, 202.26, 202.28, 202.76, 202.86, 202.96, 239.81-239.9; **For code 202.27:** 200.37, 200.47, 200.57, 200.67, 200.77, 202.20, 202.27-202.28, 202.77, 202.87, 202.97, 239.81-239.9; **For code 202.28:** 200.38, 200.48, 200.58, 200.68, 200.78, 202.20-202.28, 202.78, 202.88, 202.98, 239.81-239.9

AHA: 2Q, '99, 7

§ ✓5ᵗʰ **202.3 Malignant histiocytosis**   [CC]
[0-8]
Histiocytic medullary reticulosis
Malignant:
　reticuloendotheliosis
　reticulosis

CC Excl: For code 202.30: 200.30, 200.40, 200.50, 200.60, 200.70, 202.30-202.38, 202.70, 202.80, 202.90, 239.81-239.9; **For code 202.31:** 200.31, 200.41, 200.51, 200.61, 200.71, 202.30-202.31, 202.38, 202.71, 202.81, 202.91, 239.81-239.9; **For code 202.32:** 200.32, 200.42, 200.52, 200.62, 200.72, 202.30, 202.32, 202.38, 202.72, 202.82, 202.92, 239.81-239.9; **For code 202.33:** 200.33, 200.43, 200.53, 200.63, 200.73, 202.30, 202.33, 202.38, 202.73, 202.83, 202.93, 239.81-239.9; **For code 202.34:** 200.34, 200.44, 200.54, 200.64, 200.74, 202.30, 202.34, 202.38, 202.74, 202.84, 202.94, 239.81-239.9; **For code 202.35:** 200.35, 200.45, 200.55, 200.65, 200.75, 202.30, 202.35, 202.38, 202.75, 202.85, 202.95, 239.81-239.9; **For code 202.36:** 200.36, 200.46, 200.56, 200.66, 200.76, 202.30, 202.36, 202.38, 202.76, 202.86, 202.96, 239.81-239.9; **For code 202.37:** 200.37, 200.47, 200.57, 200.67, 200.77, 202.30, 202.37-202.38, 202.77, 202.87, 202.97, 239.81-239.9; **For code 202.38:** 200.38, 200.48, 200.58, 200.68, 200.78, 202.30-202.38, 202.78, 202.88, 202.98, 239.81-239.9

§ ✓5ᵗʰ **202.4 Leukemic reticuloendotheliosis**   [CC]
[0-8]
Hairy-cell leukemia

DEF: Chronic leukemia with large, mononuclear cells with "hairy" appearance in marrow, spleen, liver, blood.

CC Excl: For code 202.40: 200.30, 200.40, 200.50, 200.60, 200.70, 202.40-202.48, 202.70, 202.80, 202.90, 239.81-239.9; **For code 202.41:** 200.31, 200.41, 200.51, 200.61, 200.71, 202.40-202.41, 202.48, 202.71, 202.81, 202.91, 239.81-239.9; **For code 202.42:** 200.32, 200.42, 200.52, 200.62, 200.72, 202.40, 202.42, 202.48, 202.72, 202.82, 202.92, 239.81-239.9; **For code 202.43:** 200.33, 200.43, 200.53, 200.63, 200.73, 202.40, 202.43, 202.48, 202.73, 202.83, 202.93, 239.81-239.9; **For code 202.44:** 200.34, 200.44, 200.54, 200.64, 200.74, 202.40, 202.44, 202.48, 202.74, 202.84, 202.94, 239.81-239.9; **For code 202.45:** 200.35, 200.45, 200.55, 200.65, 200.75, 202.40, 202.45, 202.48, 202.75, 202.85, 202.95, 239.81-239.9; **For code 202.46:** 200.36, 200.46, 200.56, 200.66, 200.76, 202.40, 202.46, 202.48, 202.76, 202.86, 202.96, 239.81-239.9; **For code 202.47:** 200.37, 200.47, 200.57, 200.67, 200.77, 202.40, 202.47-202.48, 202.77, 202.87, 202.97, 239.81-239.9; **For code 202.48:** 200.38, 200.48, 200.58, 200.68, 200.78, 202.40-202.48, 202.78, 202.88, 202.98, 239.81-239.9

§ ✓5ᵗʰ **202.5 Letterer-Siwe disease**   [CC]
[0-8]
Acute:
　differentiated progressive histiocytosis
　histiocytosis X (progressive)
　infantile reticuloendotheliosis
　reticulosis of infancy

EXCLUDES　Hand-Schüller-Christian disease (277.89)
　　histiocytosis (acute) (chronic) (277.89)
　　histiocytosis X (chronic) (277.89)

DEF: A recessive reticuloendotheliosis of early childhood, with a hemorrhagic tendency, eczema-like skin eruption, hepatosplenomegaly, lymph node enlargement, and progressive anemia; often a fatal disease with no established cause.

CC Excl: For code 202.50: 200.30, 200.40, 200.50, 200.60, 200.70, 202.50-202.58, 202.70, 202.80, 202.90, 239.81-239.9; **For code 202.51:** 200.31, 200.41, 200.51, 200.61, 200.71, 202.50-202.51, 202.58, 202.71, 202.81, 202.91, 239.81-239.9; **For code 202.52:** 200.32, 200.42, 200.52, 200.62, 200.72, 202.50, 202.52, 202.58, 202.72, 202.82, 202.92, 239.81-239.9; **For code 202.53:** 200.33, 200.43, 200.53, 200.63, 200.73, 202.50, 202.53, 202.58, 202.73, 202.83, 202.93, 239.81-239.9; **For code 202.54:** 200.34, 200.44, 200.54, 200.64, 200.74, 202.50, 202.54, 202.58, 202.74, 202.84, 202.94, 239.81-239.9; **For code 202.55:** 200.35, 200.45, 200.55, 200.65, 200.75, 202.50, 202.55, 202.58, 202.75, 202.85, 202.95, 239.81-239.9; **For code 202.56:** 200.36, 200.46, 200.56, 200.66, 200.76, 202.50, 202.56, 202.58, 202.76, 202.86, 202.96, 239.81-239.9; **For code 202.57:** 200.37, 200.47, 200.57, 200.67, 200.77, 202.50, 202.57-202.58, 202.77, 202.87, 202.97, 239.81-239.9; **For code 202.58:** 200.38, 200.48, 200.58, 200.68, 200.78, 202.50-202.58, 202.78, 202.88, 202.98, 239.81-239.9

§　Requires fifth digit. Valid digits are in [brackets] under each code. See beginning of section 200-208 for codes and definitions.

✓4ᵗʰ / ✓5ᵗʰ Additional Digit Required　　Unacceptable PDx　　Manifestation Code　　Hospital Acquired Condition　　▶◀ Revised Text　　● New Code　　▲ Revised Code Title

Neoplasms

§ ✓5th **202.6 Malignant mast cell tumors** `CC`
[0-8]   Malignant:
                mastocytoma
                mastocytosis
             Mast cell sarcoma
             Systemic tissue mast cell disease
             EXCLUDES   mast cell leukemia (207.8)

CC Excl: For code **202.60**: 200.30, 200.40, 200.50, 200.60, 200.70, 202.60-202.70, 202.80, 202.90, 239.81-239.9; For code **202.61**: 200.31, 200.41, 200.51, 200.61, 200.71, 202.60-202.61, 202.68, 202.71, 202.81, 202.91, 239.81-239.9; For code **202.62**: 200.32, 200.42, 200.52, 200.62, 200.72, 202.60, 202.62, 202.68, 202.72, 202.82, 202.92, 239.81-239.9; For code **202.63**: 200.33, 200.43, 200.53, 200.63, 200.73, 202.60, 202.63, 202.68, 202.73, 202.83, 202.93, 239.81-239.9; For code **202.64**: 200.34, 200.44, 200.54, 200.64, 200.74, 202.60, 202.64, 202.68, 202.74, 202.84, 202.94, 239.81-239.9; For code **202.65**: 200.35, 200.45, 200.55, 200.65, 200.75, 202.60, 202.65, 202.68, 202.75, 202.85, 202.95, 239.81-239.9; For code **202.66**: 200.36, 200.46, 200.56, 200.66, 200.76, 202.60, 202.66, 202.68, 202.76, 202.86, 202.96, 239.81-239.9; For code **202.67**: 200.37, 200.47, 200.57, 200.67, 200.77, 202.60, 202.67-202.68, 202.77, 202.87, 202.97, 239.81-239.9; For code **202.68**: 200.38, 200.48, 200.58, 200.68, 200.78, 202.60-202.68, 202.78, 202.88, 202.98, 239.81-239.9

§ ✓5th **202.7 Peripheral T-cell lymphoma** `CC` `HIV`
[0-8]
Lymphoma of the T-cells circulating within the lymphatic system... affects organs of the body such as the bone marrow, liver, spleen, stomach, or bowel... disease is aggressive and may require salvage treatment and stem cell transplantation

Cutaneous T-cell lymphoma (CTCL) affects the skin.

CC Excl: For code **202.70**: 200.30-200.78, 202.70-202.90, 239.81-239.9; For code **202.71**: 200.30-200.31, 200.38-200.41, 200.48-200.51, 200.58-200.61, 200.68-200.71, 200.78, 202.70-202.71, 202.78-202.81, 202.88, 202.91, 239.81-239.9; For code **202.72**: 200.30, 200.32, 200.38-200.40, 200.42, 200.48-200.50, 200.52, 200.58-200.60, 200.62, 200.68-200.70, 200.72, 200.78, 202.70, 202.72, 202.78-202.80, 202.82, 202.88, 202.92, 239.81-239.9; For code **202.73**: 200.30, 200.33, 200.38-200.40, 200.43, 200.48-200.50, 200.53, 200.58-200.60, 200.63, 200.68-200.70, 200.73, 200.78, 202.70, 202.73, 202.78-202.80, 202.83, 202.88, 202.93, 239.81-239.9; For code **202.74**: 200.30, 200.34, 200.38-200.40, 200.44, 200.48-200.50, 200.54, 200.58-200.60, 200.64, 200.68-200.70, 200.74, 200.78, 202.70, 202.74, 202.78-202.80, 202.84, 202.88, 202.94, 239.81-239.9; For code **202.75**: 200.30, 200.35, 200.38-200.40, 200.45, 200.48-200.50, 200.55, 200.58-200.60, 200.65, 200.68-200.70, 200.75, 200.78, 202.70, 202.75, 202.78-202.80, 202.85, 202.88, 202.95, 239.81-239.9; For code **202.76**: 200.30, 200.36, 200.38-200.40, 200.46, 200.48-200.50, 200.56, 200.58-200.60, 200.66, 200.68-200.70, 200.76, 200.78, 202.70, 202.76, 202.78-202.80, 202.86, 202.88, 202.96, 239.81-239.9; For code **202.77**: 200.30, 200.37-200.40, 200.47-200.50, 200.57-200.60, 200.67-200.70, 200.77-200.78, 202.70, 202.77-202.80, 202.87-202.88, 202.97, 239.81-239.9; For code **202.78**: 200.30-200.78, 202.70-202.88, 202.98, 239.81-239.9

AHA: 4Q, '07, 66

§ ✓5th **202.8 Other lymphomas** `CC` `HIV`
[0-8]   Lymphoma (malignant):
                NOS
                diffuse
             EXCLUDES   benign lymphoma (229.0)

CC Excl: For code **202.80**: 200.30-200.78, 202.70-202.90, 239.81-239.9; For code **202.81**: 200.30-200.31, 200.38-200.41, 200.48-200.51, 200.58-200.61, 200.68-200.71, 200.78, 202.70-202.71, 202.78-202.81, 202.88, 202.91, 239.81-239.9; For code **202.82**: 200.30, 200.32, 200.38-200.40, 200.42, 200.48-200.50, 200.52, 200.58-200.60, 200.62, 200.68-200.70, 200.72, 200.78, 202.70, 202.72, 202.78-202.80, 202.82, 202.88, 202.92, 239.81-239.9; For code **202.83**: 200.30, 200.33, 200.38-200.40, 200.43, 200.48-200.50, 200.53, 200.58-200.60, 200.63, 200.68-200.70, 200.73, 200.78, 202.70, 202.73, 202.78-202.80, 202.83, 202.88, 202.93, 239.81-239.9; For code **202.84**: 200.30, 200.34, 200.38-200.40, 200.44, 200.48-200.50, 200.54, 200.58-200.60, 200.64, 200.68-200.70, 200.74, 200.78, 202.70, 202.74, 202.78-202.80, 202.84, 202.88, 202.94, 239.81-239.9; For code **202.85**: 200.30, 200.35, 200.38-200.40, 200.45, 200.48-200.50, 200.55, 200.58-200.60, 200.65, 200.68-200.70, 200.75, 200.78, 202.70, 202.75, 202.78-202.80, 202.85, 202.88, 202.95, 239.81-239.9; For code **202.86**: 200.30, 200.36, 200.38-200.40, 200.46, 200.48-200.50, 200.56, 200.58-200.60, 200.66, 200.68-200.70, 200.76, 200.78, 202.70, 202.76, 202.78-202.80, 202.86, 202.88, 202.96, 239.81-239.9; For code **202.87**: 200.30, 200.37-200.40, 200.47-200.50, 200.57-200.60, 200.67-200.70, 200.77-200.78, 202.70, 202.77-202.80, 202.87-202.88, 202.97, 239.81-239.9; For code **202.88**: 200.30-200.78, 202.70-202.88, 202.98, 239.81-239.9

AHA: 4Q, '06, 135; 2Q, '06, 20-21; 2Q, '92, 4; For code **202.80**: ▶4Q, '08, 83;◀ 1Q, '08, 16; 3Q, '07, 3

C85.70 Oth spec types non-Hodgkins lymphoma unspec site `I-10`

§ ✓5th **202.9 Other and unspecified malignant neoplasms** `CC`
[0-8]   **of lymphoid and histiocytic tissue**
             Follicular dendritic cell sarcoma
             Interdigitating dendritic cell sarcoma
             Langerhans cell sarcoma
             Malignant neoplasm of bone marrow NOS

CC Excl: For code **202.90**: 202.90-202.98, 239.81-239.9; For code **202.91**: 202.90-202.91, 202.98, 239.81-239.9; For code **202.92**: 202.90, 202.92, 202.98, 239.81-239.9; For code **202.93**: 202.90, 202.93, 202.98, 239.81-239.9; For code **202.94**: 202.90, 202.94, 202.98, 239.81-239.9; For code **202.95**: 202.90, 202.95, 202.98, 239.81-239.9; For code **202.96**: 202.90, 202.96, 202.98, 239.81-239.9; For code **202.97**: 202.90, 202.97-202.98, 239.81-239.9; For code **202.98**: 202.90-202.98, 239.81-239.9

✓4th **203 Multiple myeloma and immunoproliferative neoplasms**

AHA: ▶4Q, '08, 83-84;◀ 4Q, '91, 26

The following fifth-digit subclassification is for use with category 203:
    0 without mention of having achieved remission
        Failed remission
    1 in remission
    2 in relapse

§ ✓5th **203.0 Multiple myeloma** `CC`
[0-2]   Kahler's disease   Myelomatosis
             EXCLUDES   solitary myeloma (238.6)

CC Excl: 203.00-208.92, 239.81-239.9

AHA: 1Q, '96, 16; 4Q, '89, 10; For code **203.00**: 2Q,'07, 8; For code **203.01**: ▶4Q, '08, 91◀

C90.00 Multiple myeloma not in remission `I-10`

§ ✓5th **203.1 Plasma cell leukemia** `CC`
[0-2]   Plasmacytic leukemia
             CC Excl: See code 203.0
             AHA: 4Q, '91, 26

§ ✓5th **203.8 Other immunoproliferative neoplasms** `CC`
[0-2]   CC Excl: See code 203.0
             AHA: 4Q, '90, 26; S-O, '86, 12

§   Requires fifth digit. Valid digits are in [brackets] under each code. See appropriate category for codes and definitions.

N Newborn Age: 0   P Pediatric Age: 0-17   M Maternity Age: 12-55   A Adult Age: 15-124   `MCC` Major CC Condition   `CC` CC Condition   `HIV` HIV Related Dx

✓4ᵗʰ 204 Lymphoid leukemia

> INCLUDES   leukemia:
> lymphatic
> lymphoblastic
> lymphocytic
> lymphogenous

AHA: ▶4Q, '08, 83-84;◀ 3Q, '93, 4

> The following fifth-digit subclassification is for use with category 204:
> **0 without mention of having achieved remission**
> Failed remission
> **1 in remission**
> **2 in relapse**

§ ✓5ᵗʰ **204.0 Acute**   CC
[0-2]   EXCLUDES   *acute exacerbation of chronic lymphoid leukemia (204.1)*
   CC Excl: 203.00-208.92, 239.81-239.9
   AHA: 3Q, '99, 6

§ ✓5ᵗʰ **204.1 Chronic**   CC
[0-2]   CC Excl: See code: 204.0
   C91.10 Chronic lymphocytic leukemia not in remission   I-10

§ ✓5ᵗʰ **204.2 Subacute**   CC
[0-2]   CC Excl: See code: 204.0

§ ✓5ᵗʰ **204.8 Other lymphoid leukemia**   CC
[0-2]   Aleukemic leukemia: Aleukemic leukemia:
     lymphatic   lymphoid
     lymphocytic
   CC Excl: See code: 204.0

§ ✓5ᵗʰ **204.9 Unspecified lymphoid leukemia**   CC
[0-2]   CC Excl: See code: 204.0

✓4ᵗʰ 205 Myeloid leukemia

> INCLUDES   leukemia:
> granulocytic
> myeloblastic
> myelocytic
> myelogenous
> myelomonocytic
> myelosclerotic
> myelosis

AHA: ▶4Q, '08, 83-84;◀ 3Q, '93, 3; 4Q, '91, 26; 4Q, '90, 3; M-J, '85, 18

> The following fifth-digit subclassification is for use with category 205:
> **0 without mention of having achieved remission**
> Failed remission
> **1 in remission**
> **2 in relapse**

§ ✓5ᵗʰ **205.0 Acute**   CC
[0-2]   Acute promyelocytic leukemia
   EXCLUDES   *acute exacerbation of chronic myeloid leukemia (205.1)*
   CC Excl: 203.00-208.92, 239.81-239.9
   AHA: 2Q, '06, 20-21
   C92.00 Acute myeloid leukemia not in remission   I-10

§ ✓5ᵗʰ **205.1 Chronic**   CC
[0-2]   Eosinophilic leukemia
   Neutrophilic leukemia
   CC Excl: See code: 205.0
   AHA: 1Q, '00, 6; J-A, '85, 13; **For code 205.10:** ▶4Q, '08, 142◀

§ ✓5ᵗʰ **205.2 Subacute**   CC
[0-2]   CC Excl: See code: 205.0

§ ✓5ᵗʰ **205.3 Myeloid sarcoma**   CC
[0-2]   Chloroma
   Granulocytic sarcoma
   CC Excl: See code: 205.0

§ ✓5ᵗʰ **205.8 Other myeloid leukemia**   CC
[0-2]   Aleukemic leukemia: Aleukemic leukemia:
     granulocytic   myeloid
     myelogenous   Aleukemic myelosis
   CC Excl: See code: 205.0

§ ✓5ᵗʰ **205.9 Unspecified myeloid leukemia**   CC
[0-2]   CC Excl: See code: 205.0

✓4ᵗʰ 206 Monocytic leukemia

> INCLUDES   leukemia:
> histiocytic
> monoblastic
> monocytoid

AHA: ▶4Q, '08, 83-84◀

> The following fifth-digit subclassification is for use with category 206:
> **0 without mention of having achieved remission**
> Failed remission
> **1 in remission**
> **2 in relapse**

§ ✓5ᵗʰ **206.0 Acute**   CC
[0-2]   EXCLUDES   *acute exacerbation of chronic monocytic leukemia (206.1)*
   CC Excl: 203.00-208.92, 239.81-239.9

§ ✓5ᵗʰ **206.1 Chronic**   CC
[0-2]   CC Excl: See code: 206.0

§ ✓5ᵗʰ **206.2 Subacute**   CC
[0-2]   CC Excl: See code: 206.0

§ ✓5ᵗʰ **206.8 Other monocytic leukemia**   CC
[0-2]   Aleukemic:
     monocytic leukemia
     monocytoid leukemia
   CC Excl: See code: 206.0

§ ✓5ᵗʰ **206.9 Unspecified monocytic leukemia**   CC
[0-2]   CC Excl: See code: 206.0

✓4ᵗʰ 207 Other specified leukemia

> EXCLUDES   *leukemic reticuloendotheliosis (202.4)*
> *plasma cell leukemia (203.1)*

AHA: ▶4Q, '08, 83-85◀

> The following fifth-digit subclassification is for use with category 207:
> **0 without mention of having achieved remission**
> Failed remission
> **1 in remission**
> **2 in relapse**

§ ✓5ᵗʰ **207.0 Acute erythremia and erythroleukemia**   CC
[0-2]   Acute erythremic myelosis
   Di Guglielmo's disease
   Erythremic myelosis
   DEF: Erythremia: polycythemia vera.
   DEF: Erythroleukemia: a malignant blood dyscrasia (a myeloproliferative disorder).
   CC Excl: 203.00-208.92, 239.81-239.9

§ ✓5ᵗʰ **207.1 Chronic erythremia**   CC
[0-2]   Heilmeyer-Schöner disease
   CC Excl: See code: 207.0

§ ✓5ᵗʰ **207.2 Megakaryocytic leukemia**   CC
[0-2]   Megakaryocytic myelosis
   Thrombocytic leukemia
   CC Excl: See code: 207.0

§ ✓5ᵗʰ **207.8 Other specified leukemia**   CC
[0-2]   Lymphosarcoma cell leukemia
   CC Excl: See code: 207.0

✓4ᵗʰ 208 Leukemia of unspecified cell type

AHA: ▶4Q, '08, 83-85◀

> The following fifth-digit subclassification is for use with category 208:
> **0 without mention of having achieved remission**
> Failed remission
> **1 in remission**
> **2 in relapse**

§ ✓5ᵗʰ **208.0 Acute**   CC
[0-2]   Acute leukemia NOS
   Blast cell leukemia
   Stem cell leukemia
   EXCLUDES   *acute exacerbation of chronic unspecified leukemia (208.1)*
   CC Excl: 203.00-208.92, 239.81-239.9

---

§   Requires fifth digit. Valid digits are in [brackets] under each code. See appropriate category for codes and definitions.

✓4ᵗʰ / ✓5ᵗʰ Additional Digit Required   Unacceptable PDx   Manifestation Code   Hospital Acquired Condition   ▶◀ Revised Text   ● New Code   ▲ Revised Code Title

Neoplasms (side tab)

* Tumors are commonly classified according to the presumed embryonic site of origin, such as the foregut (bronchus and stomach), midgut (small intestine and appendix) and hindgut (colon and rectum) [handwritten annotation]

§ √5th **208.1 Chronic** CC
[0-2]
Chronic leukemia NOS
CC Excl: See code: 208.0

§ √5th **208.2 Subacute** CC
[0-2]
Subacute leukemia NOS
CC Excl: See code: 208.0

§ √5th **208.8 Other leukemia of unspecified cell type** CC
[0-2]
CC Excl: See code: 208.0

§ √5th **208.9 Unspecified leukemia** CC
[0-2]
Leukemia NOS
CC Excl: See code: 208.0

NEUROENDOCRINE TUMORS (209)

most common sites are bronchi, stomach, small intestine, appendix and rectum [handwritten annotation]

* √4th **209 Neuroendocrine tumors**
Code first any associated multiple endocrine neoplasia syndrome (258.01-258.03)

Use additional code to identify associated endocrine syndrome, such as:
carcinoid syndrome (259.2)

EXCLUDES ▶benign pancreatic islet cell tumors (211.7)◀
▶malignant◀ pancreatic islet cell tumors (157.4)

AHA: 4Q, '08, 85-89

√5th **209.0 Malignant carcinoid tumors of the small intestine**

209.00 Malignant carcinoid tumor of the small intestine, unspecified portion CC
CC Excl: 152.8-152.9, 159.0, 159.8-159.9, 176.3, 195.8, 199.0-199.2, 209.00-209.30, 209.70, 239.0, 239.81-239.9

209.01 Malignant carcinoid tumor of the duodenum CC
CC Excl: 152.0, 152.8-152.9, 159.0, 159.8-159.9, 176.3, 195.8, 199.0-199.2, 209.00-209.30, 209.70, 239.0, 239.81-239.9

209.02 Malignant carcinoid tumor of the jejunum CC
CC Excl: 152.1, 152.8-152.9, 159.0, 159.8-159.9, 176.3, 195.8, 199.0-199.2, 209.00-209.30, 209.70, 239.0, 239.81-239.9

209.03 Malignant carcinoid tumor of the ileum CC
CC Excl: 152.2, 152.8-152.9, 159.0, 159.8-159.9, 176.3, 195.8, 199.0-199.2, 209.00-209.30, 209.70, 239.0, 239.81-239.9

√5th **209.1 Malignant carcinoid tumors of the appendix, large intestine, and rectum**

209.10 Malignant carcinoid tumor of the large intestine, unspecified portion CC
Malignant carcinoid tumor of the colon NOS
CC Excl: 153.8-153.9, 159.0, 159.8-159.9, 176.3, 195.8, 199.0-199.2, 209.00-209.30, 209.70, 239.0, 239.81-239.9

209.11 Malignant carcinoid tumor of the appendix CC
CC Excl: 153.5, 153.8-153.9, 159.0, 159.8-159.9, 176.3, 195.8, 199.0-199.2, 209.00-209.30, 209.70, 239.0, 239.81-239.9

209.12 Malignant carcinoid tumor of the cecum CC
CC Excl: 153.4, 153.8-153.9, 159.0, 159.8-159.9, 176.3, 195.8, 199.0-199.2, 209.00-209.30, 209.70, 239.0, 239.81-239.9

209.13 Malignant carcinoid tumor of the ascending colon CC
CC Excl: 153.6, 153.8-153.9, 159.0, 159.8-159.9, 176.3, 195.8, 199.0-199.2, 209.00-209.30, 209.70, 239.0, 239.81-239.9

209.14 Malignant carcinoid tumor of the transverse colon CC
CC Excl: 153.1, 153.8-153.9, 159.0, 159.8-159.9, 176.3, 195.8, 199.0-199.2, 209.00-209.30, 209.70, 239.0, 239.81-239.9

209.15 Malignant carcinoid tumor of the descending colon CC
CC Excl: 153.2, 153.8-153.9, 159.0, 159.8-159.9, 176.3, 195.8, 199.0-199.2, 209.00-209.30, 209.70, 239.0, 239.81-239.9

209.16 Malignant carcinoid tumor of the sigmoid colon CC
CC Excl: 153.3, 153.8-153.9, 159.0, 159.8-159.9, 176.3, 195.8, 199.0-199.2, 209.00-209.30, 209.70, 239.0, 239.81-239.9

209.17 Malignant carcinoid tumor of the rectum CC
CC Excl: 154.1, 154.8, 159.0, 159.8-159.9, 176.3, 195.8, 199.0-199.2, 209.00-209.30, 209.70, 239.0, 239.81-239.9

√5th **209.2 Malignant carcinoid tumors of other and unspecified sites**

209.20 Malignant carcinoid tumor of the unknown primary site CC
CC Excl: 195.8, 198.89-199.2, 209.00-209.30, 209.70, 209.79, 239.81-239.9

209.21 Malignant carcinoid tumor of the bronchus and lung CC
CC Excl: 162.8-162.9, 165.8-165.9, 176.4, 195.8, 199.0-199.2, 209.00-209.30, 209.70, 239.1, 239.81-239.9

209.22 Malignant carcinoid tumor of the thymus CC
CC Excl: 164.0, 209.00-209.30

209.23 Malignant carcinoid tumor of the stomach CC
CC Excl: 151.0-151.9, 159.0, 159.8-159.9, 176.3, 195.8, 199.0-199.2, 209.00-209.30, 209.70, 239.0, 239.81-239.9
AHA: 4Q, '08, 89

209.24 Malignant carcinoid tumor of the kidney CC
CC Excl: 189.0-189.1, 189.8-189.9, 195.8, 199.0-199.2, 209.00-209.30, 209.70, 239.5, 239.81-239.9

209.25 Malignant carcinoid tumor of the foregut NOS CC
CC Excl: 151.0-151.9, 159.0, 159.8-159.9, 176.3, 195.8, 199.0-199.2, 209.00-209.30, 209.70, 239.0, 239.81-239.9

209.26 Malignant carcinoid tumor of the midgut NOS CC
CC Excl: 151.0-151.9, 159.0, 159.8-159.9, 176.3, 195.8, 199.0-199.2, 209.00-209.30, 209.70, 239.0, 239.81-239.9

209.27 Malignant carcinoid tumor of the hindgut NOS CC
CC Excl: 151.0-151.9, 159.0, 159.8-159.9, 176.3, 195.8, 199.0-199.2, 209.00-209.30, 209.70, 239.0, 239.81-239.9

209.29 Malignant carcinoid tumor of the other sites CC
CC Excl: 195.8, 198.89-199.2, 209.00-209.30, 209.70, 209.79, 239.81-239.9

√5th **209.3 Malignant poorly differentiated neuroendocrine tumors**

209.30 Malignant poorly differentiated neuroendocrine carcinoma, any site CC
High grade neuroendocrine carcinoma, any site
Malignant poorly differentiated neuroendocrine tumor NOS

EXCLUDES ▶ Merkel cell carcinoma (209.31-209.36)◀
CC Excl: 195.8, 198.89-199.2, 209.00-209.30, 209.70, 209.79, 239.81-239.9

● **209.31 Merkel cell carcinoma of the face**
Merkel cell carcinoma of the ear
Merkel cell carcinoma of the eyelid, including canthus
Merkel cell carcinoma of the lip

● **209.32 Merkel cell carcinoma of the scalp and neck**

● **209.33 Merkel cell carcinoma of the upper limb**

§ Requires fifth digit. Valid digits are in [brackets] under each code. See appropriate category for codes and definitions.

| N Newborn Age: 0 | P Pediatric Age: 0-17 | M Maternity Age: 12-55 | A Adult Age: 15-124 | MCC Major CC Condition | CC CC Condition | HIV HIV Related Dx |

● 209.34 Merkel cell carcinoma of the lower limb

● 209.35 Merkel cell carcinoma of the trunk

● 209.36 Merkel cell carcinoma of other sites
  Merkel cell carcinoma of the buttock
  Merkel cell carcinoma of the genitals
  Merkel cell carcinoma NOS

√5ᵗʰ **209.4 Benign carcinoid tumors of the small intestine**

209.40 Benign carcinoid tumor of the small intestine, unspecified portion

209.41 Benign carcinoid tumor of the duodenum

209.42 Benign carcinoid tumor of the jejunum

209.43 Benign carcinoid tumor of the ileum

√5ᵗʰ **209.5 Benign carcinoid tumors of the appendix, large intestine, and rectum**

209.50 Benign carcinoid tumor of the largeintestine, unspecified portion
  Benign carcinoid tumor of the colon NOS

209.51 Benign carcinoid tumor of the appendix

209.52 Benign carcinoid tumor of the cecum

209.53 Benign carcinoid tumor of the ascending colon

209.54 Benign carcinoid tumor of the transverse colon

209.55 Benign carcinoid tumor of the descending colon

209.56 Benign carcinoid tumor of the sigmoid colon

209.57 Benign carcinoid tumor of the rectum

√5ᵗʰ **209.6 Benign carcinoid tumors of other and unspecified sites**

209.60 Benign carcinoid tumor of unknown primary site
  Carcinoid tumor NOS
  Neuroendocrine tumor NOS

209.61 Benign carcinoid tumor of the bronchus and lung

209.62 Benign carcinoid tumor of the thymus

209.63 Benign carcinoid tumor of the stomach

209.64 Benign carcinoid tumor of the kidney

209.65 Benign carcinoid tumor of the foregut NOS

209.66 Benign carcinoid tumor of the midgut NOS

209.67 Benign carcinoid tumor of the hindgut NOS

209.69 Benign carcinoid tumors of other sites

● √5ᵗʰ **209.7 Secondary neuroendocrine tumors**
  Secondary carcinoid tumors

● 209.70 Secondary neuroendocrine tumor, unspecified site

● 209.71 Secondary neuroendocrine tumor of distant lymph nodes `CC`
  Mesentery metastasis of neuroendocrine tumor
  CC Excl: 176.5, 195.8-196.9, 199.0-199.2, 209.20, 209.29-209.30, 209.70-209.74, 209.79, 239.81-239.9

● 209.72 Secondary neuroendocrine tumor of liver `CC`
  CC Excl: 195.8, 197.7-197.8, 198.89-199.2, 209.20, 209.29-209.30, 209.70-209.74, 209.79, 239.81-239.9

● 209.73 Secondary neuroendocrine tumor of bone `CC`
  CC Excl: 195.8, 198.5, 198.89-199.2, 209.20, 209.29-209.30, 209.70-209.74, 209.79, 239.81-239.9

● 209.74 Secondary neuroendocrine tumor of peritoneum `CC`
  CC Excl: 195.8, 197.6, 197.8, 198.89-199.2, 209.20, 209.29-209.30, 209.70-209.74, 209.79, 239.81-239.9

● 209.75 Secondary Merkel cell carcinoma
  Merkel cell carcinoma nodal presentation
  Merkel cell carcinoma visceral metastatic presentation
  Secondary Merkel cell carcinoma, any site

● 209.79 Secondary neuroendocrine tumor of other sites `CC`
  CC Excl: 195.8, 198.89-199.2, 209.20, 209.29-209.30, 209.70-209.74, 209.79, 239.81-239.9

BENIGN NEOPLASMS (210-229)

√4ᵗʰ **210 Benign neoplasm of lip, oral cavity, and pharynx**
  EXCLUDES cyst (of):
    jaw (526.0-526.2, 526.89)
    oral soft tissue (528.4)
    radicular (522.8)

210.0 **Lip**
  Frenulum labii
  Lip (inner aspect) (mucosa) (vermilion border)
  EXCLUDES labial commissure (210.4)
    skin of lip (216.0)

210.1 **Tongue**
  Lingual tonsil

210.2 **Major salivary glands**
  Gland: Gland:
    parotid   submandibular
    sublingual
  EXCLUDES benign neoplasms of minor salivary glands:
    NOS (210.4)
    buccal mucosa (210.4)
    lips (210.0)
    palate (hard) (soft) (210.4)
    tongue (210.1)
    tonsil, palatine (210.5)

210.3 **Floor of mouth**

210.4 **Other and unspecified parts of mouth**
  Gingiva   Oral mucosa
  Gum (upper) (lower) Palate (hard) (soft)
  Labial commissure   Uvula
  Oral cavity NOS
  EXCLUDES benign odontogenic neoplasms of bone (213.0-213.1)
    developmental odontogenic cysts (526.0)
    mucosa of lips (210.0)
    nasopharyngeal [posterior] [superior] surface of soft palate (210.7)

210.5 **Tonsil**
  Tonsil (faucial) (palatine)
  EXCLUDES lingual tonsil (210.1)
    pharyngeal tonsil (210.7)
    tonsillar:
      fossa (210.6)
      pillars (210.6)

210.6 **Other parts of oropharynx**
  Branchial cleft or vestiges   Tonsillar:
  Epiglottis, anterior aspect   fossa
  Fauces NOS   pillars
  Mesopharynx NOS   Vallecula
  EXCLUDES epiglottis:
    NOS (212.1)
    suprahyoid portion (212.1)

210.7 **Nasopharynx**
  Adenoid tissue   Pharyngeal tonsil
  Lymphadenoid tissue   Posterior nasal septum

210.8 **Hypopharynx**
  Arytenoid fold   Postcricoid region
  Laryngopharynx   Pyriform fossa

210.9 **Pharynx, unspecified**
  Throat NOS

√4ᵗʰ **211 Benign neoplasm of other parts of digestive system**
  EXCLUDES benign stromal tumors of digestive system (215.5)

211.0 **Esophagus**

√4ᵗʰ √5ᵗʰ Additional Digit Required   Unacceptable PDx   Manifestation Code   Hospital Acquired Condition   ▶◀ Revised Text   ● New Code   ▲ Revised Code Title

2010 ICD-9-CM   **October 2009 • Volume 1 – 53**

209.34–211.0

211.1 Stomach
Body
Cardia
Fundus } of stomach
Cardiac orifice
Pylorus

> EXCLUDES benign carcinoid tumors of the stomach (209.63)

D13.1 Benign neoplasm of stomach   I-10

211.2 Duodenum, jejunum, and ileum
Small intestine NOS

> EXCLUDES ampulla of Vater (211.5)
> benign carcinoid tumors of the small intestine (209.40-209.43)
> ileocecal valve (211.3)

211.3 Colon
Appendix   Ileocecal valve
Cecum   Large intestine NOS

> EXCLUDES benign carcinoid tumors of the large intestine (209.50-209.56)
> rectosigmoid junction (211.4)

AHA: 3Q, '05, 17; 2Q, '05, 16; 4Q, '01, 56

D12.6 Benign neoplasm of colon unspecified   I-10

211.4 Rectum and anal canal
Anal canal or sphincter
Anus NOS
Rectosigmoid junction

> EXCLUDES anus:
> margin (216.5)
> skin (216.5)
> benign carcinoid tumors of the rectum (209.57)
> perianal skin (216.5)

211.5 Liver and biliary passages
Ampulla of Vater   Gallbladder
Common bile duct   Hepatic duct
Cystic duct   Sphincter of Oddi

211.6 Pancreas, except islets of Langerhans

211.7 Islets of Langerhans
Islet cell tumor
Use additional code to identify any functional activity

211.8 Retroperitoneum and peritoneum
Mesentery   Omentum
Mesocolon   Retroperitoneal tissue

211.9 Other and unspecified site
Alimentary tract NOS
Digestive system NOS
Gastrointestinal tract NOS
Intestinal tract NOS
Intestine NOS
Spleen, not elsewhere classified

√4th **212 Benign neoplasm of respiratory and intrathoracic organs**

212.0 Nasal cavities, middle ear, and accessory sinuses
Cartilage of nose   Sinus:
Eustachian tube   ethmoidal
Nares   frontal
Septum of nose   maxillary
   sphenoidal

> EXCLUDES auditory canal (external) (216.2)
> bone of:
> ear (213.0)
> nose [turbinates] (213.0)
> cartilage of ear (215.0)
> ear (external) (skin) (216.2)
> nose NOS (229.8)
> skin (216.3)
> olfactory bulb (225.1)
> polyp of:
> accessory sinus (471.8)
> ear (385.30-385.35)
> nasal cavity (471.0)
> posterior margin of septum and choanae (210.7)

212.1 Larynx
Cartilage: Epiglottis (suprahyoid
arytenoid   portion) NOS
cricoid   Glottis
cuneiform   Vocal cords (false)(true)
thyroid

> EXCLUDES epiglottis, anterior aspect (210.6)
> polyp of vocal cord or larynx (478.4)

212.2 Trachea

212.3 Bronchus and lung
Carina
Hilus of lung

> EXCLUDES benign carcinoid tumors of bronchus and lung (209.61)

212.4 Pleura

212.5 Mediastinum

212.6 Thymus

> EXCLUDES benign carcinoid tumors of thymus (209.62)

212.7 Heart

> EXCLUDES great vessels (215.4)

212.8 Other specified sites

212.9 Site unspecified
Respiratory organ NOS
Upper respiratory tract NOS

> EXCLUDES intrathoracic NOS (229.8)
> thoracic NOS (229.8)

√4th **213 Benign neoplasm of bone and articular cartilage**

> INCLUDES cartilage (articular) (joint)
> periosteum
>
> EXCLUDES cartilage of:
> ear (215.0)
> eyelid (215.0))
> larynx (212.1)
> nose (212.0)
> exostosis NOS (726.91
> synovia (215.0-215.9)

213.0 Bones of skull and face

> EXCLUDES lower jaw bone (213.1)

213.1 Lower jaw bone

213.2 Vertebral column, excluding sacrum and coccyx

213.3 Ribs, sternum, and clavicle

213.4 Scapula and long bones of upper limb

213.5 Short bones of upper limb

213.6 Pelvic bones, sacrum, and coccyx

213.7 Long bones of lower limb

213.8 Short bones of lower limb

213.9 Bone and articular cartilage, site unspecified

√4th **214 Lipoma**

> INCLUDES angiolipoma
> fibrolipoma
> hibernoma
> lipoma (fetal) (infiltrating) (intramuscular)
> myelolipoma
> myxolipoma

DEF: Benign tumor frequently composed of mature fat cells; may occasionally be composed of fetal fat cells.

214.0 Skin and subcutaneous tissue of face

214.1 Other skin and subcutaneous tissue

214.2 Intrathoracic organs

214.3 Intra-abdominal organs

214.4 Spermatic cord   ♂

214.8 Other specified sites
AHA: 3Q, '94, 7

214.9 Lipoma, unspecified site

N Newborn Age: 0   P Pediatric Age: 0-17   M Maternity Age: 12-55   A Adult Age: 15-124   MCC Major CC Condition   CC CC Condition   HIV HIV Related Dx

54 – Volume 1   **2010 ICD-9-CM**

√4th 215 Other benign neoplasm of connective and other soft tissue

INCLUDES
blood vessel
bursa
fascia
ligament
muscle
peripheral, sympathetic, and parasympathetic nerves
and ganglia
synovia
tendon (sheath)

EXCLUDES
cartilage:
articular (213.0-213.9)
larynx (212.1)
nose (212.0)
connective tissue of:
breast (217)
internal organ, except lipoma and hemangioma–
code to benign neoplasm of the site
lipoma (214.0-214.9)

215.0 Head, face, and neck

215.2 Upper limb, including shoulder

215.3 Lower limb, including hip

215.4 Thorax
EXCLUDES heart (212.7)
mediastinum (212.5)
thymus (212.6)

215.5 Abdomen
Abdominal wall
Benign stromal tumors of abdomen
Hypochondrium

215.6 Pelvis
Buttock   Inguinal region
Groin   Perineum
EXCLUDES uterine:
leiomyoma (218.0-218.9)
ligament, any (221.0)

215.7 Trunk, unspecified
Back NOS   Flank NOS

215.8 Other specified sites

215.9 Site unspecified

√4th 216 Benign neoplasm of skin

INCLUDES
blue nevus
dermatofibroma
hydrocystoma
pigmented nevus
syringoadenoma
syringoma

EXCLUDES skin of genital organs (221.0-222.9)
AHA: 1Q, '00, 21

216.0 Skin of lip
EXCLUDES vermilion border of lip (210.0)

216.1 Eyelid, including canthus
EXCLUDES cartilage of eyelid (215.0)

Types of Uterine Fibroids

Cornual — — Pedunculated
Uterine cavity — — Intramural
Subserosal — — Submucosal
— Cervical

216.2 Ear and external auditory canal
Auricle (ear)   External meatus
Auricular canal, external   Pinna
EXCLUDES cartilage of ear (215.0)

216.3 Skin of other and unspecified parts of face
Cheek, external   Nose, external
Eyebrow   Temple

216.4 Scalp and skin of neck
AHA: 3Q, '91, 12

216.5 Skin of trunk, except scrotum
Axillary fold   Skin of:
Perianal skin   buttock
Skin of: chest wall
   abdominal wall   groin
   anus   perineum
   back   Umbilicus
   breast
EXCLUDES anal canal (211.4)
anus NOS (211.4)
skin of scrotum (222.4)

216.6 Skin of upper limb, including shoulder

216.7 Skin of lower limb, including hip

216.8 Other specified sites of skin

216.9 Skin, site unspecified

217 Benign neoplasm of breast
Breast (male) (female):   Breast (male) (female):
connective tissue   soft parts
glandular tissue

EXCLUDES adenofibrosis (610.2)
benign cyst of breast (610.0)
fibrocystic disease (610.1)
skin of breast (216.5)

AHA: 1Q, '00, 4

√4th 218 Uterine leiomyoma

INCLUDES
fibroid (bleeding) (uterine)
uterine:
fibromyoma
myoma

DEF: Benign tumor primarily derived from uterine smooth muscle
tissue; may contain fibrous, fatty, or epithelial tissue; also called uterine
fibroid or myoma.

218.0 Submucous leiomyoma of uterus   ♀

218.1 Intramural leiomyoma of uterus   ♀
Interstitial leiomyoma of uterus
D25.1 Intramural leiomyoma of uterus   I-10

218.2 Subserous leiomyoma of uterus   ♀

218.9 Leiomyoma of uterus, unspecified   ♀
AHA: 1Q, '03, 4
D25.9 Leiomyoma of uterus unspecified   I-10

√4th 219 Other benign neoplasm of uterus

219.0 Cervix uteri   ♀

219.1 Corpus uteri   ♀
Endometrium   Myometrium
Fundus

219.8 Other specified parts of uterus   ♀

219.9 Uterus, part unspecified   ♀

220 Benign neoplasm of ovary   ♀
Use additional code to identify any functional activity
(256.0-256.1)
EXCLUDES cyst:
corpus albicans (620.2)
corpus luteum (620.1)
endometrial (617.1)
follicular (atretic) (620.0)
graafian follicle (620.0)
ovarian NOS (620.2)
retention (620.2)

D27.9 Benign neoplasm of ovary unspecified side   I-10

√4th √5th Additional Digit Required   Unacceptable PDx   Manifestation Code   Hospital Acquired Condition   ▶◀ Revised Text   ● New Code   ▲ Revised Code Title

2010 ICD-9-CM   **Volume 1 – 55**

Neoplasms

221–227.0

✓4th **221 Benign neoplasm of other female genital organs**

INCLUDES adenomatous polyp
benign teratoma

EXCLUDES *cyst:*
epoophoron (752.11)
fimbrial (752.11)
Gartner's duct (752.11)
parovarian (752.11)

221.0 Fallopian tube and uterine ligaments   ♀
Oviduct
Parametruim
Uterine ligament (broad) (round) (uterosacral)
Uterine tube

221.1 Vagina   ♀

221.2 Vulva   ♀
Clitoris
External female genitalia NOS
Greater vestibular [Bartholin's] gland
Labia (majora) (minora)
Pudendum
EXCLUDES *Bartholin's (duct) (gland) cyst (616.2)*

221.8 Other specified sites of female genital organs   ♀

221.9 Female genital organ, site unspecified   ♀
Female genitourinary tract NOS

✓4th **222 Benign neoplasm of male genital organs**

222.0 Testis   ♂
Use additional code to identify any functional activity

222.1 Penis   ♂
Corpus cavernosum   Prepuce
Glans penis

222.2 Prostate   ♂
EXCLUDES *adenomatous hyperplasia of prostate*
(600.20-600.21)
prostatic:
adenoma (600.20-600.21)
enlargement (600.00-600.01)
hypertrophy (600.00-600.01)

222.3 Epididymis   ♂

222.4 Scrotum   ♂
Skin of scrotum

222.8 Other specified sites of male genital organs   ♂
Seminal vesicle   Spermatic cord

222.9 Male genital organ, site unspecified   ♂
Male genitourinary tract NOS

✓4th **223 Benign neoplasm of kidney and other urinary organs**

223.0 Kidney, except pelvis
Kidney NOS
EXCLUDES *benign carcinoid tumors of kidney (209.64)*
renal:
calyces (223.1)
pelvis (223.1)

223.1 Renal pelvis

223.2 Ureter
EXCLUDES *ureteric orifice of bladder (223.3)*

223.3 Bladder

✓5th **223.8 Other specified sites of urinary organs**

223.81 Urethra
EXCLUDES *urethral orifice of bladder (223.3)*

223.89 Other
Paraurethral glands

223.9 Urinary organ, site unspecified
Urinary system NOS

Eyeball

Posterior segment
Vitreous
Optic nerve
Optic disc
Choroid
Sclera
Retina
Pars plana
Conjunctiva
Sclera
Lens
Cornea
Iris
Anterior chamber

✓4th **224 Benign neoplasm of eye**
EXCLUDES *cartilage of eyelid (215.0)*
eyelid (skin) (216.1)
optic nerve (225.1)
orbital bone (213.0)

224.0 Eyeball, except conjunctiva, cornea, retina, and choroid
Ciliary body   Sclera
Iris   Uveal tract

224.1 Orbit
EXCLUDES *bone of orbit (213.0)*

224.2 Lacrimal gland

224.3 Conjunctiva

224.4 Cornea

224.5 Retina
EXCLUDES *hemangioma of retina (228.03)*

224.6 Choroid

224.7 Lacrimal duct
Lacrimal sac   Nasolacrimal duct

224.8 Other specified parts of eye

224.9 Eye, part unspecified

✓4th **225 Benign neoplasm of brain and other parts of nervous system**
EXCLUDES *hemangioma (228.02)*
neurofibromatosis (237.7)
peripheral, sympathetic, and parasympathetic nerves
and ganglia (215.0-215.9)
retrobulbar (224.1)

225.0 Brain

225.1 Cranial nerves
Acoustic neuroma
AHA: 4Q, '04, 113

225.2 Cerebral meninges
Meninges NOS   Meningioma (cerebral)
D32.9 Benign neoplasm of meninges unspecified   I-10

225.3 Spinal cord
Cauda equina

225.4 Spinal meninges
Spinal meningioma

225.8 Other specified sites of nervous system

225.9 Nervous system, part unspecified
Nervous system (central) NOS
EXCLUDES *meninges NOS (225.2)*

226 Benign neoplasm of thyroid glands
Use additional code to identify any functional activity

✓4th **227 Benign neoplasm of other endocrine glands and related structures**
Use additional code to identify any functional activity
EXCLUDES *ovary (220)*
pancreas (211.6)
testis (222.0)

227.0 Adrenal gland
Suprarenal gland

N Newborn Age: 0   P Pediatric Age: 0-17   M Maternity Age: 12-55   A Adult Age: 15-124   MCC Major CC Condition   CC CC Condition   HIV HIV Related Dx

56 – Volume 1   2010 ICD-9-CM

227.1   **Parathyroid gland**

227.3   **Pituitary gland and craniopharyngeal duct (pouch)**
     Craniobuccal pouch   Rathke's pouch
     Hypophysis   Sella turcica

227.4   **Pineal gland**
     Pineal body

227.5   **Carotid body**

227.6   **Aortic body and other paraganglia**
     Coccygeal body   Para-aortic body
     Glomus jugulare
     AHA: N-D, '84, 17

227.8   **Other**

227.9   **Endocrine gland, site unspecified**

√4th **228 Hemangioma and lymphangioma, any site**

     INCLUDES   angioma (benign) (cavernous) (congenital) NOS
                 cavernous nevus
                 glomus tumor
                 hemangioma (benign) (congenital)

     EXCLUDES   *benign neoplasm of spleen, except hemangioma and*
                 lymphangioma (211.9)
                 glomus jugulare (227.6)
                 nevus:
                     NOS (216.0-216.9)
                     blue or pigmented (216.0-216.9)
                     vascular (757.32)

     AHA: 1Q, '00, 21

√5th **228.0 Hemangioma, any site**
     DEF: A common benign tumor usually occurring in infancy;
     composed of newly formed blood vessels due to
     malformation of angioblastic tissue.
     AHA: J-F, '85, 19

     228.00   **Of unspecified site**

     228.01   **Of skin and subcutaneous tissue**

     228.02   **Of intracranial structures**

     228.03   **Of retina**

     228.04   **Of intra-abdominal structures**
            Peritoneum   Retroperitoneal tissue

     228.09   **Of other sites**
            Systemic angiomatosis
            AHA: 3Q, '91, 20

     228.1   **Lymphangioma, any site**
          Congenital lymphangioma   Lymphatic nevus

√4th **229 Benign neoplasm of other and unspecified sites**

     229.0   **Lymph nodes**
          EXCLUDES   *lymphangioma (228.1)*

     229.8   **Other specified sites**
          Intrathoracic NOS   Thoracic NOS

     229.9   **Site unspecified**

CARCINOMA IN SITU (230-234)

     INCLUDES   Bowen's disease
                 erythroplasia
                 Queyrat's erythroplasia

     EXCLUDES   *leukoplakia–see Alphabetic Index*

     DEF: A neoplastic type; with tumor cells confined to epithelium of
     origin; without further invasion.

√4th **230 Carcinoma in situ of digestive organs**

     230.0   **Lip, oral cavity, and pharynx**
          Gingiva   Oropharynx
          Hypopharynx   Salivary gland or duct
          Mouth [any part]   Tongue
          Nasopharynx
          EXCLUDES   *aryepiglottic fold or interarytenoid fold,*
                     laryngeal aspect (231.0)
                 epiglottis:
                     NOS (231.0)
                     suprahyoid portion (231.0)
                 skin of lip (232.0)

230.1   **Esophagus**

230.2   **Stomach**
     Body
     Cardia   } of stomach
     Fundus
     Cardiac orifice
     Pylorus

230.3   **Colon**
     Appendix   Ileocecal valve
     Cecum   Large intestine NOS
     EXCLUDES   *rectosigmoid junction (230.4)*

230.4   **Rectum**
     Rectosigmoid junction

230.5   **Anal canal**
     Anal sphincter

230.6   **Anus, unspecified**
     EXCLUDES   *anus:*
                 margin (232.5)
                 skin (232.5)
              perianal skin (232.5)

230.7   **Other and unspecified parts of intestine**
     Duodenum   Jejunum
     Ileum   Small intestine NOS
     EXCLUDES   *ampulla of Vater (230.8)*

230.8   **Liver and biliary system**
     Ampulla of Vater   Gallbladder
     Common bile duct   Hepatic duct
     Cystic duct   Sphincter of Oddi

230.9   **Other and unspecified digestive organs**
     Digestive organ NOS   Pancreas
     Gastrointestinal tract NOS   Spleen

√4th **231 Carcinoma in situ of respiratory system**

     231.0   **Larynx**
          Cartilage: Epiglottis:
            arytenoid   NOS
            cricoid   posterior surface
            cuneiform   suprahyoid portion
            thyroid   Vocal cords (false)(true)
          EXCLUDES   *aryepiglottic fold or interarytenoid fold:*
                   NOS (230.0)
                   hypopharyngeal aspect (230.0)
                   marginal zone (230.0)

     231.1   **Trachea**

     231.2   **Bronchus and lung**
          Carina   Hilus of lung

     231.8   **Other specified parts of respiratory system**
          Accessory sinuses   Nasal cavities
          Middle ear   Pleura
          EXCLUDES   *ear (external) (skin) (232.2)*
                 nose NOS (234.8)
                 skin (232.3)

     231.9   **Respiratory system, part unspecified**
          Respiratory organ NOS

√4th **232 Carcinoma in situ of skin**

     INCLUDES   pigment cells
     EXCLUDES   *melanoma in situ of skin (172.0-172.9)*

     232.0   **Skin of lip**
          EXCLUDES   *vermilion border of lip (230.0)*

     232.1   **Eyelid, including canthus**

     232.2   **Ear and external auditory canal**

     232.3   **Skin of other and unspecified parts of face**

     232.4   **Scalp and skin of neck**

√4th √5th   Additional Digit Required   Unacceptable PDx   Manifestation Code   Hospital Acquired Condition   ▶◀ Revised Text   ● New Code   ▲ Revised Code Title

2010 ICD-9-CM   Volume 1 – 57

Neoplasms

232.5 Skin of trunk, except scrotum

Anus, margin	Skin of:
Axillary fold	breast
Perianal skin	buttock
Skin of:	chest wall
abdominal wall	groin
anus	perineum
back	Umbilicus

> **EXCLUDES** anal canal (230.5)
> anus NOS (230.6)
> skin of genital organs (233.30-233.39, 233.5-233.6)

232.6 Skin of upper limb, including shoulder

232.7 Skin of lower limb, including hip

232.8 Other specified sites of skin

232.9 Skin, site unspecified

√4ᵗʰ **233 Carcinoma in situ of breast and genitourinary system**

> **TIP:** For patients with carcinoma in situ found incidentally when admitted for treatment of another condition, sequence the 233 code as a secondary condition.

233.0 Breast

> **EXCLUDES** Paget's disease (174.0-174.9)
> skin of breast (232.5)

> **TIP:** Assign for tumors specified as intraductal carcinoma.

233.1 Cervix uteri ♀

Adenocarcinoma in situ of cervix
Cervical intraepithelial glandular neoplasia, grade III
Cervical intraepithelial neoplasia III [CIN III]
Severe dysplasia of cervix

> **EXCLUDES** cervical intraepithelial neoplasia II [CIN II] (622.12)
> cytologic evidence of malignancy without histologic confirmation (795.06)
> high grade squamous intraepithelial lesion (HGSIL) (795.04)
> moderate dysplasia of cervix (622.12)

> **AHA:** 3Q, '92, 7; 3Q, '92, 8; 1Q, '91, 11

233.2 Other and unspecified parts of uterus ♀

√5ᵗʰ **233.3 Other and unspecified female genital organs** ♀

> **AHA:** 4Q, '07, 67

233.30 Unspecified female genital organ ♀

233.31 Vagina ♀

Severe dysplasia of vagina
Vaginal intraepithelial neoplasia III [VAIN III]

233.32 Vulva ♀

Severe dysplasia of vulva
Vulvar intraepithelial neoplasia III [VIN III]

233.39 Other female genital organ ♀

233.4 Prostate ♂

233.5 Penis ♂

233.6 Other and unspecified male genital organs ♂

233.7 Bladder

233.9 Other and unspecified urinary organs

√4ᵗʰ **234 Carcinoma in situ of other and unspecified sites**

234.0 Eye

> **EXCLUDES** cartilage of eyelid (234.8)
> eyelid (skin) (232.1)
> optic nerve (234.8)
> orbital bone (234.8)

234.8 Other specified sites

Endocrine gland [any]

234.9 Site unspecified

Carcinoma in situ NOS

NEOPLASMS OF UNCERTAIN BEHAVIOR (235-238)

Note: Categories 235–238 classify by site certain histomorphologically well-defined neoplasms, the subsequent behavior of which cannot be predicted from the present appearance.

> **TIP:** Typically assigned for cases in which the tumor is in transition and may be undergoing malignant transformation, but continued study is required for accurate classification.

√4ᵗʰ **235 Neoplasm of uncertain behavior of digestive and respiratory systems**

> **EXCLUDES** stromal tumors of uncertain behavior of digestive system (238.1)

235.0 Major salivary glands

Gland:
parotid
sublingual
submandibular

> **EXCLUDES** minor salivary glands (235.1)

235.1 Lip, oral cavity, and pharynx

Gingiva	Nasopharynx
Hypopharynx	Oropharynx
Minor salivary glands	Tongue
Mouth	

> **EXCLUDES** aryepiglottic fold or interarytenoid fold, laryngeal aspect (235.6)
> epiglottis:
> NOS (235.6)
> suprahyoid portion (235.6)
> skin of lip (238.2)

235.2 Stomach, intestines, and rectum

235.3 Liver and biliary passages

Ampulla of Vater	Gallbladder
Bile ducts [any]	Liver

235.4 Retroperitoneum and peritoneum

235.5 Other and unspecified digestive organs

Anal:	Esophagus
canal	Pancreas
sphincter	Spleen
Anus NOS	

> **EXCLUDES** anus:
> margin (238.2)
> skin (238.2)
> perianal skin (238.2)

235.6 Larynx

> **EXCLUDES** aryepiglottic fold or interarytenoid fold:
> NOS (235.1)
> hypopharyngeal aspect (235.1)
> marginal zone (235.1)

235.7 Trachea, bronchus, and lung

235.8 Pleura, thymus, and mediastinum

235.9 Other and unspecified respiratory organs

Accessory sinuses
Middle ear
Nasal cavities
Respiratory organ NOS

> **EXCLUDES** ear (external) (skin) (238.2)
> nose (238.8)
> skin (238.2)

√4ᵗʰ **236 Neoplasm of uncertain behavior of genitourinary organs**

236.0 Uterus ♀

236.1 Placenta ♀

Chorioadenoma (destruens)
Invasive mole
Malignant hydatid (iform) mole

236.2 Ovary ♀

Use additional code to identify any functional activity

236.3 Other and unspecified female genital organs ♀

236.4 Testis ♂

Use additional code to identify any functional activity

| Ⓝ Newborn Age: 0 | Ⓟ Pediatric Age: 0-17 | Ⓜ Maternity Age: 12-55 | Ⓐ Adult Age: 15-124 | **MCC** Major CC Condition | **CC** CC Condition | **HIV** HIV Related Dx |

58 – Volume 1

2010 ICD-9-CM

236.5 Prostate ♂

236.6 Other and unspecified male genital organs ♂

236.7 Bladder

√5ᵗʰ 236.9 Other and unspecified urinary organs

236.90 Urinary organ, unspecified

236.91 Kidney and ureter

236.99 Other

√4ᵗʰ **237 Neoplasm of uncertain behavior of endocrine glands and nervous system**

237.0 Pituitary gland and craniopharyngeal duct
Use additional code to identify any functional activity

237.1 Pineal gland

237.2 Adrenal gland
Suprarenal gland
Use additional code to identify any functional activity

237.3 Paraganglia
Aortic body   Coccygeal body
Carotid body   Glomus jugulare
AHA: N-D, '84, 17

237.4 Other and unspecified endocrine glands
Parathyroid gland   Thyroid gland

237.5 Brain and spinal cord

237.6 Meninges
Meninges: Meninges:
NOS   spinal
cerebral

√5ᵗʰ 237.7 Neurofibromatosis
von Recklinghausen's disease
DEF: An inherited condition with developmental changes in the nervous system, muscles, bones and skin; multiple soft tumors (neurofibromas) distributed over the entire body.

237.70 Neurofibromatosis, unspecified

237.71 Neurofibromatosis, type 1 [von Recklinghausen's disease]

237.72 Neurofibromatosis, type 2 [acoustic neurofibromatosis]
DEF: Inherited condition with cutaneous lesions, benign tumors of peripheral nerves and bilateral 8th nerve masses.

237.9 Other and unspecified parts of nervous system
Cranial nerves
EXCLUDES peripheral, sympathetic, and parasympathetic nerves and ganglia (238.1)

√4ᵗʰ **238 Neoplasm of uncertain behavior of other and unspecified sites and tissues**

238.0 Bone and articular cartilage
EXCLUDES cartilage:
ear (238.1)
eyelid (238.1)
larynx (235.6)
nose (235.9)
synovia (238.1)
AHA: 4Q, '04, 128

238.1 Connective and other soft tissue
Peripheral, sympathetic, and parasympathetic nerves and ganglia
Stromal tumors of digestive system
EXCLUDES cartilage (of):
articular (238.0)
larynx (235.6)
nose (235.9)
connective tissue of breast (238.3)

238.2 Skin
EXCLUDES anus NOS (235.5)
skin of genital organs (236.3, 236.6)
vermilion border of lip (235.1)
TIP: Assign when documentation indicates keratocanthoma only.

238.3 Breast
EXCLUDES skin of breast (238.2)

238.4 Polycythemia vera
DEF: Abnormal proliferation of all bone marrow elements, increased red cell mass and total blood volume; unknown etiology, frequently associated with splenomegaly, leukocytosis, and thrombocythemia.
D45 Polycythemia vera [I-10]

238.5 Histiocytic and mast cells [CC]
Mast cell tumor NOS   Mastocytoma NOS
CC Excl: 238.4-238.76, 238.79, 289.83, V58.0

238.6 Plasma cells [CC]
Plasmacytoma NOS   Solitary myeloma
CC Excl: See code: 238.5

√5ᵗʰ 238.7 Other lymphatic and hematopoietic tissues
EXCLUDES acute myelogenous leukemia (205.0)
chronic myelomonocytic leukemia (205.1)
myelosclerosis NOS (289.89)
myelosis:
NOS (205.9)
megakaryocytic (207.2)
AHA: 3Q, '01, 13; 1Q, '97, 5; 2Q, '89, 8

238.71 Essential thrombocythemia
Essential hemorrhagic thrombocythemia
Essential thrombocytosis
Idiopathic (hemorrhagic) thrombocythemia
Primary thrombocytosis
AHA: 4Q, '06, 63-66
D47.3 Essential (hemorrhagic) [I-10]
thrombocythemia

238.72 Low grade myelodysplastic syndrome lesions
Refractory anemia (RA)
▶Refractory anemia with excess blasts-1 (RAEB-1)◀
Refractory anemia with ringed sideroblasts (RARS)
Refractory cytopenia with multilineage dysplasia (RCMD)
Refractory cytopenia with multilineage dysplasia and ringed sideroblasts (RCMD-RS)
DEF: Refractory anemia (RA): Form of bone marrow disorder (myelodysplastic syndrome) that interferes with red blood cell production in the bone marrow; unresponsive to hematinics; characteristic normal or hypercellular marrow with abnormal erythrocyte development and reticulocytopenia.
AHA: 4Q, '06, 63-66

238.73 High grade myelodysplastic [CC]
syndrome lesions
Refractory anemia with excess blasts-2 (RAEB-2)
CC Excl: 202.40-202.48, 203.10-203.11, 203.80-203.81, 204.00-208.92, 238.4-238.76, 238.79-238.9
AHA: 4Q, '06, 63-66

238.74 Myelodysplastic syndrome with 5q [CC]
deletion
5q minus syndrome NOS
EXCLUDES constitutional 5q deletion (758.39)
high grade myelodysplastic
syndrome with 5q deletion
(238.73)
CC Excl: See code: 238.73
AHA: 4Q, '06, 63-66

238.75 Myelodysplastic syndrome, unspecified
AHA: 4Q, '06, 63-66
D46.9 Myelodysplastic syndrome unspecified [I-10]

238.76 Myelofibrosis with myeloid metaplasia `CC`
Agnogenic myeloid metaplasia
Idiopathic myelofibrosis (chronic)
Myelosclerosis with myeloid metaplasia
Primary myelofibrosis

EXCLUDES   *myelofibrosis NOS (289.83)*
myelophthisic anemia (284.2)
myelophthisis (284.2)
secondary myelofibrosis (289.83)

CC Excl: See code: 238.73
AHA: 4Q, '06, 63-66

238.77 Post-transplant lymphoproliferative disorder [PTLD] `CC`
Code first complications of transplant (996.80-996.89)

DEF: Excessive proliferation of B-cell lymphocytes following Epstein-Barr virus infection in organ transplant patients; may progress to non-Hodgkins lymphoma.
CC Excl: 238.77, 996.80, 996.87, 997.91-997.99
AHA: 4Q, '08, 90-91

238.79 Other lymphatic and hematopoietic tissues `CC`
Lymphoproliferative disease (chronic) NOS
Megakaryocytic myelosclerosis
Myeloproliferative disease (chronic) NOS
Panmyelosis (acute)
CC Excl: 202.40-202.48, 203.10-203.11, 203.80-203.81, 204.00-208.92, 238.4-238.76, 238.79-238.9
AHA: 4Q, '06, 63-66

238.8 Other specified sites
Eye
Heart
EXCLUDES   *eyelid (skin) (238.2)*
cartilage (238.1)

238.9 Site unspecified

NEOPLASMS OF UNSPECIFIED NATURE (239)

√4ᵗʰ 239 Neoplasms of unspecified nature
Note: Category 239 classifies by site neoplasms of unspecified morphology and behavior. The term "mass," unless otherwise stated, is not to be regarded as a neoplastic growth.

INCLUDES   "growth" NOS
neoplasm NOS
new growth NOS
tumor NOS

TIP: Do not assign for inpatient cases; more information should be available.

239.0 Digestive system
EXCLUDES   *anus:*
margin (239.2)
skin (239.2)
perianal skin (239.2)

239.1 Respiratory system

239.2 Bone, soft tissue, and skin
EXCLUDES   *anal canal (239.0)*
anus NOS (239.0)
bone marrow (202.9)
cartilage:
larynx (239.1)
nose (239.1)
connective tissue of breast (239.3)
skin of genital organs (239.5)
vermilion border of lip (239.0)

239.3 Breast
EXCLUDES   *skin of breast (239.2)*

239.4 Bladder

239.5 Other genitourinary organs

239.6 Brain
EXCLUDES   *cerebral meninges (239.7)*
cranial nerves (239.7)

239.7 Endocrine glands and other parts of nervous system
EXCLUDES   *peripheral, sympathetic, and parasympathetic nerves and ganglia (239.2)*

√5ᵗʰ 239.8 Other specified sites
EXCLUDES   *eyelid (skin) (239.2)*
cartilage (239.2)
great vessels (239.2)
optic nerve (239.7)

239.81 Retina and choroid
Dark area on retina
Retinal freckle

239.89 Other specified sites

239.9 Site unspecified

3. ENDOCRINE, NUTRITIONAL AND METABOLIC DISEASES, AND IMMUNITY DISORDERS (240-279)

> **EXCLUDES** *endocrine and metabolic disturbances specific to the fetus and newborn (775.0-775.9)*

Note: All neoplasms, whether functionally active or not, are classified in Chapter 2. Codes in Chapter 3 (i.e., 242.8, 246.0, 251-253, 255-259) may be used to identify such functional activity associated with any neoplasm, or by ectopic endocrine tissue.

DISORDERS OF THYROID GLAND (240-246)

√4th **240 Simple and unspecified goiter**

> **DEF:** An enlarged thyroid gland often caused by an inadequate dietary intake of iodine.

240.0 Goiter, specified as simple

> Any condition classifiable to 240.9, specified as simple

240.9 Goiter, unspecified

> Enlargement of thyroid
> Goiter or struma:
>   NOS
>   diffuse colloid
>   endemic
> Goiter or struma:
>   hyperplastic
>   nontoxic (diffuse)
>   parenchymatous
>   sporadic
>
> **EXCLUDES** *congenital (dyshormonogenic) goiter (246.1)*

√4th **241 Nontoxic nodular goiter**

> **EXCLUDES** *adenoma of thyroid (226)*
> *cystadenoma of thyroid (226)*

241.0 Nontoxic uninodular goiter

> Thyroid nodule   Uninodular goiter (nontoxic)
>
> **DEF:** Enlarged thyroid, commonly due to decreased thyroid production, with single nodule; no clinical hypothyroidism.
>
> E04.1 Nontoxic single thyroid nodule   I-10

241.1 Nontoxic multinodular goiter

> Multinodular goiter (nontoxic)
>
> **DEF:** Enlarged thyroid, commonly due to decreased thyroid production with multiple nodules; no clinical hypothyroidism.

241.9 Unspecified nontoxic nodular goiter

> Adenomatous goiter
> Nodular goiter (nontoxic) NOS
> Struma nodosa (simplex)

√4th **242 Thyrotoxicosis with or without goiter**

> **EXCLUDES** *neonatal thyrotoxicosis (775.3)*
>
> **DEF:** A condition caused by excess quantities of thyroid hormones being introduced into the tissues

> The following fifth-digit subclassification is for use with categories 242:
> **0 without mention of thyrotoxic crisis or storm**
> **1 with mention of thyrotoxic crisis or storm**

§ √5th **242.0 Toxic diffuse goiter**   MCC 1
[0-1]

> Basedow's disease
> Exophthalmic or toxic goiter NOS
> Graves' disease
> Primary thyroid hyperplasia
>
> **DEF:** Diffuse thyroid enlargement accompanied by hyperthyroidism, bulging eyes, and dermopathy.
>
> **CC Excl:** For code 242.01: 017.50-017.56, 017.90-017.96, 240.0-246.9, 259.50-259.9

§ √5th **242.1 Toxic uninodular goiter**   MCC 1
[0-1]

> Thyroid nodule
> Uninodular goiter } toxic or with hyperthyroidism
>
> **DEF:** Symptomatic hyperthyroidism with a single nodule on the enlarged thyroid gland. Abrupt onset of symptoms; including extreme nervousness, insomnia, weight loss, tremors, and psychosis or coma.
>
> **CC Excl:** See code 242.0

§ √5th **242.2 Toxic multinodular goiter**   MCC 1
[0-1]

> Secondary thyroid hyperplasia
>
> **DEF:** Symptomatic hyperthyroidism with multiple nodules on the enlarged thyroid gland. Abrupt onset of symptoms; including extreme nervousness, insomnia, weight loss, tremors, and psychosis or coma.
>
> **CC Excl:** See code 242.0

The Endocrine System

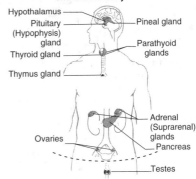

§ √5th **242.3 Toxic nodular goiter, unspecified**   MCC 1
[0-1]

> Adenomatous goiter
> Nodular goiter } toxic or with hyperthyroidism
> Struma nodosa
>
> Any condition classifiable to 241.9 specified as toxic or with hyperthyroidism
>
> **CC Excl:** See code 242.0

§ √5th **242.4 Thyrotoxicosis from ectopic thyroid nodule**   MCC 1
[0-1]   **CC Excl:** See code 242.0

§ √5th **242.8 Thyrotoxicosis of other specified origin**   MCC 1
[0-1]

> Overproduction of thyroid-stimulating hormone [TSH]
> Thyrotoxicosis:
>   factitia from ingestion of excessive thyroid material
> Use additional E code to identify cause, if drug-induced
>
> **CC Excl:** See code 242.0

§ √5th **242.9 Thyrotoxicosis without mention of goiter**   MCC 1
[0-1]   **or other cause**

> Hyperthyroidism NOS
> Thyrotoxicosis NOS
>
> **CC Excl:** See code 242.0
>
> E05.90 Thyrotoxicosis uns w/o thyrotoxic crisis or storm   I-10

243 Congenital hypothyroidism

> Congenital thyroid insufficiency
> Cretinism (athyrotic) (endemic)
>
> Use additional code to identify associated mental retardation
>
> **EXCLUDES** *congenital (dyshormonogenic) goiter (246.1)*
>
> **DEF:** Underproduction of thyroid hormone present from birth.

√4th **244 Acquired hypothyroidism**

> **INCLUDES** athyroidism (acquired)
> hypothyroidism (acquired)
> myxedema (adult) (juvenile)
> thyroid (gland) insufficiency (acquired)

244.0 Postsurgical hypothyroidism

> **DEF:** Underproduction of thyroid hormone due to surgical removal of all or part of the thyroid gland.
>
> E89.0 Postprocedural hypothyroidism   I-10

244.1 Other postablative hypothyroidism

> Hypothyroidism following therapy, such as irradiation

244.2 Iodine hypothyroidism

> Hypothyroidism resulting from administration or ingestion of iodide
>
> Use additional E code to identify drug

244.3 Other iatrogenic hypothyroidism

> Hypothyroidism resulting from:
>   P-aminosalicylic acid [PAS]
>   Phenylbutazone
>   Resorcinol
> Iatrogenic hypothyroidism NOS
> Use additional E code to identify drug

244.8 Other specified acquired hypothyroidism

> Secondary hypothyroidism NEC
>
> **AHA:** J-A, '85, 9

---

§ Requires fifth digit. Valid digits are in [brackets] under each code. See category 242 for codes and definitions.

√4th Additional Digit Required	Unacceptable PDx	Manifestation Code	Hospital Acquired Condition	►◄ Revised Text	● New Code	▲ Revised Code Title

244.9 Unspecified hypothyroidism
Hypothyroidism } primary or NOS
Myxedema

AHA: 3Q, '99, 19; 4Q, '96, 29

E03.9 Hypothyroidism unspecified   I-10

√4ᵗʰ 245 Thyroiditis

245.0 Acute thyroiditis   CC
Abscess of thyroid
Thyroiditis:
    nonsuppurative, acute
    pyogenic
    suppurative
Use additional code to identify organism
DEF: Inflamed thyroid caused by infection, with abscess and liquid puris.
CC Excl: 245.0-245.9

245.1 Subacute thyroiditis
Thyroiditis:
    de Quervain's
    giant cell
    granulomatous
    viral
DEF: Inflammation of the thyroid, characterized by fever and painful enlargement of the thyroid gland, with granulomas in the gland.

245.2 Chronic lymphocytic thyroiditis
Hashimoto's disease
Struma lymphomatosa
Thyroiditis:
    autoimmune
    lymphocytic (chronic)
DEF: Autoimmune disease of thyroid; lymphocytes infiltrate the gland and thyroid antibodies are produced; women more often affected.

245.3 Chronic fibrous thyroiditis
Struma fibrosa
Thyroiditis:
    invasive (fibrous)
    ligneous
    Riedel's
DEF: Persistent fibrosing inflammation of thyroid with adhesions to nearby structures; rare condition

245.4 Iatrogenic thyroiditis
Use additional code to identify cause
DEF: Thyroiditis resulting from treatment or intervention by physician or in a patient intervention setting.

245.8 Other and unspecified chronic thyroiditis
Chronic thyroiditis:
    NOS
    nonspecific

245.9 Thyroiditis, unspecified
Thyroiditis NOS

√4ᵗʰ 246 Other disorders of thyroid

246.0 Disorders of thyrocalcitonin secretion
Hypersecretion of calcitonin or thyrocalcitonin

246.1 Dyshormonogenic goiter
Congenital (dyshormonogenic) goiter
Goiter due to enzyme defect in synthesis of thyroid hormone
Goitrous cretinism (sporadic)

246.2 Cyst of thyroid
EXCLUDES   cystadenoma of thyroid (226)

246.3 Hemorrhage and infarction of thyroid   CC
CC Excl: 246.3

246.8 Other specified disorders of thyroid
Abnormality of thyroid-binding globulin
Atrophy of thyroid
Hyper-TBG-nemia
Hypo-TBG-nemia
AHA: 2Q, '06, 5

246.9 Unspecified disorder of thyroid
E07.9 Disorder of thyroid unspecified   I-10

DISEASES OF OTHER ENDOCRINE GLANDS (249-259)

√4ᵗʰ 249 Secondary diabetes mellitus

INCLUDES   diabetes mellitus (due to) (in) (secondary) (with):
    drug-induced or chemical induced
    infection
Use additional code to identify any associated insulin use (V58.67)

EXCLUDES   gestational diabetes (648.8)
    hyperglycemia NOS (790.29)
    neonatal diabetes mellitus (775.1)
    nonclinical diabetes (790.29)
    Type I diabetes – see category 250
    Type II diabetes – see category 250

AHA: ▶4Q, '08, 91-95◀

TIP: Do not assign a code from category 249 if the secondary DM is due to pancreatectomy; assign instead 251.3 Postsurgical hypoinsulinemia.

The following fifth-digit subclassification is for use with category 249:
    0 not stated as uncontrolled, or unspecified
    1 uncontrolled

§ √5ᵗʰ **249.0 Secondary diabetes mellitus without mention**
[0-1]   **of complication**
Secondary diabetes mellitus without mention of complication or manifestation classifiable to 249.1-249.9
Secondary diabetes mellitus NOS
E09.9 Drug/chemical induced diabetes mellitus w/o comp   I-10

§ √5ᵗʰ **249.1 Secondary diabetes mellitus with ketoacidosis**   MCC
[0-1]   Secondary diabetes mellitus with diabetic acidosis without mention of coma
Secondary diabetes mellitus with diabetic ketosis without mention of coma
CC Excl: 249.00-251.3, 259.8-259.9

§ √5ᵗʰ **249.2 Secondary diabetes mellitus with**   MCC
[0-1]   **hyperosmolarity**
Secondary diabetes mellitus with hyperosmolar (nonketotic) coma
CC Excl: See code: 249.1

§ √5ᵗʰ **249.3 Secondary diabetes mellitus with other coma**   MCC
[0-1]   Secondary diabetes mellitus with diabetic coma (with ketoacidosis)
Secondary diabetes mellitus with diabetic hypoglycemic coma
Secondary diabetes mellitus with insulin coma NOS
EXCLUDES   secondary diabetes mellitus with hyperosmolar coma (249.2)
CC Excl: See code: 249.1

§ √5ᵗʰ **249.4 Secondary diabetes mellitus with renal manifestations**
[0-1]   Use additional code to identify manifestation, as:
    chronic kidney disease (585.1-585.9)
    diabetic nephropathy NOS (583.81)
    diabetic nephrosis (581.81)
    intercapillary glomerulosclerosis (581.81)
    Kimmelstiel-Wilson syndrome (581.81)

§ √5ᵗʰ **249.5 Secondary diabetes mellitus with ophthalmic**
[0-1]   **manifestations**
Use additional code to identify manifestation, as:
    diabetic blindness (369.00-369.9)
    diabetic cataract (366.41)
    diabetic glaucoma (365.44)
    diabetic macular edema (362.07)
    diabetic retinal edema (362.07)
    diabetic retinopathy (362.01-362.07)

---

§ Requires fifth digit. Valid digits are in [brackets] under each code. See category 249 for codes and definitions.

N Newborn Age: 0   P Pediatric Age: 0-17   M Maternity Age: 12-55   A Adult Age: 15-124   MCC Major CC Condition   CC CC Condition   HIV HIV Related Dx

[handwritten at top: A diagnosis of diabetic ketoacidosis should be classified as Type 1, uncontrolled, unless the physician specifically identifies it as Type 2.]

§ ✓5th **249.6 Secondary diabetes mellitus with neurological**
[0-1] **manifestations**

Use additional code to identify manifestation, as:
diabetic amyotrophy (353.5)
diabetic gastroparalysis (536.3)
diabetic gastroparesis (536.3)
diabetic mononeuropathy (354.0-355.9)
diabetic neurogenic arthropathy (713.5)
diabetic peripheral autonomic neuropathy (337.1)
diabetic polyneuropathy (357.2)

AHA: For code 249.60: 4Q, '08, 94

§ ✓5th **249.7 Secondary diabetes mellitus with peripheral**
[0-1] **circulatory disorders**

Use additional code to identify manifestation, as:
diabetic gangrene (785.4)
diabetic peripheral angiopathy (443.81)

§ ✓5th **249.8 Secondary diabetes mellitus with other**
[0-1] **specified manifestations**

Secondary diabetic hypoglycemia in diabetes mellitus
Secondary hypoglycemic shock in diabetes mellitus

Use additional code to identify manifestation, as:
any associated ulceration (707.10-707.9)
diabetic bone changes (731.8)

§ ✓5th **249.9 Secondary diabetes mellitus with unspecified**
[0-1] **complication**

✓4th **250 Diabetes mellitus**

EXCLUDES gestational diabetes (648.8)
hyperglycemia NOS (790.29)
neonatal diabetes mellitus (775.1)
nonclinical diabetes (790.29)
secondary diabetes (249.0-249.9)

[handwritten left margin: When the type of diabetes is not documented but does indicate the patient uses insulin the default type is 2.]

[handwritten right margin: Do not code V58.67 if this is a new onset with initial insulin therapy]

The following fifth-digit subclassification is for use with category 250:

0 type II or unspecified type, not state as uncontrolled
Fifth-digit 0 is for use for type II patients, even if the patient requires insulin
Use additional code, if applicable, for associated long-term (current) insulin use (V58.67)

1 type I [juvenile type], not stated as uncontrolled

2 type II or unspecified type, uncontrolled
Fifth-digit 2 is for use for type II patients, even if the patient requires insulin
Use additional code, if applicable, for associated long-term (current) insulin use (V58.67)

3 type I [juvenile type], uncontrolled

[handwritten left margin: Do not code "uncontrolled" if documentation states "poorly controlled"]

DEF: Diabetes mellitus: Inability to metabolize carbohydrates, proteins, and fats due to insufficient secretion of insulin. Symptoms may be unremarkable, with long-term complications, involving kidneys, nerves, blood vessels, and eyes.

DEF: Uncontrolled diabetes: A nonspecific term indicating that the current treatment regimen does not keep the blood sugar level of a patient within acceptable levels.

AHA: 4Q, '04, 56; 2Q, '04, 17; 2Q, '02, 13; 2Q,'01, 16; 2Q,'98, 15; 4Q, '97, 32; 2Q, '97, 14; 3Q, '96, 5; 4Q, '93, 19; 2Q, '92, 5; 3Q, '91, 3; 2Q, '90, 22; N-D, '85, 11

TIP: Use of insulin does not ensure type I DM; if patient is on routine insulin, assign also V58.67 Long-term (current) use of insulin.

§7 ✓5th **250.0 Diabetes mellitus without mention of complication**
[0-3]
Diabetes mellitus without mention of complication or manifestation classifiable to 250.1-250.9
Diabetes (mellitus) NOS

AHA: 1Q, '06, 14; 4Q, '97, 32; 3Q, '91, 3, 12; N-D, '85, 11; **For code 250.00:** 1Q, '05, 15; 4Q, '04, 55; 4Q, '03, 105, 108; 2Q, '03, 16; 1Q, '02, 7, 11; **For code 250.01:** 4Q, '04, 55; 4Q, '03, 110; 2Q, '03, 6; **For code 250.02:** 1Q, '03, 5

E11.9 Type 2 diabetes mellitus w/o complications `I-10`

§ ✓5th **250.1 Diabetes with ketoacidosis** `MCC`
[0-3]
Diabetic:
acidosis ⎫
ketosis ⎬ without mention of coma

DEF: Diabetic hyperglycemic crisis causing ketone presence in body fluids.
CC Excl: For code 250.10: 249.00-251.3, 259.8-259.9;
For code 250.11-250.13: 249.00-251.3, 259.50-259.9
AHA: 3Q, '91, 6; **For code 250.11:** 2Q, '06, 19-20; 4Q, '03, 82; **For code 250.13:** 2Q, '06, 19-20

E10.10 Type 1 diabetes mellitus w/ketoacidosis w/o coma `I-10`

§ ✓5th **250.2 Diabetes with hyperosmolarity** `MCC`
[0-3]
Hyperosmolar (nonketotic) coma
CC Excl: For code 250.20: 249.00-251.3, 259.8-259.9;
For code 250.21-250.23: 249.00-251.3, 259.50-259.9
AHA: 4Q, '93, 19; 3Q, '91, 7

§ ✓5th **250.3 Diabetes with other coma** `MCC`
[0-3]
Diabetic coma (with ketoacidosis)
Diabetic hypoglycemic coma
Insulin coma NOS

EXCLUDES diabetes with hyperosmolar coma (250.2)

DEF: Coma (not hyperosmolar) caused by hyperglycemia or hypoglycemia as complication of diabetes.
CC Excl: For code 250.30: 249.00-251.3, 259.8-259.9; **For code 250.31-250.33:** 249.00-251.3, 259.50-259.9
AHA: 3Q, '91, 7, 12

§ ✓5th **250.4 Diabetes with renal manifestations**
[0-3]
Use additional code to identify manifestation, as:
chronic kidney disease (585.1-585.9)
diabetic:
nephropathy NOS (583.81)
nephrosis (581.81)
intercapillary glomerulosclerosis (581.81)
Kimmelstiel-Wilson syndrome (581.81)

AHA: 3Q, '91, 8, 12; S-O, '87, 9; S-O, '84, 3; **For code 250.40:** 1Q, '03, 20

E11.22 Type 2 diabetes mellitus w/diabetic ckd `I-10`

§ ✓5th **250.5 Diabetes with ophthalmic manifestations**
[0-3]
Use additional code to identify manifestation, as:
diabetic:
blindness (369.00-369.9)
cataract (366.41)
glaucoma (365.44)
macular edema (362.07)
retinal edema (362.07)
retinopathy (362.01-362.07)

AHA: 4Q, '05, 65; 3Q, '91, 8; S-O, '85, 11; **For code 250.50:** 4Q, '05, 67

E10.36 Type 1 diabetes mellitus with diabetic cataract `I-10`

§ ✓5th **250.6 Diabetes with neurological manifestations**
[0-3]
Use additional code to identify manifestation, as:
diabetic:
amyotrophy (353.5)
gastroparalysis (536.3)
gastroparesis (536.3)
mononeuropathy (354.0-355.9)
neurogenic arthropathy (713.5)
peripheral autonomic neuropathy (337.1)
polyneuropathy (357.2)

AHA: ▶2Q, '09, 13, 15;◄ 3Q, '08, 5; 2Q, '93, 6; 2Q, '92, 15; 3Q, '91, 9; N-D, '84, 9; **For code 250.60:** 4Q, '03, 105; **For code 250.61:** 2Q, '04, 7

E11.40 Type 2 diabetes mellitus w/diab neuropathy uns `I-10`

§ ✓5th **250.7 Diabetes with peripheral circulatory disorders**
[0-3]
Use additional code to identify manifestation, as:
diabetic:
gangrene (785.4)
peripheral angiopathy (443.81)

DEF: Blood vessel damage or disease, usually in the feet, legs, or hands, as a complication of diabetes.
AHA: 1Q, '96, 10; 3Q, '94, 5; 2Q, '94, 17; 3Q, '91, 10, 12; 3Q, '90, 15; **For code 250.70:** 1Q, '04, 14

E10.51 Type 1 DM w/diab periph angiopathy w/o gangrene `I-10`

---

7   Questionable admission = 0
§   Requires fifth digit. Valid digits are in [brackets] under each code. See appropriate category for codes and definitions.

✓4th/✓5th Additional Digit Required   Unacceptable PDx   Manifestation Code   Hospital Acquired Condition   ▶◀ Revised Text   ● New Code   ▲ Revised Code Title

Endocrine, Nutritional and Metabolic, Immunity

250.8–252.1

§ ✓5th **250.8 Diabetes with other specified manifestations**
[0-3]   Diabetic hypoglycemia NOS
     Hypoglycemic shock NOS

     Use additional code to identify manifestation, as:
         any associated ulceration (707.10-707.9)
         diabetic bone changes (731.8)

     AHA: 4Q, '00, 44; 4Q, '97, 43; 2Q, '97, 16; 4Q, '93, 20; 3Q, '91, 10;
     For code 250.80: 1Q, '04, 14

     TIP: Assign for diabetic osteomyelitis, along with code 731.8
     and the appropriate code from category 730.

     E11.610 Type 2 DM with diabetic neuropathic arthropathy `I-10`

§ ✓5th **250.9 Diabetes with unspecified complication**
[0-3]   **AHA:** 2Q, '92, 15; 3Q, '91, 7, 12

     TIP: Do not assign with any other code in category 250.

     E10.8 Type 1 diabetes mellitus with unspecified comp   `I-10`

✓4th **251 Other disorders of pancreatic internal secretion**

     251.0 Hypoglycemic coma   `CC`
         Iatrogenic hyperinsulinism
         Non-diabetic insulin coma

         Use additional E code to identify cause, if drug-induced

         EXCLUDES *hypoglycemic coma in diabetes mellitus
                (249.3, 250.3)*

         DEF: Coma induced by low blood sugar in non-diabetic
         patient.
         CC Excl: 2249.00-251.3, 259.50-259.9
         AHA: M-A, '85, 8

     251.1 Other specified hypoglycemia
         Hyperinsulinism:
             NOS
             ectopic
             functional
         Hyperplasia of pancreatic
             islet beta cells NOS

         Use additional E code to identify cause, if drug-induced.

         EXCLUDES *hypoglycemia:
                in diabetes mellitus (249.8, 250.8)
                in infant of diabetic mother (775.0)
             hypoglycemic coma (251.0)
             neonatal hypoglycemia (775.6)*

         DEF: Excessive production of insulin by the pancreas;
         associated with obesity and insulin-producing tumors.
         AHA: 1Q, '03, 10

     251.2 Hypoglycemia, unspecified
         Hypoglycemia: Hypoglycemia:
             NOS   spontaneous
             reactive

         EXCLUDES *hypoglycemia:
                with coma (251.0)
                in diabetes mellitus (249.8, 250.8)
                leucine-induced (270.3)*

         AHA: M-A, '85, 8

         E16.2 Hypoglycemia unspecified   `I-10`

     251.3 Postsurgical hypoinsulinemia   `CC`
         Hypoinsulinemia following complete or partial
             pancreatectomy
         Postpancreatectomy hyperglycemia

         ▶Use additional code to identify (any associated):
             acquired absence of pancreas (V45.79)
             insulin use (V58.67)
             secondary diabetes mellitus (249.00-249.91)◄

         EXCLUDES ▶*transient hyperglycemia post procedure
                (790.29)
             transient hypoglycemia post procedure
                (251.2)◄*

         CC Excl: See code: 251.0
         AHA: 3Q, '91, 6

     251.4 Abnormality of secretion of glucagon
         Hyperplasia of pancreatic islet alpha cells with glucagon
             excess

         DEF: Production malfunction of a pancreatic hormone
         secreted by cells of the islets of Langerhans.

     251.5 Abnormality of secretion of gastrin
         Hyperplasia of pancreatic alpha cells with gastrin excess
         Zollinger-Ellison syndrome

     **251.8 Other specified disorders of pancreatic internal
         secretion**
         AHA: 2Q, '98, 15; 3Q, '91, 6

         E16.8 Oth spec d/o of pancreatic internal secretion   `I-10`

     251.9 Unspecified disorder of pancreatic internal secretion
         Islet cell hyperplasia NOS

✓4th **252 Disorders of parathyroid gland**
     EXCLUDES *hungry bone syndrome (275.5)*

✓5th **252.0 Hyperparathyroidism**
     EXCLUDES *ectopic hyperparathyroidism (259.3)*

     DEF: Abnormally high secretion of parathyroid hormones
     causing bone deterioration, reduced renal function, kidney
     stones.

     252.00 Hyperparathyroidism, unspecified

         E21.3 Hyperparathyroidism unspecified   `I-10`

     252.01 Primary hyperparathyroidism
         Hyperplasia of parathyroid

         DEF: Parathyroid dysfunction commonly caused by
         hyperplasia of two or more glands; characteristic
         hypercalcemia and increased parathyroid hormone
         levels.

     252.02 Secondary hyperparathyroidism, non-renal
         EXCLUDES *secondary hyperparathyroidism (of
                renal origin) (588.81)*

         DEF: Underlying disease of nonrenal origin
         decreases blood levels of calcium causing the
         parathyroid to release increased levels of
         parathyroid hormone; parathyroid hormone levels
         return to normal once underlying condition is
         treated and blood calcium levels are normal.
         AHA: 4Q, '04, 57-59

     252.08 Other hyperparathyroidism
         Tertiary hyperparathyroidism

         DEF: Tertiary hyperparathyroidism: chronic
         secondary hyperparathyroidism with adenomatous
         parathyroid causing irreversible abnormal
         production of parathyroid hormone (PTH); PTH
         remains high after the serum calcium levels are
         brought under control.

     252.1 Hypoparathyroidism
         Parathyroiditis (autoimmune)
         Tetany:
             parathyroid
             parathyroprival

         EXCLUDES *pseudohypoparathyroidism (275.4)
                pseudopseudohypoparathyroidism (275.4)
                tetany NOS (781.7)
                transitory neonatal hypoparathyroidism
                (775.4)*

         DEF: Abnormally low secretion of parathyroid hormones
         which causes decreased calcium and increased phosphorus
         in the blood. Resulting in muscle cramps, tetany, urinary
         frequency and cataracts.

Dorsal View of Parathyroid Glands

Pharynx   Thyroid gland

Parathyroid glands

Trachea   Esophagus

Parathyroid glands
Parathyroid hormone (PTH)
Calcium in bones   Calcium in blood

---

§   Requires fifth digit. Valid digits are in [brackets] under each code. See category 250 for codes and definitions.

`N` Newborn Age: 0   `P` Pediatric Age: 0-17   `M` Maternity Age: 12-55   `A` Adult Age: 15-124   `MCC` Major CC Condition   `CC` CC Condition   `HIV` HIV Related Dx

252.8 Other specified disorders of parathyroid gland
Cyst } of parathyroid
Hemorrhage

252.9 Unspecified disorder of parathyroid gland

√4th **253 Disorders of the pituitary gland and its hypothalamic control**

INCLUDES the listed conditions whether the disorder is in the pituitary or the hypothalamus

EXCLUDES *Cushing's syndrome (255.0)*

253.0 Acromegaly and gigantism
Overproduction of growth hormone

DEF: Acromegaly: chronic, middle age condition; caused by hypersecretion of the pituitary growth hormone; enlarged parts of skeleton, especially the nose, ears, jaws, fingers and toes.

DEF: Gigantism: pituitary gigantism caused by excess growth of short flat bones; men may grow 78 to 80 inches tall.

253.1 Other and unspecified anterior pituitary hyperfunction   `CC`
Forbes-Albright syndrome

EXCLUDES *overproduction of:*
ACTH (255.3)
thyroid-stimulating hormone [TSH] (242.8)

DEF: Spontaneous galactorrhea-amenorrhea syndrome unrelated to pregnancy; usually related to presence of pituitary tumor.
CC Excl: 253.1, 253.4, 253.6
AHA: J-A, '85, 9

253.2 Panhypopituitarism   `CC`
Cachexia, pituitary   Pituitary insufficiency NOS
Necrosis of pituitary   Sheehan's syndrome
(postpartum)   Simmonds' disease

EXCLUDES *iatrogenic hypopituitarism (253.7)*

DEF: Damage to or absence of pituitary gland leading to impaired sexual function, weight loss, fatigue, bradycardia, hypotension, pallor, depression, and impaired growth in children; called Simmonds' disease if cachexia is prominent.
CC Excl: 253.0-253.9, 259.50-259.9

253.3 Pituitary dwarfism
Isolated deficiency of (human) growth hormone [HGH]
Lorain-Levi dwarfism

DEF: Dwarfism with infantile physical characteristics due to abnormally low secretion of growth hormone and gonadotropin deficiency.

253.4 Other anterior pituitary disorders
Isolated or partial deficiency of an anterior pituitary hormone, other than growth hormone
Prolactin deficiency
AHA: J-A, '85, 9

253.5 Diabetes insipidus   `CC`
Vasopressin deficiency

EXCLUDES *nephrogenic diabetes insipidus (588.1)*

DEF: Metabolic disorder causing insufficient antidiuretic hormone release; symptoms include frequent urination, thirst, ravenous hunger, loss of weight, fatigue.
CC Excl: 253.1-253.2, 253.4-253.9, 259.50-259.9

253.6 Other disorders of neurohypophysis   `CC`
Syndrome of inappropriate secretion of antidiuretic hormone [ADH]

EXCLUDES *ectopic antidiuretic hormone secretion (259.3)*
CC Excl: 253.0-253.9, 259.8-259.9
E22.2 Synd inappropriate secrectn antidiuretic hormone   `I-10`

253.7 Iatrogenic pituitary disorders
Hypopituitarism:
hormone-induced
hypophysectomy-induced
postablative
radiotherapy-induced

Use additional E code to identify cause

DEF: Pituitary dysfunction that results from drug therapy, radiation therapy, or surgery, causing mild to severe symptoms.

253.8 Other disorders of the pituitary and other syndromes of diencephalohypophyseal origin
Abscess of pituitary
Adiposogenital dystrophy
Cyst of Rathke's pouch
Fröhlich's syndrome

EXCLUDES *craniopharyngioma (237.0)*

253.9 Unspecified
Dyspituitarism

√4th **254 Diseases of thymus gland**

EXCLUDES *aplasia or dysplasia with immunodeficiency (279.2)*
hypoplasia with immunodeficiency (279.2)
myasthenia gravis (358.00-358.01)

254.0 Persistent hyperplasia of thymus
Hypertrophy of thymus

DEF: Continued abnormal growth of the twin lymphoid lobes that produce T lymphocytes.

254.1 Abscess of thymus   `CC`
CC Excl: 254.0-254.9, 259.50-259.9

254.8 Other specified diseases of thymus gland
Astrophy } of thymus
Cyst

EXCLUDES *thymoma (212.6)*

254.9 Unspecified disease of thymus gland

√4th **255 Disorders of adrenal glands**

INCLUDES the listed conditions whether the basic disorder is in the adrenals or is pituitary-induced

255.0 Cushing's syndrome   `CC`
Adrenal hyperplasia due to excess ACTH
Cushing's syndrome:
NOS
iatrogenic
idiopathic
pituitary-dependent
Ectopic ACTH syndrome
Iatrogenic syndrome of excess cortisol
Overproduction of cortisol

Use additional E code to identify cause, if drug-induced

EXCLUDES *congenital adrenal hyperplasia (255.2)*

DEF: Due to adrenal cortisol oversecretion or glucocorticoid medications; may cause excess fatty tissue of the face, neck and body; osteoporosis and curvature of spine, hypertension, diabetes mellitus, female genitourinary problems, male impotence, degeneration of muscle tissues, weakness.
CC Excl: 255.0-255.2, 259.50-259.9

√5th **255.1 Hyperaldosteronism**

DEF: Oversecretion of aldosterone causing fluid retention, hypertension.
AHA: 4Q, '03, 48

255.10 Hyperaldosteronism, unspecified
Aldosteronism NOS
Primary aldosteronism, unspecified

EXCLUDES *Conn's syndrome (255.12)*

255.11 Glucocorticoid-remediable aldosteronism
Familial aldosteronism type I

EXCLUDES *Conn's syndrome (255.12)*

DEF: Rare autosomal dominant familial form of primary aldosteronism in which the secretion of aldosterone is under the influence of adrenocortiotrophic hormone (ACTH) rather than the renin-angiotensin mechanism; moderate hypersecretion of aldosterone and suppressed plasma renin activity rapidly reversed by administration of glucosteroids; symptoms include hypertension and mild hypokalemia.

255.12 Conn's syndrome

DEF: A type of primary aldosteronism caused by an adenoma of the glomerulosa cells in the adrenal cortex; presence of hypertension.

√4th √5th Additional Digit Required   Unacceptable PDx   Manifestation Code   Hospital Acquired Condition   ▶◀ Revised Text   ● New Code   ▲ Revised Code Title

2010 ICD-9-CM   **Volume 1 – 65**

Endocrine, Nutritional and Metabolic, Immunity

255.13–257.2

255.13 Bartter's syndrome

> **DEF:** A cluster of symptoms caused by a defect in the ability of the kidney to reabsorb potassium; signs include alkalosis (hypokalemic alkalosis), increased aldosterone, increased plasma renin, and normal blood pressure; symptoms include muscle cramping, weakness, constipation, frequency of urination, and failure to grow; also known as urinary potassium wasting or juxtaglomerular cell hyperplasia.

255.14 Other secondary aldosteronism

> **AHA:** 3Q, '06, 24

255.2 Adrenogenital disorders

> Achard-Thiers syndrome
> Adrenogenital syndromes, virilizing or feminizing, whether acquired or associated with congenital adrenal hyperplasia consequent on inborn enzyme defects in hormone synthesis
> Congenital adrenal hyperplasia
> Female adrenal pseudohermaphroditism
> Male:
>> macrogenitosomia praecox
>> sexual precocity with adrenal hyperplasia
> Virilization (female) (suprarenal)
>
> **EXCLUDES** adrenal hyperplasia due to excess ACTH (255.0)
>> isosexual virilization (256.4)

255.3 Other corticoadrenal overactivity `CC`

> Acquired benign adrenal androgenic overactivity
> Overproduction of ACTH
> **CC Excl:** 017.60-017.66, 017.90-017.96, 255.3-255.9, 259.50-259.9

✓5ᵗʰ **255.4 Corticoadrenal insufficiency**

> **EXCLUDES** tuberculous Addison's disease (017.6)
>
> **DEF:** Underproduction of adrenal hormones causing low blood pressure.
> **AHA:** 4Q, '07, 68; 3Q, '06, 24

> **255.41 Glucocorticoid deficiency** `CC`
>> Addisonian crisis
>> Addison's disease NOS
>> Adrenal atrophy (autoimmune)
>> Adrenal calcification
>> Adrenal crisis
>> Adrenal hemorrhage
>> Adrenal infarction
>> Adrenal insufficiency NOS
>> Combined glucocorticoid and mineralocorticoid deficiency
>> Corticoadrenal insufficiency NOS
>>
>> **DEF:** Decreased function of the adrenal cortex resulting in insufficient production of glucocorticoid, the hormone regulating carbohydrate, fat, and protein metabolism; manifestations: hyponatremia, hyperpigmentation, orthostatic hypotension, anemia, loss of appetite, and malaise.
>> **CC Excl:** See code: 255.3
>> **AHA:** 4Q, '07, 68, 69
>>
>> **E27.1** Primary adrenocortical insufficiency `I-10`

> **255.42 Mineralocorticoid deficiency** `CC`
>> Hypoaldosteronism
>>
>> **EXCLUDES** combined glucocorticoid and mineralocorticoid deficiency (255.41)
>>
>> **DEF:** Decreased function of the adrenal cortex resulting in insufficient production of mineralocorticoid, which regulates electrolyte and water balance; manifestations: hyponatremia, hyperkalemia, and mild acidosis.
>> **CC Excl:** See code: 255.3

255.5 Other adrenal hypofunction `CC`

> Adrenal medullary insufficiency
>
> **EXCLUDES** Waterhouse-Friderichsen syndrome (meningococcal) (036.3)
>
> **CC Excl:** See code: 255.3

255.6 Medulloadrenal hyperfunction `CC`

> Catecholamine secretion by pheochromocytoma
> **CC Excl:** See code 255.3

255.8 Other specified disorders of adrenal glands

> Abnormality of cortisol-binding globulin

255.9 Unspecified disorder of adrenal glands

✓4ᵗʰ **256 Ovarian dysfunction**

> **AHA:** 4Q, '00, 51

256.0 Hyperestrogenism ♀

> **DEF:** Excess secretion of estrogen by the ovaries; characterized by ovaries containing multiple follicular cysts filled with serous fluid.

256.1 Other ovarian hyperfunction ♀

> Hypersecretion of ovarian androgens
> **AHA:** 3Q, '95, 15

256.2 Postablative ovarian failure ♀

> Ovarian failure:
>> iatrogenic
>> postirradiation
>> postsurgical
> Use additional code for states associated with artificial menopause (627.4)
>
> **EXCLUDES** acquired absence of ovary (V45.77)
>> asymptomatic age-related (natural) postmenopausal status (V49.81)
>
> **DEF:** Failed ovarian function after medical or surgical intervention.
> **AHA:** 2Q, '02, 12

✓5ᵗʰ **256.3 Other ovarian failure**

> Use additional code for states associated with natural menopause (627.2)
>
> **EXCLUDES** asymptomatic age-related (natural) postmenopausal status (V49.81)
>
> **AHA:** 4Q, '01, 41

> **256.31 Premature menopause** Ⓐ♀
>> **DEF:** Permanent cessation of ovarian function before the age of 40 occuring naturally of unknown cause.

> **256.39 Other ovarian failure** ♀
>> Delayed menarche
>> Ovarian hypofunction
>> Primary ovarian failure NOS

256.4 Polycystic ovaries ♀

> Isosexual virilization
> Stein-Leventhal syndrome
> **DEF:** Multiple serous filled cysts of ovary; symptoms of infertility, hirsutism, oligomenorrhea or amenorrhea.
> **E28.2** Polycystic ovarian syndrome `I-10`

256.8 Other ovarian dysfunction ♀

256.9 Unspecified ovarian dysfunction ♀

✓4ᵗʰ **257 Testicular dysfunction**

257.0 Testicular hyperfunction ♂

> Hypersecretion of testicular hormones

257.1 Postablative testicular hypofunction ♂

> Testicular hypofunction:
>> iatrogenic
>> postirradiation
>> postsurgical

257.2 Other testicular hypofunction

> Defective biosynthesis of testicular androgen
> Eunuchoidism:
>> NOS
>> hypogonadotropic
> Failure:
>> Leydig's cell, adult
>> seminiferous tubule, adult
> Testicular hypogonadism
>
> **EXCLUDES** azoospermia (606.0)

Ⓝ Newborn Age: 0   Ⓟ Pediatric Age: 0-17   Ⓜ Maternity Age: 12-55   Ⓐ Adult Age: 15-124   `MCC` Major CC Condition   `CC` CC Condition   `HIV` HIV Related Dx

257.8 Other testicular dysfunction
> EXCLUDES *androgen insensitivity syndromes (259.50-259.52)*

257.9 Unspecified testicular dysfunction ♂

✓4th **258 Polyglandular dysfunction and related disorders**

✓5th **258.0 Polyglandular activity in multiple endocrine adenomatosis**
Multiple endocrine neoplasia [MEN] syndromes
Use additional codes to identify any malignancies and other conditions associated with the syndromes
AHA: 4Q, '07, 70

[handwritten: When MEN syndrome is associated with neuroendocrine tumors, code first the MEN syndrome.]

258.01 Multiple endocrine neoplasia [MEN] type I
Wermer's syndrome
DEF: Wermer's syndrome: A rare hereditary condition characterized by the presence of adenomas or hyperplasia in more than one endocrine gland causing premature aging.
AHA: ▶4Q, '08, 86, 89;◀ 4Q, '07, 70, 72

258.02 Multiple endocrine neoplasia [MEN] type IIA
Sipple's syndrome
DEF: Sipple's syndrome: A hereditary disorder caused by a defect in the RET gene causing overactivity of the thyroid, adrenal, and parathyroid glands, resulting in adrenal pheochromocytoma and thyroid medullary carcinoma.

258.03 Multiple endocrine neoplasia [MEN] type IIB

258.1 Other combinations of endocrine dysfunction
Lloyd's syndrome
Schmidt's syndrome

258.8 Other specified polyglandular dysfunction

258.9 Polyglandular dysfunction, unspecified

✓4th **259 Other endocrine disorders**

259.0 Delay in sexual development and puberty, not elsewhere classified
Delayed puberty

259.1 Precocious sexual development and puberty, not elsewhere classified P
Sexual precocity: Sexual precocity:
   NOS   cryptogenic
   constitutional   idiopathic

259.2 Carcinoid syndrome CC
Hormone secretion by carcinoid tumors
DEF: Presence of carcinoid tumors that spread to liver; characterized by cyanotic flushing of skin, diarrhea, bronchospasm, acquired tricuspid and pulmonary stenosis, sudden drops in blood pressure, edema, ascites.
CC Excl: 259.2-259.3, 259.50-259.9
AHA: ▶4Q, '08, 85-86, 89◀

259.3 Ectopic hormone secretion, not elsewhere classified
Ectopic:
   antidiuretic hormone secretion [ADH]
   hyperparathyroidism
> EXCLUDES *ectopic ACTH syndrome (255.0)*
AHA: N-D, '85, 4

259.4 Dwarfism, not elsewhere classified
Dwarfism:
   NOS
   constitutional
> EXCLUDES *dwarfism:*
>   *achondroplastic (756.4)*
>   *intrauterine (759.7)*
>   *nutritional (263.2)*
>   *pituitary (253.3)*
>   *renal (588.0)*
>   *progeria (259.8)*

✓5th **259.5 Androgen insensitivity syndrome**
DEF: X chromosome abnormality that prohibits the body from recognizing androgen; XY genotype with ambiguous genitalia.
AHA: ▶4Q, '08, 95-96;◀ 4Q, '05, 53

259.50 Androgen insensitivity, unspecified

259.51 Androgen insensitivity syndrome
Complete androgen insensitivity
de Quervain's syndrome
Goldberg-Maxwell Syndrome

259.52 Partial androgen insensitivity
Partial androgen insensitivity syndrome
Reifenstein syndrome

259.8 Other specified endocrine disorders
Pineal gland dysfunction
Progeria
Werner's syndrome

259.9 Unspecified endocrine disorder
Disturbance:
   endocrine NOS
   hormone NOS
Infantilism NOS

NUTRITIONAL DEFICIENCIES (260-269)

> EXCLUDES *deficiency anemias (280.0-281.9)*

TIP: Assign first a code for the underlying condition (e.g., anorexia nervosa) if specified.

260 Kwashiorkor MCC
Nutritional edema with dyspigmentation of skin and hair
DEF: Syndrome, particularly of children; excessive carbohydrate with inadequate protein intake, inhibited growth potential, anomalies in skin and hair pigmentation, edema and liver disease.
CC Excl: 260-263.9
E40 Kwashiorkor   I-10

261 Nutritional marasmus MCC
Nutritional atrophy
Severe calorie deficiency
Severe malnutrition NOS
DEF: Protein-calorie malabsorption or malnutrition in children; characterized by tissue wasting, dehydration, and subcutaneous fat depletion; may occur with infectious disease; also called infantile atrophy.
CC Excl: See code 260
AHA: 4Q, '07, 97; 3Q, '06, 14; 2Q, '06, 12
E41 Nutritional marasmus   I-10

262 Other severe, protein-calorie malnutrition MCC
Nutritional edema without mention of dyspigmentation of skin and hair
CC Excl: See code 260
AHA: 4Q, '92, 24; J-A, '85, 12

✓4th **263 Other and unspecified protein-calorie malnutrition**
AHA: 4Q, '92, 24

263.0 Malnutrition of moderate degree
DEF: Malnutrition characterized by biochemical changes in electrolytes, lipids, blood plasma.
AHA: J-A, '85, 1

263.1 Malnutrition of mild degree
AHA: J-A, '85, 1

263.2 Arrested development following protein-calorie malnutrition CC
Nutritional dwarfism
Physical retardation due to malnutrition
CC Excl: See code 260

263.8 Other protein-calorie malnutrition CC
CC Excl: See code 260

263.9 Unspecified protein-calorie malnutrition CC
Dystrophy due to malnutrition
Malnutrition (calorie) NOS
> EXCLUDES *nutritional deficiency NOS (269.9)*
CC Excl: See code 260
AHA: 4Q, '03, 109; N-D, '84, 19
E46 Unspecified protein-calorie malnutrition   I-10

✓4th **264 Vitamin A deficiency**

264.0 With conjunctival xerosis
DEF: Vitamin A deficiency with conjunctival dryness.

✓4th ✓5th Additional Digit Required   Unacceptable PDx   Manifestation Code   Hospital Acquired Condition   ▶◀ Revised Text   ● New Code   ▲ Revised Code Title

2010 ICD-9-CM   **February 2009 · Volume 1 – 67**

264.1   **With conjunctival xerosis and Bitot's spot**
Bitot's spot in the young child
DEF: Vitamin A deficiency with conjunctival dryness, superficial spots of keratinized epithelium.

264.2   **With corneal xerosis**
DEF: Vitamin A deficiency with corneal dryness.

264.3   **With corneal ulceration and xerosis**
DEF: Vitamin A deficiency with corneal dryness, epithelial ulceration.

264.4   **With keratomalacia**
DEF: Vitamin A deficiency creating corneal dryness; progresses to corneal insensitivity, softness, necrosis; usually bilateral.

264.5   **With night blindness**
DEF: Vitamin A deficiency causing vision failure in dim light.

264.6   **With xerophthalmic scars of cornea**
DEF: Vitamin A deficiency with corneal scars from dryness.

264.7   **Other ocular manifestations of vitamin A deficiency**
Xerophthalmia due to vitamin A deficiency

264.8   **Other manifestations of vitamin A deficiency**
Follicular keratosis
Xeroderma } due to vitamin A deficiency

264.9   **Unspecified vitamin A deficiency**
Hypovitaminosis A NOS

✓4th 265   **Thiamine and niacin deficiency states**

265.0   **Beriberi**   [CC]
DEF: Inadequate vitamin B_1 (thiamine) intake, affects heart and peripheral nerves; individual may become edematous and develop cardiac disease due to the excess fluid; affects alcoholics and people with a diet of excessive polished rice.
CC Excl: 265.0-266.9, 269.1-269.9

265.1   **Other and unspecified manifestations of thiamine deficiency**   [CC]
Other vitamin B_1 deficiency states
CC Excl: See code: 265.0

265.2   **Pellagra**
Deficiency:
    niacin (-tryptophan)
    nicotinamide
    nicotinic acid
    vitamin PP
Pellagra (alcoholic)
DEF: Niacin deficiency causing dermatitis, inflammation of mucous membranes, diarrhea, and psychic disturbances.

✓4th 266   **Deficiency of B-complex components**

266.0   **Ariboflavinosis**   [CC]
Riboflavin [vitamin B_2] deficiency
DEF: Vitamin B_2 (riboflavin) deficiency marked by swollen lips and tongue fissures, corneal vascularization, scaling lesions, and anemia.
CC Excl: See code: 265.0
AHA: S-O, '86, 10

266.1   **Vitamin B_6 deficiency**
Deficiency:
    pyridoxal
    pyridoxamine
    pyridoxine
Vitamin B_6 deficiency syndrome
EXCLUDES   *vitamin B_6-responsive sideroblastic anemia (285.0)*
DEF: Vitamin B_6 deficiency causing skin, lip, and tongue disturbances, peripheral neuropathy; and convulsions in infants.

266.2   **Other B-complex deficiencies**
Deficiency:
    cyanocobalamin
    folic acid
    vitamin B_{12}
EXCLUDES   *combined system disease with anemia (281.0-281.1)*
    deficiency anemias (281.0-281.9)
    subacute degeneration of spinal cord with anemia (281.0-281.1)
E53.8 Deficiency of other specified B group vitamins [I-10]

266.9   **Unspecified vitamin B deficiency**

267   **Ascorbic acid deficiency**
Deficiency of vitamin C
Scurvy
EXCLUDES   *scorbutic anemia (281.8)*
DEF: Vitamin C deficiency causing swollen gums, myalgia, weight loss, and weakness.

✓4th 268   **Vitamin D deficiency**
EXCLUDES   *vitamin D-resistant:*
    osteomalacia (275.3)
    rickets (275.3)

268.0   **Rickets, active**   [CC]
EXCLUDES   *celiac rickets (579.0)*
    renal rickets (588.0)
DEF: Inadequate vitamin D intake, usually in pediatrics, that affects bones most involved with muscular action; may cause nodules on ends and sides of bones; delayed closure of fontanels in infants; symptoms may include muscle soreness, and profuse sweating.
CC Excl: 268.0-269.9

268.1   **Rickets, late effect**
Any condition specified as due to rickets and stated to be a late effect or sequela of rickets
Code first the nature of late effect
DEF: Distorted or demineralized bones as a result of vitamin D deficiency.

268.2   **Osteomalacia, unspecified**
DEF: Softening of bones due to decrease in calcium; marked by pain, tenderness, muscular weakness, anorexia, and weight loss.

268.9   **Unspecified vitamin D deficiency**
Avitaminosis D

✓4th 269   **Other nutritional deficiencies**

269.0   **Deficiency of vitamin K**
EXCLUDES   *deficiency of coagulation factor due to vitamin K deficiency (286.7)*
    vitamin K deficiency of newborn (776.0)

269.1   **Deficiency of other vitamins**
Deficiency:
    vitamin E
    vitamin P

269.2   **Unspecified vitamin deficiency**
Multiple vitamin deficiency NOS

269.3   **Mineral deficiency, not elsewhere classified**
Deficiency:
    calcium, dietary
    iodine
EXCLUDES   *deficiency:*
    calcium NOS (275.4)
    potassium (276.8)
    sodium (276.1)

269.8   **Other nutritional deficiency**
EXCLUDES   *adult failure to thrive (783.7)*
    failure to thrive in childhood (783.41)
    feeding problems (783.3)
    newborn ▶(779.31-779.34)◄

269.9   **Unspecified nutritional deficiency**

[N] Newborn Age: 0   [P] Pediatric Age: 0-17   [M] Maternity Age: 12-55   [A] Adult Age: 15-124   [MCC] Major CC Condition   [CC] CC Condition   [HIV] HIV Related Dx

68 – Volume 1 · October 2009   2010 ICD-9-CM

OTHER METABOLIC AND IMMUNITY DISORDERS (270-279)

Use additional code to identify any associated mental retardation

✓4ᵗʰ 270 Disorders of amino-acid transport and metabolism

> **EXCLUDES** *abnormal findings without manifest disease (790.0-796.9)*
> *disorders of purine and pyrimidine metabolism (277.1-277.2)*
> *gout ▶(274.00-274.9)◀*

270.0 Disturbances of amino-acid transport `CC`
Cystinosis
Cystinuria
Fanconi (-de Toni) (-Debré) syndrome
Glycinuria (renal)
Hartnup disease
CC Excl: 270.0-273.3, 273.8-273.9

270.1 Phenylketonuria [PKU] `CC`
Hyperphenylalaninemia
DEF: Inherited metabolic condition causing excess phenylpyruvic and other acids in urine; results in mental retardation, neurological manifestations, including spasticity and tremors, light pigmentation, eczema, and mousy odor.
CC Excl: See code: 270.0

270.2 Other disturbances of aromatic amino-acid metabolism `CC`
Albinism
Alkaptonuria
Alkaptonuric ochronosis
Disturbances of metabolism of tyrosine and tryptophan
Homogentisic acid defects
Hydroxykynureninuria
Hypertyrosinemia
Indicanuria
Kynureninase defects
Oasthouse urine disease
Ochronosis
Tyrosinosis
Tyrosinuria
Waardenburg syndrome
> **EXCLUDES** *vitamin B$_6$-deficiency syndrome (266.1)*
CC Excl: See code: 270.0
AHA: 3Q, '99, 20

270.3 Disturbances of branched-chain amino-acid metabolism `CC`
Disturbances of metabolism of leucine, isoleucine, and valine
Hypervalinemia
Intermittent branched-chain ketonuria
Leucine-induced hypoglycemia
Leucinosis
Maple syrup urine disease
CC Excl: See code: 270.0
AHA: 3Q, '00, 8

270.4 Disturbances of sulphur-bearing amino-acid metabolism `CC`
Cystathioninemia
Cystathioninuria
Disturbances of metabolism of methionine, homocystine, and cystathionine
Homocystinuria
Hypermethioninemia
Methioninemia
CC Excl: See code: 270.0
AHA: 2Q, '07, 7;1Q, '04, 6

270.5 Disturbances of histidine metabolism `CC`
Carnosinemia
Histidinemia
Hyperhistidinemia
Imidazole aminoaciduria
CC Excl: See code: 270.0

270.6 Disorders of urea cycle metabolism `CC`
Argininosuccinic aciduria
Citrullinemia
Disorders of metabolism of ornithine, citrulline, argininosuccinic acid, arginine, and ammonia
Hyperammonemia
Hyperornithinemia
CC Excl: See code: 270.0

270.7 Other disturbances of straight-chain amino-acid metabolism `CC`
Glucoglycinuria
Glycinemia (with methyl-malonic acidemia)
Hyperglycinemia
Hyperlysinemia
Other disturbances of metabolism of glycine, threonine, serine, glutamine, and lysine
Pipecolic acidemia
Saccharopinuria
CC Excl: See code: 270.0
AHA: 3Q, '00, 8

270.8 Other specified disorders of amino-acid metabolism `CC`
Alaninemia   Iminoacidopathy
Ethanolaminuria   Prolinemia
Glycoprolinuria   Prolinuria
Hydroxyprolinemia   Sarcosinemia
Hyperprolinemia
CC Excl: See code: 270.0

270.9 Unspecified disorder of amino-acid metabolism `CC`
CC Excl: See code: 270.0

✓4ᵗʰ 271 Disorders of carbohydrate transport and metabolism

> **EXCLUDES** *abnormality of secretion of glucagon (251.4)*
> *diabetes mellitus (249.0-249.9, 250.0-250.9)*
> *hypoglycemia NOS (251.2)*
> *mucopolysaccharidosis (277.5)*

271.0 Glycogenosis `CC`
Amylopectinosis
Glucose-6-phosphatase deficiency
Glycogen storage disease
McArdle's disease
Pompe's disease
von Gierke's disease
CC Excl: 270.0-273.3, 273.8-273.9
AHA: 1Q, '98, 5

271.1 Galactosemia `CC`
Galactose-1-phosphate uridyl transferase deficiency
Galactosuria
DEF: Any of three genetic disorders due to defective galactose metabolism; symptoms include failure to thrive in infancy, jaundice, liver and spleen damage, cataracts, and mental retardation.
CC Excl: See code: 271.0

271.2 Hereditary fructose intolerance
Essential benign fructosuria
Fructosemia
DEF: Chromosome recessive disorder of carbohydrate metabolism; in infants, occurs after dietary sugar introduced; characterized by enlarged spleen, yellowish cast to skin, and progressive inability to thrive.

271.3 Intestinal disaccharidase deficiencies and disaccharide malabsorption
Intolerance or malabsorption (congenital) (of):
    glucose-galactose
    lactose
    sucrose-isomaltose
E73.9 Lactose intolerance unspecified `I-10`

271.4 Renal glycosuria
Renal diabetes
DEF: Persistent abnormal levels of glucose in urine, with normal blood glucose levels; caused by failure of the renal tubules to reabsorb glucose.

✓4ᵗʰ ✓5ᵗʰ Additional Digit Required   Unacceptable PDx   Manifestation Code   Hospital Acquired Condition   ▶◀ Revised Text   ● New Code   ▲ Revised Code Title

2010 ICD-9-CM   **October 2009 • Volume 1 – 69**

271.8 Other specified disorders of carbohydrate transport and metabolism CC

Essential benign pentosuria
Fucosidosis
Glycolic aciduria
Hyperoxaluria (primary)
Mannosidosis
Oxalosis
Xylosuria
Xylulosuria

CC Excl: See code: 271.0

271.9 Unspecified disorder of carbohydrate transport and metabolism

✓4ᵗʰ **272 Disorders of lipoid metabolism**

EXCLUDES localized cerebral lipidoses (330.1)

272.0 Pure hypercholesterolemia

Familial hypercholesterolemia
Fredrickson Type IIa hyperlipoproteinemia
Hyperbetalipoproteinemia
Hyperlipidemia, Group A
Low-density-lipoid-type [LDL] hyperlipoproteinemia

AHA: 4Q, '05, 71

E78.0 Pure hypercholesterolemia I-10

272.1 Pure hyperglyceridemia

Endogenous hyperglyceridemia
Fredrickson Type IV hyperlipoproteinemia
Hyperlipidemia, Group B
Hyperprebetalipoproteinemia
Hypertriglyceridemia, essential
Very-low-density-lipoid-type [VLDL] hyperlipoproteinemia

272.2 Mixed hyperlipidemia

Broad- or floating-betalipoproteinemia
►Combined hyperlipidemia
Elevated cholesterol with elevated triglycerides NEC◄
Fredrickson Type IIb or III hyperlipoproteinemia
Hypercholesterolemia with endogenous hyperglyceridemia
Hyperbetalipoproteinemia with prebetalipoproteinemia
Tubo-eruptive xanthoma
Xanthoma tuberosum

DEF: Elevated levels of lipoprotein, a complex of fats and proteins, in blood due to inherited metabolic disorder.

272.3 Hyperchylomicronemia

Bürger-Grütz syndrome
Fredrickson type I or V hyperlipoproteinemia
Hyperlipidemia, Group D
Mixed hyperglyceridemia

272.4 Other and unspecified hyperlipidemia

Alpha-lipoproteinemia
Hyperlipidemia NOS
Hyperlipoproteinemia NOS

DEF: Hyperlipoproteinemia: elevated levels of transient chylomicrons in the blood which are a form of lipoproteins that transport dietary cholesterol and triglycerides from the small intestine to the blood.

AHA: 1Q, '05, 17

E78.4 Other hyperlipidemia I-10

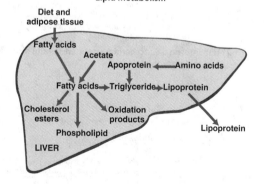

Lipid Metabolism

272.5 Lipoprotein deficiencies

Abetalipoproteinemia
Bassen-Kornzweig syndrome
High-density lipoid deficiency
Hypoalphalipoproteinemia
Hypobetalipoproteinemia (familial)

DEF: Abnormally low levels of lipoprotein, a complex of fats and protein, in the blood.

272.6 Lipodystrophy

Barraquer-Simons disease
Progressive lipodystrophy

Use additional E code to identify cause, if iatrogenic

EXCLUDES intestinal lipodystrophy (040.2)

DEF: Disturbance of fat metabolism resulting in loss of fatty tissue in some areas of the body.

272.7 Lipidoses

Chemically-induced lipidosis
Disease:
Anderson's
Fabry's
Gaucher's
I cell [mucolipidosis I]
lipoid storage NOS
Niemann-Pick
pseudo-Hurler's or mucolipdosis III
triglyceride storage, Type I or II
Wolman's or triglyceride storage, Type III
Mucolipidosis II
Primary familial xanthomatosis

EXCLUDES cerebral lipidoses (330.1)
Tay-Sachs disease (330.1)

DEF: Lysosomal storage diseases marked by an abnormal amount of lipids in reticuloendothelial cells.

272.8 Other disorders of lipoid metabolism

Hoffa's disease or liposynovitis prepatellaris
Launois-Bensaude's lipomatosis
Lipoid dermatoarthritis

272.9 Unspecified disorder of lipoid metabolism

✓4ᵗʰ **273 Disorders of plasma protein metabolism**

EXCLUDES agammaglobulinemia and
hypogammaglobulinemia (279.0-279.2)
coagulation defects (286.0-286.9)
hereditary hemolytic anemias (282.0-282.9)

273.0 Polyclonal hypergammaglobulinemia

Hypergammaglobulinemic purpura:
benign primary
Waldenström's

DEF: Elevated blood levels of gamma globulins, frequently found in patients with chronic infectious diseases.

273.1 Monoclonal paraproteinemia

Benign monoclonal hypergammaglobulinemia [BMH]
Monoclonal gammopathy:
NOS
associated with lymphoplasmacytic dyscrasias
benign
Paraproteinemia:
benign (familial)
secondary to malignant or inflammatory disease

273.2 Other paraproteinemias

Cryoglobulinemic:
purpura
vasculitis
Mixed cryoglobulinemia

AHA: 2Q, '08, 17

273.3 Macroglobulinemia

Macroglobulinemia (idiopathic) (primary)
Waldenström's macroglobulinemia

DEF: Elevated blood levels of macroglobulins (plasma globulins of high weight); characterized by malignant neoplasms of bone marrow, spleen, liver, or lymph nodes; symptoms include weakness, fatigue, bleeding disorders, and vision problems.

N Newborn Age: 0   P Pediatric Age: 0-17   M Maternity Age: 12-55   A Adult Age: 15-124   MCC Major CC Condition   CC CC Condition   HIV HIV Related Dx

70 – Volume 1 · October 2009

2010 ICD-9-CM

tophi - concentrated urate crystal deposits in and around joints and subcutaneous tissue.

273.4 Alpha-1-antitrypsin deficiency
AAT deficiency
DEF: Disorder of plasma protein metabolism that results in a deficiency of Alpha-1-antitrypsin, an acute-phase reactive protein, released into the blood in response to infection or injury to protect tissue against the harmful effect of enzymes.

273.8 Other disorders of plasma protein metabolism
Abnormality of transport protein
Bisalbuminemia
AHA: 2Q, '98, 11
E88.09 Other disorders of plasma-protein metablolis NEC `I-10`

273.9 Unspecified disorder of plasma protein metabolism

✓4ᵗʰ **274 Gout**
  EXCLUDES *lead gout (984.0-984.9)*
  DEF: Purine and pyrimidine metabolic disorders; manifested by hyperuricemia and recurrent acute inflammatory arthritis; monosodium urate or monohydrate crystals may be deposited in and around the joints, leading to joint destruction, and severe crippling.
  AHA: 2Q, '95, 4

✓5ᵗʰ **274.0 Gouty arthropathy**
  274.00 Gouty arthropathy, unspecified
   M10.00 Idiopathic gout unspecified site `I-10`

  274.01 Acute gouty arthropathy
   Acute gout
   Gout attack
   Gout flare
   Podagra

  274.02 Chronic gouty arthropathy without mention of tophus (tophi)
   Chronic gout

  274.03 Chronic gouty arthropathy with tophus (tophi)
   Chronic tophaceous gout *See Above*
   Gout with tophi NOS

✓5ᵗʰ **274.1 Gouty nephropathy**
  274.10 Gouty nephropathy, unspecified
   AHA: N-D, '85, 15

  274.11 Uric acid nephrolithiasis `CC`
   DEF: Sodium urate stones in the kidney.
   CC Excl: 016.00-016.06, 016.30-016.36, 016.90-016.96, 017.90-017.96, 078.6, 098.10, 098.19, 098.30-098.31, 098.89, 112.2, 131.00, 131.8-131.9, 249.40-249.41, 249.80-249.91, 250.40-250.43, 250.80-250.93, 274.10-274.19, 274.89, 580.0-584.9, 586-588.1, 588.9-591, 593.0-593.2, 593.89-593.9, 599.60-599.9

  274.19 Other

✓5ᵗʰ **274.8 Gout with other specified manifestations**
  274.81 Gouty tophi of ear
   DEF: Chalky sodium urate deposit in the ear due to gout; produces chronic inflammation of external ear.

  274.82 Gouty tophi of other sites
   Gouty tophi of heart
   EXCLUDES ▶*gout with tophi NOS (274.03)*
    gouty arthropathy with tophi (274.03)◀

  274.89 Other
   Use additional code to identify manifestations, as:
   gouty:
    iritis (364.11)
    neuritis (357.4)

274.9 Gout, unspecified
  M10.9 Gout unspecified `I-10`

✓4ᵗʰ **275 Disorders of mineral metabolism**
  EXCLUDES *abnormal findings without manifest disease (790.0-796.9)*

275.0 Disorders of iron metabolism
  Bronzed diabetes Pigmentary cirrhosis (of liver)
  Hemochromatosis
  EXCLUDES *anemia:*
   iron deficiency (280.0-280.9)
   sideroblastic (285.0)
  AHA: 2Q, '97, 11
  E83.10 Disorder of iron metablolism unspecified `I-10`

275.1 Disorders of copper metabolism
  Hepatolenticular degeneration
  Wilson's disease

275.2 Disorders of magnesium metabolism
  Hypermagnesemia Hypomagnesemia
  E83.40 Disorders of magnesium metabolism unspecified `I-10`

275.3 Disorders of phosphorus metabolism
  Familial hypophosphatemia
  Hypophosphatasia
  Vitamin D-resistant:
   osteomalacia
   rickets

✓5ᵗʰ **275.4 Disorders of calcium metabolism**
  EXCLUDES *hungry bone syndrome (275.5)*
   parathyroid disorders (252.00-252.9)
   vitamin D deficiency (268.0-268.9)
  AHA: 4Q, '97, 33

  275.40 Unspecified disorder of calcium metabolism

  275.41 Hypocalcemia
   DEF: Abnormally decreased blood calcium level; symptoms include hyperactive deep tendon reflexes, muscle, abdominal cramps, and carpopedal spasm.
   AHA: 3Q, '07, 5
   E83.51 Hypocalcemia `I-10`

  275.42 Hypercalcemia
   DEF: Abnormally increased blood calcium level; symptoms include muscle weakness, fatigue, nausea, depression, and constipation.
   AHA: 4Q, '03, 110

  275.49 Other disorders of calcium metabolism
   Nephrocalcinosis
   Pseudohypoparathyroidism
   Pseudopseudohypoparathyroidism
   DEF: Nephrocalcinosis: calcium phosphate deposits in the tubules of the kidney with resultant renal insufficiency.
   DEF: Pseudohypoparathyroidism: inherited hypoparathyroidism disorder; caused by inadequate response to parathyroid hormone, not hormonal deficiency; includes muscle cramps, tetany, urinary frequency, blurred vision due to cataracts, and dry scaly skin.
   DEF: Pseudopseudohypoparathyroidism: clinical manifestations of hypoparathyroidism without affecting blood calcium levels.

275.5 Hungry bone syndrome
  DEF: Marked and prolonged hypocalcemia; usually involves an extended history of elevated levels of parathyroid hormone, related bone demineralization causing the bone to sequester calcium.
  AHA: 4Q, '08, 96-97

275.8 Other specified disorders of mineral metabolism

275.9 Unspecified disorder of mineral metabolism

✓4ᵗʰ **276 Disorders of fluid, electrolyte, and acid-base balance**
  EXCLUDES *diabetes insipidus (253.5)*
   familial periodic paralysis (359.3)

276.0 Hyperosmolality and/or hypernatremia `CC`
  Sodium [Na] excess
  Sodium [Na] overload
  CC Exd: 276.0-276.9

✓4ᵗʰ Additional Digit Required Unacceptable PDx Manifestation Code Hospital Acquired Condition ▶◀ Revised Text ● New Code ▲ Revised Code Title
✓5ᵗʰ
2010 ICD-9-CM   **October 2009 • Volume 1 – 71**

Endocrine, Nutritional and Metabolic, Immunity

276.1–277.1

276.1 Hyposmolality and/or hyponatremia `CC`

Decreased Sodium level in the blood

Sodium [Na] deficiency

CC Excl: See code: 276.0

E87.1 Hypo-osmolality and hyponatremia `I-10`

276.2 Acidosis `CC`

Acidosis:
NOS
lactic
metabolic
respiratory

EXCLUDES *diabetic acidosis (249.1, 250.1)*

DEF: Disorder involves decrease of pH (hydrogen ion) concentration in blood and cellular tissues; caused by increase in acid and decrease in bicarbonate.

CC Excl: See code 276.0

AHA: J-F, '87, 15

E87.2 Acidosis `I-10`

276.3 Alkalosis `CC`

Alkalosis:
NOS
metabolic
respiratory

DEF: Increased blood alkalinity (base) without relative loss of base in body fluids; caused by increased arterial plasma bicarbonate concentration or loss of carbon dioxide due to hyperventilation.

CC Excl: See code: 276.0

276.4 Mixed acid-base balance disorder `CC`

Hypercapnia with mixed acid-base disorder

CC Excl: See code 276.0

√5th **276.5 Volume depletion**

EXCLUDES *hypovolemic shock:*
postoperative (998.0)
traumatic (958.4)

AHA: 4Q, '05, 54; 2Q, '05, 9; 1Q, '03, 5, 22; 3Q, '02, 21; 4Q, '97, 30; 2Q, '88, 9

276.50 Volume depletion, unspecified

DEF: Depletion of total body water (dehydration) and/or contraction of total intravascular plasma (hypovolemia).

E86.9 Volume depletion unspecified `I-10`

276.51 Dehydration

DEF: Depletion of total body water; blood volume may be normal while fluid is pulled from other tissues.

AHA: 1Q, '08, 10

E86.0 Dehydration `I-10`

276.52 Hypovolemia

Depletion of volume of plasma

DEF: Depletion of volume plasma; depletion of total blood volume.

276.6 Fluid overload

Fluid retention

EXCLUDES *ascites (789.51-789.59)*
localized edema (782.3)

AHA: 3Q, '07, 9; 4Q, '06, 136

276.7 Hyperpotassemia

Hyperkalemia
Potassium [K]:
excess
intoxication
overload

DEF: Elevated blood levels of potassium; symptoms include abnormal EKG readings, weakness; related to defective renal excretion.

AHA: 1Q, '05, 9; 2Q,'01, 12

E87.5 Hyperkalemia `I-10`

276.8 Hypopotassemia

Hypokalemia
Potassium [K] deficiency

DEF: Decreased blood levels of potassium; symptoms include neuromuscular disorders.

E87.6 Hypokalemia `I-10`

276.9 Electrolyte and fluid disorders not elsewhere classified

Electrolyte imbalance
Hyperchloremia
Hypochloremia

EXCLUDES *electrolyte imbalance:*
associated with hyperemesis gravidarum (643.1)
complicating labor and delivery (669.0)
following abortion and ectopic or molar pregnancy (634-638 with .4, 639.4)

AHA: J-F, '87, 15

E87.8 Oth disorders of electrolyte & fluid balance NEC `I-10`

√4th **277 Other and unspecified disorders of metabolism**

√5th **277.0 Cystic fibrosis**

Fibrocystic disease of the pancreas
Mucoviscidosis

DEF: Genetic disorder of infants, children, and young adults marked by exocrine gland dysfunction; characterized by chronic pulmonary disease with excess mucus production, pancreatic deficiency, and high levels of electrolytes in the sweat.

AHA: 4Q, '90, 16; 3Q, '90, 18

TIP: Sequencing of CF is determined by circumstances of admission. If a patient is admitted for CF, sequence the CF first. If admitted for a complication of CF (e.g., pneumothorax, acute bronchitis, or acute cor pulmonale), sequence the complication first.

277.00 Without mention of meconium ileus `CC`

Cystic fibrosis NOS

CC Excl: 277.00-277.09

AHA: 2Q, '03, 12

E84.9 Cystic fibrosis unspecified `I-10`

277.01 With meconium ileus `MCC` `N`

Meconium:
ileus (of newborn)
obstruction of intestine in mucoviscidosis

CC Excl: See code 277.00

277.02 With pulmonary manifestations `MCC`

Cystic fibrosis with pulmonary exacerbation

Use additional code to identify any infectious organism present, such as:
pseudomonas (041.7)

CC Excl: See code 277.00

277.03 With gastrointestinal manifestations `CC`

EXCLUDES *with meconium ileus (277.01)*

CC Excl: See code 277.00

AHA: 4Q, '02, 45

277.09 With other manifestations `CC`

CC Excl: See code 277.00

277.1 Disorders of porphyrin metabolism `CC`

Hematoporphyria
Hematoporphyrinuria
Hereditary coproporphyria
Porphyria
Porphyrinuria
Protocoproporphyria
Protoporphyria
Pyrroloporphyria

CC Excl: 277.1-277.2, 277.4-277.7

`N` Newborn Age: 0   `P` Pediatric Age: 0-17   `M` Maternity Age: 12-55   `A` Adult Age: 15-124   `MCC` Major CC Condition   `CC` CC Condition   `HIV` HIV Related Dx

72 – Volume 1   **2010 ICD-9-CM**

277.2 Other disorders of purine and pyrimidine metabolism `CC`
Hypoxanthine-guanine-phosphoribosyltransferase deficiency [HG-PRT deficiency]
Lesch-Nyhan syndrome
Xanthinuria

EXCLUDES gout ▶(274.00-274.9)◄
orotic aciduric anemia (281.4)

CC Excl: See code: 277.1

√5th **277.3 Amyloidosis**
DEF: Conditions of diverse etiologies characterized by the accumulation of insoluble fibrillar proteins (amyloid) in various organs and tissues of the body, compromising vital functions.
AHA: 1Q, '96, 16

277.30 Amyloidosis, unspecified `CC`
Amyloidosis NOS
CC Excl: 277.30-277.39, 277.7
AHA: 4Q, '06, 66

277.31 Familial Mediterranean fever `CC`
Benign paroxysmal peritonitis
Hereditary amyloid nephropathy
Periodic familial polyserositis
Recurrent polyserositis
DEF: Early-life onset of recurrent attacks characterized by high fevers with pain and inflammation of chest and abdominal cavities, skin and joints, also rash or vasculitis. Etiology unknown, possibly genetic, but may be precipitated by stress, trauma or exertion.
CC Excl: See code: 277.30
AHA: 4Q, '06, 66

277.39 Other amyloidosis `CC`
Hereditary cardiac amyloidosis
Inherited systemic amyloidosis
Neuropathic (Portuguese) (Swiss) amyloidosis
Secondary amyloidosis
CC Excl: See code: 277.30
AHA: ▶1Q, '09, 9;◄2Q, '08, 8; 4Q, '06, 66

277.4 Disorders of bilirubin excretion
Hyperbilirubinemia:
congenital
constitutional
Syndrome:
Crigler-Najjar
Dubin-Johnson
Gilbert's
Rotor's
EXCLUDES hyperbilirubinemias specific to the perinatal period (774.0-774.7)

277.5 Mucopolysaccharidosis `CC`
Gargoylism
Hunter's syndrome
Hurler's syndrome
Lipochondrodystrophy
Maroteaux-Lamy syndrome
Morquio-Brailsford disease
Osteochondrodystrophy
Sanfilippo's syndrome
Scheie's syndrome
DEF: Metabolic disorders evidenced by excretion of various mucopolysaccharides in urine and infiltration of these substances into connective tissue, with resulting defects of bone, cartilage and connective tissue.
CC Excl: 277.1-277.31, 277.4-277.7

277.6 Other deficiencies of circulating enzymes
Hereditary angioedema

277.7 Dysmetabolic syndrome X
Use additional code for associated manifestation, such as:
cardiovascular disease (414.00-414.07)
obesity (278.00-278.01)
DEF: A specific group of metabolic disorders that are related to the state of insulin resistance (decreased cellular response to insulin) without elevated blood sugars; often related to elevated cholesterol and triglycerides, obesity, cardiovascular disease, and high blood pressure.
AHA: 4Q, '01, 42

√5th **277.8 Other specified disorders of metabolism**
AHA: 4Q, '03, 50; 2Q, '01, 18; S-O, '87, 9

277.81 Primary carnitine deficiency

277.82 Carnitine deficiency due to inborn errors of metabolism

277.83 Iatrogenic carnitine deficiency
Carnitine deficiency due to:
hemodialysis
valproic acid therapy

277.84 Other secondary carnitine deficiency

277.85 Disorders of fatty acid oxidation `CC`
Carnitine palmitoyltransferase deficiencies (CPT1, CPT2)
Glutaric aciduria type II (type IIA, IIB, IIC)
Long chain 3-hydroxyacyl CoA dehydrogenase deficiency (LCHAD)
Long chain/very long chain acyl CoA dehydrogenase deficiency (LCAD, VLCAD)
Medium chain acyl CoA dehydrogenase deficiency (MCAD)
Short chain acyl CoA dehydrogenase deficiency (SCAD)
EXCLUDES primary carnitine deficiency (277.81)
CC Excl: 277.81-277.84, 277.86-277.87, 277.89

277.86 Peroxisomal disorders `CC`
Adrenomyeloneuropathy
Neonatal adrenoleukodystrophy
Rhizomelic chrondrodysplasia punctata
X-linked adrenoleukodystrophy
Zellweger syndrome
EXCLUDES infantile Refsum disease (356.3)
CC Excl: 277.4, 277.81-277.85, 277.87, 277.89

277.87 Disorders of mitochondrial metabolism `CC`
Kearns-Sayre syndrome
Mitochondrial Encephalopathy, Lactic Acidosis and Stroke-like episodes (MELAS syndrome)
Mitochondrial Neurogastrointestinal Encephalopathy syndrome (MNGIE)
Myoclonus with Epilepsy and with Ragged Red Fibers (MERRF syndrome)
Neuropathy, Ataxia and Retinitis Pigmentosa (NARP syndrome)
Use additional code for associated conditions
EXCLUDES disorders of pyruvate metabolism (271.8)
Leber's optic atrophy (377.16)
Leigh's subacute necrotizing encephalopathy (330.8)
Reye's syndrome (331.81)
CC Excl: 277.4, 277.81-277.86, 277.89
AHA: 4Q, '04, 62

● **277.88 Tumor lysis syndrome** `MCC`
Spontaneous tumor lysis syndrome
Tumor lysis syndrome following antineoplastic drug therapy
Use additional E code to identify cause, if drug-induced
CC Excl: 277.88, 580.0-581.0, 581.81-581.9, 583.4-584.9

[handwritten note:] Often associated with leukemias and lymphomas. Assign E code when TLS is drug induced (E933.1)

Endocrine, Nutritional and Metabolic, Immunity

277.89–279.49

277.89 Other specified disorders of metabolism `CC`
Hand-Schüller-Christian disease
Histiocytosis (acute) (chronic)
Histiocytosis X (chronic)

> **EXCLUDES** histiocytosis:
> acute differentiated progressive
> (202.5)
> X, acute (progressive) (202.5)

CC Excl: 277.4, 277.81-277.87

277.9 Unspecified disorder of metabolism
Enzymopathy NOS

✓4ᵗʰ **278 Overweight, obesity and other hyperalimentation**

> **EXCLUDES** hyperalimentation NOS (783.6)
> poisoning by vitamins NOS (963.5)
> polyphagia (783.6)

✓5ᵗʰ **278.0 Overweight and obesity**
Use additional code to identify Body Mass Index (BMI), if known (V85.0-V85.54)

> **EXCLUDES** adiposogenital dystrophy (253.8)
> obesity of endocrine origin NOS (259.9)

AHA: 4Q, '05, 97

278.00 Obesity, unspecified
Obesity NOS
DEF: BMI (body mass index) between 30.0 and 38.9.
AHA: 4Q, '01, 42; 1Q, '99, 5, 6

278.01 Morbid obesity
Severe obesity
DEF: BMI (body mass index) greater than 39.
AHA: ▶2Q, '09, 11;◀ 2Q, '06, 5-6; 3Q, '03, 6-8
E66.01 Morbid (severe) obesity due to excess `I-10`
calories

278.02 Overweight
DEF: BMI (body mass index) between 25 and 29.9.
AHA: 4Q, '05, 55
E66.3 Overweight `I-10`

278.1 Localized adiposity
Fat pad
AHA: 2Q, '06, 10

278.2 Hypervitaminosis A

278.3 Hypercarotinemia
DEF: Elevated blood carotene level due to ingesting excess carotenoids or the inability to convert carotenoids to vitamin A.

278.4 Hypervitaminosis D
DEF: Weakness, fatigue, loss of weight, and other symptoms resulting from ingesting excessive amounts of vitamin D.

278.8 Other hyperalimentation
AHA: ▶2Q, '09, 11◀

✓4ᵗʰ **279 Disorders involving the immune mechanism**

✓5ᵗʰ **279.0 Deficiency of humoral immunity**
DEF: Inadequate immune response to bacterial infections with potential reinfection by viruses due to lack of circulating immunoglobulins (acquired antibodies).

279.00 Hypogammaglobulinemia, unspecified `CC`
Agammaglobulinemia NOS
CC Excl: 279.00-279.3, 279.41-279.49, 279.8-279.9

279.01 Selective IgA immunodeficiency `CC`
CC Excl: See code: 279.00

279.02 Selective IgM immunodeficiency `CC`
CC Excl: 279.02-279.3, 279.41-279.49, 279.8-279.9

279.03 Other selective immunoglobulin deficiencies `CC`
Selective deficiency of IgG
CC Excl: See code: 279.02

279.04 Congenital hypogammaglobulinemia `CC`
Agammaglobulinemia:
Bruton's type
X-linked
CC Excl: See code 279.02

279.05 Immunodeficiency with increased IgM `CC`
Immunodeficiency with hyper-IgM:
autosomal recessive
X-linked
CC Excl: See code 279.02

279.06 Common variable immunodeficiency `CC`
Dysgammaglobulinemia (acquired) (congenital) (primary)
Hypogammaglobulinemia:
acquired primary
congenital non-sex-linked
sporadic
CC Excl: See code 279.02

279.09 Other `CC`
Transient hypogammaglobulinemia of infancy
CC Excl: See code 279.02

✓5ᵗʰ **279.1 Deficiency of cell-mediated immunity**

279.10 Immunodeficiency with predominant T-cell defect, unspecified `CC`
CC Excl: See code 279.02
AHA: S-O, '87, 10

279.11 DiGeorge's syndrome `CC`
Pharyngeal pouch syndrome
Thymic hypoplasia
DEF: Congenital hypoplasia or aplasia of the thymus, parathyroid glands; related heart defects, anomalies of the great vessels, esophageal atresia, and abnormalities of facial structures.
CC Excl: See code 279.02

279.12 Wiskott-Aldrich syndrome `CC`
DEF: A disease characterized by chronic conditions, such as eczema, suppurative otitis media and anemia; results from an X-linked recessive gene and is classified as an immune deficiency syndrome.
CC Excl: See code 279.02

279.13 Nezelof's syndrome `CC`
Cellular immunodeficiency with abnormal immunoglobulin deficiency
DEF: Immune system disorder characterized by a pathological deficiency in cellular immunity and humoral antibodies resulting in inability to fight infectious diseases.
CC Excl: See code 279.02

279.19 Other `CC`
> **EXCLUDES** ataxia-telangiectasia (334.8)

CC Excl: See code 279.02

279.2 Combined immunity deficiency `CC`
Agammaglobulinemia:
autosomal recessive
Swiss-type
x-linked recessive
Severe combined immunodeficiency [SCID]
Thymic:
alymphoplasia
aplasia or dysplasia with immunodeficiency

> **EXCLUDES** thymic hypoplasia (279.11)

DEF: Agammaglobulinemia: No immunoglobulins in the blood.
DEF: Thymic alymphoplasia: Severe combined immunodeficiency; result of failed lymphoid tissue development.
CC Excl: See code 279.02

279.3 Unspecified immunity deficiency `CC`
CC Excl: See code 279.02

✓5ᵗʰ **279.4 Autoimmune disease, not elsewhere classified**
> **EXCLUDES** transplant failure or rejection (996.80-996.89)

AHA: 3Q, 08, 5

● **279.41 Autoimmune lymphoproliferative syndrome**
ALPS

● **279.49 Autoimmune disease, not elsewhere classified**
Autoimmune disease NOS

N Newborn Age: 0   P Pediatric Age: 0-17   M Maternity Age: 12-55   A Adult Age: 15-124   MCC Major CC Condition   CC CC Condition   HIV HIV Related Dx

74 – Volume 1 · October 2009   2010 ICD-9-CM

279.5 Graft-versus-host disease

Code first underlying cause, such as:
   complication of blood transfusion ▶(999.89)◀
   complication of transplanted organ (996.80-996.89)

Use additional code to identify associated manifestations,
      such as:
   desquamative dermatitis (695.89)
   diarrhea (787.91)
   elevated bilirubin (782.4)
   hair loss (704.09)

DEF: A complication of transplantation, most commonly bone
marrow; may involve skin, GI tract, liver and cause increased
susceptibility to infection; results when donor cells
responsible for immune response attack the cells of the
transplant recipient.

AHA: 4Q, '08, 97-99, 154

279.50 Graft-versus-host disease, unspecified `CC`

CC Excl: 279.50-279.53, 996.85, 997.91-997.99
AHA: 4Q, '08, 99

279.51 Acute graft-versus-host disease `CC`

CC Excl: See code 279.50
AHA: 4Q, '08, 99

279.52 Chronic graft-versus-host disease `CC`

CC Excl: See code 279.50

279.53 Acute on chronic graft-versus-host disease `CC`

CC Excl: See code 279.50

279.8 Other specified disorders involving the immune mechanism

Single complement [C_1-C_9] deficiency or dysfunction

279.9 Unspecified disorder of immune mechanism

AHA: 3Q, '92, 13

| ✓4ᵗʰ ✓5ᵗʰ Additional Digit Required | Unacceptable PDx | Manifestation Code | Hospital Acquired Condition | ▶◀ Revised Text | ● New Code | ▲ Revised Code Title |

When neither the diagnostic statement nor review of the medical record indicates whether a blood-loss anemia is acute or chronic, code 280.0 should be assigned.

abular List   **BLOOD AND BLOOD-FORMING ORGANS**   **280–282.41**

4. DISEASES OF THE BLOOD AND BLOOD-FORMING ORGANS (280-289)

EXCLUDES *anemia complicating pregnancy or the puerperium (648.2)*

√4th 280 Iron deficiency anemias

INCLUDES anemia:
 asiderotic
 hypochromic-microcytic
 sideropenic

EXCLUDES *familial microcytic anemia (282.49)*

280.0 Secondary to blood loss (chronic)
Normocytic anemia due to blood loss

EXCLUDES *acute posthemorrhagic anemia (285.1)*

AHA: 4Q, '93, 34

280.1 Secondary to inadequate dietary iron intake

280.8 Other specified iron deficiency anemias
Paterson-Kelly syndrome
Plummer-Vinson syndrome
Sideropenic dysphagia

280.9 Iron deficiency anemia, unspecified
Anemia:
 achlorhydric
 chlorotic
 idiopathic hypochromic
 iron [Fe] deficiency NOS

√4th 281 Other deficiency anemias

281.0 Pernicious anemia
Anemia:
 Addison's
 Biermer's
 congenital pernicious
Congenital intrinsic factor [Castle's] deficiency

EXCLUDES *combined system disease without mention of anemia (266.2)*
subacute degeneration of spinal cord without mention of anemia (266.2)

DEF: Chronic progressive anemia due to Vitamin B12 malabsorption; caused by lack of a secretion of intrinsic factor, which is produced by the gastric mucosa of the stomach.

AHA: N-D, '84, 1; S-O, '84, 16

281.1 Other vitamin B$_{12}$ deficiency anemia
Anemia:
 vegan's
 vitamin B$_{12}$ deficiency (dietary)
 due to selective vitamin B$_{12}$ malabsorption with proteinuria
Syndrome:
 Imerslund's
 Imerslund-Gräsbeck

EXCLUDES *combined system disease without mention of anemia (266.2)*
subacute degeneration of spinal cord without mention of anemia (266.2)

281.2 Folate-deficiency anemia
Congenital folate malabsorption
Folate or folic acid deficiency anemia:
 NOS
 dietary
 drug-induced
Goat's milk anemia
Nutritional megaloblastic anemia (of infancy)

Use additional E code to identify drug

DEF: Macrocytic anemia resembles pernicious anemia but without absence of hydrochloric acid secretions; responsive to folic acid therapy.

281.3 Other specified megaloblastic anemias not elsewhere classified
Combined B$_{12}$ and folate-deficiency anemia
Refractory megaloblastic anemia

DEF: Megaloblasts predominant in bone marrow with few normoblasts; rare familial type associated with proteinuria and genitourinary tract anomalies.

281.4 Protein-deficiency anemia
Amino-acid-deficiency anemia

281.8 Anemia associated with other specified nutritional deficiency
Scorbutic anemia

281.9 Unspecified deficiency anemia
Anemia:
 dimorphic
 macrocytic
 megaloblastic NOS
 nutritional NOS
 simple chronic

√4th 282 Hereditary hemolytic anemias
DEF: Escalated rate of erythrocyte destruction; similar to all anemias, occurs when imbalance exists between blood loss and blood production.

282.0 Hereditary spherocytosis
Acholuric (familial) jaundice
Congenital hemolytic anemia (spherocytic)
Congenital spherocytosis
Minkowski-Chauffard syndrome
Spherocytosis (familial)

EXCLUDES *hemolytic anemia of newborn (773.0-773.5)*

DEF: Hereditary, chronic illness marked by abnormal red blood cell membrane; symptoms include enlarged spleen, jaundice; and anemia in severe cases.

282.1 Hereditary elliptocytosis
Elliptocytosis (congenital)
Ovalocytosis (congenital) (hereditary)

DEF: Genetic hemolytic anemia characterized by malformed, elliptical erythrocytes; there is increased destruction of red cells with resulting anemia.

282.2 Anemias due to disorders of glutathione metabolism
Anemia:
 6-phosphogluconic dehydrogenase deficiency
 enzyme deficiency, drug-induced
 erythrocyte glutathione deficiency
 glucose-6-phosphate dehydrogenase [G-6-PD] deficiency
 glutathione-reductase deficiency
 hemolytic nonspherocytic (hereditary), type I
Disorder of pentose phosphate pathway
Favism

282.3 Other hemolytic anemias due to enzyme deficiency
Anemia:
 hemolytic nonspherocytic (hereditary), type II
 hexokinase deficiency
 pyruvate kinase [PK] deficiency
 triosephosphate isomerase deficiency

√5th 282.4 Thalassemias
EXCLUDES *sickle-cell:*
disease (282.60-282.69)
trait (282.5)

DEF: Inherited hemolytic disorders characterized by decreased production of at least one polypeptide globin chain results in defective hemoglobin synthesis; symptoms include severe anemia, expanded marrow spaces, transfusional and absorptive iron overload, impaired growth rate, thickened cranial bones, and pathologic fractures.

AHA: 4Q, '03, 51

282.41 Sickle-cell thalassemia without crisis
Sickle-cell thalassemia NOS
Thalassemia Hb-S disease without crisis

√4th					
√5th Additional Digit Required	Unacceptable PDx	Manifestation Code	Hospital Acquired Condition	►◄ Revised Text	● New Code ▲ Revised Code Title

2010 ICD-9-CM   **Volume 1 – 77**

When the medical record indicates both terms, only the code for sickle-cell disease is assigned.

282.42 Sickle-cell thalassemia with crisis `MCC`
Sickle-cell thalassemia with vaso-occlusive pain
Thalassemia Hb-S disease with crisis
Use additional code for type of crisis, such as:
acute chest syndrome (517.3)
splenic sequestration (289.52)
CC Excl: 280.0-285.9, 289.81-289.83, 289.89-289.9, 517.3

282.49 Other thalassemia
Cooley's anemia
Hb-Bart's disease
Hereditary leptocytosis
Mediterranean anemia (with other hemoglobinopathy)
Microdrepanocytosis
Thalassemia (alpha) (beta) (intermedia) (major) (minima) (minor) (mixed) (trait) (with other hemoglobinopathy)
Thalassemia NOS

282.5 Sickle-cell trait *
Hb-AS genotype
Hemoglobin S [Hb-S] trait
Heterozygous:
hemoglobin S
Hb-S
EXCLUDES that with other hemoglobinopathy (282.60-282.69)
that with thalassemia (282.49)

Sickle-Cell "Trait" occurs when a child receives the genetic trait from only one parent.

DEF: Heterozygous genetic makeup characterized by one gene for normal hemoglobin and one for sickle-cell hemoglobin; clinical disease rarely present.
TIP: Do not assign along with another code for sickle-cell disease or thalassemia.

√5th **282.6 Sickle-cell disease** *
Sickle-cell anemia
EXCLUDES sickle-cell thalassemia (282.41-282.42)
sickle-cell trait (282.5)

Sickle-Cell "Disease" - passed to child when both parents carry the genetic trait.

DEF: Inherited blood disorder; sickle-shaped red blood cells are hard and pointed, clogging blood flow; anemia characterized by, periodic episodes of pain, acute abdominal discomfort, skin ulcerations of the legs, increased infections.

282.60 Sickle-cell disease, unspecified
Sickle-cell anemia NOS
AHA: 2Q, '97, 11

282.61 Hb-SS disease without crisis

282.62 Hb-SS disease with crisis `MCC`
Hb-SS disease with vaso-occlusive pain
Sickle-cell crisis NOS
Use additional code for type of crisis, such as:
acute chest syndrome (517.3)
splenic sequestration (289.52)
CC Excl: See code: 282.42
AHA: 4Q, '03, 56; 2Q, '98, 8; 2Q, '91, 15

282.63 Sickle-cell/Hb-C disease without crisis
Hb-S/Hb-C disease without crisis

282.64 Sickle-cell/Hb-C disease with crisis `MCC`
Hb-S/Hb-C disease with crisis
Sickle-cell/Hb-C disease with vaso-occlusive pain
Use additional code for type of crisis, such as:
acute chest syndrome (517.3)
splenic sequestration (289.52)
CC Excl: See code: 282.42
AHA: 4Q, '03, 51

282.68 Other sickle-cell disease without crisis
Hb-S/Hb-D
Hb-S/Hb-E   } diseases without
Sickle-cell/Hb-D   crisis
Sickle-cell/Hb-E
AHA: 4Q, '03, 51

282.69 Other sickle-cell disease with crisis `MCC`
Hb-S/Hb-D
Hb-S/Hb-E   } diseases with crisis
Sickle-cell/Hb-D
Sickle-cell/Hb-E
Other sickle-cell disease with vaso-occlusive pain
Use additional code for type of crisis, such as:
acute chest syndrome (517.3)
splenic sequestration (289.52)
CC Excl: 280.0-285.9, 289.81-289.83, 289.89-289.9, 517.3

282.7 Other hemoglobinopathies
Abnormal hemoglobin NOS
Congenital Heinz-body anemia
Disease:
hemoglobin C [Hb-C]
hemoglobin D [Hb-D]
hemoglobin E [Hb-E]
hemoglobin Zurich [Hb-Zurich]
Hemoglobinopathy NOS
Hereditary persistence of fetal hemoglobin [HPFH]
Unstable hemoglobin hemolytic disease
EXCLUDES familial polycythemia (289.6)
hemoglobin M [Hb-M] disease (289.7)
high-oxygen-affinity hemoglobin (289.0)
DEF: Any disorder of hemoglobin due to alteration of molecular structure; may include overt anemia.

282.8 Other specified hereditary hemolytic anemias `CC`
Stomatocytosis
CC Excl: 280.0-284.2, 284.81-285.9, 289.9, 517.3, 776.5-776.6

282.9 Hereditary hemolytic anemia, unspecified `CC`
Hereditary hemolytic anemia NOS
CC Excl: See code: 282.8

√4th **283 Acquired hemolytic anemias**
DEF: Non-heriditary anemia characterized by premature destruction of red blood cells; caused by infectious organisms, poisons, and physical agents
AHA: N-D, '84, 1

283.0 Autoimmune hemolytic anemias `CC`
Autoimmune hemolytic disease (cold type) (warm type)
Chronic cold hemagglutinin disease
Cold agglutinin disease or hemoglobinuria
Hemolytic anemia:
cold type (secondary) (symptomatic)
drug-induced
warm type (secondary) (symptomatic)
Use additional E code to identify cause, if drug-induced
EXCLUDES Evans' syndrome (287.32)
hemolytic disease of newborn (773.0-773.5)
CC Excl: 280.0-285.9, 289.81-289.83, 289.89-289.9, 517.3
AHA: ▶3Q, '08, 5◀

√5th **283.1 Non-autoimmune hemolytic anemias**
Use additional E code to identify cause
DEF: Hemolytic anemia and thrombocytopenia with acute renal failure; relatively rare condition; 50 percent of patients require renal dialysis.
AHA: 4Q, '93, 25

283.10 Non-autoimmune hemolytic anemia, unspecified `CC`
CC Excl: See code: 283.0

283.11 Hemolytic-uremic syndrome `MCC`
CC Excl: See code: 283.0

283.19 Other non-autoimmune hemolytic anemias `CC`
Hemolytic anemia:
mechanical
microangiopathic
toxic
CC Excl: See code: 283.0

`N` Newborn Age: 0   `P` Pediatric Age: 0-17   `M` Maternity Age: 12-55   `A` Adult Age: 15-124   `MCC` Major CC Condition   `CC` CC Condition   `HIV` HIV Related Dx

78 – Volume 1 • February 2009

2010 ICD-9-CM

283.2 Hemoglobinuria due to hemolysis from external causes
Acute intravascular hemolysis
Hemoglobinuria:
   from exertion
   march
   paroxysmal (cold) (nocturnal)
   due to other hemolysis
Marchiafava-Micheli syndrome
Use additional E code to identify cause

283.9 Acquired hemolytic anemia, unspecified `CC`
Acquired hemolytic anemia NOS
Chronic idiopathic hemolytic anemia
CC Excl: See code: 283.0

✓4th **284 Aplastic anemia and other bone marrow failure syndromes**
DEF: Bone marrow failure to produce the normal amount of blood components; generally non-responsive to usual therapy.
AHA: 1Q, '91, 14; N-D, '84, 1; S-0, '84, 16

✓5th **284.0 Constitutional aplastic anemia**
AHA: 1Q, '91, 14

284.01 Constitutional red blood cell aplasia `CC`
Aplasia, (pure) red cell:
   congenital
   of infants
   primary
Blackfan-Diamond syndrome
Familial hypoplastic anemia
CC Excl: 280.0-284.09, 284.81-285.9, 289.9, 776.5-776.6
AHA: 4Q, '06, 67-69

284.09 Other constitutional aplastic anemia `CC`
Fanconi's anemia
Pancytopenia with malformations
CC Excl: 280.0-284.09, 284.81-285.9, 287.30-287.39, 289.9, 776.5-776.6
AHA: 4Q, '06, 67-69

284.1 Pancytopenia `CC`
EXCLUDES pancytopenia (due to) (with):
   aplastic anemia NOS (284.9)
   bone marrow infiltration (284.2)
   constitutional red blood cell aplasia (284.01)
   drug induced (284.89)
   hairy cell leukemia (202.4)
   human immunodeficiency virus disease (042)
   leukoerythroblastic anemia (284.2)
   malformations (284.09)
   myelodysplastic syndromes (238.72-238.75)
   myeloproliferative disease (238.79)
   other constitutional aplastic anemia (284.09)
CC Excl: 284.2, 284.81-285.9, 288.00-288.09, 288.4-288.62, 288.66-288.69, 289.9, 776.6
AHA: 4Q, '06, 67-69

Acute blood loss anemia results from sudden, significant loss of blood over a brief period of time.

284.2 Myelophthisis `CC`
Leukoerythroblastic anemia
Myelophthisic anemia
Code first the underlying disorder, such as:
   malignant neoplasm of breast (174.0-174.9, 175.0-175.9)
   tuberculosis (015.0-015.9)
EXCLUDES idiopathic myelofibrosis (238.76)
   myelofibrosis NOS (289.83)
   myelofibrosis with myeloid metaplasia (238.76)
   primary myelofibrosis (238.76)
   secondary myelofibrosis (289.83)
DEF: A secondary disease process involving replacement of normal hematopoeitic tissue in the bone marrow with abnormal tissue, such as fibrous tissue or tumors. Occurs with advanced-stage neoplasms, granulomatous diseases such as miliary tuberculosis, and other inflammatory diseases.
CC Excl: 284.1-284.2, 284.81-285.9, 288.00-288.09, 288.4-288.62, 288.66-288.69, 289.9, 776.6
AHA: 4Q, '06, 67-69

✓5th **284.8 Other specified aplastic anemias**
AHA: 4Q, '07, 72; 3Q, '05, 11; 1Q, '97, 5; 1Q, '92, 15; 1Q, '91, 14

284.81 Red cell aplasia (acquired) (adult) (with thymoma) `MCC`
Red cell aplasia NOS
CC Excl: 280.0-285.9, 289.81-289.83, 289.89-289.9, 517.3

284.89 Other specified aplastic anemias `MCC`
Aplastic anemia (due to):
   chronic systemic disease
   drugs
   infection
   radiation
   toxic (paralytic)
Use additional E code to identify cause
CC Excl: See code: 284.81
AHA: ►1Q, '09, 20;◄ 2Q, '08, 6

284.9 Aplastic anemia, unspecified `CC`
Anemia:
   aplastic (idiopathic) NOS
   aregenerative
   hypoplastic NOS
   nonregenerative
Medullary hypoplasia
EXCLUDES refractory anemia (238.72)
CC Excl: See code: 284.81

✓4th **285 Other and unspecified anemias**
AHA: 1Q, '91, 14; N-D, '84, 1

285.0 Sideroblastic anemia
Anemia:
   hypochromic with iron loading
   sideroachrestic
   sideroblastic:
     acquired
     congenital
     hereditary
     primary
     secondary (drug-induced) (due to disease)
     sex-linked hypochromic
     vitamin B6-responsive
Pyridoxine-responsive (hypochromic) anemia
Use additional E code to identify cause, if drug induced
EXCLUDES refractory sideroblastic anemia (238.72)
DEF: Characterized by a disruption of final heme synthesis; results in iron overload of reticuloendothelial tissues.

285.1 Acute posthemorrhagic anemia `CC`
Anemia due to acute blood loss
EXCLUDES anemia due to chronic blood loss (280.0)
   blood loss anemia NOS (280.0)
CC Excl: 280.0-285.9, 289.81-289.83, 289.89-289.9, 517.3, 958.2
AHA: 1Q, '07, 19; 2Q, '92, 15

✓4th / ✓5th Additional Digit Required   Unacceptable PDx   Manifestation Code   Hospital Acquired Condition   ►◄ Revised Text   ● New Code   ▲ Revised Code Title

2010 ICD-9-CM   **October 2009 • Volume 1 – 79**

Blood and Blood-Forming Organs

285.2–286.5

√5ᵗʰ **285.2 Anemia of chronic disease**
Anemia in ▶(due to) (with)◀ chronic illness
AHA: 4Q, '00, 39

285.21 Anemia in chronic kidney disease
Anemia in end stage renal disease
Erythropoietin-resistant anemia (EPO resistant anemia)
TIP: Assign also a code for the chronic kidney disease (585.X).

285.22 Anemia in neoplastic disease
EXCLUDES ▶ *anemia due to antineoplastic chemotherapy (285.3)*◀
TIP: Assign also a code for the neoplasm causing the anemia. Do not assign if anemia is caused by chemotherapy drugs, which is instead reported with 285.3.

Can be used if both are documented.

285.29 Anemia of other chronic disease
Anemia in other chronic illness

● √ **285.3 Antineoplastic chemotherapy induced anemia**
Anemia due to antineoplastic chemotherapy
EXCLUDES *anemia due to drug NEC–code to type of anemia*
anemia in neoplastic disease (285.22)
aplastic anemia due to antineoplastic chemotherapy (284.89)

No E code needed to specify the drug

285.8 Other specified anemias
Anemia:
dyserythropoietic (congenital)
dyshematopoietic (congenital)
von Jaksch's
Infantile pseudoleukemia
AHA: 1Q, '91, 16

285.9 Anemia, unspecified
Anemia:
NOS
essential
normocytic, not due to blood loss
profound
progressive
secondary
Oligocythemia
EXCLUDES *anemia (due to):*
blood loss:
acute (285.1)
chronic or unspecified (280.0)
iron deficiency (280.0-280.9)
AHA: ▶1Q, '09, 17, 20;◀ 1Q. '07, 19; 1Q, '02, 14; 2Q, '92, 16; M-A, '85, 13; N-D, '84, 1
TIP: Assign for "postoperative anemia" if there is no mention of blood loss.

√4ᵗʰ **286 Coagulation defects**
AHA: 2Q, '06, 17

286.0 Congenital factor VIII disorder `MCC`
Antihemophilic globulin [AHG] deficiency
Factor VIII (functional)deficiency
Hemophilia:
NOS
A
classical
familial
hereditary
Subhemophilia
EXCLUDES *factor VIII deficiency with vascular defect (286.4)*
DEF: Hereditary, sex-linked, results in missing antihemophilic globulin (AHG) (factor VIII); causes abnormal coagulation characterized by increased bleeding, large bruises of skin, bleeding in mouth, nose, gastrointestinal tract; hemorrhages into joints, resulting in swelling and impaired function.
CC Excl: 286.0-287.9, 289.81-289.9

286.1 Congenital factor IX disorder `MCC`
Christmas disease
Deficiency:
factor IX (functional)
plasma thromboplastin component [PTC]
Hemophilia B
DEF: Deficiency of plasma thromboplastin component (PTC) (factor IX) and plasma thromboplastin antecedent (PTA); PTC deficiency clinically indistinguishable from classical hemophilia.
CC Excl: See code: 286.0

286.2 Congenital factor XI deficiency `CC`
Hemophilia C
Plasma thromboplastin antecedent [PTA] deficiency
Rosenthal's disease
CC Excl: See code: 286.0

286.3 Congenital deficiency of other clotting factors `CC`
Congenital afibrinogenemia
Deficiency:
AC globulin factor:
I [fibrinogen]
II [prothrombin]
V [labile]
VII [stable]
X [Stuart-Prower]
XII [Hageman]
XIII [fibrin stabilizing]
Laki-Lorand factor
proaccelerin
Disease
Owren's
Stuart-Prower
Dysfibrinogenemia (congenital)
Dysprothrombinemia (constitutional)
Hypoproconvertinemia
Hypoprothrombinemia (hereditary)
Parahemophilia
CC Excl: See code: 286.0

286.4 von Willebrand's disease `CC`
Angiohemophilia (A) (B)
Constitutional thrombopathy
Factor VIII deficiency with vascular defect
Pseudohemophilia type B
Vascular hemophilia
von Willebrand's (-Jürgens') disease
EXCLUDES *factor VIII deficiency:*
NOS (286.0)
with functional defect (286.0)
hereditary capillary fragility (287.8)
DEF: Abnormal blood coagulation caused by deficient blood Factor VII; congenital; symptoms include excess or prolonged bleeding.
CC Excl: See code: 286.0

286.5 Hemorrhagic disorder due to intrinsic circulating anticoagulants `CC`
Antithrombinemia
Antithromboplastinemia
Antithromboplastino-genemia
Hyperheparinemia
Increase in:
anti-VIIIa
anti-IXa
anti-Xa
anti-XIa
antithrombin
Secondary hemophilia
Systemic lupus erythematosus [SLE] inhibitor
CC Excl: See code: 286.0
AHA: 3Q, '04, 7; No.5, '93, 16; 3Q, '92, 15; 3Q, '90, 14
TIP: Do not assign for Coumadin/warfarin toxicity, poisoning or adverse effect. Follow coding guidelines for poisoning and adverse reactions.

 Newborn Age: 0   Pediatric Age: 0-17   Maternity Age: 12-55   A Adult Age: 15-124   `MCC` Major CC Condition   `CC` CC Condition   `HIV` HIV Related Dx

80 – Volume 1 · October 2009

 2010 ICD-9-CM

286.6   Defibrination syndrome `MCC`
     Afibrinogenemia, acquired
     Consumption coagulopathy
     Diffuse or disseminated intravascular coagulation [DIC
          syndrome]
     Fibrinolytic hemorrhage, acquired
     Hemorrhagic fibrinogenolysis
     Pathologic fibrinolysis
     Purpura:
          fibrinolytic
          fulminans
     EXCLUDES   *that complicating:*
                         abortion (634-638 with .1, 639.1)
                         pregnancy or the puerperium (641.3, 666.3)
                         disseminated intravascular coagulation in
                              newborn (776.2)
     DEF: Characterized by destruction of circulating fibrinogen;
     often precipitated by other conditions, such as injury, causing
     release of thromboplastic particles in blood stream.
     CC Excl: See code: 286.0
     AHA: 4Q, '93, 29

286.7   Acquired coagulation factor deficiency `CC`
     Deficiency of coagulation factor due to:
          liver disease
          vitamin K deficiency
     Hypoprothrombinemia, acquired
     Use additional E code to identify cause, if drug induced
     EXCLUDES   *vitamin K deficiency of newborn (776.0)*
     CC Excl: See code: 286.0
     AHA: 4Q, '93, 29

286.9   Other and unspecified coagulation defects `CC`
     Defective coagulation NOS   Disorder:
     Deficiency, coagulation   coagulation
          factor NOS   hemostasis
     Delay, coagulation
     EXCLUDES   *abnormal coagulation profile (790.92)*
                         hemorrhagic disease of newborn (776.0)
                         that complicating:
                              abortion (634-638 with .1, 639.1)
                              pregnancy or the puerperium (641.3, 666.3)
     CC Excl: See code: 286.0
     AHA: 4Q, '99, 22; 4Q, '93, 29

√4ᵗʰ 287 Purpura and other hemorrhagic conditions
     EXCLUDES   *hemorrhagic thrombocythemia (238.79)*
                         purpura fulminans (286.6)
     AHA: 1Q, '91, 14

287.0   Allergic purpura `CC`
     Peliosis rheumatica
     Purpura:
          anaphylactoid
          autoimmune
          Henoch's
          nonthrombocytopenic:
               hemorrhagic
               idiopathic
               rheumatica
          Schönlein-Henoch
          vascular
     Vasculitis, allergic
     EXCLUDES   *hemorrhagic purpura (287.39)*
                         purpura annularis telangiectodes (709.1)
     DEF: Any hemorrhagic condition, thrombocytic or
     nonthrombocytopenic in origin, caused by a presumed
     allergic reaction.
     CC Excl: See code: 286.0

287.1   Qualitative platelet defects
     Thrombasthenia (hemorrhagic) (hereditary)
     Thrombocytasthenia
     Thrombocytopathy (dystrophic)
     Thrombopathy (Bernard-Soulier)
     EXCLUDES   *von Willebrand's disease (286.4)*

287.2   Other nonthrombocytopenic purpuras
     Purpura:
          NOS
          senile
          simplex

√5ᵗʰ 287.3   Primary thrombocytopenia
     EXCLUDES   *thrombotic thrombocytopenic purpura (446.6)*
                         transient thrombocytopenia of newborn
                              (776.1)
     DEF: Decrease in number of blood platelets in circulating
     blood and purpural skin hemorrhages.
     AHA: 4Q, '05, 56

   287.30   Primary thrombocytopenia, unspecified
        Megakaryocytic hypoplasia

   287.31   Immune thrombocytopenic purpura `CC`
        Idiopathic thrombocytopenic purpura
        Tidal platelet dysgenesis
        DEF: Tidal platelet dysgenesis: Platelet counts
        fluctuate from normal to very low within periods of
        20 to 40 days and may involve autoimmune platelet
        destruction.
        CC Excl: See code: 286.0
        AHA: 4Q, '05, 57

   287.32   Evans' syndrome `CC`
        DEF: Combination of immunohemolytic anemia and
        autoimmune hemolytic anemia, sometimes with
        neutropenia.
        CC Excl: See code: 286.0

   287.33   Congenital and hereditary `CC`
        thrombocytopenic purpura
        Congenital and hereditary thrombocytopenia
        Thrombocytopenia with absent radii (TAR)
             syndrome
        EXCLUDES   *Wiskott-Aldrich syndrome (279.12)*
        DEF: Thrombocytopenia with absent radii (TAR)
        syndrome: autosomal recessive syndrome
        characterized by thrombocytopenia and bilateral
        radial aplasia; manifestations include skeletal,
        gastrointestinal, hematologic, and cardiac system
        abnormalities.
        CC Excl: See code: 286.0

   287.39   Other primary thrombocytopenia

287.4   Secondary thrombocytopenia
     Posttransfusion purpura
     Thrombocytopenia (due to):
          dilutional
          drugs
          extracorporeal circulation of blood
          massive blood transfusion
          platelet alloimmunization
     Use additional E code to identify cause
     EXCLUDES   *heparin-induced thrombocytopenia (HIT)*
                         (289.84)
                         transient thrombocytopenia of newborn
                              (776.1)
     DEF: Reduced number of platelets in circulating blood as
     consequence of an underlying disease or condition.
     AHA: M-A, '85, 14

287.5   Thrombocytopenia, unspecified

287.8   Other specified hemorrhagic conditions
     Capillary fragility (hereditary)
     Vascular pseudohemophilia

287.9   Unspecified hemorrhagic conditions
     Hemorrhagic diathesis (familial)

[handwritten note: Code 284.1 (pantocytopenia) if the patient has — anemia — neutropenia — thrombocytopenia]

Blood and Blood-Forming Organs

288–288.69

✓4ᵗʰ **288 Diseases of white blood cells**
    EXCLUDES *leukemia (204.0-208.9)*
    AHA: 4Q, '06, 69; 1Q, '91, 14

✓5ᵗʰ **288.0 Neutropenia**
    Decreased absolute neutrophil count [ANC]
    Use additional code for any associated:
      fever (780.61)
      mucositis (478.11, 528.00-528.09, 538, 616.81)
    EXCLUDES *neutropenic splenomegaly (289.53)*
        transitory neonatal neutropenia (776.7)
    DEF: Sudden, severe condition characterized by reduced number of white blood cells; results in sores in the throat, stomach or skin; symptoms include chills, fever.
    AHA: 4Q, '06, 69-73; 3Q, '05, 11; 3Q, '99, 6; 2Q, '99, 9; 3Q, '96, 16; 2Q, '96, 6

[handwritten margin note: If the patient has – anemia – neutropenia – thrombocytopenia Code 284.1 (pancytopenia)]

    288.00 Neutropenia, unspecified
      AHA: 4Q, '06, 69-73

    288.01 Congenital neutropenia
      Congenital agranulocytosis
      Infantile genetic agranulocytosis
      Kostmann's syndrome
      AHA: 4Q, '06, 69-73

    288.02 Cyclic neutropenia
      Cyclic hematopoiesis
      Periodic neutropenia
      AHA: 4Q, '06, 69-73

    288.03 Drug induced neutropenia
      Use additional E code to identify drug
      AHA: 4Q, '06, 69-73
      TIP: Assign for neutropenic fever due to chemotherapy drugs, along with codes for the fever, adverse effect, and the underlying malignancy.

    288.04 Neutropenia due to infection
      AHA: 4Q, '06, 69-73

    288.09 Other neutropenia
      Agranulocytosis
      Neutropenia:
        immune
        toxic
      AHA: 4Q, '06, 69-73

288.1 Functional disorders of polymorphonuclear neutrophils
    Chronic (childhood) granulomatous disease
    Congenital dysphagocytosis
    Job's syndrome
    Lipochrome histiocytosis (familial)
    Progressive septic granulomatosis

288.2 Genetic anomalies of leukocytes
    Anomaly (granulation) (granulocyte) or syndrome:
      Alder's (-Reilly)
      Chédiak-Steinbrinck (-Higashi)
      Jordan's
      May-Hegglin
      Pelger-Huet
    Hereditary:
      hypersegmentation
      hyposegmentation
      leukomelanopathy

288.3 Eosinophilia
    Eosinophilia:
      allergic
      hereditary
      idiopathic
      secondary
    Eosinophilic leukocytosis
    EXCLUDES *Löffler's syndrome (518.3)*
        pulmonary eosinophilia (518.3)
    DEF: Elevated number of eosinophils in the blood; characteristic of allergic states and various parasitic infections.
    AHA: 3Q, '00, 11

288.4 Hemophagocytic syndromes   CC
    Familial hemophagocytic lymphohistiocytosis
    Familial hemophagocytic reticulosis
    Hemophagocytic syndrome, infection-associated
    Histiocytic syndromes
    Macrophage activation syndrome
    CC Excl: 284.1-284.9, 286.6, 287.30-288.09, 288.50, 288.59, 289.84, 289.9
    AHA: 4Q, '06, 69-73

✓5ᵗʰ **288.5 Decreased white blood cell count**
    EXCLUDES *neutropenia (288.01-288.09)*

    288.50 Leukocytopenia, unspecified
      Decreased leukocytes, unspecified
      Decreased white blood cell count, unspecified
      Leukopenia NOS
      AHA: 4Q, '06, 69-73

    288.51 Lymphocytopenia
      Decreased lymphocytes
      AHA: 4Q, '06, 69-73

    288.59 Other decreased white blood cell count
      Basophilic leukopenia
      Eosinophilic leukopenia
      Monocytopenia
      Plasmacytopenia
      AHA: 4Q, '06, 69-73

✓5ᵗʰ **288.6 Elevated white blood cell count**
    EXCLUDES *eosinophilia (288.3)*

[handwritten margin note: Occurs when all white blood cells are affected.]

    288.60 Leukocytosis, unspecified
      Elevated leukocytes, unspecified
      Elevated white blood cell count, unspecified
      AHA: 4Q, '06, 69-73

    288.61 Lymphocytosis (symptomatic)
      Elevated lymphocytes
      AHA: 4Q, '06, 69-73

    288.62 Leukemoid reaction
      Basophilic leukemoid reaction
      Lymphocytic leukemoid reaction
      Monocytic leukemoid reaction
      Myelocytic leukemoid reaction
      Neutrophilic leukemoid reaction
      AHA: 4Q, '06, 69-73

    288.63 Monocytosis (symptomatic)
      EXCLUDES *infectious mononucleosis (075)*
      AHA: 4Q, '06, 69-73

    288.64 Plasmacytosis
      AHA: 4Q, '06, 69-73

    288.65 Basophilia
      AHA: 4Q, '06, 69-73

    288.66 Bandemia
      Bandemia without diagnosis of specific infection
      EXCLUDES *confirmed infection–code to infection*
        leukemia (204.00-208.9)
      DEF: Increase in early neutrophil cells, called band cells; may indicate infection.
      AHA: 4Q, '07, 73
      TIP: Do not assign based on lab values alone; physician must substantiate bandemia without evidence of corresponding infection.

    288.69 Other elevated white blood cell count
      AHA: 4Q, '06, 69-73

| N Newborn Age: 0 | P Pediatric Age: 0-17 | M Maternity Age: 12-55 | A Adult Age: 15-124 | MCC Major CC Condition | CC CC Condition | HIV HIV Related Dx |

82 – Volume 1   2010 ICD-9-CM

288.8 Other specified disease of white blood cells

> EXCLUDES decreased white blood cell counts
> (288.50-288.59)
> elevated white blood cell counts
> (288.60-288.69)
> immunity disorders (279.0-279.9)

AHA: M-A, '87, 12

288.9 Unspecified disease of white blood cells

√4ᵗʰ **289 Other diseases of blood and blood-forming organs**

289.0 Polycythemia, secondary
High-oxygen-affinity hemoglobin
Polycythemia:
    acquired
    benign
    due to:
        fall in plasma volume
        high altitude
    emotional
    erythropoietin
    hypoxemic
    nephrogenous
    relative
    spurious
    stress

> EXCLUDES polycythemia:
> neonatal (776.4)
> primary (238.4)
> vera (238.4)

DEF: Elevated number of red blood cells in circulating blood as result of reduced oxygen supply to the tissues.
D75.1 Secondary polycythemia   I-10

289.1 Chronic lymphadenitis
Chronic:
    adenitis } any lymph node, except
    lymphadenitis } mesenteric

> EXCLUDES acute lymphadenitis (683)
> mesenteric (289.2)
> enlarged glands NOS (785.6)

DEF: Persistent inflammation of lymph node tissue; origin of infection is usually elsewhere.
I88.1 Chronic lymphadenitis except mesenteric   I-10

289.2 Nonspecific mesenteric lymphadenitis
Mesenteric lymphadenitis (acute) (chronic)
DEF: Inflammation of the lymph nodes in peritoneal fold that encases abdominal organs; disease resembles acute appendicitis; unknown etiology.
I88.0 Nonspecific mesenteric lymphadenitis   I-10

289.3 Lymphadenitis, unspecified, except mesenteric
AHA: 2Q, '92, 8
I88.9 Nonspecific lymphadenitis unspecified   I-10

289.4 Hypersplenism
"Big spleen" syndrome
Dyssplenism
Hypersplenia

> EXCLUDES primary splenic neutropenia (289.53)

DEF: An overactive spleen causing a deficiency of the peripheral blood components, an increase in bone marrow cells and sometimes a notable increase in the size of the spleen.
D73.1 Hypersplenism   I-10

√5ᵗʰ **289.5 Other diseases of spleen**

289.50 Disease of spleen, unspecified
D73.9 Disease of spleen unspecified   I-10

289.51 Chronic congestive splenomegaly
D73.2 Chronic congestive splenomegaly   I-10

289.52 Splenic sequestration
Code first sickle-cell disease in crisis (282.42, 282.62, 282.64, 282.69)
DEF: Blood is entrapped in the spleen due to vessel occlusion; most often associated with sickle-cell disease; spleen becomes enlarged and there is a sharp drop in hemoglobin.
AHA: 4Q, '03, 51

289.53 Neutropenic splenomegaly
AHA: 4Q, '06, 73
D73.81 Neutropenic splenomegaly   I-10

289.59 Other
Lien migrans
Perisplenitis
Splenic:
    abscess
    atrophy
    cyst
    fibrosis
    infarction
    rupture, nontraumatic
Splenitis
Wandering spleen

> EXCLUDES bilharzial splenic fibrosis
> (120.0-120.9)
> hepatolienal fibrosis (571.5)
> splenomegaly NOS (789.2)

D73.89 Other diseases of spleen   I-10

289.6 Familial polycythemia
Familial:
    benign polycythemia
    erythrocytosis
DEF: Elevated number of red blood cells.

289.7 Methemoglobinemia   CC
Congenital NADH [DPNH]-methemoglobin- reductase deficiency
Hemoglobin M [Hb-M] disease
Methemoglobinemia:
    NOS
    acquired (with sulfhemoglobinemia)
    hereditary
    toxic
Stokvis' disease
Sulfhemoglobinemia

Use additional E code to identify cause
DEF: Presence of blood methemoglobin, a chemically altered form of hemoglobin; causes cyanosis, headache, ataxia, dyspnea, tachycardia, nausea, stupor, and coma.
CC Excl: 282.7-283.10, 283.19-283.9, 285.3-285.9, 289.7, 289.9
D74.0 Congenital methemoglobinemia   I-10

Blood and Blood-Forming Organs

289.8–289.9

√5ᵗʰ **289.8 Other specified diseases of blood and blood-forming organs**

DEF: Hypercoagulable states: a group of inherited or acquired abnormalities of specific proteins and anticoagulant factors; also called thromboembolic states or thrombotic disorders, result in abnormal development of blood clots.

AHA: 4Q, '03, 56; 1Q, '02, 16; 2Q, '89, 8; M-A, '87, 12

289.81 Primary hypercoagulable state   CC

Activated protein C resistance
Antithrombin III deficiency
Factor V Leiden mutation
Lupus anticoagulant
Protein C deficiency
Protein S deficiency
Prothrombin gene mutation

DEF: Activated protein C resistance: decreased effectiveness of protein C to degrade factor V, necessary to inhibit clotting cascade; also called Factor V Leiden mutation.

DEF: Antithrombin III deficiency: deficiency in plasma antithrombin III one of six naturally occurring antithrombins that limit coagulation.

DEF: Factor V Leiden mutation: also called activated protein C resistance.

DEF: Lupus anticoagulant: autoimmune deficiency in a circulating anticoagulant that inhibits the conversion of prothrombin into thrombin; also called anti-phospholipid syndrome.

DEF: Protein C deficiency: deficiency of activated protein C which functions to bring the blood-clotting process into balance; same outcome as factor V Leiden mutation.

DEF: Protein S deficiency: similar to protein C deficiency; protein S is a vitamin K dependent cofactor in the activation of protein C.

DEF: Prothrombin gene mutation: increased levels of prothrombin, or factor II, a plasma protein that is converted to thrombin, which acts upon fibrinogen to form the fibrin.

CC Excl: 288.00-288.9, 289.53, 289.81-289.83, 289.89-289.9

D68.59 Other primary thrombophilia   I-10

289.82 Secondary hypercoagulable state   CC

EXCLUDES heparin-induced thrombocytopenia (HIT) (289.84)

CC Excl: See code: 289.81

D68.69 Other thrombophilia   I-10

289.83 *Myelofibrosis*   CC

Myelofibrosis NOS
Secondary myelofibrosis

Code first the underlying disorder, such as:
malignant neoplasm of breast (174.0-174.9, 175.0-175.9)

Use additional code for associated therapy-related myelodysplastic syndrome, if applicable (238.72, 238.73)
Use additional external cause code if due to anti-neoplastic chemotherapy (E933.1)

EXCLUDES   *idiopathic myelofibrosis (238.76)*
leukoerythroblastic anemia (284.2)
myelofibrosis with myeloid metaplasia (238.76)
myelophthisic anemia (284.2)
myelophthisis (284.2)
primary myelofibrosis (238.76)

DEF: A progressive bone marrow disease characterized by the replacement of bone marrow with the overgrowth of neoplastic stem cells and fibrotic tissue, also progressive anemia and enlarged spleen.

CC Excl: 202.40-202.48, 203.10-203.11, 203.80-203.81, 204.00-208.92, 238.4-238.76, 238.79-238.9

AHA: 4Q, '06, 73

D75.81 Myelofibrosis   I-10

289.84 Heparin-induced thrombocytopenia [HIT]

DEF: ▶Immune-mediated reaction to heparin therapy causing an abrupt fall in platelet count and serious complications such as pulmonary embolism, stroke, AMI or DVT.◀

AHA: ▶4Q, '08, 100-101◀

289.89 Other specified diseases of blood and blood-forming organs

Hypergammaglobulinemia
Pseudocholinesterase deficiency

D75.89 Oth specified dz of blood & blood-forming organs   I-10

289.9 Unspecified diseases of blood and blood-forming organs

Blood dyscrasia NOS
Erythroid hyperplasia

AHA: M-A, '85, 14

D75.9 Disease of blood and blood-forming organs unspec I-10

N Newborn Age: 0   P Pediatric Age: 0-17   M Maternity Age: 12-55   A Adult Age: 15-124   MCC Major CC Condition   CC CC Condition   HIV HIV Related Dx

84 – Volume 1 · February 2009   **2010 ICD-9-CM**

When the diagnostic statement mentions "with dementia", "delirium", or "psychotic" (or other similar terms), the condition should be coded as psychotic

5. MENTAL DISORDERS (290-319)

PSYCHOSES (290-299)

EXCLUDES   mental retardation (317-319)

ORGANIC PSYCHOTIC CONDITIONS (290-294)

INCLUDES   psychotic organic brain syndrome
EXCLUDES   nonpsychotic syndromes of organic etiology
(310.0-310.9)
psychoses classifiable to 295-298 and without
impairment of orientation, comprehension,
calculation, learning capacity, and judgment, but
associated with physical disease, injury, or
condition affecting the brain [eg., following
childbirth] (295.0-298.8)

√4ᵗʰ 290 Dementias

Code first the associated neurological condition

EXCLUDES   dementia due to alcohol (291.0-291.2)
dementia due to drugs (292.82)
dementia not classified as senile, presenile, or
arteriosclerotic (294.10-294.11)
psychoses classifiable to 295-298 occurring in the
senium without dementia or delirium
(295.0-298.8)
senility with mental changes of nonpsychotic severity
(310.1)
transient organic psychotic conditions (293.0-293.9)

290.0 Senile dementia, uncomplicated   **A**
Senile dementia: Senile dementia:
NOS   simple type
EXCLUDES   mild memory disturbances, not amounting to
dementia, associated with senile brain
disease ▶(310.8)◄
senile dementia with:
delirium or confusion (290.3)
delusional [paranoid] features (290.20)
depressive features (290.21)

AHA: 4Q, '99, 4

F03 Unspecified dementia   **I-10**

√5ᵗʰ 290.1 Presenile dementia
Brain syndrome with presenile brain disease
EXCLUDES   arteriosclerotic dementia (290.40-290.43)
dementia associated with other cerebral
conditions (294.10-294.11)

AHA: N-D, '84, 20

290.10 Presenile dementia, uncomplicated   **A HIV**
Presenile dementia:
NOS
simple type

290.11 Presenile dementia with delirium   **CC A HIV**
Presenile dementia with acute confusional state
CC Excl: 290.0-290.12, 290.20-290.3, 290.8-290.9,
292.81, 293.0, V62.84
AHA: 1Q, '88, 3

290.12 Presenile dementia with   **CC A HIV**
delusional features
Presenile dementia, paranoid type
CC Excl: 079.82, 290.0-290.12, 290.20-290.3,
290.8-290.9, 292.81, 293.0

290.13 Presenile dementia with   **CC A HIV**
depressive features
Presenile dementia, depressed type
CC Excl: 290.0, 290.13-290.3, 296.21-296.24,
296.30-296.34, 296.43-296.44, 296.53-296.54,
296.63-296.64

√5ᵗʰ 290.2 Senile dementia with delusional or depressive features
EXCLUDES   senile dementia:
NOS (290.0)
with delirium and/or confusion (290.3)

290.20 Senile dementia with delusional   **CC A**
features
Senile dementia, paranoid type
Senile psychosis NOS
CC Excl: 290.0-290.20, 290.3

290.21 Senile dementia with depressive   **CC A**
features
CC Excl: 290.13, 290.21

290.3 Senile dementia with delirium   **CC A**
Senile dementia with acute confusional state
EXCLUDES   senile:
dementia NOS (290.0)
psychosis NOS (290.20)
CC Excl: 290.10-290.20, 290.3, V62.84

√5ᵗʰ 290.4 Vascular dementia
Multi-infarct dementia or psychosis
Use additional code to identify cerebral atherosclerosis
(437.0)
EXCLUDES   suspected cases with no clear evidence of
arteriosclerosis (290.9)
AHA: 1Q, '88, 3

290.40 Vascular dementia, uncomplicated   **A**
Arteriosclerotic dementia:
NOS
simple type
F01.50 Vascular dementia without behavioral   **I-10**
disturbance

290.41 Vascular dementia with delirium   **CC A**
Arteriosclerotic dementia with acute
confusional state
CC Excl: 290.11-290.12, 290.20, 290.3, 290.41

290.42 Vascular dementia with delusions   **CC A**
Arteriosclerotic dementia, paranoid type
CC Excl: 290.42

290.43 Vascular dementia with depressed   **CC A**
mood
Arteriosclerotic dementia, depressed type
CC Excl: 290.43

290.8 Other specified senile psychotic conditions   **CC**
Presbyophrenic psychosis
CC Excl: 290.8-291.0, 292.11, 292.81-292.82, 295.00-295.04,
295.10-295.14, 295.21-295.24, 295.31, 295.33-295.34,
295.40-295.44, 295.53-295.54, 295.63-295.64, 295.71,
295.73-295.74, 295.80-295.84, 295.91, 295.93-295.94,
296.21-296.24, 296.30-296.34

290.9 Unspecified senile psychotic condition   **CC A**
CC Excl: See code: 290.8

√4ᵗʰ 291 Alcohol induced mental disorders
EXCLUDES   alcoholism without psychosis (303.0-303.9)
AHA: 1Q, '88, 3; S-O, '86, 3

291.0 Alcohol withdrawal delirium   **CC**
Alcoholic delirium
Delirium tremens
EXCLUDES   alcohol withdrawal (291.81)
CC Excl: 291.0-294.9, 303.00-305.03, 305.20-305.93, 790.3
AHA: 2Q, '91, 11
F10.921 Alcohol use unspecified w/intoxication delirium   **I-10**

291.1 Alcohol induced persisting amnestic disorder
Alcoholic polyneuritic psychosis
Korsakoff's psychosis, alcoholic
Wernicke-Korsakoff syndrome (alcoholic)
DEF: Prominent and lasting reduced memory span, disordered
time appreciation and confabulation, occurring in alcoholics,
as sequel to acute alcoholic psychosis.
AHA: 1Q, '88, 3

when the patient is admitted in or withdrawal. When withdrawal develops after admission, the withdrawal code is designated as the principal diagnosis with additional code for alcoholism.

Additional Digit Required   Unacceptable PDx   Manifestation Code   Hospital Acquired Condition   ▶◄ Revised Text   ● New Code   ▲ Revised Code Title

2010 ICD-9-CM   **October 2009 • Volume 1 – 85**

Mental Disorders

291.2 Alcohol induced persisting dementia `CC`
Alcoholic dementia NOS
Alcoholism associated with dementia NOS
Chronic alcoholic brain syndrome
CC Excl: See code: 291.0
F10.27 Alcohol depend alcohol-induced persist dementia `I-10`

see note at 291.0

291.3 Alcohol induced psychotic disorder with `CC`
hallucinations
Alcoholic:
   hallucinosis (acute)
   psychosis with hallucinosis
EXCLUDES *alcohol withdrawal with delirium (291.0)*
schizophrenia (295.0-295.9) and paranoid
states (297.0-297.9) taking the form of
chronic hallucinosis with clear
consciousness in an alcoholic
DEF: Psychosis lasting less than six months with slight or no
clouding of consciousness in which auditory hallucinations
predominate.
CC Excl: See code: 291.0
AHA: 2Q, '91, 11

291.4 Idiosyncratic alcohol intoxication
Pathologic: Pathologic:
   alcohol intoxication   drunkenness
EXCLUDES *acute alcohol intoxication (305.0)*
in alcoholism (303.0)
simple drunkenness (305.0)
DEF: Unique behavioral patterns, like belligerence, after intake
of relatively small amounts of alcohol; behavior not due to
excess consumption.

291.5 Alcohol induced psychotic disorder with delusions
Alcoholic: Alcoholic:
   paranoia   psychosis, paranoid type
EXCLUDES *nonalcoholic paranoid states (297.0-297.9)*
schizophrenia, paranoid type (295.3)

√5th **291.8 Other specified alcohol induced mental disorders**
AHA: 3Q, '94, 13; J-A, '85, 10

291.81 Alcohol withdrawal `CC`
Alcohol:
   abstinence syndrome or symptoms
   withdrawal syndrome or symptoms
EXCLUDES *alcohol withdrawal:*
delirium (291.0)
hallucinosis (291.3)
delirium tremens (291.0)
CC Excl: See code: 291.0
AHA: 4Q, '96, 28; 2Q, '91, 11
F10.239 Alcohol dependence with withdrawal `I-10`
unspecified

see note at 291.0

291.82 Alcohol induced sleep disorders
Alcohol induced circadian rhythm sleep
   disorders
Alcohol induced hypersomnia
Alcohol induced insomnia
Alcohol induced parasomnia

291.89 Other `CC`
Alcohol induced anxiety disorder
Alcohol induced mood disorder
Alcohol induced sexual dysfunction
CC Excl: See code: 291.0

291.9 Unspecified alcohol induced mental disorders `CC`
Alcoholic:
   mania NOS
   psychosis NOS
Alcoholism (chronic) with psychosis
Alcohol related disorder NOS
CC Excl: See code: 291.0

√4th **292 Drug induced mental disorders**
INCLUDES organic brain syndrome associated with consumption
of drugs
Use additional code for any associated drug dependence
(304.0-304.9)
Use additional E code to identify drug
AHA: 3Q, '04, 8; 2Q, '91, 11; S-O, '86, 3

292.0 Drug withdrawal `CC`
Drug:
   abstinence syndrome or symptoms
   withdrawal syndrome or symptoms
CC Excl: See code: 291.0
AHA: 1Q, '97, 12; 1Q, '88, 3
TIP: Assign only for patients who suffer mental or behavioral
disturbances due to drug withdrawal, regardless of the circumstances.
F19.939 Oth psychoactive sbstnc use uns w/withdrawal `I-10`
uns

√5th **292.1 Drug induced psychotic disorders**

292.11 Drug induced psychotic disorder `CC`
with delusions
Paranoid state induced by drugs
CC Excl: See code: 291.0

292.12 Drug induced psychotic disorder with `CC`
hallucinations
Hallucinatory state induced by drugs
EXCLUDES *states following LSD or other*
hallucinogens, lasting only a
few days or less ["bad trips"]
(305.3)
CC Excl: See code: 291.0

292.2 Pathological drug intoxication
Drug reaction:
   NOS
   idiosyncratic   } resulting in brief psychotic
   pathologic   } states
EXCLUDES *expected brief psychotic reactions to*
hallucinogens ["bad trips"] (305.3)
physiological side-effects of drugs (e.g.,
dystonias)

√5th **292.8 Other specified drug induced mental disorders**

292.81 Drug induced delirium `CC`
CC Excl: 291.0-294.9, 303.00-305.03, 305.20-305.93,
790.3
AHA: 1Q, '88, 3
F19.921 Oth psychoactv sbstnc use uns `I-10`
intoxcatn delirium

292.82 Drug induced persisting dementia `CC`
CC Excl: See code: 292.81

292.83 Drug induced persisting amnestic disorder

292.84 Drug induced mood disorder
Depressive state induced by drugs

292.85 Drug induced sleep disorders
Drug induced circadian rhythm sleep disorder
Drug induced hypersomnia
Drug induced insomnia
Drug induced parasomnia

292.89 Other
Drug induced anxiety disorder
Drug induced organic personality syndrome
Drug induced sexual dysfunction
Drug intoxication

292.9 Unspecified drug induced mental disorder
Drug related disorder NOS
Organic psychosis NOS due to or associated with drugs

| `N` Newborn Age: 0 | `P` Pediatric Age: 0-17 | `M` Maternity Age: 12-55 | `A` Adult Age: 15-124 | `MCC` Major CC Condition | `CC` CC Condition | `HIV` HIV Related Dx |

86 – Volume 1   **2010 ICD-9-CM**

293–294.9

√4ᵗʰ **293 Transient mental disorders due to conditions classified elsewhere**

> **INCLUDES** transient organic mental disorders not associated with alcohol or drugs

> Code first the associated physical or neurological condition

> **EXCLUDES** confusional state or delirium superimposed on senile dementia (290.3)
> dementia due to:
>> alcohol (291.0-291.9)
>> arteriosclerosis (290.40-290.43)
>> drugs (292.82)
>> senility (290.0)

293.0 Delirium due to conditions classified elsewhere CC
> Acute:
>> confusional state
>> infective psychosis
>> organic reaction
>> posttraumatic organic psychosis
>> psycho-organic syndrome
> Acute psychosis associated with endocrine, metabolic, or cerebrovascular disorder
> Epileptic:
>> confusional state
>> twilight state
> **CC Excl:** 290.11, 290.3, 293.0, V62.84
> **AHA:** 1Q, '88, 3
> **F05** Delirium due to known physiological condition I-10

293.1 Subacute delirium CC
> Subacute:
>> confusional state
>> infective psychosis
>> organic reaction
>> posttraumatic organic psychosis
>> psycho-organic syndrome
>> psychosis associated with endocrine or metabolic disorder
> **CC Excl:** 293.0-293.1, 293.89-293.9

√5ᵗʰ **293.8 Other specified transient mental disorders due to conditions classified elsewhere**

> **293.81 Psychotic disorder with delusions in conditions classified elsewhere** CC
>> Transient organic psychotic condition, paranoid type
>> **CC Excl:** 291.0-294.9, 303.00-305.03, 305.20-305.93, 790.3

> **293.82 Psychotic disorder with hallucinations in conditions classified elsewhere** CC
>> Transient organic psychotic condition, hallucinatory type
>> **CC Excl:** See code: 293.81

> **293.83 Mood disorder in conditions classified elsewhere**
>> Transient organic psychotic condition, depressive type

> **293.84 Anxiety disorder in conditions classified elsewhere**
>> **AHA:** 4Q, '96, 29

> **293.89 Other**
>> Catatonic disorder in conditions classified elsewhere

293.9 Unspecified transient mental disorder in conditions classified elsewhere CC
> Organic psychosis:
>> infective NOS
>> posttraumatic NOS
>> transient NOS
> Psycho-organic syndrome
> **CC Excl:** See code: 293.81

√4ᵗʰ **294 Persistent mental disorders due to conditions classified elsewhere**

> **INCLUDES** organic psychotic brain syndromes (chronic), not elsewhere classified

> **AHA:** M-A, '85, 12

294.0 Amnestic disorder in conditions classified elsewhere
> Korsakoff's psychosis or syndrome (nonalcoholic)
> Code first underlying condition
> **EXCLUDES** alcoholic:
>> amnestic syndrome (291.1)
>> Korsakoff's psychosis (291.1)

√5ᵗʰ **294.1 Dementia in conditions classified elsewhere**
> Dementia of the Alzheimer's type
> *Code first any underlying physical condition, as:*
>> dementia in:
>>> Alzheimer's disease (331.0)
>>> cerebral lipidoses (330.1)
>>> dementia with Lewy bodies (331.82)
>>> dementia with Parkinsonism (331.82)
>>> epilepsy (345.0-345.9)
>>> frontal dementia (331.19)
>>> frontotemporal dementia (331.19)
>>> general paresis [syphilis] (094.1)
>>> hepatolenticular degeneration (275.1)
>>> Huntington's chorea (333.4)
>>> Jakob-Creutzfeldt disease ▶(046.11-046.19)◀
>>> multiple sclerosis (340)
>>> Pick's disease of the brain (331.11)
>>> polyarteritis nodosa (446.0)
>>> syphilis (094.1)
> **EXCLUDES** dementia:
>> arteriosclerotic (290.40-290.43)
>> presenile (290.10-290.13)
>> senile (290.0)
>> epileptic psychosis NOS (294.8)
> **AHA:** 4Q, '00, 40; 1Q, '99, 14; N-D, '85, 5

> **294.10 *Dementia in conditions classified elsewhere without behavioral disturbance***
>> Dementia in conditions classified elsewhere NOS
>> **F02.80** Dementia in oth dz class elsw w/o behavrl disturb I-10

> **294.11 *Dementia in conditions classified elsewhere with behavioral disturbance*** CC
>> Aggressive behavior
>> Combative behavior
>> Violent behavior
>> Wandering off
>> **CC Excl:** 294.11
>> **AHA:** 4Q, '00, 41
>> **TIP:** Review entire medical record for documentation of behavioral disturbance (aggressive, combative, violent behavior, wandering off); requires physician substantiation.

294.8 Other persistent mental disorders due to conditions classified elsewhere
> Amnestic disorder NOS
> Dementia NOS
> Epileptic psychosis NOS
> Mixed paranoid and affective organic psychotic states
> Use additional code for associated epilepsy (345.0-345.9)
> **EXCLUDES** mild memory disturbances, not amounting to dementia ▶(310.8)◀
> **AHA:** 3Q, '03, 14; 1Q, '88, 5
> **F06.8** Oth spec mental disord d/t known physiol cond I-10

294.9 Unspecified persistent mental disorders due to conditions classified elsewhere HIV
> Cognitive disorder NOS
> Organic psychosis (chronic)
> **AHA:** 2Q, '07, 4

Mental Disorders

295–296

OTHER PSYCHOSES (295-299)

Use additional code to identify any associated physical disease, injury, or condition affecting the brain with psychoses classifiable to 295-298

√4th **295 Schizophrenic disorders**

INCLUDES schizophrenia of the types described in 295.0-295.9 occurring in children

EXCLUDES childhood type schizophrenia (299.9)
infantile autism (299.0)

The following fifth-digit subclassification is for use with category 295:
0 unspecified
1 subchronic
2 chronic
3 subchronic with acute exacerbation
4 chronic with acute exacerbation
5 in remission

DEF: Group of disorders with disturbances in thought (delusions, hallucinations), mood (blunted, flattened, inappropriate affect), sense of self; also bizarre, purposeless behavior, repetitious activity, or inactivity.

§ √5th **295.0 Simple type** CC 0-4
[0-5] Schizophrenia simplex
EXCLUDES latent schizophrenia (295.5)
CC Excl: For codes 295.00-295.04: 295.00-301.9, 306.0-319, 339.10-339.12, 388.45, 799.23-799.24

§ √5th **295.1 Disorganized type** CC 0-4
[0-5] Hebephrenia
Hebephrenic type schizophrenia
DEF: Inappropriate behavior; results in extreme incoherence and disorganization of time, place and sense of social appropriateness; withdrawal from routine social interaction may occur.
CC Excl: For codes 295.10-295.14: 295.00-301.9, 306.0-319, 339.10-339.12, 388.45, 799.23-799.24

§ √5th **295.2 Catatonic type** CC 0-4
[0-5] Catatonic (schizophrenia):
agitation
excitation
excited type
stupor
withdrawn type
Schizophrenic:
catalepsy
catatonia
flexibilitas cerea
DEF: Extreme changes in motor activity; one extreme is decreased response or reaction to the environment and the other is spontaneous activity.
CC Excl: For codes 295.20-295.24: 295.00-301.9, 306.0-319, 339.10-339.12, 388.45, 799.23-799.24

§ √5th **295.3 Paranoid type** CC 0-4
[0-5] Paraphrenic schizophrenia
EXCLUDES involutional paranoid state (297.2)
paranoia (297.1)
paraphrenia (297.2)
DEF: Preoccupied with delusional suspicions and auditory hallucinations related to single theme; usually hostile, grandiose, overly religious, occasionally hypochondriacal.
CC Excl: For codes 295.30-295.34: 295.00-301.9, 306.0-319, 339.10-339.12, 388.45, 799.23-799.24
F20.0 Paranoid schizophrenia I-10

§ √5th **295.4 Schizophreniform disorder** CC 0-4
[0-5] Oneirophrenia   Schizophreniform:
Schizophreniform: psychosis, confusional type
attack
EXCLUDES acute forms of schizophrenia of:
catatonic type (295.2)
hebephrenic type (295.1)
paranoid type (295.3)
simple type (295.0)
undifferentiated type (295.8)
CC Excl: For codes 295.40-295.44: 295.00-301.9, 306.0-319, 339.10-339.12, 388.45, 799.23-799.24

§ √5th **295.5 Latent schizophrenia** CC 3-4
[0-5] Latent schizophrenic reaction
Schizophrenia:
borderline
incipient
prepsychotic
prodromal
pseudoneurotic
pseudopsychopathic
EXCLUDES schizoid personality (301.20-301.22)
CC Excl: For code 295.53-295.54: 295.00-295.04, 295.10-295.14, 295.21-295.24, 295.31, 295.33-295.34, 295.40-295.44, 295.53-295.54, 295.63-295.64, 295.71, 295.73-295.74, 295.80-295.84, 295.91, 295.93-295.94
AHA: For code 295.50: 1Q, '06, 10

§ √5th **295.6 Residual type** CC 0-4
[0-5] Chronic undifferentiated schizophrenia
Restzustand (schizophrenic)
Schizophrenic residual state
CC Excl: For codes 295.60-295.64: 295.00-301.9, 306.0-319, 339.10-339.12, 388.45, 799.23-799.24
AHA: For code 295.62: 4Q, '06, 78

§ √5th **295.7 Schizoaffective disorder** CC 1-4
[0-5] Cyclic schizophrenia
Mixed schizophrenic and affective psychosis
Schizo-affective psychosis
Schizophreniform psychosis, affective type
CC Excl: For codes 295.71-295.74: 295.00-301.9, 306.0-319, 339.10-339.12, 388.45, 799.23-799.24
F25.9 Schizoaffective disorder unspecified I-10

§ √5th **295.8 Other specified types of schizophrenia** CC 0-4
[0-5] Acute (undifferentiated) schizophrenia
Atypical schizophrenia
Cenesthopathic schizophrenia
EXCLUDES infantile autism (299.0)
CC Excl: For codes 295.80-295.84: 295.00-301.9, 306.0-319, 339.10-339.12, 388.45, 799.23-799.24

§ √5th **295.9 Unspecified schizophrenia** CC 1-4
[0-5] Schizophrenia:
NOS
mixed NOS
undifferentiated NOS
undifferentiated type
Schizophrenic reaction NOS
Schizophreniform psychosis NOS
CC Excl: For codes 295.91-295.94: 295.00-301.9, 306.0-319, 339.10-339.12, 388.45, 799.23-799.24
AHA: 3Q, '95, 6
F20.9 Schizophrenia unspecified I-10

√4th **296 Episodic mood disorders**

INCLUDES episodic affective disorders
EXCLUDES neurotic depression (300.4)
reactive depressive psychosis (298.0)
reactive excitation (298.1)

The following fifth-digit subclassification is for use with categories 296.0-296.6:
0 unspecified
1 mild
2 moderate
3 severe, without mention of psychotic behavior
4 severe, specified as with psychotic behavior
5 in partial or unspecified remission
6 in full remission

AHA: M-A, '85, 14

§ Requires fifth digit. Valid digits are in [brackets] under each code. See appropriate category for codes and definitions.

N Newborn Age: 0   P Pediatric Age: 0-17   M Maternity Age: 12-55   A Adult Age: 15-124   MCC Major CC Condition   CC CC Condition   HIV HIV Related Dx

88 – Volume 1   **2010 ICD-9-CM**

§ √5th **296.0 Bipolar I disorder, single manic episode** `CC 0-4`
[0-6]
Hypomania (mild) NOS
Hypomanic psychosis
Mania (momopolar) NOS
Manic-depressive psychosis or
reaction:
hypomanic
manic
} single episode or unspecified

EXCLUDES *circular type, if there was a previous attack of depression (296.4)*

DEF: Mood disorder identified by hyperactivity; may show extreme agitation or exaggerated excitability; speech and thought processes may be accelerated.

CC Excl: For codes 296.00-296.02: 295.00-301.9, 306.0-319, 388.45; **For codes 296.03:** 296.03-296.04, 296.13-296.14, 296.43-296.44, 296.53-296.54, 296.63-296.64; **For codes 296.04:** 295.00-301.9, 306.0-319, 388.45

§ √5th **296.1 Manic disorder, recurrent episode** `CC 0-4`
[0-6]
Any condition classifiable to 296.0, stated to be recurrent

EXCLUDES *circular type, if there was a previous attack of depression (296.4)*

CC Excl: For codes 296.10-296.12: 295.00-301.9, 306.0-319, 339.10-339.12, 388.45; **For codes 296.13:** 296.13-296.14, 296.43-296.44, 296.53-296.54, 296.63-296.64; **For codes 296.14:** 295.00-301.9, 306.0-319, 339.10-339.12, 388.45

§ √5th **296.2 Major depressive disorder, single episode** `CC 0-4`
[0-6]
Depressive psychosis
Endogenous depression
Involutional melancholia
Manic-depressive psychosis or
reaction, depressed type
Monopolar depression
Psychotic depression
} single episode or unspecified

EXCLUDES *circular type, if previous attack was of manic type (296.5)*
depression NOS (311)
reactive depression (neurotic) (300.4)
psychotic (298.0)

DEF: Mood disorder that produces depression; may exhibit as sadness, low self-esteem, or guilt feelings; other manifestations may be withdrawal from friends and family; interrupted sleep.

CC Excl: For code 296.20: 295.00-301.9, 306.0-319, 339.10-339.12, 388.45; **For codes 296.21-296.24:** 296.21-296.24, 296.30-296.34

F32.9 Major depressive disorder single episode uns `I-10`

§ √5th **296.3 Major depressive disorder, recurrent episode** `CC 0-4`
[0-6]
Any condition classifiable to 296.2, stated to be recurrent

EXCLUDES *circular type, if previous attack was of manic type (296.5)*
depression NOS (311)
reactive depression (neurotic) (300.4)
psychotic (298.0)

CC Excl: For codes 296.30-296.33: 296.21-296.24, 296.30-296.34; **For codes 296.34:** 295.00-301.9, 306.0-319, 339.10-339.12, 388.45

F33.2 Maj dprsv disord recur sev w/o psychot features `I-10`

§ √5th **296.4 Bipolar I disorder, most recent episode** `CC 0-4`
[0-6] **(or current) manic**
Bipolar disorder, now manic
Manic-depressive psychosis, circular type but currently manic

EXCLUDES *brief compensatory or rebound mood swings (296.99)*

CC Excl: For codes 296.40-296.42 and 296.44: 295.00-301.9, 306.0-319, 339.10-339.12, 388.45; **For code 296.43:** 296.43-296.44, 296.63-296.64, 339.10-339.12

F31.2 Bipolar d/o currnt epis mnic sev w/psychotc ftur `I-10`

§ √5th **296.5 Bipolar I disorder, most recent episode** `CC 0-4`
[0-6] **(or current) depressed**
Bipolar disorder, now depressed
Manic-depressive psychosis, circular type but currently depressed

EXCLUDES *brief compensatory or rebound mood swings (296.99)*

CC Excl: For codes 296.50-296.52 and 296.54: 295.00-301.9, 306.0-319, 339.10-339.12, 388.45; **For code 296.53:** 296.43-296.44, 296.53-296.54, 296.63-296.64

F31.30 Bipol disord currnt epis dprsd mild/mod sev uns `I-10`

§ √5th **296.6 Bipolar I disorder, most recent episode** `CC 0-4`
[0-6] **(or current) mixed**
Manic-depressive psychosis, circular type, mixed

CC Excl: For codes 296.60-296.62 and 296.64: 295.00-301.9, 306.0-319, 339.10-339.12, 388.45; **For code 296.63:** 296.43-296.44, 296.53-296.54, 296.63-296.64

296.7 Bipolar I disorder, most recent episode (or current) unspecified
Atypical bipolar affective disorder NOS
Manic-depressive psychosis, circular type, current condition not specified as either manic or depressive

DEF: Manic-depressive disorder referred to as bipolar because of the mood range from manic to depressive.

√5th **296.8 Other and unspecified bipolar disorders**

296.80 Bipolar disorder, unspecified
Bipolar disorder NOS
Manic-depressive:
reaction NOS
syndrome NOS

F31.9 Bipolar disorder unspecified `I-10`

296.81 Atypical manic disorder

296.82 Atypical depressive disorder

296.89 Other `CC`
Bipolar II disorder
Manic-depressive psychosis, mixed type

CC Excl: 295.00-301.9, 306.0-319, 339.10-339.12, 388.45

F31.81 Bipolar II disorder `I-10`

√5th **296.9 Other and unspecified episodic mood disorder**

EXCLUDES *psychogenic affective psychoses (298.0-298.8)*

296.90 Unspecified episodic mood disorder
Affective psychosis NOS
Melancholia NOS
Mood disorder NOS

AHA: M-A, '85, 14

F39 Unspecified mood [affective] disorder `I-10`

296.99 Other specified episodic mood disorder `CC`
Mood swings:
brief compensatory
rebound

CC Excl: 295.00-301.9, 306.0-319, 339.10-339.12, 388.45

√4th **297 Delusional disorders**

INCLUDES paranoid disorders
EXCLUDES *acute paranoid reaction (298.3)*
alcoholic jealousy or paranoid state (291.5)
paranoid schizophrenia (295.3)

297.0 Paranoid state, simple

297.1 Delusional disorder
Chronic paranoid psychosis
Sander's disease
Systematized delusions

EXCLUDES *paranoid personality disorder (301.0)*

F22 Delusional disorders `I-10`

§   Requires fifth digit. Valid digits are in [brackets] under each code. See category 296 for codes and definitions.

√4th/√5th **Additional Digit Required**   **Unacceptable PDx**   **Manifestation Code**   **Hospital Acquired Condition**   ▶◀ Revised Text   ● New Code   ▲ Revised Code Title

2010 ICD-9-CM   **Volume 1 – 89**

296.0–297.1

297.2 Paraphrenia
Involutional paranoid state
Late paraphrenia
Paraphrenia (involutional)

DEF: Paranoid schizophrenic disorder that persists over a prolonged period but does not distort personality despite persistent delusions.

297.3 Shared psychotic disorder
Folie à deux
Induced psychosis or paranoid disorder

DEF: Mental disorder two people share; first person with the delusional disorder convinces second person because of a close relationship and shared experiences to accept the delusions.

297.8 Other specified paranoid states
Paranoia querulans
Sensitiver Beziehungswahn
EXCLUDES   acute paranoid reaction or state (298.3)
                senile paranoid state (290.20)

297.9 Unspecified paranoid state
Paranoid:
    disorder NOS
    psychosis NOS
    reaction NOS
    state NOS
AHA: J-A, '85, 9

✓4th **298 Other nonorganic psychoses**
INCLUDES   psychotic conditions due to or provoked by:
                emotional stress
                environmental factors as major part of etiology

298.0 Depressive type psychosis   CC
Psychogenic depressive psychosis
Psychotic reactive depression
Reactive depressive psychosis
EXCLUDES   manic-depressive psychosis, depressed type
                (296.2-296.3)
                neurotic depression (300.4)
                reactive depression NOS (300.4)
CC Excl: 295.00-301.9, 306.0-319, 339.10-339.12, 388.45

298.1 Excitative type psychosis   CC
Acute hysterical psychosis
Psychogenic excitation
Reactive excitation
EXCLUDES   manic-depressive psychosis, manic type
                (296.0-296.1)
DEF: Affective disorder similar to manic-depressive psychosis, in the manic phase, seemingly brought on by stress.
CC Excl: See code: 298.0

298.2 Reactive confusion
Psychogenic confusion
Psychogenic twilight state
EXCLUDES   acute confusional state (293.0)
DEF: Confusion, disorientation, cloudiness in consciousness; brought on by severe emotional upheaval.

298.3 Acute paranoid reaction   CC
Acute psychogenic paranoid psychosis
Bouffée délirante
EXCLUDES   paranoid states (297.0-297.9)
CC Excl: See code: 298.0

298.4 Psychogenic paranoid psychosis   CC
Protracted reactive paranoid psychosis
CC Excl: See code: 298.0

298.8 Other and unspecified reactive psychosis
Brief psychotic disorder
Brief reactive psychosis NOS
Hysterical psychosis
Psychogenic psychosis NOS
Psychogenic stupor
EXCLUDES   acute hysterical psychosis (298.1)

298.9 Unspecified psychosis   HIV
Atypical psychosis
Psychosis NOS
Psychotic disorder NOS
AHA: 3Q, '06, 22
F28 Oth psych d/o not d/t sbstnc/knwn physiolog cond I-10

✓4th **299 Pervasive developmental disorders**
EXCLUDES   adult type psychoses occurring in childhood, as:
                affective disorders (296.0-296.9)
                manic-depressive disorders (296.0-296.9)
                schizophrenia (295.0-295.9)

The following fifth-digit subclassification is for use with category 299:
    0 current or active state
    1 residual state

§ ✓5th **299.0 Autistic disorder**   CC
[0-1]   Childhood autism
        Infantile psychosis
        Kanner's syndrome
EXCLUDES   disintegrative psychosis (299.1)
                Heller's syndrome (299.1)
                schizophrenic syndrome of childhood (299.9)
DEF: Severe mental disorder of children, results in impaired social behavior; abnormal development of communicative skills, appears to be unaware of the need for emotional support and little emotional response to family members.
CC Excl: 295.00-301.9, 306.0-319, 339.10-339.12, 388.45

§ ✓5th **299.1 Childhood disintegrative disorder**   CC
[0-1]   Heller's syndrome
        Use additional code to identify any associated
                neurological disorder
EXCLUDES   infantile autism (299.0)
                schizophrenic syndrome of childhood (299.9)
DEF: Mental disease of children identified by impaired development of reciprocal social skills, verbal and nonverbal communication skills, imaginative play.
CC Excl: See code: 299.0

§ ✓5th **299.8 Other specified pervasive developmental disorders** CC
[0-1]   Asperger's disorder
        Atypical childhood psychosis
        Borderline psychosis of childhood
EXCLUDES   simple stereotypes without psychotic
                disturbance (307.3)
CC Excl: See code: 299.0

§ ✓5th **299.9 Unspecified pervasive developmental disorder** CC
[0-1]   Child psychosis NOS
        Pervasive developmental disorder NOS
        Schizophrenia, childhood type NOS
        Schizophrenic syndrome of childhood NOS
EXCLUDES   schizophrenia of adult type occurring in
                childhood (295.0-295.9)
CC Excl: See code: 299.0

NEUROTIC DISORDERS, PERSONALITY DISORDERS, AND OTHER NONPSYCHOTIC MENTAL DISORDERS (300-316)

✓4th **300 Anxiety, dissociative and somatoform disorders**

✓5th **300.0 Anxiety states**
EXCLUDES   anxiety in:
                acute stress reaction (308.0)
                transient adjustment reaction (309.24)
                neurasthenia (300.5)
                psychophysiological disorders (306.0-306.9)
                separation anxiety (309.21)
DEF: Mental disorder characterized by anxiety and avoidance behavior not particularly related to any specific situation or stimulus; symptoms include emotional instability, apprehension, fatigue.

§   Requires fifth digit. Valid digits are in [brackets] under each code. See category 299 for codes and definitions.

N Newborn Age: 0   P Pediatric Age: 0-17   M Maternity Age: 12-55   A Adult Age: 15-124   MCC Major CC Condition   CC CC Condition   HIV HIV Related Dx

90 – Volume 1   **2010 ICD-9-CM**

300.00 Anxiety state, unspecified
Anxiety:
  neurosis
  reaction
  state (neurotic)
Atypical anxiety disorder
AHA: 1Q, '02, 6
TIP: For chest pain due to anxiety, assign chest pain code first, because chest pain is not integral to the diagnosis of anxiety.
F41.9 Anxiety disorder unspecified `I-10`

300.01 Panic disorder without agoraphobia
Panic:
  attack
  state
EXCLUDES panic disorder with agoraphobia (300.21)
DEF: Neurotic disorder characterized by recurrent panic or anxiety, apprehension, fear or terror; symptoms include shortness of breath, palpitations, dizziness, shakiness; fear of dying may persist.
F41.0 Panic d/o [epis paroxysmal anxiety] w/o agoraphobia `I-10`

300.02 Generalized anxiety disorder

300.09 Other

√5ᵗʰ **300.1 Dissociative, conversion and factitious disorders**
EXCLUDES adjustment reaction (309.0-309.9)
  anorexia nervosa (307.1)
  gross stress reaction (308.0-308.9)
  hysterical personality (301.50-301.59)
  psychophysiologic disorders (306.0-306.9)

300.10 Hysteria, unspecified

300.11 Conversion disorder
Astasia-abasia, hysterical
Conversion hysteria or reaction
Hysterical:
  blindness
  deafness
  paralysis
DEF: Mental disorder that impairs physical functions with no physiological basis; sensory motor symptoms include seizures, paralysis, temporary blindness; increase in stress or avoidance of unpleasant responsibilities may precipitate.
AHA: N-D, '85, 15

300.12 Dissociative amnesia
Hysterical amnesia

300.13 Dissociative fugue
Hysterical fugue
DEF: Dissociative hysteria; identified by loss of memory, flight from familiar surroundings; conscious activity is not associated with perception of surroundings, no later memory of episode.

300.14 Dissociative identity disorder

300.15 Dissociative disorder or reaction, unspecified
DEF: Hysterical neurotic episode; sudden but temporary changes in perceived identity, memory, consciousness, segregated memory patterns exist separate from dominant personality.

300.16 Factitious disorder with predominantly psychological signs and symptoms
Compensation neurosis
Ganser's syndrome, hysterical
DEF: A disorder characterized by the purposeful assumption of mental illness symptoms; which are acted out more often when another person is present.

300.19 Other and unspecified factitious illness
Factitious disorder (with combined psychological and physical signs and symptoms) (with predominantly physical signs and symptoms) NOS
EXCLUDES multiple operations or hospital addiction syndrome (301.51)

√5ᵗʰ **300.2 Phobic disorders**
EXCLUDES anxiety state not associated with a specific situation or object (300.00-300.09)
  obsessional phobias (300.3)

300.20 Phobia, unspecified
Anxiety-hysteria NOS
Phobia NOS

300.21 Agoraphobia with panic disorder
Fear of:
  open spaces
  streets } with panic attacks
  travel
Panic disorder with agoraphobia
EXCLUDES agoraphobia without panic disorder (300.22)
  panic disorder without agoraphobia (300.01)

300.22 Agoraphobia without mention of panic attacks
Any condition classifiable to 300.21 without mention of panic attacks

300.23 Social phobia
Fear of:
  eating in public
  public speaking
  washing in public

300.29 Other isolated or specific phobias
Acrophobia
Animal phobias
Claustrophobia
Fear of crowds

300.3 Obsessive-compulsive disorders
Anancastic neurosis
Compulsive neurosis
Obsessional phobia [any]
EXCLUDES obsessive-compulsive symptoms occurring in:
  endogenous depression (296.2-296.3)
  organic states (eg., encephalitis)
  schizophrenia (295.0-295.9)

300.4 Dysthymic disorder
Anxiety depression
Depression with anxiety
Depressive reaction
Neurotic depressive state
Reactive depression
EXCLUDES adjustment reaction with depressive symptoms (309.0-309.1)
  depression NOS (311)
  manic-depressive psychosis, depressed type (296.2-296.3)
  reactive depressive psychosis (298.0)
DEF: Depression without psychosis; less severe depression related to personal change or unexpected circumstances; also referred to as "reactional depression."
F34.1 Dysthymic disorder `I-10`

300.5 Neurasthenia
Fatigue neurosis
Nervous debility
Psychogenic:
  asthenia
  general fatigue
Use additional code to identify any associated physical disorder
EXCLUDES anxiety state (300.00-300.09)
  neurotic depression (300.4)
  psychophysiological disorders (306.0-306.9)
  specific nonpsychotic mental disorders following organic brain damage (310.0-310.9)
DEF: Physical and mental symptoms caused primarily by what is known as mental exhaustion; symptoms include chronic weakness, fatigue.

Mental Disorders

300.6–301.82

300.6 Depersonalization disorder
Derealization (neurotic)
Neurotic state with depersonalization episode
> **EXCLUDES** depersonalization associated with:
> anxiety (300.00-300.09)
> depression (300.4)
> manic-depressive disorder or psychosis
> (296.0-296.9)
> schizophrenia (295.0-295.9)

DEF: Dissociative disorder characterized by feelings of strangeness about self or body image; symptoms include dizziness, anxiety, fear of insanity, loss of reality of surroundings.

300.7 Hypochondriasis
Body dysmorphic disorder
> **EXCLUDES** hypochondriasis in:
> hysteria (300.10-300.19)
> manic-depressive psychosis, depressed type
> (296.2-296.3)
> neurasthenia (300.5)
> obsessional disorder (300.3)
> schizophrenia (295.0-295.9)

√5ᵗʰ 300.8 Somatoform disorders

300.81 Somatization disorder
Briquet's disorder
Severe somatoform disorder

300.82 Undifferentiated somatoform disorder
Atypical somatoform disorder
Somatoform disorder NOS
> **DEF:** Disorders in which patients have symptoms that suggest an organic disease but no evidence of physical disorder after repeated testing.
> **AHA:** 4Q, '96, 29

300.89 Other somatoform disorders
Occupational neurosis, including writers' cramp
Psychasthenia
Psychasthenic neurosis

300.9 Unspecified nonpsychotic mental disorder
Psychoneurosis NOS

√4ᵗʰ 301 Personality disorders
> **INCLUDES** character neurosis

Use additional code to identify any associated neurosis or psychosis, or physical condition
> **EXCLUDES** nonpsychotic personality disorder associated with
> organic brain syndromes (310.0-310.9)

301.0 Paranoid personality disorder
Fanatic personality
Paranoid personality (disorder)
Paranoid traits
> **EXCLUDES** acute paranoid reaction (298.3)
> alcoholic paranoia (291.5)
> paranoid schizophrenia (295.3)
> paranoid states (297.0-297.9)

AHA: J-A, '85, 9

√5ᵗʰ 301.1 Affective personality disorder
> **EXCLUDES** affective psychotic disorders (296.0-296.9)
> neurasthenia (300.5)
> neurotic depression (300.4)

301.10 Affective personality disorder, unspecified

301.11 Chronic hypomanic personality disorder
Chronic hypomanic disorder
Hypomanic personality

301.12 Chronic depressive personality disorder
Chronic depressive disorder
Depressive character or personality

301.13 Cyclothymic disorder
Cycloid personality
Cyclothymia
Cyclothymic personality

√5ᵗʰ 301.2 Schizoid personality disorder
> **EXCLUDES** schizophrenia (295.0-295.9)

301.20 Schizoid personality disorder, unspecified

301.21 Introverted personality

301.22 Schizotypal personality disorder

301.3 Explosive personality disorder
Aggressive:
personality
reaction
Aggressiveness
Emotional instability (excessive)
Pathological emotionality
Quarrelsomeness
> **EXCLUDES** dyssocial personality (301.7)
> hysterical neurosis (300.10-300.19)

301.4 Obsessive-compulsive personality disorder
Anancastic personality
Obsessional personality
> **EXCLUDES** obsessive-compulsive disorder (300.3)
> phobic state (300.20-300.29)

√5ᵗʰ 301.5 Histrionic personality disorder
> **EXCLUDES** hysterical neurosis (300.10-300.19)

DEF: Extreme emotional behavior, often theatrical; often concerned about own appeal; may demand attention, exhibit seductive behavior.

301.50 Histrionic personality disorder, unspecified
Hysterical personality NOS

301.51 Chronic factitious illness with physical   **CC**
symptoms
Hospital addiction syndrome
Multiple operations syndrome
Munchausen syndrome
> **CC Excl:** 295.00-301.9, 306.0-319, 339.10-339.12,
> 388.45

301.59 Other histrionic personality disorder
Personality:
emotionally unstable
labile
psychoinfantile

301.6 Dependent personality disorder
Asthenic personality
Inadequate personality
Passive personality
> **EXCLUDES** neurasthenia (300.5)
> passive-aggressive personality (301.84)

DEF: Overwhelming feeling of helplessness; fears of abandonment may persist; difficulty in making personal decisions without confirmation by others; low self-esteem due to irrational sensitivity to criticism.

301.7 Antisocial personality disorder
Amoral personality
Asocial personality
Dyssocial personality
Personality disorder with predominantly sociopathic or asocial manifestation
> **EXCLUDES** disturbance of conduct without specifiable
> personality disorder (312.0-312.9)
> explosive personality (301.3)

DEF: Continuous antisocial behavior that violates rights of others; social traits include extreme aggression, total disregard for traditional social rules.
AHA: S-0, '84, 16

√5ᵗʰ 301.8 Other personality disorders

301.81 Narcissistic personality disorder
> **DEF:** Grandiose fantasy or behavior, lack of social empathy, hypersensitive to the lack of others' judgment, exploits others; need for continual admiration.

301.82 Avoidant personality disorder
> **DEF:** Personality disorder marked by feelings of social inferiority; sensitivity to criticism, emotionally restrained due to fear of rejection.

N Newborn Age: 0   **P** Pediatric Age: 0-17   **M** Maternity Age: 12-55   **A** Adult Age: 15-124   **MCC** Major CC Condition   **CC** CC Condition   **HIV** HIV Related Dx

92 – Volume 1   **2010 ICD-9-CM**

301.83 Borderline personality disorder

DEF: Personality disorder characterized by unstable moods, self-image, and interpersonal relationships; uncontrolled anger, impulsive and self-destructive acts, fears of abandonment, feelings of emptiness and boredom, recurrent suicide threats or self-mutilation.

F60.3 Borderline personality disorder   I-10

301.84 Passive-aggressive personality

DEF: Pattern of procrastination and refusal to meet standards; introduce own obstacles to success and exploit failure.

301.89 Other
Personality:
eccentric
"haltlose" type
immature
masochistic
psychoneurotic

EXCLUDES *psychoinfantile personality (301.59)*

301.9 Unspecified personality disorder
Pathological personality NOS
Personality disorder NOS
Psychopathic:
constitutional state
personality (disorder)

√4ᵗʰ 302 Sexual and gender identity disorders
EXCLUDES *sexual disorder manifest in:*
organic brain syndrome (290.0-294.9, 310.0-310.9)
psychosis (295.0-298.9)

302.0 Ego-dystonic sexual orientation
Ego-dystonic lesbianism
Sexual orientation conflict disorder
EXCLUDES *homosexual pedophilia (302.2)*

302.1 Zoophilia
Bestiality
DEF: A sociodeviant disorder marked by engaging in sexual intercourse with animals.

302.2 Pedophilia
DEF: A sociodeviant condition of adults characterized by sexual activity with children.

302.3 Transvestic fetishism
EXCLUDES *trans-sexualism (302.5)*
DEF: The desire to dress in clothing of opposite sex.

302.4 Exhibitionism
DEF: Sexual deviant behavior; exposure of genitals to strangers; behavior prompted by intense sexual urges and fantasies.

√5ᵗʰ 302.5 Trans-sexualism
Sex reassignment surgery status
EXCLUDES *transvestism (302.3)*
DEF: Gender identity disturbance; overwhelming desire to change anatomic sex, due to belief that individual is a member of the opposite sex.

302.50 With unspecified sexual history
302.51 With asexual history
302.52 With homosexual history
302.53 With heterosexual history

302.6 Gender identity disorder in children
Feminism in boys
Gender identity disorder NOS
EXCLUDES *gender identity disorder in adult (302.85)*
trans-sexualism (302.50-302.53)
transvestism (302.3)

√5ᵗʰ 302.7 Psychosexual dysfunction
EXCLUDES *impotence of organic origin (607.84)*
normal transient symptoms from ruptured hymen
transient or occasional failures of erection due to fatigue, anxiety, alcohol, or drugs

302.70 Psychosexual dysfunction, unspecified
Sexual dysfunction NOS

302.71 Hypoactive sexual desire disorder
EXCLUDES *decreased sexual desire NOS (799.81)*

302.72 With inhibited sexual excitement
Female sexual arousal disorder
Frigidity
Impotence
Male erectile disorder

302.73 Female orgasmic disorder   ♀
302.74 Male orgasmic disorder   ♂
302.75 Premature ejaculation   ♂
302.76 Dyspareunia, psychogenic   ♀
DEF: Difficult or painful sex due to psychosomatic state.

302.79 With other specified psychosexual dysfunctions
Sexual aversion disorder

√5ᵗʰ 302.8 Other specified psychosexual disorders

302.81 Fetishism
DEF: Psychosexual disorder noted for intense sexual urges and arousal precipitated by fantasies; use of inanimate objects, such as clothing, to stimulate sexual arousal, orgasm.

302.82 Voyeurism
DEF: Psychosexual disorder characterized by uncontrollable impulse to observe others, without their knowledge, who are nude or engaged in sexual activity.

302.83 Sexual masochism
DEF: Psychosexual disorder noted for need to achieve sexual gratification through humiliating or hurtful acts inflicted on self.

302.84 Sexual sadism
DEF: Psychosexual disorder noted for need to achieve sexual gratification through humiliating or hurtful acts inflicted on someone else.

302.85 Gender identity disorder in adolescents or adults
Use additional code to identify sex reassignment surgery status (302.5)
EXCLUDES *gender identity disorder NOS (302.6)*
gender identity disorder in children (302.6)

302.89 Other
Frotteurism
Nymphomania
Satyriasis

302.9 Unspecified psychosexual disorder
Paraphilia NOS
Pathologic sexuality NOS
Sexual deviation NOS
Sexual disorder NOS

Mental Disorders

303–305.1

√4th **303　Alcohol dependence syndrome**

Use additional code to identify any associated condition, as:
　alcoholic psychoses (291.0-291.9)
　drug dependence (304.0-304.9)
　physical complications of alcohol, such as:
　　cerebral degeneration (331.7)
　　cirrhosis of liver (571.2)
　　epilepsy (345.0-345.9)
　　gastritis (535.3)
　　hepatitis (571.1)
　　liver damage NOS (571.3)

EXCLUDES　*drunkenness NOS (305.0)*

The following fifth-digit subclassification is for use with category 303:
　0　unspecified
　1　continuous
　2　episodic
　3　in remission

AHA: 3Q, '95, 6; 2Q, '91, 9; 4Q, '88, 8; S-O, '86, 3

TIP: The patient has become physically addicted to alcohol and often experiences withdrawal symptoms when not drinking. Do not assign both 303.0X and 303.9X on the same encounter.

Covers both acute and chronic alcoholism ←

§ √5th **303.0　Acute alcoholic intoxication**
[0-3]　　Acute drunkenness in alcoholism

§ √5th **303.9　Other and unspecified alcohol dependence**
[0-3]　　Chronic alcoholism
　　　　Dipsomania
　　AHA: 2Q, '02, 4; 2Q, '89, 9 ; For code 303.90: 2Q, '07, 6
　　F10.20 Alcohol dependence uncomplicated　I-10
　　F10.21 Alcohol dependence in remission　I-10

√4th **304　Drug dependence**

EXCLUDES　*nondependent abuse of drugs (305.1-305.9)*

The following fifth-digit subclassification is for use with category 304:
　0　unspecified
　1　continuous
　2　episodic
　3　in remission

AHA: 2Q, '91, 10; 4Q, '88, 8; S-O, '86, 3

§ √5th **304.0　Opioid type dependence**　CC 1
[0-3]　　Heroin
　　　　Meperidine
　　　　Methadone
　　　　Morphine
　　　　Opium
　　　　Opium alkaloids and their derivatives
　　　　Synthetics with morphine-like effects
　　CC Excl: For code 304.01: 291.0-292.9, 303.00-305.03,
　　305.20-305.93, 790.3
　　AHA: 2Q, '06, 7

§ √5th **304.1　Sedative, hypnotic or anxiolytic dependence**　CC 1
[0-3]　　Barbiturates
　　　　Nonbarbiturate sedatives and tranquilizers with a similar
　　　　　　effect:
　　　　　　chlordiazepoxide
　　　　　　diazepam
　　　　　　glutethimide
　　　　　　meprobamate
　　　　　　methaqualone
　　CC Excl: For code 304.11: 291.0-292.9, 303.00-305.03,
　　305.20-305.93, 790.3

§ √5th **304.2　Cocaine dependence**　CC 1
[0-3]　　Coca leaves and derivatives
　　CC Excl: For code 304.21: 291.0-292.9, 303.00-305.03,
　　305.20-305.93, 790.3
　　F14.20 Cocaine dependence uncomplicated　I-10

§ √5th **304.3　Cannabis dependence**
[0-3]　　Hashish　　　　　　Marihuana
　　　　Hemp

§ √5th **304.4　Amphetamine and other psychostimulant dependence**　CC 1
[0-3]　　Methylphenidate　　　Phenmetrazine
　　CC Excl: For code 304.41: 291.0-292.9, 303.00-305.03,
　　305.20-305.93, 790.3

§ √5th **304.5　Hallucinogen dependence**　CC 1
[0-3]　　Dimethyltryptamine [DMT]
　　　　Lysergic acid diethylamide [LSD] and derivatives
　　　　Mescaline
　　　　Psilocybin
　　CC Excl: For code 304.51: 291.0-292.9, 303.00-305.03,
　　305.20-305.93, 790.3

§ √5th **304.6　Other specified drug dependence**　CC 1
[0-3]　　Absinthe addiction
　　　　Glue sniffing
　　　　Inhalant dependence
　　　　Phencyclidine dependence
　　EXCLUDES　*tobacco dependence (305.1)*
　　CC Excl: For code 304.61: 291.0-292.9, 303.00-305.03,
　　305.20-305.93, 790.3

§ √5th **304.7　Combinations of opioid type drug with any other**　CC 1
[0-3]　　CC Excl: For code 304.71: 291.0-292.9, 303.00-305.03,
　　305.20-305.93, 790.3
　　AHA: M-A, '86, 12

§ √5th **304.8　Combinations of drug dependence excluding opioid type drug**　CC 1
[0-3]　　CC Excl: For code 304.81: 291.0-292.9, 303.00-305.03,
　　305.20-305.93, 790.3
　　AHA: M-A, '86, 12

§ √5th **304.9　Unspecified drug dependence**　CC 1
[0-3]　　Drug addiction NOS
　　　　Drug dependence NOS
　　CC Excl: For code 304.91: 291.0-292.9, 303.00-305.03,
　　305.20-305.93, 790.3
　　AHA: For code 304.90: 4Q, '03, 103

√4th **305　Nondependent abuse of drugs**

Note: Includes cases where a person, for whom no other diagnosis is possible, has come under medical care because of the maladaptive effect of a drug on which he is not dependent and that he has taken on his own initiative to the detriment of his health or social functioning.

EXCLUDES　*alcohol dependence syndrome (303.0-303.9)*
　　　　　drug dependence (304.0-304.9)
　　　　　drug withdrawal syndrome (292.0)
　　　　　poisoning by drugs or medicinal substances
　　　　　(960.0-979.9)

The following fifth-digit subclassification is for use with codes 305.0,
305.2-305.9:
　0　unspecified
　1　continuous
　2　episodic
　3　in remission

AHA: 2Q, '91, 10; 4Q, '88, 8; S-O, '86, 3

§ √5th **305.0　Alcohol abuse**　*(303.9 for dependence)*
[0-3]　　Drunkenness NOS
　　　　Excessive drinking of alcohol NOS
　　　　"Hangover" (alcohol)
　　　　Inebriety NOS
　　EXCLUDES　*acute alcohol intoxication in alcoholism*
　　　　　　(303.0)
　　　　　　alcoholic psychoses (291.0-291.9)
　　AHA: 3Q, '96, 16
　　F10.10 Alcohol abuse uncomplicated　I-10

305.1　Tobacco use disorder
　　　Tobacco dependence
　　EXCLUDES　*history of tobacco use (V15.82)*
　　　　　　smoking complicating pregnancy (649.0)
　　　　　　tobacco use disorder complicating pregnancy
　　　　　　(649.0)
　　AHA: ▶1Q, '09, 16;◀ 2Q, '96, 10; N-D, '84, 12
　　F17.210 Nicotine dependence cigarettes uncomplicated　I-10

§　Requires fifth digit. Valid digits are in [brackets] under each code. See appropriate category for codes and definitions.

N Newborn Age: 0　　P Pediatric Age: 0-17　　M Maternity Age: 12-55　　A Adult Age: 15-124　　MCC Major CC Condition　　CC CC Condition　　HIV HIV Related Dx

§ ✓5th **305.2 Cannabis abuse**
[0-3]
    F12.10 Cannabis abuse uncomplicated   I-10

§ ✓5th **305.3 Hallucinogen abuse**
[0-3]
    Acute intoxication from hallucinogens ["bad trips"]
    LSD reaction

§ ✓5th **305.4 Sedative, hypnotic or anxiolytic abuse**
[0-3]

§ ✓5th **305.5 Opioid abuse**
[0-3]

§ ✓5th **305.6 Cocaine abuse**
[0-3]
    AHA: For code 305.60: 1Q, '05, 6; 1Q, '93, 25
    F14.10 Cocaine abuse uncomplicated   I-10

§ ✓5th **305.7 Amphetamine or related acting sympathomimetic
[0-3]   abuse**
    AHA: For code 305.70: 2Q, '03, 10–11

§ ✓5th **305.8 Antidepressant type abuse**
[0-3]

§ ✓5th **305.9 Other, mixed, or unspecified drug abuse**
[0-3]
    Caffeine intoxication
    Inhalant abuse
    "Laxative habit"
    Misuse of drugs NOS
    Nonprescribed use of drugs or patent medicinals
    Phencyclidine abuse
    AHA: 3Q, '99, 20

✓4th **306 Physiological malfunction arising from mental factors**
    INCLUDES psychogenic:
            physical symptoms   } not involving tissue
            physiological   }   damage
            manifestations   }

    EXCLUDES hysteria (300.11-300.19)
            physical symptoms secondary to a psychiatric disorder
                classified elsewhere
            psychic factors associated with physical conditions
                involving tissue damage classified elsewhere (316)
            specific nonpsychotic mental disorders following organic
                brain damage (310.0-310.9)

    DEF: Functional disturbances or interruptions due to mental or
    psychological causes; no tissue damage sustained in these conditions.

    306.0 Musculoskeletal
        Psychogenic paralysis
        Psychogenic torticollis
        EXCLUDES Gilles de la Tourette's syndrome (307.23)
                paralysis as hysterical or conversion reaction
                    (300.11)
                tics (307.20-307.22)

    306.1 Respiratory
        Psychogenic: Psychogenic:
            air hunger   hyperventilation
            cough   yawning
            hiccough
        EXCLUDES psychogenic asthma (316 and 493.9)

    306.2 Cardiovascular
        Cardiac neurosis
        Cardiovascular neurosis
        Neurocirculatory asthenia
        Psychogenic cardiovascular disorder
        EXCLUDES psychogenic paroxysmal tachycardia (316 and
                    427.2)

        DEF: Neurocirculatory asthenia: functional nervous and
        circulatory irregularities with palpitations, dyspnea, fatigue,
        rapid pulse, precordial pain, fear of effort, discomfort during
        exercise, anxiety; also called DaCosta's syndrome, Effort
        syndrome, Irritable or Soldier's Heart.
        AHA: J-A, '85, 14

306.3 Skin
    Psychogenic pruritus
    EXCLUDES psychogenic:
            alopecia (316 and 704.00)
            dermatitis (316 and 692.9)
            eczema (316 and 691.8 or 692.9)
            urticaria (316 and 708.0-708.9)

306.4 Gastrointestinal
    Aerophagy
    Cyclical vomiting, psychogenic
    Diarrhea, psychogenic
    Nervous gastritis
    Psychogenic dyspepsia
    EXCLUDES cyclical vomiting NOS (536.2)
                associated with migraine (346.2)
            globus hystericus (300.11)
            mucous colitis (316 and 564.9)
            psychogenic:
                cardiospasm (316 and 530.0)
                duodenal ulcer (316 and 532.0-532.9)
                gastric ulcer (316 and 531.0-531.9)
                peptic ulcer NOS (316 and 533.0-533.9)
                vomiting NOS (307.54)

    DEF: Aerophagy: excess swallowing of air, usually
    unconscious; related to anxiety; results in distended
    abdomen or belching, often interpreted by the patient as a
    physical disorder.
    AHA: 2Q, '89, 11

✓5th **306.5 Genitourinary**
    EXCLUDES enuresis, psychogenic (307.6)
            frigidity (302.72)
            impotence (302.72)
            psychogenic dyspareunia (302.76)

    **306.50 Psychogenic genitourinary malfunction,
            unspecified**

    306.51 Psychogenic vaginismus   ♀
        Functional vaginismus
        DEF: Psychogenic response resulting in painful
        contractions of vaginal canal muscles; can be
        severe enough to prevent sexual intercourse.

    306.52 Psychogenic dysmenorrhea   ♀

    306.53 Psychogenic dysuria

    306.59 Other
        AHA: M-A, '87, 11

306.6 Endocrine

306.7 Organs of special sense
    EXCLUDES hysterical blindness or deafness (300.11)
            psychophysical visual disturbances (368.16)

306.8 Other specified psychophysiological malfunction
    Bruxism
    Teeth grinding

306.9 Unspecified psychophysiological malfunction
    Psychophysiologic disorder NOS
    Psychosomatic disorder NOS

✓4th **307 Special symptoms or syndromes, not elsewhere classified**
    Note: This category is intended for use if the psychopathology is
    manifested by a single specific symptom or group of
    symptoms which is not part of an organic illness or other
    mental disorder classifiable elsewhere.
    EXCLUDES those due to mental disorders classified elsewhere
            those of organic origin

    307.0 Stuttering
        EXCLUDES dysphasia ▶(784.59)◀
                lisping or lalling (307.9)
                retarded development of speech
                    (315.31-315.39)
                ▶stuttering (fluency disorder) due to late effect of
                    cerebrovascular accident (438.14)◀

---

§   Requires fifth digit. Valid digits are in [brackets] under each code. See appropriate category for codes and definitions.

✓4th ✓5th Additional Digit Required   Unacceptable PDx   Manifestation Code   Hospital Acquired Condition   ▶◀ Revised Text   ● New Code   ▲ Revised Code Title

Mental Disorders

307.1–307.7

307.1   **Anorexia nervosa**   `CC`

> **EXCLUDES**   *eating disturbance NOS (307.50)*
> *feeding problem (783.3)*
> *of nonorganic origin (307.59)*
> *loss of appetite (783.0)*
> *of nonorganic origin (307.59)*

> **CC Excl:** 306.4, 306.8-306.9, 307.1, 307.50-307.59, 309.22
> **AHA:** 2Q, '06, 12; 4Q, '89, 11
> **TIP:** Assign an additional code for any associated malnutrition.

✓5th   **307.2**   **Tics**

> **EXCLUDES**   *nail-biting or thumb-sucking (307.9)*
> *stereotypes occurring in isolation (307.3)*
> *tics of organic origin (333.3)*

> **DEF:** Involuntary muscle response usually confined to the face, shoulders.

307.20   **Tic disorder, unspecified**
> Tic disorder NOS

307.21   **Transient tic disorder**

307.22   **Chronic motor or vocal tic disorder**

307.23   **Tourette's disorder**
> Motor-verbal tic disorder
> **DEF:** Syndrome of facial and vocal tics in childhood; progresses to spontaneous or involuntary jerking, obscene utterances, other uncontrollable actions considered inappropriate.

307.3   **Stereotypic movement disorder**
> Body-rocking
> Head banging
> Spasmus nutans
> Stereotypes NOS

> **EXCLUDES**   *tics (307.20-307.23)*
> *of organic origin (333.3)*

✓5th   **307.4**   **Specific disorders of sleep of nonorganic origin**

> **EXCLUDES**   *narcolepsy (347.00-347.11)*
> *organic hypersomnia (327.10-327.19)*
> *organic insomnia (327.00-327.09)*
> *those of unspecified cause (780.50-780.59)*

307.40   **Nonorganic sleep disorder, unspecified**

307.41   **Transient disorder of initiating or maintaining sleep**
> Adjustment insomnia
> Hyposomnia ⎤ associated with intermittent
> Insomnia ⎬ emotional reactions or
> Sleeplessness ⎦ conflicts

307.42   **Persistent disorder of initiating or maintaining sleep**
> Hyposomnia, insomnia, or sleeplessness associated with:
> anxiety
> conditioned arousal
> depression (major) (minor)
> psychosis
> Idiopathic insomnia
> Paradoxical insomnia
> Primary insomnia
> Psychophysiological insomnia

307.43   **Transient disorder of initiating or maintaining wakefulness**
> Hypersomnia associated with acute or intermittent emotional reactions or conflicts

307.44   **Persistent disorder of initiating or maintaining wakefulness**
> Hypersomnia associated with depression (major) (minor)
> Insufficient sleep syndrome
> Primary hypersomnia

> **EXCLUDES**   *sleep deprivation (V69.4)*

307.45   **Circadian rhythm sleep disorder of nonorganic origin**

307.46   **Sleep arousal disorder**
> Night terror disorder
> Night terrors
> Sleep terror disorder
> Sleepwalking
> Somnambulism

> **DEF:** Sleepwalking marked by extreme terror, panic, screaming, confusion; no recall of event upon arousal; term may refer to simply the act of sleepwalking.

307.47   **Other dysfunctions of sleep stages or arousal from sleep**
> Nightmare disorder
> Nightmares:
> NOS
> REM-sleep type
> Sleep drunkenness

307.48   **Repetitive intrusions of sleep**
> Repetitive intrusion of sleep with:
> atypical polysomnographic features
> environmental disturbances
> repeated REM-sleep interruptions

307.49   **Other**
> "Short-sleeper"
> Subjective insomnia complaint

✓5th   **307.5**   **Other and unspecified disorders of eating**

> **EXCLUDES**   *anorexia:*
> *nervosa (307.1)*
> *of unspecified cause (783.0)*
> *overeating, of unspecified cause (783.6)*
> *vomiting:*
> *NOS (787.03)*
> *cyclical (536.2)*
> *associated with migraine (346.2)*
> *psychogenic (306.4)*

307.50   **Eating disorder, unspecified**
> Eating disorder NOS

307.51   **Bulimia nervosa**   `CC`
> Overeating of nonorganic origin
> **DEF:** Mental disorder commonly characterized by binge eating followed by self-induced vomiting; perceptions of being fat; and fear the inability to stop eating voluntarily.

> **CC Excl:** 307.1, 307.50-307.51, 307.53-307.59

307.52   **Pica**
> Perverted appetite of nonorganic origin
> **DEF:** Compulsive eating disorder characterized by craving for substances, other than food; such as paint chips or dirt.

307.53   **Rumination disorder**
> Regurgitation, of nonorganic origin, of food with reswallowing

> **EXCLUDES**   *obsessional rumination (300.3)*

307.54   **Psychogenic vomiting**

307.59   **Other**
> Feeding disorder of infancy or early childhood of nonorganic origin
> Infantile feeding ⎤ of nonorganic
> disturbances ⎬ origin
> Loss of appetite ⎦

307.6   **Enuresis**
> Enuresis (primary) (secondary) of nonorganic origin
> **EXCLUDES**   *enuresis of unspecified cause (788.3)*
> **DEF:** Involuntary urination past age of normal control; also called bedwetting; no trace to biological problem; focus on psychological issues.

307.7   **Encopresis**
> Encopresis (continuous) (discontinuous) of nonorganic origin
> **EXCLUDES**   *encopresis of unspecified cause (787.6)*
> **DEF:** Inability to control bowel movements; cause traced to psychological, not biological, problems.

N Newborn Age: 0   **P** Pediatric Age: 0-17   **M** Maternity Age: 12-55   **A** Adult Age: 15-124   **MCC** Major CC Condition   **CC** CC Condition   **HIV** HIV Related Dx

96 – Volume 1   **2010 ICD-9-CM**

✓5th **307.8 Pain disorders related to psychological factors**

307.80 Psychogenic pain, site unspecified

307.81 Tension headache

> EXCLUDES   *headache:*
> *NOS (784.0)*
> *migraine (346.0-346.9)*
> *syndromes (339.00-339.89)*
> *tension type (339.10-339.12)*

> AHA: ▶4Q, '08, 103;◀ N-D, '85, 16

307.89 Other
Code first to type or site of pain

> EXCLUDES   *pain disorder exclusively attributed to*
> *psychological factors (307.80)*
> *psychogenic pain (307.80)*

307.9 Other and unspecified special symptoms or syndromes, not elsewhere classified

Communication disorder NOS	Lisping
Hair plucking	Masturbation
Lalling	Nail-biting
	Thumb-sucking

✓4th **308 Acute reaction to stress**

> INCLUDES   catastrophic stress
> combat fatigue
> gross stress reaction (acute)
> transient disorders in response to exceptional physical or mental stress which usually subside within hours or days

> EXCLUDES   *adjustment reaction or disorder (309.0-309.9)*
> *chronic stress reaction (309.1-309.9)*

308.0 Predominant disturbance of emotions

Anxiety
Emotional crisis   } as acute reaction to exceptional
Panic state   [gross] stress

308.1 Predominant disturbance of consciousness
Fugues as acute reaction to exceptional [gross] stress

308.2 Predominant psychomotor disturbance

Agitation states } as acute reaction to exceptional
Stupor   [gross] stress

308.3 Other acute reactions to stress
Acute situational disturbance
Acute stress disorder

> EXCLUDES   *prolonged posttraumatic emotional disturbance (309.81)*

308.4 Mixed disorders as reaction to stress

308.9 Unspecified acute reaction to stress

✓4th **309 Adjustment reaction**

> INCLUDES   adjustment disorders
> reaction (adjustment) to chronic stress

> EXCLUDES   *acute reaction to major stress (308.0-308.9)*
> *neurotic disorders (300.0-300.9)*

309.0 Adjustment disorder with depressed mood
Grief reaction

> EXCLUDES   *affective psychoses (296.0-296.9)*
> *neurotic depression (300.4)*
> *prolonged depressive reaction (309.1)*
> *psychogenic depressive psychosis (298.0)*

> F43.21 Adjustment disorder with depressed mood   I-10

309.1 Prolonged depressive reaction

> EXCLUDES   *affective psychoses (296.0-296.9)*
> *brief depressive reaction (309.0)*
> *neurotic depression (300.4)*
> *psychogenic depressive psychosis (298.0)*

✓5th **309.2 With predominant disturbance of other emotions**

309.21 Separation anxiety disorder

> DEF: Abnormal apprehension by a child when physically separated from support environment; byproduct of abnormal symbiotic child-parent relationship.

309.22 Emancipation disorder of adolescence and early adult life

> DEF: Adjustment reaction of late adolescence; conflict over independence from parental supervision; symptoms include difficulty in making decisions, increased reliance on parental advice, deliberate adoption of values in opposition of parents.

309.23 Specific academic or work inhibition

309.24 Adjustment disorder with anxiety

309.28 Adjustment disorder with mixed anxiety and depressed mood
Adjustment reaction with anxiety and depression

> F43.23 Adjustment d/o w/mixed anxiety &   I-10
> depressed mood

309.29 Other
Culture shock

309.3 Adjustment disorder with disturbance of conduct

Conduct disturbance   } as adjustment reaction
Destructiveness

> EXCLUDES   *destructiveness in child (312.9)*
> *disturbance of conduct NOS (312.9)*
> *dyssocial behavior without manifest psychiatric disorder (V71.01-V71.02)*
> *personality disorder with predominantly sociopathic or asocial manifestations (301.7)*

309.4 Adjustment disorder with mixed disturbance of emotions and conduct

✓5th **309.8 Other specified adjustment reactions**

309.81 Posttraumatic stress disorder
Chronic posttraumatic stress disorder
Concentration camp syndrome
Posttraumatic stress disorder NOS
Post-traumatic stress disorder (PTSD)

> EXCLUDES   *acute stress disorder (308.3)*
> *posttraumatic brain syndrome:*
> *nonpsychotic (310.2)*
> *psychotic (293.0-293.9)*

> DEF: Preoccupation with traumatic events beyond normal experience; i.e., rape, personal assault, etc. also recurring flashbacks of trauma; symptoms include difficulty remembering, sleeping, or concentrating, and guilt feelings for surviving.

309.82 Adjustment reaction with physical symptoms

309.83 Adjustment reaction with withdrawal
Elective mutism as adjustment reaction
Hospitalism (in children) NOS

309.89 Other

309.9 Unspecified adjustment reaction
Adaptation reaction NOS
Adjustment reaction NOS

✓4th **310 Specific nonpsychotic mental disorders due to brain damage**

> EXCLUDES   *neuroses, personality disorders, or other nonpsychotic conditions occurring in a form similar to that seen with functional disorders but in association with a physical condition (300.0-300.9, 301.0-301.9)*

310.0 Frontal lobe syndrome
Lobotomy syndrome
Postleucotomy syndrome [state]

> EXCLUDES   *postcontusion syndrome (310.2)*

✓4th ✓5th Additional Digit Required   Unacceptable PDx   Manifestation Code   Hospital Acquired Condition   ▶◀ Revised Text   ● New Code   ▲ Revised Code Title

2010 ICD-9-CM   **February 2009 · Volume 1 – 97**

Mental Disorders

310.1–313.1

310.1 Personality change due to conditions classified elsewhere
Cognitive or personality change of other type, of nonpsychotic severity
Organic psychosyndrome of nonpsychotic severity
Presbyophrenia NOS
Senility with mental changes of nonpsychotic severity

EXCLUDES ▶ mild cognitive impairment (331.83)
postconcussion syndrome (310.2)
signs and symptoms involving emotional state (799.21-799.29)◀

DEF: Personality disorder caused by organic factors, such as brain lesions, head trauma, or cerebrovascular accident (CVA).
AHA: 2Q, '05, 6

310.2 Postconcussion syndrome
Postcontusion syndrome or encephalopathy
Posttraumatic brain syndrome, nonpsychotic
Status postcommotio cerebri

Use additional code to identify associated post-traumatic headache, if applicable (339.20-339.22)

EXCLUDES frontal lobe syndrome (310.0)
postencephalitic syndrome (310.8)
any organic psychotic conditions following head injury (293.0-294.0)

DEF: Nonpsychotic disorder due to brain trauma, causes symptoms unrelated to any disease process; symptoms include amnesia, serial headaches, rapid heartbeat, fatigue, disrupted sleep patterns, inability to concentrate.
AHA: 4Q, '90, 24

TIP: For treatment within 24 to 48 hours of the concussion, clarify with physician whether the concussion is still in the acute phase; if so, assign instead a code from 850.X subcategory.

310.8 Other specified nonpsychotic mental disorders following organic brain damage
Mild memory disturbance
Postencephalitic syndrome
Other focal (partial) organic psychosyndromes

EXCLUDES ▶ memory loss of unknown cause (780.93)◀

310.9 Unspecified nonpsychotic mental disorder following organic brain damage   **HIV**
AHA: 4Q, '03, 103

311 Depressive disorder, not elsewhere classified
Depressive disorder NOS   Depression NOS
Depressive state NOS

EXCLUDES acute reaction to major stress with depressive symptoms (308.0)
affective personality disorder (301.10-301.13)
affective psychoses (296.0-296.9)
brief depressive reaction (309.0)
depressive states associated with stressful events (309.0-309.1)
disturbance of emotions specific to childhood and adolescence, with misery and unhappiness (313.1)
mixed adjustment reaction with depressive symptoms (309.4)
neurotic depression (300.4)
prolonged depressive adjustment reaction (309.1)
psychogenic depressive psychosis (298.0)

AHA: 4Q, '03, 75

✓4th **312 Disturbance of conduct, not elsewhere classified**

EXCLUDES adjustment reaction with disturbance of conduct (309.3)
drug dependence (304.0-304.9)
dyssocial behavior without manifest psychiatric disorder (V71.01-V71.02)
personality disorder with predominantly sociopathic or asocial manifestations (301.7)
sexual deviations (302.0-302.9)

The following fifth-digit subclassification is for use with categories 312.0-312.2
   0   unspecified
   1   mild
   2   moderate
   3   severe

§ ✓5th **312.0 Undersocialized conduct disorder, aggressive type**
[0-3]   Aggressive outburst
Anger reaction
Unsocialized aggressive disorder
DEF: Mental condition identified by behaviors disrespectful of others' rights and of age-appropriate social norms or rules; symptoms include bullying, vandalism, verbal and physical abusiveness, lying, stealing, defiance.

§ ✓5th **312.1 Undersocialized conduct disorder, unaggressive type**
[0-3]   Childhood truancy, unsocialized
Solitary stealing
Tantrums

§ ✓5th **312.2 Socialized conduct disorder**
[0-3]   Childhood truancy, socialized
Group delinquency
EXCLUDES gang activity without manifest psychiatric disorder (V71.01)

✓5th **312.3 Disorders of impulse control, not elsewhere classified**
   312.30 Impulse control disorder, unspecified
   312.31 Pathological gambling
   312.32 Kleptomania
   312.33 Pyromania
   312.34 Intermittent explosive disorder
   312.35 Isolated explosive disorder
   312.39 Other
       Trichotillomania

312.4 Mixed disturbance of conduct and emotions
Neurotic delinquency
EXCLUDES compulsive conduct disorder (312.3)

✓5th **312.8 Other specified disturbances of conduct, not elsewhere classified**
   312.81 Conduct disorder, childhood onset type
   312.82 Conduct disorder, adolescent onset type
   312.89 Other conduct disorder
       Conduct disorder of unspecified onset

312.9 Unspecified disturbance of conduct
Delinquency (juvenile)
Disruptive behavior disorder NOS

✓4th **313 Disturbance of emotions specific to childhood and adolescence**
EXCLUDES adjustment reaction (309.0-309.9)
emotional disorder of neurotic type (300.0-300.9)
masturbation, nail-biting, thumbsucking, and other isolated symptoms (307.0-307.9)

313.0 Overanxious disorder
Anxiety and fearfulness } of childhood and
Overanxious disorder   } adolescence
EXCLUDES abnormal separation anxiety (309.21)
anxiety states (300.00-300.09)
hospitalism in children (309.83)
phobic state (300.20-300.29)

313.1 Misery and unhappiness disorder
EXCLUDES depressive neurosis (300.4)

§   Requires fifth digit. Valid digits are in [brackets] under each code. See category 312 for codes and definitions.

N Newborn Age: 0   P Pediatric Age: 0-17   M Maternity Age: 12-55   A Adult Age: 15-124   MCC Major CC Condition   CC CC Condition   HIV HIV Related Dx

98 – Volume 1 · October 2009   **2010 ICD-9-CM**

☑5th **313.2** **Sensitivity, shyness, and social withdrawal disorder**

> **EXCLUDES**   *infantile autism (299.0)*
> *schizoid personality (301.20-301.22)*
> *schizophrenia (295.0-295.9)*

313.21 **Shyness disorder of childhood**
Sensitivity reaction of childhood or adolescence

313.22 **Introverted disorder of childhood**
Social withdrawal ⎤ of childhood and
Withdrawal reaction ⎦ adolescence

313.23 **Selective mutism**

> **EXCLUDES**   *elective mutism as adjustment*
> *reaction (309.83)*

313.3 **Relationship problems**
Sibling jealousy

> **EXCLUDES**   *relationship problems associated with*
> *aggression, destruction, or other forms*
> *of conduct disturbance (312.0-312.9)*

☑5th **313.8** **Other or mixed emotional disturbances of childhood or adolescence**

313.81 **Oppositional defiant disorder**

> **DEF:** Mental disorder of children noted for pervasive opposition, defiance of authority.

313.82 **Identity disorder**
Identity problem

> **DEF:** Distress of adolescents caused by inability to form acceptable self-identity; uncertainty about career choice, sexual orientation, moral values.

313.83 **Academic underachievement disorder**

313.89 **Other** 🅿

Reactive attachment disorder of infancy or early childhood

313.9 **Unspecified emotional disturbance of** 🅿
childhood or adolescence
Mental disorder of infancy, childhood or adolescence NOS

☑4th **314** **Hyperkinetic syndrome of childhood**

> **EXCLUDES**   *hyperkinesis as symptom of underlying disorder–code*
> *the underlying disorder*

> **TIP:** These codes may be assigned for patients of any age.

☑5th **314.0** **Attention deficit disorder**
Adult
Child

> **DEF:** A behavioral disorder usually diagnosed at an early age; characterized by the inability to focus attention for a normal period of time.

314.00 **Without mention of hyperactivity**
Predominantly inattentive type

> **AHA:** 1Q, '97, 8

314.01 **With hyperactivity**
Combined type
Overactivity NOS
Predominantly hyperactive/impulsive type
Simple disturbance of attention with overactivity

> **AHA:** 1Q, '97, 8

> **F90.1** ADHD predominantly hyperactive type I-10

314.1 **Hyperkinesis with developmental delay**
Developmental disorder of hyperkinesis

> Use additional code to identify any associated neurological disorder

314.2 **Hyperkinetic conduct disorder**
Hyperkinetic conduct disorder without developmental delay

> **EXCLUDES**   *hyperkinesis with significant delays in specific*
> *skills (314.1)*

314.8 **Other specified manifestations of hyperkinetic syndrome**

314.9 **Unspecified hyperkinetic syndrome**
Hyperkinetic reaction of childhood or adolescence NOS
Hyperkinetic syndrome NOS

☑4th **315** **Specific delays in development**

> **EXCLUDES**   *that due to a neurological disorder (320.0-389.9)*

☑5th **315.0** **Specific reading disorder**

315.00 **Reading disorder, unspecified**

315.01 **Alexia**

> **DEF:** Lack of ability to understand written language; manifestation of aphasia.

315.02 **Developmental dyslexia**

> **DEF:** Serious impairment of reading skills unexplained in relation to general intelligence and teaching processes.

315.09 **Other**
Specific spelling difficulty

315.1 **Mathematics disorder**
Dyscalculia

315.2 **Other specific learning difficulties**
Disorder of written expression

> **EXCLUDES**   *specific arithmetical disorder (315.1)*
> *specific reading disorder (315.00-315.09)*

☑5th **315.3** **Developmental speech or language disorder**

315.31 **Expressive language disorder**
Developmental aphasia
Word deafness

> **EXCLUDES**   *acquired aphasia (784.3)*
> *elective mutism (309.83, 313.0,*
> *313.23)*

315.32 **Mixed receptive-expressive language disorder**
Central auditory processing disorder

> **EXCLUDES**   *acquired auditory processing*
> *disorder (388.45)*

> **AHA:** 2Q, '05, 5; 4Q, '96, 30

315.34 **Speech and language developmental delay due to hearing loss**

> **AHA:** 4Q, '07, 80, 81

315.39 **Other**
Developmental articulation disorder
Dyslalia
Phonological disorder

> **EXCLUDES**   *lisping and lalling (307.9)*
> *stammering and stuttering (307.0)*

> **AHA:** 3Q, '07, 7

315.4 **Developmental coordination disorder**
Clumsiness syndrome
Dyspraxia syndrome
Specific motor development disorder

315.5 **Mixed development disorder**

> **AHA:** 2Q, '02, 11

315.8 **Other specified delays in development**

> **F88** Other disorders of psychological development I-10

315.9 **Unspecified delay in development**
Developmental disorder NOS
Learning disorder NOS

☑4th ☑5th Additional Digit Required   Unacceptable PDx   Manifestation Code   Hospital Acquired Condition   ▶◀ Revised Text   ● New Code   ▲ Revised Code Title

2010 ICD-9-CM   **Volume 1 – 99**

Mental Disorders

316–319

316　Psychic factors associated with diseases classified elsewhere

Psychologic factors in physical conditions classified elsewhere

Use additional code to identify the associated physical condition, as:

psychogenic:
- asthma (493.9)
- dermatitis (692.9)
- duodenal ulcer (532.0-532.9)
- eczema (691.8, 692.9)
- gastric ulcer (531.0-531.9)
- mucous colitis (564.9)
- paroxysmal tachycardia (427.2)
- ulcerative colitis (556)
- urticaria (708.0-708.9)

psychosocial dwarfism (259.4)

> **EXCLUDES**　physical symptoms and physiological malfunctions, not involving tissue damage, of mental origin (306.0-306.9)

MENTAL RETARDATION (317-319)

Use additional code(s) to identify any associated psychiatric or physical condition(s)

317　Mild mental retardation

High-grade defect
IQ 50-70
Mild mental subnormality

F70 Mild mental retardation　　　　　　　　　　I-10

✓4ᵗʰ　**318　Other specified mental retardation**

318.0　Moderate mental retardation

IQ 35-49
Moderate mental subnormality

318.1　Severe mental retardation　　　　　　CC

IQ 20-34
Severe mental subnormality
CC Excl: 318.1-318.2

318.2　Profound mental retardation　　　　　CC

IQ under 20
Profound mental subnormality
CC Excl: See code: 318.1

319　Unspecified mental retardation

Mental deficiency NOS
Mental subnormality NOS

F79 Unspecified mental retardation　　　　　　I-10

N Newborn Age: 0　　P Pediatric Age: 0-17　　M Maternity Age: 12-55　　A Adult Age: 15-124　　MCC Major CC Condition　　CC CC Condition　　HIV HIV Related Dx

100 – Volume 1

2010 ICD-9-CM

6. DISEASES OF THE NERVOUS SYSTEM AND SENSE ORGANS (320-389)

INFLAMMATORY DISEASES OF THE CENTRAL NERVOUS SYSTEM (320-326)

√4th 320 Bacterial meningitis

INCLUDES | arachnoiditis
leptomeningitis
meningitis
meningoencephalitis
meningomyelitis
pachymeningitis } bacterial

DEF: Bacterial infection causing inflammation of the lining of the brain and/or spinal cord.

AHA: J-F, '87, 6

320.0 Hemophilus meningitis   MCC
Meningitis due to Hemophilus influenzae [H. influenzae]

CC Excl: 003.21, 013.00-013.16, 036.0, 047.0-047.9, 049.0-049.1, 053.0, 054.72, 072.1, 090.42, 091.81, 094.2, 098.89, 100.81, 112.83, 114.2, 115.01, 115.11, 115.91, 130.0, 249.60-249.61, 249.80-249.91, 250.60-250.63, 250.80-250.93, 320.0-322.9, 349.89-349.9, 357.0

320.1 Pneumococcal meningitis   MCC
CC Excl: See code: 320.0

320.2 Streptococcal meningitis   MCC
CC Excl: See code: 320.0

320.3 Staphylococcal meningitis   MCC
CC Excl: See code: 320.0

320.7 *Meningitis in other bacterial diseases classified elsewhere*   MCC
Code first underlying disease, as:
actinomycosis (039.8)
listeriosis (027.0)
typhoid fever (002.0)
whooping cough (033.0-033.9)

EXCLUDES | *meningitis (in):*
epidemic (036.0)
gonococcal (098.82)
meningococcal (036.0)
salmonellosis (003.21)
syphilis:
NOS (094.2)
congenital (090.42)
meningovascular (094.2)
secondary (091.81)
tuberculous (013.0)

CC Excl: See code: 320.0

√5th 320.8 Meningitis due to other specified bacteria

320.81 Anaerobic meningitis   MCC
Bacteroides (fragilis)
Gram-negative anaerobes
CC Excl: See code 320.0

320.82 Meningitis due to gram-negative bacteria, not elsewhere classified   MCC
Aerobacter aerogenes pneumoniae
Escherichia coli [E. coli]
Friedländer bacillus
Klebsiella
Proteus morganii
Pseudomonas

EXCLUDES | *gram-negative anaerobes (320.81)*

CC Excl: See code: 320.0

320.89 Meningitis due to other specified bacteria   MCC
Bacillus pyocyaneus
CC Excl: See code: 320.0

320.9 Meningitis due to unspecified bacterium   MCC
Meningitis:
bacterial NOS
purulent NOS
Meningitis:
pyogenic NOS
suppurative NOS
CC Excl: See code: 320.0

√4th 321 Meningitis due to other organisms

INCLUDES | arachnoiditis
leptomeningitis
meningitis
pachymeningitis } due to organisms other than bacterial

DEF: Infection causing inflammation of the lining of the brain and/or spinal cord, due to organisms other than bacteria.

AHA: J-F, '87, 6

321.0 *Cryptococcal meningitis*   MCC
Code first underlying disease (117.5)
CC Excl: See code: 320.0

321.1 *Meningitis in other fungal diseases*   MCC
Code first underlying disease (110.0-118)

EXCLUDES | *meningitis in:*
candidiasis (112.83)
coccidioidomycosis (114.2)
histoplasmosis (115.01, 115.11, 115.91)

CC Excl: See code: 320.0

321.2 *Meningitis due to viruses not elsewhere classified*   MCC
Code first underlying disease, as:
meningitis due to arbovirus (060.0-066.9)

EXCLUDES | *meningitis (due to):*
abacterial (047.0-047.9)
adenovirus (049.1)
aseptic NOS (047.9)
Coxsackie (virus)(047.0)
ECHO virus (047.1)
enterovirus (047.0-047.9)
herpes simplex virus (054.72)
herpes zoster virus (053.0)
lymphocytic choriomeningitis virus (049.0)
mumps (072.1)
viral NOS (047.9)
meningo-eruptive syndrome (047.1)

CC Excl: 003.21, 013.00-013.16, 036.0, 047.0-047.9, 049.0-049.1, 053.0, 054.72, 072.1, 090.42, 091.81, 094.2, 098.89, 100.81, 112.83, 114.2, 115.01, 115.11, 115.91, 130.0, 320.0-322.9, 349.89-349.9, 357.0

AHA: 4Q, '04, 51

321.3 *Meningitis due to trypanosomiasis*   MCC
Code first underlying disease (086.0-086.9)
CC Excl: See code: 320.0

321.4 *Meningitis in sarcoidosis*   MCC
Code first underlying disease (135)
CC Excl: See code: 320.0

321.8 *Meningitis due to other nonbacterial organisms classified elsewhere*   MCC
Code first underlying disease

EXCLUDES | *leptospiral meningitis (100.81)*

CC Excl: See code: 320.0

√4th 322 Meningitis of unspecified cause

INCLUDES | arachnoiditis
leptomeningitis
meningitis
pachymeningitis } with no organism specified as cause

AHA: J-F, '87, 6

DEF: Infection causing inflammation of the lining of the brain and/or spinal cord, due to unspecified cause.

322.0 Nonpyogenic meningitis   MCC
Meningitis with clear cerebrospinal fluid
CC Excl: See code: 320.0

322.1 Eosinophilic meningitis   MCC
CC Excl: See code: 320.0

322.2 Chronic meningitis   CC
CC Excl: See code: 320.0

√4th √5th Additional Digit Required   Unacceptable PDx   Manifestation Code   Hospital Acquired Condition   ▶◀ Revised Text   ● New Code   ▲ Revised Code Title

2010 ICD-9-CM   **Volume 1 – 101**

Nervous System and Sense Organs

322.9 – 323.62

322.9   Meningitis, unspecified   `MCC`
     CC Excl: See code: 320.0

√4ᵗʰ   **323   Encephalitis, myelitis, and encephalomyelitis**

     `INCLUDES`   acute disseminated encephalomyelitis
           meningoencephalitis, except bacterial
           meningomyelitis, except bacterial
           myelitis:
              ascending
              transverse

     `EXCLUDES`   *acute transverse myelitis NOS (341.20)*
           acute transverse myelitis in conditions classified
              elsewhere (341.21)
           bacterial:
              meningoencephalitis (320.0-320.9)
              meningomyelitis (320.0-320.9)
           idiopathic transverse myelitis (341.22)

     DEF: Encephalitis: inflammation of brain tissues.
     DEF: Myelitis: inflammation of the spinal cord.
     DEF: Encephalomyelitis: inflammation of brain and spinal cord.

√5ᵗʰ   **323.0   Encephalitis, myelitis, and encephalomyelitis
         in viral diseases classified elsewhere**

     Code first underlying disease, as:
       cat-scratch disease (078.3)
       infectious mononucleosis (075)
       ornithosis (073.7)

     323.01   *Encephalitis and encephalomyelitis in*   `MCC`
            viral diseases classified elsewhere

         `EXCLUDES`   *encephalitis (in):*
               arthropod-borne viral (062.0-064)
               herpes simplex (054.3)
               mumps (072.2)
               other viral diseases of central ner-
                  vous system (049.8-049.9)
               poliomyelitis (045.0-045.9)
               rubella (056.01)
               slow virus infections of central ner-
                  vous system (046.0-046.9)
               viral NOS (049.9)
               West Nile (066.41)

         CC Excl: 003.21, 013.00-013.16, 013.60-013.66, 036.0,
           046.2, 046.71-046.8, 047.0-049.8, 051.9-052.0,
           052.7-053.13, 053.19, 053.79-053.9, 054.3, 054.72,
           054.79-054.9, 056.01, 057.8-059.9, 062.0-064,
           066.2-066.49, 072.1-072.2, 073.7, 075, 078.89,
           079.81-079.82, 079.89, 079.99, 090.41-090.42,
           091.81, 094.2, 094.81, 098.89, 100.81, 112.83, 114.2,
           115.01, 115.11, 115.91, 130.0, 139.8, 290.12,
           320.0-323.9, 341.1, 349.89-349.9, 357.0, 487.8, 771.2
         AHA: 4Q, '06, 58-63

     323.02   *Myelitis in viral diseases*   `MCC`
            classified elsewhere

         `EXCLUDES`   *myelitis (in):*
               herpes simplex (054.74)
               herpes zoster (053.14)
               poliomyelitis (045.0-045.9)
               rubella (056.01)
               other viral diseases of central ner-
                  vous system (049.8-049.9)

         CC Excl: See code: 323.01
         AHA: 4Q, '06, 58-63

     323.1   *Encephalitis, myelitis, and encephalomyelitis in*   `MCC`
          rickettsial diseases classified elsewhere

       Code first underlying disease (080-083.9)

       DEF: Inflammation of the brain caused by rickettsial disease
       carried by louse, tick, or mite.
       CC Excl: 013.60-013.66, 046.2, 046.71-046.8, 048-049.0, 049.8,
       052.0, 052.2, 054.3, 054.74, 056.01, 057.8-058.29,
       059.00-059.9, 062.0-064, 066.2-066.49, 072.2, 073.7, 079.82,
       079.99, 081.9, 083.9, 090.41, 094.81, 117.5, 124, 130.0, 290.12,
       323.01-323.9, 341.1, 487.8, 771.2, 984.9

323.2   *Encephalitis, myelitis, and encephalomyelitis in*   `MCC`
       protozoal diseases classified elsewhere

     Code first underlying disease, as:
       malaria (084.0-084.9)
       trypanosomiasis (086.0-086.9)

     DEF: Inflammation of the brain caused by protozoal disease
     carried by mosquitoes and flies.
     CC Excl: 013.60-013.66, 046.2, 046.71-046.8, 048-049.0, 049.8,
     052.0, 052.2, 054.3, 054.74, 056.01, 057.8-058.29,
     059.00-059.9, 062.0-064, 066.2-066.49, 072.2, 073.7, 079.82,
     079.99, 081.9, 083.9, 084.6, 090.41, 094.81, 117.5, 124, 130.0,
     290.12, 323.01-323.9, 341.1, 487.8, 771.2, 984.9

√5ᵗʰ   **323.4   Other encephalitis, myelitis, and encephalomyelitis
         due to infection classified elsewhere**

     Code first underlying disease

     323.41   *Other encephalitis and encephalomyelitis*   `MCC`
            due to infection classified elsewhere

         `EXCLUDES`   *encephalitis (in):*
               meningococcal (036.1)
               syphilis:
                  NOS (094.81)
                  congenital (090.41)
               toxoplasmosis (130.0)
               tuberculosis (013.6)
               meningoencephalitis due to
                  free-living ameba [Naegleria]
                  (136.29)

         CC Excl: See code: 323.01
         AHA: 4Q, '06, 58-63

     323.42   *Other myelitis due to infection*   `MCC`
            classified elsewhere

         `EXCLUDES`   *myelitis (in):*
               syphilis (094.89)
               tuberculosis (013.6)

         CC Excl: See code: 323.01
         AHA: 4Q, '06, 58-63

√5ᵗʰ   **323.5   Encephalitis, myelitis, and encephalomyelitis
         following immunization procedures**

     Use additional E code to identify vaccine

     323.51   Encephalitis and encephalomyelitis   `MCC`
            following immunization procedures
         Encephalitis postimmunization or postvaccinal
         Encephalomyelitis postimmunization or
            postvaccinal

         CC Excl: See code: 323.01
         AHA: 4Q, '06, 58-63

     323.52   Myelitis following immunization   `MCC`
            procedures
         Myelitis postimmunization or postvaccinal

         CC Excl: See code: 323.01
         AHA: 4Q, '06, 58-63

√5ᵗʰ   **323.6   Postinfectious encephalitis, myelitis, and
         encephalomyelitis**

     Code first underlying disease

     DEF: Infection, inflammation of brain several weeks following
     the outbreak of a systemic infection.

     323.61   *Infectious acute disseminated*   `MCC`
            encephalomyelitis [ADEM]
         Acute necrotizing hemorrhagic encephalopathy

         `EXCLUDES`   *noninfectious acute disseminated*
               encephalo- myelitis (ADEM)
               (323.81)

         CC Excl: See code: 323.01
         AHA: 4Q, '06, 58-63

     323.62   *Other postinfectious encephalitis and*   `MCC`
            encephalomyelitis

         `EXCLUDES`   *encephalitis:*
               postchickenpox (052.0)
               postmeasles (055.0)

         CC Excl: See code: 323.01
         AHA: 4Q, '06, 58-63

`N` Newborn Age: 0   `P` Pediatric Age: 0-17   `M` Maternity Age: 12-55   `A` Adult Age: 15-124   `MCC` Major CC Condition   `CC` CC Condition   `HIV` HIV Related Dx

102 – Volume 1   **2010 ICD-9-CM**

323.63   *Postinfectious myelitis*   `MCC`

> **EXCLUDES**   postchickenpox myelitis (052.2)
> herpes simplex myelitis (054.74)
> herpes zoster myelitis (053.14)

> **CC Excl:** See code: 323.01
> **AHA:** 4Q, '06, 58-63

√5ᵗʰ 323.7   **Toxic encephalitis, myelitis, and encephalomyelitis**

> *Code first underlying cause, as:*
> carbon tetrachloride (982.1)
> hydroxyquinoline derivatives (961.3)
> lead (984.0-984.9)
> mercury (985.0)
> thallium (985.8)

> **AHA:** 2Q, '97, 8

323.71   *Toxic encephalitis and encephalomyelitis*   `MCC`

> **CC Excl:** See code: 323.01
> **AHA:** 4Q, '06, 58-63

323.72   *Toxic myelitis*   `MCC`

> **CC Excl:** See code: 323.01
> **AHA:** 4Q, '06, 58-63

√5ᵗʰ 323.8   **Other causes of encephalitis, myelitis, and encephalomyelitis**

323.81   **Other causes of encephalitis and encephalomyelitis**   `MCC` `HIV`

> Noninfectious acute disseminated encephalomyelitis (ADEM)

> **CC Excl:** See code: 323.01
> **AHA:** 4Q, '06, 58-63

323.82   **Other causes of myelitis**   `MCC` `HIV`

> Transverse myelitis NOS

> **CC Excl:** See code: 323.01
> **AHA:** 4Q, '06, 58-63

323.9   **Unspecified cause of encephalitis, myelitis, and encephalomyelitis**   `MCC` `HIV`

> **CC Excl:** 013.60-013.66, 046.2, 046.71-046.8, 048-049.0, 049.8, 052.0, 052.2, 054.3, 054.74, 056.01, 057.8-058.29, 059.00-059.9, 062.0-064, 066.2-066.49, 072.2, 073.7, 075, 078.3, 079.82, 079.99, 081.9, 083.9, 084.6, 090.41, 094.81, 117.5, 124, 130.0, 290.12, 323.01-323.9, 341.1, 382.4, 487.8, 710.0, 771.2, 984.9
> **AHA:** 1Q, '06, 8

√4ᵗʰ 324   **Intracranial and intraspinal abscess**

324.0   **Intracranial abscess**   `MCC`

> Abscess (embolic):
> cerebellar
> cerebral
> Abscess (embolic) of brain [any part]:
> epidural
> extradural
> otogenic
> subdural

> **EXCLUDES**   tuberculous (013.3)

> **CC Excl:** 006.5, 013.20-013.36, 249.60-249.61, 249.80-249.91, 250.60-250.63, 250.80-250.93, 324.0-325, 348.81-348.9

324.1   **Intraspinal abscess**   `MCC`

> Abscess (embolic) of spinal cord [any part]:
> epidural
> extradural
> subdural

> **EXCLUDES**   tuberculous (013.5)

> **CC Excl:** 0006.5, 013.20-013.36, 249.60-249.61, 249.80-249.91, 250.60-250.63, 250.80-250.93, 324.1

324.9   **Of unspecified site**   `MCC`

> Extradural or subdural abscess NOS

> **CC Excl:** 006.5, 013.20-013.36, 249.60-249.61, 249.80-249.91, 250.60-250.63, 250.80-250.93, 324.0-325

325   **Phlebitis and thrombophlebitis of intracranial venous sinuses**   `MCC`

> Embolism
> Endophlebitis
> Phlebitis, septic or suppurative   } of cavernous, lateral or other intracranial or unspecified intracranial venous sinus
> Thrombophlebitis
> Thrombosis

> **EXCLUDES**   that specified as:
> complicating pregnancy, childbirth, or the puerperium (671.5)
> of nonpyogenic origin (437.6)

> **DEF:** Inflammation and formation of blood clot in a vein within the brain or its lining.
> **CC Excl:** See code: 324.9

326   **Late effects of intracranial abscess or pyogenic infection**

> Note: This category is to be used to indicate conditions whose primary classification is to 320-325 [excluding 320.7, 321.0-321.8, 323.01-323.42, 323.6-323.7] as the cause of late effects, themselves classifiable elsewhere. The "late effects" include conditions specified as such, or as sequelae, which may occur at any time after the resolution of the causal condition.

> Use additional code to identify condition, as:
> hydrocephalus (331.4)
> paralysis (342.0-342.9, 344.0-344.9)

ORGANIC SLEEP DISORDERS (327)

> **TIP:** If the sleep disorder is not documented with the etiology related to an organic disease process, see instead subcategory 307.4.

√4ᵗʰ 327   **Organic sleep disorders**

> **AHA:** 4Q, '05, 59-64

√5ᵗʰ 327.0   **Organic disorders of initiating and maintaining sleep [Organic insomnia]**

> **EXCLUDES**   insomnia NOS (780.52)
> insomnia not due to a substance or known physiological condition (307.41-307.42)
> insomnia with sleep apnea NOS (780.51)

327.00   **Organic insomnia, unspecified**

327.01   *Insomnia due to medical condition classified elsewhere*

> *Code first underlying condition*

> **EXCLUDES**   insomnia due to mental disorder (327.02)

327.02   *Insomnia due to mental disorder*

> *Code first mental disorder*

> **EXCLUDES**   alcohol induced insomnia (291.82)
> drug induced insomnia (292.85)

327.09   **Other organic insomnia**

√5ᵗʰ 327.1   **Organic disorder of excessive somnolence [Organic hypersomnia]**

> **EXCLUDES**   hypersomnia NOS (780.54)
> hypersomnia not due to a substance or known physiological condition (307.43-307.44)
> hypersomnia with sleep apnea NOS (780.53)

327.10   **Organic hypersomnia, unspecified**

327.11   **Idiopathic hypersomnia with long sleep time**

327.12   **Idiopathic hypersomnia without long sleep time**

327.13   **Recurrent hypersomnia**

> Kleine-Levin syndrome
> Menstrual related hypersomnia

327.14   *Hypersomnia due to medical condition classified elsewhere*

> *Code first underlying condition*

> **EXCLUDES**   hypersomnia due to mental disorder (327.15)

√4ᵗʰ √5ᵗʰ Additional Digit Required   Unacceptable PDx   Manifestation Code   Hospital Acquired Condition   ▶◀ Revised Text   ● New Code   ▲ Revised Code Title

2010 ICD-9-CM   **Volume 1 – 103**

Nervous System and Sense Organs

327.15–330.3

327.15 *Hypersomnia due to mental disorder*

    Code first mental disorder

     EXCLUDES   alcohol induced hypersomnia (291.82)

          drug induced hypersomnia (292.85)

327.19   Other organic hypersomnia

✓5th **327.2**   Organic sleep apnea

     EXCLUDES   Cheyne-Stokes breathing (786.04)

          hypersomnia with sleep apnea NOS (780.53)

          insomnia with sleep apnea NOS (780.51)

          sleep apnea in newborn (770.81-770.82)

          sleep apnea NOS (780.57)

327.20   Organic sleep apnea, unspecified

327.21   Primary central sleep apnea

327.22   High altitude periodic breathing

327.23   Obstructive sleep apnea (adult) (pediatric)

     G47.33 Obstructive sleep apnea (adult) (pediatric)   **I-10**

327.24   Idiopathic sleep related nonobstructive alveolar hypoventilation

     Sleep related hypoxia

327.25   Congenital central alveolar hypoventilation syndrome

327.26   *Sleep related hypoventilation/ hypoxemia in conditions classifiable elsewhere*

     Code first underlying condition

327.27   *Central sleep apnea in conditions classified elsewhere*

     Code first underlying condition

327.29   Other organic sleep apnea

✓5th **327.3**   Circadian rhythm sleep disorder

     Organic disorder of sleep wake cycle

     Organic disorder of sleep wake schedule

     EXCLUDES   alcohol induced circadian rhythm sleep disorder (291.82)

          circadian rhythm sleep disorder of nonorganic origin (307.45)

          disruption of 24 hour sleep wake cycle NOS (780.55)

          drug induced circadian rhythm sleep disorder (292.85)

327.30   Circadian rhythm sleep disorder, unspecified

327.31   Circadian rhythm sleep disorder, delayed sleep phase type

327.32   Circadian rhythm sleep disorder, advanced sleep phase type

327.33   Circadian rhythm sleep disorder, irregular sleep-wake type

327.34   Circadian rhythm sleep disorder, free-running type

327.35   Circadian rhythm sleep disorder, jet lag type

327.36   Circadian rhythm sleep disorder, shift work type

327.37   *Circadian rhythm sleep disorder in conditions classified elsewhere*

     Code first underlying condition

327.39   Other circadian rhythm sleep disorder

✓5th **327.4**   Organic parasomnia

     EXCLUDES   alcohol induced parasomnia (291.82)

          drug induced parasomnia (292.85)

          parasomnia not due to a known physiological condition (307.47)

327.40   Organic parasomnia, unspecified

327.41   Confusional arousals

327.42   REM sleep behavior disorder

327.43   Recurrent isolated sleep paralysis

327.44   *Parasomnia in conditions classified elsewhere*

     Code first underlying condition

327.49   Other organic parasomnia

✓5th **327.5**   Organic sleep related movement disorders

     EXCLUDES   restless legs syndrome (333.94)

          sleep related movement disorder NOS (780.58)

327.51   Periodic limb movement disorder

     Periodic limb movement sleep disorder

327.52   Sleep related leg cramps

327.53   Sleep related bruxism

327.59   Other organic sleep related movement disorders

327.8   Other organic sleep disorders

     AHA: 2Q, '07, 6

HEREDITARY AND DEGENERATIVE DISEASES OF THE CENTRAL NERVOUS SYSTEM (330-337)

     EXCLUDES   hepatolenticular degeneration (275.1)

          multiple sclerosis (340)

          other demyelinating diseases of central nervous system (341.0-341.9)

✓4th **330**   Cerebral degenerations usually manifest in childhood

     Use additional code to identify associated mental retardation

330.0   Leukodystrophy   **CC**

     Krabbe's disease

     Leukodystrophy:

       NOS

       globoid cell

       metachromatic

       sudanophilic

     Pelizaeus-Merzbacher disease

     Sulfatide lipidosis

     DEF: Hereditary disease of arylsulfatase or cerebroside sulfatase; characterized by a diffuse loss of myelin in CNS; infantile form causes blindness, motor disturbances, rigidity, mental deterioration and, occasionally, convulsions.

     CC Excl: 330.0-330.9, 331.7, 348.81-348.9, 349.89-349.9

330.1   Cerebral lipidoses   **CC**

     Amaurotic (familial) idiocy

     Disease:

       Batten

       Jansky-Bielschowsky

       Kufs'

       Spielmeyer-Vogt

       Tay-Sachs

     Gangliosidosis

     DEF: Genetic disorder causing abnormal lipid accumulation in the reticuloendothelial cells of the brain.

     CC Excl: 330.1-331.2, 331.7, 331.83-331.9

330.2   *Cerebral degeneration in generalized lipidoses*   **CC**

     Code first underlying disease, as:

       Fabry's disease (272.7)

       Gaucher's disease (272.7)

       Niemann-Pick disease (272.7)

       sphingolipidosis (272.7)

     CC Excl: See code: 330.1

330.3   *Cerebral degeneration of childhood in other diseases classified elsewhere*   **CC**

     Code first underlying disease, as:

       Hunter's disease (277.5)

       mucopolysaccharidosis (277.5)

     CC Excl: See code: 330.1

N Newborn Age: 0   **P** Pediatric Age: 0-17   **M** Maternity Age: 12-55   **A** Adult Age: 15-124   **MCC** Major CC Condition   **CC** CC Condition   **HIV** HIV Related Dx

104 – Volume 1   **2010 ICD-9-CM**

330.8 Other specified cerebral degenerations in childhood `CC`

> Alpers' disease or gray-matter degeneration
> Infantile necrotizing encephalomyelopathy
> Leigh's disease
> Subacute necrotizing encephalopathy or
> encephalomyelopathy
>
> **CC Excl:** See code: 330.1
> **AHA:** N-D, '85, 5

330.9 Unspecified cerebral degeneration in childhood `CC`

> **CC Excl:** See code: 330.1

√4ᵗʰ **331 Other cerebral degenerations**

> Use additional code, where applicable, to identify dementia:
> with behavioral disturbance (294.11)
> without behavioral disturbance (294.10)

331.0 Alzheimer's disease

> **DEF:** Diffuse atrophy of cerebral cortex; causing a progressive decline in intellectual and physical functions, including memory loss, personality changes and profound dementia.
> **AHA:** 4Q, '00, 41; 4Q, '99, 7; N-D, '84, 20
>
> **G30.9** Alzheimer's disease unspecified   `I-10`

√5ᵗʰ **331.1 Frontotemporal dementia**

> **DEF:** Rare, progressive degenerative brain disease, similar to Alzheimer's; cortical atrophy affects the frontal and temporal lobes.
> **AHA:** 4Q, '03, 57

> **331.11 Pick's disease**
>
> > **DEF:** A progressive frontotemporal dementia with asymmetrical atrophy of the frontal and temporal regions of the cerebral cortex, abnormal rounded brain cells called Pick cells with the presence of abnormal staining of protein (called tau); symptoms include prominent apathy, behavioral changes such as disinhibition and restlessness, echolalia, impairment of language, memory, and intellect, increased carelessness, poor personal hygiene, and decreased attention span.

> **331.19 Other frontotemporal dementia**
> > Frontal dementia

331.2 Senile degeneration of brain

> **EXCLUDES**   senility NOS (797)

331.3 Communicating hydrocephalus `CC`

> Secondary normal pressure hydrocephalus
> **EXCLUDES**   congenital hydrocephalus (742.3)
> > idiopathic normal pressure hydrocephalus (331.5)
> > normal pressure hydrocephalus (331.5)
> > spina bifida with hydrocephalus (741.0)
>
> **DEF:** Subarachnoid hemorrhage and meningitis causing excess buildup of cerebrospinal fluid in cavities due to nonabsorption of fluid back through fluid pathways.
> **CC Excl:** 331.3-331.5
> **AHA:** S-O, '85, 12

331.4 Obstructive hydrocephalus `CC`

> Acquired hydrocephalus NOS
> **EXCLUDES**   congenital hydrocephalus (742.3)
> > idiopathic normal pressure hydrocephalus (331.5)
> > normal pressure hydrocephalus (331.5)
> > spina bifida with hydrocephalus (741.0)
>
> **DEF:** Obstruction of cerebrospinal fluid passage from brain into spinal canal.
> **CC Excl:** 249.60-249.61, 249.80-249.91, 250.60-250.63, 250.80-250.93, 331.3-331.7, 331.82-331.9, 348.81-348.9, 741.00-741.03, 742.3-742.4, 742.59-742.9
> **AHA:** 4Q, '03, 106; 1Q, '99, 9
>
> **G91.1** Obstructive hydrocephalus   `I-10`

331.5 Idiopathic normal pressure hydrocephalus [INPH] `CC`

> Normal pressure hydrocephalus NOS
> **EXCLUDES**   congenital hydrocephalus (742.3)
> > secondary normal pressure hydrocephalus (331.3)
> > spina bifida with hydrocephalus (741.0)
>
> **DEF:** Abnormal increase of cerebrospinal fluid in the brain's ventricles; results in dementia, progressive mental impairment, gait disturbance, and impaired bladder control.
> **CC Excl:** See code: 331.3
> **AHA:** 4Q, '07, 74

331.7   *Cerebral degeneration in diseases classified elsewhere*

> *Code first underlying disease, as:*
> alcoholism (303.0-303.9)
> beriberi (265.0)
> cerebrovascular disease (430-438)
> congenital hydrocephalus (741.0, 742.3)
> myxedema (244.0-244.9)
> neoplastic disease (140.0-239.9)
> vitamin B12 deficiency (266.2)
>
> **EXCLUDES**   cerebral degeneration in:
> > Jakob-Creutzfeldt disease
> > ▶(046.11-046.19)◄
> > progressive multifocal
> > leukoencephalopathy (046.3)
> > subacute spongiform encephalopathy (046.1)

√5ᵗʰ **331.8 Other cerebral degeneration**

> **331.81 Reye's syndrome**   `MCC` `P`
>
> > **DEF:** Rare childhood illness, often developed after a viral upper respiratory infection; characterized by vomiting, elevated serum transaminase, changes in liver and other viscera; brain swelling, disturbances of consciousness and seizures; can be fatal.
> > **CC Excl:** 331.81

> **331.82 Dementia with Lewy bodies**
> > Dementia with Parkinsonism
> > Lewy body dementia
> > Lewy body disease
> >
> > **DEF:** A cerebral dementia with neurophysiologic changes, increased hippocampal volume, hypoperfusion in the occipital lobes, and beta amyloid deposits with neurofibrillary tangles, atrophy of cortex and brainstem, hallmark neuropsychologic characteristics are fluctuating cognition with pronounced variation in attention and alertness; recurrent hallucinations; and parkinsonism.
> > **AHA:** 4Q, '03, 57
> >
> > **G31.83** Dementia with Lewy bodies   `I-10`

> **331.83 Mild cognitive impairment, so stated**
> > **EXCLUDES**   altered mental status (780.97)
> > > cerebral degeneration (331.0-331.9)
> > > change in mental status (780.97)
> > > cognitive deficits following (late effects of) cerebral hemorrhage or infarction (438.0)
> > > cognitive impairment due to intracranial or head injury (850-854, 959.01)
> > > cognitive impairment due to late effect of intracranial injury (907.0)
> > > ▶cognitive impairment due to skull fracture (800-801, 803-804)◄
> > > dementia (290.0-290.43, 294.8)
> > > mild memory disturbance (310.8)
> > > neurologic neglect syndrome (781.8)
> > > personality change, nonpsychotic (310.1)
> >
> > **AHA:** 4Q, '06, 75

> **331.89 Other**
> > Cerebral ataxia

331.9 Cerebral degeneration, unspecified

√4ᵗʰ √5ᵗʰ Additional Digit Required   Unacceptable PDx   Manifestation Code   Hospital Acquired Condition   ▶◄ Revised Text   ● New Code   ▲ Revised Code Title

2010 ICD-9-CM   **October 2009 • Volume 1 – 105**

Nervous System and Sense Organs

332–333.89

√4th **332 Parkinson's disease**

     EXCLUDES *dementia with Parkinsonism (331.82)*

332.0 Paralysis agitans

Parkinsonism or Parkinson's disease:
   NOS
   idiopathic
   primary

DEF: Form of progressive parkinsonism characterized by mask-like facial expressions, inability to stand or walk smoothly, muscle weakness, and involuntary trembling movement.

AHA: M-A, '87, 7

G20 Parkinson's disease   I-10

332.1 Secondary Parkinsonism   CC

Neuroleptic-induced Parkinsonism
Parkinsonism due to drugs

Use additional E code to identify drug, if drug-induced

     EXCLUDES *Parkinsonism (in):*
        Huntington's disease (333.4)
        progressive supranuclear palsy (333.0)
        Shy-Drager syndrome (333.0)
        syphilitic (094.82)

CC Excl: 332.0-332.1

√4th **333 Other extrapyramidal disease and abnormal movement disorders**

     INCLUDES other forms of extrapyramidal, basal ganglia, or striatopallidal disease

     EXCLUDES *abnormal movements of head NOS (781.0)*
        sleep related movement disorders (327.51-327.59)

333.0 Other degenerative diseases of the basal ganglia   CC

Atrophy or degeneration:
   olivopontocerebellar [Déjérine-Thomas syndrome]
   pigmentary pallidal [Hallervorden-Spatz disease]
   striatonigral
Parkinsonian syndrome associated with:
   idiopathic orthostatic hypotension
   symptomatic orthostatic hypotension
Progressive supranuclear ophthalmoplegia
Shy-Drager syndrome

CC Excl: 332.0-332.1, 335.23, 337.00-337.09, 348.30-348.39

AHA: 3Q, '96, 8

333.1 Essential and other specified forms of tremor

Benign essential tremor
Familial tremor
Medication-induced postural tremor

Use additional E code to identify drug, if drug-induced

     EXCLUDES *tremor NOS (781.0)*

333.2 Myoclonus

Familial essential myoclonus
▶Palatal myoclonus◀

     EXCLUDES ▶ *progressive myoclonic epilepsy (345.1)*
        Unverricht-Lundborg disease (345.1)◀

Use additional E code to identify drug, if drug-induced

DEF: Spontaneous movements or contractions of muscles.

AHA: 3Q, '97, 4; M-A, '87, 12

333.3 Tics of organic origin

Use additional E code to identify drug, if drug-induced

     EXCLUDES *Gilles de la Tourette's syndrome (307.23)*
        habit spasm (307.22)
        tic NOS (307.20)

333.4 Huntington's chorea   CC

DEF: Genetic disease characterized by chronic progressive men tal deterioration; dementia and death within 15 years of onset.

CC Excl: 332.0-332.1, 340-341.1, 341.8-341.9, 343.0-344.2, 348.1, 348.30-348.5, 348.81-348.9, 349.1, 349.82-349.9, 780.72

333.5 Other choreas

Hemiballism(us)
Paroxysmal choreo-athetosis

Use additional E code to identify drug, if drug-induced

     EXCLUDES *Sydenham's or rheumatic chorea (392.0-392.9)*

333.6 Genetic torsion dystonia

Dystonia:
   deformans progressiva
   musculorum deformans
   (Schwalbe-) Ziehen-Oppenheim disease

DEF: Sustained muscular contractions, causing twisting and repetitive movements that result in abnormal postures of trunk and limbs; etiology unknown.

√5th **333.7 Acquired torsion dystonia**

333.71 Athetoid cerebral palsy   CC

Double athetosis (syndrome)
Vogt's disease

     EXCLUDES *infantile cerebral palsy (343.0-343.9)*

CC Excl: 332.0-332.1, 333.71, 333.90, 333.99, 343.0-343.9, 348.30-348.39

AHA: 4Q, '06, 76-78

333.72 Acute dystonia due to drugs   CC

Acute dystonic reaction due to drugs
Neuroleptic induced acute dystonia

Use additional E code to identify drug

     EXCLUDES *blepharospasm due to drugs*
        (333.85)
        orofacial dyskinesia due to drugs
        (333.85)
        secondary Parkinsonism (332.1)
        subacute dyskinesia due to drugs
        (333.85)
        tardive dyskinesia (333.85)

CC Excl: 332.0-332.1, 333.71, 333.90, 333.99, 348.30-348.39

AHA: 4Q, '06, 76-78

333.79 Other acquired torsion dystonia   CC

CC Excl: See code: 333.72

AHA: 4Q, '06, 76-78

√5th **333.8 Fragments of torsion dystonia**

Use additional E code to identify drug, if drug-induced

333.81 Blepharospasm

     EXCLUDES *blepharospasm due to drugs*
        (333.85)

DEF: Uncontrolled winking or blinking due to orbicularis oculi muscle spasm.

333.82 Orofacial dyskinesia

     EXCLUDES *orofacial dyskinesia due to drugs*
        (333.85)

DEF: Uncontrolled movement of mouth or facial muscles.

333.83 Spasmodic torticollis

     EXCLUDES *torticollis:*
        NOS (723.5)
        hysterical (300.11)
        psychogenic (306.0)

DEF: Uncontrolled movement of head due to spasms of neck muscle.

333.84 Organic writers' cramp

     EXCLUDES *pychogenic (300.89)*

333.85 Subacute dyskinesia due to drugs

Blepharospasm due to drugs
Orofacial dyskinesia due to drugs
Tardive dyskinesia

Use additional E code to identify drug

     EXCLUDES *acute dystonia due to drugs (333.72)*
        acute dystonic reaction due to drugs
        (333.72)
        secondary Parkinsonism (332.1)

AHA: 4Q, '06, 76-78

333.89 Other

| N | Newborn Age: 0 | P Pediatric Age: 0-17 | M Maternity Age: 12-55 | A Adult Age: 15-124 | MCC Major CC Condition | CC CC Condition | HIV HIV Related Dx |

√5th 333.9 Other and unspecified extrapyramidal diseases and abnormal movement disorders

333.90 Unspecified extrapyramidal disease and abnormal movement disorder `CC`
Medication-induced movement disorders NOS
Use additional E code to identify drug, if drug-induced
CC Excl: 332.0-332.1, 333.1-333.83, 333.85-333.93, 333.99, 335.22-335.23, 340-341.1, 341.8-341.9, 343.0-344.2, 348.1, 348.30-348.5, 348.81-348.9, 349.1, 349.82-349.9, 780.72

333.91 Stiff-man syndrome `CC`
CC Excl: See code: 333.90

333.92 Neuroleptic malignant syndrome `MCC`
Use additional E code to identify drug
EXCLUDES neuroleptic induced Parkinsonism (332.1)
CC Excl: 333.0-333.93, 333.99, 342.00-342.92, 348.2-348.39
AHA: 4Q, '94, 37

333.93 Benign shuddering attacks
AHA: 4Q, '94, 37

333.94 Restless legs syndrome [RLS]
DEF: Neurological disorder of unknown etiology with an irresistible urge to move the legs, which may temporarily relieve the symptoms, is accompanied by motor restlessness and sensations of pain, burning, prickling, or tingling.
AHA: 4Q, '06, 79
TIP: Assign an additional code if the underlying cause of the RLS is specified (e.g., iron deficiency anemia).
G25.81 Restless legs syndrome `I-10`

333.99 Other
Neuroleptic-induced acute akathisia
Use additional E code to identify drug, if drug-induced
AHA: 4Q, '04, 95; 2Q, '04, 12; 4Q, '94, 37

√4th 334 Spinocerebellar disease
EXCLUDES olivopontocerebellar degeneration (333.0)
peroneal muscular atrophy (356.1)

334.0 Friedreich's ataxia `CC`
DEF: Genetic recessive disease of children; sclerosis of dorsal, lateral spinal cord columns; characterized by ataxia, speech impairment, swaying and irregular movements, with muscle paralysis, especially of lower limbs.
CC Excl: 334.0-334.9, 348.30-348.39

334.1 Hereditary spastic paraplegia `CC`
CC Excl: 333.0-333.93, 333.99-337.9, 340-344.9, 348.1, 348.30-348.39, 348.81-349.2, 349.82-349.9, 780.72

334.2 Primary cerebellar degeneration `CC`
Cerebellar ataxia:
Marie's
Sanger-Brown
Dyssynergia cerebellaris myoclonica
Primary cerebellar degeneration:
NOS
hereditary
sporadic
CC Excl: 333.0-333.93, 333.99-337.9, 340-344.9, 348.0-348.1, 348.30-348.39, 348.81-348.9, 349.82-349.9, 780.72
AHA: M-A, '87, 9

334.3 Other cerebellar ataxia `CC`
Cerebellar ataxia NOS
Use additional E code to identify drug, if drug-induced
CC Excl: See code: 334.2

334.4 Cerebellar ataxia in diseases classified elsewhere `CC`
Code first underlying disease, as:
alcoholism (303.0-303.9)
myxedema (244.0-244.9)
neoplastic disease (140.0-239.9)
CC Excl: See code: 334.2

334.8 Other spinocerebellar diseases `CC`
Ataxia-telangiectasia [Louis-Bar syndrome]
Corticostriatal-spinal degeneration
CC Excl: See code: 334.2

334.9 Spinocerebellar disease, unspecified `CC`
CC Excl: 334.0-334.9

√4th 335 Anterior horn cell disease

335.0 Werdnig-Hoffmann disease `CC`
Infantile spinal muscular atrophy
Progressive muscular atrophy of infancy
DEF: Spinal muscle atrophy manifested in prenatal period or shortly after birth; symptoms include hypotonia, atrophy of skeletal muscle; death occurs in infancy.
CC Excl: 249.60-249.61, 249.80-249.91, 250.60-250.63, 250.80-250.93, 334.8-337.9, 349.89-349.9

√5th 335.1 Spinal muscular atrophy

335.10 Spinal muscular atrophy, unspecified `CC`
CC Excl: See code: 335.0

335.11 Kugelberg-Welander disease `CC`
Spinal muscular atrophy:
familial
juvenile
DEF: Hereditary; juvenile muscle atrophy; appears during first two decades of life; due to lesions of anterior horns of spinal cord; includes wasting, diminution of lower body muscles and twitching.
CC Excl: See code: 335.0

335.19 Other `CC`
Adult spinal muscular atrophy
CC Excl: See code: 335.0

√5th 335.2 Motor neuron disease

335.20 Amyotrophic lateral sclerosis `CC` `A`
Motor neuron disease (bulbar) (mixed type)
CC Excl: See code: 335.0
AHA: 4Q, '95, 81

335.21 Progressive muscular atrophy `CC`
Duchenne-Aran muscular atrophy
Progressive muscular atrophy (pure)
CC Excl: See code: 335.0

335.22 Progressive bulbar palsy `CC`
CC Excl: See code: 335.0

335.23 Pseudobulbar palsy `CC`
CC Excl: See code: 335.0

335.24 Primary lateral sclerosis `CC`
CC Excl: See code: 335.0

335.29 Other `CC`
CC Excl: See code: 335.0

335.8 Other anterior horn cell diseases `CC`
CC Excl: See code: 335.0

335.9 Anterior horn cell disease, unspecified `CC`
CC Excl: See code: 335.0

√4th 336 Other diseases of spinal cord

336.0 Syringomyelia and syringobulbia `CC`
CC Excl: 334.8-337.9, 340-344.9, 348.30-348.39, 348.81-349.2, 349.89-349.9, 780.72
AHA: 1Q, '89, 10

Nervous System and Sense Organs

336.1–338.19

336.1 Vascular myelopathies `MCC`
Acute infarction of spinal cord (embolic) (nonembolic)
Arterial thrombosis of spinal cord
Edema of spinal cord
Hematomyelia
Subacute necrotic myelopathy
CC Excl: 249.60-249.61, 250.60-250.63, 334.8-337.9, 340-344.9, 348.1, 348.30-348.39, 349.0-349.2, 349.89-349.9, 780.72

336.2 Subacute combined degeneration of spinal cord in diseases classified elsewhere `CC`
Code first underlying disease, as:
pernicious anemia (281.0)
other vitamin B$_{12}$ deficiency anemia (281.1)
vitamin B$_{12}$ deficiency (266.2)
CC Excl: 334.8-337.9, 340-344.9, 348.1, 348.30-348.39, 349.0-349.2, 349.89-349.9, 780.72

336.3 Myelopathy in other diseases classified elsewhere `CC`
Code first underlying disease, as:
myelopathy in neoplastic disease (140.0-239.9)
EXCLUDES *myelopathy in:*
intervertebral disc disorder (722.70-722.73)
spondylosis (721.1, 721.41-721.42, 721.91)
CC Excl: See code: 336.1
AHA: 3Q, '99, 5

336.8 Other myelopathy `CC`
Myelopathy: Myelopathy:
drug-induced   radiation-induced
Use additonal E code to identify cause
CC Excl: See code: 336.1

336.9 Unspecified disease of spinal cord `CC` `HIV`
Cord compression NOS   Myelopathy NOS
EXCLUDES *myelitis (323.02, 323.1, 323.2, 323.42, 323.52,*
323.63, 323.72, 323.82, 323.9)
spinal (canal) stenosis (723.0, 724.00-724.09)
CC Excl: 249.60-249.61, 250.60-250.63, 334.1, 334.8-337.9, 340-344.9, 348.1, 348.30-348.39, 349.0-349.2, 349.89-349.9, 780.72

√4ᵗʰ 337 Disorders of the autonomic nervous system
INCLUDES disorders of peripheral autonomic, sympathetic, parasympathetic, or vegetative system
EXCLUDES *familial dysautonomia [Riley-Day syndrome] (742.8)*

√5ᵗʰ 337.0 Idiopathic peripheral autonomic neuropathy

337.00 Idiopathic peripheral autonomic neuropathy, unspecified

337.01 Carotid sinus syndrome
Carotid sinus syncope
DEF: Vagal activation caused by pressure on the carotid sinus baroreceptors; sympathetic nerve impulses may cause sinus arrest or AV block.
AHA: 4Q, '08, 101-102

337.09 Other idiopathic peripheral autonomic neuropathy
Cervical sympathetic dystrophy or paralysis

337.1 Peripheral autonomic neuropathy in disorders classified elsewhere `CC`
Code first underlying disease, as:
amyloidosis (277.30-277.39)
diabetes (249.6, 250.6)
CC Excl: 337.00-337.29, 337.9, 348.30-348.39
AHA: ▶2Q, '09, 13;◀ 2Q, '93, 6; 3Q, '91, 9; N-D, '84, 9

√5ᵗʰ 337.2 Reflex sympathetic dystrophy
DEF: Disturbance of the sympathetic nervous system evidenced by sweating, pain, pallor and edema following injury to nerves or blood vessels.
AHA: 4Q, '93, 24

337.20 Reflex sympathetic dystrophy, unspecified `CC`
Complex regional pain syndrome type I, unspecified
CC Excl: 337.20-337.29

337.21 Reflex sympathetic dystrophy of the upper limb `CC`
Complex regional pain syndrome type I of the upper limb
CC Excl: 249.60-249.61, 250.60-250.63, 334.8-337.9, 340-344.9, 348.1, 348.30-348.39, 349.0-349.2, 349.89-349.9, 780.72

337.22 Reflex sympathetic dystrophy of the lower limb `CC`
Complex regional pain syndrome type I of the lower limb
CC Excl: See code: 337.21

337.29 Reflex sympathetic dystrophy of other specified site `CC`
Complex regional pain syndrome type I of other specified site
CC Excl: See code: 337.21

337.3 Autonomic dysreflexia
Use additional code to identify the cause, such as:
pressure ulcer (707.00-707.09)
fecal impaction (560.39)
urinary tract infection (599.0)
DEF: Noxious stimuli evokes paroxysmal hypertension, bradycardia, excess sweating, headache, pilomotor responses, facial flushing, and nasal congestion due to uncontrolled parasympathetic nerve response; occurs in patients with spinal cord injury above sympathetic outflow tract (T$_6$).
AHA: 4Q, '98, 37

337.9 Unspecified disorder of autonomic nervous system

PAIN (338)

√4ᵗʰ 338 Pain, not elsewhere classified

[handwritten: Can be used as the principal diagnosis or first-listed code when pain control or pain management is the reason for the admission/encounter.]

Use additional code to identify:
pain associated with psychological factors (307.89)
EXCLUDES *generalized pain (780.96)*
headache syndromes (339.00-339.89)
localized pain, unspecified type–code to pain by site
migraines (346.0-346.9)
pain disorder exclusively attributed to psychological factors (307.80)
vulvar vestibulitis (625.71)
vulvodynia (625.70-625.79)
AHA: 2Q, '07, 12
TIP: Do not assign a 338 code if the pain is not specified as acute or chronic, unless post-thoracotomy, postoperative, neoplasm related or central pain syndrome.

338.0 Central pain syndrome
Déjérine-Roussy syndrome
Myelopathic pain syndrome
Thalamic pain syndrome (hyperesthetic)
AHA: 4Q, '06, 79-81

√5ᵗʰ 338.1 Acute pain

338.11 Acute pain due to trauma
AHA: 1Q, '07, 7; 4Q, '06, 79-81

✳ **338.12 Acute post-thoracotomy pain**
Post-thoracotomy pain NOS
AHA: 4Q, '06, 79-81

338.18 Other acute postoperative pain
Postoperative pain NOS
AHA: 4Q, '06, 79-81
G89.18 Other acute postprocedural pain `I-10`

338.19 Other acute pain
EXCLUDES *neoplasm related acute pain (338.3)*
AHA: 2Q, '07, 11; 4Q, '06, 79-81

[handwritten: ✳ pain not specified as either acute or chronic, the default is for the acute form.]

☑5th **338.2 Chronic pain**

EXCLUDES *causalgia (355.9)*
  lower limb (355.71)
  upper limb (354.4)
  chronic pain syndrome (338.4)
  myofascial pain syndrome (729.1)
  neoplasm related chronic pain (338.3)
  reflex sympathetic dystrophy (337.20-337.29)

338.21 Chronic pain due to trauma
  AHA: 4Q, '06, 79-81

✳ **338.22 Chronic post-thoracotomy pain**
  AHA: 4Q, '06, 79-81

338.28 Other chronic postoperative pain
  AHA: 4Q, '06, 79-81
  G89.28 Other chronic postprocedural pain **I-10**

338.29 Other chronic pain
  AHA: 4Q, '06, 79-81

338.3 Neoplasm related pain (acute) (chronic)
  Cancer associated pain
  Pain due to malignancy (primary) (secondary)
  Tumor associated pain
  AHA: 2Q, '07, 11; 4Q, '06, 79-81
  G89.3 Neoplasm related pain (acute) (chronic) **I-10**

338.4 Chronic pain syndrome
  Chronic pain associated with significant psychosocial dysfunction
  AHA: 2Q, '07, 11; 4Q, '06, 79-81
  G89.4 Chronic pain syndrome **I-10**

[handwritten margin note: mission for control of pain related to, associated with, or due to, malignancy. The underlying neoplasm is reported as an additional diagnosis]

OTHER HEADACHE SYNDROMES (339)

☑4th **339 Other headache syndromes**

EXCLUDES *headache:*
  NOS (784.0)
  due to lumbar puncture (349.0)
  migraine (346.0-346.9)

AHA: ▶4Q, '08, 102-105◀

☑5th **339.0 Cluster headaches and other trigeminal autonomic cephalgias**
  TACS

339.00 Cluster headache syndrome, unspecified
  Ciliary neuralgia   Lower half migraine
  Cluster headache NOS   Migrainous neuralgia
  Histamine cephalgia

339.01 Episodic cluster headache

339.02 Chronic cluster headache

339.03 Episodic paroxysmal hemicrania
  Paroxysmal hemicrania NOS

339.04 Chronic paroxysmal hemicrania

339.05 Short lasting unilateral neuralgiform headache with conjunctival injection and tearing
  SUNCT

339.09 Other trigeminal autonomic cephalgias

☑5th **339.1 Tension type headache**
  EXCLUDES *tension headache NOS (307.81)*
    tension headache related to psychological factors (307.81)
  AHA: ▶4Q, '08, 103◀

339.10 Tension type headache, unspecified

339.11 Episodic tension type headache

339.12 Chronic tension type headache

☑5th **339.2 Post-traumatic headache**
  TIP: Do not assign during the acute phase of the trauma (e.g., head injury). When assigning 339.2X, report also a late effect code (e.g., 907.0 for intracranial injury).

339.20 Post-traumatic headache, unspecified
  AHA: ▶4Q, '08, 108◀

339.21 Acute post-traumatic headache

339.22 Chronic post-traumatic headache

339.3 Drug induced headache, not elsewhere classified
  Medication overuse headache Rebound headache

☑5th **339.4 Complicated headache syndromes**

339.41 Hemicrania continua

339.42 New daily persistent headache
  NDPH

339.43 Primary thunderclap headache

339.44 Other complicated headache syndrome

☑5th **339.8 Other specified headache syndromes**

339.81 Hypnic headache

339.82 Headache associated with sexual activity
  Orgasmic headache
  Preorgasmic headache

339.83 Primary cough headache

339.84 Primary exertional headache

339.85 Primary stabbing headache

339.89 Other specified headache syndromes

OTHER DISORDERS OF THE CENTRAL NERVOUS SYSTEM (340-349)

340 Multiple sclerosis
  Disseminated or multiple sclerosis:
  NOS   cord
  brain stem   generalized
  CC Excl: 250.60-250.63, 250.80-250.93, 340, 341.8-341.9
  G35 Multiple sclerosis **I-10**

☑4th **341 Other demyelinating diseases of central nervous system**

341.0 Neuromyelitis optica **CC**
  CC Excl: 341.0, 348.30-348.39

341.1 Schilder's disease **CC**
  Baló's concentric sclerosis   Encephalitis
  Encephalitis periaxialis: periaxialis:
    concentrica [Baló's]   diffusa [Schilder's]
  DEF: Chronic leukoencephalopathy of children and adolescents; symptoms include blindness, deafness, bilateral spasticity and progressive mental deterioration.
  CC Excl: 066.40-066.49, 079.82, 348.30-348.39

☑5th **341.2 Acute (transverse) myelitis**
  EXCLUDES *acute (transverse) myelitis (in) (due to):*
    following immunization procedures (323.52)
    infection classified elsewhere (323.42)
    postinfectious (323.63)
    protozoal diseases classified elsewhere (323.2)
    rickettsial diseases classified elsewhere (323.1)
    toxic (323.72)
    viral diseases classified elsewhere (323.02)
    transverse myelitis NOS (323.82)

341.20 Acute (transverse) myelitis NOS **CC**
  CC Excl: 003.21, 013.00-013.16, 036.0, 047.0-047.9, 049.0-049.1, 053.0-053.13, 053.19, 053.79-053.9, 054.72, 054.79-054.9, 058.81-058.89, 072.1, 078.89, 079.81, 079.89, 079.99, 090.42, 091.81, 094.2, 098.89, 100.81, 112.83, 114.2, 115.01, 115.11, 115.91, 130.0, 139.8, 249.60-249.61, 250.60-250.63, 320.0-322.9, 334.8-337.9, 340-341.1, 341.8-344.9, 348.1, 348.30-348.39, 349.0-349.2, 349.89-349.9, 357.0, 780.72
  AHA: 4Q, '06, 58-63

341.21 Acute (transverse) myelitis in conditions classified elsewhere **CC**
  Code first underlying condition
  CC Excl: See code: 341.20
  AHA: 4Q, '06, 58-63

341.22 Idiopathic transverse myelitis **CC**
  CC Excl: See code: 341.20
  AHA: 4Q, '06, 58-63

Nervous System and Sense Organs

341.8–344.5

341.8 **Other demyelinating diseases of central nervous system** `CC`
Central demyelination of corpus callosum
Central pontine myelinosis
Marchiafava (-Bignami) disease
CC Excl: 333.1-333.93, 333.99-337.9, 340-344.9, 348.30-348.39, 348.81-348.9, 349.82-349.9, 780.72
AHA: N-D, '87, 6

341.9 **Demyelinating disease of central nervous system, unspecified** `CC` `HIV`
CC Excl: See code: 341.8

✓4ᵗʰ **342** **Hemiplegia and hemiparesis**
Note: This category is to be used when hemiplegia (complete) (incomplete) is reported without further specification, or is stated to be old or long-standing but of unspecified cause. The category is also for use in multiple coding to identify these types of hemiplegia resulting from any cause.
EXCLUDES *congenital (343.1)*
hemiplegia due to late effect of cerebrovascular accident (438.20-438.22)
infantile NOS (343.4)

The following fifth-diits are for use with codes 342.0-342.9:
0 **affecting unspecified side**
1 **affecting dominant side**
2 **affecting nondominant side**

AHA: 4Q, '94, 38

§ ✓5ᵗʰ **342.0** **Flaccid hemiplegia** `CC`
[0-2] **CC Excl:** 334.0-337.9, 340-344.9, 348.30-348.39, 348.81-348.9, 349.82-349.9, 780.72

§ ✓5ᵗʰ **342.1** **Spastic hemiplegia** `CC`
[0-2] **CC Excl:** See code: 342.0

§ ✓5ᵗʰ **342.8** **Other specified hemiplegia** `CC`
[0-2] **CC Excl:** See code: 342.0

§ ✓5ᵗʰ **342.9** **Hemiplegia, unspecified** `CC`
[0-2] **CC Excl:** See code: 342.0
AHA: 3Q, '06, 5; 4Q, '98, 87
G81.90 Hemiplegia unspecified affect unspecified side `I-10`

✓4ᵗʰ **343** **Infantile cerebral palsy**
INCLUDES cerebral:
palsy NOS
spastic infantile paralysis
congenital spastic paralysis (cerebral)
Little's disease
paralysis (spastic) due to birth injury:
intracranial
spinal
EXCLUDES *athetoid cerebral palsy (333.71)*
hereditary cerebral paralysis, such as:
hereditary spastic paraplegia (334.1)
Vogt's disease (333.71)
spastic paralysis specified as noncongenital or noninfantile (344.0-344.9)

343.0 **Diplegic** `CC`
Congenital diplegia   Congenital paraplegia
DEF: Paralysis affecting both sides of the body simultaneously.
CC Excl: 343.0, 348.30-348.39

343.1 **Hemiplegic** `CC`
Congenital hemiplegia
EXCLUDES *infantile hemiplegia NOS (343.4)*
CC Excl: 343.1, 348.30-348.39

343.2 **Quadriplegic** `MCC`
Tetraplegic
CC Excl: 249.60-249.61, 249.80-249.91, 250.60-250.63, 250.80-250.93, 342.00-344.9, 348.81-348.9, 349.89-349.9,742.59-742.9, 780.72

343.3 **Monoplegic**

343.4 **Infantile hemiplegia** `CC`
Infantile hemiplegia (postnatal) NOS
CC Excl: See code: 342.0

343.8 **Other specified infantile cerebral palsy**

343.9 **Infantile cerebral palsy, unspecified**
Cerebral palsy NOS
AHA: 4Q, '05, 89
G80.9 Cerebral palsy unspecified `I-10`

✓4ᵗʰ **344** **Other paralytic syndromes**
Note: This category is to be used when the listed conditions are reported without further specification or are stated to be old or long-standing but of unspecified cause. The category is also for use in multiple coding to identify these conditions resulting from any cause.
INCLUDES paralysis (complete) (incomplete), except as classifiable to 342 and 343
EXCLUDES *congenital or infantile cerebral palsy (343.0-343.9)*
hemiplegia (342.0-342.9)
congenital or infantile (343.1, 343.4)

✓5ᵗʰ **344.0** **Quadriplegia and quadriparesis**
TIP: Assign also a code from subcategory 438.5 if late effect of CVA.

344.00 **Quadriplegia unspecified** `MCC`
CC Excl: See code: 343.2
AHA: 4Q, '03, 103; 4Q, '98, 38
G82.50 Quadriplegia unspecified `I-10`

344.01 **C₁-C₄ complete** `MCC`
CC Excl: See code: 343.2

344.02 **C₁-C₄ incomplete** `MCC`
CC Excl: See code: 343.2

344.03 **C₅-C₇ complete** `MCC`
CC Excl: See code: 343.2

344.04 **C₅-C₇ incomplete** `MCC`
CC Excl: See code: 343.2

344.09 **Other** `MCC`
CC Excl: See code: 343.2
AHA: 1Q, '01, 12; 4Q, '98, 39

344.1 **Paraplegia** `CC`
Paralysis of both lower limbs
Paraplegia (lower)
CC Excl: 334.0-337.9, 340-344.9, 348.30-348.39, 348.8-348.9, 349.82-349.9, 780.72
AHA: 4Q, '03, 110;M-A, '87, 10
G82.20 Paraplegia unspecified `I-10`

344.2 **Diplegia of upper limbs** `CC`
Diplegia (upper)
Paralysis of both upper limbs
CC Excl: 344.00-344.09, 344.2, 344.81-344.9, 349.89-349.9, 780.72

✓5ᵗʰ **344.3** **Monoplegia of lower limb**
Paralysis of lower limb
EXCLUDES *monoplegia of lower limb due to late effect of cerebrovascular accident (438.40-438.42)*

344.30 **Affecting unspecified side**

344.31 **Affecting dominant side**

344.32 **Affecting nondominant side**

✓5ᵗʰ **344.4** **Monoplegia of upper limb**
Paralysis of upper limb
EXCLUDES *monoplegia of upper limb due to late effect of cerebrovascular accident (438.30-438.32)*

344.40 **Affecting unspecified side**

344.41 **Affecting dominant side**

344.42 **Affecting nondominant side**

344.5 **Unspecified monoplegia**

§   Requires fifth digit. Valid digits are in [brackets] under each code. See category 342 for codes and definitions.

N Newborn Age: 0   P Pediatric Age: 0-17   M Maternity Age: 12-55   A Adult Age: 15-124   `MCC` Major CC Condition   `CC` CC Condition   `HIV` HIV Related Dx

110 – Volume 1   **2010 ICD-9-CM**

√5ᵗʰ **344.6 Cauda equina syndrome**

> **DEF:** Dull pain and paresthesias in sacrum, perineum and bladder due to compression of spinal nerve roots; pain radiates down buttocks, back of thigh, calf of leg and into foot with prickling, burning sensations.

344.60 Without mention of neurogenic bladder `CC`

> **CC Excl:** 344.00-344.1, 344.30-344.32, 344.60-344.9, 349.89-349.9, 780.72

344.61 With neurogenic bladder `CC`

> Acontractile bladder
> Autonomic hyperreflexia of bladder
> Cord bladder
> Detrusor hyperreflexia
>
> **CC Excl:** 334.0-337.9, 340-344.9, 348.30-348.39, 348.81-348.9, 349.82-349.9, 599.60-599.69, 780.72
>
> **AHA:** M-J, '87, 12; M-A, '87, 10

√5ᵗʰ **344.8 Other specified paralytic syndromes**

344.81 Locked-in state `MCC`

> **DEF:** State of consciousness where patients are paralyzed and unable to respond to environmental stimuli; patients have eye movements, and stimuli can enter the brain but patients unable to respond.
>
> **CC Excl:** 342.00-344.9, 348.30-348.39, 348.81-348.9, 349.82-349.9, 780.72
>
> **AHA:** 4Q, '93, 24

344.89 Other specified paralytic syndrome

> **AHA:** 2Q, '99, 4

344.9 Paralysis, unspecified

√4ᵗʰ **345 Epilepsy and recurrent seizures**

> The following fifth-digit subclassification is for use with categories 345.0, .1, .4-.9:
>
>   **0 without mention of intractable eilepsy**
>   **1 with intractable epilepsy**
>   ►pharmacoresistant (pharmacologically resistant)
>   poorly controlled
>   refractory (medically)
>   treatment resistant◄

> **EXCLUDES** ►hippocampal sclerosis (348.81)
>   mesial temporal sclerosis (348.81)◄
>   progressive myoclonic epilepsy (333.2)
>   ►temporal sclerosis (348.81)◄

> **DEF:** Brain disorder characterized by electrical-like disturbances; may include occasional impairment or loss of consciousness, abnormal motor phenomena and psychic or sensory disturbances.
>
> **AHA:** 1Q, '93, 24; 2Q, '92, 8; 4Q, '92, 23

§ √5ᵗʰ **345.0 Generalized nonconvulsive epilepsy** `CC 1`
[0-1]
> Absences: Pykno-epilepsy
>   atonic   Seizures:
>   typical   akinetic
> Minor epilepsy   atonic
> Petit mal
>
> **CC Excl:** 249.60-249.61, 250.60-250.63, 345.00-345.91, 348.81-348.9, 349.89-349.9
>
> **AHA: For code 345.00:** 1Q, '04, 18

§ √5ᵗʰ **345.1 Generalized convulsive epilepsy** `CC 1`
[0-1]
> Epileptic seizures:
>   clonic
>   myoclonic
>   tonic
>   tonic-clonic
> Grand mal
> Major epilepsy
> ►Progressive myoclonic epilepsy
> Unverricht-Lundborg disease◄
>
> **EXCLUDES** convulsions:
>   NOS (780.39)
>   infantile (780.39)
>   newborn (779.0)
>   infantile spasms (345.6)
>
> **DEF:** Convulsive seizures with tension of limbs (tonic) or rhythmic contractions (clonic).
>
> **CC Excl: For code 345.11:** 249.60-249.61, 250.60-250.63, 345.00-345.91, 348.81-348.9, 349.89-349.9
>
> **AHA:** 3Q, '97, 4

345.2 Petit mal status `MCC`

> Epileptic absence status
>
> **DEF:** Minor myoclonic spasms and sudden momentary loss of consciousness in epilepsy.
>
> **CC Excl:** 249.60-249.61, 249.80-249.91, 250.60-250.63, 250.80-250.93, 345.00-345.91, 348.81-348.9, 349.89-349.9

345.3 Grand mal status `MCC`

> Status epilepticus NOS
>
> **EXCLUDES** epilepsia partialis continua (345.7)
>   status:
>   psychomotor (345.7)
>   temporal lobe (345.7)
>
> **DEF:** Sudden loss of consciousness followed by generalized convulsions in epilepsy.
>
> **CC Excl:** See code: 345.2
>
> **AHA:** 3Q, '05, 12
>
> **G40.301** Gen idiopath epilep&epi syn not intractabl w/se `I-10`

§ √5ᵗʰ **345.4 Localization-related (focal) (partial) epilepsy** `CC`
[0-1] **and epileptic syndromes with complex partial seizures**
> Epilepsy:
>   limbic system
>   partial:
>   secondarily generalized
>   with impairment of consciousness
>   with memory and ideational disturbances
>   psychomotor
>   psychosensory
>   temporal lobe
> Epileptic automatism
>
> **CC Excl: For code 345.40:** 345.00-345.91, 348.30-348.39, 348.9, 349.89-349.9; **For code 345.41:** 249.60-249.61, 250.60-250.63, 345.00-345.91, 348.81-348.9, 349.89-349.9

§ √5ᵗʰ **345.5 Localization-related (focal) (partial) epilepsy** `CC`
[0-1] **and epileptic syndromes with simple partial seizures**
> Epilepsy:
>   Bravais-Jacksonian NOS
>   focal (motor) NOS
>   Jacksonian NOS
>   motor partial
>   partial NOS:
>   without impairment of consciousness
>   sensory-induced
>   somatomotor
>   somatosensory
>   visceral
>   visual
>
> **CC Excl: For code 345.50:** 345.00-345.91, 348.30-348.39, 348.9, 349.89-349.9; **For code 345.51:** 249.60-249.61, 250.60-250.63, 345.00-345.91, 348.81-348.9, 349.89-349.9

§ √5ᵗʰ **345.6 Infantile spasms** `CC`
[0-1]
> Hypsarrhythmia   Salaam attacks
> Lightning spasms
>
> **EXCLUDES** salaam tic (781.0)
>
> **CC Excl: For code 345.60:** 345.00-345.91, 348.30-348.39, 348.9, 349.89-349.9; **For code 345.61:** 249.60-249.61, 250.60-250.63, 345.00-345.91, 348.81-348.9, 349.89-349.9
>
> **AHA:** N-D, '84, 12

§ √5ᵗʰ **345.7 Epilepsia partialis continua** `CC 0` `MCC 1`
[0-1]
> Kojevnikov's epilepsy
>
> **DEF:** Continuous muscle contractions and relaxation; result of abnormal neural discharge.
>
> **CC Excl:** 249.60-249.61, 250.60-250.63, 345.00-345.91, 348.81-348.9, 349.89-349.9

§ √5ᵗʰ **345.8 Other forms of epilepsy and recurrent seizures** `CC`
[0-1]
> Epilepsy: Epilepsy:
>   cursive [running]   gelastic
>
> **CC Excl:** 249.60-249.61, 250.60-250.63, 345.00-345.91, 348.81-348.9, 349.89-349.9

---

§   Requires fifth digit. Valid digits are in [brackets] under each code. See category 345 for codes and definitions.

√4ᵗʰ / √5ᵗʰ Additional Digit Required   Unacceptable PDx   Manifestation Code   Hospital Acquired Condition   ►◄ Revised Text   ● New Code   ▲ Revised Code Title

2010 ICD-9-CM   **October 2009 · Volume 1 – 111**

§ ✓5th **345.9 Epilepsy, unspecified** CC 1
[0-1]   Epileptic convulsions, fits, or seizures NOS
Recurrent seizures NOS
Seizure disorder NOS
EXCLUDES *convulsion (convulsive) disorder (780.39)*
convulsive seizure or fit NOS (780.39)
recurrent convulsions (780.39)
CC Excl: For code 345.91: 249.60-249.61, 250.60-250.63, 345.00-345.91, 348.81-348.9, 349.89-349.9
AHA: 1Q, '08, 17; N-D, '87, 12; **For code 345.90:** ▶2Q, '09, 10◀
G40.909 Epilepsy uns not intractbl w/o status epilepticus I-10

✓4th **346 Migraine**
EXCLUDES *headache:*
NOS (784.0)
syndromes (339.00-339.89)
AHA: 4Q, '08, 103, 105-107

The following fifth-digit subclassification is for use with category 346:
0 without mention of intractable migraine without mention of status migrainosus
1 with intractable migraine, so stated without mention of status migrainosus
2 without mention of intractable migraine with status migrainosus
3 with intractable migraine, so stated, with status migrainosus

Status migrainosus - severe migraine attack that lasts for more than 12 hours [handwritten annotation]

DEF: Benign vascular headache of extreme pain; commonly associated with irritability, nausea, vomiting and often photophobia; premonitory visual hallucination of a crescent in the visual field (scotoma).

§ ✓5th **346.0 Migraine with aura**
[0-3]   Basilar migraine
Classic migraine
Migraine preceded or accompanied by transient focal neurological phenomena
Migraine triggered seizures
Migraine with acute-onset aura
Migraine with aura without headache (migraine equivalents)
Migraine with prolonged aura
Migraine with typical aura
Retinal migraine
EXCLUDES *persistent migraine aura (346.5, 346.6)*

§ ✓5th **346.1 Migraine without aura**
[0-3]   Common migraine

§ ✓5th **346.2 Variants of migraine, not elsewhere classified**
[0-3]   Abdominal migraine
Cyclical vomiting associated with migraine
Ophthalmoplegic migraine
Periodic headache syndromes in child or adolescent
EXCLUDES *cyclical vomiting NOS (536.2)*
psychogenic cyclical vomiting (306.4)

§ ✓5th **346.3 Hemiplegic migraine**
[0-3]   Familial migraine   Sporadic migraine

§ ✓5th **346.4 Menstrual migraine**   ♀
[0-3]   Menstrual headache
Menstrually related migraine
Premenstrual headache
Premenstrual migraine
Pure menstrual migraine

§ ✓5th **346.5 Persistent migraine aura without cerebral**
[0-3]   **infarction**
Persistent migraine aura NOS

§ ✓5th **346.6 Persistent migraine aura with cerebral infarction** CC
[0-3]   **CC Excl: For code 346.60:** 346.60-346.63, 433.00-434.91; **For code 346.61, 346.62, 346.63:** 346.60-346.63, 433.00-434.91, 436
AHA: For code 346.60: 4Q, '08, 108
TIP: Assign also a code for the specific type of cerebral infarction.

§ ✓5th **346.7 Chronic migraine without aura**
[0-3]   Transformed migraine without aura

§ ✓5th **346.8 Other forms of migraine**
[0-3]

§ ✓5th **346.9 Migraine, unspecified**
[0-3]   **AHA:** N-D, '85, 16
G43.90 Migraine unspecified not intractable I-10

✓4th **347 Cataplexy and narcolepsy**
DEF: Cataplexy: Sudden onset of muscle weakness with loss of tone and strength; caused by aggressive or spontaneous emotions.
DEF: Narcolepsy: Brief, recurrent, uncontrollable episodes of sound sleep.

✓5th **347.0 Narcolepsy**
347.00 Without cataplexy
Narcolepsy NOS
347.01 With cataplexy

✓5th **347.1 Narcolepsy in conditions classified elsewhere**
Code first underlying condition
347.10 Without cataplexy
347.11 With cataplexy

✓4th **348 Other conditions of brain**
348.0 Cerebral cysts
Arachnoid cyst   Porencephaly, acquired
Porencephalic cyst   Pseudoporencephaly
EXCLUDES *porencephaly (congenital) (742.4)*

348.1 Anoxic brain damage CC
Use additional E code to identify cause
EXCLUDES *that occurring in:*
abortion (634-638 with .7, 639.8)
ectopic or molar pregnancy (639.8)
labor or delivery (668.2, 669.4)
that of newborn (767.0, 768.0-768.9, 772.1-772.2)
DEF: Brain injury due to lack of oxygen, other than birth trauma.
CC Excl: 249.60-249.61, 249.80-249.91, 250.60-250.63, 250.80-250.93, 348.1-348.2, 349.89-349.9
G93.1 Anoxic brain damage not elsewhere classified I-10

348.2 Benign intracranial hypertension
Pseudotumor cerebri
EXCLUDES *hypertensive encephalopathy (437.2)*
DEF: Elevated pressure in brain due to fluid retention in brain cavities.

✓5th **348.3 Encephalopathy, not elsewhere classified**
AHA: 4Q, '03, 58; 3Q, '97, 4

348.30 Encephalopathy, unspecified MCC HIV
CC Excl: 333.92, 344.81, 348.31-348.39
G93.40 Encephalopathy unspecified I-10

348.31 Metabolic encephalopathy MCC HIV
Septic encephalopathy
EXCLUDES *toxic metabolic encephalopathy (349.82)*
CC Excl: 333.92, 344.81, 348.30, 348.39
TIP: Physician documentation may include "acute confusional state," usually denoting delirium secondary to the encephalopathy.

348.39 Other encephalopathy MCC HIV
EXCLUDES *encephalopathy:*
alcoholic (291.2)
hepatic (572.2)
hypertensive (437.2)
toxic (349.82)
CC Excl: 333.92, 344.81, 348.30-348.31

---

§   Requires fifth digit. Valid digits are in [brackets] under each code. See appropriate category for codes and definitions.

348.4　Compression of brain　　`MCC`

Compression
Herniation } brain (stem)

Posterior fossa compression syndrome
DEF: Elevated pressure in brain due to blood clot, tumor, fracture, abscess, other condition.
CC Excl: 342.90
AHA: 4Q, '94, 37
TIP: Assign for Arnold-Chiari syndrome, Type I. For Type II, III, or IV, refer to categories 741 and 742.

348.5　Cerebral edema　　`MCC`

DEF: Elevated pressure in the brain due to fluid retention in brain tissues.
CC Excl: 348.5
G93.6 Cerebral edema　`I-10`

√5ᵗʰ **348.8　Other conditions of brain**
AHA: S-O, '87, 9

348.81　Temporal sclerosis
Hippocampal sclerosis
Mesial temporal sclerosis

348.89　Other conditions of brain
Cerebral:
calcification
fungus

348.9　Unspecified condition of brain　`HIV`

√4ᵗʰ **349　Other and unspecified disorders of the nervous system**
AHA: 4Q, '08, 109

349.0　Reaction to spinal or lumbar puncture
Headache following lumbar puncture
AHA: 2Q, '99, 9; 3Q, '90, 18
G97.1 Other reaction to spinal and lumbar puncture　`I-10`

349.1　Nervous system complications from　`CC`
surgically implanted device
　　EXCLUDES　immediate postoperative complications
　　　　　　　　(997.00-997.09)
　　　　　　　　mechanical complications of nervous system
　　　　　　　　device (996.2)
CC Excl: 2249.60-249.61, 249.80-249.91, 250.60-250.63, 250.80-250.93, 349.1, 349.89-349.9

349.2　Disorders of meninges, not elsewhere classified
Adhesions, meningeal (cerebral) (spinal)
Cyst, spinal meninges
Meningocele, acquired
Pseudomeningocele, acquired
AHA: 1Q, '06, 15; 2Q, '98, 18; 3Q, '94, 4

√5ᵗʰ **349.3　Dural tear**

349.31　Accidental puncture or laceration　`CC`
of dura during a procedure
Incidental (inadvertent) durotomy
CC Excl: 349.31-349.39, 997.91-997.99, 998.2, 998.81, 998.83-998.9
AHA: 4Q, '08, 109-110
TIP: Do not assign code 998.2 Accidental puncture or laceration during a procedure, for an incidental dural tear.

349.39　Other dural tear　`CC`
CC Excl: 349.31-349.39, 997.91-997.99, 998.2, 998.81, 998.83-998.9

√5ᵗʰ **349.8　Other specified disorders of nervous system**

349.81　Cerebrospinal fluid rhinorrhea　`CC`
　　EXCLUDES　cerebrospinal fluid otorrhea (388.61)
DEF: Cerebrospinal fluid discharging from the nose; caused by fracture of frontal bone with tearing of dura mater and arachnoid.
CC Excl: 249.60-249.61, 249.80-249.91, 250.60-250.63, 250.80-250.93, 349.81, 349.89-349.9

349.82　Toxic encephalopathy　　`MCC`
Toxic metabolic encephalopathy
Use additional E code to identify cause
DEF: Brain tissue degeneration due to toxic substance.
CC Excl: 013.60-013.66, 017.90-017.96, 036.1, 049.8-049.9, 052.0, 054.3, 058.21-058.29, 062.0-063.9, 072.2, 090.41, 094.81, 130.0, 249.60-249.61, 249.80-249.91, 250.60-250.63, 250.80-250.93, 323.01-323.9, 341.20-341.22, 348.30-348.39, 348.81-348.9, 349.82-349.9
AHA: 4Q, '93, 29
G92 Toxic encephalopathy　`I-10`

349.89　Other

349.9　Unspecified disorders of nervous system　`HIV`
Disorder of nervous system (central) NOS

DISORDERS OF THE PERIPHERAL NERVOUS SYSTEM (350-359)

EXCLUDES　diseases of:
　　　　　　acoustic [8th] nerve (388.5)
　　　　　　oculomotor [3rd, 4th, 6th] nerves (378.0-378.9)
　　　　　　optic [2nd] nerve (377.0-377.9)
　　　　　　peripheral autonomic nerves (337.0-337.9)
　　　　　neuralgia
　　　　　neuritis　　} NOS or "rheumatic" (729.2)
　　　　　radiculitis
　　　　　peripheral neuritis in pregnancy (646.4)

√4ᵗʰ **350　Trigeminal nerve disorders**
INCLUDES　disorders of 5th cranial nerve

350.1　Trigeminal neuralgia
Tic douloureux　　　　　Trigeminal neuralgia NOS
Trifacial neuralgia
　　EXCLUDES　postherpetic (053.12)
G50.0 Trigeminal neuralgia　`I-10`

350.2　Atypical face pain

350.8　Other specified trigeminal nerve disorders

350.9　Trigeminal nerve disorder, unspecified

√4ᵗʰ **351　Facial nerve disorders**
INCLUDES　disorders of 7th cranial nerve
EXCLUDES　that in newborn (767.5)

351.0　Bell's palsy
Facial palsy
DEF: Unilateral paralysis of face due to lesion on facial nerve; produces facial distortion.
G51.0 Bell's palsy　`I-10`

351.1　Geniculate ganglionitis
Geniculate ganglionitis NOS
　　EXCLUDES　herpetic (053.11)
DEF: Inflammation of tissue at bend in facial nerve.

351.8　Other facial nerve disorders
Facial myokymia　　　　Melkersson's syndrome
AHA: 3Q, '02, 13

351.9　Facial nerve disorder, unspecified

Trigeminal and Facial Nerve Branches

Temporal branches
Zygomatic branches
Buccal branches
Mandibular branch
Cervical branch
Branches of Facial Nerve (above)
Maxillary (V2)
Divisions of Trigeminal Nerve (below)
Ophthalmic (V1)
Trigeminal nerve (CN V)
Mandibulary (V3)

√4ᵗʰ
√5ᵗʰ　Additional Digit Required　　Unacceptable PDx　　Manifestation Code　　Hospital Acquired Condition　　▶◀ Revised Text　　● New Code　　▲ Revised Code Title

2010 ICD-9-CM　　　　　　　　　　　　　　　　　　　　　　　**October 2009 • Volume 1 – 113**

Nervous System and Sense Organs

352–354.9

Cranial Nerves

- Olfactory bulb (I)
- Optic nerve (II)
- Oculomotor nerve (III)
- Trochlear nerve (IV)
- Trigeminal nerve (V)
- Abducens nerve (VI)
- Facial nerve (VII)
- Vestibulocochlear nerve (VIII)
- Glossopharyngeal nerve (IX)
- Vagus nerve (X)
- Accessory nerve (XI)
- Hypoglossal nerve (XII)

Pons

Peripheral Nervous System

- Brain
- Spinal cord
- Brachial plexus
- Musculocutaneous
- Intercostal
- Subcostal
- Radial
- Median
- Lumbar plexus
- Deep branch of radial
- Superficial branch of radial
- Ulnar
- Sacral plexus
- Femoral
- Sciatic
- Muscular branches of femoral
- Saphenous
- Common peroneal
- Tibial
- Deep peroneal
- Superficial peroneal

✓4th 352 Disorders of other cranial nerves

352.0 Disorders of olfactory [lst] nerve

352.1 Glossopharyngeal neuralgia
> **DEF:** Pain between throat and ear along petrosal and jugular ganglia.
> **AHA:** 2Q, '02, 8

352.2 Other disorders of glossopharyngeal [9th] nerve

352.3 Disorders of pneumogastric [10th] nerve
> Disorders of vagal nerve
> **EXCLUDES** paralysis of vocal cords or larynx (478.30-478.34)
> **DEF:** Nerve disorder affecting ear, tongue, pharynx, larynx, esophagus, viscera and thorax.

352.4 Disorders of accessory [11th] nerve
> **DEF:** Nerve disorder affecting palate, pharynx, larynx, thoracic viscera, sternocleidomastoid and trapezius muscles.

352.5 Disorders of hypoglossal [12th] nerve
> **DEF:** Nerve disorder affecting tongue muscles.

352.6 Multiple cranial nerve palsies
> Collet-Sicard syndrome
> Polyneuritis cranialis

352.9 Unspecified disorder of cranial nerves

✓4th 353 Nerve root and plexus disorders
> **EXCLUDES** conditions due to:
> intervertebral disc disorders (722.0-722.9)
> spondylosis (720.0-721.9)
> vertebrogenic disorders (723.0-724.9)

353.0 Brachial plexus lesions
> Cervical rib syndrome
> Costoclavicular syndrome
> Scalenus anticus syndrome
> Thoracic outlet syndrome
> **EXCLUDES** brachial neuritis or radiculitis NOS (723.4)
> that in newborn (767.6)
> **DEF:** Acquired disorder in tissue along nerves in shoulder; causes corresponding motor and sensory dysfunction.
> **AHA:** 3Q, '06, 12

353.1 Lumbosacral plexus lesions
> **DEF:** Acquired disorder in tissue along nerves in lower back; causes corresponding motor and sensory dysfunction.

353.2 Cervical root lesions, not elsewhere classified

353.3 Thoracic root lesions, not elsewhere classified

353.4 Lumbosacral root lesions, not elsewhere classified

353.5 Neuralgic amyotrophy
> Parsonage-Aldren-Turner syndrome
> Code first any associated underlying disease, such as:
> diabetes mellitus (249.6, 250.6)

353.6 Phantom limb (syndrome)
> **DEF:** Abnormal tingling or a burning sensation, transient aches, and intermittent or continuous pain perceived as originating in the absent limb.

353.8 Other nerve root and plexus disorders

353.9 Unspecified nerve root and plexus disorder

✓4th 354 Mononeuritis of upper limb and mononeuritis multiplex
> **DEF:** Inflammation of a single nerve; known as mononeuritis multiplex when several nerves in unrelated body areas are affected.

354.0 Carpal tunnel syndrome
> Median nerve entrapment
> Partial thenar atrophy
> **DEF:** Compression of median nerve by tendons; causes pain, tingling, numbness and burning sensation in hand.
> **G56.00** Carpal tunnel syndrome unspecified side   I-10

354.1 Other lesion of median nerve
> Median nerve neuritis

354.2 Lesion of ulnar nerve
> Cubital tunnel syndrome
> Tardy ulnar nerve palsy

354.3 Lesion of radial nerve
> Acute radial nerve palsy
> **AHA:** N-D, '87, 6

354.4 Causalgia of upper limb
> Complex regional pain syndrome type II of the upper limb
> **EXCLUDES** causalgia:
> NOS (355.9)
> lower limb (355.71)
> complex regional pain syndrome type II of the lower limb (355.71)
> **DEF:** Peripheral nerve damage, upper limb; usually due to injury; causes burning sensation and trophic skin changes.

354.5 Mononeuritis multiplex
> Combinations of single conditions classifiable to 354 or 355

354.8 Other mononeuritis of upper limb

354.9 Mononeuritis of upper limb, unspecified

N Newborn Age: 0   P Pediatric Age: 0-17   M Maternity Age: 12-55   A Adult Age: 15-124   MCC Major CC Condition   CC CC Condition   HIV HIV Related Dx

114 – Volume 1   2010 ICD-9-CM

√4ᵗʰ **355 Mononeuritis of lower limb**

355.0 Lesion of sciatic nerve
> EXCLUDES *sciatica NOS (724.3)*
>
> **DEF:** Acquired disorder of sciatic nerve; causes motor and sensory dysfunction in back, buttock and leg.
>
> **AHA:** 2Q, '89, 12

355.1 Meralgia paresthetica
> Lateral cutaneous femoral nerve of thigh compression or syndrome
>
> **DEF:** Inguinal ligament entraps lateral femoral cutaneous nerve; causes tingling, pain and numbness along outer thigh.

355.2 Other lesion of femoral nerve

355.3 Lesion of lateral popliteal nerve
> Lesion of common peroneal nerve

355.4 Lesion of medial popliteal nerve

355.5 Tarsal tunnel syndrome
> **DEF:** Compressed, entrapped posterior tibial nerve; causes tingling, pain and numbness in sole of foot.

355.6 Lesion of plantar nerve
> Morton's metatarsalgia, neuralgia, or neuroma

√5ᵗʰ **355.7 Other mononeuritis of lower limb**

> **355.71 Causalgia of lower limb**
> > EXCLUDES *causalgia:*
> > *NOS (355.9)*
> > *upper limb (354.4)*
> > *complex regional pain syndrome*
> > *type II of upper limb (354.4)*
> >
> > **DEF:** Dysfunction of lower limb peripheral nerve, usually due to injury; causes burning pain and trophic skin changes.
>
> **355.79 Other mononeuritis of lower limb**

355.8 Mononeuritis of lower limb, unspecified

355.9 Mononeuritis of unspecified site
> Causalgia NOS
> Complex regional pain syndrome NOS
> > EXCLUDES *causalgia:*
> > *lower limb (355.71)*
> > *upper limb (354.4)*
> > *complex regional pain syndrome:*
> > *lower limb (355.71)*
> > *upper limb (354.4)*
>
> G58.9 Mononeuropathy unspecified I-10

√4ᵗʰ **356 Hereditary and idiopathic peripheral neuropathy**

356.0 Hereditary peripheral neuropathy
> Déjérine-Sottas disease

356.1 Peroneal muscular atrophy
> Charcôt-Marie-Tooth disease
> Neuropathic muscular atrophy
>
> **DEF:** Genetic disorder, in muscles innervated by peroneal nerves; symptoms include muscle wasting in lower limbs and locomotor difficulties.

356.2 Hereditary sensory neuropathy
> **DEF:** Inherited disorder in dorsal root ganglia, optic nerve, and cerebellum, causing sensory losses, shooting pains, and foot ulcers.

356.3 Refsum's disease CC
> Heredopathia atactica polyneuritiformis
>
> **DEF:** Genetic disorder of lipid metabolism; causes persistent, painful inflammation of nerves and retinitis pigmentosa.
>
> **CC Excl:** 350.1-357.9

356.4 Idiopathic progressive polyneuropathy

356.8 Other specified idiopathic peripheral neuropathy
> Supranuclear paralysis

356.9 Unspecified
> G60.9 Hereditary & idiopathic neuropathy unspecified I-10

√4ᵗʰ **357 Inflammatory and toxic neuropathy**

357.0 Acute infective polyneuritis CC
> Guillain-Barré syndrome
> Postinfectious polyneuritis
>
> **DEF:** Guillain-Barré syndrome: acute demyelinatry polyneuropathy preceded by viral illness (i.e., herpes, cytomegalovirus [CMV], Epstein-Barr virus [EBV]) or a bacterial illness; areflexic motor paralysis with mild sensory disturbance and acellular rise in spinal fluid protein.
>
> **CC Excl:** 003.21, 013.00-013.16, 036.0, 036.89-036.9, 041.81-041.9, 047.0-047.9, 049.0-049.1, 053.0, 054.72, 072.1, 090.42, 091.81, 094.2, 098.89, 100.81, 112.83, 114.2, 115.01, 115.11, 115.91, 130.0, 139.8, 320.0-322.9, 349.89-349.9, 357.0
>
> **AHA:** 2Q, '98, 12

357.1 Polyneuropathy in collagen vascular disease
> *Code first underlying disease, as:*
> *disseminated lupus erythematosus (710.0)*
> *polyarteritis nodosa (446.0)*
> *rheumatoid arthritis (714.0)*

357.2 Polyneuropathy in diabetes
> *Code first underlying disease (249.6, 250.6)*
>
> **AHA:** ▶2Q, '09, 13, 15;◀ 3Q, '08, 5; 4Q, '03, 105; 2Q, '92, 15; 3Q, '91, 9

357.3 Polyneuropathy in malignant disease
> *Code first underlying disease (140.0-208.9)*

357.4 Polyneuropathy in other diseases classified elsewhere
> *Code first underlying disease, as:*
> *amyloidosis (277.30-277.39)*
> *beriberi (265.0)*
> *chronic uremia (585.9)*
> *deficiency of B vitamins (266.0-266.9)*
> *diphtheria (032.0-032.9)*
> *hypoglycemia (251.2)*
> *pellagra (265.2)*
> *porphyria (277.1)*
> *sarcoidosis (135)*
> *uremia NOS (586)*
> > EXCLUDES *polyneuropathy in:*
> > *herpes zoster (053.13)*
> > *mumps (072.72)*
>
> **AHA:** 2Q, '08, 8; 2Q, '98, 15
> G63 Polyneuropathy in diseases classified elsewhere I-10

357.5 Alcoholic polyneuropathy

357.6 Polyneuropathy due to drugs
> Use additional E code to identify drug

357.7 Polyneuropathy due to other toxic agents
> Use additional E code to identify toxic agent

√5ᵗʰ **357.8 Other**
> **AHA:** 4Q, '02, 47; 2Q, '98, 12

> **357.81 Chronic inflammatory demyelinating polyneuritis** CC
> > **DEF:** Inflammation of peripheral nerves resulting in destruction of myelin sheath; associated with diabetes mellitus, dysproteinemias, renal failure and malnutrition; symptoms are tingling, numbness, burning pain, diminished tendon reflexes, weakness, of lower extremities.
> >
> > **CC Excl:** 351.0-353.5, 353.8-356.9, 357.81-357.89

> **357.82 Critical illness polyneuropathy** CC
> > Acute motor neuropathy
> >
> > **DEF:** An acute axonal neuropathy, both sensory and motor, that is associated with Systemic Inflammatory Response Syndrome (SIRS).
> >
> > **CC Excl:** 351.0-353.5, 353.8-356.9, 357.81-357.9
> >
> > **AHA:** 4Q, '03, 111

> **357.89 Other inflammatory and toxic neuropathy**

357.9 Unspecified

√4ᵗʰ / √5ᵗʰ Additional Digit Required | Unacceptable PDx | Manifestation Code | Hospital Acquired Condition | ▶◀ Revised Text | ● New Code | ▲ Revised Code Title

2010 ICD-9-CM

October 2009 • Volume 1 – 115
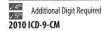

Nervous System and Sense Organs

358–359.9

✓4th **358 Myoneural disorders**

✓5th **358.0 Myasthenia gravis**

DEF: Autoimmune disorder of acetylcholine at neuromuscular junction; causing fatigue of voluntary muscles.
AHA: 4Q, '03, 59

358.00 Myasthenia gravis without (acute) exacerbation
Myasthenia gravis NOS

G70.00 Myathenia gravis without (acute) [I-10]
exacerbation

358.01 Myasthenia gravis with (acute) [MCC] exacerbation
Myasthenia gravis in crisis

CC Excl: 249.60-249.61, 249.80-249.91, 250.60-250.63, 250.80-250.93, 349.89-349.9, 358.00-358.1
AHA: 4Q, '07, 109; 1Q, '05, 4; 4Q, '04, 139

358.1 Myasthenic syndromes in diseases classified [CC] *elsewhere*
Eaton-Lambert syndrome from stated cause classified elsewhere

Code first underlying disease, as:
botulism (005.1, 040.41-040.42)
hypothyroidism (244.0-244.9)
malignant neoplasm (140.0-208.9)
pernicious anemia (281.0)
thyrotoxicosis (242.0-242.9)

CC Excl: See code: 358.01

358.2 Toxic myoneural disorders
Use additional E code to identify toxic agent

358.8 Other specified myoneural disorders

358.9 Myoneural disorders, unspecified
AHA: 2Q, '02, 16

✓4th **359 Muscular dystrophies and other myopathies**
EXCLUDES idiopathic polymyositis (710.4)

359.0 Congenital hereditary muscular dystrophy [CC]
Benign congenital myopathy
Central core disease
Centronuclear myopathy
Myotubular myopathy
Nemaline body disease
EXCLUDES arthrogryposis multiplex congenita (754.89)
DEF: Genetic disorder; causing progressive or nonprogressive muscle weakness.
CC Excl: 249.60-249.61, 249.80-249.91, 250.60-250.63, 250.80-250.93, 349.89-349.9, 359.0-359.1

359.1 Hereditary progressive muscular dystrophy [CC]
Muscular dystrophy:
NOS
distal
Duchenne
Erb's
fascioscapulohumeral
Gower's
Landouzy-Déjérine
limb-girdle
ocular
oculopharyngeal
DEF: Genetic degenerative, muscle disease; causes progressive weakness, wasting of muscle with no nerve involvement.
CC Excl: See code: 359.0

✓5th **359.2 Myotonic disorders**
EXCLUDES periodic paralysis (359.3)
DEF: Impaired movement due to spasmatic, rigid muscles.
AHA: 4Q, '07, 75

359.21 Myotonic muscular dystrophy
Dystrophia myotonica
Myotonia atrophica
Myotonic dystrophy
Proximal myotonic myopathy [PROMM]
Steinert's disease

359.22 Myotonia congenita
Acetazolamide responsive myotonia congenita
Dominant form [Thomsen's disease]
▶Myotonia levior◀
Recessive form [Becker's disease]

359.23 Myotonic chondrodystrophy
Congenital myotonic chondrodystrophy
Schwartz-Jampel disease

359.24 Drug induced myotonia
Use additional E code to identify drug

359.29 Other specified myotonic disorder
Myotonia fluctuans
Myotonia permanens
Paramyotonia congenita (of von Eulenburg)

359.3 Periodic paralysis
Familial periodic paralysis
Hypokalemic familial periodic paralysis
Hyperkalemic periodic paralysis
Hypokalemic periodic paralysis
Potassium sensitive periodic paralysis
EXCLUDES paramyotonia congenita (of von Eulenburg) (359.29)
DEF: Genetic disorder; characterized by rapidly progressive flaccid paralysis; attacks often occur after exercise or exposure to cold or dietary changes.

359.4 Toxic myopathy [CC]
Use additional E code to identify toxic agent
DEF: Muscle disorder caused by toxic agent.
CC Excl: 349.89-349.9, 358.00-359.6, 359.81-359.9
AHA: 1Q, '88, 5

359.5 Myopathy in endocrine diseases classified elsewhere
Code first underlying disease, as:
Addison's disease (255.41)
Cushing's syndrome (255.0)
hypopituitarism (253.2)
myxedema (244.0-244.9)
thyrotoxicosis (242.0-242.9)
DEF: Muscle disorder secondary to dysfunction in hormone secretion.

359.6 Symptomatic inflammatory myopathy in diseases [CC] *classified elsewhere*
Code first underlying disease, as:
amyloidosis (277.30-277.39)
disseminated lupus erythematosus (710.0)
malignant neoplasm (140.0-208.9)
polyarteritis nodosa (446.0)
rheumatoid arthritis (714.0)
sarcoidosis (135)
scleroderma (710.1)
Sjögren's disease (710.2)
CC Excl: 249.60-249.61, 249.80-249.91, 250.60-250.63, 250.80-250.93, 349.89-349.9, 358.00-359.6, 359.81-359.9

● ✓5th **359.7 Inflammatory and immune myopathies, NEC**
●   **359.71 Inclusion body myositis**
IBM

●   **359.79 Other inflammatory and immune myopathies, NEC**
Inflammatory myopathy NOS

✓5th **359.8 Other myopathies**
AHA: 4Q, '02, 47; 3Q, '90, 17

359.81 Critical illness myopathy [CC]
Acute necrotizing myopathy
Acute quadriplegic myopathy
Intensive care (ICU) myopathy
Myopathy of critical illness
CC Excl: 358.1-359.6, 359.81-359.9

359.89 Other myopathies

359.9 Myopathy, unspecified

[N] Newborn Age: 0   [P] Pediatric Age: 0-17   [M] Maternity Age: 12-55   [A] Adult Age: 15-124   [MCC] Major CC Condition   [CC] CC Condition   [HIV] HIV Related Dx

116 – Volume 1 • October 2009   2010 ICD-9-CM

Eye

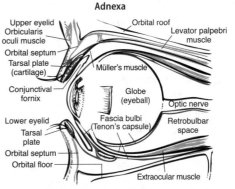

Adnexa

DISORDERS OF THE EYE AND ADNEXA (360-379)

Use additional external cause code, if applicable, to identify the cause of the eye condition

√4ᵗʰ **360 Disorders of the globe**

     INCLUDES   disorders affecting multiple structures of eye

√5ᵗʰ **360.0 Purulent endophthalmitis**

     EXCLUDES   *bleb associated endophthalmitis (379.63)*

   360.00 Purulent endophthalmitis, unspecified `CC`
     CC Excl: 360.00-360.04, 360.13, 360.19, 364.05

   360.01 Acute endophthalmitis `CC`
     CC Excl: See code 360.00

   360.02 Panophthalmitis `CC`
     CC Excl: See code 360.00

   360.03 Chronic endophthalmitis

   360.04 Vitreous abscess `CC`
     CC Excl: 360.00-360.19

√5ᵗʰ **360.1 Other endophthalmitis**

     EXCLUDES   *bleb associated endophthalmitis (379.63)*

   360.11 Sympathetic uveitis `CC`
     DEF: Inflammation of vascular layer of uninjured eye; follows injury to other eye.
     CC Excl: 360.11-360.12

   360.12 Panuveitis `CC`
     DEF: Inflammation of entire vascular layer of eye, including choroid, iris and ciliary body.
     CC Excl: 360.11-360.12

   360.13 Parasitic endophthalmitis NOS `CC`
     DEF: Parasitic infection causing inflammation of the entire eye.
     CC Excl: 360.00-360.04, 360.13, 360.19, 364.05

   360.14 Ophthalmia nodosa
     DEF: Conjunctival inflammation caused by embedded hairs.

   360.19 Other `CC`
     Phacoanaphylactic endophthalmitis
     CC Excl: 360.00-360.04, 360.13, 360.19, 364.05

√5ᵗʰ **360.2 Degenerative disorders of globe**
     AHA: 3Q, '91, 3

   360.20 Degenerative disorder of globe, unspecified

   360.21 Progressive high (degenerative) myopia
     Malignant myopia
     DEF: Severe, progressive nearsightedness in adults, complicated by serious disease of the choroid; leads to retinal detachment and blindness.

   360.23 Siderosis
     DEF: Iron pigment deposits within tissue of eyeball; caused by high iron content of blood.

   360.24 Other metallosis
     Chalcosis
     DEF: Metal deposits, other than iron, within eyeball tissues.

   360.29 Other
     EXCLUDES   *xerophthalmia (264.7)*

√5ᵗʰ **360.3 Hypotony of eye**

   360.30 Hypotony, unspecified
     DEF: Low osmotic pressure causing lack of tone, tension and strength.

   360.31 Primary hypotony

   360.32 Ocular fistula causing hypotony
     DEF: Low intraocular pressure due to leak through abnormal passage.

   360.33 Hypotony associated with other ocular disorders

   360.34 Flat anterior chamber
     DEF: Low pressure behind cornea, causing compression.

√5ᵗʰ **360.4 Degenerated conditions of globe**

   360.40 Degenerated globe or eye, unspecified

   360.41 Blind hypotensive eye
     Atrophy of globe
     Phthisis bulbi
     DEF: Vision loss due to extremely low intraocular pressure.

   360.42 Blind hypertensive eye
     Absolute glaucoma
     DEF: Vision loss due to painful, high intraocular pressure.

   360.43 Hemophthalmos, except current injury
     EXCLUDES   *traumatic (871.0-871.9, 921.0-921.9)*
     DEF: Pool of blood within eyeball, not from current injury.

   360.44 Leucocoria
     DEF: Whitish mass or reflex in the pupil behind lens; also called cat's eye reflex; often indicative of retinoblastoma.

√5ᵗʰ **360.5 Retained (old) intraocular foreign body, magnetic**
     EXCLUDES   *current penetrating injury with magnetic foreign body (871.5)*
     retained (old) foreign body of orbit (376.6)

   360.50 Foreign body, magnetic, intraocular, unspecified

   360.51 Foreign body, magnetic, in anterior chamber

   360.52 Foreign body, magnetic, in iris or ciliary body

√4ᵗʰ √5ᵗʰ Additional Digit Required   Unacceptable PDx   Manifestation Code   Hospital Acquired Condition   ▶◀ Revised Text   ● New Code   ▲ Revised Code Title

2010 ICD-9-CM   **Volume 1 – 117**

Nervous System and Sense Organs

360.53–362.06

360.53   Foreign body, magnetic, in lens

360.54   Foreign body, magnetic, in vitreous

360.55   Foreign body, magnetic, in posterior wall

360.59   Foreign body, magnetic, in other or multiple sites

√5th   360.6   Retained (old) intraocular foreign body, nonmagnetic
Retained (old) foreign body:
    NOS
    nonmagnetic
    EXCLUDES   current penetrating injury with (nonmagnetic) foreign body (871.6)
            retained (old) foreign body in orbit (376.6)

360.60   Foreign body, intraocular, unspecified

360.61   Foreign body in anterior chamber

360.62   Foreign body in iris or ciliary body

360.63   Foreign body in lens

360.64   Foreign body in vitreous

360.65   Foreign body in posterior wall

360.69   Foreign body in other or multiple sites

√5th   360.8   Other disorders of globe

360.81   Luxation of globe
      DEF: Displacement of eyeball.

360.89   Other

360.9   Unspecified disorder of globe

√4th   **361**   **Retinal detachments and defects**
    DEF: Light-sensitive layer at back of eye, separates from blood supply; disrupting vision.

√5th   361.0   Retinal detachment with retinal defect
Rhegmatogenous retinal detachment
    EXCLUDES   detachment of retinal pigment epithelium (362.42-362.43)
            retinal detachment (serous) (without defect) (361.2)

361.00   Retinal detachment with retinal defect, unspecified

361.01   Recent detachment, partial, with single defect

361.02   Recent detachment, partial, with multiple defects

361.03   Recent detachment, partial, with giant tear

361.04   Recent detachment, partial, with retinal dialysis
      Dialysis (juvenile) of retina (with detachment)

361.05   Recent detachment, total or subtotal

361.06   Old detachment, partial
      Delimited old retinal detachment

361.07   Old detachment, total or subtotal

√5th   361.1   Retinoschisis and retinal cysts
    EXCLUDES   juvenile retinoschisis (362.73)
            microcystoid degeneration of retina (362.62)
            parasitic cyst of retina (360.13)

361.10   Retinoschisis, unspecified
      DEF: Separation of retina due to degenerative process of aging; should not be confused with acute retinal detachment.

361.11   Flat retinoschisis
      DEF: Slow, progressive split of retinal sensory layers

361.12   Bullous retinoschisis
      DEF: Fluid retention between split retinal sensory layers.

361.13   Primary retinal cysts

361.14   Secondary retinal cysts

361.19   Other
      Pseudocyst of retina

361.2   Serous retinal detachment   `CC`
Retinal detachment without retinal defect
    EXCLUDES   central serous retinopathy (362.41)
            retinal pigment epithelium detachment (362.42-362.43)
    CC Excl: 361.00-361.9, 362.40-362.43

√5th   361.3   Retinal defects without detachment
    EXCLUDES   chorioretinal scars after surgery for detachment (363.30-363.35)
            peripheral retinal degeneration without defect (362.60-362.66)

361.30   Retinal defect, unspecified
      Retinal break(s) NOS

361.31   Round hole of retina without detachment

361.32   Horseshoe tear of retina without detachment
      Operculum of retina without mention of detachment

361.33   Multiple defects of retina without detachment

√5th   361.8   Other forms of retinal detachment

361.81   Traction detachment of retina   `CC`
      Traction detachment with vitreoretinal organization
      CC Excl: 361.00-361.9, 362.40-362.43

361.89   Other   `CC`
      CC Excl: 361.00-361.9, 362.40-362.43
      AHA: 3Q, '99, 12

361.9   Unspecified retinal detachment   `CC`
      CC Excl: 361.00-361.9, 362.40-362.43
      AHA: N-D, '87, 10

√4th   **362**   **Other retinal disorders**
    EXCLUDES   chorioretinal scars (363.30-363.35)
            chorioretinitis (363.0-363.2)

√5th   362.0   Diabetic retinopathy
    Code first diabetes (249.5, 250.5)
    DEF: Retinal changes in diabetes of long duration; causes hemorrhages, microaneurysms, waxy deposits and proliferative noninflammatory degenerative disease of retina.
    AHA: 4Q, '05, 65; 3Q, '91, 8

362.01   *Background diabetic retinopathy*
      Diabetic retinal microaneurysms
      Diabetic retinopathy NOS

362.02   *Proliferative diabetic retinopathy*
      DEF: Occurrence of the ischemic effects of vessel blockages result in neovascularization; new blood vessels begin to form to compensate for restricted blood flow; multiple areas of the retina and inner vitreous may be affected.
      AHA: 3Q, '96, 5

362.03   *Nonproliferative diabetic retinopathy NOS*

362.04   *Mild nonproliferative diabetic retinopathy*
      DEF: Early stages of degenerative condition of the retina due to diabetes; microaneurysm formation; small balloon-like swelling of the retinal vessels.

362.05   *Moderate nonproliferative diabetic retinopathy*
      DEF: Stage of degenerative condition of the retina due to diabetes with pronounced microaneurysms; vessel blockages can occur.

362.06   *Severe nonproliferative diabetic retinopathy*
      DEF: Stage of degenerative condition of the retina due to diabetes in which vascular breakdown in the retina results in multiple vascular blockages, or "beadings," with intraretinal hemorrhages.
      AHA: 4Q, '05, 67

`N` Newborn Age: 0   `P` Pediatric Age: 0-17   `M` Maternity Age: 12-55   `A` Adult Age: 15-124   `MCC` Major CC Condition   `CC` CC Condition   `HIV` HIV Related Dx

118 – Volume 1   2010 ICD-9-CM

362.07   *Diabetic macular edema*
> Note: Code 362.07 must be used with a code for diabetic retinopathy (362.01-362.06)
> Diabetic retinal edema
> **DEF:** Leakage from retinal blood vessels causes swelling of the macula and impaired vision; exudates or plaques may develop in the posterior pole of the retina due to the breakdown of retinal vasculature.

✓5th 362.1 **Other background retinopathy and retinal vascular changes**

362.10 **Background retinopathy, unspecified**
> **AHA:** 1Q, '06, 12

362.11 **Hypertensive retinopathy**
> **DEF:** Retinal irregularities caused by systemic hypertension.
> **AHA:** 3Q, '90, 3

362.12 **Exudative retinopathy**
> Coats' syndrome
> **AHA:** 3Q, '99, 12

362.13 **Changes in vascular appearance**
> Vascular sheathing of retina
> Use additional code for any associated atherosclerosis (440.8)

362.14 **Retinal microaneurysms NOS**
> **DEF:** Microscopic dilation of retinal vessels in nondiabetic.

362.15 **Retinal telangiectasia**
> **DEF:** Dilation of blood vessels of the retina.

362.16 **Retinal neovascularization NOS**
> Neovascularization: Neovascularization:
>   choroidal   subretinal
> **DEF:** New and abnormal vascular growth in the retina.

362.17 **Other intraretinal microvascular abnormalities**
> Retinal sclerosis   Retinal varices

362.18 **Retinal vasculitis**
> Eales' disease   Retinal:
> Retinal: perivasculitis
>   arteritis   phlebitis
>   endarteritis
> **DEF:** Inflammation of retinal blood vessels.

✓5th 362.2 **Other proliferative retinopathy**
> **AHA:** ▶4Q, '08, 110-111◀

362.20 **Retinopathy of prematurity, unspecified**
> Retinopathy of prematurity NOS

362.21 **Retrolental fibroplasia**
> Cicatricial retinopathy of prematurity
> **DEF:** Fibrous tissue in vitreous, from retina to lens, causing blindness; associated with premature infants requiring high amounts of oxygen.

362.22 **Retinopathy of prematurity, stage 0**

362.23 **Retinopathy of prematurity, stage 1**

362.24 **Retinopathy of prematurity, stage 2**

362.25 **Retinopathy of prematurity, stage 3**

362.26 **Retinopathy of prematurity, stage 4**

362.27 **Retinopathy of prematurity, stage 5**

362.29 **Other nondiabetic proliferative retinopathy**
> **AHA:** 3Q, '96, 5

✓5th 362.3 **Retinal vascular occlusion**
> **DEF:** Obstructed blood flow to and from retina.

362.30 **Retinal vascular occlusion, unspecified**   CC
> **CC Excl:** 362.30-362.37

362.31 **Central retinal artery occlusion**   CC
> **CC Excl:** See code: 362.30

362.32 **Arterial branch occlusion**   CC
> **CC Excl:** See code: 362.30

362.33 **Partial arterial occlusion**   CC
> Hollenhorst plaque
> Retinal microembolism
> **CC Excl:** See code: 362.30

362.34 **Transient arterial occlusion**   CC
> Amaurosis fugax
> **CC Excl:** See code: 362.30
> **AHA:** 1Q, '00, 16

362.35 **Central retinal vein occlusion**   CC
> **CC Excl:** See code: 362.30
> **AHA:** 2Q, '93, 6

362.36 **Venous tributary (branch) occlusion**

362.37 **Venous engorgement**
> Occlusion:
>   incipient ⎫
>   partial   ⎬ of retinal vein

✓5th 362.4 **Separation of retinal layers**
> **EXCLUDES**   retinal detachment (serous) (361.2)
>   rhegmatogenous (361.00-361.07)

362.40 **Retinal layer separation, unspecified**   CC
> **CC Excl:** 361.00-361.9, 362.40-362.43

362.41 **Central serous retinopathy**
> **DEF:** Serous-filled blister causing detachment of retina from pigment epithelium.

362.42 **Serous detachment of retinal pigment epithelium**   CC
> Exudative detachment of retinal pigment epithelium
> **CC Excl:** See code: 362.40
> **DEF:** Blister of fatty fluid causing detachment of retina from pigment epithelium.

362.43 **Hemorrhagic detachment of retinal pigment epithelium**   CC
> **CC Excl:** See code: 362.40
> **DEF:** Blood-filled blister causing detachment of retina from pigment epithelium.

✓5th 362.5 **Degeneration of macula and posterior pole**
> **EXCLUDES**   degeneration of optic disc (377.21-377.24)
>   hereditary retinal degeneration [dystrophy] (362.70-362.77)

362.50 **Macular degeneration (senile), unspecified**

362.51 **Nonexudative senile macular degeneration**
> Senile macular degeneration:
>   atrophic
>   dry

362.52 **Exudative senile macular degeneration**
> Kuhnt-Junius degeneration
> Senile macular degeneration:
>   disciform
>   wet
> **DEF:** Leakage in macular blood vessels with loss of visual acuity.

362.53 **Cystoid macular degeneration**
> Cystoid macular edema
> **DEF:** Retinal swelling and cyst formation in macula.

362.54 **Macular cyst, hole, or pseudohole**

362.55 **Toxic maculopathy**
> Use additional E code to identify drug, if drug induced

362.56 **Macular puckering**
> Preretinal fibrosis

362.57 **Drusen (degenerative)**
> **DEF:** White, hyaline deposits on Bruch's membrane (lamina basalis choroideae).

■4th Additional Digit Required   Unacceptable PDx   Manifestation Code   Hospital Acquired Condition   ▶◀ Revised Text   ● New Code   ▲ Revised Code Title
■5th
2010 ICD-9-CM   **February 2009 • Volume 1 – 119**

✓5th **362.6 Peripheral retinal degenerations**

> EXCLUDES   hereditary retinal degeneration [dystrophy]
> (362.70-362.77)
> retinal degeneration with retinal defect
> (361.00-361.07)

362.60 Peripheral retinal degeneration, unspecified

362.61 Paving stone degeneration
> **DEF:** Degeneration of peripheral retina; causes thinning through which choroid is visible.

362.62 Microcystoid degeneration
> Blessig's cysts   Iwanoff's cysts

362.63 Lattice degeneration
> Palisade degeneration of retina
> **DEF:** Degeneration of retina; often bilateral, usually benign; characterized by lines intersecting at irregular intervals in peripheral retina; retinal thinning and retinal holes may occur.

362.64 Senile reticular degeneration
> **DEF:** Net-like appearance of retina; sign of degeneration.

362.65 Secondary pigmentary degeneration
> Pseudoretinitis pigmentosa

362.66 Secondary vitreoretinal degenerations

✓5th **362.7 Hereditary retinal dystrophies**
> **DEF:** Genetically induced progressive changes in retina.

362.70 Hereditary retinal dystrophy, unspecified

362.71 Retinal dystrophy in systemic or cerebroretinal lipidoses

> Code first underlying disease, as:
> cerebroretinal lipidoses (330.1)
> systemic lipidoses (272.7)

362.72 Retinal dystrophy in other systemic disorders and syndromes

> Code first underlying disease, as:
> Bassen-Kornzweig syndrome (272.5)
> Refsum's disease (356.3)

362.73 Vitreoretinal dystrophies
> Juvenile retinoschisis

362.74 Pigmentary retinal dystrophy
> Retinal dystrophy, albipunctate
> Retinitis pigmentosa

362.75 Other dystrophies primarily involving the sensory retina
> Progressive cone(-rod) dystrophy
> Stargardt's disease

362.76 Dystrophies primarily involving the retinal pigment epithelium
> Fundus flavimaculatus   Vitelliform dystrophy

362.77 Dystrophies primarily involving Bruch's membrane
> Dystrophy:
> hyaline
> pseudoinflammatory foveal
> Hereditary drusen

✓5th **362.8 Other retinal disorders**

> EXCLUDES   chorioretinal inflammations (363.0-363.2)
> chorioretinal scars (363.30-363.35)

362.81 Retinal hemorrhage
> Hemorrhage:
> preretinal
> retinal (deep) (superficial)
> subretinal
> **AHA:** 4Q, '96, 43

362.82 Retinal exudates and deposits

362.83 Retinal edema
> Retinal:
> cotton wool spots
> edema (localized) (macular) (peripheral)
> **DEF:** Retinal swelling due to fluid accumulation.

362.84 Retinal ischemia `CC`
> **CC Excl:** 362.81-362.89
> **DEF:** Reduced retinal blood supply.

362.85 Retinal nerve fiber bundle defects

362.89 Other retinal disorders

362.9 Unspecified retinal disorder

✓4th **363 Chorioretinal inflammations, scars, and other disorders of choroid**

✓5th **363.0 Focal chorioretinitis and focal retinochoroiditis**

> EXCLUDES   focal chorioretinitis or retinochoroiditis in:
> histoplasmosis (115.02, 115.12, 115.92)
> toxoplasmosis (130.2)
> congenital infection (771.2)

363.00 Focal chorioretinitis, unspecified
> Focal:
> choroiditis or chorioretinitis NOS
> retinitis or retinochoroiditis NOS

363.01 Focal choroiditis and chorioretinitis, juxtapapillary

363.03 Focal choroiditis and chorioretinitis of other posterior pole

363.04 Focal choroiditis and chorioretinitis, peripheral

363.05 Focal retinitis and retinochoroiditis, juxtapapillary
> Neuroretinitis

363.06 Focal retinitis and retinochoroiditis, macular or paramacular

363.07 Focal retinitis and retinochoroiditis of other posterior pole

363.08 Focal retinitis and retinochoroiditis, peripheral

✓5th **363.1 Disseminated chorioretinitis and disseminated retinochoroiditis**

> EXCLUDES   disseminated choroiditis or chorioretinitis in:
> secondary syphilis (091.51)
> neurosyphilitic disseminated retinitis or
> retinochoroiditis (094.83)
> retinal (peri)vasculitis (362.18)

363.10 Disseminated chorioretinitis, unspecified `CC`
> Disseminated:
> choroiditis or chorioretinitis NOS
> retinitis or retinochoroiditis NOS
> **CC Excl:** 363.00-363.22

363.11 Disseminated choroiditis and chorioretinitis, posterior pole `CC`
> **CC Excl:** See code: 363.10

363.12 Disseminated choroiditis and chorioretinitis, peripheral `CC`
> **CC Excl:** See code: 363.10

363.13 Disseminated choroiditis and chorioretinitis, generalized `CC`
> Code first any underlying disease, as:
> tuberculosis (017.3)
> **CC Excl:** See code: 363.10

363.14 Disseminated retinitis and retinochoroiditis, metastatic `CC`
> **CC Excl:** See code: 363.10

363.15 Disseminated retinitis and retinochoroiditis, pigment epitheliopathy `CC`
> Acute posterior multifocal placoid pigment epitheliopathy
> **DEF:** Widespread inflammation of retina and choroid; characterized by pigmented epithelium involvement.
> **CC Excl:** See code: 363.10

N Newborn Age: 0   P Pediatric Age: 0-17   M Maternity Age: 12-55   A Adult Age: 15-124   MCC Major CC Condition   CC CC Condition   HIV HIV Related Dx

120 – Volume 1   **2010 ICD-9-CM**

Nervous System and Sense Organs

362.6–363.15

√5ᵗʰ 363.2 Other and unspecified forms of chorioretinitis and retinochoroiditis

> **EXCLUDES** panophthalmitis (360.02)
> sympathetic uveitis (360.11)
> uveitis NOS (364.3)

363.20 Chorioretinitis, unspecified `CC`
Choroiditis NOS
Retinitis NOS
Uveitis, posterior NOS
CC Excl: See code: 363.10

363.21 Pars planitis
Posterior cyclitis
DEF: Inflammation of peripheral retina and ciliary body; characterized by bands of white cells.

363.22 Harada's disease
DEF: Retinal detachment and bilateral widespread exudative choroiditis; symptoms include headache, vomiting, increased lymphocytes in cerebrospinal fluid; with temporary or permanent deafness.

√5ᵗʰ 363.3 Chorioretinal scars
Scar (postinflammatory) (postsurgical) (posttraumatic):
choroid
retina

363.30 Chorioretinal scar, unspecified

363.31 Solar retinopathy
DEF: Retinal scarring caused by solar radiation.

363.32 Other macular scars

363.33 Other scars of posterior pole

363.34 Peripheral scars

363.35 Disseminated scars

√5ᵗʰ 363.4 Choroidal degenerations

363.40 Choroidal degeneration, unspecified
Choroidal sclerosis NOS

363.41 Senile atrophy of choroid
DEF: Wasting away of choroid; due to aging.

363.42 Diffuse secondary atrophy of choroid
DEF: Wasting away of choroid in systemic disease.

363.43 Angioid streaks of choroid
DEF: Degeneration of choroid; characterized by dark brown steaks radiating from optic disk; occurs with pseudoxanthoma, elasticum or Paget's disease.

√5ᵗʰ 363.5 Hereditary choroidal dystrophies
Hereditary choroidal atrophy:
partial [choriocapillaris]
total [all vessels]

363.50 Hereditary choroidal dystrophy or atrophy, unspecified

363.51 Circumpapillary dystrophy of choroid, partial

363.52 Circumpapillary dystrophy of choroid, total
Helicoid dystrophy of choroid

363.53 Central dystrophy of choroid, partial
Dystrophy, choroidal:
central areolar
circinate

363.54 Central choroidal atrophy, total
Dystrophy, choroidal:　　Dystrophy, choroidal:
central gyrate　　　　　serpiginous

363.55 Choroideremia
DEF: Hereditary choroid degeneration, occurs in first decade; characterized by constricted visual field and ultimately blindness in males; less debilitating in females.

363.56 Other diffuse or generalized dystrophy, partial
Diffuse choroidal sclerosis

363.57 Other diffuse or generalized dystrophy, total
Generalized gyrate atrophy, choroid

√5ᵗʰ 363.6 Choroidal hemorrhage and rupture

363.61 Choroidal hemorrhage, unspecified

363.62 Expulsive choroidal hemorrhage

363.63 Choroidal rupture `CC`
CC Excl: 363.61-363.9

√5ᵗʰ 363.7 Choroidal detachment

363.70 Choroidal detachment, unspecified `CC`
CC Excl: See code: 363.63

363.71 Serous choroidal detachment `CC`
DEF: Detachment of choroid from sclera; due to blister of serous fluid.
CC Excl: See code: 363.63

363.72 Hemorrhagic choroidal detachment `CC`
DEF: Detachment of choroid from sclera; due to blood-filled blister.
CC Excl: See code: 363.63

363.8 Other disorders of choroid
AHA: 1Q, '06, 12

363.9 Unspecified disorder of choroid

√4ᵗʰ 364 Disorders of iris and ciliary body

√5ᵗʰ 364.0 Acute and subacute iridocyclitis
Anterior uveitis
Cylitis
Iridocyclitis　　} acute, subacute
Iritis

> **EXCLUDES** gonococcal (098.41)
> herpes simplex (054.44)
> herpes zoster (053.22)

364.00 Acute and subacute iridocyclitis, unspecified `CC`
CC Excl: 364.00-364.3

364.01 Primary iridocyclitis `CC`
CC Excl: See code: 364.00

364.02 Recurrent iridocyclitis `CC`
CC Excl: See code: 364.00

364.03 Secondary iridocyclitis, infectious `CC`
CC Excl: See code: 364.00

364.04 Secondary iridocyclitis, noninfectious
Aqueous:　　　　　Aqueous:
cells　　　　　　flare
fibrin

364.05 Hypopyon
DEF: Accumulation of white blood cells between cornea and lens.

√5ᵗʰ 364.1 Chronic iridocyclitis
> **EXCLUDES** posterior cyclitis (363.21)

364.10 Chronic iridocyclitis, unspecified

364.11 Chronic iridocyclitis in diseases classified elsewhere
Code first underlying disease, as:
sarcoidosis (135)
tuberculosis (017.3)
> **EXCLUDES** syphilitic iridocyclitis (091.52)
DEF: Persistent inflammation of iris and ciliary body; due to underlying disease or condition.

√5ᵗʰ 364.2 Certain types of iridocyclitis
> **EXCLUDES** posterior cyclitis (363.21)
> sympathetic uveitis (360.11)

364.21 Fuchs' heterochromic cyclitis
DEF: Chronic cyclitis characterized by differences in the color of the two irises; the lighter iris appears in the inflamed eye.

364.22 Glaucomatocyclitic crises `CC`
DEF: An uncommon inflammatory unilateral eye condition, characteristic recurrent episodes of high intraocular pressure accompanied by mild inflammation.
CC Excl: See code: 364.00

Nervous System and Sense Organs

364.23–365.04

364.23 Lens-induced iridocyclitis
DEF: Inflammation of iris; due to immune reaction to proteins in lens following trauma or other lens abnormality.

364.24 Vogt-Koyanagi syndrome
DEF: Uveomeningitis with exudative iridocyclitis and choroiditis; causes depigmentation of hair and skin, detached retina; tinnitus and loss of hearing.

364.3 Unspecified iridocyclitis `CC`
Uveitis NOS
CC Excl: See code: 364.00-364.3

√5ᵗʰ 364.4 Vascular disorders of iris and ciliary body

364.41 Hyphema
Hemorrhage of iris or ciliary body
DEF: Hemorrhage in anterior chamber; also called hyphemia or "blood shot" eyes.

364.42 Rubeosis iridis
Neovascularization of iris or ciliary body
DEF: Blood vessel and connective tissue formation on surface of iris; symptomatic of diabetic retinopathy, central retinal vein occlusion and retinal detachment.

√5ᵗʰ 364.5 Degenerations of iris and ciliary body

364.51 Essential or progressive iris atrophy

364.52 Iridoschisis
DEF: Splitting of the iris into two layers.

364.53 Pigmentary iris degeneration
Acquired heterochromia
Pigment dispersion syndrome } of iris
Translucency

364.54 Degeneration of pupillary margin
Atrophy of sphincter
Ectropion of pigment epithelium } of iris

364.55 Miotic cysts of pupillary margin
DEF: Serous-filled sacs in pupillary margin of iris.

364.56 Degenerative changes of chamber angle

364.57 Degenerative changes of ciliary body

364.59 Other iris atrophy
Iris atrophy (generalized) (sector shaped)

√5ᵗʰ 364.6 Cysts of iris, ciliary body, and anterior chamber
EXCLUDES   miotic pupillary cyst (364.55)
parasitic cyst (360.13)

364.60 Idiopathic cysts
DEF: Fluid-filled sacs in iris or ciliary body; unknown etiology.

364.61 Implantation cysts
Epithelial down-growth, anterior chamber
Implantation cysts (surgical) (traumatic)

364.62 Exudative cysts of iris or anterior chamber

364.63 Primary cyst of pars plana
DEF: Fluid-filled sacs of outermost ciliary ring.

364.64 Exudative cyst of pars plana
DEF: Protein, fatty-filled sacs of outermost ciliary ring; due to fluid lead from blood vessels.

√5ᵗʰ 364.7 Adhesions and disruptions of iris and ciliary body
EXCLUDES   flat anterior chamber (360.34)

364.70 Adhesions of iris, unspecified
Synechiae (iris) NOS

364.71 Posterior synechiae
DEF: Adhesion binding iris to lens.

364.72 Anterior synechiae
DEF: Adhesion binding the iris to cornea.

364.73 Goniosynechiae
Peripheral anterior synechiae
DEF: Adhesion binding the iris to cornea at the angle of the anterior chamber.

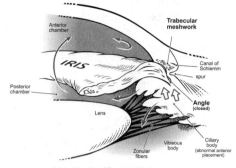

▶Plateau Iris Syndrome◀

364.74 Pupillary membranes
Iris bombé   Pupillary:
Pupillary: seclusion
occlusion
DEF: Membrane traversing the pupil and blocking vision.

364.75 Pupillary abnormalities
Deformed pupil   Rupture of sphincter,
Ectopic pupil   pupil

364.76 Iridodialysis
DEF: Separation of the iris from the ciliary body base; due to trauma or surgical accident.

364.77 Recession of chamber angle
DEF: Receding of anterior chamber angle of the eye; restricts vision.

√5ᵗʰ 364.8 Other disorders of iris and ciliary body
AHA: 2Q, '07, 9

364.81 Floppy iris syndrome
Intraoperative floppy iris syndrome [IFIS]
Use additional E code to identify cause, such as: sympatholytics [antiadrenergics] causing adverse effect in therapeutic use (E941.3)
DEF: Condition complicating cataract surgery for patients who have received alpha blocker treatment for urinary retention problems; iris dilator muscle fails to dilate, and the iris may billow or flap.
AHA: 4Q, '07, 77, 79

364.82 Plateau iris syndrome
DEF: ▶A postoperative chronic angle-closure glaucoma characterized by closing of the anterior chamber angle secondary to a large or anteriorly positioned ciliary body that impairs the normal flow of aqueous fluid.◀
AHA: ▶4Q, '08, 112◀

364.89 Other disorders of iris and ciliary body
Prolapse of iris NOS
EXCLUDES   prolapse of iris in recent wound (871.1)

364.9 Unspecified disorder of iris and ciliary body

√4ᵗʰ 365 Glaucoma
EXCLUDES   blind hypertensive eye [absolute glaucoma] (360.42)
congenital glaucoma (743.20-743.22)
DEF: Rise in intraocular pressure restricting blood flow; multiple causes.

√5ᵗʰ 365.0 Borderline glaucoma [glaucoma suspect]
AHA: 1Q, '90, 8

365.00 Preglaucoma, unspecified

365.01 Open angle with borderline findings
Open angle with:
borderline intraocular pressure
cupping of optic discs
DEF: Minor block of aqueous outflow from eye.

365.02 Anatomical narrow angle

365.03 Steroid responders

365.04 Ocular hypertension
DEF: High fluid pressure within eye; no clear cause.

▶Normal Aqueous Flow◀

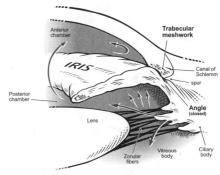

▶Angle-Closure Glaucoma◀

√5th **365.1　Open-angle glaucoma**

365.10　Open-angle glaucoma, unspecified
Wide-angle glaucoma NOS

365.11　Primary open angle glaucoma
Chronic simple glaucoma
DEF: High intraocular pressure, despite free flow of aqueous.

365.12　Low tension glaucoma

365.13　Pigmentary glaucoma
DEF: High intraocular pressure; due to iris pigment granules blocking aqueous flow.

365.14　Glaucoma of childhood
Infantile or juvenile glaucoma

365.15　Residual stage of open angle glaucoma

√5th **365.2　Primary angle-closure glaucoma**
DEF: ▶Glaucoma caused by a shift in the position of the iris of the eye that blocks the surface of the trabecular meshwork causing impairment of the normal flow of aqueous fluid.◀

365.20　Primary angle-closure glaucoma, unspecified

365.21　Intermittent angle-closure glaucoma
Angle-closure glaucoma:
　interval
　subacute
DEF: Recurring attacks of high intraocular pressure; due to blocked aqueous flow.

365.22　Acute angle-closure glaucoma　　`CC`
DEF: Sudden, severe rise in intraocular pressure due to blockage in aqueous drainage.
CC Excl: See code: 365.22

365.23　Chronic angle-closure glaucoma
AHA: 2Q, '98, 16

365.24　Residual stage of angle-closure glaucoma

√5th **365.3　Corticosteroid-induced glaucoma**
DEF: Elevated intraocular pressure; due to long-term corticosteroid therapy.

365.31　Glaucomatous stage

365.32　Residual stage

√5th **365.4　Glaucoma associated with congenital anomalies, dystrophies, and systemic syndromes**

365.41　Glaucoma associated with chamber angle anomalies

365.42　Glaucoma associated with anomalies of iris

365.43　Glaucoma associated with other anterior segment anomalies

365.44　Glaucoma associated with systemic syndromes

Code first associated disease, as
　neurofibromatosis (237.7)
　Sturge-Weber (-Dimitri) syndrome (759.6)

√5th **365.5　Glaucoma associated with disorders of the lens**

365.51　Phacolytic glaucoma
DEF: Elevated intraocular pressure; due to lens protein blocking aqueous flow.

365.52　Pseudoexfoliation glaucoma
DEF: Glaucoma characterized by small grayish particles deposited on the lens.

365.59　Glaucoma associated with other lens disorders

√5th **365.6　Glaucoma associated with other ocular disorders**

365.60　Glaucoma associated with unspecified ocular disorder

365.61　Glaucoma associated with pupillary block
DEF: Acute, open-angle glaucoma caused by mature cataract; aqueous flow is blocked by lens material and macrophages.

365.62　Glaucoma associated with ocular inflammations

365.63　Glaucoma associated with vascular disorders

365.64　Glaucoma associated with tumors or cysts

365.65　Glaucoma associated with ocular trauma

√5th **365.8　Other specified forms of glaucoma**

365.81　Hypersecretion glaucoma

365.82　Glaucoma with increased episcleral venous pressure

365.83　Aqueous misdirection
Malignant glaucoma
DEF: A form of secondary angle-closure glaucoma that occurs when aqueous humor flows into the posterior chamber of the eye (vitreous) rather than through the normal recycling channels.
AHA: 4Q, '02, 48

365.89　Other specified glaucoma
AHA: 2Q, '98, 16

365.9　Unspecified glaucoma
AHA: 3Q, '03, 14; 2Q, '01, 16
H40.9 Unspecified glaucoma　　`I-10`

√4th **366　Cataract**
EXCLUDES　*congenital cataract (743.30-743.34)*
DEF: A variety of conditions that create a cloudy, or calcified lens that obstructs vision.

√5th **366.0　Infantile, juvenile, and presenile cataract**

366.00　Nonsenile cataract, unspecified

366.01　Anterior subcapsular polar cataract
DEF: Defect within the front, center lens surface.

366.02　Posterior subcapsular polar cataract
DEF: Defect within the rear, center lens surface.

366.03　Cortical, lamellar, or zonular cataract
DEF: Opacities radiating from center to edge of lens; appear as thin, concentric layers of lens.

366.04　Nuclear cataract

366.09　Other and combined forms of nonsenile cataract

Nervous System and Sense Organs

366.1–367.53

Cataract

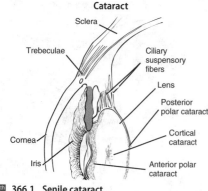

Labels: Sclera, Trebeculae, Ciliary suspensory fibers, Lens, Posterior polar cataract, Cortical cataract, Cornea, Iris, Anterior polar cataract

√5ᵗʰ **366.1 Senile cataract**
> AHA: 3Q, '91, 9; S-O, '85, 10

366.10 Senile cataract, unspecified Ⓐ
> AHA: 1Q, '03, 5

366.11 Pseudoexfoliation of lens capsule Ⓐ

366.12 Incipient cataract Ⓐ
> Cataract: Cataract:
> coronary   punctate
> immature NOS   Water clefts
> **DEF:** Minor disorders of lens not affecting vision; due to aging.

366.13 Anterior subcapsular polar senile cataract Ⓐ

366.14 Posterior subcapsular polar senile cataract Ⓐ

366.15 Cortical senile cataract Ⓐ

366.16 Nuclear sclerosis Ⓐ
> Cataracta brunescens
> Nuclear cataract
> **AHA:** 4Q, '07, 79

366.17 Total or mature cataract Ⓐ

366.18 Hypermature cataract Ⓐ
> Morgagni cataract

366.19 Other and combined forms of senile cataract Ⓐ

√5ᵗʰ **366.2 Traumatic cataract**

366.20 Traumatic cataract, unspecified

366.21 Localized traumatic opacities
> Vossius' ring

366.22 Total traumatic cataract

366.23 Partially resolved traumatic cataract

√5ᵗʰ **366.3 Cataract secondary to ocular disorders**

366.30 Cataracta complicata, unspecified

366.31 Glaucomatous flecks (subcapsular)
> Code first underlying glaucoma (365.0-365.9)

366.32 Cataract in inflammatory disorders
> Code first underlying condition, as:
> chronic choroiditis (363.0-363.2)

366.33 Cataract with neovascularization
> Code first underlying condition, as:
> chronic iridocyclitis (364.10)

366.34 Cataract in degenerative disorders
> Sunflower cataract
> Code first underlying condition, as:
> chalcosis (360.24)
> degenerative myopia (360.21)
> pigmentary retinal dystrophy (362.74)

√5ᵗʰ **366.4 Cataract associated with other disorders**

366.41   *Diabetic cataract*
> Code first diabetes (249.5, 250.5)
> **AHA:** 3Q, '91, 9; S-O, '85, 11

366.42   *Tetanic cataract*
> Code first underlying disease, as:
> calcinosis (275.4)
> hypoparathyroidism (252.1)

366.43   *Myotonic cataract*
> Code first underlying disorder (359.21, 359.23)

366.44   *Cataract associated with other syndromes*
> Code first underlying condition, as:
> craniofacial dysostosis (756.0)
> galactosemia (271.1)

366.45 Toxic cataract
> Drug-induced cataract
> Use additional E code to identify drug or other toxic substance

366.46 Cataract associated with radiation and other physical influences
> Use additional E code to identify cause

√5ᵗʰ **366.5 After-cataract**

366.50 After-cataract, unspecified
> Secondary cataract NOS

366.51 Soemmering's ring
> **DEF:** A donut-shaped lens remnant and a capsule behind the pupil as a result of cataract surgery or trauma.

366.52 Other after-cataract, not obscuring vision

366.53 After-cataract, obscuring vision

366.8 Other cataract
> Calcification of lens

366.9 Unspecified cataract
> H26.9 Unspecified cataract   🔟

√4ᵗʰ **367 Disorders of refraction and accommodation**

367.0 Hypermetropia
> Far-sightedness   Hyperopia
> **DEF:** Refraction error, called also hyperopia, focal point is posterior to retina; abnormally short anteroposterior diameter or subnormal refractive power; causes farsightedness.

367.1 Myopia
> Near-sightedness
> **DEF:** Refraction error, focal point is anterior to retina; causes near-sightedness.

√5ᵗʰ **367.2 Astigmatism**

367.20 Astigmatism, unspecified

367.21 Regular astigmatism

367.22 Irregular astigmatism

√5ᵗʰ **367.3 Anisometropia and aniseikonia**

367.31 Anisometropia
> **DEF:** Eyes with refractive powers that differ by at least one diopter.

367.32 Aniseikonia
> **DEF:** Eyes with unequal retinal imaging; usually due to refractive error.

367.4 Presbyopia
> **DEF:** Loss of crystalline lens elasticity; causes errors of accommodation; due to aging.

√5ᵗʰ **367.5 Disorders of accommodation**

367.51 Paresis of accommodation
> Cycloplegia
> **DEF:** Partial paralysis of ciliary muscle; causing focus problems.

367.52 Total or complete internal ophthalmoplegia
> **DEF:** Total paralysis of ciliary muscle; large pupil incapable of focus.

367.53 Spasm of accommodation
> **DEF:** Abnormal contraction of ciliary muscle; causes focus problems.

Ⓝ Newborn Age: 0   Ⓟ Pediatric Age: 0-17   Ⓜ Maternity Age: 12-55   Ⓐ Adult Age: 15-124   MCC Major CC Condition   CC CC Condition   HIV HIV Related Dx

124 – Volume 1   **2010 ICD-9-CM**

√5th **367.8 Other disorders of refraction and accommodation**

     367.81 Transient refractive change

     367.89 Other

         Drug-induced } disorders of refraction and
         Toxic   accommodation

     367.9 Unspecified disorder of refraction and accommodation

√4th **368 Visual disturbances**

     EXCLUDES *electrophysiological disturbances (794.11-794.14)*

√5th **368.0 Amblyopia ex anopsia**

     DEF: Vision impaired due to disuse; esotropia often cause.

     368.00 Amblyopia, unspecified

     368.01 Strabismic amblyopia

         Suppression amblyopia

     368.02 Deprivation amblyopia

         DEF: Decreased vision associated with suppressed retinal image of one eye.

     368.03 Refractive amblyopia

√5th **368.1 Subjective visual disturbances**

     368.10 Subjective visual disturbance, unspecified

     368.11 Sudden visual loss   `CC`

         CC Excl: 368.10-368.12, 368.16

     368.12 Transient visual loss   `CC`

         Concentric fading   Scintillating scotoma

         CC Excl: See code: 368.11

     368.13 Visual discomfort

         Asthenopia   Photophobia
         Eye strain

     368.14 Visual distortions of shape and size

         Macropsia   Micropsia
         Metamorphopsia

     368.15 Other visual distortions and entoptic phenomena

         Photopsia   Refractive:
         Refractive: polyopia
         diplopia   Visual halos

     368.16 Psychophysical visual disturbances

         Prosopagnosia
         Visual:
              agnosia
              disorientation syndrome
              hallucinations
              object agnosia

     368.2 Diplopia

         Double vision

         H53.2 Diplopia   `I-10`

√5th **368.3 Other disorders of binocular vision**

     368.30 Binocular vision disorder, unspecified

     368.31 Suppression of binocular vision

     368.32 Simultaneous visual perception without fusion

     368.33 Fusion with defective stereopsis

         DEF: Faulty depth perception though normal ability to focus.

     368.34 Abnormal retinal correspondence

√5th **368.4 Visual field defects**

     368.40 Visual field defect, unspecified

     368.41 Scotoma involving central area

         Scotoma: Scotoma:
              central   paracentral
              centrocecal

         DEF: Vision loss (blind spot) in central five degrees of visual field.

     368.42 Scotoma of blind spot area

         Enlarged: Paracecal scotoma
              angioscotoma
              blind spot

     368.43 Sector or arcuate defects

         Scotoma: Scotoma:
              arcuate   Seidel
              Bjerrum

         DEF: Arc-shaped blind spot caused by retinal nerve damage.

     368.44 Other localized visual field defect

         Scotoma: Visual field defect:
              NOS   nasal step
              ring   peripheral

     368.45 Generalized contraction or constriction

     368.46 Homonymous bilateral field defects

         Hemianopsia (altitudinal) (homonymous)
         Quadrant anopia

         DEF: Disorders found in the corresponding vertical halves of the visual fields of both eyes.

     368.47 Heteronymous bilateral field defects

         Hemianopsia: Hemianopsia:
              binasal   bitemporal

         DEF: Disorders in the opposite halves of the visual fields of both eyes.

√5th **368.5 Color vision deficiencies**

     Color blindness

     368.51 Protan defect

         Protanomaly   Protanopia

         DEF: Mild difficulty distinguishing green and red hues with shortened spectrum; sex-linked affecting one percent of males.

     368.52 Deutan defect

         Deuteranomaly   Deuteranopia

         DEF: Male-only disorder; difficulty in distinguishing green and red, no shortened spectrum.

     368.53 Tritan defect

         Tritanomaly   Tritanopia

         DEF: Difficulty in distinguishing blue and yellow; occurs often due to drugs, retinal detachment and central nervous system diseases.

     368.54 Achromatopsia

         Monochromatism (cone) (rod)

         DEF: Complete color blindness; caused by disease, injury to retina, optic nerve or pathway.

     368.55 Acquired color vision deficiencies

     368.59 Other color vision deficiencies

√5th **368.6 Night blindness**

     Nyctalopia

     DEF: Nyctalopia: disorder of vision in dim light or night blindness.

     368.60 Night blindness, unspecified

     368.61 Congenital night blindness

         Hereditary night blindness
         Oguchi's disease

     368.62 Acquired night blindness

         EXCLUDES *that due to vitamin A deficiency (264.5)*

     368.63 Abnormal dark adaptation curve

         Abnormal threshold } of cones or rods
         Delayed adaptation

     368.69 Other night blindness

     368.8 Other specified visual disturbances

     Blurred vision NOS

     AHA: 4Q, '02, 56

     368.9 Unspecified visual disturbance

     AHA: 3Q, '06, 22; 1Q, '04, 15

√4th √5th **Additional Digit Required**   **Unacceptable PDx**   **Manifestation Code**   **Hospital Acquired Condition**   ►◄ **Revised Text**   ● **New Code**   ▲ **Revised Code Title**

2010 ICD-9-CM   **Volume 1 – 125**

√4ᵗʰ **369 Blindness and low vision**

Note: Visual impairment refers to a functional limitation of the eye (e.g., limited visual acuity or visual field). It should be distinguished from visual disability, indicating a limitation of the abilities of the individual (e.g., limited reading skills, vocational skills), and from visual handicap, indicating a limitation of personal and socioeconomic independence (e.g., limited mobility, limited employability).

The levels of impairment defined in the table on the next page are based on the recommendations of the WHO Study Group on Prevention of Blindness (Geneva, November 6-10, 1972; WHO Technical Report Series 518), and of the International Council of Ophthalmology (1976).

Note that definitions of blindness vary in different settings.

For international reporting WHO defines blindness as profound impairment. This definition can be applied to blindness of one eye (369.1, 369.6) and to blindness of the individual (369.0).

For determination of benefits in the U.S.A., the definition of legal blindness as severe impairment is often used. This definition applies to blindness of the individual only.

EXCLUDES *correctable impaired vision due to refractive errors (367.0-367.9)*

√5ᵗʰ **369.0 Profound impairment, both eyes**

369.00 Impairment level not further specified
Blindness:
NOS according to WHO definition
both eyes

369.01 Better eye: total impairment; lesser eye: total impairment

369.02 Better eye: near-total impairment; lesser eye: not further specified

369.03 Better eye: near-total impairment; lesser eye: total impairment

369.04 Better eye: near-total impairment; lesser eye: near-total impairment

369.05 Better eye: profound impairment; lesser eye: not further specified

369.06 Better eye: profound impairment; lesser eye: total impairment

369.07 Better eye: profound impairment; lesser eye: near-total impairment

369.08 Better eye: profound impairment; lesser eye: profound impairment

√4ᵗʰ **369.1 Moderate or severe impairment, better eye, profound impairment lesser eye**

369.10 Impairment level not further specified
Blindness, one eye, low vision other eye

369.11 Better eye: severe impairment; lesser eye: blind, not further specified

369.12 Better eye: severe impairment; lesser eye: total impairment

369.13 Better eye: severe impairment; lesser eye: near-total impairment

369.14 Better eye: severe impairment; lesser eye: profound impairment

369.15 Better eye: moderate impairment; lesser eye: blind, not further specified

369.16 Better eye: moderate impairment; lesser eye: total impairment

369.17 Better eye: moderate impairment; lesser eye: near-total impairment

369.18 Better eye: moderate impairment; lesser eye: profound impairment

√5ᵗʰ **369.2 Moderate or severe impairment, both eyes**

369.20 Impairment level not further specified
Low vision, both eyes NOS

369.21 Better eye: severe impairment; lesser eye: not further specified

369.22 Better eye: severe impairment; lesser eye: severe impairment

369.23 Better eye: moderate impairment; lesser eye: not further specified

369.24 Better eye: moderate impairment; lesser eye: severe impairment

369.25 Better eye: moderate impairment; lesser eye: moderate impairment

369.3 Unqualified visual loss, both eyes
EXCLUDES *blindness NOS:
legal [U.S.A. definition] (369.4)
WHO definition (369.00)*

369.4 Legal blindness, as defined in U.S.A.
Blindness NOS according to U.S.A. definition
EXCLUDES *legal blindness with specification of impairment level (369.01-369.08, 369.11-369.14, 369.21-369.22)*
H54.8 Legal blindness as defined in USA   I-10

√5ᵗʰ **369.6 Profound impairment, one eye**

369.60 Impairment level not further specified
Blindness, one eye

369.61 One eye: total impairment; other eye: not specified

369.62 One eye: total impairment; other eye: near normal vision

369.63 One eye: total impairment; other eye: normal vision

369.64 One eye: near-total impairment; other eye: not specified

369.65 One eye: near-total impairment; other eye: near-normal vision

369.66 One eye: near-total impairment; other eye: normal vision

369.67 One eye: profound impairment; other eye: not specified

369.68 One eye: profound impairment; other eye: near-normal vision

369.69 One eye: profound impairment; other eye: normal vision

√5ᵗʰ **369.7 Moderate or severe impairment, one eye**

369.70 Impairment level not further specified
Low vision, one eye

369.71 One eye: severe impairment; other eye: not specified

369.72 One eye: severe impairment; other eye: near-normal vision

369.73 One eye: severe impairment; other eye: normal vision

369.74 One eye: moderate impairment; other eye: not specified

369.75 One eye: moderate impairment; other eye: near-normal vision

369.76 One eye: moderate impairment; other eye: normal vision

369.8 Unqualified visual loss, one eye

369.9 Unspecified visual loss
AHA: 4Q, '02, 114; 3Q, '02, 20

√4ᵗʰ **370 Keratitis**

√5ᵗʰ **370.0 Corneal ulcer**
EXCLUDES *that due to vitamin A deficiency (264.3)*

370.00 Corneal ulcer, unspecified

370.01 Marginal corneal ulcer

Ⓝ Newborn Age: 0   Ⓟ Pediatric Age: 0-17   Ⓜ Maternity Age: 12-55   Ⓐ Adult Age: 15-124   **MCC** Major CC Condition   **CC** CC Condition   **HIV** HIV Related Dx

126 – Volume 1   2010 ICD-9-CM

Classification		LEVELS OF VISUAL IMPAIRMENT	Additional descriptors which may be encountered
"legal"	WHO	Visual acuity and/or visual field limitation (whichever is worse)	
	(NEAR-) NORMAL VISION	RANGE OF NORMAL VISION 20/10　20/13　20/16　20/20　20/25 2.0　　1.6　　1.25　　1.0　　0.8	
		NEAR-NORMAL VISION 20/30　20/40　20/50　20/60 0.7　　0.6　　0.5　　0.4　　0.3	
	LOW VISION	MODERATE VISUAL IMPAIRMENT 20/70　20/80　20/100　20/125 20/160 0.25　0.20　0.16　0.12	Moderate low vision
		SEVERE VISUAL IMPAIRMENT 20/200　20/250　20/320　20/400 0.10　0.08　0.06　0.05 Visual field: 20 degrees or less	Severe low vision, "Legal" blindness
LEGAL BLINDNESS (U.S.A.) both eyes	BLINDNESS (WHO) one or both eyes	PROFOUND VISUAL IMPAIRMENT 20/500　20/630　20/800　20/1000 0.04　0.03　0.025　0.02 Count fingers at:　less than 3m (10 ft.) Visual field:　10 degrees or less	Profound low vision, Moderate blindness
		NEAR-TOTAL VISUAL IMPAIRMENT Visual acuity: less than 0.02 (20/1000) Count fingers at:　1m (3 ft.) or less Hand movements:　5m (15 ft.) or less Light projection, light perception Visual field:　5 degrees or less	Severe blindness Near-total blindness
		TOTAL VISUAL IMPAIRMENT No light perception (NLP)	Total blindness

Visual acuity refers to best achievable acuity with correction.
Non-listed Snellen fractions may be classified by converting to the nearest decimal equivalent, e.g. 10/200 = 0.05, 6/30 = 0.20.
CF (count fingers) without designation of distance, may be classified to profound impairment.
HM (hand motion) without designation of distance, may be classified to near-total impairment.
Visual field measurements refer to the largest field diameter for a 1/100 white test object.

370.02　**Ring corneal ulcer**

370.03　**Central corneal ulcer**

370.04　**Hypopyon ulcer**
　　　　Serpiginous ulcer
　　　　DEF: Corneal ulcer with an accumulation of pus in the eye's anterior chamber.

370.05　**Mycotic corneal ulcer**
　　　　DEF: Fungal infection causing corneal tissue loss.

370.06　**Perforated corneal ulcer**
　　　　DEF: Tissue loss through all layers of cornea.

370.07　**Mooren's ulcer**
　　　　DEF: Tissue loss, with chronic inflammation, at junction of cornea and sclera; seen in elderly.

√5th　370.2　**Superficial keratitis without conjunctivitis**
　　　　EXCLUDES　dendritic [herpes simplex] keratitis (054.42)

370.20　**Superficial keratitis, unspecified**

370.21　**Punctate keratitis**
　　　　Thygeson's superficial punctate keratitis
　　　　DEF: Formation of cellular and fibrinous deposits (keratic precipitates) on posterior surface; deposits develop after injury or iridocyclitis.

370.22　**Macular keratitis**
　　　　Keratitis:　　　　　Keratitis:
　　　　　areolar　　　　　　stellate
　　　　　nummular　　　　　striate

370.23　**Filamentary keratitis**
　　　　DEF: Keratitis characterized by twisted filaments of mucoid material on the cornea's surface.

370.24　**Photokeratitis**
　　　　Snow blindness
　　　　Welders' keratitis
　　　　DEF: Painful, inflamed cornea; due to extended exposure to ultraviolet light.
　　　　AHA: 3Q, '96, 6

√5th　370.3　**Certain types of keratoconjunctivitis**

370.31　**Phlyctenular keratoconjunctivitis**
　　　　Phlyctenulosis
　　　　Use additional code for any associated tuberculosis (017.3)
　　　　DEF: Miniature blister on conjunctiva or cornea; associated with tuberculosis and malnutrition disorders.

370.32　**Limbar and corneal involvement in vernal conjunctivitis**
　　　　Use additional code for vernal conjunctivitis (372.13)
　　　　DEF: Corneal itching and inflammation in conjunctivitis; often limited to lining of eyelids.

370.33　**Keratoconjunctivitis sicca, not specified as Sjögren's**
　　　　EXCLUDES　Sjögren's syndrome (710.2)
　　　　DEF: Inflammation of conjunctiva and cornea; characterized by "horny" looking tissue and excess blood in these areas; decreased flow of lacrimal (tear) is a contributing factor.

370.34　**Exposure keratoconjunctivitis**
　　　　DEF: Incomplete closure of eyelid causing dry, inflamed eye.
　　　　AHA: 3Q, '96, 6

370.35　**Neurotrophic keratoconjunctivitis**

√5th　370.4　**Other and unspecified keratoconjunctivitis**

370.40　**Keratoconjunctivitis, unspecified**
　　　　Superficial keratitis with conjunctivitis NOS

370.44　***Keratitis or keratoconjunctivitis in exanthema***
　　　　Code first underlying condition (050.0-052.9)
　　　　EXCLUDES　herpes simplex (054.43)
　　　　　　　　　　herpes zoster (053.21)
　　　　　　　　　　measles (055.71)

370.49　**Other**
　　　　EXCLUDES　epidemic keratoconjunctivitis (077.1)

√5th　370.5　**Interstitial and deep keratitis**

370.50　**Interstitial keratitis, unspecified**

370.52　**Diffuse interstitial keratitis**
　　　　Cogan's syndrome
　　　　DEF: Inflammation of cornea; with deposits in middle corneal layers; may obscure vision.

370.54　**Sclerosing keratitis**
　　　　DEF: Chronic corneal inflammation leading to opaque scarring.

370.55　**Corneal abscess**
　　　　DEF: Pocket of pus and inflammation on the cornea.

370.59　**Other**
　　　　EXCLUDES　disciform herpes simplex keratitis (054.43)
　　　　　　　　　　syphilitic keratitis (090.3)

√5th　370.6　**Corneal neovascularization**

370.60　**Corneal neovascularization, unspecified**

370.61　**Localized vascularization of cornea**
　　　　DEF: Limited infiltration of cornea by new blood vessels.

370.62　**Pannus (corneal)**
　　　　DEF: Buildup of superficial vascularization and granulated tissue under epithelium of cornea.
　　　　AHA: 3Q, '02, 20

370.63　**Deep vascularization of cornea**
　　　　DEF: Deep infiltration of cornea by new blood vessels.

370.64　**Ghost vessels (corneal)**

370.02–370.64

√4th √5th　Additional Digit Required　　Unacceptable PDx　　Manifestation Code　　Hospital Acquired Condition　　▶◀ Revised Text　　● New Code　　▲ Revised Code Title

2010 ICD-9-CM　　　　　　　　　　　　　　　　　　　　　　　　　　　　　　　　　　　　　　Volume 1 – 127

370.8 Other forms of keratitis
Code first underlying condition, such as:
Acanthamoeba (136.21)
Fusarium (118)
AHA: ▶4Q, '08, 80-81;◀ 3Q, '94, 5

370.9 Unspecified keratitis

✓4th **371 Corneal opacity and other disorders of cornea**

✓5th **371.0 Corneal scars and opacities**
EXCLUDES   that due to vitamin A deficiency (264.6)

371.00 Corneal opacity, unspecified
Corneal scar NOS

371.01 Minor opacity of cornea
Corneal nebula

371.02 Peripheral opacity of cornea
Corneal macula not interfering with central vision

371.03 Central opacity of cornea
Corneal:
leucoma   } interfering with central
macula   } vision

371.04 Adherent leucoma
DEF: Dense, opaque corneal growth adhering to the iris; also spelled as leukoma.

371.05 Phthisical cornea
Code first underlying tuberculosis (017.3)

✓5th **371.1 Corneal pigmentations and deposits**

371.10 Corneal deposit, unspecified

371.11 Anterior pigmentations
Stähli's lines

371.12 Stromal pigmentations
Hematocornea

371.13 Posterior pigmentations
Krukenberg spindle

371.14 Kayser-Fleischer ring
DEF: Copper deposits forming ring at outer edge of cornea; seen in Wilson's disease and other liver disorders.

371.15 Other deposits associated with metabolic disorders

371.16 Argentous deposits
DEF: Silver deposits in cornea.

✓5th **371.2 Corneal edema**

371.20 Corneal edema, unspecified

371.21 Idiopathic corneal edema
DEF: Corneal swelling and fluid retention of unknown cause.

371.22 Secondary corneal edema
DEF: Corneal swelling and fluid retention caused by an underlying disease, injury, or condition.

371.23 Bullous keratopathy
DEF: Corneal degeneration; characterized by recurring, rupturing epithelial "blisters;" ruptured blebs expose corneal nerves; occurs in glaucoma, iridocyclitis and Fuchs' epithelial dystrophy.

371.24 Corneal edema due to wearing of contact lenses

✓5th **371.3 Changes of corneal membranes**

371.30 Corneal membrane change, unspecified

371.31 Folds and rupture of Bowman's membrane

371.32 Folds in Descemet's membrane

371.33 Rupture in Descemet's membrane

✓5th **371.4 Corneal degenerations**

371.40 Corneal degeneration, unspecified

371.41 Senile corneal changes
Arcus senilis   Hassall-Henle bodies

371.42 Recurrent erosion of cornea
EXCLUDES   Mooren's ulcer (370.07)

371.43 Band-shaped keratopathy
DEF: Horizontal bands of superficial corneal calcium deposits.

371.44 Other calcerous degenerations of cornea

371.45 Keratomalacia NOS
EXCLUDES   that due to vitamin A deficiency (264.4)
DEF: Destruction of the cornea by keratinization of the epithelium with ulceration and perforation of the cornea; seen in cases of vitamin A deficiency.

371.46 Nodular degeneration of cornea
Salzmann's nodular dystrophy

371.48 Peripheral degenerations of cornea
Marginal degeneration of cornea [Terrien's]

371.49 Other
Discrete colliquative keratopathy

✓5th **371.5 Hereditary corneal dystrophies**
DEF: Genetic disorder; leads to opacities, edema or lesions of cornea.

371.50 Corneal dystrophy, unspecified

371.51 Juvenile epithelial corneal dystrophy

371.52 Other anterior corneal dystrophies
Corneal dystrophy: Corneal dystrophy:
microscopic cystic   ring-like

371.53 Granular corneal dystrophy

371.54 Lattice corneal dystrophy

371.55 Macular corneal dystrophy

371.56 Other stromal corneal dystrophies
Crystalline corneal dystrophy

371.57 Endothelial corneal dystrophy
Combined corneal dystrophy
Cornea guttata
Fuchs' endothelial dystrophy

371.58 Other posterior corneal dystrophies
Polymorphous corneal dystrophy

✓5th **371.6 Keratoconus**
DEF: Bilateral bulging protrusion of anterior cornea; often due to noninflammatory thinning.

371.60 Keratoconus, unspecified

371.61 Keratoconus, stable condition

371.62 Keratoconus, acute hydrops

✓5th **371.7 Other corneal deformities**

371.70 Corneal deformity, unspecified

371.71 Corneal ectasia
DEF: Bulging protrusion of thinned, scarred cornea.

371.72 Descemetocele
DEF: Protrusion of Descemet's membrane into cornea.

371.73 Corneal staphyloma
DEF: Protrusion of cornea into adjacent tissue.

✓5th **371.8 Other corneal disorders**

371.81 Corneal anesthesia and hypoesthesia
DEF: Decreased or absent sensitivity of cornea.

371.82 Corneal disorder due to contact lens
EXCLUDES   corneal edema due to contact lens (371.24)
DEF: Contact lens wear causing cornea disorder, excluding swelling.

371.89 Other
AHA: 3Q, '99, 12

371.9 Unspecified corneal disorder

√4th 372 Disorders of conjunctiva
> **EXCLUDES** *keratoconjunctivitis (370.3-370.4)*

√5th 372.0 Acute conjunctivitis

372.00 Acute conjunctivitis, unspecified

372.01 Serous conjunctivitis, except viral
> **EXCLUDES** *viral conjunctivitis NOS (077.9)*
>
> **AHA:** 3Q, '08, 6

372.02 Acute follicular conjunctivitis
Conjunctival folliculosis NOS
> **EXCLUDES** *conjunctivitis:*
> *adenoviral (acute follicular)*
> *(077.3)*
> *epidemic hemorrhagic (077.4)*
> *inclusion (077.0)*
> *Newcastle (077.8)*
> *epidemic keratoconjunctivitis (077.1)*
> *pharyngoconjunctival fever (077.2)*
>
> **DEF:** Severe conjunctival inflammation with dense infiltrations of lymphoid tissues of inner eyelids; may be traced to a viral or chlamydial etiology.

372.03 Other mucopurulent conjunctivitis
Catarrhal conjunctivitis
> **EXCLUDES** *blennorrhea neonatorum*
> *(gonococcal) (098.40)*
> *neonatal conjunctivitis(771.6)*
> *ophthalmia neonatorum NOS*
> *(771.6)*

372.04 Pseudomembranous conjunctivitis
Membranous conjunctivitis
> **EXCLUDES** *diphtheritic conjunctivitis (032.81)*
>
> **DEF:** Severe inflammation of conjunctiva; false membrane develops on inner surface of eyelid; membrane can be removed without harming epithelium, due to bacterial infections, toxic and allergic factors, and viral infections.

372.05 Acute atopic conjunctivitis
> **DEF:** Sudden, severe conjunctivitis due to allergens.

372.06 Acute chemical conjunctivitis
Acute toxic conjunctivitis
Use additional E code to identify the chemical or toxic agent
> **EXCLUDES** *burn of eye and adnexa*
> *(940.0-940.9)*
> *chemical corrosion injury of eye*
> *(940.2-940.3)*

√5th 372.1 Chronic conjunctivitis

372.10 Chronic conjunctivitis, unspecified

372.11 Simple chronic conjunctivitis

372.12 Chronic follicular conjunctivitis
> **DEF:** Persistent conjunctival inflammation with dense, localized infiltrations of lymphoid tissues of inner eyelids.

372.13 Vernal conjunctivitis
> **AHA:** 3Q, '96, 8

372.14 Other chronic allergic conjunctivitis
> **AHA:** 3Q, '96, 8

372.15 *Parasitic conjunctivitis*
> *Code first underlying disease, as:*
> *filariasis (125.0-125.9)*
> *mucocutaneous leishmaniasis (085.5)*

√5th 372.2 Blepharoconjunctivitis

372.20 Blepharoconjunctivitis, unspecified

372.21 Angular blepharoconjunctivitis
> **DEF:** Inflammation at junction of upper and lower eyelids; may block lacrimal secretions.

372.22 Contact blepharoconjunctivitis

√5th 372.3 Other and unspecified conjunctivitis

372.30 Conjunctivitis, unspecified
> H10.9 Unspecified conjunctivitis `I-10`

372.31 *Rosacea conjunctivitis*
> *Code first underlying rosacea dermatitis (695.3)*

372.33 *Conjunctivitis in mucocutaneous disease*
> *Code first underlying disease, as:*
> *erythema multiforme (695.10-695.19)*
> *Reiter's disease (099.3)*
>
> **EXCLUDES** *ocular pemphigoid (694.61)*

372.34 Pingueculitis
> **EXCLUDES** ► *pinguecula (372.51)*◄
>
> **AHA:** 4Q, '08, 112-113

372.39 Other
> **AHA:** 2Q, '07, 9

√5th 372.4 Pterygium
> **EXCLUDES** *pseudopterygium (372.52)*
>
> **DEF:** Wedge-shaped, conjunctival thickening that advances from the inner corner of the eye toward the cornea.

372.40 Pterygium, unspecified

372.41 Peripheral pterygium, stationary

372.42 Peripheral pterygium, progressive

372.43 Central pterygium

372.44 Double pterygium

372.45 Recurrent pterygium

√5th 372.5 Conjunctival degenerations and deposits

372.50 Conjunctival degeneration, unspecified

372.51 Pinguecula
> **EXCLUDES** ► *pingueculitis (372.34)*◄
>
> **DEF:** Proliferative spot on the bulbar conjunctiva located near the sclerocorneal junction, usually on the nasal side; it is seen in elderly people.

372.52 Pseudopterygium
> **DEF:** Conjunctival scar joined to the cornea; it looks like a pterygium but is not attached to the tissue.

372.53 Conjunctival xerosis
> **EXCLUDES** *conjunctival xerosis due to vitamin A deficiency (264.0, 264.1, 264.7)*
>
> **DEF:** Dry conjunctiva due to vitamin A deficiency; related to Bitot's spots; may develop into xerophthalmia and keratomalacia.

372.54 Conjunctival concretions
> **DEF:** Calculus or deposit on conjunctiva.

372.55 Conjunctival pigmentations
Conjunctival argyrosis
> **DEF:** Color deposits in conjunctiva.

372.56 Conjunctival deposits

√5th 372.6 Conjunctival scars

372.61 Granuloma of conjunctiva

372.62 Localized adhesions and strands of conjunctiva
> **DEF:** Abnormal fibrous connections in conjunctiva.

372.63 Symblepharon
Extensive adhesions of conjunctiva
> **DEF:** Adhesion of the eyelids to the eyeball.

372.64 Scarring of conjunctiva
Contraction of eye socket (after enucleation)

√5th 372.7 Conjunctival vascular disorders and cysts

372.71 Hyperemia of conjunctiva
> **DEF:** Conjunctival blood vessel congestion causing eye redness.

372.72 Conjunctival hemorrhage
Hyposphagma
Subconjunctival hemorrhage

√4th
√5th Additional Digit Required Unacceptable PDx Manifestation Code Hospital Acquired Condition ►◄ Revised Text ● New Code ▲ Revised Code Title

2010 ICD-9-CM **October 2009 · Volume 1 – 129**

Nervous System and Sense Organs

372.73–374.34

372.73 Conjunctival edema
Chemosis of conjunctiva
Subconjunctival edema
DEF: Fluid retention and swelling in conjunctival tissue.

372.74 Vascular abnormalities of conjunctiva
Aneurysm(ata) of conjunctiva

372.75 Conjunctival cysts
DEF: Abnormal sacs of fluid in conjunctiva.

√5th **372.8 Other disorders of conjunctiva**

372.81 Conjunctivochalasis
AHA: 4Q, '00, 41
DEF: Bilateral condition of redundant conjunctival tissue between globe and lower eyelid margin; may cover lower punctum, interferring with normal tearing.

372.89 Other disorders of conjunctiva

372.9 Unspecified disorder of conjunctiva

√4th **373 Inflammation of eyelids**

√5th **373.0 Blepharitis**
EXCLUDES *blepharoconjunctivitis (372.20-372.22)*

373.00 Blepharitis, unspecified

373.01 Ulcerative blepharitis

373.02 Squamous blepharitis

√5th **373.1 Hordeolum and other deep inflammation of eyelid**
DEF: Purulent, localized, staphylococcal infection in sebaceous glands of eyelids.

373.11 Hordeolum externum
Hordeolum NOSStye
DEF: Infection of the oil glands in the eyelash follicles.

373.12 Hordeolum internum
Infection of meibomian gland
DEF: Infection of the oil gland of the eyelid margin.

373.13 Abscess of eyelid
Furuncle of eyelid
DEF: Inflamed pocket of pus on the eyelid.

373.2 Chalazion
Meibomian (gland) cyst
EXCLUDES *infected meibomian gland (373.12)*
DEF: Chronic inflammation of the meibomian gland, causing an eyelid mass.

√5th **373.3 Noninfectious dermatoses of eyelid**

373.31 Eczematous dermatitis of eyelid

373.32 Contact and allergic dermatitis of eyelid

373.33 Xeroderma of eyelid

373.34 Discoid lupus erythematosus of eyelid

373.4 Infective dermatitis of eyelid of types resulting in deformity
Code first underlying disease, as:
leprosy (030.0-030.9)
lupus vulgaris (tuberculous) (017.0)
yaws (102.0-102.9)

373.5 Other infective dermatitis of eyelid
Code first underlying disease, as:
actinomycosis (039.3)
impetigo (684)
mycotic dermatitis (110.0-111.9)
vaccinia (051.0)
postvaccination (999.0)
EXCLUDES *herpes:*
simplex (054.41)
zoster (053.20)

Entropion and Ectropion

Ectropion

Normal eyelashes

Entropion

373.6 Parasitic infestation of eyelid
Code first underlying disease, as:
leishmaniasis (085.0-085.9)
loiasis (125.2)
onchocerciasis (125.3)
pediculosis (132.0)

373.8 Other inflammations of eyelids

373.9 Unspecified inflammation of eyelid

√4th **374 Other disorders of eyelids**

√5th **374.0 Entropion and trichiasis of eyelid**
DEF: Entropion: turning inward of eyelid edge toward eyeball.
DEF: Trichiasis: ingrowing eyelashes marked by irritation with possible distortion of sight.

374.00 Entropion, unspecified

374.01 Senile entropion   Ⓐ

374.02 Mechanical entropion

374.03 Spastic entropion

374.04 Cicatricial entropion

374.05 Trichiasis without entropion

√5th **374.1 Ectropion**
DEF: Turning outward (eversion) of eyelid edge; exposes palpebral conjunctiva; dryness irritation result.

374.10 Ectropion, unspecified

374.11 Senile ectropion   Ⓐ

374.12 Mechanical ectropion

374.13 Spastic ectropion

374.14 Cicatricial ectropion

√5th **374.2 Lagophthalmos**
DEF: Incomplete closure of eyes; causes dry eye and other complications.

374.20 Lagophthalmos, unspecified

374.21 Paralytic lagophthalmos

374.22 Mechanical lagophthalmos

374.23 Cicatricial lagophthalmos

√5th **374.3 Ptosis of eyelid**

374.30 Ptosis of eyelid, unspecified
AHA: 2Q, '96, 11

374.31 Paralytic ptosis
DEF: Drooping of upper eyelid due to nerve disorder.

374.32 Myogenic ptosis
DEF: Drooping of upper eyelid due to muscle disorder.

374.33 Mechanical ptosis
DEF: Outside force causes drooping of upper eyelid.

374.34 Blepharochalasis
Pseudoptosis
DEF: Loss of elasticity, thickened or indurated skin of eyelids associated with recurrent episodes of idiopathic edema causing intracellular tissue atrophy.

Ⓝ Newborn Age: 0   Ⓟ Pediatric Age: 0-17   Ⓜ Maternity Age: 12-55   Ⓐ Adult Age: 15-124   MCC Major CC Condition   CC CC Condition   HIV HIV Related Dx

130 – Volume 1   2010 ICD-9-CM

√5ᵗʰ **374.4   Other disorders affecting eyelid function**

EXCLUDES   *blepharoclonus (333.81)*
blepharospasm (333.81)
facial nerve palsy (351.0)
third nerve palsy or paralysis (378.51-378.52)
tic (psychogenic) (307.20-307.23)
organic (333.3)

374.41   Lid retraction or lag

374.43   Abnormal innervation syndrome
Jaw-blinking
Paradoxical facial movements

374.44   Sensory disorders

374.45   Other sensorimotor disorders
Deficient blink reflex

374.46   Blepharophimosis
Ankyloblepharon
DEF: Narrowing of palpebral fissure horizontally;
caused by laterally displaced inner canthi; either
acquired or congenital.

√5ᵗʰ **374.5   Degenerative disorders of eyelid and periocular area**

374.50   Degenerative disorder of eyelid, unspecified

374.51   Xanthelasma
Xanthoma (planum) (tuberosum) of eyelid
Code first underlying condition (272.0-272.9)
DEF: Fatty tumors of the eyelid linked to high fat
content of blood.

374.52   Hyperpigmentation of eyelid
Chloasma
Dyspigmentation
DEF: Excess pigment of eyelid.

374.53   Hypopigmentation of eyelid
Vitiligo of eyelid
DEF: Lack of color pigment of the eyelid.

374.54   Hypertrichosis of eyelid
DEF: Excessive eyelash growth.

374.55   Hypotrichosis of eyelid
Madarosis of eyelid
DEF: Less than normal, or absent, eyelashes.

**374.56   Other degenerative disorders of skin affecting
eyelid**

√5ᵗʰ **374.8   Other disorders of eyelid**

374.81   Hemorrhage of eyelid
EXCLUDES   *black eye (921.0)*

374.82   Edema of eyelid
Hyperemia of eyelid
DEF: Swelling and fluid retention in eyelid.
AHA: ▶4Q, '08, 131◀

374.83   Elephantiasis of eyelid
DEF: Filarial disease causing dermatitis and
enlargement of eyelid.

374.84   Cysts of eyelids
Sebaceous cyst of eyelid

374.85   Vascular anomalies of eyelid

374.86   Retained foreign body of eyelid

374.87   Dermatochalasis
DEF: Acquired form of connective tissue disorder
associated with decreased elastic tissue and
abnormal elastin formation resulting in loss of
elasticity of the skin of the eyelid, generally
associated with aging.

374.89   Other disorders of eyelid

374.9   Unspecified disorder of eyelid

Lacrimal System

Superior and
inferior lobes
of lacrimal
gland

Medial
angle

Lacrimal
ducts

Lacrimal
canaliculi

Nasolacrimal
sac

Lacrimal
caruncle

Superior,
inferior
lacrimal
puncta

Left eye

√4ᵗʰ **375   Disorders of lacrimal system**

√5ᵗʰ **375.0   Dacryoadenitis**

375.00   Dacryoadenitis, unspecified

375.01   Acute dacryoadenitis
DEF: Severe, sudden inflammation of the lacrimal
gland.

375.02   Chronic dacryoadenitis
DEF: Persistent inflammation of the lacrimal gland.

375.03   Chronic enlargement of lacrimal gland

√5ᵗʰ **375.1   Other disorders of lacrimal gland**

375.11   Dacryops
DEF: Overproduction and constant flow of tears;
may cause distended lacrimal duct.

375.12   Other lacrimal cysts and cystic degeneration

375.13   Primary lacrimal atrophy

375.14   Secondary lacrimal atrophy
DEF: Wasting away of the lacrimal gland due to
another disease.

375.15   Tear film insufficiency, unspecified
Dry eye syndrome
AHA: 3Q, '96, 6
DEF: Eye dryness and irritation from insufficient tear
production.

375.16   Dislocation of lacrimal gland

√5ᵗʰ **375.2   Epiphora**
DEF: Abnormal development of tears due to stricture of
lacrimal passages.

375.20   Epiphora, unspecified as to cause

375.21   Epiphora due to excess lacrimation
DEF: Tear overflow due to overproduction.

375.22   Epiphora due to insufficient drainage
DEF: Tear overflow due to blocked drainage.

√5ᵗʰ **375.3   Acute and unspecified inflammation of lacrimal
passages**
EXCLUDES   *neonatal dacryocystitis (771.6)*

375.30   Dacryocystitis, unspecified

375.31   Acute canaliculitis, lacrimal

375.32   Acute dacryocystitis
Acute peridacryocystitis

375.33   Phlegmonous dacryocystitis
DEF: Infection of the tear sac with pockets of pus.

√5ᵗʰ **375.4   Chronic inflammation of lacrimal passages**

375.41   Chronic canaliculitis

375.42   Chronic dacryocystitis

375.43   Lacrimal mucocele

√5ᵗʰ **375.5   Stenosis and insufficiency of lacrimal passages**

375.51   Eversion of lacrimal punctum
DEF: Abnormal turning outward of the tear duct.

375.52   Stenosis of lacrimal punctum
DEF: Abnormal narrowing of the tear duct.

375.53   Stenosis of lacrimal canaliculi

√4ᵗʰ √5ᵗʰ   Additional Digit Required   Unacceptable PDx   Manifestation Code   Hospital Acquired Condition   ▶◀ Revised Text   ● New Code   ▲ Revised Code Title

2010 ICD-9-CM   **February 2009 · Volume 1 – 131**

Nervous System and Sense Organs

375.54–377.03

375.54 Stenosis of lacrimal sac
DEF: Abnormal narrowing of the tear sac.

375.55 Obstruction of nasolacrimal duct, neonatal
EXCLUDES   congenital anomaly of nasola-crimal duct (743.65)
DEF: Acquired, abnormal obstruction of tear drainage system from the eye to the nose; in an infant.

375.56 Stenosis of nasolacrimal duct, acquired

375.57 Dacryolith
DEF: Concretion or stone anywhere in lacrimal system.

√5th **375.6 Other changes of lacrimal passages**

375.61 Lacrimal fistula
DEF: Abnormal communication from the lacrimal system.

375.69 Other

√5th **375.8 Other disorders of lacrimal system**

375.81 Granuloma of lacrimal passages
DEF: Abnormal nodules within lacrimal system.

375.89 Other

375.9 Unspecified disorder of lacrimal system

√4th **376 Disorders of the orbit**

√5th **376.0 Acute inflammation of orbit**

376.00 Acute inflammation of orbit, unspecified

376.01 Orbital cellulitis   CC
Abscess of orbit
DEF: Infection of tissue between the orbital bone and eyeball.
CC Excl: 376.00-376.04

376.02 Orbital periostitis   CC
DEF: Inflammation of connective tissue covering the orbital bone.
CC Excl: 003.24, 015.50-015.56, 015.70-015.76, 015.90-015.96, 017.90-017.96, 376.02, 730.00-730.39, 730.80-730.99

376.03 Orbital osteomyelitis   CC
DEF: Inflammation of the orbital bone.
CC Excl: 003.24, 015.50-015.56, 015.70-015.76, 015.90-015.96, 017.90-017.96, 376.03, 730.00-730.39, 730.80-730.99

376.04 Tenonitis

√5th **376.1 Chronic inflammatory disorders of orbit**

376.10 Chronic inflammation of orbit, unspecified

376.11 Orbital granuloma
Pseudotumor (inflammatory) of orbit
DEF: Abnormal nodule between orbital bone and eyeball.

376.12 Orbital myositis
DEF: Painful inflammation of the muscles of the eye.

376.13 Parasitic infestation of orbit
Code first underlying disease, as:
hydatid infestation of orbit (122.3, 122.6, 122.9)
myiasis of orbit (134.0)

√5th **376.2 Endocrine exophthalmos**
Code first underlying thyroid disorder (242.0-242.9)

376.21 Thyrotoxic exophthalmos
DEF: Painful inflammation of eye muscles.

376.22 Exophthalmic ophthalmoplegia
DEF: Inability to rotate eye as a result of bulging eyes.

√5th **376.3 Other exophthalmic conditions**

376.30 Exophthalmos, unspecified
DEF: Abnormal protrusion of eyeball.

376.31 Constant exophthalmos
DEF: Continuous, abnormal protrusion or bulging of eyeball.

376.32 Orbital hemorrhage
DEF: Bleeding behind the eyeball, causing it to bulge forward.

376.33 Orbital edema or congestion
DEF: Fluid retention behind eyeball, causing forward bulge.

376.34 Intermittent exophthalmos

376.35 Pulsating exophthalmos
DEF: Bulge or protrusion; associated with a carotid-cavernous fistula.

376.36 Lateral displacement of globe
DEF: Abnormal displacement of the eyeball away from nose, toward temple.

√5th **376.4 Deformity of orbit**

376.40 Deformity of orbit, unspecified

376.41 Hypertelorism of orbit
DEF: Abnormal increase in interorbital distance; associated with congenital facial deformities; may be accompanied by mental deficiency.

376.42 Exostosis of orbit
DEF: Abnormal bony growth of orbit.

376.43 Local deformities due to bone disease
DEF: Acquired abnormalities of orbit; due to bone disease.

376.44 Orbital deformities associated with craniofacial deformities

376.45 Atrophy of orbit
DEF: Wasting away of bone tissue of orbit.

376.46 Enlargement of orbit

376.47 Deformity due to trauma or surgery

√5th **376.5 Enophthalmos**
DEF: Recession of eyeball deep into eye socket.

376.50 Enophthalmos, unspecified as to cause

376.51 Enophthalmos due to atrophy of orbital tissue

376.52 Enophthalmos due to trauma or surgery

376.6 Retained (old) foreign body following penetrating wound of orbit
Retrobulbar foreign body

√5th **376.8 Other orbital disorders**

376.81 Orbital cysts
Encephalocele of orbit
AHA: 3Q, '99, 13

376.82 Myopathy of extraocular muscles
DEF: Disease in the muscles that control eyeball movement.

376.89 Other

376.9 Unspecified disorder of orbit

√4th **377 Disorders of optic nerve and visual pathways**

√5th **377.0 Papilledema**

377.00 Papilledema, unspecified   CC
CC Excl: 017.30-017.36, 017.90-017.96, 036.81, 249.50-249.51, 249.80-249.91, 250.50-250.53, 250.80-250.93, 377.00-377.03, 377.14, 377.24, 379.60-379.90, 379.99, 743.8-743.9

377.01 Papilledema associated with increased   CC
intracranial pressure
CC Excl: See code: 377.00

377.02 Papilledema associated with decreased ocular pressure

377.03 Papilledema associated with retinal disorder

N Newborn Age: 0   P Pediatric Age: 0-17   M Maternity Age: 12-55   A Adult Age: 15-124   MCC Major CC Condition   CC CC Condition   HIV HIV Related Dx

132 – Volume 1   2010 ICD-9-CM

377.04 Foster-Kennedy syndrome
DEF: Retrobulbar optic neuritis, central scotoma and optic atrophy; caused by tumors in frontal lobe of brain that press downward.

√5th **377.1 Optic atrophy**

377.10 Optic atrophy, unspecified

377.11 Primary optic atrophy
EXCLUDES neurosyphilitic optic atrophy (094.84)

377.12 Postinflammatory optic atrophy
DEF: : Adverse effect of inflammation causing wasting away of eye.

377.13 Optic atrophy associated with retinal dystrophies
DEF: Progressive changes in retinal tissue due to metabolic disorder causing wasting away of eye.

377.14 Glaucomatous atrophy [cupping] of optic disc

377.15 Partial optic atrophy
Temporal pallor of optic disc

377.16 Hereditary optic atrophy
Optic atrophy:
    dominant hereditary
    Leber's

√5th **377.2 Other disorders of optic disc**

377.21 Drusen of optic disc

377.22 Crater-like holes of optic disc

377.23 Coloboma of optic disc
DEF: Ocular malformation caused by the failure of fetal fissure of optic stalk to close.

377.24 Pseudopapilledema

√5th **377.3 Optic neuritis**
EXCLUDES meningococcal optic neuritis (036.81)

377.30 Optic neuritis, unspecified `CC`
CC Excl: 377.30-377.39

377.31 Optic papillitis `CC`
CC Excl: See code: 377.30
DEF: Swelling and inflammation of the optic disc.

377.32 Retrobulbar neuritis (acute) `CC`
EXCLUDES syphilitic retrobulbar neuritis (094.85)
CC Excl: See code: 377.30
DEF: Inflammation of optic nerve immediately behind the eyeball.

377.33 Nutritional optic neuropathy
DEF: Malnutrition causing optic nerve disorder.

377.34 Toxic optic neuropathy
Toxic amblyopia
DEF: Toxic substance causing optic nerve disorder.

377.39 Other `CC`
EXCLUDES ischemic optic neuropathy (377.41)
CC Excl: See code: 377.30

√5th **377.4 Other disorders of optic nerve**

377.41 Ischemic optic neuropathy
DEF: Decreased blood flow affecting optic nerve.

377.42 Hemorrhage in optic nerve sheaths
DEF: Bleeding in meningeal lining of optic nerve.

377.43 Optic nerve hypoplasia
AHA: 4Q, '06, 81

377.49 Other
Compression of optic nerve

√5th **377.5 Disorders of optic chiasm**

377.51 Associated with pituitary neoplasms and `CC`
disorders
CC Excl: 377.51-377.63
DEF: Abnormal pituitary growth causing disruption in nerve chain from retina to brain.

377.52 Associated with other neoplasms `CC`
CC Excl: See code: 377.51
DEF: Abnormal growth, other than pituitary, causing disruption in nerve chain from retina to brain.

377.53 Associated with vascular disorders `CC`
CC Excl: See code: 377.51
DEF: Vascular disorder causing disruption in nerve chain from retina to brain.

377.54 Associated with inflammatory disorders `CC`
CC Excl: See code: 377.51
DEF: Inflammatory disease causing disruption in nerve chain from retina to brain.

√5th **377.6 Disorders of other visual pathways**

377.61 Associated with neoplasms `CC`
CC Excl: See code: 377.51

377.62 Associated with vascular disorders `CC`
CC Excl: See code: 377.51

377.63 Associated with inflammatory `CC`
disorders
CC Excl: See code: 377.51

√5th **377.7 Disorders of visual cortex**
EXCLUDES visual:
    agnosia (368.16)
    hallucinations (368.16)
    halos (368.15)

377.71 Associated with neoplasms `CC`
CC Excl: 377.71-377.9

377.72 Associated with vascular disorders `CC`
CC Excl: See code: 377.71

377.73 Associated with inflammatory `CC`
disorders
CC Excl: See code: 377.71

377.75 Cortical blindness
DEF: Blindness due to brain disorder, rather than eye disorder.

377.9 Unspecified disorder of optic nerve and visual pathways

√4th **378 Strabismus and other disorders of binocular eye movements**
EXCLUDES nystagmus and other irregular eye movements (379.50-379.59)
DEF: Misalignment of the eyes due to imbalance in extraocular muscles.

√5th **378.0 Esotropia**
Convergent concomitant strabismus
EXCLUDES intermittent esotropia (378.20-378.22)
DEF: Visual axis deviation created by one eye fixing upon an image and the other eye deviating inward.

378.00 Esotropia, unspecified

378.01 Monocular esotropia

378.02 Monocular esotropia with A pattern

378.03 Monocular esotropia with V pattern

Eye Musculature

Superior rectus
Superior oblique
Lateral rectus
Medial rectus
Inferior oblique
Inferior rectus
Muscles and actions (right eye)

R.   L.
Monocular (one eye only) esotropia (inward)

Monocular exotropia (outward)

Monocular hypertropia (upward)

378.04 Monocular esotropia with other noncomitancies
Monocular esotropia with X or Y pattern

378.05 Alternating esotropia

378.06 Alternating esotropia with A pattern

378.07 Alternating esotropia with V pattern

378.08 Alternating esotropia with other noncomitancies
Alternating esotropia with X or Y pattern

√5ᵗʰ **378.1 Exotropia**
Divergent concomitant strabismus
EXCLUDES *intermittent exotropia (378.20, 378.23-378.24)*
DEF: Visual axis deviation created by one eye fixing upon an image and the other eye deviating outward.

378.10 Exotropia, unspecified

378.11 Monocular exotropia

378.12 Monocular exotropia with A pattern

378.13 Monocular exotropia with V pattern

378.14 Monocular exotropia with other noncomitancies
Monocular exotropia with X or Y pattern

378.15 Alternating exotropia

378.16 Alternating exotropia with A pattern

378.17 Alternating exotropia with V pattern

378.18 Alternating exotropia with other noncomitancies
Alternating exotropia with X or Y pattern

√5ᵗʰ **378.2 Intermittent heterotropia**
EXCLUDES *vertical heterotropia (intermittent) (378.31)*
DEF: Deviation of eyes seen only at intervals; it is also called strabismus.

378.20 Intermittent heterotropia, unspecified
Intermittent:
esotropia NOS
exotropia NOS

378.21 Intermittent esotropia, monocular

378.22 Intermittent esotropia, alternating

378.23 Intermittent exotropia, monocular

378.24 Intermittent exotropia, alternating

√5ᵗʰ **378.3 Other and unspecified heterotropia**

378.30 Heterotropia, unspecified

378.31 Hypertropia
Vertical heterotropia (constant) (intermittent)

378.32 Hypotropia

378.33 Cyclotropia

378.34 Monofixation syndrome
Microtropia

378.35 Accommodative component in esotropia

√5ᵗʰ **378.4 Heterophoria**
DEF: Deviation occurring only when the other eye is covered.

378.40 Heterophoria, unspecified

378.41 Esophoria

378.42 Exophoria

378.43 Vertical heterophoria

378.44 Cyclophoria

378.45 Alternating hyperphoria

√5ᵗʰ **378.5 Paralytic strabismus**
DEF: Deviation of the eye due to nerve paralysis affecting muscle.

378.50 Paralytic strabismus, unspecified

378.51 Third or oculomotor nerve palsy, partial
AHA: 3Q, '91, 9

378.52 Third or oculomotor nerve palsy, total
AHA: 2Q, '89, 12

378.53 Fourth or trochlear nerve palsy
AHA: 2Q, '01, 21

378.54 Sixth or abducens nerve palsy
AHA: 2Q, '89, 12

378.55 External ophthalmoplegia

378.56 Total ophthalmoplegia

√5ᵗʰ **378.6 Mechanical strabismus**
DEF: Deviation of the eye due to an outside force upon the extraocular muscles.

378.60 Mechanical strabismus, unspecified

378.61 Brown's (tendon) sheath syndrome
DEF: Congenital or acquired shortening of the anterior sheath of superior oblique muscle; eye is unable to move upward and inward; usually unilateral.

378.62 Mechanical strabismus from other musculofascial disorders

378.63 Limited duction associated with other conditions

√5ᵗʰ **378.7 Other specified strabismus**

378.71 Duane's syndrome
DEF: Congenital, affects one eye; due to abnormal fibrous bands attached to rectus muscle; inability to abduct affected eye with retraction of globe.

378.72 Progressive external ophthalmoplegia
DEF: Paralysis progressing from one eye muscle to another.

378.73 Strabismus in other neuromuscular disorders

√5ᵗʰ **378.8 Other disorders of binocular eye movements**
EXCLUDES *nystagmus (379.50-379.56)*

378.81 Palsy of conjugate gaze
DEF: Paralysis progressing from one eye muscle to another.

378.82 Spasm of conjugate gaze
DEF: Muscle contractions impairing parallel movement of eye.

378.83 Convergence insufficiency or palsy

378.84 Convergence excess or spasm

378.85 Anomalies of divergence

378.86 Internuclear ophthalmoplegia
DEF: Eye movement anomaly due to brainstem lesion.

378.87 Other dissociated deviation of eye movements
Skew deviation

378.9 Unspecified disorder of eye movements
Ophthalmoplegia NOS   Strabismus NOS
AHA: 2Q, '01, 21

√4ᵗʰ **379 Other disorders of eye**

√5ᵗʰ **379.0 Scleritis and episcleritis**
EXCLUDES *syphilitic episcleritis (095.0)*

379.00 Scleritis, unspecified
Episcleritis NOS

379.01 Episcleritis periodica fugax
DEF: Hyperemia (engorgement) of the sclera and overlying conjunctiva characterized by a sudden onset and short duration.

379.02 Nodular episcleritis
DEF: Inflammation of the outermost layer of the sclera, with formation of nodules.

379.03 Anterior scleritis

379.04 Scleromalacia perforans
DEF: Scleral thinning, softening and degeneration; seen with rheumatoid arthritis.

Ⓝ Newborn Age: 0   Ⓟ Pediatric Age: 0-17   Ⓜ Maternity Age: 12-55   Ⓐ Adult Age: 15-124   **MCC** Major CC Condition   **CC** CC Condition   **HIV** HIV Related Dx

379.05 Scleritis with corneal involvement
Scleroperikeratitis

379.06 Brawny scleritis
DEF: Severe scleral inflammation with thickening corneal margins.

379.07 Posterior scleritis
Sclerotenonitis

379.09 Other
Scleral abscess

√5th **379.1 Other disorders of sclera**
EXCLUDES blue sclera (743.47)

379.11 Scleral ectasia
Scleral staphyloma NOS
DEF: Protrusion of the contents of the eyeball where the sclera has thinned.

379.12 Staphyloma posticum
DEF: Ring-shaped protrusion or bulging of sclera and uveal tissue at posterior pole of eye.

379.13 Equatorial staphyloma
DEF: Ring-shaped protrusion or bulging of sclera and uveal tissue midway between front and back of eye.

379.14 Anterior staphyloma, localized

379.15 Ring staphyloma

379.16 Other degenerative disorders of sclera

379.19 Other

√5th **379.2 Disorders of vitreous body**
DEF: Disorder of clear gel that fills space between retina and lens.

379.21 Vitreous degeneration
Vitreous: Vitreous:
  cavitation   liquefaction
  detachment

379.22 Crystalline deposits in vitreous
Asteroid hyalitis   Synchysis scintillans

379.23 Vitreous hemorrhage
AHA: 3Q, '91, 15

379.24 Other vitreous opacities
Vitreous floaters

379.25 Vitreous membranes and strands

379.26 Vitreous prolapse
DEF: Slipping of vitreous from normal position.

379.29 Other disorders of vitreous
EXCLUDES vitreous abscess (360.04)
AHA: 1Q, '99, 11

√5th **379.3 Aphakia and other disorders of lens**
EXCLUDES after-cataract (366.50-366.53)

379.31 Aphakia
EXCLUDES cataract extraction status (V45.61)
DEF: Absence of eye's crystalline lens.

379.32 Subluxation of lens

379.33 Anterior dislocation of lens
DEF: Lens displaced toward iris.

379.34 Posterior dislocation of lens
DEF: Lens displaced backward toward vitreous.

379.39 Other disorders of lens

√5th **379.4 Anomalies of pupillary function**

379.40 Abnormal pupillary function, unspecified

379.41 Anisocoria
DEF: Unequal pupil diameter.

379.42 Miosis (persistent), not due to miotics
DEF: Abnormal contraction of pupil less than 2 mil.

379.43 Mydriasis (persistent), not due to mydriatics
DEF: Morbid dilation of pupil.

379.45 Argyll Robertson pupil, atypical
Argyll Robertson phenomenon or pupil, nonsyphilitic
EXCLUDES Argyll Robertson pupil (syphilitic) (094.89)
DEF: Failure of pupil to respond to light; affects both eyes; may be caused by diseases such as syphilis of the central nervous system or miosis.

379.46 Tonic pupillary reaction
Adie's pupil or syndrome

379.49 Other
Hippus
Pupillary paralysis

√5th **379.5 Nystagmus and other irregular eye movements**

379.50 Nystagmus, unspecified
AHA: 4Q, '02, 68; 2Q, '01, 21
DEF: Involuntary, rapid, rhythmic movement of eyeball; vertical, horizontal, rotatory or mixed; cause may be congenital, acquired, physiological, neurological, myopathic, or due to ocular diseases.

379.51 Congenital nystagmus

379.52 Latent nystagmus

379.53 Visual deprivation nystagmus

379.54 Nystagmus associated with disorders of the vestibular system

379.55 Dissociated nystagmus

379.56 Other forms of nystagmus

379.57 Deficiencies of saccadic eye movements
Abnormal optokinetic response
DEF: Saccadic eye movements; small, rapid, involuntary movements by both eyes simultaneously, due to changing point of fixation on visualized object.

379.58 Deficiencies of smooth pursuit movements

379.59 Other irregularities of eye movements
Opsoclonus

√5th **379.6 Inflammation (infection) of postprocedural bleb**
Postprocedural blebitis

379.60 Inflammation (infection) of postprocedural bleb, unspecified
AHA: 4Q, '06, 82

379.61 Inflammation (infection) of postprocedural bleb, stage 1
AHA: 4Q, '06, 82

379.62 Inflammation (infection) of postprocedural bleb, stage 2
AHA: 4Q, '06, 82

379.63 Inflammation (infection) of postprocedural bleb, stage 3
Bleb associated endophthalmitis
AHA: 4Q, '06, 82

379.8 Other specified disorders of eye and adnexa

√5th **379.9 Unspecified disorder of eye and adnexa**

379.90 Disorder of eye, unspecified

379.91 Pain in or around eye

379.92 Swelling or mass of eye

379.93 Redness or discharge of eye

379.99 Other ill-defined disorders of eye
EXCLUDES blurred vision NOS (368.8)

√4th √5th Additional Digit Required   Unacceptable PDx   Manifestation Code   Hospital Acquired Condition   ▶◀ Revised Text   ● New Code   ▲ Revised Code Title

2010 ICD-9-CM　　　　　　　　　　　　　　　　　　　　　　　　　　　　　　　　　　　　**Volume 1 – 135**

Nervous System and Sense Organs

380–381.10

Ear and Mastoid Process

Helix

External auditory meatus

Antihelix

Concha

Tragus

Mastoid process

Antitragus

DISEASES OF THE EAR AND MASTOID PROCESS (380-389)

Use additional external cause code, if applicable, to identify the cause of the ear condition

✓4ᵗʰ **380 Disorders of external ear**

✓5ᵗʰ **380.0 Perichondritis and chondritis of pinna**
Chondritis of auricle   Perichondritis of auricle

380.00 Perichondritis of pinna, unspecified

380.01 Acute perichondritis of pinna

380.02 Chronic perichondritis of pinna

380.03 Chondritis of pinna
AHA: 4Q, '04, 76
DEF: Infection that has progressed into the cartilage; presents as indurated and edematous skin over the pinna; vascular compromise occurs with tissue necrosis and deformity.

✓5ᵗʰ **380.1 Infective otitis externa**

380.10 Infective otitis externa, unspecified
Otitis externa (acute):
NOS
circumscribed
diffuse
hemorrhagica
infective NOS

380.11 Acute infection of pinna
EXCLUDES   *furuncular otitis externa (680.0)*

380.12 Acute swimmers' ear
Beach ear   Tank ear
DEF: Otitis externa due to swimming.

380.13 Other acute infections of external ear
Code first underlying disease, as:
erysipelas (035)
impetigo (684)
seborrheic dermatitis (690.10-690.18)
EXCLUDES   *herpes simplex (054.73)*
herpes zoster (053.71)

380.14 Malignant otitis externa   **CC**
CC Excl: 380.14, 383.00-383.1
DEF: Severe necrotic otitis externa; due to bacteria.

380.15 Chronic mycotic otitis externa
Code first underlying disease, as:
aspergillosis (117.3)
otomycosis NOS (111.9)
EXCLUDES   *candidal otitis externa (112.82)*

380.16 Other chronic infective otitis externa
Chronic infective otitis externa NOS

✓5ᵗʰ **380.2 Other otitis externa**

380.21 Cholesteatoma of external ear
Keratosis obturans of external ear (canal)
EXCLUDES   *cholesteatoma NOS (385.30-385.35)*
postmastoidectomy (383.32)
DEF: Cystlike mass filled with debris, including cholesterol; rare, congenital condition.

380.22 Other acute otitis externa
Acute otitis externa: Acute otitis externa:
actinic   eczematoid
chemical   reactive
contact

380.23 Other chronic otitis externa
Chronic otitis externa NOS

✓5ᵗʰ **380.3 Noninfectious disorders of pinna**

380.30 Disorder of pinna, unspecified

380.31 Hematoma of auricle or pinna

380.32 Acquired deformities of auricle or pinna
EXCLUDES   *cauliflower ear (738.7)*
AHA: 3Q, '03, 12

380.39 Other
EXCLUDES   *gouty tophi of ear (274.81)*

380.4 Impacted cerumen
Wax in ear

✓5ᵗʰ **380.5 Acquired stenosis of external ear canal**
Collapse of external ear canal

380.50 Acquired stenosis of external ear canal, unspecified as to cause

380.51 Secondary to trauma
DEF: Narrowing of the external ear canal; due to trauma.

380.52 Secondary to surgery
DEF: Postsurgical narrowing of the external ear canal.

380.53 Secondary to inflammation
DEF: Narrowing of the external ear canal; due to chronic inflammation.

✓5ᵗʰ **380.8 Other disorders of external ear**

380.81 Exostosis of external ear canal

380.89 Other

380.9 Unspecified disorder of external ear

✓4ᵗʰ **381 Nonsuppurative otitis media and Eustachian tube disorders**

✓5ᵗʰ **381.0 Acute nonsuppurative otitis media**
Acute tubotympanic catarrh
Otitis media, acute or subacute:
catarrhal
exudative
transudative
with effusion
EXCLUDES   *otitic barotrauma (993.0)*

381.00 Acute nonsuppurative otitis media, unspecified

381.01 Acute serous otitis media
Acute or subacute secretory otitis media
DEF: Sudden, severe infection of the middle ear.

381.02 Acute mucoid otitis media
Acute or subacute seromucinous otitis media
Blue drum syndrome
DEF: Sudden, severe infection of the middle ear, with mucous.

381.03 Acute sanguinous otitis media
DEF: Sudden, severe infection of the middle ear, with blood.

381.04 Acute allergic serous otitis media

381.05 Acute allergic mucoid otitis media

381.06 Acute allergic sanguinous otitis media

✓5ᵗʰ **381.1 Chronic serous otitis media**
Chronic tubotympanic catarrh

381.10 Chronic serous otitis media, simple or unspecified
DEF: Persistent infection of the middle ear, without pus.

N Newborn Age: 0   **P** Pediatric Age: 0-17   **M** Maternity Age: 12-55   **A** Adult Age: 15-124   **MCC** Major CC Condition   **CC** CC Condition   **HIV** HIV Related Dx

136 – Volume 1   **2010 ICD-9-CM**

381.19 Other
Serosanguinous chronic otitis media

✓5th 381.2 Chronic mucoid otitis media
Glue ear
EXCLUDES adhesive middle ear disease (385.10-385.19)
DEF: Chronic condition; characterized by viscous fluid in middle ear; due to obstructed Eustachian tube.

381.20 Chronic mucoid otitis media, simple or unspecified

381.29 Other
Mucosanguinous chronic otitis media

381.3 Other and unspecified chronic nonsuppurative otitis media
Otitis media, chronic:
allergic
exudative
secretory
Otitis media, chronic:
seromucinous
transudative
with effusion

381.4 Nonsuppurative otitis media, not specified as acute or chronic
Otitis media:
allergic
catarrhal
exudative
mucoid
Otitis media:
secretory
seromucinous
serous
transudative
with effusion

✓5th 381.5 Eustachian salpingitis

381.50 Eustachian salpingitis, unspecified

381.51 Acute Eustachian salpingitis
DEF: Sudden, severe inflammation of the Eustachian tube.

381.52 Chronic Eustachian salpingitis
DEF: Persistent inflammation of the Eustachian tube.

✓5th 381.6 Obstruction of Eustachian tube
Stenosis
Stricture } of Eustachian tube

381.60 Obstruction of Eustachian tube, unspecified

381.61 Osseous obstruction of Eustachian tube
Obstruction of Eustachian tube from cholesteatoma, polyp, or other osseous lesion

381.62 Intrinsic cartilaginous obstruction of Eustachian tube
DEF: Blockage of Eustachian tube; due to cartilage overgrowth.

381.63 Extrinsic cartilaginous obstruction of Eustachian tube
Compression of Eustachian tube

381.7 Patulous Eustachian tube
DEF: Distended, oversized Eustachian tube.

✓5th 381.8 Other disorders of Eustachian tube

381.81 Dysfunction of Eustachian tube

381.89 Other

381.9 Unspecified Eustachian tube disorder

✓4th 382 Suppurative and unspecified otitis media

✓5th 382.0 Acute suppurative otitis media
Otitis media, acute:
necrotizing NOS
Otitis media, acute:
purulent

382.00 Acute suppurative otitis media without spontaneous rupture of ear drum
DEF: Sudden, severe inflammation of middle ear, with pus.

382.01 Acute suppurative otitis media with spontaneous rupture of ear drum
DEF: Sudden, severe inflammation of middle ear, with pressure tearing ear drum tissue.

382.02 Acute suppurative otitis media in diseases classified elsewhere
Code first underlying disease, as:
influenza (487.8)
scarlet fever (034.1)
EXCLUDES postmeasles otitis (055.2)

382.1 Chronic tubotympanic suppurative otitis media
Benign chronic suppurative otitis media
Chronic tubotympanic disease } (with anterior perforation of ear drum)
DEF: Inflammation of tympanic cavity and auditory tube; with pus formation.

382.2 Chronic atticoantral suppurative otitis media
Chronic atticoantral disease
Persistent mucosal disease } (with posterior or superior marginal perforation of ear drum)
DEF: Inflammation of upper tympanic membrane and mastoid antrum with pus formation.

382.3 Unspecified chronic suppurative otitis media
Chronic purulent otitis media
EXCLUDES tuberculous otitis media (017.4)

382.4 Unspecified suppurative otitis media
Purulent otitis media NOS

382.9 Unspecified otitis media
Otitis media:
NOS
acute NOS
Otitis media:
chronic NOS
AHA: N-D, '84, 16
H66.93 Otitis media unspecified bilateral   `I-10`

✓4th 383 Mastoiditis and related conditions

✓5th 383.0 Acute mastoiditis
Abscess of mastoid   Empyema of mastoid

383.00 Acute mastoiditis without complications   `CC`
DEF: Sudden, severe inflammation of mastoid air cells.
CC Excl: 015.60-015.66, 017.40-017.46, 017.90-017.96, 383.00-383.9, 388.71-388.9, 744.00, 744.02, 744.09, 744.29-744.3

383.01 Subperiosteal abscess of mastoid   `CC`
DEF: Pocket of pus within the mastoid bone.
CC Excl: See code: 383.00

383.02 Acute mastoiditis with other complications   `CC`
Gradenigo's syndrome
CC Excl: See code: 383.00

383.1 Chronic mastoiditis
Caries of mastoid   Fistula of mastoid
EXCLUDES tuberculous mastoiditis (015.6)
DEF: Persistent inflammation of the mastoid air cells.

✓5th 383.2 Petrositis
Coalescing osteitis
Inflammation
Osteomyelitis } of petrous bone

383.20 Petrositis, unspecified

383.21 Acute petrositis
DEF: Sudden, severe inflammation of dense bone behind the ear.

383.22 Chronic petrositis
DEF: Persistent inflammation of dense bone behind the ear.

✓5th 383.3 Complications following mastoidectomy

383.30 Postmastoidectomy complication, unspecified

383.31 Mucosal cyst of postmastoidectomy cavity
DEF: Mucous-lined cyst cavity following removal of mastoid bone.

383.32 Recurrent cholesteatoma of postmastoidectomy cavity
DEF: Cystlike mass of cell debris in cavity following removal of mastoid bone.

Nervous System and Sense Organs

383.33–385.33

383.33   **Granulations of postmastoidectomy cavity**
Chronic inflammation of postmastoidectomy cavity
DEF: Granular tissue in cavity following removal of mastoid bone.

√5th **383.8**   **Other disorders of mastoid**

383.81   **Postauricular fistula**
DEF: Abnormal passage behind mastoid cavity.

383.89   **Other**

383.9   **Unspecified mastoiditis**

√4th **384**   **Other disorders of tympanic membrane**

√5th **384.0**   **Acute myringitis without mention of otitis media**

384.00   **Acute myringitis, unspecified**
Acute tympanitis NOS
DEF: Sudden, severe inflammation of ear drum.

384.01   **Bullous myringitis**
Myringitis bullosa hemorrhagica
DEF: Type of viral otitis media characterized by the appearance of serous or hemorrhagic blebs on the tympanic membrane.

384.09   **Other**

384.1   **Chronic myringitis without mention of otitis media**
Chronic tympanitis
DEF: Persistent inflammation of ear drum; with no evidence of middle ear infection.

√5th **384.2**   **Perforation of tympanic membrane**
Perforation of ear drum:
   NOS
   persistent posttraumatic
   postinflammatory
EXCLUDES   otitis media with perforation of tympanic membrane (382.00-382.9)
traumatic perforation [current injury] (872.61)

384.20   **Perforation of tympanic membrane, unspecified**

384.21   **Central perforation of tympanic membrane**

384.22   **Attic perforation of tympanic membrane**
Pars flaccida

384.23   **Other marginal perforation of tympanic membrane**

384.24   **Multiple perforations of tympanic membrane**

384.25   **Total perforation of tympanic membrane**

√5th **384.8**   **Other specified disorders of tympanic membrane**

384.81   **Atrophic flaccid tympanic membrane**
Healed perforation of ear drum

384.82   **Atrophic nonflaccid tympanic membrane**

384.9   **Unspecified disorder of tympanic membrane**

√4th **385**   **Other disorders of middle ear and mastoid**
EXCLUDES   mastoiditis (383.0-383.9)

√5th **385.0**   **Tympanosclerosis**

385.00   **Tympanosclerosis, unspecified as to involvement**

385.01   **Tympanosclerosis involving tympanic membrane only**
DEF: Tough, fibrous tissue impeding functions of ear drum.

385.02   **Tympanosclerosis involving tympanic membrane and ear ossicles**
DEF: Tough, fibrous tissue impeding functions of middle ear bones (stapes, malleus, incus).

385.03   **Tympanosclerosis involving tympanic membrane, ear ossicles, and middle ear**
DEF: Tough, fibrous tissue impeding functions of ear drum, middle ear bones and middle ear canal.

385.09   **Tympanosclerosis involving other combination of structures**

Middle and Inner Ear

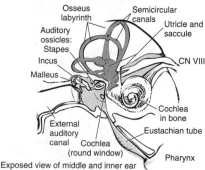

Exposed view of middle and inner ear

√5th **385.1**   **Adhesive middle ear disease**
Adhesive otitis   Otitis media:
Otitis media: fibrotic
  chronic adhesive
EXCLUDES   glue ear (381.20-381.29)
DEF: Adhesions of middle ear structures.

385.10   **Adhesive middle ear disease, unspecified as to involvement**

385.11   **Adhesions of drum head to incus**

385.12   **Adhesions of drum head to stapes**

385.13   **Adhesions of drum head to promontorium**

385.19   **Other adhesions and combinations**

√5th **385.2**   **Other acquired abnormality of ear ossicles**

385.21   **Impaired mobility of malleus**
Ankylosis of malleus

385.22   **Impaired mobility of other ear ossicles**
Ankylosis of ear ossicles, except malleus

385.23   **Discontinuity or dislocation of ear ossicles**
DEF: Disruption in auditory chain; created by malleus, incus and stapes.

385.24   **Partial loss or necrosis of ear ossicles**
DEF: Tissue loss in malleus, incus and stapes.

√5th **385.3**   **Cholesteatoma of middle ear and mastoid**
Cholesterosis
Epidermosis
Keratosis   } of (middle) ear
Polyp
EXCLUDES   cholesteatoma:
external ear canal (380.21)
recurrent of postmastoidectomy cavity (383.32)
DEF: Cystlike mass of middle ear and mastoid antrum filled with debris, including cholesterol.

385.30   **Cholesteatoma, unspecified**

385.31   **Cholesteatoma of attic**

385.32   **Cholesteatoma of middle ear**

385.33   **Cholesteatoma of middle ear and mastoid**
DEF: Cystlike mass of cell debris in middle ear and mastoid air cells behind ear.
AHA: 3Q, '00, 10

Cholesteatoma

Ⓝ Newborn Age: 0   Ⓟ Pediatric Age: 0-17   Ⓜ Maternity Age: 12-55   Ⓐ Adult Age: 15-124   **MCC** Major CC Condition   **CC** CC Condition   **HIV** HIV Related Dx

138 – Volume 1   **2010 ICD-9-CM**

385.35　Diffuse cholesteatosis

√5ᵗʰ　385.8　Other disorders of middle ear and mastoid

385.82　Cholesterin granuloma

DEF: Granuloma formed of fibrotic tissue; contains cholesterol crystals surrounded by foreign-body cells; found in the middle ear and mastoid area.

385.83　Retained foreign body of middle ear

AHA: 3Q, '94, 7; N-D, '87, 9

385.89　Other

385.9　Unspecified disorder of middle ear and mastoid

√4ᵗʰ　**386　Vertiginous syndromes and other disorders of vestibular system**

EXCLUDES　vertigo NOS (780.4)

AHA: M-A, '85, 12 k

386.0　Ménière's disease

Endolymphatic hydrops
Lermoyez's syndrome
Ménière's syndrome or vertigo

DEF: Distended membranous labyrinth of middle ear from endolymphatic hydrops; causes ischemia, failure of nerve function; hearing and balance dysfunction; symptoms include fluctuating deafness, ringing in ears and dizziness.

386.00　Ménière's disease, unspecified

Ménière's disease (active)

H81.03 Ménière's disease bilateral　　**I-10**

386.01　Active Ménière's disease, cochleovestibular

386.02　Active Ménière's disease, cochlear

386.03　Active Ménière's disease, vestibular

386.04　Inactive Ménière's disease

Ménière's disease in remission

√5ᵗʰ　386.1　Other and unspecified peripheral vertigo

EXCLUDES　epidemic vertigo (078.81)

386.10　Peripheral vertigo, unspecified

386.11　Benign paroxysmal positional vertigo

Benign paroxysmal positional nystagmus

386.12　Vestibular neuronitis

Acute (and recurrent) peripheral vestibulopathy

DEF: Transient benign vertigo, unknown cause; characterized by response to caloric stimulation on one side, nystagmus with rhythmic movement of eyes; normal auditory function present.

386.19　Other

Aural vertigo
Otogenic vertigo

386.2　Vertigo of central origin

Central positional nystagmus
Malignant positional vertigo

√5ᵗʰ　386.3　Labyrinthitis

386.30　Labyrinthitis, unspecified

386.31　Serous labyrinthitis

Diffuse labyrinthitis

DEF: Inflammation of labyrinth; with fluid buildup.

386.32　Circumscribed labyrinthitis

Focal labyrinthitis

386.33　Suppurative labyrinthitis

Purulent labyrinthitis

DEF: Inflammation of labyrinth; with pus.

386.34　Toxic labyrinthitis

DEF: Inflammation of labyrinth; due to toxic reaction.

386.35　Viral labyrinthitis

√5ᵗʰ　386.4　Labyrinthine fistula

386.40　Labyrinthine fistula, unspecified

386.41　Round window fistula

386.42　Oval window fistula

386.43　Semicircular canal fistula

386.48　Labyrinthine fistula of combined sites

√5ᵗʰ　386.5　Labyrinthine dysfunction

386.50　Labyrinthine dysfunction, unspecified

386.51　Hyperactive labyrinth, unilateral

DEF: Abnormal increased sensitivity of labyrinth to stimuli such as sound, pressure or gravitational change, affecting one ear.

386.52　Hyperactive labyrinth, bilateral

DEF: Abnormal increased sensitivity of labyrinth to stimuli such as sound, pressure or gravitational change, affecting both ears.

386.53　Hypoactive labyrinth, unilateral

DEF: Abnormal decreased sensitivity of labyrinth to stimuli such as sound, pressure or gravitational change, affecting one ear.

386.54　Hypoactive labyrinth, bilateral

DEF: Abnormal decreased sensitivity of labyrinth to stimuli such as sound, pressure or gravitational change, affecting both ears.

386.55　Loss of labyrinthine reactivity, unilateral

DEF: Decreased function of the labyrinth sensors, affecting one ear

386.56　Loss of labyrinthine reactivity, bilateral

DEF: Decreased function of the labyrinth sensors, affecting both ears

386.58　Other forms and combinations

386.8　Other disorders of labyrinth

386.9　Unspecified vertiginous syndromes and labyrinthine disorders

√4ᵗʰ　**387　Otosclerosis**

INCLUDES　otospongiosis

DEF: Synonym for otospongiosis, spongy bone formation in the labyrinth bones of the ear; it causes progressive hearing impairment.

387.0　Otosclerosis involving oval window, nonobliterative

DEF: Tough, fibrous tissue impeding functions of oval window.

387.1　Otosclerosis involving oval window, obliterative

DEF: Tough, fibrous tissue blocking oval window.

387.2　Cochlear otosclerosis

Otosclerosis involving:
otic capsule
round window

DEF: Tough, fibrous tissue impeding functions of cochlea.

387.8　Other otosclerosis

387.9　Otosclerosis, unspecified

√4ᵗʰ　**388　Other disorders of ear**

√5ᵗʰ　388.0　Degenerative and vascular disorders of ear

388.00　Degenerative and vascular disorders, unspecified

388.01　Presbyacusis

DEF: Progressive, bilateral perceptive hearing loss caused by advancing age; it is also known as presbycusis.

388.02　Transient ischemic deafness

DEF: Restricted blood flow to auditory organs causing temporary hearing loss.

√5ᵗʰ　388.1　Noise effects on inner ear

388.10　Noise effects on inner ear, unspecified

388.11　Acoustic trauma (explosive) to ear

Otitic blast injury

388.12　Noise-induced hearing loss

388.2　Sudden hearing loss, unspecified

√5ᵗʰ　388.3　Tinnitus

DEF: Abnormal noises in ear; may be heard by others beside the affected individual; noises include ringing, clicking, roaring and buzzing.

388.30　Tinnitus, unspecified

√4ᵗʰ Additional Digit Required　　Unacceptable PDx　　Manifestation Code　　Hospital Acquired Condition　　►◄ Revised Text　　● New Code　　▲ Revised Code Title

Nervous System and Sense Organs

388.31–389.9

388.31 **Subjective tinnitus**

388.32 **Objective tinnitus**

√5th 388.4 **Other abnormal auditory perception**

388.40 **Abnormal auditory perception, unspecified**

388.41 **Diplacusis**
> **DEF:** Perception of a single auditory sound as two sounds at two different levels of intensity.

388.42 **Hyperacusis**
> **DEF:** Exceptionally acute sense of hearing caused by such conditions as Bell's palsy; this term may also refer to painful sensitivity to sounds.

388.43 **Impairment of auditory discrimination**
> **DEF:** Impaired ability to distinguish tone of sound.

388.44 **Recruitment**
> **DEF:** Perception of abnormally increased loudness caused by a slight increase in sound intensity; it is a term used in audiology.

388.45 **Acquired auditory processing disorder**
Auditory processing disorder NOS
> **EXCLUDES** central auditory processing disorder (315.32)
>
> **DEF:** Difficulty in recognizing and interpreting sounds; a failure of the brain to process auditory information; due to neurological problems due to injury, infection, and degenerative conditions.
> **AHA:** 4Q, '07, 79

388.5 **Disorders of acoustic nerve**
Acoustic neuritis
Degeneration } of acoustic or eighth nerve
Disorder
> **EXCLUDES** acoustic neuroma (225.1)
> syphilitic acoustic neuritis (094.86)
>
> **AHA:** M-A, '87, 8

√5th 388.6 **Otorrhea**

388.60 **Otorrhea, unspecified**
Discharging ear NOS

388.61 **Cerebrospinal fluid otorrhea** `CC`
> **EXCLUDES** cerebrospinal fluid rhinorrhea (349.81)
>
> **CC Excl:** 388.61-388.69
> **DEF:** Spinal fluid leakage from ear.

388.69 **Other**
Otorrhagia

√5th 388.7 **Otalgia**

388.70 **Otalgia, unspecified**
Earache NOS

388.71 **Otogenic pain**

388.72 **Referred pain**

388.8 **Other disorders of ear**

388.9 **Unspecified disorder of ear**

√4th 389 **Hearing loss**

√5th 389.0 **Conductive hearing loss**
Conductive deafness
> **EXCLUDES** mixed conductive and sensorineural hearing loss (389.20-389.22)
>
> **DEF:** Dysfunction in sound-conducting structures of external or middle ear causing hearing loss.
> **AHA:** 4Q, '07, 80; 4Q, '89, 5

389.00 **Conductive hearing loss, unspecified**

389.01 **Conductive hearing loss, external ear**

389.02 **Conductive hearing loss, tympanic membrane**

389.03 **Conductive hearing loss, middle ear**

389.04 **Conductive hearing loss, inner ear**

389.05 **Conductive hearing loss, unilateral**

389.06 **Conductive hearing loss, bilateral**
> **AHA:** 4Q, '07, 81

389.08 **Conductive hearing loss of combined types**

√5th 389.1 **Sensorineural hearing loss**
Perceptive hearing loss or deafness
> **EXCLUDES** abnormal auditory perception (388.40-388.44)
> mixed conductive and sensorineural hearing loss (389.20-389.22)
> psychogenic deafness (306.7)
>
> **DEF:** Nerve conduction causing hearing loss.
> **AHA:** 4Q, '07, 80; 4Q, '89, 5

389.10 **Sensorineural hearing loss, unspecified**
> **AHA:** 1Q, '93, 29

389.11 **Sensory hearing loss, bilateral**

389.12 **Neural hearing loss, bilateral**

389.13 **Neural hearing loss, unilateral**

389.14 **Central hearing loss**

389.15 **Sensorineural hearing loss, unilateral**
> **AHA:** 4Q, '06, 84

389.16 **Sensorineural hearing loss, asymmetrical**
> **AHA:** 4Q, '06, 84

389.17 **Sensory hearing loss, unilateral**

389.18 **Sensorineural hearing loss, bilateral**
> **AHA:** 4Q, '06, 84

√5th 389.2 **Mixed conductive and sensorineural hearing loss**
Deafness or hearing loss of type classifiable to 389.00-389.08 with type classifiable to 389.10-389.18
> **AHA:** 4Q, '07, 80

389.20 **Mixed hearing loss, unspecified**

389.21 **Mixed hearing loss, unilateral**

389.22 **Mixed hearing loss, bilateral**

389.7 **Deaf, non-speaking, not elsewhere classifiable**

389.8 **Other specified forms of hearing loss**

389.9 **Unspecified hearing loss**
Deafness NOS
> **AHA:** 1Q, '04, 15
> **H91.93** Unspecified hearing loss bilateral `I-10`

 `N` Newborn Age: 0 `P` Pediatric Age: 0-17 `M` Maternity Age: 12-55 `A` Adult Age: 15-124 `MCC` Major CC Condition `CC` CC Condition `HIV` HIV Related Dx

140 – Volume 1 2010 ICD-9-CM

7. DISEASES OF THE CIRCULATORY SYSTEM (390-459)

ACUTE RHEUMATIC FEVER (390-392)

DEF: Febrile disease occurs mainly in children or young adults following throat infection by group A *streptococci;* symptoms include fever, joint pain, lesions of heart, blood vessels and joint connective tissue, abdominal pain, skin changes, and chorea.

390 Rheumatic fever without mention of heart involvement
Arthritis, rheumatic, acute or subacute
Rheumatic fever (active) (acute)
Rheumatism, articular, acute or subacute
> **EXCLUDES**   that with heart involvement (391.0-391.9)

✓4ᵗʰ 391 Rheumatic fever with heart involvement
> **EXCLUDES**   chronic heart diseases of rheumatic origin (393-398.99) unless rheumatic fever is also present or there is evidence of recrudescence or activity of the rheumatic process

391.0 Acute rheumatic pericarditis   CC
Rheumatic:
    fever (active) (acute) with pericarditis
    pericarditis (acute)
Any condition classifiable to 390 with pericarditis
> **EXCLUDES**   that not specified as rheumatic (420.0-420.9)

DEF: Sudden, severe inflammation of heart lining due to rheumatic fever.
CC Excl: 074.21, 093.81, 391.0, 393, 420.0-420.99, 423.3-423.9, 459.89-459.9

391.1 Acute rheumatic endocarditis   CC
Rheumatic:
    endocarditis, acute
    fever (active) (acute) with endocarditis or valvulitis
    valvulitis acute
Any condition classifiable to 390 with endocarditis or valvulitis
DEF: Sudden, severe inflammation of heart cavities due to rheumatic fever.
CC Excl: 002.0, 036.42, 074.22, 083.0, 093.20-093.24, 098.84, 112.81, 115.94, 390, 391.1, 391.8-392.0, 394.0-395.9, 396.9-397.9, 398.90, 398.99, 421.0-421.9, 424.0-424.99, 425.3, 459.89-459.9, 746.09, 746.89, 996.61

391.2 Acute rheumatic myocarditis   CC
Rheumatic fever (active) (acute) with myocarditis
Any condition classifiable to 390 with myocarditis
DEF: Sudden, severe inflammation of heart muscles due to rheumatic fever.
CC Excl: 074.20, 074.22-074.23, 093.82, 390, 391.2-391.9, 398.0-398.90, 398.99, 422.0-422.99, 429.0, 429.71-429.79, 459.89-459.9

391.8 Other acute rheumatic heart disease   CC
Rheumatic:
    fever (active) (acute) with other or multiple types of heart involvement
    pancarditis, acute
Any condition classifiable to 390 with other or multiple types of heart involvement
CC Excl: 391.0-398.99, 428.20-428.43

391.9 Acute rheumatic heart disease, unspecified   CC
Rheumatic:
    carditis, acute
    fever (active) (acute) with unspecified type of heart involvement
    heart disease, active or acute
Any condition classifiable to 390 with unspecified type of heart involvement
CC Excl: 391.0-398.99

✓4ᵗʰ 392 Rheumatic chorea
> **INCLUDES**   Sydenham's chorea
> **EXCLUDES**   chorea:
>   NOS (333.5)
>   Huntington's (333.4)

DEF: Childhood disease linked with rheumatic fever and streptococcal infections; symptoms include spasmodic, involuntary movements of limbs or facial muscles, psychic symptoms, and irritability.

392.0 With heart involvement   CC
Rheumatic chorea with heart involvement of any type classifiable to 391
CC Excl: See code: 391.8

392.9 Without mention of heart involvement   CC
CC Excl: See code: 391.9

CHRONIC RHEUMATIC HEART DISEASE (393-398)

393 Chronic rheumatic pericarditis   CC
Adherent pericardium, rheumatic
Chronic rheumatic:
    mediastinopericarditis
    myopericarditis
> **EXCLUDES**   pericarditis NOS or not specified as rheumatic (423.0-423.9)

DEF: Persistent inflammation of heart lining due to rheumatic heart disease.
CC Excl: 074.21, 093.81, 391.0, 393, 420.0-420.99, 423.3-423.9, 459.89-459.9

✓4ᵗʰ 394 Diseases of mitral valve
> **EXCLUDES**   that with aortic valve involvement (396.0-396.9)

394.0 Mitral stenosis
Mitral (valve):
    obstruction (rheumatic)
    stenosis NOS
DEF: Narrowing, of mitral valve between left atrium and left ventricle; due to rheumatic heart disease.
TIP: Assign when documentation indicates mitral valve stenosis or obstruction with no further specification of cause.

394.1 Rheumatic mitral insufficiency
Rheumatic mitral:
    incompetence
    regurgitation
> **EXCLUDES**   that not specified as rheumatic (424.0)

DEF: Malfunction of mitral valve between left atrium and left ventricle; due to rheumatic heart disease.
AHA: 2Q, '05, 14

394.2 Mitral stenosis with insufficiency
Mitral stenosis with incompetence or regurgitation
DEF: A narrowing or stricture of the mitral valve situated between the left atrium and left ventricle; valve does not completely close, is insufficient (inadequate) in preventing regurgitation into the atrium; also called incompetence.
AHA: 1Q, '07, 11

394.9 Other and unspecified mitral valve diseases
Mitral (valve):
    disease (chronic)
    failure

✓4ᵗʰ 395 Diseases of aortic valve
> **EXCLUDES**   that not specified as rheumatic (424.1)
>   that with mitral valve involvement (396.0-396.9)

395.0 Rheumatic aortic stenosis
Rheumatic aortic (valve) obstruction
DEF: Narrowing of the aortic valve; results in backflow into ventricle; due to rheumatic heart disease.
AHA: 4Q, '88, 8

395.1 Rheumatic aortic insufficiency
Rheumatic aortic:
    incompetence
    regurgitation
DEF: Malfunction of the aortic valve; results in backflow into left ventricle; due to rheumatic heart disease.

395.2 Rheumatic aortic stenosis with insufficiency
Rheumatic aortic stenosis with incompetence or regurgitation
DEF: Malfunction and narrowing, of the aortic valve; results in backflow into left ventricle; due to rheumatic heart disease.

395.9 Other and unspecified rheumatic aortic diseases
Rheumatic aortic (valve) disease

✓4ᵗʰ ✓5ᵗʰ Additional Digit Required   Unacceptable PDx   Manifestation Code   Hospital Acquired Condition   ►◄ Revised Text   ● New Code   ▲ Revised Code Title

2010 ICD-9-CM   **Volume 1 – 141**

390–395.9

Circulatory System

396–402.91

√4th **396 Diseases of mitral and aortic valves**

INCLUDES   involvement of both mitral and aortic valves, whether specified as rheumatic or not

AHA: N-D, '87, 8

396.0 Mitral valve stenosis and aortic valve stenosis
Atypical aortic (valve) stenosis
Mitral and aortic (valve) obstruction (rheumatic)

396.1 Mitral valve stenosis and aortic valve insufficiency

396.2 Mitral valve insufficiency and aortic valve stenosis
AHA: ▶2Q, '09, 17; 1Q, '09, 18;◀ 2Q, '00, 16

396.3 Mitral valve insufficiency and aortic valve insufficiency
Mitral and aortic (valve):
incompetence
regurgitation
I08.0 Rheumatic d/o of both mitral & aortic valves   I-10

396.8 Multiple involvement of mitral and aortic valves
Stenosis and insufficiency of mitral or aortic valve with stenosis or insufficiency, or both, of the other valve

396.9 Mitral and aortic valve diseases, unspecified

√4th **397 Diseases of other endocardial structures**

397.0 Diseases of tricuspid valve
Tricuspid (valve) (rheumatic):
disease
insufficiency
obstruction
regurgitation
stenosis
DEF: Malfunction of the valve between right atrium and right ventricle; due to rheumatic heart disease.
AHA: 3Q, '06, 7; 2Q, '00, 16
I07.2 Rheumatic tricuspid stenosis and insufficiency   I-10

397.1 Rheumatic diseases of pulmonary valve
EXCLUDES   that not specified as rheumatic (424.3)

397.9 Rheumatic diseases of endocardium, valve unspecified
Rheumatic: Rheumatic:
endocarditis (chronic)   valvulitis (chronic)
EXCLUDES   that not specified as rheumatic (424.90-424.99)

√4th **398 Other rheumatic heart disease**

398.0 Rheumatic myocarditis   CC
Rheumatic degeneration of myocardium
EXCLUDES   myocarditis not specified as rheumatic (429.0)
DEF: Chronic inflammation of heart muscle; due to rheumatic heart disease.
CC Excl: 390, 391.2-391.9, 398.0-398.90, 398.99, 422.0-422.99, 429.0, 429.71-429.79, 459.89-459.9

√5th **398.9 Other and unspecified rheumatic heart diseases**

398.90 Rheumatic heart disease, unspecified
Rheumatic: Rheumatic:
carditis   heart disease NOS
EXCLUDES   carditis not specified as rheumatic (429.89)
heart disease NOS not specified as rheumatic (429.9)

398.91 Rheumatic heart failure (congestive)   CC
Rheumatic left ventricular failure
DEF: Decreased cardiac output, edema and hypertension; due to rheumatic heart disease.
CC Excl: 398.90-398.99, 402.01, 402.11, 402.91, 428.0-428.9, 459.89-459.9
AHA: 2Q, '05, 14; 1Q, '95, 6; 3Q, '88, 3
I09.81 Rheumatic heart failure   I-10

[handwritten: A diagnosis of heart failure in a patient who has rheumatic heart disease is classified as rheumatic heart failure, unless the physician specifies a different cause.]

398.99 Other

HYPERTENSIVE DISEASE (401-405)

EXCLUDES   that complicating pregnancy, childbirth, or the puerperium (642.0-642.9)
that involving coronary vessels (410.00-414.9)
AHA: 3Q, '90, 3; 2Q, '89, 12; S-O, '87, 9; J-A, '84, 11

√4th **401 Essential hypertension** – *[handwritten: also known as primary hypertension, hypertensive vascular dis. and systolic hypertension]*
INCLUDES   high blood pressure
hyperpiesia
hyperpiesis
hypertension (arterial) (essential) (primary) (systemic)
hypertensive vascular:
degeneration
disease
EXCLUDES   elevated blood pressure without diagnosis of hypertension (796.2)
pulmonary hypertension (416.0-416.9)
that involving vessels of:
brain (430-438)
eye (362.11)
DEF: Hypertension that occurs without apparent organic cause; idiopathic.
AHA: 2Q, '92, 5

401.0 Malignant   CC
[handwritten: Includes hypertension described as accelerated or necrotizing]
DEF: Severe high arterial blood pressure; results in necrosis in kidney, retina, etc.; hemorrhages occur and death commonly due to uremia or rupture of cerebral vessel.
CC Excl: 401.0-405.99, 459.89-459.9
AHA: M-J, '85, 19

401.1 Benign
[handwritten: mild degree of hypertension of chronic or prolonged duration]
DEF: Mildly elevated arterial blood pressure.

401.9 Unspecified
AHA: ▶1Q, '09, 16;◀ 2Q, '08, 16; 4Q, '05, 71; 3Q, '05, 8; 4Q, '04, 78; 4Q, '03, 105, 108, 111; 3Q, '03, 14; 2Q, '03, 16; 4Q, '97, 37
I10 Essential (primary) hypertension   I-10

√4th **402 Hypertensive heart disease** – *[handwritten: Congestive Heart Failure Code 428]*
INCLUDES   hypertensive:
[handwritten: myocarditis, and degeneration of the myocardium]
cardiomegaly
cardiopathy
cardiovascular disease
heart (disease) (failure)
any condition classifiable to 429.0-429.3, 429.8, 429.9 due to hypertension
Use additional code to specify type of heart failure (428.0-428.43), if known
AHA: 4Q, '02, 49; 2Q, '93, 9; N-D, '84, 18
TIP: Assign when a cardiac condition is stated (due to hypertension) or implied (hypertensive).

√5th **402.0 Malignant**

402.00 Without heart failure   CC
CC Excl: See code: 401.0

402.01 With heart failure   CC
CC Excl: 398.91, 401.0-405.99, 428.0-428.9, 459.89-459.9
AHA: 4Q, '08, 180

√5th **402.1 Benign**

402.10 Without heart failure

402.11 With heart failure

√5th **402.9 Unspecified**

402.90 Without heart failure
I11.9 Hypertensive heart disease without heart failure   I-10

402.91 With heart failure
AHA: 4Q, '02, 52; 1Q, '93, 19; 2Q, '89, 12

| N Newborn Age: 0 | P Pediatric Age: 0-17 | M Maternity Age: 12-55 | A Adult Age: 15-124 | MCC Major CC Condition | CC CC Condition | HIV HIV Related Dx |

142 – Volume 1 • October 2009

2010 ICD-9-CM

√4ᵗʰ **403 Hypertensive chronic kidney disease**

> INCLUDES   arteriolar nephritis
> arteriosclerosis of:
>   kidney
>   renal arterioles
> arteriosclerotic nephritis (chronic) (interstitial)
> hypertensive:
>   nephropathy
>   renal failure
>   uremia (chronic)
> nephrosclerosis
> renal sclerosis with hypertension
> any condition classifiable to 585 with any condition
>   classifiable to 401
>
> EXCLUDES   *acute ▶kidney◀ failure (584.5-584.9)*
> *renal disease stated as not due to hypertension*
> *renovascular hypertension (405.0-405.9 with*
>   *fifth-digit 1)*

> The following fifth-digit subclassification is for use with category 403:
> **0 with chronic kidney disease stage I through stage IV, or unspecified**
>   Use additional code to identify the stage of chronic kidney disease (585.1-585.4, 585.9)
> **1 with chronic kidney disease stage V or end stage renal disease**
>   Use additional code to identify the stage of chronic kidney disease (585.5, 585.6)

AHA: 4Q, '06, 84-86; 4Q, '05, 68; 4Q, '92, 22; 2Q, '92, 5

TIP: Assign whenever a patient has both chronic kidney disease and hypertension (presumed cause-and-effect relationship).

§ √5ᵗʰ **403.0 Malignant**   CC
[0-1]   **CC Excl:** 401.0-405.99, 459.89-459.9

§ √5ᵗʰ **403.1 Benign**   CC 1
[0-1]   **CC Excl: For code 403.11:** See code 403.0

§ √5ᵗʰ **403.9 Unspecified**   CC 1
[0-1]   **CC Excl: For code 403.91:** 401.0-415.99, 459.89-459.9
   AHA: For code 403.90: 1Q, '08, 10; 2Q, '07, 3; 4Q, '06, 86; **For code 403.91:** 1Q, '08, 7; 4Q, '05, 69; 1Q, '04, 14; 1Q, '03, 20; 2Q, '01, 11; 3Q, '91, 8
   I12.9 HTN CKD w/stage I thru IV CKD/UNS CKD   I-10

√4ᵗʰ **404 Hypertensive heart and chronic kidney disease**

> INCLUDES   disease:
>   cardiorenal
>   cardiovascular renal
> any condition classifiable to 402 with any condition
>   classifiable to 403

Use additional code to specify type of heart failure (428.0-428.43), if known

> The following fifth-digit subclassification is for use with category 404:
> **0 without heart failure and with chronic kidney disease stage I through stage IV, or unspecified**
>   Use additional code to identify the stage of chronic kidney disease (585.1-585.4, 585.9)
> **1 with heart failure and with chronic kidney disease stage I through stage IV, or unspecified**
>   Use additional code to identify the stage of chronic kidney disease (585.1-585.4, 585.9)
> **2 without heart failure and with chronic kidney disease stage V or end stage renal disease**
>   Use additional code to identify the stage of chronic kidney disease (585.5, 585.6)
> **3 with heart failure and chronic kidney disease stage V or end stage renal disease**
>   Use additional code to identify the stage of chronic kidney disease (585.5, 585.6)

AHA: 4Q, '06, 84-86; 4Q, '05, 68; 4Q, '02, 49; 3Q, '90, 3; J-A, '84, 14

§ √5ᵗʰ **404.0 Malignant**   CC
[0-3]   **CC Excl:** 401.0-405.99, 459.89-459.9

§ √5ᵗʰ **404.1 Benign**   CC 1-3
[0-3]   **CC Excl: For codes 404.11-404.13:** 401.0-405.99, 459.89-459.9

§ √5ᵗʰ **404.9 Unspecified**   CC 1-3
[0-3]   **CC Excl: For codes 404.91-404.93:** 401.0-405.99, 459.89-459.9
   I13.0 HTN heart & CKD HF & stage I thru IV CKD/UNS CKD   I-10

√4ᵗʰ **405 Secondary hypertension**

> **DEF:** High arterial blood pressure due to or with a variety of primary diseases, such as renal disorders, CNS disorders, endocrine, and vascular diseases.
> **AHA:** 3Q, '90, 3; S-O, '87, 9, 11; J-A, '84, 14

√5ᵗʰ **405.0 Malignant**

    405.01 Renovascular   CC
       CC Excl: See code: 404.0

    405.09 Other   CC
       CC Excl: See code: 404.0

√5ᵗʰ **405.1 Benign**

    405.11 Renovascular

    405.19 Other

√5ᵗʰ **405.9 Unspecified**

    405.91 Renovascular

    405.99 Other
       AHA: 3Q, '00, 4

ISCHEMIC HEART DISEASE (410-414)

> INCLUDES   that with mention of hypertension
> Use additional code to identify presence of hypertension (401.0-405.9)
> **AHA:** 3Q, '91, 10; J-A, '84, 5

[handwritten margin notes:] AKA — Arteriosclerotic heart disease (ASHD) — Coronary ischemia — Coronary Artery Disease — Coronary Arterio sclerosis (Atherosclerosis)

√4ᵗʰ **410 Acute myocardial infarction**

> INCLUDES   cardiac infarction
> coronary (artery):
>   embolism
>   occlusion
>   rupture
>   thrombosis
> infarction of heart, myocardium, or ventricle
> rupture of heart, myocardium, or ventricle
> ST elevation (STEMI) and non-ST elevation (NSTEMI)
>   myocardial infarction
> any condition classifiable to 414.1-414.9 specified as
>   acute or with a stated duration of 8 weeks or
>   less

> The following fifth-digit subclassification is for use with category 410:
> **0 episode of care unspecified**
>   Use when the source document does not contain sufficient information for the assigment of fifth-digit 1 or 2.
> **1 initial episode of care**
>   Use fifth-digit 1 to designate the first episode of care (regardless of facility site) for a newly diagnosed myocardial infarction. The fifth-digit 1 is assigned regardless of the number of times a patient may be transferred during the initial episode of care.
> **2 subsequent episode of care**
>   Use fifth-digit 2 to designate an episode of care following the initial episode when the patient is admitted for further observation, evaluation or treatment for a myocardial infarction that has received initial treatment, but is still less than 8 weeks old.

> **DEF:** A sudden insufficiency of blood supply to an area of the heart muscle; usually due to a coronary artery occlusion.
> **AHA:** 2Q, '06, 9; 4Q, '05, 69; 3Q, '01, 21; 3Q, '98, 15; 4Q, '97, 37; 3Q, '95, 9; 4Q, 92, 24; 1Q, '92, 10; 3Q, '91, 18; 1Q, '91, 14; 3Q, '89, 3

§ √5ᵗʰ **410.0 Of anterolateral wall**   MCC 1
[0-2]   ST elevation myocardial infarction (STEMI) of anterolateral wall
   CC Excl: For code 410.01 410.00-410.92, 459.89-459.9
   AHA: For code 410.01: 4Q, '08, 72

---

§   Requires fifth digit. Valid digits are in [brackets] under each code. See appropriate category for codes and definitions.

√4ᵗʰ / √5ᵗʰ Additional Digit Required   Unacceptable PDx   Manifestation Code   Hospital Acquired Condition   ▶◀ Revised Text   ● New Code   ▲ Revised Code Title

Circulatory System

ॐ

410.1–411.89

Acute Myocardial Infarction

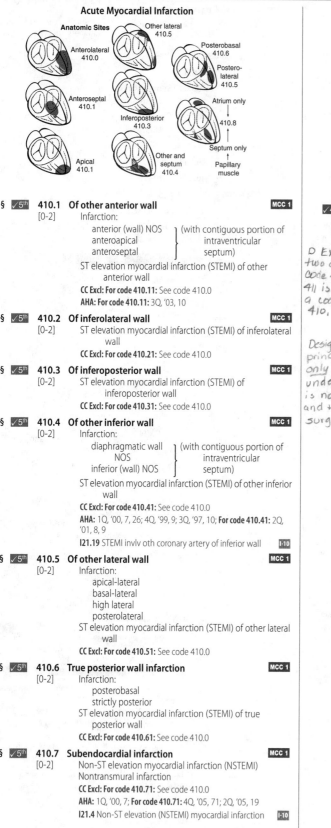

Anatomic Sites

Anterolateral 410.0

Other lateral 410.5

Posterobasal 410.6

Postero-lateral 410.5

Anteroseptal 410.1

Atrium only

410.8

Inferoposterior 410.3

Septum only

Apical 410.1

Other and septum 410.4

Papillary muscle

§ ✓5ᵗʰ **410.1 Of other anterior wall**   MCC 1
[0-2]   Infarction:
     anterior (wall) NOS } (with contiguous portion of
     anteroapical   intraventricular
     anteroseptal   septum)
   ST elevation myocardial infarction (STEMI) of other anterior wall
   CC Excl: For code 410.11: See code 410.0
   AHA: For code 410.11: 3Q, '03, 10

§ ✓5ᵗʰ **410.2 Of inferolateral wall**   MCC 1
[0-2]   ST elevation myocardial infarction (STEMI) of inferolateral wall
   CC Excl: For code 410.21: See code 410.0

§ ✓5ᵗʰ **410.3 Of inferoposterior wall**   MCC 1
[0-2]   ST elevation myocardial infarction (STEMI) of inferoposterior wall
   CC Excl: For code 410.31: See code 410.0

§ ✓5ᵗʰ **410.4 Of other inferior wall**   MCC 1
[0-2]   Infarction:
     diaphragmatic wall } (with contiguous portion of
     NOS   intraventricular
     inferior (wall) NOS   septum)
   ST elevation myocardial infarction (STEMI) of other inferior wall
   CC Excl: For code 410.41: See code 410.0
   AHA: 1Q, '00, 7, 26; 4Q, '99, 9; 3Q, '97, 10; **For code 410.41:** 2Q, '01, 8, 9
   I21.19 STEMI invlv oth coronary artery of inferior wall   I-10

§ ✓5ᵗʰ **410.5 Of other lateral wall**   MCC 1
[0-2]   Infarction:
     apical-lateral
     basal-lateral
     high lateral
     posterolateral
   ST elevation myocardial infarction (STEMI) of other lateral wall
   CC Excl: For code 410.51: See code 410.0

§ ✓5ᵗʰ **410.6 True posterior wall infarction**   MCC 1
[0-2]   Infarction:
     posterobasal
     strictly posterior
   ST elevation myocardial infarction (STEMI) of true posterior wall
   CC Excl: For code 410.61: See code 410.0

§ ✓5ᵗʰ **410.7 Subendocardial infarction**   MCC 1
[0-2]   Non-ST elevation myocardial infarction (NSTEMI)
   Nontransmural infarction
   CC Excl: For code 410.71: See code 410.0
   AHA: 1Q, '00, 7; **For code 410.71:** 4Q, '05, 71; 2Q, '05, 19
   I21.4 Non-ST elevation (NSTEMI) myocardial infarction   I-10

§ ✓5ᵗʰ **410.8 Of other specified sites**   MCC 1
[0-2]   Infarction of:
     atrium
     papillary muscle
     septum alone
   ST elevation myocardial infarction (STEMI) of other specified sites
   CC Excl: For code 410.81: See code 410.0

§ ✓5ᵗʰ **410.9 Unspecified site**   MCC 1
[0-2]   Acute myocardial infarction NOS
   Coronary occlusion NOS
   Myocardial infarction NOS
   CC Excl: For code 410.91: See code 410.0
   AHA: 1Q, '96, 17; 1Q, '92, 9; **For code 410.91:** 2Q, '05, 18; 3Q, '02, 5
   I21.3 ST elevation myocardial infarction of uns site   I-10

✓4ᵗʰ **411 Other acute and subacute forms of ischemic heart disease**
   AHA: 4Q, '94, 55; 3Q, '91, 24

411.0 Postmyocardial infarction syndrome   CC
   Dressler's syndrome
   DEF: Complication developing several days/weeks after myocardial infarction; symptoms include fever, leukocytosis, chest pain, pericarditis, pleurisy, and pneumonitis; tendency to recur.
   CC Excl: 411.0, 411.81-411.89, 459.89-459.9

411.1 Intermediate coronary syndrome   CC
   Impending infarction
   Preinfarction angina
   Preinfarction syndrome
   Unstable angina
   EXCLUDES   angina (pectoris) (413.9)
                decubitus (413.0)
   DEF: A condition representing an intermediate stage between angina of effort and acute myocardial infarction. It is often documented by the physician as "unstable angina."
   CC Excl: 398.91, 402.01, 402.11, 402.91, 404.01, 404.03, 404.11, 404.13, 404.91, 404.93, 410.00-410.92, 411.1-411.89, 413.0-414.00, 414.2-414.9, 428.0-428.1, 428.9, 459.89-459.9, 785.50-785.51
   AHA: 3Q, '07, 9; 4Q, '05, 105; 2Q, '04, 3; 1Q, '03, 12; 3Q, '01, 15; 2Q, '01, 7, 9; 4Q, '98, 86; 2Q, '96, 10; 3Q, '91, 24; 1Q, '91, 14; 3Q, '90, 6; 4Q, '89, 10
   TIP: Do not assign code 411.1 on the same episode of care as an acute myocardial infarction (category 410). Assign 411.1 for accelerated angina.
   I20.0 Unstable angina   I-10

✓5ᵗʰ **411.8 Other**
   AHA: 3Q, '91, 18; 3Q, '89, 4

411.81 Acute coronary occlusion without myocardial infarction   CC
   Acute coronary (artery):
     embolism } without or not
     obstruction   resulting in
     occlusion   myocardial
     thrombosis   infarction
   EXCLUDES   obstruction without infarction due to atherosclerosis (414.00-414.07)
                occlusion without infarction due to atherosclerosis (414.00-414.07)
   DEF: Interrupted blood flow to a portion of the heart; without tissue death.
   CC Excl: 410.00-411.89, 413.0-413.9, 414.8-414.9, 459.89-459.9
   AHA: 3Q, '91, 24; 1Q, '91, 14

411.89 Other   CC
   Coronary insufficiency (acute)
   Subendocardial ischemia
   CC Excl: See code: 411.81
   AHA: 3Q, '01, 14; 1Q, '92, 9

(handwritten note) D Except for these two conditions, no code from category 411 is assigned with a code from category 410.

(handwritten note) Designated as the principal diagnosis only when the underlying condition is not identified and there is no surgical intervention.

§   Requires fifth digit. Valid digits are in [brackets] under each code. See category 410 for codes and definitions.

N Newborn Age: 0   P Pediatric Age: 0-17   M Maternity Age: 12-55   A Adult Age: 15-124   MCC Major CC Condition   CC CC Condition   HIV HIV Related Dx

144 – Volume 1   **2010 ICD-9-CM**

[handwritten margin note: will not be assigned on current ischemic heart disease is present assigned as an additional code if as some significance the current episode of care.]

412 Old myocardial infarction
Healed myocardial infarction
Past myocardial infarction diagnosed on ECG [EKG] or other special investigation, but currently presenting no symptoms
AHA: 2Q, '03, 10; 2Q, '01, 9; 3Q, '98, 15; 2Q, '91, 22; 3Q, '90, 7
TIP: Assign for any acute myocardial infarction stated to be older than 8 weeks.
125.2 Old myocardial infarction   `I-10`

✓4th 413 Angina pectoris
DEF: Severe constricting pain in the chest, often radiating from the precordium to the left shoulder and down the arm, due to ischemia of the heart muscle; usually caused by coronary disease; pain is often precipitated by effort or excitement.

413.0 Angina decubitus   `CC`
Nocturnal angina
DEF: Angina occurring only in the recumbent position.
CC Excl: 410.00-410.92, 411.1-411.89, 413.0-413.9, 414.8-414.9, 459.89-459.9

413.1 Prinzmetal angina   `CC`
Variant angina pectoris
DEF: Angina occurring when patient is recumbent; associated with ST-segment elevations.
CC Excl: See code: 413.0
AHA: 3Q, '06, 23

413.9 Other and unspecified angina pectoris
Angina: Anginal syndrome
   NOS   Status anginosus
   cardiac   Stenocardia
   ▶equivalent◀   Syncope anginosa
   of effort
▶Use additional code(s) for symptoms associated with angina equivalent◀
   EXCLUDES   preinfarction angina (411.1)
AHA: 2Q, '08, 16; 3Q, '02, 4; 3Q, '91, 16; 3Q, '90, 6
TIP: For patients with both angina and coronary artery disease, sequence the CAD (subcategory 414.0) code first.
120.9 Angina pectoris unspecified   `I-10`

✓4th 414 Other forms of chronic ischemic heart disease
   EXCLUDES   arteriosclerotic cardiovascular disease [ASCVD] (429.2)
     cardiovascular:
       arteriosclerosis or sclerosis (429.2)
       degeneration or disease (429.2)

[handwritten margin note: includes atherosclerosis, chronic coronary insufficiency, myocardial ischemia, and aneurysm.]

✓5th 414.0 Coronary atherosclerosis
Arteriosclerotic heart disease [ASHD]
Atherosclerotic heart disease
Coronary (artery):
   arteriosclerosis
   arteritis or endarteritis
   atheroma
   sclerosis
   stricture
Use additional code, if applicable, to identify chronic total occlusion of coronary artery (414.2)
   EXCLUDES   embolism of graft (996.72)
     occlusion NOS of graft (996.72)
     thrombus of graft (996.72)
DEF: A chronic condition marked by thickening and loss of elasticity of the coronary artery; caused by deposits of plaque containing cholesterol, lipoid material and lipophages.
AHA: 2Q, '97, 13; 2Q, '95, 17; 4Q, '94, 49; 2Q, '94, 13; 1Q, '94, 6; 3Q, '90, 7

414.00 Of unspecified type of vessel, native or graft   `A`
AHA: 1Q, '04, 24; 2Q, '03, 16; 3Q, '01, 15; 4Q, '99, 4; 3Q, '97, 15; 4Q, '96, 31

414.01 Of native coronary artery   `A`
DEF: Plaque deposits in natural heart vessels.
AHA: 3Q, '08, 10; 2Q, '08, 16; 3Q, '06, 25; 4Q, '05, 71; 2Q, '04, 3; 4Q, '03, 108; 3Q, '03, 9, 14; 3Q, '02, 4-9; 3Q, '01, 15; 2Q, '01, 8, 9; 3Q, '97, 15; 2Q, '96, 10; 4Q, '96, 31
TIP: Assign for documentation of CAD NOS in a patient with no history of coronary artery bypass procedure.
125.10 ASHD of native cor artery w/o angina pectoris   `I-10`

✳ 414.02 Of autologous vein bypass graft   `CC` `A`
DEF: Plaque deposit in grafted vein originating within patient.
CC Excl: 414.00-414.05, 414.07, 414.2-414.3

✳ 414.03 Of nonautologous biological bypass graft   `CC` `A`
DEF: Plaque deposits in grafted vessel originating outside patient.
CC Excl: See code: 414.02

[handwritten margin note: ✳ A history of previous bypass, when information indicating the material used in the bypass is available.]

✳ 414.04 Of artery bypass graft   `CC` `A`
Internal mammary artery
DEF: Plaque deposits in grafted artery originating within patient.
CC Excl: See code: 414.02
AHA: 4Q, '96, 31

414.05 Of unspecified type of bypass graft   `A`
Bypass graft NOS
AHA: 3Q, '97, 15; 4Q, '96, 31

414.06 Of native coronary artery of transplanted heart   `CC`
CC Excl: 414.00-414.07, 414.2-414.3
AHA: 4Q, '03, 60; 4Q, '02, 53

414.07 Of bypass graft (artery) (vein) of transplanted heart   `CC` `A`
CC Excl: 414.00-414.06, 414.2-414.3

✓5th 414.1 Aneurysm and dissection of heart
AHA: 4Q, '02, 54

414.10 Aneurysm of heart (wall)   `CC`
Aneurysm (arteriovenous):
   mural
   ventricular
CC Excl: 414.10-414.11, 414.19

414.11 Aneurysm of coronary vessels
Aneurysm (arteriovenous) of coronary vessels
DEF: Dilatation of all three-vessel wall layers forming a sac filled with blood.
AHA: 3Q, '03, 10; 1Q, '99, 17

414.12 Dissection of coronary artery   `MCC`
DEF: A tear in the intimal arterial wall of a coronary artery resulting in the sudden intrusion of blood within the layers of the wall.
CC Excl: 414.12, 443.29, 447.2, 447.5-447.9

414.19 Other aneurysm of heart   `CC`
Arteriovenous fistula, acquired, of heart
CC Excl: See code: 414.10

Arteries of the Heart

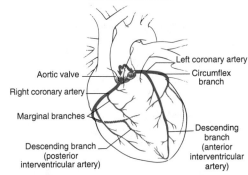

Aortic valve
Right coronary artery
Marginal branches
Descending branch (posterior interventricular artery)
Left coronary artery
Circumflex branch
Descending branch (anterior interventricular artery)

`✓4th` Additional Digit Required   Unacceptable PDx   Manifestation Code   Hospital Acquired Condition   ▶◀ Revised Text   ● New Code   ▲ Revised Code Title
`✓5th`

2010 ICD-9-CM   **October 2009 • Volume 1 – 145**

Circulatory System

414.2–420.0

414.2 Chronic total occlusion of coronary artery
Complete occlusion of coronary artery
Total occlusion of coronary artery
Code first coronary atherosclerosis (414.00-414.07)
EXCLUDES *acute coronary occlusion with myocardial infarction (410.00-410.92)*
acute coronary occlusion without myocardial infarction (411.81)
DEF: Complete blockage of coronary artery due to plaque accumulation over an extended period of time; results in substantial reduction of blood flow.
AHA: 4Q, '07, 82

414.3 Coronary atherosclerosis due to lipid rich plaque A
Code first coronary atherosclerosis (414.00-414.07)
AHA: 4Q, '08, 113

414.8 Other specified forms of chronic ischemic heart disease
Chronic coronary insufficiency
Ischemia, myocardial (chronic)
Any condition classifiable to 410 specified as chronic, or presenting with symptoms after 8 weeks from date of infarction
EXCLUDES *coronary insufficiency (acute) (411.89)*
AHA: 3Q, '01, 15; 1Q, '92, 10; 3Q, '90, 7, 15; 2Q, '90, 19
I25.89 Other forms of chronic ischemic heart disease I-10

414.9 Chronic ischemic heart disease, unspecified
Ischemic heart disease NOS

DISEASES OF PULMONARY CIRCULATION (415-417)

√4ᵗʰ **415 Acute pulmonary heart disease**

415.0 Acute cor pulmonale MCC
EXCLUDES *cor pulmonale NOS (416.9)*
DEF: A heart-lung disease marked by dilation and failure of the right side of heart; due to pulmonary embolism; ventilatory function is impaired and pulmonary hypertension results.
CC Excl: 415.0, 416.8-416.9, 459.89-459.9

√5ᵗʰ **415.1 Pulmonary embolism and infarction**
Acute Pulmonary embolism [handwritten annotation]
Pulmonary (artery) (vein):   Pulmonary (artery) (vein):
  apoplexy   infarction (hemorrhagic)
  embolism   thrombosis
EXCLUDES ▶ *chronic pulmonary embolism (416.2)*
personal history of pulmonary embolism (V12.51) ◀
that complicating:
abortion (634-638 with .6, 639.6)
ectopic or molar pregnancy (639.6)
pregnancy, childbirth, or the puerperium (673.0-673.8)
DEF: Embolism: Closure of the pulmonary artery or branch; due to thrombosis (blood clot).
DEF: Infarction: Necrosis of lung tissue; due to obstructed arterial blood supply, most often by pulmonary embolism.
AHA: 4Q, '90, 25

415.11 Iatrogenic pulmonary embolism and infarction MCC
Use additional code for associated septic pulmonary embolism, if applicable, 415.12
CC Excl: 415.11-415.19, 416.2, 459.89-459.9
AHA: 4Q, '95, 58
TIP: Do not assign additional code of 997.39 Other respiratory complications, with code 415.11.

415.12 Septic pulmonary embolism MCC
Septic embolism NOS
Code first underlying infection, such as:
septicemia (038.0-038.9)
EXCLUDES *septic arterial embolism (449)*
CC Excl: See code: 415.11
AHA: 4Q, '07, 84-86

415.19 Other MCC
CC Excl: See code: 415.11
I26.99 Other pulmonary embolism w/o acute cor pulmonale I-10

√4ᵗʰ **416 Chronic pulmonary heart disease**

416.0 Primary pulmonary hypertension CC
Idiopathic pulmonary arteriosclerosis
Pulmonary hypertension (essential) (idiopathic) (primary)
DEF: A rare increase in pulmonary circulation, often resulting in right ventricular failure or fatal syncope.
CC Excl: 416.0, 416.8-416.9, 417.8-417.9, 459.89-459.9
I27.0 Primary pulmonary hypertension I-10

416.1 Kyphoscoliotic heart disease CC
DEF: High blood pressure within the lungs as a result of curvature of the spine.
CC Excl: 416.0-416.1, 416.8-416.9

● **416.2 Chronic pulmonary embolism** CC
or recurrent ← [handwritten annotation]
Use additional code, if applicable, for associated long-term (current) use of anticoagulants (V58.61)
EXCLUDES *personal history of pulmonary embolism (V12.51)*
CC Excl: 415.11-415.19, 416.2, 459.89-459.9

416.8 Other chronic pulmonary heart diseases
Pulmonary hypertension, secondary
I27.89 Other specified pulmonary heart diseases I-10

416.9 Chronic pulmonary heart disease, unspecified
Chronic cardiopulmonary disease
Cor pulmonale (chronic) NOS

√4ᵗʰ **417 Other diseases of pulmonary circulation**

417.0 Arteriovenous fistula of pulmonary vessels CC
EXCLUDES *congenital arteriovenous fistula (747.3)*
DEF: Abnormal communication between blood vessels within lung.
CC Excl: 417.0-417.9

417.1 Aneurysm of pulmonary artery CC
EXCLUDES *congenital aneurysm (747.3)*
CC Excl: See code: 417.0

417.8 Other specified diseases of pulmonary circulation
Pulmonary:
arteritis
endarteritis
Rupture } of pulmonary vessel
Stricture

417.9 Unspecified disease of pulmonary circulation

OTHER FORMS OF HEART DISEASE (420-429)

√4ᵗʰ **420 Acute pericarditis**
INCLUDES acute:
mediastinopericarditis
myopericarditis
pericardial effusion
pleuropericarditis
pneumopericarditis
EXCLUDES *acute rheumatic pericarditis (391.0)*
postmyocardial infarction syndrome [Dressler's] (411.0)
DEF: Inflammation of the pericardium (heart sac); pericardial friction rub results from this inflammation and is heard as a scratchy or leathery sound.

420.0 Acute pericarditis in diseases classified elsewhere CC
Code first underlying disease, as:
actinomycosis (039.8)
amebiasis (006.8)
chronic uremia (585.9)
nocardiosis (039.8)
tuberculosis (017.9)
uremia NOS (586)
EXCLUDES *pericarditis (acute) (in):*
Coxsackie (virus) (074.21)
gonococcal (098.83)
histoplasmosis (115.0-115.9 with fifth-digit 3)
meningococcal infection (036.41)
syphilitic (093.81)
CC Excl: 391.0, 393, 420.0-420.99, 423.3-423.9, 459.89-459.9

N Newborn Age: 0   P Pediatric Age: 0-17   M Maternity Age: 12-55   A Adult Age: 15-124   MCC Major CC Condition   CC CC Condition   HIV HIV Related Dx

146 – Volume 1 • October 2009   2010 ICD-9-CM

√5th **420.9** **Other and unspecified acute pericarditis**

420.90 **Acute pericarditis, unspecified** `CC`
Pericarditis (acute):
NOS
infective NOS
sicca
CC Excl: See code: 420.0
AHA: 2Q, '89, 12

420.91 **Acute idiopathic pericarditis** `CC`
Pericarditis, acute:
benign
nonspecific
viral
CC Excl: See code: 420.0

420.99 **Other** `CC`
Pericarditis (acute):
pneumococcal
purulent
staphylococcal
streptococcal
suppurative
Pneumopyopericardium
Pyopericardium
EXCLUDES *pericarditis in diseases classified elsewhere (420.0)*
CC Excl: See code: 420.0

√4th **421** **Acute and subacute endocarditis**
DEF: Bacterial inflammation of the endocardium (intracardiac area); major symptoms include fever, fatigue, heart murmurs, splenomegaly, embolic episodes and areas of infarction.

421.0 **Acute and subacute bacterial endocarditis** `MCC` `HIV`
Endocarditis (acute)(chronic) (subacute):
bacterial
infective NOS
lenta
malignant
purulent
septic
ulcerative
vegetative
Infective aneurysm
Subacute bacterial endocarditis [SBE]
Use additional code to identify infectious organism [e.g., Streptococcus 041.0, Staphylococcus 041.1]
CC Excl: 391.1, 397.9, 421.0-421.9, 424.90-424.99, 459.89-459.9
AHA: ▶4Q, '08, 73;◀ 1Q, '99, 12; 1Q, '91, 15
I33.0 Acute and subacute infective endocarditis `I-10`

421.1 *Acute and subacute infective endocarditis in diseases classified elsewhere* `MCC`
Code first underlying disease, as:
blastomycosis (116.0)
Q fever (083.0)
typhoid (fever) (002.0)
EXCLUDES *endocarditis (in):*
Coxsackie (virus) (074.22)
gonococcal (098.84)
histoplasmosis (115.0-115.9 with fifth-digit 4)
meningococcal infection (036.42)
monilial (112.81)
CC Excl: See code: 421.0

421.9 **Acute endocarditis, unspecified** `MCC` `HIV`
Endocarditis
Myoendocarditis } acute or subacute
Periendocarditis
EXCLUDES *acute rheumatic endocarditis (391.1)*
CC Excl: See code: 421.0

Anatomy

Blood Flow

√4th **422** **Acute myocarditis**
EXCLUDES *acute rheumatic myocarditis (391.2)*
DEF: Acute inflammation of the muscular walls of the heart (myocardium).

422.0 *Acute myocarditis in diseases classified elsewhere* `MCC`
Code first underlying disease, as:
myocarditis (acute):
influenzal (487.8)
tuberculous (017.9)
EXCLUDES *myocarditis (acute) (due to):*
aseptic, of newborn (074.23)
Coxsackie (virus) (074.23)
diphtheritic (032.82)
meningococcal infection (036.43)
syphilitic (093.82)
toxoplasmosis (130.3)
CC Excl: 391.2, 398.0, 422.0-422.99, 429.0, 429.71-429.79, 459.89-459.9

√5th **422.9** **Other and unspecified acute myocarditis**

422.90 **Acute myocarditis, unspecified** `MCC` `HIV`
Acute or subacute (interstitial) myocarditis
CC Excl: See code: 422.0

422.91 **Idiopathic myocarditis** `MCC` `HIV`
Myocarditis (acute or subacute):
Fiedler's
giant cell
isolated (diffuse) (granulomatous)
nonspecific granulomatous
CC Excl: See code: 422.0

422.92 **Septic myocarditis** `MCC` `HIV`
Myocarditis, acute or subacute:
pneumococcal
staphylococcal
Use additional code to identify infectious organism [e.g., Staphylococcus 041.1]
EXCLUDES *myocarditis, acute or subacute:*
in bacterial diseases classified elsewhere (422.0)
streptococcal (391.2)
CC Excl: See code 422.0

422.93 Toxic myocarditis `MCC` `HIV`
DEF: Inflammation of the heart muscle due to an adverse reaction to certain drugs or chemicals reaching the heart through the bloodstream.
CC Excl: See code: 422.0

422.99 Other `MCC` `HIV`
CC Excl: See code: 422.0

`✓4th` **423 Other diseases of pericardium**
EXCLUDES that specified as rheumatic (393)

423.0 Hemopericardium `CC`
DEF: Blood in the pericardial sac (pericardium).
CC Excl: 423.0-423.9, 459.89-459.9

423.1 Adhesive pericarditis `CC`
Adherent pericardium
Fibrosis of pericardium
Milk spots
Pericarditis:
adhesive
obliterative
Soldiers' patches
DEF: Two layers of serous pericardium adhere to each other by fibrous adhesions.
CC Excl: See code: 423.0

423.2 Constrictive pericarditis `CC`
Concato's disease
Pick's disease of heart (and liver)
DEF: Inflammation identified by a rigid, thickened and sometimes calcified pericardium; ventricles of the heart not adequately filled; congestive heart failure may result.
CC Excl: See code: 423.0

423.3 Cardiac tamponade (AKA Pericardial Tamponade) `CC`
Code first the underlying cause
DEF: Life-threatening condition in which fluid or blood accumulates between the muscle of the heart (myocardium) and the outer sac (pericardium), resulting in compression of the heart, which decreases cardiac output.
CC Excl: 074.21, 093.81, 391.0, 393, 420.0-420.99, 423.3-423.9, 459.89-459.9
AHA: 4Q, '07, 86, 87

423.8 Other specified diseases of pericardium `CC`
Calcification
Fistula } of pericardium
CC Excl: See code: 423.3
AHA: 2Q, '89, 12

423.9 Unspecified disease of pericardium `CC`
CC Excl: See code: 423.3
AHA: 1Q, '07, 11

Cardiac Tamponade

Normal   Cardiac Tamponade

Serous pericardium (visceral layer)
Excessive fluid in pericardial space
Fibrous pericardium
Pericardial space (potential)
Serous pericardium (parietal layer)
constricted areas

`✓4th` **424 Other diseases of endocardium**
EXCLUDES bacterial endocarditis (421.0-421.9)
rheumatic endocarditis (391.1, 394.0-397.9)
syphilitic endocarditis (093.20-093.24)

424.0 Mitral valve disorders
Mitral (valve):
incompetence
insufficiency } NOS of specified cause, except rheumatic
regurgitation
EXCLUDES mitral (valve):
disease (394.9)
failure (394.9)
stenosis (394.0)
the listed conditions:
specified as rheumatic (394.1)
unspecified as to cause but with mention of:
diseases of aortic valve (396.0-396.9)
mitral stenosis or obstruction (394.2)
AHA: 3Q, '06, 7; 2Q, '00, 16; 3Q, '98, 11; N-D, '87, 8; N-D, '84, 8
I34.8 Other nonrheumatic mitral valve disorders `I-10`

424.1 Aortic valve disorders
Aortic (valve):
incompetence
insufficiency } NOS of specified cause, except rheumatic
regurgitation
stenosis
EXCLUDES hypertrophic subaortic stenosis (425.1)
that specified as rheumatic (395.0-395.9)
that of unspecified cause but with mention of diseases of mitral valve (396.0-396.9)
AHA: ▶4Q, '08, 179;◀ 4Q, '88, 8; N-D, '87, 8

424.2 Tricuspid valve disorders, specified as nonrheumatic
Tricuspid valve:
incompetence
insufficiency } of specified cause, except rheumatic
regurgitation
stenosis
EXCLUDES rheumatic or of unspecified cause (397.0)

Heart Valve Disorders

Incompetent valve (trouble closing)
causes regurgitation (backflow of blood)
Valve stenosis (trouble opening)
Insufficient valve (unable to close completely)
Shortened, fused chorda tendinae
Ventricular hypertrophy

Normal Heart Valve Function

Atrium contracts
Valve leaflet (cusp)
Chorda tendinae
Papillary muscle
Great artery (aorta or pulmonary artery)
Ventricle fills
Great vein (vena cava or pulmonary vein)
Atrium fills
Ventricle contracts
Great artery (blood to body or lungs)

`N` Newborn Age: 0   `P` Pediatric Age: 0-17   `M` Maternity Age: 12-55   `A` Adult Age: 15-124   `MCC` Major CC Condition   `CC` CC Condition   `HIV` HIV Related Dx

148 – Volume 1 • February 2009   2010 ICD-9-CM

424.3 Pulmonary valve disorders
Pulmonic:
incompetence NOS
insufficiency NOS
regurgitation NOS
stenosis NOS
EXCLUDES that specified as rheumatic (397.1)

√5th **424.9 Endocarditis, valve unspecified**

424.90 Endocarditis, valve unspecified, unspecified cause `CC`
Endocarditis (chronic):
NOS
nonbacterial thrombotic
Valvular:
incompetence
insufficiency } of unspecified valve,
regurgitation } unspecified cause
stenosis
Valvulitis (chronic)
CC Excl: 424.90-424.99, 459.89-459.9
I38 Endocarditis valve unspecified `I-10`

424.91 Endocarditis in diseases classified elsewhere `CC`
Code first underlying disease as:
atypical verrucous endocarditis [Libman-Sacks] (710.0)
disseminated lupus erythematosus (710.0)
tuberculosis (017.9)
EXCLUDES syphilitic (093.20-093.24)
CC Excl: See code: 424.90

424.99 Other `CC`
Any condition classifiable to 424.90 with specified cause, except rheumatic
EXCLUDES endocardial fibroelastosis (425.3)
that specified as rheumatic (397.9)
CC Excl: See code: 424.90

√4th **425 Cardiomyopathy** – clinical picture of a dialated heart, flabby heart muscles, and normal coronary arteries.
INCLUDES myocardiopathy
AHA: J-A, '85, 15

ssociated /CHF...if ɔ, the heart ailure (428.0 – 28.43) is designated ɔ the principal agnosis, ᵗʰ an dditional de for the ardiomyopathy.

425.0 Endomyocardial fibrosis `CC`
CC Excl: 398.91, 402.01, 402.11, 402.91, 404.01, 404.03, 404.11, 404.13, 404.91, 404.93, 414.00-414.07, 414.2-414.9, 425.0-425.9, 426.10-426.13, 426.50-426.54, 426.81-426.89, 427.31-427.42, 427.60-427.89, 428.0-428.1, 428.9, 459.89-459.9, 746.86, 785.0-785.1, 785.50-785.51

425.1 Hypertrophic obstructive cardiomyopathy `CC`
Hypertrophic subaortic stenosis (idiopathic)
DEF: Cardiomyopathy marked by left ventricle hypertrophy, enlarged septum; results in obstructed blood flow.
CC Excl: See code: 425.0

425.2 Obscure cardiomyopathy of Africa `CC`
Becker's disease
Idiopathic mural endomyocardial disease
CC Excl: See code: 425.0

425.3 Endocardial fibroelastosis `CC`
Elastomyofibrosis
DEF: A condition marked by left ventricle hypertrophy and conversion of the endocardium into a thick fibroelastic coat; capacity of the ventricle may be reduced, but is often increased.
CC Excl: See code: 425.0

425.4 Other primary cardiomyopathies `CC`
Cardiomyopathy: Cardiomyopathy:
NOS idiopathic
congestive nonobstructive
constrictive obstructive
familial restrictive
hypertrophic Cardiovascular collagenosis
CC Excl: See code: 425.0
AHA: 1Q, '07, 20; 2Q, '05, 14; 1Q, '00, 22; 4Q, '97, 55; 2Q, '90, 19
TIP: For congestive cardiomyopathy, assign first a code for the CHF (category 428) if the treatment is directed toward the CHF.
I42.8 Other cardiomyopathies `I-10`

425.5 Alcoholic cardiomyopathy `CC`
DEF: Heart disease as result of excess alcohol consumption.
CC Excl: See code: 425.0
AHA: S-O, '85, 15

425.7 Nutritional and metabolic cardiomyopathy `CC`
Code first underlying disease, as:
amyloidosis (277.30-277.39)
beriberi (265.0)
cardiac glycogenosis (271.0)
mucopolysaccharidosis (277.5)
thyrotoxicosis (242.0-242.9)
EXCLUDES gouty tophi of heart (274.82)
CC Excl: See code 425.0

425.8 Cardiomyopathy in other diseases classified elsewhere `CC`
Code first underlying disease, as:
Friedreich's ataxia (334.0)
myotonia atrophica (359.21)
progressive muscular dystrophy (359.1)
sarcoidosis (135)
EXCLUDES cardiomyopathy in Chagas' disease (086.0)
CC Excl: See code 425.0
AHA: 2Q, '93, 9
I43 Cardiomyopathy in diseases classified elsewhere `I-10`

425.9 Secondary cardiomyopathy, unspecified `CC`
CC Excl: See code 425.0

√4th **426 Conduction disorders**
DEF: Disruption or disturbance in the electrical impulses that regulate heartbeats.

426.0 Atrioventricular block, complete `CC`
Third degree atrioventricular block
CC Excl: 426.0-427.5, 427.89, 459.89-459.9
AHA: 2Q, '06, 14
TIP: Assign if documentation indicates intermittent complete heart block.

√5th **426.1 Atrioventricular block, other and unspecified**
TIP: Assign separate codes for each type of AV block documented.

426.10 Atrioventricular block, unspecified
Atrioventricular [AV] block (incomplete) (partial)
AHA: 2Q, '06, 14

Nerve Conduction of the Heart

Sinoatrial node (pacemaker)
Bachmann's bundle
Internodal tracts:
Anterior
Middle
Posterior
Left bundle branch block
Atrioventricular node
Left bundle branch:
Anterior fascicle
Posterior fascicle
Common bundle (of His)
Atrioventricular block
Accessory bundle (of Kent)
Left bundle branch hemiblock
Right bundle branch
Right bundle branch block
Moderator band
Purkinje fibers

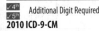

Circulatory System

426.11 First degree atrioventricular block
Incomplete atrioventricular block, first degree
Prolonged P-R interval NOS

I44.0 Atrioventricular block first degree   `I-10`

426.12 Mobitz (type) II atrioventricular   `CC`
block
Incomplete atrioventricular block:
Mobitz (type) II
second degree, Mobitz (type) II
DEF: Impaired conduction of excitatory impulse
from cardiac atrium to ventricle through AV node.
CC Excl: See code: 426.0

426.13 Other second degree atrioventricular block
Incomplete atrioventricular block:
Mobitz (type) I [Wenckebach's]
second degree:
NOS
Mobitz (type) I
with 2:1 atrioventricular response [block]
Wenckebach's phenomenon
DEF: Wenckebach's phenomenon: impulses
generated at constant rate to sinus node, P-R
interval lengthens; results in cycle of ventricular
inadequacy and shortened P-R interval;
second-degree A-V block commonly called "Mobitz
type 1."

426.2 Left bundle branch hemiblock
Block:
left anterior fascicular
left posterior fascicular

426.3 Other left bundle branch block
Left bundle branch block:
NOS
anterior fascicular with posterior fascicular
complete
main stem

I44.7 Left bundle-branch block unspecified   `I-10`

426.4 Right bundle branch block
AHA: 3Q, '00, 3

I45.10 Unspecified right bundle-branch block   `I-10`

`√5ᵗʰ` **426.5 Bundle branch block, other and unspecified**

426.50 Bundle branch block, unspecified

426.51 Right bundle branch block and left posterior
fascicular block

426.52 Right bundle branch block and left anterior
fascicular block

426.53 Other bilateral bundle branch block   `CC`
Bifascicular block NOS
Bilateral bundle branch block NOS
Right bundle branch with left bundle branch
block (incomplete) (main stem)
CC Excl: 426.0-427.5, 427.89, 459.89-459.9

426.54 Trifascicular block   `CC`
CC Excl: 426.0-427.5, 427.89, 459.89-459.9

Normal and Long QT Electrocardiogram

426.6 Other heart block
Intraventricular block: Sinoatrial block
NOS   Sinoauricular block
diffuse
myofibrillar

426.7 Anomalous atrioventricular excitation
Atrioventricular conduction:
accelerated
accessory
pre-excitation
Ventricular pre-excitation
Wolff-Parkinson-White syndrome
DEF: Wolff-Parkinson-White: normal conduction pathway is
bypassed; results in short P-R interval on EKG; tendency to
supraventricular tachycardia.

`√5ᵗʰ` **426.8 Other specified conduction disorders**

426.81 Lown-Ganong-Levine syndrome
Syndrome of short P-R interval, normal QRS
complexes, and supraventricular
tachycardias

426.82 Long QT syndrome
DEF: Condition characterized by recurrent syncope,
malignant arrhythmias, and sudden death;
characteristic prolonged Q-T interval on
electrocardiogram.
AHA: 4Q, '05, 72

426.89 Other   `CC`
Dissociation:
atrioventricular [AV]
interference
isorhythmic
Nonparoxysmal AV nodal tachycardia
CC Excl: 426.0-426.5, 427.89, 459.89-459.9

426.9 Conduction disorder, unspecified
Heart block NOS
Stokes-Adams syndrome

`√4ᵗʰ` **427 Cardiac dysrhythmias**
`EXCLUDES`   *that complicating:*
abortion (634-638 with .7, 639.8)
ectopic or molar pregnancy (639.8)
labor or delivery (668.1, 669.4)
DEF: Disruption or disturbance in the rhythm of heartbeats.
AHA: J-A, '85, 15

427.0 Paroxysmal supraventricular tachycardia   `CC`
Paroxysmal tachycardia: Paroxysmal tachycardia:
atrial [PAT]   junctional
atrioventricular [AV]   nodal
DEF: Rapid atrial rhythm.
CC Excl: See code: 426.89

427.1 Paroxysmal ventricular tachycardia   `CC`
Ventricular tachycardia (paroxysmal)
DEF: Rapid ventricular rhythm.
CC Excl: See code: 426.89
AHA: ▶2Q, '09, 14;◀1Q, '08, 14; 2Q, '06, 15-16; 3Q, '95, 9;
M-A, '86, 11
TIP: If a ventricular tachycardia is documented as sustained or
nonsustained but is induced during an EP study, assign 427.1.

I47.2 Ventricular tachycardia   `I-10`

427.2 Paroxysmal tachycardia, unspecified
Bouveret-Hoffmann syndrome
Paroxysmal tachycardia:
essential
NOS

`√5ᵗʰ` **427.3 Atrial fibrillation and flutter**
TIP: Assign V58.61 Long-term (current) use of anticoagulants,
as a secondary diagnosis if the patient is maintained on Coumadin.

427.31 Atrial fibrillation
DEF: Irregular, rapid atrial contractions.
AHA: 4Q, '08, 135; 3Q, '05, 8; 4Q, '04, 78, 121; 3Q, '04,
7; 4Q, '03, 95, 105; 1Q, '03, 8; 2Q, '99, 17; 3Q '95, 8

I48.0 Atrial fibrillation   `I-10`

`N` Newborn Age: 0   `P` Pediatric Age: 0-17   `M` Maternity Age: 12-55   `A` Adult Age: 15-124   `MCC` Major CC Condition   `CC` CC Condition   `HIV` HIV Related Dx

(handwritten note at top) ICD-9 presumes a disorder affecting the mitral and aortic valves is rheumatic in origin. A diagnosis of heart failure in a patient who has rheumatic heart disease is classified as 398.91 (rheumatic heart failure) unless the physician specifies a different cause.

427.32 Atrial flutter [CC]
DEF: Regular, rapid atrial contractions.
CC Excl: See code: 426.89
AHA: 4Q, '03, 94
148.1 Atrial flutter [I-10]

✓5ᵗʰ 427.4 Ventricular fibrillation and flutter

¹ 427.41 Ventricular fibrillation [MCC]
DEF: Irregular, rapid ventricular contractions.
CC Excl: See code: 426.89
AHA: ▶2Q, '09, 14-15;◀3Q, '02, 5

427.42 Ventricular flutter [MCC]
DEF: Regular, rapid ventricular contractions.
CC Excl: See code: 426.89

¹ 427.5 Cardiac arrest [MCC]
Cardiorespiratory arrest
CC Excl: 427.0-427.5, 459.89-459.9
AHA: 3Q, '02, 5; 2Q, '00, 12; 3Q, '95, 8; 2Q, '88, 8
146.9 Cardiac arrest cause unspecified [I-10]

(handwritten note in left margin) – Do not code when the patient is not resuscitated (patient dies)

(handwritten note in left margin) ...signed as principal ...ly when patient ...ives in State of ...rdiac arrest and ...nnot be ...suscitated ... is resuscitated ...fly – and ...onounced dead – ...fore the ...derlying cause ... the arrest ... identified.

✓5ᵗʰ 427.6 Premature beats

427.60 Premature beats, unspecified
Ectopic beats
Extrasystoles
Extrasystolic arrhythmia
Premature contractions or systoles NOS

427.61 Supraventricular premature beats
Atrial premature beats, contractions, or systoles

427.69 Other
Ventricular premature beats, contractions, or systoles
AHA: 4Q, '93, 42

✓5ᵗʰ 427.8 Other specified cardiac dysrhythmias

427.81 Sinoatrial node dysfunction
Sinus bradycardia:
  persistent
  severe
Syndrome:
  sick sinus
  tachycardia-bradycardia
EXCLUDES   sinus bradycardia NOS (427.89)
DEF: Complex cardiac arrhythmia; appears as severe sinus bradycardia, sinus bradycardia with tachycardia, or sinus bradycardia with atrioventricular block.
AHA: 3Q, '00, 8
149.5 Sick sinus syndrome [I-10]

427.89 Other
Rhythm disorder:
  coronary sinus
  ectopic
  nodal
Wandering (atrial) pacemaker
EXCLUDES   carotid sinus syncope (337.0)
  neonatal bradycardia (779.81)
  neonatal tachycardia (779.82)
  reflex bradycardia (337.0)
  tachycardia NOS (785.0)
149.8 Other specified cardiac arrhythmias [I-10]

427.9 Cardiac dysrhythmia, unspecified
Arrhythmia (cardiac) NOS
AHA: 2Q, '89, 10

Echocardiography of Heart Failure

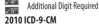

Four-chamber echocardiograms, two-dimensional views.
LV: Left ventricle
RV: Right ventricle
RA: Right atrium
LA: Left atrium

Systolic dysfunction with dilated LV

Diastolic dysfunction with LV hypertrophy

✓4ᵗʰ 428 Heart failure
Code, if applicable, heart failure due to hypertension first (402.0-402.9, with fifth-digit 1 or 404.0-404.9 with fifth-digit 1 or 3)
EXCLUDES   following cardiac surgery (429.4)
  rheumatic (398.91)
  that complicating:
    abortion (634-638 with .7, 639.8)
    ectopic or molar pregnancy (639.8)
    labor or delivery (668.1, 669.4)
AHA: 4Q, '02, 49; 3Q, '98, 5; 2Q, '90, 16; 2Q, '90, 19; 2Q, '89, 10; 3Q, '88, 3

(handwritten note left) Pulmonary edema is included in codes 428.X, no additional code is needed.

428.0 Congestive heart failure, unspecified
Congestive heart disease
Right heart failure (secondary to left heart failure)
EXCLUDES   fluid overload NOS (276.6)
DEF: Mechanical inadequacy; caused by inability of heart to pump and circulate blood; results in fluid collection in lungs, hypertension, congestion and edema of tissue.
AHA: ▶1Q, '09, 8, 18;◀4Q, '08, 72, 180, 182; 3Q, '08, 12; 3Q, '07, 9; 1Q, 07, 20; 3Q, '06, 7; 4Q, '05, 120; 3Q, '05, 8; 1Q, '05, 5, 9; 1Q, '05, 5, 9; 4Q, '04, 140; 3Q, '04, 7;4Q, '03, 109; 1Q, '03, 9; 4Q, '02, 52; 2Q, '01, 13; 4Q, '00, 48; 2Q, '00, 16; 1Q, '00, 22; 4Q, '99, 4; 1Q, '99, 11; 4Q, '97, 55; 3Q, '97, 10; 3Q, '96, 9; 3Q, '91, 18; 3Q, '91, 19; 2Q, '89, 12
TIP: Assign additional code(s) from subcategory 428.2, 428.3, or 428.4 to specify the type of heart failure.
150.9 Heart failure unspecified [I-10]

(handwritten note) – Hypertensive Heart Failure code 402

(handwritten note left) Includes any left-sided failure that is present, therefore, codes 428.0 and 428.1 are not assigned for the same episode of care, code 428.0 takes precedence.

428.1 Left heart failure [CC]
Acute edema of lung } with heart disease NOS or
Acute pulmonary edema } heart failure
Cardiac asthma
Left ventricular failure
DEF: Mechanical inadequacy of left ventricle; causing fluid in lungs.
CC Excl: 398.91, 402.01, 402.11, 402.91, 428.0-428.9, 459.89-459.9

(handwritten note left) Includes associated conditions such as dyspnea, orthopnea, bronchospasms, and acute pulmonary edema. No additional codes are assigned.

✓5ᵗʰ 428.2 Systolic heart failure
EXCLUDES   combined systolic and diastolic heart failure (428.40-428.43)
DEF: Heart failure due to a defect in expulsion of blood caused by an abnormality in systolic function, or ventricular contractile dysfunction.

(handwritten note left) Occurs when the ability of the heart to contract decreases.

428.20 Unspecified [CC]
CC Excl: 398.91, 402.01, 402.11, 402.91, 428.0-428.9, 459.89-459.9, 518.4
150.20 Unspecified systolic congestive heart failure [I-10]

428.21 Acute [MCC]
CC Excl: See code: 428.20
150.21 Acute systolic congestive heart failure [I-10]

428.22 Chronic [CC]
CC Excl: See code: 428.20
AHA: 4Q, '05, 120

428.23 Acute on chronic [MCC]
CC Excl: See code: 428.20
AHA: ▶1Q, '09, 8, 18;◀1Q, '03, 9

---

¹ MCC = Only if patient is discharged alive.

✓4ᵗʰ✓5ᵗʰ Additional Digit Required   Unacceptable PDx   Manifestation Code   Hospital Acquired Condition   ▶◀ Revised Text   ● New Code   ▲ Revised Code Title

2010 ICD-9-CM   October 2009 • Volume 1 – 151

√5th **428.3** <u>Diasto</u>lic heart failure

> **EXCLUDES** *combined systolic and diastolic heart failure (428.40-428.43)*

Occurs when the heart has a problem relaxing between contractions (diastole) to allow enough blood to enter the ventricles.

> **DEF:** Heart failure due to resistance to ventricular filling caused by an abnormality in the diastolic function.

428.30 Unspecified `CC`

> **CC Excl:** See code: 428.20
> **AHA:** 4Q, '02, 52
> **I50.30** Unspecified diastolic congestive heart failure `I-10`

428.31 Acute `MCC`

> **CC Excl:** See code: 428.20

428.32 Chronic `CC`

> **CC Excl:** See code: 428.20
> **AHA:** ▶3Q, '08, 12◀
> **I50.32** Chronic diastolic congestive heart failure `I-10`

428.33 Acute on chronic `MCC`

> **CC Excl:** See code: 428.20
> **AHA:** ▶3Q, '08, 12;◀1Q, '07, 20
> **I50.33** Acute on chronic diastolic heart failure `I-10`

√5th **428.4 Combined systolic and diastolic heart failure**

428.40 Unspecified `CC`

> **CC Excl:** See code: 428.20

428.41 Acute `MCC`

> **CC Excl:** See code: 428.20
> **AHA:** 4Q, '04, 140

428.42 Chronic `CC`

> **CC Excl:** See code: 428.20

428.43 Acute on chronic `MCC`

> **CC Excl:** See code: 428.20
> **AHA:** 3Q, '06, 7; 4Q, '02, 52

428.9 Heart failure, unspecified

> Cardiac failure NOS
> Heart failure NOS
> Myocardial failure NOS
> Weak heart
> **AHA:** 2Q, '89, 10; N-D, '85, 14

√4th **429 Ill-defined descriptions and complications of heart disease**

429.0 Myocarditis, unspecified

> Myocarditis:
> NOS
> chronic (interstitial)　⎫ (with mention of
> fibroid　　　　　　　⎬ arteriosclerosis)
> senile　　　　　　　⎭
> Use additional code to identify presence of arteriosclerosis
>
> **EXCLUDES** *acute or subacute (422.0-422.9)*
> *rheumatic (398.0)*
> *acute (391.2)*
> *that due to hypertension (402.0-402.9)*

429.1 Myocardial degeneration

> Degeneration of heart or　⎫
> myocardium:　　　　　⎪
> fatty　　　　　　　　⎪
> mural　　　　　　　⎬ (with mention of
> muscular　　　　　⎪ arteriosclerosis)
> Myocardial:　　　　⎪
> degeneration　　　⎪
> disease　　　　　⎭
> Use additional code to identify presence of arteriosclerosis
>
> **EXCLUDES** *that due to hypertension (402.0-402.9)*

429.2 Cardiovascular disease, unspecified

> Arteriosclerotic cardiovascular disease [ASCVD]
> Cardiovascular arteriosclerosis
> Cardiovascular:　　⎫
> degeneration　　⎪ (with mention of
> disease　　　　⎬ arteriosclerosis)
> sclerosis　　　⎭
> Use additional code to identify presence of arteriosclerosis
>
> **EXCLUDES** *that due to hypertension (402.0-402.9)*

429.3 Cardiomegaly

> Cardiac:
> dilatation
> hypertrophy
> Ventricular dilatation
>
> **EXCLUDES** *that due to hypertension (402.0-402.9)*
>
> **I51.7** Cardiomegaly `I-10`

429.4 Functional disturbances following cardiac surgery

> Cardiac insufficiency　⎫ following cardiac surgery or
> Heart failure　　　　⎬ due to presthesis
> Postcardiotomy syndrome
> Postvalvulotomy syndrome
>
> **EXCLUDES** *cardiac failure in the immediate postoperative period (997.1)*
>
> **AHA:** 2Q, '02, 12; N-D, '85, 6

429.5 Rupture of chordae tendineae `MCC`

> **DEF:** Torn tissue, between heart valves and papillary muscles.
> **CC Excl:** 429.5, 429.71-429.79, 459.89-459.9

429.6 Rupture of papillary muscle `MCC`

> **DEF:** Torn muscle, between chordae tendineae and heart wall.
> **CC Excl:** 429.6-429.81, 459.89-459.9

√5th **429.7 Certain sequelae of myocardial infarction, not elsewhere classified**

> Use additional code to identify the associated myocardial infarction:
> with onset of 8 weeks or less (410.00-410.92)
> with onset of more than 8 weeks (414.8)
>
> **EXCLUDES** *congenital defects of heart (745, 746)*
> *coronary aneurysm (414.11)*
> *disorders of papillary muscle (429.6, 429.81)*
> *postmyocardial infarction syndrome (411.0)*
> *rupture of chordae tendineae (429.5)*
>
> **AHA:** 3Q, '89, 5

429.71 Acquired cardiac septal defect `CC` `A`

> **EXCLUDES** *acute septal infarction (410.00-410.92)*
>
> **DEF:** Abnormal communication, between opposite heart chambers; due to defect of septum; not present at birth.
> **CC Excl:** 422.0-422.99, 429.0, 429.4-429.82, 459.89-459.9, 745.0-745.9, 746.89-746.9, 747.83-747.9, 759.7-759.89

429.79 Other `CC` `A`

> Mural thrombus (atrial) (ventricular), acquired, following myocardial infarction
> **CC Excl:** See code: 429.71
> **AHA:** 1Q, '92, 10

√5th **429.8 Other ill-defined heart diseases**

429.81 Other disorders of papillary muscle `CC`

> Papillary muscle:
> atrophy
> degeneration
> dysfunction
> incompetence
> incoordination
> scarring
> **CC Excl:** 429.6-429.81, 459.89-459.9

`N` Newborn Age: 0　　`P` Pediatric Age: 0-17　　`M` Maternity Age: 12-55　　`A` Adult Age: 15-124　　`MCC` Major CC Condition　　`CC` CC Condition　　`HIV` HIV Related Dx

429.82 Hyperkinetic heart disease `CC`

DEF: Condition of unknown origin in young adults; marked by increased cardiac output at rest, increased rate of ventricular ejection; may lead to heart failure.

CC Excl: 429.71-429.79, 429.82, 459.89-459.9

429.83 Takotsubo syndrome `CC`

Broken heart syndrome
Reversible left ventricular dysfunction following sudden emotional stress
Stress induced cardiomyopathy
Transient left ventricular apical ballooning syndrome

CC Excl: 398.91, 402.01, 402.11, 402.91, 428.0-428.9, 429.83, 429.9, 459.89-459.9

AHA: 4Q, '06, 87

429.89 Other

Carditis

> *EXCLUDES*   *that due to hypertension (402.0-402.9)*

AHA: 2Q, '06, 18; 3Q, '05, 14; 1Q, '92, 10

429.9 Heart disease, unspecified

Heart disease (organic) NOS
Morbus cordis NOS

> *EXCLUDES*   *that due to hypertension (402.0-402.9)*

Systolic or diastolic dysfunction without mention of heart failure. [handwritten]

AHA: ▶1Q, '09, 7;◀1Q, '93, 19

I51.9 Heart disease unspecified `I-10`

CEREBROVASCULAR DISEASE (430-438)

> *INCLUDES*   with mention of hypertension (conditions classifiable to 401-405)

Use additional code to identify presence of hypertension

> *EXCLUDES*   *any condition classifiable to 430-434, 436, 437 occurring during pregnancy, childbirth, or the puerperium, or specified as puerperal (674.0)*
> *iatrogenic cerebrovascular infarction or hemorrhage (997.02)*

AHA: 1Q, '93, 27; 3Q, '91, 10; 3Q, '90, 3; 2Q, '89, 8; M-A, '85, 6

430 Subarachnoid hemorrhage `MCC`

Meningeal hemorrhage
Ruptured:
   berry aneurysm
   (congenital) cerebral aneurysm NOS

> *EXCLUDES*   *syphilitic ruptured cerebral aneurysm (094.87)*

DEF: Bleeding in space between brain and lining.

CC Excl: 430-432.9, 459.89-459.9, 780.01-780.09, 800.00-801.99, 803.00-804.96, 850.0-852.19, 852.21-854.19

AHA: 4Q, '04, 77

431 Intracerebral hemorrhage `MCC`

Hemorrhage (of):   Hemorrhage (of):
  basilar   internal capsule
  bulbar   intrapontine
  cerebellar   pontine
  cerebral   subcortical
  cerebromeningeal   ventricular
  cortical   Rupture of blood vessel in brain

DEF: Bleeding within the brain.

CC Excl: See code: 430

AHA: 3Q, '07, 4; 4Q, '04, 77

I61.9 Nontraumatic intracerebral hemorrhage unspec `I-10`

√4ᵗʰ 432 Other and unspecified intracranial hemorrhage

AHA: 4Q, '04, 7

432.0 Nontraumatic extradural hemorrhage `MCC`

Nontraumatic epidural hemorrhage

DEF: Bleeding, nontraumatic, between skull and brain lining.

CC Excl: See code: 430

432.1 Subdural hemorrhage `MCC`

Subdural hematoma, nontraumatic

DEF: Bleeding, between outermost and other layers of brain lining.

CC Excl: See code: 430

Berry Aneurysms

432.9 Unspecified intracranial hemorrhage `CC`

Intracranial hemorrhage NOS

CC Excl: See code: 430

√4ᵗʰ 433 Occlusion and stenosis of precerebral arteries

> *INCLUDES*   embolism   ⎫
>   narrowing   ⎬ of basilar, carotid, and vertebral
>   obstruction ⎪   arteries
>   thrombosis   ⎭

Use additional code, if applicable, to identify status post administration of tPA (rtPA) in a different facility within the last 24 hours prior to admission to current facility (V45.88)

> *EXCLUDES*   *insufficiency NOS of precerebral arteries (435.0-435.9)*

> The following fifth-digit subclassification is for use with category 433:
>   **0 without mention of cerebral infarction**
>   **1 with cerebral infarction**

DEF: Blockage, stricture, arteries branching into brain.

AHA: 2Q, '95, 14; 3Q, '90, 16

§ √5ᵗʰ 433.0 Basilar artery `MCC 1`

[0-1]   **CC Excl: For code 433.01:** 249.70-249.91, 250.70-250.93, 346.60-346.63, 433.00-433.91, 435.0, 459.89-459.9

§ √5ᵗʰ 433.1 Carotid artery `MCC 1`

[0-1]   **CC Excl: For code 433.11:** 249.70-249.91, 250.70-250.93, 346.60-346.63, 433.00-433.91, 459.89-459.9

AHA: 1Q, '00, 16; **For code 433.10:** 1Q, '06, 17; 1Q, '02, 7, 10

I65.29 Occlusion and stenosis of unspec carotid artery `I-10`

§ √5ᵗʰ 433.2 Vertebral artery `MCC 1`

[0-1]   **CC Excl: For code 433.21:** 249.70-249.91, 250.70-250.93, 346.60-346.63, 433.00-433.91, 435.1, 459.89-459.9

§ √5ᵗʰ 433.3 Multiple and bilateral `MCC 1`

[0-1]   **CC Excl: For code 433.31:** 249.70-249.91, 250.70-250.93, 346.60-346.63, 433.00-433.91, 459.89-459.9

AHA: 2Q, '02, 19

§ √5ᵗʰ 433.8 Other specified precerebral artery `MCC 1`

[0-1]   **CC Excl: For code 433.81:** 249.70-249.91, 250.70-250.93, 346.60-346.63, 433.00-433.91, 435.0, 459.89-459.9

§ √5ᵗʰ 433.9 Unspecified precerebral artery `MCC 1`

[0-1]   Precerebral artery NOS

CC Excl: For code 433.91: 249.70-249.91, 250.70-250.93, 346.60-346.63, 433.00-433.91, 435.0, 459.89-459.9

√4ᵗʰ 434 Occlusion of cerebral arteries

Use additional code, if applicable, to identify status post administration of tPA (rtPA) in a different facility within the last 24 hours prior to admission to current facility (V45.88)

> The following fifth-digit subclassification is for use with category 434:
>   **0 without mention of cerebral infarction**
>   **1 with cerebral infarction**

AHA: 2Q, '95, 14

§ √5ᵗʰ 434.0 Cerebral thrombosis `MCC 1`

[0-1]   Thrombosis of cerebral arteries

CC Excl: For code 434.01: 249.70-249.91, 250.70-250.93, 346.60-346.63, 434.00-434.91, 436, 459.89-459.9

AHA: For code 434.01: 4Q, '04, 77

---

§   Requires fifth digit. Valid digits are in [brackets] under each code. See category 433 or 434 for codes and definitions.

√4ᵗʰ Additional Digit Required   Unacceptable PDx   Manifestation Code   Hospital Acquired Condition   ▶◀ Revised Text   ● New Code   ▲ Revised Code Title

2010 ICD-9-CM   **October 2009 • Volume 1 – 153**

Cerebrovascular Arteries

Posterior parietal
Parietal-occipital
Calcarine
Posterior cerebral
Anterior inferior cerebellar
Posterior inferior cerebellar
Basilar
Vertebral
Callosal-marginal
Pericallosal
Anterior cerebral
Anterior communicating
Middle cerebral
Ophthalmic
Posterior communicating
External carotid
Internal carotid
Aorta

§ ✓5th **434.1** **Cerebral embolism** `MCC 1`
[0-1]   CC Excl: For code 434.11: 249.70-249.91, 250.70-250.93, 346.60-346.63, 433.00-433.91, 435.0, 459.89-459.9
AHA: For code 434.11: 4Q, '04, 77; 3Q, '97, 11
I63.449 Cerbral infarct d/t embo of uns cerebellar art `I-10`

§ ✓5th **434.9** **Cerebral artery occlusion, unspecified** `MCC 1`
[0-1]   CC Excl: For code 434.91: 249.70-249.91, 250.70-250.93, 346.60-346.63, 433.00-433.91, 435.0, 459.89-459.9
See above
AHA: For code 434.91: 4Q, '08, 108; 3Q, '07, 9; 1Q, '07, 23; 4Q, '04, 77-78; 4Q, '98, 87

✓4th **435** **Transient cerebral ischemia**
INCLUDES cerebrovascular insufficiency (acute) with trans- ient focal neurological signs and symptoms
insufficiency of basilar, carotid, and vertebral arteries
spasm of cerebral arteries
EXCLUDES acute cerebrovascular insufficiency NOS (437.1)
that due to any condition classifiable to 433 (433.0-433.9)

435.0 **Basilar artery syndrome** `CC`
CC Excl: 249.70-249.91, 250.70-250.93, 433.00-433.91, 435.0-435.9, 459.89-459.9

435.1 **Vertebral artery syndrome** `CC`
CC Excl: See code: 435.0

435.2 **Subclavian steal syndrome** `CC`
DEF: Cerebrovascular insufficiency, due to occluded subclavian artery; symptoms include pain in mastoid and posterior head regions, flaccid paralysis of arm and diminished or absent radial pulse on affected side.
CC Excl: See code: 435.0

435.3 **Vertebrobasilar artery syndrome** `CC`
DEF: Transient ischemic attack; due to brainstem dysfunction; symptoms include confusion, vertigo, binocular blindness, diplopia, unilateral or bilateral weakness and paresthesis of extremities.
CC Excl: See code: 435.0
AHA: 4Q, '95, 60

435.8 **Other specified transient cerebral ischemias** `CC`
CC Excl: See code: 435.0

435.9 **Unspecified transient cerebral ischemia** `CC`
Impending cerebrovascular accident
Intermittent cerebral ischemia
Transient ischemic attack [TIA]
CC Excl: See code: 435.0
AHA: N-D, '85, 12
G45.9 Transient cerebral ischemic attack unspecified `I-10`

436 **Acute, but ill-defined, cerebrovascular disease** `CC`
Apoplexy, apoplectic:
NOS
attack
cerebral
seizure
Cerebral seizure
EXCLUDES any condition classifiable to categories 430-435
cerebrovascular accident (434.91)
CVA (ischemic) (434.91)
embolic (434.11)
hemorrhagic (430, 431, 432.0-432.9)
thrombotic (434.01)
postoperative cerebrovascular accident (997.02)
stroke (ischemic) (434.91)
embolic (434.11)
hemorrhagic (430, 431, 432.0-432.9)
thrombotic (434.01)
CC Excl: 249.70-249.91, 250.70-250.93, 346.60-346.63, 430-432.9, 434.00-434.91, 436, 459.89-459.9, 780.01-780.09, 800.00-801.99, 803.00-804.96, 850.0-852.19, 852.21-854.19
AHA: 4Q, '04, 77; 4Q, '99, 3
TIP: Do not assign when documentation indicates "CVA, stroke, or cerebral infarction." See instead default code 434.91.

✓4th **437** **Other and ill-defined cerebrovascular disease**

437.0 **Cerebral atherosclerosis** `A`
Atheroma of cerebral arteries
Cerebral arteriosclerosis
I67.2 Cerebral atherosclerosis `I-10`

437.1 **Other generalized ischemic cerebrovascular disease** `CC`
Acute cerebrovascular insufficiency NOS
Cerebral ischemia (chronic)
CC Excl: 249.70-249.91, 250.70-250.93, 430-432.9, 434.00-436, 437.1, 459.89-459.9
AHA: ▶1Q, '09, 8◀

437.2 **Hypertensive encephalopathy** `CC`
DEF: Cerebral manifestations (such as visual disturbances and headache) due to high blood pressure.
CC Excl: 249.70-249.91, 250.70-250.93, 437.2, 459.89-459.9
AHA: J-A, '84, 14

437.3 **Cerebral aneurysm, nonruptured**
Internal carotid artery, intracranial portion
Internal carotid artery NOS
EXCLUDES congenital cerebral aneurysm, nonruptured (747.81)
internal carotid artery, extracranial portion (442.81)
AHA: ▶2Q, '09, 12◀

437.4 **Cerebral arteritis** `CC`
DEF: Inflammation of a cerebral artery or arteries.
CC Excl: 249.70-249.91, 250.70-250.93, 437.4, 459.89-459.9
AHA: 4Q, '99, 21

437.5 **Moyamoya disease** `CC`
DEF: Cerebrovascular ischemia; vessels occlude and rupture causing tiny hemorrhages at base of brain; predominantly affects Japanese.
CC Excl: 249.70-249.91, 250.70-250.93, 437.5, 459.89-459.9

437.6 **Nonpyogenic thrombosis of intracranial venous sinus** `CC`
EXCLUDES pyogenic (325)
CC Excl: 249.70-249.91, 250.70-250.93, 437.6, 459.89-459.9

437.7 **Transient global amnesia**
DEF: Episode of short-term memory loss, not often recurrent; pathogenesis unknown; with no signs or symptoms of neurological disorder.
AHA: 4Q, '92, 20

437.8 **Other**

437.9 **Unspecified**
Cerebrovascular disease or lesion NOS
AHA: ▶1Q, '09, 9◀

§   Requires fifth digit. Valid digits are in [brackets] under each code. See category 434 for codes and definitions.

`N` Newborn Age: 0   `P` Pediatric Age: 0-17   `M` Maternity Age: 12-55   `A` Adult Age: 15-124   `MCC` Major CC Condition   `CC` CC Condition   `HIV` HIV Related Dx

154 – Volume 1 · October 2009   2010 ICD-9-CM

(Handwritten margin notes at top:) 438- can be assigned as principal when the purpose of the admission is to deal with the late effect. V57- if admission is for the purpose of rehabilitation code V57 and an additional code from 438. Residual effects still present at discharge are coded as additional diagnosis but not as late effects,

Tabular List

√4th 438 Late effects of cerebrovascular disease

Note: This category is to be used to indicate conditions in 430-437 as the cause of late effects. The "late effects" include conditions specified as such, as sequelae, which may occur at any time after the onset of the causal condition.

EXCLUDES personal history of:
cerebral infarction without residual deficits (V12.54)
PRIND [Prolonged reversible ischemic neurologic deficit] (V12.54)
RIND [Reversible ischemic neurological deficit] (V12.54)
transient ischemic attack [TIA] (V12.54)

AHA: 3Q, '06, 3-4, 6; 4Q, '99, 4, 6, 7; 4Q, '98, 39, 88; 4Q, '97, 35, 37; 4Q, '92, 21;N-D,'86, 12; M-A, '86, 7

TIP: Assign instead code V12.54 TIA and cerebral infarction without residual effects, if no residual deficits are present.

438.0 Cognitive deficits

√5th **438.1 Speech and language deficits**

438.10 Speech and language deficit, unspecified

438.11 Aphasia
DEF: Impairment or absence of the ability to communicate by speech, writing or signs or to comprehend the spoken or written language due to disease or injury to the brain.
AHA: 4Q, '03, 105; 4Q, '97, 36

438.12 Dysphasia
DEF: Impaired speech; marked by inability to sequence language.
AHA: 4Q, '99, 3, 9

438.13 Dysarthria

438.14 Fluency disorder
Stuttering

438.19 Other speech and language deficits

√5th **438.2 Hemiplegia/hemiparesis**
DEF: Paralysis of one side of the body.

438.20 Hemiplegia affecting unspecified side CC
CC Excl: 438.20
AHA: 4Q, '07, 94; 4Q, '03, 105; 4Q, '99, 3, 9
I69.959 Hempl & hemiparesis flw uns CVD affect uns side I-10

438.21 Hemiplegia affecting dominant side CC
CC Excl: 438.21

438.22 Hemiplegia affecting nondominant side CC
CC Excl: 438.22
AHA: 4Q, '03, 105; 1Q, '02, 16

√5th **438.3 Monoplegia of upper limb**
DEF: Paralysis of one limb or one muscle group.

438.30 Monoplegia of upper limb affecting unspecified side

438.31 Monoplegia of upper limb affecting dominant side

438.32 Monoplegia of upper limb affecting nondominant side

√5th **438.4 Monoplegia of lower limb**

438.40 Monoplegia of lower limb affecting unspecified side

438.41 Monoplegia of lower limb affecting dominant side

438.42 Monoplegia of lower limb affecting nondominant side

√5th **438.5 Other paralytic syndrome**
Use additional code to identify type of paralytic syndrome, such as:
locked-in state (344.81)
quadriplegia (344.00-344.09)

EXCLUDES late effects of cerebrovascular accident with:
hemiplegia/hemiparesis (438.20-438.22)
monoplegia of lower limb (438.40-438.42)
monoplegia of upper limb (438.30-438.32)

438.50 Other paralytic syndrome affecting unspecified side

438.51 Other paralytic syndrome affecting dominant side

438.52 Other paralytic syndrome affecting nondominant side

438.53 Other paralytic syndrome, bilateral
AHA: 4Q, '98, 39

438.6 Alterations of sensations
Use additional code to identify the altered sensation

438.7 Disturbances of vision
Use additional code to identify the visual disturbance
AHA: 4Q, '02, 56

√5th **438.8 Other late effects of cerebrovascular disease**

438.81 Apraxia
DEF: Inability to activate learned movements; no known sensory or motor impairment.

438.82 Dysphagia
Use additional code to identify the type of dysphagia, if known (787.20-787.29)
DEF: Inability or difficulty in swallowing.
AHA: 4Q, '07, 94
I69.991 Dysphagia following uns cerebrovascular disease I-10

438.83 Facial weakness
Facial droop

438.84 Ataxia
AHA: 4Q, '02, 56

438.85 Vertigo

438.89 Other late effects of cerebrovascular disease
Use additional code to identify the late effect
AHA: ▶2Q, '09, 10;◀1Q, '05, 13; 4Q, '98, 39
TIP: Assign 438.89 and 728.87 Muscle weakness, for residual weakness secondary to late effect of CVA.
I69.998 Other sequelae flw uns cerebrovascular disease I-10

438.9 Unspecified late effects of cerebrovascular disease

DISEASES OF ARTERIES, ARTERIOLES, AND CAPILLARIES (440-449)

√4th 440 Atherosclerosis

INCLUDES arteriolosclerosis
arteriosclerosis (obliterans) (senile)
arteriosclerotic vascular disease
atheroma
degeneration:
arterial
arteriovascular
vascular
endarteritis deformans or obliterans
senile:
arteritis
endarteritis

EXCLUDES atheroembolism (445.01-445.89)
atherosclerosis of bypass graft of the extremities (440.30-440.32)

DEF: Stricture and reduced elasticity of an artery; due to plaque deposits.

440.0 Of aorta A
AHA: 2Q, '93, 7; 2Q, '93, 8; 4Q, '88, 8

(Handwritten margin notes, left column:) significant for the current episode of care... V1254 if the patient has history of CVA w/no residual conditions, when new CVA is present and deficits from earlier episode remain.

440.1   **Of renal artery**   A
    EXCLUDES   atherosclerosis of renal arterioles (403.00-403.91)

√5ᵗʰ 440.2   **Of native arteries of the extremities**
Use additional code, if applicable, to identify chronic total occlusion of artery of the extremities (440.4)
    EXCLUDES   atherosclerosis of bypass graft of the extremities (440.30-440.32)
AHA: 4Q, '94, 49; 4Q, '93, 27; 4Q, '92, 25; 3Q, '90, 15; M-A, '87, 6

TIP: Codes are listed in order of increasing severity; all patients who have gangrene (regardless of whether ulceration, rest pain, and/or intermittent claudication are present) are coded to 440.24. Patients without gangrene, but with ulceration (regardless of whether they also suffer from rest pain or intermittent claudication) are coded to 440.23.

440.20   **Atherosclerosis of the extremities, unspecified**   A
    I70.209 Uns atherosclero natv art of extrem uns extrem   I-10

440.21   **Atherosclerosis of the extremities with intermittent claudication**   A
    DEF: Atherosclerosis; marked by pain, tension and weakness after walking; no symptoms while at rest.
    I70.219 Atherosclerosis native arteries ext w/interm claud uns ext   I-10

440.22   **Atherosclerosis of the extremities with rest pain**   A
    INCLUDES   any condition classifiable to 440.21
    DEF: Atherosclerosis, marked by pain, tension and weakness while at rest.

440.23   **Atherosclerosis of the extremities with ulceration**   A
    INCLUDES   any condition classifiable to 440.21 and 440.22
Use additional code for any associated ulceration (707.10-707.9)
    AHA: 4Q, '00, 44
    I70.249 Atherosclero natv art lt leg ulceration uns site   I-10

440.24   **Atherosclerosis of the extremities with gangrene**   CC
    INCLUDES   any condition classifiable to 440.21, 440.22, and 440.23 with ischemic gangrene 785.4
Use additional code for any associated ulceration (707.10-707.9)
    EXCLUDES   gas gangrene (040.0)
    CC Excl: 338.0-338.4, 440.24, 780.91-780.99, 785.4, 799.81-799.89
    AHA: 4Q, '03, 109; 3Q, '03, 14; 4Q, '95, 54; 1Q, '95, 11

440.29   **Other**   A

√5ᵗʰ 440.3   **Of bypass graft of extremities**
    EXCLUDES   atherosclerosis of native arteries of the extremities (440.21-440.24)
       embolism [occlusion NOS] [thrombus] of graft (996.74)
    AHA: 4Q, '94, 49

440.30   **Of unspecified graft**   A

Map of Major Arteries

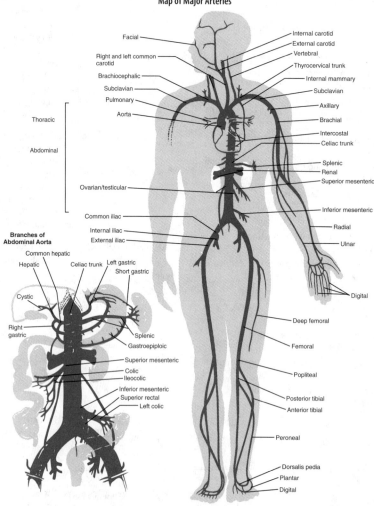

N Newborn Age: 0   P Pediatric Age: 0-17   M Maternity Age: 12-55   A Adult Age: 15-124   MCC Major CC Condition   CC CC Condition   HIV HIV Related Dx

156 – Volume 1   2010 ICD-9-CM

440.31 Of autologous vein bypass graft `A`

440.32 Of nonautologous biological bypass graft `A`

440.4 **Chronic total occlusion of artery of the extremities**
Complete occlusion of artery of the extremities
Total occlusion of artery of the extremities
Code first atherosclerosis of arteries of the extremities
(440.20-440.29, 440.30-440.32)

> **EXCLUDES** acute occlusion of artery of extremity
> (444.21-444.22)

AHA: 4Q, '07, 82

440.8 **Of other specified arteries** `A`

> **EXCLUDES** basilar (433.0)
> carotid (433.1)
> cerebral (437.0)
> coronary (414.00-414.07)
> mesenteric (557.1)
> precerebral (433.0-433.9)
> pulmonary (416.0)
> vertebral (433.2)

440.9 **Generalized and unspecified atherosclerosis** `A`
Arteriosclerotic vascular disease NOS

> **EXCLUDES** arteriosclerotic cardiovascular disease [ASCVD]
> (429.2)

I70.91 Generalized atherosclerosis `I-10`

√4th **441 Aortic aneurysm and dissection**

> **EXCLUDES** syphilitic aortic aneurysm (093.0)
> traumatic aortic aneurysm (901.0, 902.0)

√5th **441.0 Dissection of aorta**
AHA: 4Q, '89, 10
DEF: Dissection or splitting of wall of the aorta; due to blood
entering through intimal tear or interstitial hemorrhage.

441.00 **Unspecified site** `MCC`
CC Excl: 249.70-249.91, 250.70-250.93, 441.00-441.9,
459.89-459.9

441.01 **Thoracic** `MCC`
CC Excl: See code: 441.00
AHA: ▶1Q, '09, 16;◀ 4Q, '07, 87

441.02 **Abdominal** `MCC`
CC Excl: See code: 441.00

441.03 **Thoracoabdominal** `MCC`
CC Excl: See code: 441.00

441.1 **Thoracic aneurysm, ruptured** `MCC`
CC Excl: See code: 441.00

441.2 **Thoracic aneurysm without mention of rupture**
AHA: 3Q, '92, 10
I71.2 Thoracic aortic aneurysm without rupture `I-10`

441.3 **Abdominal aneurysm, ruptured** `MCC`
CC Excl: See code: 441.00

441.4 **Abdominal aneurysm without mention of rupture**
AHA: 4Q, '00, 64; 1Q, '99, 15, 16, 17; 3Q, '92, 10
I71.4 Abdominal aortic aneurysm without rupture `I-10`

441.5 **Aortic aneurysm of unspecified site, ruptured** `MCC`
Rupture of aorta NOS
CC Excl: See code: 441.00

441.6 **Thoracoabdominal aneurysm, ruptured** `MCC`
CC Excl: See code: 441.00

441.7 **Thoracoabdominal aneurysm, without mention of
rupture**
AHA: 2Q, '06, 16

Thoracic and Abdominal Aortic Aneurysm

441.9 **Aortic aneurysm of unspecified site without mention of
rupture**
Aneurysm
Dilatation } of aorta
Hyaline necrosis

√4th **442 Other aneurysm**

> **INCLUDES** aneurysm (ruptured) (cirsoid) (false) (varicose)
> aneurysmal varix

> **EXCLUDES** arteriovenous aneurysm or fistula:
> acquired (447.0)
> congenital (747.60-747.69)
> traumatic (900.0-904.9)

DEF: Dissection or splitting of arterial wall; due to blood entering
through intimal tear or interstitial hemorrhage.

442.0 **Of artery of upper extremity**

442.1 **Of renal artery**

442.2 **Of iliac artery**
AHA: 1Q, '99, 16, 17

442.3 **Of artery of lower extremity**
Aneurysm:
femoral artery
popliteal artery
AHA: 2Q, '08, 13; 3Q, '02, 24-26; 1Q, '99, 16

√5th **442.8 Of other specified artery**

442.81 **Artery of neck**
Aneurysm of carotid artery (common) (external)
(internal, extracranial portion)

> **EXCLUDES** internal carotid artery, intra- cranial
> portion (437.3)

442.82 **Subclavian artery**

442.83 **Splenic artery**

442.84 **Other visceral artery**
Aneurysm:
celiac
gastroduodenal
gastroepiploic } artery
hepatic
pancreaticoduodenal
superior mesenteric

442.89 **Other**
Aneurysm:
mediastinal artery
spinal artery

> **EXCLUDES** cerebral (nonruptured) (437.3)
> congenital (747.81)
> ruptured (430)
> coronary (414.11)
> heart (414.10)
> pulmonary (417.1)

442.9 **Of unspecified site**

Circulatory System

443–444.81

✓4ᵗʰ **443 Other peripheral vascular disease**

443.0 Raynaud's syndrome
Raynaud's:
    disease
    phenomenon (secondary)
Use additional code to identify gangrene (785.4)
DEF: Constriction of the arteries, due to cold or stress; bilateral ischemic attacks of fingers, toes, nose or ears; symptoms include pallor, paresthesia and pain.
I73.00 Raynaud's syndrome without gangrene   I-10

443.1 Thromboangiitis obliterans [Buerger's disease]
Presenile gangrene
DEF: Inflammatory disease of extremity blood vessels, mainly the lower; occurs primarily in young men and leads to tissue ischemia and gangrene.

✓5ᵗʰ **443.2 Other arterial dissection**
EXCLUDES   dissection of aorta (441.00-441.03)
           dissection of coronary arteries (414.12)
AHA: 4Q, '02, 54

  443.21 Dissection of carotid artery   MCC
     CC Excl: 447.2, 447.5-447.9

  443.22 Dissection of iliac artery   MCC
     CC Excl: See code: 443.21

  443.23 Dissection of renal artery   MCC
     CC Excl: See code: 443.21

  443.24 Dissection of vertebral artery   MCC
     CC Excl: See code: 443.21

  443.29 Dissection of other artery   MCC
     CC Excl: See code: 443.21

✓5ᵗʰ **443.8 Other specified peripheral vascular diseases**

  443.81 *Peripheral angiopathy in diseases classified elsewhere*
     Code first underlying disease, as:
       diabetes mellitus (249.7, 250.7)
     AHA: 1Q, '04, 14; 3Q, '91, 10
     I79.8 Oth d/o art arterioles & cap in dz class elsw   I-10

  443.82 Erythromelalgia
     DEF: Rare syndrome of paroxysmal vasodilation; maldistribution of blood flow causes redness, pain, increased skin temperature, and burning sensations in various parts of the body.
     AHA: 4Q, '05, 73

  443.89 Other
     Acrocyanosis
     Acroparesthesia:
       simple [Schultze's type]
       vasomotor [Nothnagel's type]
     Erythrocyanosis
     EXCLUDES   chilblains (991.5)
               frostbite (991.0-991.3)
               immersion foot (991.4)
     AHA: 4Q, '07, 124
     I73.89 Other specified peripheral vascular disease   I-10

443.9 Peripheral vascular disease, unspecified
Intermittent claudication NOS
Peripheral:
   angiopathy NOS
   vascular disease NOS
Spasm of artery
EXCLUDES   atherosclerosis of the arteries of the extremities
               (440.20-440.22)
            spasm of cerebral artery (435.0-435.9)
AHA: 4Q, '92, 25; 3Q, '91, 10
I73.9 Peripheral vascular disease unspecified   I-10

Arterial Diseases and Disorders

Lipids
Calcium deposits

Atherosclerosis narrowing lumen   Thrombus (clot) forming in lumen

Organization of thrombus and recanalization

Intimal proliferation

Aneurysm bypasses lumen or...

Embolus (from elsewhere) occluding lumen

...bulges from arterial wall

Arteriovenous fistula

✓4ᵗʰ **444 Arterial embolism and thrombosis**

INCLUDES   infarction:
       embolic
       thrombotic
     occlusion

EXCLUDES   atheroembolism (445.01-445.89)
      that complicating:
       abortion (634-638 with .6, 639.6)
       ectopic or molar pregnancy (639.6)
       pregnancy, childbirth, or the pueperium (673.0-673.8)
      septic arterial embolism (449)
AHA: 2Q, '92, 11; 4Q, '90, 27

444.0 Of abdominal aorta   CC
Aortic bifurcation syndrome
Aortoiliac obstruction
Leriche's syndrome
Saddle embolus
CC Excl: 249.70-249.91, 250.70-250.93, 444.0, 444.89-444.9, 449, 459.89-459.9
AHA: 2Q, '93, 7; 4Q, '90, 27

444.1 Of thoracic aorta   CC
Embolism or thrombosis of aorta (thoracic)
CC Excl: 249.70-249.91, 250.70-250.93, 444.1, 444.89-444.9, 449, 459.89-459.9

✓5ᵗʰ **444.2 Of arteries of the extremities**
AHA: M-A, '87, 6

  444.21 Upper extremity   CC
     CC Excl: 249.70-249.91, 250.70-250.93, 444.21, 444.89-444.9, 449, 459.89-459.9

  444.22 Lower extremity   CC
     Arterial embolism or thrombosis:
       femoral
       peripheral NOS
       popliteal
     EXCLUDES   iliofemoral (444.81)
     CC Excl: 249.70-249.91, 250.70-250.93, 444.22, 444.89-444.9, 449, 459.89-459.9
     AHA: 4Q, '07, 85; 3Q, '03, 10; 1Q, '03, 17; 3Q, '90, 16
     I74.3 Embo & thromb of arteries of the low extremities   I-10

✓5ᵗʰ **444.8 Of other specified artery**

  444.81 Iliac artery   CC
     CC Excl: 249.70-249.91, 250.70-250.93, 444.81-444.9, 449, 459.89-459.9
     AHA: 1Q, '03, 16

N Newborn Age: 0   P Pediatric Age: 0-17   M Maternity Age: 12-55   A Adult Age: 15-124   MCC Major CC Condition   CC CC Condition   HIV HIV Related Dx

158 – Volume 1   **2010 ICD-9-CM**

444.89 Other `CC`
 EXCLUDES *basilar (433.0)*
carotid (433.1)
cerebral (434.0-434.9)
coronary (410.00-410.92)
mesenteric (557.0)
ophthalmic (362.30-362.34)
precerebral (433.0-433.9)
pulmonary (415.19)
renal (593.81)
retinal (362.30-362.34)
vertebral (433.2)
 CC Excl: 249.70-249.91, 250.70-250.93, 444.89-444.9, 449, 459.89-459.9

444.9 Of unspecified artery `CC`
 CC Excl: See code: 444.89

445 Atheroembolism
 INCLUDES atherothrombotic microembolism
cholesterol embolism
 AHA: 4Q, '02, 57

445.0 Of extremities
445.01 Upper extremity `CC`
 CC Excl: 249.70-249.91, 250.70-250.93, 444.89-445.01, 449, 459.89-459.9

445.02 Lower extremity `CC`
 CC Excl: 249.70-249.91, 250.70-250.93, 444.89-444.9, 445.02, 449, 459.89-459.9

445.8 Of other sites
445.81 Kidney `CC`
 Use additional code for any associated acute
 ▶kidney◀ failure or chronic kidney
 disease (584, 585)
 CC Excl: 249.70-249.91, 250.70-250.93, 444.89-444.9, 445.81, 449, 459.89-459.9

445.89 Other site `CC`
 CC Excl: 249.70-249.91, 250.70-250.93, 444.89-444.9, 445.89, 449, 459.89-459.9

446 Polyarteritis nodosa and allied conditions

446.0 Polyarteritis nodosa `CC`
 Disseminated necrotizing periarteritis
 Necrotizing angiitis
 Panarteritis (nodosa)
 Periarteritis (nodosa)
 DEF: Inflammation of small and mid-size arteries; symptoms related to involved arteries in kidneys, muscles, gastrointestinal tract and heart; results in tissue death.
 CC Excl: 249.70-249.91, 250.70-250.93, 446.0-446.7, 459.89-459.9

446.1 Acute febrile mucocutaneous lymph node syndrome [MCLS] `CC`
 Kawasaki disease
 DEF: Acute febrile disease of children; marked by erythema of conjunctiva and mucous membranes of upper respiratory tract, skin eruptions and edema.
 CC Excl: 446.0-446.29, 446.4-446.7, 459.89-459.9

446.2 Hypersensitivity angiitis
 EXCLUDES *antiglomerular basement membrane disease without pulmonary hemorrhage (583.89)*

446.20 Hypersensitivity angiitis, unspecified `CC`
 CC Excl: See code: 446.0

446.21 Goodpasture's syndrome `CC`
 Antiglomerular basement membrane antibody-mediated nephritis with pulmonary hemorrhage
 Use additional code to identify renal disease (583.81)
 DEF: Glomerulonephritis associated with hematuria, progresses rapidly; results in death from renal failure.
 CC Excl: See code: 446.0

446.29 Other specified hypersensitivity angiitis `CC`
 CC Excl: See code: 446.0
 AHA: 1Q, '95, 3

446.3 Lethal midline granuloma `CC`
 Malignant granuloma of face
 DEF: Granulomatous lesion; in nose or paranasal sinuses; often fatal; occurs chiefly in males.
 CC Excl: See code: 446.0

446.4 Wegener's granulomatosis `CC`
 Necrotizing respiratory granulomatosis
 Wegener's syndrome
 DEF: A disease occurring mainly in men; marked by necrotizing granulomas and ulceration of the upper respiratory tract; cause is a vasculitis affecting small vessels due to an immune disorder.
 CC Excl: See code: 446.0
 AHA: 3Q, '00, 11

446.5 Giant cell arteritis `CC`
 Bagratuni's syndrome
 Cranial arteritis
 Horton's disease
 Temporal arteritis
 DEF: Inflammation of arteries; due to giant cells affecting carotid artery branches, resulting in occlusion; symptoms include fever, headache and neurological problems.
 M31.6 Other giant cell arteritis `I-10`

446.6 Thrombotic microangiopathy `MCC`
 Moschcowitz's syndrome
 Thrombotic thrombocytopenic purpura
 DEF: Blockage of small blood vessels; due to hyaline deposits; symptoms include purpura, CNS disorders; results in protracted disease or rapid death.
 CC Excl: See code: 446.0

446.7 Takayasu's disease `CC`
 Aortic arch arteritis
 Pulseless disease
 DEF: Progressive obliterative arteritis of brachiocephalic trunk, left subclavian, and left common carotid arteries above aortic arch; results in ischemia in brain, heart and arm.
 CC Excl: See code: 446.0

447 Other disorders of arteries and arterioles

447.0 Arteriovenous fistula, acquired
 Arteriovenous aneurysm, acquired
 EXCLUDES *cerebrovascular (437.3)*
coronary (414.19)
pulmonary (417.0)
surgically created arteriovenous shunt or fistula:
 complication (996.1, 996.61-996.62)
 status or presence (V45.11)
traumatic (900.0-904.9)
 DEF: Communication between an artery and vein caused by error in healing.

447.1 Stricture of artery
 AHA: 2Q, '93, 8; M-A, '87, 6
 I77.1 Stricture of artery `I-10`

447.2 Rupture of artery `CC`
 Erosion
 Fistula, except arteriovenous } of artery
 Ulcer
 EXCLUDES *traumatic rupture of artery (900.0-904.9)*
 CC Excl: 249.70-249.91, 250.70-250.93, 446.0-446.7, 459.89-459.9

447.3 Hyperplasia of renal artery
 Fibromuscular hyperplasia of renal artery
 DEF: Overgrowth of cells in muscular lining of renal artery.

447.4 Celiac artery compression syndrome `CC`
 Celiac axis syndrome
 Marable's syndrome
 CC Excl: 447.4

447.5 Necrosis of artery `CC`
 CC Excl: 447.5

447.6 Arteritis, unspecified
Aortitis NOS
Endarteritis NOS

> **EXCLUDES**   arteritis, endarteritis:
>   aortic arch (446.7)
>   cerebral (437.4)
>   coronary (414.00-414.07)
>   deformans (440.0-440.9)
>   obliterans (440.0-440.9)
>   pulmonary (417.8)
>   senile (440.0-440.9)
>   polyarteritis NOS (446.0)
>   syphilitic aortitis (093.1)

AHA: 1Q, '95, 3

447.8 Other specified disorders of arteries and arterioles
Fibromuscular hyperplasia of arteries, except renal

447.9 Unspecified disorders of arteries and arterioles

✓4ᵗʰ **448 Disease of capillaries**

448.0 Hereditary hemorrhagic telangiectasia
Rendu-Osler-Weber disease

DEF: Genetic disease with onset after puberty; results in multiple telangiectases, dilated venules on skin and mucous membranes; recurrent bleeding may occur.

448.1 Nevus, non-neoplastic
Nevus: Nevus:
  araneus   spider
  senile   stellar

> **EXCLUDES**   neoplastic (216.0-216.9)
>   port wine (757.32)
>   strawberry (757.32)

DEF: Enlarged or malformed blood vessels of skin; results in reddish swelling, skin patch, or birthmark.

448.9 Other and unspecified capillary diseases
Capillary:
  hemorrhage
  hyperpermeability
  thrombosis

> **EXCLUDES**   capillary fragility (hereditary) (287.8)

449 Septic arterial embolism   CC
Code first underlying infection, such as:
  infective endocarditis (421.0)
  lung abscess (513.0)
Use additional code to identify the site of the embolism (433.0-433.9, 444.0-444.9)

> **EXCLUDES**   septic pulmonary embolism (415.12)

CC Excl: 249.70-249.91, 250.70-250.93, 444.89-444.9, 449, 459.89-459.9
AHA: 4Q, '07, 84-85

DISEASES OF VEINS AND LYMPHATICS, AND OTHER DISEASES OF CIRCULATORY SYSTEM (451-459)

✓4ᵗʰ **451 Phlebitis and thrombophlebitis**

> **INCLUDES**   endophlebitis
>   inflammation, vein
>   periphlebitis
>   suppurative phlebitis

Use additional E code to identify drug, if drug-induced

> **EXCLUDES**   that complicating:
>   abortion (634-638 with .7, 639.8)
>   ectopic or molar pregnancy (639.8)
>   pregnancy, childbirth, or the puerperium (671.0-671.9)
>   that due to or following:
>   implant or catheter device (996.61-996.62)
>   infusion, perfusion, or transfusion (999.2)

DEF: Inflammation of a vein (phlebitis) with formation of a thrombus (thrombophlebitis).
AHA: 1Q, '92, 16
TIP: Do not assign an additional code from category 453 for thrombosis; if both conditions are present, assign only a code from category 451.

[handwritten margin note: Thrombosis - clot has formed. Thrombophlebitis - clot has become inflamed]

451.0 Of superficial vessels of lower extremities
Saphenous vein (greater) (lesser)
AHA: 3Q, '91, 16

✓5ᵗʰ **451.1 Of deep vessels of lower extremities**
AHA: 3Q, '91, 16

451.11 Femoral vein (deep) (superficial)   CC
CC Excl: 249.70-249.91, 250.70-250.93, 451.0-451.9, 459.89-459.9

451.19 Other   CC
Femoropopliteal vein
Popliteal vein
Tibial vein
CC Excl: 249.70-249.91, 250.70-250.93, 451.0-451.9, 459.89-459.9

451.2 Of lower extremities, unspecified
AHA: 4Q, '04, 80

✓5ᵗʰ **451.8 Of other sites**
> **EXCLUDES**   intracranial venous sinus (325)
>   nonpyogenic (437.6)
>   portal (vein) (572.1)

451.81 Iliac vein   CC
CC Excl: See code: 451.19

451.82 Of superficial veins of upper extremities
Antecubital vein
Basilic vein
Cephalic vein

451.83 Of deep veins of upper extremities   CC
Brachial vein
Radial vein
Ulnar vein
CC Excl: 451.0-451.2, 451.83, 451.89-451.9

451.84 Of upper extremities, unspecified

451.89 Other   CC
Axillary vein
Jugular vein
Subclavian vein
Thrombophlebitis of breast (Mondor's disease)
CC Excl: 451.0-451.2, 451.89-451.9

451.9 Of unspecified site

452 Portal vein thrombosis   MCC
Portal (vein) obstruction
> **EXCLUDES**   hepatic vein thrombosis (453.0)
>   phlebitis of portal vein (572.1)

DEF: Formation of a blood clot in main vein of liver.
CC Excl: 249.70-249.91, 250.70-250.93, 452, 453.40-453.79, 453.81-453.9, 459.89-459.9

✓4ᵗʰ **453 Other venous embolism and thrombosis**
> **EXCLUDES**   that complicating:
>   abortion (634-638 with .7, 639.8)
>   ectopic or molar pregnancy (639.8)
>   pregnancy, childbirth, or the puerperium (671.0-671.9)

AHA: 1Q, '92, 16

453.0 Budd-Chiari syndrome   MCC
Hepatic vein thrombosis
DEF: Thrombosis or other obstruction of hepatic vein; symptoms include enlarged liver, extensive collateral vessels, intractable ascites and severe portal hypertension.
CC Excl: 249.70-249.91, 250.70-250.93, 453.0, 453.40-453.79, 453.81-453.9, 459.89-459.9

453.1 Thrombophlebitis migrans   CC
DEF: Slow, advancing thrombophlebitis; appearing first in one vein then another.
CC Excl: 249.70-249.91, 250.70-250.93, 453.1, 453.40-453.79, 453.81-453.9, 459.89-459.9

▲ **453.2 Of inferior vena cava**   MCC
CC Excl: 249.70-249.91, 250.70-250.93, 453.2, 453.40-453.79, 453.81-453.9, 459.89-459.9

453.3 Of renal vein   CC
CC Excl: 249.70-249.91, 250.70-250.93, 453.3-453.79, 453.81-453.9, 459.89-459.9

N Newborn Age: 0   P Pediatric Age: 0-17   M Maternity Age: 12-55   A Adult Age: 15-124   MCC Major CC Condition   CC CC Condition   HIV HIV Related Dx

160 – Volume 1 • October 2009

2010 ICD-9-CM

Map of Major Veins

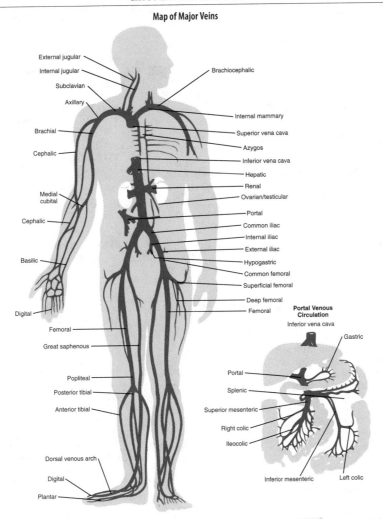

▲ ☑5th **453.4 Acute venous embolism and thrombosis of deep vessels of lower extremity**

AHA: 3Q, '08, 16

▲   **453.40 Acute venous embolism and thrombosis** CC **of unspecified deep vessels of lower extremity**

← Deep vein thrombosis NOS

Also referred to as venous thromboembolism

DVT NOS

CC Excl: 249.70-249.91, 250.70-250.93, 453.40-453.79, 453.81-453.9, 459.89-459.9

I82.40 Embo & thrombo of uns deep veins of I-10 lower extrem

▲   **453.41 Acute venous embolism and thrombosis** CC **of deep vessels of proximal lower extremity**

Femoral
Iliac
Popliteal
Thigh
Upper leg NOS

CC Excl: See code: 453.40

AHA: 4Q, '04, 79

▲   **453.42 Acute venous embolism and thrombosis** CC **of deep vessels of distal lower extremity**

Calf
Lower leg NOS
Peroneal
Tibial

CC Excl: See code: 453.40

● ☑5th **453.5 Chronic venous embolism and thrombosis of deep vessels of lower extremity**

Use additional code, if applicable, for associated long-term (current) use of anticoagulants (V58.61)

EXCLUDES *personal history of venous thrombosis and embolism (V12.51)*

●   **453.50 Chronic venous embolism and thrombosis** CC **of unspecified deep vessels of lower extremity**

CC Excl: See code: 453.40

●   **453.51 Chronic venous embolism and thrombosis** CC **of deep vessels of proximal lower extremity**

CC Excl: See code: 453.40

●   **453.52 Chronic venous embolism and thrombosis** CC **of deep vessels of distal lower extremity**

CC Excl: See code: 453.40

● **453.6 Venous embolism and thrombosis of superficial** CC **vessels of lower extremity**

Saphenous vein (greater) (lesser)

CC Excl: See code: 453.40

● ☑5th **453.7 Chronic venous embolism and thrombosis of other specified vessels**

Use additional code, if applicable, for associated long-term (current) use of anticoagulants (V58.61)

EXCLUDES *personal history of venous thrombosis and embolism (V12.51)*

●   **453.71 Chronic venous embolism and thrombosis** CC **of superficial veins of upper extremity**

Antecubital vein
Basilic vein
Cephalic vein

CC Excl: See code: 453.40

☑4th ☑5th Additional Digit Required   Unacceptable PDx   Manifestation Code   Hospital Acquired Condition   ►◄ Revised Text   ● New Code   ▲ Revised Code Title

2010 ICD-9-CM   **October 2009 • Volume 1 – 161**

453.72 Chronic venous embolism and thrombosis `CC` of deep veins of upper extremity
    Brachial vein
    Radial vein
    Ulnar vein
    CC Excl: 249.70-249.91, 250.70-250.93, 453.40-453.79, 453.81-453.9, 459.89-459.9

453.73 Chronic venous embolism and thrombosis `CC` of upper extremity, unspecified
    CC Excl: See code: 453.72

453.74 Chronic venous embolism and thrombosis `CC` of axillary veins
    CC Excl: See code: 453.72

453.75 Chronic venous embolism and thrombosis `CC` of subclavian veins
    CC Excl: See code: 453.72

453.76 Chronic venous embolism and thrombosis `CC` of internal jugular veins
    CC Excl: See code: 453.72

453.77 Chronic venous embolism and thrombosis `CC` of other thoracic veins
    Brachiocephalic (innominate)
    Superior vena cava
    CC Excl: See code: 453.72

453.79 Chronic venous embolism and thrombosis `CC` of other specified veins
    CC Excl: See code: 453.72

▲ ✓5th **453.8** Acute venous embolism and thrombosis of other specified veins
    EXCLUDES cerebral (434.0-434.9)
      coronary (410.00-410.92)
      intracranial venous sinus (325)
        nonpyogenic (437.6)
      mesenteric (557.0)
      portal (452)
      precerebral (433.0-433.9)
      pulmonary (415.19)
    AHA: 3Q, '91, 16; M-A, '87, 6

453.81 Acute venous embolism and thrombosis `CC` of superficial veins of upper extremity
    Antecubital vein
    Basilic vein
    Cephalic vein
    CC Excl: 249.70-249.91, 250.70-250.93, 453.40-453.79, 453.81-453.9, 459.89-459.9

453.82 Acute venous embolism and thrombosis `CC` of deep veins of upper extremity
    Brachial vein
    Radial vein
    Ulnar vein
    CC Excl: See code: 453.81

453.83 Acute venous embolism and thrombosis `CC` of upper extremity, unspecified
    CC Excl: See code: 453.81

453.84 Acute venous embolism and thrombosis `CC` of axillary veins
    CC Excl: See code: 453.81

453.85 Acute venous embolism and thrombosis `CC` of subclavian veins
    CC Excl: See code: 453.81

453.86 Acute venous embolism and thrombosis `CC` of internal jugular veins
    CC Excl: See code: 453.81

453.87 Acute venous embolism and thrombosis `CC` of other thoracic veins
    Brachiocephalic (innominate)
    Superior vena cava
    CC Excl: See code: 453.81

453.89 Acute venous embolism and thrombosis `CC` of other specified veins
    CC Excl: See code: 453.81
    I82.89 Embolism and thrombosis of other `I-10` specified veins

453.9 Of unspecified site `CC`
    Embolism of vein
    Thrombosis (vein)
    CC Excl: See code: 453.81

✓4th **454** Varicose veins of lower extremities
    EXCLUDES that complicating pregnancy, childbirth, or the puerperium (671.0)
    DEF: Dilated leg veins; due to incompetent vein valves that allow reversed blood flow and cause tissue erosion or weakness of wall; may be painful.
    AHA: 2Q, '91, 20

454.0 With ulcer `A`
    Varicose ulcer (lower extremity, any part)
    Varicose veins with ulcer of lower extremity [any part] or of unspecified site
    Any condition classifiable to 454.9 with ulcer or specified as ulcerated
    AHA: 4Q, '99, 18

454.1 With inflammation `A`
    Stasis dermatitis
    Varicose veins with inflammation of lower extremity [any part] or of unspecified site
    Any condition classifiable to 454.9 with inflammation or specified as inflamed

454.2 With ulcer and inflammation `CC` `A`
    Varicose veins with ulcer and inflammation of lower extremity [any part] or of unspecified site
    Any condition classifiable to 454.9 with ulcer and inflammation
    CC Excl: 454.0-454.2, 454.9

454.8 With other complications
    Edema
    Pain
    Swelling
    AHA: 4Q, '02, 58

454.9 Asymptomatic varicose veins `A`
    Phlebectasia
    Varicose veins   } of lower extremity [any part] or of unspecified site
    Varix
    Varicose veins NOS
    AHA: 4Q, '02, 58
    TIP: Do not assign if patient seen for surgical treatment of varicose veins; query physician for specific symptom (inflammation, pain, edema, swelling).

✓4th **455** Hemorrhoids
    INCLUDES hemorrhoids (anus) (rectum)
      piles
      varicose veins, anus or rectum
    EXCLUDES that complicating pregnancy, childbirth, or the puerperium (671.8)
    DEF: Varicose condition of external hemorrhoidal veins causing painful swellings at the anus.

455.0 Internal hemorrhoids without mention of complication
    AHA: 3Q, '05, 17
    I84.21 Internal hemorrhoids without complication `I-10`

455.1 Internal thrombosed hemorrhoids

455.2 Internal hemorrhoids with other complication
    Internal hemorrhoids:
      bleeding
      prolapsed
      strangulated
      ulcerated
    AHA: 3Q, '05, 17; 1Q, '03, 8
    I84.111 Internal bleeding hemorrhoids `I-10`

455.3 External hemorrhoids without mention of complication
    AHA: 1Q, '07, 13; 3Q, '05, 17
    I84.22 External hemorrhoids without complicaton `I-10`

455.4 External thrombosed hemorrhoids

N Newborn Age: 0   P Pediatric Age: 0-17   M Maternity Age: 12-55   A Adult Age: 15-124   MCC Major CC Condition   CC CC Condition   HIV HIV Related Dx

162 – Volume 1 • October 2009   2010 ICD-9-CM

455.5   **External hemorrhoids with other complication**
External hemorrhoids:
  bleeding
  prolapsed
  strangulated
  ulcerated
AHA: 3Q, '05, 17; 1Q, '03, 8

455.6   **Unspecified hemorrhoids without mention of complication**
Hemorrhoids NOS

455.7   **Unspecified thrombosed hemorrhoids**
Thrombosed hemorrhoids, unspecified whether internal or external

455.8   **Unspecified hemorrhoids with other complication**
Hemorrhoids, unspecified whether internal or external:
  bleeding
  prolapsed
  strangulated
  ulcerated

455.9   **Residual hemorrhoidal skin tags**
Skin tags, anus or rectum

✓4ᵗʰ 456 Varicose veins of other sites

456.0   **Esophageal varices with bleeding**   `MCC`
DEF: Distended, tortuous, veins of lower esophagus, usually due to portal hypertension.
CC Excl: 251.5, 456.0, 456.20, 459.89-459.9, 530.20-530.21, 530.7, 530.82, 530.85, 531.00-534.91, 535.01, 535.11, 535.21, 535.31, 535.41, 535.51, 535.61, 537.83, 562.02-562.03, 562.12-562.13, 569.3, 569.85, 578.0-578.9

456.1   **Esophageal varices without mention of bleeding**   `CC`
CC Excl: 251.5, 456.0-456.20, 459.89-459.9, 530.7, 530.82, 531.00-534.91, 535.01, 535.11, 535.21, 535.31, 535.41, 535.51, 535.61, 537.83, 578.0-578.9

✓5ᵗʰ 456.2   **Esophageal varices in diseases classified elsewhere**
Code first underlying cause, as:
  cirrhosis of liver (571.0-571.9)
  portal hypertension (572.3)

    456.20   *With bleeding*   `MCC`
       CC Excl: 456.0, 456.20, 459.89-459.9, 530.82
       AHA: N-D, '85, 14
       I85.11 Secondary esophageal varices with bleeding   `I-10`

    456.21   *Without mention of bleeding*   `CC`
       CC Excl: 251.5, 456.0, 456.20-456.21, 459.89-459.9, 530.7, 530.82, 531.00-534.91, 535.01, 535.11, 535.21, 535.31, 535.41, 535.51, 535.61, 537.83, 578.0-578.9
       AHA: 3Q, '05, 15; 2Q, '02, 4

456.3   **Sublingual varices**
DEF: Distended, tortuous veins beneath tongue.

456.4   **Scrotal varices**   ♂
Varicocele

456.5   **Pelvic varices**
Varices of broad ligament

456.6   **Vulval varices**   ♀
Varices of perineum
EXCLUDES *that complicating pregnancy, childbirth, or the puerperium (671.1)*

456.8   **Varices of other sites**
Varicose veins of nasal septum (with ulcer)
EXCLUDES *placental varices (656.7)*
retinal varices (362.17)
varicose ulcer of unspecified site (454.0)
varicose veins of unspecified site (454.9)
AHA: 2Q, '02, 4

✓4ᵗʰ 457 Noninfectious disorders of lymphatic channels

457.0   **Postmastectomy lymphedema syndrome**   `A`
Elephantiasis
Obliteration of lymphatic vessel } due to mastectomy
DEF: Reduced lymphatic circulation following mastectomy; symptoms include swelling of the arm on the operative side.
AHA: 2Q, '02, 12

457.1   **Other lymphedema**
Elephantiasis (nonfilarial) NOS
Lymphangiectasis
Lymphedema:
  acquired (chronic)
  praecox
  secondary
Obliteration, lymphatic vessel
EXCLUDES *elephantiasis (nonfilarial):*
congenital (757.0)
eyelid (374.83)
vulva (624.8)
DEF: Fluid retention due to reduced lymphatic circulation; due to other than mastectomy.
AHA: 3Q, '04, 5
I89.0 Lymphedema not elsewhere classified   `I-10`

457.2   **Lymphangitis**
Lymphangitis:
  NOS
  chronic
  subacute
EXCLUDES *acute lymphangitis (682.0-682.9)*

457.8   **Other noninfectious disorders of lymphatic channels**
Chylocele (nonfilarial)
Chylous:
  ascites
  cyst
Lymph node or vessel:
  fistula
  infarction
  rupture
EXCLUDES *chylocele:*
filarial (125.0-125.9)
tunica vaginalis (nonfilarial) (608.84)
AHA: 1Q, '04, 5; 3Q, '03, 17

457.9   **Unspecified noninfectious disorder of lymphatic channels**

✓4ᵗʰ 458 Hypotension
INCLUDES hypopiesis
EXCLUDES *cardiovascular collapse (785.50)*
maternal hypotension syndrome (669.2)
shock (785.50-785.59)
Shy-Drager syndrome (333.0)

458.0   **Orthostatic hypotension**
Hypotension:
  orthostatic (chronic)
  postural
DEF: Low blood pressure; occurs when standing.
AHA: 3Q, '00, 8; 3Q, '91, 9
I95.1 Orthostatic hypotension   `I-10`

458.1   **Chronic hypotension**
Permanent idiopathic hypotension
DEF: Persistent low blood pressure.

✓5ᵗʰ 458.2   **Iatrogenic hypotension**
DEF: Abnormally low blood pressure; due to medical treatment.
AHA: 4Q, '03, 60; 3Q, '02, 12; 4Q, '95, 57

    458.21   **Hypotension of hemodialysis**
       Intra-dialytic hypotension
       AHA: 4Q, '03, 61

    458.29   **Other iatrogenic hypotension**
       Postoperative hypotension
       I95.81 Postprocedural hypotension   `I-10`

| ✓4ᵗʰ ✓5ᵗʰ Additional Digit Required | Unacceptable PDx | Manifestation Code | Hospital Acquired Condition | ►◄ Revised Text | ● New Code | ▲ Revised Code Title |

2010 ICD-9-CM   **Volume 1 – 163**

455.5–458.29

458.8 Other specified hypotension
AHA: 4Q, '97, 37

458.9 Hypotension, unspecified
Hypotension (arterial) NOS
I95.9 Hypotension unspecified   I-10

✓4ᵗʰ **459 Other disorders of circulatory system**

459.0 Hemorrhage, unspecified
Rupture of blood vessel NOS
Spontaneous hemorrhage NEC
EXCLUDES *hemorrhage:*
gastrointestinal NOS (578.9)
in newborn NOS (772.9)
secondary or recurrent following trauma
(958.2)
traumatic rupture of blood vessel
(900.0-904.9)
nontraumatic hematoma of soft tissue
(729.92)
AHA: 4Q, '90, 26
R58 Hemorrhage not elsewhere classified   I-10

✓5ᵗʰ **459.1 Postphlebitic syndrome**
Chronic venous hypertension due to deep vein
thrombosis
EXCLUDES *chronic venous hypertension without deep*
vein thrombosis (459.30-459.39)
DEF: Various conditions following deep vein thrombosis;
including edema, pain, stasis dermatitis, cellulitis, varicose
veins and ulceration of the lower leg.
AHA: 4Q, '02, 58; 2Q, '91, 20

**459.10 Postphlebitic syndrome without
complications**
Asymptomatic postphlebitic syndrome
Postphlebitic syndrome NOS

459.11 Postphlebitic syndrome with ulcer   CC
CC Excl: 451.0-451.9

459.12 Postphlebitic syndrome with inflammation

**459.13 Postphlebitic syndrome with ulcer and   CC
inflammation**
CC Excl: See code: 459.11

**459.19 Postphlebitic syndrome with other
complication**

459.2 Compression of vein   CC
Stricture of vein
Vena cava syndrome (inferior) (superior)
CC Excl: 459.2

✓5ᵗʰ **459.3 Chronic venous hypertension (idiopathic)**
Stasis edema
EXCLUDES *chronic venous hypertension due to deep vein*
thrombosis (459.10-459.9)
varicose veins (454.0-454.9)
AHA: 4Q, '02, 59

**459.30 Chronic venous hypertension without
complications**
Asymptomatic chronic venous hypertension
Chronic venous hypertension NOS

**459.31 Chronic venous hypertension   CC
with ulcer**
CC Excl: 454.0-454.2, 454.9, 459.81-459.9
AHA: 4Q, '02, 43

**459.32 Chronic venous hypertension with
inflammation**

**459.33 Chronic venous hypertension with   CC
ulcer and inflammation**
CC Excl: See code: 459.31

**459.39 Chronic venous hypertension with other
complication**

✓5ᵗʰ **459.8 Other specified disorders of circulatory system**

459.81 Venous (peripheral) insufficiency, unspecified
Chronic venous insufficiency NOS
Use additional code for any associated
ulceration (707.10-707.9)
DEF: Insufficient drainage, venous blood, any part of
body, results in edema or dermatosis.
AHA: 3Q, '04, 5; 2Q, '91, 20; M-A, '87, 6
TIP: Assign for stasis dermatitis without varicose
veins or past DVT.
I87.2 Venous insufficiency (chronic) (peripheral) I-10

459.89 Other
Collateral circulation (venous), any site
Phlebosclerosis
Venofibrosis

459.9 Unspecified circulatory system disorder

N Newborn Age: 0   P Pediatric Age: 0-17   M Maternity Age: 12-55   A Adult Age: 15-124   MCC Major CC Condition   CC CC Condition   HIV HIV Related Dx

164 – Volume 1

2010 ICD-9-CM

8. DISEASES OF THE RESPIRATORY SYSTEM (460-519)

Use additional code to identify infectious organism

ACUTE RESPIRATORY INFECTIONS (460-466)

EXCLUDES *pneumonia and influenza (480.0-488)*

460 Acute nasopharyngitis [common cold]
Coryza (acute)
Nasal catarrh, acute
Nasopharyngitis:
  NOS
  acute
  infective NOS
Rhinitis:
  acute
  infective

EXCLUDES *nasopharyngitis, chronic (472.2)*
pharyngitis:
  acute or unspecified (462)
  chronic (472.1)
rhinitis:
  allergic (477.0-477.9)
  chronic or unspecified (472.0)
sore throat:
  acute or unspecified (462)
  chronic (472.1)

DEF: Acute inflammation of mucous membranes; extends from nares to pharynx.
AHA: 1Q, '88, 12

✓4ᵗʰ 461 Acute sinusitis
INCLUDES abscess
  empyema
  infection   } acute, of sinus (accessory)
  inflammation   (nasal)
  suppuration

EXCLUDES *chronic or unspecified sinusitis (473.0-473.9)*

461.0 Maxillary
  Acute antritis

461.1 Frontal

461.2 Ethmoidal

461.3 Sphenoidal

461.8 Other acute sinusitis
  Acute pansinusitis

461.9 Acute sinusitis, unspecified
  Acute sinusitis NOS
  J01.90 Acute sinusitis unspecified   `I-10`

462 Acute pharyngitis
Acute sore throat NOS   Pharyngitis (acute):
Pharyngitis (acute):   staphylococca
  NOS   suppurative
  gangrenous   ulcerative
  infective   Sore throat (viral) NOS
  phlegmonous   Viral pharyngitis
  pneumococcal

EXCLUDES *abscess:*
  peritonsillar [quinsy] (475)
  pharyngeal NOS (478.29)
  retropharyngeal (478.24)
chronic pharyngitis (472.1)
infectious mononucleosis (075)
that specified as (due to):
  Coxsackie (virus) (074.0)
  gonococcus (098.6)
  herpes simplex (054.79)
  influenza (487.1)
  septic (034.0)
  streptococcal (034.0)

AHA: 4Q, '99, 26; S-O, '85, 8
J02.9 Acute pharyngitis unspecified   `I-10`

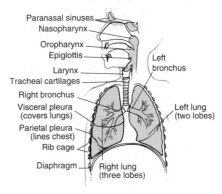

Respiratory System

Paranasal sinuses
Nasopharynx
Oropharynx
Epiglottis   Left
Larynx   bronchus
Tracheal cartilages
Right bronchus
Visceral pleura   Left lung
(covers lungs)   (two lobes)
Parietal pleura
(lines chest)
Rib cage
Diaphragm   Right lung
               (three lobes)

463 Acute tonsillitis
Tonsillitis (acute):
  NOS
  follicular
  gangrenous
  infective
  pneumococcal
  septic
  staphylococcal
  suppurative
  ulcerative
  viral

EXCLUDES *chronic tonsillitis (474.0)*
hypertrophy of tonsils (474.1)
peritonsillar abscess [quinsy] (475)
sore throat:
  acute or NOS (462)
  septic (034.0)
streptococcal tonsillitis (034.0)

AHA: N-D, '84, 16

✓4ᵗʰ 464 Acute laryngitis and tracheitis
EXCLUDES *that associated with influenza (487.1)*
that due to Streptococcus (034.0)

✓5ᵗʰ 464.0 Acute laryngitis
Laryngitis (acute):
  NOS
  edematous
  Hemophilus influenzae [H. influenzae]
  pneumococcal
  septic
  suppurative
  ulcerative

EXCLUDES *chronic laryngitis (476.0-476.1)*
influenzal laryngitis (487.1)

464.00 Without mention of obstruction

464.01 With obstruction   `MCC`
  CC Excl: 012.20-012.86, 464.00-464.31, 579.8-519.9

✓5ᵗʰ 464.1 Acute tracheitis
Tracheitis (acute):
  NOS
  catarrhal
  viral

EXCLUDES *chronic tracheitis (491.8)*

464.10 Without mention of obstruction

464.11 With obstruction   `MCC`
  CC Excl: 012.20-012.86, 017.90-017.96,
  464.00-464.31, 519.8-519.9

✓5ᵗʰ 464.2 Acute laryngotracheitis
Laryngotracheitis (acute)
Tracheitis (acute) with laryngitis (acute)

EXCLUDES *chronic laryngotracheitis (476.1)*

464.20 Without mention of obstruction

464.21 With obstruction   `MCC`
  CC Excl: See code 464.11

Respiratory System

464.3–472.0

☑5ᵗʰ **464.3** **Acute epiglottitis**
Viral epiglottitis
EXCLUDES *epiglottitis, chronic (476.1)*

464.30 **Without mention of obstruction** `CC`
CC Excl: 464.01, 464.30-464.31, 464.51

464.31 **With obstruction** `MCC`
CC Excl: See code 464.11

464.4 **Croup**
Croup syndrome
DEF: Acute laryngeal obstruction due to allergy, foreign body or infection; symptoms include barking cough, hoarseness and harsh, persistent high-pitched respiratory sound.
J05.0 Acute obstructive laryngitis [croup] `I-10`

☑5ᵗʰ **464.5** **Supraglottitis, unspecified**
DEF: A rapidly advancing generalized upper respiratory infection of the lingual tonsillar area, epiglottic folds, false vocal cords, and the epiglottis.
AHA: 4Q, '01, 42

464.50 **Without mention of obstruction**
AHA: 4Q, '01, 43

464.51 **With obstruction** `MCC`
CC Excl: 012.20-012.86, 017.90-017.96, 464.00-464.31, 519.8-519.9

☑4ᵗʰ **465** **Acute upper respiratory infections of multiple or unspecified sites**
EXCLUDES *upper respiratory infection due to:*
influenza (487.1)
Streptococcus (034.0)

465.0 **Acute laryngopharyngitis**
DEF: Acute infection of the vocal cords and pharynx.

465.8 **Other multiple sites**
Multiple URI
AHA: 4Q, '07, 85

465.9 **Unspecified site**
Acute URI NOS
Upper respiratory infection (acute)
J06.9 Acute upper respiratory infection unspecified `I-10`

☑4ᵗʰ **466** **Acute bronchitis and bronchiolitis**
INCLUDES that with:
bronchospasm
obstruction

466.0 **Acute bronchitis**
Bronchitis, acute or subacute:
fibrinous
membranous
pneumococcal
purulent
septic
viral
with tracheitis
Croupous bronchitis
Tracheobronchitis, acute
EXCLUDES *acute bronchitis with chronic obstructive pulmonary disease (491.22)*

DEF: Acute inflammation of main branches of bronchial tree due to infectious or irritant agents; symptoms include cough with a varied production of sputum, fever, substernal soreness, and lung rales.
AHA: 4Q, '04, 137; 1Q, '04, 3; 4Q, '02, 46; 4Q, '96, 28; 4Q, '91, 24; 1Q, '88, 12
TIP: If documented with COPD, assign only 491.22 Obstructive chronic bronchitis with acute bronchitis.
J20.9 Acute bronchitis unspecified `I-10`

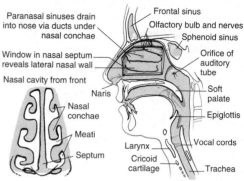

Upper Respiratory System

Paranasal sinuses drain into nose via ducts under nasal conchae
Frontal sinus
Olfactory bulb and nerves
Sphenoid sinus
Window in nasal septum reveals lateral nasal wall
Orifice of auditory tube
Nasal cavity from front
Soft palate
Naris
Nasal conchae
Epiglottis
Meati
Vocal cords
Larynx
Septum
Cricoid cartilage
Trachea

☑5ᵗʰ **466.1** **Acute bronchiolitis**
Bronchiolitis (acute)
Capillary pneumonia
DEF: Acute inflammation of main branches of bronchial tree due to infectious or irritant agents; symptoms include cough, tachycardia, labored breathing, and lung crackles.

466.11 **Acute bronchiolitis due to respiratory** `CC`
syncytial virus (RSV)
CC Excl: 466.11
AHA: 1Q, '05, 10; 4Q, '96, 27
J21.0 Acute bronchiolitis d/t resp syncytial virus `I-10`

466.19 **Acute bronchiolitis due to other infectious** `CC`
organisms
Use additional code to identify organism
CC Excl: 466.0-466.19
J21.8 Acute bronchiolitis d/t oth specified `I-10`
organisms

OTHER DISEASES OF THE UPPER RESPIRATORY TRACT (470-478)

470 **Deviated nasal septum**
Deflected septum (nasal) (acquired)
EXCLUDES *congenital (754.0)*

☑4ᵗʰ **471** **Nasal polyps**
EXCLUDES *adenomatous polyps (212.0)*

471.0 **Polyp of nasal cavity**
Polyp:
choanal
nasopharyngeal

471.1 **Polypoid sinus degeneration**
Woakes' syndrome or ethmoiditis

471.8 **Other polyp of sinus**
Polyp of sinus::
accessory
ethmoidal
maxillary
sphenoidal

471.9 **Unspecified nasal polyp**
Nasal polyp NOS

☑4ᵗʰ **472** **Chronic pharyngitis and nasopharyngitis**

472.0 **Chronic rhinitis**
Ozena
Rhinitis:
NOS
atrophic
granulomatous
hypertrophic
obstructive
purulent
ulcerative
EXCLUDES *allergic rhinitis (477.0-477.9)*
DEF: Persistent inflammation of mucous membranes of nose.

`N` Newborn Age: 0   `P` Pediatric Age: 0-17   `M` Maternity Age: 12-55   `A` Adult Age: 15-124   `MCC` Major CC Condition   `CC` CC Condition   `HIV` HIV Related Dx

166 – Volume 1   **2010 ICD-9-CM**

472.1 Chronic pharyngitis
Chronic sore throat
Pharyngitis:
  atrophic
  granular (chronic)
  hypertrophic

472.2 Chronic nasopharyngitis
> **EXCLUDES** *acute or unspecified nasopharyngitis (460)*

DEF: Persistent inflammation of mucous membranes extending from nares to pharynx.

✓4th 473 Chronic sinusitis
> **INCLUDES** abscess
> empyema   (chronic) of sinus
> infection   (accessory) (nasal)
> suppuration

> **EXCLUDES** *acute sinusitis (461.0-461.9)*

473.0 Maxillary
Antritis (chronic)
J32.0 Chronic maxillary sinusitis   I-10

473.1 Frontal

473.2 Ethmoidal
> **EXCLUDES** *Woakes' ethmoiditis (471.1)*

473.3 Sphenoidal

473.8 Other chronic sinusitis
Pansinusitis (chronic)

473.9 Unspecified sinusitis (chronic)
Sinusitis (chronic) NOS
J32.9 Chronic sinusitis unspecified   I-10

✓4th 474 Chronic disease of tonsils and adenoids

✓5th 474.0 Chronic tonsillitis and adenoiditis
> **EXCLUDES** *acute or unspecified tonsillitis (463)*

AHA: 4Q, '97, 38

474.00 Chronic tonsillitis

474.01 Chronic adenoiditis

474.02 Chronic tonsillitis and adenoiditis

✓5th 474.1 Hypertrophy of tonsils and adenoids
Enlargement
Hyperplasia   of tonsils or adenoids
Hypertrophy

> **EXCLUDES** *that with:*
> *adenoiditis (474.01)*
> *adenoiditis and tonsillitis (474.02)*
> *tonsillitis (474.00)*

474.10 Tonsils with adenoids
AHA: 2Q, '05, 16

474.11 Tonsils alone

474.12 Adenoids alone

474.2 Adenoid vegetations
DEF: Fungus-like growth of lymph tissue between the nares and pharynx.

474.8 Other chronic disease of tonsils and adenoids
Amygdalolith
Calculus, tonsil
Cicatrix of tonsil (and adenoid)
Tonsillar tag
Ulcer, tonsil

474.9 Unspecified chronic disease of tonsils and adenoids
Disease (chronic) of tonsils (and adenoids)

475 Peritonsillar abscess   CC
Abscess of tonsil
Peritonsillar cellulitis
Quinsy
> **EXCLUDES** *tonsillitis:*
> *acute or NOS (463)*
> *chronic (474.0)*

CC Excl: 475, 519.8-519.9
J36 Peritonsillar abscess   I-10

Paranasal Sinuses

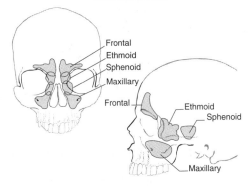

✓4th 476 Chronic laryngitis and laryngotracheitis

476.0 Chronic laryngitis
Laryngitis:
  catarrhal
  hypertrophic
  sicca

476.1 Chronic laryngotracheitis
Laryngitis, chronic, with tracheitis (chronic)
Tracheitis, chronic, with laryngitis
> **EXCLUDES** *chronic tracheitis (491.8)*
> *laryngitis and tracheitis, acute or unspecified*
> *(464.00-464.51)*

✓4th 477 Allergic rhinitis
> **INCLUDES** allergic rhinitis (nonseasonal) (seasonal)
> hay fever
> spasmodic rhinorrhea

> **EXCLUDES** *allergic rhinitis with asthma (bronchial) (493.0)*

DEF: True immunoglobulin E (IgE)-mediated allergic reaction of nasal mucosa; seasonal (typical hay fever) or perennial (year-round allergens: dust, food, dander).

477.0 Due to pollen
Pollinosis

477.1 Due to food
AHA: 4Q, '00, 42

477.2 Due to animal (cat) (dog) hair and dander

477.8 Due to other allergen

477.9 Cause unspecified
AHA: 2Q, '97, 9
J30.9 Allergic rhinitis unspecified   I-10

✓4th 478 Other diseases of upper respiratory tract

478.0 Hypertrophy of nasal turbinates
DEF: Overgrowth, enlargement of shell-shaped bones, in nasal cavity.

✓5th 478.1 Other diseases of nasal cavity and sinuses
> **EXCLUDES** *varicose ulcer of nasal septum (456.8)*

478.11 Nasal mucositis (ulcerative)
Use additional E code to identify adverse effects of therapy, such as:
  antineoplastic and immunosuppressive drugs (E930.7, E933.1)
  radiation therapy (E879.2)
AHA: 4Q, '06, 88-90

478.19 Other diseases of nasal cavity and sinuses
Abscess
Necrosis   of nose (septum)
Ulcer

Cyst or mucocele of sinus (nasal)
Rhinolith
AHA: 4Q, '06, 88-90
J34.1 Cyst and mucocele of nose and nasal   I-10
sinus

✓4th / ✓5th Additional Digit Required   Unacceptable PDx   Manifestation Code   Hospital Acquired Condition   ►◄ Revised Text   ● New Code   ▲ Revised Code Title

2010 ICD-9-CM   **Volume 1 – 167**

Respiratory System

478.2–481

√5ᵗʰ **478.2 Other diseases of pharynx, not elsewhere classified**

478.20 Unspecified disease of pharynx

478.21 Cellulitis of pharynx or nasopharynx `CC`
CC Excl: 478.20-478.24, 519.8-519.9

478.22 Parapharyngeal abscess `CC`
CC Excl: See code: 478.21

478.24 Retropharyngeal abscess `CC`
DEF: Purulent infection, behind pharynx and front of precerebral fascia.
CC Excl: See code 478.21

478.25 Edema of pharynx or nasopharynx

478.26 Cyst of pharynx or nasopharynx

478.29 Other
Abscess of pharynx or nasopharynx
EXCLUDES ulcerative pharyngitis (462)

√5ᵗʰ **478.3 Paralysis of vocal cords or larynx**
DEF: Loss of motor ability of vocal cords or larynx; due to nerve or muscle damage.

478.30 Paralysis, unspecified
Laryngoplegia   Paralysis of glottis

478.31 Unilateral, partial

478.32 Unilateral, complete

478.33 Bilateral, partial

478.34 Bilateral, complete `CC`
CC Excl: 478.30-478.34, 478.5, 478.70, 519.8-519.9

478.4 Polyp of vocal cord or larynx
EXCLUDES adenomatous polyps (212.1)

478.5 Other diseases of vocal cords
Abscess
Cellulitis } of vocal cords
Granuloma
Leukoplakia
Chorditis (fibrinous) (nodosa) (tuberosa)
Singers' nodes

478.6 Edema of larynx
Edema (of):   Edema (of):
glottis   supraglottic
subglottic

√5ᵗʰ **478.7 Other diseases of larynx, not elsewhere classified**

478.70 Unspecified disease of larynx

478.71 Cellulitis and perichondritis of larynx `CC`
DEF: Inflammation of deep soft tissues or lining of bone of the larynx.
CC Excl: 478.70-478.71, 478.79

478.74 Stenosis of larynx

478.75 Laryngeal spasm
Laryngismus (stridulus)
DEF: Involuntary muscle contraction of the larynx.

478.79 Other
Abscess
Necrosis
Obstruction } of larynx
Pachyderma
Ulcer
EXCLUDES ulcerative laryngitis (464.00-464.01)
AHA: 3Q, '91, 20

478.8 Upper respiratory tract hypersensitivity reaction, site unspecified
EXCLUDES hypersensitivity reaction of lower respiratory tract, as:
extrinsic allergic alveolitis (495.0-495.9)
pneumoconiosis (500-505)

Lungs

Right Lung (Three Lobes)   Trachea   Left Lung (Two Lobes)
Bronchopulmonary   Primary bronchus
segments: S1 S3   Secondary bronchus
Upper lobe   S2   S1,2   S3 Upper lobe
          S5   S4   S4
          S5
Middle lobe   S6
          S4   S7,8
Lower   S8   S9 Lower lobe
lobe
Diaphragm   S9 S10   S7 S10

478.9 Other and unspecified diseases of upper respiratory tract
Abscess
Cicatrix } of trachea

PNEUMONIA AND INFLUENZA (480-488)

EXCLUDES pneumonia:
allergic or eosinophilic (518.3)
aspiration:
NOS (507.0)
newborn (770.18)
solids and liquids (507.0-507.8)
congenital (770.0)
lipoid (507.1)
passive (514)
rheumatic (390)
ventilator-associated (997.31)

Do not assign separate code for organism if included in pneumonia code.

√4ᵗʰ **480 Viral pneumonia**

480.0 Pneumonia due to adenovirus `MCC`
CC Excl: 011.00-012.16, 012.80-012.86, 017.90-017.96, 020.3-020.5, 021.3, 022.1, 031.0, 039.1, 073.0, 115.05, 115.15, 115.95, 122.1, 130.4, 136.3, 480.0-487.1, 488, 495.0-495.9, 500-508.9, 517.1, 517.8, 518.89, 519.8-519.9

480.1 Pneumonia due to respiratory syncytial virus `MCC`
CC Excl: See code: 480.0
AHA: 4Q, '96, 28; 1Q, '88, 12

480.2 Pneumonia due to parainfluenza virus `MCC`
CC Excl: See code: 480.0

480.3 Pneumonia due to SARS-associated coronavirus `MCC`
DEF: A severe adult respiratory syndrome caused by the coronavirus, specified as inflammation of the lungs with consolidation.
CC Excl: 011.00-012.16, 012.80-012.86, 017.90-017.96, 021.2, 031.0, 039.1, 115.05, 115.15, 115.95, 122.1, 130.4, 136.3, 480.0-487.1, 488, 494.0-508.9, 517.1, 517.8, 518.89, 519.8-519.9, 748.61
AHA: 4Q, '03, 46-47

480.8 Pneumonia due to other virus not elsewhere classified `MCC` `HIV`
EXCLUDES congenital rubella pneumonitis (771.0)
influenza with pneumonia, any form (487.0)
pneumonia complicating viral diseases classified elsewhere (484.1-484.8)
CC Excl: See code: 480.0

480.9 Viral pneumonia, unspecified `MCC` `HIV`
CC Excl: See code: 480.0
AHA: 3Q, '98, 5

481 Pneumococcal pneumonia [Streptococcus pneumoniae pneumonia] `MCC` `HIV`
Lobar pneumonia, organism unspecified
CC Excl: 011.00-012.16, 012.80-012.86, 017.90-017.96, 021.2, 031.0, 039.1, 115.05, 115.15, 115.95, 122.1, 130.4, 136.3, 480.0-480.2, 480.8-487.1, 488, 494.0-508.9, 517.1, 517.8, 518.89, 519.8-519.9, 748.61
AHA: 2Q, '98, 7; 4Q, '92, 19; 1Q, '92, 18; 1Q, '91, 13; 1Q, '88, 13; M-A, '85, 6

A diagnosis of lobar pneumonia does not refer to the lobe affected but a particular type of pneumonia.

N Newborn Age: 0   P Pediatric Age: 0-17   M Maternity Age: 12-55   A Adult Age: 15-124   MCC Major CC Condition   CC CC Condition   HIV HIV Related Dx

168 – Volume 1   2010 ICD-9-CM

√4th **482 Other bacterial pneumonia**
   AHA: 4Q, '93, 39

   482.0 Pneumonia due to Klebsiella pneumoniae   `MCC` `HIV`
      CC Excl: See code 481

   482.1 Pneumonia due to Pseudomonas   `MCC` `HIV`
      CC Excl: See code 481

   482.2 Pneumonia due to Hemophilus influenzae [H. influenzae]   `MCC` `HIV`
      CC Excl: See code 481
      AHA: 2Q, '05, 19

   √5th **482.3 Pneumonia due to Streptococcus**
      EXCLUDES   *Streptococcus pneumoniae (481)*
      AHA: 1Q, '88, 13

      482.30 Streptococcus, unspecified   `MCC` `HIV`
         CC Excl: See code 481

      482.31 Group A   `MCC` `HIV`
         CC Excl: See code 481

      482.32 Group B   `MCC` `HIV`
         CC Excl: See code 481

      482.39 Other Streptococcus   `MCC` `HIV`
         CC Excl: See code 481

   √5th **482.4 Pneumonia due to Staphylococcus**
      AHA: 3Q, '91, 16

      482.40 Pneumonia due to Staphylococcus, unspecified   `MCC` `HIV`
         CC Excl: See code 481

      482.41 Methicillin susceptible pneumonia due to Staphylococcus aureus   `MCC` `HIV`
         Staphylococcus aureus
         MSSA pneumonia
         Pneumonia due to Staphylococcus aureus NOS
         CC Excl: See code 481
         J15.21 Pneumonia due to staphylococcus aureus   `I-10`

      482.42 Methicillin resistant pneumonia due to Staphylococcus aureus   `MCC` `HIV`
         CC Excl: See code 481
         AHA: ▶4Q, '08, 69, 71, 72◀

      482.49 Other Staphylococcus pneumonia   `MCC` `HIV`
         CC Excl: See code 481

   √5th **482.8 Pneumonia due to other specified bacteria**
      EXCLUDES   *pneumonia, complicating infectious disease classified elsewhere (484.1-484.8)*
      AHA: 3Q, '88, 11

      482.81 Anaerobes   `MCC` `HIV`
         Bacteroides (melaninogenicus)
         Gram-negative anaerobes
         CC Excl: See code 481

      482.82 Escherichia coli [E. coli]   `MCC` `HIV`
         CC Excl: See code 481

      482.83 Other gram-negative bacteria   `MCC` `HIV`
         Gram-negative pneumonia NOS
         Proteus
         Serratia marcescens
         EXCLUDES   *gram-negative anaerobes (482.81)*
                        Legionnaires' disease (482.84)
         CC Excl: See code 481
         AHA: 2Q, '98, 5; 3Q, '94, 9
         TIP: Do not assign based solely on laboratory findings of gram-negative bacteria on gram-stain. Physician substantiation is required.
         J15.6 Pneumonia d/t oth aerobic Gram-negative bacteria   `I-10`

   482.84 Legionnaires' disease   `MCC` `HIV`
      DEF: Severe and often fatal infection by Legionella pneumophilia; symptoms include high fever, gastrointestinal pain, headache, myalgia, dry cough, and pneumonia; usually transmitted airborne via air conditioning systems.
      CC Excl: See code 481
      AHA: 4Q, '97, 38

An additional code should be assigned for the responsible organism.

   482.89 Other specified bacteria   `MCC` `HIV`
      CC Excl: See code 481
      AHA: 2Q, '97, 6
      TIP: Do not assign based on documentation of "mixed bacterial pneumonia" or "gram-positive pneumonia." See instead 482.9.

   482.9 Bacterial pneumonia unspecified   `MCC` `HIV`
      CC Excl: See code 481
      AHA: 2Q, '98, 6; 2Q, '97, 6; 1Q, '94, 17
      J15.9 Unspecified bacterial pneumonia   `I-10`

√4th **483 Pneumonia due to other specified organism**
   AHA: N-D, '87, 5
   TIP: Do not assign if pneumonia due to candidiasis; see instead code 112.4.

   483.0 Mycoplasma pneumoniae   `MCC`
      Eaton's agent
      Pleuropneumonia-like organism [PPLO]
      CC Excl: See code 481

   483.1 Chlamydia   `MCC`
      CC Excl: See code 481
      AHA: 4Q, '96, 31

   483.8 Other specified organism   `MCC`
      CC Excl: See code 481

√4th **484 Pneumonia in infectious diseases classified elsewhere**
   EXCLUDES   *influenza with pneumonia, any form (487.0)*

   484.1 Pneumonia in cytomegalic inclusion disease   `MCC`
      Code first underlying disease (078.5)
      CC Excl: See code 481

   484.3 Pneumonia in whooping cough   `MCC`
      Code first underlying disease (033.0-033.9)
      CC Excl: See code 481

   484.5 Pneumonia in anthrax   `MCC`
      Code first underlying disease (022.1)
      CC Excl: See code 481

   484.6 Pneumonia in aspergillosis   `MCC`
      Code first underlying disease (117.3)
      CC Excl: See code 481
      AHA: 4Q, '97, 40

   484.7 Pneumonia in other systemic mycoses   `MCC`
      Code first underlying disease
      EXCLUDES   *pneumonia in:*
                     candidiasis (112.4)
                     coccidioidomycosis (114.0)
                     histoplasmosis (115.0-115.9 with fifth-digit 5)
      CC Excl: See code 481

Respiratory System

484.8 *Pneumonia in other infectious diseases classified elsewhere* `MCC`

Code first underlying disease, as:
Q fever (083.0)
typhoid fever (002.0)

EXCLUDES pneumonia in:
actinomycosis (039.1)
measles (055.1)
nocardiosis (039.1)
ornithosis (073.0)
Pneumocystis carinii (136.3)
salmonellosis (003.22)
toxoplasmosis (130.4)
tuberculosis (011.6)
tularemia (021.2)
varicella (052.1)

CC Excl: See code 481

485 Bronchopneumonia, organism unspecified `MCC`

Bronchopneumonia:
hemorrhagic
terminal
Pleurobronchopneumonia
Pneumonia:
lobular
segmental

EXCLUDES bronchiolitis (acute) (466.11-466.19)
chronic (491.8)
lipoid pneumonia (507.1)

CC Excl: See code 481

486 Pneumonia, organism unspecified `MCC` `HIV`

EXCLUDES hypostatic or passive pneumonia (514)
influenza with pneumonia, any form (487.0)
inhalation or aspiration pneumonia due to foreign materials (507.0-507.8)
pneumonitis due to fumes and vapors (506.0)

CC Excl: 011.00-012.16, 012.80-012.86, 017.90-017.96, 021.2, 031.0, 039.1, 115.05, 115.15, 115.95, 122.1, 130.4, 136.3, 480.0-480.2, 480.8-487.1, 488, 494.0-508.9, 517.1, 517.8, 518.89, 519.8-519.9, 748.61

AHA: 4Q, '08, 142; 4Q, '99, 6; 3Q, '99, 9; 3Q, '98, 7; 2Q, '98, 4, 5; 1Q, '98, 8; 3Q, '97, 9; 3Q, '94, 10; 3Q, '88, 11

TIP: Never assume a causal organism based on laboratory or radiology findings alone.

J18.9 Pneumonia unspecified organism `I-10`

✓4ᵗʰ 487 Influenza

▶Influenza caused by unspecified influenza virus◀

EXCLUDES Hemophilus influenzae [H. influenzae]:
infection NOS (041.5)
▶influenza due to 2009 H1N1 [swine] influenza virus (488.1)
influenza due to identified avian influenza virus (488.0)
influenza due to identified novel H1N1 influenza virus (488.1)◀
laryngitis (464.00-464.01)
meningitis (320.0)

487.0 With pneumonia `MCC`

Influenza with pneumonia, any form
Influenzal:
bronchopneumonia
pneumonia

Use additional code to identify the type of pneumonia (480.0-480.9, 481, 482.0-482.9, 483.0-483.8, 485)

CC Excl: See code 486
AHA: 1Q, '06, 18; 2Q, '05, 18

487.1 With other respiratory manifestations

Influenza NOS
Influenzal:
laryngitis
pharyngitis
respiratory infection (upper) (acute)

AHA: 1Q, '06, 18; 2Q, '05, 18; 4Q, '99, 26

TIP: Selection of the principal diagnosis will be dependent on the circumstances of admission.

J10.1 Influenza d/t oth influenza virus w/resp manifestations `I-10`

Bronchioli and Alveoli

To trachea
Pulmonary arteriole
Terminal bronchiolus
Elastic fibers
Capillary network over all alveoli
Alveoli
Alveolus

487.8 With other manifestations

Encephalopathy due to influenza
Influenza with involvement of gastrointestinal tract

EXCLUDES "intestinal flu" [viral gastroenteritis] (008.8)

▲ ✓4ᵗʰ 488 Influenza due to certain identified influenza viruses

EXCLUDES ▶influenza caused by unspecified influenza viruses (487.0-487.8)◀

● 488.0 Influenza due to identified avian influenza virus

Avian influenza
Bird flu
Influenza A/H5N1

DEF: Infection caused by contact with bird influenza viruses; results in flu-like symptoms that may progress to other severe and life-threatening complications.

AHA: 4Q, '07, 87

TIP: Assign only if identified avian influenza virus is confirmed; coding may be based on provider diagnostic statement.

[handwritten note: Neither code is assigned when the diagnostic statement indicates that the infection is "suspected" "likely" "possible" or "questionable"]

● 488.1 Influenza due to identified novel H1N1 influenza virus

2009 H1N1 [swine] influenza virus
Novel 2009 influenza H1N1
Novel H1N1 influenza
Novel influenza A/H1N1
Swine flu

CHRONIC OBSTRUCTIVE PULMONARY DISEASE AND ALLIED CONDITIONS (490-496)

AHA: 3Q, '88, 5

TIP: Due to the overlapping nature of conditions that make up COPD, it's essential that the coder review all instructional notes carefully.

490 Bronchitis, not specified as acute or chronic

Bronchitis NOS:
catarrhal
with tracheitis NOS
Tracheobronchitis NOS

EXCLUDES bronchitis:
allergic NOS (493.9)
asthmatic NOS (493.9)
due to fumes and vapors (506.0)

J40 Bronchitis not specified as acute or chronic `I-10`

✓4ᵗʰ 491 Chronic bronchitis

EXCLUDES chronic obstructive asthma (493.2)

491.0 Simple chronic bronchitis

Catarrhal bronchitis, chronic
Smokers' cough

J41.0 Simple chronic bronchitis `I-10`

491.1 Mucopurulent chronic bronchitis

Bronchitis (chronic) (recurrent):
fetid
mucopurulent
purulent

DEF: Chronic bronchial infection characterized by both mucus and pus secretions in the bronchial tree; recurs after asymptomatic periods; signs are coughing, expectoration and secondary changes in the lung.

AHA: 3Q, '88, 12

`N` Newborn Age: 0   `P` Pediatric Age: 0-17   `M` Maternity Age: 12-55   `A` Adult Age: 15-124   `MCC` Major CC Condition   `CC` CC Condition   `HIV` HIV Related Dx

170 – Volume 1 • October 2009

2010 ICD-9-CM

[Handwritten note at top:] Other terms for status asthmaticus:
- Intractable Asthma Attack
- Refractory Asthma
- Severe, intractable wheezing
- Airway obstruction not relieved by bronchodilators
- Severe, prolonged asthmatic attack

Interrelationship Between Chronic Airway Obstruction, Chronic Bronchitis, and Emphysema

Chronic Bronchitis 491

Chronic Airway Obstruction (COPD, NOS) 496

Emphysema 492

Shaded area:
Obstructive Chronic Bronchitis (Chronic Bronchitis with COPD) 491.20-491.21

√5ᵗʰ **491.2 Obstructive chronic bronchitis**
Bronchitis:
  emphysematous
  obstructive (chronic) (diffuse)
Bronchitis with:
  chronic airway obstruction
  emphysema

EXCLUDES asthmatic bronchitis (acute) NOS (493.9)
  chronic obstructive asthma (493.2)

AHA: 3Q, '97, 9; 4Q, '91, 25; 2Q, '91, 21

491.20 Without exacerbation
Emphysema with chronic bronchitis

AHA: 3Q, '97, 9

J44.9 Chronic obstructive pulmonary disease, unspec   I-10

491.21 With (acute) exacerbation   CC
Acute exacerbation of chronic obstructive pulmonary disease [COPD]
Decompensated chronic obstructive pulmonary disease [COPD]
Decompensated chronic obstructive pulmonary disease [COPD] with exacerbation

EXCLUDES chronic obstructive asthma with acute exacerbation (493.22)

CC Excl: 491.1-491.9, 493.20-493.21

AHA: 1Q, '04, 3; 3Q, '02, 18, 19; 4Q, '01, 43; 2Q, '96, 10

J44.1 Chronic obst pulmonary disease with exacerbation   I-10

[Handwritten note in left margin:] terms include:
COPD in exacerbation
severe COPD in exacerbation
→ endstage COPD in exacerbation
decompensated COPD
exacerbation of COPD
acute exacerbation of chronic obstructive bronchitis

491.22 With acute bronchitis   CC
CC Excl: See code 491.21
AHA: 3Q, '06, 20; 4Q, '04, 82
J44.0 Chronic obst pulm dz acute lower respiratory inf   I-10

491.8 Other chronic bronchitis
Chronic:
  tracheitis
  tracheobronchitis

491.9 Unspecified chronic bronchitis
J42 Unspecified chronic bronchitis   I-10

√4ᵗʰ **492 Emphysema**
AHA: 2Q, '91, 21

492.0 Emphysematous bleb
Giant bullous emphysema
Ruptured emphysematous bleb
Tension pneumatocele
Vanishing lung
DEF: Formation of vesicle or bulla in emphysematous lung, more than one millimeter; contains serum or blood.
AHA: 2Q, '93, 3

492.8 Other emphysema
Emphysema (lung or pulmonary):
  NOS
  centriacinar
  centrilobular
  obstructive
  panacinar
  panlobular
  unilateral
  vesicular
MacLeod's syndrome
Swyer-James syndrome
Unilateral hyperlucent lung

EXCLUDES emphysema:
  with chronic bronchitis (491.20-491.22)
  compensatory (518.2)
  due to fumes and vapors (506.4)
  interstitial (518.1)
    newborn (770.2)
  mediastinal (518.1)
  surgical (subcutaneous) (998.81)
  traumatic (958.7)

AHA: 4Q, '08, 175; 1Q, '05, 4; 4Q, '93, 41; J-A, '84, 17

J43.9 Emphysema unspecified   I-10

√4ᵗʰ **493 Asthma**

EXCLUDES wheezing NOS (786.07)

The following fifth-digit subclassification is for use with codes 493.0-493.2, 493.9:
  0 unspecified
  [handwritten: See above ←] 1 with status asthmaticus
  2 with (acute) exacerbation

DEF: Status asthmaticus: severe, intractable episode of asthma unresponsive to normal therapeutic measures.

AHA: 4Q, '04, 137; 4Q, '03, 62; 4Q, '01, 43; 4Q, '00, 42; 1Q, '91, 13; 3Q, '88, 9; J-A, '85, 8; N-D, '84, 17

TIP: If documentation indicates both exacerbation and status asthmaticus, assign only the code for status asthmaticus.

§ √5ᵗʰ **493.0 Extrinsic asthma**   CC 1-2
[0-2]   Asthma:
  allergic with stated cause
  atopic
  childhood
  hay
  platinum
Hay fever with asthma

EXCLUDES asthma:
  allergic NOS (493.9)
  detergent (507.8)
  miners' (500)
  wood (495.8)

DEF: Transient stricture of airway diameters of bronchi; due to environmental factor; also called allergic (bronchial) asthma.

CC Excl: For code 493.01 and 493.02: 493.00-493.92, 517.8, 518.89, 519.8-519.9

J45.20 Mild intermittent asthma uncomplicated   I-10

§ √5ᵗʰ **493.1 Intrinsic asthma**   CC 1-2
[0-2]   Late-onset asthma

DEF: Transient stricture, of airway diameters of bronchi; due to pathophysiological disturbances.

CC Excl: For code 493.11 and 493.12: See code 493.01

AHA: 3Q, '88, 9; M-A, '85, 7

§ √5ᵗʰ **493.2 Chronic obstructive asthma**   CC 1-2
[0-2]   Asthma with chronic obstructive pulmonary disease [COPD]
Chronic asthmatic bronchitis

EXCLUDES acute bronchitis (466.0)
  chronic obstructive bronchitis (491.20-491.22)

DEF: Persistent narrowing of airway diameters in the bronchial tree, restricting airflow and causing constant labored breathing.

CC Excl: For code 493.21: 491.1-493.92, 517.8, 518.89, 519.8-519.9; **For code 493.22:** 493.00-493.92, 517.8, 518.89, 519.8-519.9

AHA: 2Q, '91, 21; 2Q, '90, 20; **For code 493.20:** 4Q, '03, 108; **For code 493.22:** ►1Q, '09, 17;◄ 3Q, '06, 20

§   Requires fifth digit. Valid digits are in [brackets] under each code. See category 493 for codes and definitions.

√4ᵗʰ √5ᵗʰ Additional Digit Required   Unacceptable PDx   Manifestation Code   Hospital Acquired Condition   ►◄ Revised Text   ● New Code   ▲ Revised Code Title

2010 ICD-9-CM   **October 2009 • Volume 1 – 171**

491.2–493.2

√5th **493.8** **Other forms of asthma**
AHA: 4Q, '03, 62

493.81 **Exercise induced bronchospasm**

493.82 **Cough variant asthma**

§ √5th **493.9** **Asthma, unspecified** `CC 1-2`
[0-2] Asthma (bronchial) (allergic NOS)
Bronchitis:
allergic
asthmatic
CC Excl: For code 493.91 and 493.92: 493.00-493.92, 517.8, 518.89, 519.8-519.9
AHA: 4Q, '97, 40, For code 493.90: 4Q, '04, 137; 4Q, '03, 108; 4Q, '99, 25; 1Q, '97, 7; **For code 493.91:** 1Q, '05, 5; **For code 493.92:** 1Q, '03, 9
J45.909 Unspecified asthma uncomplicated `I-10`
J45.901 Unspecified asthma with acute exacerbation `I-10`

494 **Bronchiectasis**
Bronchiectasis (fusiform) (postinfectious) (recurrent)
Bronchiolectasis
EXCLUDES congenital (748.61)
tuberculous bronchiectasis (current disease) (011.5)
DEF: Dilation of bronchi; due to infection or chronic conditions; causes decreased lung capacity and recurrent infections of lungs.
AHA: 4Q, '00, 42
J47.9 Bronchiectasis uncomplicated `I-10`

494.0 **Bronchiectasis without acute exacerbation**

494.1 **Bronchiectasis with acute exacerbation** `CC`
CC Excl: 017.90-017.96, 487.1, 488, 494.1, 496, 506.1, 506.4-506.9, 748.61

√4th **495** **Extrinsic allergic alveolitis**
`INCLUDES` allergic alveolitis and pneumonitis due to inhaled organic dust particles of fungal, thermophilic actinomycete, or other origin
DEF: Pneumonitis due to particles inhaled into lung, often at workplace; symptoms include cough, chills, fever, increased heart and respiratory rates; develops within hours of exposure.

495.0 **Farmers' lung**

495.1 **Bagassosis**

495.2 **Bird-fanciers' lung**
Budgerigar-fanciers' disease or lung
Pigeon-fanciers' disease or lung

495.3 **Suberosis**
Cork-handlers' disease or lung

495.4 **Malt workers' lung**
Alveolitis due to Aspergillus clavatus

495.5 **Mushroom workers' lung**

495.6 **Maple bark-strippers' lung**
Alveolitis due to Cryptostroma corticale

495.7 **"Ventilation" pneumonitis** `CC`
Allergic alveolitis due to fungal, thermophilic actinomycete, and other organisms growing in ventilation [air conditioning] systems
CC Excl: 011.00-012.16, 012.80-012.86, 017.90-017.96, 021.2, 031.0, 039.1, 115.05, 115.15, 115.95, 122.1, 130.4, 136.3, 480.0-480.2, 480.8-487.1, 488, 494.0-508.9, 517.1, 517.8, 518.89, 519.8-519.9, 748.61

495.8 **Other specified allergic alveolitis and pneumonitis** `CC`
Cheese-washers' lung
Coffee workers' lung
Fish-meal workers' lung
Furriers' lung
Grain-handlers' disease or lung
Pituitary snuff-takers' disease
Sequoiosis or red-cedar asthma
Wood asthma
CC Excl: See code 495.7

495.9 **Unspecified allergic alveolitis and pneumonitis** `CC`
Alveolitis, allergic (extrinsic)
Hypersensitivity pneumonitis
CC Excl: See code 495.7

496 **Chronic airway obstruction, not elsewhere classified**
Note: This code is not to be used with any code from categories 491-493
Chronic:
nonspecific lung disease
obstructive lung disease
obstructive pulmonary disease [COPD] NOS
EXCLUDES chronic obstructive lung disease [COPD] specified (as) (with):
allergic alveolitis (495.0-495.9)
asthma (493.20-493.22)
bronchiectasis (494.0-494.1)
bronchitis (491.20-491.22)
with emphysema (491.20-491.22)
decompensated (491.21)
emphysema (492.0-492.8)
AHA: ▶1Q, '09, 16;◀ 3Q, '07, 10; 4Q, '03, 109; 2Q, '00, 15; 2Q, '92, 16; 2Q, '91, 21; 3Q, '88, 56
TIP: COPD is a nonspecific term that encompasses many different respiratory conditions; review medical record and query physician for more specific documentation of emphysema, bronchitis, asthma, etc.
J44.9 Chronic obstructive pulmonary disease unspec `I-10`

PNEUMOCONIOSES AND OTHER LUNG DISEASES DUE TO EXTERNAL AGENTS (500-508)
DEF: Permanent deposits of particulate matter, within lungs; due to occupational or environmental exposure; results in chronic induration and fibrosis. (See specific listings in 500-508 code range)

500 **Coal workers' pneumoconiosis** `A`
Anthracosilicosis
Anthracosis
Black lung disease
Coal workers' lung
Miner's asthma

501 **Asbestosis** `A`

502 **Pneumoconiosis due to other silica or silicates**
Pneumoconiosis due to talc
Silicotic fibrosis (massive) of lung
Silicosis (simple) (complicated)

503 **Pneumoconiosis due to other inorganic dust**
Aluminosis (of lung)
Baritosis
Bauxite fibrosis (of lung)
Berylliosis
Graphite fibrosis (of lung)
Siderosis
Stannosis

504 **Pneumonopathy due to inhalation of other dust**
Byssinosis
Cannabinosis
Flax-dressers' disease
EXCLUDES allergic alveolitis (495.0-495.9)
asbestosis (501)
bagassosis (495.1)
farmers' lung (495.0)

505 **Pneumoconiosis, unspecified**

√4th **506** **Respiratory conditions due to chemical fumes and vapors**
Use additional E code to identify cause

506.0 **Bronchitis and pneumonitis due to fumes and vapors** `CC`
Chemical bronchitis (acute)
CC Excl: 011.00-012.16, 012.80-012.86, 017.90-017.96, 021.2, 031.0, 039.1, 115.05, 115.15, 115.95, 122.1, 130.4, 136.3, 480.0-480.2, 480.8-487.1, 488, 494.0-508.9, 517.1, 517.8, 518.89, 519.8-519.9, 748.61
AHA: 3Q, '08, 7

§ Requires fifth digit. Valid digits are in [brackets] under each code. See category 493 for codes and definitions.

`N` Newborn Age: 0 `P` Pediatric Age: 0-17 `M` Maternity Age: 12-55 `A` Adult Age: 15-124 `MCC` Major CC Condition `CC` CC Condition `HIV` HIV Related Dx

172 – Volume 1 · October 2009

2010 ICD-9-CM

506.1   Acute pulmonary edema due to fumes and vapors   `MCC`

Chemical pulmonary edema (acute)

> **EXCLUDES**   acute pulmonary edema NOS (518.4)
> chronic or unspecified pulmonary edema (514)

CC Excl: See code 506.0

AHA: 3Q, '88, 4

506.2   Upper respiratory inflammation due to fumes and vapors

AHA: 3Q, '05, 10

506.3   Other acute and subacute respiratory conditions due to fumes and vapors

506.4   Chronic respiratory conditions due to fumes and vapors

Emphysema (diffuse) (chronic) ⎤ due to inhalation of
Obliterative bronchiolitis   ⎬ chemical
   (chronic) (subacute)   ⎟ fumes and
Pulmonary fibrosis (chronic) ⎦ vapors

506.9   Unspecified respiratory conditions due to fumes and vapors

Silo-fillers' disease

√4ᵗʰ 507   Pneumonitis due to solids and liquids

> **EXCLUDES**   fetal aspiration pneumonitis (770.18)

AHA: 3Q, '91, 16

507.0   Due to inhalation of food or vomitus   `MCC`

Aspiration pneumonia (due to):
   NOS
   food (regurgitated)
   gastric secretions
   milk
   saliva
   vomitus

CC Excl: See code 506.0

AHA: 1Q, '08, 18;1Q, '89, 10

TIP: Assign an additional code for pneumonia due to a specific organism if that documentation is provided in addition to aspiration pneumonia.

J69.0 Pneumonitis due to inhalation of food and vomit   `I-10`

507.1   Due to inhalation of oils and essences   `MCC`

Lipoid pneumonia (exogenous)

> **EXCLUDES**   endogenous lipoid pneumonia (516.8)

CC Excl: See code 506.0

507.8   Due to other solids and liquids   `MCC`

Detergent asthma

CC Excl: See code 506.0

√4ᵗʰ 508   Respiratory conditions due to other and unspecified external agents

Use additional E code to identify cause

508.0   Acute pulmonary manifestations due to radiation   `CC`

Radiation pneumonitis

CC Excl: See code 506.0

AHA: 2Q, '88, 4

508.1   Chronic and other pulmonary manifestations due to radiation   `CC`

Fibrosis of lung following radiation

CC Excl: See code 506.0

508.8   Respiratory conditions due to other specified external agents

508.9   Respiratory conditions due to unspecified external agent

OTHER DISEASES OF RESPIRATORY SYSTEM (510-519)

√4ᵗʰ 510   Empyema

Use additional code to identify infectious organism (041.0-041.9)

> **EXCLUDES**   abscess of lung (513.0)

DEF: Purulent infection; within pleural space.

510.0   With fistula   `MCC`

Fistula:
   bronchocutaneous
   bronchopleural
   hepatopleural
   mediastinal
   pleural
   thoracic

Any condition classifiable to 510.9 with fistula

DEF: Purulent infection of respiratory cavity; with communication from cavity to another structure.

CC Excl: 510.0-510.9, 517.8, 518.89, 519.8-519.9

510.9   Without mention of fistula   `MCC`

Abscess:
   pleura
   thorax
Empyema (chest) (lung) (pleura)
Fibrinopurulent pleurisy
Pleurisy:
   purulent
   septic
   seropurulent
   suppurative
Pyopneumothorax
Pyothorax

CC Excl: See code: 510.0

AHA: 4Q, '07, 113; 3Q, '94, 6

J86.9 Pyothorax without fistula   `I-10`

√4ᵗʰ 511   Pleurisy

> **EXCLUDES**   pleurisy with mention of tuberculosis, current disease (012.0)

DEF: Inflammation of serous membrane of lungs and lining of thoracic cavity; causes exudation in cavity or membrane surface.

511.0   Without mention of effusion or current tuberculosis

Adhesion, lung or pleura
Calcification of pleura
Pleurisy (acute) (sterile):
   diaphragmatic
   fibrinous
   interlobar
Pleurisy:
   NOS
   pneumococcal
   staphylococcal
   streptococcal
Thickening of pleura

AHA: 3Q, '94, 5

511.1   With effusion, with mention of a bacterial cause other than tuberculosis   `MCC`

Pleurisy with effusion (exudative) (serous):
   pneumococcal
   staphylococcal
   streptococcal
   other specified nontuberculous bacterial cause

CC Excl: 011.00-012.16, 012.80-012.86, 017.90-017.96, 511.0-511.9, 517.8, 518.89, 519.8-519.9

[handwritten note: When pleural effusion is due to bacterial infection, an additional code for the responsible organism.]

√5ᵗʰ 511.8   Other specified forms of effusion, except tuberculous

> **EXCLUDES**   traumatic (860.2-860.5, 862.29, 862.39)

AHA: ▶4Q, '08, 113-114;◀1Q, '97, 10

[handwritten note: Obstruction of drainage system...regulation of reabsorption of fluid in the pleural space.]

511.81   Malignant pleural effusion   `CC`

Code first malignant neoplasm, if known

CC Excl: 195.8, 197.2-197.3, 198.89-199.2, 209.20, 209.29-209.30, 209.70, 209.79, 239.81-239.9, 511.81-511.89

J91.0 Malignant pleural effusion   `I-10`

√4ᵗʰ √5ᵗʰ Additional Digit Required   Unacceptable PDx   Manifestation Code   Hospital Acquired Condition   ▶◀ Revised Text   ● New Code   ▲ Revised Code Title

2010 ICD-9-CM   **February 2009 • Volume 1 – 173**

Respiratory System

511.89–517.1

511.89 Other specified forms of effusion, except tuberculous `CC`
Encysted pleurisy
Hemopneumothorax
Hemothorax
Hydropneumothorax
Hydrothorax
CC Excl: 011.00-012.16, 012.80-012.86, 017.90-017.96, 511.0-511.9, 517.8, 518.89, 519.8-519.9

511.9 Unspecified pleural effusion `CC`
Pleural effusion NOS   Pleurisy:
Pleurisy: serous
  exudative   with effusion NOS
  serofibrinous
CC Excl: 011.00-012.16, 012.80-012.86, 017.90-017.96, 511.0-511.9, 517.8, 518.89, 519.8-519.9
AHA: 2Q, '03, 7; 3Q, '91, 19; 4Q, '89, 11

TIP: Do not assign when the pleural effusion is a symptom of CHF and no therapeutic treatment (e.g., thoracentesis) is directed towards the pleural effusion.
J90 Pleural effusion not elsewhere classified `I-10`

✓4ᵗʰ **512 Pneumothorax**
DEF: Collapsed lung; due to gas or air in pleural space.

512.0 Spontaneous tension pneumothorax `MCC`
DEF: Leaking air from lung into lining causing collapse.
CC Excl: 512.0-512.8, 517.8, 518.89, 519.8-519.9
AHA: 3Q, '94, 5

512.1 Iatrogenic pneumothorax `CC`
Postoperative pneumothorax
DEF: Air trapped in the lining of the lung following surgery.
CC Excl: See code 512.0
AHA: 4Q, '94, 40

TIP: Pneumothorax is a known risk associated with most thoracic surgery; do not assign based on radiology findings alone, without physician substantiation.
J95.81 Postprocedural pneumothorax `I-10`

512.8 Other spontaneous pneumothorax `CC`
Pneumothorax:
  NOS
  acute
  chronic
EXCLUDES pneumothorax:
  congenital (770.2)
  traumatic (860.0-860.1, 860.4-860.5)
  tuberculous, current disease (011.7)
CC Excl: See code 512.0
AHA: 2Q, '93, 3
J93.9 Pneumothorax unspecified `I-10`

✓4ᵗʰ **513 Abscess of lung and mediastinum**

513.0 Abscess of lung `MCC`
Abscess (multiple) of lung
Gangrenous or necrotic pneumonia
Pulmonary gangrene or necrosis
CC Excl: 006.4, 011.00-012.16, 012.80-012.86, 017.90-017.96, 513.0, 519.8-519.9
AHA: 4Q, '07, 85; 2Q, '98, 7

513.1 Abscess of mediastinum `MCC`
CC Excl: 513.1, 519.8-519.9

514 Pulmonary congestion and hypostasis `CC`
Hypostatic:
  bronchopneumonia
  pneumonia
Passive pneumonia
Pulmonary congestion (chronic) (passive)
Pulmonary edema:
  NOS
  chronic
EXCLUDES acute pulmonary edema:
  NOS (518.4)
  with mention of heart disease or failure (428.1)
  hypostatic pneumonia due to or specified as a specific type of pneumonia–code to the type of pneumonia (480.0-480.9, 481, 482.0-482.49, 483.0-483.8, 485, 486, 487.0)
DEF: Excessive retention of interstitial fluid in the lungs and pulmonary vessels; due to poor circulation.
CC Excl: 514, 517.8, 518.89, 519.8-519.9
AHA: 2Q, '98, 6; 3Q, '88, 5
J81.1 Chronic pulmonary edema `I-10`

515 Postinflammatory pulmonary fibrosis
Cirrhosis of lung
Fibrosis of lung (atrophic) (confluent)
  (massive) (perialveolar)   } chronic or unspecified
  (peribronchial)
Induration of lung
DEF: Fibrosis and scarring of the lungs due to inflammatory reaction.
J84.1 Other interstitial pulmonary diseases w/fibrosis `I-10`

✓4ᵗʰ **516 Other alveolar and parietoalveolar pneumonopathy**

516.0 Pulmonary alveolar proteinosis `CC`
DEF: Reduced ventilation; due to proteinaceous deposits on alveoli; symptoms include dyspnea, cough, chest pain, weakness, weight loss, and hemoptysis.
CC Excl: 011.00-012.16, 012.80-012.86, 017.90-017.96, 494.0-508.9, 515-516.9, 517.2, 517.8, 518.89, 519.8-519.9, 748.61

516.1 Idiopathic pulmonary hemosiderosis `CC`
Code first underlying disease (275.0)
Essential brown induration of lung
DEF: Fibrosis of alveolar walls; marked by abnormal amounts hemosiderin in lungs; primarily affects children; symptoms include anemia, fluid in lungs, and blood in sputum; etiology unknown.
CC Excl: See code: 516.0

516.2 Pulmonary alveolar microlithiasis `CC`
DEF: Small calculi in pulmonary alveoli resembling sand-like particles on x-ray.
CC Excl: See code: 516.0

516.3 Idiopathic fibrosing alveolitis `CC`
Alveolar capillary block
Diffuse (idiopathic) (interstitial) pulmonary fibrosis
Hamman-Rich syndrome
CC Excl: See code: 516.0

516.8 Other specified alveolar and parietoalveolar pneumonopathies `CC`
Endogenous lipoid pneumonia
Interstitial pneumonia (desquamative) (lymphoid)
EXCLUDES lipoid pneumonia, exogenous or unspecified (507.1)
CC Excl: See code: 516.0
AHA: 2Q, '06, 20; 1Q, '92, 12

516.9 Unspecified alveolar and parietoalveolar pneumonopathy `CC`
CC Excl: See code: 516.0

✓4ᵗʰ **517 Lung involvement in conditions classified elsewhere**
EXCLUDES rheumatoid lung (714.81)

517.1 Rheumatic pneumonia `CC`
Code first underlying disease (390)
CC Excl: 011.00-012.16, 012.80-012.86, 017.90-017.96, 480.0-480.2, 480.8-487.1, 488, 494.0-508.9, 515-517.2, 517.8, 518.89, 519.8-519.9, 748.61

`N` Newborn Age: 0   `P` Pediatric Age: 0-17   `M` Maternity Age: 12-55   `A` Adult Age: 15-124   `MCC` Major CC Condition   `CC` CC Condition   `HIV` HIV Related Dx

174 – Volume 1

2010 ICD-9-CM

517.2 Lung involvement in systemic sclerosis `CC`

    Code first underlying disease (710.1)

    CC Excl: 011.00-012.16, 012.80-012.86, 017.90-017.96, 494.0-508.9, 515-516.9, 517.2, 517.8, 518.89, 519.8-519.9, 748.61

517.3 Acute chest syndrome `CC`

    Code first sickle-cell disease in crisis (282.42, 282.62, 282.64, 282.69)

    CC Excl: 280.0-282.3, 282.5-282.63, 282.69-284.2, 284.81-285.9, 289.9, 776.5-776.6

    AHA: 4Q, '03, 51, 56

517.8 Lung involvement in other diseases classified elsewhere

    Code first underlying disease, as:
        amyloidosis (277.30-277.39)
        polymyositis (710.4)
        sarcoidosis (135)
        Sjögren's disease (710.2)
        systemic lupus erythematosus (710.0)

    EXCLUDES *syphilis (095.1)*

    AHA: 2Q, '03, 7

✓4ᵗʰ 518 Other diseases of lung

518.0 Pulmonary collapse `CC`

    Atelectasis
    Collapse of lung
    Middle lobe syndrome

    EXCLUDES *atelectasis:*
        congenital (partial) (770.5)
        primary (770.4)
        tuberculous, current disease (011.8)

    CC Excl: 518.0, 519.8-519.9

    AHA: 4Q, '90, 25

    J98.11 Atelectasis `I-10`

518.1 Interstitial emphysema

    Mediastinal emphysema

    EXCLUDES *surgical (subcutaneous) emphysema (998.81)*
        that in fetus or newborn (770.2)
        traumatic emphysema (958.7)

    DEF: Escaped air from the alveoli trapped in the interstices of the lung; trauma or cough may cause the disease.

518.2 Compensatory emphysema

    DEF: Distention of all or part of the lung caused by disease processes or surgical intervention that decreased volume in another part of the lung; overcompensation reaction to the loss of capacity in another part of the lung.

518.3 Pulmonary eosinophilia `CC`

    Eosinophilic asthma
    Loffler's syndrome
    Pneumonia:
        allergic
        eosinophilic
    Tropical eosinophilia

    DEF: Infiltration, into pulmonary parenchyma of eosinophilia; results in cough, fever, and dyspnea.

    CC Excl: 011.00-012.16, 012.80-012.86, 017.90-017.96, 020.3-020.5, 021.3, 022.1, 031.0, 039.1, 073.0, 115.05, 115.15, 115.95, 122.1, 130.4, 136.3, 480.0-480.2, 480.8-482.41, 482.49-487.1, 488, 494.0-495.9, 500-508.9, 517.1, 517.8, 518.3, 518.89, 519.8-519.9, 748.61

518.4 Acute edema of lung, unspecified `MCC`

    Acute pulmonary edema NOS
    Pulmonary edema, postoperative

    EXCLUDES *pulmonary edema:*
        acute, with mention of heart disease or failure (428.1)
        chronic or unspecified (514)
        due to external agents (506.0-508.9)

    DEF: Severe, sudden fluid retention within lung tissues.

    CC Excl: 398.91, 428.0-428.9, 518.4, 519.8-519.9

    TIP: Do not assign separately if associated with CHF or heart disease; it is incorporated into those codes.

[handwritten note: Any mention of drug dependence or abuse should also be coded.]

518.5 Pulmonary insufficiency following trauma and surgery `MCC`

    Adult respiratory distress syndrome
    Pulmonary insufficiency following:
        shock
        surgery
        trauma
    Shock lung

    EXCLUDES *adult respiratory distress syndrome associated with other conditions (518.82)*
        pneumonia:
        aspiration (507.0)
        hypostatic (514)
        respiratory failure in other conditions (518.81, 518.83-518.84)

    CC Excl: 518.5, 519.8-519.9

    AHA: 4Q, '04, 139; 3Q, '88, 3; 3Q, '88, 7; S-O, '87, 1

    J95.82 Postprocedural respiratory failure `I-10`

518.6 Allergic bronchopulmonary aspergillosis `CC`

    DEF: Noninvasive hypersensitive reaction; due to allergic reaction to *Aspergillus fumigatus* (mold).

    CC Excl: 518.6, 519.8-519.9

    AHA: 4Q, '97, 39

518.7 Transfusion related acute lung injury [TRALI] `CC`

    DEF: A relatively rare, but serious pulmonary complication of blood transfusion, with acute respiratory distress, noncardiogenic pulmonary edema, cyanosis, hypoxemia, hypotension, fever and chills.

    CC Excl: 518.7, 997.31-997.39, 997.91-997.99, 998.81, 998.83-998.9

    AHA: 4Q, '06, 91

✓5ᵗʰ 518.8 Other diseases of lung

518.81 Acute respiratory failure `MCC`

    Respiratory failure NOS

    EXCLUDES *acute and chronic respiratory failure (518.84)*
        acute respiratory distress (518.82)
        chronic respiratory failure (518.83)
        respiratory arrest (799.1)
        respiratory failure, newborn (770.84)

    CC Excl: 518.81-518.84, 519.8-519.9, 799.1

    AHA: ▶2Q, '09, 11;◀ 1Q, '08, 18; 3Q, '07, 6; 2Q, '06, 25; 4Q, '05, 96; 2Q, '05, 19; 1Q, '05, 3-8; 1Q, '05, 3–8; 4Q, '04, 139; 1Q, '03, 15; 4Q, '98, 41; 3Q, '91, 14; 2Q, '91, 3; 4Q, '90, 25; 2Q, '90, 20; 3Q, '88, 7; 3Q, '88, 10; S-O, '87, 1

    TIP: If both respiratory failure and another acute condition are responsible for admission, either may be sequenced as principal diagnosis.

    J96.0 Acute respiratory failure `I-10`

[handwritten note: May be assigned as the principal diagnosis when it is the condition established after study to be chiefly responsible for occasioning the admission to the hospital. Respiratory failure may be listed as a secondary diagnosis if it develops after admission.]

518.82 Other pulmonary insufficiency, not elsewhere classified `CC`

    Acute respiratory distress
    Acute respiratory insufficiency
    Adult respiratory distress syndrome NEC

    EXCLUDES *adult respiratory distress syndrome associated with trauma and surgery (518.5)*
        pulmonary insufficiency following trauma and surgery (518.5)
        respiratory distress:
        NOS (786.09)
        newborn (770.89)
        syndrome, newborn (769)
        shock lung (518.5)

    CC Excl: See code: 518.81

    AHA: 4Q, '03, 105; 2Q, '91, 21; 3Q, '88, 7

    J80 Acute respiratory distress syndrome `I-10`

518.83 Chronic respiratory failure `CC`

    CC Excl: See code: 518.81

    AHA: 4Q, '05, 96; 4Q, '03, 103, 111

    J96.1 Chronic respiratory failure `I-10`

✓4ᵗʰ ✓5ᵗʰ Additional Digit Required   Unacceptable PDx   Manifestation Code   Hospital Acquired Condition   ▶◀ Revised Text   ● New Code   ▲ Revised Code Title

2010 ICD-9-CM   **October 2009 • Volume 1 – 175**

Respiratory System

518.84   **Acute and chronic respiratory failure** `MCC`
Acute on chronic respiratory failure
CC Excl: See code: 518.81

     J96.2 Acute and chronic respiratory failure   `I-10`

518.89   **Other diseases of lung, not elsewhere classified**
Broncholithiasis
Calcification of lung
Lung disease NOS
Pulmolithiasis
DEF: Broncholithiasis: calculi in lumen of transbronchial tree.
DEF: Pulmolithiasis: calculi in lung.
AHA: 3Q, '90, 18; 4Q, '88, 6

     J98.4 Other disorders of lung   `I-10`

✓4ᵗʰ **519**   **Other diseases of respiratory system**

  ✓5ᵗʰ **519.0**   **Tracheostomy complications**

    519.00   **Tracheostomy complication, unspecified** `CC`
CC Excl: 519.00-519.19, 519.8-519.9

    519.01   **Infection of tracheostomy** `CC`
Use additional code to identify type of infection, such as:
  abscess or cellulitis of neck (682.1)
  septicemia (038.0-038.9)
Use additional code to identify organism (041.00-041.9)
CC Excl: See code 519.00
AHA: 4Q, '98, 41

    519.02   **Mechanical complication of tracheostomy** `CC`
Tracheal stenosis due to tracheostomy
CC Excl: See code 519.00

    519.09   **Other tracheostomy complications** `CC`
Hemorrhage due to tracheostomy
Tracheoesophageal fistula due to tracheostomy
CC Excl: See code 519.00

✓5ᵗʰ **519.1**   **Other diseases of trachea and bronchus, not elsewhere classified**
AHA: 3Q, '02, 18; 3Q, '88, 6

    519.11   **Acute bronchospasm**
Bronchospasm NOS
EXCLUDES   acute bronchitis with bronchospasm (466.0)
    asthma (493.00-493.92)
    exercise induced bronchospasm (493.81)
AHA: 4Q, '06, 92

[handwritten note: Bronchospasm is an integral part of asthma or other type of chronic airway obstruction, but no additional code is assigned to indicate its presence. Code 519.11 is assigned only when the underlying cause has not been identified.]

    519.19   **Other diseases of trachea and bronchus**
Calcification ⎫
Stenosis   ⎬ of bronchus or trachea
Ulcer   ⎭
AHA: 4Q, '06, 92

[9] **519.2**   **Mediastinitis**   `MCC`
DEF: Inflammation of tissue between organs behind sternum.
CC Excl: 519.2-519.3, 519.8-519.9

519.3   **Other diseases of mediastinum, not elsewhere classified**
Fibrosis   ⎫
Hernia   ⎬ of mediastinum
Retraction ⎭

519.4   **Disorders of diaphragm**
Diaphragmitis
Paralysis of diaphragm
Relaxation of diaphragm
EXCLUDES   congenital defect of diaphragm (756.6)
    diaphragmatic hernia (551-553 with .3)
      congenital (756.6)

519.8   **Other diseases of respiratory system, not elsewhere classified**
AHA: 4Q, '89, 12

519.9   **Unspecified disease of respiratory system**
Respiratory disease (chronic) NOS

---

9   HAC = when in combination with a procedure code from 36.10-36.19.

`N` Newborn Age: 0	`P` Pediatric Age: 0-17	`M` Maternity Age: 12-55	`A` Adult Age: 15-124	`MCC` Major CC Condition	`CC` CC Condition	`HIV` HIV Related Dx

9. DISEASES OF THE DIGESTIVE SYSTEM (520-579)

DISEASES OF ORAL CAVITY, SALIVARY GLANDS, AND JAWS (520-529)

✓4ᵗʰ **520 Disorders of tooth development and eruption**

520.0 Anodontia
Absence of teeth (complete) (congenital) (partial)
Hypodontia
Oligodontia
EXCLUDES *acquired absence of teeth (525.10-525.19)*

520.1 Supernumerary teeth
Distomolar
Fourth molar
Mesiodens
Paramolar
Supplemental teeth
EXCLUDES *supernumerary roots (520.2)*

520.2 Abnormalities of size and form
Concrescence ⎫
Fusion   ⎬ of teeth
Gemination ⎭

Dens evaginatus
Dens in dente
Dens invaginatus
Enamel pearls
Macrodontia
Microdontia
Peg-shaped [conical] teeth
Supernumerary roots
Taurodontism
Tuberculum paramolare
EXCLUDES *that due to congenital syphilis (090.5)*
tuberculum Carabelli, which is regarded as a normal variation

520.3 Mottled teeth
Mottling of enamel
Dental fluorosis
Nonfluoride enamel opacities

Digestive System

The Oral Cavity

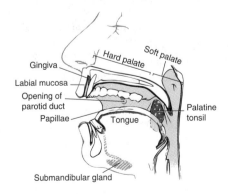

Teeth

Labial frenulum
Mucosa
Vestibule
Gingiva
Upper lip
Hard palate
Uvula
Tongue

Enamel
Dentine
Gingiva (gum)
Root canal
Cementum

Section of molar

Maxillary view

Uvula
Tongue
Gingiva
Lower lip
Mucosa
Vestibule
Frenulum

Enamel
Dentin
Pulp cavity
Alveolar bone
Mandible

Section of incisor

Mandibular view

520.4 Disturbances of tooth formation
Aplasia and hypoplasia of cementum
Dilaceration of tooth
Enamel hypoplasia (neonatal) (postnatal) (prenatal)
Horner's teeth
Hypocalcification of teeth
Regional odontodysplasia
Turner's tooth
EXCLUDES *Hutchinson's teeth and mulberry molars in congenital syphilis (090.5)*
mottled teeth (520.3)

520.5 Hereditary disturbances in tooth structure, not elsewhere classified
Amelogenesis   ⎫
Dentinogenesis ⎬ imperfecta
Odontogenesis ⎭

Dentinal dysplasia
Shell teeth

520.6 Disturbances in tooth eruption
Teeth: Tooth eruption:
    embedded   late
    impacted   obstructed
    natal   premature
    neonatal
    prenatal
    primary [deciduous]:
        persistent
        shedding, premature
EXCLUDES *exfoliation of teeth (attributable to disease of surrounding tissues) (525.0-525.19)*
AHA: 1Q, '06, 18; 2Q, '05, 15

520.7 Teething syndrome

520.8 Other specified disorders of tooth development and eruption
Color changes during tooth formation
Pre-eruptive color changes
EXCLUDES *posteruptive color changes (521.7)*

520.9 Unspecified disorder of tooth development and eruption

✓4ᵗʰ Additional Digit Required   Unacceptable PDx   Manifestation Code   Hospital Acquired Condition   ▶◀ Revised Text   ● New Code   ▲ Revised Code Title
✓5ᵗʰ
2010 ICD-9-CM   **Volume 1 – 177**

520–520.9

✓4ᵗʰ **521 Diseases of hard tissues of teeth**

✓5ᵗʰ **521.0 Dental caries**
AHA: 4Q, '01, 44

521.00 Dental caries, unspecified

521.01 Dental caries limited to enamel
Initial caries
White spot lesion

521.02 Dental caries extending into dentine

521.03 Dental caries extending into pulp

521.04 Arrested dental caries

521.05 Odontoclasia
Infantile melanodontia
Melanodontoclasia

EXCLUDES *internal and external resorption of teeth (521.40-521.49)*

DEF: A pathological dental condition described as stained areas, loss of tooth substance, and hypoplasia linked to nutritional deficiencies during tooth development and to cariogenic oral conditions.

521.06 Dental caries pit and fissure
Primary dental caries, pit and fissure origin

521.07 Dental caries of smooth surface
Primary dental caries, smooth surface origin

521.08 Dental caries of root surface
Primary dental caries, root surface

521.09 Other dental caries
AHA: 3Q, '02, 14

✓5ᵗʰ **521.1 Excessive attrition (approximal wear) (occlusal wear)**

521.10 Excessive attrition, unspecified

521.11 Excessive attrition, limited to enamel

521.12 Excessive attrition, extending into dentine

521.13 Excessive attrition, extending into pulp

521.14 Excessive attrition, localized

521.15 Excessive attrition, generalized

✓5ᵗʰ **521.2 Abrasion**
Abrasion:
  dentifrice
  habitual
  occupational   } of teeth
  ritual
  traditional
  Wedge defect NOS

521.20 Abrasion, unspecified

521.21 Abrasion, limited to enamel

521.22 Abrasion, extending into dentine

521.23 Abrasion, extending into pulp

521.24 Abrasion, localized

521.25 Abrasion, generalized

✓5ᵗʰ **521.3 Erosion**
Erosion of teeth:
  NOS
  due to:
    medicine
    persistent vomiting
  idiopathic
  occupational

521.30 Erosion, unspecified

521.31 Erosion, limited to enamel

521.32 Erosion, extending into dentine

521.33 Erosion, extending into pulp

521.34 Erosion, localized

521.35 Erosion, generalized

✓5ᵗʰ **521.4 Pathological resorption**
DEF: Loss of dentin and cementum due to disease process.

521.40 Pathological resorption, unspecified

521.41 Pathological resorption, internal

521.42 Pathological resorption, external

521.49 Other pathological resorption
Internal granuloma of pulp

521.5 Hypercementosis
Cementation hyperplasia
DEF: Excess deposits of cementum, on tooth root. Primary dental caries, root surface

521.6 Ankylosis of teeth
DEF: Adhesion of tooth to surrounding bone.

521.7 Intrinsic posteruptive color changes
Staining [discoloration] of teeth:
  NOS
  due to:
    drugs
    metals
    pulpal bleeding

EXCLUDES *accretions [deposits] on teeth (523.6)*
extrinsic color changes (523.6)
pre-eruptive color changes (520.8)

✓5ᵗʰ **521.8 Other specified diseases of hard tissues of teeth**

521.81 Cracked tooth

EXCLUDES *asymptomatic craze lines in enamel*
— omit code
broken tooth due to trauma (873.63, 873.73)
fractured tooth due to trauma (873.63, 873.73)

521.89 Other specified diseases of hard tissues of teeth
Irradiated enamel
Sensitive dentin

521.9 Unspecified disease of hard tissues of teeth

✓4ᵗʰ **522 Diseases of pulp and periapical tissues**

522.0 Pulpitis   CC
Pulpal:
  abscess
  polyp
Pulpitis:
  acute
  chronic (hyperplastic) (ulcerative)
  suppurative
CC Excl: 520.0-525.9

522.1 Necrosis of the pulp
Pulp gangrene
DEF: Death of pulp tissue.

522.2 Pulp degeneration
Denticles
Pulp calcifications
Pulp stones

522.3 Abnormal hard tissue formation in pulp
Secondary or irregular dentin

522.4 Acute apical periodontitis of pulpal origin   CC
DEF: Severe inflammation of periodontal ligament due to pulpal inflammation or necrosis.
CC Excl: See code: 522.0

522.5 Periapical abscess without sinus
Abscess:
  dental
  dentoalveolar
EXCLUDES *periapical abscess with sinus (522.7)*

522.6 Chronic apical periodontitis
Apical or periapical granuloma
Apical periodontitis NOS

N Newborn Age: 0   P Pediatric Age: 0-17   M Maternity Age: 12-55   A Adult Age: 15-124   MCC Major CC Condition   CC CC Condition   HIV HIV Related Dx

178 – Volume 1

2010 ICD-9-CM

522.7 Periapical abscess with sinus
Fistula:
  alveolar process
  dental

522.8 Radicular cyst
Cyst:
  apical (periodontal)
  periapical
  radiculodental
  residual radicular
  EXCLUDES *lateral developmental or lateral periodontal cyst (526.0)*
  DEF: Cyst in tissue around tooth apex due to chronic infection of granuloma around root.

522.9 Other and unspecified diseases of pulp and periapical tissues

√4th **523 Gingival and periodontal diseases**

√5th **523.0 Acute gingivitis**
  EXCLUDES *acute necrotizing ulcerative gingivitis (101)*
  herpetic gingivostomatitis (054.2)

  523.00 Acute gingivitis, plaque induced
  Acute gingivitis NOS

  523.01 Acute gingivitis, non-plaque induced

√5th **523.1 Chronic gingivitis**
Gingivitis (chronic):
  desquamative
  hyperplastic
  simple marginal
  ulcerative
  EXCLUDES *herpetic gingivostomatitis (054.2)*

  523.10 Chronic gingivitis, plaque induced
  Chronic gingivitis NOS
  Gingivitis NOS

  523.11 Chronic gingivitis, non-plaque induced

√5th **523.2 Gingival recession**
Gingival recession (postinfective) (postoperative)

  523.20 Gingival recession, unspecified
  523.21 Gingival recession, minimal
  523.22 Gingival recession, moderate
  523.23 Gingival recession, severe
  523.24 Gingival recession, localized
  523.25 Gingival recession, generalized

√5th **523.3 Aggressive and acute periodontitis**
Acute:
  pericementitis
  pericoronitis
  EXCLUDES *acute apical periodontitis (522.4)*
  periapical abscess (522.5, 522.7)
  DEF: Severe inflammation, of tissues supporting teeth.

  523.30 Aggressive periodontitis, unspecified
  523.31 Aggressive periodontitis, localized
  Periodontal abscess
  523.32 Aggressive periodontitis, generalized
  523.33 Acute periodontitis

√5th **523.4 Chronic periodontitis**
Chronic pericoronitis
Pericementitis (chronic)
Periodontitis:
  complex
  simplex
  NOS
  EXCLUDES *chronic apical periodontitis (522.6)*

  523.40 Chronic periodontitis, unspecified
  523.41 Chronic periodontitis, localized
  523.42 Chronic periodontitis, generalized

523.5 Periodontosis

523.6 Accretions on teeth
Dental calculus:
  subgingival
  supragingival
Deposits on teeth:
  betel
  materia alba
  soft
  tartar
  tobacco
Extrinsic discoloration of teeth
  EXCLUDES *intrinsic discoloration of teeth (521.7)*
  DEF: Foreign material on tooth surface, usually plaque or calculus.

523.8 Other specified periodontal diseases
Giant cell:
  epulis
  peripheral granuloma
Gingival:
  cysts
  enlargement NOS
  fibromatosis
Gingival polyp
Periodontal lesions due to traumatic occlusion
Peripheral giant cell granuloma
  EXCLUDES *leukoplakia of gingiva (528.6)*

523.9 Unspecified gingival and periodontal disease
  AHA: 3Q ,'02, 14

√4th **524 Dentofacial anomalies, including malocclusion**

√5th **524.0 Major anomalies of jaw size**
  EXCLUDES *hemifacial atrophy or hypertrophy (754.0)*
  unilateral condylar hyperplasia or hypoplasia of mandible (526.89)

  524.00 Unspecified anomaly
  DEF: Unspecified deformity of jaw size.

  524.01 Maxillary hyperplasia
  DEF: Overgrowth or over development of upper jaw bone.

  524.02 Mandibular hyperplasia
  DEF: Overgrowth or over development of lower jaw bone.

  524.03 Maxillary hypoplasia
  DEF: Incomplete or underdeveloped, upper jaw bone.

  524.04 Mandibular hypoplasia
  DEF: Incomplete or underdeveloped, lower jaw bone.

  524.05 Macrogenia
  DEF: Enlarged, jaw, especially chin; affects bone, soft tissue, or both.

  524.06 Microgenia
  DEF: Underdeveloped mandible, characterized by an extremely small chin.

  524.07 Excessive tuberosity of jaw
  Entire maxillary tuberosity

  524.09 Other specified anomaly

√5th **524.1 Anomalies of relationship of jaw to cranial base**

  524.10 Unspecified anomaly
  Prognathism
  Retrognathism
  DEF: Prognathism: protrusion of lower jaw.
  DEF: Retrognathism: jaw is located posteriorly to a normally positioned jaw; backward position of mandible.

  524.11 Maxillary asymmetry
  DEF: Absence of symmetry of maxilla.

  524.12 Other jaw asymmetry

  524.19 Other specified anomaly

√4th √5th Additional Digit Required   Unacceptable PDx   Manifestation Code   Hospital Acquired Condition   ▶◀ Revised Text   ● New Code   ▲ Revised Code Title

2010 ICD-9-CM   **Volume 1 – 179**

Angle's Classification of Malocclusion

Normal occlusion

Class I Malocclusion

Class II Malocclusion

Class III Malocclusion

√5ᵗʰ **524.2 Anomalies of dental arch relationship**
Anomaly of dental arch
EXCLUDES *hemifacial atrophy or hypertrophy (754.0)*
soft tissue impingement (524.81-524.82)
unilateral condylar hyperplasia or hypoplasia of mandible (526.89)

524.20 Unspecified anomaly of dental arch relationship

524.21 Malocclusion, Angle's class I
Neutro-occlusion

524.22 Malocclusion, Angle's class II
Disto-occlusion Division I
Disto-occlusion Division II

524.23 Malocclusion, Angle's class III
Mesio-occlusion

524.24 Open anterior occlusal relationship
Anterior open bite

524.25 Open posterior occlusal relationship
Posterior open bite

524.26 Excessive horizontal overlap
Excessive horizontal overjet

524.27 Reverse articulation
Anterior articulation
Crossbite
Posterior articulation

524.28 Anomalies of interarch distance
Excessive interarch distance
Inadequate interarch distance

524.29 Other anomalies of dental arch relationship
Other anomalies of dental arch

√5ᵗʰ **524.3 Anomalies of tooth position of fully erupted teeth**
EXCLUDES *impacted or embedded teeth with abnormal position of such teeth or adjacent teeth (520.6)*

524.30 Unspecified anomaly of tooth position
Diastema of teeth NOS
Displacement of teeth NOS
Transposition of teeth NOS

524.31 Crowding of teeth

524.32 Excessive spacing of teeth

524.33 Horizontal displacement of teeth
Tipped teeth
Tipping of teeth

524.34 Vertical displacement of teeth
Extruded tooth
Infraeruption of teeth
Intruded tooth
Supraeruption of teeth

524.35 Rotation of tooth/teeth

524.36 Insufficient interocclusal distance of teeth (ridge)
Lack of adequate intermaxillary vertical dimension

524.37 Excessive interocclusal distance of teeth
Excessive intermaxillary vertical dimension
Loss of occlusal vertical dimension

524.39 Other anomalies of tooth position

524.4 Malocclusion, unspecified
DEF: Malposition of top and bottom teeth; interferes with chewing.

√5ᵗʰ **524.5 Dentofacial functional abnormalities**

524.50 Dentofacial functional abnormality, unspecified

524.51 Abnormal jaw closure

524.52 Limited mandibular range of motion

524.53 Deviation in opening and closing of the mandible

524.54 Insufficient anterior guidance
Insufficient anterior occlusal guidance

524.55 Centric occlusion maximum intercuspation discrepancy
Centric occlusion of teeth discrepancy

524.56 Non-working side interference
Balancing side interference

524.57 Lack of posterior occlusal support

524.59 Other dentofacial functional abnormalities
Abnormal swallowing
Mouth breathing
Sleep postures
Tongue, lip, or finger habits

√5ᵗʰ **524.6 Temporomandibular joint disorders**
EXCLUDES *current temporomandibular joint:*
dislocation (830.0-830.1)
strain (848.1)

524.60 Temporomandibular joint disorders, unspecified
Temporomandibular joint-pain- dysfunction syndrome [TMJ]

524.61 Adhesions and ankylosis (bony or fibrous)
DEF: Stiffening or union of temporomandibular joint due to bony or fibrous union across joint.

524.62 Arthralgia of temporomandibular joint
DEF: Pain in temporomandibular joint; not inflammatory in nature.

524.63 Articular disc disorder (reducing or non-reducing)

524.64 Temporomandibular joint sounds on opening and/or closing the jaw

524.69 Other specified temporomandibular joint disorders

√5ᵗʰ **524.7 Dental alveolar anomalies**

524.70 Unspecified alveolar anomaly

524.71 Alveolar maxillary hyperplasia
DEF: Excessive tissue formation in the dental alveoli of upper jaw.

524.72 Alveolar mandibular hyperplasia
DEF: Excessive tissue formation in the dental alveoli of lower jaw.

524.73 Alveolar maxillary hypoplasia
DEF: Incomplete or underdeveloped, alveolar tissue of upper jaw.

524.74 Alveolar mandibular hypoplasia
DEF: Incomplete or underdeveloped, alveolar tissue of lower jaw.

524.75 Vertical displacement of alveolus and teeth
Extrusion of alveolus and teeth

Ⓝ Newborn Age: 0   Ⓟ Pediatric Age: 0-17   Ⓜ Maternity Age: 12-55   Ⓐ Adult Age: 15-124   **MCC** Major CC Condition   **CC** CC Condition   **HIV** HIV Related Dx

180 – Volume 1

2010 ICD-9-CM

524.76   Occlusal plane deviation

524.79   Other specified alveolar anomaly

√5th   **524.8**   **Other specified dentofacial anomalies**

524.81   Anterior soft tissue impingement

524.82   Posterior soft tissue impingement

524.89   Other specified dentofacial anomalies

524.9   **Unspecified dentofacial anomalies**

√4th   **525**   **Other diseases and conditions of the teeth and supporting structures**

525.0   **Exfoliation of teeth due to systemic causes**
> **DEF:** Deterioration of teeth and surrounding structures due to systemic disease.

√5th   **525.1**   **Loss of teeth due to trauma, extraction, or periodontal disease**
> *Code first class of edentulism (525.40-525.44, 525.50-525.54)*
> **AHA:** 4Q, '05, 74; 4Q, '01, 44

525.10   *Acquired absence of teeth, unspecified*
> Tooth extraction status, NOS

525.11   *Loss of teeth due to trauma*

525.12   *Loss of teeth due to periodontal disease*

525.13   *Loss of teeth due to caries*

525.19   *Other loss of teeth*

√5th   **525.2**   **Atrophy of edentulous alveolar ridge**

525.20   Unspecified atrophy of edentulous alveolar ridge
> Atrophy of the mandible NOS
> Atrophy of the maxilla NOS

525.21   Minimal atrophy of the mandible

525.22   Moderate atrophy of the mandible

525.23   Severe atrophy of the mandible

525.24   Minimal atrophy of the maxilla

525.25   Moderate atrophy of the maxilla

525.26   Severe atrophy of the maxilla

525.3   **Retained dental root**

√5th   **525.4**   **Complete edentulism**
> Use additional code to identify cause of edentulism (525.10-525.19)
> **AHA:** 4Q, '05, 74

525.40   Complete edentulism, unspecified
> Edentulism NOS

525.41   Complete edentulism, class I

525.42   Complete edentulism, class II

525.43   Complete edentulism, class III

525.44   Complete edentulism, class IV

√5th   **525.5**   **Partial edentulism**
> Use additional code to identify cause of edentulism (525.10-525.19)
> **AHA:** 4Q, '05, 74

525.50   Partial edentulism, unspecified

525.51   Partial edentulism, class I

525.52   Partial edentulism, class II

525.53   Partial edentulism, class III

525.54   Partial edentulism, class IV

√5th   **525.6**   **Unsatisfactory restoration of tooth**
> Defective bridge, crown, fillings
> Defective dental restoration
> **EXCLUDES**   *dental restoration status (V45.84)*
>   *unsatisfactory endodontic treatment (526.61-526.69)*

525.60   Unspecified unsatisfactory restoration of tooth
> Unspecified defective dental restoration

525.61   Open restoration margins
> Dental restoration failure of marginal integrity
> Open margin on tooth restoration

525.62   Unrepairable overhanging of dental restorative materials
> Overhanging of tooth restoration

525.63   Fractured dental restorative material without loss of material
> **EXCLUDES**   *cracked tooth (521.81)*
>   *fractured tooth (873.63, 873.73)*

525.64   Fractured dental restorative material with loss of material
> **EXCLUDES**   *cracked tooth (521.81)*
>   *fractured tooth (873.63, 873.73)*

525.65   Contour of existing restoration of tooth biologically incompatible with oral health
> Dental restoration failure of periodontal anatomical integrity
> Unacceptable contours of existing restoration
> Unacceptable morphology of existing restoration

525.66   Allergy to existing dental restorative material
> Use additional code to identify the specific type of allergy

525.67   Poor aesthetics of existing restoration
> Dental restoration aesthetically inadequate or displeasing

525.69   Other unsatisfactory restoration of existing tooth

√5th   **525.7**   **Endosseous dental implant failure**

525.71   Osseointegration failure of dental implant
> Failure of dental implant due to infection
> Failure of dental implant due to unintentional loading
> Failure of dental implant osseointegration due to premature loading
> Failure of dental implant to osseointegrate prior to intentional prosthetic loading
> Hemorrhagic complications of dental implant placement
> Iatrogenic osseointegration failure of dental implant
> Osseointegration failure of dental implant due to complications of systemic disease
> Osseointegration failure of dental implant due to poor bone quality
> Pre-integration failure of dental implant NOS
> Pre-osseointegration failure of dental implant

525.72   Post-osseointegration biological failure of dental implant
> Failure of dental implant due to lack of attached gingiva
> Failure of dental implant due to occlusal trauma (caused by poor prosthetic design)
> Failure of dental implant due to parafunctional habits
> Failure of dental implant due to periodontal infection (peri-implantitis)
> Failure of dental implant due to poor oral hygiene
> Failure of dental implant to osseointegrate following intentional prosthetic loading
> Iatrogenic post-osseointegration failure of dental implant
> Post-osseointegration failure of dental implant due to complications of systemic disease

---

√4th √5th   Additional Digit Required   Unacceptable PDx   Manifestation Code   Hospital Acquired Condition   ▶◀ Revised Text   ● New Code   ▲ Revised Code Title

Digestive System

525.73 Post-osseointegration mechanic failure of dental implant

    Failure of dental prosthesis causing loss of dental implant

    Fracture of dental implant

    Mechanical failure of dental implant NOS

    EXCLUDES *cracked tooth (521.81)*
        fractured dental restorative material with loss of material (525.64)
        fractured dental restorative material without loss of material (525.63)
        fractured tooth (873.63, 873.73)

525.79 Other endosseous dental implant failure

    Dental implant failure NOS

525.8 Other specified disorders of the teeth and supporting structures

    Enlargement of alveolar ridge NOS

    Irregular alveolar process

525.9 Unspecified disorder of the teeth and supporting structures

✓4th **526 Diseases of the jaws**

526.0 Developmental odontogenic cysts

    Cyst:
        dentigerous
        eruption
        follicular
        lateral developmental
        lateral periodontal
        primordial
    Keratocyst
    EXCLUDES *radicular cyst (522.8)*

526.1 Fissural cysts of jaw

    Cyst:
        globulomaxillary
        incisor canal
        median anterior maxillary
        median palatal
        nasopalatine
        palatine of papilla
    EXCLUDES *cysts of oral soft tissues (528.4)*

526.2 Other cysts of jaws

    Cyst of jaw:
        NOS
        aneurysmal
        hemorrhagic
        traumatic

526.3 Central giant cell (reparative) granuloma

    EXCLUDES *peripheral giant cell granuloma (523.8)*

526.4 Inflammatory conditions

    Abscess
    Osteitis } of jaw (acute) (chronic)
    Osteomyelitis (neonatal) } (suppurative)
    Periostitis

    Sequestrum of jaw bone
    EXCLUDES *alveolar osteitis (526.5)*
        osteonecrosis of jaw (733.45)

526.5 Alveolitis of jaw

    Alveolar osteitis
    Dry socket
    DEF: Inflammation, of alveoli or tooth socket.

✓5th **526.6 Periradicular pathology associated with previous endodontic treatment**

526.61 Perforation of root canal space

526.62 Endodontic overfill

526.63 Endodontic underfill

526.69 Other periradicular pathology associated with previous endodontic treatment

✓5th **526.8 Other specified diseases of the jaws**

526.81 Exostosis of jaw

    Torus mandibularis
    Torus palatinus
    DEF: Spur or bony outgrowth on the jaw.

526.89 Other

    Cherubism
    Fibrous dysplasia } of jaw(s)
    Latent bone cyst
    Osteoradionecrosis

    Unilateral condylar hyperplasia or hypoplasia of mandible

526.9 Unspecified disease of the jaws

✓4th **527 Diseases of the salivary glands**

527.0 Atrophy

    DEF: Wasting away, necrosis of salivary gland tissue.

527.1 Hypertrophy

    DEF: Overgrowth or overdeveloped salivary gland tissue.

527.2 Sialoadenitis

    Parotitis:
        NOS
        allergic
        toxic
    Sialoangitis
    Sialodochitis
    EXCLUDES *epidemic or infectious parotitis (072.0-072.9)*
        uveoparotid fever (135)
    DEF: Inflammation of salivary gland.

527.3 Abscess   `CC`

    CC Excl: 527.0-527.9, 537.89-538

527.4 Fistula   `CC`

    EXCLUDES *congenital fistula of salivary gland (750.24)*
    CC Excl: See code: 527.3

527.5 Sialolithiasis

    Calculus } of salivary gland or duct
    Stone
    Sialodocholithiasis

527.6 Mucocele

    Mucous:
        extravasation cyst of salivary gland
        retention cyst of salivary gland
    Ranula
    DEF: Dilated salivary gland cavity filled with mucous.

527.7 Disturbance of salivary secretion

    Hyposecretion
    Ptyalism
    Sialorrhea
    Xerostomia

527.8 Other specified diseases of the salivary glands

    Benign lymphoepithelial lesion of salivary gland
    Sialectasia
    Sialosis
    Stenosis } of salivary duct
    Stricture

527.9 Unspecified disease of the salivary glands

`N` Newborn Age: 0	`P` Pediatric Age: 0-17	`M` Maternity Age: 12-55	`A` Adult Age: 15-124	`MCC` Major CC Condition	`CC` CC Condition `HIV` HIV Related Dx

✓4ᵗʰ **528 Diseases of the oral soft tissues, excluding lesions specific for gingiva and tongue**

✓5ᵗʰ **528.0 Stomatitis and mucositis (ulcerative)**

EXCLUDES cellulitis and abscess of mouth (528.3)
diphtheritic stomatitis (032.0)
epizootic stomatitis (078.4)
gingivitis (523.0-523.1)
oral thrush (112.0)
Stevens-Johnson syndrome (695.13)
stomatitis:
  acute necrotizing ulcerative (101)
  aphthous (528.2)
  gangrenous (528.1)
  herpetic (054.2)
  Vincent's (101)

DEF: Stomatitis: Inflammation of oral mucosa; labial and buccal mucosa, tongue, palate, floor of the mouth, and gingivae.

AHA: 2Q, '99, 9

TIP: Do not assign if documented as fungal oral thrush, or as due to candidiasis. See instead 112.0.

528.00 Stomatitis and mucositis, unspecified
Mucositis NOS
Ulcerative mucositis NOS
Ulcerative stomatitis NOS
Vesicular stomatitis NOS
AHA: 4Q, '06, 88-90

528.01 Mucositis (ulcerative) due to antineoplastic therapy
Use additional E code to identify adverse effects of therapy, such as:
  antineoplastic and immunosuppressive drugs (E930.7, E933.1)
  radiation therapy (E879.2)
AHA: 4Q, '06, 88-90

528.02 Mucositis (ulcerative) due to other drugs
Use additional E code to identify drug
AHA: 4Q, '06, 88-90

528.09 Other stomatitis and mucositis (ulcerative)
AHA: 4Q, '06, 88-90

528.1 Cancrum oris
Gangrenous stomatitis
Noma
DEF: A severely gangrenous lesion of mouth due to fusospirochetal infection; destroys buccal, labial and facial tissues; can be fatal; found primarily in debilitated and malnourished children.

528.2 Oral aphthae
Aphthous stomatitis
Canker sore
Periadenitis mucosa necrotica recurrens
Recurrent aphthous ulcer
Stomatitis herpetiformis
EXCLUDES herpetic stomatitis (054.2)
DEF: Small oval or round ulcers of the mouth marked by a grayish exudate and a red halo effect.

528.3 Cellulitis and abscess   **CC**
Cellulitis of mouth (floor)
Ludwig's angina
Oral fistula
EXCLUDES abscess of tongue (529.0)
cellulitis or abscess of lip (528.5)
fistula (of):
  dental (522.7)
  lip (528.5)
gingivitis (523.00-523.11)
CC Excl: 528.00-528.09, 528.3, 529.0, 529.2

528.4 Cysts
Dermoid cyst ⎫
Epidermoid cyst ⎪
Epstein's pearl ⎬ or mouth
Lymphoepithelial cyst ⎪
Nasoalveolar cyst ⎪
Nasolabial cyst ⎭
EXCLUDES cyst:
  gingiva (523.8)
  tongue (529.8)

528.5 Diseases of lips
Abscess ⎫
Cellulitis ⎬ of lips
Fistula ⎪
Hypertrophy ⎭
Cheilitis:
  NOS
  angular
Cheilodynia
Cheilosis
EXCLUDES actinic cheilitis (692.79)
congenital fistula of lip (750.25)
leukoplakia of lips (528.6)
AHA: S-O, '86, 10

528.6 Leukoplakia of oral mucosa, including tongue
Leukokeratosis of oral mucosa
Leukoplakia of:
  gingiva
  lips
  tongue
EXCLUDES carcinoma in situ (230.0, 232.0)
leukokeratosis nicotina palati (528.79)
DEF: Thickened white patches of epithelium on mucous membranes of mouth.

✓5ᵗʰ **528.7 Other disturbances of oral epithelium, including tongue**
EXCLUDES carcinoma in situ (230.0, 232.0)
leukokeratosis NOS (702.8)

528.71 Minimal keratinized residual ridge mucosa
Minimal keratinization of alveolar ridge mucosa

528.72 Excessive keratinized residual ridge mucosa
Excessive keratinization of alveolar ridge mucosa

528.79 Other disturbances of oral epithelium, including tongue
Erythroplakia of mouth or tongue
Focal epithelial hyperplasia of mouth or tongue
Leukoedema of mouth or tongue
Leukokeratosis nicotina palate
Other oral epithelium disturbances

528.8 Oral submucosal fibrosis, including of tongue

528.9 Other and unspecified diseases of the oral soft tissues
Cheek and lip biting
Denture sore mouth
Denture stomatitis
Melanoplakia
Papillary hyperplasia of palate
Eosinophilic granuloma ⎫
Irritative hyperplasisa ⎬ of oral mucosa
Pyogenic granuloma ⎪
Ulcer (traumatic) ⎭

✓4ᵗʰ **529 Diseases and other conditions of the tongue**

529.0 Glossitis
Abscess ⎫
Ulceration (traumatic) ⎬ of tongue
EXCLUDES glossitis:
  benign migratory (529.1)
  Hunter's (529.4)
  median rhomboid (529.2)
  Moeller's (529.4)

Digestive System

528–529.0

Digestive System

529.1–530.4

529.1 Geographic tongue
Benign migratory glossitis
Glossitis areata exfoliativa
DEF: Chronic glossitis; marked by filiform papillae atrophy and inflammation; no known etiology.

529.2 Median rhomboid glossitis
DEF: A noninflammatory, congenital disease characterized by rhomboid-like lesions at the middle third of the tongue's dorsal surface.

529.3 Hypertrophy of tongue papillae
Black hairy tongue
Coated tongue
Hypertrophy of foliate papillae
Lingua villosa nigra

529.4 Atrophy of tongue papillae
Bald tongue
Glazed tongue
Glossitis:
    Hunter's
    Moeller's
Glossodynia exfoliativa
Smooth atrophic tongue

529.5 Plicated tongue
Fissured ⎫
Furrowed ⎬ tongue
Scrotal ⎭
EXCLUDES fissure of tongue, congenital (750.13)
DEF: Cracks, fissures or furrows, on dorsal surface of tongue.

529.6 Glossodynia
Glossopyrosis
Painful tongue
EXCLUDES glossodynia exfoliativa (529.4)

529.8 Other specified conditions of the tongue
Atrophy ⎫
Crenated ⎪
Enlargement ⎬ (of) tongue
Hypertrophy ⎭
Glossocele
Glossoptosis
EXCLUDES erythroplasia of tongue (528.79)
        leukoplakia of tongue (528.6)
        macroglossia (congenital) (750.15)
        microglossia (congenital) (750.16)
        oral submucosal fibrosis (528.8)

529.9 Unspecified condition of the tongue

DISEASES OF ESOPHAGUS, STOMACH, AND DUODENUM
(530-538)

√4ᵗʰ **530 Diseases of esophagus**
EXCLUDES esophageal varices (456.0-456.2)

530.0 Achalasia and cardiospasm
Achalasia (of cardia)
Aperistalsis of esophagus
Megaesophagus
EXCLUDES congenital cardiospasm (750.7)
DEF: Failure of smooth muscle fibers to relax, at gastrointestinal junctures; such as esophagogastric sphincter when swallowing.

√5ᵗʰ **530.1 Esophagitis**
Esophagitis: Esophagitis:
    chemical   postoperative
    peptic   regurgitant
Use additional E code to identify cause, if induced by chemical
EXCLUDES tuberculous esophagitis (017.8)
AHA: 4Q, '93, 27; 1Q, '92, 17; 3Q, '91, 20
TIP: Do not assign if esophagitis due to candidiasis; see instead code 112.84.

530.10 Esophagitis, unspecified
Esophagitis NOS
AHA: 3Q, '05, 17

Esophagus

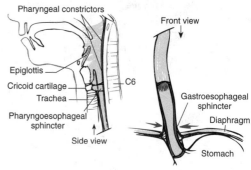

530.11 Reflux esophagitis
DEF: Inflammation of lower esophagus; due to regurgitated gastric acid.
AHA: 4Q, '95, 82
K21.0 Gastro-esophageal reflux disease w/esophagitis `I-10`

530.12 Acute esophagitis `CC`
DEF: An acute inflammation of the mucous lining or submucosal coat of the esophagus.
CC Excl: 530.10-530.19-530.21, 530.4, 530.7, 530.82, 530.85-530.89
AHA: 4Q, '01, 45

530.13 Eosinophilic esophagitis
AHA: ▶4Q, '08, 115-116◄

530.19 Other esophagitis
Abscess of esophagus
AHA: 3Q, '01, 10
K20 Esophagitis `I-10`

√5ᵗʰ **530.2 Ulcer of esophagus**
Ulcer of esophagus:
    fungal
    peptic
Ulcer of esophagus due to ingestion of:
    aspirin
    chemicals
    medicines
Use additional E code to identify cause, if induced by chemical or drug
AHA: 4Q, '03, 63

530.20 Ulcer of esophagus without bleeding `CC`
Ulcer of esophagus NOS
CC Excl: 530.21, 530.89-530.9, 537.84

530.21 Ulcer of esophagus with bleeding `MCC`
EXCLUDES bleeding esophageal varices (456.0, 456.20)
CC Excl: 251.5, 456.0, 530.20-530.21, 530.7, 530.82, 530.85, 531.00-534.91, 535.01, 535.11, 535.21, 535.31, 535.41, 535.51, 535.61, 537.83, 537.89-538, 562.02-562.03, 562.12-562.13, 569.3, 569.85, 578.0-578.9

530.3 Stricture and stenosis of esophagus
Compression of esophagus
Obstruction of esophagus
EXCLUDES congenital stricture of esophagus (750.3)
AHA: 2Q, '01, 4; 2Q, '97, 3; 1Q, '88, 13
TIP: If esophageal obstruction is due to impacted foreign body, such as meat or other substance, assign instead code 935.1.
K22.2 Esophageal obstruction `I-10`

530.4 Perforation of esophagus `MCC`
Rupture of esophagus
EXCLUDES traumatic perforation of esophagus (862.22, 862.32, 874.4-874.5)
CC Excl: 530.4, 530.7-530.81, 530.83-530.84, 530.89-530.9

`N` Newborn Age: 0   `P` Pediatric Age: 0-17   `M` Maternity Age: 12-55   `A` Adult Age: 15-124   `MCC` Major CC Condition   `CC` CC Condition   `HIV` HIV Related Dx

184 – Volume 1 · February 2009   **2010 ICD-9-CM**

530.5   **Dyskinesia of esophagus**

Corkscrew esophagus   Esophagospasm
Curling esophagus   Spasm of esophagus

EXCLUDES   *cardiospasm (530.0)*

DEF: Difficulty performing voluntary esophageal movements.

AHA: 1Q, '88, 13; N-D, '84, 19

530.6   **Diverticulum of esophagus, acquired**

Diverticulum, acquired:
    epiphrenic
    pharyngoesophageal
    pulsion
    subdiaphragmatic
    traction
    Zenker's (hypopharyngeal)
Esophageal pouch, acquired
Esophagocele, acquired

EXCLUDES   *congenital diverticulum of esophagus (750.4)*

AHA: J-F, '85, 3

530.7   **Gastroesophageal laceration-hemorrhage syndrome**   `MCC`

Mallory-Weiss syndrome

DEF: Laceration of distal esophagus and proximal stomach due to vomiting, hiccups or other sustained activity.

CC Excl: 251.5, 456.0, 530.20-530.21, 530.4, 530.7-530.85, 530.89-534.91, 535.01, 535.11, 535.21, 535.31, 535.41, 535.51, 535.61, 537.83, 562.02-562.03, 562.12-562.13, 569.3, 569.85, 578.0-578.9

√5ᵗʰ 530.8   **Other specified disorders of esophagus**

530.81   **Esophageal reflux**

Gastroesophageal reflux

EXCLUDES   *reflux esophagitis (530.11)*

DEF: Regurgitation of the gastric contents into esophagus and possibly pharynx.

AHA: 2Q, '01, 4; 1Q, '95, 7; 4Q, '92, 27

K21.9 Gastro-esophageal reflux dz w/o esophagitis   `I-10`

530.82   **Esophageal hemorrhage**   `MCC`

EXCLUDES   *hemorrhage due to esophageal varices (456.0-456.2)*

CC Excl: 251.5, 456.0, 456.20, 459.89-459.9, 530.20-530.21, 530.7, 530.82, 530.85, 531.00-534.91, 535.01, 535.11, 535.21, 535.31, 535.41, 535.51, 535.61, 537.83, 562.02-562.03, 562.12-562.13, 569.3, 569.85, 578.0-578.9

AHA: 1Q, '05, 17

530.83   **Esophageal leukoplakia**

530.84   **Tracheoesophageal fistula**   `MCC`

EXCLUDES   *congenital tracheoesophageal fistula (750.3)*

CC Excl: 530.4, 530.7-530.81, 530.83-530.84, 530.89-530.9

530.85   **Barrett's esophagus**

DEF: A metaplastic disorder in which specialized columnar epithelial cells replace the normal squamous epithelial cells; secondary to chronic gastroesophageal reflux damage to the mucosa; increases risk of developing adenocarcinoma.

AHA: 4Q, '03, 63

K22.7 Barrett's esophagus   `I-10`

530.86   **Infection of esophagostomy**   `CC`

Use additional code to specify infection

CC Excl: 530.86-530.87, 536.40-536.49, 569.71-569.79, 997.4, 997.71, 997.91-997.99, 998.81, 998.83-998.9

530.87   **Mechanical complication of esophagostomy**   `CC`

Malfunction of esophagostomy

CC Excl: See code: 530.86

530.89   **Other**

EXCLUDES   *Paterson-Kelly syndrome (280.8)*

530.9   **Unspecified disorder of esophagus**

Stomach

√4ᵗʰ 531   **Gastric ulcer**

INCLUDES   ulcer (peptic):
    prepyloric
    pylorus
    stomach

Use additional E code to identify drug, if drug-induced

EXCLUDES   *peptic ulcer NOS (533.0-533.9)*

The following fifth-digit subclassification is for use with category 531:
   0 without mention of obstruction
   1 with obstruction

DEF: Destruction of tissue in lumen of stomach due to action of gastric acid and pepsin on gastric mucosa decreasing resistance to ulcers.

AHA: 1Q, '91, 15; 4Q, '90, 27

§ **√5ᵗʰ 531.0**   **Acute with hemorrhage**   `MCC`
[0-1]

CC Excl: 251.5, 456.0, 530.20-530.21, 530.7, 530.82, 530.85, 531.00-534.91, 535.01, 535.11, 535.21, 535.31, 535.41, 535.51, 535.61, 537.83, 537.89-538, 562.02-562.03, 562.12-562.13, 569.3, 569.85, 578.0-578.9

AHA: N-D, '84, 15

§ **√5ᵗʰ 531.1**   **Acute with perforation**   `MCC`
[0-1]

CC Excl: See code 531.0

§ **√5ᵗʰ 531.2**   **Acute with hemorrhage and perforation**   `MCC`
[0-1]

CC Excl: See code 531.0

§ **√5ᵗʰ 531.3**   **Acute without mention of hemorrhage or perforation**   `MCC 1` `CC 0`
[0-1]

CC Excl: See code 531.0

§ **√5ᵗʰ 531.4**   **Chronic or unspecified with hemorrhage**   `MCC`
[0-1]

CC Excl: See code 531.0

AHA: 4Q, '90, 22

K25.4 Chronic/unspecified gastric ulcer w/hemorrhage   `I-10`

§ **√5ᵗʰ 531.5**   **Chronic or unspecified with perforation**   `MCC`
[0-1]

CC Excl: See code 531.0

§ **√5ᵗʰ 531.6**   **Chronic or unspecified with hemorrhage and perforation**   `MCC`
[0-1]

CC Excl: See code 531.0

§ **√5ᵗʰ 531.7**   **Chronic without mention of hemorrhage or perforation**   `MCC 1`
[0-1]

CC Excl: For code 531.71: see code 531.0

§ **√5ᵗʰ 531.9**   **Unspecified as acute or chronic, without mention of hemorrhage or perforation**   `MCC 1`
[0-1]

CC Excl: For code 531.91: see code 531.0

K25.9 Gastric ulcer uns acute/chronic w/o hem/perf   `I-10`

530.5–531.9

---

§   Requires fifth digit. Valid digits are in [brackets] under each code. See category 531 for codes and definitions.

`√4ᵗʰ` Additional Digit Required   Unacceptable PDx   Manifestation Code   Hospital Acquired Condition   ►◄ Revised Text   ● New Code   ▲ Revised Code Title

2010 ICD-9-CM   **Volume 1 – 185**

Digestive System

532–534.9

✓4ᵗʰ **532 Duodenal ulcer**

INCLUDES   erosion (acute) of duodenum
ulcer (peptic):
    duodenum
    postpyloric

Use additional E code to identify drug, if drug-induced

EXCLUDES   *peptic ulcer NOS (533.0-533.9)*

The following fifth-digit subclassification is for use with category 532:
   0 **without mention of obstruction**
   1 **with obstruction**

DEF: Ulcers in duodenum due to action of gastric acid and pepsin on mucosa decreasing resistance to ulcers.
AHA: 4Q, '90, 27; 1Q, '91, 15

§ ✓5ᵗʰ **532.0 Acute with hemorrhage**   MCC
[0-1]   **CC Excl:** 251.5, 456.0, 530.20-530.21, 530.7, 530.82, 530.85, 531.00-534.91, 535.01, 535.11, 535.21, 535.31, 535.41, 535.51, 535.61, 537.3, 537.83, 537.89-538, 562.02-562.03, 562.12-562.13, 569.3, 569.85, 578.0-578.9
     AHA: 4Q, '90, 22

§ ✓5ᵗʰ **532.1 Acute with perforation**   MCC
[0-1]   **CC Excl:** See code 532.0

§ ✓5ᵗʰ **532.2 Acute with hemorrhage and perforation**   MCC
[0-1]   **CC Excl:** See code 532.0

§ ✓5ᵗʰ **532.3 Acute without mention of hemorrhage**   MCC 1   CC 0
[0-1]   **or perforation**
     CC Excl: For code 532.30: 251.5, 456.0, 530.7, 530.82, 531.00-534.91, 535.01, 535.11, 535.21, 535.31, 535.41, 535.51, 535.61, 537.3, 537.83-538, 562.02-562.03, 562.12-562.13, 569.3, 569.85, 578.0-578.9; **For code 532.31:** 251.5, 456.0, 530.20-530.21, 530.7, 530.82, 530.85, 531.00-534.91, 535.01, 535.11, 535.21, 535.31, 535.41, 535.51, 535.61, 537.3, 537.83, 537.89-538, 562.02-562.03, 562.12-562.13, 569.3, 569.85, 578.0-578.9

§ ✓5ᵗʰ **532.4 Chronic or unspecified with hemorrhage**   MCC
[0-1]   **CC Excl:** See code 532.0
     K26.4 Chronic/unspecified duodenal ulcer w/hemorrhage   I-10

§ ✓5ᵗʰ **532.5 Chronic or unspecified with perforation**   MCC
[0-1]   **CC Excl:** See code 532.0

§ ✓5ᵗʰ **532.6 Chronic or unspecified with hemorrhage**   MCC
[0-1]   **and perforation**
     CC Excl: See code 532.0

§ ✓5ᵗʰ **532.7 Chronic without mention of hemorrhage**   MCC 1
[0-1]   **or perforation**
     CC Excl: For code 532.71: See code 532.0

§ ✓5ᵗʰ **532.9 Unspecified as acute or chronic, without**   MCC 1
[0-1]   **mention of hemorrhage or perforation**
     CC Excl: For code 532.91: See code 532.0
     K26.9 Duodenal ulcer uns acute/chronic w/o hem/perf   I-10

✓4ᵗʰ **533 Peptic ulcer, site unspecified**

INCLUDES   gastroduodenal ulcer NOS
peptic ulcer NOS
stress ulcer NOS

Use additional E code to identify drug, if drug-induced

EXCLUDES   *peptic ulcer:*
    duodenal (532.0-532.9)
    gastric (531.0-531.9)

The following fifth-digit subclassification is for use with category 533:
   0 **without mention of obstruction**
   1 **with obstruction**

DEF: Ulcer of mucous membrane of esophagus, stomach or duodenum due to gastric acid secretion.
AHA: 1Q, '91, 15; 4Q, '90, 27

§ ✓5ᵗʰ **533.0 Acute with hemorrhage**   MCC
[0-1]   **CC Excl:** See code 532.0

§ ✓5ᵗʰ **533.1 Acute with perforation**   MCC
[0-1]   **CC Excl:** See code 533.0

§ ✓5ᵗʰ **533.2 Acute with hemorrhage and perforation**   MCC
[0-1]   **CC Excl:** See code 533.0

§ ✓5ᵗʰ **533.3 Acute without mention of hemorrhage**   MCC 1   CC 0
[0-1]   **and perforation**
     CC Excl: See code: 533.0

§ ✓5ᵗʰ **533.4 Chronic or unspecified with hemorrhage**   MCC
[0-1]   **CC Excl:** See code 533.0

§ ✓5ᵗʰ **533.5 Chronic or unspecified with perforation**   MCC
[0-1]   **CC Excl:** See code 533.0

§ ✓5ᵗʰ **533.6 Chronic or unspecified with hemorrhage**   MCC
[0-1]   **and perforation**
     CC Excl: See code 533.0

§ ✓5ᵗʰ **533.7 Chronic without mention of hemorrhage or**   MCC 1
[0-1]   **perforation**
     CC Excl: For code 533.71: See code 533.0
     AHA: 2Q, '89, 16

§ ✓5ᵗʰ **533.9 Unspecified as acute or chronic, without**   MCC 1
[0-1]   **mention of hemorrhage or perforation**
     CC Excl: For code 533.91: See code 533.0

✓4ᵗʰ **534 Gastrojejunal ulcer**

INCLUDES   ulcer (peptic) or erosion:
    anastomotic
    gastrocolic
    gastrointestinal
    gastrojejunal
    jejunal
    marginal
    stomal

EXCLUDES   *primary ulcer of small intestine (569.82)*

The following fifth-digit subclassification is for use with category 534:
   0 **without mention of obstruction**
   1 **with obstruction**

AHA: 1Q, '91, 15; 4Q, '90, 27

§ ✓5ᵗʰ **534.0 Acute with hemorrhage**   MCC
[0-1]   **CC Excl:** 251.5, 456.0, 530.20-530.21, 530.7, 530.82, 530.85, 531.00-534.91, 535.01, 535.11, 535.21, 535.31, 535.41, 535.51, 535.61, 537.83, 537.89-538, 562.02-562.03, 562.12-562.13, 569.3, 569.85, 578.0-578.9

§ ✓5ᵗʰ **534.1 Acute with perforation**   MCC
[0-1]   **CC Excl:** See code 534.0

§ ✓5ᵗʰ **534.2 Acute with hemorrhage and perforation**   MCC
[0-1]   **CC Excl:** See code 534.0

§ ✓5ᵗʰ **534.3 Acute without mention of hemorrhage**   MCC 1   CC 0
[0-1]   **or perforation**
     CC Excl:: See code 534.0

§ ✓5ᵗʰ **534.4 Chronic or unspecified with hemorrhage**   MCC
[0-1]   **CC Excl:** See code 534.0

§ ✓5ᵗʰ **534.5 Chronic or unspecified with perforation**   MCC
[0-1]   **CC Excl:** See code 534.0

§ ✓5ᵗʰ **534.6 Chronic or unspecified with hemorrhage**   MCC
[0-1]   **and perforation**
     CC Excl: See code 534.0

§ ✓5ᵗʰ **534.7 Chronic without mention of hemorrhage**   MCC 1
[0-1]   **or perforation**
     CC Excl: For code 534.71: See code 534.0

§ ✓5ᵗʰ **534.9 Unspecified as acute or chronic, without**   MCC 1
[0-1]   **mention of hemorrhage or perforation**
     CC Excl: For code 534.91: See code 534.0

---

§   Requires fifth digit. Valid digits are in [brackets] under each code. See appropriate category for codes and definitions.

Ⓝ Newborn Age: 0   Ⓟ Pediatric Age: 0-17   Ⓜ Maternity Age: 12-55   Ⓐ Adult Age: 15-124   MCC Major CC Condition   CC CC Condition   HIV HIV Related Dx

√4ᵗʰ **535 Gastritis and duodenitis**

> The following fifth-digit subclassification is for use with category 535:
> 0 **without mention of hemorrhage**
> 1 **with hemorrhage**

AHA: 2Q, '92, 9; 4Q, '91, 25

§ √5ᵗʰ **535.0 Acute gastritis** `MCC 1`
[0-1]   **DEF:** Inflammation of stomach, with mucous membrane atrophy and peptic gland destruction.
CC Excl: For code 535.01: 251.5, 456.0,530.20-530.21, 530.7, 530.82, 530.85,531.00-534.91, 535.01, 535.11, 535.21, 535.31, 535.41, 535.51, 535.61, 535.71, 537.83, 562.02-562.03, 562.12-562.13, 569.3, 569.85, 578.0-578.9
AHA: 2Q, '92, 8; N-D, '86, 9

§ √5ᵗʰ **535.1 Atrophic gastritis** `MCC 1`
[0-1]   Gastritis: Gastritis:
   atrophic-hyperplastic   chronic (atrophic)
CC Excl: For code 535.11: See code 535.01
AHA: 1Q, '94, 18
K29.50 Unspecified chronic gastritis without bleeding `I-10`

§ √5ᵗʰ **535.2 Gastric mucosal hypertrophy** `MCC 1`
[0-1]   Hypertrophic gastritis
CC Excl: For code 535.21: See code 535.01

§ √5ᵗʰ **535.3 Alcoholic gastritis** `MCC 1`
[0-1]   **CC Excl: For code 535.31:** See code 535.01

§ √5ᵗʰ **535.4 Other specified gastritis** `MCC 1`
[0-1]   Gastritis: Gastritis:
   allergic   superficial
   bile induced   toxic
   irritant
   EXCLUDES *eosinophilic gastritis (535.7)*
CC Excl: For code 535.41: See code 535.01
AHA: 4Q, '90, 27

§ √5ᵗʰ **535.5 Unspecified gastritis and gastroduodenitis** `MCC 1`
[0-1]   **CC Excl: For code 535.51:** See code 535.01
AHA: For code 535.50: 3Q, '05, 17; 4Q, '99, 25

§ √5ᵗʰ **535.6 Duodenitis** `MCC 1`
[0-1]   **DEF:** Inflammation of intestine, between pylorus and jejunum.
CC Excl: For code 535.61: See code 535.01
AHA: For code 535.60: 3Q, '05, 17
K29.80 Duodenitis without bleeding `I-10`

§ √5ᵗʰ **535.7 Eosinophilic gastritis** `MCC 1`
[0-1]   **CC Excl: For code 535.71:** See code 535.01
AHA: 4Q, '08, 115-116

√4ᵗʰ **536 Disorders of function of stomach**
   EXCLUDES *functional disorders of stomach specified as psychogenic (306.4)*

536.0 Achlorhydria
   DEF: Absence of gastric acid due to gastric mucosa atrophy; unresponsive to histamines; also known as gastric anacidity.

536.1 Acute dilatation of stomach `CC`
   Acute distention of stomach
   CC Excl: 536.1

536.2 Persistent vomiting
   Cyclical vomiting
   Habit vomiting
   Persistent vomiting [not of pregnancy]
   Uncontrollable vomiting
   EXCLUDES ►*bilious emesis (vomiting) (787.04)*◄
       excessive vomiting in pregnancy (643.0-643.9)
       vomiting NOS (787.03)
         cyclical, associated with migraine (346.2)
       ►*vomiting of fecal matter (569.87)*◄

536.3 Gastroparesis
   Gastroparalysis
   Code first underlying disease, such as: diabetes mellitus (249.6, 250.6)
   DEF: Slight degree of paralysis within muscular coat of stomach.
   AHA: 4Q, '08, 94; 2Q, '04, 7; 2Q, '01, 4; 4Q, '94, 42

√5ᵗʰ **536.4 Gastrostomy complications**
AHA: 4Q, '98, 42
TIP: Do not assign code 997.4 Digestive system complications, for any gastrostomy complications.

536.40 Gastrostomy complication, unspecified

536.41 Infection of gastrostomy `CC`
   Use additional code to specify type of infection, such as:
     abscess or cellulitis of abdomen (682.2)
     septicemia (038.0-038.9)
   Use additional code to identify organism (041.00-041.9)
   CC Excl: 530.86-530.87, 536.40-536.49, 569.71-569.79, 997.4, 997.71, 997.91-997.99, 998.81, 998.83-998.9
   AHA: 4Q, '98, 42

536.42 Mechanical complication of gastrostomy `CC`
   CC Excl: See code 536.41

536.49 Other gastrostomy complications
   AHA: 4Q, '98, 42

536.8 Dyspepsia and other specified disorders of function of stomach
   Achylia gastrica   Hyperchlorhydria
   Hourglass contraction   Hypochlorhydria
     of stomach   Indigestion
   Hyperacidity   Tachygastria
   EXCLUDES *achlorhydria (536.0)*
       heartburn (787.1)
   AHA: 2Q, '93, 6; 2Q, '89, 16; N-D, '84, 9
   K30 Dyspepsia `I-10`

536.9 Unspecified functional disorder of stomach
   Functional gastrointestinal:
     disorder
     disturbance
     irritation

√4ᵗʰ **537 Other disorders of stomach and duodenum**

537.0 Acquired hypertrophic pyloric stenosis `CC`
   Constriction ⎫
   Obstruction ⎬ of pylorus, acquired or adult
   Stricture   ⎭
   EXCLUDES *congenital or infantile pyloric stenosis (750.5)*
   CC Excl: 536.3, 536.8-537.0, 537.3, 750.5, 750.8-750.9, 751.1, 751.5
   AHA: 2Q, '01, 4; J-F, '85, 14

537.1 Gastric diverticulum
   EXCLUDES *congenital diverticulum of stomach (750.7)*
   DEF: Herniated sac or pouch, within stomach or duodenum.
   AHA: J-F, '85, 4

537.2 Chronic duodenal ileus
   DEF: Persistent obstruction between pylorus and jejunum.

537.3 Other obstruction of duodenum `CC`
   Cicatrix   ⎫
   Stenosis   ⎬ of duodenum
   Stricture   ⎪
   Volvulus   ⎭
   EXCLUDES *congenital obstruction of duodenum (751.1)*
   CC Excl: 537.3, 750.8-750.9, 751.1, 751.5

537.4 Fistula of stomach or duodenum `CC`
   Gastrocolic fistula
   Gastrojejunocolic fistula
   CC Excl: 537.4, 750.8-750.9, 751.5

537.5 Gastroptosis
   DEF: Downward displacement of stomach.

537.6 Hourglass stricture or stenosis of stomach
   Cascade stomach
   EXCLUDES *congenital hourglass stomach (750.7)*
       hourglass contraction of stomach (536.8)

§   Requires fifth digit. Valid digits are in [brackets] under each code. See appropriate category for codes and definitions.

√4ᵗʰ / √5ᵗʰ Additional Digit Required   Unacceptable PDx   Manifestation Code   Hospital Acquired Condition   ►◄ Revised Text   ● New Code   ▲ Revised Code Title

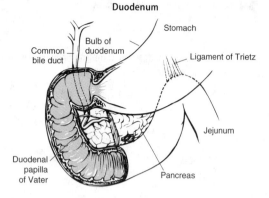

Duodenum

Stomach

Bulb of duodenum

Common bile duct

Ligament of Trietz

Jejunum

Pancreas

Duodenal papilla of Vater

☑5th **537.8 Other specified disorders of stomach and duodenum**
AHA: 4Q, '91, 25

537.81 Pylorospasm
EXCLUDES *congenital pylorospasm (750.5)*
DEF: Spasm of the pyloric sphincter.

537.82 Angiodysplasia of stomach and duodenum (without mention of hemorrhage)
AHA: 2Q, '07, 7; 3Q, '96, 10; 4Q, '90, 4

537.83 Angiodysplasia of stomach and duodenum with hemorrhage `MCC`
CC Excl: 251.5, 456.0, 530.20-530.21, 530.7, 530.82, 530.85, 531.00-534.91, 535.01, 535.11, 535.21, 535.31, 535.41, 535.51, 535.61, 537.83, 562.02-562.03, 562.12-562.13, 569.3, 569.85, 578.0-578.9
DEF: Bleeding of stomach and duodenum due to vascular abnormalities.
AHA: 2Q, '07, 7

537.84 Dieulafoy lesion (hemorrhagic) of stomach and duodenum `MCC`
CC Excl: 251.5, 456.0, 530.20-530.21, 530.7, 530.82, 530.85, 531.00-534.91, 535.01, 535.11, 535.21, 535.31, 535.41, 535.51, 535.61, 537.83-537.84, 562.02-562.03, 562.12-562.13, 569.3, 569.85, 578.0-578.9
DEF: An abnormally large and convoluted submucosal artery protruding through a defect in the mucosa in the stomach or intestines that can erode the epithelium causing hemorrhaging.
AHA: 4Q, '02, 60

537.89 Other
Gastric or duodenal:
prolapse
rupture
Intestinal metaplasia of gastric mucosa
Passive congestion of stomach
EXCLUDES *diverticula of duodenum (562.00-562.01)*
gastrointestinal hemorrhage (578.0-578.9)
AHA: 3Q, '05, 15; N-D, '84, 7
TIP: Assign for congestive portal gastropathy or portal hypertensive gastropathy.

537.9 Unspecified disorder of stomach and duodenum

538 Gastrointestinal mucositis (ulcerative) `CC`
Use additional E code to identify adverse effects of therapy, such as:
antineoplastic and immunosuppressive drugs (E930.7, E933.1)
radiation therapy (E879.2)
EXCLUDES *mucositis (ulcerative) of mouth and oral soft tissue (528.00- 528.09)*
CC Excl: 251.5, 456.0, 530.20-530.21, 530.7, 530.82, 530.85, 531.00-534.91, 535.01, 535.11, 535.21, 535.31, 535.41, 535.51, 535.61, 537.83, 537.89-538, 562.02-562.03, 562.12-562.13, 569.3, 569.85, 578.0-578.9
AHA: 4Q, '06, 88-90

APPENDICITIS (540-543)

☑4th **540 Acute appendicitis**
DEF: Inflammation of vermiform appendix due to fecal obstruction, neoplasm or foreign body of appendiceal lumen; causes infection, edema and infarction of appendiceal wall; may result in mural necrosis, and perforation.
AHA: N-D, '84, 19

540.0 With generalized peritonitis `MCC`
Appendicitis (acute) with: { perforation peritonitis (generalized) rupture } { fulminating gangrenous obstructive }
Cecitis (acute) with perforation, peritonitis (generalized), rupture
Rupture of appendix
EXCLUDES *acute appendicitis with peritoneal abscess (540.1)*
CC Excl: 537.89-543.9
K35.0 Acute appendicitis w/generalized peritonitis `I-10`

540.1 With peritoneal abscess `MCC`
Abscess of appendix
With generalized peritonitis
CC Excl: See code 540.0
AHA: N-D, '84, 19

540.9 Without mention of peritonitis `CC`
Acute appendicitis without mention of perforation, peritonitis, or rupture:
fulminating
gangrenous
inflamed
obstructive
Acute cecitis without mention of perforation, peritonitis, or rupture
CC Excl: See code 540.0
AHA: 1Q, '01, 15; 4Q, '97, 52
K35.9 Acute appendicitis unspecified `I-10`

541 Appendicitis, unqualified
AHA: 2Q, '90, 26
TIP: Do not assign for normal appendix found at appendectomy. Assign instead symptom code (e.g., abdominal pain).

542 Other appendicitis
Appendicitis: | Appendicitis:
chronic | relapsing
recurrent | subacute
EXCLUDES *hyperplasia (lymphoid) of appendix (543.0)*
AHA: 1Q, '01, 15

Appendix

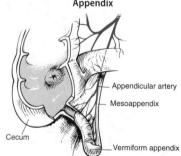

Appendicular artery

Mesoappendix

Cecum

Vermiform appendix

N Newborn Age: 0   P Pediatric Age: 0-17   M Maternity Age: 12-55   A Adult Age: 15-124   `MCC` Major CC Condition   `CC` CC Condition   `HIV` HIV Related Dx

188 – Volume 1   **2010 ICD-9-CM**

√4th **543 Other diseases of appendix**

543.0 **Hyperplasia of appendix (lymphoid)**
   DEF: Proliferation of cells in appendix tissue.

543.9 **Other and unspecified diseases of appendix**
   Appendicular or appendiceal:
      colic
      concretion
      fistula
   Diverticulum ⎫
   Fecalith   ⎪
   Intussusception ⎬ of appendix
   Mucocele   ⎪
   Stercolith   ⎭

HERNIA OF ABDOMINAL CAVITY (550-553)

[INCLUDES] hernia:
      acquired
      congenital, except diaphragmatic or hiatal

√4th **550 Inguinal hernia**

[INCLUDES] bubonocele
      inguinal hernia (direct) (double) (indirect) (oblique)
         (sliding)
      scrotal hernia

The following fifth-digit subclassification is for use with category 550:
   0 unilateral or unspecified (not specified as recurrent)
      Unilateral NOS
   1 unilateral or unspecified, recurrent
   2 bilateral (not specified as recurrent)
      Bilateral NOS
   3 bilateral, recurrent

DEF: Hernia protrusion of an abdominal organ or tissue through inguinal canal.
DEF: Indirect inguinal hernia: (external or oblique) leaves abdomen through deep inguinal ring, passes through inguinal canal lateral to the inferior epigastric artery.
DEF: Direct inguinal hernia: (internal) emerges between inferior epigastric artery and rectus muscle edge.
AHA: N-D, '85, 12

§ √5th **550.0 Inguinal hernia, with gangrene**   MCC
   [0-3]   Inguinal hernia with gangrene (and obstruction)
         CC Excl: 537.89-538, 550.00-550.93, 552.8-552.9, 553.8-553.9

§ √5th **550.1 Inguinal hernia, with obstruction, without**   CC
   [0-3]   **mention of gangrene**
         Inguinal hernia with mention of incarceration,
            irreducibility, or strangulation
         CC Excl: See code 550.0

§ √5th **550.9 Inguinal hernia, without mention of**
   [0-3]   **obstruction or gangrene**
         Inguinal hernia NOS
         AHA: For code 550.91: 3Q, '03, 10; 1Q, '03, 4
         K40.90 Uni ingin hernia w/o obst/gangrene not spec   I-10
            recur

Hernias of Abdominal Cavity

Hiatal hernia
Diaphragm
Epigastric hernia
Incisional hernia
Umbilical hernia
Inguinal hernia

√4th **551 Other hernia of abdominal cavity, with gangrene**
   [INCLUDES] that with gangrene (and obstruction)

√5th **551.0 Femoral hernia with gangrene**

551.00 **Unilateral or unspecified (not specified**   MCC
         as recurrent)
         Femoral hernia NOS with gangrene
         CC Excl: 537.89-538, 551.00-551.03, 552.8-553.03,
            553.8-553.9

551.01 **Unilateral or unspecified, recurrent**   MCC
         CC Excl: See code 551.00

551.02 **Bilateral (not specified as recurrent)**   MCC
         CC Excl: See code 551.00

551.03 **Bilateral, recurrent**   MCC
         CC Excl: See code 551.00

551.1 **Umbilical hernia with gangrene**   MCC
      Parumbilical hernia specified as gangrenous
      CC Excl: 537.89-538, 551.1-551.29, 552.1-552.29, 552.8-552.9,
         553.1-553.29, 553.8-553.9

√5th **551.2 Ventral hernia with gangrene**

551.20 **Ventral, unspecified, with gangrene**   MCC
         CC Excl: See code 551.1

551.21 **Incisional, with gangrene**   MCC
         Hernia:
            postoperative ⎫ specified as
            recurrent, ventral ⎬ gangrenous
         CC Excl: See code 551.1

551.29 **Other**   MCC
         Epigastric hernia specified as gangrenous
         CC Excl: See code 551.1

551.3 **Diaphragmatic hernia with gangrene**   MCC
      Hernia:
         hiatal (esophageal) (sliding) ⎫ specified as
         paraesophageal   ⎬ gangrenous
         Thoracic stomach   ⎭
      [EXCLUDES] congenital diaphragmatic hernia (756.6)
      CC Excl: 551.3, 552.3-552.9, 553.3-553.9

551.8 **Hernia of other specified sites, with gangrene**   MCC
      Any condition classifiable to 553.8 if specified as
         gangrenous
      CC Excl: 537.89-538, 550.00-553.9

Inguinal Hernias

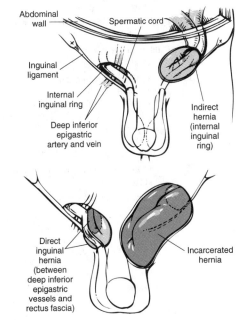

Abdominal wall
Spermatic cord
Inguinal ligament
Internal inguinal ring
Deep inferior epigastric artery and vein
Indirect hernia (internal inguinal ring)
Direct inguinal hernia (between deep inferior epigastric vessels and rectus fascia)
Incarcerated hernia

543–551.8

§ Requires fifth digit. Valid digits are in [brackets] under each code. See category 550 for codes and definitions.

√4th Additional Digit Required   Unacceptable PDx   Manifestation Code   Hospital Acquired Condition   ▶◀ Revised Text   ● New Code   ▲ Revised Code Title
√5th

2010 ICD-9-CM   **Volume 1 – 189**

Femoral Hernia

Diaphragmatic Hernias

551.9 **Hernia of unspecified site, with gangrene**   `MCC`
Any condition classifiable to 553.9 if specified as gangrenous
CC Excl: See code 551.8

√4th **552** **Other hernia of abdominal cavity, with obstruction, but without mention of gangrene**
EXCLUDES that with mention of gangrene (551.0-551.9)

√5th **552.0** **Femoral hernia with obstruction**
Femoral hernia specified as incarcerated, irreducible, strangulated, or causing obstruction

552.00 **Unilateral or unspecified (not specified as recurrent)**   `CC`
CC Excl: 537.89-538, 551.00-551.03, 552.00-552.03, 552.8-553.03, 553.8-553.9

552.01 **Unilateral or unspecified, recurrent**   `CC`
CC Excl: See code 552.00

552.02 **Bilateral (not specified as recurrent)**   `CC`
CC Excl: See code 552.00

552.03 **Bilateral, recurrent**   `CC`
CC Excl: See code 552.00

552.1 **Umbilical hernia with obstruction**   `CC`
Parumbilical hernia specified as incarcerated, irreducible, strangulated, or causing obstruction
CC Excl: 551.1-551.29, 552.1-552.29, 552.8-552.9, 553.8-553.9

√5th **552.2** **Ventral hernia with obstruction**
Ventral hernia specified as incarcerated, irreducible, strangulated, or causing obstruction

552.20 **Ventral, unspecified, with obstruction**   `CC`
CC Excl: See code 552.1

552.21 **Incisional, with obstruction**   `CC`
Hernia:
postoperative   } specified as incarcerated,
recurrent,   irreducible,
ventral   strangulated, or
                           causing obstruction

CC Excl: See code 552.1
AHA: 3Q, '03, 11

552.29 **Other**   `CC`
Epigastric hernia specified as incarcerated, irreducible, strangulated, or causing obstruction
CC Excl: See code 552.1

552.3 **Diaphragmatic hernia with obstruction**   `CC`
Hernia:
hiatal (esophageal)   } specified as caracerated,
(sliding)   irreducible, strangulated,
paraesophageal   or causing obstruction
Thoracic stomach
EXCLUDES congenital diaphragmatic hernia (756.6)
CC Excl: 551.3, 552.3-552.9, 553.3-553.9

552.8 **Hernia of other specified sites, with obstruction**   `CC`
Any condition classifiable to 553.8 if specified as incarcerated, irreducible, strangulated, or causing obstruction
EXCLUDES hernia due to adhesion with obstruction (560.81)
CC Excl: 550.00-553.9
AHA: 1Q, '04, 10

552.9 **Hernia of unspecified site, with obstruction**   `CC`
Any condition classifiable to 553.9 if specified as incarcerated, irreducible, strangulated, or causing obstruction
CC Excl: See code: 552.8

√4th **553** **Other hernia of abdominal cavity without mention of obstruction or gangrene**
EXCLUDES the listed conditions with mention of:
gangrene (and obstruction) (551.0-551.9)
obstruction (552.0-552.9)

√5th **553.0** **Femoral hernia**

553.00 **Unilateral or unspecified (not specified as recurrent)**
Femoral hernia NOS

553.01 **Unilateral or unspecified, recurrent**

553.02 **Bilateral (not specified as recurrent)**

553.03 **Bilateral, recurrent**

553.1 **Umbilical hernia**
Parumbilical hernia
K42.9 Umbilical hernia without obstruction/gangrene   `I-10`

√5th **553.2** **Ventral hernia**

553.20 **Ventral, unspecified**
AHA: 2Q, '06, 10; 3Q, '03, 6

553.21 **Incisional**
Hernia:
postoperative
recurrent, ventral
AHA: 3Q, '03, 6
K43.91 Incisional hernia w/o obstruction or gangrene   `I-10`

553.29 **Other**
Hernia:
epigastric
spigelian

553.3 **Diaphragmatic hernia**
Hernia: Thoracic stomach
hiatal (esophageal)
(sliding)
paraesophageal
EXCLUDES congenital:
diaphragmatic hernia (756.6)
hiatal hernia (750.6)
esophagocele (530.6)
AHA: 2Q, '01, 6; 1Q, '00, 6
K44.9 Diaphragmatic hernia w/o obstruction/gangrene   `I-10`

`N` Newborn Age: 0   `P` Pediatric Age: 0-17   `M` Maternity Age: 12-55   `A` Adult Age: 15-124   `MCC` Major CC Condition   `CC` CC Condition   `HIV` HIV Related Dx

190 – Volume 1   2010 ICD-9-CM

553.8　Hernia of other specified sites
Hernia:
ischiatic
ischiorectal
lumbar
obturator
Hernia:
pudendal
retroperitoneal
sciatic

Other abdominal hernia of specified site
EXCLUDES　*vaginal enterocele (618.6)*

553.9　Hernia of unspecified site
Enterocele
Epiplocele
Hernia:
　NOS
　interstitial
Hernia:
　intestinal
　intra-abdominal
Rupture (nontraumatic)
Sarcoepiplocele

NONINFECTIOUS ENTERITIS AND COLITIS (555-558)

√4ᵗʰ　**555　Regional enteritis**
INCLUDES　Crohn's disease
granulomatous enteritis
EXCLUDES　*ulcerative colitis (556)*
DEF: Inflammation of intestine; classified to site.
TIP: Assign separate code for fistula, if present. Sequence 555 code as first-listed/principal diagnosis (if underlying cause of fistula).

555.0　Small intestine　　`CC`
Ileitis:
　regional
　segmental
　terminal
Regional enteritis or Crohn's disease of:
　duodenum
　ileum
　jejunum
CC Excl: 555.0-556.9

555.1　Large intestine　　`CC`
Colitis:
　granulmatous
　regional
　transmural
Regional enteritis or Crohn's disease of:
　colon
　large bowel
　rectum
CC Excl: See code: 555.0
AHA: 3Q, '99, 8

555.2　Small intestine with large intestine　　`CC`
Regional ileocolitis
CC Excl: See code: 555.0
AHA: 1Q, '03, 18

555.9　Unspecified site　　`CC`
Crohn's disease NOS
Regional enteritis NOS
CC Excl: 555.0-555.9
AHA: ▶1Q, '09, 5;◀ 2Q, '05, 11; 3Q, '99, 8; 4Q, '97, 42; 2Q, '97, 3
K50.90 Crohns disease unspecified w/o complications　`I-10`

Large Intestine

Splenic flexure
Hepatic flexure
Transverse colon
Ascending colon
Descending colon
Cecum
Sigmoid colon

√4ᵗʰ　**556　Ulcerative colitis**
DEF: Chronic inflammation of mucosal lining of intestinal tract; may be single area or entire colon.
AHA: 3Q, '99, 8

556.0　Ulcerative (chronic) enterocolitis　　`CC`
CC Excl: 555.0-556.9

556.1　Ulcerative (chronic) ileocolitis　　`CC`
CC Excl: 555.0-556.9

556.2　Ulcerative (chronic) proctitis　　`CC`
CC Excl: 555.0-556.9

556.3　Ulcerative (chronic) proctosigmoiditis　　`CC`
CC Excl: 555.0-556.9

556.4　Pseudopolyposis of colon　　`CC`
CC Excl: 555.0-556.9

556.5　Left-sided ulcerative (chronic) colitis　　`CC`
CC Excl: 555.0-556.9

556.6　Universal ulcerative (chronic) colitis　　`CC`
Pancolitis
CC Excl: 555.0-556.9

556.8　Other ulcerative colitis　　`CC`
CC Excl: 555.0-556.9

556.9　Ulcerative colitis, unspecified　　`CC`
Ulcerative enteritis NOS
CC Excl: 555.0-556.9
AHA: 1Q, '03, 10
K51.90 Ulcerative colitis unspecified w/o complications　`I-10`

√4ᵗʰ　**557　Vascular insufficiency of intestine**
EXCLUDES　*necrotizing enterocolitis of the newborn (777.50-777.53)*
DEF: Inadequacy of intestinal vessels.

557.0　Acute vascular insufficiency of intestine　　`MCC`
Acute:
　hemorrhagic enterocolitis
　ischemic colitis, enteritis, or enterocolitis
　massive necrosis of intestine
Bowel infarction
Embolism of mesenteric artery
Fulminant enterocolitis
Hemorrhagic necrosis of intestine
Infarction of appendices epiploicae
Intestinal gangrene
Intestinal infarction (acute) (agnogenic) (hemorrhagic) (nonocclusive)
Mesenteric infarction (embolic) (thrombotic)
Necrosis of intestine
Terminal hemorrhagic enteropathy
Thrombosis of mesenteric artery
CC Excl: 557.0-557.1
AHA: 2Q, '08, 15; 4Q, '01, 53
TIP: Do not assign an additional code for GI bleeding; it is inherent in 557.0.
K55.0 Acute vascular disorders of intestine　`I-10`

557.1　Chronic vascular insufficiency of intestine　　`CC`
Angina, abdominal
Chronic ischemic colitis, enteritis, or enterocolitis
Ischemic stricture of intestine
Mesenteric:
　angina
　artery syndrome (superior)
　vascular insufficiency
CC Excl: 557.0-557.9
AHA: 3Q, '96, 9; 4Q, '90, 4; N-D, '86, 11; N-D, '84, 7

557.9　Unspecified vascular insufficiency of intestine　　`CC`
Alimentary pain due to vascular insufficiency
Ischemic colitis, enteritis, or enterocolitis NOS
CC Excl: 557.0-557.9
K55.9 Vascular disorder of intestine unspecified　`I-10`

√4ᵗʰ √5ᵗʰ　Additional Digit Required　　Unacceptable PDx　　Manifestation Code　　Hospital Acquired Condition　　▶◀ Revised Text　　● New Code　　▲ Revised Code Title

2010 ICD-9-CM　　　　　　　　　　　　　　　　　　　　　　　　　　　**October 2009 • Volume 1 – 191**

✓4ᵗʰ **558 Other and unspecified noninfectious gastroenteritis and colitis**

    EXCLUDES *infectious:*

        colitis, enteritis, or gastroenteritis (009.0-009.1)
        diarrhea (009.2-009.3)

558.1 Gastroenteritis and colitis due to radiation `CC`
    Radiation enterocolitis
    CC Excl: 558.1

558.2 Toxic gastroenteritis and colitis `CC`
    Use additional E code to identify cause
    CC Excl: 558.2

558.3 Allergic gastroenteritis and colitis
    Use additional code to identify type of food allergy
    (V15.01-V15.05)
    DEF: True immunoglobulin E (IgE)-mediated allergic reaction of the lining of the stomach, intestines, or colon to food proteins; causes nausea, vomiting, diarrhea, and abdominal cramping.
    AHA: ▶4Q, '08, 116;◀ 1Q, '03, 12; 4Q, '00, 42

✓5ᵗʰ **558.4 Eosinophilic gastroenteritis and colitis**
    AHA: ▶4Q, '08, 115-116◀

    558.41 Eosinophilic gastroenteritis
        Eosinophilic enteritis

    558.42 Eosinophilic colitis

558.9 Other and unspecified noninfectious gastroenteritis and colitis

    Colitis
    Enteritis
    Gastroenteritis
    Ileitis   } NOS, dietetic, or noninfectious
    Jejunitis
    Sigmoiditis

    AHA: 2Q, '08, 10; 1Q, '08, 10; 3Q, '99, 4, 6; N-D, '87, 7
    K52.9 Noninfective gastroenteritis & colitis unspec `I-10`

OTHER DISEASES OF INTESTINES AND PERITONEUM (560-569)

✓4ᵗʰ **560 Intestinal obstruction without mention of hernia**

    EXCLUDES *duodenum (537.2-537.3)*
        inguinal hernia with obstruction (550.1)
        intestinal obstruction complicating hernia (552.0-552.9)
        mesenteric:
            embolism (557.0)
            infarction (557.0)
            thrombosis (557.0)
        neonatal intestinal obstruction (277.01, 777.1-777.2, 777.4)

    TIP: If intestinal obstruction is due to abdominal carcinomatosis or Crohn's disease, sequence that condition first.

560.0 Intussusception `CC`
    Intussusception (colon) (intestine) (rectum)
    Invagination of intestine or colon
    EXCLUDES *intussusception of appendix (543.9)*
    CC Excl: 560.0-560.9, 569.87-569.9
    AHA: 4Q, '98, 82

560.1 Paralytic ileus `CC`
    Adynamic ileus
    Ileus (of intestine) (of bowel) (of colon)
    Paralysis of intestine or colon
    EXCLUDES *gallstone ileus (560.31)*
    DEF: Obstruction of ileus due to inhibited bowel motility.
    CC Excl: See code 560.0
    AHA: J-F, '87, 13
    K56.0 Paralytic ileus `I-10`

Volvulus and Diverticulitis

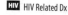

Knotted intestine (volvulus)

Diverticulum

560.2 Volvulus `MCC`
    Knotting
    Strangulation
    Torsion   } if intestine, bowel, or colon
    Twist
    DEF: Entanglement of bowel; causes obstruction; may compromise bowel circulation.
    CC Excl: See code 560.0

✓5ᵗʰ **560.3 Impaction of intestine**

    560.30 Impaction of intestine, unspecified `CC`
        Impaction of colon
        CC Excl: See code 560.0

    560.31 Gallstone ileus `CC`
        Obstruction of intestine by gallstone
        CC Excl: See code 560.0

    560.39 Other `CC`
        Concretion of intestine
        Fecal impaction
        Enterolith
        CC Excl: See code 560.0
        AHA: 4Q, '98, 38
        K56.4 Other impaction of intestine `I-10`

✓5ᵗʰ **560.8 Other specified intestinal obstruction**

    560.81 Intestinal or peritoneal adhesions with obstruction (postoperative) (postinfection) `CC`
        EXCLUDES *adhesions without obstruction (568.0)*
        DEF: Obstruction of peritoneum or intestine due to abnormal union of tissues.
        CC Excl: See code 560.0
        AHA: 4Q, '95, 55; 3Q, '95, 6; N-D, '87, 9
        TIP: Do not assign additional code 997.4 Digestive system complications.
        K56.5 Intestinal adhes [bands] w/obst (postproc) (postinfec) `I-10`

    560.89 Other `CC`
        Acute pseudo-obstruction of intestine
        Mural thickening causing obstruction
        EXCLUDES *ischemic stricture of intestine (557.1)*
        CC Excl: See code 560.0
        AHA: 2Q, '97, 3; 1Q, '88, 6

560.9 Unspecified intestinal obstruction `CC`
    Enterostenosis
    Obstruction
    Occlusion
    Stenosis   } of intestine or colon
    Stricture
    EXCLUDES *congenital stricture or stenosis of intestine (751.1-751.2)*
    CC Excl: See code 560.0
    K56.60 Unspecified intestinal obstruction `I-10`

`N` Newborn Age: 0   `P` Pediatric Age: 0-17   `M` Maternity Age: 12-55   `A` Adult Age: 15-124   `MCC` Major CC Condition   `CC` CC Condition   `HIV` HIV Related Dx

192 – Volume 1 · February 2009   **2010 ICD-9-CM**

√4th **562　Diverticula of intestine**

Use additional code to identify any associated:
peritonitis (567.0–567.9)

EXCLUDES *congenital diverticulum of colon (751.5)*
diverticulum of appendix (543.9)
Meckel's diverticulum (751.0)

AHA: 4Q, '91, 25; J-F, '85, 1

[handwritten left margin: diagnosis of diverticulitis assumes the presence of diverticula; only the code for diverticulitis is assigned, as indicated in the alphabetic Index, even when both conditions are mentioned in the physician's diagnostic statement.]

√5th **562.0　Small intestine**

562.00　Diverticulosis of small intestine (without mention of hemorrhage)

Diverticulosis:
duodenum ⎫
ileum　⎬ without mention of diverticulitis
jejunum ⎭

DEF: Saclike herniations of mucous lining of small intestine.

562.01　Diverticulitis of small intestine (without mention of hemorrhage) `CC`

Diverticulitis (with diverticulosis):
duodenum
ileum
jejunum
small intestine

DEF: Inflamed saclike herniations of mucous lining of small intestine

CC Excl: 562.00–562.03

562.02　Diverticulosis of small intestine with hemorrhage `MCC`

CC Excl: 251.5, 456.0, 530.20–530.21, 530.7, 530.82, 530.85, 531.00–534.91, 535.01, 535.11, 535.21, 535.31, 535.41, 535.51, 535.61, 537.83, 562.02–562.03, 562.12–562.13, 569.3, 569.85, 578.0–578.9

562.03　Diverticulitis of small intestine with hemorrhage `MCC`

CC Excl: See code 562.02

√5th **562.1　Colon**

562.10　Diverticulosis of colon (without mention of hemorrhage)

Diverticulosis:
NOS　　　　　⎫
intestine (large) ⎬ without mention of diverticulitis

Diverticular disease (colon) without mention of diverticulitis

DEF: Saclike herniations of mucous lining of large intestine.

AHA: 3Q, '05, 17; 3Q, '02, 15; 4Q, '90, 21; J-F, '85, 5

K57.90 Divrticulos intest part uns w/o perf/absc w/o bldg `I-10`

562.11　Diverticulitis of colon (without mention of hemorrhage) `CC`

Diverticulitis (with diverticulosis):
NOS
colon
intestine (large)

DEF: Inflamed saclike herniations of mucosal lining of large intestine.

CC Excl: 562.10–562.13

AHA: 1Q, '96, 14; J-F, '85, 5

K57.92 Divrticulit intest part uns w/o perf/absc w/o bldg `I-10`

562.12　Diverticulosis of colon with hemorrhage `MCC`

CC Excl: See code 562.02

562.13　Diverticulitis of colon with hemorrhage `MCC`

CC Excl: See code 562.02

√4th **564　Functional digestive disorders, not elsewhere classified**

EXCLUDES *functional disorders of stomach (536.0–536.9)*
those specified as psychogenic (306.4)

√5th **564.0　Constipation**

AHA: 4Q, '01, 45

564.00　Constipation, unspecified

K59.00 Constipation unspecified `I-10`

564.01　Slow transit constipation

DEF: Delay in the transit of fecal material through the colon secondary to smooth muscle dysfunction or decreased peristaltic contractions along the colon: also called colonic inertia or delayed transit.

564.02　Outlet dysfunction constipation

DEF: Failure to relax the paradoxical contractions of the striated pelvic floor muscles during the attempted defecation.

564.09　Other constipation

564.1　Irritable bowel syndrome

Irritable colon
Spastic colon

DEF: Functional gastrointestinal disorder (FGID); symptoms include diarrhea, constipation, abdominal pain; gas, distended abdomen, nausea, vomiting, emotional distress, and depression.

AHA: 1Q, '88, 6

K58.9 Irritable bowel syndrome without diarrhea `I-10`

564.2　Postgastric surgery syndromes

Dumping syndrome
Jejunal syndrome
Postgastrectomy syndrome
Postvagotomy syndrome

EXCLUDES *malnutrition following gastrointestinal surgery (579.3)*
postgastrojejunostomy ulcer (534.0–534.9)

AHA: 1Q, '95, 11

564.3　Vomiting following gastrointestinal surgery

Vomiting (bilious) following gastrointestinal surgery

564.4　Other postoperative functional disorders

Diarrhea following gastrointestinal surgery

EXCLUDES *colostomy and enterostomy complications (569.60–569.69)*

564.5　Functional diarrhea

EXCLUDES *diarrhea:*
NOS (787.91)
psychogenic (306.4)

DEF: Diarrhea with no detectable organic cause.

564.6　Anal spasm

Proctalgia fugax

564.7　Megacolon, other than Hirschsprung's `CC`

Dilatation of colon

EXCLUDES *megacolon:*
congenital [Hirschsprung's] (751.3)
toxic (556)

DEF: Enlarged colon; congenital or acquired; can occur acutely or become chronic.

CC Excl: 564.1–564.9

√5th **564.8　Other specified functional disorders of intestine**

EXCLUDES *malabsorption (579.0–579.9)*

AHA: 1Q, '88, 6

564.81　Neurogenic bowel `CC`

DEF: Disorder of bowel due to spinal cord lesion above conus medullaris; symptoms include precipitous micturition, nocturia, headache, sweating, nasal obstruction and spastic contractions.

CC Excl: See code: 564.7

AHA: 1Q, '01, 12; 4Q, '98, 45

564.89　Other functional disorders of intestine

Atony of colon

564.9　Unspecified functional disorder of intestine

√4th √5th **Additional Digit Required**　　**Unacceptable PDx**　　**Manifestation Code**　　**Hospital Acquired Condition**　　►◄ Revised Text　　● New Code　　▲ Revised Code Title

2010 ICD-9-CM　　　　　　　　　　　　　　　　　　　　　　　　　　　　　　　　　　　　　　　**Volume 1 – 193**

562–564.9

Digestive System

565–567.89

Anal Fistula and Abscess

Labels: Urethra, Fistula, Bladder, Abscess, Rectum

Psoas Muscle Abscess

Labels: Psoas minor muscle, Psoas major muscle, Small intestine (ilium), Peritoneal cavity, Abscess, Ascending colon, Pelvic bone, Psoas major muscle, Erector spinae muscles, Small intestine (jejunum), Ascending colon, Psoas major muscle, Spinous process of L4

√4th **565 Anal fissure and fistula**

565.0 **Anal fissure**

> **EXCLUDES** anal sphincter tear (healed) (non-traumatic) (old) (569.43)
> traumatic (863.89, 863.99)

> **DEF:** Ulceration of cleft at anal mucosa; causes pain, itching, bleeding, infection, and sphincter spasm; may occur with hemorrhoids.

565.1 **Anal fistula**

Fistula:
- anorectal
- rectal
- rectum to skin

> **EXCLUDES** fistula of rectum to internal organs—see Alphabetic Index
> ischiorectal fistula (566)
> rectovaginal fistula (619.1)

> **DEF:** Abnormal opening on cutaneous surface near anus; may lack connection with rectum.

> **AHA:** 1Q, '07, 13

566 Abscess of anal and rectal regions   `CC`

Abscess:
- ischiorectal
- perianal
- perirectal

Cellulitis:
- anal

Cellulitis:
- perirectal
- rectal
- Ischiorectal fistula

CC Excl: 566

√4th **567 Peritonitis and retroperitoneal infections**

> **EXCLUDES** peritonitis:
> benign paroxysmal (277.31)
> pelvic, female (614.5, 614.7)
> periodic familial (277.31)
> puerperal ▶(670.8)◀
> with or following:
> abortion (634-638 with .0, 639.0)
> appendicitis (540.0-540.1)
> ectopic or molar pregnancy (639.0)

> **DEF:** Inflammation of the peritoneal cavity.

567.0 **Peritonitis in infectious diseases classified elsewhere**   `MCC`

> Code first underlying disease
> **EXCLUDES** peritonitis:
> gonococcal (098.86)
> syphilitic (095.2)
> tuberculous (014.0)

> **CC Excl:** 567.0-567.29, 567.38-567.9, 569.87-569.9

567.1 **Pneumococcal peritonitis**   `MCC`

> **CC Excl:** See code: 567.0

√5th 567.2 **Other suppurative peritonitis**

> **AHA:** 4Q, '05, 74; 2Q, '01, 11, 12; 3Q, '99, 9; 2Q, '98, 19

567.21 **Peritonitis (acute) generalized**   `MCC`

> Pelvic peritonitis, male
> **CC Excl:** See code 567.0
> **TIP:** For pelvic peritonitis in a female patient, refer to code 614.5.

567.22 **Peritoneal abscess**   `MCC`

> Abscess (of):
> abdominopelvic
> mesenteric
> omentum
> peritoneum
> retrocecal
> subdiaphragmatic
> subhepatic
> subphrenic

> **CC Excl:** See code 567.0
> **K65.1** Peritoneal abscess   `I-10`

567.23 **Spontaneous bacterial peritonitis**   `MCC`

> **EXCLUDES** bacterial peritonitis NOS (567.29)
> **CC Excl:** See code 567.0

567.29 **Other suppurative peritonitis**   `MCC`

> Subphrenic peritonitis
> **CC Excl:** See code 567.0

√5th 567.3 **Retroperitoneal infections**

> **AHA:** 4Q, '05, 74

567.31 **Psoas muscle abscess**   `MCC`

> **DEF:** Infection that extends into or around the psoas muscle that connects the lumbar vertebrae to the femur.
> **CC Excl:** 567.31, 728.0, 728.11-728.3, 728.81, 728.86

567.38 **Other retroperitoneal abscess**   `MCC`

> **AHA:** 4Q, '05, 77
> **CC Excl:** See code 567.0

567.39 **Other retroperitoneal infections**   `MCC`

> **CC Excl:** See code 567.0

√5th 567.8 **Other specified peritonitis**

> **AHA:** 4Q, '05, 74

567.81 **Choleperitonitis**   `MCC`

> Peritonitis due to bile
> **DEF:** Inflammation or infection due to presence of bile in the peritoneum resulting from rupture of the bile passages or gallbladder.
> **CC Excl:** See code 567.0

567.82 **Sclerosing mesenteritis**   `CC`

> Fat necrosis of peritoneum
> (Idiopathic) sclerosing mesenteric fibrosis
> Mesenteric lipodystrophy
> Mesenteric panniculitis
> Retractile mesenteritis

> **DEF:** Inflammatory processes involving the mesenteric fat; progresses to fibrosis and necrosis of tissue.
> **CC Excl:** See code 567.0
> **AHA:** 4Q, '05, 77

567.89 **Other specified peritonitis**   `MCC`

> Chronic proliferative peritonitis
> Mesenteric saponification
> Peritonitis due to urine
> **CC Excl:** See code 567.0

`N` Newborn Age: 0   `P` Pediatric Age: 0-17   `M` Maternity Age: 12-55   `A` Adult Age: 15-124   `MCC` Major CC Condition   `CC` CC Condition   `HIV` HIV Related Dx

194 – Volume 1 · October 2009   2010 ICD-9-CM

567.9   **Unspecified peritonitis**   `MCC`
     Peritonitis NOS
     Peritonitis of unspecified cause
     CC Excl: See code 567.0
     AHA: 1Q, '04, 10

✓4ᵗʰ **568**   **Other disorders of peritoneum**

   568.0   **Peritoneal adhesions (postoperative) (postinfection)**

Adhesions (of):	Adhesions (of):
abdominal (wall)	mesenteric
diaphragm	omentum
intestine	stomach
male pelvis	Adhesive bands

     EXCLUDES   *adhesions:*
         pelvic, female (614.6)
         with obstruction:
           duodenum (537.3)
           intestine (560.81)

     DEF: Abnormal union of tissues in peritoneum.
     AHA: 3Q, '03, 7, 11; 4Q, '95, 55; 3Q, '95, 7; S-O, '85, 11
     TIP: Do not assign additional code 997.4 Digestive system complications.
     K66.0 Peritoneal adhesns (postprocedural) (postinfection) `I-10`

  ✓5ᵗʰ **568.8**   **Other specified disorders of peritoneum**

     568.81   **Hemoperitoneum (nontraumatic)**   `MCC`
         CC Excl: 568.81

     568.82   **Peritoneal effusion (chronic)**   `CC`
         EXCLUDES   *ascites NOS (789.51-789.59)*
         DEF: Persistent leakage of fluid within peritoneal cavity.
         CC Excl: 568.82

     568.89   **Other**

Peritoneal:	Peritoneal:
cyst	granuloma

   568.9   **Unspecified disorder of peritoneum**

✓4ᵗʰ **569**   **Other disorders of intestine**

   569.0   **Anal and rectal polyp**
     Anal and rectal polyp NOS
     EXCLUDES   *adenomatous anal and rectal polyp (211.4)*

   569.1   **Rectal prolapse**

Procidentia:	Prolapse:
anus (sphincter)	anal canal
rectum (sphincter)	rectal mucosa
Proctoptosis	

     EXCLUDES   *prolapsed hemorrhoids (455.2, 455.5)*

   569.2   **Stenosis of rectum and anus**
     Stricture of anus (sphincter)

   569.3   **Hemorrhage of rectum and anus**   `CC`
     EXCLUDES   *gastrointestinal bleeding NOS (578.9)*
           melena (578.1)
     CC Excl: 251.5, 456.0, 530.20-530.21, 530.7, 530.82, 530.85, 531.00-534.91, 535.01, 535.11, 535.21, 535.31, 535.41, 535.51, 535.61, 537.83, 562.02-562.03, 562.12-562.13, 569.3, 569.85, 578.0-578.9
     AHA: 3Q, '05, 17
     K62.5 Hemorrhage of anus and rectum   `I-10`

Rectum and Anus

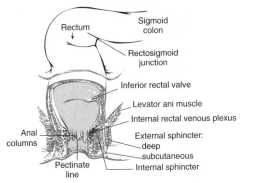

✓5ᵗʰ **569.4**   **Other specified disorders of rectum and anus**

   569.41   **Ulcer of anus and rectum**   `CC`

Solitary ulcer	⎱ of anus (sphincter) or
Stercoral ulcer	⎰ rectum (sphincter)

     CC Excl: 569.41

   569.42   **Anal or rectal pain**
     AHA: 1Q, '03, 8; 1Q, '96, 13

   569.43   **Anal sphincter tear (healed) (old)**
     Tear of anus, nontraumatic
     Use additional code for any associated fecal incontinence (787.6)
     EXCLUDES   *anal fissure (565.0)*
           anal sphincter tear (healed) (old)
             complicating delivery (654.8)
     AHA: 4Q, '07, 88

   569.44   **Dysplasia of anus**
     Anal intraepithelial neoplasia I and II
       (AIN I and II) (histologically confirmed)
     Dysplasia of anus NOS
     Mild and moderate dysplasia of anus
       (histologically confirmed)
     EXCLUDES   *abnormal results from anal cytologic*
           examination without
           histologic confirmation
           (796.70-796.79)
           anal intraepithelial neoplasia III
           (230.5, 230.6)
           carcinoma in situ of anus (230.5,
           230.6)
           HGSIL of anus (796.74)
           severe dysplasia of anus (230.5,
           230.6)
     AHA: ▶4Q, '08, 117◀

   569.49   **Other**

Granuloma	⎱ of rectum (sphincter)
Rupture	⎰

     Hypertrophy of anal papillae
     Proctitis NOS
     EXCLUDES   *fistula of rectum to:*
           internal organs–see Alphabetic
             Index
           skin (565.1)
           hemorrhoids (455.0-455.9)
           incontinence of sphincter ani (787.6)

   569.5   **Abscess of intestine**   `CC`
     EXCLUDES   *appendiceal abscess (540.1)*
     CC Excl: 569.5
     K63.0 Abscess of intestine   `I-10`

✓5ᵗʰ **569.6**   **Colostomy and enterostomy complications**
     DEF: Complication in a surgically created opening, from intestine to surface skin.
     AHA: 4Q, '95, 58
     TIP: Do not assign additional code 997.4 Digestive system complications.

   569.60   **Colostomy and enterostomy complication, unspecified**

   569.61   **Infection of colostomy or enterostomy**   `CC`
     Use additional code to identify organism
       (041.00-041.9)
     Use additional code to specify type of infection, such as:
       abscess or cellulitis of abdomen (682.2)
       septicemia (038.0-038.9)
     CC Excl: 569.60-569.69

   569.62   **Mechanical complication of colostomy and enterostomy**   `CC`
     Malfunction of colostomy and enterostomy
     CC Excl: 530.86-530.87, 536.40-536.49, 569.60-569.79, 997.4, 997.71, 997.91-997.99, 998.81, 998.83-998.9
     AHA: 2Q, '05, 11 ; 1Q, '03, 10; 4Q, '98, 44

✓4ᵗʰ ✓5ᵗʰ Additional Digit Required	Unacceptable PDx	Manifestation Code	Hospital Acquired Condition	▶◀ Revised Text	● New Code	▲ Revised Code Title

569.69 Other complication `CC`
Fistula   Prolapse
Hernia
CC Excl: See code: 569.61
AHA: 3Q, '98, 16

● √5ᵗʰ **569.7 Complications of intestinal pouch**
●
569.71 Pouchitis `CC`
Inflammation of internal ileoanal pouch
CC Excl: 30.86-530.87, 536.40-536.49, 569.71-569.79, 997.4, 997.71, 997.91-997.99, 998.81, 998.83-998.9

● **569.79 Other complications of intestinal pouch** `CC`
CC Excl: See code: 569.71

√5ᵗʰ **569.8 Other specified disorders of intestine**
AHA: 4Q, '91, 25

569.81 Fistula of intestine, excluding rectum and anus `CC`
Fistula: Fistula:
   abdominal wall   enteroenteric
   enterocolic   ileorectal
EXCLUDES   fistula of intestine to internal organs–see Alphabetic Index
persistent postoperative fistula (998.6)
CC Excl: 569.81
AHA: 3Q, '99, 8

569.82 Ulceration of intestine `CC`
Primary ulcer of intestine
Ulceration of colon
EXCLUDES   that with perforation (569.83)
CC Excl: 569.82

569.83 Perforation of intestine `MCC`
CC Excl: 569.83

569.84 Angiodysplasia of intestine (without mention of hemorrhage)
DEF: Small vascular abnormalities of the intestinal tract without bleeding problems.
AHA: 3Q, '96, 10; 4Q, '90, 4; 4Q, '90, 21
TIP: Assign code 569.84 or 569.85 for documentation of either intestinal arteriovenous (AV) malformation or angiodysplasia.

569.85 Angiodysplasia of intestine with hemorrhage `MCC`
DEF: Small vascular abnormalities of the intestinal tract with bleeding problems.
CC Excl: 251.5, 456.0, 530.20-530.21, 530.7, 530.82, 530.85, 531.00-534.91, 535.01, 535.11, 535.21, 535.31, 535.41, 535.51, 535.61, 537.83, 562.02-562.03, 562.12-562.13, 569.3, 569.85, 578.0-578.9
AHA: 3Q, '96, 9

569.86 Dieulafoy lesion (hemorrhagic) of intestine `MCC`
CC Excl: 251.5, 456.0, 530.20-530.21, 530.7, 530.82, 530.85, 531.00-534.91, 535.01, 535.11, 535.21, 535.31, 535.41, 535.51, 535.61, 537.83, 562.02-562.03, 562.12-562.13, 569.3, 569.85-569.86, 578.0-578.9
AHA: 4Q, '02, 60-61

● **569.87 Vomiting of fecal matter**

569.89 Other
Enteroptosis
Granuloma   ⎫
Prolapse   ⎬ of intestine
           ⎭
Pericolitis
Perisigmoiditis
Visceroptosis
EXCLUDES   gangrene of intestine, mesentery, or omentum (557.0)
hemorrhage of intestine NOS (578.9)
obstruction of intestine (560.0-560.9)
AHA: 3Q, '96, 9

569.9 Unspecified disorder of intestine

OTHER DISEASES OF DIGESTIVE SYSTEM (570-579)

570 Acute and subacute necrosis of liver `MCC`
Acute hepatic failure
Acute or subacute hepatitis, not specified as infective
Necrosis of liver (acute) (diffuse) (massive) (subacute)
Parenchymatous degeneration of liver
Yellow atrophy (liver) (acute) (subacute)
EXCLUDES   icterus gravis of newborn (773.0-773.2)
serum hepatitis (070.2-070.3)
that with:
   abortion (634-638 with .7, 639.8)
   ectopic or molar pregnancy (639.8)
   pregnancy, childbirth, or the puerperium (646.7)
viral hepatitis (070.0-070.9)
CC Excl: 570, 573.4-573.9
AHA: 2Q, '05, 9; 1Q, '00, 22
K72.00 Acute and subacute hepatic failure without coma `I-10`

√4ᵗʰ **571 Chronic liver disease and cirrhosis**

571.0 Alcoholic fatty liver `A`

571.1 Acute alcoholic hepatitis `A`
Acute alcoholic liver disease
AHA: 2Q, '02, 4

571.2 Alcoholic cirrhosis of liver `A`
Florid cirrhosis
Laennec's cirrhosis (alcoholic)
DEF: Fibrosis and dysfunction, of liver; due to alcoholic liver disease.
AHA: 3Q, '07, 7; 2Q, '07, 6; 2Q, '02, 4; 1Q, '02, 3; N-D, '85, 14
TIP: For a patient admitted for bleeding esophageal varices due to alcoholic liver cirrhosis, sequence the liver cirrhosis first.
K70.30 Alcoholic cirrhosis of liver without ascites `I-10`

571.3 Alcoholic liver damage, unspecified `A`

√5ᵗʰ **571.4 Chronic hepatitis**
EXCLUDES   viral hepatitis (acute) (chronic) (070.0-070.9)

571.40 Chronic hepatitis, unspecified

571.41 Chronic persistent hepatitis

571.42 Autoimmune hepatitis
AHA: 4Q, '08, 120

571.49 Other
Chronic hepatitis:
   active
   aggressive
Recurrent hepatitis
AHA: 3Q, '99, 19; N-D, '85, 14

Liver

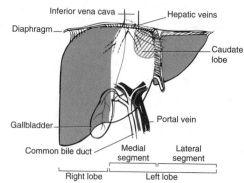

Inferior vena cava — Hepatic veins
Diaphragm —
       Caudate lobe
Gallbladder — Portal vein
Common bile duct — Medial segment | Lateral segment
Right lobe | Left lobe

N Newborn Age: 0   **P** Pediatric Age: 0-17   **M** Maternity Age: 12-55   **A** Adult Age: 15-124   **MCC** Major CC Condition   **CC** CC Condition   **HIV** HIV Related Dx

196 – Volume 1 · October 2009   **2010 ICD-9-CM**

571.5 Cirrhosis of liver without mention of alcohol

Cirrhosis of liver:
 NOS
 cryptogenic
 macronodular
 micronodular
 posthepatitic
 postnecrotic

Healed yellow atrophy (liver)
Portal cirrhosis

Code first, if applicable, viral hepatitis (acute) (chronic) (070.0–070.9)

DEF: Fibrosis and dysfunction of liver; not alcohol related.

AHA: 3Q, '07, 7; 2Q, '07, 5

TIP: For a patient admitted for bleeding esophageal varices due to liver cirrhosis, sequence the liver cirrhosis first.

571.6 Biliary cirrhosis
Chronic nonsuppurative destructive cholangitis
Cirrhosis:
 cholangitic
 cholestatic

571.8 Other chronic nonalcoholic liver disease
Chronic yellow atrophy (liver)
Fatty liver, without mention of alcohol

AHA: 2Q, '96, 12

571.9 Unspecified chronic liver disease without mention of alcohol

✓4ᵗʰ 572 Liver abscess and sequelae of chronic liver disease

572.0 Abscess of liver   MCC
EXCLUDES amebic liver abscess (006.3)
CC Excl: 006.3, 572.0-572.1, 573.8-573.9

572.1 Portal pyemia   MCC
Phlebitis of portal vein
Portal thrombophlebitis
Pylephlebitis
Pylethrombophlebitis
DEF: Inflammation of portal vein or branches; may be due to intestinal disease; symptoms include fever, chills, jaundice, sweating, and abscess in various body parts.
CC Excl: See code 572.0

▲ 572.2 Hepatic encephalopathy   MCC
►Hepatic coma◄
Hepatocerebral intoxication
Portal-systemic encephalopathy
EXCLUDES hepatic coma associated with viral hepatitis–see category 070
CC Excl: 572.2, 573.8-573.9
AHA: 2Q, '07, 5; 2Q, '05, 9; 1Q, '02, 3; 3Q, '95, 14
TIP: Do not assign if hepatic coma is documented with viral hepatitis; see category 070 with fourth digit indicating hepatic coma.
K72.91 Hepatic failure unspecified with coma   I-10

572.3 Portal hypertension   CC
DEF: Abnormally high blood pressure in the portal vein.
CC Excl: 572.2-572.3, 573.8-573.9
AHA: 3Q, '05, 15
K76.6 Portal hypertension   I-10

572.4 Hepatorenal syndrome   MCC
EXCLUDES that following delivery (674.8)
DEF: Hepatic and renal failure characterized by cirrhosis with ascites or obstructive jaundice, oliguria, and low sodium concentration.
CC Excl: 572.4, 573.8-573.9
AHA: 3Q, '93, 15

572.8 Other sequelae of chronic liver disease

✓4ᵗʰ 573 Other disorders of liver
EXCLUDES amyloid or lardaceous degeneration of liver (277.39)
congenital cystic disease of liver (751.62)
glycogen infiltration of liver (271.0)
hepatomegaly NOS (789.1)
portal vein obstruction (452)

573.0 Chronic passive congestion of liver
DEF: Blood accumulation in liver tissue.

573.1 Hepatitis in viral diseases classified elsewhere   CC
Code first underlying disease as:
 Coxsackie virus disease (074.8)
 cytomegalic inclusion virus disease (078.5)
 infectious mononucleosis (075)
EXCLUDES hepatitis (in):
 mumps (072.71)
 viral (070.0-070.9)
 yellow fever (060.0-060.9)
CC Excl: 573.1-573.3, 573.8-573.9

573.2 Hepatitis in other infectious diseases classified elsewhere   CC
Code first underlying disease, as:
 malaria (084.9)
EXCLUDES hepatitis in:
 late syphilis (095.3)
 secondary syphilis (091.62)
 toxoplasmosis (130.5)
CC Excl: See code: 573.1

573.3 Hepatitis, unspecified
Toxic (noninfectious) hepatitis
Use additional E code to identify cause
AHA: 3Q, '98, 3, 4; 4Q, '90, 26
K75.9 Inflammatory liver disease unspecified   I-10

573.4 Hepatic infarction   MCC
CC Excl: 570, 573.4-573.9

573.8 Other specified disorders of liver
Hepatoptosis

573.9 Unspecified disorder of liver

✓4ᵗʰ 574 Cholelithiasis

The following fifth-digit subclassification is for use with category 574:
 0 without mention of obstruction
 1 with obstruction

§ ✓5ᵗʰ 574.0 Calculus of gallbladder with acute cholecystitis   CC
[0-1]
Biliary calculus
Calculus of cystic duct } with acute cholecystitis
Cholelithiasis

Any condition classifiable to 574.2 with acute cholecystitis
CC Excl: For code 574.00: 574.00-574.21, 574.40, 574.60-574.61, 574.80-574.81, 575.0-575.12, 575.9, 576.8-576.9; **For code 574.01:** 574.00-574.21, 574.60-574.61, 574.80-574.81, 575.0-575.12, 575.9, 576.8-576.9
AHA: 4Q, '96, 32
K80.00 Calculus of GB w/acute cholecystitis w/o obst   I-10

Gallbladder and Bile Ducts

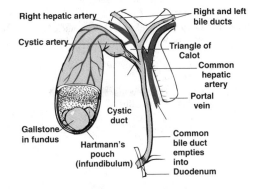

571.5 Cirrhosis of liver without mention of alcohol

§   Requires fifth digit. Valid digits are in [brackets] under each code. See category 574 for codes and definitions.

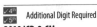

✓4ᵗʰ / ✓5ᵗʰ Additional Digit Required   Unacceptable PDx   Manifestation Code   Hospital Acquired Condition   ►◄ Revised Text   ● New Code   ▲ Revised Code Title

2010 ICD-9-CM   **October 2009 · Volume 1 – 197**

Digestive System

574.1–575.6

§ ✓5ᵗʰ **574.1 Calculus of gallbladder with other cholecystitis** `CC`
[0-1]
Billiary calculus
Calculus of cystic duct } with cholecystitis
Choleithiasis

Cholecystitis with cholelithiasis NOS

Any condition classifiable to 574.2 with cholecystitis
(chronic)

CC Excl: See code 574.01

AHA: 3Q, '99, 9; 4Q, '96, 32, 69; 2Q, '96, 13; **For code 574.10:** 1Q, '03, 5

K80.10 Calculus of GB w/chronic cholecystitis w/o obst `I-10`

§ ✓5ᵗʰ **574.2 Calculus of gallbladder without mention of** `CC 1`
[0-1] **cholecystitis**
Biliary:
calculus NOS
colic NOS
Calculus of cystic duct
Cholelithiasis NOS
Colic (recurrent) of gallbladder
Gallstone (impacted)

CC Excl: For code 574.21: See code 574.01

AHA: For code 574.20: 1Q, '88, 14

K80.20 Calculus of GB w/o cholecystitis w/o obst `I-10`

§ ✓5ᵗʰ **574.3 Calculus of bile duct with acute cholecystitis** `CC`
[0-1]
Calculus of bile duct (any) } with acute cholecystitis
Choledocholithiasis

Any condition classifiable to 574.5 with acute cholecystitis

CC Excl: 574.30-575.12, 576.8-576.9

§ ✓5ᵗʰ **574.4 Calculus of bile duct with other cholecystitis** `CC`
[0-1]
Calculus of bile duct
(any) } with cholecystitis (chronic)
Choledocholithiasis

Any condition classifiable to 574.5 with cholecystitis
(chronic)

CC Excl: See code 574.3

§ ✓5ᵗʰ **574.5 Calculus of bile duct without mention of** `CC 1`
[0-1] **cholecystitis**
Calculus of:
bile duct [any]
common duct
hepatic duct
Choledocholithiasis
Hepatic:
colic (recurrent)
lithiasis

CC Excl: For code 574.51: 574.30-575.12, 576.8-576.9

AHA: 3Q, '94, 11

§ ✓5ᵗʰ **574.6 Calculus of gallbladder and bile duct with** `CC`
[0-1] **acute cholecystitis**
Any condition classifiable to 574.0 and 574.3

CC Excl: 574.60-574.61, 575.0-575.12, 575.9, 576.8-576.9

AHA: 4Q, '96, 32

§ ✓5ᵗʰ **574.7 Calculus of gallbladder and bile duct with** `CC`
[0-1] **other cholecystitis**
Any condition classifiable to 574.1 and 574.4

CC Excl: 574.30-575.12, 576.8-576.9

AHA: 4Q, '96, 32

§ ✓5ᵗʰ **574.8 Calculus of gallbladder and bile duct** `MCC 1` `CC 0`
[0-1] **with acute and chronic cholecystitis**
Any condition classifiable to 574.6 and 574.7

CC Excl: 574.80-574.81, 575.0-575.12, 575.9, 576.8-576.9

AHA: 4Q, '96, 32

§ ✓5ᵗʰ **574.9 Calculus of gallbladder and bile duct** `CC 1`
[0-1] **without cholecystitis**
Any condition classifiable to 574.2 and 574.5

CC Excl: For code 574.91: 574.30-575.12, 576.8-576.9

AHA: 4Q, '96, 32

✓4ᵗʰ **575 Other disorders of gallbladder**

TIP: Do not assign a separate cholecystitis code from category 575 with a code from category 574; cholecystitis is inherent.

575.0 Acute cholecystitis `CC`
Abscess of gallbladder
Angiocholecystitis
Cholecystitis:
emphysematous (acute) } without mention of
gangrenous   calculus
suppurative
Empyema of gallbladder
Gangrene of gallbladder

EXCLUDES that with:
acute and chronic cholecystitis (575.12)
choledocholithiasis (574.3)
choledocholithiasis and cholelithiasis
(574.6)
cholelithiasis (574.0)

CC Excl: 574.60-574.61, 574.80-574.81, 575.0-575.12, 575.9, 576.8-576.9

AHA: 3Q, '91, 17

K81.0 Acute cholecystitis `I-10`

✓5ᵗʰ **575.1 Other cholecystitis**
Cholecystitis:
NOS } without mention of calculus
chronic

EXCLUDES that with:
choledocholithiasis (574.4)
choledocholithiasis and cholelithiasis
(574.8)
cholelithiasis (574.1)

AHA: 4Q, '96, 32

575.10 Cholecystitis, unspecified
Cholecystitis NOS

575.11 Chronic cholecystitis
K81.1 Chronic cholecystitis `I-10`

575.12 Acute and chronic cholecystitis `CC`
CC Excl: 575.0-575.12, 575.9, 576.8-576.9
AHA: 4Q, '97, 52; 4Q, '96, 32

575.2 Obstruction of gallbladder `CC`
Occlusion } of cystic duct or gallbladder without
Stenosis   mention of calculus
Stricture

Assigned only when there is obstruction but no calculi are present.

EXCLUDES that with calculus (574.0-574.2 with
fifth-digit 1)

CC Excl: 575.2-575.9, 576.8-576.9

575.3 Hydrops of gallbladder `CC`
Mucocele of gallbladder
DEF: Serous fluid accumulation in bladder.
CC Excl: See code 575.2
AHA: 2Q, '89, 13

575.4 Perforation of gallbladder `MCC`
Rupture of cystic duct or gallbladder
CC Excl: See code 575.2

575.5 Fistula of gallbladder `CC`
Fistula:
cholecystoduodenal
cholecystoenteric
CC Excl: See code 575.2

575.6 Cholesterolosis of gallbladder
Strawberry gallbladder
DEF: Cholesterol deposits in gallbladder tissue.
AHA: 4Q, '90, 17

Should not be coded when other gallbladder pathology is present. Incidental finding of gallbladder pathology.

---

§   Requires fifth digit. Valid digits are in [brackets] under each code. See category 574 for codes and definitions.

| `N` Newborn Age: 0 | `P` Pediatric Age: 0-17 | `M` Maternity Age: 12-55 | `A` Adult Age: 15-124 | `MCC` Major CC Condition | `CC` CC Condition | `HIV` HIV Related Dx |

575.8 **Other specified disorders of gallbladder**

Adhesions
Atrophy
Cyst
Hypertrophy
Nonfunctioning
Ulcer
} of cystic duct or gallbladder

Biliary dyskinesia

EXCLUDES *Hartmann's pouch of intestine (V44.3)*
nonvisualization of gallbladder (793.3)

AHA: 4Q, '90, 26; 2Q, '89, 13

575.9 **Unspecified disorder of gallbladder**

✓4th 576 **Other disorders of biliary tract**

EXCLUDES *that involving the:*
cystic duct (575.0-575.9)
gallbladder (575.0-575.9)

576.0 **Postcholecystectomy syndrome**

DEF: Jaundice or abdominal pain following cholecystectomy.

AHA: 1Q, '88, 10

TIP: Do not assign additional code 997.4 Digestive system complications.

576.1 **Cholangitis** `CC`

Cholangitis:
NOS
acute
ascending
chronic
primary
recurrent
sclerosing
secondary
stenosing
suppurative

CC Excl: 576.1, 576.8-576.9

AHA: 2Q, '99, 13

K83.0 Cholangitis `I-10`

576.2 **Obstruction of bile duct** `MCC`

Occlusion
Stenosis
Stricture
} of bile duct, except cystic duct, without mention of calculus

Assigned only when there is an obstruction but no calculi are present.

EXCLUDES *congenital (751.61)*
that with calculus (574.3-574.5 with fifth-digit 1)

CC Excl: 574.31, 574.41, 574.51, 576.2, 576.8-576.9, 751.61

AHA: 3Q, '03, 17-18; 1Q, '01, 8; 2Q, '99, 13

K83.1 Obstruction of bile duct `I-10`

576.3 **Perforation of bile duct** `MCC`

Rupture of bile duct, except cystic duct

CC Excl: 576.3-576.4, 576.8-576.9

576.4 **Fistula of bile duct** `CC`

Choledochoduodenal fistula

CC Excl: See code: 576.3

576.5 **Spasm of sphincter of Oddi**

576.8 **Other specified disorders of biliary tract**

Adhesions
Atrophy
Cyst
Hypertrophy
Nonfunctioning
Ulcer
} of bile duct (any)

EXCLUDES *congenital choledochal cyst (751.69)*

AHA: 3Q, '03, 17; 2Q, '99, 14

576.9 **Unspecified disorder of biliary tract**

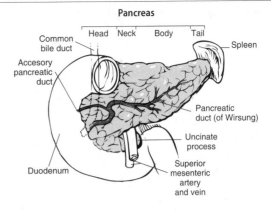

Pancreas

✓4th 577 **Diseases of pancreas**

577.0 **Acute pancreatitis** `MCC`

Abscess of pancreas
Necrosis of pancreas:
acute
infective
Pancreatitis:
NOS
acute (recurrent)
apoplectic
hemorrhagic
subacute
suppurative

EXCLUDES *mumps pancreatitis (072.3)*

CC Excl: 577.0-577.1, 577.8-577.9

AHA: 3Q, '99, 9; 2Q, '98, 19; 2Q, '96, 13; 2Q, '89, 9

K85.0 Idiopathic acute pancreatitis `I-10`

577.1 **Chronic pancreatitis** `CC`

Chronic pancreatitis: Pancreatitis:
NOS   painless
infectious   recurrent
interstitial   relapsing

CC Excl: 251.8, 577.0-577.9

AHA: 1Q, '01, 8; 2Q, '96, 13; 3Q, '94, 11

K86.1 Other chronic pancreatitis `I-10`

577.2 **Cyst and pseudocyst of pancreas** `CC`

CC Excl: 577.2-577.9

K86.2 Cyst of pancreas `I-10`

577.8 **Other specified diseases of pancreas**

Atrophy
Calculus
Cirrhosis
Fibrosis
} of pancreas

Pancreatic:
infantilism
necrosis:
NOS
aseptic
fat
Pancreatolithiasis

EXCLUDES *fibrocystic disease of pancreas (277.00-277.09)*
islet cell tumor of pancreas (211.7)
pancreatic steatorrhea (579.4)

AHA: 1Q, '01, 8

577.9 **Unspecified disease of pancreas**

✓4th ✓5th Additional Digit Required | Unacceptable PDx | Manifestation Code | Hospital Acquired Condition | ►◄ Revised Text | ● New Code | ▲ Revised Code Title

2010 ICD-9-CM | **Volume 1 – 199**

575.8–577.9

✓4ᵗʰ **578 Gastrointestinal hemorrhage**

> **EXCLUDES** *that with mention of:*
> *angiodysplasia of stomach and duodenum*
> *(537.83)*
> *angiodysplasia of intestine (569.85)*
> *diverticulitis, intestine:*
> *large (562.13)*
> *small (562.03)*
> *diverticulosis, intestine:*
> *large (562.12)*
> *small (562.02)*
> *gastritis and duodenitis (535.0-535.6)*
> *ulcer:*
> *duodenal, gastric, gastrojejunal or peptic*
> *(531.00-534.91)*

AHA: 2Q, '92, 9; 4Q, '90, 20

578.0 Hematemesis `CC`

Vomiting of blood

CC Excl: 251.5, 456.0, 530.20-530.21, 530.7, 530.82, 530.85, 531.00-534.91, 535.01, 535.11, 535.21, 535.31, 535.41, 535.51, 535.61, 537.83, 562.02-562.03, 562.12-562.13, 569.3, 569.85, 578.0-578.9

AHA: 2Q, '02, 4

578.1 Blood in stool `CC`

Melena

> **EXCLUDES** *melena of the newborn (772.4, 777.3)*
> *occult blood (792.1)*

CC Excl: See code 578.0

AHA: 2Q, '06, 17; 2Q, '92, 8

K92.1 Melena `I-10`

578.9 Hemorrhage of gastrointestinal tract, unspecified `CC`

Gastric hemorrhage
Intestinal hemorrhage

CC Excl: See code 578.0

AHA: 4Q, '06, 91; 3Q, '05, 17; N-D, '86, 9

TIP: Assign 578.9 if the physician does not establish a causal link between GI bleeding and any possible causes found on endoscopy.

K92.2 Gastrointestinal hemorrhage unspecified `I-10`

✓4ᵗʰ **579 Intestinal malabsorption**

579.0 Celiac disease

Celiac:
crisis
infantilism
rickets
Gee (-Herter) disease
Gluten enteropathy
Idiopathic steatorrhea
Nontropical sprue

DEF: Malabsorption syndrome due to gluten consumption; symptoms include fetid, bulky, frothy, oily stools; distended abdomen, gas, asthenia, electrolyte depletion and vitamin B, D and K deficiency.

579.1 Tropical sprue `CC`

Sprue:
NOS
tropical
Tropical steatorrhea

DEF: Diarrhea, occurs in tropics; may be due to enteric infection and malnutrition.

CC Excl: 277.03, 579.0-579.9

579.2 Blind loop syndrome `CC`

Postoperative blind loop syndrome

DEF: Obstruction or impaired passage in small intestine due to alterations, from strictures or surgery; causes stasis, abnormal bacterial flora, diarrhea, weight loss, multiple vitamin deficiency, and megaloblastic anemia.

CC Excl: See code: 579.1

TIP: Do not assign additional code 997.4 Digestive system complications.

579.3 Other and unspecified postsurgical nonabsorption `CC`

Hypoglycemia
Malnutrition } following gastrointestinal surgery

CC Excl: 579.3-579.9

AHA: 4Q, '03, 104

579.4 Pancreatic steatorrhea `CC`

DEF: Excess fat in feces due to absence of pancreatic juice in intestine.

CC Excl: See code: 579.1

579.8 Other specified intestinal malabsorption `CC`

Enteropathy:
exudative
protein-losing
Steatorrhea (chronic)

CC Excl: See code: 579.1

AHA: 1Q, '88, 6

579.9 Unspecified intestinal malabsorption `CC`

Malabsorption syndrome NOS

CC Excl: See code: 579.1

AHA: 4Q, '04, 59

N Newborn Age: 0   P Pediatric Age: 0-17   M Maternity Age: 12-55   A Adult Age: 15-124   MCC Major CC Condition   CC CC Condition   HIV HIV Related Dx

200 – Volume 1

2010 ICD-9-CM

10. DISEASES OF THE GENITOURINARY SYSTEM (580-629)

NEPHRITIS, NEPHROTIC SYNDROME, AND NEPHROSIS (580-589)

EXCLUDES *hypertensive chronic kidney disease (403.00-403.91, 404.00-404.93)*

√4th 580 Acute glomerulonephritis

INCLUDES acute nephritis

DEF: Acute, severe inflammation in tuft of capillaries that filter the kidneys.

580.0 With lesion of proliferative glomerulonephritis `MCC`
Acute (diffuse) proliferative glomerulonephritis
Acute poststreptococcal glomerulonephritis
CC Excl: 016.00-016.06, 016.30-016.36, 016.90-016.96, 017.90-017.96, 098.10, 098.19, 098.30-098.31, 098.89, 112.2, 131.00, 131.8-131.9, 249.40-249.41, 249.80-249.91, 250.40-250.43, 250.80-250.93, 274.10, 274.19, 277.88, 580.0-591, 593.0-593.2, 593.89-593.9, 599.70-599.9

580.4 With lesion of rapidly progressive glomerulonephritis `MCC`
Acute nephritis with lesion of necrotizing glomerulitis
DEF: Acute glomerulonephritis; progresses to ESRD with diffuse epithelial proliferation.
CC Excl: See code 580.0

√5th 580.8 With other specified pathological lesion in kidney

580.81 *Acute glomerulonephritis in diseases classified elsewhere* `MCC`
Code first underlying disease, as:
infectious hepatitis (070.0-070.9)
mumps (072.79)
subacute bacterial endocarditis (421.0)
typhoid fever (002.0)
CC Excl: See code 580.0

580.89 Other `MCC`
Glomerulonephritis, acute, with lesion of:
exudative nephritis
interstitial (diffuse) (focal) nephritis
CC Excl: 016.00-016.06, 016.30-016.36, 016.90-016.96, 017.90-017.96, 098.10, 098.19, 098.30-098.31, 098.89, 112.2, 131.00, 131.8-131.9, 274.10, 274.19, 277.88, 580.0-591, 593.0-593.2, 593.89-593.9, 599.70-599.9

580.9 Acute glomerulonephritis with unspecified pathological lesion in kidney `MCC`
Glomerulonephritis
NOS
hemorrhagic } specified as acute
Nephritis
Nephropathy
CC Excl: See code: 580.0

√4th 581 Nephrotic syndrome

DEF: Disease process marked by symptoms such as; extensive edema, notable proteinuria, hypoalbuminemia, and susceptibility to intercurrent infections.

581.0 With lesion of proliferative glomerulonephritis `CC`
CC Excl: 016.00-016.06, 016.30-016.36, 016.90-016.96, 017.90-017.96, 098.10, 098.19, 098.30-098.31, 098.89, 112.2, 131.00, 131.8-131.9, 249.40-249.41, 249.80-249.91, 250.40-250.43, 250.80-250.93, 274.10, 274.19, 277.88, 580.0-591, 593.0-593.2, 593.89-593.9, 599.70-599.9

581.1 With lesion of membranous glomerulonephritis `CC`
Epimembranous nephritis
Idiopathic membranous glomerular disease
Nephrotic syndrome with lesion of:
focal glomerulosclerosis
sclerosing membranous glomerulonephritis
segmental hyalinosis
CC Excl: See code: 581.0

Kidney

Fibrous capsule
Renal cortex
Nephron
Medulla (pyramid)
Renal column
Renal sinus
Pelvis
Renal hilum
Major calyx
Minor calyx
Ureter

581.2 With lesion of membranoproliferative glomerulonephritis `CC`
Nephrotic syndrome with lesion (of):
endothelial
hypocomplementemic
persistent
lobular   } glomerulonephritis
mesangiocapillary
mixed membranous and
proliferative
DEF: Glomerulonephritis combined with clinical features of nephrotic syndrome; characterized by uneven thickening of glomerular capillary walls and mesangial cell increase; slowly progresses to ESRD.
CC Excl: See code: 581.0

581.3 With lesion of minimal change glomerulonephritis `CC`
Foot process disease
Lipoid nephrosis
Minimal change:
glomerular disease
glomerulitis
nephrotic syndrome
CC Excl: See code: 581.0
AHA: 1Q, '07, 23

√5th 581.8 With other specified pathological lesion in kidney

581.81 *Nephrotic syndrome in diseases classified elsewhere* `CC`
Code first underlying disease, as:
amyloidosis (277.30-277.39)
diabetes mellitus (249.4, 250.4)
malaria (084.9)
polyarteritis (446.0)
systemic lupus erythematosus (710.0)
EXCLUDES *nephrosis in epidemic hemorrhagic fever (078.6)*
CC Excl: See code: 581.0
AHA: 3Q, '91, 8, 12; S-O, '85, 3

581.89 Other `CC`
Glomerulonephritis with edema and lesion of:
exudative nephritis
interstitial (diffuse) (focal) nephritis
CC Excl: See code: 581.0

Nephron

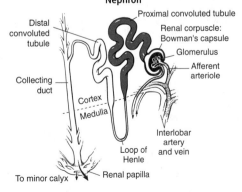

Distal convoluted tubule
Proximal convoluted tubule
Renal corpuscle: Bowman's capsule
Glomerulus
Afferent arteriole
Collecting duct
Cortex
Medulla
Interlobar artery and vein
Loop of Henle
Renal papilla
To minor calyx

Genitourinary System

581.9–583.81

581.9 **Nephrotic syndrome with unspecified pathological lesion in kidney** CC
Glomerulonephritis with edema NOS
Nephritis:
nephrotic NOS
with edema NOS
Nephrosis NOS
Renal disease with edema NOS
CC Excl: See code 581.0

✓4th **582** **Chronic glomerulonephritis**
INCLUDES chronic nephritis
DEF: Slow progressive type of nephritis characterized by inflammation of the capillary loops in the glomeruli of the kidney, which leads to renal failure.

582.0 **With lesion of proliferative glomerulonephritis** CC
Chronic (diffuse) proliferative glomerulonephritis
CC Excl: 016.00-016.06, 016.30-016.36, 016.90-016.96, 017.90-017.96, 078.6, 098.10, 098.19, 098.30-098.31, 098.89, 112.2, 131.00, 131.8-131.9, 249.40-249.41, 249.80-249.91, 250.40-250.43, 250.80-250.93, 274.10, 274.19, 580.0-584.9, 586-591, 593.0-593.2, 593.89-593.9, 599.70-599.9

582.1 **With lesion of membranous glomerulonephritis** CC
Chronic glomerulonephritis:
membranous
sclerosing
Focal glomerulosclerosis
Segmental hyalinosis
CC Excl: See code: 582.0
AHA: S-O, '84, 16

582.2 **With lesion of membranoproliferative glomerulonephritis** CC
Chronic glomerulonephritis:
endothelial
hypocomplementemic persistent
lobular
membranoproliferative
mesangiocapillary
mixed membranous and proliferative
DEF: Chronic glomerulonephritis with mesangial cell proliferation.
CC Excl: See code: 582.0

582.4 **With lesion of rapidly progressive glomerulonephritis** CC
Chronic nephritis with lesion of necrotizing glomerulitis
DEF: Chronic glomerulonephritisrapidly progresses to ESRD; marked by diffuse epithelial proliferation.
CC Excl: See code: 582.0

✓5th **582.8** **With other specified pathological lesion in kidney**
582.81 *Chronic glomerulonephritis in diseases classified elsewhere* CC
Code first underlying disease, as:
amyloidosis (277.30-277.39)
systemic lupus erythematosus (710.0)
CC Excl: See code: 582.0

582.89 **Other** CC
Chronic glomerulonephritis with lesion of:
exudative nephritis
interstitial (diffuse) (focal) nephritis
CC Excl: See code: 582.0

582.9 **Chronic glomerulonephritis with unspecified pathological lesion in kidney** CC
Glomerulonephritis:
NOS
hemorrhagic }specified as chronic
Nephritis
Nephropathy
CC Excl: See code: 582.0
AHA: 2Q, '01, 12

✓4th **583** **Nephritis and nephropathy, not specified as acute or chronic**
INCLUDES "renal disease" so stated, not specified as acute or chronic but with stated pathology or cause

583.0 **With lesion of proliferative glomerulonephritis** CC
Proliferative:
glomerulonephritis (diffuse) NOS
nephritis NOS
nephropathy NOS
CC Excl: See code: 582.0

583.1 **With lesion of membranous glomerulonephritis** CC
Membranous:
glomerulonephritis NOS
nephritis NOS
Membranous nephropathy NOS
DEF: Kidney inflammation or dysfunction with deposits on glomerular capillary basement membranes.
CC Excl: See code: 582.0
N05.2 Uns nephritic syndr w/ diffuse membranous gln I-10

583.2 **With lesion of membranoproliferative glomerulonephritis** CC
Membranoproliferative:
glomerulonephritis NOS
nephritis NOS
nephropathy NOS
Nephritis NOS, with lesion of:
hypocomplementemic
persistant
lobular }glomerulonephritis
mesangiocapillary
mixed membranous and
proliferative
DEF: Kidney inflammation or dysfunction with mesangial cell proliferation.
CC Excl: See code: 582.0

583.4 **With lesion of rapidly progressive glomerulonephritis** MCC
Necrotizing or rapidly progressive:
glomerulitis NOS
glomerulonephritis NOS
nephritis NOS
nephropathy NOS
Nephritis, unspecified, with lesion of necrotizing glomerulitis
DEF: Kidney inflammation or dysfunction; rapidly progresses to ESRD marked by diffuse epithelial proliferation.
CC Excl: 016.00-016.06, 016.30-016.36, 016.90-016.96, 017.90-017.96, 098.10, 098.19, 098.30-098.31, 098.89, 112.2, 131.00, 131.8-131.9, 249.40-249.41, 249.80-249.91, 250.40-250.43, 250.80-250.93, 274.10, 274.19, 277.88, 580.0-591, 593.0-593.2, 593.89-593.9, 599.70-599.9

583.6 **With lesion of renal cortical necrosis** MCC
Nephritis, NOS }with (renal) cortical necrosis
Nephropathy NS
Renal cortical necrosis NOS
CC Excl: 277.88, 583.6, 588.81-588.89

583.7 **With lesion of renal medullary necrosis** CC
Nephritis, NOS }with (renal) medullary
Nephropathy NOS }[papillary] necrosis
CC Excl: 277.88, 583.7, 588.81-588.89

✓5th **583.8** **With other specified pathological lesion in kidney**
583.81 *Nephritis and nephropathy, not specified as acute or chronic, in diseases classified elsewhere*
Code first underlying disease, as:
amyloidosis (277.30-277.39)
diabetes mellitus (249.4, 250.4)
gonococcal infection (098.19)
Goodpasture's syndrome (446.21)
systemic lupus erythematosus (710.0)
tuberculosis (016.0)
EXCLUDES *gouty nephropathy (274.10)*
syphilitic nephritis (095.4)
AHA: 2Q, '03, 7; 3Q, '91, 8; S-O, '85, 3

583.89 Other

Glomerulitis
Glomerulonephritis   } with lesions of:
Nephritis   exudative nephritis
Nephropathy   interstitial nephritis
Renal disease

583.9 With unspecified pathological lesion in kidney

Glomerulitis
Glomerulonephritis } NOS
Nephritis
Nephropathy

> **EXCLUDES** *nephropathy complicating pregnancy, labor,*
> *or the puerperium (642.0-642.9, 646.2)*
> *renal disease NOS with no stated cause (593.9)*

▲ ✓4th **584 Acute kidney failure**

INCLUDES ►acute renal failure◄

EXCLUDES *following labor and delivery (669.3)*
posttraumatic (958.5)
that complicating:
  abortion (634-638 with .3, 639.3)
  ectopic or molar pregnancy (639.3)

DEF: State resulting from increasing urea and related substances from the blood (azotemia), often with urine output of less than 500 ml per day.

AHA: 1Q, '93, 18; 2Q, '92, 5; 4Q, '92, 22

TIP: Do not assign combination code for hypertensive renal disease unless chronic kidney disease is also present.

▲ **584.5 Acute kidney failure with lesion of tubular**   MCC
necrosis

Lower nephron nephrosis
Renal failure with (acute) tubular necrosis
Tubular necrosis:
  NOS
  acute

DEF: Acute decline in kidney efficiency with destruction of tubules.

CC Excl: 249.40-249.41, 249.80-249.91, 250.40-250.43, 250.80-250.93, 274.10, 274.19, 277.88, 580.0-591, 593.0-593.2, 593.89-593.9, 599.70-599.9, 753.0-753.3, 753.9

N17.0 Acute renal failure with tubular necrosis   I-10

▲ **584.6 Acute kidney failure with lesion of renal cortical**   MCC
necrosis

DEF: Acute decline in kidney efficiency with destruction of renal tissues that filter blood.

CC Excl: See code: 584.5

▲ **584.7 Acute kidney failure with lesion of renal**   MCC
medullary [papillary] necrosis

Necrotizing renal papillitis

DEF: Acute decline in kidney efficiency with destruction of renal tissues that collect urine.

CC Excl: See code: 584.5

▲ **584.8 Acute kidney failure with other specified**   MCC
pathological lesion in kidney

CC Excl: 249.40-249.41, 249.80-249.91, 250.40-250.43, 250.80-250.93, 274.10, 274.19, 277.88, 580.0-591, 593.0-593.2, 593.89-593.9, 599.70-599.9

AHA: N-D, '85, 1

▲ **584.9 Acute kidney failure, unspecified**   MCC

Acute kidney injury (nontraumatic)

EXCLUDES *traumatic kidney injury (866.00-866.13)*

CC Excl: See code: 584.5

AHA: 4Q, '08, 192; 4Q, '07, 97; 2Q, '05, 18; 2Q, '03, 7; 1Q, '03, 22; 3Q, '02, 21, 28; 2Q, '01, 14; 1Q, '00, 22; 3Q, '96, 9; 4Q, '88, 1

N17.9 Acute renal failure unspecified   I-10

✓4th **585 Chronic kidney disease [CKD]**

Chronic uremia

Code first hypertensive chronic kidney disease, if applicable, (403.00-403.91, 404.00-404.93)

Use additional code to identify kidney transplant status, if applicable (V42.0)

Use additional code to identify manifestation as:
uremic:
  neuropathy (357.4)
  pericarditis (420.0)

AHA: 4Q, '06, 84-86; 4Q, '05, 68, 77; 1Q, '04, 5; 4Q, '03, 61, 111; 2Q, '03, 7; 2Q, '01, 12, 13; 1Q, '01, 3; 4Q, '98, 55; 3Q, '98, 6, 7; 2Q, '98, 20; 3Q, '96, 9; 1Q, '93, 18; 3Q, '91, 8; 4Q, '89, 1; N-D, '85, 15; S-O, '84, 3

[handwritten: If due to diabetic neuropathy, code 250.4X first]

585.1 Chronic kidney disease, Stage I

DEF: Some kidney damage; normal or slightly increased GFR (> 90).

585.2 Chronic kidney disease, Stage II (mild)

DEF: Kidney damage with mild decrease in GFR (60–89).

585.3 Chronic kidney disease, Stage III (moderate)

DEF: Kidney damage with moderate decrease in GFR (30–59).

AHA: 4Q, '05, 69

N18.3 Chronic kidney disease stage III moderate   I-10

585.4 Chronic kidney disease, Stage IV (severe)   CC

DEF: Kidney damage with severe decrease in GFR (15–29).

CC Excl: See code: 584.5

N18.4 Chronic kidney disease stage IV severe   I-10

585.5 Chronic kidney disease, Stage V   CC

EXCLUDES *chronic kidney disease, stage V requiring*
chronic dialysis (585.6)

DEF: Kidney failure with GFR value of less than 15.

CC Excl: See code 584.5

585.6 End stage renal disease   MCC

Chronic kidney disease requiring chronic dialysis

DEF: Federal government indicator of a stage V CKD patient undergoing treatment by dialysis or transplantation.

CC Excl: See code 584.5

AHA: 4Q, '08, 193; 1Q, '08, 7; 4Q, '07, 86; 3Q, '07, 5, 9; 4Q, '06, 136; 4Q, '05, 79

N18.6 End stage renal disease   I-10

585.9 Chronic kidney disease, unspecified

Chronic renal disease
Chronic renal failure NOS
Chronic renal insufficiency

AHA: 1Q, '08, 10; 2Q, '07, 3; 4Q, '06, 86; 4Q, '05, 79

N18.9 Chronic kidney disease unspecified   I-10

586 Renal failure, unspecified

Uremia NOS

EXCLUDES *following labor and delivery (669.3)*
posttraumatic renal failure (958.5)
that complicating:
  abortion (634-638 with .3, 639.3)
  ectopic or molar pregnancy (639.3)
uremia:
  extrarenal (788.9)
  prerenal (788.9)

DEF: Renal failure: kidney functions cease; malfunction may be due to inability to excrete metabolized substances or retain level of electrolytes.

DEF: Uremia: excess urea, creatinine and other nitrogenous products of protein and amino acid metabolism in blood due to reduced excretory function in bilateral kidney disease; also called azotemia.

AHA: 3Q, '98, 6; 1Q, '93, 18; 1Q, '88, 3

N19 Unspecified renal failure   I-10

587 Renal sclerosis, unspecified

Atrophy of kidney
Contracted kidney
Renal:
  cirrhosis
  fibrosis

✓4th ✓5th Additional Digit Required   Unacceptable PDx   Manifestation Code   Hospital Acquired Condition   ►◄ Revised Text   ● New Code   ▲ Revised Code Title

2010 ICD-9-CM   **October 2009 · Volume 1 – 203**

583.89-587

Genitourinary System

✓4ᵗʰ 588 Disorders resulting from impaired renal function

588.0 Renal osteodystrophy
Azotemic osteodystrophy
Phosphate-losing tubular disorders
Renal:
dwarfism
infantilism
rickets

DEF: Condition resulting from chronic renal failure results in osteomalacia, osteoporosis or osteosclerosis; an abnormal level of phosphorus in the blood and impaired stimulation of the parathyroid.

588.1 Nephrogenic diabetes insipidus `CC`
EXCLUDES *diabetes insipidus NOS (253.5)*

DEF: Type of diabetes due to renal tubules inability to reabsorb water; not responsive to vasopressin; may develop into chronic renal insufficiency.

CC Excl: 016.00-016.06, 016.30-016.36, 016.90-016.96, 017.90-017.96, 078.6, 098.10, 098.19, 098.30-098.31, 098.89, 112.2, 131.00, 131.8-131.9, 249.40-249.41, 249.80-249.91, 250.40-250.43, 250.80-250.93, 274.10, 274.19, 580.0-584.9, 585.3-585.6, 586-591, 593.0-593.2, 593.89-593.9, 599.70-599.9

✓5ᵗʰ 588.8 Other specified disorders resulting from impaired renal function
EXCLUDES *secondary hypertension (405.0-405.9)*

588.81 Secondary hyperparathyroidism (of renal origin) `CC`
Secondary hyperparathyroidism NOS

DEF: Parathyroid dysfunction caused by chronic renal failure; phosphate clearance is impaired, phosphate is released from bone, vitamin D is not produced, intestinal calcium absorption is low, and blood levels of calcium are lowered causing excessive production of parathyroid hormone.

CC Excl: 016.00-016.06, 016.30-016.36, 016.90-016.96, 017.90-017.96, 078.6, 098.10, 098.19, 098.30-098.31, 098.89, 112.2, 131.00, 131.8-131.9, 249.40-249.41, 249.80-249.91, 250.40-250.43, 250.80-250.93, 274.10, 274.19, 580.0-584.9, 586-588.1, 588.89-591, 593.0-593.2, 593.89-593.9, 599.70-599.9

AHA: 4Q, '04, 58-59

N25.81 Secondary hyperparathyroidism of renal origin `I-10`

588.89 Other specified disorders resulting from impaired renal function
Hypokalemic nephropathy

588.9 Unspecified disorder resulting from impaired renal function

✓4ᵗʰ 589 Small kidney of unknown cause

589.0 Unilateral small kidney

589.1 Bilateral small kidneys

589.9 Small kidney, unspecified

OTHER DISEASES OF URINARY SYSTEM (590-599)

✓4ᵗʰ 590 Infections of kidney
Use additional code to identify organism, such as Escherichia coli [E. coli] (041.4)

✓5ᵗʰ 590.0 Chronic pyelonephritis
Chronic pyelitis
Chronic pyonephrosis
Code if applicable, any causal condition first

590.00 Without lesion of renal medullary necrosis

590.01 With lesion of renal medullary necrosis `CC`
CC Excl: 016.00-016.06, 016.30-016.36, 016.90-016.96, 017.90-017.96, 078.6, 098.10, 098.19, 098.30-098.31, 098.89, 112.2, 131.00, 131.8-131.9, 249.40-249.41, 249.80-249.91, 250.40-250.43, 250.80-250.93, 274.10, 274.19, 580.0-584.9, 586-591, 593.0-593.2, 593.89-593.9, 599.70-599.9, 646.61-646.64

Genitourinary System

Inferior vena cava — Aorta — Left kidney — Right kidney — Ureter — Anterior division of internal iliac artery — Ovarian or testicular artery and vein — Superior and Inferior vesicular arteries — Urinary bladder — Ureteral orifice — Urogenital diaphragm — Urethra

✓5ᵗʰ 590.1 Acute pyelonephritis
Acute pyelitis
Acute pyonephrosis

⁸ 590.10 Without lesion of renal medullary necrosis `CC`
CC Excl: 016.00-016.06, 016.30-016.36, 016.90-016.96, 017.90-017.96, 098.10, 098.19, 098.30-098.31, 098.89, 112.2, 131.00, 131.8-131.9, 249.40-249.41, 249.80-249.91, 250.40-250.43, 250.80-250.93, 274.10, 274.19, 580.0-591, 593.0-593.2, 593.89-593.9, 599.0, 599.70-599.9

⁸ 590.11 With lesion of renal medullary necrosis `MCC`
CC Excl: See code 590.10

⁸ 590.2 Renal and perinephric abscess `MCC`
Abscess:
kidney
nephritic
perirenal
Carbuncle of kidney
CC Excl: See code 590.10

⁸ 590.3 Pyeloureteritis cystica `CC`
Infection of renal pelvis and ureter
Ureteritis cystica

DEF: Inflammation and formation of submucosal cysts in the kidney, pelvis, and ureter.

CC Excl: 016.00-016.06, 016.30-016.36, 016.90-016.96, 017.90-017.96, 098.10, 098.19, 098.30-098.31, 098.89, 112.2, 131.00, 131.8-131.9, 274.10, 274.19, 580.0-591, 593.0-593.2, 593.89-593.9, 599.0, 599.70-599.9

✓5ᵗʰ 590.8 Other pyelonephritis or pyonephrosis, not specified as acute or chronic

⁸ 590.80 Pyelonephritis, unspecified `CC`
Pyelitis NOS
Pyelonephritis NOS
CC Excl: See code 590.3
AHA: 1Q, '98, 10; 4Q, '97, 40
N11.9 Chronic tubulo-interstitial nephritis uns `I-10`

⁸ 590.81 *Pyelitis or pyelonephritis in diseases classified elsewhere* `CC`
Code first underlying disease, as:
tuberculosis (016.0)
CC Excl: See code 590.3

590.9 Infection of kidney, unspecified
EXCLUDES *urinary tract infection NOS (599.0)*

591 Hydronephrosis `CC`
Hydrocalycosis   Hydroureteronephrosis
Hydronephrosis
EXCLUDES *congenital hydronephrosis (753.29)*
hydroureter (593.5)

DEF: Distention of kidney and pelvis, with urine build-up due to ureteral obstruction; pyonephrosis may result.
CC Excl: See code 590.3
AHA: 2Q, '98, 9
TIP: Hydronephrosis is not inherent in urinary obstructions and should be coded separately.
N13.30 Unspecified hydronephrosis `I-10`

⁸ CC/MCC except when in combination with 996.64 and POA = N

N Newborn Age: 0   **P** Pediatric Age: 0-17   **M** Maternity Age: 12-55   **A** Adult Age: 15-124   **MCC** Major CC Condition   **CC** CC Condition   **HIV** HIV Related Dx

204 – Volume 1   2010 ICD-9-CM

✓4th **592 Calculus of kidney and ureter**
- **EXCLUDES** *nephrocalcinosis (275.4)*

592.0 Calculus of kidney
Nephrolithiasis NOS   Staghorn calculus
Renal calculus or stone   Stone in kidney
- **EXCLUDES** *uric acid nephrolithiasis (274.11)*
- **AHA:** 1Q, '00, 4
- **N20.0** Calculus of kidney   I-10

592.1 Calculus of ureter   CC
Ureteric stone   Ureterolithiasis
- **CC Excl:** 592.0-592.9, 593.3-593.5, 593.89-594.9, 599.60-599.9
- **AHA:** 2Q, '98, 9; 1Q, '98, 10; 1Q, '91, 11
- **N20.1** Calculus of ureter   I-10

592.9 Urinary calculus, unspecified
- **AHA:** 1Q, '98, 10; 4Q, '97, 40

✓4th **593 Other disorders of kidney and ureter**

593.0 Nephroptosis
Floating kidney
Mobile kidney

593.1 Hypertrophy of kidney

593.2 Cyst of kidney, acquired
Cyst (multiple) (solitary) of kidney, not congenital
Peripelvic (lymphatic) cyst
- **EXCLUDES** *calyceal or pyelogenic cyst of kidney (591)*
  congenital cyst of kidney (753.1)
  polycystic (disease of) kidney (753.1)
- **DEF:** Abnormal, fluid-filled sac in the kidney, not present at birth.
- **AHA:** 4Q, '90, 3
- **N28.1** Cyst of kidney acquired   I-10

593.3 Stricture or kinking of ureter
Angulation ⎫
Constriction ⎬ of ureter (post-operative)
Stricture of pelviureteric junction
- **DEF:** Stricture or knot in tube connecting kidney to bladder.
- **AHA:** 2Q, '98, 9

593.4 Other ureteric obstruction   CC
Idiopathic retroperitoneal fibrosis
Occlusion NOS of ureter
- **EXCLUDES** *that due to calculus (592.1)*
- **CC Excl:** 593.3-593.5, 593.89-593.9, 595.0-595.9, 596.8-596.9, 599.0, 599.60-599.9, 753.4-753.5, 753.9, V45.74
- **AHA:** 2Q, '97, 4

593.5 Hydroureter   CC
- **EXCLUDES** *congenital hydroureter (753.22)*
  hydroureteronephrosis (591)
- **CC Excl:** 593.3-593.5, 593.89-593.9, 595.0-595.9, 596.8-596.9, 599.0, 599.60-599.9, 753.4-753.5, 753.9

593.6 Postural proteinuria
Benign postural proteinuria   Orthostatic proteinuria
- **EXCLUDES** *proteinuria NOS (791.0)*
- **DEF:** Excessive amounts of serum protein in the urine caused by the body position, e.g., orthostatic and lordotic.

✓5th **593.7 Vesicoureteral reflux**
- **DEF:** Backflow of urine, from bladder into ureter due to obstructed bladder neck.
- **AHA:** 4Q, '94, 42

593.70 Unspecified or without reflux nephropathy

593.71 With reflux nephropathy, unilateral

593.72 With reflux nephropathy, bilateral

593.73 With reflux nephropathy NOS

✓5th **593.8 Other specified disorders of kidney and ureter**

593.81 Vascular disorders of kidney   CC
Renal (artery):   Renal (artery):
  embolism   thrombosis
  hemorrhage   Renal infarction
- **CC Excl:** 593.70-593.81, 593.9

593.82 Ureteral fistula   CC
Intestinoureteral fistula
- **EXCLUDES** *fistula between ureter and female genital tract (619.0)*
- **DEF:** Abnormal communication, between tube connecting kidney to bladder and another structure.
- **CC Excl:** 593.82-593.9

593.89 Other
Adhesions, kidney or ureter
Periureteritis
Polyp of ureter
Pyelectasia
Ureterocele
- **EXCLUDES** *tuberculosis of ureter (016.2)*
  ureteritis cystica (590.3)

593.9 Unspecified disorder of kidney and ureter
Acute renal disease
Acute renal insufficiency
Renal disease NOS
Salt-losing nephritis or syndrome
- **EXCLUDES** *chronic renal insufficiency (585.9)*
  cystic kidney disease (753.1)
  nephropathy, so stated (583.0-583.9)
  renal disease:
    arising in pregnancy or the puerperium (642.1-642.2, 642.4-642.7, 646.2)
    not specified as acute or chronic, but with stated pathology or cause (583.0-583.9)
- **AHA:** 4Q, '05, 79; 1Q, '93, 17
- **N28.9** Disorder of kidney and ureter unspecified   I-10

✓4th **594 Calculus of lower urinary tract**

594.0 Calculus in diverticulum of bladder
- **DEF:** Stone or mineral deposit in abnormal sac on the bladder wall.

594.1 Other calculus in bladder
Urinary bladder stone
- **EXCLUDES** *staghorn calculus (592.0)*
- **DEF:** Stone or mineral deposit in bladder.

594.2 Calculus in urethra
- **DEF:** Stone or mineral deposit in tube that empties urine from bladder.

594.8 Other lower urinary tract calculus
- **AHA:** J-F, '85, 16

594.9 Calculus of lower urinary tract, unspecified
- **EXCLUDES** *calculus of urinary tract NOS (592.9)*

✓4th **595 Cystitis**
- **EXCLUDES** *prostatocystitis (601.3)*
- Use additional code to identify organism, such as Escherichia coli [E. coli] (041.4)

8 **595.0 Acute cystitis**   CC
- **EXCLUDES** *trigonitis (595.3)*
- **DEF:** Acute inflammation of bladder.
- **CC Excl:** 016.10-016.16, 016.30-016.36, 016.90-016.96, 017.90-017.96, 098.0, 098.11, 098.2, 098.39, 098.89, 112.2, 131.00, 131.8-131.9, 593.3-593.5, 593.89-593.9, 595.0-595.9, 596.8-596.9, 599.0, 599.60-599.9
- **AHA:** 2Q, '99, 15
- **N30.00** Acute cystitis without hematuria   I-10

595.1 Chronic interstitial cystitis
Hunner's ulcer
Panmural fibrosis of bladder
Submucous cystitis
- **DEF:** Inflamed lesion affecting bladder wall; symptoms include urinary frequency, pain on bladder filling, nocturia, and distended bladder.

595.2 Other chronic cystitis
Chronic cystitis NOS   Subacute cystitis
- **EXCLUDES** *trigonitis (595.3)*
- **DEF:** Persistent inflammation of bladder.

---

8 CC/MCC except when in combination with 996.64 and POA = N

✓4th
✓5th Additional Digit Required   Unacceptable PDx   Manifestation Code   Hospital Acquired Condition   ▶◀ Revised Text   ● New Code   ▲ Revised Code Title

2010 ICD-9-CM   **Volume 1 – 205**

Genitourinary System

595.3–596.59

595.3 Trigonitis
Follicular cystitis
Trigonitis (acute) (chronic)
Urethrotrigonitis
DEF: Inflammation of the triangular area of the bladder called the trigonum vesicae.

595.4 Cystitis in diseases classified elsewhere
Code first underlying disease, as:
actinomycosis (039.8)
amebiasis (006.8)
bilharziasis (120.0-120.9)
Echinococcus infestation (122.3, 122.6)
EXCLUDES   *cystitis:*
diphtheritic (032.84)
gonococcal (098.11, 098.31)
monilial (112.2)
trichomonal (131.09)
tuberculous (016.1)

√5th **595.8 Other specified types of cystitis**

595.81 Cystitis cystica
DEF: Inflammation of the bladder characterized by formation of multiple cysts.

595.82 Irradiation cystitis   **CC**
Use additional E code to identify cause
DEF: Inflammation of the bladder due to effects of radiation.
CC Excl: see code 595.0

595.89 Other
Abscess of bladder
Cystitis:
bullous
emphysematous
glandularis

595.9 Cystitis, unspecified

√4th **596 Other disorders of bladder**
Use additional code to identify urinary incontinence (625.6, 788.30-788.39)
AHA: M-A, '87, 10

596.0 Bladder neck obstruction
Contracture (acquired)   } of bladder neck or
Obstruction (acquired)   } vesicourethral orifice
Stenosis (acquired)
EXCLUDES   *congenital (753.6)*
DEF: Bladder outlet and vesicourethral obstruction; occurs as a consequence of benign prostatic hypertrophy or prostatic cancer; may also occur in either sex due to strictures, following radiation, cystoscopy, catheterization, injury, infection, blood clots, bladder cancer, impaction or disease compressing bladder neck.
AHA: 3Q, '02, 28; 2Q, '01, 14; N-D, '86, 10
N32.0 Bladder-neck obstruction   **I-10**

596.1 Intestinovesical fistula   **CC**
Fistula: Fistula:
enterovesical   vesicoenteric
vesicocolic   vesicorectal
DEF: Abnormal communication, between intestine and bladder.
CC Excl: 098.0, 098.2, 098.39, 098.89, 596.1-596.2, 596.8-596.9, 599.70-599.9, 788.1

596.2 Vesical fistula, not elsewhere classified   **CC**
Fistula: Fistula:
bladder NOS   vesicocutaneous
urethrovesical   vesicoperineal
EXCLUDES   *fistula between bladder and female genital tract (619.0)*
DEF: Abnormal communication between bladder and another structure.
CC Excl: See code: 596.1

Bladder
Anterior View

Lateral View

596.3 Diverticulum of bladder
Diverticulitis   }
Diverticulum (acquired) (false) } of bladder
EXCLUDES   *that with calculus in diverticulum of bladder (594.0)*
DEF: Abnormal pouch in bladder wall.

596.4 Atony of bladder
High compliance bladder
Hypotonicity } of bladder
Inertia   }
EXCLUDES   *neurogenic bladder (596.54)*
DEF: Distended, bladder with loss of expulsive force; linked to CNS disease.

√5th **596.5 Other functional disorders of bladder**
EXCLUDES   *cauda equina syndrome with neurogenic bladder (344.61)*

596.51 Hypertonicity of bladder
Hyperactivity   Overactive bladder
DEF: Abnormal tension of muscular wall of bladder; may appear after surgery of voluntary nerve.
N32.81 Overactive bladder   **I-10**

596.52 Low bladder compliance
DEF: Low bladder capacity; causes increased pressure and frequent urination.

596.53 Paralysis of bladder
DEF: Impaired bladder motor function due to nerve or muscle damage.

596.54 Neurogenic bladder NOS
DEF: Unspecified dysfunctional bladder due to lesion of central, peripheral nervous system; may result in incontinence, residual urine retention, urinary infection, stones and renal failure.
AHA: 1Q, '01, 12
N31.9 Neuromuscular dysfunction of   **I-10**
bladder unspecified

596.55 Detrusor sphincter dyssynergia
DEF: Instability of the urinary bladder sphincter muscle associated with urinary incontinence..

596.59 Other functional disorder of bladder
Detrusor instability
DEF: Detrusor instability: instability of bladder; marked by uninhibited contractions often leading to incontinence.

N Newborn Age: 0   **P** Pediatric Age: 0-17   **M** Maternity Age: 12-55   **A** Adult Age: 15-124   **MCC** Major CC Condition   **CC** CC Condition   **HIV** HIV Related Dx

206 – Volume 1   **2010 ICD-9-CM**

596.6   **Rupture of bladder, nontraumatic**   `MCC`
     CC Excl: 596.6-596.9, 599.70-599.9, 788.1

596.7   **Hemorrhage into bladder wall**   `CC`
     Hyperemia of bladder
     EXCLUDES   *acute hemorrhagic cystitis (595.0)*
     CC Excl: See code: 596.6

596.8   **Other specified disorders of bladder**
     Bladder: Bladder:
       calcified   hemorrhage
       contracted   hypertrophy
     EXCLUDES   *cystocele, female (618.01-618.02, 618.09, 618.2-618.4)*
                 hernia or prolapse of bladder, female (618.01-618.02, 618.09, 618.2-618.4)
     AHA: J-F, '85, 8

596.9   **Unspecified disorder of bladder**
     AHA: J-F, '85, 8

√4th   **597**   **Urethritis, not sexually transmitted, and urethral syndrome**
     EXCLUDES   *nonspecific urethritis, so stated (099.4)*

8 **597.0**   **Urethral abscess**   `CC`
     Abscess:
       periurethral
       urethral (gland)
     Abscess of:
       bulbourethral gland
       Cowper's gland
       Littré's gland
     Periurethral cellulitis
     EXCLUDES   *urethral caruncle (599.3)*
     DEF: Pocket of pus in tube that empties urine from the bladder.
     CC Excl: 098.0, 098.2, 098.39, 098.89, 099.40-099.49, 112.2, 131.00, 131.02, 131.8-131.9, 597.0-598.01, 598.8-599.0, 599.60-599.9, 607.1-607.83, 607.85-607.9, 608.4-608.81, 608.85, 608.87-608.89, 752.61-752.69, 752.81-752.9, 753.6-753.9, 788.1

√5th   **597.8**   **Other urethritis**

     597.80   **Urethritis, unspecified**

     597.81   **Urethral syndrome NOS**

     597.89   **Other**
            Adenitis, Skene's glands
            Cowperitis
            Meatitis, urethral
            Ulcer, urethra (meatus)
            Verumontanitis
            EXCLUDES   *trichomonal (131.02)*

√4th   **598**   **Urethral stricture**
     Use additional code to identify urinary incontinence (625.6, 788.30-788.39)
     INCLUDES   pinhole meatus
              stricture of urinary meatus
     EXCLUDES   *congenital stricture of urethra and urinary meatus (753.6)*
     DEF: Narrowing of tube that empties urine from bladder.

√5th   **598.0**   **Urethral stricture due to infection**

     598.00   **Due to unspecified infection**

     598.01   **Due to infective diseases classified elsewhere**
            Code first underlying disease, as:
               gonococcal infection (098.2)
               schistosomiasis (120.0-120.9)
               syphilis (095.8)

     598.1   **Traumatic urethral stricture**
            Stricture of urethra:
               late effect of injury
               postobstetric
            EXCLUDES   *postoperative following surgery on genitourinary tract (598.2)*

598.2   **Postoperative urethral stricture**
     Postcatheterization stricture of urethra
     AHA: 3Q, '97, 6

598.8   **Other specified causes of urethral stricture**
     AHA: N-D, '84, 9

598.9   **Urethral stricture, unspecified**

√4th   **599**   **Other disorders of urethra and urinary tract**

8 **599.0**   **Urinary tract infection, site not specified**   `CC`
     EXCLUDES   *candidiasis of urinary tract (112.2)*
                 urinary tract infection of newborn (771.82)
     Use additional code to identify organism, such as Escherichia coli [E. coli] (041.4)
     CC Excl: 098.2, 098.39, 098.89, 099.40-099.49, 112.2, 131.00, 131.8-131.9, 590.10-591, 593.89-593.9, 595.0-595.9, 599.0, 599.60-599.9, 788.1, 996.64
     AHA: 3Q, '05, 12; 2Q, '04, 13; 4Q, '03, 79; 4Q, '99, 6; 2Q, '99, 15; 1Q, '98, 5; 2Q, '96, 7; 4Q, '96, 33; 2Q, '95, 7; 1Q, '92, 13
     TIP: Do not assign if UTI due to candidiasis; see instead code 112.2.
     N39.0 Urinary tract infection site not specified   `I-10`

599.1   **Urethral fistula**   `CC`
     Fistula:
       urethroperineal
       urethrorectal
     Urinary fistula NOS
     EXCLUDES   *fistula:*
                  urethroscrotal (608.89)
                  urethrovaginal (619.0)
                  urethrovesicovaginal (619.0)
     CC Excl: 597.0-598.9, 599.1-599.9, 607.1-607.83, 607.85-607.9, 608.4-608.81, 608.85, 608.87-608.89, 752.61-752.69, 752.81-752.9, 753.9, 788.1
     AHA: 3Q, '97, 6

599.2   **Urethral diverticulum**
     DEF: Abnormal pouch in urethral wall.

599.3   **Urethral caruncle**
     Polyp of urethra

599.4   **Urethral false passage**
     DEF: Abnormal opening in urethra due to surgery; trauma or disease.

599.5   **Prolapsed urethral mucosa**
     Prolapse of urethra
     Urethrocele
     EXCLUDES   *urethrocele, female (618.03, 618.09, 618.2-618.4)*

√5th   **599.6**   **Urinary obstruction**
     Use additional code to identify urinary incontinence (625.6, 788.30-788.39)
     EXCLUDES   *obstructive nephropathy NOS (593.89)*
     AHA: 4Q, '05, 80

     599.60   **Urinary obstruction, unspecified**
            Obstructive uropathy NOS
            Urinary (tract) obstruction NOS
            N13.9 Obstructive and reflux uropathy unspec   `I-10`

     599.69   **Urinary obstruction, not elsewhere classified**
            Code, if applicable, any causal condition first, such as:
               hyperplasia of prostate (600.0-600.9 with fifth-digit 1)
            AHA: 4Q, '06, 93

√5th   **599.7**   **Hematuria** (blood in the urine)
     Hematuria (benign) (essential)
     EXCLUDES   *hemoglobinuria (791.2)*
     AHA: ▶4Q, '08, 121;◀ 1Q, '00, 5; 3Q, '95, 8

     599.70   **Hematuria, unspecified**
            R31.9 Hematuria unspecified   `I-10`

     599.71   **Gross hematuria**

     599.72   **Microscopic hematuria**

[handwritten margin note:] many genitourinary conditions have Hematuria as an integral associated symptom.

√4th √5th Additional Digit Required   Unacceptable PDx   Manifestation Code   Hospital Acquired Condition   ▶◀ Revised Text   ● New Code   ▲ Revised Code Title

Genitourinary System

599.8–600.90

√5ᵗʰ **599.8** **Other specified disorders of urethra and urinary tract**

Use additional code to identify urinary incontinence (625.6, 788.30-788.39), if present

EXCLUDES *symptoms and other conditions classifiable to 788.0-788.2, 788.4-788.9, 791.0-791.9*

599.81 **Urethral hypermobility**
DEF: Hyperactive urethra.

599.82 **Intrinsic (urethral) sphincter deficiency [ISD]**
DEF: Malfunctioning urethral sphincter.
AHA: 2Q, '96, 15

599.83 **Urethral instability**
DEF: Inconsistent functioning of urethra.

599.84 **Other specified disorders of urethra**
Rupture of urethra (nontraumatic)
Urethral:
    cyst
    granuloma
DEF: Rupture of urethra due to herniation or breaking down of tissue; not due to trauma.
DEF: Urethral cyst: abnormal sac in urethra; usually fluid filled.
DEF: Granuloma: inflammatory cells forming small nodules in urethra.
AHA:▶1Q, '09, 15◀

599.89 **Other specified disorders of urinary tract**

599.9 **Unspecified disorder of urethra and urinary tract**

DISEASES OF MALE GENITAL ORGANS (600-608)

√4ᵗʰ **600** **Hyperplasia of prostate**
INCLUDES enlarged prostate
DEF: Fibrostromal proliferation in periurethral glands, causes blood in urine; etiology unknown.
AHA: 3Q, '05, 20; 4Q, '00, 43; 3Q, '94, 12; 3Q, '92, 7; N-D, '86, 10

√5ᵗʰ **600.0** **Hypertrophy (benign) of prostate**
Benign prostatic hypertrophy
Enlargement of prostate
Smooth enlarged prostate
Soft enlarged prostate
AHA: 4Q, '06, 93-95; 3Q, '05, 20; 4Q, '03, 63; 1Q, '03, 6; 3Q, '02, 28; 2Q, '01, 14

600.00 **Hypertrophy (benign) of prostate without urinary obstruction and other lower urinary tract symptoms [LUTS]**   A♂
Hypertrophy (benign) of prostate NOS
N40.0 Enlarged prostate without LUTS   I-10

600.01 **Hypertrophy (benign) of prostate with urinary obstruction and other lower urinary tract symptoms [LUTS]**   A♂
Hypertrophy (benign) of prostate with urinary retention
Use additional code to identify symptoms:
    incomplete bladder emptying (788.21)
    nocturia (788.43)
    straining on urination (788.65)
    urinary frequency (788.41)
    urinary hesitancy (788.64)
    urinary incontinence (788.30-788.39)
    urinary obstruction (599.69)
    urinary retention (788.20)
    urinary urgency (788.63)
    weak urinary stream (788.62)
AHA: 4Q, '06, 93-95; 4Q, '03, 64

√5ᵗʰ **600.1** **Nodular prostate**
Hard, firm prostate
Multinodular prostate
EXCLUDES *malignant neoplasm of prostate (185)*
DEF: Hard, firm nodule in prostate.
AHA: 4Q, '03, 63

600.10 **Nodular prostate without urinary obstruction**   A♂
Nodular prostate NOS

Male Pelvic Organs

600.11 **Nodular prostate with urinary obstruction**   A♂
Nodular prostate with urinary retention

√5ᵗʰ **600.2** **Benign localized hyperplasia of prostate**
Adenofibromatous hypertrophy of prostate
Adenoma of prostate
Fibroadenoma of prostate
Fibroma of prostate
Myoma of prostate
Polyp of prostate
EXCLUDES *benign neoplasms of prostate (222.2)*
hypertrophy of prostate (600.00-600.01)
malignant neoplasm of prostate (185)
DEF: Benign localized hyperplasia clearly defined epithelial tumor.
AHA: 4Q, '06, 93-95; 4Q, '03, 63

600.20 **Benign localized hyperplasia of prostate without urinary obstruction and other lower urinary tract symptoms [LUTS]**   A♂
Benign localized hyperplasia of prostate NOS

600.21 **Benign localized hyperplasia of prostate with urinary obstruction and other lower urinary tract symptoms [LUTS]**   A♂
Benign localized hyperplasia of prostate with urinary retention
Use additional code to identify symptoms:
    incomplete bladder emptying (788.21)
    nocturia (788.43)
    straining on urination (788.65)
    urinary frequency (788.41)
    urinary hesitancy (788.64)
    urinary incontinence (788.30-788.39)
    urinary obstruction (599.69)
    urinary retention (788.20)
    urinary urgency (788.63)
    weak urinary stream (788.62)

600.3 **Cyst of prostate**   A♂
DEF: Sacs of fluid, which differentiate this from either nodular or adenomatous tumors.

√5ᵗʰ **600.9** **Hyperplasia of prostate, unspecified**
Median bar
Prostatic obstruction NOS
AHA: 4Q, '06, 93-95; 4Q, '03, 63

600.90 **Hyperplasia of prostate, unspecified, without urinary obstruction and other lower urinary tract symptoms [LUTS]**   A♂
Hyperplasia of prostate NOS

N Newborn Age: 0 | P Pediatric Age: 0-17 | M Maternity Age: 12-55 | A Adult Age: 15-124 | MCC Major CC Condition | CC CC Condition | HIV HIV Related Dx

600.91 Hyperplasia of prostate, unspecified ▲ ♂
with urinary obstruction and other lower
urinary tract symptoms [LUTS]
Hyperplasia of prostate, unspecified, with
urinary retention

Use additional code to identify symptoms:
incomplete bladder emptying (788.21)
nocturia (788.43)
straining on urination (788.65)
urinary frequency (788.41)
urinary hesitancy (788.64)
urinary incontinence (788.30-788.39)
urinary obstruction (599.69)
urinary retention (788.20)
urinary urgency (788.63)
weak urinary stream (788.62)

✓4ᵗʰ **601 Inflammatory diseases of prostate**
Use additional code to identify organism, such as Staphylococcus
(041.1), or Streptococcus (041.0)

601.0 Acute prostatitis CC A ♂
CC Excl: 098.12, 098.32, 098.89, 112.2, 131.00, 131.03,
131.8-131.9, 600.00-602.9

601.1 Chronic prostatitis A ♂

601.2 Abscess of prostate CC A ♂
CC Excl: See code: 601.0

601.3 Prostatocystitis A ♂

601.4 *Prostatitis in diseases classified elsewhere* A ♂
Code first underlying disease, as:
actinomycosis (039.8)
blastomycosis (116.0)
syphilis (095.8)
tuberculosis (016.5)

EXCLUDES *prostatitis:*
gonococcal (098.12, 098.32)
monilial (112.2)
trichomonal (131.03)

601.8 Other specified inflammatory diseases of A ♂
prostate
Prostatitis:
cavitary
diverticular
granulomatous

601.9 Prostatitis, unspecified A ♂
Prostatitis NOS

✓4ᵗʰ **602 Other disorders of prostate**

602.0 Calculus of prostate A ♂
Prostatic stone
DEF: Stone or mineral deposit in prostate.

602.1 Congestion or hemorrhage of prostate A ♂
DEF: Bleeding or fluid collection in prostate.

602.2 Atrophy of prostate A ♂

602.3 Dysplasia of prostate ♂
Prostatic intraepithelial neoplasia I (PIN I)
Prostatic intraepithelial neoplasia II (PIN II)
EXCLUDES *prostatic intraepithelial neoplasia III (PIN III)*
(233.4)
DEF: Abnormality of shape and size of the intraepithelial
tissues of the prostate; premalignant condition characterized
by stalks and absence of a basilar cell layer; synonyms are
intraductal dysplasia, large acinar atypical hyperplasia,
atypical primary hyperplasia, hyperplasia with malignant
changes, marked atypia, or duct-acinar dysplasia.
AHA: 4Q, '01, 46

602.8 Other specified disorders of prostate A ♂
Fistula
Infarction ⎫ of prostate
Stricture ⎭
Periprostatic adhesions

602.9 Unspecified disorder of prostate A ♂

Common Inguinal Canal Anomalies

✓4ᵗʰ **603 Hydrocele**
INCLUDES hydrocele of spermatic cord, testis or tunica vaginalis
EXCLUDES *congenital (778.6)*
DEF: Circumscribed collection of fluid in tunica vaginalis, spermatic cord
or testis.

603.0 Encysted hydrocele ♂

603.1 Infected hydrocele CC ♂
Use additional code to identify organism
CC Excl: 112.2, 131.00, 131.8-131.9, 603.0-603.9

603.8 Other specified types of hydrocele ♂

603.9 Hydrocele, unspecified ♂

✓4ᵗʰ **604 Orchitis and epididymitis**
Use additional code to identify organism, such as Escherichia coli
[E. coli] (041.4), Staphylococcus (041.1), or Streptococcus
(041.0)

604.0 Orchitis, epididymitis, and epididymoorchitis, CC ♂
with abscess
Abscess of epididymis or testis
CC Excl: 072.0, 098.13-098.14, 098.33-098.34, 098.89, 112.2,
131.00, 131.8-131.9, 604.0-604.99

✓5ᵗʰ **604.9 Other orchitis, epididymitis, and epididymo-orchitis,**
without mention of abscess

604.90 Orchitis and epididymitis, ♂
unspecified

604.91 *Orchitis and epididymitis in diseases* ♂
classified elsewhere
Code first underlying disease, as:
diphtheria (032.89)
filariasis (125.0-125.9)
syphilis (095.8)

EXCLUDES *orchitis:*
gonococcal (098.13, 098.33)
mumps (072.0)
tuberculous (016.5)
tuberculous epididymitis (016.4)

604.99 Other ♂

605 Redundant prepuce and phimosis ♂
Adherent prepuce   Phimosis (congenital)
Paraphimosis   Tight foreskin
DEF: Constriction of preputial orifice causing inability of the prepuce to
be drawn back over the glans; it may be congenital or caused by
infection.
AHA: ▶3Q, '08, 9◀

✓4ᵗʰ **606 Infertility, male**
AHA: 2Q, '96, 9

606.0 Azoospermia A ♂
Absolute infertility
Infertility due to:
germinal (cell) aplasia
spermatogenic arrest (complete)
DEF: Absence of spermatozoa in the semen or inability to
produce spermatozoa.

606.1 Oligospermia 🅰 ♂
Infertility due to:
germinal cell desquamation
hypospermatogenesis
incomplete spermatogenic arrest
DEF: Insufficient number of sperm in semen.

606.8 Infertility due to extratesticular causes 🅰 ♂
Infertility due to:
drug therapy
infection
obstruction of efferent ducts
radiation
systemic disease

606.9 Male infertility, unspecified 🅰 ♂

√4ᵗʰ **607 Disorders of penis**
EXCLUDES phimosis (605)

607.0 Leukoplakia of penis ♂
Kraurosis of penis
EXCLUDES carcinoma in situ of penis (233.5)
erythroplasia of Queyrat (233.5)
DEF: White, thickened patches on glans penis.

607.1 Balanoposthitis ♂
Balanitis
Use additional code to identify organism
DEF: Inflammation of glans penis and prepuce.

607.2 Other inflammatory disorders of penis ♂
Abscess
Boil
Carbuncle } of corpus cavernosum or penis
Cellulitis
Cavernitis (penis)
Use additional code to identify organism
EXCLUDES herpetic infection (054.13)

607.3 Priapism cc ♂
Painful erection
DEF: Prolonged penile erection without sexual stimulation.
CC Excl: 607.0-607.9

√5ᵗʰ **607.8 Other specified disorders of penis**

607.81 Balanitis xerotica obliterans ♂
Induratio penis plastica
DEF: Inflammation of the glans penis, caused by
stricture of the opening of the prepuce.

607.82 Vascular disorders of penis cc ♂
Embolism
Hematoma
(nontraumatic) } of corpus
Hemorrhage   cavernosum
Thrombosis   or penis
CC Excl: 607.82-607.83

607.83 Edema of penis ♂
DEF: Fluid retention within penile tissues.

607.84 Impotence of organic origin 🅰 ♂
EXCLUDES nonorganic (302.72)
DEF: Physiological cause interfering with erection.
AHA: 3Q, '91, 11
TIP: If impotence is a result of previous radical pros-
tatectomy, assign also 997.99.

607.85 Peyronie's disease ♂
DEF: A severe curvature of the erect penis due to
fibrosis of the cavernous sheaths.
AHA: 4Q, '03, 64

607.89 Other ♂
Atrophy
Fibrosis } of corpus
Hypertrophy   cavernosum
Ulcer (chronic) or penis

607.9 Unspecified disorder of penis ♂

Torsion of the Testis

√4ᵗʰ **608 Other disorders of male genital organs**

608.0 Seminal vesiculitis ♂
Abscess
Cellulitis } of seminal vesicle
Vesiculitis (seminal)
Use additional code to identify organism
EXCLUDES gonococcal infection (098.14, 098.34)
DEF: Inflammation of seminal vesicle.

608.1 Spermatocele ♂
DEF: Cystic enlargement of the epididymis or the testis; the
cysts contain spermatozoa.

√5ᵗʰ **608.2 Torsion of testis**
DEF: Twisted or rotated testis; may compromise blood flow.

608.20 Torsion of testis, unspecified cc ♂
CC Excl: 608.20-608.24
AHA: 4Q, '06, 95

608.21 Extravaginal torsion of spermatic cord cc ♂
DEF: Torsion of the spermatic cord just below the
tunica vaginalis attachments.
CC Excl: See code: 608.20
AHA: 4Q, '06, 95

608.22 Intravaginal torsion of spermatic cord cc ♂
Torsion of spermatic cord NOS
DEF: Torsion within the tunica vaginalis also called
the "bell-clapper" anomaly. It usually occurs in older
children.
CC Excl: See code: 608.20
AHA: 4Q, '06, 95

608.23 Torsion of appendix testis cc ♂
DEF: Torsion of small solid projection of tissue on the
upper outer surface of the testis (hydatid of
Morgagni); a remnant of the embryologic mullerian
duct.
CC Excl: See code: 608.20
AHA: 4Q, '06, 95

608.24 Torsion of appendix epididymis cc ♂
DEF: Torsion of small stalked appendage of the head
of the epididymis (pedunculated hydatid); a
detached embryologic efferent duct.
CC Excl: See code: 608.20
AHA: 4Q, '06, 95

608.3 Atrophy of testis ♂

**608.4 Other inflammatory disorders of male
genital organs** ♂
Abscess
Boil } of scrotum, spermatic cord, testis
Carbuncle   [except abscess], tunica
Cellulitis   vaginalis, or vas deferens
Vasitis
Use additional code to identify organism
EXCLUDES abscess of testis (604.0)

N Newborn Age: 0   **P** Pediatric Age: 0-17   **M** Maternity Age: 12-55   **A** Adult Age: 15-124   **MCC** Major CC Condition   **CC** CC Condition   **HIV** HIV Related Dx

210 – Volume 1   **2010 ICD-9-CM**

√5th **608.8 Other specified disorders of male genital organs**

     608.81 ***Disorders of male genital organs in***   ♂
             diseases classified elsewhere

           Code first underlying disease, as:
              filariasis (125.0-125.9)
              tuberculosis (016.5)

     608.82 Hematospermia   ♂
           DEF: Presence of blood in the ejaculate; relatively common, affecting men of any age after puberty; cause is often the result of a viral or bacterial infection and inflammation.
           AHA: 4Q, '01, 46

     608.83 Vascular disorders   ♂
           Hematoma
             (non-   } of seminal vessel, spermatic
             traumatic)   cord, testis, scrotum,
           Hemorrhage   tunica vaginalis, or
           Thrombosis   vas deferens
           Hematocele NOS, male
           AHA: 4Q, '03, 110
           TIP: Assign for Fournier's gangrene, which is a result of an infection in the genital area.

     608.84 Chylocele of tunica vaginalis   ♂
           DEF: Chylous effusion into tunica vaginalis; due to infusion of lymphatic fluids.

     608.85 Stricture   ♂
           Stricture of: Stricture of:
             spermatic cord   vas deferens
             tunica vaginalis

     608.86 Edema   ♂

     608.87 Retrograde ejaculation   ♂
           DEF: Condition where the semen travels to the bladder rather than out through the urethra due to damaged nerves causing the bladder neck to remain open during ejaculation.
           AHA: 4Q, '01, 46

     608.89 Other   ♂
           Atrophy   } of seminal vessel, spermatic
           Fibrosis   cord, testis, scrotum,
           Hypertrophy   tunica vaginalis, or vas
           Ulcer   deferens
           EXCLUDES *atrophy of testis (608.3)*

   608.9 Unspecified disorder of male genital organs   ♂

DISORDERS OF BREAST (610-612)

√4th **610 Benign mammary dysplasias**

     610.0 Solitary cyst of breast
           Cyst (solitary) of breast

     610.1 Diffuse cystic mastopathy   A
           Chronic cystic mastitis
           Cystic breast
           Fibrocystic disease of
             breast
           DEF: Extensive formation of nodular cysts in breast tissue; symptoms include tenderness, change in size and hyperplasia of ductal epithelium.
           AHA: 2Q, '06, 10
           TIP: Assign in addition to screening mammography V code; is a normal variant, commonly found in normal breasts and not a pathological condition.

     610.2 Fibroadenosis of breast
           Fibroadenosis of breast: Fibroadenosis of breast:
             NOS   diffuse
             chronic   periodic
             cystic   segmental
           DEF: Non-neoplastic nodular condition of breast.

     610.3 Fibrosclerosis of breast
           DEF: Fibrous tissue in breast.

     610.4 Mammary duct ectasia
           Comedomastitis   Mastitis:
           Duct ectasia   periductal
                                plasma cell
           DEF: Atrophy of duct epithelium; causes distended collecting ducts of mammary gland; drying up of breast secretion, intraductal inflammation and periductal and interstitial chronic inflammatory reaction.

     610.8 Other specified benign mammary dysplasias
           Mazoplasia   Sebaceous cyst of breast
           AHA: ▶2Q, '09, 9◀

     610.9 Benign mammary dysplasia, unspecified

√4th **611 Other disorders of breast**
       EXCLUDES *that associated with lactation or the puerperium (675.0-676.9)*

     611.0 Inflammatory disease of breast
           Abscess (acute) (chronic) (nonpuerperal) of:
             areola
             breast
           Mammillary fistula
           Mastitis (acute) (subacute) (nonpuerperal):
             NOS
             infective
             retromammary
             submammary
           EXCLUDES *carbuncle of breast (680.2)*
                           chronic cystic mastitis (610.1)
                           neonatal infective mastitis (771.5)
                           thrombophlebitis of breast [Mondor's disease] (451.89)

     611.1 Hypertrophy of breast
           Gynecomastia
           Hypertrophy of breast:
             NOS
             massive pubertal
           EXCLUDES *breast engorgement in newborn (778.7)*
                           disproportion of reconstructed breast (612.1)

     611.2 Fissure of nipple

     611.3 Fat necrosis of breast
           Fat necrosis (segmental) of breast
           Code first breast necrosis due to breast graft (996.79)
           DEF: Splitting of neutral fats in adipose tissue cells as a result of trauma; a firm circumscribed mass is then formed in the breast.

     611.4 Atrophy of breast

     611.5 Galactocele

     611.6 Galactorrhea not associated with childbirth

√5th **611.7 Signs and symptoms in breast**

         611.71 Mastodynia
               Pain in breast

         611.72 Lump or mass in breast
               AHA: 2Q, '03, 4-5
               TIP: Do not assign if the underlying cause of the breast lump or mass is determined and documented during the episode of care.

         611.79 Other
               Induration of breast
               Inversion of nipple
               Nipple discharge
               Retraction of nipple

√5th **611.8 Other specified disorders of breast**
         AHA: 4Q, '08, 121-122

         611.81 Ptosis of breast   A
              EXCLUDES *ptosis of native breast in relation to reconstructed breast (612.1)*

√4th √5th **Additional Digit Required**   **Unacceptable PDx**   **Manifestation Code**   **Hospital Acquired Condition**   ▶◀ Revised Text   ● New Code   ▲ Revised Code Title

2010 ICD-9-CM   **October 2009 · Volume 1 – 211**

Genitourinary System

611.82 **Hypoplasia of breast** ▢A
Micromastia

> EXCLUDES ▶congenital absence of breast
> (757.6)◀
> hypoplasia of native breast in
> relation to reconstructed
> breast (612.1)

611.83 **Capsular contracture of breastimplant** ▢A
TIP: Do not assign additional code from category
996 Complications peculiar to certain specified procedures.

611.89 **Other specified disorders of breast**
Hematoma (nontraumatic) of breast
Infarction of breast
Occlusion of breast duct
Subinvolution of breast (postlactational)
(postpartum)

611.9 **Unspecified breast disorder**

✓4ᵗʰ **612** **Deformity and disproportion of reconstructed breast**
AHA: 4Q, '08, 123

612.0 **Deformity of reconstructed breast** ▢A
Contour irregularity in reconstructed breast
Excess tissue in reconstructed breast
Misshapen reconstructed breast

612.1 **Disproportion of reconstructed breast** ▢A
Breast asymmetry between native breast and
reconstructed breast
Disproportion between native breast and reconstructed
breast

INFLAMMATORY DISEASE OF FEMALE PELVIC ORGANS (614-616)

Use additional code to identify organism, such as Staphylococcus
(041.1), or Streptococcus (041.0)

> EXCLUDES that associated with pregnancy, abortion, childbirth, or
> the puerperium (630-676.9)

✓4ᵗʰ **614** **Inflammatory disease of ovary, fallopian tube, pelvic
cellular tissue, and peritoneum**

> EXCLUDES endometritis (615.0-615.9)
> major infection following delivery ▶(670.0-670.8)◀
> that complicating:
> abortion (634-638 with .0, 639.0)
> ectopic or molar pregnancy (639.0)
> pregnancy or labor (646.6)

614.0 **Acute salpingitis and oophoritis** cc ♀
Any condition classifiable to 614.2, specified as acute or
subacute
DEF: Acute inflammation, of ovary and fallopian tube.
CC Excl: 016.60-016.96, 017.90-017.96, 098.15-098.17,
098.35-098.37, 098.89, 112.2, 131.00, 131.8-131.9,
614.0-615.9, 616.81-616.9, 625.70, 625.79-625.9, 629.20-629.9,
752.81-752.9

614.1 **Chronic salpingitis and oophoritis** ♀
Hydrosalpinx
Salpingitis:
follicularis
isthmica nodosa
Any condition classifiable to 614.2, specified as chronic
DEF: Persistent inflammation of ovary and fallopian tube.

614.2 **Salpingitis and oophoritis not specified as
acute, subacute, or chronic** ♀
Abscess (of):   Perisalpingitis
  fallopian tube   Pyosalpinx
  ovary   Salpingitis
  tubo-ovarian   Salpingo-oophoritis
Oophoritis   Tubo-ovarian inflammatory
Perioophoritis   disease

> EXCLUDES gonococcal infection (chronic) (098.37)
> acute (098.17)
> tuberculous (016.6)

AHA: 2Q, '91, 5

614.3 **Acute parametritis and pelvic cellulitis** cc ♀
Acute inflammatory pelvic disease
Any condition classifiable to 614.4, specified as acute
DEF: Parametritis: inflammation of the parametrium; pelvic
cellulitis is a synonym for parametritis.
CC Excl: See code 614.0

614.4 **Chronic or unspecified parametritis and
pelvic cellulitis** ♀
Abscess (of):
  broad ligament
  parametrium ⎫
  pelvis, femal ⎬ chronic or NOS
  pouch of Douglas ⎭
Chronic inflammatory pelvic disease
Pelvic cellulitis, female

> EXCLUDES tuberculous (016.7)

614.5 **Acute or unspecified pelvic peritonitis, female** mcc ♀
CC Excl: See code 614.0
AHA: 4Q, '05, 74
TIP: For pelvic peritonitis in a male patient, refer to code
567.21.

614.6 **Pelvic peritoneal adhesions, female (postoperative)** ♀
(postinfection)
Adhesions:
  peritubal
  tubo-ovarian
Use additional code to identify any associated infertility
(628.2)
DEF: Fibrous scarring abnormally joining structures within
abdomen.
AHA: 3Q, '03, 6; 1Q, '03, 4; 3Q, '95, 7; 3Q, '94, 12
N73.6 Female pelvic peritoneal adhesions (postinfective) I-10

614.7 **Other chronic pelvic peritonitis, female** cc ♀

> EXCLUDES tuberculous (016.7)
CC Excl: See code: 614.0

614.8 **Other specified inflammatory disease of
female pelvic organs and tissues** ♀

614.9 **Unspecified inflammatory disease of female
pelvic organs and tissues** ♀
Pelvic infection or inflammation, female NOS
Pelvic inflammatory disease [PID]

✓4ᵗʰ **615** **Inflammatory diseases of uterus, except cervix**

> EXCLUDES following delivery ▶(670.0-670.8)◀
> hyperplastic endometritis ▶(621.30-621.35)◀
> that complicating:
> abortion (634-638 with .0, 639.0)
> ectopic or molar pregnancy (639.0)
> pregnancy or labor (646.6)

615.0 **Acute** cc ♀
Any condition classifiable to 615.9, specified as acute or
subacute
CC Excl: 016.60-016.96, 017.90-017.96, 098.15-098.17,
098.35-098.37, 098.89, 112.2, 131.00, 131.8-131.9,
614.0-616.0, 616.81-616.9, 621.8-621.9, 625.70, 625.79-625.9,
629.20-629.9, 752.81-752.9

615.1 **Chronic** ♀
Any condition classifiable to 615.9, specified as chronic

615.9 **Unspecified inflammatory disease of uterus** ♀
Endometritis   Myometritis
Endomyometritis   Perimetritis
Intrauterine infection Pyometra
Metritis   Uterine abscess
N71.9 Inflammatory disease of uterus unspecified I-10

▢N Newborn Age: 0 ▢P Pediatric Age: 0-17 ▢M Maternity Age: 12-55 ▢A Adult Age: 15-124 mcc Major CC Condition cc CC Condition HIV HIV Related Dx

212 – Volume 1 · October 2009

2010 ICD-9-CM

✓4ᵗʰ 616 Inflammatory disease of cervix, vagina, and vulva

> **EXCLUDES** *that complicating:*
> *abortion (634-638 with .0, 639.0)*
> *ectopic or molar pregnancy (639.0)*
> *pregnancy, childbirth, or the puerperium (646.6)*

616.0 Cervicitis and endocervicitis ♀

Cervicitis ⎱ with or without mention of
Endocervicitis ⎰ erosion or ectropion

Nabothian (gland) cyst or follicle

> **EXCLUDES** *erosion or ectropion without mention of cervicitis (622.0)*

N72 Inflammatory disease of cervix uteri |I-10|

✓5ᵗʰ 616.1 Vaginitis and vulvovaginitis

> **EXCLUDES** *vulvar vestibulitis (625.71)*

DEF: Inflammation or infection of vagina or external female genitalia.

616.10 Vaginitis and vulvovaginitis, unspecified ♀
Vaginitis:
 NOS
 postirradiation
Vulvitis NOS
Vulvovaginitis NOS

Use additional code to identify organism, such as Escherichia coli [E. coli] (041.4), Staphylococcus (041.1), or Streptococcus (041.0)

> **EXCLUDES** *noninfective leukorrhea (623.5)*
> *postmenopausal or senile vaginitis (627.3)*

616.11 *Vaginitis and vulvovaginitis in diseases classified elsewhere* ♀

> *Code first underlying disease, as:*
> pinworm vaginitis (127.4)

> **EXCLUDES** *herpetic vulvovaginitis (054.11)*
> *monilial vulvovaginitis (112.1)*
> *trichomonal vaginitis or vulvovaginitis (131.01)*

616.2 Cyst of Bartholin's gland ♀
Bartholin's duct cyst
DEF: Fluid-filled sac within gland of vaginal orifice.

616.3 Abscess of Bartholin's gland |CC| ♀
Vulvovaginal gland abscess
CC Excl: 016.70-016.96, 017.90-017.96, 112.1-112.2, 131.00-131.01, 131.8-131.9, 616.10-616.9, 624.3-624.9, 625.70-625.9, 629.20-629.9, 752.81-752.9

616.4 Other abscess of vulva |CC| ♀
Abscess ⎱
Carbuncle ⎰ of vulva
Furuncle
CC Excl: See code 616.3

✓5ᵗʰ 616.5 Ulceration of vulva

616.50 Ulceration of vulva, unspecified ♀
Ulcer NOS of vulva

616.51 *Ulceration of vulva in diseases classified elsewhere* ♀

> *Code first underlying disease, as:*
> Behçet's syndrome (136.1)
> tuberculosis (016.7)

> **EXCLUDES** *vulvar ulcer (in):*
> *gonococcal (098.0)*
> *herpes simplex (054.12)*
> *syphilitic (091.0)*

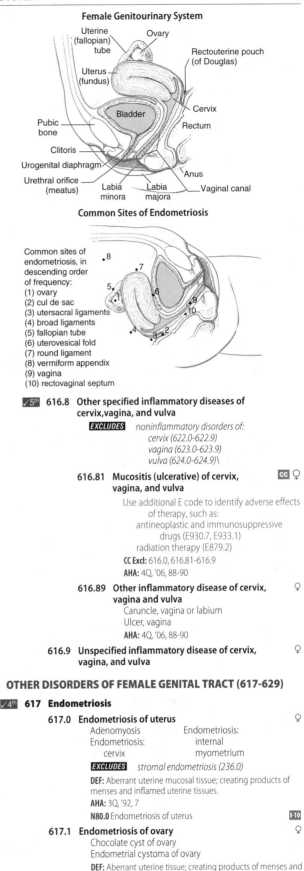

Female Genitourinary System

Uterine (fallopian) tube · Ovary · Rectouterine pouch (of Douglas) · Uterus (fundus) · Cervix · Bladder · Rectum · Pubic bone · Clitoris · Urogenital diaphragm · Anus · Urethral orifice (meatus) · Labia minora · Labia majora · Vaginal canal

Common Sites of Endometriosis

Common sites of endometriosis, in descending order of frequency:
(1) ovary
(2) cul de sac
(3) utersacral ligaments
(4) broad ligaments
(5) fallopian tube
(6) uterovesical fold
(7) round ligament
(8) vermiform appendix
(9) vagina
(10) rectovaginal septum

✓5ᵗʰ 616.8 Other specified inflammatory diseases of cervix, vagina, and vulva

> **EXCLUDES** *noninflammatory disorders of:*
> *cervix (622.0-622.9)*
> *vagina (623.0-623.9)*
> *vulva (624.0-624.9)*

616.81 Mucositis (ulcerative) of cervix, vagina, and vulva |CC| ♀

Use additional E code to identify adverse effects of therapy, such as:
 antineoplastic and immunosuppressive drugs (E930.7, E933.1)
 radiation therapy (E879.2)

CC Excl: 616.0, 616.81-616.9
AHA: 4Q, '06, 88-90

616.89 Other inflammatory disease of cervix, vagina and vulva ♀
Caruncle, vagina or labium
Ulcer, vagina
AHA: 4Q, '06, 88-90

616.9 Unspecified inflammatory disease of cervix, vagina, and vulva ♀

OTHER DISORDERS OF FEMALE GENITAL TRACT (617-629)

✓4ᵗʰ 617 Endometriosis

617.0 Endometriosis of uterus ♀
Adenomyosis Endometriosis:
Endometriosis: internal
 cervix myometrium

> **EXCLUDES** *stromal endometriosis (236.0)*

DEF: Aberrant uterine mucosal tissue; creating products of menses and inflamed uterine tissues.
AHA: 3Q, '92, 7
N80.0 Endometriosis of uterus |I-10|

617.1 Endometriosis of ovary ♀
Chocolate cyst of ovary
Endometrial cystoma of ovary
DEF: Aberrant uterine tissue; creating products of menses and inflamed ovarian tissues.
N80.1 Endometriosis of ovary |I-10|

| ✓4ᵗʰ ✓5ᵗʰ Additional Digit Required | Unacceptable PDx | Manifestation Code | Hospital Acquired Condition | ▶◀ Revised Text | ● New Code | ▲ Revised Code Title |

2010 ICD-9-CM **Volume 1 – 213**

616–617.1

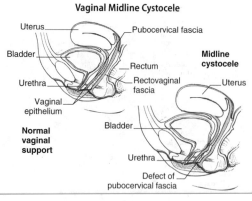

Vaginal Midline Cystocele

Vaginal Lateral Cystocele

Types of Vaginal Hernias

617.2   **Endometriosis of fallopian tube**   ♀
> **DEF:** Aberrant uterine tissue; creating products of menses and inflamed tissues of fallopian tubes.

617.3   **Endometriosis of pelvic peritoneum**   ♀
> Endometriosis:
>> broad ligament
>> cul-de-sac (Douglas')
>> parametrium
>> round ligament
>
> **DEF:** Aberrant uterine tissue; creating products of menses and inflamed peritoneum tissues.

617.4   **Endometriosis of rectovaginal septum and vagina**   ♀
> **DEF:** Aberrant uterine tissue; creating products of menses and inflamed tissues in and behind vagina.

617.5   **Endometriosis of intestine**   ♀
> Endometriosis: Endometriosis:
>> appendix   rectum
>> colon
>
> **DEF:** Aberrant uterine tissue; creating products of menses and inflamed intestinal tissues.

617.6   **Endometriosis in scar of skin**   ♀

617.8   **Endometriosis of other specified sites**   ♀
> Endometriosis:
>> bladder
>> lung
>> umbilicus
>> vulva

617.9   **Endometriosis, site unspecified**   ♀

√4ᵗʰ   **618**   **Genital prolapse**
> Use additional code to identify urinary incontinence (625.6, 788.31, 788.33-788.39)
>
> **EXCLUDES**   that complicating pregnancy, labor, or delivery (654.4)

√5ᵗʰ   **618.0**   **Prolapse of vaginal walls without mention of uterine prolapse**
> **EXCLUDES**   that with uterine prolapse (618.2-618.4)
>> enterocele (618.6)
>> vaginal vault prolapse following hysterectomy (618.5)

> **618.00**   **Unspecified prolapse of vaginal walls**   ♀
>> Vaginal prolapse NOS

> **618.01**   **Cystocele, midline**   ♀
>> Cystocele NOS
>>
>> **DEF:** Defect in the pubocervical fascia, the supportive layer of the bladder, causing bladder drop and herniated into the vagina along the midline.
>>
>> **N81.11** Cystocele midline   I-10

> **618.02**   **Cystocele, lateral**   ♀
>> Paravaginal
>>
>> **DEF:** Loss of support of the lateral attachment of the vagina at the arcus tendinous results in bladder drop; bladder herniates into the vagina laterally.

> **618.03**   **Urethrocele**   ♀

> **618.04**   **Rectocele**   ♀
>> Proctocele
>>
>> **N81.6** Rectocele   I-10

> **618.05**   **Perineocele**   ♀

> **618.09**   **Other prolapse of vaginal walls without mention of uterine prolapse**   ♀
>> Cystourethrocele

618.1   **Uterine prolapse without mention of vaginal wall prolapse**   ♀
> Descensus uteri
> Uterine prolapse:
>> NOS
>> complete
>> first degree
>> second degree
>> third degree
>
> **EXCLUDES**   that with mention of cystocele, urethrocele, or rectocele (618.2-618.4)

618.2   **Uterovaginal prolapse, incomplete**   ♀
> **DEF:** Downward displacement of uterus downward into vagina.
>
> **N81.2** Incomplete uterovaginal prolapse   I-10

618.3   **Uterovaginal prolapse, complete**   ♀
> **DEF:** Downward displacement of uterus exposed within external genitalia.

618.4   **Uterovaginal prolapse, unspecified**   ♀
> **N81.4** Uterovaginal prolapse unspecified   I-10

618.5   **Prolapse of vaginal vault after hysterectomy**   ♀
> **N99.3** Prolapse of vaginal vault after hysterectomy   I-10

618.6   **Vaginal enterocele, congenital or acquired**   ♀
> Pelvic enterocele, congenital or acquired
>
> **DEF:** Vaginal vault hernia formed by the loop of the small intestine protruding into the rectal vaginal pouch; can also accompany uterine prolapse or follow hysterectomy.
>
> **N81.5** Vaginal enterocele   I-10

618.7   **Old laceration of muscles of pelvic floor**   ♀

☒ Newborn Age: 0   ☒ Pediatric Age: 0-17   ☒ Maternity Age: 12-55   ☒ Adult Age: 15-124   **MCC** Major CC Condition   **CC** CC Condition   **HIV** HIV Related Dx

214 – Volume 1   **2010 ICD-9-CM**

√5th **618.8** Other specified genital prolapse

618.81 Incompetence or weakening of pubocervical tissue ♀

618.82 Incompetence or weakening of rectovaginal tissue ♀

618.83 Pelvic muscle wasting ♀
Disuse atrophy of pelvic muscles and anal sphincter

618.84 Cervical stump prolapse ♀
AHA: 4Q, '06, 97

618.89 Other specified genital prolapse ♀

618.9 Unspecified genital prolapse ♀

√4th **619** **Fistula involving female genital tract**
EXCLUDES *vesicorectal and intestinovesical fistula (596.1)*

619.0 Urinary-genital tract fistula, female CC ♀
Fistula:
cervicovesical
ureterovaginal
urethrovaginal
urethrovesicovaginal
ureterouteric
uterovesical
vesicocervicovaginal
vesicovaginal
CC Excl: 619.0-619.9

619.1 Digestive-genital tract fistula, female CC ♀
Fistula: Fistula:
intestinouterine   rectovulval
intestinovaginal   sigmoidovaginal
rectovaginal   uterorectal
CC Excl: See code: 619.0

619.2 Genital tract-skin fistula, female CC ♀
Fistula:
uterus to abdominal wall
vaginoperineal
CC Excl: See code: 619.0

619.8 Other specified fistulas involving female genital tract CC ♀
Fistula:
cervix
cul-de-sac (Douglas')
uterus
vagina
CC Excl: See code: 619.0

619.9 Unspecified fistula involving female genital tract CC ♀
CC Excl: see code 619.0

√4th **620** **Noninflammatory disorders of ovary, fallopian tube, and broad ligament**
EXCLUDES *hydrosalpinx (614.1)*

620.0 Follicular cyst of ovary ♀
Cyst of graafian follicle
DEF: Fluid-filled, encapsulated cyst due to occluded follicle duct that secretes hormones into ovaries.
N83.0 Follicular cyst of ovary I-10

620.1 Corpus luteum cyst or hematoma ♀
Corpus luteum hemorrhage or rupture
Lutein cyst
DEF: Fluid-filled cyst due to serous developing from corpus luteum or clotted blood.
N83.1 Corpus luteum cyst I-10

Uterus and Ovaries

620.2 Other and unspecified ovarian cyst ♀
Cyst:
NOS
corpus albicans
retention NOS } of ovary
serous
theca-lutein
Simple cystoma of ovary
EXCLUDES *cystadenoma (benign) (serous) (220)*
developmental cysts (752.0)
neoplastic cysts (220)
polycystic ovaries (256.4)
Stein-Leventhal syndrome (256.4)
N83.20 Unspecified ovarian cysts I-10

620.3 Acquired atrophy of ovary and fallopian tube ♀
Senile involution of ovary

620.4 Prolapse or hernia of ovary and fallopian tube ♀
Displacement of ovary and fallopian tube
Salpingocele

620.5 Torsion of ovary, ovarian pedicle, or fallopian tube CC ♀
Torsion:
accessory tube
hydatid of Morgagni
CC Excl: 620.0-620.9

620.6 Broad ligament laceration syndrome ♀
Masters-Allen syndrome

620.7 Hematoma of broad ligament ♀
Hematocele, broad ligament
DEF: Blood within peritoneal fold that supports uterus.

620.8 Other noninflammatory disorders of ovary, fallopian tube, and broad ligament ♀
Cyst   } of broad ligament or fallopian
Polyp   } tube
Infarction } of ovary or fallopian tube
Rupture }
Hematosalpinx
EXCLUDES *hematosalpinx in ectopic pregnancy (639.2)*
peritubal adhesions (614.6)
torsion of ovary, ovarian pedicle, or fallopian tube (620.5)

620.9 Unspecified noninflammatory disorder of ovary, fallopian tube, and broad ligament ♀

√4th **621** **Disorders of uterus, not elsewhere classified**

621.0 Polyp of corpus uteri ♀
Polyp:
endometrium
uterus NOS
EXCLUDES *cervical polyp NOS (622.7)*
N84.0 Polyp of corpus uteri I-10

√4th √5th Additional Digit Required   Unacceptable PDx   Manifestation Code   Hospital Acquired Condition   ►◄ Revised Text   ● New Code   ▲ Revised Code Title

621.1 Chronic subinvolution of uterus ♀
> **EXCLUDES** *puerperal (674.8)*
>
> **DEF:** Abnormal size of uterus after delivery; the uterus does not return to its normal size after the birth of a child.
>
> **AHA:** 1Q, '91, 11

621.2 Hypertrophy of uterus ♀
> Bulky or enlarged uterus
> **EXCLUDES** *puerperal (674.8)*

✓5ᵗʰ **621.3 Endometrial hyperplasia**
> **DEF:** Abnormal cystic overgrowth of endometrial tissue.

> **621.30 Endometrial hyperplasia, unspecified** ♀
> Endometrial hyperplasia NOS
> ▶Hyperplasia (adenomatous) (cystic) (glandular) of endometrium
> Hyperplastic endometritis◀

> **621.31 Simple endometrial hyperplasia without atypia** ♀
> **EXCLUDES** ▶ *benign endometrial hyperplasia (621.34)*◀

> **621.32 Complex endometrial hyperplasia without atypia** ♀
> **EXCLUDES** ▶ *benign endometrial hyperplasia (621.34)*◀

> **621.33 Endometrial hyperplasia with atypia** ♀
> **EXCLUDES** ▶ *endometrial intraepithelial neoplasia [EIN] (621.35)*◀

● **621.34 Benign endometrial hyperplasia** ♀
● **621.35 Endometrial intraepithelial neoplasia [EIN]** ♀
> **EXCLUDES** *malignant neoplasm of endometrium with endometrial intraepithelial neoplasia [EIN] (182.0)*

621.4 Hematometra ♀
> Hemometra
> **EXCLUDES** *that in congenital anomaly (752.2-752.3)*
> **DEF:** Accumulated blood in uterus.

621.5 Intrauterine synechiae ♀
> Adhesions of uterus Band(s) of uterus

621.6 Malposition of uterus ♀
> Anteversion
> Retroflexion } of uterus
> Retroversion
> **EXCLUDES** *malposition complicating pregnancy, labor, or delivery (654.3-654.4)*

621.7 Chronic inversion of uterus ♀
> **EXCLUDES** *current obstetrical trauma (665.2)*
> *prolapse of uterus (618.1-618.4)*

621.8 Other specified disorders of uterus, not elsewhere classified ♀
> Atrophy, acquired
> Cyst
> Fibrosis NOS } of uterus
> Old laceration (postpartum)
> Ulcer
> **EXCLUDES** *bilharzial fibrosis (120.0-120.9)*
> *endometriosis (617.0)*
> *fistulas (619.0-619.8)*
> *inflammatory diseases (615.0-615.9)*

621.9 Unspecified disorder of uterus ♀

✓4ᵗʰ **622 Noninflammatory disorders of cervix**
> **EXCLUDES** *abnormality of cervix complicating pregnancy, labor, or delivery (654.5-654.6)*
> *fistula (619.0-619.8)*

622.0 Erosion and ectropion of cervix ♀
> Eversion
> Ulcer } of cervix
> **EXCLUDES** *that in chronic cervicitis (616.0)*
> **DEF:** Ulceration or turning outward of uterine cervix.

✓5ᵗʰ **622.1 Dysplasia of cervix (uteri)**
> **EXCLUDES** *abnormal results from cervical cytologic examination without histologic confirmation (795.00-795.09)*
> *carcinoma in situ of cervix (233.1)*
> *cervical intraepithelial neoplasia III [CIN III] (233.1)*
> *HGSIL of cervix (795.04)*
> **DEF:** Abnormal cell structures in portal between uterus and vagina.
> **AHA:** 1Q, '91, 11

> **622.10 Dysplasia of cervix, unspecified** ♀
> Anaplasia of cervix
> Cervical atypism
> Cervical dysplasia NOS

> **622.11 Mild dysplasia of cervix** ♀
> Cervical intraepithelial neoplasia I [CIN I]

> **622.12 Moderate dysplasia of cervix** ♀
> Cervical intraepithelial neoplasia II [CIN II]
> **EXCLUDES** *carcinoma in situ of cervix (233.1)*
> *cervical intraepithelial neo-plasia III [CIN III] (233.1)*
> *severe dysplasia (233.1)*

622.2 Leukoplakia of cervix (uteri) ♀
> **EXCLUDES** *carcinoma in situ of cervix (233.1)*
> **DEF:** Thickened, white patches on portal between uterus and vagina.

622.3 Old laceration of cervix ♀
> Adhesions
> Band(s) } of cervix
> Cicatrix (postpartum)
> **EXCLUDES** *current obstetrical trauma (665.3)*
> **DEF:** Scarring or other evidence of old wound on cervix.

622.4 Stricture and stenosis of cervix ♀
> Atresia (acquired)
> Contracture } of cervix
> Occlusion
> Pinpoint os uteri
> **EXCLUDES** *congenital (752.49)*
> *that complicating labor (654.6)*

622.5 Incompetence of cervix ♀
> **EXCLUDES** *complicating pregnancy (654.5)*
> *that affecting fetus or newborn (761.0)*
> **DEF:** Inadequate functioning of cervix; marked by abnormal widening during pregnancy; causing miscarriage.

622.6 Hypertrophic elongation of cervix ♀
> **DEF:** Overgrowth of cervix tissues extending down into vagina.

622.7 Mucous polyp of cervix ♀
> Polyp NOS of cervix
> **EXCLUDES** *adenomatous polyp of cervix (219.0)*

622.8 Other specified noninflammatory disorders of cervix ♀
> Atrophy (senile)
> Cyst
> Fibrosis } of cervix
> Hemorrhage
> **EXCLUDES** *endometriosis (617.0)*
> *fistula (619.0-619.8)*
> *inflammatory diseases (616.0)*

622.9 Unspecified noninflammatory disorder of cervix ♀

N Newborn Age: 0   P Pediatric Age: 0-17   M Maternity Age: 12-55   A Adult Age: 15-124   MCC Major CC Condition   CC CC Condition   HIV HIV Related Dx

216 – Volume 1 • October 2009

2010 ICD-9-CM

✓4th 623 Noninflammatory disorders of vagina

> **EXCLUDES**   *abnormality of vagina complicating pregnancy, labor, or delivery (654.7)*
> *congenital absence of vagina (752.49)*
> *congenital diaphragm or bands (752.49)*
> *fistulas involving vagina (619.0-619.8)*

623.0 Dysplasia of vagina   ♀
> Mild and moderate dysplasia of vagina
> Vaginal intraepithelial neoplasia I and II [VAIN I and II]
> **EXCLUDES**   *abnormal results from vaginal cytological examination without histologic confirmation (795.10-795.19)*
> *carcinoma in situ of vagina (233.31)*
> *HGSIL of vagina (795.14)*
> *severe dysplasia of vagina (233.31)*
> *vaginal intraepithelial neoplasia III [VAIN III] (233.31)*

623.1 Leukoplakia of vagina   ♀
> **DEF:** Thickened white patches on vaginal canal.

623.2 Stricture or atresia of vagina   ♀
> Adhesions (postoperative) (postradiation) of vagina
> Occlusion of vagina
> Stenosis, vagina
> Use additional E code to identify any external cause
> **EXCLUDES**   *congenital atresia or stricture (752.49)*

623.3 Tight hymenal ring   ♀
> Rigid hymen
> Tight hymenal ring } acquired or congenital
> Tight introitus
> **EXCLUDES**   *imperforate hymen (752.42)*

623.4 Old vaginal laceration   ♀
> **EXCLUDES**   *old laceration involving muscles of pelvic floor (618.7)*
> **DEF:** Scarring or other evidence of old wound on vagina.

623.5 Leukorrhea, not specified as infective   ♀
> Leukorrhea NOS of vagina
> Vaginal discharge NOS
> **EXCLUDES**   *trichomonal (131.00)*
> **DEF:** Viscid whitish discharge, from vagina.

623.6 Vaginal hematoma   ♀
> **EXCLUDES**   *current obstetrical trauma (665.7)*

623.7 Polyp of vagina   ♀

623.8 Other specified noninflammatory disorders of vagina   ♀
> Cyst } of vagina
> Hemorrhage

623.9 Unspecified noninflammatory disorder of vagina   ♀

✓4th 624 Noninflammatory disorders of vulva and perineum

> **EXCLUDES**   *abnormality of vulva and perineum complicating pregnancy, labor, or delivery (654.8)*
> *condyloma acuminatum ▶(078.11)◀*
> *fistulas involving:*
> *perineum–see Alphabetic Index*
> *vulva (619.0-619.8)*
> *vulval varices (456.6)*
> *vulvar involvement in skin conditions (690-709.9)*

✓5th 624.0 Dystrophy of vulva
> **EXCLUDES**   *carcinoma in situ of vulva (233.32)*
> *severe dysplasia of vulva (233.32)*
> *vulvar intraepithelial neoplasia III [VIN III] (233.32)*
> **AHA:** 4Q, '07, 90

624.01 Vulvar intraepithelial neoplasia I [VIN I]   ♀
> Mild dysplasia of vulva

624.02 Vulvar intraepithelial neoplasia II [VIN II]   ♀
> Moderate dysplasia of vulva
> **AHA:** 4Q, '07, 91

624.09 Other dystrophy of vulva   ♀
> Kraurosis of vulva
> Leukoplakia of vulva

624.1 Atrophy of vulva   ♀

624.2 Hypertrophy of clitoris   ♀
> **EXCLUDES**   *that in endocrine disorders (255.2, 256.1)*

624.3 Hypertrophy of labia   ♀
> Hypertrophy of vulva NOS
> **DEF:** Overgrowth of fleshy folds on either side of vagina.

624.4 Old laceration or scarring of vulva   ♀
> **DEF:** Scarring or other evidence of old wound on external female genitalia.

624.5 Hematoma of vulva   ♀
> **EXCLUDES**   *that complicating delivery (664.5)*
> **DEF:** Blood in tissue of external genitalia.

624.6 Polyp of labia and vulva   ♀

624.8 Other specified noninflammatory disorders of vulva and perineum   ♀
> Cyst
> Edema } of vulva
> Stricture
> **AHA:** 1Q, '03, 13; 1Q, '95, 8

624.9 Unspecified noninflammatory disorder of vulva and perineum   ♀

✓4th 625 Pain and other symptoms associated with female genital organs

625.0 Dyspareunia   ♀
> **EXCLUDES**   *psychogenic dyspareunia (302.76)*
> **DEF:** Difficult or painful sexual intercourse.

625.1 Vaginismus   ♀
> Colpospasm
> Vulvismus
> **EXCLUDES**   *psychogenic vaginismus (306.51)*
> **DEF:** Vaginal spasms; due to involuntary contraction of musculature; prevents intercourse.

625.2 Mittelschmerz   ♀
> Intermenstrual pain
> Ovulation pain
> **DEF:** Pain occurring between menstrual periods.

625.3 Dysmenorrhea   ♀
> Painful menstruation
> **EXCLUDES**   *psychogenic dysmenorrhea (306.52)*
> **AHA:** 2Q, '94, 12
> N94.6 Dysmenorrhea unspecified   [I-10]

625.4 Premenstrual tension syndromes   ♀
> Menstrual molimen
> Premenstrual dysphoric disorder
> Premenstrual syndrome
> Premenstrual tension NOS
> **EXCLUDES**   *menstrual migraine (346.4)*
> **AHA:** 4Q, '03, 116

625.5 Pelvic congestion syndrome   ♀
> Congestion-fibrosis syndrome
> Taylor's syndrome
> **DEF:** Excessive accumulation of blood in vessels of pelvis; may occur after orgasm; causes abnormal menstruation, lower back pain and vaginal discharge.

625.6 Stress incontinence, female   ♀
> **EXCLUDES**   *mixed incontinence (788.33)*
> *stress incontinence, male (788.32)*
> **DEF:** Involuntary leakage of urine due to insufficient sphincter control; occurs upon sneezing, laughing, coughing, sudden movement or lifting.
> N39.3 Stress incontinence (female) (male)   [I-10]

✓5th 625.7 Vulvodynia   ♀
> **DEF:** Vulvar pain without an identifiable cause that persists for three months or longer.
> **AHA:** 4Q, '08, 124

625.70 Vulvodynia, unspecified   ♀
> Vulvodynia NOS

625.71 Vulvar vestibulitis   ♀

625.79 Other vulvodynia   ♀

✓4th / ✓5th   Additional Digit Required   Unacceptable PDx   Manifestation Code   Hospital Acquired Condition   ▶◀ Revised Text   ● New Code   ▲ Revised Code Title

2010 ICD-9-CM   **October 2009 · Volume 1 – 217**

Genitourinary System

625.8–629.20

625.8 Other specified symptoms associated with female genital organs ♀
AHA: N-D, '85, 16

625.9 Unspecified symptom associated with female genital organs ♀
AHA: 4Q, '06, 110
R39.8 Oth symptoms & signs involv genitourinary system `I-10`

✓4th **626 Disorders of menstruation and other abnormal bleeding from female genital tract**
EXCLUDES *menopausal and premenopausal bleeding (627.0)*
pain and other symptoms associated with menstrual cycle (625.2-625.4)
postmenopausal bleeding (627.1)

626.0 Absence of menstruation ♀
Amenorrhea (primary) (secondary)

626.1 Scanty or infrequent menstruation ♀
Hypomenorrhea   Oligomenorrhea

626.2 Excessive or frequent menstruation ♀
Heavy periods
Menometrorrhagia
Menorrhagia
Plymenorrhea
EXCLUDES *premenopausal (627.0)*
that in puberty (626.3)
N92.0 Excess & frequent menstruation w/regular cycle `I-10`

626.3 Puberty bleeding ♀
Excessive bleeding associated with onset of menstrual periods
Pubertal menorrhagia

626.4 Irregular menstrual cycle ♀
Irregular:
bleeding NOS
menstruation
periods

626.5 Ovulation bleeding ♀
Regular intermenstrual bleeding

626.6 Metrorrhagia ♀
Bleeding unrelated to menstrual cycle
Irregular intermenstrual bleeding

626.7 Postcoital bleeding ♀
DEF: Bleeding from vagina after sexual intercourse.

626.8 Other ♀
Dysfunctional or functional uterine hemorrhage NOS
Menstruation:
retained
suppression of
N92.5 Other specified irregular menstruation `I-10`

626.9 Unspecified ♀

✓4th **627 Menopausal and postmenopausal disorders**
EXCLUDES *asymptomatic age-related (natural) postmenopausal status (V49.81)*

627.0 Premenopausal menorrhagia ♀
Excessive bleeding associated with onset of menopause
Menorrhagia:
climacteric
menopausal
preclimacteric

627.1 Postmenopausal bleeding ♀
N95.0 Postmenopausal bleeding `I-10`

627.2 Symptomatic menopausal or female climacteric states ♀
Symptoms, such as flushing, sleeplessness, headache, lack of concentration, associated with the menopause

627.3 Postmenopausal atrophic vaginitis ♀
Senile (atrophic) vaginitis

627.4 Symptomatic states associated with artificial menopause ♀
Postartificial menopause syndromes
Any condition classifiable to 627.1, 627.2, or 627.3 which follows induced menopause
DEF: Conditions arising after hysterectomy.

627.8 Other specified menopausal and postmenopausal disorders ♀
EXCLUDES *premature menopause NOS (256.31)*

627.9 Unspecified menopausal and postmenopausal disorder ♀

✓4th **628 Infertility, female**
INCLUDES primary and secondary sterility
DEF: Infertility: inability to conceive for at least one year with regular intercourse.
DEF: Primary infertility: occurring in patients who have never conceived.
DEF: Secondary infertility: occurring in patients who have previously conceived.
AHA: 2Q, '96, 9; 1Q, '95, 7

628.0 Associated with anovulation
Anovulatory cycle
Use additional code for any associated Stein-Leventhal syndrome (256.4)

628.1 *Of pituitary-hypothalamic origin* ♀
Code first underlying cause, as:
adiposogenital dystrophy (253.8)
anterior pituitary disorder (253.0-253.4)

628.2 Of tubal origin ♀
Infertility associated with congenital anomaly of tube
Tubal:
block
occlusion
stenosis
Use additional code for any associated peritubal adhesions (614.6)

628.3 Of uterine origin ♀
Infertility associated with congenital anomaly of uterus
Nonimplantation
Use additional code for any associated tuberculous endometritis (016.7)

628.4 Of cervical or vaginal origin ♀
Infertility associated with:
anomaly of cervical mucus
congenital structural anomaly
dysmucorrhea

628.8 Of other specified origin ♀

628.9 Of unspecified origin ♀

✓4th **629 Other disorders of female genital organs**

629.0 Hematocele, female, not elsewhere classified
EXCLUDES *hematocele or hematoma:*
broad ligament (620.7)
fallopian tube (620.8)
that associated with ectopic pregnancy (633.00-633.91)
uterus (621.4)
vagina (623.6)
vulva (624.5)

629.1 Hydrocele, canal of Nuck
Cyst of canal of Nuck (acquired)
EXCLUDES *congenital (752.41)*

✓5th **629.2 Female genital mutilation status**
Female circumcision status
Female genital cutting
AHA: 4Q, '04, 88

629.20 Female genital mutilation status, unspecified ♀
Female genital cutting status, unspecified
Female genital mutilation status NOS

N Newborn Age: 0   P Pediatric Age: 0-17   M Maternity Age: 12-55   A Adult Age: 15-124   MCC Major CC Condition   CC CC Condition   HIV HIV Related Dx

218 – Volume 1   2010 ICD-9-CM

629.21 **Female genital mutilation Type I status**   ♀
Clitorectomy status
Female genital cutting Type I status
DEF: Female genital mutilation involving
clitorectomy, with part or all of the clitoris removed.

629.22 **Female genital mutilation Type II status**   ♀
Clitorectomy with excision of labia
minora status
Female genital cutting Type II status
DEF: Female genital mutilation involving clitoris and
the labia minora amputation.
AHA: 4Q, '04, 90

629.23 **Female genital mutilation Type III status**   ♀
Female genital cutting Type III status
Infibulation status
DEF: Female genital mutilation involving removal,
most or all of the labia minora excised, labia majora
incised which is then made into a hood of skin over
the urethral and vaginal opening.
AHA: 4Q, '04, 90

629.29 **Other female genital mutilation status**   ♀
Female genital cutting Type IV status
Female genital mutilation Type IV status
Other female genital cutting status
AHA: 4Q, '06, 97

√5ᵗʰ **629.8** **Other specified disorders of female genital organs**

629.81 **Habitual aborter without current pregnancy**   ♀
EXCLUDES   *habitual aborter with current
pregnancy (646.3)*
AHA: 4Q, '06, 98

629.89 **Other specified disorders of female genital organs**   ♀
AHA: 4Q, '06, 98

629.9 **Unspecified disorder of female genital organs**   ♀

Any condition that occurs during pregnancy, childbirth, or the puerperium is considered to be a complication unless the attending physician specifically documents that it neither affects the pregnancy nor is affected by the pregnancy. When the encounter is for a condition totally unrelated to the pregnancy - and the physician so documents - the code for the condition is listed first, V22.2 (pregnant state, incidental) assigned as an additional code.

Chapter 11 codes relate to the Mother only and are never assigned to the newborn's records.

11. COMPLICATIONS OF PREGNANCY, CHILDBIRTH, AND THE PUERPERIUM (630–679)

ECTOPIC AND MOLAR PREGNANCY (630–633)

Use additional code from category 639 to identify any complications

630 Hydatidiform mole   M♀

Trophoblastic disease NOS
Vesicular mole

> **EXCLUDES**   chorioadenoma (destruens) (236.1)
> chorionepithelioma (181)
> malignant hydatidiform mole (236.1)

DEF: Abnormal product of pregnancy; marked by mass of cysts resembling bunch of grapes due to chorionic villi proliferation, and dissolution; must be surgically removed.

631 Other abnormal product of conception   M♀

Blighted ovum   Mole:
Mole: fleshy
   NOS   stone
   carneous

632 Missed abortion   M♀

Early fetal death before completion of 22 weeks' gestation with retention of dead fetus
Retained products of conception, not following spontaneous or induced abortion or delivery

> **EXCLUDES**   failed induced abortion (638.0-638.9)
> fetal death (intrauterine) (late) (656.4)
> missed delivery (656.4)
> that with abnormal product of conception (630, 631)

AHA: 1Q, '01, 5

002.1 Missed abortion   I-10

√4th 633 Ectopic pregnancy

> **INCLUDES**   ruptured ectopic pregnancy

DEF: Fertilized egg develops outside uterus.
AHA: 4Q, '02, 61

√5th 633.0 Abdominal pregnancy

Intraperitoneal pregnancy

633.00 Abdominal pregnancy without intrauterine pregnancy   CC M♀
   CC Excl: 633.01, 633.11-633.91

633.01 Abdominal pregnancy with intrauterine pregnancy   CC M♀
   CC Excl: 633.00-633.91

√5th 633.1 Tubal pregnancy

Fallopian pregnancy
Rupture of (fallopian) tube due to pregnancy
Tubal abortion
AHA: 2Q, '90, 27

633.10 Tubal pregnancy without intrauterine pregnancy   CC M♀
   CC Excl: See code: 633.01

000.1 Tubal pregnancy   I-10

633.11 Tubal pregnancy with intrauterine pregnancy   CC M♀
   CC Excl: See code: 633.01

√5th 633.2 Ovarian pregnancy

633.20 Ovarian pregnancy without intrauterine pregnancy   CC M♀
   CC Excl: See code: 633.01

633.21 Ovarian pregnancy with intrauterine pregnancy   CC M♀
   CC Excl: See code: 633.01

√5th 633.8 Other ectopic pregnancy

Pregnancy: Pregnancy:
   cervical   intraligamentous
   combined   mesometric
   cornual   mural

633.80 Other ectopic pregnancy without intrauterine pregnancy   CC M♀
   CC Excl: See code: 633.01

633.81 Other ectopic pregnancy with intrauterine pregnancy   CC M♀
   CC Excl: See code: 633.01

√5th 633.9 Unspecified ectopic pregnancy

633.90 Unspecified ectopic pregnancy without intrauterine pregnancy   CC M♀
   CC Excl: See code: 633.01

633.91 Unspecified ectopic pregnancy with intrauterine pregnancy   CC M♀
   CC Excl: See code: 633.01

OTHER PREGNANCY WITH ABORTIVE OUTCOME (634–639)

The following fourth-digit subdivisions are for use with categories 634-638:

.0 Complicated by genital tract and pelvic infection

Endometritis
Salpingo-oophoritis
Sepsis NOS
Septicemia NOS

Any condition classifiable to 639.0 with condition classifiable to 634-638
   EXCLUDES urinary tract infection (634-638 with .7)

.1 Complicated by delayed or excessive hemorrhage

Afibrinogenemia
Defibrination syndrome
Intravascular hemolysis

Any condition classifiable to 639.1 with condition classifiable to 634-638

.2 Complicated by damage to pelvic organs and tissues

Laceration, perforation, or tear of:
   bladder
   uterus

Any condition classifiable to 639.2 with condition classifiable to 634-638

.3 Complicated by renal failure

Oliguria
Uremia

Any condition classifiable to 639.3, with condition classifiable to 634-638

.4 Complicated by metabolic disorder

Electrolyte imbalance with conditions classfiable to 634-638

.5 Complicated by shock

Circulatory collapse
Shock (postoperative) (septic)

Any condition classifiable to 639.5 with condition classifiable to 634-638

.6 Complicated by embolism

Embolism:
   NOS
   amniotic fluid
   pulmonary

Any condition classifiable to 639.6, with condition classifiable to 634-638

.7 With other specified complications

Cardiac arrest or failure
Urinary tract infection

Any condition classiable to 639.8 with condition classifiable to 634-638

.8 With unspecified complication
.9 Without mention of complication

Ectopic Pregnancy Sites

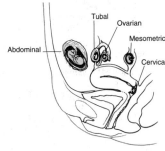

Tubal
Ovarian
Mesometric
Abdominal
Cervical

√4th Additional Digit Required   Unacceptable PDx   Manifestation Code   Hospital Acquired Condition   ►◄ Revised Text   ● New Code   ▲ Revised Code Title
√5th

2010 ICD-9-CM   **Volume 1 – 221**

Complications of Pregnancy, Childbirth & Puerperium

634–636.5

§ ✓4ᵗʰ **634 Spontaneous abortion**

Requires fifth digit. to identify stage:
- 0 unspecified
- 1 incomplete
- 2 complete

INCLUDES   miscarriage
            spontaneous abortion

DEF: Spontaneous premature expulsion of the products of conception from the uterus.

AHA: 2Q, '91, 16

§§ ✓5ᵗʰ **634.0 Complicated by genital tract and pelvic infection**   CC M♀
[0-2]
     CC Excl: 634.00-638.9, 640.00-641.23, 646.80-646.93, 648.90-649.64, 650, 669.40-669.44, 669.80-669.94, 679.00-679.04, 679.12, 679.14

§§ ✓5ᵗʰ **634.1 Complicated by delayed or excessive hemorrhage**   M♀
[0-2]
     AHA: For Code 634.11: 1Q, '03, 6

§§ ✓5ᵗʰ **634.2 Complicated by damage to pelvic organs or tissues**   CC M♀
[0-2]
     CC Excl: See code: 634.0

§§ ✓5ᵗʰ **634.3 Complicated by renal failure**   MCC M♀
[0-2]
     CC Excl: See code: 634.0

§§ ✓5ᵗʰ **634.4 Complicated by metabolic disorder**   CC M♀
[0-2]
     CC Excl: See code: 634.0

§§ ✓5ᵗʰ **634.5 Complicated by shock**   MCC M♀
[0-2]
     CC Excl: See code: 634.0

§§ ✓5ᵗʰ **634.6 Complicated by embolism**   MCC 1-2 CC 0 M♀
[0-2]
     CC Excl: See code: 634.0

§§ ✓5ᵗʰ **634.7 With other specified complications**   CC M♀
[0-2]
     CC Excl: See code: 634.0

§§ ✓5ᵗʰ **634.8 With unspecified complication**   CC M♀
[0-2]
     CC Excl: See code: 634.0

§§ ✓5ᵗʰ **634.9 Without mention of complication**   M♀
[0-2]

§ ✓4ᵗʰ **635 Legally induced abortion**

Requires fifth digit. to identify stage:
- 0 unspecified
- 1 incomplete
- 2 complete

INCLUDES   abortion or termination of pregnancy:
            elective
            legal
            therapeutic

EXCLUDES   *menstrual extraction or regulation (V25.3)*

DEF: Intentional expulsion of products of conception from uterus performed by medical professionals inside boundaries of law.

AHA: 2Q, '94, 14

§§ ✓5ᵗʰ **635.0 Complicated by genital tract and pelvic infection**   CC M♀
.[0-2]
     CC Excl: 634.00-635.02, 635.20-635.22, 635.70-638.9, 640.00-641.23, 646.80-646.93, 648.90-649.64, 650, 669.40-669.44, 669.80-669.94, 679.00-679.04, 679.12, 679.14

§§ ✓5ᵗʰ **635.1 Complicated by delayed or excessive hemorrhage**   M♀
[0-2]

§§ ✓5ᵗʰ **635.2 Complicated by damage to pelvic organs or tissues**   CC M♀
[0-2]
     CC Excl: For code 635.20: 634.00-638.9, 640.00-641.23, 646.80-646.93, 648.90-649.64, 650, 669.40-669.44, 669.80-669.94, 679.00-679.04, 679.12, 679.14; For code 635.21: 634.00-635.62, 638.5-638.9, 640.00-641.00; For code 635.22: 635.22

§§ ✓5ᵗʰ **635.3 Complicated by renal failure**   MCC M♀
[0-2]
     CC Excl: For code 635.30: 635.30-635.32; For code 635.31: 635.30-635.32, 637.11-638.9, 640.00-641.23, 646.80-646.93, 648.90-649.64, 650, 669.40-669.44, 669.80-669.94, 679.00-679.04, 679.12, 679.14; For code 635.32: 634.00-634.92, 635.30-635.32, 635.70-638.9, 640.00-641.23, 646.80-646.93, 648.90-649.64, 650, 669.40-669.44, 669.80-669.94, 679.00-679.04, 679.12, 679.144

§§ ✓5ᵗʰ **635.4 Complicated by metabolic disorder**   CC M♀
[0-2]
     CC Excl: 634.00-638.9, 640.00-641.23, 646.80-646.93, 648.90-649.64, 650, 669.40-669.44, 669.80-669.94, 679.00-679.04, 679.12, 679.14

§§ ✓5ᵗʰ **635.5 Complicated by shock**   MCC M♀
[0-2]
     CC Excl: 634.00-634.92, 635.50-635.52, 635.70-638.9, 640.00-641.23, 646.80-646.93, 648.90-649.64, 650, 669.40-669.44, 669.80-669.94, 679.00-679.04, 679.12, 679.14

§§ ✓5ᵗʰ **635.6 Complicated by embolism**   MCC M♀
[0-2]
     CC Excl: 634.00-634.92, 635.60-638.9, 640.00-641.23, 646.80-646.93, 648.90-649.64, 650, 669.40-669.44, 669.80-669.94, 679.00-679.04, 679.12, 679.14

§§ ✓5ᵗʰ **635.7 With other specified complications**   CC M♀
[0-2]
     CC Excl: 634.00-638.9, 640.00-641.23, 646.80-646.93, 648.90-649.64, 650, 669.40-669.44, 669.80-669.94, 679.00-679.04, 679.12, 679.14

§§ ✓5ᵗʰ **635.8 With unspecified complication**   CC M♀
[0-2]
     CC Excl: 634.00-638.9, 640.00-641.23, 646.80-646.93, 648.90-649.64, 650, 669.40-669.44, 669.80-669.94, 679.00-679.04, 679.12, 679.14

§§ ✓5ᵗʰ **635.9 Without mention of complication**   M♀
[0-2]
     AHA: For code 635.92: 2Q, '94, 14

§ ✓4ᵗʰ **636 Illegally induced abortion**

Requires fifth digit. to identify stage:
- 0 unspecified
- 1 incomplete
- 2 complete

INCLUDES   abortion:
            criminal
            illegal
            self-induced

DEF: Intentional expulsion of products of conception from uterus; outside boundaries of law.

§§ ✓5ᵗʰ **636.0 Complicated by genital tract and pelvic infection**   CC M♀
[0-2]
     CC Excl: 634.00-636.02, 636.70-638.9, 640.00-641.23, 646.80-646.93, 648.90-649.64, 650, 669.40-669.44, 669.80-669.94, 679.00-679.04, 679.12, 679.14

§§ ✓5ᵗʰ **636.1 Complicated by delayed or excessive hemorrhage**   M♀
[0-2]

§§ ✓5ᵗʰ **636.2 Complicated by damage to pelvic organs or tissues**   CC M♀
[0-2]
     CC Excl: 634.00-638.9, 640.00-641.23, 646.80-646.93, 648.90-649.64, 650, 669.40-669.44, 669.80-669.94, 679.00-679.04, 679.12, 679.14

§§ ✓5ᵗʰ **636.3 Complicated by renal failure**   MCC M♀
[0-2]
     CC Excl: 634.00-635.92, 636.30-636.32, 636.70-638.9, 640.00-641.23, 646.80-646.93, 648.90-649.64, 650, 669.40-669.44, 669.80-669.94, 679.00-679.04, 679.12, 679.14

§§ ✓5ᵗʰ **636.4 Complicated by metabolic disorder**   CC M♀
[0-2]
     CC Excl: 634.00-635.92, 636.30-636.32, 636.70-638.9, 640.00-641.23, 646.80-646.93, 648.90-649.64, 650, 669.40-669.44, 669.80-669.94, 679.00-679.04, 679.12, 679.14

§§ ✓5ᵗʰ **636.5 Complicated by shock**   MCC M♀
[0-2]
     CC Excl: For codes 636.50 and 636.51: 634.00-635.92, 636.50-636.52, 636.70-638.9, 640.00-641.23, 646.80-646.93, 648.90-649.64, 650, 669.40-669.44, 669.80-669.94, 679.00-679.04, 679.12, 679.14; For code 636.52: 634.00-635.92, 636.50-636.52, 636.70-636.92, 637.50-637.52, 637.70-637.92, 638.5, 638.7-638.9, 640.00-641.23, 646.80-646.93, 648.90-649.64, 650, 669.40-669.44, 669.80-669.94, 679.00-679.04, 679.12, 679.14

§   See beginning of section 634-639 for fourth-digit definitions.
§§   Requires fifth digit. Valid digits are in [brackets] under each code. See appropriate category for codes and definitions.

N Newborn Age: 0   P Pediatric Age: 0-17   M Maternity Age: 12-55   A Adult Age: 15-124   MCC Major CC Condition   CC CC Condition   HIV HIV Related Dx

§§ ✓5th **636.6 Complicated by embolism** `MCC` `M♀`
[0-2] CC Excl: 634.00-635.92, 636.60-638.9, 640.00-641.23, 646.80-646.93, 648.90-649.64, 650, 669.40-669.44, 669.80-669.94, 679.00-679.04, 679.12, 679.14

§§ ✓5th **636.7 With other specified complications** `CC` `M♀`
[0-2] CC Excl: 634.00-638.9, 640.00-641.23, 646.80-646.93, 648.90-649.64, 650, 669.40-669.44, 669.80-669.94, 679.00-679.04, 679.12, 679.14

§§ ✓5th **636.8 With unspecified complication** `CC` `M♀`
[0-2] CC Excl: See code: 636.2

§§ ✓5th **636.9 Without mention of complication** `M♀`
[0-2]

§ ✓4th **637 Unspecified abortion**

Requires fifth digit. to identify stage:
0 unspecified
1 incomplete
2 complete

INCLUDES abortion NOS
retained products of conception following abortion, not classifiable elsewhere

§§ ✓5th **637.0 Complicated by genital tract and pelvic infection** `CC` `M♀`
[0-2] CC Excl: 634.00-637.02, 637.70-638.9, 640.00-641.23, 646.80-646.93, 648.90-649.64, 650, 669.40-669.44, 669.80-669.94, 679.00-679.04, 679.12, 679.14

§§ ✓5th **637.1 Complicated by delayed or excessive hemorrhage** `M♀`
[0-2]

§§ ✓5th **637.2 Complicated by damage to pelvic organs or tissues** `CC` `M♀`
[0-2] CC Excl: 634.00-636.92, 637.30-637.32, 637.70-638.9, 640.00-641.23, 646.80-646.93, 648.90-649.64, 650, 669.40-669.44, 669.80-669.94, 679.00-679.04, 679.12, 679.14

§§ ✓5th **637.3 Complicated by renal failure** `MCC` `M♀`
[0-2] CC Excl: 634.00-636.92, 637.30-637.32, 637.70-638.9, 640.00-641.23, 646.80-646.93, 648.90-649.64, 650, 669.40-669.44, 669.80-669.94, 679.00-679.04, 679.12, 679.14

§§ ✓5th **637.4 Complicated by metabolic disorder** `CC` `M♀`
[0-2] CC Excl: See code: 637.2

§§ ✓5th **637.5 Complicated by shock** `MCC` `M♀`
[0-2] CC Excl: 634.00-636.92, 637.50-637.52, 637.70-638.9, 640.00-641.23, 646.80-646.93, 648.90-649.64, 650, 669.40-669.44, 669.80-669.94, 679.00-679.04, 679.12, 679.14

§§ ✓5th **637.6 Complicated by embolism** `MCC` `M♀`
[0-2] CC Excl: For codes 637.60 and 637.61: 634.00-636.92, 637.60-638.9, 640.00-641.23, 646.80-646.93, 648.90-649.64, 650, 669.40-669.44, 669.80-669.94, 679.00-679.04, 679.12, 679.14; For code 637.62: 634.00-636.92, 637.60-638.9, 640.00-641.23, 646.80-646.93, 648.90-649.64, 650, 669.40-669.44, 669.80-669.94, 679.00-679.04, 679.12, 679.14

§§ ✓5th **637.7 With other specified complications** `CC` `M♀`
[0-2] CC Excl: See code: 637.2

§§ ✓5th **637.8 With unspecified complication** `CC` `M♀`
[0-2] CC Excl: For codes 637.80 and 637.82: 634.00-638.9, 640.00-641.23, 646.80-646.93, 648.90-649.64, 650, 669.40-669.44, 669.80-669.94, 679.00-679.04, 679.12, 679.14; For code 637.81: 634.00-635.32, 635.41-638.9, 640.00-641.23, 646.80-646.93, 648.90-649.64, 650, 669.40-669.44, 669.80-669.94, 679.00-679.04, 679.12, 679.14

§§ ✓5th **637.9 Without mention of complication** `M♀`
[0-2]

§ ✓4th **638 Failed attempted abortion**
INCLUDES failure of attempted induction of (legal) abortion
EXCLUDES incomplete abortion (634.0-637.9)
DEF: Continued pregnancy despite an attempted legal abortion.

638.0 Complicated by genital tract and pelvic infection `CC` `M♀`
CC Excl: 634.00-638.0, 638.7-638.9, 640.00-641.23, 646.80-646.93, 648.90-649.64, 650, 669.40-669.44, 669.80-669.94, 679.00-679.04, 679.12, 679.14

638.1 Complicated by delayed or excessive hemorrhage `CC` `M♀`
CC Excl: 634.00-637.92, 638.1, 638.7-638.9, 640.00-641.23, 646.80-646.93, 648.90-649.64, 650, 669.40-669.44, 669.80-669.94, 679.00-679.04, 679.12, 679.14

638.2 Complicated by damage to pelvic organs or tissues `CC` `M♀`
CC Excl: 634.00-637.92, 638.2, 638.7-638.9, 640.00-641.23, 646.80-646.93, 648.90-649.64, 650, 669.40-669.44, 669.80-669.94, 679.00-679.04, 679.12, 679.14

638.3 Complicated by renal failure `MCC` `M♀`
CC Excl: 634.00-637.92, 638.3, 638.7-638.9, 640.00-641.23, 646.80-646.93, 648.90-649.64, 650, 669.40-669.44, 669.80-669.94, 679.00-679.04, 679.12, 679.14

638.4 Complicated by metabolic disorder `CC` `M♀`
CC Excl: 634.00-638.9, 640.00-641.23, 646.80-646.93, 648.90-649.64, 650, 669.40-669.44, 669.80-669.94, 679.00-679.04, 679.12, 679.14

638.5 Complicated by shock `MCC` `M♀`
CC Excl: 634.00-637.12, 637.21-637.92, 638.4-638.5, 638.7-638.9, 640.00-641.23, 646.80-646.93, 648.90-649.64, 650, 669.40-669.44, 669.80-669.94, 679.00-679.04, 679.12, 679.14

638.6 Complicated by embolism `MCC` `M♀`
CC Excl: 634.00-637.92, 638.6-638.9, 640.00-641.23, 646.80-646.93, 648.90-649.64, 650, 669.40-669.44, 669.80-669.94, 679.00-679.04, 679.12, 679.14

638.7 With other specified complications `CC` `M♀`
CC Excl: See code: 638.4

638.8 With unspecified complication `CC` `M♀`
CC Excl: See code: 638.4

638.9 Without mention of complication `M♀`

✓4th **639 Complications following abortion and ectopic and molar pregnancies**
Note: This category is provided for use when it is required to classify separately the complications classifiable to the fourth-digit level in categories 634-638; for example:
a) when the complication itself was responsible for an episode of medical care, the abortion, ectopic or molar pregnancy itself having been dealt with at a previous episode
b) when these conditions are immediate complications of ectopic or molar pregnancies classifiable to 630-633 where they cannot be identified at fourth-digit level.

639.0 Genital tract and pelvic infection `CC` `M♀`
Endometritis
Parametritis
Pelvic peritonitis } following conditions classifiable to 630-638
Salpingitis
Salpingo-oophoritis
Sepsis NOS
Septicemia NOS

EXCLUDES urinary tract infection (639.8)
CC Excl: 639.0, 639.2-641.23, 646.80-646.93, 648.90-649.64, 650, 669.40-669.44, 669.80-669.94, 679.00-679.04, 679.12, 679.14

639.1 Delayed or excessive hemorrhage `CC` `M♀`
Afibrinogenemia } following conditions classfiable to 630-638
Defibrination syndrome
Intravascular
CC Excl: 639.1-641.23, 646.80-646.93, 648.90-649.64, 650, 669.40-669.44, 669.80-669.94, 679.00-679.04, 679.12, 679.14

639.2 Damage to pelvic organs and tissues `CC` `M♀`
Laceration, perforation, or tear of:
bladder
bowel
broad ligament } following conditions classifiable to 630-638
cervix
periurethral tissue
uterus
vagina
CC Excl: 639.2-641.23, 646.80-646.93, 648.90-649.64, 650, 669.40-669.44, 669.80-669.94, 679.00-679.04, 679.12, 679.14

§ See beginning of section 634-639 for fourth-digit definitions.
§§ Requires fifth digit. Valid digits are in [brackets] under each code. See appropriate category for codes and definitions.

✓4th Additional Digit Required   Unacceptable PDx   Manifestation Code   Hospital Acquired Condition   ►◄ Revised Text   ● New Code   ▲ Revised Code Title
✓5th
2010 ICD-9-CM   **Volume 1 – 223**

▲

639.3 Kidney failure   `MCC` `M`♀
Oliguria
Renal ►(kidney)◄:
   failure (acute)
   shutdown   } following conditions
   tubular necrosis   } classifiable to 630-638
Uremia
CC Excl: See code: 639.2

639.4 Metabolic disorders   `CC` `M`♀
Electrolyte imbalance following conditions classifiable to
630-638
CC Excl: See code: 639.2

639.5 Shock   `MCC` `M`♀
Circulatory collapse   } following conditions
Shock (postoperative)   } classifiable to
  (septic)   } 630-638
CC Excl: See code: 639.2

639.6 Embolism   `MCC` `M`♀
Embolism:
  NOS
  air
  amniotic fluid
  blood-clot
  fat   } following conditions classifiable
  pulmonary   } to 630-638
  pyemic
  septic
  soap
CC Excl: See code: 639.2

639.8 Other specified complications following   `CC` `M`♀
abortion or ectopic and molar pregnancy
Acute yellow atrophy or
  necrosis of liver   } following conditons
Cardiac arrest or failure } classifiable to
Cerebral anoxia   } 630-638
Urinary tract infection
CC Excl: See code: 639.2

639.9 Unspecified complication following   `CC` `M`♀
abortion or ectopic and molar pregnancy
Complication(s) not further specified following conditions
classifiable to 630-638
CC Excl: See code: 639.2

Placenta Previa

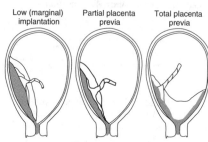

Low (marginal) implantation   Partial placenta previa   Total placenta previa

Abruptio Placentae

Partial separation (concealed bleeding)   Partial separation (apparent hemorrhage)   Complete separation (concealed hemorrhage)

COMPLICATIONS MAINLY RELATED TO PREGNANCY (640-649)

`INCLUDES`   the listed conditions even if they arose or were present during labor, delivery, or the puerperium

AHA: 2Q, '90, 11

The following fifth-digit subclassification is for use with categories 640-649 to denote the current episode of care. Valid fifth-digits are in [brackets] under each code.

  0 unspecified as to episode of care or not applicable
  1 <u>delivered</u>, with or without mention of antepartum condition
    Antepartum condition with delivery
    Delivery NOS (with mention of antepartum complication during current episode of care)
    Intrapartum obstetric condition (with mention of antepartum complication during current episode of care)
    Pregnancy, delivered (with mention of antepartum complication during current episode of care)
  2 <u>delivered</u>, with mention of postpartum complication *[handwritten: same admission as delivery]*
    Delivery with mention of puerperal complication during current episode of care
  3 <u>antepartum</u> condition or complication
    Antepartum obstetric condtion, <u>not delivered</u> during the current episode of care
  4 <u>postpartum</u> condition of complication *[handwritten: after discharge]*
    Postpartum or puerperal obstetric condition or complication following delivery that occurred:
      during previous episode of care
      outside hospital, with subsequent admission for observation or care

✓4ᵗʰ **640 Hemorrhage in early pregnancy**
  `INCLUDES`   hemorrhage before completion of 22 weeks' gestation

§ ✓5ᵗʰ **640.0 Threatened abortion**   `CC` `1,3` `M`♀
[0,1,3]   **DEF:** Bloody discharge during pregnancy; cervix may be dilated and pregnancy is threatened, but the pregnancy is not terminated.
  CC Excl: For codes **640.01 and 640.03:** 640.00-641.13, 646.80-646.93, 648.90-649.64, 650, 669.40-669.44, 669.80-669.94, 679.00-679.04, 679.12, 679.14

§ ✓5ᵗʰ **640.8 Other specified hemorrhage in early**   `M`♀
[0,1,3] **pregnancy**

§ ✓5ᵗʰ **640.9 Unspecified hemorrhage in early pregnancy**   `CC 3` `M`♀
[0,1,3]   **CC Excl:** For code **640.93:** 640.00-641.13, 646.80-646.93, 648.90-649.64, 650, 669.40-669.44, 669.80-669.94, 679.00-679.04, 679.12, 679.14

✓4ᵗʰ **641 Antepartum hemorrhage, abruptio placentae, and placenta previa**

§ ✓5ᵗʰ **641.0 Placenta previa without hemorrhage**   `CC 1,3` `M`♀
[0,1,3]   Low implantation of placenta
  Placenta previa noted: } without hemorrhage
    during pregnancy
    before labor (and delivered by caesarean delivery)
  DEF: Placenta implanted in lower segment of uterus; commonly causes hemorrhage in the last trimester of pregnancy.
  CC Excl: For codes **641.01 and 641.03:** 640.00-641.13, 646.80-646.93, 648.90-649.64, 650, 669.40-669.44, 669.80-669.94, 679.00-679.04, 679.12, 679.14

§ ✓5ᵗʰ **641.1 Hemorrhage from placenta previa**   `MCC 1,3` `M`♀
[0,1,3]   Low-lying placenta
  Placenta previa   } NOS or with hemorrhage
    incomplete   } (intrapartum)
    marginal
    partial
    total
  EXCLUDES   hemorrhage from vasa previa (663.5)
  CC Excl: For codes **641.11 and 641.13:** 640.00-641.13, 646.80-646.93, 648.90-649.64, 650, 669.40-669.44, 669.80-669.94, 679.00-679.04, 679.12, 679.14

---

§   Requires fifth digit. Valid digits are in [brackets] under each code. See beginning of section 640-649 for codes and definitions.

`N` Newborn Age: 0   `P` Pediatric Age: 0-17   `M` Maternity Age: 12-55   `A` Adult Age: 15-124   `MCC` Major CC Condition   `CC` CC Condition   `HIV` HIV Related Dx

Complications of Pregnancy, Childbirth & Puerperium

641.2–643.8

§ ✓5th **641.2 Premature separation of placenta** `MCC 1` `CC 3` M♀
[0,1,3]
    Ablatio placentae
    Abruptio placentae
    Accidental antepartum hemorrhage
    Couvelaire uterus
    Detachment of placenta (premature)
    Premature separation of normally implanted placenta

    DEF: Abruptio placentae: premature detachment of the placenta, characterized by shock, oliguria and decreased fibrinogen.

    CC Excl: For code 641.21: 640.00-641.13, 641.21, 646.80-646.93, 648.90-649.64, 650, 669.40-669.44, 669.80-669.94, 679.00-679.04, 679.12, 679.14; **For code 641.23:** 640.00-641.13, 641.23, 646.80-646.93, 648.90-649.64, 650, 669.40-669.44, 669.80-669.94, 679.00-679.04, 679.12, 679.14

    045.90 Premature sep of placenta unspec, uns trimester `I-10`

§ ✓5th **641.3 Antepartum hemorrhage associated** `MCC 1, 3` M♀
[0,1,3] **with coagulation defects**
    Antepartum or intrapartum hemorrhage associated with:
      afibrinogenemia
      hyperfibrinolysis
      hypofibrinogenemia

    EXCLUDES *coagulation defects not associated with antepartum hemorrhage (649.3)*

    DEF: Uterine hemorrhage prior to delivery.

    CC Excl: For codes 641.31 and 641.33: 641.30-641.93, 646.80-646.93, 648.90-649.64, 650, 669.40-669.44, 669.80-669.94, 679.00-679.04, 679.12, 679.14

§ ✓5th **641.8 Other antepartum hemorrhage** M♀
[0,1,3]
    Antepartum or intrapartum hemorrhage associated with:
      trauma
      uterine leiomyoma

§ ✓5th **641.9 Unspecified antepartum hemorrhage** M♀
[0,1,3]
    Hemorrhage: Hemorrhage:
      antepartum NOS   of pregnancy NOS
      intrapartum NOS

✓4th **642 Hypertension complicating pregnancy, childbirth, and the puerperium**

§ ✓5th **642.0 Benign essential hypertension** `CC 1-3` M♀
[0-4] **complicating pregnancy, childbirth, and the puerperium**

    Hypertension   ⎫ specified as complicating, or as
      benign essential   ⎪ reason for obstetric care
      chronic NOS   ⎬ during pregnancy,
      essential   ⎪ childbirth, or the
      pre-existing NOS   ⎭ puerperium

    CC Excl: For codes 642.01, 642.02, 642.03: 642.00-642.94, 646.10-646.14, 646.80-646.93, 648.90-649.64, 650, 669.40-669.44, 669.80-669.94, 679.00-679.04, 679.12, 679.14

    010.02 Pre-exist essential hypertension comp childbirth `I-10`

§ ✓5th **642.1 Hypertension secondary to renal** `MCC 1-2` `CC 3-4` ♀
[0-4] **disease, complicating pregnancy, childbirth, and the puerperium**
    Hypertension secondary to renal disease, specified as complicating, or as a reason for obstetric care during pregnancy, childbirth, or the puerperium

    CC Excl: For codes 642.11-642.14: See code: 642.01

§ ✓5th **642.2 Other pre-existing hypertension complicating** M♀
[0-4] **pregnancy, childbirth, and the puerperium**

    Hypertensive   ⎫ specified as complicating,
      chronic kidney disease   ⎪ or as a reason for
      heart and chronic   ⎪ obstetric care during
           kidney disease   ⎬ pregnancy,
      heart disease   ⎪ childbirth, or the
      Malignant hypertension   ⎭ puerperium

§ ✓5th **642.3 Transient hypertension of pregnancy** `CC 1-2` M♀
[0-4]
    Gestational hypertension
    Transient hypertension, so described, in pregnancy, childbirth, or the puerperium

    CC Excl: For codes 642.31, 642.32: See code: 642.01

    AHA: 3Q, '90, 4

    013.9 Gestatnl pg-inducd HTN w/o sig protnuria uns tri `I-10`

§ ✓5th **642.4 Mild or unspecified pre-eclampsia** `MCC 2` `CC 1, 3, 4`
[0-4]   M♀
    Hypertension in pregnancy, childbirth, or the puerperium, not specified as pre-existing, with either albuminuria or edema, or both; mild or unspecified
    Pre-eclampsia:
      NOS
      mild
    Toxemia (pre-eclamptic):
      NOS
      mild

    EXCLUDES *albuminuria in pregnancy, without mention of hypertension (646.2)*
                      edema in pregnancy, without mention of hypertension (646.1)

    CC Excl: For codes 642.41-642.44: See code: 642.01

    014.00 Mild pre-eclampsia unspecified trimester `I-10`

§ ✓5th **642.5 Severe pre-eclampsia** `MCC 1-4` M♀
[0-4]
    Hypertension in pregnancy, childbirth, or the puerperium, not specified as pre-existing, with either albuminuria or edema, or both; specified as severe
    Pre-eclampsia, severe
    Toxemia (pre-eclamptic), severe

    CC Excl: For codes 642.51-642.54: See code: 642.01

    AHA: N-D, '85, 3

§ ✓5th **642.6 Eclampsia** `MCC 1-4` M♀
[0-4]
    Toxemia:
      eclamptic
      with convulsions

    CC Excl: For codes 642.61-642.64: See code: 642.01

§ ✓5th **642.7 Pre-eclampsia or eclampsia** `MCC 1-4` M♀
[0-4] **superimposed on pre-existing hypertension**
    Conditions classifiable to 642.4-642.6, with conditions classifiable to 642.0-642.2

    CC Excl: For codes 642.71-642.74: See code: 642.01

§ ✓5th **642.9 Unspecified hypertension complicating** `CC 1-4` M♀
[0-4] **pregnancy, childbirth, or the puerperium**
    Hypertension NOS, without mention of albuminuria or edema, complicating pregnancy, childbirth, or the puerperium

    CC Excl: For codes 642.91, 642.92: 640.00-641.13, 646.80-646.93, 648.90-649.64, 650, 669.40-669.44, 669.80-669.94, 679.00-679.04, 679.12, 679.14; **For codes 642.93, 642.94:** 642.01-642.44, 642.61-642.94

    AHA: For code 642.94: ▶1Q, '09, 17◀

✓4th **643 Excessive vomiting in pregnancy**

    INCLUDES   hyperemesis   ⎫
                vomiting: ⎪
                   persistent   ⎬ arising during pregnancy
                   vicious   ⎪
              hyperemesis gravidarum   ⎭

§ ✓5th **643.0 Mild hyperemesis gravidarum** M♀
[0,1,3]
    Hyperemesis gravidarum, mild or unspecified, starting before the end of the 22nd week of gestation

    DEF: Treatment Site Detrimental vomiting and nausea.

§ ✓5th **643.1 Hyperemesis gravidarum with metabolic** M♀
[0,1,3] **disturbance**
    Hyperemesis gravidarum, starting before the end of the 22nd week of gestation, with metabolic disturbance, such as:
      carbohydrate depletion
      dehydration
      electrolyte imbalance

§ ✓5th **643.2 Late vomiting of pregnancy** M♀
[0,1,3]
    Excessive vomiting starting after 22 completed weeks of gestation

§ ✓5th **643.8 Other vomiting complicating pregnancy** M♀
[0,1,3]
    Vomiting due to organic disease or other cause, specified as complicating pregnancy, or as a reason for obstetric care during pregnancy
    Use additional code to specify cause

---

§   Requires fifth digit. Valid digits are in [brackets] under each code. See beginning of section 640-649 for codes and definitions.

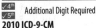

Complications of Pregnancy, Childbirth & Puerperium

643.9–647.4

§ ✓5ᵗʰ **643.9 Unspecified vomiting of pregnancy** M♀
[0,1,3] Vomiting as a reason for care during pregnancy, length of gestation unspecified

✓4ᵗʰ **644 Early or threatened labor**

§ ✓5ᵗʰ **644.0 Threatened premature labor** MCC 3 M♀
[0,3] Premature labor after 22 weeks, but before 37 completed weeks of gestation without delivery
EXCLUDES *that occurring before 22 completed weeks of gestation (640.0)*
CC Excl: For code 644.03: 644.00-644.21, 646.80-646.93, 648.90-649.64, 650, 669.40-669.44, 669.80-669.94, 679.00-679.04, 679.12, 679.14
060.00 Preterm labor without delivery unspec trimester I-10

§ ✓5ᵗʰ **644.1 Other threatened labor** CC 3 M♀
[0,3] False labor:
NOS
after 37 completed weeks of gestation } without delivery
Threatened labor NOS
CC Excl: For code 644.13: See code 644.03

§ ✓5ᵗʰ **644.2 Early onset of delivery** MCC 1 CC 0 M♀
[0,1] Onset (spontaneous) of delivery } before 37 completed weeks of gestation
Premature labor with onset of delivery
CC Excl: See code: 644.03
AHA: 2Q, '91, 16
TIP: Assign if an attempted termination of pregnancy results in a liveborn fetus.
060.14x0 Pt labor 3rd tri w/pt del 3rd tri not applic/uns I-10

✓4ᵗʰ **645 Late pregnancy**
AHA: 4Q, '00, 43; 4Q, '91, 26

§ ✓5ᵗʰ **645.1 Post term pregnancy** M♀
[0,1,3] Pregnancy over 40 completed weeks to 42 completed weeks gestation
048.0 Post-term pregnancy I-10

§ ✓5ᵗʰ **645.2 Prolonged pregnancy** M♀
[0,1,3] Pregnancy which has advanced beyond 42 completed weeks gestation

✓4ᵗʰ **646 Other complications of pregnancy, not elsewhere classified**
Use additional code(s) to further specify complication
AHA: 4Q, '95, 59

§ ✓5ᵗʰ **646.0 Papyraceous fetus** M♀
[0,1,3] **DEF:** Fetus that dies in the second trimester of pregnancy and is retained in the uterus, with subsequent atrophy and mummification; commonly occurs in twin pregnancy, nonviable fetus becomes compressed by growth of living twin.

§ ✓5ᵗʰ **646.1 Edema or excessive weight gain in** M♀
[0-4] **pregnancy, without mention of hypertension**
Gestational edema
Maternal obesity syndrome
EXCLUDES *that with mention of hypertension (642.0-642.9)*

§ ✓5ᵗʰ **646.2 Unspecified renal disease in** CC 1-4 M♀
[0-4] **pregnancy, without mention of hypertension**
Albuminuria } in pregnancy or the
Nephropathy NOS puerperium, without
Renal disease NOS mention of
Uremia hypertension
Gestational proteinuria
EXCLUDES *that with mention of hypertension (642.0-642.9)*
CC Excl: For codes 646.21- 646.24: 646.21-646.24

§ ✓5ᵗʰ **646.3 Habitual aborter** CC 1 M♀
[0,1,3] EXCLUDES *with current abortion (634.0-634.9)*
without current pregnancy (629.81)
DEF: Treatment Site Three or more consecutive spontaneous abortions.
CC Excl: For code 646.31: 646.31

§ ✓5ᵗʰ **646.4 Peripheral neuritis in pregnancy** M♀
[0-4]

§ ✓5ᵗʰ **646.5 Asymptomatic bacteriuria in pregnancy** M♀
[0-4]

§ ✓5ᵗʰ **646.6 Infections of genitourinary tract in** CC 1-4 M♀
[0-4] **pregnancy**
Conditions classifiable to 590, 595, 597, 599.0, 616 complicating pregnancy, childbirth, or the puerperium
Conditions classifiable to 614.0-614.5, 614.7-614.9, 615 complicating pregnancy or labor
EXCLUDES *major puerperal infection ▶(670.0-670.8)◀*
CC Excl: For code 646.61-646.64: 646.60-646.64, 646.80-646.93, 648.90-649.64, 650, 669.40-669.44, 669.80-669.94, 679.00-679.04, 679.12, 679.14
AHA: For code 646.63: 4Q, '04, 90
023.90 Unspec GU tract infection in pregnancy uns tri I-10

(handwritten note: Assign as additional codes)

§ ✓5ᵗʰ **646.7 Liver disorders in pregnancy** CC 1,3 M♀
[0,1,3] Acute yellow atrophy of liver (obstetric) (true) } of pregnancy
Icterus gravis
Necrosis of liver
EXCLUDES *hepatorenal syndrome following delivery (674.8)*
viral hepatitis (647.6)
CC Excl: For code 646.71, 646.73: 646.70-646.93, 648.90-649.64, 650, 669.40-669.44, 669.80-669.94, 679.00-679.04, 679.12, 679.14

§ ✓5ᵗʰ **646.8 Other specified complications of pregnancy** M♀
[0-4] Fatigue during pregnancy
Herpes gestationis
Insufficient weight gain of pregnancy
AHA: 3Q, '98, 16; J-F, '85, 15

§ ✓5ᵗʰ **646.9 Unspecified complication of pregnancy** M♀
[0,1,3]

✓4ᵗʰ **647 Infectious and parasitic conditions in the mother classifiable elsewhere, but complicating pregnancy, childbirth, or the puerperium**
INCLUDES the listed conditions when complicating the pregnant state, aggravated by the pregnancy, or when a main reason for obstetric care
EXCLUDES *those conditions in the mother known or suspected to have affected the fetus (655.0-655.9)*
Use additional code(s) to further specify complication

§ ✓5ᵗʰ **647.0 Syphilis** CC 1-4 ♀
[0-4] Conditions classifiable to 090-097
CC Excl: For code 647.01- 647.04: 646.81-647.24, 679.12, 679.14

§ ✓5ᵗʰ **647.1 Gonorrhea** CC 1-4 M♀
[0-4] Conditions classifiable to 098
CC Excl: For code 647.11-647.14: See code: 647.01

§ ✓5ᵗʰ **647.2 Other venereal diseases** CC 1-4 M♀
[0-4] Conditions classifiable to 099
CC Excl: For code 647.21-647.24: See code: 647.01

§ ✓5ᵗʰ **647.3 Tuberculosis** CC 1-4 M♀
[0-4] Conditions classifiable to 010-018
CC Excl: For code 647.31-647.34: 646.80-646.93, 647.30-647.34, 648.90-649.64, 650, 669.40-669.44, 669.80-669.94, 679.00-679.04, 679.12, 679.14

§ ✓5ᵗʰ **647.4 Malaria** CC 1-4 ♀
[0-4] Conditions classifiable to 084
CC Excl: For code 647.41-647.44: 646.80-646.93, 647.40-647.44, 648.90-649.64, 650, 669.40-669.44, 669.80-669.94, 679.00-679.04, 679.12, 679.14

§ Requires fifth digit. Valid digits are in [brackets] under each code. See beginning of section 640-649 for codes and definitions.

N Newborn Age: 0   P Pediatric Age: 0-17   M Maternity Age: 12-55   A Adult Age: 15-124   MCC Major CC Condition   CC CC Condition   HIV HIV Related Dx

Infants born to Diabetic mothers but does not display manifestation of diabetes should include with V30.xx the code V29.3 to indicate observation.

§ ✓5th **647.5 Rubella**   CC 1-4 M ♀
[0-4]   Conditions classifiable to 056
      CC Excl: For code 647.51-647.54: 647.51-647.94

§ ✓5th **647.6 Other viral diseases**   CC 1-4 M ♀
[0-4]   Conditions classifiable to 042, 050-055, 057-079, 795.05, 795.15, 796.75
      CC Excl: For code 647.61-647.64: See code 647.51
      AHA: J-F, '85, 15
      TIP: Assign when pregnant patient has any HIV-related condition or is stated to have an asymptomatic HIV infection.
      098.52 Other viral diseases complicating childbirth   I-10

§ ✓5th **647.8 Other specified infectious and parasitic diseases**   CC 1-4 M ♀
[0-4]   CC Excl: For code 647.81-647.84: See code 647.51

§ ✓5th **647.9 Unspecified infection or infestation**   CC 1-4 M ♀
[0-4]   CC Excl: For code 647.91-647.94: See code 647.51

✓4th **648 Other current conditions in the mother classifiable elsewhere, but complicating pregnancy, childbirth, or the puerperium**
     INCLUDES   the listed conditions when complicating the pregnant state, aggravated by the pregnancy, or when a main reason for obstetric care
     EXCLUDES   *those conditions in the mother known or suspected to have affected the fetus (655.0-655.9)*
     Use additional code(s) to identify the condition

§ ✓5th **648.0 Diabetes mellitus**   MCC 1-2 CC 0, 3, 4 M ♀
[0-4]   Conditions classifiable to 249, 250
     EXCLUDES   *gestational diabetes (648.8)*
      CC Excl: 646.80-646.93, 648.00-648.04, 648.90-649.64, 650, 669.40-669.44, 669.80-669.94, 679.00-679.04, 679.12, 679.14
      AHA: 3Q, '91, 5, 11
      024.32 Uns pre-existing diabetes mellitus in childbirth   I-10

additional codes from [?]9 or 250 fully [de]scribe patients [co]ndition. [V]58.67 - Insulin

§ ✓5th **648.1 Thyroid dysfunction**   M ♀
[0-4]   Conditions classifiable to 240-246

§ ✓5th **648.2 Anemia**   M ♀
[0-4]   Conditions classifiable to 280-285
      AHA: For Code 648.22: 1Q, '02, 14; For code 648.24: ▶1Q, '09, 17◀
      TIP: Assign with fifth digit 2 for postpartum anemia.
      099.013 Anemia complicating pregnancy third trimester   I-10

§ ✓5th **648.3 Drug dependence**   CC 1-4 M ♀
[0-4]   Conditions classifiable to 304
      CC Excl: For code 648.31-648.34: 646.80-646.93, 648.30-648.34, 648.90-649.64, 650, 669.40-669.44, 669.80-669.94, 679.00-679.04, 679.12, 679.14
      AHA: 2Q, '98, 13; 4Q, '88, 8

§ ✓5th **648.4 Mental disorders**   M ♀
[0-4]   Conditions classifiable to 290-303, 305.0, 305.2-305.9, 306-316, 317-319
      AHA: 2Q, '98, 13; 4Q, '95, 63
      099.314 Alcohol use complicating childbirth   I-10

§ ✓5th **648.5 Congenital cardiovascular disorders**   CC 1-4 M ♀
[0-4]   Conditions classifiable to 745-747
      CC Excl: For code 648.51, 648.52, 648.53, 648.54: 646.80-646.93, 648.50-648.64, 648.90-649.64, 650, 669.40-669.44, 669.80-669.94, 679.00-679.04, 679.12, 679.14

§ ✓5th **648.6 Other cardiovascular diseases**   CC 1-4 M ♀
[0-4]   Conditions classifiable to 390-398, 410-429
     EXCLUDES   *cerebrovascular disorders in the puerperium (674.0)*
         peripartum cardiomyopathy (674.5)
         venous complications (671.0-671.9)
      CC Excl: For code 648.61, 648.62, 648.63, 648.64: 646.80-646.93, 648.50-648.64, 648.90-649.64, 650, 669.40-669.44, 669.80-669.94, 679.00-679.04, 679.12, 679.14
      AHA: 3Q, '98, 11

§ ✓5th **648.7 Bone and joint disorders of back, pelvis, and lower limbs**   CC 1-4 M ♀
[0-4]   Conditions classifiable to 720-724, and those classifiable to 711-719 or 725-738, specified as affecting the lower limbs
      CC Excl: For code 648.71, 648.72, 648.73, 648.74: 648.71-648.74

§ ✓5th **648.8 Abnormal glucose tolerance**   M ♀
[0-4]   Conditions classifiable to 790.21-790.29
      <u>Gestational diabetes</u>
      Use additional code, if applicable, for associated long-term (current) insulin use (V58.67)
      DEF: Treatment Site Glucose intolerance arising in pregnancy, resolving at end of pregnancy.
      AHA: 3Q, '91, 5; For code 648.83: 4Q, '04, 56
      TIP: Do not assign if patient was diabetic before becoming pregnant; should never be assigned in combination with code 648.0X.
      024.429 Gestational diab mellitus childbirth uns cntrl   I-10

§ ✓5th **648.9 Other current conditions classifiable elsewhere**   M ♀
[0-4]   Conditions classifiable to 440-459, 795.01-795.04, 795.06, 795.10-795.14, 795.16, 796.70-796.74, 796.76
      Nutritional deficiencies [conditions classifiable to 260-269]
      AHA: 3Q, '06, 14; 4Q, '04, 88; N-D, '87, 10; For code 648.91: 1Q, '02, 14; For code 648.93: 4Q, '04, 90; For code 648.94: ▶1Q, '09, 17◀
      TIP: Assign for group B streptococcus carrier patients, along with code V02.51 Carrier or suspected carrier of infectious diseases.

✓4th **649 Other conditions or status of the mother complicating pregnancy, childbirth, or the puerperium**
      AHA: 4Q, '06, 99

§ ✓5th **649.0 Tobacco use disorder complicating pregnancy, childbirth, or the puerperium**   M ♀
[0-4]   Smoking complicating pregnancy, childbirth, or the puerperium
      AHA: 4Q, '06, 99
      099.334 Smoking tobacco complicating childbirth   I-10

§ ✓5th **649.1 Obesity complicating pregnancy, childbirth, or the puerperium**   M ♀
[0-4]   Use additional code to identify the obesity (278.00, 278.01)
      AHA: 4Q, '06, 99
      099.214 Obesity complicating childbirth   I-10

§ ✓5th **649.2 Bariatric surgery status complicating pregnancy, childbirth, or the puerperium**   M ♀
[0-4]   Gastric banding status complicating pregnancy, childbirth, or the puerperium
      Gastric bypass status for obesity complicating pregnancy, childbirth, or the puerperium
      Obesity surgery status complicating pregnancy, childbirth, or the puerperium
      AHA: 4Q, '06, 99, 118

§ ✓5th **649.3 Coagulation defects complicating pregnancy, childbirth, or the puerperium**   CC M ♀
[0-4]   Conditions classifiable to ▶286, 287, 289◀
      Use additional code to identify the specific coagulation defect ▶(286.0-286.9, 287.0-287.9, 289.0-289.9)◀
     EXCLUDES   *coagulation defects causing antepartum hemorrhage (641.3)*
         postpartum coagulation defects (666.3)
      CC Excl: For code 649.30: 648.90; For codes 649.31, 649.32, 649.33, 649.34: 648.91-648.94
      AHA: 4Q, '06, 99

§ ✓5th **649.4 Epilepsy complicating pregnancy, childbirth, or the puerperium**   CC 1-4 M ♀
[0-4]   Conditions classifiable to ▶286, 287, 289◀
      Use additional code to identify specific type of epilepsy (345.00-345.91)
     EXCLUDES   *eclampsia (642.6)*
      CC Excl: For codes 649.41, 649.42, 649.43, 649.44: 648.91-648.94
      AHA: 4Q, '06, 99

§   Requires fifth digit. Valid digits are in [brackets] under each code. See beginning of section 640-649 for codes and definitions.

| ✓4th ✓5th Additional Digit Required | Unacceptable PDx | Manifestation Code | Hospital Acquired Condition | ▶◀ Revised Text | ● New Code | ▲ Revised Code Title |

§ ✓5th **649.5 Spotting complicating pregnancy** M♀
[0,1,3] **EXCLUDES** antepartum hemorrhage (641.0-641.9)
hemorrhage in early pregnancy (640.0-640.9)
AHA: 4Q, '06, 99

§ ✓5th **649.6 Uterine size date discrepancy** M♀
[0-4] **EXCLUDES** suspected problem with fetal growth not found (V89.04)
AHA: 4Q, '06, 99

§ ✓5th **649.7 Cervical shortening** M CC ♀
[0,1,3] **EXCLUDES** suspected cervical shortening not found (V89.05)
DEF: A cervix that has shortened to < 25 mm in length by the 16th week of pregnancy; warning sign for impending premature delivery; treated by cervical cerclage placement or progesterone.
CC Excl: For codes 649.70, 649.71, 649.73: 649.70-649.73, 654.51-654.54
AHA: ▶4Q, '08, 124-125; **For Code 649.73:** 4Q '08, 125◀

NORMAL DELIVERY, AND OTHER INDICATIONS FOR CARE IN PREGNANCY, LABOR, AND DELIVERY (650-659)

The following fifth-digit subclassification is for use with categories 651-659 to denote the current episode of care. Valid fifth-digits are in [brackets] under each code.
0 unspecified as to episode of care or not applicable
1 delivered, with or without mention of antepartum condition
2 delivered, with mention of postpartum complication
3 antepartum condition or complication
4 postpartum condition or complication

650 Normal delivery M♀
Delivery requiring minimal or no assistance, with or without episiotomy, without fetal manipulation [e.g., rotation version] or instrumentation [forceps] of spontaneous, cephalic, vaginal, full-term, single, live-born infant. This code is for use as a single diagnosis code and is not to be used with any other code in the range 630-676.
Use additional code to indicate outcome of delivery (V27.0)
EXCLUDES breech delivery (assisted) (spontaneous) NOS (652.2)
delivery by vacuum extractor, forceps, cesarean section, or breech extraction, without specified complication (669.5-669.7)
AHA: 2Q, '02, 10; 3Q, '01, 12; 3Q, '00, 5; 4Q, '95, 28, 59
TIP: Code 650 is to be assigned only for the episode of care during which the patient delivers and may be assigned if the patient is admitted for induction of labor.
080 Encounter for full-term uncomplicated delivery I-10

Presentation at delivery can only be head or occipital. Terms ROA, LOA, ROP, LOP and vertex describe occipital presentation. Single birth only

✓4th **651 Multiple gestation**

§ ✓5th **651.0 Twin pregnancy** CC 1 M♀
[0,1,3] **EXCLUDES** fetal conjoined twins (678.1)
CC Excl: For code 651.01: 650-651.63, 651.71-652.20, 652.23-652.93
AHA: 3Q, '06, 16
030.009 Twin pregnancy unspecified, unspecified trimester I-10

§ ✓5th **651.1 Triplet pregnancy** CC 1,3 M♀
[0,1,3] **CC Excl: For code 651.11, 651.13:** 650-651.63, 651.71-652.93

§ ✓5th **651.2 Quadruplet pregnancy** CC 1,3 M♀
[0,1,3] **CC Excl: For code 651.21, 651.23:** See code 651.11

§ ✓5th **651.3 Twin pregnancy with fetal loss and** M♀
[0,1,3] **retention of one fetus**
Vanishing twin syndrome (651.33)

§ ✓5th **651.4 Triplet pregnancy with fetal loss and** CC 1,3 M♀
[0,1,3] **retention of one or more fetus(es)**
CC Excl: For code 651.41, 651.43: See code 651.11

§ ✓5th **651.5 Quadruplet pregnancy with fetal loss** CC 1,3 M♀
[0,1,3] **and retention of one or more fetus(es)**
CC Excl: For code 651.51, 651.53: See code 651.11

§ ✓5th **651.6 Other multiple pregnancy with fetal loss** M♀
[0,1,3] **and retention of one or more fetus(es)**

Malposition and Malpresentation

Breech | Shoulder (arm prolapse) | Mother's pelvis | Compound (extremity together with head) | Face (mentum) | Oblique

§ ✓5th **651.7 Multiple gestation following (elective)** M♀
[0,1,3] **fetal reduction**
Fetal reduction of multiple fetuses reduced to single fetus
AHA: 3Q, '06, 18; **For code 651.71:** 4Q, '05, 81

§ ✓5th **651.8 Other specified multiple gestation** CC 1,3 M♀
[0,1,3] **CC Excl: For code 651.81, 651.83:** See code 651.11

§ ✓5th **651.9 Unspecified multiple gestation** M♀
[0,1,3]

✓4th **652 Malposition and malpresentation of fetus**
Code first any associated obstructed labor (660.0)

§ ✓5th **652.0 Unstable lie** M♀
[0,1,3] **DEF:** Changing fetal position.

§ ✓5th **652.1 Breech or other malpresentation** M♀
[0,1,3] **successfully converted to cephalic presentation**
Cephalic version NOS

§ ✓5th **652.2 Breech presentation without mention of version** M♀
[0,1,3] Breech delivery (assisted) (spontaneous) NOS
Buttocks presentation
Complete breech
Frank breech
EXCLUDES footling presentation (652.8)
incomplete breech (652.8)
DEF: Fetal presentation of buttocks or feet at birth canal.
032.1xx0 Maternal care breech presentation not applic/uns I-10

§ ✓5th **652.3 Transverse or oblique presentation** M♀
[0,1,3] Oblique lie   Transverse lie
EXCLUDES transverse arrest of fetal head (660.3)

§ ✓5th **652.4 Face or brow presentation** M♀
[0,1,3] Mentum presentation

§ ✓5th **652.5 High head at term** M♀
[0,1,3] Failure of head to enter pelvic brim
032.4xx0 Maternal care high head at term not applic/uns I-10

§ ✓5th **652.6 Multiple gestation with malpresentation** M♀
[0,1,3] **of one fetus or more**

§ ✓5th **652.7 Prolapsed arm** M♀
[0,1,3]

§ ✓5th **652.8 Other specified malposition or** M♀
[0,1,3] **malpresentation**
Compound presentation

§ ✓5th **652.9 Unspecified malposition or** M♀
[0,1,3] **malpresentation**

✓4th **653 Disproportion**
Code first any associated obstructed labor (660.1)

§ ✓5th **653.0 Major abnormality of bony pelvis, not** M♀
[0,1,3] **further specified**
Pelvic deformity NOS

§ ✓5th **653.1 Generally contracted pelvis** M♀
[0,1,3] Contracted pelvis NOS

§ ✓5th **653.2 Inlet contraction of pelvis** M♀
[0,1,3] Inlet contraction (pelvis)

§ Requires fifth digit. Valid digits are in [brackets] under each code. See beginning of section 640-649 for codes and definitions.

N Newborn Age: 0   P Pediatric Age: 0-17   M Maternity Age: 12-55   A Adult Age: 15-124   MCC Major CC Condition   CC CC Condition   HIV HIV Related Dx

Cephalopelvic Disproportion

Pubic symphysis

Cephalopelvic disproportion due to: Contraction of pelvic inlet, or large fetus, or hydrocephalus

Ischial tuberosity

Contraction of pelvic outlet (from below)

Pubic symphysis

Pelvic inlet from above

§ ✓5th **653.3 Outlet contraction of pelvis** Ⓜ♀
[0,1,3]   Outlet contraction (pelvis)

§ ✓5th **653.4 Fetopelvic disproportion** Ⓜ♀
[0,1,3]   Cephalopelvic disproportion NOS
    Disproportion of mixed maternal and fetal origin, with normally formed fetus
    033.4xx0 Mtrn care dispropor mtrn&fetal orig not applic `I-10`

§ ✓5th **653.5 Unusually large fetus causing disproportion** Ⓜ♀
[0,1,3]   Disproportion of fetal origin with normally formed fetus
    Fetal disproportion NOS
    EXCLUDES that when the reason for medical care was concern for the fetus (656.6)

§ ✓5th **653.6 Hydrocephalic fetus causing disproportion** Ⓜ♀
[0,1,3]   **EXCLUDES** that when the reason for medical care was concern for the fetus (655.0)

§ ✓5th **653.7 Other fetal abnormality causing disproportion** Ⓜ♀
[0,1,3]   Fetal:
      ascites
      hydrops
      myelomeningocele
      sacral teratoma
      tumor
    EXCLUDES conjoined twins causing disproportion (678.1)

§ ✓5th **653.8 Disproportion of other origin** Ⓜ♀
[0,1,3]   **EXCLUDES** shoulder (girdle) dystocia (660.4)

§ ✓5th **653.9 Unspecified disproportion** Ⓜ♀
[0,1,3]

✓4th **654 Abnormality of organs and soft tissues of pelvis**
    INCLUDES the listed conditions during pregnancy, childbirth, or the puerperium
    Code first any associated obstructed labor (660.2)
    EXCLUDES trauma to perineum and vulva complicating current delivery (664.0-664.9)

§ ✓5th **654.0 Congenital abnormalities of uterus** Ⓜ♀
[0-4]   Double uterus
    Uterus bicornis

§ ✓5th **654.1 Tumors of body of uterus** Ⓜ♀
[0-4]   Uterine fibroids

§ ✓5th **654.2 Previous cesarean delivery** Ⓜ♀
[0,1,3]   Uterine scar from previous cesarean delivery
    AHA: 1Q, '92, 8
    034.21 Maternal care for scar from prev cesarean del `I-10`

§ ✓5th **654.3 Retroverted and incarcerated gravid uterus** Ⓜ♀
[0-4]   **DEF:** Treatment Site Retroverted: tilted back uterus; no change in angle of longitudinal axis.
    DEF: Treatment Site Incarcerated: immobile, fixed uterus.

§ ✓5th **654.4 Other abnormalities in shape or position of gravid uterus and of neighboring structures** Ⓜ♀
[0-4]   Cystocele
    Pelvic floor repair
    Pendulous abdomen
    Prolapse of gravid uterus
    Rectocele
    Rigid pelvic floor

§ ✓5th **654.5 Cervical incompetence** `MCC 1-4` Ⓜ♀
[0-4]   Presence of Shirodkar suture with or without mention of cervical incompetence
    DEF: Abnormal cervix; tendency to dilate in second trimester; causes premature fetal expulsion.
    DEF: Shirodkar suture: purse-string suture used to artificially close incompetent cervix.
    CC Excl: For code 654.51-654.54: 649.70-649.73, 654.51-654.54

§ ✓5th **654.6 Other congenital or acquired abnormality of cervix** Ⓜ♀
[0-4]   Cicatricial cervix
    Polyp of cervix
    Previous surgery to cervix
    Rigid cervix (uteri)
    Stenosis or stricture of cervix
    Tumor of cervix

§ ✓5th **654.7 Congenital or acquired abnormality of vagina** Ⓜ♀
[0-4]   Previous surgery to vagina
    Septate vagina
    Stenosis of vagina (acquired) (congenital)
    Stricture of vagina
    Tumor of vagina

§ ✓5th **654.8 Congenital or acquired abnormality of vulva** Ⓜ♀
[0-4]   Anal sphincter tear (healed) (old) complicating delivery
    Fibrosis of perineum
    Persistent hymen
    Previous surgery to perineum or vulva
    Rigid perineum
    Tumor of vulva
    EXCLUDES anal sphincter tear (healed) (old) not associated with delivery (569.43)
      varicose veins of vulva (671.1)
    AHA: 1Q, '03, 14

§ ✓5th **654.9 Other and unspecified** Ⓜ♀
[0-4]   Uterine scar NEC

✓4th **655 Known or suspected fetal abnormality affecting management of mother** – only
    INCLUDES the listed conditions in the fetus as a reason for observation or obstetrical care of the mother, or for termination of pregnancy
    AHA: 3Q, '90, 4
    TIP: Only assign when the fetal condition affects the management of the mother. Assign on mother's chart when in utero procedures are performed on the fetus.

§ ✓5th **655.0 Central nervous system malformation in fetus** Ⓜ♀
[0,1,3]   Fetal or suspected fetal:
      anencephaly
      hydrocephalus
      spina bifida (with myelomeningocele)

§ ✓5th **655.1 Chromosomal abnormality in fetus** Ⓜ♀
[0,1,3]

§ ✓5th **655.2 Hereditary disease in family possibly affecting fetus** Ⓜ♀
[0,1,3]

§ ✓5th **655.3 Suspected damage to fetus from viral disease in the mother** Ⓜ♀
[0,1,3]   Suspected damage to fetus from maternal rubella

§ ✓5th **655.4 Suspected damage to fetus from other disease in the mother** Ⓜ♀
[0,1,3]   Suspected damage to fetus from maternal:
      alcohol addiction
      listeriosis
      toxoplasmosis

§ ✓5th **655.5 Suspected damage to fetus from drugs** Ⓜ♀
[0,1,3]

§ ✓5th **655.6 Suspected damage to fetus from radiation** Ⓜ♀
[0,1,3]

§ ✓5th **655.7 Decreased fetal movements** Ⓜ♀
[0,1,3]   **AHA:** 4Q, '97, 41

§   Requires fifth digit. Valid digits are in [brackets] under each code. See beginning of section 640-649 for codes and definitions.

Complications of Pregnancy, Childbirth & Puerperium

655.8–659.2

§ ✓5ᵗʰ **655.8 Other known or suspected fetal**   M♀
[0,1,3] **abnormality, not elsewhere classified**
Suspected damage to fetus from:
     environmental toxins
     intrauterine contraceptive device
AHA: 3Q, '06, 16, 18

§ ✓5ᵗʰ **655.9 Unspecified**   M♀
[0,1,3]

✓4ᵗʰ **656 Other known or suspected fetal and placental problems**
affecting management of mother –only!
EXCLUDES *fetal hematologic conditions (678.0)*
suspected placental problems not found (V89.02)

§ ✓5ᵗʰ **656.0 Fetal-maternal hemorrhage**   M♀
[0,1,3] Leakage (microscopic) of fetal blood into maternal
     circulation

§ ✓5ᵗʰ **656.1 Rhesus isoimmunization**   CC 3 M♀
[0,1,3] Anti-D [Rh] antibodies
Rh incompatibility
DEF: Antibodies developing against Rh factor; mother with Rh
negative develops antibodies against Rh positive fetus.
CC Excl: For code 656.13: 656.11-656.13
036.0190 Mtrn care anti-D Rh antibods uns tri not applic   I-10

§ ✓5ᵗʰ **656.2 Isoimmunization from other and**   M♀
[0,1,3] **unspecified blood-group incompatibility**
ABO isoimmunization
AHA: 4Q, '06, 135

§ ✓5ᵗʰ **656.3 Fetal distress**   CC 1 M♀
[0,1,3] Fetal metabolic acidemia
EXCLUDES *abnormal fetal acid-base balance (656.8)*
abnormality in fetal heart rate or rhythm
(659.7)
fetal bradycardia (659.7)
fetal tachycardia (659.7)
meconium in liquor (656.8)
DEF: Life-threatening disorder; fetal anoxia, hemolytic disease
and other miscellaneous diseases cause fetal distress.
CC Excl: For code 656.31: 656.31-656.33, 659.71, 763.82
AHA: N-D, '86, 4

§ ✓5ᵗʰ **656.4 Intrauterine death**   CC 1,3 M♀
[0,1,3] Fetal death:
     NOS
     after completion of 22 weeks' gestation
     late
Missed delivery
EXCLUDES *missed abortion (632)*
CC Excl: For code 656.41: 656.41-656.43; **For code 656.43:** 656.43

§ ✓5ᵗʰ **656.5 Poor fetal growth**   CC 1 M♀
[0,1,3] "Light-for-dates"
"Placental insufficiency"
"Small-for-dates"
CC Excl: For code 656.51: 656.51-656.53
036.5190 Mtrn care known/spct placental insuff uns tri   I-10

§ ✓5ᵗʰ **656.6 Excessive fetal growth**   M♀
[0,1,3] "Large-for-dates"
036.60x0 Mtrn care excess fetl grwth uns tri not applic   I-10

§ ✓5ᵗʰ **656.7 Other placental conditions**   M♀
[0,1,3] Abnormal placenta
Placental infarct
EXCLUDES *placental polyp (674.4)*
placentitis (658.4)

§ ✓5ᵗʰ **656.8 Other specified fetal and placental**   M♀
[0,1,3] **problems**
Abnormal acid-base balance
Intrauterine acidosis
Lithopedian
Meconium in liquor
Subchorionic hematoma
DEF: Lithopedion: Calcified fetus; not expelled by mother.
036.20x0 Mtrn care hydrops fetalis uns tri not applic/uns   I-10

§ ✓5ᵗʰ **656.9 Unspecified fetal and placental problem**   M♀
[0,1,3]

✓4ᵗʰ **657 Polyhydramnios**   CC 1 M♀
[0,1,3]

§ ✓5ᵗʰ Use 0 as fourth-digit for this category
Hydramnios
EXCLUDES *suspected polyhydramnios not found (V89.01)*
DEF: Excess amniotic fluid.
CC Excl: For code 657.01: 657.01-657.03
AHA: 3Q, '06, 16; 4Q, '91, 26
040.9xx0 Polyhydraminos uns trimester not applicable/uns   I-10

✓4ᵗʰ **658 Other problems associated with amniotic cavity and**
membranes
EXCLUDES *amniotic fluid embolism (673.1)*
suspected problems with amniotic cavity and
membranes not found (V89.01)

§ ✓5ᵗʰ **658.0 Oligohydramnios**   CC 1,3 M♀
[0,1,3] Oligohydramnios without mention of
     rupture of membranes
DEF: Deficient amount of amniotic fluid.
CC Excl: For code 658.01, 658.03: 658.01-658.03
AHA: 3Q, '06, 16
041.00x0 Oligohydraminos uns trimester not   I-10
applicable/uns

§ ✓5ᵗʰ **658.1 Premature rupture of membranes**   M♀
[0,1,3] Rupture of amniotic sac less than 24
     hours prior to the onset of labor
AHA: For code 658.13: 1Q, '01, 5; 4Q, '98, 77
042.00 Prmat rom ool w/in 24 hrs of rup uns wks gestatn   I-10

§ ✓5ᵗʰ **658.2 Delayed delivery after spontaneous or**   M♀
[0,1,3] **unspecified rupture of membranes**
Prolonged rupture of membranes NOS
Rupture of amniotic sac 24 hours or more prior to the
     onset of labor

§ ✓5ᵗʰ **658.3 Delayed delivery after artificial rupture**   M♀
[0,1,3] **of membranes**

§ ✓5ᵗʰ **658.4 Infection of amniotic cavity**   MCC 1,3 M♀
[0,1,3] Amnionitis
Chorioamnionitis
Membranitis
Placentitis
CC Excl: For code 658.41, 658.43: 658.41-658.43
041.1090 Inf amniotic sac & memb uns, uns tri not   I-10
applic/uns

§ ✓5ᵗʰ **658.8 Other**   CC 1 M♀
[0,1,3] Amnion nodosum
Amniotic cyst
CC Excl: For code 658.81: 658.81

§ ✓5ᵗʰ **658.9 Unspecified**   M♀
[0,1,3]

✓4ᵗʰ **659 Other indications for care or intervention related to labor**
and delivery, not elsewhere classified

§ ✓5ᵗʰ **659.0 Failed mechanical induction**   M♀
[0,1,3] Failure of induction of labor by surgical
     or other instrumental methods

§ ✓5ᵗʰ **659.1 Failed medical or unspecified induction**   M♀
[0,1,3] Failed induction NOS
Failure of induction of labor by medical
     methods, such as oxytocic drugs
061.9 Failed induction of labor unspecified   I-10

§ ✓5ᵗʰ **659.2 Maternal pyrexia during labor,**   CC 1 M♀
[0,1,3] **unspecified**
DEF: Fever during labor.
CC Excl: For code 659.21: 659.21-659.23
075.2 Pyrexia during labor not elsewhereclassified   I-10

---

§   Requires fifth digit. Valid digits are in [brackets] under each code. See beginning of section 640-649 for codes and definitions.

N Newborn Age: 0   P Pediatric Age: 0-17   M Maternity Age: 12-55   A Adult Age: 15-124   MCC Major CC Condition   CC CC Condition   HIV HIV Related Dx

230 – Volume 1   2010 ICD-9-CM

§ ✓5ᵗʰ **659.3 Generalized infection during labor**   MCC 1,3   M♀
[0,1,3]   Septicemia during labor
   CC Excl: For code 659.31, 659.33: 646.80-646.93, 648.90-649.64, 650, 659.30-659.33, 669.40-669.44, 669.80-669.94, 679.00-679.04, 679.12, 679.14

§ ✓5ᵗʰ **659.4 Grand multiparity**   M♀
[0,1,3]   **EXCLUDES**   supervision only, in pregnancy (V23.3)
         without current pregnancy (V61.5)
   DEF: Having borne six or more children previously.

§ ✓5ᵗʰ **659.5 Elderly primigravida**   M♀
[0,1,3]   First pregnancy in a woman who will be 35 years of age or older at expected date of delivery
   EXCLUDES   supervision only, in pregnancy (V23.81)
   AHA: 3Q, '01, 12
   009.519 Supervisn of elderly primigravida uns trimester   I-10

§ ✓5ᵗʰ **659.6 Elderly multigravida**   M♀
[0,1,3]   Second or more pregnancy in a woman who will be 35 years of age or older at expected date of delivery
   EXCLUDES   elderly primigravida 659.5
         supervision only, in pregnancy (V23.82)
   AHA: 3Q, '01, 12
   009.529 Supervisn of elderly multigravida uns trimester   I-10

§ ✓5ᵗʰ **659.7 Abnormality in fetal heart rate or rhythm**   M♀
[0,1,3]   Depressed fetal heart tones
   Fetal:
     bradycardia
     tachycardia
   Fetal heart rate decelerations
   Non-reassuring fetal heart rate or rhythm
   AHA: 4Q, '98, 48
   076 Abn in fetal heart rate & rhythm comp L&D   I-10

§ ✓5ᵗʰ **659.8 Other specified indications for care or intervention related to labor and delivery**   M♀
[0,1,3]   Pregnancy in a female less than 16 years old at expected date of delivery
   Very young maternal age
   AHA: 3Q, '01, 12

§ ✓5ᵗʰ **659.9 Unspecified indication for care or intervention related to labor and delivery**   M♀
[0,1,3]

COMPLICATIONS OCCURRING MAINLY IN THE COURSE OF LABOR AND DELIVERY (660-669)

The following fifth-digit subclassification is for use with categories 660-669 to denote the current episode of care. Valid fifth-digits are in [brackets] under each code.
   0 unspecified as to episode of care or not applicable
   1 delivered, with or without mention of antepartum condition
   2 delivered, with mention of postpartum complication
   3 antepartum condition or complication
   4 postpartum condition or complication

✓4ᵗʰ **660 Obstructed labor**
   AHA: 3Q, '95, 10

§ ✓5ᵗʰ **660.0 Obstruction caused by malposition of fetus at onset of labor**   CC 3   M♀
[0,1,3]   Any condition classifiable to 652, causing obstruction during labor
   Use additional code from 652.0-652.9 to identify condition
   CC Excl: For code 660.03: 646.80-646.93, 648.90-649.64, 650, 655.70-655.73, 660.03, 665.00-665.11, 665.50-665.54, 665.80-665.94, 669.40-669.44, 669.80-669.94, 679.00-679.04, 679.12, 679.14

§ ✓5ᵗʰ **660.1 Obstruction by bony pelvis**   M♀
[0,1,3]   Any condition classifiable to 653, causing obstruction during labor
   Use additional code from 653.0-653.9 to identify condition

§ ✓5ᵗʰ **660.2 Obstruction by abnormal pelvic soft tissues**   M♀
[0,1,3]   Prolapse of anterior lip of cervix
   Any condition classifiable to 654, causing obstruction during labor
   Use additional code from 654.0-654.9 to identify condition

§ ✓5ᵗʰ **660.3 Deep transverse arrest and persistent occipitoposterior position**   M♀
[0,1,3]   **064.0xx0** Obst labor incpl rotat of fetal head not applic   I-10

§ ✓5ᵗʰ **660.4 Shoulder (girdle) dystocia**   M♀
[0,1,3]   Impacted shoulders
   DEF: Obstructed labor due to impacted fetal shoulders.
   066.0 Obstructed labor due to shoulder dystocia   I-10

§ ✓5ᵗʰ **660.5 Locked twins**   M♀
[0,1,3]

§ ✓5ᵗʰ **660.6 Failed trial of labor, unspecified**   M♀
[0,1,3]   Failed trial of labor, without mention of condition or suspected condition

§ ✓5ᵗʰ **660.7 Failed forceps or vacuum extractor, unspecified**   M♀
[0,1,3]   Application of ventouse or forceps, without mention of condition

§ ✓5ᵗʰ **660.8 Other causes of obstructed labor**   M♀
[0,1,3]   Use additional code to identify condition
   AHA: 4Q, '04, 88

§ ✓5ᵗʰ **660.9 Unspecified obstructed labor**   M♀
[0,1,3]   Dystocia:
     NOS
     fetal NOS
     maternal NOS

✓4ᵗʰ **661 Abnormality of forces of labor**

§ ✓5ᵗʰ **661.0 Primary uterine inertia**   M♀
[0,1,3]   Failure of cervical dilation
   Hypotonic uterine dysfunction, primary
   Prolonged latent phase of labor
   DEF: Lack of efficient contractions during labor causing prolonged labor.
   062.0 Primary inadequate contractions   I-10

§ ✓5ᵗʰ **661.1 Secondary uterine inertia**   M♀
[0,1,3]   Arrested active phase of labor
   Hypotonic uterine dysfunction, secondary
   062.1 Secondary uterine inertia   I-10

§ ✓5ᵗʰ **661.2 Other and unspecified uterine inertia**   M♀
[0,1,3]   Atony of uterus without hemorrhage
   Desultory labor
   Irregular labor
   Poor contractions
   Slow slope active phase of labor
   EXCLUDES   atony of uterus with hemorrhage (666.1)
         postpartum atony of uterus without hemorrhage (669.8)

[handwritten: Failure of the uterine muscle to contract adequately after the delivery.]

§ ✓5ᵗʰ **661.3 Precipitate labor**   M♀
[0,1,3]   **DEF:** Rapid labor and delivery.

§ ✓5ᵗʰ **661.4 Hypertonic, incoordinate, or prolonged uterine contractions**   M♀
[0,1,3]   Cervical spasm
   Contraction ring (dystocia)
   Dyscoordinate labor
   Hourglass contraction of uterus
   Hypertonic uterine dysfunction
   Incoordinate uterine action
   Retraction ring (Bandl's) (pathological)
   Tetanic contractions
   Uterine dystocia NOS
   Uterine spasm

§ ✓5ᵗʰ **661.9 Unspecified abnormality of labor**   M♀
[0,1,3]

§   Requires fifth digit. Valid digits are in [brackets] under each code. See beginning of section 640-649 for codes and definitions.

✓4ᵗʰ / ✓5ᵗʰ   Additional Digit Required   Unacceptable PDx   Manifestation Code   Hospital Acquired Condition   ►◄ Revised Text   ● New Code   ▲ Revised Code Title

2010 ICD-9-CM   **Volume 1 – 231**

Complications of Pregnancy, Childbirth & Puerperium

662–665.2

Perineal Lacerations

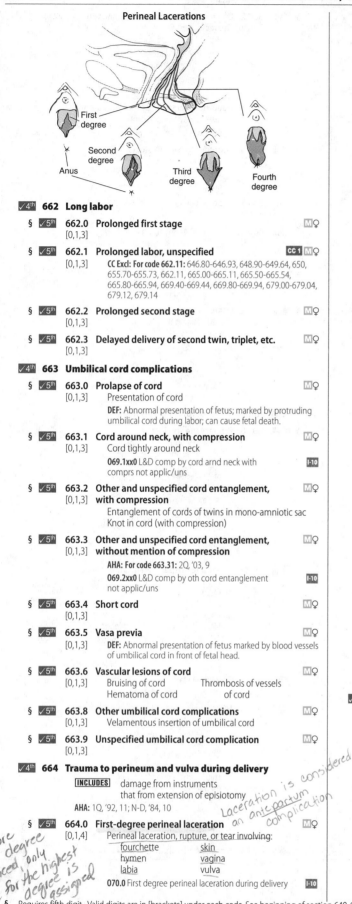

✓4th **662** **Long labor**

§ ✓5th **662.0** **Prolonged first stage**   M♀
[0,1,3]

§ ✓5th **662.1** **Prolonged labor, unspecified**   CC 1 M♀
[0,1,3]   CC Excl: For code 662.11: 646.80-646.93, 648.90-649.64, 650,
      655.70-655.73, 662.11, 665.00-665.11, 665.50-665.54,
      665.80-665.94, 669.40-669.44, 669.80-669.94, 679.00-679.04,
      679.12, 679.14

§ ✓5th **662.2** **Prolonged second stage**   M♀
[0,1,3]

§ ✓5th **662.3** **Delayed delivery of second twin, triplet, etc.**   M♀
[0,1,3]

✓4th **663** **Umbilical cord complications**

§ ✓5th **663.0** **Prolapse of cord**   M♀
[0,1,3]   Presentation of cord
     DEF: Abnormal presentation of fetus; marked by protruding
     umbilical cord during labor; can cause fetal death.

§ ✓5th **663.1** **Cord around neck, with compression**   M♀
[0,1,3]   Cord tightly around neck

     069.1xx0 L&D comp by cord arnd neck with   I-10
     comprs not applic/uns

§ ✓5th **663.2** **Other and unspecified cord entanglement,**   M♀
[0,1,3] **with compression**
     Entanglement of cords of twins in mono-amniotic sac
     Knot in cord (with compression)

§ ✓5th **663.3** **Other and unspecified cord entanglement,**   M♀
[0,1,3] **without mention of compression**
     AHA: For code 663.31: 2Q, '03, 9

     069.2xx0 L&D comp by oth cord entanglement   I-10
     not applic/uns

§ ✓5th **663.4** **Short cord**   M♀
[0,1,3]

§ ✓5th **663.5** **Vasa previa**   M♀
[0,1,3]   **DEF:** Abnormal presentation of fetus marked by blood vessels
     of umbilical cord in front of fetal head.

§ ✓5th **663.6** **Vascular lesions of cord**   M♀
[0,1,3]   Bruising of cord   Thrombosis of vessels
     Hematoma of cord   of cord

§ ✓5th **663.8** **Other umbilical cord complications**   M♀
[0,1,3]   Velamentous insertion of umbilical cord

§ ✓5th **663.9** **Unspecified umbilical cord complication**   M♀
[0,1,3]

✓4th **664** **Trauma to perineum and vulva during delivery**
   INCLUDES damage from instruments
      that from extension of episiotomy
   AHA: 1Q, '92, 11; N-D, '84, 10

§ ✓5th **664.0** **First-degree perineal laceration**   M♀
[0,1,4]   Perineal laceration, rupture, or tear involving:
     fourchette   skin
     hymen   vagina
     labia   vulva

     070.0 First degree perineal laceration during delivery   I-10

(handwritten note: When more than one degree is referenced only the code for the highest degree is assigned)

§ ✓5th **664.1** **Second-degree perineal laceration**   M♀
[0,1,4]   Perineal laceration, rupture, or tear (following episiotomy)
     involving:
     pelvic floor
     perineal muscles
     vaginal muscles
     EXCLUDES *that involving anal sphincter (664.2)*
     AHA: For code 664.11: ▶4Q, '08, 192◀
     070.1 Second degree perineal laceration dur delivery   I-10

§ ✓5th **664.2** **Third-degree perineal laceration**   CC 1 M♀
[0,1,4]   Perineal laceration, rupture, or tear
     (following episiotomy) involving:
     anal sphincter
     rectovaginal septum
     sphincter NOS
     EXCLUDES *anal sphincter tear during delivery not*
       associated with third-degree perineal
       laceration (664.6)
       that with anal or rectal mucosal laceration
       (664.3)
     CC Excl: For code 664.21: 646.80-646.93, 648.90-649.64, 650,
      655.70-655.73, 664.21, 664.61, 665.00-665.11, 665.50-665.54,
      665.80- 665.94, 669.40-669.44, 669.80-669.94, 679.00-679.04,
      679.12, 679.14
     070.2 Third degree perineal laceration during delivery   I-10

§ ✓5th **664.3** **Fourth-degree perineal laceration**   CC 1 M♀
[0,1,4]   Perineal laceration, rupture, or tear as
     classifiable to 664.2 and involving also:
     anal mucosa
     rectal mucosa
     CC Excl: For code 664.31: 646.80-646.93, 648.90-649.64, 650,
      655.70-655.73, 664.31, 665.00-665.11, 665.50-665.54,
      665.80-665.94, 669.40-669.44, 669.80-669.94, 679.00-679.04,
      679.12, 679.14

§ ✓5th **664.4** **Unspecified perineal laceration**   M♀
[0,1,4]   Central laceration
     AHA: 1Q, '92, 8

§ ✓5th **664.5** **Vulval and perineal hematoma**   M♀
[0,1,4]   **AHA:** N-D, '84, 10

§ ✓5th **664.6** **Anal sphincter tear complicating delivery,**   CC 1,4
[0,1,4] **not associated with third-degree perineal**   M♀
   laceration
     EXCLUDES *third-degree perineal laceration (664.2)*
     CC Excl: For code 664.61, 664.64: 646.80-646.93, 648.90-649.64,
      650, 655.70-655.73, 664.21, 664.60-664.64, 665.00-665.11,
      665.50-665.54, 665.80-665.94, 669.40-669.44, 669.80-669.94,
      679.00-679.04, 679.12, 679.14
     AHA: For code 664.61: 4Q, '07, 88, 90

§ ✓5th **664.8** **Other specified trauma to perineum**   M♀
[0,1,4] **and vulva**
     AHA: For code 664.81: 4Q, '07, 125
     TIP: Assign when documentation indicates periurethral lacer-
     ation only.

§ ✓5th **664.9** **Unspecified trauma to perineum and vulva**   M♀
[0,1,4]

✓4th **665** **Other obstetrical trauma**
   INCLUDES damage from instruments

§ ✓5th **665.0** **Rupture of uterus before onset of**   MCC 1,3 M♀
[0,1,3] **labor**
     CC Excl: For code 665.01, 665.03: 646.80-646.93, 648.90-649.64,
      650, 655.70-655.73, 665.00-665.11, 665.50-665.54,
      665.80-665.94, 669.40-669.44, 669.80-669.94, 679.00-679.04,
      679.12, 679.14

§ ✓5th **665.1** **Rupture of uterus during labor**   MCC 1 M♀
[0,1]   Rupture of uterus NOS
     CC Excl: For code 665.11: See code 665.01

§ ✓5th **665.2** **Inversion of uterus**   CC 2 M♀
[0,2,4]   CC Excl: For code 665.22: 646.80-646.93, 648.90-649.64, 650,
      655.70-655.73, 665.00-665.11, 665.22, 665.50-665.54,
      665.80-665.94, 669.40-669.44, 669.80-669.94, 679.00-679.04,
      679.12, 679.14

(handwritten note: Laceration is considered an antepartum complication)

§   Requires fifth digit. Valid digits are in [brackets] under each code. See beginning of section 640-649 for codes and definitions.

N Newborn Age: 0   P Pediatric Age: 0-17   M Maternity Age: 12-55   A Adult Age: 15-124   MCC Major CC Condition   CC CC Condition   HIV HIV Related Dx

232 – Volume 1 · February 2009   2010 ICD-9-CM

§ ✓5ᵗʰ **665.3 Laceration of cervix**   CC 1 M ♀
[0,1,4]
   CC Excl: For code 665.31: 646.80-646.93, 648.90-649.64, 650, 655.70-655.73, 665.00-665.11, 665.31, 665.50-665.54, 665.80-665.94, 669.40-669.44, 669.80-669.94, 679.00-679.04, 679.12, 679.14

§ ✓5ᵗʰ **665.4 High vaginal laceration**   CC 1 M ♀
[0,1,4]
   Laceration of vaginal wall or sulcus without mention of perineal laceration
   CC Excl: For code 665.41: 646.80-646.93, 648.90-649.64, 650, 655.70-655.73, 665.00-665.11, 665.41, 665.50-665.54, 665.80-665.94, 669.40-669.44, 669.80-669.94, 679.00-679.04, 679.12, 679.14
   071.4 Obstetric high vaginal laceration alone   I-10

§ ✓5ᵗʰ **665.5 Other injury to pelvic organs**   CC 1 M ♀
[0,1,4]
   Injury to:
     bladder
     urethra
   CC Excl: For code 665.51: See code 665.01
   AHA: M-A, '87, 10
   071.5 Other obstetric injury to pelvic organs   I-10

§ ✓5ᵗʰ **665.6 Damage to pelvic joints and ligaments**   CC 1 M ♀
[0,1,4]
   Avulsion of inner symphyseal cartilage
   Damage to coccyx
   Separation of symphysis (pubis)
   CC Excl: For code 665.61: 646.80-646.93, 648.90-649.64, 650, 655.70-655.73, 665.00-665.11, 665.50-665.54, 665.61, 665.80-665.94, 669.40-669.44, 669.80-669.94, 679.00-679.04, 679.12, 679.14
   AHA: N-D, '84, 12

§ ✓5ᵗʰ **665.7 Pelvic hematoma**   CC 1-2 M ♀
[0,1,2,4]
   Hematoma of vagina
   CC Excl: For code 665.71: 646.80-646.93, 648.90-649.64, 650, 655.70-655.73, 665.00-665.11, 665.50-665.54, 665.71, 665.80-665.94, 669.40-669.44, 669.80-669.94, 679.00-679.04, 679.12, 679.14; **For code 665.72:** 646.80-646.93, 648.90-649.64, 650, 655.70-655.73, 665.00-665.11, 665.50-665.54, 665.72, 665.80-665.94, 669.40-669.44, 669.80-669.94, 679.00-679.04, 679.12, 679.14

§ ✓5ᵗʰ **665.8 Other specified obstetrical trauma**   M ♀
[0-4]

§ ✓5ᵗʰ **665.9 Unspecified obstetrical trauma**   M ♀
[0-4]

✓4ᵗʰ **666 Postpartum hemorrhage**
   AHA: 1Q, '88, 14

§ ✓5ᵗʰ **666.0 Third-stage hemorrhage**   CC 2,4 ♀
[0,2,4]
   Hemorrhage associated with retained, trapped, or adherent placenta
   Retained placenta NOS
   CC Excl: For code 666.02: 646.80-646.93, 648.90-649.64, 650, 655.70-655.73, 665.00-665.11, 665.50-665.54, 665.80-665.94, 666.02, 669.40-669.44, 669.80-669.94, 679.00-679.04, 679.12, 679.14; **For code 666.04:** 646.80-646.93, 648.90-649.64, 650, 655.70-655.73, 665.00-665.11, 665.50-665.54, 665.80-665.94, 666.04, 669.40-669.44, 669.80-669.94, 679.00-679.04, 679.12, 679.14

§ ✓5ᵗʰ **666.1 Other immediate postpartum hemorrhage**   CC 2,4 M ♀
[0,2,4]
   Atony of uterus with hemorrhage
   Hemorrhage within the first 24 hours following delivery of placenta
   Postpartum atony of uterus with hemorrhage
   Postpartum hemorrhage (atonic) NOS
   EXCLUDES atony of uterus without hemorrhage (661.2)
     postpartum atony of uterus without hemorrhage (669.8)
   CC Excl: For code 666.12: 646.80-646.93, 648.90-649.64, 650, 655.70-655.73, 665.00-665.11, 665.50-665.54, 665.80- 665.94, 666.12, 669.40-669.44, 669.80-669.94, 679.00-679.04, 679.12, 679.14; **For code 666.14:** 666.10-666.14
   072.1 Other immediate postpartum hemorrhage   I-10

[handwritten: w/o hemorrhage 661.2]

§ ✓5ᵗʰ **666.2 Delayed and secondary postpartum**   CC 2,4 M ♀
[0,2,4] **hemorrhage**
   Hemorrhage:
     after the first 24 hours following delivery
     associated with retained portions of placenta or membranes
   Postpartum hemorrhage specified as delayed or secondary
   Retained products of conception NOS, following delivery
   CC Excl: For code 666.22: 646.80-646.93, 648.90-649.64, 650, 655.70-655.73, 665.00-665.11, 665.50-665.54, 665.80- 665.94, 666.22, 669.40-669.44, 669.80-669.94, 679.00-679.04, 679.12, 679.14; **For code 666.24:** 666.20-666.24

§ ✓5ᵗʰ **666.3 Postpartum coagulation defects**   CC 2 M ♀
[0,2,4]
   Postpartum:
     afibrinogenemia
     fibrinolysis
   CC Excl: For code 666.32: 646.80-646.93, 648.90-649.64, 650, 666.00-666.34, 669.40-669.44, 669.80-669.94, 679.00-679.04, 679.12, 679.14

✓4ᵗʰ **667 Retained placenta or membranes, without hemorrhage**
   DEF: Postpartum condition resulting from failure to expel placental membrane tissues due to failed contractions of uterine wall.
   AHA: 1Q, '88, 14
   TIP: A retained placenta is one that has not separated or been expelled within one hour after completion of the second stage of labor (birth of the fetus).

§ ✓5ᵗʰ **667.0 Retained placenta without hemorrhage**   M ♀
[0,2,4]
   Placenta accreta
   Retained placenta: } without hemorrhage
     NOS
     total
   073.0 Retained placenta without hemorrhage   I-10

§ ✓5ᵗʰ **667.1 Retained portions of placenta or membranes,**   M ♀
[0,2,4] **without hemorrhage**
   Retained products of conception following delivery, without hemorrhage

✓4ᵗʰ **668 Complications of the administration of anesthetic or other sedation in labor and delivery**
   INCLUDES complications arising from the administration of a general or local anesthetic, analgesic, or other sedation in labor and delivery
   EXCLUDES reaction to spinal or lumbar puncture (349.0)
     spinal headache (349.0)
   Use additional code(s) to further specify complication

§ ✓5ᵗʰ **668.0 Pulmonary complications**   M ♀
[0-4]
   Inhalation (aspiration) of stomach contents or secretions } following anesthesia or other sedation in labor or delivery
   Mendelson's syndrome
   Pressure collapse of lung

§ ✓5ᵗʰ **668.1 Cardiac complications**   M ♀
[0-4]
   Cardiac arrest or failure following anesthesia or other sedation in labor and delivery

§ ✓5ᵗʰ **668.2 Central nervous system complications**   M ♀
[0-4]
   Cerebral anoxia following anesthesia or other sedation in labor and delivery

§ ✓5ᵗʰ **668.8 Other complications of anesthesia or other**   M ♀
[0-4] **sedation in labor and delivery**
   AHA: 2Q, '99, 9

§ ✓5ᵗʰ **668.9 Unspecified complication of anesthesia**   M ♀
[0-4] **and other sedation**

✓4ᵗʰ **669 Other complications of labor and delivery, not elsewhere classified**

§ ✓5ᵗʰ **669.0 Maternal distress**   M ♀
[0-4]
   Metabolic disturbance in labor and delivery

---

§ Requires fifth digit. Valid digits are in [brackets] under each code. See beginning of section 640-649 for codes and definitions.

Complications of Pregnancy, Childbirth & Puerperium

669.1–671.3

(handwritten note, top right:) Begins immediately after birth and includes the subsequent 4 weeks following

§ ✓5th **669.1** **Shock during or following labor and delivery** `MCC 1-4` M♀
[0-4]
Obstetric shock
CC Excl: For codes 669.11-669.14: 646.80-646.93, 648.90-649.64, 650, 669.10-669.14, 669.40-669.44, 669.80-669.94, 679.00-679.04, 679.12, 679.14

§ ✓5th **669.2** **Maternal hypotension syndrome** `MCC 1-2` `CC 4` M♀
[0-4]
DEF: Low arterial blood pressure, in mother, during labor and delivery.
CC Excl: For code 669.21: 646.80-646.93, 648.90-649.64, 650, 669.10-669.14, 669.21, 669.40-669.44, 669.80-669.94, 679.00-679.04, 679.12, 679.14; For code 669.22: 646.80-646.93, 648.90-649.64, 650, 669.10-669.14, 669.22, 669.40-669.44, 669.80-669.94, 679.00-679.04, 679.12, 679.14; For code 669.24: 646.80-646.93, 648.90-649.64, 650, 669.10-669.14, 669.24, 669.40-669.44, 669.80-669.94, 679.00-679.04, 679.12, 679.14

▲ § ✓5th **669.3** **Acute kidney failure following labor and delivery** `MCC 2,4` M♀
[0,2,4]
CC Excl: For codes 669.32, 669.34: 646.80-646.93, 648.90-649.64, 650, 669.30-669.44, 669.80-669.94, 679.00-679.04, 679.12, 679.14

§ ✓5th **669.4** **Other complications of obstetrical surgery and procedures** M♀
[0-4]
Cardiac:
arrest
failure   } following cesarean or other obstetrical surgery or procedure, including delivery NOS
Cerebral anoxia
EXCLUDES complications of obstetrical surgical wounds (674.1-674.3)

§ ✓5th **669.5** **Forceps or vacuum extractor delivery without mention of indication** M♀
[0,1]
Delivery by ventouse, without mention of indication

§ ✓5th **669.6** **Breech extraction, without mention of indication** M♀
[0,1]
EXCLUDES breech delivery NOS (652.2)

§ ✓5th **669.7** **Cesarean delivery, without mention of indication** M♀
[0,1]
AHA: For code 669.71: 1Q, '01, 11
O82 Encounter for cesarean delivery w/o indication `I-10`

§ ✓5th **669.8** **Other complications of labor and delivery** M♀
[0-4]
AHA: 4Q, '06, 135

§ ✓5th **669.9** **Unspecified complication of labor and delivery** M♀
[0-4]

(handwritten note, bottom left:) If the patient was admitted with a condition that resulted in the performance of a cesarean procedure, that condition should be selected as the principal diagnosis.

(handwritten note, bottom center:) Sepsis requires secondary code for causal organism - do not code 995.91, but may code 995.92 if severe sepsis.

COMPLICATIONS OF THE PUERPERIUM (670-677)

Note: Categories 671 and 673-676 include the listed conditions even if they occur during pregnancy or childbirth.

The following fifth-digit subclassification is for use with categories 670-676 to denote the current episode of care. Valid fifth-digits are in [brackets] under each code.
0 unspecified as to episode of care or not applicable
1 delivered, with or without mention of antepartum condition
2 delivered, with mention of postpartum complication - *(handwritten:)* same admission as delivery
3 antepartum condition or complication - *(handwritten:)* after discharge
4 postpartum condition or complication

✓4th **670** **Major puerperal infection**
EXCLUDES infection following abortion (639.0)
minor genital tract infection following delivery (646.6)
puerperal pyrexia NOS (672)
puerperal fever NOS (672)
puerperal pyrexia of unknown origin (672)
urinary tract infection following delivery (646.6)
DEF: Infection and inflammation, following childbirth.
AHA: 4Q, '91, 26; 2Q, '91, 7

▲ § ✓5th **670.0** **Major puerperal infection, unspecified** `MCC 2,4` M♀
[0,2,4]
AHA: For codes 670.02 and 670.04: 3Q, '07, 8
CC Excl: 646.80-646.93, 648.90-649.64, 650, 669.40-669.44, 669.80-670.84, 679.00-679.04, 679.12, 679.14

● § ✓5th **670.1** **Puerperal endometritis** `CC` M♀
[0,2,4]
CC Excl: See code: 670.0

● § ✓5th **670.2** **Puerperal sepsis** `CC 0` `MCC 2,4` M♀
[0,2,4]
Puerperal pyemia
CC Excl: See code: 670.0

● § ✓5th **670.3** **Puerperal septic thrombophlebitis** `CC 0` `MCC 2,4` M♀
[0,2,4]
CC Excl: See code: 670.0

● § ✓5th **670.8** **Other major puerperal infection** `MCC` M♀
[0,2,4]
Puerperal:
pelvic cellulitis
peritonitis
salpingitis
CC Excl: See code: 670.0

✓4th **671** **Venous complications in pregnancy and the puerperium**
EXCLUDES ▶personal history of venous complications prior to pregnancy, such as:
thrombophlebitis (V12.52)
thrombosis and embolism (V12.51)◀

§ ✓5th **671.0** **Varicose veins of legs** M♀
[0-4]
Varicose veins NOS
DEF: Distended, tortuous veins on legs associated with pregnancy.

§ ✓5th **671.1** **Varicose veins of vulva and perineum** M♀
[0-4]
DEF: Distended, tortuous veins on external female genitalia associated with pregnancy.

§ ✓5th **671.2** **Superficial thrombophlebitis** `CC` M♀
[0-4]
▶Phlebitis NOS◀
Thrombophlebitis (superficial)
▶Thrombosis NOS◀
CC Excl: 646.80-646.93, 648.90-649.64, 650, 669.40-669.44, 669.80-669.94, 671.20-671.94, 679.00-679.04, 679.12, 679.14

§ ✓5th **671.3** **Deep phlebothrombosis, antepartum** `MCC 1,3` `CC 0`
[0,1,3] M♀
Deep vein thrombosis antepartum
▶Use additional code to identify the deep vein thrombosis (453.40-453.42, 453.50-453.52, 453.72-453.79, 453.82-453.89)◀
▶Use additional code for long term (current) use of anticoagulants, if applicable (V58.61)◀
CC Excl: See code: 671.2

§ Requires fifth digit. Valid digits are in [brackets] under each code. See beginning of section 640-649 for codes and definitions.

N Newborn Age: 0   P Pediatric Age: 0-17   M Maternity Age: 12-55   A Adult Age: 15-124   `MCC` Major CC Condition   `CC` CC Condition   `HIV` HIV Related Dx

234 – Volume 1 · October 2009   2010 ICD-9-CM

§ ✓5th **671.4 Deep phlebothrombosis, postpartum**　　MCC 2,4 | CC 0 | M♀
　[0,2,4]　Deep-vein thrombosis, postpartum
　　　　Pelvic thrombophlebitis, postpartum
　　　　Phlegmasia alba dolens (puerperal)
　　　　▶Use additional code to identify the deep vein
　　　　　thrombosis (453.40-453.42, 453.50-453.52,
　　　　　453.72-453.79, 453.82-453.89)◀
　　　　▶Use additional code for long term (current) use of
　　　　　anticoagulants, if applicable (V58.61)◀
　　　　CC Excl: See code: 671.2

§ ✓5th **671.5 Other phlebitis and thrombosis**　　CC | M♀
　[0-4]　Cerebral venous thrombosis
　　　　Thrombosis of intracranial venous sinus
　　　　CC Excl: See code: 671.2

§ ✓5th **671.8 Other venous complications**　　CC | M♀
　[0-4]　Hemorrhoids
　　　　CC Excl: For codes 671.80-671.83: 646.80-646.93, 648.90-649.64,
　　　　650, 669.40-669.44, 669.80-669.94, 671.20-671.94,
　　　　679.00-679.04, 679.12, 679.14; For code 671.84: 671.80-671.84

§ ✓5th **671.9 Unspecified venous complication**　　CC 0-2 | M♀
　[0-4]　CC Excl: For code 671.90-671.92: 646.80-646.93, 648.90-649.64,
　　　　650, 669.40-669.44, 669.80-669.94, 671.20-671.94,
　　　　679.00-679.04, 679.12, 679.14

✓4th **672 Pyrexia of unknown origin during the**　　CC 2,4 | M♀
　[0,2,4] **puerperium**

§ ✓5th 　Use 0 as fourth-digit for this category
　　　Postpartum fever NOS
　　　Puerperal fever NOS
　　　Puerperal pyrexia NOS
　　　DEF: Fever of unknown origin experienced by the mother after childbirth.
　　　CC Excl: For code 672.02: 646.80-646.93, 648.90-649.64, 650,
　　　669.40-669.44, 669.80-669.94, 671.20, 671.23-671.30, 671.33-671.40,
　　　671.50, 671.53-671.80, 671.83-671.90, 671.93-671.94, 672.02,
　　　679.00-679.04, 679.12, 679.14; For code 672.04: 672.02-672.04
　　　AHA: 4Q, '91, 26
　　　086.4 Pyrexia of unknown origin following delivery　　I-10

✓4th **673 Obstetrical pulmonary embolism**
　　INCLUDES pulmonary emboli in pregnancy, childbirth, or the puerperium, or specified as puerperal
　　EXCLUDES embolism following abortion (639.6)

§ ✓5th **673.0 Obstetrical air embolism**　　MCC 1-4 | M♀
　[0-4]　**DEF:** Sudden blocking of pulmonary artery with air or nitrogen bubbles during puerperium.
　　　　CC Excl: 646.80-646.93, 648.90-649.64, 650, 669.40-669.44,
　　　　669.80-669.94, 673.00-673.84, 679.00-679.04, 679.12, 679.14

§ ✓5th **673.1 Amniotic fluid embolism**　　MCC 1-4 | M♀
　[0-4]　**DEF:** Sudden onset of pulmonary artery blockage from amniotic fluid entering the mother's circulation near the end of pregnancy due to strong uterine contractions.
　　　　CC Excl: For code 673.11-673.14: See code: 673.0

§ ✓5th **673.2 Obstetrical blood-clot embolism**　　MCC 1-4 | M♀
　[0-4]　Puerperal pulmonary embolism NOS
　　　　DEF: Blood clot blocking artery in the lung; associated with pregnancy.
　　　　CC Excl: For code 673.21-673.24: See code: 673.0
　　　　AHA: For code 673.24: 1Q, '05, 6
　　　　TIP: If a pregnant or postpartum patient develops a pulmonary embolism that progresses to acute respiratory failure, the code for the pregnancy/delivery complication (673.2X) should be sequenced first.

§ ✓5th **673.3 Obstetrical pyemic and septic embolism**　　MCC 1-4
　[0-4]　CC Excl: See code: 673.0　　CC 0 | M♀

§ ✓5th **673.8 Other pulmonary embolism**　　MCC 1-4 | M♀
　[0-4]　Fat embolism
　　　　CC Excl: For code 673.81-673.84: See code: 673.0

✓4th **674 Other and unspecified complications of the puerperium, not elsewhere classified**

§ ✓5th **674.0 Cerebrovascular disorders in the**　　MCC 1 | CC 2-4
　[0-4] **puerperium**　　M♀
　　　　Any condition classifiable to 430-434, 436-437 occurring during pregnancy, childbirth, or the puerperium, or specified as puerperal
　　　　EXCLUDES intracranial venous sinus thrombosis (671.5)
　　　　CC Excl: For code 674.01-674.04: 646.80-646.93, 648.90-649.64,
　　　　650, 669.40-669.44, 669.80-669.94, 674.00-674.04,
　　　　674.50-674.54, 679.00-679.04, 679.12, 679.14

§ ✓5th **674.1 Disruption of cesarean wound**　　M♀
　[0,2,4]　Dehiscence or disruption of uterine wound
　　　　EXCLUDES uterine rupture before onset of labor (665.0)
　　　　　　　　uterine rupture during labor (665.1)

§ ✓5th **674.2 Disruption of perineal wound**　　M♀
　[0,2,4]　Breakdown of perineum
　　　　Disruption of wound of:
　　　　　episiotomy
　　　　　perineal laceration
　　　　Secondary perineal tear
　　　　AHA: For code 674.24: 1Q, '97, 9

§ ✓5th **674.3 Other complications of obstetrical**　　M♀
　[0,2,4] **surgical wounds**
　　　　Hematoma ⎫
　　　　Hemorrhage ⎬ of cesarean section or perineal wound
　　　　Infection ⎭
　　　　EXCLUDES damage from instruments in delivery (664.0-665.9)
　　　　AHA: 2Q, '91, 7

§ ✓5th **674.4 Placental polyp**　　M♀
　[0,2,4]

§ ✓5th **674.5 Peripartum cardiomyopathy**　　MCC | M♀
　[0-4]　Postpartum cardiomyopathy
　　　　DEF: Any structural or functional abnormality of the ventricular myocardium, non-inflammatory disease of obscure or unknown etiology with onset during the postpartum period.
　　　　CC Excl: See code: 674.01
　　　　AHA: 4Q, '03, 65

§ ✓5th **674.8 Other**　　M♀
　[0,2,4]　Hepatorenal syndrome, following delivery
　　　　Postpartum:
　　　　　subinvolution of uterus
　　　　　uterine hypertrophy
　　　　AHA: 3Q, '98, 16

§ ✓5th **674.9 Unspecified**　　M♀
　[0,2,4]　Sudden death of unknown cause during the puerperium

✓4th **675 Infections of the breast and nipple associated with childbirth**
　　INCLUDES the listed conditions during pregnancy, childbirth, or the puerperium

§ ✓5th **675.0 Infections of nipple**　　M♀
　[0-4]　Abscess of nipple

§ ✓5th **675.1 Abscess of breast**　　CC 1-2 | M♀
　[0-4]　Abscess:
　　　　　mammary
　　　　　subareolar
　　　　　submammary
　　　　　purulent
　　　　　retromammary
　　　　　submammary
　　　　CC Excl: For codes 675.11-675.12: 646.80-646.93, 648.90-649.64,
　　　　650, 669.40-669.44, 669.80-669.94, 675.00-675.94,
　　　　679.00-679.04, 679.12, 679.14

§ ✓5th **675.2 Nonpurulent mastitis**　　M♀
　[0-4]　Lymphangitis of breast
　　　　Mastitis:
　　　　　NOS
　　　　　interstitial
　　　　　parenchymatous

§ 　Requires fifth digit. Valid digits are in [brackets] under each code. See beginning of section 640-649 for codes and definitions.

| ✓4th ✓5th Additional Digit Required | Unacceptable PDx | Manifestation Code | Hospital Acquired Condition | ▶◀ Revised Text | ● New Code | ▲ Revised Code Title |

Lactation Process: Ejection Reflex Arc

§ ✓5ᵗʰ **675.8** **Other specified infections of the breast** Ⓜ♀
[0-4] **and nipple**

§ ✓5ᵗʰ **675.9** **Unspecified infection of the breast** Ⓜ♀
[0-4] **and nipple**

✓4ᵗʰ **676** **Other disorders of the breast associated with childbirth and disorders of lactation**

     INCLUDES   the listed conditions during pregnancy, the puerperium, or lactation

§ ✓5ᵗʰ **676.0** **Retracted nipple** Ⓜ♀
[0-4]

§ ✓5ᵗʰ **676.1** **Cracked nipple** Ⓜ♀
[0-4] Fissure of nipple

§ ✓5ᵗʰ **676.2** **Engorgement of breasts** Ⓜ♀
[0-4] **DEF:** Abnormal accumulation of milk in ducts of breast.

§ ✓5ᵗʰ **676.3** **Other and unspecified disorder of breast** Ⓜ♀
[0-4]

§ ✓5ᵗʰ **676.4** **Failure of lactation** Ⓜ♀
[0-4] Agalactia
DEF: Abrupt ceasing of milk secretion by breast.

§ ✓5ᵗʰ **676.5** **Suppressed lactation** Ⓜ♀
[0-4]

§ ✓5ᵗʰ **676.6** **Galactorrhea** Ⓜ♀
[0-4]   **EXCLUDES**   galactorrhea not associated with childbirth (611.6)
DEF: Excessive or persistent milk secretion by breast; may be in absence of nursing.

§ ✓5ᵗʰ **676.8** **Other disorders of lactation** Ⓜ♀
[0-4] Galactocele
DEF: Galactocele: Obstructed mammary gland, creating retention cyst, results in milk-filled cysts enlarging mammary gland.

§ ✓5ᵗʰ **676.9** **Unspecified disorder of lactation** Ⓜ♀
[0-4]

677 **Late effect of complication of pregnancy, childbirth, and the puerperium** ♀

Note: This category is to be used to indicate conditions in 632-648.9 and 651-676.9 as the cause of the late effect, themselves classifiable elsewhere. The "late effects" include conditions specified as such, or as sequelae, which may occur at any time after puerperium.

Code first any sequelae
AHA: 1Q, '97, 9; 4Q, '94, 42

TIP: Sequence as a secondary diagnosis, after the code for the late effect complication. May be assigned at any time after the initial postpartum period (six weeks following delivery).

OTHER MATERNAL AND FETAL COMPLICATIONS (678-679)

The following fifth-digit subclassification is for use with categories 678-679 to denote the current episode of care. Valid fifth-digits are in [brackets] under each code.

0   unspecified as to episode of care or not applicable
1   delivered, with or without mention of antepartum condition
2   delivered, with mention of postpartum complication
3   antepartum condition or complication
4   postpartum condition or complication

✓4ᵗʰ **678** **Other fetal conditions**

§ ✓5ᵗʰ **678.0** **Fetal hematologic conditions** Ⓜ♀
[0,1,3] Fetal anemia
Fetal thrombocytopenia
Fetal twin to twin transfusion
   EXCLUDES   fetal and neonatal hemorrhage (772.0-772.9)
fetal hematologic disorders affecting newborn (776.0-776.9)
fetal-maternal hemorrhage (656.00-656.03)
isoimmunization incompatibility (656.10-656.13, 656.20-656.23)
AHA: ▶4Q, '08, 125-127◀

§ ✓5ᵗʰ **678.1** **Fetal conjoined twins** Ⓜ♀
[0,1,3] **AHA:** ▶4Q, '08, 125-127◀

✓4ᵗʰ **679** **Complications of in utero procedures**
AHA: ▶4Q, '08, 127-128, 158◀

§ ✓5ᵗʰ ✳ **679.0** **Maternal complications from in utero** Ⓜ♀
[0-4] **procedure**
   EXCLUDES   maternal history of in utero procedure during previous pregnancy (V23.86)

§ ✓5ᵗʰ ✳ **679.1** **Fetal complications from in utero** Ⓜ♀
[0-4] **procedure**
Fetal complications from amniocentesis
   EXCLUDES   newborn affected by in utero procedure (760.61-760.64)
TIP: Assign only on the mother's record. Although there is a fetal complication, it affects the mother's pregnancy.

✳ Use V23.86 as additional code if the patient has a past history of in utero surgery during a previous pregnancy.

---

§   Requires fifth digit. Valid digits are in [brackets] under each code. See beginning of section 640-649 for codes and definitions.

Ⓝ Newborn Age: 0   Ⓟ Pediatric Age: 0-17   Ⓜ Maternity Age: 12-55   Ⓐ Adult Age: 15-124   **MCC** Major CC Condition   **CC** CC Condition   **HIV** HIV Related Dx

236 – Volume 1 · February 2009   **2010 ICD-9-CM**

12. DISEASES OF THE SKIN AND SUBCUTANEOUS TISSUE
(680-709)

INFECTIONS OF SKIN AND SUBCUTANEOUS TISSUE (680-686)

EXCLUDES *certain infections of skin classified under "Infectious and Parasitic Diseases," such as:*
erysipelas (035)
erysipeloid of Rosenbach (027.1)
herpes:
    simplex (054.0-054.9)
    zoster (053.0-053.9)
molluscum contagiosum (078.0)
viral warts ▶(078.10-078.19)◀

✓4th **680 Carbuncle and furuncle**

INCLUDES boil
    furunculosis

DEF: Carbuncle: necrotic boils in skin and subcutaneous tissue of neck or back mainly due to staphylococcal infection.
DEF: Furuncle: circumscribed inflammation of corium and subcutaneous tissue due to staphylococcal infection.

680.0 Face
Ear [any part]
Face [any part, except eye]
Nose (septum)
Temple (region)
EXCLUDES *eyelid (373.13)*
lacrimal apparatus (375.31)
orbit (376.01)

680.1 Neck

680.2 Trunk
Abdominal wall
Back [any part, except buttocks]
Breast
Chest wall
Flank
Groin
Pectoral region
Perineum
Umbilicus
EXCLUDES *buttocks (680.5)*
external genital organs:
    female (616.4)
    male (607.2, 608.4)

680.3 Upper arm and forearm
Arm [any part, except hand]
Axilla
Shoulder

680.4 Hand
Finger [any]
Thumb
Wrist

680.5 Buttock
Anus
Gluteal region

680.6 Leg, except foot
Ankle
Hip
Knee
Thigh

680.7 Foot
Heel
Toe

680.8 Other specified sites
Head [any part, except face]
Scalp
EXCLUDES *external genital organs:*
    female (616.4)
    male (607.2, 608.4)

680.9 Unspecified site
Boil NOS
Carbuncle NOS
Furuncle NOS

Skin and Subcutaneous Layer

Hair follicle
Epidermis
Dermis
Hypodermis (subcutaneous layer)
Bulb
Sebaceous gland
Arrector pili muscle
Thick-skin epidermis
Hair shaft
Pacinian corpuscle
Hair matrix
Sweat (eccrine gland)
Sensory nerve
Blood vessels

✓4th **681 Cellulitis and abscess of finger and toe**

INCLUDES that with lymphangitis

Use additional code to identify organism, such as Staphylococcus (041.1)

DEF: Acute suppurative inflammation and edema in subcutaneous tissue or muscle of finger or toe.
AHA: 2Q, '91, 5; J-F, '87, 12
TIP: Coding of cellulitis due to superficial injury, burn, or frostbite requires two codes, one for the injury and one for the cellulitis. Sequencing depends on the circumstances of the admission.

✓5th **681.0 Finger**

681.00 Cellulitis and abscess, unspecified
L03.019 Cellulitis of unspecified finger   I-10

681.01 Felon
Pulp abscess
Whitlow
EXCLUDES *herpetic whitlow (054.6)*
DEF: Painful abscess of fingertips caused by infection in the closed space of terminal phalanx.

681.02 Onychia and paronychia of finger
Panaritium ⎫
Perionychia ⎬ of finger
DEF: Onychia: inflammation of nail matrix; causes nail loss.
DEF: Paronychia: inflammation of tissue folds around nail.

✓5th **681.1 Toe**

681.10 Cellulitis and abscess, unspecified
AHA: 1Q, '05, 14
L03.039 Cellulitis of unspecified toe   I-10

681.11 Onychia and paronychia of toe
Panaritium ⎫
Perionychia ⎬ of toe

681.9 Cellulitis and abscess of unspecified digit
Infection of nail NOS

✓4th **682 Other cellulitis and abscess**

INCLUDES abscess (acute ⎫
cellulitis (diffuse ⎬ (with lymphangitis) except
lymphangitis, acute ⎭ of finger or toe

Use additional code to identify organism, such as Staphylococcus (041.1)

EXCLUDES *lymphangitis (chronic) (subacute) (457.2)*

DEF: Cellulitis: Acute suppurative inflammation of deep subcutaneous tissue and sometimes muscle due to infection of wound, burn or other lesion.
AHA: 2Q, '91, 5; J-F, '87, 12; S-O, '85, 10
TIP: Coding of cellulitis due to superficial injury, burn, or frostbite requires two codes, one for the injury and one for the cellulitis. Sequencing depends on the circumstances of the admission.

Skin and Subcutaneous Tissue

682.0–686

Lymphatic System of Head and Neck

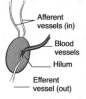

Afferent vessels (in)
Blood vessels
Hilum
Efferent vessel (out)

Schematic of lymph node

Jugulodigastric
Superficial parotid
Submental
Occipital
Submandibular
Jugulomyohyoid
Anterior cervical

Lymphatic drainage of the head, neck, and face

682.0 Face [CC]

Cheek, external	Nose, external
Chin	Submandibular
Forehead	Temple (region)

EXCLUDES ear [any part] (380.10-380.16)
eyelid (373.13)
lacrimal apparatus (375.31)
lip (528.5)
mouth (528.3)
nose (internal) (478.1)
orbit (376.01)

CC Excl: 017.00-017.06, 017.90-017.96, 040.82-041.9, 682.0, 682.8-682.9, 686.00-686.9, 705.83, 709.8, V09.0-V09.91

L03.211 Cellulitis of face [I-10]

682.1 Neck [CC]

CC Excl: 017.00-017.06, 017.90-017.96, 040.82-041.9, 682.1, 682.8-682.9, 686.00-686.9, 705.83, 709.8, V09.0-V09.91

L03.221 Cellulitis of neck [I-10]

682.2 Trunk [CC]

Abdominal wall
Back [any part, except buttock]
Chest wall
Flank
Groin
Pectoral region
Perineum
Umbilicus, except newborn

EXCLUDES anal and rectal regions (566)
breast:
NOS (611.0)
puerperal (675.1)
external genital organs:
female (616.3-616.4)
male (604.0, 607.2, 608.4)
umbilicus, newborn (771.4)

CC Excl: 017.00-017.06, 017.90-017.96, 040.82-041.9, 682.2, 682.8-682.9, 686.00-686.9, 705.83, 709.8, V09.0-V09.91

AHA: 4Q, '98, 42

L03.319 Cellulitis of trunk unspecified [I-10]

682.3 Upper arm and forearm [CC]

Arm [any part, except hand]
Axilla
Shoulder

EXCLUDES hand (682.4)

CC Excl: 017.00-017.06, 017.90-017.96, 040.82-041.9, 682.3, 682.8-682.9, 686.00-686.9, 705.83, 709.8, V09.0-V09.91

AHA: 2Q, '03, 7

L03.113 Cellulitis of right upper limb [I-10]

682.4 Hand, except fingers and thumb [CC]

Wrist

EXCLUDES finger and thumb (681.00-681.02)

CC Excl: 017.00-017.06, 017.90-017.96, 040.82-041.9, 682.4, 682.8-682.9, 686.00-686.9, 705.83, 709.8, V09.0-V09.91

682.5 Buttock [CC]

Gluteal region

EXCLUDES anal and rectal regions (566)

CC Excl: 017.00-017.06, 017.90-017.96, 040.82-041.9, 682.5, 682.8-682.9, 686.00-686.9, 705.83, 709.8, V09.0-V09.91

L03.317 Cellulitis of buttock [I-10]

682.6 Leg, except foot [CC]

Ankle
Hip
Knee
Thigh

CC Excl: 017.00-017.06, 017.90-017.96, 040.82-041.9, 682.6, 682.8-682.9, 686.00-686.9, 705.83, 709.8, V09.0-V09.91

AHA: ▶1Q, '09, 10;◀ 3Q, '04, 5; 4Q, '03, 108

L03.115 Cellulitis of right lower limb [I-10]

682.7 Foot, except toes [CC]

Heel

EXCLUDES toe (681.10-681.11)

CC Excl: 017.00-017.06, 017.90-017.96, 040.82-041.9, 682.7-682.9, 686.00-686.9, 705.83, 709.8, V09.0-V09.91

682.8 Other specified sites [CC]

Head [except face]
Scalp

EXCLUDES face (682.0)

CC Excl: 017.00-017.06, 017.90-017.96, 040.82-041.9, 682.8-682.9, 686.00-686.9, 705.83, 709.8, V09.0-V09.91

682.9 Unspecified site [CC]

Abscess NOS
Cellulitis NOS
Lymphangitis, acute NOS

EXCLUDES lymphangitis NOS (457.2)

CC Excl: See code: 682.8

683 Acute lymphadenitis

Abscess (acute)
Adenitis, acute } lymph gland or node, except mesenteric
Lymphadenitis, acute

Use additional code to identify organism, such as Staphylococcus (041.1)

EXCLUDES enlarged glands NOS (785.6)
lymphadenitis:
chronic or subacute, except mesenteric (289.1)
mesenteric (acute) (chronic) (subacute) (289.2)
unspecified (289.3)

DEF: Acute inflammation of lymph nodes due to primary infection located elsewhere in the body.

684 Impetigo

Impetiginization of other dermatoses
Impetigo (contagiosa) [any site] [any organism]:
bullous
circinate
neonatorum
simplex
Pemphigus neonatorum

EXCLUDES impetigo herpetiformis (694.3)

DEF: Infectious skin disease commonly occurring in children; caused by group A streptococci or *Staphylococcus aureus;* skin lesions usually appear on the face and consist of subcorneal vesicles and bullae that burst and form yellow crusts.

√4ᵗʰ 685 Pilonidal cyst

INCLUDES fistula } coccygeal or pilonidal
sinus

DEF: Hair-containing cyst or sinus in the tissues of the sacrococcygeal area; often drains through opening at the postanal dimple.

685.0 With abscess [CC]

CC Excl: 685.0-685.1, 709.8

685.1 Without mention of abscess

√4ᵗʰ 686 Other local infections of skin and subcutaneous tissue

Use additional code to identify any infectious organism (041.0-041.8)

[N] Newborn Age: 0   [P] Pediatric Age: 0-17   [M] Maternity Age: 12-55   [A] Adult Age: 15-124   [MCC] Major CC Condition   [CC] CC Condition   [HIV] HIV Related Dx

238 – Volume 1 · October 2009   2010 ICD-9-CM

Stages of Pilonidal Disease

- Normal follicle
- Stretched follicle
- Infected follicle
- Acute abscess
- Chronic abscess
- Epithelial tube

√5ᵗʰ **686.0 Pyoderma**
Dermatitis:
  purulent
  septic
  suppurative
DEF: Nonspecific purulent skin disease related most to furuncles, pustules, or possibly carbuncles.

686.00 Pyoderma, unspecified

686.01 Pyoderma gangrenosum [CC]
DEF: Persistent debilitating skin disease, characterized by irregular, boggy, blue-red ulcerations, with central healing and undermined edges.
CC Excl: 686.00-686.09
AHA: 4Q, '97, 42

686.09 Other pyoderma

686.1 Pyogenic granuloma
Granuloma:
  septic
  suppurative
  telangiectaticum
EXCLUDES *pyogenic granuloma of oral mucosa (528.9)*
DEF: Solitary polypoid capillary hemangioma often asociated with local irritation, trauma, and superimposed inflammation; located on the skin and gingival or oral mucosa.

686.8 Other specified local infections of skin and subcutaneous tissue
Bacterid (pustular)
Dermatitis vegetans
Ecthyma
Perlèche
EXCLUDES *dermatitis infectiosa eczematoides (690.8)*
panniculitis (729.30-729.39)

686.9 Unspecified local infection of skin and subcutaneous tissue
Fistula of skin NOS
Skin infection NOS
EXCLUDES *fistula to skin from internal organs – see Alphabetic Index*

OTHER INFLAMMATORY CONDITIONS OF SKIN AND SUBCUTANEOUS TISSUE (690-698)
EXCLUDES *panniculitis (729.30-729.39)*

√4ᵗʰ **690 Erythematosquamous dermatosis**
EXCLUDES *eczematous dermatitis of eyelid (373.31)*
parakeratosis variegata (696.2)
psoriasis (696.0-696.1)
seborrheic keratosis (702.11-702.19)

√5ᵗʰ **690.1 Seborrheic dermatitis**
AHA: 4Q, '95, 58

690.10 Seborrheic dermatitis, unspecified
Seborrheic dermatitis NOS
  L21.9 Seborrheic dermatitis unspecified [I-10]

690.11 Seborrhea capitis [P]
Cradle cap

690.12 Seborrheic infantile dermatitis [P]

690.18 Other seborrheic dermatitis

690.8 Other erythematosquamous dermatosis

√4ᵗʰ **691 Atopic dermatitis and related conditions**
DEF: Atopic dermatitis: chronic, pruritic, inflammatory skin disorder found on the face and antecubital and popliteal fossae; often accompanied by allergic rhinitis, hay fever, asthma, and extreme itching; also called allergic dermatitis, or disseminated neurodermatitis.

691.0 Diaper or napkin rash
Ammonia dermatitis
Diaper or napkin:
  dermatitis
  erythema
  rash
Psoriasiform napkin eruption

691.8 Other atopic dermatitis and related conditions
Atopic dermatitis
Besnier's prurigo
Eczema:
  atopic
  flexural
  intrinsic (allergic)
Neurodermatitis:
  atopic
  diffuse (of Brocq)

√4ᵗʰ **692 Contact dermatitis and other eczema**
INCLUDES dermatitis:
  NOS
  contact
  occupational
  venenata
eczema (acute) (chronic):
  NOS
  allergic
  erythematous
  occupational
EXCLUDES *allergy NOS (995.3)*
contact dermatitis of eyelids (373.32)
dermatitis due to substances taken internally (693.0-693.9)
eczema of external ear (380.22)
perioral dermatitis (695.3)
urticarial reactions (708.0-708.9, 995.1)
DEF: Contact dermatitis: acute or chronic dermatitis caused by initial irritant effect of a substance, or by prior sensitization to a substance coming once again in contact with skin.

692.0 Due to detergents

692.1 Due to oils and greases

692.2 Due to solvents
Dermatitis due to solvents of:
  chlorocompound ⎫
  cyclohexane   ⎪
  ester   ⎬ group
  glycol   ⎪
  hydrocarbon   ⎪
  ketone   ⎭

692.3 Due to drugs and medicines in contact with skin
Dermatitis (allergic) (contact) due to:
  arnica
  fungicides
  iodine
  keratolytics
  mercurials
  neomycin
  pediculocides
  phenols
  scabicides
  any drug applied to skin
Dermatitis medicamentosa due to drug applied to skin
Use additional E code to identify drug
EXCLUDES *allergy NOS due to drugs (995.27)*
dermatitis due to ingested drugs (693.0)
dermatitis medicamentosa NOS (693.0)

√4ᵗʰ Additional Digit Required   Unacceptable PDx   Manifestation Code   Hospital Acquired Condition   ▶◀ Revised Text   ● New Code   ▲ Revised Code Title

√5ᵗʰ
2010 ICD-9-CM   **Volume 1 – 239**

Skin and Subcutaneous Tissue

692.4–692.9

692.4   Due to other chemical products
Dermatitis due to:
  acids
  adhesive plaster
  alkalis
  caustics
  dichromate
  insecticide
  nylon
  plastic
  rubber

AHA: ▶3Q, '08, 6-7;◀ 2Q, '89, 16

692.5   Due to food in contact with skin
Dermatitis, contact, due to:
  cereals
  fish
  flour
  fruit
  meat
  milk

EXCLUDES   dermatitis due to:
                dyes (692.89)
                ingested foods (693.1)
                preservatives (692.89)

692.6   Due to plants [except food]
Dermatitis due to:
  lacquer tree [Rhus verniciflua]
  poison:
    ivy [Rhus toxicodendron]
    oak [Rhus diversiloba]
    sumac [Rhus venenata]
    vine [Rhus radicans]
  primrose [Primula]
  ragweed [Senecio jacobae]
  other plants in contact with the skin

EXCLUDES   allergy NOS due to pollen (477.0)
             nettle rash (708.8)

✓5ᵗʰ **692.7   Due to solar radiation**

EXCLUDES   sunburn due to other ultraviolet radiation
             exposure (692.82)

692.70   Unspecified dermatitis due to sun

692.71   Sunburn
First degree sunburn
Sunburn NOS

AHA: 4Q, '01, 47

TIP: Do not assign if sunburn is due to tanning bed
use; see instead code 692.82.

692.72   Acute dermatitis due to solar radiation
Acute solar skin damage NOS
Berloque dermatitis
Photoallergic response
Phototoxic response
Polymorphus light eruption

Use additional E code to identify drug, if drug
  induced

EXCLUDES   sunburn (692.71, 692.76-692.77)

DEF: Berloque dermatitis: Phytophotodermatitis due
to sun exposure after use of a product containing
bergamot oil; causes red patches, that turn brown.
DEF: Photoallergic response: Dermatitis due to
hypersensitivity to the sun; causes papulovesicular,
eczematous or exudative eruptions.
DEF: Phototoxic response: Chemically induced
sensitivity to sun causes burn-like reaction,
occasionally vesiculation and subsequent
hyperpigmentation.
DEF: Polymorphous light eruption: Inflammatory
skin eruptions due to sunlight exposure; eruptions
differ in size and shape.
DEF: Acute solar skin damage (NOS): Rapid,
unspecified injury to skin from sun.

692.73   Actinic reticuloid and actinic granuloma
DEF: Actinic reticuloid: Dermatosis aggravated by
light, causes chronic eczema-like eruption on
exposed skin which extends to other unexposed
surfaces; occurs in the eldery.
DEF: Actinic granuloma: Inflammatory response of
skin to sun causing small nodule of microphages.

692.74   Other chronic dermatitis due to solar radiation
Chronic solar skin damage NOS
Solar elastosis

EXCLUDES   actinic [solar] keratosis (702.0)

DEF: Solar elastosis: Premature aging of skin of
light-skinned people; causes inelasticity, thinning or
thickening, wrinkling, dryness, scaling and
hyperpigmentation.
DEF: Chronic solar skin damage (NOS): Chronic skin
impairment due to exposure to the sun, not
otherwise specified.

**692.75   Disseminated superficial actinic
porokeratosis [DSAP]**
DEF: Autosomal dominant skin condition occurring
in skin that has been overexposed to the sun;
characterized by superficial annular, keratotic,
brownish-red spots or thickenings with depressed
centers and sharp, ridged borders, may evolve into
squamous cell carcinoma.
AHA: 4Q, '00, 43

692.76   Sunburn of second degree
AHA: 4Q, '01, 47
TIP: Do not assign if sunburn is due to tanning bed
use; see instead code 692.82.

692.77   Sunburn of third degree
AHA: 4Q, '01, 47
TIP: Do not assign if sunburn is due to tanning bed
use; see instead code 692.82.

692.79   Other dermatitis due to solar radiation
Hydroa aestivale
Photodermatitis   ⎫
Photosensitiveness   ⎬ (due to sun)
                       ⎭
Solar skin damage NOS

✓5ᵗʰ **692.8   Due to other specified agents**

692.81   Dermatitis due to cosmetics

692.82   Dermatitis due to other radiation
Infrared rays
Light, except from sun
Radiation NOS
Tanning bed
Ultraviolet rays, except from sun
X-rays

EXCLUDES   solar radiation (692.70-692.79)
AHA: 4Q, '01, 47; 3Q, '00, 5

692.83   Dermatitis due to metals
Jewelry

692.84   Due to animal (cat) (dog) dander
Due to animal (cat) (dog) hair

692.89   Other
Dermatitis due to: Dermatitis due to:
  cold weather   hot weather
  dyes   preservatives

EXCLUDES   allergy (NOS) (rhinitis) due to animal
             hair or dander (477.2)
             allergy to dust (477.8)
             sunburn (692.71, 692.76-692.77)

692.9   Unspecified cause
Dermatitis:
  NOS
  contact NOS
  venenata NOS
Eczema NOS

L23.9 Allergic contact dermatitis unspecified cause   I-10

Ⓝ Newborn Age: 0   Ⓟ Pediatric Age: 0-17   Ⓜ Maternity Age: 12-55   Ⓐ Adult Age: 15-124   MCC Major CC Condition   CC CC Condition   HIV HIV Related Dx

240 – Volume 1 • February 2009   2010 ICD-9-CM

✓4th 693 Dermatitis due to substances taken internally

> **EXCLUDES**   adverse effect NOS of drugs and medicines (995.20)
> allergy NOS (995.3)
> contact dermatitis (692.0-692.9)
> urticarial reactions (708.0-708.9, 995.1)

DEF: Inflammation of skin due to ingested substance.

693.0 Due to drugs and medicines
Dermatitis medicamentosa NOS

Use additional E code to identify drug

> **EXCLUDES**   that due to drugs in contact with skin (692.3)

AHA: 2Q, '07, 8

TIP: Assign for palmar plantar erythrodysesthesia (PPE) or hand-foot syndrome due to chemotherapy drugs.

L27.0 Gen skin eruption d/t Rx & med taken internally   `I-10`

693.1 Due to food

693.8 Due to other specified substances taken internally

693.9 Due to unspecified substance taken internally

> **EXCLUDES**   dermatitis NOS (692.9)

✓4th 694 Bullous dermatoses

694.0 Dermatitis herpetiformis
Dermatosis herpetiformis   Hydroa herpetiformis
Duhring's disease

> **EXCLUDES**   herpes gestationis (646.8)
> dermatitis herpetiformis:
>   juvenile (694.2)
>   senile (694.5)

DEF: Chronic, multisystem disease manifested in the cutaneous system; seen as an extremely pruritic eruption of various lesions that frequently heal leaving hyperpigmentation or hypopigmentation and occasionally scarring; usually associated with an asymptomatic gluten-sensitive enteropathy, and immunogenic factors .

694.1 Subcorneal pustular dermatosis
Sneddon-Wilkinson disease or syndrome

DEF: Chronic relapses of sterile pustular blebs beneath the horny skin layer of the trunk and skin folds; resembles dermatitis herpetiformis.

694.2 Juvenile dermatitis herpetiformis
Juvenile pemphigoid

694.3 Impetigo herpetiformis

DEF: Rare dermatosis associated with pregnancy; marked by itching pustules in third trimester, hypocalcemia, tetany, fever and lethargy; may result in maternal or fetal death.

694.4 Pemphigus   `CC`
Pemphigus: Pemphigus:
   NOS   malignant
   erythematosus   vegetans
   foliaceus   vulgaris

> **EXCLUDES**   pemphigus neonatorum (684)

CC Excl: 694.4-694.9, 709.8

DEF: Chronic, relapsing, sometimes fatal skin diseases; causes vesicles, bullae; autoantibodies against intracellular connections cause acantholysis.

694.5 Pemphigoid   `CC`
Benign pemphigus NOS
Bullous pemphigoid
Herpes circinatus bullosus
Senile dermatitis herpetiformis

CC Excl: See code 694.4

✓5th 694.6 Benign mucous membrane pemphigoid
Cicatricial pemphigoid
Mucosynechial atrophic bullous dermatitis

694.60 Without mention of ocular involvement

694.61 With ocular involvement
Ocular pemphigus

DEF: Mild self-limiting, subepidermal blistering of mucosa including the conjunctiva, seen predominantly in the elderly, produces adhesions and scarring.

694.8 Other specified bullous dermatoses

> **EXCLUDES**   herpes gestationis (646.8)

694.9 Unspecified bullous dermatoses

✓4th 695 Erythematous conditions

695.0 Toxic erythema   `CC`
Erythema venenatum

CC Excl: 695.0-695.4, 709.8

✓5th 695.1 Erythema multiforme
Use additional code to identify associated manifestations, such as:
   arthropathy associated with dermatological disorders (713.3)
   conjunctival edema (372.73)
   conjunctivitis (372.04, 372.33)
   corneal scars and opacities (371.00-371.05)
   corneal ulcer (370.00-370.07)
   edema of eyelid (374.82)
   inflammation of eyelid (373.8)
   keratoconjunctivitis sicca (370.33)
   mechanical lagophthalmos (374.22)
   mucositis (478.11, 528.00, 538, 616.81)
   stomatitis (528.00)
   symblepharon (372.63)

Use additional E code to identify drug, if drug-induced

Use additional code to identify percentage of skin exfoliation (695.50-695.59)

> **EXCLUDES**   (Staphylococcal) scalded skin syndrome (695.81)

DEF: Symptom complex with varied skin eruption pattern of macular, bullous, papular, nodose, or vesicular lesions on the neck, face, and legs; gastritis and rheumatic pains; secondary to number of factors, including infections, ingestants, physical agents, malignancy and pregnancy.

AHA: ▶4Q, '08, 128-130◀

695.10 Erythema multiforme, unspecified
Erythema iris
Herpes iris

695.11 Erythema multiforme minor

695.12 Erythema multiforme major   `CC`
CC Excl: 695.0-695.4, 695.81-695.9, 709.8

695.13 Stevens-Johnson syndrome   `CC`
CC Excl: See code 695.12

695.14 Stevens-Johnson syndrome-toxic   `CC`
epidermal necrolysis overlap syndrome
SJS-TEN overlap syndrome
CC Excl: See code 695.12
AHA: ▶4Q, '08, 131◀

695.15 Toxic epidermal necrolysis   `CC`
Lyell's syndrome
CC Excl: See code 695.12

695.19 Other erythema multiforme

695.2 Erythema nodosum

> **EXCLUDES**   tuberculous erythema nodosum (017.1)

DEF: Panniculitis (an inflammatory reaction of the subcutaneous fat) of women, usually seen as a hypersensitivity reaction to infections, drugs, sarcoidosis, and specific enteropathies; the acute stage associated with fever, malaise, and arthralgia; the lesions are pink to blue in color as tender nodules found on the front of the legs below the knees.

695.3 Rosacea
Acne: Perioral dermatitis
   erythematosa   Rhinophyma
   rosacea

DEF: Chronic skin disease, usually of the face, characterized by persistent erythema and telangiectasis with acute episodes of edema, engorgement papules, and pustules.

✓4th / ✓5th   Additional Digit Required   Unacceptable PDx   Manifestation Code   Hospital Acquired Condition   ▶◀ Revised Text   ● New Code   ▲ Revised Code Title

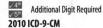

Skin and Subcutaneous Tissue

693–695.3

695.4 Lupus erythematosus
Lupus:
   erythematodes (discoid)
   erythematosus (discoid), not disseminated
   EXCLUDES lupus (vulgaris) NOS (017.0)
                 systemic [disseminated] lupus erythematosus
                    (710.0)
   DEF: Group of connective tissue disorders occurring as various
   cutaneous diseases of unknown origin; it primarily affects
   women between the ages of 20 and 40.

✓5ᵗʰ **695.5 Exfoliation due to erythematous conditions according
to extent of body surface involved**
   Code first erythematous condition causing exfoliation,
      such as:
      Ritter's disease (695.81)
      (Staphylococcal) scalded skin syndrome (695.81)
      Stevens-Johnson syndrome (695.13)
      Stevens-Johnson syndrome-toxic epidermal
         necrolysis overlap syndrome (695.14)
      toxic epidermal necrolysis (695.15)
   AHA: ▶4Q, '08, 128-131◀

   **695.50 Exfoliation due to erythematous condition
   involving less than 10 percent of body
   surface**
      Exfoliation due to erythematous condition NOS

   **695.51 Exfoliation due to erythematous condition
   involving 10-19 percent of body surface**

   **695.52 Exfoliation due to erythematous condition
   involving 20-29 percent of body surface**

   **695.53 Exfoliation due to erythematous
   condition involving 30-39 percent of
   body surface**   CC
      CC Excl: 695.53
      AHA: ▶4Q, '08, 131◀

   **695.54 Exfoliation due to erythematous
   condition involving 40-49 percent of
   body surface**   CC
      CC Excl: 695.54

   **695.55 Exfoliation due to erythematous
   condition involving 50-59 percent of
   body surface**   CC
      CC Excl: 695.55

   **695.56 Exfoliation due to erythematous
   condition involving 60-69 percent of
   body surface**   CC
      CC Excl: 695.56

   **695.57 Exfoliation due to erythematous
   condition involving 70-79 percent of
   body surface**   CC
      CC Excl: 695.57

   **695.58 Exfoliation due to erythematous
   condition involving 80-89 percent of
   body surface**   CC
      CC Excl: 695.58

   **695.59 Exfoliation due to erythematous
   condition involving 90 percent or more
   of body surface**   CC
      CC Excl: 695.59

✓5ᵗʰ **695.8 Other specified erythematous conditions**

   695.81 Ritter's disease
      Dermatitis exfoliativa neonatorum
      (Staphylococcal) Scalded skin syndrome
      Use additional code to identify percentage of
         skin exfoliation (695.50-695.59)
      DEF: Infectious skin disease of young children
      marked by eruptions ranging from a localized
      bullous to widespread easily ruptured fine vesicles
      and bullae; results in exfoliation of large planes of
      skin and leaves raw areas.

   695.89 Other
      Erythema intertrigo   Pityriasis rubra
      Intertrigo   (Hebra)
      EXCLUDES mycotic intertrigo (111.0-111.9)
      AHA: S-O, '86, 10

695.9 Unspecified erythematous condition
   Erythema NOS   Erythroderma (secondary)

✓4ᵗʰ **696 Psoriasis and similar disorders**

   696.0 Psoriatic arthropathy
      DEF: Psoriasis associated with inflammatory arthritis; often
      involves interphalangeal joints.

   696.1 Other psoriasis
      Acrodermatitis continua   Psoriasis:
      Dermatitis repens   NOS
      Psoriasis: any type, except
         arthropathic
      EXCLUDES psoriatic arthropathy (696.0)
      L40.9 Psoriasis unspecified   I-10

   696.2 Parapsoriasis
      Parakeratosis variegata
      Parapsoriasis lichenoides chronica
      Pityriasis lichenoides et varioliformis
      DEF: Erythrodermas similar to lichen, planus and psoriasis;
      symptoms include redness and itching; resistant to treatment.

   696.3 Pityriasis rosea
      Pityriasis circinata (et maculata)
      DEF: Common, self-limited rash of unknown etiology marked
      by a solitary erythematous, salmon or fawn-colored herald
      plaque on the trunk, arms or thighs; followed by
      development of papular or macular lesions that tend to peel
      and form a scaly collarette.

   696.4 Pityriasis rubra pilaris
      Devergie's disease   Lichen ruber acuminatus
      EXCLUDES pityriasis rubra (Hebra) (695.89)
      DEF: Inflammatory disease of hair follicles; marked by firm, red
      lesions topped by horny plugs; may form patches; occurs on
      fingers elbows, knees.

   696.5 Other and unspecified pityriasis
      Pityriasis: Pityriasis:
         NOS   streptogenes
         alba
      EXCLUDES pityriasis:
                    simplex (690.18)
                    versicolor (111.0)

   696.8 Other

✓4ᵗʰ **697 Lichen**
      EXCLUDES lichen:
                    obtusus corneus (698.3)
                    pilaris (congenital) (757.39)
                    ruber acuminatus (696.4)
                    sclerosus et atrophicus (701.0)
                    scrofulosus (017.0)
                    simplex chronicus (698.3)
                    spinulosus (congenital) (757.39)
                    urticatus (698.2)

   697.0 Lichen planus
      Lichen: Lichen:
         planopilaris   ruber planus
      DEF: Inflammatory, pruritic skin disease; marked by angular,
      flat-top, violet-colored papules; may be acute and
      widespread or chronic and localized.

   697.1 Lichen nitidus
      Pinkus' disease
      DEF: Chronic, inflammatory, asymptomatic skin disorder,
      characterized by numerous glistening, flat-topped, discrete,
      skin-colored micropapules most often on penis, lower
      abdomen, inner thighs, wrists, forearms, breasts and buttocks.

   697.8 Other lichen, not elsewhere classified
      Lichen: Lichen:
         ruber moniliforme   striata

   697.9 Lichen, unspecified

N Newborn Age: 0   P Pediatric Age: 0-17   M Maternity Age: 12-55   A Adult Age: 15-124   MCC Major CC Condition   CC CC Condition   HIV HIV Related Dx

242 – Volume 1 • February 2009   2010 ICD-9-CM

√4ᵗʰ **698 Pruritus and related conditions**

> EXCLUDES *pruritus specified as psychogenic (306.3)*
>
> **DEF:** Pruritus: Intense, persistent itching due to irritation of sensory nerve endings from organic or psychogenic causes.

698.0 Pruritus ani
Perianal itch

698.1 Pruritus of genital organs

698.2 Prurigo
Lichen urticatus   Prurigo:
Prurigo: mitis
   NOS   simplex
   Hebra's   Urticaria papulosa (Hebra)

> EXCLUDES *prurigo nodularis (698.3)*

698.3 Lichenification and lichen simplex chronicus
Hyde's disease
Neurodermatitis (circumscripta) (local)
Prurigo nodularis

> EXCLUDES *neurodermatitis, diffuse (of Brocq) (691.8)*
>
> **DEF:** Lichenification: thickening of skin due to prolonged rubbing or scratching.
>
> **DEF:** Lichen simplex chronicus: eczematous dermatitis, of face, neck, extremities, scrotum, vulva, and perianal region due to repeated itching, rubbing and scratching; spontaneous or evolves with other dermatoses.

698.4 Dermatitis factitia [artefacta]
Dermatitis ficta   Neurotic excoriation

Use additional code to identify any associated mental disorder

> **DEF:** Various types of self-inflicted skin lesions characterized in appearance as an erythema to a gangrene.

698.8 Other specified pruritic conditions
Pruritus: Winter itch
   hiemalis
   senilis

698.9 Unspecified pruritic disorder
Itch NOS   Pruritus NOS

L29.9 Pruritus unspecified   ⏺I-10

OTHER DISEASES OF SKIN AND SUBCUTANEOUS TISSUE (700-709)

> EXCLUDES *conditions confined to eyelids (373.0-374.9)*
> *congenital conditions of skin, hair, and nails (757.0-757.9)*

700 Corns and callosities
Callus   Clavus

> **DEF:** Corns: Conical or horny thickening of skin on toes, due to friction, pressure from shoes and hosiery; pain and inflammation may develop.
>
> **DEF:** Callosities: Localized overgrowth (hyperplasia) of the horny epidermal layer due to pressure or friction.

√4ᵗʰ **701 Other hypertrophic and atrophic conditions of skin**

> EXCLUDES *dermatomyositis (710.3)*
> *hereditary edema of legs (757.0)*
> *scleroderma (generalized) (710.1)*

701.0 Circumscribed scleroderma
Addison's keloid
Dermatosclerosis, localized
Lichen sclerosus et atrophicus
Morphea
Scleroderma, circumscribed or localized

> **DEF:** Thickened, hardened, skin and subcutaneous tissue; may involve musculoskeletal system.

701.1 Keratoderma, acquired
Acquired:
   ichthyosis
   keratoderma palmaris et plantaris
Elastosis perforans serpiginosa
Hyperkeratosis:
   NOS
   follicularis in cutem penetrans
   palmoplantaris climacterica
Keratoderma:
   climactericum
   tylodes, progressive
Keratosis (blennorrhagica)

> EXCLUDES *Darier's disease [keratosis follicularis]*
> *(congenital) (757.39)*
> *keratosis:*
> *arsenical (692.4)*
> *gonococcal (098.81)*

AHA: 4Q, '94, 48

701.2 Acquired acanthosis nigricans
Keratosis nigricans

> **DEF:** Diffuse velvety hyperplasia of the spinous skin layer of the axilla and other body folds marked by gray, brown, or black pigmentation; in adult form often associated with malignant acanthosis nigricans in a benign, nevoid form relatively generalized.

701.3 Striae atrophicae
Atrophic spots of skin
Atrophoderma maculatum
Atrophy blanche (of Milian)
Degenerative colloid atrophy
Senile degenerative atrophy
Striae distensae

> **DEF:** Bands of atrophic, depressed, wrinkled skin associated with stretching of skin from pregnancy, obesity, or rapid growth during puberty.

701.4 Keloid scar
Cheloid
Hypertrophic scar
Keloid

> **DEF:** Overgrowth of scar tissue due to excess amounts of collagen during connective tissue repair; occurs mainly on upper trunk, face.

701.5 Other abnormal granulation tissue
Excessive granulation

701.8 Other specified hypertrophic and atrophic conditions of skin
Acrodermatitis atrophicans chronica
Atrophia cutis senilis
Atrophoderma neuriticum
Confluent and reticulate papillomatosis
Cutis laxa senilis
Elastosis senilis
Folliculitis ulerythematosa reticulata
Gougerot-Carteaud syndrome or disease

AHA: 1Q, '08, 7

> **TIP:** Assign for nephrogenic fibrosing dermopathy (NFD) or nephrogenic systemic dermopathy (NSD), a systemic condition occurring only in patients with kidney disease.

701.9 Unspecified hypertrophic and atrophic conditions of skin
Atrophoderma
Skin tag

√4ᵗʰ **702 Other dermatoses**

> EXCLUDES *carcinoma in situ (232.0-232.9)*

702.0 Actinic keratosis

> **DEF:** Wart-like growth, red or skin-colored; may form a cutaneous horn.
>
> **AHA:** 1Q, '92, 18

√5ᵗʰ **702.1 Seborrheic keratosis**

> **DEF:** Common, benign, lightly pigmented, warty growth composed of basaloid cells.

702.11 Inflamed seborrheic keratosis

> **AHA:** 4Q, '94, 48

Skin and Subcutaneous Tissue

702.19   Other seborrheic keratosis
Seborrheic keratosis NOS

702.8   Other specified dermatoses

√4ᵗʰ 703   Diseases of nail
EXCLUDES   congenital anomalies (757.5)
onychia and paronychia (681.02, 681.11)

703.0   Ingrowing nail
Ingrowing nail with infection
Unguis incarnatus
EXCLUDES   infection, nail NOS (681.9)

703.8   Other specified diseases of nail
Dystrophia unguium
Hypertrophy of nail
Koilonychia
Leukonychia (punctata) (striata)
Onychauxis
Onychogryposis
Onycholysis

703.9   Unspecified disease of nail

√4ᵗʰ 704   Diseases of hair and hair follicles
EXCLUDES   congenital anomalies (757.4)

√5ᵗʰ 704.0   Alopecia
EXCLUDES   madarosis (374.55)
syphilitic alopecia (091.82)
DEF: Lack of hair, especially on scalp; often called baldness; may be partial or total; occurs at any age.

704.00   Alopecia, unspecified
Baldness
Loss of hair

704.01   Alopecia areata
Ophiasis
DEF: Alopecia areata: usually reversible, inflammatory, patchy hair loss found in beard or scalp.
DEF: Ophiasis: alopecia areata of children; marked by band around temporal and occipital scalp margins.

704.02   Telogen effluvium
DEF: Shedding of hair from premature telogen development in follicles due to stress, including shock, childbirth, surgery, drugs or weight loss.

704.09   Other
Folliculitis decalvans
Hypotrichosis:
NOS
postinfectional NOS
Pseudopelade

704.1   Hirsutism
Hypertrichosis:
NOS
lanuginosa, acquired
Polytrichia
EXCLUDES   hypertrichosis of eyelid (374.54)
DEF: Excess hair growth; often in unexpected places and amounts.

704.2   Abnormalities of the hair
Atrophic hair
Clastothrix
Fragilitas crinium
Trichiasis:
NOS
cicatrical
Trichorrhexis (nodosa)
EXCLUDES   trichiasis of eyelid (374.05)

704.3   Variations in hair color
Canities (premature)
Grayness, hair (premature)
Heterochromia of hair
Poliosis:
NOS
circumscripta, acquired

704.8   Other specified diseases of hair and hair follicles
Folliculitis:
NOS
abscedens et suffodiens
pustular
Perifolliculitis:
NOS
capitis abscedens et suffodiens
scalp
Sycosis:
NOS
barbae [not parasitic]
lupoid
vulgaris

704.9   Unspecified disease of hair and hair follicles

√4ᵗʰ 705   Disorders of sweat glands

705.0   Anhidrosis
Hypohidrosis
Oligohidrosis
DEF: Lack or deficiency of ability to sweat.

705.1   Prickly heat
Heat rash
Miliaria rubra (tropicalis)
Sudamina

√5ᵗʰ 705.2   Focal hyperhidrosis
EXCLUDES   generalized (secondary) hyperhidrosis (780.8)

705.21   Primary focal hyperhidrosis
Focal hyperhidrosis NOS
Hyperhidrosis NOS
Hyperhidrosis of:
axilla
face
palms
soles
DEF: A rare disorder of the sweat glands resulting in excessive production of sweat; occurs in the absence of any underlying condition, almost always focal, confined to one or more specific areas of the body.
AHA: 4Q, '04, 91

705.22   Secondary focal hyperhidrosis
Frey's syndrome
DEF: Secondary focal hyperhidrosis: a symptom of an underlying disease process resulting in excessive sweating beyond what the body requires to maintain thermal control, confined to one or more specific areas of the body.
DEF: Frey's syndrome: an auriculotemporal syndrome due to lesion on the parotid gland; characteristic redness and excessive sweating on the cheek in connection with eating.
AHA: 4Q, '04, 91

√5ᵗʰ 705.8   Other specified disorders of sweat glands

705.81   Dyshidrosis
Cheiropompholyx
Pompholyx
DEF: Vesicular eruption, on hands, feet causing itching and burning.

705.82   Fox-Fordyce disease
DEF: Chronic, usually pruritic disease evidenced by small follicular papular eruptions, especially in the axillary and pubic areas; develops from the closure and rupture of the affected apocrine glands' intraepidermal portion of the ducts.

705.83   Hidradenitis
Hidradenitis suppurativa
DEF: Inflamed sweat glands.

705.89   Other
Bromhidrosis
Chromhidrosis
Granulosis rubra nasi
Urhidrosis

> **EXCLUDES**   generalized hyperhidrosis (780.8)
> hidrocystoma (216.0-216.9)

DEF: Bromhidrosis: foul-smelling axillary sweat due to decomposed bacteria.
DEF: Chromhidrosis: secretion of colored sweat.
DEF: Granulosis rubra nasi: ideopathic condition of children; causes redness, sweating around nose, face and chin; tends to end by puberty.
DEF: Urhidrosis: urinous substance, such as uric acid, in sweat; occurs in uremia.

705.9   Unspecified disorder of sweat glands
Disorder of sweat glands NOS

✓4th **706   Diseases of sebaceous glands**

706.0   Acne varioliformis
Acne: Acne:
frontalis   necrotica

DEF: Rare form of acne characterized by persistent brown papulo-pustules usually on the brow and temporoparietal part of the scalp.

706.1   Other acne
Acne: Blackhead
NOS   Comedo
conglobata
cystic
pustular
vulgaris

> **EXCLUDES**   acne rosacea (695.3)

706.2   Sebaceous cyst
Atheroma, skin
Keratin cyst
Wen

DEF: Benign epidermal cyst, contains sebum and keratin; presents as firm, circumscribed nodule.

706.3   Seborrhea

> **EXCLUDES**   seborrhea:
> capitis (690.11)
> sicca (690.18)
> seborrheic
> dermatitis (690.10)
> keratosis (702.11-702.19)

DEF: Seborrheic dermatitis marked by excessive secretion of sebum; the sebum forms an oily coating, crusts, or scales on the skin; it is also called hypersteatosis.

706.8   Other specified diseases of sebaceous glands
Asteatosis (cutis)
Xerosis cutis

706.9   Unspecified disease of sebaceous glands

✓4th **707   Chronic ulcer of skin**

> **INCLUDES**   non-infected sinus of skin
> non-healing ulcer
> **EXCLUDES**   varicose ulcer (454.0, 454.2)

AHA: 4Q, '04, 92

✓5th **707.0   Pressure ulcer**
Bed sore
Decubitus ulcer
Plaster ulcer

Use additional code to identify pressure ulcer stage (707.20-707.25)

AHA: 4Q, '08, 132-133; 1Q, '04, 14; 4Q, '03, 110; 4Q, '99, 20; 1Q, '96, 15; 3Q, '90, 15; N-D, '87, 9

707.00   Unspecified site

707.01   Elbow

707.02   Upper back
Shoulder blades

Four Stages of Pressure Ulcers

First Stage
Persistent focal erythema

Second Stage
Partial thickness skin loss involving epidermis, dermis, or both

Third Stage
Full thickness skin loss extending through subcutaneous tissue

Fourth Stage
Necrosis of soft tissue extending to muscle and bone

707.03   Lower back
►Coccyx◄
Sacrum
AHA: 3Q, '08, 17; 1Q, '05, 16
L89.159 Pressure ulcer of sacral region uns stage   [I-10]

707.04   Hip
L89.209 Pressure ulcer of unspecified hip uns stage   [I-10]

707.05   Buttock
L89.309 Pressure ulcer of unspecified buttock uns stage   [I-10]

707.06   Ankle

707.07   Heel
AHA: 1Q, '05, 16
L89.609 Pressure ulcer of unspecified heel uns stage   [I-10]

707.09   Other site
Head
L89.899 Pressure ulcer of other site unspecified stage   [I-10]

✓5th **707.1   Ulcer of lower limbs, except pressure ulcer**
Ulcer, chronic:
neurogenic } of lower limb
trophic

Code, if applicable, any causal condition first:
atherosclerosis of the extremities with ulceration (440.23)
chronic venous hypertension with ulcer (459.31)
chronic venous hypertension with ulcer and inflammation (459.33)
diabetes mellitus (249.80-249.81, 250.80-250.83)
postphlebitic syndrome with ulcer (459.11)
postphlebitic syndrome with ulcer and inflammation (459.13)

AHA: 4Q, '00, 44; 4Q, '99, 15

707.10   Ulcer of lower limb, unspecified   [CC]
CC Excl: 440.23, 707.10-707.19, 707.8-707.9, 709.8
AHA: 3Q, '04, 5; 4Q, '02, 43
L97.901 Non-prss chr ulcr uns part uns lw leg brkdwn skn   [I-10]

707.11   Ulcer of thigh   [CC]
CC Excl: See code 707.10

707.12   Ulcer of calf   [CC]
CC Excl: See code 707.10
L97.229 Non-press chronic ulcer left calf w/uns severity   [I-10]

707.13   Ulcer of ankle   [CC]
CC Excl: See code 707.10
L97.309 Non-press chronic ulcer uns ankle uns severity   [I-10]

707.14   Ulcer of heel and midfoot   [CC]
Plantar surface of midfoot
CC Excl: See code 707.10
L97.409 Non-press chr ulcer uns heel & midft uns sevrity   [I-10]

✓4th / ✓5th   Additional Digit Required   Unacceptable PDx   Manifestation Code   Hospital Acquired Condition   ►◄ Revised Text   ● New Code   ▲ Revised Code Title

2010 ICD-9-CM   October 2009 • Volume 1 – 245

Skin and Subcutaneous Tissue

707.15–709.4

707.15   Ulcer of other part of foot
Toes

L97.509 Non-press chr ulcer oth part uns ft uns severity   `I-10`

707.19   Ulcer of other part of lower limb   `CC`
CC Excl: See code 707.10

L97.819 Non-press chr ulcer oth part rt low leg uns sevr   `I-10`

√5ᵗʰ **707.2   Pressure ulcer stages**
Code first site of pressure ulcer (707.00-707.09)
AHA: ▶4Q, '08, 132-134◀

TIP: Pressure ulcer stage codes should be assigned only with codes for pressure ulcers; do not assign with other types of skin ulcers.

TIP: If a pressure ulcer progresses during an admission from one stage to another, assign only the code for the higher stage.

707.20   Pressure ulcer, unspecified stage
Healing pressure ulcer NOS
Healing pressure ulcer, unspecified stage

707.21   Pressure ulcer stage I
Healing pressure ulcer, stage I
Pressure pre-ulcer skin changes limited to persistent focal erythema

707.22   Pressure ulcer stage II
Healing pressure ulcer, stage II
Pressure ulcer with abrasion, blister, partial thickness skin loss involving epidermis and/or dermis

707.23   Pressure ulcer stage III   `MCC`
Healing pressure ulcer, stage III
Pressure ulcer with full thickness skin loss involving damage or necrosis of subcutaneous tissue
CC Excl: 707.00-707.24, 707.8-707.9

707.24   Pressure ulcer stage IV   `MCC`
Healing pressure ulcer, stage IV
Pressure ulcer with necrosis of soft tissues through to underlying muscle, tendon, or bone
CC Excl: See code 707.23

707.25   Pressure ulcer, unstageable
TIP: Assign only if ulcer is covered by eschar, has been treated with skin or other graft, or is documented as a deep tissue injury but not documented as due to trauma.

707.8   Chronic ulcer of other specified sites
Ulcer, chronic:
neurogenic ⎱ of other specified sites
trophic ⎰

L98.499 Non-press chr ulcer skin oth sites uns severity   `I-10`

707.9   Chronic ulcer of unspecified site
Chronic ulcer NOS
Trophic ulcer NOS
Tropical ulcer NOS
Ulcer of skin NOS

Cutaneous Lesions

Surface Lesions
Fissure   Polyp growth   Ulcer
Solid Lesions
Flat macule   Slightly elevated wheal   Solid papule
Sac Lesions
Cyst   Clear fluid vesicle   Pustule

√4ᵗʰ **708   Urticaria**
EXCLUDES   edema:
angioneurotic (995.1)
Quincke's (995.1)
hereditary angioedema (277.6)
urticaria:
giant (995.1)
papulosa (Hebra) (698.2)
pigmentosa (juvenile) (congenital) (757.33)
DEF: Skin disorder marked by raised edematous patches of skin or mucous membrane with intense itching; also called hives.

708.0   Allergic urticaria

708.1   Idiopathic urticaria

708.2   Urticaria due to cold and heat
Thermal urticaria

708.3   Dermatographic urticaria
Dermatographia
Factitial urticaria

708.4   Vibratory urticaria

708.5   Cholinergic urticaria

708.8   Other specified urticaria
Nettle rash
Urticaria:
chronic
recurrent periodic

708.9   Urticaria, unspecified
Hives NOS

√4ᵗʰ **709   Other disorders of skin and subcutaneous tissue**

√5ᵗʰ **709.0   Dyschromia**
EXCLUDES   albinism (270.2)
pigmented nevus (216.0-216.9)
that of eyelid (374.52-374.53)
DEF: Pigment disorder of skin or hair.

709.00   Dyschromia, unspecified

709.01   Vitiligo
DEF: Persistent, progressive development of nonpigmented white patches on otherwise normal skin.

709.09   Other

709.1   Vascular disorders of skin
Angioma serpiginosum
Purpura (primary)annularis telangiectodes

709.2   Scar conditions and fibrosis of skin
Adherent scar (skin)
Cicatrix
Disfigurement (due to scar)
Fibrosis, skin NOS
Scar NOS
EXCLUDES   keloid scar (701.4)
AHA: N-D, '84, 19

709.3   Degenerative skin disorders
Calcinosis:
circumscripta
cutis
Colloid milium
Degeneration, skin
Deposits, skin
Senile dermatosis NOS
Subcutaneous calcification

709.4   Foreign body granuloma of skin and subcutaneous tissue
EXCLUDES   residual foreign body without granuloma of skin and subcutaneous tissue (729.6)
that of muscle (728.82)

`N` Newborn Age: 0   `P` Pediatric Age: 0-17   `M` Maternity Age: 12-55   `A` Adult Age: 15-124   `MCC` Major CC Condition   `CC` CC Condition   `HIV` HIV Related Dx

246 – Volume 1 • February 2009

2010 ICD-9-CM

709.8 **Other specified disorders of skin**
Epithelial hyperplasia
Menstrual dermatosis
Vesicular eruption

DEF: Epithelial hyperplasia: increased number of epitheleal cells.

DEF: Vesicular eruption: liquid-filled structures appearing through skin.

AHA: ▶4Q, '08, 99;◀ N-D, '87, 6

L98.8 Other spec disorders skin & subcutaneous tissue `I-10`

709.9 **Unspecified disorder of skin and subcutaneous tissue**
Dermatosis NOS

✓4ᵗʰ ✓5ᵗʰ Additional Digit Required   Unacceptable PDx   Manifestation Code   Hospital Acquired Condition   ▶◀ Revised Text   ● New Code   ▲ Revised Code Title

2010 ICD-9-CM   **February 2009 • Volume 1 – 247**

13. DISEASES OF THE MUSCULOSKELETAL SYSTEM AND CONNECTIVE TISSUE (710-739)

Use additional external cause code, if applicable, to identify the cause of the musculoskeletal condition

The following fifth-digit subclassification is for use with categories 711-712, 715-716, 718-719, and 730:

0 site unspecified
1 shoulder region
  Acromioclavicular joint(s)
  Clavicle
  Glenohumeral joint(s)
  Scapula
  Sternoclavicular joint(s)
2 upper arm
  Elbow joint
  Humerus
3 forearm
  Radius
  Ulna
  Wrist joint
4 hand
  Carpus
  Metacarpus
  Phalanges [fingers]
5 pelvic region and thigh
  Buttock
  Femur
  Hip (joint)

6 lower leg
  Fibula
  Knee joint
  Patella
  Tibia
7 ankle and foot
  Ankle joint
  Digits [toes]
  Metatarsus
  Phalanges, foot
  Tarsus
  Other joints in foot
8 other specified sites
  Head
  Neck
  Ribs
  Skull
  Trunk
  Vertebral column
9 multiple sites

ARTHROPATHIES AND RELATED DISORDERS (710-719)

> **EXCLUDES** *disorders of spine (720.0-724.9)*

✅4ᵗʰ **710 Diffuse diseases of connective tissue**

> **INCLUDES** all collagen diseases whose effects are not mainly confined to a single system

> **EXCLUDES** *those affecting mainly the cardiovascular system, i.e., polyarteritis nodosa and allied conditions (446.0-446.7)*

710.0 Systemic lupus erythematosus
  Disseminated lupus erythematosus
  Libman-Sacks disease
  Use additional code to identify manifestation, as:
    endocarditis (424.91)
    nephritis (583.81)
      chronic (582.81)
    nephrotic syndrome (581.81)

> **EXCLUDES** *lupus erythematosus (discoid) NOS (695.4)*

  DEF: A chronic multisystemic inflammatory disease affecting connective tissue; marked by anemia, leukopenia, muscle and joint pains, fever, rash of a butterfly pattern around cheeks and forehead area; of unknown etiology.
  AHA: 2Q, '03, 7-8; 2Q, '97, 8
  M32.9 Systemic lupus erythematosus unspecified [I-10]

710.1 Systemic sclerosis
  Acrosclerosis
  CRST syndrome
  Progressive systemic sclerosis
  Scleroderma
  Use additional code to identify manifestation, as:
    lung involvement (517.2)
    myopathy (359.6)

> **EXCLUDES** *circumscribed scleroderma (701.0)*

  DEF: Systemic disease, involving excess fibrotic collagen build-up; symptoms include thickened skin; fibrotic degenerative changes in various organs; and vascular abnormalities; condition occurs more often in females.
  AHA: 1Q, '88, 6

710.2 Sicca syndrome
  Keratoconjunctivitis sicca
  Sjögren's disease
  DEF: Autoimmune disease; associated with keratoconjunctivitis, laryngopharyngitis, rhinitis, dry mouth, enlarged parotid gland, and chronic polyarthritis.

Joint Structures

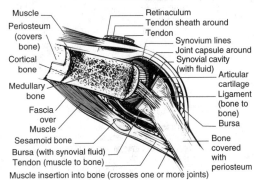

Muscle
Periosteum (covers bone)
Cortical bone
Medullary bone
Fascia over Muscle
Sesamoid bone
Bursa (with synovial fluid)
Tendon (muscle to bone)
Muscle insertion into bone (crosses one or more joints)
Retinaculum
Tendon sheath around Tendon
Synovium lines
Joint capsule around
Synovial cavity (with fluid)
Articular cartilage
Ligament (bone to bone)
Bursa
Bone covered with periosteum

710.3 Dermatomyositis [cc]
  Poikilodermatomyositis
  Polymyositis with skin involvement
  DEF: Polymyositis characterized by flat-top purple papules on knuckles; upper eyelid rash, edema of eyelids and orbit area, red rash on forehead, neck, shoulders, trunk and arms; symptoms include fever, weight loss, aching muscles; visceral cancer.
  CC Excl: 710.3

710.4 Polymyositis [cc]
  DEF: Chronic, progressive, inflammatory skeletal muscle disease; causes weakness of limb girdles, neck, pharynx; may precede or follow scleroderma, Sjogren's disease, systemic lupus erythematosus, arthritis, or malignancy.
  CC Excl: 710.4

710.5 Eosinophilia myalgia syndrome [cc]
  Toxic oil syndrome
  Use additional E code to identify drug, if drug induced
  DEF: Eosinophilia myalgia syndrome (EMS): inflammatory, multisystem fibrosis; associated with ingesting elementary L-tryptophan; symptoms include myalgia, weak limbs and bulbar muscles, distal sensory loss, areflexia, arthralgia, cough, fever, fatigue, skin rashes, myopathy, and eosinophil counts greater than 1000/microliter.
  DEF: Toxic oil syndrome: syndrome similar to EMS due to ingesting contaminated cooking oil.
  CC Excl: 292.0-293.9, 710.5
  AHA: 4Q, '92, 21

710.8 Other specified diffuse diseases of connective tissue [cc]
  Multifocal fibrosclerosis (idiopathic) NEC
  Systemic fibrosclerosing syndrome
  CC Excl: 359.71-359.79, 710.8
  AHA: M-A, '87, 12

710.9 Unspecified diffuse connective tissue disease
  Collagen disease NOS

✅4ᵗʰ **711 Arthropathy associated with infections**

> **INCLUDES**
>   arthritis
>   arthropathy
>   polyarthritis
>   polyarthropathy
> } associated with conditions classifiable below

> **EXCLUDES** *rheumatic fever (390)*

The following fifth-digit subclassification is for use with category 711; valid digits are in [brackets] under each code. See list at beginning of chapter for definitions.

0 site unspecified
1 shoulder region
2 upper arm
3 forearm
4 hand
5 pelvic region and thigh
6 lower leg
7 ankle and foot
8 other specified sites
9 multiple sites

AHA: 1Q, '92, 17

✅4ᵗʰ ✅5ᵗʰ Additional Digit Required   Unacceptable PDx   Manifestation Code   Hospital Acquired Condition   ▶◀ Revised Text   ● New Code   ▲ Revised Code Title

2010 ICD-9-CM   **Volume 1 – 249**

Musculoskeletal System and Connective Tissue

711.0–711.2

§ √5ᵗʰ **711.0 Pyogenic arthritis** CC
[0-9]
Arthritis or polyarthritis (due to):
coliform [Escherichia coli]
Hemophilus influenzae [H. influenzae]
pneumococcal
Pseudomonas
staphylococcal
streptococcal
Pyarthrosis
Use additional code to identify infectious organism (041.0-041.8)

DEF: Infectious arthritis caused by various bacteria; marked by inflamed synovial membranes, and purulent effusion in joints.

CC Excl: For codes 711.00, 711.08-711.09: 015.80-015.96, 017.90-017.96, 036.82, 056.71, 098.50-098.51, 098.59, 098.89, 711.00-714.0, 715.00, 715.09-715.10, 715.18-716.99, 718.00-718.08, 719.00-719.10, 719.18-719.99; **For code 711.01:** 015.80-015.96, 017.90-017.96, 036.82, 056.71, 098.50-098.51, 098.59, 098.89, 711.00-711.01, 711.08-711.11, 711.18-711.21, 711.28-711.31, 711.38-711.41, 711.48-711.51, 711.58-711.61, 711.68-711.71, 711.78-711.81, 711.88-711.91, 711.98-712.11, 712.18-712.21, 712.28-712.31, 712.38-712.81, 712.88-712.91, 712.98-714.0, 715.00, 715.09-715.11, 715.18-715.21, 715.28-715.31, 715.38-715.91, 715.98-716.01, 716.08-716.11, 716.18-716.21, 716.28-716.31, 716.38-716.41, 716.48-716.51, 716.58-716.61, 716.68-716.81, 716.88-716.91, 716.98-716.99, 718.00-718.01, 718.08, 719.00-719.01, 719.08-719.11, 719.18-719.21, 719.28-719.31, 719.38-719.41, 719.48-719.51, 719.58-719.61, 719.68-719.81, 719.88-719.91, 719.98-719.99; **For code 711.02:** 015.80-015.96, 017.90-017.96, 036.82, 056.71, 098.50-098.51, 098.59, 098.89, 711.00, 711.02, 711.08-711.10, 711.12, 711.18-711.20, 711.22, 711.28-711.30, 711.32, 711.38-711.40, 711.42, 711.48-711.50, 711.52, 711.58-711.60, 711.62, 711.68-711.70, 711.72, 711.78-711.80, 711.82, 711.88-711.90, 711.92, 711.98-712.10, 712.12, 712.18-712.20, 712.22, 712.28-712.30, 712.32, 712.38-712.80, 712.82, 712.88-712.90, 712.92, 712.98-714.0, 715.00, 715.09-715.10, 715.12, 715.18-715.20, 715.22, 715.28-715.30, 715.32, 715.38-715.90, 715.92, 715.98-716.00, 716.02, 716.08-716.10, 716.12, 716.18-716.20, 716.22, 716.28-716.30, 716.32, 716.38-716.40, 716.42, 716.48-716.50, 716.52, 716.58-716.60, 716.62, 716.68-716.80, 716.82, 716.88-716.90, 716.92, 716.98-716.99, 718.00, 718.02, 718.08, 719.00, 719.02, 719.08-719.10, 719.12, 719.18-719.20, 719.22, 719.28-719.30, 719.32, 719.38-719.40, 719.42, 719.48-719.50, 719.52, 719.58-719.60, 719.62, 719.68-719.80, 719.82, 719.88-719.90, 719.92, 719.98-719.99; **For code 711.03:** 015.80-015.96, 017.90-017.96, 036.82, 056.71, 098.50-098.51, 098.59, 098.89, 711.00, 711.03, 711.08-711.10, 711.13, 711.18-711.20, 711.23, 711.28-711.30, 711.33, 711.38-711.40, 711.43, 711.48-711.50, 711.53, 711.58-711.60, 711.63, 711.68-711.70, 711.73, 711.78-711.80, 711.83, 711.88-711.90, 711.93, 711.98-712.10, 712.13, 712.18-712.20, 712.23, 712.28-712.30, 712.33, 712.38-712.80, 712.83, 712.88-712.90, 712.93, 712.98-714.0, 715.00, 715.09-715.10, 715.13, 715.18-715.20, 715.23, 715.28-715.30, 715.33, 715.38-715.90, 715.93, 715.98-716.00, 716.03, 716.08-716.10, 716.13, 716.18-716.20, 716.23, 716.28-716.30, 716.33, 716.38-716.40, 716.43, 716.48-716.50, 716.53, 716.58-716.60, 716.63, 716.68-716.80, 716.83, 716.88-716.90, 716.93, 716.98-716.99, 718.00, 718.03, 718.08, 719.00, 719.03, 719.08-719.10, 719.13, 719.18-719.20, 719.23, 719.28-719.30, 719.33, 719.38-719.40, 719.43, 719.48-719.50, 719.53, 719.58-719.60, 719.63, 719.68-719.80, 719.83, 719.88-719.90, 719.93, 719.98-719.99; **For code 711.04:** 015.80-015.96, 017.90-017.96, 036.82, 056.71, 098.50-098.51, 098.59, 098.89, 711.00, 711.04, 711.08-711.10, 711.14, 711.18-711.20, 711.24, 711.28-711.30, 711.34, 711.38-711.40, 711.44, 711.48-711.50, 711.54, 711.58-711.60, 711.64, 711.68-711.70, 711.74, 711.78-711.80, 711.84, 711.88-711.90, 711.94, 711.98-712.10, 712.14, 712.18-712.20, 712.24, 712.28-712.30, 712.34, 712.38-712.80, 712.84, 712.88-712.90, 712.94, 712.98-714.0, 715.00-715.10, 715.14, 715.18-715.20, 715.24, 715.28-715.30, 715.34, 715.38-715.90, 715.94, 715.98-716.00, 716.04, 716.08-716.10, 716.14, 716.18-716.20, 716.24, 716.28-716.30, 716.34, 716.38-716.40, 716.44, 716.48-716.50, 716.54, 716.58-716.60, 716.64, 716.68-716.80, 716.84, 716.88-716.90, 716.94, 716.98-716.99, 718.00, 718.04, 718.08, 719.00, 719.04, 719.08-719.10, 719.14, 719.18-719.20, 719.24, 719.28-719.30, 719.34, 719.38-719.40, 719.44, 719.48-719.50, 719.54, 719.58-719.60, 719.64, 719.68-719.80, 719.84, 719.88-719.90, 719.94, 719.98-719.99; **For code 711.05:** 015.80-015.96, 017.90-017.96, 036.82, 056.71, 098.50-098.51, 098.59, 098.89, 711.00, 711.05, 711.08-711.10, 711.15, 711.18-711.20, 711.25, 711.28-711.30, 711.35, 711.38-711.40, 711.45, 711.48-711.50, 711.55, 711.58-711.60, 711.65, 711.68-711.70, 711.75, 711.78-711.80, 711.85, 711.88-711.90, 711.95, 711.98-712.10, 712.15, 712.18-712.20, 712.25, 712.28-712.30, 712.35, 712.38-712.80,

712.85, 712.88-712.90, 712.95, 712.98-714.0, 715.00, 715.09-715.10, 715.15, 715.18-715.20, 715.25, 715.28-715.30, 715.35, 715.38-715.90, 715.95, 715.98-716.00, 716.05, 716.08-716.10, 716.15, 716.18-716.20, 716.25, 716.28-716.30, 716.35, 716.38-716.40, 716.45, 716.48-716.50, 716.55, 716.58-716.60, 716.65, 716.68-716.80, 716.85, 716.88-716.90, 716.95, 716.98-716.99, 718.00, 718.05, 718.08, 719.00, 719.05, 719.08-719.10, 719.15, 719.18-719.20, 719.25, 719.28-719.30, 719.35, 719.38-719.40, 719.45, 719.48-719.50, 719.55, 719.58-719.60, 719.65, 719.68-719.80, 719.85, 719.88-719.90, 719.95, 719.98-719.99; **For code 711.06:** 015.80-015.96, 017.90-017.96, 036.82, 056.71, 098.50-098.51, 098.59, 098.89, 711.00, 711.06, 711.08-711.10, 711.16, 711.18-711.20, 711.26, 711.28-711.30, 711.36, 711.38-711.40, 711.46, 711.48-711.50, 711.56, 711.58-711.60, 711.66, 711.68-711.70, 711.76, 711.78-711.80, 711.86, 711.88-711.90, 711.96, 711.98-712.10, 712.16, 712.18-712.20, 712.26, 712.28-712.30, 712.36, 712.38-712.80, 712.86, 712.88-712.90, 712.96, 712.98-714.0, 715.00, 715.09-715.10, 715.16, 715.18-715.20, 715.26, 715.28-715.30, 715.36, 715.38-715.90, 715.96, 715.98-716.00, 716.06, 716.08-716.10, 716.16, 716.18-716.20, 716.26, 716.28-716.30, 716.36, 716.38-716.40, 716.46, 716.48-716.50, 716.56, 716.58-716.60, 716.66, 716.68-716.80, 716.86, 716.88-716.90, 716.96, 716.98-716.99, 718.00, 718.08, 719.00, 719.06, 719.08-719.10, 719.16, 719.18-719.20, 719.26, 719.28-719.30, 719.36, 719.38-719.40, 719.46, 719.48-719.50, 719.56, 719.58-719.60, 719.66, 719.68-719.80, 719.86, 719.88-719.90, 719.96, 719.98-719.99; **For code 711.07:** 015.80-015.96, 017.90-017.96, 036.82, 056.71, 098.50-098.51, 098.59, 098.89, 711.00, 711.07-711.10, 711.17-711.20, 711.27-711.30, 711.37-711.40, 711.47-711.50, 711.57-711.60, 711.67-711.70, 711.77-711.80, 711.87-711.90, 711.97-712.10, 712.17-712.20, 712.27-712.30, 712.37-712.80, 712.87-712.90, 712.97-714.0, 715.00, 715.09-715.10, 715.17-715.20, 715.27-715.30, 715.37-715.90, 715.97-716.00, 716.07-716.10, 716.17-716.20, 716.27-716.30, 716.37-716.40, 716.47-716.50, 716.57-716.60, 716.67-716.80, 716.87-716.90, 716.97-716.99, 718.00, 718.07-718.08, 719.00, 719.07-719.10, 719.17-719.20, 719.27-719.30, 719.37-719.40, 719.47-719.50, 719.57-719.60, 719.67-719.80, 719.87-719.90, 719.97-719.99

AHA: 1Q, '92, 16; 1Q, '91, 15

M00.869 Arthritis due to other bacteria unspecified knee [I-10]

§ √5ᵗʰ **711.1 Arthropathy associated with Reiter's disease** CC
[0-9] **and nonspecific urethritis**
Code first underlying disease as:
nonspecific urethritis (099.4)
Reiter's disease (099.3)

DEF: Reiter's disease: joint disease marked by diarrhea, urethritis, conjunctivitis, keratosis and arthritis; of unknown etiology; affects young males.
DEF: Urethritis: inflamed urethra.

CC Excl: 003.23, 015.80-015.96, 017.90-017.96, 036.82, 056.71, 098.50-098.51, 098.59, 098.89, 711.00-714.0, 715.00, 715.09-715.10, 715.18-716.99, 718.00-718.08, 719.00-719.10, 719.18-719.69, 719.80-719.99

§ √5ᵗʰ **711.2 Arthropathy in Behçet's syndrome** CC
[0-9]
Code first underlying disease (136.1)

DEF: Behçet's syndrome: Chronic inflammatory disorder, of unknown etiology; affects small blood vessels; causes ulcers of oral and pharyngeal mucous membranes and genitalia, skin lesions, retinal vasculitis, optic atrophy and severe uveitis.
CC Excl: 003.23, 015.80-015.96, 017.90-017.96, 036.82, 056.71, 098.50-098.51, 098.59, 098.89, 711.00-714.0, 715.00, 715.09-715.10, 715.18-716.99, 718.00-718.08, 719.00-719.10, 719.18-719.69, 719.80-719.99

§ Requires fifth digit. Valid digits are in [brackets] under each code. See beginning of section 710-739 for codes and defintions.

N Newborn Age: 0   P Pediatric Age: 0-17   M Maternity Age: 12-55   A Adult Age: 15-124   MCC Major CC Condition   CC CC Condition   HIV HIV Related Dx

250 – Volume 1   2010 ICD-9-CM

§ ✓5th **711.3** **Postdysenteric arthropathy**
[0-9]

    Code first underlying disease as:
      dysentery (009.0)
      enteritis, infectious (008.0-009.3)
      paratyphoid fever (002.1-002.9)
      typhoid fever (002.0)

    EXCLUDES   *salmonella arthritis (003.23)*

    CC Excl: For codes 711.30-711.35, 711.37, and 711.39: 003.23, 015.80-015.96, 017.90-017.96, 036.82, 056.71, 098.50-098.51, 098.59, 098.89, 711.00-714.0, 715.00, 715.09-715.10, 715.18-716.99, 718.00-718.08, 719.00-719.10, 719.18-719.69, 719.80-719.99; **For code 711.36:** 003.23, 015.80-015.96, 017.90-017.96, 036.82, 056.71, 098.50-098.51, 098.59, 098.89, 711.00-714.0, 715.00, 715.09-715.10, 715.18-716.07, 716.09-716.99, 718.00-718.08, 719.00-719.10, 719.18-719.69, 719.80-719.99; **For code 711.38:** 003.23, 015.80-015.96, 017.90-017.96, 036.82, 056.71, 098.50-098.51, 098.59, 098.89, 711.00-714.0, 715.00, 715.09-715.10, 715.18-716.57, 716.59-716.99, 718.00-718.08, 719.00-719.10, 719.18-719.69, 719.80-719.99

§ ✓5th **711.4** **Arthropathy associated with other**
[0-9] **bacterial diseases**

    Code first underlying disease as:
      diseases classifiable to 010-040, 090-099, except as in
        711.1, 711.3, and 713.5
      leprosy (030.0-030.9)
      tuberculosis (015.0-015.9)

    EXCLUDES   *gonococcal arthritis (098.50)*
             meningococcal arthritis (036.82)

    CC Excl: For codes 711.40, 711.42-711.49: 003.23, 015.80-015.96, 017.90-017.96, 036.82, 056.71, 098.50-098.51, 098.59, 098.89, 711.00-714.0, 715.00, 715.09-715.10, 715.18-716.99, 718.00-718.08, 719.00-719.10, 719.18-719.69, 719.80-719.99; **For code 711.41:** 003.23, 015.80-015.96, 017.90-017.96, 036.82, 056.71, 098.50-098.51, 098.59, 098.89, 711.00-714.0, 715.00, 715.09-715.10, 715.18-716.99, 718.00-718.08, 719.00-719.10, 719.18-719.39, 719.41-719.69, 719.80-719.99

§ ✓5th **711.5** **Arthropathy associated with other viral**
[0-9] **diseases**

    Code first underlying disease as:
      diseases classifiable to 045-049, 050-079, 480, 487
      O'nyong nyong (066.3)

    EXCLUDES   *that due to rubella (056.71)*

    CC Excl: 003.23, 015.80-015.96, 017.90-017.96, 036.82, 056.71, 098.50-098.51, 098.59, 098.89, 711.00-714.0, 715.00, 715.09-715.10, 715.18-716.99, 718.00-718.08, 719.00-719.10, 719.18-719.69, 719.80-719.99

§ ✓5th **711.6** **Arthropathy associated with mycoses**
[0-9]   *Code first underlying disease (110.0-118)*

    CC Excl: For codes 711.60, 711.68-711.69: 015.80-015.96, 017.90-017.96, 036.82, 056.71, 098.50-098.51, 098.59, 098.89, 711.00-714.0, 715.00, 715.09-715.10, 715.18-716.99, 718.00-718.08, 719.00-719.10, 719.18-719.99; **For code 711.61:** 015.80-015.96, 017.90-017.96, 036.82, 056.71, 098.50-098.51, 098.59, 098.89, 711.00-714.0, 715.00, 715.09-715.10, 715.18-716.99, 718.00-718.08, 719.00-719.10, 719.18-719.99; **For code 711.62:** 015.80-015.96, 017.90-017.96, 036.82, 056.71, 098.50-098.51, 098.59, 098.89, 711.00-711.01, 711.08-711.11, 711.18-711.21, 711.28-711.31, 711.38-711.41, 711.48-711.51, 711.58-711.61, 711.68-711.71, 711.78-711.81, 711.88-711.91, 711.98-712.11, 712.18-712.21, 712.28-712.31, 712.38-712.81, 712.88-712.91, 712.98-714.0, 715.00, 715.09-715.11, 715.18-715.21, 715.28-715.31, 715.38-715.91, 715.98-716.01, 716.08-716.11, 716.18-716.21, 716.28-716.31, 716.38-716.41, 716.48-716.51, 716.58-716.61, 716.68-716.81, 716.88-716.91, 716.98-716.99, 718.00-718.01, 718.08, 719.00-719.01, 719.08-719.11, 719.18-719.21, 719.28-719.31, 719.38-719.41, 719.48-719.51, 719.58-719.61, 719.68-719.81, 719.88-719.91, 719.98-719.99; **For code 711.63:** 015.80-015.96, 017.90-017.96, 036.82, 056.71, 098.50-098.51, 098.59, 098.89, 711.00, 711.02, 711.08-711.10, 711.12, 711.18-711.20, 711.22, 711.28-711.30, 711.32, 711.38-711.40, 711.42, 711.48-711.50, 711.52, 711.58-711.60, 711.62, 711.68-711.70, 711.72, 711.78-711.80, 711.82, 711.88-711.90, 711.92, 711.98-712.10, 712.12, 712.18-712.20, 712.22, 712.28-712.30, 712.32, 712.38-712.80, 712.82, 712.88-712.90, 712.92, 712.98-714.0, 715.00, 715.09-715.10, 715.12, 715.18-715.20, 715.22, 715.28-715.30, 715.32, 715.38-715.90, 715.92, 715.98-716.00, 716.02, 716.08-716.10, 716.12, 716.18-716.20, 716.22, 716.28-716.30, 716.32, 716.38-716.40, 716.42, 716.48-716.50, 716.52, 716.58-716.60, 716.62, 716.68-716.80, 716.82,

716.88-716.90, 716.92, 716.98-716.99, 718.00, 718.02, 718.08, 719.00, 719.02, 719.08-719.10, 719.12, 719.18-719.20, 719.22, 719.28-719.30, 719.32, 719.38-719.40, 719.42, 719.48-719.50, 719.52, 719.58-719.60, 719.62, 719.68-719.80, 719.82, 719.88-719.90, 719.92, 719.98-719.99; **For code 711.64:** 015.80-015.96, 017.90-017.96, 036.82, 056.71, 098.50-098.51, 098.59, 098.89, 711.00, 711.03, 711.08-711.10, 711.13, 711.18-711.20, 711.23, 711.28-711.30, 711.33, 711.38-711.40, 711.43, 711.48-711.50, 711.53, 711.58-711.60, 711.63, 711.68-711.70, 711.73, 711.78-711.80, 711.83, 711.88-711.90, 711.93, 711.98-712.10, 712.13, 712.18-712.20, 712.23, 712.28-712.30, 712.33, 712.38-712.80, 712.83, 712.88-712.90, 712.93, 712.98-714.0, 715.00, 715.09-715.10, 715.13, 715.18-715.20, 715.23, 715.28-715.30, 715.33, 715.38-715.90, 715.93, 715.98-716.00, 716.03, 716.08-716.10, 716.13, 716.18-716.20, 716.23, 716.28-716.30, 716.33, 716.38-716.40, 716.43, 716.48-716.50, 716.53, 716.58-716.60, 716.63, 716.68-716.80, 716.83, 716.88-716.90, 716.93, 716.98-716.99, 718.00, 718.03, 718.08, 719.00, 719.03, 719.08-719.10, 719.13, 719.18-719.20, 719.23, 719.28-719.30, 719.33, 719.38-719.40, 719.43, 719.48-719.50, 719.53, 719.58-719.60, 719.63, 719.68-719.80, 719.83, 719.88-719.90, 719.93, 719.98-719.99; **For code 711.65:** 015.80-015.96, 017.90-017.96, 036.82, 056.71, 098.50-098.51, 098.59, 098.89, 711.00, 711.04, 711.08-711.10, 711.14, 711.18-711.20, 711.24, 711.28-711.30, 711.34, 711.38-711.40, 711.44, 711.48-711.50, 711.54, 711.58-711.60, 711.64, 711.68-711.70, 711.74, 711.78-711.80, 711.84, 711.88-711.90, 711.94, 711.98-712.10, 712.14, 712.18-712.20, 712.24, 712.28-712.30, 712.34, 712.38-712.80, 712.84, 712.88-712.90, 712.94, 712.98-714.0, 715.00-715.10, 715.14, 715.18-715.20, 715.24, 715.28-715.30, 715.34, 715.38-715.90, 715.94, 715.98-716.00, 716.04, 716.08-716.10, 716.14, 716.18-716.20, 716.24, 716.28-716.30, 716.34, 716.38-716.40, 716.44, 716.48-716.50, 716.54, 716.58-716.60, 716.64, 716.68-716.80, 716.84, 716.88-716.90, 716.94, 716.98-716.99, 718.00, 718.04, 718.08, 719.00, 719.04, 719.08-719.10, 719.14, 719.18-719.20, 719.24, 719.28-719.30, 719.34, 719.38-719.40, 719.44, 719.48-719.50, 719.54, 719.58-719.60, 719.64, 719.68-719.80, 719.84, 719.88-719.90, 719.94, 719.98-719.99; **For code 711.66:** 015.80-015.96, 017.90-017.96, 036.82, 056.71, 098.50-098.51, 098.59, 098.89, 711.00, 711.05, 711.08-711.10, 711.15, 711.18-711.20, 711.25, 711.28-711.30, 711.35, 711.38-711.40, 711.45, 711.48-711.50, 711.55, 711.58-711.60, 711.65, 711.68-711.70, 711.75, 711.78-711.80, 711.85, 711.88-711.90, 711.95, 711.98-712.10, 712.15, 712.18-712.20, 712.25, 712.28-712.30, 712.35, 712.38-712.80, 712.85, 712.88-712.90, 712.95, 712.98-714.0, 715.00, 715.09-715.10, 715.15, 715.18-715.20, 715.25, 715.28-715.30, 715.35, 715.38-715.90, 715.95, 715.98-716.00, 716.05, 716.08-716.10, 716.15, 716.18-716.20, 716.25, 716.28-716.30, 716.35, 716.38-716.40, 716.45, 716.48-716.50, 716.55, 716.58-716.60, 716.65, 716.68-716.80, 716.85, 716.88-716.90, 716.95, 716.98-716.99, 718.00, 718.05, 718.08, 719.00, 719.05, 719.08-719.10, 719.15, 719.18-719.20, 719.25, 719.28-719.30, 719.35, 719.38-719.40, 719.45, 719.48-719.50, 719.55, 719.58-719.60, 719.65, 719.68-719.80, 719.85, 719.88-719.90, 719.95, 719.98-719.99; **For code 711.67:** 015.80-015.96, 017.90-017.96, 036.82, 056.71, 098.50-098.51, 098.59, 098.89, 711.00, 711.06, 711.08-711.10, 711.16, 711.18-711.20, 711.26, 711.28-711.30, 711.36, 711.38-711.40, 711.46, 711.48-711.50, 711.56, 711.58-711.60, 711.66, 711.68-711.70, 711.76, 711.78-711.80, 711.86, 711.88-711.90, 711.96, 711.98-712.10, 712.16, 712.18-712.20, 712.26, 712.28-712.30, 712.36, 712.38-712.80, 712.86, 712.88-712.90, 712.96, 712.98-714.0, 715.00, 715.09-715.10, 715.16, 715.18-715.20, 715.26, 715.28-715.30, 715.36, 715.38-715.90, 715.96, 715.98-716.00, 716.06, 716.08-716.10, 716.16, 716.18-716.20, 716.26, 716.28-716.30, 716.36, 716.38-716.40, 716.46, 716.48-716.50, 716.56, 716.58-716.60, 716.66, 716.68-716.80, 716.86, 716.88-716.90, 716.96, 716.98-716.99, 718.00, 718.08, 719.00, 719.06, 719.08-719.10, 719.16, 719.18-719.20, 719.26, 719.28-719.30, 719.36, 719.38-719.40, 719.46, 719.48-719.50, 719.56, 719.58-719.60, 719.66, 719.68-719.80, 719.86, 719.88-719.90, 719.96, 719.98-719.99 **For code 711.68:** 015.80-015.96, 017.90-017.96, 036.82, 056.71, 098.50-098.51, 098.59, 098.89, 711.00-711.99, 712.10-712.99, 713.0-713.8, 714.0, 715.00, 715.09-715.10, 715.18-715.98, 716.00-716.99, 718.00-718.08, 719.00-719.10, 719.18-719.99 **For code 711.69:** See code 711.68

§ Requires fifth digit. Valid digits are in [brackets] under each code. See beginning of section 710-739 for codes and defintions.

✓4th ✓5th **Additional Digit Required**   **Unacceptable PDx**   **Manifestation Code**   **Hospital Acquired Condition**   ▶◀ Revised Text   ● New Code   ▲ Revised Code Title

2010 ICD-9-CM   **Volume 1 – 251**

§ ✓5th   711.7   Arthropathy associated with helminthiasis   `CC`
[0-9]
> *Code first underlying disease as:*
> filariasis (125.0-125.9)

CC Excl: For codes 711.70-711.74, 711.76, 711.78-711.79: 003.23, 015.80-015.96, 017.90-017.96, 036.82, 056.71, 098.50-098.51, 098.59, 098.89, 711.00-714.0, 715.00, 715.09-715.10, 715.18-716.99, 718.00-718.08, 719.00-719.10, 719.18-719.69, 719.80-719.99; **For codes 711.75:** 003.23, 015.80-015.96, 017.90-017.96, 036.82, 056.71, 098.50-098.51, 098.59, 098.89, 711.00-714.0, 715.00, 715.09-715.10, 715.18-716.99, 718.00-718.08, 719.00-719.10, 719.18-719.43, 719.45-719.69, 719.80-719.99; **For code 711.77:** 003.23, 015.80-015.96, 017.90-017.96, 036.82, 056.71, 098.50-098.51, 098.59, 098.89, 711.00-714.0, 715.00, 715.09-715.10, 715.18-716.99, 718.00-718.08, 719.00-719.10, 719.18-719.69, 719.80-719.97, 719.99

§ ✓5th   711.8   Arthropathy associated with other infectious and parasitic diseases   `CC`
[0-9]
> *Code first underlying disease as:*
> diseases classifiable to 080-088, 100-104, 130-136

> **EXCLUDES**   *arthropathy associated with sarcoidosis (713.7)*

CC Excl: For codes 711.80, 711.82-711.89: 003.23, 015.80-015.96, 017.90-017.96, 036.82, 056.71, 098.50-098.51, 098.59, 098.89, 711.00-714.0, 715.00, 715.09-715.10, 715.18-716.99, 718.00-718.08, 719.00-719.10, 719.18-719.69, 719.80-719.99; **For code 711.81:** 003.23, 015.80-015.96, 017.90-017.96, 036.82, 056.71, 098.50-098.51, 098.59, 098.89, 711.00-711.41, 711.43-714.0, 715.00, 715.09-715.10, 715.18-716.99, 718.00-718.08, 719.00-719.10, 719.18-719.69, 719.80-719.99

AHA: 4Q, '91, 15; 3Q, '90, 14

§ ✓5th   711.9   Unspecified infective arthritis   `CC`
[0-9]
Infective arthritis or polyarthritis (acute) (chronic) (subacute) NOS

CC Excl: 003.23, 015.80-015.96, 017.90-017.96, 036.82, 056.71, 098.50-098.51, 098.59, 098.89, 711.00-714.0, 715.00, 715.09-715.10, 715.18-716.99, 718.00-718.08, 719.00-719.10, 719.18-719.69, 719.80-719.99

✓4th   712   Crystal arthropathies

> **INCLUDES**   crystal-induced arthritis and synovitis
> **EXCLUDES**   *gouty arthropathy ▶(274.00-274.03)◀*

DEF: Joint disease due to urate crystal deposit in joints or synovial membranes.

The following fifth-digit subclassification is for use with category 712; valid digits are in [brackets] under each code. See list at beginning of chapter for definitions.

   0   **site unspecified**
   1   **shoulder region**
   2   **upper arm**
   3   **forearm**
   4   **hand**
   5   **pelvic region and thigh**
   6   **lower leg**
   7   **ankle and foot**
   8   **other specified sites**
   9   **multiple sites**

§ ✓5th   712.1   Chondrocalcinosis due to dicalcium phosphate crystals
[0-9]
Chondrocalcinosis due to dicalcium phosphate crystals (with other crystals)
> *Code first underlying disease (275.4)*

§ ✓5th   712.2   Chondrocalcinosis due to pyrophosphate crystals
[0-9]
> *Code first underlying disease (275.4)*

§ ✓5th   712.3   Chondrocalcinosis, unspecified
[0-9]
> *Code first underlying disease (275.4)*

§ ✓5th   712.8   Other specified crystal arthropathies
[0-9]

§ ✓5th   712.9   Unspecified crystal arthropathy
[0-9]

✓4th   713   Arthropathy associated with other disorders classified elsewhere

> **INCLUDES**   arthritis
> arthropathy   } associated with conditions
> polyarthritis   classifiable below
> polyarthropathy

713.0   Arthropathy associated with other endocrine and metabolic disorders
> *Code first underlying disease as:*
> acromegaly (253.0)
> hemochromatosis (275.0)
> hyperparathyroidism (252.00-252.08)
> hypogammaglobulinemia (279.00-279.09)
> hypothyroidism (243-244.9)
> lipoid metabolism disorder (272.0-272.9)
> ochronosis (270.2)

> **EXCLUDES**   *arthropathy associated with:*
> *amyloidosis (713.7)*
> *crystal deposition disorders, except gout (712.1-712.9)*
> *diabetic neuropathy (713.5)*
> *▶gout (274.00-274.03)◀*

713.1   Arthropathy associated with gastrointestinal conditions other than infections
> *Code first underlying disease as:*
> regional enteritis (555.0-555.9)
> ulcerative colitis (556)

713.2   Arthropathy associated with hematological disorders
> *Code first underlying disease as:*
> hemoglobinopathy (282.4-282.7)
> hemophilia (286.0-286.2)
> leukemia (204.0-208.9)
> malignant reticulosis (202.3)
> multiple myelomatosis (203.0)

> **EXCLUDES**   *arthropathy associated with Henoch-Schönlein purpura (713.6)*

713.3   Arthropathy associated with dermatological disorders
> *Code first underlying disease as:*
> erythema multiforme (695.10-695.19)
> erythema nodosum (695.2)

> **EXCLUDES**   *psoriatic arthropathy (696.0)*

713.4   Arthropathy associated with respiratory disorders
> *Code first underlying disease as:*
> diseases classifiable to 490-519

> **EXCLUDES**   *arthropathy associated with respiratory infections (711.0, 711.4-711.8)*

713.5   Arthropathy associated with neurological disorders

Charcôt's arthropathy   } associated with diseases
Neuropathic arthritis   classifiable elsewhere

> *Code first underlying disease as:*
> neuropathic joint disease [Charcôt's joints]:
>   NOS (094.0)
>   diabetic (249.6, 250.6)
>   syringomyelic (336.0)
>   tabetic [syphilitic] (094.0)

713.6   Arthropathy associated with hypersensitivity reaction
> *Code first underlying disease as:*
> Henoch (-Schönlein) purpura (287.0)
> serum sickness (999.5)

> **EXCLUDES**   *allergic arthritis NOS (716.2)*

713.7   Other general diseases with articular involvement
> *Code first underlying disease as:*
> amyloidosis (277.30-277.39)
> familial Mediterranean fever (277.31)
> sarcoidosis (135)

AHA: 2Q, '97, 12

---

§   Requires fifth digit. Valid digits are in [brackets] under each code. See beginning of section 710-739 for codes and defintions.

`N` Newborn Age: 0   `P` Pediatric Age: 0-17   `M` Maternity Age: 12-55   `A` Adult Age: 15-124   `MCC` Major CC Condition   `CC` CC Condition   `HIV` HIV Related Dx

713.8   ***Arthropathy associated with other condition classifiable elsewhere***

> *Code first underlying disease as:*
> conditions classifiable elsewhere except as in 711.1-711.8, 712, and 713.0-713.7

✓4th 714   Rheumatoid arthritis and other inflammatory polyarthropathies

EXCLUDES rheumatic fever (390)
rheumatoid arthritis of spine NOS (720.0)

AHA: 2Q, '95, 3

714.0   Rheumatoid arthritis
Arthritis or polyarthritis:
   atrophic
   rheumatic (chronic)
Use additional code to identify manifestation, as:
   myopathy (359.6)
   polyneuropathy (357.1)

EXCLUDES juvenile rheumatoid arthritis NOS (714.30)

DEF: Chronic systemic disease principally of joints, manifested by inflammatory changes in articular structures and synovial membranes, atrophy, and loss in bone density.

AHA: 2Q, '06, 20; 1Q, '90, 5

M06.9 Rheumatoid arthritis unspecified   I-10

714.1   Felty's syndrome
Rheumatoid arthritis with splenoadenomegaly and leukopenia

DEF: Syndrome marked by rheumatoid arthritis, splenomegaly, leukopenia, pigmented spots on lower extremity skin, anemia, and thrombocytopenia.

714.2   Other rheumatoid arthritis with visceral or systemic involvement
Rheumatoid carditis

✓5th 714.3   Juvenile chronic polyarthritis

DEF: Rheumatoid arthritis of more than one joint; lasts longer than six weeks in age 17 or younger; symptoms include fever, erythematous rash, weight loss, lymphadenopathy, hepatosplenomegaly and pericarditis.

714.30   Polyarticular juvenile rheumatoid arthritis, chronic or unspecified
Juvenile rheumatoid arthritis NOS
Still's disease

714.31   Polyarticular juvenile rheumatoid arthritis, acute   **CC**
CC Excl: 036.82, 056.71, 711.00-714.4, 715.00, 715.09-715.10, 715.18-716.99, 718.00-718.08, 719.00-719.10, 719.18-719.99

714.32   Pauciarticular juvenile rheumatoid arthritis

714.33   Monoarticular juvenile rheumatoid arthritis

714.4   Chronic postrheumatic arthropathy
Chronic rheumatoid nodular fibrositis
Jaccoud's syndrome

DEF: Persistent joint disorder; follows previous rheumatic infection.

✓5th 714.8   Other specified inflammatory polyarthropathies

714.81   Rheumatoid lung
Caplan's syndrome
Diffuse interstitial rheumatoid disease of lung
Fibrosing alveolitis, rheumatoid

DEF: Lung disorders associated with rheumatoid arthritis.

714.89   Other

714.9   Unspecified inflammatory polyarthropathy
Inflammatory polyarthropathy or polyarthritis NOS

EXCLUDES polyarthropathy NOS (716.5)

✓4th 715   Osteoarthrosis and allied disorders

Note: Localized, in the subcategories below, includes bilateral involvement of the same site.

INCLUDES arthritis or polyarthritis:
   degenerative
   hypertrophic
   degenerative joint disease
   osteoarthritis

EXCLUDES Marie-Strümpell spondylitis (720.0)
osteoarthrosis [osteoarthritis] of spine (721.0-721.9)

> The following fifth-digit subclassification is for use with category 715; valid digits are in [brackets] under each code. See list at beginning of chapter for definitions.
> 0 site unspecified
> 1 shoulder region
> 2 upper arm
> 3 forearm
> 4 hand
> 5 pelvic region and thigh
> 6 lower leg
> 7 ankle and foot
> 8 other specified sites
> 9 multiple sites

§ ✓5th 715.0   Osteoarthrosis, generalized
[0,4,9] Degenerative joint disease, involving multiple joints
Primary generalized hypertrophic osteoarthrosis

DEF: Chronic noninflammatory arthritis; marked by degenerated articular cartilage and enlarged bone; symptoms include pain and stiffness with activity.

§ ✓5th 715.1   Osteoarthrosis, localized, primary
[0-8] Localized osteoarthropathy, idiopathic
M17.0 Bilateral primary osteoarthritis of knee   I-10

§ ✓5th 715.2   Osteoarthrosis, localized, secondary
[0-8] Coxae malum senilis

§ ✓5th 715.3   Osteoarthrosis, localized, not specified whether
[0-8] **primary or secondary**
Otto's pelvis
AHA: For code 715.35: 3Q, '04, 12; 2Q, '04, 15; **For code 715.36:** 4Q, '03, 118; 2Q, '95, 5
M16.9 Osteoarthritis of hip unspecified   I-10

§ ✓5th 715.8   Osteoarthrosis involving, or with mention of
[0,9] **more than one site, but not specified as generalized**

§ ✓5th 715.9   Osteoarthrosis, unspecified whether
[0-8] **generalized or localized**
AHA: For code 715.90: 2Q, '97, 12
M19.90 Unspecified osteoarthritis unspecified site   I-10
M17.9 Osteoarthritis of knee unspecified   I-10

✓4th 716   Other and unspecified arthropathies

EXCLUDES cricoarytenoid arthropathy (478.79)

> The following fifth-digit subclassification is for use with category 716; valid digits are in [brackets] under each code. See list at beginning of chapter for definitions.
> 0 site unspecified
> 1 shoulder region
> 2 upper arm
> 3 forearm
> 4 hand
> 5 pelvic region and thigh
> 6 lower leg
> 7 ankle and foot
> 8 other specified sites
> 9 multiple sites

AHA: 2Q, '95, 3

§ ✓5th 716.0   Kaschin-Beck disease
[0-9] Endemic polyarthritis
DEF: Chronic degenerative disease of spine and peripheral joints; occurs in eastern Siberian, northern Chinese, and Korean youth; may be a mycotoxicosis caused by eating cereals infected with fungus.

§ ✓5th 716.1   Traumatic arthropathy
[0-9] **AHA: For Code 716.11:** 1Q, '02, 9; **For Code 716.15:** ▶2Q, '09, 11◀

§ Requires fifth digit. Valid digits are in [brackets] under each code. See beginning of section 710-739 for codes and defintions.

Musculoskeletal System and Connective Tissue

716.2–718.0

Disruption and Tears of Meniscus

Bucket-handle

Flap-type

Radial
Peripheral

Horizontal cleavage

Vertical

Congenital discoid meniscus

Internal Derangements of Knee

Disruptions of Cruciate Ligament

Anterior

Posterior

Chondromalacia of Patella

"Kissing" lesion of femur

§ ✓5th **716.2 Allergic arthritis**
[0-9] **EXCLUDES** *arthritis associated with Henoch-Schönlein purpura or serum sickness (713.6)*

§ ✓5th **716.3 Climacteric arthritis**   ♀
[0-9] Menopausal arthritis
  DEF: Ovarian hormone deficiency; causes pain in small joints, shoulders, elbows or knees; affects females at menopause; also called arthropathia ovaripriva.

§ ✓5th **716.4 Transient arthropathy**
[0-9] **EXCLUDES** *palindromic rheumatism (719.3)*

§ ✓5th **716.5 Unspecified polyarthropathy or polyarthritis**
[0-9]

§ ✓5th **716.6 Unspecified monoarthritis**
[0-8] Coxitis

§ ✓5th **716.8 Other specified arthropathy**
[0-9]

§ ✓5th **716.9 Arthropathy, unspecified**
[0-9] Arthritis
  Arthropathy } (acute) (chronic) (subacute)
  Articular rheumatism (chronic)
  Inflammation of joint NOS
  M12.9 Arthropathy unspecified   I-10

✓4th **717 Internal derangement of knee**
  INCLUDES degeneration
  rupture, old } of articular cartilage or meniscus of knee
  tear, old
  EXCLUDES *acute derangement of knee (836.0-836.6)*
  ankylosis (718.5)
  contracture (718.4)
  current injury (836.0-836.6)
  deformity (736.4-736.6)
  recurrent dislocation (718.3)

  717.0 Old bucket handle tear of medial meniscus
  Old bucket handle tear of unspecified cartilage

  717.1 Derangement of anterior horn of medial meniscus

  717.2 Derangement of posterior horn of medial meniscus

  717.3 Other and unspecified derangement of medial meniscus
  Degeneration of internal semilunar cartilage

✓5th **717.4 Derangement of lateral meniscus**

  717.40 Derangement of lateral meniscus, unspecified

  717.41 Bucket handle tear of lateral meniscus

  717.42 Derangement of anterior horn of lateral meniscus

  717.43 Derangement of posterior horn of lateral meniscus

  717.49 Other

717.5 Derangement of meniscus, not elsewhere classified
  Congenital discoid meniscus
  Cyst of semilunar cartilage
  Derangement of semilunar cartilage NOS

717.6 Loose body in knee
  Joint mice, knee
  Rice bodies, knee (joint)
  DEF: The presence in the joint synovial area of a small, frequently calcified, loose body created from synovial membrane, organized fibrin fragments of articular cartilage or arthritis osteophytes.

717.7 Chondromalacia of patella
  Chondromalacia patellae
  Degeneration [softening] of articular cartilage of patella
  DEF: Softened patella cartilage.
  AHA: M-A, '85, 14; N-D, '84, 9

✓5th **717.8 Other internal derangement of knee**

  717.81 Old disruption of lateral collateral ligament

  717.82 Old disruption of medial collateral ligament

  717.83 Old disruption of anterior cruciate ligament

  717.84 Old disruption of posterior cruciate ligament

  717.85 Old disruption of other ligaments of knee
  Capsular ligament of knee

  717.89 Other
  Old disruption of ligaments NOS

717.9 Unspecified internal derangement of knee
  Derangement NOS of knee

✓4th **718 Other derangement of joint**
  EXCLUDES *current injury (830.0-848.9)*
  jaw (524.60-524.69)

  The following fifth-digit subclassification is for use with category 718; valid digits are in [brackets] under each code. See list at beginning of chapter for definitions.
  0 site unspecified
  1 shoulder region
  2 upper arm
  3 forearm
  4 hand
  5 pelvic region and thigh
  6 lower leg
  7 ankle and foot
  8 other specified sites
  9 multiple sites

§ ✓5th **718.0 Articular cartilage disorder**
[0-5,7-9] Meniscus:
  disorder
  rupture, old
  tear, old
  Old rupture of ligament(s) of joint NOS
  EXCLUDES *articular cartilage disorder:*
  in ochronosis (270.2)
  knee (717.0-717.9)
  chondrocalcinosis (275.4)
  metastatic calcification (275.4)

§ Requires fifth digit. Valid digits are in [brackets] under each code. See beginning of section 710-739 for codes and defintions.

N Newborn Age: 0   P Pediatric Age: 0-17   M Maternity Age: 12-55   A Adult Age: 15-124   MCC Major CC Condition   CC CC Condition   HIV HIV Related Dx

254 – Volume 1   **2010 ICD-9-CM**

Joint Derangements and Disorders

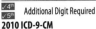

Loose body in joint

Dislocation of joint

Joint contracture   Ankylosis of joint   Synovial effusion (fluid)   Hemarthrosis (blood)

§ ✓5th **718.1 Loose body in joint**
[0-5,7-9]   Joint mice
    EXCLUDES   knee (717.6)
    DEF: Calcified loose bodies in synovial fluid; due to arthritic osteophytes.
    AHA: For code 718.17: 2Q, '01, 15

§ ✓5th **718.2 Pathological dislocation**
[0-9]   Dislocation or displacement of joint, not recurrent and not current injury
    Spontaneous dislocation (joint)

§ ✓5th **718.3 Recurrent dislocation of joint**
[0-9]   **AHA:** N-D, '87, 7

§ ✓5th **718.4 Contracture of joint**
[0-9]   **AHA:** 4Q, '98, 40
    TIP: Assign an additional code from category 438 if the contracture is a result of a CVA.

§ ✓5th **718.5 Ankylosis of joint**
[0-9]   Ankylosis of joint (fibrous) (osseous)
    EXCLUDES   spine (724.9)
              stiffness of joint without mention of ankylosis (719.5)
    DEF: Immobility and solidification, of joint; due to disease, injury or surgical procedure.

§ ✓5th **718.6 Unspecified intrapelvic protrusion of acetabulum**
[0,5]   Protrusio acetabuli, unspecified
    DEF: Sinking of the floor of acetabulum; causing femoral head to protrude, limits hip movement; of unknown etiology.

§ ✓5th **718.7 Developmental dislocation of joint**
[0-9]   *EXCLUDES*   congenital dislocation of joint (754.0-755.8)
              traumatic dislocation of joint (830-839)
    AHA: 4Q, '01, 48

§ ✓5th **718.8 Other joint derangement, not elsewhere classified**
[0-9]   Flail joint (paralytic)   Instability of joint
    EXCLUDES   deformities classifiable to 736 (736.0-736.9)
    AHA: For code 718.81: 2Q, '00, 14
    TIP: Assign 718.81 for multidirectional shoulder instability.

§ ✓5th **718.9 Unspecified derangement of joint**
[0-5,7-9]   *EXCLUDES*   knee (717.9)

✓4th **719 Other and unspecified disorders of joint**
    EXCLUDES   jaw (524.60-524.69)

    The following fifth-digit subclassification is for use with codes 719.0-719.6, 719.8-719.9; valid digits are in [brackets] under each code. See list at beginning of chapter for definitions.
    0   site unspecified
    1   shoulder region
    2   upper arm
    3   forearm
    4   hand
    5   pelvic region and thigh
    6   lower leg
    7   ankle and foot
    8   other specified sites
    9   multiple sites

§ ✓5th **719.0 Effusion of joint**
[0-9]   Hydrarthrosis
    Swelling of joint, with or without pain
    EXCLUDES   intermittent hydrarthrosis (719.3)
    M25.469 Effusion unspecified knee   `I-10`

§ ✓5th **719.1 Hemarthrosis**   `CC`
[0-9]   *EXCLUDES*   current injury (840.0-848.9)
    CC Excl: For codes: 719.10, 719.15, 719.18-719.19: 719.10-719.19, 958.91-958.92; **For code 719.11:** 719.10-719.13, 719.18-719.19, 958.91; **For code 719.12:** 719.10-719.12, 719.18-719.19, 958.91; **For code 719.13:** 719.10, 719.12-719.14, 719.18-719.19, 958.91; **For code 719.14:** 719.10, 719.13-719.14, 719.18-719.19, 958.91; **For codes 719.16-719.17:** 719.10, 719.16-719.19, 958.92

§ ✓5th **719.2 Villonodular synovitis**
[0-9]   **DEF:** Overgrowth of synovial tissue, especially at knee joint; due to macrophage infiltration of giant cells in synovial villi and fibrous nodules.

§ ✓5th **719.3 Palindromic rheumatism**
[0-9]   Hench-Rosenberg syndrome
    Intermittent hydrarthrosis
    DEF: Recurrent episodes of afebrile arthritis and periarthritis marked by their complete disappearance after a few days or hours; causes swelling, redness, and disability usually affecting only one joint; no known cause.

§ ✓5th **719.4 Pain in joint**
[0-9]   Arthralgia
    AHA: For code 719.46: 1Q, '01, 3
    TIP: Assign 719.46 for patellofemoral syndrome, a chronic knee pain common among athletes.
    M25.519 Pain in unspecified shoulder   `I-10`
    M25.552 Pain in left hip   `I-10`

§ ✓5th **719.5 Stiffness of joint, not elsewhere classified**
[0-9]

§ ✓5th **719.6 Other symptoms referable to joint**
[0-9]   Joint crepitus
    Snapping hip
    AHA: 1Q, '94, 15; **For code 719.66:** 2Q, '07, 6
    TIP: Assign 719.66 for patellar clunk syndrome, which is a fibrous reaction caused by chronic pressure on the patella, S/P knee replacement surgery.

    719.7 Difficulty in walking
    EXCLUDES   abnormality of gait (781.2)
    AHA: 2Q, '04, 15; 4Q, '03, 66
    R26.2 Difficulty in walking not elsewhere classified   `I-10`

§ ✓5th **719.8 Other specified disorders of joint**
[0-9]   Calcification of joint
    Fistula of joint
    EXCLUDES   temporomandibular joint-pain-dysfunction syndrome [Costen's syndrome] (524.60)

§ ✓5th **719.9 Unspecified disorder of joint**
[0-9]

DORSOPATHIES (720-724)

    EXCLUDES   curvature of spine (737.0-737.9)
              osteochondrosis of spine (juvenile) (732.0)
              adult (732.8)

✓4th **720 Ankylosing spondylitis and other inflammatory spondylopathies**

    720.0 Ankylosing spondylitis
    Rheumatoid arthritis of spine NOS
    Spondylitis:
       Marie-Strümpell
       rheumatoid
    DEF: Rheumatoid arthritis of spine and sacroiliac joints; fusion and deformity in spine follows; affects mainly males; cause unknown.

    720.1 Spinal enthesopathy
    Disorder of peripheral ligamentous or muscular attachments of spine
    Romanus lesion
    DEF: Tendinous or muscular vertebral bone attachment abnormality.

§   Requires fifth digit. Valid digits are in [brackets] under each code. See beginning of section 710-739 for codes and defintions.

✓4th ✓5th   Additional Digit Required   Unacceptable PDx   Manifestation Code   Hospital Acquired Condition   ▶◀ Revised Text   ● New Code   ▲ Revised Code Title

2010 ICD-9-CM   **Volume 1 – 255**

Musculoskeletal System and Connective Tissue

720.2–722.2

720.2 Sacroiliitis, not elsewhere classified
Inflammation of sacroiliac joint NOS
DEF: Pain due to inflammation in joint, at juncture of sacrum and hip.

√5ᵗʰ **720.8 Other inflammatory spondylopathies**

720.81 Inflammatory spondylopathies in diseases classified elsewhere
Code first underlying disease as:
tuberculosis (015.0)

720.89 Other

720.9 Unspecified inflammatory spondylopathy
Spondylitis NOS

√4ᵗʰ **721 Spondylosis and allied disorders**
DEF: Degenerative changes in spinal joint.
AHA: 2Q, '89, 14

721.0 Cervical spondylosis without myelopathy
Cervical or cervicodorsal:
arthritis
osteoarthritis
spondylarthritis

721.1 Cervical spondylosis with myelopathy `CC`
Anterior spinal artery compression syndrome
Spondylogenic compression of cervical spinal cord
Vertebral artery compression syndrome
CC Excl: 721.0-721.1
M47.12 Other spondylosis w/myelopathy cervical region `I-10`

721.2 Thoracic spondylosis without myelopathy
Thoracic:
arthritis
osteoarthritis
spondylarthritis

721.3 Lumbosacral spondylosis without myelopathy
Lumbar or lumbosacral:
arthritis
osteoarthritis
spondylarthritis
AHA: 4Q, '02, 107
M47.817 Spondylosis w/o myelopath/radiculopath lumboscrl `I-10`

√5ᵗʰ **721.4 Thoracic or lumbar spondylosis with myelopathy**

721.41 Thoracic region `CC`
Spondylogenic compression of thoracic spinal cord
CC Excl: 721.41

721.42 Lumbar region `CC`
Spondylogenic compression of lumbar spinal cord
CC Excl: 721.3, 721.42, 722.10, 722.2, 722.32, 722.52-722.70, 722.73, 722.83-722.90, 722.93

721.5 Kissing spine
Baastrup's syndrome
DEF: Compression of spinous processes of adjacent vertebrae; due to mutual contact.

721.6 Ankylosing vertebral hyperostosis

721.7 Traumatic spondylopathy `CC`
Kümmell's disease or spondylitis
CC Excl: 721.7

721.8 Other allied disorders of spine

√5ᵗʰ **721.9 Spondylosis of unspecified site**

721.90 Without mention of myelopathy
Spinal:
arthritis (deformans) (degenerative) (hypertrophic)
osteoarthritis NOS
Spondylarthrosis NOS

721.91 With myelopathy `CC`
Spondylogenic compression of spinal cord NOS
CC Excl: 721.0-721.91

Anatomy of Vertebral Disc

Spinal canal · Spinal cord in dural sac · Lamina · Ligamentum flavum · Intervertebral disk · Annulus · Nucleus pulposus · Vertebral body · Spinal nerve · Disk annulus · Nucleus pulposus

Normal Top View · **Normal Side View**

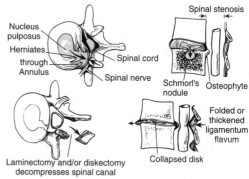

Derangement of Vertebral Disc

Spinal stenosis · Nucleus pulposus · Herniates through Annulus · Spinal cord · Spinal nerve · Schmorl's nodule · Osteophyte · Folded or thickened ligamentum flavum · Collapsed disk · Laminectomy and/or diskectomy decompresses spinal canal

√4ᵗʰ **722 Intervertebral disc disorders**
AHA: 1Q, '88, 10

722.0 Displacement of cervical intervertebral disc without myelopathy
Neuritis (brachial) or radiculitis due to displacement or rupture of cervical intervertebral disc
Any condition classifiable to 722.2 of the cervical or cervicothoracic intervertebral disc
M50.20 Other cerv disc displacement uns cerv region `I-10`

√5ᵗʰ **722.1 Displacement of thoracic or lumbar intervertebral disc without myelopathy**

722.10 Lumbar intervertebral disc without myelopathy
Lumbago or sciatica due to displacement of intervertebral disc
Neuritis or radiculitis due to displacement or rupture of lumbar intervertebral disc
Any condition classifiable to 722.2 of the lumbar or lumbosacral intervertebral disc
AHA: ▶4Q, '08, 184;◀ 1Q, '07, 9; 3Q, '03, 12; 1Q, '03, 7; 4Q, '02, 107
M51.26 Oth intervertebral disc displcmnt lumbar region `I-10`

722.11 Thoracic intervertebral disc without myelopathy
Any condition classifiable to 722.2 of thoracic intervertebral disc

722.2 Displacement of intervertebral disc, site unspecified, without myelopathy
Discogenic syndrome NOS
Herniation of nucleus pulposus NOS
Intervertebral disc NOS:
extrusion
prolapse
protrusion
rupture
Neuritis or radiculitis due to displacement or rupture of intervertebral disc

`N` Newborn Age: 0   `P` Pediatric Age: 0-17   `M` Maternity Age: 12-55   `A` Adult Age: 15-124   `MCC` Major CC Condition   `CC` CC Condition   `HIV` HIV Related Dx

256 – Volume 1 • February 2009

2010 ICD-9-CM

√5th **722.3 Schmorl's nodes**
> **DEF:** Irregular bone defect in the margin of the vertebral body; causes herniation into end plate of vertebral body.

722.30 Unspecified region

722.31 Thoracic region

722.32 Lumbar region

722.39 Other

722.4 Degeneration of cervical intervertebral disc
> Degeneration of cervicothoracic intervertebral disc
> **M50.30** Other cerv disc degeneration uns cerv region `I-10`

√5th **722.5 Degeneration of thoracic or lumbar intervertebral disc**

722.51 Thoracic or thoracolumbar intervertebral disc

722.52 Lumbar or lumbosacral intervertebral disc
> **AHA:** 2Q, '06, 18; 4Q, '04, 133
> **M51.37** Oth intervertebral disc degen lumbosacral region `I-10`

722.6 Degeneration of intervertebral disc, site unspecified
> Degenerative disc disease NOS
> Narrowing of intervertebral disc or space NOS

√5th **722.7 Intervertebral disc disorder with myelopathy**

722.70 Unspecified region

722.71 Cervical region `CC`
> **CC Excl:** 722.0, 722.71

722.72 Thoracic region `CC`
> **CC Excl:** 722.11, 722.72

722.73 Lumbar region `CC`
> **CC Excl:** 722.11, 722.73

√5th **722.8 Postlaminectomy syndrome**
> **DEF:** Spinal disorder due to spinal laminectomy surgery.
> **AHA:** J-F, '87, 7
> **TIP:** Assign if documentation indicates that scar tissue has formed following disc surgery.

722.80 Unspecified region

722.81 Cervical region

722.82 Thoracic region

722.83 Lumbar region
> **AHA:** 2Q, '97, 15
> **M96.1** Postlaminectomy syndrome NEC `I-10`

√5th **722.9 Other and unspecified disc disorder**
> Calcification of intervertebral cartilage or disc
> Discitis

722.90 Unspecified region
> **AHA:** N-D, '84, 19

722.91 Cervical region

722.92 Thoracic region

722.93 Lumbar region
> **M51.86** Other intervertebral disc disorder lumbar region `I-10`

√4th **723 Other disorders of cervical region**
> **EXCLUDES** conditions due to:
>   intervertebral disc disorders (722.0-722.9)
>   spondylosis (721.0-721.9)
> **AHA:** 3Q, '94, 14; 2Q, '89, 14

723.0 Spinal stenosis in cervical region
> **AHA:** 4Q, '03, 101
> **M48.02** Spinal stenosis cervical region `I-10`

723.1 Cervicalgia
> Pain in neck
> **DEF:** Pain in cervical spine or neck region.
> **M54.2** Cervicalgia `I-10`

723.2 Cervicocranial syndrome
> Barré-Liéou syndrome
> Posterior cervical sympathetic syndrome
> **DEF:** Neurologic disorder of upper cervical spine and nerve roots.

723.3 Cervicobrachial syndrome (diffuse)
> **DEF:** Complex of symptoms due to scalenus anterior muscle compressing the brachial plexus; pain radiates from shoulder to arm or back of neck.
> **AHA:** N-D, '85, 12

723.4 Brachial neuritis or radiculitis NOS
> Cervical radiculitis
> Radicular syndrome of upper limbs

723.5 Torticollis, unspecified
> Contracture of neck
> **EXCLUDES** congenital (754.1)
>   due to birth injury (767.8)
>   hysterical (300.11)
>   ocular torticollis (781.93)
>   psychogenic (306.0)
>   spasmodic (333.83)
>   traumatic, current (847.0)
> **DEF:** Abnormally positioned neck relative to head; due to cervical muscle or fascia contractions; also called wryneck.
> **AHA:** 2Q, '01, 21; 1Q, '95, 7

723.6 Panniculitis specified as affecting neck
> **DEF:** Inflammation of the panniculus adiposus (subcutaneous fat) in the neck.

723.7 Ossification of posterior longitudinal ligament in cervical region

723.8 Other syndromes affecting cervical region
> Cervical syndrome NEC
> Klippel's disease
> Occipital neuralgia
> **AHA:** 1Q, '00, 7

723.9 Unspecified musculoskeletal disorders and symptoms referable to neck
> Cervical (region) disorder NOS

√4th **724 Other and unspecified disorders of back**
> **EXCLUDES** collapsed vertebra (code to cause, e.g., osteoporosis, 733.00-733.09)
>   conditions due to:
>   intervertebral disc disorders (722.0-722.9)
>   spondylosis (721.0-721.9)
> **AHA:** 2Q, '89, 14

√5th **724.0 Spinal stenosis, other than cervical**

724.00 Spinal stenosis, unspecified region
> **M48.00** Spinal stenosis site unspecified `I-10`

724.01 Thoracic region

724.02 Lumbar region
> **AHA:** ▶4Q, '08, 109;◀ 4Q, '07, 120; 1Q, '07, 10, 20; 4Q, '99, 13
> **M48.06** Spinal stenosis lumbar region `I-10`

724.09 Other

Stenosis in Cervical Region

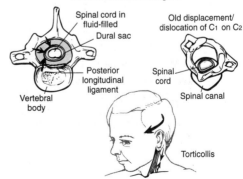

724.1   Pain in thoracic spine

724.2   Lumbago
Low back pain
Low back syndrome
Lumbalgia
AHA: 2Q, '07, 11; N-D, '85, 12
M54.5 Low back pain   `I-10`

724.3   Sciatica
Neuralgia or neuritis of sciatic nerve
EXCLUDES   *specified lesion of sciatic nerve (355.0)*
AHA: 2Q, '89, 12
M54.30 Sciatica unspecified side   `I-10`

724.4   Thoracic or lumbosacral neuritis or radiculitis, unspecified
Radicular syndrome of lower limbs
AHA: 2Q, '99, 3
M51.14 Intervertebral disc d/o w/radiculopathy thoracic   `I-10`

724.5   Backache, unspecified
Vertebrogenic (pain) syndrome NOS
M54.9 Dorsalgia unspecified   `I-10`

724.6   Disorders of sacrum
Ankylosis }
Instability } lumbosacral or sacroiliac (joint)

√5th 724.7   Disorders of coccyx

     724.70   Unspecified disorder of coccyx

     724.71   Hypermobility of coccyx

     724.79   Other
         Coccygodynia

724.8   Other symptoms referable to back
Ossification of posterior longitudinal ligament NOS
Panniculitis specified as sacral or affecting back

724.9   Other unspecified back disorders
Ankylosis of spine NOS
Compression of spinal nerve root NEC
Spinal disorder NOS
EXCLUDES   *sacroiliitis (720.2)*

RHEUMATISM, EXCLUDING THE BACK (725-729)

INCLUDES   disorders of muscles and tendons and their attachments, and of other soft tissues

725   Polymyalgia rheumatica
DEF: Joint and muscle pain, pelvis, and shoulder girdle stiffness, high sedimentation rate and temporal arteritis; occurs in elderly.
M35.3 Polymyalgia rheumatica   `I-10`

√4th 726   Peripheral enthesopathies and allied syndromes
Note: Enthesopathies are disorders of peripheral ligamentous or muscular attachments.
EXCLUDES   *spinal enthesopathy (720.1)*

726.0   Adhesive capsulitis of shoulder

√5th 726.1   Rotator cuff syndrome of shoulder and allied disorders

     726.10   Disorders of bursae and tendons in shoulder region, unspecified
         Rotator cuff syndrome NOS
         Supraspinatus syndrome NOS
         AHA: 2Q, '01, 11
         M75.11 Rotator cuff syndrome right shoulder   `I-10`

     726.11   Calcifying tendinitis of shoulder

     726.12   Bicipital tenosynovitis

     726.19   Other specified disorders
         EXCLUDES   *complete rupture of rotator cuff, nontraumatic (727.61)*

726.2   Other affections of shoulder region, not elsewhere classified
Periarthritis of shoulder
Scapulohumeral fibrositis

√5th 726.3   Enthesopathy of elbow region

     726.30   Enthesopathy of elbow, unspecified

     726.31   Medial epicondylitis

     726.32   Lateral epicondylitis
         Epicondylitis NOS
         Golfers' elbow
         Tennis elbow

     726.33   Olecranon bursitis
         Bursitis of elbow

     726.39   Other

726.4   Enthesopathy of wrist and carpus
Bursitis of hand or wrist
Periarthritis of wrist

726.5   Enthesopathy of hip region
Bursitis of hip
Gluteal tendinitis
Iliac crest spur
Psoas tendinitis
Trochanteric tendinitis

√5th 726.6   Enthesopathy of knee

     726.60   Enthesopathy of knee, unspecified
         Bursitis of knee NOS

     726.61   Pes anserinus tendinitis or bursitis
         DEF: Inflamed tendons of sartorius, gracilis and semitendinosus muscles of medial aspect of knee.

     726.62   Tibial collateral ligament bursitis
         Pellegrini-Stieda syndrome

     726.63   Fibular collateral ligament bursitis

     726.64   Patellar tendinitis

     726.65   Prepatellar bursitis
         AHA: 2Q, '06, 15

     726.69   Other
         Bursitis:
           infrapatellar
           subpatellar

√5th 726.7   Enthesopathy of ankle and tarsus

     726.70   Enthesopathy of ankle and tarsus, unspecified
         Metatarsalgia NOS
         EXCLUDES   *Morton's metatarsalgia (355.6)*

     726.71   Achilles bursitis or tendinitis

     726.72   Tibialis tendinitis
         Tibialis (anterior) (posterior) tendinitis

     726.73   Calcaneal spur
         DEF: Overgrowth of calcaneous bone; causes pain on walking; due to chronic avulsion injury of plantar fascia from calcaneus.

     726.79   Other
         Peroneal tendinitis

726.8   Other peripheral enthesopathies

√5th 726.9   Unspecified enthesopathy

     726.90   Enthesopathy of unspecified site
         Capsulitis NOS
         Periarthritis NOS
         Tendinitis NOS

     726.91   Exostosis of unspecified site
         Bone spur NOS
         AHA: 2Q, '01, 15

√4th 727   Other disorders of synovium, tendon, and bursa

√5th 727.0   Synovitis and tenosynovitis

     727.00   Synovitis and tenosynovitis, unspecified
         Synovitis NOS
         Tenosynovitis NOS
         M65.9 Synovitis and tenosynovitis unspecified   `I-10`

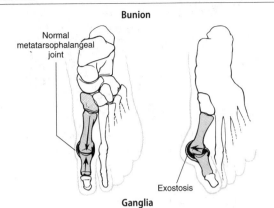

Bunion

Normal
metatarsophalangeal
joint

Exostosis

Ganglia

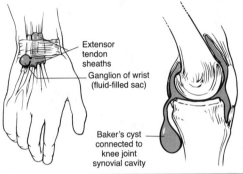

Extensor
tendon
sheaths

Ganglion of wrist
(fluid-filled sac)

Baker's cyst
connected to
knee joint
synovial cavity

727.01 *Synovitis and tenosynovitis in diseases classified elsewhere*

Code first underlying disease as:
tuberculosis (015.0-015.9)

EXCLUDES *crystal-induced (275.4)*
gonococcal (098.51)
▶*gout (274.00-274.03)*◀
syphilitic (095.7)

727.02 **Giant cell tumor of tendon sheath**

727.03 **Trigger finger (acquired)**

DEF: Stenosing tenosynovitis or nodule in flexor tendon; cessation of flexion or extension movement in finger, followed by snapping into place.

727.04 **Radial styloid tenosynovitis**
de Quervain's disease

727.05 **Other tenosynovitis of hand and wrist**

727.06 **Tenosynovitis of foot and ankle**

727.09 **Other**

727.1 **Bunion**

DEF: Enlarged first metatarsal head due to inflamed bursa; results in laterally displaced great toe.

727.2 **Specific bursitides often of occupational origin**
Beat:
elbow
hand
knee
Chronic crepitant synovitis of wrist
Miners':
elbow
knee

727.3 **Other bursitis**
Bursitis NOS

EXCLUDES *bursitis:*
gonococcal (098.52)
subacromial (726.19)
subcoracoid (726.19)
subdeltoid (726.19)
syphilitic (095.7)
"frozen shoulder" (726.0)

√5th **727.4** **Ganglion and cyst of synovium, tendon, and bursa**

727.40 **Synovial cyst, unspecified**

EXCLUDES *that of popliteal space (727.51)*
AHA: 2Q, '97, 6

727.41 **Ganglion of joint**

727.42 **Ganglion of tendon sheath**

727.43 **Ganglion, unspecified**

727.49 **Other**
Cyst of bursa

√5th **727.5** **Rupture of synovium**

727.50 **Rupture of synovium, unspecified**

727.51 **Synovial cyst of popliteal space**
Baker's cyst (knee)

727.59 **Other**

√5th **727.6** **Rupture of tendon, nontraumatic**

727.60 **Nontraumatic rupture of unspecified tendon**

727.61 **Complete rupture of rotator cuff**

727.62 **Tendons of biceps (long head)**

727.63 **Extensor tendons of hand and wrist**

727.64 **Flexor tendons of hand and wrist**

727.65 **Quadriceps tendon**

727.66 **Patellar tendon**

727.67 **Achilles tendon**

727.68 **Other tendons of foot and ankle**

727.69 **Other**

√5th **727.8** **Other disorders of synovium, tendon, and bursa**

727.81 **Contracture of tendon (sheath)**
Short Achilles tendon (acquired)

727.82 **Calcium deposits in tendon and bursa**
Calcification of tendon NOS
Calcific tendinitis NOS

EXCLUDES *peripheral ligamentous or muscular attachments (726.0-726.9)*

727.83 **Plica syndrome**
Plica knee

DEF: A fold in the synovial tissue formed before birth, creating a septum between two pockets of synovial tissue; most common are the medial patellar plica and the suprapatellar plica. Plica syndrome, or plica knee, refers to symptomatic plica.
AHA: 4Q, '00, 44

727.89 **Other**
Abscess of bursa or tendon

EXCLUDES *xanthomatosis localized to tendons (272.7)*

AHA: 2Q, '89, 15

727.9 **Unspecified disorder of synovium, tendon, and bursa**

√4th **728** **Disorders of muscle, ligament, and fascia**

EXCLUDES *enthesopathies (726.0-726.9)*
muscular dystrophies (359.0-359.1)
myoneural disorders (358.00-358.9)
myopathies (359.2-359.9)
nontraumatic hematoma of muscle (729.92)
old disruption of ligaments of knee (717.81-717.89)

728.0 **Infective myositis**   CC
Myositis:
purulent
suppurative

EXCLUDES *myositis:*
epidemic (074.1)
interstitial (728.81)
syphilitic (095.6)
tropical (040.81)

CC Excl: 567.31, 728.0, 728.11-728.3, 728.81, 728.86
DEF: Inflamed connective septal tissue of muscle.

√4th √5th Additional Digit Required   Unacceptable PDx   Manifestation Code   Hospital Acquired Condition   ▶◀ Revised Text   ● New Code   ▲ Revised Code Title

2010 ICD-9-CM   **October 2009 • Volume 1 – 259**

Musculoskeletal System and Connective Tissue

728.1–729.31

√5th **728.1 Muscular calcification and ossification**

    728.10 Calcification and ossification, unspecified
        Massive calcification (paraplegic)

    728.11 Progressive myositis ossificans
        DEF: Progressive myositic disease; marked by bony tissue formed by voluntary muscle; occurs among very young.

    728.12 Traumatic myositis ossificans
        Myositis ossificans (circumscripta)

    728.13 Postoperative heterotopic calcification
        DEF: Abnormal formation of calcium deposits in muscular tissue after surgery, marked by a corresponding loss of muscle tone and tension.

    728.19 Other
        Polymyositis ossificans

728.2 Muscular wasting and disuse atrophy, not elsewhere classified
    Amyotrophia NOS
    Myofibrosis
    EXCLUDES   *neuralgic amyotrophy (353.5)*
        pelvic muscle wasting and disuse atrophy (618.83)
        progressive muscular atrophy (335.0-335.9)

728.3 Other specific muscle disorders
    Arthrogryposis
    Immobility syndrome (paraplegic)
    EXCLUDES   *arthrogryposis multiplex congenita (754.89)*
        stiff-man syndrome (333.91)

728.4 Laxity of ligament

728.5 Hypermobility syndrome

728.6 Contracture of palmar fascia   A
    Dupuytren's contracture
    DEF: Dupuytren's contracture: flexion deformity of finger, due to shortened, thickened fibrosing of palmar fascia; cause unknown; associated with long-standing epilepsy.

√5th **728.7 Other fibromatoses**

    728.71 Plantar fascial fibromatosis
        Contracture of plantar fascia
        Plantar fasciitis (traumatic)
        DEF: Plantar fascia fibromatosis; causes nodular swelling and pain; not associated with contractures.

    728.79 Other
        Garrod's or knuckle pads
        Nodular fasciitis
        Pseudosarcomatous fibromatosis (proliferative) (subcutaneous)
        DEF: Knuckle pads: Pea-size nodules on dorsal surface of interphalangeal joints; new growth of fibrous tissue with thickened dermis and epidermis.

√5th **728.8 Other disorders of muscle, ligament, and fascia**

    728.81 Interstitial myositis
        DEF: Inflammation of septal connective parts of muscle tissue.

    728.82 Foreign body granuloma of muscle
        Talc granuloma of muscle

    728.83 Rupture of muscle, nontraumatic

    728.84 Diastasis of muscle
        Diastasis recti (abdomen)
        EXCLUDES   *diastasis recti complicating pregnancy, labor, and delivery (665.8)*
        DEF: Muscle separation, such as recti abdominis after repeated pregnancies.

    728.85 Spasm of muscle
        M62.838 Other muscle spasm   I-10

    728.86 Necrotizing fasciitis   MCC
        Use additional code to identify:
          infectious organism (041.00-041.89)
          gangrene (785.4), if applicable
        DEF: Fulminating infection begins with extensive cellulitis, spreads to superficial and deep fascia; causes thrombosis of subcutaneous vessels, and gangrene of underlying tissue.
        CC Excl: 567.31, 728.0, 728.11-728.3, 728.81, 728.86
        AHA: 4Q, '95, 54

    728.87 Muscle weakness (generalized)
        EXCLUDES   *generalized weakness (780.79)*
        AHA: 1Q, '05, 13; 4Q, '03, 66
        TIP: Assign an additional code from category 438 if the weakness is a result of a CVA.

    728.88 Rhabdomyolysis   CC
        DEF: A disintegration or destruction of muscle; an acute disease characterized by the excretion of myoglobin into the urine.
        CC Excl: 567.31, 728.0, 728.11-728.3, 728.81, 728.86, 728.88
        AHA: 4Q, '03, 66

    728.89 Other
        Eosinophilic fasciitis
        Use additional E code to identify drug, if drug induced
        DEF: Eosinophilic fasciitis: inflammation of fascia of extremities associated with eosinophilia, edema, and swelling; occurs alone or as part of myalgia syndrome.
        AHA: 3Q, '06, 13; 3Q, '02, 28; 2Q, '01, 14, 15

728.9 Unspecified disorder of muscle, ligament, and fascia
    AHA: 4Q, '88, 11

√4th **729 Other disorders of soft tissues**
    EXCLUDES   *acroparesthesia (443.89)*
        carpal tunnel syndrome (354.0)
        disorders of the back (720.0-724.9)
        entrapment syndromes (354.0-355.9)
        palindromic rheumatism (719.3)
        periarthritis (726.0-726.9)
        psychogenic rheumatism (306.0)

729.0 Rheumatism, unspecified and fibrositis
    DEF: General term describes diseases of muscle, tendon, nerve, joint, or bone; symptoms include pain and stiffness.

729.1 Myalgia and myositis, unspecified
    Fibromyositis NOS
    DEF: Myalgia: muscle pain.
    DEF: Myositis: inflamed voluntary muscle.
    DEF: Fibromyositis: inflamed fibromuscular tissue.
    M79.1 Myalgia   I-10

729.2 Neuralgia, neuritis, and radiculitis, unspecified
    EXCLUDES   *brachial radiculitis (723.4)*
        cervical radiculitis (723.4)
        lumbosacral radiculitis (724.4)
        mononeuritis (354.0-355.9)
        radiculitis due to intervertebral disc involvement (722.0-722.2, 722.7)
        sciatica (724.3)
    DEF: Neuralgia: paroxysmal pain along nerve; symptoms include brief pain and tenderness at point nerve exits.
    DEF: Neuritis: inflamed nerve, symptoms include paresthesia, paralysis and loss of reflexes at nerve site.
    DEF: Radiculitis: inflamed nerve root.

√5th **729.3 Panniculitis, unspecified**
    DEF: Inflammatory reaction of subcutaneous fat; causes nodules; often develops in abdominal region.

    729.30 Panniculitis, unspecified site
        Weber-Christian disease
        DEF: Febrile, nodular, nonsuppurative, relapsing inflammation of subcutaneous fat.

    729.31 Hypertrophy of fat pad, knee
        Hypertrophy of infrapatellar fat pad

N Newborn Age: 0   P Pediatric Age: 0-17   M Maternity Age: 12-55   A Adult Age: 15-124   MCC Major CC Condition   CC CC Condition   HIV HIV Related Dx

260 – Volume 1   **2010 ICD-9-CM**

729.39   Other site

> EXCLUDES   panniculitis specified as (affecting):
> back (724.8)
> neck (723.6)
> sacral (724.8)

729.4   Fasciitis, unspecified

> EXCLUDES   necrotizing fasciitis (728.86)
> nodular fasciitis (728.79)

AHA: 2Q, '94, 13

729.5   Pain in limb

AHA: 2Q, '07, 11

M79.609 Pain in unspecified limb   `I-10`

729.6   Residual foreign body in soft tissue

> EXCLUDES   foreign body granuloma:
> muscle (728.82)
> skin and subcutaneous tissue (709.4)

√5ᵗʰ 729.7   Nontraumatic compartment syndrome

Code first, if applicable, postprocedural complication (998.89)

> EXCLUDES   compartment syndrome NOS (958.90)
> traumatic compartment syndrome (958.90-958.99)

DEF: Compression of nerves and blood vessels within an enclosed space, leading to impaired blood flow and muscle and nerve damage.

729.71   Nontraumatic compartment syndrome of upper extremity   `CC`

Nontraumatic compartment syndrome of shoulder, arm, forearm, wrist, hand, and fingers

CC Excl: 729.81, 729.89-729.99, 903.8, 904.9

AHA: 4Q, '06, 100-102

729.72   Nontraumatic compartment syndrome of lower extremity   `CC`

Nontraumatic compartment syndrome of hip, buttock, thigh, leg, foot, and toes

CC Excl: 729.81, 729.89-729.99, 904.7, 904.9

AHA: 4Q, '06, 100-102

729.73   Nontraumatic compartment syndrome of abdomen   `CC`

CC Excl: 863.0-867.3, 867.5-868.14, 869.0-869.1, 879.2-879.9, 929.0-929.9, 958.8, 959.8-959.9

AHA: 4Q, '06, 100-102

729.79   Nontraumatic compartment syndrome of other sites   `CC`

CC Excl: 868.03-868.10, 868.13-869.1

AHA: 4Q, '06, 100-102

√5ᵗʰ 729.8   Other musculoskeletal symptoms referable to limbs

729.81   Swelling of limb

AHA: 4Q, '88, 6

TIP: Assign for pseudothrombophlebitis, which involves painful swelling of the lower extremity and mimics deep vein thrombosis (DVT).

729.82   Cramp

729.89   Other

> EXCLUDES   abnormality of gait (781.2)
> tetany (781.7)
> transient paralysis of limb (781.4)

AHA: 4Q, '88, 12

R29.898 Oth symptoms & signs involv musculoskeletal sys   `I-10`

√5ᵗʰ 729.9   Other and unspecified disorders of soft tissue

AHA: ▶4Q, '08, 134-136◀

729.90   Disorders of soft tissue, unspecified

729.91   Post-traumatic seroma

> EXCLUDES   seroma complicating a procedure (998.13)

729.92   Nontraumatic hematoma of soft tissue

Nontraumatic hematoma of muscle

AHA: ▶4Q, '08, 135◀

TIP: Assign an additional E code for a drug adverse effect if caused by Coumadin or other anticoagulants.

729.99   Other disorders of soft tissue

Polyalgia

OSTEOPATHIES, CHONDROPATHIES, AND ACQUIRED MUSCULOSKELETAL DEFORMITIES (730-739)

√4ᵗʰ 730   Osteomyelitis, periostitis, and other infections involving bone

> EXCLUDES   jaw (526.4-526.5)
> petrous bone (383.2)

Use additional code to identify organism, such as Staphylococcus (041.1)

The following fifth-digit subclassification is for use with category 730; valid digits are in [brackets] under each code. See list at beginning of chapter for definitions.

0 site unspecified
1 shoulder region
2 upper arm
3 forearm
4 hand
5 pelvic region and thigh
6 lower leg
7 ankle and foot
8 other specified sites
9 multiple sites

DEF: Osteomyelitis: bacterial inflammation of bone tissue and marrow.
DEF: Periostitis: inflammation of specialized connective tissue; causes swelling of bone and aching pain.

AHA: 4Q, '97, 43

§ √5ᵗʰ 730.0   Acute osteomyelitis   `CC`
[0-9]

Abscess of any bone except accessory sinus, jaw, or mastoid

Acute or subacute osteomyelitis, with or without mention of periostitis

Use additional code to identify major osseous defect, if applicable (731.3)

CC Excl: For code 730.00: 015.50-015.56, 015.70-015.76, 015.90-015.96, 017.90-017.96, 730.00-730.39, 730.80-730.99 For code 730.01: 015.50-015.56, 015.70-015.76, 015.90-015.96, 017.90-017.96, 730.00, 730.08-730.11, 730.18-730.21, 730.28-730.31, 730.38-730.39, 730.80-730.81, 730.88-730.91, 730.98-730.99 For code 730.02: 015.50-015.56, 015.70-015.76, 015.90-015.96, 017.90-017.96, 730.00, 730.08-730.10, 730.12, 730.18-730.20, 730.22, 730.28-730.30, 730.32, 730.38-730.39, 730.80, 730.82, 730.88-730.90, 730.92, 730.98-730.99 For code 730.03: 015.50-015.56, 015.70-015.76, 015.90-015.96, 017.90-017.96, 730.00, 730.08-730.10, 730.13, 730.18-730.20, 730.23, 730.28-730.30, 730.33, 730.38-730.39, 730.80, 730.83, 730.88-730.90, 730.93, 730.98-730.99: For code 730.04: 015.50-015.56, 015.70-015.76, 015.90-015.96, 017.90-017.96, 730.00, 730.08-730.10, 730.14, 730.18-730.20, 730.24, 730.28-730.30, 730.34, 730.38-730.39, 730.80, 730.84, 730.88-730.90, 730.94, 730.98-730.99 For code 730.05: 015.10-015.16, 015.50-015.56, 015.70-015.76, 015.90-015.96, 017.90-017.96, 730.00, 730.08-730.10, 730.15, 730.18-730.20, 730.25, 730.28-730.30, 730.35, 730.38-730.39, 730.80, 730.85, 730.88-730.90, 730.95, 730.98-730.99: For code 730.06: 015.20-015.56, 015.70-015.76, 015.90-015.96, 017.90-017.96, 730.00, 730.08-730.10, 730.16, 730.18-730.20, 730.26, 730.28-730.30, 730.36, 730.38-730.39, 730.80, 730.86, 730.88-730.90, 730.96, 730.98-730.99: For code 730.07: 015.50-015.56, 015.70-015.76, 015.90-015.96, 017.90-017.96, 730.00, 730.08-730.10, 730.17-730.20, 730.27-730.30, 730.37-730.39, 730.80, 730.87-730.90, 730.97-730.99: For code 730.08: 015.00-015.06, 015.50-015.56, 015.70-015.76, 015.90-015.96, 017.90-017.96, 730.00-730.39, 730.80-730.99: For code 730.09: 015.50-015.56, 015.70-015.76, 015.90-015.96, 017.90-017.96, 730.00-730.39, 730.80-730.99

AHA: 4Q, '06, 103; For code 730.06: 1Q, '02, 4; For code 730.07: 1Q, '04, 14

§ Requires fifth digit. Valid digits are in [brackets] under each code. See beginning of section 710-739 for codes and defintions.

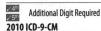

2010 ICD-9-CM   Unacceptable PDx   Manifestation Code   Hospital Acquired Condition   ▶◀ Revised Text   ● New Code   ▲ Revised Code Title

February 2009 • Volume 1 – 261

Musculoskeletal System and Connective Tissue

730.1–732.0

§ ✓5ᵗʰ **730.1 Chronic osteomyelitis**   CC
[0-9]
Brodie's abscess
Chronic or old osteomyelitis, with or without mention of periostitis
Sequestrum of bone
Sclerosing osteomyelitis of Garré
Use additional code to identify major osseous defect, if applicable (731.3)
EXCLUDES aseptic necrosis of bone (733.40-733.49)
CC Excl: For code 730.10: 730.10-730.39, 730.80-731.1; For codes 730.11-730.19: 003.24, 015.50-015.56, 015.70-015.76, 015.90-015.96, 017.90-017.96, 730.00-730.39, 730.80-730.99
AHA: 4Q, '06, 103; For code 730.17: 3Q, '00, 4

§ ✓5ᵗʰ **730.2 Unspecified osteomyelitis**   CC
[0-9]
Osteitis or osteomyelitis NOS, with or without mention of periostitis
Use additional code to identify major osseous defect, if applicable (731.3)
CC Excl: For code 730.20: 730.10-730.39, 730.80-731.1; For codes 730.21-730.29: 003.24, 015.50-015.56, 015.70-015.76, 015.90-015.96, 017.90-017.96, 730.00-730.39, 730.80-730.99
AHA: 4Q, '06, 103;
M86.9 Osteomyelitis unspecified   I-10

§ ✓5ᵗʰ **730.3 Periostitis without mention of osteomyelitis**
[0-9]
Abscess of periosteum } without mention of
Periostosis } osteomyelitis
EXCLUDES that in secondary syphilis (091.61)

§ ✓5ᵗʰ **730.7 Osteopathy resulting from poliomyelitis**
[0-9]
Code first underlying disease (045.0-045.9)

§ ✓5ᵗʰ **730.8 Other infections involving bone in diseases classified elsewhere**   CC
[0-9]
Code first underlying disease as:
tuberculosis (015.0-015.9)
typhoid fever (002.0)
EXCLUDES syphilis of bone NOS (095.5)
CC Excl: For codes 730.80, 730.89: 015.50-015.56, 015.70-015.76, 015.90-015.96, 017.90-017.96, 730.00-730.39, 730.80-730.99; For code 730.81: 015.50-015.56, 015.70-015.76, 015.90-015.96, 017.90-017.96, 730.00-730.01, 730.08-730.11, 730.18-730.21, 730.28-730.31, 730.38-730.39, 730.80, 730.88-730.91, 730.98-730.99; For code 730.82: 015.50-015.56, 015.70-015.76, 015.90-015.96, 017.90-017.96, 730.00, 730.02, 730.08-730.10, 730.12, 730.18-730.20, 730.22, 730.28-730.30, 730.32, 730.38-730.39, 730.80, 730.88-730.90, 730.92, 730.98-730.99; For code 730.83: 015.50-015.56, 015.70-015.76, 015.90-015.96, 017.90-017.96, 730.00, 730.03, 730.08-730.10, 730.13, 730.18-730.20, 730.23, 730.28-730.30, 730.33, 730.38-730.39, 730.80, 730.88-730.90, 730.93, 730.98-730.99; For code 730.84: 015.50-015.56, 015.70-015.76, 015.90-015.96, 017.90-017.96, 730.00, 730.04, 730.08-730.10, 730.14, 730.18-730.20, 730.24, 730.28-730.30, 730.34, 730.38-730.39, 730.80, 730.88-730.90, 730.94, 730.98-730.99; For code 730.85: 015.10-015.16, 015.50-015.56, 015.70-015.76, 015.90-015.96, 017.90-017.96, 730.00, 730.05, 730.08-730.10, 730.15, 730.18-730.20, 730.25, 730.28-730.30, 730.35, 730.38-730.39, 730.80, 730.88-730.90, 730.95, 730.98-730.99; For code 730.86: 015.20-015.56, 015.70-015.76, 015.90-015.96, 017.90-017.96, 730.00, 730.06, 730.08-730.10, 730.16, 730.18-730.20, 730.26, 730.28-730.30, 730.36, 730.38-730.39, 730.80, 730.88-730.90, 730.96, 730.98-730.99; For code 730.87: 015.50-015.56, 015.70-015.76, 015.90-015.96, 017.90-017.96, 730.00, 730.07-730.10, 730.17-730.20, 730.27-730.30, 730.37-730.39, 730.80, 730.88-730.90, 730.97-730.99; For code 730.88: 015.00-015.06, 015.50-015.56, 015.70-015.76, 015.90-015.96, 017.90-017.96, 730.00-730.39, 730.80-730.99
AHA: 2Q, '97, 16; 3Q, '91, 10

§ ✓5ᵗʰ **730.9 Unspecified infection of bone**   CC
[0-9]
CC Excl: For codes 730.90, 730.99: 015.50-015.56, 015.70-015.76, 015.90-015.96, 017.90-017.96, 730.00-730.39, 730.80-730.99; For code 730.91: 015.50-015.56, 015.70-015.76, 015.90-015.96, 017.90-017.96, 730.00-730.01, 730.08-730.11, 730.18-730.21, 730.28-730.31, 730.38-730.39, 730.80-730.81, 730.88-730.90, 730.98-730.99; For code 730.92: 015.50-015.56, 015.70-015.76, 015.90-015.96, 017.90-017.96, 730.00, 730.02, 730.08-730.10, 730.12, 730.18-730.20, 730.22, 730.28-730.30, 730.32, 730.38-730.39, 730.80, 730.82, 730.88-730.90, 730.98-730.99; For code 730.93: 015.50-015.56, 015.70-015.76, 015.90-015.96, 017.90-017.96, 730.00, 730.03, 730.08-730.10, 730.13, 730.18-730.20, 730.23, 730.28-730.30, 730.33, 730.38-730.39, 730.80, 730.83, 730.88-730.90, 730.98-730.99; For code 730.94: 015.50-015.56, 015.70-015.76, 015.90-015.96, 017.90-017.96, 730.00, 730.04, 730.08-730.10, 730.14, 730.18-730.20, 730.24, 730.28-730.30, 730.34, 730.38-730.39, 730.80, 730.84, 730.88-730.90, 730.98-730.99; For code 730.95: 015.10-015.16, 015.50-015.56, 015.70-015.76, 015.90-015.96, 017.90-017.96, 730.00, 730.05, 730.08-730.10, 730.15, 730.18-730.20, 730.25, 730.28-730.30, 730.35, 730.38-730.39, 730.80, 730.85, 730.88-730.90, 730.98-730.99; For code 730.96: 015.20-015.56, 015.70-015.76, 015.90-015.96, 017.90-017.96, 730.00, 730.06, 730.08-730.10, 730.16, 730.18-730.20, 730.26, 730.28-730.30, 730.36, 730.38-730.39, 730.80, 730.86, 730.88-730.90, 730.98-730.99; For code 730.97: 015.50-015.56, 015.70-015.76, 015.90-015.96, 017.90-017.96, 730.00, 730.07-730.10, 730.17-730.20, 730.27-730.30, 730.37-730.39, 730.80, 730.87-730.90, 730.98-730.99; For code 730.98: 0015.00-015.06, 015.50-015.56, 015.70-015.76, 015.90-015.96, 017.90-017.96, 730.00-730.39, 730.80-730.99

✓4ᵗʰ **731 Osteitis deformans and osteopathies associated with other disorders classified elsewhere**
DEF: Osteitis deformans: Bone disease marked by episodes of increased bone loss, excessive repair attempts; causes weakened, deformed bones with increased mass, bowed long bones, deformed flat bones, pain and pathological fractures; may be fatal if associated with congestive heart failure, giant cell tumors or bone sarcoma; also called Paget's disease.

731.0 Osteitis deformans without mention of bone tumor
Paget's disease of bone

731.1 Osteitis deformans in diseases classified elsewhere
Code first underlying disease as:
malignant neoplasm of bone (170.0-170.9)

731.2 Hypertrophic pulmonary osteoarthropathy
Bamberger-Marie disease
DEF: Clubbing, of fingers and toes; related to enlarged ends of long bones; due to chronic lung and heart disease.

731.3 Major osseous defects
Code first underlying disease, if known, such as:
aseptic necrosis (733.40-733.49)
malignant neoplasm of bone (170.0-170.9)
osteomyelitis (730.00-730.29)
osteoporosis (733.00-733.09)
peri-prosthetic osteolysis (996.45)
AHA: 4Q, '06, 103

731.8 Other bone involvement in diseases classified elsewhere
Code first underlying disease as:
diabetes mellitus (249.8, 250.8)
Use additional code to specify bone condition, such as:
acute osteomyelitis (730.00-730.09)
AHA: 1Q, '04, 14; 4Q, '97, 43; 2Q, '97, 16
TIP: For diabetic osteomyelitis, assign a total of three codes: 250.8X, 731.8, and a code from category 730.
M90.89 Osteopathy dz classified elsewhere multiple site   I-10

✓4ᵗʰ **732 Osteochondropathies**
DEF: Conditions related to both bone and cartilage, or conditions in which cartilage is converted to bone (enchondral ossification).

732.0 Juvenile osteochondrosis of spine
Juvenile osteochondrosis (of):
marginal or vertebral epiphysis (of Scheuermann)
spine NOS
Vertebral epiphysitis
EXCLUDES adolescent postural kyphosis (737.0)

§ Requires fifth digit. Valid digits are in [brackets] under each code. See beginning of section 710-739 for codes and defintions.

N Newborn Age: 0   P Pediatric Age: 0-17   M Maternity Age: 12-55   A Adult Age: 15-124   MCC Major CC Condition   CC CC Condition   HIV HIV Related Dx

262 – Volume 1   2010 ICD-9-CM

732.1 Juvenile osteochondrosis of hip and pelvis
Coxa plana
Ischiopubic synchondrosis (of van Neck)
Osteochondrosis (juvenile) of:
    acetabulum
    head of femur (of Legg-Calvé-Perthes)
    iliac crest (of Buchanan)
    symphysis pubis (of Pierson)
Pseudocoxalgia

732.2 Nontraumatic slipped upper femoral epiphysis
Slipped upper femoral epiphysis NOS

732.3 Juvenile osteochondrosis of upper extremity
Osteochondrosis (juvenile) of:
    capitulum of humerus (of Panner)
    carpal lunate (of Kienbock)
    hand NOS
    head of humerus (of Haas)
    heads of metacarpals (of Mauclaire)
    lower ulna (of Burns)
    radial head (of Brailsford)
    upper extremity NOS

732.4 Juvenile osteochondrosis of lower extremity, excluding foot
Osteochondrosis (juvenile) of:
    lower extremity NOS
    primary patellar center (of Köhler)
    proximal tibia (of Blount)
    secondary patellar center (of Sinding-Larsen)
    tibial tubercle (of Osgood-Schlatter)
Tibia vara

732.5 Juvenile osteochondrosis of foot
Calcaneal apophysitis
Epiphysitis, os calcis
Osteochondrosis (juvenile) of:
    astragalus (of Diaz)
    calcaneum (of Sever)
    foot NOS
    metatarsal
        second (of Freiberg)
        fifth (of Iselin)
    os tibiale externum (of Haglund)
    tarsal navicular (of Köhler)

732.6 Other juvenile osteochondrosis
Apophysitis ⎫
Epiphysitis ⎬ specified as juvenile, of other
Osteochondritis ⎪   site, or site NOS
Osteochondrosis ⎭

732.7 Osteochondritis dissecans

732.8 Other specified forms of osteochondropathy
Adult osteochondrosis of spine

732.9 Unspecified osteochondropathy
Apophysitis ⎫ NOS
Epiphysitis ⎬ not specified as adult or
Osteochondritis ⎪   juvenile, of unspecified
Osteochondrosis ⎭   site

Slipped Femoral Epiphysis

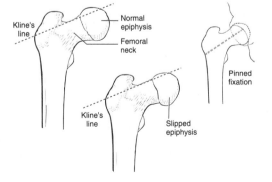

Kline's line — Normal epiphysis
— Femoral neck
Pinned fixation
Kline's line — Slipped epiphysis

✓4ᵗʰ 733 Other disorders of bone and cartilage
> **EXCLUDES** bone spur (726.91)
> cartilage of, or loose body in, joint (717.0-717.9, 718.0-718.9)
> giant cell granuloma of jaw (526.3)
> osteitis fibrosa cystica generalisata (252.01)
> osteomalacia (268.2)
> polyostotic fibrous dysplasia of bone (756.54)
> prognathism, retrognathism (524.1)
> xanthomatosis localized to bone (272.7)

✓5ᵗʰ 733.0 Osteoporosis
Use additional code to identify major osseous defect, if applicable (731.3)
Use additional code to identify personal history of pathologic (healed) fracture (V13.51)
DEF: Bone mass reduction that ultimately results in fractures after minimal trauma; dorsal kyphosis or loss of height often occur.
AHA: 4Q, '06, 103

733.00 Osteoporosis, unspecified
Wedging of vertebra NOS
AHA: 4Q, '07, 92;1Q, '07, 22; 3Q, '01, 19; 2Q, '98, 12
M81.8 Other osteoporosis w/o current **I-10** pathological fx

733.01 Senile osteoporosis
Postmenopausal osteoporosis
AHA: 1Q, '07, 5, 6

733.02 Idiopathic osteoporosis

733.03 Disuse osteoporosis

733.09 Other
Drug-induced osteoporosis
Use additional E code to identify drug
AHA: 4Q, '03, 108

✓5ᵗʰ 733.1 Pathologic fracture
▶Chronic fracture◀
Spontaneous fracture
> **EXCLUDES** stress fracture (733.93-733.95)
> traumatic fracture (800-829)

DEF: Fracture due to bone structure weakening by pathological processes (e.g., osteoporosis, neoplasms and osteomalacia).
AHA: 4Q, '08, 158; 1Q, '07, 3-4; 4Q, '93, 25; N-D, '86, 10; N-D, '85, 16
TIP: Assign only for newly diagnosed fractures; refer to V code aftercare categories if patient is receiving routine care during healing or recovery phase.

733.10 Pathologic fracture, unspecified site **CC**
CC Excl: 733.10-733.19, 733.93-733.95

733.11 Pathologic fracture of humerus **CC**
CC Excl: See code 733.10

733.12 Pathologic fracture of distal radius and ulna **CC**
Wrist NOS
CC Excl: See code 733.10

733.13 Pathologic fracture of vertebrae **CC**
Collapse of vertebra NOS
CC Excl: See code 733.10
AHA: 3Q, '08, 4; 1Q, '07, 5, 6, 22; 3Q, '99, 5
TIP: Assign for a chronic vertebral pathological fracture for which the patient is receiving medication.
M48.53xA Collapsed vertebra NEC **I-10** cervicothorac initial enc

733.14 Pathologic fracture of neck of femur **CC**
Femur NOS
Hip NOS
CC Excl: See code 733.10
AHA: 1Q, '01, 1; 1Q, '96, 16

733.15 Pathologic fracture of other specified part of femur **CC**
CC Excl: See code 733.10
AHA: 2Q, '98, 12

Musculoskeletal System and Connective Tissue

733.16–733.99

733.16 **Pathologic fracture of tibia or fibula** `CC`
Ankle NOS
CC Excl: See code 733.10

733.19 **Pathologic fracture of other specified site** `CC`
CC Excl: See code 733.10

✓5th **733.2** **Cyst of bone**

733.20 **Cyst of bone (localized), unspecified**

733.21 **Solitary bone cyst**
Unicameral bone cyst

733.22 **Aneurysmal bone cyst**
DEF: Solitary bone lesion, bulges into periosteum; marked by calcified rim.

733.29 **Other**
Fibrous dysplasia (monostotic)
EXCLUDES   cyst of jaw (526.0-526.2, 526.89)
osteitis fibrosa cystica (252.01)
polyostotic fibrousdyplasia of bone (756.54)

733.3 **Hyperostosis of skull**
Hyperostosis interna frontalis
Leontiasis ossium
DEF: Abnormal bone growth on inner aspect of cranial bones.

✓5th **733.4** **Aseptic necrosis of bone**
Use additional code to identify major osseous defect, if applicable (731.3)
EXCLUDES   osteochondropathies (732.0-732.9)
DEF: Infarction of bone tissue due to a nonfectious etiology, such as a fracture, ischemic disorder or administration of immunosuppressive drugs; leads to degenerative joint disease or nonunion of fractures.
AHA: 4Q, '06, 103

733.40 **Aseptic necrosis of bone, site unspecified** `CC`
CC Excl: 733.40-733.49

733.41 **Head of humerus** `CC`
CC Excl: 733.40-733.41, 733.45-733.49

733.42 **Head and neck of femur** `CC`
Femur NOS
EXCLUDES   Legg-Calvé-Perthes disease (732.1)
CC Excl: 733.40, 733.42, 733.45-733.49
M87.256 Osteonecrosis due to previous trauma uns femur `I-10`

733.43 **Medial femoral condyle** `CC`
CC Excl: 733.40, 733.43, 733.45-733.49

733.44 **Talus** `CC`
CC Excl: 733.40, 733.44-733.49

733.45 **Jaw** `CC`
Use additional E code to identify drug, if drug-induced
EXCLUDES   osteoradionecrosis of jaw (526.89)
CC Excl: See code: 733.40
AHA: 4Q, '07, 91

733.49 **Other** `CC`
CC Excl: See code: 733.40

733.5 **Osteitis condensans**
Piriform sclerosis of ilium
DEF: Idiopathic condition marked by low back pain; associated with oval or triangular sclerotic, opaque bone next to sacroiliac joints in the ileum.

733.6 **Tietze's disease**
Costochondral junction syndrome
Costochondritis
DEF: Painful, idiopathic, nonsuppurative, swollen costal cartilage sometimes confused with cardiac symptoms because the anterior chest pain resembles that of coronary artery disease.
M94.0 Chondrocostal junction syndrome (Tietze dz) `I-10`

733.7 **Algoneurodystrophy**
Disuse atrophy of bone
Sudeck's atrophy

✓5th **733.8** **Malunion and nonunion of fracture**
AHA: 2Q, '94, 5

733.81 **Malunion of fracture** `CC`
CC Excl: 733.81-733.82

733.82 **Nonunion of fracture** `CC`
Pseudoarthrosis (bone)
CC Excl: See code: 733.81

✓5th **733.9** **Other unspecified disorders of bone and cartilage**
AHA: ▶4Q, '08, 136-137◀

733.90 **Disorder of bone and cartilage**
M89.9 Disorder of bone, unspecified `I-10`

733.91 **Arrest of bone development or growth**
Epiphyseal arrest

733.92 **Chondromalacia**
Chondromalacia:
NOS
localized, except patella
systemic
tibial plateau
EXCLUDES   chondromalacia of patella (717.7)
DEF: Articular cartilage softening.

733.93 **Stress fracture of tibia or fibula**
Stress reaction of tibia or fibula
Use additional external cause code(s) to identify the cause of the stress fracture
AHA: ▶4Q, '08, 158;◀ 4Q, '01, 48

733.94 **Stress fracture of the metatarsals**
Stress reaction of metatarsals
Use additional external cause code(s) to identify the cause of the stress fracture
AHA: ▶4Q, '08, 158;◀ 4Q, '01, 48

733.95 **Stress fracture of other bone**
Stress reaction of other bone
Use additional external cause code(s) to identify the cause of the stress fracture
EXCLUDES   stress fracture of:
femoral neck (733.96)
fibula (733.93)
metatarsals (733.94)
pelvis (733.98)
shaft of femur (733.97)
tibia (733.93)
AHA: ▶4Q, '08, 158;◀ 4Q, '01, 48

733.96 **Stress fracture of femoral neck**
Stress reaction of femoral neck
Use additional external cause code(s) to identify the cause of the stress fracture
AHA: ▶4Q, '08, 158◀

733.97 **Stress fracture of shaft of femur**
Stress reaction of shaft of femur
Use additional external cause code(s) to identify the cause of the stress fracture
AHA: ▶4Q, '08, 158◀

733.98 **Stress fracture of pelvis**
Stress reaction of pelvis
Use additional external cause code(s) to identify the cause of the stress fracture
AHA: ▶4Q, '08, 158◀

733.99 **Other**
Diaphysitis
Hypertrophy of bone
Relapsing polychondritis
AHA: J-F, '87, 14

`N` Newborn Age: 0   `P` Pediatric Age: 0-17   `M` Maternity Age: 12-55   `A` Adult Age: 15-124   `MCC` Major CC Condition   `CC` CC Condition   `HIV` HIV Related Dx

Acquired Deformities of Toe

Acquired Deformities of Forearm

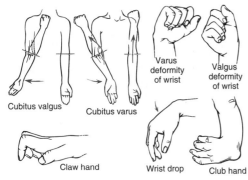

734   Flat foot
Pes planus (acquired)
Talipes planus (acquired)
EXCLUDES   congenital (754.61)
rigid flat foot (754.61)
spastic (everted) flat foot (754.61)

✓4th 735   Acquired deformities of toe
EXCLUDES   congenital (754.60-754.69, 755.65-755.66)

735.0   Hallux valgus (acquired)
DEF: Angled displacement of the great toe, causing it to ride over or under other toes.

735.1   Hallux varus (acquired)
DEF: Angled displacement of the great toe toward the body midline, away from the other toes.

735.2   Hallux rigidus
DEF: Limited flexion movement at metatarsophalangeal joint of great toe; due to degenerative joint disease.

735.3   Hallux malleus
DEF: Extended proximal phalanx, flexed distal phalanges, of great toe; foot resembles claw or hammer.

735.4   Other hammer toe (acquired)

735.5   Claw toe (acquired)
DEF: Hyperextended proximal phalanges, flexed middle and distal phalanges

735.8   Other acquired deformities of toe
AHA: 4Q, '07, 123
TIP: Assign for hallux limitus, a deformity of the first metatarsophalangeal joint, which restricts the range of motion and can lead to stiffness and pain in the joint.

735.9   Unspecified acquired deformity of toe

✓4th 736   Other acquired deformities of limbs
EXCLUDES   congenital (754.3-755.9)

✓5th 736.0   Acquired deformities of forearm, excluding fingers

736.00   Unspecified deformity
Deformity of elbow, forearm, hand, or wrist (acquired) NOS

736.01   Cubitus valgus (acquired)
DEF: Deviation of the elbow away from the body midline upon extension; it occurs when the palm is turning outward.

736.02   Cubitus varus (acquired)
DEF: Elbow joint displacement angled laterally; when the forearm is extended, it is deviated toward the midline of the body; also called "gun stock" deformity.

736.03   Valgus deformity of wrist (acquired)
DEF: Abnormal angulation away from the body midline.

736.04   Varus deformity of wrist (acquired)
DEF: Abnormal angulation toward the body midline.

736.05   Wrist drop (acquired)
DEF: Inability to extend the hand at the wrist due to extensor muscle paralysis

736.06   Claw hand (acquired)
DEF: Flexion and atrophy of the hand and fingers; found in ulnar nerve lesions, syringomyelia, and leprosy.

736.07   Club hand, acquired
DEF: Twisting of the hand out of shape or position; caused by the congenital absence of the ulna or radius.

736.09   Other

736.1   Mallet finger
DEF: Permanently flexed distal phalanx.

✓5th 736.2   Other acquired deformities of finger

736.20   Unspecified deformity
Deformity of finger (acquired) NOS

736.21   Boutonniere deformity
DEF: A deformity of the finger caused by flexion of the proximal interphalangeal joint and hyperextension of the distal joint; also called buttonhole deformity.

736.22   Swan-neck deformity
DEF: Flexed distal and hyperextended proximal interphalangeal joint.

736.29   Other
EXCLUDES   trigger finger (727.03)
AHA: 2Q, '05, 7; 2Q, '89, 13

✓5th 736.3   Acquired deformities of hip

736.30   Unspecified deformity
Deformity of hip (acquired) NOS

736.31   Coxa valga (acquired)
DEF: Increase of at least 140 degrees in the angle formed by the axis of the head and the neck of the femur, and the axis of its shaft.

736.32   Coxa vara (acquired)
DEF: The bending downward of the neck of the femur: causing difficulty in movement; a right angle or less may be formed by the axis of the head and neck of the femur, and the axis of its shaft.

736.39   Other
AHA: 2Q, '08, 4; 2Q, '91, 18
TIP: Assign as principal diagnosis for follow-up visit for patient with hip methylmethacrylate cement spacer, following removal of infected joint prosthesis.

Acquired Deformities of Hip

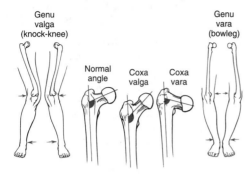

Deformities of Lower Limb

Kyphosis and Lordosis

736.79 Other
Acquired:
pes
talipes } not elsewhere classified

✓5ᵗʰ **736.8 Acquired deformities of other parts of limbs**

736.81 Unequal leg length (acquired)

736.89 Other
Deformity (acquired):
arm or leg, not elsewhere classified
shoulder
AHA: 2Q, '08, 5
TIP: Assign as principal diagnosis for follow-up visit for patient with humeral methylmethacrylate cement spacer, following removal of infected joint prosthesis.

736.9 Acquired deformity of limb, site unspecified

✓4ᵗʰ **737 Curvature of spine**
EXCLUDES *congenital (754.2)*

737.0 Adolescent postural kyphosis
EXCLUDES *osteochondrosis of spine (juvenile) (732.0)*
adult (732.8)

✓5ᵗʰ **737.1 Kyphosis (acquired)**

737.10 Kyphosis (acquired) (postural)
M40.05 Postural kyphosis thoracolumbar region   I-10

737.11 Kyphosis due to radiation

737.12 Kyphosis, postlaminectomy
AHA: J-F, '87, 7
M96.3 Postlaminectomy kyphosis   I-10

737.19 Other
EXCLUDES *that associated with conditions classifiable elsewhere (737.41)*
AHA: 1Q, '07, 20

✓5ᵗʰ **737.2 Lordosis (acquired)**
DEF: Swayback appearance created by an abnormally increased spinal curvature; it is also referred to as "hollow back" or "saddle back."

737.20 Lordosis (acquired) (postural)

737.21 Lordosis, postlaminectomy

737.22 Other postsurgical lordosis

737.29 Other
EXCLUDES *that associated with conditions classifiable elsewhere (737.42)*

✓5ᵗʰ **736.4 Genu valgum or varum (acquired)**

736.41 Genu valgum (acquired)
DEF: Abnormally close together and an abnormally large space between the ankles; also called "knock-knees."

736.42 Genu varum (acquired)
DEF: Abnormally separated knees and the inward bowing of the legs; it is also called "bowlegs."

736.5 Genu recurvatum (acquired)
DEF: Hyperextended knees; also called "backknee."

736.6 Other acquired deformities of knee
Deformity of knee (acquired) NOS

✓5ᵗʰ **736.7 Other acquired deformities of ankle and foot**
EXCLUDES *deformities of toe (acquired) (735.0-735.9)*
pes planus (acquired) (734)

736.70 Unspecified deformity of ankle and foot, acquired

736.71 Acquired equinovarus deformity
Clubfoot, acquired
EXCLUDES *clubfoot not specified as acquired (754.5-754.7)*

736.72 Equinus deformity of foot, acquired
DEF: A plantar flexion deformity that forces people to walk on their toes.

736.73 Cavus deformity of foot
EXCLUDES *that with claw foot (736.74)*
DEF: Abnormally high longitudinal arch of the foot.

736.74 Claw foot, acquired
DEF: High foot arch with hyperextended toes at metatarsophalangeal joint and flexed toes at distal joints; also called "main en griffe."

736.75 Cavovarus deformity of foot, acquired
DEF: Inward turning of the heel from the midline of the leg and an abnormally high longitudinal arch.

736.76 Other calcaneus deformity

N Newborn Age: 0   P Pediatric Age: 0-17   M Maternity Age: 12-55   A Adult Age: 15-124   MCC Major CC Condition   CC CC Condition   HIV HIV Related Dx

266 – Volume 1   **2010 ICD-9-CM**

Scoliosis and Kyphoscoliosis

Scoliosis　　　　Kyphoscoliosis

√5ᵗʰ 737.3 Kyphoscoliosis and scoliosis
> **DEF:** Kyphoscoliosis: backward and lateral curvature of the spinal column; it is found in vertebral osteochondrosis.
> **DEF:** Scoliosis: an abnormal deviation of the spine to the left or right of the midline

737.30 Scoliosis [and kyphoscoliosis], idiopathic
> **AHA:** 3Q, '03, 19
> **M41.115** Juvenile idiopathic scoliosis thoracolumbar region　　`I-10`

737.31 Resolving infantile idiopathic scoliosis

737.32 Progressive infantile idiopathic scoliosis
> **AHA:** 3Q, '02, 12

737.33 Scoliosis due to radiation

737.34 Thoracogenic scoliosis

737.39 Other
> **EXCLUDES** that associated with conditions classifiable elsewhere (737.43) that in kyphoscoliotic heart disease (416.1)
> **AHA:** 2Q, '02, 16

√5ᵗʰ 737.4 Curvature of spine associated with other conditions
> *Code first associated condition as:*
> Charcôt-Marie-Tooth disease (356.1)
> mucopolysaccharidosis (277.5)
> neurofibromatosis (237.7)
> osteitis deformans (731.0)
> osteitis fibrosa cystica (252.01)
> osteoporosis (733.00-733.09)
> poliomyelitis (138)
> tuberculosis [Pott's curvature] (015.0)

737.40 Curvature of spine, unspecified

737.41 Kyphosis

737.42 Lordosis

737.43 Scoliosis

737.8 Other curvatures of spine

737.9 Unspecified curvature of spine
> Curvature of spine (acquired) (idiopathic) NOS
> Hunchback, acquired
> **EXCLUDES** deformity of spine NOS (738.5)

√4ᵗʰ 738 Other acquired deformity
> **EXCLUDES** congenital (754.0-756.9, 758.0-759.9)
> dentofacial anomalies (524.0-524.9)

738.0 Acquired deformity of nose
> Deformity of nose (acquired)
> Overdevelopment of nasal bones
> **EXCLUDES** deflected or deviated nasal septum (470)

√5ᵗʰ 738.1 Other acquired deformity of head

738.10 Unspecified deformity

738.11 Zygomatic hyperplasia
> **DEF:** Abnormal enlargement of the zygoma (processus zygomaticus temporalis).

738.12 Zygomatic hypoplasia
> **DEF:** Underdevelopment of the zygoma (processus zygomaticus temporalis).

738.19 Other specified deformity
> **AHA:** 1Q, '06, 6; 2Q, '03, 13

738.2 Acquired deformity of neck

738.3 Acquired deformity of chest and rib
> Deformity:
> chest (acquired)
> rib (acquired)
> Pectus:
> carinatum, acquired
> excavatum, acquired

738.4 Acquired spondylolisthesis
> Degenerative spondylolisthesis
> Spondylolysis, acquired
> **EXCLUDES** congenital (756.12)
> **DEF:** Vertebra displaced forward over another; due to bilateral defect in vertebral arch, eroded articular surface of posterior facts and elongated pedicle between fifth lumbar vertebra and sacrum.
> **AHA:** 4Q, '07, 120; 1Q, '07, 10
> **M43.10** Spondylolisthesis site unspecified　　`I-10`

738.5 Other acquired deformity of back or spine
> Deformity of spine NOS
> **EXCLUDES** curvature of spine (737.0-737.9)
> **AHA:** 1Q, '08, 11
> **TIP:** Assign for post procedural flat back syndrome, which may be the result of a previous spinal fusion surgery. Do not assign a surgical complication code.

738.6 Acquired deformity of pelvis
> Pelvic obliquity
> **EXCLUDES** intrapelvic protrusion of acetabulum (718.6)
> that in relation to labor and delivery (653.0-653.4, 653.8-653.9)
> **DEF:** Pelvic obliquity: slanting or inclination of the pelvis at an angle between 55 and 60 degrees between the plane of the pelvis and the horizontal plane.

738.7 Cauliflower ear
> **DEF:** Abnormal external ear; due to injury, subsequent perichondritis.

738.8 Acquired deformity of other specified site
> Deformity of clavicle
> **AHA:** 2Q, '01, 15

738.9 Acquired deformity of unspecified site

√4ᵗʰ 739 Nonallopathic lesions, not elsewhere classified
> **INCLUDES** segmental dysfunction
> somatic dysfunction
> **DEF:** Disability, loss of function or abnormality of a body part that is neither classifiable to a particular system nor brought about therapeutically to counteract another disease.

739.0 Head region
> Occipitocervical region

739.1 Cervical region
> Cervicothoracic region

739.2 Thoracic region
> Thoracolumbar region

739.3 Lumbar region
> Lumbosacral region

739.4 Sacral region
> Sacrococcygeal region
> Sacroiliac region

739.5 Pelvic region
    Hip region
    Pubic region

739.6 Lower extremities

739.7 Upper extremities
    Acromioclavicular region
    Sternoclavicular region

739.8 Rib cage
    Costochondral region
    Costovertebral region
    Sternochondral region

739.9 Abdomen and other
    AHA: 2Q, '89, 14

N Newborn Age: 0   P Pediatric Age: 0-17   M Maternity Age: 12-55   A Adult Age: 15-124   MCC Major CC Condition   CC CC Condition   HIV HIV Related Dx

268 – Volume 1   2010 ICD-9-CM

14. CONGENITAL ANOMALIES (740-759)

TIP: Codes from chapter 14 may be assigned throughout the life of the patient, whenever the congenital anomaly is diagnosed.

✓4th 740 Anencephalus and similar anomalies

740.0 Anencephalus `MCC`
Acrania
Amyelencephalus
Hemicephaly
Hemianencephaly
DEF: Fetus without cerebrum, cerebellum and flat bones of skull.
CC Excl: 740.0-740.2

740.1 Craniorachischisis `MCC`
DEF: Congenital slit in cranium and vertebral column
CC Excl: See code: 740.0

740.2 Iniencephaly `MCC`
DEF: Spinal cord passes through enlarged occipital bone (foramen magnum); absent vertebral bone layer and spinal processes; resulting in both reduction in number and proper fusion of the vertebrae.
CC Excl: See code: 740.0

✓4th 741 Spina bifida

EXCLUDES spina bifida occulta (756.17)

The following fifth-digit subclassification is for use with category 741:
0 unspecified region
1 cervical region
2 dorsal [thoracic] region
3 lumbar region

DEF: Lack of closure of spinal cord's bony encasement; marked by cord protrusion into lumbosacral area; evident by elevated alpha-fetoprotein of amniotic fluid
AHA: 3Q, '94, 7
TIP: For Arnold-Chiari syndrome, Type I, refer to code 348.4.

§ ✓5th **741.0 With hydrocephalus** `CC`
[0-3] Arnold-Chiari syndrome, type II
Chiari malformation, type II
Any condition classifiable to 741.9 with any condition classifiable to 742.3
CC Excl: 741.00-741.93, 742.59-742.9, 759.7-759.89
AHA: 4Q, '97, 51; 4Q, '94, 37; S-O, '87, 10
Q05.4 Unspecified spina bifida with hydrocephalus `I-10`

§ ✓5th **741.9 Without mention of hydrocephalus**
[0-3] Hydromeningocele (spinal)
Hydromyelocele
Meningocele (spinal)
Meningomyelocele
Myelocele
Myelocystocele
Rachischisis
Spina bifida (aperta)
Syringomyelocele
Q05.8 Sacral spina bifida without hydrocephalus `I-10`

✓4th 742 Other congenital anomalies of nervous system

EXCLUDES congenital central alveolar hypoventilation syndrome (327.25)

742.0 Encephalocele `CC`
Encephalocystocele
Encephalomyelocele
Hydroencephalocele
Hydromeningocele, cranial
Meningocele, cerebral
Meningoencephalocele
DEF: Brain tissue protrudes through skull defect.
CC Excl: 742.0-742.2, 742.4
AHA: 4Q, '94, 37

742.1 Microcephalus
Hydromicrocephaly
Micrencephaly
DEF: Extremely small head or brain.

Spina Bifida

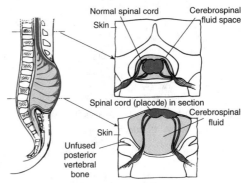

742.2 Reduction deformities of brain `MCC`
Absence
Agenesis
Aplasia   } of part of brain
Hypoplasia
Agyria
Arhinencephaly
Holoprosencephaly
Microgyria
CC Excl: See code 742.0
AHA: 3Q, '03, 15; 4Q, '94, 37
TIP: Assign for septo-optic dysplasia.

742.3 Congenital hydrocephalus
Aqueduct of Sylvius:
anomaly
obstruction, congenital
stenosis
Atresia of foramina of Magendie and Luschka
Hydrocephalus in newborn
EXCLUDES hydrocephalus:
acquired (331.3-331.4)
due to congenital toxoplasmosis (771.2)
with any condition classifiable to 741.9 (741.0)
DEF: Fluid accumulation within the skull; involves subarachnoid (external) or ventricular (internal) brain spaces.
AHA: 4Q, '05, 83
Q03.9 Congenital hydrocephalus unspecified `I-10`

Normal Ventricles and Hydrocephalus

§ Requires fifth digit. Valid digits are in [brackets] under each code. See category 741 for codes and defintions.

✓4th / ✓5th Additional Digit Required   Unacceptable PDx   Manifestation Code   Hospital Acquired Condition   ►◄ Revised Text   ● New Code   ▲ Revised Code Title

2010 ICD-9-CM   **Volume 1 – 269**

Congenital Anomalies

742.4–743.51

742.4 Other specified anomalies of brain `CC`
Congenital cerebral cyst
Macroencephaly
Macrogyria
Megalencephaly
Multiple anomalies of brain NOS
Porencephaly
Ulegyria
CC Excl: 742.4
AHA: 1Q, '99, 9; 3Q, '92, 12

✓5ᵗʰ **742.5 Other specified anomalies of spinal cord**

742.51 Diastematomyelia
DEF: Congenital anomaly often associated with spina bifida; the spinal cord is separated into halves by a bony tissue resembling a "spike" (a spicule), each half surrounded by a dural sac.

742.53 Hydromyelia
Hydrorhachis
DEF: Dilated central spinal cord canal; characterized by increased fluid accumulation.

742.59 Other
Amyelia
Atelomyelia
Congenital anomaly of spinal meninges
Defective development of cauda equina
Hypoplasia of spinal cord
Myelatelia
Myelodysplasia
AHA: 2Q, '91, 14; 1Q, '89, 10
TIP: Assign for tethered spinal cord syndrome, regardless of when it is diagnosed.

742.8 Other specified anomalies of nervous system
Agenesis of nerve
Displacement of brachial plexus
Familial dysautonomia
Jaw-winking syndrome
Marcus-Gunn syndrome
Riley-Day syndrome
EXCLUDES neurofibromatosis (237.7)

742.9 Unspecified anomaly of brain, spinal cord, and nervous system
Anomaly
Congenital:
  disease } of: { brain
  lesion   nervous system
Deformity   spinal cord

✓4ᵗʰ **743 Congenital anomalies of eye**

✓5ᵗʰ **743.0 Anophthalmos**
DEF: Complete absence of the eyes or the presence of vestigial eyes.

743.00 Clinical anophthalmos, unspecified
Agenesis   } of eye
Congenital absence
Anophthalmos NOS

743.03 Cystic eyeball, congenital

743.06 Cryptophthalmos
DEF: Skin is continuous over eyeball, results in apparent absence of eyelids.

✓5ᵗʰ **743.1 Microphthalmos**
Dysplasia } of eye
Hypoplasia
Rudimentary eye
DEF: Abnormally small eyeballs, may be opacities of cornea and lens, scarring of choroid and retina.

743.10 Microphthalmos, unspecified

743.11 Simple microphthalmos

743.12 Microphthalmos associated with other anomalies of eye and adnexa

✓5ᵗʰ **743.2 Buphthalmos**
Glaucoma:
  congenital
  newborn
Hydrophthalmos
EXCLUDES glaucoma of childhood (365.14)
            traumatic glaucoma due to birth injury (767.8)
DEF: Distended, enlarged fibrous coats of eye; due to intraocular pressure of congenital glaucoma.

743.20 Buphthalmos, unspecified

743.21 Simple buphthalmos

743.22 Buphthalmos associated with other ocular anomalies
Keratoglobus, congenital } associated with
Megalocornea   buphthalmos

✓5ᵗʰ **743.3 Congenital cataract and lens anomalies**
EXCLUDES infantile cataract (366.00-366.09)
DEF: Opaque eye lens.

743.30 Congenital cataract, unspecified

743.31 Capsular and subcapsular cataract

743.32 Cortical and zonular cataract

743.33 Nuclear cataract

743.34 Total and subtotal cataract, congenital

743.35 Congenital aphakia
Congenital absence of lens

743.36 Anomalies of lens shape
Microphakia
Spherophakia

743.37 Congenital ectopic lens

743.39 Other

✓5ᵗʰ **743.4 Coloboma and other anomalies of anterior segment**
DEF: Coloboma: ocular tissue defect associated with defect of ocular fetal intraocular fissure; may cause small pit on optic disk, major defects of iris, ciliary body, choroid, and retina.

743.41 Anomalies of corneal size and shape
Microcornea
EXCLUDES that associated with buphthalmos (743.22)

743.42 Corneal opacities, interfering with vision, congenital

743.43 Other corneal opacities, congenital

743.44 Specified anomalies of anterior chamber, chamber angle, and related structures
Anomaly:
  Axenfeld's
  Peters'
  Rieger's

743.45 Aniridia
DEF: Incompletely formed or absent iris; affects both eyes; dominant trait; also called congenital hyperplasia of iris.
AHA: 3Q, '02, 20

743.46 Other specified anomalies of iris and ciliary body
Anisocoria, congenital   Coloboma of iris
Atresia of pupil   Corectopia

743.47 Specified anomalies of sclera

743.48 Multiple and combined anomalies of anterior segment

743.49 Other

✓5ᵗʰ **743.5 Congenital anomalies of posterior segment**

743.51 Vitreous anomalies
Congenital vitreous opacity

N Newborn Age: 0   P Pediatric Age: 0-17   M Maternity Age: 12-55   A Adult Age: 15-124   MCC Major CC Condition   CC CC Condition   HIV HIV Related Dx

270 – Volume 1   **2010 ICD-9-CM**

743.52　**Fundus coloboma**
　　DEF: Absent retinal and choroidal tissue; occurs in
　　lower fundus; a bright white ectatic zone of
　　exposed sclera extends into and changes the optic
　　disk.

743.53　**Chorioretinal degeneration, congenital**

743.54　**Congenital folds and cysts of posterior
　　　　segment**

743.55　**Congenital macular changes**

743.56　**Other retinal changes, congenital**
　　AHA: 3Q, '99, 12

743.57　**Specified anomalies of optic disc**
　　Coloboma of optic disc (congenital)

743.58　**Vascular anomalies**
　　Congenital retinal aneurysm

743.59　**Other**

√5th　743.6　**Congenital anomalies of eyelids, lacrimal system, and
　　　　orbit**

743.61　**Congenital ptosis**
　　DEF: Drooping of eyelid.

743.62　**Congenital deformities of eyelids**
　　Ablepharon
　　Absence of eyelid
　　Accessory eyelid
　　Congenital:
　　　　ectropion
　　　　entropion
　　AHA: 1Q, '00, 22
　　TIP: Assign for epiblepharon, in which a redundant
　　horizontal skin fold under the eyelid causes an
　　abnormal vertical orientation of the eyelashes; may
　　result in the eyelashes touching the eyeball.

743.63　**Other specified congenital anomalies of eyelid**
　　Absence, agenesis, of cilia

743.64　**Specified congenital anomalies of lacrimal
　　　　gland**

743.65　**Specified congenital anomalies of lacrimal
　　　　passages**
　　Absence, agenesis of:
　　　　lacrimal apparatus
　　　　punctum lacrimale
　　Accessory lacrimal canal

743.66　**Specified congenital anomalies of orbit**

743.69　**Other**
　　Accessory eye muscles

743.8　**Other specified anomalies of eye**
　　EXCLUDES　*congenital nystagmus (379.51)*
　　　　　　　　ocular albinism (270.2)
　　　　　　　　optic nerve hypoplasia (377.43)
　　　　　　　　retinitis pigmentosa (362.74)

743.9　**Unspecified anomaly of eye**
　　Congenital:
　　　　anomaly NOS　⎫
　　　　deformity NOS　⎬ of eye (any part)

√4th　744　**Congenital anomalies of ear, face, and neck**
　　EXCLUDES　*anomaly of:*
　　　　　　　　cervical spine (754.2, 756.10-756.19)
　　　　　　　　larynx (748.2-748.3)
　　　　　　　　nose (748.0-748.1)
　　　　　　　　parathyroid gland (759.2)
　　　　　　　　thyroid gland (759.2)
　　　　　　　　cleft lip (749.10-749.25)

√5th　744.0　**Anomalies of ear causing impairment of hearing**
　　EXCLUDES　*congenital deafness without mention of cause
　　　　　　　　(389.0-389.9)*

744.00　**Unspecified anomaly of ear with impairment
　　　　of hearing**

744.01　**Absence of external ear**
　　Absence of:
　　　　auditory canal (external)
　　　　auricle (ear) (with stenosis or atresia of
　　　　　　auditory canal)

744.02　**Other anomalies of external ear with
　　　　impairment of hearing**
　　Atresia or stricture of auditory canal (external)

744.03　**Anomaly of middle ear, except ossicles**
　　Atresia or stricture of osseous meatus (ear)

744.04　**Anomalies of ear ossicles**
　　Fusion of ear ossicles

744.05　**Anomalies of inner ear**
　　Congenital anomaly of:
　　　　membranous labyrinth
　　　　organ of Corti

744.09　**Other**
　　Absence of ear, congenital

744.1　**Accessory auricle**
　　Accessory tragus
　　Polyotia
　　Preauricular appendage
　　Supernumerary:
　　　　ear
　　　　lobule
　　DEF: Redundant tissue or structures of ear.

√5th　744.2　**Other specified anomalies of ear**
　　EXCLUDES　*that with impairment of hearing
　　　　　　　　(744.00-744.09)*

744.21　**Absence of ear lobe, congenital**

744.22　**Macrotia**
　　DEF: Abnormally large pinna of ear.

744.23　**Microtia**
　　DEF: Hypoplasia of pinna; associated with absent or
　　closed auditory canal.

744.24　**Specified anomalies of Eustachian tube**
　　Absence of Eustachian tube

744.29　**Other**
　　Bat ear
　　Darwin's tubercle
　　Pointed ear
　　Prominence of auricle
　　Ridge ear
　　EXCLUDES　*preauricular sinus (744.46)*

744.3　**Unspecified anomaly of ear**
　　Congenital:
　　　　anomaly NOS　⎫
　　　　deformity NOS　⎬ of ear, not elsewhere classified

√5th　744.4　**Branchial cleft cyst or fistula; preauricular sinus**

744.41　**Branchial cleft sinus or fistula**
　　Branchial:
　　　　sinus (external) (internal)
　　　　vestige
　　DEF: Cyst due to failed closure of embryonic
　　branchial cleft.

744.42　**Branchial cleft cyst**

744.43　**Cervical auricle**

744.46　**Preauricular sinus or fistula**

744.47　**Preauricular cyst**

744.49　**Other**
　　Fistula (of):
　　　　auricle, congenital
　　　　cervicoaural

744.5　**Webbing of neck**
　　Pterygium colli
　　DEF: Thick, triangular skinfold, stretches from lateral side of
　　neck across shoulder; associated with Turner's and Noonan's
　　syndromes.

Congenital Anomalies

744.8–745.9

☑5th **744.8 Other specified anomalies of face and neck**

     744.81 Macrocheilia
         Hypertrophy of lip, congenital
         DEF: Abnormally large lips.

     744.82 Microcheilia
         DEF: Abnormally small lips.

     744.83 Macrostomia
         DEF: Bilateral or unilateral anomaly, of mouth due to malformed maxillary and mandibular processes; results in mouth extending toward ear.

     744.84 Microstomia
         DEF: Abnormally small mouth.

     744.89 Other
         EXCLUDES   *congenital fistula of lip (750.25)*
                   musculoskeletal anomalies (754.0-754.1, 756.0)

744.9 Unspecified anomalies of face and neck
     Congenital:
         anomaly NOS   } of face [any part] or neck [any
         deformity NOS }   part]

☑4th **745 Bulbus cordis anomalies and anomalies of cardiac septal closure**

     745.0 Common truncus   `MCC`
         Absent septum   } between aorta and
         Communication (abnormal) }   pulmonary artery
         Aortic septal defect
         Common aortopulmonary trunk
         Persistent truncus arteriosus
         CC Excl: 429.71-429.79, 745.0-745.9, 746.89-746.9, 747.83-747.9, 759.7-759.89

☑5th **745.1 Transposition of great vessels**

     745.10 Complete transposition of great vessels   `MCC`
         Transposition of great vessels:
            NOS
            classical
         CC Excl: See code 745.0

     745.11 Double outlet right ventricle   `MCC`
         Dextratransposition of aorta
         Incomplete transposition of great vessels
         Origin of both great vessels from right ventricle
         Taussig-Bing syndrome or defect
         CC Excl: See code 745.0

     745.12 Corrected transposition of great vessels   `CC`
         CC Excl: See code 745.0

     745.19 Other   `MCC`
         CC Excl: See code 745.0

     745.2 Tetralogy of Fallot   `MCC`
         Fallot's pentalogy
         Ventricular septal defect with pulmonary stenosis or atresia, dextraposition of aorta, and hypertrophy of right ventricle
         EXCLUDES   *Fallot's triad (746.09)*
         DEF: Obstructed cardiac outflow causes pulmonary stenosis, interventricular septal defect and right ventricular hypertrophy.
         CC Excl: See code 745.0

     745.3 Common ventricle   `MCC`
         Cor triloculare biatriatum
         Single ventricle
         CC Excl: See code 745.0

Heart Defects

745.4 Ventricular septal defect   `CC`
     Eisenmenger's defect or complex
     Gerbo dedefect
     Interventricular septal defect
     Left ventricular-right atrial communication
     Roger's disease
     EXCLUDES   *common atrioventricular canal type (745.69)*
                 single ventricle (745.3)
     CC Excl: See code 745.0
     Q21.0 Ventricular septal defect   `I-10`

745.5 Ostium secundum type atrial septal defect   `CC`
     Defect:
         atrium secundum
         fossa ovalis
     Lutembacher's syndrome
     Patent or persistent:
         foramen ovale
         ostium secundum
     DEF: Opening in atrial septum due to failure of the septum secundum and the endocardial cushions to fuse; there is a rim of septum surrounding the defect.
     CC Excl: 429.71-429.79, 745.0-745.3, 745.5-745.9, 746.89-746.9, 747.89-747.9, 759.7, 759.89
     Q21.1 Atrial septal defect   `I-10`

☑5th **745.6 Endocardial cushion defects**
     DEF: Atrial and/or ventricular septal defects causing abnormal fusion of cushions in atrioventricular canal.

     745.60 Endocardial cushion defect, unspecified type   `CC`
         DEF: Septal defect due to imperfect fusion of endocardial cushions.
         CC Excl: See code 745.0

     745.61 Ostium primum defect   `CC`
         Persistent ostium primum
         DEF: Opening in low, posterior septum primum; causes cleft in basal portion of atrial septum; associated with cleft mitral valve.
         CC Excl: See code: 745.0

     745.69 Other   `CC`
         Absence of atrial septum
         Atrioventricular canal type ventricular septal defect
         Common atrioventricular canal
         Common atrium
         CC Excl: See code 745.0

745.7 Cor biloculare   `MCC`
     Absence of atrial and ventricular septa
     DEF: Atrial and ventricular septal defect; marked by heart with two cardiac chambers (one atrium, one ventricle), and one atrioventricular valve.
     CC Excl: See code 745.0

745.8 Other

745.9 Unspecified defect of septal closure
     Septal defect NOS

`N` Newborn Age: 0   `P` Pediatric Age: 0-17   `M` Maternity Age: 12-55   `A` Adult Age: 15-124   `MCC` Major CC Condition   `CC` CC Condition   `HIV` HIV Related Dx

272 – Volume 1   **2010 ICD-9-CM**

Congenital Anomalies

746–746.9

✓4ᵗʰ **746**   **Other congenital anomalies of heart**
    EXCLUDES   endocardial fibroelastosis (425.3)

✓5ᵗʰ **746.0**   **Anomalies of pulmonary valve**
    EXCLUDES   infundibular or subvalvular pulmonic stenosis (746.83)
       tetralogy of Fallot (745.2)

746.00   **Pulmonary valve anomaly, unspecified** `CC`
    CC Excl: 746.00-746.09, 746.89-746.9, 747.89-747.9, 759.7, 759.89

746.01   **Atresia, congenital** `MCC`
    Congenital absence of pulmonary valve
    CC Excl: 746.00-746.09, 746.89-746.9, 747.89-747.9, 759.7, 759.89

746.02   **Stenosis, congenital** `CC`
    DEF: Stenosis of opening between pulmonary artery and right ventricle; causes obstructed blood outflow from right ventricle.
    CC Excl: See code 746.01
    AHA: 1Q, '04, 16

746.09   **Other** `CC`
    Congenital insufficiency of pulmonary valve
    Fallot's triad or trilogy
    CC Excl: See code: 746.00

746.1   **Tricuspid atresia and stenosis, congenital** `MCC`
    Absence of tricuspid valve
    CC Excl: 746.1-746.7, 746.89-746.9, 747.83-747.9, 759.7-759.89

746.2   **Ebstein's anomaly** `MCC`
    DEF: Malformation of the tricuspid valve characterized by septal and posterior leaflets attaching to the wall of the right ventricle; causing the right ventricle to fuse with the atrium into a large right atrium and a small ventricle; causes heart failure and abnormal cardiac rhythm.
    CC Excl: See code 746.1

746.3   **Congenital stenosis of aortic valve** `CC`
    Congenital aortic stenosis
    EXCLUDES   congenital:
       subaortic stenosis (746.81)
       supravalvular aortic stenosis (747.22)
    DEF: Stenosis of orifice of aortic valve; obstructs blood outflow from left ventricle.
    CC Excl: See code 746.1
    AHA: 4Q, '88, 8

746.4   **Congenital insufficiency of aortic valve** `CC`
    Bicuspid aortic valve
    Congenital aortic insufficiency
    DEF: Impaired functioning of aortic valve due to incomplete closure; causes backflow (regurgitation) of blood from aorta to left ventricle.
    CC Excl: See code 746.1
    Q23.1 Congenital insufficiency of aortic valve `I-10`

746.5   **Congenital mitral stenosis** `CC`
    Fused commissure
    Parachute deformity } of mitral valve
    Supernumerary cusps
    DEF: Stenosis of left atrioventricular orifice.
    CC Excl: See code 746.1
    AHA: 3Q, '07, 3

746.6   **Congenital mitral insufficiency** `CC`
    DEF: Impaired functioning of mitral valve due to incomplete closure; causes backflow of blood from left ventricle to left atrium.
    CC Excl: See code 746.1

746.7   **Hypoplastic left heart syndrome** `MCC`
    Atresia, or marked hypoplasia, of aortic orifice or valve, with hypoplasia of ascending aorta and defective development of left ventricle (with mitral valve atresia)
    CC Excl: See code 746.1

✓5ᵗʰ **746.8**   **Other specified anomalies of heart**

746.81   **Subaortic stenosis** `MCC`
    DEF: Stenosis, of left ventricular outflow tract due to fibrous tissue ring or septal hypertrophy below aortic valve.
    CC Excl: 746.81-746.84, 746.89-746.9, 747.83-747.9, 759.7-759.89
    AHA: 3Q, '07, 3

746.82   **Cor triatriatum** `MCC`
    DEF: Transverse septum divides left atrium due to failed resorption of embryonic common pulmonary vein; results in three atrial chambers.
    CC Excl: See code 746.81

746.83   **Infundibular pulmonic stenosis** `CC`
    Subvalvular pulmonic stenosis
    DEF: Stenosis of right ventricle outflow tract within infundibulum due to fibrous diaphragm below valve or long, narrow fibromuscular channel.
    CC Excl: See code 746.81

746.84   **Obstructive anomalies of heart, not elsewhere classified** `MCC`
    Shone's syndrome
    Uhl's disease
    Use additional code for associated anomalies, such as:
       coarctation of aorta (747.10)
       congenital mitral stenosis (746.5)
       subaortic stenosis (746.81)
    CC Excl: See code: 746.81

746.85   **Coronary artery anomaly** `CC`
    Anomalous origin or communication of coronary artery
    Arteriovenous malformation of coronary artery
    Coronary artery:
       absence
       arising from aorta or pulmonary trunk
       single
    CC Excl: 746.85, 746.89-746.9
    AHA: N-D, '85, 3

746.86   **Congenital heart block** `MCC`
    Complete or incomplete atrioventricular [AV] block
    DEF: Impaired conduction of electrical impulses; due to maldeveloped junctional tissue.
    CC Excl: 746.86, 746.89-746.9, 747.83-747.9, 759.7-759.89

746.87   **Malposition of heart and cardiac apex** `CC`
    Abdominal heart
    Dextrocardia
    Ectopia cordis
    Levocardia (isolated)
    Mesocardia
    EXCLUDES   dextrocardia with complete transposition of viscera (759.3)
    CC Excl: 746.81-746.84, 746.87-746.9, 747.89-747.9, 759.7, 759.89

746.89   **Other**
    Atresia } of cardiac vein
    Hypoplasia
    Congenital:
       cardiomegaly
       diverticulum, left ventricle
       pericardial defect
    AHA: 3Q, '00, 3; 1Q, '99, 11; J-F, '85, 3
    TIP: Assign for Brugada syndrome, and also for congenital long QT syndrome. Additional codes may be required.
    Q24.8 Oth specified congenital malformations of heart `I-10`

746.9   **Unspecified anomaly of heart**
    Congenital:
       anomaly of heart NOS
       heart disease NOS

✓4ᵗʰ Additional Digit Required   ✓5ᵗʰ   Unacceptable PDx   Manifestation Code   Hospital Acquired Condition   ▶◀ Revised Text   ● New Code   ▲ Revised Code Title

2010 ICD-9-CM   **Volume 1 – 273**

Congenital Anomalies

747–747.81

✓4th **747   Other congenital anomalies of circulatory system**

747.0   Patent ductus arteriosus   `CC`
Patent ductus Botalli
Persistent ductus arteriosus
DEF: Open lumen in ductus arteriosus causes arterial blood recirculation in lungs; inhibits blood supply to aorta; symptoms such as shortness of breath more noticeable upon activity.
CC Excl: 747.0, 747.89
Q25.0 Patent ductus arteriosus   `I-10`

✓5th **747.1   Coarctation of aorta**
DEF: Localized deformity of aortic media seen as a severe constriction of the vessel lumen; major symptom is high blood pressure in the arms and low pressure in the legs; may result in a CVA, rupture of the aorta, bacterial endocarditis or congestive heart failure.

747.10   Coarctation of aorta (preductal) (postductal)   `CC`
Hypoplasia of aortic arch
CC Excl: 747.10-747.22, 747.89-747.9, 759.7, 759.89
AHA: 3Q, '07, 3; 1Q, '99, 11; 4Q, '88, 8

747.11   Interruption of aortic arch   `MCC`
CC Excl: 747.10-747.22, 747.83-747.9, 759.7-759.89

✓5th **747.2   Other anomalies of aorta**

747.20   Anomaly of aorta, unspecified   `CC`
CC Excl: 747.10-747.22, 747.89-747.9, 759.7, 759.89

747.21   Anomalies of aortic arch   `CC`
Anomalous origin, right subclavian artery
Dextraposition of aorta
Double aortic arch
Kommerell's diverticulum
Overriding aorta
Persistent:
  convolutions, aortic arch
  right aortic arch
Vascular ring
EXCLUDES   *hypoplasia of aortic arch (747.10)*
CC Excl: See code: 747.20
AHA: 1Q, '03, 15

747.22   Atresia and stenosis of aorta   `CC`
Absence ⎫
Aplasia ⎬ of aorta
Hypoplasia ⎪
Stricture ⎭
Supra (valvular)-aortic stenosis
EXCLUDES   *congenital aortic (valvular) stenosis or stricture, so stated (746.3)*
hypoplasia of aorta in hypoplastic left heart syndrome (746.7)
CC Excl: 747.10-747.22, 747.83-747.9, 759.7-759.89

747.29   Other   `CC`
Aneurysm of sinus of Valsalva
Congenital:
  aneurysm ⎫
  dilation ⎬ of aorta
CC Excl: 747.10-747.29, 747.89-747.9, 759.7, 759.89

747.3   Anomalies of pulmonary artery   `MCC`
Agenesis ⎫
Anomaly ⎪
Atresia ⎬ of pulmonary artery
Coarctation ⎪
Hypoplasia ⎪
Stenosis ⎭
Pulmonary arteriovenous aneurysm
CC Excl: 747.3, 747.89-747.9
AHA: 1Q, '04, 16; 1Q, '94, 15; 4Q, '88, 8
Q25.7 Oth congenital malformations pulmonary artery   `I-10`

✓5th **747.4   Anomalies of great veins**

747.40   Anomaly of great veins, unspecified   `CC`
Anomaly NOS of:
  pulmonary veins
  vena cava
CC Excl: 747.40, 747.89-747.9

747.41   Total anomalous pulmonary venous connection   `CC`
Total anomalous pulmonary venous return [TAPVR]:
  subdiaphragmatic
  supradiaphragmatic
CC Excl: 747.41, 747.89-747.9

747.42   Partial anomalous pulmonary venous connection   `CC`
Partial anomalous pulmonary venous return
CC Excl: 747.42, 747.89-747.9

747.49   Other anomalies of great veins   `CC`
Absence ⎫
Congenital ⎬ of vena cava (inferior)
stenosis ⎭ (superior)
Persistent:
  left posterior cardinal vein
  left superior vena cava
Scimitar syndrome
Transposition of pulmonary veins NOS
CC Excl: 747.49, 747.89-747.9

747.5   Absence or hypoplasia of umbilical artery
Single umbilical artery

✓5th **747.6   Other anomalies of peripheral vascular system**
Absence ⎫
Anomaly ⎬ of artery or vein, NEC
Atresia ⎭
Arteriovenous aneurysm (peripheral)
Arteriovenous malformation of the peripheral vascular system
Congenital:
  aneurysm (peripheral)
  phlebectasia
  stricture, artery
  varix
Multiple renal arteries
EXCLUDES   *anomalies of:*
   cerebral vessels (747.81)
   pulmonary artery (747.3)
   congenital retinal aneurysm (743.58)
   hemangioma (228.00-228.09)
   lymphangioma (228.1)

747.60   Anomaly of the peripheral vascular system, unspecified site

747.61   Gastrointestinal vessel anomaly
AHA: 3Q, '96, 10
TIP: Do not assign for gastric or intestinal AV malformation or angiodysplasia not stated to be congenital. See instead code 537.82, 537.83, 569.84, or 569.85.

747.62   Renal vessel anomaly

747.63   Upper limb vessel anomaly

747.64   Lower limb vessel anomaly

747.69   Anomalies of other specified sites of peripheral vascular system

✓5th **747.8   Other specified anomalies of circulatory system**

747.81   Anomalies of cerebrovascular system   `MCC`
Arteriovenous malformation of brain
Cerebral arteriovenous aneurysm, congenital
Congenital anomalies of cerebral vessels
EXCLUDES   *ruptured cerebral (arteriovenous) aneurysm (430)*
CC Excl: 747.81, 747.89-747.9
Q28.3 Other malformations of cerebral vessels   `I-10`

`N` Newborn Age: 0   `P` Pediatric Age: 0-17   `M` Maternity Age: 12-55   `A` Adult Age: 15-124   `MCC` Major CC Condition   `CC` CC Condition   `HIV` HIV Related Dx

Persistent Fetal Circulation

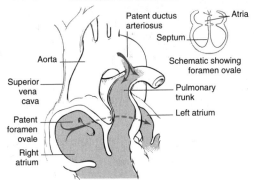

747.82 Spinal vessel anomaly `CC`
Arteriovenous malformation of spinal vessel
CC Excl: 747.82, 747.89-747.9
AHA: 3Q, '95, 5

747.83 Persistent fetal circulation `MCC` `N`
Persistent pulmonary hypertension
Primary pulmonary hypertension of newborn
DEF: A return to fetal circulation due to constriction of pulmonary arterioles and opening of the ductus arteriosus and foramen ovale, right-to-left shunting, oxygenation of the blood does not occur, and the lungs remain constricted after birth; is seen in term or post-term infants causes include asphyxiation, meconium aspiration syndrome, acidosis, sepsis, and developmental immaturity.
CC Excl: 416.0, 416.8-416.9
AHA: 4Q, '02, 62

747.89 Other `CC`
Aneurysm, congenital, specified site not elsewhere classified
> *EXCLUDES* *congenital aneurysm:*
> *coronary (746.85)*
> *peripheral (747.6)*
> *pulmonary (747.3)*
> *retinal (743.58)*

CC Excl: 745.0-745.9, 747.89
AHA: 4Q, '02, 63

747.9 Unspecified anomaly of circulatory system `CC`
CC Excl: 745.0-747.82, 747.89-747.9

`√4th` **748 Congenital anomalies of respiratory system**
> *EXCLUDES* *congenital central alveolar hypoventilation syndrome (327.25)*
> *congenital defect of diaphragm (756.6)*

748.0 Choanal atresia
Atresia
Congenital stenosis } of nares (anterior) (posterior)
DEF: Occluded posterior nares (choana), bony or membranous due to failure of embryonic bucconasal membrane to rupture.

748.1 Other anomalies of nose
Absent nose
Accessory nose
Cleft nose
Congenital:
  deformity of nose
  notching of tip of nose
  perforation of wall of nasal sinus
Deformity of wall of nasal sinus
> *EXCLUDES* *congenital deviation of nasal septum (754.0)*

748.2 Web of larynx
Web of larynx: Web of larynx:
  NOS   subglottic
  glottic
DEF: Malformed larynx; marked by thin, translucent, or thick, fibrotic spread between vocal folds; affects speech.

748.3 Other anomalies of larynx, trachea, and bronchus `CC`
Absence or agenesis of: Congenital:
  bronchus   dilation, trachea
  larynx   stenosis:
  trachea   larynx
Anomaly (of):   trachea
  cricoid cartilage   tracheocele
  epiglottis   Diverticulum:
  thyroid cartilage   bronchus
  tracheal cartilage   trachea
Atresia (of):   Fissure of epiglottis
  epiglottis   Laryngocele
  glottis   Posterior cleft of cricoid
  larynx   cartilage (congenital)
  trachea   Rudimentary tracheal bronchus
Cleft thyroid, cartilage, Stridor, laryngeal, congenital
  congenital
CC Excl: 493.81, 519.19, 748.3, 748.8-748.9
AHA: 1Q, '99, 14
`I-10` **Q32.4** Other congenital malformations of bronchus

748.4 Congenital cystic lung `CC`
Disease, lung:
  cystic, congenital
  polycystic, congenital
Honeycomb lung, congenital
> *EXCLUDES* *acquired or unspecified cystic lung (518.89)*

DEF: Enlarged air spaces of lung parenchyma.
CC Excl: 748.4-748.9

748.5 Agenesis, hypoplasia, and dysplasia of lung `MCC`
Absence of lung (fissures) (lobe) (lobe)
Aplasia of lung
Hypoplasia of lung
Sequestration of lung
CC Excl: See code 748.4

`√5th` **748.6 Other anomalies of lung**

748.60 Anomaly of lung, unspecified

748.61 Congenital bronchiectasis `CC`
CC Excl: 494.0-494.1, 496, 506.1,506.4-506.9, 748.61

748.69 Other
Accessory lung (lobe)
Azygos lobe (fissure), lung

748.8 Other specified anomalies of respiratory system
Abnormal communication between pericardial and pleural sacs
Anomaly, pleural folds
Atresia of nasopharynx
Congenital cyst of mediastinum

748.9 Unspecified anomaly of respiratory system
Anomaly of respiratory system NOS

`√4th` **749 Cleft palate and cleft lip**

`√5th` **749.0 Cleft palate**

749.00 Cleft palate, unspecified

749.01 Unilateral, complete

749.02 Unilateral, incomplete
Cleft uvula

749.03 Bilateral, complete

749.04 Bilateral, incomplete

`√5th` **749.1 Cleft lip**
Cheiloschisis
Congenital fissure of lip
Harelip
Labium leporinum

749.10 Cleft lip, unspecified

749.11 Unilateral, complete

749.12 Unilateral, incomplete

749.13 Bilateral, complete

749.14 Bilateral, incomplete

`√4th` `√5th` Additional Digit Required   Unacceptable PDx   Manifestation Code   Hospital Acquired Condition   ►◄ Revised Text   ● New Code   ▲ Revised Code Title

2010 ICD-9-CM   **Volume 1 – 275**

Congenital Anomalies

749.2–751.0

Cleft Lip and Palate

Unilateral cleft lip

No cleft palate

Cleft lip with cleft alveolar ridge

No cleft palate

Unilateral cleft lip and cleft palate

Alveolar ridge

Cleft palate

Prolabium

Bilateral cleft lip and cleft palate

Isolated cleft palate

√5th **749.2   Cleft palate with cleft lip**
Cheilopalatoschisis

749.20   **Cleft palate with cleft lip, unspecified**

749.21   **Unilateral, complete**

749.22   **Unilateral, incomplete**

749.23   **Bilateral, complete**
AHA: 1Q, '96, 14

749.24   **Bilateral, incomplete**

749.25   **Other combinations**

√4th **750   Other congenital anomalies of upper alimentary tract**
EXCLUDES   dentofacial anomalies (524.0-524.9)

750.0   **Tongue tie**
Ankyloglossia
DEF: Restricted tongue movement due to lingual frenum extending toward tip of tongue. Tongue may be fused to mouth floor affecting speech.

√5th **750.1   Other anomalies of tongue**

750.10   **Anomaly of tongue, unspecified**

750.11   **Aglossia**
DEF: Absence of tongue.

750.12   **Congenital adhesions of tongue**

750.13   **Fissure of tongue**
Bifid tongue
Double tongue

750.15   **Macroglossia**
Congenital hypertrophy of tongue

750.16   **Microglossia**
Hypoplasia of tongue

750.19   **Other**

√5th **750.2   Other specified anomalies of mouth and pharynx**

750.21   **Absence of salivary gland**

750.22   **Accessory salivary gland**

750.23   **Atresia, salivary duct**
Imperforate salivary duct

750.24   **Congenital fistula of salivary gland**

750.25   **Congenital fistula of lip**
Congenital (mucus) lip pits

750.26   **Other specified anomalies of mouth**
Absence of uvula

750.27   **Diverticulum of pharynx**
Pharyngeal pouch

750.29   **Other specified anomalies of pharynx**
Imperforate pharynx

750.3   **Tracheoesophageal fistula, esophageal atresia and stenosis**   `MCC`
Absent esophagus
Atresia of esophagus
Congenital:
esophageal ring
stenosis of esophagus
stricture of esophagus
Congenital fistula:
esophagobronchial
esophagotracheal
Imperforate esophagus
Webbed esophagus
CC Excl: 530.84, 750.3-750.4, 751.8-751.9

750.4   **Other specified anomalies of esophagus**   `CC`
Dilatation, congenital
Displacement, congenital
Diverticulum   } (of) esophagus
Duplication
Giant

Esophageal pouch
EXCLUDES   congenital hiatus hernia (750.6)
CC Excl: 750.4, 751.8-751.9
AHA: J-F, '85, 3

750.5   **Congenital hypertrophic pyloric stenosis**
Congenital or infantile:
constriction
hypertrophy
spasm   } of pylorus
stenosis
stricture

DEF: Obstructed pylorus due to overgrowth of pyloric muscle.
Q40.0 Congenital hypertrophic pyloric stenosis   `I-10`

750.6   **Congenital hiatus hernia**
Displacement of cardia through esophageal hiatus
EXCLUDES   congenital diaphragmatic hernia (756.6)

750.7   **Other specified anomalies of stomach**
Congenital:
cardiospasm
hourglass stomach
Displacement of stomach
Diverticulum of stomach, congenital
Duplication of stomach
Megalogastria
Microgastria
Transposition of stomach

750.8   **Other specified anomalies of upper alimentary tract**

750.9   **Unspecified anomaly of upper alimentary tract**
Congenital:
anomaly NOS   } of upper alimentary tract [any part,
deformity NOS }   except tongue]

√4th **751   Other congenital anomalies of digestive system**

751.0   **Meckel's diverticulum**
Meckel's diverticulum (displaced) (hypertrophic)
Persistent:
omphalomesenteric duct
vitelline duct
DEF: Malformed sacs or appendages of ileum of small intestine; can cause strangulation, volvulus and intussusception.
AHA: 1Q, '04, 10
TIP: Assign for mesodiverticular band, a fibrous band connecting the tip of the diverticulum to the mesentery; can cause small bowel herniation and obstruction.

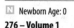 Newborn Age: 0   `P` Pediatric Age: 0-17   `M` Maternity Age: 12-55   `A` Adult Age: 15-124   `MCC` Major CC Condition   `CC` CC Condition   `HIV` HIV Related Dx

276 – Volume 1   **2010 ICD-9-CM**

751.1 Atresia and stenosis of small intestine `CC` `P`
Atresia of:
   duodenum
   ileum
   intestine NOS
Congenital:
   absence
   obstruction   } of small intestine or intestine
   stenosis   NOS
   stricture

Imperforate jejunum
CC Excl: 751.1, 751.8-751.9

751.2 Atresia and stenosis of large intestine `CC` `P`
rectum, and anal canal
Absence:
   anus (congenital)
   appendix, congenital
   large intestine, congenital
   rectum
Atresia of:
   anus
   colon
   rectum
Congenital or infantile:
   obstruction of large intestine
   occlusion of anus
   stricture of anus
Imperforate:
   anus
   rectum
Stricture of rectum, congenital
CC Excl: 751.2, 751.8-751.9
AHA: 2Q, '98, 16

751.3 Hirschsprung's disease and other congenital `CC`
functional disorders of colon
Aganglionosis
Congenital dilation of colon
Congenital megacolon
Macrocolon
DEF: Hirschsprung's disease: enlarged or dilated colon
(megacolon), with absence of ganglion cells in the narrowed
wall distally; causes inability to defecate.
CC Excl: 751.3, 751.8-751.9

751.4 Anomalies of intestinal fixation `CC`
Congenital adhesions:
   omental, anomalous
   peritoneal
Jackson's membrane
Malrotation of colon
Rotation of cecum or colon:
   failure of
   incomplete
   insufficient
Universal mesentery
CC Excl: 751.4-751.5

751.5 Other anomalies of intestine `CC`
Congenital diverticulum, colon
Dolichocolon
Duplication of:
   anus
   appendix
   cecum
   intestine
Ectopic anus
Megaloappendix
Megaloduodenum
Microcolon
Persistent cloaca
Transposition of:
   appendix
   colon
   intestine
CC Excl: 751.0-751.5
AHA: 3Q, '02, 11; 3Q, '01, 8
Q43.9 Congenital malformation of intestine unspecified `I-10`

✓5th **751.6 Anomalies of gallbladder, bile ducts, and liver**

751.60 Unspecified anomaly of gallbladder, `CC`
bile ducts, and liver
CC Excl: 751.60

751.61 Biliary atresia `MCC` `P`
Congenital:
   absence
   hypoplasia } of bile duct (common)
   obstruction   of passage
   stricture
CC Excl: 751.61, 751.8-751.9
AHA: S-O, '87, 8

751.62 Congenital cystic disease of liver `CC`
Congenital polycystic disease of liver
Fibrocystic disease of liver
CC Excl: 751.62-751.69

751.69 Other anomalies of gallbladder, bile `CC`
ducts, and liver
Absence of:
   gallbladder, congenital
   liver (lobe)
Accessory:
   hepatic ducts
   liver
Congenital:
   choledochal cyst
   hepatomegaly
Duplication of:
   biliary duct
   cystic duct
   gallbladder
   liver
Floating:
   gallbladder
   liver
Intrahepatic gallbladder
CC Excl: 751.60-751.69
AHA: S-O, '87, 8

751.7 Anomalies of pancreas `CC`
Absence
Accessory
Agenesis   } (of) pancreas
Annular
Hypoplasia
Ectopic pancreatic tissue
Pancreatic heterotopia
EXCLUDES   *diabetes mellitus (249.0-249.9, 250.0-250.9)*
        fibrocystic disease of pancreas (277.00-277.09)
        neonatal diabetes mellitus (775.1)
CC Excl: 751.7-751.9

751.8 Other specified anomalies of digestive system
Absence (complete) (partial) of alimentary tract NOS
Duplication   } of digestive organs NOS
Malposition, congenital
EXCLUDES   *congenital diaphragmatic hernia (756.6)*
        congenital hiatus hernia (750.6)

751.9 Unspecified anomaly of digestive system
Congenital:
   anomaly NOS   } of digestive system NOS
   deformity NOS

✓4th **752 Congenital anomalies of genital organs**
EXCLUDES   *syndromes associated with anomalies in the number*
        and form of chromosomes (758.0-758.9)

752.0 Anomalies of ovaries ♀
Absence, congenital
Accessory   } (of) ovary
Ectopic
Streak

✓5th **752.1 Anomalies of fallopian tubes and broad ligaments**

752.10 Unspecified anomaly of fallopian ♀
tubes and broad ligaments

✓4th
✓5th   Additional Digit Required   Unacceptable PDx   Manifestation Code   Hospital Acquired Condition   ▶◀ Revised Text   ● New Code   ▲ Revised Code Title
2010 ICD-9-CM   **Volume 1 – 277**

Congenital Anomalies

752.11–752.9

Hypospadias and Epispadias

Glans penis
Glandular hypospadias
Penile hypospadias
Penile raphe
Scrotal hypospadias
Scrotum
Scrotal raphe

Hypospadias (ventral view)

Normal external urethral orifice
Glans penis
Foreskin (retracted)
Epispadias

Epispadias (dorsal view)

752.11 Embryonic cyst of fallopian tubes and broad ligaments ♀
Cyst:
epoophoron
fimbrial
parovarian
AHA: S-O, '85, 13

752.19 Other ♀
Absence
Accessory } (of) fallopian tube or broad
Atresia } ligament

752.2 Doubling of uterus ♀
Didelphic uterus
Doubling of uterus [any degree] (associated with doubling of cervix and vagina)

752.3 Other anomalies of uterus ♀
Absence, congenital
Agenesis
Aplasia } (of) uterus
Bicornuate
Uterus unicornis
Uterus with only one functioning horn
AHA: 3Q, '06, 18

✓5th **752.4 Anomalies of cervix, vagina, and external female genitalia**

752.40 Unspecified anomaly of cervix, vagina, and external female genitalia ♀

752.41 Embryonic cyst of cervix, vagina, and external female genitalia ♀
Cyst of:
canal of Nuck, congenital
Gartner's duct
vagina, embryonal
vulva, congenital
DEF: Embryonic fluid-filled cysts, of cervix, vagina or external female genitalia.

752.42 Imperforate hymen ♀
DEF: Complete closure of membranous fold around external opening of vagina.

752.49 Other anomalies of cervix, vagina, and external female genitalia ♀
Absence
Agenesis } of cervix, clitoris, vagina, or vulva
Congenital stenosis or stricture of:
cervical canal
vagina
EXCLUDES double vagina associated with total duplication (752.2)
AHA: 3Q, '06, 18

✓5th **752.5 Undescended and retractile testicle**
AHA: 4Q, '96, 33

752.51 Undescended testis ♂
Cryptorchism   Ectopic testis
Q53.20 Undescended testicle unspecified bilateral   I-10

752.52 Retractile testis ♂

✓5th **752.6 Hypospadias and epispadias and other penile anomalies**
AHA: 4Q, '96, 34, 35

752.61 Hypospadias ♂
DEF: Abnormal opening of urethra on the ventral surface of the penis or perineum; also a rare defect of vagina.
AHA: 4Q, '03, 67-68; 3Q, '97, 6
Q54.1 Hypospadias penile   I-10

752.62 Epispadias ♂
Anaspadias
DEF: Urethra opening on dorsal surface of penis; in females appears as a slit in the upper wall of urethra.

752.63 Congenital chordee ♂
DEF: Ventral bowing of penis due to fibrous band along corpus spongiosum; occurs with hypospadias.

752.64 Micropenis ♂

752.65 Hidden penis ♂

752.69 Other penile anomalies ♂

752.7 Indeterminate sex and pseudohermaphroditism
Gynandrism
Hermaphroditism
Ovotestis
Pseudohermaphroditism (male) (female)
Pure gonadal dysgenesis
EXCLUDES androgen insensitivity (259.50-259.52)
pseudohermaphroditism:
female, with adrenocortical disorder (255.2)
male, with gonadal disorder (257.8)
with specified chromosomal anomaly (758.0-758.9)
testicular feminization syndrome (259.50-259.52)
DEF: Pseudohermaphroditism: presence of gonads of one sex and external genitalia of other sex.

✓5th **752.8 Other specified anomalies of genital organs**
EXCLUDES congenital hydrocele (778.6)
penile anomalies (752.61-752.69)
phimosis or paraphimosis (605)

752.81 Scrotal transposition ♂
AHA: 4Q, '03, 67-68

752.89 Other specified anomalies of genital organs
Absence of:
prostate
spermatic cord
vas deferens
Anorchism
Aplasia (congenital) of:
prostate
round ligament
testicle
Atresia of:
ejaculatory duct
vas deferens
Fusion of testes
Hypoplasia of testis
Monorchism
Polyorchism

752.9 Unspecified anomaly of genital organs
Congenital:
anomaly NOS } of genital organ, not
deformity NOS } elsewhere classified

N Newborn Age: 0   P Pediatric Age: 0-17   M Maternity Age: 12-55   A Adult Age: 15-124   MCC Major CC Condition   CC CC Condition   HIV HIV Related Dx

278 – Volume 1   **2010 ICD-9-CM**

√4ᵗʰ **753 Congenital anomalies of urinary system**

753.0 **Renal agenesis and dysgenesis** `CC`
Atrophy of kidney:
   congenital
   infantile
Congenital absence of kidney(s)
Hypoplasia of kidney(s)
CC Excl: 599.60-599.69, 753.0
Q60.2 Renal agenesis unspecified `I-10`

√5ᵗʰ 753.1 **Cystic kidney disease**
EXCLUDES acquired cyst of kidney (593.2)
AHA: 4Q, '90, 3

753.10 **Cystic kidney disease, unspecified** `CC`
CC Excl: 599.60-599.69, 753.10
Q61.9 Cystic kidney disease unspecified `I-10`

753.11 **Congenital single renal cyst** `CC`
CC Excl: 599.60-599.69, 753.11

753.12 **Polycystic kidney, unspecified type** `CC`
CC Excl: 599.60-599.69, 753.12-753.14
Q61.3 Polycystic kidney unspecified `I-10`

753.13 **Polycystic kidney, autosomal dominant** `CC`
DEF: Slow progressive disease characterized by bilateral cysts causing increased kidney size and impaired function.
CC Excl: See code: 753.12

753.14 **Polycystic kidney, autosomal recessive** `CC`
DEF: Rare disease characterized by multiple cysts involving kidneys and liver, producing renal and hepatic failure in childhood or adolescence.
CC Excl: See code: 753.12

753.15 **Renal dysplasia** `CC`
CC Excl: 599.60-599.69, 753.15

753.16 **Medullary cystic kidney** `CC`
Nephronopthisis
DEF: Diffuse kidney disease results in uremia onset prior to age 20.
CC Excl: 599.60-599.69, 753.16-753.19

753.17 **Medullary sponge kidney** `CC`
DEF: Dilated collecting tubules; usually asymptomatic but calcinosis in tubules may cause renal insufficiency.
CC Excl: See code: 753.16

753.19 **Other specified cystic kidney disease** `CC`
Multicystic kidney
CC Excl: See code: 753.16

√5ᵗʰ 753.2 **Obstructive defects of renal pelvis and ureter**
AHA: 4Q, '96, 35

753.20 **Unspecified obstructive defect of renal pelvis and ureter** `CC`
CC Excl: 599.60-599.69, 753.20-753.22, 753.29

753.21 **Congenital obstruction of ureteropelvic junction** `CC`
DEF: Stricture at junction of ureter and renal pelvis.
CC Excl: See code: 753.20

753.22 **Congenital obstruction of ureterovesical junction** `CC`
Adynamic ureter
Congenital hydroureter
DEF: Stricture at junction of ureter and bladder.
CC Excl: See code: 753.20

753.23 **Congenital ureterocele** `CC`
CC Excl: See code: 753.20

753.29 **Other** `CC`
CC Excl: See code: 753.20
Q62.39 Other obstructive defects renal pelvis & ureter `I-10`

753.3 **Other specified anomalies of kidney**
Accessory kidney
Congenital:
   calculus of kidney
   displaced kidney
Discoid kidney
Double kidney with double pelvis
Ectopic kidney
Fusion of kidneys
Giant kidney
Horseshoe kidney
Hyperplasia of kidney
Lobulation of kidney
Malrotation of kidney
Trifid kidney (pelvis)
AHA: 1Q, '07, 23
TIP: Assign for Finnish-type congenital nephrosis, along with code 581.3 Nephrotic syndrome.
Q63.8 Oth specified congenital malformations of kidney `I-10`

753.4 **Other specified anomalies of ureter**
Absent ureter
Accessory ureter
Deviation of ureter
Displaced ureteric orifice
Double ureter
Ectopic ureter
Implantation, anomalous of ureter

753.5 **Exstrophy of urinary bladder** `CC`
Ectopia vesicae
Extroversion of bladder
DEF: Absence of lower abdominal and anterior bladder walls with posterior bladder wall protrusion.
CC Excl: 599.60-599.69, 753.5, 753.9

753.6 **Atresia and stenosis of urethra and bladder neck** `CC`
Congenital obstruction:
   bladder neck
   urethra
Congenital stricture of:
   urethra (valvular)
   urinary meatus
   vesicourethral orifice
Imperforate urinary meatus
Impervious urethra
Urethral valve formation
CC Excl: 599.60-599.69, 753.6, 753.9

753.7 **Anomalies of urachus**
Cyst
Fistula } (of) urachussinus
Patent
Persistent umbilical sinus

753.8 **Other specified anomalies of bladder and urethra**
Absence, congenital of:
   bladder
   urethra
Accessory:
   bladder
   urethra
Congenital:
   diverticulum of bladder
   hernia of bladder
   urethrorectal fistula
   prolapse of:
      bladder (mucosa)
      urethra
Double:
   urethra
   urinary meatus

753.9 **Unspecified anomaly of urinary system**
Congenital:
   anomaly NOS } of urinary system [any part,
   deformity NOS } except urachus]

Congenital Anomalies

754–755.21

✓4th **754 Certain congenital musculoskeletal deformities**

> INCLUDES   nonteratogenic deformities which are considered to be due to intrauterine malposition and pressure

754.0 Of skull, face, and jaw
Asymmetry of face
Compression facies
Depressions in skull
Deviation of nasal septum, congenital
Dolichocephaly
Plagiocephaly
Potter's facies
Squashed or bent nose, congenital
> EXCLUDES   dentofacial anomalies (524.0-524.9)
> syphilitic saddle nose (090.5)

754.1 Of sternocleidomastoid muscle
Congenital sternomastoid torticollis
Congenital wryneck
Contracture of sternocleidomastoid (muscle)
Sternomastoid tumor

754.2 Of spine   CC
Congenital postural:
lordosis
scoliosis
CC Excl: 754.2

✓5th **754.3 Congenital dislocation of hip**

754.30 Congenital dislocation of hip, unilateral
Congenital dislocation of hip NOS

754.31 Congenital dislocation of hip, bilateral

754.32 Congenital subluxation of hip, unilateral
Congenital flexion deformity, hip or thigh
Predislocation status of hip at birth
Preluxation of hip, congenital

754.33 Congenital subluxation of hip, bilateral

754.35 Congenital dislocation of one hip with subluxation of other hip

✓5th **754.4 Congenital genu recurvatum and bowing of long bones of leg**

754.40 Genu recurvatum
DEF: Backward curving of knee joint.

754.41 Congenital dislocation of knee (with genu recurvatum)

754.42 Congenital bowing of femur

754.43 Congenital bowing of tibia and fibula

754.44 Congenital bowing of unspecified long bones of leg

✓5th **754.5 Varus deformities of feet**
> EXCLUDES   acquired (736.71, 736.75, 736.79)

754.50 Talipes varus
Congenital varus deformity of foot, unspecified
Pes varus
DEF: Inverted foot marked by outer sole resting on ground.

754.51 Talipes equinovarus
Equinovarus (congenital)
DEF: Elevated, outward rotation of heel; also called clubfoot.

754.52 Metatarsus primus varus
DEF: Malformed first metatarsal bone, with bone angled toward body.

754.53 Metatarsus varus

754.59 Other
Talipes calcaneovarus

✓5th **754.6 Valgus deformities of feet**
> EXCLUDES   valgus deformity of foot (acquired) (736.79)

754.60 Talipes valgus
Congenital valgus deformity of foot, unspecified

754.61 Congenital pes planus
Congenital rocker bottom flat foot
Flat foot, congenital
> EXCLUDES   pes planus (acquired) (734)

754.62 Talipes calcaneovalgus

754.69 Other
Talipes:
equinovalgus
planovalgus

✓5th **754.7 Other deformities of feet**
> EXCLUDES   acquired (736.70-736.79)

754.70 Talipes, unspecified
Congenital deformity of foot NOS

754.71 Talipes cavus
Cavus foot (congenital)

754.79 Other
Asymmetric talipes
Talipes:
calcaneus
equinus

✓5th **754.8 Other specified nonteratogenic anomalies**

754.81 Pectus excavatum
Congenital funnel chest

754.82 Pectus carinatum
Congenital pigeon chest [breast]

754.89 Other   CC
Club hand (congenital)
Congenital:
deformity of chest wall
dislocation of elbow
Generalized flexion contractures of lower limb joints, congenital
Spade-like hand (congenital)
CC Excl: 754.81-754.89

✓4th **755 Other congenital anomalies of limbs**
> EXCLUDES   those deformities classifiable to 754.0-754.8

✓5th **755.0 Polydactyly**

755.00 Polydactyly, unspecified digits
Supernumerary digits

755.01 Of fingers
Accessory fingers

755.02 Of toes
Accessory toes

✓5th **755.1 Syndactyly**
Symphalangy
Webbing of digits

755.10 Of multiple and unspecified sites

755.11 Of fingers without fusion of bone

755.12 Of fingers with fusion of bone

755.13 Of toes without fusion of bone

755.14 Of toes with fusion of bone

✓5th **755.2 Reduction deformities of upper limb**

755.20 Unspecified reduction deformity of upper limb
Ectromelia NOS ⎫
Hemimelia NOS ⎭ of upper limb
Shortening of arm, congenital

755.21 Transverse deficiency of upper limb
Amelia of upper limb
Congenital absence of:
fingers, all (complete or partial)
forearm, including hand and fingers
upper limb, complete
Congenital amputation of upper limb
Transverse hemimelia of upper limb

N Newborn Age: 0   P Pediatric Age: 0-17   M Maternity Age: 12-55   A Adult Age: 15-124   MCC Major CC Condition   CC CC Condition   HIV HIV Related Dx

755.22 Longitudinal deficiency of upper limb, not elsewhere classified
     Phocomelia NOS of upper limb
     Rudimentary arm

755.23 Longitudinal deficiency, combined, involving humerus, radius, and ulna (complete or incomplete)
     Congenital absence of arm and forearm (complete or incomplete) with or without metacarpal deficiency and/or phalangeal deficiency, incomplete
     Phocomelia, complete, of upper limb

755.24 Longitudinal deficiency, humeral, complete or partial (with or without distal deficiencies, incomplete)
     Congenital absence of humerus (with or without absence of some [but not all] distal elements)
     Proximal phocomelia of upper limb

755.25 Longitudinal deficiency, radioulnar, complete or partial (with or without distal deficiencies, incomplete)
     Congenital absence of radius and ulna (with or without absence of some [but not all] distal elements)
     Distal phocomelia of upper limb

755.26 Longitudinal deficiency, radial, complete or partial (with or without distal deficiencies, incomplete)
     Agenesis of radius
     Congenital absence of radius (with or without absence of some [but not all] distal elements)

755.27 Longitudinal deficiency, ulnar, complete or partial (with or without distal deficiencies, incomplete)
     Agenesis of ulna
     Congenital absence of ulna (with or without absence of some [but not all] distal elements)

755.28 Longitudinal deficiency, carpals or metacarpals, complete or partial (with or without incomplete phalangeal deficiency)

755.29 Longitudinal deficiency, phalanges, complete or partial
     Absence of finger, congenital
     Aphalangia of upper limb, terminal, complete or partial

     EXCLUDES   *terminal deficiency of all five digits (755.21)*
                  transverse deficiency of phalanges (755.21)

✓5ᵗʰ **755.3 Reduction deformities of lower limb**

755.30 Unspecified reduction deformity of lower limb
     Ectromelia NOS ⎫
     Hemimelia NOS ⎬ of lower limb
     Shortening of leg, congenital

755.31 Transverse deficiency of lower limb
     Amelia of lower limb
     Congenital absence of:
         foot
         leg, including foot and toes
         lower limb, complete
         toes, all, complete
     Transverse hemimelia of lower limb

755.32 Longitudinal deficiency of lower limb, not elsewhere classified
     Phocomelia NOS of lower limb

755.33 Longitudinal deficiency, combined, involving femur, tibia, and fibula (complete or incomplete)
     Congenital absence of thigh and (lower) leg (complete or incomplete) with or without metacarpal deficiency and/or phalangeal deficiency, incomplete
     Phocomelia, complete, of lower limb

755.34 Longitudinal deficiency, femoral, complete or partial (with or without distal deficiencies, incomplete)
     Congenital absence of femur (with or without absence of some [but not all] distal elements)
     Proximal phocomelia of lower limb

755.35 Longitudinal deficiency, tibiofibular, complete or partial (with or without distal deficiencies, incomplete)
     Congenital absence of tibia and fibula (with or without absence of some [but not all] distal elements)
     Distal phocomelia of lower limb

755.36 Longitudinal deficiency, tibia, complete or partial (with or without distal deficiencies, incomplete)
     Agenesis of tibia
     Congenital absence of tibia (with or without absence of some [but not all] distal elements)

755.37 Longitudinal deficiency, fibular, complete or partial (with or without distal deficiencies, incomplete)
     Agenesis of fibula
     Congenital absence of fibula (with or without absence of some [but not all] distal elements)

755.38 Longitudinal deficiency, tarsals or metatarsals, complete or partial (with or without incomplete phalangeal deficiency)

755.39 Longitudinal deficiency, phalanges, complete or partial
     Absence of toe, congenital
     Aphalangia of lower limb, terminal, complete or partial

     EXCLUDES   *terminal deficiency of all five digits (755.31)*
                  transverse deficiency of phalanges (755.31)

755.4 Reduction deformities, unspecified limb
     Absence, congenital (complete or partial) of limb NOS
     Amelia ⎫
     Ectromelia ⎬ of unspecified limb
     Hemimelia ⎪
     Phocomelia ⎭

✓5ᵗʰ **755.5 Other anomalies of upper limb, including shoulder girdle**

755.50 Unspecified anomaly of upper limb

755.51 Congenital deformity of clavicle

755.52 Congenital elevation of scapula
     Sprengel's deformity

755.53 Radioulnar synostosis
     DEF: Osseous adhesion of radius and ulna.

755.54 Madelung's deformity
     DEF: Distal ulnar overgrowth or radial shortening; also called carpus curvus.

755.55 Acrocephalosyndactyly   MCC
     Apert's syndrome
     DEF: Premature cranial suture fusion (craniostenosis); marked by cone-shaped or pointed (acrocephaly) head and webbing of the fingers (syndactyly); similar to craniofacial dysostosis.
     CC Excl: 755.50, 755.55, 755.59

✓4ᵗʰ
✓5ᵗʰ   Additional Digit Required   Unacceptable PDx   Manifestation Code   Hospital Acquired Condition   ▶◀ Revised Text   ● New Code   ▲ Revised Code Title

2010 ICD-9-CM   **Volume 1 – 281**

Congenital Anomalies

755.56–756.3

755.56 Accessory carpal bones

755.57 Macrodactylia (fingers)
> **DEF:** Abnormally large fingers, toes.

755.58 Cleft hand, congenital
> Lobster-claw hand
> **DEF:** Extended separation between fingers into metacarpus; also may refer to large fingers and absent middle fingers of hand.

755.59 Other
> Cleidocranial dysostosis
> Cubitus:
> > valgus, congenital
> > varus, congenital
>
> **EXCLUDES** club hand (congenital) (754.89)
> congenital dislocation of elbow (754.89)

✓5th **755.6 Other anomalies of lower limb, including pelvic girdle**

755.60 Unspecified anomaly of lower limb

755.61 Coxa valga, congenital
> **DEF:** Abnormally wide angle between the neck and shaft of the femur.

755.62 Coxa vara, congenital
> **DEF:** Diminished angle between neck and shaft of femur.

755.63 Other congenital deformity of hip (joint)
> Congenital anteversion of femur (neck)
> **EXCLUDES** congenital dislocation of hip (754.30-754.35)
> **AHA:** 1Q, '94, 15; S-O, '84, 15
> **Q65.9** Congenital deformity of hip unspecified   I-10

755.64 Congenital deformity of knee (joint)
> Congenital:
> > absence of patella
> > genu valgum [knock-knee]
> > genu varum [bowleg]
> Rudimentary patella

755.65 Macrodactylia of toes
> **DEF:** Abnormally large toes.

755.66 Other anomalies of toes
> Congenital:
> > hallux valgus
> > hallux varus
> > hammer toe

755.67 Anomalies of foot, not elsewhere classified
> Astragaloscaphoid synostosis
> Calcaneonavicular bar
> Coalition of calcaneus
> Talonavicular synostosis
> Tarsal coalitions

755.69 Other
> Congenital:
> > angulation of tibia
> > deformity (of):
> > > ankle (joint)
> > > sacroiliac (joint)
> > fusion of sacroiliac joint

755.8 Other specified anomalies of unspecified limb

755.9 Unspecified anomaly of unspecified limb
> Congenital:
> > anomaly NOS } of unspecified limb
> > deformity NOS
> **EXCLUDES** reduction deformity of unspecified limb (755.4)

✓4th **756 Other congenital musculoskeletal anomalies**
> **EXCLUDES** congenital myotonic chondrodystrophy (359.23)
> those deformities classifiable to 754.0-754.8

756.0 Anomalies of skull and face bones
> Absence of skull bones
> Acrocephaly
> Congenital deformity of forehead
> Craniosynostosis
> Crouzon's disease
> Hypertelorism
> Imperfect fusion of skull
> Oxycephaly
> Platybasia
> Premature closure of cranial sutures
> Tower skull
> Trigonocephaly
> **EXCLUDES** acrocephalosyndactyly [Apert's syndrome] (755.55)
> dentofacial anomalies (524.0-524.9)
> skull defects associated with brain anomalies, such as:
> > anencephalus (740.0)
> > encephalocele (742.0)
> > hydrocephalus (742.3)
> > microcephalus (742.1)
> **AHA:** 3Q, '98, 9; 3Q, '96, 15
> **TIP:** Assign for Nager syndrome (preaxial acrofacial dysostosis), along with codes for any additional features that are not captured in the code.
> **Q75.8** Other spec cong malformations skull & face bones   I-10

✓5th **756.1 Anomalies of spine**

756.10 Anomaly of spine, unspecified

756.11 Spondylolysis, lumbosacral region
> Prespondylolisthesis (lumbosacral)
> **DEF:** Bilateral or unilateral defect through the pars interarticularis of a vertebra causes spondylolisthesis.

756.12 Spondylolisthesis
> **DEF:** Downward slipping of lumbar vertebra over next vertebra; usually related to pelvic deformity.
> **Q76.2** Congenital spondylolisthesis   I-10

756.13 Absence of vertebra, congenital   CC
> **CC Excl:** 756.10-756.19

756.14 Hemivertebra
> **DEF:** Incomplete development of one side of a vertebra.

756.15 Fusion of spine [vertebra], congenital

756.16 Klippel-Feil syndrome
> **DEF:** Short, wide neck; limits range of motion due to abnormal number of cervical vertebra or fused hemivertebrae.

756.17 Spina bifida occulta
> **EXCLUDES** spina bifida (aperta) (741.0-741.9)
> **DEF:** Spina bifida marked by a bony spinal canal defect without a protrusion of the cord or meninges; it is diagnosed by radiography and has no symptoms.

756.19 Other
> Platyspondylia
> Supernumerary vertebra

756.2 Cervical rib
> Supernumerary rib in the cervical region
> **DEF:** Costa cervicalis: extra rib attached to cervical vertebra.

756.3 Other anomalies of ribs and sternum   CC
> Congenital absence of:
> > rib
> > sternum
> Congenital:
> > fissure of sternum
> > fusion of ribs
> Sternum bifidum
> **EXCLUDES** nonteratogenic deformity of chest wall (754.81-754.89)
> **CC Excl:** 756.2-756.3

N Newborn Age: 0   P Pediatric Age: 0-17   M Maternity Age: 12-55   A Adult Age: 15-124   MCC Major CC Condition   CC CC Condition   HIV HIV Related Dx

282 – Volume 1   2010 ICD-9-CM

756.4 Chondrodystrophy
Achondroplasia
Chondrodystrophia (fetalis)
Dyschondroplasia
Enchondromatosis
Ollier's disease

> **EXCLUDES** congenital myotonic chondrodystrophy (359.23)
> lipochondrodystrophy [Hurler's syndrome] (277.5)
> Morquio's disease (277.5)

DEF: Abnormal development of cartilage.
AHA: 2Q, '02, 16; S-O, '87, 10
TIP: Assign for Jeune's syndrome, and also for cartilage-hair syndrome (cartilage-hair hypoplasia).

√5th **756.5 Osteodystrophies**

756.50 Osteodystrophy, unspecified

756.51 Osteogenesis imperfecta `CC`
Fragilitas ossium
Osteopsathyrosis

DEF: A collagen disorder commonly characterized by brittle, osteoporotic, easily fractured bones, hypermobility of joints, blue sclerae, and a tendency to hemorrhage.
CC Excl: 756.50-756.59

756.52 Osteopetrosis `CC`
DEF: Abnormally dense bone, optic atrophy, hepatosplenomegaly, deafness; sclerosing depletes bone marrow and nerve foramina of skull; often fatal.
CC Excl: See code: 756.51

756.53 Osteopoikilosis
DEF: Multiple sclerotic foci on ends of long bones, stippling in round, flat bones; identified by x-ray.

756.54 Polyostotic fibrous dysplasia of bone
DEF: Fibrous tissue displaces bone results in segmented ragged-edge café-au-lait spots; occurs in girls of early puberty.

756.55 Chondroectodermal dysplasia
Ellis-van Creveld syndrome
DEF: Inadequate enchondral bone formation; impaired development of hair and teeth, polydactyly, and cardiac septum defects.

756.56 Multiple epiphyseal dysplasia

756.59 Other
Albright (-McCune)-Sternberg syndrome

756.6 Anomalies of diaphragm `MCC`
Absence of diaphragm
Congenital hernia:
   diaphragmatic
   foramen of Morgagni
Eventration of diaphragm

> **EXCLUDES** congenital hiatus hernia (750.6)

CC Excl: 750.6, 756.6

√5th **756.7 Anomalies of abdominal wall**

756.70 Anomaly of abdominal wall, unspecified `MCC`
CC Excl: 756.70-756.79

756.71 Prune belly syndrome `MCC`
Eagle-Barrett syndrome
Prolapse of bladder mucosa
DEF: Prune belly syndrome: absence of lower rectus abdominis muscle and lower and medial oblique muscles; results in dilated bladder and ureters, dysplastic kidneys and hydronephrosis; common in male infants with undescended testicles.
CC Excl: See code: 756.70
AHA: 4Q, '97, 44

● **756.72 Omphalocele** `MCC`
Exomphalos
DEF: Exomphalos: umbilical hernia prominent navel.
DEF: Omphalocele: hernia of umbilicus due to impaired abdominal wall; results in membrane-covered intestine protruding through peritoneum and amnion.
CC Excl: See code: 756.70

● **756.73 Gastroschisis** `MCC`
DEF: Fissure of abdominal wall, results in protruding small or large intestine.
CC Excl: See code: 756.70

756.79 Other congenital anomalies of `MCC`
abdominal wall

> **EXCLUDES** umbilical hernia (551-553 with .1)

CC Excl: See code: 756.70

√5th **756.8 Other specified anomalies of muscle, tendon, fascia, and connective tissue**

756.81 Absence of muscle and tendon
Absence of muscle (pectoral)

756.82 Accessory muscle

756.83 Ehlers-Danlos syndrome `CC`
DEF: Danlos syndrome: connective tissue disorder causes hyperextended skin and joints; results in fragile blood vessels with bleeding, poor wound healing and subcutaneous pseudotumors.
CC Excl: 756.83-756.89

756.89 Other
Amyotrophia congenita
Congenital shortening of tendon
AHA: 3Q, '99, 16
TIP: Assign for Stickler's syndrome, a hereditary progressive arthro-ophthalmopathy, along with codes for the specific manifestations.

756.9 Other and unspecified anomalies of musculoskeletal system
Congenital:
   anomaly NOS } of musculoskeletal system, not
   deformity NOS } elsewhere classified

√4th **757 Congenital anomalies of the integument**

> **INCLUDES** anomalies of skin, subcutaneous tissue, hair, nails, and breast
> **EXCLUDES** hemangioma (228.00-228.09)
> pigmented nevus (216.0-216.9)

757.0 Hereditary edema of legs
Congenital lymphedema
Hereditary trophedema
Milroy's disease

757.1 Ichthyosis congenita
Congenital ichthyosis
Harlequin fetus
Ichthyosiform erythroderma
DEF: Overproduction of skin cells causes scaling of skin; may result in stillborn fetus or death soon after birth.

757.2 Dermatoglyphic anomalies
Abnormal palmar creases
DEF: Abnormal skin-line patterns of fingers, palms, toes and soles; initial finding of possible chromosomal abnormalities.

√5th **757.3 Other specified anomalies of skin**

757.31 Congenital ectodermal dysplasia
DEF: Tissues and structures originate in embryonic ectoderm; includes anhidrotic and hidrotic ectodermal dysplasia and EEC syndrome.

757.32 Vascular hamartomas
Birthmarks
Port-wine stain
Strawberry nevus
DEF: Benign tumor of blood vessels; due to malformed angioblastic tissues.
Q82.5 Congenital non-neoplastic nevus `I-10`

√4th √5th   Additional Digit Required   Unacceptable PDx   Manifestation Code   Hospital Acquired Condition   ►◄ Revised Text   ● New Code   ▲ Revised Code Title

2010 ICD-9-CM   **October 2009 • Volume 1 – 283**

757.33 Congenital pigmentary anomalies of skin
Congenital poikiloderma
Urticaria pigmentosa
Xeroderma pigmentosum
EXCLUDES albinism (270.2)

Q82.2 Mastocytosis [I-10]

757.39 Other
Accessory skin tags, congenital
Congenital scar
Epidermolysis bullosa
Keratoderma (congenital)
EXCLUDES pilonidal cyst (685.0-685.1)

Q82.8 Other specified congenital [I-10]
malformations of skin

757.4 Specified anomalies of hair
Congenital:
  alopecia
  atrichosis
  beaded hair
  hypertrichosis
  monilethrix
Persistent lanugo

757.5 Specified anomalies of nails
Anonychia
Congenital:
  clubnail
  koilonychia
  leukonychia
  onychauxis
  pachyonychia

▲ **757.6 Specified congenital anomalies of breast**
Accessory
▶Congenital absent◀ } breast or nipple
Supernumerary
EXCLUDES absence of pectoral muscle (756.81)
hypoplasia of breast (611.82)
▶micromastia (611.82)◀

757.8 Other specified anomalies of the integument

757.9 Unspecified anomaly of the integument
Congenital:
  anomaly NOS } of integument
  deformity NOS

✓4ᵗʰ 758 Chromosomal anomalies
INCLUDES syndromes associated with anomalies in the number
and form of chromosomes
Use additional codes for conditions associated with the
chromosomal anomalies

758.0 Down's syndrome
Mongolism
Translocation Down's syndrome
Trisomy:
  21 or 22
  G
Q90.9 Down's syndrome unspecified [I-10]

758.1 Patau's syndrome [CC]
Trisomy:
  13
  D₁
DEF: Trisomy of 13th chromosome; characteristic failure to
thrive, severe mental impairment, seizures, abnormal eyes,
low-set ears and sloped forehead.
CC Excl: 758.0-758.9

758.2 Edwards' syndrome [CC]
Trisomy:
  18
  E₃
DEF: Trisomy of 18th chromosome; characteristic mental and
physical impairments; mainly affects females.
CC Excl: See code: 758.1

✓5ᵗʰ 758.3 Autosomal deletion syndromes

758.31 Cri-du-chat syndrome [CC]
Deletion 5p
DEF: Hereditary congenital syndrome caused by a
microdeletion of short arm of chromosome 5;
characterized by catlike cry in newborn,
microencephaly, severe mental deficiency, and
hypertelorism.
CC Excl: 758.0-758.2, 758.32-758.9

758.32 Velo-cardio-facial syndrome [MCC]
Deletion 22q11.2
DEF: Microdeletion syndrome affecting multiple
organs; characteristic cleft palate, heart defects,
elongated face with almond-shaped eyes, wide
nose, small ears, weak immune systems, weak
musculature, hypothyroidism, short stature, and
scoliosis; deletion at q11.2 on the long arm of the
chromosome 22.
CC Excl: 758.0-758.31, 758.33-758.9

758.33 Other microdeletions [CC]
Miller-Dieker syndrome
Smith-Magenis syndrome
DEF: Miller-Dieker syndrome: deletion from the
short arm of chromosome 17; characteristic mental
retardation, speech and motor development delays,
neurological complications, and multiple
abnormalities affecting the kidneys, heart,
gastrointestinal tract; death in infancy or early
childhood.
DEF: Smith-Magenis syndrome: deletion in a certain
area of chromosome 17 that results in craniofacial
changes, speech delay, hoarse voice, hearing loss,
and behavioral problems, such as self-destructive
head banging, wrist biting, and tearing at nails.
CC Excl: 758.0-758.32, 758.39-758.9

758.39 Other autosomal deletions [CC]
CC Excl: 758.0-758.33, 758.4-758.9

758.4 Balanced autosomal translocation in normal individual

758.5 Other conditions due to autosomal anomalies
Accessory autosomes NEC

758.6 Gonadal dysgenesis
Ovarian dysgenesis   XO syndrome
Turner's syndrome
EXCLUDES pure gonadal dysgenesis (752.7)

758.7 Klinefelter's syndrome ♂
XXY syndrome
DEF: Impaired embryonic development of seminiferous tubes;
results in small testes, azoospermia, infertility and enlarged
mammary glands.

✓5ᵗʰ 758.8 Other conditions due to chromosome anomalies

**758.81 Other conditions due to sex chromosome
anomalies**

758.89 Other
Q99.8 Other specified chromosome [I-10]
abnormalities

758.9 Conditions due to anomaly of unspecified chromosome

✓4ᵗʰ 759 Other and unspecified congenital anomalies

759.0 Anomalies of spleen [CC]
Aberrant
Absent } spleen
Accessory
Congenital splenomegaly
Ectopic spleen
Lobulation of spleen
CC Excl: 759.0, 759.9

759.1 Anomalies of adrenal gland
Aberrant
Absent } adrenal gland
Accessory
EXCLUDES adrenogenital disorders (255.2)
congenital disorders of steroid metabolism
(255.2)

[N] Newborn Age: 0   [P] Pediatric Age: 0-17   [M] Maternity Age: 12-55   [A] Adult Age: 15-124   [MCC] Major CC Condition   [CC] CC Condition   [HIV] HIV Related Dx

284 – Volume 1 · October 2009

2010 ICD-9-CM

759.2 Anomalies of other endocrine glands
  Absent parathyroid gland
  Accessory thyroid gland
  Persistent thyroglossal or thyrolingual duct
  Thyroglossal (duct) cyst
  EXCLUDES congenital:
    goiter (246.1)
    hypothyroidism (243)

759.3 Situs inversus `CC`
  Situs inversus or transversus:
    abdominalis
    thoracis
  Transposition of viscera:
    abdominal
    thoracic
  EXCLUDES dextrocardia without mention of complete
    transposition (746.87)
  DEF: Laterally transposed thoracic and abdominal viscera.
  CC Excl: 759.3, 759.7, 759.9

759.4 Conjoined twins `MCC`
  Craniopagus
  Dicephalus
  Pygopagus
  Thoracopagus
  Xiphopagus
  CC Excl: 759.4, 759.7, 759.9

759.5 Tuberous sclerosis `CC`
  Bourneville's disease
  Epiloia
  DEF: Hamartomas of brain, retina and viscera, impaired mental
    ability, seizures and adenoma sebaceum.
  CC Excl: 759.5-759.7, 759.9

759.6 Other hamartoses, not elsewhere classified `CC`
  Syndrome:
    Peutz-Jeghers
    Sturge-Weber (-Dimitri)
    von Hippel-Lindau
  EXCLUDES neurofibromatosis (237.7)
  DEF: Peutz-Jeghers: hereditary syndrome characterized by
    hamartomas of small intestine.
  DEF: Sturge-Weber: congenital syndrome characterized by
    unilateral port-wine stain over trigeminal nerve, underlying
    meninges and cerebral cortex.
  DEF: von Hipple-Lindau: hereditary syndrome of congenital
    angiomatosis of the retina and cerebellum.
  CC Excl: 759.6, 759.9
  AHA: 3Q, '92, 12

759.7 Multiple congenital anomalies, so described `CC`
  Congenital:
    anomaly, multiple NOS
    deformity, multiple NOS
  CC Excl: See code: 759.3

√5ᵗʰ **759.8 Other specified anomalies**
  AHA: S-O, '87, 9; S-O, '85, 11

  759.81 Prader-Willi syndrome `CC`
    CC Excl: 759.6-759.9

  759.82 Marfan syndrome `CC`
    CC Excl: See code: 759.81
    AHA: 3Q, '93, 11

  759.83 Fragile X syndrome
    AHA: 4Q, '94, 41

  759.89 Other `CC`
    Congenital malformation syndromes affecting
      multiple systems, not elsewhere classified
    Laurence-Moon-Biedl syndrome
    CC Excl: 759.81-759.89
    AHA: ▶3Q, '08, 3;◀ 3Q, '06, 21; 2Q, '05, 17; 2Q, '04,
      12; 1Q, '01, 3; 3Q, '99, 17, 18; 3Q, '98, 8
    TIP: Assign for the following syndromes: cardiofa-
      ciocutaneous (CFC), Borjeson-Forssman-Lehmann
      syndrome (BFLS), Alagille syndrome, startle disease,
      Alport's syndrome, branchio-oto-renal (BOR) syn-
      drome, Costello syndrome, Williams syndrome, Ant-
      ley-Bixler syndrome, and multiple pterygium
      syndrome. Assign additional codes for any docu-
      mented manifestations.

759.9 Congenital anomaly, unspecified

[handwritten:] Codes do not apply for fetal conditions requiring in utero surgery.

15. CERTAIN CONDITIONS ORIGINATING IN THE PERINATAL PERIOD (760-779)

INCLUDES   conditions which have their origin in the perinatal period, before birth through the first 28 days after birth, even though death or morbidity occurs later

Use additional code(s) to further specify condition

TIP: A newborn condition is clinically significant when it has implications for the newborn's *future* health care. This is an exception to the UHDDS guidelines.

MATERNAL CAUSES OF PERINATAL MORBIDITY AND MORTALITY (760-763)

AHA: 2Q, '89, 14; 3Q, '90, 5

√4ᵗʰ **760 Fetus or newborn affected by maternal conditions which may be unrelated to present pregnancy**

INCLUDES   the listed maternal conditions only when specified as a cause of mortality or morbidity of the fetus or newborn

EXCLUDES   *maternal endocrine and metabolic disorders affecting fetus or newborn (775.0-775.9)*

AHA: 1Q, '94, 8; 2Q, '92, 12; N-D, '84, 11

TIP: Do not assign unless the mother's condition has actually affected the fetus or newborn.

760.0 Maternal hypertensive disorders
Fetus or newborn affected by maternal conditions classifiable to 642

760.1 Maternal renal and urinary tract diseases
Fetus or newborn affected by maternal conditions classifiable to 580-599

760.2 Maternal infections
Fetus or newborn affected by maternal infectious disease classifiable to 001-136 and 487, but fetus or newborn not manifesting that disease

EXCLUDES   *congenital infectious diseases (771.0-771.8)*
maternal genital tract and other localized infections (760.8)

760.3 Other chronic maternal circulatory and respiratory diseases
Fetus or newborn affected by chronic maternal conditions classifiable to 390-459, 490-519, 745-748

760.4 Maternal nutritional disorders
Fetus or newborn affected by:
maternal disorders classifiable to 260-269
maternal malnutrition NOS

EXCLUDES   *fetal malnutrition (764.10-764.29)*

760.5 Maternal injury
Fetus or newborn affected by maternal conditions classifiable to 800-995

√5ᵗʰ **760.6 Surgical operation on mother and fetus**

EXCLUDES   *cesarean section for present delivery (763.4)*
damage to placenta from amniocentesis, cesarean section, or surgical induction (762.1)

AHA: ▶4Q, '08, 137-138◀

TIP: These codes include existing conditions present at the time of birth that are related to procedures performed before the time of delivery.

760.61 Newborn affected by amniocentesis
EXCLUDES   *fetal complications from amniocentesis (679.1)*

760.62 Newborn affected by other in utero procedure
EXCLUDES   *fetal complications of in utero procedure (679.1)*

760.63 Newborn affected by other surgical operations on mother during pregnancy
EXCLUDES   *newborn affected by previous surgical procedure on mother not associated with pregnancy (760.64)*

760.64 Newborn affected by previous surgical procedure on mother not associated with pregnancy

√5ᵗʰ **760.7 Noxious influences affecting fetus or newborn via placenta or breast milk**
Fetus or newborn affected by noxious substance transmitted via placenta or breast milk

EXCLUDES   *anesthetic and analgesic drugs administered during labor and delivery (763.5)*
drug withdrawal syndrome in newborn (779.5)

AHA: 3Q, '91, 21

760.70 Unspecified noxious substance
Fetus or newborn affected by:
Drug NEC

760.71 Alcohol
Fetal alcohol syndrome

760.72 Narcotics

760.73 Hallucinogenic agents

760.74 Anti-infectives
Antibiotics
Antifungals

760.75 Cocaine
AHA: 3Q, '94, 6; 2Q, '92, 12; 4Q, '91, 26

TIP: If documentation indicates drug withdrawal in the newborn, also assign code 779.5 Drug withdrawal syndrome in newborn.

760.76 Diethylstilbestrol [DES]
AHA: 4Q, '94, 45

760.77 Anticonvulsants   N
Carbamazepine
Phenobarbital
Phenytoin
Valproic acid
AHA: 4Q, '05, 82

760.78 Antimetabolic agents   N
Methotrexate
Retinoic acid
Statins
AHA: 4Q, '05, 82-83

760.79 Other
Fetus or newborn affected by:
immune sera ⎫ transmitted via
medicinal agents NEC ⎬ placenta
toxic substance NEC ⎭ or breast

P04.8 Newborn (suspected) affected by oth   I-10
maternl noxious substnce

760.8 Other specified maternal conditions affecting fetus or newborn
Maternal genital tract and other localized infection affecting fetus or newborn, but fetus or newborn not manifesting that disease

EXCLUDES   *maternal urinary tract infection affecting fetus or newborn (760.1)*

760.9 Unspecified maternal condition affecting fetus or newborn

√4ᵗʰ **761 Fetus or newborn affected by maternal complications of pregnancy**

INCLUDES   the listed maternal conditions only when specified as a cause of mortality or morbidity of the fetus or newborn

761.0 Incompetent cervix
DEF: Inadequate functioning of uterine cervix.

761.1 Premature rupture of membranes

√4ᵗʰ Additional Digit Required   Unacceptable PDx   Manifestation Code   Hospital Acquired Condition   ▶◀ Revised Text   ● New Code   ▲ Revised Code Title
√5ᵗʰ

2010 ICD-9-CM   **February 2009 • Volume 1 – 287**

Conditions in the Perinatal Period

761.2–763.83

761.2 Oligohydramnios

> **EXCLUDES** *that due to premature rupture of membranes (761.1)*

DEF: Deficient amniotic fluid.

761.3 Polyhydramnios

Hydramnios (acute) (chronic)

DEF: Excess amniotic fluid.

761.4 Ectopic pregnancy

Pregnancy: Pregnancy:
   abdominal   tubal
   intraperitoneal

761.5 Multiple pregnancy

Triplet (pregnancy)
Twin (pregnancy)

761.6 Maternal death

761.7 Malpresentation before labor

Breech presentation
External version
Oblique lie   } before labor
Transverse lie
Unstable lie

761.8 Other specified maternal complications of pregnancy affecting fetus or newborn

Spontaneous abortion, fetus

761.9 Unspecified maternal complication of pregnancy affecting fetus or newborn

✓4ᵗʰ 762 Fetus or newborn affected by complications of placenta, cord, and membranes

> **INCLUDES** the listed maternal conditions only when specified as a cause of mortality or morbidity in the fetus or newborn

AHA: 1Q, '94, 8

762.0 Placenta previa   N

DEF: Placenta developed in lower segment of uterus; causes hemorrhaging in last trimester.

762.1 Other forms of placental separation and hemorrhage   N

Abruptio placentae
Antepartum hemorrhage
Damage to placenta from amniocentesis, cesarean section, or surgical induction
Maternal blood loss
Premature separation of placenta
Rupture of marginal sinus

762.2 Other and unspecified morphological and functional abnormalities of placenta   N

Placental: Placental:
   dysfunction   insufficiency
   infarction

762.3 Placental transfusion syndromes   N

Placental and cord abnormality resulting in twin-to-twin or other transplacental transfusion

Use additional code to indicate resultant condition in newborn:
   fetal blood loss (772.0)
   polycythemia neonatorum (776.4)

762.4 Prolapsed cord   N

Cord presentation

762.5 Other compression of umbilical cord   N

Cord around neck   Knot in cord
Entanglement of cord   Torsion of cord

AHA: 2Q, '03, 9

TIP: Assign only if the cord compression or entanglement was documented as having affected the fetus/newborn.

P02.5 Newborn (suspected) affected by oth compression I-10 umb cord

762.6 Other and unspecified conditions of umbilical cord   N

Short cord

Thrombosis
Varices   } of umbilical cord
Velamentous insertion
Vasa previa

> **EXCLUDES** *infection of umbilical cord (771.4)*
> *single umbilical artery (747.5)*

P02.69 Newborn (suspected) affected by oth cond I-10 umbili cord

762.7 Chorioamnionitis   N

Amnionitis   Placentitis
Membranitis

DEF: Inflamed fetal membrane.

762.8 Other specified abnormalities of chorion and amnion   N

762.9 Unspecified abnormality of chorion and amnion

✓4ᵗʰ 763 Fetus or newborn affected by other complications of labor and delivery

> **INCLUDES** the listed conditions only when specified as a cause of mortality or morbidity in the fetus or newborn
> **EXCLUDES** *newborn affected by surgical procedures on mother (760.61-760.64)*

AHA: 1Q, '94, 8

763.0 Breech delivery and extraction   N

763.1 Other malpresentation, malposition, and disproportion during labor and delivery   N

Fetus or newborn affected by:
   abnormality of bony pelvis
   contracted pelvis
   persistent occipitoposterior position
   shoulder presentation
   transverse lie
Fetus or newborn affected by conditions classifiable to 652, 653, and 660

763.2 Forceps delivery   N

Fetus or newborn affected by forceps extraction

763.3 Delivery by vacuum extractor   N

763.4 Cesarean delivery   N

> **EXCLUDES** *placental separation or hemorrhage from cesarean section (762.1)*

763.5 Maternal anesthesia and analgesia   N

Reactions and intoxications from maternal opiates and tranquilizers during labor and delivery

> **EXCLUDES** *drug withdrawal syndrome in newborn (779.5)*

763.6 Precipitate delivery   N

Rapid second stage

763.7 Abnormal uterine contractions   N

Fetus or newborn affected by:
   contraction ring
   hypertonic labor
   hypotonic uterine dysfunction
   uterine inertia or dysfunction
Fetus or newborn affected by conditions classifiable to 661, except 661.3

✓5ᵗʰ 763.8 Other specified complications of labor and delivery affecting fetus or newborn

AHA: 4Q, '98, 46

763.81 Abnormality in fetal heart rate or rhythm before the onset of labor   N

763.82 Abnormality in fetal heart rate or rhythm during labor   N

AHA: 4Q, '98, 46

763.83 Abnormality in fetal heart rate or rhythm, unspecified as to time of onset   N

N Newborn Age: 0   P Pediatric Age: 0-17   M Maternity Age: 12-55   A Adult Age: 15-124   **MCC** Major CC Condition   **CC** CC Condition   **HIV** HIV Related Dx

763.84　Meconium passage during delivery N

> EXCLUDES　*meconium aspiration (770.11, 770.12)*
> *meconium staining (779.84)*
>
> **DEF:** Fetal intestinal activity that increases in response to a distressed state during delivery; anal sphincter relaxes, and meconium is passed into the amniotic fluid.
>
> **AHA:** 4Q, '05, 83
>
> **TIP:** If the meconium was documented as aspirated or had any effect on the newborn, see codes 770.11 and 770.12.

763.89　Other specified complications of labor and delivery affecting fetus or newborn N

> Fetus or newborn affected by:
> > abnormality of maternal soft tissues
> > destructive operation on live fetus to facilitate delivery
> > induction of labor (medical)
> > other procedures used in labor and delivery
> Fetus or newborn affected by other conditions classifiable to 650-699

763.9　Unspecified complication of labor and delivery affecting fetus or newborn N

OTHER CONDITIONS ORIGINATING IN THE PERINATAL PERIOD (764-779)

The following fifth-digit subclassification is for use with category 764 and codes 765.0-765.1 to denote birthweight:

> **0　unspecified [weight]**
> **1　less than 500 grams**
> **2　500-749 grams**
> **3　750-999 grams**
> **4　1,000-1,249 grams**
> **5　1,250-1,499 grams**
> **6　1,500-1,749 grams**
> **7　1,750-1,999 grams**
> **8　2,000-2,499 grams**
> **9　2,500 grams and over**

✓4ᵗʰ **764　Slow fetal growth and fetal malnutrition**

> **AHA:** ▶1Q, '09, 13◀ 3Q, '04, 4; 4Q, '02, 63; 1Q,'94, 8; 2Q, '91, 19; 2Q, '89, 15

§ ✓5ᵗʰ **764.0　"Light-for-dates" without mention of fetal** N
[0-9]　**malnutrition**

> Infants underweight for gestational age
> "Small-for-dates"
>
> P07.18 Other low birth weight newborn 2000-2499 grams　I-10

§ ✓5ᵗʰ **764.1　"Light-for-dates" with signs of fetal malnutrition** N
[0-9]

> Infants "light-for-dates" classifiable to 764.0, who in addition show signs of fetal malnutrition, such as dry peeling skin and loss of subcutaneous tissue

§ ✓5ᵗʰ **764.2　Fetal malnutrition without mention of** N
[0-9]　**"light-for-dates"**

> Infants, not underweight for gestational age, showing signs of fetal malnutrition, such as dry peeling skin and loss of subcutaneous tissue
> Intrauterine malnutrition

§ ✓5ᵗʰ **764.9　Fetal growth retardation, unspecified** N
[0-9]

> Intrauterine growth retardation
> **AHA:** For code 764.97: 1Q, '97, 6

✓4ᵗʰ **765　Disorders relating to short gestation and low birthweight**

> INCLUDES　the listed conditions, without further specification, as causes of mortality, morbidity, or additional care, in fetus or newborn
>
> **AHA:** 1Q, '97, 6; 1Q, '94, 8; 2Q, '91, 19; 2Q, '89, 15

§ ✓5ᵗʰ **765.0　Extreme immaturity** N
[0-9]

> Note: Usually implies a birthweight of less than 1000 grams.
>
> Use additional code for weeks of gestation (765.20-765.29)
>
> **AHA:** ▶1Q, '09, 13◀ 3Q, '04, 4; 4Q, '02, 63; **For code 765.03:** 4Q, '01, 51

§ ✓5ᵗʰ **765.1　Other preterm infants** N
[0-9]

> Note: Usually implies a birthweight of 1000-2499 grams.
> Prematurity NOS
> Prematurity or small size, not classifiable to 765.0 or as "light-for-dates" in 764
>
> Use additional code for weeks of gestation (765.20-765.29)
>
> **AHA:** ▶1Q, '09, 13◀ 3Q, '04, 4; 4Q, '02, 63; **For code 765.10:** ▶1Q, '09, 15;◀ 1Q, '94, 14; **For code 765.17:** 4Q, '08, 139; 1Q, '97, 6; **For code 765.18:** 4Q, '02, 64
>
> P07.10 Other low birth weight newborn uns weight　I-10

✓5ᵗʰ **765.2　Weeks of gestation**

> **AHA:** 3Q, '04, 4; 4Q, '02, 63
>
> **TIP:** Assign as an additional code with category 764 and codes from 765.0 and 765.1, as documented by the provider.

765.20　Unspecified weeks of gestation N

765.21　Less than 24 completed weeks of gestation N

765.22　24 completed weeks of gestation N

765.23　25-26 completed weeks of gestation N

> **AHA:** ▶1Q, '09, 14◀

765.24　27-28 completed weeks of gestation N

765.25　29-30 completed weeks of gestation N

> P07.31 Other preterm newborn 28-31 complete weeks

765.26　31-32 completed weeks of gestation N

> **AHA:** ▶1Q, '09, 14;◀ 4Q, '08, 139

765.27　33-34 completed weeks of gestation N

765.28　35-36 completed weeks of gestation N

> **AHA:** 4Q, '02, 64
>
> P07.32 Other preterm newborn 32-36 complete weeks　I-10

765.29　37 or more completed weeks of gestation N

✓4ᵗʰ **766　Disorders relating to long gestation and high birthweight**

> INCLUDES　the listed conditions, without further specification, as causes of mortality, morbidity, or additional care, in fetus or newborn

766.0　Exceptionally large baby N

> Note: Usually implies a birthweight of 4500 grams or more.

766.1　Other "heavy-for-dates" infants N

> Other fetus or infant "heavy-" or "large-for-dates" regardless of period of gestation
>
> P08.1 Other heavy for gestational age newborn　I-10

✓5ᵗʰ **766.2　Late infant, not "heavy-for-dates"**

> **AHA:** 2Q, '06, 12
>
> **TIP:** May be assigned based on gestational age alone, without documentation of any related specific condition or disorder.

766.21　Post-term infant N

> Infant with gestation period over 40 completed weeks to 42 completed weeks
>
> **AHA:** ▶1Q, '09, 12;◀ 4Q, '03, 69
>
> P08.21 Post-term newborn　I-10

766.22　Prolonged gestation of infant N

> Infant with gestation period over 42 completed weeks
> Postmaturity NOS
> **AHA:** ▶1Q, '09, 12◀

---

§　Requires fifth digit. Valid digits are in [brackets] under each code. See beginning of section 764-779 for fifth digit definitions.

✓4ᵗʰ／✓5ᵗʰ　Additional Digit Required　　Unacceptable PDx　　Manifestation Code　　Hospital Acquired Condition　　▶◀ Revised Text　　● New Code　　▲ Revised Code Title

2010 ICD-9-CM　　　　　**October 2009 • Volume 1 – 289**

✓4th **767 Birth trauma**

767.0 Subdural and cerebral hemorrhage `MCC` `N`
Subdural and cerebral hemorrhage, whether described as due to birth trauma or to intrapartum anoxia or hypoxia
Subdural hematoma (localized)
Tentorial tear
Use additional code to identify cause
> `EXCLUDES` intraventricular hemorrhage (772.10-772.14)
> subarachnoid hemorrhage (772.2)
CC Excl: 767.0, 767.8-767.9, 779.81-779.84, 779.89

✓5th **767.1 Injuries to scalp**
AHA: 4Q, '03, 69

767.11 Epicranial subaponeurotic hemorrhage `CC` `N`
(massive)
Subgaleal hemorrhage
DEF: A hemorrhage that occurs within the space between the galea aponeurotica, or epicranial aponeurosis, a thin tendinous structure that is attached to the skull laterally, and the periosteum of the skull.
CC Excl: 767.0-767.11, 767.8-767.9, 779.81-779.84, 779.89

767.19 Other injuries to scalp `N`
Caput succedaneum
Cephalhematoma
Chignon (from vacuum extraction)
P12.89 Other birth injuries to scalp `I-10`

767.2 Fracture of clavicle `N`

767.3 Other injuries to skeleton `N`
Fracture of:
long bones
skull
> `EXCLUDES` congenital dislocation of hip (754.30-754.35)
> fracture of spine, congenital (767.4)

767.4 Injury to spine and spinal cord `N`
Dislocation ⎫
Fracture ⎬ of spine or spinal cord due to
Laceration ⎪   birth trauma
Rupture   ⎭

767.5 Facial nerve injury `N`
Facial palsy

767.6 Injury to brachial plexus `N`
Palsy or paralysis:
brachial
Erb (-Duchenne)
Klumpke (-Déjérine)

767.7 Other cranial and peripheral nerve injuries `N`
Phrenic nerve paralysis

767.8 Other specified birth trauma `N`
Eye damage
Hematoma of:
liver (subcapsular)
testes
vulva
Rupture of:
liver
spleen
Scalpel wound
Traumatic glaucoma
> `EXCLUDES` hemorrhage classifiable to 772.0-772.9

767.9 Birth trauma, unspecified `N`
Birth injury NOS

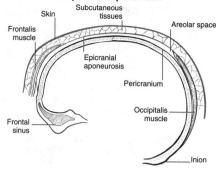

Epicranial Aponeurosis

✓4th **768 Intrauterine hypoxia and birth asphyxia**
Use only when associated with newborn morbidity classifiable elsewhere
> `EXCLUDES` acidemia NOS of newborn (775.81)
> acidosis NOS of newborn (775.81)
> cerebral ischemia NOS (779.2)
> hypoxia NOS of newborn (770.88)
> mixed metabolic and respiratory acidosis of newborn (775.81)
> respiratory arrest of newborn (770.87)
DEF: Oxygen intake insufficiency due to interrupted placental circulation or premature separation of placenta.
AHA: 4Q, '92, 20

768.0 Fetal death from asphyxia or anoxia before `N`
onset of labor or at unspecified time

768.1 Fetal death from asphyxia or anoxia during labor `N`

768.2 Fetal distress before onset of labor, in `N`
liveborn infant
Fetal metabolic acidemia before onset of labor, in liveborn infant

768.3 Fetal distress first noted during labor and `N`
delivery, in liveborn infant
Fetal metabolic acidemia first noted during labor and delivery, in liveborn infant

768.4 Fetal distress, unspecified as to time of `N`
onset, in liveborn infant
Fetal metabolic acidemia unspecified as to time of onset, in liveborn infant
AHA: N-D, '86, 10

768.5 Severe birth asphyxia `MCC` `N`
Birth asphyxia with neurologic involvement
> `EXCLUDES` hypoxic-ischemic encephalopathy [HIE]
> ▶(768.70-768.73)◀
CC Excl: 768.5-768.6, 768.9-770.86, 770.89-770.9, 779.81-779.84, 779.89
AHA: N-D, '86, 3

768.6 Mild or moderate birth asphyxia `N`
Birth asphyxia (without mention of neurologic involvement)
> `EXCLUDES` hypoxic-ischemic encephalopathy [HIE]
> ▶(768.70-768.73)◀
AHA: N-D, '86, 3

✓5th **768.7 Hypoxic-ischemic encephalopathy [HIE]**
AHA: 4Q, '06, 104

● **768.70 Hypoxic-ischemic encephalopathy,** `CC` `N`
unspecified
CC Excl: 768.5-768.6, 768.70-768.9

● **768.71 Mild hypoxic-ischemic encephalopathy** `CC` `N`
CC Excl: See code: 768.70

● **768.72 Moderate hypoxic-ischemic** `CC` `N`
encephalopathy
CC Excl: See code: 768.70

● **768.73 Severe hypoxic-ischemic** `MCC` `N`
encephalopathy
CC Excl: See code: 768.70

`N` Newborn Age: 0   `P` Pediatric Age: 0-17   `M` Maternity Age: 12-55   `A` Adult Age: 15-124   `MCC` Major CC Condition   `CC` CC Condition   `HIV` HIV Related Dx

768.9   Unspecified birth asphyxia in liveborn infant N
   Anoxia
   Asphyxia } NOS, in liveborn infant

769   Respiratory distress syndrome MCC N
   Cardiorespiratory distress syndrome of newborn
   Hyaline membrane disease (pulmonary)
   Idiopathic respiratory distress syndrome [IRDS or RDS] of newborn
   Pulmonary hypoperfusion syndrome
   EXCLUDES *transient tachypnea of newborn (770.6)*
   DEF: Severe chest contractions upon air intake and expiratory grunting; infant appears blue due to oxygen deficiency and has rapid respiratory rate; formerly called hyaline membrane disease.
   CC Excl: 768.5-768.6, 768.9-770.86, 770.89-770.9, 779.81-779.84, 779.89
   AHA: 1Q, '89, 10; N-D, '86, 6
   TIP: Do not assign if documentation specifies Type II respiratory distress syndrome, which usually resolves within six to 24 hours after birth; see instead 770.6.
   P22.0 Respiratory distress syndrome of newborn   I-10

√4ᵗʰ **770   Other respiratory conditions of fetus and newborn**

770.0   Congenital pneumonia MCC N
   Infective pneumonia acquired prenatally
   EXCLUDES *pneumonia from infection acquired after birth (480.0-486)*
   CC Excl: 768.5-768.6, 768.9-770.86, 770.89-770.9, 779.81-779.84, 779.89
   AHA: 1Q, '05, 10

√5ᵗʰ **770.1   Fetal and newborn aspiration**
   EXCLUDES *aspiration of postnatal stomach contents (770.85, 770.86)*
   meconium passage during delivery (763.84)
   meconium staining (779.84)
   AHA: 4Q, '05, 83

770.10   Fetal and newborn aspiration, unspecified N

770.11   Meconium aspiration without respiratory N **symptoms**
   Meconium aspiration NOS

770.12   Meconium aspiration with respiratory MCC N **symptoms**
   Meconium aspiration pneumonia
   Meconium aspiration pneumonitis
   Meconium aspiration syndrome NOS
   Use additional code to identify any secondary pulmonary hypertension (416.8), if applicable
   DEF: Meconium aspiration syndrome: aspiration of fetal intestinal material during or prior to delivery, usually a complication of placental insufficiency, causing pneumonitis and bronchial obstruction (inflammatory reaction of lungs).
   CC Excl: See code: 770.0

770.13   Aspiration of clear amniotic fluid without N **respiratory symptoms**
   Aspiration of clear amniotic fluid NOS

770.14   Aspiration of clear amniotic MCC N **fluid with respiratory symptoms**
   Aspiration of clear amniotic fluid with pneumonia
   Aspiration of clear amniotic fluid with pneumonitis
   Use additional code to identify any secondary pulmonary hypertension (416.8), if applicable
   CC Excl: See code: 770.0

770.15   Aspiration of blood without respiratory N **symptoms**
   Aspiration of blood NOS

770.16   Aspiration of blood with respiratory MCC N **symptoms**
   Aspiration of blood with pneumonia
   Aspiration of blood with pneumonitis
   Use additional code to identify any secondary pulmonary hypertension (416.8), if applicable
   CC Excl: See code: 770.0

770.17   Other fetal and newborn aspiration N **without respiratory symptoms**

770.18   Other fetal and newborn MCC N **aspiration with respiratory symptoms**
   Other aspiration pneumonia
   Other aspiration pneumonitis
   Use additional code to identify any secondary pulmonary hypertension (416.8), if applicable
   CC Excl: See code: 770.0

770.2   Interstitial emphysema and related conditions MCC N
   Pneumomediastinum
   Pneumopericardium } originating in the perinatal period
   Pneumothorax
   CC Excl: See code: 770.0
   P25.0 Interstitial emphysema origin perinatal period   I-10

770.3   Pulmonary hemorrhage MCC N
   Hemorrhage:
      alveolar (lung)
      intra-alveolar (lung) } originating in the perinatal period
      massive pulmonary
   CC Excl: See code: 770.0

770.4   Primary atelectasis CC N
   Pulmonary immaturity NOS
   DEF: Alveoli fail to expand causing insufficient air intake by newborn.
   CC Excl: See code: 770.0

770.5   Other and unspecified atelectasis CC N
   Atelectasis:
      NOS
      partial } originating in the perinatal period
      secondary
   Pulmonary collapse
   CC Excl: See code: 770.0

770.6   Transitory tachypnea of newborn N
   Idiopathic tachypnea of newborn
   Wet lung syndrome
   EXCLUDES *respiratory distress syndrome (769)*
   DEF: Quick, shallow breathing of newborn; short-term problem.
   AHA: 4Q, '95, 4; 1Q, '94, 12; 3Q, '93, 7; 1Q, '89, 10; N-D, '86, 6
   P22.1 Transient tachypnea of newborn   I-10

770.7   Chronic respiratory disease arising in the MCC **perinatal period**
   Bronchopulmonary dysplasia
   Interstitial pulmonary fibrosis of prematurity
   Wilson-Mikity syndrome
   CC Excl: See code: 770.0
   AHA: 2Q, '91, 19; N-D, '86, 11
   P27.8 Other chronic resp dz origin perinatal period   I-10

√5ᵗʰ **770.8   Other respiratory problems after birth**
   EXCLUDES *mixed metabolic and respiratory acidosis of newborn (775.81)*
   AHA: 4Q, '02, 65; 2Q, '98, 10; 2Q, '96, 10

770.81   Primary apnea of newborn CC N
   Apneic spells of newborn NOS
   Essential apnea of newborn
   Sleep apnea of newborn
   DEF: Cessation of breathing when a neonate makes no respiratory effort for 15 seconds, resulting in cyanosis and bradycardia.
   CC Excl: 770.82-770.83, 770.87-770.9, 786.03
   P28.3 Primary sleep apnea of newborn   I-10

770.82 **Other apnea of newborn**   CC N
Obstructive apnea of newborn
CC Excl: 770.81-770.83, 770.87-770.9, 786.03

770.83 **Cyanotic attacks of newborn**   CC N
CC Excl: 770.81-770.83, 770.87-770.9, 782.5, 786.03

770.84 **Respiratory failure of newborn**   MCC N
EXCLUDES *respiratory distress syndrome (769)*
CC Excl: 768.5-768.6, 768.9-770.86, 770.89-770.9, 779.81-779.84, 779.89
AHA: 4Q, '08, 99

770.85 **Aspiration of postnatal stomach contents without respiratory symptoms**   N
Aspiration of postnatal stomach contents NOS
AHA: 4Q, '05, 83

770.86 **Aspiration of postnatal stomach contents with respiratory symptoms**   MCC N
Aspiration of postnatal stomach contents with pneumonia
Aspiration of postnatal stomach contents with pneumonitis
Use additional code to identify any secondary pulmonary hypertension (416.8), if applicable
CC Excl: See code: 770.84
AHA: 4Q, '05, 83

770.87 **Respiratory arrest of newborn**   MCC N
CC Excl: 770.11, 770.13, 770.15, 770.17, 770.6, 770.81-770.85, 770.88-770.9, 779.85, 786.03, 799.1
AHA: 4Q, '06, 104-106

770.88 **Hypoxemia of newborn**   N
Hypoxia NOS of newborn
AHA: 4Q, '06, 104-106

770.89 **Other respiratory problems after birth**   N
P28.89 Oth specified respiratory conditions   I-10
of newborn

770.9 **Unspecified respiratory condition of fetus and newborn**   N

✓4th **771** **Infections specific to the perinatal period**
INCLUDES infections acquired before or during birth or via the umbilicus or during the first 28 days after birth
EXCLUDES *congenital pneumonia (770.0)*
congenital syphilis (090.0-090.9)
infant botulism (040.41)
maternal infectious disease as a cause of mortality or morbidity in fetus or newborn, but fetus or newborn not manifesting the disease (760.2)
ophthalmia neonatorum due to gonococcus (098.40)
other infections not specifically classified to this category
AHA: N-D, '85, 4

771.0 **Congenital rubella**   CC N
Congenital rubella pneumonitis
CC Excl: 771.0-771.2, 779.81-779.84, 779.89

771.1 **Congenital cytomegalovirus infection**   MCC N
Congenital cytomegalic inclusion disease
CC Excl: See code: 771.0

771.2 **Other congenital infections**   MCC N
Congenital: Congenital:
   herpes simplex   toxoplasmosis
   listeriosis   tuberculosis
   malaria
CC Excl: 013.60-013.66, 046.2, 046.71-046.8, 048-049.0, 049.8, 052.0, 052.2, 054.3, 054.74, 056.01, 057.8-058.29, 059.00-059.9, 062.0-064, 066.2-066.49, 072.2, 073.7, 075, 078.3, 079.82, 079.99, 081.9, 083.9, 084.6, 090.41, 094.81, 117.5, 124, 130.0, 290.12, 323.01-323.9, 341.1, 382.4, 487.8, 710.0, 771.2, 984.9

771.3 **Tetanus neonatorum**   MCC N
Tetanus omphalitis
EXCLUDES *hypocalcemic tetany (775.4)*
DEF: Severe infection of central nervous system; due to exotoxin of tetanus bacillus from navel infection prompted by nonsterile technique during umbilical ligation.
CC Excl: 771.3, 779.81-779.84, 779.89

771.4 **Omphalitis of the newborn**   CC N
Infection:
   navel cord
   umbilical stump
EXCLUDES *tetanus omphalitis (771.3)*
DEF: Inflamed umbilicus.
CC Excl: 771.89

771.5 **Neonatal infective mastitis**   CC N
EXCLUDES *noninfective neonatal mastitis (778.7)*
CC Excl: See code: 771.4

771.6 **Neonatal conjunctivitis and dacryocystitis**   N
Ophthalmia neonatorum NOS
EXCLUDES *ophthalmia neonatorum due to gonococcus (098.40)*

771.7 **Neonatal Candida infection**   N
Neonatal moniliasis
Thrush in newborn

✓5th **771.8** **Other infection specific to the perinatal period**
Use additional code to identify organism (041.00-041.9)
AHA: 4Q, '02, 66

771.81 **Septicemia [sepsis] of newborn**   MCC N
Use additional codes to identify severe sepsis (995.92) and any associated acute organ dysfunction, if applicable
CC Excl: 771.4-771.89, 776.0-776.9, 779.81-779.84, 779.89
AHA: 4Q, '08, 99
TIP: Assign instead of 038 or 995.91. Assign also a code to identify severe sepsis (995.92) or any acute organ dysfunction, or a code from category 041 to specify the organism.
P36.9 Bacterial sepsis newborn unspecified   I-10

771.82 **Urinary tract infection of newborn**   CC N
CC Excl: 041.9, 590.00-590.9, 593.89-593.9, 595.0-595.81, 595.89-595.9, 599.0, 599.9, 771.89, 788.1, 996.64

771.83 **Bacteremia of newborn**   CC N
CC Excl: See code: 771.81

771.89 **Other infections specific to the perinatal period**   CC N
Intra-amniotic infection of fetus NOS
Infection of newborn NOS
CC Excl: 003.1, 020.2, 022.3, 036.2, 038.0-038.9, 040.89-041.11, 041.19-041.9, 054.5, 139.8, 771.82-771.89, 779.9, 790.7

✓4th **772** **Fetal and neonatal hemorrhage**
EXCLUDES ▶*fetal hematologic conditions complicating pregnancy (678.0)*◄
hematological disorders of fetus and newborn (776.0-776.9)

▲ **772.0** **Fetal blood loss affecting newborn**   N
Fetal blood loss from:
   cut end of co-twin's cord
   placenta
   ruptured cord
   vasa previa
Fetal exsanguination
Fetal hemorrhage into:
   co-twin
   mother's circulation

✓5th **772.1** **Intraventricular hemorrhage**
Intraventricular hemorrhage from any perinatal cause
AHA: 4Q, '01, 49; 3Q, '92, 8; 4Q, '88, 8

N Newborn Age: 0   P Pediatric Age: 0-17   M Maternity Age: 12-55   A Adult Age: 15-124   MCC Major CC Condition   CC CC Condition   HIV HIV Related Dx

292 – Volume 1 • October 2009   **2010 ICD-9-CM**

772.10 Unspecified grade `CC` `N`
CC Excl: 772.0-772.2, 772.8-772.9, 776.0-776.9, 779.81-779.84, 779.89

772.11 Grade I `CC` `N`
Bleeding into germinal matrix
CC Excl: See code: 772.10

772.12 Grade II `CC` `N`
Bleeding into ventricle
CC Excl: See code 772.10

772.13 Grade III `MCC` `N`
Bleeding with enlargement of ventricle
CC Excl: See code 772.10
AHA: 4Q, '01, 51

772.14 Grade IV `MCC` `N`
Bleeding into cerebral cortex
CC Excl: See code 772.10

772.2 Subarachnoid hemorrhage `MCC` `N`
Subarachnoid hemorrhage from any perinatal cause
EXCLUDES *subdural and cerebral hemorrhage (767.0)*
CC Excl: 772.0-772.2, 772.8-772.9, 776.0-776.9, 779.7-779.84, 779.89

772.3 Umbilical hemorrhage after birth `N`
Slipped umbilical ligature

772.4 Gastrointestinal hemorrhage `MCC` `N`
EXCLUDES *swallowed maternal blood (777.3)*
CC Excl: 772.0, 772.4-772.5, 772.8-772.9, 776.0-776.9, 779.81-779.84, 779.89

772.5 Adrenal hemorrhage `CC` `N`
CC Excl: See code: 772.4

772.6 Cutaneous hemorrhage `N`
Bruising
Ecchymoses } in fetus or newborn
Petechiae
Superficial hematoma
P54.5 Neonatal cutaneous hemorrhage `I-10`

772.8 Other specified hemorrhage of fetus or newborn `N`
EXCLUDES *hemorrhagic disease of newborn (776.0)*
pulmonary hemorrhage (770.3)

772.9 Unspecified hemorrhage of newborn `N`

✓4th 773 Hemolytic disease of fetus or newborn, due to isoimmunization
DEF: Hemolytic anemia of fetus or newborn due to maternal antibody formation against fetal erythrocytes; infant blood contains nonmaternal antigen.
TIP: Do not assign unless the physician substantiates confirmation by a positive Coomb's (direct antibody or direct antiglobulin) test.

773.0 Hemolytic disease due to Rh isoimmunization `N`
Anemia
Erythroblastosis (fetalis) } due to RH:
Hemolytic disease (fetus)   antibodies
   (newborn)   isoimmunization
     maternal/fetal
Jaundice   incompatibility
Rh hemolytic disease
Rh isoimmunization

773.1 Hemolytic disease due to ABO isoimmunization `N`
ABO hemolytic disease
ABO isoimmunization
Anemia   } due to ABO:
Erythroblastosis (fetalis)   antibodies
Hemolytic disease (fetus)   isoimmunization
   (newborn)   maternal/fetal
Jaundice   incompatibility
DEF: Incompatible Rh fetal-maternal blood grouping; prematurely destroys red blood cells; detected by Coombs test.
AHA: 3Q, '92, 8
P55.1 ABO isoimmunization of newborn `I-10`

773.2 Hemolytic disease due to other and unspecified isoimmunization `N`
Erythroblastosis (fetalis) (neonatorum) NOS
Hemolytic disease (fetus) (newborn) NOS
Jaundice or anemia due to other and unspecified blood-group incompatibility
AHA: 1Q, '94, 13
P55.9 Hemolytic disease of newborn unspecified `I-10`

773.3 Hydrops fetalis due to isoimmunization `MCC` `N`
Use additional code to identify type of isoimmunization (773.0-773.2)
DEF: Massive edema of entire body and severe anemia; may result in fetal death or stillbirth.
CC Excl: 773.0-773.5, 779.81-779.84, 779.89

773.4 Kernicterus due to isoimmunization `MCC` `N`
Use additional code to identify type of isoimmunization (773.0-773.2)
DEF: Complication of erythroblastosis fetalis associated with severe neural symptoms, high blood bilirubin levels and nerve cell destruction; results in bilirubin-pigmented gray matter of central nervous system.
CC Excl: See code: 773.3

773.5 Late anemia due to isoimmunization `N`

✓4th 774 Other perinatal jaundice

774.0 *Perinatal jaundice from hereditary hemolytic anemias* `N`
Code first underlying disease (282.0-282.9)

774.1 Perinatal jaundice from other excessive hemolysis `N`
Fetal or neonatal jaundice from:
   bruising
   drugs or toxins transmitted from mother
   infection
   polycythemia
   swallowed maternal blood
Use additional code to identify cause
EXCLUDES *jaundice due to isoimmunization (773.0-773.2)*

774.2 Neonatal jaundice associated with preterm delivery `N`
Hyperbilirubinemia of prematurity
Jaundice due to delayed conjugation associated with preterm delivery
AHA: 3Q, '91, 21
P59.0 Neonatal jaundice associated w/preterm delivery `I-10`

✓5th 774.3 Neonatal jaundice due to delayed conjugation from other causes

774.30 Neonatal jaundice due to delayed conjugation, cause unspecified `N`
DEF: Jaundice of newborn with abnormal bilirubin metabolism; causes excess accumulated unconjugated bilirubin in blood.

774.31 *Neonatal jaundice due to delayed conjugation in diseases classified elsewhere* `N`
Code first underlying diseases as:
   congenital hypothyroidism (243)
   Crigler-Najjar syndrome (277.4)
   Gilbert's syndrome (277.4)

774.39 Other `N`
Jaundice due to delayed conjugation from causes, such as:
   breast milk inhibitors
   delayed development of conjugating system

774.4 Perinatal jaundice due to hepatocellular damage `MCC` `N`
Fetal or neonatal hepatitis   Inspissated bile syndrome
Giant cell hepatitis
CC Excl: 774.0-774.7, 779.81-779.84, 779.89

774.5 *Perinatal jaundice from other causes* `N`
Code first underlying cause as:
   congenital obstruction of bile duct (751.61)
   galactosemia (271.1)
   mucoviscidosis (277.00-277.09)

Conditions in the Perinatal Period

774.6–777.2

774.6 Unspecified fetal and neonatal jaundice [N]
Icterus neonatorum
Neonatal hyperbilirubinemia (transient)
Physiologic jaundice NOS in newborn
> **EXCLUDES** *that in preterm infants (774.2)*
> AHA: 1Q, '94, 13; 2Q, '89, 15
> P59.9 Neonatal jaundice unspecified   [I-10]

774.7 Kernicterus not due to isoimmunization [MCC] [N]
Bilirubin encephalopathy
Kernicterus of newborn NOS
> **EXCLUDES** *kernicterus due to isoimmunization (773.4)*
> CC Excl: See code: 774.4

✓4th **775 Endocrine and metabolic disturbances specific to the fetus and newborn**
> **INCLUDES** transitory endocrine and metabolic disturbances caused by the infant's response to maternal endocrine and metabolic factors, its removal from them, or its adjustment to extrauterine existence

775.0 Syndrome of "infant of a diabetic mother" [N]
Maternal diabetes mellitus affecting fetus or newborn (with hypoglycemia)
> AHA: 1Q, '04, 7-8; 3Q, '91, 5
> **TIP:** Do not assign if the infant has no manifestations or symptoms of the syndrome; refer instead to code V18.0 Family history, diabetes mellitus.
> P70.1 Syndrome of infant of diabetic mother   [I-10]

[handwritten: Includes transient decrease in blood sugar or hyperglycemia]

775.1 Neonatal diabetes mellitus [CC] [N]
Diabetes mellitus syndrome in newborn infant
> CC Excl: 775.0-775.7, 775.9, 779.81-779.84, 779.89
> AHA: 3Q, '91, 6

[handwritten: Includes transient hypoglycemia]

775.2 Neonatal myasthenia gravis [CC] [N]
> CC Excl: See code: 775.1

775.3 Neonatal thyrotoxicosis [CC] [N]
Neonatal hyperthyroidism (transient)
> CC Excl: See code 775.1

775.4 Hypocalcemia and hypomagnesemia of newborn [CC] [N]
Cow's milk hypocalcemia
Hypocalcemic tetany, neonatal
Neonatal hypoparathyroidism
Phosphate-loading hypocalcemia
> CC Excl: See code 775.1

775.5 Other transitory neonatal electrolyte disturbances [N]
Dehydration, neonatal
> AHA: 1Q, '05, 9
> **TIP:** If the patient has neonatal hyperkalemia, assign also code 276.7 Hyperpotassemia.
> P74.1 Dehydration of newborn   [I-10]

775.6 Neonatal hypoglycemia [N]
> **EXCLUDES** *infant of mother with diabetes mellitus (775.0)*
> AHA: 1Q, '94, 8
> P70.4 Other neonatal hypoglycemia   [I-10]

775.7 Late metabolic acidosis of newborn [MCC] [N]
> CC Excl: See code 775.1

775.8 Other neonatal endocrine and metabolic disturbances

775.81 Other acidosis of newborn [CC] [N]
Acidemia NOS of newborn
Acidosis of newborn NOS
Mixed metabolic and respiratory acidosis of newborn
> CC Excl: 775.5, 775.7, 775.9
> AHA: 4Q, '06, 104-106

775.89 Other neonatal endocrine and metabolic disturbances [CC] [N]
Amino-acid metabolic disorders described as transitory
> CC Excl: 775.0-775.7, 775.9
> AHA: 4Q, '06, 104-106

775.9 Unspecified endocrine and metabolic disturbances specific to the fetus and newborn [N]

✓4th **776 Hematological disorders of newborn**
> **INCLUDES** disorders specific to the newborn though possibly originating in utero
> **EXCLUDES** *fetal hematologic conditions (678.0)*

776.0 Hemorrhagic disease of newborn [CC] [N]
Hemorrhagic diathesis of newborn
Vitamin K deficiency of newborn
> **EXCLUDES** *fetal or neonatal hemorrhage (772.0-772.9)*
> CC Excl: 776.0-776.9, 779.81-779.84, 779.89

776.1 Transient neonatal thrombocytopenia [MCC] [N]
Neonatal thrombocytopenia due to:
   exchange transfusion
   idiopathic maternal thrombocytopenia
   isoimmunization
> **DEF:** Temporary decrease in blood platelets of newborn.
> CC Excl: See code 776.0
> P61.0 Transient neonatal thrombocytopenia   [I-10]

776.2 Disseminated intravascular coagulation in newborn [MCC] [N]
> **DEF:** Disseminated intravascular coagulation of newborn: clotting disorder due to excess thromboplastic agents in blood as a result of disease or trauma; causes blood clotting within vessels and reduces available elements necessary for blood coagulation.
> CC Excl: See code 776.0

776.3 Other transient neonatal disorders of coagulation [CC] [N]
Transient coagulation defect, newborn
> CC Excl: See code 776.0

776.4 Polycythemia neonatorum [N]
Plethora of newborn
Polycythemia due to:
   donor twin transfusion
   maternal-fetal transfusion
> **DEF:** Abnormal increase of total red blood cells of newborn.

776.5 Congenital anemia [CC] [N]
Anemia following fetal blood loss
> **EXCLUDES** *anemia due to isoimmunization (773.0-773.2, 773.5)*
>   *hereditary hemolytic anemias (282.0-282.9)*
> CC Excl: 280.0-282.3, 282.5-284.2, 284.81-285.9, 289.9, 517.3, 776.5-776.6

776.6 Anemia of prematurity [CC] [N]
> CC Excl: See code: 776.5
> P61.2 Anemia of prematurity   [I-10]

776.7 Transient neonatal neutropenia [MCC] [N]
Isoimmune neutropenia
Maternal transfer neutropenia
> **EXCLUDES** *congenital neutropenia (nontransient) (288.01)*
> **DEF:** Decreased neutrophilic leukocytes in blood of newborn.
> CC Excl: 280.1-281.9, 282.5-282.63, 282.69-282.7, 283.0, 283.11, 284.01-284.2, 284.81-285.0, 285.21-285.9, 289.9, 776.7-776.9

776.8 Other specified transient hematological disorders [N]

▲ **776.9 Unspecified hematological disorder specific to newborn** [N]

✓4th **777 Perinatal disorders of digestive system**
> **INCLUDES** disorders specific to the fetus and newborn
> **EXCLUDES** *intestinal obstruction classifiable to 560.0-560.9*

777.1 Meconium obstruction [N]
Congenital fecaliths
Delayed passage of meconium
Meconium ileus NOS
Meconium plug syndrome
> **EXCLUDES** *meconium ileus in cystic fibrosis (277.01)*
> **DEF:** Meconium blocked digestive tract of newborn.

777.2 Intestinal obstruction due to inspissated milk [N]

[N] Newborn Age: 0   [P] Pediatric Age: 0-17   [M] Maternity Age: 12-55   [A] Adult Age: 15-124   [MCC] Major CC Condition   [CC] CC Condition   [HIV] HIV Related Dx

777.3 Hematemesis and melena due to swallowed maternal blood [N]
Swallowed blood syndrome in newborn
> **EXCLUDES** *that not due to swallowed maternal blood (772.4)*

777.4 Transitory ileus of newborn [CC][N]
> **EXCLUDES** *Hirschsprung's disease (751.3)*
CC Excl: 777.1-777.9

√5th **777.5 Necrotizing enterocolitis in newborn**
> **DEF:** Serious intestinal infection and inflammation in preterm infants; severity is measured by stages and may progress to life-threatening perforation or peritonitis; resection surgical treatment may be necessary.
AHA: 4Q, '08, 138-140

   777.50 Necrotizing enterocolitis in newborn, unspecified [MCC][N]
Necrotizing enterocolitis in newborn, NOS
CC Excl: 777.1-777.9, 779.81-779.84, 779.89

   777.51 Stage I necrotizing enterocolitis in newborn [MCC][N]
> ►Necrotizing enterocolitis without pneumatosis, without perforation◄
> **DEF:** Broad-spectrum symptoms with non-specific signs including feeding intolerance, sepsis, gastroenteritis, ileus, metabolic abnormalities.
CC Excl: 777.1-777.9, 779.81-779.84, 779.89

   777.52 Stage II necrotizing enterocolitis in newborn [MCC][N]
Necrotizing enterocolitis with pneumatosis, without perforation
> **DEF:** Proven NEC via abdominal radiographs showing intestinal dilatation and pneumatosis intestinalis.
CC Excl: 777.1-777.9, 779.81-779.84, 779.89

   777.53 Stage III necrotizing enterocolitis in newborn [MCC][N]
Necrotizing enterocolitis with perforation
Necrotizing enterocolitis with pneumatosis and perforation
> **DEF:** Advanced stage in which infant demonstrates signs of bowel perforation, septic shock, metabolic acidosis, ascites, disseminated intravascular coagulopathy, neutropenia.
AHA: 4Q, '08, 139
CC Excl: 777.1-777.9, 779.81-779.84, 779.89

777.6 Perinatal intestinal perforation [MCC][N]
Meconium peritonitis
CC Excl: See code: 777.50

777.8 Other specified perinatal disorders of digestive system [N]

777.9 Unspecified perinatal disorder of digestive system [N]

√4th **778 Conditions involving the integument and temperature regulation of fetus and newborn**

778.0 Hydrops fetalis not due to isoimmunization [MCC][N]
Idiopathic hydrops
> **EXCLUDES** *hydrops fetalis due to isoimmunization (773.3)*
> **DEF:** Edema of entire body, unrelated to immune response.
CC Excl: 778.0, 779.81-779.84, 779.89

778.1 Sclerema neonatorum [CC][N]
Subcutaneous fat necrosis
> **DEF:** Diffuse, rapidly progressing white, waxy, nonpitting hardening of tissue, usually of legs and feet, life-threatening; found in preterm or debilitated infants; unknown etiology.
CC Excl: 778.1, 778.5

778.2 Cold injury syndrome of newborn [N]

778.3 Other hypothermia of newborn [N]

778.4 Other disturbances of temperature regulation of newborn [N]
Dehydration fever in newborn
Environmentally-induced pyrexia
Hyperthermia in newborn
Transitory fever of newborn
P81.9 Disturbance of temp regulation newborn uns [I-10]

778.5 Other and unspecified edema of newborn [CC][N]
Edema neonatorum
CC Excl: 778.1-778.5

778.6 Congenital hydrocele
Congenital hydrocele of tunica vaginalis
P83.5 Congenital hydrocele [I-10]

778.7 Breast engorgement in newborn [N]
Noninfective mastitis of newborn
> **EXCLUDES** *infective mastitis of newborn (771.5)*

778.8 Other specified conditions involving the integument of fetus and newborn [N]
Urticaria neonatorum
> **EXCLUDES** *impetigo neonatorum (684)*
> *pemphigus neonatorum (684)*
P83.8 Oth spec conditions integument specific newborn [I-10]

778.9 Unspecified condition involving the integument and temperature regulation of fetus and newborn [N]

√4th **779 Other and ill-defined conditions originating in the perinatal period**

779.0 Convulsions in newborn [MCC][N]
Fits } in newborn
Seizures
CC Excl: 779.0-779.1, 779.81-779.84, 779.89
AHA: N-D, '84, 11
TIP: Clarify with the physician that convulsions are not actually infantile spasms; if so, refer to subcategory 345.6.

779.1 Other and unspecified cerebral irritability in newborn [N]

779.2 Cerebral depression, coma, and other abnormal cerebral signs [MCC][N]
Cerebral ischemia NOS of newborn
CNS dysfunction in newborn NOS
> **EXCLUDES** *cerebral ischemia due to birth trauma (767.0)*
> *intrauterine cerebral ischemia (768.2-768.9)*
> *intraventricular hemorrhage (772.10-772.14)*
CC Excl: 779.0-779.2

▲ √5th **779.3 Disorder of stomach function and feeding problems in newborn**
AHA: 2Q, '89, 15

   ● **779.31 Feeding problems in newborn** [N]
Slow feeding in newborn
> **EXCLUDES** *feeding problem in child over 28 days old (783.3)*
P92.9 Feeding problem of newborn unspecified [I-10]

   ● **779.32 Bilious vomiting in newborn** [MCC][N]
> **EXCLUDES** *bilious vomiting in child over 28 days old (787.04)*
CC Excl: 779.32-779.33

   ● **779.33 Other vomiting in newborn** [N]
Regurgitation of food in newborn
> **EXCLUDES** *vomiting in child over 28 days old (536.2, 787.01-787.04)*

   ● **779.34 Failure to thrive in newborn** [N]
> **EXCLUDES** *failure to thrive in child over 28 days old (783.41)*

779.4 Drug reactions and intoxications specific to newborn [CC][N]
Gray syndrome from chloramphenicol administration in newborn
> **EXCLUDES** *fetal alcohol syndrome (760.71)*
> *reactions and intoxications from maternal opiates and tranquilizers (763.5)*
CC Excl: 779.4-779.5

Conditions in the Perinatal Period

779.5–779.9

779.5 Drug withdrawal syndrome in newborn `CC` `N`
Drug withdrawal syndrome in infant of dependent
mother
EXCLUDES   *fetal alcohol syndrome (760.71)*
CC Excl: See code: 779.4
AHA: 3Q, '94, 6
TIP: If the infant is asymptomatic but has a positive drug
screen (e.g., for cocaine), assign instead 760.75.

779.6 Termination of pregnancy (fetus) `N`
Fetal death due to:
induced abortion
termination of pregnancy
EXCLUDES   *spontaneous abortion (fetus) (761.8)*

779.7 Periventricular leukomalacia `MCC`
DEF: Necrosis of white matter adjacent to lateral ventricles
with the formation of cysts; cause of PVL has not been firmly
established, but thought to be related to inadequate blood
flow in certain areas of the brain.
CC Excl: 772.0-772.2, 772.8-772.9, 776.0-776.9, 779.7-779.84,
779.89
AHA: 4Q, '01, 50, 51

√5ᵗʰ **779.8 Other specified conditions originating in the
perinatal period**
AHA: 4Q, '02, 67; 1Q, '94, 15

     779.81 Neonatal bradycardia `N`
EXCLUDES   *abnormality in fetal heart rate or
rhythm complicating labor
and delivery (763.81-763.83)
bradycardia due to birth asphyxia
(768.5-768.9)*

         P29.12 Neonatal bradycardia `I-10`

     779.82 Neonatal tachycardia `N`
EXCLUDES   *abnormality in fetal heart rate or
rhythm complicating labor
and delivery (763.81-763.83)*

779.83 Delayed separation of umbilical cord `N`
AHA: 4Q, '03, 71

779.84 Meconium staining `N`
EXCLUDES   *meconium aspiration (770.11,
770.12)
meconium passage during delivery
(763.84)*
AHA: 4Q, '05, 83, 88
P96.83 Meconium staining `I-10`

779.85 Cardiac arrest of newborn `MCC` `N`
CC Excl: 779.85
AHA: 4Q, '06, 104-106

**779.89 Other specified conditions
originating in the perinatal period** `N`
Use additional code to specify condition
AHA: 1Q, '06, 18; 2Q, '05, 15; 1Q, '05, 9
P96.89 Oth spec conditions originating `I-10`
perinatal period

**779.9 Unspecified condition originating in the
perinatal period** `N`
Congenital debility NOS
Stillbirth NEC

`N` Newborn Age: 0   `P` Pediatric Age: 0-17   `M` Maternity Age: 12-55   `A` Adult Age: 15-124   `MCC` Major CC Condition   `CC` CC Condition   `HIV` HIV Related Dx

296 – Volume 1   **2010 ICD-9-CM**

16. SYMPTOMS, SIGNS, AND ILL-DEFINED CONDITIONS (780-799)

This section includes symptoms, signs, abnormal results of laboratory or other investigative procedures, and ill-defined conditions regarding which no diagnosis classifiable elsewhere is recorded.

Signs and symptoms that point rather definitely to a given diagnosis are assigned to some category in the preceding part of the classification. In general, categories 780-796 include the more ill-defined conditions and symptoms that point with perhaps equal suspicion to two or more diseases or to two or more systems of the body, and without the necessary study of the case to make a final diagnosis. Practically all categories in this group could be designated as "not otherwise specified," or as "unknown etiology," or as "transient." The Alphabetic Index should be consulted to determine which symptoms and signs are to be allocated here and which to more specific sections of the classification; the residual subcategories numbered .9 are provided for other relevant symptoms which cannot be allocated elsewhere in the classification.

The conditions and signs or symptoms included in categories 780-796 consist of: (a) cases for which no more specific diagnosis can be made even after all facts bearing on the case have been investigated; (b) signs or symptoms existing at the time of initial encounter that proved to be transient and whose causes could not be determined; (c) provisional diagnoses in a patient who failed to return for further investigation or care; (d) cases referred elsewhere for investigation or treatment before the diagnosis was made; (e) cases in which a more precise diagnosis was not available for any other reason; (f) certain symptoms which represent important problems in medical care and which it might be desired to classify in addition to a known cause.

SYMPTOMS (780-789)

AHA: 1Q, '91, 12; 2Q, '90, 3; 2Q, '90, 5; 2Q, '90, 15; M-A, '85, 3

✓4th **780 General symptoms**

✓5th **780.0 Alteration of consciousness**

> **EXCLUDES** ▶alteration of consciousness due to:
>   intracranial injuries (850.0-854.19)
>   skull fractures (800.00-801.99,
>   803.00-804.99)◄
> coma:
>   diabetic (249.2-249.3, 250.2-250.3)
>   hepatic (572.2)
>   originating in the perinatal period (779.2)

AHA: 4Q, '92, 20

780.01 Coma `MCC`

> **DEF:** State of unconsciousness from which the patient cannot be awakened.
> **CC Excl:** 070.0-070.9, 249.00-251.3, 338.0-338.4, 348.81-348.9, 349.89-349.9, 430-432.9, 572.2, 780.01-780.09, 780.2, 780.4, 780.64-780.65, 780.91-780.99, 799.81-799.89, 800.00-801.99, 803.00-804.96, 850.0-852.19, 852.21-854.19
> **AHA:** 3Q, '96, 16

780.02 Transient alteration of awareness

> **DEF:** Temporary, recurring spells of reduced consciousness.

780.03 Persistent vegetative state `CC`

> **DEF:** Persistent wakefulness without consciousness due to nonfunctioning cerebral cortex.
> **CC Excl:** See code: 780.01

780.09 Other

> Drowsiness   Stupor
> Semicoma   Unconsciousness
> Somnolence

> **R40.1** Stupor   `I-10`

780.1 Hallucinations `CC`

Hallucinations:
  NOS
  auditory
  gustatory
  olfactory
  tactile

> **EXCLUDES** those associated with mental disorders, as
>   functional psychoses (295.0-298.9)
>   organic brain syndromes (290.0-294.9,
>   310.0-310.9)
>   visual hallucinations (368.16)

DEF: Perception of external stimulus in absence of stimulus; inability to distinguish between real and imagined.
CC Excl: 338.0-338.4, 780.1, 780.4, 780.91-780.99, 799.81-799.89

780.2 Syncope and collapse

Blackout
Fainting
(Near) (Pre) syncope
Vasovagal attack

> **EXCLUDES** carotid sinus syncope (337.0)
>   heat syncope (992.1)
>   neurocirculatory asthenia (306.2)
>   orthostatic hypotension (458.0)
>   shock NOS (785.50)

DEF: Sudden unconsciousness due to reduced blood flow to brain.
AHA: 1Q, '02, 6; 3Q, '00, 12; 4Q, '95, 42; 3Q, '95, 14; N-D, '85, 12

> **R55** Syncope and collapse   `I-10`

✓5th **780.3 Convulsions**

> **EXCLUDES** convulsions:
>   epileptic (345.10-345.91)
>   in newborn (779.0)

DEF: Sudden, involuntary contractions of the muscles.
AHA: 2Q, '97, 8; 1Q, '97, 12; 3Q, '94, 9; 1Q, '93, 24; 4Q, '92, 23; N-D, '87, 12

780.31 Febrile convulsions (simple), unspecified `CC`

recurrent

> Febrile seizure NOS
> **CC Excl:** 338.0-338.4, 345.00-345.91, 348.81-348.9, 349.89-349.9, 779.0-779.1, 780.31-780.39, 780.64-780.65, 780.91-780.99, 799.81-799.89
> **AHA:** 4Q, '97, 45

780.32 Complex febrile convulsions `CC`

> Febrile seizure:
>   atypical
>   complex
>   complicated

> **EXCLUDES** status epilepticus (345.3)
> **CC Excl:** See code: 780.31
> **AHA:** 4Q, '06, 106

780.39 Other convulsions

> Convulsive disorder NOS
> Fit NOS
> Recurrent convulsions NOS
> Seizure NOS

> **AHA:** 1Q, '08, 17; 3Q, '06, 22; 4Q, '04, 51; 1Q, '03, 7; 2Q, '99, 17; 4Q, '98, 39

> **R56.9** Unspecified convulsions   `I-10`

780.4 Dizziness and giddiness

Light-headedness
Vertigo NOS

> **EXCLUDES** Ménière's disease and other specified
>   vertiginous syndromes (386.0-386.9)

DEF: Whirling sensations in head with feeling of falling.
AHA: 2Q, '03, 11; 3Q, '00, 12; 2Q, '97, 9; 2Q, '91, 17

> **R42** Dizziness and giddiness   `I-10`

✓4th ✓5th Additional Digit Required   Unacceptable PDx   Manifestation Code   Hospital Acquired Condition   ▶◄ Revised Text   ● New Code   ▲ Revised Code Title

2010 ICD-9-CM   October 2009 • Volume 1 – 297

Symptoms, Signs, and Ill-Defined Conditions

780.5–780.79

✓5ᵗʰ **780.5 Sleep disturbances**

EXCLUDES *circadian rhythm sleep disorders*
(327.30-327.39)
organic hypersomnia (327.10-327.19)
organic insomnia (327.00-327.09)
organic sleep apnea (327.20-327.29)
organic sleep related movement disorders
(327.51-327.59)
parasomnias (327.40-327.49)
that of nonorganic origin (307.40-307.49)

AHA: 4Q, '05, 59

780.50 Sleep disturbance, unspecified

780.51 Insomnia with sleep apnea, unspecified

DEF: Transient cessation of breathing disturbing sleep.

780.52 Insomnia, unspecified

DEF: Inability to maintain adequate sleep cycle.

G47.00 Insomnia unspecified   `I-10`

780.53 Hypersomnia with sleep apnea, unspecified

DEF: Autonomic response inhibited during sleep; causes insufficient oxygen intake, acidosis and pulmonary hypertension.

AHA: 1Q, '93, 28; N-D, '85, 4

780.54 Hypersomnia, unspecified

DEF: Prolonged sleep cycle.

780.55 Disruptions of 24 hour sleep wake cycle, unspecified

780.56 Dysfunctions associated with sleep stages or arousal from sleep

780.57 Unspecified sleep apnea

AHA: 1Q, '01, 6 ; 1Q, '97, 5; 1Q, '93, 28

G47.30 Sleep apnea unspecified   `I-10`

780.58 Sleep related movement disorder, unspecified

EXCLUDES *restless legs syndrome (333.94)*

AHA: 4Q, '04, 95

780.59 Other

✓5ᵗʰ **780.6 Fever and other physiologic disturbances of temperature regulation**

EXCLUDES *effects of reduced environmental temperature*
(991.0-991.9)
effects of heat and light (992.0-992.9)
fever, chills or hypothermia associated with
confirmed infection – code to infection

AHA: ▶4Q, '08, 140-142;◀ 3Q, '05, 16; 3Q, '00,13; 4Q, '99, 26; 2Q, '91, 8

780.60 Fever, unspecified

Chills with fever
Fever NOS
Fever of unknown origin (FUO)
Hyperpyrexia NOS
Pyrexia NOS
Pyrexia of unknown origin

EXCLUDES *chills without fever (780.64)*
neonatal fever (778.4)
pyrexia of unknown origin (during):
in newborn (778.4)
labor (659.2)
the puerperium (672)

R50.9 Fever unspecified   `I-10`

780.61 Fever presenting with conditions classified elsewhere

Code first underlying condition when associated fever is present, such as with:
leukemia (conditions classifiable to 204-208)
neutropenia (288.00-288.09)
sickle-cell disease (282.60-282.69)

AHA: ▶4Q, '08, 142◀

780.62 Postprocedural fever

EXCLUDES *postvaccination fever (780.63)*

TIP: Do not assign a code from category 998 for post-procedural fever.

780.63 Postvaccination fever

Postimmunization fever

780.64 Chills (without fever)

Chills NOS

EXCLUDES *chills with fever (780.60)*

780.65 Hypothermia not associated with low environmental temperature

EXCLUDES *hypothermia:*
associated with low environmen-
tal temperature (991.6)
due to anesthesia (995.89)
of newborn (778.2, 778.3)

✓5ᵗʰ **780.7 Malaise and fatigue**

EXCLUDES *debility, unspecified (799.3)*
fatigue (during):
combat (308.0-308.9)
heat (992.6)
pregnancy (646.8)
neurasthenia (300.5)
senile asthenia (797)

AHA: 4Q, '88, 12; M-A, '87, 8

780.71 Chronic fatigue syndrome

DEF: Persistent fatigue, symptoms include weak muscles, sore throat, lymphadenitis, headache, depression and mild fever; no known cause; also called chronic mononucleosis, benign myalgic encephalomyelitis, Iceland disease and neurosthenia.

AHA: 4Q, '98, 48

780.72 Functional quadriplegia   `MCC`

Complete immobility due to severe physical disability or frailty

EXCLUDES *hysterical paralysis (300.11)*
immobility syndrome (728.3)
neurologic quadriplegia
(344.00-344.09)
quadriplegia NOS (344.00)

DEF: ▶Inability to move due to another condition such as dementia, severe contractures, or arthritis, not a physiologic one; no mental ability to move independently; typically found in severely demented patients.◀

CC Excl: 249.60-249.61, 249.80-249.91, 250.60-250.63, 250.80-250.93, 342.00-344.9, 348.8-348.9, 349.89-349.9, 742.59-742.9, 780.72

AHA: ▶4Q, '08, 143◀

TIP: The functional quadriplegic patient typically has severe dementia and the quadriplegia will be due to a nonneurologic condition.

780.79 Other malaise and fatigue

Asthenia NOS
Lethargy
Postviral (asthenic) syndrome
Tiredness

DEF: Asthenia: Any weakness, lack of strength or loss of energy, especially neuromuscular.

DEF: Lethargy: Listlessness, drowsiness, stupor and apathy.

DEF: Malaise: Vague feeling of debility or lack of good health.

DEF: Postviral (asthenic) syndrome: Listlessness, drowsiness, stupor and apathy; follows acute viral infection.

DEF: Tiredness: General exhaustion or fatigue.

AHA: 4Q, '04, 78; 1Q, '00, 6; 4Q, '99, 26

R53.83 Other fatigue   `I-10`

 Newborn Age: 0   📄 Pediatric Age: 0-17   📄 Maternity Age: 12-55   📄 Adult Age: 15-124   **MCC** Major CC Condition   **CC** CC Condition   **HIV** HIV Related Dx

298 – Volume 1 • February 2009   **2010 ICD-9-CM**

780.8 Generalized hyperhidrosis
Diaphoresis   Secondary hyperhidrosis
Excessive sweating
> EXCLUDES   focal (localized) (primary) (secondary)
> hyperhidrosis (705.21-705.22)
> Frey's syndrome (705.22)

DEF: Excessive sweating, appears as droplets on skin; general or localized.

TIP: Do not assign if documentation indicates a specific diagnosis of focal hyperhidrosis (primary or secondary); see subcategory 705.2.

√5th **780.9 Other general symptoms**
> EXCLUDES   hypothermia:
> NOS (accidental) (991.6)
> due to anesthesia (995.89)
> of newborn (778.2-778.3)
> memory disturbance as part of a pattern of
> mental disorder

AHA: 4Q, '02, 67; 4Q, '99, 10; 3Q, '93, 11; N-D, '85, 12

780.91 Fussy infant (baby) P

780.92 Excessive crying of infant (baby) N
> EXCLUDES   excessive crying of child, adolescent
> or adult (780.95)

780.93 Memory loss
Amnesia (retrograde)
Memory loss NOS
> EXCLUDES   ►memory loss due to:
> intracranial injuries (850.0-854.19)
> skull fractures (800.00-801.99,
> 803.00-804.99)◄
> mild memory disturbance due to
> organic brain damage
> ►(310.8)◄
> transient global amnesia (437.7)

AHA: 4Q, '03, 71

780.94 Early satiety
DEF: The premature feeling of being full; mechanism of satiety is mutlifactorial.
AHA: 4Q, '03, 72

780.95 Excessive crying of child, adolescent, or adult
> EXCLUDES   excessive crying of infant (baby)
> (780.92)

AHA: 4Q, '05, 89

780.96 Generalized pain
Pain NOS
AHA: 4Q, '06, 79-81
TIP: For pain syndromes, refer to category 338; if site is specified, refer to index.

780.97 Altered mental status
Change in mental status
> EXCLUDES   altered level of consciousness
> (780.01-780.09)
> altered mental status due to known
> condition–code to condition
> delirium NOS (780.09)

If the condition causing the change in mental status is known, do not assign 780.97; code the condition instead.

AHA: 4Q, '06, 107
R41.82 Altered mental status unspecified I-10

780.99 Other general symptoms
AHA: 4Q, '03, 103

√4th **781 Symptoms involving nervous and musculoskeletal systems**
> EXCLUDES   depression NOS (311)
> disorders specifically relating to:
> back (724.0-724.9)
> hearing (388.0-389.9)
> joint (718.0-719.9)
> limb (729.0-729.9)
> neck (723.0-723.9)
> vision (368.0-369.9)
> pain in limb (729.5)

781.0 Abnormal involuntary movements
Abnormal head movements
Fasciculation
Spasms NOS
Tremor NOS
> EXCLUDES   abnormal reflex (796.1)
> chorea NOS (333.5)
> infantile spasms (345.60-345.61)
> spastic paralysis (342.1, 343.0-344.9)
> specified movement disorders classifiable to
> 333 (333.0-333.9)
> that of nonorganic origin (307.2-307.3)

R25.9 Unspecified abnormal involuntary movements I-10

781.1 Disturbances of sensation of smell and taste
Anosmia
Parageusia
Parosmia
DEF: Anosmia: loss of sense of smell due to organic factors, including loss of olfactory nerve conductivity, cerebral disease, nasal fossae formation and peripheral olfactory nerve diseases; can also be psychological disorder.
DEF: Parageusia: distorted sense of taste, or bad taste in mouth.
DEF: Parosmia: distorted sense of smell.

781.2 Abnormality of gait
Gait:
ataxic
paralytic
spastic
staggering
> EXCLUDES   ataxia:
> NOS (781.3)
> locomotor (progressive) (094.0)
> difficulty in walking (719.7)

DEF: Abnormal, asymmetric gait.
AHA: 2Q, '05, 6; 2Q, '04, 15
TIP: If the patient's gait abnormality is due to a joint problem, refer to code 719.7 Difficulty in walking.
R26.9 Unspecified abnormalities of gait and mobility I-10

781.3 Lack of coordination
Ataxia NOS
Muscular incoordination
> EXCLUDES   ataxic gait (781.2)
> cerebellar ataxia (334.0-334.9)
> difficulty in walking (719.7)
> vertigo NOS (780.4)

AHA: 4Q, '04, 51; 3Q, '97, 12

781.4 Transient paralysis of limb CC
Monoplegia, transient NOS
> EXCLUDES   paralysis (342.0-344.9)

CC Excl: 781.4, 781.94

781.5 Clubbing of fingers
DEF: Enlarged soft tissue of distal fingers.

781.6 Meningismus CC
Dupré's syndrome
Meningism
DEF: Condition with signs and symptoms that resemble meningeal irritation; it is associated with febrile illness and dehydration with no evidence of infection.
CC Excl: 781.4, 781.94
AHA: 3Q, '00,13; J-F, '87, 7

Symptoms, Signs, and Ill-Defined Conditions

781.7–783.22

781.7 Tetany `CC`
Carpopedal spasm
EXCLUDES tetanus neonatorum (771.3)
tetany:
  hysterical (300.11)
  newborn (hypocalcemic) (775.4)
  parathyroid (252.1)
  psychogenic (306.0)
DEF: Nerve and muscle hyperexcitability; symptoms include muscle spasms, twitching, cramps, laryngospasm with inspiratory stridor, hyperreflexia and choreiform movements.
CC Excl: 037, 332.0-333.93, 333.99-334.4, 338.0-338.4, 342.10-342.12, 771.3, 780.91-780.99, 781.7, 799.81-799.89

781.8 Neurologic neglect syndrome `CC`
Asomatognosia
Hemi-akinesia
Hemi-inattention
Hemispatial neglect
Left-sided neglect
Sensory extinction
Sensory neglect
Visuospatial neglect
CC Excl: 781.8-781.92, 781.94-781.99
AHA: 4Q, '94, 37
TIP: If documented as sequelae of a CVA, assign also a code from category 438.

√5ᵗʰ **781.9 Other symptoms involving nervous and musculoskeletal systems**
AHA: 4Q, '00, 45

781.91 Loss of height
EXCLUDES osteoporosis (733.00-733.09)

781.92 Abnormal posture

781.93 Ocular torticollis
DEF: Abnormal head posture as a result of a contracted state of cervical muscles to correct a visual disturbance; either double vision or a visual field defect.
AHA: 4Q, '02, 68

781.94 Facial weakness
Facial droop
EXCLUDES facial weakness due to late effect of cerebrovascular accident (438.83)
AHA: 4Q, '03, 72
TIP: Do not assign if facial droop or weakness is due to Bell's palsy; see instead code 351.0.
R29.810 Facial weakness `I-10`

781.99 Other symptoms involving nervous and musculoskeletal systems

√4ᵗʰ **782 Symptoms involving skin and other integumentary tissue**
EXCLUDES symptoms relating to breast (611.71-611.79)

782.0 Disturbance of skin sensation
Anesthesia of skin
Burning or prickling sensation
Hyperesthesia
Hypoesthesia
Numbness
Paresthesia
Tingling
R20.9 Unspecified disturbances of skin sensation `I-10`

782.1 Rash and other nonspecific skin eruption
Exanthem
EXCLUDES vesicular eruption (709.8)
AHA: ▶4Q, '08, 99◄

782.2 Localized superficial swelling, mass, or lump
Subcutaneous nodules
EXCLUDES localized adiposity (278.1)

782.3 Edema
Anasarca   Localized edema NOS
Dropsy
EXCLUDES ascites (789.51-789.59)
edema of:
  newborn NOS (778.5)
  pregnancy (642.0-642.9, 646.1)
fluid retention (276.6)
hydrops fetalis (773.3, 778.0)
hydrothorax (511.81-511.89)
nutritional edema (260, 262)
DEF: Edema: excess fluid in intercellular body tissue.
DEF: Anasarca: massive edema in all body tissues.
DEF: Dropsy: serous fluid accumulated in body cavity or cellular tissue.
DEF: Localized edema: edema in specific body areas.
AHA: 2Q, '00, 18
R60.9 Edema unspecified `I-10`

782.4 Jaundice, unspecified, not of newborn `CC`
Cholemia NOS
Icterus NOS
EXCLUDES jaundice in newborn (774.0-774.7)
  due to isoimmunization (773.0-773.2, 773.4)
DEF: Bilirubin deposits of skin, causing yellow cast.
CC Excl: 774.0-774.7, 782.4, 782.9
R17 Unspecified jaundice `I-10`

782.5 Cyanosis
EXCLUDES newborn (770.83)
DEF: Deficient oxygen of blood; causes blue cast to skin.

√5ᵗʰ **782.6 Pallor and flushing**

782.61 Pallor

782.62 Flushing
Excessive blushing

782.7 Spontaneous ecchymoses
Petechiae
EXCLUDES ecchymosis in fetus or newborn (772.6)
  purpura (287.0-287.9)
DEF: Hemorrhagic spots of skin; resemble freckles.

782.8 Changes in skin texture
Induration
Thickening   } of skin

782.9 Other symptoms involving skin and integumentary tissues

√4ᵗʰ **783 Symptoms concerning nutrition, metabolism, and development**

783.0 Anorexia
Loss of appetite
EXCLUDES anorexia nervosa (307.1)
  loss of appetite of nonorganic origin (307.59)
R63.0 Anorexia `I-10`

783.1 Abnormal weight gain
EXCLUDES excessive weight gain in pregnancy (646.1)
  obesity (278.00)
  morbid (278.01)

√5ᵗʰ **783.2 Abnormal loss of weight and underweight**
Use additional code to identify Body Mass Index (BMI), if known (V85.0-V85.54)
AHA: 4Q, '00, 45

783.21 Loss of weight
AHA: 4Q, '05, 96
R63.4 Abnormal weight loss `I-10`

783.22 Underweight
AHA: 4Q, '05, 96

N Newborn Age: 0   P Pediatric Age: 0-17   M Maternity Age: 12-55   A Adult Age: 15-124   MCC Major CC Condition   CC CC Condition   HIV HIV Related Dx

300 – Volume 1 · February 2009   2010 ICD-9-CM

783.3 Feeding difficulties and mismanagement
Feeding problem (elderly) (infant)
> **EXCLUDES** *feeding disturbance or problems:*
> *in newborn ▶(779.31-779.34)◀*
> *of nonorganic origin (307.50-307.59)*

AHA: 3Q, '97, 12

√5ᵗʰ 783.4 Lack of expected normal physiological development in childhood
> **EXCLUDES** *delay in sexual development and puberty (259.0)*
> *gonadal dysgenesis (758.6)*
> *pituitary dwarfism (253.3)*
> *slow fetal growth and fetal malnutrition (764.00-764.99)*
> *specific delays in mental development (315.0-315.9)*

AHA: 4Q, '00, 45; 3Q, '97, 4

783.40 Lack of normal physiological development, unspecified
Inadequate development
Lack of development

783.41 Failure to thrive P
Failure to gain weight
> **EXCLUDES** ▶*failure to thrive in newborn (779.34)◀*

DEF: Organic failure to thrive: acute or chronic illness that interferes with nutritional intake, absorption, metabolism excretion and energy requirements. Nonorganic FTT is symptom of neglect or abuse.
AHA: 1Q, '03, 12

783.42 Delayed milestones P
Late talker
Late walker

783.43 Short stature
Growth failure
Growth retardation
Lack of growth
Physical retardation
DEF: Constitutional short stature: stature inconsistent with chronological age. Genetic short stature is when skeletal maturation matches chronological age.

783.5 Polydipsia
Excessive thirst

783.6 Polyphagia
Excessive eating
Hyperalimentation NOS
> **EXCLUDES** *disorders of eating of nonorganic origin (307.50-307.59)*

783.7 Adult failure to thrive A
R62.7 Adult failure to thrive I-10

783.9 Other symptoms concerning nutrition, metabolism, and development
Hypometabolism
> **EXCLUDES** *abnormal basal metabolic rate (794.7)*
> *dehydration (276.51)*
> *other disorders of fluid, electrolyte, and acid-base balance (276.0-276.9)*

AHA: 2Q, '04, 3

√4ᵗʰ 784 Symptoms involving head and neck
> **EXCLUDES** *encephalopathy NOS (348.30)*
> *specific symptoms involving neck classifiable to 723 (723.0-723.9)*

784.0 Headache
Facial pain
Pain in head NOS
> **EXCLUDES** *atypical face pain (350.2)*
> *migraine (346.0-346.9)*
> *tension headache (307.81)*

AHA: 3Q, '06, 22; 2Q, '06, 17; 3Q, '00, 13; 1Q, '90, 4; 3Q, '92, 14
TIP: Do not assign if headache syndrome has been diagnosed, refer to category 339.
R51 Headache I-10

784.1 Throat pain
> **EXCLUDES** *dysphagia (787.20-787.29)*
> *neck pain (723.1)*
> *sore throat (462)*
> *chronic (472.1)*

784.2 Swelling, mass, or lump in head and neck
Space-occupying lesion, intracranial NOS
AHA: 1Q, '03, 8

784.3 Aphasia CC
> **EXCLUDES** *aphasia due to late effects of cerebrovascular disease (438.11)*
> *developmental aphasia (315.31)*

DEF: Inability to communicate through speech, written word, or sign language.
CC Excl: 315.31, 432.0-434.91, 436, 784.3-784.49, 784.51-784.59
AHA: 4Q, '04, 78; 4Q, '98, 87; 3Q, '97, 12
R47.01 Aphasia I-10

▲ √5ᵗʰ 784.4 Voice and resonance disorders
▲ 784.40 Voice and resonance disorder, unspecified
784.41 Aphonia
Loss of voice
● 784.42 Dysphonia
Hoarseness
● 784.43 Hypernasality
● 784.44 Hyponasality
▲ 784.49 Other voice and resonance disorders
Change in voice

√5ᵗʰ 784.5 Other speech disturbance
> **EXCLUDES** ▶*speech disorder due to late effect of cerebrovascular accident (438.10-438.19)◀*
> *stammering and stuttering (307.0)*
> *that of nonorganic origin (307.0, 307.9)*

● 784.51 Dysarthria
> **EXCLUDES** *dysarthria due to late effect of cerebrovascular accident (438.13)*

● 784.59 Other speech disturbance
Dysphasia
Slurred speech
Speech disturbance NOS
R47.89 Other speech disturbances I-10

√5ᵗʰ 784.6 Other symbolic dysfunction
> **EXCLUDES** *developmental learning delays (315.0-315.9)*

784.60 Symbolic dysfunction, unspecified
784.61 Alexia and dyslexia
Alexia (with agraphia)
DEF: Alexia: Inability to understand written word due to central brain lesion.
DEF: Dyslexia: Ability to recognize letters but inability to read, spell, and write words; genetic.

784.69 Other
Acalculia   Agraphia NOS
Agnosia   Apraxia

Symptoms, Signs, and Ill-Defined Conditions

784.7–786.04

784.7   **Epistaxis**
Hemorrhage from nose   Nosebleed
AHA: 3Q, '04, 7
R04.0 Epistaxis   I-10

784.8   **Hemorrhage from throat**
EXCLUDES   *hemoptysis (786.3)*

√5th **784.9**   **Other symptoms involving head and neck**

784.91   **Postnasal drip**
AHA: 4Q, '06, 108

784.99   **Other symptoms involving head and neck**
Choking sensation
Feeling of foreign body in throat
Halitosis
Mouth breathing
Sneezing
EXCLUDES   *foreign body in throat (933.0)*
AHA: 4Q, '06, 108

√4th **785**   **Symptoms involving cardiovascular system**
EXCLUDES   *heart failure NOS (428.9)*

785.0   **Tachycardia, unspecified**
Rapid heart beat
EXCLUDES   *neonatal tachycardia (779.82)*
      paroxysmal tachycardia (427.0-427.2)
DEF: Excessively rapid heart rate.
AHA: 2Q, '03, 11
R00.0 Tachycardia unspecified   I-10

785.1   **Palpitations**
Awareness of heart beat
EXCLUDES   *specified dysrhythmias (427.0-427.9)*
R00.2 Palpitations   I-10

785.2   **Undiagnosed cardiac murmurs**
Heart murmurs NOS
AHA: 4Q, '92, 16
R01.1 Cardiac murmur unspecified   I-10

785.3   **Other abnormal heart sounds**
Cardiac dullness, increased or decreased
Friction fremitus, cardiac
Precordial friction

785.4   **Gangrene**   CC
Gangrene:
NOS
spreading cutaneous
Gangrenous cellulitis
Phagedena
Code first any associated underlying condition
EXCLUDES   *gangrene of certain sites – see Alphabetic Index*
      gangrene with atherosclerosis of the extremities (440.24)
      gas gangrene (040.0
DEF: Gangrene: necrosis of skin tissue due to bacterial infection, diabetes, embolus and vascular supply loss.
DEF: Gangrenous cellulitis: group A streptococcal infection; begins with severe cellulitis, spreads to superficial and deep fascia; produces gangrene of underlying tissues.
CC Excl: 338.0-338.4, 440.24, 780.91-780.99, 785.4, 799.81-799.89
AHA: 1Q, '04, 14; 3Q, '91, 12; 3Q, '90, 15; M-A, '86, 12
I96 Gangrene not elsewhere classified   I-10

√5th **785.5**   **Shock without mention of trauma**

785.50   **Shock, unspecified**   CC
Failure of peripheral circulation
DEF: Peripheral circulatory failure due to heart insufficiencies.
CC Excl: 338.0-338.4, 780.91-780.99, 785.50-785.59, 785.9, 799.81-799.89
AHA: 2Q, '96, 10

[1] **785.51**   **Cardiogenic shock**   MCC
DEF: Shock syndrome: associated with myocardial infarction, cardiac tamponade and massive pulmonary embolism; symptoms include mental confusion, reduced blood pressure, tachycardia, pallor and cold, clammy skin.
CC Excl: See code: 785.50
AHA: ▶4Q, '08, 182; ◀3Q, '05, 14
R57.0 Cardiogenic shock   I-10

785.52   **Septic shock**   MCC
Shock:
endotoxic
gram-negative
Code first:
    systemic inflammatory response syndrome due to infectious process with organ dysfunction (995.92)
CC Excl: See code 785.50
AHA: ▶4Q, '08, 99; ◀4Q, '06, 113; 2Q, '05, 18-19; 4Q, '03, 73, 79
TIP: The diagnosis of septic shock indicates the presence of severe sepsis; code 785.52 should not be assigned without first assigning code 995.92.

[1] **785.59**   **Other**   MCC
Shock:
hypovolemic
EXCLUDES   *shock (due to):*
    anesthetic (995.4)
    anaphylactic (995.0)
    due to serum (999.4)
    electric (994.8)
    following abortion (639.5)
    lightning (994.0)
    obstetrical (669.1)
    postoperative (998.0)
    traumatic (958.4)
CC Excl: see code 785.50
AHA: 2Q, '00, 3

785.6   **Enlargement of lymph nodes**
Lymphadenopathy
"Swollen glands"
EXCLUDES   *lymphadenitis (chronic) (289.1-289.3)*
    acute (683)
R59.9 Enlarged lymph nodes unspecified   I-10

785.9   **Other symptoms involving cardiovascular system**
Bruit (arterial)
Weak pulse

√4th **786**   **Symptoms involving respiratory system and other chest symptoms**

√5th **786.0**   **Dyspnea and respiratory abnormalities**

786.00   **Respiratory abnormality, unspecified**

786.01   **Hyperventilation**
EXCLUDES   *hyperventilation, psychogenic (306.1)*
DEF: Rapid breathing causes carbon dioxide loss from blood.

786.02   **Orthopnea**
DEF: Difficulty breathing except in upright position.

786.03   **Apnea**
EXCLUDES   *apnea of newborn (770.81, 770.82)*
    sleep apnea (780.51, 780.53, 780.57)
DEF: Cessation of breathing.
AHA: 4Q, '98, 50

786.04   **Cheyne-Stokes respiration**   CC
DEF: Rhythmic increase of depth and frequency of breathing with apnea; occurs in frontal lobe and diencephalic dysfunction.
CC Excl: 518.81-518.84, 519.8-519.9, 786.03-786.04, 799.1
AHA: 4Q, '98, 50

[1] MCC = Only if patient discharged alive.

N Newborn Age: 0   P Pediatric Age: 0-17   M Maternity Age: 12-55   A Adult Age: 15-124   MCC Major CC Condition   CC CC Condition   HIV HIV Related Dx

302 – Volume 1 · February 2009   2010 ICD-9-CM

786.05 Shortness of breath
  DEF: Inability to take in sufficient oxygen.
  AHA: 4Q, '99, 25; 1Q, '99, 6; 4Q, '98, 50
  R06.02 Shortness of breath `I-10`

786.06 Tachypnea
  EXCLUDES transitory tachypnea of newborn (770.6)
  DEF: Abnormal rapid respiratory rate; called hyperventilation.
  AHA: 4Q, '98, 50

786.07 Wheezing
  EXCLUDES asthma (493.00-493.92)
  DEF: Stenosis of respiratory passageway; causes whistling sound; due to asthma, coryza, croup, emphysema, hay fever, edema, and pleural effusion.
  AHA: 4Q, '98, 50

786.09 Other
  Respiratory:
    distress
    insufficiency
  EXCLUDES respiratory distress:
      following trauma and surgery (518.5)
      newborn (770.89)
      syndrome (newborn) (769)
        adult (518.5)
      respiratory failure (518.81, 518.83-518.84)
      newborn (770.84)
  AHA: 4Q, '05, 90; 2Q, '98, 10; 1Q, '97, 7; 1Q, '90, 9
  R06.82 Tachypnea not elsewhere classified `I-10`

786.1 Stridor
  EXCLUDES congenital laryngeal stridor (748.3)
  DEF: Obstructed airway causes harsh sound.

786.2 Cough
  EXCLUDES cough:
      psychogenic (306.1)
      smokers' (491.0)
      with hemorrhage (786.3)
  AHA: 4Q, '99, 26
  R05 Cough `I-10`

786.3 Hemoptysis `CC`
  Cough with hemorrhage
  Pulmonary hemorrhage NOS
  EXCLUDES pulmonary hemorrhage of newborn (770.3)
  DEF: Coughing up blood or blood-stained sputum.
  CC Excl: 338.0-338.4, 780.91-780.99, 786.3-786.4, 786.9, 799.81-799.89
  AHA: 2Q, '06, 17; 4Q, '90, 26
  R04.2 Hemoptysis `I-10`

786.4 Abnormal sputum
  Abnormal:
    amount
    color   } sputum
    odor
  Excessive septum

✓5th **786.5 Chest pain**

  786.50 Chest pain, unspecified
    AHA: 1Q, '07, 19; 2Q, '06, 7; 1Q, '03, 6; 1Q, '02, 4; 4Q, '99, 25
    R07.9 Chest pain unspecified `I-10`

  786.51 Precordial pain
    DEF: Chest pain over heart and lower thorax.

786.52 Painful respiration
  Pain:
    anterior chest wall
    pleuritic
  Pleurodynia
  EXCLUDES epidemic pleurodynia (074.1)
  AHA: N-D, '84, 17
  TIP: Assign for musculoskeletal chest pain with no indication of underlying cause.
  R07.1 Chest pain on breathing `I-10`

786.59 Other
  Discomfort
  Pressure   } in chest
  Tightness
  EXCLUDES pain in breast (611.71)
  AHA: 1Q, '02, 6
  TIP: Assign for chest pain due to anxiety, along with an additional code for anxiety. Chest pain is not integral to the diagnosis of anxiety.
  R07.89 Other chest pain `I-10`

786.6 Swelling, mass, or lump in chest
  EXCLUDES lump in breast (611.72)
  R22.2 Localized swelling, mass, lump, trunk `I-10`

786.7 Abnormal chest sounds
  Abnormal percussion, chest
  Friction sounds, chest
  Rales
  Tympany, chest
  EXCLUDES wheezing (786.07)

786.8 Hiccough
  EXCLUDES psychogenic hiccough (306.1)

786.9 Other symptoms involving respiratory system and chest
  Breath-holding spell

✓4th **787 Symptoms involving digestive system**
  EXCLUDES constipation (564.00-564.09)
      pylorospasm (537.81)
        congenital (750.5)

✓5th **787.0 Nausea and vomiting**
  Emesis
  EXCLUDES hematemesis NOS (578.0)
      vomiting:
        bilious, following gastrointestinal surgery (564.3)
        cyclical (536.2)
          associated with migraine (346.2)
          psychogenic (306.4)
        excessive, in pregnancy (643.0-643.9)
        ►fecal matter (569.87)◄
          habit (536.2)
        of newborn ►(779.32, 779.33)◄
        ►persistent (536.2)◄
          psychogenic NOS (307.54)
  AHA: M-A, '85, 11

  787.01 Nausea with vomiting
    AHA: 1Q, '03, 5
    R11.0 Nausea with vomiting `I-10`

  787.02 Nausea alone
    AHA: 3Q, '00, 12; 2Q, '97, 9
    R11.1 Nausea alone `I-10`

  787.03 Vomiting alone

● **787.04 Bilious emesis**
    Bilious vomiting
    EXCLUDES bilious emesis (vomiting) in newborn (779.32)

Symptoms, Signs, and Ill-Defined Conditions

787.1–788.32

Phases of Swallowing

Oral phase

Oropharyngeal phase

Pharyngeal phase

Pharyngeoesophageal phase

787.1 Heartburn
Pyrosis
Waterbrash
EXCLUDES *dyspepsia or indigestion (536.8)*
AHA: 2Q, '01, 6

√5th **787.2 Dysphagia**
Code first, if applicable, dysphagia due to late effect of cerebrovascular accident (438.82)
AHA: 4Q, '07, 92-94; 3Q, '07, 7; 4Q, '03, 103, 109; 2Q, '01, 4

  787.20 Dysphagia, unspecified
  Difficulty in swallowing NOS

  787.21 Dysphagia, oral phase

  787.22 Dysphagia, oropharyngeal phase
  AHA: 4Q, '07, 94

  787.23 Dysphagia, pharyngeal phase

  787.24 Dysphagia, pharyngoesophageal phase

  787.29 Other dysphagia
  Cervical dysphagia
  Neurogenic dysphagia
  R13.19 Other dysphagia   I-10

787.3 Flatulence, eructation, and gas pain
Abdominal distention (gaseous)
Bloating
Tympanites (abdominal) (intestinal)
EXCLUDES *aerophagy (306.4)*
DEF: Flatulence: excess air or gas in intestine or stomach.
DEF: Eructation: belching, expelling gas through mouth.
DEF: Gas pain: gaseous pressure affecting gastrointestinal system.

787.4 Visible peristalsis
Hyperperistalsis
DEF: Increase in involuntary movements of intestines.

787.5 Abnormal bowel sounds
Absent bowel sounds
Hyperactive bowel sounds

787.6 Incontinence of feces
Encopresis NOS
Incontinence of sphincter ani
EXCLUDES *that of nonorganic origin (307.7)*
AHA: 1Q, '97, 9

787.7 Abnormal feces
Bulky stools
EXCLUDES *abnormal stool content (792.1)*
          melena:
            NOS (578.1)
            newborn (772.4, 777.3)

√5th **787.9 Other symptoms involving digestive system**
EXCLUDES *gastrointestinal hemorrhage (578.0-578.9)*
          intestinal obstruction (560.0-560.9)
          specific functional digestive disorders:
            esophagus (530.0-530.9)
            stomach and duodenum (536.0-536.9)
            those not elsewhere classified
              (564.00-564.9)

  787.91 Diarrhea
  Diarrhea NOS
  AHA: 4Q, '08, 99; 4Q, '95, 54
  R19.7 Diarrhea unspecified   I-10

  787.99 Other
  Change in bowel habits
  Tenesmus (rectal)
  DEF: Tenesmus: Painful, ineffective straining at the rectum with limited passage of fecal matter.

√4th **788 Symptoms involving urinary system**
EXCLUDES *hematuria (599.70-599.72)*
          nonspecific findings on examination of the urine
            (791.0-791.9)
          small kidney of unknown cause (589.0-589.9)
          uremia NOS (586)
          urinary obstruction (599.60, 599.69)

788.0 Renal colic
Colic (recurrent) of:
  kidney
  ureter
DEF: Kidney pain.
AHA: 3Q, '04, 8
TIP: Do not assign if renal colic is due to calculus; see category 592.

788.1 Dysuria
Painful urination
Strangury

√5th **788.2 Retention of urine**
Code, if applicable, any causal condition first, such as:
  hyperplasia of prostate (600.0-600.9 with fifth-digit 1)
DEF: Accumulation of urine in the bladder due to inability to void

  788.20 Retention of urine, unspecified
  AHA: 4Q, '06, 93, 95; 2Q, '04, 18; 3Q, '03, 12-13; 1Q, '03, 6; 3Q, '96, 10
  R33.9 Retention of urine unspecified   I-10

  788.21 Incomplete bladder emptying
  AHA: 4Q, '06, 93

  788.29 Other specified retention of urine

√5th **788.3 Urinary incontinence**
Code, if applicable, any causal condition first, such as:
  congenital ureterocele (753.23)
  genital prolapse (618.00-618.9)
  hyperplasia of prostate (600.0-600.9 with fifth-digit 1)
EXCLUDES *functional urinary incontinence (788.91)*
          that of nonorganic origin (307.6)
          urinary incontinence associated with cognitive
            impairment (788.91)
AHA: 4Q, '06, 93; 4Q, '92, 22

  788.30 Urinary incontinence, unspecified
  Enuresis NOS
  AHA: ►1Q, '09, 15◄
  R32 Unspecified urinary incontinence   I-10

  788.31 Urge incontinence
  DEF: Inability to control urination, upon urge to urinate.
  AHA: 1Q, '00, 19

  788.32 Stress incontinence, male   ♂
  EXCLUDES *stress incontinence, female (625.6)*
  DEF: Inability to control urination associated with weak sphincter in males.

N Newborn Age: 0   P Pediatric Age: 0-17   M Maternity Age: 12-55   A Adult Age: 15-124   MCC Major CC Condition   CC CC Condition   HIV HIV Related Dx

304 – Volume 1 · October 2009   2010 ICD-9-CM

788.33 Mixed incontinence, (male) (female)
Urge and stress
DEF: Urge, stress incontinence: involuntary discharge of urine due to anatomic displacement.

788.34 Incontinence without sensory awareness
DEF: Involuntary discharge of urine without sensory warning.

788.35 Post-void dribbling
DEF: Involuntary discharge of residual urine after voiding.

788.36 Nocturnal enuresis
DEF: Involuntary discharge of urine during the night.

788.37 Continuous leakage
DEF: Continuous, involuntary urine seepage.

788.38 Overflow incontinence
DEF: Leakage caused by pressure of retained urine in the bladder after the bladder has fully contracted due to weakened bladder muscles or an obstruction of the urethra.

788.39 Other urinary incontinence

√5th **788.4 Frequency of urination and polyuria**
Code, if applicable, any causal condition first, such as:
hyperplasia of prostate (600.0-600.9 with fifth-digit 1)

788.41 Urinary frequency
Frequency of micturition
AHA: 4Q, '06, 93

788.42 Polyuria
DEF: Excessive urination.

788.43 Nocturia
DEF: Urination affecting sleep patterns.
AHA: 4Q, '06, 93

788.5 Oliguria and anuria
Deficient secretion of urine
Suppression of urinary secretion
EXCLUDES that complicating:
abortion (634-638 with .3, 639.3)
ectopic or molar pregnancy (639.3)
pregnancy, childbirth, or the puerperium
(642.0-642.9, 646.2)
DEF: Oliguria: diminished urinary secretion related to fluid intake.
DEF: Anuria: lack of urinary secretion due to renal failure or obstructed urinary tract.

√5th **788.6 Other abnormality of urination**
Code, if applicable, any causal condition first, such as:
hyperplasia of prostate (600.0-600.9 with fifth-digit 1)

788.61 Splitting of urinary stream
Intermittent urinary stream

788.62 Slowing of urinary stream
Weak stream
AHA: 4Q, '06, 93

788.63 Urgency of urination
EXCLUDES urge incontinence (788.31, 788.33)
DEF: Feeling of intense need to urinate; abrupt sensation of imminent urination.
AHA: 4Q, '06, 93; 4Q, '03, 74

788.64 Urinary hesitancy
AHA: 4Q, '06, 93, 109

788.65 Straining on urination
AHA: 4Q, '06, 93, 109

788.69 Other

788.7 Urethral discharge
Penile discharge
Urethrorrhea

788.8 Extravasation of urine   CC
DEF: Leaking or infiltration of urine into tissues.
CC Excl: 788.8-788.99

√5th **788.9 Other symptoms involving urinary system**
AHA: 1Q, '05, 12; 4Q, '88, 1

788.91 Functional urinary incontinence
Urinary incontinence due to cognitive impairment, or severe physical disability or immobility
EXCLUDES urinary incontinence due to physiologic condition (788.30-788.39)
AHA: ▶4Q, '08, 144-145◀

788.99 Other symptoms involving urinary system
Extrarenal uremia   Vesical:
Vesical.   tenesmus
pain

√4th **789 Other symptoms involving abdomen and pelvis**
EXCLUDES symptoms referable to genital organs:
female (625.0-625.9)
male (607.0-608.9)
psychogenic (302.70-302.79))

The following fifth-digit subclassification is to be used for codes 789.0. 789.3, 789.4, 789.6:
0 **unspecified site**
1 **right upper quadrant**
2 **left upper quadrant**
3 **right lower quadrant**
4 **left lower quadrant**
5 **periumbilic**
6 **epigastric**
7 **generalized**
9 **other specified site**
   Multiple sites

§ √5th **789.0 Abdominal pain**
[0-7, 9]   Cramps, abdominal
AHA: 1Q, '95, 3; **For code 789.06:** 1Q, '02, 5
R10.9 Unspecified abdominal pain   I-10
R10.31 Right lower quadrant pain   I-10
R10.13 Epigastric pain   I-10
R10.84 Generalized abdominal pain   I-10

789.1 Hepatomegaly
Enlargement of liver

789.2 Splenomegaly
Enlargement of spleen

§ √5th **789.3 Abdominal or pelvic swelling, mass, or lump**
[0-7, 9]   Diffuse or generalized swelling or mass:
abdominal NOS
umbilical
EXCLUDES abdominal distention (gaseous) (787.3)
ascites (789.51-789.59)

§ √5th **789.4 Abdominal rigidity**
[0-7, 9]

√5th **789.5 Ascites**
Fluid in peritoneal cavity
DEF: Serous fluid effusion and accumulation in abdominal cavity.
AHA: 4Q, '07, 95; 2Q, '05, 8; 4Q, '89, 11

789.51 Malignant ascites   CC
Code first malignancy, such as:
malignant neoplasm of ovary (183.0)
secondary malignant neoplasm of retroperitoneum and peritoneum (197.6)
AHA: 4Q, '07, 96
CC Excl: 338.0-338.4, 780.91-780.99, 789.30-789.49, 789.51-789.59, 789.9, 799.81-799.89
R18.0 Malignant ascities   I-10

789.59 Other ascites   CC
CC Excl: See code: 789.51
AHA: 4Q, '08, 99
R18.8 Other ascites   I-10

(handwritten margin notes)
Abnormal buildup of fluid in the abdomen caused by a malignancy.
coding sequence:
- malignancy
- ascites
- underlying cause of ascites
- diagnostic testing/procedures

---

§   Requires fifth digit. Valid digits are in [brackets] under each code. See category 789 for codes and definitions.

| √4th Additional Digit Required | Unacceptable PDx | Manifestation Code | Hospital Acquired Condition | ▶◀ Revised Text | ● New Code | ▲ Revised Code Title |

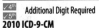

§ ✓5th **789.6 Abdominal tenderness**
[0-7, 9]   Rebound tenderness

● **789.7 Colic**
Colic NOS
Infantile colic
EXCLUDES   *colic in adult and child over 12 months old*
(789.0)
renal colic (788.0)

789.9 Other symptoms involving abdomen and pelvis
Umbilical:
bleeding
discharge

NONSPECIFIC ABNORMAL FINDINGS (790-796)
AHA: 2Q, '90, 16

✓4th **790 Nonspecific findings on examination of blood**
EXCLUDES   *abnormality of:*
platelets (287.0-287.9)
thrombocytes (287.0-287.9)
white blood cells (288.00-288.9)

✓5th **790.0 Abnormality of red blood cells**
EXCLUDES   *anemia:*
congenital (776.5)
newborn, due to isoimmunization
(773.0-773.2, 773.5)
of premature infant (776.6)
other specified types (280.0-285.9)
hemoglobin disorders (282.5-282.7)
polycythemia:
familial (289.6)
neonatorum (776.4)
secondary (289.0)
vera (238.4)
AHA: 4Q, '00, 46

790.01 Precipitous drop in hematocrit   CC
Drop in hematocrit
▶Drop in hemoglobin◀
CC Excl: 285.1, 285.3-285.9
TIP: Typically reported as a reason for encounter at a
dialysis center.

790.09 Other abnormality of red blood cells
Abnormal red cell morphology NOS
Abnormal red cell volume NOS
Anisocytosis
Poikilocytosis

790.1 Elevated sedimentation rate

✓5th **790.2 Abnormal glucose**
EXCLUDES   *diabetes mellitus (249.00-249.91,*
250.00-250.93)
dysmetabolic syndrome X (277.7)
gestational diabetes (648.8)
glycosuria (791.5)
hypoglycemia (251.2)
that complicating pregnancy, childbirth, or
puerperium (648.8)
AHA: 4Q, '03, 74; 3Q, '91, 5
TIP: These codes are typically assigned on encounters before a
patient is diagnosed with diabetes mellitus.

790.21 Impaired fasting glucose
Elevated fasting glucose

790.22 Impaired glucose tolerance test (oral)
Elevated glucose tolerance test

790.29 Other abnormal glucose
Abnormal glucose NOS
Abnormal non-fasting glucose
Hyperglycemia NOS
Pre-diabetes NOS
AHA: 2Q, '05, 21
R73.09 Other abnormal glucose   I-10

790.3 Excessive blood level of alcohol
Elevated blood-alcohol
AHA: S-O, '86, 3

**790.4 Nonspecific elevation of levels of transaminase or lactic
acid dehydrogenase [LDH]**
R74.0 Nonspecific elevation levels transaminase & LDH   I-10

790.5 Other nonspecific abnormal serum enzyme levels
Abnormal serum level of:
acid phosphatase
alkaline phosphatase
amylase
lipase
EXCLUDES   *deficiency of circulating enzymes (277.6)*
R74.8 Abnormal levels of other serum enzymes   I-10

790.6 Other abnormal blood chemistry

Abnormal blood level of:	Abnormal blood level of:
cobalt	lithium
copper	magnesium
iron	mineral
lead	zinc

EXCLUDES   *abnormality of electrolyte or acid-base balance*
(276.0-276.9)
hypoglycemia NOS (251.2)
lead poisoning (984.0-984.9)
specific finding indicating abnormality of:
amino-acid transport and metabolism
(270.0-270.9)
carbohydrate transport and metabolism
(271.0-271.9)
lipid metabolism (272.0-272.9)
uremia NOS (586)
AHA: 4Q, '88, 1
TIP: If only azotemia is documented (indexed to 790.6), clarify
with physician; if due to uremia or renal failure, code to those
conditions instead.
R78.89 Finding oth spec substances not norm found   I-10
blood

790.7 Bacteremia   CC
EXCLUDES   *bacteremia of newborn (771.83)*
septicemia (038)
Use additional code to identify organism (041)
DEF: Laboratory finding of bacteria in the blood in the
absence of two or more signs of sepsis; transient in nature,
progresses to septicemia with severe infectious process.
CC Excl: 338.0-338.4, 780.91-780.99, 790.7-790.99,
799.81-799.89
AHA: 2Q, '03, 7; 4Q, '93, 29; 3Q, '88, 12
TIP: If clinical signs or symptoms indicating systemic disease
exist, query physician for the presence of sepsis; code to category 038 if documented.

[handwritten: The presence of bacteria in the bloodstream after a trauma or mild infection.]

790.8 Viremia, unspecified
DEF: Presence of a virus in the blood stream.
AHA: 4Q, '88, 10

✓5th **790.9 Other nonspecific findings on examination of blood**
AHA: 4Q, '93, 29

790.91 Abnormal arterial blood gases

790.92 Abnormal coagulation profile
Abnormal or prolonged:
bleeding time
coagulation time
partial thromboplastin time [PTT]
prothrombin time [PT]
EXCLUDES   *coagulation (hemorrhagic) disorders*
(286.0-286.9)
R79.1 Abnormal coagulaton profile   I-10

**790.93 Elevated prostate specific antigen,
[PSA]**   A♂

790.94 Euthyroid sick syndrome
DEF: Transient alteration of thyroid hormone
metabolism due to nonthyroid illness or stress.
AHA: 4Q, '97, 45

§   Requires fifth digit. Valid digits are in [brackets] under each code. See category 789 for codes and definitions.

N Newborn Age: 0   P Pediatric Age: 0-17   M Maternity Age: 12-55   A Adult Age: 15-124   MCC Major CC Condition   CC CC Condition   HIV HIV Related Dx

306 – Volume 1 · October 2009

2010 ICD-9-CM

790.95 Elevated C-reactive protein [CRP]

DEF: Inflammation in an arterial wall results in elevated C-reactive protein (CRP) in the blood; CRP is a recognized risk factor in cardiovascular disease.

790.99 Other

AHA: 2Q, '03, 14

✓4th 791 Nonspecific findings on examination of urine

EXCLUDES hematuria NOS (599.70-599.72)
specific findings indicating abnormality of:
amino-acid transport and metabolism (270.0-270.9)
carbohydrate transport and metabolism
(271.0-271.9)

791.0 Proteinuria
Albuminuria
Bence-Jones proteinuria
EXCLUDES postural proteinuria (593.6)
that arising during pregnancy or the
puerperium (642.0-642.9, 646.2)
DEF: Excess protein in urine.
AHA: 3Q, '91, 8

791.1 Chyluria   `CC`
EXCLUDES filarial (125.0-125.9)
DEF: Excess chyle in urine.
CC Excl: 338.0-338.4, 780.91-780.99, 791.1, 791.9,
799.81-799.89

791.2 Hemoglobinuria
DEF: Free hemoglobin in blood due to rapid hemolysis of red
blood cells.

791.3 Myoglobinuria   `CC`
DEF: Myoglobin (oxygen-transporting pigment) in urine.
CC Excl: 338.0-338.4, 780.91-780.99, 791.2-791.3, 791.9,
799.81-799.89

791.4 Biliuria
DEF: Bile pigments in urine.

791.5 Glycosuria
EXCLUDES renal glycosuria (271.4)
DEF: Sugar in urine.

791.6 Acetonuria
Ketonuria
DEF: Excess acetone in urine.

791.7 Other cells and casts in urine

791.9 Other nonspecific findings on examination of urine
Crystalluria
Elevated urine levels of:
17-ketosteroids
catecholamines
indolacetic acid
vanillylmandelic acid [VMA]
Melanuria
AHA: 1Q, '05, 12

✓4th 792 Nonspecific abnormal findings in other body substances

EXCLUDES that in chromosomal analysis (795.2)

792.0 Cerebrospinal fluid

792.1 Stool contents
Abnormal stool color   Occult stool
Fat in stool   Pus in stool
Mucus in stool
EXCLUDES blood in stool [melena] (578.1)
newborn (772.4, 777.3)
AHA: 2Q, '92, 9

792.2 Semen   ♂
Abnormal spermatozoa
EXCLUDES azoospermia (606.0)
oligospermia (606.1)

792.3 Amniotic fluid   M ♀
DEF: Nonspecific abnormal findings in amniotic fluid.
AHA: N-D, '86, 4

792.4 Saliva
EXCLUDES that in chromosomal analysis (795.2)

792.5 Cloudy (hemodialysis) (peritoneal) dialysis effluent
AHA: 4Q, '00, 46

792.9 Other nonspecific abnormal findings in body substances
Peritoneal fluid   Synovial fluid
Pleural fluid   Vaginal fluids

▲ ✓4th 793 Nonspecific (abnormal) findings on radiological and other examination of body structure

INCLUDES nonspecific abnormal findings of:
thermography
ultrasound examination [echogram]
x-ray examination
EXCLUDES abnormal results of function studies and radioisotope
scans (794.0-794.9)

793.0 Skull and head
EXCLUDES nonspecific abnormal echoencephalogram
(794.01)
AHA: 3Q, '06, 22

793.1 Lung field
Coin lesion ⎫
Shadow ⎬ (of) lung
DEF: Coin lesion of lung: coin-shaped, solitary pulmonary
nodule.

793.2 Other intrathoracic organ
Abnormal:
echocardiogram
heart shadow
ultrasound cardiogram
Mediastinal shift

793.3 Biliary tract
Nonvisualization of gallbladder

793.4 Gastrointestinal tract

793.5 Genitourinary organs
Filling defect:
bladder
kidney
ureter

793.6 Abdominal area, including retroperitoneum

793.7 Musculoskeletal system

✓5th 793.8 Breast
AHA: 4Q, '01, 51

793.80 Abnormal mammogram, unspecified

793.81 Mammographic microcalcification
EXCLUDES mammographic calcification
(793.89)
mammographic calculus (793.89)
DEF: Calcium and cellular debris deposits in the
breast that cannot be felt but can be detected on a
mammogram; can be a sign of cancer, benign
conditions, or changes in the breast tissue as a
result of inflammation, injury, or obstructed duct.

● 793.82 Inconclusive mammogram
Dense breasts NOS
Inconclusive mammogram NEC
Inconclusive mammography due to dense
breasts
Inconclusive mammography NEC

[handwritten margin note: Nothing found on mammogram but issues such as dense breasts require further testing to confirm that no malignant condition exists.]

▲ 793.89 Other (abnormal) findings on radiological examination of breast
Mammographic calcification
Mammographic calculus

Symptoms, Signs, and Ill-Defined Conditions

793.9–795.08

√5ᵗʰ **793.9 Other**

> EXCLUDES   *abnormal finding by radioisotope localization of placenta (794.9)*

> **TIP:** Sequence a code for the sign or symptom that was the reason for the imaging or radiological test first.

793.91 Image test inconclusive due to excess body fat

> Use additional code to identify Body Mass Index (BMI), if known (V85.0-V85.54)
>
> AHA: 4Q, '06, 109

▲   **793.99 Other nonspecific (abnormal) findings on radiological and other examinations of body structure**

> Abnormal:
>   placental finding by x-ray or ultrasound method
>   radiological findings in skin and subcutaneous tissue
>
> AHA: 4Q, '06, 109

√4ᵗʰ **794 Nonspecific abnormal results of function studies**

> INCLUDES   radioisotope:
>   scans
>   uptake studies
>   scintiphotography

√5ᵗʰ **794.0 Brain and central nervous system**

794.00 Abnormal function study, unspecified

794.01 Abnormal echoencephalogram

794.02 Abnormal electroencephalogram [EEG]

794.09 Other

> Abnormal brain scan

√5ᵗʰ **794.1 Peripheral nervous system and special senses**

794.10 Abnormal response to nerve stimulation, unspecified

794.11 Abnormal retinal function studies

> Abnormal electroretinogram [ERG]

794.12 Abnormal electro-oculogram [EOG]

794.13 Abnormal visually evoked potential

794.14 Abnormal oculomotor studies

794.15 Abnormal auditory function studies

> AHA: 1Q, '04, 15-16
>
> **TIP:** If the reason for the encounter was for a hearing examination, sequence a code from subcategory V72.1 first. When nonspecific hearing loss is documented, assign 389.9 instead of 794.15.

794.16 Abnormal vestibular function studies

794.17 Abnormal electromyogram [EMG]

> EXCLUDES   *that of eye (794.14)*

794.19 Other

794.2 Pulmonary

> Abnormal lung scan
> Reduced:
>   ventilatory capacity
>   vital capacity

√5ᵗʰ **794.3 Cardiovascular**

794.30 Abnormal function study, unspecified

794.31 Abnormal electrocardiogram [ECG] [EKG]

> EXCLUDES   *long QT syndrome (426.82)*
>
> **R94.31** Abnormal electrocardiogram [ECG] [EKG]   I-10

794.39 Other

> Abnormal:
>   ballistocardiogram
>   phonocardiogram
>   vectorcardiogram
>
> **R94.39** Abnormal result oth cardiovasculr function study   I-10

794.4 Kidney

> Abnormal renal function test

794.5 Thyroid

> Abnormal thyroid:
>   scan
>   uptake

794.6 Other endocrine function study

794.7 Basal metabolism

> Abnormal basal metabolic rate [BMR]

794.8 Liver

> Abnormal liver scan
>
> **R94.5** Abnormal results of liver function studies   I-10

794.9 Other

> Bladder
> Pancreas
> Placenta
> Spleen

√4ᵗʰ **795 Other and nonspecific abnormal cytological, histological, immunological and DNA test findings**

> EXCLUDES   *abnormal cytologic smear of anus and anal HPV (796.70-796.79)*
>   *nonspecific abnormalities of red blood cells (790.01-790.09)*

√5ᵗʰ **795.0 Abnormal Papanicolaou smear of cervix and cervical HPV**

> Abnormal thin preparation smear of cervix
> Abnormal cervical cytology
>
> EXCLUDES   *abnormal cytologic smear of vagina and vaginal I IPV (795.10-795.19)*
>   *carcinoma ▶in situ◀ of cervix (233.1)*
>   *cervical intraepithelial neoplasia I (CIN I) (622.11)*
>   *cervical intraepithelial neoplasia II (CIN II) (622.12)*
>   *cervical intraepithelial neoplasia III (CIN III) (233.1)*
>   *dysplasia (histologically confirmed) of cervix (uteri) NOS (622.10)*
>   *mild cervical dysplasia (histologically confirmed) (622.11)*
>   *moderate cervical dysplasia (histologically confirmed) (622.12)*
>   *severe cervical dysplasia (histologically confirmed) (233.1)*
>
> AHA: 4Q, '08, 145-146; 4Q, '02, 69

795.00 Abnormal glandular Papanicolaou smear of cervix   ♀

> Atypical endocervical cells NOS
> Atypical endometrial cells NOS
> Atypical cervical glandular cells NOS

795.01 Papanicolaou smear of cervix with atypical squamous cells of undetermined significance [ASC-US]   ♀

> AHA: 2Q, '06, 4

795.02 Papanicolaou smear of cervix with atypical squamous cells cannot exclude high grade squamous intraepithelial lesion [ASC-H]   ♀

795.03 Papanicolaou smear of cervix with low grade squamous intraepithelial lesion [LGSIL]   ♀

795.04 Papanicolaou smear of cervix with high grade squamous intraepithelial lesion [HGSIL]   ♀

795.05 Cervical high risk human papillomavirus [HPV] DNA test positive   ♀

795.06 Papanicolaou smear of cervix with cytologic evidence of malignancy   ♀

> AHA: 4Q, '06, 110

795.07 Satisfactory cervical smear but lacking transformation zone   ♀

795.08 Unsatisfactory cervical cytology smear   ♀

> Inadequate cervical cytology sample
>
> AHA: 2Q, '06, 4

Ⓝ Newborn Age: 0   Ⓟ Pediatric Age: 0-17   Ⓜ Maternity Age: 12-55   Ⓐ Adult Age: 15-124   MCC Major CC Condition   CC CC Condition   HIV HIV Related Dx

795.09 Other abnormal Papanicolaou smear of cervix and cervical HPV ♀
Cervical low risk human papillomavirus (HPV) DNA test positive
Use additional code for associated human papillomavirus (079.4)

> EXCLUDES *encounter for Papanicolaou cervical smear to confirm findings of recent normal smear following initial abnormal smear (V72.32)*

√5th **795.1 Abnormal Papanicolaou smear of vagina and vaginal HPV**
Abnormal thin preparation smear of vagina NOS
Abnormal vaginal cytology NOS
Use additional code to identify acquired absence of uterus and cervix, if applicable (V88.01-V88.03)

> EXCLUDES *abnormal cytologic smear of cervix and cervical HPV (795.00-795.09)*
> *carcinoma in situ of vagina (233.31)*
> *carcinoma in situ of vulva (233.32)*
> *dysplasia (histologically confirmed) of vagina NOS (623.0, 233.31)*
> *dysplasia (histologically confirmed) of vulva NOS (624.01, 624.02, 233.32)*
> *mild vaginal dysplasia (histologically confirmed) (623.0)*
> *mild vulvar dysplasia (histologically confirmed) (624.01)*
> *moderate vaginal dysplasia (histologically confirmed) (623.0)*
> *moderate vulvar dysplasia (histologically confirmed) (624.02)*
> *severe vaginal dysplasia (histologically confirmed) (233.31)*
> *severe vulvar dysplasia (histologically confirmed) (233.32)*
> *vaginal intraepithelial neoplasia I (VAIN I) (623.0)*
> *vaginal intraepithelial neoplasia II (VAIN II) (623.0)*
> *vaginal intraepithelial neoplasia III (VAIN III) (233.31)*
> *vulvar intraepithelial neoplasia I (VIN I) (624.01)*
> *vulvar intraepithelial neoplasia II (VIN II) (624.02)*
> *vulvar intraepithelial neoplasia III (VIN III) (233.32)*

AHA: 4Q, '08, 145-148

795.10 Abnormal glandular Papanicolaou smear of vagina ♀
Atypical vaginal glandular cells NOS

795.11 Papanicolaou smear of vagina with atypical squamous cells of undetermined significance [ASC-US] ♀

795.12 Papanicolaou smear of vagina with atypical squamous cells cannot exclude high grade squamous intraepithelial lesion [ASC-H] ♀

795.13 Papanicolaou smear of vagina with low grade squamous intraepithelial lesion [LGSIL] ♀

795.14 Papanicolaou smear of vagina with high grade squamous intraepithelial lesion [HGSIL] ♀

795.15 Vaginal high risk human papillomavirus [HPV] DNA test positive ♀

> EXCLUDES *condyloma acuminatum (078.11)*
> *genital warts (078.11)*

795.16 Papanicolaou smear of vagina with cytologic evidence of malignancy ♀

795.18 Unsatisfactory vaginal cytology smear ♀
Inadequate vaginal cytology sample

795.19 Other abnormal Papanicolaou smear of vagina and vaginal HPV ♀
Vaginal low risk human papillomavirus (HPV) DNA test positive
Use additional code for associated human papillomavirus (079.4)

795.2 Nonspecific abnormal findings on chromosomal analysis
Abnormal karyotype

√5th **795.3 Nonspecific positive culture findings**
Positive culture findings in:
nose
throat
sputum
wound

> EXCLUDES *that of:*
> *blood (790.7-790.8)*
> *urine (791.9)*

795.31 Nonspecific positive findings for anthrax
Positive findings by nasal swab
AHA: 4Q, '02, 70
TIP: If the patient has been exposed only to anthrax, assign instead V01.81. If a patient has not been exposed but fears anthrax and tests negative, assign instead V71.82.

795.39 Other nonspecific positive culture findings
> EXCLUDES ▶*colonization status (V02.0-V02.9)*◀

795.4 Other nonspecific abnormal histological findings

795.5 Nonspecific reaction to tuberculin skin test without active tuberculosis
Abnormal result of Mantoux test
PPD positive
Tuberculin (skin test):
positive
reactor

795.6 False positive serological test for syphilis
False positive Wassermann reaction

√5th **795.7 Other nonspecific immunological findings**
> EXCLUDES *abnormal tumor markers (795.81-795.89)*
> *elevated prostate specific antigen [PSA] (790.93)*
> *elevated tumor associated antigens (795.81-795.89)*
> *isoimmunization, in pregnancy (656.1-656.2)*
> *affecting fetus or newborn (773.0-773.2)*

AHA: 2Q, '93, 6

795.71 Nonspecific serologic evidence of human immunodeficiency virus [HIV]
Inclusive human immunodeficiency [HIV] test (adult) (infant)
Note: This code is **only** to be used when a test finding is reported as nonspecific. Asymptomatic positive findings are coded to V08. If any HIV infection symptom or condition is present, see code 042. Negative findings are not coded.

> EXCLUDES *acquired immunodeficiency syndrome [AIDS] (042)*
> *asymptomatic human immunodeficiency virus, [HIV] infection status (V08)*
> *HIV infection, symptomatic (042)*
> *human immunodeficiency virus [HIV] disease (042)*
> *positive (status) NOS (V08)*

AHA: 2Q, '04, 11; 1Q, '93, 21; 1Q, '93, 22; 2Q, '92, 11; J-A, '87, 24

795.79 Other and unspecified nonspecific immunological findings
Raised antibody titer
Raised level of immunoglobulins

[handwritten annotations: "Inconclusive findings only"; "Asymptomatic positive V08"; "symptomatic or condition is present 042"]

Symptoms, Signs, and Ill-Defined Conditions

795.8–799.02

√5th **795.8 Abnormal tumor markers**
Elevated tumor associated antigens [TAA]
Elevated tumor specific antigens [TSA]
EXCLUDES   elevated prostate specific antigen [PSA] (790.93)

795.81 Elevated carcinoembryonic antigen [CEA]
AHA: 4Q, '06, 111

795.82 Elevated cancer antigen 125 [CA 125]   ♀
AHA: 4Q, '06, 111

795.89 Other abnormal tumor markers
AHA: 4Q, '06, 111

√4th **796 Other nonspecific abnormal findings**

796.0 Nonspecific abnormal toxicological findings
Abnormal levels of heavy metals or drugs in blood, urine, or other tissue
EXCLUDES   excessive blood level of alcohol (790.3)
AHA: 1Q, '97, 16

796.1 Abnormal reflex

796.2 Elevated blood pressure reading without diagnosis of hypertension
Note: This category is to be used to record an episode of elevated blood pressure in a patient in whom no formal diagnosis of hypertension has been made, or as an incidental finding.
AHA: 2Q, '03, 11; 3Q, '90, 4; J-A, '84, 12
TIP: Assign an additional E code for poisoning or adverse effect of a drug if the documentation indicates it's the underlying cause of the elevated blood pressure.
R03.0 Elevated blood-pressure reading without dx HTN   I-10

796.3 Nonspecific low blood pressure reading

796.4 Other abnormal clinical findings
AHA: 1Q, '97, 16

796.5 Abnormal finding on antenatal screening   ♀ M
AHA: 4Q, '97, 46

796.6 Abnormal findings on neonatal screening   N
EXCLUDES   nonspecific serologic evidence of human immunodeficiency virus [HIV] (795.71)
AHA: 4Q, '04, 99

√5th **796.7 Abnormal cytologic smear of anus and anal HPV**
EXCLUDES   abnormal cytologic smear of cervix and cervical HPV (795.00-795.09)
abnormal cytologic smear of vagina and vaginal HPV (795.10-795.19)
anal intraepithelial neoplasia I (AIN I) (569.44)
anal intraepithelial neoplasia II (AIN II) (569.44)
anal intraepithelial neoplasia III (AIN III) (230.5, 230.6)
carcinoma in situ of anus (230.5, 230.6)
dysplasia (histologically confirmed) of anus NOS (569.44)
mild anal dysplasia (histologically confirmed) (569.44)
moderate anal dysplasia (histologically confirmed) (569.44)
severe anal dysplasia (histologically confirmed) ▶(230.5, 230.6)◀
AHA: 4Q, '08, 117-119

796.70 Abnormal glandular Papanicolaou smear of anus
Atypical anal glandular cells NOS

796.71 Papanicolaou smear of anus with atypical squamous cells of undetermined significance [ASC-US]

796.72 Papanicolaou smear of anus with atypical squamous cells cannot exclude high grade squamous intraepithelial lesion [ASC-H]

796.73 Papanicolaou smear of anus with low grade squamous intraepithelial lesion [LGSIL]

796.74 Papanicolaou smear of anus with high grade squamous intraepithelial lesion [HGSIL]

796.75 Anal high risk human papillomavirus [HPV] DNA test positive

796.76 Papanicolaou smear of anus with cytologic evidence of malignancy

796.77 Satisfactory anal smear but lacking transformation zone

796.78 Unsatisfactory anal cytology smear
Inadequate anal cytology sample

796.79 Other abnormal Papanicolaou smear of anus and anal HPV
Anal low risk human papillomavirus (HPV) DNA test positive
Use additional code for associated human papillomavirus (079.4)

796.9 Other

ILL-DEFINED AND UNKNOWN CAUSES OF MORBIDITY AND MORTALITY (797-799)

797 Senility without mention of psychosis
Frailty
Old age
Senescence
Senile asthenia
Senile:
   debility
   exhaustion
EXCLUDES   senile psychoses (290.0-290.9)

√4th **798 Sudden death, cause unknown**

798.0 Sudden infant death syndrome   P
Cot death
Crib death
Sudden death of nonspecific cause in infancy
DEF: Death of infant under age one due to nonspecific cause.

798.1 Instantaneous death

798.2 Death occurring in less than 24 hours from onset of symptoms, not otherwise explained
Death known not to be violent or instantaneous, for which no cause could be discovered
Died without sign of disease

798.9 Unattended death
Death in circumstances where the body of the deceased was found and no cause could be discovered
Found dead

√4th **799 Other ill-defined and unknown causes of morbidity and mortality**

√5th **799.0 Asphyxia and hypoxemia**
EXCLUDES   asphyxia and hypoxemia (due to):
   carbon monoxide (986)
   hypercapnia (786.09)
   inhalation of food or foreign body (932-934.9)
   newborn (768.0-768.9)
   traumatic (994.7)

799.01 Asphyxia   CC
DEF: Lack of oxygen in inspired air, causing a deficiency of oxygen in tissues (hypoxia) and elevated levels of arterial carbon dioxide (hypercapnia).
CC Excl: 338.0-338.4, 518.81-518.84, 780.91-780.99, 798.0, 799.01-799.1, 799.81-799.89
AHA: 4Q, '05, 90

799.02 Hypoxemia
DEF: Deficient oxygenation of the blood.
AHA: 2Q, '06, 24, 25; 4Q, '05, 90
R09.02 Hypoxemia   I-10

N Newborn Age: 0   P Pediatric Age: 0-17   M Maternity Age: 12-55   A Adult Age: 15-124   MCC Major CC Condition   CC CC Condition   HIV HIV Related Dx

310 – Volume 1 · October 2009   2010 ICD-9-CM

[1] **799.1 Respiratory arrest**   `MCC`
Cardiorespiratory failure
   EXCLUDES   *cardiac arrest (427.5)*
           failure of peripheral circulation (785.50)
           respiratory distress:
             NOS (786.09)
             acute (518.82)
             following trauma and surgery (518.5)
             newborn (770.89)
             syndrome (newborn) (769)
               adult (following trauma and surgery)
                 (518.5)
             other (518.82)
           respiratory failure (518.81, 518.83-518.84)
            newborn (770.84)
           respiratory insufficiency (786.09)
            acute (518.82)
   CC Excl: See code: 799.01

▲   ✓5ᵗʰ   **799.2 Signs and symptoms involving emotional state**
   EXCLUDES ▶*anxiety (293.84, 300.00-300.09)*
          depression (311)◀

●   **799.21 Nervousness**
      Nervous

●   **799.22 Irritability**
      Irritable

●   **799.23 Impulsiveness**
      Impulsive
      EXCLUDES   *impulsive neurosis (300.3)*

●   **799.24 Emotional lability**

●   **799.25 Demoralization and apathy**
      Apathetic

●   **799.29 Other signs and symptoms involving emotional state**

   799.3 Debility, unspecified
      EXCLUDES   *asthenia (780.79)*
           nervous debility (300.5)
           neurasthenia (300.5)
           senile asthenia (797)

799.4 Cachexia   `CC`
Wasting disease
Code first underlying condition, if known
DEF: General ill health and poor nutrition.
CC Excl: 338.0-338.4, 780.91-780.99, 799.3-799.89
AHA: 3Q, '06, 14, 15; 3Q, '90, 17
TIP: Assign an additional code for any associated malnutrition, if documented.
R64 Cachexia   `I-10`

✓5ᵗʰ   **799.8 Other ill-defined conditions**

   799.81 Decreased libido   `A`
      Decreased sexual desire
      EXCLUDES   *psychosexual dysfunction with inhibited sexual desire (302.71)*
      AHA: 4Q, '03, 75

●   **799.82 Apparent life threatening event in infant**
      ALTE
      Apparent life threatening event in newborn and infant
      Use additional code(s) for associated signs and symptoms
      EXCLUDES   *signs and symptoms associated with a confirmed diagnosis–code to confirmed diagnosis*

   799.89 Other ill-defined conditions

799.9 Other unknown and unspecified cause
      Undiagnosed disease, not specified as to site or system involved
      Unknown cause of morbidity or mortality
      AHA: 1Q, '98,.4; 1Q, '90, 20

---

[1] MCC = Only if patient discharged alive.

✓4ᵗʰ / ✓5ᵗʰ   Additional Digit Required   Unacceptable PDx   Manifestation Code   Hospital Acquired Condition   ▶◀ Revised Text   ● New Code   ▲ Revised Code Title

2010 ICD-9-CM   **October 2009 • Volume 1 – 311**

Injuries are classified in the following sections:

Fractures   800-829
Dislocations   830-839
Sprains and strains   840-848
Intracranial injuries   850-854
Internal injuries   860-869
Open wounds   870-897
Blood vessel injuries   900-904
Late effects of injuries   905-909
Superficial injuries   910-919
Contusions   920-924
Crushing injuries   925-929
Foreign body entering through orfice   930-939
Burns   940-949
Nerve and spinal cord injuries   950-957
Early complications of trauma   958

If admission is due to injury and several injuries are present, the code for the most severe injury is designated as the principal diagnosis.

Fractures
Skull 800-804
Neck/trunk 805-809
Upper extremity 810-819
Lower extremity 820-829

*Open "fracture... bone is present... aka "compound", "infected" "missle", "puncture" and "with foreign body."
"closed" fracture... no bone is present... aka "comminuted", "elevated", "greenstick", "spiral", "simple"*

17. INJURY AND POISONING (800-999)

Use E code(s) to identify the cause and intent of the injury or poisoning (E800-E999)

Note:

1. The principle of multiple coding of injuries should be followed wherever possible. Combination categories for multiple injuries are provided for use when there is insufficient detail as to the nature of the individual conditions, or for primary tabulation purposes when it is more convenient to record a single code; otherwise, the component injuries should be coded separately.

   Where multiple sites of injury are specified in the titles, the word "with" indicates involvement of both sites, and the word "and" indicates involvement of either or both sites. The word "finger" includes thumb.

2. Categories for "late effect" of injuries are to be found at 905-909.

FRACTURES (800-829)

> **EXCLUDES**   malunion (733.81)
> nonunion (733.82)
> pathological or spontaneous fracture (733.10-733.19)
> stress fractures (733.93-733.95)

a diagnostic statement containing terms that relate to both open and closed fractures... the code for the open fracture always takes precedence.

The terms "condyle," "coronoid process," "ramus," and "symphysis" indicate the portion of the bone fractured, not the name of the bone involved.

The descriptions "closed" and "open" used in the fourth-digit subdivisions include the following terms:

closed (with or without delayed healing):

comminuted	impacted
depressed	linear
elevated	simple
fissured	slipped epiphysis
fracture NOS	spiral
greenstick	

open (with or without delayed healing):

compound	puncture
infected	with foreign body
missile	

Note: A fracture not indicated as closed or open should be classified as closed.

AHA: 4Q, '08, 158;1Q, '07, 3-4; 4Q, '90, 26; 3Q, '90, 5; 3Q, '90, 13; 2Q, '90, 7; 2Q, '89, 15, S-O, '85, 3

TIP: Assign the acute fracture codes only while the patient is receiving active treatment for the fracture, such as during surgical care, an ED encounter, or evaluation and treatment by a new physician. Otherwise, refer to aftercare category V54.

FRACTURE OF SKULL (800-804)

> **INCLUDES** ▶traumatic brain injury due to fracture of skull◀

The following fifth-digit subclassification is for use with the appropriate codes in category 800, 801, 803, and 804:
  0   unspecified state of consciousness
  1   with no loss of consciousness
  2   with brief [less than one hour] loss of consciousness
  3   with moderate [1-24 hours] loss of consciousness
  4   with prolonged [more than 24 hours] loss of consciousness and return to pre-existing conscious level
  5   with prolonged [more than 24 hours] loss of consciousness, without return to pre-existing conscious level
     Use fifth-digit 5 to designate when a patient is unconscious and dies before regaining consciousness, regardless of the duration of the loss of consciousness
  6   with loss of consciousness of unspecified duration
  9   with concussion, unspecified

✓4th   **800   Fracture of vault of skull**

> **INCLUDES**   frontal bone
> parietal bone
> **DEF:** Fracture of bone that forms skull dome and protects brain.
> **AHA:** 4Q,'96, 36

§   ✓5th   **800.0   Closed without mention of**   MCC 3-5
    [0-6, 9]   **intracranial injury**   CC 0-2, 6, 9
      CC Excl: 800.00-801.99, 803.00-804.99, 829.0-829.1, 850.0-852.19, 852.21-854.19, 873.8-873.9, 879.8-879.9, 905.0, 925.1-925.2, 929.0-929.9, 958.8-959.09, 959.8-959.9

Fractures

§   ✓5th   **800.1   Closed with cerebral laceration and contusion**   MCC
    [0-6, 9]   **CC Excl:** See code 800.0

§   ✓5th   **800.2   Closed with subarachnoid, subdural, and**   MCC
    [0-6, 9]   **extradural hemorrhage**
      CC Excl: See code 800.0

§   ✓5th   **800.3   Closed with other and unspecified**   MCC
    [0-6, 9]   **intracranial hemorrhage**
      CC Excl: See code 800.0

§   ✓5th   **800.4   Closed with intracranial injury of**   MCC 3-5
    [0-6, 9]   **other and unspecified nature**   CC 0-2, 6, 9
      CC Excl: See code 800.0

§   ✓5th   **800.5   Open without mention of intracranial injury**   MCC
    [0-6, 9]   **CC Excl:** See code 800.0

§   ✓5th   **800.6   Open with cerebral laceration and contusion**   MCC
    [0-6, 9]   **CC Excl:** See code 800.0

§   ✓5th   **800.7   Open with subarachnoid, subdural, and**   MCC
    [0-6, 9]   **extradural hemorrhage**
      CC Excl: See code 800.0

§   ✓5th   **800.8   Open with other and unspecified**   MCC
    [0-6, 9]   **intracranial hemorrhage**
      CC Excl: See code 800.0

§   ✓5th   **800.9   Open with intracranial injury of other and**   MCC
    [0-6, 9]   **unspecified nature**
      CC Excl: See code 800.0

✓4th   **801   Fracture of base of skull**

> **INCLUDES**   fossa:
>   anterior
>   middle
>   posterior
> occiput bone
> orbital roof
> sinus:
>   ethmoid
>   frontal
> sphenoid bone
> temporal bone
> **DEF:** Fracture of bone that forms skull floor.
> **AHA:** 4Q, '96, 36

§   ✓5th   **801.0   Closed without mention of intracranial**   MCC 3-5
    [0-6, 9]   **injury**   CC 0-2, 6, 9
      CC Excl: 800.00-801.99, 803.00-804.99, 829.0-829.1, 850.0-852.19, 852.21-854.19, 873.8-873.9, 879.8-879.9, 905.0, 925.1-925.2, 929.0-929.9, 958.8-959.09, 959.8-959.9

§   ✓5th   **801.1   Closed with cerebral laceration and contusion**   MCC
    [0-6, 9]   **CC Excl:** See code: 801.0
      AHA: 4Q, '96, 36

§   ✓5th   **801.2   Closed with subarachnoid, subdural, and**   MCC
    [0-6, 9]   **extradural hemorrhage**
      CC Excl: See code: 801.0

§   ✓5th   **801.3   Closed with other and unspecified intracranial**   MCC
    [0-6, 9]   **hemorrhage**
      CC Excl: See code: 801.0

---

§   Requires fifth digit. Valid digits are in [brackets] under each code. See beginning of section 800-804 for codes and definitions.

✓4th ✓5th   Additional Digit Required   Unacceptable PDx   Manifestation Code   Hospital Acquired Condition   ▶◀ Revised Text   ● New Code   ▲ Revised Code Title

2010 ICD-9-CM   **October 2009 • Volume 1 – 313**

Injury and Poisoning

801.4–802.9

Skull

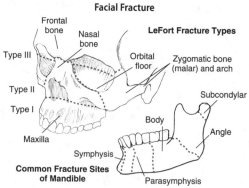

Facial Fracture

§ ☑5th **801.4** **Closed with intracranial injury of other**   `MCC 3-5`
[0-6, 9] **and unspecified nature**   `CC 0-2, 6, 9`
     CC Excl: See code 801.0

§ ☑5th **801.5** **Open without mention of intracranial injury**   `MCC`
[0-6, 9]   CC Excl: See code: 801.0

§ ☑5th **801.6** **Open with cerebral laceration and contusion**   `MCC`
[0-6, 9]   CC Excl: See code: 801.0

§ ☑5th **801.7** **Open with subarachnoid, subdural, and**   `MCC`
[0-6, 9] **extradural hemorrhage**
     CC Excl: See code: 801.0

§ ☑5th **801.8** **Open with other and unspecified intracranial**   `MCC`
[0-6, 9] **hemorrhage**
     CC Excl: See code: 801.0

§ ☑5th **801.9** **Open with intracranial injury of other and**   `MCC`
[0-6, 9] **unspecified nature**
     CC Excl: See code: 801.0

☑4th **802** **Fracture of face bones**
     AHA: 4Q, '96, 36

802.0 **Nasal bones, closed**
     S02.2xxA Fracture nasal bones initial encounter closed fx   `I-10`

802.1 **Nasal bones, open**   `CC`
     CC Excl: 800.00–802.1, 803.00–804.99, 829.0–829.1,
     850.0–852.19, 852.21–854.19, 873.8–873.9, 879.8–879.9, 905.0,
     925.1–925.2, 929.0–929.9, 958.8–959.09, 959.8–959.9

☑5th **802.2** **Mandible, closed**
     Inferior maxilla
     Lower jaw (bone)

     802.20 **Unspecified site**   `CC`
         CC Excl: 800.00–801.99, 802.20–802.5, 803.00–804.99,
         829.0–830.1, 850.0–852.19, 852.21–854.19,
         873.8–873.9, 879.8–879.9, 905.0, 925.1–925.2,
         929.0–929.9, 958.8–959.09, 959.8–959.9

     802.21 **Condylar process**   `CC`
         CC Excl: See code 802.20

     802.22 **Subcondylar**   `CC`
         CC Excl: See code 802.20

     802.23 **Coronoid process**   `CC`
         CC Excl: See code 802.20

     802.24 **Ramus, unspecified**   `CC`
         CC Excl: See code 802.20

     802.25 **Angle of jaw**   `CC`
         CC Excl: See code 802.20

     802.26 **Symphysis of body**   `CC`
         CC Excl: See code 802.20

     802.27 **Alveolar border of body**   `CC`
         CC Excl: See code 802.20

     802.28 **Body, other and unspecified**   `CC`
         CC Excl: See code 802.20

     802.29 **Multiple sites**   `CC`
         CC Excl: See code 802.20

☑5th **802.3** **Mandible, open**

     802.30 **Unspecified site**   `CC`
         CC Excl: See code 802.20

     802.31 **Condylar process**   `CC`
         CC Excl: See code 802.20

     802.32 **Subcondylar**   `CC`
         CC Excl: See code 802.20

     802.33 **Coronoid process**   `CC`
         CC Excl: See code 802.20

     802.34 **Ramus, unspecified**   `CC`
         CC Excl: See code 802.20

     802.35 **Angle of jaw**   `CC`
         CC Excl: See code 802.20

     802.36 **Symphysis of body**   `CC`
         CC Excl: See code 802.20

     802.37 **Alveolar border of body**   `CC`
         CC Excl: See code 802.20

     802.38 **Body, other and unspecified**   `CC`
         CC Excl: See code 802.20

     802.39 **Multiple sites**   `CC`
         CC Excl: See code 802.20

802.4 **Malar and maxillary bones, closed**   `CC`
     Superior maxilla
     Upper jaw (bone)
     Zygoma
     Zygomatic arch
     CC Excl: See code 802.20
     S02.40xA Fx malar max & zygoma uns initial enc closed fx   `I-10`

802.5 **Malar and maxillary bones, open**   `CC`
     CC Excl: See code 802.20

802.6 **Orbital floor (blow-out), closed**   `CC`
     CC Excl: 800.00–801.99, 802.6–804.99, 829.0–829.1,
     850.0–852.19, 852.21–854.19, 873.8–873.9, 879.8–879.9, 905.0,
     925.1–925.2, 929.0–929.9, 958.8–959.09, 959.8–959.9
     S02.3xxA Fracture orbital floor initial encounter clos fx   `I-10`

802.7 **Orbital floor (blow-out), open**   `CC`
     CC Excl: See code 802.6

802.8 **Other facial bones, closed**   `CC`
     Alveolus
     Orbit:
       NOS
       part other than roof or floor
     Palate
     EXCLUDES *orbital:*
               floor (802.6)
               roof (801.0-801.9)
     CC Excl: See code 802.6
     S02.89xA Fx oth skull & face bones initial enc closed fx   `I-10`

802.9 **Other facial bones, open**   `CC`
     CC Excl: See code 802.6

---

§   Requires fifth digit. Valid digits are in [brackets] under each code. See beginning of section 800-804 for codes and definitions.

`N` Newborn Age: 0   `P` Pediatric Age: 0-17   `M` Maternity Age: 12-55   `A` Adult Age: 15-124   `MCC` Major CC Condition   `CC` CC Condition   `HIV` HIV Related Dx

✓4ᵗʰ **803　Other and unqualified skull fractures**

> INCLUDES　skull NOS
> 　　　　　　skull multiple NOS
>
> AHA: 4Q, '96, 36

§ ✓5ᵗʰ **803.0　Closed without mention of**　`MCC 3-5` `CC 0-2, 6, 9`
　[0-6, 9]　**intracranial injury**

> **CC Excl:** 800.00-801.99, 803.00-804.99, 829.0-829.1,
> 850.0-852.19, 852.21-854.19, 873.8-873.9, 879.8-879.9, 905.0,
> 925.1-925.2, 929.0-929.9, 958.8-959.09, 959.8-959.9

§ ✓5ᵗʰ **803.1　Closed with cerebral laceration and contusion**　`MCC`
　[0-6, 9]　**CC Excl:** See code 803.0

§ ✓5ᵗʰ **803.2　Closed with subarachnoid, subdural, and**　`MCC`
　[0-6, 9]　**extradural hemorrhage**

> **CC Excl:** See code 803.0

§ ✓5ᵗʰ **803.3　Closed with other and unspecified**　`MCC`
　[0-6, 9]　**intracranial hemorrhage**

> **CC Excl:** See code 803.0

§ ✓5ᵗʰ **803.4　Closed with intracranial injury of**　`MCC 3-5` `CC 0-2, 6, 9`
　[0-6, 9]　**other and unspecified nature**

> **CC Excl:** See code 803.0

§ ✓5ᵗʰ **803.5　Open without mention of intracranial injury**　`MCC`
　[0-6, 9]　**CC Excl:** See code 803.0

§ ✓5ᵗʰ **803.6　Open with cerebral laceration and contusion**　`MCC`
　[0-6, 9]　**CC Excl:** See code 803.0

§ ✓5ᵗʰ **803.7　Open with subarachnoid, subdural, and**　`MCC`
　[0-6, 9]　**extradural hemorrhage**

> **CC Excl:** See code 803.0

§ ✓5ᵗʰ **803.8　Open with other and unspecified**　`MCC`
　[0-6, 9]　**intracranial hemorrhage**

> **CC Excl:** See code 803.0

§ ✓5ᵗʰ **803.9　Open with intracranial injury of other and**　`MCC`
　[0-6, 9]　**unspecified nature**

> **CC Excl:** See code 803.0

✓4ᵗʰ **804　Multiple fractures involving skull or face with other bones**

> AHA: 4Q, '96, 36

§ ✓5ᵗʰ **804.0　Closed without mention of**　`MCC 3-5` `CC 0-2, 6, 9`
　[0-6, 9]　**intracranial injury**

> **CC Excl:** 800.00-801.99, 803.00-804.99, 829.0-829.1,
> 850.0-852.19, 852.21-854.19, 873.8-873.9, 879.8-879.9, 905.0,
> 925.1-925.2, 929.0-929.9, 958.8-959.09, 959.8-959.9

§ ✓5ᵗʰ **804.1　Closed with cerebral laceration and contusion**　`MCC`
　[0-6, 9]　**CC Excl:** See code: 804.0
> AHA: For code 804.10: 1Q, '06, 6

§ ✓5ᵗʰ **804.2　Closed with subarachnoid, subdural, and**　`MCC`
　[0-6, 9]　**extradural hemorrhage**

> **CC Excl:** See code 804.0

§ ✓5ᵗʰ **804.3　Closed with other and unspecified**　`MCC`
　[0-6, 9]　**intracranial hemorrhage**

> **CC Excl:** See code 804.0

§ ✓5ᵗʰ **804.4　Closed with intracranial injury of**　`MCC 3-5` `CC 0-2, 6, 9`
　[0-6, 9]　**other and unspecified nature**

> **CC Excl:** See code 804.0

§ ✓5ᵗʰ **804.5　Open without mention of**　`MCC 3-5` `CC 0-2, 6, 9`
　[0-6, 9]　**intracranial injury**

> **CC Excl:** See code 804.0

§ ✓5ᵗʰ **804.6　Open with cerebral laceration and contusion**　`MCC`
　[0-6, 9]　**CC Excl:** See code 804.0

§ ✓5ᵗʰ **804.7　Open with subarachnoid, subdural, and**　`MCC`
　[0-6, 9]　**extradural hemorrage**

> **CC Excl:** See code 804.0

§ ✓5ᵗʰ **804.8　Open with other and unspecified**　`MCC`
　[0-6, 9]　**intracranial hemorrhage**

> **CC Excl:** See code 804.0

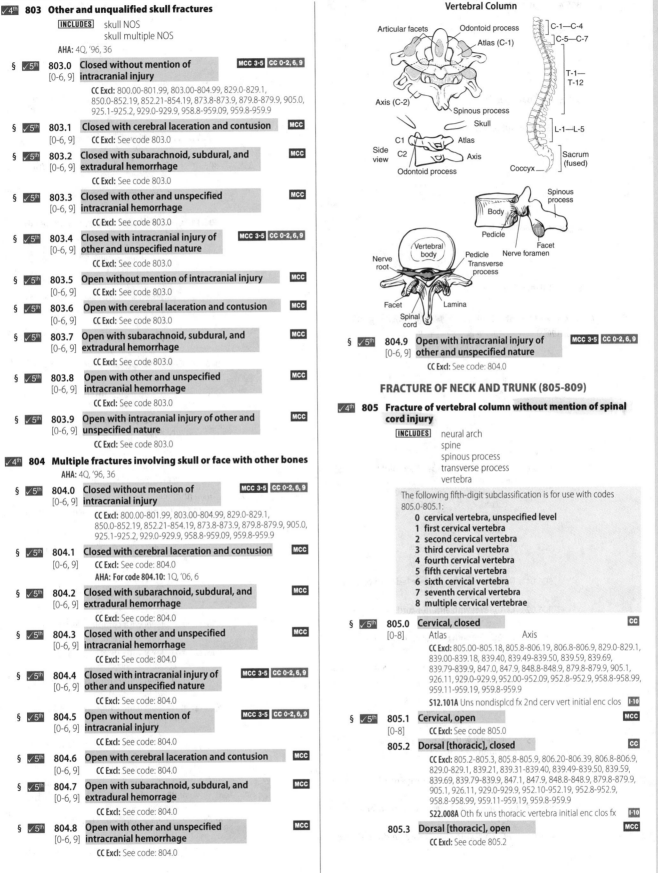

Vertebral Column

§ ✓5ᵗʰ **804.9　Open with intracranial injury of**　`MCC 3-5` `CC 0-2, 6, 9`
　[0-6, 9]　**other and unspecified nature**

> **CC Excl:** See code: 804.0

FRACTURE OF NECK AND TRUNK (805-809)

✓4ᵗʰ **805　Fracture of vertebral column without mention of spinal cord injury**

> INCLUDES　neural arch
> 　　　　　　spine
> 　　　　　　spinous process
> 　　　　　　transverse process
> 　　　　　　vertebra

> The following fifth-digit subclassification is for use with codes 805.0-805.1:
>
> 　0　cervical vertebra, unspecified level
> 　1　first cervical vertebra
> 　2　second cervical vertebra
> 　3　third cervical vertebra
> 　4　fourth cervical vertebra
> 　5　fifth cervical vertebra
> 　6　sixth cervical vertebra
> 　7　seventh cervical vertebra
> 　8　multiple cervical vertebrae

§ ✓5ᵗʰ **805.0　Cervical, closed**　`CC`
　[0-8]　　Atlas　　　　　　　　Axis

> **CC Excl:** 805.00-805.18, 805.8-806.19, 806.8-806.9, 829.0-829.1,
> 839.00-839.18, 805.8-806.19, 839.31-839.40, 839.49-839.50, 839.59, 839.69,
> 839.79-839.9, 847.0, 847.9, 848.8-848.9, 879.8-879.9, 905.1,
> 926.11, 929.0-929.9, 952.00-952.09, 952.8-952.9, 958.8-958.99,
> 959.11-959.19, 959.8-959.9
>
> **S12.101A** Uns nondisplcd fx 2nd cerv vert initial enc clos　`I-10`

§ ✓5ᵗʰ **805.1　Cervical, open**　`MCC`
　[0-8]　　**CC Excl:** See code 805.0

805.2　Dorsal [thoracic], closed　`CC`

> **CC Excl:** 805.2-805.3, 805.8-805.9, 806.20-806.39, 806.8-806.9,
> 829.0-829.1, 839.21, 839.31-839.40, 839.49-839.50, 839.59,
> 839.69, 839.79-839.9, 847.1, 847.9, 848.8-848.9, 879.8-879.9,
> 905.1, 926.11, 929.0-929.9, 952.10-952.19, 952.8-952.9,
> 958.8-958.99, 959.11-959.19, 959.8-959.9
>
> **S22.008A** Oth fx uns thoracic vertebra initial enc clos fx　`I-10`

805.3　Dorsal [thoracic], open　`MCC`

> **CC Excl:** See code 805.2

---

§　Requires fifth digit. Valid digits are in [brackets] under each code. See appropriate category for codes and definitions.

`✓4ᵗʰ`/`✓5ᵗʰ` **Additional Digit Required**　　**Unacceptable PDx**　　**Manifestation Code**　　**Hospital Acquired Condition**　　►◄ Revised Text　　● New Code　　▲ Revised Code Title

2010 ICD-9-CM　　　　　　　　　　　　　　　　　　　　　　　　　　　　　　　**Volume 1 – 315**

Injury and Poisoning

805.4–806.27

805.4 Lumbar, closed `CC`

CC Excl: 805.4-805.5, 805.8-805.9, 806.4-806.5, 806.8-806.9, 829.0-829.1, 839.20, 839.30, 839.40, 839.49-839.50, 839.59, 839.69, 839.79-839.9, 847.2, 847.9, 848.8-848.9, 879.8-879.9, 905.1, 926.11, 929.0-929.9, 952.2, 952.8-952.9, 958.8-958.99, 959.11-959.19, 959.8-959.9

AHA: 1Q, '07, 7; 4Q, '99, 12

S32.008A Oth fx uns lumbar vertebra initial enc closed fx `I-10`

805.5 Lumbar, open `MCC`

CC Excl: See code 805.4

805.6 Sacrum and coccyx, closed `CC`

CC Excl: 805.6-805.9, 806.60-806.9, 829.0-829.1, 839.40-839.59, 839.69, 839.79-839.9, 846.0-846.9, 847.3-847.9, 848.5-848.9, 879.8-879.9, 905.1, 926.11, 929.0-929.9, 952.3-952.9, 958.8-958.99, 959.11-959.19, 959.8-959.9

S32.19xA Other fx of sacrum initial encounter closed fx `I-10`

805.7 Sacrum and coccyx, open `MCC`

CC Excl: See code 805.6

805.8 Unspecified, closed `CC`

CC Excl: 733.10-733.19, 733.93-733.95, 805.00-806.9, 829.0-829.1, 839.00-839.59, 839.69, 839.79-839.9, 846.0-847.9, 848.5-848.9, 879.8-879.9, 905.1, 926.11, 929.0-929.9, 952.00-952.9, 958.8-958.99, 959.11-959.19, 959.8-959.9

805.9 Unspecified, open `MCC`

CC Excl: See code 805.8

√4th **806 Fracture of vertebral column with spinal cord injury**

INCLUDES   any condition classifiable to 805 with:
      complete or incomplete transverse lesion (of cord)
      hematomyelia
      injury to:
           cauda equina
           nerve
      paralysis
      paraplegia
      quadriplegia
      spinal concussion

√5th **806.0 Cervical, closed**

806.00 C_1-C_4 level with unspecified spinal cord injury `MCC`

Cervical region NOS with spinal cord injury NOS

CC Excl: 733.10-733.19, 733.93-733.95, 805.00-805.18, 805.8-806.19, 806.8-806.9, 829.0-829.1, 839.00-839.18, 839.40, 839.49-839.50, 839.59, 839.69, 839.79-839.9, 847.9, 848.8-848.9, 879.8-879.9, 905.1, 926.11, 929.0-929.9, 952.00-952.09, 952.8-952.9, 958.8-958.99, 959.11-959.19, 959.8-959.9

806.01 C_1-C_4 level with complete lesion of cord `MCC`
CC Excl: See code 806.00

806.02 C_1-C_4 level with anterior cord syndrome `MCC`
CC Excl: See code 806.00

806.03 C_1-C_4 level with central cord syndrome `MCC`
CC Excl: See code 806.00

806.04 C_1-C_4 level with other specified spinal cord injury `MCC`
C_1-C_4 level with:
     incomplete spinal cord lesion NOS
     posterior cord syndrome
CC Excl: See code 806.00

806.05 C_5-C_7 level with unspecified spinal cord injury `MCC`
CC Excl: See code 806.00

806.06 C_5-C_7 level with complete lesion of cord `MCC`
CC Excl: See code 806.00

806.07 C_5-C_7 level with anterior cord syndrome `MCC`
CC Excl: See code 806.00

806.08 C_5-C_7 level with central cord syndrome `MCC`
CC Excl: See code 806.00

806.09 C_5-C_7 level with other specified spinal cord injury `MCC`
C_5-C_7 level with:
     incomplete spinal cord lesion NOS
     posterior cord syndrome
CC Excl: See code 806.00

√5th **806.1 Cervical, open**

806.10 C_1-C_4 level with unspecified spinal cord injury `MCC`
CC Excl: See code 806.00

806.11 C_1-C_4 level with complete lesion of cord `MCC`
CC Excl: See code 806.00

806.12 C_1-C_4 level with anterior cord syndrome `MCC`
CC Excl: See code 806.00

806.13 C_1-C_4 level with central cord syndrome `MCC`
CC Excl: See code 806.00

806.14 C_1-C_4 level with other specified spinal cord injury `MCC`
C_1-C_4 level with:
     incomplete spinal cord lesion NOS
     posterior cord syndrome
CC Excl: See code 806.00

806.15 C_5-C_7 level with unspecified spinal cord injury `MCC`
CC Excl: See code 806.00

806.16 C_5-C_7 level with complete lesion of cord `MCC`
CC Excl: See code 806.00

806.17 C_5-C_7 level with anterior cord syndrome `MCC`
CC Excl: See code 806.00

806.18 C_5-C_7 level with central cord syndrome `MCC`
CC Excl: See code 806.00

806.19 C_5-C_7 level with other specified spinal cord injury `MCC`
C_5-C_7 level with:
     incomplete spinal cord lesion NOS
     posterior cord syndrome
CC Excl: See code 806.00

√5th **806.2 Dorsal [thoracic], closed**

806.20 T_1-T_6 level with unspecified spinal cord injury `MCC`
Thoracic region NOS with spinal cord injury NOS

CC Excl: 733.10-733.19, 733.93-733.95, 805.2-805.3, 805.8-805.9, 806.20-806.39, 806.8-806.9, 829.0-829.1, 839.21, 839.31-839.40, 839.49-839.50, 839.59, 839.69, 839.79-839.9, 847.1, 847.9, 848.8-848.9, 879.8-879.9, 905.1, 926.11, 929.0-929.9, 952.10-952.19, 952.8-952.9, 958.8-958.99, 959.11-959.19, 959.8-959.9

806.21 T_1-T_6 level with complete lesion of cord `MCC`
CC Excl: See code 806.20

806.22 T_1-T_6 level with anterior cord syndrome `MCC`
CC Excl: See code 806.20

806.23 T_1-T_6 level with central cord syndrome `MCC`
CC Excl: See code 806.20

806.24 T_1-T_6 level with other specified spinal cord injury `MCC`
T_1-T_6 level with:
     incomplete spinal cord lesion NOS
     posterior cord syndrome
CC Excl: See code 806.20

806.25 T_7-T_{12} level with unspecified spinal cord injury `MCC`
CC Excl: See code 806.20

806.26 T_7-T_{12} level with complete lesion of cord `MCC`
CC Excl: See code 806.20

806.27 T_7-T_{12} level with anterior cord syndrome `MCC`
CC Excl: See code 806.20

`N` Newborn Age: 0   `P` Pediatric Age: 0-17   `M` Maternity Age: 12-55   `A` Adult Age: 15-124   `MCC` Major CC Condition   `CC` CC Condition   `HIV` HIV Related Dx

316 – Volume 1   2010 ICD-9-CM

806.28 T$_7$-T$_{12}$ level with central cord syndrome `MCC`
CC Excl: See code 806.20

806.29 T$_7$-T$_{12}$ level with other specified spinal cord injury `MCC`
T$_7$-T$_{12}$ level with:
incomplete spinal cord lesion NOS
posterior cord syndrome
CC Excl: See code 806.20

√5th **806.3** Dorsal [thoracic], open

806.30 T$_1$-T$_6$ level with unspecified spinal cord injury `MCC`
CC Excl: See code 806.20

806.31 T$_1$-T$_6$ level with complete lesion of cord `MCC`
CC Excl: See code 806.20

806.32 T$_1$-T$_6$ level with anterior cord syndrome `MCC`
CC Excl: See code 806.20

806.33 T$_1$-T$_6$ level with central cord syndrome `MCC`
CC Excl: See code 806.20

806.34 T$_1$-T$_6$ level with other specified spinal cord injury `MCC`
T$_1$-T$_6$ level with:
incomplete spinal cord lesion NOS
posterior cord syndrome
CC Excl: See code 806.20

806.35 T$_7$-T$_{12}$ level with unspecified spinal cord injury `MCC`
CC Excl: See code 806.20

806.36 T$_7$-T$_{12}$ level with complete lesion of cord `MCC`
CC Excl: See code 806.20

806.37 T$_7$-T$_{12}$ level with anterior cord syndrome `MCC`
CC Excl: See code 806.20

806.38 T$_7$-T$_{12}$ level with central cord syndrome `MCC`
CC Excl: See code 806.20

806.39 T$_7$-T$_{12}$ level with other specified spinal cord injury `MCC`
T$_7$-T$_{12}$ level with:
incomplete spinal cord lesion NOS
posterior cord syndrome
CC Excl: See code 806.20

806.4 Lumbar, closed `MCC`
CC Excl: 733.10-733.19, 733.93-733.95, 805.4-805.5, 805.8-805.9, 806.4-806.5, 806.8-806.9, 829.0-829.1, 839.20, 839.30, 839.40, 839.49-839.50, 839.59, 839.69, 839.79-839.9, 847.2, 847.9, 848.8-848.9, 879.8-879.9, 905.1, 926.11, 929.0-929.9, 952.2, 952.8-952.9, 958.8-958.99, 959.11-959.19, 959.8-959.9
AHA: 4Q, '99, 11, 13

806.5 Lumbar, open `MCC`
CC Excl: See code 806.4

√5th **806.6** Sacrum and coccyx, closed

806.60 With unspecified spinal cord injury `MCC`
CC Excl: 733.10-733.19, 733.93-733.95, 805.6-805.9, 806.60-806.9, 829.0-829.1, 839.40-839.59, 839.69, 839.79-839.9, 846.0-847.0, 847.3-847.9, 848.5-848.9, 879.8-879.9, 905.1, 926.11, 929.0-929.9, 952.3-952.9, 958.8-958.99, 959.11-959.19, 959.8-959.9

806.61 With complete cauda equina lesion `MCC`
CC Excl: See code 806.60

806.62 With other cauda equina injury `MCC`
CC Excl: See code 806.60

806.69 With other spinal cord injury `MCC`
CC Excl: See code 806.60

√5th **806.7** Sacrum and coccyx, open

806.70 With unspecified spinal cord injury `MCC`
CC Excl: See code 806.60

806.71 With complete cauda equina lesion `MCC`
CC Excl: See code 806.60

806.72 With other cauda equina injury `MCC`
CC Excl: See code 806.60

Ribs, Sternum, Larynx, and Trachea

806.79 With other spinal cord injury `MCC`
CC Excl: See code 806.60

806.8 Unspecified, closed `MCC`
CC Excl: 733.10-733.19, 733.93-733.95, 805.00-806.9, 829.0-829.1, 839.00-839.59, 839.69, 839.79-839.9, 846.0-847.9, 848.5-848.9, 879.8-879.9, 905.1, 926.11, 929.0-929.9, 952.00-952.9, 958.8-958.99, 959.11-959.19, 959.8-959.9

806.9 Unspecified, open `MCC`
CC Excl: See code 806.

√4th **807** Fracture of rib(s), sternum, larynx, and trachea

The following fifth-digit subclassification is for use with codes 807.0-807.1:

0 rib(s) unspecifed
1 one rib
2 two ribs
3 three ribs
4 four ribs
5 five ribs
6 six ribs
7 seven ribs
8 eight or more ribs
9 multiple ribs, unspecified

§ √5th **807.0** Rib(s), closed `CC`
[0-9]
CC Excl: For codes 807.00-807.02: 807.00-807.4, 819.0-819.1, 828.0-829.1, 848.8-848.9, 879.8-879.9, 929.0-929.9, 958.8-958.99, 959.8-959.9; For code 807.03: 807.00-807.19, 807.4, 819.0-819.1, 828.0-829.1, 848.8-848.9, 929.0-929.9, 958.8, 959.8-959.9; For codes 807.04-807.09: 807.00-807.19, 807.4, 819.0-819.1, 828.0-829.1, 848.8-848.9, 879.8-879.9, 929.0-929.9, 958.8-958.99, 959.8-959.9

S22.31xA Fracture rib right initial encounter closed fx `I-10`
S22.43xG Mx fx ribs bilat subseqnt enc fx delayed healing `I-10`

§ √5th **807.1** Rib(s), open `MCC`
[0-9]
CC Excl: 807.00-807.19, 807.4, 819.0-819.1, 828.0-829.1, 848.8-848.9, 879.8-879.9, 929.0-929.9, 958.8-958.99, 959.8-959.9

807.2 Sternum, closed `CC`
DEF: Break in flat bone (breast bone) in anterior thorax.
CC Excl: 807.2-807.4, 829.0-829.1, 848.8-848.9, 879.8-879.9, 929.0-929.9, 958.8-958.99, 959.8-959.9

807.3 Sternum, open `MCC`
DEF: Break, with open wound, in flat bone in mid anterior thorax.
CC Excl: See code: 807.2

807.4 Flail chest `MCC`
CC Excl: 807.00-807.4, 829.0-829.1, 848.8-848.9, 879.8-879.9, 929.0-929.9, 958.8-958.99, 959.8-959.9

807.5 Larynx and trachea, closed `MCC`
Hyoid bone
Thyroid cartilage
Trachea
CC Excl: 807.5-807.6, 829.0-829.1, 848.8-848.9, 879.8-879.9, 929.0-929.9, 958.8-958.99, 959.8-959.9

807.6 Larynx and trachea, open `MCC`
CC Excl: See code 807.5

§ Requires fifth digit. Valid digits are in [brackets] under each code. See category 807 for codes and definitions.

√4th √5th Additional Digit Required | Unacceptable PDx | Manifestation Code | Hospital Acquired Condition | ▶◀ Revised Text | ● New Code | ▲ Revised Code Title

Injury and Poisoning

808–812.0

Pelvis and Pelvic Fractures

Fractures Disrupting Pelvic Circle — Pelvic circle — Stable — Unstable (two-place fracture)

Iliac crest — Ilium — Anterior superior iliac spine — Ischial spine — Acetabulum — Femur — Ischial tuberosity — Pubic symphysis — L5 — Sacrum — Coccyx — Pubis

Pelvic Bones

Acetabular Fractures — Posterior pillar — Transverse

Right Clavicle and Scapula, Anterior View

Acromion — Acromial end — Clavicle — Coracoid process — Shaft — Humerus — Sternal end — Body of scapula — First rib — Glenoid fossa — Neck of scapula

√4th 808 Fracture of pelvis

808.0 Acetabulum, closed   MCC
CC Excl: 733.10-733.19, 733.93-733.95, 808.0-808.1, 808.43-808.49, 808.53-809.1, 829.0-829.1, 835.00-835.13, 843.0-843.9, 846.0-846.9, 848.5-848.9, 879.8-879.9, 929.0-929.9, 958.8-958.99, 959.6, 959.8-959.9

808.1 Acetabulum, open   MCC
CC Excl: 808.0-808.1, 808.43-808.49, 808.53-809.1, 829.0-829.1, 835.00-835.13, 843.0-843.9, 846.0-846.9, 848.5-848.9, 879.8-879.9, 929.0-929.9, 958.8-958.99, 959.6, 959.8-959.9

808.2 Pubis, closed   CC
AHA: 1Q, '08, 9
CC Excl: 733.10-733.19, 733.93-733.95, 808.2-808.3, 808.43-808.49, 808.53-809.1, 829.0-829.1, 835.00-835.13, 843.0-843.9, 846.0-846.9, 848.5-848.9, 879.8-879.9, 929.0-929.9, 958.8-958.99, 959.6, 959.8-959.9
S32.50xA Fracture pubis initial encounter closed fracture   I-10

808.3 Pubis, open   MCC
CC Excl: See code 808.2

√5th 808.4 Other specified part, closed

808.41 Ilium   CC
CC Excl: 733.10, 733.19, 808.0-809.1, 829.0-829.1, 835.00-835.13, 843.0-843.9, 846.0-846.9, 848.5-848.9, 879.8-879.9, 929.0-929.9, 958.8, 958.99, 959.6, 959.8-959.9

808.42 Ischium   CC
CC Excl: 808.42

808.43 Multiple pelvic fractures with disruption of pelvic circle   CC
AHA: 1Q, '08, 9
TIP: To assign, documentation must indicate multiple pelvic fractures with complete disruption of the pelvic circle.
CC Excl: 733.10-733.19, 733.93-733.95, 808.0-809.1, 829.0-829.1, 835.00-835.13, 843.0-843.9, 846.0-846.9, 848.5-848.9, 879.8-879.9, 929.0-929.9, 958.8-958.99, 959.6, 959.8-959.9

808.49 Other   CC
Innominate bone
Pelvic rim
CC Excl: See code: 808.43

√5th 808.5 Other specified part, open

808.51 Ilium   MCC
CC Excl: 733.10-733.19, 733.93-733.95, 808.41, 808.43-808.51, 808.53-809.1, 829.0-829.1, 835.00-835.13, 843.0-843.9, 846.0-846.9, 848.5-848.9, 879.8-879.9, 929.0-929.9, 958.8-958.99, 959.6, 959.8-959.9

808.52 Ischium   MCC
CC Excl: 733.10-733.19, 733.93-733.95, 808.42-808.49, 808.52-809.1, 829.0-829.1, 835.00-835.13, 843.0-843.9, 846.0-846.9, 848.5-848.9, 879.8-879.9, 929.0-929.9, 958.8-958.99, 959.6, 959.8-959.9

808.53 Multiple pelvic fractures with disruption of pelvic circle   MCC
CC Excl: See code: 808.43

808.59 Other   MCC
CC Excl: See code: 808.43

808.8 Unspecified, closed   CC
CC Excl: See code: 808.43

808.9 Unspecified, open   MCC
CC Excl: See code: 808.43

√4th 809 Ill-defined fractures of bones of trunk

INCLUDES   bones of trunk with other bones except those of skull and face
multiple bones of trunk

EXCLUDES   multiple fractures of:
pelvic bones alone (808.0-808.9)
ribs alone (807.0-807.1, 807.4)
ribs or sternum with limb bones (819.0-819.1, 828.0-828.1)
skull or face with other bones (804.0-804.9)

809.0 Fracture of bones of trunk, closed   CC
CC Excl: 733.10, 733.19, 808.0-809.1, 829.0-829.1, 835.00-835.13, 843.0-843.9, 846.0-846.9, 848.5-848.9, 879.8-879.9, 929.0-929.9, 958.8, 958.99, 959.6, 959.8-959.9

809.1 Fracture of bones of trunk, open   MCC
CC Excl: See code: 809.0

FRACTURE OF UPPER LIMB (810-819)

√4th 810 Fracture of clavicle
INCLUDES   collar bone
interligamentous part of clavicle

The following fifth-digit subclassification is for use with category 810:
   0 unspecified part
     Clavicle NOS
   1 sternal end of clavicle
   2 shaft of clavicle
   3 acromial end of clavicle

§ √5th **810.0 Closed**
[0-3]

§ √5th **810.1 Open**   CC
[0-3]   CC Excl: 810.00-810.13, 818.0-819.1

√4th 811 Fracture of scapula
INCLUDES   shoulder blade

The following fifth-digit subclassification is for use with category 811:
   0 unspecified part
   1 acromial process
     Acromion (process)
   2 coracoid process
   3 glenoid cavity and neck of scapula
   9 other

§ √5th **811.0 Closed**
[0-3, 9]

§ √5th **811.1 Open**   CC
[0-3, 9]   CC Excl: 811.00-811.19, 818.0-819.1

√4th 812 Fracture of humerus

√5th 812.0 Upper end, closed

§   Requires fifth digit. Valid digits are in [brackets] under each code. See appropriate category for codes and definitions.

N Newborn Age: 0   P Pediatric Age: 0-17   M Maternity Age: 12-55   A Adult Age: 15-124   MCC Major CC Condition   CC CC Condition   HIV HIV Related Dx

ICD-9 makes no provision for distinguishing between unilateral and bilateral fractures of the same site in the upper or lower limbs when assigning diagnosis codes, however, the procedure code can be reported twice when bilateral fracture procedures are carried out to reflect more accurately the resources used.

Tabular List   **INJURY AND POISONING**   **812.00–813.17**

Injury and Poisoning

812.00–813.17

Right Humerus, Anterior View

812.00 Upper end, unspecified part   `CC`
Proximal end
Shoulder
CC Excl: 812.00-812.59, 819.0-819.1

812.01 Surgical neck   `CC`
Neck of humerus NOS
CC Excl: See code: 812.00
S42.214A Uns nondsplcd fx surg neck rt humerus inital clo fx   `I-10`

812.02 Anatomical neck   `CC`
CC Excl: See code: 812.00

812.03 Greater tuberosity   `CC`
CC Excl: See code: 812.00

812.09 Other   `CC`
Head   Upper epiphysis
Lesser tuberosity
CC Excl: See code: 812.00
S42.294A Oth nondsplcd fx up end rt humerus initial clos fx   `I-10`

√5th **812.1 Upper end, open**

812.10 Upper end, unspecified part   `MCC`
CC Excl: 812.10-812.59, 818.0-819.1

812.11 Surgical neck   `MCC`
CC Excl: See code: 812.10

812.12 Anatomical neck   `MCC`
CC Excl: See code: 812.10

812.13 Greater tuberosity   `MCC`
CC Excl: See code: 812.10

812.19 Other   `MCC`
CC Excl: See code: 812.10

√5th **812.2 Shaft or unspecified part, closed**

812.20 Unspecified part of humerus   `CC`
Humerus NOS
Lesser tuberosity
Upper arm NOS
CC Excl: See code: 812.00

812.21 Shaft of humerus   `CC`
CC Excl: 812.21
AHA: 4Q, '05, 129; 3Q, '99, 14

√5th **812.3 Shaft or unspecified part, open**

812.30 Unspecified part of humerus   `MCC`
CC Excl: See code: 812.10

812.31 Shaft of humerus   `MCC`
CC Excl: See code: 812.10

√5th **812.4 Lower end, closed**
Distal end of humerus
Elbow

812.40 Lower end, unspecified part   `CC`
CC Excl: 812.00-812.59, 819.0-819.1

812.41 Supracondylar fracture of humerus   `CC`
CC Excl: See code: 812.40

812.42 Lateral condyle   `CC`
External condyle
CC Excl: See code: 812.40

812.43 Medial condyle   `CC`
Internal epicondyle
CC Excl: See code: 812.40

812.44 Condyle(s), unspecified   `CC`
Articular process NOS
Lower epiphysis NOS
CC Excl: See code: 812.40

812.49 Other   `CC`
Multiple fractures of lower end
Trochlea
CC Excl: See code: 812.40

√5th **812.5 Lower end, open**

812.50 Lower end, unspecified part   `MCC`
CC Excl: 812.00-812.59, 819.0-819.1

812.51 Supracondylar fracture of humerus   `MCC`
CC Excl: See code: 812.50

812.52 Lateral condyle   `MCC`
CC Excl: See code: 812.50

812.53 Medial condyle   `MCC`
CC Excl: See code: 812.50

812.54 Condyle(s), unspecified   `MCC`
CC Excl: See code: 812.50

812.59 Other   `MCC`
CC Excl: See code: 812.50

√4th **813 Fracture of radius and ulna**

√5th **813.0 Upper end, closed**
Proximal end

813.00 Upper end of forearm, unspecified

813.01 Olecranon process of ulna

813.02 Coronoid process of ulna

813.03 Monteggia's fracture
DEF: Fracture near the head of the ulnar shaft, causing dislocation of the radial head.

813.04 Other and unspecified fractures of proximal end of ulna (alone)
Multiple fractures of ulna, upper end

813.05 Head of radius

813.06 Neck of radius

813.07 Other and unspecified fractures of proximal end of radius (alone)
Multiple fractures of radius, upper end

813.08 Radius with ulna, upper end [any part]

√5th **813.1 Upper end, open**

813.10 Upper end of forearm, unspecified   `MCC`
CC Excl: 813.10-813.44, 813.50-813.93, 818.0-819.1

813.11 Olecranon process of ulna   `MCC`
CC Excl: 813.10-813.40, 813.42-813.44, 813.50-813.93, 818.0-819.1

813.12 Coronoid process of ulna   `MCC`
CC Excl: See code: 813.10

813.13 Monteggia's fracture   `MCC`
CC Excl: See code: 813.10

813.14 Other and unspecified fractures of proximal end of ulna   `MCC`
CC Excl: See code: 813.10

813.15 Head of radius   `MCC`
CC Excl: See code: 813.10

813.16 Neck of radius   `MCC`
CC Excl: See code: 813.10

813.17 Other and unspecified fractures of proximal end of radius (alone)   `MCC`
CC Excl: See code: 813.10

√4th √5th Additional Digit Required   Unacceptable PDx   Manifestation Code   Hospital Acquired Condition   ▶◀ Revised Text   ● New Code   ▲ Revised Code Title

2010 ICD-9-CM   **Volume 1 – 319**

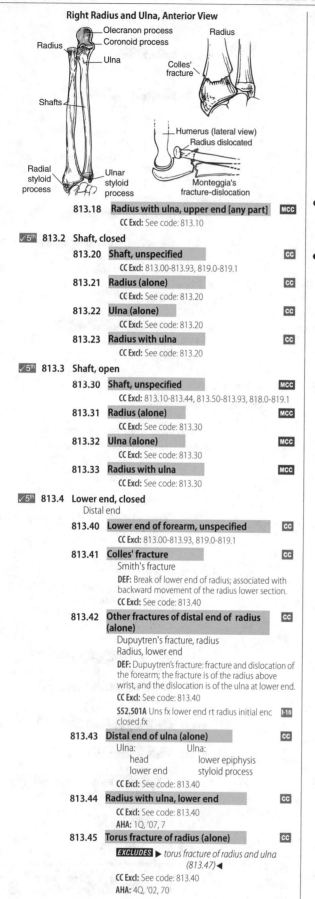

Right Radius and Ulna, Anterior View

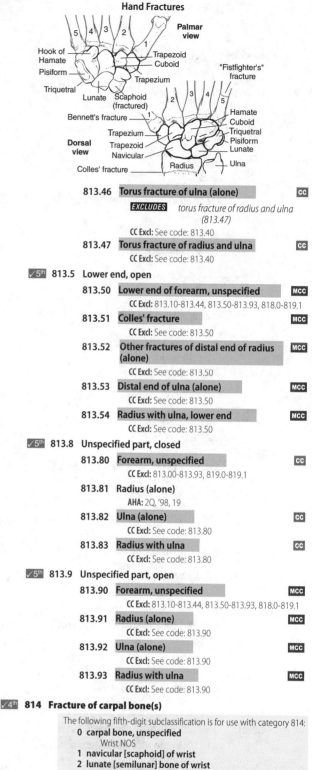

Hand Fractures

813.18 **Radius with ulna, upper end [any part]** `MCC`
CC Excl: See code: 813.10

✓5ᵗʰ **813.2** Shaft, closed

813.20 **Shaft, unspecified** `CC`
CC Excl: 813.00-813.93, 819.0-819.1

813.21 **Radius (alone)** `CC`
CC Excl: See code: 813.20

813.22 **Ulna (alone)** `CC`
CC Excl: See code: 813.20

813.23 **Radius with ulna** `CC`
CC Excl: See code: 813.20

✓5ᵗʰ **813.3** Shaft, open

813.30 **Shaft, unspecified** `MCC`
CC Excl: 813.10-813.44, 813.50-813.93, 818.0-819.1

813.31 **Radius (alone)** `MCC`
CC Excl: See code: 813.30

813.32 **Ulna (alone)** `MCC`
CC Excl: See code: 813.30

813.33 **Radius with ulna** `MCC`
CC Excl: See code: 813.30

✓5ᵗʰ **813.4** Lower end, closed
Distal end

813.40 **Lower end of forearm, unspecified** `CC`
CC Excl: 813.00-813.93, 819.0-819.1

813.41 **Colles' fracture** `CC`
Smith's fracture
DEF: Break of lower end of radius; associated with backward movement of the radius lower section.
CC Excl: See code: 813.40

813.42 **Other fractures of distal end of radius** `CC`
(alone)
Dupuytren's fracture, radius
Radius, lower end
DEF: Dupuytren's fracture: fracture and dislocation of the forearm; the fracture is of the radius above wrist, and the dislocation is of the ulna at lower end.
CC Excl: See code: 813.40
S52.501A Uns fx lower end rt radius initial enc `I-10`
closed fx

813.43 **Distal end of ulna (alone)** `CC`
Ulna: Ulna:
head   lower epiphysis
lower end   styloid process
CC Excl: See code: 813.40

813.44 **Radius with ulna, lower end** `CC`
CC Excl: See code: 813.40
AHA: 1Q, '07, 7

▲ **813.45** **Torus fracture of radius (alone)** `CC`
EXCLUDES ▶ torus fracture of radius and ulna
(813.47)◀
CC Excl: See code: 813.40
AHA: 4Q, '02, 70

● **813.46** **Torus fracture of ulna (alone)** `CC`
EXCLUDES torus fracture of radius and ulna
(813.47)
CC Excl: See code: 813.40

● **813.47** **Torus fracture of radius and ulna** `CC`
CC Excl: See code: 813.40

✓5ᵗʰ **813.5** Lower end, open

813.50 **Lower end of forearm, unspecified** `MCC`
CC Excl: 813.10-813.44, 813.50-813.93, 818.0-819.1

813.51 **Colles' fracture** `MCC`
CC Excl: See code: 813.50

813.52 **Other fractures of distal end of radius** `MCC`
(alone)
CC Excl: See code: 813.50

813.53 **Distal end of ulna (alone)** `MCC`
CC Excl: See code: 813.50

813.54 **Radius with ulna, lower end** `MCC`
CC Excl: See code: 813.50

✓5ᵗʰ **813.8** Unspecified part, closed

813.80 **Forearm, unspecified** `CC`
CC Excl: 813.00-813.93, 819.0-819.1

813.81 **Radius (alone)**
AHA: 2Q, '98, 19

813.82 **Ulna (alone)** `CC`
CC Excl: See code: 813.80

813.83 **Radius with ulna** `CC`
CC Excl: See code: 813.80

✓5ᵗʰ **813.9** Unspecified part, open

813.90 **Forearm, unspecified** `MCC`
CC Excl: 813.10-813.44, 813.50-813.93, 818.0-819.1

813.91 **Radius (alone)** `MCC`
CC Excl: See code: 813.90

813.92 **Ulna (alone)** `MCC`
CC Excl: See code: 813.90

813.93 **Radius with ulna** `MCC`
CC Excl: See code: 813.90

✓4ᵗʰ **814** **Fracture of carpal bone(s)**

The following fifth-digit subclassification is for use with category 814:
0 carpal bone, unspecified
   Wrist NOS
1 navicular [scaphoid] of wrist
2 lunate [semilunar] bone of wrist
3 triquetral [cuneiform] bone of wrist
4 pisiform
5 trapezium bone [larger multangular]
6 trapezoid bone [smaller multangular]
7 capitate bone [os magnum]
8 hamate [unciform] bone
9 other

§ ✓5ᵗʰ **814.0** **Closed**
[0-9]

§ Requires fifth digit. Valid digits are in [brackets] under each code. See appropriate category for codes and definitions.

`N` Newborn Age: 0   `P` Pediatric Age: 0-17   `M` Maternity Age: 12-55   `A` Adult Age: 15-124   `MCC` Major CC Condition   `CC` CC Condition   `HIV` HIV Related Dx

320 – Volume 1 • October 2009   2010 ICD-9-CM

§ ✓5th **814.1** **Open** CC
[0-9] **CC Excl:** 814.00-814.19, 819.0-819.1

✓4th **815** **Fracture of metacarpal bone(s)**
INCLUDES hand [except finger]
metacarpus

The following fifth-digit subclassification is for use with category 815:
0 metacarpal bone(s), site unspecified
1 base of thumb [first] metacarpal
Bennett's fracture
2 base of other metacarpal bone(s)
3 shaft of metacarpal bone(s)
4 neck of metacarpal bone(s)
9 multiple sites of metacarpus

§ ✓5th **815.0** **Closed**
[0-4, 9]

§ ✓5th **815.1** **Open** CC
[0-4, 9] **CC Excl:** 815.00-815.19, 817.0-817.1

✓4th **816** **Fracture of one or more phalanges of hand**
INCLUDES finger(s)
thumb

The following fifth-digit subclassification is for use with category 816:
0 phalanx or phalanges, unspecified
1 middle or proximal phalanx or phalanges
2 distal phalanx or phalanges
3 multiple sites

TIP: If phalangeal fracture(s) are due to crushing injury, sequence that code (927.3) first.

§ ✓5th **816.0** **Closed**
[0-3]

§ ✓5th **816.1** **Open** CC
[0-3] **CC Excl: For codes 816.10-816.12:** 816.00-817.1; **For code 816.13:** 816.00-816.13, 818.0-819.1
AHA: For code 816.12: 4Q, '03, 77

✓4th **817** **Multiple fractures of hand bones**
INCLUDES metacarpal bone(s) with phalanx or phalanges of same hand

817.0 **Closed**

817.1 **Open** CC
CC Excl: 814.00-819.1

✓4th **818** **Ill-defined fractures of upper limb**
INCLUDES arm NOS
multiple bones of same upper limb
EXCLUDES multiple fractures of:
metacarpal bone(s) with phalanx or phalanges (817.0-817.1)
phalanges of hand alone (816.0-816.1)
radius with ulna (813.0-813.9)

818.0 **Closed**

818.1 **Open** CC
CC Excl: 812.00-813.44, 813.50-819.1

✓4th **819** **Multiple fractures involving both upper limbs, and upper limb with rib(s) and sternum**
INCLUDES arm(s) with rib(s) or sternum
both arms [any bones]

819.0 **Closed** CC
CC Excl: 807.00-807.4, 812.00-813.44, 813.50-819.1

819.1 **Open** CC
CC Excl: See code: 819.0

FRACTURE OF LOWER LIMB (820-829)

✓4th **820** **Fracture of neck of femur**

✓5th **820.0** **Transcervical fracture, closed**

820.00 **Intracapsular section, unspecified** MCC
CC Excl: 733.10-733.19, 733.93-733.95, 820.00-821.39, 827.0-829.1, 843.0-843.9, 848.8-848.9, 879.8-879.9, 929.0-929.9, 958.8-958.99, 959.6, 959.8-959.9

820.01 **Epiphysis (separation) (upper)** MCC
Transepiphyseal
CC Excl: See code 820.00

820.02 **Midcervical section** MCC
Transcervical NOS
CC Excl: See code 820.00
AHA: 3Q, '03, 12

820.03 **Base of neck** MCC
Cervicotrochanteric section
CC Excl: See code 820.00

820.09 **Other** MCC
Head of femur
Subcapital
CC Excl: See code 820.00
S72.064A Nondsplcd art fx head rt femur initial enc clos fx I-10

✓5th **820.1** **Transcervical fracture, open**

820.10 **Intracapsular section, unspecified** MCC
CC Excl: See code 820.00

820.11 **Epiphysis (separation) (upper)** MCC
CC Excl: See code 820.00

820.12 **Midcervical section** MCC
CC Excl: See code 820.00

820.13 **Base of neck** MCC
CC Excl: See code 820.00

820.19 **Other** MCC
CC Excl: See code 820.00

✓5th **820.2** **Pertrochanteric fracture, closed**

820.20 **Trochanteric section, unspecified** MCC
Trochanter: Trochanter:
NOS   lesser
greater
CC Excl: See code 820.00

820.21 **Intertrochanteric section** MCC
CC Excl: See code 820.00

820.22 **Subtrochanteric section** MCC
CC Excl: See code 820.00
S72.25xA Nondsplcd subtrochant fx lt femur inital enc clo fx I-10

✓5th **820.3** **Pertrochanteric fracture, open**

820.30 **Trochanteric section, unspecified** MCC
CC Excl: See code 820.00

820.31 **Intertrochanteric section** MCC
CC Excl: See code 820.00

820.32 **Subtrochanteric section** MCC
CC Excl: See code 820.00

820.8 **Unspecified part of neck of femur, closed** MCC
Hip NOS   Neck of femur NOS
CC Excl: See code 820.00
S72.002A Fx uns part neck left femur initial enc clos fx I-10

820.9 **Unspecified part of neck of femur, open** MCC
CC Excl: See code 820.00

§ Requires fifth digit. Valid digits are in [brackets] under each code. See appropriate category for codes and definitions.

✓4th / ✓5th **Additional Digit Required**   **Unacceptable PDx**   **Manifestation Code**   **Hospital Acquired Condition**   ►◄ Revised Text   ● New Code   ▲ Revised Code Title

2010 ICD-9-CM   **Volume 1 – 321**

Injury and Poisoning

821–824.0

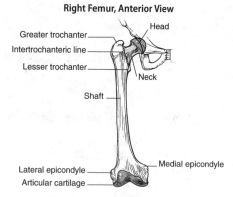

Right Femur, Anterior View

Head
Greater trochanter
Intertrochanteric line
Lesser trochanter
Neck
Shaft
Lateral epicondyle
Medial epicondyle
Articular cartilage

Right Tibia and Fibula, Anterior View

Patella
Tibial plateau
Tibial tubercle
Shaft of fibula
Tibia
Pott's fracture
Lateral (fibular) malleolus
Medial (tibial) malleolus

√4ᵗʰ **821 Fracture of other and unspecified parts of femur**

√5ᵗʰ **821.0 Shaft or unspecified part, closed**

821.00 Unspecified part of femur   `MCC`
Thigh
Upper leg

EXCLUDES hip NOS (820.8)

CC Excl: 733.10-733.19, 733.93-733.95,
820.00-821.39, 827.0-829.1, 843.0-843.9,
848.8-848.9, 879.8-879.9, 929.0-929.9, 958.8-958.99,
959.6, 959.8-959.9

821.01 Shaft   `MCC`
CC Excl: See code: 821.00
AHA: 1Q, '07, 4; 1Q, '99, 5

S72.331A Displaced obl fx shaft rt femur initial   `I-10`
enc clos fx

√5ᵗʰ **821.1 Shaft or unspecified part, open**

821.10 Unspecified part of femur   `MCC`
CC Excl: See code: 821.00

821.11 Shaft   `MCC`
CC Excl: See code: 821.00

√5ᵗʰ **821.2 Lower end, closed**
Distal end

821.20 Lower end, unspecified part   `CC`
CC Excl: 733.10, 733.14-733.15, 733.19,
820.00-821.39, 827.0-829.1, 843.0-843.9,
848.8-848.9, 879.8-879.9, 929.0-929.9, 958.99,
959.6, 959.8-959.9

821.21 Condyle, femoral   `CC`
CC Excl: See code: 821.20

821.22 Epiphysis, lower (separation)   `CC`
CC Excl: See code: 821.20

821.23 Supracondylar fracture of femur   `CC`
CC Excl: See code: 821.20

821.29 Other   `CC`
Multiple fractures of lower end
CC Excl: See code: 821.20

√5ᵗʰ **821.3 Lower end, open**

821.30 Lower end, unspecified part   `MCC`
CC Excl: See code: 821.20

821.31 Condyle, femoral   `MCC`
CC Excl: See code: 821.20

821.32 Epiphysis, lower (separation)   `MCC`
CC Excl: See code: 821.20

821.33 Supracondylar fracture of femur   `MCC`
CC Excl: See code: 821.20

821.39 Other   `MCC`
CC Excl: 733.10, 733.14-733.15, 733.19, 821.39-822.1,
827.0-829.1, 843.0-843.9, 848.8-848.9, 879.8-879.9,
929.0-929.9, 958.8, 958.99, 959.6, 959.8-959.9

√4ᵗʰ **822 Fracture of patella**

822.0 Closed   `CC`
CC Excl: 822.0-822.1, 828.0-828.1

S82.001A Uns fx right patella initial encounter closed fx   `I-10`

822.1 Open   `CC`
CC Excl: 733.10, 733.19, 822.1-823.32, 823.80-823.92,
827.0-829.1, 843.0-843.9, 848.8-848.9, 879.8-879.9,
929.0-929.9, 958.8, 958.99, 959.6, 959.8-959.9

√4ᵗʰ **823 Fracture of tibia and fibula**

EXCLUDES Dupuytren's fracture (824.4-824.5)
ankle (824.4-824.5)
radius (813.42, 813.52)
Pott's fracture (824.4-824.5)
that involving ankle (824.0-824.9)

The following fifth-digit subclassification is for use with category 823:
0 tibia alone
1 fibula alone
2 fibula with tibia

§ √5ᵗʰ **823.0 Upper end, closed**   `CC 0,2`
[0-2]   Head   Tibia:
        Proximal end   condyles
                     tuberosity

CC Excl: For codes 823.00, 823.02: 733.10, 733.16-733.19,
823.00-823.32, 823.80-823.92, 827.0-829.1, 843.0-843.9,
848.8-848.9, 879.8-879.9, 929.0-929.9, 958.8, 958.99, 959.6,
959.8-959.9

S82.121A Displcd fx lat condyle rt tibia initial enc clos fx   `I-10`

§ √5ᵗʰ **823.1 Upper end, open**   `MCC`
[0-2]   CC Excl: See code: 823.00

§¹⁰ √5ᵗʰ **823.2 Shaft, closed**   `CC 0,2`
[0-2]   CC Excl: See code: 823.00

§ √5ᵗʰ **823.3 Shaft, open**   `MCC`
[0-2]   CC Excl: See code: 823.00

§¹⁰ √5ᵗʰ **823.4 Torus fracture**   `CC 0,2`
[0-2]   DEF: A bone deformity in children, occurring commonly in the
tibia and fibula, in which the bone bends and buckles but
does not fracture.
CC Excl: See code: 823.00
AHA: 4Q, '02, 70

§¹⁰ √5ᵗʰ **823.8 Unspecified part, closed**   `CC 0,2`
[0-2]   Lower leg NOS
CC Excl: For code 823.80: 823.00-823.92; For code 823.82: 733.10,
733.16-733.19, 823.00-823.32, 823.80-823.92, 827.0-829.1,
843.0-843.9, 848.8-848.9, 879.8-879.9, 929.0-929.9, 958.8,
958.99, 959.6, 959.8-959.9
AHA: For code 823.82: 1Q, '97, 8

§ √5ᵗʰ **823.9 Unspecified part, open**   `MCC`
[0-2]   CC Excl: See code: 823.00

√4ᵗʰ **824 Fracture of ankle**

TIP: If ankle fracture also includes syndesmotic injury, assign also code
845.03 Sprains and strains of tibiofibular (ligament), distal.

824.0 Medial malleolus, closed
Tibia involving:
ankle
malleolus
AHA: 1Q, '04, 9

---

¹⁰ HAC = only for valid CC or MCC codes.
§   Requires fifth digit. Valid digits are in [brackets] under each code. See category 823 for codes and definitions.

Ⓝ Newborn Age: 0   Ⓟ Pediatric Age: 0-17   Ⓜ Maternity Age: 12-55   Ⓐ Adult Age: 15-124   `MCC` Major CC Condition   `CC` CC Condition   `HIV` HIV Related Dx

322 – Volume 1   **2010 ICD-9-CM**

Torus Fracture

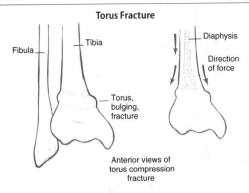

Anterior views of torus compression fracture

Right Foot, Dorsal

824.1 Medial malleolus, open   `CC`

> CC Excl: 733.10, 733.16-733.19, 824.1-824.9, 827.0-829.1,
> 843.0-843.9, 848.8-848.9, 879.8-879.9, 929.0-929.9, 958.8,
> 958.99, 959.6, 959.8-959.9

824.2 Lateral malleolus, closed

> Fibula involving:
>   ankle
>   malleolus
>
> **AHA:** 2Q, '02, 3

824.3 Lateral malleolus, open   `CC`

> CC Excl: See code: 824.1

824.4 Bimalleolar, closed

> Dupuytren's fracture, fibula
> Pott's fracture
>
> **DEF:** Bimalleolar, closed: Breaking of both nodules (malleoli)
> on either side of ankle joint, without an open wound.
>
> **DEF:** Dupuytren's fracture (Pott's fracture): The breaking of the
> farthest end of the lower leg bone (fibula), with injury to the
> farthest end joint of the other lower leg bone (tibia).
>
> **S82.841A** Displcd bimalleolar fx rt lw leg intial enc clos fx `I-10`

824.5 Bimalleolar, open   `CC`

> CC Excl: See code: 824.1

824.6 Trimalleolar, closed

> Lateral and medial malleolus with anterior or posterior lip
> of tibia
>
> **S82.855G** Nondsplcd trimalleolr lft lw leg fx subsq clo fx `I-10`
> delay healing

824.7 Trimalleolar, open   `CC`

> CC Excl: See code: 824.1

824.8 Unspecified, closed

> Ankle NOS
>
> **AHA:** 3Q, '00, 12
>
> **S89.302A** Uns physeal fx low end lt fibula initial enc clo fx `I-10`

824.9 Unspecified, open   `CC`

> CC Excl: See code: 824.1

√4ᵗʰ **825 Fracture of one or more tarsal and metatarsal bones**

825.0 Fracture of calcaneus, closed

> Heel bone
> Os calcis

825.1 Fracture of calcaneus, open   `CC`

> CC Excl: 733.10, 733.16-733.19, 825.1-825.39, 827.0-829.1,
> 843.0-843.9, 848.8-848.9, 879.8-879.9, 929.0-929.9, 958.8,
> 958.99, 959.6, 959.8-959.9

√5ᵗʰ **825.2 Fracture of other tarsal and metatarsal bones, closed**

    825.20 Unspecified bone(s) of foot [except toes]
>   Instep

    825.21 Astragalus
>   Talus

    825.22 Navicular [scaphoid], foot

    825.23 Cuboid

    825.24 Cuneiform, foot

    825.25 Metatarsal bone(s)

    825.29 Other
>   Tarsal with metatarsal bone(s) only
>
>   ***EXCLUDES*** calcaneus (825.0)

√5ᵗʰ **825.3 Fracture of other tarsal and metatarsal bones, open**

    825.30 Unspecified bone(s) of foot [except toes] `CC`
>   CC Excl: 825.0-826.1

    825.31 Astragalus `CC`
>   CC Excl: 733.10, 733.19, 825.1-825.39, 827.0-829.1,
>   843.0-843.9, 848.8-848.9, 879.8-879.9, 929.0-929.9,
>   958.8, 958.99, 959.6, 959.8-959.9

    825.32 Navicular [scaphoid], foot `CC`
>   CC Excl: See code: 825.31

    825.33 Cuboid `CC`
>   CC Excl: See code: 825.31

    825.34 Cuneiform, foot `CC`
>   CC Excl: See code: 825.31

    825.35 Metatarsal bone(s) `CC`
>   CC Excl: See code: 825.31

    825.39 Other `CC`
>   CC Excl: See code: 825.31

√4ᵗʰ **826 Fracture of one or more phalanges of foot**

> ***INCLUDES*** toe(s)

826.0 Closed

826.1 Open

√4ᵗʰ **827 Other, multiple, and ill-defined fractures of lower limb**

> ***INCLUDES*** leg NOS
>   multiple bones of same lower limb
>
> ***EXCLUDES*** multiple fractures of:
>   ankle bones alone (824.4-824.9)
>   phalanges of foot alone (826.0-826.1)
>   tarsal with metatarsal bones (825.29, 825.39)
>   tibia with fibula (823.0-823.9 with fifth-digit 2)

827.0 Closed

827.1 Open   `CC`

> CC Excl: 820.00-823.32, 823.80-829.1

√4ᵗʰ **828 Multiple fractures involving both lower limbs, lower with upper limb, and lower limb(s) with rib(s) and sternum**

> ***INCLUDES*** arm(s) with leg(s) [any bones]
>   both legs [any bones]
>   leg(s) with rib(s) or sternum

828.0 Closed   `MCC`

> CC Excl: See code: 827.1

828.1 Open   `MCC`

> CC Excl: See code: 827.1

√4ᵗʰ **829 Fracture of unspecified bones**

829.0 Unspecified bone, closed

829.1 Unspecified bone, open

√4ᵗʰ √5ᵗʰ Additional Digit Required   Unacceptable PDx   Manifestation Code   Hospital Acquired Condition   ▶◀ Revised Text   ● New Code   ▲ Revised Code Title

2010 ICD-9-CM   **Volume 1 – 323**

Injury and Poisoning

830–836.50

DISLOCATION (830-839)

| INCLUDES | displacement |
| | subluxation |

EXCLUDES	congenital dislocation (754.0-755.8)
	pathological dislocation (718.2)
	recurrent dislocation (718.3)

The descriptions "closed" and "open," used in the fourth-digit subdivisions, include the following terms:

closed: open:
complete   compound
dislocation NOS   infected
partial   with foreign body
simple
uncomplicated

A dislocation not indicated as closed or open should be classified as closed.

AHA: 3Q, '90, 12

TIP: Do not assign if documentation indicates developmental dislocation; see instead subcategory 718.7.

Unless otherwise directed, dislocations that occur with fractures of the same site should not be coded separately; assign only the fracture code.

✓4th 830 Dislocation of jaw

INCLUDES	jaw (cartilage) (meniscus)
	mandible
	maxilla (inferior)
	temporomandibular (joint)

830.0 Closed dislocation

830.1 Open dislocation   CC
     CC Excl: 830.0-830.1, 839.69, 839.79-839.9

✓4th 831 Dislocation of shoulder

| EXCLUDES | sternoclavicular joint (839.61, 839.71) |
| | sternum (839.61, 839.71) |

The following fifth-digit subclassification is for use with category 831:
- 0 shoulder, unspecified
  - Humerus NOS
- 1 anterior dislocation of humerus
- 2 posterior dislocation of humerus
- 3 inferior dislocation of humerus
- 4 acromioclavicular (joint)
  - Clavicle
- 9 other
  - Scapula

TIP: Do not assign if documentation indicates recurrent shoulder dislocation; see instead code 718.31.

§ ✓5th **831.0 Closed dislocation**
[0-4, 9]

§ ✓5th **831.1 Open dislocation**   CC
[0-4, 9]   **CC Excl: For code 831.10:** 831.10, 839.69, 839.79-839.9; **For code 831.11:** 831.11, 839.69, 839.79-839.9; **For code 831.12:** 831.12, 839.69, 839.79-839.9; **For code 831.13:** 831.13, 839.69, 839.79-839.9; **For code 831.14:** 831.14, 839.69, 839.79-839.9; **For code 831.19:** 831.19, 839.69, 839.79-839.9

✓4th 832 Dislocation of elbow

The following fifth-digit subclassification is for use with ▶subcategories 832.0 and 832.1◀:
- 0 elbow, unspecified
- 1 anterior dislocation of elbow
- 2 posterior dislocation of elbow
- 3 medial dislocation of elbow
- 4 lateral dislocation of elbow
- 9 other

§ ✓5th **832.0 Closed dislocation**
[0-4, 9]

§ ✓5th **832.1 Open dislocation**   CC
[0-4, 9]   **CC Excl: For code 832.10:** 832.10; **For code 832.11:** 832.11; **For code 832.12:** 832.12; **For code 832.13:** 832.13; **For code 832.14:** 832.14; **For code 832.19:** 832.19

● **832.2 Nursemaid's elbow**
     Subluxation of radial head

Usually caused by Sudden pull on the hand/arm... commonly seen in children under the age of 5.

✓4th 833 Dislocation of wrist

The following fifth-digit subclassification is for use with category 833:
- 0 wrist unspecified part
  - Carpal (bone)
  - Radius, distal end
- 1 radioulnar (joint), distal
- 2 radiocarpal (joint)
- 3 midcarpal (joint)
- 4 carpometacarpal (joint)
- 5 metacarpal (bone), proximal end
- 9 other
  - Ulna, distal end

§ ✓5th **833.0 Closed dislocation**
[0-5, 9]

§ ✓5th **833.1 Open dislocation**   CC
[0-5, 9]   **CC Excl: For codes 833.10, 833.13-833.19:** 833.00-833.19; **For code 833.11:** 833.11; **For code 833.12:** 833.12

✓4th 834 Dislocation of finger

INCLUDES	finger(s)
	phalanx of hand
	thumb

The following fifth-digit subclassification is for use with category 834:
- 0 finger unspecified part
- 1 metacarpophalangeal (joint)
  - Metacarpal (bone), distal end
- 2 interphalangeal (joint), hand

§ ✓5th **834.0 Closed dislocation**
[0-2]

§ ✓5th **834.1 Open dislocation**
[0-2]

✓4th 835 Dislocation of hip

The following fifth-digit subclassification is for use with category 835:
- 0 dislocation of hip, unspecified
- 1 posterior dislocation
- 2 obturator dislocation
- 3 other anterior dislocation

§ ✓5th **835.0 Closed dislocation**   CC
[0-3]   **CC Excl: For code 835.00:** 835.00, 839.69, 839.79-839.9; **For code 835.01:** 835.01, 839.69, 839.79-839.9; **For code 835.02:** 835.02, 839.69, 839.79-839.9; **For code 835.03:** 835.03, 839.69, 839.79-839.9

§ ✓5th **835.1 Open dislocation**   MCC
[0-3]   **CC Excl: For code 835.10:** 835.10, 839.69, 839.79-839.9; **For code 835.11:** 835.11, 839.69, 839.79-839.9; **For code 835.12:** 835.12, 839.69, 839.79-839.9; **For code 835.13:** 835.13, 839.69, 839.79-839.9

✓4th 836 Dislocation of knee

EXCLUDES	dislocation of knee:
	old or pathological (718.2)
	recurrent (718.3)
	internal derangement of knee joint (717.0-717.5, 717.8-717.9)
	old tear of cartilage or meniscus of knee (717.0-717.5, 717.8-717.9)

836.0 Tear of medial cartilage or meniscus of knee, current
Bucket handle tear:
NOS   } current injury
medial meniscus

836.1 Tear of lateral cartilage or meniscus of knee, current

836.2 Other tear of cartilage or meniscus of knee, current
Tear of:
cartilage (semilunar) } current injury, not specified as
meniscus   medial or lateral

836.3 Dislocation of patella, closed

836.4 Dislocation of patella, open   CC
     CC Excl: 836.3-836.4

✓5th **836.5 Other dislocation of knee, closed**

836.50 Dislocation of knee, unspecified

§   Requires fifth digit. Valid digits are in [brackets] under each code. See appropriate category for codes and definitions.

| N Newborn Age: 0 | P Pediatric Age: 0-17 | M Maternity Age: 12-55 | A Adult Age: 15-124 | MCC Major CC Condition | CC CC Condition | HIV HIV Related Dx |

324 – Volume 1 · October 2009   2010 ICD-9-CM

836.51 **Anterior dislocation of tibia, proximal end**
Posterior dislocation of femur, distal end

836.52 **Posterior dislocation of tibia, proximal end**
Anterior dislocation of femur, distal end

836.53 **Medial dislocation of tibia, proximal end**

836.54 **Lateral dislocation of tibia, proximal end**

836.59 **Other**

√5th 836.6 **Other dislocation of knee, open**

836.60 **Dislocation of knee, unspecified** `CC`
CC Excl: 717.0-717.9, 718.26, 718.36, 836.60, 839.69, 839.79-839.9

836.61 **Anterior dislocation of tibia, proximal end** `CC`
CC Excl: 836.61, 839.69, 839.79-839.9

836.62 **Posterior dislocation of tibia, proximal end** `CC`
CC Excl: 836.62, 839.69, 839.79-839.9

836.63 **Medial dislocation of tibia, proximal end** `CC`
CC Excl: 836.63, 839.69, 839.79-839.9

836.64 **Lateral dislocation of tibia, proximal end** `CC`
CC Excl: 836.64, 839.69, 839.79-839.9

836.69 **Other** `CC`
CC Excl: 836.69, 839.69, 839.79-839.9

√4th **837 Dislocation of ankle**
INCLUDES astragalus
fibula, distal end
navicular, foot
scaphoid, foot
tibia, distal end

837.0 **Closed dislocation**

837.1 **Open dislocation** `CC`
CC Excl: 837.1, 839.69, 839.79-839.9

√4th **838 Dislocation of foot**

The following fifth-digit subclassification is for use with category 838:
0 foot unspecified
1 tarsal (bone), joint unspecified
2 midtarsal (joint)
3 tarsometatarsal (joint)
4 metatarsal (bone), joint unspecified
5 metatarsophalangeal (joint)
6 interphalangeal (joint), foot
9 other
Phalanx of foot
Toe(s)

§ √5th 838.0 **Closed dislocation**
[0-6, 9]

§ √5th 838.1 **Open dislocation**
[0-6, 9]

√4th **839 Other, multiple, and ill-defined dislocations**

√5th 839.0 **Cervical vertebra, closed**
Cervical spine
Neck

839.00 **Cervical vertebra, unspecified** `CC`
CC Excl: 805.00-805.18, 806.00-806.19, 806.8-806.9, 839.00-839.18, 847.0, 848.8-848.9, 879.8-879.9, 929.0-929.9, 952.00-952.09, 958.8-958.99, 959.8-959.9

839.01 **First cervical vertebra** `CC`
CC Excl: See code 839.00

839.02 **Second cervical vertebra** `CC`
CC Excl: See code 839.00

839.03 **Third cervical vertebra** `CC`
CC Excl: See code 839.00

839.04 **Fourth cervical vertebra** `CC`
CC Excl: See code 839.00

839.05 **Fifth cervical vertebra** `CC`
CC Excl: See code 839.00

839.06 **Sixth cervical vertebra** `CC`
CC Excl: See code 839.00

839.07 **Seventh cervical vertebra** `CC`
CC Excl: See code 839.00

839.08 **Multiple cervical vertebrae** `CC`
CC Excl: See code 839.00

√5th 839.1 **Cervical vertebra, open**

839.10 **Cervical vertebra, unspecified** `MCC`
CC Excl: See code 839.00

839.11 **First cervical vertebra** `MCC`
CC Excl: See code 839.00

839.12 **Second cervical vertebra** `MCC`
CC Excl: See code 839.00

839.13 **Third cervical vertebra** `MCC`
CC Excl: See code 839.00

839.14 **Fourth cervical vertebra** `MCC`
CC Excl: See code 839.00

839.15 **Fifth cervical vertebra** `MCC`
CC Excl: See code 839.00

839.16 **Sixth cervical vertebra** `MCC`
CC Excl: See code 839.00

839.17 **Seventh cervical vertebra** `MCC`
CC Excl: See code 839.00

839.18 **Multiple cervical vertebrae** `MCC`
CC Excl: See code 839.00

√5th 839.2 **Thoracic and lumbar vertebra, closed**

839.20 **Lumbar vertebra**

839.21 **Thoracic vertebra**
Dorsal [thoracic] vertebra

√5th 839.3 **Thoracic and lumbar vertebra, open**

839.30 **Lumbar vertebra** `MCC`
CC Excl: 839.30

839.31 **Thoracic vertebra** `MCC`
CC Excl: 839.21, 839.31

√5th 839.4 **Other vertebra, closed**

839.40 **Vertebra, unspecified site**
Spine NOS

839.41 **Coccyx**

839.42 **Sacrum**
Sacroiliac (joint)

839.49 **Other**

√5th 839.5 **Other vertebra, open**

839.50 **Vertebra, unspecified site** `MCC`
CC Excl: 839.10-839.18, 839.30-839.31, 839.50-839.59, 839.79, 839.9

839.51 **Coccyx** `CC`
CC Excl: 839.51

839.52 **Sacrum** `CC`
CC Excl: 839.52

839.59 **Other** `MCC`
CC Excl: See code: 839.50

√5th 839.6 **Other location, closed**

839.61 **Sternum** `CC`
Sternoclavicular joint
CC Excl: 839.61, 839.71

839.69 **Other**
Pelvis

√5th 839.7 **Other location, open**

839.71 **Sternum** `MCC`
CC Excl: See code: 839.61

§ Requires fifth digit. Valid digits are in [brackets] under each code. See category 838 for codes and definitions.

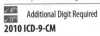

839.79 **Other** `CC`

CC Excl: 830.1, 831.10-831.19, 832.10-832.19, 833.10-833.19, 834.10-834.12, 835.10-835.13, 836.4, 836.60-836.69, 837.1, 838.10-838.19, 839.10-839.18, 839.30-839.31, 839.50-839.59, 839.71-839.79, 839.9

839.8 **Multiple and ill-defined, closed**
Arm
Back
Hand
Multiple locations, except fingers or toes alone
Other ill-defined locations
Unspecified location

839.9 **Multiple and ill-defined, open** `CC`

CC Excl: See code: 839.79

SPRAINS AND STRAINS OF JOINTS AND ADJACENT MUSCLES (840-848)

INCLUDES
avulsion
hemarthrosis
laceration } of:
rupture
sprain
strain
tear

joint capsule
ligament
muscle
tendon

EXCLUDES *laceration of tendon in open wounds (880-884 and 890-894 with .2)*

✓4th **840 Sprains and strains of shoulder and upper arm**

840.0 **Acromioclavicular (joint) (ligament)**

840.1 **Coracoclavicular (ligament)**

840.2 **Coracohumeral (ligament)**

840.3 **Infraspinatus (muscle) (tendon)**

840.4 **Rotator cuff (capsule)**
EXCLUDES *complete rupture of rotator cuff, nontraumatic (727.61)*

840.5 **Subscapularis (muscle)**

840.6 **Supraspinatus (muscle) (tendon)**

840.7 **Superior glenoid labrum lesion**
SLAP lesion
DEF: Detachment injury of the superior aspect of the glenoid labrum which is the ring of fibrocartilage attached to the rim of the glenoid cavity of the scapula.
AHA: 4Q,'01, 52

840.8 **Other specified sites of shoulder and upper arm**

840.9 **Unspecified site of shoulder and upper arm**
Arm NOS   Shoulder NOS

✓4th **841 Sprains and strains of elbow and forearm**

841.0 **Radial collateral ligament**

841.1 **Ulnar collateral ligament**

841.2 **Radiohumeral (joint)**

841.3 **Ulnohumeral (joint)**

841.8 **Other specified sites of elbow and forearm**

841.9 **Unspecified site of elbow and forearm**
Elbow NOS

✓4th **842 Sprains and strains of wrist and hand**

✓5th 842.0 **Wrist**

842.00 **Unspecified site**

842.01 **Carpal (joint)**

842.02 **Radiocarpal (joint) (ligament)**

842.09 **Other**
Radioulnar joint, distal

✓5th 842.1 **Hand**

842.10 **Unspecified site**

842.11 **Carpometacarpal (joint)**

842.12 **Metacarpophalangeal (joint)**

842.13 **Interphalangeal (joint)**

842.19 **Other**
Midcarpal (joint)

✓4th **843 Sprains and strains of hip and thigh**

843.0 **Iliofemoral (ligament)**

843.1 **Ischiocapsular (ligament)**

843.8 **Other specified sites of hip and thigh**

843.9 **Unspecified site of hip and thigh**
Hip NOS
Thigh NOS

✓4th **844 Sprains and strains of knee and leg**

844.0 **Lateral collateral ligament of knee**

844.1 **Medial collateral ligament of knee**

844.2 **Cruciate ligament of knee**

844.3 **Tibiofibular (joint) (ligament), superior**

844.8 **Other specified sites of knee and leg**

844.9 **Unspecified site of knee and leg**
Knee NOS
Leg NOS

✓4th **845 Sprains and strains of ankle and foot**

✓5th 845.0 **Ankle**

845.00 **Unspecified site**
AHA: 2Q, '02, 3

845.01 **Deltoid (ligament), ankle**
Internal collateral (ligament), ankle

845.02 **Calcaneofibular (ligament)**

845.03 **Tibiofibular (ligament), distal**
AHA: 1Q, '04, 9

845.09 **Other**
Achilles tendon

✓5th 845.1 **Foot**

845.10 **Unspecified site**

845.11 **Tarsometatarsal (joint) (ligament)**

845.12 **Metatarsophalangeal (joint)**

845.13 **Interphalangeal (joint), toe**

845.19 **Other**

✓4th **846 Sprains and strains of sacroiliac region**

846.0 **Lumbosacral (joint) (ligament)**

846.1 **Sacroiliac ligament**

846.2 **Sacrospinatus (ligament)**

846.3 **Sacrotuberous (ligament)**

846.8 **Other specified sites of sacroiliac region**

846.9 **Unspecified site of sacroiliac region**

✓4th **847 Sprains and strains of other and unspecified parts of back**
EXCLUDES *lumbosacral (846.0)*

847.0 **Neck**
Anterior longitudinal (ligament), cervical
Atlanto-axial (joints)
Atlanto-occipital (joints)
Whiplash injury
EXCLUDES *neck injury NOS (959.0)*
thyroid region (848.2)
S13.4xxA Sprain ligaments cervical spine initial encounter `I-10`

847.1 **Thoracic**

847.2 **Lumbar**

847.3 **Sacrum**
Sacrococcygeal (ligament)

847.4 **Coccyx**

847.9 **Unspecified site of back**
Back NOS

N Newborn Age: 0   P Pediatric Age: 0-17   M Maternity Age: 12-55   A Adult Age: 15-124   MCC Major CC Condition   CC CC Condition   HIV HIV Related Dx

326 – Volume 1   **2010 ICD-9-CM**

848 Other and ill-defined sprains and strains

848.0 Septal cartilage of nose

848.1 Jaw
Temporomandibular (joint) (ligament)

848.2 Thyroid region
Cricoarytenoid (joint) (ligament)
Cricothyroid (joint) (ligament)
Thyroid cartilage

848.3 Ribs
Chondrocostal (joint) ⎫
Costal cartilage ⎭ without mention of injury to sternum

√5th **848.4 Sternum**

848.40 Unspecified site

848.41 Sternoclavicular (joint) (ligament)

848.42 Chondrosternal (joint)

848.49 Other
Xiphoid cartilage

848.5 Pelvis
Symphysis pubis
EXCLUDES *that in childbirth (665.6)*

848.8 Other specified sites of sprains and strains

848.9 Unspecified site of sprain and strain

INTRACRANIAL INJURY, EXCLUDING THOSE WITH SKULL FRACTURE (850-854)

INCLUDES ►traumatic brain injury without skull fracture◄
*open wound of head without intracranial injury (870.0-873.9)
skull fracture alone (800-801 and 803-804 with .0, .5)*

EXCLUDES *intracranial injury with skull fracture (800-801 and 803-804, except .0 and .5)*

Note: The description "with open intracranial wound," used in the fourth-digit subdivisions, includes those specified as open or with mention of infection or foreign body.

The following fifth-digit subclassification is for use with categories 851-854:
 0 unspecified state of consciousness
 1 with no loss of consciousness
 2 with brief [less than one hour] loss of consciousness
 3 with moderate [1-24 hours] loss of consciousness
 4 with prolonged [more than 24 hours] loss of consciousness and return to pre-existing conscious level
 5 with prolonged [more than 24 hours] loss of consciousness without return to pre-existing conscious level
    Use fifth-digit 5 to designate when a patient is unconscious and dies before regaining consciousness, regardless of the duration of the loss of consciousness
 6 with loss of consciousness of unspecified duration
 9 with concussion, unspecified

AHA: 1Q, '93, 22

TIP: If documentation specifies only "head injury," with no further specificity, and is self-limiting, assign instead code 959.01 Head injury, unspecified.

850 Concussion

cerebral bruising that sometimes leads to transient unconsciousness, often followed by brief amnesia, vertigo, nausea, and weak pulse, may experience severe headace and blurred vision after regaining consciousness.

INCLUDES commotio cerebri
EXCLUDES *concussion with:
    cerebral laceration or contusion (851.0-851.9)
    cerebral hemorrhage (852-853)
    head injury NOS (959.01)*   *post-concussion syndrome 310.2*

AHA: 2Q, '96, 6; 4Q, '90, 24

TIP: When a patient is treated for symptoms within 24 to 48 hours of the concussion, clarify with the physician whether the concussion is still in the acute phase or is a postconcussion syndrome; if so, assign instead code 310.2.

850.0 With no loss of consciousness
Concussion with mental confusion or disorientation, without loss of consciousness

√5th **850.1 With brief loss of consciousness**
Loss of consciousness for less than one hour
AHA: 4Q, '03, 76; 1Q, '99, 10; 2Q, '92, 5

850.11 With loss of consciousness of 30 minutes or less   CC
CC Excl: 800.00-801.99, 803.00-804.99, 850.0-852.19, 852.21-854.19, 873.8-873.9, 879.8-879.9, 905.0, 925.1-925.2, 929.0-929.9, 958.8-959.09, 959.8-959.9
S06.0x1A Concussion w/loc 30 min/less initial encounter   I-10

850.12 With loss of consciousness from 31 to 59 minutes   CC
CC Excl: See code: 850.11

850.2 With moderate loss of consciousness   CC
Loss of consciousness for 1-24 hours
CC Excl: See code: 850.11

850.3 With prolonged loss of consciousness and return to pre-existing conscious level   CC
Loss of consciousness for more than 24 hours with complete recovery
CC Excl: See code: 850.11

850.4 With prolonged loss of consciousness, without return to pre-existing conscious level   MCC
CC Excl: See code: 850.11

850.5 With loss of consciousness of unspecified duration   CC
CC Excl: See code: 850.11
S06.0x9A Concussion w/loc uns duration initial encounter   I-10

850.9 Concussion, unspecified

851 Cerebral laceration and contusion
AHA: 4Q, '96, 36; 1Q, '93, 22; 4Q, '90, 24

§10 √5th **851.0 Cortex (cerebral) contusion without**   MCC 5 CC 2-4, 6
[0-6, 9] **mention of open intracranial wound**
CC Excl: For codes 851.02-851.06: 800.00-801.99, 803.00-804.99, 850.0-852.19, 852.21-854.19, 873.8-873.9, 879.8-879.9, 905.0, 925.1-925.2, 929.0-929.9, 958.8-959.09, 959.8-959.9

Brain

Corpus callosum
Cerebrum
Hypothalamus
Interventricular foramen
Fornix
Third ventricle
Pineal body
Optic chiasm
Corpora quadrigemina
Cerebral aqueduct
Hypophysis
Pons
Vermis
Mamillary body
Fourth ventricle
Peduncle
Median aperture
Medulla oblangata
Spinal cord

Precentral gyrus (motor)
Central sulcus
Postcentral gyrus (sensory)
Anterior horn of lateral ventricle
Body and posterior horn of lateral ventricle
Intraventricular foramen
Third ventricle
Lateral sulcus
Inferior horn of lateral ventricle
Fourth ventricle
Cerebral aqueduct
Median aperture
Lateral aperture

10 HAC = only for valid CC or MCC codes.
§ Requires fifth digit. Valid digits are in [brackets] under each code. See beginning of section 850–854 for codes and definitions.

√4th Additional Digit Required   Unacceptable PDx   Manifestation Code   Hospital Acquired Condition   ►◄ Revised Text   ● New Code   ▲ Revised Code Title

Injury and Poisoning

851.1–854.1

§ ✓5ᵗʰ **851.1** **Cortex (cerebral) contusion with open**   `MCC`
[0-6, 9] **intracranial wound**

> CC Excl: 800.00-801.99, 803.00-804.99, 850.0-852.19,
> 852.21-854.19, 873.8-873.9, 879.8-879.9, 905.0, 925.1-925.2,
> 929.0-929.9, 958.8-959.09, 959.8-959.9
> AHA: 1Q, '92, 9

§ ✓5ᵗʰ **851.2** **Cortex (cerebral) laceration without mention**   `MCC`
[0-6, 9] **of open intracranial wound**

> CC Excl: See code: 851.1

§ ✓5ᵗʰ **851.3** **Cortex (cerebral) laceration with open**   `MCC`
[0-6, 9] **intracranial wound**

> CC Excl: See code: 851.1

§¹⁰ ✓5ᵗʰ **851.4** **Cerebellar or brain stem contusion**   `MCC 5` `CC 2-4, 6`
without mention of open intracranial
wound

> CC Excl: For codes 851.42-851.46: 800.00-801.99, 803.00-804.99,
> 850.0-852.19, 852.21-854.19, 873.8-873.9, 879.8-879.9, 905.0,
> 925.1-925.2, 929.0-929.9, 958.8-959.09, 959.8-959.9

§ ✓5ᵗʰ **851.5** **Cerebellar or brain stem contusion with**   `MCC`
[0-6, 9] **open intracranial wound**

> CC Excl: See code: 851.1

§ ✓5ᵗʰ **851.6** **Cerebellar or brain stem laceration without**   `MCC`
[0-6, 9] **mention of open intracranial wound**

> CC Excl: See code: 851.1

§ ✓5ᵗʰ **851.7** **Cerebellar or brain stem laceration with**   `MCC`
[0-6, 9] **open intracranial wound**

> CC Excl: See code: 851.1

§ ✓5ᵗʰ **851.8** **Other and unspecified cerebral laceration and**   `MCC`
[0-6, 9] **contusion, without mention of open**
intracranial wound

> Brain (membrane) NOS
> CC Excl: See code: 851.1
> AHA: 4Q, '96, 37

§ ✓5ᵗʰ **851.9** **Other and unspecified cerebral laceration and**   `MCC`
[0-6, 9] **contusion, with open intracranial wound**

> CC Excl: See code: 851.1

✓4ᵗʰ **852** **Subarachnoid, subdural, and extradural hemorrhage,**
following injury

> **EXCLUDES**   *Cerebral contusion or laceration (with hemorrhage)*
> *(851.0-851.9)*
> **DEF:** Bleeding from lining of brain; due to injury.

§ ✓5ᵗʰ **852.0** **Subarachnoid hemorrhage following injury**   `MCC`
[0-6, 9] **without mention of open intracranial wound**

> Middle meningeal hemorrhage following injury
> CC Excl: 800.00-801.99, 803.00-804.99, 850.0-852.19,
> 852.21-854.19, 873.8-873.9, 879.8-879.9, 905.0, 925.1-925.2,
> 929.0-929.9, 958.8-959.09, 959.8-959.9

§ ✓5ᵗʰ **852.1** **Subarachnoid hemorrhage following injury**   `MCC`
[0-6, 9] **with open intracranial wound**

> CC Excl: See code: 852.0

§ ✓5ᵗʰ **852.2** **Subdural hemorrhage following injury without**   `MCC`
[0-6, 9] **mention of open intracranial wound**

> CC Excl: For code 852.20: 800.00-801.99, 803.00-804.99,
> 850.0-854.19, 873.8-873.9, 879.8-879.9, 905.0, 925.1-925.2,
> 929.0-929.9, 958.8-959.09, 959.8-959.9; **For codes**
> **852.21-852.29:** 800.00-801.99, 803.00-804.99, 850.0-852.19,
> 852.21-854.19, 873.8-873.9, 879.8-879.9, 905.0, 925.1-925.2,
> 929.0-929.9, 958.8-959.09, 959.8-959.9
> AHA: 4Q, '96, 43; **For codes 852.21-852.29:** 4Q, '07, 107
> **S06.5x0A** Traumatic subdurl hemorrhage w/o   `I-10`
> loc initial enc

§ ✓5ᵗʰ **852.3** **Subdural hemorrhage following injury with**   `MCC`
[0-6, 9] **open intracranial wound**

> CC Excl: See code: 852.0

§ ✓5ᵗʰ **852.4** **Extradural hemorrhage following injury**   `MCC`
[0-6, 9] **without mention of open intracranial wound**

> Epidural hematoma following injury
> CC Excl: See code: 852.0

§ ✓5ᵗʰ **852.5** **Extradural hemorrhage following injury**   `MCC`
[0-6, 9] **with open intracranial wound**

> CC Excl: See code: 852.0

✓4ᵗʰ **853** **Other and unspecified intracranial hemorrhage following**
injury

§ ✓5ᵗʰ **853.0** **Without mention of open intracranial wound**   `MCC`
[0-6, 9]

> Cerebral compression due to injury
> Intracranial hematoma following injury
> Traumatic cerebral hemorrhage
> CC Excl: 800.00-801.99, 803.00-804.99, 850.0-852.19,
> 852.21-854.19, 873.8-873.9, 879.8-879.9, 905.0, 925.1-925.2,
> 929.0-929.9, 958.8-959.09, 959.8-959.9
> AHA: 3Q, '90, 14

§ ✓5ᵗʰ **853.1** **With open intracranial wound**   `MCC`
[0-6, 9]   CC Excl: See code: 853.0

✓4ᵗʰ **854** **Intracranial injury of other and unspecified nature**

> **INCLUDES** ▶injury:
>   brain NOS
>   cavernous sinus
>   intracranial
>   traumatic brain NOS◀
> **EXCLUDES**   *any condition classifiable to 850-853*
> *head injury NOS (959.01)*
> AHA: 1Q, '99, 10; 2Q, '92, 6
> **TIP:** Assign a code from category 854 for traumatic brain injury (TBI)
> with diffuse axonal injury (DAI), also known as a shear injury.

§¹⁰ ✓5ᵗʰ **854.0** **Without mention of open intracranial**   `MCC 5` `CC 2-4, 6`
[0-6, 9] **wound**

> CC Excl: For codes 854.02-854.06: 800.00-801.99, 803.00-804.99,
> 850.0-852.19, 852.21-854.19, 873.8-873.9, 879.8-879.9, 905.0,
> 925.1-925.2, 929.0-929.9, 958.8-959.09, 959.8-959.9
> AHA: For code 854.00: 2Q, '05, 6

§ ✓5ᵗʰ **854.1** **With open intracranial wound**   `MCC`
[0-6, 9]

> CC Excl: 800.00-801.99, 803.00-804.99, 850.0-852.19,
> 852.21-854.19, 873.8-873.9, 879.8-879.9, 905.0, 925.1-925.2,
> 929.0-929.9, 958.8-959.09, 959.8-959.9

---

¹⁰   HAC = only for valid CC or MCC codes.
§   Requires fifth digit. Valid digits are in [brackets] under each code. See beginning of section 850–854 for codes and definitions.

`N` Newborn Age: 0   `P` Pediatric Age: 0-17   `M` Maternity Age: 12-55   `A` Adult Age: 15-124   `MCC` Major CC Condition   `CC` CC Condition   `HIV` HIV Related Dx

328 – Volume 1 • October 2009   **2010 ICD-9-CM**

INTERNAL INJURY OF THORAX, ABDOMEN, AND PELVIS (860-869)

INCLUDES
blast injuries
blunt trauma
bruise
concussion injuries (except cerebral)
crushing   of internal
hematoma   organs
laceration
puncture
tear
traumatic rupture

EXCLUDES
concussion NOS (850.0-850.9)
flail chest (807.4)
foreign body entering through orifice (930.0-939.9)
injury to blood vessels (901.0-902.9)

Note: The description "with open wound," used in the fourth-digit subdivisions, includes those with mention of infection or foreign body.

√4th **860   Traumatic pneumothorax and hemothorax**
DEF: Traumatic pneumothorax: air or gas leaking into pleural space of lung due to trauma.
DEF: Traumatic hemothorax: blood buildup in pleural space of lung due to trauma.
AHA: 2Q, '93, 4
TIP: If there's no mention of trauma associated with pneumothorax, see instead category 512.

860.0   **Pneumothorax without mention of open**   CC
wound into thorax
CC Excl: 860.0-860.5, 861.20-861.32, 862.29, 862.39-862.9, 875.0-875.1, 879.8-879.9, 929.0-929.9, 958.7-958.99, 959.8-959.9
S27.0xxA Traumatic pneumothorax initial encounter   I-10

860.1   **Pneumothorax with open wound into thorax**   MCC
CC Excl: See code 860.0

860.2   **Hemothorax without mention of open**   MCC
wound into thorax
CC Excl: See code 860.0

860.3   **Hemothorax with open wound into thorax**   MCC
CC Excl: See code 860.0

860.4   **Pneumohemothorax without mention of**   MCC
open wound into thorax
CC Excl: See code 860.0

860.5   **Pneumohemothorax with open wound into thorax** MCC
CC Excl: See code 860.0

√4th **861   Injury to heart and lung**
EXCLUDES   injury to blood vessels of thorax (901.0-901.9)

√5th   861.0   **Heart, without mention of open wound into thorax**
AHA: 1Q, '92, 9

861.00   **Unspecified injury**   CC
CC Excl: 861.00-861.13, 862.29, 862.39-862.9, 959.9

861.01   **Contusion**   CC
Cardiac contusion
Myocardial contusion
DEF: Bruising within the pericardium with no mention of open wound.
CC Excl: 861.00-861.13, 862.29, 862.39-862.9, 875.0-875.1, 879.8-879.9, 929.0-929.9, 958.7-958.99, 959.8-959.9

861.02   **Laceration without penetration of**   MCC
heart chambers
DEF: Tearing injury of heart tissue, without penetration of chambers; no open wound.
CC Excl: See code 861.01

861.03   **Laceration with penetration of**   MCC
heart chambers
CC Excl: See code 861.01

√5th   861.1   **Heart, with open wound into thorax**

861.10   **Unspecified injury**   MCC
CC Excl: See code 861.01

861.11   **Contusion**   MCC
CC Excl: See code 861.01

861.12   **Laceration without penetration of**   MCC
heart chambers
CC Excl: See code 861.01

861.13   **Laceration with penetration of**   MCC
heart chambers
CC Excl: See code 861.01

√5th   861.2   **Lung, without mention of open wound into thorax**

861.20   **Unspecified injury**   CC
CC Excl: 861.20-861.32, 862.29, 862.39-862.9, 875.0-875.1, 879.8-879.9, 929.0-929.9, 958.7-958.8, 958.99, 959.8-959.9

861.21   **Contusion**   CC
DEF: Bruising of lung without mention of open wound.
CC Excl: See code: 861.20
S27.321A Contusion of lung unilateral initial encounter   I-10

861.22   **Laceration**   MCC
CC Excl: 861.20-861.32, 862.29, 862.39-862.9, 875.0-875.1, 879.8-879.9, 929.0-929.9, 958.7-958.99, 959.8-959.9

√5th   861.3   **Lung, with open wound into thorax**

861.30   **Unspecified injury**   MCC
CC Excl: See code 861.22

861.31   **Contusion**   MCC
CC Excl: See code 861.22

861.32   **Laceration**   MCC
CC Excl: See code 861.22

√4th **862   Injury to other and unspecified intrathoracic organs**
EXCLUDES   injury to blood vessels of thorax (901.0-901.9)

862.0   **Diaphragm, without mention of open wound**   CC
into cavity
CC Excl: 862.0-862.1, 862.29, 862.39-862.9, 875.0-875.1, 879.8-879.9, 929.0-929.9, 958.7-958.8, 958.99, 959.8-959.9

862.1   **Diaphragm, with open wound into cavity**   MCC
CC Excl: 862.0-862.1, 862.29, 862.39-862.9, 875.0-875.1, 879.8-879.9, 929.0-929.9, 958.7-958.99, 959.8-959.9

√5th   862.2   **Other specified intrathoracic organs, without mention of open wound into cavity**

862.21   **Bronchus**   MCC
CC Excl: 862.21, 862.29-862.31, 862.39-862.9, 875.0-875.1, 879.8-879.9, 929.0-929.9, 958.7-958.99, 959.8-959.9

862.22   **Esophagus**   MCC
CC Excl: 862.22-862.29, 862.32-862.9, 875.0-875.1, 879.8-879.9, 929.0-929.9, 958.7-958.99, 959.8-959.9

862.29   **Other**   CC
Pleura   Thymus gland
CC Excl: 862.29, 862.39-862.9, 875.0-875.1, 879.8-879.9, 929.0-929.9, 958.7-958.99, 959.8-959.9

√5th   862.3   **Other specified intrathoracic organs, with open wound into cavity**

862.31   **Bronchus**   MCC
CC Excl: See code: 862.21

862.32   **Esophagus**   MCC
CC Excl: See code: 862.22

862.39   **Other**   MCC
CC Excl: See code: 862.29

862.8   **Multiple and unspecified intrathoracic**   CC
organs, without mention of open wound into cavity
Crushed chest
Multiple intrathoracic organs
CC Excl: 862.29, 862.39-862.9, 875.0-875.1, 879.8-879.9, 929.0-929.9, 958.7-958.8, 958.93-958.99, 959.8-959.9

√4th
√5th   Additional Digit Required   Unacceptable PDx   Manifestation Code   Hospital Acquired Condition   ▶◀ Revised Text   ● New Code   ▲ Revised Code Title
2010 ICD-9-CM   **Volume 1 – 329**

860–862.8

Injury and Poisoning

862.9–863.99

862.9 Multiple and unspecified intrathoracic organs, with open wound into cavity `MCC`
CC Excl: See code: 862.29

√4ᵗʰ **863 Injury to gastrointestinal tract**
EXCLUDES anal sphincter laceration during delivery (664.2)
bile duct (868.0-868.1 with fifth-digit 2)
gallbladder (868.0-868.1 with fifth-digit 2)

863.0 Stomach, without mention of open wound into cavity `CC`
CC Excl: 729.73, 863.0-863.1, 863.80, 863.89-863.90, 863.99, 868.00, 868.03-868.10, 868.13-869.1, 879.2-879.9, 929.0-929.9, 958.8, 958.93-958.99, 959.8-959.9

863.1 Stomach, with open wound into cavity `MCC`
CC Excl: 863.0-863.1, 863.80, 863.89-863.90, 863.99, 868.00, 868.03-868.10, 868.13-869.1, 879.2-879.9, 929.0-929.9, 958.8-958.99, 959.8-959.9

√5ᵗʰ **863.2 Small intestine, without mention of open wound into cavity**

863.20 Small intestine, unspecified site `CC`
CC Excl: 729.73, 863.20-863.39, 863.80, 863.89-863.90, 863.99, 868.00, 868.03-868.10, 868.13-869.1, 879.2-879.9, 929.0-929.9, 958.8, 958.93-958.99, 959.8-959.9

863.21 Duodenum `CC`
CC Excl: See code: 863.20

863.29 Other `CC`
CC Excl: See code: 863.20

√5ᵗʰ **863.3 Small intestine, with open wound into cavity**

863.30 Small intestine, unspecified site `MCC`
CC Excl: 863.20-863.39, 863.80, 863.89-863.90, 863.99, 868.00, 868.03-868.10, 868.13-869.1, 879.2-879.9, 929.0-929.9, 958.8-958.99, 959.8-959.9

863.31 Duodenum `MCC`
CC Excl: 863.21, 863.31-863.39, 863.80, 863.89-863.90, 863.99, 868.00, 868.03-868.10, 868.13-869.1, 879.2-879.9, 929.0-929.9, 958.8-958.99, 959.8-959.9

863.39 Other `MCC`
CC Excl: See code: 863.30

√5ᵗʰ **863.4 Colon or rectum, without mention of open wound into cavity**

863.40 Colon, unspecified site `CC`
CC Excl: 729.73, 863.40-863.80, 863.89-863.90, 863.99, 868.00, 868.03-868.10, 868.13-869.1, 879.2-879.9, 929.0-929.9, 958.8, 958.93-958.99, 959.8-959.9

863.41 Ascending [right] colon `CC`
CC Excl: See code: 863.40

863.42 Transverse colon `CC`
CC Excl: See code: 863.40

863.43 Descending [left] colon `CC`
CC Excl: See code: 863.40

863.44 Sigmoid colon `CC`
CC Excl: See code: 863.40

863.45 Rectum `CC`
CC Excl: See code: 863.40

863.46 Multiple sites in colon and rectum `CC`
CC Excl: See code: 863.40

863.49 Other `CC`
CC Excl: See code: 863.40

√5ᵗʰ **863.5 Colon or rectum, with open wound into cavity**

863.50 Colon, unspecified site `MCC`
CC Excl: 863.40-863.80, 863.89-863.90, 863.99, 868.00, 868.03-868.10, 868.13-869.1, 879.2-879.9, 929.0-929.9, 958.8-958.99, 959.8-959.9

863.51 Ascending [right] colon `MCC`
CC Excl: See code 863.50

863.52 Transverse colon `MCC`
CC Excl: See code 863.50

863.53 Descending [left] colon `MCC`
CC Excl: See code 863.50

863.54 Sigmoid colon `MCC`
CC Excl: See code 863.50

863.55 Rectum `MCC`
CC Excl: See code 863.50

863.56 Multiple sites in colon and rectum `MCC`
CC Excl: See code 863.50

863.59 Other `MCC`
CC Excl: See code 863.50

√5ᵗʰ **863.8 Other and unspecified gastrointestinal sites, without mention of open wound into cavity**

863.80 Gastrointestinal tract, unspecified site `CC`
CC Excl: 729.73, 863.0-863.80, 863.89-863.90, 863.99, 868.00, 868.03-868.10, 868.13-869.1, 879.2-879.9, 929.0-929.9, 958.8, 958.93-958.99, 959.8-959.9

863.81 Pancreas, head `CC`
CC Excl: 729.73, 863.80-863.84, 863.91-863.94, 863.99, 868.00, 868.03-868.10, 868.13-869.1, 879.2-879.9, 929.0-929.9, 958.8, 958.93-958.99, 959.8-959.9

863.82 Pancreas, body `CC`
CC Excl: See code: 863.81

863.83 Pancreas, tail `CC`
CC Excl: See code: 863.81

863.84 Pancreas, multiple and unspecified sites `CC`
CC Excl: See code: 863.81

863.85 Appendix `CC`
CC Excl: 729.73, 863.40-863.80, 863.85-863.90, 863.99, 868.00, 868.03-868.10, 868.13-869.1, 879.2-879.9, 929.0-929.9, 958.8, 958.93-958.99, 959.8-959.9

863.89 Other `CC`
Intestine NOS
CC Excl: 729.73, 863.0-863.84, 863.89-863.94, 863.99, 868.00, 868.03-868.10, 868.13-869.1, 879.2-879.9, 929.0-929.9, 958.8-958.90, 958.93-958.99, 959.8-959.9

√5ᵗʰ **863.9 Other and unspecified gastrointestinal sites, with open wound into cavity**

863.90 Gastrointestinal tract, unspecified site `MCC`
CC Excl: 863.80-863.84, 863.89-863.94, 863.99, 868.00, 868.03-868.10, 868.13-869.1, 879.2-879.9, 929.0-929.9, 958.8-958.99, 959.8-959.9

863.91 Pancreas, head `MCC`
CC Excl: 863.80-863.84, 863.91-863.94, 863.99, 868.00, 868.03-868.10, 868.13-869.1, 879.2-879.9, 929.0-929.9, 958.8-958.99, 959.8-959.9

863.92 Pancreas, body `MCC`
CC Excl: See code 863.91

863.93 Pancreas, tail `MCC`
CC Excl: See code 863.91

863.94 Pancreas, multiple and unspecified sites `MCC`
CC Excl: See code 863.91

863.95 Appendix `MCC`
CC Excl: 863.80, 863.85, 863.95-863.99, 868.00, 868.03-868.10, 868.13-869.1, 879.2-879.9, 929.0-929.9, 958.8-958.99, 959.8-959.9

863.99 Other `MCC`
CC Excl: 863.80, 863.99, 868.00, 868.03-868.10, 868.13-869.1, 879.2-879.9, 929.0-929.9, 958.8-958.99, 959.8-959.9

✓4ᵗʰ 864 Injury to liver

The following fifth-digit subclassification is for use with category 864:
- **0 unspecified injury**
- **1 hematoma and contusion**
- **2 laceration, minor**
  Laceration involving capsule only, or without significant involvement of hepatic parenchyma [i.e., less than 1 cm deep]
- **3 laceration, moderate**
  Laceration involving parenchyma but without major disruption of parenchyma [i.e., less than 10 cm long and less than 3 cm deep]
- **4 laceration, major**
  Laceration with significant disruption of hepatic parenchyma [i.e., 10 cm long and 3 cm deep]
  Multiple moderate lacerations, with or without hematoma
  Stellate lacerations of liver
- **5 laceration, unspecified**
- **9 other**

§ ✓5ᵗʰ **864.0 Without mention of open wound**   `MCC 3-4` `CC 0-2, 5, 9`
[0-5, 9] **into cavity**

    CC Excl: 863.80, 863.99-864.19, 868.00, 868.03-868.10, 868.13-869.1, 879.2-879.9, 929.0-929.9, 958.8-958.99, 959.8-959.9

§ ✓5ᵗʰ **864.1 With open wound into cavity**   `MCC`
[0-5, 9] **CC Excl:** See code 864.0

✓4ᵗʰ 865 Injury to spleen

The following fifth-digit subclassification is for use with category 865:
- **0 unspecified injury**
- **1 hematoma without rupture of capsule**
- **2 capsular tears, without major disruption of parenchyma**
- **3 laceration extending into parenchyma**
- **4 massive parenchymal disruption**
- **9 other**

§ ✓5ᵗʰ **865.0 Without mention of wound into**   `MCC 3-4` `CC 0-2, 9`
[0-4, 9] **cavity**

    CC Excl: 865.00-865.19, 868.00, 868.03-868.10, 868.13-869.1, 879.2-879.9, 929.0-929.9, 958.8-958.99, 959.8-959.9

§ ✓5ᵗʰ **865.1 With open wound into cavity**   `MCC`
[0-4, 9] **CC Excl:** See code 865.0

✓4ᵗʰ 866 Injury to kidney

    `EXCLUDES` *acute kidney injury (nontraumatic) (584.9)*

    AHA: ▶4Q, '08, 192◀

The following fifth-digit subclassification is for use with category 866:
- **0 unspecified injury**
- **1 hematoma without rupture of capsule**
- **2 laceration**
- **3 complete disruption of kidney parenchyma**

§ ✓5ᵗʰ **866.0 Without mention of open wound**   `MCC 3` `CC 0-2`
[0-3] **into cavity**

    CC Excl: 866.00-866.13, 868.00, 868.03-868.10, 868.13-869.1, 879.2-879.9, 929.0-929.9, 958.8-958.99, 959.8-959.9

§ ✓5ᵗʰ **866.1 With open wound into cavity**   `MCC`
[0-3] **CC Excl:** See code 866.0

✓4ᵗʰ 867 Injury to pelvic organs

    `EXCLUDES` *injury during delivery (664.0-665.9)*

867.0 Bladder and urethra, without mention of   `CC`
open wound into cavity

    CC Excl: 867.0-867.1, 867.6-868.00, 868.03-868.10, 868.13-869.1, 879.2-879.9, 929.0-929.9, 958.8-958.99, 959.8-959.9

    AHA: N-D, '85, 15

    TIP: Assign for urethral injury due to senile patient's pulling out indwelling urinary catheter.

    S37.20xA Unspecified injury of bladder initial encounter   `I-10`

867.1 Bladder and urethra, with open wound   `MCC`
into cavity

    CC Excl: See code 867.0

867.2 Ureter, without mention of open wound   `CC`
into cavity

    CC Excl: 867.2-867.3, 867.6-868.00, 868.03-868.10, 868.13-869.1, 879.2-879.9, 929.0-929.9, 958.8-958.99, 959.8-959.9

867.3 Ureter, with open wound into cavity   `MCC`

    CC Excl: See code 867.2

867.4 Uterus, without mention of open wound   `CC` ♀
into cavity

    CC Excl: 867.4-868.00, 868.03-868.10, 868.13-869.1, 879.2-879.9, 929.0-929.9, 958.8-958.99, 959.8-959.9

867.5 Uterus, with open wound into cavity   `MCC` ♀

    CC Excl: See code 867.4

867.6 Other specified pelvic organs, without   `CC`
mention of open wound into cavity

    Fallopian tube   Seminal vesicle
    Ovary   Vas deferens
    Prostate

    CC Excl: 867.6-868.00, 868.03-868.10, 868.13-869.1, 879.2-879.9, 929.0-929.9, 958.8-958.99, 959.8-959.9

867.7 Other specified pelvic organs, with open   `MCC`
wound into cavity

    CC Excl: See code 867.6

867.8 Unspecified pelvic organ, without mention   `CC`
of open wound into cavity

    CC Excl: See code 867.6

867.9 Unspecified pelvic organ, with open wound   `MCC`
into cavity

    CC Excl: See code 867.6

✓4ᵗʰ 868 Injury to other intra-abdominal organs

The following fifth-digit subclassification is for use with category 868:
- **0 unspecified intra-abdominal organ**
- **1 adrenal gland**
- **2 bile duct and gallbladder**
- **3 peritoneum**
- **4 retroperitoneum**
- **9 other and multiple intra-abdominal organs**

§ ✓5ᵗʰ **868.0 Without mention of open wound into cavity**   `CC`
[0-4, 9] **CC Excl: For codes 868.00, 868.03-863.09:** 868.00, 868.03-868.10, 868.13-869.1, 879.2-879.9, 929.0-929.9, 958.8-958.99, 959.8-959.9; **For code 868.01:** 868.00-868.01, 868.03-868.11, 868.13-869.1, 879.2-879.9, 929.0-929.9, 958.8-958.99, 959.8-959.9; **For code 868.02:** 868.00, 868.02-868.10, 868.13-869.1, 879.2-879.9, 929.0-929.9, 958.8-958.99, 959.8-959.9

§ ✓5ᵗʰ **868.1 With open wound into cavity**   `MCC`
[0-4, 9] **CC Excl: For codes 868.10, 868.13-868.19:** 868.00, 868.03-868.10, 868.13-869.1, 879.2-879.9, 929.0-929.9, 958.8-958.99, 959.8-959.9; **For code 868.11:** 868.00-868.01, 868.03-868.11, 868.13-869.1, 879.2-879.9, 929.0-929.9, 958.8-958.99, 959.8-959.9; **For code 868.12:** 868.00, 868.03-868.10, 868.12-869.1, 879.2-879.9, 929.0-929.9, 958.8-958.99, 959.8-959.9

✓4ᵗʰ 869 Internal injury to unspecified or ill-defined organs

    `INCLUDES`   internal injury NOS
                multiple internal injury NOS

869.0 Without mention of open wound into cavity   `CC`

    CC Excl: 868.00, 868.03-868.10, 868.13-869.1, 879.2-879.9, 929.0-929.9, 958.8-958.99, 959.8-959.9

869.1 With open wound into cavity   `MCC`

    CC Excl: See code: 869.0

    AHA: 2Q, '89, 15

---

§   Requires fifth digit. Valid digits are in [brackets] under each code. See appropriate category for codes and definitions.

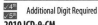

✓4ᵗʰ / ✓5ᵗʰ Additional Digit Required   Unacceptable PDx   Manifestation Code   Hospital Acquired Condition   ▶◀ Revised Text   ● New Code   ▲ Revised Code Title

Injury and Poisoning

870–872.9

OPEN WOUND (870-897)

INCLUDES	animal bite
	avulsion
	cut
	laceration
	puncture wound
	traumatic amputation
EXCLUDES	*burn (940.0-949.5)*
	crushing (925-929.9)
	puncture of internal organs (860.0-869.1)
	superficial injury (910.0-919.9)
	that incidental to:
	dislocation (830.0-839.9)
	fracture (800.0-829.1)
	internal injury (860.0-869.1)
	intracranial injury (851.0-854.1)

Note: The description "complicated" used in the fourth-digit subdivisions includes those with mention of delayed healing, delayed treatment, foreign body, or infection.

AHA: 4Q, '01, 52

TIP: Do not assign a code designated as "complicated" based only on physician documentation of complicated. For coding purposes, there must be indications of delayed healing, delayed treatment, infection, or foreign body.

OPEN WOUND OF HEAD, NECK, AND TRUNK (870-879)

√4th **870   Open wound of ocular adnexa**

870.0   Laceration of skin of eyelid and periocular area

870.1   Laceration of eyelid, full-thickness, not involving lacrimal passages

870.2   Laceration of eyelid involving lacrimal passages   `CC`
CC Excl: 870.0-871.9, 879.8-879.9, 929.0-929.9, 958.8, 959.8-959.9

870.3   Penetrating wound of orbit, without mention of foreign body   `CC`
CC Excl: 870.0-871.9, 879.8-879.9, 929.0-929.9, 958.8-958.99, 959.8-959.9

870.4   Penetrating wound of orbit with foreign body   `CC`
EXCLUDES   *retained (old) foreign body in orbit (376.6)*
CC Excl: See code 870.3

870.8   Other specified open wounds of ocular adnexa   `CC`
CC Excl: See code 870.3

870.9   Unspecified open wound of ocular adnexa   `CC`
CC Excl: See code 870.3

√4th **871   Open wound of eyeball**
EXCLUDES   *2nd cranial nerve [optic] injury (950.0-950.9)*
     3rd cranial nerve [oculomotor] injury (951.0)

871.0   Ocular laceration without prolapse of intraocular tissue   `CC`
DEF: Tear in ocular tissue without displacing structures.
CC Excl: See code 870.3
AHA: 3Q, '96, 7

871.1   Ocular laceration with prolapse or exposure of intraocular tissue   `CC`
CC Excl: See code 870.3

871.2   Rupture of eye with partial loss of intraocular tissue   `CC`
DEF: Forcible tearing of eyeball, with tissue loss.
CC Excl: See code 870.3

871.3   Avulsion of eye   `CC`
Traumatic enucleation
DEF: Traumatic extraction of eyeball from socket.
CC Excl: See code 870.3

871.4   Unspecified laceration of eye

871.5   Penetration of eyeball with magnetic foreign body   `CC`
EXCLUDES   *retained (old) magnetic foreign body in globe (360.50-360.59)*
CC Excl: 870.0-871.9, 879.8-879.9, 929.0-929.9, 958.8, 959.8-959.9

871.6   Penetration of eyeball with (nonmagnetic) foreign body   `CC`
EXCLUDES   *retained (old) (nonmagnetic) foreign body in globe (360.60-360.69)*
CC Excl: 870.0-871.9, 879.8-879.9, 929.0-929.9, 958.8, 959.8-959.9

871.7   Unspecified ocular penetration

871.9   Unspecified open wound of eyeball   `CC`
CC Excl: See code: 870.3

√4th **872   Open wound of ear**

√5th **872.0   External ear, without mention of complication**

872.00   External ear, unspecified site

872.01   Auricle, ear
Pinna
DEF: Open wound of fleshy, outer ear.

872.02   Auditory canal
DEF: Open wound of passage from external ear to eardrum.

√5th **872.1   External ear, complicated**

872.10   External ear, unspecified site

872.11   Auricle, ear

872.12   Auditory canal   `CC`
CC Excl: 872.00-872.9, 879.8-879.9, 929.0-929.9, 958.8, 959.8-959.9

√5th **872.6   Other specified parts of ear, without mention of complication**

872.61   Ear drum   `CC`
Drumhead
Tympanic membrane
CC Excl: See code: 872.12

872.62   Ossicles   `CC`
CC Excl: See code: 872.12

872.63   Eustachian tube   `CC`
DEF: Open wound of channel between nasopharynx and tympanic cavity.
CC Excl: See code: 872.12

872.64   Cochlea   `CC`
DEF: Open wound of snail shell shaped tube of inner ear.
CC Excl: See code: 872.12

872.69   Other and multiple sites   `CC`
CC Excl: See code 872.12

√5th **872.7   Other specified parts of ear, complicated**

872.71   Ear drum   `CC`
CC Excl: See code: 872.12

872.72   Ossicles   `CC`
CC Excl: 872.00-872.9, 879.8-879.9, 929.0-929.9, 958.8-958.99, 959.8-959.9

872.73   Eustachian tube   `CC`
CC Excl: See code: 872.72

872.74   Cochlea   `CC`
CC Excl: See code 872.72

872.79   Other and multiple sites   `CC`
CC Excl: See code: 872.12

872.8   Ear, part unspecified, without mention of complication
Ear NOS

872.9   Ear, part unspecified, complicated

| N Newborn Age: 0 | P Pediatric Age: 0-17 | M Maternity Age: 12-55 | A Adult Age: 15-124 | MCC Major CC Condition | CC CC Condition | HIV HIV Related Dx |

332 – Volume 1   **2010 ICD-9-CM**

✓4th 873   Other open wound of head

    873.0   Scalp, without mention of complication
       S01.01xA Laceration w/o foreign body scalp initial enc   `I-10`

    873.1   Scalp, complicated

    ✓5th 873.2   Nose, without mention of complication

       873.20   Nose, unspecified site

       873.21   Nasal septum
          DEF: Open wound between nasal passages.

       873.22   Nasal cavity
          DEF: Open wound of nostrils.

       873.23   Nasal sinus   `CC`
          DEF: Open wound of mucous-lined respiratory cavities.
          CC Excl: 873.20-873.39, 879.8-879.9, 929.0-929.9, 958.8, 959.8-959.9

       873.29   Multiple sites

    ✓5th 873.3   Nose, complicated

       873.30   Nose, unspecified site

       873.31   Nasal septum

       873.32   Nasal cavity

       873.33   Nasal sinus   `CC`
          CC Excl: 873.20-873.39, 879.8-879.9, 929.0-929.9, 958.8-958.99, 959.8-959.9

       873.39   Multiple sites

    ✓5th 873.4   Face, without mention of complication

       873.40   Face, unspecified site

       873.41   Cheek

       873.42   Forehead
          Eyebrow
          AHA: 4Q, '96, 43
          S01.81xA Laceration w/o FB other part head initial enc   `I-10`

       873.43   Lip

       873.44   Jaw

       873.49   Other and multiple sites

    ✓5th 873.5   Face, complicated

       873.50   Face, unspecified site

       873.51   Cheek

       873.52   Forehead

       873.53   Lip

       873.54   Jaw

       873.59   Other and multiple sites

    ✓5th 873.6   Internal structures of mouth, without mention of complication

       873.60   Mouth, unspecified site

       873.61   Buccal mucosa
          DEF: Open wound of inside of cheek.

       873.62   Gum (alveolar process)

       873.63   Tooth (broken) (fractured) (due to trauma)
          EXCLUDES   cracked tooth (521.81)
          AHA: 1Q, '04, 17

       873.64   Tongue and floor of mouth

       873.65   Palate
          DEF: Open wound of roof of mouth.

       873.69   Other and multiple sites

    ✓5th 873.7   Internal structures of mouth, complicated

       873.70   Mouth, unspecified site

       873.71   Buccal mucosa

       873.72   Gum (alveolar process)

       873.73   Tooth (broken) (fractured) (due to trauma)
          EXCLUDES   cracked tooth (521.81)
          AHA: 1Q, '04, 17

       873.74   Tongue and floor of mouth

       873.75   Palate

       873.79   Other and multiple sites

    873.8   Other and unspecified open wound of head without mention of complication
       Head NOS

    873.9   Other and unspecified open wound of head, complicated

✓4th 874   Open wound of neck

    ✓5th 874.0   Larynx and trachea, without mention of complication

       874.00   Larynx with trachea   `MCC`
          CC Excl: 847.0, 874.00-874.12, 874.8-874.9, 879.8-879.9, 929.0-929.9, 958.8-958.99, 959.8-959.9

       874.01   Larynx   `MCC`
          CC Excl: See code 874.00

       874.02   Trachea   `MCC`
          CC Excl: See code 874.00

    ✓5th 874.1   Larynx and trachea, complicated

       874.10   Larynx with trachea   `MCC`
          CC Excl: See code 874.00

       874.11   Larynx   `MCC`
          CC Excl: See code 874.00

       874.12   Trachea   `MCC`
          CC Excl: See code 874.00

    874.2   Thyroid gland, without mention of complication   `CC`
       CC Excl: 847.0, 874.2-874.3, 874.8-874.9, 879.8-879.9, 929.0-929.9, 958.8, 959.8-959.9

    874.3   Thyroid gland, complicated   `CC`
       CC Excl: 847.0, 874.2-874.3, 874.8-874.9, 879.8-879.9, 929.0-929.9, 958.8-958.99, 959.8-959.9

    874.4   Pharynx, without mention of complication   `CC`
       Cervical esophagus
       CC Excl: 847.0, 874.4-874.9, 879.8-879.9, 929.0-929.9, 958.8, 959.8-959.9

    874.5   Pharynx, complicated   `CC`
       CC Excl: 847.0, 874.4-874.9, 879.8-879.9, 929.0-929.9, 958.8-958.99, 959.8-959.9

    874.8   Other and unspecified parts, without mention of complication
       Nape of neck
       Supraclavicular region
       Throat NOS

    874.9   Other and unspecified parts, complicated

✓4th 875   Open wound of chest (wall)
    EXCLUDES   open wound into thoracic cavity (860.0-862.9)
          traumatic pneumothorax and hemothorax (860.1, 860.3, 860.5)
    AHA: 3Q, '95, 17; 3Q, '93, 17

    875.0   Without mention of complication   `CC`
       CC Excl: 847.1, 862.29, 862.39-862.9, 875.0-875.1, 879.8-879.9, 929.0-929.9, 958.7-958.99, 959.8-959.9

    875.1   Complicated   `CC`
       CC Excl: See code 875.0

✓4th 876   Open wound of back
    `INCLUDES`   loin
          lumbar region
    EXCLUDES   open wound into thoracic cavity (860.0-862.9)
          traumatic pneumothorax and hemothorax (860.1, 860.3, 860.5)

    876.0   Without mention of complication

    876.1   Complicated

✓4th Additional Digit Required   Unacceptable PDx   Manifestation Code   Hospital Acquired Condition   ▶◀ Revised Text   ● New Code   ▲ Revised Code Title

✓5th

2010 ICD-9-CM   **Volume 1 – 333**

Injury and Poisoning

877–886.1

√4ʰ **877 Open wound of buttock**

     INCLUDES   sacroiliac region

     877.0 Without mention of complication

     877.1 Complicated

√4ʰ **878 Open wound of genital organs (external), including traumatic amputation**

     EXCLUDES   *injury during delivery (664.0-665.9)*
                   internal genital organs (867.0-867.9)

     878.0 Penis, without mention of complication   ♂

     878.1 Penis, complicated   ♂

     878.2 Scrotum and testes, without mention of complication   ♂

     878.3 Scrotum and testes, complicated   ♂

     878.4 Vulva, without mention of complication   ♀
             Labium (majus) (minus)

     878.5 Vulva, complicated   ♀

     878.6 Vagina, without mention of complication   ♀

     878.7 Vagina, complicated   ♀

     878.8 Other and unspecified parts, without mention of complication

     878.9 Other and unspecified parts, complicated

√4ʰ **879 Open wound of other and unspecified sites, except limbs**

     879.0 Breast, without mention of complication

     879.1 Breast, complicated

     879.2 Abdominal wall, anterior, without mention of complication
             Abdominal wall NOS
             Epigastric region
             Hypogastric region
             Pubic region
             Umbilical region
             AHA: 2Q, '91, 22; 3Q, '90, 5
             TIP: If the abdominal wall open wound results in aortic rupture, sequence code 902.0 first.

     879.3 Abdominal wall, anterior, complicated

     879.4 Abdominal wall, lateral, without mention of complication
             Flank
             Groin
             Hypochondrium
             Iliac (region)
             Inguinal region

     879.5 Abdominal wall, lateral, complicated

     879.6 Other and unspecified parts of trunk, without mention of complication
             Pelvic region
             Perineum
             Trunk NOS

     879.7 Other and unspecified parts of trunk, complicated

     879.8 Open wound(s) (multiple) of unspecified site(s) without mention of complication
             Multiple open wounds NOS
             Open wound NOS

     879.9 Open wound(s) (multiple) of unspecified site(s), complicated

OPEN WOUND OF UPPER LIMB (880-887)

AHA: N-D, '85, 5

TIP: For degloving injuries, assign code for open wound of the specified site, most often involving extremities.

√4ʰ **880 Open wound of shoulder and upper arm**

     The following fifth-digit subclassification is for use with category 880:
        0   shoulder region
        1   scapular region
        2   axillary region
        3   upper arm
        9   multiple sites

§ √5ʰ **880.0 Without mention of complication**
     [0-3,9]

§ √5ʰ **880.1 Complicated**
     [0-3,9]   **AHA: For code 880.13:** 2Q, '06, 7

§ √5ʰ **880.2 With tendon involvement**   CC
     [0-3,9]   **CC Excl:** 880.00-880.29

√4ʰ **881 Open wound of elbow, forearm, and wrist**

     The following fifth-digit subclassification is for use with category 881:
        0   forearm
        1   elbow
        2   wrist

§ √5ʰ **881.0 Without mention of complication**
     [0-2]

§ √5ʰ **881.1 Complicated**
     [0-2]

§ √5ʰ **881.2 With tendon involvement**   CC
     [0-2]   **CC Excl:** 881.00-881.22

√4ʰ **882 Open wound of hand except finger(s) alone**

     882.0 Without mention of complication

     882.1 Complicated
             AHA: ▶4Q, '08, 152◀

     882.2 With tendon involvement   CC
             CC Excl: 882.0-882.2

√4ʰ **883 Open wound of finger(s)**

     INCLUDES   fingernail
                   thumb (nail)

     883.0 Without mention of complication

     883.1 Complicated

     883.2 With tendon involvement   CC
             CC Excl: 883.0-883.2

√4ʰ **884 Multiple and unspecified open wound of upper limb**

     INCLUDES   arm NOS
                   multiple sites of one upper limb
                   upper limb NOS

     884.0 Without mention of complication

     884.1 Complicated

     884.2 With tendon involvement   CC
             CC Excl: 884.0-884.2

√4ʰ **885 Traumatic amputation of thumb (complete) (partial)**

     INCLUDES   thumb(s) (with finger(s) of either hand)

     885.0 Without mention of complication
             AHA: 1Q, '03, 7

     885.1 Complicated

√4ʰ **886 Traumatic amputation of other finger(s) (complete) (partial)**

     INCLUDES   finger(s) of one or both hands, without mention of thumb(s)

     886.0 Without mention of complication

     886.1 Complicated

---

§   Requires fifth digit. Valid digits are in [brackets] under each code. See appropriate category for codes and definitions.

N Newborn Age: 0   P Pediatric Age: 0-17   M Maternity Age: 12-55   A Adult Age: 15-124   MCC Major CC Condition   CC CC Condition   HIV HIV Related Dx

✓4ᵗʰ **887 Traumatic amputation of arm and hand (complete) (partial)**

887.0   Unilateral, below elbow, without mention of complication   **CC**
     CC Excl: 880.00-887.7, 929.0-929.9, 958.8-958.99, 959.8-959.9

887.1   Unilateral, below elbow, complicated   **CC**
     CC Excl: See code 887.0

887.2   Unilateral, at or above elbow, without mention of complication   **CC**
     CC Excl: See code 887.0

887.3   Unilateral, at or above elbow, complicated   **CC**
     CC Excl: See code 887.0

887.4   Unilateral, level not specified, without mention of complication   **CC**
     CC Excl: See code 887.0

887.5   Unilateral, level not specified, complicated   **CC**
     CC Excl: See code 887.0

887.6   Bilateral [any level], without mention of complication   **MCC**
     One hand and other arm
     CC Excl: See code 887.0

887.7   Bilateral [any level], complicated   **MCC**
     CC Excl: See code 887.0

OPEN WOUND OF LOWER LIMB (890-897)

AHA: N-D, '85, 5

✓4ᵗʰ **890 Open wound of hip and thigh**

890.0   Without mention of complication

890.1   Complicated

890.2   With tendon involvement   **CC**
     CC Excl: 890.0-890.2

✓4ᵗʰ **891 Open wound of knee, leg [except thigh], and ankle**

   INCLUDES   leg NOS
          multiple sites of leg, except thigh
   EXCLUDES   that of thigh (890.0-890.2)
          with multiple sites of lower limb (894.0-894.2)

891.0   Without mention of complication
     S81.031A Puncture wound w/o FB rt knee initial encounter   **I-10**

891.1   Complicated

891.2   With tendon involvement   **CC**
     CC Excl: 891.0-891.2

✓4ᵗʰ **892 Open wound of foot except toe(s) alone**

   INCLUDES   heel

892.0   Without mention of complication

892.1   Complicated

892.2   With tendon involvement   **CC**
     CC Excl: 892.0-892.2

✓4ᵗʰ **893 Open wound of toe(s)**

   INCLUDES   toenail

893.0   Without mention of complication

893.1   Complicated
     AHA: ▶4Q, '08, 73◀

893.2   With tendon involvement   **CC**
     CC Excl: 893.0-893.2

✓4ᵗʰ **894 Multiple and unspecified open wound of lower limb**

   INCLUDES   lower limb NOS
          multiple sites of one lower limb, with thigh

894.0   Without mention of complication

894.1   Complicated

894.2   With tendon involvement   **CC**
     CC Excl: 894.0-894.2

✓4ᵗʰ **895 Traumatic amputation of toe(s) (complete) (partial)**

   INCLUDES   toe(s) of one or both feet

895.0   Without mention of complication

895.1   Complicated

✓4ᵗʰ **896 Traumatic amputation of foot (complete) (partial)**

896.0   Unilateral, without mention of complication   **CC**
     CC Excl: 890.0-897.7, 929.0-929.9, 958.8-958.99, 959.8-959.9

896.1   Unilateral, complicated   **CC**
     CC Excl: See code 896.0

896.2   Bilateral, without mention of complication   **MCC**
     EXCLUDES   one foot and other leg (897.6-897.7)
     CC Excl: See code 896.0

896.3   Bilateral, complicated   **MCC**
     CC Excl: See code 896.0

✓4ᵗʰ **897 Traumatic amputation of leg(s) (complete) (partial)**

897.0   Unilateral, below knee, without mention of complication   **CC**
     CC Excl: See code 896.0

897.1   Unilateral, below knee, complicated   **CC**
     CC Excl: See code 896.0

897.2   Unilateral, at or above knee, without mention of complication   **CC**
     CC Excl: See code 896.0

897.3   Unilateral, at or above knee, complicated   **CC**
     CC Excl: See code 896.0

897.4   Unilateral, level not specified, without mention of complication   **CC**
     CC Excl: See code 896.0

897.5   Unilateral, level not specified, complicated   **CC**
     CC Excl: See code 896.0

897.6   Bilateral [any level], without mention of complication   **MCC**
     One foot and other leg
     CC Excl: See code 896.0

897.7   Bilateral [any level], complicated   **MCC**
     CC Excl: See code 896.0
     AHA: 3Q, '90, 5

INJURY TO BLOOD VESSELS (900-904)

   INCLUDES   arterial hematoma
          avulsion
          cut
          laceration
          rupture
          traumatic aneurysm or fistula (arteriovenous)
     } of blood vessel secondary to other injuries, e.g.; fracture or open wound

   EXCLUDES   accidental puncture or laceration during medical procedure (998.2)
          intracranial hemorrhage following injury (851.0-854.1)

AHA: 3Q, '90, 5

✓4ᵗʰ **900 Injury to blood vessels of head and neck**

✓5ᵗʰ   900.0   Carotid artery

900.00   Carotid artery, unspecified   **CC**
     CC Excl: 900.00, 900.82-900.9, 904.9, 929.0-929.9, 958.8-958.99, 959.8-959.9

900.01   Common carotid artery   **CC**
     CC Excl: See code 900.00

900.02   External carotid artery   **CC**
     CC Excl: See code 900.00

900.03   Internal carotid artery   **CC**
     CC Excl: See code 900.00

900.1   Internal jugular vein   **CC**
     CC Excl: 900.82-900.9, 904.9, 929.0-929.9, 958.8-958.99, 959.8-959.9

✓4ᵗʰ Additional Digit Required   Unacceptable PDx   Manifestation Code   Hospital Acquired Condition   ▶◀ Revised Text   ● New Code   ▲ Revised Code Title
✓5ᵗʰ
2010 ICD-9-CM   **February 2009 • Volume 1 – 335**

Injury and Poisoning

900.8–902.51

✓5ᵗʰ **900.8 Other specified blood vessels of head and neck**

900.81 External jugular vein `CC`
Jugular vein NOS
CC Excl: See code 900.1

900.82 Multiple blood vessels of head and neck `CC`
CC Excl: See code 900.1

900.89 Other `CC`
CC Excl: See code 900.1

900.9 Unspecified blood vessel of head and neck `CC`
CC Excl: See code 900.1

✓4ᵗʰ **901 Injury to blood vessels of thorax**
EXCLUDES   traumatic hemothorax (860.2-860.5)

901.0 Thoracic aorta `MCC`
CC Excl: 901.0, 904.9, 929.0-929.9, 958.8-958.99, 959.8-959.9

901.1 Innominate and subclavian arteries `MCC`
CC Excl: 901.1, 904.9, 929.0-929.9, 958.8-958.99, 959.8-959.9

901.2 Superior vena cava `MCC`
CC Excl: 901.2, 904.9, 929.0-929.9, 958.8-958.99, 959.8-959.9

901.3 Innominate and subclavian veins `MCC`
CC Excl: 901.3, 904.9, 929.0-929.9, 958.8-958.99, 959.8-959.9

✓5ᵗʰ **901.4 Pulmonary blood vessels**

901.40 Pulmonary vessel(s), unspecified `MCC`
CC Excl: 901.40-901.41, 904.9, 929.0-929.9, 958.8-958.90, 958.99, 959.8-959.9

901.41 Pulmonary artery `MCC`
CC Excl: 901.40-901.41, 904.9, 929.0-929.9, 958.8-958.99, 959.8-959.9

901.42 Pulmonary vein `MCC`
CC Excl: 901.40, 901.42, 904.9, 929.0-929.9, 958.8-958.99, 959.8-959.9

✓5ᵗʰ **901.8 Other specified blood vessels of thorax**

901.81 Intercostal artery or vein `CC`
CC Excl: 901.81, 901.83-901.89

901.82 Internal mammary artery or vein `CC`
CC Excl: 901.82-901.89

901.83 Multiple blood vessels of thorax `MCC`
CC Excl: 904.9, 929.0-929.9, 958.8-958.99, 959.8-959.9

901.89 Other `CC`
Azygos vein
Hemiazygos vein
CC Excl: 901.0-901.9

901.9 Unspecified blood vessel of thorax `CC`
CC Excl: See code: 901.89

✓4ᵗʰ **902 Injury to blood vessels of abdomen and pelvis**

902.0 Abdominal aorta `MCC`
CC Excl: 902.0, 902.87-902.9, 904.9, 929.0-929.9, 958.8-958.99, 959.8-959.9

✓5ᵗʰ **902.1 Inferior vena cava**

902.10 Inferior vena cava, unspecified `MCC`
CC Excl: 902.10, 902.87-902.9, 904.9, 929.0-929.9, 958.8-958.99, 959.8-959.9

902.11 Hepatic veins `MCC`
CC Excl: 902.11, 902.87-902.9, 904.9, 929.0-929.9, 958.8-958.99, 959.8-959.9

902.19 Other `MCC`
CC Excl: 902.19, 902.87-902.9, 904.9, 929.0-929.9, 958.8-958.99, 959.8-959.9

✓5ᵗʰ **902.2 Celiac and mesenteric arteries**

902.20 Celiac and mesenteric arteries, unspecified `MCC`
CC Excl: 902.20, 902.87-902.9, 904.9, 929.0-929.9, 958.8-958.99, 959.8-959.9

902.21 Gastric artery `MCC`
CC Excl: 902.21, 902.87-902.9, 904.9, 929.0-929.9, 958.8-958.90, 958.93-958.99, 959.8-959.9

902.22 Hepatic artery `MCC`
CC Excl: 902.22, 902.87-902.9, 904.9, 929.0-929.9, 958.8-958.99, 959.8-959.9

902.23 Splenic artery `MCC`
CC Excl: 902.23, 902.87-902.9, 904.9, 929.0-929.9, 958.8-958.99, 959.8-959.9

902.24 Other specified branches of celiac axis `MCC`
CC Excl: 902.24, 902.87-902.9, 904.9, 929.0-929.9, 958.8-958.99, 959.8-959.9

902.25 Superior mesenteric artery (trunk) `MCC`
CC Excl: 902.25, 902.87-902.9, 904.9, 929.0-929.9, 958.8-958.99, 959.8-959.9

902.26 Primary branches of superior mesenteric artery `MCC`
Ileocolic artery
CC Excl: 902.26, 902.87-902.9, 904.9, 929.0-929.9, 958.8-958.99, 959.8-959.9

902.27 Inferior mesenteric artery `MCC`
CC Excl: 902.27, 902.87-902.9, 904.9, 929.0-929.9, 958.8-958.99, 959.8-959.9

902.29 Other `MCC`
CC Excl: 902.29, 902.87-902.9, 904.9, 929.0-929.9, 958.8-958.99, 959.8-959.9

✓5ᵗʰ **902.3 Portal and splenic veins**

902.31 Superior mesenteric vein and primary subdivisions `MCC`
Ileocolic vein
CC Excl: 902.31, 902.87-902.9, 904.9, 929.0-929.9, 958.8-958.99, 959.8-959.9

902.32 Inferior mesenteric vein `MCC`
CC Excl: 902.32, 902.87-902.9, 904.9, 929.0-929.9, 958.8-958.99, 959.8-959.9

902.33 Portal vein `MCC`
CC Excl: 902.33, 902.87-902.9, 904.9, 929.0-929.9, 958.8-958.99, 959.8-959.9

902.34 Splenic vein `MCC`
CC Excl: 902.34, 902.87-902.9, 904.9, 929.0-929.9, 958.8-958.99, 959.8-959.9

902.39 Other `MCC`
Cystic vein
Gastric vein
CC Excl: 902.39, 902.87-902.9, 904.9, 929.0-929.9, 958.8-958.99, 959.8-959.9

✓5ᵗʰ **902.4 Renal blood vessels**

902.40 Renal vessel(s), unspecified `MCC`
CC Excl: 902.40, 902.87-902.9, 904.9, 929.0-929.9, 958.8-958.99, 959.8-959.9

902.41 Renal artery `MCC`
CC Excl: 902.41, 902.87-902.9, 904.9, 929.0-929.9, 958.8-958.99, 959.8-959.9

902.42 Renal vein `MCC`
CC Excl: 902.42, 902.87-902.9, 904.9, 929.0-929.9, 958.8-958.99, 959.8-959.9

902.49 Other `MCC`
Suprarenal arteries
CC Excl: 902.49, 902.87-902.9, 904.9, 929.0-929.9, 958.8-958.99, 959.8-959.9

✓5ᵗʰ **902.5 Iliac blood vessels**

902.50 Iliac vessel(s), unspecified `MCC`
CC Excl: 902.50, 902.53-902.54, 902.59, 902.87-902.9, 904.9, 929.0-929.9, 958.8-958.99, 959.8-959.9

902.51 Hypogastric artery `MCC`
CC Excl: 902.51, 902.87-902.9, 904.9, 929.0-929.9, 958.8-958.99, 959.8-959.9

| N Newborn Age: 0 | P Pediatric Age: 0-17 | M Maternity Age: 12-55 | A Adult Age: 15-124 | `MCC` Major CC Condition | `CC` CC Condition | `HIV` HIV Related Dx |

Injury and Poisoning

902.52 Hypogastric vein `MCC`
  CC Excl: 902.52, 902.87-902.9, 904.9, 929.0-929.9,
  958.8-958.99, 959.8-959.9

902.53 Iliac artery `MCC`
  CC Excl: 902.50, 902.53, 902.59, 902.87-902.9, 904.9,
  929.0-929.9, 958.8-958.99, 959.8-959.9

902.54 Iliac vein `MCC`
  CC Excl: 902.50, 902.54, 902.59, 902.87-902.9, 904.9,
  929.0-929.9, 958.8-958.99, 959.8-959.9

902.55 Uterine artery `CC` ♀
  CC Excl: 902.55, 902.59, 902.87-902.9, 904.9,
  929.0-929.9, 958.8-958.90, 958.93-958.99,
  959.8-959.9

902.56 Uterine vein `CC` ♀
  CC Excl: 902.56-902.59, 902.87-902.9, 904.9,
  929.0-929.9, 958.8-958.90, 958.93-958.99,
  959.8-959.9

902.59 Other `MCC`
  CC Excl: See code: 902.50

✓5th **902.8 Other specified blood vessels of abdomen and pelvis**

902.81 Ovarian artery `CC` ♀
  CC Excl: 902.81, 902.87-902.9, 904.9, 929.0-929.9,
  958.8-958.90, 958.93-958.99, 959.8-959.9

902.82 Ovarian vein `CC` ♀
  CC Excl: 902.82-902.9, 904.9, 929.0-929.9,
  958.8-958.90, 958.93-958.99, 959.8-959.9

902.87 Multiple blood vessels of abdomen and pelvis `MCC`
  CC Excl: 902.87-902.9, 904.9, 929.0-929.9,
  958.8-958.99, 959.8-959.9

902.89 Other `CC`
  CC Excl: 902.87-902.9, 904.9, 929.0-929.9,
  958.8-958.90, 958.93-958.99, 959.8-959.9

902.9 Unspecified blood vessel of abdomen and pelvis `CC`
  CC Excl: 902.0-902.9, 904.9, 929.0-929.9, 958.8-958.90,
  958.93-958.99, 959.8-959.9

✓4th **903 Injury to blood vessels of upper extremity**

✓5th **903.0 Axillary blood vessels**

903.00 Axillary vessel(s), unspecified `MCC`
  CC Excl: 903.00-903.02, 903.8-903.9, 904.9

903.01 Axillary artery `MCC`
  CC Excl: 903.00-903.01, 903.8-903.9, 904.9

903.02 Axillary vein `MCC`
  CC Excl: 903.00, 903.02, 903.8-903.9, 904.9

903.1 Brachial blood vessels `CC`
  CC Excl: 903.1, 903.8-903.9, 904.9

903.2 Radial blood vessels `CC`
  CC Excl: 903.2, 903.8-903.9, 904.9

903.3 Ulnar blood vessels `CC`
  CC Excl: 903.3, 903.8-903.9, 904.9

903.4 Palmar artery `CC`
  CC Excl: 903.4, 903.8-903.9, 904.9

903.5 Digital blood vessels `CC`
  CC Excl: 903.5-903.9, 904.9

903.8 Other specified blood vessels of upper extremity `CC`
  Multiple blood vessels of upper extremity
  CC Excl: 903.3-903.9, 904.9

903.9 Unspecified blood vessel of upper extremity `CC`
  CC Excl: See code: 903.8

✓4th **904 Injury to blood vessels of lower extremity and unspecified sites**

904.0 Common femoral artery `MCC`
  Femoral artery above profunda origin
  CC Excl: 904.0, 904.7-904.9

904.1 Superficial femoral artery `MCC`
  CC Excl: 904.1, 904.7-904.9

904.2 Femoral veins `MCC`
  CC Excl: 904.2, 904.7-904.9

904.3 Saphenous veins `CC`
  Saphenous vein (greater) (lesser)
  CC Excl: 904.3, 904.7-904.9

✓5th **904.4 Popliteal blood vessels**

904.40 Popliteal vessel(s), unspecified `MCC`
  CC Excl: 904.40, 904.7-904.9

904.41 Popliteal artery `MCC`
  CC Excl: 904.41, 904.7-904.9

904.42 Popliteal vein `MCC`
  CC Excl: 904.42, 904.7-904.9

✓5th **904.5 Tibial blood vessels**

904.50 Tibial vessel(s), unspecified `CC`
  CC Excl: 904.50, 904.7-904.9

904.51 Anterior tibial artery `CC`
  CC Excl: 904.51, 904.7-904.9

904.52 Anterior tibial vein `CC`
  CC Excl: 904.52, 904.7-904.9

904.53 Posterior tibial artery `CC`
  CC Excl: 904.53, 904.7-904.9

904.54 Posterior tibial vein `CC`
  CC Excl: 904.54, 904.7-904.9

904.6 Deep plantar blood vessels `CC`
  CC Excl: 904.6-904.9

904.7 Other specified blood vessels of lower extremity `CC`
  Multiple blood vessels of lower extremity
  CC Excl: 729.72, 904.0-904.9

904.8 Unspecified blood vessel of lower extremity `CC`
  CC Excl: See code: 904.7

904.9 Unspecified site `CC`
  Injury to blood vessel NOS
  CC Excl: 729.71-729.72, 900.00-904.9

LATE EFFECTS OF INJURIES, POISONINGS, TOXIC EFFECTS, AND OTHER EXTERNAL CAUSES (905-909)

[handwritten: Include late affect E codes, as applicable]

Note: These categories are to be used to indicate conditions classifiable to 800-999 as the cause of late effects, which are themselves classified elsewhere. The "late effects" include those specified as such, or as sequelae, which may occur at any time after the acute injury.

✓4th **905 Late effects of musculoskeletal and connective tissue injuries**
  AHA: 1Q, '95, 10; 2Q, '94, 3

[handwritten: When coding injuries the residual condition (malunion, nonunion, deformity or paralysis) is sequenced first.]

905.0 Late effect of fracture of skull and face bones
  Late effect of injury classifiable to 800-804
  AHA: 3Q, '97, 12

905.1 Late effect of fracture of spine and trunk without mention of spinal cord lesion
  Late effect of injury classifiable to 805, 807-809
  AHA: 1Q, '07, 20

905.2 Late effect of fracture of upper extremities
  Late effect of injury classifiable to 810-819

905.3 Late effect of fracture of neck of femur
  Late effect of injury classifiable to 820

905.4 Late effect of fracture of lower extremities
  Late effect of injury classifiable to 821-827
  S79.001S Uns physeal fx upper end right femur sequela `I-10`

905.5 Late effect of fracture of multiple and unspecified bones
  Late effect of injury classifiable to 828-829

905.6 Late effect of dislocation
  Late effect of injury classifiable to 830-839

905.7 Late effect of sprain and strain without mention of tendon injury
  Late effect of injury classifiable to 840-848, except tendon injury

902.52–905.7

✓4th ✓5th Additional Digit Required   Unacceptable PDx   Manifestation Code   Hospital Acquired Condition   ►◄ Revised Text   ● New Code   ▲ Revised Code Title

2010 ICD-9-CM   Volume 1 – 337

905.8   Late effect of tendon injury
  Late effect of tendon injury due to:
    open wound [injury classifiable to 880-884
      with .2, 890-894 with .2]
    sprain and strain [injury classifiable to 840-848]
  AHA: 2Q, '89, 13; 2Q, '89, 15

905.9   Late effect of traumatic amputation
  Late effect of injury classifiable to 885-887, 895-897
  EXCLUDES   *late amputation stump complication*
           (997.60-997.69)

✓4ᵗʰ **906   Late effects of injuries to skin and subcutaneous tissues**

906.0   Late effect of open wound of head, neck, and trunk
  Late effect of injury classifiable to 870-879

**906.1   Late effect of open wound of extremities without
        mention of tendon injury**
  Late effect of injury classifiable to 880-884, 890-894
    except .2

906.2   Late effect of superficial injury
  Late effect of injury classifiable to 910-919

906.3   Late effect of contusion
  Late effect of injury classifiable to 920-924

906.4   Late effect of crushing
  Late effect of injury classifiable to 925-929

906.5   Late effect of burn of eye, face, head, and neck
  Late effect of injury classifiable to 940-941
  AHA: 4Q, '04, 76

906.6   Late effect of burn of wrist and hand
  Late effect of injury classifiable to 944
  AHA: 4Q, '94, 22

906.7   Late effect of burn of other extremities
  Late effect of injury classifiable to 943 or 945
  AHA: 4Q, '94, 22

906.8   Late effect of burns of other specified sites
  Late effect of injury classifiable to 942, 946-947
  AHA: 4Q, '94, 22

906.9   Late effect of burn of unspecified site
  Late effect of injury classifiable to 948-949
  AHA: 4Q, '94, 22

✓4ᵗʰ **907   Late effects of injuries to the nervous system**

**907.0   Late effect of intracranial injury without mention of
        skull fracture**
  Late effect of injury classifiable to 850-854
  AHA: ▶4Q, '08, 108;◀ 4Q, '03, 103; 3Q, '90, 14
  S06.2x1S Diffuse traumatic brain inj loc 30 min/less seq   I-10

907.1   Late effect of injury to cranial nerve
  Late effect of injury classifiable to 950-951

907.2   Late effect of spinal cord injury
  Late effect of injury classifiable to 806, 952
  AHA: 4Q, '03, 103; 4Q, '98, 38
  S34.114S Complete lesion L4 of lumbar spinal cord   I-10
  sequela

**907.3   Late effect of injury to nerve root(s), spinal
        plexus(es), and other nerves of trunk**
  Late effect of injury classifiable to 953-954
  AHA: 2Q, '07, 11

**907.4   Late effect of injury to peripheral nerve of shoulder
        girdle and upper limb**
  Late effect of injury classifiable to 955

**907.5   Late effect of injury to peripheral nerve of pelvic girdle
        and lower limb**
  Late effect of injury classifiable to 956

907.9   Late effect of injury to other and unspecified nerve
  Late effect of injury classifiable to 957

✓4ᵗʰ **908   Late effects of other and unspecified injuries**

908.0   Late effect of internal injury to chest
  Late effect of injury classifiable to 860-862

**908.1   Late effect of internal injury to intra-abdominal
        organs**
  Late effect of injury classifiable to 863-866, 868

908.2   Late effect of internal injury to other internal organs
  Late effect of injury classifiable to 867 or 869

**908.3   Late effect of injury to blood vessel of head, neck, and
        extremities**
  Late effect of injury classifiable to 900, 903-904

**908.4   Late effect of injury to blood vessel of thorax,
        abdomen, and pelvis**
  Late effect of injury classifiable to 901-902

908.5   Late effect of foreign body in orifice
  Late effect of injury classifiable to 930-939

908.6   Late effect of certain complications of trauma
  Late effect of complications classifiable to 958

908.9   Late effect of unspecified injury
  Late effect of injury classifiable to 959
  AHA: 3Q, '00, 4

✓4ᵗʰ **909   Late effects of other and unspecified external causes**

**909.0   Late effect of poisoning due to drug, medicinal or
        biological substance**
  Late effect of conditions classifiable to 960-979
  EXCLUDES   *late effect of adverse effect of drug, medicinal*
           or biological substance (909.5)
  AHA: 4Q, '03, 103

909.1   Late effect of toxic effects of nonmedical substances
  Late effect of conditions classifiable to 980-989

909.2   Late effect of radiation
  Late effect of conditions classifiable to 990

**909.3   Late effect of complications of surgical and
        medical care**
  Late effect of conditions classifiable to 996-999
  AHA: 1Q, '93, 29

909.4   Late effect of certain other external causes
  Late effect of conditions classifiable to 991-994

**909.5   Late effect of adverse effect of drug, medical or
        biological substance**
  EXCLUDES   *late effect of poisoning due to drug, medicinal*
           or biological substance (909.0)
  AHA: 4Q, '94, 48

909.9   Late effect of other and unspecified external causes

SUPERFICIAL INJURY (910-919)
  EXCLUDES   *burn (blisters) (940.0-949.5)*
           contusion (920-924.9)
           foreign body:
             granuloma (728.82)
             inadvertently left in operative wound (998.4)
             residual in soft tissue (729.6)
           insect bite, venomous (989.5)
           open wound with incidental foreign body (870.0-897.7)
  AHA: 2Q, '89, 15
  TIP: Do not code separately when associated with more severe injuries
  of the same site.

✓4ᵗʰ **910   Superficial injury of face, neck, and scalp except eye**
  INCLUDES   cheek
           ear
           gum
           lip
           nose
           throat
  EXCLUDES   *eye and adnexa (918.0-918.9)*

910.0   Abrasion or friction burn without mention of infection
  S00.01xA Abrasion of scalp initial encounter   I-10

910.1   Abrasion or friction burn, infected

910.2   Blister without mention of infection

910.3   Blister, infected

N Newborn Age: 0   P Pediatric Age: 0-17   M Maternity Age: 12-55   A Adult Age: 15-124   MCC Major CC Condition   CC CC Condition   HIV HIV Related Dx

338 – Volume 1 · February 2009   2010 ICD-9-CM

910.4 Insect bite, nonvenomous, without mention of infection

910.5 Insect bite, nonvenomous, infected

910.6 Superficial foreign body (splinter) without major open wound and without mention of infection

910.7 Superficial foreign body (splinter) without major open wound, infected

910.8 Other and unspecified superficial injury of face, neck, and scalp without mention of infection

910.9 Other and unspecified superficial injury of face, neck, and scalp, infected

✓4th **911 Superficial injury of trunk**

INCLUDES
abdominal wall	interscapular region
anus	labium (majus) (minus)
back	penis
breast	perineum
buttock	scrotum
chest wall	testis
flank	vagina
groin	vulva

EXCLUDES *hip (916.0-916.9)*
          scapular region (912.0-912.9)

911.0 Abrasion or friction burn without mention of infection
AHA: 3Q, '01, 10

911.1 Abrasion or friction burn, infected

911.2 Blister without mention of infection

911.3 Blister, infected

911.4 Insect bite, nonvenomous, without mention of infection

911.5 Insect bite, nonvenomous, infected

911.6 Superficial foreign body (splinter) without major open wound and without mention of infection

911.7 Superficial foreign body (splinter) without major open wound, infected

911.8 Other and unspecified superficial injury of trunk without mention of infection

911.9 Other and unspecified superficial injury of trunk, infected

✓4th **912 Superficial injury of shoulder and upper arm**

INCLUDES axilla
          scapular region

912.0 Abrasion or friction burn without mention of infection

912.1 Abrasion or friction burn, infected

912.2 Blister without mention of infection

912.3 Blister, infected

912.4 Insect bite, nonvenomous, without mention of infection

912.5 Insect bite, nonvenomous, infected

912.6 Superficial foreign body (splinter) without major open wound and without mention of infection

912.7 Superficial foreign body (splinter) without major open wound, infected

912.8 Other and unspecified superficial injury of shoulder and upper arm without mention of infection

912.9 Other and unspecified superficial injury of shoulder and upper arm, infected

✓4th **913 Superficial injury of elbow, forearm, and wrist**

913.0 Abrasion or friction burn without mention of infection

913.1 Abrasion or friction burn, infected

913.2 Blister without mention of infection

913.3 Blister, infected

913.4 Insect bite, nonvenomous, without mention of infection

913.5 Insect bite, nonvenomous, infected

913.6 Superficial foreign body (splinter) without major open wound and without mention of infection

913.7 Superficial foreign body (splinter) without major open wound, infected

913.8 Other and unspecified superficial injury of elbow, forearm, and wrist without mention of infection

913.9 Other and unspecified superficial injury of elbow, forearm, and wrist, infected

✓4th **914 Superficial injury of hand(s) except finger(s) alone**

914.0 Abrasion or friction burn without mention of infection

914.1 Abrasion or friction burn, infected

914.2 Blister without mention of infection

914.3 Blister, infected

914.4 Insect bite, nonvenomous, without mention of infection

914.5 Insect bite, nonvenomous, infected

914.6 Superficial foreign body (splinter) without major open wound and without mention of infection

914.7 Superficial foreign body (splinter) without major open wound, infected

914.8 Other and unspecified superficial injury of hand without mention of infection

914.9 Other and unspecified superficial injury of hand, infected

✓4th **915 Superficial injury of finger(s)**

INCLUDES fingernail
          thumb (nail)

915.0 Abrasion or friction burn without mention of infection

915.1 Abrasion or friction burn, infected

915.2 Blister without mention of infection

915.3 Blister, infected

915.4 Insect bite, nonvenomous, without mention of infection

915.5 Insect bite, nonvenomous, infected

915.6 Superficial foreign body (splinter) without major open wound and without mention of infection

915.7 Superficial foreign body (splinter) without major open wound, infected

915.8 Other and unspecified superficial injury of fingers without mention of infection
AHA: 3Q, '01, 10

915.9 Other and unspecified superficial injury of fingers, infected

✓4th **916 Superficial injury of hip, thigh, leg, and ankle**

916.0 Abrasion or friction burn without mention of infection
S80.812A Abrasion left lower leg initial encounter   I-10

916.1 Abrasion or friction burn, infected

916.2 Blister without mention of infection

916.3 Blister, infected

916.4 Insect bite, nonvenomous, without mention of infection

916.5 Insect bite, nonvenomous, infected

916.6 Superficial foreign body (splinter) without major open wound and without mention of infection

916.7 Superficial foreign body (splinter) without major open wound, infected

916.8 Other and unspecified superficial injury of hip, thigh, leg, and ankle without mention of infection

916.9 Other and unspecified superficial injury of hip, thigh, leg, and ankle, infected

Injury and Poisoning

917–923.11

✓4ᵗʰ **917 Superficial injury of foot and toe(s)**

> INCLUDES   heel
> toenail

917.0 Abrasion or friction burn without mention of infection

917.1 Abrasion or friction burn, infected

917.2 Blister without mention of infection

917.3 Blister, infected

917.4 Insect bite, nonvenomous, without mention of infection

917.5 Insect bite, nonvenomous, infected

917.6 Superficial foreign body (splinter) without major open wound and without mention of infection

917.7 Superficial foreign body (splinter) without major open wound, infected

917.8 Other and unspecified superficial injury of foot and toes without mention of infection

> AHA: 1Q, '03, 13

917.9 Other and unspecified superficial injury of foot and toes, infected

> AHA: 1Q, '03, 13
>
> TIP: Assign for hair strangulation of toe, with infection.

✓4ᵗʰ **918 Superficial injury of eye and adnexa**

> EXCLUDES   burn (940.0-940.9)
> foreign body on external eye (930.0-930.9)

918.0 Eyelids and periocular area
Abrasion
Insect bite
Superficial foreign body (splinter)

918.1 Cornea
Corneal abrasion
Superficial laceration

> EXCLUDES   corneal injury due to contact lens (371.82)

918.2 Conjunctiva

918.9 Other and unspecified superficial injuries of eye
Eye (ball) NOS

✓4ᵗʰ **919 Superficial injury of other, multiple, and unspecified sites**

> EXCLUDES   multiple sites classifiable to the same three-digit category (910.0-918.9)

919.0 Abrasion or friction burn without mention of infection

919.1 Abrasion or friction burn, infected

919.2 Blister without mention of infection

919.3 Blister, infected

919.4 Insect bite, nonvenomous, without mention of infection

919.5 Insect bite, nonvenomous, infected

919.6 Superficial foreign body (splinter) without major open wound and without mention of infection

919.7 Superficial foreign body (splinter) without major open wound, infected

919.8 Other and unspecified superficial injury without mention of infection

919.9 Other and unspecified superficial injury, infected

CONTUSION WITH INTACT SKIN SURFACE (920-924)

> INCLUDES   bruise   } without fracture or open
> hematoma   } wound

> EXCLUDES   concussion (850.0-850.9)
> hemarthrosis (840.0-848.9)
> internal organs (860.0-869.1)
> that incidental to:
>   crushing injury (925-929.9)
>   dislocation (830.0-839.9)
>   fracture (800.0-829.1)
>   internal injury (860.0-869.1)
>   intracranial injury (850.0-854.1)
>   nerve injury (950.0-957.9)
>   open wound (870.0-897.7)

920 Contusion of face, scalp, and neck except eye(s)

Cheek	Mandibular joint area
Ear (auricle)	Nose
Gum	Throat
Lip	

> S00.33xA Contusion of nose initial encounter   I-10

✓4ᵗʰ **921 Contusion of eye and adnexa**

921.0 Black eye, not otherwise specified

921.1 Contusion of eyelids and periocular area

921.2 Contusion of orbital tissues

921.3 Contusion of eyeball

> AHA: J-A, '85, 16
>
> TIP: If iridodialysis (rupture of the root of the iris) is present and is due to the eyeball contusion, assign also code 364.76.

921.9 Unspecified contusion of eye
Injury of eye NOS

✓4ᵗʰ **922 Contusion of trunk**

922.0 Breast

922.1 Chest wall

> S20.212A Contusion left front wall thorax initial enc   I-10

922.2 Abdominal wall
Flank   Groin

✓5ᵗʰ **922.3** Back

> AHA: 4Q, '96, 39

     922.31 Back

> > EXCLUDES   interscapular region (922.33)
> > AHA: 3Q, '99, 14

     922.32 Buttock

     922.33 Interscapular region

922.4 Genital organs

Labium (majus) (minus)	Testis
Penis	Vagina
Perineum	Vulva
Scrotum	

922.8 Multiple sites of trunk

922.9 Unspecified part
Trunk NOS

✓4ᵗʰ **923 Contusion of upper limb**

✓5ᵗʰ **923.0** Shoulder and upper arm

     923.00 Shoulder region

     923.01 Scapular region

     923.02 Axillary region

     923.03 Upper arm

     923.09 Multiple sites

✓5ᵗʰ **923.1** Elbow and forearm

     923.10 Forearm

     923.11 Elbow

| N Newborn Age: 0 | P Pediatric Age: 0-17 | M Maternity Age: 12-55 | A Adult Age: 15-124 | MCC Major CC Condition | CC CC Condition | HIV HIV Related Dx |

340 – Volume 1   2010 ICD-9-CM

√5ᵗʰ 923.2 **Wrist and hand(s), except finger(s) alone**

     923.20 **Hand(s)**

     923.21 **Wrist**

923.3 **Finger**
     Fingernail
     Thumb (nail)

923.8 **Multiple sites of upper limb**

923.9 **Unspecified part of upper limb**
     Arm NOS

√4ᵗʰ 924 **Contusion of lower limb and of other and unspecified sites**

  √5ᵗʰ 924.0 **Hip and thigh**

     924.00 **Thigh**
       AHA: ▶1Q, '09, 10◀

     924.01 **Hip**
       S70.02xA Contusion of left hip initial encounter I-10

  √5ᵗʰ 924.1 **Knee and lower leg**

     924.10 **Lower leg**

     924.11 **Knee**

  √5ᵗʰ 924.2 **Ankle and foot, excluding toe(s)**

     924.20 **Foot**
       Heel

     924.21 **Ankle**

924.3 **Toe**
     Toenail

924.4 **Multiple sites of lower limb**

924.5 **Unspecified part of lower limb**
     Leg NOS

924.8 **Multiple sites, not elsewhere classified**
     AHA: 1Q, '03, 7
     S70.10xA Contusion of unspecified thigh initial encounter I-10

924.9 **Unspecified site**

CRUSHING INJURY (925-929)

Use additional code to identify any associated injuries, such as:
     fractures (800-829)
     internal injuries (860.0-869.1)
     intracranial injuries (850.0-854.1)
AHA: 4Q, '03, 77; 2Q, '93, 7

√4ᵗʰ 925 **Crushing injury of face, scalp, and neck**
     Cheek   Pharynx
     Ear   Throat
     Larynx

     925.1 **Crushing injury of face and scalp**   CC
       Cheek   Ear
       CC Excl: 873.8-873.9, 905.0, 925.1-925.2, 929.0-929.9, 958.8-959.09, 959.8-959.9

     925.2 **Crushing injury of neck**   CC
       Larynx   Throat
       Pharynx
       CC Excl: See code: 925.1

√4ᵗʰ 926 **Crushing injury of trunk**

     926.0 **External genitalia**
       Labium (majus) (minus)   Testis
       Penis   Vulva
       Scrotum

  √5ᵗʰ 926.1 **Other specified sites**

     926.11 **Back**

     926.12 **Buttock**

     926.19 **Other**
       Breast

926.8 **Multiple sites of trunk**

926.9 **Unspecified site**
     Trunk NOS

√4ᵗʰ 927 **Crushing injury of upper limb**

  √5ᵗʰ 927.0 **Shoulder and upper arm**

     927.00 **Shoulder region**

     927.01 **Scapular region**

     927.02 **Axillary region**

     927.03 **Upper arm**

     927.09 **Multiple sites**

  √5ᵗʰ 927.1 **Elbow and forearm**

     927.10 **Forearm**

     927.11 **Elbow**

  √5ᵗʰ 927.2 **Wrist and hand(s), except finger(s) alone**

     927.20 **Hand(s)**

     927.21 **Wrist**

     927.3 **Finger(s)**
       AHA: 4Q, '03, 77

     927.8 **Multiple sites of upper limb**

     927.9 **Unspecified site**
       Arm NOS

√4ᵗʰ 928 **Crushing injury of lower limb**

  √5ᵗʰ 928.0 **Hip and thigh**

     928.00 **Thigh**   CC
       CC Excl: 928.00, 928.8-929.9

     928.01 **Hip**   CC
       CC Excl: 928.01, 928.8-929.9

  √5ᵗʰ 928.1 **Knee and lower leg**

     928.10 **Lower leg**

     928.11 **Knee**

  √5ᵗʰ 928.2 **Ankle and foot, excluding toe(s) alone**

     928.20 **Foot**
       Heel

     928.21 **Ankle**

928.3 **Toe(s)**

928.8 **Multiple sites of lower limb**

928.9 **Unspecified site**
     Leg NOS

√4ᵗʰ 929 **Crushing injury of multiple and unspecified sites**

929.0 **Multiple sites, not elsewhere classified**

929.9 **Unspecified site**

EFFECTS OF FOREIGN BODY ENTERING THROUGH ORIFICE (930-939)

EXCLUDES   foreign body:
     granuloma (728.82)
     inadvertently left in operative wound (998.4, 998.7)
     in open wound (800-839, 851-897)
     residual in soft tissues (729.6)
     superficial without major open wound (910-919 with .6 or .7)

√4ᵗʰ 930 **Foreign body on external eye**
     EXCLUDES   foreign body in penetrating wound of:
       eyeball (871.5-871.6)
       retained (old) (360.5-360.6)
       ocular adnexa (870.4)
       retained (old) (376.6)

930.0 **Corneal foreign body**

930.1 **Foreign body in conjunctival sac**

930.2 **Foreign body in lacrimal punctum**

930.8 **Other and combined sites**

930.9 **Unspecified site**
     External eye NOS

| √4ᵗʰ√5ᵗʰ Additional Digit Required | Unacceptable PDx | Manifestation Code | Hospital Acquired Condition | ▶◀ Revised Text | ● New Code | ▲ Revised Code Title |

[handwritten note at top:] Skin layers:
– Epidermis
– Dermis
– Subcutaneous tissue

Injury and Poisoning

931–941.5

931   Foreign body in ear
Auditory canal
Auricle

932   Foreign body in nose
Nasal sinus
Nostril

✓4th **933   Foreign body in pharynx and larynx**

933.0   **Pharynx**
Nasopharynx
Throat NOS

933.1   **Larynx**
Asphyxia due to foreign body
Choking due to:
    food (regurgitated)
    phlegm
TIP: Assign for mucous plug causing asphyxia; otherwise, for tracheobronchial, refer to code 519.19 Other diseases of trachea and bronchus.

✓4th **934   Foreign body in trachea, bronchus, and lung**

934.0   **Trachea**   `CC`
CC Excl: 934.0

934.1   **Main bronchus**   `CC`
CC Excl: 934.0-934.9
AHA: 3Q, '02, 18

934.8   **Other specified parts**   `CC`
Bronchioles
Lung
CC Excl: See code: 934.1

934.9   **Respiratory tree, unspecified**
Inhalation of liquid or vomitus, lower respiratory tract NOS

✓4th **935   Foreign body in mouth, esophagus, and stomach**

935.0   **Mouth**

935.1   **Esophagus**
AHA: 1Q, '88, 13
TIP: If esophageal obstruction is due to stenosis, caustic stricture (e.g., lye ingestion), or tumor, assign instead code 530.3.

935.2   **Stomach**

936   Foreign body in intestine and colon

937   Foreign body in anus and rectum
Rectosigmoid (junction)

938   Foreign body in digestive system, unspecified
Alimentary tract NOS
Swallowed foreign body

✓4th **939   Foreign body in genitourinary tract**

939.0   **Bladder and urethra**

939.1   **Uterus, any part**   ♀
EXCLUDES   *intrauterine contraceptive device:*
               complications from (996.32, 996.65)
               presence of (V45.51)

939.2   **Vulva and vagina**   ♀

939.3   **Penis**   ♂

939.9   **Unspecified site**

BURNS (940-949)

[handwritten note:] Classified according to the highest degree recorded in the diagnosis... sequence highest degree (severity) first with additional codes for other sites.

INCLUDES   burns from:
    electrical heating appliance
    electricity
    flame
    hot object
    lightning
    radiation
  chemical burns (external) (internal)
  scalds

EXCLUDES   *friction burns (910-919 with .0, .1)*
                sunburn (692.71, 692.76-692.77)

AHA: 4Q, 94, 22; 2Q, '90, 7; 4Q, '88, 3; M-A, '86, 9
TIP: Nonhealing burns are coded as acute burns, as is necrosis of burned skin. Assign code 958.3 for any documented infected burn site.

✓4th **940   Burn confined to eye and adnexa**

940.0   **Chemical burn of eyelids and periocular area**

940.1   **Other burns of eyelids and periocular area**

940.2   **Alkaline chemical burn of cornea and conjunctival sac**

940.3   **Acid chemical burn of cornea and conjunctival sac**

940.4   **Other burn of cornea and conjunctival sac**

940.5   **Burn with resulting rupture and destruction of eyeball**   `CC`
CC Excl: No exclusions

940.9   **Unspecified burn of eye and adnexa**

✓4th **941   Burn of face, head, and neck**
EXCLUDES   *mouth (947.0)*

The following fifth-digit subclassification is for use with category 941:
  0   face and head, unspecified site
  1   ear [any part]
  2   eye (with other parts of face, head, and neck)
  3   lip(s)
  4   chin
  5   nose (septum)
  6   scalp [any part]
       Temple (region)
  7   forehead and cheek
  8   neck
  9   multiple sites [except with eye] of face, head, and neck

AHA: 4Q, '94, 22; M-A, '86, 9

§ ✓5th **941.0   Unspecified degree**
[0-9]

§ ✓5th **941.1   Erythema [first degree]**
[0-9]   **AHA: For code 941.19:** 3Q, '05, 10

§ ✓5th **941.2   Blisters, epidermal loss [second degree]**
[0-9]

§ ✓5th **941.3   Full-thickness skin loss [third degree NOS]**   `CC`
[0-9]   **CC Excl: For code 941.30:** 941.30, 941.39; **For code 941.31:** 941.31, 941.39; **For code 941.32:** 941.32, 941.39; **For code 941.33:** 941.33, 941.39; **For code 941.34:** 941.34, 941.39; **For code 941.35:** 941.35, 941.39; **For code 941.36:** 941.36, 941.39; **For code 941.37:** 941.37, 941.39; **For code 941.38:** 941.38-941.39; **For code 941.39:** 941.30-941.39

§ ✓5th **941.4   Deep necrosis of underlying tissues [deep third degree] without mention of loss of a body part**   `CC`
[0-9]   **CC Excl: For code 941.40, 941.49:** 941.40, 941.49; **For code 941.41:** 941.40-941.41, 941.49; **For code 941.42:** 941.40, 941.42, 941.49; **For code 941.43:** 941.40, 941.43, 941.49; **For code 941.44:** 941.40, 941.44, 941.49; **For code 941.45:** 941.40, 941.45, 941.49; **For code 941.46:** 941.40, 941.46, 941.49; **For code 941.47:** 941.40, 941.47, 941.49; **For code 941.48:** 941.40, 941.48-941.49

§ ✓5th **941.5   Deep necrosis of underlying tissues [deep third degree] with loss of a body part**   `CC`
[0-9]   **CC Excl: For code 941.50, 941.59:** 941.50, 941.59; **For code 941.51:** 941.50-941.51, 941.59; **For code 941.52:** 941.50, 941.52, 941.59; **For code 941.53:** 941.50, 941.53, 941.59; **For code 941.54:** 941.50, 941.54, 941.59; **For code 941.55:** 941.50, 941.55, 941.59; **For code 941.56:** 941.50, 941.56, 941.59; **For code 941.57:** 941.50, 941.57, 941.59; **For code 941.58:** 941.50, 941.58-941.59

---

§   Requires fifth digit. Valid digits are in [brackets] under each code. See appropriate category for codes and definitions.

N Newborn Age: 0   P Pediatric Age: 0-17   M Maternity Age: 12-55   A Adult Age: 15-124   MCC Major CC Condition   CC CC Condition   HIV HIV Related Dx

342 – Volume 1   2010 ICD-9-CM

√4ᵗʰ **942 Burn of trunk**

> **EXCLUDES** *scapular region (943.0-943.5 with fifth-digit 6)*
>
> The following fifth-digit subclassificaiton is for use with category 942:
> 0 trunk, unspecified
> 1 breast
> 2 chest wall, excluding breast and nipple
> 3 abdominal wall
> > Flank
> > Groin
> 4 back [any part]
> > Buttock
> > Interscapular region
> 5 genitalia
> > Labium (majus) (minus)
> > Penis
> > Perineum
> > Scrotum
> > Testis
> > Vulva
> 9 other and multiple sites of trunk

> **AHA:** 4Q, '94, 22; M-A, '86, 9

§ √5ᵗʰ **942.0 Unspecified degree**
[0-5, 9]

§ √5ᵗʰ **942.1 Erythema [first degree]**
[0-5, 9]

§ √5ᵗʰ **942.2 Blisters, epidermal loss [second degree]**
[0-5, 9]

§ √5ᵗʰ **942.3 Full-thickness skin loss [third degree NOS]** CC
[0-5, 9]
> CC Excl: For code 942.30, 942.39: 942.30, 942.39; For code 942.31: 942.30-942.31, 942.39; For code 942.32: 942.30, 942.32, 942.39; For code 942.33: 942.30, 942.33, 942.39; For code 942.34: 942.30, 942.34, 942.39; For code 942.35: 942.30, 942.35-942.39

§ √5ᵗʰ **942.4 Deep necrosis of underlying tissues [deep third degree] without mention of loss of a body part** CC
[0-5, 9]
> CC Excl: For code 942.40: 942.40, 942.49; For code 942.41: 942.40-942.41, 942.49; For code 942.42: 942.40, 942.42, 942.49; For code 942.43: 942.40, 942.43, 942.49; For code 942.44: 942.40, 942.44, 942.49; For code 942.45: 942.40, 942.45-942.49; For code 942.49: 942.40-942.49

§ √5ᵗʰ **942.5 Deep necrosis of underlying tissues [deep third degree] with loss of a body part** CC
[0-5, 9]
> CC Excl: For code 942.50: 942.50, 942.59; For code 942.51: 942.50-942.51, 942.59; For code 942.52: 942.50, 942.52, 942.59; For code 942.53: 942.50, 942.53, 942.59; For code 942.54: 942.50, 942.54, 942.59; For code 942.55: 942.50, 942.55-942.59; For code 942.59: 942.50, 942.59

√4ᵗʰ **943 Burn of upper limb, except wrist and hand**

> The following fifth-digit subclassificaiton is for use with category 943:
> 0 upper limb, unspecified site
> 1 forearm
> 2 elbow
> 3 upper arm
> 4 axilla
> 5 shoulder
> 6 scapular region
> 9 multiple sites of upper limb, except wrist and hand

> **AHA:** 4Q, '94, 22; M-A, '86, 9

§ √5ᵗʰ **943.0 Unspecified degree**
[0-6, 9]

§ √5ᵗʰ **943.1 Erythema [first degree]**
[0-6, 9]

§ √5ᵗʰ **943.2 Blisters, epidermal loss [second degree]**
[0-6, 9]

§ √5ᵗʰ **943.3 Full-thickness skin loss [third degree NOS]** CC
[0-6, 9]
> CC Excl: For code 943.30, 943.39: 943.30, 943.39; For code 943.31: 943.30-943.31, 943.39; For code 943.32: 943.30, 943.32, 943.39; For code 943.33: 943.30, 943.33, 943.39; For code 943.34: 943.30, 943.34, 943.39; For code 943.35: 943.30, 943.35, 943.39; For code 943.36: 943.30, 943.36-943.39

§ √5ᵗʰ **943.4 Deep necrosis of underlying tissues [deep third degree] without mention of loss of a body part** CC
[0-6, 9]
> CC Excl: For code 943.40, 943.49: 943.40, 943.49; For code 943.41: 943.40-943.41, 943.49; For code 943.42: 943.40, 943.42, 943.49; For code 943.43: 943.40, 943.43, 943.49; For code 943.44: 943.40, 943.44, 943.49; For code 943.45: 943.40, 943.45, 943.49; For code 943.46: 943.40, 943.46-943.49

§ √5ᵗʰ **943.5 Deep necrosis of underlying tissues [deep third degree] with loss of a body part** CC
[0-6, 9]
> CC Excl: For code 943.50, 943.59: 943.50, 943.59; For code 943.51: 943.50-943.51, 943.59; For code 943.52: 943.50, 943.52, 943.59; For code 943.53: 943.50, 943.53, 943.59; For code 943.54: 943.50, 943.54, 943.59; For code 943.55: 943.50, 943.55, 943.59; For code 943.56: 943.50, 943.56-943.59

√4ᵗʰ **944 Burn of wrist(s) and hand(s)**

> The following fifth-digit subclassification is for use with category 944:
> 0 hand, unspecified site
> 1 single digit [finger (nail)] other than thumb
> 2 thumb (nail)
> 3 two or more digits, not including thumb
> 4 two or more digits including thumb
> 5 palm
> 6 back of hand
> 7 wrist
> 8 multiple sites of wrist(s) and hand(s)

§ √5ᵗʰ **944.0 Unspecified degree**
[0-8]

§ √5ᵗʰ **944.1 Erythema [first degree]**
[0-8]

§ √5ᵗʰ **944.2 Blisters, epidermal loss [second degree]**
[0-8]

§ √5ᵗʰ **944.3 Full-thickness skin loss [third degree NOS]** CC
[0-8]
> CC Excl: For code 944.30, 944.38: 944.30, 944.38; For code 944.31: 944.30-944.31, 944.38; For code 944.32: 944.30, 944.32, 944.38; For code 944.33: 944.30, 944.33, 944.38; For code 944.34: 944.30, 944.34, 944.38; For code 944.35: 944.30, 944.35, 944.38; For code 944.36: 944.30, 944.36, 944.38; For code 944.37: 944.30, 944.37-944.38

§ √5ᵗʰ **944.4 Deep necrosis of underlying tissues [deep third degree] without mention of loss of a body part** CC
[0-8]
> CC Excl: For code 944.40, 944.48: 944.40, 944.48; For code 944.41: 944.40-944.41, 944.48; For code 944.42: 944.40, 944.42, 944.48; For code 944.43: 944.40, 944.43, 944.48; For code 944.44: 944.40, 944.44, 944.48; For code 944.45: 944.40, 944.45, 944.48; For code 944.46: 944.40, 944.46, 944.48; For code 944.47: 944.40, 944.47-944.48

§ √5ᵗʰ **944.5 Deep necrosis of underlying tissues [deep third degree] with loss of a body part** CC
[0-8]
> CC Excl: For code 944.50, 944.58: 944.50, 944.58; For code 944.51: 944.50-944.51, 944.58; For code 944.52: 944.50, 944.52, 944.58; For code 944.53: 944.50, 944.53, 944.58; For code 944.54: 944.50, 944.54, 944.58; For code 944.55: 944.50, 944.55, 944.58; For code 944.56: 944.50, 944.56, 944.58; For code 944.57: 944.50, 944.57-944.58

√4ᵗʰ **945 Burn of lower limb(s)**

> The following fifth-digit subclassification is for use with category 945:
> 0 lower limb [leg], unspecified site
> 1 toe(s) (nail)
> 2 foot
> 3 ankle
> 4 lower leg
> 5 knee
> 6 thigh [any part]
> 9 multiple sites of lower limb(s)

> **AHA:** 4Q, '94, 22; M-A, '86, 9

§ √5ᵗʰ **945.0 Unspecified degree**
[0-6, 9]

§ √5ᵗʰ **945.1 Erythema [first degree]**
[0-6, 9]

§ √5ᵗʰ **945.2 Blisters, epidermal loss [second degree]**
[0-6, 9]

---

§   Requires fifth digit. Valid digits are in [brackets] under each code. See appropriate category for codes and definitions.

√4ᵗʰ √5ᵗʰ Additional Digit Required   Unacceptable PDx   Manifestation Code   Hospital Acquired Condition   ▶◀ Revised Text   ● New Code   ▲ Revised Code Title

§ ✓5ᵗʰ **945.3** **Full-thickness skin loss [third degree NOS]** CC
[0-6, 9]   CC Excl: For code 945.30, 945.39: 945.30, 945.39; For code 945.31: 945.30-945.31, 945.39; For code 945.32: 945.30, 945.32, 945.39; For code 945.33: 945.30, 945.33, 945.39; For code 945.34: 945.30, 945.34, 945.39; For code 945.35: 945.30, 945.35, 945.39; For code 945.36: 945.30, 945.36-945.39

§ ✓5ᵗʰ **945.4** **Deep necrosis of underlying tissues [deep third** CC
[0-6, 9] **degree] without mention of loss of a body part**
   CC Excl: For code 945.40, 945.49: 945.40, 945.49; For code 945.41: 945.40-945.41, 945.49; For code 945.42: 945.40, 945.42, 945.49; For code 945.43: 945.40, 945.43, 945.49; For code 945.44: 945.40, 945.44, 945.49; For code 945.45: 945.40, 945.45, 945.49; For code 945.46: 945.40, 945.46-945.49

§ ✓5ᵗʰ **945.5** **Deep necrosis of underlying tissues [deep third** CC
[0-6, 9] **degree] with loss of a body part**
   CC Excl: For code 945.50, 945.59: 945.50, 945.59; For code 945.51: 945.50-945.51, 945.59; For code 945.52: 945.50, 945.52, 945.59; For code 945.53: 945.50, 945.53, 945.59; For code 945.54: 945.50, 945.54, 945.59; For code 945.55: 945.50, 945.55, 945.59; For code 945.56: 945.50, 945.56-945.59

✓4ᵗʰ **946** **Burns of multiple specified sites**
   INCLUDES   burns of sites classifiable to more than one three-digit category in 940-945
   EXCLUDES   *multiple burns NOS (949.0-949.5)*
   AHA: 4Q, '94, 22; M-A, '86, 9
   TIP: Only assign if the specific sites of the multiple burns are not specified.

   946.0   **Unspecified degree**

   946.1   **Erythema [first degree]**

   946.2   **Blisters, epidermal loss [second degree]**

   946.3   **Full-thickness skin loss [third degree NOS]** CC
      CC Excl: 946.3

   946.4   **Deep necrosis of underlying tissues [deep third** CC
      degree] without mention of loss of a body part
      CC Excl: 946.4

   946.5   **Deep necrosis of underlying tissues [deep third** CC
      degree] with loss of a body part
      CC Excl: 946.5

✓4ᵗʰ **947** **Burn of internal organs**
   INCLUDES   burns from chemical agents (ingested)
   AHA: 4Q, '94, 22; M-A, '86, 9

   947.0   **Mouth and pharynx**
      Gum
      Tongue

   947.1   **Larynx, trachea, and lung** CC
      CC Excl: 947.1, 947.8-947.9

   947.2   **Esophagus** CC
      CC Excl: 947.2, 947.8-947.9

   947.3   **Gastrointestinal tract** CC
      Colon   Small intestine
      Rectum   Stomach
      CC Excl: 947.3, 947.8-947.9

   947.4   **Vagina and uterus** CC ♀
      CC Excl: 947.4-947.9

   947.8   **Other specified sites**

   947.9   **Unspecified site**

✓4ᵗʰ **948** **Burns classified according to extent of body surface involved**
   Note: This category is to be used when the site of the burn is unspecified, or with categories 940-947 when the site is specified.
   EXCLUDES   *sunburn (692.71, 692.76-692.77)*
   The following fifth-digit subclassification is for use with category 948 to indicate the percent of body surface with third degree burn; valid digits are in [brackets] under each code:
     0 less than 10 percent or unspecified
     1 10-19%
     2 20-29%
     3 30-39%
     4 40-49%
     5 50-59%
     6 60-69%
     7 70-79%
     8 80-89%
     9 90% or more of body surface
   AHA: 4Q, '94, 22; 4Q, '88, 3; M-A, '86, 9; N-D, '84, 13

§ ✓5ᵗʰ **948.0** **Burn [any degree] involving less than 10**
[0] **percent of body surface**
      T31.0 Burns involving less than 10% of body surface   I-10

§¹⁰ ✓5ᵗʰ **948.1** **10-19 percent of body surface** CC 0-1
[0-1]   CC Excl: 948.00-948.99

§¹⁰ ✓5ᵗʰ **948.2** **20-29 percent of body surface** MCC 1-2 CC 0
[0-2]   CC Excl: See code: 948.1

§¹⁰ ✓5ᵗʰ **948.3** **30-39 percent of body surface** MCC 1-3 CC 0
[0-3]   CC Excl: See code: 948.1

§¹⁰ ✓5ᵗʰ **948.4** **40-49 percent of body surface** MCC 1-4 CC 0
[0-4]   CC Excl: See code: 948.1

§¹⁰ ✓5ᵗʰ **948.5** **50-59 percent of body surface** MCC 1-5 CC 0
[0-5]   CC Excl: See code: 948.1

§¹⁰ ✓5ᵗʰ **948.6** **60-69 percent of body surface** MCC 1-6 CC 0
[0-6]   CC Excl: See code: 948.1

§¹⁰ ✓5ᵗʰ **948.7** **70-79 percent of body surface** MCC 1-7 CC 0
[0-7]   CC Excl: See code: 948.1

§¹⁰ ✓5ᵗʰ **948.8** **80-89 percent of body surface** MCC 1-8 CC 0
[0-8]   CC Excl: See code: 948.1

§¹⁰ ✓5ᵗʰ **948.9** **90 percent or more of body surface** MCC 1-9 CC 0
[0-9]   CC Excl: See code: 948.1

Burns

Degrees of Burns

First (redness)   Second (blistering)   Third (fill thickness)   Deep Third (deep necrosis)   Eschar

Rule of Nines
Estimation of Total Body Surface Burned

Each arm 9%
Anterior trunk 18%
Genitalia 1%
Anterior leg 9%

Head and neck 9%
Posterior trunk 18%
Posterior leg 9%

---

§ Requires fifth digit. Valid digits are in [brackets] under each code. See category 948 for codes and definitions.
¹⁰ HAC = only for valid CC or MCC codes.

N Newborn Age: 0   P Pediatric Age: 0-17   M Maternity Age: 12-55   A Adult Age: 15-124   MCC Major CC Condition   CC CC Condition   HIV HIV Related Dx

344 – Volume 1   2010 ICD-9-CM

✓4th **949 Burn, unspecified**

> INCLUDES   burn NOS
> multiple burns NOS
>
> EXCLUDES   *burn of unspecified site but with statement of the extent of body surface involved (948.0-948.9)*

> AHA: 4Q, '94, 22; M-A, '86, 9

949.0 Unspecified degree

949.1 Erythema [first degree]

949.2 Blisters, epidermal loss [second degree]

949.3 Full-thickness skin loss [third degree NOS] `CC`

> CC Excl: 941.30-941.39, 942.30-942.39, 944.30-944.38, 945.30-945.39, 946.3, 949.3

949.4 Deep necrosis of underlying tissues [deep third degree] without mention of loss of a body part `CC`

> CC Excl: 941.40-941.49, 942.40-942.49, 944.40-944.48, 945.40-945.49, 946.4, 949.4

949.5 Deep necrosis of underlying tissues [deep third degree] with loss of a body part `CC`

> CC Excl: 946.5, 949.5

INJURY TO NERVES AND SPINAL CORD (950-957)

> INCLUDES   division of nerve
> lesion in continuity   } (with open
> traumatic neuroma   wound)
> traumatic transient paralysis
>
> EXCLUDES   *accidental puncture or laceration during medical procedure (998.2)*

[handwritten in margin: Primary injury first, with sequenced codes, from additional codes, 950-957 and/or 900-904]

✓4th **950 Injury to optic nerve and pathways**

950.0 Optic nerve injury `CC`
> Second cranial nerve
> CC Excl: 950.0-950.9, 951.8-951.9

950.1 Injury to optic chiasm `CC`
> CC Excl: See code: 950.0

950.2 Injury to optic pathways `CC`
> CC Excl: See code: 950.0

950.3 Injury to visual cortex `CC`
> CC Excl: See code: 950.0

950.9 Unspecified `CC`
> Traumatic blindness NOS
> CC Excl: See code: 950.0

✓4th **951 Injury to other cranial nerve(s)**

951.0 Injury to oculomotor nerve `CC`
> Third cranial nerve
> CC Excl: 951.0, 951.8-951.9

951.1 Injury to trochlear nerve `CC`
> Fourth cranial nerve
> CC Excl: 951.1, 951.8-951.9

951.2 Injury to trigeminal nerve `CC`
> Fifth cranial nerve
> CC Excl: 951.2, 951.8-951.9

951.3 Injury to abducens nerve `CC`
> Sixth cranial nerve
> CC Excl: 951.3, 951.8-951.9

951.4 Injury to facial nerve `CC`
> Seventh cranial nerve
> CC Excl: 951.4, 951.8-951.9

951.5 Injury to acoustic nerve `CC`
> Auditory nerve
> Eighth cranial nerve
> Traumatic deafness NOS
> CC Excl: 951.5, 951.8-951.9

951.6 Injury to accessory nerve `CC`
> Eleventh cranial nerve
> CC Excl: 951.6, 951.8-951.9

951.7 Injury to hypoglossal nerve `CC`
> Twelfth cranial nerve
> CC Excl: 951.7-951.9

951.8 Injury to other specified cranial nerves `CC`
> Glossopharyngeal [9th cranial] nerve
> Olfactory [1st cranial] nerve
> Pneumogastric [10th cranial] nerve
> Traumatic anosmia NOS
> Vagus [10th cranial] nerve
> CC Excl: 951.8-951.9

951.9 Injury to unspecified cranial nerve `CC`
> CC Excl: See code: 951.8

✓4th **952 Spinal cord injury without evidence of spinal bone injury**

✓5th **952.0 Cervical**

952.00 C_1-C_4 level with unspecified spinal cord injury `MCC`
> Spinal cord injury, cervical region NOS
> CC Excl: 805.00-805.18, 805.8-806.19, 806.8-806.9, 839.00-839.18, 839.40, 839.49-839.50, 839.59, 839.69, 839.79-839.9, 847.9, 905.1, 926.11, 952.00-952.09, 952.8-952.9, 958.8-958.99, 959.11-959.19, 959.8-959.9

952.01 C_1-C_4 level with complete lesion of spinal cord `MCC`
> CC Excl: See code 952.00

952.02 C_1-C_4 level with anterior cord syndrome `MCC`
> CC Excl: See code 952.00

952.03 C_1-C_4 level with central cord syndrome `MCC`
> CC Excl: See code 952.00

952.04 C_1-C_4 level with other specified spinal cord injury `MCC`
> Incomplete spinal cord lesion at C_1-C_4 level:
>   NOS
>   with posterior cord syndrome
> CC Excl: See code 952.00

952.05 C_5-C_7 level with unspecified spinal cord injury `MCC`
> CC Excl: See code 952.00

952.06 C_5-C_7 level with complete lesion of spinal cord `MCC`
> CC Excl: See code 952.00

952.07 C_5-C_7 level with anterior cord syndrome `MCC`
> CC Excl: See code 952.00

952.08 C_5-C_7 level with central cord syndrome `MCC`
> CC Excl: See code 952.00

952.09 C_5-C_7 level with other specified spinal cord injury `MCC`
> Incomplete spinal cord lesion at C_5-C_7 level:
>   NOS
>   with posterior cord syndrome
> CC Excl: See code 952.00

✓5th **952.1 Dorsal [thoracic]**

952.10 T_1-T_6 level with unspecified spinal cord injury `MCC`
> Spinal cord injury, thoracic region NOS
> CC Excl: 805.8-805.9, 806.20-806.39, 839.40, 839.49-839.50, 839.59, 839.69, 839.79-839.9, 847.9, 905.1, 926.11, 952.10-952.19, 952.8-952.9, 958.8-958.99, 959.11-959.19, 959.8-959.9

Spinal Nerve Roots

Gray matter, White matter, Rootlets, Anterior (ventral) root, Rami communicantes, Dorsal root ganglion, Posterior (dorsal) root, Posterior primary ramus, C_1, C_7, T_1, T_{12}, L_1, L_5, Cervical Nerve Roots, Thoracic Nerve Roots, Lumbar Nerve Roots, Cauda equina, Sacrum, Filum terminale

✓4th Additional Digit Required   Unacceptable PDx   Manifestation Code   Hospital Acquired Condition   ▶◀ Revised Text   ● New Code   ▲ Revised Code Title

2010 ICD-9-CM   Volume 1 – 345

Injury and Poisoning

952.11–958.2

952.11 T_1-T_6 level with complete lesion of spinal cord   `MCC`
     CC Excl: See code 952.10

952.12 T_1-T_6 level with anterior cord syndrome   `MCC`
     CC Excl: See code 952.10

952.13 T_1-T_6 level with central cord syndrome   `MCC`
     CC Excl: See code 952.10

952.14 T_1-T_6 level with other specified spinal cord injury   `MCC`
     Incomplete spinal cord lesion at T_1-T_6 level:
       NOS
       with posterior cord syndrome
     CC Excl: See code 952.10

952.15 T_7-T_{12} level with unspecified spinal cord injury   `MCC`
     CC Excl: See code 952.10

952.16 T_7-T_{12} level with complete lesion of spinal cord   `MCC`
     CC Excl: See code 952.10

952.17 T_7-T_{12} level with anterior cord syndrome   `MCC`
     CC Excl: See code 952.10

952.18 T_7-T_{12} level with central cord syndrome   `MCC`
     CC Excl: See code 952.10

952.19 T_7-T_{12} level with other specified spinal cord injury   `MCC`
     Incomplete spinal cord lesion at T_7-T_{12} level:
       NOS
       with posterior cord syndrome
     CC Excl: See code 952.10

952.2   **Lumbar**   `MCC`
     CC Excl: 805.8-805.9, 806.4-806.5, 839.40, 839.49-839.50, 839.59, 839.69, 839.79-839.9, 847.9, 905.1, 926.11, 952.2, 952.8-952.9,958.8-958.99, 959.11-959.19, 959.8-959.9

952.3   **Sacral**   `MCC`
     CC Excl: 805.8-805.9, 806.60-806.79, 839.40, 839.49-839.50, 839.59, 839.69, 839.79-839.9, 847.9, 905.1, 926.11, 952.3-952.9, 958.8-958.99, 959.11-959.19, 959.8-959.9

952.4   **Cauda equina**   `MCC`
     CC Excl: See code 952.3

952.8   **Multiple sites of spinal cord**   `MCC`
     CC Excl: 805.8-805.9, 839.40, 839.49-839.50, 839.59, 839.69, 839.79-839.9, 847.9, 905.1, 926.11, 952.8-952.9, 958.8-958.99, 959.11-959.19, 959.8-959.9

952.9   **Unspecified site of spinal cord**

√4ᵗʰ **953**   **Injury to nerve roots and spinal plexus**

953.0   **Cervical root**

953.1   **Dorsal root**

953.2   **Lumbar root**

953.3   **Sacral root**

953.4   **Brachial plexus**

953.5   **Lumbosacral plexus**

953.8   **Multiple sites**

953.9   **Unspecified site**

√4ᵗʰ **954**   **Injury to other nerve(s) of trunk, excluding shoulder and pelvic girdles**

954.0   **Cervical sympathetic**

954.1   **Other sympathetic**
     Celiac ganglion or plexus
     Inferior mesenteric plexus
     Splanchnic nerve(s)
     Stellate ganglion

954.8   **Other specified nerve(s) of trunk**

954.9   **Unspecified nerve of trunk**

√4ᵗʰ **955**   **Injury to peripheral nerve(s) of shoulder girdle and upper limb**

955.0   **Axillary nerve**

955.1   **Median nerve**

955.2   **Ulnar nerve**

955.3   **Radial nerve**

955.4   **Musculocutaneous nerve**

955.5   **Cutaneous sensory nerve, upper limb**

955.6   **Digital nerve**

955.7   **Other specified nerve(s) of shoulder girdle and upper limb**

955.8   **Multiple nerves of shoulder girdle and upper limb**

955.9   **Unspecified nerve of shoulder girdle and upper limb**

√4ᵗʰ **956**   **Injury to peripheral nerve(s) of pelvic girdle and lower limb**

956.0   **Sciatic nerve**

956.1   **Femoral nerve**

956.2   **Posterior tibial nerve**

956.3   **Peroneal nerve**

956.4   **Cutaneous sensory nerve, lower limb**

956.5   **Other specified nerve(s) of pelvic girdle and lower limb**

956.8   **Multiple nerves of pelvic girdle and lower limb**

956.9   **Unspecified nerve of pelvic girdle and lower limb**

√4ᵗʰ **957**   **Injury to other and unspecified nerves**

957.0   **Superficial nerves of head and neck**

957.1   **Other specified nerve(s)**

957.8   **Multiple nerves in several parts**
     Multiple nerve injury NOS

957.9   **Unspecified site**
     Nerve injury NOS

CERTAIN TRAUMATIC COMPLICATIONS AND UNSPECIFIED INJURIES (958-959)

√4ᵗʰ **958**   **Certain early complications of trauma**
     EXCLUDES   *adult respiratory distress syndrome (518.5)*
       flail chest (807.4)
       post-traumatic seroma (729.91)
       shock lung (518.5)
       that occurring during or following medical procedures (996.0-999.9)

958.0   **Air embolism**   `MCC`
     Pneumathemia
     EXCLUDES   *that complicating:*
       abortion (634-638 with .6, 639.6)
       ectopic or molar pregnancy (639.6)
       pregnancy, childbirth, or the puerperium (673.0)
     DEF: Arterial obstruction due to introduction of air bubbles into the veins following surgery or trauma.
     CC Excl: 958.0, 958.8-958.99, 959.8-959.9, 997.91-997.99, 998.81, 998.83-998.9, 999.1

958.1   **Fat embolism**   `MCC`
     EXCLUDES   *that complicating:*
       abortion (634-638 with .6, 639.6)
       pregnancy, childbirth, or the puerperium (673.8)
     DEF: Arterial blockage due to the entrance of fat in circulatory system, after fracture of large bones or administration of corticosteroids.
     CC Excl: 958.1, 958.8-958.99, 959.8-959.9, 997.91-997.99, 998.81, 998.83-998.9

958.2   **Secondary and recurrent hemorrhage**   `CC`
     CC Excl: 958.2, 958.8-958.99, 959.8-959.9, 997.91-997.99, 998.81, 998.83-998.9

N Newborn Age: 0   P Pediatric Age: 0-17   M Maternity Age: 12-55   A Adult Age: 15-124   `MCC` Major CC Condition   `CC` CC Condition   `HIV` HIV Related Dx

346 – Volume 1   **2010 ICD-9-CM**

958.3 Posttraumatic wound infection, not elsewhere classified `CC`

> _EXCLUDES_ infected open wounds-code to complicated open wound of site
>
> **CC Excl:** 958.3, 958.8-958.99, 959.8-959.9, 997.91-997.99, 998.81, 998.83-998.9
>
> **AHA:** 4Q, '01, 53; S-O, '85, 10
>
> **TIP:** Do not assign if the infection is documented as due to cellulitis; see instead categories 681 and 682 and complicated wound codes.

958.4 Traumatic shock `MCC`
Shock (immediate) (delayed) following injury

> _EXCLUDES_ shock:
> anaphylactic (995.0)
> due to serum (999.4)
> anesthetic (995.4)
> electric (994.8)
> following abortion (639.5)
> lightning (994.0)
> nontraumatic NOS (785.50)
> obstetric (669.1)
> postoperative (998.0)
>
> **DEF:** Shock, immediate or delayed following injury.
> **CC Excl:** 958.4, 958.8-958.99, 959.8-959.9, 997.91-997.99, 998.81, 998.83-998.9

958.5 Traumatic anuria `MCC`
Crush syndrome
Renal failure following crushing

> _EXCLUDES_ that due to a medical procedure (997.5)
> **DEF:** Complete suppression of urinary secretion by kidneys due to trauma.
> **CC Excl:** 958.5, 958.8-958.99, 959.8-959.9, 995.4, 997.91-998.13, 998.81, 998.83-998.9

958.6 Volkmann's ischemic contracture
Posttraumatic muscle contracture

> **DEF:** Muscle deterioration due to loss of blood supply from injury or tourniquet; causes muscle contraction and results in inability to extend the muscles fully.

958.7 Traumatic subcutaneous emphysema `CC`

> _EXCLUDES_ subcutaneous emphysema resulting from a procedure (998.81)
> **CC Excl:** 860.0-860.5, 861.20-862.1, 862.29-862.9, 875.0-875.1, 958.7-958.99, 959.8-959.9, 997.91-997.99, 998.81, 998.83-998.9

958.8 Other early complications of trauma
> **AHA:** 2Q, '92, 13

958.9 Traumatic compartment syndrome `√5th`

> _EXCLUDES_ nontraumatic compartment syndrome (729.71-729.79)
> **DEF:** Compression of nerves and blood vessels within an enclosed space due to previous trauma, which leads to impaired blood flow and muscle and nerve damage.
> **TIP:** If the compartment syndrome is specified as chronic or exercise-induced, see instead subcategory 729.7.

[handwritten margin note: Acute traumatic compartment syndrome is usually a sequelae of a serious injury to lower/upper extremities and can lead to significant motor and sensory deficits, pain, stiffness, and deformity when untreated.]

958.90 Compartment syndrome, unspecified `CC`
> **CC Excl:** 868.03-868.10, 868.13-869.1
> **AHA:** 4Q, '06, 100-102

958.91 Traumatic compartment syndrome of upper extremity `CC`
Traumatic compartment syndrome of shoulder, arm, forearm, wrist, hand, and fingers
> **CC Excl:** 729.81, 729.89-729.99
> **AHA:** 4Q, '06, 100-102

958.92 Traumatic compartment syndrome of lower extremity `CC`
Traumatic compartment syndrome of hip, buttock, thigh, leg, foot, and toes
> **CC Excl:** See code: 958.91
> **AHA:** 4Q, '06, 100-102

958.93 Traumatic compartment syndrome of abdomen `CC`
> **CC Excl:** 863.0-867.3, 867.5-869.1, 879.2-879.9, 929.0-929.9, 958.8, 959.8-959.9
> **AHA:** 4Q, '06, 100-102

958.99 Traumatic compartment syndrome of other sites `CC`
> **CC Excl:** 868.03-868.10, 868.13-869.1
> **AHA:** 4Q, '06, 100-102

959 Injury, other and unspecified `√4th`
> _INCLUDES_ injury NOS
> _EXCLUDES_ injury NOS of:
> blood vessels (900.0-904.9)
> eye (921.0-921.9)
> internal organs (860.0-869.1)
> intracranial sites (854.0-854.1)
> nerves (950.0-951.9, 953.0-957.9)
> spinal cord (952.0-952.9)

959.0 Head, face and neck `√5th`

959.01 Head injury, unspecified
> _EXCLUDES_ concussion (850.1-850.9)
> with head injury NOS (850.1-850.9)
> head injury NOS with loss of consciousness (850.1-850.5)
> specified intracranial injuries (850.0-854.1)
> **AHA:** ▶4Q, '08, 108;◀ 4Q, '97, 46
> **S09.90xA** Unspecified injury of head initial encounter `I-10`

959.09 Injury of face and neck
Cheek   Mouth
Ear   Nose
Eyebrow Throat
Lip
> **AHA:** 4Q, '97, 46

959.1 Trunk `√5th`
> _EXCLUDES_ scapular region (959.2)
> **AHA:** 4Q, '03, 78; 1Q, '99, 10

959.11 Other injury of chest wall
959.12 Other injury of abdomen
959.13 Fracture of corpus cavernosum penis ♂
959.14 Other injury of external genitals
959.19 Other injury of other sites of trunk
Injury of trunk NOS

959.2 Shoulder and upper arm
Axilla
Scapular region

959.3 Elbow, forearm, and wrist
> **AHA:** 1Q, '97, 8

959.4 Hand, except finger

959.5 Finger
Fingernail
Thumb (nail)

959.6 Hip and thigh
Upper leg

959.7 Knee, leg, ankle, and foot

959.8 Other specified sites, including multiple
> _EXCLUDES_ multiple sites classifiable to the same four-digit category (959.0-959.7)

959.9 Unspecified site

Injury and Poisoning

960–962.3

POISONING BY DRUGS, MEDICINAL AND BIOLOGICAL SUBSTANCES (960-979)

INCLUDES   overdose of these substances
wrong substance given or taken in error

Use additional code to specify the effects of the poisoning

EXCLUDES   *adverse effects ["hypersensitivity," "reaction," etc.] of correct substance properly administered. Such cases are to be classified according to the nature of the adverse effect, such as:*
adverse effect NOS (995.20)
allergic lymphadenitis (289.3)
aspirin gastritis (535.4)
blood disorders (280.0-289.9)
dermatitis:
  contact (692.0-692.9)
  due to ingestion (693.0-693.9)
nephropathy (583.9)
[The drug giving rise to the adverse effect may be identified by use of categories E930-E949.]
drug dependence (304.0-304.9)
drug reaction and poisoning affecting the newborn (760.0-779.9)
nondependent abuse of drugs (305.0-305.9)
pathological drug intoxication (292.2)

AHA: 2Q, '90, 11

TIP: Assign a poisoning code for interaction between prescribed drug and alcohol or prescribed drug and other nonprescribed drug or medicinal agent. Sequence poisoning code first, then code for manifestation of poisoning.

If respiratory failure is due to a poisoning, the poisoning code must be sequenced first.

✓4th 960 Poisoning by antibiotics

EXCLUDES   *antibiotics:*
ear, nose, and throat (976.6)
eye (976.5)
local (976.0)

960.0 Penicillins
Ampicillin   Cloxacillin
Carbenicillin   Penicillin G

960.1 Antifungal antibiotics
Amphotericin B   Nystatin
Griseofulvin   Trichomycin
> **EXCLUDES**   *preparations intended for topical use (976.0-976.9)*

960.2 Chloramphenicol group
Chloramphenicol
Thiamphenicol

960.3 Erythromycin and other macrolides
Oleandomycin
Spiramycin

960.4 Tetracycline group
Doxycycline   Oxytetracycline
Minocycline

960.5 Cephalosporin group
Cephalexin   Cephaloridine
Cephaloglycin   Cephalothin

960.6 Antimycobacterial antibiotics
Cycloserine   Rifampin
Kanamycin   Streptomycin

960.7 Antineoplastic antibiotics
Actinomycin such as: Actinomycin such as:
  Bleomycin   Daunorubicin
  Cactinomycin   Mitomycin
  Dactinomycin

960.8 Other specified antibiotics

960.9 Unspecified antibiotic

✓4th 961 Poisoning by other anti-infectives

EXCLUDES   *anti-infectives:*
ear, nose, and throat (976.6)
eye (976.5)
local (976.0)

961.0 Sulfonamides
Sulfadiazine   Sulfamethoxazole
Sulfafurazole

961.1 Arsenical anti-infectives

961.2 Heavy metal anti-infectives
Compounds of: Compounds of:
  antimony   lead
  bismuth   mercury
> **EXCLUDES**   *mercurial diuretics (974.0)*

961.3 Quinoline and hydroxyquinoline derivatives
Chiniofon
Diiodohydroxyquin
> **EXCLUDES**   *antimalarial drugs (961.4)*

961.4 Antimalarials and drugs acting on other blood protozoa
Chloroquine   Proguanil [chloroguanide]
Cycloguanil   Pyrimethamine
Primaquine   Quinine

961.5 Other antiprotozoal drugs
Emetine

961.6 Anthelmintics
Hexylresorcinol   Thiabendazole
Piperazine

961.7 Antiviral drugs
Methisazone
> **EXCLUDES**   *amantadine (966.4)*
> *cytarabine (963.1)*
> *idoxuridine (976.5)*

961.8 Other antimycobacterial drugs
Ethambutol
Ethionamide
Isoniazid
Para-aminosalicylic acid derivatives
Sulfones

961.9 Other and unspecified anti-infectives
Flucytosine
Nitrofuran derivatives

✓4th 962 Poisoning by hormones and synthetic substitutes

EXCLUDES   *oxytocic hormones (975.0)*

962.0 Adrenal cortical steroids
Cortisone derivatives
Desoxycorticosterone derivatives
Fluorinated corticosteroids

962.1 Androgens and anabolic congeners
Methandriol   Oxymetholone
Nandrolone   Testosterone

962.2 Ovarian hormones and synthetic substitutes
Contraceptives, oral
Estrogens
Estrogens and progestogens, combined
Progestogens

962.3 Insulins and antidiabetic agents
Acetohexamide
Biguanide derivatives, oral
Chlorpropamide
Glucagon
Insulin
Phenformin
Sulfonylurea derivatives, oral
Tolbutamide

AHA: 4Q, '93, 19; M-A, '85, 8

TIP: Assign only if documentation indicates overdose of insulin; if due to diabetic adjusting dosage, assign instead 250.8X or 249.8X and E932.3 for adverse reaction to insulin, if applicable.

N Newborn Age: 0   **P** Pediatric Age: 0-17   **M** Maternity Age: 12-55   **A** Adult Age: 15-124   **MCC** Major CC Condition   **CC** CC Condition   **HIV** HIV Related Dx

348 – Volume 1   **2010 ICD-9-CM**

Injury and Poisoning

962.4 Anterior pituitary hormones
Corticotropin
Gonadotropin
Somatotropin [growth hormone]

962.5 Posterior pituitary hormones
Vasopressin
EXCLUDES *oxytocic hormones (975.0)*

962.6 Parathyroid and parathyroid derivatives

962.7 Thyroid and thyroid derivatives
Dextrothyroxin   Liothyronine
Levothyroxine sodium   Thyroglobulin

962.8 Antithyroid agents
Iodides
Thiouracil
Thiourea

962.9 Other and unspecified hormones and synthetic substitutes

✓4th **963 Poisoning by primarily systemic agents**

963.0 Antiallergic and antiemetic drugs
Antihistamines   Diphenylpyraline
Chlorpheniramine   Thonzylamine
Diphenhydramine   Tripelennamine
EXCLUDES *phenothiazine-based tranquilizers (969.1)*

963.1 Antineoplastic and immunosuppressive drugs
Azathioprine   Cytarabine
Busulfan   Fluorouracil
Chlorambucil   Mercaptopurine
Cyclophosphamide   thio-TEPA
EXCLUDES *antineoplastic antibiotics (960.7)*

963.2 Acidifying agents

963.3 Alkalizing agents

963.4 Enzymes, not elsewhere classified
Penicillinase

963.5 Vitamins, not elsewhere classified
Vitamin A
Vitamin D
EXCLUDES *nicotinic acid (972.2)*
vitamin K (964.3)

963.8 Other specified systemic agents
Heavy metal antagonists

963.9 Unspecified systemic agent

✓4th **964 Poisoning by agents primarily affecting blood constituents**

964.0 Iron and its compounds
Ferric salts
Ferrous sulfate and other ferrous salts

964.1 Liver preparations and other antianemic agents
Folic acid

964.2 Anticoagulants
Coumarin   Phenindione
Heparin   Warfarin sodium
AHA: 1Q, '94, 22
TIP: If documentation indicates an adverse reaction to Coumadin, assign instead manifestation (e.g., hematuria or epistaxis), code 790.92 if abnormal coagulation profile is documented, and E934.2.

964.3 Vitamin K [phytonadione]

964.4 Fibrinolysis-affecting drugs
Aminocaproic acid   Streptokinase
Streptodornase   Urokinase

964.5 Anticoagulant antagonists and other coagulants
Hexadimethrine
Protamine sulfate

964.6 Gamma globulin

964.7 Natural blood and blood products
Blood plasma   Packed red cells
Human fibrinogen   Whole blood
EXCLUDES *transfusion reactions (999.4-999.8)*

964.8 Other specified agents affecting blood constituents
Macromolecular blood substitutes
Plasma expanders

964.9 Unspecified agent affecting blood constituents

✓4th **965 Poisoning by analgesics, antipyretics, and antirheumatics**
EXCLUDES *drug dependence (304.0-304.9)*
nondependent abuse (305.0-305.9)

✓5th **965.0 Opiates and related narcotics**

965.00 Opium (alkaloids), unspecified
AHA: 3Q, '07, 6

965.01 Heroin
Diacetylmorphine

965.02 Methadone

965.09 Other
Codeine [methylmorphine]
Meperidine [pethidine]
Morphine
AHA: 3Q, '07, 6
T40.4x1A Poisoning oth synthetic narc accidnt I-10 initial enc

965.1 Salicylates
Acetylsalicylic acid [aspirin]
Salicylic acid salts
AHA: N-D, '94, 15

965.4 Aromatic analgesics, not elsewhere classified
Acetanilid
Paracetamol [acetaminophen]
Phenacetin [acetophenetidin]

965.5 Pyrazole derivatives
Aminophenazone [aminopyrine]
Phenylbutazone

✓5th **965.6 Antirheumatics [antiphlogistics]**
EXCLUDES *salicylates (965.1)*
steroids (962.0-962.9)
AHA: 4Q, '98, 50

965.61 Propionic acid derivatives
Fenoprofen   Ketoprofen
Flurbiprofen   Naproxen
Ibuprofen   Oxaprozin
AHA: 4Q, '98, 50

965.69 Other antirheumatics
Gold salts
Indomethacin

965.7 Other non-narcotic analgesics
Pyrabital

965.8 Other specified analgesics and antipyretics
Pentazocine

965.9 Unspecified analgesic and antipyretic

✓4th **966 Poisoning by anticonvulsants and anti-Parkinsonism drugs**

966.0 Oxazolidine derivatives
Paramethadione
Trimethadione

966.1 Hydantoin derivatives
Phenytoin

966.2 Succinimides
Ethosuximide
Phensuximide

966.3 Other and unspecified anticonvulsants
Primidone
EXCLUDES *barbiturates (967.0)*
sulfonamides (961.0)

966.4 Anti-Parkinsonism drugs
Amantadine
Ethopropazine [profenamine]
Levodopa [L-dopa]

Injury and Poisoning

967–970.9

✓4th **967 Poisoning by sedatives and hypnotics**
    EXCLUDES   *drug dependence (304.0-304.9)*
                nondependent abuse (305.0-305.9)

  967.0 **Barbiturates**
      Amobarbital [amylobarbitone]
      Barbital [barbitone]
      Butabarbital [butabarbitone]
      Pentobarbital [pentobarbitone]
      Phenobarbital [phenobarbitone]
      Secobarbital [quinalbarbitone]
      EXCLUDES   *thiobarbiturate anesthetics (968.3)*

  967.1 **Chloral hydrate group**

  967.2 **Paraldehyde**

  967.3 **Bromine compounds**
      Bromide
      Carbromal (derivatives)

  967.4 **Methaqualone compounds**

  967.5 **Glutethimide group**

  967.6 **Mixed sedatives, not elsewhere classified**

  967.8 **Other sedatives and hypnotics**

  967.9 **Unspecified sedative or hypnotic**
      Sleeping:
        drug
        pill   } NOS
        tablet

✓4th **968 Poisoning by other central nervous system depressants and anesthetics**
    EXCLUDES   *drug dependence (304.0-304.9)*
                nondependent abuse (305.0-305.9)

  968.0 **Central nervous system muscle-tone depressants**
      Chlorphenesin (carbamate)
      Mephenesin
      Methocarbamol

  968.1 **Halothane**

  968.2 **Other gaseous anesthetics**
      Ether
      Halogenated hydrocarbon derivatives, except halothane
      Nitrous oxide

  968.3 **Intravenous anesthetics**
      Ketamine
      Methohexital [methohexitone]
      Thiobarbiturates, such as thiopental sodium

  968.4 **Other and unspecified general anesthetics**

  968.5 **Surface [topical] and infiltration anesthetics**
      Cocaine
      Lidocaine [lignocaine]
      Procaine
      Tetracaine
      AHA: 1Q, '93, 25

  968.6 **Peripheral nerve- and plexus-blocking anesthetics**

  968.7 **Spinal anesthetics**

  968.9 **Other and unspecified local anesthetics**
      T41.44xA Poisoning uns anesthetic undetermind initial   **I-10** enc

✓4th **969 Poisoning by psychotropic agents**
    EXCLUDES   *drug dependence (304.0-304.9)*
                nondependent abuse (305.0-305.9)

✓5th   969.0 **Antidepressants**

  ●   969.00 **Antidepressant, unspecified**
        AHA: 3Q, '07, 6; #5, '94, 9; 3Q, '91, 14; N-D, '84, 14

  ●   969.01 **Monoamine oxidase inhibitors**
        MAOI

●   969.02 **Selective serotonin and norepinephrine reuptake inhibitors**
      SSNRI antidepressants
      TIP: Assign for serotonin syndrome due to poisoning, along with 333.99 and E854.0, for accidental poisoning.

●   969.03 **Selective serotonin reuptake inhibitors**
      SSRI antidepressants
      TIP: Assign for serotonin syndrome due to poisoning, along with 333.99 and E854.0, for accidental poisoning.

●   969.04 **Tetracyclic antidepressants**

●   969.05 **Tricyclic antidepressants**

●   969.09 **Other antidepressants**

  969.1 **Phenothiazine-based tranquilizers**
      Chlorpromazine   Prochlorperazine
      Fluphenazine   Promazine

  969.2 **Butyrophenone-based tranquilizers**
      Haloperidol
      Spiperone
      Trifluperidol

  969.3 **Other antipsychotics, neuroleptics, and major tranquilizers**

  969.4 **Benzodiazepine-based tranquilizers**
      Chlordiazepoxide
      Diazepam
      Flurazepam
      Lorazepam
      Medazepam
      Nitrazepam
      T42.4x1D Poisoning benzodiazepines accidental subseq   **I-10** enc

  969.5 **Other tranquilizers**
      Hydroxyzine
      Meprobamate

  969.6 **Psychodysleptics [hallucinogens]**
      Cannabis (derivatives)
      Lysergide [LSD]
      Marihuana (derivatives)
      Mescaline
      Psilocin
      Psilocybin

✓5th   969.7 **Psychostimulants**
      EXCLUDES   *central appetite depressants (977.0)*

  ●   969.70 **Psychostimulant, unspecified**
        AHA: 2Q, '03, 11

  ●   969.71 **Caffeine**

  ●   969.72 **Amphetamines**
        Methamphetamines
        TIP: Assign for overdose and poisoning of the club drug ecstasy.

  ●   969.73 **Methylphenidate**

  ●   969.79 **Other psychostimulants**

  969.8 **Other specified psychotropic agents**

  969.9 **Unspecified psychotropic agent**

✓4th **970 Poisoning by central nervous system stimulants**

  970.0 **Analeptics**
      Lobeline
      Nikethamide

  970.1 **Opiate antagonists**
      Levallorphan
      Nalorphine
      Naloxone

  970.8 **Other specified central nervous system stimulants**
      AHA: 1Q, '05, 6

  970.9 **Unspecified central nervous system stimulant**

N Newborn Age: 0   P Pediatric Age: 0-17   M Maternity Age: 12-55   A Adult Age: 15-124   **MCC** Major CC Condition   **CC** CC Condition   **HIV** HIV Related Dx

350 – Volume 1 • October 2009

2010 ICD-9-CM

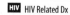

✓4th 971 Poisoning by drugs primarily affecting the autonomic nervous system

971.0 **Parasympathomimetics [cholinergics]**
Acetylcholine
Anticholinesterase:
organophosphorus
reversible
Pilocarpine

971.1 **Parasympatholytics [anticholinergics and antimuscarinics] and spasmolytics**
Atropine
Homatropine
Hyoscine [scopolamine]
Quaternary ammonium derivatives
EXCLUDES *papaverine (972.5)*

971.2 **Sympathomimetics [adrenergics]**
Epinephrine [adrenalin]
Levarterenol [noradrenalin]

971.3 **Sympatholytics [antiadrenergics]**
Phenoxybenzamine
Tolazolinehydrochloride

971.9 **Unspecified drug primarily affecting autonomic nervous system**

✓4th 972 Poisoning by agents primarily affecting the cardiovascular system

972.0 **Cardiac rhythm regulators**
Practolol
Procainamide
Propranolol
Quinidine
EXCLUDES *lidocaine (968.5)*

972.1 **Cardiotonic glycosides and drugs of similar action**
Digitalis glycosides
Digoxin
Strophanthins

972.2 **Antilipemic and antiarteriosclerotic drugs**
Clofibrate
Nicotinic acid derivatives

972.3 **Ganglion-blocking agents**
Pentamethonium bromide

972.4 **Coronary vasodilators**
Dipyridamole
Nitrates [nitroglycerin]
Nitrites

972.5 **Other vasodilators**
Cyclandelate
Diazoxide
Papaverine
EXCLUDES *nicotinic acid (972.2)*

972.6 **Other antihypertensive agents**
Clonidine
Guanethidine
Rauwolfia alkaloids
Reserpine

972.7 **Antivaricose drugs, including sclerosing agents**
Sodium morrhuate
Zinc salts

972.8 **Capillary-active drugs**
Adrenochrome derivatives
Metaraminol

972.9 **Other and unspecified agents primarily affecting the cardiovascular system**

✓4th 973 Poisoning by agents primarily affecting the gastrointestinal system

973.0 **Antacids and antigastric secretion drugs**
Aluminum hydroxide
Magnesium trisilicate
AHA: 1Q, '03, 19

973.1 **Irritant cathartics**
Bisacodyl
Castor oil
Phenolphthalein

973.2 **Emollient cathartics**
Dioctyl sulfosuccinates

973.3 **Other cathartics, including intestinal atonia drugs**
Magnesium sulfate

973.4 **Digestants**
Pancreatin
Papain
Pepsin

973.5 **Antidiarrheal drugs**
Kaolin
Pectin
EXCLUDES *anti-infectives (960.0-961.9)*

973.6 **Emetics**

973.8 **Other specified agents primarily affecting the gastrointestinal system**

973.9 **Unspecified agent primarily affecting the gastrointestinal system**

✓4th 974 Poisoning by water, mineral, and uric acid metabolism drugs

974.0 **Mercurial diuretics**
Chlormerodrin   Mersalyl
Mercaptomerin

974.1 **Purine derivative diuretics**
Theobromine
Theophylline
EXCLUDES *aminophylline [theophylline ethylenediamine] (975.7)*
caffeine ▶(969.71)◀

974.2 **Carbonic acid anhydrase inhibitors**
Acetazolamide

974.3 **Saluretics**
Benzothiadiazides
Chlorothiazide group

974.4 **Other diuretics**
Ethacrynic acid
Furosemide

974.5 **Electrolytic, caloric, and water-balance agents**

974.6 **Other mineral salts, not elsewhere classified**

974.7 **Uric acid metabolism drugs**
Allopurinol   Probenecid
Colchicine

✓4th 975 Poisoning by agents primarily acting on the smooth and skeletal muscles and respiratory system

975.0 **Oxytocic agents**
Ergot alkaloids
Oxytocin
Prostaglandins

975.1 **Smooth muscle relaxants**
Adiphenine
Metaproterenol [orciprenaline]
EXCLUDES *papaverine (972.5)*

975.2 **Skeletal muscle relaxants**

975.3 **Other and unspecified drugs acting on muscles**

975.4 **Antitussives**
Dextromethorphan
Pipazethate

975.5 **Expectorants**
Acetylcysteine
Guaifenesin
Terpin hydrate

975.6 **Anti-common cold drugs**

975.7 **Antiasthmatics**
Aminophylline [theophylline ethylenediamine]

975.8 **Other and unspecified respiratory drugs**

Injury and Poisoning

976–983.1

☑4ᵗʰ **976 Poisoning by agents primarily affecting skin and mucous membrane, ophthalmological, otorhinolaryngological, and dental drugs**

976.0 **Local anti-infectives and anti-inflammatory drugs**

976.1 **Antipruritics**

976.2 **Local astringents and local detergents**

976.3 **Emollients, demulcents, and protectants**

976.4 **Keratolytics, keratoplastics, other hair treatment drugs and preparations**

976.5 **Eye anti-infectives and other eye drugs**
Idoxuridine

976.6 **Anti-infectives and other drugs and preparations for ear, nose, and throat**

976.7 **Dental drugs topically applied**
EXCLUDES *anti-infectives (976.0)*
local anesthetics (968.5)

976.8 **Other agents primarily affecting skin and mucous membrane**
Spermicides [vaginal contraceptives]

976.9 **Unspecified agent primarily affecting skin and mucous membrane**

☑4ᵗʰ **977 Poisoning by other and unspecified drugs and medicinal substances**

977.0 **Dietetics**
Central appetite depressants

977.1 **Lipotropic drugs**

977.2 **Antidotes and chelating agents, not elsewhere classified**

977.3 **Alcohol deterrents**

977.4 **Pharmaceutical excipients**
Pharmaceutical adjuncts

977.8 **Other specified drugs and medicinal substances**
Contrast media used for diagnostic x-ray procedures
Diagnostic agents and kits

977.9 **Unspecified drug or medicinal substance**

☑4ᵗʰ **978 Poisoning by bacterial vaccines**

978.0 **BCG**

978.1 **Typhoid and paratyphoid**

978.2 **Cholera**

978.3 **Plague**

978.4 **Tetanus**

978.5 **Diphtheria**

978.6 **Pertussis vaccine, including combinations with a pertussis component**

978.8 **Other and unspecified bacterial vaccines**

978.9 **Mixed bacterial vaccines, except combinations with a pertussis component**

☑4ᵗʰ **979 Poisoning by other vaccines and biological substances**
EXCLUDES *gamma globulin (964.6)*

979.0 **Smallpox vaccine**

979.1 **Rabies vaccine**

979.2 **Typhus vaccine**

979.3 **Yellow fever vaccine**

979.4 **Measles vaccine**

979.5 **Poliomyelitis vaccine**

979.6 **Other and unspecified viral and rickettsial vaccines**
Mumps vaccine

979.7 **Mixed viral-rickettsial and bacterial vaccines, except combinations with a pertussis component**
EXCLUDES *combinations with a pertussis component (978.6)*

979.9 **Other and unspecified vaccines and biological substances**

TOXIC EFFECTS OF SUBSTANCES CHIEFLY NONMEDICINAL AS TO SOURCE (980-989)

Use additional code to specify the nature of the toxic effect
EXCLUDES *burns from chemical agents (ingested) (947.0-947.9)*
localized toxic effects indexed elsewhere (001.0-799.9)
respiratory conditions due to external agents (506.0-508.9)

☑4ᵗʰ **980 Toxic effect of alcohol**

980.0 **Ethyl alcohol**
Denatured alcohol   Grain alcohol
Ethanol
Use additional code to identify any associated:
acute alcohol intoxication (305.0)
in alcoholism (303.0)
drunkenness (simple) (305.0)
pathological (291.4)
AHA: 3Q, '96, 16
T51.0x1A Toxic effect ethanol accidental initial encountr I-10

980.1 **Methyl alcohol**
Methanol
Wood alcohol

980.2 **Isopropyl alcohol**
Dimethyl carbinol
Isopropanol
Rubbing alcohol

980.3 **Fusel oil**
Alcohol:
amyl
butyl
propyl

980.8 **Other specified alcohols**

980.9 **Unspecified alcohol**

981 Toxic effect of petroleum products
Benzine
Gasoline
Kerosene
Paraffin wax
Petroleum:
ether
naphtha
spirit

☑4ᵗʰ **982 Toxic effect of solvents other than petroleum-based**

982.0 **Benzene and homologues**

982.1 **Carbon tetrachloride**

982.2 **Carbon disulfide**
Carbon bisulfide

982.3 **Other chlorinated hydrocarbon solvents**
Tetrachloroethylene
Trichloroethylene
EXCLUDES *chlorinated hydrocarbon preparations other than solvents (989.2)*
AHA: ▶3Q, '08, 6-7◀

982.4 **Nitroglycol**

982.8 **Other nonpetroleum-based solvents**
Acetone

☑4ᵗʰ **983 Toxic effect of corrosive aromatics, acids, and caustic alkalis**

983.0 **Corrosive aromatics**
Carbolic acid or phenol
Cresol

983.1 **Acids**
Acid:
hydrochloric
nitric
sulfuric

N Newborn Age: 0   P Pediatric Age: 0-17   M Maternity Age: 12-55   A Adult Age: 15-124   MCC Major CC Condition   CC CC Condition   HIV HIV Related Dx

352 – Volume 1 • February 2009   2010 ICD-9-CM

983.2 **Caustic alkalis**
Lye
Potassium hydroxide
Sodium hydroxide

983.9 **Caustic, unspecified**

√4th 984 **Toxic effect of lead and its compounds (including fumes)**

INCLUDES   that from all sources except medicinal substances

984.0 **Inorganic lead compounds**
Lead dioxide
Lead salts

984.1 **Organic lead compounds**
Lead acetate
Tetraethyl lead

984.8 **Other lead compounds**

984.9 **Unspecified lead compound**

√4th 985 **Toxic effect of other metals**

INCLUDES   that from all sources except medicinal substances

985.0 **Mercury and its compounds**
Minamata disease

985.1 **Arsenic and its compounds**

985.2 **Manganese and its compounds**

985.3 **Beryllium and its compounds**

985.4 **Antimony and its compounds**

985.5 **Cadmium and its compounds**

985.6 **Chromium**

985.8 **Other specified metals**

Brass fumes	Iron compounds
Copper salts	Nickel compounds

AHA: 1Q, '88, 5

TIP: Assign for aluminum overloading or excessive concentration of aluminum in the body, along with E879.1 if due to renal dialysis and E879.8 if due to total parenteral nutrition.

985.9 **Unspecified metal**

986 **Toxic effect of carbon monoxide**
Carbon monoxide from any source

√4th 987 **Toxic effect of other gases, fumes, or vapors**

987.0 **Liquefied petroleum gases**
Butane
Propane

987.1 **Other hydrocarbon gas**

987.2 **Nitrogen oxides**
Nitrogen dioxide
Nitrous fumes

987.3 **Sulfur dioxide**

987.4 **Freon**
Dichloromonofluoromethane

987.5 **Lacrimogenic gas**
Bromobenzyl cyanide
Chloroacetophenone
Ethyliodoacetate

987.6 **Chlorine gas**

987.7 **Hydrocyanic acid gas**

987.8 **Other specified gases, fumes, or vapors**
Phosgene
Polyester fumes

987.9 **Unspecified gas, fume, or vapor**

AHA: 3Q, '05, 10

TIP: Assign for smoke inhalation, along with the appropriate E code describing the source of the smoke and fumes.

√4th 988 **Toxic effect of noxious substances eaten as food**

EXCLUDES   *allergic reaction to food, such as:*
gastroenteritis (558.3)
rash (692.5, 693.1)
food poisoning (bacterial) (005.0-005.9)
toxic effects of food contaminants, such as:
aflatoxin and other mycotoxin (989.7)
mercury (985.0)

988.0 **Fish and shellfish**

988.1 **Mushrooms**

988.2 **Berries and other plants**

988.8 **Other specified noxious substances eaten as food**

988.9 **Unspecified noxious substance eaten as food**

√4th 989 **Toxic effect of other substances, chiefly nonmedicinal as to source**

989.0 **Hydrocyanic acid and cyanides**
Potassium cyanide
Sodium cyanide

EXCLUDES   *gas and fumes (987.7)*

989.1 **Strychnine and salts**

989.2 **Chlorinated hydrocarbons**
Aldrin
Chlordane
DDT
Dieldrin

EXCLUDES   *chlorinated hydrocarbon solvents (982.0-982.3)*

989.3 **Organophosphate and carbamate**
Carbaryl
Dichlorvos
Malathion
Parathion
Phorate
Phosdrin

989.4 **Other pesticides, not elsewhere classified**
Mixtures of insecticides

989.5 **Venom**
Bites of venomous snakes, lizards, and spiders
Tick paralysis

989.6 **Soaps and detergents**

989.7 **Aflatoxin and other mycotoxin [food contaminants]**

√5th 989.8 **Other substances, chiefly nonmedicinal as to source**

AHA: 4Q, '95, 60

989.81 **Asbestos**

EXCLUDES   *asbestosis (501)*
exposure to asbestos (V15.84)

989.82 **Latex**

989.83 **Silicone**

EXCLUDES   *silicone used in medical devices, implants and grafts (996.00-996.79)*

989.84 **Tobacco**

989.89 **Other**

989.9 **Unspecified substance, chiefly nonmedicinal as to source**

√4th √5th Additional Digit Required   Unacceptable PDx   Manifestation Code   Hospital Acquired Condition   ▶◀ Revised Text   ● New Code   ▲ Revised Code Title

2010 ICD-9-CM   Volume 1 – 353

Injury and Poisoning

990–994.6

OTHER AND UNSPECIFIED EFFECTS OF EXTERNAL CAUSES
(990-995)

990 Effects of radiation, unspecified
Complication of:
  phototherapy
  radiation therapy
Radiation sickness

[The type of radiation giving rise to the adverse effect may be identified by use of the E codes.]

> **EXCLUDES**   *specified adverse effects of radiation. Such conditions are to be classified according to the nature of the adverse effect, as:*
> *burns (940.0-949.5)*
> *dermatitis (692.7-692.8)*
> *leukemia (204.0-208.9)*
> *pneumonia (508.0)*
> *sunburn (692.71, 692.76-692.77)*

✓4ᵗʰ **991 Effects of reduced temperature**

991.0 Frostbite of face   **CC**
CC Excl: 991.0, 991.3

991.1 Frostbite of hand   **CC**
CC Excl: 991.1, 991.3

991.2 Frostbite of foot   **CC**
CC Excl: 991.2-991.3

991.3 Frostbite of other and unspecified sites   **CC**
CC Excl: 991.0-991.4

991.4 Immersion foot   **CC**
Trench foot
DEF: Paresthesia, edema, blotchy cyanosis of foot, the skin is soft (macerated), pale and wrinkled, and the sole is swollen with surface ridging and following sustained immersion in water.
CC Excl: 991.3-991.4

991.5 Chilblains
Erythema pernio
Perniosis
DEF: Red, swollen, itchy skin; follows damp cold exposure; also associated with pruritus and a burning feeling, in hands, feet, ears, and face in children, legs and toes in women, and hands and fingers in men.

991.6 Hypothermia
Hypothermia (accidental)
> **EXCLUDES**   *hypothermia following anesthesia (995.89)*
> *hypothermia not associated with low environmental temperature (780.65)*

DEF: Reduced body temperature due to low environmental temperatures.

991.8 Other specified effects of reduced temperature

991.9 Unspecified effect of reduced temperature
Effects of freezing or excessive cold NOS

✓4ᵗʰ **992 Effects of heat and light**
> **EXCLUDES**   *burns (940.0-949.5)*
> *diseases of sweat glands due to heat (705.0-705.9)*
> *malignant hyperpyrexia following anesthesia (995.86)*
> *sunburn (692.71, 692.76-692.77)*

992.0 Heat stroke and sunstroke   **CC**
Heat apoplexy
Heat pyrexia
Ictus solaris
Siriasis
Thermoplegia
DEF: Headache, vertigo, cramps and elevated body temperature due to high environmental temperatures.
CC Excl: 992.0-992.9

992.1 Heat syncope
Heat collapse

992.2 Heat cramps

992.3 Heat exhaustion, anhydrotic
Heat prostration due to water depletion
> **EXCLUDES**   *that associated with salt depletion (992.4)*

992.4 Heat exhaustion due to salt depletion
Heat prostration due to salt (and water) depletion

992.5 Heat exhaustion, unspecified
Heat prostration NOS

992.6 Heat fatigue, transient

992.7 Heat edema
DEF: Fluid retention due to high environmental temperatures.

992.8 Other specified heat effects

992.9 Unspecified

✓4ᵗʰ **993 Effects of air pressure**

993.0 Barotrauma, otitic
Aero-otitis media
Effects of high altitude on ears
DEF: Ringing ears, deafness, pain and vertigo due to air pressure changes.

993.1 Barotrauma, sinus
Aerosinusitis
Effects of high altitude on sinuses

993.2 Other and unspecified effects of high altitude
Alpine sickness
Andes disease
Anoxia due to high altitude
Hypobaropathy
Mountain sickness
AHA: 3Q, '88, 4

993.3 Caisson disease   **CC**
Bends
Compressed-air disease
Decompression sickness
Divers' palsy or paralysis
DEF: Rapid reduction in air pressure while breathing compressed air; symptoms include skin lesions, joint pains, respiratory and neurological problems.
CC Excl: 993.3-993.9

993.4 Effects of air pressure caused by explosion

993.8 Other specified effects of air pressure

993.9 Unspecified effect of air pressure

✓4ᵗʰ **994 Effects of other external causes**
> **EXCLUDES**   *certain adverse effects not elsewhere classified (995.0-995.8)*

994.0 Effects of lightning
Shock from lightning
Struck by lightning NOS
> **EXCLUDES**   *burns (940.0-949.5)*

994.1 Drowning and nonfatal submersion   **CC**
Bathing cramp
Immersion
CC Excl: 994.1
AHA: 3Q, '88, 4
TIP: When near-drowning results in acute respiratory edema, assign also code 518.5 Post-traumatic pulmonary insufficiency.

994.2 Effects of hunger
Deprivation of food
Starvation

994.3 Effects of thirst
Deprivation of water

994.4 Exhaustion due to exposure

994.5 Exhaustion due to excessive exertion
Exhaustion due to overexertion

994.6 Motion sickness
Air sickness
Seasickness
Travel sickness

N Newborn Age: 0   P Pediatric Age: 0-17   M Maternity Age: 12-55   A Adult Age: 15-124   **MCC** Major CC Condition   **CC** CC Condition   **HIV** HIV Related Dx

994.7 Asphyxiation and strangulation `CC`

Suffocation (by):   Suffocation (by):
bedclothes   plastic bag
cave-in   pressure
constriction   strangulation
mechanical

> **EXCLUDES** asphyxia from:
>   carbon monoxide (986)
>   inhalation of food or foreign body
>   (932-934.9)
>   other gases, fumes, and vapors
>   (987.0-987.9)

CC Excl: 994.7

994.8 Electrocution and nonfatal effects of electric current

Shock from electric current
Shock from electroshock gun (taser)

> **EXCLUDES** electric burns (940.0-949.5)

994.9 Other effects of external causes

Effects of:
abnormal gravitational [G] forces or states
weightlessness

✓4ᵗʰ 995 Certain adverse effects not elsewhere classified

> **EXCLUDES** complications of surgical and medical care (996.0-999.9)

995.0 Other anaphylactic shock `CC`

Allergic shock   ⎫ NOS or due to adverse effect of
Anaphylactic   ⎬   correct medicinal
    reaction   ⎪   substance properly
Anaphylaxis   ⎭   administered

Use additional E code to identify external cause, such as:
adverse effects of correct medicinal substance
properly administered [E930-E949]

> **EXCLUDES** anaphylactic reaction to serum (999.4)
>   anaphylactic shock due to adverse food
>   reaction (995.60-995.69)

DEF: Immediate sensitivity response after exposure to specific antigen; results in life-threatening respiratory distress; usually followed by vascular collapse, shock , urticaria, angioedema and pruritus.

CC Excl: 995.60-995.69

AHA: 4Q, '93, 30

995.1 Angioneurotic edema

Giant urticaria

> **EXCLUDES** urticaria:
>   due to serum (999.5)
>   other specified (698.2, 708.0-708.9, 757.33)

DEF: Circulatory response of deep dermis, subcutaneous or submucosal tissues; causes localized edema and wheals.

✓5ᵗʰ 995.2 Other and unspecified adverse effect of drug, medicinal and biological substance (due) to correct medicinal substance properly administered

Adverse effect   ⎫ (due) to correct medicinal
Allergic reaction   ⎬   substance properly
Hypersensitivity   ⎪   administered
Idiosyncrasy   ⎭

Drug:
hypersensitivity NOS
reaction NOS

> **EXCLUDES** pathological drug intoxication (292.2)

AHA: 2Q, '97, 12; 3Q, '95, 13; 3Q, '92, 16

TIP: Codes from this subcategory should not be assigned for inpatient cases; their use is limited to certain outpatient cases in which there is no documentation of specific symptoms associated with the adverse effect.

995.20 Unspecified adverse effect of unspecified drug, medicinal and biological substance

AHA: 4Q, '06, 112

995.21 Arthus phenomenon

Arthus reaction

AHA: 4Q, '06, 112

995.22 Unspecified adverse effect of anesthesia

AHA: 4Q, '06, 112

995.23 Unspecified adverse effect of insulin

AHA: 4Q, '06, 112

● **995.24 Failed moderate sedation during procedure**

Failed conscious sedation during procedure

995.27 Other drug allergy

Drug allergy NOS
Drug hypersensitivity NOS

AHA: 4Q, '06, 112

995.29 Unspecified adverse effect of other drug,medicinal and biological substance

AHA: 4Q, '06, 112

995.3 Allergy, unspecified

Allergic reaction NOS
Hypersensitivity NOS
Idiosyncrasy NOS

> **EXCLUDES** allergic reaction NOS to correct medicinal
>   substance properly administered
>   (995.27)
>   allergy to existing dental restorative materials
>   (525.66)
>   specific types of allergic reaction, such as:
>   allergic diarrhea (558.3)
>   dermatitis (691.0-693.9)
>   hayfever (477.0-477.9)

995.4 Shock due to anesthesia `CC`

Shock due to anesthesia in which the correct substance
was properly administered

> **EXCLUDES** complications of anesthesia in labor or delivery
>   (668.0-668.9)
>   overdose or wrong substance given
>   (968.0-969.9)
>   postoperative shock NOS (998.0)
>   specified adverse effects of anesthesia classified
>   elsewhere, such as:
>   anoxic brain damage (348.1)
>   hepatitis (070.0-070.9), etc.
>   unspecified adverse effect of anesthesia
>   (995.22)

CC Excl: 958.4, 995.4, 997.91-998.13, 998.81, 998.83-998.9

✓5ᵗʰ 995.5 Child maltreatment syndrome

Use additional code(s), if applicable, to identify any
associated injuries

Use additional E code to identify:
nature of abuse (E960-E968)
perpetrator (E967.0-E967.9)

AHA: 1Q, '98, 11

TIP: Although separate codes for any associated injuries should be assigned, codes from this subcategory may be assigned alone if there are no documented injuries or associated conditions.

995.50 Child abuse, unspecified `CC` `P`

CC Excl: 995.50-995.59, 995.80-995.85

995.51 Child emotional/psychological abuse `CC` `P`

CC Excl: See code: 995.50

AHA: 4Q, '96, 38, 40

995.52 Child neglect (nutritional) `CC` `P`

CC Excl: See code: 995.50

AHA: 4Q, '96, 38, 40

995.53 Child sexual abuse `CC` `P`

CC Excl: See code: 995.50

AHA: 4Q, '96, 39, 40

995.54 Child physical abuse `CC` `P`

Battered baby or child syndrome

> **EXCLUDES** shaken infant syndrome (995.55)

CC Excl: See code: 995.50

AHA: 3Q, '99, 14; 4Q, '96, 39, 40

995.55 Shaken infant syndrome `CC` `P`

Use additional code(s) to identify any associated
injuries

CC Excl: See code: 995.50

AHA: 4Q, '96, 40, 43

✓4ᵗʰ Additional Digit Required | Unacceptable PDx | Manifestation Code | Hospital Acquired Condition | ►◄ Revised Text | ● New Code | ▲ Revised Code Title

2010 ICD-9-CM   **October 2009 • Volume 1 – 355**

995.59 Other child abuse and neglect `CC` `P`
Multiple forms of abuse
CC Excl: See code: 995.50

✓5ᵗʰ **995.6 Anaphylactic shock due to adverse food reaction**
Anaphylactic reaction due to food
Anaphylactic shock due to nonpoisonous foods
AHA: 4Q, '93, 30

TIP: Codes from this subcategory may be assigned not only
for anaphylactic shock, but also for any documentation of
anaphylactic reaction to food.

995.60 Due to unspecified food `CC`
CC Excl: 995.60-995.69

995.61 Due to peanuts `CC`
CC Excl: See code: 995.60

995.62 Due to crustaceans `CC`
CC Excl: See code: 995.60

995.63 Due to fruits and vegetables `CC`
CC Excl: See code: 995.60

995.64 Due to tree nuts and seeds `CC`
AHA: 1Q, '08, 12
CC Excl: See code: 995.60

995.65 Due to fish `CC`
CC Excl: See code: 995.60

995.66 Due to food additives `CC`
CC Excl: See code: 995.60

995.67 Due to milk products `CC`
CC Excl: See code: 995.60

995.68 Due to eggs `CC`
CC Excl: See code: 995.60

995.69 Due to other specified food `CC`
CC Excl: See code: 995.60

**995.7 Other adverse food reactions, not elsewhere
classified**
Use additional code to identify the type of reaction,
such as:
hives (708.0)
wheezing (786.07)

> **EXCLUDES** anaphylactic shock due to adverse food
> reaction (995.60-995.69)
> asthma (493.0, 493.9)
> dermatitis due to food (693.1)
> in contact with skin (692.5)
> gastroenteritis and colitis due to food (558.3)
> rhinitis due to food (477.1)

✓5ᵗʰ **995.8 Other specified adverse effects, not elsewhere
classified**

995.80 Adult maltreatment, unspecified `CC` `A`
Abused person NOS
Use additional code to identify:
any associated injury
perpetrator (E967.0-E967.9)
CC Excl: 995.80
AHA: 4Q, '96, 41, 43

995.81 Adult physical abuse `CC` `A`
Battered:
person syndrome NEC
man
spouse
woman
Use additional code to identify:
any association injury
nature of abuse (E960-E968)
perpetrator (E967.0-E967.9)
CC Excl: 995.50-995.59, 995.80-995.85
AHA: 4Q, '96, 42, 43

995.82 Adult emotional/psychological abuse `A`
Use additional E code to identify perpetrator
(E967.0-E967.9)

995.83 Adult sexual abuse `CC` `A`
Use additional code(s) to identify:
any associated injury
perpetrator (E967.0-E967.9)
CC Excl: See code: 995.81

995.84 Adult neglect (nutritional) `CC` `A`
Use additional code(s) to identify:
intent of neglect (E904.0, E968.4)
perpetrator (E967.0-E967.9)
CC Excl: See code: 995.81

995.85 Other adult abuse and neglect `CC` `A`
Multiple forms of abuse and neglect
Use additional code(s) to identify
any associated injury
intent of neglect (E904.0, E968.4)
nature of abuse (E960-E968)
perpetrator (E967.0-E967.9)
CC Excl: See code: 995.81

995.86 Malignant hyperthermia `CC`
Malignant hyperpyrexia due to anesthesia
CC Excl: 958.4, 995.4, 995.86, 997.91-998.13, 998.81,
998.83-998.9
AHA: 4Q, '98, 51

995.89 Other
Hypothermia due to anesthesia
AHA: 2Q, '04, 18; 3Q, '03, 12

✓5ᵗʰ **995.9 Systemic inflammatory response syndrome (SIRS)**
DEF: Clinical response to infection or trauma that can trigger
an acute inflammatory reaction and progresses to
coagulation, impaired fibrinolysis, and organ failure;
manifested by two or more of the following symptoms: fever,
tachycardia, tachypnea, leukocytosis or leukopenia.
AHA: 4Q, '06, 113-116; 2Q, '04, 16; 4Q, '02, 71

TIP: Coding these conditions requires a minimum of two
codes: the underlying cause (e.g., Infection or trauma) is
sequenced first, followed by a code from subcategory 995.9.

[handwritten: Systemic response to infection, trauma, burns, or other insult (such as a cancer)]

[handwritten: Code can never be assigned as a principal diagnosis]

**995.90 Systemic inflammatory response
syndrome, unspecified** `CC`
SIRS NOS
CC Excl: 003.1, 020.2, 036.2, 038.0-038.9,
040.82-041.9, 054.5, 139.8, 995.90-995.94,
V09.0-V09.91

995.91 Sepsis `MCC`
Systemic inflammatory response syndrome due
to infectious process without acute organ
dysfunction
Code first underlying infection

> **EXCLUDES** sepsis with acute organ dysfunction
> (995.92)
> sepsis with multiple organ
> dysfunction (995.92)
> severe sepsis (995.92)

CC Excl: See code 995.90
AHA: ►4Q, '08, 72;◄ 4Q, '07, 86; 4Q, '06, 113-116;
2Q, '04, 16; 4Q, '03, 79

Continuum of Illness Due to Infection

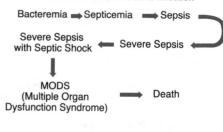

`N` Newborn Age: 0   `P` Pediatric Age: 0-17   `M` Maternity Age: 12-55   `A` Adult Age: 15-124   `MCC` Major CC Condition   `CC` CC Condition   `HIV` HIV Related Dx

356 – Volume 1 • February 2009   **2010 ICD-9-CM**

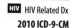

995.92 Severe sepsis   `MCC`

Sepsis with acute organ dysfunction
Sepsis with multiple organ dysfunction (MOD)
Systemic inflammatory response syndrome due to infectious process with acute organ dysfunction

Code first underlying infection

Use additional code to specify acute organ dysfunction, such as:
acute ►kidney◄ failure (584.5-584.9)
acute respiratory failure (518.81)
critical illness myopathy (359.81)
critical illness polyneuropathy (357.82)
disseminated intravascular coagulopathy [DIC] (286.6)
encephalopathy (348.31)
hepatic failure (570)
septic shock (785.52)

CC Excl: See code 995.90

AHA: 4Q, '08, 99; 4Q, '07, 97; 4Q, '06, 113-116; 2Q, '05, 18-19; 1Q, '05, 7; 1Q, '05, 7; 2Q, '04, 16; 4Q, '03, 73, 79

R65.21 Severe sepsis with septic shock   `I-10`

995.93 Systemic inflammatory response syndrome due to noninfectious process without acute organ dysfunction   `CC`

Code first underlying conditions, such as:
acute pancreatitis (577.0)
trauma

> **EXCLUDES**   systemic inflammatory response syndrome due to noninfectious process with acute organ dysfunction (995.94)

CC Excl: See code 995.90

AHA: 4Q, '06, 113-116

995.94 Systemic inflammatory response syndrome due to noninfectious process with acute organ dysfunction   `MCC`

Code first underlying conditions, such as:
acute pancreatitis (577.0)
trauma

Use additional code to specify acute organ dysfunction, such as:
acute ►kidney◄ failure (584.5-584.9)
acute respiratory failure (518.81)
critical illness myopathy (359.81)
critical illness polyneuropathy (357.82)
disseminated intravascular coagulopathy [DIC] syndrome (286.6)
encephalopathy (348.31)
hepatic failure (570)

> **EXCLUDES**   severe sepsis (995.92)

CC Excl: See code 995.90

AHA: 4Q, '06, 113-116; 4Q, '03, 79

COMPLICATIONS OF SURGICAL AND MEDICAL CARE, NOT ELSEWHERE CLASSIFIED (996-999)

> **EXCLUDES**   adverse effects of medicinal agents (001.0-799.9, 995.0-995.8)
> burns from local applications and irradiation (940.0-949.5)
> complications of:
>   conditions for which the procedure was performed
>   surgical procedures during abortion, labor, and delivery (630-676.9)
> poisoning and toxic effects of drugs and chemicals (960.0-989.9)
> postoperative conditions in which no complications are present, such as:
>   artificial opening status (V44.0-V44.9)
>   closure of external stoma (V55.0-V55.9)
>   fitting of prosthetic device (V52.0-V52.9)
> specified complications classified elsewhere
>   anesthetic shock (995.4)
>   electrolyte imbalance (276.0-276.9)
>   postlaminectomy syndrome (722.80-722.83)
>   postmastectomy lymphedema syndrome (457.0)
>   postoperative psychosis (293.0-293.9)
>   any other condition classified elsewhere in the Alphabetic Index when described as due to a procedure

√4ᵗʰ 996 Complications peculiar to certain specified procedures

> **INCLUDES**   complications, not elsewhere classified, in the use of artificial substitutes [e.g., Dacron, metal, Silastic, Teflon] or natural sources [e.g., bone] involving:
>   anastomosis (internal)
>   graft (bypass) (patch)
>   implant
>   internal device:
>   catheter
>   electronic
>   fixation
>   prosthetic
>   reimplant
>   transplant

> **EXCLUDES**   accidental puncture or laceration during procedure (998.2)
> capsular contracture of breast implant (611.83)
> complications of internal anastomosis of:
>   gastrointestinal tract (997.4)
>   urinary tract (997.5)
> endosseous dental implant failures (525.71-525.79)
> intraoperative floppy iris syndrome [IFIS] (364.81)
> mechanical complication of respirator (V46.14)
> other specified complications classified elsewhere, such as:
>   hemolytic anemia (283.1)
>   functional cardiac disturbances (429.4)
>   serum hepatitis (070.2-070.3)

AHA: 1Q, '94, 3

√5ᵗʰ 996.0 Mechanical complication of cardiac device, implant, and graft

Breakdown (mechanical)
Displacement
Leakage
Obstruction, mechanical
Perforation
Protrusion

AHA: 2Q, '08, 9; 2Q, '93, 9

TIP: If the documentation indicates that the cardiac device (e.g., pacemaker, heart valve prosthesis) has reached its normally occurring end of life, do not assign a complication code; see instead subcategory V53.3.

996.00 Unspecified device, implant, and graft   `CC`

CC Excl: 996.00, 996.04, 996.61-996.62, 996.70-996.74, 997.91-997.99, 998.81, 998.83-998.9

996.01 Due to cardiac pacemaker (electrode)   `CC`

CC Excl: 996.01, 997.91-997.99, 998.81, 998.83-998.9

AHA: 2Q, '06, 15; 2Q, '99, 11

T82.120A Displacement cardiac electrode initial encounter   `I-10`

√4ᵗʰ √5ᵗʰ Additional Digit Required   Unacceptable PDx   Manifestation Code   Hospital Acquired Condition   ►◄ Revised Text   ● New Code   ▲ Revised Code Title

2010 ICD-9-CM   **October 2009 • Volume 1 – 357**

996.02   **Due to heart valve prosthesis**   `CC`
CC Excl: 996.02, 997.91-997.99, 998.81, 998.83-998.9

996.03   **Due to coronary bypass graft**   `CC`
> EXCLUDES   atherosclerosis of graft (414.02, 414.03)
> embolism [occlusion NOS] [thrombus] of graft (996.72)

CC Excl: 996.03, 997.91-997.99, 998.81, 998.83-998.9
AHA: 2Q, '95, 17; N-D, '86, 5

996.04   **Due to automatic implantable cardiac defibrillator**   `CC`
CC Excl: 996.04, 997.91-997.99, 998.81, 998.83-998.9
AHA: 2Q, '05, 3

996.09   **Other**   `CC`
CC Excl: 996.09, 997.91-997.99, 998.81, 998.83-998.9
AHA: 2Q, '93, 9

996.1   **Mechanical complication of other vascular device, implant, and graft**   `CC`
Mechanical complications involving:
aortic (bifurcation) graft (replacement)
arteriovenous:
    dialysis catheter
    fistula   } surgically created
    shunt
balloon (counterpulsation) device, intra-aortic
carotid artery bypass graft
femoral-popliteal bypass graft
umbrella device, vena cava
> EXCLUDES   atherosclerosis of biological graft (440.30-440.32)
> embolism [occlusion NOS] [thrombus] of (biological) (synthetic) graft (996.74)
> peritoneal dialysis catheter (996.56)

CC Excl: 996.1, 997.91-997.99, 998.81, 998.83-998.9
AHA: 1Q, '06, 10; 2Q, '05, 8; 1Q, '02, 13; 1Q, '95, 3
TIP: Assign for a nonmaturing AV fistula and also for postprocedural reduction in transjugular intrahepatic portosystemic shunt flow in a patient with a TIPS catheter.
T82.330A Leakage aortic bifurcation graft initial enc   `I-10`

996.2   **Mechanical complication of nervous system device, implant, and graft**   `CC`
Mechanical complications involving:
dorsal column stimulator
electrodes implanted in brain [brain "pacemaker"]
peripheral nerve graft
ventricular (communicating) shunt
CC Excl: 996.2, 996.63, 996.75, 997.91-997.99, 998.81, 998.83-998.9
AHA: 2Q, '99, 4; S-O, '87, 10

✓5ᵗʰ   **996.3**   **Mechanical complication of genitourinary device, implant, and graft**
AHA: 3Q, '01, 13; S-O, '85, 3

996.30   **Unspecified device, implant, and graft**   `CC`
CC Excl: 996.30, 996.64-996.65, 996.76, 997.91-997.99, 998.81, 998.83-998.9

996.31   **Due to urethral [indwelling] catheter**

996.32   **Due to intrauterine contraceptive device**   ♀

996.39   **Other**   `CC`
Cystostomy catheter
Prosthetic reconstruction of vas deferens
Repair (graft) of ureter without mention of resection
> EXCLUDES   complications due to:
> external stoma of urinary tract (997.5)
> internal anastomosis of urinary tract (997.5)

CC Excl: 996.39, 996.64-996.65, 996.76, 997.91-997.99, 998.81, 998.83-998.9

✓5ᵗʰ   **996.4**   **Mechanical complication of internal orthopedic device, implant, and graft**
Mechanical complications involving:
external (fixation) device utilizing internal screw(s), pin(s) or other methods of fixation
grafts of bone, cartilage, muscle, or tendon
internal (fixation) device such as nail, plate, rod, etc.
Use additional code to identify prosthetic joint with mechanical complication (V43.60-V43.69)
> EXCLUDES   complications of external orthopedic device, such as:
> pressure ulcer due to cast (707.00-707.09)

AHA: 4Q, '05, 91; 2Q, '99, 10; 2Q, '98, 19; 2Q, '96, 11; 3Q, '95, 16; N-D, '85, 11
TIP: Since these codes may be used for any joint device complications, assign an additional code from subcategory V43.6 to specify the joint involved.

996.40   **Unspecified mechanical complication of internal orthopedic device, implant, and graft**   `CC`
CC Excl: 996.40-996.49, 996.66-996.67, 996.77-996.78, 997.91-997.99, 998.81, 998.83-998.9

996.41   **Mechanical loosening of prosthetic joint**   `CC`
Aseptic loosening
CC Excl: See code: 996.40
AHA: 4Q, '05, 112
T84.031A Mech loosening int lt hip prosth jnt initial enc   `I-10`

996.42   **Dislocation of prosthetic joint**   `CC`
Instability of prosthetic joint
Subluxation of prosthetic joint
CC Excl: See code 996.40
T84.020D Displacment internal right hip prosth subsqt enc   `I-10`

996.43   **Broken prosthetic joint implant**   `CC`
Breakage (fracture) of prosthetic joint
CC Excl: See code 996.40

996.44   **Peri-prosthetic fracture around prosthetic joint**   `CC`
CC Excl: See code 996.40
AHA: 4Q, '05, 93

996.45   **Peri-prosthetic osteolysis**   `CC`
Use additional code to identify major osseous defect, if applicable (731.3)
CC Excl: See code 996.40
AHA: 4Q, '06, 103

996.46   **Articular bearing surface wear of prosthetic joint**   `CC`
CC Excl: See code 996.40

996.47   **Other mechanical complication of prosthetic joint implant**   `CC`
Mechanical complication of prosthetic joint NOS
▶Prosthetic joint implant failure NOS◀
CC Excl: See code 996.40

996.49   **Other mechanical complication of other internal orthopedic device, implant, and graft**   `CC`
Breakage of internal fixation device in bone
Dislocation of internal fixation device in bone
> EXCLUDES   mechanical complication of prosthetic joint implant (996.41-996.47)

CC Excl: See code 996.40

N Newborn Age: 0   P Pediatric Age: 0-17   M Maternity Age: 12-55   A Adult Age: 15-124   MCC Major CC Condition   CC CC Condition   HIV HIV Related Dx

358 – Volume 1 · October 2009   2010 ICD-9-CM

√5ᵗʰ 996.5 Mechanical complication of other specified prosthetic device, implant, and graft
 Mechanical complications involving:
  prosthetic implant in:
   bile duct
   breast
   chin
   orbit of eye
  nonabsorbable surgical material NOS
  other graft, implant, and internal device, not
   elsewhere classified
 AHA: 1Q, '98, 11

996.51 Due to corneal graft `CC`
 CC Excl: 996.51, 997.91-997.99

996.52 Due to graft of other tissue, not elsewhere `CC` **classified**
 Skin graft failure or rejection
  EXCLUDES *failure of artificial skin graft (996.55)*
   failure of decellularized allodermis (996.55)
   sloughing of temporary skin allografts or xenografts (pigskin) — omit code
 CC Excl: 996.52, 996.55, 997.91-997.99
 AHA: 1Q, '96, 10

996.53 Due to ocular lens prosthesis `CC`
  EXCLUDES *contact lenses–code to condition*
 CC Excl: 996.53, 997.91-997.99
 AHA: 1Q, '00, 9

996.54 Due to breast prosthesis `CC`
 Breast capsule (prosthesis)
 Mammary implant
 CC Excl: 996.54, 997.91-997.99
 AHA: 2Q, '98, 14; 3Q, '92, 4
 TIP: If documentation indicates capsular contracture of breast implant, see instead code 611.83.

996.55 Due to artificial skin graft and `CC` **decellularized allodermis**
 Dislodgement
 Displacement
 Failure
 Non-adherence
 Poor incorporation
 Shearing
 CC Excl: 996.52, 996.55-996.60, 996.68-996.70, 996.79, 997.91-997.99
 AHA: 4Q, '98, 52

996.56 Due to peritoneal dialysis catheter `CC`
  EXCLUDES *mechanical complication of arteriovenous dialysis catheter (996.1)*
 CC Excl: 996.56-996.60, 996.68-996.70, 996.79, 997.91-997.99
 AHA: 4Q, '98, 54

996.57 Due to insulin pump `CC`
 CC Excl: 996.00-996.30, 996.39-996.79, 997.91-997.99, 998.81, 998.83-998.9
 AHA: 4Q, '03, 81-82

996.59 Due to other implant and internal `CC` **device, not elsewhere classified**
 Nonabsorbable surgical material NOS
 Prosthetic implant in:
  bile duct
  chin
  orbit of eye
 CC Excl: See code: 996.56
 AHA: 2Q, '99, 13; 3Q, '94, 7
 TIP: Assign for clogged biliary stent and also for nonfunctioning pressure equalization (PE) tubes.

√5ᵗʰ 996.6 Infection and inflammatory reaction due to internal prosthetic device, implant, and graft
 Infection (causing ⎱ due to (presence of) any device,
  obstruction) ⎰ implant, and graft
 Inflammation   classifiable to 996.0-996.5
 Use additional code to identify specified infections
 AHA: 2Q, '89, 16; J-F, '87, 14

996.60 Due to unspecified device, implant, `CC` **and graft**
 CC Excl: See code: 996.57

996.61 Due to cardiac device, implant, and graft `CC`
 Cardiac pacemaker or defibrillator:
  electrode(s), lead(s)
  pulse generator
  subcutaneous pocket
 Coronary artery bypass graft
 Heart valve prosthesis
 CC Excl: 996.00-996.1, 996.52, 996.55-996.62, 996.68-996.74, 996.79, 997.91-997.99, 998.81, 998.83-998.9

996.62 Due to other vascular device, implant, `CC` **and graft**
 Arterial graft
 Arteriovenous fistula or shunt
 Infusion pump
 Vascular catheter (arterial) (dialysis) (peripheral venous)
  EXCLUDES *infection due to:*
   central venous catheter (999.31)
   Hickman catheter (999.31)
   peripherally inserted central catheter [PICC] (999.31)
   portacath (port-a-cath) (999.31)
   triple lumen catheter (999.31)
   umbilical venous catheter (999.31)
 CC Excl: See code 996.61
 AHA: 4Q, '07, 86; 2Q, '04, 16; 1Q, '04, 5; 4Q, '03, 107, 111; 2Q, '03, 7; 2Q, '94, 13
 T82.7xxA Inf & inflam react oth card vasc dev `I-10` gft initial enc

996.63 Due to nervous system device, `CC` **implant, and graft**
 Electrodes implanted in brain
 Peripheral nerve graft
 Spinal canal catheter
 Ventricular (communicating) shunt (catheter)
 CC Excl: 996.2, 996.52, 996.55-996.60, 996.63, 996.68-996.70, 996.75, 996.79, 997.91-997.99, 998.81, 998.83-998.9

996.64 Due to indwelling urinary catheter `CC`
 Use additional code to identify specified infections, such as:
  cystitis (595.0-595.9)
  sepsis (038.0-038.9)
 CC Excl: 599.0, 996.30, 996.39, 996.56-996.60, 996.64-996.65, 996.68-996.70, 996.76, 996.79, 997.91-997.99, 998.81, 998.83-998.9
 AHA: 3Q, '93, 6
 T83.51xD Inf & inflam react indwll urinary cath `I-10` subsq enc

996.65 Due to other genitourinary device, `CC` **implant, and graft**
 Intrauterine contraceptive device
 CC Excl: 996.30, 996.39, 996.52, 996.55-996.60, 996.64-996.65, 996.68-996.70, 996.76, 996.79, 997.91-997.99, 998.81, 998.83-998.9
 AHA: 1Q, '00, 15

Injury and Poisoning

996.66–996.81

996.66 Due to internal joint prosthesis `CC`
> Use additional code to identify infected
> prosthetic joint (V43.60-V43.69)
>
> **CC Excl:** 996.40-996.49, 996.52, 996.55-996.60,
> 996.66-996.70, 996.77-996.79, 997.91-997.99,
> 998.81, 998.83-998.9
>
> **AHA:** 2Q, '08, 3-5; 2Q, '07, 7; 4Q, '05, 91, 113;
> 2Q, '91, 18
>
> **TIP:** Do not assign for the second admission of a
> staged procedure whereby the infected prosthesis
> has been previously removed and the patient now
> returns for placement of a new prosthesis; see
> instead codes from category 736.
>
> **T84.51xA** Inf & inflam reaction int rt hip pros `I-10`
> initial enc

996.67 Due to other internal orthopedic device, `CC`
implant, and graft
> Bone growth stimulator (electrode)
> Internal fixation device (pin) (rod) (screw)
> **CC Excl:** See code: 996.66

996.68 Due to peritoneal dialysis catheter `CC`
> Exit-site infection or inflammation
> **CC Excl:** 996.56-996.60, 996.68-996.70, 996.79,
> 997.91-997.99
>
> **AHA:** 4Q, '98, 54

996.69 Due to other internal prosthetic device, `CC`
implant, and graft
> Breast prosthesis
> Ocular lens prosthesis
> Prosthetic orbital implant
> **CC Excl:** 996.00-996.30, 996.39-996.79,
> 997.91-997.99, 998.81, 998.83-998.9
>
> **AHA:** 2Q, '08, 11; 4Q, '03, 108; 4Q, '98, 52

√5th **996.7 Other complications of internal (biological) (synthetic)**
prosthetic device, implant, and graft

> Complication NOS
> Occlusion NOS
> Embolism
> Fibrosis   due to (presence of) any device,
> Hemorrhage   implant, and graft
> Pain   classifiable to 996.0-996.5
> Stenosis
> Thrombus
>
> Use additional code to identify complication, such as:
> pain due to presence of device, implant or graft
> (338.18-338.19, 338.28-338.29)
> ▶venous embolism and thrombosis (453.2-453.9)◀
> **EXCLUDES** disruption (dehiscence) of internal suture
> material (998.31)
> transplant rejection (996.8)
> **AHA:** 2Q, '07, 12; 4Q, '05, 94; 1Q, '89, 9; N-D, '86, 5

996.70 Due to unspecified device, implant, and graft

996.71 Due to heart valve prosthesis `CC`
> **CC Excl:** 996.00, 996.02, 996.09-996.1, 996.52,
> 996.55-996.62, 996.68-996.74, 996.79,
> 997.91-997.99, 998.81, 998.83-998.9

996.72 Due to other cardiac device, implant, `CC`
and graft
> Cardiac pacemaker or defibrillator:
> electrode(s), lead(s)
> subcutaneous pocket
> Coronary artery bypass (graft)
> **EXCLUDES** occlusion due to atherosclerosis
> (414.02-414.06)
> **CC Excl:** 996.00-996.02, 996.04-996.1, 996.52,
> 996.55-996.62, 996.68-996.74, 996.79,
> 997.91-997.99, 998.81, 998.83-998.9
>
> **AHA:** 3Q, '08, 10; 3Q, '06, 8, 25; 3Q, '01, 20
>
> **TIP:** Assign for in-stent stenosis of previously placed
> coronary artery stent.
>
> **T82.847A** Pain cardiac prosth devc impl graft `I-10`
> initial enc

996.73 Due to renal dialysis device, implant, `CC`
and graft
> **CC Excl:** 996.1, 996.52, 996.55-996.60, 996.68-996.70,
> 996.73, 996.79, 997.91-997.99, 998.81, 998.83-998.9
>
> **AHA:** 2Q, '91, 18
>
> **T82.858A** Stenosis vasc prosth devc impl graft `I-10`
> initial enc

996.74 Due to other vascular device, implant, `CC`
and graft
> **EXCLUDES** occlusion of biological graft due to
> atherosclerosis
> (440.30-440.32)
> **CC Excl:** 996.00-996.1, 996.52, 996.55-996.62, 996.68-
> 996.74, 996.79, 997.91-997.99, 998.81, 998.83-998.9
>
> **AHA:** 1Q, '03, 16, 17

996.75 Due to nervous system device, implant, `CC`
and graft
> **CC Excl:** 996.2, 996.52, 996.55-996.60, 996.63,
> 996.68-996.70, 996.75, 996.79, 997.91-997.99,
> 998.81, 998.83-998.9

996.76 Due to genitourinary device, implant, `CC`
and graft
> **CC Excl:** 996.30, 996.39, 996.52, 996.55-996.60,
> 996.64-996.65, 996.68-996.70, 996.76, 996.79,
> 997.91-997.99, 998.81, 998.83-998.9
>
> **AHA:** ▶1Q, '09, 15;◀ 1Q, '00, 15
>
> **T83.83xA** Hemorrhage GU prosth devc impl `I-10`
> graft initial enc

996.77 Due to internal joint prosthesis `CC`
> Use additional code to identify prosthetic joint
> (V43.60-V43.69)
> **CC Excl:** 996.40-996.49, 996.52, 996.55-996.60,
> 996.66-996.70, 996.77-996.79, 997.91-997.99,
> 998.81, 998.83-998.9
>
> **AHA:** 4Q, '05, 91
>
> **T84.84xA** Pain int ortho prosth devc impl gft `I-10`
> initial enc

996.78 Due to other internal orthopedic device, `CC`
implant, and graft
> **CC Excl:** 996.40-996.49, 996.52, 996.55-996.60,
> 996.66-996.70, 996.77-996.79, 997.91-997.99,
> 998.81, 998.83-998.9
>
> **AHA:** 2Q, '03, 14

996.79 Due to other internal prosthetic device, `CC`
implant, and graft
> **CC Excl:** 996.00-996.30, 996.39-996.79,
> 997.91-997.99, 998.81, 998.83-998.9
>
> **AHA:** 2Q, '04, 7; 1Q'01, 8; 3Q, '95, 14; 3Q, '92, 4

√5th **996.8 Complications of transplanted organ**
> Transplant failure or rejection
> Use additional code to identify nature of complication,
> such as:
> cytomegalovirus (CMV) infection (078.5)
> graft-versus-host disease (279.50-279.53)
> malignancy associated with organ transplant (199.2)
> post-transplant lymphoproliferative disorder (PTLD)
> (238.77)
>
> **AHA:** 4Q, '08, 82-83; 3Q, '01, 12; 3Q, '93, 3, 4; 2Q, '93, 11; 1Q, '93,
> 24
>
> **TIP:** Assign only if the complication affects the function of the
> transplanted organ. Assign also a code for the specific compli-
> cation.

996.80 Transplanted organ, unspecified `CC`
> **CC Excl:** 238.77, 996.80, 996.87, 997.91-997.99

996.81 Kidney `CC`
> **CC Excl:** 996.81, 997.91-997.99
>
> **AHA:** 4Q, '08, 83; 3Q, '03, 16; 3Q, '98, 6, 7; 3Q, '94; 8;
> 2Q, '94, 9; 1Q, '93, 24
>
> **TIP:** Do not assign for chronic kidney disease (CKD)
> status following kidney transplant. The provider
> must indicate transplant failure, rejection, or other
> complication to support assignment of this code.
>
> **T86.11** Kidney transplant rejection `I-10`

`N` Newborn Age: 0   `P` Pediatric Age: 0-17   `M` Maternity Age: 12-55   `A` Adult Age: 15-124   `MCC` Major CC Condition   `CC` CC Condition   `HIV` HIV Related Dx

360 – Volume 1 · October 2009   2010 ICD-9-CM

996.82 Liver `CC`
CC Excl: 996.82, 997.91-997.99
AHA: 4Q, '08, 82, 99; 3Q, '03, 17; 3Q, '98, 3, 4

996.83 Heart `CC`
CC Excl: 996.83, 997.91-997.99
AHA: 3Q, '03, 16; 4Q, '02, 53; 3Q, '98, 5

996.84 Lung `CC`
CC Excl: 996.84, 997.91-997.99
AHA: 2Q, '03, 12; 3Q, '98, 5

996.85 Bone marrow `CC`
CC Excl: 279.50-279.53, 996.85, 997.91-997.99
AHA: 4Q, '08, 91x; 4Q, '90, 4

996.86 Pancreas `CC`
CC Excl: 996.86, 997.91-997.99

996.87 Intestine `CC`
CC Excl: 238.77, 996.80, 996.87, 997.91-997.99

996.89 Other specified transplanted organ `CC`
CC Excl: 996.89, 997.91-997.99
AHA: 3Q, '94, 5

√5ᵗʰ **996.9 Complications of reattached extremity or body part**

996.90 Unspecified extremity `CC`
CC Excl: 996.90, 997.91-997.99, 998.81, 998.83-998.9

996.91 Forearm `CC`
CC Excl: 996.91, 997.91-997.99, 998.81, 998.83-998.9

996.92 Hand `CC`
CC Excl: 996.92, 997.91-997.99, 998.81, 998.83-998.9

996.93 Finger(s) `CC`
CC Excl: 996.93, 997.91-997.99, 998.81, 998.83-998.9

996.94 Upper extremity, other and unspecified `CC`
CC Excl: 996.94, 997.91-997.99, 998.81, 998.83-998.9

996.95 Foot and toe(s) `CC`
CC Excl: 996.95, 997.91-997.99, 998.81, 998.83-998.9

996.96 Lower extremity, other and unspecified `CC`
CC Excl: 996.96, 997.91-997.99, 998.81, 998.83-998.9

996.99 Other specified body part `CC`
CC Excl: 996.99, 997.91-997.99, 998.81, 998.83-998.9

√4ᵗʰ **997 Complications affecting specified body systems, not elsewhere classified**
Use additional code to identify complications
EXCLUDES　the listed conditions when specified as:
　causing shock (998.0)
　complications of:
　　anesthesia:
　　　adverse effect (001.0-799.9, 995.0-995.8)
　　　in labor or delivery (668.0-668.9)
　　　poisoning (968.0-969.9)
　　implanted device or graft (996.0-996.9)
　　obstetrical procedures (669.0-669.4)
　　reattached extremity (996.90-996.96)
　　transplanted organ (996.80-996.89)
AHA: 1Q, '94, 4; 1Q, '93, 26

√5ᵗʰ **997.0 Nervous system complications**

997.00 Nervous system complication, unspecified

997.01 Central nervous system complication `CC`
Anoxic brain damage
Cerebral hypoxia
EXCLUDES　cerebrovascular hemorrhage or
　　　　　infarction (997.02)
CC Excl: 997.00-997.09, 997.91-997.99, 998.81, 998.83-998.9
AHA: 1Q, '07, 22; 1Q, '06, 15
TIP: Assign for hyperperfusion syndrome, a compli-
cation of carotid endarterectomy.

997.02 Iatrogenic cerebrovascular infarction or hemorrhage `CC`
Postoperative stroke
CC Excl: See code: 997.01
AHA: 3Q, '06, 6; 2Q, '04, 8; 4Q, '95, 57
TIP: Assign an additional code to specify the type of postoperative stroke involved.
I97.810 Intraop cerebrvascular infarct during card surg `I-10`

997.09 Other nervous system complications `CC`
CC Excl: See code: 997.01
G97.0 Cerebrospinal fluid leak from spinal puncture `I-10`

997.1 Cardiac complications `CC`
Cardiac:
　arrest
　insufficiency ⎫
Cardiorespiratory failure ⎬ during or resulting from a procedure
Heart failure ⎭
EXCLUDES　the listed conditions as long-term effects of
　　　　　cardiac surgery or due to the presence of
　　　　　cardiac prosthetic device (429.4)
CC Excl: 997.1, 997.91-997.99, 998.81, 998.83-998.9
AHA: 4Q, '08, 179; 2Q, '02, 12
I97.711 Intraoperative cardiac arrest during oth surgery `I-10`

997.2 Peripheral vascular complications `CC`
Phlebitis or thrombophlebitis during or resulting from a procedure
EXCLUDES　the listed conditions due to:
　　　　　implant or catheter device (996.62)
　　　　　infusion, perfusion, or transfusion (999.2)
　　　　　complications affecting blood vessels
　　　　　(997.71-997.79)
CC Excl: 997.2, 997.79-997.99, 998.81, 998.83-998.9
AHA: 1Q, '03, 6; 3Q, '02, 24-26
T81.72xA Complication of vein following a procedure NEC intl enc `I-10`

√5ᵗʰ **997.3 Respiratory complications**
EXCLUDES　iatrogenic [postoperative] pneumothorax
　　　　　(512.1)
　　　　　iatrogenic pulmonary embolism (415.11)
　　　　　Mendelson's syndrome in labor and delivery
　　　　　(668.0)
　　　　　specified complications classified elsewhere,
　　　　　such as:
　　　　　　adult respiratory distress syndrome (518.5)
　　　　　　pulmonary edema, postoperative (518.4)
　　　　　　respiratory insufficiency, acute,
　　　　　　　postoperative (518.5)
　　　　　　shock lung (518.5)
　　　　　　tracheostomy complications (519.00-519.09)
　　　　　　transfusion related acute lung injury [TRALI]
　　　　　　(518.7)
DEF: Mendelson's syndrome: acid pneumonitis due to aspiration of gastric acids, may occur after anesthesia or sedation.
AHA: 1Q, '97, 10; 2Q, '93, 3; 2Q, '93, 9; 4Q, '90, 25

997.31 Ventilator associated pneumonia `CC`
▶Ventilator associated pneumonitis◀
Use additional code to identify organism
CC Excl: 518.7, 997.31-997.39, 997.91-997.99, 998.81, 998.83-998.9
AHA: 4Q, '08, 148-149
TIP: Do not assign unless the provider has docu-
mented the relationship between the pneumonia
and ventilation status.

997.39 Other respiratory complications `CC`
Mendelson's syndrome resulting from a procedure
Pneumonia (aspiration) resulting from a procedure
CC Excl: See code 997.31
J95.4 Chem pneumonitis d/t anesthesia [Mendelson's syndrm] `I-10`

Injury and Poisoning

997.4–998.11

997.4 Digestive system complications `CC`
Complications of:
  intestinal (internal) anastomosis and bypass, not
   elsewhere classified, except that involving
   urinary tract
  Hepatic failure ⎫
  Hepatorenal syndrome ⎬ specified as due to a
  Intestinal obstruction NOS ⎭ procedure

  EXCLUDES *gastrostomy complications (536.40-536.49)*
   specified gastrointestinal complications
    classified elsewhere, such as:
    blind loop syndrome (579.2)
    colostomy and enterostomy complications
     (569.60-569.69)
    ▶*complications of intestinal pouch*
     (569.71-569.79)◀
    gastrojejunal ulcer (534.0-534.9)
    infection of esophagostomy (530.86)
    infection of external stoma (569.61)
    mechanical complication of
     esophagostomy (530.87)
    pelvic peritoneal adhesions, female (614.6)
    peritoneal adhesions (568.0)
    peritoneal adhesions with obstruction
     (560.81)
    postcholecystectomy syndrome (576.0)
    postgastric surgery syndromes (564.2)
    ▶*pouchitis (569.71)*◀
    vomiting following gastrointestinal surgery
     (564.3)

  CC Excl: 530.86-530.87, 536.40-536.49, 569.71-569.79, 997.4,
  997.71, 997.91-997.99, 998.81, 998.83-998.9
  AHA: 2Q, '01, 4-6; 3Q, '99, 4; 2Q, '99, 14; 3Q, '97, 7; 1Q, '97, 11;
  2Q, '95, 7; 1Q, '93, 26; 3Q, '92, 15; 2Q, '89, 15; 1Q, '88, 14
  K91.3 Postprocedural intestinal obstruction `I-10`

997.5 Urinary complications
Complications of:
  external stoma of urinary tract
  internal anastomosis and bypass of urinary tract,
   including that involving intestinal tract
  Oliguria or anuria ⎫
  Renal ▶(kidney):◀ ⎬
   failure (acute) ⎬ specified as due to
   insufficiency (acute) ⎬ procedure
  Tubular necrosis (acute) ⎭

  EXCLUDES *specified complications classified elsewhere,*
   such as:
   postoperative stricture of:
    ureter (593.3)
    urethra (598.2)

  AHA: 3Q, '03, 13; 3Q, '96, 10, 15; 4Q, '95, 73; 1Q, '92, 13; 2Q, '89,
  16; M-A, '87, 10; S-O, '85, 3
  TIP: If a urinary tract infection is specified as a postoperative
  complication, assign both 997.5 and 599.0.
  N99.0 Postprocedural (acute) (chronic) renal failure `I-10`

√5ᵗʰ 997.6 Amputation stump complication
  EXCLUDES *admission for treatment for a current*
   traumatic amputation – code to
   complicated traumatic amputation
   phantom limb (syndrome) (353.6)
  AHA: 4Q, '95, 82

997.60 Unspecified complication

997.61 Neuroma of amputation stump
  DEF: Hyperplasia generated nerve cell mass
  following amputation.

997.62 Infection (chronic) `CC`
  Use additional code to identify the organism
  CC Excl: 997.60, 997.62-997.69, 997.91-997.99,
  998.81, 998.83-998.9
  AHA: 1Q, '05, 15 4Q, '96, 46
  TIP: If cellulitis is specified as a manifestation of the
  infection, assign an additional code from category
  681 or 682.
  T87.43 Infection amputation stump right `I-10`
  lower extremity

997.69 Other
  AHA: 1Q, '05, 15

√5ᵗʰ 997.7 Vascular complications of other vessels
  EXCLUDES *peripheral vascular complications (997.2)*

997.71 Vascular complications of `CC`
mesenteric artery
  CC Excl: 997.2, 997.71-997.99, 998.81, 998.83-998.9
  AHA: 4Q, '01, 53
  TIP: For postoperative mesenteric artery embolism,
  assign also code 557.0 Acute vascular insufficiency
  of intestine.

997.72 Vascular complications of renal artery `CC`
  CC Excl: See code 997.71

997.79 Vascular complications of other vessels `CC`
  CC Excl: See code 997.71

**√5ᵗʰ 997.9 Complications affecting other specified body systems,
not elsewhere classified**
  EXCLUDES *specified complications classified elsewhere,*
   such as:
   broad ligament laceration syndrome
    (620.6)
   postartificial menopause syndrome (627.4)
   postoperative stricture of vagina (623.2)

Such as — true postoperative hypertension

997.91 Hypertension
  EXCLUDES *essential hypertension (401.0-401.9)*
  AHA: 4Q, '95, 57

997.99 Other `CC`
  Vitreous touch syndrome
  DEF: Vitreous touch syndrome: vitreous protruding
  through pupil and attaches to corneal epithelium;
  causes aqueous fluid in vitreous body; marked by
  corneal edema, loss of lucidity; complication of
  cataract surgery.
  CC Excl: 997.91-997.99, 998.81, 998.83-998.9
  AHA: 2Q, '94, 12; 1Q, '94, 17

**√4ᵗʰ 998 Other complications of procedures, not elsewhere
classified**
  AHA: 1Q, '94, 4

998.0 Postoperative shock `CC`
  Collapse NOS ⎫
  Shock (endotoxic) ⎬ during or resulting from a
   (hypovolemic septic) ⎭ surgical procedure
  EXCLUDES *shock:*
   anaphylactic due to serum (999.4)
   anesthetic (995.4)
   electric (994.8)
   following abortion (639.5)
   obstetric (669.1)
   traumatic (958.4)
  CC Excl: 958.4, 995.4, 997.91-998.13, 998.81,
  998.83-998.9

**√5ᵗʰ 998.1 Hemorrhage or hematoma or seroma complicating a
procedure**
  EXCLUDES *hemorrhage, hematoma, or seroma:*
   complicating cesarean section or puerperal
    perineal wound (674.3)
   due to implanted device or graft
    (996.70-996.79)

998.11 Hemorrhage complicating a procedure `CC`
  CC Excl: 456.0, 456.20, 530.81-530.83, 530.89,
  531.00-531.01, 531.20-531.21, 531.40-531.41,
  531.60-531.61, 532.00-532.01, 532.20-532.21,
  532.40-532.41, 532.60-532.61, 533.00-533.01,
  533.20-533.21, 533.40-533.41, 533.60-533.61,
  534.00-534.01, 534.20-534.21, 534.40-534.41,
  534.60-534.61, 535.01, 535.11, 535.21, 535.31,
  535.41, 535.51, 535.61, 537.83, 562.02-562.03,
  562.12-562.13, 569.3, 569.85, 578.0-578.9, 772.4,
  997.91-998.13, 998.81, 998.89-998.9
  AHA: 3Q, '03, 13; 1Q, '03, 4; 4Q, '97, 52; 1Q, '97, 10
  I97.410 Intraop hemorrhage circ sys organ `I-10`
  comp card cath

N Newborn Age: 0   P Pediatric Age: 0-17   M Maternity Age: 12-55   A Adult Age: 15-124   `MCC` Major CC Condition   `CC` CC Condition   **HIV** HIV Related Dx

362 – Volume 1 • October 2009   **2010 ICD-9-CM**

998.12 Hematoma complicating a procedure `CC`
CC Excl: see code 998.11
AHA: 3Q, '06, 12; 1Q, '03, 6; 3Q, '02, 24, 26

998.13 Seroma complicating a procedure `CC`
CC Excl: See code 998.11
AHA: 4Q, '96, 46; 1Q, '93, 26; 2Q, '92, 15; S-O, '87, 8

998.2 Accidental puncture or laceration during a procedure `CC`
Accidental perforation by catheter or other instrument during a procedure on:
blood vessel
nerve
organ
EXCLUDES *iatrogenic [postoperative] pneumothorax (512.1)*
puncture or laceration caused by implanted device intentionally left in operation wound (996.0-996.5)
specified complications classified elsewhere, such as:
broad ligament laceration syndrome (620.6)
dural tear (349.31)
incidental durotomy (349.31)
trauma from instruments during delivery (664.0-665.9)
CC Excl: 997.91-997.99, 998.2, 998.81, 998.83-998.9
AHA: 2Q, '07, 9; 1Q, '06, 15; 3Q, '02, 24, 26; 3Q, '94, 6; 3Q, '90, 17; 3Q, '90, 18
I97.51 Accidentl punct lac circ sys organ dur circ proc `I-10`

√5ᵗʰ 998.3 Disruption of wound
Dehiscence } of operation wound
Rupture
Disruption of any suture materials or other closure method
EXCLUDES *disruption of:*
cesarean wound (674.1)
perineal wound, puerperal (674.2)
AHA: 4Q, '08,149-152; 4Q, '02, 73; 1Q, '93, 19

998.30 Disruption of wound, unspecified `CC`
Disruption of wound NOS
CC Excl: 997.91-997.99, 998.30-998.33, 998.81, 998.83-998.9

998.31 Disruption of internal operation (surgical) wound `CC`
Disruption or dehiscence of closure of:
fascia, superficial or muscular
internal organ
muscle or muscle flap
ribs or rib cage
skull or craniotomy
sternum or sternotomy
tendon or ligament
Deep disruption or dehiscence of operation wound NOS
EXCLUDES *complications of internal anastomosis of:*
gastrointestinal tract (997.4)
urinary tract (997.5)
CC Excl: See code 998.30

998.32 Disruption of external operation (surgical) wound `CC`
Disruption of operation wound NOS
Disruption or dehiscence of closure of:
cornea
mucosa
skin
subcutaneous tissue
Full-thickness skin disruption or dehiscence
Superficial disruption or dehiscence of operation wound
CC Excl: See code 998.30
AHA: 1Q, '06, 8; 1Q, '05, 11; 4Q, '03, 104, 106
T81.31xA Disruption ext operation wound NEC initial enc `I-10`

998.33 Disruption of traumatic injury wound repair `CC`
Disruption or dehiscence of closure of traumatic laceration (external) (internal)
CC Excl: See code 998.30
AHA: 4Q, '08, 151, 152

998.4 Foreign body accidentally left during a procedure `CC`
Adhesions } due to foreign body accidentally left in operative wound or body cavity during a procedure
Obstruction
Perforation
EXCLUDES *obstruction or perforation caused by implanted device intentionally left in body (996.0-996.5)*
CC Excl: 997.91-997.99, 998.4, 998.81, 998.83-998.9
AHA: ►1Q, '09,18◄ 1Q, '89, 9

√5ᵗʰ 998.5 Postoperative infection
EXCLUDES *bleb associated endophthalmitis (379.63)*
infection due to:
implanted device (996.60-996.69)
infusion, perfusion, or transfusion (999.31-999.39)
postoperative obstetrical wound infection (674.3)

998.51 Infected postoperative seroma `CC`
Use additional code to identify organism
CC Excl: 997.91-997.99, 998.51-998.59, 998.81, 998.89-998.9
AHA: 4Q, '96, 46

998.59 Other postoperative infection `CC`
Abscess:
intra-abdominal
stitch
subphrenic } postoperative
wound
Septicemia
Use additional code to identify infection
CC Excl: See code: 998.51
AHA: 2Q, '06, 23; 4Q, '04, 76; 4Q, '03, 104, 106-107; 3Q, '98, 3; 3Q, '95, 5; 2Q, '95, 7; 3Q, '94, 6; 1Q, '93, 19; J-F, '87, 14
TIP: Do not assign if the infection is related to an internal prosthetic device, implant, or graft; see instead subcategory 996.6.
T81.4xxA Infection following procedure initial encounter `I-10`

998.6 Persistent postoperative fistula `CC`
CC Excl: 997.91-997.99, 998.6, 998.81, 998.83-998.9
AHA: J-F, '87, 14
T81.83xD Persistent postprocedural fistula subsequent enc `I-10`

998.7 Acute reaction to foreign substance accidentally left during a procedure `CC`
Peritonitis:
aseptic
chemical
CC Excl: 997.91-997.99, 998.7-998.81, 998.83-998.9

✓5th **998.8 Other specified complications of procedures, not elsewhere classified**

AHA: 4Q, '94, 46; 1Q, '89, 9

998.81 Emphysema (subcutaneous) (surgical) resulting from a procedure

998.82 Cataract fragments in eye following cataract surgery

998.83 Non-healing surgical wound `CC`

CC Excl: 997.91-997.99, 998.81, 998.83-998.9

AHA: 4Q, '96, 47

998.89 Other specified complications

AHA: ▶2Q, '09, 11;◀ 3Q, '06, 9; 3Q, '05, 16; 3Q, '99, 13; 2Q, '98, 16

TIP: Assign for cases in which a procedure is performed on the wrong body site (e.g., right leg versus left leg), along with E876.5-E876.7.

T81.89 Other complications of procedures NEC `I-10`

998.9 Unspecified complication of procedure, not elsewhere classified

Postoperative complication NOS

EXCLUDES   *complication NOS of obstetrical, surgery or procedure (669.4)*

AHA: 4Q, '93, 37

✓4th **999 Complications of medical care, not elsewhere classified**

INCLUDES   complications, not elsewhere classified, of:
dialysis (hemodialysis) (peritoneal) (renal)
extracorporeal circulation
hyperalimentation therapy
immunization
infusion
inhalation therapy
injection
inoculation
perfusion
transfusion
vaccination
ventilation therapy

Use additional code, where applicable, to identify specific complication

EXCLUDES   *specified complications classified elsewhere such as:*
complications of implanted device (996.0-996.9)
contact dermatitis due to drugs (692.3)
dementia dialysis (294.8)
transient (293.9)
dialysis disequilibrium syndrome (276.0-276.9)
poisoning and toxic effects of drugs and chemicals (960.0-989.9)
postvaccinal encephalitis (323.51)
water and electrolyte imbalance (276.0-276.9)

999.0 Generalized vaccinia `CC`

EXCLUDES   *vaccinia not from vaccine (051.02)*

DEF: Skin eruption, self-limiting; follows vaccination; due to transient viremia with virus localized in skin.

CC Excl: 999.0

999.1 Air embolism `MCC`

Air embolism to any site following infusion, perfusion, or transfusion

EXCLUDES   *embolism specified as:*
complicating:
abortion (634-638 with .6, 639.6)
ectopic or molar pregnancy (639.6)
pregnancy, childbirth, or the puerperium (673.0)
due to implanted device (996.7)
traumatic (958.0)

CC Excl: 958.0, 999.1

999.2 Other vascular complications `CC`

Phlebitis
Thromboembolism } following infusion, perfusion, or transfusion
Thrombophlebitis

EXCLUDES   *extravasation of vesicant drugs (999.81, 999.82)*
the listed conditions when specified as:
due to implanted device (996.61-996.62. 996.72-996.74)
postoperative NOS (997.2, 997.71-997.79)

CC Excl: 999.2, 999.81-999.88

AHA: 2Q, '97, 5

TIP: Do not assign for IV infiltration; if the infiltration is severe enough to cause other complications, a code for the specific complication should be assigned. For chemotherapy extravasation, see code 999.81.

T80.1xxA Vasc comp follw inf transfusn tx inj initial enc `I-10`

✓5th **999.3 Other infection**

Infection
Sepsis } following infusion, injection, transfusion, or vaccination
Septicemia

Use additional code to identify the specified infection, such as:
septicemia (038.0-038.9)

EXCLUDES   *the listed conditions when specified as:*
due to implanted device (996.60-996.69)
postoperative NOS (998.51-998.59)

AHA: 4Q, '07, 96; 2Q, '01, 11, 12; 2Q, '97, 5; J-F, '87, 14

999.31 Infection due to central venous catheter `CC`

Catheter-related bloodstream infection (CRBSI) NOS
Infection due to:
Hickman catheter
peripherally inserted central catheter (PICC)
portacath (port-a-cath)
triple lumen catheter
umbilical venous catheter

EXCLUDES   *infection due to:*
arterial catheter (996.62)
catheter NOS (996.69)
peripheral venous catheter (996.62)
urinary catheter (996.64)

CC Excl: 996.62, 999.31-999.39

AHA: 4Q, '08, 72, 193; 4Q, '07, 97

T80.21xD Inf due to central venous cath subsequent enc `I-10`

999.39 Infection following other infusion, injection, transfusion, or vaccination `CC`

CC Excl: 996.62, 999.31-999.39

AHA: 4Q, '08, 99

999.4 Anaphylactic shock due to serum `CC`

Anaphylactic reaction due to serum

EXCLUDES   *shock:*
allergic NOS (995.0)
anaphylactic:
NOS (995.0)
due to drugs and chemicals (995.0)

DEF: Life-threatening hypersensitivity to foreign serum; causes respiratory distress, vascular collapse, and shock.

CC Excl: 999.4

999.5 Other serum reaction `CC`

Intoxication by serum
Protein sickness
Serum rash
Serum sickness
Urticaria due to serum

EXCLUDES   *serum hepatitis (070.2-070.3)*

DEF: Serum sickness: Hypersensitivity to foreign serum; causes fever, hives, swelling, and lymphadenopathy.

CC Excl: 999.5

`N` Newborn Age: 0   `P` Pediatric Age: 0-17   `M` Maternity Age: 12-55   `A` Adult Age: 15-124   `MCC` Major CC Condition   `CC` CC Condition   `HIV` HIV Related Dx

364 – Volume 1 • October 2009   2010 ICD-9-CM

999.6 **ABO incompatibility reaction** `CC`
Incompatible blood transfusion
Reaction to blood group incompatibility in infusion or transfusion

> **EXCLUDES** ►minor blood group antigens reactions (Duffy) (E) (K(ell)) (Kidd) (Lewis) (M) (N) (P) (S) (999.89)◄

CC Excl: 999.6

999.7 **Rh incompatibility reaction** `CC`
Elevation of Rh titer
Reactions due to Rh factor in infusion or transfusion

CC Excl: 999.7

✓5ᵗʰ **999.8** **Other infusion and transfusion reaction**

> **EXCLUDES** postoperative shock (998.0)
> transfusion related acute lung injury [TRALI] (518.7)

AHA: 4Q, '08, 152-155; 3Q, '00, 9

999.81 **Extravasation of vesicant chemotherapy** `CC`
Infiltration of vesicant chemotherapy
CC Excl: 999.2, 999.81-999.88
AHA: 4Q, '08, 155

999.82 **Extravasation of other vesicant agent** `CC`
Infiltration of other vesicant agent
CC Excl: 999.2, 999.81-999.88

999.88 **Other infusion reaction**

999.89 **Other transfusion reaction**
Transfusion reaction NOS
Use additional code to identify graft-versus-host reaction (279.5)
AHA: 4Q, '08, 99, 154

999.9 **Other and unspecified complications of medical care, not elsewhere classified**
Complications, not elsewhere classified, of:
electroshock
inhalation
ultrasound } therapy
ventilation

Unspecified misadventure of medical care

> **EXCLUDES** unspecified complication of:
> phototherapy (990)
> radiation therapy (999)
> ventilator associated pneumonia (997.31)

AHA: 3Q, '06, 25; 1Q, '03, 19; 2Q, '97, 5

Aftercare visit codes V51-58

Special Screening
        examinations   V73-V82

Personal history of   V10-V15
    a previous
    condition

Family history   V16-V19

Continuing condition   V40-V49
    or health status that
    may influence care

Problems that may   V60-V63
    affect patient care

Procedures/Services not carried
out as scheduled — V64

V57 is assigned as the principal
diagnosis when the patient is admitted
for the purpose of rehabilitation following
previous illness or injury, with the
fourth digit indicating the focus of
treatment. An additional code is
assigned for the residual condition
requiring rehabilitation.

V58.6X - long-term (current) drug use

V71 - suspected conditions not found
        (observation and evaluation)

V29 - observation of a newborn

V89 - suspected conditions not found
        (maternal/fetus)

V66 - convalesence/palliative care
    V66.7 - end of life/hospice/terminal
            care

V72.8 pre-operative examinations

V84 - genetic susceptibility to disease

V15.X - past history of psychological trauma
        (including physical/emotional abuse/neglect)

V61.XX - counseling codes

V54.X - Fracture aftercare codes

SUPPLEMENTARY CLASSIFICATION OF FACTORS INFLUENCING HEALTH STATUS AND CONTACT WITH HEALTH SERVICES (V01-V89)

This classification is provided to deal with occasions when circumstances other than a disease or injury classifiable to categories 001-999 (the main part of ICD) are recorded as "diagnoses" or "problems." This can arise mainly in three ways:

a) When a person who is not currently sick encounters the health services for some specific purpose, such as to act as a donor of an organ or tissue, to receive prophylactic vaccination, or to discuss a problem which is in itself not a disease or injury. This will be a fairly rare occurrence among hospital inpatients, but will be relatively more common among hospital outpatients and patients of family practitioners, health clinics, etc.

b) When a person with a known disease or injury, whether it is current or resolving, encounters the health care system for a specific treatment of that disease or injury (e.g., dialysis for renal disease; chemotherapy for malignancy; cast change).

c) When some circumstance or problem is present which influences the person's health status but is not in itself a current illness or injury. Such factors may be elicited during population surveys, when the person may or may not be currently sick, or be recorded as an additional factor to be borne in mind when the person is receiving care for some current illness or injury classifiable to categories 001-999.

In the latter circumstances the V code should be used only as a supplementary code and should not be the one selected for use in primary, single cause tabulations. Examples of these circumstances are a personal history of certain diseases, or a person with an artificial heart valve in situ.

AHA: J-F, '87, 8

PERSONS WITH POTENTIAL HEALTH HAZARDS RELATED TO COMMUNICABLE DISEASES (V01-V06)

     EXCLUDES *family history of infectious and parasitic diseases (V18.8)*
personal history of infectious and parasitic diseases (V12.0)

√4ᵗʰ **V01 Contact with or exposure to communicable diseases**
     TIP: Do not assign if the patient shows signs or symptoms of the disease to which he or she was exposed.

V01.0 Cholera
     Conditions classifiable to 001

V01.1 Tuberculosis
     Conditions classifiable to 010-018

V01.2 Poliomyelitis
     Conditions classifiable to 045

V01.3 Smallpox
     Conditions classifiable to 050

V01.4 Rubella
     Conditions classifiable to 056

V01.5 Rabies
     Conditions classifiable to 071

V01.6 Venereal diseases
     Conditions classifiable to 090-099
     AHA: 4Q, '07, 125

√5ᵗʰ **V01.7 Other viral diseases**
     Conditions classifiable to 042-078 and V08, except as above
     AHA: 2Q, '92, 11

   ² **V01.71 Varicella**

   ² **V01.79 Other viral diseases**

√5ᵗʰ **V01.8 Other communicable diseases**
     Conditions classifiable to 001-136, except as above
     AHA: J-A, '87, 24

V01.81 Anthrax
     AHA: 4Q, '02, 70, 78

   ² **V01.82 Exposure to SARS-associated coronavirus**
     AHA: 4Q, '03, 46-47

   ² **V01.83 Escherichia coli (E. coli)**

   ² **V01.84 Meningococcus**
     Z20.811 Contact with and exposure to   **I-10**
     meningococcus

V01.89 Other communicable diseases

V01.9 Unspecified communicable diseases

√4ᵗʰ **V02 Carrier or suspected carrier of infectious diseases**
     INCLUDES colonization status
     AHA: 3Q, '95, 18; 3Q, '94, 4

V02.0 Cholera

V02.1 Typhoid

V02.2 Amebiasis

V02.3 Other gastrointestinal pathogens

V02.4 Diphtheria

√5ᵗʰ **V02.5 Other specified bacterial diseases**

V02.51 Group B streptococcus
     AHA: 3Q, '06, 14; 1Q, '02, 14; 4Q, '98, 56

V02.52 Other streptococcus

V02.53 Methicillin susceptible Staphylococcus aureus
     MSSA colonization
     AHA: ▶4Q, '08, 69, 71, 156◀

V02.54 Methicillin resistant Staphylococcus aureus
     MRSA colonization
     AHA: ▶4Q, '08, 69, 71, 72, 156◀

V02.59 Other specified bacterial diseases
     Meningococcal
     Staphylococcal

√5ᵗʰ **V02.6 Viral hepatitis**
     Hepatitis Australian-antigen [HAA] [SH] carrier
     Serum hepatitis carrier

V02.60 Viral hepatitis carrier, unspecfied
     AHA: 4Q, '97, 47

V02.61 Hepatitis B carrier
     AHA: 4Q, '97, 47

     Z22.51 Carrier of viral hepatitis B   **I-10**

V02.62 Hepatitis C carrier
     AHA: 4Q, '97, 47

V02.69 Other viral hepatitis carrier
     AHA: 4Q, '97, 47

V02.7 Gonorrhea

V02.8 Other veneral diseases

V02.9 Other specified infectious organism
     AHA: 3Q, '95, 18; 1Q, '93, 22; J-A, '87, 24

√4ᵗʰ **V03 Need for prophylactic vaccination and inoculation against bacterial diseases**
     EXCLUDES *vaccination not carried out (V64.00-V64.09)*
vaccines against combinations of diseases (V06.0-V06.9)

V03.0 Cholera alone

V03.1 Typhoid-paratyphoid alone [TAB]

V03.2 Tuberculosis [BCG]

V03.3 Plague

V03.4 Tularemia

V03.5 Diphtheria alone

V03.6 Pertussis alone

V03.7 Tetanus toxoid alone

√5ᵗʰ **V03.8 Other specified vaccinations against single bacterial diseases**

V03.81 Hemophilus influenza, type B [Hib]

V03.82 Streptococcus pneumoniae [pneumococcus]

---

² These V codes may be used as principal diagnosis on Medicare patients.

√4ᵗʰ √5ᵗʰ **Additional Digit Required**   **Unacceptable PDx**   **Manifestation Code**   **Hospital Acquired Condition**   ▶◀ Revised Text   ● New Code   ▲ Revised Code Title

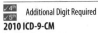

2010 ICD-9-CM   **February 2009 • Volume 1 – 367**

V01–V03.82

V03.89   **Other specified vaccination**
    AHA: 2Q, '00, 9
    TIP: Assign for vaccination against Lyme disease.

V03.9   **Unspecified single bacterial disease**

√4ᵗʰ **V04**   **Need for prophylactic vaccination and inoculation against certain viral diseases**
    EXCLUDES   *vaccines against combinations of diseases (V06.0-V06.9)*

V04.0   **Poliomyelitis**

V04.1   **Smallpox**

V04.2   **Measles alone**

V04.3   **Rubella alone**

V04.4   **Yellow fever**

V04.5   **Rabies**

V04.6   **Mumps alone**

V04.7   **Common cold**

√5ᵗʰ V04.8   **Other viral diseases**
    AHA: 4Q, '03, 83

V04.81   **Influenza**

V04.82   **Respiratory syncytial virus (RSV)**
    AHA: ▶1Q, '09, 14◀

V04.89   **Other viral diseases**
    AHA: 2Q, '07, 9
    TIP: Assign for vaccination against human papilloma virus (HPV).

√4ᵗʰ **V05**   **Need for other prophylactic vaccination and inoculation against single diseases**
    EXCLUDES   *vaccines against combinations of diseases (V06.0-V06.9)*

V05.0   **Athropod-borne viral encephalitis**

V05.1   **Other arthropod-borne viral diseases**

V05.2   **Leshmaniasis**

V05.3   **Viral hepatitis**

V05.4   **Varicella**
    Chickenpox

V05.8   **Other specified disease**
    AHA: 1Q, '01, 4; 3Q, '91, 20

V05.9   **Unspecified single disease**

√4ᵗʰ **V06**   **Need for prophylactic vaccination and inoculation against combinations of diseases**
    Note: Use additional single vaccination codes from categories V03-V05 to identify any vaccinations not included in a combination code.

V06.0   **Cholera with typhoid-paratyphoid [cholera+TAB]**

V06.1   **Diphtheria-tetanus-pertussis, combined [DTP] [DTaP]**
    AHA: 4Q, '03, 83; 3Q, '98, 13

V06.2   **Diphtheria-tetanus-pertussis with typhoid-paratyphoid [DTP+TAB]**

V06.3   **Diphtheria-tetanus-pertussis with poliomyelitis [DTP+polio]**

V06.4   **Measles-mumps-rubella [MMR]**

V06.5   **Tetanus-diphtheria [Td] [DT]**
    AHA: 4Q, '03, 83

V06.6   **Streptococcus pneumoniae [pneumococcus] and influenza**

V06.8   **Other combinations**
    EXCLUDES   *multiple single vaccination codes (V03.0-V05.9)*
    AHA: 1Q, '94, 19

V06.9   **Unspecified combined vaccine**

PERSONS WITH NEED FOR ISOLATION, OTHER POTENTIAL HEALTH HAZARDS AND PROPHYLACTIC MEASURES (V07-V09)

√4ᵗʰ **V07**   **Need for isolation and other prophylactic measures**
    EXCLUDES   *prophylactic organ removal (V50.41-V50.49)*

² V07.0   **Isolation**
    Admission to protect the individual from his surroundings or for isolation of individual after contact with infectious diseases

V07.1   **Desensitization to allergens**

V07.2   **Prophylactic immunotherapy**
    Administration of:
      antivenin
      immune sera [gamma globulin]
      RhoGAM
      tetanus antitoxin

√5ᵗʰ V07.3   **Other prophylactic chemotherapy**

V07.31   **Prophylactic fluoride administration**

² V07.39   **Other prophylactic chemotherapy**
    EXCLUDES   *maintenance chemotherapy following disease (V58.11)*

V07.4   **Hormone replacement therapy (postmenopausal)** ♀
    Z79.890 Hormone replacement therapy postmenopausal   I-10

√5ᵗʰ V07.5   **Prophylactic use of agents affecting estrogen receptors and estrogen levels**
    Code first, if applicable:
      malignant neoplasm of breast (174.0-174.9, 175.0-175.9)
      malignant neoplasm of prostate (185)
    Use additional code, if applicable, to identify:
      estrogen receptor positive status (V86.0)
      family history of breast cancer (V16.3)
      genetic susceptibility to cancer (V84.01-V84.09)
      personal history of breast cancer (V10.3)
      personal history of prostate cancer (V10.46)
      postmenopausal status (V49.81)
    EXCLUDES   *hormone replacement therapy (postmenopausal) (V07.4)*
    AHA: 4Q, '08, 156

V07.51   **Prophylactic use of selective estrogen receptor modulators [SERMs]**
    Prophylactic use of:
      raloxifene (Evista)
      tamoxifen (Nolvadex)
      toremifene (Fareston)
    Z79.81 Long term (current) use agent affecting estrogen receptors   I-10

V07.52   **Prophylactic use of aromatase inhibitors**
    Prophylactic use of:
      anastrozole (Arimidex)
      ▶exemestane◀ (Aromasin)
      letrozole (Femara)

V07.59   **Prophylactic use of other agents affecting estrogen receptors and estrogen levels**
    Prophylactic use of:
      estrogen receptor downregulators
      fulvestrant (Faslodex)
      gonadotropin-releasing hormone (GnRH) agonist
      goserelin acetate (Zoladex)
      leuprolide acetate (leuprorelin) (Lupron)
      megestrol acetate (Megace)

² V07.8   **Other specified prophylactic measure**
    AHA: 1Q, '92, 11
    TIP: Assign for patients having prophylactic breast removal because of a strong family history of breast cancer, along with code V16.3 Family history of breast cancer.

V07.9   **Unspecified prophylactic measure**

² These V codes may be used as principal diagnosis on Medicare patients.

N Newborn Age: 0   P Pediatric Age: 0-17   M Maternity Age: 12-55   A Adult Age: 15-124   MCC Major CC Condition   CC CC Condition   HIV HIV Related Dx

368 – Volume 1 • October 2009   2010 ICD-9-CM

V10.X... aka "status post"

V08 Asymptomatic human immunodeficiency virus [HIV] infection status
HIV positive NOS
Note: This code is only to be used when no HIV infection symptoms or conditions are present. If any HIV infection symptoms or conditions are present, see code 042.

EXCLUDES AIDS (042)
human immunodeficiency virus [HIV] disease (042)
exposure to HIV (V01.79)
nonspecific serologic evidence of HIV (795.71)
symptomatic human immunodeficiency virus [HIV] infection (042)

AHA: 2Q, '04, 11; 2Q, '99, 8; 3Q, '95, 18

Z21 Asymptomatic HIV infection status   I-10

√4ᵗʰ V09 Infection with drug-resistant microorganisms
Note: This category is intended for use as an additional code for infectious conditions classified elsewhere to indicate the presence of drug-resistance of the infectious organism.

AHA: 3Q, '94, 4; 4Q, '93, 22

Assigned as additional codes and only when the physician specifically documents an infection that has become drug resistant.

V09.0 Infection with microorganisms resistant to penicillins
AHA: 2Q, '06, 16; 4Q, '03, 104, 106

V09.1 Infection with microorganisms resistant to cephalosporins and other B-lactam antibiotics

V09.2 Infection with microorganisms resistant to macrolides

V09.3 Infection with microorganisms resistant to tetracyclines

V09.4 Infection with microorganisms resistant to aminoglycosides

√5ᵗʰ V09.5 Infection with microorganisms resistant to quinolones and fluoroquinolones

V09.50 Without mention of resistance to multiple quinolones and fluoroquinoles

V09.51 With resistance to multiple quinolones and fluoroquinoles

V09.6 Infection with microorganisms resistant to sulfonamides

√5ᵗʰ V09.7 Infection with microorganisms resistant to other specified antimycobacterial agents

EXCLUDES Amikacin (V09.4)
Kanamycin (V09.4)
Streptomycin [SM] (V09.4)

V09.70 Without mention of resistance to multiple antimycobacterial agents

V09.71 With resistance to multiple antimycobacterial agents

√5ᵗʰ V09.8 Infection with microorganisms resistant to other specified drugs
Vancomycin (glycopeptide) intermediate staphylococcus aureus (VISA/GISA)
Vancomycin (glycopeptide) resistant enterococcus (VRE)
Vancomycin (glycopeptide) resistant staphylococcus aureus (VRSA/GRSA)

V09.80 Without mention of resistance to multiple drugs

V09.81 With resistance to multiple drugs

√5ᵗʰ V09.9 Infection with drug-resistant microorganisms, unspecified
Drug resistance, NOS

V09.90 Without mention of multiple drug resistance
Z16 Infection with drug resistant microorganisms   I-10

V09.91 With multiple drug resistance
Multiple drug resistance NOS

PERSONS WITH POTENTIAL HEALTH HAZARDS RELATED TO PERSONAL AND FAMILY HISTORY (V10-V19)

EXCLUDES obstetric patients where the possibility that the fetus might be affected is the reason for observation or management during pregnancy (655.0-655.9)

AHA: J-F, '87, 1

√4ᵗʰ V10 Personal history of malignant neoplasm
AHA: 4Q, '02, 80; 4Q, '98, 69; 1Q, '95, 4; 3Q, '92, 5; M-J, '85, 10; 2Q, '90, 9
TIP: Assign the codes in this category only for a personal history of primary malignancy (not metastatic malignancies).

√5ᵗʰ V10.0 Gastrointestinal tract
History of conditions classifiable to 140-159

EXCLUDES ► personal history of malignant carcinoid tumor (V10.91)
personal history of malignant neuroendocrine tumor (V10.91)◄

V10.00 Gastrointestinal tract, unspecified

V10.01 Tongue

V10.02 Other and unspecified oral cavity and pharynx

V10.03 Esophagus

V10.04 Stomach

V10.05 Large intestine
AHA: 3Q, '99, 7; 1Q, '95, 4

Z85.03 Personal hx prim malig neoplasm large intestine   I-10

V10.06 Rectum, rectosigmoid junction, and anus

V10.07 Liver

V10.09 Other
AHA: 4Q, '03, 111

√5ᵗʰ V10.1 Trachea, bronchus, and lung
History of conditions classifiable to 162

EXCLUDES ► personal history of malignant carcinoid tumor (V10.91)
personal history of malignant neuroendocrine tumor (V10.91)◄

V10.11 Bronchus and lung

V10.12 Trachea

√5ᵗʰ V10.2 Other respiratory and intrathoracic organs
History of conditions classifiable to 160, 161, 163-165

V10.20 Respiratory organ, unspecified

V10.21 Larynx
AHA: 4Q, '03, 108, 110

V10.22 Nasal cavities, middle ear, and accessory sinuses

V10.29 Other

V10.3 Breast
History of conditions classifiable to 174 and 175
AHA: 3Q, '07, 4; 1Q, '07, 6; 2Q, '03, 5; 4Q, '01, 66; 4Q, '98, 65; 4Q, '97, 50; 1Q, '91, 16; 1Q, '90, 21
Z85.3 Personal history primary malig neoplasm breast   I-10

√5ᵗʰ V10.4 Genital organs
History of conditions classifiable to 179-187

V10.40 Female genital organ, unspecfied   ♀

V10.41 Cervix uteri   ♀
AHA: 4Q, '07, 99

V10.42 Other parts of uterus   ♀

V10.43 Ovary   ♀

V10.44 Other female genital organs   ♀

V10.45 Male genital organ, unspecfied   ♂

V10.46 Prostate   ♂
AHA: ►1Q, '09,15◄

V10.47 Testis   ♂
Z85.47 Personal history primary malig neoplasm testis   I-10

√4ᵗʰ √5ᵗʰ Additional Digit Required | Unacceptable PDx | Manifestation Code | Hospital Acquired Condition | ►◄ Revised Text | ● New Code | ▲ Revised Code Title

2010 ICD-9-CM | October 2009 • Volume 1 – 369

V10.48   **Epididymis** ♂

V10.49   **Other male genital organs** ♂

✓5th **V10.5 Urinary organs**
History of conditions classifiable to 188 and 189

V10.50   **Urinary organ, unspecified**

V10.51   **Bladder**

V10.52   **Kidney**
AHA: 2Q, '04, 4
EXCLUDES   *renal pelvis (V10.53)*

V10.53   **Renal pelvis**
AHA: 4Q, '01, 55

V10.59   **Other**

✓5th **V10.6 Leukemia**
Conditions classifiable to 204-208
EXCLUDES   *leukemia in remission (204-208)*
AHA: 2Q, '92, 13; 4Q, '91, 26; 4Q, '90, 3

V10.60   **Leukemia, unspecified**

V10.61   **Lymphoid leukemia**

V10.62   **Myeloid leukemia**

V10.63   **Monocytic leukemia**

V10.69   **Other**

✓5th **V10.7 Other lymphatic and hematopoietic neoplasms**
Conditions classifiable to 200-203
EXCLUDES   *listed conditions in 200-203 in remission*
AHA: M-J, '85, 18

V10.71   **Lymphosarcoma and reticulosarcoma**

V10.72   **Hodgkin's disease**

V10.79   **Other**

✓5th **V10.8 Personal history of malignant neoplasm of other sites**
History of conditions classifiable to 170-173, 190-195
EXCLUDES   ▶*personal history of malignant carcinoid tumor (V10.91)*
personal history of malignant neuroendocrine tumor (V10.91)◀

V10.81   **Bone**
AHA: 2Q, '03, 13

V10.82   **Malignant melanoma of skin**

V10.83   **Other malignant neoplasm of skin**

V10.84   **Eye**

V10.85   **Brain**
AHA: 1Q, '01, 6

V10.86   **Other parts of the nervous system**
EXCLUDES   *peripheral sympathetic, and parasympathetic nerves (V10.89)*

V10.87   **Thyroid**

V10.88   **Other endocrine glands and related structures**

V10.89   **Other**

▲ ✓5th **V10.9 Other and unspecified personal history of malignant neoplasm**

● V10.90   **Personal history of unspecified malignant neoplasm**
Personal history of malignant neoplasm NOS
EXCLUDES   *personal history of malignant carcinoid tumor (V10.91)*
personal history of malignant neuroendocrine tumor (V10.91)
personal history of Merkel cell carcinoma (V10.91)

● V10.91   **Personal history of malignant neuroendocrine tumor**
Personal history of malignant carcinoid tumor NOS
Personal history of malignant neuroendocrine tumor NOS
Personal history of Merkel cell carcinoma NOS
Code first any continuing functional activity, such as:
carcinoid syndrome (259.2)

✓4th **V11 Personal history of mental disorder**

V11.0   **Schizophrenia**
EXCLUDES   *that in remission (295.0-295.9 with fifth-digit 5)*

V11.1   **Affective disorders**
Personal history of manic-depressive psychosis
EXCLUDES   *that in remission (296.0-296.6 with fifth-digit 5, 6)*

V11.2   **Neurosis**

V11.3   **Alcoholism**

V11.8   **Other mental disorders**

V11.9   **Unspecified mental disorder**

✓4th **V12 Personal history of certain other diseases**
AHA: 3Q, '92, 11

✓5th **V12.0 Infectious and parasitic diseases**
EXCLUDES   *personal history of infectious diseases specific to a body system*

V12.00   **Unspecified infectious and parasitic disease**

V12.01   **Tuberculosis**

V12.02   **Poliomyelitis**
Z86.12 Personal history of poliomyelitis   **I-10**

V12.03   **Malaria**

V12.04   **Methicillin resistant Staphylococcus aureus**
MRSA
AHA: 4Q, '08, 69, 71

V12.09   **Other**

V12.1   **Nutritional deficiency**

V12.2   **Endocrine, metabolic, and immunity disorders**
EXCLUDES   *history of allergy (V14.0-V14.9, V15.01-V15.09)*
AHA: 3Q, '07, 5

V12.3   **Diseases of blood and blood-forming organs**

✓5th **V12.4 Disorders of nervous system and sense organs**

V12.40   **Unspecified disorder of nervous system and sense organs**

V12.41   **Benign neoplasm of the brain**
AHA: 4Q, '97, 48
TIP: Benign neoplasms of the brain are tracked separately because, besides being potentially life-threatening, they often recur and can be difficult to treat.

[handwritten: No history code is assigned for prior benign neoplasm except V12.41]

V12.42   **Infections of the central nervous system**
Encephalitis Meningitis
AHA: 4Q, '05, 95

V12.49   **Other disorders of nervous system and sense organs**
AHA: 4Q, '98, 59

✓5th **V12.5 Diseases of circulatory system**
AHA: 4Q, '95, 61
EXCLUDES   *old myocardial infarction (412)*
postmyocardial infarction syndrome (411.0)

V12.50   **Unspecified circulatory disease**

V12.51   **Venous thrombosis and embolism**
Pulmonary embolism
AHA: 3Q, '06, 12; 4Q, '03, 108; 1Q, '02, 15

N Newborn Age: 0   **P** Pediatric Age: 0-17   **M** Maternity Age: 12-55   **A** Adult Age: 15-124   **MCC** Major CC Condition   **CC** CC Condition   **HIV** HIV Related Dx

V12.52 Thrombophlebitis

V12.53 Sudden cardiac arrest
Sudden cardiac death successfully resuscitated
AHA: 4Q, '07, 98

V12.54 Transient ischemic attack [TIA], and cerebral infarction without residual deficits
Prolonged reversible ischemic neurological deficit [PRIND]
Reversible ischemic neurologic deficit [RIND]
Stroke NOS without residual deficits

> EXCLUDES ▶ history of traumatic brain injury (V15.52)◀
> late effects of cerebrovascular disease (438.0-438.9)

AHA: 4Q, '07, 98
TIP: Assign for old CVA for which the patient has no residual deficits; if deficits are present, see category 438.
Z86.73 Personal hx TIA & cerebral infarct w/o deficits   I-10

V12.59 Other
AHA: 2Q, '07, 3; 4Q, '99, 4; 4Q, '98, 88; 4Q, '97, 37

✓5th **V12.6 Diseases of respiratory system**
> EXCLUDES tuberculosis (V12.01)

V12.60 Unspecified disease of respiratory system

V12.61 Pneumonia (recurrent)
AHA: 4Q, '05, 95

V12.69 Other diseases of respiratory system

✓5th **V12.7 Diseases of digestive system**
AHA: 1Q, '95, 3; 2Q, '89, 16

V12.70 Unspecified digestive disease

V12.71 Peptic ulcer disease

V12.72 Colonic polyps
AHA: 3Q, '02, 15
Z86.010 Personal history of colonic polyps   I-10

V12.79 Other

✓4th **V13 Personal history of other diseases**

✓5th **V13.0 Disorders of urinary system**

V13.00 Unspecified urinary disorder

V13.01 Urinary calculi

V13.02 Urinary (tract) infection
AHA: 4Q, '05, 95

V13.03 Nephrotic syndrome
AHA: 4Q, '05, 95

V13.09 Other

V13.1 Trophoblastic disease   ♀
> EXCLUDES supervision during a current pregnancy (V23.1)

✓5th **V13.2 Other genital system and obstetric disorders**
> EXCLUDES habitual aborter (646.3)
> without current pregnancy (629.81)
> supervision during a current pregnancy of a woman with poor obstetric history (V23.0-V23.9)

V13.21 Personal history of pre-term labor   ♀
> EXCLUDES current pregnancy with history of pre-term labor (V23.41)

AHA: 4Q, '02, 78

V13.22 Personal history of cervical dysplasia   ♀
Personal history of conditions classifiable to 622.10-622.12
> EXCLUDES personal history of malignant neoplasm of cervix uteri (V10.41)

AHA: 4Q, '07, 98

V13.29 Other genital system and obstetric disorders   ♀

V13.3 Diseases of skin and subcutaneous tissue

V13.4 Arthritis

✓5th **V13.5 Other musculoskeletal disorders**
AHA: 4Q, '08, 158
TIP: Personal histories of pathological, stress, or traumatic fractures are separately classified because a patient with such a history is at much higher risk of refracture of the same site.

V13.51 Pathologic fracture
Healed pathologic fracture
> EXCLUDES personal history of traumatic fracture (V15.51)

V13.52 Stress fracture
Healed stress fracture
> EXCLUDES personal history of traumatic fracture (V15.51)

V13.59 Other musculoskeletal disorders

✓5th **V13.6 Congenital malformations**
AHA: 4Q, '98, 63

V13.61 Hypospadias   ♂

V13.69 Other congenital malformations
AHA: 1Q, '04, 16

V13.7 Perinatal problems
> EXCLUDES low birth weight status (V21.30-V21.35)

V13.8 Other specified diseases

V13.9 Unspecified disease
AHA: 4Q, '06, 117

✓4th **V14 Personal history of allergy to medicinal agents**

V14.0 Penicillin
Z88.0 Allergy status to penicillin   I-10

V14.1 Other antibiotic agent

V14.2 Sulfonamides

V14.3 Other anti-infective agent

V14.4 Anesthetic age

V14.5 Narcotic agent

V14.6 Analgesic agent

V14.7 Serum or vaccine

V14.8 Other specified medicinal agents

V14.9 Unspecified medicinal agent

✓4th **V15 Other personal history presenting hazards to health**
> EXCLUDES personal history of drug therapy (V87.41-V87.49)

✓5th **V15.0 Allergy, other than to medicinal agents**
> EXCLUDES allergy to food substance used as base for medicinal agent (V14.0-V14.9)

AHA: 4Q, '00, 42, 49
TIP: A person who has had an allergic episode to a substance in the past should always be considered allergic to the substance.

V15.01 Allergy to peanuts
Z91.010 Allergy to peanuts   I-10

V15.02 Allergy to milk products
> EXCLUDES lactose intolerance (271.3)

AHA: 1Q, '03, 12

V15.03 Allergy to eggs

V15.04 Allergy to seafood
Seafood (octopus) (squid) ink
Shellfish

V15.05 Allergy to other foods
Food additives   Nuts other than peanuts

▲ **V15.06 Allergy to insects and arachnids**
Bugs
Insect bites and stings
Spiders

V15.07 Allergy to latex
Latex sensitivity

✓4th ✓5th Additional Digit Required   Unacceptable PDx   Manifestation Code   Hospital Acquired Condition   ▶◀ Revised Text   ● New Code   ▲ Revised Code Title

2010 ICD-9-CM   **October 2009 • Volume 1 – 371**

V12.52–V15.07

V15.08 Allergy to radiographic dye
Contrast media used for diagnostic x-ray procedures

V15.09 Other allergy, other than to medicinal agents

V15.1 Surgery to heart and great vessels
EXCLUDES replacement by transplant or other means (V42.1-V42.2, V43.2-V43.4)
AHA: 1Q, '04, 16

√5th **V15.2 Surgery to other organs**
EXCLUDES replacement by transplant or other means (V42.0-V43.8)l
AHA: 4Q, '08, 158

V15.21 Personal history of undergoing in utero procedure during pregnancy ♀
AHA: 4Q, '08, 158

V15.22 Personal history of undergoing in utero procedure while a fetus
AHA: 4Q, '08, 158

V15.29 Surgery to other organs

V15.3 Irradiation
Previous exposure to therapeutic or other ionizing radiation

√5th **V15.4 Psychological trauma**
EXCLUDES history of condition classifiable to 290-316 (V11.0-V11.9)

V15.41 History of physical abuse
Rape
AHA: 3Q, '99, 15

V15.42 History of emotional abuse
Neglect
AHA: 3Q, '99, 15

V15.49 Other
AHA: 3Q, '99, 15

√5th **V15.5 Injury**
AHA: 4Q, '08, 158

V15.51 Traumatic fracture
Healed traumatic fracture
EXCLUDES personal history of pathologic and stress fracture (V13.51, V13.52)
TIP: Personal histories of pathological, stress, or traumatic fractures are separately classified because a patient with such a history is at much higher risk of refracture of the same site.

● **V15.52 History of traumatic brain injury**
EXCLUDES personal history of cerebrovascular accident (cerebral infarction) without residual deficits (V12.54)

V15.59 Other injury

V15.6 Poisoning

V15.7 Contraception
EXCLUDES current contraceptive management (V25.0-V25.4)
presence of intrauterine contraceptive device as incidental finding (V45.5)

√5th **V15.8 Other specified personal history presenting hazards to health**
EXCLUDES contact with and (suspected) exposure to: aromatic compounds and dyes (V87.11-V87.19)
arsenic and other metals (V87.01-V87.09)
molds (V87.31)
AHA: 4Q, '95, 62

● **V15.80 History of failed moderate sedation**
History of failed conscious sedation

V15.81 Noncompliance with medical treatment
EXCLUDES noncompliance with renal dialysis (V45.12)
AHA: 3Q, '07, 9; 4Q, '06, 136; 2Q, '03, 7; 2Q, '01, 11, 12, 13; 2Q, '99, 17; 2Q, '97, 11; 1Q, '97, 12; 3Q, '96, 9

V15.82 History of tobacco use
EXCLUDES tobacco dependence (305.1)
AHA: ►1Q, '09, 17◄
Z87.82 Personal history of nicotine dependence I-10

● **V15.83 Underimmunization status**
Delinquent immunization status
Lapsed immunization schedule status

▲ **V15.84 Contact with and (suspected) exposure to asbestos**

▲ **V15.85 Contact with and (suspected) exposure to potentially hazardous body fluids**

▲ **V15.86 Contact with and (suspected) exposure to lead**

V15.87 History of extracorporeal membrane oxygenation [ECMO]
AHA: 4Q, '03, 84

V15.88 History of fall
At risk for falling
AHA: 4Q, '05, 95
Z91.81 History of falling I-10

V15.89 Other
EXCLUDES contact with and (suspected) exposure to other potentially hazardous:
chemicals (V87.2)
substances (V87.39)
AHA: 3Q, '08, 7; 3Q, '07, 5; 1Q, '90, 21; N-D, '84, 12

V15.9 Unspecified personal history presenting hazards to health

√4th **V16 Family history of malignant neoplasm**

V16.0 Gastrointestinal tract
Family history of condition classifiable to 140-159
AHA: 1Q, '99, 4
TIP: Family history of colon cancer is a condition that meets the criteria of "high risk" for a screening colonoscopy.

V16.1 Trachea, bronchus, and lung
Family history of condition classifiable to 162

V16.2 Other respiratory and intrathoracic organs
Family history of condition classifiable to 160-161, 163-165

V16.3 Breast
Family history of condition classifiable to 174
AHA: 4Q, '04, 107; 2Q, '03, 4; 2Q, '00, 8; 1Q, '92, 11
Z80.3 Family history of malignant neoplasm of breast I-10

√5th **V16.4 Genital organs**
Family history of condition classifiable to 179-187
AHA: 4Q, '97, 48

V16.40 Genital organ, unspecified

V16.41 Ovary

V16.42 Prostate
Z80.42 Family history of malignant neoplasm of prostate I-10

V16.43 Testis

V16.49 Other
AHA: 2Q, '06, 2

√5th **V16.5 Urinary organs**
Family history of condition classifiable to 188-189

V16.51 Kidney

V16.52 Bladder
AHA: 4Q, '07, 98

V16.59 Other

N Newborn Age: 0   P Pediatric Age: 0-17   M Maternity Age: 12-55   A Adult Age: 15-124   MCC Major CC Condition   CC CC Condition   HIV HIV Related Dx

372 – Volume 1 • October 2009   **2010 ICD-9-CM**

V16.6 Leukemia
Family history of condition classifiable to 204-208

V16.7 Other lymphatic and hematopoietic neoplasms
Family history of condition classifiable to 200-203

V16.8 Other specified malignant neoplasm
Family history of other condition classifiable to 140-199

V16.9 Unspecified malignant neoplasm

✓4th **V17 Family history of certain chronic disabling diseases**

V17.0 Psychiatric condition
> EXCLUDES *family history of mental retardation (V18.4)*

V17.1 Stroke (cerebrovascular)
Z82.3 Family history of stroke   I-10

V17.2 Other neurological diseases
Epilepsy   Huntington's chorea

V17.3 Ischemic heart disease

✓5th **V17.4 Other cardiovascular diseases**
AHA: 1Q, '04, 6

V17.41 Family history of sudden cardiac death [SCD]
> EXCLUDES *family history of ischemic heart disease (V17.3)*
> *family history of myocardial infarction (V17.3)*
AHA: 4Q, '07, 98

V17.49 Family history of other cardiovascular diseases
Family history of cardiovascular disease NOS

V17.5 Asthma

V17.6 Other chronic respiratory conditions

V17.7 Arthritis

✓5th **V17.8 Other musculoskeletal diseases**

V17.81 Osteoporosis
AHA: 4Q, '05, 95

V17.89 Other musculoskeletal diseases

✓4th **V18 Family history of certain other specific conditions**

V18.0 Diabetes mellitus
AHA: 1Q, '04, 8
TIP: Assign for a normal infant born to a diabetic mother who presents with no manifestations of the syndrome.

✓5th **V18.1 Other endocrine and metabolic diseases**

V18.11 Multiple endocrine neoplasia [MEN] syndrome
AHA: 4Q, '07, 98, 100

V18.19 Other endocrine and metabolic diseases

V18.2 Anemia

V18.3 Other blood disorders

V18.4 Mental retardation

✓5th **V18.5 Digestive disorders**

V18.51 Colonic polyps
> EXCLUDES *family history of malignant neoplasm of gastrointestinal tract (V16.0)*
AHA: 4Q, '06, 117
Z83.71 Family history of colonic polyps   I-10

V18.59 Other digestive disorders

✓5th **V18.6 Kidney diseases**

V18.61 Polycystic kidney

V18.69 Other kidney diseases

V18.7 Other genitourinary diseases

V18.8 Infectious and parasitic diseases

V18.9 Genetic disease carrier
AHA: 4Q, '05, 95

✓4th **V19 Family history of other conditions**

V19.0 Blindness or visual loss

V19.1 Other eye disorders

V19.2 Deafness or hearing loss

V19.3 Other ear disorders

V19.4 Skin conditions

V19.5 Congenital anomalies

V19.6 Allergic disorders

V19.7 Consanguinity

V19.8 Other condition

PERSONS ENCOUNTERING HEALTH SERVICES IN CIRCUMSTANCES RELATED TO REPRODUCTION AND DEVELOPMENT (V20-V29)

✓4th **V20 Health supervision of infant or child**

² **V20.0 Foundling**   P

V20.1 Other healthy infant or child receiving care   P
Medical or nursing care supervision of healthy infant in cases of:
maternal illness, physical or psychiatric
socioeconomic adverse condition at home
too many children at home preventing or interfering with normal care
AHA: 1Q, '00, 25; 3Q, '89, 14

V20.2 Routine infant or child health check   P
Developmental testing of infant or child
►Health check for child over 28 days old◄
Immunizations appropriate for age
Routine vision and hearing testing
Use additional code(s) to identify:
special screening examination(s) performed (V73.0-V82.9)
> EXCLUDES ► *health check for child under 29 days old (V20.31-V20.32)*
> *newborn health supervision (V20.31-V20.32)*◄
> *special screening for developmental handicaps (V79.3)*
AHA: ►1Q, '09, 15;◄ 1Q, '04, 15

● ✓5th **V20.3 Newborn health supervision**
Health check for child under 29 days old
> EXCLUDES *health check for child over 28 days old (V20.2)*

● **V20.31 Health supervision for newborn under 8 days old**   N
Health check for newborn under 8 days old

● **V20.32 Health supervision for newborn 8 to 28 days old**   N
Health check for newborn 8 to 28 days old
Newborn weight check

✓4th **V21 Constitutional states in development**

V21.0 Period of rapid growth in childhood

V21.1 Puberty

V21.2 Other adolecsence

✓5th **V21.3 Low birth weight status**
> EXCLUDES *history of perinatal problems*
AHA: 4Q, '00, 51
TIP: There are no age restrictions on these V codes after the perinatal period; assign for patients without the initial condition who may continue to manifest the consequences of it.

V21.30 Low birth weight status, unspecified

V21.31 Low birth weight status, less than 500 grams

V21.32 Low birth weight status, 500-999 grams

V21.33 Low birth weight status, 1000-1499 grams

V21.34 Low birth weight status, 1500-1999 grams

V21.35 Low birth weight status, 2000-2500 grams

V21.8 Other specified constitutional states in development

V21.9 Unspecified constitutional state in development

² These V codes may be used as principal diagnosis on Medicare patients.

✓4th Additional Digit Required   Unacceptable PDx   Manifestation Code   Hospital Acquired Condition   ►◄ Revised Text   ● New Code   ▲ Revised Code Title
✓5th
2010 ICD-9-CM   October 2009 · Volume 1 – 373

✓4th **V22 Normal pregnancy**

> EXCLUDES   pregnancy examination or test, pregnancy unconfirmed (V72.40)

AHA: 4Q, '07, 125

TIP: Do not assign with any code from chapter 11, "Complications of Pregnancy, Childbirth, and the Puerperium."

These codes are assigned only as principal DX- no chapter 11 codes used

V22.0 Supervision of normal first pregnancy ♀

AHA: 3Q, '99, 16

Z34.00 Encounter suprvisn norm 1 pregnancy uns trimestr   I-10

V22.1 Supervision of other normal pregnancy ♀

AHA: 3Q, '99, 16

Never assigned as principal DX and no chapter 11 codes used

V22.2 Pregnant state, incidental ♀

Pregnant state NOS

✓4th **V23 Supervision of high-risk pregnancy**

AHA: 1Q, '90, 10

Can be used as principal or additional codes, chapter 11 codes can be used.

V23.0 Pregnancy with history of infertility M ♀

V23.1 Pregnancy with history of trophoblastic disease M ♀

Pregnancy with history of:
     hydatidiform mole
     vesicular mole

> EXCLUDES   that without current pregnancy (V13.1)

V23.2 Pregnancy with history of abortion M ♀

Pregnancy with history of conditions classifiable to 634-638

Not assigned to pregnant patient... see

> EXCLUDES   habitual aborter:
>   care during pregnancy (646.3)
>   that without current pregnancy (629.81)

V23.3 Grand multiparity M ♀

> EXCLUDES   care in relation to labor and delivery (659.4)
>   that without current pregnancy (V61.5)

✓5th **V23.4 Pregnancy with other poor obstetric history**

Pregnancy with history of other conditions classifiable to 630-676

V23.41 Pregnancy with history of pre-term labor M ♀

AHA: 4Q, '02, 79

V23.49 Pregnancy with other poor obstetric history M ♀

V23.5 Pregnancy with other poor reproductive history M ♀

Pregnancy with history of stillbirth or neonatal death

V23.7 Insufficient prenatal care M ♀

History of little or no prenatal care

✓5th **V23.8 Other high-risk pregnancy –** *Supervision*

AHA: 4Q, '08, 158; 4Q, '98, 56, 63

V23.81 Elderly primigravida M ♀

First pregnancy in a woman who will be 35 years of age or older at expected date of delivery

> EXCLUDES   elderly primigravida complicating pregnancy (659.5)

Complications due to patient's age – see 659.XX

V23.82 Elderly multigravida M ♀

Second or more pregnancy in a woman who will be 35 years of age or older at expected date of delivery

> EXCLUDES   elderly multigravida complicating pregnancy (659.6)

V23.83 Young primigravida M ♀

First pregnancy in a female less than 16 years old at expected date of delivery

> EXCLUDES   young primigravida complicating pregnancy (659.8)

V23.84 Young multigravida M ♀

Second or more pregnancy in a female less than 16 years old at expected date of delivery

> EXCLUDES   young multigravida complicating pregnancy (659.8)

V23.85 Pregnancy resulting from assisted reproductive technology M ♀

Pregnancy resulting from in vitro fertilization

AHA: 4Q, '08, 160

V23.86 Pregnancy with history of in utero procedure during previous pregnancy M ♀

> EXCLUDES   management of pregnancy affected by in utero procedure during current pregnancy
> ▶(679.0-679.1)◄

AHA: 4Q, '08, 158, 160

V23.89 Other high-risk pregnancy M ♀

AHA: 3Q, '06, 14

V23.9 Unspecified high-risk pregnancy M ♀

✓4th **V24 Postpartum care and examination**

Coded as principal diagnosis unless postpartum complication is present

[2] **V24.0 Immediately after delivery** M ♀

Care and observation in uncomplicated cases

AHA: 3Q, '06, 11

V24.1 Lactating mother ♀

Supervision of lactation

V24.2 Routine postpartum follow-up ♀

✓4th **V25 Encounter for contraceptive management**

AHA: 4Q, '92, 24

✓5th **V25.0 General counseling and advice**

V25.01 Prescription of oral contraceptives ♀

V25.02 Initiation of other contraceptive measures

Fitting of diaphragm
Prescription of foams, creams, or other agents

AHA: 3Q, '97, 7

V25.03 Encounter for emergency contraceptive counseling and prescription

Encounter for postcoital contraceptive counseling and prescription

AHA: 4Q, '03, 84

V25.04 Counseling and instruction in natural family planning to avoid pregnancy

AHA: 4Q, '07, 99

Z30.02 Counsel & instruct natural family plan avoid pg   I-10

V25.09 Other

Family planning advice

V25.1 Insertion of intrauterine contraceptive device ♀

[2] **V25.2 Sterilization**

Admission for interruption of fallopian tubes or vas deferens

Can be used as solo diagnosis code unless part of other treatment

[2] **V25.3 Menstrual extraction** ♀

Menstrual regulation

✓5th **V25.4 Surveillance of previously prescribed contraceptive methods**

Checking, reinsertion, or removal of contraceptive device
Repeat prescription for contraceptive method
Routine examination in connection with contraceptive maintenance

> EXCLUDES   presence of intrauterine contraceptive device as incidental finding (V45.5)

V25.40 Contraceptive surveillance, unspecified

V25.41 Contraceptive pill ♀

V25.42 Intrauterine contraceptive device ♀

Checking, reinsertion, or removal of intrauterine device

V25.43 Implantable subdermal contraceptive ♀

V25.49 Other contraceptive method

AHA: 3Q, '97, 7

V25.5 Insertion of implantable subdermal contraceptive ♀

AHA: 3Q, '92, 9

[2] These V codes may be used as principal diagnosis on Medicare patients.

N Newborn Age: 0   P Pediatric Age: 0-17   M Maternity Age: 12-55   A Adult Age: 15-124   MCC Major CC Condition   CC CC Condition   HIV HIV Related Dx

V25.8   **Other specified contraceptive management**
    Postvasectomy sperm count
    EXCLUDES   *sperm count following sterilization reversal (V26.22)*
                  sperm count for fertility testing (V26.21)
    AHA: 3Q, '96, 9

V25.9   **Unspecified contraceptive management**

✓4th **V26**   **Procreative management**

[2] **V26.0**   **Tuboplasty or vasoplasty after previous sterilization**
    AHA: 2Q, '95, 10
    TIP: Assign for encounters for tubal ligation or vasectomy reversal procedures.

V26.1   **Artificial insemination**   ♀

✓5th **V26.2**   **Investigation and testing**
    EXCLUDES   *postvasectomy sperm count (V25.8)*
    AHA: 4Q, '00, 56

    V26.21   **Fertility testing**
         Fallopian insufflation
         Sperm count for fertility testing
         EXCLUDES   *genetic counseling and testing (V26.31-V26.39)*

    V26.22   **Aftercare following sterilization reversal**
         Fallopian insufflation following sterilization reversal
         Sperm count following sterilization reversal

    V26.29   **Other investigation and testing**
         AHA: 2Q, '96, 9; N-D, '85, 15

✓5th **V26.3**   **Genetic counseling and testing**
    EXCLUDES   *fertility testing (V26.21)*
                  nonprocreative genetic screening (V82.71, V82.79)
    AHA: 4Q, '05, 96

    V26.31   **Testing of female for genetic disease carrier status**   ♀
         AHA: 4Q, '06, 117

    V26.32   **Other genetic testing of female**   ♀
         Use additional code to identify habitual aborter (629.81, 646.3)
         AHA: 4Q, '06, 117
         Z31.438 Encounter oth genetic test female procreative mngmnt   I-10

    V26.33   **Genetic counseling**

    V26.34   **Testing of male for genetic disease carrier status**   ♂
         AHA: 4Q, '06, 117

    V26.35   **Encounter for testing of male partner of habitual aborter**   ♂
         AHA: 4Q, '06, 117

    V26.39   **Other genetic testing of male**   ♂
         AHA: 4Q, '06, 117

✓5th **V26.4**   **General counseling and advice**

    V26.41   **Procreative counseling and advice using natural family planning**
         AHA: 4Q, '07, 99

    V26.42   **Encounter for fertility preservation counseling**
         Encounter for fertility preservation counseling prior to cancer therapy
         Encounter for fertility preservation counseling prior to surgical removal of gonads

    V26.49   **Other procreative management, counseling and advice**

✓5th **V26.5**   **Sterilization status**

    V26.51   **Tubal ligation status**   ♀
         EXCLUDES   *infertility not due to previous tubal ligation (628.0-628.9)*
         Z98.51 Tubal ligation status   I-10

    V26.52   **Vasectomy status**   ♂

✓5th **V26.8**   **Other specified procreative management**

    V26.81   **Encounter for assisted reproductive fertility procedure cycle**   ♀
         Patient undergoing in vitro fertilization cycle
         Use additional code to identify the type of infertility
         EXCLUDES   *pre-cycle diagnosis and testing—code to reason for encounter*
         AHA: 4Q, '07, 99

    V26.82   **Encounter for fertility preservation procedure**
         Encounter for fertility preservation procedure prior to cancer therapy
         Encounter for fertility preservation procedure prior to surgical removal of gonads

    V26.89   **Other specified procreative management**

V26.9   **Unspecified procreative management**

✓4th **V27**   **Outcome of delivery**
    Note: This category is intended for the coding of the outcome of delivery on the mother's record.
    AHA: 2Q, '91, 16
    TIP: Assign on the maternal chart for every admission during which a delivery occurs.

V27.0   **Single liveborn**   M ♀
    AHA: 4Q, '08, 192; 4Q, '05, 81; 2Q, '03, 9; 2Q, '02, 10; 1Q, '01, 10; 3Q, '00, 5; 4Q, '98, 77; 4Q, '95, 59; 1Q, '92, 9
    Z37.0 Single live birth   I-10

V27.1   **Single stillborn**   M ♀

V27.2   **Twins, both liveborn**   M ♀
    Z37.2 Twins both liveborn   I-10

V27.3   **Twins, one liveborn and one stillborn**   M ♀

V27.4   **Twins, both stillborn**   M ♀

V27.5   **Other multiple birth, all liveborn**   M ♀

V27.6   **Other multiple birth, some liveborn**   M ♀

V27.7   **Other multiple birth, all stillborn**   M ♀

V27.9   **Unspecified outcome of delivery**   M ♀
    Single birth }
    Multiple birth } outcome to infant unspecified

✓4th **V28**   **Encounter for antenatal screening of mother**
    EXCLUDES   *abnormal findings on screening — code to findings*
                  routine prenatal care (V22.0-V23.9)
                  suspected fetal conditions affecting management of pregnancy (655.00-655.93, 656.00-656.93, 657.00-657.03, 658.00-658.93)
                  suspected fetal conditions not found (V89.01-V89.09)
    AHA: 4Q, '06, 117; 1Q, '04, 11

V28.0   **Screening for chromosomal anomalies by amniocentesis**   M ♀

V28.1   **Screening for raised alpha-fetoprotein levels in amniotic fluid**   M ♀

V28.2   **Other screening based on amniocentesis**   M ♀

V28.3   **Encounter for routine screening for malformation using ultrasonics**
    Encounter for routine fetal ultrasound NOS
    EXCLUDES   *encounter for fetal anatomic survey (V28.81)*
                  genetic counseling and testing (V26.31-V26.39)

V28.4   **Screening for fetal growth retardation using ultrasonics**   ♀

---

[2]   These V codes may be used as principal diagnosis on Medicare patients.

✓4th / ✓5th   Additional Digit Required   Unacceptable PDx   Manifestation Code   Hospital Acquired Condition   ►◄ Revised Text   ● New Code   ▲ Revised Code Title

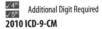

2010 ICD-9-CM   **October 2009 · Volume 1 – 375**

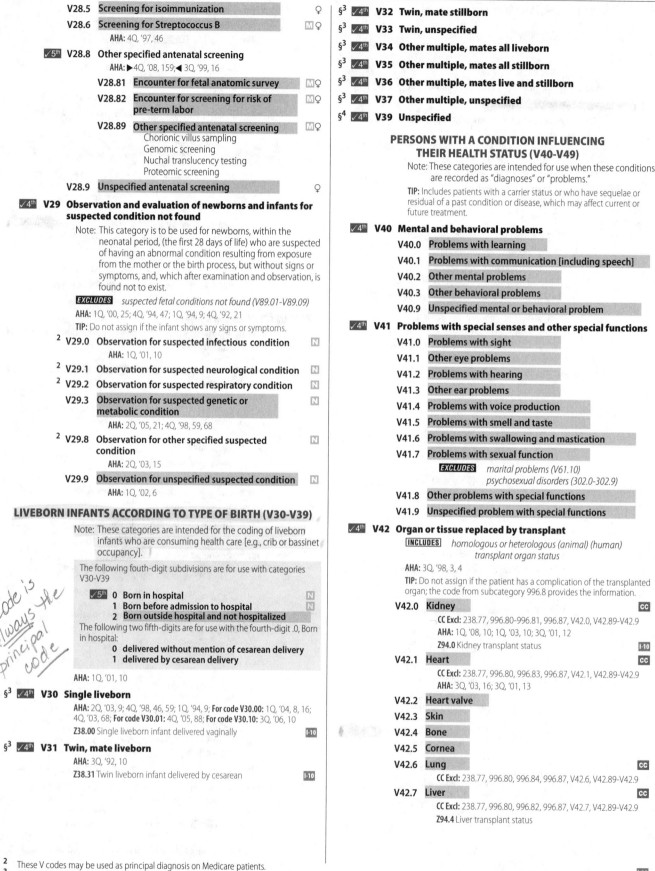

2 These V codes may be used as principal diagnosis on Medicare patients.
3 These codes with a fourth-digit of 0 or 1 may be used as a principal diagnosis for Medicare patients
4 These codes with a fourth-digit of 0 may be used as a prinicpal diagnosis for Medicare patients
§ Requires fourth- and fifth-digit. See beginning of section V30-V39 for codes and definitions.

N Newborn Age: 0   P Pediatric Age: 0-17   M Maternity Age: 12-55   A Adult Age: 15-124   MCC Major CC Condition   CC CC Condition   HIV HIV Related Dx

376 – Volume 1 · February 2009   2010 ICD-9-CM

V42.8 Other specified organ or tissue
AHA: 4Q, '98, 64; 4Q, '97, 49

V42.81 Bone marrow `CC`
CC Excl: 238.77, 279.50-279.53, 996.80, 996.85, 996.87, V42.9

V42.82 Peripheral stem cells `CC`
CC Excl: 238.77, 996.80, 996.87, V42.9

V42.83 Pancreas `CC`
CC Excl: 238.77, 996.80, 996.86-996.87, V42.83, V42.9
AHA: 1Q, '03, 10; 2Q, '01, 16

V42.84 Intestines `CC`
CC Excl: 238.77, 996.80, 996.89, V42.84-V42.9
AHA: 4Q, '00, 48, 50

V42.89 Other

V42.9 Unspecified organ or tissue

V43 Organ or tissue replaced by other means `√4th`
INCLUDES organ or tissue assisted by other means
replacement of organ by:
artificial device
mechanical device
prosthesis
EXCLUDES cardiac pacemaker in situ (V45.01)
fitting and adjustment of prosthetic device (V52.0-V52.9)
renal dialysis status (V45.11)

V43.0 Eye globe

V43.1 Lens
Pseudophakos
AHA: 4Q, '98, 65

V43.2 Heart `√5th`
AHA: 4Q, '03, 85

V43.21 Heart assist device `CC`
CC Excl: 238.77, 996.80, 996.83, 996.87, V42.1, V43.21-V43.22

V43.22 Fully implantable artificial heart `CC`
CC Excl: See code: V43.21

V43.3 Heart valve
AHA: 3Q, '06, 7; 3Q, '02, 13, 14
TIP: If the status post heart valve replacement information includes "porcine" or mention of other homologous or heterologous tissue, assign instead V42.2.
Z95.2 Presence of prosthetic heart valve `I-10`

V43.4 Blood vessel

V43.5 Bladder

V43.6 Joint `√5th`
AHA: 4Q, '05, 91

V43.60 Unspecified joint

V43.61 Shoulder

V43.62 Elbow

V43.63 Wrist

V43.64 Hip
AHA: ▶1Q, '09, 6;◀ 2Q, '08, 3-5; 3Q, '06, 4, 5; 4Q, '05, 93, 112; 2Q, '04, 15
Z96.641 Presence of right artificial hip joint `I-10`

V43.65 Knee
AHA: 3Q, '06, 5

V43.66 Ankle

V43.69 Other

V43.7 Limb

V43.8 Other organ or tissue `√5th`

V43.81 Larynx
AHA: 4Q, '95, 55

V43.82 Breast
AHA: 4Q, '95, 55
Z98.82 Breast implant status `I-10`

V43.83 Artificial skin

V43.89 Other

V44 Artificial opening status `√4th`
EXCLUDES artificial openings requiring attention or management (V55.0-V55.9)
TIP: Do not assign if the patient has a complication of the artificial opening, such as infection or obstruction; assign only the complication code.

V44.0 Tracheostomy
AHA: 4Q, '03, 103, 107, 111; 1Q, '01, 6

V44.1 Gastrostomy
AHA: 4Q, '03, 103, 107-108, 110; 1Q, '01, 12; 3Q, '97, 12; 1Q, '93, 26

V44.2 Ileostomy

V44.3 Colostomy
AHA: 4Q, '03, 110
Z93.3 Colostomy status `I-10`

V44.4 Other artificial opening of gastrointestinal tract

V44.5 Cystostomy `√5th`

V44.50 Cystostomy, unspecified

V44.51 Cutaneous-vesicostomy

V44.52 Appendico-vesicostomy

V44.59 Other cystostomy

V44.6 Other artificial opening of urinary tract
Nephrostomy
Ureterostomy
Urethrostomy

V44.7 Artificial vagina

V44.8 Other artificial opening status

V44.9 Unspecified artificial opening status

V45 Other postprocedural states `√4th`
EXCLUDES aftercare management (V51-V58.9)
malfunction or other complication — code to condition
AHA: 4Q, '03, 85

V45.0 Cardiac device in situ `√5th`
EXCLUDES artificial heart (V43.22)
heart assist device (V43.21)

V45.00 Unspecified cardiac device

V45.01 Cardiac pacemaker

V45.02 Automatic implantable cardiac defibrillator
Z95.810 Presence auto implantable cardiac defibrillator `I-10`

V45.09 Other specified cardiac device
Carotid sinus pacemaker in situ

V45.1 Renal dialysis status `√5th`
EXCLUDES admission for dialysis treatment or session (V56.0)
AHA: 4Q, '08, 157; 1Q, '08, 10; 4Q, '07, 86; 3Q, '07, 9; 4Q, '06, 136; 4Q, '05, 96; 2Q, '03, 7; 2Q, '01, 12, 13

V45.11 Renal dialysis status
Hemodialysis status
Patient requiring intermittent renal dialysis
Peritoneal dialysis status
Presence of arterial-venous shunt (for dialysis)
AHA: 4Q, '08, 157, 193
Z99.2 Dependence on renal dialysis `I-10`

V45.12 Noncompliance with renal dialysis

V45.2 Presence of cerebrospinal fluid drainage device
Cerebral ventricle (communicating) shunt, valve, or device in situ
EXCLUDES malfunction (996.2)
AHA: 4Q, '03, 106

√4th √5th Additional Digit Required | Unacceptable PDx | Manifestation Code | Hospital Acquired Condition | ▶◀ Revised Text | ● New Code | ▲ Revised Code Title

V45.3 **Intestinal bypass or anastomosis status**
> **EXCLUDES** *bariatric surgery status (V45.86)*
> *gastric bypass status (V45.86)*
> *obesity surgery status (V45.86)*

V45.4 **Arthrodesis status**
> **AHA:** N-D, '84, 18
> **TIP:** If there is a complication of the fusion graft site that requires refusion or revision, assign instead a code from subcategory 996.4.

√5ᵗʰ **V45.5** **Presence of contraceptive device**
> **EXCLUDES** *checking, reinsertion, or removal of device (V25.42)*
> *complication from device (996.32)*
> *insertion of device (V25.1)*

V45.51 **Intrauterine contraceptive device** ♀
> **Z97.5** Presence of intrauterine contraceptive device ⃞I-10

V45.52 **Subdermal contraceptive implant**

V45.59 **Other**

√5ᵗʰ **V45.6** **States following surgery of eye and adnexa**
> Cataract extraction
> Filtering bleb ⎫ state following eye
> Surgical eyelid adhesion ⎭ surgery
>
> **EXCLUDES** *aphakia (379.31)*
> *artificial eye globe (V43.0)*
> **AHA:** 4Q, '98, 65; 4Q, '97, 49

V45.61 **Cataract extraction status**
> Use additional code for associated artificial lens status (V43.1)

V45.69 **Other states following surgery of eye and adnexa**
> **AHA:** 2Q, '01, 16; 1Q, '98, 10; 4Q, '97, 19

√5ᵗʰ **V45.7** **Acquired absence of organ**
> **AHA:** 4Q, '98, 65; 4Q, '97, 50

² **V45.71** **Acquired absence of breast and nipple**
> **EXCLUDES** ▶ *congenital absence of breast and nipple (757.6)*◀
> **AHA:** 4Q, '08, 159; 4Q, '01, 66; 4Q, '97, 50

V45.72 **Acquired absence of intestine (large) (small)**

V45.73 **Acquired absence of kidney**

V45.74 **Other parts of urinary tract**
> Bladder
> **AHA:** 4Q, '00, 51

V45.75 **Stomach**
> **AHA:** 4Q, '00, 51

V45.76 **Lung**
> **AHA:** 4Q, '00, 51

V45.77 **Genital organs**
> **EXCLUDES** *acquired absence of cervix and uterus (V88.01-V88.03)*
> *female genital mutilation status (629.20-629.29)*
> **AHA:** 1Q, '03, 13, 14; 4Q, '00, 51

V45.78 **Eye**
> **AHA:** 4Q, '00, 51

V45.79 **Other acquired absence of organ**
> **AHA:** 4Q, '00, 51

√5ᵗʰ **V45.8** **Other postprocedural status**

V45.81 **Aortocoronary bypass status**
> **AHA:** 4Q, '03, 105; 3Q, '01, 15; 3Q, '97, 16

V45.82 **Percutaneous transluminal coronary angioplasty status**

V45.83 **Breast implant removal status**
> **AHA:** 4Q, '95, 55

V45.84 **Dental restoration status**
> Dental crowns status
> Dental fillings status
> **AHA:** 4Q, '01, 54

V45.85 **Insulin pump status**

V45.86 **Bariatric surgery status**
> Gastric banding status
> Gastric bypass status for obesity
> Obesity surgery status
>
> **EXCLUDES** *bariatric surgery status complicating pregnancy, childbirth or the puerperium (649.2)* •
> *intestinal bypass or anastomosis status (V45.3)*
> **AHA:** ▶2Q, '09, 10;◀ 4Q, '06, 118
> **Z98.84** Bariatric surgery status ⃞I-10

V45.87 **Transplanted organ removal status** ●
> Transplanted organ previously removed due to complication, failure, rejection or infection
>
> **EXCLUDES** *encounter for removal of transplanted organ — code to complication of transplanted organ (996.80-996.89)*
> **AHA:** 4Q, '08, 157

V45.88 **Status post administration of tPA (rtPA) in a different facility within the last 24 hours prior to admission to current facility**
> Code first condition requiring tPA administration, such as:
> acute cerebral infarction (433.0-433.9 with fifth- digit 1, 434.0-434.9 with fifth digit 1)
> acute myocardial infarction (410.00-410.92)
> **AHA:** 4Q, '08, 157
> **TIP:** Assign only on receiving facility record; assign even if the patient is still receiving tPA at the time of transfer.

V45.89 **Other**
> Presence of neuropacemaker or other electronic device
>
> **EXCLUDES** *artificial heart valve in situ (V43.3)*
> *vascular prosthesis in situ (V43.4)*
> **AHA:** 1Q, '95, 11

√4ᵗʰ **V46** **Other dependence on machines and devices**

V46.0 **Aspirator**

√5ᵗʰ **V46.1** **Respirator [Ventilator]**
> Iron lung
> **AHA:** 4Q, '05, 96; 4Q, '03, 103; 1Q, '01, 12; J-F, '87, 7 3

² **V46.11** **Dependence on respirator, status** ⃞CC
> **CC Excl:** V46.0-V46.2, V46.8-V46.9
> **AHA:** 4Q, '04, 100
> **Z99.11** Dependence on respirator ventilator status ⃞I-10

² **V46.12** **Encounter for respirator dependence during power failure** ⃞CC
> **CC Excl:** See code V46.11
> **AHA:** 4Q, '04, 100

² **V46.13** **Encounter for weaning from respirator [ventilator]** ⃞CC
> **CC Excl:** See code V46.11

² **V46.14** **Mechanical complication of respirator [ventilator]** ⃞CC
> Mechanical failure of respirator [ventilator]
> **CC Excl:** See code V46.11

V46.2 **Supplemental oxygen**
> Long-term oxygen therapy
> **AHA:** 4Q, '03, 108; 4Q, '02, 79

---

² These V codes may be used as principal diagnosis on Medicare patients.

⃞N Newborn Age: 0 ⃞P Pediatric Age: 0-17 ⃞M Maternity Age: 12-55 ⃞A Adult Age: 15-124 ⃞MCC Major CC Condition ⃞CC CC Condition ⃞HIV HIV Related Dx

V46.3   **Wheelchair dependence**
Wheelchair confinement status
Code first cause of dependence, such as:
muscular dystrophy (359.1)
obesity (278.00, 278.01)
AHA: 4Q, '08, 157

V46.8   **Other enabling machines**
Hyperbaric chamber
Possum [Patient-Operated-Selector-Mechanism]
EXCLUDES   cardiac pacemaker (V45.0)
kidney dialysis machine (V45.11)

V46.9   **Unspecified machine dependence**
AHA: 4Q, '06, 117

✓4ᵗʰ **V47**   **Other problems with internal organs**

V47.0   **Deficiencies of internal organs**

V47.1   **Mechanical and motor problems with internal organs**

V47.2   **Other cardiorespiratory problems**
Cardiovascular exercise intolerance with pain (with):
at rest
less than ordinary activity
ordinary activity

V47.3   **Other digestive problems**

V47.4   **Other urinary problems**

V47.5   **Other genital problems**

V47.9   **Unspecified**

✓4ᵗʰ **V48**   **Problems with head, neck, and trunk**

V48.0   **Deficiencies of head**
EXCLUDES   deficiencies of ears, eyelids, and nose (V48.8)

V48.1   **Deficiencies of neck and trunk**

V48.2   **Mechanical and motor problems with head**

V48.3   **Mechanical and motor problems with neck and trunk**

V48.4   **Sensory problem with head**

V48.5   **Sensory problem with neck and trunk**

V48.6   **Disfigurements of head**

V48.7   **Disfigurements of neck and trunk**

V48.8   **Other problems with head, neck, and trunk**

V48.9   **Unspecified problem with head, neck, or trunk**

V49   **Other conditions influencing health status**

V49.0   **Deficiencies of limbs**

V49.1   **Mechanical problems with limbs**

V49.2   **Motor problems with limbs**

V49.3   **Sensory problems with limbs**

V49.4   **Disfigurements of limbs**

V49.5   **Other problems of limbs**

✓5ᵗʰ **V49.6**   **Upper limb amputation status**
AHA: 4Q, '05, 94; 4Q, '98, 42; 4Q, '94, 39

V49.60   **Unspecified level**
Z89.201 Acquired absence of right upper   I-10
limb uns level

V49.61   **Thumb**

V49.62   **Other finger(s)**
AHA: 2Q, '05, 7

V49.63   **Hand**

V49.64   **Wrist**
Disarticulation of wrist

V49.65   **Below elbow**

V49.66   **Above elbow**
Disarticulation of elbow

V49.67   **Shoulder**
Disarticulation of shoulder

✓5ᵗʰ **V49.7**   **Lower limb amputation status**
AHA: 3Q, '06, 5; 4Q, '05, 94; 4Q, '98, 42; 4Q, '94, 39

V49.70   **Unspecified level**

V49.71   **Great toe**

V49.72   **Other toe(s)**

V49.73   **Foot**

V49.74   **Ankle**
Disarticulation of ankle

V49.75   **Below knee**
Z89.52 Acquired absence of left leg below   I-10
knee

V49.76   **Above knee**
Disarticulation of knee
AHA: 2Q, '05, 14

V49.77   **Hip**
Disarticulation of hip

✓5ᵗʰ **V49.8**   **Other specified conditions influencing health status**
AHA: 4Q, '00, 51

V49.81   **Asymptomatic postmenopausal status (age-related) (natural)**   A ♀
EXCLUDES   menopausal and premenopausal
disorder (627.0-627.9)
postsurgical menopause (256.2)
premature menopause (256.31)
symptomatic menopause
(627.0-627.9)
AHA: 4Q, '02, 79; 4Q, '00, 54

V49.82   **Dental sealant status**
AHA: 4Q, '01, 54

V49.83   **Awaiting organ transplant status**

V49.84   **Bed confinement status**
AHA: 4Q, '05, 96

V49.85   **Dual sensory impairment**
Blindness with deafness
Combined visual hearing impairment
Code first:
hearing impairment (389.00-389.9)
visual impairment (369.00-369.9)
AHA: 4Q, '07, 100

V49.89   **Other specified conditions influencing health status**
AHA: 4Q, '05, 94

V49.9   **Unspecified**

PERSONS ENCOUNTERING HEALTH SERVICES FOR SPECIFIC PROCEDURES AND AFTERCARE (V50-V59)

Note: Categories V51-V59 are intended for use to indicate a reason for care in patients who may have already been treated for some disease or injury not now present, or who are receiving care to consolidate the treatment, to deal with residual states, or to prevent recurrence.
EXCLUDES   follow-up examination for medical surveillance
following treatment (V67.0-V67.9)

✓4ᵗʰ **V50**   **Elective surgery for purposes other than remedying health states**

² **V50.0**   **Hair transplant**

² **V50.1**   **Other plastic surgery for unacceptable cosmetic appearance**
Breast augmentation or reduction
Face-lift
EXCLUDES   encounter for breast reduction (611.1)
plastic surgery following healed injury or
operation (V51.0-V51.8)

² **V50.2**   **Routine or ritual circumcision**   ♂
Circumcision in the absence of significant medical
indication

V50.3   **Ear piercing**

²   These V codes may be used as principal diagnosis on Medicare patients.

[handwritten top margin:] For encounters specifically for prophylactic removal of breasts, ovaries, or other organs due to genetic susceptibility or family history of cancer — use as principal diagnosis

[handwritten left margin:] Genetic Susceptibility V 84.XX — Family History V16.XX

✓5th V50.4 Prophylactic organ removal

> EXCLUDES organ donations (V59.0-V59.9)
> therapeutic organ removal — code to condition

AHA: 4Q, '94, 44

TIP: Assign an additional code, such as one from category V16 Family history of malignant neoplasm, to indicate the reason for the prophylactic organ removal.

2 V50.41 Breast

AHA: 4Q, '04, 107

2 V50.42 Ovary ♀

2 V50.49 Other

V50.8 Other

Z40.8 Encounter for other prophylactic surgery [I-10]

V50.9 Unspecified

✓4th V51 Aftercare involving the use of plastic surgery

Plastic surgery following healed injury or operation

> EXCLUDES cosmetic plastic surgery (V50.1)
> plastic surgery as treatment for current condition or injury — code to condition or injury
> repair of scarred tissue — code to scar

AHA: 4Q, '08, 159

[handwritten left margin:] Inappropriate for burn patients admitted for repair of scar tissue, skin contracture, or other sequela. Code for condition being treated.

2 V51.0 Encounter for breast reconstruction following mastectomy [A]

> EXCLUDES deformity and disproportion of reconstructed breast (612.0-612.1)

AHA: 4Q, '08, 159-160

2 V51.8 Other aftercare involving the use of plastic surgery

✓4th V52 Fitting and adjustment of prosthetic device and implant

> INCLUDES removal of device
> EXCLUDES malfunction or complication of prosthetic device (996.0-996.7)
> status only, without need for care (V43.0-V43.8)

AHA: 4Q, '05, 94; 4Q, '95, 55 ; 1Q, '90, 7

2 V52.0 Artificial arm (complete) (partial)

2 V52.1 Artificial leg (complete) (partial)

2 V52.2 Artificial eye

2 V52.3 Dental prosthetic device

2 V52.4 Breast prosthesis and implant ♀

Elective implant exchange (different material) (different size)

Removal of tissue expander without synchronous insertion of permanent implant

> EXCLUDES admission for initial breast implant insertion for breast augmentation (V50.1)
> complications of breast implant (996.54, 996.69, 996.79)
> encounter for breast reconstruction following mastectomy (V51.0)

AHA: 4Q, '95, 80, 81

2 V52.8 Other specified prosthetic device

AHA: 2Q, '02, 12, 16

V52.9 Unspecified prosthetic device

✓4th V53 Fitting and adjustment of other device

> INCLUDES removal of device
> replacement of device
> EXCLUDES status only, without need for care (V45.0-V45.8)

✓5th V53.0 Devices related to nervous system and special senses

AHA: 4Q, '98, 66; 4Q, '97, 51

2 V53.01 Fitting and adjustment of cerebral ventricular (communicating) shunt

AHA: 4Q, '97, 51

2 V53.02 Neuropacemaker (brain) (peripheral nerve) (spinal cord)

2 V53.09 Fitting and adjustment of other devices related to nervous system and special senses

Auditory substitution device
Visual substitution device

AHA: 2Q, '99, 4

V53.1 Spectacles and contact lenses

V53.2 Hearing aid

✓5th V53.3 Cardiac device

Reprogramming

AHA: 3Q, '92, 3; 1Q, '90, 7; M-J, '87, 8 ; N-D, '84, 18

TIP: Assign for cardiac device replacement when the device has reached normal end-of-life parameters.

[handwritten:] Excludes mechanical complications (996.04)

V53.31 Cardiac pacemaker

> EXCLUDES mechanical complication of cardiac pacemaker (996.01)

AHA: 1Q, '02, 3

V53.32 Automatic implantable cardiac defibrillator

AHA: 3Q, '05, 8

V53.39 Other cardiac device

AHA: 2Q, '08, 9; 1Q, '07, 20

V53.4 Orthodontic devices

▲ **✓5th V53.5 Other gastrointestinal appliance and device**

> EXCLUDES colostomy (V55.3)
> ileostomy (V55.2)
> other artificial opening of digestive tract (V55.4)

● **V53.50 Fitting and adjustment of intestinal appliance and device**

● **V53.51 Fitting and adjustment of gastric lap band**

● **V53.59 Fitting and adjustment of other gastrointestinal appliance and device**

V53.6 Urinary devices

Urinary catheter

> EXCLUDES cystostomy (V55.5)
> nephrostomy (V55.6)
> ureterostomy (V55.6)
> urethrostomy (V55.6)

V53.7 Orthopedic devices

Orthopedic: Orthopedic
  brace   corset
  cast   shoes

> EXCLUDES other orthopedic aftercare (V54)

V53.8 Wheelchair

✓5th V53.9 Other and unspecified device

AHA: 2Q, '03, 6

V53.90 Unspecified device

V53.91 Fitting and adjustment of insulin pump

Insulin pump titration

V53.99 Other device

AHA: ▶2Q, '09, 10◀

✓4th V54 Other orthopedic aftercare

> EXCLUDES fitting and adjustment of orthopedic devices (V53.7)
> malfunction of internal orthopedic device (996.40-996.49)
> other complication of nonmechanical nature (996.60-996.79)

AHA: 4Q, '08, 158; 1Q, '07, 3-4; 3Q, '95, 3

✓5th V54.0 Aftercare involving internal fixation device

> EXCLUDES malfunction of internal orthopedic device (996.40-996.49)
> other complication of nonmechanical nature (996.60-996.79)
> removal of external fixation device (V54.89)

AHA: 4Q, '03, 87

[handwritten:] Do not code current fracture

2 V54.01 Encounter for removal of internal fixation device

2 These V codes may be used as principal diagnosis on Medicare patients.

[N] Newborn Age: 0   [P] Pediatric Age: 0-17   [M] Maternity Age: 12-55   [A] Adult Age: 15-124   [MCC] Major CC Condition   [CC] CC Condition   [HIV] HIV Related Dx

380 – Volume 1 · October 2009   2010 ICD-9-CM

(2) **V54.02** Encounter for lengthening/adjustment of growth rod

(2) **V54.09** Other aftercare involving internal fixation device

√5th **V54.1** **Aftercare for healing traumatic fracture**
> **EXCLUDES** ▶ aftercare following joint replacement (V54.81)◀
> aftercare for amputation stump (V54.89)

> AHA: 4Q, '02, 80

> **TIP:** Assign for follow-up and treatment during the healing phase of the fracture; an aftercare code should be used for all subsequent encounters after the initial encounter for care of a fracture.

² **V54.10** Aftercare for healing traumatic fracture of arm, unspecified

² **V54.11** Aftercare for healing traumatic fracture of upper arm

² **V54.12** Aftercare for healing traumatic fracture of lower arm
> AHA: 1Q, '07, 7

² **V54.13** Aftercare for healing traumatic fracture of hip
> AHA: ▶1Q, '09, 6;◀ 4Q, '03, 103, 105; 2Q, '03, 16

² **V54.14** Aftercare for healing traumatic fracture of leg, unspecified

² **V54.15** Aftercare for healing traumatic fracture of upper leg
> **EXCLUDES** aftercare for healing traumatic fracture of hip (V54.13)

> AHA: 3Q, '06, 6

² **V54.16** Aftercare for healing traumatic fracture of lower leg

² **V54.17** Aftercare for healing traumatic fracture of vertebrae

² **V54.19** Aftercare for healing traumatic fracture of other bone
> AHA: 1Q, '05, 13; 4Q, '02, 80

√5th **V54.2** **Aftercare for healing pathologic fracture**
> **EXCLUDES** ▶ aftercare following joint replacement (V54.81)◀

> AHA: 4Q, '02, 80

² **V54.20** Aftercare for healing pathologic fracture of arm, unspecified

² **V54.21** Aftercare for healing pathologic fracture of upper arm

² **V54.22** Aftercare for healing pathologic fracture of lower arm

² **V54.23** Aftercare for healing pathologic fracture of hip

² **V54.24** Aftercare for healing pathologic fracture of leg, unspecified

² **V54.25** Aftercare for healing pathologic fracture of upper leg
> **EXCLUDES** aftercare for healing pathologic fracture of hip (V54.23)

² **V54.26** Aftercare for healing pathologic fracture of lower leg

² **V54.27** Aftercare for healing pathologic fracture of vertebrae
> AHA: 1Q, '07, 6; 4Q, '03, 108

² **V54.29** Aftercare for healing pathologic fracture of other bone
> AHA: 4Q, '02, 80

√5th **V54.8** **Other orthopedic aftercare**
> AHA: 3Q, '01, 19; 4Q, '99, 5

² **V54.81** Aftercare following joint replacement
> Use additional code to identify joint replacement site (V43.60-V43.69)
> AHA: ▶1Q, '09, 6;◀ 3Q, '06, 4; 2Q, '04, 15; 4Q, '02, 80

² **V54.89** Other orthopedic aftercare
> Aftercare for healing fracture NOS

V54.9 Unspecified orthopedic aftercare

√4th **V55** **Attention to artificial openings**
> **INCLUDES** adjustment or repositioning of catheter
> closure
> passage of sounds or bougies
> reforming
> removal or replacement of catheter
> toilet or cleansing
> **EXCLUDES** complications of external stoma (519.00-519.09, 569.60-569.69, 997.4, 997.5)
> status only, without need for care (V44.0-V44.9)

² **V55.0** Tracheostomy

² **V55.1** Gastrostomy   CC
> **CC Excl:** V55.1
> AHA: 4Q, '99, 9; 3Q, '97, 7, 8; 1Q, '96, 14; 3Q, '95, 13
> **TIP:** Assign for gastrostomy or PEG tube that has been dislodged or clogged, for which simple irrigation or replacement is performed.

² **V55.2** Ileostomy

² **V55.3** Colostomy
> AHA: ▶1Q, '09, 5;◀ 2Q, '05, 4; 3Q, '97, 9
> Z43.3 Encounter for attention to colostomy   I-10

² **V55.4** Other artificial opening of digestive tract
> AHA: 2Q, '05, 14; 1Q, '03, 10

² **V55.5** Cystostomy

² **V55.6** Other artificial opening of urinary tract
> Nephrostomy   Urethrostomy
> Ureterostomy

² **V55.7** Artificial vagina

² **V55.8** Other specified artificial opening

V55.9 Unspecified artificial opening

√4th **V56** **Encounter for dialysis and dialysis catheter care**
> Use additional code to identify the associated condition
> **EXCLUDES** dialysis preparation — code to condition
> AHA: 4Q, '98, 66; 1Q, '93, 29

Can be principal diagnosis with additional code for associated condition

² **V56.0** Extracorporeal dialysis
> Dialysis (renal) NOS
> **EXCLUDES** dialysis status (V45.11)
> AHA: 4Q, '05, 79; 1Q, '04, 23; 4Q, '00, 40; 3Q, '98, 6; 2Q, '98, 20

² **V56.1** Fitting and adjustment of extracorporeal dialysis catheter
> Removal or replacement of catheter
> Toilet or cleansing
> Use additional code for any concurrent extracorporeal dialysis (V56.0)
> AHA: 2Q, '98, 20

V56.2 Fitting and adjustment of peritoneal dialysis catheter
> Use additional code for any concurrent peritoneal dialysis (V56.8)
> AHA: 4Q, '98, 55

√5th **V56.3** Encounter for adequacy testing for dialysis
> AHA: 4Q, '00, 55

V56.31 Encounter for adequacy testing for hemodialysis

V56.32 Encounter for adequacy testing for peritoneal dialysis
> Peritoneal equilibration test

² These V codes may be used as principal diagnosis on Medicare patients.
⁵ Rehabilitation codes acceptable as a principal diagnosis when accompanied by a secondary diagnosis reflecting the condition treated.

√4th √5th Additional Digit Required   Unacceptable PDx   Manifestation Code   Hospital Acquired Condition   ▶◀ Revised Text   ● New Code   ▲ Revised Code Title

2010 ICD-9-CM   **October 2009 • Volume 1 – 381**

² V56.8 Other dialysis
Peritoneal dialysis
AHA: 4Q, '98, 55

Handwritten note: Can be used as principal diagnosis. See notes at beginning of this section.

√4ᵗʰ V57 Care involving use of rehabilitation procedures
Use additional code to identify underlying condition
AHA: 3Q, '06, 3; 1Q, '02, 19; 3Q, '97, 12; 1Q, '90, 6; S-O, '86, 3
TIP: Assign codes from this category for episodes of care related to rehabilitation.

V57.0 Breathing exercises

⁵ V57.1 Other physical therapy
Therapeutic and remedial exercises, except breathing
AHA: 3Q, '06, 4; 2Q, '04, 15; 4Q, '02, 56; 4Q, '99, 5

√5ᵗʰ V57.2 Occupational therapy and vocational rehabilitation

⁵ V57.21 Encounter for occupational therapy
AHA: 4Q, '99, 7

⁵ V57.22 Encounter for vocational therapy

▲ **⁵ V57.3 Speech-language therapy**
AHA: 4Q, '97, 36

V57.4 Orthoptic training

√5ᵗʰ V57.8 Other specified rehabilitation procedure

V57.81 Orthotic training
Gait training in the use of artificial limbs

⁵ V57.89 Other
Multiple training or therapy
AHA: 4Q, '07, 94; 3Q, '06, 6; 4Q, '03, 105-106, 108; 2Q, '03, 16; 1Q '02, 16; 3Q, '01, 21; 3Q, '97, 11, 12; S-O, '86, 4

⁵ V57.9 Unspecified rehabilitation procedure

√4ᵗʰ V58 Encounter for other and unspecified procedures and aftercare
EXCLUDES convalescence and palliative care (V66)
TIP: If a patient is admitted for both radiation therapy and chemotherapy, either code V58.0 or V58.11 may be sequenced as the principal diagnosis.

² V58.0 Radiotherapy
Encounter or admission for radiotherapy
EXCLUDES encounter for radioactive implant — code to condition
radioactive iodine therapy — code to condition
AHA: 3Q, '92, 5; 2Q, '90, 7; J-F, '87, 13
Z51.0 Encounter for antineoplastic radiation therapy **I-10**

√5ᵗʰ V58.1 Encounter for antineoplastic chemotherapy and immunotherapy
Encounter or admission for chemotherapy
EXCLUDES chemotherapy and immunotherapy for nonneoplastic conditions — code to condition
AHA: 1Q, '04, 13; 2Q, '03, 16; 3Q, '93, 4; 2Q, '92, 6; 2Q, '91, 17; 2Q, '90, 7; S-O, '84, 5

² V58.11 Encounter for antineoplastic chemotherapy
AHA: 4Q, '08, 82, 155; 4Q, '07, 104; 2Q, '06, 20-21; 4Q, '05, 98
Z51.11 Encounter for antineoplastic chemotherapy **I-10**

² V58.12 Encounter for antineoplastic immunotherapy
AHA: 4Q, '05, 98

V58.2 Blood transfusion, without reported diagnosis

Handwritten notes: Can only be used as principal diagnosis. Include also 99.25...infusion of cancer chemo substance. V58.11 Not assigned for Intra-Operative Election Radiation Therapy (IOERT)...use 92.41

√5ᵗʰ V58.3 Attention to dressings and sutures
Change or removal of wound packing
EXCLUDES attention to drains (V58.49)
planned postoperative wound closure (V58.41)
AHA: 2Q, '05, 14

V58.30 Encounter for change or removal of nonsurgical wound dressing
Encounter for change or removal of wound dressing NOS
AHA: 4Q, '06, 117

V58.31 Encounter for change or removal of surgical wound dressing
AHA: 4Q, '06, 117
Z48.01 Encounter change/removal surgical wound dressing **I-10**

V58.32 Encounter for removal of sutures
Encounter for removal of staples
AHA: 4Q, '06, 117
Z48.02 Encounter for removal of sutures **I-10**

√5ᵗʰ V58.4 Other aftercare following surgery
Note: Codes from this subcategory should be used in conjunction with other aftercare codes to fully identify the reason for the aftercare encounter
EXCLUDES aftercare following sterilization reversal surgery (V26.22)
attention to artificial openings (V55.0-V55.9)
orthopedic aftercare (V54.0-V54.9)
AHA: 4Q, '99, 9; N-D, '87, 9

⁶ V58.41 Encounter for planned postoperative wound closure
EXCLUDES disruption of operative wound (998.31-998.32)
encounter for dressings and suture aftercare (V58.30-V58.32)
AHA: 4Q, '99, 15

⁶ V58.42 Aftercare following surgery for neoplasm
Conditions classifiable to 140-239
AHA: 4Q, '02, 80

⁶ V58.43 Aftercare following surgery for injury and trauma
Conditions classifiable to 800-999
EXCLUDES aftercare for healing traumatic fracture (V54.10-V54.19)
AHA: 4Q, '02, 80

⁶ V58.44 Aftercare following organ transplant
Use additional code to identify the organ transplanted (V42.0-V42.9)
AHA: 4Q, '04, 101

⁶ V58.49 Other specified aftercare following surgery
Change or removal of drains
AHA: 1Q, '96, 8, 9

⁶ V58.5 Orthodontics
EXCLUDES fitting and adjustment of orthodontic device (V53.4)

---

² These V codes may be used as principal diagnosis on Medicare patients.
⁵ Rehabilitation codes acceptable as a principal diagnosis when accompanied by a secondary diagnosis reflecting the condition treated.
⁶ These V codes are acceptable as principal diagnosis and group to DRGs 949-950.

N Newborn Age: 0   P Pediatric Age: 0-17   M Maternity Age: 12-55   A Adult Age: 15-124   **MCC** Major CC Condition   **CC** CC Condition   **HIV** HIV Related Dx

√5th **V58.6 Long-term (current) drug use**

> **EXCLUDES** *drug abuse and dependence complicating pregnancy (648.3-648.4)*
> *drug abuse (305.00-305.93)*
> *drug dependence (304.00-304.93)*
> *hormone replacement therapy (postmenopausal) (V07.4)*
> *prophylactic use of agents affecting estrogen receptors and estrogen levels (V07.51-V07.59)*

> **AHA:** 4Q, '08, 159; 4Q, '03, 85; 4Q, '02, 84; 3Q, '02, 15; 4Q, '95, 61

> **TIP:** Do not assign for patients on detoxification drugs or maintenance programs to prevent withdrawal symptoms related to drug dependence; assign instead drug dependence code(s).

6 **V58.61 Long-term (current) use of anticoagulants**

> **EXCLUDES** *long-term (current) use of aspirin (V58.66)*

> **AHA:** 4Q, '08, 135; 3Q, '06, 13; 3Q, '04, 7; 4Q, '03, 108; 3Q, '02, 13-16; 1Q, '02, 15, 16

> **Z79.01** Long term (current) use of anticoagulants   `I-10`

V58.62 Long-term (current) use of antibiotics

> **AHA:** 4Q, '98, 59

V58.63 Long-term (current) use of antiplatelets/antithrombotics

> **EXCLUDES** *long-term (current) use of aspirin (V58.66)*

V58.64 Long-term (current) use of non-steroidal anti-inflammatories (NSAID)

> **EXCLUDES** *long-term (current) use of aspirin (V58.66)*

V58.65 Long-term (current) use of steroids

> **Z79.5** Long term (current) use of steroids   `I-10`

V58.66 Long-term (current) use of aspirin

> **AHA:** 4Q, '04, 102

V58.67 Long-term (current) use of insulin

> **AHA:** 4Q, '04, 55-56, 103

> **Z79.4** Long term (current) use of insulin   `I-10`

6 **V58.69 Long-term (current) use of other medications**

> Other high-risk medications
> Long term current use of methadone
> Long term current use of opiate analgesic

> **AHA:** 4Q, '08, 156; 2Q, '04, 10; 1Q, '04, 13; 1Q, '03, 11; 2Q, '00, 8; 3Q, '99, 13; 2Q, '99, 17; 1Q, '97, 12; 2Q, '96, 7

√5th **V58.7 Aftercare following surgery to specified body systems, not elsewhere classified**

> Note: Codes from this subcategory should be used in conjunction with other aftercare codes to fully identify the reason for the aftercare encounter

> **EXCLUDES** *aftercare following organ transplant (V58.44)*
> *aftercare following surgery for neoplasm (V58.42)*

> **AHA:** 4Q, '03, 104; 4Q, '02, 80

6 **V58.71 Aftercare following surgery of the sense organs, NEC**

> Conditions classifiable to 360-379, 380-389

6 **V58.72 Aftercare following surgery of the nervous system, NEC**

> Conditions classifiable to 320-359

> **EXCLUDES** *aftercare following surgery of the sense organs, NEC (V58.71)*

6 **V58.73 Aftercare following surgery of the circulatory system, NEC**

> Conditions classifiable to 390-459

> **AHA:** ▶2Q, '09, 12;◀ 4Q, '03, 105

6 **V58.74 Aftercare following surgery of the respiratory system, NEC**

> Conditions classifiable to 460-519

6 **V58.75 Aftercare following surgery of the teeth, oral cavity and digestive system, NEC**

> Conditions classifiable to 520-579

> **AHA:** 2Q, '05, 14

6 **V58.76 Aftercare following surgery of the genitourinary system, NEC**

> Conditions classifiable to 580-629

> **EXCLUDES** *aftercare following sterilization reversal (V26.22)*

> **AHA:** 1Q, '05, 11-12

6 **V58.77 Aftercare following surgery of the skin and subcutaneous tissue, NEC**

> Conditions classifiable to 680-709

6 **V58.78 Aftercare following surgery of the musculoskeletal system, NEC**

> Conditions classifiable to 710-739

> **EXCLUDES** *orthopedic aftercare (V54.01-V54.9)*

√5th **V58.8 Other specified procedures and aftercare**

> **AHA:** 4Q, '94, 45; 2Q, '94, 8

6 **V58.81 Fitting and adjustment of vascular catheter**

> Removal or replacement of catheter
> Toilet or cleansing

> **EXCLUDES** *complication of renal dialysis (996.73)*
> *complication of vascular catheter (996.74)*
> *dialysis preparation — code to condition*
> *encounter for dialysis (V56.0-V56.8)*
> *fitting and adjustment of dialysis catheter (V56.1)*

6 **V58.82 Fitting and adjustment of nonvascular catheter, NEC**

> Removal or replacement of catheter
> Toilet or cleansing

> **EXCLUDES** *fitting and adjustment of peritoneal dialysis catheter (V56.2)*
> *fitting and adjustment of urinary catheter (V53.6)*

6 **V58.83 Encounter for therapeutic drug monitoring**

> Use additional code for any associated long-term (current) drug use (V58.61-V58.69)

> **EXCLUDES** *blood-drug testing for medicolegal reasons (V70.4)*

> **DEF:** Drug monitoring: Measurement of the level of a specific drug in the body or measurement of a specific function to assess effectiveness of a drug.

> **AHA:** 4Q, '08, 156; 2Q, '04, 10; 1Q, '04, 13; 4Q, '03, 85; 4Q, '02, 84; 3Q, '02, 13-16

6 **V58.89 Other specified aftercare**

> **AHA:** 4Q, '98, 59

6 **V58.9 Unspecified aftercare**

√4th **V59 Donors**

> **EXCLUDES** *examination of potential donor (V70.8)*
> *self-donation of organ or tissue — code to condition*

> **AHA:** 4Q, '95, 62; 1Q, '90, 10; N-D, '84, 8

> **TIP:** Assign only for living donations to other individuals, not for self-donation or for cadaveric donations.

√5th **V59.0 Blood**

> **V59.01 Whole blood**
> **V59.02 Stem cells**
> **V59.09 Other**

2 **V59.1 Skin**

2 **V59.2 Bone**

2 **V59.3 Bone marrow**

2 **V59.4 Kidney**

---

2   These V codes may be used as principal diagnosis on Medicare patients.
6   These V codes are acceptable as principal diagnosis and group to DRGs 949-950.

√4th √5th   Additional Digit Required   Unacceptable PDx   Manifestation Code   Hospital Acquired Condition   ▶◀ Revised Text   ● New Code   ▲ Revised Code Title

² **V59.5** Cornea

² **V59.6** Liver

✓5th **V59.7** **Egg (oocyte) (ovum)**
      AHA: 4Q, '05, 99

      V59.70 **Egg (oocyte) (ovum) donor, unspecified** ♀

      V59.71 **Egg (oocyte) (ovum) donor, under age 35, anonymous recipient** ♀
           Egg donor, under age 35 NOS

      V59.72 **Egg (oocyte) (ovum) donor, under age 35, designated recipient** ♀

      V59.73 **Egg (oocyte) (ovum) donor, age 35 and over, anonymous recipient** ♀
           Egg donor, age 35 and over NOS

      V59.74 **Egg (oocyte) (ovum) donor, age 35 and over, designated recipient** ♀

² **V59.8** Other specified organ or tissue
      AHA: 3Q, '02, 20

² **V59.9** Unspecified organ or tissue

PERSONS ENCOUNTERING HEALTH SERVICES IN OTHER CIRCUMSTANCES (V60-V69)

✓4th **V60** **Housing, household, and economic circumstances**

      V60.0 **Lack of housing**
           Hobos
           Social migrants
           Tramps
           Transients
           Vagabonds

      V60.1 **Inadequate housing**
           Lack of heating
           Restriction of space
           Technical defects in home preventing adequate care

      V60.2 **Inadequate material resources**
           Economic problem
           Poverty NOS

      V60.3 **Person living alone**

      V60.4 **No other household member able to render care**
           Person requiring care (has) (is):
              family member too handicapped, ill, or otherwise unsuited to render care
              partner temporarily away from home
              temporarily away from usual place of abode
           EXCLUDES   *holiday relief care (V60.5)*

      V60.5 **Holiday relief care**
           Provision of health care facilities to a person normally cared for at home, to enable relatives to take a vacation

      V60.6 **Person living in residential institution**
           Boarding school resident

✓5th **V60.8** **Other specified housing or economic circumstances**

      V60.81 **Foster care (status)**

      V60.89 **Other specified housing or economic circumstances**

      V60.9 **Unspecified housing or economic circumstance**

✓4th **V61** **Other family circumstances**

      INCLUDES   when these circumstances or fear of them, affecting the person directly involved or others, are mentioned as the reason, justified or not, for seeking or receiving medical advice or care

      AHA: 1Q, '90, 9

✓5th **V61.0** **Family disruption**
      AHA: 4Q, '08, 160

      V61.01 **Family disruption due to family member on military deployment**
           Individual or family affected by other family member being on deployment
           EXCLUDES ▶ *family disruption due to family member on non-military extended absence from home (V61.08)*◀

      V61.02 **Family disruption due to return of family member from military deployment**
           Individual or family affected by other family member having returned from deployment (current or past conflict)

      V61.03 **Family disruption due to divorce or legal separation**

      V61.04 **Family disruption due to parent-child estrangement**
           EXCLUDES   *other family estrangement (V61.09)*

      V61.05 **Family disruption due to child in welfare custody**

      V61.06 **Family disruption due to child in foster care or in care of non-parental family member**

      V61.07 **Family disruption due to death of family member**
           EXCLUDES   *bereavement (V62.82)*

      V61.08 **Family disruption due to other extended absence of family member**
           EXCLUDES   *family disruption due to family member on military deployment (V61.01)*

      V61.09 **Other family disruption**
           Family estrangement NOS

✓5th **V61.1** **Counseling for marital and partner problems**
      EXCLUDES   *problems related to:*
           psychosexual disorders (302.0-302.9)
           sexual function (V41.7)

      V61.10 **Counseling for marital and partner problems, unspecified**
           Marital conflict
           Marital relationship problem
           Partner conflict
           Partner relationship problem

      V61.11 **Counseling for victim of spousal and partner abuse**
           EXCLUDES   *encounter for treatment of current injuries due to abuse (995.80-995.85)*

      V61.12 **Counseling for perpetrator of spousal and partner abuse**

✓5th **V61.2** **Parent-child problems**

      V61.20 **Counseling for parent-child problem, unspecified**
           Concern about behavior of child
           Parent-child conflict
           Parent-child relationship problem

² **V61.21** **Counseling for victim of child abuse**
           Child battering
           Child neglect
           EXCLUDES   *current injuries due to abuse (995.50-995.59)*

      V61.22 **Counseling for perpetrator of parental child abuse**
           EXCLUDES   *counseling for non-parental abuser (V62.83)*

---

² These V codes may be used as principal diagnosis on Medicare patients.

N Newborn Age: 0   P Pediatric Age: 0-17   M Maternity Age: 12-55   A Adult Age: 15-124   **MCC** Major CC Condition   **CC** CC Condition   **HIV** HIV Related Dx

384 – Volume 1 · October 2009   **2010 ICD-9-CM**

● V61.23 **Counseling for parent-biological child problem**
Concern about behavior of biological child
Parent-biological child conflict
Parent-biological child relationship problem

● V61.24 **Counseling for parent-adopted child problem**
Concern about behavior of adopted child
Parent-adopted child conflict
Parent-adopted child relationship problem

● V61.25 **Counseling for parent (guardian)-foster child problem**
Concern about behavior of foster child
Parent (guardian)-foster child conflict
Parent (guardian)-foster child relationship problem

▲ V61.29 **Other parent-child problems**
AHA: 3Q, '99, 16

V61.3 **Problems with aged parents or in-laws**

√5th V61.4 **Health problems within family**

V61.41 **Alcoholism in family**

V61.42 **Substance abuse in family**

V61.49 **Other**
Care of ⎫ sick or handicapped person in
Presence of ⎬ family or household

V61.5 **Multiparity**

V61.6 **Illegitimacy or illegitimate pregnancy** Ⓜ ♀

V61.7 **Other unwanted pregnancy** Ⓜ ♀

V61.8 **Other specified family circumstances**
Problems with family members NEC
Sibling relationship problem

V61.9 **Unspecified family circumstance**

√4th **V62 Other psychosocial circumstances**
INCLUDES those circumstances or fear of them, affecting the person directly involved or others, mentioned as the reason, justified or not, for seeking or receiving medical advice or care
EXCLUDES *previous psychological trauma (V15.41-V15.49)*

V62.0 **Unemployment**
EXCLUDES *circumstances when main problem is economic inadequacy or poverty (V60.2)*

V62.1 **Adverse effects of work environment**

√5th V62.2 **Other occupational circumstances or maladjustment**
AHA: 4Q, '08, 160

V62.21 **Personal current military deployment status** Ⓐ
Individual (civilian or military) currently deployed in theater or in support of military war, peacekeeping and humanitarian operations

V62.22 **Personal history of return from military deployment** Ⓐ
Individual (civilian or military) with past history of military war, peacekeeping and humanitarian deployment (current or past conflict)

V62.29 **Other occupational circumstances or maladjustment** Ⓐ
Career choice problem
Dissatisfaction with employment
Occupational problem

V62.3 **Educational circumstances**
Academic problem
Dissatisfaction with school environment
Educational handicap

V62.4 **Social maladjustment**
Acculturation problem
Cultural deprivation
Political, religious, or sex discrimination
Social:
isolation
persecution

V62.5 **Legal circumstances**
Imprisonment   Litigation
Legal investigation   Prosecution

V62.6 **Refusal of treatment for reasons of religion or conscience**

√5th V62.8 **Other psychological or physical stress, not elsewhere classified**

V62.81 **Interpersonal problems, not elsewhere classified**
Relational problem NOS

V62.82 **Bereavement, uncomplicated**
EXCLUDES ►*family disruption due to death of family member (V61.07)*◄

V62.83 **Counseling for perpetrator of physical/sexual abuse**
EXCLUDES *counseling for perpetrator of parental child abuse (V61.22)*
counseling for perpetrator of spousal and partner abuse (V61.12)

2 V62.84 **Suicidal ideation** CC
EXCLUDES *suicidal tendencies (300.9)*
DEF: Thoughts of committing suicide; no actual attempt at suicide has been made.
CC Excl: 290.11, 290.3, 293.0
AHA: 4Q, '05, 96
TIP: Assign as a secondary diagnosis for patients who have not attempted suicide, and who may not be considered a suicide risk, but who have indicated thoughts about suicide.
R45.85 Suicidal ideation I-10

V62.89 **Other**
Borderline intellectual functioning
Life circumstance problems
Phase of life problems
Religious or spiritual problem

V62.9 **Unspecified psychosocial circumstance**

√4th **V63 Unavailability of other medical facilities for care**
AHA: 1Q, '91, 21

V63.0 **Residence remote from hospital or other health care facility**

V63.1 **Medical services in home not available**
EXCLUDES *no other household member able to render care (V60.4)*
AHA: 4Q, '01, 67; 1Q, '01, 12

V63.2 **Person awaiting admission to adequate facility elsewhere**

V63.8 **Other specified reasons for unavailability of medical facilities**
Person on waiting list undergoing social agency investigation

V63.9 **Unspecified reason for unavailability of medical facilities**

√4th **V64 Persons encountering health services for specific procedures, not carried out**

√5th V64.0 **Vaccination not carried out**
AHA: 4Q, '05, 99

V64.00 **Vaccination not carried out, unspecified reason**

V64.01 **Vaccination not carried out because of acute illness**

V64.02 **Vaccination not carried out because of chronic illness or condition**

2 These V codes may be used as principal diagnosis on Medicare patients.

V64.03 Vaccination not carried out because of immune compromised state

V64.04 Vaccination not carried out because of allergy to vaccine or component

> **Z28.04** Immunization not carried out pt allergy vaccine `I-10`

V64.05 Vaccination not carried out because of caregiver refusal

> Guardian refusal   Parent refusal
>
> **EXCLUDES** *vaccination not carried out because of caregiver refusal for religious reasons (V64.07)*
>
> **AHA:** 1Q, '07, 12

V64.06 Vaccination not carried out because of patient refusal

V64.07 Vaccination not carried out for religious reasons

V64.08 Vaccination not carried out because patient had disease being vaccinated against

V64.09 Vaccination not carried out for other reason

V64.1 Surgical or other procedure not carried out because of contraindication

> **TIP:** Assign an additional code to indicate the contraindication (reason the surgery or other procedure was canceled).

V64.2 Surgical or other procedure not carried out because of patient's decision

> **AHA:** 2Q, '01, 8

V64.3 Procedure not carried out for other reasons

✓5ᵗʰ **V64.4** Closed surgical procedure converted to open procedure

> **AHA:** 4Q, '03, 87; 4Q, '98, 68; 4Q, '97, 52

V64.41 Laparoscopic surgical procedure converted to open procedure

V64.42 Thoracoscopic surgical procedure converted to open procedure

V64.43 Arthroscopic surgical procedure converted to open procedure

✓4ᵗʰ **V65** Other persons seeking consultation

² **V65.0** Healthy person accompanying sick person
> Boarder

✓5ᵗʰ **V65.1** Person consulting on behalf of another person
> Advice or treatment for nottending third party
>
> **EXCLUDES** *concern (normal) about sick person in family (V61.41-V61.49)*
>
> **AHA:** 4Q, '03, 84

▲ **V65.11** Pediatric pre-birth visit for expectant parent(s)
> ▶Pre-adoption visit for adoptive parent(s)◀

V65.19 Other person consulting on behalf of another person

² **V65.2** Person feigning illiness
> Malingerer   Peregrinating patient
>
> **AHA:** 3Q, '99, 20
>
> **TIP:** Assign for patients engaged in what is documented as "drug- seeking behavior."

V65.3 Dietary surveillance and counseling

> Dietary surveillance and counseling (in):
> NOS
> colitis
> diabetes mellitus
> food allergies or intolerance
> gastritis
> hypercholesterolemia
> hypoglycemia
> obesity
>
> Use additional code to identify Body Mass Index (BMI), if known (V85.0-V85.54)
>
> **AHA:** 4Q, '05, 96

✓5ᵗʰ **V65.4** Other counseling, not elsewhere classified

> Health: Health:
> advice   instruction
> education
>
> **EXCLUDES** *counseling (for):*
> *contraception (V25.40-V25.49)*
> *genetic (V26.31-V26.39)*
> *on behalf of third party (V65.11-V65.19)*
> *procreative management (V26.41-V26.49)*

V65.40 Counseling NOS

V65.41 Exercise counseling

V65.42 Counseling on substance use and abuse
> **Z71.6** Tobacco abuse counseling `I-10`

V65.43 Counseling on injury prevention

V65.44 Human immunodeficiency virus [HIV] counseling

V65.45 Counseling on other sexually transmitted diseases

V65.46 Encounter for insulin pump training
> **Z71.82** Insulin pump counseling and training `I-10`

V65.49 Other specified counseling
> **AHA:** 4Q, '08, 156; 2Q, '00, 8

V65.5 Person with feared complaint in whom no diagnosis was made
> Feared condition not demonstrated
> Problem was normal state
> "Worried well"

V65.8 Other reasons for seeking consultation
> **EXCLUDES** *specified symptoms*
>
> **AHA:** 3Q, '92, 4

V65.9 Unspecified reason for consultation

✓4ᵗʰ **V66** Convalescence and palliative care

² **V66.0** Following surgery

² **V66.1** Following radiotherapy

² **V66.2** Following chemotherapy

² **V66.3** Following psychotherapy and other treatment for mental disorder

² **V66.4** Following treatment of fracture

V66.5 Following other treatment

² **V66.6** Following combined treatment

V66.7 Encounter for palliative care
> End of life care   Terminal care
> Hospice care
>
> Code first underlying disease
>
> **AHA:** 3Q, '08, 13; 2Q, '05, 9; 4Q, '03, 107; 1Q, '98, 11; 4Q, '96, 47, 48
>
> **TIP:** Assign as secondary diagnosis when treatment is focused on management of pain and symptoms in a patient with an incurable disease.
>
> **Z51.5** Encounter for palliative care `I-10`

[handwritten annotation: "Can never be listed as principal diagnosis" with arrow pointing to V66.7]

V66.9 Unspecified convalescence
> **AHA:** 4Q, '99, 8

---

² These V codes may be used as principal diagnosis on Medicare patients.

N Newborn Age: 0   P Pediatric Age: 0-17   M Maternity Age: 12-55   A Adult Age: 15-124   MCC Major CC Condition   CC CC Condition   HIV HIV Related Dx

386 – Volume 1 • October 2009

2010 ICD-9-CM

Assigned as principal diagnosis or reason for encounter when a patient is admitted for the purpose of surveillance after the initial treatment of disease/injury has been completed.

✓4ᵗʰ **V67 Follow-up examination**

    INCLUDES   surveillance only following completed treatment

    EXCLUDES   *surveillance of contraception (V25.40-V25.49)*

    AHA: 4Q, '08, 157; 2Q, '03, 5

   ✓5ᵗʰ **V67.0 Following surgery**

     AHA: 4Q, '00, 56; 4Q, '98, 69; 4Q, '97, 50; 2Q, '95, 8;1Q, '95, 4; 3Q, '92, 11

    ⁶ **V67.00 Following surgery, unspecified**

    ⁶ **V67.01 Follow-up vaginal pap smear**   ♀

      Vaginal pap smear, status-post hysterectomy for malignant condition

      Use additional code to identify:
       acquired absence of uterus (V88.01-V88.03)
       personal history of malignant neoplasm (V10.40-V10.44)

      EXCLUDES   *vaginal pap smear status-post hysterectomy for non-malignant condition (V76.47)*

      AHA: 4Q, '08, 157

    ⁶ **V67.09 Following other surgery**

      EXCLUDES   *sperm count following sterilization reversal (V26.22)*
                  sperm count for fertility testing (V26.21)

      AHA: 3Q, '08, 6; 3Q, '03, 16; 3Q, '02, 15

   ² **V67.1 Following radiotherapy**

   ² **V67.2 Following chemotherapy**

     Cancer chemotherapy follow-up

   ² **V67.3 Following psychotherapy and other treatment for mental disorder**

   ⁶ **V67.4 Following treatment of healed fracture**

     EXCLUDES   *current (healing) fracture aftercare (V54.0-V54.9)*

     AHA: ▶1Q, '09, 6;◀ 1Q, '90, 7

   ✓5ᵗʰ **V67.5 Following other treatment**

    ² **V67.51 Following completed treatment with high-risk medications, not elsewhere classified**

      EXCLUDES   *long-term (current) drug use (V58.61-V58.69)*

      AHA: 1Q, '99, 5, 6; 4Q, '95, 61; 1Q, '90, 18

    ² **V67.59 Other**

   ² **V67.6 Following combined treatment**

    V67.9 Unspecified follow-up examination

✓4ᵗʰ **V68 Encounters for administrative purposes**

   ✓5ᵗʰ **V68.0 Issue of medical certificates**

     EXCLUDES   *encounter for general medical examination (V70.0-V70.9)*

    V68.01 Disability examination

      Use additional code(s) to identify specific examination(s), screening and testing performed (V72.0-V82.9)

      AHA: 4Q, '07, 101

    V68.09 Other issue of medical certificates

    V68.1 Issue of repeat prescriptions

     Issue of repeat prescription for:
      appliance
      glasses
      medications

     EXCLUDES   *repeat prescription for contraceptives (V25.41-V25.49)*

    V68.2 Request for expert evidence

   ✓5ᵗʰ **V68.8 Other specified administrative purpose**

    V68.81 Referral of patient without examination or treatment

    V68.89 Other

    V68.9 Unspecified administrative purpose

✓4ᵗʰ **V69 Problems related to lifestyle**

    AHA: 4Q, '94, 48

    V69.0 Lack of physical exercise

    V69.1 Inappropriate diet and eating habits

     EXCLUDES   *anorexia nervosa (307.1)*
                bulimia (783.6)
                malnutrition and other nutritional deficiencies (260-269.9)
                other and unspecified eating disorders (307.50-307.59)

    V69.2 High-risk sexual behavior

    V69.3 Gambling and betting

     EXCLUDES   *pathological gambling (312.31)*

   ² **V69.4 Lack of adequate sleep**

     Sleep deprivation

     EXCLUDES   *insomnia (780.52)*

    V69.5 Behavioral insomnia of childhood   P

     DEF: Behaviors on the part of the child or caregivers that cause negative compliance with a child's sleep schedule; results in lack of adequate sleep.

     AHA: 4Q, '05, 99

    V69.8 Other problems related to lifestyle

     Self-damaging behavior

    V69.9 Problem related to lifestyle, unspecified

PERSONS WITHOUT REPORTED DIAGNOSIS ENCOUNTERED DURING EXAMINATION AND INVESTIGATION OF INDIVIDUALS AND POPULATIONS (V70-V82)

    Note: Nonspecific abnormal findings disclosed at the time of these examinations are classifiable to categories 790-796.

✓4ᵗʰ **V70 General medical examination**

    Use additional code(s) to identify any special screening examination(s) performed (V73.0-V82.9)

    V70.0 Routine general medical examination at a health care facility

     Health checkup

     EXCLUDES   *health checkup of infant or child ▶over 28 days old◀ (V20.2)*
                ▶health supervision of newborn 8 to 28 days old (V20.32)
                health supervision of newborn under 8 days old (V20.31)◀
                pre-procedural general physical examination (V72.83)

   ² **V70.1 General psychiatric examination, requested by the authority**

    V70.2 General psychiatric examination, other and unspecified

---

² These V codes may be used as principal diagnosis on Medicare patients.
⁶ These V codes are acceptable as principal diagnosis and group to DRGs 949-950.

| ✓4ᵗʰ ✓5ᵗʰ Additional Digit Required | Unacceptable PDx | Manifestation Code | Hospital Acquired Condition | ▶◀ Revised Text | ● New Code | ▲ Revised Code Title |

V70.3 Other medical examination for administrative purposes
General medical examination for:
admission to old age home
adoption
camp
driving license
immigration and naturalization
insurance certification
marriage
prison
school admission
sports competition

> **EXCLUDES** attendance for issue of medical certificates (V68.0)
> pre-employment screening (V70.5)

AHA: 3Q, '08, 6; 1Q, '90, 6

Z02.6 Encounter for exam for insurance purposes   I-10

2 V70.4 Examination for medicolegal reasons
Blood-alcohol tests   Paternity testing
Blood-drug tests

> **EXCLUDES** examination and observation following:
> accidents (V71.3, V71.4)
> assault (V71.6)
> rape (V71.5)

2 V70.5 Health examination of defined subpopulations
Armed forces personnel
Inhabitants of institutions
Occupational healthexaminations
Pre-employment screening
Preschool children
Prisoners
Prostitutes
Refugees
School children
Students

V70.6 Health examination in population surveys

> **EXCLUDES** special screening (V73.0-V82.9)

2 V70.7 Examination of participant in clinical trial
Examination of participant or control in clinical research

AHA: 2Q, '06, 5-6; 4Q, '01, 55

V70.8 Other specified general medical examinations
Examination of potential donor of organ or tissue

V70.9 Unspecified general medical examination

√4th V71 Observation and evaluation for suspected conditions not found

> **INCLUDES** This category is to be used when persons without a diagnosis are suspected of having an abnormal condition, without signs or symptoms, which requires study, but after examination and observation, is found not to exist. This category is also for use for administrative and legal observation status.

> **EXCLUDES** suspected maternal and fetal conditions not found (V89.01-V89.09)

AHA: 4Q, '94, 47; 2Q, '90, 5; M-A, '87, 1

TIP: Assign observation codes only as principal/first-listed diagnosis and only if there is no documentation of any signs or symptoms.

(handwritten: Can be assigned only as principal diagnosis or reason for encounter – never as a secondary diagnosis)

√5th V71.0 Observation for suspected mental condition

2 V71.01 Adult antisocial behavior A
Dyssocial behavior or gang activity in adult without manifest psychiatric disorder

2 V71.02 Childhood or adolescent antisocial behavior
Dyssocial behavior or gang activity in child or adolescent without manifest psychiatric disorder

2 V71.09 Other suspected mental condition

2 V71.1 Observation for suspected malignant neoplasm

2 V71.2 Observation for suspected tuberculosis

2 V71.3 Observation following accident at work

2 V71.4 Observation following other accident
Examination of individual involved in motor vehicle traffic accident
AHA: 1Q, '06, 9

2 V71.5 Observation following alleged rape or seduction
Examination of victim or culprit

2 V71.6 Observation following other inflicted injury
Examination of victim or culprit

2 V71.7 Observation for suspected cardiovascular disease
AHA: 1Q, '04, 6; 3Q, '90, 10; S-O, '87, 10

√5th V71.8 Observation and evaluation for other specified suspected conditions

> **EXCLUDES** contact with and (suspected) exposure to (potentially) hazardous substances (V15.84-V15.86, V87.0-V87.31)

AHA: 4Q, '00, 54 ; 1Q, '90, 19

2 V71.81 Abuse and neglect

> **EXCLUDES** adult abuse and neglect (995.80-995.85)
> child abuse and neglect (995.50-995.59)

AHA: 4Q, '00, 55

2 V71.82 Observation and evaluation for suspected exposure to anthrax
AHA: 4Q, '02, 70, 85

2 V71.83 Observation and evaluation for suspected exposure to other biological agent
AHA: 4Q, '03, 47

2 V71.89 Other specified suspected conditions
AHA: 3Q, '08, 7; 2Q, '03, 15

V71.9 Observation for unspecified suspected condition
AHA: 1Q, '02, 6

√4th V72 Special investigations and examinations

> **INCLUDES** routine examination of specific system

Use additional code(s) to identify any special screening examination(s) performed (V73.0-V82.9)

> **EXCLUDES** general medical examination (V70.0-V70.4)
> general screening examination of defined population groups (V70.5, V70.6, V70.7)
> ►health supervision of newborn 8 to 28 days old (V20.32)
> health supervision of newborn under 8 days old (V20.31)◄
> routine examination of infant or child ►over 28 days old (V20.2)◄

2 V72.0 Examination of eyes and vision
AHA: 1Q, '04, 15

√5th V72.1 Examination of ears and hearing
AHA: 1Q, '04, 15

V72.11 Encounter for hearing examination following failed hearing screening
AHA: 4Q, '06, 118
Z01.110 Encounter hearing exam follow failed hearing scr   I-10

V72.12 Encounter for hearing conservation and treatment
AHA: 4Q, '07, 100

V72.19 Other examination of ears and hearing

V72.2 Dental examination

√5th V72.3 Gynecological examination

> **EXCLUDES** cervical Papanicolaou smear without general gynecological examination (V76.2)
> routine examination in contraceptive management (V25.40-V25.49)

2 These V codes may be used as principal diagnosis on Medicare patients.

N Newborn Age: 0   P Pediatric Age: 0-17   M Maternity Age: 12-55   A Adult Age: 15-124   MCC Major CC Condition   CC CC Condition   HIV HIV Related Dx

388 – Volume 1 • October 2009   2010 ICD-9-CM

² **V72.31 Routine gynecological examination**   ♀
General gynecological examination with or
without Papanicolaou cervical smear
Pelvic examination (annual) (periodic)
Use additional code to identify:
human papillomavirus (HPV) screening
(V73.81)
routine vaginal Papanicolaou smear (V76.47)
AHA: 2Q, '06, 2-3; 4Q, '05, 9

² **V72.32 Encounter for Papanicolaou cervical**   ♀
smear to confirm findings of recent normal
smear following initial abnormal smear
AHA: 2Q, '06, 4

✓5th **V72.4 Pregnancy examination or test**
AHA: 4Q, '05, 98

² **V72.40 Pregnancy examination or test,**   ♀
pregnancy unconfirmed
Possible pregnancy, not (yet) confirmed

² **V72.41 Pregnancy examination or test,**   ♀
negative result

² **V72.42 Pregnancy examination or test,**   ♀ Ⓜ
positive result

V72.5 Radiological examination, not elsewhere classified
Routine chest x-ray
EXCLUDES ▶*radiologic examinations as part of*
pre-procedural testing
(V72.81-V72.84)◀
AHA: 1Q, '90, 19

V72.6 Laboratory examination
▶Encounters for blood and urine testing◀
AHA: 2Q, '06, 4; 1Q, '90, 22

● **V72.60 Laboratory examination, unspecified**
● **V72.61 Antibody response examination**
Immunity status testing
EXCLUDES *encounter for allergy testing (V72.7)*

● **V72.62 Laboratory examination ordered as part**
of a routine general medical examination
Blood tests for routine general physical
examination

● **V72.63 Pre-procedural laboratory examination**
Blood tests prior to treatment or procedure
Pre-operative laboratory examination

● **V72.69 Other laboratory examination**

V72.7 Diagnostic skin and sensitization tests
Allergy tests
Skin tests for hypersensitivity
EXCLUDES *diagnostic skin tests for bacterial diseases*
(V74.0-V74.9)

✓5th **V72.8 Other specified examinations**
EXCLUDES ▶*pre-procedural laboratory examinations*
(V72.63)◀

² **V72.81 Pre-operative cardiovascular examination**
Pre-procedural cardiovascular examination
Z01.810 Encounter for preprocedural   Ⓘ-10
cardiovascular exam

² **V72.82 Pre-operative respiratory examination**
Pre-procedural respiratory examination
AHA: 3Q, '96, 14

² **V72.83 Other specified pre-operative examination**
▶Examination prior to chemotherapy◀
Other pre-procedural examination
Pre-procedural general physical examination
EXCLUDES *routine general medical examination*
(V70.0)
AHA: 3Q, '96, 14

V72.84 Pre-operative examination, unspecified
Pre-procedural examination, unspecified

V72.85 Other specified examination
AHA: 4Q, '05, 96; 1Q, '04, 12

² These V codes may be used as principal diagnosis on Medicare patients.

V72.86 Encounter for blood typing

V72.9 Unspecified examination
AHA: 4Q, '06, 117

✓4th **V73 Special screening examination for viral and chlamydial diseases**
AHA: 1Q, '04, 11

V73.0 Poliomyelitis
V73.1 Smallpox
V73.2 Measles
V73.3 Rubella
V73.4 Yellow fever
V73.5 Other arthropod-borne viral diseases
Dengue fever   Viral encephalitis:
Hemorrhagic fever   tick-borne
Viral encephalitis:
mosquito-borne

V73.6 Trachoma

✓5th **V73.8 Other specified viral and chlamydial diseases**

V73.81 Human papillomavirus [HPV]
AHA: 4Q, '07, 100

V73.88 Other specified chlamydial diseases
AHA: 4Q, '07, 124

V73.89 Other specified viral diseases

✓5th **V73.9 Unspecified viral and chlamydial disease**

V73.98 Unspecified chlamydial disease
V73.99 Unspecified viral disease

✓4th **V74 Special screening examination for bacterial and spirochetal diseases**
INCLUDES diagnostic skin tests for these diseases
AHA: 1Q, '04, 11

V74.0 Cholera
V74.1 Pulmonary tuberculosis
V74.2 Leprosy [Hansen's disease]
V74.3 Diphtheria
V74.4 Bacterial conjunctivitis
V74.5 Venereal disease
Screening for bacterial and spirochetal sexually
transmitted diseases
Screening for sexually transmitted diseases NOS
EXCLUDES *special screening for nonbacterial sexually*
transmitted diseases (V73.81-V73.89,
V75.4, V75.8)
AHA: 4Q, '07, 124

V74.6 Yaws
V74.8 Other specified bacterial and spirochetal diseases
Brucellosis   Tetanus
Leptospirosis   Whooping cough
Plague

V74.9 Unspecified bacterial and spirochetal disease

✓4th **V75 Special screening examination for other infectious diseases**
AHA: 1Q, '04, 11

V75.0 Rickettsial diseases
V75.1 Malaria
V75.2 Leishmaniasis
V75.3 Trypanosomiasis
Chagas' disease
Sleeping sickness

V75.4 Mycotic infections
V75.5 Schistosomiasis
V75.6 Filariasis
V75.7 Intestinal helminthiasis

| ✓4th
✓5th Additional Digit Required | Unacceptable PDx | Manifestation Code | Hospital Acquired Condition | ▶◀ Revised Text | ● New Code | ▲ Revised Code Title |

2010 ICD-9-CM   **October 2009 • Volume 1 – 389**

V75.8   Other specified parasitic infections

V75.9   Unspecified infectious disease

☑4ᵗʰ **V76 Special screening for malignant neoplasms**

     AHA: 1Q, '04, 11

     TIP: Whenever a screening examination is performed, the screening code is the first-listed code, regardless of the findings or any procedure that is performed as a result of the findings.

V76.0   Respiratory organs

☑5ᵗʰ V76.1   Breast

     AHA: 4Q, '98, 67

     V76.10   Breast screening, unspecified

     V76.11   Screening mammogram for high-risk patient   ♀

         AHA: 2Q, '03, 4

     V76.12   Other screening mammogram

         AHA: 2Q, '06, 10; 2Q, '03, 3-4

     V76.19   Other screening breast examination

V76.2   Cervix   ♀

     Routine cervical Papanicolaou smear

     EXCLUDES   *special screening for human papillomavirus (V73.81)*

                   that as part of a general gynecological examination (V72.31)

V76.3   Bladder

☑5ᵗʰ V76.4   Other sites

     V76.41   Rectum

     V76.42   Oral cavity

     V76.43   Skin

     ² V76.44   Prostate   ♂

         Z12.5 Encounter screening malignant neoplasm prostate   **I-10**

     V76.45   Testis   ♂

     V76.46   Ovary   ♀

         AHA: 4Q, '00, 52

     V76.47   Vagina   ♀

         Vaginal pap smear status-post hysterectomy for non-malignant condition

         Use additional code to identify acquired absence of uterus (V88.01-V88.03)

         EXCLUDES   *vaginal pap smear status-post hysterectomy for malignant condition (V67.01)*

         AHA: 4Q, '08, 157; 4Q, '00, 52

     V76.49   Other sites

         AHA: 1Q, '99, 4

☑5ᵗʰ V76.5   Intestine

     AHA: 4Q, '00, 52

     V76.50   Intestine, unspecified

     V76.51   Colon

         EXCLUDES   *rectum (V76.41)*

         AHA: 4Q, '01, 56

         Z12.11 Encounter screening malignant neoplasm of colon   **I-10**

     V76.52   Small intestine

☑5ᵗʰ V76.8   Other neoplasm

     AHA: 4Q, '00, 52

     V76.81   Nervous system

     V76.89   Other neoplasm

V76.9   Unspecified

☑4ᵗʰ **V77 Special screening for endocrine, nutritional, metabolic, and immunity disorders**

     AHA: 1Q, '04, 11

V77.0   Thyroid disorders

V77.1   Diabetes mellitus

V77.2   Malnutrition

V77.3   Phenylketonuria [PKU]

V77.4   Galactosemia

V77.5   Gout

V77.6   Cystic fibrosis

     Screening for mucoviscidosis

V77.7   Other inborn errors of metabolism

V77.8   Obesity

☑5ᵗʰ V77.9   Other and unspecified endocrine, nutritional, metabolic, and immunity disorders

     AHA: 4Q, '00, 53

     V77.91   Screening for lipoid disorders

         Screening for cholesterol level

         Screening for hypercholesterolemia

         Screening for hyperlipidemia

     V77.99   Other and unspecified endocrine, nutritional, metabolic, and immunity disorders

☑4ᵗʰ **V78 Special screening for disorders of blood and blood-forming organs**

     AHA: 1Q, '04, 11

V78.0   Iron deficiency anemia

V78.1   Other and unspecified deficiency anemia

V78.2   Sickle cell disease or trait

V78.3   Other hemoglobinopathies

V78.8   Other disorders of blood and blood-forming organs

V78.9   Unspecified disorder of blood and blood-forming organs

☑4ᵗʰ **V79 Special screening for mental disorders and developmental handicaps**

     AHA: 1Q, '04, 11

V79.0   Depression

V79.1   Alcoholism

V79.2   Mental retardation

V79.3   Developmental handicaps in early childhood

V79.8   Other specified mental disorders and developmental handicaps

V79.9   Unspecified mental disorder and developmental handicap

☑4ᵗʰ **V80 Special screening for neurological, eye, and ear diseases**

     AHA: 1Q, '04, 11

☑5ᵗʰ V80.0   Neurological conditions

     ● V80.01   Traumatic brain injury

     ● V80.09   Other neurological conditions

V80.1   Glaucoma

V80.2   Other eye conditions

     Screening for: Screening for:

     cataract   senile macular

     congenital anomaly of eye   lesions

     EXCLUDES   *general vision examination (V72.0)*

V80.3   Ear diseases

     EXCLUDES   *general hearing examination (V72.11-V72.19)*

☑4ᵗʰ **V81 Special screening for cardiovascular, respiratory, and genitourinary diseases**

     AHA: 1Q, '04, 11

V81.0   Ischemic heart disease

V81.1   Hypertension

V81.2   Other and unspecified cardiovascular conditions

V81.3   Chronic bronchitis and emphysema

---

² These V codes may be used as principal diagnosis on Medicare patients.

N Newborn Age: 0   **P** Pediatric Age: 0-17   **M** Maternity Age: 12-55   **A** Adult Age: 15-124   **MCC** Major CC Condition   **CC** CC Condition   **HIV** HIV Related Dx

390 – Volume 1 • October 2009   **2010 ICD-9-CM**

V81.4 Other and unspecified respiratory conditions
> **EXCLUDES**   screening for:
> > lung neoplasm (V76.0)
> > pulmonary tuberculosis (V74.1)

V81.5 Nephropathy
> Screening for asymptomatic bacteriuria

V81.6 Other and unspecified
> genitourinary conditions

√4th **V82** Special screening for other conditions
> AHA: 1Q, '04, 11

V82.0 Skin conditions

V82.1 Rheumatoid arthritis

V82.2 Other rheumatic disorders

V82.3 Congenital dislocation of hip

V82.4 Maternal postnatal screening for ♀
> chromosomal anomalies
> > **EXCLUDES**   antenatal screening by amniocentesis (V28.0)

V82.5 Chemical poisoning and other contamination
> Screening for:
> > heavy metal poisoning
> > ingestion of radioactive substance
> > poisoning from contaminated water supply
> > radiation exposure

V82.6 Multiphasic screening

√5th **V82.7** Genetic screening
> **EXCLUDES**   genetic testing for procreative management
> (V26.31-V26.39)

> **V82.71** Screening for genetic disease carrier status
> > AHA: 4Q, '06, 118

> **V82.79** Other genetic screening
> > AHA: 4Q, '06, 118

√5th **V82.8** Other specified conditions
> AHA: 4Q, '00, 53

> **V82.81** Osteoporosis
> > Use additional code to identify:
> > hormone replacement therapy
> > (postmenopausal) status (V07.4)
> > postmenopausal (age-related) (natural)
> > status (V49.81)
> > AHA: 4Q, '00, 54

> **V82.89** Other specified conditions

V82.9 Unspecified condition

GENETICS (V83-V84)

√4th **V83** Genetic carrier status
> AHA: 4Q, '02, 79; 4Q, '01, 54
> **TIP:** The patient does not have the disease or carry a risk of developing it, but may genetically pass it to offspring who then may develop it.

√5th **V83.0** Hemophilia A carrier
> **V83.01** Asymptomatic hemophilia A carrier
> **V83.02** Symptomatic hemophilia A carrier

√5th **V83.8** Other genetic carrier status
> **V83.81** Cystic fibrosis gene carrier
> **V83.89** Other genetic carrier status

√4th **V84** Genetic susceptibility to disease
> **INCLUDES**   confirmed abnormal gene
> Use additional code, if applicable, for any associated family history of the disease (V16-V19)
> AHA: 4Q, '04, 106
> **TIP:** The patient has a gene that increases the risk of developing a specific disease; assign only as a secondary condition.

√5th **V84.0** Genetic susceptibility to malignant neoplasm
> Code first, if applicable, any current malignant neoplasms (140.0-195.8, 200.0-208.9, 230.0-234.9)
> Use additional code, if applicable, for any personal history of malignant neoplasm (V10.0-V10.9)

> **V84.01** Genetic susceptibility to
> > malignant neoplasm of breast
> > AHA: 4Q, '04, 107
> > Z15.01 Genetic susceptibility malignant   I-10
> > neoplasm breast

> **V84.02** Genetic susceptibility to ♀
> > malignant neoplasm of ovary

> **V84.03** Genetic susceptibility to malignant ♂
> > neoplasm of prostate

> **V84.04** Genetic susceptibility to malignant ♀
> > neoplasm of endometrium

> **V84.09** Genetic susceptibility to other malignant
> > neoplasm

√5th **V84.8** Genetic susceptibility to other disease
> **V84.81** Genetic susceptibility to multiple
> > endocrine neoplasia [MEN]
> > AHA: 4Q, '07, 100

> **V84.89** Genetic susceptibility to other disease

BODY MASS INDEX (V85)

√4th **V85** Body Mass Index [BMI]
> Kilograms per meters squared
> Note: BMI adult codes are for use for persons over 20 years old
> AHA: ▶4Q, '08, 191;◀ 4Q, '05, 97
> **TIP:** While BMI may be coded from dietician or other caregiver documentation, the diagnosis of being overweight or obese must be coded from physician documentation.

> **V85.0** Body Mass Index less than 19, adult   CC A
> > CC Excl: 278.00-278.01, V77.8, V85.0-V85.54

> **V85.1** Body Mass Index between 19-24, adult   A

√5th **V85.2** Body Mass Index between 25-29, adult
> **V85.21** Body Mass Index 25.0-25.9, adult   A
> **V85.22** Body Mass Index 26.0-26.9, adult   A
> **V85.23** Body Mass Index 27.0-27.9, adult   A
> **V85.24** Body Mass Index 28.0-28.9, adult   A
> **V85.25** Body Mass Index 29.0-29.9, adult   A

√5th **V85.3** Body Mass Index between 30-39, adult
> **V85.30** Body Mass Index 30.0-30.9, adult   A
> **V85.31** Body Mass Index 31.0-31.9, adult   A
> **V85.32** Body Mass Index 32.0-32.9, adult   A
> **V85.33** Body Mass Index 33.0-33.9, adult   A
> **V85.34** Body Mass Index 34.0-34.9, adult   A
> **V85.35** Body Mass Index 35.0-35.9, adult   A
> **V85.36** Body Mass Index 36.0-36.9, adult   A
> **V85.37** Body Mass Index 37.0-37.9, adult   A
> **V85.38** Body Mass Index 38.0-38.9, adult   A
> **V85.39** Body Mass Index 39.0-39.9, adult   A

> **V85.4** Body Mass Index 40 and over, adult   CC A
> > CC Excl: 278.00-278.01, 278.1, V85.0-V85.39, V85.51-V85.54
> > Z68.4 Body mass index BMI 40 or greater adult   I-10

√4th √5th Additional Digit Required   Unacceptable PDx   Manifestation Code   Hospital Acquired Condition   ▶◀ Revised Text   ● New Code   ▲ Revised Code Title

2010 ICD-9-CM   **February 2009 · Volume 1 – 391**

√5th **V85.5 Body Mass Index, pediatric**
  Note: BMI pediatric codes are for use for persons age 2-20 years old. These percentiles are based on the growth charts published by the Centers for Disease Control and Prevention (CDC)
  AHA: 4Q, '06, 118

  V85.51 Body Mass Index, pediatric, less than 5th percentile for age P

  V85.52 Body Mass Index, pediatric, 5th percentile to less than 85th percentile for age P

  V85.53 Body Mass Index, pediatric, 85th percentile to less than 95th percentile for age P

  V85.54 Body Mass Index, pediatric, greater than or equal to 95th percentile for age P
    Z68.54 Body mass index ped >/equal to 95 % for age I-10

ESTROGEN RECEPTOR STATUS (V86)

√4th **V86 Estrogen receptor status**
  Code first malignant neoplasm of breast (174.0-174.9, 175.0-175.9)
  AHA: 4Q, '06, 118

  V86.0 Estrogen receptor positive status [ER+]

  V86.1 Estrogen receptor negative status [ER-]

OTHER SPECIFIED PERSONAL EXPOSURES AND HISTORY PRESENTING HAZARDS TO HEALTH (V87)

√4th **V87 Other specified personal exposures and history presenting hazards to health**

  √5th **V87.0 Contact with and (suspected) exposure to hazardous metals**
    EXCLUDES   exposure to lead (V15.86)
               toxic effect of metals (984.0-985.9)
    AHA: 4Q, '08, 158

    V87.01 Arsenic

    V87.09 Other hazardous metals
      Chromium compounds
      Nickel dust

  √5th **V87.1 Contact with and (suspected) exposure to hazardous aromatic compounds**
    EXCLUDES   toxic effects of aromatic compounds (982.0, 983.0)
    AHA: 4Q, '08, 158

    V87.11 Aromatic amines

    V87.12 Benzene

    V87.19 Other hazardous aromatic compounds
      Aromatic dyes NOS
      Polycyclic aromatic hydrocarbons

  V87.2 Contact with and (suspected) exposure to other potentially hazardous chemicals
    Dyes NOS
    EXCLUDES   exposure to asbestos (V15.84)
               toxic effect of chemicals (980-989)
    AHA: 4Q, '08, 158

  √5th **V87.3 Contact with and (suspected) exposure to other potentially hazardous substances**
    EXCLUDES   contact with and (suspected) exposure to potentially hazardous body fluids (V15.85)
               toxic effect of substances (980-989)

    V87.31 Exposure to mold

    V87.32 Contact with and (suspected) exposure to algae bloom

    V87.39 Contact with and (suspected) exposure to other potentially hazardous substances

√5th **V87.4 Personal history of drug therapy**
  EXCLUDES   long-term (current) drug use (V58.61-V58.69)
  AHA: 4Q, '08, 159

  V87.41 Personal history of antineoplastic chemotherapy
    Z92.6 Personal hx chemotherapy for neoplastic disease I-10

  V87.42 Personal history of monoclonal drug therapy

  V87.43 Personal history of estrogen therapy

  V87.44 Personal history of inhaled steroid therapy

  V87.45 Personal history of systemic steroid therapy
    Personal history of steroid therapy NOS

  V87.46 Personal history of immunosuppression therapy
    EXCLUDES   personal history of steroid therapy (V87.44, V87.45)

  V87.49 Personal history of other drug therapy

ACQUIRED ABSENCE OF OTHER ORGANS AND TISSUE (V88)

√4th **V88 Acquired absence of other organs and tissue**

  √5th **V88.0 Acquired absence of cervix and uterus**
    AHA: 4Q, '08, 157

    V88.01 Acquired absence of both cervix and uterus ♀
      Acquired absence of uterus NOS
      Status post total hysterectomy

    V88.02 Acquired absence of uterus with remaining cervical stump ♀
      Status post partial hysterectomy with remaining cervical stump

    V88.03 Acquired absence of cervix with remaining uterus ♀

OTHER SUSPECTED CONDITIONS NOT FOUND (V89)

√4th **V89 Other suspected conditions not found**

  √5th **V89.0 Suspected maternal and fetal conditions not found**
    EXCLUDES   known or suspected fetal anomalies affecting management of mother, not ruled out (655.00, 655.93, 656.00-656.93, 657.00-657.03, 658.00-658.93)
               newborn and perinatal conditions — code to condition
    AHA: 4Q, '08, 159
    TIP: These investigations are performed while the fetus is in utero; the codes should be assigned only on the mother's medical record.

    V89.01 Suspected problem with amniotic cavity and membrane not found M♀
      Suspected oligohydramnios not found
      Suspected polyhydramnios not found

    V89.02 Suspected placental problem not found M♀

    V89.03 Suspected fetal anomaly not found M♀

    V89.04 Suspected problem with fetal growth not found M♀

    V89.05 Suspected cervical shortening not found M♀

    V89.09 Other suspected maternal and fetal condition not found M♀

N Newborn Age: 0   P Pediatric Age: 0-17   M Maternity Age: 12-55   A Adult Age: 15-124   MCC Major CC Condition   CC CC Condition   HIV HIV Related Dx

392 – Volume 1 • October 2009   2010 ICD-9-CM

Definition of poisoning: Error, Overdose, Non-prescribed drug taken with correctly prescribed and administered drug, Interaction between alcohol and drugs (considered poisoning with new 2010 guidelines)

SUPPLEMENTARY CLASSIFICATION OF EXTERNAL CAUSES OF INJURY AND POISONING ▶(E000-E999)◀

This section is provided to permit the classification of environmental events, circumstances, and conditions as the cause of injury, poisoning, and other adverse effects. Where a code from this section is applicable, it is intended that it shall be used in addition to a code from one of the main chapters of ICD-9-CM, indicating the nature of the condition. Certain other conditions which may be stated to be due to external causes are classified in Chapters 1 to 16 of ICD-9-CM. For these, the "E" code classification should be used as an additional code for more detailed analysis.

▶Machinery accidents [other than those connected with transport] are classifiable to category E919, in which the fourth digit allows a broad classification of the type of machinery involved. ◀

Categories for "late effects" of accidents and other external causes are to be found at E929, E959, E969, E977, E989, and E999.

▶EXTERNAL CAUSE STATUS (E000)◀

Note: A code from category E000 may be used in conjunction with the external cause code(s) assigned to a record to indicate the status of the person at the time the event occurred. A single code from category E000 should be assigned for an encounter.

- ✓4ᵗʰ **E000 External cause status**
- **E000.0 Civilian activity done for income or pay**
  Civilian activity done for financial or other compensation
  EXCLUDES *military activity (E000.1)*
- **E000.1 Military activity**
  EXCLUDES *activity of off-duty military personnel (E000.8)*
- **E000.8 Other external cause status**
  Activity NEC
  Hobby not done for income
  Leisure activity
  Off-duty activity of military personnel
  Recreation or sport not for income or while a student
  Student activity
  Volunteer activity
  EXCLUDES *civilian activity done for income or compensation (E000.0)*
  military activity (E000.1)
- **E000.9 Unspecified external cause status**

▶ACTIVITY (E001-E030)◀

Note: Categories E001 to E030 are provided for use to indicate the activity of the person seeking healthcare for an injury or health condition, such as a heart attack while shoveling snow, which resulted from, or was contributed to, by the activity. These codes are appropriate for use for both acute injuries, such as those from chapter 17, and conditions that are due to the long-term, cumulative affects of an activity, such as those from chapter 13. They are also appropriate for use with external cause codes for cause and intent if identifying the activity provides additional information on the event.

These codes should be used in conjunction with other external cause codes for external cause status (E000) and place of occurrence (E849).

This section contains the following broad activity categories:

E001 Activities involving walking and running
E002 Activities involving water and water craft
E003 Activities involving ice and snow
E004 Activities involving climbing, rappelling, and jumping off
E005 Activities involving dancing and other rhythmic movement
E006 Activities involving other sports and athletics played individually
E007 Activities involving other sports and athletics played as a team or group
E008 Activities involving other specified sports and athletics
E009 Activity involving other cardiorespiratory exercise
E010 Activity involving other muscle strengthening exercises
E011 Activities involving computer technology and electronic devices
E012 Activities involving arts and handcrafts
E013 Activities involving personal hygiene and household maintenance
E014 Activities involving person providing caregiving
E015 Activities involving food preparation, cooking and grilling

E016 Activities involving property and land maintenance, building and construction
E017 Activities involving roller coasters and other types of external motion
E018 Activities involving playing musical instrument
E019 Activities involving animal care
E029 Other activity
E030 Unspecified activity

- ✓4ᵗʰ **E001 Activities involving walking and running**
  EXCLUDES *walking an animal (E019.0)*
  walking or running on a treadmill (E009.0)
- **E001.0 Walking, marching and hiking**
  Walking, marching and hiking on level or elevated terrain
  EXCLUDES *mountain climbing (E004.0)*
- **E001.1 Running**

- ✓4ᵗʰ **E002 Activities involving water and water craft**
  EXCLUDES *activities involving ice (E003.0-E003.9)*
  boating and other watercraft transport accidents (E830-E838)
- **E002.0 Swimming**
- **E002.1 Springboard and platform diving**
- **E002.2 Water polo**
- **E002.3 Water aerobics and water exercise**
- **E002.4 Underwater diving and snorkeling**
  SCUBA diving
- **E002.5 Rowing, canoeing, kayaking, rafting and tubing**
  Canoeing, kayaking, rafting and tubing in calm and turbulent water
- **E002.6 Water skiing and wake boarding**
- **E002.7 Surfing, windsurfing and boogie boarding**
- **E002.8 Water sliding**
- **E002.9 Other activity involving water and watercraft**
  Activity involving water NOS
  Parasailing
  Water survival training and testing

- ✓4ᵗʰ **E003 Activities involving ice and snow**
  EXCLUDES *shoveling ice and snow (E016.0)*
- **E003.0 Ice skating**
  Figure skating (singles) (pairs)
  Ice dancing
  EXCLUDES *ice hockey (E003.1)*
- **E003.1 Ice hockey**
- **E003.2 Snow (alpine) (downhill) skiing, snow boarding, sledding, tobogganing and snow tubing**
  EXCLUDES *cross country skiing (E003.3)*
- **E003.3 Cross country skiing**
  Nordic skiing
- **E003.9 Other activity involving ice and snow**
  Activity involving ice and snow NOS

- ✓4ᵗʰ **E004 Activities involving climbing, rappelling, and jumping off**
  EXCLUDES *hiking on level or elevated terrain (E001.0)*
  jumping rope (E006.5)
  sky diving (E840-E844)
  trampoline jumping (E005.3)
- **E004.0 Mountain climbing, rock climbing and wall climbing**
- **E004.1 Rappelling**
- **E004.2 BASE jumping**
  Building, Antenna, Span, Earth jumping
- **E004.3 Bungee jumping**
- **E004.4 Hang gliding**
- **E004.9 Other activity involving climbing, rappelling and jumping off**

- ✓4ᵗʰ **E005 Activities involving dancing and other rhythmic movement**
  EXCLUDES *martial arts (E008.4)*
- **E005.0 Dancing**
- **E005.1 Yoga**

✓4ᵗʰ Fourth-digit Required ▶◀ Revised Text ● New Code ▲ Revised Code TitleDx

E005.2–E013.2

- ● E005.2 **Gymnastics**
  Rhythmic gymnastics
  EXCLUDES   trampoline (E005.3)
- ● E005.3 **Trampoline**
- ● E005.4 **Cheerleading**
- ● E005.9 **Other activity involving dancing and other rhythmic movements**
- ● ✓4th E006 **Activities involving other sports and athletics played individually**
  EXCLUDES   dancing (E005.0)
              gymnastic (E005.2)
              trampoline (E005.3)
              yoga (E005.1)
- ● E006.0 **Roller skating (inline) and skateboarding**
- ● E006.1 **Horseback riding**
- ● E006.2 **Golf**
- ● E006.3 **Bowling**
- ● E006.4 **Bike riding**
  EXCLUDES   transport accident involving bike riding
              (E800-E829)
- ● E006.5 **Jumping rope**
- ● E006.6 **Non-running track and field events**
  EXCLUDES   running (any form) (E001.1)
- ● E006.9 **Other activity involving other sports and athletics played individually**
  EXCLUDES   activities involving climbing, rappelling, and
              jumping (E004.0-E004.9)
              activities involving ice and snow
              (E003.0-E003.9)
              activities involving walking and running
              (E001.0-E001.9)
              activities involving water and watercraft
              (E002.0-E002.9)
- ● ✓4th E007 **Activities involving other sports and athletics played as a team or group**
  EXCLUDES   ice hockey (E003.1)
              water polo (E002.2)
- ● E007.0 **American tackle football**
  Football NOS
- ● E007.1 **American flag or touch football**
- ● E007.2 **Rugby**
- ● E007.3 **Baseball**
  Softball
- ● E007.4 **Lacrosse and field hockey**
- ● E007.5 **Soccer**
- ● E007.6 **Basketball**
- ● E007.7 **Volleyball (beach) (court)**
- ● E007.8 **Physical games generally associated with school recess, summer camp and children**
  Capture the flag
  Dodge ball
  Four square
  Kickball
- ● E007.9 **Other activity involving other sports and athletics played as a team or group**
  Cricket
- ● ✓4th E008 **Activities involving other specified sports and athletics**
- ● E008.0 **Boxing**
- ● E008.1 **Wrestling**
- ● E008.2 **Racquet and hand sports**
  Handball
  Racquetball
  Squash
  Tennis
- ● E008.3 **Frisbee**
  Ultimate frisbee
- ● E008.4 **Martial arts**
  Combatives

- ● E008.9 **Other specified sports and athletics activity**
  EXCLUDES   sports and athletics activities specified in
              categories E001-E007
- ● ✓4th E009 **Activity involving other cardiorespiratory exercise**
  Activity involving physical training
- ● E009.0 **Exercise machines primarily for cardiorespiratory conditioning**
  Elliptical and stepper machines
  Stationary bike
  Treadmill
- ● E009.1 **Calisthenics**
  Jumping jacks
  Warm up and cool down
- ● E009.2 **Aerobic and step exercise**
- ● E009.3 **Circuit training**
- ● E009.4 **Obstacle course**
  Challenge course
  Confidence course
- ● E009.5 **Grass drills**
  Guerilla drills
- ● E009.9 **Other activity involving cardiorespiratory exercise**
  EXCLUDES   activities involving cardiorespiratory exercise
              specified in categories E001-E008
- ● ✓4th E010 **Activity involving other muscle strengthening exercises**
- ● E010.0 **Exercise machines primarily for muscle strengthening**
- ● E010.1 **Push-ups, pull-ups, sit-ups**
- ● E010.2 **Free weights**
  Barbells
  Dumbbells
- ● E010.3 **Pilates**
- ● E010.9 **Other activity involving other muscle strengthening exercises**
  EXCLUDES   activities involving muscle strengthening
              specified in categories E001-E009
- ● ✓4th E011 **Activities involving computer technology and electronic devices**
  EXCLUDES   electronic musical keyboard or instruments (E018.0)
- ● E011.0 **Computer keyboarding**
  Electronic game playing using keyboard or other
  stationary device
- ● E011.1 **Hand held interactive electronic device**
  Cellular telephone and communication device
  Electronic game playing using interactive device
  EXCLUDES   electronic game playing using keyboard or
              other stationary device (E011.0)
- ● E011.9 **Other activity involving computer technology and electronic devices**
- ● ✓4th E012 **Activities involving arts and handcrafts**
  EXCLUDES   activities involving playing musical instrument
              (E018.0-E018.3)
- ● E012.0 **Knitting and crocheting**
- ● E012.1 **Sewing**
- ● E012.2 **Furniture building and finishing**
  Furniture repair
- ● E012.9 **Activity involving other arts and handcrafts**
- ● ✓4th E013 **Activities involving personal hygiene and household maintenance**
  EXCLUDES   activities involving cooking and grilling (E015.0-E015.9)
              activities involving property and land maintenance,
              building and construction (E016.0-E016.9)
              activity involving persons providing caregiving
              (E014.0-E014.9)
              dishwashing (E015.0)
              food preparation (E015.0)
              gardening (E016.1)
- ● E013.0 **Personal bathing and showering**
- ● E013.1 **Laundry**
- ● E013.2 **Vacuuming**

✓4th Fourth-digit Required   ►◄ Revised Text   ● New Code   ▲ Revised Code TitleDx

- E013.3 Ironing
- E013.4 Floor mopping and cleaning
- E013.5 Residential relocation
      Packing up and unpacking involved in moving to a new residence
- E013.8 Other personal hygiene activity
- E013.9 Other household maintenance
- ✓4ᵗʰ **E014 Activities involving person providing caregiving**
  - E014.0 Caregiving involving bathing
  - E014.1 Caregiving involving lifting
  - E014.9 Other activity involving person providing caregiving
- ✓4ᵗʰ **E015 Activities involving food preparation, cooking and grilling**
  - E015.0 Food preparation and clean up
        Dishwasing
  - E015.1 Grilling and smoking food
  - E015.2 Cooking and baking
        Use of stove, oven and microwave oven
  - E015.9 Other activity involving cooking and grilling
- ✓4ᵗʰ **E016 Activities involving property and land maintenance, building and construction**
  - E016.0 Digging, shoveling and raking
        Dirt digging
        Raking leaves
        Snow shoveling
  - E016.1 Gardening and landscaping
        Pruning, trimming shrubs, weeding
  - E016.2 Building and construction
  - E016.9 Other activity involving property and land maintenance, building and construction
- ✓4ᵗʰ **E017 Activities involving roller coasters and other types of external motion**
  - E017.0 Roller coaster riding
  - E017.9 Other activity involving external motion
- ✓4ᵗʰ **E018 Activities involving playing musical instrument**
      Activity involving playing electric musical instrument
  - E018.0 Piano playing
        Musical keyboard (electronic) playing
  - E018.1 Drum and other percussion instrument playing
  - E018.2 String instrument playing
  - E018.3 Wind and brass instrument playing
- ✓4ᵗʰ **E019 Activities involving animal care**
      EXCLUDES horseback riding (E006.1)
  - E019.0 Walking an animal
  - E019.1 Milking an animal
  - E019.2 Grooming and shearing an animal
  - E019.9 Other activity involving animal care
- ✓4ᵗʰ **E029 Other activity**
  - E029.0 Refereeing a sports activity
  - E029.1 Spectator at an event
  - E029.2 Rough housing and horseplay
  - E029.9 Other activity
- **E030 Unspecified activity**

▶TRANSPORT ACCIDENTS (E800-E848)◀

DEFINITIONS AND EXAMPLES RELATED TO TRANSPORT ACCIDENTS

(a) A **transport accident** (E800-E848) is any accident involving a device designed primarily for, or being used at the time primarily for, conveying persons or goods from one place to another.

INCLUDES accidents involving:
       aircraft and spacecraft (E840-E845)
       watercraft (E830-E838)
       motor vehicle (E810-E825)
       railway (E800-E807)
       other road vehicles (E826-E829)

In classifying accidents which involve more than one kind of transport, the above order of precedence of transport accidents should be used.

Accidents involving agricultural and construction machines, such as tractors, cranes, and bulldozers, are regarded as transport accidents only when these vehicles are under their own power on a highway [otherwise the vehicles are regarded as machinery]. Vehicles which can travel on land or water, such as hovercraft and other amphibious vehicles, are regarded as watercraft when on the water, as motor vehicles when on the highway, and as off-road motor vehicles when on land, but off the highway.

EXCLUDES accidents:
       in sports which involve the use of transport but where the transport vehicle itself was not involved in the accident
       involving vehicles which are part of industrial equipment used entirely on industrial premises
       occurring during transportation but unrelated to the hazards associated with the means of transportation [e.g., injuries received in a fight on board ship; transport vehicle involved in a cataclysm such as an earthquake]
       to persons engaged in the maintenance or repair of transport equipment or vehicle not in motion, unlesss injured by another vehicle in motion

(b) A **railway accident** is a transport accident involving a railway train or other railway vehicle operated on rails, whether in motion or not.

EXCLUDES *accidents:*
       in repair shops
       in roundhouse or on turntable
       on railway premises but not involving a train or other railway vehicle

(c) A **railway train** or **railway vehicle** is any device with or without cars coupled to it, desiged for traffic on a railway.

INCLUDES interurban:
       electric car ⎱ (operated chiefly on its own
       street car   ⎰ right-of-way, not open to other traffic)
       railway train, any power [diesel] [electric] [steam]
       funicular
       monorail or two-rail
       subterranean or elevated
       other vehicle designed to run on a railway track

EXCLUDES *interurban electric cars [streetcars] specified to be operating on a right-of-way that forms part of the public street or highway [definition (h)]*

(d) A **railway** or **railroad** is a right-of-way designed for traffic on rails, which is used by carriages or wagons transporting passengers or freight, and by other rolling stock, and which is not open to other public vehicular traffic.

(e) A **motor vehicle accident** is a transport accident involving a motor vehicle. It is defined as a motor vehicle traffic accident or as a motor vehicle nontraffic accident according to whether the accident occurs on a public highway or elsewhere.

EXCLUDES *injury or damage due to cataclysm*
       injury or damage while a motor vehicle, not under its own power, is being loaded on, or unloaded from, another conveyance

(f) A **motor vehicle traffic accident** is any motor vehicle accident occurring on a public highway [i.e., originating, terminating, or involving a vehicle partially on the highway]. A motor vehicle accident is assumed to have occurred on the highway unless another place is specified, except in the case of accidents involving only off-road motor vehicles which are classified as nontraffic accidents unless the contrary is stated.

(g) A **motor vehicle nontraffic accident** is any motor vehicle accident which occurs entirely in any place other than a public highway.

(h) A **public highway [trafficway]** or **street** is the entire width between property lines [or other boundary lines] of every way or place, of which any part is open to the use of the public for purposes of vehicular traffic as a matter of right or custom. A **roadway** is that part of the public highway designed, improved, and ordinarily used, for vehicular travel.

> **INCLUDES** approaches (public) to:
>> docks
>> public building
>> station
>
> *EXCLUDES* *driveway (private)*
> *parking lot*
> *ramp*
> *roads in:*
>> *airfield*
>> *farm*
>> *industrial premises*
>> *mine*
>> *private grounds*
>> *quarry*

(i) A **motor vehicle** is any mechanically or electrically powered device, not operated on rails, upon which any person or property may be transported or drawn upon a highway. Any object such as a trailer, coaster, sled, or wagon being towed by a motor vehicle is considered a part of the motor vehicle.

> **INCLUDES** automobile [any type]
> bus
> construction machinery, farm and industrial machinery, steam roller, tractor, army tank, highway grader, or similar vehicle on wheels or treads, while in transport under own power
> fire engine (motorized)
> motorcycle
> motorized bicycle [moped] or scooter
> trolley bus not operating on rails
> truck
> van
>
> *EXCLUDES* *devices used solely to move persons or materials within the confines of a building and its premises, such as:*
>> *building elevator*
>> *coal car in mine*
>> *electric baggage or mail truck used solely within a railroad station*
>> *electric truck used solely within an industrial plant*
>> *moving overhead crane*

(j) A **motorcycle** is a two-wheeled motor vehicle having one or two riding saddles and sometimes having a third wheel for the support of a sidecar. The sidecar is considered part of the motorcycle.

> **INCLUDES** motorized:
>> bicycle [moped]
>> scooter
>> tricycle

(k) An **off-road motor vehicle** is a motor vehicle of special design, to enable it to negotiate rough or soft terrain or snow. Examples of special design are high construction, special wheels and tires, driven by treads, or support on a cushion of air.

> **INCLUDES** all terrain vehicle [ATV]
> army tank
> hovercraft, on land or swamp
> snowmobile

(l) A **driver** of a motor vehicle is the occupant of the motor vehicle operating it or intending to operate it. A **motorcyclist** is the driver of a motorcycle. Other authorized occupants of a motor vehicle are **passengers**.

(m) An **other road vehicle** is any device, except a motor vehicle, in, on, or by which any person or property may be transported on a highway.

> **INCLUDES** animal carrying a person or goods
> animal-drawn vehicles
> animal harnessed to conveyance
> bicycle [pedal cycle]
> streetcar
> tricycle (pedal)
>
> *EXCLUDES* *pedestrian conveyance [definition (q)]*

(n) A **streetcar** is a device designed and used primarily for transporting persons within a municipality, running on rails, usually subject to normal traffic control signals, and operated principally on a right-of-way that forms part of the traffic way. A trailer being towed by a streetcar is considered a part of the streetcar.

> **INCLUDES** interurban or intraurban electric or streetcar, when specified to be operating on a street or public highway
> tram (car)
> trolley (car)

(o) A **pedal cycle** is any road transport vehicle operated solely by pedals.

> **INCLUDES** bicycle
> pedal cycle
> tricycle
>
> *EXCLUDES* *motorized bicycle [definition (j)]*

(p) A **pedal cyclist** is any person riding on a pedal cycle or in a sidecar attached to such a vehicle.

(q) A **pedestrian conveyance** is any human powered device by which a pedestrian may move other than by walking or by which a walking person may move another pedestrian.

> **INCLUDES** baby carriage
> coaster wagon
> heelies, wheelies
> ice skates
> perambulator
> pushcart
> pushchair
> roller skates
> scooter
> skateboard
> skis
> sled
> wheelchair

(r) A **pedestrian** is any person involved in an accident who was not at the time of the accident riding in or on a motor vehicle, railroad train, streetcar, animal-drawn or other vehicle, or on a bicycle or animal.

> **INCLUDES** person:
>> changing tire of vehicle
>> in or operating a pedestrian conveyance
>> making adjustment to motor of vehicle
>> on foot

(s) A **watercraft** is any device for transporting passengers or goods on the water.

(t) A **small boat** is any watercraft propelled by paddle, oars, or small motor, with a passenger capacity of less than ten.

> **INCLUDES** boat NOS
> canoe
> coble
> dinghy
> punt
> raft
> rowboat
> rowing shell
> scull
> skiff
> small motorboat
>
> *EXCLUDES* *barge*
> *lifeboat (used after abandoning ship)*
> *raft (anchored) being used as a diving platform*
> *yacht*

(u) An **aircraft** is any device for transporting passengers or goods in the air.

> **INCLUDES**   airplane [any type]
> balloon
> bomber
> dirigible
> glider (hang)
> military aircraft
> parachute

(v) A **commercial transport aircraft** is any device for collective passenger or freight transportation by air, whether run on commercial lines for profit or by government authorities, with the exception of military craft.

RAILWAY ACCIDENTS (E800-E807)

Note: For definitions of railway accident and related terms see definitions (a) to (d).

> **EXCLUDES**   *accidents involving railway train and:*
> *aircraft (E840.0-E845.9)*
> *motor vehicle (E810.0-E825.9)*
> *watercraft (E830.0-E838.9)*

The following fourth-digit subdivisions are for use with categories E800-E807 to identify the injured person:

.0 Railway employee
Any person who by virtue of his employment in connection with a railway, whether by the railway company or not, is at increased risk of involvement in a railway accident, such as:
catering staff of train
driver
guard
porter
postal staff on train
railway fireman
shunter
sleeping car attendant

.1 Passenger on railway
Any authorized person traveling on a train, except a railway employee.
> **EXCLUDES** *intending passenger waiting at station (.8)*
> *unauthorized rider on railway vehicle (.8)*

.2 Pedestrian
See definition (r)

.3 Pedal cyclist
See definition (p)

.8 Other specified person
Intending passenger or bystander waiting at station
Unauthorized rider on railway vehicle

.9 Unspecified person

§ ☑4th **E800 Railway accident involving collision with rolling stock**

> **INCLUDES**   collision between railway trains or railway vehicles, any kind
> collision NOS on railway
> derailment with antecedent collision with rolling stock or NOS

§ ☑4th **E801 Railway accident involving collision with other object**

> **INCLUDES**   collision of railway train with:
> buffers
> fallen tree on railway
> gates
> platform
> rock on railway
> streetcar
> other nonmotor vehicle
> other object
> **EXCLUDES** *collision with:*
> *aircraft (E840.0-E842.9)*
> *motor vehicle (E810.0-E810.9, E820.0-E822.9)*

§ ☑4th **E802 Railway accident involving derailment without antecedent collision**

§ ☑4th **E803 Railway accident involving explosion, fire, or burning**

> **EXCLUDES** *explosion or fire, with antecedent derailment (E802.0-E802.9)*
> *explosion or fire, with mention of antecedent collision (E800.0-E801.9)*

§ ☑4th **E804 Fall in, on, or from railway train**

> **INCLUDES**   fall while alighting from or boarding railway train
> **EXCLUDES** *fall related to collision, derailment, or explosion of railway train (E800.0-E803.9)*

§ ☑4th **E805 Hit by rolling stock**

> **INCLUDES**   crushed
> injured
> killed   } by railway train or part
> knocked down
> run over
> **EXCLUDES** *pedestrian hit by object set in motion by railway train (E806.0-E806.9)*

§ ☑4th **E806 Other specified railway accident**

> **INCLUDES**   hit by object falling in railway train
> injured by door or window on railway train
> nonmotor road vehicle or pedestrian hit by object set in motion by railway train
> railway train hit by falling:
> earth NOS
> rock
> tree
> other object
> **EXCLUDES** *railway accident due to cataclysm (E908-E909)*

§ ☑4th **E807 Railway accident of unspecified nature**

> **INCLUDES**   found dead   } on railway right-of-way NOS
> injured
> railway accident NOS

MOTOR VEHICLE TRAFFIC ACCIDENTS (E810-E819)

Note: For definitions of motor vehicle traffic accident, and related terms, see definitions (e) to (k).

> **EXCLUDES** *accidents involving motor vehicle and aircraft (E840.0-E845.9)*

The following fourth-digit subdivisions are for use with categories E810-E819 to identify the injured person:

.0 Driver of motor vehicle other than motorcycle
See definition (l)

.1 Passenger in motor vehicle other than motorcycle
See definition (l)

.2 Motorcyclist
See definition (l)

.3 Passenger on motorcycle
See definition (l)

.4 Occupant of streetcar

.5 Rider of animal; occupant of animal-drawn vehicle

.6 Pedal cyclist
See definition (p)

.7 Pedestrian
See definition (r)

.8 Other specified person
Occupant of vehicle other than above
Person in railway train involved in accident
Unauthorized rider of motor vehicle

.9 Unspecified person

§ ☑4th **E810 Motor vehicle traffic accident involving collision with train**

> **EXCLUDES** *motor vehicle collision with object set in motion by railway train (E815.0-E815.9)*
> *railway train hit by object set in motion by motor vehicle (E818.0-E818.9)*

§ ☑4th **E811 Motor vehicle traffic accident involving re-entrant collision with another motor vehicle**

> **INCLUDES**   collision between motor vehicle which accidentally leaves the roadway then re-enters the same roadway, or the opposite roadway on a divided highway, and another motor vehicle
> **EXCLUDES** *collision on the same roadway when none of the motor vehicles involved have left and re-entered the highway (E812.0-E812.9)*

§ Requires fourth-digit. See beginning of appropriate section for codes and definitions.

§ ✓4ᵗʰ **E812 Other motor vehicle traffic accident involving collision with motor vehicle**

> INCLUDES   collision with another motor vehicle parked, stopped, stalled, disabled, or abandoned on the highway
> motor vehicle collision NOS
>
> EXCLUDES   *collision with object set in motion by another motor vehicle (E815.0-E815.9)*
> *re-entrant collision with another motor vehicle (E811.0-E811.9)*

§ ✓4ᵗʰ **E813 Motor vehicle traffic accident involving collision with other vehicle**

> INCLUDES   collision between motor vehicle, any kind, and:
> other road (nonmotor transport) vehicle, such as:
> animal carrying a person
> animal-drawn vehicle
> pedal cycle
> streetcar
>
> EXCLUDES   *collision with:*
> *object set in motion by nonmotor road vehicle (E815.0-E815.9)*
> *pedestrian (E814.0-E814.9)*
> *nonmotor road vehicle hit by object set in motion by motor vehicle (E818.0-E818.9)*

§ ✓4ᵗʰ **E814 Motor vehicle traffic accident involving collision with pedestrian**

> INCLUDES   collision between motor vehicle, any kind, and pedestrian
> pedestrian dragged, hit, or run over by motor vehicle, any kind
>
> EXCLUDES   *pedestrian hit by object set in motion by motor vehicle (E818.0-E818.9)*

§ ✓4ᵗʰ **E815 Other motor vehicle traffic accident involving collision on the highway**

> INCLUDES   collision (due to loss of control) (on highway) between motor vehicle, any kind, and:
> abutment (bridge) (overpass)
> animal (herded) (unattended)
> fallen stone, traffic sign, tree, utility pole
> guard rail or boundary fence
> interhighway divider
> landslide (not moving)
> object set in motion by railway train or road vehicle (motor) (nonmotor)
> object thrown in front of motor vehicle
> other object, fixed, movable, or moving
> safety island
> temporary traffic sign or marker
> wall of cut made for road
>
> EXCLUDES   *collision with:*
> *any object off the highway (resulting from loss of control) (E816.0-E816.9)*
> *any object which normally would have been off the highway and is not stated to have been on it (E816.0-E816.9)*
> *motor vehicle parked, stopped, stalled, disabled, or abandoned on highway (E812.0-E812.9)*
> *moving landslide (E909)*
> *motor vehicle hit by object:*
> *set in motion by railway train or road vehicle (motor) (nonmotor) (E818.0-E818.9)*
> *thrown into or on vehicle (E818.0-E818.9)*

§ ✓4ᵗʰ **E816 Motor vehicle traffic accident due to loss of control, without collision on the highway**

> INCLUDES   motor vehicle:
> failing to make curve
> going out of control (due to):
> blowout   and:
> burst tire   coliding with object
> driver falling asleep   off the highway
> drive inattention   overturning
> excessive speed   stopping abruptly
> failure of mechanical part   off the highway
>
> EXCLUDES   *collision on highway following loss of control (E810.0-E815.9)*
> *loss of control of motor vehicle following collision on the highway (E810.0-E815.9)*

§ ✓4ᵗʰ **E817 Noncollision motor vehicle traffic accident while boarding or alighting**

> INCLUDES   fall down stairs of motor bus
> fall from car in street
> injured by moving part of the vehicle   while boarding or alighting
> trapped by door of motor bus

§ ✓4ᵗʰ **E818 Other noncollision motor vehicle traffic accident**

> INCLUDES   accidental poisoning from exhaust gas generated by
> breakage of any part of
> explosion of any part of
> fall, jump, or being accidentally pushed from
> fire starting in   motor vehicle while in motion
> hit by object thrown into or on
> injured by being thrown against some part of, or object in
> injury from moving part of
> object falling in or on
> object thrown on
>
> collision of railway train or road vehicle except motor vehicle, with object set in motion by motor vehicle
> motor vehicle hit by object set in motion by railway train or road vehicle (motor) (nonmotor)
> pedestrian, railway train, or road vehicle (motor) (non-motor) hit by object set in motion by motor vehicle
>
> EXCLUDES   *collision between motor vehicle and:*
> *object set in motion by railway train or road vehicle (motor) (nonmotor) (E815.0-E815.9)*
> *object thrown towards the motor vehicle (E815.0-E815.9)*
> *person overcome by carbon monoxide generated by stationary motor vehicle off the roadway with motor running (E868.2)*

§ ✓4ᵗʰ **E819 Motor vehicle traffic accident of unspecified nature**

> INCLUDES   motor vehicle traffic accident NOS
> traffic accident NOS

---

§   Requires fourth-digit. See beginning of appropriate section for codes and definitions.

✓4ᵗʰ Fourth-digit Required   ►◄ Revised Text   ● New Code   ▲ Revised Code TitleDx

MOTOR VEHICLE NONTRAFFIC ACCIDENTS (E820-E825)

Note: For definitions of motor vehicle nontraffic accident and related terms see definition (a) to (k).

INCLUDES accidents involving motor vehicles being used in recreational or sporting activities off the highway
collision and noncollision motor vehicle acci- dents occurring entirely off the highway

EXCLUDES *accidents involving motor vehicle and:*
aircraft (E840.0-E845.9)
watercraft (E830.0-E838.9)
accidents, not on the public highway, involving agricultural and construction machinery but not involving another motor vehicle (E919.0, E919.2, E919.7)

The following fourth-digit subdivisions are for use with categories E820-E825 to identify the injured person:

.0 **Driver of motor vehicle other than motorcycle**
See definition (l)
.1 **Passenger in motor vehicle other than motorcycle**
See definition (l)
.2 **Motorcyclist**
See definition (l)
.3 **Passenger on motorcycle**
See definition (l)
.4 **Occupant of streetcar**
.5 **Rider of animal; occupant of animal-drawn vehicle**
.6 **Pedal cyclist**
See definition (p)
.7 **Pedestrian**
See definition (r)
.8 **Other specified person**
Occupant of vehicle other than above
Person in railway train involved in accident
Unauthorized rider of motor vehicle
.9 **Unspecified person**

§ ✓4ᵗʰ **E820 Nontraffic accident involving motor-driven snow vehicle**

INCLUDES breakage of part of ⎫
fall from ⎬ motor-driven snow
hit by ⎪ vehicle (not on
overturning of ⎪ public highway)
run over or dragged by ⎭

collision of motor-driven snow vehicle with:
animal (being ridden) (-drawn vehicle)
another off-road motor vehicle
other motor vehicle, not on public highway
railway train
other object, fixed or movable
injury caused by rough landing of motor-driven snow vehicle (after leaving ground on rough terrain)

EXCLUDES *accident on the public highway involving motor driven snow vehicle (E810.0-E819.9)*

§ ✓4ᵗʰ **E821 Nontraffic accident involving other off-road motor vehicle**

INCLUDES breakage of part of ⎫
fall from ⎪
hit by ⎪ off-road motorvehicle
overturning of ⎬ except snow
run over or dragged by ⎪ vehicle (not on
thrown against some part ⎪ public highway
of or object in ⎭

collision with:
animal (being ridden) (-drawn vehicle)
another off-road motor vehicle, except snow vehicle
other motor vehicle, not on public highway
other object, fixed or movable

EXCLUDES *accident on public highway involving off-road motor vehicle (E810.0-E819.9)*
collision between motor driven snow vehicle and other off-road motor vehicle (E820.0-E820.9)
hovercraft accident on water (E830.0-E838.9)

§ ✓4ᵗʰ **E822 Other motor vehicle nontraffic accident involving collision with moving object**

INCLUDES collision, not on public highway, between motor vehicle, except off-road motor vehicle and:
animal
nonmotor vehicle
other motor vehicle, except off-road motor vehicle
pedestrian
railway train
other moving object

EXCLUDES *collision with:*
motor-driven snow vehicle (E820.0-E820.9)
other off-road motor vehicle (E821.0-E821.9)

§ ✓4ᵗʰ **E823 Other motor vehicle nontraffic accident involving collision with stationary object**

INCLUDES collision, not on public highway, between motor vehicle, except off-road motor vehicle, and any object, fixed or movable, but not in motion

§ ✓4ᵗʰ **E824 Other motor vehicle nontraffic accident while boarding and alighting**

INCLUDES
fall ⎫ while boarding or alighting
injury from oving part ⎬ from motor vehicle,
of motor vehicle ⎪ except off-road motor
trapped by door of ⎪ vehicle, not on public
motor vehhicle ⎭ highway

§ ✓4ᵗʰ **E825 Other motor vehicle nontraffic accident of other and unspecified nature**

INCLUDES accidental poisoning from ⎫
carbon monoxide ⎪
generated by ⎪
breakage of any part of ⎪
explosion of any part of ⎪
fall, jump, or being ⎪
accidentally pushed ⎪ motor vehicle while in
from ⎬ motion, not on
fire starting in ⎪ public highway
hit by object thrown into, ⎪
towards, or on ⎪
injured by being thrown ⎪
against some part of, ⎪
or object in ⎪
injury from moving part of ⎪
object falling in or on ⎭

motor vehicle nontraffic accident NOS

EXCLUDES *fall from or in stationary motor vehicle (E884.9, E885.9)*
overcome by carbon monoxide or exhaust gas generated by stationary motor vehicle off the roadway with motor running (E868.2)
struck by falling object from or in stationary motor vehicle (E916)

---

§ Requires fourth-digit. See beginning of appropriate section for codes and definitions.

OTHER ROAD VEHICLE ACCIDENTS (E826-E829)

Note: Other road vehicle accidents are transport accidents involving road vehicles other than motor vehicles. For definitions of other road vehicle and related terms see definitions (m) to (o).

INCLUDES   accidents involving other road vehicles being used in recreational or sporting activities

EXCLUDES   *collision of other road vehicle [any] with:*
aircraft (E840.0-E845.9)
motor vehicle (E813.0-E813.9, E820.0-E822.9)
railway train (E801.0-E801.9))

The following fourth-digit subdivisions are for use with categories E826-E829 to identify the injured person:
- .0 **Pedestrian**
  - See definition (r)
- .1 **Pedal cyclist**
  - See definition (p)
- .2 **Rider of animal**
- .3 **Occupant of animal-drawn vehicle**
- .4 **Occupant of streetcar**
- .8 **Other specified person**
- .9 **Unspecified person**

§ ✓4th **E826   Pedal cycle accident**
[0-9]   **INCLUDES**   breakage of any part of pedal cycle
collision between pedal cycle and:
    animal (being ridden) (herded) (unattended)
    another pedal cycle
    any pedestrian
    nonmotor road vehicle
    other object, fixed, movable, or moving, not set in
       motion by motor vehicle, railway train, or
       aircraft
entanglement in wheel of pedal cycle
fall from pedal cycle
hit by object falling or thrown on the pedal cycle
pedal cycle accident NOS
pedal cycle overturned

§ ✓4th **E827   Animal-drawn vehicle accident**
[0,2,4,8,9] **INCLUDES**   breakage of any part of vehicle
collision between animal-drawn vehicle and:
    animal (being ridden) (herded) (unattended)
    nonmotor road vehicle, except pedal cycle
    pedestrian, pedestrian conveyance, or pedestrian
       vehicle
    other object, fixed, movable, or moving, not set in
       motion by motor vehicle, railway train, or
       aircraft

fall from
knocked down by
overturning of   } animal drawn vehicle
running over by
thrown from

EXCLUDES   *collision of animal-drawn vehicle with pedal cycle*
(E826.0-E826.9)

§ ✓4th **E828   Accident involving animal being ridden**
[0,2,4,8,9] **INCLUDES**   collision between animal being ridden and:
    another animal
    nonmotor road vehicle, except pedal cycle, and
       animal-drawn vehicle
    pedestrian, pedestrian conveyance, or pedestrian
       vehicle
    other object, fixed, movable, or moving, not set in
       motion by motor vehicle, railway train, or
       aircraft

fall from
knocked down by
thrown from   } animal being ridden
trampled by

ridden animal stumbled and fell

EXCLUDES   *collision of animal being ridden with:*
animal-drawn vehicle (E827.0-E827.9)
pedal cycle (E826.0-E826.9)

§ ✓4th **E829   Other road vehicle accidents**
[0,4,8,9]   **INCLUDES**

accident while boarding or
    alighting from
blow from object in
breakage of any part of   } streetcar
caught in door of   nonmotor road
derailment of   vehicle not
fall in, on, or from   classifiable to
fire in   E826-E828

collision between streetcar or nonmotor road vehicle,
       except as in E826-E828, and:
    animal (not being ridden)
    another nonmotor road vehicle not classifiable to
       E826-E828
    pedestrian
    other object, fixed, movable, or moving, not set in
       motion by motor vehicle, railway train, or
       aircraft
nonmotor road vehicle accident NOS
streetcar accident NOS

EXCLUDES   *collision with:*
animal being ridden (E828.0-E828.9)
animal-drawn vehicle (E827.0-E827.9)
pedal cycle (E826.0-E826.9)

WATER TRANSPORT ACCIDENTS (E830-E838)

Note: For definitions of water transport accident and related terms see definitions (a), (s), and (t).

INCLUDES   watercraft accidents in the course of recreational activities

EXCLUDES   *accidents involving both aircraft, including objects set in motion by aircraft, and watercraft (E840.0-E845.9)*

The following fourth-digit subdivisions are for use with categories E830-E838 to identify the injured person:
- .0 **Occupant of small boat, unpowered**
- .1 **Occupant of small boat, powered**
  - See definition (t)
  - **EXCLUDES**   *water skier (.4)*
- .2 **Occupant of other watercraft – crew**
  - Persons:
  - engaged in operation of watercraft
  - providing passenger services [cabin attendants, ship's physician, catering personnel]
  - working on ship during voyage in other capacity [musician in band, operators of shops and beauty parlors
- .3 **Occupant of other watercraft – other than crew**
  - Passenger
  - Occupant of lifeboat, other than crew, after abandoning ship
- .4 **Water skier**
- .5 **Swimmer**
- .6 **Dockers, stevedores**
  - Longshoreman employed on the dock in loading and unloading ships
- ▶.7 **Occupant of military watercraft, any type◀**
- .8 **Other specified person**
  - Immigration and custom officials on board ship
  - Person:
  - accompanying passenger or member of crew visiting boat
  - Pilot (guiding ship into port)
- .9 **Unspecified person**

§ ✓4th **E830   Accident to watercraft causing submersion**
INCLUDES   submersion and drowning due to:
    boat overturning
    boat submerging
    falling or jumping from burning ship
    falling or jumping from crushed watercraft
    ship sinking
    other accident to watercraft

---

§   Requires fourth-digit. Valid digits are in [brackets] under each code. See beginning of appropriate section for codes and definitions.

✓4th Fourth-digit Required   ▶◀ Revised Text   ● New Code   ▲ Revised Code TitleDx

§ ☑4ᵗʰ **E831 Accident to watercraft causing other injury**

INCLUDES   any injury, except submersion and drowning, as a
result of an accident to watercraft
burned while ship on fire
crushed between ships in collision
crushed by lifeboat after abandoning ship
fall due to collision or other accident to watercraft
hit by falling object due to accident to watercraft
injured in watercraft accident involving collision
struck by boat or part thereof after fall or jump from
damaged boat

EXCLUDES   *burns from localized fire or explosion on board ship
(E837.0-E837.9)*

§ ☑4ᵗʰ **E832 Other accidental submersion or drowning in water
transport accident**

INCLUDES   submersion or drowning as a result of an accident
other than accident to the watercraft, such as:
fall:
from gangplank
from ship
overboard
thrown overboard by motion of ship
washed overboard

EXCLUDES   *submersion or drowning of swimmer or diver who
voluntarily jumps from boat not involved in an
accident (E910.0-E910.9)*

§ ☑4ᵗʰ **E833 Fall on stairs or ladders in water transport**

EXCLUDES   *fall due to accident to watercraft (E831.0-E831.9)*

§ ☑4ᵗʰ **E834 Other fall from one level to another in water transport**

EXCLUDES   *fall due to accident to watercraft (E831.0-E831.9)*

§ ☑4ᵗʰ **E835 Other and unspecified fall in water transport**

EXCLUDES   *fall due to accident to watercraft (E831.0-E831.9)*

§ ☑4ᵗʰ **E836 Machinery accident in water transport**

INCLUDES   injuries in water transport caused by:
deck
engine room
galley   } machinery
laundry
loading

§ ☑4ᵗʰ **E837 Explosion, fire, or burning in watercraft**

INCLUDES   explosion of boiler on steamship
localized fire on ship

EXCLUDES   *burning ship (due to collision or explosion) resulting in:
submersion or drowning (E830.0-E830.9)
other injury (E831.0-E831.9)*

§ ☑4ᵗʰ **E838 Other and unspecified water transport accident**

INCLUDES   accidental poisoning by gases or fumes on ship
atomic power plant malfunction in watercraft
crushed between ship and stationary object [wharf]
crushed between ships without accident to watercraft
crushed by falling object on ship or while loading or
unloading
hit by boat while water skiing
struck by boat or part thereof (after fall from boat)
watercraft accident NOS

AIR AND SPACE TRANSPORT ACCIDENTS (E840-E845)

Note: For definition of aircraft and related terms see definitions (u)
and (v).

The following fourth-digit subdivisions are for use with categories
E840-E845 to identify the injured person. Valid fourth digits are in
[brackets] under codes E842-E845:

.0 **Occupant of spacecraft**
.1 **Occupant of military aircraft, any**
Crew in military aircraft [air force] [army] [national guard]
[navy]
Passenger (civilian) (military) in military aircraft [air force]
[army] [national guard] [navy]
Troops in military aircraft [air force] [army] [national guard]
[navy]

EXCLUDES   *occupants of aircraft operated under
jurisdiction of police departments (.5)
parachutist (.7)*

.2 **Crew of commercial aircraft (powered) in surface to surface
transport**
.3 **Other occupant of commercial aircraft (powered) in surface to
surface transport**
Flight personnel:
not part of crew
on familiarization flight
Passenger on aircraft (powered) NOS
.4 **Occupant of commercial aircraft (powered) in surface to air
transport**
Occupant [crew] [passenger] of aircraft (powered)
engaged in activities, such as:
aerial spraying (crops) (fire retardants)
air drops of emergency supplies
air drops of parachutists, except from military craft
crop dusting
lowering of construction material [bridge or telephone
pole]
sky writing
.5 **Occupant of other powered aircraft**
Occupant [crew] [passenger] of aircraft (powered)
engaged in activities, such as:
aerobatic flying
aircraft racing
rescue operation
storm surveillance
traffic surveillance
Occupant of private plane NOS
.6 **Occupant of unpowered aircraft, except parachutist**
Occupant of aircraft classifiable to E842
.7 **Parachutist (military) (other)**
Person making voluntary descent
EXCLUDES   *person making descent after accident to
aircraft (.1-.6)*
.8 **Ground crew, airline employee**
Persons employed at airfields (civil) (military) or launching
pads, not occupants of aircraft
.9 **Other person**

§ ☑4ᵗʰ **E840 Accident to powered aircraft at takeoff or landing**

INCLUDES   collision of aircraft with any
object, fixed, movable, or
moving
crash   } while taking off or
explosion on aircraft   landing
fire on aircraft
forced landing

§ ☑4ᵗʰ **E841 Accident to powered aircraft, other and unspecified**

INCLUDES   aircraft accident NOS
aircraft crash or wreck NOS
any accident to powered aircraft while in transit or
when not specified whether in transit, taking
off, or landing
collision of aircraft with another aircraft, bird, or any
object, while in transit
explosion on aircraft while in transit
fire on aircraft while in transit

§   Requires fourth-digit. See beginning of appropriate section for codes and definitions.

§ ☑4ᵗʰ **E842 Accident to unpowered aircraft**

    [6-9]   **INCLUDES**   any accident, except collision with powered aircraft, to:
                            balloon
                            glider
                            hang glider
                            kite carrying a person
                            hit by object falling from unpowered aircraft

§ ☑4ᵗʰ **E843 Fall in, on, or from aircraft**

    [0-9]   **INCLUDES**   accident in boarding or alighting from aircraft, any kind
                          fall in, on, or from aircraft [any kind], while in transit, taking off, or landing, except when as a result of an accident to aircraft

§ ☑4ᵗʰ **E844 Other specified air transport accidents**

    [0-9]   **INCLUDES**   hit by:
                          aircraft
                          object falling from aircraft
                 injury by or from:
                          machinery of aircraft
                          rotating propellar   without accident
                          voluntary parachute descent   to aircraft
                 poisoning by carbon monoxide
                          from aircraft while in transit
                 sucked into jet

                 any accident involving other transport vehicle (motor) (nonmotor) due to being hit by object set in motion by aircraft (powered)

         EXCLUDES   *air sickness (E903)*
                          effects of:
                              high altitude (E902.0-E902.1)
                              pressure change (E902.0-E902.1)
                          injury in parachute descent due to accident to aircraft (E840.0-E842-9)

§ ☑4ᵗʰ **E845 Accident involving spacecraft**

    [0,8,9]   **INCLUDES**   launching pad accident
             EXCLUDES   *effects of weightlessness in spacecraft (E928.0)*

VEHICLE ACCIDENTS NOT ELSEWHERE CLASSIFIABLE (E846-E848)

E846 Accidents involving powered vehicles used solely within the buildings and premises of industrial or commercial establishment

     Accident to, on, or involving:
         battery powered airport passenger vehicle
         battery powered trucks (baggage) (mail)
         coal car in mine
         logging car
         self propelled truck, industrial
         station baggage truck (powered)
         tram, truck, or tub (powered) in mine or quarry
     Collision with:
         pedestrian
         other vehicle or object within premises
     Explosion of
     Fall from   } powered vehicle, industrial or
     Overturning of   } commercial
     Struck by

         EXCLUDES   *accidental poisoning by exhaust gas from vehicle not elsewhere classifiable (E868.2)*
                          injury by crane, lift (fork), or elevator (E919.2)

E847 Accidents involving cable cars not running on rails

     Accident to, on, or involving:
         cable car, not on rails
         ski chair-lift
         ski-lift with gondola
         téléférique
     Breakage of cable
     Caught or dragged by
     Fall or jump from   } cable car, not on rails
     Object thrown from or in

E848 Accidents involving other vehicles, not elsewhere classifiable

     Accident to, on, or involving:
         ice yacht
         land yacht
         nonmotor, nonroad vehicle NOS

☑4ᵗʰ **E849 Place of occurrence**

     The following category is for use to denote the place where the injury or poisoning occurred.

E849.0 Home

         Apartment
         Boarding house
         Farm house
         Home premises
         House (residential)
         Noninstitutional place of residence
         Private:
             driveway
             garage
             garden
             home
             walk
         Swimming pool in private house or garden
         Yard of home
         EXCLUDES   *home under construction but not yet occupied (E849.3)*
                          institutional place of residence (E849.7)

E849.1 Farm

         Farm:
             buildings
             land under cultivation
         EXCLUDES   *farm house and home premises of farm (E849.0)*

E849.2 Mine and quarry

         Gravel pit
         Sand pit
         Tunnel under construction

E849.3 Industrial place and premises

         Building under construction
         Dockyard
         Dry dock
         Factory
             building
             premises
         Garage (place of work)
         Industrial yard
         Loading platform (factory) (store)
         Plant, industrial
         Railway yard
         Shop (place of work)
         Warehouse
         Workhouse

E849.4 Place for recreation and sport

         Amusement park   *Playground, including school*
         Baseball field   *playground*
         Basketball court   *Public park*
         Beach resort   *Racecourse*
         Cricket ground   *Resort NOS*
         Fives court   *Riding school*
         Football field   *Rifle range*
         Golf course   *Seashore resort*
         Gymnasium   *Skating rink*
         Hockey field   *Sports palace*
         Holiday camp   *Stadium*
         Ice palace   *Swimming pool, public*
         Lake resort   *Tennis court*
         Mountain resort   *Vacation resort*
         EXCLUDES   *that in private house or garden (E849.0)*

E849.5 Street and highway

---

§   Requires fourth-digit. Valid digits are in [brackets] under each code. See beginning of appropriate section for codes and definitions.

E849.6 Public building
> Building (including adjacent grounds) used by the general
> public or by a particular group of the public, such as:
>> airport
>> bank
>> café
>> casino
>> church
>> cinema
>> clubhouse
>> courthouse
>> dance hall
>> garage building (for car storage)
>> hotel
>> market (grocery or other commodity)
>> movie house
>> music hall
>> nightclub
>> office
>> office building
>> opera house
>> post office
>> public hall
>> radio broadcasting station
>> restaurant
>> school (state) (public) (private)
>> shop, commercial
>> station (bus) (railway)
>> store
>> theater

> **EXCLUDES**   home garage (E849.0)
>> industrial building or workplace (E849.3)

E849.7 Residential institution
> Children's home
> Dormitory
> Hospital
> Jail
> Old people's home
> Orphanage
> Prison
> Reform school

E849.8 Other specified places

Beach NOS	Pond or pool (natural)
Canal	Prairie
Caravan site NOS	Public place NOS
Derelict house	Railway line
Desert	Reservoir
Dock	River
Forest	Sea
Harbor	Seashore NOS
Hill	Stream
Lake NOS	Swamp
Mountain	Trailer court
Parking lot	Woods
Parking place	

E849.9 Unspecified place

ACCIDENTAL POISONING BY DRUGS, MEDICINAL SUBSTANCES, AND BIOLOGICALS (E850-E858)

> **INCLUDES**   accidental overdose of drug, wrong drug given or
>> taken in error, and drug taken inadvertently
>> accidents in the use of drugs and biologicals in medi-
>> cal and surgical procedures

> **EXCLUDES**   administration with suicidal or homicidal intent or intent
>> to harm, or in circumstances classifiable to
>> E980-E989 (E950.0-E950.5, E962.0, E980.0-E980.5)
>> correct drug properly administered in therapeutic or
>> prophylactic dosage, as the cause of adverse effect
>> (E930.0-E949.9)

> See Alphabetic Index for more complete list of specific drugs to be
> classified under the fourth-digit subdivisions. The American
> Hospital Formulary numbers can be used to classify new
> drugs listed by the American Hospital Formulary Service
> (AHFS). See Appendix C.

√4ᵗʰ E850 Accidental poisoning by analgesics, antipyretics, and antirheumatics

E850.0 Heroin
> Diacetylmorphine

E850.1 Methadone

E850.2 Other opiates and related narcotics
> Codeine [methylmorphine]
> Meperidine [pethidine]
> Morphine
> Opium (alkaloids)

E850.3 Salicylates
> Acetylsalicylic acid [aspirin]
> Amino derivatives of salicylic acid
> Salicylic acid salts

E850.4 Aromatic analgesics, not elsewhere classified
> Acetanilid
> Paracetamol [acetaminophen]
> Phenacetin [acetophenetidin]

E850.5 Pyrazole derivatives
> Aminophenazone [amidopyrine]
> Phenylbutazone

E850.6 Antirheumatics [antiphlogistics]
> Gold salts
> Indomethacin
> **EXCLUDES**   salicylates (E850.3)
>> steroids (E858.0)

E850.7 Other non-narcotic analgesics
> Pyrabital

E850.8 Other specified analgesics and antipyretics
> Pentazocine

E850.9 Unspecified analgesic or antipyretic

E851 Accidental poisoning by barbiturates
> Amobarbital [amylobarbitone]
> Barbital [barbitone]
> Butabarbital [butabarbitone]
> Pentobarbital [pentobarbitone]
> Phenobarbital [phenobarbitone]
> Secobarbital [quinalbarbitone]
> **EXCLUDES**   thiobarbiturates (E855.1)

√4ᵗʰ E852 Accidental poisoning by other sedatives and hypnotics

E852.0 Chloral hydrate group

E852.1 Paraldehyde

E852.2 Bromine compounds
> Bromides
> Carbromal (derivatives)

E852.3 Methaqualone compounds

E852.4 Glutethimide group

E852.5 Mixed sedatives, not elsewhere classified

E852.8 Other specified sedatives and hypnotics

E852.9 Unspecified sedative or hypnotic
> Sleeping:
>> drug
>> pill   } NOS
>> tablet

√4ᵗʰ E853 Accidental poisoning by tranquilizers

E853.0 Phenothiazine-based tranquilizers

Chlorpromazine	Prochlorperazine
Fluphenazine	Promazine

E853.1 Butyrophenone-based tranquilizers

Haloperidol	Trifluperidol
Spiperone	

E853.2 Benzodiazepine-based tranquilizers

Chlordiazepoxide	Lorazepam
Diazepam	Medazepam
Flurazepam	Nitrazepam

E853.8 Other specified tranquilizers

Hydroxyzine	Meprobamate

E853.9 Unspecified tranquilizer

☑4ᵗʰ **E854 Accidental poisoning by other psychotropic agents**

E854.0 Antidepressants
Amitriptyline
Imipramine
Monoamine oxidase [MAO] inhibitors

E854.1 Psychodysleptics [hallucinogens]
Cannabis derivatives   Mescaline
Lysergide [LSD]   Psilocin
Marihuana (derivatives)   Psilocybin

E854.2 Psychostimulants
Amphetamine
Caffeine
> **EXCLUDES** *central appetite depressants (E858.8)*

E854.3 Central nervous system stimulants
Analeptics
Opiate antagonists

E854.8 Other psychotropic agents

☑4ᵗʰ **E855 Accidental poisoning by other drugs acting on central and autonomic nervous system**

E855.0 Anticonvulsant and anti-Parkinsonism drugs
Amantadine
Hydantoin derivatives
Levodopa [L-dopa]
Oxazolidine derivatives [paramethadione]
          [trimethadione]
Succinimides

E855.1 Other central nervous system depressants
Ether
Gaseous anesthetics
Halogenated hydrocarbon derivatives
Intravenous anesthetics
Thiobarbiturates, such as thiopental sodium

E855.2 Local anesthetics
Cocaine   Procaine
Lidocaine [lignocaine]   Tetracaine

E855.3 Parasympathomimetics [cholinergics]
Acetylcholine   Anticholinesterase:
Anticholinesterase: reversible
     organophosphorus   Pilocarpine

E855.4 Parasympatholytics [anticholinergics and antimuscarinics] and spasmolytics
Atropine   Hyoscine [scopolamine]
Homatropine   Quaternary ammonium
                          derivatives

E855.5 Sympathomimetics [adrenergics]
Epinephrine [adrenalin]
Levarterenol [noradrenalin]

E855.6 Sympatholytics [antiadrenergics]
Phenoxybenzamine
Tolazoline hydrochloride

E855.8 Other specified drugs acting on central and autonomic nervous systems

E855.9 Unspecified drug acting on central and autonomic nervous systems

E856 Accidental poisoning by antibiotics

E857 Accidental poisoning by other anti-infectives

☑4ᵗʰ **E858 Accidental poisoning by other drugs**

E858.0 Hormones and synthetic substitutes

E858.1 Primarily systemic agents

E858.2 Agents primarily affecting blood constituents

E858.3 Agents primarily affecting cardiovascular system

E858.4 Agents primarily affecting gastrointestinal system

E858.5 Water, mineral, and uric acid metabolism drugs

E858.6 Agents primarily acting on the smooth and skeletal muscles and respiratory system

E858.7 Agents primarily affecting skin and mucous membrane, ophthalmological, otorhinolaryngological, and dental drugs

E858.8 Other specified drugs
Central appetite depressants

E858.9 Unspecified drug

ACCIDENTAL POISONING BY OTHER SOLID AND LIQUID SUBSTANCES, GASES, AND VAPORS (E860-E869)
Note: Categories in this section are intended primarily to indicate the external cause of poisoning states classifiable to 980-989. They may also be used to indicate external causes of localized effects classifiable to 001-799.

☑4ᵗʰ **E860 Accidental poisoning by alcohol, not elsewhere classified**

E860.0 Alcoholic beverages
Alcohol in preparations intended for consumption

E860.1 Other and unspecified ethyl alcohol and its products
Denatured alcohol   Grain alcohol NOS
Ethanol NOS   Methylated spirit

E860.2 Methyl alcohol
Methanol   Wood alcohol

E860.3 Isopropyl alcohol
Dimethyl carbinol   Rubbing alcohol subsitute
Isopropanol   Secondary propyl alcohol

E860.4 Fusel oil
Alcohol: Alcohol:
   amyl   propyl
   butyl

E860.8 Other specified alcohols

E860.9 Unspecified alcohol

☑4ᵗʰ **E861 Accidental poisoning by cleansing and polishing agents, disinfectants, paints, and varnishes**

E861.0 Synthetic detergents and shampoos

E861.1 Soap products

E861.2 Polishes

E861.3 Other cleansing and polishing agents
Scouring powders

E861.4 Disinfectants
Household and other disinfectants not ordinarily used on the person
> **EXCLUDES** *carbolic acid or phenol (E864.0)*

E861.5 Lead paints

E861.6 Other paints and varnishes
Lacquers   Paints, other than lead
Oil colors   White washes

E861.9 Unspecified

☑4ᵗʰ **E862 Accidental poisoning by petroleum products, other solvents and their vapors, not elsewhere classified**

E862.0 Petroleum solvents
Petroleum: Petroleum:
   ether   naphtha
   benzine

E862.1 Petroleum fuels and cleaners
Antiknock additives   Gasoline or petrol
   to petroleum fuels   Kerosene
Gas oils
> **EXCLUDES** *kerosene insecticides (E863.4)*

E862.2 Lubricating oils

E862.3 Petroleum solids
Paraffin wax

E862.4 Other specified solvents
Benzene

E862.9 Unspecified solvent

☑4ᵗʰ Fourth-digit Required   ▶◀ Revised Text   ● New Code   ▲ Revised Code TitleDx

☑4ᵗʰ **E863 Accidental poisoning by agricultural and horticultural chemical and pharmaceutical preparations other than plant foods and fertilizers**

> **EXCLUDES** *plant foods and fertilizers (E866.5)*

E863.0 Insecticides of organochlorine compounds

Benzene hexachloride	Dieldrin
Chlordane	Endrine
DDT	Toxaphene

E863.1 Insecticides of organophosphorus compounds

Demeton	Parathion
Diazinon	Phenylsulphthion
Dichlorvos	Phorate
Malathion	Phosdrin
Methyl parathion	

E863.2 Carbamates

Aldicarb	Propoxur
Carbaryl	

E863.3 Mixtures of insecticides

E863.4 Other and unspecified insecticides
Kerosene insecticides

E863.5 Herbicides
2, 4-Dichlorophenoxyacetic acid [2, 4-D]
2, 4, 5-Trichlorophenoxyacetic acid [2, 4, 5-T]
Chlorates
Diquat
Mixtures of plant foods and fertilizers with herbicides
Paraquat

E863.6 Fungicides
Organic mercurials (used in seed dressing)
Pentachlorophenols

E863.7 Rodenticides

Fluoroacetates	Warfarin
Squill and derivatives	Zinc phosphide
Thallium	

E863.8 Fumigants

Cyanides	Phosphine
Methyl bromide	

E863.9 Other and unspecified

☑4ᵗʰ **E864 Accidental poisoning by corrosives and caustics, not elsewhere classified**

> **EXCLUDES** *those as components of disinfectants (E861.4)*

E864.0 Corrosive aromatics
Carbolic acid or phenol

E864.1 Acids

Acid:	Acid:
hydrochloric	sulfuric
nitric	

E864.2 Caustic alkalis
Lye

E864.3 Other specified corrosives and caustics

E864.4 Unspecified corrosives and caustics

☑4ᵗʰ **E865 Accidental poisoning from poisonous foodstuffs and poisonous plants**

> **INCLUDES** any meat, fish, or shellfish
> plants, berries, and fungi eaten as, or in mistake for, food, or by a child
>
> **EXCLUDES** *anaphylactic shock due to adverse food reaction (995.60-995.69)*
> *food poisoning (bacterial) (005.0-005.9)*
> *poisoning and toxic reactions to venomous plants (E905.6-E905.7)*

E865.0 Meat

E865.1 Shellfish

E865.2 Other fish

E865.3 Berries and seeds

E865.4 Other specified plants

E865.5 Mushrooms and other fungi

E865.8 Other specified foods

E865.9 Unspecified foodstuff or poisonous plant

☑4ᵗʰ **E866 Accidental poisoning by other and unspecified solid and liquid substances**

> **EXCLUDES** *these substances as a component of:*
> *medicines (E850.0-E858.9)*
> *paints (E861.5-E861.6)*
> *pesticides (E863.0-E863.9)*
> *petroleum fuels (E862.1)*

E866.0 Lead and its compounds and fumes

E866.1 Mercury and its compounds and fumes

E866.2 Antimony and its compounds and fumes

E866.3 Arsenic and its compounds and fumes

E866.4 Other metals and their compounds and fumes
Beryllium (compounds)
Brass fumes
Cadmium (compounds)
Copper salts
Iron (compounds)
Manganese (compounds)
Nickel (compounds)
Thallium (compounds)

E866.5 Plant foods and fertilizers

> **EXCLUDES** *mixtures with herbicides (E863.5)*

E866.6 Glues and adhesives

E866.7 Cosmetics

E866.8 Other specified solid or liquid substances

E866.9 Unspecified solid or liquid substance

E867 Accidental poisoning by gas distributed by pipeline
Carbon monoxide from incomplete combustion of piped gas
Coal gas NOS
Liquefied petroleum gas distributed through pipes (pure or mixed with air)
Piped gas (natural) (manufactured)

☑4ᵗʰ **E868 Accidental poisoning by other utility gas and other carbon monoxide**

E868.0 Liquefied petroleum gas distributed in mobile containers

Butane	⎱ or carbon monoxide
Liquefied hydrocarbon gas NOS	⎰ from incomplete
	conbustion of
Propane	these gases

E868.1 Other and unspecified utility gas

Acetylene	⎱ or carbon monoxide
Gas NOS used for lighting, heating, or cooking	⎰ from incomplete conbustion of
Water gas	these gases

E868.2 Motor vehicle exhaust gas
Exhaust gas from:
any type of combustion engine not in watercraft
farm tractor, not in transit
gas engine
motor pump
motor vehicle, not in transit

> **EXCLUDES** *poisoning by carbon monoxide from:*
> *aircraft while in transit (E844.0-E844.9)*
> *motor vehicle while in transit (E818.0-E818.9)*
> *watercraft whether or not in transit (E838.0-E838.9)*

E868.3 Carbon monoxide from incomplete combustion of other domestic fuels
Carbon monoxide from incomplete combustion of:

coal	⎱
coke	⎰ in domestic stove or fireplace
kerosene	
wood	

> **EXCLUDES** *carbon monoxide from smoke and fumes due to conflagration (E890.0-E893.9)*

E868.8 Carbon monoxide from other sources
> Carbon monoxide from:
>> blast furnace gas
>> incomplete combustion of fuels in industrial use
>> kiln vapor

E868.9 Unspecified carbon monoxide

✓4ᵗʰ **E869 Accidental poisoning by other gases and vapors**

> EXCLUDES   *effects of gases used as anesthetics (E855.1, E938.2)*
> *fumes from heavy metals (E866.0-E866.4)*
> *smoke and fumes due to conflagration or explosion (E890.0-E899)*

E869.0 Nitrogen oxides

E869.1 Sulfur dioxide

E869.2 Freon

E869.3 Lacrimogenic gas [tear gas]
> Bromobenzyl cyanide
> Chloroacetophenone
> Ethyliodoacetate

E869.4 Second-hand tobacco smoke

E869.8 Other specified gases and vapors
> Chlorine
> Hydrocyanic acid gas

E869.9 Unspecified gases and vapors

MISADVENTURES TO PATIENTS DURING SURGICAL AND MEDICAL CARE (E870-E876)

> EXCLUDES   *accidental overdose of drug and wrong drug given in error (E850.0-E858.9)*
> *surgical and medical procedures as the cause of abnormal reaction by the patient, without mention of misadventure at the time of procedure (E878.0-E879.9)*

✓4ᵗʰ **E870 Accidental cut, puncture, perforation, or hemorrhage during medical care**

E870.0 Surgical operation

E870.1 Infusion or transfusion

E870.2 Kidney dialysis or other perfusion

E870.3 Injection or vaccination

E870.4 Endoscopic examination

E870.5 Aspiration of fluid or tissue, puncture, and catheterization
> Abdominal paracentesis
> Aspirating needle biopsy
> Blood sampling
> Lumbar puncture
> Thoracentesis
>> EXCLUDES   *heart catheterization (E870.6)*

E870.6 Heart catheterization

E870.7 Administration of enema

E870.8 Other specified medical care

E870.9 Unspecified medical care

✓4ᵗʰ **E871 Foreign object left in body during procedure**

E871.0 Surgical operation

E871.1 Infusion or transfusion

E871.2 Kidney dialysis or other perfusion

E871.3 Injection or vaccination

E871.4 Endoscopic examination

E871.5 Aspiration of fluid or tissue, puncture, and catheterization
> Abdominal paracentesis
> Aspiration needle biopsy
> Blood sampling
> Lumbar puncture
> Thoracentesis
>> EXCLUDES   *heart catheterization (E871.6)*

E871.6 Heart catheterization

E871.7 Removal of catheter or packing

E871.8 Other specified procedures

E871.9 Unspecified procedure

✓4ᵗʰ **E872 Failure of sterile precautions during procedure**

E872.0 Surgical operation

E872.1 Infusion or transfusion

E872.2 Kidney dialysis and other perfusion

E872.3 Injection or vaccination

E872.4 Endoscopic examination

E872.5 Aspiration of fluid or tissue, puncture, and catheterization
> Abdominal paracentesis
> Aspiration needle biopsy
> Blood sampling
> Lumbar puncture
> Thoracentesis
>> EXCLUDES   *heart catheterization (E872.6)*

E872.6 Heart catheterization

E872.8 Other specified procedures

E872.9 Unspecified procedure

✓4ᵗʰ **E873 Failure in dosage**

> EXCLUDES   *accidental overdose of drug, medicinal or biological substance (E850.0-E858.9)*

E873.0 Excessive amount of blood or other fluid during transfusion or infusion

E873.1 Incorrect dilution of fluid during infusion

E873.2 Overdose of radiation in therapy

E873.3 Inadvertent exposure of patient to radiation during medical care

E873.4 Failure in dosage in electroshock or insulin-shock therapy

E873.5 Inappropriate [too hot or too cold] temperature in local application and packing

E873.6 Nonadministration of necessary drug or medicinal substance

E873.8 Other specified failure in dosage

E873.9 Unspecified failure in dosage

✓4ᵗʰ **E874 Mechanical failure of instrument or apparatus during procedure**

E874.0 Surgical operation

E874.1 Infusion and transfusion
> Air in system

E874.2 Kidney dialysis and other perfusion

E874.3 Endoscopic examination

E874.4 Aspiration of fluid or tissue, puncture, and catheterization
> Abdominal paracentesis   Lumbar puncture
> Aspiration needle biopsy   Thoracentesis
> Blood sampling
>> EXCLUDES   *heart catheterization (E874.5)*

E874.5 Heart catheterization

E874.8 Other specified procedures

E874.9 Unspecified procedure

✓4ᵗʰ **E875 Contaminated or infected blood, other fluid, drug, or biological substance**

> INCLUDES   presence of:
>> bacterial pyrogens
>> endotoxin-producing bacteria
>> serum hepatitis-producing agent

E875.0 Contaminated substance transfused or infused

E875.1 Contaminated substance injected or used for vaccination

E875.2 Contaminated drug or biological substance administered by other means

E875.8 Other

E875.9 Unspecified

√4th **E876 Other and unspecified misadventures during medical care**

E876.0 Mismatched blood in transfusion

E876.1 Wrong fluid in infusion

E876.2 Failure in suture and ligature during surgical operation

E876.3 Endotracheal tube wrongly placed during anesthetic procedure

E876.4 Failure to introduce or to remove other tube or instrument
> EXCLUDES   *foreign object left in body during procedure (E871.0-E871.9)*

▲   * E876.5 Performance of wrong operation (procedure) on correct patient
> ▶Wrong device implanted into correct surgical site◀
> EXCLUDES ▶*correct operation (procedure) performed on wrong body part (E876.7)*◀

●   * E876.6 Performance of operation (procedure) on patient not scheduled for surgery
> Performance of operation (procedure) intended for another patient
> Performance of operation (procedure) on wrong patient

●   * E876.7 Performance of correct operation (procedure) on wrong side/body part
> Performance of correct operation (procedure) on wrong side
> Performance of correct operation (procedure) on wrong site

E876.8 Other specified misadventures during medical care
> Performance of inappropriate treatment NEC

E876.9 Unspecified misadventure during medical care

SURGICAL AND MEDICAL PROCEDURES AS THE CAUSE OF ABNORMAL REACTION OF PATIENT OR LATER COMPLICATION, WITHOUT MENTION OF MISADVENTURE AT THE TIME OF PROCEDURE (E878-E879)

> INCLUDES   procedures as the cause of abnormal reaction, such as:
> displacement or malfunction of prosthetic device
> hepatorenal failure, postoperative
> malfunction of external stoma
> postoperative intestinal obstruction
> rejection of transplanted organ

> EXCLUDES   *anesthetic management properly carried out as the cause of adverse effect (E937.0-E938.9)*
> *infusion and transfusion, without mention of misadventure in the technique of procedure (E930.0-E949.9)*

√4th **E878 Surgical operation and other surgical procedures as the cause of abnormal reaction of patient, or of later complication, without mention of misadventure at the time of operation**

E878.0 Surgical operation with transplant of whole organ
> Transplantation of: Transplantation of:
> heart   liver
> kidney

E878.1 Surgical operation with implant of artificial internal device
> Cardiac pacemaker
> Electrodes implanted in brain
> Heart valve prosthesis
> Internal orthopedic device

E878.2 Surgical operation with anastomosis, bypass, or graft, with natural or artificial tissues used as implant
> Anastomosis:
> arteriovenous
> gastrojejunal
> Graft of blood vessel, tendon, or skin
> EXCLUDES   *external stoma (E878.3)*

E878.3 Surgical operation with formation of external stoma
> Colostomy   Gastrostomy
> Cystostomy   Ureterostomy
> Duodenostomy

E878.4 Other restorative surgery

E878.5 Amputation of limb(s)

E878.6 Removal of other organ (partial) (total)

E878.8 Other specified surgical operations and procedures

E878.9 Unspecified surgical operations and procedures

√4th **E879 Other procedures, without mention of misadventure at the time of procedure, as the cause of abnormal reaction of patient, or of later complication**

E879.0 Cardiac catheterization

E879.1 Kidney dialysis

E879.2 Radiological procedure and radiotherapy
> EXCLUDES   *radio-opaque dyes for diagnostic x-ray procedures (E947.8)*

E879.3 Shock therapy
> Electroshock therapy   Insulin-shock therapy

E879.4 Aspiration of fluid
> Lumbar puncture   Thoracentesis

E879.5 Insertion of gastric or duodenal sound

E879.6 Urinary catheterization

E879.7 Blood sampling

E879.8 Other specified procedures
> Blood transfusion

E879.9 Unspecified procedure

ACCIDENTAL FALLS (E880-E888)

> EXCLUDES   *falls (in or from):*
> *burning building (E890.8, E891.8)*
> *into fire (E890.0-E899)*
> *into water (with submersion or drowning) (E910.0-E910.9)*
> *machinery (in operation) (E919.0-E919.9)*
> *on edged, pointed, or sharp object (E920.0-E920.9)*
> *transport vehicle (E800.0-E845.9)*
> *vehicle not elsewhere classifiable (E846-E848)*

√4th **E880 Fall on or from stairs or steps**

E880.0 Escalator

E880.1 Fall on or from sidewalk curb
> EXCLUDES   *fall from moving sidewalk (E885.9)*

E880.9 Other stairs or steps

√4th **E881 Fall on or from ladders or scaffolding**

E881.0 Fall from ladder

E881.1 Fall from scaffolding

E882 Fall from or out of building or other structure
> Fall from: Fall from:
> balcony   turret
> bridge   viaduct
> building   wall
> flagpole   window
> tower   Fall through roof
> EXCLUDES   *collapse of a building or structure (E916)*
> *fall or jump from burning building (E890.8, E891.8)*

---

*   Wrong surgery edit applies.

√4th Fourth-digit Required   ▶◀ Revised Text   ● New Code   ▲ Revised Code TitleDx

E Codes

E883–E891.3

√4ᵗʰ **E883 Fall into hole or other opening in surface**

> INCLUDES   fall into: fall into:
>   cavity   shaft
>   dock   swimming pool
>   hole   tank
>   pit   well
>   quarry
>
> EXCLUDES   *fall into water NOS (E910.9)*
>   *that resulting in drowning or submersion without*
>   *mention of injury (E910.0-E910.9)*

    E883.0 Accident from diving or jumping into water [swimming pool]
> Strike or hit:
>   against bottom when jumping or diving into water
>   wall or board of swimming pool
>   water surface
>   EXCLUDES   *diving with insufficient air supply (E913.2)*
>   *effects of air pressure from diving (E902.2)*

    E883.1 Accidental fall into well

    E883.2 Accidental fall into storm drain or manhole

    E883.9 Fall into other hole or other opening in surface

√4ᵗʰ **E884 Other fall from one level to another**

    E884.0 Fall from playground equipment
>   EXCLUDES   *recreational machinery (E919.8)*

    E884.1 Fall from cliff

    E884.2 Fall from chair

    E884.3 Fall from wheelchair

    E884.4 Fall from bed

    E884.5 Fall from other furniture

    E884.6 Fall from commode
> Toilet

    E884.9 Other fall from one level to another
> Fall from: Fall from:
>   embankment   stationary vehicle
>   haystack   tree

√4ᵗʰ **E885 Fall on same level from slipping, tripping, or stumbling**

    E885.0 Fall from (nonmotorized) scooter

    E885.1 Fall from roller skates
> Heelies
> In-line skates
> Wheelies

    E885.2 Fall from skateboard

    E885.3 Fall from skis

    E885.4 Fall from snowboard

    E885.9 Fall from other slipping, tripping, or stumbling
> Fall on moving sidewalk

√4ᵗʰ **E886 Fall on same level from collision, pushing, or shoving, by or with other person**
> EXCLUDES   *crushed or pushed by a crowd or human stampede*
>   *(E917.1, E917.6)*

    E886.0 In sports
> Tackles in sports
>   EXCLUDES   *kicked, stepped on, struck by object, in sports*
>   *(E917.0, E917.5)*

    E886.9 Other and unspecified
> Fall from collision of pedestrian (conveyance) with
>   another pedestrian (conveyance)

    E887 Fracture, cause unspecified

√4ᵗʰ **E888 Other and unspecified fall**
> Accidental fall NOS
> Fall on same level NOS

    E888.0 Fall resulting in striking against sharp object
> Use additional external cause code to identify object
>   (E920)

    E888.1 Fall resulting in striking against other object

    E888.8 Other fall

    E888.9 Unspecified fall
> Fall NOS

ACCIDENTS CAUSED BY FIRE AND FLAMES (E890-E899)

> INCLUDES   asphyxia or poisoning due to conflagration or ignition
>   burning by fire
>   secondary fires resulting from explosion
>
> EXCLUDES   *arson (E968.0)*
>   *fire in or on:*
>   *machinery (in operation) (E919.0-E919.9)*
>   *transport vehicle other than stationary vehicle*
>   *(E800.0-E845.9)*
>   *vehicle not elsewhere classifiable (E846-E848)*

√4ᵗʰ **E890 Conflagration in private dwelling**

> INCLUDES   conflagration in:
>   apartment
>   boarding house
>   camping place
>   caravan
>   farmhouse
>   house
>   lodging house
>   mobile home
>   private garage
>   rooming house
>   tenement
>   conflagration originating from sources classifiable to
>   E893-E898 in the above buildings

    E890.0 Explosion caused by conflagration

    E890.1 Fumes from combustion of polyvinylchloride [PVC] and similar material in conflagration

    E890.2 Other smoke and fumes from conflagration
> Carbon monoxide   } from conflagration in private
> Fumes NOS   building
> Smoke NOS

    E890.3 Burning caused by conflagration

    E890.8 Other accident resulting from conflagration
> Collapse of
> Fall from   } burning private
> Hit by object falling from   building
> Jump from

    E890.9 Unspecified accident resulting from conflagration in private dwelling

√4ᵗʰ **E891 Conflagration in other and unspecified building or structure**
> Conflagration in:
>   barn
>   church
>   convalescent and other residential home
>   dormitory of educational institution
>   factory
>   farm outbuildings
>   hospital
>   hotel
>   school
>   store
>   theater
> Conflagration originating from sources classifiable to E893-E898, in
>   the above buildings

    E891.0 Explosion caused by conflagration

    E891.1 Fumes from combustion of polyvinylchloride [PVC] and similar material in conflagration

    E891.2 Other smoke and fumes from conflagration
> Carbon monoxide   } from conflagration in private
> Fumes NOS   building or structure
> Smoke NOS

    E891.3 Burning caused by conflagration

√4ᵗʰ Fourth-digit Required   ▶◀ Revised Text   ● New Code   ▲ Revised Code TitleDx

E891.8 Other accident resulting from conflagration

Collapse of
Fall from
Hit by object falling from
Jump from
} burning private building or structure

E891.9 Unspecified accident resulting from conflagration of other and unspecified building or structure

E892 Conflagration not in building or structure

Fire (uncontrolled) (in) (of):
forest
grass
hay
lumber
mine
prairie
transport vehicle [any], except while in transit
tunnel

✓4th E893 Accident caused by ignition of clothing

EXCLUDES *ignition of clothing:*
from highly inflammable material (E894)
with conflagration (E890.0-E892)

E893.0 From controlled fire in private dwelling

Ignition of clothing from:

normal fire (charcoal) (coal) (electric) (gas) (wood) in:
brazier
fireplace
furnace
stove
} in private dwelling (as listed in E890)

E893.1 From controlled fire in other building or structure

Ignition of clothing from:

normal fire (charcoal) (coal) (electric) (gas) (wood) in:
brazier
fireplace
furnace
stove
} in other building or structure (as listed in E891)

E893.2 From controlled fire not in building or structure

Ignition of clothing from:
bonfire (controlled)
brazier fire (controlled), not in building or structure
trash fire (controlled)

EXCLUDES *conflagration not in building (E892)*
trash fire out of control (E892)

E893.8 From other specified sources

Ignition of clothing from:
blowlamp
blowtorch
burning bedspread
candle
cigar

Ignition of clothing from:
cigarette
lighter
matches
pipe
welding torch

E893.9 Unspecified source

Ignition of clothing (from controlled fire NOS) (in building NOS) NOS

E894 Ignition of highly inflammable material

Ignition of:
benzine
gasoline
fat
kerosene
paraffin
petrol
} (with ignition of clothing)

EXCLUDES *ignition of highly inflammable material with:*
conflagration (E890.0-E892)
explosion (E923.0-E923.9)

E895 Accident caused by controlled fire in private dwelling

Burning by (flame of) normal fire (charcoal) (coal) (electric) (gas) (wood) in:
brazier
fireplace
furnace
stove
} in private dwelling (as listed in E890)

EXCLUDES *burning by hot objects not producing fire or flames (E924.0-E924.9)*
ignition of clothing from these sources (E893.0)
poisoning by carbon monoxide from incomplete combustion of fuel (E867-E868.9)
that with conflagration (E890.0-E890.9)

E896 Accident caused by controlled fire in other and unspecified building or structure

Burning by (flame of) normal fire (charcoal) (coal)(electric)(gas)(wood) in:
brazier
fireplace
furnace
stove
} in other building or structure (as listed in E891)

EXCLUDES *burning by hot objects not producing fire or flames (E924.0-E924.9)*
ignition of clothing from these sources (E893.1)
poisoning by carbon monoxide from incomplete combustion of fuel (E867-E868.9)
that with conflagration (E891.0-E891.9)

E897 Accident caused by controlled fire not in building or structure

Burns from flame of:
bonfire
brazier fire, not in building or structure
trash fire
} controlled

EXCLUDES *ignition of clothing from these sources (E893.2)*
trash fire out of control (E892)
that with conflagration (E892)

✓4th E898 Accident caused by other specified fire and flames

EXCLUDES *conflagration (E890.0-E892)*
that with ignition of:
clothing (E893.0-E893.9)
highly inflammable material (E894)

E898.0 Burning bedclothes

Bed set on fire NOS

E898.1 Other

Burning by:
blowlamp
blowtorch
candle
cigar
cigarette
fire in room NOS

Burning by:
lamp
lighter
matches
pipe
welding torch

E899 Accident caused by unspecified fire

Burning NOS

ACCIDENTS DUE TO NATURAL AND ENVIRONMENTAL FACTORS (E900-E909)

✓4th E900 Excessive heat

E900.0 Due to weather conditions

Excessive heat as the external cause of:
ictus solaris
siriasis
sunstroke

E900.1 Of man-made origin

Heat (in):
boiler room
drying room
factory
furnace room
generated in transport vehicle
kitchen

E900.9 Of unspecified origin

☑4ᵗʰ **E901 Excessive cold**

E901.0 Due to weather conditions
Excessive cold as the cause of:
chilblains NOS
immersion foot

E901.1 Of man-made origin

Contact with or
inhalation of:
dry ice
liquid air
liquid hydrogen
liquid nitrogen

Prolonged exposure in:
deep freeze unit
refrigerator

E901.8 Other specified origin

E901.9 Of unspecified origin

☑4ᵗʰ **E902 High and low air pressure and changes in air pressure**

E902.0 Residence or prolonged visit at high altitude
Residence or prolonged visit at high altitude as the cause of:
Acosta syndrome
Alpine sickness
altitude sickness
Andes disease
anoxia, hypoxia
barotitis, barodontalgia, barosinusitis, otitic barotrauma
hypobarism, hypobaropathy
mountain sickness
range disease

E902.1 In aircraft
Sudden change in air pressure in aircraft during ascent or descent as the cause of:
aeroneurosis
aviators' disease

E902.2 Due to diving

High air pressure from rapid
descent in water
Reduction in atmospheric
pressure while surfacing
from deep water diving

} as the cause of:
caisson disease
divers' disease
divers' palsy or
paralysis

E902.8 Due to other specified causes
Reduction in atmospheric pressure whilesurfacing from underground

E902.9 Unspecified cause

E903 Travel and motion

☑4ᵗʰ **E904 Hunger, thirst, exposure, and neglect**
EXCLUDES *any condition resulting from homicidal intent (E968.0-E968.9)*
hunger, thirst, and exposure resulting from accidents connected with transport (E800.0-E848)

E904.0 Abandonment or neglect of infants and helpless persons

Exposure to weather
conditions
Hunger or thirst

} resulting from
abandonment or
neglect

Desertion of newborn
Inattention at or after birth
Lack of care (helpless person) (infant)
EXCLUDES *criminal [purposeful] neglect (E968.4)*

E904.1 Lack of food
Lack of food as the cause of:
inanition
insufficient nourishment
starvation
EXCLUDES *hunger resulting from abandonment or neglect (E904.0)*

E904.2 Lack of water
Lack of water as the cause of:
dehydration
inanition
EXCLUDES *dehydration due to acute fluid loss (276.51)*

E904.3 Exposure (to weather conditions), not elsewhere classifiable
Exposure NOS
Humidity
Struck by hailstones
EXCLUDES *struck by lightning (E907)*

E904.9 Privation, unqualified
Destitution

☑4ᵗʰ **E905 Venomous animals and plants as the cause of poisoning and toxic reactions**
INCLUDES chemical released by animal
insects
release of venom through fangs, hairs, spines, tentacles, and other venom apparatus
EXCLUDES *eating of poisonous animals or plants (E865.0-E865.9)*

E905.0 Venomous snakes and lizards

Cobra
Copperhead snake
Coral snake
Fer de lance
Gila monster
Krait

Mamba
Rattlesnake
Sea snake
Snake (venomous)
Viper
Water moccasin

EXCLUDES *bites of snakes and lizards known to be nonvenomous (E906.2)*

E905.1 Venomous spiders
Black widow spider
Brown spider
Tarantula (venomous)

E905.2 Scorpion

E905.3 Hornets, wasps, and bees
Yellow jacket

E905.4 Centipede and venomous millipede (tropical)

E905.5 Other venomous arthropods
Sting of:
ant
caterpillar

E905.6 Venomous marine animals and plants
Puncture by sea urchin spine
Sting of:
coral
jelly fish
nematocysts
sea anemone
sea cucumber
other marine animal or plant
EXCLUDES *bites and other injuries caused by nonvenomous marine animal (E906.2-E906.8)*
bite of sea snake (venomous) (E905.0)

E905.7 Poisoning and toxic reactions caused by other plants
Injection of poisons or toxins into or through skin by plant thorns, spines, or other mechanisms
EXCLUDES *puncture wound NOS by plant thorns or spines (E920.8)*

E905.8 Other specified

E905.9 Unspecified
Sting NOS
Venomous bite NOS

☑4ᵗʰ **E906 Other injury caused by animals**
EXCLUDES *poisoning and toxic reactions caused by venomous animals and insects (E905.0-E905.9)*
road vehicle accident involving animals (E827.0-E828.9)
tripping or falling over an animal (E885.9)

E906.0 Dog bite

E906.1 Rat bite

☑4ᵗʰ Fourth-digit Required   ▶◀ Revised Text   ● New Code   ▲ Revised Code TitleDx

E906.2 Bite of nonvenomous snakes and lizards

E906.3 Bite of other animal except arthropod
  Cats   Rodents, except rats
  Moray eel   Shark

E906.4 Bite of nonvenomous arthropod
  Insect bite NOS

E906.5 Bite by unspecified animal
  Animal bite NOS

E906.8 Other specified injury caused by animal
  Butted by animal
  Fallen on by horse or other animal, not being ridden
  Gored by animal
  Implantation of quills of porcupine
  Pecked by bird
  Run over by animal, not being ridden
  Stepped on by animal, not being ridden
  EXCLUDES *injury by animal being ridden (E828.0-E828.9)*

E906.9 Unspecified injury caused by animal

E907 Lightning
  EXCLUDES *injury from:*
              fall of tree or other object caused by lightning (E916)
              fire caused by lightning (E890.0-E892)

✓4ᵗʰ **E908 Cataclysmic storms, and floods resulting from storms**
  EXCLUDES *collapse of dam or man-made structure causing flood*
              (E909.3)

  E908.0 Hurricane
    Storm surge
    "Tidal wave" caused by storm action
    Typhoon

  E908.1 Tornado
    Cyclone
    Twisters

  E908.2 Floods
    Torrential rainfall
    Flash flood
    EXCLUDES *collapse of dam or man-made structure*
                causing flood (E909.3)

  E908.3 Blizzard (snow)(ice)

  E908.4 Dust storm

  E908.8 Other cataclysmic storms
    Cloudburst

  E908.9 Unspecified cataclysmic storms, and floods resulting
         from storms
    Storm NOS

✓4ᵗʰ **E909 Cataclysmic earth surface movements and eruptions**

  E909.0 Earthquakes

  E909.1 Volcanic eruptions
    Burns from lava
    Ash inhalation

  E909.2 Avalanche, landslide, or mudslide

  E909.3 Collapse of dam or man-made structure

  E909.4 Tidalwave caused by earthquake
    Tidalwave NOS
    Tsunami
    EXCLUDES *tidalwave caused by tropical storm (E908.0)*

  E909.8 Other cataclysmic earth surface movements and
         eruptions

  E909.9 Unspecified cataclysmic earth surface movements and
         eruptions

ACCIDENTS CAUSED BY SUBMERSION, SUFFOCATION, AND FOREIGN BODIES (E910-E915)

✓4ᵗʰ **E910 Accidental drowning and submersion**
  INCLUDES immersion
               swimmers' cramp
  EXCLUDES *diving accident (NOS) (resulting in injury except*
              drowning) (E883.0)
              diving with insufficient air supply (E913.2)
              drowning and submersion due to:
              cataclysm (E908-E909)
              machinery accident (E919.0-E919.9)
              transport accident (E800.0-E845.9)
              effect of high and low air pressure (E902.2)
              injury from striking against objects while in running
              water (E917.2)

  E910.0 While water-skiing
    Fall from water skis with submersion or drowning
    EXCLUDES *accident to water-skier involving a watercraft*
                and resulting in submersion or other
                injury (E830.4, E831.4)

  E910.1 While engaged in other sport or recreational activity
         with diving equipment
    Scuba diving NOS
    Skin diving NOS
    Underwater spear fishing NOS

  E910.2 While engaged in other sport or recreational activity
         without diving equipment
    Fishing or hunting, except from boat or with diving
      equipment
    Ice skating
    Playing in water
    Surfboarding
    Swimming NOS
    Voluntarily jumping from boat, not involved in accident,
      for swim NOS
    Wading in water
    EXCLUDES *jumping into water to rescue another person*
                (E910.3)

  E910.3 While swimming or diving for purposes other than
         recreation or sport
    Marine salvage   ⎫
    Pearl diving   ⎪
    Placement of fishing nets ⎬ (with diving
    Rescue (attempt) of another ⎪   equipment)
      person   ⎪
    Underwater construction or ⎭
      repairs

  E910.4 In bathtub

  E910.8 Other accidental drowning or submersion
    Drowning in:
      quenching tank
      swimming pool

  E910.9 Unspecified accidental drowning or submersion
    Accidental fall into water NOS
    Drowning NOS

E911 Inhalation and ingestion of food causing obstruction of respiratory tract or suffocation
  Aspiration and inhalation of food [any] (into respiratory tract) NOS
  Asphyxia by   ⎫ food [including bone, seed in food,
  Choked on   ⎬   regurgitated food]
  Suffocation by   ⎭

  Compression of trachea   ⎫
  Interruption of respiration ⎬ by food lodged in
  Obstruction of respiration ⎭   esophagus

  Obstruction of pharynx by food (bolus)
  EXCLUDES *injury, except asphyxia and obstruction of respiratory*
              passage, caused by food (E915)
              obstruction of esophagus by food without mention of
              asphyxia or obstruction of respiratory passage
              (E915)

E912 Inhalation and ingestion of other object causing obstruction of respiratory tract or suffocation

Aspiration and inhalation of foreign body except food (into respiratory tract) NOS
Foreign object [bean] [marble] in nose
Obstruction of pharynx by foreign body
Compression ⎫
Interruption of respiration ⎬ by foreign body in esophagus
Obstruction of respiration ⎭

EXCLUDES injury, except asphyxia and obstruction of respiratory passage, caused by foreign body (E915)
obstruction of esophagus by foreign body without mention of asphyxia or obstruction in respiratory passage (E915)

✓4th E913 Accidental mechanical suffocation

EXCLUDES mechanical suffocation from or by:
accidental inhalation or ingestion of:
food (E911)
foreign object (E912)
cataclysm (E908-E909)
explosion (E921.0-E921.9, E923.0-E923.9)
machinery accident (E919.0-E919.9)

E913.0 In bed or cradle
EXCLUDES suffocation by plastic bag (E913.1)

E913.1 By plastic bag

E913.2 Due to lack of air (in closed place)
Accidentally closed up in refrigerator or other airtight enclosed space
Diving with insufficient air supply
EXCLUDES suffocation by plastic bag (E913.1)

E913.3 By falling earth or other substance
Cave-in NOS
EXCLUDES cave-in caused by cataclysmic earth surface movements and eruptions (E909)
struck by cave-in without asphyxiation or suffocation (E916)

E913.8 Other specified means
Accidental hanging, except in bed or cradle

E913.9 Unspecified means
Asphyxia, mechanical NOS
Strangulation NOS
Suffocation NOS

E914 Foreign body accidentally entering eye and adnexa
EXCLUDES corrosive liquid (E924.1)

E915 Foreign body accidentally entering other orifice
EXCLUDES aspiration and inhalation of foreign body, any, (into respiratory tract) NOS (E911-E912)

OTHER ACCIDENTS (E916-E928)

E916 Struck accidentally by falling object
Collapse of building, except on fire
Falling:
rock
snowslide NOS
stone
tree
Object falling from:
machine, not in operation
stationary vehicle
Code first:
collapse of building on fire (E890.0-E891.9)
falling object in:
cataclysm (E908-E909)
machinery accidents (E919.0-E919.9)
transport accidents (E800.0-E845.9)
vehicle accidents not elsewhere classifiable (E846-E848)
object set in motion by:
explosion (E921.0-E921.9, E923.0-E923.9)
firearm (E922.0-E922.9)
projected object (E917.0-E917.9)

✓4th E917 Striking against or struck accidentally by objects or persons

INCLUDES bumping into or against ⎫
colliding with ⎪ object (moving) (projected) (stationary)
kicking against ⎬ pedestrian conveyance
stepping on ⎪ person
struck by ⎭

EXCLUDES fall from:
collision with another person, except when caused by a crowd (E886.0-E886.9)
stumbling over object (E885.9)
fall resulting in striking against object (E888.0, E888.1)
injury caused by:
assault (E960.0-E960.1, E967.0-E967.9)
cutting or piercing instrument (E920.0-E920.9)
explosion (E921.0-E921.9, E923.0-E923.9)
firearm (E922.0-E922.9)
machinery (E919.0-E919.9)
transport vehicle (E800.0-E845.9)
vehicle not elsewhere classifiable (E846-E848)

E917.0 In sports without subsequent fall
Kicked or stepped on during game (football) (rugby)
Struck by hit or thrown ball
Struck by hockey stick or puck

E917.1 Caused by a crowd, by collective fear or panic without subsequent fall
Crushed ⎫
Pushed ⎬ by crowd or human stampede
Stepped on ⎭

E917.2 In running water without subsequent fall
EXCLUDES drowning or submersion (E910.0-E910.9)
that in sports (E917.0, E917.5)

E917.3 Furniture without subsequent fall
EXCLUDES fall from furniture (E884.2, E884.4-E884.5)

E917.4 Other stationary object without subsequent fall
Bath tub
Fence
Lamp-post

E917.5 Object in sports with subsequent fall
Knocked down while boxing

E917.6 Caused by a crowd, by collective fear or panic with subsequent fall

E917.7 Furniture with subsequent fall
EXCLUDES fall from furniture (E884.2, E884.4-E884.5)

E917.8 Other stationary object with subsequent fall
Bath tub
Fence
Lamp-post

E917.9 Other striking against with or without subsequent fall

E918 Caught accidentally in or between objects
Caught, crushed, jammed, or pinched in or between moving or stationary objects, such as:
escalator
folding object
hand tools, appliances, or implements
sliding door and door frame
under packing crate
washing machine wringer
EXCLUDES injury caused by:
cutting or piercing instrument (E920.0-E920.9)
machinery (E919.0-E919.9)
▶mechanism or component of firearm and air gun (E928.7)◀
transport vehicle (E800.0-E845.9)
vehicle not elsewhere classifiable (E846-E848)
struck accidentally by:
falling object (E916)
object (moving) (projected) (E917.0-E917.9)

☑4ᵗʰ **E919 Accidents caused by machinery**

    INCLUDES

burned by	
caught in (moving parts of)	
collapse of	
crushed by	
cut or pierced by	
drowning or submersion	
caused by	
expolosion of, on, in	
fall from or into moving part	
of	
fire starting in or on	machinery (accident)
mechanical suffocation	
caused by	
object falling from, on, in	
motion by	
overturning of	
pinned under	
run over by	
struck by	
thrown from	

  caught between machinery and other object
  machinery accident NOS

    EXCLUDES   *accidents involving machinery, not in operation (E884.9,*
             E916-E918)
        injury caused by:
          electric current in connection with machinery
             (E925.0-E925.9)
          escalator (E880.0, E918)
          explosion of pressure vessel in connection with
             machinery (E921.0-E921.9)
          ▶*mechanism or component of firearm and air gun*
             (E928.7)◀
          moving sidewalk (E885.9)
          powered hand tools, appliances, and implements
             (E916-E918, E920.0-E921.9, E923.0-E926.9)
          transport vehicle accidents involving machinery
             (E800.0-E848)
          poisoning by carbon monoxide generated by machine
             (E868.8)

E919.0 Agricultural machines

Animal-powered	Farm tractor
agricultural machine	Harvester
Combine	Hay mower or rake
Derrick, hay	Reaper
Farm machinery NOS	Thresher

    EXCLUDES   *that in transport under own power on the*
          highway (E810.0-E819.9)
          that being towed by another vehicle on the
             highway (E810.0-E819.9, E827.0-E827.9,
             E829.0-E829.9)
          that involved in accident classifiable to
             E820-E829 (E820.0-E829.9)

E919.1 Mining and earth-drilling machinery

  Bore or drill (land) (seabed)
  Shaft hoist
  Shaft lift
  Under-cutter

    EXCLUDES   *coal car, tram, truck, and tub in mine (E846)*

E919.2 Lifting machines and appliances

Chain hoist	
Crane	
Derrick	
Elevator (building) (grain)	except in agricultural or
Forklift truck	mining
Lift	operations
Pulley block	
Winch	

    EXCLUDES   *that being towed by another vehicle on the*
          highway (E810.0-E819.9, E827.0-E827.9,
             E829.0-829.9)
          that in transport under own power on the
           highway (E810.0-E819.9)
           that involved in accident classifiable to
             E820-E829 (E820.0-E829.9)

E919.3 Metalworking machines

Abrasive wheel	Metal:
Forging machine	milling machine
Lathe	power press
Mechanical shears	rolling-mill
Metal:	sawing machine
drilling machine	

E919.4 Woodworking and forming machines

Band saw	Overhead plane
Bench saw	Powered saw
Circular saw	Radial saw
Molding machine	Sander

    EXCLUDES   *hand saw (E920.1)*

E919.5 Prime movers, except electrical motors

  Gas turbine
  Internal combustion engine
  Steam engine
  Water driven turbine

    EXCLUDES   *that being towed by other vehicle on the*
          highway (E810.0-E819.9, E827.0-E827.9,
             E829.0-E829.9)
          that in transport under own power on the
           highway (E810.0-E819.9)

E919.6 Transmission machinery

Transmission:	Transmission:
belt	pinion
cable	pulley
chain	shaft
gear	

E919.7 Earth moving, scraping, and other excavating machines

Bulldozer	Steam shovel
Road scraper	

    EXCLUDES   *that being towed by other vehicle on the*
          highway (E810.0-E819.9, E827.0-E827.9,
             E829.0-E829.9)
          that in transport under own power on the
           highway (E810.0-E819.9)

E919.8 Other specified machinery

  Machines for manufacture of:
    clothing
    foodstuffs and beverages
    paper
  Printing machine
  Recreational machinery
  Spinning, weaving, and textile machines

E919.9 Unspecified machinery

☑4ᵗʰ **E920 Accidents caused by cutting and piercing instruments or objects**

    INCLUDES

	edged
accidental injury (by) object	pointed
	sharp

    EXCLUDES ▶*injury caused by mechanism or component of firearm*
           and air gun (E928.7)◀

E920.0 Powered lawn mower

E920.1 Other powered hand tools

  Any powered hand tool [compressed air] [electric]
    [explosive cartridge] [hydraulic power], such as:
    drill
    hand saw
    hedge clipper
    rivet gun
    snow blower
    staple gun

    EXCLUDES   *band saw (E919.4)*
          bench saw (E919.4)

E920.2 Powered household appliances and implements

Blender	Electric:
Electric:	knife
beater or mixer	sewing machine
can opener	Garbage disposal appliance
fan	

E920.3 Knives, swords, and daggers

E920.4 Other hand tools and implements

Axe	Paper cutter
Can opener NOS	Pitchfork
Chisel	Rake
Fork	Scissors
Hand saw	Screwdriver
Hoe	Sewing machine, not powered
Ice pick	Shovel
Needle (sewing)	

E920.5 Hypodermic needle
Contaminated needle
Needle stick

E920.8 Other specified cutting and piercing instruments or objects

Arrow	Nail
Broken glass	Plant thorn
Dart	Splinter
Edge of stiff paper	Tin can lid
Lathe turnings	

    EXCLUDES   animal spines or quills (E906.8)
                       flying glass due to explosion (E921.0-E923.9)

E920.9 Unspecified cutting and piercing instrument or object

✓4th E921 Accident caused by explosion of pressure vessel
    INCLUDES   accidental explosion of pressure vessels, whether or not part of machinery
    EXCLUDES   explosion of pressure vessel on transport vehicle (E800.0-E845.9)

E921.0 Boilers

E921.1 Gas cylinders
Air tank   Pressure gas tank

E921.8 Other specified pressure vessels
Aerosol can   Tin can lid
Automobile tire

E921.9 Unspecified pressure vessel

✓4th E922 Accident caused by firearm, and air gun missile
    EXCLUDES   ►injury caused by mechanism or component of firearm and air gun (E928.7)◄

E922.0 Handgun
Pistol   Revolver
    EXCLUDES   Verey pistol (E922.8)

E922.1 Shotgun (automatic)

E922.2 Hunting rifle

E922.3 Military firearms
Army rifle   Machine gun

E922.4 Air gun
BB gun   Pellet gun

E922.5 Paintball gun

E922.8 Other specified firearm missile
Verey pistol [flare]

E922.9 Unspecified firearm missile
Gunshot wound NOS
Shot NOS

✓4th E923 Accident caused by explosive material
    INCLUDES   flash burns and other injuries resulting from explosion of explosive material
                   ignition of highly explosive material with explosion
    EXCLUDES   explosion:
                 in or on machinery (E919.0-E919.9)
                 on any transport vehicle, except stationary motor vehicle (E800.0-E848)
                 with conflagration (E890.0, E891.0,E892)
                 ►injury caused by mechanism or component of firearm and air gun (E928.7)◄
                 secondary fires resulting from explosion (E890.0-E899)

E923.0 Fireworks

E923.1 Blasting materials
Blasting cap	Dynamite
Detonator	Explosive [any] used in blasting operations

E923.2 Explosive gases
Acetylene	Fire damp
Butane	Gasoline fumes
Coal gas	Methane
Explosion in mine NOS	Propane

E923.8 Other explosive materials
Bomb	Torpedo
Explosive missile	Explosion in munitions:
Grenade	dump
Mine	factory
Shell	

E923.9 Unspecified explosive material
Explosion NOS

✓4th E924 Accident caused by hot substance or object, caustic or corrosive material, and steam
    EXCLUDES   burning NOS (E899)
                 chemical burn resulting from swallowing a corrosive substance (E860.0-E864.4)
                 fire caused by these substances and objects (E890.0-E894)
                 radiation burns (E926.0-E926.9)
                 therapeutic misadventures (E870.0-E876.9)

E924.0 Hot liquids and vapors, including steam
Burning or scalding by:
     boiling water
     hot or boiling liquids not primarily caustic or corrosive
     liquid metal
     steam
     other hot vapor
    EXCLUDES   hot (boiling) tap water (E924.2)

E924.1 Caustic and corrosive substances
Burning by:
     acid [any kind]
     ammonia
     caustic oven cleaner or other substance
     corrosive substance
     lye
     vitriol

E924.2 Hot (boiling) tap water

E924.8 Other
Burning by:
     heat from electric heating appliance
     hot object NOS
     light bulb
     steam pipe

E924.9 Unspecified

✓4th E925 Accident caused by electric current
    INCLUDES   electric current from exposed wire, faulty appliance, high voltage cable, live rail, or open electric socket as the cause of:
                 burn
                 cardiac fibrillation
                 convulsion
                 electric shock
                 electrocution
                 puncture wound
                 respiratory paralysis
    EXCLUDES   burn by heat from electrical appliance (E924.8)
                 lightning (E907)

E925.0 Domestic wiring and appliances

E925.1 Electric power generating plants, distribution stations, transmission lines
Broken power line

E925.2 Industrial wiring, appliances, and electrical machinery
Conductors
Control apparatus
Electrical equipment and machinery
Transformers

E925.8 Other electric current
  Wiring and appliances in or on:
    farm [not farmhouse]
    outdoors
    public building
    residential institutions
    schools

E925.9 Unspecified electric current
  Burns or other injury from electric current NOS
  Electric shock NOS
  Electrocution NOS

☑4ᵗʰ **E926 Exposure to radiation**
  EXCLUDES *abnormal reaction to or complication of treatment*
            without mention of misadventure (E879.2)
            atomic power plant malfunction in water transport
            (E838.0-E838.9)
            misadventure to patient in surgical and medical
            procedures (E873.2-E873.3)
            use of radiation in war operations (E996-E997.9)

E926.0 Radiofrequency radiation

  Overexposure to: from:
    microwave radiation   high-powered radio and
    radar radiation   television
    radiofrequency   transmitters
    radiofrequency   industrial radiofrequency
    radiation [any]   induction heaters
                                radar installations

E926.1 Infrared heaters and lamps
  Exposure to infrared radiation from heaters and lamps as
    the cause of:
    blistering
    burning
    charring
    inflammatory change
  EXCLUDES *physical contact with heater or lamp (E924.8)*

E926.2 Visible and ultraviolet light sources
  Arc lamps
  Black light sources
  Electrical welding arc
  Oxygas welding torch
  Sun rays
  Tanning bed
  EXCLUDES *excessive heat from these sources*
            (E900.1-E900.9)

E926.3 X-rays and other electromagnetic ionizing radiation
  Gamma rays
  X-rays (hard) (soft)

E926.4 Lasers

E926.5 Radioactive isotopes
  Radiobiologicals
  Radiopharmaceuticals

E926.8 Other specified radiation
  Artificially accelerated beams of ionized particles
    generated by:
    betatrons
    synchrotrons

E926.9 Unspecified radiation
  Radiation NOS

☑4ᵗʰ **E927 Overexertion and strenuous and repetitive movements or
loads**
  ►Use additional code to identify activity (E001-E030)◄

E927.0 Overexertion from sudden strenuous movement
  Sudden trauma from strenuous movement

E927.1 Overexertion from prolonged static position
  Overexertion from maintaining prolonged positions, such
    as:
    holding
    sitting
    standing

E927.2 Excessive physical exertion from prolonged activity

E927.3 Cumulative trauma from repetitive motion
  Cumulative trauma from repetitive movements

E927.4 Cumulative trauma from repetitive impact

**E927.8 Other overexertion and strenuous and repetitive
movements or loads**

**E927.9 Unspecified overexertion and strenuous and repetitive
movements or loads**

☑4ᵗʰ **E928 Other and unspecified environmental and accidental
causes**

E928.0 Prolonged stay in weightless environment
  Weightlessness in spacecraft (simulator)

E928.1 Exposure to noise
  Noise (pollution)
  Sound waves
  Supersonic waves

E928.2 Vibration

E928.3 Human bite

E928.4 External constriction caused by hair

E928.5 External constriction caused by other object

E928.6 Environmental exposure to harmful algae and toxins
  Algae bloom NOS   Florida red tide
  Blue-green algae bloom   Harmful algae bloom
  Brown tide   Pfiesteria piscicida
  Cyanobacteria bloom   Red tide

● **E928.7 Mechanism or component of firearm and air gun**
  Injury due to:
    explosion of gun parts
    recoil
  Pierced, cut, crushed, or pinched by slide, trigger
    mechanism, scope, or other gun part
  Powder burn from firearm or air gun
  EXCLUDES *accident caused by firearm and air gun missile*
            (E922.0-E922.9)

E928.8 Other

E928.9 Unspecified accident
  Accident NOS   }
  Blow NOS   } stated as accidentally
  Casualty (not due to war) }   inflicted
  Decapitation   }

  Knocked down   }
  Killed   } stated as accidentally
  Injury [any part of body, or }   inflicted, but not
    unspecified]   }   otherwise
  Mangled   }   specified
  Wound   }
  EXCLUDES *fracture, cause unspecified (E887)*
            injuries undetermined whether accidentally or
            purposely inflicted (E980.0-E989)

LATE EFFECTS OF ACCIDENTAL INJURY (E929)

Note: This category is to be used to indicate accidental injury as
      the cause of death or disability from late effects, which are
      themselves classifiable elsewhere. The "late effects" include
      conditions reported as such, or as sequelae which may occur
      at any time after the attempted suicide or self-inflicted
      injury.

☑4ᵗʰ **E929 Late effects of accidental injury**
  EXCLUDES *late effects of:*
            surgical and medical procedures (E870.0-E879.9)
            therapeutic use of drugs and medicines
            (E930.0-E949.9)

E929.0 Late effects of motor vehicle accident
  Late effects of accidents classifiable to E810-E825

E929.1 Late effects of other transport accident
  Late effects of accidents classifiable to E800-E807,
    E826-E838, E840-E848

E929.2 Late effects of accidental poisoning
  Late effects of accidents classifiable to E850-E858,
    E860-E869

E Codes

E929.3 Late effects of accidental fall
Late effects of accidents classifiable to E880-E888

E929.4 Late effects of accident caused by fire
Late effects of accidents classifiable to E890-E899

E929.5 Late effects of accident due to natural and environmental factors
Late effects of accidents classifiable to E900-E909

E929.8 Late effects of other accidents
Late effects of accidents classifiable to E910-E928.8

E929.9 Late effects of unspecified accident
Late effects of accidents classifiable to E928.9

DRUGS, MEDICINAL AND BIOLOGICAL SUBSTANCES CAUSING ADVERSE EFFECTS IN THERAPEUTIC USE (E930-E949)

INCLUDES correct drug properly administered in therapeutic or prophylactic dosage, as the cause of any adverse effect including allergic or hypersensitivity reactions

EXCLUDES *accidental overdose of drug and wrong drug given or taken in error (E850.0-E858.9)*
accidents in the technique of administration of drug or biological substance, such as accidental puncture during injection, or contamination of drug (E870.0-E876.9)
administration with suicidal or homicidal intent or intent to harm, or in circumstances classifiable to E950.0-E950.5, E962.0, E980.0-E980.5

See Alphabetic Index for more complete list of specific drugs to be classified under the fourth-digit subdivisions. The American Hospital Formulary numbers can be used to classify new drugs listed by the American Hospital Formulary Service (AHFS). See Appendix C.

√4ᵗʰ **E930 Antibiotics**

EXCLUDES *that used as eye, ear, nose, and throat [ENT], and local anti-infectives (E946.0-E946.9)*

E930.0 Penicillins
Natural	Semisynthetic, such as:
Synthetic	cloxacillin
Semisynthetic, such as:	nafcillin
ampicillin	oxacillin

E930.1 Antifungal antibiotics
Amphotericin B	Hachimycin [trichomycin]
Griseofulvin	Nystatin

E930.2 Chloramphenicol group
Chloramphenicol	Thiamphenicol

E930.3 Erythromycin and other macrolides
Oleandomycin	Spiramycin

E930.4 Tetracycline group
Doxycycline	Oxytetracycline
Minocycline	

E930.5 Cephalosporin group
Cephalexin	Cephaloridine
Cephaloglycin	Cephalothin

E930.6 Antimycobacterial antibiotics
Cycloserine	Rifampin
Kanamycin	Streptomycin

E930.7 Antineoplastic antibiotics
Actinomycins, such as:
Bleomycin
Cactinomycin
Dactinomycin
Daunorubicin
Mitomycin

EXCLUDES *other antineoplastic drugs (E933.1)*

E930.8 Other specified antibiotics

E930.9 Unspecified antibiotic

√4ᵗʰ **E931 Other anti-infectives**

EXCLUDES *ENT, and local anti-infectives (E946.0-E946.9)*

E931.0 Sulfonamides
Sulfadiazine
Sulfafurazole
Sulfamethoxazole

E931.1 Arsenical anti-infectives

E931.2 Heavy metal anti-infectives
Compounds of:
antimony
bismuth
lead
mercury

EXCLUDES *mercurial diuretics (E944.0)*

E931.3 Quinoline and hydroxyquinoline derivatives
Chiniofon
Diiodohydroxyquin

EXCLUDES *antimalarial drugs (E931.4)*

E931.4 Antimalarials and drugs acting on other blood protozoa
Chloroquine phosphate	Proguanil [chloroguanide]
Cycloguanil	Pyrimethamine
Primaquine	Quinine (sulphate)

E931.5 Other antiprotozoal drugs
Emetine

E931.6 Anthelmintics
Hexylresorcinol	Piperazine
Male fern oleoresin	Thiabendazole

E931.7 Antiviral drugs
Methisazone

EXCLUDES *amantadine (E936.4)*
cytarabine (E933.1)
idoxuridine (E946.5)

E931.8 Other antimycobacterial drugs
Ethambutol
Ethionamide
Isoniazid
Para-aminosalicylic acid derivatives
Sulfones

E931.9 Other and unspecified anti-infectives
Flucytosine
Nitrofuranderivatives

√4ᵗʰ **E932 Hormones and synthetic substitutes**

E932.0 Adrenal cortical steroids
Cortisone derivatives
Desoxycorticosterone derivatives
Fluorinated corticosteroid

E932.1 Androgens and anabolic congeners
Nandrolone phenpropionate
Oxymetholone
Testosterone and preparations

E932.2 Ovarian hormones and synthetic substitutes
Contraceptives, oral
Estrogens
Estrogens and progestogens combined
Progestogens

E932.3 Insulins and antidiabetic agents
Acetohexamide
Biguanide derivatives, oral
Chlorpropamide
Glucagon
Insulin
Phenformin
Sulfonylurea derivatives, oral
Tolbutamide

EXCLUDES *adverse effect of insulin administered for shock therapy (E879.3)*

E932.4 Anterior pituitary hormones
Corticotropin
Gonadotropin
Somatotropin [growth hormone]

√4ᵗʰ Fourth-digit Required   ▶◀ Revised Text   ● New Code   ▲ Revised Code TitleDx

E932.5 Posterior pituitary hormones
Vasopressin
EXCLUDES   *oxytocic agents (E945.0)*

E932.6 Parathyroid and parathyroid derivatives

E932.7 Thyroid and thyroid derivatives
Dextrothyroxine
Levothyroxine sodium
Liothyronine
Thyroglobulin

E932.8 Antithyroid agents
Iodides
Thiouracil
Thiourea

E932.9 Other and unspecified hormones and synthetic substitutes

✓4th **E933 Primarily systemic agents**

E933.0 Antiallergic and antiemetic drugs
Antihistamines   Diphenylpyraline
Chlorpheniramine   Thonzylamine
Diphenhydramine   Tripelennamine
EXCLUDES   *phenothiazine-based tranquilizers (E939.1)*

E933.1 Antineoplastic and immunosuppressive drugs
Azathioprine
Busulfan
Chlorambucil
Cyclophosphamide
Cytarabine
Fluorouracil
Mechlorethamine hydrochloride
Mercaptopurine
Triethylenethiophosphoramide [thio-TEPA]
EXCLUDES   *antineoplastic antibiotics (E930.7)*

E933.2 Acidifying agents

E933.3 Alkalizing agents

E933.4 Enzymes, not elsewhere classified
Penicillinase

E933.5 Vitamins, not elsewhere classified
Vitamin A
Vitamin D
EXCLUDES   *nicotinic acid (E942.2)*
            vitamin K (E934.3)

E933.6 Oral bisphosphonates

E933.7 Intravenous bisphosphonates

E933.8 Other systemic agents, not elsewhere classified
Heavy metal antagonists

E933.9 Unspecified systemic agent

✓4th **E934 Agents primarily affecting blood constituents**

E934.0 Iron and its compounds
Ferric salts
Ferrous sulphate and other ferrous salts

E934.1 Liver preparations and other antianemic agents
Folic acid

E934.2 Anticoagulants
Coumarin
Heparin
Phenindione
Prothrombin synthesis inhibitor
Warfarin sodium

E934.3 Vitamin K [phytonadione]

E934.4 Fibrinolysis-affecting drugs
Aminocaproic acid   Streptokinase
Streptodornase   Urokinase

E934.5 Anticoagulant antagonists and other coagulants
Hexadimethrine bromide
Protamine sulfate

E934.6 Gamma globulin

E934.7 Natural blood and blood products
Blood plasma
Human fibrinogen
Packed red cells
Whole blood

E934.8 Other agents affecting blood constituents
Macromolecular blood substitutes

E934.9 Unspecified agent affecting blood constituents

✓4th **E935 Analgesics, antipyretics, and antirheumatics**

E935.0 Heroin
Diacetylmorphine

E935.1 Methadone

E935.2 Other opiates and related narcotics
Codeine [methylmorphine]
Meperidine [pethidine]
Morphine
Opium (alkaloids)

E935.3 Salicylates
Acetylsalicylic acid [aspirin]
Amino derivatives of salicylic acid
Salicylic acid salts

E935.4 Aromatic analgesics, not elsewhere classified
Acetanilid
Paracetamol [acetaminophen]
Phenacetin [acetophenetidin]

E935.5 Pyrazole derivatives
Aminophenazone [aminopyrine]
Phenylbutazone

E935.6 Antirheumatics [antiphlogistics]
Gold salts
Indomethacin
EXCLUDES   *salicylates (E935.3)*
            steroids (E932.0)

E935.7 Other non-narcotic analgesics
Pyrabital

E935.8 Other specified analgesics and antipyretics
Pentazocine

E935.9 Unspecified analgesic and antipyretic

✓4th **E936 Anticonvulsants and anti-Parkinsonism drugs**

E936.0 Oxazolidine derivatives
Paramethadione
Trimethadione

E936.1 Hydantoin derivatives
Phenytoin

E936.2 Succinimides
Ethosuximide
Phensuximide

E936.3 Other and unspecified anticonvulsants
Beclamide
Primidone

E936.4 Anti-Parkinsonism drugs
Amantadine
Ethopropazine [profenamine]
Levodopa [L-dopa]

✓4th **E937 Sedatives and hypnotics**

E937.0 Barbiturates
Amobarbital [amylobarbitone]
Barbital [barbitone]
Butabarbital [butabarbitone]
Pentobarbital [pentobarbitone]
Phenobarbital [phenobarbitone]
Secobarbital [quinalbarbitone]
EXCLUDES   *thiobarbiturates (E938.3)*

E937.1 Chloral hydrate group

E937.2 Paraldehyde

E937.3 Bromine compounds
Bromide
Carbromal (derivatives)

✓4th Fourth-digit Required   ▶◀ Revised Text   ● New Code   ▲ Revised Code TitleDx

E Codes

E937.4 Methaqualone compounds

E937.5 Glutethimide group

E937.6 Mixed sedatives, not elsewhere classified

E937.8 Other sedatives and hypnotics

E937.9 Unspecified
Sleeping:
drug
pill   } NOS
tablet

✓4ᵗʰ **E938 Other central nervous system depressants and anesthetics**

E938.0 Central nervous system muscle-tone depressants
Chlorphenesin (carbamate)
Mephenesin
Methocarbamol

E938.1 Halothane

E938.2 Other gaseous anesthetics
Ether
Halogenated hydrocarbon derivatives, except halothane
Nitrous oxide

E938.3 Intravenous anesthetics
Ketamine
Methohexital [methohexitone]
Thiobarbiturates, such as thiopental sodium

E938.4 Other and unspecified general anesthetics

E938.5 Surface and infiltration anesthetics
Cocaine
Lidocaine [lignocaine]
Procaine
Tetracaine

E938.6 Peripheral nerve- and plexus-blocking anesthetics

E938.7 Spinal anesthetics

E938.9 Other and unspecified local anesthetics

✓4ᵗʰ **E939 Psychotropic agents**

E939.0 Antidepressants
Amitriptyline
Imipramine
Monoamine oxidase [MAO] inhibitors

E939.1 Phenothiazine-based tranquilizers
Chlorpromazine   Prochlorperazine
Fluphenazine   Promazine
Phenothiazine

E939.2 Butyrophenone-based tranquilizers
Haloperidol
Spiperone
Trifluperidol

E939.3 Other antipsychotics, neuroleptics, and major tranquilizers

E939.4 Benzodiazepine-based tranquilizers
Chlordiazepoxide   Lorazepam
Diazepam   Medazepam
Flurazepam   Nitrazepam

E939.5 Other tranquilizers
Hydroxyzine
Meprobamate

E939.6 Psychodysleptics [hallucinogens]
Cannabis (derivatives)   Mescaline
Lysergide [LSD]   Psilocin
Marihuana (derivatives) Psilocybin

E939.7 Psychostimulants
Amphetamine
Caffeine
EXCLUDES central appetite depressants (E947.0)

E939.8 Other psychotropic agents

E939.9 Unspecified psychotropic agent

✓4ᵗʰ **E940 Central nervous system stimulants**

E940.0 Analeptics
Lobeline
Nikethamide

E940.1 Opiate antagonists
Levallorphan
Nalorphine
Naloxone

E940.8 Other specified central nervous system stimulants

E940.9 Unspecified central nervous system stimulant

✓4ᵗʰ **E941 Drugs primarily affecting the autonomic nervous system**

E941.0 Parasympathomimetics [cholinergics]
Acetylcholine
Anticholinesterase:
organophosphorus
reversible
Pilocarpine

E941.1 Parasympatholytics [anticholinergics and antimuscarinics] and spasmolytics
Atropine
Homatropine
Hyoscine [scopolamine]
Quaternary ammonium derivatives
EXCLUDES papaverine (E942.5)

E941.2 Sympathomimetics [adrenergics]
Epinephrine [adrenalin]
Levarterenol [noradrenalin]

E941.3 Sympatholytics [antiadrenergics]
Phenoxybenzamine
Tolazolinehydrochloride

E941.9 Unspecified drug primarily affecting the autonomic nervous system

✓4ᵗʰ **E942 Agents primarily affecting the cardiovascular system**

E942.0 Cardiac rhythm regulators
Practolol   Propranolol
Procainamide   Quinidine

E942.1 Cardiotonic glycosides and drugs of similar action
Digitalis glycosides   Strophanthins
Digoxin

E942.2 Antilipemic and antiarteriosclerotic drugs
Cholestyramine   Nicotinic acid derivatives
Clofibrate   Sitosterols
EXCLUDES dextrothyroxine (E932.7)

E942.3 Ganglion-blocking agents
Pentamethonium bromide

E942.4 Coronary vasodilators
Dipyridamole   Nitrites
Nitrates [nitroglycerin]   Prenylamine

E942.5 Other vasodilators
Cyclandelate   Hydralazine
Diazoxide   Papaverine

E942.6 Other antihypertensive agents
Clonidine   Rauwolfia alkaloids
Guanethidine   Reserpine

E942.7 Antivaricose drugs, including sclerosing agents
Monoethanolamine
Zinc salts

E942.8 Capillary-active drugs
Adrenochrome derivatives
Bioflavonoids
Metaraminol

E942.9 Other and unspecified agents primarily affecting the cardiovascular system

✓4ᵗʰ **E943 Agents primarily affecting gastrointestinal system**

E943.0 Antacids and antigastric secretion drugs
Aluminum hydroxide
Magnesium trisilicate

E943.1 **Irritant cathartics**
    Bisacodyl
    Castor oil
    Phenolphthalein

E943.2 **Emollient cathartics**
    Sodium dioctyl sulfosuccinate

E943.3 **Other cathartics, including intestinal atonia drugs**
    Magnesium sulfate

E943.4 **Digestants**
    Pancreatin
    Papain
    Pepsin

E943.5 **Antidiarrheal drugs**
    Bismuth subcarbonate Pectin or Kaolin
    EXCLUDES *anti-infectives (E930.0-E931.9)*

E943.6 **Emetics**

E943.8 **Other specified agents primarily affecting the gastrointestinal system**

E943.9 **Unspecified agent primarily affecting the gastrointestinal system**

√4ᵗʰ **E944 Water, mineral, and uric acid metabolism drugs**

E944.0 **Mercurial diuretics**
    Chlormerodrin   Mercurophylline
    Mercaptomerin   Mersalyl

E944.1 **Purine derivative diuretics**
    Theobromine
    Theophylline
    EXCLUDES *aminophylline [theophylline ethylenediamine] (E945.7)*

E944.2 **Carbonic acid anhydrase inhibitors**
    Acetazolamide

E944.3 **Saluretics**
    Benzothiadiazides   Chlorothiazide group

E944.4 **Other diuretics**
    Ethacrynic acid   Furosemide

E944.5 **Electrolytic, caloric, and water-balance agents**

E944.6 **Other mineral salts, not elsewhere classified**

E944.7 **Uric acid metabolism drugs**
    Cinchophen and congeners
    Colchicine
    Phenoquin
    Probenecid

√4ᵗʰ **E945 Agents primarily acting on the smooth and skeletal muscles and respiratory system**

E945.0 **Oxytocic agents**
    Ergot alkaloids
    Prostaglandins

E945.1 **Smooth muscle relaxants**
    Adiphenine
    Metaproterenol [orciprenaline]
    EXCLUDES *papaverine (E942.5)*

E945.2 **Skeletal muscle relaxants**
    Alcuronium chloride
    Suxamethonium chloride

E945.3 **Other and unspecified drugs acting on muscles**

E945.4 **Antitussives**
    Dextromethorphan
    Pipazethate hydrochloride

E945.5 **Expectorants**
    Acetylcysteine
    Cocillana
    Guaifenesin [glyceryl guaiacolate]
    Ipecacuanha
    Terpin hydrate

E945.6 **Anti-common cold drugs**

E945.7 **Antiasthmatics**
    Aminophylline [theophylline ethylenediamine]

E945.8 **Other and unspecified respiratory drugs**

√4ᵗʰ **E946 Agents primarily affecting skin and mucous membrane, ophthalmological, otorhinolaryngological, and dental drugs**

E946.0 **Local anti-infectives and anti-inflammatory drugs**

E946.1 **Antipruritics**

E946.2 **Local astringents and local detergents**

E946.3 **Emollients, demulcents, and protectants**

E946.4 **Keratolytics, kerstoplastics, other hair treatment drugs and preparations**

E946.5 **Eye anti-infectives and other eye drugs**
    Idoxuridine

E946.6 **Anti-infectives and other drugs and preparations for ear, nose, and throat**

E946.7 **Dental drugs topically applied**

E946.8 **Other agents primarily affecting skin and mucous membrane**
    Spermicides

E946.9 **Unspecified agent primarily affecting skin and mucous membrane**

√4ᵗʰ **E947 Other and unspecified drugs and medicinal substances**

E947.0 **Dietetics**

E947.1 **Lipotropic drugs**

E947.2 **Antidotes and chelating agents, not elsewhere classified**

E947.3 **Alcohol deterrents**

E947.4 **Pharmaceutical excipients**

E947.8 **Other drugs and medicinal substances**
    Contrast media used for diagnostic x-ray procedures
    Diagnostic agents and kits

E947.9 **Unspecified drug or medicinal substance**

√4ᵗʰ **E948 Bacterial vaccines**

E948.0 **BCG vaccine**

E948.1 **Typhoid and paratyphoid**

E948.2 **Cholera**

E948.3 **Plague**

E948.4 **Tetanus**

E948.5 **Diphtheria**

E948.6 **Pertussis vaccine, including combinations with a pertussis component**

E948.8 **Other and unspecified bacterial vaccines**

E948.9 **Mixed bacterial vaccines, except combinations with a pertussis component**

√4ᵗʰ **E949 Other vaccines and biological substances**
    EXCLUDES *gamma globulin (E934.6)*

E949.0 **Smallpox vaccine**

E949.1 **Rabies vaccine**

E949.2 **Typhus vaccine**

E949.3 **Yellow fever vaccine**

E949.4 **Measles vaccine**

E949.5 **Poliomyelitis vaccine**

E949.6 **Other and unspecified viral and rickettsial vaccines**
    Mumps vaccine

E949.7 **Mixed viral-rickettsial and bacterial vaccines, except combinations with a pertussis component**
    EXCLUDES *combinations with a pertussis component (E948.6)*

E949.9 **Other and unspecified vaccines and biological substances**

SUICIDE AND SELF-INFLICTED INJURY (E950-E959)

> **INCLUDES**   injuries in suicide and attempted suicide
> self-inflicted injuries specified as intentional

☑4th E950 Suicide and self-inflicted poisoning by solid or liquid substances

E950.0 Analgesics, antipyretics, and antirheumatics

E950.1 Barbiturates

E950.2 Other sedatives and hypnotics

E950.3 Tranquilizers and other psychotropic agents

E950.4 Other specified drugs and medicinal substances

E950.5 Unspecified drug or medicinal substance

E950.6 Agricultural and horticultural chemical and pharmaceutical preparations other than plant foods and fertilizers

E950.7 Corrosive and caustic substances
> Suicide and self-inflicted poisoning by substances classifiable to E864

E950.8 Arsenic and its compounds

E950.9 Other and unspecified solid and liquid substances

☑4th E951 Suicide and self-inflicted poisoning by gases in domestic use

E951.0 Gas distributed by pipeline

E951.1 Liquefied petroleum gas distributed in mobile containers

E951.8 Other utility gas

☑4th E952 Suicide and self-inflicted poisoning by other gases and vapors

E952.0 Motor vehicle exhaust gas

E952.1 Other carbon monoxide

E952.8 Other specified gases and vapors

E952.9 Unspecified gases and vapors

☑4th E953 Suicide and self-inflicted injury by hanging, strangulation, and suffocation

E953.0 Hanging

E953.1 Suffocation by plastic bag

E953.8 Other specified means

E953.9 Unspecified means

E954 Suicide and self-inflicted injury by submersion [drowning]

☑4th E955 Suicide and self-inflicted injury by firearms, air guns and explosives

E955.0 Handgun

E955.1 Shotgun

E955.2 Hunting rifle

E955.3 Military firearms

E955.4 Other and unspecified firearm
> Gunshot NOS
> Shot NOS

E955.5 Explosives

E955.6 Air gun
> BB gun
> Pellet gun

E955.7 Paintball gun

E955.9 Unspecified

E956 Suicide and self-inflicted injury by cutting and piercing instrument

☑4th E957 Suicide and self-inflicted injuries by jumping from high place

E957.0 Residential premises

E957.1 Other man-made structures

E957.2 Natural sites

E957.9 Unspecified

☑4th E958 Suicide and self-inflicted injury by other and unspecified means

E958.0 Jumping or lying before moving object

E958.1 Burns, fire

E958.2 Scald

E958.3 Extremes of cold

E958.4 Electrocution

E958.5 Crashing of motor vehicle

E958.6 Crashing of aircraft

E958.7 Caustic substances, except poisoning
> **EXCLUDES**   poisoning by caustic substance (E950.7)

E958.8 Other specified means

E958.9 Unspecified means

E959 Late effects of self-inflicted injury
> Note: This category is to be used to indicate circumstances classifiable to E950-E958 as the cause of death or disability from late effects, which are themselves classifiable elsewhere. The "late effects" include conditions reported as such, or as sequelae which may occur at any time after the attempted suicide or self-inflicted injury.

HOMICIDE AND INJURY PURPOSELY INFLICTED BY OTHER PERSONS (E960-E969)

> **INCLUDES**   injuries inflicted by another person with intent to injure or kill, by any means
>
> **EXCLUDES**   injuries due to:
> legal intervention (E970-E978)
> operations of war (E990-E999)
> terrorism (E979)

☑4th E960 Fight, brawl, rape

E960.0 Unarmed fight or brawl
> Beatings NOS
> Brawl or fight with hands, fists, feet
> Injured or killed in fight NOS
> **EXCLUDES**   homicidal:
> injury by weapons (E965.0-E966, E969)
> strangulation (E963)
> submersion (E964)

E960.1 Rape

E961 Assault by corrosive or caustic substance, except poisoning
> Injury or death purposely caused by corrosive or caustic substance, such as:
> acid [any]
> corrosive substance
> vitriol
> **EXCLUDES**   burns from hot liquid (E968.3)
> chemical burns from swallowing a corrosive substance (E962.0-E962.9)

☑4th E962 Assault by poisoning

E962.0 Drugs and medicinal substances
> Homicidal poisoning by any drug or medicinal substance

E962.1 Other solid and liquid substances

E962.2 Other gases and vapors

E962.9 Unspecified poisoning

E963 Assault by hanging and strangulation
> Homicidal (attempt):
> garrotting or ligature
> hanging
> strangulation
> suffocation

☑4th Fourth-digit Required   ▶◀ Revised Text   ● New Code   ▲ Revised Code TitleDx

E964 Assault by submersion [drowning]

✓4th **E965 Assault by firearms and explosives**

E965.0 Handgun
> Pistol
> Revolver

E965.1 Shotgun

E965.2 Hunting rifle

E965.3 Military firearms

E965.4 Other and unspecified firearm

E965.5 Antipersonnel bomb

E965.6 Gasoline bomb

E965.7 Letter bomb

E965.8 Other specified explosive
> Bomb NOS (placed in):
>> car
>> house
> Dynamite

E965.9 Unspecified explosive

E966 Assault by cutting and piercing instrument
> Assassination (attempt), homicide (attempt) by any instrument classifiable under E920
> Homicidal:
>> cut
>> puncture } any part of the body
>> stab
> Stabbed any part of the body

✓4th **E967 Perpetrator of child and adult abuse**
> Note: Selection of the correct perpetrator code is based on the relationship between the perpetrator and the victim

E967.0 By father, stepfather, or boyfriend
> Male partner of child's parent or guardian

E967.1 By other specified person

E967.2 By mother, stepmother, or girlfriend
> Female partner of child's parent or guardian

E967.3 By spouse or partner
> Abuse of spouse or partner by ex-spouse or ex-partner

E967.4 By child

E967.5 By sibling

E967.6 By grandparent

E967.7 By other relative

E967.8 By non-related caregiver

E967.9 By unspecified person

✓4th **E968 Assault by other and unspecified means**

E968.0 Fire
> Arson
> Homicidal burns NOS
> **EXCLUDES** *burns from hot liquid (E968.3)*

E968.1 Pushing from a high place

E968.2 Striking by blunt or thrown object

E968.3 Hot liquid
> Homicidal burns by scalding

E968.4 Criminal neglect
> Abandonment of child, infant, or other helpless person with intent to injure or kill

E968.5 Transport vehicle
> Being struck by other vehicle or run down with intent to injure
> Pushed in front of, thrown from, or dragged by moving vehicle with intent to injure

E968.6 Air gun
> BB gun
> Pellet gun

E968.7 Human bite

E968.8 Other specified means

E968.9 Unspecified means
> Assassination (attempt) NOS
> Homicidal (attempt):
>> injury NOS
>> wound NOS
> Manslaughter (nonaccidental)
> Murder (attempt) NOS
> Violence, non-accidental

E969 Late effects of injury purposely inflicted by other person
> Note: This category is to be used to indicate circumstances classifiable to E960-E968 as the cause of death or disability from late effects, which are themselves classifiable elsewhere. The "late effects" include conditions reported as such, or as sequelae which may occur at any time after injury purposely inflicted by another person.

LEGAL INTERVENTION (E970-E978)

INCLUDES injuries inflicted by the police or other law-enforcing agents, including military on duty, in the course of arresting or attempting to arrest lawbreakers, suppressing disturbances, maintaining order, and other legal action
> legal execution

EXCLUDES *injuries caused by civil insurrections (E990.0-E999)*

E970 Injury due to legal intervention by firearms
> Gunshot wound
> Injury by:
>> machine gun
>> revolver
>> rifle pellet or rubber bullet
>> shot NOS

E971 Injury due to legal intervention by explosives
> Injury by:
>> dynamite
>> explosive shell
>> grenade
>> mortar bomb

E972 Injury due to legal intervention by gas
> Asphyxiation by gas
> Injury by tear gas
> Poisoning by gas

E973 Injury due to legal intervention by blunt object
> Hit, struck by:
>> baton (nightstick)
>> blunt object
>> stave

E974 Injury due to legal intervention by cutting and piercing instrument
> Cut
> Incised wound
> Injured by bayonet
> Stab wound

E975 Injury due to legal intervention by other specified means
> Blow
> Manhandling

E976 Injury due to legal intervention by unspecified means

E977 Late effects of injuries due to legal intervention
> Note: This category is to be used to indicate circumstances classifiable to E970-E976 as the cause of death or disability from late effects, which are themselves classifiable elsewhere. The "late effects" include conditions reported as such, or as sequelae, which may occur at any time after the injury due to legal intervention.

E978 **Legal execution**

All executions performed at the behest of the judiciary or ruling authority [whether permanent or temporary] as:
asphyxiation by gas
beheading, decapitation (by guillotine)
capital punishment
electrocution
hanging
poisoning
shooting
other specified means

TERRORISM (E979)

✓4ᵗʰ E979 **Terrorism**

Injuries resulting from the unlawful use of force or violence against persons or property to intimidate or coerce a Government, the civilian population, or any segment thereof, in furtherance of political or social objective

E979.0 **Terrorism involving explosion of marine weapons**
Depth-charge
Marine mine
Mine NOS, at sea or in harbour
Sea-based artillery shell
Torpedo
Underwater blast

E979.1 **Terrorism involving destruction of aircraft**
Aircraft used as a weapon
Aircraft:
burned
exploded
shot down
Crushed by falling aircraft

E979.2 **Terrorism involving other explosions and fragments**
Antipersonnel bomb (fragments)
Blast NOS
Explosion (of):
artillery shell
breech-block
cannon block
mortar bomb
munitions being used in terrorism
NOS
Fragments from:
artillery shell
bomb
grenade
guided missile
land-mine
rocket
shell
shrapnel
Mine NOS

E979.3 **Terrorism involving fires, conflagration and hot substances**
Burning building or structure:
collapse of
fall from
hit by falling object in
jump from
Conflagration NOS
Fire (causing):
Asphyxia
Burns
NOS
Other injury
Melting of fittings and furniture in burning
Petrol bomb
Smouldering building or structure

E979.4 **Terrorism involving firearms**
Bullet:
carbine
machine gun
pistol
rifle
rubber (rifle)
Pellets (shotgun)

E979.5 **Terrorism involving nuclear weapons**
Blast effects
Exposure to ionizing radiation from nuclear weapon
Fireball effects
Heat from nuclear weapon
Other direct and secondary effects of nuclear weapons

E979.6 **Terrorism involving biological weapons**
Anthrax
Cholera
Smallpox

E979.7 **Terrorism involving chemical weapons**
Gases, fumes, chemicals
Hydrogen cyanide
Phosgene
Sarin

E979.8 **Terrorism involving other means**
Drowning and submersion
Lasers
Piercing or stabbing instruments
Terrorism NOS

E979.9 **Terrorism, secondary effects**

Note: This code is for use to identify conditions occurring subsequent to a terrorist attack not those that are due to the initial terrorist act

EXCLUDES *late effect of terrorist attack (E999.1)*

INJURY UNDETERMINED WHETHER ACCIDENTALLY OR PURPOSELY INFLICTED (E980-E989)

Note: Categories E980-E989 are for use when it is unspecified or it cannot be determined whether the injuries are accidental (unintentional), suicide (attempted), or assault.

✓4ᵗʰ E980 **Poisoning by solid or liquid substances, undetermined whether accidentally or purposely inflicted**

E980.0 **Analgesics, antipyretics, and antirheumatics**

E980.1 **Barbiturates**

E980.2 **Other sedatives and hypnotics**

E980.3 **Tranquilizers and other psychotropic agents**

E980.4 **Other specified drugs and medicinal substances**

E980.5 **Unspecified drug or medicinal substance**

E980.6 **Corrosive and caustic substances**
Poisoning, undetermined whether accidental or purposeful, by substances classifiable to E864

E980.7 **Agricultural and horticultural chemical and pharmaceutical preparations other than plant foods and fertilizers**

E980.8 **Arsenic and its compounds**

E980.9 **Other and unspecified solid and liquid substances**

✓4ᵗʰ E981 **Poisoning by gases in domestic use, undetermined whether accidentally or purposely inflicted**

E981.0 **Gas distributed by pipeline**

E981.1 **Liquefied petroleum gas distributed in mobile containers**

E981.8 **Other utility gas**

✓4ᵗʰ E982 **Poisoning by other gases, undetermined whether accidentally or purposely inflicted**

E982.0 **Motor vehicle exhaust gas**

E982.1 **Other carbon monoxide**

E982.8 **Other specified gases and vapors**

E982.9 **Unspecified gases and vapors**

☑4ᵗʰ **E983 Hanging, strangulation, or suffocation, undetermined whether accidentally or purposely inflicted**

   E983.0 Hanging

   E983.1 Suffocation by plastic bag

   E983.8 Other specified means

   E983.9 Unspecified means

E984 Submersion [drowning], undetermined whether accidentally or purposely inflicted

☑4ᵗʰ **E985 Injury by firearms, air guns and explosives, undetermined whether accidentally or purposely inflicted**

   E985.0 Handgun

   E985.1 Shotgun

   E985.2 Hunting rifle

   E985.3 Military firearms

   E985.4 Other and unspecified firearm

   E985.5 Explosives

   E985.6 Air gun
       BB gun   Pellet gun

   E985.7 Paintball gun

E986 Injury by cutting and piercing instruments, undetermined whether accidentally or purposely inflicted

☑4ᵗʰ **E987 Falling from high place, undetermined whether accidentally or purposely inflicted**

   E987.0 Residential premises

   E987.1 Other man-made structures

   E987.2 Natural sites

   E987.9 Unspecified site

☑4ᵗʰ **E988 Injury by other and unspecified means, undetermined whether accidentally or purposely inflicted**

   E988.0 Jumping or lying before moving object

   E988.1 Burns, fire

   E988.2 Scald

   E988.3 Extremes of cold

   E988.4 Electrocution

   E988.5 Crashing of motor vehicle

   E988.6 Crashing of aircraft

   E988.7 Caustic substances, except poisoning

   E988.8 Other specified means

   E988.9 Unspecified means

E989 Late effects of injury, undetermined whether accidentally or purposely inflicted

   Note: This category is to be used to indicate circumstances classifiable to E980-E988 as the cause of death or disability from late effects, which are themselves classifiable elsewhere. The "late effects" include conditions reported as such, or as sequelae, which may occur at any time after injury, undetermined whether accidentally or purposely inflicted.

INJURY RESULTING FROM OPERATIONS OF WAR (E990-E999)

   INCLUDES injuries to military personnel and civilians caused by war and civil insurrections and occurring during the time of war and insurrection, ▶and peacekeeping missions◀

   EXCLUDES *accidents during training of military personnel manufacture of war material and transport, unless attributable to enemy action*

☑4ᵗʰ **E990 Injury due to war operations by fires and conflagrations**

   INCLUDES asphyxia, burns, or other injury originating from fire caused by a fire-producing device or indirectly by any conventional weapon

   E990.0 From gasoline bomb
      ▶Incendiary bomb◀

●   E990.1 From flamethrower

●   E990.2 From incendiary bullet

●   E990.3 From fire caused indirectly from conventional weapon
      EXCLUDES *fire aboard military aircraft (E994.3)*

●   E990.9 From other and unspecified source

☑4ᵗʰ **E991 Injury due to war operations by bullets and fragments**

   EXCLUDES *▶injury due to bullets and fragments due to war operations, but occurring after cessation of hostilities (E998.0)*
      injury due to explosion of artillery shells and mortars (E993.2)
      injury due to explosion of improvised explosive device [IED] (E993.3-E993.5)
      injury due to sea-based artillery shell (E992.3)◀

   E991.0 Rubber bullets (rifle)

   E991.1 Pellets (rifle)

   E991.2 Other bullets
      Bullet [any, except rubber bullets and pellets]
        carbine
        machine gun
        pistol
        rifle
        shotgun

   E991.3 Antipersonnel bomb (fragments)

●   E991.4 Fragments from munitions
      Fragments from:
        artillery shell
        bombs, except antipersonnel
        detonation of unexploded ordnance [UXO]
        grenade
        guided missile
        land mine
        rockets
        shell

●   E991.5 Fragments from person-borne improvised explosive device [IED]

●   E991.6 Fragments from vehicle-borne improvised explosive device [IED]
      IED borne by land, air, or water transport vehicle

●   E991.7 Fragments from other improvised explosive device [IED]
      Roadside IED

●   E991.8 Fragments from weapons
      Fragments from:
        artillery
        autocannons
        automatic grenade launchers
        missile launchers
        mortars
        small arms

   E991.9 Other and unspecified fragments
      Shrapnel ▶NOS◀

☑4ᵗʰ **E992 Injury due to war operations by explosion of marine weapons**

●   E992.0 Torpedo

●   E992.1 Depth charge

●   E992.2 Marine mines
      Marine mines at sea or in harbor

●   E992.3 Sea-based artillery shell

●   E992.8 Other marine weapons

●   E992.9 Unspecified marine weapon
      Underwater blast NOS

☑4ᵗʰ **E993 Injury due to war operations by other explosion**
   ▶Injuries due to direct or indirect pressure or air blast of an explosion occurring during war operations◀

      EXCLUDES *▶injury due to fragments resulting from an explosion (E991.0-E991.9)*
      injury due to detonation of unexploded ordnance but occurring after cessation of hostilities (E998.0-E998.9)
      injury due to nuclear weapons (E996.0-E996.9)◀

    ☑4ᵗʰ Fourth-digit Required   ▶◀ Revised Text   ● New Code   ▲ Revised Code TitleDx

E Codes

E993.0–E999.1

- **E993.0 Aerial bomb**
- **E993.1 Guided missile**
- **E993.2 Mortar**
  Artillery shell
- **E993.3 Person-borne improvised explosive device [IED]**
- **E993.4 Vehicle-borne improvised explosive device [IED]**
  IED borne by land, air, or water transport vehicle
- **E993.5 Other improvised explosive device [IED]**
  Roadside IED
- **E993.6 Unintentional detonation of own munitions**
  Unintentional detonation of own ammunition (artillery) (mortars)
- **E993.7 Unintentional discharge of own munitions launch device**
  Unintentional explosion of own:
    autocannons
    automatic grenade launchers
    missile launchers
    small arms
- **E993.8 Other specified explosion**
  Bomb
  Grenade
  Land mine
- **E993.9 Unspecified explosion**
  Air blast NOS
  Blast NOS
  Blast wave NOS
  Blast wind NOS
  Explosion NOS

☑4ᵗʰ **E994 Injury due to war operations by destruction of aircraft**
- **E994.0 Destruction of aircraft due to enemy fire or explosives**
  Air to air missile
  Explosive device placed on aircraft
  Rocket propelled grenade [RPG]
  Small arms fire
  Surface to air missile
- **E994.1 Unintentional destruction of aircraft due to own onboard explosives**
- **E994.2 Destruction of aircraft due to collision with other aircraft**
- **E994.3 Destruction of aircraft due to onboard fire**
- **E994.8 Other destruction of aircraft**
- **E994.9 Unspecified destruction of aircraft**

☑4ᵗʰ **E995 Injury due to war operations by other and unspecified forms of conventional warfare**
- **E995.0 Unarmed hand-to-hand combat**
  EXCLUDES   intentional restriction of airway (E995.3)
- **E995.1 Struck by blunt object**
  Baton (nightstick)
  Stave
- **E995.2 Piercing object**
  Bayonet
  Knife
  Sword
- **E995.3 Intentional restriction of air and airway**
  Intentional submersion
  Strangulation
  Suffocation
- **E995.4 Unintentional drowning due to inability to surface or obtain air**
  Submersion
- **E995.8 Other forms of conventional warfare**
- **E995.9 Unspecified form of conventional warfare**

☑4ᵗʰ **E996 Injury due to war operations by nuclear weapons**
▶Dirty bomb NOS◀
  EXCLUDES ▶late effects of injury due to nuclear weapons (E999.0, E999.1)◀
- **E996.0 Direct blast effect of nuclear weapon**
  Injury to bodily organs due to blast pressure
- **E996.1 Indirect blast effect of nuclear weapon**
  Injury due to being thrown by blast
  Injury due to being struck or crushed by blast debris
- **E996.2 Thermal radiation effect of nuclear weapon**
  Burns due to thermal radiation
  Fireball effects
  Flash burns
  Heat effects
- **E996.3 Nuclear radiation effects**
  Acute radiation exposure
  Beta burns
  Fallout exposure
  Radiation sickness
  Secondary effects of nuclear weapons
- **E996.8 Other effects of nuclear weapons**
- **E996.9 Unspecified effect of nuclear weapon**

☑4ᵗʰ **E997 Injury due to war operations by other forms of unconventional warfare**
- **E997.0 Lasers**
- **E997.1 Biological warfare**
- **E997.2 Gases, fumes, and chemicals**
- **E997.3 Weapon of mass destruction [WMD], unspecified**
- **E997.8 Other specified forms of unconventional warfare**
- **E997.9 Unspecified form of unconventional warfare**

☑4ᵗʰ **E998 Injury due to war operations but occurring after cessation of hostilities**
  Injuries due to operations of war but occurring after cessation of hostilities by any means classifiable under E990-E997
  Injuries by explosion of bombs or mines placed in the course of operations of war, if the explosion occurred after cessation of hostilities
- **E998.0 Explosion of mines**
- **E998.1 Explosion of bombs**
- **E998.8 Injury due to other war operations but occurring after cessation of hostilities**
- **E998.9 Injury due to unspecified war operations but occurring after cessation of hostilities**

☑4ᵗʰ **E999 Late effect of injury due to war operations and terrorism**
  Note: This category is to be used to indicate circumstances classifiable to E979, E990-E998 as the cause of death or disability from late effects, which are themselves classifiable elsewhere. The "late effects" include conditions reported as such, or as sequelae, which may occur at any time after the injury, resulting from operations of war or terrorism
- **E999.0 Late effect of injury due to war operations**
- **E999.1 Late effect of injury due to terrorism**

Order of Sequencing E Codes:
(1) child and adult abuse
(2) terrorism
(3) cataclysmic events
(4) transport accidents

Activity codes are always listed last

Official ICD-9-CM Government Appendixes

MORPHOLOGY OF NEOPLASMS

The World Health Organization has published an adaptation of the International Classification of Diseases for oncology (ICD-O). It contains a coded nomenclature for the morphology of neoplasms, which is reproduced here for those who wish to use it in conjunction with Chapter 2 of the International Classification of Diseases, 9th Revision, Clinical Modification.

The morphology code numbers consist of five digits; the first four identify the histological type of the neoplasm and the fifth indicates its behavior. The one-digit behavior code is as follows:

/0 Benign
/1 Uncertain whether benign or malignant
   Borderline malignancy
/2 Carcinoma in situ
   Intraepithelial
   Noninfiltrating
   Noninvasive
/3 Malignant, primary site
/6 Malignant, metastatic site
   Secondary site
/9 Malignant, uncertain whether primary or
   metastatic site

In the nomenclature below, the morphology code numbers include the behavior code appropriate to the histological type of neoplasm, but this behavior code should be changed if other reported information makes this necessary. For example, "chordoma (M9370/3)" is assumed to be malignant; the term "benign chordoma" should be coded M9370/0. Similarly, "superficial spreading adenocarcinoma (M8143/3)" described as "noninvasive" should be coded M8143/2 and "melanoma (M8720/3)" described as "secondary" should be coded M8720/6.

The following table shows the correspondence between the morphology code and the different sections of Chapter 2:

Morphology Code Histology/Behavior		ICD-9-CM Chapter 2
Any	0	210-229 Benign neoplasms
M8000-M8004	1	239 Neoplasms of unspecified nature
M8010+	1	235-238 Neoplasms of uncertain behavior
Any	2	230-234 Carcinoma in situ
Any	3	140-195 200-208 Malignant neoplasms, stated or presumed to be primary
Any	6	196-198 Malignant neoplasms, stated or presumed to be secondary

The ICD-O behavior digit /9 is inapplicable in an ICD context, since all malignant neoplasms are presumed to be primary (/3) or secondary (/6) according to other information on the medical record.the first-listed term of the full ICD-O morphology nomenclature appears against each code number in the list below. The ICD-9-CM Alphabetical Index (Volume 2), however, includes all the ICD-O synonyms as well as a number of other morphological names still likely to be encountered on medical records but omitted from ICD-O as outdated or otherwise undesirable.

A coding difficulty sometimes arises where a morphological diagnosis contains two qualifying adjectives that have different code numbers. An example is "transitional cell epidermoid carcinoma."

"Transitional cell carcinoma NOS" is M8120/3 and "epidermoid carcinoma NOS" is M8070/3. In such circumstances, the higher number (M8120/3 in this example) should be used, as it is usually more specific.

CODED NOMENCLATURE FOR MORPHOLOGY OF NEOPLASMS

M800 Neoplasms NOS
M8000/0 Neoplasm, benign
M8000/1 Neoplasm, uncertain whether benign or malignant
M8000/3 Neoplasm, malignant
M8000/6 Neoplasm, metastatic
M8000/9 Neoplasm, malignant, uncertain whether primary or metastatic
M8001/0 Tumor cells, benign
M8001/1 Tumor cells, uncertain whether benign or malignant
M8001/3 Tumor cells, malignant
M8002/3 Malignant tumor, small cell type
M8003/3 Malignant tumor, giant cell type
M8004/3 Malignant tumor, fusiform cell type

M801-M804 Epithelial neoplasms NOS
M8010/0 Epithelial tumor, benign
M8010/2 Carcinoma in situ NOS
M8010/3 Carcinoma NOS
M8010/6 Carcinoma, metastatic NOS
M8010/9 Carcinomatosis
M8011/0 Epithelioma, benign
M8011/3 Epithelioma, malignant
M8012/3 Large cell carcinoma NOS
M8020/3 Carcinoma, undifferentiated type NOS
M8021/3 Carcinoma, anaplastic type NOS
M8022/3 Pleomorphic carcinoma
M8030/3 Giant cell and spindle cell carcinoma
M8031/3 Giant cell carcinoma
M8032/3 Spindle cell carcinoma
M8033/3 Pseudosarcomatous carcinoma
M8034/3 Polygonal cell carcinoma
M8035/3 Spheroidal cell carcinoma
M8040/1 Tumorlet
M8041/3 Small cell carcinoma NOS
M8042/3 Oat cell carcinoma
M8043/3 Small cell carcinoma, fusiform cell type

M805-M808 Papillary and squamous cell neoplasms
M8050/0 Papilloma NOS (except Papilloma of urinary bladder M8120/1)
M8050/2 Papillary carcinoma in situ
M8050/3 Papillary carcinoma NOS
M8051/0 Verrucous papilloma
M8051/3 Verrucous carcinoma NOS
M8052/0 Squamous cell papilloma
M8052/3 Papillary squamous cell carcinoma
M8053/0 Inverted papilloma
M8060/0 Papillomatosis NOS
M8070/2 Squamous cell carcinoma in situ NOS
M8070/3 Squamous cell carcinoma NOS
M8070/6 Squamous cell carcinoma, metastatic NOS
M8071/3 Squamous cell carcinoma, keratinizing type NOS
M8072/3 Squamous cell carcinoma, large cell, nonkeratinizing type
M8073/3 Squamous cell carcinoma, small cell, nonkeratinizing type
M8074/3 Squamous cell carcinoma, spindle cell type
M8075/3 Adenoid squamous cell carcinoma
M8076/2 Squamous cell carcinoma in situ with questionable stromal invasion

M8076/3 Squamous cell carcinoma, microinvasive
M8080/2 Queyrat's erythroplasia
M8081/2 Bowen's disease
M8082/3 Lymphoepithelial carcinoma

M809-M811 Basal cell neoplasms
M8090/1 Basal cell tumor
M8090/3 Basal cell carcinoma NOS
M8091/3 Multicentric basal cell carcinoma
M8092/3 Basal cell carcinoma, morphea type
M8093/3 Basal cell carcinoma, fibroepithelial type
M8094/3 Basosquamous carcinoma
M8095/3 Metatypical carcinoma
M8096/0 Intraepidermal epithelioma of Jadassohn
M8100/0 Trichoepithelioma
M8101/0 Trichofolliculoma
M8102/0 Tricholemmoma
M8110/0 Pilomatrixoma

M812-M813 Transitional cell papillomas and carcinomas
M8120/0 Transitional cell papilloma NOS
M8120/1 Urothelial papilloma
M8120/2 Transitional cell carcinoma in situ
M8120/3 Transitional cell carcinoma NOS
M8121/0 Schneiderian papilloma
M8121/1 Transitional cell papilloma, inverted type
M8121/3 Schneiderian carcinoma
M8122/3 Transitional cell carcinoma, spindle cell type
M8123/3 Basaloid carcinoma
M8124/3 Cloacogenic carcinoma
M8130/3 Papillary transitional cell carcinoma

M814-M838 Adenomas and adenocarcinomas
M8140/0 Adenoma NOS
M8140/1 Bronchial adenoma NOS
M8140/2 Adenocarcinoma in situ
M8140/3 Adenocarcinoma NOS
M8140/6 Adenocarcinoma, metastatic NOS
M8141/3 Scirrhous adenocarcinoma
M8142/3 Linitis plastica
M8143/3 Superficial spreading adenocarcinoma
M8144/3 Adenocarcinoma, intestinal type
M8145/3 Carcinoma, diffuse type
M8146/0 Monomorphic adenoma
M8147/0 Basal cell adenoma
M8150/0 Islet cell adenoma
M8150/3 Islet cell carcinoma
M8151/0 Insulinoma NOS
M8151/3 Insulinoma, malignant
M8152/0 Glucagonoma NOS
M8152/3 Glucagonoma, malignant
M8153/1 Gastrinoma NOS
M8153/3 Gastrinoma, malignant
M8154/3 Mixed islet cell and exocrine adenocarcinoma
M8160/0 Bile duct adenoma
M8160/3 Cholangiocarcinoma
M8161/0 Bile duct cystadenoma
M8161/3 Bile duct cystadenocarcinoma
M8170/0 Liver cell adenoma
M8170/3 Hepatocellular carcinoma NOS
M8180/0 Hepatocholangioma, benign
M8180/3 Combined hepatocellular carcinoma and cholangiocarcinoma
M8190/0 Trabecular adenoma
M8190/3 Trabecular adenocarcinoma
M8191/0 Embryonal adenoma
M8200/0 Eccrine dermal cylindroma

M8200/3	Adenoid cystic carcinoma	M8373/0	Adrenal cortical adenoma, clear cell type	**M850-M854**	**Ductal, lobular, and medullary neoplasms**
M8201/3	Cribriform carcinoma	M8374/0	Adrenal cortical adenoma, glomerulosa cell type	M8500/2	Intraductal carcinoma, noninfiltrating NOS
M8210/0	Adenomatous polyp NOS				
M8210/3	Adenocarcinoma in adenomatous polyp	M8375/0	Adrenal cortical adenoma, mixed cell type	M8500/3	Infiltrating duct carcinoma
M8211/0	Tubular adenoma NOS	M8380/0	Endometrioid adenoma NOS	M8501/2	Comedocarcinoma, noninfiltrating
M8211/3	Tubular adenocarcinoma	M8380/1	Endometrioid adenoma, borderline malignancy	M8501/3	Comedocarcinoma NOS
M8220/0	Adenomatous polyposis coli			M8502/3	Juvenile carcinoma of the breast
M8220/3	Adenocarcinoma in adenomatous polyposis coli	M8380/3	Endometrioid carcinoma	M8503/0	Intraductal papilloma
		M8381/0	Endometrioid adenofibroma NOS	M8503/2	Noninfiltrating intraductal papillary adenocarcinoma
M8221/0	Multiple adenomatous polyps	M8381/1	Endometrioid adenofibroma, borderline malignancy		
M8230/0	Solid carcinoma NOS			M8504/0	Intracystic papillary adenoma
M8231/3	Carcinoma simplex	M8381/3	Endometrioid adenofibroma, malignant	M8504/2	Noninfiltrating intracystic carcinoma
M8240/1	Carcinoid tumor NOS			M8505/0	Intraductal papillomatosis NOS
M8240/3	Carcinoid tumor, malignant			M8506/0	Subareolar duct papillomatosis
M8241/1	Carcinoid tumor, argentaffin NOS	**M839-M842**	**Adnexal and skin appendage neoplasms**	M8510/3	Medullary carcinoma NOS
M8241/3	Carcinoid tumor, argentaffin, malignant	M8390/0	Skin appendage adenoma	M8511/3	Medullary carcinoma with amyloid stroma
		M8390/3	Skin appendage carcinoma		
M8242/1	Carcinoid tumor, nonargentaffin NOS	M8400/0	Sweat gland adenoma	M8512/3	Medullary carcinoma with lymphoid stroma
M8242/3	Carcinoid tumor, nonargentaffin, malignant	M8400/1	Sweat gland tumor NOS		
		M8400/3	Sweat gland adenocarcinoma	M8520/2	Lobular carcinoma in situ
M8243/3	Mucocarcinoid tumor, malignant	M8401/0	Apocrine adenoma	M8520/3	Lobular carcinoma NOS
M8244/3	Composite carcinoid	M8401/3	Apocrine adenocarcinoma	M8521/3	Infiltrating ductular carcinoma
M8250/1	Pulmonary adenomatosis	M8402/0	Eccrine acrospiroma	M8530/3	Inflammatory carcinoma
M8250/3	Bronchiolo-alveolar adenocarcinoma	M8403/0	Eccrine spiradenoma	M8540/3	Paget's disease, mammary
M8251/0	Alveolar adenoma	M8404/0	Hidrocystoma	M8541/3	Paget's disease and infiltrating duct carcinoma of breast
M8251/3	Alveolar adenocarcinoma	M8405/0	Papillary hydradenoma		
M8260/0	Papillary adenoma NOS	M8406/0	Papillary syringadenoma	M8542/3	Paget's disease, extramammary (except Paget's disease of bone)
M8260/3	Papillary adenocarcinoma NOS	M8407/0	Syringoma NOS		
M8261/1	Villous adenoma NOS	M8410/0	Sebaceous adenoma		
M8261/3	Adenocarcinoma in villous adenoma	M8410/3	Sebaceous adenocarcinoma	**M855**	**Acinar cell neoplasms**
M8262/3	Villous adenocarcinoma	M8420/0	Ceruminous adenoma	M8550/0	Acinar cell adenoma
M8263/3	Tubulovillous adenoma	M8420/3	Ceruminous adenocarcinoma	M8550/1	Acinar cell tumor
M8270/0	Chromophobe adenoma			M8550/3	Acinar cell carcinoma
M8270/3	Chromophobe carcinoma	**M843**	**Mucoepidermoid neoplasms**	**M856-M858**	**Complex epithelial neoplasms**
M8280/0	Acidophil adenoma	M8430/1	Mucoepidermoid tumor	M8560/3	Adenosquamous carcinoma
M8280/3	Acidophil carcinoma	M8430/3	Mucoepidermoid carcinoma	M8561/0	Adenolymphoma
M8281/0	Mixed acidophil-basophil adenoma			M8570/3	Adenocarcinoma with squamous metaplasia
M8281/3	Mixed acidophil-basophil carcinoma	**M844-M849**	**Cystic, mucinous, and serous neoplasms**		
M8290/0	Oxyphilic adenoma	M8440/0	Cystadenoma NOS	M8571/3	Adenocarcinoma with cartilaginous and osseous metaplasia
M8290/3	Oxyphilic adenocarcinoma	M8440/3	Cystadenocarcinoma NOS		
M8300/0	Basophil adenoma	M8441/0	Serous cystadenoma NOS	M8572/3	Adenocarcinoma with spindle cell metaplasia
M8300/3	Basophil carcinoma	M8441/1	Serous cystadenoma, borderline malignancy		
M8310/0	Clear cell adenoma			M8573/3	Adenocarcinoma with apocrine metaplasia
M8310/3	Clear cell adenocarcinoma NOS	M8441/3	Serous cystadenocarcinoma NOS		
M8311/1	Hypernephroid tumor	M8450/0	Papillary cystadenoma NOS	M8580/0	Thymoma, benign
M8312/3	Renal cell carcinoma	M8450/1	Papillary cystadenoma, borderline malignancy	M8580/3	Thymoma, malignant
M8313/3	Clear cell adenofibroma			**M859-M867**	**Specialized gonadal neoplasms**
M8320/3	Granular cell carcinoma	M8450/3	Papillary cystadenocarcinoma NOS	M8590/1	Sex cord-stromal tumor
M8321/0	Chief cell adenoma	M8460/0	Papillary serous cystadenoma NOS	M8600/0	Thecoma NOS
M8322/0	Water-clear cell adenoma	M8460/1	Papillary serous cystadenoma, borderline malignancy	M8600/3	Theca cell carcinoma
M8322/3	Water-clear cell adenocarcinoma			M8610/0	Luteoma NOS
M8323/0	Mixed cell adenoma	M8460/3	Papillary serous cystadenocarcinoma	M8620/1	Granulosa cell tumor NOS
M8323/3	Mixed cell adenocarcinoma	M8461/0	Serous surface papilloma NOS	M8620/3	Granulosa cell tumor, malignant
M8324/0	Lipoadenoma	M8461/1	Serous surface papilloma, borderline malignancy	M8621/1	Granulosa cell-theca cell tumor
M8330/0	Follicular adenoma			M8630/0	Androblastoma, benign
M8330/3	Follicular adenocarcinoma NOS	M8461/3	Serous surface papillary carcinoma	M8630/1	Androblastoma NOS
M8331/3	Follicular adenocarcinoma, well differentiated type	M8470/0	Mucinous cystadenoma NOS	M8630/3	Androblastoma, malignant
		M8470/1	Mucinous cystadenoma, borderline malignancy	M8631/0	Sertoli-Leydig cell tumor
M8332/3	Follicular adenocarcinoma, trabecular type			M8632/1	Gynandroblastoma
		M8470/3	Mucinous cystadenocarcinoma NOS	M8640/0	Tubular androblastoma NOS
M8333/0	Microfollicular adenoma	M8471/0	Papillary mucinous cystadenoma NOS	M8640/0	Sertoli cell carcinoma
M8334/0	Macrofollicular adenoma	M8471/1	Papillary mucinous cystadenoma, borderline malignancy	M8641/0	Tubular androblastoma with lipid storage
M8340/3	Papillary and follicular adenocarcinoma				
		M8471/3	Papillary mucinous cystadenocarcinoma	M8650/0	Leydig cell tumor, benign
M8350/3	Nonencapsulated sclerosing carcinoma			M8650/1	Leydig cell tumor NOS
M8360/1	Multiple endocrine adenomas	M8480/0	Mucinous adenoma	M8650/3	Leydig cell tumor, malignant
M8361/1	Juxtaglomerular tumor	M8480/3	Mucinous adenocarcinoma	M8660/0	Hilar cell tumor
M8370/0	Adrenal cortical adenoma NOS	M8480/6	Pseudomyxoma peritonei	M8670/0	Lipid cell tumor of ovary
M8370/3	Adrenal cortical carcinoma	M8481/3	Mucin-producing adenocarcinoma	M8671/0	Adrenal rest tumor
M8371/0	Adrenal cortical adenoma, compact cell type	M8490/3	Signet ring cell carcinoma	**M868-M871**	**Paragangliomas and glomus tumors**
		M8490/6	Metastatic signet ring cell carcinoma		
M8372/0	Adrenal cortical adenoma, heavily pigmented variant			M8680/1	Paraganglioma NOS
				M8680/3	Paraganglioma, malignant
				M8681/1	Sympathetic paraganglioma

M8682/1	Parasympathetic paraganglioma	M8830/1	Atypical fibrous histiocytoma	M9000/3	Brenner tumor, malignant
M8690/1	Glomus jugulare tumor	M8830/3	Fibrous histiocytoma, malignant	M9010/0	Fibroadenoma NOS
M8691/1	Aortic body tumor	M8831/0	Fibroxanthoma NOS	M9011/0	Intracanalicular fibroadenoma NOS
M8692/1	Carotid body tumor	M8831/1	Atypical fibroxanthoma	M9012/0	Pericanalicular fibroadenoma
M8693/1	Extra-adrenal paraganglioma NOS	M8831/3	Fibroxanthoma, malignant	M9013/0	Adenofibroma NOS
M8693/3	Extra-adrenal paraganglioma, malignant	M8832/0	Dermatofibroma NOS	M9014/0	Serous adenofibroma
		M8832/1	Dermatofibroma protuberans	M9015/0	Mucinous adenofibroma
M8700/0	Pheochromocytoma NOS	M8832/3	Dermatofibrosarcoma NOS	M9020/0	Cellular intracanalicular fibroadenoma

M884　　　Myxomatous neoplasms

Code	Description
M8682/1	Parasympathetic paraganglioma
M8690/1	Glomus jugulare tumor
M8691/1	Aortic body tumor
M8692/1	Carotid body tumor
M8693/1	Extra-adrenal paraganglioma NOS
M8693/3	Extra-adrenal paraganglioma, malignant
M8700/0	Pheochromocytoma NOS
M8700/3	Pheochromocytoma, malignant
M8710/3	Glomangiosarcoma
M8711/0	Glomus tumor
M8712/0	Glomangioma

M872-M879　　Nevi and melanomas

Code	Description
M8720/0	Pigmented nevus NOS
M8720/3	Malignant melanoma NOS
M8721/3	Nodular melanoma
M8722/0	Balloon cell nevus
M8722/3	Balloon cell melanoma
M8723/0	Halo nevus
M8724/0	Fibrous papule of the nose
M8725/0	Neuronevus
M8726/0	Magnocellular nevus
M8730/0	Nonpigmented nevus
M8730/3	Amelanotic melanoma
M8740/0	Junctional nevus
M8740/3	Malignant melanoma in junctional nevus
M8741/2	Precancerous melanosis NOS
M8741/3	Malignant melanoma in precancerous melanosis
M8742/2	Hutchinson's melanotic freckle
M8742/3	Malignant melanoma in Hutchinson's melanotic freckle
M8743/3	Superficial spreading melanoma
M8750/0	Intradermal nevus
M8760/0	Compound nevus
M8761/1	Giant pigmented nevus
M8761/3	Malignant melanoma in giant pigmented nevus
M8770/0	Epithelioid and spindle cell nevus
M8771/3	Epithelioid cell melanoma
M8772/3	Spindle cell melanoma NOS
M8773/3	Spindle cell melanoma, type A
M8774/3	Spindle cell melanoma, type B
M8775/3	Mixed epithelioid and spindle cell melanoma
M8780/0	Blue nevus NOS
M8780/3	Blue nevus, malignant
M8790/0	Cellular blue nevus

M880　　　Soft tissue tumors and sarcomas NOS

Code	Description
M8800/0	Soft tissue tumor, benign
M8800/3	Sarcoma NOS
M8800/9	Sarcomatosis NOS
M8801/3	Spindle cell sarcoma
M8802/3	Giant cell sarcoma (except of bone M9250/3)
M8803/3	Small cell sarcoma
M8804/3	Epithelioid cell sarcoma

M881-M883　　Fibromatous neoplasms

Code	Description
M8810/0	Fibroma NOS
M8810/3	Fibrosarcoma NOS
M8811/0	Fibromyxoma
M8811/3	Fibromyxosarcoma
M8812/0	Periosteal fibroma
M8812/3	Periosteal fibrosarcoma
M8813/0	Fascial fibroma
M8813/3	Fascial fibrosarcoma
M8814/3	Infantile fibrosarcoma
M8820/0	Elastofibroma
M8821/1	Aggressive fibromatosis
M8822/1	Abdominal fibromatosis
M8823/1	Desmoplastic fibroma
M8830/0	Fibrous histiocytoma NOS

Code	Description
M8830/1	Atypical fibrous histiocytoma
M8830/3	Fibrous histiocytoma, malignant
M8831/0	Fibroxanthoma NOS
M8831/1	Atypical fibroxanthoma
M8831/3	Fibroxanthoma, malignant
M8832/0	Dermatofibroma NOS
M8832/1	Dermatofibroma protuberans
M8832/3	Dermatofibrosarcoma NOS

M884　　　Myxomatous neoplasms

Code	Description
M8840/0	Myxoma NOS
M8840/3	Myxosarcoma

M885-M888　　Lipomatous neoplasms

Code	Description
M8850/0	Lipoma NOS
M8850/3	Liposarcoma NOS
M8851/0	Fibrolipoma
M8851/3	Liposarcoma, well differentiated type
M8852/0	Fibromyxolipoma
M8852/3	Myxoid liposarcoma
M8853/3	Round cell liposarcoma
M8854/3	Pleomorphic liposarcoma
M8855/3	Mixed type liposarcoma
M8856/0	Intramuscular lipoma
M8857/0	Spindle cell lipoma
M8860/0	Angiomyolipoma
M8860/3	Angiomyoliposarcoma
M8861/0	Angiolipoma NOS
M8861/1	Angiolipoma, infiltrating
M8870/0	Myelolipoma
M8880/0	Hibernoma
M8881/0	Lipoblastomatosis

M889-M892　　Myomatous neoplasms

Code	Description
M8890/0	Leiomyoma NOS
M8890/1	Intravascular leiomyomatosis
M8890/3	Leiomyosarcoma NOS
M8891/1	Epithelioid leiomyoma
M8891/3	Epithelioid leiomyosarcoma
M8892/1	Cellular leiomyoma
M8893/0	Bizarre leiomyoma
M8894/0	Angiomyoma
M8894/3	Angiomyosarcoma
M8895/0	Myoma
M8895/3	Myosarcoma
M8900/0	Rhabdomyoma NOS
M8900/3	Rhabdomyosarcoma NOS
M8901/3	Pleomorphic rhabdomyosarcoma
M8902/3	Mixed type rhabdomyosarcoma
M8903/0	Fetal rhabdomyoma
M8904/0	Adult rhabdomyoma
M8910/3	Embryonal rhabdomyosarcoma
M8920/3	Alveolar rhabdomyosarcoma

M893-M899　　Complex mixed and stromal neoplasms

Code	Description
M8930/3	Endometrial stromal sarcoma
M8931/1	Endolymphatic stromal myosis
M8932/0	Adenomyoma
M8940/0	Pleomorphic adenoma
M8940/3	Mixed tumor, malignant NOS
M8950/3	Mullerian mixed tumor
M8951/3	Mesodermal mixed tumor
M8960/0	Mesoblastic nephroma
M8960/3	Nephroblastoma NOS
M8961/3	Epithelial nephroblastoma
M8962/3	Mesenchymal nephroblastoma
M8970/3	Hepatoblastoma
M8980/3	Carcinosarcoma NOS
M8981/3	Carcinosarcoma, embryonal type
M8982/0	Myoepithelioma
M8990/0	Mesenchymoma, benign
M8990/1	Mesenchymoma NOS
M8990/3	Mesenchymoma, malignant
M8991/3	Embryonal sarcoma

M900-M903　　Fibroepithelial neoplasms

Code	Description
M9000/0	Brenner tumor NOS
M9000/1	Brenner tumor, borderline malignancy

Code	Description
M9000/3	Brenner tumor, malignant
M9010/0	Fibroadenoma NOS
M9011/0	Intracanalicular fibroadenoma NOS
M9012/0	Pericanalicular fibroadenoma
M9013/0	Adenofibroma NOS
M9014/0	Serous adenofibroma
M9015/0	Mucinous adenofibroma
M9020/0	Cellular intracanalicular fibroadenoma
M9020/1	Cystosarcoma phyllodes NOS
M9020/3	Cystosarcoma phyllodes, malignant
M9030/0	Juvenile fibroadenoma

M904　　　Synovial neoplasms

Code	Description
M9040/0	Synovioma, benign
M9040/3	Synovial sarcoma NOS
M9041/3	Synovial sarcoma, spindle cell type
M9042/3	Synovial sarcoma, epithelioid cell type
M9043/3	Synovial sarcoma, biphasic type
M9044/3	Clear cell sarcoma of tendons and aponeuroses

M905　　　Mesothelial neoplasms

Code	Description
M9050/0	Mesothelioma, benign
M9050/3	Mesothelioma, malignant
M9051/0	Fibrous mesothelioma, benign
M9051/3	Fibrous mesothelioma, malignant
M9052/0	Epithelioid mesothelioma, benign
M9052/3	Epithelioid mesothelioma, malignant
M9053/0	Mesothelioma, biphasic type, benign
M9053/3	Mesothelioma, biphasic type, malignant
M9054/0	Adenomatoid tumor NOS

M906-M909　　Germ cell neoplasms

Code	Description
M9060/3	Dysgerminoma
M9061/3	Seminoma NOS
M9062/3	Seminoma, anaplastic type
M9063/3	Spermatocytic seminoma
M9064/3	Germinoma
M9070/3	Embryonal carcinoma NOS
M9071/3	Endodermal sinus tumor
M9072/3	Polyembryoma
M9073/1	Gonadoblastoma
M9080/0	Teratoma, benign
M9080/1	Teratoma NOS
M9080/3	Teratoma, malignant NOS
M9081/3	Teratocarcinoma
M9082/3	Malignant teratoma, undifferentiated type
M9083/3	Malignant teratoma, intermediate type
M9084/0	Dermoid cyst
M9084/3	Dermoid cyst with malignant transformation
M9090/0	Struma ovarii NOS
M9090/3	Struma ovarii, malignant
M9091/1	Strumal carcinoid

M910　　　Trophoblastic neoplasms

Code	Description
M9100/0	Hydatidiform mole NOS
M9100/1	Invasive hydatidiform mole
M9100/3	Choriocarcinoma
M9101/3	Choriocarcinoma combined with teratoma
M9102/3	Malignant teratoma, trophoblastic

M911　　　Mesonephromas

Code	Description
M9110/0	Mesonephroma, benign
M9110/1	Mesonephric tumor
M9110/3	Mesonephroma, malignant
M9111/1	Endosalpingioma

M912-M916　　Blood vessel tumors

Code	Description
M9120/0	Hemangioma NOS
M9120/3	Hemangiosarcoma
M9121/0	Cavernous hemangioma
M9122/0	Venous hemangioma
M9123/0	Racemose hemangioma
M9124/3	Kupffer cell sarcoma
M9130/0	Hemangioendothelioma, benign

M9130/1	Hemangioendothelioma NOS		M9320/0	Odontogenic myxoma		M9534/0	Angiomatous meningioma
M9130/3	Hemangioendothelioma, malignant		M9321/0	Odontogenic fibroma NOS		M9535/0	Hemangioblastic meningioma
M9131/0	Capillary hemangioma		M9330/0	Ameloblastic fibroma		M9536/0	Hemangiopericytic meningioma
M9132/0	Intramuscular hemangioma		M9330/3	Ameloblastic fibrosarcoma		M9537/0	Transitional meningioma
M9140/3	Kaposi's sarcoma		M9340/0	Calcifying epithelial odontogenic		M9538/1	Papillary meningioma
M9141/0	Angiokeratoma			tumor		M9539/3	Meningeal sarcomatosis

M917 **Lymphatic vessel tumors**

M918-M920 **Osteomas and osteosarcomas**

M921-M924 **Chondromatous neoplasms**

M925 **Giant cell tumors**

M926 **Miscellaneous bone tumors**

M927-M934 **Odontogenic tumors**

M935-M937 **Miscellaneous tumors**

M938-M948 **Gliomas**

M949-M952 **Neuroepitheliomatous neoplasms**

M953 **Meningiomas**

M954-M957 **Nerve sheath tumor**

M958 **Granular cell tumors and alveolar soft part sarcoma**

M959-M963 **Lymphomas, NOS or diffuse**

M964 **Reticulosarcomas**

M965-M966 **Hodgkin's disease**

M9142/0	Verrucous keratotic hemangioma
M9150/0	Hemangiopericytoma, benign
M9150/1	Hemangiopericytoma NOS
M9150/3	Hemangiopericytoma, malignant
M9160/0	Angiofibroma NOS
M9161/1	Hemangioblastoma
M9170/0	Lymphangioma NOS
M9170/3	Lymphangiosarcoma
M9171/0	Capillary lymphangioma
M9172/0	Cavernous lymphangioma
M9173/0	Cystic lymphangioma
M9174/0	Lymphangiomyoma
M9174/1	Lymphangiomyomatosis
M9175/0	Hemolymphangioma
M9180/0	Osteoma NOS
M9180/3	Osteosarcoma NOS
M9181/3	Chondroblastic osteosarcoma
M9182/3	Fibroblastic osteosarcoma
M9183/3	Telangiectatic osteosarcoma
M9184/3	Osteosarcoma in Paget's disease of bone
M9190/3	Juxtacortical osteosarcoma
M9191/0	Osteoid osteoma NOS
M9200/0	Osteoblastoma
M9210/0	Osteochondroma
M9210/1	Osteochondromatosis NOS
M9220/0	Chondroma NOS
M9220/1	Chondromatosis NOS
M9220/3	Chondrosarcoma NOS
M9221/0	Juxtacortical chondroma
M9221/3	Juxtacortical chondrosarcoma
M9230/0	Chondroblastoma NOS
M9230/3	Chondroblastoma, malignant
M9240/3	Mesenchymal chondrosarcoma
M9241/0	Chondromyxoid fibroma
M9250/1	Giant cell tumor of bone NOS
M9250/3	Giant cell tumor of bone, malignant
M9251/1	Giant cell tumor of soft parts NOS
M9251/3	Malignant giant cell tumor of soft parts
M9260/3	Ewing's sarcoma
M9261/3	Adamantinoma of long bones
M9262/0	Ossifying fibroma
M9270/0	Odontogenic tumor, benign
M9270/1	Odontogenic tumor NOS
M9270/3	Odontogenic tumor, malignant
M9271/0	Dentinoma
M9272/0	Cementoma NOS
M9273/0	Cementoblastoma, benign
M9274/0	Cementifying fibroma
M9275/0	Gigantiform cementoma
M9280/0	Odontoma NOS
M9281/0	Compound odontoma
M9282/0	Complex odontoma
M9290/0	Ameloblastic fibro-odontoma
M9290/3	Ameloblastic odontosarcoma
M9300/0	Adenomatoid odontogenic tumor
M9301/0	Calcifying odontogenic cyst
M9310/0	Ameloblastoma NOS
M9310/3	Ameloblastoma, malignant
M9311/0	Odontoameloblastoma
M9312/0	Squamous odontogenic tumor

M9350/1	Craniopharyngioma
M9360/1	Pinealoma
M9361/1	Pineocytoma
M9362/3	Pineoblastoma
M9363/0	Melanotic neuroectodermal tumor
M9370/3	Chordoma
M9380/3	Glioma, malignant
M9381/3	Gliomatosis cerebri
M9382/3	Mixed glioma
M9383/1	Subependymal glioma
M9384/1	Subependymal giant cell astrocytoma
M9390/0	Choroid plexus papilloma NOS
M9390/3	Choroid plexus papilloma, malignant
M9391/3	Ependymoma NOS
M9392/3	Ependymoma, anaplastic type
M9393/1	Papillary ependymoma
M9394/1	Myxopapillary ependymoma
M9400/3	Astrocytoma NOS
M9401/3	Astrocytoma, anaplastic type
M9410/3	Protoplasmic astrocytoma
M9411/3	Gemistocytic astrocytoma
M9420/3	Fibrillary astrocytoma
M9421/3	Pilocytic astrocytoma
M9422/3	Spongioblastoma NOS
M9423/3	Spongioblastoma polare
M9430/3	Astroblastoma
M9440/3	Glioblastoma NOS
M9441/3	Giant cell glioblastoma
M9442/3	Glioblastoma with sarcomatous component
M9443/3	Primitive polar spongioblastoma
M9450/3	Oligodendroglioma NOS
M9451/3	Oligodendroglioma, anaplastic type
M9460/3	Oligodendroblastoma
M9470/3	Medulloblastoma NOS
M9471/3	Desmoplastic medulloblastoma
M9472/3	Medullomyoblastoma
M9480/3	Cerebellar sarcoma NOS
M9481/3	Monstrocellular sarcoma
M9490/0	Ganglioneuroma
M9490/3	Ganglioneuroblastoma
M9491/0	Ganglioneuromatosis
M9500/3	Neuroblastoma NOS
M9501/3	Medulloepithelioma NOS
M9502/3	Teratoid medulloepithelioma
M9503/3	Neuroepithelioma NOS
M9504/3	Spongioneuroblastoma
M9505/1	Ganglioglioma
M9506/0	Neurocytoma
M9507/0	Pacinian tumor
M9510/3	Retinoblastoma NOS
M9511/3	Retinoblastoma, differentiated type
M9512/3	Retinoblastoma, undifferentiated type
M9520/3	Olfactory neurogenic tumor
M9521/3	Esthesioneurocytoma
M9522/3	Esthesioneuroblastoma
M9523/3	Esthesioneuroepithelioma
M9530/0	Meningioma NOS
M9530/1	Meningiomatosis NOS
M9530/3	Meningioma, malignant
M9531/0	Meningotheliomatous meningioma
M9532/0	Fibrous meningioma
M9533/0	Psammomatous meningioma

M9540/0	Neurofibroma NOS
M9540/1	Neurofibromatosis NOS
M9540/3	Neurofibrosarcoma
M9541/0	Melanotic neurofibroma
M9550/0	Plexiform neurofibroma
M9560/0	Neurilemmoma NOS
M9560/1	Neurinomatosis
M9560/3	Neurilemmoma, malignant
M9570/0	Neuroma NOS
M9580/0	Granular cell tumor NOS
M9580/3	Granular cell tumor, malignant
M9581/3	Alveolar soft part sarcoma
M9590/0	Lymphomatous tumor, benign
M9590/3	Malignant lymphoma NOS
M9591/3	Malignant lymphoma, non Hodgkin's type
M9600/3	Malignant lymphoma, undifferentiated cell type NOS
M9601/3	Malignant lymphoma, stem cell type
M9602/3	Malignant lymphoma, convoluted cell type NOS
M9610/3	Lymphosarcoma NOS
M9611/3	Malignant lymphoma, lymphoplasma-cytoid type
M9612/3	Malignant lymphoma, immunoblastic type
M9613/3	Malignant lymphoma, mixed lympho-cytic-histiocytic NOS
M9614/3	Malignant lymphoma, centroblas-tic-centrocytic, diffuse
M9615/3	Malignant lymphoma, follicular center cell NOS
M9620/3	Malignant lymphoma, lymphocytic, well differentiated NOS
M9621/3	Malignant lymphoma, lymphocytic, intermediate differentiation NOS
M9622/3	Malignant lymphoma, centrocytic
M9623/3	Malignant lymphoma, follicular center cell, cleaved NOS
M9630/3	Malignant lymphoma, lymphocytic, poorly differentiated NOS
M9631/3	Prolymphocytic lymphosarcoma
M9632/3	Malignant lymphoma, centroblastic type NOS
M9633/3	Malignant lymphoma, follicular center cell, noncleaved NOS
M9640/3	Reticulosarcoma NOS
M9641/3	Reticulosarcoma, pleomorphic cell type
M9642/3	Reticulosarcoma, nodular
M9650/3	Hodgkin's disease NOS
M9651/3	Hodgkin's disease, lymphocytic pre-dominance
M9652/3	Hodgkin's disease, mixed cellularity
M9653/3	Hodgkin's disease, lymphocytic deple-tion NOS
M9654/3	Hodgkin's disease, lymphocytic deple-tion, diffuse fibrosis
M9655/3	Hodgkin's disease, lymphocytic deple-tion, reticular type
M9656/3	Hodgkin's disease, nodular sclerosis NOS

M9657/3	*Hodgkin's disease, nodular sclerosis, cellular phase*
M9660/3	*Hodgkin's paragranuloma*
M9661/3	*Hodgkin's granuloma*
M9662/3	*Hodgkin's sarcoma*

M969   **Lymphomas, nodular or follicular**

M9690/3	*Malignant lymphoma, nodular NOS*
M9691/3	*Malignant lymphoma, mixed lympho-cytic-histiocytic, nodular*
M9692/3	*Malignant lymphoma, centroblas-tic-centrocytic, follicular*
M9693/3	*Malignant lymphoma, lymphocytic, well differentiated, nodular*
M9694/3	*Malignant lymphoma, lymphocytic, intermediate differentiation, nodular*
M9695/3	*Malignant lymphoma, follicular center cell, cleaved, follicular*
M9696/3	*Malignant lymphoma, lymphocytic, poorly differentiated, nodular*
M9697/3	*Malignant lymphoma, centroblastic type, follicular*
M9698/3	*Malignant lymphoma, follicular center cell, noncleaved, follicular*

M970   **Mycosis fungoides**

M9700/3	*Mycosis fungoides*
M9701/3	*Sezary's disease*

M971-M972   **Miscellaneous reticuloendothelial neoplasms**

M9710/3	*Microglioma*
M9720/3	*Malignant histiocytosis*
M9721/3	*Histiocytic medullary reticulosis*
M9722/3	*Letterer-Siwe's disease*

M973   **Plasma cell tumors**

M9730/3	*Plasma cell myeloma*

M9731/0	*Plasma cell tumor, benign*
M9731/1	*Plasmacytoma NOS*
M9731/3	*Plasma cell tumor, malignant*

M974   **Mast cell tumors**

M9740/1	*Mastocytoma NOS*
M9740/3	*Mast cell sarcoma*
M9741/3	*Malignant mastocytosis*

M975   **Burkitt's tumor**

M9750/3	*Burkitt's tumor*

M980-M994   **Leukemias NOS**

M9800/3	*Leukemias NOS*
M9800/3	*Leukemia NOS*
M9801/3	*Acute leukemia NOS*
M9802/3	*Subacute leukemia NOS*
M9803/3	*Chronic leukemia NOS*
M9804/3	*Aleukemic leukemia NOS*

M981   **Compound leukemias**

M9810/3	*Compound leukemia*

M982   **Lymphoid leukemias**

M9820/3	*Lymphoid leukemia NOS*
M9821/3	*Acute lymphoid leukemia*
M9822/3	*Subacute lymphoid leukemia*
M9823/3	*Chronic lymphoid leukemia*
M9824/3	*Aleukemic lymphoid leukemia*
M9825/3	*Prolymphocytic leukemia*

M983   **Plasma cell leukemias**

M9830/3	*Plasma cell leukemia*

M984   **Erythroleukemias**

M9840/3	*Erythroleukemia*
M9841/3	*Acute erythremia*
M9842/3	*Chronic erythremia*

M985   **Lymphosarcoma cell leukemias**

M9850/3	*Lymphosarcoma cell leukemia*

M986   **Myeloid leukemias**

M9860/3	*Myeloid leukemia NOS*
M9861/3	*Acute myeloid leukemia*
M9862/3	*Subacute myeloid leukemia*
M9863/3	*Chronic myeloid leukemia*
M9864/3	*Aleukemic myeloid leukemia*
M9865/3	*Neutrophilic leukemia*
M9866/3	*Acute promyelocytic leukemia*

M987   **Basophilic leukemias**

M9870/3	*Basophilic leukemia*

M988   **Eosinophilic leukemias**

M9880/3	*Eosinophilic leukemia*

M989   **Monocytic leukemias**

M9890/3	*Monocytic leukemia NOS*
M9891/3	*Acute monocytic leukemia*
M9892/3	*Subacute monocytic leukemia*
M9893/3	*Chronic monocytic leukemia*
M9894/3	*Aleukemic monocytic leukemia*

M990-M994   **Miscellaneous leukemias**

M9900/3	*Mast cell leukemia*
M9910/3	*Megakaryocytic leukemia*
M9920/3	*Megakaryocytic myelosis*
M9930/3	*Myeloid sarcoma*
M9940/3	*Hairy cell leukemia*

M995-M997   **Miscellaneous myeloproliferative and lymphoproliferative disorders**

M9950/1	*Polycythemia vera*
M9951/1	*Acute panmyelosis*
M9960/1	*Chronic myeloproliferative disease*
M9961/1	*Myelosclerosis with myeloid metapla-sia*
M9962/1	*Idiopathic thrombocythemia*
M9970/1	*Chronic lymphoproliferative disease*

APPENDIX B
WAS OFFICIALLY DELETED
OCTOBER 1, 2004

CLASSIFICATION OF DRUGS BY AMERICAN HOSPITAL FORMULARY SERVICE LIST NUMBER AND THEIR ICD-9-CM EQUIVALENTS

The coding of adverse effects of drugs is keyed to the continually revised Hospital Formulary of the American Hospital Formulary Service (AHFS) published under the direction of the American Society of Hospital Pharmacists.

The following section gives the ICD-9-CM diagnosis code for each AHFS list.

AHFS* List		ICD-9-CM Diagnosis Code
4:00	ANTIHISTAMINE DRUGS	963.0
8:00	ANTI-INFECTIVE AGENTS	
8:04	Amebacides	961.5
	hydroxyquinoline derivatives	961.3
	arsenical anti-infectives	961.1
	quinoline derivatives	961.3
8:12.04	Antifungal Antibiotics	960.1
	nonantibiotics	961.9
8:12.06	Cephalosporins	960.5
8:12.08	Chloramphenicol	960.2
8:12.12	The Erythromycins	960.3
8:12.16	The Penicillins	960.0
8:12.20	The Streptomycins	960.6
8:12.24	The Tetracyclines	960.4
8:12.28	Other Antibiotics	960.8
	antimycobacterial antibiotics	960.6
	macrolides	960.3
8:16	Antituberculars	961.8
	antibiotics	960.6
8:18	Antivirals	961.7
8:20	Plasmodicides (antimalarials)	961.4
8:24	Sulfonamides	961.0
8:26	The Sulfones	961.8
8:28	Treponemicides	961.2
8:32	Trichomonacides	961.5
	hydroxyquinoline derivatives	961.3
	nitrofuran derivatives	961.9
8:36	Urinary Germicides	961.9
	quinoline derivatives	961.3
8:40	Other Anti-Infectives	961.9
10:00	ANTINEOPLASTIC AGENTS	963.1
	antibiotics	960.7
	progestogens	962.2
12:00	AUTONOMIC DRUGS	
12:04	Parasympathomimetic (Cholinergic) Agents	971.0
12:08	Parasympatholytic (Cholinergic Blocking Agents	971.1
12:12	Sympathomimetic (Adrenergic) Agents	971.2
12:16	Sympatholytic (Adrenergic Blocking) Agents	971.3
12:20	Skeletal Muscle Relaxants	975.2
	central nervous system muscle-tone depressants	968.0
16:00	BLOOD DERIVATIVES	964.7
20:00	BLOOD FORMATION AND COAGULATION	
20:04	Antianemia Drugs	964.1
20:04.04	Iron Preparations	964.0
20:04.08	Liver and Stomach Preparations	964.1
20:12.04	Anticoagulants	964.2
20:12.08	Antiheparin Agents	964.5
20:12.12	Coagulants	964.5
20:12.16	Hemostatics	964.5
	capillary-active drugs	972.8
	fibrinolysis-affecting agents	964.4
	natural products	964.7
24:00	CARDIOVASCULAR DRUGS	
24:04	Cardiac Drugs	972.9
	cardiotonic agents	972.1
	rhythm regulators	972.0
24:06	Antilipemic Agents	972.2
	thyroid derivatives	962.7

AHFS* List		ICD-9-CM Diagnosis Code
24:08	Hypotensive Agents	972.6
	adrenergic blocking agents	971.3
	ganglion-blocking agents	972.3
	vasodilators	972.5
24:12	Vasodilating Agents	972.5
	coronary	972.4
	nicotinic acid derivatives	972.2
24:16	Sclerosing Agents	972.7
28:00	CENTRAL NERVOUS SYSTEM DRUGS	
28:04	General Anesthetics	968.4
	gaseous anesthetics	968.2
	halothane	968.1
	intravenous anesthetics	968.3
28:08	Analgesics and Antipyretics	965.9
	antirheumatics	965.61-965.69
	aromatic analgesics	965.4
	non-narcotics NEC	965.7
	opium alkaloids	965.00
	heroin	965.01
	methadone	965.02
	specified type NEC	965.09
	pyrazole derivatives	965.5
	salicylates	965.1
	specified type NEC	965.8
28:10	Narcotic Antagonists	970.1
28:12	Anticonvulsants	966.3
	barbiturates	967.0
	benzodiazepine-based tranquilizers	969.4
	bromides	967.3
	hydantoin derivatives	966.1
	oxazolidine derivative	966.0
	succinimides	966.2
28:16.04	Antidepressants	969.0
28:16.08	Tranquilizers	969.5
	benzodiazepine-based	969.4
	butyrophenone-based	969.2
	major NEC	969.3
	phenothiazine-based	969.1
28:16.12	Other Psychotherapeutic Agents	969.8
28:20	Respiratory and Cerebral Stimulants	970.9
	analeptics	970.0
	anorexigenic agents	977.0
	psychostimulants	969.7
	specified type NEC	970.8
28:24	Sedatives and Hypnotics	967.9
	barbiturates	967.0
	benzodiazepine-based tranquilizers	969.4
	chloral hydrate group	967.1
	glutethamide group	967.5
	intravenous anesthetics	968.3
	methaqualone	967.4
	paraldehyde	967.2
	phenothiazine-based tranquilizers	969.1
	specified type NEC	967.8
	thiobarbiturates	968.3
	tranquilizer NEC	969.5
36:00	DIAGNOSTIC AGENTS	977.8
40:00	ELECTROLYTE, CALORIC, AND WATER BALANCE AGENTS NEC	974.5
40:04	Acidifying Agents	963.2
40:08	Alkalinizing Agents	963.3
40:10	Ammonia Detoxicants	974.5
40:12	Replacement Solutions NEC	974.5
	plasma volume expanders	964.8
40:16	Sodium-Removing Resins	974.5
40:18	Potassium-Removing Resins	974.5
40:20	Caloric Agents	974.5
40:24	Salt and Sugar Substitutes	974.5

AHFS* List		ICD-9-CM Diagnosis Code
40:28	Diuretics NEC	974.4
	carbonic acid anhydrase inhibitors	974.2
	mercurials	974.0
	purine derivatives	974.1
	saluretics	974.3
40:36	Irrigating Solutions	974.5
40:40	Uricosuric Agents	974.7
44:00	ENZYMES NEC	963.4
	fibrinolysis-affecting agents	964.4
	gastric agents	973.4
48:00	EXPECTORANTS AND COUGH PREPARATIONS	
	antihistamine agents	963.0
	antitussives	975.4
	codeine derivatives	965.09
	expectorants	975.5
	narcotic agents NEC	965.09
52:00	EYE, EAR, NOSE, AND THROAT PREPARATIONS	
52:04	Anti-Infectives	
	ENT	976.6
	ophthalmic	976.5
52:04.04	Antibiotics	
	ENT	976.6
	ophthalmic	976.5
52:04.06	Antivirals	
	ENT	976.6
	ophthalmic	976.5
52:04.08	Sulfonamides	
	ENT	976.6
	ophthalmic	976.5
52:04.12	Miscellaneous Anti-Infectives	
	ENT	976.6
	ophthalmic	976.5
52:08	Anti-Inflammatory Agents	
	ENT	976.6
	ophthalmic	976.5
52:10	Carbonic Anhydrase Inhibitors	974.2
52:12	Contact Lens Solutions	976.5
52:16	Local Anesthetics	968.5
52:20	Miotics	971.0
52:24	Mydriatics	
	adrenergics	971.2
	anticholinergics	971.1
	antimuscarinics	971.1
	parasympatholytics	971.1
	spasmolytics	971.1
	sympathomimetics	971.2
52:28	Mouth Washes and Gargles	976.6
52:32	Vasoconstrictors	971.2
52:36	Unclassified Agents	
	ENT	976.6
	ophthalmic	976.5
56:00	GASTROINTESTINAL DRUGS	
56:04	Antacids and Absorbents	973.0
56:08	Anti-Diarrhea Agents	973.5
56:10	Antiflatulents	973.8
56:12	Cathartics NEC	973.3
	emollients	973.2
	irritants	973.1
56:16	Digestants	973.4
56:20	Emetics and Antiemetics	
	antiemetics	963.0
	emetics	973.6
56:24	Lipotropic Agents	977.1
60:00	GOLD COMPOUNDS	965.69
64:00	HEAVY METAL ANTAGONISTS	963.8
68:00	HORMONES AND SYNTHETIC SUBSTITUTES	
68:04	Adrenals	962.0
68:08	Androgens	962.1
68:12	Contraceptives	962.2
68:16	Estrogens	962.2

AHFS* List		ICD-9-CM Diagnosis Code
68:18	Gonadotropins	962.4
68:20	Insulins and Antidiabetic Agents	962.3
68:20.08	Insulins	962.3
68:24	Parathyroid	962.6
68:28	Pituitary	
	anterior	962.4
	posterior	962.5
68:32	Progestogens	962.2
68:34	Other Corpus Luteum Hormones	962.2
68:36	Thyroid and Antithyroid	
	antithyroid	962.8
	thyroid	962.7
72:00	LOCAL ANESTHETICS NEC	968.9
	topical (surface) agents	968.5
	infiltrating agents (intradermal) (subcutaneous) (submucosal)	968.5
	nerve blocking agents (peripheral) (plexus) (regional)	968.6
	spinal	968.7
76:00	OXYTOCICS	975.0
78:00	RADIOACTIVE AGENTS	990
80:00	SERUMS, TOXOIDS, AND VACCINES	
80:04	Serums	979.9
	immune globulin (gamma) (human)	964.6
80:08	Toxoids NEC	978.8
	diphtheria	978.5
	and tetanus	978.9
	with pertussis component	978.6
	tetanus	978.4
	and diphtheria	978.9
	with pertussis component	978.6
80:12	Vaccines NEC	979.9
	bacterial NEC	978.8
	with other bacterial component	978.9
	pertussis component	978.6
	viral and rickettsial component	979.7
	rickettsial NEC	979.6
	with bacterial component	979.7
	pertussis component	978.6
	viral component	979.7
	viral NEC	979.6
	with bacterial component	979.7
	pertussis component	978.6
	rickettsial component	979.7
84:00	SKIN AND MUCOUS MEMBRANE PREPARATIONS	
84:04	Anti-Infectives	976.0
84:04.04	Antibiotics	976.0
84:04.08	Fungicides	976.0
84:04.12	Scabicides and Pediculicides	976.0
84:04.16	Miscellaneous Local Anti-Infectives	976.0
84:06	Anti-Inflammatory Agents	976.0
84:08	Antipruritics and Local Anesthetics	
	antipruritics	976.1
	local anesthetics	968.5
84:12	Astringents	976.2
84:16	Cell Stimulants and Proliferants	976.8
84:20	Detergents	976.2
84:24	Emollients, Demulcents, and Protectants	976.3
84:28	Keratolytic Agents	976.4
84:32	Keratoplastic Agents	976.4
84:36	Miscellaneous Agents	976.8
86:00	SPASMOLYTIC AGENTS	975.1
	antiasthmatics	975.7
	papaverine	972.5
	theophyllin	974.1
88:00	VITAMINS	
88:04	Vitamin A	963.5

AHFS* List	ICD-9-CM Diagnosis Code	AHFS* List	ICD-9-CM Diagnosis Code
88:08 Vitamin B Complex	963.5	88:16 Vitamin D	963.5
hematopoietic vitamin	964.1	88:20 Vitamin E	963.5
nicotinic acid derivatives	972.2	88:24 Vitamin K Activity	964.3
88:12 Vitamin C	963.5	88:28 Multivitamin Preparations	963.5
		92:00 UNCLASSIFIED THERAPEUTIC AGENTS	977.8

* American Hospital Formulary Service

CLASSIFICATION OF INDUSTRIAL ACCIDENTS ACCORDING TO AGENCY

Annex B to the Resolution concerning Statistics of Employment Injuries adopted by the Tenth International Conference of Labor Statisticians on 12 October 1962

1 MACHINES

11   *Prime-Movers, except Electrical Motors*
111   *Steam engines*
112   *Internal combustion engines*
119   *Others*
12   *Transmission Machinery*
121   *Transmission shafts*
122   *Transmission belts, cables, pulleys, pinions, chains, gears*
129   *Others*
13   *Metalworking Machines*
131   *Power presses*
132   *Lathes*
133   *Milling machines*
134   *Abrasive wheels*
135   *Mechanical shears*
136   *Forging machines*
137   *Rolling-mills*
139   *Others*
14   *Wood and Assimilated Machines*
141   *Circular saws*
142   *Other saws*
143   *Molding machines*
144   *Overhand planes*
149   *Others*
15   *Agricultural Machines*
151   *Reapers (including combine reapers)*
152   *Threshers*
159   *Others*
16   *Mining Machinery*
161   *Under-cutters*
169   *Others*
19   *Other Machines Not Elsewhere Classified*
191   *Earth-moving machines, excavating and scraping machines, except means of transport*
192   *Spinning, weaving and other textile machines*
193   *Machines for the manufacture of food- stuffs and beverages*
194   *Machines for the manufacture of paper*
195   *Printing machines*
199   *Others*

2 MEANS OF TRANSPORT AND LIFTING EQUIPMENT

21   *Lifting Machines and Appliances*
211   *Cranes*
212   *Lifts and elevators*
213   *Winches*
214   *Pulley blocks*
219   *Others*
22   *Means of Rail Transport*
221   *Inter-urban railways*
222   *Rail transport in mines, tunnels, quarries, industrial establishments, docks, etc.*
229   *Others*
23   *Other Wheeled Means of Transport, Excluding Rail Transport*
231   *Tractors*
232   *Lorries*
233   *Trucks*
234   *Motor vehicles, not elsewhere classified*
235   *Animal-drawn vehicles*
236   *Hand-drawn vehicles*
239   *Others*
24   *Means of Air Transport*
25   *Means of Water Transport*
251   *Motorized means of water transport*
252   *Non-motorized means of water transport*
26   *Other Means of Transport*
261   *Cable-cars*
262   *Mechanical conveyors, except cable-cars*
269   *Others*

3 OTHER EQUIPMENT

31   *Pressure Vessels*
311   *Boilers*
312   *Pressurized containers*
313   *Pressurized piping and accessories*
314   *Gas cylinders*
315   *Caissons, diving equipment*
319   *Others*
32   *Furnaces, Ovens, Kilns*
321   *Blast furnaces*
322   *Refining furnaces*
323   *Other furnaces*
324   *Kilns*
325   *Ovens*
33   *Refrigerating Plants*
34   *Electrical Installations, Including Electric Motors, but Excluding Electric Hand Tools*
341   *Rotating machines*
342   *Conductors*
343   *Transformers*
344   *Control apparatus*
349   *Others*
35   *Electric Hand Tools*
36   *Tools, Implements, and Appliances, Except Electric Hand Tools*
361   *Power-driven hand tools, except electrichand tools*
362   *Hand tools, not power-driven*
369   *Others*
37   *Ladders, Mobile Ramps*
38   *Scaffolding*
39   *Other Equipment, Not Elsewhere Classified*

4 MATERIALS, SUBSTANCES AND RADIATIONS

41   *Explosives*
42   *Dusts, Gases, Liquids and Chemicals, Excluding Explosives*
421   *Dusts*
422   *Gases, vapors, fumes*
423   *Liquids, not elsewhere classified*
424   *Chemicals, not elsewhere classified*
43   *Flying Fragments*
44   *Radiations*
441   *Ionizing radiations*
449   *Others*
49   *Other Materials and Substances Not Elsewhere Classified*

5 WORKING ENVIRONMENT

51   *Outdoor*
511   *Weather*
512   *Traffic and working surfaces*
513   *Water*
519   *Others*
52   *Indoor*
521   *Floors*
522   *Confined quarters*
523   *Stairs*
524   *Other traffic and working surfaces*
525   *Floor openings and wall openings*
526   *Environmental factors (lighting, ventilation, temperature, noise, etc.)*
529   *Others*
53   *Underground*
531   *Roofs and faces of mine roads and tunnels, etc.*
532   *Floors of mine roads and tunnels, etc.*
533   *Working-faces of mines, tunnels, etc.*
534   *Mine shafts*
535   *Fire*
536   *Water*
539   *Others*

6 OTHER AGENCIES, NOT ELSEWHERE CLASSIFIED

61   *Animals*
611   *Live animals*
612   *Animal products*
69   *Other Agencies, Not Elsewhere Classified*

7 AGENCIES NOT CLASSIFIED FOR LACK OF SUFFICIENT DATA

LIST OF THREE-DIGIT CATEGORIES

1. INFECTIOUS AND PARASITIC DISEASES

Intestinal infectious diseases (001-009)
001 Cholera
002 Typhoid and paratyphoid fevers
003 Other salmonella infections
004 Shigellosis
005 Other food poisoning (bacterial)
006 Amebiasis
007 Other protozoal intestinal diseases
008 Intestinal infections due to other organisms
009 Ill-defined intestinal infections

Tuberculosis (010-018)
010 Primary tuberculous infection
011 Pulmonary tuberculosis
012 Other respiratory tuberculosis
013 Tuberculosis of meninges and central nervous system
014 Tuberculosis of intestines, peritoneum, and mesenteric glands
015 Tuberculosis of bones and joints
016 Tuberculosis of genitourinary system
017 Tuberculosis of other organs
018 Miliary tuberculosis

Zoonotic bacterial diseases (020-027)
020 Plague
021 Tularemia
022 Anthrax
023 Brucellosis
024 Glanders
025 Melioidosis
026 Rat-bite fever
027 Other zoonotic bacterial diseases

Other bacterial diseases (030-042)
030 Leprosy
031 Diseases due to other mycobacteria
032 Diphtheria
033 Whooping cough
034 Streptococcal sore throat and scarlatina
035 Erysipelas
036 Meningococcal infection
037 Tetanus
038 Septicemia
039 Actinomycotic infections
040 Other bacterial diseases
041 Bacterial infection in conditions classified elsewhere and of unspecified site

Human immunodeficiency virus (042)
042 Human immunodeficiency virus [HIV] disease

Poliomyelitis and other non-arthropod-borne viral diseases and prion diseases of central nervous system (045-049)
045 Acute poliomyelitis
046 Slow virus infections and prion diseases of central nervous system
047 Meningitis due to enterovirus
048 Other enterovirus diseases of central nervous system
049 Other non-arthropod-borne viral diseases of central nervous system

Viral diseases generally accompanied by exanthem (050-058)
050 Smallpox
051 Cowpox and paravaccinia
052 Chickenpox
053 Herpes zoster
054 Herpes simplex
055 Measles
056 Rubella
057 Other viral exanthemata
058 Other human herpesvirus

059 Other poxvirus infections

Arthropod-borne viral diseases (060-066)
060 Yellow fever
061 Dengue
062 Mosquito-borne viral encephalitis
063 Tick-borne viral encephalitis
064 Viral encephalitis transmitted by other and unspecified arthropods
065 Arthropod-borne hemorrhagic fever
066 Other arthropod-borne viral diseases

Other diseases due to viruses and Chlamydiae (070-079)
070 Viral hepatitis
071 Rabies
072 Mumps
073 Ornithosis
074 Specific diseases due to Coxsackievirus
075 Infectious mononucleosis
076 Trachoma
077 Other diseases of conjunctiva due to viruses and Chlamydiae
078 Other diseases due to viruses and Chlamydiae
079 Viral infection in conditions classified elsewhere and of unspecified site

Rickettsioses and other arthropod-borne diseases (080-088)
080 Louse-borne [epidemic] typhus
081 Other typhus
082 Tick-borne rickettsioses
083 Other rickettsioses
084 Malaria
085 Leishmaniasis
086 Trypanosomiasis
087 Relapsing fever
088 Other arthropod-borne diseases

Syphilis and other venereal diseases (090-099)
090 Congenital syphilis
091 Early syphilis, symptomatic
092 Early syphilis, latent
093 Cardiovascular syphilis
094 Neurosyphilis
095 Other forms of late syphilis, with symptoms
096 Late syphilis, latent
097 Other and unspecified syphilis
098 Gonococcal infections
099 Other venereal diseases

Other spirochetal diseases (100-104)
100 Leptospirosis
101 Vincent's angina
102 Yaws
103 Pinta
104 Other spirochetal infection

Mycoses (110-118)
110 Dermatophytosis
111 Dermatomycosis, other and unspecified
112 Candidiasis
114 Coccidioidomycosis
115 Histoplasmosis
116 Blastomycotic infection
117 Other mycoses
118 Opportunistic mycoses

Helminthiases (120-129)
120 Schistosomiasis [bilharziasis]
121 Other trematode infections
122 Echinococcosis
123 Other cestode infection
124 Trichinosis
125 Filarial infection and dracontiasis
126 Ancylostomiasis and necatoriasis
127 Other intestinal helminthiases
128 Other and unspecified helminthiases
129 Intestinal parasitism, unspecified

Other infectious and parasitic diseases (130-136)
130 Toxoplasmosis
131 Trichomoniasis
132 Pediculosis and phthirus infestation
133 Acariasis
134 Other infestation
135 Sarcoidosis
136 Other and unspecified infectious and parasitic diseases

Late effects of infectious and parasitic diseases (137-139)
137 Late effects of tuberculosis
138 Late effects of acute poliomyelitis
139 Late effects of other infectious and parasitic diseases

2. NEOPLASMS

Malignant neoplasm of lip, oral cavity, and pharynx (140-149)
140 Malignant neoplasm of lip
141 Malignant neoplasm of tongue
142 Malignant neoplasm of major salivary glands
143 Malignant neoplasm of gum
144 Malignant neoplasm of floor of mouth
145 Malignant neoplasm of other and unspecified parts of mouth
146 Malignant neoplasm of oropharynx
147 Malignant neoplasm of nasopharynx
148 Malignant neoplasm of hypopharynx
149 Malignant neoplasm of other and ill-defined sites within the lip, oral cavity, and pharynx

Malignant neoplasm of digestive organs and peritoneum (150-159)
150 Malignant neoplasm of esophagus
151 Malignant neoplasm of stomach
152 Malignant neoplasm of small intestine, including duodenum
153 Malignant neoplasm of colon
154 Malignant neoplasm of rectum, rectosigmoid junction, and anus
155 Malignant neoplasm of liver and intrahepatic bile ducts
156 Malignant neoplasm of gallbladder and extrahepatic bile ducts
157 Malignant neoplasm of pancreas
158 Malignant neoplasm of retroperitoneum and peritoneum
159 Malignant neoplasm of other and ill-defined sites within the digestive organs and peritoneum

Malignant neoplasm of respiratory and intrathoracic organs (160-165)
160 Malignant neoplasm of nasal cavities, middle ear, and accessory sinuses
161 Malignant neoplasm of larynx
162 Malignant neoplasm of trachea, bronchus, and lung
163 Malignant neoplasm of pleura
164 Malignant neoplasm of thymus, heart, and mediastinum
165 Malignant neoplasm of other and ill-defined sites within the respiratory system and intrathoracic organs

Malignant neoplasm of bone, connective tissue, skin, and breast (170-176)
170 Malignant neoplasm of bone and articular cartilage
171 Malignant neoplasm of connective and other soft tissue
172 Malignant melanoma of skin
173 Other malignant neoplasm of skin
174 Malignant neoplasm of female breast
175 Malignant neoplasm of male breast

176   Kaposi's sarcoma

Malignant neoplasm of genitourinary organs (179-189)

179   Malignant neoplasm of uterus, part unspecified
180   Malignant neoplasm of cervix uteri
181   Malignant neoplasm of placenta
182   Malignant neoplasm of body of uterus
183   Malignant neoplasm of ovary and other uterine adnexa
184   Malignant neoplasm of other and unspecified female genital organs
185   Malignant neoplasm of prostate
186   Malignant neoplasm of testis
187   Malignant neoplasm of penis and other male genital organs
188   Malignant neoplasm of bladder
189   Malignant neoplasm of kidney and other unspecified urinary organs

Malignant neoplasm of other and unspecified sites (190-199)

190   Malignant neoplasm of eye
191   Malignant neoplasm of brain
192   Malignant neoplasm of other and unspecified parts of nervous system
193   Malignant neoplasm of thyroid gland
194   Malignant neoplasm of other endocrine glands and related structures
195   Malignant neoplasm of other and ill-defined sites
196   Secondary and unspecified malignant neoplasm of lymph nodes
197   Secondary malignant neoplasm of respiratory and digestive systems
198   Secondary malignant neoplasm of other specified sites
199   Malignant neoplasm without specification of site

Malignant neoplasm of lymphatic and hematopoietic tissue (200-208)

200   Lymphosarcoma and reticulosar-coma and other specified malignant tumors of lymphatic tissue
201   Hodgkin's disease
202   Other malignant neoplasm of lymphoid and histiocytic tissue
203   Multiple myeloma and immunoproliferative neoplasms
204   Lymphoid leukemia
205   Myeloid leukemia
206   Monocytic leukemia
207   Other specified leukemia
208   Leukemia of unspecified cell type

Neuroendocrine tumors (209)

209   Neuroendocrine tumors

Benign neoplasms (210-229)

210   Benign neoplasm of lip, oral cavity, and pharynx
211   Benign neoplasm of other parts of digestive system
212   Benign neoplasm of respiratory and intrathoracic organs
213   Benign neoplasm of bone and articular cartilage
214   Lipoma
215   Other benign neoplasm of connective and other soft tissue
216   Benign neoplasm of skin
217   Benign neoplasm of breast
218   Uterine leiomyoma
219   Other benign neoplasm of uterus
220   Benign neoplasm of ovary

221   Benign neoplasm of other female genital organs
222   Benign neoplasm of male genital organs
223   Benign neoplasm of kidney and other urinary organs
224   Benign neoplasm of eye
225   Benign neoplasm of brain and other parts of nervous system
226   Benign neoplasm of thyroid gland
227   Benign neoplasm of other endocrine glands and related structures
228   Hemangioma and lymphangioma, any site
229   Benign neoplasm of other and unspecified sites

Carcinoma in situ (230-234)

230   Carcinoma in situ of digestive organs
231   Carcinoma in situ of respiratory system
232   Carcinoma in situ of skin
233   Carcinoma in situ of breast and genitourinary system
234   Carcinoma in situ of other and unspecified sites

Neoplasms of uncertain behavior (235-238)

235   Neoplasm of uncertain behavior of digestive and respiratory systems
236   Neoplasm of uncertain behavior of genitourinary organs
237   Neoplasm of uncertain behavior of endocrine glands and nervous system
238   Neoplasm of uncertain behavior of other and unspecified sites and tissues

Neoplasms of unspecified nature (239)

239   Neoplasm of unspecified nature

3. ENDOCRINE, NUTRITIONAL AND METABOLIC DISEASES, AND IMMUNITY DISORDERS

Disorders of thyroid gland (240-246)

240   Simple and unspecified goiter
241   Nontoxic nodular goiter
242   Thyrotoxicosis with or without goiter
243   Congenital hypothyroidism
244   Acquired hypothyroidism
245   Thyroiditis
246   Other disorders of thyroid

Diseases of other endocrine glands (249-259)

249   Secondary diabetes mellitus
250   Diabetes mellitus
251   Other disorders of pancreatic internal secretion
252   Disorders of parathyroid gland
253   Disorders of the pituitary gland and its hypothalamic control
254   Diseases of thymus gland
255   Disorders of adrenal glands
256   Ovarian dysfunction
257   Testicular dysfunction
258   Polyglandular dysfunction and related disorders
259   Other endocrine disorders

Nutritional deficiencies (260-269)

260   Kwashiorkor
261   Nutritional marasmus
262   Other severe protein-calorie malnutrition
263   Other and unspecified protein-calorie malnutrition
264   Vitamin A deficiency
265   Thiamine and niacin deficiency states
266   Deficiency of B-complex components
267   Ascorbic acid deficiency
268   Vitamin D deficiency
269   Other nutritional deficiencies

Other metabolic disorders and immnity disorders (270-279)

270   Disorders of amino-acid transport and metabolism
271   Disorders of carbohydrate transport and metabolism
272   Disorders of lipoid metabolism
273   Disorders of plasma protein metabolism
274   Gout
275   Disorders of mineral metabolism
276   Disorders of fluid, electrolyte, and acid-base balance
277   Other and unspecified disorders of metabolism
278   Overweight, obesity and other hyperalimentation
279   Disorders involving the immune mechanism

4. DISEASES OF BLOOD AND BLOOD-FORMING ORGANS (280-289)

280   Iron deficiency anemias
281   Other deficiency anemias
282   Hereditary hemolytic anemias
283   Acquired hemolytic anemias
284   Aplastic anemia
285   Other and unspecified anemias
286   Coagulation defects
287   Purpura and other hemorrhagic conditions
288   Diseases of white blood cells
289   Other diseases of blood and blood-forming organs

5. MENTAL DISORDERS

Organic psychotic conditions (290-294)

290   Senile and presenile organic psychotic conditions
291   Alcoholic psychoses
292   Drug psychoses
293   Transient organic psychotic conditions
294   Other organic psychotic conditions (chronic)

Other psychoses (295-299)

295   Schizophrenic psychoses
296   Affective psychoses
297   Paranoid states
298   Other nonorganic psychoses
299   Psychoses with origin specific to childhood

Neurotic disorders, personality disorders, and other nonpsychotic mental disorders (300-316)

300   Neurotic disorders
301   Personality disorders
302   Sexual and gender identity disorders
303   Alcohol dependence syndrome
304   Drug dependence
305   Nondependent abuse of drugs
306   Physiological malfunction arising from mental factors
307   Special symptoms or syndromes, not elsewhere classified
308   Acute reaction to stress
309   Adjustment reaction
310   Specific nonpsychotic mental disorders following organic brain damage
311   Depressive disorder, not elsewhereclassified
312   Disturbance of conduct, not elsewhere classified
313   Disturbance of emotions specific tochildhood and adolescence
314   Hyperkinetic syndrome of childhood
315   Specific delays in development
316   Psychic factors associated with diseases classified elsewhere

Mental retardation (317-319)

317   Mild mental retardation
318   Other specified mental retardation

319	Unspecified mental retardation	

6. DISEASES OF THE NERVOUS SYSTEM AND SENSE ORGANS

Inflammatory diseases of the central nervous system (320-326)
320 Bacterial meningitis
321 Meningitis due to other organisms
322 Meningitis of unspecified cause
323 Encephalitis, myelitis, and encephalomyelitis
324 Intracranial and intraspinal abscess
325 Phlebitis and thrombophlebitis of intracranial venous sinuses
326 Late effects of intracranial abscess or pyogenic infection

Organic Sleep Disorders (327)
327 Organic sleep disorders

Hereditary and degenerative diseases of the central nervous system (330-337)
330 Cerebral degenerations usually manifest in childhood
331 Other cerebral degenerations
332 Parkinson's disease
333 Other extrapyramidal diseases and abnormal movement disorders
334 Spinocerebellar disease
335 Anterior horn cell disease
336 Other diseases of spinal cord
337 Disorders of the autonomic nervous system

Pain (338)
338 Pain, not elsewhere classified

Other headache syndromes (339)
339 Other headache syndromes

Other disorders of the central nervous system (340-349)
340 Multiple sclerosis
341 Other demyelinating diseases of central nervous system
342 Hemiplegia and hemiparesis
343 Infantile cerebral palsy
344 Other paralytic syndromes
345 Epilepsy and recurrent seizures
346 Migraine
347 Cataplexy and narcolepsy
348 Other conditions of brain
349 Other and unspecified disorders of the nervous system

Disorders of the peripheral nervous system (350-359)
350 Trigeminal nerve disorders
351 Facial nerve disorders
352 Disorders of other cranial nerves
353 Nerve root and plexus disorders
354 Mononeuritis of upper limb and mononeuritis multiplex
355 Mononeuritis of lower limb
356 Hereditary and idiopathic peripheral neuropathy
357 Inflammatory and toxic neuropathy
358 Myoneural disorders
359 Muscular dystrophies and other myopathies

Disorders of the eye and adnexa (360-379)
360 Disorders of the globe
361 Retinal detachments and defects
362 Other retinal disorders
363 Chorioretinal inflammations and scars and other disorders of choroid
364 Disorders of iris and ciliary body
365 Glaucoma
366 Cataract
367 Disorders of refraction and accommodation
368 Visual disturbances

369 Blindness and low vision
370 Keratitis
371 Corneal opacity and other disorders of cornea
372 Disorders of conjunctiva
373 Inflammation of eyelids
374 Other disorders of eyelids
375 Disorders of lacrimal system
376 Disorders of the orbit
377 Disorders of optic nerve and visual pathways
378 Strabismus and other disorders of binocular eye movements
379 Other disorders of eye

Diseases of the ear and mastoid process (380-389)
380 Disorders of external ear
381 Nonsuppurative otitis media and Eustachian tube disorders
382 Suppurative and unspecified otitis media
383 Mastoiditis and related conditions
384 Other disorders of tympanic membrane
385 Other disorders of middle ear and mastoid
386 Vertiginous syndromes and other disorders of vestibular system
387 Otosclerosis
388 Other disorders of ear
389 Hearing loss

7. DISEASES OF THE CIRCULATORY SYSTEM

Acute rheumatic fever (390-392)
390 Rheumatic fever without mention of heart involvement
391 Rheumatic fever with heart involvement
392 Rheumatic chorea

Chronic rheumatic heart disease (393-398)
393 Chronic rheumatic pericarditis
394 Diseases of mitral valve
395 Diseases of aortic valve
396 Diseases of mitral and aortic valves
397 Diseases of other endocardial structures
398 Other rheumatic heart disease

Hypertensive disease (401-405)
401 Essential hypertension
402 Hypertensive heart disease
403 Hypertensive kidney disease
404 Hypertensive heart and kidney disease
405 Secondary hypertension

Ischemic heart disease (410-414)
410 Acute myocardial infarction
411 Other acute and subacute form of ischemic heart disease
412 Old myocardial infarction
413 Angina pectoris
414 Other forms of chronic ischemic heart disease

Diseases of pulmonary circulation (415-417)
415 Acute pulmonary heart disease
416 Chronic pulmonary heart disease
417 Other diseases of pulmonary circulation

Other forms of heart disease (420-429)
420 Acute pericarditis
421 Acute and subacute endocarditis
422 Acute myocarditis
423 Other diseases of pericardium
424 Other diseases of endocardium
425 Cardiomyopathy
426 Conduction disorders
427 Cardiac dysrhythmias
428 Heart failure
429 Ill-defined descriptions and complications of heart disease

Cerebrovascular disease (430-438)
430 Subarachnoid hemorrhage
431 Intracerebral hemorrhage

432 Other and unspecified intracranial hemorrhage
433 Occlusion and stenosis of precerebral arteries
434 Occlusion of cerebral arteries
435 Transient cerebral ischemia
436 Acute but ill-defined cerebrovascular disease
437 Other and ill-defined cerebrovascular disease
438 Late effects of cerebrovascular disease

Diseases of arteries, arterioles, and capillaries (440-449)
440 Atherosclerosis
441 Aortic aneurysm and dissection
442 Other aneurysm
443 Other peripheral vascular disease
444 Arterial embolism and thrombosis
445 Atheroembolism
446 Polyarteritis nodosa and allied conditions
447 Other disorders of arteries and arterioles
448 Diseases of capillaries
449 Septic arterial embolism

Diseases of veins and lymphatics, and other diseases of circulatory system (451-459)
451 Phlebitis and thrombophlebitis
452 Portal vein thrombosis
453 Other venous embolism and thrombosis
454 Varicose veins of lower extremities
455 Hemorrhoids
456 Varicose veins of other sites
457 Noninfective disorders of lymphatic channels
458 Hypotension
459 Other disorders of circulatory system

8. DISEASES OF THE RESPIRATORY SYSTEM

Acute respiratory infections (460-466)
460 Acute nasopharyngitis [common cold]
461 Acute sinusitis
462 Acute pharyngitis
463 Acute tonsillitis
464 Acute laryngitis and tracheitis
465 Acute upper respiratory infections of multiple or unspecified sites
466 Acute bronchitis and bronchiolitis

Other diseases of upper respiratory tract (470-478)
470 Deviated nasal septum
471 Nasal polyps
472 Chronic pharyngitis and nasopharyngitis
473 Chronic sinusitis
474 Chronic disease of tonsils and adenoids
475 Peritonsillar abscess
476 Chronic laryngitis and aryngotracheitis
477 Allergic rhinitis
478 Other diseases of upper respiratory tract

Pneumonia and influenza (480-488)
480 Viral pneumonia
481 Pneumococcal pneumonia [Streptococcus pneumoniae pneumonia]
482 Other bacterial pneumonia
483 Pneumonia due to other specified organism
484 Pneumonia in infectious diseases classified elsewhere
485 Bronchopneumonia, organism unspecified
486 Pneumonia, organism unspecified
487 Influenza
488 Influenza due to certain identified influenza viruses

Chronic obstructive pulmonary disease and allied conditions (490-496)
490 Bronchitis, not specified as acute or chronic
491 Chronic bronchitis
492 Emphysema
493 Asthma
494 Bronchiectasis

495 Extrinsic allergic alveolitis
496 Chronic airways obstruction, not elsewhere classified

Pneumoconioses and other lung diseases due to external agents (500-508)
500 Coal workers' pneumoconiosis
501 Asbestosis
502 Pneumoconiosis due to other silica or silicates
503 Pneumoconiosis due to other inorganic dust
504 Pneumopathy due to inhalation of other dust
505 Pneumoconiosis, unspecified
506 Respiratory conditions due to chemical fumes and vapors
507 Pneumonitis due to solids and liquids
508 Respiratory conditions due to other and unspecified external agents

Other diseases of respiratory system (510-519)
510 Empyema
511 Pleurisy
512 Pneumothorax
513 Abscess of lung and mediastinum
514 Pulmonary congestion and hypostasis
515 Postinflammatory pulmonary fibrosis
516 Other alveolar and parietoalveolar pneumopathy
517 Lung involvement in conditions classified elsewhere
518 Other diseases of lung
519 Other diseases of respiratory system

9. DISEASES OF THE DIGESTIVE SYSTEM

Diseases of oral cavity, salivary glands, and jaws (520-529)
520 Disorders of tooth development and eruption
521 Diseases of hard tissues of teeth
522 Diseases of pulp and periapical tissues
523 Gingival and periodontal diseases
524 Dentofacial anomalies, including malocclusion
525 Other diseases and conditions of the teeth and supporting structures
526 Diseases of the jaws
527 Diseases of the salivary glands
528 Diseases of the oral soft tissues, excluding lesions specific for gingiva and tongue
529 Diseases and other conditions of the tongue

Diseases of esophagus, stomach, and duodenum (530-538)
530 Diseases of esophagus
531 Gastric ulcer
532 Duodenal ulcer
533 Peptic ulcer, site unspecified
534 Gastrojejunal ulcer
535 Gastritis and duodenitis
536 Disorders of function of stomach
537 Other disorders of stomach and duodenum
538 Gastrointestinal mucositis (ulcerative)

Appendicitis (540-543)
540 Acute appendicitis
541 Appendicitis, unqualified
542 Other appendicitis
543 Other diseases of appendix

Hernia of abdominal cavity (550-553)
550 Inguinal hernia
551 Other hernia of abdominal cavity, with gangrene
552 Other hernia of abdominal cavity, with ob-struction, but without mention of gangrene
553 Other hernia of abdominal cavity without mention of obstruction or gangrene

Noninfective enteritis and colitis (555-558)
555 Regional enteritis
556 Ulcerative colitis
557 Vascular insufficiency of intestine
558 Other noninfective gastroenteritis and colitis

Other diseases of intestines and peritoneum (560-569)
560 Intestinal obstruction without mention of hernia
562 Diverticula of intestine
564 Functional digestive disorders, not elsewhere classified
565 Anal fissure and fistula
566 Abscess of anal and rectal regions
567 Peritonitis and retroperitoneal infections
568 Other disorders of peritoneum
569 Other disorders of intestine

Other diseases of digestive system (570-579)
570 Acute and subacute necrosis of liver
571 Chronic liver disease and cirrhosis
572 Liver abscess and sequelae of chronic liver disease
573 Other disorders of liver
574 Cholelithiasis
575 Other disorders of gallbladder
576 Other disorders of biliary tract
577 Diseases of pancreas
578 Gastrointestinal hemorrhage
579 Intestinal malabsorption

10. DISEASES OF THE GENITOURINARY SYSTEM

Nephritis, nephrotic syndrome, and nephrosis (580-589)
580 Acute glomerulonephritis
581 Nephrotic syndrome
582 Chronic glomerulonephritis
583 Nephritis and nephropathy, not specified as acute or chronic
584 Acute kidney failure
585 Chronic kidney disease (CKD)
586 Renal failure, unspecified
587 Renal sclerosis, unspecified
588 Disorders resulting from impaired renal function
589 Small kidney of unknown cause

Other diseases of urinary system (590-599)
590 Infections of kidney
591 Hydronephrosis
592 Calculus of kidney and ureter
593 Other disorders of kidney and ureter
594 Calculus of lower urinary tract
595 Cystitis
596 Other disorders of bladder
597 Urethritis, not sexually transmitted, and urethral syndrome
598 Urethral stricture
599 Other disorders of urethra and urinary tract

Diseases of male genital organs (600-608)
600 Hyperplasia of prostate
601 Inflammatory diseases of prostate
602 Other disorders of prostate
603 Hydrocele
604 Orchitis and epididymitis
605 Redundant prepuce and phimosis
606 Infertility, male
607 Disorders of penis
608 Other disorders of male genital organs

Disorders of breast (610-612)
610 Benign mammary dysplasias
611 Other disorders of breast
612 Deformity and disproportion of reconstructed breast

Inflammatory disease of female pelvic organs (614-616)
614 Inflammatory disease of ovary, fallopian tube, pelvic cellular tissue, and peritoneum
615 Inflammatory diseases of uterus, except cervix
616 Inflammatory disease of cervix, vagina, and vulva

Other disorders of female genital tract (617-629)
617 Endometriosis
618 Genital prolapse
619 Fistula involving female genital tract
620 Noninflammatory disorders of ovary, fallopian tube, and broad ligament
621 Disorders of uterus, not elsewhere classified
622 Noninflammatory disorders of cervix
623 Noninflammatory disorders of vagina
624 Noninflammatory disorders of vulva and perineum
625 Pain and other symptoms associated with female genital organs
626 Disorders of menstruation and other abnormal bleeding from female genital tract
627 Menopausal and postmenopausal disorders
628 Infertility, female
629 Other disorders of female genital organs

11. COMPLICATIONS OF PREGNANCY, CHILDBIRTH AND THE PUERPERIUM

Ectopic and molar pregnancy and other pregnancy with abortive outcome (630-639)
630 Hydatidiform mole
631 Other abnormal product of conception
632 Missed abortion
633 Ectopic pregnancy
634 Spontaneous abortion
635 Legally induced abortion
636 Illegally induced abortion
637 Unspecified abortion
638 Failed attempted abortion
639 Complications following abortion and ectopic and molar pregnancies

Complications mainly related to pregnancy (640-649)
640 Hemorrhage in early pregnancy
641 Antepartum hemorrhage, abruptio placentae, and placenta previa
642 Hypertension complicating pregnancy, childbirth, and the puerperium
643 Excessive vomiting in pregnancy
644 Early or threatened labor
645 Prolonged pregnancy
646 Other complications of pregnancy, not elsewhere classified
647 Infective and parasitic conditions in the mother classifiable elsewhere but complicating pregnancy, childbirth, and the puerperium
648 Other current conditions in the mother classifiable elsewhere but complicating pregnancy, childbirth, and the puerperium
649 Other conditions or status of the mother complicating pregnancy, childbirth, or puerperium

Normal delivery, and other indications for care in pregnancy, labor, and delivery (650-659)
650 Normal delivery
651 Multiple gestation
652 Malposition and malpresentation of fetus
653 Disproportion
654 Abnormality of organs and soft tissues of pelvis
655 Known or suspected fetal abnormality affecting management of mother

656 Other fetal and placental problems affecting management of mother
657 Polyhydramnios
658 Other problems associated with amniotic cavity and membranes
659 Other indications for care or intervention related to labor and delivery and not elsewhere classified

Complications occurring mainly in the course of labor and delivery (660-669)
660 Obstructed labor
661 Abnormality of forces of labor
662 Long labor
663 Umbilical cord complications
664 Trauma to perineum and vulva during delivery
665 Other obstetrical trauma
666 Postpartum hemorrhage
667 Retained placenta or membranes, without hemorrhage
668 Complications of the administration of anesthetic or other sedation in labor and delivery
669 Other complications of labor and delivery, not elsewhere classified

Complications of the puerperium (670-679)
670 Major puerperal infection
671 Venous complications in pregnancy and the puerperium
672 Pyrexia of unknown origin during the puerperium
673 Obstetrical pulmonary embolism
674 Other and unspecified complications of the puerperium, not elsewhere classified
675 Infections of the breast and nipple associated with childbirth
676 Other disorders of the breast associated with childbirth, and disorders of lactation
677 Late effect of complication of pregnancy, childbirth, and the puerperium
678 Other fetal conditions
679 Complications of in utero procedures

12. DISEASES OF THE SKIN AND SUBCUTANEOUS TISSUE

Infections of skin and subcutaneous tissue (680-686)
680 Carbuncle and furuncle
681 Cellulitis and abscess of finger and toe
682 Other cellulitis and abscess
683 Acute lymphadenitis
684 Impetigo
685 Pilonidal cyst
686 Other local infections of skin and subcutaneous tissue

Inflammatory conditions of skin and subcutaneous tissue (690-698)
690 Erythematosquamous dermatosis
691 Atopic dermatitis and related conditions
692 Contact dermatitis and other eczema
693 Dermatitis due to substances taken internally
694 Bullous dermatoses
695 Erythematous conditions
696 Psoriasis and similar disorders
697 Lichen
698 Pruritus and related conditions

Other diseases of skin and subcutaneous tissue (700-709)
700 Corns and callosities
701 Other hypertrophic and atrophic conditions of skin
702 Other dermatoses
703 Diseases of nail
704 Diseases of hair and hair follicles
705 Disorders of sweat glands
706 Diseases of sebaceous glands
707 Chronic ulcer of skin
708 Urticaria
709 Other disorders of skin and subcutaneous tissue

13. DISEASES OF THE MUSCULOSKELETAL SYSTEM AND CONNECTIVE TISSUE

Arthropathies and related disorders (710-719)
710 Diffuse diseases of connective tissue
711 Arthropathy associated with infections
712 Crystal arthropathies
713 Arthropathy associated with other disorders classified elsewhere
714 Rheumatoid arthritis and other inflammatory polyarthropathies
715 Osteoarthrosis and allied disorders
716 Other and unspecified arthropathies
717 Internal derangement of knee
718 Other derangement of joint
719 Other and unspecified disorder of joint

Dorsopathies (720-724)
720 Ankylosing spondylitis and other inflammatory spondylopathies
721 Spondylosis and allied disorders
722 Intervertebral disc disorders
723 Other disorders of cervical region
724 Other and unspecified disorders of back

Rheumatism, excluding the back (725-729)
725 Polymyalgia rheumatica
726 Peripheral enthesopathies and allied syndromes
727 Other disorders of synovium, tendon, and bursa
728 Disorders of muscle, ligament, and fascia
729 Other disorders of soft tissues

Osteopathies, chondropathies, and acquired musculoskeletal deformities (730-739)
730 Osteomyelitis, periostitis, and other infections involving bone
731 Osteitis deformans and osteopathies associated with other disorders classified elsewhere
732 Osteochondropathies
733 Other disorders of bone and cartilage
734 Flat foot
735 Acquired deformities of toe
736 Other acquired deformities of limbs
737 Curvature of spine
738 Other acquired deformity
739 Nonallopathic lesions, not elsewhere classified

14. CONGENITAL ANOMALIES

740 Anencephalus and similar anomalies
741 Spina bifida
742 Other congenital anomalies of nervous system
743 Congenital anomalies of eye
744 Congenital anomalies of ear, face, and neck
745 Bulbus cordis anomalies and anomalies of cardiac septal closure
746 Other congenital anomalies of heart
747 Other congenital anomalies of circulatory system
748 Congenital anomalies of respiratory system
749 Cleft palate and cleft lip
750 Other congenital anomalies of upper alimentary tract
751 Other congenital anomalies of digestive system
752 Congenital anomalies of genital organs
753 Congenital anomalies of urinary system
754 Certain congenital musculoskeletal deformities
755 Other congenital anomalies of limbs
756 Other congenital musculoskeletal anomalies
757 Congenital anomalies of the integument
758 Chromosomal anomalies
759 Other and unspecified congenital anomalies

15. CERTAIN CONDITIONS ORIGINATING IN THE PERINATAL PERIOD

Maternal causes of perinatal morbidity and mortality (760-763)
760 Fetus or newborn affected by maternal conditions which may be unrelated to present pregnancy
761 Fetus or newborn affected by maternal complications of pregnancy
762 Fetus or newborn affected by complications of placenta, cord, and membranes
763 Fetus or newborn affected by other complications of labor and delivery

Other conditions originating in the perinatal period (764-779)
764 Slow fetal growth and fetal malnutrition
765 Disorders relating to short gestation and unspecified low birthweight
766 Disorders relating to long gestation and high birthweight
767 Birth trauma
768 Intrauterine hypoxia and birth asphyxia
769 Respiratory distress syndrome
770 Other respiratory conditions of fetus and newborn
771 Infections specific to the perinatal period
772 Fetal and neonatal hemorrhage
773 Hemolytic disease of fetus or newborn, due to isoimmunization
774 Other perinatal jaundice
775 Endocrine and metabolic disturbances specific to the fetus and newborn
776 Hematological disorders of newborn
777 Perinatal disorders of digestive system
778 Conditions involving the integument and temperature regulation of fetus and newborn
779 Other and ill-defined conditions originating in the perinatal period

16. SYMPTOMS, SIGNS, AND ILL-DEFINED CONDITIONS

Symptoms (780-789)
780 General symptoms
781 Symptoms involving nervous and musculoskeletal systems
782 Symptoms involving skin and other integumentary tissue
783 Symptoms concerning nutrition, metabolism, and development
784 Symptoms involving head and neck
785 Symptoms involving cardiovascular system
786 Symptoms involving respiratory system and other chest symptoms
787 Symptoms involving digestive system
788 Symptoms involving urinary system
789 Other symptoms involving abdomen and pelvis

Nonspecific abnormal findings (790-796)
790 Nonspecific findings on examination of blood
791 Nonspecific findings on examination of urine
792 Nonspecific abnormal findings in other body substances
793 Nonspecific (abnormal) findings on radiological and other examination of body structure
794 Nonspecific abnormal results of function studies

| 795 | Nonspecific abnormal histological and immunological findings |
| 796 | Other nonspecific abnormal findings |

Ill-defined and unknown causes of morbidity and mortality (797-799)

797	Senility without mention of psychosis
798	Sudden death, cause unknown
799	Other ill-defined and unknown causes of morbidity and mortality

17. INJURY AND POISONING

Fracture of skull (800-804)

800	Fracture of vault of skull
801	Fracture of base of skull
802	Fracture of face bones
803	Other and unqualified skull fractures
804	Multiple fractures involving skull or face with other bones

Fracture of spine and trunk (805-809)

805	Fracture of vertebral column without mention of spinal cord lesion
806	Fracture of vertebral column with spinal cord lesion
807	Fracture of rib(s), sternum, larynx, and trachea
808	Fracture of pelvis
809	Ill-defined fractures of bones of trunk

Fracture of upper limb (810-819)

810	Fracture of clavicle
811	Fracture of scapula
812	Fracture of humerus
813	Fracture of radius and ulna
814	Fracture of carpal bone(s)
815	Fracture of metacarpal bone(s)
816	Fracture of one or more phalanges of hand
817	Multiple fractures of hand bones
818	Ill-defined fractures of upper limb
819	Multiple fractures involving both upper limbs, and upper limb with rib(s) and sternum

Fracture of lower limb (820-829)

820	Fracture of neck of femur
821	Fracture of other and unspecified parts of femur
822	Fracture of patella
823	Fracture of tibia and fibula
824	Fracture of ankle
825	Fracture of one or more tarsal and metatarsal bones
826	Fracture of one or more phalanges of foot
827	Other, multiple, and ill-defined fractures of lower limb
828	Multiple fractures involving both lower limbs, lower with upper limb, and lower limb(s) with rib(s) and sternum
829	Fracture of unspecified bones

Dislocation (830-839)

830	Dislocation of jaw
831	Dislocation of shoulder
832	Dislocation of elbow
833	Dislocation of wrist
834	Dislocation of finger
835	Dislocation of hip
836	Dislocation of knee
837	Dislocation of ankle
838	Dislocation of foot
839	Other, multiple, and ill-defined dislocations

Sprains and strains of joints and adjacent muscles (840-848)

840	Sprains and strains of shoulder and upper arm
841	Sprains and strains of elbow and forearm
842	Sprains and strains of wrist and hand
843	Sprains and strains of hip and thigh
844	Sprains and strains of knee and leg
845	Sprains and strains of ankle and foot
846	Sprains and strains of sacroiliac region
847	Sprains and strains of other and unspecified parts of back
848	Other and ill-defined sprains and strains

Intracranial injury, excluding those with skull fracture (850-854)

850	Concussion
851	Cerebral laceration and contusion
852	Subarachnoid, subdural, and extradural hemorrhage, following injury
853	Other and unspecified intracranial hemorrhage following injury
854	Intracranial injury of other and unspecified nature

Internal injury of chest, abdomen, and pelvis (860-869)

860	Traumatic pneumothorax and hemothorax
861	Injury to heart and lung
862	Injury to other and unspecified intrathoracic organs
863	Injury to gastrointestinal tract
864	Injury to liver
865	Injury to spleen
866	Injury to kidney
867	Injury to pelvic organs
868	Injury to other intra-abdominal organs
869	Internal injury to unspecified or ill-defined organs

Open wound of head, neck, and trunk (870-879)

870	Open wound of ocular adnexa
871	Open wound of eyeball
872	Open wound of ear
873	Other open wound of head
874	Open wound of neck
875	Open wound of chest (wall)
876	Open wound of back
877	Open wound of buttock
878	Open wound of genital organs (external), including traumatic amputation
879	Open wound of other and unspecified sites, except limbs

Open wound of upper limb (880-887)

880	Open wound of shoulder and upper arm
881	Open wound of elbow, forearm, and wrist
882	Open wound of hand except finger(s) alone
883	Open wound of finger(s)
884	Multiple and unspecified open wound of upper limb
885	Traumatic amputation of thumb (complete) (partial)
886	Traumatic amputation of other finger(s) (complete) (partial)
887	Traumatic amputation of arm and hand (complete) (partial)

Open wound of lower limb (890-897)

890	Open wound of hip and thigh
891	Open wound of knee, leg [except thigh], and ankle
892	Open wound of foot except toe(s) alone
893	Open wound of toe(s)
894	Multiple and unspecified open wound of lower limb
895	Traumatic amputation of toe(s) (complete) (partial)
896	Traumatic amputation of foot (complete) (partial)
897	Traumatic amputation of leg(s) (complete) (partial)

Injury to blood vessels (900-904)

900	Injury to blood vessels of head and neck
901	Injury to blood vessels of thorax
902	Injury to blood vessels of abdomen and pelvis
903	Injury to blood vessels of upper extremity
904	Injury to blood vessels of lower extremity and unspecified sites

Late effects of injuries, poisonings, toxic effects, and other external causes (905-909)

905	Late effects of musculoskeletal and connective tissue injuries
906	Late effects of injuries to skin and subcutaneous tissues
907	Late effects of injuries to the nervous system
908	Late effects of other and unspecified injuries
909	Late effects of other and unspecified external causes

Superficial injury (910-919)

910	Superficial injury of face, neck, and scalp except eye
911	Superficial injury of trunk
912	Superficial injury of shoulder and upper arm
913	Superficial injury of elbow, forearm, and wrist
914	Superficial injury of hand(s) except finger(s) alone
915	Superficial injury of finger(s)
916	Superficial injury of hip, thigh, leg, and ankle
917	Superficial injury of foot and toe(s)
918	Superficial injury of eye and adnexa
919	Superficial injury of other, multiple, and unspecified sites

Contusion with intact skin surface (920-924)

920	Contusion of face, scalp, and neck except eye(s)
921	Contusion of eye and adnexa
922	Contusion of trunk
923	Contusion of upper limb
924	Contusion of lower limb and of other and unspecified sites

Crushing injury (925-929)

925	Crushing injury of face, scalp, and neck
926	Crushing injury of trunk
927	Crushing injury of upper limb
928	Crushing injury of lower limb
929	Crushing injury of multiple and unspecified sites

Effects of foreign body entering through orifice (930-939)

930	Foreign body on external eye
931	Foreign body in ear
932	Foreign body in nose
933	Foreign body in pharynx and larynx
934	Foreign body in trachea, bronchus, and lung
935	Foreign body in mouth, esophagus, and stomach
936	Foreign body in intestine and colon
937	Foreign body in anus and rectum
938	Foreign body in digestive system, unspecified
939	Foreign body in genitourinary tract

Burns (940-949)

940	Burn confined to eye and adnexa
941	Burn of face, head, and neck
942	Burn of trunk
943	Burn of upper limb, except wrist and hand
944	Burn of wrist(s) and hand(s)
945	Burn of lower limb(s)
946	Burns of multiple specified sites
947	Burn of internal organs
948	Burns classified according to extent of body surface involved
949	Burn, unspecified

Injury to nerves and spinal cord (950-957)

950	Injury to optic nerve and pathways
951	Injury to other cranial nerve(s)
952	Spinal cord injury without evidence of spinal bone injury

953	Injury to nerve roots and spinal plexus
954	Injury to other nerve(s) of trunk excluding shoulder and pelvic girdles
955	Injury to peripheral nerve(s) of shoulder girdle and upper limb
956	Injury to peripheral nerve(s) of pelvic girdle and lower limb
957	Injury to other and unspecified nerves

Certain traumatic complications and unspecified injuries (958-959)

958	Certain early complications of trauma
959	Injury, other and unspecified

Poisoning by drugs, medicinals and biological substances (960-979)

960	Poisoning by antibiotics
961	Poisoning by other anti-infectives
962	Poisoning by hormones and synthetic substitutes
963	Poisoning by primarily systemic agents
964	Poisoning by agents primarily affecting blood constituents
965	Poisoning by analgesics, antipyretics, and antirheumatics
966	Poisoning by anticonvulsants and anti-Parkinsonism drugs
967	Poisoning by sedatives and hypnotics
968	Poisoning by other central nervous system depressants and anesthetics
969	Poisoning by psychotropic agents
970	Poisoning by central nervous system stimulants
971	Poisoning by drugs primarily affecting the autonomic nervous system
972	Poisoning by agents primarily affecting the cardiovascular system
973	Poisoning by agents primarily affecting the gastrointestinal system
974	Poisoning by water, mineral, and uric acid metabolism drugs
975	Poisoning by agents primarily acting on the smooth and skeletal muscles and respiratory system
976	Poisoning by agents primarily affecting skin and mucous membrane, ophthalmological, otorhinolaryngological, and dental drugs
977	Poisoning by other and unspecified drugs and medicinals
978	Poisoning by bacterial vaccines
979	Poisoning by other vaccines and biological substances

Toxic effects of substances chiefly nonmedicinal as to source (980-989)

980	Toxic effect of alcohol
981	Toxic effect of petroleum products
982	Toxic effect of solvents other than petroleum-based
983	Toxic effect of corrosive aromatics, acids, and caustic alkalis
984	Toxic effect of lead and its compounds (including fumes)
985	Toxic effect of other metals
986	Toxic effect of carbon monoxide
987	Toxic effect of other gases, fumes, or vapors
988	Effect of noxious substances eaten as food
989	Toxic effect of other substances, chiefly nonmedicinal as to source

Other and unspecified effects of external causes (990-995)

990	Effects of radiation, unspecified
991	Effects of reduced temperature
992	Effects of heat and light
993	Effects of air pressure
994	Effects of other external causes

995	Certain adverse effects, not elsewhere classified

Complications of surgical and medical care, not elsewhere classified (996-999)

996	Complications peculiar to certain specified procedures
997	Complications affecting specified body systems, not elsewhere classified
998	Other complications of procedures, not elsewhere classified
999	Complications of medical care, not elsewhere classified

SUPPLEMENTARY CLASSIFICATION OF FACTORS INFLUENCING HEALTH STATUS AND CONTACT WITH HEALTH SERVICES

Persons with potential health hazards related to communicable diseases (V01-V09)

V01	Contact with or exposure to communicable diseases
V02	Carrier or suspected carrier of infectious diseases
V03	Need for prophylactic vaccination and inoculation against bacterial diseases
V04	Need for prophylactic vaccination and inoculation against certain viral diseases
V05	Need for other prophylactic vaccination and inoculation against single diseases
V06	Need for prophylactic vaccination and inoculation against combinations of diseases
V07	Need for isolation and other prophylactic measures
V08	Asymptomatic human immunodeficiency virus [HIV] infection status
V09	Infection with drug-resistant microorganisms

Persons with potential health hazards related to personal and family history (V10-V19)

V10	Personal history of malignant neoplasm
V11	Personal history of mental disorder
V12	Personal history of certain other diseases
V13	Personal history of other diseases
V14	Personal history of allergy to medicinal agents
V15	Other personal history presenting hazards to health
V16	Family history of malignant neoplasm
V17	Family history of certain chronic disabling diseases
V18	Family history of certain other specific conditions
V19	Family history of other conditions

Persons encountering health services in circumstances related to reproduction and development (V20-V29)

V20	Health supervision of infant or child
V21	Constitutional states in development
V22	Normal pregnancy
V23	Supervision of high-risk pregnancy
V24	Postpartum care and examination
V25	Encounter for contraceptive management
V26	Procreative management
V27	Outcome of delivery
V28	Antenatal screening
V29	Observation and evaluation of newborns and infants for suspected condition not found

Liveborn infants according to type of birth (V30-V39)

V30	Single liveborn
V31	mate liveborn
V32	Twin, mate stillborn
V33	Twin, unspecified
V34	Other multiple, mates all liveborn
V35	Other multiple, mates all stillborn
V36	Other multiple, mates live- and stillborn

V37	Other multiple, unspecified
V39	Unspecified

Persons with a condition influencing their health status (V40-V49)

V40	Mental and behavioral problems
V41	Problems with special senses and other special functions
V42	Organ or tissue replaced by transplant
V43	Organ or tissue replaced by other means
V44	Artificial opening status
V45	Other postprocedural states
V46	Other dependence on machines
V47	Other problems with internal organs
V48	Problems with head, neck, and trunk
V49	Other conditions influencing health status

Persons encountering health services for specific procedures and aftercare (V50-V59)

V50	Elective surgery for purposes other than remedying health states
V51	Aftercare involving the use of plastic surgery
V52	Fitting and adjustment of prosthetic device
V53	Fitting and adjustment of other device
V54	Other orthopedic aftercare
V55	Attention to artificial openings
V56	Encounter for dialysis and dialysis catheter care
V57	Care involving use of rehabilitation procedures
V58	Encounter for other and unspecified procedures and aftercare
V59	Donors

Persons encountering health services in other circumstances (V60-V69)

V60	Housing, household, and economic circumstances
V61	Other family circumstances
V62	Other psychosocial circumstances
V63	Unavailability of other medical facilities for care
V64	Persons encountering health services for specific procedures, not carried out
V65	Other persons seeking consultation
V66	Convalescence and palliative care
V67	Follow-up examination
V68	Encounters for administrative purposes
V69	Problems related to lifestyle

Persons without reported diagnosis encountered during examination and investigation of individuals and populations (V70-V82)

V70	General medical examination
V71	Observation and evaluation for suspected conditions not found
V72	Special investigations and examinations
V73	Special screening examination for viral and chlamydial diseases
V74	Special screening examination for bacterial and spirochetal diseases
V75	Special screening examination for other infectious diseases
V76	Special screening for malignant neoplasms
V77	Special screening for endocrine, nutritional, metabolic, and immunity disorders
V78	Special screening for disorders of blood and blood-forming organs
V79	Special screening for mental disorders and developmental handicaps
V80	Special screening for neurological, eye, and ear diseases
V81	Special screening for cardiovascular, respiratory, and genitourinary diseases
V82	Special screening for other conditions

Genetics (V83-V84)

V83	Genetic carrier status

V84   Genetic susceptibility to disease

Body mass index (V85)
V85   Body Mass Index

Estrogen receptor status (V86)
V86   Estrogen receptor status

Other specified personal exposures and history presenting hazards to health (V87)
V87   Other specified personal exposures and history presenting hazards to health

Acquired absence of other organs and tissue (V88)
V88   Acquired absence of other organs and tissue

Other suspected conditions not found (V89)
V89   Other suspected conditions not found

SUPPLEMENTARY CLASSIFICATION OF EXTERNAL CAUSES OF INJURY AND POISONING

External Cause Status (E000)
E000   External cause status

Activity (E001-E030)
E001   Activities involving walking and running
E002   Activities involving water and water craft
E003   Activities involving ice and snow
E004   Activities involving climbing, rappelling, and jumping off
E005   Activities involving dancing and other rhythmic movement
E006   Activities involving other sports and athletics played individually
E007   Activities involving other sports and athletics played as a team or group
E008   Activities involving other specified sports and athletics
E009   Activity involving other cardiorespiratory exercise
E010   Activity involving other muscle strengthening exercises
E011   Activities involving computer technology and electronic devices
E012   Activities involving arts and handcrafts
E013   Activities involving personal hygiene and household maintenance
E014   Activities involving person providing caregiving
E015   Activities involving food preparation, cooking and grilling
E016   Activities involving property and land maintenance, building and construction
E017   Activities involving roller coasters and other types of external motion
E018   Activities involving playing musical instrument
E019   Activities involving animal care
E029   Other activity
E030   Unspecified activity

Transport Accidents (E800-E848)

Railway accidents (E800-E807)
E800   Railway accident involving collision with roling stock
E801   Railway accident involving collision with other object
E802   Railway accident involving derailment without antecedent collision
E803   Railway accident involving explosion, fire, or burning
E804   Fall in, on, or from railway train
E805   Hit by rolling stock
E806   Other specified railway accident
E807   Railway accident of unspecified nature

Motor vehicle traffic accidents (E810-E819)
E810   Motor vehicle traffic accident involving collision with train
E811   Motor vehicle traffic accident involving re-entrant collision with another motor vehicle
E812   Other motor vehicle traffic accident involving collision with another motor vehicle
E813   Motor vehicle traffic accident involving collision with other vehicle
E814   Motor vehicle traffic accident involving collision with pedestrian
E815   Other motor vehicle traffic accident involving collision on the highway
E816   Motor vehicle traffic accident due to loss of control, without collision on the highway
E817   Noncollision motor vehicle traffic accident while boarding or alighting
E818   Other noncollision motor vehicle traffic accident
E819   Motor vehicle traffic accident of unspecified nature

Motor vehicle nontraffic accidents (E820-E825)
E820   Nontraffic accident involving motor-driven snow vehicle
E821   Nontraffic accident involving other off-road motor vehicle
E822   Other motor vehicle nontraffic accident involving collision with moving object
E823   Other motor vehicle nontraffic accident involving collision with stationary object
E824   Other motor vehicle nontraffic accident while boarding and alighting
E825   Other motor vehicle nontraffic accident of other and unspecified nature

Other road vehicle accidents (E826-E829)
E826   Pedal cycle accident
E827   Animal-drawn vehicle accident
E828   Accident involving animal being ridden
E829   Other road vehicle accidents

Water transport accidents (E830-E838)
E830   Accident to watercraft causing submersion
E831   Accident to watercraft causing other injury
E832   Other accidental submersion or drowning in water transport accident
E833   Fall on stairs or ladders in water transport
E834   Other fall from one level to another in water transport
E835   Other and unspecified fall in water transport
E836   Machinery accident in water transport
E837   Explosion, fire, or burning in watercraft
E838   Other and unspecified water transport accident

Air and space transport accidents (E840-E845)
E840   Accident to powered aircraft at takeoff or landing
E841   Accident to powered aircraft, other and unspecified
E842   Accident to unpowered aircraft
E843   Fall in, on, or from aircraft
E844   Other specified air transport accidents
E845   Other involving spacecraft

Vehicle accidents, not elsewhere classfiable (E846-E849)
E846   Accidents involving powered vehicles used solely within the buildings and premises of an industrial or commercial establishment
E847   Accidents involving cable cars not running on rails
E848   Accidents involving other vehicles, not elsewhere classifiable
E849   Place of occurrence

Accidental poisoning by drugs, medicinal substances, and biologicals (E850-E858)
E850   Accidental poisoning by analgesics, antipyretics, and antirheumatics
E851   Accidental poisoning by barbiturates
E852   Accidental poisoning by other sedatives and hypnotics
E853   Accidental poisoning by tranquilizers
E854   Accidental poisoning by other psychotropic agents
E855   Accidental poisoning by other drugs acting on central and autonomic nervous systems
E856   Accidental poisoning by antibiotics
E857   Accidental poisoning by anti-infectives
E858   Accidental poisoning by other drugs

Accidental poisoning by other solid and liquid substances, gases, and vapors (E860-E869)
E860   Accidental poisoning by alcohol, not elsewhere classified
E861   Accidental poisoning by cleansing and polishing agents, disinfectants, paints, and varnishes
E862   Accidental poisoning by petroleum products, other solvents and their vapors, not elsewhere classified
E863   Accidental poisoning by agricultural and horticultural chemical and pharmaceutical preparations other than plant foods and fertilizers
E864   Accidental poisoning by corrosives and caustics, not elsewhere classified
E865   Accidental poisoning from poisonous foodstuffs and poisonous plants
E866   Accidental poisoning by other and unspecified solid and liquid substances
E867   Accidental poisoning by gas distributed by pipeline
E868   Accidental poisoning by other utility gas and other carbon monoxide
E869   Accidental poisoning by other gases and vapors

Misadventures to patients during surgical and medical care (E870-E876)
E870   Accidental cut, puncture, perforation, or hemorrhage during medical care
E871   Foreign object left in body during procedure
E872   Failure of sterile precautions during procedure
E873   Failure in dosage
E874   Mechanical failure of instrument or apparatus during procedure
E875   Contaminated or infected blood, other fluid, drug, or biological substance
E876   Other and unspecified misadventures during medical care

Surgical and medical procedures as the cause of abnormal reaction of patient or later complication, without mention of misadventure at the time of procedure (E878-E879)
E878   Surgical operation and other surgical procedures as the cause of abnormal reaction of patient, or of later complication, without mention of misadventure at the time of operation
E879   Other procedures, without mention of misadventure at the time of procedure, as the cause of abnormal reaction of patient, or of later complication

Accidental falls (E880-E888)
E880   Fall on or from stairs or steps
E881   Fall on or from ladders or scaffolding
E882   Fall from or out of building or other structure
E883   Fall into hole or other opening in surface
E884   Other fall from one level to another

E885   Fall on same level from slipping, tripping, or stumbling

E886   Fall on same level from collision, pushing or shoving, by or with other person

E887   Fracture, cause unspecified

E888   Other and unspecified fall

Accidents caused by fire and flames (E890-E899)

E890   Conflagration in private dwelling

E891   Conflagration in other and unspecified building or structure

E892   Conflagration not in building or structure

E893   Accident caused by ignition of clothing

E894   Ignition of highly inflammable material

E895   Accident caused by controlled fire in private dwelling

E896   Accident caused by controlled fire in other and unspecified building or structure

E897   Accident caused by controlled fire not in building or structure

E898   Accident caused by other specified fire and flames

E899   Accident caused by unspecified fire

Accidents due to natural and environmental factors (E900-E909)

E900   Excessive heat

E901   Excessive cold

E902   High and low air pressure and changes in air pressure

E903   Travel and motion

E904   Hunger, thirst, exposure, and neglect

E905   Venomous animals and plants as the cause of poisoning and toxic reactions

E906   Other injury caused by animals

E907   Lightning

E908   Cataclysmic storms, and floods resulting from storms

E909   Cataclysmic earth surface movements and eruptions

Accidents caused by submersion, suffocation, and foreign bodies (E910-E915)

E910   Accidental drowning and submersion

E911   Inhalation and ingestion of food causing obstruction of respiratory tract or suffocation

E912   Inhalation and ingestion of other object causing obstruction of respiratory tract or suffocation

E913   Accidental mechanical suffocation

E914   Foreign body accidentally entering eye and adnexa

E915   Foreign body accidentally entering other orifice

Other accidents (E916-E928)

E916   Struck accidentally by falling object

E917   Striking against or struck accidentally by objects or persons

E918   Caught accidentally in or between objects

E919   Accidents caused by machinery

E920   Accidents caused by cutting and piercing instruments or objects

E921   Accident caused by explosion of pressure vessel

E922   Accident caused by firearm missile

E923   Accident caused by explosive material

E924   Accident caused by hot substance or object, caustic or corrosive material, and steam

E925   Accident caused by electric current

E926   Exposure to radiation

E927   Overexertion and strenuous movements

E928   Other and unspecified environmental and accidental causes

Late effects of accidental injury (E929)

E929   Late effects of accidental injury

Drugs, medicinal and biological substances causing adverse effects in therapeutic use (E930-E949)

E930   Antibiotics

E931   Other anti-infectives

E932   Hormones and synthetic substitutes

E933   Primarily systemic agents

E934   Agents primarily affecting blood constituents

E935   Analgesics, antipyretics, and antirheumatics

E936   Anticonvulsants and anti-Parkinsonism drugs

E937   Sedatives and hypnotics

E938   Other central nervous system depressants and anesthetics

E939   Psychotropic agents

E940   Central nervous system stimulants

E941   Drugs primarily affecting the autonomic nervous system

E942   Agents primarily affecting the cardiovascular system

E943   Agents primarily affecting gastrointestinal system

E944   Water, mineral, and uric acid metabolism drugs

E945   Agents primarily acting on the smooth and skeletal muscles and respiratory system

E946   Agents primarily affecting skin and mucous membrane, ophthalmological, otorhinolaryngological, and dental drugs

E947   Other and unspecified drugs and medicinal substances

E948   Bacterial vaccines

E949   Other vaccines and biological substances

Suicide and self-inflicted injury (E950-E959)

E950   Suicide and self-inflicted poisoning by solid or liquid substances

E951   Suicide and self-inflicted poisoning by gases in domestic use

E952   Suicide and self-inflicted poisoning by other gases and vapors

E953   Suicide and self-inflicted injury by hanging, strangulation, and suffocation

E954   Suicide and self-inflicted injury by submersion [drowning]

E955   Suicide and self-inflicted injury by firearms and explosives

E956   Suicide and self-inflicted injury by cutting and piercing instruments

E957   Suicide and self-inflicted injuries by jumping from high place

E958   Suicide and self-inflicted injury by other and unspecified means

E959   Late effects of self-inflicted injury

Homicide and injury purposely inflicted by other persons (E960-E969)

E960   Fight, brawl, and rape

E961   Assault by corrosive or caustic substance, except poisoning

E962   Assault by poisoning

E963   Assault by hanging and strangulation

E964   Assault by submersion [drowning]

E965   Assault by firearms and explosives

E966   Assault by cutting and piercing instrument

E967   Child and adult battering and other maltreatment

E968   Assault by other and unspecified means

E969   Late effects of injury purposely inflicted by other person

Legal intervention (E970-E978)

E970   Injury due to legal intervention by firearms

E971   Injury due to legal intervention by explosives

E972   Injury due to legal intervention by gas

E973   Injury due to legal intervention by blunt object

E974   Injury due to legal intervention by cutting and piercing instruments

E975   Injury due to legal intervention by other specified means

E976   Injury due to legal intervention by unspecified means

E977   Late effects of injuries due to legal intervention

E978   Legal execution

Terrorism (E979)

E979   Terrorism

Injury undetermined whether accidentally or purposely inflicted (E980-E989)

E980   Poisoning by solid or liquid substances, undetermined whether accidentally or purposely inflicted

E981   Poisoning by gases in domestic use, undetermined whether accidentally or purposely inflicted

E982   Poisoning by other gases, undetermined whether accidentally or purposely inflicted

E983   Hanging, strangulation, or suffocation, undetermined whether accidentally or purposely inflicted

E984   Submersion [drowning], undetermined whether accidentally or purposely inflicted

E985   Injury by firearms and explosives, undetermined whether accidentally or purposely inflicted

E986   Injury by cutting and piercing instruments, undetermined whether accidentally or purposely inflicted

E987   Falling from high place, undetermined whether accidentally or purposely inflicted

E988   Injury by other and unspecified means, undetermined whether accidentally or purposely inflicted

E989   Late effects of injury, undetermined whether accidentally or purposely inflicted

Injury resulting from operations of war (E990-E999)

E990   Injury due to war operations by fires and conflagrations

E991   Injury due to war operations by bullets and fragments

E992   Injury due to war operations by explosion of marine weapons

E993   Injury due to war operations by other explosion

E994   Injury due to war operations by destruction of aircraft

E995   Injury due to war operations by other and unspecified forms of conventional warfare

E996   Injury due to war operations by nuclear weapons

E997   Injury due to war operations by other forms of unconventional warfare

E998   Injury due to war operations but occurring after cessation of hostilities

E999   Late effects of injury due to war operations

☑ Additional Digit Required — Refer to the Tabular List for Digit Selection   ☜ Subterms under main terms may continue to next column or page

2010 ICD-9-CM   ▶◀ Revised Text   ● New Line   ▲ Revised Code   October 2009 • Volume 3 — 1

Index

Amputation — Angiectomy

Amputation — continued
  supracondyler, above-knee 84.17
  supramalleolar, foot 84.14
  Syme's (ankle amputation through malleoli of tibia and fibula) 84.14
  thigh 84.17
  thumb 84.02
  toe (through metatarsophalangeal joint) 84.11
  transcarpal 84.03
  transmetatarsal 84.12
  upper limb NEC (see also Amputation, arm) 84.00
  wrist (disarticulation) 84.04
Amygdalohippocampotomy 01.39
Amygdalotomy 01.39
Analysis
  cardiac rhythm device (CRT-D) (CRT-P) (AICD) (pacemaker) — see Interrogation
  character 94.03
  gastric 89.39
  psychologic 94.31
  transactional
    group 94.44
    individual 94.39
Anastomosis
  abdominal artery to coronary artery 36.17
  accessory-facial nerve 04.72
  accessory-hypoglossal nerve 04.73
  anus (with formation of endorectal ileal pouch) 45.95
  aorta (descending)-pulmonary (artery) 39.0
  aorta-renal artery 39.24
  aorta-subclavian artery 39.22
  aortoceliac 39.26
  aorto(ilio)femoral 39.25
  aortomesenteric 39.26
  appendix 47.99
  arteriovenous NEC 39.29
    for renal dialysis 39.27
  artery (suture of distal to proximal end) 39.31
    with
      bypass graft 39.29
        extracranial-intracranial [EC-IC] 39.28
      excision or resection of vessel — see Arteriectomy, with anastomosis, by site
    revision 39.49
  bile ducts 51.39
  bladder NEC 57.88
    with
      isolated segment of intestine 57.87 [45.50]
        colon (sigmoid) 57.87 [45.52]
        ileum 57.87 [45.51]
        open loop of ileum 57.87 [45.51]
      to intestine 57.88
        ileum 57.87 [45.51]
  bowel (see also Anastomosis, intestine) 45.90
  bronchotracheal 33.48
  bronchus 33.48
  carotid-subclavian artery 39.22
  caval-mesenteric vein 39.1
  caval-pulmonary artery 39.21
  cervicoesophageal 42.59
  colohypopharyngeal (intrathoracic) 42.55
    antesternal or antethoracic 42.65
  common bile duct 51.39
  common pulmonary trunk and left atrium (posterior wall) 35.82
  cystic bile duct 51.39
  cystocolic 57.88
  epididymis to vas deferens 63.83
  esophagocolic (intrathoracic) NEC 42.56
    with interposition 42.55
    antesternal or antethoracic NEC 42.66
      with interposition 42.65
  esophagocologastric (intrathoracic) 42.55
    antesternal or antethoracic 42.65
  esophagoduodenal (intrathoracic) NEC 42.54
    with interposition 42.53
  esophagoenteric (intrathoracic) NEC (see also Anastomosis, esophagus, to intestinal segment) 42.54

Anastomosis — continued
  esophagoenteric (see also Anastomosis, esophagus, to intestinal segment) — continued
    antesternal or antethoracic NEC (see also Anastomosis, esophagus, antesternal, to intestinal segment) 42.64
  esophagoesophageal (intrathoracic) 42.51
    antesternal or antethoracic 42.61
  esophagogastric (intrathoracic) 42.52
    antesternal or antethoracic 42.62
  esophagus (intrapleural) (intrathoracic) (retrosternal) NEC 42.59
    with
      gastrectomy (partial) 43.5
        complete or total 43.99
      interposition (of) NEC 42.58
        colon 42.55
        jejunum 42.53
        small bowel 42.53
    antesternal or antethoracic NEC 42.69
      with
        interposition (of) NEC 42.68
          colon 42.65
          jejunal loop 42.63
          small bowel 42.63
          rubber tube 42.68
      to intestinal segment NEC 42.64
        with interposition 42.68
          colon NEC 42.66
            with interposition 42.65
          small bowel NEC 42.64
            with interposition 42.63
    to intestinal segment (intrathoracic) NEC 42.54
      with interposition 42.58
      antesternal or antethoracic NEC 42.64
        with interposition 42.68
        colon (intrathoracic) NEC 42.56
          with interposition 42.55
          antesternal or antethoracic 42.66
            with interposition 42.65
        small bowel NEC 42.54
          with interposition 42.53
          antesternal or antethoracic 42.64
            with interposition 42.63
  facial-accessory nerve 04.72
  facial-hypoglossal nerve 04.71
  fallopian tube 66.73
    by reanastomosis 66.79
  gallbladder 51.35
    to
      hepatic ducts 51.31
      intestine 51.32
      pancreas 51.33
      stomach 51.34
  gastroepiploic artery to coronary artery 36.17
  hepatic duct 51.39
  hypoglossal-accessory nerve 04.73
  hypoglossal-facial nerve 04.71
  ileal loop to bladder 57.87 [45.51]
  ileoanal 45.95
  ileorectal 45.93
  inferior vena cava and portal vein 39.1
  internal mammary artery (to)
    coronary artery (single vessel) 36.15
      double vessel 36.16
    myocardium 36.2
  intestine 45.90
    large-to-anus 45.95
    large-to-large 45.94
    large-to-rectum 45.94
    large-to-small 45.93
    small-to-anus 45.95
    small-to-large 45.93
    small-to-rectal stump 45.92
    small-to-small 45.91
  intrahepatic 51.79
  intrathoracic vessel NEC 39.23
  kidney (pelvis) 55.86
  lacrimal sac to conjunctiva 09.82
  left-to-right (systemic-pulmonary artery) 39.0
  lymphatic (channel) (peripheral) 40.9
  mesenteric-caval 39.1
  mesocaval 39.1
  nasolacrimal 09.81

Anastomosis — continued
  nerve (cranial) (peripheral) NEC 04.74
    accessory-facial 04.72
    accessory-hypoglossal 04.73
    hypoglossal-facial 04.71
  pancreas (duct) (to) 52.96
    bile duct 51.39
    gall bladder 51.33
    intestine 52.96
    jejunum 52.96
    stomach 52.96
  pleurothecal (with valve) 03.79
  portacaval 39.1
  portal vein to inferior vena cava 39.1
  pulmonary-aortic (Pott's) 39.0
  pulmonary artery and superior vena cava 39.21
  pulmonary-innominate artery (Blalock) 39.0
  pulmonary-subclavian artery (Blalock-Taussig) 39.0
  pulmonary vein and azygos vein 39.23
  pyeloileocutaneous 56.51
  pyeloureterovesical 55.86
  radial artery 36.19
  rectum, rectal NEC 48.74
    stump to small intestine 45.92
  renal (pelvis) 55.86
    vein and splenic vein 39.1
  renoportal 39.1
  salpingothecal (with valve) 03.79
  splenic to renal veins 39.1
  splenorenal (venous) 39.1
    arterial 39.26
  subarachnoid-peritoneal (with valve) 03.71
  subarachnoid-ureteral (with valve) 03.72
  subclavian-aortic 39.22
  superior vena cava to pulmonary artery 39.21
  systemic-pulmonary artery 39.0
  thoracic artery (to)
    coronary artery (single) 36.15
      double 36.16
    myocardium 36.2
  ureter (to) NEC 56.79
    bladder 56.74
    colon 56.71
    ileal pouch (bladder) 56.51
    ileum 56.71
    intestine 56.71
    skin 56.61
  ureterocalyceal 55.86
  ureterocolic 56.71
  ureterovesical 56.74
  urethra (end-to-end) 58.44
  vas deferens 63.82
  veins (suture of proximal to distal end) (with bypass graft) 39.29
    with excision or resection of vessel — see Phlebectomy, with anastomosis, by site
    mesenteric to vena cava 39.1
    portal to inferior vena cava 39.1
    revision 39.49
    splenic and renal 39.1
  ventricle, ventricular (intracerebral) (with valve) (see also Shunt, ventricular) 02.2
  ventriculoatrial (with valve) 02.32
  ventriculocaval (with valve) 02.32
  ventriculomastoid (with valve) 02.31
  ventriculopleural (with valve) 02.33
  vesicle — see Anastomosis, bladder
Anderson operation (tibial lengthening) 78.37
Anel operation (dilation of lacrimal duct) 09.42
Anesthesia
  acupuncture for 99.91
  cryoanalgesia, nerve (cranial) (peripheral) 04.2
  spinal — omit code
Aneurysmectomy 38.60
  with
    anastomosis 38.30
      abdominal
        artery 38.36
        vein 38.37
      aorta (arch) (ascending) (descending) 38.34
      head and neck NEC 38.32
      intracranial NEC 38.31

Aneurysmectomy — continued
  with — continued
    anastomosis — continued
      lower limb
        artery 38.38
        vein 38.39
      thoracic NEC 38.35
      upper limb (artery) (vein) 38.33
    graft replacement (interposition) 38.40
      abdominal
        aorta
          endovascular approach 39.71
          open approach 38.44
          Zenith® Renu™ AAA graft 39.71
        artery 38.46
        vein 38.47
      aorta (arch) (ascending) (descending thoracic)
        abdominal 38.44
        thoracic 38.45
        thoracoabdominal 38.45 [38.44]
      head and neck NEC 38.42
      intracranial NEC 38.41
      lower limb
        artery 38.48
        vein 38.49
      thoracic NEC 38.45
      upper limb (artery) (vein) 38.43
  abdominal
    artery 38.66
    vein 38.67
  aorta (arch) (ascending) (descending) 38.64
  atrial, auricular 37.32
  head and neck NEC 38.62
  heart 37.32
  intracranial NEC 38.61
  lower limb
    artery 38.68
    vein 38.69
  sinus of Valsalva 35.39
  thoracic NEC 38.65
  upper limb (artery) (vein) 38.63
  ventricle (myocardium) 37.32
Aneurysmoplasty — see Aneurysmorrhaphy
Aneurysmorrhaphy NEC 39.52
  by or with
    anastomosis — see Aneurysmectomy, with anastomosis, by site
    clipping 39.51
    coagulation 39.52
    electrocoagulation 39.52
    endovascular graft
      abdominal aorta 39.71
      lower extremity artery(s) 39.79
      thoracic aorta 39.73
      upper extremity artery(s) 39.79
    excision or resection (see also Aneurysmectomy, by site)
      with
        anastomosis — see Aneurysmectomy, with anastomosis, by site
        graft replacement — see Aneurysmectomy, with graft replacement, by site
    filipuncture 39.52
    graft replacement — see Aneurysmectomy, with graft replacement, by site
    methyl methacrylate 39.52
    suture 39.52
    wiring 39.52
    wrapping 39.52
  Matas' 39.52
Aneurysmotomy — see Aneurysmectomy
Angiectomy
  with
    anastomosis 38.30
      abdominal
        artery 38.36
        vein 38.37
      aorta (arch) (ascending) (descending) 38.34
      head and neck NEC 38.32
      intracranial NEC 38.31
      lower limb
        artery 38.38

☑ Additional Digit Required — Refer to the Tabular List for Digit Selection   Subterms under main terms may continue to next column or page

2 — Volume 3   ▶◀ Revised Text   ● New Line   ▲ Revised Code   **2010 ICD-9-CM**

☑ Additional Digit Required — Refer to the Tabular List for Digit Selection   Subterms under main terms may continue to next column or page

2010 ICD-9-CM   ▶◀ Revised Text   ● New Line   ▲ Revised Code   **Volume 3 — 3**

Arrest — *continued*
  bone growth — *continued*
    by stapling — *see* Stapling, epiphyseal plate
      femur 78.25
      fibula 78.27
      humerus 78.22
      radius 78.23
      tibia 78.27
      ulna 78.23
  cardiac, induced (anoxic) (circulatory) 39.63
  circulatory, induced (anoxic) 39.63
  hemorrhage — *see* Control, hemorrhage
Arslan operation (fenestration of inner ear) 20.61
Arteriectomy 38.60
  with
    anastomosis 38.30
      abdominal 38.36
      aorta (arch) (ascending) (descending thoracic) 38.34
      head and neck NEC 38.32
      intracranial NEC 38.31
      lower limb 38.38
      thoracic NEC 38.35
      upper limb 38.33
    graft replacement (interposition) 38.40
      abdominal
        aorta 38.44
      aorta (arch) (ascending) (descending thoracic)
        abdominal 38.44
        thoracic 38.45
        thoracoabdominal 38.45 *[38.44]*
      head and neck NEC 38.42
      intracranial NEC 38.41
      lower limb 38.48
      thoracic NEC 38.45
      upper limb 38.43
  abdominal 38.66
  aorta (arch) (ascending) (descending) 38.64
  head and neck NEC 38.62
  intracranial NEC 38.61
  lower limb 38.68
  thoracic NEC 38.65
  upper limb 38.63
Arteriography (contrast) (fluoroscopic) (retrograde) 88.40
  by
    radioisotope — *see* Scan, radioisotope
    ultrasound (Doppler) — *see* Ultrasonography, by site
  aorta (arch) (ascending) (descending) 88.42
  basilar 88.41
  brachial 88.49
  carotid (internal) 88.41
  cerebral (posterior circulation) 88.41
  coronary (direct) (selective) NEC 88.57
    double catheter technique (Judkins) (Ricketts and Abrams) 88.56
    intra-operative fluorescence vascular 88.59
    single catheter technique (Sones) 88.55
  Doppler (ultrasonic) — *see* Ultrasonography, by site
  femoral 88.48
  head and neck 88.41
  intra-abdominal NEC 88.47
  intrathoracic NEC 88.44
  lower extremity 88.48
  placenta 88.46
  pulmonary 88.43
  radioisotope — *see* Scan, radioisotope
  renal 88.45
  specified site NEC 88.49
  SPY 88.59
  superior mesenteric artery 88.47
  transfemoral 88.48
  ultrasound — *see* Ultrasonography, by site
  upper extremity 88.49
Arterioplasty — *see* Repair, artery
Arteriorrhaphy 39.31
Arteriotomy 38.00
  abdominal 38.06
  aorta (arch) (ascending) (descending) 38.04
  head and neck NEC 38.02
  intracranial NEC 38.01
  lower limb 38.08

Arteriotomy — *continued*
  thoracic NEC 38.05
  upper limb 38.03
Arteriovenostomy 39.29
  for renal dialysis 39.27
Arthrectomy 80.90
  ankle 80.97
  elbow 80.92
  foot and toe 80.98
  hand and finger 80.94
  hip 80.95
  intervertebral disc — *see* category 80.5 ☑
  knee 80.96
    semilunar cartilage 80.6
  shoulder 80.91
  specified site NEC 80.99
  spine NEC 80.99
  wrist 80.93
Arthrocentesis 81.91
  for arthrography — *see* Arthrogram
Arthrodesis (compression) (extra-articular) (intra-articular) (with bone graft) (with fixation device) 81.20
  ankle 81.11
  carporadial 81.25
  cricoarytenoid 31.69
  elbow 81.24
  finger 81.28
  foot NEC 81.17
  hip 81.21
  interphalangeal
    finger 81.28
    toe NEC 77.58
      claw toe repair 77.57
      hammer toe repair 77.56
  ischiofemoral 81.21
  knee 81.22
  lumbosacral, lumbar NEC 81.08
    ALIF (anterior lumbar interbody fusion) 81.06
    anterior (interbody), anterolateral technique 81.06
    lateral transverse process technique 81.07
    PLIF (posterior lumbar interbody fusion) 81.08
    posterior (interbody), posterolateral technique 81.08
    TLIF (transforaminal lumbar interbody fusion) 81.08
  McKeever (metatarsophalangeal) 81.16
  metacarpocarpal 81.26
  metacarpophalangeal 81.27
  metatarsophalangeal 81.16
  midtarsal 81.14
  pantalar 81.11
  sacroiliac 81.08
  shoulder 81.23
  specified joint NEC 81.29
  spinal (*see also* Fusion, spinal) 81.00
  subtalar 81.11
  tarsometatarsal 81.15
  tibiotalar 81.11
  toe NEC 77.58
    claw toe repair 77.57
    hammer toe repair 77.56
  triple 81.12
  wrist 81.26
Arthroendoscopy — *see* Arthroscopy
Arthroereisis, subtalar joint 81.18
Arthrogram, arthrography 88.32
  temporomandibular 87.13
Arthrolysis 93.26
Arthroplasty (with fixation device) (with traction) 81.96
  ankle 81.49
  carpals 81.75
    with prosthetic implant 81.74
  carpocarpal, carpometacarpal 81.75
    with prosthetic implant 81.74
  Carroll and Taber (proximal interphalangeal joint) 81.72
  cup (partial hip) 81.52
  Curtis (interphalangeal joint) 81.72
  elbow 81.85
    with prosthetic replacement ▶(partial)◄ (total) 81.84

Arthroplasty — *continued*
  femoral head NEC 81.40
    with prosthetic implant 81.52
  finger(s) 81.72
    with prosthetic implant 81.71
  foot (metatarsal) with joint replacement 81.57
  Fowler (metacarpophalangeal joint) 81.72
  hand (metacarpophalangeal) (interphalangeal) 81.72
    with prosthetic implant 81.71
  hip (with bone graft) 81.40
    cup (partial hip) 81.52
    femoral head NEC 81.40
      with prosthetic implant 81.52
        with total replacement 81.51
    partial replacement 81.52
    total replacement 81.51
  interphalangeal joint 81.72
    with prosthetic implant 81.71
  Kessler (carpometacarpal joint) 81.74
  knee (*see also* Repair, knee) 81.47
    prosthetic replacement (bicompartmental) (hemijoint) (partial) (total) (tricompartmental) (unicompartmental) 81.54
    revision 81.55
  metacarpophalangeal joint 81.72
    with prosthetic implant 81.71
  shoulder 81.83
    for recurrent dislocation 81.82
    prosthetic replacement (partial) 81.81
      total 81.80
  temporomandibular 76.5
  toe NEC 77.58
    for hallux valgus repair 77.59
    with prosthetic replacement 81.57
  wrist 81.75
    with prosthetic implant 81.74
      total replacement 81.73
Arthroscopy 80.20
  ankle 80.27
  elbow 80.22
  finger 80.24
  foot 80.28
  hand 80.24
  hip 80.25
  knee 80.26
  shoulder 80.21
  specified site NEC 80.29
  toe 80.28
  wrist 80.23
Arthrostomy — *see also* Arthrotomy 80.10
Arthrotomy 80.10
  as operative approach — *omit code*
  with
    arthrography — *see* Arthrogram
    arthroscopy — *see* Arthroscopy
    injection of drug 81.92
    removal of prosthesis ▶without replacement◄ (*see* Removal, prosthesis, joint structures)
  ankle 80.17
  elbow 80.12
  foot and toe 80.18
  hand and finger 80.14
  hip 80.15
  knee 80.16
  shoulder 80.11
  specified site NEC 80.19
  spine 80.19
  wrist 80.13
Artificial
  heart 37.52
    AbioCor® 37.52
    CardioWest™ (TAH-t) 37.52
  insemination 69.92
  kidney 39.95
  rupture of membranes 73.09
Arytenoidectomy 30.29
Arytenoidopexy 31.69
Asai operation (larynx) 31.75
Aspiration
  abscess — *see* Aspiration, by site
  anterior chamber, eye (therapeutic) 12.91
    diagnostic 12.21
  aqueous (eye) (humor) (therapeutic) 12.91

Aspiration — *continued*
  aqueous — *continued*
    diagnostic 12.21
  ascites 54.91
  Bartholin's gland (cyst) (percutaneous) 71.21
  biopsy — *see* Biopsy, by site
  bladder (catheter) 57.0
    percutaneous (needle) 57.11
  bone marrow (for biopsy) 41.31
    from donor for transplant 41.91
    stem cell 99.79
  branchial cleft cyst 29.0
  breast 85.91
  bronchus 96.05
    with lavage 96.56
  bursa (percutaneous) 83.94
    hand 82.92
  calculus, bladder 57.0
  cataract 13.3
    with
      phacoemulsification 13.41
      phacofragmentation 13.43
        posterior route 13.42
  chest 34.91
  cisternal 01.01
  cranial (puncture) 01.09
  craniobuccal pouch 07.72
  craniopharyngioma 07.72
  cul-de-sac (abscess) 70.0
  curettage, uterus 69.59
    after abortion or delivery 69.52
    diagnostic 69.59
    to terminate pregnancy 69.51
  cyst — *see* Aspiration, by site
  diverticulum, pharynx 29.0
  endotracheal 96.04
    with lavage 96.56
  extradural 01.09
  eye (anterior chamber) (therapeutic) 12.91
    diagnostic 12.21
  fallopian tube 66.91
  fascia 83.95
    hand 82.93
  gallbladder (percutaneous) 51.01
  hematoma (*see also* Aspiration, by site)
    obstetrical 75.92
      incisional 75.91
  hydrocele, tunica vaginalis 61.91
  hygroma — *see* Aspiration, by site
  hyphema 12.91
  hypophysis 07.72
  intracranial space (epidural) (extradural) (subarachnoid) (subdural) (ventricular) 01.09
    through previously implanted catheter or reservoir (Ommaya) (Rickham) 01.02
  joint 81.91
    for arthrography — *see* Arthrogram
  kidney (cyst) (pelvis) (percutaneous) (therapeutic) 55.92
    diagnostic 55.23
  liver (percutaneous) 50.91
  lung (percutaneous) (puncture) (needle) (trocar) 33.93
  middle ear 20.09
    with intubation 20.01
  muscle 83.95
    hand 82.93
  nail 86.01
  nasal sinus 22.00
    by puncture 22.01
    through natural ostium 22.02
  nasotracheal 96.04
    with lavage 96.56
  orbit, diagnostic 16.22
  ovary 65.91
  percutaneous — *see* Aspiration, by site
  pericardium (wound) 37.0
  pituitary gland 07.72
  pleural cavity 34.91
  prostate (percutaneous) 60.91
  Rathke's pouch 07.72
  seminal vesicles 60.71
  seroma — *see* Aspiration, by site
  skin 86.01

☑ Additional Digit Required — Refer to the Tabular List for Digit Selection   ▭ Subterms under main terms may continue to next column or page

4 — Volume 3 · October 2009   ▶◀ Revised Text   ● New Line   ▲ Revised Code   **2010 ICD-9-CM**

Index   Arrest — Aspiration

Aspiration — *continued*
soft tissue NEC 83.95
hand 82.93
spermatocele 63.91
spinal (puncture) 03.31
spleen (cyst) 41.1
stem cell 99.79
subarachnoid space (cerebral) 01.09
subcutaneous tissue 86.01
subdural space (cerebral) 01.09
tendon 83.95
hand 82.93
testis 62.91
thymus 07.92
thoracoscopic 07.95
thyroid (field) (gland) 06.01
postoperative 06.02
trachea 96.04
with lavage 96.56
percutaneous 31.99
tunica vaginalis (hydrocele) (percutaneous) 61.91
vitreous (and replacement) 14.72
diagnostic 14.11
Assessment
fitness to testify 94.11
mental status 94.11
nutritional status 89.39
personality 94.03
temperament 94.02
vocational 93.85
Assistance
cardiac (*see also* Resuscitation, cardiac)
extracorporeal circulation 39.61
endotracheal respiratory — *see* category 96.7 ☑
hepatic, extracorporeal 50.92
respiratory (endotracheal) (mechanical) — *see* Ventilation, mechanical
Astragalectomy 77.98
Asymmetrogammagram — *see* Scan, radioisotope
Atherectomy
cerebrovascular — *see* Angioplasty
coronary — *see* Angioplasty
peripheral 39.50
Atriocommissuropexy (mitral valve) 35.12
Atrioplasty NEC 37.99
combined with repair of valvular and ventricular septal defects — *see* Repair, endocardial cushion defect
septum (heart) NEC 35.71
Atrioseptopexy — *see also* Repair, atrial septal defect 35.71
Atrioseptoplasty — *see also* Repair, atrial septal defect 35.71
Atrioseptostomy (balloon) 35.41
Atriotomy 37.11
Atrioventriculostomy (cerebral-heart) 02.32
Attachment
abutment (screw) for prosthetic ear device
percutaneous 20.99
eye muscle
orbicularis oculi to eyebrow 08.36
rectus to frontalis 15.9
pedicle (flap) graft 86.74
hand 86.73
lip 27.57
mouth 27.57
pharyngeal flap (for cleft palate repair) 27.62
secondary or subsequent 27.63
prosthetic ear device, abutment 20.99
retina — *see* Reattachment, retina
Atticoantrostomy (ear) 20.49
Atticoantrotomy (ear) 20.49
Atticotomy (ear) 20.23
Audiometry (Békésy 5-tone) (impedance) (stapedial reflex response) (subjective) 95.41
Augmentation
bladder 57.87
breast — *see* Mammoplasty, augmentation
buttock ("fanny-lift") 86.89
chin 76.68
genioplasty 76.68

Augmentation — *continued*
mammoplasty — *see* Mammoplasty, augmentation
outflow tract (pulmonary valve) (gusset type) 35.26
in total repair of tetralogy of Fallot 35.81
vocal cord(s) 31.0
Auriculectomy 18.39
Autograft — *see* Graft
Autologous — *see* Blood, transfusion
Autopsy 89.8
Autotransfusion (whole blood) — *see* Blood, transfusion
Autotransplant, autotransplantation — *see also* Reimplantation
adrenal tissue (heterotopic) (orthotopic) 07.45
kidney 55.61
lung — *see* Transplant, transplantation, lung 33.5 ☑
ovary 65.72
laparoscopic 65.75
pancreatic tissue 52.81
parathyroid tissue (heterotopic) (orthotopic) 06.95
thyroid tissue (heterotopic) (orthotopic) 06.94
tooth 23.5
Avulsion, nerve (cranial) (peripheral) NEC 04.07
acoustic 04.01
phrenic 33.31
sympathetic 05.29
Azygography 88.63

B

Bacterial smear — *see* Examination, microscopic
Baffes operation (interatrial transposition of venous return) 35.91
Baffle, atrial or interatrial 35.91
Balanoplasty 64.49
Baldy-Webster operation (uterine suspension) 69.22
Ball operation
herniorrhaphy — *see* Repair, hernia, inguinal
undercutting 49.02
Bandage 93.57
elastic 93.56
Banding
gastric 44.68
vertical 44.68
pulmonary artery 38.85
Bankhart operation (capsular repair into glenoid, for shoulder dislocation) 81.82
Bardenheuer operation (ligation of innominate artery) 38.85
Barium swallow 87.61
Barkan operation (goniotomy) 12.52
with goniopuncture 12.53
Barr operation (transfer of tibialis posterior tendon) 83.75
Barsky operation (closure of cleft hand) 82.82
Basal metabolic rate 89.39
Basiotripsy 73.8
Bassett operation (vulvectomy with inguinal lymph node dissection) 71.5 [40.3]
Bassini operation — *see* Repair, hernia, inguinal
Batch-Spittler-McFaddin operation (knee disarticulation) 84.16
Batista operation (partial ventriculectomy) (ventricular reduction) (ventricular remodeling) 37.35
Bearing surface, hip
ceramic-on-ceramic 00.76
ceramic-on-polyethylene 00.77
metal-on-metal 00.75
metal-on-polyethylene 00.74
Beck-Jianu operation (permanent gastrostomy) 43.19
Beck operation
aorta-coronary sinus shunt 36.39
epicardial poudrage 36.39
Behavior modification 94.33

Bell-Beuttner operation (subtotal abdominal hysterectomy) 68.39
laparoscopic 68.31
Belsey operation (esophagogastric sphincter) 44.65
Benenenti operation (rotation of bulbous urethra) 58.49
Berke operation (levator resection of eyelid) 08.33
Bicuspidization of heart valve 35.10
aortic 35.11
mitral 35.12
Bicycle dynamometer 93.01
Biesenberger operation (size reduction of breast, bilateral) 85.32
unilateral 85.31
Bifurcation, bone — *see also* Osteotomy 77.30
Bigelow operation (litholapaxy) 57.0
Bililite therapy (ultraviolet) 99.82
Billroth I operation (partial gastrectomy with gastroduodenostomy) 43.6
Billroth II operation (partial gastrectomy with gastrojejunostomy) 43.7
Binnie operation (hepatopexy) 50.69
Biofeedback, psychotherapy 94.39
Biopsy
abdominal wall 54.22
adenoid 28.11
adrenal gland NEC 07.11
closed 07.11
open 07.12
percutaneous (aspiration) (needle) 07.11
alveolus 24.12
anus 49.23
appendix 45.26
artery (any site) 38.21
aspiration — *see* Biopsy, by site
bile ducts 51.14
closed (endoscopic) 51.14
open 51.13
percutaneous (needle) 51.12
bladder 57.33
closed 57.33
open 57.34
transurethral 57.33
blood vessel (any site) 38.21
bone 77.40
carpal, metacarpal 77.44
clavicle 77.41
facial 76.11
femur 77.45
fibula 77.47
humerus 77.42
marrow 41.31
patella 77.46
pelvic 77.49
phalanges (foot) (hand) 77.49
radius 77.43
scapula 77.41
specified site NEC 77.49
tarsal, metatarsal 77.48
thorax (ribs) (sternum) 77.41
tibia 77.47
ulna 77.43
vertebrae 77.49
bowel — *see* Biopsy, intestine
brain NEC 01.13
closed 01.13
open 01.14
percutaneous (needle) 01.13
breast 85.11
blind 85.11
closed 85.11
open 85.12
percutaneous (needle) (Vimm-Silverman) 85.11
bronchus NEC 33.24
brush 33.24
closed (endoscopic) 33.24
open 33.25
transbronchoscopic needle aspiration ● (TBNA) 33.24
Wang needle (transbronchoscopic) 33.24 ●
washings 33.24
bursa 83.21
cardioesophageal (junction) 44.14

Biopsy — *continued*
cardioesophageal — *continued*
closed (endoscopic) 44.14
open 44.15
cecum 45.25
brush 45.25
closed (endoscopic) 45.25
open 45.26
cerebral meninges NEC 01.11
closed 01.11
open 01.12
percutaneous (needle) 01.11
cervix (punch) 67.12
conization (sharp) 67.2
chest wall 34.23
clitoris 71.11
colon 45.25
brush 45.25
closed (endoscopic) 45.25
open 45.26
conjunctiva 10.21
cornea 11.22
cul-de-sac 70.23
diaphragm 34.27
duodenum 45.14
brush 45.14
closed (endoscopic) 45.14
open 45.15
ear (external) 18.12
middle or inner 20.32
endocervix 67.11
endometrium NEC 68.16
by
aspiration curettage 69.59
dilation and curettage 69.09
closed (endoscopic) 68.16
open 68.13
epididymis 63.01
esophagus 42.24
closed (endoscopic) 42.24
open 42.25
extraocular muscle or tendon 15.01
eye 16.23
muscle (oblique) (rectus) 15.01
eyelid 08.11
fallopian tube 66.11
fascia 83.21
fetus 75.33
gallbladder 51.12
closed (endoscopic) 51.14
open 51.13
percutaneous (needle) 51.12
ganglion (cranial) (peripheral) NEC 04.11
closed 04.11
open 04.12
percutaneous (needle) 04.11
sympathetic nerve 05.11
gum 24.11
heart 37.25
hypophysis (*see also* Biopsy, pituitary gland) 07.15
ileum 45.14
brush 45.14
closed (endoscopic) 45.14
open 45.15
intestine NEC 45.27
large 45.25
brush 45.25
closed (endoscopic) 45.25
open 45.26
small 45.14
brush 45.14
closed (endoscopic) 45.14
open 45.15
intra-abdominal mass 54.24
closed 54.24
percutaneous (needle) 54.24
iris 12.22
jejunum 45.14
brush 45.14
closed (endoscopic) 45.14
open 45.15
joint structure (aspiration) 80.30
ankle 80.37
elbow 80.32
foot and toe 80.38

Aspiration — Biopsy

☑ Additional Digit Required — Refer to the Tabular List for Digit Selection   ₩₩₩ Subterms under main terms may continue to next column or page

2010 ICD-9-CM   ▶◀ Revised Text   ● New Line   ▲ Revised Code   **October 2009 • Volume 3 — 5**

☑ Additional Digit Required — Refer to the Tabular List for Digit Selection   ▽ Subterms under main terms may continue to next column or page

☑ Additional Digit Required — Refer to the Tabular List for Digit Selection
▽ Subterms under main terms may continue to next column or page
8 — Volume 3 • October 2009
▶◀ Revised Text ● New Line ▲ Revised Code
2010 ICD-9-CM

Index

Cauterization — Closure

Closure — see also Repair — continued
aorticopulmonary fenestration (fistula) 39.59
appendicostomy 47.92
artificial opening
  bile duct 51.79
  bladder 57.82
  bronchus 33.42
  common duct 51.72
  esophagus 42.83
  gallbladder 51.92
  hepatic duct 51.79
  intestine 46.50
    large 46.52
    small 46.51
  kidney 55.82
  larynx 31.62
  rectum 48.72
  stomach 44.62
  thorax 34.72
  trachea 31.72
  ureter 56.83
  urethra 58.42
atrial septal defect (see also Repair, atrial septal
    defect) 35.71
  with umbrella device (King-Mills type)
    35.52
  combined with repair of valvular and ven-
    tricular septal defects — see Repair,
    endocardial cushion defect
bronchostomy 33.42
cecostomy 46.52
cholecystostomy 51.92
cleft hand 82.82
colostomy 46.52
cystostomy 57.82
diastema (alveolar) (dental) 24.8
disrupted abdominal wall (postoperative)
    54.61
duodenostomy 46.51
encephalocele 02.12
endocardial cushion defect (see also Repair,
    endocardial cushion defect) 35.73
enterostomy 46.50
esophagostomy 42.83
fenestration
  aorticopulmonary 39.59
  septal, heart (see also Repair, heart, sep-
    tum) 35.70
filtering bleb, corneoscleral (postglaucoma)
    12.66
fistula
  abdominothoracic 34.83
  anorectal 48.73
  anovaginal 70.73
  antrobuccal 22.71
  anus 49.73
  aorticopulmonary (fenestration) 39.59
  aortoduodenal 39.59
  appendix 47.92
  biliary tract 51.79
  bladder NEC 57.84
  branchial cleft 29.52
  bronchocutaneous 33.42
  bronchoesophageal 33.42
  bronchomediastinal 34.73
  bronchopleural 34.73
  bronchopleurocutaneous 34.73
  bronchopleuromediastinal 34.73
  bronchovisceral 33.42
  bronchus 33.42
  cecosigmoidal 46.76
  cerebrospinal fluid 02.12
  cervicoaural 18.79
  cervicosigmoidal 67.62
  cervicovesical 57.84
  cervix 67.62
  cholecystocolic 51.93
  cholecystoduodenal 51.93
  cholecystoenteric 51.93
  cholecystogastric 51.93
  cholecystojejunal 51.93
  cisterna chyli 40.63
  colon 46.76
  colovaginal 70.72
  common duct 51.72
  cornea 11.49

Closure — see also Repair — continued
fistula — continued
  cornea — continued
    with lamellar graft (homograft) 11.62
      autograft 11.61
  diaphragm 34.83
  duodenum 46.72
  ear drum 19.4
  ear, middle 19.9
  enterocolic 46.74
  enterocutaneous 46.74
  enterouterine 69.42
  enterovaginal 70.74
  enterovesical 57.83
  esophagobronchial 33.42
  esophagocutaneous 42.84
  esophagopleurocutaneous 34.73
  esophagotracheal 31.73
  esophagus NEC 42.84
  fecal 46.79
  gallbladder 51.93
  gastric NEC 44.63
  gastrocolic 44.63
  gastroenterocolic 44.63
  gastroesophageal 42.84
  gastrojejunal 44.63
  gastrojejunocolic 44.63
  heart valve — see Repair, heart, valve
  hepatic duct 51.79
  hepatopleural 34.73
  hepatopulmonary 34.73
  ileorectal 46.74
  ileosigmoidal 46.74
  ileovesical 57.83
  ileum 46.74
  in ano 49.73
  intestine 46.79
    large 46.76
    small NEC 46.74
  intestinocolonic 46.74
  intestinoureteral 56.84
  intestinouterine 69.42
  intestinovaginal 70.74
  intestinovesical 57.83
  jejunum 46.74
  kidney 55.83
  lacrimal 09.99
  laryngotracheal 31.62
  larynx 31.62
  lymphatic duct, left (thoracic) 40.63
  mastoid (antrum) 19.9
  mediastinobronchial 34.73
  mediastinocutaneous 34.73
  mouth (external) 27.53
  nasal 21.82
    sinus 22.71
  nasolabial 21.82
  nasopharyngeal 21.82
  oroantral 22.71
  oronasal 21.82
  oval window (ear) 20.93
  pancreaticoduodenal 52.95
  perilymph 20.93
  perineorectal 48.73
  perineosigmoidal 46.76
  perineourethroscrotal 58.43
  perineum 71.72
  perirectal 48.93
  pharyngoesophageal 29.53
  pharynx NEC 29.53
  pleura, pleural NEC 34.93
  pleurocutaneous 34.73
  pleuropericardial 37.49
  pleuroperitoneal 34.83
  pulmonoperitoneal 34.83
  rectolabial 48.73
  rectoureteral 56.84
  rectourethral 58.43
  rectovaginal 70.73
  rectovesical 57.83
  rectovesicovaginal 57.83
  rectovulvar 48.73
  rectum NEC 48.73
  renal 55.83
  reno-intestinal 55.83
  round window 20.93

Closure — see also Repair — continued
fistula — continued
  salivary (gland) (duct) 26.42
  scrotum 61.42
  sigmoidovaginal 70.74
  sigmoidovesical 57.83
  splenocolic 41.95
  stomach NEC 44.63
  thoracic duct 40.63
  thoracoabdominal 34.83
  thoracogastric 34.83
  thoracointestinal 34.83
  thorax NEC 34.73
  trachea NEC 31.73
  tracheoesophageal 31.73
  tympanic membrane (see also Tym-
    panoplasty) 19.4
  umbilicourinary 57.51
  ureter 56.84
  ureterocervical 56.84
  ureterorectal 56.84
  ureterosigmoidal 56.84
  ureterovaginal 56.84
  ureterovesical 56.84
  urethra 58.43
  urethroperineal 58.43
  urethroperineovesical 57.84
  urethrorectal 58.43
  urethroscrotal 58.43
  urethrovaginal 58.43
  uteroenteric 69.42
  uterointestinal 69.42
  uterorectal 69.42
  uteroureteric 56.84
  uterovaginal 69.42
  uterovesical 57.84
  vagina 70.75
  vaginocutaneous 70.75
  vaginoenteric 70.74
  vaginoperineal 70.75
  vaginovesical 57.84
  vesicocervicovaginal 57.84
  vesicocolic 57.83
  vesicocutaneous 57.84
  vesicoenteric 57.83
  vesicometrorectal 57.83
  vesicoperineal 57.84
  vesicorectal 57.83
  vesicosigmoidal 57.83
  vesicosigmoidovaginal 57.83
  vesicoureteral 56.84
  vesicoureterovaginal 56.84
  vesicourethral 57.84
  vesicourethrorectal 57.83
  vesicouterine 57.84
  vesicovaginal 57.84
  vulva 71.72
  vulvorectal 48.73
foramen ovale (patent) 35.71
  with
    prosthesis (open heart technique)
      35.51
      closed heart technique 35.52
    tissue graft 35.61
gastroduodenostomy 44.5
gastrojejunostomy 44.5
gastrostomy 44.62
ileostomy 46.51
jejunostomy 46.51
laceration (see also Suture, by site)
  liver 50.61
laparotomy, delayed 54.62
meningocele (spinal) 03.51
  cerebral 02.12
myelomeningocele 03.52
nephrostomy 55.82
palmar cleft 82.82
patent ductus arteriosus 38.85
pelviostomy 55.82
peptic ulcer (bleeding) (perforated) 44.40
perforation
  ear drum (see also Tympanoplasty) 19.4
  esophagus 42.82
  nasal septum 21.88
  tympanic membrane (see also Tym-
    panoplasty) 19.4

Closure — see also Repair — continued
proctostomy 48.72
punctum, lacrimal (papilla) 09.91
pyelostomy 55.82
rectostomy 48.72
septum defect (heart) (see also Repair, heart,
    septum) 35.70
sigmoidostomy 46.52
skin (V-Y type) 86.59
stoma
  bile duct 51.79
  bladder 57.82
  bronchus 33.42
  common duct 51.72
  esophagus 42.83
  gallbladder 51.92
  hepatic duct 51.79
  intestine 46.50
    large 46.52
    small 46.51
  kidney 55.82
  larynx 31.62
  rectum 48.72
  stomach 44.62
  thorax 34.72
  trachea 31.72
  ureter 56.83
  urethra 58.42
thoracostomy 34.72
tracheostomy 31.72
ulcer (bleeding) (peptic) (perforated) 44.40
  duodenum 44.42
  gastric 44.41
  intestine (perforated) 46.79
  skin 86.59
  stomach 44.41
ureterostomy 56.83
urethrostomy 58.42
vagina 70.8
vascular
  percutaneous puncture — omit code
vesicostomy 57.22
wound (see also Suture, by site)
  with graft — see Graft
  with tissue adhesive 86.59
Coagulation, electrocoagulation — see also
    Destruction, lesion, by site
aneurysm (cerebral) (peripheral vessel) 39.52
arteriovenous fistula 39.53
brain tissue (incremental) (radio-frequency)
    01.59
broad ligament 69.19
cervix 67.32
ear
  external 18.29
  inner 20.79
  middle 20.51
fallopian tube 66.61
gasserian ganglion 04.05
nose for epistaxis (with packing) 21.03
ovary 65.29
  laparoscopic 65.25
pharynx (by diathermy) 29.39
prostatic bed 60.94
rectum (polyp) 48.32
  radical 48.31
retina (for)
  destruction of lesion 14.21
  reattachment 14.51
  repair of tear 14.31
round ligament 69.19
semicircular canals 20.79
spinal cord (lesion) 03.4
urethrovesical junction, transurethral 57.49
uterosacral ligament 69.19
uterus 68.29
vagina 70.33
vulva 71.3
Coating, aneurysm of brain 39.52
Cobalt-60 therapy (treatment) 92.23
Coccygectomy (partial) 77.89
  total 77.99
Coccygotomy 77.39
"Cocked hat" procedure (metacarpal lengthen-
    ing and transfer of local flap) 82.69

Cockett operation (varicose vein)
  lower limb 38.59
  upper limb 38.53
Cody tack (perforation of footplate) 19.0
Coffey operation (uterine suspension) (Meig's modification) 69.22
Colectomy (partial) (segmental) (subtotal)
  cecum (with terminal ileum)
    laparoscopic 17.32
    open and other 45.72
  laparoscopic 17.39
  left (Hartmann) (lower) (radical)
    laparoscopic 17.35
    open and other 45.75
  multiple segmental
    laparoscopic 17.31
    open and other 45.71
  open and other 45.79
  right (radical)
    laparoscopic 17.33
    open and other 45.73
  sigmoid
    laparoscopic 17.36
    open and other 45.76
  terminal ileum with cecum
    laparoscopic 17.32
    open and other 45.72
  total
    laparoscopic 45.81
    open 45.82
    other 45.83
    unspecified 45.83
  transverse
    laparoscopic 17.34
    open and other 45.74
Cole operation (anterior tarsal wedge osteotomy) 77.28
Collapse, lung, surgical 33.39
  by
    destruction of phrenic nerve 33.31
    pneumoperitoneum 33.33
    pneumothorax, artificially-induced 33.32
    thoracoplasty 33.34
Collection, sperm for artificial insemination 99.96
Collis-Nissen operation (hiatal hernia repair with esophagogastroplasty) 53.80
Colocentesis 45.03
Colocolostomy 45.94
  proximal to distal segment 45.79
Colocystoplasty 57.87 *[45.52]*
Colofixation 46.64
Coloileotomy 45.00
Colonna operation
  adductor tenotomy (first stage) 83.12
  hip arthroplasty (second stage) 81.40
  reconstruction of hip (second stage) 81.40
Colonoscopy 45.23
  with
    biopsy 45.25
      rectum 48.24
    stent — see Insertion, stent, colon
  fiberoptic (flexible) 45.23
  intraoperative 45.21
  through stoma (artificial) 45.22
  transabdominal 45.21
Colopexy 46.63
Coloplication 46.64
Coloproctostomy 45.94
Colorectosigmoidostomy 45.94
Colorectostomy 45.94
Colorrhaphy 46.75
Coloscopy — see Colonoscopy
Colosigmoidostomy 45.94
Colostomy (ileo-ascending) (ileo-transverse) (perineal) (transverse) 46.10
  with anterior rectal resection 48.62
  delayed opening 46.14
  loop 46.03
  permanent (magnetic) 46.13
  temporary 46.11
Colotomy 45.03
Colpectomy 70.4
Colpoceliocentesis 70.0
Colpocentesis 70.0
Colpocleisis (complete) (partial) 70.8

Colpohysterectomy 68.59
  laparoscopically assisted (LAVH) 68.51
Colpoperineoplasty 70.79
  with repair of urethrocele 70.51
    with graft or prosthesis 70.53
Colpoperineorrhaphy 70.71
  following delivery 75.69
Colpopexy 70.77
  with graft or prosthesis 70.78
Colpoplasty 70.79
Colpopoiesis 70.61
  vaginal construction 70.61
    with graft or prosthesis 70.63
Colporrhaphy 70.71
  for repair of
    cystocele 70.51
      with rectocele 70.50
        with graft or prosthesis 70.53
    enterocele 70.92
      with graft or prosthesis 70.93
    rectocele 70.52
      with cystocele 70.50
        with graft or prosthesis 70.53
    urethrocele 70.51
      with graft or prosthesis 70.54
    anterior (cystocele repair) 70.51
      with graft or prosthesis 70.54
    posterior (rectocele repair) 70.52
      with graft or prosthesis 70.55
Colposcopy 70.21
Colpotomy 70.14
  for pelvic peritoneal drainage 70.12
Commando operation (radical glossectomy) 25.4
Commissurotomy
  closed heart technique — see Valvulotomy, heart
  open heart technique — see Valvuloplasty, heart
Compression, trigeminal nerve 04.02
Conchectomy 21.69
Conchotomy 21.1
Conduction study, nerve 89.15
Conduitogram, ileum 87.78
Condylectomy — see category 77.8 ☑
  mandible 76.5
Condylotomy NEC — see also Division, joint capsule 80.40
  mandible (open) 76.62
    closed 76.61
Conization
  cervix (knife) (sharp) (biopsy) 67.2
    by
      cryosurgery 67.33
      electroconization 67.32
Conjunctivocystorhinostomy 09.82
  with insertion of tube or stent 09.83
Conjunctivodacryocystorhinostomy (CDCR) 09.82
  with insertion of tube or stent 09.83
● **Conjunctivodacryocystostomy** 09.82
●   with insertion of tube or stent 09.83
● **Conjunctivoplasty** 10.49
Conjunctivorhinostomy 09.82
  with insertion of tube or stent 09.83
Constriction of globe, for scleral buckling — see also Buckling, scleral 14.49
Construction
  auricle, ear (with graft) (with implant) 18.71
  ear
    auricle (with graft) (with implant) 18.71
    meatus (osseous) (skin-lined) 18.6
  endorectal ileal pouch (J-pouch) (H-pouch) (S-pouch) (with anastomosis to anus) 45.95
  esophagus, artificial — see Anastomosis, esophagus
  ileal bladder (open) 56.51
    closed 57.87 *[45.51]*
  ileal conduit 56.51
  larynx, artificial 31.75
  patent meatus (ear) 18.6
  penis (rib graft) (skin graft) (myocutaneous flap) 64.43
  pharyngeal valve, artificial 31.75
  urethra 58.46
  vagina, artificial 70.61

Construction — *continued*
  vagina, artificial — *continued*
    with graft or prosthesis 70.63
  venous valves (peripheral) 39.59
Consultation 89.09
  comprehensive 89.07
  limited (single organ system) 89.06
  specified type NEC 89.08
Continuous positive airway pressure [CPAP] (non-invasive) 93.90
  delivered by
    endotracheal tube — *see* category 96.7 ☑
    tracheostomy — *see* category 96.7 ☑
Control
  atmospheric pressure and composition NEC 93.98
    antigen-free air conditioning 93.98
    decompression chamber 93.97
    mountain sanatorium 93.98
  epistaxis 21.00
    by
      cauterization (and packing) 21.03
      coagulation (with packing) 21.03
      electrocoagulation (with packing) 21.03
      excision of nasal mucosa with grafting 21.07
      ligation of artery 21.09
        ethmoidal 21.04
        external carotid 21.06
        maxillary (transantral) 21.05
      packing (nasal) (anterior) 21.01
      posterior (and anterior) 21.02
    specified means NEC 21.09
  hemorrhage 39.98
    abdominal cavity 54.19
    adenoids (postoperative) 28.7
    anus (postoperative) 49.95
    bladder (postoperative) 57.93
    chest 34.09
    colon 45.49
      endoscopic 45.43
    duodenum (ulcer) 44.49
      by
        embolization (transcatheter) 44.44
        suture (ligation) 44.42
      endoscopic 44.43
    esophagus 42.39
      endoscopic 42.33
    gastric (ulcer) 44.49
      by
        embolization (transcatheter) 44.44
        suture (ligation) 44.41
      endoscopic 44.43
    intrapleural 34.09
      postoperative (recurrent) 34.03
    laparotomy site 54.12
    nose (see also Control, epistaxis) 21.00
    peptic (ulcer) 44.49
      by
        embolization (transcatheter) 44.44
        suture (ligation) 44.40
      endoscopic 44.43
    pleura, pleural cavity 34.09
      postoperative (recurrent) 34.03
    postoperative NEC 39.98
    postvascular surgery 39.41
    prostate 60.94
    specified site NEC 39.98
    stomach — *see* Control, hemorrhage, gastric
    thorax NEC 34.09
      postoperative (recurrent) 34.03
    thyroid (postoperative) 06.02
    tonsils (postoperative) 28.7
Conversion
  anastomosis — *see* Revision, anastomosis
  atrial rhythm (to sinus rhythm) 99.61 ●
  cardiac rhythm NEC 99.69
    to sinus rhythm 99.62
  gastrostomy to jejunostomy (endoscopic) for feeding tube placement 46.32
  obstetrical position — *see* Version
Cooling, gastric 96.31
CorCap™ 37.41
Cordectomy, vocal 30.22

Cordopexy, vocal 31.69
Cordotomy
  spinal (bilateral) NEC 03.29
    percutaneous 03.21
  vocal 31.3
Corectomy 12.12
Corelysis 12.35
Coreoplasty 12.35
Corneoconjunctivoplasty 11.53
Corpectomy, (vertebral) 80.99
  with diskectomy 80.99
Correction — *see also* Repair
  atresia
    esophageal 42.85
      by magnetic forces 42.99
    external meatus (ear) 18.6
    nasopharynx, nasopharyngeal 29.4
    rectum 48.0
    tricuspid 35.94
  atrial septal defect (*see also* Repair, atrial septal defect) 35.71
    combined with repair of valvular and ventricular septal defects — *see* Repair, endocardial cushion defect
  blepharoptosis (*see also* Repair, blepharoptosis) 08.36
  bunionette (with osteotomy) 77.54
  chordee 64.42
  claw toe 77.57
  cleft
    lip 27.54
    palate 27.62
  clubfoot NEC 83.84
  coarctation of aorta
    with
      anastomosis 38.34
      graft replacement 38.44
  cornea NEC 11.59
    refractive NEC 11.79
      epikeratophakia 11.76
      keratomileusis 11.71
      keratophakia 11.72
      radial keratotomy 11.75
  esophageal atresia 42.85
    by magnetic forces 42.99
  everted lacrimal punctum 09.71
  eyelid
    ptosis (*see also* Repair, blepharoptosis) 08.36
    retraction 08.38
  fetal defect 75.36
  forcible, of musculoskeletal deformity NEC 93.29
  hammer toe 77.56
  hydraulic pressure, open surgery for penile inflatable prosthesis 64.99
  urinary artificial sphincter 58.99
  intestinal malrotation 46.80
    large 46.82
    small 46.81
  inverted uterus — *see* Repair, inverted uterus
  lymphedema (of limb) 40.9
    excision with graft 40.9
    obliteration of lymphatics 40.9
    transplantation of autogenous lymphatics 40.9
  nasopharyngeal atresia 29.4
  overlapping toes 77.58
  palate (cleft) 27.62
  prognathism NEC 76.64
  prominent ear 18.5
  punctum (everted) 09.71
  spinal pseudarthrosis — *see* Refusion, spinal
  syndactyly 86.85
  tetralogy of Fallot
    one-stage 35.81
    partial — *see* specific procedure
    total 35.81
  total anomalous pulmonary venous connection
    one-stage 35.82
    partial — *see* specific procedure
    total 35.82
  transposition, great arteries, total 35.84
  tricuspid atresia 35.94

☑ Additional Digit Required — Refer to the Tabular List for Digit Selection   ▦ Subterms under main terms may continue to next column or page

Correction — *see also* Repair — *continued*
  truncus arteriosus
    one-stage 35.83
    partial — *see* specific procedure
    total 35.83
  ureteropelvic junction 55.87
  ventricular septal defect (*see also* Repair, ventricular septal defect) 35.72
    combined with repair of valvular and atrial septal defects — *see* Repair, endocardial cushion defect
Costectomy 77.91
  with lung excision — *see* Excision, lung
  associated with thoracic operation — *omit code*
Costochondrectomy 77.91
  associated with thoracic operation — *omit code*
Costosternoplasty (pectus excavatum repair) 34.74
Costotomy 77.31
Costotransversectomy 77.91
  associated with thoracic operation — *omit code*
Counseling (for) NEC 94.49
  alcoholism 94.46
  drug addiction 94.45
  employers 94.49
  family (medical) (social) 94.49
  marriage 94.49
  ophthalmologic (with instruction) 95.36
  pastoral 94.49
Countershock, cardiac NEC 99.62
Coventry operation (tibial wedge osteotomy) 77.27
CPAP (continuous positive airway pressure) 93.90
  delivered by
    endotracheal tube — *see* category 96.7 ☑
    tracheostomy — *see* category 96.7 ☑
Craniectomy 01.25
  linear (opening of cranial suture) 02.01
  reopening of site 01.23
  strip (opening of cranial suture) 02.01
Cranioclasis, fetal 73.8
Cranioplasty 02.06
  with synchronous repair of encephalocele 02.12
Craniotomy 01.24
  as operative approach — *omit code*
  for decompression of fracture 02.02
  fetal 73.8
  reopening of site 01.23
Craterization, bone — *see also* Excision, lesion, bone 77.60
Crawford operation (tarso-frontalis sling of eyelid) 08.32
Creation — *see also* Formation
  cardiac device (defibrillator) (pacemaker) pocket
    with initial insertion of cardiac device — *omit code*
    new site (skin) (subcutaneous) 37.79
  conduit
    ileal (urinary) 56.51
    left ventricle and aorta 35.93
    right atrium and pulmonary artery 35.94
    right ventricle and pulmonary (distal) artery 35.92
      in repair of
        pulmonary artery atresia 35.92
        transposition of great vessels 35.92
        truncus arteriosus 35.83
  endorectal ileal pouch (J-pouch) (H-pouch) (S-pouch) (with anastomosis to anus) 45.95
  esophagogastric sphincteric competence NEC 44.66
    laparoscopic 44.67
  Hartmann pouch — *see* Colectomy, by site
  interatrial fistula 35.42
  pericardial window 37.12
  pleural window, for drainage 34.09

Creation — *see also* Formation — *continued*
  pocket
    cardiac device (defibrillator) (pacemaker)
      with initial insertion of cardiac device — *omit code*
      new site (skin) (subcutaneous) 37.79
    loop recorder 37.79
    thalamic stimulator pulse generator
      with initial insertion of battery package — *omit code*
      new site (skin) (subcutaneous) 86.09
  shunt (*see also* Shunt)
    arteriovenous fistula, for dialysis 39.93
    left-to-right (systemic to pulmonary circulation) 39.0
  subcutaneous tunnel for esophageal anastomosis 42.86
    with anastomosis — *see* Anastomosis, esophagus, antesternal
  syndactyly (finger) (toe) 86.89
  thalamic stimulator pulse generator pocket
    with initial insrtion of battery package — *omit code*
    new site (skin) (subcutaneous) 86.09
  tracheoesophageal fistula 31.95
  window
    pericardial 37.12
    pleura, for drainage 34.09
Credé maneuver 73.59
Cricoidectomy 30.29
Cricothyreotomy (for assistance in breathing) 31.1
Cricothyroidectomy 30.29
Cricothyrostomy 31.1
Cricothyrotomy (for assistance in breathing) 31.1
Cricotomy (for assistance in breathing) 31.1
Cricotracheotomy (for assistance in breathing) 31.1
Crisis intervention 94.35
Croupette, croup tent 93.94
Crown, dental (ceramic) (gold) 23.41
Crushing
  bone — *see* category 78.4 ☑
  calculus
    bile (hepatic) passage 51.49
      endoscopic 51.88
    bladder (urinary) 57.0
    pancreatic duct 52.09
      endoscopic 52.94
  fallopian tube (*see also* Ligation, fallopian tube) 66.39
  ganglion — *see* Crushing, nerve
  hemorrhoids 49.45
  nasal septum 21.88
  nerve (cranial) (peripheral) NEC 04.03
    acoustic 04.01
    auditory 04.01
    phrenic 04.03
      for collapse of lung 33.31
    sympathetic 05.0
    trigeminal 04.02
    vestibular 04.01
  vas deferens 63.71
Cryoablation — *see* Ablation
Cryoanalgesia
  nerve (cranial) (peripheral) 04.2
Cryoconization, cervix 67.33
Cryodestruction — *see* Destruction, lesion, by site
Cryoextraction, lens — *see also* Extraction, cataract, intracapsular 13.19
Cryohypophysectomy (complete) (total) — *see also* Hypophysectomy 07.69
Cryoleucotomy 01.32
Cryopexy, retinal — *see* Cryotherapy, retina
Cryoprostatectomy 60.62
Cryoretinopexy (for)
  reattachment 14.52
  repair of tear or defect 14.32
Cryosurgery — *see* Cryotherapy
Cryothalamectomy 01.41
Cryotherapy — *see also* Destruction, lesion, by site
  bladder 57.59
  brain 01.59
  cataract 13.19

Cryotherapy — *see also* Destruction, lesion, by site — *continued*
  cervix 67.33
  choroid — *see* Cryotherapy, retina
  ciliary body 12.72
  corneal lesion (ulcer) 11.43
    to reshape cornea 11.79
  ear
    external 18.29
    inner 20.79
  esophagus 42.39
    endoscopic 42.33
  eyelid 08.25
  hemorrhoids 49.44
  iris 12.41
  nasal turbinates 21.61
  palate (bony) 27.31
  prostate 60.62
  retina (for)
    destruction of lesion 14.22
    reattachment 14.52
    repair of tear 14.32
  skin 86.3
  stomach 43.49
    endoscopic 43.41
  subcutaneous tissue 86.3
  turbinates (nasal) 21.61
  warts 86.3
    genital 71.3
Cryptectomy (anus) 49.39
  endoscopic 49.31
Cryptorchidectomy (unilateral) 62.3
  bilateral 62.41
Cryptotomy (anus) 49.39
  endoscopic 49.31
Cuirass 93.99
Culdocentesis 70.0
Culdoplasty 70.92
  with graft or prosthesis 70.93
Culdoscopy (exploration) (removal of foreign body or lesion) 70.22
Culdotomy 70.12
Culp-Deweerd operation (spiral flap pyeloplasty) 55.87
Culp-Scardino operation (ureteral flap pyeloplasty) 55.87
Culture (and sensitivity) — *see* Examination, microscopic
Curettage (with packing) (with secondary closure) — *see also* Dilation and curettage
  adenoids 28.6
  anus 49.39
    endoscopic 49.31
  bladder 57.59
    transurethral 57.49
  bone (*see also* Excision, lesion, bone) 77.60
  brain 01.59
  bursa 83.39
    hand 82.29
  cartilage (*see also* Excision, lesion, joint) 80.80
  cerebral meninges 01.51
  chalazion 08.25
  conjunctiva (trachoma follicles) 10.33
  corneal epithelium 11.41
    for smear or culture 11.21
  ear, external 18.29
  eyelid 08.25
  joint (*see also* Excision, lesion, joint) 80.80
  meninges (cerebral) 01.51
    spinal 03.4
  muscle 83.32
    hand 82.22
  nerve (peripheral) 04.07
    sympathetic 05.29
  sclera 12.84
  skin 86.3
  spinal cord (meninges) 03.4
  subgingival 24.31
  tendon 83.39
    sheath 83.31
      hand 82.21
  uterus (with dilation) 69.09
    aspiration (diagnostic) NEC 69.59
      after abortion or delivery 69.52
      to terminate pregnancy 69.51
    following delivery or abortion 69.02

Curette evacuation, lens 13.2
Curtis operation (interphalangeal joint arthroplasty) 81.72
Cutaneolipectomy 86.83
Cutdown, venous 38.94
Cutting
  nerve (cranial) (peripheral) NEC 04.03
    acoustic 04.01
    auditory 04.01
    root, spinal 03.1
    sympathetic 05.0
    trigeminal 04.02
    vestibular 04.01
  pedicle (flap) graft 86.71
  pylorus (with wedge resection) 43.3
  spinal nerve root 03.1
  ureterovesical orifice 56.1
  urethral sphincter 58.5
CVP (central venous pressure monitoring) 89.62
Cyclectomy (ciliary body) 12.44
  eyelid margin 08.20
Cyclicotomy 12.55
Cycloanemization 12.74
Cyclocryotherapy 12.72
Cyclodialysis (initial) (subsequent) 12.55
Cyclodiathermy (penetrating) (surface) 12.71
Cycloelectrolysis 12.71
Cyclophotocoagulation 12.73
Cyclotomy 12.55
Cystectomy — *see also* Excision, lesion, by site
  gallbladder — *see* Cholecystectomy
  urinary (partial) (subtotal) 57.6
    complete (with urethrectomy) 57.79
    radical 57.71
      with pelvic exenteration (female) 68.8
    total (with urethrectomy) 57.79
Cystocolostomy 57.88
Cystogram, cystography NEC 87.77
Cystolithalapaxy 57.0
Cystolithotomy 57.19
Cystometrogram 89.22
Cystopexy NEC 57.89
Cystoplasty NEC 57.89
Cystoproctostomy 57.88
Cystoprostatectomy, radical 57.71
Cystopyelography 87.74
Cystorrhaphy 57.81
Cystoscopy (transurethral) 57.32
  for
    control of hemorrhage
      bladder 57.93
      prostate 60.94
    retrograde pyelography 87.74
  with biopsy 57.33
  ileal conduit 56.35
  through stoma (artificial) 57.31
Cystostomy
  closed (suprapubic) (percutaneous) 57.17
  open (suprapubic) 57.18
  percutaneous (closed) (suprapubic) 57.17
  suprapubic
    closed 57.17
    open 57.18
Cystotomy (open) (for removal of calculi) 57.19
Cystourethrogram (retrograde) (voiding) 87.76
Cystourethropexy (by) 59.79
  levator muscle sling 59.71
  retropubic suspension 59.5
  suprapubic suspension 59.4
Cystourethroplasty 57.85
Cystourethroscopy 57.32
  with biopsy
    bladder 57.33
    ureter 56.33
Cytology — *see* Examination, microscopic

D

Dacryoadenectomy 09.20
  partial 09.22
  total 09.23
Dacryoadenotomy 09.0
Dacryocystectomy (complete) (partial) 09.6
Dacryocystogram 87.05
Dacryocystorhinostomy (DCR) (by intubation) (external) (intranasal) 09.81
Dacryocystostomy 09.53

▽ Subterms under main terms may continue to next column or page

Dacryocystosyringotomy 09.53
Dacryocystotomy 09.53
Dahlman operation (excision of esophageal diverticulum) 42.31
Dana operation (posterior rhizotomy) 03.1
Danforth operation (fetal) 73.8
Darrach operation (ulnar resection) 77.83
da Vinci® (S HD) Surgical System — see category 17.4 ☑
Davis operation (intubated ureterotomy) 56.2
Deaf training 95.49
Debridement
　abdominal wall 54.3
　bone (see also Excision, lesion, bone) 77.60
　　fracture — see Debridement, open fracture
　brain 01.59
　burn (skin) 86.28
　　excisional 86.22
　　nonexcisional 86.28
　bursa 83.5
　cerebral meninges 01.51
　dental 96.54
　fascia 83.39
　flap graft 86.75
　graft (flap) (pedicle) 86.75
　heart valve (calcified) — see Valvuloplasty, heart
　infection (skin) 86.28
　　excisional 86.22
　　nail (bed) (fold) 86.27
　　nonexcisional 86.28
　joint — see Excision, lesion, joint
　meninges (cerebral) 01.51
　　spinal 03.4
　muscle 83.45
　　hand 82.36
　nail (bed) (fold) 86.27
　nerve (peripheral) 04.07
　open fracture (compound) 79.60
　　arm NEC 79.62
　　carpal, metacarpal 79.63
　　facial bone 76.2
　　femur 79.65
　　fibula 79.66
　　foot NEC 79.67
　　hand NEC 79.63
　　humerus 79.61
　　leg NEC 79.66
　　phalanges
　　　foot 79.68
　　　hand 79.64
　　radius 79.62
　　specified site NEC 79.69
　　tarsal, metatarsal 79.67
　　tibia 79.66
　　ulna 79.62
　patella 77.66
　pedicle graft 86.75
　skin or subcutaneous tissue (burn) (infection) (wound) 86.28
　　cardioverter/defibrillator (automatic) pocket 37.79
　　excisional 86.22
　　graft 86.75
　　nail, nail bed, or nail fold 86.27
　　nonexcisional 86.28
　　pacemaker pocket 37.79
　　pocket
　　　cardiac device NEC 37.79
　　　cardiac pacemaker 37.79
　　　cardioverter/defibrillator (automatic) 37.79
　skull 01.25
　　compound fracture 02.02
　spinal cord (meninges) 03.4
　tendon 83.39
　VersaJet™ 86.28
　wound (skin) 86.28
　　excisional 86.22
　　nonexcisional 86.28
Decapitation, fetal 73.8
Decapsulation, kidney 55.91
Declotting — see also Removal, thrombus
　arteriovenous cannula or shunt 39.49
Decompression
　anus (imperforate) 48.0

Decompression — continued
　biliary tract 51.49
　　by intubation 51.43
　　　endoscopic 51.87
　　　percutaneous 51.98
　brain 01.24
　carpal tunnel 04.43
　cauda equina 03.09
　chamber 93.97
　colon 96.08
　　by incision 45.03
　　endoscopic (balloon) 46.85
　common bile duct 51.42
　　by intubation 51.43
　　　endoscopic 51.87
　　　percutaneous 51.98
　cranial 01.24
　　for skull fracture 02.02
　endolymphatic sac 20.79
　ganglion (peripheral) NEC 04.49
　　cranial NEC 04.42
　gastric 96.07
　heart 37.0
　intestine 96.08
　　by incision 45.00
　　endoscopic (balloon) 46.85
　intracranial 01.24
　labyrinth 20.79
　laminectomy 03.09
　laminotomy 03.09
　median nerve 04.43
　muscle 83.02
　　hand 82.02
　nerve (peripheral) NEC 04.49
　　auditory 04.42
　　cranial NEC 04.42
　　median 04.43
　　trigeminal (root) 04.41
　orbit (see also Orbitotomy) 16.09
　pancreatic duct 52.92
　　endoscopic 52.93
　pericardium 37.0
　rectum 48.0
　skull fracture 02.02
　spinal cord (canal) 03.09
　tarsal tunnel 04.44
　tendon (sheath) 83.01
　　hand 82.01
　thoracic outlet
　　by
　　　myotomy (division of scalenus anticus muscle) 83.19
　　　tenotomy 83.13
　trigeminal (nerve root) 04.41
Decortication
　arterial 05.25
　brain 01.51
　cerebral meninges 01.51
　heart 37.31
　kidney 55.91
　lung (partial) (total) 34.51
　　thoracoscopic 34.52
　nasal turbinates — see Turbinectomy
　nose 21.89
　ovary 65.29
　　laparoscopic 65.25
　periarterial 05.25
　pericardium 37.31
　ventricle, heart (complete) 37.31
Decoy, E2F 00.16
Deepening
　alveolar ridge 24.5
　buccolabial sulcus 24.91
　lingual sulcus 24.91
Defatting, flap or pedicle graft 86.75
Defibrillation, electric (external) (internal) 99.62
　automatic cardioverter/defibrillator — see category 37.9 ☑
de Grandmont operation (tarsectomy) 08.35
Delaying of pedicle graft 86.71
Delivery (with)
　assisted spontaneous 73.59
　breech extraction (assisted) 72.52
　　partial 72.52
　　　with forceps to aftercoming head 72.51
　　total 72.54

Delivery — continued
　breech extraction — continued
　　total — continued
　　　with forceps to aftercoming head 72.53
　　　unassisted (spontaneous delivery) — omit code
　cesarean section — see Cesarean section
　Credé maneuver 73.59
　De Lee maneuver 72.4
　forceps 72.9
　　application to aftercoming head (Piper) 72.6
　　with breech extraction
　　　partial 72.51
　　　total 72.53
　　Barton's 72.4
　　failed 73.3
　　high 72.39
　　　with episiotomy 72.31
　　low (outlet) 72.0
　　　with episiotomy 72.1
　　mid 72.29
　　　with episiotomy 72.21
　　outlet (low) 72.0
　　　with episiotomy 72.1
　　rotation of fetal head 72.4
　　trial 73.3
　instrumental NEC 72.9
　　specified NEC 72.8
　key-in-lock rotation 72.4
　Kielland rotation 72.4
　Malström's extraction 72.79
　　with episiotomy 72.71
　manually assisted (spontaneous) 73.59
　spontaneous (unassisted) 73.59
　　assisted 73.59
　vacuum extraction 72.79
　　with episiotomy 72.71
Delorme operation
　pericardiectomy 37.31
　proctopexy 48.76
　repair of prolapsed rectum 48.76
　thoracoplasty 33.34
Denervation
　aortic body 39.8
　carotid body 39.8
　facet, percutaneous (radiofrequency) 03.96
　ovarian 65.94
　paracervical uterine 69.3
　uterosacral 69.3
Denker operation (radical maxillary antrotomy) 22.31
Dennis-Barco operation — see Repair, hernia, femoral
Denonvillier operation (limited rhinoplasty) 21.86
Densitometry, bone (serial) (radiographic) 88.98
Depilation, skin 86.92
Derlacki operation (tympanoplasty) 19.4
Dermabond 86.59
Dermabrasion (laser) 86.25
　for wound debridement 86.28
Derotation — see Reduction, torsion
Desensitization
　allergy 99.12
　psychologic 94.33
Desmotomy — see also Division, ligament 80.40
Destruction
　breast 85.20
　chorioretinopathy (see also Destruction, lesion, choroid) 14.29
　ciliary body 12.74
　epithelial downgrowth, anterior chamber 12.93
　fallopian tube 66.39
　　with
　　　crushing (and ligation) 66.31
　　　　by endoscopy (laparoscopy) 66.21
　　　division (and ligation) 66.32
　　　　by endoscopy (culdoscopy) (hysteroscopy) (laparoscopy) (peritoneoscopy) 66.22
　　　ligation 66.39
　　　　with
　　　　　crushing 66.31

Destruction — continued
　fallopian tube — continued
　　with — continued
　　　ligation — continued
　　　　with — continued
　　　　　crushing — continued
　　　　　　by endoscopy (laparoscopy) 66.21
　　　　　division 66.32
　　　　　　by endoscopy (culdoscopy) (hysteroscopy) (laparoscopy) (peritoneoscopy) 66.22
　fetus 73.8
　hemorrhoids 49.49
　　by
　　　cryotherapy 49.44
　　　sclerotherapy 49.42
　inner ear NEC 20.79
　　by injection 20.72
　intervertebral disc (NOS) 80.50
　　by injection 80.52
　　by other specified method 80.59
　　herniated (nucleus pulposus) 80.51
　LAA 37.36
　lacrimal sac 09.6
　left atrial appendage 37.36
　lesion (local)
　　anus 49.39
　　　endoscopic 49.31
　　Bartholin's gland 71.24
　　　by
　　　　aspiration 71.21
　　　　excision 71.24
　　　　incision 71.22
　　　　marsupialization 71.23
　　biliary ducts 51.69
　　　endoscopic 51.64
　　bladder 57.59
　　　transurethral 57.49
　　bone — see Excision, lesion, bone
　　bowel — see Destruction, lesion, intestine
　　brain (transtemporal approach) NEC 01.59
　　　by stereotactic radiosurgery 92.30
　　　　cobalt 60 92.32
　　　　linear accelerator (LINAC) 92.31
　　　　multi-source 92.32
　　　　particle beam 92.33
　　　　particulate 92.33
　　　　radiosurgery NEC 92.39
　　　　single source photon 92.31
　　breast NEC 85.20
　　bronchus NEC 32.09
　　　endoscopic 32.01
　　cerebral NEC 01.59
　　　meninges 01.51
　　cervix 67.39
　　　by
　　　　cauterization 67.32
　　　　cryosurgery, cryoconization 67.33
　　　　electroconization 67.32
　　choroid 14.29
　　　by
　　　　cryotherapy 14.22
　　　　diathermy 14.21
　　　　implantation of radiation source 14.27
　　　　photocoagulation 14.25
　　　　　laser 14.24
　　　　　xenon arc 14.23
　　　　radiation therapy 14.26
　　ciliary body (nonexcisional) 12.43
　　　by excision 12.44
　　conjunctiva 10.32
　　　by excision 10.31
　　cornea NEC 11.49
　　　by
　　　　cryotherapy 11.43
　　　　electrocauterization 11.42
　　　　thermocauterization 11.42
　　cul-de-sac 70.32
　　duodenum NEC 45.32
　　　by excision 45.31
　　　endoscopic 45.30
　　　endoscopic 45.30

Destruction — *continued*
lesion — *continued*
esophagus (chemosurgery) (cryosurgery) (electroresection) (fulguration) NEC 42.39
by excision 42.32
endoscopic 42.33
endoscopic 42.33
eye NEC 16.93
eyebrow 08.25
eyelid 08.25
excisional — *see* Excision, lesion, eyelid
heart
by catheter ablation 37.34
by endovascular approach 37.34
by open approach 37.33
left atrial appendage 37.36
intestine (large) 45.49
by excision 45.41
endoscopic 45.43
polypectomy 45.42
endoscopic 45.43
polypectomy 45.42
small 45.34
by excision 45.33
intranasal 21.31
iris (nonexcisional) NEC 12.41
by excision 12.42
kidney 55.39
by marsupialization 55.31
lacrimal sac 09.6
larynx 30.09
liver 50.29
lung 32.29
endoscopic 32.28
meninges (cerebral) 01.51
spinal 03.4
nerve (peripheral) 04.07
sympathetic 05.29
nose 21.30
intranasal 21.31
specified NEC 21.32
ovary
by
aspiration 65.91
excision 65.29
laparoscopic 65.25
cyst by rupture (manual) 65.93
palate (bony) (local) 27.31
wide 27.32
pancreas 52.22
by marsupialization 52.3
endoscopic 52.21
pancreatic duct 52.22
endoscopic 52.21
penis 64.2
pharynx (excisional) NEC 29.39
pituitary gland
by stereotactic radiosurgery 92.30
cobalt 60 92.32
linear accelerator (LINAC) 92.31
multi-source 92.32
particle beam 92.33
particulate 92.33
radiosurgery NEC 92.39
single source photon 92.31
rectum (local) 48.32
by
cryosurgery 48.34
electrocoagulation 48.32
excision 48.35
fulguration 48.32
laser (Argon) 48.33
polyp 48.36
radical 48.31
retina 14.29
by
cryotherapy 14.22
diathermy 14.21
implantation of radiation source 14.27
photocoagulation 14.25
laser 14.24
xenon arc 14.23
radiation therapy 14.26
salivary gland NEC 26.29

Destruction — *continued*
lesion — *continued*
salivary gland — *continued*
by marsupialization 26.21
sclera 12.84
scrotum 61.3
skin NEC 86.3
sphincter of Oddi 51.69
endoscopic 51.64
spinal cord (meninges) 03.4
spleen 41.42
by marsupialization 41.41
stomach NEC 43.49
by excision 43.42
endoscopic 43.41
endoscopic 43.41
subcutaneous tissue NEC 86.3
testis 62.2
tongue 25.1
urethra (excisional) 58.39
endoscopic 58.31
uterus 68.29
nerve (cranial) (peripheral) (by cryoanalgesia) (by radiofrequency) 04.2
sympathetic, by injection of neurolytic agent 05.32
neuroma
acoustic 04.01
by craniotomy 04.01
by stereotactic radiosurgery 92.30
cobalt 60 92.32
linear accelerator (LINAC) 92.31
multi-source 92.32
particle beam 92.33
particulate 92.33
radiosurgery NEC 92.39
single source photon 92.31
cranial 04.07
Morton's 04.07
peripheral
Morton's 04.07
prostate (prostatic tissue)
by
cryotherapy 60.62
microwave 60.96
radiofrequency 60.97
transurethral microwave thermotherapy (TUMT) 60.96
transurethral needle ablation (TUNA) 60.97
TULIP (transurethral) (ultrasound) guided laser induced prostatectomy 60.21
TUMT (transurethral microwave thermotherapy) 60.96
TUNA (transurethral needle ablation) 60.97
semicircular canals, by injection 20.72
vestibule, by injection 20.72
Detachment, uterosacral ligaments 69.3
Determination
mental status (clinical) (medicolegal) (psychiatric) NEC 94.11
psychologic NEC 94.09
vital capacity (pulmonary) 89.37
Detorsion
intestine (twisted) (volvulus) 46.80
large 46.82
endoscopic (balloon) 46.85
small 46.81
kidney 55.84
ovary 65.95
spermatic cord 63.52
with orchiopexy 62.5
testis 63.52
with orchiopexy 62.5
volvulus 46.80
endoscopic (balloon) 46.85
Detoxification therapy 94.25
alcohol 94.62
with rehabilitation 94.63
combined alcohol and drug 94.68
with rehabilitation 94.69
drug 94.65
with rehabilitation 94.66
combined alcohol and drug 94.68
with rehabilitation 94.69
Devascularization, stomach 44.99

Device
CorCap™ 37.41
external fixator — *see* Fixator, external
Dewebbing
esophagus 42.01
syndactyly (fingers) (toes) 86.85
Dextrorotation — *see* Reduction, torsion
Dialysis
hemodiafiltration, hemofiltration (extracorporeal) 39.95
kidney (extracorporeal) 39.95
liver 50.92
peritoneal 54.98
renal (extracorporeal) 39.95
Diaphanoscopy
nasal sinuses 89.35
skull (newborn) 89.16
Diaphysectomy — *see* category 77.8 ☑
Diathermy 93.34
choroid — *see* Diathermy, retina
nasal turbinates 21.61
retina
for
destruction of lesion 14.21
reattachment 14.51
repair of tear 14.31
surgical — *see* Destruction, lesion, by site
turbinates (nasal) 21.61
Dickson-Diveley operation (tendon transfer and arthrodesis to correct claw toe) 77.57
Dickson operation (fascial transplant) 83.82
Dieffenbach operation (hip disarticulation) 84.18
Dilation
achalasia 42.92
ampulla of Vater 51.81
endoscopic 51.84
anus, anal (sphincter) 96.23
biliary duct
endoscopic 51.84
pancreatic duct 52.99
endoscopic 52.98
percutaneous (endoscopy) 51.98
sphincter
of Oddi 51.81
endoscopic 51.84
pancreatic 51.82
endoscopic 51.85
bladder 96.25
neck 57.92
bronchus 33.91
cervix (canal) 67.0
obstetrical 73.1
to assist delivery 73.1
choanae (nasopharynx) 29.91
colon (endoscopic) (balloon) 46.85
with insertion of colonic stent ●
endoscopic 46.86 ●
other 46.87 ●
colostomy stoma 96.24
duodenum (endoscopic) (balloon) 46.85
with insertion of colonic stent ●
endoscopic 46.86 ●
other 46.87 ●
endoscopic — *see* Dilation, by site
enterostomy stoma 96.24
esophagus (by bougie) (by sound) 42.92
fallopian tube 66.96
foreskin (newborn) 99.95
frontonasal duct 96.21
gastrojejunostomy site, endoscopic 44.22
heart valve — *see* Valvulotomy, heart
ileostomy stoma 96.24
ileum (endoscopic) (balloon) 46.85
with insertion of colonic stent ●
endoscopic 46.86 ●
other 46.87 ●
intestinal stoma (artificial) 96.24
intestine (endoscopic) (balloon) 46.85
with insertion of colonic stent ●
endoscopic 46.86 ●
other 46.87 ●
jejunum (endoscopic) (balloon) 46.85
with insertion of colonic stent ●
endoscopic 46.86 ●
other 46.87 ●

Dilation — *continued*
lacrimal
duct 09.42
punctum 09.41
larynx 31.98
lymphatic structure(s) (peripheral) 40.9
nares 21.99
nasolacrimal duct (retrograde) 09.43
with insertion of tube or stent 09.44
nasopharynx 29.91
pancreatic duct 52.99
endoscopic 52.98
pharynx 29.91
prostatic urethra (transurethral) (balloon) 60.95
punctum, lacrimal papilla 09.41
pylorus
by incision 44.21
endoscopic 44.22
rectum 96.22
salivary duct 26.91
sphenoid ostia 22.52
sphincter
anal 96.23
cardiac 42.92
of Oddi 51.81
endoscopic 51.84
pancreatic 51.82
endoscopic 51.85
pylorus, endoscopic 44.22
by incision 44.21
Stenson's duct 26.91
trachea 31.99
ureter 59.8
meatus 56.91
ureterovesical orifice 59.8
urethra 58.6
prostatic (transurethral) (balloon) 60.95
urethrovesical junction 58.6
vagina (instrumental) (manual) NEC 96.16
vesical neck 57.92
Wharton's duct 26.91
Wirsung's duct 52.99
endoscopic 52.98
Dilation and curettage, uterus (diagnostic) 69.09
after
abortion 69.02
delivery 69.02
to terminate pregnancy 69.01
Diminution, ciliary body 12.74
Disarticulation 84.91
ankle 84.13
elbow 84.06
finger, except thumb 84.01
thumb 84.02
hip 84.18
knee 84.16
shoulder 84.08
thumb 84.02
toe 84.11
wrist 84.04
● **Discectomy** — *see* Diskectomy
● **Discission**
capsular membrane 13.64
cataract (Wheeler knife) (Ziegler knife) 13.2
congenital 13.69
secondary membrane 13.64
iris 12.12
lens (capsule) (Wheeler knife) (Ziegler knife) (with capsulotomy) 13.2
orbitomaxillary, radical 16.51
pupillary 13.2
secondary membrane (after cataract) 13.64
vitreous strands (posterior approach) 14.74
anterior approach 14.73
Discogram, diskogram 87.21
Discolysis (by injection) 80.52
Diskectomy (discectomy), intervertebral 80.51
with corpectomy 80.99
herniated (nucleus pulposus) 80.51
percutaneous 80.59
Dispensing (with fitting)
contact lens 95.32
low vision aids NEC 95.33
spectacles 95.31

☑ Additional Digit Required — Refer to the Tabular List for Digit Selection

Subterms under main terms may continue to next column or page

Disruption
blood brain barrier via infusion [BBBD] 00.19
Dissection — *see also* Excision
aneurysm 38.60
artery-vein-nerve bundle 39.91
branchial cleft fistula or sinus 29.52
bronchus 32.1
femoral hernia 53.29
groin, radical 40.54
larynx block (en bloc) 30.3
mediastinum with pneumonectomy 32.59
thoracoscopic 32.50
neck, radical 40.40
with laryngectomy 30.4
bilateral 40.42
unilateral 40.41
orbital fibrous bands 16.92
pterygium (with reposition) 11.31
radical neck — *see* Dissection, neck, radical
retroperitoneal NEC 59.00
thoracic structures (block) (en bloc) (radical)
(brachial plexus, bronchus, lobe of
lung, ribs, and sympathetic nerves) 32.6
vascular bundle 39.91
Distention, bladder (therapeutic) (intermittent)
96.25
Diversion
biliopancreatic (BPD) 43.7 *[45.51] [45.91]*
with duodenal switch 43.89 *[45.51] [45.91]*
urinary
cutaneous 56.61
ileal conduit 56.51
internal NEC 56.71
uretero-ileostomy 56.51
ureter to
intestine 56.71
skin 56.61
Diversional therapy 93.81
Diverticulectomy
bladder (suprapubic) 57.59
transurethral approach 57.49
duodenum 45.31
endoscopic 45.30
esophagomyotomy 42.7
esophagus 42.31
endoscopic 42.33
hypopharyngeal (by cricopharyngeal myotomy) 29.32
intestine
large 45.41
endoscopic 45.43
small 45.33
kidney 55.39
Meckel's 45.33
pharyngeal (by cricopharyngeal myotomy)
29.32
pharyngoesophageal (by cricopharyngeal
myotomy) 29.32
stomach 43.42
endoscopic 43.41
urethra 58.39
endoscopic 58.31
Division
Achilles tendon 83.11
adductor tendon (hip) 83.12
adhesions — *see* Lysis, adhesions
angle of mandible (open) 76.62
closed 76.61
anterior synechiae 12.32
aponeurosis 83.13
arcuate ligament (spine) — *omit code*
arteriovenous fistula (with ligation) 39.53
artery (with ligation) 38.80
abdominal 38.86
aorta (arch) (ascending) (descending)
38.84
head and neck NEC 38.82
intracranial NEC 38.81
lower limb 38.88
thoracic NEC 38.85
upper limb 38.83
bladder neck 57.91
blepharorrhaphy 08.02
blood vessels, cornea 10.1
bone (*see also* Osteotomy) 77.30
brain tissue 01.32

Division — *continued*
brain tissue — *continued*
cortical adhesions 02.91
canaliculus 09.52
canthorrhaphy 08.02
cartilage 80.40
ankle 80.47
elbow 80.42
foot and toe 80.48
hand and finger 80.44
hip 80.45
knee 80.46
shoulder 80.41
specified site NEC 80.49
spine 80.49
wrist 80.43
cerebral tracts 01.32
chordae tendineae 35.32
common wall between posterior left atrium
and coronary sinus (with roofing of resultant defect with patch graft) 35.82
congenital web
larynx 31.98
pharynx 29.54
endometrial synechiae 68.21
fallopian tube — *see* Ligation, fallopian tube
fascia 83.14
hand 82.12
frenulum, frenum
labial 27.91
lingual 25.91
tongue 25.91
ganglion, sympathetic 05.0
glossopharyngeal nerve 29.92
goniosynechiae 12.31
hypophyseal stalk (*see also* Hypophysectomy,
partial) 07.63
iliotibial band 83.14
isthmus
horseshoe kidney 55.85
thyroid 06.91
joint capsule 80.40
ankle 80.47
elbow 80.42
foot and toe 80.48
hand and finger 80.44
hip 80.45
knee 80.46
shoulder 80.41
specified site NEC 80.49
wrist 80.43
labial frenum 27.91
lacrimal ductules 09.0
laryngeal nerve (external) (recurrent) (superior)
31.91
ligament 80.40
ankle 80.47
arcuate (spine) — *omit code*
canthal 08.36
elbow 80.42
foot and toe 80.48
hand and finger 80.44
hip 80.45
knee 80.46
palpebrae 08.36
shoulder 80.41
specified site NEC 80.49
spine 80.49
arcuate — *omit code*
flavum — *omit code*
uterosacral 69.3
wrist 80.43
ligamentum flavum (spine) — *omit code*
meninges (cerebral) 01.31
muscle 83.19
hand 82.19
nasolacrimal duct stricture (with drainage)
09.59
nerve (cranial) (peripheral) NEC 04.03
acoustic 04.01
adrenal gland 07.42
auditory 04.01
glossopharyngeal 29.92
lacrimal branch 05.0
laryngeal (external) (recurrent) (superior)
31.91

Division — *continued*
nerve — *continued*
phrenic 04.03
for collapse of lung 33.31
root, spinal or intraspinal 03.1
sympathetic 05.0
tracts
cerebral 01.32
spinal cord 03.29
percutaneous 03.21
trigeminal 04.02
vagus (*see also* Vagotomy) 44.00
vestibular 04.01
otosclerotic process or material, middle ear
19.0
papillary muscle (heart) 35.31
patent ductus arteriosus 38.85
penile adhesions 64.93
posterior synechiae 12.33
pylorus (with wedge resection) 43.3
rectum (stricture) 48.91
scalenus anticus muscle 83.19
Skene's gland 71.3
soft tissue NEC 83.19
hand 82.19
sphincter
anal (external) (internal) 49.59
left lateral 49.51
posterior 49.52
cardiac 42.7
of Oddi 51.82
endoscopic 51.85
pancreatic 51.82
endoscopic 51.85
spinal
cord tracts 03.29
percutaneous 03.21
nerve root 03.1
symblepharon (with insertion of conformer)
10.5
synechiae
endometrial 68.21
iris (posterior) 12.33
anterior 12.32
tarsorrhaphy 08.02
tendon 83.13
Achilles 83.11
adductor (hip) 83.12
hand 82.11
trabeculae carneae cordis (heart) 35.35
tympanum 20.23
uterosacral ligaments 69.3
vaginal septum 70.14
vas deferens 63.71
vein (with ligation) 38.80
abdominal 38.87
head and neck NEC 38.82
intracranial NEC 38.81
lower limb 38.89
varicose 38.59
thoracic NEC 38.85
upper limb 38.83
varicose 38.50
abdominal 38.57
head and neck NEC 38.52
intracranial NEC 38.51
lower limb 38.59
thoracic NEC 38.55
upper limb 38.53
vitreous, cicatricial bands (posterior approach)
14.74
anterior approach 14.73
Doleris operation (shortening of round ligaments) 69.22
D'Ombrain operation (excision of pterygium
with corneal graft) 11.32
Domestic tasks therapy 93.83
Dopplergram, Doppler flow mapping — *see
also* Ultrasonography
aortic arch 88.73
head and neck 88.71
heart 88.72
thorax NEC 88.73
Dorrance operation (push-back operation for
cleft palate) 27.62

Dotter operation (transluminal angioplasty)
39.59
Douche, vaginal 96.44
Douglas' operation (suture of tongue to lip for
micrognathia) 25.59
Downstream® System (AO therapy) (aqueous
oxygen) 00.49
Doyle operation (paracervical uterine denervation) 69.3
Drainage
by
anastomosis — *see* Anastomosis
aspiration — *see* Aspiration
incision — *see* Incision
abdomen 54.19
percutaneous 54.91
abscess (*see also* Drainage, by site *and* Incision,
by site)
appendix 47.2
with appendectomy 47.09
laparoscopic 47.01
parapharyngeal (oral) (transcervical) 28.0
peritonsillar (oral) (transcervical) 28.0
retropharyngeal (oral) (transcervical) 28.0
thyroid (field) (gland) 06.09
percutaneous (needle) 06.01
postoperative 06.02
tonsil, tonsillar (oral) (transcervical) 28.0
antecubital fossa 86.04
appendix 47.91
with appendectomy 47.09
laparoscopic 47.01
abscess 47.2
with appendectomy 47.09
laparoscopic 47.01
axilla 86.04
bladder (without incision) 57.0
by indwelling catheter 57.94
percutaneous suprapubic (closed)
57.17
suprapubic NEC 57.18
buccal space 27.0
bursa 83.03
by aspiration 83.94
hand 82.92
hand 82.03
by aspiration 82.92
radial 82.03
ulnar 82.03
cerebrum, cerebral (meninges) (ventricle) (incision) (trephination) 01.39
by
anastomosis — *see* Shunt, ventricular
aspiration 01.09
through previously implanted
catheter 01.02
chest (closed) 34.04
open (by incision) 34.09
thoracoscopic 34.06
cranial sinus (incision) (trephination) 01.21
by aspiration 01.09
cul-de-sac 70.12
by aspiration 70.0
cyst (*see also* Drainage, by site *and* Incision, by
site)
pancreas (by catheter) 52.01
by marsupialization 52.3
internal (anastomosis) 52.4
pilonidal 86.03
spleen, splenic (by marsupialization) 41.41
duodenum (tube) 46.39
by incision 45.01
ear
external 18.09
inner 20.79
middle (by myringotomy) 20.09
with intubation 20.01
epidural space, cerebral (incision) (trephination) 01.24
by aspiration 01.09
extradural space, cerebral (incision) (trephination) 01.24
by aspiration 01.09
extraperitoneal 54.0
facial region 27.0
fascial compartments, head and neck 27.0

Drainage — *continued*
  fetal hydrocephalic head (needling) (trocar) 73.8
  gallbladder 51.04
    by
      anastomosis 51.35
      aspiration 51.01
      incision 51.04
  groin region (abdominal wall) (inguinal) 54.0
    skin 86.04
    subcutaneous tissue 86.04
  hematoma — *see* Drainage, by site *and* Incision, by site
  hydrocephalic head (needling) (trocar) 73.8
  hypochondrium 54.0
    intra-abdominal 54.19
  iliac fossa 54.0
  infratemporal fossa 27.0
  intracranial space (epidural) (extradural) (incision) (trephination) 01.24
    by aspiration 01.09
    subarachnoid or subdural (incision) (trephination) 01.31
      by aspiration 01.09
  intraperitoneal 54.19
    percutaneous 54.91
  kidney (by incision) 55.01
    by
      anastomosis 55.86
      catheter 59.8
      pelvis (by incision) 55.11
  liver 50.0
    by aspiration 50.91
  Ludwig's angina 27.0
  lung (by incision) 33.1
    by punch (needle) (trocar) 33.93
  midpalmar space 82.04
  mouth floor 27.0
  mucocele, nasal sinus 22.00
    by puncture 22.01
    through natural ostium 22.02
  omentum 54.19
    percutaneous 54.91
  ovary (aspiration) 65.91
    by incision 65.09
    laparoscopic 65.01
  palmar space (middle) 82.04
  pancreas (by catheter) 52.01
    by anastomosis 52.96
  parapharyngeal 28.0
  paronychia 86.04
  parotid space 27.0
  pelvic peritoneum (female) 70.12
    male 54.19
  pericardium 37.0
  perigastric 54.19
    percutaneous 54.91
  perineum
    female 71.09
    male 86.04
  perisplenic tissue 54.19
    percutaneous 54.91
  peritoneum 54.19
    pelvic (female) 70.12
    percutaneous 54.91
  peritonsillar 28.0
  pharyngeal space, lateral 27.0
  pilonidal cyst or sinus 86.03
  pleura (closed) 34.04
    open (by incision) 34.09
    thoracoscopic 34.06
  popliteal space 86.04
  postural 93.99
  postzygomatic space 27.0
  pseudocyst, pancreas 52.3
    by anastomosis 52.4
  pterygopalatine fossa 27.0
  retropharyngeal 28.0
  scrotum 61.0
  skin 86.04
  spinal (canal) (cord) 03.09
    by anastomosis — *see* Shunt, spinal
    diagnostic 03.31
  spleen 41.2
    cyst (by marsupialization) 41.41

Drainage — *continued*
  subarachnoid space, cerebral (incision) (trephination) 01.31
    by aspiration 01.09
  subcutaneous tissue 86.04
  subdiaphragmatic 54.19
    percutaneous 54.91
  subdural space, cerebral (incision) (trephination) 01.31
    by aspiration 01.09
  subhepatic space 54.19
    percutaneous 54.91
  sublingual space 27.0
  submental space 27.0
  subphrenic space 54.19
    percutaneous 54.91
  supraclavicular fossa 86.04
  temporal pouches 27.0
  tendon (sheath) 83.01
    hand 82.01
  thenar space 82.04
  thorax (closed) 34.04
    open (by incision) 34.09
    thoracoscopic 34.06
  thyroglossal tract (by incision) 06.09
    by aspiration 06.01
  thyroid (field) (gland) (by incision) 06.09
    by aspiration 06.01
    postoperative 06.02
  tonsil 28.0
  tunica vaginalis 61.0
  ureter (by catheter) 59.8
    by
      anastomosis NEC (*see also* Anastomosis, ureter) 56.79
      incision 56.2
  ventricle (cerebral) (incision) NEC 02.39
    by
      anastomosis — *see* Shunt, ventricular
      aspiration 01.09
        through previously implanted catheter 01.02
  vertebral column 03.09
Drawing test 94.08
Dressing
  burn 93.57
  ulcer 93.56
  wound 93.57
Drilling
  bone (*see also* Incision, bone) 77.10
  ovary 65.99
Drotrecogin alfa (activated), infusion 00.11
Ductogram, mammary 87.35
Duhamel operation (abdominoperineal pull-through) 48.65
Dührssen's
  incisions (cervix, to assist delivery) 73.93
  operation (vaginofixation of uterus) 69.22
Dunn operation (triple arthrodesis) 81.12
Duodenectomy 45.62
  with
    gastrectomy — *see* Gastrectomy
    pancreatectomy — *see* Pancreatectomy
Duodenocholedochotomy 51.51
Duodenoduodenostomy 45.91
  proximal to distal segment 45.62
Duodenoileostomy 45.91
Duodenojejunostomy 45.91
Duodenoplasty 46.79
Duodenorrhaphy 46.71
Duodenoscopy 45.13
  through stoma (artificial) 45.12
  transabdominal (operative) 45.11
Duodenostomy 46.39
Duodenotomy 45.01
Dupuytren operation
  fasciectomy 82.35
  fasciotomy 82.12
    with excision 82.35
  shoulder disarticulation 84.08
Durabond 86.59
Duraplasty 02.12
Durham (-Caldwell) operation (transfer of biceps femoris tendon) 83.75
DuToit and Roux operation (staple capsulorrhaphy of shoulder) 81.82

DuVries operation (tenoplasty) 83.88
Dwyer operation
  fasciotomy 83.14
  soft tissue release NEC 83.84
  wedge osteotomy, calcaneus 77.28

E

E2F decoy 00.16
Eagleton operation (extrapetrosal drainage) 20.22
ECG — *see* Electrocardiogram
Echocardiography 88.72
  intracardiac (heart chambers) (ICE) 37.28
  intravascular (coronary vessels) 00.24
  transesophageal 88.72
    monitoring (Doppler) (ultrasound) 89.68
Echoencephalography 88.71
Echography — *see* Ultrasonography
Echogynography 88.79
Echoplacentogram 88.78
EC-IC vascular bypass 39.28
ECMO (extracorporeal membrane oxygenation) 39.65
Eden-Hybinette operation (glenoid bone block) 78.01
Educational therapy (bed-bound children) (handicapped) 93.82
EEG (electroencephalogram) 89.14
  monitoring (radiographic) (video) 89.19
Effler operation (heart) 36.2
Effleurage 93.39
EGD (esophagogastroduodenoscopy) 45.13
  with closed biopsy 45.16
Eggers operation
  tendon release (patellar retinacula) 83.13
  tendon transfer (biceps femoris tendon) (hamstring tendon) 83.75
EKG — *see also* Electrocardiogram 89.52
Elastic hosiery 93.59
Electrocardiogram (with 12 or more leads) 89.52
  with vectorcardiogram 89.53
  fetal (scalp), intrauterine 75.32
  rhythm (with one to three leads) 89.51
Electrocautery — *see also* Cauterization
  cervix 67.32
  corneal lesion (ulcer) 11.42
  esophagus 42.39
    endoscopic 42.33
Electrocoagulation — *see also* Destruction, lesion, by site
  aneurysm (cerebral) (peripheral vessels) 39.52
  cervix 67.32
  cystoscopic 57.49
  ear
    external 18.29
    inner 20.79
    middle 20.51
  fallopian tube (lesion) 66.61
    for tubal ligation — *see* Ligation, fallopian tube
  gasserian ganglion 04.02
  nasal turbinates 21.61
  nose, for epistaxis (with packing) 21.03
  ovary 65.29
    laparoscopic 65.25
  prostatic bed 60.94
  rectum (polyp) 48.32
    radical 48.31
  retina (for)
    destruction of lesion 14.21
    reattachment 14.51
    repair of tear 14.31
  round ligament 69.19
  semicircular canals 20.79
  urethrovesical junction, transurethral 57.49
  uterine ligament 69.19
  uterosacral ligament 69.19
  uterus 68.29
  vagina 70.33
  vulva 71.3
Electrocochleography 20.31
Electroconization, cervix 67.32
Electroconvulsive therapy (ECT) 94.27
Electroencephalogram (EEG) 89.14
  monitoring (radiographic) (video) 89.19
Electrogastrogram 44.19

Electrokeratotomy 11.49
Electrolysis
  ciliary body 12.71
  hair follicle 86.92
  retina (for)
    destruction of lesion 14.21
    reattachment 14.51
    repair of tear 14.31
  skin 86.92
  subcutaneous tissue 86.92
Electromyogram, electromyography (EMG) (muscle) 93.08
  eye 95.25
  urethral sphincter 89.23
Electronarcosis 94.29
Electronic gaiter 93.59
Electronystagmogram (ENG) 95.24
Electro-oculogram (EOG) 95.22
Electroresection — *see also* Destruction, lesion, by site
  bladder neck (transurethral) 57.49
  esophagus 42.39
    endoscopic 42.33
  prostate (transurethral) 60.29
  stomach 43.49
    endoscopic 43.41
Electroretinogram (ERG) 95.21
Electroshock therapy (EST) 94.27
  subconvulsive 94.26
Elevation
  bone fragments (fractured)
    orbit 76.79
    sinus (nasal)
      frontal 22.79
      maxillary 22.79
    skull (with debridement) 02.02
    spinal 03.53
  pedicle graft 86.71
Elliot operation (scleral trephination with iridectomy) 12.61
Ellis Jones operation (repair of peroneal tendon) 83.88
Ellison operation (reinforcement of collateral ligament) 81.44
Elmslie-Cholmeley operation (tarsal wedge osteotomy) 77.28
Eloesser operation
  thoracoplasty 33.34
  thoracostomy 34.09
Elongation — *see* Lengthening
Embolectomy 38.00
  with endarterectomy — *see* Endarterectomy
  abdominal
    artery 38.06
    vein 38.07
  aorta (arch) (ascending) (descending) 38.04
  arteriovenous shunt or cannula 39.49
  bovine graft 39.49
  head and neck NEC 38.02
  intracranial NEC 38.01
  lower limb
    artery 38.08
    vein 38.09
  mechanical
    endovascular
      head and neck 39.74
  pulmonary (artery) (vein) 38.05
  thoracic NEC 38.05
  upper limb (artery) (vein) 38.03
Embolization (transcatheter)
  adhesive (glue) 39.79
    head and neck 39.72
  arteriovenous fistula 39.53
    endovascular 39.72
  artery (selective) 38.80
    by
      endovascular approach 39.79
        head and neck vessels
          bare coils 39.75 ●
          bioactive coils 39.76 ●
        percutaneous transcatheter infusion 99.29
    abdominal NEC 38.86
      duodenal (transcatheter) 44.44
      gastric (transcatheter) 44.44
      renal (transcatheter) 38.86

☑ Additional Digit Required — Refer to the Tabular List for Digit Selection   Subterms under main terms may continue to next column or page

☑ Additional Digit Required — Refer to the Tabular List for Digit Selection   ▽ Subterms under main terms may continue to next column or page

16 — Volume 3 · October 2009   ▶◀ Revised Text   ● New Line   ▲ Revised Code   2010 ICD-9-CM

☑ Additional Digit Required — Refer to the Tabular List for Digit Selection ⓦ Subterms under main terms may continue to next column or page

2010 ICD-9-CM ▶◀ Revised Text ● New Line ▲ Revised Code Volume 3 — 17

Excision — *continued*
breast (*see also* Mastectomy) — *continued*
    accessory 85.24
    ectopic 85.24
    nipple 85.25
        accessory 85.24
    segmental 85.23
    supernumerary 85.24
    wedge 85.21
broad ligament 69.19
bronchogenic cyst 32.09
    endoscopic 32.01
bronchus (wide sleeve) NEC 32.1
buccal mucosa 27.49
bulbourethral gland 58.92
bulbous tuberosities (mandible) (maxilla) (fibrous) (osseous) 24.31
bunion (*see also* Bunionectomy) 77.59
bunionette (with osteotomy) 77.54
bursa 83.5
    hand 82.31
canal of Nuck 69.19
cardioma 37.33
carotid body (lesion) (partial) (total) 39.8
cartilage (*see also* Chondrectomy) 80.90
    intervertebral — see category 80.5 ☑
    knee (semilunar) 80.6
    larynx 30.29
    nasal (submucous) 21.5
caruncle, urethra 58.39
    endoscopic 58.31
cataract (*see also* Extraction, cataract) 13.19
    secondary membrane (after cataract) 13.65
cervical
    rib 77.91
    stump 67.4
cervix (stump) NEC 67.4
    cold (knife) 67.2
    conization 67.2
    cryoconization 67.33
    electroconizaton 67.32
chalazion (multiple) (single) 08.21
cholesteatoma — *see* Excision, lesion, by site
choroid plexus 02.14
cicatrix (skin) 86.3
cilia base 08.20
ciliary body, prolapsed 12.98
clavicle (head) (partial) 77.81
    total (complete) 77.91
clitoris 71.4
coarctation of aorta (end-to-end anastomosis) 38.64
    with
        graft replacement (interposition) abdominal 38.44
            thoracic 38.45
            thoracoabdominal 38.45 [38.44]
common
    duct 51.63
    wall between posterior and coronary sinus (with roofing of resultant defect with patch graft) 35.82
condyle — *see* category 77.8 ☑
    mandible 76.5
conjunctival ring 10.31
cornea 11.49
    epithelium (with chemocauterization) 11.41
        for smear or culture 11.21
costal cartilage 80.99
cul-de-sac (Douglas') 70.92
    with graft or prosthesis 70.93
cusp, heart valve 35.10
    aortic 35.11
    mitral 35.12
    tricuspid 35.14
cyst (*see also* Excision, lesion, by site)
    apical (tooth) 23.73
        with root canal therapy 23.72
    Baker's (popliteal) 83.39
    breast 85.21
    broad ligament 69.19
    bronchogenic 32.09
        endoscopic 32.01
    cervix 67.39
    dental 24.4

Excision — *continued*
cyst (*see also* Excision, lesion, by site) — *continued*
    dentigerous 24.4
    epididymis 63.2
    fallopian tube 66.61
    Gartner's duct 70.33
    hand 82.29
    labia 71.3
    lung 32.29
        endoscopic 32.28
        thoracoscopic 32.20
    mesonephric duct 69.19
    Morgagni
        female 66.61
        male 62.2
    Müllerian duct 60.73
    nasolabial 27.49
    nasopalatine 27.31
        by wide excision 27.32
    ovary 65.29
        laparoscopic 65.25
    parovarian 69.19
    pericardium 37.31
    periodontal (apical) (lateral) 24.4
    popliteal (Baker's), knee 83.39
    radicular 24.4
    spleen 41.42
    synovial (membrane) 83.39
    thyroglossal (with resection of hyoid bone) 06.7
    urachal (bladder) 57.51
        abdominal wall 54.3
    vagina (Gartner's duct) 70.33
cystic
    duct remnant 51.61
    hygroma 40.29
dentinoma 24.4
diaphragm 34.81
disc, intervertebral (NOS) 80.50
    herniated (nucleus pulposus) 80.51
    other specified (diskectomy) 80.51
diverticulum
    ampulla of Vater 51.62
    anus 49.39
        endoscopic 49.31
    bladder 57.59
        transurethral 57.49
    duodenum 45.31
        endoscopic 45.30
    esophagus (local) 42.31
        endoscopic 42.33
    hypopharyngeal (by cricopharyngeal myotomy) 29.32
    intestine
        large 45.41
            endoscopic 45.43
        small NEC 45.33
    Meckel's 45.33
    pharyngeal (by cricopharyngeal myotomy) 29.32
    pharyngoesophageal (by cricopharyngeal myotomy) 29.32
    stomach 43.42
        endoscopic 43.41
    urethra 58.39
        endoscopic 58.31
    ventricle, heart 37.33
duct
    Müllerian 69.19
    paramesonephric 69.19
    thyroglossal (with resection of hyoid bone) 06.7
ear, external (complete) NEC 18.39
    partial 18.29
    radical 18.31
ectopic
    abdominal fetus 74.3
    tissue (*see also* Excision, lesion, by site of tissue origin)
        bone, from muscle 83.32
        breast 85.24
        lung 32.29
            endoscopic 32.28
            thoracoscopic 32.20
        spleen 41.93

Excision — *continued*
empyema pocket, lung 34.09
epididymis 63.4
epiglottis 30.21
epithelial downgrowth, anterior chamber (eye) 12.93
epulis (gingiva) 24.31
esophagus (*see also* Esophagectomy) 42.40
exostosis (*see also* Excision, lesion, bone) 77.60
    auditory canal, external 18.29
    facial bone 76.2
    first metatarsal (hallux valgus repair) — *see* Bunionectomy
eye 16.49
    with implant (into Tenon's capsule) 16.42
        with attachment of muscles 16.41
eyelid 08.20
    redundant skin 08.86
falciform ligament 54.4
fallopian tube — *see* Salpingectomy
fascia 83.44
    for graft 83.43
        hand 82.34
    hand 82.35
        for graft 82.34
fat pad NEC 86.3
    knee (infrapatellar) (prepatellar) 86.3
    scalene 40.21
fibroadenoma, breast 85.21
fissure, anus 49.39
    endoscopic 49.31
fistula (*see also* Fistulectomy)
    anal 49.12
    arteriovenous (*see also* Aneurysmectomy) 38.60
    ileorectal 46.74
    lacrimal
        gland 09.21
        sac 09.6
    rectal 48.73
    vesicovaginal 57.84
frenulum, frenum
    labial (lip) 27.41
    lingual (tongue) 25.92
ganglion (hand) (tendon sheath) (wrist) 82.21
    gasserian 04.05
    site other than hand or nerve 83.31
    sympathetic nerve 05.29
    trigeminal nerve 04.05
gastrocolic ligament 54.4
gingiva 24.31
glomus jugulare tumor 20.51
goiter — *see* Thyroidectomy
gum 24.31
hallux valgus (*see also* Bunionectomy)
    with prosthetic implant 77.59
hamartoma, mammary 85.21
heart assist system — *see* Removal
hematocele, tunica vaginalis 61.92
hematoma — *see* Drainage, by site
hemorrhoids (external) (internal) (tag) 49.46
heterotopic bone, from
    muscle 83.32
        hand 82.22
    skin 86.3
    tendon 83.31
        hand 82.21
hydatid cyst, liver 50.29
hydatid of Morgagni
    female 66.61
    male 62.2
hydrocele
    canal of Nuck (female) 69.19
    male 63.1
    round ligament 69.19
    spermatic cord 63.1
    tunica vaginalis 61.2
hygroma, cystic 40.29
hymen (tag) 70.31
hymeno-urethral fusion 70.31
intervertebral disc — *see* Excision, disc, intervertebral (NOS) 80.50
intestine (*see also* Resection, intestine)
    for interposition 45.50
        large 45.52
        small 45.51

Excision — *continued*
intestine (*see also* Resection, intestine) — *continued*
    large (total)
        for interposition 45.52
        laparoscopic 45.81
        local 45.41
            endoscopic 45.43
        open 45.82
        other 45.83
        segmental
            laparoscopic 17.39
            multiple
                laparoscopic 17.31
                open and other 45.71
            open and other 45.79
        unspecified 45.83
    small (total) 45.63
        for interposition 45.51
        local 45.33
        partial 45.62
        segmental 45.62
            multiple 45.61
intraductal papilloma 85.21
iris prolapse 12.13
joint (*see also* Arthrectomy) 80.90
keloid (scar), skin 86.3
LAA 37.36
labia — *see* Vulvectomy
lacrimal
    gland 09.20
        partial 09.22
        total 09.23
    passage 09.6
    sac 09.6
left atrial appendage 37.36
lesion (local)
    abdominal wall 54.3
    accessory sinus — *see* Excision, lesion, nasal sinus
    adenoids 28.92
    adrenal gland(s) 07.21
    alveolus 24.4
    ampulla of Vater 51.62
    anterior chamber (eye) NEC 12.40
    anus 49.39
        endoscopic 49.31
    apocrine gland 86.3
    artery 38.60
        abdominal 38.66
        aorta (arch) (ascending) (descending) thoracic) 38.64
            with end-to-end anastomosis 38.45
                abdominal 38.44
                thoracic 38.45
                thoracoabdominal 38.45 [38.44]
            with graft interposition graft replacement 38.45
                abdominal 38.44
                thoracic 38.45
                thoracoabdominal 38.45 [38.44]
        head and neck NEC 38.62
        intracranial NEC 38.61
        lower limb 38.68
        thoracic NEC 38.65
        upper limb 38.63
    atrium 37.33
    auditory canal or meatus, external 18.29
        radical 18.31
    auricle, ear 18.29
        radical 18.31
    biliary ducts 51.69
        endoscopic 51.64
    bladder (transurethral) 57.49
        open 57.59
        suprapubic 57.59
    blood vessel 38.60
        abdominal
            artery 38.66
            vein 38.67
        aorta (arch) (ascending) (descending) 38.64
        head and neck NEC 38.62
        intracranial NEC 38.61
        lower limb
            artery 38.68

☑ Additional Digit Required — Refer to the Tabular List for Digit Selection   ⵣ Subterms under main terms may continue to next column or page

18 — Volume 3   ▶◀ Revised Text   ● New Line   ▲ Revised Code   **2010 ICD-9-CM**

Excision — *continued*
  lesion — *continued*
    blood vessel — *continued*
      lower limb — *continued*
        vein 38.69
        thoracic NEC 38.65
        upper limb (artery) (vein) 38.63
    bone 77.60
      carpal, metacarpal 77.64
      clavicle 77.61
      facial 76.2
      femur 77.65
      fibula 77.67
      humerus 77.62
      jaw 76.2
        dental 24.4
      patella 77.66
      pelvic 77.69
      phalanges (foot) (hand) 77.69
      radius 77.63
      scapula 77.61
      skull 01.6
      specified site NEC 77.69
      tarsal, metatarsal 77.68
      thorax (ribs) (sternum) 77.61
      tibia 77.67
      ulna 77.63
      vertebrae 77.69
    brain (transtemporal approach) NEC 01.59
      by stereotactic radiosurgery 92.30
        cobalt 60 92.32
        linear accelerator (LINAC) 92.31
        multi-source 92.32
        particle beam 92.33
        particulate 92.33
        radiosurgery NEC 92.39
        single source photon 92.31
    breast (segmental) (wedge) 85.21
    broad ligament 69.19
    bronchus NEC 32.09
      endoscopic 32.01
    cerebral (cortex) NEC 01.59
      meninges 01.51
    cervix (myoma) 67.39
    chest wall 34.4
    choroid plexus 02.14
    ciliary body 12.44
    colon 45.41
      endoscopic NEC 45.43
        polypectomy 45.42
    conjunctiva 10.31
    cornea 11.49
    cranium 01.6
    cul-de-sac (Douglas') 70.32
    dental (jaw) 24.4
    diaphragm 34.81
    duodenum (local) 45.31
      endoscopic 45.30
    ear, external 18.29
      radical 18.31
    endometrium 68.29
    epicardium 37.31
    epididymis 63.3
    epiglottis 30.09
    esophagus NEC 42.32
      endoscopic 42.33
    eyebrow (skin) 08.20
    eye, eyeball 16.93
      anterior segment NEC 12.40
    eyelid 08.20
      by
        halving procedure 08.24
        wedge resection 08.24
      major
        full-thickness 08.24
        partial-thickness 08.23
      minor 08.22
    fallopian tube 66.61
    fascia 83.39
      hand 82.29
    groin region (abdominal wall) (inguinal) 54.3
      skin 86.3
      subcutaneous tissue 86.3
    gum 24.31
    heart 37.33

Excision — *continued*
  lesion — *continued*
    hepatic duct 51.69
    inguinal canal 54.3
    intestine
      large 45.41
        endoscopic NEC 45.43
          polypectomy 45.42
      small NEC 45.33
    intracranial NEC 01.59
    intranasal 21.31
    intraspinal 03.4
    iris 12.42
    jaw 76.2
      dental 24.4
    joint 80.80
      ankle 80.87
      elbow 80.82
      foot and toe 80.88
      hand and finger 80.84
      hip 80.85
      knee 80.86
      shoulder 80.81
      specified site NEC 80.89
      spine 80.89
      wrist 80.83
    kidney 55.39
      with partial nephrectomy 55.4
    labia 71.3
    lacrimal
      gland (frontal approach) 09.21
      passage 09.6
      sac 09.6
    larynx 30.09
    ligament (joint) (*see also* Excision, lesion, joint) 80.80
      broad 69.19
      round 69.19
      uterosacral 69.19
    lip 27.43
      by wide excision 27.42
    liver 50.29
    lung NEC 32.29
      by lung volume reduction surgery 32.22
      by wide excision 32.39
        thoracoscopic 32.30
      endoscopic 32.28
      thoracoscopic 32.20
    lymph structure(s) (channel) (vessel) NEC 40.29
      node — *see* Excision, lymph, node
    mammary duct 85.21
    mastoid (bone) 20.49
    mediastinum 34.3
    meninges (cerebral) 01.51
      spinal 03.4
    mesentery 54.4
    middle ear 20.51
    mouth NEC 27.49
    muscle 83.32
      hand 82.22
      ocular 15.13
    myocardium 37.33
    nail 86.23
    nasal sinus 22.60
      antrum 22.62
        with Caldwell-Luc approach 22.61
        specified approach NEC 22.62
      ethmoid 22.63
      frontal 22.42
      maxillary 22.62
        with Caldwell-Luc approach 22.61
        specified approach NEC 22.62
      sphenoid 22.64
    nasopharynx 29.3 ☑
    nerve (cranial) (peripheral) 04.07
      sympathetic 05.29
    nonodontogenic 24.31
    nose 21.30
      intranasal 21.31
        polyp 21.31
      skin 21.32
      specified site NEC 21.32
    odontogenic 24.4
    omentum 54.4

Excision — *continued*
  lesion — *continued*
    orbit 16.92
    ovary 65.29
      by wedge resection 65.22
        laparoscopic 65.24
      that by laparoscope 65.25
    palate (bony) 27.31
      by wide excision 27.32
      soft 27.49
    pancreas (local) 52.22
      endoscopic 52.21
    parathyroid 06.89
    parotid gland or duct NEC 26.29
    pelvic wall 54.3
    pelvirectal tissue 48.82
    penis 64.2
    pericardium 37.31
    perineum (female) 71.3
      male 86.3
    periprostatic tissue 60.82
    perirectal tissue 48.82
    perirenal tissue 59.91
    peritoneum 54.4
    perivesical tissue 59.91
    pharynx 29.39
      diverticulum 29.32
    pineal gland 07.53
    pinna 18.29
      radical 18.31
    pituitary (gland) (*see also* Hypophysectomy, partial) 07.63
      by stereotactic radiosurgery 92.30
        cobalt 60 92.32
        linear accelerator (LINAC) 92.31
        multi-source 92.32
        particle beam 92.33
        particulate 92.33
        radiosurgery NEC 92.39
        single source photon 92.31
    pleura 34.59
    pouch of Douglas 70.32
    preauricular (ear) 18.21
    presacral 54.4
    prostate (transurethral) 60.61
    pulmonary (fibrosis) 32.29
      endoscopic 32.28
      thoracoscopic 32.20
    rectovaginal septum 48.82
    rectum 48.35
      polyp (endoscopic) 48.36
    retroperitoneum 54.4
    salivary gland or duct NEC 26.29
      en bloc 26.32
    sclera 12.84
    scrotum 61.3
    sinus (nasal) — *see* Excision, lesion, nasal sinus
    Skene's gland 71.3
    skin 86.3
      breast 85.21
      nose 21.32
      radical (wide) (involving underlying or adjacent structure) (with flap closure) 86.4
      scrotum 61.3
    skull 01.6
    soft tissue NEC 83.39
      hand 82.29
    spermatic cord 63.3
    sphincter of Oddi 51.62
      endoscopic 51.64
    spinal cord (meninges) 03.4
    spleen (cyst) 41.42
    stomach NEC 43.42
      endoscopic 43.41
        polyp 43.41
      polyp (endoscopic) 43.41
    subcutaneous tissue 86.3
      breast 85.21
    subgingival 24.31
    sweat gland 86.3
    tendon 83.39
      hand 82.29
      ocular 15.13
      sheath 83.31

Excision — *continued*
  lesion — *continued*
    tendon — *continued*
      sheath — *continued*
        hand 82.21
    testis 62.2
    thorax 34.4
    thymus
      partial (open) (other) 07.81
        thoracoscopic 07.83
      total (open) (other) 07.82
        thoracoscopic 07.84
    thyroid 06.31
      substernal or transsternal route 06.51
    tongue 25.1
    tonsil 28.92
    trachea 31.5
    tunica vaginalis 61.92
    ureter 56.41
    urethra 58.39
      endoscopic 58.31
    uterine ligament 69.19
    uterosacral ligament 69.19
    uterus 68.29
    vagina 70.33
    vein 38.60
      abdominal 38.67
      head and neck NEC 38.62
      intracranial NEC 38.61
      lower limb 38.69
      thoracic NEC 38.65
      upper limb 38.63
    ventricle (heart) 37.33
    vocal cords 30.09
    vulva 71.3
  ligament (*see also* Arthrectomy) 80.90
    broad 69.19
    round 69.19
    uterine 69.19
    uterosacral 69.19
  ligamentum flavum (spine) — omit code
  lingual tonsil 28.5
  lip 27.43
  liver (partial) 50.22
  loose body
    bone — *see* Sequestrectomy, bone
    joint 80.10
  lung (with mediastinal dissection) 32.59
    accessory or ectopic tissue 32.29
      endoscopic 32.28
      thoracoscopic 32.20
    segmental 32.39
      thoracoscopic 32.30
    specified type NEC 32.29
      endoscopic 32.28
      thoracoscopic 32.20
    thoracoscopic 32.50
    volume reduction surgery 32.22
      biologic lung volume reduction (BLVR) — *see* category 33.7 ☑
    wedge 32.29
      thoracoscopic 32.20
  lymphangioma (simple) (*see also* Excision, lymph, lymphatic node) 40.29
  lymph, lymphatic
    drainage area 40.29
      radical — *see* Excision, lymph, node, radical
      regional (with lymph node, skin, subcutaneous tissue, and fat) 40.3
    node (simple) NEC 40.29
      with
        lymphatic drainage area (including skin, subcutaneous tissue, and fat) 40.3
        mastectomy — *see* Mastectomy, radical
        muscle and deep fascia — *see* Excision, lymph, node, radical
      axillary 40.23
        radical 40.51
        regional (extended) 40.3
      cervical (deep) (with excision of scalene fat pad) 40.21
        with laryngectomy 30.4

Excision — Excision

☑ Additional Digit Required — Refer to the Tabular List for Digit Selection   ▽ Subterms under main terms may continue to next column or page

2010 ICD-9-CM   ▶◀ Revised Text   ● New Line   ▲ Revised Code   **Volume 3 — 21**

Exploration — Extraction

Extraction — *continued*
  tooth — *continued*
    deciduous 23.01
    surgical NEC (*see also* Removal, tooth, surgical) 23.19
    vacuum, fetus 72.79
      with episiotomy 72.71
  vitreous (*see also* Removal, vitreous) 14.72

F

Face lift 86.82
Facetectomy 77.89
Facilitation, intraocular circulation NEC 12.59
Failed (trial) forceps 73.3
Family
  counselling (medical) (social) 94.49
  therapy 94.42
Farabeuf operation (ischiopubiotomy) 77.39
Fasanella-Servatt operation (blepharoptosis repair) 08.35
Fasciaplasty — *see* Fascioplasty
Fascia sling operation — *see* Operation, sling
Fasciectomy 83.44
  for graft 83.43
    hand 82.34
  hand 82.35
    for graft 82.34
  palmar (release of Dupuytren's contracture) 82.35
Fasciodesis 83.89
  hand 82.89
Fascioplasty — *see also* Repair, fascia 83.89
  hand (*see also* Repair, fascia, hand) 82.89
Fasciorrhaphy — *see* Suture, fascia
Fasciotomy 83.14
  Dupuytren's 82.12
    with excision 82.35
  Dwyer 83.14
  hand 82.12
  Ober-Yount 83.14
  orbital (*see also* Orbitotomy) 16.09
  palmar (release of Dupuytren's contracture) 82.12
    with excision 82.35
Fenestration
  aneurysm (dissecting), thoracic aorta 39.54
  aortic aneurysm 39.54
  cardiac valve 35.10
  chest wall 34.01
  ear
    inner (with graft) 20.61
      revision 20.62
    tympanic 19.55
  labyrinth (with graft) 20.61
  Lempert's (endaural) 19.9
  operation (aorta) 39.54
  oval window, ear canal 19.55
  palate 27.1
  pericardium 37.12
  semicircular canals (with graft) 20.61
  stapes foot plate (with vein graft) 19.19
    with incus replacement 19.11
  tympanic membrane 19.55
  vestibule (with graft) 20.61
Ferguson operation (hernia repair) 53.00
Fetography 87.81
Fetoscopy 75.31
Fiberoscopy — *see* Endoscopy, by site
Fibroidectomy, uterine 68.29
Fick operation (perforation of foot plate) 19.0
Filipuncture (aneurysm) (cerebral) 39.52
Filleting
  hammer toe 77.56
  pancreas 52.3
Filling, tooth (amalgam) (plastic) (silicate) 23.2
  root canal (*see also* therapy, root canal) 23.70
Fimbriectomy — *see also* Salpingectomy, partial 66.69
  Uchida (with tubal ligation) 66.32
Finney operation (pyloroplasty) 44.29
Fissurectomy, anal 49.39
  endoscopic 49.31
  skin (subcutaneous tissue) 49.04
Fistulectomy — *see also* Closure, fistula, by site
  abdominothoracic 34.83
  abdominouterine 69.42

Fistulectomy — *see also* Closure, fistula, by site — *continued*
  anus 49.12
  appendix 47.92
  bile duct 51.79
  biliary tract NEC 51.79
  bladder (transurethral approach) 57.84
  bone (*see also* Excision, lesion, bone) 77.60
  branchial cleft 29.52
  bronchocutaneous 33.42
  bronchoesophageal 33.42
  bronchomediastinal 34.73
  bronchopleural 34.73
  bronchopleurocutaneous 34.73
  bronchopleuromediastinal 34.73
  bronchovisceral 33.42
  cervicosigmoidal 67.62
  cholecystogastroenteric 51.93
  cornea 11.49
  diaphragm 34.83
  enterouterine 69.42
  esophagopleurocutaneous 34.73
  esophagus NEC 42.84
  fallopian tube 66.73
  gallbladder 51.93
  gastric NEC 44.63
  hepatic duct 51.79
  hepatopleural 34.73
  hepatopulmonary 34.73
  intestine
    large 46.76
    small 46.74
  intestinouterine 69.42
  joint (*see also* Excision, lesion, joint) 80.80
  lacrimal
    gland 09.21
    sac 09.6
  laryngotracheal 31.62
  larynx 31.62
  mediastinocutaneous 34.73
  mouth NEC 27.53
  nasal 21.82
    sinus 22.71
  nasolabial 21.82
  nasopharyngeal 21.82
  oroantral 22.71
  oronasal 21.82
  pancreas 52.95
  perineorectal 71.72
  perineosigmoidal 71.72
  perirectal, not opening into rectum 48.93
  pharyngoesophageal 29.53
  pharynx NEC 29.53
  pleura 34.73
  rectolabial 71.72
  rectourethral 58.43
  rectouterine 69.42
  rectovaginal 70.73
  rectovesical 57.83
  rectovulvar 71.72
  rectum 48.73
  salivary (duct) (gland) 26.42
  scrotum 61.42
  skin 86.3
  stomach NEC 44.63
  subcutaneous tissue 86.3
  thoracoabdominal 34.83
  thoracogastric 34.83
  thoracointestinal 34.83
  thorax NEC 34.73
  trachea NEC 31.73
  tracheoesophageal 31.73
  ureter 56.84
  urethra 58.43
  uteroenteric 69.42
  uterointestinal 69.42
  uterorectal 69.42
  uterovaginal 69.42
  vagina 70.75
  vesicosigmoidovaginal 57.83
  vocal cords 31.62
  vulvorectal 71.72
Fistulization
  appendix 47.91
  arteriovenous 39.27
  cisterna chyli 40.62

Fistulization — *continued*
  endolymphatic sac (for decompression) 20.79
  esophagus, external 42.10
    cervical 42.11
    specified technique NEC 42.19
  interatrial 35.41
  labyrinth (for decompression) 20.79
  lacrimal sac into nasal cavity 09.81
  larynx 31.29
  lymphatic duct, left (thoracic) 40.62
  orbit 16.09
  peritoneal 54.93
  salivary gland 26.49
  sclera 12.69
    by trephination 12.61
    with iridectomy 12.65
  sinus, nasal NEC 22.9
  subarachnoid space 02.2
  thoracic duct 40.62
  trachea 31.29
  tracheoesophageal 31.95
  urethrovaginal 58.0
  ventricle, cerebral (*see also* Shunt, ventricular) 02.2
Fistulogram
  abdominal wall 88.03
  chest wall 87.38
  retroperitoneum 88.14
  specified site NEC 88.49
Fistulotomy, anal 49.11
Fitting
  arch bars (orthodontic) 24.7
    for immobilization (fracture) 93.55
  artificial limb 84.40
  contact lens 95.32
  denture (total) 99.97
    bridge (fixed) 23.42
      removable 23.43
    partial (fixed) 23.42
      removable 23.43
  hearing aid 95.48
  obturator (orthodontic) 24.7
  ocular prosthetics 95.34
  orthodontic
    appliance 24.7
    obturator 24.7
    wiring 24.7
  orthotic device 93.23
  periodontal splint (orthodontic) 24.7
  prosthesis, prosthetic device
    above knee 84.45
    arm 84.43
      lower (and hand) 84.42
      upper (and shoulder) 84.41
    below knee 84.46
    hand (and lower arm) 84.42
    leg 84.47
      above knee 84.45
      below knee 84.46
    limb NEC 84.40
    ocular 95.34
    penis (external) 64.94
    shoulder (and upper arm) 84.41
  spectacles 95.31
Five-in-one repair, knee 81.42
Fixation
  bone
    external, without reduction 93.59
      with fracture reduction — *see* Reduction, fracture
    cast immobilization NEC 93.53
    external fixator — *see* Fixator, external
    splint 93.54
    traction (skeletal) NEC 93.44
      intermittent 93.43
    internal (without fracture reduction) 78.50
      with fracture reduction — *see* Reduction, fracture
      carpal, metacarpal 78.54
      clavicle 78.51
      femur 78.55
      fibula 78.57
      humerus 78.52
      patella 78.56
      pelvic 78.59
      phalanges (foot) (hand) 78.59

Fixation — *continued*
  bone — *continued*
    internal — *continued*
      radius 78.53
      scapula 78.51
      specified site NEC 78.59
      tarsal, metatarsal 78.58
      thorax (ribs) (sternum) 78.51
      tibia 78.57
      ulna 78.53
      vertebrae 78.59
  breast (pendulous) 85.6
  cardinal ligaments 69.22
  cervical collar 93.52
  duodenum 46.62
    to abdominal wall 46.61
  external (without manipulation for reduction) 93.59
    with fracture reduction — *see* Reduction, fracture
    cast immobilization NEC 93.53
    pressure dressing 93.56
    splint 93.54
    strapping (non-traction) 93.59
    traction (skeletal) NEC 93.44
      intermittent 93.43
  hip 81.40
  ileum 46.62
    to abdominal wall 46.61
  internal
    with fracture reduction — *see* Reduction, fracture
    without fracture reduction — *see* Fixation, bone, internal
  intestine 46.60
    large 46.64
      to abdominal wall 46.63
    small 46.62
      to abdominal wall 46.61
    to abdominal wall 46.60
  iris (bombé) 12.11
  jejunum 46.62
    to abdominal wall 46.61
  joint — *see* Arthroplasty
  kidney 55.7
  ligament
    cardinal 69.22
    palpebrae 08.36
  omentum 54.74
  parametrial 69.22
  plaster jacket 93.51
    other cast 93.53
  rectum (sling) 48.76
  spine, with fusion (*see also* Fusion, spinal) 81.00
  spleen 41.95
  splint 93.54
  tendon 83.88
    hand 82.85
  testis in scrotum 62.5
  tongue 25.59
  urethrovaginal (to Cooper's ligament) 70.77
    with graft or prosthesis 70.78
  uterus (abdominal) (vaginal) (ventrofixation) 69.22
  vagina 70.77
    with graft or prosthesis 70.78
Fixator, external
  computer assisted (dependent) 84.73
  hybrid device or system 84.73
  Ilizarov type 84.72
  monoplanar system 84.71
  ring device or system 84.72
  Sheffield type 84.72
Flooding (psychologic desensitization) 94.33
Flowmetry, Doppler (ultrasonic) — *see also* Ultrasonography
  aortic arch 88.73
  head and neck 88.71
  heart 88.72
  thorax NEC 88.73
Fluoroscopy — *see* Radiography
Fog therapy (respiratory) 93.94
Folding, eye muscle 15.22
  multiple (two or more muscles) 15.4
Foley operation (pyeloplasty) 55.87

☑ Additional Digit Required — Refer to the Tabular List for Digit Selection   ▽ Subterms under main terms may continue to next column or page

22 — Volume 3   ▶◀ Revised Text   ● New Line   ▲ Revised Code   2010 ICD-9-CM

☑ Additional Digit Required — Refer to the Tabular List for Digit Selection ☒ Subterms under main terms may continue to next column or page

2010 ICD-9-CM ▶◀ Revised Text ● New Line ▲ Revised Code **Volume 3 — 23**

Ganglionectomy — continued
  nerve — continued
    sympathetic 05.29
    sphenopalatine (Meckel's) 05.21
    tendon sheath (wrist) 82.21
      site other than hand 83.31
    trigeminal 04.05
Ganglionotomy, trigeminal (radiofrequency) 04.02
Gant operation (wedge osteotomy of trochanter) 77.25
Garceau operation (tibial tendon transfer) 83.75
Gardner operation (spinal meningocele repair) 03.51
Gas endarterectomy 38.10
  abdominal 38.16
  aorta (arch) (ascending) (descending) 38.14
  coronary artery 36.09
  head and neck NEC 38.12
  intracranial NEC 38.11
  lower limb 38.18
  thoracic NEC 38.15
  upper limb 38.13
Gastrectomy (partial) (subtotal) NEC 43.89
  with
    anastomosis (to) NEC 43.89
      duodenum 43.6
      esophagus 43.5
      gastrogastric 43.89
      jejunum 43.7
    esophagogastrostomy 43.5
    gastroduodenostomy (bypass) 43.6
    gastroenterostomy (bypass) 43.7
    gastrogastrostomy (bypass) 43.89
    gastrojejunostomy (bypass) 43.7
    jejunal transposition 43.81
  complete NEC 43.99
    with intestinal interposition 43.91
  distal 43.6
  Hofmeister 43.7
  Polya 43.7
  proximal 43.5
  radical NEC 43.99
    with intestinal interposition 43.91
  total NEC 43.99
    with intestinal interposition 43.91
Gastrocamera 44.19
Gastroduodenectomy — see Gastrectomy
Gastroduodenoscopy 45.13
  through stoma (artificial) 45.12
  transabdominal (operative) 45.11
Gastroduodenostomy (bypass) (Jaboulay's) 44.39
  with partial gastrectomy 43.6
  laparoscopic 44.38
Gastroenterostomy (bypass) NEC 44.39
  with partial gastrectomy 43.7
  laparoscopic 44.38
Gastrogastrostomy (bypass) 44.39
  with partial gastrectomy 43.89
  laparoscopic 44.38
Gastrojejunostomy (bypass) 44.39
  with partial gastrectomy 43.7
  laparoscopic 44.38
  percutaneous (endoscopic)
    for bypass 44.32
    for feeding tube placement 46.32
Gastrolysis 54.59
  laparoscopic 54.51
Gastropexy 44.64
Gastroplasty NEC 44.69
  laparoscopic 44.68
  vertical banded gastroplasty (VBG) 44.68
Gastroplication 44.69
  laparoscopic 44.68
Gastropylorectomy 43.6
Gastrorrhaphy 44.61
Gastroscopy NEC 44.13
  through stoma (artificial) 44.12
  transabdominal (operative) 44.11
Gastrostomy (Brunschwig's) (decompression) (fine caliber tube) (Kader) (permanent) (Stamm) (Stamm-Kader) (temporary) (tube) (Witzel) 43.19
  Beck-Jianu 43.19
  Frank's 43.19

Gastrostomy — continued
  Janeway 43.19
  percutaneous (endoscopic) (PEG) 43.11
  Spivack's 43.19
  Ssabanejew-Frank 43.19
Gastrotomy 43.0
  for control of hemorrhage 44.49
Gavage, gastric 96.35
Gelman operation (release of clubfoot) 83.84
Genioplasty (augmentation) (with graft) (with implant) 76.68
  reduction 76.67
Ghormley operation (hip fusion) 81.21
Gifford operation
  destruction of lacrimal sac 09.6
  keratotomy (delimiting) 11.1
    radial (refractive) 11.75
Gilliam operation (uterine suspension) 69.22
Gill operation
  arthrodesis of shoulder 81.23
  laminectomy 03.09
Gill-Stein operation (carporadial arthrodesis) 81.25
Gingivectomy 24.31
Gingivoplasty (with bone graft) (with soft tissue graft) 24.2
Girdlestone operation
  laminectomy with spinal fusion 81.00
  muscle transfer for claw toe repair 77.57
  resection of femoral head and neck (without insertion of joint prosthesis) 77.85
    with replacement prosthesis — see Implant, joint, hip
  resection of hip prosthesis 80.05
    with replacement prosthesis — see Implant, joint, hip
Girdlestone-Taylor operation (muscle transfer for claw toe repair) 77.57
Glenn operation (anastomosis of superior vena cava to right pulmonary artery) 39.21
Glenoplasty, shoulder 81.83
  for recurrent dislocation 81.82
  with
    partial replacement 81.81
    total replacement 81.80
Glomectomy
  carotid 39.8
  jugulare 20.51
Glossectomy (complete) (total) 25.3
  partial or subtotal 25.2
  radical 25.4
Glossopexy 25.59
Glossoplasty NEC 25.59
Glossorrhaphy 25.51
Glossotomy NEC 25.94
  for tongue tie 25.91
Glycoprotein IIb/IIIa inhibitor 99.20
Goebel-Frangenheim-Stoeckel operation (urethrovesical suspenion) 59.4
Goldner operation (clubfoot release) 80.48
Goldthwaite operation
  ankle stabilization 81.11
  patellar stabilization 81.44
  tendon transfer for stabilization of patella 81.44
Gonadectomy
  ovary
    bilateral 65.51
      laparoscopic 65.53
    unilateral 65.39
      laparoscopic 65.31
  testis 62.3
    bilateral 62.41
    unilateral 62.3
Goniopuncture 12.51
  with goniotomy 12.53
Gonioscopy 12.29
Goniospasis 12.59
Goniotomy (Barkan's) 12.52
  with goniopuncture 12.53
Goodal-Power operation (vagina) 70.8
Gordon-Taylor operation (hindquarter amputation) 84.19
GP IIb/IIIa inhibitor, infusion 99.20
Graber-Duvernay operation (drilling of femoral head) 77.15

Graft, grafting
  aneurysm 39.52
    endovascular
      abdominal aorta 39.71
      lower extremity artery(s) 39.79
      thoracic aorta 39.73
      upper extremity artery(s) 39.79
  artery, arterial (patch) 39.58
    with
      excision or resection of vessel — see Arteriectomy, with graft replacement
      synthetic patch (Dacron) (Teflon) 39.57
      tissue patch (vein) (autogenous) (homograft) 39.56
  blood vessel (patch) 39.58
    with
      excision or resection of vessel — see Angiectomy, with graft replacement
      synthetic patch (Dacron) (Teflon) 39.57
      tissue patch (vein) (autogenous) (homograft) 39.56
  bone (autogenous) (bone bank) (dual onlay) (heterogenous) (inlay) (massive onlay) (multiple) (osteoperiosteal) (peg) (subperiosteal) (with metallic fixation) 78.00
    with
      arthrodesis — see Arthrodesis
      arthroplasty — see Arthroplasty
      gingivoplasty 24.2
      lengthening — see Lengthening, bone
    carpals, metacarpals 78.04
    clavicle 78.01
    facial NEC 76.91
      with total ostectomy 76.44
    femur 78.05
    fibula 78.07
    humerus 78.02
    joint — see Arthroplasty
    mandible 76.91
      with total mandibulectomy 76.41
    marrow — see Transplant, bone, marrow
    nose — see Graft, nose
    patella 78.06
    pelvic 78.09
    pericranial 02.04
    phalanges (foot) (hand) 78.09
    radius 78.03
    scapula 78.01
    skull 02.04
    specified site NEC 78.09
    spine 78.09
      with fusion — see Fusion, spinal
    tarsal, metatarsal 78.08
    thorax (ribs) (sternum) 78.01
    thumb (with transfer of skin flap) 82.69
    tibia 78.07
    ulna 78.03
    vertebrae 78.09
      with fusion — see Fusion, spinal
  breast (see also Mammoplasty) 85.89
  buccal sulcus 27.99
  cartilage (joint) (see also Arthroplasty)
    nose — see Graft, nose
  chest wall (mesh) (silastic) 34.79
  conjunctiva (free) (mucosa) 10.44
    for symblepharon repair 10.41
  cornea (see also Keratoplasty) 11.60
  dermal-fat 86.69
  dermal regenerative 86.67
  dura 02.12
  ear
    auricle 18.79
  esophagus NEC 42.87
    with interposition (intrathoracic) NEC 42.58
      antesternal or antethoracic NEC 42.68
    colon (intrathoracic) 42.55
      antesternal or antethoracic 42.65
    small bowel (intrathoracic) 42.53
      antesternal or antethoracic 42.63
  external auditory meatus 18.6
    inner 20.61
    pedicle preparation 86.71

Graft, grafting — continued
  eyebrow (see also Reconstruction, eyelid, with graft) 08.69
  eyelid (see also Reconstruction, eyelid, with graft) 08.69
    free mucous membrane 08.62
  eye socket (skin) (cartilage) (bone) 16.63
  fallopian tube 66.79
  fascia 83.82
    with hernia repair — see Repair, hernia
    eyelid 08.32
    hand 82.72
    tarsal cartilage 08.69
  fat pad NEC 86.89
    with skin graft — see Graft, skin, full-thickness
  flap (advanced) (rotating) (sliding) (see also Graft, skin, pedicle)
    tarsoconjunctival 08.64
  hair-bearing skin 86.64
  hand
    fascia 82.72
    free skin 86.62
    muscle 82.72
    pedicle (flap) 86.73
    tendon 82.79
  heart, for revascularization — see category 36.3 ✓
  joint — see Arthroplasty
  larynx 31.69
  lip 27.56
    full-thickness 27.55
  lymphatic structure(s) (channel) (node) (vessel) 40.9
  mediastinal fat to myocardium 36.39
  meninges (cerebral) 02.12
  mouth, except palate 27.56
    full-thickness 27.55
  muscle 83.82
    hand 82.72
  myocardium, for revascularization 36.39
  nasolabial flaps 21.86
  nerve (cranial) (peripheral) 04.5
  nipple 85.86
  nose 21.89
    with
      augmentation 21.85
      rhinoplasty — see Rhinoplasty
      total reconstruction 21.83
    septum 21.88
    tip 21.86
  omentum 54.74
    to myocardium 36.39
  orbit (bone) (cartilage) (skin) 16.63
  outflow tract (patch) (pulmonary valve) 35.26
    in total repair of tetralogy of Fallot 35.81
  ovary 65.92
  palate 27.69
    for cleft palate repair 27.62
  pedicle — see Graft, skin, pedicle
  penis (rib) (skin) 64.49
  pigskin 86.65
  pinch — see Graft, skin, free
  pocket — see Graft, skin, pedicle
  porcine 86.65
  postauricular (Wolff) 18.79
  razor — see Graft, skin, free
  rope — see Graft, skin, pedicle
  saphenous vein in aortocoronary bypass — see Bypass, aortocoronary
  scrotum 61.49
  skin (partial-thickness) (split-thickness) 86.69
    amnionic membrane 86.66
    auditory meatus (ear) 18.6
    dermal-fat 86.69
      for breast augmentation 85.50
    dermal regenerative 86.67
    ear
      auditory meatus 18.6
      postauricular 18.79
    eyelid 08.61
    flap — see Graft, skin, pedicle
    free (autogenous) NEC 86.60

Index

Ganglionectomy — Graft, grafting

☑ Additional Digit Required — Refer to the Tabular List for Digit Selection
▷◁ Revised Text ● New Line ▲ Revised Code
Subterms under main terms may continue to next column or page
2010 ICD-9-CM
October 2009 • Volume 3 — 25

☑ Additional Digit Required — Refer to the Tabular List for Digit Selection
Ⓥ Subterms under main terms may continue to next column or page
2010 ICD-9-CM ►◄ Revised Text ● New Line ▲ Revised Code **October 2009 · Volume 3 — 27**

Implant, implantation — *continued*
  prosthesis, prosthetic device — *continued*
    joint — *continued*
      knee — *continued*
        revision — *continued*
          partial
            femoral component 00.82
            patellar component 00.83
            tibial component 00.81
            tibial insert 00.84
          patellar component 00.83
          tibial component 00.81
          tibial insert 00.84
          total (all components) 00.80
      metacarpophalangeal 81.71
      shoulder (partial) 81.81
        total 81.80
      spine NEC 84.59
        interspinous process decompression device
      toe 81.57
        for hallux valgus repair 77.59
      wrist (partial) 81.74
        total 81.73
    leg (bioelectric) (cineplastic) (kineplastic) 84.48
    lens 13.91
    outflow tract (heart) (gusset type)
      in
        pulmonary valvuloplasty 35.26
        total repair of tetralogy of Fallot 35.81
    penis (internal) (non-inflatable) 64.95
      inflatable (internal) 64.97
    skin (dermal regenerative) (matrix) 86.67
    testicular (bilateral) (unilateral) 62.7
  pulsation balloon (phase-shift) 37.61
  pump, infusion 86.06
  radial artery 36.19
  radioactive isotope 92.27
  radium (radon) 92.27
  retinal attachment 14.41
    with buckling 14.41
  Rheos™ carotid sinus baroreflex activation device 39.8
  Rickham reservoir 02.2
  silicone
    breast (bilateral) 85.54
      unilateral 85.53
    skin (for filling of defect) 86.02
      for augmentation NEC 86.89
  spine NEC 84.59
    facet replacement device(s) 84.84
    interspinous process decompression device 84.80
    pedicle-based dynamic stabilization device(s) 84.82
    posterior motion preservation device(s) — *see* category 84.8
  stimoceiver — *see* Implant, neurostimulator, by site
  stimulator
    carotid sinus 39.8
  subdural
    grids 02.93
    strips 02.93
  Swanson prosthesis (joint) (silastic) NEC 81.96
    carpocarpal, carpometacarpal 81.74
    finger 81.71
    hand (metacarpophalangeal) (interphalangeal) 81.71
    interphalangeal 81.71
    knee (partial) (total) 81.54
      revision 81.55
    metacarpophalangeal 81.71
    toe 81.57
      for hallux valgus repair 77.59
    wrist (partial) 81.74
      total 81.73
  systemic arteries into myocardium (Vineberg type operation) 36.2
  Tandem™ heart 37.68
  telescope (IMT) (miniature) 13.91
  testicular prosthesis (bilateral) (unilateral) 62.7
  tissue expander (skin) NEC 86.93
    breast 85.95

Implant, implantation — *continued*
  tissue mandril (for vascular graft) 39.99
    with
      blood vessel repair 39.56
      vascular bypass or shunt — *see* Bypass, vascular
  tooth (bud) (germ) 23.5
    prosthetic 23.6
  umbrella, vena cava 38.7
  ureters into
    bladder 56.74
    intestine 56.71
      external diversion 56.51
    skin 56.61
  urethra
    for repair of urinary stress incontinence
      collagen 59.72
      fat 59.72
      polytef 59.72
  urethral sphincter, artificial (inflatable) 58.93
  urinary sphincter, artificial (inflatable) 58.93
  vascular access device 86.07
  vitreous (silicone) 14.75
    for retinal reattachment 14.41
      with buckling 14.41
  vocal cord(s) (paraglottic) 31.98
  X Stop™ 84.80
Implosion (psychologic desensitization) 94.33
Incision (and drainage)
  with
    exploration — *see* Exploration
    removal of foreign body — *see* Removal, foreign body
  abdominal wall 54.0
    as operative approach — *omit code*
  abscess (*see also* Incision, by site)
    antecubital fossa 86.04
    appendix 47.2
      with appendectomy 47.09
        laparoscopic 47.01
    axilla 86.04
    cheek 86.04
    extraperitoneal 54.0
    face 86.04
    gluteal 86.04
    groin region (abdominal wall) (inguinal) 54.0
      skin 86.04
      subcutaneous tissue 86.04
    hair follicle 86.04
    ischiorectal 49.01
    lip 27.0
    nailbed or nailfold 86.04
    neck 86.04
    omental 54.19
    paronychia 86.04
    perianal 49.01
    perigastric 54.19
    perineum (female) 71.09
      male 86.04
    perisplenic 54.19
    peritoneal NEC 54.19
      pelvic (female) 70.12
    popliteal space 86.04
    retroperitoneal 54.0
    sclera 12.89
    skin 86.04
    subcutaneous tissue 86.04
    subdiaphragmatic 54.19
    subhepatic 54.19
    submaxillary 86.04
    subphrenic 54.19
    supraclavicular fossa 86.04
    vas deferens 63.6
  adrenal gland 07.41
  alveolus, alveolar bone 24.0
  antecubital fossa 86.09
  anus NEC 49.93
    fistula 49.11
    septum 49.91
  appendix 47.2
  artery 38.00
    abdominal 38.06
      aorta (arch) (ascending) (descending) 38.04
    head and neck NEC 38.02

Incision — *continued*
  artery — *continued*
    intracranial NEC 38.01
    lower limb 38.08
    thoracic NEC 38.05
    upper limb 38.03
  atrium (heart) 37.11
  auditory canal or meatus, external 18.02
  auricle 18.09
  axilla 86.09
  Bartholin's gland or cyst 71.22
  bile duct (with T or Y tube insertion) NEC 51.59
    for
      exploration 51.59
      relief of obstruction 51.49
    common (exploratory) 51.51
      for
        relief of obstruction NEC 51.42
        removal of calculus 51.41
  bladder 57.19
    neck (transurethral) 57.91
    percutaneous suprapubic (closed) 57.17
    suprapubic NEC 57.18
  blood vessel (*see also* Angiotomy) 38.00
  bone 77.10
    alveolus, alveolar 24.0
    carpals, metacarpals 77.14
    clavicle 77.11
    facial 76.09
    femur 77.15
    fibula 77.17
    humerus 77.12
    patella 77.16
    pelvic 77.19
    phalanges (foot) (hand) 77.19
    radius 77.13
    scapula 77.11
    skull 01.24
    specified site NEC 77.19
    tarsals, metatarsals 77.18
    thorax (ribs) (sternum) 77.11
    tibia 77.17
    ulna 77.13
    vertebrae 77.19
  brain 01.39
    cortical adhesions 02.91
  breast (skin) 85.0
    with removal of tissue expander 85.96
  bronchus 33.0
  buccal space 27.0
  bulbourethral gland 58.91
  bursa 83.03
    hand 82.03
    pharynx 29.0
  carotid body 39.8
  cerebral (meninges) 01.39
    epidural or extradural space 01.24
    subarachnoid or subdural space 01.31
  cerebrum 01.39
  cervix 69.95
    to
      assist delivery 73.93
      replace inverted uterus 75.93
  chalazion 08.09
    with removal of capsule 08.21
  cheek 86.09
  chest wall (for extrapleural drainage) (for removal of foreign body) 34.01
    as operative approach — *omit code*
  common bile duct (for exploration) 51.51
    for
      relief of obstruction 51.42
      removal of calculus 51.41
  common wall between posterior left atrium and coronary sinus (with roofing of resultant defect with patch graft) 35.82
  conjunctiva 10.1
  cornea 11.1
    radial (refractive) 11.75
  cranial sinus 01.21
  craniobuccal pouch 07.72
  cul-de-sac 70.12
  cyst
    dentigerous 24.0
    radicular (apical) (periapical) 24.0
  Dührssen's (cervix, to assist delivery) 73.93

Incision — *continued*
  duodenum 45.01
  ear
    external 18.09
    inner 20.79
    middle 20.23
  endocardium 37.11
  endolymphatic sac 20.79
  epididymis 63.92
  epidural space, cerebral 01.24
  epigastric region 54.0
    intra-abdominal 54.19
  esophagus, esophageal NEC 42.09
    web 42.01
  exploratory — *see* Exploration
  extradural space (cerebral) 01.24
  extrapleural 34.01
  eyebrow 08.09
  eyelid 08.09
    margin (trichiasis) 08.01
  face 86.09
  fallopian tube 66.01
  fascia 83.09
    with division 83.14
      hand 82.12
    hand 82.09
      with division 82.12
  fascial compartments, head and neck 27.0
  fistula, anal 49.11
  flank 54.0
  furuncle — *see* Incision, by site
  gallbladder 51.04
  gingiva 24.0
  gluteal 86.09
  groin region (abdominal wall) (inguinal) 54.0
    skin 86.09
    subcutaneous tissue 86.09
  gum 24.0
  hair follicles 86.09
  heart 37.10
    valve — *see* Valvulotomy
  hematoma (*see also* Incision, by site)
    axilla 86.04
    broad ligament 69.98
    ear 18.09
    episiotomy site 75.91
    fossa (superficial) NEC 86.04
    groin region (abdominal wall) (inguinal) 54.0
      skin 86.04
      subcutaneous tissue 86.04
    laparotomy site 54.12
    mediastinum 34.1
    perineum (female) 71.09
      male 86.04
    popliteal space 86.04
    scrotum 61.0
    skin 86.04
    space of Retzius 59.19
    subcutaneous tissue 86.04
    vagina (cuff) 70.14
      episiotomy site 75.91
      obstetrical NEC 75.92
  hepatic ducts 51.59
  hordeolum 08.09
  hygroma (*see also* Incision, by site)
    cystic 40.0
  hymen 70.11
  hypochondrium 54.0
    intra-abdominal 54.19
  hypophysis 07.72
  iliac fossa 54.0
  infratemporal fossa 27.0
  ingrown nail 86.09
  intestine 45.00
    large 45.03
    small 45.02
  intracerebral 01.39
  intracranial (epidural space) (extradural space) 01.24
    subarachnoid or subdural space 01.31
  intraperitoneal 54.19
  ischiorectal tissue 49.02
    abscess 49.01
  joint structures (*see also* Arthrotomy) 80.10
  kidney 55.01

☑ Additional Digit Required — Refer to the Tabular List for Digit Selection
▽ Subterms under main terms may continue to next column or page

28 — Volume 3
►◄ Revised Text
● New Line
▲ Revised Code
2010 ICD-9-CM

Incision — *continued*
kidney — *continued*
  pelvis 55.11
labia 71.09
lacrimal
  canaliculus 09.52
  gland 09.0
  passage NEC 09.59
  punctum 09.51
  sac 09.53
larynx NEC 31.3
ligamentum flavum (spine) — *omit code*
liver 50.0
lung 33.1
lymphangioma 40.0
lymphatic structure (channel) (node) (vessel) 40.0
mastoid 20.21
mediastinum 34.1
meibomian gland 08.09
meninges (cerebral) 01.31
  spinal 03.09
midpalmar space 82.04
mouth NEC 27.92
  floor 27.0
muscle 83.02
  with division 83.19
    hand 82.19
  hand 82.02
    with division 82.19
myocardium 37.11
nailbed or nailfold 86.09
nasolacrimal duct (stricture) 09.59
neck 86.09
nerve (cranial) (peripheral) NEC 04.04
  root (spinal) 03.1
nose 21.1
omentum 54.19
orbit (*see also* Orbitotomy) 16.09
ovary 65.09
  laparoscopic 65.01
palate 27.1
palmar space (middle) 82.04
pancreas 52.09
pancreatic sphincter 51.82
  endoscopic 51.85
parapharyngeal (oral) (transcervical) 28.0
paronychia 86.09
parotid
  gland or duct 26.0
  space 27.0
pelvirectal tissue 48.81
penis 64.92
perianal (skin) (tissue) 49.02
  abscess 49.01
perigastric 54.19
perineum (female) 71.09
  male 86.09
peripheral vessels
  lower limb
    artery 38.08
    vein 38.09
  upper limb (artery) (vein) 38.03
periprostatic tissue 60.81
perirectal tissue 48.81
perirenal tissue 59.09
perisplenic 54.19
peritoneum 54.95
  by laparotomy 54.19
  pelvic (female) 70.12
    male 54.19
periureteral tissue 59.09
periurethral tissue 58.91
perivesical tissue 59.19
petrous pyramid (air cells) (apex) (mastoid) 20.22
pharynx, pharyngeal (bursa) 29.0
  space, lateral 27.0
pilonidal sinus (cyst) 86.03
pineal gland 07.52
pituitary (gland) 07.72
pleura NEC 34.09
popliteal space 86.09
postzygomatic space 27.0
pouch of Douglas 70.12

Incision — *continued*
prostate (perineal approach) (transurethral approach) 60.0
pterygopalatine fossa 27.0
pulp canal (tooth) 24.0
Rathke's pouch 07.72
rectovaginal septum 48.81
rectum 48.0
  stricture 48.91
renal pelvis 55.11
retroperitoneum 54.0
retropharyngeal (oral) (transcervical) 28.0
salivary gland or duct 26.0
sclera 12.89
scrotum 61.0
sebaceous cyst 86.04
seminal vesicle 60.72
sinus — *see* Sinusotomy
Skene's duct or gland 71.09
skin 86.09
  with drainage 86.04
  breast 85.0
  cardiac pacemaker pocket, new site 37.79
  ear 18.09
  nose 21.1
  subcutaneous tunnel for pulse generator lead wire 86.99
    with initial procedure — *omit code*
  thalamic stimulator pulse generator pocket, new site 86.09
    with initial insertion of battery package — *omit code*
  tunnel, subcutaneous for pulse generator lead wire 86.99
    with initial procedure — *omit code*
skull 01.24
soft tissue NEC 83.09
  with division 83.19
    hand 82.19
  hand 82.09
    with division 82.19
space of Retzius 59.19
spermatic cord 63.93
sphincter of Oddi 51.82
  endoscopic 51.85
spinal
  cord 03.09
  nerve root 03.1
spleen 41.2
stomach 43.0
stye 08.09
subarachnoid space, cerebral 01.31
subcutaneous tissue 86.09
  with drainage 86.04
  tunnel
    esophageal 42.86
      with anastomosis — *see* Anastomosis, esophagus, antesternal
    pulse generator lead wire 86.99
      with initial procedure — *omit code*
subdiaphragmatic space 54.19
subdural space, cerebral 01.31
sublingual space 27.0
submandibular space 27.0
submaxillary 86.09
  with drainage 86.04
submental space 27.0
subphrenic space 54.19
supraclavicular fossa 86.09
  with drainage 86.04
sweat glands, skin 86.04
temporal pouches 27.0
tendon (sheath) 83.01
  with division 83.13
    hand 82.11
  hand 82.01
    with division 82.11
testis 62.0
thenar space 82.04
thymus (open) (other) 07.92
  thoracoscopic 07.95
thyroid (field) (gland) NEC 06.09
  postoperative 06.02
tongue NEC 25.94
  for tongue tie 25.91
tonsil 28.0

Incision — *continued*
trachea NEC 31.3
tunica vaginalis 61.0
umbilicus 54.0
urachal cyst 54.0
ureter 56.2
urethra 58.0
uterus (corpus) 68.0
  for termination of pregnancy 74.91
  cervix 69.95
  septum (congenital) 68.22
uvula 27.71
vagina (cuff) (septum) (stenosis) 70.14
  for
    incisional hematoma (episiotomy) 75.91
    obstetrical hematoma NEC 75.92
    pelvic abscess 70.12
vas deferens 63.6
vein 38.00
  abdominal 38.07
  head and neck NEC 38.02
  intracranial NEC 38.01
  lower limb 38.09
  thoracic NEC 38.05
  upper limb 38.03
vertebral column 03.09
vulva 71.09
  obstetrical 75.92
web, esophageal 42.01
Incudectomy NEC 19.3
  with
    stapedectomy (*see also* Stapedectomy) 19.19
    tympanoplasty — *see* Tympanoplasty
Incudopexy 19.19
Incudostapediopexy 19.19
  with incus replacement 19.11
Indentation, sclera, for buckling — *see also* Buckling, scleral 14.49
Indicator dilution flow measurement 89.68
Induction
  abortion
    by
      D and C 69.01
      insertion of prostaglandin suppository 96.49
      intra-amniotic injection (prostaglandin) (saline) 75.0
  labor
    medical 73.4
    surgical 73.01
      intra- and extra-amniotic injection 73.1
      stripping of membranes 73.1
Inflation
  belt wrap 93.99
  Eustachian tube 20.8
  fallopian tube 66.8
    with injection of therapeutic agent 66.95
Infolding, sclera, for buckling — *see also* Buckling, scleral 14.49
Infraction, turbinates (nasal) 21.62
Infundibulectomy
  hypophyseal (*see also* Hypophysectomy, partial) 07.63
  ventricle (heart) (right) 35.34
    in total repair of tetralogy of Fallot 35.81
Infusion (intra-arterial) (intravenous)
  with
    disruption of blood brain barrier [BBBD] 00.19
  Abciximab 99.20
  antibiotic
    oxazolidinone class 00.14
  antineoplastic agent (chemotherapeutic) 99.25
    biological response modifier [BRM] 99.28
    cintredekin besudotox 99.28
    CLO 17.70 ●
    clofarabine 17.70 ●
    CLOLAR® 17.70 ●
    high-dose interleukin-2 00.15
    low-dose interleukin-2 99.28
  biological response modifier [BRM], antineoplastic agent 99.28
    cintredekin besudotox 99.28
    high-dose interleukin-2 00.15

Infusion — *continued*
  biological response modifier [BRM], antineoplastic agent — *continued*
    low-dose interleukin-2 99.28
  cancer chemotherapy agent NEC 99.25
  cintredekin besudotox 99.28
  CLO 17.70 ●
  clofarabine 17.70 ●
  CLOLAR® 17.70 ●
  drotrecogin alfa (activated) 00.11
  electrolytes 99.18
  enzymes, thrombolytic (streptokinase) (tissue plasminogen activator) (TPA) (urokinase)
    direct coronary artery 36.04
    intravenous 99.10
  Eptifibatide 99.20
  gamma globulin 99.14
  GP IIb/IIIa inhibitor 99.20
  hormone substance NEC 99.24
  human B-type natriuretic peptide (hBNP) 00.13
  immunosuppressive antibody therapy 00.18
  interleukin-2
    high-dose 00.15
    low-dose 99.28
  nesiritide 00.13
  neuroprotective agent 99.75
  nimodipine 99.75
  nutritional substance — *see* Nutrition
  platelet inhibitor
    direct coronary artery 36.04
    intravenous 99.20
  Proleukin (low-dose) 99.28
    high-dose 00.15
  prophylactic substance NEC 99.29
  radioimmunoconjugate 92.28
  radioimmunotherapy 92.28
  radioisotope (liquid brachytherapy) (liquid I-125) 92.20
  recombinant protein 00.11
  reteplase 99.10
  therapeutic substance NEC 99.29
  thrombolytic agent (enzyme) (streptokinase) 99.10
    with percutaneous transluminal angioplasty

Note: Also use 00.40, 00.41, 00.42, or 00.43 to show the total number of vessels treated.

      coronary 00.66
      non-coronary vessel(s) 39.50
      specified site NEC 39.50
    direct intracoronary artery 36.04
  tirofiban (HCl) 99.20
  vaccine
    tumor 99.28
  vasopressor 00.17
Injection (into) (hypodermically) (intramuscularly) (intravenously) (acting locally or systemically)
  Actinomycin D, for cancer chemotherapy 99.25
  adhesion barrier substance 99.77
  alcohol
    nerve — *see* Injection, nerve
    spinal 03.8
  anterior chamber, eye (air) (liquid) (medication) 12.92
  antibiotic 99.21
    oxazolidinone class 00.14
  anticoagulant 99.19
  anti-D (Rhesus) globulin 99.11
  antidote NEC 99.16
  anti-infective NEC 99.22
  antineoplastic agent (chemotherapeutic) NEC 99.25
    biological response modifier [BRM] 99.28
    cintredekin besudotox 99.28
    high-dose interleukin-2 00.15
    low-dose interleukin-2 99.28
  antivenin 99.16
  barrier substance, adhesion 99.77
  BCG
    for chemotherapy 99.25
    vaccine 99.33
  biological response modifier [BRM], antineoplastic agent 99.28
    cintredekin besudotox 99.28

☑ Additional Digit Required — Refer to the Tabular List for Digit Selection   ▼ Subterms under main terms may continue to next column or page

2010 ICD-9-CM   ▶◀ Revised Text   ● New Line   ▲ Revised Code   October 2009 • Volume 3 — 29

☑ Additional Digit Required — Refer to the Tabular List for Digit Selection   ▽ Subterms under main terms may continue to next column or page

30 — Volume 3 • October 2009   ▶◀ Revised Text   ● New Line   ▲ Revised Code   **2010 ICD-9-CM**

☑ Additional Digit Required — Refer to the Tabular List for Digit Selection   ▽ Subterms under main terms may continue to next column or page

2010 ICD-9-CM   ►◄ Revised Text   ● New Line   ▲ Revised Code   **October 2009 • Volume 3 — 31**

Insertion — *continued*
  prosthesis, prosthetic device — *continued*
    acetabulum — *continued*
      hip — *continued*
        revision — *continued*
          acetabular and femoral compo-
            nents (total) 00.70
          acetabular component only
            00.71
          acetabular liner and/or femoral
            head only 00.73
          femoral component only 00.72
          femoral head only and/or ac-
            etabular liner 00.73
          partial
            acetabular component only
              00.71
            acetabular liner and/or
              femoral head only
              00.73
            femoral component only
              00.72
            femoral head only and/or
              acetabular liner
              00.73
          total (acetabular and femoral
            components) 00.70
    revision 81.53
  ankle (total) 81.56
  arm (bioelectric) (cineplastic) (kineplastic)
    84.44
  biliary tract 51.99
  breast (bilateral) 85.54
    unilateral 85.53
  cardiac support device (CSD) (CorCap™)
    37.41
  chin (polyethylene) (silastic) 76.68
  elbow (total) 81.84
    revision 81.97
  extremity (bioelectric) (cineplastic) (kine-
    plastic) 84.40
    lower 84.48
    upper 84.44
  fallopian tube 66.93
  femoral head (Austin-Moore) (bipolar)
    (Eicher) (Thompson) 81.52
  hip (partial) 81.52
    revision NOS 81.53
      acetabular and femoral compo-
        nents (total) 00.70
      acetabular component only 00.71
      acetabular liner and/or femoral
        head only 00.73
      femoral component only 00.72
      femoral head only and/or acetabu-
        lar liner 00.73
      partial
        acetabular component only
          00.71
        acetabular liner and/or femoral
          head only 00.73
        femoral component only 00.72
        femoral head only and/or ac-
          etabular liner 00.73
      total (acetabular and femoral com-
        ponents) 00.70
    total 81.51
      revision
        acetabular and femoral compo-
          nents (total) 00.70
        total (acetabular and femoral
          components) 00.70
  joint — *see* Arthroplasty
  knee (partial) (total) 81.54
    revision NOS 81.55
      femoral component 00.82
      partial
        femoral component 00.82
        patellar component 00.83
        tibial component 00.81
        tibial insert 00.84
      patellar component 00.83
      tibial component 00.81
      tibial insert 00.84
      total (all components) 00.80

Insertion — *continued*
  prosthesis, prosthetic device — *continued*
    leg (bioelectric) (cineplastic) (kineplastic)
      84.48
    lens 13.91
    ocular (secondary) 16.61
      with orbital exenteration 16.42
    outflow tract (gusset type) (heart)
      in
        pulmonary valvuloplasty 35.26
        total repair of tetralogy of Fallot
          35.81
    penis (internal) (noninflatable) 64.95
      with
        construction 64.43
        reconstruction 64.44
      inflatable (internal) 64.97
    Rosen (for urinary incontinence) 59.79
    shoulder
      partial 81.81
      revision 81.97
      total 81.80
    spine
      artificial disc, NOS 84.60
        cervical 84.62
          nucleus 84.61
          partial 84.61
          total 84.62
        lumbar, lumbosacral 84.65
          nucleus 84.64
          partial 84.64
          total 84.65
        thoracic (partial) (total) 84.63
      other device 84.59
    testicular (bilateral) (unilateral) 62.7
    toe 81.57
      hallux valgus repair 77.59
    vagina
      synthetic 70.95
  pseudophakos (*see also* Insertion, lens) 13.70
  pump, infusion 86.06
  radioactive isotope 92.27
  radium 92.27
  radon seeds 92.27
  Reuter bobbin (with intubation) 20.01
  Rickham reservoir 02.2
  Rosen prosthesis (for urinary incontinence)
    59.79
  Scribner shunt 39.93
  Sengstaken-Blakemore tube 96.06
  sensor (lead)
    intra-aneurysm sac pressure monitoring
      device 00.58
    intra-arterial, for continuous blood gas
      monitoring 89.60
    intracardiac ►or great vessel◄ hemody-
      namic monitoring 00.56
  shunt — *see* Shunt   ●
  sieve, vena cava 38.7
  skeletal muscle stimulator 83.92
  skull
    plate 02.05
    stereotactic frame 93.59
    tongs (Barton) (caliper) (Garder Wells)
      (Vinke) (with synchronous skeletal
      traction) 02.94
  spacer (cement) (joint) (methylmethacrylate)
    84.56
    spine 84.51
  sphenoidal electrodes 02.96
  spine
    bone void filler
      that with percutaneous vertebral aug-
        mentation 81.66
      that with percutaneous vertebroplasty
        81.65
    cage (BAK) 84.51
    facet replacement device(s) 84.84
    interbody spinal fusion device 84.51
    interspinous process decompression de-
      vice 84.80
    non-fusion stabilization device — *see* cat-
      egory 84.8
    pedicle-based dynamic stabilization de-
      vice(s) 84.82

Insertion — *continued*
  spine — *continued*
    posterior motion preservation device(s) —
      see category 84.8
    spacer 84.51
  Spitz-Holter valve 02.2
  Steinmann pin 93.44
    with reduction of fracture or dislocation
      — *see* Reduction, fracture *and* Re-
      duction, dislocation
  stent(s) (stent graft)
    artery (bare) (bonded) (drug-coated) (non-
      drug-eluting)

> *Note* — Also use 00.40, 00.41, 00.42, or
> 00.43 to show the total number of vessels
> treated. Use code 00.44 once to show proce-
> dure on a bifurcated vessel. In addition, use
> 00.45, 00.46, 00.47, or 00.48 to show the
> number of vascular stents inserted.

      basilar 00.64
      carotid 00.63
      cerebrovascular
        cerebral (intracranial) 00.65
        precerebral (extracranial) 00.64
          carotid 00.63
      coronary (bare) (bonded) (drug-coat-
        ed) (non-drug-eluting) 36.06
        drug-eluting 36.07
      extracranial 00.64
        carotid 00.63
      intracranial 00.65
      non-coronary vessel
        basilar 00.64
        carotid 00.63
        extracranial 00.64
        intracranial 00.65
        peripheral 39.90
          bare, drug-coated 39.90
          drug-eluting 00.55
        vertebral 00.64
    bile duct 51.43
      endoscopic 51.87
      percutaneous transhepatic 51.98
    colon   ●
      endoscopic (fluoroscopic guidance) ●
        46.86   ●
      other 46.87   ●
    coronary (artery) (bare) (bonded) (drug-
      coated) (non-drug-eluting) 36.06

> *Note* — Also use 00.40, 00.41, 00.42, or
> 00.43 to show the total number of vessels
> treated. Use code 00.44 once to show proce-
> dure on a bifurcated vessel. In addition, use
> 00.45, 00.46, 00.47, or 00.48 to show the
> number of vascular stents inserted.

      drug-eluting 36.07
    esophagus (endoscopic) (fluoroscopic)
      42.81
    mesenteric 39.90
      bare, drug-coated 39.90
      drug-eluting 00.55
    non-coronary vessel

> *Note* — Also use 00.40, 00.41, 00.42, or
> 00.43 to show the total number of vessels
> treated. Use code 00.44 once to show proce-
> dure on a bifurcated vessel. In addition, use
> 00.45, 00.46, 00.47, or 00.48 to show the
> number of vascular stents inserted.

      with angioplasty or atherectomy 39.50
      with bypass — *omit code*
      basilar 00.64
      carotid 00.63
      extracranial 00.64
      intracranial 00.65
      mesenteric 39.90
        bare, drug-coated 39.90
        drug-eluting 00.55
      peripheral 39.90
        bare, drug-coated 39.90
        drug-eluting 00.55
      renal 39.90
        bare, drug-coated 39.90
        drug-eluting 00.55
      vertebral 00.64

Insertion — *continued*
  stent(s) — *continued*
    pancreatic duct 52.92
      endoscopic 52.93
    peripheral vessel 39.90

> *Note* — Also use 00.40, 00.41, 00.42, or
> 00.43 to show the total number of vessels
> treated. Use code 00.44 once to show proce-
> dure on a bifurcated vessel. In addition, use
> 00.45, 00.46, 00.47, or 00.48 to show the
> number of vascular stents inserted.

      bare, drug-coated 39.90
      drug-eluting 00.55
    precerebral 00.64

> *Note* — Also use 00.40, 00.41, 00.42, or
> 00.43 to show the total number of vessels
> treated. Use code 00.44 once to show proce-
> dure on a bifurcated vessel. In addition, use
> 00.45, 00.46, 00.47, or 00.48 to show the
> number of vascular stents inserted.

    renal 39.90
      bare, drug-coated 39.90
      drug-eluting 00.55
    subclavian 39.90

> *Note* — Also use 00.40, 00.41, 00.42, or
> 00.43 to show the total number of vessels
> treated. Use code 00.44 once to show proce-
> dure on a bifurcated vessel In addition, use
> 00.45, 00.46, 00.47, or 00.48 to show the
> number of vascular stents inserted.

      bare, drug-coated 39.90
      drug-eluting 00.55
    tracheobronchial 96.05
    vertebral 00.64

> *Note* — Also use 00.40, 00.41, 00.42, or
> 00.43 to show the total number of vessels
> treated. Use code 00.44 once to show proce-
> dure on a bifurcated vessel. In addition, use
> 00.45, 00.46, 00.47, or 00.48 to show the
> number of vascular stents inserted.

  stimoceiver — *see* Implant, neurostimulator,
    by site
  stimulator for bone growth — *see* category
    78.9 ☑
  subdural
    grids 02.93
    strips 02.93
  suppository
    prostaglandin (for abortion) 96.49
    vagina 96.49
  Swan-Ganz catheter (pulmonary) 89.64
  tampon
    esophagus 96.06
    uterus 69.91
    vagina 96.14
      after delivery or abortion 75.8
  Tandem™ heart 37.68
  telescope (IMT) (miniature) 13.91
  testicular prosthesis (bilateral) (unilateral) 62.7
  tissue expander (skin) NEC 86.93
    breast 85.95
  tissue mandril (peripheral vessel) (Dacron)
    (Spark's type) 39.99
    with
      blood vessel repair 39.56
      vascular bypass or shunt — *see* Bypass,
        vascular
  tongs, skull (with synchronous skeletal trac-
    tion) 02.94
  totally implanted device for bone growth (in-
    vasive) — *see* category 78.9 ☑
  tube (*see also* Catheterization and Intubation)
    bile duct 51.43
      endoscopic 51.87
    chest 34.04
      revision (with lysis of adhesions) 34.04
        thoracoscopic 34.06
      thoracoscopic 34.06
    endotracheal 96.04
    esophagus (nonoperative) (Sengstaken)
      96.06
      permanent (silicone) (Souttar) 42.81

☑ Additional Digit Required — Refer to the Tabular List for Digit Selection   Subterms under main terms may continue to next column or page

32 — Volume 3 • October 2009   ▶◀ Revised Text   ● New Line   ▲ Revised Code   2010 ICD-9-CM

Insertion — *continued*
tube (*see also* Catheterization and Intubation)
— *continued*
feeding
esophageal 42.81
gastric 96.6
nasogastric 96.6
gastric
by gastrostomy — *see category*
43.1 ☑
for
decompression, intestinal 96.07
feeding 96.6
intercostal catheter (with water seal), for
drainage 34.04
revision (with lysis of adhe-sions) 34.04
thoracoscopic 34.06
thoracoscopic 34.06
Miller-Abbott (for intestinal decompression) 96.08
nasobiliary (drainage) 51.86
nasogastric (for intestinal decompression)
NEC 96.07
naso-intestinal 96.08
nasopancreatic drainage (endoscopic)
52.97
pancreatic duct 52.92
endoscopic 52.93
rectum 96.09
stomach (nasogastric) (for intestinal decompression) NEC 96.07
for feeding 96.6
tracheobronchial 96.05
umbrella device
atrial septum (King-Mills) 35.52
vena cava (Mobitz-Uddin) 38.7
ureteral stent (transurethral) 59.8
with ureterotomy 59.8 *[56.2]*
urinary sphincter, artificial (AUS) (inflatable)
58.93
vaginal mold 96.15
valve(s)
bronchus
multiple lobes 33.73 ●
single lobe 33.71 ●
Holter 02.2
Hufnagel — *see* Replacement, heart valve
pharyngeal (artificial) 31.75
Spitz-Holter 02.2
vas deferens 63.95
vascular access device, totally implantable
86.07
vena cava sieve or umbrella 38.7
Vinke tongs (skull) (with synchronous skeletal
traction) 02.94
X Stop™ 84.80
Instillation
bladder 96.49
digestive tract, except gastric gavage 96.43
genitourinary NEC 96.49
radioisotope (intracavitary) (intravenous) 92.28
thoracic cavity 34.92
Insufflation
Eustachian tube 20.8
fallopian tube (air) (dye) (gas) (saline) 66.8
for radiography — *see* Hysterosalpingog-
raphy
therapeutic substance 66.95
lumbar retroperitoneal, bilateral 88.15
Intercricothyroidotomy (for assistance in
breathing) 31.1
Interleukin-2, infusion
high-dose 00.15
low-dose 99.28
Intermittent positive pressure breathing (IPPB)
93.91
Interposition operation
antesternal or antethoracic NEC (*see also*
Anastomosis, esophagus, antesternal,
with, interposition) 42.68
esophageal reconstruction (intrathoracic)
(retrosternal) NEC (*see also* Anastomosis, esophagus, with, interposition)
42.58
uterine suspension 69.21

Interrogation
cardioverter-defibrillator, automatic (AICD)
with catheter based invasive electrophysiologic testing 37.26
with NIPS (arrhythmia induction) 37.20
interrogation only (bedside device check)
89.49
CRT-D (cardiac resynchronization defibrillator)
with catheter based invasive electrophysiologic testing 37.26
with NIPS (arrhythmia induction) 37.20
interrogation only (bedside device check)
89.49
CRT-P (cardiac resynchronization pacemaker)
with catheter based invasive electrophysiologic testing 37.26
with NIPS (arrhythmia induction) 37.20
interrogation only (bedside device check)
89.45
pacemaker
with catheter based invasive electrophysiologic testing 37.26
with NIPS (arrhythmia induction) 37.20
interrogation only (bedside device check)
89.45
Interruption
vena cava (inferior) (superior) 38.7
Interview (evaluation) (diagnostic)
medical, except psychiatric 89.05
brief (abbreviated history) 89.01
comprehensive (history and evaluation of
new problem) 89.03
limited (interval history) 89.02
specified type NEC 89.04
psychiatric NEC 94.19
follow-up 94.19
initial 94.19
pre-commitment 94.13
Intimectomy 38.10
abdominal 38.16
aorta (arch) (ascending) (descending) 38.14
head and neck NEC 38.12
intracranial NEC 38.11
lower limb 38.18
thoracic NEC 38.15
upper limb 38.13
Intraoperative anesthetic effect monitoring ●
and titration (IAEMT) 00.94 *[89.14]* ●
Introduction
orthodontic appliance 24.7
therapeutic substance (acting locally or systemically) NEC 99.29
bursa 83.96
hand 82.94
fascia 83.98
hand 82.96
heart 37.92
joint 81.92
temporomandibular 76.96
ligament (joint) 81.92
pericardium 37.93
soft tissue NEC 83.98
hand 82.96
tendon 83.97
hand 82.95
vein 39.92
Intubation — *see also* Catheterization and Insertion
bile duct(s) 51.59
common 51.51
endoscopic 51.87
endoscopic 51.87
esophagus (nonoperative) (Sengstaken) 96.06
permanent tube (silicone) (Souttar) 42.81
Eustachian tube 20.8
intestine (for decompression) 96.08
lacrimal for
dilation 09.42
tear drainage, intranasal 09.81
larynx 96.05
nasobiliary (drainage) 51.86
nasogastric
for
decompression, intestinal 96.07
feeding 96.6
naso-intestinal 96.08

Intubation — *see also* Catheterization and
Insertion — *continued*
nasolacrimal (duct) (with irrigation) 09.44
nasopancreatic drainage (endoscopic) 52.97
respiratory tract NEC 96.05
small intestine (Miller-Abbott) 96.08
stomach (nasogastric) (for intestinal decompression) NEC 96.07
for feeding 96.6
trachea 96.04
ventriculocisternal 02.2
Invagination, diverticulum
gastric 44.69
laparoscopic 44.68
pharynx 29.59
stomach 44.69
laparoscopic 44.68
Inversion
appendix 47.99
diverticulum
gastric 44.69
laparoscopic 44.68
intestine
large 45.49
endoscopic 45.43
small 45.34
stomach 44.69
laparoscopic 44.68
tunica vaginalis 61.49
IOERT (intra-operative electron radiation therapy)
92.41
IOM (intra-operative neurophysiologic monitoring) 00.94
Ionization, medical 99.27
Iontherapy 99.27
Iontophoresis 99.27
Iridectomy (basal) (buttonhole) (optical) (peripheral) (total) 12.14
with
capsulectomy 13.65
cataract extraction — *see* Extraction,
cataract
filtering operation (for glaucoma) NEC
12.65
scleral
fistulization 12.65
thermocauterization 12.62
trephination 12.61
Iridencleisis 12.63
Iridesis 12.63
Irido-capsulectomy 13.65
Iridocyclectomy 12.44
Iridocystectomy 12.42
Iridodesis 12.63
Iridoplasty NEC 12.39
Iridosclerectomy 12.65
Iridosclerotomy 12.69
Iridotasis 12.63
Iridotomy 12.12
by photocoagulation 12.12
for iris bombé 12.11
with transfixion 12.11
specified type NEC 12.12
Iron lung 93.99
Irradiation
gamma, stereotactic 92.32
Irrigation
anterior chamber (eye) 12.91
bronchus NEC 96.56
canaliculus 09.42
catheter
ureter 96.46
urinary, indwelling NEC 96.48
vascular 96.57
ventricular 02.41
wound 96.58
cholecystostomy 96.41
cornea 96.51
with removal of foreign body 98.21
corpus cavernosum 64.98
cystostomy 96.47
ear (removal of cerumen) 96.52
enterostomy 96.36
eye 96.51
with removal of foreign body 98.21
gastrostomy 96.36

Irrigation — *continued*
lacrimal
canaliculi 09.42
punctum 09.41
muscle 83.02
hand 82.02
nasal
passages 96.53
sinus 22.00
nasolacrimal duct 09.43
with insertion of tube or stent 09.44
nephrostomy 96.45
peritoneal 54.25
pyelostomy 96.45
rectal 96.39
stomach 96.33
tendon (sheath) 83.01
hand 82.01
trachea NEC 96.56
traumatic cataract 13.3
tube
biliary NEC 96.41
nasogastric NEC 96.34
pancreatic 96.42
ureterostomy 96.46
ventricular shunt 02.41
wound (cleaning) NEC 96.59
Irving operation (tubal ligation) 66.32
Irwin operation — *see also* Osteotomy 77.30
Ischiectomy (partial) 77.89
total 77.99
Ischiopubiotomy 77.39
Isolation
after contact with infectious disease 99.84
ileal loop 45.51
intestinal segment or pedicle flap
large 45.52
small 45.51
Isthmectomy, thyroid — *see also* Thyroidectomy, partial 06.39
IVUS — *see* Ultrasound, intravascular, by site ●

J

Jaboulay operation (gastroduodenostomy)
44.39
laparoscopic 44.38
Janeway operation (permanent gastrostomy)
43.19
Jatene operation (arterial switch) 35.84
Jejunectomy 45.62
Jejunocecostomy 45.93
Jejunocholecystostomy 51.32
Jejunocolostomy 45.93
Jejunoileostomy 45.91
Jejunojejunostomy 45.91
Jejunopexy 46.61
Jejunorrhaphy 46.73
Jejunostomy (feeding) 46.39
delayed opening 46.31
loop 46.01
percutaneous (endoscopic) (PEJ) 46.32
revision 46.41
Jejunotomy 45.02
Johanson operation (urethral reconstruction)
58.46
Jones operation
claw toe (transfer of extensor hallucis longus
tendon) 77.57
modified (with arthrodesis) 77.57
dacryocystorhinostomy 09.81
hammer toe (interphalangeal fusion) 77.56
modified (tendon transfer with arthrodesis)
77.57
repair of peroneal tendon 83.88
Joplin operation (exostectomy with tendon
transfer) 77.53

K

Kader operation (temporary gastrostomy) 43.19
Kasai portoenterostomy 51.37
Kaufman operation (for urinary stress inconti-
nence) 59.79
Kazanjiian operation (buccal vestibular sulcus
extension) 24.91
Kehr operation (hepatopexy) 50.69

☑ Additional Digit Required — Refer to the Tabular List for Digit Selection
▼ Subterms under main terms may continue to next column or page

2010 ICD-9-CM
▶◀ Revised Text
● New Line
▲ Revised Code
October 2009 • Volume 3 — 33

Keller operation (bunionectomy) 77.59
Kelly (-Kennedy) operation (urethrovesical plication) 59.3
Kelly-Stoeckel operation (urethrovesical plication) 59.3
Kelotomy 53.9
Keratectomy (complete) (partial) (superficial) 11.49
  for pterygium 11.39
    with corneal graft 11.32
Keratocentesis (for hyphema) 12.91
Keratomileusis 11.71
Keratophakia 11.72
Keratoplasty (tectonic) (with autograft) (with homograft) 11.60
  lamellar (nonpenetrating) (with homograft) 11.62
    with autograft 11.61
  penetrating (full-thickness) (with homograft) 11.64
    with autograft 11.63
  perforating — see Keratoplasty, penetrating
  refractive 11.71
  specified type NEC 11.69
Keratoprosthesis 11.73
Keratotomy (delimiting) (posterior) 11.1
  radial (refractive) 11.75
Kerr operation (low cervical cesarean section) 74.1
Kessler operation (arthroplasty, carpometacarpal joint) 81.74
Kidner operation (excision of accessory navicular bone) (with tendon transfer) 77.98
Killian operation (frontal sinusotomy) 22.41
Kineplasty — see Cineplasty
King-Steelquist operation (hind-quarter amputation) 84.19
Kirk operation (amputation through thigh) 84.17
Kockogram (ileal conduitogram) 87.78
Kockoscopy 45.12
Kock pouch
  bowel anastomosis — omit code
  continent ileostomy 46.22
  cutaneous uretero-ileostomy 56.51
  ESWL (extracorporeal shockwave lithotripsy) 98.51
  removal, calculus 57.19
  revision, cutaneous uretero-ileostomy 56.52
  urinary diversion procedure 56.51
Kondoleon operation (correction of lymphedema) 40.9
Krause operation (sympathetic denervation) 05.29
Kroener operation (partial salpingectomy) 66.69
Kroenlein operation (lateral orbitotomy) 16.01
Krönig operation (low cervical cesarean section) 74.1
Krukenberg operation (reconstruction of below-elbow amputation) 82.89
Kuhnt-Szymanowski operation (ectropion repair with lid reconstruction) 08.44
Kyphoplasty 81.66

L

Labbe operation (gastrotomy) 43.0
Labiectomy (bilateral) 71.62
  unilateral 71.61
Labyrinthectomy (transtympanic) 20.79
Labyrinthotomy (transtympanic) 20.79
Ladd operation (mobilization of intestine) 54.95
Lagrange operation (iridosclerectomy) 12.65
Lambrinudi operation (triple arthrodesis) 81.12
Laminectomy (decompression) (for exploration) 03.09
  as operative approach — omit code
  with
    excision of herniated intervertebral disc (nucleus pulposus) 80.51
    excision of other intraspinal lesion (tumor) 03.4
  reopening of site 03.02
Laminography — see Radiography
Laminoplasty, expansile 03.09
Laminotomy (decompression) (for exploration) 03.09

Laminotomy — continued
  as operative approach — omit code
  reopening of site 03.02
Langenbeck operation (cleft palate repair) 27.62
Laparoamnioscopy 75.31
Laparorrhaphy 54.63
Laparoscopy 54.21
  with
    biopsy (intra-abdominal) 54.24
      uterine ligaments 68.15
      uterus 68.16
    destruction of fallopian tubes — see Destruction, fallopian tube
Laparotomy NEC 54.19
  as operative approach — omit code
  exploratory (pelvic) 54.11
  reopening of recent operative site (for control of hemorrhage) (for exploration) (for incision of hematoma) 54.12
Laparotrachelotomy 74.1
Lapidus operation (bunionectomy with metatarsal osteotomy) 77.51
Larry operation (shoulder disarticulation) 84.08
Laryngectomy
  with radical neck dissection (with synchronous thyroidectomy) (with synchronous tracheostomy) 30.4
  complete (with partial laryngectomy) (with synchronous tracheostomy) 30.3
    with radical neck dissection (with synchronous thyroidectomy) (with synchronous tracheostomy) 30.4
  frontolateral partial (extended) 30.29
  glottosupraglottic partial 30.29
  lateral partial 30.29
  partial (frontolateral) (glottosupraglottic) (lateral) (submucous) (supraglottic) (vertical) 30.29
  radical (with synchronous thyroidectomy) (with synchronous tracheostomy) 30.4
  submucous (partial) 30.29
  supraglottic partial 30.29
  total (with partial pharyngectomy) (with synchronous tracheostomy) 30.3
    with radical neck dissection (with synchronous thyroidectomy) (with synchronous tracheostomy) 30.4
  vertical partial 30.29
  wide field 30.3
Laryngocentesis 31.3
Laryngoesophagectomy 30.4
Laryngofissure 30.29
Laryngogram 87.09
  contrast 87.07
Laryngopharyngectomy (with synchronous tracheostomy) 30.3
  radical (with synchronous thyroidectomy) 30.4
Laryngopharyngoesophagectomy (with synchronous tracheostomy) 30.3
  with radical neck dissection (with synchronous thyroidectomy) 30.4
Laryngoplasty 31.69
Laryngorrhaphy 31.61
Laryngoscopy (suspension) (through artificial stoma) 31.42
Laryngostomy (permanent) 31.29
  revision 31.63
  temporary (emergency) 31.1
Laryngotomy 31.3
Laryngotracheobronchoscopy 33.23
  with biopsy 33.24
Laryngotracheoscopy 31.42
Laryngotracheostomy (permanent) 31.29
  temporary (emergency) 31.1
Laryngotracheotomy (temporary) 31.1
  permanent 31.29
Laser — see also Coagulation, Destruction, and Photocoagulation by site
  angioplasty, percutaneous transluminal 39.59
  coronary — see Angioplasty, coronary
Laser interstitial thermal therapy (LITT) under guidance ●
  lesion ●
    brain 17.61 ●
    breast 17.69 ●
    head and neck 17.62 ●

Laser interstitial thermal therapy (LITT) under guidance — continued
  lesion — continued
    liver 17.63 ●
    lung 17.69 ●
    prostate 17.69 ●
    thyroid 17.62 ●
Lash operation
  internal cervical os repair 67.59
  laparoscopic supracervical hysterectomy 68.31
LASIK (laser-assisted in situ keratomileusis) 11.71
Latzko operation
  cesarean section 74.2
  colpocleisis 70.8
Lavage
  antral 22.00
  bronchus NEC 96.56
    diagnostic (endoscopic) bronchoalveolar lavage (BAL) 33.24
  endotracheal 96.56
  gastric 96.33
  lung (total) (whole) 33.99
    diagnostic (endoscopic) bronchoalveolar lavage (BAL) 33.24
  nasal sinus(es) 22.00
    by puncture 22.01
    through natural ostium 22.02
  peritoneal (diagnostic) 54.25
  trachea NEC 96.56
Leadbetter operation (urethral reconstruction) 58.46
Leadbetter-Politano operation (ureteroneocystostomy) 56.74
LEEP (loop electrosurgical excision procedure) of cervix 67.32
Le Fort operation (colpocleisis) 70.8
LeMesurier operation (cleft lip repair) 27.54
Lengthening
  bone (with bone graft) 78.30
    for reconstruction of thumb 82.69
    femur 78.35
    specified site NEC (see also category 78.3 ☑)
    tibia 78.37
    ulna 78.33
  extraocular muscle NEC 15.21
    multiple (two or more muscles) 15.4
  fascia 83.89
    hand 82.89
  hamstring NEC 83.85
  heel cord 83.85
  leg
    femur 78.35
    tibia 78.37
  levator palpebrae muscle 08.38
  muscle 83.85
    extraocular 15.21
      multiple (two or more muscles) 15.4
    hand 82.55
  palate 27.62
    secondary or subsequent 27.63
  tendon 83.85
    for claw toe repair 77.57
    hand 82.55
Leriche operation (periarterial sympathectomy) 05.25
Leucotomy, leukotomy 01.32
Leukopheresis, therapeutic 99.72
Lid suture operation (blepharoptosis) 08.31
Ligation
  adrenal vessel (artery) (vein) 07.43
  aneurysm 39.52
  appendages, dermal 86.26
  arteriovenous fistula 39.53
    coronary artery 36.99
  artery 38.80
    for control of epistaxis — see Control, epistaxis
    abdominal 38.86
    adrenal 07.43
    aorta (arch) (ascending) (descending) 38.84
    coronary (anomalous) 36.99
    ethmoidal 21.04
    external carotid 21.06
    head and neck NEC 38.82

Ligation — continued
  artery — continued
    intracranial NEC 38.81
    lower limb 38.88
    maxillary (transantral) 21.05
    middle meningeal 02.13
    thoracic NEC 38.85
    thyroid 06.92
    upper limb 38.83
  atrium, heart 37.99
  auricle, heart 37.99
  bleeding vessel — see Control, hemorrhage
  blood vessel 38.80
    abdominal
      artery 38.86
      vein 38.87
    adrenal 07.43
    aorta (arch) (ascending) (descending) 38.84
    esophagus 42.91
      endoscopic 42.33
    head and neck NEC 38.82
    intracranial NEC 38.81
    lower limb
      artery 38.88
      vein 38.89
    meningeal (artery) (longitudinal sinus) 02.13
    thoracic NEC 38.85
    thyroid 06.92
    upper limb (artery) (vein) 38.83
  bronchus 33.92
  cisterna chyli 40.64
  coronary
    artery (anomalous) 36.99
    sinus 36.39
  dermal appendage 86.26
  ductus arteriosus, patent 38.85
  esophageal vessel 42.91
    endoscopic 42.33
  ethmoidal artery 21.04
  external carotid artery 21.06
  fallopian tube (bilateral) (remaining) (solitary) 66.39
    by endoscopy (culdoscopy) (hysteroscopy) (laparoscopy) (peritoneoscopy) 66.29
    with
      crushing 66.31
        by endoscopy (laparoscopy) 66.21
      division 66.32
        by endoscopy (culdoscopy) (laparoscopy) (peritoneoscopy) 66.22
      Falope ring 66.39
        by endoscopy (laparoscopy) 66.29
    unilateral 66.92
  fistula, arteriovenous 39.53
    coronary artery 36.99
  gastric
    artery 38.86
    varices 44.91
      endoscopic 43.41
  hemorrhoids 49.45
  longitudinal sinus (superior) 02.13
  lymphatic (channel) (peripheral) 40.9
    thoracic duct 40.64
  maxillary artery 21.05
  meningeal vessel 02.13
  spermatic
    cord 63.72
      varicocele 63.1
    vein (high) 63.1
  splenic vessels 38.86
  subclavian artery 38.85
  superior longitudinal sinus 02.13
  supernumerary digit 86.26
  thoracic duct 40.64
  thyroid vessel (artery) (vein) 06.92
  toes (supernumerary) 86.26
  tooth 93.55
    impacted 24.6
  ulcer (peptic) (base) (bed) (bleeding vessel) 44.40
    duodenal 44.42
    gastric 44.41

☑ Additional Digit Required — Refer to the Tabular List for Digit Selection   ▽ Subterms under main terms may continue to next column or page

34 — Volume 3 • October 2009   ▶◀ Revised Text   ● New Line   ▲ Revised Code   2010 ICD-9-CM

☑ Additional Digit Required — Refer to the Tabular List for Digit Selection
▽ Subterms under main terms may continue to next column or page
2010 ICD-9-CM
►◄ Revised Text
● New Line
▲ Revised Code
October 2009 • Volume 3 — 35

☑ Additional Digit Required — Refer to the Tabular List for Digit Selection   ▽ Subterms under main terms may continue to next column or page

36 — Volume 3 • October 2009   ▶◀ Revised Text   ● New Line   ▲ Revised Code   **2010 ICD-9-CM**

Side tab: Index / Mammoplasty — Monitoring

Monitoring — *continued*
　cardiac output — *continued*
　　transesophageal (Doppler) (ultrasound) 89.68
　central venous pressure 89.62
　circulatory NEC 89.69
　continuous intra-arterial blood gas 89.60
　coronary blood flow (coincidence counting technique) 89.69
　　fractional flow reserve (FFR) 00.59
　　intravascular pressure measurement 00.59
　electroencephalographic 89.19
　　radio-telemetered 89.19
　　video 89.19
　fetus (fetal heart)
　　antepartum
　　　nonstress (fetal activity acceleration determinations) 75.34
　　　oxytocin challenge (contraction stress test) 75.35
　　　ultrasonography (early pregnancy) (Doppler) 88.78
　　intrapartum (during labor) (extrauterine) (external) 75.34
　　　ausculatory (stethoscopy) — omit code
　　　internal (with contraction measurements) (ECG) 75.32
　　　intrauterine (direct) (ECG) 75.32
　　　phonocardiographic (extrauterine) 75.34
　　　pulsed ultrasound (Doppler) 88.78
　　　transcervical fetal oxygen saturation monitoring 75.38
　　　transcervical fetal SpO$_2$ monitoring 75.38
　Holter-type device (cardiac) 89.50
　IAEMT (intraoperative anesthetic effect monitoring and titration) 00.94 [89.14] •
　intra-aneurysm sac pressure 00.58
　intracranial oxygen 01.16
　intracranial pressure 01.10
　intraoperative anesthetic effect monitoring ● and titration (IAEMT) 00.94 [89.14] ●
　intravascular pressure 00.69
　　coronary 00.59
　　iliac 00.69
　　intra-abdominal 00.69
　　intrathoracic 00.67
　　　aorta 00.67
　　　aortic arch 00.67
　　　carotid 00.67
　　mesenteric 00.69
　　peripheral 00.68
　　renal 00.69
　neurophysiologic
　　intra-operative 00.94
　partial pressure of brain oxygen (PbtO$_2$) 01.16
　pulmonary artery
　　pressure 89.63
　　wedge 89.64
　sleep (recording) — see categories 89.17-89.18
　systemic arterial pressure 89.61
　　intra-aneurysm sac pressure 00.58
　telemetry (cardiac) 89.54
　transesophageal cardiac output (Doppler) 89.68
　ventricular pressure (cardiac) 89.62
Moore operation (arthroplasty) 81.52
Moschowitz
　enterocele repair 70.92
　　with graft or prosthesis 70.93
　herniorrhaphy — see Repair, hernia, femoral
　sigmoidopexy 46.63
Mountain resort sanitarium 93.98
Mouth-to-mouth resuscitation 93.93
Moxibustion 93.35
MRI — see Imaging, magnetic resonance
Muller operation (banding of pulmonary artery) 38.85
Multiple sleep latency test (MSLT) 89.18
Mumford operation (partial claviculectomy) 77.81
Musculoplasty — see also Repair, muscle 83.87
　hand (see also Repair, muscle, hand) 82.89
Music therapy 93.84

Mustard operation (interatrial transposition of venous return) 35.91
Myectomy 83.45
　for graft 83.43
　　hand 82.34
　anorectal 48.92
　eye muscle 15.13
　　multiple 15.3
　　hand 82.36
　　　for graft 82.34
　levator palpebrae 08.33
　rectal 48.92
Myelogram, myelography (air) (gas) 87.21
　posterior fossa 87.02
Myelotomy
　spine, spinal (cord) (tract) (one-stage) (two-stage) 03.29
　percutaneous 03.21
Myocardiectomy (infarcted area) 37.33
Myocardiotomy 37.11
Myoclasis 83.99
　hand 82.99
Myomectomy (uterine) 68.29
　broad ligament 69.19
Myoplasty — see also Repair, muscle 83.87
　hand (see also Repair, muscle, hand) 82.89
　mastoid 19.9
Myorrhaphy 83.65
　hand 82.46
Myosuture 83.65
　hand 82.46
Myotasis 93.27
Myotenontoplasty — see also Repair, tendon 83.88
　hand 82.86
Myotenoplasty — see also Repair, tendon 83.88
　hand 82.86
Myotenotomy 83.13
　hand 82.11
Myotomy 83.02
　with division 83.19
　　hand 82.19
　colon NEC 46.92
　　sigmoid 46.91
　cricopharyngeal 29.31
　　that for pharyngeal (pharyngoesophageal) diverticulectomy 29.32
　esophagus 42.7
　eye (oblique) (rectus) 15.21
　　multiple (two or more muscles) 15.4
　hand 82.02
　　with division 82.19
　levator palpebrae 08.38
　sigmoid (colon) 46.91
Myringectomy 20.59
Myringodectomy 20.59
Myringomalleolabyrinthopexy 19.52
Myringoplasty (epitympanic, type I) (by cauterization) (by graft) 19.4
　revision 19.6
Myringostapediopexy 19.53
Myringostomy 20.01
Myringotomy (with aspiration) (with drainage) 20.09
　with insertion of tube or drainage device (button) (grommet) 20.01

N

Nailing, intramedullary — see Reduction, fracture with internal fixation
　with fracture reduction — see Reduction, fracture with internal fixation
　internal (without fracture reduction) 78.50
Narcoanalysis 94.21
Narcosynthesis 94.21
Narrowing, palpebral fissure 08.51
Nasopharyngogram 87.09
　contrast 87.06
Necropsy 89.8
Needleoscopy (fetus) 75.31
Needling
　Bartholin's gland (cyst) 71.21
　cataract (secondary) 13.64
　fallopian tube 66.91
　hydrocephalic head 73.8
　lens (capsule) 13.2

Needling — *continued*
　pupillary membrane (iris) 12.35
Nephrectomy (complete) (total) (unilateral) 55.51
　bilateral 55.54
　partial (wedge) 55.4
　remaining or solitary kidney 55.52
　removal transplanted kidney 55.53
Nephrocolopexy 55.7
Nephrocystanastomosis NEC 56.73
Nephrolithotomy 55.01
Nephrolysis 59.02
　laparoscopic 59.03
Nephropexy 55.7
Nephroplasty 55.89
Nephropyeloplasty 55.87
Nephropyeloureterostomy 55.86
Nephrorrhaphy 55.81
Nephroscopy 55.21
Nephrostolithotomy, percutaneous 55.03
Nephrostomy (with drainage tube) 55.02
　closure 55.82
　percutaneous 55.03
　　with fragmentation (ultrasound) 55.04
Nephrotomogram, nephrotomography NEC 87.72
Nephrotomy 55.01
Nephroureterectomy (with bladder cuff) 55.51
Nephroureterocystectomy 55.51 [57.79]
Nerve block (cranial) (peripheral) NEC — see also Block, by site 04.81
Neurectasis (cranial) (peripheral) 04.91
Neurectomy (cranial) (infraorbital) (occipital) (peripheral) (spinal) NEC 04.07
　gastric (vagus) (see also Vagotomy) 44.00
　opticociliary 12.79
　paracervical 05.22
　presacral 05.24
　retrogasserian 04.07
　sympathetic — see Sympathectomy
　trigeminal 04.07
　tympanic 20.91
Neuroexeresis NEC 04.07
Neuroablation
　radiofrequency 04.2
Neuroanastomosis (cranial) (peripheral) NEC 04.74
　accessory-facial 04.72
　accessory-hypoglossal 04.73
　hypoglossal-facial 04.71
Neurolysis (peripheral nerve) NEC 04.49
　carpal tunnel 04.43
　cranial nerve NEC 04.42
　spinal (cord) (nerve roots) 03.6
　tarsal tunnel 04.44
　trigeminal nerve 04.41
Neuromonitoring
　intra-operative 00.94
Neuroplasty (cranial) (peripheral) NEC 04.79
　of old injury (delayed repair) 04.76
　revision 04.75
Neurorrhaphy (cranial) (peripheral) 04.3
Neurotomy (cranial) (peripheral) (spinal) NEC 04.04
　acoustic 04.01
　glossopharyngeal 29.92
　lacrimal branch 05.0
　retrogasserian 04.02
　sympathetic 05.0
　vestibular 04.01
Neurotripsy (peripheral) NEC 04.03
　trigeminal 04.02
Nicola operation (tenodesis for recurrent dislocation of shoulder) 81.82
Nimodipine, infusion 99.75
NIPS (non-invasive programmed electrical stimulation) 37.20
Nissen operation (fundoplication of stomach) 44.66
　laparoscopic 44.67
Noble operation (plication of small intestine) 46.62
Norman Miller operation (vaginopexy) 70.77
　with graft or prosthesis 70.78
Norton operation (extraperitoneal cesarean section) 74.2

Nuclear magnetic resonance imaging — see Imaging, magnetic resonance
Nutrition, concentrated substances
　enteral infusion (of) 96.6
　parenteral, total 99.15
　peripheral parenteral 99.15

O

Ober (-Yount) operation (gluteal-iliotibial fasciotomy) 83.14
Obliteration
　bone cavity (see also Osteoplasty) 78.40
　calyceal diverticulum 55.39
　canaliculi 09.6
　cerebrospinal fistula 02.12
　cul-de-sac 70.92
　　with graft or prosthesis 70.93
　frontal sinus (with fat) 22.42
　lacrimal punctum 09.91
　lumbar pseudomeningocele 03.51
　lymphatic structure(s) (peripheral) 40.9
　maxillary sinus 22.31
　meningocele (sacral) 03.51
　pelvic 68.8
　pleural cavity 34.6
　sacral meningocele 03.51
　Skene's gland 71.3
　tympanomastoid cavity 19.9
　vagina, vaginal (partial) (total) 70.4
　vault 70.8
Occlusal molds (dental) 89.31
Occlusion
　artery
　　by embolization — see Embolization, artery
　　by endovascular approach — see Embolization, artery
　　by ligation — see Ligation, artery
　fallopian tube — see Ligation, fallopian tube
　patent ductus arteriosus (PDA) 38.85
　vein
　　by embolization — see Embolization, vein
　　by endovascular approach — see Embolization, vein
　　by ligation — see Ligation, vein
　vena cava (surgical) 38.7
Occupational therapy 93.83
OCT (optical coherence tomography) (intravascular imaging) ●
　coronary vessel(s) 38.24 ●
　non-coronary vessel(s) 38.25 ●
O'Donoghue operation (triad knee repair) 81.43
Odontectomy NEC — see also Removal, tooth, surgical 23.19
Oleothorax 33.39
Olshausen operation (uterine suspension) 69.22
Omentectomy 54.4
Omentofixation 54.74
Omentopexy 54.74
Omentoplasty 54.74
Omentorrhaphy 54.74
Omentotomy 54.19
Omphalectomy 54.3
Onychectomy 86.23
Onychoplasty 86.86
Onychotomy 86.09
　with drainage 86.04
Oophorectomy (unilateral) 65.39
　with salpingectomy 65.49
　　laparoscopic 65.41
　bilateral (same operative episode) 65.51
　　with salpingectomy 65.61
　　　laparoscopic 65.63
　　laparoscopic 65.53
　　laparoscopic 65.31
　partial 65.29
　　laparoscopic 65.25
　　wedge 65.22
　　　that by laparoscope 65.24
　remaining ovary 65.52
　　with tube 65.62
　　　laparoscopic 65.64
　　laparoscopic 65.54
Oophorocystectomy 65.29
　laparoscopic 65.25
Oophoropexy 65.79

Operation — Operation

☑ Additional Digit Required — Refer to the Tabular List for Digit Selection   ▽ Subterms under main terms may continue to next column or page

2010 ICD-9-CM   ▶◀ Revised Text   ● New Line   ▲ Revised Code   **Volume 3 — 39**

Index

Operation — Operation

☑ Additional Digit Required — Refer to the Tabular List for Digit Selection   ▽ Subterms under main terms may continue to next column or page

40 — Volume 3   ▶◀ Revised Text   ● New Line   ▲ Revised Code   2010 ICD-9-CM

☑ Additional Digit Required — Refer to the Tabular List for Digit Selection   Ⓦ Subterms under main terms may continue to next column or page

2010 ICD-9-CM   ▶◀ Revised Text   ● New Line   ▲ Revised Code   October 2009 · Volume 3 — 41

Procedure — *see also* specific procedure — *continued*
  diagnostic — *continued*
    spine, spinal (canal) (cord) (meninges) (structure) 03.39
    spleen 41.39
    stomach 44.19
    subcutaneous tissue 86.19
    sympathetic nerve 05.19
    tarsus 09.19
    tendon NEC 83.29
      extraocular 15.09
    testicle 62.19
    thalamus 01.18
    thoracic duct 40.19
    thorax 34.28
    thymus 07.19
    thyroid gland 06.19
    tongue 25.09
    tonsils 28.19
    tooth 24.19
    trachea 31.49
    tunica vaginalis 61.19
    ureter 56.39
    urethra 58.29
    uterus and supporting structures 68.19
    uvula 27.29
    vagina 70.29
    vas deferens 63.09
    vesical 57.39
    vessel (blood) (any site) 38.29
    vitreous 14.19
    vulva 71.19
  fistulizing, sclera NEC 12.69
  miscellaneous (nonoperative) NEC 99.99
  respiratory (nonoperative) NEC 93.99
  surgical — *see* Operation
Proctectasis 96.22
Proctectomy (partial) — *see also* Resection, rectum 48.69
  abdominoperineal, NOS 48.50
    laparoscopic 48.51
    open 48.52
    other 48.59
  complete (Miles) (Rankin), NOS 48.50
    laparoscopic 48.51
    open 48.52
    other 48.59
  pull-through
    laparoscopic 48.42
    not otherwise specified 48.40
    open 48.43
    other 48.49
Proctoclysis 96.37
Proctolysis 48.99
Proctopexy (Delorme) 48.76
  abdominal (Ripstein) 48.75
Proctoplasty 48.79
Proctorrhaphy 48.71
Proctoscopy 48.23
  with biopsy 48.24
  through stoma (artificial) 48.22
  transabdominal approach 48.21
Proctosigmoidectomy — *see also* Resection, rectum 48.69
Proctosigmoidopexy 48.76
Proctosigmoidoscopy (rigid) 48.23
  with biopsy 48.24
  flexible 45.24
  through stoma (artificial) 48.22
  transabdominal approach 48.21
Proctostomy 48.1
Proctotomy (decompression) (linear) 48.0
Production — *see also* Formation and Creation
  atrial septal defect 35.42
  subcutaneous tunnel for esophageal anastomosis 42.86
    with anastomosis — *see* Anastomosis, esophagus, antesternal
Prognathic recession 76.64
Prophylaxis, dental (scaling) (polishing) 96.54
Prostatectomy (complete) (partial) NEC 60.69
  loop 60.29
  perineal 60.62
  radical (any approach) 60.5
  retropubic (punch) (transcapsular) 60.4

Prostatectomy — *continued*
  suprapubic (punch) (transvesical) 60.3
  transcapsular NEC 60.69
    retropubic 60.4
  transperineal 60.62
  transurethral 60.29
    ablation (contact) (noncontact) by laser 60.21
    electrovaporization 60.29
    enucleative 60.29
    resection of prostate (TURP) 60.29
    ultrasound guided laser induced (TULIP) 60.21
  transvesical punch (suprapubic) 60.3
Prostatocystotomy 60.0
Prostatolithotomy 60.0
Prostatotomy (perineal) 60.0
Prostatovesiculectomy 60.5
Protection (of)
  individual from his surroundings 99.84
  surroundings from individual 99.84
Psychoanalysis 94.31
Psychodrama 94.43
Psychotherapy NEC 94.39
  biofeedback 94.39
  exploratory verbal 94.37
  group 94.44
    for psychosexual dysfunctions 94.41
  play 94.36
  psychosexual dysfunctions 94.34
  supportive verbal 94.38
PTCA (percutaneous transluminal coronary angioplasty) — *see* Angioplasty, balloon, coronary
Ptyalectasis 26.91
Ptyalithotomy 26.0
Ptyalolithotomy 26.0
Pubiotomy 77.39
  assisting delivery 73.94
Pubococcygeoplasty 59.71
Puestow operation (pancreaticojejunostomy) 52.96
Pull-through
  abdomino-anal 48.49
  abdominoperineal 48.49
    Duhamel type 48.65
  endorectal 48.41
Pulmowrap 93.99
Pulpectomy — *see also* Therapy, root canal 23.70
Pulpotomy — *see also* Therapy, root canal 23.70
Pump-oxygenator, for extracorporeal circulation 39.61
  percutaneous 39.66
Punch
  operation
    bladder neck, transurethral 57.49
    prostate — *see* Prostatectomy
  resection, vocal cords 30.22
Puncture
  antrum (nasal) (bilateral) (unilateral) 22.01
  artery NEC 38.98
    for
      arteriography (*see also* Arteriography) 88.40
      coronary arteriography (*see also* Arteriography, coronary) 88.57
    percutaneous vascular closure — *omit code*
  bladder, suprapubic (for drainage) NEC 57.18
    needle 57.11
    percutaneous (suprapubic) 57.17
  bursa 83.94
    hand 82.92
  cisternal 01.01
    with contrast media 87.02
  cranial 01.09
    with contrast media 87.02
  craniobuccal pouch 07.72
  craniopharyngioma 07.72
  fallopian tube 66.91
  fontanel, anterior 01.09
  heart 37.0
    for intracardiac injection 37.92
  hypophysis 07.72
  iris 12.12
  joint 81.91

Puncture — *continued*
  kidney (percutaneous) 55.92
  larynx 31.98
  lumbar (diagnostic) (removal of dye) 03.31
  lung (for aspiration) 33.93
  nasal sinus 22.01
  pericardium 37.0
  pituitary gland 07.72
  pleural cavity 34.91
  Rathke's pouch 07.72
  spinal 03.31
  spleen 41.1
    for biopsy 41.32
  sternal (for bone marrow biopsy) 41.31
    donor for bone marrow transplant 41.91
  vein NEC 38.99
    for
      phlebography (*see also* Phlebography) 88.60
      transfusion — *see* Transfusion
  ventricular shunt tubing 01.02
Pupillotomy 12.35
Push-back operation (cleft palate repair) 27.62
Putti-Platt operation (capsulorrhaphy of shoulder for recurrent dislocation) 81.82
pVAD (percutaneous ventricular assist device) 37.68
Pyelogram (intravenous) 87.73
  infusion (continuous) (diuretic) 87.73
  percutaneous 87.75
  retrograde 87.74
Pyeloileostomy 56.71
Pyelolithotomy 55.11
Pyeloplasty 55.87
Pyelorrhaphy 55.81
Pyeloscopy 55.22
Pyelostolithotomy, percutaneous 55.03
Pyelostomy 55.12
  closure 55.82
Pyelotomy 55.11
Pyeloureteroplasty 55.87
Pylorectomy 43.6
Pyloroduodenotomy — *see* category 44.2 ☑
Pyloromyotomy (Ramstedt) (with wedge resection) 43.3
Pyloroplasty (Finney) (Heineke-Mikulicz) 44.29
  dilation, endoscopic 44.22
    by incision 44.21
  not elsewhere classified 44.29
  revision 44.29
Pylorostomy — *see* Gastrostomy

Q

Quadrant resection of breast 85.22
Quadricepsplasty (Thompson) 83.86
Quarantine 99.84
Quenuthoracoplasty 77.31
Quotient, respiratory 89.38

R

Rabbit ear (Tudor) **operation** 59.79
Rachicentesis 03.31
Rachitomy 03.09
Radiation therapy — *see also* Therapy, radiation
  teleradiotherapy — *see* Teleradiotherapy
Radical neck dissection — *see* Dissection, neck
Radicotomy 03.1
Radiculectomy 03.1
Radiculotomy 03.1
Radiography (diagnostic) NEC 88.39
  abdomen, abdominal (flat plate) NEC 88.19
    wall (soft tissue) NEC 88.09
  adenoid 87.09
  ankle (skeletal) 88.28
    soft tissue 88.37
  bone survey 88.31
  bronchus 87.49
  chest (routine) 87.44
    wall NEC 87.39
  clavicle 87.43
  computer assisted surgery (CAS) with fluoroscopy 00.33
  contrast (air) (gas) (radio-opaque substance) NEC
    abdominal wall 88.03

Radiography — *continued*
  contrast — *continued*
    arteries (by fluoroscopy) — *see* Arteriography
    bile ducts NEC 87.54
    bladder NEC 87.77
    brain 87.02
    breast 87.35
    bronchus NEC (transcricoid) 87.32
      endotracheal 87.31
    epididymis 87.93
    esophagus 87.61
    fallopian tubes
      gas 87.82
      opaque dye 87.83
    fistula (sinus tract) (*see also* Radiography, contrast, by site)
      abdominal wall 88.03
      chest wall 87.38
    gallbladder NEC 87.59
    intervertebral disc(s) 87.21
    joints 88.32
    larynx 87.07
    lymph — *see* Lymphangiogram
    mammary ducts 87.35
    mediastinum 87.33
    nasal sinuses 87.15
    nasolacrimal ducts 87.05
    nasopharynx 87.06
    orbit 87.14
    pancreas 87.66
    pelvis
      gas 88.12
      opaque dye 88.11
    peritoneum NEC 88.13
    retroperitoneum NEC 88.15
    seminal vesicles 87.91
    sinus tract (*see also* Radiography, contrast, by site)
      abdominal wall 88.03
      chest wall 87.38
      nose 87.15
    skull 87.02
    spinal disc(s) 87.21
    trachea 87.32
    uterus
      gas 87.82
      opaque dye 87.83
    vas deferens 87.94
    veins (by fluoroscopy) — *see* Phlebography
    vena cava (inferior) (superior) 88.51
  dental NEC 87.12
  diaphragm 87.49
  digestive tract NEC 87.69
    barium swallow 87.61
    lower GI series 87.64
    small bowel series 87.63
    upper GI series 87.62
  elbow (skeletal) 88.22
    soft tissue 88.35
  epididymis NEC 87.95
  esophagus 87.69
    barium-swallow 87.61
  eye 95.14
  face, head, and neck 87.09
  facial bones 87.16
  fallopian tubes 87.85
  foot 88.28
  forearm (skeletal) 88.22
    soft tissue 88.35
  frontal area, facial 87.16
  genital organs
    female NEC 87.89
    male NEC 87.99
  hand (skeletal) 88.23
    soft tissue 88.35
  head NEC 87.09
  heart 87.49
  hip (skeletal) 88.26
    soft tissue 88.37
  intestine NEC 87.65
  kidney-ureter-bladder (KUB) 87.79
  knee (skeletal) 88.27
    soft tissue 88.37
  KUB (kidney-ureter-bladder) 87.79

☑ Additional Digit Required — Refer to the Tabular List for Digit Selection   Subterms under main terms may continue to next column or page

44 — Volume 3   ▶◀ Revised Text   ● New Line   ▲ Revised Code   **2010 ICD-9-CM**

Index (left margin)

Reduction — Release (left margin)

Reduction — *continued*
fracture (bone) (with cast) (with splint) (with traction device) (closed) 79.00
  with internal fixation 79.10
  alveolar process (with stabilization of teeth)
    mandible (closed) 76.75
      open 76.77
    maxilla (closed) 76.73
      open 76.77
      open 76.77
  ankle — *see* Reduction, fracture, leg
  arm (closed) NEC 79.02
    with internal fixation 79.12
    open 79.22
      with internal fixation 79.32
  blow-out — *see* Reduction, fracture, orbit
  carpal, metacarpal (closed) 79.03
    with internal fixation 79.13
    open 79.23
      with internal fixation 79.33
  epiphysis — *see* Reduction, separation
  facial (bone) NEC 76.70
    closed 76.78
    open 76.79
  femur (closed) 79.05
    with internal fixation 79.15
    open 79.25
      with internal fixation 79.35
  fibula (closed) 79.06
    with internal fixation 79.16
    open 79.26
      with internal fixation 79.36
  foot (closed) NEC 79.07
    with internal fixation 79.17
    open 79.27
      with internal fixation 79.37
  hand (closed) NEC 79.03
    with internal fixation 79.13
    open 79.23
      with internal fixation 79.33
  humerus (closed) 79.01
    with internal fixation 79.11
    open 79.21
      with internal fixation 79.31
  jaw (lower) (*see also* Reduction, fracture, mandible)
    upper — *see* Reduction, fracture, maxilla
  larynx 31.64
  leg (closed) NEC 79.06
    with internal fixation 79.16
    open 79.26
      with internal fixation 79.36
  malar (closed) 76.71
    open 76.72
  mandible (with dental wiring) (closed) 76.75
    open 76.76
  maxilla (with dental wiring) (closed) 76.73
    open 76.74
  nasal (closed) 21.71
    open 21.72
  open 79.20
    with internal fixation 79.30
    specified site NEC 79.29
      with internal fixation 79.39
  orbit (rim) (wall) (closed) 76.78
    open 76.79
  patella (open) (with internal fixation) 79.36
  phalanges
    foot (closed) 79.08
      with internal fixation 79.18
      open 79.28
        with internal fixation 79.38
    hand (closed) 79.04
      with internal fixation 79.14
      open 79.24
        with internal fixation 79.34
  radius (closed) 79.02
    with internal fixation 79.12
    open 79.22
      with internal fixation 79.32
  skull 02.02
  specified site (closed) NEC 79.09
    with internal fixation 79.19
    open 79.29

Reduction — *continued*
fracture — *continued*
  specified site — *continued*
    open — *continued*
      with internal fixation 79.39
    spine 03.53
    tarsal, metatarsal (closed) 79.07
      with internal fixation 79.17
      open 79.27
        with internal fixation 79.37
    tibia (closed) 79.06
      with internal fixation 79.16
      open 79.26
        with internal fixation 79.36
    ulna (closed) 79.02
      with internal fixation 79.12
      open 79.22
        with internal fixation 79.32
    vertebra 03.53
    zygoma, zygomatic arch (closed) 76.71
      open 76.72
  fracture-dislocation — *see* Reduction, fracture
heart volume 37.35
hemorrhoids (manual) 49.41
hernia (*see also* Repair, hernia)
  manual 96.27
intussusception (open) 46.80
  with
    fluoroscopy 96.29
    ionizing radiation enema 96.29
    ultrasonography guidance 96.29
  hydrostatic 96.29
  large intestine 46.82
    endoscopic (balloon) 46.85
  pneumatic 96.29
  small intestine 46.81
lung volume 32.22
  biologic lung volume reduction (BLVR) — *see* category 33.7 ☑
malrotation, intestine (manual) (surgical) 46.80
  large 46.82
    endoscopic (balloon) 46.85
  small 46.81
mammoplasty (bilateral) 85.32
  unilateral 85.31
prolapse
  anus (operative) 49.94
  colostomy (manual) 96.28
  enterostomy (manual) 96.28
  ileostomy (manual) 96.28
  rectum (manual) 96.26
  uterus
    by pessary 96.18
    surgical 69.22
ptosis overcorrection 08.37
retroversion, uterus by pessary 96.18
separation, epiphysis (with internal fixation) (closed) 79.40
  femur (closed) 79.45
    open 79.55
  fibula (closed) 79.46
    open 79.56
  humerus (closed) 79.41
    open 79.51
  open 79.50
  specified site (closed) NEC (*see also* category) 79.4 ☑
    open — *see* category 79.5 ☑
  tibia (closed) 79.46
    open 79.56
size
  abdominal wall (adipose) (pendulous) 86.83
  arms (adipose) (batwing) 86.83
  breast (bilateral) 85.32
    unilateral 85.31
  buttocks (adipose) 86.83
  finger (macrodactyly repair) 82.83
  skin 86.83
  subcutaneous tissue 86.83
  thighs (adipose) 86.83
torsion
  intestine (manual) (surgical) 46.80
    large 46.82
      endoscopic (balloon) 46.85
    small 46.81

Reduction — *continued*
torsion — *continued*
  kidney pedicle 55.84
  omentum 54.74
  spermatic cord 63.52
    with orchiopexy 62.5
  testis 63.52
    with orchiopexy 62.5
  uterus NEC 69.98
    gravid 75.99
  ventricular 37.35
volvulus
  intestine 46.80
    large 46.82
      endoscopic (balloon) 46.85
    small 46.81
  stomach 44.92
Reefing, joint capsule — *see also* Arthroplasty 81.96
Re-entry operation (aorta) 39.54
Re-establishment, continuity — *see also* Anastomosis
  bowel 46.50
  fallopian tube 66.79
  vas deferens 63.82
Referral (for)
  psychiatric aftercare (halfway house) (outpatient clinic) 94.52
  psychotherapy 94.51
  rehabilitation
    alcoholism 94.53
    drug addiction 94.54
    psychologic NEC 94.59
    vocational 94.55
Reformation
  cardiac pacemaker pocket, new site (skin) (subcutaneous) 37.79
  cardioverter/defibrillator (automatic) pocket, new site (skin) (subcutaneous) 37.79
  chamber of eye 12.99
Refracture
  bone (for faulty union) (*see also* Osteoclasis) 78.70
  nasal bones 21.88
Refusion
  spinal, NOS 81.30

> Note: Also use either 81.62, 81.63, or 81.64 as an additional code to show the total number of vertebrae fused

  atlas-axis (anterior) (transoral) (posterior) 81.31
  cervical (C_2 level or below) NEC 81.32
    anterior (interbody), anterolateral technique 81.32
    C_1-C_2 level (anterior) (posterior) 81.31
    posterior (interbody), posterolateral technique 81.33
  craniocervical (anterior) (transoral) (posterior) 81.31
  dorsal, dorsolumbar NEC 81.35
    anterior (interbody) anterolateral technique 81.34
    posterior (interbody), posterolateral technique 81.35
  lumbar, lumbosacral NEC 81.38
    anterior (interbody), anterolateral technique 81.36
    anterior lumbar interbody fusion (ALIF) 81.36
    lateral transverse process technique 81.37
    posterior lumbar interbody fusion (PLIF) 81.38
    posterior (interbody), posterolateral technique 81.38
    transforaminal lumbar interbody fusion (TLIF) 81.38
  number of vertebrae — *see* codes 81.62-81.64
  occiput — C_2 (anterior) (transoral) (posterior) 81.31
  refusion NEC 81.39
Regional blood flow study 92.05
Regulation, menstrual 69.6
Rehabilitation programs NEC 93.89

Rehabilitation programs — *continued*
  alcohol 94.61
    with detoxification 94.63
    combined alcohol and drug 94.67
      with detoxification 94.69
  drug 94.64
    with detoxification 94.66
    combined drug and alcohol 94.67
      with detoxification 94.69
  sheltered employment 93.85
  vocational 93.85
Reimplantation
  adrenal tissue (heterotopic) (orthotopic) 07.45
  artery 39.59
    renal, aberrant 39.55
  bile ducts following excision of ampulla of Vater 51.62
  extremity — *see* Reattachment, extremity
  fallopian tube into uterus 66.74
  kidney 55.61
  lung 33.5 ☑
  ovary 65.72
    laparoscopic 65.75
  pancreatic tissue 52.81
  parathyroid tissue (heterotopic) (orthotopic) 06.95
  pulmonary artery for hemitruncus repair 35.83
  renal vessel, aberrant 39.55
  testis in scrotum 62.5
  thyroid tissue (heterotopic) (orthotopic) 06.94
  tooth 23.5
  ureter into bladder 56.74
Reinforcement — *see also* Repair, by site
  sclera NEC 12.88
    with graft 12.87
Reinsertion — *see also* Insertion or Revision
  cystostomy tube 59.94
  fixation device (internal) (*see also* Fixation, bone, internal) 78.50
  heart valve (prosthetic) 35.95
  Holter (-Spitz) valve 02.42
  implant (expelled) (extruded)
    eyeball (with conjunctival graft) 16.62
    orbital 16.62
  nephrostomy tube 55.93
  pyelostomy tube 55.94
  ureteral stent (transurethral) 59.8
    with ureterotomy 59.8 [56.2]
  ureterostomy tube 59.93
  valve
    heart (prosthetic) 35.95
    ventricular (cerebral) 02.42
Relaxation — *see also* Release training 94.33
Release
  carpal tunnel (for nerve decompression) 04.43
  celiac artery axis 39.91
  central slip, extensor tendon hand (mallet finger repair) 82.84
  chordee 64.42
  clubfoot NEC 83.84
  de Quervain's tenosynovitis 82.01
  Dupuytren's contracture (by palmar fasciectomy) 82.35
    by fasciotomy (subcutaneous) 82.12
      with excision 82.35
  Fowler (mallet finger repair) 82.84
  joint (capsule) (adherent) (constrictive) (*see also* Division, joint capsule) 80.40
  laryngeal 31.92
  ligament (*see also* Division, ligament) 80.40
    median arcuate 39.91
  median arcuate ligament 39.91
  muscle (division) 83.19
    hand 82.19
  nerve (peripheral) NEC 04.49
    cranial NEC 04.42
    trigeminal 04.41
  pressure, intraocular 12.79
  scar tissue
    skin 86.84
    stoma — *see* Revision, stoma
  tarsal tunnel 04.44
  tendon 83.13
    hand 82.11
      extensor, central slip (repair mallet finger) 82.84

☑ Additional Digit Required — Refer to the Tabular List for Digit Selection   ⬛ Subterms under main terms may continue to next column or page

Release — *continued*
tendon — *continued*
  sheath 83.01
    hand 82.01
  tenosynovitis 83.01
    abductor pollicis longus 82.01
    de Quervain's 82.01
    external pollicis brevis 82.01
    hand 82.01
torsion
  intestine 46.80
    large 46.82
      endoscopic (balloon) 46.85
    small 46.81
  kidney pedicle 55.84
  ovary 65.95
  testes 63.52
transverse carpal ligament (for nerve decompression) 04.43
trigger finger or thumb 82.01
urethral stricture 58.5
Volkmann's contracture
  excision of scar, muscle 83.32
  fasciotomy 83.14
  muscle transplantation 83.77
web contracture (skin) 86.84
Relief — *see* Release
Relocation — *see also* Revision
cardiac device (CRT-D) (CRT-P) (defibrillator) (pacemaker) pocket, new site (skin) (subcutaneous) 37.79
  CRT-D pocket 37.79
  CRT-P pocket 37.79
subcutaneous device pocket NEC 86.09
Remobilization
joint 93.16
stapes 19.0
Remodel
ventricle 37.35
Removal — *see also* Excision
Abrams bar (chest wall) 34.01
abscess — *see* Incision, by site
adenoid tag(s) 28.6
anal sphincter
  with revision 49.75
  without revision 49.76
arch bars (orthodontic) 24.8
  immobilization device 97.33
arterial graft or prosthesis 39.49
arteriovenous shunt (device) 39.43
  with creation of new shunt 39.42
artificial heart
  internal biventricular replacement system 37.55
Barton's tongs (skull) 02.95
  with synchronous replacement 02.94
bladder sphincter, artificial 58.99
  with replacement 58.93
blood clot (*see also* Incision, by site)
  bladder (by incision) 57.19
    without incision 57.0
  kidney (without incision) 56.0
    by incision 55.01
  ureter
    by incision 56.2
bone fragment (chip) (*see also* Incision, bone) 77.10
  joint (*see also* Arthrotomy) 80.10
  necrotic (*see also* Sequestrectomy, bone) 77.00
    joint (*see also* Arthrotomy) 80.10
  skull 01.25
    with debridement compound fracture 02.02
bone growth stimulator — *see* category 78.6 ☑
bony spicules, spinal canal 03.53
brace 97.88
breast implant 85.94
  tissue expander 85.96
bronchial device or substance
  endoscopic 33.78
calcareous deposit
  bursa 83.03
    hand 82.03
  tendon, intratendinous 83.39

Removal — *see also* Excision — *continued*
calcareous deposit — *continued*
  tendon, intratendinous — *continued*
    hand 82.29
calcification, heart valve leaflets — *See* Valvuloplasty, heart
calculus
  bile duct (by incision) 51.49
    endoscopic 51.88
    laparoscopic 51.88
    percutaneous 51.98
  bladder (by incision) 57.19
    without incision 57.0
  common duct (by incision) 51.41
    endoscopic 51.88
    laparoscopic 51.88
    percutaneous 51.96
  gallbladder 51.04
    endoscopic 51.88
    laparoscopic 51.88
  kidney (by incision) 55.01
    without incision (transurethral) 56.0
    percutaneous 55.03
      with fragmentation (ultrasound) 55.04
    renal pelvis (by incision) 55.11
      percutaneous nephrostomy 55.03
        with fragmentation 55.04
      transurethral 56.0
  lacrimal
    canaliculi 09.42
      by incision 09.52
    gland 09.3
      by incision 09.0
    passage(s) 09.49
      by incision 09.59
    punctum 09.41
      by incision 09.51
    sac 09.49
      by incision 09.53
  pancreatic duct (by incision) 52.09
    endoscopic 52.94
  perirenal tissue 59.09
  pharynx 29.39
  prostate 60.0
  salivary gland (by incision) 26.0
    by probe 26.91
  ureter (by incision) 56.2
    without incision 56.0
  urethra (by incision) 58.0
    without incision 58.6
caliper tongs (skull) 02.95
cannula
  for extracorporeal membrane oxygenation (ECMO) — omit code
cardiac pacemaker (device) (initial) (permanent) (cardiac resynchronization device, CRT-P) 37.89
  with replacement
    cardiac resynchronization pacemaker (CRT-P)
      device only 00.53
      total system 00.50
    dual-chamber 37.87
    single-chamber device 37.85
      rate responsive 37.86
cardioverter/defibrillator pulse generator
  without replacement (cardiac resynchronization defibrillator device (CRT-D) 37.79
cast 97.88
  with reapplication 97.13
  lower limb 97.12
  upper limb 97.11
catheter (indwelling) (*see also* Removal, tube)
  bladder 97.64
  cranial cavity 01.27
  middle ear (tympanum) 20.1
  ureter 97.62
  urinary 97.64
  ventricular (cerebral) 02.43
    with synchronous replacement 02.42
  CCM (cardiac contractility modulation) ●
    without replacement (rechargeable ●
    pulse generator) (total system) 37.79 ●
cerclage material, cervix 69.96

Removal — *see also* Excision — *continued*
cerumen, ear 96.52
corneal epithelium 11.41
  for smear or culture 11.21
coronary artery obstruction (thrombus) 36.09
  direct intracoronary artery infusion 36.04
  open chest approach 36.03
  percutaneous transluminal (balloon) 00.66

Note — Also use 00.40, 00.41, 00.42, or 00.43 to show the total number of vessels treated. Use code 00.44 once to show procedure on a bifurcated vessel. In addition, use 00.45, 00.46, 00.47, or 00.48 to show the number of vascular stents inserted.

Crutchfield tongs (skull) 02.95
  with synchronous replacement 02.94
cyst (*see also* Excision, lesion, by site)
  dental 24.4
  lung 32.29
    endoscopic 32.28
    thoracoscopic 32.20
cystic duct remnant 51.61
decidua (by)
  aspiration curettage 69.52
  curettage (D and C) 69.02
  manual 75.4
dental wiring (immobilization device) 97.33
  orthodontic 24.8
device (therapeutic) NEC 97.89
  for musculoskeletal immobilization NEC 97.88
  abdomen NEC 97.86
  bronchus 33.78
    valve 33.78
  digestive system NEC 97.59
  drainage — *see* Removal, tube
  external fixation device 97.88
    mandibular NEC 97.36
    minifixator (bone) — *see* category 78.6 ☑
  genital tract NEC 97.79
  head and neck NEC 97.39
  intrauterine contraceptive 97.71
  spine 80.09
  thorax NEC 97.49
  trunk NEC 97.87
  urinary system NEC 97.69
diaphragm, vagina 97.73
drainage device — *see* Removal, tube
dye, spinal canal 03.31
ectopic fetus (from) 66.02
  abdominal cavity 74.3
  extraperitoneal (intraligamentous) 74.3
  fallopian tube (by salpingostomy) 66.02
    by salpingotomy 66.01
    with salpingectomy 66.62
  intraligamentous 74.3
  ovarian 74.3
  peritoneal (following uterine or tubal rupture) 74.3
  site NEC 74.3
  tubal (by salpingostomy) 66.02
    by salpingotomy 66.01
    with salpingectomy 66.62
electrodes
  bone growth stimulator — *see* category 78.6 ☑
  brain 01.22
    depth 01.22
      with synchronous replacement 02.93
    foramen ovale 01.22
      with synchronous replacement 02.93
    sphenoidal — *omit code*
      with synchronous replacement 02.96
  cardiac pacemaker (atrial) (transvenous) (ventricular) 37.77
    with replacement 37.76
  carotid sinus 04.93
    with synchronous replacement 04.92
  depth 01.22
    with synchronous replacement 02.93
  epicardial (myocardial) 37.77

Removal — *see also* Excision — *continued*
electrodes — *continued*
  epicardial — *continued*
    with replacement (by)
      atrial and/or ventricular lead(s) (electrode) 37.76
      epicardial lead 37.74
  epidural pegs 01.22
    with synchronous replacement 02.93
  foramen ovale 01.22
    with synchronous replacement 02.93
  gastric 04.93
    with synchronous replacement 04.92
  intracranial 01.22
    with synchronous replacement 02.93
  peripheral nerve 04.93
    with synchronous replacement 04.92
  sacral nerve 04.93
  sphenoidal — *omit code*
    with synchronous replacement 02.96
  spinal 03.94
    with synchronous replacement 03.93
  temporary transvenous pacemaker system — *omit code*
electroencephalographic receiver (brain) (intracranial) 01.22
  with synchronous replacement 02.93
electronic
  stimulator — *see* Removal, neurostimulator, by site
    bladder 57.98
    bone 78.6 ☑
      skeletal muscle 83.93
        with synchronous replacement 83.92
    ureter 56.94
electrostimulator — *see* Removal, electronic, stimulator, by site
embolus 38.00
  with endarterectomy — *see* Endarterectomy
  abdominal
    artery 38.06
    vein 38.07
  aorta (arch) (ascending) (descending) 38.04
  arteriovenous shunt or cannula 39.49
  bovine graft 39.49
  head and neck vessel
    endovascular approach 39.74
    open approach, intracranial vessels 38.01
    open approach, other vessels of head and neck 38.02
  intracranial vessel
    endovascular approach 39.74
    open approach, intracranial vessels 38.01
    open approach, other vessels of head and neck 38.02
  lower limb
    artery 38.08
    vein 38.09
  pulmonary (artery) (vein) 38.05
  thoracic vessel NEC 38.05
  upper limb (artery) (vein) 38.03
embryo — *see* Removal, ectopic fetus
encircling tube, eye (episcleral) 14.6
epithelial downgrowth, anterior chamber 12.93
external fixation device 97.88
  mandibular NEC 97.36
  minifixator (bone) — *see* category 78.6 ☑
extrauterine embryo — *see* Removal, ectopic fetus
eyeball 16.49
  with implant 16.42
    with attachment of muscles 16.41
fallopian tube — *see* Salpingectomy
feces (impacted) (by flushing) (manual) 96.38
fetus, ectopic — *see* Removal, ectopic fetus
fingers, supernumerary 86.26
fixation device
  external 97.88
    mandibular NEC 97.36

Removal — see also Excision — continued
fixation device — continued
external — continued
minifixator (bone) — see category 78.6 ☑
internal 78.60
carpal, metacarpal 78.64
clavicle 78.61
facial (bone) 76.97
femur 78.65
fibula 78.67
humerus 78.62
patella 78.66
pelvic 78.69
phalanges (foot) (hand) 78.69
radius 78.63
scapula 78.61
specified site NEC 78.69
tarsal, metatarsal 78.68
thorax (ribs) (sternum) 78.61
tibia 78.67
ulna 78.63
vertebrae 78.69
foreign body NEC (see also Incision, by site) 98.20
abdominal (cavity) 54.92
wall 54.0
adenoid 98.13
by incision 28.91
alveolus, alveolar bone 98.22
by incision 24.0
antecubital fossa 98.27
by incision 86.05
anterior chamber 12.00
by incision 12.02
with use of magnet 12.01
anus (intraluminal) 98.05
by incision 49.93
artifical stoma (intraluminal) 98.18
auditory canal, external 18.02
axilla 98.27
by incision 86.05
bladder (without incision) 57.0
by incision 57.19
bone, except fixation device (see also Incision, bone) 77.10
alveolus, alveolar 98.22
by incision 24.0
brain 01.39
without incision into brain 01.24
breast 85.0
bronchus (intraluminal) 98.15
by incision 33.0
bursa 83.03
hand 82.03
canthus 98.22
by incision 08.51
cerebral meninges 01.31
cervix (intraluminal) NEC 98.16
penetrating 69.97
choroid (by incision) 14.00
with use of magnet 14.01
without use of magnet 14.02
ciliary body (by incision) 12.00
with use of magnet 12.01
without use of magnet 12.02
conjunctiva (by magnet) 98.22
by incision 10.0
cornea 98.21
by
incision 11.1
magnet 11.0
duodenum 98.03
by incision 45.01
ear (intraluminal) 98.11
with incision 18.09
epididymis 63.92
esophagus (intraluminal) 98.02
by incision 42.09
extrapleural (by incision) 34.01
eye, eyeball (by magnet) 98.21
anterior segment (by incision) 12.00
with use of magnet 12.01
without use of magnet 12.02
posterior segment (by incision) 14.00
with use of magnet 14.01

Removal — see also Excision — continued
foreign body (see also Incision, by site) — continued
eye, eyeball — continued
posterior segment — continued
without use of magnet 14.02
superficial 98.21
eyelid 98.22
by incision 08.09
fallopian tube
by salpingostomy 66.02
by salpingotomy 66.01
fascia 83.09
hand 82.09
foot 98.28
gall bladder 51.04
groin region (abdominal wall) (inguinal) 54.0
gum 98.22
by incision 24.0
hand 98.26
head and neck NEC 98.22
heart 37.11
internal fixation device — see Removal, fixation device, internal
intestine
by incision 45.00
large (intraluminal) 98.04
by incision 45.03
small (intraluminal) 98.03
by incision 45.02
intraocular (by incision) 12.00
with use of magnet 12.01
without use of magnet 12.02
iris (by incision) 12.00
with use of magnet 12.01
without use of magnet 12.02
joint structures (see also Arthrotomy) 80.10
kidney (transurethral) (by endoscopy) 56.0
by incision 55.01
pelvis (transurethral) 56.0
by incision 55.11
labia 98.23
by incision 71.09
lacrimal
canaliculi 09.42
by incision 09.52
gland 09.3
by incision 09.0
passage(s) 09.49
by incision 09.59
punctum 09.41
by incision 09.51
sac 09.49
by incision 09.53
large intestine (intraluminal) 98.04
by incision 45.03
larynx (intraluminal) 98.14
by incision 31.3
lens 13.00
by incision 13.02
with use of magnet 13.01
liver 50.0
lower limb, except foot 98.29
foot 98.28
lung 33.1
mediastinum 34.1
meninges (cerebral) 01.31
spinal 03.01
mouth (intraluminal) 98.01
by incision 27.92
muscle 83.02
hand 82.02
nasal sinus 22.50
antrum 22.2
with Caldwell-Luc approach 22.39
ethmoid 22.51
frontal 22.41
maxillary 22.2
with Caldwell-Luc approach 22.39
sphenoid 22.52
nerve (cranial) (peripheral) NEC 04.04
root 03.01
nose (intraluminal) 98.12
by incision 21.1
oral cavity (intraluminal) 98.01

Removal — see also Excision — continued
foreign body (see also Incision, by site) — continued
oral cavity — continued
by incision 27.92
orbit (by magnet) 98.21
by incision 16.1
palate (penetrating) 98.22
by incision 27.1
pancreas 52.09
penis 98.24
by incision 64.92
pericardium 37.12
perineum (female) 98.23
by incision 71.09
male 98.25
by incision 86.05
perirenal tissue 59.09
peritoneal cavity 54.92
perivesical tissue 59.19
pharynx (intraluminal) 98.13
by pharyngotomy 29.0
pleura (by incision) 34.09
popliteal space 98.29
by incision 86.05
rectum (intraluminal) 98.05
by incision 48.0
renal pelvis (transurethral) 56.0
by incision 56.1
retina (by incision) 14.00
with use of magnet 14.01
without use of magnet 14.02
retroperitoneum 54.92
sclera (by incision) 12.00
with use of magnet 12.01
without use of magnet 12.02
scrotum 98.24
by incision 61.0
sinus (nasal) 22.50
antrum 22.2
with Caldwell-Luc approach 22.39
ethmoid 22.51
frontal 22.41
maxillary 22.2
with Caldwell-Luc approach 22.39
sphenoid 22.52
skin NEC 98.20
by incision 86.05
skull 01.24
with incision into brain 01.39
small intestine (intraluminal) 98.03
by incision 45.02
soft tissue NEC 83.09
hand 82.09
spermatic cord 63.93
spinal (canal) (cord) (meninges) 03.01
stomach (intraluminal) 98.03
by incision 43.0
bubble (balloon) 44.94
subconjunctival (by magnet) 98.22
by incision 10.0
subcutaneous tissue NEC 98.20
by incision 86.05
supraclavicular fossa 98.27
by incision 86.05
tendon (sheath) 83.01
hand 82.01
testis 62.0
thorax (by incision) 34.09
thyroid (field) (gland) (by incision) 06.09
tonsil 98.13
by incision 28.91
trachea (intraluminal) 98.15
by incision 31.3
trunk NEC 98.25
tunica vaginalis 98.24
upper limb, except hand 98.27
hand 98.26
ureter (transurethral) 56.0
by incision 56.2
urethra (intraluminal) 98.19
by incision 58.0
uterus (intraluminal) 98.16
vagina (intraluminal) 98.17
by incision 70.14
vas deferens 63.6

Removal — see also Excision — continued
foreign body (see also Incision, by site) — continued
vitreous (by incision) 14.00
with use of magnet 14.01
without use of magnet 14.02
vulva 98.23
by incision 71.09
gallstones
bile duct (by incision) NEC 51.49
endoscopic 51.88
common duct (by incision) 51.41
endoscopic 51.88
percutaneous 51.96
duodenum 45.01
gallbladder 51.04
endoscopic 51.88
laparoscopic 51.88
hepatic ducts 51.49
endoscopic 51.88
intestine 45.00
large 45.03
small NEC 45.02
liver 50.0
Gardner Wells tongs (skull) 02.95
with synchronous replacement 02.94
gastric band (adjustable), laparoscopic 44.97
gastric bubble (balloon) 44.94
granulation tissue (see also Excision, lesion, by site)
with repair — see Repair, by site
cranial 01.6
skull 01.6
halo traction device (skull) 02.95
with synchronous replacement 02.94
heart assist system
with replacement 37.63
intra-aortic balloon pump (IABP) 97.44
nonoperative 97.44
open removal 37.64
percutaneous external device 97.44
heart replacement system
internal biventricular 37.55
hematoma — see Drainage, by site
Hoffman minifixator device (bone) — see category 78.6 ☑
hydatidiform mole 68.0
impacted
feces (rectum) (by flushing) (manual) 96.38
tooth 23.19
from nasal sinus (maxillary) 22.61
implant
breast 85.94
cochlear prosthetic device 20.99
cornea 11.92
lens (prosthetic) 13.8
middle ear NEC 20.99
ocular 16.71
posterior segment 14.6
orbit 16.72
retina 14.6
tympanum 20.1
implantable hemodynamic sensor (lead) and monitor device 37.79
internal biventricular heart replacement system 37.55
internal fixation device — see Removal, fixation device, internal
intra-aortic balloon pump (IABP) 97.44
intrauterine contraceptive device (IUD) 97.71
joint (structure) NOS 80.90
ankle 80.97
elbow 80.92
foot and toe 80.98
hand and finger 80.94
hip 80.95
knee 80.96
other specified sites 80.99
shoulder 80.91
spine 80.99
toe 80.98
wrist 80.93
Kantrowitz heart pump 37.64
nonoperative 97.44
keel (tantalum plate), larynx 31.98
kidney (see also Nephrectomy)

[handwritten] Prophylactic Organ Removal V 50.4... genetic susceptibility V84.0 X and family history V16.X

Removal — see also Excision — continued
kidney (see also Nephrectomy) — continued
  mechanical 55.98
  transplanted or rejected 55.53
laminaria (tent), uterus 97.79
leads (cardiac) — see Removal, electrodes, cardiac pacemaker
lesion — see Excision, lesion, by site
ligamentum flavum (spine) — omit code
ligature
  fallopian tube 66.79
  ureter 56.86
  vas deferens 63.84
limb lengthening device, internal — see category 78.6 ☑
loop recorder 86.05
loose body
  bone — see Sequestrectomy, bone
  joint 80.10
  mesh (surgical) — see Removal, foreign body, by site
lymph node — see Excision, lymph, node
minifixator device (bone) — see category 78.6 ☑
  external fixation device 97.88
Mulligan hood, fallopian tube 66.94
  with synchronous replacement 66.93
muscle stimulator (skeletal) 83.93
  with replacement 83.92
myringotomy device or tube 20.1
nail (bed) (fold) 86.23
  internal fixation device — see Removal, fixation device, internal
necrosis
  skin 86.28
    excisional 86.22
neuropacemaker — see Removal, neurostimulator, by site
neurostimulator
  brain 01.22
    with synchronous replacement 02.93
  electrodes
    brain 01.22
      with synchronous replacement 02.93
    carotid sinus 04.93
      with synchronous replacement 04.92
    gastric 04.93
      with synchronous replacement 04.92
    intracranial 01.22
      with synchronous replacement 02.93
    peripheral nerve 04.93
      with synchronous replacement 04.92
    sacral nerve 04.93
      with synchronous replacement 04.92
    spinal 03.94
      with synchronous replacement 03.93
  intracranial 01.22
    with synchronous replacement 02.93
  peripheral nerve 04.93
    with synchronous replacement 04.92
  pulse generator (single array, dual array) 86.05
    with synchronous replacement 86.96
      dual array 86.95
        rechargeable 86.98
      single array 86.94
        rechargeable 86.97
  spinal 03.94
    with synchronous replacement 03.93
nonabsorbable surgical material NEC — see Removal, foreign body, by site
odontoma (tooth) 24.4
orbital implant 16.72
osteocartilagenous loose body, joint structures (see also Arthrotomy) 80.10
outer attic wall (middle ear) 20.59
ovo-testis (unilateral) 62.3
  bilateral 62.41

Removal — see also Excision — continued
pacemaker
  brain (intracranial) — see Removal, neurostimulator
  cardiac (device) (initial) (permanent) 37.89
    with replacement
      dual-chamber device 37.87
      single-chamber device 37.85
        rate responsive 37.86
    electrodes (atrial) (transvenous) (ventricular) 37.77
      with replacement 37.76
    epicardium (myocardium) 37.77
      with replacement (by)
        atrial and/or ventricular lead(s) (electrode) 37.76
        epicardial lead 37.74
    temporary transvenous pacemaker system — omit code
  intracranial — see Removal, neurostimulator
  neural — see Removal, neurostimulator
  peripheral nerve — see Removal, neurostimulator
  spine — see Removal, neurostimulator
pack, packing
  dental 97.34
  intrauterine 97.72
  nasal 97.32
  rectum 97.59
  trunk NEC 97.85
  vagina 97.75
  vulva 97.75
pantopaque dye, spinal canal 03.31
patella (complete) 77.96
  partial 77.86
pectus deformity implant device 34.01
pelvic viscera, en masse (female) 68.8
  male 57.71
pessary, vagina NEC 97.74
pharynx (partial) 29.33
phlebolith — see Removal, embolus
placenta (by)
  aspiration curettage 69.52
  D and C 69.02
  manual 75.4
plaque, dental 96.54
plate, skull 02.07
  with synchronous replacement 02.05
polyp (see also Excision, lesion, by site)
  esophageal 42.32
    endoscopic 42.33
  gastric (endoscopic) 43.41
  intestine 45.41
    endoscopic 45.42
  nasal 21.31
prosthesis
  bile duct 51.95
    nonoperative 97.55
  cochlear prosthetic device 20.99
  dental 97.35
  eye 97.31
  facial bone 76.99
  fallopian tube 66.94
    with synchronous replacement 66.93
  joint structures
    with replacement — see Revision, joint replacement, by site
    without replacement ●
      ankle 80.07 ●
      elbow 80.02 ●
      foot and toe 80.08 ●
      hand and finger 80.04 ●
      hip 80.05 ●
      knee 80.06 ●
      shoulder 80.01 ●
      specified site NEC 80.09 ●
      spine 80.09 ●
      unspecified site 80.00 ●
      wrist 80.03 ●
  lens 13.8
  penis (internal) without replacement 64.96
  Rosen (urethra) 59.99
  testicular, by incision 62.0
  urinary sphincter, artificial 58.99
    with replacement 58.93

Removal — see also Excision — continued
pseudophakos 13.8
pterygium 11.39
  with corneal graft 11.32
pulse generator
  cardiac pacemaker 37.86
  cardioverter/defibrillator 37.79
  neurostimulator — see Removal, neurostimulator, pulse generator
pump assist device, heart 37.64
  with replacement 37.63
  nonoperative 97.44
radioactive material — see Removal, foreign body, by site
redundant skin, eyelid 08.86
rejected organ
  kidney 55.53
  testis 62.42
reservoir, ventricular (Ommaya) (Rickham) 02.43
  with synchronous replacement 02.42
retained placenta (by)
  aspiration curettage 69.52
  D and C 69.02
  manual 75.4
retinal implant 14.6
Rheos™ carotid sinus baroreflex activation device 86.05
rhinolith 21.31
rice bodies, tendon sheaths 83.01
  hand 82.01
Roger-Anderson minifixator device (bone) — see category 78.6 ☑
root, residual (tooth) (buried) (retained) 23.11
Rosen prosthesis (urethra) 59.99
scleral buckle or implant 14.6
Scribner shunt 39.43
secondary membranous cataract (with iridectomy) 13.65
secundines (by)
  aspiration curettage 69.52
  D and C 69.02
  manual 75.4
sequestrum — see Sequestrectomy
seton, anus 49.93
Shepard's tube (ear) 20.1
Shirodkar suture, cervix 69.96
shunt
  arteriovenous 39.43
    with creation of new shunt 39.42
  lumbar-subarachnoid NEC 03.98
  pleurothecal 03.98
  salpingothecal 03.98
  spinal (thecal) NEC 03.98
  subarachnoid-peritoneal 03.98
  subarachnoid-ureteral 03.98
silastic tubes
  ear 20.1
  fallopian tubes 66.94
    with synchronous replacement 66.93
skin
  necrosis or slough 86.28
    excisional 86.22
    superficial layer (by dermabrasion) 86.25
skull tongs 02.95
  with synchronous replacement 02.94
spacer (cement) (joint) (methylmethacrylate) 84.57
splint 97.88
stent
  bile duct 97.55
  larynx 31.98
  ureteral 97.62
  urethral 97.65
stimoceiver — see Removal, neurostimulator
subdural
  grids 01.22
  strips 01.22
supernumerary digit(s) 86.26
suture(s) NEC 97.89
  by incision — see Incision, by site
  abdominal wall 97.83
  genital tract 97.79
  head and neck 97.38
  thorax 97.43

Removal — see also Excision — continued
suture(s) — continued
  trunk NEC 97.84
symblepharon — see Repair, symblepharon
temporary transvenous pacemaker system — omit code
testis (unilateral) 62.3
  bilateral 62.41
  remaining or solitary 62.42
thrombus 38.00
  with endarterectomy — see Endarterectomy
  abdominal
    artery 38.06
    vein 38.07
  aorta (arch) (ascending) (descending) 38.04
  arteriovenous shunt or cannula 39.49
  bovine graft 39.49
  coronary artery 36.09
  head and neck vessel NEC 38.02
  intracranial vessel NEC 38.01
  lower limb
    artery 38.08
    vein 38.09
  pulmonary (artery) (vein) 38.05
  thoracic vessel NEC 38.05
  upper limb (artery) (vein) 38.03
tissue expander (skin) NEC 86.05
  breast 85.96
toes, supernumerary 86.26
tongs, skull 02.95
  with synchronous replacement 02.94
tonsil tag 28.4
tooth (by forceps) (multiple) (single) NEC 23.09
  deciduous 23.01
  surgical NEC 23.19
    impacted 23.19
    residual root 23.11
    root apex 23.73
      with root canal therapy 23.72
trachoma follicles 10.33
T-tube (bile duct) 97.55
tube
  appendix 97.53
  bile duct (T-tube) NEC 97.55
  cholecystostomy 97.54
  cranial cavity 01.27
  cystostomy 97.63
  ear (button) 20.1
  gastrostomy 97.51
  large intestine 97.53
  liver 97.55
  mediastinum 97.42
  nephrostomy 97.61
  pancreas 97.56
  peritoneum 97.82
  pleural cavity 97.41
  pyelostomy 97.61
  retroperitoneum 97.81
  small intestine 97.52
  thoracotomy 97.41
  tracheostomy 97.37
  tympanostomy 20.1
  tympanum 20.1
  ureterostomy 97.62
ureteral splint (stent) 97.62
urethral sphincter, artificial 58.99
  with replacement 58.93
urinary sphincter, artificial 58.99
  with replacement 58.93
utricle 20.79
valve
  vas deferens 63.85
  ventricular (cerebral) 02.43
vascular graft or prosthesis 39.49
ventricular shunt or reservoir 02.43
  with synchronous replacement 02.42
Vinke tongs (skull) 02.95
  with synchronous replacement 02.94
vitreous (with replacement) 14.72
  anterior approach (partial) 14.71
  open sky technique 14.71
Wagner-Brooker minifixator device (bone) — see category 78.6 ☑
wiring, dental (immobilization device) 97.33

☑ Additional Digit Required — Refer to the Tabular List for Digit Selection

📖 Subterms under main terms may continue to next column or page

Removal — see also Excision — continued
  wiring, dental — continued
    orthodontic 24.8
Renipuncture (percutaneous) 55.92
Renogram 92.03
Renotransplantation NEC 55.69

> Note — To report donor source:
> cadaver 00.93
> live non-related donor 00.92
> live related donor 00.91
> live unrelated donor 00.92

Reopening — see also Incision, by site
  blepharorrhaphy 08.02
  canthorrhaphy 08.02
  cilia base 08.71
  craniotomy or craniectomy site 01.23
  fallopian tube (divided) 66.79
  iris in anterior chambers 12.97
  laminectomy or laminotomy site 03.02
  laparotomy site 54.12
  osteotomy site (see also Incision, bone) 77.10
    facial bone 76.09
  tarsorrhaphy 08.02
  thoracotomy site (for control of hemorrhage) (for examination) (for exploration) 34.03
  thyroid field wound (for control of hemorrhage) (for examination) (for exploration) (for removal of hematoma) 06.02

Repacking — see Replacement, pack, by site
Repair
  abdominal wall 54.72
  adrenal gland 07.44
  alveolus, alveolar (process) (ridge) (with graft) (with implant) 24.5
  anal sphincter 49.79
    artificial sphincter
      implantation 49.75
      revision 49.75
    laceration (by suture) 49.71
      obstetric (current) 75.62
        old 49.79
  aneurysm (false) (true) 39.52
    by or with
      clipping 39.51
      coagulation 39.52
      coil, ▶NEC◀ (endovascular approach) 39.79
        head and neck
          bare coils 39.75 ●
          bioactive coils 39.76 ●
      electrocoagulation 39.52
      with
        anastomosis — see Aneurysmectomy, with anastomosis, by site
        graft replacement — see Aneurysmectomy, with graft replacement, by site
        excision or resection of vessel (see also Aneurysmectomy, by site)
      endovascular graft 39.79
        abdominal aorta 39.71
        head and neck 39.72
        lower extremity artery(s) 39.79
        thoracic aorta 39.73
        upper extremity artery(s) 39.79
      filipuncture 39.52
      graft replacement — see Aneurysmectomy, with graft replacement, by site
      ligation 39.52
      liquid tissue adhesive (glue) 39.79
        endovascular approach 39.79
          head and neck 39.72
      methyl methacrylate 39.52
        endovascular approach 39.79
          head and neck 39.72
      occlusion 39.52
        endovascular approach 39.79
          head and neck 39.72
      suture 39.52
      trapping 39.52

Repair — continued
  aneurysm — continued
    by or with — continued
      wiring 39.52
      wrapping (gauze) (methyl methacrylate) (plastic) 39.52
    coronary artery 36.91
    heart 37.32
    sinus of Valsalva 35.39
    thoracic aorta (dissecting), by fenestration 39.54
  anomalous pulmonary venous connection (total)
    one-stage 35.82
    partial — see specific procedure
    total 35.82
  anular disc 80.54
    with graft or prosthesis 80.53
  anulus fibrosus 80.54
    with graft or prosthesis 80.53
  anus 49.79
    laceration (by suture) 49.71
      obstetric (current) 75.62
        old 49.79
  aorta 39.31
  aorticopulmonary window 39.59
  arteriovenous fistula 39.53
    by or with
      clipping 39.53
      coagulation 39.53
      coil, ▶NEC◀ (endovascular approach) 39.79
        head and neck vessels
          bare coils 39.75 ●
          bioactive coils 39.76 ●
      division 39.53
      excision or resection (see also Aneurysmectomy, by site)
        with
          anastomosis — see Aneurysmectomy, with anastomosis, by site
          graft replacement — see Aneurysmectomy, with graft replacement, by site
      ligation 39.53
        coronary artery 36.99
      occlusion 39.53
        endovascular approach 39.79
          head and neck 39.72
      suture 39.53
  artery NEC 39.59
    by
      endovascular approach
        abdominal aorta 39.71
        head and neck (embolization or occlusion) 39.72
        other repair (of aneurysm) 39.79
        percutaneous repair of intracranial vessel(s) (for stent insertion) 00.62

> Note — Also use 00.40, 00.41, 00.42, or 00.43 to show the total number of vessels treated. Use code 00.44 once to show procedure on a bifurcated vessel. In addition, use 00.45, 00.46, 00.47, or 00.48 to show the number of vascular stents inserted.

        percutaneous repair of precerebral (extracranial) vessel(s) (for stent insertion) 00.61

> Note — Also use 00.40, 00.41, 00.42, or 00.43 to show the total number of vessels treated. Use code 00.44 once to show procedure on a bifurcated vessel. In addition, use 00.45, 00.46, 00.47, or 00.48 to show the number of vascular stents inserted.

        thoracic aorta 39.73

Repair — continued
  artery — continued
    by — continued
      non-coronary percutaneous transluminal angioplasty or atherectomy

> Note — Also use 00.40, 00.41, 00.42, or 00.43 to show the total number of vessels treated. Use code 00.44 once to show procedure on a bifurcated vessel. In addition, use 00.45, 00.46, 00.47, or 00.48 to show the number of vascular stents inserted.

        basilar 00.61
        carotid 00.61
        femoropopliteal 39.50
        iliac 39.50
        lower extremity NOS 39.50
        mesenteric 39.50
        renal 39.50
        upper extremity NOS 39.50
        vertebral 00.61
    with
      patch graft 39.58
        with excision or resection of vessel — see Arteriectomy, with graft replacement, by site
        synthetic (Dacron) (Teflon) 39.57
        tissue (vein) (autogenous) (homograft) 39.56
      suture 39.31
    coronary NEC 36.99
      by angioplasty — see Angioplasty, coronary
      by atherectomy — see Angioplasty, coronary
  artificial opening — see Repair, stoma
  atrial septal defect 35.71
    with
      prosthesis (open heart technique) 35.51
        closed heart technique 35.52
      tissue graft 35.61
    combined with repair of valvular and ventricular septal defects — see Repair, endocardial cushion defect
    in total repair of total anomalous pulmonary venous connection 35.82
  atrioventricular canal defect (any type) 35.73
    with
      prosthesis 35.54
      tissue graft 35.63
  bifid digit (finger) 82.89
  bile duct NEC 51.79
    laceration (by suture) NEC 51.79
      common bile duct 51.71
  bladder NEC 57.89
    for stress incontinence — see Repair, stress incontinence
    exstrophy 57.86
    laceration (by suture) 57.81
      obstetric (current) 75.61
        old 57.89
    neck 57.85
  blepharophimosis 08.59
  blepharoptosis 08.36
    by
      frontalis muscle technique (with)
        fascial sling 08.32
        suture 08.31
      levator muscle technique 08.34
        with resection or advancement 08.33
      orbicularis oculi muscle sling 08.36
      tarsal technique 08.35
  blood vessel NEC 39.59
    with
      patch graft 39.58
        with excision or resection — see Angiectomy, with graft replacement
        synthetic (Dacron) (Teflon) 39.57
        tissue (vein) (autogenous) (homograft) 39.56
      resection — see Angiectomy
      suture 39.30
    coronary artery NEC 36.99
      by angioplasty — see Angioplasty, coronary

Repair — continued
  blood vessel — continued
    coronary artery — continued
      by atherectomy — see Angioplasty, coronary
    peripheral vessel NEC 39.59
      by angioplasty 39.50

> Note — Also use 00.40, 00.41, 00.42, or 00.43 to show the total number of vessels treated. Use code 00.44 once to show procedure on a bifurcated vessel. In addition, use 00.45, 00.46, 00.47, or 00.48 to show the number of vascular stents inserted.

      by atherectomy 39.50

> Note — Also use 00.40, 00.41, 00.42, or 00.43 to show the total number of vessels treated. Use code 00.44 once to show procedure on a bifurcated vessel. In addition, use 00.45, 00.46, 00.47, or 00.48 to show the number of vascular stents inserted.

      by endovascular approach 39.79
  bone NEC (see also Osteoplasty) — see category 78.4 ☑
    by synostosis technique — see Arthrodesis
    for malunion, nonunion, or delayed union of fracture — see Repair, fracture, malunion or nonunion
    accessory sinus 22.79
    cranium NEC 02.06
      with
        flap (bone) 02.03
        graft (bone) 02.04
    nasal 21.89
    skull NEC 02.06
      with
        flap (bone) 02.03
        graft (bone) 02.04
  bottle, hydrocele of tunica vaginalis 61.2
  brain (trauma) NEC 02.92
  breast (plastic) (see also Mammoplasty) 85.89
  broad ligament 69.29
  bronchus NEC 33.48
    laceration (by suture) 33.41
  bunionette (with osteotomy) 77.54
  canaliculus, lacrimal 09.73
  canthus (lateral) 08.59
  cardiac pacemaker NEC 37.89
    electrode(s) (lead) NEC 37.75
  cardioverter/defibrillator (automatic) pocket (skin) (subcutaneous) 37.99
  cerebral meninges 02.12
  cervix 67.69
    internal os 67.59
      transabdominal 67.51
      transvaginal 67.59
    laceration (by suture) 67.61
      obstetric (current) 75.51
        old 67.69
  chest wall (mesh) (silastic) NEC 34.79
  chordae tendineae 35.32
  choroid NEC 14.9
    with retinal repair — see Repair, retina
  cisterna chyli 40.69
  claw toe 77.57
  cleft
    hand 82.82
    laryngotracheal 31.69
    lip 27.54
    palate 27.62
      secondary or subsequent 27.63
  coarctation of aorta — see Excision, coarctation of aorta
  cochlear prosthetic device 20.99
    external components only 95.49
  cockup toe 77.58
  colostomy 46.43
  conjunctiva NEC 10.49
    with scleral repair 12.81
    laceration 10.6
      with repair of sclera 12.81
    late effect of trachoma 10.49
  cornea NEC 11.59
    with
      conjunctival flap 11.53
      transplant — see Keratoplasty

☑ Additional Digit Required — Refer to the Tabular List for Digit Selection   ▽ Subterms under main terms may continue to next column or page

Repair — *continued*
  hernia — *continued*
    diaphragmatic — *continued*
      thoracic, thoracoabdominal approach — *continued*
        laparoscopic 53.83
        other and open 53.84
    epigastric 53.59
      with prosthesis or graft 53.69
    esophageal hiatus
      abdominal approach
        laparoscopic 53.71
        other and open 53.72
        unspecified 53.75
      thoracic, thoracoabdominal approach 53.80
    fascia 83.89
      hand 82.89
    femoral (unilateral) 53.29
      with prosthesis or graft 53.21
      bilateral 53.39
        with prosthesis or graft 53.31
    Ferguson 53.00
    Halsted 53.00
    Hill-Allison (hiatal hernia repair, transpleural approach) 53.80
    hypogastric 53.59
      with prosthesis or graft 53.69
    incisional 53.51
      laparoscopic with prosthesis or graft 53.62
      other open with prosthesis or graft 53.61
    inguinal (unilateral) 53.00
      with prosthesis or graft 53.05
      bilateral 53.10
        with prosthesis or graft 53.1/
          laparoscopic 17.24
        direct
          laparoscopic with graft or prosthesis 17.21
          other and open 53.11
            with prosthesis or graft 53.14
        direct and indirect
          laparoscopic with graft or prosthesis 17.23
          other and open 53.13
            with prosthesis or graft 53.16
        indirect
          laparoscopic with graft or prosthesis 17.22
          other and open 53.12
            with prosthesis or graft 53.15
      direct (unilateral)
        with prosthesis or graft 53.03
      and indirect (unilateral)
        laparoscopic with graft or prosthesis 17.11
        other and open 53.01
          with prosthesis or graft 53.03
        laparoscopic with graft or prosthesis 17.11
        other and open 53.01
          with prosthesis or graft 53.03
      indirect (unilateral)
        laparoscopic with graft or prosthesis 17.12
        other and open 53.02
          with prosthesis or graft 53.04
    internal 53.9
    ischiatic 53.9
    ischiorectal 53.9
    laparoscopic with graft or prosthesis, NOS 17.13
    lumbar 53.9
    manual 96.27
    obturator 53.9
    omental 53.9
    paraesophageal
      laparoscopic 53.71
      other and open 53.72
      unspecified 53.75

Repair — *continued*
  hernia — *continued*
    parahiatal
      laparoscopic 53.71
      other and open 53.72
      unspecified 53.75
    paraileostomy 46.41
    parasternal 53.82
    paraumbilical
      laparoscopic 53.43
        with graft or prosthesis 53.42
      other and open with graft or prosthesis 53.41
      other open 53.49
    pericolostomy 46.42
    perineal (enterocele) 53.9
    preperitoneal 53.29
    pudendal 53.9
    retroperitoneal 53.9
    sciatic 53.9
    scrotal — *see* Repair, hernia, inguinal
    spigelian 53.59
      with prosthesis or graft 53.69
    umbilical
      laparoscopic 53.43
        with graft or prosthesis 53.42
      other and open with graft or prosthesis 53.41
      other open 53.49
    uveal 12.39
    ventral 53.59
      with prosthesis or graft
        laparoscopic 53.63
        other and open 53.69
      incisional 53.51
        other open with prosthesis or graft 53.61
  hydrocele
    round ligament 69.19
    spermatic cord 63.1
    tunica vaginalis 61.2
  hymen 70.76
  hypospadias 58.45
  ileostomy 46.41
  ingrown toenail 86.23
  intestine, intestinal NEC 46.79
    fistula — *see* Closure, fistula, intestine
    laceration
      large intestine 46.75
      small intestine NEC 46.73
    stoma — *see* Repair, stoma
  inverted uterus NEC 69.29
    manual
      nonobstetric 69.94
      obstetric 75.94
    obstetrical
      manual 75.94
      surgical 75.93
    vaginal approach 69.23
  iris (rupture) NEC 12.39
  jejunostomy 46.41
  joint (capsule) (cartilage) NEC (*see also* Arthroplasty) 81.96
  kidney NEC 55.89
  knee (joint) NEC 81.47
    collateral ligaments 81.46
    cruciate ligaments 81.45
    five-in-one 81.42
    triad 81.43
  labia — *see* Repair, vulva
  laceration — *see* Suture, by site
  lacrimal system NEC 09.99
    canaliculus 09.73
    punctum 09.72
      for eversion 09.71
  laryngostomy 31.62
  laryngotracheal cleft 31.69
  larynx 31.69
    fracture 31.64
    laceration 31.61
  leads (cardiac) NEC 37.75
  ligament (*see also* Arthroplasty) 81.96
    broad 69.29
    collateral, knee NEC 81.46
    cruciate, knee NEC 81.45
    round 69.29

Repair — *continued*
  ligament (*see also* Arthroplasty) — *continued*
    uterine 69.29
  lip NEC 27.59
    cleft 27.54
    laceration (by suture) 27.51
  liver NEC 50.69
    laceration 50.61
  lop ear 18.79
  lung NEC 33.49
  lymphatic (channel) (peripheral) NEC 40.9
    duct, left (thoracic) NEC 40.69
  macrodactyly 82.83
  mallet finger 82.84
  mandibular ridge 76.64
  mastoid (antrum) (cavity) 19.9
  meninges (cerebral) NEC 02.12
    spinal NEC 03.59
      meningocele 03.51
      myelomeningocele 03.52
  meningocele (spinal) 03.51
    cranial 02.12
  mesentery 54.75
  mouth NEC 27.59
    laceration NEC 27.52
  muscle NEC 83.87
    by
      graft or implant (fascia) (muscle) 83.82
        hand 82.72
      tendon 83.81
        hand 82.79
      suture (direct) 83.65
        hand 82.46
      transfer or transplantation (muscle) 83.77
        hand 82.58
    hand 82.89
      by
        graft or implant NEC 82.79
          fascia 82.72
        suture (direct) 82.46
        transfer or transplantation (muscle) 82.58
  musculotendinous cuff, shoulder 83.63
  myelomeningocele 03.52
  nasal
    septum (perforation) NEC 21.88
    sinus NEC 22.79
      fistula 22.71
  nasolabial flaps (plastic) 21.86
  nasopharyngeal atresia 29.4
  nerve (cranial) (peripheral) NEC 04.79
    old injury 04.76
    revision 04.75
    sympathetic 05.81
  nipple NEC 85.87
  nose (external) (internal) (plastic) NEC (*see also* Rhinoplasty) 21.89
    laceration (by suture) 21.81
  notched lip 27.59
  omentum 54.74
  omphalocele
    laparoscopic 53.43
      with graft or prosthesis 53.42
    other and open with graft or prosthesis 53.41
    other open 53.49
  orbit 16.89
    wound 16.81
  ostium
    primum defect 35.73
      with
        prosthesis 35.54
        tissue graft 35.63
    secundum defect 35.71
      with
        prosthesis (open heart technique) 35.51
          closed heart technique 35.52
        tissue graft 35.61
  ovary 65.79
    with tube 65.73
      laparoscopic 65.76
  overlapping toe 77.58

Repair — *continued*
  pacemaker
    cardiac
      device (permanent) 37.89
      electrode(s) (leads) NEC 37.75
      pocket (skin) (subcutaneous) 37.79
  palate NEC 27.69
    cleft 27.62
      secondary or subsequent 27.63
    laceration (by suture) 27.61
  pancreas NEC 52.95
    Wirsung's duct 52.99
  papillary muscle (heart) 35.31
  patent ductus arteriosus 38.85
  pectus deformity (chest) (carinatum) (excavatum) 34.74
  pelvic floor NEC 70.79
    obstetric laceration (current) 75.69
      old 70.79
  penis NEC 64.49
    for epispadias or hypospadias 58.45
    inflatable prosthesis 64.99
    laceration 64.41
  pericardium 37.49
  perineum (female) 71.79
    laceration (by suture) 71.71
      obstetric (current) 75.69
        old 71.79
    male NEC 86.89
      laceration (by suture) 86.59
  peritoneum NEC 54.73
    by suture 54.64
  pharynx NEC 29.59
    laceration (by suture) 29.51
    plastic 29.4
  pleura NEC 34.93
  postcataract wound dehiscence 11.52
    with conjunctival flap 11.53
  pouch of Douglas 70.52
  primum ostium defect 35.73
    with
      prosthesis 35.54
      tissue graft 35.63
  prostate 60.93
  ptosis, eyelid — *see* Repair, blepharoptosis
  punctum, lacrimal NEC 09.72
    for correction of eversion 09.71
  quadriceps (mechanism) 83.86
  rectocele (posterior colporrhaphy) 70.52
    with graft or prosthesis 70.55
    and cystocele 70.50
      with graft or prosthesis 70.53
  rectum NEC 48.79
    laceration (by suture) 48.71
    prolapse NEC 48.76
      abdominal, approach 48.75
    STARR procedure 48.74
  retina, retinal
    detachment 14.59
      by
        cryotherapy 14.52
        diathermy 14.51
        photocoagulation 14.55
          laser 14.54
          xenon arc 14.53
        scleral buckling (*see also* Buckling, scleral) 14.49
    tear or defect 14.39
      by
        cryotherapy 14.32
        diathermy 14.31
        photocoagulation 14.35
          laser 14.34
          xenon arc 14.33
  retroperitoneal tissue 54.73
  rotator cuff (graft) (suture) 83.63
  round ligament 69.29
  ruptured tendon NEC 83.88
    hand 82.86
  salivary gland or duct NEC 26.49
  sclera, scleral 12.89
    fistula 12.82
    staphyloma NEC 12.86
      with graft 12.85
  scrotum 61.49

☑ Additional Digit Required — Refer to the Tabular List for Digit Selection   Subterms under main terms may continue to next column or page

2010 ICD-9-CM   ▶◀ Revised Text   ● New Line   ▲ Revised Code   October 2009 · Volume 3 — 53

☑ Additional Digit Required — Refer to the Tabular List for Digit Selection

▼ Subterms under main terms may continue to next column or page

2010 ICD-9-CM

▶◀ Revised Text   ● New Line   ▲ Revised Code

Volume 3 — 55

Resection — Resection

Resection — see also Excision, by site — continued
 tooth root — continued
  apex (abscess) 23.73
   with root canal therapy 23.72
  residual or retained 23.11
 trachea 31.5
 transurethral
  bladder NEC 57.49
  prostate 60.29
 transverse colon
  laparoscopic 17.34
  open and other 45.74
 turbinates — see Turbinectomy
 ureter (partial) 56.41
  total 56.42
 uterus — see Hysterectomy
 vein — see Phlebectomy
 ventricle (heart) 37.35
  infundibula 35.34
 vesical neck 57.59
  transurethral 57.49
 vocal cords (punch) 30.22
Respirator, volume-controlled (Bennett) (Byrd) — see Ventilation
Restoration
 cardioesophageal angle 44.66
  laparoscopic 44.67
 dental NEC 23.49
  by
   application of crown (artificial) 23.41
   insertion of bridge (fixed) 23.42
    removable 23.43
 extremity — see Reattachment, extremity
 eyebrow 08.70
  with graft 08.63
 eye socket 16.64
  with graft 16.63
 tooth NEC 23.2
  by
   crown (artificial) 23.41
   filling (amalgam) (plastic) (silicate) 23.2
   inlay 23.3
Restrictive
 gastric band, laparoscopic 44.95
Resurfacing, hip 00.86
 acetabulum 00.87
  with femoral head 00.85
 femoral head 00.86
  with acetabulum 00.85
 partial NOS 00.85
  acetabulum 00.87
  femoral head 00.86
 total (acetabulum and femoral head) 00.85
Resuscitation
 artificial respiration 93.93
 cardiac 99.60
  cardioversion 99.62
   atrial 99.61
  defibrillation 99.62
  external massage 99.63
   open chest 37.91
   intracardiac injection 37.92
 cardiopulmonary 99.60
 endotracheal intubation 96.04
 manual 93.93
 mouth-to-mouth 93.93
 pulmonary 93.93
Resuture
 abdominal wall 54.61
 cardiac septum prosthesis 35.95
 chest wall 34.71
 heart valve prosthesis (poppet) 35.95
 wound (skin and subcutaneous tissue) (without graft) NEC 86.59
Retavase, infusion 99.10
Reteplase, infusion 99.10
Retightening (noninvasive) ●
 external fixator device — omit code ●
Retinaculotomy NEC — see also Division, ligament 80.40
 carpal tunnel (flexor) 04.43
Retraining
 cardiac 93.36
 vocational 93.85
Retrogasserian neurotomy 04.02

Revascularization
 cardiac (heart muscle) (myocardium) (direct) 36.10
  with
   bypass anastomosis
    abdominal artery to coronary artery 36.17
    aortocoronary (catheter stent) (homograft) (prosthesis) (saphenous vein graft) 36.10
     one coronary vessel 36.11
     two coronary vessels 36.12
     three coronary vessels 36.13
     four coronary vessels 36.14
    gastroepiploic artery to coronary artery 36.17
    internal mammary-coronary artery (single vessel) 36.15
     double vessel 36.16
    specified type NEC 36.19
    thoracic artery-coronary artery (single vessel) 36.15
     double vessel 36.16
   implantation of artery into heart (muscle) (myocardium) (ventricle) 36.2
  indirect 36.2
  specified type NEC 36.39
  transmyocardial
   endoscopic 36.33
   endovascular 36.34
   open chest 36.31
   percutaneous 36.34
   specified type NEC 36.32
   thoracoscopic 36.33
Reversal, intestinal segment 45.50
 large 45.52
 small 45.51
Revision
 amputation stump 84.3
  current traumatic — see Amputation
 anastomosis
  biliary tract 51.94
  blood vessel 39.49
  gastric, gastrointestinal (with jejunal interposition) 44.5
  intestine (large) 46.94
   small 46.93
  pleurothecal 03.97
  pyelointestinal 56.72
  salpingotheral 03.97
  subarachnoid-peritoneal 03.97
  subarachnoid-ureteral 03.97
  ureterointestinal 56.72
 ankle replacement (prosthesis) 81.59
 anterior segment (eye) wound (operative) NEC 12.83
 arteriovenous shunt (cannula) (for dialysis) 39.42
 arthroplasty — see Arthroplasty
 bone flap, skull 02.06
 breast implant 85.93
 bronchostomy 33.42
 bypass graft (vascular) 39.49
  abdominal-coronary artery 36.17
  aortocoronary (catheter stent) (with prosthesis) (with saphenous vein graft) (with vein graft) 36.10
   one coronary vessel 36.11
   three coronary vessels 36.13
   four coronary vessels 36.14
   two coronary vessels 36.12
  CABG — see Revision, aortocoronary bypass graft
  chest tube — see intercostal catheter
  coronary artery bypass graft (CABG) — see Revision, aortocoronary bypass graft, abdominal-coronary artery bypass, and internal mammary-coronary artery bypass
  intercostal catheter (with lysis of adhesions) 34.04
   thoracoscopic 34.06
  internal mammary-coronary artery (single) 36.15
   double vessel 36.16

Revision — continued
 cannula, vessel-to-vessel (arteriovenous) 39.94
 canthus, lateral 08.59
 cardiac pacemaker
  device (permanent) 37.89
  electrode(s) (atrial) (transvenous) (ventricular) 37.75
  pocket 37.79
 cardiac resynchronization defibrillator (CRT-D)
  device 37.79
  electrode(s) 37.75
  pocket 37.79
 cardiac resynchronization pacemaker (CRT-P)
  device (permanent) 37.89
  electrode(s) (atria) (transvenous) (ventricular) 37.75
  pocket 37.79
 cardioverter/defibrillator (automatic) pocket 37.79
 cholecystostomy 51.99
 cleft palate repair 27.63
 colostomy 46.43
 conduit, urinary 56.52
 cystostomy (stoma) 57.22
 disc — see Revision, intervertebral disc
 elbow replacement (prosthesis) 81.97
 enterostomy (stoma) 46.40
  large intestine 46.43
  small intestine 46.41
 enucleation socket 16.64
  with graft 16.63
 esophagostomy 42.83
 exenteration cavity 16.66
  with secondary graft 16.65
 extraocular muscle surgery 15.6
 fenestration, inner ear 20.62
 filtering bleb 12.66
 fixation device (broken) (displaced) (see also Fixation, bone, internal) 78.50
 flap or pedicle graft (skin) 86.75
 foot replacement (prosthesis) 81.59
 gastric anastomosis (with jejunal interposition) 44.5
 gastric band, laparoscopic 44.96
 gastric port device
  laparoscopic 44.96
 gastroduodenostomy (with jejunal interposition) 44.5
 gastrointestinal anastomosis (with jejunal interposition) 44.5
 gastrojejunostomy 44.5
 gastrostomy 44.69
  laparoscopic 44.68
 hand replacement (prosthesis) 81.97
 heart procedure NEC 35.95
 hip replacement NOS 81.53
  acetabular and femoral components (total) 00.70
  acetabular component only 00.71
  acetabular liner and/or femoral head only 00.73
  femoral component only 00.72
  femoral head only and/or acetabular liner 00.73
  partial
   acetabular component only 00.71
   acetabular liner and/or femoral head only 00.73
   femoral component only 00.72
   femoral head only and/or acetabular liner 00.73
  total (acetabular and femoral components) 00.70
 Holter (-Spitz) valve 02.42
 ileal conduit 56.52
 ileostomy 46.41
 intervertebral disc, artificial (partial) (total) NOS 84.69
  cervical 84.66
  lumbar, lumbosacral 84.68
  thoracic 84.67
 jejunoileal bypass 46.93
 jejunostomy 46.41
 joint replacement
  acetabular and femoral components (total) 00.70

Revision — continued
 joint replacement — continued
  acetabular component only 00.71
  acetabular liner and/or femoral head only 00.73
  ankle 81.59
  elbow 81.97
  femoral component only 00.72
  femoral head only and/or acetabular liner 00.73
  foot 81.59
  hand 81.97
  hip 81.53
   acetabular and femoral components (total) 00.70
   acetabular component only 00.71
   acetabular liner and/or femoral head only 00.73
   femoral component only 00.72
   femoral head only and/or acetabular liner 00.73
   partial
    acetabular component only 00.71
    acetabular liner and/or femoral head only 00.73
    femoral component only 00.72
    femoral head only and/or acetabular liner 00.73
   total (acetabular and femoral components) 00.70
  knee replacement NOS 81.55
   femoral component 00.82
   partial
    femoral component 00.82
    patellar component 00.83
    tibial component 00.81
    tibial insert 00.84
   patellar component 00.83
   tibial component 00.81
   tibial insert 00.84
   total (all components) 00.80
  lower extremity NEC 81.59
  toe 81.59
  upper extremity 81.97
  wrist 81.97
 knee replacement (prosthesis) NOS 81.55
  femoral component 00.82
  partial
   femoral component 00.82
   patellar component 00.83
   tibial component 00.81
   tibial insert 00.84
  patellar component 00.83
  tibial component 00.81
  tibial insert 00.84
  total (all components) 00.80
 laryngostomy 31.63
 lateral canthus 08.59
 mallet finger 82.84
 mastoid antrum 19.9
 mastoidectomy 20.92
 nephrostomy 55.89
 neuroplasty 04.75
 ocular implant 16.62
 orbital implant 16.62
 pocket
  cardiac device (defibrillator) (pacemaker)
   with initial insertion of cardiac device — omit code
   new site (cardiac device pocket) (skin) (subcutaneous) 37.79
  intracardiac hemodynamic monitoring 37.79
  subcutaneous device pocket NEC
   with initial insertion of generator or device — omit code
   new site 86.09
  thalamic stimulator pulse generator
   with initial insertion of battery package — omit code
   new site (skin) (subcutaneous) 86.09
 previous mastectomy site — see category 85.0-85.99
 proctostomy 48.79

☑ Additional Digit Required — Refer to the Tabular List for Digit Selection   ▽ Subterms under main terms may continue to next column or page

2010 ICD-9-CM   ▶◀ Revised Text   ● New Line   ▲ Revised Code   Volume 3 — 57

☑ Additional Digit Required — Refer to the Tabular List for Digit Selection   ▽ Subterms under main terms may continue to next column or page

58 — Volume 3 • October 2009   ▶◀ Revised Text   ● New Line   ▲ Revised Code   2010 ICD-9-CM

Sling — *see also* Operation, sling — *continued*
fascial — *continued*
mouth 86.81
orbicularis (mouth) 86.81
tongue 25.59
levator muscle (urethrocystopexy) 59.71
pubococcygeal 59.71
rectum (puborectalis) 48.76
tongue (fascial) 25.59

Slitting
canaliculus for
passage of tube 09.42
removal of streptothrix 09.42
lens 13.2
prepuce (dorsal) (lateral) 64.91

Slocum operation (pes anserinus transfer) 81.47
Sluder operation (tonsillectomy) 28.2
Small bowel series (x-ray) 87.63
Smith operation (open osteotomy of mandible) 76.62
Smith-Peterson operation (radiocarpal arthrodesis) 81.25
Smithwick operation (sympathectomy) 05.29
Snaring, polyp, colon (endoscopic) 45.42
Snip, punctum (with dilation) 09.51
Soave operation (endorectal pull-through) 48.41
Somatotherapy, psychiatric NEC 94.29
Sonneberg operation (inferior maxillary neurectomy) 04.07
Sorondo-Ferré operation (hindquarter amputation) 84.19
Soutter operation (iliac crest fasciotomy) 83.14
Spaulding-Richardson operation (uterine suspension) 69.22
Spectrophotometry NEC 89.39
blood 89.39
placenta 89.29
urine 89.29
Spectroscopy
intravascular 38.23
near infrared (NIR) 38.23
Speech therapy NEC 93.75
Spermatocelectomy 63.2
Spermatocystectomy 60.73
Spermatocystotomy 60.72
Sphenoidectomy 22.64
Sphenoidotomy 22.52
Sphincterectomy, anal 49.6
Sphincteroplasty
anal 49.79
obstetrical laceration (current) 75.62
old 49.79
bladder neck 57.85
pancreas 51.83
sphincter of Oddi 51.83
Sphincterorrhaphy, anal 49.71
obstetrical laceration (current) 75.62
old 49.79
Sphincterotomy
anal (external) (internal) 49.59
left lateral 49.51
posterior 49.52
bladder (neck) (transurethral) 57.91
choledochal 51.82
endoscopic 51.85
iris 12.12
pancreatic 51.82
endoscopic 51.85
sphincter of Oddi 51.82
endoscopic 51.85
transduodenal ampullary 51.82
endoscopic 51.85
Spinal anesthesia — *omit code*
Spinelli operation (correction of inverted uterus) 75.93
Spineoplasty 81.66
Spirometry (incentive) (respiratory) 89.37
Spivack operation (permanent gastrostomy) 43.19
Splanchnicectomy 05.29
Splanchnicotomy 05.0
Splenectomy (complete) (total) 41.5
partial 41.43
Splenogram 88.64
radioisotope 92.05

Splenolysis 54.59
laparoscopic 54.51
Splenopexy 41.95
Splenoplasty 41.95
Splenoportogram (by splenic arteriography) 88.64
Splenorrhaphy 41.95
Splenotomy 41.2
Splinting
dental (for immobilization) 93.55
orthodontic 24.7
musculoskeletal 93.54
ureteral 56.2
Splitting — *see also* Division
canaliculus 09.52
lacrimal papilla 09.51
spinal cord tracts 03.29
percutaneous 03.21
tendon sheath 83.01
hand 82.01
Spondylosyndesis — *see also* Fusion, spinal 81.00
S.P. Rogers operation (knee disarticulation) 84.16
Ssabanejew-Frank operation (permanent gastrostomy) 43.19
Stabilization, joint — *see also* Arthrodesis patella (for recurrent dislocation) 81.44
Stab, intercostal 34.09
Stacke operation (simple mastoidectomy) 20.41
Stallard operation (conjunctivocystorhinostomy) 09.82
with insertion of tube or stent 09.83
Stamm (-Kader) operation (temporary gastrostomy) 43.19
Stapedectomy 19.19
with incus replacement (homograft) (prosthesis) 19.11
revision 19.29
with incus replacement 19.21
Stapediolysis 19.0
Stapling
artery 39.31
blebs, lung (emphysematous) 32.21
diaphysis (*see also* Stapling, epiphyseal plate) 78.20
epiphyseal plate 78.20
femur 78.25
fibula 78.27
humerus 78.22
radius 78.23
specified site NEC 78.29
tibia 78.27
ulna 78.23
gastric varices 44.91
graft — *see* Graft
left atrial appendage 37.36
vein 39.32
STARR (stapled transanal rectal resection) 48.74
StaXx® FX Structural Kyphoplasty System 81.66
Steinberg operation 44.5
Steindler operation
fascia stripping (for cavus deformity) 83.14
flexorplasty (elbow) 83.77
muscle transfer 83.77
Stereotactic head frame application 93.59
Stereotactic radiosurgery 92.30
cobalt 60 92.32
linear accelerator (LINAC) 92.31
multi-source 92.32
particle beam 92.33
particulate 92.33
radiosurgery NEC 92.39
single source photon 92.31
Sterilization
female (*see also* specific operation) 66.39
male NEC (*see also* Ligation, vas deferens) 63.70
Sternotomy 77.31
as operative approach — *omit code*
for bone marrow biopsy 41.31
Stewart operation (renal plication with pyeloplasty) 55.87
Stimulation (electronic) — *see also* Implant, electronic stimulator

Stimulation — *see also* Implant, electronic stimulator — *continued*
bone growth (percutaneous) — *see* category 78.9 ☑
transcutaneous (surface) 99.86
cardiac (external) 99.62
internal 37.91
carotid sinus 99.64
CaverMap™ 89.58
defibrillator
as part of intraoperative testing — *omit code*
catheter based invasive electrophysiologic testing 37.26
device interrogation only without arrhythmia induction (bedside check) 89.45-89.49
non-invasive programmed electrical stimulation (NIPS) 37.20
electrophysiologic, cardiac
as part of intraoperative testing — *omit code*
catheter based invasive electrophysiologic testing 37.26
device interrogation only without arrhythmia induction (bedside check) 89.45-89.49
noninvasive programmed electrical stimulation (NIPS) 37.20
nerve
CaverMap™ 89.58
penile 89.58
peripheral or spinal cord, transcutaneous 93.39
Stitch, Kelly-Stoeckel (urethra) 59.3
Stomatoplasty 27.59
Stomatorrhaphy 27.52
Stone operation (anoplasty) 49.79
Strapping (non-traction) 93.59
Strassman operation (metroplasty) 69.49
Strayer operation (gastrocnemius recession) 83.72
Stretching
eyelid (with elongation) 08.71
fascia 93.28
foreskin 99.95
iris 12.63
muscle 93.27
nerve (cranial) (peripheral) 04.91
tendon 93.27
Stripping
bone (*see also* Incision, bone) 77.10
carotid sinus 39.8
cranial suture 02.01
fascia 83.14
hand 82.12
membranes for surgical induction of labor 73.1
meninges (cerebral) 01.51
spinal 03.4
saphenous vein, varicose 38.59
subdural membrane (cerebral) 01.51
spinal 03.4
varicose veins (lower limb) 38.59
upper limb 38.53
vocal cords 30.09
Stromeyer-Little operation (hepatotomy) 50.0
Strong operation (unbridling of celiac artery axis) 39.91
Stryker frame 93.59
Study
bone mineral density 88.98
bundle of His 37.29
color vision 95.06
conduction, nerve (median) 89.15
dark adaptation, eye 95.07
electrophysiologic stimulation and recording, cardiac
as part of intraoperative testing — *omit code*
catheter based invasive electrophysiologic testing 37.26
device interrogation only without arrhythmia induction (bedside check) 89.45-89.49
noninvasive programmed electrical stimulation (NIPS) 37.20

Study — *continued*
function (*see also* Function, study)
radioisotope — *see* Scan, radioisotope
lacrimal flow (radiographic) 87.05
ocular motility 95.15
pulmonary
airway flow measurement, endoscopic 33.72
function — *see* categories 89.37-89.38
radiographic — *see* Radiography
radio-iodinated triolein 92.04
renal clearance 92.03
spirometer 89.37
tracer (*see also* Scan, radioisotope eye (P^{32})) 95.16
ultrasonic — *see* Ultrasonography
visual field 95.05
xenon flow NEC 92.19
cardiovascular 92.05
pulmonary 92.15
Sturmdorf operation (conization of cervix) 67.2
Submucous resection
larynx 30.29
nasal septum 21.5
Summerskill operation (dacryocystorhinostomy by intubation) 09.81
Surgery
computer assisted (CAS) 00.39
with robotics — *see* category 17.4 ☑
CAS with CT/CTA 00.31
CAS with fluoroscopy 00.33
CAS with MR/MRA 00.32
CAS with multiple datasets 00.35
imageless 00.34
other CAS 00.39
IGS — *see* Surgery, computer assisted
image guided — *see* Surgery, computer assisted
navigation (CT-free, IGN image guided, imageless) — *see* Surgery, computer assisted
robotic assisted — *see* category 17.4 ☑
Surmay operation (jejunostomy) 46.39
Suspension
balanced, for traction 93.45
bladder NEC 57.89
diverticulum, pharynx 29.59
kidney 55.7
Olshausen (uterus) 69.22
ovary 65.79
paraurethral (Pereyra) 59.6
periurethral 59.6
urethra (retropubic) (sling) 59.5
urethrovesical
Goebel-Frangenheim-Stoeckel 59.4
gracilis muscle transplant 59.71
levator muscle sling 59.71
Marshall-Marchetti (-Krantz) 59.5
Millin-Read 59.4
suprapubic 59.4
uterus (abdominal or vaginal approach) 69.22
vagina 70.77
with graft or prosthesis 70.78
Suture (laceration)
abdominal wall 54.63
secondary 54.61
adenoid fossa 28.7
adrenal (gland) 07.44
aneurysm (cerebral) (peripheral) 39.52
anus 49.71
obstetric laceration (current) 75.62
old 49.79
aorta 39.31
aponeurosis (*see also* Suture, tendon) 83.64
arteriovenous fistula 39.53
artery 39.31
percutaneous puncture closure — *omit code*
bile duct 51.79
bladder 57.81
obstetric laceration (current) 75.61
blood vessel NEC 39.30
artery 39.31
percutaneous puncture closure — *omit code*
vein 39.32
breast (skin) 85.81

☑ Additional Digit Required — Refer to the Tabular List for Digit Selection ⬧ Subterms under main terms may continue to next column or page

60 — Volume 3 • October 2009 ▶◀ Revised Text ● New Line ▲ Revised Code 2010 ICD-9-CM

☑ Additional Digit Required — Refer to the Tabular List for Digit Selection   Subterms under main terms may continue to next column or page

2010 ICD-9-CM   ▶◀ Revised Text   ● New Line   ▲ Revised Code   October 2009 • Volume 3 — 61

Take-down — Therapy

Therapy — *continued*
  respiratory — *continued*
    other continuous invasive (unspecified duration) 96.70
      for 96 consecutive hours or more 96.72
      for less than 96 consecutive hours 96.71
    positive end expiratory pressure [PEEP]
      invasive — *see* category 96.7 ☑
      non-invasive [NIPPV] 93.90
  root canal 23.70
    with
      apicoectomy 23.72
      irrigation 23.71
  shock
    chemical 94.24
    electric 94.27
      subconvulsive 94.26
    insulin 94.24
  speech 93.75
    for correction of defect 93.74
  SuperOxygenation (SSO₂) 00.49
  SuperSaturated oxygen 00.49
  ultrasound
    heat therapy 93.35
    hyperthermia for cancer treatment 99.85
    physical therapy 93.35
    therapeutic — *see* Ultrasound
  ultraviolet light 99.82
Thermocautery — *see* Cauterization
Thermography 88.89
  blood vessel 88.86
  bone 88.83
  breast 88.85
  cerebral 88.81
  eye 88.82
  lymph gland 88.89
  muscle 88.84
  ocular 88.82
  osteoarticular 88.83
  specified site NEC 88.89
  vein, deep 88.86
Thermokeratoplasty 11.74
Thermosclerectomy 12.62
Thermotherapy (hot packs) (paraffin bath) NEC 93.35
  prostate
    by
      microwave 60.96
      radiofrequency 60.97
      transurethral microwave thermotherapy (TUMT) 60.96
      transurethral needle ablation (TUNA) 60.97
      TUMT (transurethral microwave thermotherapy) 60.96
      TUNA (transurethral needle ablation) 60.97
Thiersch operation
  anus 49.79
  skin graft 86.69
  hand 86.62
Thompson operation
  cleft lip repair 27.54
  correction of lymphedema 40.9
  quadricepsplasty 83.86
  thumb apposition with bone graft 82.69
Thoracectomy 34.09
  for lung collapse 33.34
Thoracentesis 34.91
Thoracocentesis 34.91
Thoracolysis (for collapse of lung) 33.39
Thoracoplasty (anterior) (extrapleural) (paravertebral) (posterolateral) (complete) (partial) 33.34
Thoracoscopy, transpleural (for exploration) 34.21
Thoracostomy 34.09
  for lung collapse 33.32
Thoracotomy (with drainage) 34.09
  as operative approach — *omit code*
  exploratory 34.02
Thoratec® implantable ventricular assist device (IVAD™) 37.66
Thoratec® ventricular assist device (VAD) system 37.66
Three-snip operation, punctum 09.51
Thrombectomy 38.00

Thrombectomy — *continued*
  with endarterectomy — *see* Endarterectomy
  abdominal
    artery 38.06
    vein 38.07
  aorta (arch) (ascending) (descending) 38.04
  arteriovenous shunt or cannula 39.49
  bovine graft 39.49
  coronary artery 36.09
  head and neck vessel NEC 38.02
  intracranial vessel NEC 38.01
  lower limb
    artery 38.08
    vein 38.09
  mechanical
    endovascular
      head and neck 39.74
  pulmonary vessel 38.05
  thoracic vessel NEC 38.05
  upper limb (artery) (vein) 38.03
Thromboendarterectomy 38.10
  abdominal 38.16
  aorta (arch) (ascending) (descending) 38.14
  coronary artery 36.09
    open chest approach 36.03
  head and neck NEC 38.12
  intracranial NEC 38.11
  lower limb 38.18
  thoracic NEC 38.15
  upper limb 38.13
Thymectomy 07.80
  partial (open) (other) 07.81
    thoracoscopic 07.83
  total (open) (other) 07.82
    thoracoscopic 07.84
  transcervical 07.99
Thyrochondrotomy 31.3
Thyrocricoidectomy 30.29
Thyrocricotomy (for assistance in breathing) 31.1
Thyroidectomy NEC 06.39
  by mediastinotomy (*see also* Thyroidectomy, substernal) 06.50
  with laryngectomy — *see* Laryngectomy
  complete or total 06.4
    substernal (by mediastinotomy) (transsternal route) 06.52
    transoral route (lingual) 06.6
  lingual (complete) (partial) (subtotal) (total) 06.6
  partial or subtotal NEC 06.39
    with complete removal of remaining lobe 06.2
    submental route (lingual) 06.6
    substernal (by mediastinotomy) (transsternal route) 06.51
  remaining tissue 06.4
  submental route (lingual) 06.6
  substernal (by mediastinotomy) (transsternal route) 06.50
    complete or total 06.52
    partial or subtotal 06.51
  transoral route (lingual) 06.6
  transsternal route (*see also* Thyroidectomy, substernal) 06.50
  unilateral (with removal of isthmus) (with removal of portion of other lobe) 06.2
Thyroidorrhaphy 06.93
Thyroidotomy (field) (gland) NEC 06.09
  postoperative 06.02
Thyrotomy 31.3
  with tantalum plate 31.69
Tirofiban (HCl), infusion 99.20
Toilette
  skin — *see* Debridement, skin or subcutaneous tissue
  tracheostomy 96.55
Token economy (behavior therapy) 94.33
Tomkins operation (metroplasty) 69.49
Tomography — *see also* Radiography
  abdomen NEC 88.02
  cardiac 87.42
  computerized axial NEC 88.38
    abdomen 88.01
    bone 88.38
      quantitative 88.98
    brain 87.03

Tomography — *see also* Radiography — *continued*
  computerized axial — *continued*
    cardiac 87.41
    coronary 87.41
    head 87.03
    kidney 87.71
    skeletal 88.38
      quantitative 88.98
    thorax 87.41
  head NEC 87.04
  kidney NEC 87.72
  lung 87.42
  optical coherence (intravascular imaging) ●
    coronary vessel(s) 38.24 ●
    non-coronary vessel(s) 38.25 ●
  thorax NEC 87.42
Tongue tie operation 25.91
Tonography 95.26
Tonometry 89.11
Tonsillectomy 28.2
  with adenoidectomy 28.3
Tonsillotomy 28.0
Topectomy 01.32
Torek (-Bevan) operation (orchidopexy) (first stage) (second stage) 62.5
Torkildsen operation (ventriculocisternal shunt) 02.2
Torpin operation (cul-de-sac resection) 70.92
Toti operation (dacryocystorhinostomy) 09.81
Touchas operation 86.83
Touroff operation (ligation of subclavian artery) 38.85
Toxicology — *see* Examination, microscopic
TPN (total parenteral nutrition) 99.15
Trabeculectomy ab externo 12.64
Trabeculodialysis 12.59
Trabeculotomy ab externo 12.54
Trachelectomy 67.4
Trachelopexy 69.22
Tracheloplasty 67.69
Trachelorrhaphy (Emmet) (suture) 67.61
  obstetrical 75.51
Trachelotomy 69.95
  obstetrical 73.93
Tracheocricotomy (for assistance in breathing) 31.1
Tracheofissure 31.1
Tracheography 87.32
Tracheolaryngotomy (emergency) 31.1
  permanent opening 31.29
Tracheoplasty 31.79
  with artificial larynx 31.75
Tracheorrhaphy 31.71
Tracheoscopy NEC 31.42
  through tracheotomy (stoma) 31.41
Tracheostomy (emergency) (temporary) (for assistance in breathing) 31.1
  mediastinal 31.21
  percutaneous dilatational
    other permanent 31.29
    temporary 31.1
  permanent NEC 31.29
  revision 31.74
Tracheotomy (emergency) (temporary) (for assistance in breathing) 31.1
  percutaneous dilatational
    other permanent 31.29
    temporary 31.1
  permanent 31.29
Tracing, carotid pulse with ECG lead 89.56
Traction
  with reduction of fracture or dislocation — *see* Reduction, fracture *and* Reduction, dislocation
  adhesive tape (skin) 93.46
  boot 93.46
  Bryant's (skeletal) 93.44
  Buck's 93.46
  caliper tongs 93.41
    with synchronous insertion of device 02.94
  Cortel's (spinal) 93.42
  Crutchfield tongs 93.41
    with synchronous insertion of device 02.94
  Dunlop's (skeletal) 93.44
  gallows 93.46

Traction — *continued*
  Gardner Wells 93.41
    with synchronous insertion of device 02.94
  halo device, skull 93.41
    with synchronous insertion of device 02.94
  Lyman Smith (skeletal) 93.44
  manual, intermittent 93.21
  mechanical, intermittent 93.21
  Russell's (skeletal) 93.44
  skeletal NEC 93.44
    intermittent 93.43
  skin, limbs NEC 93.46
  spinal NEC 93.42
    with skull device (halo) (caliper) (Crutchfield) (Gardner Wells) (Vinke) (tongs) 93.41
      with synchronous insertion of device 02.94
  Thomas' splint 93.45
  Vinke tongs 93.41
    with synchronous insertion of device 02.94
Tractotomy
  brain 01.32
  medulla oblongata 01.32
  mesencephalon 01.32
  percutaneous 03.21
  spinal cord (one-stage) (two-stage) 03.29
  trigeminal (percutaneous) (radiofrequency) 04.02
Training (for) (in)
  ADL (activities of daily living) 93.83
    for the blind 93.78
  ambulation 93.22
  braille 93.77
  crutch walking 93.24
  dyslexia 93.71
  dysphasia 93.72
  esophageal speech (postlaryngectomy) 93.73
  gait 93.22
  joint movements 93.14
  lip reading 93.75
  Moon (blind reading) 93.77
  orthoptic 95.35
  prenatal (natural childbirth) 93.37
  prosthetic or orthotic device usage 93.24
  relaxation 94.33
  speech NEC 93.75
    for correction of defect 93.74
    esophageal 93.73
  use of lead dog for the blind 93.76
  vocational 93.85
TRAM (transverse rectus abdominis musculocutaneous) flap of breast
  free 85.73
  pedicled 85.72
Transactional analysis
  group 94.44
  individual 94.39
Transection — *see also* Division
  artery (with ligation) (*see also* Division, artery) 38.80
    renal, aberrant (with reimplantation) 39.55
  bone (*see also* Osteotomy) 77.30
  fallopian tube (bilateral) (remaining) (solitary) 66.39
    by endoscopy 66.22
    unilateral 66.92
  isthmus, thyroid 06.91
  muscle 83.19
    eye 15.13
      multiple (two or more muscles) 15.3
    hand 82.19
  nerve (cranial) (peripheral) NEC 04.03
    acoustic 04.01
    root (spinal) 03.1
    sympathetic 05.0
    tracts in spinal cord 03.29
    trigeminal 04.02
    vagus (transabdominal) (*see also* Vagotomy) 44.00
  pylorus (with wedge resection) 43.3
  renal vessel, aberrant (with reimplantation) 39.55
  spinal
    cord tracts 03.29
    nerve root 03.1

☑ Additional Digit Required — Refer to the Tabular List for Digit Selection   ∭ Subterms under main terms may continue to next column or page

2010 ICD-9-CM   ▶◀ Revised Text   ● New Line   ▲ Revised Code   Volume 3 — 63

Ultrasonography — *continued*
  total body 88.79
  urinary system 88.75
  uterus 88.79
    gravid 88.78
Ultrasound
  diagnostic — *see* Ultrasonography
  fragmentation (of)
    cataract (with aspiration) 13.41
    urinary calculus, stones (Kock pouch) 59.95
  heart (intravascular) 88.72
    intracardiac (heart chambers) (ICE) 37.28
    intravascular (coronary vessels) (IVUS) 00.24
    non-invasive 88.72
  inner ear 20.79
  intravascular (IVUS) ▶(VH™-IVUS)◀ 00.29
    aorta 00.22
    aortic arch 00.22
    cerebral vessel, extracranial 00.21
    coronary vessel 00.24
    intrathoracic vessel 00.22
    other specified vessel 00.28
    peripheral vessel 00.23
    renal vessel 00.25
    vena cava (inferior) (superior) 00.22
  therapeutic
    head 00.01
    heart 00.02
    neck 00.01
    other therapeutic ultrasound 00.09
    peripheral vascular vessels 00.03
    vessels of head and neck 00.01
  therapy 93.35
  VH™-IVUS — *see* Ultrasound, intravascular, ●
    by site ●
  virtual histology intravascular ultrasound — ●
    see Ultrasound, intravascular, by site ●
Umbilectomy 54.3
Unbridling
  blood vessel, peripheral 39.91
  celiac artery axis 39.91
Uncovering — *see* Incision, by site
Undercutting
  hair follicle 86.09
  perianal tissue 49.02
Unroofing — *see also* Incision, by site
  external
    auditory canal 18.02
      ear NEC 18.09
  kidney cyst 55.39
UPP (urethral pressure profile) 89.25
Upper GI series (x-ray) 87.62
UPPP (uvulopalatopharyngoplasty) 27.69 *[29.4]*
Uranoplasty (for cleft palate repair) 27.62
Uranorrhaphy (for cleft palate repair) 27.62
Uranostaphylorrhaphy 27.62
Urban operation (mastectomy) (unilateral) 85.47
  bilateral 85.48
Ureterectomy 56.40
  with nephrectomy 55.51
  partial 56.41
  total 56.42
Ureterocecostomy 56.71
Ureterocelectomy 56.41
Ureterocolostomy 56.71
Ureterocystostomy 56.74
Ureteroenterostomy 56.71
Ureteroileostomy (internal diversion) 56.71
  external diversion 56.51
Ureterolithotomy 56.2
Ureterolysis 59.02
  with freeing or repositioning of ureter 59.02
  laparoscopic 59.03
Ureteroneocystostomy 56.74
Ureteropexy 56.85
Ureteroplasty 56.89
Ureteroplication 56.89
Ureteroproctostomy 56.71
Ureteropyelography (intravenous) (diuretic infusion) 87.73
  percutaneous 87.75
  retrograde 87.74
Ureteropyeloplasty 55.87
Ureteropyelostomy 55.86
Ureterorrhaphy 56.82

Ureteroscopy 56.31
  with biopsy 56.33
Ureterosigmoidostomy 56.71
Ureterostomy (cutaneous) (external) (tube) 56.61
  closure 56.83
  ileal 56.51
Ureterotomy 56.2
Ureteroureterostomy (crossed) 56.75
  lumbar 56.41
  resection with end-to-end anastomosis 56.41
  spatulated 56.41
Urethral catheterization, indwelling 57.94
Urethral pressure profile (UPP) 89.25
Urethrectomy (complete) (partial) (radical) 58.39
  with
    complete cystectomy 57.79
    pelvic exenteration 68.8
    radical cystectomy 57.71
Urethrocystography (retrograde) (voiding) 87.76
Urethrocystopexy (by) 59.79
  levator muscle sling 59.71
  retropubic suspension 59.5
  suprapubic suspension 59.4
Urethrolithotomy 58.0
Urethrolysis 58.5
Urethropexy 58.49
  anterior 59.79
Urethroplasty 58.49
  augmentation 59.79
  collagen implant 59.72
  fat implant 59.72
  injection (endoscopic) of implant into urethra 59.72
  polytef implant 59.72
Urethrorrhaphy 58.41
Urethroscopy 58.22
  for control of hemorrhage of prostate 60.94
  perineal 58.21
Urethrostomy (perineal) 58.0
Urethrotomy (external) 58.0
  internal (endoscopic) 58.5
Uroflowmetry (UFR) 89.24
Urography (antegrade) (excretory) (intravenous) 87.73
  retrograde 87.74
Uteropexy (abdominal approach) (vaginal approach) 69.22
UVP (uvulopalatopharyngoplasty) 27.69 *[29.4]*
Uvulectomy 27.72
Uvulopalatopharyngoplasty (UPPP) 27.69 *[29.4]*
Uvulotomy 27.71

V

Vaccination (prophylactic) (against) 99.59
  anthrax 99.55
  brucellosis 99.55
  cholera 99.31
  common cold 99.51
  disease NEC 99.55
    arthropod-borne viral NEC 99.54
  encephalitis, arthropod-borne viral 99.53
  German measles 99.47
  hydrophobia 99.44
  infectious parotitis 99.46
  influenza 99.52
  measles 99.45
  mumps 99.46
  paratyphoid fever 99.32
  pertussis 99.37
  plague 99.34
  poliomyelitis 99.41
  rabies 99.44
  Rocky Mountain spotted fever 99.55
  rubella 99.47
  rubeola 99.45
  smallpox 99.42
  Staphylococcus 99.55
  Streptococcus 99.55
  tuberculosis 99.33
  tularemia 99.35
  tumor 99.28
  typhoid 99.32
  typhus 99.55
  undulant fever 99.55
  yellow fever 99.43
Vacuum extraction, fetal head 72.79

Vacuum extraction, fetal head — *continued*
  with episiotomy 72.71
VAD
  vascular access device — *see* Vascular access device, totally implantable
  ventricular assist device — *see* Implant, heart assist system
Vagectomy (subdiaphragmatic) — *see also* Vagotomy 44.00
Vaginal douche 96.44
Vaginectomy 70.4
Vaginofixation 70.77
  with graft or prosthesis 70.78
Vaginoperineotomy 70.14
Vaginoplasty 70.79
Vaginorrhaphy 70.71
  obstetrical 75.69
Vaginoscopy 70.21
Vaginotomy 70.14
  for
    culdocentesis 70.0
    pelvic abscess 70.12
Vagotomy (gastric) 44.00
  parietal cell 44.02
  selective NEC 44.03
    highly 44.02
    Holle's 44.02
    proximal 44.02
  truncal 44.01
Valvotomy — *see* Valvulotomy
Valvulectomy, heart — *see* Valvuloplasty, heart
Valvuloplasty
  heart (open heart technique) (without valve replacement) 35.10
    with prosthesis or tissue graft — *see* Replacement, heart, valve, by site
    aortic valve 35.11
      percutaneous (balloon) 35.96
    combined with repair of atrial and ventricular septal defects — *see* Repair, endocardial cushion defect
    mitral valve 35.12
    percutaneous (balloon) 35.96
    pulmonary valve 35.13
      in total repair of tetralogy of Fallot 35.81
      percutaneous (balloon) 35.96
    tricuspid valve 35.14
Valvulotomy
  heart (closed heart technique) (transatrial) (transventricular) 35.00
    aortic valve 35.01
    mitral valve 35.02
    open heart technique — *see* Valvuloplasty, heart
    pulmonary valve 35.03
      in total repair of tetralogy of Fallot 35.81
    tricuspid valve 35.04
Varicocelectomy, spermatic cord 63.1
Varicotomy, peripheral vessels (lower limb) 38.59
  upper limb 38.53
Vascular access device, totally implantable 86.07
Vascular closure, percutaneous puncture — *omit code*
Vascularization — *see* Revascularization
Vasectomy (complete) (partial) 63.73
Vasogram 87.94
Vasoligation 63.71
  gastric 38.86
Vasorrhaphy 63.81
Vasostomy 63.6
Vasotomy 63.6
Vasotripsy 63.71
Vasovasostomy 63.82
Vectorcardiogram (VCG) (with ECG) 89.53
Vectra® vascular access graft 86.07
Venectomy — *see* Phlebectomy
Venipuncture NEC 38.99
  for injection of contrast material — *see* Phlebography
Venography — *see* Phlebography
Venorrhaphy 39.32

Venotomy 38.00
  abdominal 38.07
  head and neck NEC 38.02
  intracranial NEC 38.01
  lower limb 38.09
  thoracic NEC 38.05
  upper limb 38.03
Venotripsy 39.98
Venovenostomy 39.29
Ventilation
  bi-level positive airway pressure [BiPAP] 93.90
    delivered by
      endotracheal tube — *see* category 96.7 ☑
      tracheostomy — *see* category 96.7 ☑
  continuous positive airway pressure [CPAP] 93.90
    delivered by
      endotracheal tube — *see* category 96.7 ☑
      tracheostomy — *see* category 96.7 ☑
  endotracheal respiratory assistance — *see* category 96.7 ☑
  intermittent positive pressure breathing [IPPB] 93.91
  mechanical, NOS 93.90
    by endotracheal tube — *see* category 96.7 ☑
    by tracheostomy — *see* category 96.7 ☑
    endotracheal respiratory assistance — *see* category 96.7 ☑
    invasive — *see* category 96.7 ☑
    non-invasive [NIPPV] 93.90
    other continuous invasive (unspecified duration) 96.70
      for 96 consecutive hours or more 96.72
      for less than 96 consecutive hours 96.71
    positive end expiratory pressure [PEEP]
      invasive — *see* category 96.7 ☑
      non-invasive [NIPPV] 93.90
  negative pressure (continuous) [CNP] 93.99
  non-invasive positive pressure (NIPPV) 93.90
Ventriculectomy, heart
  partial 37.35
Ventriculocholecystostomy 02.34
Ventriculocisternostomy 02.2
Ventriculocordectomy 30.29
Ventriculogram, ventriculography (cerebral) 87.02
  cardiac
    left ventricle (outflow tract) 88.53
      combined with right heart 88.54
    right ventricle (outflow tract) 88.52
      combined with left heart 88.54
    radionuclide cardiac 92.05
Ventriculomyocardiotomy 37.11
Ventriculoperitoneostomy 02.34
Ventriculopuncture 01.09
  through previously implanted catheter or reservoir (Ommaya) (Rickham) 01.02
Ventriculoseptopexy — *see* Repair, ventricular septal defect 35.72
Ventriculoseptoplasty — *see also* Repair, ventricular septal defect 35.72
Ventriculostomy 02.2
Ventriculotomy
  cerebral 02.2
  heart 37.11
Ventriculoureterostomy 02.35
Ventriculovenostomy 02.32
Ventrofixation, uterus 69.22
Ventrohysteropexy 69.22
Ventrosuspension, uterus 69.22
VEP (visual evoked potential) 95.23
Version, obstetrical (bimanual) (cephalic) (combined) (internal) (podalic) 73.21
  with extraction 73.22
  Braxton Hicks 73.21
    with extraction 73.22
  external (bipolar) 73.91
  Potter's (podalic) 73.21
    with extraction 73.22
  Wigand's (external) 73.91
  Wright's (cephalic) 73.21
    with extraction 73.22

☑ Additional Digit Required — Refer to the Tabular List for Digit Selection   ▼ Subterms under main terms may continue to next column or page

64 — Volume 3 • October 2009   ▶◀ Revised Text   ● New Line   ▲ Revised Code   **2010 ICD-9-CM**

☑ Additional Digit Required — Refer to the Tabular List for Digit Selection   ▽ Subterms under main terms may continue to next column or page

2010 ICD-9-CM   ▶◀ Revised Text   ● New Line   ▲ Revised Code   October 2009 • Volume 3 — 65

Arteries coded in aorta coronary bypass grafts (CABG):

- Right coronary artery (RCA)
  - Right marginal
  - Right posterior descending (PDA)
- Left main coronary artery (LMCA)
  - Left anterior descending branch (LAD)
  - Diagonal
  - Septal
  - Circumflex (LCX)
  - Obtuse marginal (OM)
  - Posterior descending
  - Posterolateral

00. PROCEDURES AND INTERVENTIONS, NOT ELSEWHERE CLASSIFIED (00)

√3ʳᵈ **00 Procedures and interventions, not elsewhere classified**

√4ᵗʰ **00.0 Therapeutic ultrasound**

 EXCLUDES *diagnostic ultrasound (non-invasive) (88.71-88.79)*
 intracardiac echocardiography [ICE] (heart chamber(s)) (37.28)
 intravascular imaging (adjunctive) (00.21-00.29)

DEF: Interventional treatment modality using lower frequency and higher intensity levels of ultrasound energy than used in diagnostic ultrasound modality for the purpose of limiting intimal hyperplasia, or restenosis, associated with atherosclerotic vascular disease.
AHA: 4Q, '02, 90

00.01 Therapeutic ultrasound of vessels of head and neck

 Anti-restenotic ultrasound
 Intravascular non-ablative ultrasound
 EXCLUDES *diagnostic ultrasound of:*
  eye (95.13)
  head and neck (88.71)
  that of inner ear (20.79)
 ultrasonic:
  angioplasty of non-coronary vessel (39.50)
  embolectomy (38.01, 38.02)
  endarterectomy (38.11, 38.12)
  thrombectomy (38.01, 38.02)

00.02 Therapeutic ultrasound of heart

 Anti-restenotic ultrasound
 Intravascular non-ablative ultrasound
 EXCLUDES *diagnostic ultrasound of heart (88.72)*
 ultrasonic ablation of heart lesion (37.34)
 ultrasonic angioplasty of coronary vessels (00.66, 36.09)

00.03 Therapeutic ultrasound of peripheral vascular vessels

 Anti-restenotic ultrasound
 Intravascular non-ablative ultrasound
 EXCLUDES *diagnostic ultrasound of peripheral vascular system (88.77)*
 ultrasonic angioplasty of: non-coronary vessel (39.50)

00.09 Other therapeutic ultrasound

 EXCLUDES *ultrasonic:*
  fragmentation of urinary stones (59.95)
  percutaneous nephrostomy with fragmentation (55.04)
  physical therapy (93.35)
  transurethral guided laser induced prostatectomy (TULIP) (60.21)

√4ᵗʰ **00.1 Pharmaceuticals**

00.10 Implantation of chemotherapeutic agent

 Brain wafer chemotherapy
 Interstitial/intracavitary
 EXCLUDES *injection or infusion of cancer chemotherapeutic substance (99.25)*

DEF: Brain wafer chemotherapy: Placement of wafers containing antineoplastic agent against the wall of the resection cavity subsequent to the surgeon completing a tumor excision to deliver chemotherapy directly to the tumor site; used to treat glioblastoma multiforme (GBM).
AHA: 4Q, '02, 93

00.11 Infusion of drotrecogin alfa (activated)

 Infusion of recombinant protein
 AHA: 4Q, '02, 93

 TIP: A recombinant version of naturally occurring activated protein C (APC), required to ensure the control of inflammation and clotting in blood vessels; used for patients with severe sepsis.

00.12 Administration of inhaled nitric oxide

 Nitric oxide therapy
 AHA: 4Q, '02, 94

00.13 Injection or infusion of nesiritide

 Human B-type natriuretic peptide (hBNP)
 AHA: 4Q, '02, 94

 TIP: Used for the treatment of acutely decompensated congestive heart failure with dyspnea at rest or with minimal activity; is administered intravenously by infusion or bolus.

00.14 Injection or infusion of oxazolidinone class of antibiotics

 Linezolid injection
 AHA: 4Q, '02, 95

00.15 High-dose infusion interleukin-2 [IL-2]

 Infusion (IV bolus, CIV) interleukin
 Injection of aldesleukin
 EXCLUDES *low-dose infusion interleukin-2 (99.28)*

 DEF: A high-dose anti-neoplastic therapy using a biological response modifier (BRM); the body naturally produces substances called interleukins, which are multi-function cytokines in the generation of an immune response.
 AHA: 4Q, '03, 92

00.16 Pressurized treatment of venous bypass graft [conduit] with pharmaceutical substance

 Ex-vivo treatment of vessel
 Hyperbaric pressurized graft [conduit]
 DEF: Ex-vivo process of delivering small nucleic acid molecules that block protein transcription factors essential for the expression of genes controlling cell proliferation into graft tissue under nondistending pressure; reduces intimal hyperplasia and vein graft failure.

00.17 Infusion of vasopressor agent

00.18 Infusion of immunosuppressive antibody therapy

 Monoclonal antibody therapy
 Polyclonal antibody therapy
 INCLUDES *during induction phase of solid organ transplantation*

 AHA: 4Q, '05, 101

00.19 Disruption of blood brain barrier via infusion [BBBD]

 Infusion of substance to disrupt blood brain barrier

 Code also chemotherapy (99.25)
 EXCLUDES *other perfusion (39.97)*

 DEF: Infusion of chemotherapy drug that temporarily allows the transport of materials into the brain through the blood brain barrier (BBB), which is the protective mechanism that limits transport of toxins while allowing necessary nutrients to pass from the blood vessels into the brain tissue; used in the treatment of brain cancers.
 AHA: 4Q, '07, 103-104

✓4ᵗʰ 00.2 Intravascular imaging of blood vessels

Note: Real-time imaging of lumen of blood vessel(s) using sound waves
Endovascular ultrasonography
Intravascular [ultrasound] imaging of blood vessels
Intravascular ultrasound (IVUS)
▶Virtual histology intravascular ultrasound [VH-IVUS]◀
Code also any synchronous diagnostic or therapeutic procedures

EXCLUDES adjunct vascular system procedures, number of vessels treated (00.40-00.43)
diagnostic procedures on blood vessels (38.21-38.29)
diagnostic ultrasound of peripheral vascular system (88.77)
▶intravascular imaging of vessel(s) by OCT (38.24-38.25)◀
magnetic resonance imaging (MRI) (88.91-88.97)
therapeutic ultrasound (00.01-00.09)

00.21 Intravascular imaging of extracranial cerebral vessels

Common carotid vessels and branches
Intravascular ultrasound (IVUS), extracranial cerebral vessels
EXCLUDES diagnostic ultrasound (non-invasive) of head and neck (88.71)

00.22 Intravascular imaging of intrathoracic vessels

Aorta and aortic arch
Intravascular ultrasound (IVUS), intrathoracic vessels
Vena cava (superior) (inferior)
EXCLUDES diagnostic ultrasound (non-invasive) of other sites of thorax (88.73)

00.23 Intravascular imaging of peripheral vessels

Imaging of:
vessels of arm(s)
vessels of leg(s)
Intravascular ultrasound (IVUS), peripheral vessels
EXCLUDES diagnostic ultrasound (non-invasive) of peripheral vascular system (88.77)

00.24 Intravascular imaging of coronary vessels

Intravascular ultrasound (IVUS), coronary vessels
EXCLUDES diagnostic ultrasound (non-invasive) of heart (88.72)
intracardiac echocardiography [ICE] (ultrasound of heart chamber(s)) (37.28)
AHA: 3Q, '06, 8

00.25 Intravascular imaging of renal vessels

Intravascular ultrasound (IVUS), renal vessels
Renal artery
EXCLUDES diagnostic ultrasound (non-invasive) of urinary system (88.75)

00.28 Intravascular imaging, other specified vessel(s)

00.29 Intravascular imaging, unspecified vessel(s)

✓4ᵗʰ 00.3 Computer assisted surgery [CAS]

CT-free navigation
Image guided navigation (IGN)
Image guided surgery (IGS)
Imageless navigation
That without the use of robotic(s) technology
Code also diagnostic or therapeutic procedure
EXCLUDES robotic assisted procedures (17.41-17.49)
stereotactic frame application only (93.59)
TIP: CAS includes three key activities: surgical planning, registration, and navigation; typically used in brain; cranial; ear, nose and throat (ENT); spinal; and orthopaedic surgeries.

00.31 Computer assisted surgery with CT/CTA
    AHA: 4Q, '04, 113

00.32 Computer assisted surgery with MR/MRA
    AHA: 4Q, '04, 113

00.33 Computer assisted surgery with fluoroscopy

00.34 Imageless computer assisted surgery

00.35 Computer assisted surgery with multiple datasets

00.39 Other computer assisted surgery
Computer assisted surgery NOS

✓4ᵗʰ 00.4 Adjunct vascular system procedures

Note: These codes can apply to both coronary and peripheral vessels. These codes are to be used in conjunction with other therapeutic procedure codes to provide additional information on the number of vessels upon which a procedure was performed and/or the number of stents inserted. As appropriate, code both the number of vessels operated on (00.40-00.43), and the number of stents inserted (00.45-00.48).
Code also any:
angioplasty or atherectomy (00.61-00.62, 00.66, 39.50)
endarterectomy (38.10-38.18)
insertion of vascular stent(s) (00.55, 00.63-00.65, 36.06-36.07, 39.90)
other removal of coronary artery obstruction (36.09)
AHA: 4Q, '05, 101

00.40 Procedure on single vessel
Number of vessels, unspecified
EXCLUDES (aorto)coronary bypass (36.10-36.19)
intravascular imaging of blood vessels (00.21-00.29)
AHA: ▶2Q, '09, 12;◀ 1Q, '07, 17; 3Q, '06, 8; 4Q, '05, 71, 106

00.41 Procedure on two vessels
EXCLUDES (aorto)coronary bypass (36.10-36.19)
intravascular imaging of blood vessels (00.21-00.29)
AHA: 4Q, '06, 119; 4Q, '05, 105

00.42 Procedure on three vessels
EXCLUDES (aorto)coronary bypass (36.10-36.19)
intravascular imaging of blood vessels (00.21-00.29)

00.43 Procedure on four or more vessels
EXCLUDES (aorto)coronary bypass (36.10-36.19)
intravascular imaging of blood vessels (00.21-00.29)

00.44 Procedure on vessel bifurcation
Note: This code is to be used to identify the presence of a vessel bifurcation; it does not describe a specific bifurcation stent. Use this code only once per operative episode, irrespective of the number of bifurcations in vessels.
AHA: 4Q, '06, 119

00.45 Insertion of one vascular stent
Number of stents, unspecified
AHA: 4Q, '05, 71

00.46 Insertion of two vascular stents
AHA: ▶2Q, '09, 12;◀ 4Q, '05, 105-106

00.47 Insertion of three vascular stents
AHA: 4Q, '06, 119

00.48 Insertion of four or more vascular stents

Stenting Techniques on Vessel Bifurcation

[handwritten note:] Bifurcation: A separation into two branches; the point of forking.

BI Bilateral Procedure   **NC** Non-covered Procedure   **LC** Limited Coverage Procedure   ▶◀ Revised Text   ● New Code   ▲ Revised Code Title

68 – Volume 3 • October 2009   **2010 ICD-9-CM**

Cardiac Resynchronization Therapy (CRT) – different from pacemaker therapy or implantable cardioverter-defibrillators (ICD) because it requires the implantation of a special electrode within the coronary vein to attach the device to the exterior wall of the left ventricle.

00.49 SuperSaturated oxygen therapy

Aqueous oxygen (AO) therapy
SSO_2
SuperOxygenation infusion therapy

Code also any:
- injection or infusion of thrombolytic agent (99.10)
- insertion of coronary artery stent(s) (36.06-36.07)
- intracoronary artery thrombolytic infusion (36.04)
- number of vascular stents inserted (00.45-00.48)
- number of vessels treated (00.40-00.43)
- open chest coronary artery angioplasty (36.03)
- other removal of coronary obstruction (36.09)
- percutaneous transluminal coronary angioplasty [PTCA] (00.66)
- procedure on vessel bifurcation (00.44)

EXCLUDES *other oxygen enrichment (93.96)*
other perfusion (39.97)

DEF: ▶Method of reducing myocardial tissue damage via infusion of super-oxygenated blood directly to oxygen-deprived myocardial tissue in MI patients; typically performed as an adjunct procedure during PTCA or stent insertion.◀

AHA: ▶4Q, '08, 162◀

✓4th 00.5 Other cardiovascular procedures
AHA: 4Q, '02, 95

00.50 Implantation of cardiac resynchronization pacemaker without mention of defibrillation, total system [CRT-P]

Note: Device testing during procedure — *omit code*
Biventricular pacemaker
Biventricular pacing without internal cardiac defibrillator
BiV pacemaker
Implantation of cardiac resynchronization (biventricular) pulse generator pacing device, formation of pocket, transvenous leads including placement of lead into left ventricular coronary venous system, and intraoperative procedures for evaluation of lead signals
That with CRT-P generator and one or more leads

EXCLUDES *implantation of cardiac resynchronization defibrillator, total system [CRT-D] (00.51)*
insertion or replacement of any type pacemaker device (37.80-37.87)
replacement of cardiac resynchronization:
defibrillator, pulse generator only [CRT-D] (00.54)
pacemaker, pulse generator only [CRT-P] (00.53)

DEF: Cardiac resynchronization pacemaker: CRT-P, or bi-ventricular pacing, adds a third lead to traditional pacemaker designs that connects to the left ventricle. The device provides electrical stimulation and coordinates ventricular contractions to improve cardiac output.
AHA: 3Q, '05, 3-9; 4Q, '02, 100

00.53/00.54 Cardiac Resynchronization Therapy (CRT) ... similar to conventional pacemaker therapy.

00.51 Implantation of cardiac resynchronization defibrillator, total system [CRT-D]

Note: Device testing during procedure — *omit code*
BiV defibrillator
Biventricular defibrillator
Biventricular pacing with internal cardiac defibrillator
BiV ICD
BiV pacemaker with defibrillator
BiV pacing with defibrillator
Implantation of cardiac resynchronization (biventricular) pulse generator with defibrillator [AICD], formation of pocket, transvenous leads, including placement of lead into left ventricular coronary venous system, intraoperative procedures for evaluation of lead signals, and obtaining defibrillator threshold measurements
That with CRT-D generator and one or more leads

EXCLUDES *implantation of cardiac resynchronization pacemaker, total system [CRT-P] (00.50)*
implantation or replacement of automatic cardioverter/defibrillator, total system [AICD] (37.94)
replacement of cardiac resynchronization defibrillator, pulse generator only [CRT-D] (00.54)

AHA: ▶3Q, '08, 18;◀ 1Q, '07, 16, 17; 3Q, '05, 3-9; 4Q, '02, 99, 100

TIP: If an angiogram or a venogram is performed in conjunction with CRT-D placement, it should be coded separately; refer to subcategories 88.5 and 88.6.

00.52 Implantation or replacement of transvenous lead [electrode] into left ventricular coronary venous system

EXCLUDES *implantation of cardiac resynchronization:*
defibrillator, total system [CRT-D] (00.51)
pacemaker, total system [CRT-P] (00.50)
initial insertion of transvenous lead [electrode] (37.70-37.72)
replacement of transvenous atrial and/or ventricular lead(s) [electrodes] (37.76)

00.53 Implantation or replacement of cardiac resynchronization pacemaker, pulse generator only [CRT-P]

Note: Device testing during procedure — *omit code*
Implantation of CRT-P device with removal of any existing CRT-P or other pacemaker device

EXCLUDES *implantation of cardiac resynchronization pacemaker, total system [CRT-P] (00.50)*
implantation or replacement of cardiac resynchronization defibrillator, pulse generator only [CRT-D] (00.54)
insertion or replacement of any type pacemaker device (37.80-37.87)

AHA: 3Q, '05, 3-9

00.54   **Implantation or replacement of cardiac resynchronization defibrillator, pulse generator device only [CRT-D]**

Note: Device testing during procedure — *omit code*

Implantation of CRT-D device with removal of any existing CRT-D, CRT-P, pacemaker, or defibrillator device

EXCLUDES   *implantation of automatic cardioverter/defibrillator pulse generator only (37.96)*

implantation of cardiac resynchronization defibrillator, total system [CRT-D] (00.51)

implantation or replacement of cardiac resynchronization pacemaker, pulse generator only [CRT-P] (00.53)

AHA: 3Q, '05, 3-9; 4Q, '02, 100

00.55   **Insertion of drug-eluting peripheral vessel stent(s)**

Endograft(s)

Endovascular graft(s)

Stent graft(s)

Code also any:

angioplasty or atherectomy of other non-coronary vessel(s) (39.50)

number of vascular stents inserted (00.45-00.48)

number of vessels treated (00.40-00.43)

procedure on vessel bifurcation (00.44)

EXCLUDES   *drug-coated peripheral stents, e.g., heparin coated (39.90)*

insertion of cerebrovascular stent(s) (00.63-00.65)

insertion of drug-eluting coronary artery stent (36.07)

insertion of non-drug-eluting stent(s): coronary artery (36.06) peripheral vessel (39.90) that for aneurysm repair (39.71-39.79)

AHA: 4Q, '02, 101

TIP: Drug-eluting stents gradually release a drug, such as Sirolimus, Taxol, or Paclitaxel into the vessel wall tissue over a period of 30 to 45 days to prevent the build-up of scar tissue that can narrow the reopened artery.

▲ **00.56**   **Insertion or replacement of implantable pressure sensor [lead] for intracardiac or great vessel hemodynamic monitoring**

Code also any associated implantation or replacement of monitor (00.57)

EXCLUDES   *circulatory monitoring (blood gas, arterial or venous pressure, cardiac output and coronary blood flow) (89.60-89.69)*

DEF: Insertion of an implantable device consisting of a data storage system, a single lead with a pressure sensor tip and a wireless antenna that continuously collects data on heart rate, pressures, physical activity and temperature.

AHA: 4Q, '06, 119

▲ **00.57**   **Implantation or replacement of subcutaneous device for intracardiac or great vessel hemodynamic monitoring**

Implantation of monitoring device with formation of subcutaneous pocket and connection to intracardiac pressure sensor (lead)

Code also any associated insertion or replacement of implanted pressure sensor (lead) (00.56)

AHA: 4Q, '06, 119

00.58   **Insertion of intra-aneurysm sac pressure monitoring device (intraoperative)**

Insertion of pressure sensor during endovascular repair of abdominal or thoracic aortic aneurysm(s)

DEF: Placement of a device in an aortic aneurysm sac during aneurysm repair to evaluate sac pressure before and after stent graft placement; helps detect endoleaks and prevents serious aneurysm complications.

AHA: 4Q, '08, 163-165

00.59   **Intravascular pressure measurement of coronary arteries**

INCLUDES   fractional flow reserve (FFR)

Code also any synchronous diagnostic or therapeutic procedures

EXCLUDES   *intravascular pressure meas- urement of intrathoracic arteries (00.67)*

AHA: 4Q, '08, 163

✓4ᵗʰ **00.6**   **Procedures on blood vessels**

00.61   **Percutaneous angioplasty or atherectomy of precerebral (extracranial) vessel(s)**

Basilar   Vertebral

Carotid

Code also any:

injection or infusion of thrombolytic agent (99.10)

number of vascular stents inserted (00.45-00.48)

number of vessels treated (00.40-00.43)

percutaneous insertion of carotid artery stent(s) (00.63)

percutaneous insertion of other precerebral artery stent(s) (00.64)

procedure on vessel bifurcation (00.44)

EXCLUDES   *angioplasty or atherectomy of other non-coronary vessel(s) (39.50)*

removal of cerebrovascular obstruction of vessel(s) by open approach (38.01-38.02, 38.11-38.12, 38.31-38.32, 38.41-38.42)

⁷ **00.62**   **Percutaneous angioplasty or atherectomy** NC **intracranial vessel(s)**

Code also any:

injection or infusion of thrombolytic agent (99.10)

number of vascular stents inserted (00.45-00.48)

number of vessels treated (00.40-00.43)

percutaneous insertion of intracranial stent(s) (00.65)

procedure on vessel bifurcation (00.44)

EXCLUDES   *angioplasty or atherectomy of other non-coronary vessel(s) (39.50)*

removal of cerebrovascular obstruction of vessel(s) by open approach (38.01-38.02, 38.11-38.12, 38.31-38.32, 38.41-38.42)

00.63   **Percutaneous insertion of carotid artery stent(s)**

Includes the use of any embolic protection device, distal protection device, filter device, or stent delivery system

Non-drug-eluting stent

Code also any:

number of vascular stents inserted (00.45-00.48)

number of vessels treated (00.40-00.43)

percutaneous angioplasty or atherectomy of precerebral vessel(s) (00.61)

procedure on vessel bifurcation (00.44)

EXCLUDES   *angioplasty or atherectomy of other non-coronary vessel(s) (39.50)*

insertion of drug-eluting periph- eral vessel stent(s) (00.55)

---

⁷ Noncovered except when reported with code 00.65.

BI Bilateral Procedure   **NC** Non-covered Procedure   **LC** Limited Coverage Procedure   ▶◀ Revised Text   ● New Code   ▲ Revised Code Title

70 – Volume 3 · October 2009   2010 ICD-9-CM

✳ Minor intimal tears often occur during angioplasty; these are considered to be an unavoidable part of the procedure and are not classified as complications.

00.64   **Percutaneous insertion of other precerebral (extracranial) artery stent(s)**

Includes the use of any embolic protection device, distal protection device, filter device, or stent delivery system

Basilar stent
Vertebral stent

Code also any:
number of vascular stents inserted (00.45-00.48)
number of vessels treated (00.40-00.43)
percutaneous angioplasty or atherectomy of precerebral vessel(s) (00.61)
procedure on vessel bifurcation (00.44)

EXCLUDES   *angioplasty or atherectomy of other non-coronary vessel(s) (39.50)*
insertion of drug-eluting peripheral vessel stent(s) (00.55)

00.65   **Percutaneous insertion of intracranial vascular stent(s)**

Includes the use of any embolic protection device, distal protection device, filter device, or stent delivery system

Code also any:
number of vascular stents inserted (00.45-00.48)
number of vessels treated (00.40-00.43)
percutaneous angioplasty or atherectomy of intracranial vessel(s) (00.62)
procedure on vessel bifurcation (00.44)

EXCLUDES   *angioplasty or atherectomy of other non-coronary vessel(s) (39.50)*
insertion of drug-eluting peripheral vessel stent(s) (00.55)

✳ **00.66**   **Percutaneous transluminal coronary angioplasty [PTCA] or coronary atherectomy**

Balloon angioplasty of coronary artery
Coronary atherectomy
Percutaneous coronary angioplasty NOS
PTCA NOS

Code also any:
injection or infusion of thrombolytic agent (99.10)
insertion of coronary artery stent(s) (36.06-36.07)
intracoronary artery thrombolytic infusion (36.04)
number of vascular stents inserted (00.45-00.48)
number of vessels treated (00.40-00.43)
procedure on vessel bifurcation (00.44)
SuperSaturated oxygen therapy (00.49)

DEF: Balloon angioplasty: Insertion of catheter with inflation of balloon to flatten plaque and widen vessels.

AHA: ▶2Q, '09, 12;◀ 1Q, '07, 17; 3Q, '06, 8; 4Q, '05, 71, 101; **The following references pertain to deleted PTCA codes (36.01, 36.02, 36.05):** 1Q, '04, 10; 3Q, '03, 9; 4Q, '02, 114; 3Q, '02, 19; 1Q, '01, 9; 2Q, '01, 24; 1Q, '00, 11; 1Q, '99, 17; 4Q, '98, 74, 85; 1Q, '97, 3; 1Q, '94, 3; 3Q, '91, 24

00.67   **Intravascular pressure measurement of intrathoracic arteries**

Assessment of: Assessment of:
aorta and aortic arch   carotid

Code also any synchronous diagnostic or therapeutic procedures

AHA: 4Q, '08, 163-164

00.68   **Intravascular pressure measurement of peripheral arteries**

Assessment of: Assessment of:
other peripheral vessels   vessels of leg(s)
vessels of arm(s)

Code also any synchronous diagnostic or therapeutic procedures

AHA: 4Q, '08, 163-164

PTCA (Balloon Angioplasty)

Aorta
Left coronary artery
Right coronary artery
Plaque
Inflated balloon

00.69   **Intravascular pressure measurement, other specified and unspecified vessels**

Assessment of: Assessment of:
iliac vessels   mesenteric vessels
intra-abdominal vessels   renal vessels

Code also any synchronous diagnostic or therapeutic procedures

EXCLUDES   *intravascular pressure measurement of:*
coronary arteries (00.59)
intrathoracic arteries (00.67)
peripheral arteries (00.68)

AHA: 4Q, '08, 163-164

✓4ᵗʰ **00.7**   **Other hip procedures**
AHA: 4Q, '05, 106

00.70   **Revision of hip replacement, both acetabular and femoral components**   BI

Total hip revision

Code also any:
removal of (cement) (joint) spacer (84.57)
type of bearing surface, if known (00.74-00.77)

EXCLUDES   *revision of hip replacement, acetabular component only (00.71)*
revision of hip replacement, fem- oral component only (00.72)
revision of hip replacement, not otherwise specified (81.53)
revision with replacement of acetabular liner and/or femoral head only (00.73)

AHA: 2Q, '08, 3, 4; 1Q, '08, 6; 4Q, '05, 113

TIP: Assign for a conversion from a previously placed hip hemiarthroplasty to a total hip joint replacement procedure.

00.71   **Revision of hip replacement, acetabular component**

Partial, acetabular component only
That with:
exchange of acetabular cup and liner
exchange of femoral head

Code also any type of bearing surface, if known (00.74-00.77)

EXCLUDES   *revision of hip replacement, both acetabular and femoral components (00.70)*
revision of hip replacement, femoral component (00.72)
revision of hip replacement, not otherwise specified (81.53)
revision with replacement of acetabular liner and/or femoral head only (00.73)

AHA: 4Q, '05, 112

Procedures and Interventions, NEC

00.72–00.94

00.72   **Revision of hip replacement, femoral component**

Partial, femoral component only

That with:
     exchange of acetabular liner
     exchange of femoral stem and head

Code also any type of bearing surface, if known (00.74-00.77)

EXCLUDES   *revision of hip replacement, acetabular component (00.71)*
revision of hip replacement, both acetabular and femoral components (00.70)
revision of hip replacement, not otherwise specified (81.53)
revision with replacement of acetabular liner and/or femoral head only (00.73)

00.73   **Revision of hip replacement, acetabular liner and/or femoral head only**

Code also any type of bearing surface, if known (00.74-00.77)

00.74   **Hip bearing surface, metal-on- polyethylene**

00.75   **Hip bearing surface, metal-on-metal**

AHA: 4Q, '06, 121

00.76   **Hip bearing surface, ceramic-on-ceramic**

AHA: 4Q, '05, 112

00.77   **Hip bearing surface, ceramic-on- polyethylene**

AHA: 4Q, '06, 120

✓4ᵗʰ **00.8**   **Other knee and hip procedures**

Note: Report up to two components using 00.81-00.83 to describe revision of knee replacements. If all three components are revised, report 00.80.

AHA: 4Q, '05, 113

00.80   **Revision of knee replacement, total (all components)**   **BI**

Replacement of femoral, tibial, and patellar components (all components)

Code also any removal of (cement) (joint) spacer (84.57)

EXCLUDES   *revision of only one or two components (tibial, femoral or patellar component) (00.81-00.84)*

AHA: 1Q, '08, 6

TIP: Assign for the revision of a unicompartment knee replacement to total knee arthroplasty; the procedure is still considered a revision, even though part of the component is being replaced for the first time.

00.81   **Revision of knee replacement, tibial component**

Replacement of tibial baseplate and tibial insert (liner)

EXCLUDES   *revision of knee replacement, total (all components) (00.80)*

AHA: 4Q, '05, 117

00.82   **Revision of knee replacement, femoral component**

That with replacement of tibial insert (liner)

EXCLUDES   *revision of knee replacement, total (all components) (00.80)*

AHA: 3Q, '06, 9; 4Q, '05, 117

00.83   **Revision of knee replacement, patellar component**

EXCLUDES   *revision of knee replacement, total (all components) (00.80)*

00.84   **Revision of total knee replacement, tibial insert (liner)**

Replacement of tibial insert (liner)

EXCLUDES   *that with replacement of tibial component (tibial base plate and liner) (00.81)*

00.85   **Resurfacing hip, total, acetabulum and femoral head**

Hip resurfacing arthroplasty, total

AHA: 4Q, '06, 121

00.86   **Resurfacing hip, partial, femoral head**

Hip resurfacing arthroplasty, NOS

Hip resurfacing arthroplasty, partial, femoral head

EXCLUDES   *that with resurfacing of acetabulum (00.85)*

AHA: 4Q, '06, 121

00.87   **Resurfacing hip, partial, acetabulum**

Hip resurfacing arthroplasty, partial, acetabulum

EXCLUDES   *that with resurfacing of femoral head (00.85)*

AHA: 4Q, '06, 121

✓4ᵗʰ **00.9**   **Other procedures and interventions**

00.91   **Transplant from live related donor**

Code also organ transplant procedure

00.92   **Transplant from live non-related donor**

Code also organ transplant procedure

AHA: 2Q, '08, 8; 4Q, '04, 117

00.93   **Transplant from cadaver**

Code also organ transplant procedure

00.94   **Intra-operative neurophysiologic monitoring**

Intra-operative neurophysiologic testing

IOM

Nerve monitoring

Neuromonitoring

INCLUDES   Cranial nerve, peripheral nerve and spinal cord testing performed intra-operatively

EXCLUDES   *brain temperature monitoring (01.17)*
intracranial oxygen monitoring (01.16)
intracranial pressure monitoring (01.10)
plethysmogram (89.58)

DEF: Real-time testing techniques used in brain, spinal cord, and nerve procedures to assist in lesion excision and provide ongoing neurological functioning information and/or warning of impending neural structure injury.

AHA:▶2Q, '09, 4;◀ 4Q, '07, 104

BI Bilateral Procedure   **NC** Non-covered Procedure   **LC** Limited Coverage Procedure   ▶◀ Revised Text   ● New Code   ▲ Revised Code Title

1. OPERATIONS ON THE NERVOUS SYSTEM (01-05)

√3ʳᵈ **01   Incision and excision of skull, brain, and cerebral meninges**

√4ᵗʰ **01.0   Cranial puncture**

01.01   Cisternal puncture
Cisternal aspiration
Cisternal tap
EXCLUDES   pneumocisternogram (87.02)
DEF: Needle insertion through subarachnoid space to withdraw cerebrospinal fluid.

01.02   Ventriculopuncture through previously implanted catheter
Puncture of ventricular shunt tubing
DEF: Piercing of artificial, fluid-diverting tubing in the brain for withdrawal of cerebrospinal fluid.

01.09   Other cranial puncture
Aspiration of:
subarachnoid space
subdural space
Cranial aspiration NOS
Puncture of anterior fontanel
Subdural tap (through fontanel)
AHA: 4Q, '07, 107
TIP: Assign for aspiration of a subdural hematoma.

√4ᵗʰ **01.1   Diagnostic procedures on skull, brain, and cerebral meninges**

01.10   Intracranial pressure monitoring
INCLUDES   insertion of catheter or probe for monitoring
AHA: 4Q, '07, 105, 107
TIP: Several different devices are available that are connected to a catheter inserted via ventriculostomy, subarachnoid bolt, or screw; used to monitor intracranial pressure in patients with traumatic brain injury (TBI) or other serious brain disorders.

01.11   Closed [percutaneous] [needle] biopsy of cerebral meninges
Burr hole approach
DEF: Needle excision of tissue sample through skin into cerebral membranes; no other procedure performed.

01.12   Open biopsy of cerebral meninges
DEF: Open surgical excision of tissue sample from cerebral membrane.

01.13   Closed [percutaneous] [needle] biopsy of brain
Burr hole approach
Stereotactic method
DEF: Removal by needle of brain tissue sample through skin.
AHA: M-A, '87, 9

01.14   Open biopsy of brain
DEF: Open surgical excision of brain tissue sample.

01.15   Biopsy of skull

01.16   Intracranial oxygen monitoring
Partial pressure of brain oxygen (PbtO₂)
INCLUDES   insertion of catheter or probe for monitoring
AHA: 4Q, '07, 105, 107

01.17   Brain temperature monitoring
INCLUDES   insertion of catheter or probe for monitoring
AHA: 4Q, '07, 105

01.18   Other diagnostic procedures on brain and cerebral meninges
EXCLUDES   brain temperature monitoring (01.17)
cerebral:
arteriography (88.41)
thermography (88.81)
contrast radiogram of brain (87.01-87.02)
echoencephalogram (88.71)
electroencephalogram (89.14)
intracranial oxygen monitoring (01.16)
intracranial pressure monitoring (01.10)
microscopic examination of specimen from nervous system and of spinal fluid (90.01-90.09)
neurologic examination (89.13)
phlebography of head and neck (88.61)
pneumoencephalogram (87.01)
radioisotope scan:
cerebral (92.11)
head NEC (92.12)
tomography of head:
C.A.T. scan (87.03)
other (87.04)
AHA: 3Q, '98, 12

01.19   Other diagnostic procedures on skull
EXCLUDES   transillumination of skull (89.16)
x-ray of skull (87.17)

√4ᵗʰ **01.2   Craniotomy and craniectomy**
EXCLUDES   decompression of skull fracture (02.02)
exploration of orbit (16.01-16.09)
that as operative approach — omit code
DEF: Craniotomy: Incision into skull.
DEF: Craniectomy: Excision of part of skull.
AHA: 1Q, '91, 1

01.21   Incision and drainage of cranial sinus
DEF: Incision for drainage, including drainage of air cavities in skull bones.

01.22   Removal of intracranial neurostimulator lead(s)
Code also any removal of neurostimulator pulse generator (86.05)
EXCLUDES   removal with synchronous replacement (02.93)

01.23   Reopening of craniotomy site
DEF: Reopening of skull incision.

01.24   Other craniotomy
Cranial:
decompression
exploration
trephination
Craniotomy NOS
Craniotomy with removal of:
epidural abscess
extradural hematoma
foreign body of skull
EXCLUDES   removal of foreign body with incision into brain (01.39)
AHA: 2Q, '91, 14

01.25   Other craniectomy
Debridement of skull NOS
Sequestrectomy of skull
EXCLUDES   debridement of compound fracture of skull (02.02)
strip craniectomy (02.01)
AHA: 1Q, '06, 6

Operations on the Nervous System

01.26–02.14

01.26   **Insertion of catheter(s) into cranial cavity or tissue**
Code also any concomitant procedure (e.g. resection (01.59))
EXCLUDES   *placement of intracerebral catheter(s) via burr hole(s) (01.28)*
AHA: 4Q, '05, 117-118
TIP: Assign for balloon catheter placement in brain for infusion of liquid brachytherapy radioisotope for malignancy treatment; see also code 92.20 for infusion procedure.

01.27   **Removal of catheter(s) from cranial cavity or tissue**
AHA: 4Q, '05, 117-118

01.28   **Placement of intracerebral catheter(s) via burr hole(s)**
Convection enhanced delivery
Stereotactic placement of intracerebral catheter(s)
Code also infusion of medication
EXCLUDES   *insertion of catheter(s) into cranial cavity or tissue(s) (01.26)*
DEF: The strategic neurosurgical placement of catheters via burr holes into targeted brain tissue, through which therapeutic agents such as antineoplastics are microinfused.
AHA: 4Q, '06, 122

√4th **01.3**   **Incision of brain and cerebral meninges**

01.31   **Incision of cerebral meninges**
Drainage of:
intracranial hygroma
subarachnoid abscess (cerebral)
subdural empyema

01.32   **Lobotomy and tractotomy**
Division of:
brain tissue
cerebral tracts
Percutaneous (radiofrequency) cingulotomy
DEF: Lobotomy: Incision of nerve fibers of brain lobe, usually frontal.
DEF: Tractotomy: Severing of a nerve fiber group to relieve pain.

01.39   **Other incision of brain**
Amygdalohippocampotomy
Drainage of intracerebral hematoma
Incision of brain NOS
EXCLUDES   *division of cortical adhesions (02.91)*

√4th **01.4**   **Operations on thalamus and globus pallidus**

01.41   **Operations on thalamus**
Chemothalamectomy
Thalamotomy
EXCLUDES   *that by stereotactic radiosurgery (92.30-92.39)*

01.42   **Operations on globus pallidus**
Pallidoansectomy
Pallidotomy
EXCLUDES   *that by stereotactic radiosurgery (92.30-92.39)*

√4th **01.5**   **Other excision or destruction of brain and meninges**
AHA: 4Q, '93, 33

01.51   **Excision of lesion or tissue of cerebral meninges**
Decortication
Resection   } of (cerebral)
Stripping of subdural   meninges
membrane
EXCLUDES   *biopsy of cerebral meninges (01.11-01.12)*

01.52   **Hemispherectomy**
DEF: Removal of one half of the brain. Most often performed for malignant brain tumors or intractable epilepsy.

01.53   **Lobectomy of brain**
DEF: Excision of a brain lobe.

01.59   **Other excision or destruction of lesion or tissue of brain**
Curettage of brain
Debridement of brain
Marsupialization of brain cyst
Transtemporal (mastoid) excision of brain tumor
EXCLUDES   *biopsy of brain (01.13-01.14)*
▶*laser interstitial thermal therapy [LITT] of lesion or tissue of brain under guidance (17.61)*◀
that by stereotactic radiosurgery (92.30-92.39)
AHA: 4Q, '05, 118; 3Q, '99, 7; 1Q, '99, 9; 3Q, '98, 12; 1Q, '98, 6

01.6   **Excision of lesion of skull**
Removal of granulation tissue of cranium
EXCLUDES   *biopsy of skull (01.15)*
sequestrectomy (01.25)

√3rd **02**   **Other operations on skull, brain, and cerebral meninges**

√4th **02.0**   **Cranioplasty**
EXCLUDES   *that with synchronous repair of encephalocele (02.12)*

02.01   **Opening of cranial suture**
Linear craniectomy
Strip craniectomy
DEF: Opening of the lines of junction between the bones of the skull for removal of strips of skull bone.

02.02   **Elevation of skull fracture fragments**
Debridement of compound fracture of skull
Decompression of skull fracture
Reduction of skull fracture
Code also any synchronous debridement of brain (01.59)
EXCLUDES   *debridement of skull NOS (01.25)*
removal of granulation tissue of cranium (01.6)

02.03   **Formation of cranial bone flap**
Repair of skull with flap

02.04   **Bone graft to skull**
Pericranial graft (autogenous) (heterogenous)

02.05   **Insertion of skull plate**
Replacement of skull plate

02.06   **Other cranial osteoplasty**
Repair of skull NOS
Revision of bone flap of skull
DEF: Plastic surgery repair of skull bones.
AHA: 1Q, '06, 6; 1Q, '05, 11; 3Q, '98, 9

02.07   **Removal of skull plate**
EXCLUDES   *removal with synchronous replacement (02.05)*

√4th **02.1**   **Repair of cerebral meninges**
EXCLUDES   *marsupialization of cerebral lesion (01.59)*

02.11   **Simple suture of dura mater of brain**

02.12   **Other repair of cerebral meninges**
Closure of fistula of cerebrospinal fluid
Dural graft
Repair of encephalocele including synchronous cranioplasty
Repair of meninges NOS
Subdural patch

02.13   **Ligation of meningeal vessel**
Ligation of:
longitudinal sinus
middle meningeal artery

02.14   **Choroid plexectomy**
Cauterization of choroid plexus
DEF: Excision or destruction of the ependymal cells that form the membrane lining in the third, fourth, and lateral ventricles of the brain and secrete cerebrospinal fluid.

02.2　Ventriculostomy

Anastomosis of ventricle to:
　cervical subarachnoid space
　cisterna magna
Insertion of Holter valve
Ventriculocisternal intubation

DEF: Surgical creation of an opening of ventricle; often performed to drain cerebrospinal fluid in treating hydrocephalus.

✓4ᵗʰ　02.3　Extracranial ventricular shunt

INCLUDES　that with insertion of valve

DEF: Placement of shunt or creation of artificial passage leading from skull cavities to site outside skull to relieve excess cerebrospinal fluid created in the chorioid plexuses of the third and fourth ventricles of the brain.

02.31　Ventricular shunt to structure in head and neck

Ventricle to nasopharynx shunt
Ventriculomastoid anastomosis

02.32　Ventricular shunt to circulatory system

Ventriculoatrial anastomosis
Ventriculocaval shunt

02.33　Ventricular shunt to thoracic cavity

Ventriculopleural anastomosis

02.34　Ventricular shunt to abdominal cavity and organs

Ventriculocholecystostomy
Ventriculoperitoneostomy

02.35　Ventricular shunt to urinary system

Ventricle to ureter shunt

02.39　Other operations to establish drainage of ventricle

Ventricle to bone marrow shunt
Ventricular shunt to extracranial site NEC

✓4ᵗʰ　02.4　Revision, removal, and irrigation of ventricular shunt

EXCLUDES　revision of distal catheter of ventricular shunt (54.95)

02.41　Irrigation and exploration of ventricular shunt

Exploration of ventriculoperitoneal shunt at ventricular site
Re-programming of ventriculoperitoneal shunt

02.42　Replacement of ventricular shunt

Reinsertion of Holter valve
Replacement of ventricular catheter
Revision of ventriculoperitoneal shunt at ventricular site

AHA: N-D, '86, 8

TIP: If a ventriculoperitoneal shunt is explored or revised at the peritoneal site, assign instead code 54.95.

02.43　Removal of ventricular shunt

AHA: N-D, '86, 8

✓4ᵗʰ　02.9　Other operations on skull, brain, and cerebral meninges

EXCLUDES　operations on:
　pineal gland (07.17, 07.51-07.59)
　pituitary gland [hypophysis] (07.13-07.15, 07.61-07.79)

02.91　Lysis of cortical adhesions

DEF: Breaking up of fibrous structures in brain outer layer.

02.92　Repair of brain

02.93　Implantation or replacement of intracranial neurostimulator lead(s)

Implantation, insertion, placement, or replacement of intracranial:
　brain pacemaker [neuropacemaker]
　depth electrodes
　epidural pegs
　electroencephalographic receiver
　foramen ovale electrodes
　intracranial electrostimulator
　subdural grids
　subdural strips

Code also any insertion of neurostimulator pulse generator (86.94-86.98)

AHA: 4Q, '97, 57; 4Q, '92, 28

02.94　Insertion or replacement of skull tongs or halo traction device

DEF: Halo traction device: Metal or plastic band encircles the head or neck secured to the skull with four pins and attached to a metal chest plate by rods; provides support and stability for the head and neck.

DEF: Skull tongs: Device inserted into each side of the skull used to apply parallel traction to the long axis of the cervical spine.

AHA: 3Q, '01, 8; 3Q, '96, 14

02.95　Removal of skull tongs or halo traction device

02.96　Insertion of sphenoidal electrodes

AHA: 4Q, '92, 28

02.99　Other

EXCLUDES　chemical shock therapy (94.24)
　electroshock therapy:
　　subconvulsive (94.26)
　　other (94.27)

✓3ʳᵈ　03　Operations on spinal cord and spinal canal structures

Code also any application or administration of an adhesion barrier substance (99.77)

✓4ᵗʰ　03.0　Exploration and decompression of spinal canal structures

03.01　Removal of foreign body from spinal canal

03.02　Reopening of laminectomy site

03.09　Other exploration and decompression of spinal canal

Decompression:
　laminectomy
　laminotomy
Expansile laminoplasty
Exploration of spinal nerve root
Foraminotomy

Code also any synchronous insertion, replacement and revision of posterior spinal motion preservation device(s), if performed (84.80-84.85)

EXCLUDES　drainage of spinal fluid by anastomosis (03.71-03.79)
　laminectomy with excision of intervertebral disc (80.51)
　spinal tap (03.31)
　that as operative approach — omit code

DEF: Decompression of spinal canal: Excision of bone pieces, hematoma or other lesion to relieve spinal cord pressure.

DEF: Expansile laminoplasty: Lamina is incised at the level of the pedicle to relieve pressure; no tissue is excised.

DEF: Foraminotomy: Removal of root opening between vertebrae to relieve nerve root pressure.

AHA: ▶4Q, '08, 109;◀ 2Q, '08, 12; 4Q, '07, 117, 120; 1Q, '07, 10; 3Q, '04, 6; 4Q, '02, 109; 2Q, '02, 15; 4Q, '99, 14; 2Q, '97, 6; 2Q, '95, 9; 2Q, '95, 10; 2Q, '90, 22; S-Q, '86, 12

TIP: Assign for expansile laminoplasty; when the lamina is incised at the level of the pedicle, relieving pressure without tissue excision, along with code 78.59 for the internal bone fixation.

✓3ʳᵈ
✓4ᵗʰ　Additional Digit Required　　　　Valid OR Procedure　　　　Non-OR Procedure　　　　Adjunct Code

Operations on the Nervous System

03.1–03.91

Laminotomy with Decompression

Laminotomy decompresses spinal nerve

Lumbar Spinal Puncture

03.1 Division of intraspinal nerve root
Rhizotomy

DEF: Rhizotomy: Surgical severing of spinal nerve roots within spinal canal for pain relief.

✓4th **03.2 Chordotomy**

DEF: Chordotomy: Surgical cutting of lateral spinothalamic tract of spinal cord to relieve pain.

03.21 Percutaneous chordotomy
Stereotactic chordotomy

DEF: Percutaneous chordotomy: Insertion of hollow needle through skin to interrupt spinal nerve root.

DEF: Stereotactic chordotomy: Use of three-dimensional imaging to locate spinal nerve root for surgical interruption.

03.29 Other chordotomy
Chordotomy NOS
Tractotomy (one-stage) (two-stage) of spinal cord
Transection of spinal cord tracts

DEF: Tractotomy (one stage) (two stages) of the spinal cord: Surgical incision or severing of a nerve tract of spinal cord.

DEF: Transection of spinal cord tracts: Use of transverse incision to divide spinal nerve root.

✓4th **03.3 Diagnostic procedures on spinal cord and spinal canal structures**

03.31 Spinal tap
Lumbar puncture for removal of dye
EXCLUDES lumbar puncture for injection of dye [myelogram] (87.21)

DEF: Puncture into lumbar subarachnoid space to tap cerebrospinal fluid.

AHA: 2Q, '90, 22

03.32 Biopsy of spinal cord or spinal meninges

03.39 Other diagnostic procedures on spinal cord and spinal canal structures
EXCLUDES microscopic examination of specimen from nervous system or of spinal fluid (90.01-90.09)
x-ray of spine (87.21-87.29)

03.4 Excision or destruction of lesion of spinal cord or spinal meninges
Curettage
Debridement
Marsupialization of cyst
Resection
} of spinal cord or spinal meninges

EXCLUDES biopsy of spinal cord or meninges (03.32)
AHA: 2Q, '08, 10; 3Q, '95, 5

TIP: A laminectomy is inherent to the excision of a spinal cord tumor; do not assign 03.09 separately.

✓4th **03.5 Plastic operations on spinal cord structures**

03.51 Repair of spinal meningocele
Repair of meningocele NOS

DEF: Restoration of hernial protrusion of spinal meninges through defect in vertebral column.

03.52 Repair of spinal myelomeningocele

DEF: Restoration of hernial protrusion of spinal cord and meninges through defect in vertebral column.

03.53 Repair of vertebral fracture
Elevation of spinal bone fragments
Reduction of fracture of vertebrae
Removal of bony spicules from spinal canal
EXCLUDES percutaneous vertebral augmentation (81.66)
percutaneous vertebroplasty (81.65)
AHA: 1Q, '07, 20; 4Q, '04, 126; 2Q, '02, 14; 4Q, '99, 11, 12, 13; 3Q, '96, 14

03.59 Other repair and plastic operations on spinal cord structures

Repair of: Repair of:
diastematomyelia   spinal meninges NOS
spina bifida NOS   vertebral arch defect
spinal cord NOS

AHA: ►4Q, '08, 109◄

TIP: Assign for repair of dural tears occurring during spinal surgery.

03.6 Lysis of adhesions of spinal cord and nerve roots
AHA: 2Q, '98, 18

✓4th **03.7 Shunt of spinal theca**
INCLUDES that with valve

DEF: Surgical passage created from spinal cord dura mater to another channel.

03.71 Spinal subarachnoid-peritoneal shunt

03.72 Spinal subarachnoid-ureteral shunt

03.79 Other shunt of spinal theca
Lumbar-subarachnoid shunt NOS
Pleurothecal anastomosis
Salpingothecal anastomosis
AHA: 1Q, '97, 7

03.8 Injection of destructive agent into spinal canal

✓4th **03.9 Other operations on spinal cord and spinal canal structures**

03.90 Insertion of catheter into spinal canal for infusion of therapeutic or palliative substances
Insertion of catheter into epidural, subarachnoid, or subdural space of spine with intermittent or continuous infusion of drug (with creation of any reservoir)

Code also any implantation of infusion pump (86.06)

03.91 Injection of anesthetic into spinal canal for analgesia
EXCLUDES that for operative anesthesia — omit code
AHA: 3Q, '00, 15; 1Q, '99, 8; 2Q, '98, 18

B1 Bilateral Procedure   NC Non-covered Procedure   LC Limited Coverage Procedure   ►◄ Revised Text   ● New Code   ▲ Revised Code Title

76 – Volume 3 • February 2009   **2010 ICD-9-CM**

03.92 **Injection of other agent into spinal canal**
Intrathecal injection of steroid
Subarachnoid perfusion of refrigerated saline
EXCLUDES   *injection of:*
contrast material for myelogram
(87.21)
destructive agent into spinal canal
(03.8)
AHA: 2Q, '03, 6; 3Q, '00, 15; 2Q, '98, 18
TIP: Assign, along with code 99.23 for a steroid injection into the spinal canal; if both steroid and other anesthetic agent are injected, assign 03.91, 03.92, and 99.23.

03.93 **Implantation or replacement of spinal neurostimulator lead(s)**
Code also any insertion of neurostimulator pulse generator (86.94-86.98)
AHA: 1Q, '00, 19

03.94 **Removal of spinal neurostimulator lead(s)**
Code also any removal of neurostimulator pulse generator (86.05)

03.95 **Spinal blood patch**
DEF: Injection of blood into epidural space to patch hole in outer spinal membrane when blood clots.

03.96 **Percutaneous denervation of facet**

03.97 **Revision of spinal thecal shunt**
AHA: 2Q, '99, 4

03.98 **Removal of spinal thecal shunt**

03.99 **Other**

√3rd **04** **Operations on cranial and peripheral nerves**

√4th **04.0** **Incision, division, and excision of cranial and peripheral nerves**
EXCLUDES   *opticociliary neurectomy (12.79)*
sympathetic ganglionectomy (05.21-05.29)

04.01 **Excision of acoustic neuroma**
That by craniotomy
EXCLUDES   *that by stereotactic radiosurgery (92.3)*
AHA: 2Q, '98, 20; 2Q, '95, 8; 4Q, '92, 26

04.02 **Division of trigeminal nerve**
Retrogasserian neurotomy
DEF: Transection of sensory root fibers of trigeminal nerve for relief of trigeminal neuralgia.

04.03 **Division or crushing of other cranial and peripheral nerves**
EXCLUDES   *that of:*
glossopharyngeal nerve (29.92)
laryngeal nerve (31.91)
nerves to adrenal glands (07.42)
phrenic nerve for collapse of lung
(33.31)
vagus nerve (44.00-44.03)
AHA: 2Q, '98, 20

04.04 **Other incision of cranial and peripheral nerves**

04.05 **Gasserian ganglionectomy**

04.06 **Other cranial or peripheral ganglionectomy**
EXCLUDES   *sympathetic ganglionectomy*
(05.21-05.29)

04.07 **Other excision or avulsion of cranial and peripheral nerves**
Curettage ⎫
Debridement ⎬ of peripheral nerve
Resection ⎭
Excision of peripheral neuroma [Morton's]
EXCLUDES   *biopsy of cranial or peripheral nerve*
(04.11-04.12)
AHA: 2Q, '95, 8; 4Q, '92, 26

√4th **04.1** **Diagnostic procedures on peripheral nervous system**

04.11 **Closed [percutaneous] [needle] biopsy of cranial or peripheral nerve or ganglion**

04.12 **Open biopsy of cranial or peripheral nerve or ganglion**

Release of Carpal Tunnel

Median nerve

(Deep) transverse carpal ligament being cut

04.19 **Other diagnostic procedures on cranial and peripheral nerves and ganglia**
EXCLUDES   *microscopic examination of specimen*
from nervous system
(90.01-90.09)
neurologic examination (89.13)

04.2 **Destruction of cranial and peripheral nerves**
Destruction of cranial or peripheral nerves by:
cryoanalgesia
injection of neurolytic agent
radiofrequency
Radiofrequency ablation
DEF: Radiofrequency ablation: High frequency radio waves are applied to injure the nerve resulting in interruption of the pain signal.
AHA: 3Q, '02, 10, 11; 4Q, '95, 74

04.3 **Suture of cranial and peripheral nerves**

√4th **04.4** **Lysis of adhesions and decompression of cranial and peripheral nerves**

04.41 **Decompression of trigeminal nerve root**

04.42 **Other cranial nerve decompression**
AHA: 3Q, '02, 13

04.43 **Release of carpal tunnel**

04.44 **Release of tarsal tunnel**

04.49 **Other peripheral nerve or ganglion decompression or lysis of adhesions**
Peripheral nerve neurolysis NOS

04.5 **Cranial or peripheral nerve graft**

04.6 **Transposition of cranial and peripheral nerves**
Nerve transplantation
DEF: Relocation of cranial or peripheral nerves without detaching or severing them.

√4th **04.7** **Other cranial or peripheral neuroplasty**

04.71 **Hypoglossal-facial anastomosis**
DEF: Surgical connection of hypoglossal nerve to facial nerve.

04.72 **Accessory-facial anastomosis**
DEF: Surgical connection of accessory nerve to facial nerve.

04.73 **Accessory-hypoglossal anastomosis**
DEF: Surgical connection of accessory nerve to hypoglossal nerve.

04.74 **Other anastomosis of cranial or peripheral nerve**

04.75 **Revision of previous repair of cranial and peripheral nerves**

04.76 **Repair of old traumatic injury of cranial and peripheral nerves**

04.79 **Other neuroplasty**
AHA: 1Q, '06, 11
TIP: Assign for application of a NeuraWrap nerve protector, an absorbable collagen implant that provides a nonconstricting encasement for injured peripheral nerves.

Operations on the Nervous System

04.8–05.9

✓4th **04.8 Injection into peripheral nerve**

     EXCLUDES   *destruction of nerve (by injection of neurolytic agent) (04.2)*

     04.80 Peripheral nerve injection, not otherwise specified

     04.81 Injection of anesthetic into peripheral nerve for analgesia

         EXCLUDES   *that for operative anesthesia — omit code*

         AHA: 1Q, '00, 7

     04.89 Injection of other agent, except neurolytic

         EXCLUDES   *injection of neurolytic agent (04.2)*

✓4th **04.9 Other operations on cranial and peripheral nerves**

     04.91 Neurectasis

         DEF: Surgical stretching of peripheral or cranial nerve.

     04.92 Implantation or replacement of peripheral neurostimulator lead(s)

         Code also any insertion of neurostimulator pulse generator (86.94-86.98)

         DEF: Placement of or removal and replacement of neurostimulator lead(s) during the same episode.

         AHA: 2Q, '07, 8; 2Q, '06, 5; 2Q, '04, 7; 3Q, '01, 16; 2Q, '00, 22; 3Q, '96, 12

         TIP: Assign for insertion of the Rheos Baroreflex Hypertension Therapy System, along with codes 39.8 and 86.96.

     04.93 Removal of peripheral neurostimulator lead(s)

         Code also any removal of neurostimulator pulse generator (86.05)

         AHA: 3Q, '01, 16

     04.99 Other

✓3rd **05 Operations on sympathetic nerves or ganglia**

     EXCLUDES   *paracervical uterine denervation (69.3)*

     05.0 Division of sympathetic nerve or ganglion

         EXCLUDES   *that of nerves to adrenal glands (07.42)*

✓4th **05.1 Diagnostic procedures on sympathetic nerves or ganglia**

     05.11 Biopsy of sympathetic nerve or ganglion

     05.19 Other diagnostic procedures on sympathetic nerves or ganglia

✓4th **05.2 Sympathectomy**

     DEF: Sympathectomy: Division of nerve pathway at a specific site of a sympathetic nerve.

     05.21 Sphenopalatine ganglionectomy

     05.22 Cervical sympathectomy

     05.23 Lumbar sympathectomy

         DEF: Excision, resection of lumber chain nerve group to relieve causalgia, Raynaud's disease, or lower extremity thromboangiitis.

     05.24 Presacral sympathectomy

         DEF: Excision or resection of hypogastric nerve network.

     05.25 Periarterial sympathectomy

         DEF: Removal of arterial sheath containing sympathetic nerve fibers.

     05.29 Other sympathectomy and ganglionectomy

         Excision or avulsion of sympathetic nerve NOS

         Sympathetic ganglionectomy NOS

         EXCLUDES   *biopsy of sympathetic nerve or ganglion (05.11)*

                 opticociliary neurectomy (12.79)

                 periarterial sympathectomy (05.25)

                 tympanosympathectomy (20.91)

✓4th **05.3 Injection into sympathetic nerve or ganglion**

     EXCLUDES   *injection of ciliary sympathetic ganglion (12.79)*

     05.31 Injection of anesthetic into sympathetic nerve for analgesia

     05.32 Injection of neurolytic agent into sympathetic nerve

     05.39 Other injection into sympathetic nerve or ganglion

✓4th **05.8 Other operations on sympathetic nerves or ganglia**

     05.81 Repair of sympathetic nerve or ganglion

     05.89 Other

     05.9 Other operations on nervous system

BI Bilateral Procedure   **NC** Non-covered Procedure   **LC** Limited Coverage Procedure   ▶◀ Revised Text   ● New Code   ▲ Revised Code Title

78 – Volume 3   **2010 ICD-9-CM**

2. OPERATIONS ON THE ENDOCRINE SYSTEM (06-07)

√3ʳᵈ **06 Operations on thyroid and parathyroid glands**
    INCLUDES incidental resection of hyoid bone

√4ᵗʰ **06.0 Incision of thyroid field**
    EXCLUDES *division of isthmus (06.91)*

    06.01 Aspiration of thyroid field
      Percutaneous or needle drainage of thyroid field
      EXCLUDES *aspiration biopsy of thyroid (06.11)*
             drainage by incision (06.09)
             postoperative aspiration of field (06.02)

    06.02 Reopening of wound of thyroid field
      Reopening of wound of thyroid field for:
        control of (postoperative) hemorrhage
        examination
        exploration
        removal of hematoma

    06.09 Other incision of thyroid field
      Drainage of hematoma
      Drainage of thyroglossal tract
      Exploration
        neck   } by incision
        thyroid (field)
      Removal of foreign body
      Thyroidotomy NOS
      EXCLUDES *postoperative exploration (06.02)*
             removal of hematoma by aspiration (06.01)

√4ᵗʰ **06.1 Diagnostic procedures on thyroid and parathyroid glands**

    06.11 Closed [percutaneous] [needle] biopsy of thyroid gland
      Aspiration biopsy of thyroid
      DEF: Insertion of needle-type device for removal of thyroid tissue sample.

    06.12 Open biopsy of thyroid gland

    06.13 Biopsy of parathyroid gland

    06.19 Other diagnostic procedures on thyroid and parathyroid glands
      EXCLUDES *radioisotope scan of:*
             parathyroid (92.13)
             thyroid (92.01)
             soft tissue x-ray of thyroid field (87.09)

06.2 Unilateral thyroid lobectomy
    Complete removal of one lobe of thyroid (with removal of isthmus or portion of other lobe)
    Hemithyroidectomy
    EXCLUDES *partial substernal thyroidectomy (06.51)*
    DEF: Excision of thyroid lobe.

√4ᵗʰ **06.3 Other partial thyroidectomy**

    06.31 Excision of lesion of thyroid
      EXCLUDES *biopsy of thyroid (06.11-06.12)*
             ▶*laser interstitial thermal therapy [LITT] of lesion or tissue of neck under guidance (17.62)*◀
      DEF: Removal of growth on thyroid.

    06.39 Other
      Isthmectomy
      Partial thyroidectomy NOS
      EXCLUDES *partial substernal thyroidectomy (06.51)*

06.4 Complete thyroidectomy
    EXCLUDES *complete substernal thyroidectomy (06.52)*
             that with laryngectomy (30.3-30.4)

√4ᵗʰ **06.5 Substernal thyroidectomy**
    DEF: Removal of thyroid tissue below breastbone.

    06.50 Substernal thyroidectomy, not otherwise specified

    06.51 Partial substernal thyroidectomy

    06.52 Complete substernal thyroidectomy

Thyroidectomy

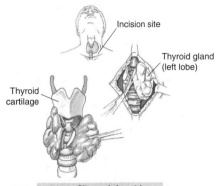

Incision site
Thyroid gland (left lobe)
Thyroid cartilage

06.6 Excision of lingual thyroid
    Excision of thyroid by: Excision of thyroid by:
      submental route   transoral route
    DEF: Excision of thyroid tissue at base of tongue.

06.7 Excision of thyroglossal duct or tract

√4ᵗʰ **06.8 Parathyroidectomy**
    DEF: Removal of parathyroid glands.

    06.81 Complete parathyroidectomy

    06.89 Other parathyroidectomy
      Parathyroidectomy NOS
      Partial parathyroidectomy
      EXCLUDES *biopsy of parathyroid (06.13)*

√4ᵗʰ **06.9 Other operations on thyroid (region) and parathyroid**

    06.91 Division of thyroid isthmus
      Transection of thyroid isthmus
      DEF: Cutting or division of tissue at narrowest point of thyroid.

    06.92 Ligation of thyroid vessels

    06.93 Suture of thyroid gland

    06.94 Thyroid tissue reimplantation
      Autotransplantation of thyroid tissue
      DEF: Placement of thyroid tissue graft into functional site.
      DEF: Autotransplantation of thyroid tissue: Tissue graft from patient thyroid tissue to another site on thyroid.

    06.95 Parathyroid tissue reimplantation
      Autotransplantation of parathyroid tissue
      DEF: Placement of parathyroid tissue graft into functional site.
      DEF: Autotransplantation of parathyroid tissue: Use of patient parathyroid tissue for graft.

    06.98 Other operations on thyroid glands

    06.99 Other operations on parathyroid glands

√3ʳᵈ **07 Operations on other endocrine glands**
    INCLUDES operations on:
        adrenal glands
        pineal gland
        pituitary gland
        thymus
    EXCLUDES *operations on:*
        aortic and carotid bodies (39.8)
        ovaries (65.0-65.99)
        pancreas (52.01-52.99)
        testes (62.0-62.99)

√4ᵗʰ **07.0 Exploration of adrenal field**
    EXCLUDES *incision of adrenal (gland) (07.41)*

    07.00 Exploration of adrenal field, not otherwise specified

    07.01 Unilateral exploration of adrenal field
      DEF: Investigation of one adrenal gland for diagnostic reasons.

    07.02 Bilateral exploration of adrenal field
      DEF: Investigation of both adrenal glands for diagnostic reasons.

Operations on the Endocrine System

07.1–07.82

√4ᵗʰ **07.1　Diagnostic procedures on adrenal glands, pituitary gland, pineal gland, and thymus**

07.11　**Closed [percutaneous] [needle] biopsy of adrenal gland**

07.12　**Open biopsy of adrenal gland**

07.13　**Biopsy of pituitary gland, transfrontal approach**
　　　　DEF: Excision of pituitary gland tissue for exam through frontal bone.

07.14　**Biopsy of pituitary gland, transsphenoidal approach**
　　　　DEF: Excision of pituitary gland tissue for exam through sphenoid bone.

07.15　**Biopsy of pituitary gland, unspecified approach**

07.16　**Biopsy of thymus**

07.17　**Biopsy of pineal gland**

07.19　**Other diagnostic procedures on adrenal glands, pituitary gland, pineal gland, and thymus**
　　　　EXCLUDES　microscopic examination of specimen from endocrine gland (90.11-90.19)
　　　　　　　　　radioisotope scan of pituitary gland (92.11)

√4ᵗʰ **07.2　Partial adrenalectomy**

07.21　**Excision of lesion of adrenal gland**
　　　　EXCLUDES　biopsy of adrenal gland (07.11-07.12)

07.22　**Unilateral adrenalectomy**
　　　　Adrenalectomy NOS
　　　　EXCLUDES　excision of remaining adrenal gland (07.3)
　　　　DEF: Excision of one adrenal gland.

07.29　**Other partial adrenalectomy**
　　　　Partial adrenalectomy NOS
　　　　AHA: 2Q, '05, 4
　　　　TIP: Assign in addition to a code from subcategory 55.5 if the documentation specifies radical nephrectomy, which includes adrenal gland resection.

07.3　**Bilateral adrenalectomy**
　　　Excision of remaining adrenal gland
　　　EXCLUDES　bilateral partial adrenalectomy (07.29)

√4ᵗʰ **07.4　Other operations on adrenal glands, nerves, and vessels**

07.41　**Incision of adrenal gland**
　　　　Adrenalotomy (with drainage)

07.42　**Division of nerves to adrenal glands**

07.43　**Ligation of adrenal vessels**

07.44　**Repair of adrenal gland**

07.45　**Reimplantation of adrenal tissue**
　　　　Autotransplantation of adrenal tissue
　　　　DEF: Autotransplantation of adrenal tissue: Use of tissue graft from the patient's own body.

07.49　**Other**

√4ᵗʰ **07.5　Operations on pineal gland**

07.51　**Exploration of pineal field**
　　　　EXCLUDES　that with incision of pineal gland (07.52)

07.52　**Incision of pineal gland**

07.53　**Partial excision of pineal gland**
　　　　EXCLUDES　biopsy of pineal gland (07.17)

07.54　**Total excision of pineal gland**
　　　　Pinealectomy (complete) (total)

07.59　**Other operations on pineal gland**

√4ᵗʰ **07.6　Hypophysectomy**
　　　DEF: Excision, destruction of pituitary gland.

07.61　**Partial excision of pituitary gland, transfrontal approach**
　　　　Cryohypophysectomy, partial
　　　　Division of hypophyseal stalk
　　　　Excision of lesion of pituitary ⎤ transfrontal
　　　　　[hypophysis] 　　　　　　　　│ approach
　　　　Hypophysectomy subtotal
　　　　Infundibulectomy, hypophyseal ⎦
　　　　EXCLUDES　biopsy of pituitary gland, transfrontal approach (07.13)
　　　　DEF: Removal of pituitary gland, partial, through frontal bone.

07.62　**Partial excision of pituitary gland, transsphenoidal approach**
　　　　EXCLUDES　biopsy of pituitary gland, transsphenoidal approach (07.14)
　　　　DEF: Removal of pituitary gland, partial, through sphenoid bone.

07.63　**Partial excision of pituitary gland, unspecified approach**
　　　　EXCLUDES　biopsy of pituitary gland NOS (07.15)

07.64　**Total excision of pituitary gland, transfrontal approach**
　　　　Ablation of pituitary by ⎤
　　　　　implantation 　　　　　│ transfrontal
　　　　　(strontium-yttrium)(Y) ├ approach
　　　　Cryohypophysectomy, 　　│
　　　　　complete 　　　　　　　⎦
　　　　DEF: Removal of pituitary gland, total, through frontal bone.

07.65　**Total excision of pituitary gland, transsphenoidal approach**
　　　　DEF: Removal of pituitary gland, total, through sphenoid bone.

07.68　**Total excision of pituitary gland, other specified approach**
　　　　DEF: Destroy or remove pituitary gland by a specified approach, other than those listed.

07.69　**Total excision of pituitary gland, unspecified approach**
　　　　Hypophysectomy NOS
　　　　Pituitectomy NOS

√4ᵗʰ **07.7　Other operations on hypophysis**

07.71　**Exploration of pituitary fossa**
　　　　EXCLUDES　exploration with incision of pituitary gland (07.72)
　　　　DEF: Exploration of region of pituitary gland.

07.72　**Incision of pituitary gland**
　　　　Aspiration of:
　　　　　craniobuccal pouch
　　　　　craniopharyngioma
　　　　　hypophysis
　　　　　pituitary gland
　　　　　Rathke's pouch

07.79　**Other**
　　　　Insertion of pack into sella turcica

√4ᵗʰ **07.8　Thymectomy**

07.80　**Thymectomy, not otherwise specified**

07.81　**Other partial excision of thymus**
　　　　Open partial excision of thymus
　　　　EXCLUDES　biopsy of thymus (07.16)
　　　　　　　　　thoracoscopic partial excision of thymus (07.83)

07.82　**Other total excision of thymus**
　　　　Open total excision of thymus
　　　　EXCLUDES　thoracoscopic total excision of thymus (07.84)

BI Bilateral Procedure　　NC Non-covered Procedure　　LC Limited Coverage Procedure　　►◄ Revised Text　　● New Code　　▲ Revised Code Title

80 – Volume 3　　　　　　　　　　　　　　　　　　　　　　　　　　　　　　　　　　　2010 ICD-9-CM

07.83 **Thoracoscopic partial excision of thymus**
     EXCLUDES   *other partial excision of thymus (07.81)*
     AHA: 4Q, '07, 108

07.84 **Thoracoscopic total excision of thymus**
     EXCLUDES   *other total excision of thymus (07.82)*
     AHA: 4Q, '07, 108, 109

✓4ᵗʰ **07.9** **Other operations on thymus**

07.91 **Exploration of thymus field**
     EXCLUDES   *exploration with incision of thymus (07.92)*

07.92 **Other incision of thymus**
     Open incision of thymus
     EXCLUDES   *thoracoscopic incision of thymus (07.95)*

07.93 **Repair of thymus**

07.94 **Transplantation of thymus**
     DEF: Placement of thymus tissue grafts into functional area of gland.

07.95 **Thoracoscopic incision of thymus**
     EXCLUDES   *other incision of thymus (07.92)*
     AHA: 4Q, '07, 108

07.98 **Other and unspecified thoracoscopic operations on thymus**
     AHA: 4Q, '07, 108

07.99 **Other and unspecified operations on thymus**
     Transcervical thymectomy
     EXCLUDES   *other thoracoscopic operations on thymus (07.98)*

Operations on the Endocrine System

07.83–07.99

✓3ʳᵈ
✓4ᵗʰ   Additional Digit Required   Valid OR Procedure   Non-OR Procedure   Adjunct Code
2010 ICD-9-CM   **Volume 3 – 81**

Operations on the Eye

08–08.74

3. OPERATIONS ON THE EYE (08-16)

√3rd **08 Operations on eyelids**

> INCLUDES operations on the eyebrow

√4th **08.0 Incision of eyelid**

08.01 Incision of lid margin

> DEF: Cutting into eyelid edge.

08.02 Severing of blepharorrhaphy

> DEF: Freeing of eyelids previously sutured shut.

08.09 Other incision of eyelid

√4th **08.1 Diagnostic procedures on eyelid**

08.11 Biopsy of eyelid

08.19 Other diagnostic procedures on eyelid

√4th **08.2 Excision or destruction of lesion or tissue of eyelid**

> Code also any synchronous reconstruction (08.61-08.74)
> EXCLUDES biopsy of eyelid (08.11)

08.20 Removal of lesion of eyelid, not otherwise specified

> Removal of meibomian gland NOS

08.21 Excision of chalazion

08.22 Excision of other minor lesion of eyelid

> Excision of:
> verruca
> wart

08.23 Excision of major lesion of eyelid, partial-thickness

> Excision involving one-fourth or more of lid margin, partial-thickness
> DEF: Excision of lesion not in all eyelid layers.

08.24 Excision of major lesion of eyelid, full-thickness

> Excision involving one-fourth or more of lid margin, full-thickness
> Wedge resection of eyelid
> DEF: Excision of growth in all eyelid layers, full thickness.

08.25 Destruction of lesion of eyelid

√4th **08.3 Repair of blepharoptosis and lid retraction**

08.31 Repair of blepharoptosis by frontalis muscle technique with suture

> DEF: Correction of drooping upper eyelid with suture of frontalis muscle.

08.32 Repair of blepharoptosis by frontalis muscle technique with fascial sling

> DEF: Correction of drooping upper eyelid with fascial tissue sling of frontalis muscle.

08.33 Repair of blepharoptosis by resection or advancement of levator muscle or aponeurosis

> DEF: Correction of drooping upper eyelid with levator muscle, extended, cut, or by expanded tendon.

08.34 Repair of blepharoptosis by other levator muscle techniques

08.35 Repair of blepharoptosis by tarsal technique

> DEF: Correction of drooping upper eyelid with tarsal muscle.

08.36 Repair of blepharoptosis by other techniques

> Correction of eyelid ptosis NOS
> Orbicularis oculi muscle sling for correction of blepharoptosis

08.37 Reduction of overcorrection of ptosis

> DEF: Correction, release of previous plastic repair of drooping eyelid.

08.38 Correction of lid retraction

> DEF: Fixing of withdrawn eyelid into normal position.

√4th **08.4 Repair of entropion or ectropion**

08.41 Repair of entropion or ectropion by thermocauterization

> DEF: Restoration of eyelid margin to normal position with heat cautery.

08.42 Repair of entropion or ectropion by suture technique

> DEF: Restoration of eyelid margin to normal position by suture.

08.43 Repair of entropion or ectropion with wedge resection

> DEF: Restoration of eyelid margin to normal position by removing tissue.

08.44 Repair of entropion or ectropion with lid reconstruction

> DEF: Reconstruction of eyelid margin.

08.49 Other repair of entropion or ectropion

√4th **08.5 Other adjustment of lid position**

08.51 Canthotomy

> DEF: Incision into outer canthus of eye.

08.52 Blepharorrhaphy

> Canthorrhaphy   Tarsorrhaphy
> DEF: Suture together of eyelids, partial or repair; done to shorten palpebral fissure or protect cornea.

08.59 Other

> Canthoplasty NOS
> Repair of epicanthal fold

√4th **08.6 Reconstruction of eyelid with flaps or grafts**

> EXCLUDES that associated with repair of entropion and ectropion (08.44)

08.61 Reconstruction of eyelid with skin flap or graft

> DEF: Rebuild of eyelid by graft or flap method.

08.62 Reconstruction of eyelid with mucous membrane flap or graft

> DEF: Rebuild of eyelid with mucous membrane by graft or flap method.

08.63 Reconstruction of eyelid with hair follicle graft

> DEF: Rebuild of eyelid with hair follicle graft.

08.64 Reconstruction of eyelid with tarsoconjunctival flap

> Transfer of tarsoconjunctival flap from opposing lid
> DEF: Recreation of eyelid with tarsoconjunctival tissue.

08.69 Other reconstruction of eyelid with flaps or grafts

√4th **08.7 Other reconstruction of eyelid**

> EXCLUDES that associated with repair of entropion and ectropion (08.44)
> TIP: Assign these codes twice for bilateral blepharoplasty procedures; ensure documentation indicates any visual field loss.

08.70 Reconstruction of eyelid, not otherwise specified

> AHA: 2Q, '96, 11

08.71 Reconstruction of eyelid involving lid margin, partial-thickness

> DEF: Repair of eyelid margin not using all lid layers.

08.72 Other reconstruction of eyelid, partial-thickness

> DEF: Reshape of eyelid not using all lid layers.

08.73 Reconstruction of eyelid involving lid margin, full-thickness

> DEF: Repair of eyelid and margin using all tissue layers.

08.74 Other reconstruction of eyelid, full-thickness

> DEF: Other repair of eyelid using all tissue layers.

BI Bilateral Procedure   NC Non-covered Procedure   LC Limited Coverage Procedure   ▶◀ Revised Text   ● New Code   ▲ Revised Code Title

82 – Volume 3   2010 ICD-9-CM

✓4ᵗʰ 08.8 **Other repair of eyelid**

08.81 **Linear repair of laceration of eyelid or eyebrow**

08.82 **Repair of laceration involving lid margin, partial-thickness**
DEF: Repair of laceration not involving all layers of eyelid margin.

08.83 **Other repair of laceration of eyelid, partial thickness**
DEF: Repair of eyelid tear not involving all eyelid layers.

08.84 **Repair of laceration involving lid margin, full-thickness**
DEF: Repair of eyelid margin tear involving all margin layers.

08.85 **Other repair of laceration of eyelid, full-thickness**
DEF: Repair of eyelid tear involving all layers.

08.86 **Lower eyelid rhytidectomy**
DEF: Removal of wrinkles from lower eyelid.

08.87 **Upper eyelid rhytidectomy**
DEF: Removal of wrinkles from upper eyelid.
AHA: 2Q, '96, 11

08.89 **Other eyelid repair**
AHA: 1Q, '00, 22

✓4ᵗʰ 08.9 **Other operations on eyelids**

08.91 **Electrosurgical epilation of eyelid**
DEF: Electrical removal of eyelid hair roots.

08.92 **Cryosurgical epilation of eyelid**
DEF: Removal of eyelid hair roots by freezing.

08.93 **Other epilation of eyelid**

08.99 **Other**

✓3ʳᵈ 09 **Operations on lacrimal system**

09.0 **Incision of lacrimal gland**
Incision of lacrimal cyst (with drainage)

✓4ᵗʰ 09.1 **Diagnostic procedures on lacrimal system**

09.11 **Biopsy of lacrimal gland**

09.12 **Biopsy of lacrimal sac**

09.19 **Other diagnostic procedures on lacrimal system**
EXCLUDES contrast dacryocystogram (87.05)
soft tissue x-ray of nasolacrimal duct (87.09)

✓4ᵗʰ 09.2 **Excision of lesion or tissue of lacrimal gland**

09.20 **Excision of lacrimal gland, not otherwise specified**

09.21 **Excision of lesion of lacrimal gland**
EXCLUDES biopsy of lacrimal gland (09.11)

09.22 **Other partial dacryoadenectomy**
EXCLUDES biopsy of lacrimal gland (09.11)
DEF: Excision, partial, of tear gland.

09.23 **Total dacryoadenectomy**
DEF: Excision, total, of tear gland.

09.3 **Other operations on lacrimal gland**

✓4ᵗʰ 09.4 **Manipulation of lacrimal passage**
INCLUDES removal of calculus
that with dilation
EXCLUDES contrast dacryocystogram (87.05)

09.41 **Probing of lacrimal punctum**
DEF: Exploration of tear duct entrance with flexible rod.

09.42 **Probing of lacrimal canaliculi**
DEF: Exploration of tear duct with flexible rod.

09.43 **Probing of nasolacrimal duct**
EXCLUDES that with insertion of tube or stent (09.44)
DEF: Exploration of passage between tear sac and nose with flexible rod.

09.44 **Intubation of nasolacrimal duct**
Insertion of stent into nasolacrimal duct
AHA: 2Q, '94, 11

09.49 **Other manipulation of lacrimal passage**

✓4ᵗʰ 09.5 **Incision of lacrimal sac and passages**

09.51 **Incision of lacrimal punctum**

09.52 **Incision of lacrimal canaliculi**

09.53 **Incision of lacrimal sac**
DEF: Cutting into lacrimal pouch of tear gland.

09.59 **Other incision of lacrimal passages**
Incision (and drainage) of nasolacrimal duct NOS

09.6 **Excision of lacrimal sac and passage**
EXCLUDES biopsy of lacrimal sac (09.12)
DEF: Removal of pouch and passage of tear gland.

✓4ᵗʰ 09.7 **Repair of canaliculus and punctum**
EXCLUDES repair of eyelid (08.81–08.89)

09.71 **Correction of everted punctum**
DEF: Repair of an outwardly turned tear duct entrance.

09.72 **Other repair of punctum**

09.73 **Repair of canaliculus**

✓4ᵗʰ 09.8 **Fistulization of lacrimal tract to nasal cavity**

09.81 **Dacryocystorhinostomy [DCR]**
DEF: Creation of entrance between tear gland and nasal passage for tear flow.

09.82 **Conjunctivocystorhinostomy**
Conjunctivodacryocystorhinostomy [CDCR]
EXCLUDES that with insertion of tube or stent (09.83)
DEF: Creation of tear drainage path from lacrimal sac to nasal cavity through conjunctiva.

09.83 **Conjunctivorhinostomy with insertion of tube or stent**
DEF: Creation of passage between eye sac membrane and nasal cavity with tube or stent.

✓4ᵗʰ 09.9 **Other operations on lacrimal system**

09.91 **Obliteration of lacrimal punctum**
DEF: Destruction, total of tear gland opening in eyelid.

09.99 **Other**
AHA: 2Q, '94, 11
TIP: Assign for removal of nasolacrimal stent.

✓3ʳᵈ 10 **Operations on conjunctiva**

10.0 **Removal of embedded foreign body from conjunctiva by incision**
EXCLUDES removal of:
embedded foreign body without incision (98.22)
superficial foreign body (98.21)

10.1 **Other incision of conjunctiva**

✓4ᵗʰ 10.2 **Diagnostic procedures on conjunctiva**

10.21 **Biopsy of conjunctiva**

10.29 **Other diagnostic procedures on conjunctiva**

✓4ᵗʰ 10.3 **Excision or destruction of lesion or tissue of conjunctiva**

10.31 **Excision of lesion or tissue of conjunctiva**
Excision of ring of conjunctiva around cornea
EXCLUDES biopsy of conjunctiva (10.21)
DEF: Removal of growth or tissue from eye membrane.
AHA: 4Q, '00, 41; 3Q, '96, 7
TIP: Assign for excision of conjunctivochalasis.

10.32 **Destruction of lesion of conjunctiva**
EXCLUDES excision of lesion (10.31)
thermocauterization for entropion (08.41)
DEF: Destruction of eye membrane growth; not done by excision.

10.33 **Other destructive procedures on conjunctiva**
Removal of trachoma follicles

Operations on the Eye

10.4–12.02

✓4th **10.4 Conjunctivoplasty**
> **DEF:** Correction of conjunctiva by plastic surgery.

10.41 Repair of symblepharon with free graft
> AHA: 3Q, '96, 7

10.42 Reconstruction of conjunctival cul-de-sac with free graft
> **EXCLUDES** revision of enucleation socket with graft (16.63)
> **DEF:** Rebuilding of eye membrane fold with graft of unattached tissue.

10.43 Other reconstruction of conjunctival cul-de-sac
> **EXCLUDES** revision of enucleation socket (16.64)

10.44 Other free graft to conjunctiva

10.49 Other conjunctivoplasty
> **EXCLUDES** repair of cornea with conjunctival flap (11.53)

10.5 Lysis of adhesions of conjunctiva and eyelid
> Division of symblepharon (with insertion of conformer)

10.6 Repair of laceration of conjunctiva
> **EXCLUDES** that with repair of sclera (12.81)

✓4th **10.9 Other operations on conjunctiva**

10.91 Subconjunctival injection
> AHA: 3Q, '96, 7

10.99 Other

✓3rd **11 Operations on cornea**

11.0 Magnetic removal of embedded foreign body from cornea
> **EXCLUDES** that with incision (11.1)

11.1 Incision of cornea
> Incision of cornea for removal of foreign body

✓4th **11.2 Diagnostic procedures on cornea**

11.21 Scraping of cornea for smear or culture

11.22 Biopsy of cornea

11.29 Other diagnostic procedures on cornea

✓4th **11.3 Excision of pterygium**

11.31 Transposition of pterygium
> **DEF:** Cutting into membranous structure extending from eye membrane to cornea and suturing it in a downward position.

11.32 Excision of pterygium with corneal graft
> **DEF:** Surgical removal and repair of membranous structure extending from eye membrane to cornea using corneal tissue transplant.

11.39 Other excision of pterygium

✓4th **11.4 Excision or destruction of tissue or other lesion of cornea**

11.41 Mechanical removal of corneal epithelium
> That by chemocauterization
> **EXCLUDES** that for smear or culture (11.21)
> **DEF:** Removal of outer layer of cornea by mechanical means.
> AHA: 3Q, '02, 20

11.42 Thermocauterization of corneal lesion
> **DEF:** Destruction of corneal lesion by electrical cautery.

11.43 Cryotherapy of corneal lesion
> **DEF:** Destruction of corneal lesion with cold therapy.

11.49 Other removal or destruction of corneal lesion
> Excision of cornea NOS
> **EXCLUDES** biopsy of cornea (11.22)

✓4th **11.5 Repair of cornea**

11.51 Suture of corneal laceration
> AHA: 3Q, '96, 7

11.52 Repair of postoperative wound dehiscence of cornea
> **DEF:** Repair of ruptured postoperative corneal wound.

11.53 Repair of corneal laceration or wound with conjunctival flap
> **DEF:** Correction corneal wound or tear with conjunctival tissue.

11.59 Other repair of cornea

✓4th **11.6 Corneal transplant**
> **EXCLUDES** excision of pterygium with corneal graft (11.32)

11.60 Corneal transplant, not otherwise specified
> Note: To report donor sources – see codes 00.91-00.93
> Keratoplasty NOS

11.61 Lamellar keratoplasty with autograft
> **DEF:** Restoration of sight using patient's own corneal tissue, partial thickness.

11.62 Other lamellar keratoplasty
> **DEF:** Restoration of sight using donor corneal tissue, partial thickness.
> AHA: S-O, '85, 6

11.63 Penetrating keratoplasty with autograft
> Perforating keratoplasty with autograft
> **TIP:** Penetrating keratoplasty infers a full-thickness corneal transplant grafting procedure.

11.64 Other penetrating keratoplasty
> Perforating keratoplasty (with homograft)

11.69 Other corneal transplant

✓4th **11.7 Other reconstructive and refractive surgery on cornea**

11.71 Keratomileusis NC
> **DEF:** Restoration of corneal shape by removing portion of cornea, freezing, reshaping curve and reattaching it.

11.72 Keratophakia NC
> **DEF:** Correction of eye lens loss by dissecting the central zone of the cornea and replacing it with a thickened graft of the cornea.

11.73 Keratoprosthesis
> **DEF:** Placement of corneal artificial implant.

11.74 Thermokeratoplasty
> **DEF:** Reshaping and reforming cornea by heat application.

11.75 Radial keratotomy NC
> **DEF:** Incisions around cornea radius to correct nearsightedness.

11.76 Epikeratophakia NC
> **DEF:** Repair lens loss by cornea graft sutured to central corneal zone.

11.79 Other

✓4th **11.9 Other operations on cornea**

11.91 Tattooing of cornea

11.92 Removal of artificial implant from cornea

11.99 Other
> AHA: 3Q, '02, 20
> **TIP:** Assign for keratolimbal stem cell transplant, typically performed for aniridia and decreasing vision with deep vascular pannus of the eye.

✓3rd **12 Operations on iris, ciliary body, sclera, and anterior chamber**
> **EXCLUDES** operations on cornea (11.0-11.99)

✓4th **12.0 Removal of intraocular foreign body from anterior segment of eye**

12.00 Removal of intraocular foreign body from anterior segment of eye, not otherwise specified

12.01 Removal of intraocular foreign body from anterior segment of eye with use of magnet

12.02 Removal of intraocular foreign body from anterior segment of eye without use of magnet

BI Bilateral Procedure   NC Non-covered Procedure   LC Limited Coverage Procedure   ▶◀ Revised Text   ● New Code   ▲ Revised Code Title

84 – Volume 3   2010 ICD-9-CM

✓4th **12.1　Iridotomy and simple iridectomy**

> **EXCLUDES** *iridectomy associated with:*
> *cataract extraction (13.11-13.69)*
> *removal of lesion (12.41-12.42)*
> *scleral fistulization (12.61-12.69)*

12.11　Iridotomy with transfixion

12.12　Other iridotomy
Corectomy
Discission of iris
Iridotomy NOS
DEF: Corectomy: Incision into iris (also called iridotomy).

12.13　Excision of prolapsed iris
DEF: Removal of downwardly placed portion of iris.

12.14　Other iridectomy
Iridectomy (basal) (peripheral) (total)
DEF: Removal, partial or total of iris.

✓4th **12.2　Diagnostic procedures on iris, ciliary body, sclera, and anterior chamber**

12.21　Diagnostic aspiration of anterior chamber of eye
DEF: Suction withdrawal of fluid from anterior eye chamber for diagnostic reasons.

12.22　Biopsy of iris

12.29　Other diagnostic procedures on iris, ciliary body, sclera, and anterior chamber

✓4th **12.3　Iridoplasty and coreoplasty**
DEF: Correction or abnormal iris or pupil by plastic surgery.

12.31　Lysis of goniosynechiae
Lysis of goniosynechiae by injection of air or liquid
DEF: Freeing of fibrous structures between cornea and iris by injecting air or liquid.

12.32　Lysis of other anterior synechiae
Lysis of anterior synechiae:
NOS
by injection of air or liquid

12.33　Lysis of posterior synechiae
Lysis of iris adhesions NOS

12.34　Lysis of corneovitreal adhesions
DEF: Release of adhesions of cornea and vitreous body.

12.35　Coreoplasty
Needling of pupillary membrane
DEF: Correction of an iris defect.

12.39　Other iridoplasty

✓4th **12.4　Excision or destruction of lesion of iris and ciliary body**

12.40　Removal of lesion of anterior segment of eye, not otherwise specified

12.41　Destruction of lesion of iris, nonexcisional
Destruction of lesion of iris by:
cauterization
cryotherapy
photocoagulation

12.42　Excision of lesion of iris
> **EXCLUDES** *biopsy of iris (12.22)*

12.43　Destruction of lesion of ciliary body, nonexcisional

12.44　Excision of lesion of ciliary body

✓4th **12.5　Facilitation of intraocular circulation**

12.51　Goniopuncture without goniotomy
DEF: Stab incision into anterior chamber of eye to relieve optic pressure.

12.52　Goniotomy without goniopuncture
DEF: Incision into Schlemm's canal to drain aqueous and relieve pressure.

12.53　Goniotomy with goniopuncture

12.54　Trabeculotomy ab externo
DEF: Incision into supporting connective tissue strands of eye capsule, via exterior approach.

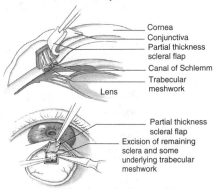

Trabeculectomy Ab Externo

Cornea
Conjunctiva
Partial thickness scleral flap
Canal of Schlemm
Trabecular meshwork
Lens

Partial thickness scleral flap
Excision of remaining sclera and some underlying trabecular meshwork

12.55　Cyclodialysis
DEF: Creation of passage between anterior chamber and suprachoroidal space.

12.59　Other facilitation of intraocular circulation

✓4th **12.6　Scleral fistulization**
> **EXCLUDES** *exploratory sclerotomy (12.89)*

12.61　Trephination of sclera with iridectomy
DEF: Cut around sclerocornea to remove part of the iris.

12.62　Thermocauterization of sclera with iridectomy
DEF: Destruction of outer eyeball layer with partial excision of iris using heat.

12.63　Iridencleisis and iridotasis
DEF: Creation of permanent drain in iris by transposing or stretching iris tissue.

12.64　Trabeculectomy ab externo
DEF: Excision of supporting connective tissue strands of eye capsule, via exterior approach.

12.65　Other scleral fistulization with iridectomy
Holth's sclerectomy
DEF: Creation of outer eyeball layer passage with partial excision of iris.

12.66　Postoperative revision of scleral fistulization procedure
Revision of filtering bleb
> **EXCLUDES** *repair of fistula (12.82)*
AHA: 2Q, '01, 16

12.69　Other fistulizing procedure

✓4th **12.7　Other procedures for relief of elevated intraocular pressure**

12.71　Cyclodiathermy
DEF: Destruction of ciliary body tissue with heat.

12.72　Cyclocryotherapy
DEF: Destruction of ciliary body tissue by freezing.

12.73　Cyclophotocoagulation
DEF: Destruction of ciliary body tissue by high energy light source.

12.74　Diminution of ciliary body, not otherwise specified

12.79　Other glaucoma procedures
AHA: 2Q, '98, 16
TIP: Assign for suture lysis performed for elevated intraocular pressure status post trabeculectomy.

✓4th **12.8　Operations on sclera**
> **EXCLUDES** *those associated with:*
> *retinal reattachment (14.41-14.59)*
> *scleral fistulization (12.61-12.69)*

12.81　Suture of laceration of sclera
Suture of sclera with synchronous repair of conjunctiva

12.82　Repair of scleral fistula
> **EXCLUDES** *postoperative revision of scleral fistulization procedure (12.66)*

12.83   **Revision of operative wound of anterior segment, not elsewhere classified**

> **EXCLUDES**   *postoperative revision of scleral fistulization procedure (12.66)*

12.84   **Excision or destruction of lesion of sclera**

12.85   **Repair of scleral staphyloma with graft**

> **DEF:** Repair of protruding outer eyeball layer with a graft.

12.86   **Other repair of scleral staphyloma**

12.87   **Scleral reinforcement with graft**

> **DEF:** Restoration of outer eyeball shape with tissue graft.

12.88   **Other scleral reinforcement**

12.89   **Other operations on sclera**

> Exploratory sclerotomy

√4ᵗʰ **12.9**   **Other operations on iris, ciliary body, and anterior chamber**

12.91   **Therapeutic evacuation of anterior chamber**

> Paracentesis of anterior chamber
>
> **EXCLUDES**   *diagnostic aspiration (12.21)*

12.92   **Injection into anterior chamber**

> Injection of:
> air ⎫
> liquid ⎬ into anterior chamber
> medication ⎭
>
> **AHA:** J-A, '84, 1

12.93   **Removal or destruction of epithelial downgrowth from anterior chamber**

> **EXCLUDES**   *that with iridectomy (12.41-12.42)*
>
> **DEF:** Excision or destruction of epithelial overgrowth in anterior eye chamber.

12.97   **Other operations on iris**

12.98   **Other operations on ciliary body**

12.99   **Other operations on anterior chamber**

√3ʳᵈ **13**   **Operations on lens**

√4ᵗʰ **13.0**   **Removal of foreign body from lens**

> **EXCLUDES**   *removal of pseudophakos (13.8)*

13.00   **Removal of foreign body from lens, not otherwise specified**

13.01   **Removal of foreign body from lens with use of magnet**

13.02   **Removal of foreign body from lens without use of magnet**

√4ᵗʰ **13.1**   **Intracapsular extraction of lens**

> Code also any synchronous insertion of pseudophakos (13.71)
>
> **AHA:** S-O, '85, 6

13.11   **Intracapsular extraction of lens by temporal inferior route**

> **DEF:** Extraction of lens and capsule via anterior approach through outer side of eyeball.

13.19   **Other intracapsular extraction of lens**

> Cataract extraction NOS
> Cryoextraction of lens
> Erysiphake extraction of cataract
> Extraction of lens NOS

13.2   **Extracapsular extraction of lens by linear extraction technique**

> ▶Code also any synchronous insertion of pseudophakos (13.71)◀
>
> **DEF:** Excision of lens without the posterior capsule at junction between the cornea and outer eyeball layer by means of a linear incision.
>
> **AHA:** S-O, '85, 6

Extraction of Lens (with insertion of intraocular lens prosthesis)

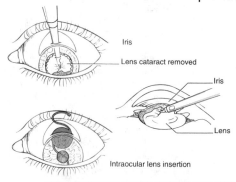

Iris
Lens cataract removed
Iris
Lens
Intraocular lens insertion

13.3   **Extracapsular extraction of lens by simple aspiration (and irrigation) technique**

> Irrigation of traumatic cataract
>
> ▶Code also any synchronous insertion of pseudophakos (13.71)◀
>
> **DEF:** Removal of lens without the posterior capsule by suctioning and flushing out the area.
>
> **AHA:** S-O, '85, 6

√4ᵗʰ **13.4**   **Extracapsular extraction of lens by fragmentation and aspiration technique**

> ▶Code also any synchronous insertion of pseudophakos (13.71)◀
>
> **DEF:** Removal of lens after division into smaller pieces with posterior capsule left intact.
>
> **AHA:** S-O, '85, 6
>
> **TIP:** Assign an additional code from subcategory 14.7 if a vitrectomy procedure is also performed with cataract extraction procedures.

13.41   **Phacoemulsification and aspiration of cataract**

> **AHA:** 3Q, '96, 4; 1Q, '94, 16

13.42   **Mechanical phacofragmentation and aspiration of cataract by posterior route**

> Code also any synchronous vitrectomy (14.74)

13.43   **Mechanical phacofragmentation and other aspiration of cataract**

√4ᵗʰ **13.5**   **Other extracapsular extraction of lens**

> Code also any synchronous insertion of pseudophakos (13.71)
>
> **AHA:** S-O, '85, 6

13.51   **Extracapsular extraction of lens by temporal inferior route**

> **DEF:** Removal of lens through outer eyeball with posterior capsule left intact.

13.59   **Other extracapsular extraction of lens**

√4ᵗʰ **13.6**   **Other cataract extraction**

> Code also any synchronous insertion of pseudophakos (13.71)
>
> **AHA:** S-O, '85, 6

13.64   **Discission of secondary membrane [after cataract]**

> **DEF:** Breaking up of fibrotic lens capsule developed after previous lens extraction.

13.65   **Excision of secondary membrane [after cataract]**

> Capsulectomy
>
> **DEF:** Capsulectomy: Excision of lens capsule membrane after previous lens extraction.

13.66   **Mechanical fragmentation of secondary membrane [after cataract]**

> **DEF:** Breaking up and removal of fibrotic lens capsule developed after previous lens extraction.

13.69   **Other cataract extraction**

■BI Bilateral Procedure   ■NC Non-covered Procedure   ■LC Limited Coverage Procedure   ▶◀ Revised Text   ● New Code   ▲ Revised Code Title

86 – Volume 3 · October 2009   **2010 ICD-9-CM**

√4th **13.7 Insertion of prosthetic lens [pseudophakos]**

EXCLUDES *implantation of intraocular telescope prosthesis (13.91)*

DEF: Insertion of ocular implant, following lens extraction.
AHA: J-A, '84, 1

13.70 Insertion of pseudophakos, not otherwise specified

13.71 Insertion of intraocular lens prosthesis at time of cataract extraction, one-stage

Code also synchronous extraction of cataract (13.11-13.69)

AHA: 3Q, '96, 4

13.72 Secondary insertion of intraocular lens prosthesis

13.8 Removal of implanted lens

Removal of pseudophakos

√4th **13.9 Other operations on lens**
AHA: 1Q, '00, 9

13.90 Operation on lens, not elsewhere classified

AHA: 4Q, '06, 123

13.91 Implantation of intraocular telescope prosthesis

Implantable miniature telescope
INCLUDES removal of lens, any method
EXCLUDES *secondary insertion of ocular implant (16.61)*

AHA: 4Q, '06, 123

TIP: This device is implanted in one eye, providing central vision; the nonimplanted eye can continue to provide peripheral vision for orientation and mobility.

√3rd **14 Operations on retina, choroid, vitreous, and posterior chamber**

√4th **14.0 Removal of foreign body from posterior segment of eye**
EXCLUDES *removal of surgically implanted material (14.6)*

14.00 Removal of foreign body from posterior segment of eye, not otherwise specified

14.01 Removal of foreign body from posterior segment of eye with use of magnet

14.02 Removal of foreign body from posterior segment of eye without use of magnet

√4th **14.1 Diagnostic procedures on retina, choroid, vitreous, and posterior chamber**

14.11 Diagnostic aspiration of vitreous

14.19 Other diagnostic procedures on retina, choroid, vitreous, and posterior chamber

√4th **14.2 Destruction of lesion of retina and choroid**

INCLUDES destruction of chorioretinopathy or isolated chorioretinal lesion
EXCLUDES *that for repair of retina (14.31-14.59)*
DEF: Destruction of damaged retina and choroid tissue.

14.21 Destruction of chorioretinal lesion by diathermy

14.22 Destruction of chorioretinal lesion by cryotherapy

14.23 Destruction of chorioretinal lesion by xenon arc photocoagulation

Laser Surgery (YAG)

Scleral Buckling with Implant

14.24 Destruction of chorioretinal lesion by laser photocoagulation

14.25 Destruction of chorioretinal lesion by photocoagulation of unspecified type

14.26 Destruction of chorioretinal lesion by radiation therapy

14.27 Destruction of chorioretinal lesion by implantation of radiation source

14.29 Other destruction of chorioretinal lesion

Destruction of lesion of retina and choroid NOS

√4th **14.3 Repair of retinal tear**

INCLUDES repair of retinal defect
EXCLUDES *repair of retinal detachment (14.41-14.59)*

14.31 Repair of retinal tear by diathermy

14.32 Repair of retinal tear by cryotherapy

14.33 Repair of retinal tear by xenon arc photocoagulation

14.34 Repair of retinal tear by laser photocoagulation
AHA: 1Q, '94, 17

14.35 Repair of retinal tear by photocoagulation of unspecified type

14.39 Other repair of retinal tear

√4th **14.4 Repair of retinal detachment with scleral buckling and implant**

DEF: Placement of material around eye to indent sclera and close a hole or tear or to reduce vitreous traction.

14.41 Scleral buckling with implant
AHA: 3Q, '96, 6

14.49 Other scleral buckling
Scleral buckling with:
air tamponade
resection of sclera
vitrectomy
AHA: 1Q, '94, 16

√4th **14.5 Other repair of retinal detachment**

INCLUDES that with drainage

14.51 Repair of retinal detachment with diathermy

14.52 Repair of retinal detachment with cryotherapy

14.53 Repair of retinal detachment with xenon arc photocoagulation

14.54 Repair of retinal detachment with laser photocoagulation
AHA: N-D, '87, 10

14.55 Repair of retinal detachment with photocoagulation of unspecified type

14.59 Other

14.6 Removal of surgically implanted material from posterior segment of eye

Operations on the Eye

14.7–16.23

✓4th **14.7** **Operations on vitreous**

14.71 **Removal of vitreous, anterior approach**
Open sky technique
Removal of vitreous, anterior approach (with replacement)
DEF: Removal of all or part of the eyeball fluid via the anterior segment of the eyeball.

14.72 **Other removal of vitreous**
Aspiration of vitreous by posterior sclerotomy

14.73 **Mechanical vitrectomy by anterior approach**
DEF: Removal of abnormal tissue in eyeball fluid to control fibrotic overgrowth in severe intraocular injury.
AHA: 3Q, '96, 4, 5

14.74 **Other mechanical vitrectomy**
Posterior approach
AHA: 3Q, '96, 4, 5

14.75 **Injection of vitreous substitute**
EXCLUDES *that associated with removal (14.71-14.72)*
AHA: 1Q, '98, 6; 3Q, '96, 4, 5; 1Q, '94, 17

14.79 **Other operations on vitreous**
AHA: 3Q, '99, 12; 1Q, '99, 11; 1Q, '98, 6
TIP: Assign for an endoscopic vitreous washout and reinjection of silicone oil.

14.9 **Other operations on retina, choroid, and posterior chamber**
AHA: 3Q, '96, 5
TIP: Assign for epiretinal membrane peeling, which is typically performed with vitrectomy but is not an inherent component.

✓3rd **15** **Operations on extraocular muscles**
TIP: If a procedure is performed on the same muscle in both eyes, assign the appropriate code twice from subcategory 15.1 or 15.2.

✓4th **15.0** **Diagnostic procedures on extraocular muscles or tendons**

15.01 **Biopsy of extraocular muscle or tendon**

15.09 **Other diagnostic procedures on extraocular muscles and tendons**

✓4th **15.1** **Operations on one extraocular muscle involving temporary detachment from globe**

15.11 **Recession of one extraocular muscle**
DEF: Detachment of exterior eye muscle with posterior reattachment to correct strabismus.
AHA: 3Q, '96, 3

15.12 **Advancement of one extraocular muscle**
DEF: Detachment of exterior eye muscle with forward reattachment to correct strabismus.

15.13 **Resection of one extraocular muscle**

15.19 **Other operations on one extraocular muscle involving temporary detachment from globe**
EXCLUDES *transposition of muscle (15.5)*

Lengthening Procedure on One Extraocular Muscle

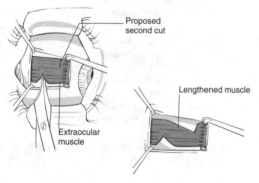

Shortening Procedure on One Extraocular Muscle

✓4th **15.2** **Other operations on one extraocular muscle**

15.21 **Lengthening procedure on one extraocular muscle**
DEF: Extension of exterior eye muscle length.

15.22 **Shortening procedure on one extraocular muscle**
DEF: Shortening of exterior eye muscle.

15.29 **Other**

15.3 **Operations on two or more extraocular muscles involving temporary detachment from globe, one or both eyes**
AHA: 3Q, '96, 3

15.4 **Other operations on two or more extraocular muscles, one or both eyes**

15.5 **Transposition of extraocular muscles**
EXCLUDES *that for correction of ptosis (08.31-08.36)*
DEF: Relocation of exterior eye muscle to a more functional site.

15.6 **Revision of extraocular muscle surgery**
DEF: Repair of previous exterior eye muscle surgery.

15.7 **Repair of injury of extraocular muscle**
Freeing of entrapped extraocular muscle
Lysis of adhesions of extraocular muscle
Repair of laceration of extraocular muscle, tendon, or Tenon's capsule

15.9 **Other operations on extraocular muscles and tendons**

✓3rd **16** **Operations on orbit and eyeball**
EXCLUDES *reduction of fracture of orbit (76.78-76.79)*

✓4th **16.0** **Orbitotomy**

16.01 **Orbitotomy with bone flap**
Orbitotomy with lateral approach
DEF: Incision into orbital bone with insertion of small bone piece.

16.02 **Orbitotomy with insertion of orbital implant**
EXCLUDES *that with bone flap (16.01)*

16.09 **Other orbitotomy**

16.1 **Removal of penetrating foreign body from eye, not otherwise specified**
EXCLUDES *removal of nonpenetrating foreign body (98.21)*
DEF: Removal of foreign body from an unspecified site in eye.

✓4th **16.2** **Diagnostic procedures on orbit and eyeball**

16.21 **Ophthalmoscopy**

16.22 **Diagnostic aspiration of orbit**

16.23 **Biopsy of eyeball and orbit**

BI Bilateral Procedure   NC Non-covered Procedure   LC Limited Coverage Procedure   ▶◀ Revised Text   ● New Code   ▲ Revised Code Title

88 – Volume 3   **2010 ICD-9-CM**

Operations on the Eye

16.29 **Other diagnostic procedures on orbit and eyeball**
> **EXCLUDES** examination of form and structure of
> eye (95.11-95.16)
> general and subjective eye
> examination (95.01-95.09)
> microscopic examination of specimen
> from eye (90.21-90.29)
> objective functional tests of eye
> (95.21-95.26)
> ocular thermography (88.82)
> tonometry (89.11)
> x-ray of orbit (87.14, 87.16)

✓4th **16.3** **Evisceration of eyeball**
> **DEF:** Removal of eyeball, leaving sclera and occasionally cornea.

16.31 **Removal of ocular contents with synchronous implant into scleral shell**
> **DEF:** Removal of eyeball leaving outer eyeball layer with ocular implant into shell.

16.39 **Other evisceration of eyeball**

✓4th **16.4** **Enucleation of eyeball**
> **DEF:** Removal of entire eyeball after severing eye muscles and optic nerves.

16.41 **Enucleation of eyeball with synchronous implant into Tenon's capsule with attachment of muscles**
> Integrated implant of eyeball
> **DEF:** Removal of eyeball with insertion of ocular implant and muscle attachment.

16.42 **Enucleation of eyeball with other synchronous implant**

16.49 **Other enucleation of eyeball**
> Removal of eyeball NOS

✓4th **16.5** **Exenteration of orbital contents**

16.51 **Exenteration of orbit with removal of adjacent structures**
> Radical orbitomaxillectomy
> **DEF:** Removal of contents of bony cavity of eye as well as related tissues and structures.
> **DEF:** Radical orbitomaxillectomy: Removal of contents of bony cavity of eye, related tissues and structures, and a portion of maxillary bone.

16.52 **Exenteration of orbit with therapeutic removal of orbital bone**

16.59 **Other exenteration of orbit**
> Evisceration of orbit NOS
> Exenteration of orbit with temporalis muscle transplant

✓4th **16.6** **Secondary procedures after removal of eyeball**
> **EXCLUDES** that with synchronous:
> enucleation of eyeball (16.41-16.42)
> evisceration of eyeball (16.31)

16.61 **Secondary insertion of ocular implant**
> **DEF:** Insertion of ocular implant after previous eye removal.

16.62 **Revision and reinsertion of ocular implant**
> **DEF:** Reimplant or correction of ocular implant.

16.63 **Revision of enucleation socket with graft**
> **DEF:** Implant of tissue to correct socket after eye removal.

16.64 **Other revision of enucleation socket**

16.65 **Secondary graft to exenteration cavity**
> **DEF:** Implant of tissue in place of eye after removal.

16.66 **Other revision of exenteration cavity**

16.69 **Other secondary procedures after removal of eyeball**

✓4th **16.7** **Removal of ocular or orbital implant**

16.71 **Removal of ocular implant**

16.72 **Removal of orbital implant**

✓4th **16.8** **Repair of injury of eyeball and orbit**

16.81 **Repair of wound of orbit**
> **EXCLUDES** reduction of orbital fracture
> (76.78-76.79)
> repair of extraocular muscles (15.7)

16.82 **Repair of rupture of eyeball**
> Repair of multiple structures of eye
> **EXCLUDES** repair of laceration of:
> cornea (11.51-11.59)
> sclera (12.81)

16.89 **Other repair of injury of eyeball or orbit**

✓4th **16.9** **Other operations on orbit and eyeball**
> **EXCLUDES** irrigation of eye (96.51)
> prescription and fitting of low vision aids
> (95.31-95.33)
> removal of:
> eye prosthesis NEC (97.31)
> nonpenetrating foreign body from eye
> without incision (98.21)

16.91 **Retrobulbar injection of therapeutic agent**
> **EXCLUDES** injection of radiographic contrast
> material (87.14)
> opticociliary injection (12.79)

16.92 **Excision of lesion of orbit**
> **EXCLUDES** biopsy of orbit (16.23)

16.93 **Excision of lesion of eye, unspecified structure**
> **EXCLUDES** biopsy of eye NOS (16.23)

16.98 **Other operations on orbit**

16.99 **Other operations on eyeball**

16.29–16.99

✳ CCM; three leads are implanted into the heart... two are placed in the right ventricular septum; the third is placed in the right atrium.

17–17.63   MISCELLANEOUS DIAGNOSTIC AND THERAPEUTIC PROCEDURES   Tabular List

Miscellaneous Diagnostic and Therapeutic Procedures

17–17.63

3A. OTHER MISCELLANEOUS DIAGNOSTIC AND THERAPEUTIC PROCEDURES (17)

√3rd **17   Other miscellaneous procedures**

√4th **17.1   Laparoscopic unilateral repair of inguinal hernia**
EXCLUDES   *other and open unilateral repair of hernia (53.00-53.05)*
AHA: 4Q, '08, 165-166

17.11   Laparoscopic repair of direct inguinal hernia with graft or prosthesis
Laparoscopic repair of direct and indirect inguinal hernia with graft or prosthesis

17.12   Laparoscopic repair of indirect inguinal hernia with graft or prosthesis

17.13   Laparoscopic repair of inguinal hernia with graft or prosthesis, not otherwise specified

√4th **17.2   Laparoscopic bilateral repair of inguinal hernia**
EXCLUDES   *other and open bilateral repair of hernia (53.10-53.17)*
AHA: 4Q, '08, 165-166

17.21   Laparoscopic bilateral repair of direct inguinal hernia with graft or prosthesis

17.22   Laparoscopic bilateral repair of indirect inguinal hernia with graft or prosthesis

17.23   Laparoscopic bilateral repair of inguinal hernia, one direct and one indirect, with graft or prosthesis

17.24   Laparoscopic bilateral repair of inguinal hernia with graft or prosthesis, not otherwise specified

17.3   Laparoscopic partial excision of large intestine
EXCLUDES   *other and open partial excision of large intestine (45.71-45.79)*
AHA: 4Q, '08, 169-170

17.31   Laparoscopic multiple segmental resection of large intestine

17.32   Laparoscopic cecectomy

17.33   Laparoscopic right hemicolectomy

17.34   Laparoscopic resection of transverse colon

17.35   Laparoscopic left hemicolectomy

17.36   Laparoscopic sigmoidectomy

17.39   Other laparoscopic partial excision of large intestine

√4th **17.4   Robotic assisted procedures**
Note: This category includes use of a computer console with (3-D) imaging, software, camera(s), visualization and instrumentation *combined* with the use of robotic arms, device(s), or system(s) at the time of the procedure.
Computer assisted robotic surgery
Computer-enhanced robotic surgery
Robotic procedure with computer assistance
Surgeon-controlled robotic surgery
Code first primary procedure
EXCLUDES   *computer assisted surgery (00.31-00.35, 00.39)*
AHA: 4Q, '08, 172-174

17.41   Open robotic assisted procedure
Robotic assistance in open procedure

17.42   Laparoscopic robotic assisted procedure
Robotic assistance in laparoscopic procedure
AHA: 4Q, '08, 174

17.43   Percutaneous robotic assisted procedure
Robotic assistance in percutaneous procedure

17.44   Endoscopic robotic assisted procedure
Robotic assistance in endoscopic procedure

17.45   Thoracoscopic robotic assisted procedure
Robotic assistance in thoracoscopic procedure

17.49   Other and unspecified robotic assisted procedure
Robotic assistance in other and unspecified procedure
EXCLUDES   *endoscopic robotic assisted procedure (17.44)*
laparoscopic robotic assisted procedure (17.42)
open robotic assisted procedure (17.41)
percutaneous robotic assisted procedure (17.43)
thoracoscopic robotic assisted procedure (17.45)

● √4th **17.5   Additional cardiovascular procedures**

● **17.51   Implantation of rechargeable cardiac contractility modulation [CCM], total system**
Note: Device testing during procedure — *omit code*
Implantation of CCM system includes formation of pocket, transvenous leads, including placement of leads, placement of catheter into left ventricle, intraoperative procedures for evaluation of lead signals, obtaining sensing threshold measurements, obtaining defibrillator threshold measurements.
Includes implantation of device with removal of existing device
Code also any concomitant:
coronary bypass (36.10-36.19)
extracorporeal circulation (39.61)
insertion or replacement of automatic cardioverter/defibrillator, total system [AICD] 37.94
EXCLUDES   *implantation of CCM pulse generator only (17.52)*

● **17.52   Implantation or replacement of cardiac contractility modulation [CCM] rechargeable pulse generator only**
Note: Device testing during procedure — *omit code*
Implantation of CCM device with removal of any existing CCM device
Code also any concomitant:
revision of device pocket (37.79)
revision of lead [electrode] (37.75)

● √4th **17.6   Laser interstitial thermal therapy [LITT] under guidance**
Focused laser interstitial thermal therapy [f-LITT] under MRI guidance
MRI-guided LITT

● **17.61   Laser interstitial thermal therapy [LITT] of lesion or tissue of brain under guidance**
Focused laser interstitial thermal therapy [f-LITT] under MRI guidance
MRI-guided LITT of lesion or tissue of brain
EXCLUDES   *laser interstitial thermal therapy [LITT] of lesion or tissue of head under guidance (17.62)*

● **17.62   Laser interstitial thermal therapy [LITT] of lesion or tissue of head and neck under guidance**
Focused laser interstitial thermal therapy [f-LITT] under MRI guidance
MRI-guided LITT of lesion or tissue of head and neck
EXCLUDES   *laser interstitial thermal therapy [LITT] of lesion or tissue of brain under guidance (17.61)*

● **17.63   Laser interstitial thermal therapy [LITT] of lesion or tissue of liver under guidance**
Focused laser interstitial thermal therapy [f-LITT] under MRI guidance
MRI-guided LITT of lesion or tissue of liver

BI Bilateral Procedure   NC Non-covered Procedure   LC Limited Coverage Procedure   ►◄ Revised Text   ● New Code   ▲ Revised Code Title

90 – Volume 3 • October 2009   2010 ICD-9-CM

- 17.69 **Laser interstitial thermal therapy [LITT] of lesion or tissue of other and unspecified site under guidance**
  Focused laser interstitial thermal therapy [f-LITT] under MRI guidance
  MRI-guided LITT of lesion or tissue of breast
  MRI-guided LITT of lesion or tissue of lung
  MRI-guided LITT of lesion or tissue of prostate
  EXCLUDES *laser interstitial thermal therapy [LITT] of lesion or tissue of brain under guidance (17.61)*
  laser interstitial thermal therapy [LITT] of lesion or tissue of head and neck under guidance (17.62)
  laser interstitial thermal therapy [LITT] of lesion or tissue of liver under guidance (17.63)

- √4th 17.7 **Other diagnostic and therapeutic procedures**
- 17.70 **Intravenous infusion of clofarabine**
  EXCLUDES *injection or infusion of cancer chemotherapeutic substance (99.25)*

√3rd
√4th Additional Digit Required

Valid OR Procedure

Non-OR Procedure

Adjunct Code

2010 ICD-9-CM

October 2009 • Volume 3 – 91

Operations on the Ear

18–19.3

4. OPERATIONS ON THE EAR (18-20)

√3rd **18**   **Operations on external ear**

> **INCLUDES**   operations on:
> external auditory canal
> skin and cartilage of:
>   auricle
>   meatus

√4th **18.0**   **Incision of external ear**

> **EXCLUDES**   *removal of intraluminal foreign body (98.11)*

   18.01   **Piercing of ear lobe**
> Piercing of pinna

   18.02   **Incision of external auditory canal**

   18.09   **Other incision of external ear**

√4th **18.1**   **Diagnostic procedures on external ear**

   18.11   **Otoscopy**
> **DEF:** Exam of the ear with instrument designed for visualization.

   18.12   **Biopsy of external ear**

   18.19   **Other diagnostic procedures on external ear**
> **EXCLUDES**   *microscopic examination of specimen from ear (90.31-90.39)*

√4th **18.2**   **Excision or destruction of lesion of external ear**

   18.21   **Excision of preauricular sinus**
> Radical excision of preauricular sinus or cyst
> **EXCLUDES**   *excision of preauricular remnant [appendage] (18.29)*
>
> **DEF:** Excision of preauricular sinus or cyst with adjacent tissues.

   18.29   **Excision or destruction of other lesion of external ear**

> Cauterization
> Coagulation
> Cryosurgery   } of external ear
> Curettage
> Electrocoagulation
> Enucleation
>
> Excision of:
>   exostosis of external auditory canal
>   preauricular remnant [appendage]
> Partial excision of ear
> **EXCLUDES**   *biopsy of external ear (18.12)*
>   *radical excision of lesion (18.31)*
>   *removal of cerumen (96.52)*

√4th **18.3**   **Other excision of external ear**

> **EXCLUDES**   *biopsy of external ear (18.12)*

   18.31   **Radical excision of lesion of external ear**
> **EXCLUDES**   *radical excision of preauricular sinus (18.21)*
>
> **DEF:** Removal of damaged, diseased ear and adjacent tissue.

   18.39   **Other**
> Amputation of external ear
> **EXCLUDES**   *excision of lesion (18.21-18.29, 18.31)*

   18.4   **Suture of laceration of external ear**

   18.5   **Surgical correction of prominent ear**
> Ear:
>   pinning
>   setback
> **DEF:** Reformation of protruding outer ear.

   18.6   **Reconstruction of external auditory canal**
> Canaloplasty of external auditory meatus
> Construction [reconstruction] of external meatus of ear:
>   osseous portion
>   skin-lined portion (with skin graft)
> **DEF:** Repair of outer ear canal.

√4th **18.7**   **Other plastic repair of external ear**

   18.71   **Construction of auricle of ear**
> Prosthetic appliance for absent ear
> Reconstruction:
>   auricle
>   ear
> **DEF:** Reformation or repair of external ear flap.

   18.72   **Reattachment of amputated ear**

   18.79   **Other plastic repair of external ear**
> Otoplasty NOS
> Postauricular skin graft
> Repair of lop ear
> **DEF:** Postauricular skin graft: Graft repair behind ear.
> **DEF:** Repair of lop ear: Reconstruction of ear that is at right angle to head.
> **AHA:** 3Q, '03, 12

   18.9   **Other operations on external ear**
> **EXCLUDES**   *irrigation of ear (96.52)*
>   *packing of external auditory canal (96.11)*
>   *removal of:*
>   *cerumen (96.52)*
>   *foreign body (without incision) (98.11)*

√3rd **19**   **Reconstructive operations on middle ear**

   19.0   **Stapes mobilization**
> Division, otosclerotic: Remobilization of stapes
>   material   Stapediolysis
>   process   Transcrural stapes mobilization
> **EXCLUDES**   *that with synchronous stapedectomy (19.11-19.19)*
>
> **DEF:** Repair of innermost bone of middle ear to enable movement and response to sound.

√4th **19.1**   **Stapedectomy**
> **EXCLUDES**   *revision of previous stapedectomy (19.21-19.29)*
>   *stapes mobilization only (19.0)*
>
> **DEF:** Removal of innermost bone of middle ear.

   19.11   **Stapedectomy with incus replacement**
> Stapedectomy with incus:
>   homograft
>   prosthesis
> **DEF:** Removal of innermost bone of middle ear with autograft or prosthesis replacement.

   19.19   **Other stapedectomy**

√4th **19.2**   **Revision of stapedectomy**

   19.21   **Revision of stapedectomy with incus replacement**

   19.29   **Other revision of stapedectomy**

   19.3   **Other operations on ossicular chain**
> Incudectomy NOS
> Ossiculectomy NOS
> Reconstruction of ossicles, second stage
> **DEF:** Incudectomy: Excision of middle bone of middle ear, not otherwise specified.
> **DEF:** Ossiculectomy: Excision of middle ear bones, not otherwise specified.
> **DEF:** Reconstruction of ossicles, second stage: Repair of middle ear bones following previous surgery.

Stapedectomy with Incus Replacement

Incus

Stapes with footplate in oval window

Malleus

Handle of malleus

Wire piston

Tympanic membrane

Cochlea

▓ Area excised   Tissue seal on oval window

BI Bilateral Procedure   **NC** Non-covered Procedure   **LC** Limited Coverage Procedure   ▶◀ Revised Text   ● New Code   ▲ Revised Code Title

92 – Volume 3   **2010 ICD-9-CM**

19.4 **Myringoplasty**

Epitympanic, type I
Myringoplasty by:
   cauterization
   graft
Tympanoplasty (type I)

DEF: Epitympanic, type I: Repair over or upon eardrum.

DEF: Myringoplasty by cauterization: Plastic repair of tympanic membrane of eardrum by heat.

DEF: Graft: Plastic repair using implanted tissue.

DEF: Tympanoplasty (type I): Reconstruction of eardrum to restore hearing.

√4ᵗʰ 19.5 **Other tympanoplasty**

19.52 **Type II tympanoplasty**

Closure of perforation with graft against incus or malleus

19.53 **Type III tympanoplasty**

Graft placed in contact with mobile and intact stapes

AHA: M-A, '85, 15

TIP: Assign for a total ossicular replacement prosthesis (TORP) procedure.

19.54 **Type IV tympanoplasty**

Mobile footplate left exposed with air pocket between round window and graft

19.55 **Type V tympanoplasty**

Fenestra in horizontal semicircular canal covered by graft

19.6 **Revision of tympanoplasty**

DEF: Repair or correction of previous plastic surgery on eardrum.

19.9 **Other repair of middle ear**

Closure of mastoid fistula
Mastoid myoplasty
Obliteration of tympanomastoid cavity

DEF: Closure of mastoid fistula: Closing of abnormal channel in mastoid.

DEF: Mastoid myoplasty: Restoration or repair of mastoid muscle.

DEF: Obliteration of tympanomastoid cavity: Removal, total, of functional elements of middle ear.

√3ʳᵈ **20** **Other operations on middle and inner ear**

√4ᵗʰ 20.0 **Myringotomy**

DEF: Myringotomy: Puncture of tympanic membrane or eardrum, also called tympanocentesis

20.01 **Myringotomy with insertion of tube**

Myringostomy

20.09 **Other myringotomy**

Aspiration of middle ear NOS

20.1 **Removal of tympanostomy tube**

√4ᵗʰ 20.2 **Incision of mastoid and middle ear**

20.21 **Incision of mastoid**

20.22 **Incision of petrous pyramid air cells**

20.23 **Incision of middle ear**

Atticotomy
Division of tympanum
Lysis of adhesions of middle ear

EXCLUDES *division of otosclerotic process (19.0)*
stapediolysis (19.0)
that with stapedectomy (19.11-19.19)

√4ᵗʰ 20.3 **Diagnostic procedures on middle and inner ear**

20.31 **Electrocochleography**

DEF: Measure of electric potential of eighth cranial nerve by electrode applied sound.

20.32 **Biopsy of middle and inner ear**

20.39 **Other diagnostic procedures on middle and inner ear**

EXCLUDES *auditory and vestibular function tests (89.13, 95.41-95.49)*
microscopic examination of specimen from ear (90.31-90.39)

√4ᵗʰ 20.4 **Mastoidectomy**

Code also any:
   skin graft (18.79)
   tympanoplasty (19.4-19.55)

EXCLUDES *that with implantation of cochlear prosthetic device (20.96-20.98)*

DEF: Mastoidectomy: Excision of bony protrusion behind ear.

20.41 **Simple mastoidectomy**

20.42 **Radical mastoidectomy**

20.49 **Other mastoidectomy**

Atticoantrostomy
Mastoidectomy:
   NOS
   modified radical

DEF: Atticoantrotomy: Opening of cavity of mastoid bone and middle ear.

√4ᵗʰ 20.5 **Other excision of middle ear**

EXCLUDES *that with synchronous mastoidectomy (20.41-20.49)*

20.51 **Excision of lesion of middle ear**

EXCLUDES *biopsy of middle ear (20.32)*

20.59 **Other**

Apicectomy of petrous pyramid
Tympanectomy

√4ᵗʰ 20.6 **Fenestration of inner ear**

20.61 **Fenestration of inner ear (initial)**

Fenestration of:
   labyrinth
   semicircular canals } with graft (skin)
   vestibule (vein)

EXCLUDES *that with tympanoplasty, type V (19.55)*

DEF: Creation of inner ear opening.

20.62 **Revision of fenestration of inner ear**

√4ᵗʰ 20.7 **Incision, excision, and destruction of inner ear**

20.71 **Endolymphatic shunt**

DEF: Insertion of tube to drain fluid in inner ear cavities.

20.72 **Injection into inner ear**

Destruction by injection (alcohol):
   inner ear
   semicircular canals
   vestibule

20.79 **Other incision, excision, and destruction of inner ear**

Decompression of labyrinth
Drainage of inner ear
Fistulization:
   endolymphatic sac
   labyrinth
Incision of endolymphatic sac
Labyrinthectomy (transtympanic)
Opening of bony labyrinth
Perilymphatic tap

EXCLUDES *biopsy of inner ear (20.32)*

DEF: Decompression of labyrinth: Controlled relief of pressure in cavities of inner ear.

DEF: Drainage of inner ear: Removal of fluid from inner ear.

DEF: Fistulization of endolymphatic sac: Creation of passage to fluid sac in inner ear cavities.

DEF: Fistulization of labyrinth: Creation of passage to inner ear cavities.

DEF: Incision of endolymphatic sac: Cutting into fluid sac in inner ear cavities.

DEF: Labyrinthectomy (transtympanic): Excision of cavities across eardrum.

DEF: Opening of bony labyrinth: Cutting into inner ear bony cavities.

DEF: Perilymphatic tap: Puncture or incision into fluid sac of inner ear cavities.

√3ʳᵈ
√4ᵗʰ Additional Digit Required   Valid OR Procedure   Non-OR Procedure   Adjunct Code
2010 ICD-9-CM   **Volume 3 – 93**

Operations on the Ear

20.8 **Operations on Eustachian tube**

Catheterization
Inflation
Injection (Teflon paste)
Insufflation (boric
   acid-salicylic acid)   } of Eustachian tube
Intubation
Politzerization

DEF: Catheterization: Passing catheter into passage between pharynx and middle ear.

DEF: Inflation: Blowing air, gas or liquid into passage between pharynx and middle ear to inflate.

DEF: Injection (Teflon paste): Forcing fluid (Teflon paste) into passage between pharynx and middle ear.

DEF: Insufflation (boric acid-salicylic acid): Blowing gas or liquid into passage between pharynx and middle ear.

DEF: Intubation: Placing tube into passage between pharynx and middle ear.

DEF: Politzerization: Inflating passage between pharynx and middle ear with Politzer bag.

✓4ᵗʰ **20.9** **Other operations on inner and middle ear**

20.91 **Tympanosympathectomy**

DEF: Excision or chemical suppression of impulses of middle ear nerves.

20.92 **Revision of mastoidectomy**

AHA: 2Q, '98, 20

DEF: Correction of previous removal of mastoid cells from temporal or mastoid bone.

20.93 **Repair of oval and round windows**

Closure of fistula:
   oval window
   perilymph
   round window

DEF: Restoration of middle ear openings.

20.94 **Injection of tympanum**

20.95 **Implantation of electromagnetic hearing device**

Bone conduction hearing device

EXCLUDES cochlear prosthetic device (20.96-20.98)

AHA: 3Q, '07, 4; 4Q, '89, 5

20.96 **Implantation or replacement of cochlear prosthetic device, not otherwise specified**

Implantation of receiver (within skull) and insertion of electrode(s) in the cochlea

INCLUDES mastoidectomy

EXCLUDES electromagnetic hearing device (20.95)

AHA: 4Q, '89, 5

20.97 **Implantation or replacement of cochlear prosthetic device, single channel**

Implantation of receiver (within skull) and insertion of electrode in the cochlea

INCLUDES mastoidectomy

EXCLUDES electromagnetic hearing device (20.95)

AHA: 4Q, '89, 5

20.98 **Implantation or replacement of cochlear prosthetic device, multiple channel**

Implantation of receiver (within skull) and insertion of electrodes in the cochlea

INCLUDES mastoidectomy

EXCLUDES electromagnetic hearing device (20.95)

AHA: 4Q, '89, 5

20.99 **Other operations on middle and inner ear**

Attachment of percutaneous abutment (screw) for prosthetic device

Repair or removal of cochlear prosthetic device (receiver) (electrode)

EXCLUDES adjustment (external components) of cochlear prosthetic device (95.49)

fitting of hearing aid (95.48)

AHA: 3Q, '07, 4; 4Q, '89, 7

BI Bilateral Procedure   **NC** Non-covered Procedure   **LC** Limited Coverage Procedure   ▶◀ Revised Text   ● New Code   ▲ Revised Code Title

94 – Volume 3   **2010 ICD-9-CM**

5. OPERATIONS ON THE NOSE, MOUTH, AND PHARYNX (21-29)

√3ʳᵈ **21 Operations on nose**

INCLUDES operations on:
   bone
   skin } of nose

AHA: 1Q, '94, 5

√4ᵗʰ **21.0 Control of epistaxis**

21.00 Control of epistaxis, not otherwise specified

21.01 Control of epistaxis by anterior nasal packing

21.02 Control of epistaxis by posterior (and anterior) packing

21.03 Control of epistaxis by cauterization (and packing)

21.04 Control of epistaxis by ligation of ethmoidal arteries

21.05 Control of epistaxis by (transantral) ligation of the maxillary artery

21.06 Control of epistaxis by ligation of the external carotid artery

21.07 Control of epistaxis by excision of nasal mucosa and skin grafting of septum and lateral nasal wall

21.09 Control of epistaxis by other means

21.1 Incision of nose
   Chondrotomy
   Incision of skin of nose
   Nasal septotomy
   DEF: Chondrotomy: Incision or division of nasal cartilage.
   DEF: Nasal septotomy: Incision into bone dividing nose into two chambers.

√4ᵗʰ **21.2 Diagnostic procedures on nose**

21.21 Rhinoscopy
   DEF: Visualization of nasal passage with nasal speculum.

21.22 Biopsy of nose

21.29 Other diagnostic procedures on nose
   EXCLUDES microscopic examination of specimen from nose (90.31-90.39)
      nasal:
         function study (89.12)
         x-ray (87.16)
      rhinomanometry (89.12)

√4ᵗʰ **21.3 Local excision or destruction of lesion of nose**
   EXCLUDES biopsy of nose (21.22)
      nasal fistulectomy (21.82)

21.30 Excision or destruction of lesion of nose, not otherwise specified

21.31 Local excision or destruction of intranasal lesion
   Nasal polypectomy

21.32 Local excision or destruction of other lesion of nose
   AHA: 2Q, '89, 16

21.4 Resection of nose
   Amputation of nose

21.5 Submucous resection of nasal septum
   DEF: Resection, partial, of nasal septum with mucosa reimplanted after excision.

√4ᵗʰ **21.6 Turbinectomy**
   DEF: Removal, partial, or total of turbinate bones; inferior turbinate is most often excised.

21.61 Turbinectomy by diathermy or cryosurgery
   DEF: Destruction of turbinate bone by heat or freezing.

21.62 Fracture of the turbinates
   DEF: Surgical breaking of turbinate bones.

Excision of Turbinate

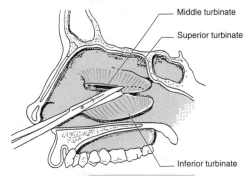

- Middle turbinate
- Superior turbinate
- Inferior turbinate

21.69 Other turbinectomy
   EXCLUDES turbinectomy associated with sinusectomy (22.31-22.39, 22.42, 22.60-22.64)

√4ᵗʰ **21.7 Reduction of nasal fracture**

21.71 Closed reduction of nasal fracture

21.72 Open reduction of nasal fracture

√4ᵗʰ **21.8 Repair and plastic operations on the nose**

21.81 Suture of laceration of nose

21.82 Closure of nasal fistula
   Nasolabial
   Nasopharyngeal } fistulectomy
   Oronasal
   DEF: Sealing off crack or hole between nose and lip, nose and pharynx, or nose and mouth.

21.83 Total nasal reconstruction
   Reconstruction of nose with:
      arm flap
      forehead flap
   DEF: Reformation, plastic, of nasal structure with tissue flap from arm or forehead.

21.84 Revision rhinoplasty
   Rhinoseptoplasty
   Twisted nose rhinoplasty
   DEF: Rhinoseptoplasty: Repair of nose and the bone dividing the nose into two chambers.
   DEF: Twisted nose rhinoplasty: Repair of nose alignment following reconstructive surgery.

21.85 Augmentation rhinoplasty
   Augmentation rhinoplasty with:
      graft
      synthetic implant
   DEF: Implant of tissue or synthetic graft to enlarge nose.

21.86 Limited rhinoplasty
   Plastic repair of nasolabial flaps
   Tip rhinoplasty
   DEF: Plastic repair of nasolabial flaps: Reconstruction of nasal area above lips.
   DEF: Tip rhinoplasty: Reconstruction or restoration of nasal tip.

21.87 Other rhinoplasty
   Rhinoplasty NOS

21.88 Other septoplasty
   Crushing of nasal septum
   Repair of septal perforation
   EXCLUDES septoplasty associated with submucous resection of septum (21.5)
   DEF: Crushing of nasal septum: Division and reconstruction of defects in bone dividing nasal chambers.
   DEF: Repair of septal perforation: Repair of hole in bone dividing nasal chambers with adjacent tissue.

21.89 Other repair and plastic operations on nose
   Reattachment of amputated nose

√3ʳᵈ / √4ᵗʰ Additional Digit Required   Valid OR Procedure   Non-OR Procedure   Adjunct Code

Operations on the Nose, Mouth, and Pharynx   *21.9–24.2*

✓4ᵗʰ **21.9** **Other operations on nose**

21.91 **Lysis of adhesions of nose**
Posterior nasal scrub

DEF: Posterior nasal scrub: Clearing out of abnormal adhesions in posterior nasal area.

21.99 **Other**

EXCLUDES *dilation of frontonasal duct (96.21)*
irrigation of nasal passages (96.53)
removal of:
    intraluminal foreign body without
      incision (98.12)
    nasal packing (97.32)
    replacement of nasal packing (97.21)

✓3ʳᵈ **22** **Operations on nasal sinuses**

✓4ᵗʰ **22.0** **Aspiration and lavage of nasal sinus**

22.00 **Aspiration and lavage of nasal sinus, not otherwise specified**

22.01 **Puncture of nasal sinus for aspiration or lavage**

22.02 **Aspiration or lavage of nasal sinus through natural ostium**

DEF: Withdrawal of fluid and washing of nasal cavity through natural opening.

✓4ᵗʰ **22.1** **Diagnostic procedures on nasal sinus**

22.11 **Closed [endoscopic] [needle] biopsy of nasal sinus**

22.12 **Open biopsy of nasal sinus**

22.19 **Other diagnostic procedures on nasal sinuses**
Endoscopy without biopsy

EXCLUDES *transillumination of sinus (89.35)*
x-ray of sinus (87.15-87.16)

22.2 **Intranasal antrotomy**

EXCLUDES *antrotomy with external approach (22.31-22.39)*

DEF: Incision of intranasal sinus.

✓4ᵗʰ **22.3** **External maxillary antrotomy**

22.31 **Radical maxillary antrotomy**
Removal of lining membrane of maxillary sinus using Caldwell-Luc approach

DEF: Caldwell-Luc approach: Removal of membrane lining the maxillary cavity through incision above canine teeth.

22.39 **Other external maxillary antrotomy**
Exploration of maxillary antrum with Caldwell-Luc approach

✓4ᵗʰ **22.4** **Frontal sinusotomy and sinusectomy**

22.41 **Frontal sinusotomy**

22.42 **Frontal sinusectomy**
Excision of lesion of frontal sinus
Obliteration of frontal sinus (with fat)

EXCLUDES *biopsy of nasal sinus (22.11-22.12)*

✓4ᵗʰ **22.5** **Other nasal sinusotomy**

22.50 **Sinusotomy, not otherwise specified**

22.51 **Ethmoidotomy**

22.52 **Sphenoidotomy**

22.53 **Incision of multiple nasal sinuses**

✓4ᵗʰ **22.6** **Other nasal sinusectomy**

INCLUDES *that with incidental turbinectomy*
EXCLUDES *biopsy of nasal sinus (22.11-22.12)*

22.60 **Sinusectomy, not otherwise specified**

22.61 **Excision of lesion of maxillary sinus with Caldwell-Luc approach**

22.62 **Excision of lesion of maxillary sinus with other approach**

22.63 **Ethmoidectomy**

DEF: Removal of ethmoid cells and bone, partial or total includes excising mucosal lining, partial or total.

22.64 **Sphenoidectomy**

DEF: Removal of wedge shaped sphenoid bone at base of brain.

✓4ᵗʰ **22.7** **Repair of nasal sinus**

22.71 **Closure of nasal sinus fistula**
Repair of oro-antral fistula

22.79 **Other repair of nasal sinus**
Reconstruction of frontonasal duct
Repair of bone of accessory sinus

22.9 **Other operations on nasal sinuses**
Exteriorization of maxillary sinus
Fistulization of sinus

EXCLUDES *dilation of frontonasal duct (96.21)*

DEF: Exteriorization of maxillary sinus: Creation of external maxillary cavity opening.

DEF: Fistulization of sinus: Creation of fistula canal in nasal cavity.

✓3ʳᵈ **23** **Removal and restoration of teeth**

✓4ᵗʰ **23.0** **Forceps extraction of tooth**

23.01 **Extraction of deciduous tooth**

23.09 **Extraction of other tooth**
Extraction of tooth NOS

✓4ᵗʰ **23.1** **Surgical removal of tooth**

23.11 **Removal of residual root**

23.19 **Other surgical extraction of tooth**
Odontectomy NOS
Removal of impacted tooth
Tooth extraction with elevation of mucoperiosteal flap

23.2 **Restoration of tooth by filling**

23.3 **Restoration of tooth by inlay**

DEF: Restoration of tooth by cementing in a molded filling.

✓4ᵗʰ **23.4** **Other dental restoration**

23.41 **Application of crown**

23.42 **Insertion of fixed bridge**

23.43 **Insertion of removable bridge**

23.49 **Other**

23.5 **Implantation of tooth**

DEF: Insertion of a sound tooth to replace extracted tooth.

23.6 **Prosthetic dental implant**
Endosseous dental implant

DEF: Implant of artificial denture within bone covering tooth socket.

✓4ᵗʰ **23.7** **Apicoectomy and root canal therapy**

23.70 **Root canal, not otherwise specified**

23.71 **Root canal therapy with irrigation**

23.72 **Root canal therapy with apicoectomy**

DEF: Removal of tooth root to treat damaged root canal tissue.

23.73 **Apicoectomy**

✓3ʳᵈ **24** **Other operations on teeth, gums, and alveoli**

24.0 **Incision of gum or alveolar bone**
Apical alveolotomy

✓4ᵗʰ **24.1** **Diagnostic procedures on teeth, gums, and alveoli**

24.11 **Biopsy of gum**

24.12 **Biopsy of alveolus**

24.19 **Other diagnostic procedures on teeth, gums, and alveoli**

EXCLUDES *dental:*
    examination (89.31)
    x-ray:
      full-mouth (87.11)
      other (87.12)
    microscopic examination of dental
      specimen (90.81-90.89)

24.2 **Gingivoplasty**
Gingivoplasty with bone or soft tissue graft

DEF: Repair of gum tissue.

BI Bilateral Procedure   **NC** Non-covered Procedure   **LC** Limited Coverage Procedure   ▶◀ Revised Text   ● New Code   ▲ Revised Code Title

√4ᵗʰ 24.3 Other operations on gum

24.31 **Excision of lesion or tissue of gum**
  EXCLUDES *biopsy of gum (24.11)*
  excision of odontogenic lesion (24.4)

24.32 **Suture of laceration of gum**

24.39 **Other**

24.4 Excision of dental lesion of jaw
  Excision of odontogenic lesion

24.5 Alveoloplasty
  Alveolectomy (interradicular) (intraseptal) (radical) (simple)
  (with graft or implant)
  EXCLUDES *biopsy of alveolus (24.12)*
  en bloc resection of alveolar process and palate
  (27.32)
  DEF: Repair or correction of bony tooth socket.

24.6 Exposure of tooth

24.7 Application of orthodontic appliance
  Application, insertion, or fitting of:
  arch bars
  orthodontic obturator
  orthodontic wiring
  periodontal splint
  EXCLUDES *nonorthodontic dental wiring (93.55)*

24.8 Other orthodontic operation
  Closure of diastema (alveolar) (dental)
  Occlusal adjustment
  Removal of arch bars
  Repair of dental arch
  EXCLUDES *removal of nonorthodontic wiring (97.33)*

√4ᵗʰ 24.9 Other dental operations

24.91 **Extension or deepening of buccolabial or lingual sulcus**

24.99 **Other**
  EXCLUDES *dental:*
  debridement (96.54)
  examination (89.31)
  prophylaxis (96.54)
  scaling and polishing (96.54)
  wiring (93.55)
  fitting of dental appliance [denture]
  (99.97)
  microscopic examination of dental
  specimen (90.81-90.89)
  removal of dental:
  packing (97.34)
  prosthesis (97.35)
  wiring (97.33)
  replacement of dental packing (97.22)

√3ʳᵈ 25 Operations on tongue

√4ᵗʰ 25.0 Diagnostic procedures on tongue

25.01 **Closed [needle] biopsy of tongue**

25.02 **Open biopsy of tongue**
  Wedge biopsy

25.09 **Other diagnostic procedures on tongue**

25.1 Excision or destruction of lesion or tissue of tongue
  EXCLUDES *biopsy of tongue (25.01-25.02)*
  frenumectomy:
  labial (27.41)
  lingual (25.92)
  AHA: 2Q, '02, 5
  TIP: Assign for tongue-based somnoplasty procedure, a temperature-controlled radiofrequency-based technology, used for treatment of obstructive sleep apnea.

25.2 Partial glossectomy

25.3 Complete glossectomy
  Glossectomy NOS
  Code also any neck dissection (40.40-40.42)

25.4 Radical glossectomy
  Code also any:
  neck dissection (40.40-40.42)
  tracheostomy (31.1-31.29)

√4ᵗʰ 25.5 Repair of tongue and glossoplasty

25.51 **Suture of laceration of tongue**

25.59 **Other repair and plastic operations on tongue**
  Fascial sling of tongue
  Fusion of tongue (to lip)
  Graft of mucosa or skin to tongue
  EXCLUDES *lysis of adhesions of tongue (25.93)*
  AHA: 1Q, '97, 5
  TIP: Assign for genioglossus advancement, which may be performed in association with uvulopalatopharyngoplasty (UPPP).

√4ᵗʰ 25.9 Other operations on tongue

25.91 **Lingual frenotomy**
  EXCLUDES *labial frenotomy (27.91)*
  DEF: Extension of groove between cheek and lips or cheek and tongue.

25.92 **Lingual frenectomy**
  EXCLUDES *labial frenectomy (27.41)*
  DEF: Frenectomy: Removal of vertical membrane attaching tongue to floor of mouth.

25.93 **Lysis of adhesions of tongue**

25.94 **Other glossotomy**

25.99 **Other**

√3ʳᵈ 26 Operations on salivary glands and ducts
  INCLUDES operations on:
  lesser salivary
  parotid } gland and duct
  sublingual
  submaxillry
  Code also any neck dissection (40.40-40.42)

26.0 Incision of salivary gland or duct

√4ᵗʰ 26.1 Diagnostic procedures on salivary glands and ducts

26.11 **Closed [needle] biopsy of salivary gland or duct**

26.12 **Open biopsy of salivary gland or duct**

26.19 **Other diagnostic procedures on salivary glands and ducts**
  EXCLUDES *x-ray of salivary gland (87.09)*

√4ᵗʰ 26.2 Excision of lesion of salivary gland

26.21 **Marsupialization of salivary gland cyst**
  DEF: Creation of pouch of salivary gland cyst to drain and promote healing.

26.29 **Other excision of salivary gland lesion**
  EXCLUDES *biopsy of salivary gland (26.11-26.12)*
  salivary fistulectomy (26.42)

√4ᵗʰ 26.3 Sialoadenectomy
  DEF: Removal of salivary gland.

26.30 **Sialoadenectomy, not otherwise specified**

26.31 **Partial sialoadenectomy**

26.32 **Complete sialoadenectomy**
  En bloc excision of salivary gland lesion
  Radical sialoadenectomy

√4ᵗʰ 26.4 Repair of salivary gland or duct

26.41 **Suture of laceration of salivary gland**

26.42 **Closure of salivary fistula**
  DEF: Closing of abnormal opening in salivary gland.

26.49 **Other repair and plastic operations on salivary gland or duct**
  Fistulization of salivary gland
  Plastic repair of salivary gland or duct NOS
  Transplantation of salivary duct opening

√4ᵗʰ 26.9 Other operations on salivary gland or duct

26.91 **Probing of salivary duct**

26.99 **Other**

Operations on the Nose, Mouth, and Pharynx

27–27.99

√3rd **27 Other operations on mouth and face**

INCLUDES operations on:
  lips
  palate
  soft tissue of face and mouth, except tongue and gingiva
EXCLUDES operations on:
  gingiva (24.0-24.99)
  tongue (25.01-25.99)

27.0 Drainage of face and floor of mouth
Drainage of:
  facial region (abscess)
  fascial compartment of face
  Ludwig's angina
EXCLUDES drainage of thyroglossal tract (06.09)

27.1 Incision of palate

√4th **27.2 Diagnostic procedures on oral cavity**

27.21 Biopsy of bony palate

27.22 Biopsy of uvula and soft palate

27.23 Biopsy of lip

27.24 Biopsy of mouth, unspecified structure

27.29 Other diagnostic procedures on oral cavity
EXCLUDES soft tissue x-ray (87.09)

√4th **27.3 Excision of lesion or tissue of bony palate**

27.31 Local excision or destruction of lesion or tissue of bony palate
Local excision or destruction of palate by:
  cautery
  chemotherapy
  cryotherapy
EXCLUDES biopsy of bony palate (27.21)

27.32 Wide excision or destruction of lesion or tissue of bony palate
En bloc resection of alveolar process and palate

√4th **27.4 Excision of other parts of mouth**

27.41 Labial frenectomy
EXCLUDES division of labial frenum (27.91)
DEF: Removal of mucous membrane fold of lip.

27.42 Wide excision of lesion of lip

27.43 Other excision of lesion or tissue of lip

27.49 Other excision of mouth
EXCLUDES biopsy of mouth NOS (27.24)
  excision of lesion of:
    palate (27.31-27.32)
    tongue (25.1)
    uvula (27.72)
  fistulectomy of mouth (27.53)
  frenectomy of:
    lip (27.41)
    tongue (25.92)

AHA: 2Q, '05, 8

TIP: Assign for "composite resection," which includes the mandible and floor of the mouth, performed for mandibular carcinoma. Codes for bone and lymph node resection should also be assigned.

▲ √4th **27.5 Plastic repair of lip and mouth**
EXCLUDES palatoplasty (27.61-27.69)

27.51 Suture of laceration of lip

27.52 Suture of laceration of other part of mouth

27.53 Closure of fistula of mouth
EXCLUDES fistulectomy:
  nasolabial (21.82)
  oro-antral (22.71)
  oronasal (21.82)

27.54 Repair of cleft lip

27.55 Full-thickness skin graft to lip and mouth

27.56 Other skin graft to lip and mouth

27.57 Attachment of pedicle or flap graft to lip and mouth
AHA: 1Q, '96, 14
DEF: Repair of lip or mouth with tissue pedicle or flap still connected to original vascular base.

27.59 Other plastic repair of mouth

√4th **27.6 Palatoplasty**

27.61 Suture of laceration of palate

27.62 Correction of cleft palate
Correction of cleft palate by push-back operation
EXCLUDES revision of cleft palate repair (27.63)

27.63 Revision of cleft palate repair
Secondary:
  attachment of pharyngeal flap
  lengthening of palate
AHA: 1Q, '96, 14

27.64 Insertion of palatal implant
DEF: Nonabsorbable polyester implants into the soft palate at the back of the roof of the mouth; one implant placed at the soft palate midline and two are positioned on either side; to support and stiffen the palate reducing vibration (snoring).

27.69 Other plastic repair of palate
Code also any insertion of palatal implant (27.64)
EXCLUDES fistulectomy of mouth (27.53)
AHA: 3Q, '99, 22; 1Q, '97, 14; 3Q, '92, 18
TIP: Assign for uvulopalatopharyngoplasty (UPPP), along with code 29.4 Plastic operation on pharynx, along with additional codes for hyoid suspension and genioglossus advancement, if performed.

√4th **27.7 Operations on uvula**

27.71 Incision of uvula

27.72 Excision of uvula
EXCLUDES biopsy of uvula (27.22)

27.73 Repair of uvula
EXCLUDES that with synchronous cleft palate repair (27.62)
  uranostaphylorrhaphy (27.62)

27.79 Other operations on uvula
AHA: 3Q, '92, 18

√4th **27.9 Other operations on mouth and face**

27.91 Labial frenotomy
Division of labial frenum
EXCLUDES lingual frenotomy (25.91)
DEF: Division of labial frenum: Cutting and separating mucous membrane fold of lip.

27.92 Incision of mouth, unspecified structure
EXCLUDES incision of:
  gum (24.0)
  palate (27.1)
  salivary gland or duct (26.0)
  tongue (25.94)
  uvula (27.71)

27.99 Other operations on oral cavity
Graft of buccal sulcus
EXCLUDES removal of:
  intraluminal foreign body (98.01)
  penetrating foreign body from mouth without incision (98.22)
DEF: Graft of buccal sulcus: Implant of tissue into groove of interior cheek lining.

√3rd **28 Operations on tonsils and adenoids**

28.0 **Incision and drainage of tonsil and peritonsillar structures**
Drainage (oral) (transcervical) of:
parapharyngeal
peritonsillar ⎱ abscess
retropharyngeal ⎰
tonsillar

√4th 28.1 **Diagnostic procedures on tonsils and adenoids**

28.11 **Biopsy of tonsils and adenoids**

28.19 **Other diagnostic procedures on tonsils and adenoids**
EXCLUDES   *soft tissue x-ray (87.09)*

28.2 **Tonsillectomy without adenoidectomy**
AHA: 1Q, '97, 5; 2Q, '90, 23

28.3 **Tonsillectomy with adenoidectomy**
AHA: 2Q, '05, 16

28.4 **Excision of tonsil tag**

28.5 **Excision of lingual tonsil**

28.6 **Adenoidectomy without tonsillectomy**
Excision of adenoid tag

28.7 **Control of hemorrhage after tonsillectomy and adenoidectomy**
AHA: 2Q, '05, 16

√4th 28.9 **Other operations on tonsils and adenoids**

28.91 **Removal of foreign body from tonsil and adenoid by incision**
EXCLUDES   *that without incision (98.13)*

28.92 **Excision of lesion of tonsil and adenoid**
EXCLUDES   *biopsy of tonsil and adenoid (28.11)*

28.99 **Other**

√3rd **29 Operations on pharynx**
INCLUDES   operations on:
hypopharynx
nasopharynx
oropharynx
pharyngeal pouch
pyriform sinus

29.0 **Pharyngotomy**
Drainage of pharyngeal bursa
EXCLUDES   *incision and drainage of retropharyngeal abscess (28.0)*
removal of foreign body (without incision) (98.13)

√4th 29.1 **Diagnostic procedures on pharynx**

29.11 **Pharyngoscopy**

29.12 **Pharyngeal biopsy**
Biopsy of supraglottic mass

29.19 **Other diagnostic procedures on pharynx**
EXCLUDES   *x-ray of nasopharynx:*
contrast (87.06)
other (87.09)

29.2 **Excision of branchial cleft cyst or vestige**
EXCLUDES   *branchial cleft fistulectomy (29.52)*

√4th 29.3 **Excision or destruction of lesion or tissue of pharynx**
AHA: 2Q, '89, 18

29.31 **Cricopharyngeal myotomy**
EXCLUDES   *that with pharyngeal diverticulectomy (29.32)*
DEF: Removal of outward pouching of throat.

29.32 **Pharyngeal diverticulectomy**

29.33 **Pharyngectomy (partial)**
EXCLUDES   *laryngopharyngectomy (30.3)*

29.39 **Other excision or destruction of lesion or tissue of pharynx**

29.4 **Plastic operation on pharynx**
Correction of nasopharyngeal atresia
EXCLUDES   *pharyngoplasty associated with cleft palate repair (27.62-27.63)*
AHA: 3Q, '99, 22; 1Q, '97, 5; 3Q, '92, 18
DEF: Correction of nasopharyngeal atresia: Construction of normal opening for throat stricture behind nose.
TIP: Assign for uvulopalatopharyngoplasty (UPPP), secondary to code 27.69 Other plastic repair of the palate. Report additional codes for hyoid suspension and genioglossus advancement, if performed.

√4th 29.5 **Other repair of pharynx**

29.51 **Suture of laceration of pharynx**

29.52 **Closure of branchial cleft fistula**
DEF: Sealing off an abnormal opening of the branchial fissure in throat.

29.53 **Closure of other fistula of pharynx**
Pharyngoesophageal fistulectomy

29.54 **Lysis of pharyngeal adhesions**

29.59 **Other**
AHA: 2Q, '89, 18

√4th 29.9 **Other operations on pharynx**

29.91 **Dilation of pharynx**
Dilation of nasopharynx

29.92 **Division of glossopharyngeal nerve**

29.99 **Other**
EXCLUDES   *insertion of radium into pharynx and nasopharynx (92.27)*
removal of intraluminal foreign body (98.13)

Operations on the Respiratory System

30–31.72

6. OPERATIONS ON THE RESPIRATORY SYSTEM (30-34)

√3ʳᵈ 30   Excision of larynx

  √4ᵗʰ 30.0   Excision or destruction of lesion or tissue of larynx

    30.01   Marsupialization of laryngeal cyst
      DEF: Incision of cyst of larynx with the edges sutured open to create pouch.

    30.09   Other excision or destruction of lesion or lesion or tissue of larynx
      Stripping of vocal cords
      EXCLUDES   *biopsy of larynx (31.43)*
           laryngeal fistulectomy (31.62)
           laryngotracheal fistulectomy (31.62)

  30.1   Hemilaryngectomy
    DEF: Excision of one side (half) of larynx.

  √4ᵗʰ 30.2   Other partial laryngectomy

    30.21   Epiglottidectomy

    30.22   Vocal cordectomy
      Excision of vocal cords

    30.29   Other partial laryngectomy
      Excision of laryngeal cartilage

  30.3   Complete laryngectomy
    Block dissection of larynx (with thyroidectomy) (with synchronous tracheostomy)
    Laryngopharyngectomy
    EXCLUDES   *that with radical neck dissection (30.4)*

  30.4   Radical laryngectomy
    Complete [total] laryngectomy with radical neck dissection (with thyroidectomy) (with synchronous tracheostomy)

√3ʳᵈ 31   Other operations on larynx and trachea

  31.0   Injection of larynx
    Injection of inert material into larynx or vocal cords

  31.1   Temporary tracheostomy
    Temporary percutaneous dilatational tracheostomy [PDT]
    Tracheotomy for assistance in breathing
    Code also any synchronous bronchoscopy, if performed (33.21-33.24, 33.27)
    AHA: 1Q, '97, 6
    TIP: Assign for a procedure described as a mini-tracheostomy.

  √4ᵗʰ 31.2   Permanent tracheostomy

    31.21   Mediastinal tracheostomy
      DEF: Placement of artificial breathing tube in windpipe through mediastinum, for long-term use.

    31.29   Other permanent tracheostomy
      Permanent percutaneous dilatational tracheostomy [PDT]
      Code also any synchronous bronchoscopy, if performed (33.21-33.24, 33.27)
      EXCLUDES   *that with laryngectomy (30.3-30.4)*
      AHA: 2Q, '05, 8; 2Q, '02, 6

  31.3   Other incision of larynx or trachea
    EXCLUDES   *that for assistance in breathing (31.1-31.29)*

Temporary Tracheostomy

Trachea

Tracheostomy tube

In place

Closed Endoscopic Biopsy of Larynx

Laryngoscope

Trachea

Palate

Growth on vocal cord

  √4ᵗʰ 31.4   Diagnostic procedures on larynx and trachea

    31.41   Tracheoscopy through artificial stoma
      EXCLUDES   *that with biopsy (31.43-31.44)*
      DEF: Exam by scope of trachea through an artificial opening.

    31.42   Laryngoscopy and other tracheoscopy
      EXCLUDES   *that with biopsy (31.43-31.44)*

    31.43   Closed [endoscopic] biopsy of larynx

    31.44   Closed [endoscopic] biopsy of trachea

    31.45   Open biopsy of larynx or trachea

    31.48   Other diagnostic procedures on larynx
      EXCLUDES   *contrast laryngogram (87.07)*
           microscopic examination of specimen from larynx (90.31-90.39)
           soft tissue x-ray of larynx NEC (87.09)

    31.49   Other diagnostic procedures on trachea
      EXCLUDES   *microscopic examination of specimen from trachea (90.41-90.49)*
           x-ray of trachea (87.49)

  31.5   Local excision or destruction of lesion or tissue of trachea
    EXCLUDES   *biopsy of trachea (31.44-31.45)*
           laryngotracheal fistulectomy (31.62)
           tracheoesophageal fistulectomy (31.73)

  √4ᵗʰ 31.6   Repair of larynx

    31.61   Suture of laceration of larynx

    31.62   Closure of fistula of larynx
      Laryngotracheal fistulectomy
      Take-down of laryngostomy
      DEF: Laryngotracheal fistulectomy: Excision and closing of passage between voice box and trachea.
      DEF: Take-down of laryngostomy: Removal of laryngostomy tube and restoration of voice box.

    31.63   Revision of laryngostomy

    31.64   Repair of laryngeal fracture
      DEF: Alignment and positioning of harder structures of larynx such as hyoid bone; following fracture.

    31.69   Other repair of larynx
      Arytenoidopexy
      Cordopexy
      Graft of larynx
      Transposition of vocal cords
      EXCLUDES   *construction of artificial larynx (31.75)*
      DEF: Arytenoidopexy: Fixation of pitcher-shaped cartilage in voice box.
      DEF: Graft of larynx: Implant of graft tissue into voice box.
      DEF: Transposition of the vocal cords: Placement of vocal cords into more functional positions.

  √4ᵗʰ 31.7   Repair and plastic operations on trachea

    31.71   Suture of laceration of trachea

    31.72   Closure of external fistula of trachea
      Closure of tracheotomy

BI Bilateral Procedure   **NC** Non-covered Procedure   **LC** Limited Coverage Procedure   ▶◀ Revised Text   ● New Code   ▲ Revised Code Title

100 – Volume 3   2010 ICD-9-CM

31.73 Closure of other fistula of trachea
Tracheoesophageal fistulectomy
EXCLUDES *laryngotracheal fistulectomy (31.62)*
DEF: Tracheoesophageal fistulectomy: Excision and closure of abnormal opening between windpipe and esophagus.

31.74 Revision of tracheostomy

31.75 Reconstruction of trachea and construction of artificial larynx
Tracheoplasty with artificial larynx

31.79 Other repair and plastic operations on trachea

✓4th **31.9** Other operations on larynx and trachea

31.91 Division of laryngeal nerve

31.92 Lysis of adhesions of trachea or larynx

31.93 Replacement of laryngeal or tracheal stent
DEF: Removal and substitution of tubed molding into larynx or trachea.

31.94 Injection of locally-acting therapeutic substance into trachea

31.95 Tracheoesophageal fistulization
DEF: Creation of passage between trachea and esophagus.

31.98 Other operations on larynx
Dilation
Division of congenital web ⎫ of larynx
Removal of keel or stent ⎭
EXCLUDES *removal of intraluminal foreign body from larynx without incision (98.14)*
DEF: Dilation: Increasing larynx size by stretching.
DEF: Division of congenital web: Cutting and separating congenital membranes around larynx.
DEF: Removal of keel or stent: Removal of prosthetic device from larynx.

31.99 Other operations on trachea
EXCLUDES *removal of:*
intraluminal foreign body from trachea without incision (98.15)
tracheostomy tube (97.37)
replacement of tracheostomy tube (97.23)
tracheostomy toilette (96.55)
AHA: 1Q, '97, 14
TIP: Assign for tracheal dilation associated with insertion of tracheobronchial endoprosthesis performed for treating benign tracheobronchial strictures or strictures produced by malignant neoplasms.

✓3rd **32** **Excision of lung and bronchus**
INCLUDES rib section ⎫
sternotomy ⎪ as operative
sternum-splitting incision ⎬ approach
thoracotomy ⎭
Code also any synchronous bronchoplasty (33.48)
DEF: Rib resection: Cutting of ribs to access operative field.
DEF: Sternotomy: Cut through breastbone as an operative approach.
DEF: Sternum-splitting incision: Breaking through breastbone to access operative field.

✓4th **32.0** Local excision or destruction of lesion or tissue of bronchus
EXCLUDES *biopsy of bronchus (33.24-33.25)*
bronchial fistulectomy (33.42)
AHA: 4Q, '88, 11

32.01 Endoscopic excision or destruction of lesion or tissue of bronchus

32.09 Other local excision or destruction of lesion or tissue of bronchus
EXCLUDES *that by endoscopic approach (32.01)*

32.1 Other excision of bronchus
Resection (wide sleeve) of bronchus
EXCLUDES *radical dissection [excision] of bronchus (32.6)*
DEF: Resection (wide sleeve) of bronchus: Excision and partial, lengthwise removal of a lung branch.Lung Volume Reduction

Lung Volume Reduction

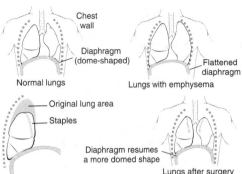

✓4th **32.2** Local excision or destruction of lesion or tissue of lung

32.20 Thoracoscopic excision of lesion or tissue of lung
Thoracoscopic wedge resection
AHA: 4Q, '07, 109, 110

32.21 Plication of emphysematous bleb
DEF: Stitching of a swollen vesicle into folds or tuck.

32.22 Lung volume reduction surgery **LC**
DEF: Excision of portion of lung(s) to reduce respiratory effort in moderate to severe emphysema.
AHA: 1Q, '97, 6; 3Q, '96, 20; 4Q, '95, 64

32.23 Open ablation of lung lesion or tissue
AHA: 4Q, '06, 124

32.24 Percutaneous ablation of lung lesion or tissue
AHA: 4Q, '06, 124

32.25 Thoracoscopic ablation of lung lesion or tissue
EXCLUDES *thoracoscopic excision of lesion or tissue of lung (32.20)*
AHA: 4Q, '06, 124

32.26 Other and unspecified ablation of lung lesion or tissue
AHA: 4Q, '06, 124

32.28 Endoscopic excision or destruction of lesion or tissue of lung
EXCLUDES *ablation of lung lesion or tissue:*
open (32.23)
other (32.26)
percutaneous (32.24)
thoracoscopic (32.25)
biopsy of lung (33.26-33.27)

32.29 Other local excision or destruction of lesion or tissue of lung
Resection of lung:
NOS
wedge
EXCLUDES *ablation of lung lesion or tissue:*
open (32.23)
other (32.26)
percutaneous (32.24)
thoracoscopic (32.25)
biopsy of lung (33.26-33.27)
▶*laser interstitial thermal therapy [LITT] of lesion or tissue of lung under guidance (17.69)*◀
that by endoscopic approach (32.28)
thoracoscopic excision of lesion or tissue of lung (32.20)
wide excision of lesion of lung (32.3)
AHA: 3Q, '99, 3

✓4th **32.3** Segmental resection of lung
Partial lobectomy
AHA: 4Q, '07, 109

32.30 Thoracoscopic segmental resection of lung
AHA: 4Q, '07, 110

32.39   Other and unspecified segmental resection of lung

> EXCLUDES   *thoracoscopic segmental resection of lung (32.30)*

✓4th **32.4   Lobectomy of lung**

Lobectomy with segmental resection of adjacent lobes of lung

> EXCLUDES   *that with radical dissection [excision] of thoracic structures (32.6)*

AHA: 4Q, '07, 109

32.41   Thoracoscopic lobectomy of lung

AHA: 4Q, '07, 110

32.49   Other lobectomy of lung

> EXCLUDES   *thoracoscopic lobectomy of lung (32.41)*

✓4th **32.5   Pneumonectomy**

Excision of lung NOS
Pneumonectomy (with mediastinal dissection)

AHA: 1Q, '99, 6

32.50   Thoracoscopic pneumonectomy

AHA: 4Q, '07, 110

32.59   Other and unspecified pneumonectomy

> EXCLUDES   *thoracoscopic pneumonectomy (32.50)*

32.6   Radical dissection of thoracic structures

Block [en bloc] dissection of bronchus, lobe of lung, brachial plexus, intercostal structure, ribs (transverse process), and sympathetic nerves

32.9   Other excision of lung

> EXCLUDES   *biopsy of lung and bronchus (33.24-33.27)*
> *pulmonary decortication (34.51)*

✓3rd **33   Other operations on lung and bronchus**

> INCLUDES   rib section
> sternotomy   } as operative
> sternum-splitting incision   approach
> thoracotomy

33.0   Incision of bronchus

33.1   Incision of lung

> EXCLUDES   *puncture of lung (33.93)*

✓4th **33.2   Diagnostic procedures on lung and bronchus**

33.20   Thoracoscopic lung biopsy

> EXCLUDES   *closed endoscopic biopsy of lung (33.27)*
> *closed [percutaneous] [needle] biopsy of lung (33.26)*
> *open biopsy of lung (33.28)*

AHA: 4Q, '07, 110

33.21   Bronchoscopy through artificial stoma

> EXCLUDES   *that with biopsy (33.24, 33.27)*

DEF: Visual exam of lung and its branches via tube through artificial opening.

33.22   Fiber-optic bronchoscopy

> EXCLUDES   *that with biopsy (33.24, 33.27)*

DEF: Exam of lung and bronchus via flexible optical instrument for visualization.

AHA: 1Q, '04, 4

Bronchoscopy with Bite Biopsy

33.23   Other bronchoscopy

> EXCLUDES   *that for:*
> *aspiration (96.05)*
> *biopsy (33.24, 33.27)*

AHA: 3Q, '02, 18; 1Q, '99, 6

33.24   Closed [endoscopic] biopsy of bronchus

Bronchoscopy (fiberoptic) (rigid) with:
   brush biopsy of "lung"
   brushing or washing for specimen collection
   excision (bite) biopsy
Diagnostic bronchoalveolar lavage [BAL]
▶Transbronchoscopic needle aspiration [TBNA]◀

> EXCLUDES   *closed biopsy of lung, other than brush biopsy of "lung" (33.26, 33.27)*
> *whole lung lavage (33.99)*

DEF: Bronchoalveolar lavage (BAL): Saline is introduced into the subsegment of a lobe and retrieved using gentle suction; also called 'liquid biopsy'.

DEF: Brush biopsy: Obtaining cell or tissue samples via bristled instrument without incision.

AHA: ▶2Q, '09, 9, 16;◀ 2Q, '06, 20; 3Q, '04, 9; 3Q, '02, 16; 4Q, '92, 27; 3Q, '91, 15

33.25   Open biopsy of bronchus

> EXCLUDES   *open biopsy of lung (33.28)*

33.26   Closed [percutaneous] [needle] biopsy of lung

Fine needle aspiration [FNA] of lung
Transthoracic needle biopsy of lung [TTNB]

> EXCLUDES   *endoscopic biopsy of lung (33.27)*
> *thoracoscopic lung biopsy (33.20)*

AHA: 3Q, '92, 12

33.27   Closed endoscopic biopsy of lung

Fiber-optic (flexible) bronchoscopy with fluoroscopic guidance with biopsy
Transbronchial lung biopsy

> EXCLUDES   *brush biopsy of "lung" (33.24)*
> *percutaneous biopsy of lung (33.26)*
> *thoracoscopic lung biopsy (33.20)*

AHA: ▶2Q, '09, 9, 16;◀ 3Q, '04, 9; 3Q, '02, 16; 4Q, '92, 27; 3Q, '91, 15; S-O, '86, 11

TIP: Transbronchial lung biopsy involves a biopsy taken endoscopically through the bronchus into the lung alveoli; if separate biopsies are taken of the bronchial and/or tracheal tissue, assign also 33.24.

33.28   Open biopsy of lung

AHA: 3Q, '99, 3; 3Q, '92, 12

| BI | Bilateral Procedure | NC | Non-covered Procedure | LC | Limited Coverage Procedure | ▶◀ Revised Text | ● New Code | ▲ Revised Code Title |

102 – Volume 3 • October 2009   **2010 ICD-9-CM**

33.29   **Other diagnostic procedures on lung and bronchus**

> EXCLUDES   *contrast bronchogram:*
> *   endotracheal (87.31)*
> *   other (87.32)*
> *endoscopic pulmonary airway flow*
> *   measurement (33.72)*
> *lung scan (92.15)*
> *magnetic resonance imaging (88.92)*
> *microscopic examination of specimen*
> *   from bronchus or lung*
> *   (90.41-90.49)*
> *routine chest x-ray (87.44)*
> *ultrasonography of lung (88.73)*
> *vital capacity determination (89.37)*
> *x-ray of bronchus or lung NOS (87.49)*

✓4ᵗʰ   **33.3**   **Surgical collapse of lung**

33.31   **Destruction of phrenic nerve for collapse of lung**
> DEF: Therapeutic deadening or destruction of diaphragmatic nerve to collapse the lung.

33.32   **Artificial pneumothorax for collapse of lung**
Thoracotomy for collapse of lung
> DEF: Forcing air or gas into diaphragmatic space to achieve therapeutic collapse of lung.
> DEF: Thoracotomy for collapse of lung: Incision into chest for therapeutic collapse of lung.

33.33   **Pneumoperitoneum for collapse of lung**
> DEF: Forcing air or gas into abdominal serous membrane to achieve therapeutic collapse of lung.

33.34   **Thoracoplasty**
> DEF: Removal of ribs for therapeutic collapse of lungs.

33.39   **Other surgical collapse of lung**
Collapse of lung NOS

✓4ᵗʰ   **33.4**   **Repair and plastic operation on lung and bronchus**

33.41   **Suture of laceration of bronchus**

33.42   **Closure of bronchial fistula**
Closure of bronchostomy
Fistulectomy:
   bronchocutaneous
   bronchoesophageal
   bronchovisceral

> EXCLUDES   *closure of fistula:*
> *   bronchomediastinal (34.73)*
> *   bronchopleural (34.73)*
> *   bronchopleuromediastinal (34.73)*

> DEF: Closure of bronchostomy: Removal of bronchostomy tube and repair of surgical wound.
> DEF: Fistulectomy: Closure of abnormal passage.
> Bronchocutaneous: Between skin and lung branch.
> Bronchoesophagus: Between esophagus and lung branch.
> Bronchovisceral: Between an internal organ and lung branch.

33.43   **Closure of laceration of lung**

33.48   **Other repair and plastic operations on bronchus**

33.49   **Other repair and plastic operations on lung**
> EXCLUDES   *closure of pleural fistula (34.73)*

✓4ᵗʰ   **33.5**   **Lung transplant**
Note: To report donor source – *see* codes 00.91-00.93
Code also cardiopulmonary bypass [extracorporeal circulation] [heart-lung machine] [39.61]
> EXCLUDES   *combined heart-lung transplantation (33.6)*
AHA: 4Q, '95, 75

33.50   **Lung transplantation, not otherwise specified**   LC

33.51   **Unilateral lung transplantation**   LC

33.52   **Bilateral lung transplantation**   LC
Double-lung transplantation
En bloc transplantation
> DEF: Sequential excision and implant of both lungs.

33.6   **Combined heart-lung transplantation**   LC
Note: To report donor source – *see* codes 00.91-00.93
Code also cardiopulmonary bypass [extracorporeal circulation] [heart-lung machine] (39.61)

✓4ᵗʰ   **33.7**   **Other endoscopic procedures in bronchus or lung**
> EXCLUDES   *insertion of tracheobronchial stent (96.05)*

▲   **33.71**   **Endoscopic insertion or replacement of bronchial valve(s), single lobe**
Endobronchial airflow redirection valve
Intrabronchial airflow redirection valve
> EXCLUDES   ▶*endoscopic insertion or replacement of bronchial valve(s), multiple lobes (33.73)*◀

> AHA: 4Q, '08, 175; 4Q, '06, 126
> TIP: Bronchial valve placement is a less invasive treatment than lung volume reduction surgery (LVRS) or lung transplant in a patient with severe or end-stage emphysema or COPD.

33.72   **Endoscopic pulmonary airway flow measurement**
Assessment of pulmonary airway flow
Code also any diagnostic or therapeutic procedure, if performed
> AHA: 4Q, '08, 174-175

•   **33.73**   **Endoscopic insertion or replacement of bronchial valve(s), multiple lobes**
> EXCLUDES   *endoscopic insertion or replacement of bronchial valve(s), single lobe (33.71)*

33.78   **Endoscopic removal of bronchial device(s) or substances**
> AHA: 4Q, '06, 126

33.79   **Endoscopic insertion of other bronchial device or substances**
Biologic lung volume reduction NOS (BLVR)
> AHA: 4Q, '06, 126

✓4ᵗʰ   **33.9**   **Other operations on lung and bronchus**

33.91   **Bronchial dilation**
> AHA: 1Q, '97, 14

33.92   **Ligation of bronchus**
> DEF: Tying off of a lung branch.

33.93   **Puncture of lung**
> EXCLUDES   *needle biopsy (33.26)*
> DEF: Piercing of lung with surgical instrument.

33.98   **Other operations on bronchus**
> EXCLUDES   *bronchial lavage (96.56)*
> *removal of intraluminal foreign body from bronchus without incision (98.15)*

33.99   **Other operations on lung**
Whole lung lavage
> EXCLUDES   *other continuous mechanical ventilation (96.70-96.72)*
> *respiratory therapy (93.90-93.99)*

> AHA: 3Q, '02, 17

✓3ʳᵈ   **34**   **Operations on chest wall, pleura, mediastinum, and diaphragm**
> EXCLUDES   *operations on breast (85.0-85.99)*

✓4ᵗʰ   **34.0**   **Incision of chest wall and pleura**
> EXCLUDES   *that as operative approach — omit code*

34.01   **Incision of chest wall**
Extrapleural drainage
> EXCLUDES   *incision of pleura (34.09)*
> DEF: Extrapleural drainage: Incision to drain fluid from external pleura.
> AHA: 3Q, '00, 12; 1Q, '92, 13
> TIP: Assign for removal of a broken sternal wire (S/P CABG procedure) when no replacement is implanted.

34.02   **Exploratory thoracotomy**

34.03   **Reopening of recent thoracotomy site**

34.04 Insertion of intercostal catheter for drainage
Chest tube
Closed chest drainage
Revision of intercostal catheter (chest tube) (with lysis of adhesions)
EXCLUDES *thoracoscopic drainage of pleural cavity (34.06)*

DEF: Insertion of catheter between ribs for drainage.
AHA: 2Q, '03, 7; 1Q, '99, 10; 2Q, '99, 12; 1Q, '95, 5; 1Q, '92, 12

34.05 Creation of pleuroperitoneal shunt
AHA: 4Q, '94, 50

34.06 Thoracoscopic drainage of pleural cavity
Evacuation of empyema
AHA: 4Q, '07, 110, 112

34.09 Other incision of pleura
Creation of pleural window for drainage
Intercostal stab
Open chest drainage
EXCLUDES *thoracoscopy (34.21)*
thoracotomy for collapse of lung (33.32)

DEF: Creation of pleural window: Creation of circumscribed drainage hole in serous membrane of chest.
DEF: Intercostal stab: Creation of penetrating stab wound between ribs.
DEF: Open chest drainage: Insertion of tube through ribs and serous membrane of chest for drainage.
AHA: 1Q, '07,14; 3Q, '02, 22; 1Q, '94, 7; 4Q, '94, 50
TIP: Assign for placement of either a Denver or a LeVeen pleuroperitoneal shunt, used for treating refractory pleural effusion or chylothorax.

34.1 Incision of mediastinum
► Code also any biopsy, if performed ◄
EXCLUDES *mediastinoscopy (34.22)*
mediastinotomy associated with pneumonectomy (32.5)

✓4ᵗʰ 34.2 Diagnostic procedures on chest wall, pleura, mediastinum, and diaphragm

34.20 Thoracoscopic pleural biopsy
AHA: 4Q, '07, 110

34.21 Transpleural thoracoscopy
DEF: Exam of chest through serous membrane using scope.
AHA: 3Q, '02, 27

34.22 Mediastinoscopy
► Code also any biopsy, if performed ◄
DEF: Exam of lung cavity and heart using scope.

34.23 Biopsy of chest wall

34.24 Other pleural biopsy
EXCLUDES *thoracoscopic pleural biopsy (34.20)*
AHA: 3Q, '02, 22, 27; 1Q, '92, 14

34.25 Closed [percutaneous] [needle] biopsy of mediastinum

34.26 Open biopsy of mediastinum

34.27 Biopsy of diaphragm

34.28 Other diagnostic procedures on chest wall, pleura, and diaphragm
EXCLUDES *angiocardiography (88.50-88.58)*
aortography (88.42)
arteriography of:
intrathoracic vessels NEC (88.44)
pulmonary arteries (88.43)
microscopic examination of specimen from chest wall, pleura, and diaphragm (90.41-90.49)
phlebography of:
intrathoracic vessels NEC (88.63)
pulmonary veins (88.62)
radiological examinations of thorax:
C.A.T. scan (87.41)
diaphragmatic x-ray (87.49)
intrathoracic lymphangiogram (87.34)
routine chest x-ray (87.44)
sinogram of chest wall (87.38)
soft tissue x-ray of chest wall NEC (87.39)
tomogram of thorax NEC (87.42)
ultrasonography of thorax (88.73)

34.29 Other diagnostic procedures on mediastinum
EXCLUDES *mediastinal:*
pneumogram (87.33)
x-ray NEC (87.49)

34.3 Excision or destruction of lesion or tissue of mediastinum
EXCLUDES *biopsy of mediastinum (34.25-34.26)*
mediastinal fistulectomy (34.73)

34.4 Excision or destruction of lesion of chest wall
Excision of lesion of chest wall NOS (with excision of ribs)
EXCLUDES *biopsy of chest wall (34.23)*
costectomy not incidental to thoracic procedure (77.91)
excision of lesion of:
breast (85.20-85.25)
cartilage (80.89)
skin (86.2-86.3)
fistulectomy (34.73)

✓4ᵗʰ 34.5 Pleurectomy

34.51 Decortication of lung
EXCLUDES *thoracoscopic decortication of lung (34.52)*
DEF: Removal of thickened serous membrane for lung expansion.

34.52 Thoracoscopic decortication of lung
AHA: 4Q, '07, 111, 113

34.59 Other excision of pleura
Excision of pleural lesion
EXCLUDES *biopsy of pleura (34.24)*
pleural fistulectomy (34.73)

34.6 Scarification of pleura
Pleurosclerosis
EXCLUDES *injection of sclerosing agent (34.92)*
DEF: Destruction of fluid-secreting serous membrane cells of chest.
AHA: 1Q, '92, 12

✓4ᵗʰ 34.7 Repair of chest wall

34.71 Suture of laceration of chest wall
EXCLUDES *suture of skin and subcutaneous tissue alone (86.59)*

34.72 Closure of thoracostomy

34.73 Closure of other fistula of thorax
Closure of:
bronchopleural
bronchopleurocutaneous } fistula
bronchopleuromediastinal

34.74 **Repair of pectus deformity**

Repair of:

pectus carinatum
pectus excavatum } (with implant)

DEF: Pectus carinatum repair: Restoration of prominent chest bone defect with implant.

DEF: Pectus excavatum: Restoration of depressed chest bone defect with implant.

AHA: 2Q, '04, 6

34.79 **Other repair of chest wall**

Repair of chest wall NOS

AHA: 2Q, '04, 6; J-F, '87, 13

TIP: Assign for removal and replacement of broken sternal wires (S/P CABG procedure), along with code 77.61 if sternal bone debridement was also performed.

√4ᵗʰ 34.8 **Operations on diaphragm**

34.81 **Excision of lesion or tissue of diaphragm**

EXCLUDES *biopsy of diaphragm (34.27)*

34.82 **Suture of laceration of diaphragm**

34.83 **Closure of fistula of diaphragm**

Thoracicoabdominal
Thoracicogastric } fistulectomy
Thoracicointestinal

DEF: Fistulectomy: Closure of abnormal passage.

34.84 **Other repair of diaphragm**

EXCLUDES *repair of diaphragmatic hernia (53.7-53.82)*

34.85 **Implantation of diaphragmatic pacemaker**

34.89 **Other operations on diaphragm**

√4ᵗʰ 34.9 **Other operations on thorax**

34.91 **Thoracentesis**

DEF: Puncture of pleural cavity for fluid aspiration, also called pleurocentesis.

AHA: S-O, '85, 6

34.92 **Injection into thoracic cavity**

Chemical pleurodesis
Injection of cytotoxic agent or tetracycline
Instillation into thoracic cavity

Requires additional code for any cancer chemotherapeutic substance (99.25)

EXCLUDES *that for collapse of lung (33.32)*

DEF: Chemical pleurodesis: Tetracycline hydrochloride injections to create adhesions between parietal and visceral pleura for treatment of pleural effusion.

AHA: 4Q, '07, 112; 1Q, '07, 14; 1Q, '92, 12; 2Q, '89, 17

TIP: Assign for installation of biological glue and/or talc into the pleural cavity.

34.93 **Repair of pleura**

34.99 **Other**

EXCLUDES *removal of:*
mediastinal drain (97.42)
sutures (97.43)
thoracotomy tube (97.41)

DEF: Pleural tent: Extrapleural mobilization of parietal pleura that allows draping of membrane over visceral pleura to eliminate intrapleural dead space and seal visceral pleura.

AHA: 1Q, '00, 17; 1Q, '88, 9

TIP: Assign for formation of a pleural tent, which involves extrapleural mobilization of the parietal pleura in the apex of the chest cavity.

Operations on the Cardiovascular System

35–35.41

7. OPERATIONS ON THE CARDIOVASCULAR SYSTEM (35-39)

√3ʳᵈ **35 Operations on valves and septa of heart**

INCLUDES   sternotomy (median)
(tranverse)   } as operative approach
thoracotomy

Code also cardiopulmonary bypass [extracorporeal circulation] [heart-lung machine] (39.61)

√4ᵗʰ **35.0 Closed heart valvotomy**

EXCLUDES   percutaneous (balloon) valvuloplasty (35.96)

DEF: Incision into valve to restore function.

35.00 Closed heart valvotomy, unspecified valve

35.01 Closed heart valvotomy, aortic valve

35.02 Closed heart valvotomy, mitral valve

35.03 Closed heart valvotomy, pulmonary valve

35.04 Closed heart valvotomy, tricuspid valve

√4ᵗʰ **35.1 Open heart valvuloplasty without replacement**

INCLUDES   open heart valvotomy

Code also cardiopulmonary bypass, if performed [extracorporeal circulation] [heart-lung machine] (39.61)

EXCLUDES   that associated with repair of:
endocardial cushion defect
(35.54,35.63,35.73)
percutaneous (balloon) valvuloplasty (35.96)
valvular defect associated with atrial and ventricular septal defects (35.54, 35.63, 35.73)

DEF: Incision into heart for plastic repair of valve without replacing valve.

35.10 Open heart valvuloplasty without replacement, unspecified valve

35.11 Open heart valvuloplasty of aortic valve without replacement

AHA: 2Q, '08, 13

TIP: Assign for resuspension of aortic valve, in which 4-0 Prolene sutures are used to lift the valve into correct anatomical position, and a double layer of felt is placed on the inside and outside of the valve.

35.12 Open heart valvuloplasty of mitral valve without replacement

AHA: 1Q, '97, 13

35.13 Open heart valvuloplasty of pulmonary valve without replacement

35.14 Open heart valvuloplasty of tricuspid valve without replacement

√4ᵗʰ **35.2 Replacement of heart valve**

INCLUDES   excision of heart valve with replacement

Code also cardiopulmonary bypass [extracorporeal circulation] [heart-lung machine] (39.61)

EXCLUDES   that associated with repair of:
endocardial cushion defect (35.54,35.63, 35.73)
valvular defect associated with atrial and ventricular septal defects (35.54, 35.63, 35.73)

DEF: Removal and replacement of valve with tissue from patient, animal, other human, or prosthetic (synthetic) valve.

35.20 Replacement of unspecified heart valve

Repair of unspecified heart valve with tissue graft or prosthetic implant

35.21 Replacement of aortic valve with tissue graft

Repair of aortic valve with tissue graft (autograft) (heterograft) (homograft)

AHA: 2Q, '97, 8

35.22 Other replacement of aortic valve

Repair of aortic valve with replacement:
NOS
prosthetic (partial) (synthetic) (total)

AHA: ▶4Q, '08, 179;◀ 1Q, '96, 11

35.23 Replacement of mitral valve with tissue graft

Repair of mitral valve with tissue graft (autograft) (heterograft) (homograft)

35.24 Other replacement of mitral valve

Repair of mitral valve with replacement:
NOS
prosthetic (partial) (synthetic) (total)

AHA: 4Q, '97, 55

35.25 Replacement of pulmonary valve with tissue graft

Repair of pulmonary valve with tissue graft (autograft) (heterograft) (homograft)

AHA: 1Q, '07, 14; 1Q, '04, 16; 2Q, '97, 8

TIP: Assign for a Ross procedure, in which a patient's aortic valve is replaced by utilizing the pulmonary valve and the pulmonary valve is replaced with a homograft. Also assign code 35.21 for the aortic valve replacement.

35.26 Other replacement of pulmonary valve

Repair of pulmonary valve with replacement:
NOS
prosthetic (partial) (synthetic) (total)

35.27 Replacement of tricuspid valve with tissue graft

Repair of tricuspid valve with tissue graft (autograft) (heterograft) (homograft)

35.28 Other replacement of tricuspid valve

Repair of tricuspid valve with replacement:
NOS
prosthetic (partial) (synthetic) (total)

√4ᵗʰ **35.3 Operations on structures adjacent to heart valves**

Code also cardiopulmonary bypass [extracorporeal circulation] [heart-lung machine] (39.61)

35.31 Operations on papillary muscle

Division
Reattachment } of papillary muscle
Repair

35.32 Operations on chordae tendineae

Division
Repair } chordae tendineae

35.33 Annuloplasty

Plication of annulus

DEF: Plication of annulus: Tuck stitched in valvular ring for tightening.

AHA: 1Q, '97, 13; 1Q, '88, 10

TIP: Do not assign unless the annuloplasty is the only procedure performed; if it included an operation on the leaflet as well, refer to valvuloplasty codes, which include the annuloplasty.

35.34 Infundibulectomy

Right ventricular infundibulectomy

DEF: Infundibulectomy: Excision of funnel-shaped heart passage.

DEF: Right ventricular infundibulectomy: Excision of funnel-shaped passage in right upper heart chamber.

35.35 Operations on trabeculae carneae cordis

Division
Excision } of trabeculae carneae cordis

Excision of aortic subvalvular ring

35.39 Operations on other structures adjacent to valves of heart

Repair of sinus of Valsalva (aneurysm)

√4ᵗʰ **35.4 Production of septal defect in heart**

35.41 Enlargement of existing atrial septal defect

Rashkind procedure
Septostomy (atrial) (balloon)

DEF: Enlargement of partition wall defect in lower heart chamber to improve function.

DEF: Rashkind procedure: Enlargement of partition wall defect between the two lower heart chambers by balloon catheter.

BI Bilateral Procedure   NC Non-covered Procedure   LC Limited Coverage Procedure   ▶◀ Revised Text   ● New Code   ▲ Revised Code Title

106 – Volume 3 · February 2009   2010 ICD-9-CM

35.42   **Creation of septal defect in heart**
Blalock-Hanlon operation
DEF: Blalock-Hanlon operation: Removal of partition wall defect in lower heart chamber.

√4ᵗʰ **35.5**   **Repair of atrial and ventricular septa with prosthesis**
INCLUDES   repair of septa with synthetic implant or patch
Code also cardiopulmonary bypass [extracorporeal circulation] [heart-lung machine] (39.61)

35.50   **Repair of unspecified septal defect of heart with prosthesis**
EXCLUDES   that associated with repair of:
endocardial cushion defect (35.54)
septal defect associated with valvular defect (35.54)

35.51   **Repair of atrial septal defect with prosthesis, open technique**
Atrioseptoplasty
Correction of atrial septal defect
Repair: } with prosthesis
foramen ovale (patent)
ostium secundum defect
EXCLUDES   that associated with repair of:
atrial septal defect associated with valvular and ventricular septal defects (35.54)
endocardial cushion defect (35.54)
DEF: Repair of opening or weakening in septum separating the atria; prosthesis implanted through heart incision.

35.52   **Repair of atrial septal defect with prosthesis, closed technique**
Insertion of atrial septal umbrella [King-Mills]
DEF: Correction of partition wall defect in lower heart chamber with artificial material; without incision into heart.
DEF: Insertion of atrial septal umbrella (King-Mills): Correction of partition wall defect in lower heart chamber with atrial septal umbrella.
AHA: 2Q, '05, 17; 3Q, '98, 11
TIP: Assign for Amplatzer balloon occlusion, used to repair cardiac anomalies; is implanted at the site of the defect via a catheter; typically performed in the cardiac catheterization lab.

35.53   **Repair of ventricular septal defect with prosthesis, open technique**
Correction of ventricular septal defect   } with prosthesis
Repair of supracristal defect
EXCLUDES   that associated with repair of:
endocardial cushion defect (35.54)
ventricular defect associated with valvular and atrial septal defects (35.54)
AHA: 1Q, '07, 14

35.54   **Repair of endocardial cushion defect with prosthesis**
Repair:
atrioventricular canal
ostium primum defect
valvular defect associated with atrial and ventricular septal defects   } with prosthesis (grafted to septa)
EXCLUDES   repair of isolated:
atrial septal defect (35.51-35.52)
valvular defect (35.20, 35.22, 35.24, 35.26, 35.28)
ventricular septal defect (35.53)

35.55   **Repair of ventricular septal defect with prosthesis, closed technique**

√4ᵗʰ **35.6**   **Repair of atrial and ventricular septa with tissue graft**
Code also cardiopulmonary bypass [extracorporeal circulation] [heart-lung machine] (39.61)

35.60   **Repair of unspecified septal defect of heart with tissue graft**
EXCLUDES   that associated with repair of:
endocardial cushion defect (35.63)
septal defect associated with valvular defect (35.63)

35.61   **Repair of atrial septal defect with tissue graft**
Atrioseptoplasty
Correction of atrial septal defect   } with tissue graft
Repair:
foramen ovale (patent)
ostium secundum defect
EXCLUDES   that associated with repair of:
atrial septal defect associated with valvular and ventricular septal defects (35.63)
endocardial cushion defect (35.63)

35.62   **Repair of ventricular septal defect with tissue graft**
Correction of ventricular septal defect   } with tissue graft
Repair of supracristal defect
EXCLUDES   that associated with repair of:
endocardial cushion defect (35.63)
ventricular defect associated with valvular and atrial septal defects (35.63)

35.63   **Repair of endocardial cushion defect with tissue graft**
Repair of:
artrioventricular canal
ostium primum defect
valvular defect associated with atrial and ventricular septal defects   } with tissue graft
EXCLUDES   repair of isolated:
atrial septal defect (35.61)
valvular defect (35.20-35.21, 35.23, 35.25, 35.27)
ventricular septal defect (35.62)

√4ᵗʰ **35.7**   **Other and unspecified repair of atrial and ventricular septa**
Code also cardiopulmonary bypass [extracorporeal circulation] [heart-lung machine] (39.61)

35.70   **Other and unspecified repair of unspecified septal defect of heart**
Repair of septal defect NOS
EXCLUDES   that associated with repair of:
endocardial cushion defect (35.73)
septal defect associated with valvular defect (35.73)

35.71   **Other and unspecified repair of atrial septal defect**
Repair NOS:
atrial septum
foramen ovale (patent)
ostium secundum defect
EXCLUDES   that associated with repair of:
atrial septal defect associated with valvular and ventricular septal defects (35.73)
endocardial cushion defect (35.73)

35.72   **Other and unspecified repair of ventricular septal defect**
Repair NOS: Repair NOS:
supracristal defect   ventricular septum
EXCLUDES   that associated with repair of:
endocardial cushion defect (35.73)
ventricular septal defect associated with valvular and atrial septal defects (35.73)

Operations on the Cardiovascular System

35.73–35.99

35.73 Other and unspecified repair of endocardial cushion defect

Repair NOS:
   atrioventricular canal
   ostium primum defect
   valvular defect associated with atrial and ventricular septal defects

> *EXCLUDES*   *repair of isolated:*
>   *atrial septal defect (35.71)*
>   *valvular defect (35.20, 35.22, 35.24, 35.26, 35.28)*
>   *ventricular septal defect (35.72)*

✓4th 35.8 Total repair of certain congenital cardiac anomalies

Note: For partial repair of defect [e.g. repair of atrial septal defect in tetralogy of Fallot] – code to specific procedure

35.81 Total repair of tetralogy of Fallot

One-stage total correction of tetralogy of Fallot with or without:
   commissurotomy of pulmonary valve
   infundibulectomy
   outflow tract prosthesis
   patch graft of outflow tract
   prosthetic tube for pulmonary artery
   repair of ventricular septal defect (with prosthesis)
   take-down of previous systemic-pulmonary artery anastomosis

35.82 Total repair of total anomalous pulmonary venous connection

One-stage total correction of total anomalous pulmonary venous connection with or without:
   anastomosis between (horizontal) common pulmonary trunk and posterior wall of left atrium (side-to-side)
   enlargement of foramen ovale
   incision [excision] of common wall between posterior left atrium and coronary sinus and roofing of resultant defect with patch graft (synthetic)
   ligation of venous connection (descending anomalous vein) (to left innominate vein) (to superior vena cava)
   repair of atrial septal defect (with prosthesis)

35.83 Total repair of truncus arteriosus

One-stage total correction of truncus arteriosus with or without:
   construction (with aortic homograft) (with prosthesis) of a pulmonary artery placed from right ventricle to arteries supplying the lung
   ligation of connections between aorta and pulmonary artery
   repair of ventricular septal defect (with prosthesis)

35.84 Total correction of transposition of great vessels, not elsewhere classified

Arterial switch operation [Jatene]
Total correction of transposition of great arteries at the arterial level by switching the great arteries, including the left or both coronary arteries, implanted in the wall of the pulmonary artery

> *EXCLUDES*   *baffle operation [Mustard] [Senning] (35.91)*
>   *creation of shunt between right ventricle and pulmonary artery [Rastelli] (35.92)*

✓4th 35.9 Other operations on valves and septa of heart

Code also cardiopulmonary bypass, if performed [extracorporeal circulation] [heart-lung machine] (39.61)

35.91 Interatrial transposition of venous return

Baffle:
   atrial
   interatrial
Mustard's operation
Resection of atrial septum and insertion of patch to direct systemic venous return to tricuspid valve and pulmonary venous return to mitral valve

DEF: Atrial baffle: Correction of venous flow of abnormal or deviated lower heart chamber.

DEF: Interatrial baffle: Correction of venous flow between abnormal lower heart chambers.

DEF: Mustard's operation: Creates intra-atrial baffle using pericardial tissue to correct transposition of the great vessels.

35.92 Creation of conduit between right ventricle and pulmonary artery

Creation of shunt between right ventricle and (distal) pulmonary artery

> *EXCLUDES*   *that associated with total repair of truncus arteriosus (35.83)*

AHA: 1Q, '07, 14

35.93 Creation of conduit between left ventricle and aorta

Creation of apicoaortic shunt
Shunt between apex of left ventricle and aorta

AHA: ▶2Q, '09, 8◀

35.94 Creation of conduit between atrium and pulmonary artery

Fontan procedure

35.95 Revision of corrective procedure on heart

Replacement of prosthetic heart valve poppet
Resuture of prosthesis of:
   septum
   valve

> *EXCLUDES*   *complete revision – code to specific procedure*
>   *replacement of prosthesis or graft of:*
>   *septum (35.50-35.63)*
>   *valve (35.20-35.28)*

DEF: Replacement of prosthetic heart valve poppet: Removal and replacement of valve-supporting prosthesis.

DEF: Resuture of prosthesis of septum: Restitching of prosthesis in partition wall.

DEF: Resuture of prosthesis of valve: Restitching of prosthetic valve.

35.96 Percutaneous valvuloplasty

Percutaneous balloon valvuloplasty (PBPV) *[handwritten: ← Non-invasive treatment for pulmonary valve stenosis]*

DEF: Repair of valve with catheter.

DEF: Percutaneous balloon valvuloplasty: Repair of valve with inflatable catheter.

AHA: 3Q, '04, 10; M-J, '86, 6; N-D, '85, 10

35.98 Other operations on septa of heart

AHA: 1Q, '07, 11

35.99 Other operations on valves of heart

BI Bilateral Procedure   NC Non-covered Procedure   LC Limited Coverage Procedure   ▶◀ Revised Text   ● New Code   ▲ Revised Code Title

108 – Volume 3 • October 2009   2010 ICD-9-CM

Coronary circulation consists of two main arteries - right and left— each with several branches which are counted as arteries in coding aortocoronary bypass grafts; See beginning of procedure codes for list.

√3rd **36 Operations on vessels of heart**

    INCLUDES   sternotomy (median)
                       (transverse)   } as operative approach
                       thoracotomy

Code also any:
    injection or infusion of platelet inhibitor (99.20)
    injection or infusion of thrombolytic agent (99.10)
Code also cardiopulmonary bypass, if performed [extra- corporeal
    circulation] [heart-lung machine] (39.61)

√4th **36.0 Removal of coronary artery obstruction and insertion of stent(s)**

    AHA: 4Q, '95, 66; 2Q, '94, 13; 1Q, '94, 3; 2Q, '90, 23; N-D, '86, 8

    36.03   **Open chest coronary artery angioplasty**

            Coronary (artery):
                endarterectomy (with patch graft)
                thromboendarterectomy (with patch graft)
            Open surgery for direct relief of coronary artery
                obstruction

            Code also any:
                insertion of drug-eluting coronary stent(s)
                    (36.07)
                insertion of non-drug-eluting coronary stent(s)
                    (36.06)
                number of vascular stents inserted
                    (00.45-00.48)
                number of vessels treated (00.40-00.43)
                procedure on vessel bifurcation (00.44)

            EXCLUDES   *that with coronary artery bypass graft (36.10-36.19)*

            DEF: Endarterectomy (with patch graft): Excision of thickened material within coronary artery; repair with patch graft.
            DEF: Thromboendarterectomy (with patch graft): Excision of blood clot and thickened material within coronary artery; repair with patch graft.
            DEF: Open surgery for direct relief of coronary artery obstruction: Removal of coronary artery obstruction through opening in chest.
            AHA: 2Q, '01, 24; 3Q, '93, 7
            TIP: Do not assign if the procedure was performed percutaneously; see instead code 00.66.

    36.04   **Intracoronary artery thrombolytic infusion**

            Enzyme infusion
            Platelet inhibitor
            That by direct coronary artery injection, infusion,
                or catheterization

            EXCLUDES   *infusion of platelet inhibitor (99.20)*
                       infusion of thrombolytic agent (99.10)
                       that associated with any procedure in 36.03

            DEF: Infusion of clot breaking solution into intracoronary artery.
            AHA: 4Q, '05, 102; 4Q, '02, 114; 3Q, '02, 20; 2Q, '01, 24; 4Q, '98, 85; 1Q, '97, 3; 4Q, '95, 67
            TIP: If tPA infusion was performed in another facility within the previous 24 hours prior to arrival in the current facility, assign also diagnosis code V45.88.

    36.06   **Insertion of non-drug-eluting coronary artery stent(s)**

            Bare stent(s)   Endograft(s)
            Bonded stent(s)   Endovascular graft(s)
            Drug-coated stent(s),e.g.,   Stent graft(s)
                heparin coated

            Code also any:
                number of vascular stents inserted (00.45-00.48)
                number of vessels treated (00.40-00.43)
                open chest coronary artery angioplasty (36.03)
                percutaneous transluminal coronary
                    angioplasty [PTCA] or coronary
                    atherectomy (00.66)
                procedure on vessel bifurcation (00.44)

            EXCLUDES   *insertion of drug-eluting coronary artery stent(s) (36.07)*

            DEF: Percutaneous implant via catheter of metal stent, to enlarge, maintain lumen size of coronary artery.
            AHA: ▶2Q, '09, 12;◄ 4Q, '05, 71; 2Q, '04, 3; 4Q, '02, 101; 1Q,'01, 9; 2Q, '01, 24; 1Q, '00, 11; 1Q, '99, 17

36.07   **Insertion of drug-eluting coronary artery stent(s)**

    Endograft(s)   Stent graft(s)
    Endovascular graft(s)

    Code also any:
        number of vascular stents inserted
            (00.45-00.48)
        number of vessels treated (00.40-00.43)
        open chest coronary artery angioplasty (36.03)
        percutaneous transluminal coronary
            angioplasty [PTCA] or coronary
            atherectomy (00.66)
        procedure on vessel bifurcation (00.44)

    EXCLUDES   *drug-coated stents, e.g., heparin coated (36.06)*
                  insertion of non-drug-eluting coronary artery stent(s) (36.06)

    DEF: Drug-eluting stent technology developed to prevent the accumulation of scar tissue that can narrow reopened coronary arteries. A special polymer is used to coat the drug onto the stent, which slowly releases into the coronary artery wall tissue.
    AHA: 4Q, '05, 105-106; 4Q, '02, 101

36.09   **Other removal of coronary artery obstruction**

    Coronary angioplasty NOS

    Code also any:
        number of vascular stents inserted
            (00.45-00.48)
        number of vessels treated (00.40-00.43)
        procedure on vessel bifurcation (00.44)

    EXCLUDES   *that by open angioplasty (36.03)*
                  that by percutaneous transluminal coronary angioplasty [PTCA] or coronary atherectomy (00.66)

√4th **36.1 Bypass anastomosis for heart revascularization**

    Note: Do not assign codes from series 00.40-00.43 with codes from series 36.10-36.19

    Code also:
        cardiopulmonary bypass [extracorporeal circulation] [heart-lung machine] (39.61)
        pressurized treatment of venous bypass graft [conduit] with pharmaceutical substance, if performed (00.16)

    DEF: Insertion of tube to bypass blocked coronary artery, correct coronary blood flow.
    AHA: 4Q, '07, 121; 2Q, '96, 7; 3Q, '95, 7; 3Q, '93, 8; 1Q, '91, 7; 2Q, '90, 24; 4Q, '89, 3
    TIP: The determining factor for coding an aortocoronary artery bypass graft operation is the number of coronary arteries involved rather than the number of grafts; the use of the sequential technique does not affect the code assignment.

36.10   **Aortocoronary bypass for heart revascularization, not otherwise specified**

    Direct revascularization:
        cardiac
        coronary   } with catheter stent,
        hear muscle   prosthesis, or vein
        myocardial   graft

    Heart revascularization NOS
    AHA: 2Q, '96, 7

Coronary Bypass

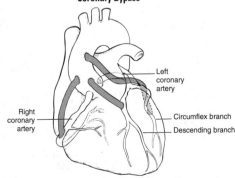

Procedures such as hypothermia, cardioplegia, intra operative pacing, and chest tube insertions are considered integral to bypass surgery; no separate codes are assigned.

√3rd Additional Digit Required   Valid OR Procedure   Non-OR Procedure   Adjunct Code
√4th
2010 ICD-9-CM   **October 2009 · Volume 3 – 109**

The fact that a detached segment of the internal mammary artery is used as graft material instead of saphenous vein in performing aortocoronary bypass does not make it an internal mammary-coronary artery bypass. The internal mammary-coronary artery bypass involves the use of the internal mammary itself as a still vascularized conduit for the blood supply and does not involve the aorta.

Operations on the Cardiovascular System

36.11–37.24

36.11 (Aorto)coronary bypass of one coronary artery
AHA: 3Q, '02, 4, 9; 4Q, '89, 3

36.12 (Aorto)coronary bypass of two coronary arteries
AHA: 3Q, '02, 8; 4Q, '99, 15; 2Q, '96, 7; 3Q, '97, 14; 4Q, '89, 3

36.13 (Aorto)coronary bypass of three coronary arteries
AHA: 3Q, '02, 6, 7, 9; 2Q, '96, 7; 4Q, '89, 3

36.14 (Aorto)coronary bypass of four or more coronary arteries
AHA: 3Q, '02, 5; 2Q, '96, 7; 4Q, '89, 3

✳ 36.15 Single internal mammary-coronary artery bypass
Anastomosis (single):
  mammary artery to coronary artery
  thoracic artery to coronary artery
AHA: 3Q, '02, 4-9; 4Q, '99, 15; 3Q, '97, 14; 2Q, '96, 7

✳ 36.16 Double internal mammary-coronary artery bypass
Anastomosis, double:
  mammary artery to coronary artery
  thoracic artery to coronary artery
AHA: 3Q, '02, 6, 8, 9; 2Q, '96, 7

36.17 Abdominal-coronary artery bypass
Anastomosis:
  gastroepiploic artery to coronary artery
AHA: 3Q, '97, 14; 4Q, '96, 64

Abdominal artery such as the gastric or gastroepiploic artery is used for the graft.

36.19 Other bypass anastomosis for heart revascularization
AHA: 2Q, '96, 7

36.2 Heart revascularization by arterial implant
Implantation of:
  aortic branches [ascending aortic branches] into heart muscle
  blood vessels into myocardium
  internal mammary artery [internal thoracic artery] into:
    heart muscle
    myocardium
    ventricle
    ventricular wall
  Indirect heart revascularization NOS

✓4th 36.3 Other heart revascularization

36.31 Open chest transmyocardial revascularization
DEF: Transmyocardial revascularization (TMR): Laser creation of channels through myocardium allows oxygenated blood flow from sinusoids to myocardial tissue.

36.32 Other transmyocardial revascularization
AHA: 4Q, '98, 74

36.33 Endoscopic transmyocardial revascularization
Thoracoscopic transmyocardial revascularization
AHA: 4Q, '06, 127

36.34 Percutaneous transmyocardial revascularization
Endovascular transmyocardial revascularization
AHA: 4Q, '06, 127

Transmyocardial Revascularization

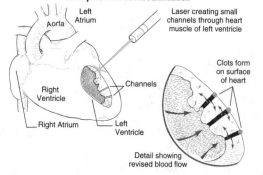

Aorta — Left Atrium
Laser creating small channels through heart muscle of left ventricle
Right Ventricle
Channels
Right Atrium
Left Ventricle
Clots form on surface of heart
Detail showing revised blood flow

36.39 Other heart revascularization
Abrasion of epicardium
Cardio-omentopexy
Intrapericardial poudrage
Myocardial graft:
  mediastinal fat
  omentum
  pectoral muscles
DEF: Cardio-omentopexy: Suture of omentum segment to heart after drawing segment through incision in diaphragm to improve blood supply.
DEF: Intrapericardial poudrage: Application of powder to heart lining to promote fusion.

✓4th 36.9 Other operations on vessels of heart
Code also cardiopulmonary bypass [extracorporeal circulation] [heart-lung machine] (39.61)

36.91 Repair of aneurysm of coronary vessel

36.99 Other operations on vessels of heart
Exploration
Incision } of coronary artery
Ligation
Repair of arteriovenous fistula
AHA: 3Q, '03, 18; 1Q, '94, 3

✓3rd 37 Other operations on heart and pericardium
Code also any injection or infusion of platelet inhibitor (99.20)

37.0 Pericardiocentesis
DEF: Puncture of the heart lining to withdraw fluid.
AHA: 1Q, '07, 11

✓4th 37.1 Cardiotomy and pericardiotomy
Code also cardiopulmonary bypass [extracorporeal circulation] [heart-lung machine] (39.61)

37.10 Incision of heart, not otherwise specified
Cardiolysis NOS

37.11 Cardiotomy
Incision of:
  atrium
  endocardium
Incision of:
  myocardium
  ventricle

37.12 Pericardiotomy
Pericardial window operation
Pericardiolysis
Pericardiotomy
DEF: Pericardial window operation: Incision into heart lining for drainage.
DEF: Pericardiolysis: Destruction of heart tissue lining.

✓4th 37.2 Diagnostic procedures on heart and pericardium

37.20 Non-invasive programmed electrical stimulation [NIPS]
EXCLUDES catheter based invasive electro-physiologic testing (37.26)
device interrogation only without arrhythmia induction (bedside check) (89.45-89.49)
that as part of intraoperative testing — omit code
DEF: Non-invasive testing of a previously implanted cardioverter-defibrillator to ensure proper lead placement and system function.
AHA: 4Q, '06, 128

37.21 Right heart cardiac catheterization
Cardiac catheterization NOS
EXCLUDES that with catheterization of left heart (37.23)
AHA: 3Q, '04, 10; 3Q, '03, 9; 2Q, '90, 23; M-J, '87, 11

37.22 Left heart cardiac catheterization
EXCLUDES that with catheterization of right heart (37.23)
AHA: 4Q, '05, 71; 3Q, '05, 14; 3Q, '04, 10; 2Q, '04, 3; 1Q, '00, 21; 2Q, '90, 23; 4Q, '88, 4; M-J, '87, 11

37.23 Combined right and left heart cardiac catheterization
AHA: 1Q, '07, 11; 2Q, '05, 17; 3Q, '04, 10; 2Q, '01, 8; 1Q, '00, 20; 3Q, '98, 11; 2Q, '90, 23; M-J, '87, 11

37.24 Biopsy of pericardium

BI Bilateral Procedure   NC Non-covered Procedure   LC Limited Coverage Procedure   ►◄ Revised Text   ● New Code   ▲ Revised Code Title

110 – Volume 3   2010 ICD-9-CM

His bundle: atrioventricular (AV) bundle, a group of modified muscle fibers (the Purkinje fibers) forming a part of the impulse-conducting system of the heart.

37.25 Biopsy of heart
AHA: 3Q, '03, 16; 3Q, '94, 8

37.26 Catheter based invasive electrophysiologic testing
Electrophysiologic studies [EPS]

EPS: performed as part of the diagnosis and therapeutic management of patients with ventricular tachycardia or ventricular fibrillation (a treatable, but lethal dysrhythmia, marked on EKG by rapid, chaotic, nonrepetitive waveforms).

Code also any concomitant procedure

EXCLUDES   *device interrogation only without arrhythmia induction (bedside check) (89.45-89.49)*
His bundle recording (37.29)
non-invasive programmed electrical stimulation (NIPS) (37.20)
that as part of intraoperative testing — omit code

DEF: Diagnostic mapping and measurement of intracardiac electrical activity; requires inserting three to six catheters into heart blood vessels and positioning catheters under fluoroscopic guidance to determine site of the tachycardia or abnormal impulse pathway; may also be used to terminate arrhythmias.

AHA: 3Q, '03, 23; 2Q, '03, 19; 1Q, '02, 8, 9; 1Q, '99, 3; 2Q, '97, 10; 3Q, '90, 11

37.26 is not assigned for an "intraoperative EP study performed for device testing during implantation of an AICD (37.94)

37.27 Cardiac mapping
Code also any concomitant procedure

EXCLUDES   *electrocardiogram (89.52)*
His bundle recording (37.29)

37.28 Intracardiac echocardiography
Echocardiography of heart chambers
ICE

Code also any synchronous Doppler flow mapping (88.72)

EXCLUDES   *intravascular imaging of coronary vessels (intravascular ultra-sound) (IVUS) (00.24)*

DEF: Creation of a two-dimensional graphic of heart using endoscopic echocardiographic equipment.
AHA: 4Q, '01, 62

37.29 Other diagnostic procedures on heart and pericardium

His bundle study... if performed in conjunction with cardiac cath, the code for cardiac cath would be sequenced first.

EXCLUDES   *angiocardiography (88.50-88.58)*
cardiac function tests (89.41-89.69)
cardiovascular radioisotopic scan and function study (92.05)
coronary arteriography (88.55-88.57)
diagnostic pericardiocentesis (37.0)
diagnostic ultrasound of heart (88.72)
x-ray of heart (87.49)

AHA: S-O, '87, 3

✓4th 37.3 Pericardiectomy and excision of lesion of heart
Code also cardiopulmonary bypass [extracorporeal circulation] [heart-lung machine] (39.61)

37.31 Pericardiectomy
Excision of:
  adhesions of pericardium
  constricting scar of:
    epicardium
    pericardium
DEF: Excision of a portion of heart lining.

Intracardiac Echocardiography

Ventricular Reduction Surgery

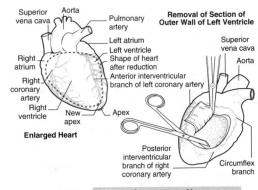

Enlarged Heart — Removal of Section of Outer Wall of Left Ventricle

37.32 Excision of aneurysm of heart
Repair of aneurysm of heart

37.33 Excision or destruction of other lesion or tissue of heart, open approach
Ablation of heart tissue (cryoablation) (electrocurrent) (laser) (microwave) (radiofrequency) (resection), open chest approach
Cox-maze procedure
Maze procedure
Modified maze procedure, transthoracic approach

EXCLUDES   *ablation, excision or destruction of lesion or tissue of heart, endovascular approach (37.34)*
excision or destruction of left atrial appendage (LAA) (37.36)

AHA: 3Q, '06, 13; 4Q, '03, 93-94; 2Q, '94, 12

37.34 Excision or destruction of other lesion or tissue of heart, other approach
Ablation of heart tissue (cryoablation) (electrocurrent) (laser) (microwave) (radiofrequency) (resection), via peripherally inserted catheter
Modified maze procedure, endovascular approach

DEF: Destruction of heart tissue or lesion by freezing, electric current or resection.
AHA: 4Q, '03, 93-95; 1Q, '00, 20

TIP: If the ablation is performed via a right and left cardiac catheterization, report also code 37.23 and any associated procedures (e.g., angiography).

37.35 Partial ventriculectomy   NC
Ventricular reduction surgery
Ventricular remodeling

Code also any synchronous:
  mitral valve repair (35.02, 35.12)
  mitral valve replacement (35.23-35.24)

DEF: Removal of elliptical slice of ventricle between anterior and posterior papillary muscle; also called Batiste operation.
AHA: 4Q, '97, 54, 55

37.36 Excision or destruction of left atrial appendage [LAA]
INCLUDES   thoracoscopic approach, minithoracotomy approach

Clipping of left atrial appendage
Exclusion of left atrial appendage
Oversewing of left atrial appendage
Stapling of left atrial appendage
Code also any concomitant procedure performed

EXCLUDES   *ablation, excision or destruction of lesion or tissue of heart, endovascular approach (37.34)*

DEF: ▶Closure of LAA tissue via use of stapler, clip, or suture; performed for patients with atrial fibrillation for whom traditional anticoagulant therapies are contraindicated; prevents strokes and other embolic events.◄
AHA: ▶4Q, '08, 176◄

▶Total Internal Biventricular Heart Replacement System◀

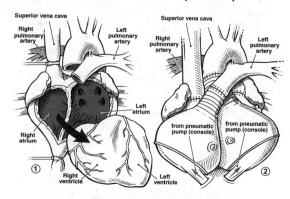

✓4th **37.4 Repair of heart and pericardium**
AHA: 2Q, '90, 24

37.41 Implantation of prosthetic cardiac support device around the heart
Cardiac support device [CSD]
Epicardial support device
Fabric (textile) (mesh) device
Ventricular support device on surface of heart

Code also any:
cardiopulmonary bypass [extracorporeal circulation] [heart-lung machine] if performed (39.61)
mitral valve repair (35.02, 35.12)
mitral valve replacement (35.23-35.24)
transesophageal echocardiography (88.72)
EXCLUDES   circulatory assist systems (37.61-37.68)

DEF: Cardiac support device: any device implanted around the ventricles of the heart for cardiac support

DEF: Fabric (textile) (mesh) device: textile mesh net sutured around the heart for support.

AHA: 4Q, '05, 119-120

37.49 Other repair of heart and pericardium
AHA: 3Q, '08, 9

TIP: Assign for surgical ventricular restoration (SVR), performed to remodel or restore the left ventricle to a more normal size and shape in patients with akinetic parts of the heart.

✓4th **37.5 Heart replacement procedures**
AHA: 4Q, '03, 96

37.51 Heart transplantation   LC
Donor heart
EXCLUDES   combined heart-lung transplantation (33.6)

AHA: ▶4Q, '08, 182;◀ 2Q, '05, 14

[12] **37.52 Implantation of total internal biventricular heart replacement system**   LC
artificial heart
Note: This procedure includes substantial removal of part or all of the biological heart. Both ventricles are resected, and the native heart is no longer intact. Ventriculectomy is included in this procedure; do not code separately.
Artificial heart
EXCLUDES   implantation of heart assist system [VAD] (37.62, 37.65, 37.66, 37.68)

AHA: ▶4Q, '08, 181◀

37.53 Replacement or repair of thoracic unit of (total) replacement heart system   NC
EXCLUDES   replacement and repair of heart assist system [VAD] (37.63)

AHA: ▶4Q, '08, 181◀

37.54 Replacement or repair of other implantable component of (total) replacement heart system   NC
Implantable battery
Implantable controller
Transcutaneous energy transfer [TET] device
EXCLUDES   replacement and repair of heart assist system [VAD] (37.63)
replacement or repair of thoracic unit of (total) replacement heart system (37.53)

AHA: ▶4Q, '08, 181◀

37.55 Removal of internal biventricular heart replacement system
Explantation of artificial heart
Code also any concomitant procedure, such as:
combined heart-lung transplantation (33.6)
heart transplantation (37.51)
implantation of internal biventricular heart replacement system (37.52)
EXCLUDES   explantation [removal] of external heart assist system (37.64)
explantation [removal] of percutaneous external heart assist device (97.44)
nonoperative removal of heart assist system (97.44)
that with replacement or repair of heart replacement system (37.53, 37.54)

AHA: ▶4Q, '08, 180-182◀

✓4th **37.6 Implantation of heart and circulatory assist system(s)**
EXCLUDES   implantation of prosthetic cardiac support system (37.41)

DEF: Implant of device for assisting heart in circulating blood.
AHA: ▶4Q, '08, 177-179;◀ 4Q, '95, 68

V53.31
Fitting and adjustment of a cardiac pacemaker

37.60 Implantation or insertion of biventricular external heart assist system
Note: Device (outside the body but connected to heart) with external circulation pump. Ventriculotomy is included; do not code separately.
INCLUDES   open chest (sternotomy) procedure for cannulae attachments

Temporary cardiac support for both left and right ventricles, inserted in the same operative episode
EXCLUDES   implantation of internal biventricular heart replacement system (artificial heart) (37.52)
implant of pulsation balloon (37.61)
insertion of percutaneous external heart assist device (37.68)
insertion of temporary non-implantable extracorporeal circulatory assist device (37.62)

AHA: ▶4Q, '08, 179◀

▶Ventricular Assist Devices◀

VAD   pVAD   IABP

[12] Limited coverage only when reported in combination with diagnosis code V70.7.

BI Bilateral Procedure   NC Non-covered Procedure   LC Limited Coverage Procedure   ▶◀ Revised Text   ● New Code   ▲ Revised Code Title

112 – Volume 3 · February 2009   2010 ICD-9-CM

37.61　Implant of pulsation balloon
AHA: 3Q, '05, 14

37.62　Insertion of temporary non-implantable extracorporeal circulatory assist device
Note: Includes explantation of this device; do not code separately.
Acute circulatory support device
Insertion of heart assist system, NOS
Insertion of heart pump
Short-term circulatory support (up to six hours)
EXCLUDES　*implantation of total internal biventricular heart replacement system [artificial heart] (37.52)*
implant of external heart assist system (37.65)
insertion of implantable extracorporeal heart assist system (37.66)
insertion of percutaneous external heart assist device (37.68)
removal of heart assist system (37.64)
AHA: 4Q, '03, 116; 2Q, '90, 25

37.63　Repair of heart assist system
Replacement of parts of an existing ventricular assist device (VAD)
EXCLUDES　*replacement or repair of other implantable component of (total) replacement heart system [artificial heart] (37.54)*
replacement or repair of thoracic unit of (total) replacement heart system [artificial heart] (37.53)

37.64　Removal of external heart assist system(s) or device(s)
Explantation of external device(s) providing left and right ventricular support
Explantation of single external device and cannulae
EXCLUDES　*explantation [removal] of percutaneous external heart assist device (97.44)*
nonoperative removal of heart assist system (97.44)
temporary non-implantable extracorporeal circulatory assist device (37.62)
that with replacement of implant (37.63)
AHA: ▶4Q, '08, 177-178, 180◀

37.65　Implant of single ventricular (extracorporeal) external heart assist system
Note: Device (outside the body but connected to heart) with external circulation and pump
Note: Insertion or implantation of one external VAD for left or right heart support
INCLUDES　open chest (sternotomy) procedure for cannulae attachments
Insertion of one device into one ventricle
EXCLUDES　*implantation of total internal biventricular heart replacement system (37.52)*
implant of pulsation balloon (37.61)
insertion of implantable heart assist system (37.66)
insertion or implantation of two external VADs for simultaneous right and left heart support (37.60)
insertion of percutaneous external heart assist device (37.68)
that without sternotomy (37.62)
DEF: Insertion of short-term circulatory support device with pump outside body.

37.66　Insertion of implantable heart assist system　`LC`
Note: Device directly connected to the heart and implanted in the upper left quadrant of peritoneal cavity. This device can be used for either destination therapy (DT) or bridge-to-transplant (BTT).
Axial flow heart assist system
Diagonal pump heart assist system
Left ventricular assist device (LVAD)
Pulsatile heart assist system
Right ventricular assist device (RVAD)
Rotary pump heart assist system
Transportable, implantable heart assist system
Ventricular assist device (VAD) not otherwise specified
EXCLUDES　*implantation of total internal biventricular heart replacement system [artificial heart] (37.52)*
implant of pulsation balloon (37.61)
insertion of percutaneous external heart assist device (37.68)
DEF: Insertion of long-term circulatory support device with pump in body.
AHA: 4Q, '03, 116; 1Q, '98, 8

37.67　Implantation of cardiomyostimulation system
Note: Two-step open procedure consisting of tranfer of one end of the latissimus dorsi muscle; wrapping it around the heart; rib resection; implantation of epicardial cardiac pacing leads into the right ventricle; tunneling and pocket creation for the cardiomyostimulator.
AHA: 4Q, '98, 75; 1Q, '98, 8

37.68　Insertion of percutaneous external heart assist device
Circulatory assist device
Extrinsic heart assist device
pVAD
Percutaneous heart assist device
EXCLUDES　*percutaneous [femoral] insertion of cannulae attachments*
AHA: 2Q, '08, 12
TIP: Assign for placement of the Orqis device, an extracorporeal, minimally invasive cardiac system designed to increase blood velocity down the thoracic aorta; used for patients with CHF who respond poorly to medical treatment.

`√4th` **37.7　Insertion, revision, replacement, and removal of leads; insertion of temporary pacemaker system; or revision of cardiac device pocket**
Code also any insertion and replacement of pacemaker device (37.80-37.87)
EXCLUDES　*implantation or replacement of transvenous lead [electrode] into left ventricular cardiac venous system (00.52)*
AHA: 1Q, '94, 16; 3Q, '92, 3; M-J, '87, 1

[handwritten: 37.71–37.74 Indicates insertion of leads for initial insertion of a permanent pacemaker]

[1] **37.70　Initial insertion of lead [electrode], not otherwise specified**
EXCLUDES　*insertion of temporary transvenous pacemaker system (37.78)*
replacement of atrial and/or ventricular lead(s) (37.76)

[1] **37.71　Initial insertion of transvenous lead [electrode] into ventricle**
EXCLUDES　*insertion of temporary transvenous pacemaker system (37.78)*
replacement of atrial and/or ventricular lead(s) (37.76)

[2] **37.72　Initial insertion of transvenous leads [electrodes] into atrium and ventricle**
EXCLUDES　*insertion of temporary transvenous pacemaker system (37.78)*
replacement of atrial and/or ventricular lead(s) (37.76)
AHA: ▶4Q, '08, 102;◀ 2Q, '97, 4

[1] Valid OR procedure code if accompanied by one of the following codes: 37.80, 37.81, 37.82, 37.85, 37.86, 37.87
[2] Valid OR procedure code if accompanied by one of the following codes: 37.80, 37.83

When an existing pacemaker device is replaced with a new device, the type of device being removed does not effect the code; only the type of new device should be coded.

Operations on the Cardiovascular System

37.73–37.87

[1] **37.73 Initial insertion of transvenous lead [electrode] into atrium**

> EXCLUDES   insertion of temporary transvenous pacemaker system (37.78)
> replacement of atrial and/or ventricular lead(s) (37.76)

[4] **37.74 Insertion or replacement of epicardial lead [electrode] into epicardium**

> Insertion or replacement of epicardial lead by:
>   sternotomy
>   thoracotomy
> EXCLUDES   replacement of atrial and/or ventricular lead(s) (37.76)

AHA: 1Q, '07, 20; 3Q, '05, 3-9

37.75 Revision of lead [electrode]

> Repair of electrode [removal with re-insertion]
> Repositioning of lead(s) (AICD) (cardiac device) (CRT-D) (CRT-P) (defibrillator) (pacemaker) (pacing) (sensing) [electrode]
> Revision of lead NOS
> EXCLUDES   repositioning of temporary transvenous pacemaker system — omit code

AHA: 3Q, '05, 8; 2Q, '99, 11

Two codes are required for total replacement of permanent pacemaker... 37.74 or 37.74 and 37.85–37.87

[3] **37.76 Replacement of transvenous atrial and/or ventricular lead(s) [electrode]**

> Removal or abandonment of existing transvenous or epicardial lead(s) with transvenous lead(s) replacement
> EXCLUDES   replacement of epicardial lead [electrode] (37.74)

AHA: 3Q, '05, 3-9

37.77 Removal of lead(s) [electrode] without replacement

> Removal:
>   epicardial lead (transthoracic approach)
>   transvenous lead(s)
> EXCLUDES   removal of temporary transvenous pacemaker system — omit code
> that with replacement of:
>   atrial and/or ventricular lead(s) [electrode] (37.76)
>   epicardial lead [electrode] (37.74)

37.78 Insertion of temporary transvenous pacemaker system

> EXCLUDES   intraoperative cardiac pacemaker (39.64)

AHA: 3Q, '05, 7; 3Q, '93, 12; 1Q, '89, 2

Insertion of Pacemaker

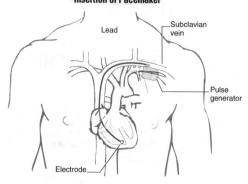

Lead — Subclavian vein — Pulse generator — Electrode

37.79 Revision or relocation of cardiac device pocket

> Debridement and reforming pocket (skin and subcutaneous tissue)
> Insertion of loop recorder
> Relocation of pocket [creation of new pocket] pacemaker or CRT-P
> Removal of cardiac device/pulse generator without replacement
> Removal of the implantable hemodynamic pressure sensor [lead] and monitor device
> Removal without replacement of cardiac resynchronization defibrillator device
> Repositioning of implantable hemodynamic pressure sensor [lead] and monitor device
> Repositioning of pulse generator
> Revision of cardioverter/defibrillator (automatic) pocket
> Revision of pocket for intracardiac hemodynamic monitoring
> Revision or relocation of CRT-D pocket
> Revision or relocation of pacemaker, defibrillator, or other implanted cardiac device pocket
> EXCLUDES   removal of loop recorder (86.05)

AHA: 3Q, '05, 3-9

Also includes creation of a pocket for an implantable, patient-activated cardiac event recorder.

[✓4th] **37.8 Insertion, replacement, removal, and revision of pacemaker device**

> Note: Device testing during procedure — omit code
> Code also any lead insertion, lead replacement, lead removal and/or lead revision (37.70-37.77)
> EXCLUDES   implantation of cardiac resynchronization pacemaker, total system [CRT-P] (00.50)
> implantation or replacement of cardiac resynchronization pacemaker pulse generator only [CRT-P] (00.53)

AHA: M-J, '87, 1

37.80 Insertion of permanent pacemaker, initial or replacement, type of device not specified

[5] **37.81 Initial insertion of single-chamber device, not specified as rate responsive**

> EXCLUDES   replacement of existing pacemaker device (37.85-37.87)

[5] **37.82 Initial insertion of single-chamber device, rate responsive**

> Rate responsive to physiologic stimuli other than atrial rate
> EXCLUDES   replacement of existing pacemaker device (37.85-37.87)

[6] **37.83 Initial insertion of dual-chamber device**

> Atrial ventricular sequential device
> EXCLUDES   replacement of existing pacemaker device (37.85-37.87)

AHA: 4Q, '08, 102; 2Q, '97, 4

37.85 Replacement of any type pacemaker device with single-chamber device, not specified as rate responsive

37.86 Replacement of any type pacemaker device with single-chamber device, rate responsive

> Rate responsive to physiologic stimuli other than atrial rate

37.87 Replacement of any type pacemaker device with dual-chamber device

> Atrial ventricular sequential device

37.81–37.83 Indicates the type of device (aka pulse generator) for initial insertion of permanent pacemaker

Device Only

Rate Responsive: device in which the pacing rate is determined by physiological variable other than the atrial rate.

---

[1] Valid OR procedure code if accompanied by one of the following codes: 37.80, 37.81, 37.82, 37.85, 37.86, 37.87
[3] Valid OR procedure code if accompanied by one of the following codes: 37.80, 37.85, 37.86, 37.87
[4] Valid OR procedure code if accompanied by one of the following codes: 37.80, 37.81, 37.82, 37.83, 37.85, 37.86, 37.87
[5] Valid OR procedure code if accompanied by one of the following codes: 37.70, 37.71, 37.73, 37.74
[6] Valid OR procedure code if accompanied by one of the following codes: 37.72, 37.74

BI Bilateral Procedure   **NC** Non-covered Procedure   **LC** Limited Coverage Procedure   ▶◀ Revised Text   ● New Code   ▲ Revised Code Title

If the AICD is in combination with CCM, use this code for AICD and 17.51 for implantation of CCM

37.89　**Revision or removal of pacemaker device**

Removal without replacement of cardiac re-synchronization pacemaker device [CRT-P]

Repair of pacemaker device

> **EXCLUDES**　removal of temporary transvenous pacemaker system — omit code
>
> replacement of existing pacemaker device (37.85-37.87)
>
> replacement of existing pacemaker device with CRT-P pacemaker device (00.53)

AHA: N-D, '86, 1

√4th　37.9　**Other operations on heart and pericardium**
AHA: 3Q, '90, 11

37.90　**Insertion of left atrial appendage device**

Left atrial filter

Left atrial occluder

Transseptal catheter technique

DEF: Implantation of a filtering device within the left atrial appendage (LAA) to block emboli from exiting the LAA causing stroke or systemic thromboembolism.

AHA: 4Q, '04, 121

37.91　**Open chest cardiac massage**

> **EXCLUDES**　closed chest cardiac massage (99.63)

DEF: Massage of heart through opening in chest wall to reinstate or maintain circulation.

AHA: 4Q, '88, 12

37.92　**Injection of therapeutic substance into heart**

37.93　**Injection of therapeutic substance into pericardium**

37.94　**Implantation or replacement of automatic cardioverter/defibrillator, total system [AICD]**

Note: Device testing during procedure — omit code

Implantation of defibrillator with leads (epicardial patches), formation of pocket (abdominal fascia) (subcutaneous), any transvenous leads, intra-operative procedures for evaluation of lead signals, and obtaining defibrillator threshold measurements　*[total procedure]*

Techniques:
  lateral thoracotomy
  medial sternotomy
  subxiphoid procedure

Code also extracorporeal circulation, if performed (39.61)

▶Code also any concomitant procedure [e.g., coronary bypass (36.10-36.19) or CCM, total system (17.51)]◀

> **EXCLUDES**　implantation of cardiac resynchronization defibrillator, total system [CRT-D] (00.51)

DEF: Direct insertion, of defibrillator/cardioverter system to deliver shock and restore heart rhythm.

AHA: 2Q, '03, 19; 3Q, '01, 5-7; 3Q, '99, 12; 1Q, '99, 3; 3Q, '90, 11; S-O, '87, 5

TIP: Assign for AICD placement, regardless of approach, whether by thoracotomy or by cephalic vein cutdown.

37.95　**Implantation of automatic cardioverter/defibrillator lead(s) only**　*Stage I*

AHA: 3Q, '90, 11

37.96　**Implantation of automatic cardioverter/defibrillator pulse generator only**　*Stage II*

Note: Device testing during procedure — omit code

> **EXCLUDES**　implantation or replacement of cardiac resynchronization defibrillator, pulse generator device only [CRT-D] (00.54)

AHA: 3Q, '90, 11

Left Atrial Appendage Device Insertion

Automatic Implantable Cardioverter/Defibrillator

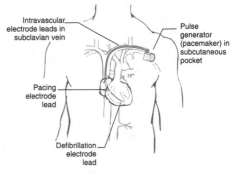

37.97　**Replacement of automatic cardioverter/defibrillator lead(s) only**

> **EXCLUDES**　replacement of epicardial lead [electrode] into epicardium (37.74)
>
> replacement of transvenous lead [electrode] into left ventricular coronary venous system (00.52)

AHA: 3Q, '05, 3-9; 3Q, '90, 11

37.98　**Replacement of automatic cardioverter defibrillator pulse generator only**

Note: Device testing during procedure — omit code

> **EXCLUDES**　replacement of cardiac resynchronization defibrillator, pulse generator device only [CRT-D] (00.54)

AHA: 1Q, '99, 3; 3Q, '90, 11

37.99　**Other**

> **EXCLUDES**　cardiac retraining (93.36)
>
> conversion of cardiac rhythm (99.60-99.69)
>
> implantation of prosthetic cardiac support device (37.41)
>
> insertion of left atrial appendage device (37.90)
>
> maze procedure (Cox-maze), open (37.33)
>
> maze procedure, endovascular approach (37.34)
>
> repositioning of pulse generator (37.79)
>
> revision of lead(s) (37.75)
>
> revision or relocation of pacemaker, defibrillator or other implanted cardiac device pocket (37.79)

AHA: 3Q, '05, 5; 2Q, '05, 14; 1Q, '97, 12; 1Q, '94, 19; 3Q, '90, 11; 1Q, '89, 11

AICD: an electronic device designed to detect and treat life-threatening tachyarrhythmias by means of countershocks.

During surgery to implant the AICD, the device is tested by inducing ventricular fibrillation (VF)...shocks are delivered and normal sinus rythm is restored. A diagnosis of VF is not coded when it is induced by the defibrillator (shocking) to make sure the AICD recognized the VF. The arrhythmia is being induced to check the functioning of the device.

Operations on the Cardiovascular System

38–38.3

√3rd **38**   **Incision, excision, and occlusion of vessels**

Code also any application or administration of an adhesion barrier substance (99.77)

Code also cardiopulmonary bypass [extracorporeal circulation] [heart-lung machine] (39.61)

EXCLUDES   *that of coronary vessels (00.66, 36.03, 36.04, 36.09, 36.10-36.99)*

The following fourth-digit subclassification is for use with appropriate categories in section 38.0, 38.1, 38.3, 38.5, 38.6, and 38.8 according to site. Valid fourth-digits are in [brackets] under each code.

0   **unspecified**
1   **intracranial vessels**
    Cerebral (anterior) (middle)
    Circle of Willis
    Posterior communicating artery
2   **other vessels of head and neck**
    Carotid artery (common) (external) (internal)
    Jugular vein (external) (internal)
3   **upper limb vessels**

Axillary	Radial
Brachial	Ulnar

4   **aorta**
5   **other thoracic vessels**

Innominate	Subclavian
Pulmonary (artery) (vein)	Vena cava, superior

6   **abdominal arteries**

Celiac	Mesenteric
Gastric	Renal
Hepatic	Splenic
Iliac	Umbilical

    EXCLUDES   *abdominal aorta (4)*
7   **abdominal veins**

Iliac	Splenic
Portal	Vena cava (inferior)
Renal	

8   **lower limb arteries**

Femoral (common)	Popliteal
(superficial)	Tibial

9   **lower limb veins**

Femoral	Saphenous
Popliteal	Tibial

§ √4th **38.0**   **Incision of vessel**
[0-9]   Embolectomy
    Thrombectomy
    EXCLUDES   *endovascular removal of obstruction from head and neck vessel(s) (39.74)*
       puncture or catheterization of any:
         artery (38.91, 38.98)
         vein (38.92-38.95, 38.99)
    AHA: 2Q, '98, 23; **For code 38.08 and 38.09:** 1Q, '03, 17

§ √4th **38.1**   **Endarterectomy**
[0-6,8]   Endarterectomy with:
       embolectomy
       patch graft
       temporary bypass during procedure
       thrombectomy
    Code also any:
       number of vascular stents inserted (00.45-00.48)
       number of vessels treated (00.40-00.43)
       procedure on vessel bifurcation (00.44)
    DEF: Excision of tunica intima of artery to relieve arterial walls thickened by plaque or chronic inflammation.
    AHA: 1Q, '00, 16; 2Q, '99, 5; 2Q, '95, 16; **For code 38.12:** 3Q, '06, 20; 1Q, '02, 10

√4th **38.2**   **Diagnostic procedures on blood vessels**
    EXCLUDES   *adjunct vascular system procedures (00.40-00.43)*

    38.21   **Biopsy of blood vessel**

    38.22   **Percutaneous angioscopy**
       EXCLUDES   *angioscopy of eye (95.12)*
       DEF: Exam, with fiberoptic catheter inserted through peripheral artery to visualize inner lining of blood vessels.

Endarterectomy of Aortic Bifurcation

- Aorta (shown sectioned)
- Plaque
- Femoral artery
- Plaque removed

38.23   **Intravascular spectroscopy**
    INCLUDES   ►spectroscopy of both coronary and peripheral vessels◄
    Intravascular chemography
    Near infrared (NIR) spectroscopy
    EXCLUDES   *intravascular imaging of:*
       coronary vessels ►(00.24, 38.24)
       peripheral vessels (00.23, 38.25)◄
    DEF: Method of identifying the chemical composition of coronary plaques by shining a near infrared (NIR) light at the plaque and measuring the amount of light reflected at different wavelengths.
       peripheral vessels (00.23)
    AHA: 4Q, '08, 182-183

● **38.24**   **Intravascular imaging of coronary vessel(s) by optical coherence tomography [OCT]**

● **38.25**   **Intravascular imaging of non-coronary vessel(s) by optical coherence tomography [OCT]**
       EXCLUDES   *intravascular imaging of coronary vessel(s) by OCT (38.24)*

38.29   **Other diagnostic procedures on blood vessels**
    EXCLUDES   *blood vessel thermography (88.86)*
       circulatory monitoring (89.61-89.69)
       contrast:
         angiocardiography (88.50-88.58)
         arteriography (88.40-88.49)
         phlebography (88.60-88.67)
       impedance phlebography (88.68)
       peripheral vascular ultrasonography (88.77)
       plethysmogram (89.58)
    AHA: 3Q, '00, 16; 1Q, '99, 7
    TIP: Assign for an artery test occlusion, performed to determine the feasibility of coil occlusion of an aneurysm.

§ √4th **38.3**   **Resection of vessel with anastomosis**
[0-9]   Angiectomy
    Excision of:
       aneurysm (arteriovenous) } with anastomosis
       blood vessel (lesion)
    DEF: Reconstruction and reconnection of vessel after partial excision.

Methods of Vessel Anastomoses

End-to-end	Side-to-side
Oblique cut	Fish mouth
Funnelization	End-to-side

§   Requires fourth digit. See category 38 for definitions.

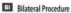

BI Bilateral Procedure   NC Non-covered Procedure   LC Limited Coverage Procedure   ►◄ Revised Text   ● New Code   ▲ Revised Code Title

§§ ✓4th **38.4** **Resection of vessel with replacement**
[0-9]

Angiectomy

Excision of:

aneurysm (arteriovenous) or   } with replacement
blood vessel (lesion)

Partial resection with replacement

EXCLUDES *endovascular repair of aneurysm (39.71-39.79)*

Subcategory 38.4 requires the use of one of the following fourth-digit subclassifications to identify site:

0 unspecified
1 intracranial vessels
    Cerebral (anterior) (middle)
    Circle of Willis
    Posterior communicating artery
2 other vessels of head and neck
    Carotid artery (common) (external) (internal)
    Jugular vein (external) (internal)
3 upper limb vessels
    Axilllary   Radial
    Brachial   Ulnar
4 aorta, abdominal
    Code also any thoracic vessel involvement (thoracoabdominal
        procedure) (38.45)
5 other thoracic vessels
    Aorta (thoracic)   Subclavian
    Innominate   Vena cava, superior
    Pulmonary (artery) (vein)
    Code also any abdominal aorta involvement
        (thoracoabdominal procedure) (38.44)
6 abdominal arteries
    Celiac   Mesenteric
    Gastric   Renal
    Hepatic   Splenic
    Iliac   Umbilical
    EXCLUDES *abdominal aorta (4)*
7 abdominal veins
    Iliac   Splenic
    Portal   Vena cava (inferior)
    Renal
8 lower limb arteries
    Femoral (common)(superficial)
    Tibial
9 lower limb veins
    Femoral   Saphenous
    Popliteal   Tibial

    DEF: Excision of aneurysm (arteriovenous): Excision and replacement of segment of stretched or bulging blood vessel.
    DEF: Excision of blood vessel (lesion): Excision and replacement of segment of vessel containing lesion.
    AHA: 2Q, '99, 5, 6; **For code 38.44:** 3Q, '06, 15; **For code 38.45:** 2Q, '08, 13; **For code 38.48:** 2Q, '08, 13

§ ✓4th **38.5** **Ligation and stripping of varicose veins**
[0-3,5,7,9] **EXCLUDES** *ligation of varices:*
                    esophageal (42.91)
                    gastric (44.91)

    DEF: Ligation of varicose veins: Typing off vein with thread or wire to eliminate blood flow; stripping involves excising length of vein.
    AHA: For code 38.59: 2Q, '97, 7

    TIP: Do not assign a separate code for subfascial endoscopic perforator vein interruption, which is an integral part of the procedure.

§ ✓4th **38.6** **Other excision of vessels**
[0-9]

Excision of blood vessel (lesion) NOS

    EXCLUDES *excision of vessel for aortocoronary bypass*
                    (36.10-36.14)
               excision with:
                    anastomosis (38.30-38.39)
                    graft replacement (38.40-38.49)
                    implant (38.40-38.49)
    AHA: 3Q, '90, 17

        38.7 **Interruption of the vena cava**

    Insertion of implant or sieve in vena cava
    Ligation of vena cava (inferior) (superior)
    Plication of vena cava

[handwritten: Insertion of femoral tulip filter]

    DEF: Interruption of the blood flow through the venous heart vessels to prevent clots from reaching the chambers of the heart by means of implanting a sieve or implant, separating off a portion or by narrowing the venous blood vessels.
    AHA: 2Q, '07, 4; 2Q, '94, 9; S-O, '85, 5
    TIP: Assign this code for placement of a vena cava sieve, umbrella, or filter, regardless of the approach (open or percutaneous).

§ ✓4th **38.8** **Other surgical occlusion of vessels**
[0-9]

Clamping   }
Division   }
Ligation   } of blood vessel
Occlusion   }

    EXCLUDES *adrenal vessels (07.43)*
                 esophageal varices (42.91)
                 gastric or duodenal vessel for ulcer (44.40-44.49)
                 gastric varices (44.91)
                 meningeal vessel (02.13)
                 percutaneous transcatheter infusion
                    embolization (99.29)
                 spermatic vein for varicocele (63.1)
                 surgical occlusion of vena cava (38.7)
                 that for chemoembolization (99.25)
                 that for control of (postoperative) hemorrhage:
                    anus (49.95)
                    bladder (57.93)
                    following vascular procedure (39.41)
                    nose (21.00-21.09)
                    prostate (60.94)
                    tonsil (28.7)
                    thyroid vessel (06.92)
                 transcatheter (infusion) 99.29
    AHA: 2Q, '90, 23; M-A, '87, 9; **For code 38.85:** 1Q, '03, 15; **For code 38.86:** 1Q, '05, 14; N-D, '87, 4

✓4th **38.9** **Puncture of vessel**
    EXCLUDES *that for circulatory monitoring (89.60-89.69)*

    38.91 **Arterial catheterization**
        AHA: 1Q, '05, 14; 1Q, '97, 3; 1Q, '95, 3; 2Q, '91, 15; 2Q, '90, 23

    38.92 **Umbilical vein catheterization**

    38.93 **Venous catheterization, not elsewhere classified**

[handwritten: AKA Heparin lock]

        EXCLUDES *that for cardiac catheterization*
                    (37.21-37.23)
                 that for renal dialysis (38.95)
        AHA: 3Q, '00, 9; 2Q, '98, 24; 1Q, '96, 3; 2Q, '96, 15; 3Q, '91, 13; 4Q, '90, 14; 2Q, '90, 24; 3Q, '88, 13

    38.94 **Venous cutdown**
        DEF: Incision of vein to place needle or catheter.

    38.95 **Venous catheterization for renal dialysis**
        EXCLUDES *insertion of totally implantable*
                    vascular access device [VAD]
                    (86.07)
        AHA: ▶4Q, '08, 193;◀ 3Q, '98, 13; 2Q, '94, 11
        TIP: Do not assign for vessel-to-vessel cannula (AV dialysis graft) insertion; see instead code 39.93.

Typical Venous Cutdown

Vein mobilized, opened by oblique cut, catheter inserted

Distal vein tied

Saphenous vein (typical site) accessed by transverse incision

---

§   Requires fourth digit. Valid digits are in [brackets] under each code. See category 38 for definitions.
§§   Requires fourth digit. Valid digits are in [brackets] under each code. See subcategory 38.4 for definitions

 Additional Digit Required   Valid OR Procedure   Non-OR Procedure   Adjunct Code
2010 ICD-9-CM   **February 2009 • Volume 3 – 117**

Operations on the Cardiovascular System

38.98–39.43

38.98 Other puncture of artery
> *EXCLUDES*   that for:
> > arteriography (88.40-88.49)
> > coronary arteriography
> > (88.55-88.57)

38.99 Other puncture of vein
Phlebotomy
> *EXCLUDES*   that for:
> > angiography of veins (88.60-88.68)
> > extracorporeal circulation (39.61, 50.92)
> > injection or infusion of:
> > sclerosing solution (39.92)
> > therapeutic or prophylactic sub-stance (99.11-99.29)
> > perfusion (39.96, 39.97)
> > phlebography 88.60-88.68)
> > transfusion (99.01-99.09)

AHA: 4Q, '94, 50; 1Q, '88, 11

√3rd **39 Other operations on vessels**
> *EXCLUDES*   those on coronary vessels (36.03-36.99)

39.0 Systemic to pulmonary artery shunt

Descending aorta-pulmonary
    artery
Left to right   } anastomosis (graft)
Subclavian-pulmonary

Code also cardiopulmonary bypass [extracorporeal circulation] [heart-lung machine] (39.61)

DEF: Descending aorta-pulmonary artery anastomosis (graft): Connection of descending main heart artery to pulmonary artery.
DEF: Left to right anastomosis (graft): Connection of systemic arterial blood vessel to venous pulmonary system.
DEF: Subclavian-pulmonary anastomosis (graft): Connection of subclavian artery to pulmonary artery

39.1 Intra-abdominal venous shunt

Anastomosis:
   mesocaval
   portacaval
   portal vein to inferior vena cava
   splenic and renal veins
   transjugular intrahepatic portosystemic shunt [TIPS]
> *EXCLUDES*   peritoneovenous shunt (54.94)

DEF: Connection of two venous blood vessels within abdominal cavity.
AHA: 2Q, '02, 4; 4Q, '94, 50; 4Q, '93, 31; 2Q, '93, 8

√4th **39.2 Other shunt or vascular bypass**
Code also pressurized treatment of venous bypass graft [conduit] with pharmaceutical substance, if performed (00.16)

DEF: Creation of supplemental blood flow to area with inadequate blood supply due to disease or injury of vessels.
TIP: Assign separate codes for any concomitant procedures performed, such as arterial or venous thrombectomy or arteriography.

39.21 Caval-pulmonary artery anastomosis
Code also cardiopulmonary bypass (39.61)

39.22 Aorta-subclavian-carotid bypass
Bypass (arterial):
   aorta to carotid and brachial
   aorta to subclavian and carotid
   carotid to subclavian

39.23 Other intrathoracic vascular shunt or bypass
Intrathoracic (arterial) bypass graft NOS
> *EXCLUDES*   coronary artery bypass (36.10-36.19)

39.24 Aorta-renal bypass

39.25 Aorta-iliac-femoral bypass
Bypass:
   aortofemoral
   aortoiliac
   aortoiliac to popliteal
   aortopopliteal
   iliofemoral [iliac-femoral]
AHA: 1Q, '03, 16; 4Q, '90, 27; 1Q, '88, 10

39.26 Other intra-abdominal vascular shunt or bypass
Bypass:
   aortoceliac
   aortic-superior mesenteric
   common hepatic-common iliac-renal
Intra-abdominal arterial bypass graft NOS
> *EXCLUDES*   peritoneovenous shunt (54.94)

39.27 Arteriovenostomy for renal dialysis
Anastomosis for renal dialysis
Formation of (peripheral) arteriovenous fistula for renal [kidney] dialysis
Code also any renal dialysis (39.95)
AHA: 1Q, '07, 18; 1Q, '06, 10
TIP: Assign for arteriovenostomy for renal dialysis; includes transposition of the basilic vein.

39.28 Extracranial-intracranial (EC-IC) vascular bypass   NC
AHA: 2Q, '92, 7; 4Q, '91, 22

39.29 Other (peripheral) vascular shunt or bypass
Bypass (graft):
   axillary-brachial
   axillary-femoral [axillofemora] (superficial)
   brachial
   femoral-femoral
   femoroperoneal
   femoropopliteal (arteries)
   femorotibial (anterior) (posterior)
   popliteal
   vascular NOS
> *EXCLUDES*   peritoneovenous shunt (54.94)
AHA: 1Q, '03, 17; 2Q, '02, 8; 1Q, '02, 13; S-O, '85, 13

√4th **39.3 Suture of vessel**
Repair of laceration of blood vessel
> *EXCLUDES*   any other vascular puncture closure device — omit code
> > suture of aneurysm (39.52)
> > that for control of hemorrhage (postoperative):
> > anus (49.95)
> > bladder (57.93)
> > following vascular procedure (39.41)
> > nose (21.00-21.09)
> > prostate (60.94)
> > tonsil (28.7)

39.30 Suture of unspecified blood vessel

39.31 Suture of artery
AHA: 3Q, '06, 9

39.32 Suture of vein

√4th **39.4 Revision of vascular procedure**
39.41 Control of hemorrhage following vascular surgery
> *EXCLUDES*   that for control of hemorrhage (postoperative):
> > anus (49.95)
> > bladder (57.93)
> > nose (21.00-21.09)
> > prostate (60.94)
> > tonsil (28.7)

39.42 Revision of arteriovenous shunt for renal dialysis
Conversion of renal dialysis:
   end-to-end anastomosis to end-to-side
   end-to-side anastomosis to end-to-end
   vessel-to-vessel cannula to arteriovenous shunt
Removal of old arteriovenous shunt and creation of new shunt
> *EXCLUDES*   replacement of vessel-to-vessel cannula (39.94)
AHA: 2Q, '94, 15; 4Q, '93, 33

39.43 Removal of arteriovenous shunt for renal dialysis
> *EXCLUDES*   that with replacement [revision] of shunt (39.42)

BI Bilateral Procedure   **NC** Non-covered Procedure   **LC** Limited Coverage Procedure   ►◄ Revised Text   ● New Code   ▲ Revised Code Title

118 – Volume 3   **2010 ICD-9-CM**

39.49   **Other revision of vascular procedure**

Declotting (graft)

Revision of:

anastomosis of blood vessel

vascular procedure (previous)

DEF: Declotting (graft): Removal of clot from graft.

AHA: 2Q, '98, 17; 1Q, '97, 3; 2Q, '94, 15

TIP: Do not assign if a declotting procedure of an AV dialysis graft is performed as a component of a revision procedure; see instead code 39.42.

✓4ᵗʰ **39.5**   **Other repair of vessels**

39.50   **Angioplasty or atherectomy of other non-coronary vessel(s)**

Percutaneous transluminal angioplasty (PTA) of non-coronary vessels:

lower extremity vessels

mesenteric artery

renal artery

upper extremity vessels

Code also any:

injection or infusion of thrombolytic agent (99.10)

▶insertion of drug-eluting peripheral vessel stent (00.55)◀

▶insertion of non-drug-eluting peripheral vessel stent(s) or stent grafts(s) (39.90)◀

number of vascular stents inserted (00.45-00.48)

number of vessels treated (00.40-00.43)

procedure on vessel bifurcation (00.44)

EXCLUDES   percutaneous angioplasty or atherectomy of precerebral or cerebral vessel(s) (00.61-00.62)

AHA: 4Q, '06, 119; 3Q, '03, 10; 1Q, '02, 13; 2Q, '01, 23; 2Q, '00, 10; 1Q, '00, 12; 2Q, '98, 17; 1Q, '97, 3; 4Q, '96, 63; 4Q, '95, 66

39.51   **Clipping of aneurysm**

EXCLUDES   clipping of arteriovenous fistula (39.53)

39.52   **Other repair of aneurysm**

Repair of aneurysm by:

coagulation

electrocoagulation

filipuncture

methyl methacrylate

suture

wiring

wrapping

EXCLUDES   endovascular repair of aneurysm (39.71-39.79)

re-entry operation (aorta) (39.54)

that with:

graft replacement (38.40-38.49)

resection (38.30-38.49, 38.60-38.69)

DEF: Application of device in abnormally stretched blood vessel to prevent movement of material collected in vessel.

DEF: Repair of aneurysm by: Coagulation: Clotting or solidifying. Electrocoagulation: Electrically produced clotting. Filipuncture: Insertion of wire or thread. Methyl methacrylate: Injection or insertion of plastic material. Suture: Stitching. Wiring: Insertion of wire. Wrapping: Compression.

AHA: 3Q, '06, 15-16; 3Q, '02, 25, 26; 1Q, '99, 15, 16, 17; 1Q, '88, 10

TIP: Do not assign if any type of grafting material was used in the aneurysm repair; see instead subcategory 38.4 or endovascular repair subcategory 39.7.

39.53   **Repair of arteriovenous fistula**

Embolization of carotid cavernous fistula

Repair of arteriovenous fistula by:

clipping

coagulation

ligation and division

EXCLUDES   repair of:

arteriovenous shunt for renal dialysis (39.42)

head and neck vessels, endovascular approach (39.72)

that with:

graft replacement (38.40-38.49)

resection (38.30-38.49, 38.60-38.69)

DEF: Correction of arteriovenous fistula by application of clamps, causing coagulation or by tying off and dividing the connection.

AHA: 1Q, '00, 8

TIP: Do not assign for an embolization procedure performed by interventional radiologists via radiological guidance; it is not considered a surgical procedure; see instead code 99.29.

39.54   **Re-entry operation (aorta)**

Fenestration of dissecting aneurysm of thoracic aorta

Code also cardiopulmonary bypass [extracorporeal circulation] [heart-lung machine] (39.61)

DEF: Re-entry operation: Creation of passage between stretched wall of the vessel and major arterial channel to heart.

DEF: Fenestration of dissecting aneurysm of thoracic aorta: Creation of passage between stretched arterial heart vessel and functional part of vessel.

39.55   **Reimplantation of aberrant renal vessel**

DEF: Reimplant of renal vessel into normal position.

39.56   **Repair of blood vessel with tissue patch graft**

EXCLUDES   that with resection (38.40-38.49)

AHA: 1Q, '04, 16

39.57   **Repair of blood vessel with synthetic patch graft**

EXCLUDES   that with resection (38.40-38.49)

39.58   **Repair of blood vessel with unspecified type of patch graft**

EXCLUDES   that with resection (38.40-38.49)

39.59   **Other repair of vessel**

Aorticopulmonary window operation

Arterioplasty NOS

Construction of venous valves (peripheral)

Plication of vein (peripheral)

Reimplantation of artery

Code also cardiopulmonary bypass [extracorporeal circulation] [heart-lung machine] (39.61)

EXCLUDES   interruption of the vena cava (38.7)

reimplantation of renal artery (39.55)

that with:

graft (39.56-39.58)

resection (38.30-38.49, 38.60-38.69)

DEF: Aorticopulmonary window operation: Repair of abnormal opening between major heart arterial vessel above valves and pulmonary artery.

DEF: Construction of venous valves (peripheral): Reconstruction of valves within peripheral veins.

DEF: Plication of vein (peripheral): Shortening of peripheral vein.

DEF: Reimplantation of artery: Reinsertion of artery into its normal position.

AHA: 4Q, '93, 31; 2Q, '89, 17; N-D, '86, 8; S-O, '85, 5; M-A, '85, 15

Operations on the Cardiovascular System

39.49–39.59

Operations on the Cardiovascular System

39.6–39.73

✓4ᵗʰ **39.6** **Extracorporeal circulation and procedures auxiliary to heart surgery**
AHA: 1Q, '95, 5

39.61 **Extracorporeal circulation auxiliary to open heart surgery**
Artificial heart and lung   Pump oxygenator
Cardiopulmonary bypass
EXCLUDES   extracorporeal hepatic assistance (50.92)
extracorporeal membrane oxygenation [ECMO] (39.65)
hemodialysis (39.95)
percutaneous cardiopulmonary bypass (39.66)

AHA: ▶2Q, '09, 8;◀ 3Q, '08, 9; 2Q, '08, 13; 1Q, '04, 16; 3Q, '02, 5; 4Q, '97, 55; 3Q, '97, 14; 2Q, '97, 8; 2Q, '90, 24

39.62 **Hypothermia (systemic) incidental to open heart surgery**

39.63 **Cardioplegia**
Arrest: Arrest:
    anoxic   circulatory
DEF: Purposely inducing electromechanical cardiac arrest.

39.64 **Intraoperative cardiac pacemaker**
Temporary pacemaker used during and immediately following cardiac surgery
AHA: 1Q, '89, 2; M-J, '87, 3

[handwritten note: No codes are assigned for insertion of the leads or for removal of a temporary or intraoperative pacemaker.]

39.65 **Extracorporeal membrane oxygenation [ECMO]**
EXCLUDES   extracorporeal circulation auxiliary to open heart surgery (39.61)
percutaneous cardiopulmonary bypass (39.66)
DEF: Creation of closed-chest, heart-lung bypass or Bard cardiopulmonary assist system with tube insertion.
AHA: 2Q, '90, 23; 2Q, '89, 17; 4Q, '88, 5

39.66 **Percutaneous cardiopulmonary bypass**
Closed chest
EXCLUDES   extracorporeal circulation auxiliary to open heart surgery (39.61)
extracorporeal hepatic assistance (50.92)
extracorporeal membrane oxygenation [ECMO] (39.65)
hemodialysis (39.95)
DEF: Use of mechanical pump system to oxygenate and pump blood throughout the body via catheter in the femoral artery and vein.
AHA: 3Q, '96, 11

▲ ✓4ᵗʰ **39.7** **Endovascular procedures on vessel(s)**
▶Embolization◀
Endoluminal repair
▶Implantation
Occlusion
Removal
Repair◀
EXCLUDES   angioplasty or atherectomy of other non-coronary vessel(s) (39.50)
insertion of non-drug-eluting peripheral vessel stent(s) (39.90)
other repair of aneurysm (39.52)
percutaneous insertion of carotid artery stent(s) (00.63)
percutaneous insertion of intracranial stent(s) (00.65)
percutaneous insertion of other precerebral artery stent(s) (00.64)
resection of abdominal aorta with replacement (38.44)
resection of lower limb arteries with replacement (38.48)
resection of thoracic aorta with replacement (38.45)
resection of upper limb vessels with replacement (38.43)

Endovascular Repair of Abdominal Aortic Aneurysm

Renal arteries
Stent
Abdominal aortic aneurysm
Common iliac arteries

39.71 **Endovascular implantation of graft in abdominal aorta**
Endovascular repair of abdominal aortic aneurysm with graft
Stent graft(s)
Code also intra-aneurysm sac pressure monitoring (intraoperative) (00.58)
DEF: Replacement of a section of abdominal aorta with mesh graft; via catheters inserted through femoral arteries.
AHA: 1Q, '02, 13; 4Q, '00, 63, 64

▲ **39.72** **Endovascular embolization or occlusion of head and neck vessels**
Endograft(s)
Endovascular graft(s)
Liquid tissue adhesive (glue) embolization or occlusion
Other implant or substance for repair, embolization or occlusion
That for repair of aneurysm, arteriovenous malformation [AVM] or fistula
EXCLUDES   ▶embolization of head or neck vessels using bare coils (39.75)
embolization of head or neck vessels using bioactive coils (39.76)◀
mechanical thrombectomy of precerebral and cerebral vessels (39.74)
DEF: Coil embolization or occlusion: Utilizing x-ray guidance a neuro-microcatheter is guided from entry in the femoral artery in the groin to the site of the aneurysm of the head and neck vessels for delivery of micro-coils that stop blood flow to the arteriovenous malformation (AVM).
AHA: 4Q, '02, 103

39.73 **Endovascular implantation of graft in thoracic aorta**
Endograft(s)
Endovascular graft(s)
Endovascular repair of defect of thoracic aorta with graft(s) or device(s)
Stent graft(s) or device(s)
That for repair of aneurysm, dissection, or injury
Code also intra-aneurysm sac pressure monitoring (intraoperative) (00.58)
EXCLUDES   fenestration of dissecting aneurysm of thoracic aorta (39.54)
DEF: Intravascular transcatheter deployment of an expanding stent-graft for repair of thoracic aortic aneurysm, performed without opening the chest.
AHA: 4Q, '05, 120

BI Bilateral Procedure   **NC** Non-covered Procedure   **LC** Limited Coverage Procedure   ▶◀ Revised Text   ● New Code   ▲ Revised Code Title

120 – Volume 3 · October 2009   **2010 ICD-9-CM**

39.74　Endovascular removal of obstruction from head and neck vessel(s)

Endovascular embolectomy

Endovascular thrombectomy of pre-cerebral and cerebral vessels

Mechanical embolectomy or thrombectomy

Code also:

any injection or infusion of thrombolytic agent (99.10)

number of vessels treated (00.40-00.43)

procedure on vessel bifurcation (00.44)

EXCLUDES　endarterectomy of intracranial vessels and other vessels of head and neck (38.11-38.12)

▶occlusive endovascular embolization of head or neck vessels using bare coils (39.75)

occlusive endovascular embolization of head or neck vessel(s) using bioactive coils (39.76)◀

open embolectomy or thrombectomy (38.01-38.02)

AHA: 4Q, '06, 129

TIP: Mechanical thrombectomy represented by this code may also be documented as mechanical embolus removal in cerebral ischemia (MERCI®) extraction.

● **39.75　Endovascular embolization or occlusion of vessel(s) of head or neck using bare coils**

Bare metal coils

Bare platinum coils [BPC]

That for treatment of aneurysm, arteriovenous malformation [AVM] or fistula

● **39.76　Endovascular embolization or occlusion of vessel(s) of head or neck using bioactive coils**

Biodegradable inner luminal polymer coils

Coil embolization or occlusion utilizing bioactive coils

Coils containing polyglycolic acid [PGA]

That for treatment of aneurysm, arteriovenous malformation [AVM] or fistula

▲ **39.79　Other endovascular procedures on other vessels**

Endograft(s)

Endovascular graft(s)

Liquid tissue adhesive (glue) embolization or occlusion

▶Other coil embolization or occlusion◀

Other implant or substance for repair, embolization or occlusion

▶Repair of aneurysm◀

EXCLUDES　▶abdominal aortic aneurysm resection [AAA] (38.44)

endovascular implantation of graft in abdominal aorta (39.71)◀

endovascular implantation of graft in thoracic aorta (39.73)

▶endovascular embolization or occlusion of head and neck vessels, bare metal coils (39.75)

endovascular embolization or occlusion of head and neck vessels, bioactive coils (39.76)◀

insertion of drug-eluting peripheral vessel stent(s) (00.55)

insertion of non-drug-eluting peripheral vessel stent(s) (for other than aneurysm repair) (39.90)

non-endovascular repair of arteriovenous fistula (39.53)

other surgical occlusion of vessels – see category 38.8

percutaneous transcatheter infusion (99.29)

▶thoracic aortic aneurysm resection (38.45)◀

transcatheter embolization for gastric or duodenal bleeding (44.44)

AHA: ▶2Q, '09, 7-8;◀ 2Q, '06, 22, 23; 4Q, '02, 103; 3Q, '01, 17,18; 4Q, '00, 64

39.8　Operations on carotid body, carotid sinus and other vascular bodies

Chemodectomy

Denervation of:

aortic body

carotid body

Electronic stimulator

Glomectomy, carotid

Implantation or replacement of carotid sinus baroreflex activation device

EXCLUDES　excision of glomus jugulare (20.51)

replacement of carotid sinus lead(s) only (04.92)

DEF: Chemodectomy: Removal of a chemoreceptor vascular body.

DEF: Denervation of aortic body: Destruction of nerves attending the major heart blood vessels.

DEF: Denervation of carotid body: Destruction of nerves of carotid artery.

DEF: Glomectomy, carotid: Removal of the carotid artery framework.

AHA: 2Q, '07, 8

✓4ᵗʰ **39.9　Other operations on vessels**

▲ **39.90　Insertion of non-drug-eluting peripheral (non-coronary) vessel stent(s)**

Bare stent(s)

Bonded stent(s)

Drug-coated stent(s), i.e., heparin coated

Endograft(s)

Endovascular graft(s)

Endovascular recanalization techniques

Stent graft(s)

Code also any:

non-coronary angioplasty or atherectomy (39.50)

number of vascular stents inserted (00.45-00.48)

number of vessels treated (00.40-00.43)

procedure on vessel bifurcation (00.44)

EXCLUDES　insertion of drug-eluting, peripheral vessel stent(s) (00.55)

percutaneous insertion of carotid artery stent(s) (00.63)

percutaneous insertion of intracranial stent(s) (00.65)

percutaneous insertion of other precerebral artery stent(s) (00.64)

that for aneurysm repair (39.71-39.79)

AHA: 4Q, '06, 119; 4Q, '02, 101; 1Q, '00, 12; 4Q, '96, 63

39.91　Freeing of vessel

Dissection and freeing of adherent tissue:

artery-vein-nerve bundle

vascular bundle

AHA: 3Q, '02, 12

39.92　Injection of sclerosing agent into vein

EXCLUDES　injection:

esophageal varices (42.33)

hemorrhoids (49.42)

AHA: 2Q, '92, 17

39.93　Insertion of vessel-to-vessel cannula

Formation of:

arteriovenous:

fistula ⎫
　　　 ⎬ by external cannula
shunt ⎭

Code also any renal dialysis (39.95)

AHA: 3Q, '88, 13; S-O, '85, 5, 12

TIP: If the AV fistula or shunt catheter or device is considered totally implantable, assign instead 86.07.

39.94　Replacement of vessel-to-vessel cannula

Revision of vessel-to-vessel cannula

External Arteriovenous Shunt

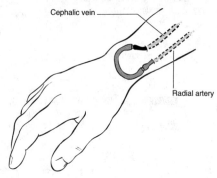

Cephalic vein

Radial artery

39.95 Hemodialysis
Artificial kidney
Hemodiafiltration
Hemofiltration
Renal dialysis
EXCLUDES peritoneal dialysis (54.98)
DEF: Filtration process to treat acute and chronic renal failure by eliminating toxic end products of nitrogen metabolism from blood.
AHA: ▶4Q, '08, 193◀ 3Q, '07, 9; 1Q, '04, 22; 4Q, '03, 111; 2Q, '01, 2-14; 4Q, '00, 40; 2Q, '98, 20; S-O, '86, 11

39.96 Total body perfusion
Code also substance perfused (99.21-99.29)

39.97 Other perfusion
Perfusion NOS
Perfusion, local [regional] of:
carotid artery
coronary artery
head
lower limb
neck
upper limb
Code also substance perfused (99.21-99.29)
EXCLUDES perfusion of:
kidney (55.95)
large intestine (46.96)
liver (50.93)
small intestine (46.95)
SuperSaturated oxygen therapy (00.49)
AHA: 3Q, '96, 11

39.98 Control of hemorrhage, not otherwise specified
Angiotripsy
Control of postoperative hemorrhage NOS
Venotripsy
EXCLUDES control of hemorrhage (postoperative):
anus (49.95)
bladder (57.93)
following vascular procedure (39.41)
nose (21.00-21.09)
prostate (60.94)
tonsil (28.7)
that by:
ligation (38.80-38.89)
suture (39.30-39.32)
DEF: Angiotripsy: Clamping of tissue to stop arterial blood flow.
DEF: Venotripsy: Clamping of tissue to stop venous blood flow.

39.99 Other operations on vessels
EXCLUDES injection or infusion of therapeutic or prophylactic substance (99.11-99.29)
transfusion of blood and blood components (99.01-99.09)
AHA: 1Q, '89, 11
TIP: Assign for removal of a vena cava filter via percutaneous transluminal approach via the jugular vein.

8. OPERATIONS ON THE HEMIC AND LYMPHATIC SYSTEMS (40-41)

√3rd 40   Operations on lymphatic system

40.0   Incision of lymphatic structures

√4th 40.1   Diagnostic procedures on lymphatic structures

  40.11   Biopsy of lymphatic structure

    AHA: 4Q, '08, 91

  40.19   Other diagnostic procedures on lymphatic structures

    EXCLUDES   *lymphangiogram:*
      abdominal (88.04)
      cervical (87.08)
      intrathoracic (87.34)
      lower limb (88.36)
      upper limb (88.34)
    microscopic examination of specimen (90.71-90.79)
    radioisotope scan (92.16)
    thermography (88.89)

√4th 40.2   Simple excision of lymphatic structure

  EXCLUDES   *biopsy of lymphatic structure (40.11)*

  DEF: Removal of lymphatic structure only.

  40.21   Excision of deep cervical lymph node

    AHA: 4Q, '99, 16

  40.22   Excision of internal mammary lymph node

  40.23   Excision of axillary lymph node

    AHA: 2Q, '02, 7

  40.24   Excision of inguinal lymph node

  40.29   Simple excision of other lymphatic structure

    Excision of:
      cystic hygroma
      lymphangioma
    Simple lymphadenectomy

    DEF: Lymphangioma: Removal of benign congenital lymphatic malformation.
    DEF: Simple lymphadenectomy: Removal of lymph node.
    AHA: 1Q, '99, 6

40.3   Regional lymph node excision

  Extended regional lymph node excision
  Regional lymph node excision with excision of lymphatic drainage area including skin, subcutaneous tissue, and fat

  DEF: Extended regional lymph node excision: Removal of lymph node group, including area around nodes.
  AHA: 2Q, '92, 7

√4th 40.4   Radical excision of cervical lymph nodes

  Resection of cervical lymph nodes down to muscle and deep fascia

  EXCLUDES   *that associated with radical laryngectomy (30.4)*

  TIP: Assign a code from this subcategory for procedures described as modified radical neck dissection.

  40.40   Radical neck dissection, not otherwise specified

  40.41   Radical neck dissection, unilateral

    AHA: 2Q, '05, 8; 2Q, '99, 6

    DEF: Dissection, total, of cervical lymph nodes on one side of neck.

  40.42   Radical neck dissection, bilateral

    DEF: Dissection, total, of cervical lymph nodes on both sides of neck.

√4th 40.5   Radical excision of other lymph nodes

  EXCLUDES   *that associated with radical mastectomy (85.45-85.48)*

  40.50   Radical excision of lymph nodes, not otherwise specified

    Radical (lymph) node dissection NOS

  40.51   Radical excision of axillary lymph nodes

  40.52   Radical excision of periaortic lymph nodes

  40.53   Radical excision of iliac lymph nodes

  40.54   Radical groin dissection

  40.59   Radical excision of other lymph nodes

    EXCLUDES   *radical neck dissection (40.40-40.42)*

√4th 40.6   Operations on thoracic duct

  40.61   Cannulation of thoracic duct

    DEF: Placement of cannula in main lymphatic duct of chest.

  40.62   Fistulization of thoracic duct

    DEF: Creation of passage in main lymphatic duct of chest.

  40.63   Closure of fistula of thoracic duct

    DEF: Closure of fistula in main lymphatic duct of chest.

  40.64   Ligation of thoracic duct

    DEF: Tying off main lymphatic duct of chest.

  40.69   Other operations on thoracic duct

40.9   Other operations on lymphatic structures

  Anastomosis
  Dilation
  Ligation
  Obliteration   } of peripheral lymphatics
  Reconstruction
  Repair
  Transplantation

  Correction of lymphedema of limb, NOS

  EXCLUDES   *reduction of elephantiasis of scrotum (61.3)*

√3rd 41   Operations on bone marrow and spleen

√4th 41.0   Bone marrow or hematopoietic stem cell transplant

  Note: To report donor source – see codes 00.91-00.93
  EXCLUDES   *aspiration of bone marrow from donor (41.91)*
  AHA: 4Q, '00, 64; 1Q, '91, 3; 4Q, '91, 26

  41.00   Bone marrow transplant, not otherwise specified

  8 41.01   Autologous bone marrow transplant without purging   NC

    EXCLUDES   *that with purging (41.09)*

    DEF: Transplant of patient's own bone marrow.

  9 41.02   Allogeneic bone marrow transplant with purging   NC

    Allograft of bone marrow with in vitro removal (purging) of T-cells

    DEF: Transplant of bone marrow from donor to patient after donor marrow purged of undesirable cells.

  9 41.03   Allogeneic bone marrow transplant without purging   NC

    Allograft of bone marrow NOS

  8 41.04   Autologous hematopoietic stem cell transplant without purging   NC

    EXCLUDES   *that with purging (41.07)*

    AHA: 4Q, '94, 52

  9 41.05   Allogeneic hematopoietic stem cell transplant without purging   NC

    EXCLUDES   *that with purging (41.08)*

    AHA: ▶1Q, '09, 9;◀ 4Q, '97, 55

  41.06   Cord blood stem cell transplant

    AHA: 4Q, '97, 56

  8 41.07   Autologous hematopoietic stem cell transplant with purging   NC

    Cell depletion

    AHA: 2Q, '06, 20-22

    TIP: Assign for autologous peripheral blood stem cell boost reinfusion.

  9 41.08   Allogeneic hematopoietic stem cell transplant with purging   NC

    Cell depletion

---

8   Noncovered procedure only when the following diagnoses are present as either principal or secondary diagnosis: 204.00, 205.00, 205.10, 205.11, 206.00, 207.00, 208.00
9   Noncovered procedure only when the following diagnoses are present as either principal or secondary diagnosis: 203.00, 203.01

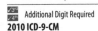

Operations on the Hemic and Lymphatic Systems

41.09–41.99

Partial Splenectomy

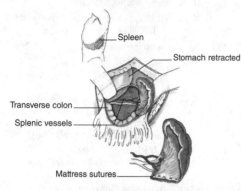

- Spleen
- Stomach retracted
- Transverse colon
- Splenic vessels
- Mattress sutures

Total Splenectomy

- Ligated splenic artery
- Splenic vein
- Pancreas
- Gastro-splenic ligament
- Short gastric vessels ligated
- Ruptured spleen

[9] **41.09   Autologous bone marrow transplant with purging**   `NC`

With extracorporeal purging of malignant cells from marrow
Cell depletion

41.1   Puncture of spleen

EXCLUDES   *aspiration biopsy of spleen (41.32)*

41.2   Splenotomy

✓4th   **41.3   Diagnostic procedures on bone marrow and spleen**

41.31   Biopsy of bone marrow

41.32   Closed [aspiration] [percutaneous] biopsy of spleen

Needle biopsy of spleen

41.33   Open biopsy of spleen

41.38   Other diagnostic procedures on bone marrow

EXCLUDES   *microscopic examination of specimen from bone marrow (90.61-90.69)*
radioisotope scan (92.05)

41.39   Other diagnostic procedures on spleen

EXCLUDES   *microscopic examination of specimen from spleen (90.61-90.69)*
radioisotope scan (92.05)

✓4th   **41.4   Excision or destruction of lesion or tissue of spleen**

Code also any application or administration of an adhesion barrier substance (99.77)

EXCLUDES   *excision of accessory spleen (41.93)*

41.41   Marsupialization of splenic cyst

DEF: Incision of cyst of spleen with edges sutured open to create pouch.

41.42   Excision of lesion or tissue of spleen

EXCLUDES   *biopsy of spleen (41.32-41.33)*

41.43   Partial splenectomy

DEF: Removal of spleen, partial.

41.5   Total splenectomy

Splenectomy NOS

Code also any application or administration of an adhesion barrier substance (99.77)

✓4th   **41.9   Other operations on spleen and bone marrow**

Code also any application or administration of an adhesion barrier substance (99.77)

41.91   Aspiration of bone marrow from donor for transplant

EXCLUDES   *biopsy of bone marrow (41.31)*

AHA: 1Q, '91, 3

41.92   Injection into bone marrow

EXCLUDES   *bone marrow transplant (41.00-41.03)*

AHA: 3Q, '96, 17

TIP: Assign for intraosseous IV access, performed emergently for a dehydrated infant whose peripheral vein cannot be accessed.

41.93   Excision of accessory spleen

41.94   Transplantation of spleen

41.95   Repair and plastic operations on spleen

41.98   Other operations on bone marrow

AHA: ▶3Q, '08, 19◀

41.99   Other operations on spleen

---

[9] Noncovered procedure only when the following diagnoses are present as either principal or secondary diagnosis: 203.00, 203.01

`BI` Bilateral Procedure   `NC` Non-covered Procedure   `LC` Limited Coverage Procedure   ▶◀ Revised Text   ● New Code   ▲ Revised Code Title

124 – Volume 3 • February 2009   **2010 ICD-9-CM**

9. OPERATIONS ON THE DIGESTIVE SYSTEM (42-54)

√3rd **42**   **Operations on esophagus**

   √4th   **42.0**   **Esophagotomy**

     42.01   **Incision of esophageal web**

       DEF: Cutting into congenital esophageal membrane.

     42.09   **Other incision of esophagus**

       Esophagotomy NOS

       EXCLUDES   *esophagomyotomy (42.7)*
                 esophagostomy (42.10-42.19)

   √4th   **42.1**   **Esophagostomy**

     42.10   **Esophagostomy, not otherwise specified**

     42.11   **Cervical esophagostomy**

       DEF: Creation of opening into upper region of esophagus.

     42.12   **Exteriorization of esophageal pouch**

       DEF: Transfer of section of esophageal pouch to exterior of the body.

     42.19   **Other external fistulization of esophagus**

       Thoracic esophagostomy

       Code also any resection (42.40-42.42)

   √4th   **42.2**   **Diagnostic procedures on esophagus**

     42.21   **Operative esophagoscopy by incision**

       DEF: Esophageal examination with an endoscope through incision.

     42.22   **Esophagoscopy through artificial stoma**

       EXCLUDES   *that with biopsy (42.24)*

     42.23   **Other esophagoscopy**

       EXCLUDES   *that with biopsy (42.24)*

       AHA: 1Q, '00, 20; 3Q, '98, 11

       TIP: Assign in addition to code 88.72 Diagnostic ultrasound of heart, for transesophageal echocardiography (TEE).

     42.24   **Closed [endoscopic] biopsy of esophagus**

       Brushing or washing for specimen collection

       Esophagoscopy with biopsy

       Suction biopsy of the esophagus

       EXCLUDES   *esophagogastroduodenoscopy [EGD]*
                 with closed biopsy (45.16)

       DEF: Scope passed through mouth and throat to obtain biopsy specimen, usually by brushing and swabbing.

     42.25   **Open biopsy of esophagus**

     42.29   **Other diagnostic procedures on esophagus**

       EXCLUDES   *barium swallow (87.61)*
                 esophageal manometry (89.32)
                 microscopic examination of specimen
                     from esophagus (90.81-90.89)

       AHA: 3Q, '96, 12

   √4th   **42.3**   **Local excision or destruction of lesion or tissue of esophagus**

     42.31   **Local excision of esophageal diverticulum**

     42.32   **Local excision of other lesion or tissue of esophagus**

       EXCLUDES   *biopsy of esophagus (42.24-42.25)*
                 esophageal fistulectomy (42.84)

     42.33   **Endoscopic excision or destruction of lesion or tissue of esophagus**

       Ablation of esophageal neoplasm ⎫
       Control of esophageal bleeding   ⎬ by endoscopic approach
       Esophageal polypectomy   ⎪
       Esophageal varices   ⎪
       Injection of esophageal varies   ⎭

       EXCLUDES   *biopsy of esophagus (42.24-42.25)*
                 fistulectomy (42.84)
                 open ligation of esophageal varices
                     (42.91)

       TIP: Assign for endoscopic sclerotherapy for bleeding esophageal varices.

     42.39   **Other destruction of lesion or tissue of esophagus**

       EXCLUDES   *that by endoscopic approach (42.33)*

   √4th   **42.4**   **Excision of esophagus**

     EXCLUDES   *esophagogastrectomy NOS 43.99)*

     42.40   **Esophagectomy, not otherwise specified**

     42.41   **Partial esophagectomy**

       Code also any synchronous:
         anastomosis other than end-to-end
             (42.51-42.69)
         esophagostomy (42.10-42.19)
         gastrostomy (43.11-43.19)

       DEF: Surgical removal of any part of esophagus.

     42.42   **Total esophagectomy**

       Code also any synchronous:
         gastrostomy (43.11-43.19)
         interposition or anastomosis other than
            end-to-end (42.51-42.69)

       EXCLUDES   *esophagogastrectomy (43.99)*

       AHA: 4Q, '88, 11

       DEF: Surgical removal of entire esophagus.

   √4th   **42.5**   **Intrathoracic anastomosis of esophagus**

     Code also any synchronous:
       esophagectomy (42.40-42.42)
       gastrostomy (43.1)

     DEF: Connection of esophagus to conduit within chest.

     42.51   **Intrathoracic esophagoesophagostomy**

       DEF: Connection of both ends of esophagus within chest cavity.

     42.52   **Intrathoracic esophagogastrostomy**

       DEF: Connection of esophagus to stomach within chest; follows esophagogastrectomy.

     42.53   **Intrathoracic esophageal anastomosis with interposition of small bowel**

     42.54   **Other intrathoracic esophagoenterostomy**

       Anastomosis of esophagus to intestinal segment NOS

     42.55   **Intrathoracic esophageal anastomosis with interposition of colon**

     42.56   **Other intrathoracic esophagocolostomy**

       Esophagocolostomy NOS

     42.58   **Intrathoracic esophageal anastomosis with other interposition**

       Construction of artificial esophagus

       Retrosternal formation of reversed gastric tube

       DEF: Construction of artificial esophagus: Creation of artificial esophagus.

       DEF: Retrosternal anastomosis of reversed gastric tube: Formation of gastric tube behind breastbone.

     42.59   **Other intrathoracic anastomosis of esophagus**

       AHA: 4Q, '88, 11

   √4th   **42.6**   **Antesternal anastomosis of esophagus**

     Code also any synchronous:
       esophagectomy (42.40-42.42)
       gastrostomy (43.1)

     42.61   **Antesternal esophagoesophagostomy**

     42.62   **Antesternal esophagogastrostomy**

     42.63   **Antesternal esophageal anastomosis with interposition of small bowel**

     42.64   **Other antesternal esophagoenterostomy**

       Antethoracic:
         esophagoenterostomy
         esophagoileostomy
         esophagojejunostomy

     42.65   **Antesternal esophageal anastomosis with interposition of colon**

       DEF: Connection of esophagus with colon segment.

     42.66   **Other antesternal esophagocolostomy**

       Antethoracic esophagocolostomy

     42.68   **Other antesternal esophageal anastomosis with interposition**

     42.69   **Other antesternal anastomosis of esophagus**

Operations on the Digestive System

42.7–43.89

42.7   Esophagomyotomy
> DEF: Division of esophageal muscle, usually distal.

✓4th **42.8   Other repair of esophagus**

42.81   Insertion of permanent tube into esophagus
> AHA: 1Q, '97, 15

42.82   Suture of laceration of esophagus

42.83   Closure of esophagostomy

42.84   Repair of esophageal fistula, not elsewhere classified
> EXCLUDES   repair of fistula:
> bronchoesophageal (33.42)
> esophagopleurocutaneous (34.73)
> pharyngoesophageal (29.53)
> tracheoesophageal (31.73)

42.85   Repair of esophageal stricture

42.86   Production of subcutaneous tunnel without esophageal anastomosis
> DEF: Surgical formation of esophageal passage, without cutting, and reconnection.

42.87   Other graft of esophagus
> EXCLUDES   antesternal esophageal anastomosis
> with interposition of:
> colon (42.65)
> small bowel (42.63)
> antesternal esophageal anastomosis
> with other interposition (42.68)
> intrathoracic esophageal anastomosis
> with
> interposition of:
> colon (42.55)
> small bowel (42.53)
> intrathoracic esophageal anastomosis
> with other interposition (42.58)

42.89   Other repair of esophagus

✓4th **42.9   Other operations on esophagus**

42.91   Ligation of esophageal varices
> EXCLUDES   that by endoscopic approach (42.33)
> DEF: Destruction of dilated veins by suture strangulation.

42.92   Dilation of esophagus
> Dilation of cardiac sphincter
> EXCLUDES   intubation of esophagus (96.03, 96.06-96.08)
> DEF: Passing of balloon or hydrostatic dilators through esophagus to enlarge esophagus and relieve obstruction.

42.99   Other
> EXCLUDES   insertion of Sengstaken tube (96.06)
> intubation of esophagus (96.03, 96.06-96.08)
> removal of intraluminal foreign body
> from esophagus without
> incision (98.02)
> tamponade of esophagus (96.06)

✓3rd **43   Incision and excision of stomach**
> Code also any application or administration of an adhesion barrier substance (99.77)

43.0   Gastrotomy
> EXCLUDES   gastrostomy (43.11-43.19)
> that for control of hemorrhage (44.49)
> AHA: 3Q, '89, 14

✓4th **43.1   Gastrostomy**
> AHA: S-O, '85, 5

43.11   Percutaneous [endoscopic] gastrostomy [PEG]
> Percutaneous transabdominal gastrostomy
> DEF: Endoscopic positioning of tube through abdominal wall into stomach.

43.19   Other gastrostomy
> EXCLUDES   percutaneous [endoscopic]
> gastrostomy [PEG] (43.11)
> AHA: 1Q, '92, 14; 3Q, '89, 14

Partial Gastrectomy with Anastomosis to Duodenum

43.3   Pyloromyotomy
> DEF: Cutting into longitudinal and circular muscular membrane between stomach and small intestine.

✓4th **43.4   Local excision or destruction of lesion or tissue of stomach**

43.41   Endoscopic excision or destruction of lesion or tissue of stomach
> Gastric polypectomy by endoscopic approach
> Gastric varices by endoscopic approach
> EXCLUDES   biopsy of stomach (44.14-44.15)
> control of hemorrhage (44.43)
> open ligation of gastric varices (44.91)
> AHA: 3Q, '96, 10

43.42   Local excision of other lesion or tissue of stomach
> EXCLUDES   biopsy of stomach (44.14-44.15)
> gastric fistulectomy (44.62-44.63)
> partial gastrectomy (43.5-43.89)

43.49   Other destruction of lesion or tissue of stomach
> EXCLUDES   that by endoscopic approach (43.41)
> AHA: N-D, '87, 5; S-O, '85, 6

43.5   Partial gastrectomy with anastomosis to esophagus
> Proximal gastrectomy

43.6   Partial gastrectomy with anastomosis to duodenum
> Billroth I operation
> Distal gastrectomy
> Gastropylorectomy

43.7   Partial gastrectomy with anastomosis to jejunum
> Billroth II operation
> AHA: 3Q, '03, 7

✓4th **43.8   Other partial gastrectomy**

43.81   Partial gastrectomy with jejunal transposition
> Henley jejunal transposition operation
> Code also any synchronous intestinal resection (45.51)

43.89   Other
> Partial gastrectomy with bypass gastrogastrostomy
> Sleeve resection of stomach
> AHA: 3Q, '03, 6-8

Biliopancreatic Diversion Without Duodenal Switch

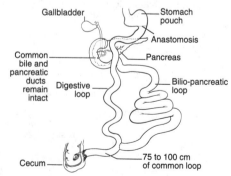

BI Bilateral Procedure   NC Non-covered Procedure   LC Limited Coverage Procedure   ►◄ Revised Text   ● New Code   ▲ Revised Code Title

126 – Volume 3   2010 ICD-9-CM

Biliopancreatic Diversion with Duodenal Switch

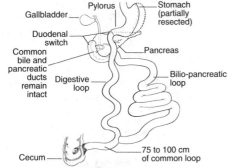

Roux-en-Y Operation (Gastrojejunostomy without gastrectomy)

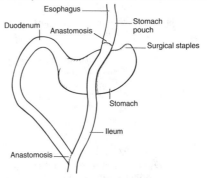

√4th **43.9 Total gastrectomy**

   43.91   Total gastrectomy with intestinal interposition

   43.99   Other total gastrectomy

      Complete gastroduodenectomy
      Esophagoduodenostomy with complete
         gastrectomy
      Esophagogastrectomy NOS
      Esophagojejunostomy with complete
         gastrectomy
      Radical gastrectomy

√3rd **44 Other operations on stomach**

   Code also any application or administration of an adhesion barrier
   substance (99.77)

√4th **44.0 Vagotomy**

   44.00   Vagotomy, not otherwise specified

      Division of vagus nerve NOS

      DEF: Cutting of vagus nerve to reduce acid
      production.

   44.01   Truncal vagotomy

      DEF: Surgical removal of vagus nerve segment near
      stomach branches.

   44.02   Highly selective vagotomy

      Parietal cell vagotomy
      Selective proximal vagotomy

      DEF: Cutting select gastric branches of vagus nerve to
      reduce acid production and preserve other nerve
      functions.

   44.03   Other selective vagotomy

√4th **44.1 Diagnostic procedures on stomach**

   44.11   Transabdominal gastroscopy

      Intraoperative gastroscopy
      EXCLUDES   *that with biopsy (44.14)*

   44.12   Gastroscopy through artificial stoma
      EXCLUDES   *that with biopsy (44.14)*

   44.13   Other gastroscopy
      EXCLUDES   *that with biopsy (44.14)*

      AHA: 1Q, '88, 15; N-D, '87, 5

   44.14   Closed [endoscopic] biopsy of stomach

      Brushing or washing for specimen collection
      EXCLUDES   *esophagogastroduodenoscopy [EGD]*
         with closed biopsy (45.16)

      AHA: 1Q, '88, 15; N-D, '87, 5

Types of Vagotomy Procedures

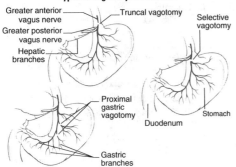

   44.15   Open biopsy of stomach

   44.19   Other diagnostic procedures on stomach
      EXCLUDES   *gastric lavage (96.33)*
         microscopic examination of specimen
           from stomach (90.81-90.89)
         upper GI series (87.62)

√4th **44.2 Pyloroplasty**

   44.21   Dilation of pylorus by incision

      DEF: Cutting and suturing pylorus to relieve
      obstruction.

   44.22   Endoscopic dilation of pylorus

      Dilation with balloon endoscope
      Endoscopic dilation of gastrojejunostomy site

      AHA: 2Q, '01, 17

      TIP: Assign for stent placement across an extrinsic
      obstruction of a gastrojejunostomy.

   44.29   Other pyloroplasty

      Pyloroplasty NOS
      Revision of pylorus

      AHA: 3Q, '99, 3

√4th **44.3 Gastroenterostomy without gastrectomy**

   44.31   High gastric bypass

      Printen and Mason gastric bypass

      DEF: Connection of middle part of small intestine to
      upper stomach to divert food passage from upper
      intestine.

      AHA: M-J, '85, 17

   44.32   Percutaneous [endoscopic] gastrojejunostomy

      Bypass:
         gastroduodenostomy
      PEGJJ
      EXCLUDES   *percutaneous (endoscopic) feeding*
         jejunostomy (46.32)

      DEF: Percutaneous placement of a thin feeding tube
      through a gastrostomy tube and then pulling the
      tube into the proximal end of the jejunum.

   44.38   Laparoscopic gastroenterostomy

      Bypass:
         gastroduodenostomy
         gastroenterostomy
         gastrogastrostomy
      Laparoscopic gastrojejunostomy without
         gastrectomy NEC
      EXCLUDES   *gastroenterostomy, open approach*
         (44.39)

   44.39   Other gastroenterostomy

      Bypass:
         gastroduodenostomy
         gastroenterostomy
         gastrogastrostomy
      Gastrojejunostomy without gastrectomy NOS

      AHA: 3Q, '03, 6; 1Q, '01, 16, 17

√4th **44.4 Control of hemorrhage and suture of ulcer of stomach or duodenum**

   44.40   Suture of peptic ulcer, not otherwise specified

   44.41   Suture of gastric ulcer site

      EXCLUDES   *ligation of gastric varices (44.91)*

Operations on the Digestive System

44.42–45.03

44.42   **Suture of duodenal ulcer site**
> AHA: J-F, '87, 11

44.43   **Endoscopic control of gastric or duodenal bleeding**
> AHA: 2Q, '04, 12; 2Q, '92, 17; N-D, '87, 4

44.44   **Transcatheter embolization for gastric or duodenal bleeding**
> EXCLUDES   *surgical occlusion of abdominal vessels (38.86-38.87)*
>
> DEF: Therapeutic blocking of stomach or upper small intestine blood vessel to stop hemorrhaging; accomplished by introducing various substances using a catheter.
> AHA: 1Q, '88, 15; N-D, '87, 4

44.49   **Other control of hemorrhage of stomach or duodenum**
> That with gastrotomy

44.5   **Revision of gastric anastomosis**
> Closure of:
>   gastric anastomosis
>   gastroduodenostomy
>   gastrojejunostomy
> Pantaloon operation

√4th **44.6**   **Other repair of stomach**

44.61   **Suture of laceration of stomach**
> EXCLUDES   *that of ulcer site (44.41)*

44.62   **Closure of gastrostomy**

44.63   **Closure of other gastric fistula**
> Closure of:
>   gastrocolic fistula
>   gastrojejunocolic fistula

44.64   **Gastropexy**
> DEF: Suturing of stomach into position.
> AHA: M-J, '85, 17

44.65   **Esophagogastroplasty**
> Belsey operation
> Esophagus and stomach cardioplasty
> AHA: M-J, '85, 17

44.66   **Other procedures for creation of esophagogastric sphincteric competence**
> Fundoplication
> Gastric cardioplasty
> Nissen's fundoplication
> Restoration of cardio-esophageal angle
> EXCLUDES   *that by laparoscopy (44.67)*
> AHA: 2Q, '03, 12; 2Q, '01, 3, 5, 6; 3Q, '98, 10; M-J, '85, 17
> TIP: Assign for endoscopic suturing of the esophago-gastric junction, performed to relieve the symptoms of gastroesophageal reflux.

44.67   **Laparoscopic procedures for creation of esophagogastric sphincteric competence**
> Fundoplication
> Gastric cardioplasty
> Nissen's fundoplication
> Restoration of cardio-esophageal angle

44.68   **Laparoscopic gastroplasty**
> Banding
> Silastic vertical banding
> Vertical banded gastroplasty (VBG)
> Code also any synchronous laparoscopic gastroenterostomy (44.38)
> EXCLUDES   *insertion, laparoscopic adjustable gastric band (restrictive procedure) (44.95)*
>   *other repair of stomach, open approach (44.61-44.65, 44.69)*

44.69   **Other**
> Inversion of gastric diverticulum
> Repair of stomach NOS
> DEF: Inversion of gastric diverticulum: Turning stomach inward to repair outpouch of wall.
> AHA: 3Q, '03, 8; 2Q, '01, 3; 3Q, '99, 3; M-J, '85, 17; N-D, '84, 13

√4th **44.9**   **Other operations on stomach**

44.91   **Ligation of gastric varices**
> EXCLUDES   *that by endoscopic approach (43.41)*
> DEF: Destruction of dilated veins by suture or strangulation.

44.92   **Intraoperative manipulation of stomach**
> Reduction of gastric volvulus

44.93   **Insertion of gastric bubble (balloon)**   NC

44.94   **Removal of gastric bubble (balloon)**

44.95   **Laparoscopic gastric restrictive procedure**
> Adjustable gastric band and port insertion
> EXCLUDES   *laparoscopic gastroplasty (44.68)*
>   *other repair of stomach (44.69)*

44.96   **Laparoscopic revision of gastric restrictive procedure**
> Revision or replacement of:
>   adjustable gastric band
>   subcutaneous gastric port device

44.97   **Laparoscopic removal of gastric restrictive device(s)**
> Removal of either or both:
>   adjustable gastric band
>   subcutaneous port device
> EXCLUDES   *nonoperative removal of gastric restrictive device(s) (97.86)*
>   *open removal of gastric restrictive device(s) (44.99)*

44.98   **(Laparoscopic) adjustment of size of adjustable gastric restrictive device**
> Infusion of saline for device tightening
> Withdrawal of saline for device loosening
> Code also any:
>   abdominal ultrasound (88.76)
>   abdominal wall fluoroscopy (88.09)
>   barium swallow (87.61)

44.99   **Other**
> EXCLUDES   *change of gastrostomy tube (97.02)*
>   *dilation of cardiac sphincter (42.92)*
>   *gastric:*
>   *cooling (96.31)*
>   *freezing (96.32)*
>   *gavage (96.35)*
>   *hypothermia (96.31)*
>   *lavage (96.33)*
>   *insertion of nasogastric tube (96.07)*
>   *irrigation of gastrostomy (96.36)*
>   *irrigation of nasogastric tube (96.34)*
>   *removal of:*
>   *gastrostomy tube (97.51)*
>   *intraluminal foreign body from stomach without incision (98.03)*
>   *replacement of:*
>   *gastrostomy tube (97.02)*
>   *(naso-)gastric tube (97.01)*
> AHA: 3Q, '04, 5
> TIP: Assign for balloon dilatation of a gastric stricture.

√3rd **45**   **Incision, excision, and anastomosis of intestine**
> Code also any application or administration of an adhesion barrier substance (99.77)

√4th **45.0**   **Enterotomy**
> EXCLUDES   *duodenocholedochotomy (51.41-51.42, 51.51)*
>   *that for destruction of lesion (45.30-45.34)*
>   *that of exteriorized intestine (46.14, 46.24, 46.31)*

45.00   **Incision of intestine, not otherwise specified**

45.01   **Incision of duodenum**

45.02   **Other incision of small intestine**

45.03   **Incision of large intestine**
> EXCLUDES   *proctotomy (48.0)*

BI **Bilateral Procedure**   NC **Non-covered Procedure**   LC **Limited Coverage Procedure**   ▶◀ **Revised Text**   ● **New Code**   ▲ **Revised Code Title**

128 – Volume 3   **2010 ICD-9-CM**

Esophagogastroduodenoscopy

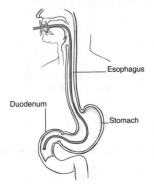

Esophagus

Duodenum

Stomach

✓4th 45.1 Diagnostic procedures on small intestine
Code also any laparotomy (54.11-54.19)

45.11 Transabdominal endoscopy of small intestine
Intraoperative endoscopy of small intestine
EXCLUDES   that with biopsy (45.14)
DEF: Endoscopic exam of small intestine through abdominal wall.
DEF: Intraoperative endoscope of small intestine: Endoscopic exam of small intestine during surgery.

45.12 Endoscopy of small intestine through artificial stoma
EXCLUDES   that with biopsy (45.14)
AHA: M-J, '85, 17

45.13 Other endoscopy of small intestine
Esophagogastroduodenoscopy [EGD]
EXCLUDES   that with biopsy (45.14, 45.16)
AHA: 3Q, '04, 5; N-D, '87, 5

45.14 Closed [endoscopic] biopsy of small intestine
Brushing or washing for specimen collection
EXCLUDES   esophagogastroduodenoscopy [EGD] with closed biopsy (45.16)

45.15 Open biopsy of small intestine
AHA: 2Q, '05, 12

45.16 Esophagogastroduodenoscopy [EGD] with closed biopsy
Biopsy of one or more sites involving esophagus, stomach, and/or duodenum
AHA: 3Q, '05, 17; 2Q, '01, 9

45.19 Other diagnostic procedures on small intestine
EXCLUDES   microscopic examination of specimen from small intestine (90.91-90.99)
radioisotope scan (92.04)
ultrasonography (88.74)
x-ray (87.61-87.69)

✓4th 45.2 Diagnostic procedures on large intestine
Code also any laparotomy (54.11-54.19)

45.21 Transabdominal endoscopy of large intestine
Intraoperative endoscopy of large intestine
EXCLUDES   that with biopsy (45.25)
DEF: Endoscopic exam of large intestine through abdominal wall.
DEF: Intraoperative endoscopy of large intestine: Endoscopic exam of large intestine during surgery.

45.22 Endoscopy of large intestine through artificial stoma
EXCLUDES   that with biopsy (45.25)
DEF: Endoscopic exam of large intestine lining from rectum to cecum via colostomy stoma.

45.23 Colonoscopy
Flexible fiberoptic colonoscopy
EXCLUDES   endoscopy of large intestine through artificial stoma (45.22)
flexible sigmoidoscopy (45.24)
rigid proctosigmoidoscopy (48.23)
transabdominal endoscopy of large intestine (45.21)
DEF: Endoscopic exam of descending colon, splenic flexure, transverse colon, hepatic flexure and cecum.
AHA: 3Q, '05, 17; S-O, '85, 5

45.24 Flexible sigmoidoscopy
Endoscopy of descending colon
EXCLUDES   rigid proctosigmoidoscopy (48.23)
DEF: Endoscopic exam of anus, rectum and sigmoid colon.

45.25 Closed [endoscopic] biopsy of large intestine
Biopsy, closed, of unspecified intestinal site
Brushing or washing for specimen collection
Colonoscopy with biopsy
EXCLUDES   proctosigmoidoscopy with biopsy (48.24)
AHA: 1Q, '03, 10

45.26 Open biopsy of large intestine

45.27 Intestinal biopsy, site unspecified

45.28 Other diagnostic procedures on large intestine

45.29 Other diagnostic procedures on intestine, site unspecified
EXCLUDES   microscopic examination of specimen (90.91-90.99)
scan and radioisotope function study (92.04)
ultrasonography (88.74)
x-ray (87.61-87.69)

✓4th 45.3 Local excision or destruction of lesion or tissue of small intestine

45.30 Endoscopic excision or destruction of lesion of duodenum
EXCLUDES   biopsy of duodenum (45.14-45.15)
control of hemorrhage (44.43)
fistulectomy (46.72)

45.31 Other local excision of lesion of duodenum
EXCLUDES   biopsy of duodenum (45.14-45.15)
fistulectomy (46.72)
multiple segmental resection (45.61)
that by endoscopic approach (45.30)

45.32 Other destruction of lesion of duodenum
EXCLUDES   that by endoscopic approach (45.30)
AHA: N-D, '87, 5; S-O, '85, 6

45.33 Local excision of lesion or tissue of small intestine, except duodenum
Excision of redundant mucosa of ileostomy
EXCLUDES   biopsy of small intestine (45.14-45.15)
fistulectomy (46.74)
multiple segmental resection (45.61)

45.34 Other destruction of lesion of small intestine, except duodenum

✓4th 45.4 Local excision or destruction of lesion or tissue of large intestine
AHA: N-D, '87, 11

45.41 Excision of lesion or tissue of large intestine
Excision of redundant mucosa of colostomy
EXCLUDES   biopsy of large intestine (45.25-45.27)
endoscopic polypectomy of large intestine (45.42)
fistulectomy (46.76)
multiple segmental resection (17.31, 45.71)
that by endoscopic approach (45.42-45.43)

45.42 Endoscopic polypectomy of large intestine
> EXCLUDES *that by open approach (45.41)*
> DEF: Endoscopic removal of polyp from large intestine.
> AHA: 2Q, '05, 16; 2Q, '90, 25

45.43 Endoscopic destruction of other lesion or tissue of large intestine
> Endoscopic ablation of tumor of large intestine
> Endoscopic control of colonic bleeding
> EXCLUDES *endoscopic polypectomy of large intestine (45.42)*
>
> AHA: 4Q, '02, 61
> TIP: Assign for endoscopic treatment of a Dieulafoy lesion of the large intestine, regardless of technique.

45.49 Other destruction of lesion of large intestine
> EXCLUDES *that by endoscopic approach (45.43)*

✓4ᵗʰ **45.5 Isolation of intestinal segment**
> Code also any synchronous:
> anastomosis other than end-to-end (45.90-45.94)
> enterostomy (46.10-46.39)

45.50 Isolation of intestinal segment, not otherwise specified
> Isolation of intestinal pedicle flap
> Reversal of intestinal segment
> DEF: Isolation of small intestinal pedicle flap: Separation of intestinal pedicle flap.
> DEF: Reversal of intestinal segment: Separation of intestinal segment.

45.51 Isolation of segment of small intestine
> Isolation of ileal loop
> Resection of small intestine for interposition
> AHA: 2Q, '05, 12; 3Q, '03, 6-8; 2Q, '03, 11; 3Q, '00, 7

45.52 Isolation of segment of large intestine
> Resection of colon for interposition

✓4ᵗʰ **45.6 Other excision of small intestine**
> Code also any synchronous:
> anastomosis other than end-to-end (45.90-45.93, 45.95)
> colostomy (46.10-46.13)
> enterostomy (46.10-46.39)
> EXCLUDES *cecectomy (17.32, 45.72)*
> *enterocolectomy (17.39, 45.79)*
> *gastroduodenectomy (43.6-43.99)*
> *ileocolectomy (17.33, 45.73)*
> *pancreatoduodenectomy (52.51-52.7)*

45.61 Multiple segmental resection of small intestine
> Segmental resection for multiple traumatic lesions of small intestine

45.62 Other partial resection of small intestine
> Duodenectomy   Jejunectomy
> Ileectomy
> EXCLUDES *duodenectomy with synchronous pancreatectomy (52.51-52.7)*
> *resection of cecum and terminal ileum (17.32, 45.72)*
> AHA: 1Q, '04, 10; 1Q, '03, 18

45.63 Total removal of small intestine

✓4ᵗʰ **45.7 Open and other partial excision of large intestine**
> Code also any synchronous:
> anastomosis other than end-to-end (45.92-45.94)
> enterostomy (46.10-46.39)
> EXCLUDES *laparoscopic partial excision of large intestine (17.31-17.39)*
>
> AHA: 4Q, '92, 27

45.71 Open and other multiple segmental resection of large intestine
> Segmental resection for multiple traumatic lesions of large intestine

45.72 Open and other cecectomy
> Resection of cecum and terminal ileum

45.73 Open and other right hemicolectomy
> Ileocolectomy
> Right radical colectomy
> AHA: 3Q, '99, 10

45.74 Open and other resection of transverse colon

45.75 Open and other left hemicolectomy
> EXCLUDES *proctosigmoidectomy (48.41-48.69)*
> *second stage Mikulicz operation (46.04)*
> DEF: Excision of left descending large intestine.
> TIP: Assign for Hartmann procedure, typically involving resection of the sigmoid colon with the proximal end terminated as a colostomy and the distal end (rectum) oversewn. A true Hartmann procedure is done on the left side only.

45.76 Open and other sigmoidectomy
> AHA: 1Q, '96, 9; 3Q, '89, 15

45.79 Other and unspecified partial excision of large intestine
> Enterocolectomy NEC
> AHA: ▶1Q, '09, 5;◀1Q, '03, 18; 3Q, '97, 9; 2Q, '91, 16

✓4ᵗʰ **45.8 Total intra-abdominal colectomy**
> Excision of cecum, colon, and sigmoid
> EXCLUDES *coloproctectomy (48.41-48.69)*
> AHA: 4Q, '08, 169-170

45.81 Laparoscopic total intra-abdominal colectomy

45.82 Open total intra-abdominal colectomy

45.83 Other and unspecified total intra-abdominal colectomy

✓4ᵗʰ **45.9 Intestinal anastomosis**
> Code also any synchronous resection (45.31-45.8, 48.41-48.69)
> EXCLUDES *end-to-end anastomosis — omit code*

45.90 Intestinal anastomosis, not otherwise specified

45.91 Small-to-small intestinal anastomosis
> AHA: 3Q, '03, 6-8; M-J, '85, 17

45.92 Anastomosis of small intestine to rectal stump
> Hampton procedure

45.93 Other small-to-large intestinal anastomosis
> AHA: 1Q, '03, 18; N-D, '86, 11

Colectomy

Intestinal Anastomosis

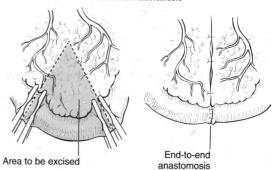

BI Bilateral Procedure   NC Non-covered Procedure   LC Limited Coverage Procedure   ▶◀ Revised Text   ● New Code   ▲ Revised Code Title

130 – Volume 3 · October 2009   2010 ICD-9-CM

45.94 **Large-to-large intestinal anastomosis**
  EXCLUDES   rectorectostomy (48.74)
  AHA: ▶1Q, '09, 5;◀ 3Q, '89, 15

45.95 **Anastomosis to anus**
  Formation of endorectal ileal pouch (J-pouch)
  (H-pouch) (S-pouch) with anastomosis of
  small intestine to anus
  AHA: 2Q, '05, 13

√3ʳᵈ **46 Other operations on intestine**
  Code also any application or administration of an adhesion barrier
  substance (99.77)

√4ᵗʰ **46.0 Exteriorization of intestine**
  INCLUDES   loop enterostomy
  multiple stage resection of intestine
  DEF: Bringing intestinal segment to body surface.

  46.01 **Exteriorization of small intestine**
    Loop ileostomy

  46.02 **Resection of exteriorized segment of
  small intestine**

  46.03 **Exteriorization of large intestine**
    Exteriorization of intestine NOS
    First stage Mikulicz exteriorization of intestine
    Loop colostomy

  46.04 **Resection of exteriorized segment of large
  intestine**
    Resection of exteriorized segment of intestine
    NOS
    Second stage Mikulicz operation

√4ᵗʰ **46.1 Colostomy**
  Code also any synchronous resection (45.49, 45.71-45.79,
  45.8)
  EXCLUDES   loop colostomy (46.03)
    that with abdominoperineal resection of rectum
    (48.5)
    that with synchronous anterior rectal resection
    (48.62)
  DEF: Creation of opening from large intestine through
  abdominal wall to body surface.

  46.10 **Colostomy, not otherwise specified**
  46.11 **Temporary colostomy**
  46.13 **Permanent colostomy**
  46.14 **Delayed opening of colostomy**

√4ᵗʰ **46.2 Ileostomy**
  Code also any synchronous resection (45.34, 45.61-45.63)
  EXCLUDES   loop ileostomy (46.01)
  DEF: Creation of artificial anus by bringing ileum through
  abdominal wall to body surface.

  46.20 **Ileostomy, not otherwise specified**
  46.21 **Temporary ileostomy**
  46.22 **Continent ileostomy**
    DEF: Creation of opening from third part of small
    intestine through abdominal wall, with pouch
    outside abdomen.
    AHA: M-J, '85, 17

  46.23 **Other permanent ileostomy**
  46.24 **Delayed opening of ileostomy**

√4ᵗʰ **46.3 Other enterostomy**
  Code also any synchronous resection (45.61-45.8)

  46.31 **Delayed opening of other enterostomy**
  46.32 **Percutaneous (endoscopic) jejunostomy [PEJ]**
    Endoscopic conversion of gastrostomy to
    jejunostomy
    Percutaneous (endoscopic) feeding enterostomy
    EXCLUDES   percutaneous [endoscopic]
      gastrojejunostomy (bypass)
      (44.32)
    DEF: Endoscopic placement of tube in midsection of
    small intestine through abdominal wall.

  46.39 **Other**
    Duodenostomy   Feeding enterostomy
    AHA: 3Q, '89, 15

√4ᵗʰ **46.4 Revision of intestinal stoma**
  DEF: Revision of opening surgically created from intestine
  through abdominal wall, to skin surface.

  46.40 **Revision of intestinal stoma, not
  otherwise specified**
    Plastic enlargement of intestinal stoma
    Reconstruction of stoma of intestine
    Release of scar tissue of intestinal stoma
    EXCLUDES   excision of redundant mucosa (45.41)

  46.41 **Revision of stoma of small intestine**
    EXCLUDES   excision of redundant mucosa (45.33)
    AHA: 2Q, '05, 11

  46.42 **Repair of pericolostomy hernia**

  46.43 **Other revision of stoma of large intestine**
    EXCLUDES   excision of redundant mucosa (45.41)
    AHA: 2Q, '02, 9
    TIP: Assign for a relocation of a stoma.

√4ᵗʰ **46.5 Closure of intestinal stoma**
  Code also any synchronous resection (45.34, 45.49,
  45.61-45.8)

  46.50 **Closure of intestinal stoma, not otherwise
  specified**

  46.51 **Closure of stoma of small intestine**

  46.52 **Closure of stoma of large intestine**
    Closure or take-down of cecostomy
    Closure or take-down of colostomy
    Closure or take-down of sigmoidostomy
    AHA: ▶1Q, '09, 5;◀ 2Q, '05, 4; 3Q, '97, 9; 2Q, '91, 16;
    N-D, '87, 8

√4ᵗʰ **46.6 Fixation of intestine**

  46.60 **Fixation of intestine, not otherwise
  specified**
    Fixation of intestine to abdominal wall

  46.61 **Fixation of small intestine to abdominal wall**
    Ileopexy

  46.62 **Other fixation of small intestine**
    Noble plication of small intestine
    Plication of jejunum
    DEF: Noble plication of small intestine: Fixing small
    intestine into place with tuck in small intestine.
    DEF: Plication of jejunum: Fixing small intestine into
    place with tuck in midsection.

  46.63 **Fixation of large intestine to
  abdominal wall**
    Cecocoloplicopexy
    Sigmoidopexy (Moschowitz)

  46.64 **Other fixation of large intestine**
    Cecofixation
    Colofixation

√4ᵗʰ **46.7 Other repair of intestine**
  EXCLUDES   closure of:
    ulcer of duodenum (44.42)
    vesicoenteric fistula (57.83)

  46.71 **Suture of laceration of duodenum**
  46.72 **Closure of fistula of duodenum**
  46.73 **Suture of laceration of small
  intestine, except duodenum**
  46.74 **Closure of fistula of small intestine,
  except duodenum**
    EXCLUDES   closure of:
      artificial stoma (46.51)
      vaginal fistula (70.74)
      repair of gastrojejunocolic fistula
      (44.63)

  46.75 **Suture of laceration of large intestine**

√3ʳᵈ
√4ᵗʰ Additional Digit Required   Valid OR Procedure   Non-OR Procedure   Adjunct Code

Operations on the Digestive System

46.76–47.99

46.76   **Closure of fistula of large intestine**
     EXCLUDES   closure of:
         gastrocolic fistula (44.63)
         rectal fistula (48.73)
         sigmoidovesical fistula (57.83)
         stoma (46.52)
         vaginal fistula (70.72-70.73)
         vesicocolic fistula (57.83)
         vesicosigmoidovaginal fistula
           (57.83)
     AHA: 3Q, '99, 8

46.79   **Other repair of intestine**
     Duodenoplasty
     AHA: 3Q, '02, 11
     TIP: Assign for duodenoplasty, typically performed for infants with congenital duodenal webs and stenosis.

√4th **46.8**   **Dilation and manipulation of intestine**
     AHA: 1Q, '03, 14

46.80   **Intra-abdominal manipulation of intestine, not otherwise specified**
     Correction of intestinal malrotation
     Reduction of:
         intestinal torsion
         intestinal volvulus
         intussusception
     EXCLUDES   *reduction of intussusception with:*
         fluoroscopy (96.29)
         ionizing radiation enema (96.29)
         ultrasonography guidance (96.29)
     DEF: Correction of intestinal malrotation: Repair of abnormal rotation.
     DEF: Reduction of: Intestinal torsion: Repair of twisted segment. Intestinal volvulus: Repair of a knotted segment. Intussusception: Repair of prolapsed segment.
     AHA: 4Q, '98, 82
     TIP: Do not assign if the documentation indicates only "running or milking the bowel." This is an integral component of other procedures.

46.81   **Intra-abdominal manipulation of small intestine**

46.82   **Intra-abdominal manipulation of large intestine**

46.85   **Dilation of intestine**
     Dilation (balloon) of duodenum
     Dilation (balloon) of jejunum
     Endoscopic dilation (balloon) of large intestine
     That through rectum or colostomy
     EXCLUDES   ▶*with insertion of colonic stent*
         (46.86-46.87)◀
     AHA: 3Q, '07, 5; 3Q, '89, 15

● **46.86**   **Endoscopic insertion of colonic stent(s)**
     Colonoscopy (flexible) (through stoma) with transendoscopic stent placement
     Combined with fluoroscopic-guided insertion
     Stent endoprosthesis of colon
     Through the scope [TTS] technique
     EXCLUDES   *other non-endoscopic insertion of colonic stent (46.87)*

● **46.87**   **Other insertion of colonic stent(s)**
     INCLUDES   that by:
         fluoroscopic guidance only
         rectal guiding tube
     Non-endoscopic insertion
     Code also any synchronous diagnostic procedure(s)
     EXCLUDES   *endoscopic insertion of colonic stent (46.86)*

√4th **46.9**   **Other operations on intestines**

46.91   **Myotomy of sigmoid colon**

46.92   **Myotomy of other parts of colon**

46.93   **Revision of anastomosis of small intestine**

46.94   **Revision of anastomosis of large intestine**

46.95   **Local perfusion of small intestine**
     Code also substance perfused (99.21-99.29)

46.96   **Local perfusion of large intestine**
     Code also substance perfused (99.21-99.29)

46.97   **Transplant of intestine**   LC
     Note: To report donor source – see codes 00.91-00.93
     AHA: 4Q, '00, 66

46.99   **Other**
     Ileoentectomy
     EXCLUDES   *diagnostic procedures on intestine (45.11-45.29)*
         dilation of enterostomy stoma (96.24)
         intestinal intubation (96.08)
         removal of:
           intraluminal foreign body from large intestine without incision (98.04)
           intraluminal foreign body from small intestine without incision (98.03)
           tube from large intestine (97.53)
           tube from small intestine (97.52)
          replacement of:
           large intestine tube or enterostomy device (97.04)
           small intestine tube or enterostomy device (97.03)
     AHA: 3Q, '99, 11; 1Q, '89, 11

√3rd **47**   **Operations on appendix**
     INCLUDES   appendiceal stump
     Code also any application or administration of an adhesion barrier substance (99.77)

√4th **47.0**   **Appendectomy**
     EXCLUDES   *incidental appendectomy, so described*
         laparoscopic (47.11)
         other (47.19)
     AHA: 4Q, '96, 64; 3Q, '92, 12

47.01   **Laparoscopic appendectomy**
     AHA: 1Q, '01, 15; 4Q, '96, 64

47.09   **Other appendectomy**
     AHA: 4Q, '97, 52

√4th **47.1**   **Incidental appendectomy**
     DEF: Removal of appendix during abdominal surgery as prophylactic measure, without significant appendiceal pathology.

47.11   **Laparoscopic incidental appendectomy**

47.19   **Other incidental appendectomy**
     AHA: 4Q, '96, 65

47.2   **Drainage of appendiceal abscess**
     EXCLUDES   *that with appendectomy (47.0)*

√4th **47.9**   **Other operations on appendix**

47.91   **Appendicostomy**

47.92   **Closure of appendiceal fistula**

47.99   **Other**
     Anastomosis of appendix
     EXCLUDES   *diagnostic procedures on appendix (45.21-45.29)*
     AHA: 3Q, '01, 16
     TIP: Assign for a Malone antegrade continence enema procedure, in which the appendix is sutured to the abdominal wall, creating an orifice through which the patient can administer enemas via a small catheter through the appendix and into the cecum.

BI Bilateral Procedure   NC Non-covered Procedure   LC Limited Coverage Procedure   ▶◀ Revised Text   ● New Code   ▲ Revised Code Title

132 – Volume 3 • October 2009   2010 ICD-9-CM

√3rd **48** **Operations on rectum, rectosigmoid, and perirectal tissue**
Code also any application or administration of an adhesion barrier substance (99.77)

48.0 **Proctotomy**
Decompression of imperforate anus
Panas' operation [linear proctotomy]
EXCLUDES   *incision of perirectal tissue (48.81)*
DEF: Incision into rectal portion of large intestine.
DEF: Decompression of imperforate anus: opening a closed anus by means of an incision.
DEF: Panas' operation (linear proctotomy): Linear incision into rectal portion of large intestine
AHA: 3Q, '99, 8

48.1 **Proctostomy**

√4th **48.2** **Diagnostic procedures on rectum, rectosigmoid, and perirectal tissue**

48.21 **Transabdominal proctosigmoidoscopy**
Intraoperative proctosigmoidoscopy
EXCLUDES   *that with biopsy (48.24)*

48.22 **Proctosigmoidoscopy through artificial stoma**
EXCLUDES   *that with biopsy (48.24)*

48.23 **Rigid proctosigmoidoscopy**
EXCLUDES   *flexible sigmoidoscopy (45.24)*
DEF: Endoscopic exam of anus, rectum and lower sigmoid colon.
AHA: 1Q, '01, 8

48.24 **Closed [endoscopic] biopsy of rectum**
Brushing or washing for specimen collection
Proctosigmoidoscopy with biopsy
AHA: 1Q, '03, 14

48.25 **Open biopsy of rectum**

48.26 **Biopsy of perirectal tissue**

48.29 **Other diagnostic procedures on rectum, rectosigmoid, and perirectal tissue**
EXCLUDES   *digital examination of rectum (89.34)*
lower GI series (87.64)
microscopic examination of specimen from rectum (90.91-90.99)

√4th **48.3** **Local excision or destruction of lesion or tissue of rectum**

48.31 **Radical electrocoagulation of rectal lesion or tissue**
DEF: Destruction of lesion or tissue of large intestine, rectal part.

48.32 **Other electrocoagulation of rectal lesion or tissue**
AHA: 2Q, '98, 18

48.33 **Destruction of rectal lesion or tissue by laser**

48.34 **Destruction of rectal lesion or tissue by cryosurgery**

48.35 **Local excision of rectal lesion or tissue**
EXCLUDES   *biopsy of rectum (48.24-48.25)*
[endoscopic] polypectomy of rectum (48.36)
excision of perirectal tissue (48.82)
hemorrhoidectomy (49.46)
rectal fistulectomy (48.73)

48.36 **[Endoscopic] polypectomy of rectum**
AHA: 4Q, '95, 65

√4th **48.4** **Pull-through resection of rectum**
Code also any synchronous anastomosis other than end-to-end (45.90, 45.92-45.95)
AHA: ▶4Q, '08, 169-171◀

48.40 **Pull-through resection of rectum, not otherwise specified**
Pull-through resection NOS
EXCLUDES   *abdominoperineal pull-through NOS (48.50)*

48.41 **Soave submucosal resection of rectum**
Endorectal pull-through operation
DEF: Soave submucosal resection: Resection of submucosal rectal part of large intestine by pull-through technique.
DEF: Endorectal pull-through operation: Resection of interior large intestine by pull-through technique.

48.42 **Laparoscopic pull-through resection of rectum**

48.43 **Open pull-through resection of rectum**

48.49 **Other pull-through resection of rectum**
Abdominoperineal pull-through
Altemeier operation
Swenson proctectomy
EXCLUDES   *Duhamel abdominoperineal pull-through (48.65)*
laparoscopic pull-through resection of rectum (48.42)
open pull-through resection of rectum (48.43)
pull-through resection of rectum, not otherwise specified (48.40)
DEF: Abdominoperineal pull-through: Resection of large intestine, latter part, by pull-through of abdomen, scrotum or vulva and anus.
DEF: Swenson proctatectomy: Excision of large intestine, rectal by pull-through and preserving muscles that close the anus.
AHA: 3Q, '01, 8; 2Q, '99, 13

√4th **48.5** **Abdominoperineal resection of rectum**
INCLUDES   with synchronous colostomy
Combined abdominoendorectal resection
Complete proctectomy
Code also any synchronous anastomosis other than end-to-end (45.90, 45.92-45.95)
EXCLUDES   *Duhamel abdominoperineal pull-through (48.65)*
that as part of pelvic exenteration (68.8)
DEF: Rectal excision through cavities formed by abdomen, anus, vulva or scrotum.
AHA: ▶4Q, '08, 169-172;◀ 2Q, '97, 5

48.50 **Abdominoperineal resection of the rectum, not otherwise specified**

48.51 **Laparoscopic abdominoperineal resection of the rectum**

48.52 **Open abdominoperineal resection of the rectum**

48.59 **Other abdominoperineal resection of the rectum**
EXCLUDES   *abdominoperineal resection of the rectum, NOS (48.50)*
laparoscopic abdominoperineal resection of the rectum (48.51)
open abdominoperineal resection of the rectum (48.52)

√4th **48.6** **Other resection of rectum**
Code also any synchronous anastomosis other than end-to-end (45.90, 45.92-45.95)

48.61 **Transsacral rectosigmoidectomy**
DEF: Excision through sacral bone area of sigmoid and last parts of large intestine.

48.62 **Anterior resection of rectum with synchronous colostomy**
DEF: Resection of front terminal end of large intestine and creation of colostomy.

48.63 **Other anterior resection of rectum**
EXCLUDES   *that with synchronous colostomy (48.62)*
AHA: 1Q, '96, 9

48.64 **Posterior resection of rectum**

48.65 **Duhamel resection of rectum**
Duhamel abdominoperineal pull-through

48.69 **Other**
Partial proctectomy   Rectal resection NOS
AHA: 2Q, '05, 13; J-F, '87, 11; N-D, '86, 11

Operations on the Digestive System

48.7–49.47

√4ᵗʰ **48.7　Repair of rectum**
  EXCLUDES *repair of:*
     current obstetric laceration (75.62)
     vaginal rectocele (70.50, 70.52, 70.53, 70.55)

48.71　Suture of laceration of rectum

48.72　Closure of proctostomy

48.73　Closure of other rectal fistula
  EXCLUDES *fistulectomy:*
     perirectal (48.93)
     rectourethral (58.43)
     rectovaginal (70.73)
     rectovesical (57.83)
     rectovesicovaginal (57.83)

48.74　Rectorectostomy
  Rectal anastomosis NOS
  Stapled transanal rectal resection (STARR)
  DEF: Rectal anastomosis: Connection of two cut portions of large intestine, rectal end.

48.75　Abdominal proctopexy
  Frickman procedure
  Ripstein repair of rectal prolapse
  DEF: Fixation of rectum to adjacent abdominal structures.

48.76　Other proctopexy
  Delorme repair of prolapsed rectum
  Proctosigmoidopexy
  Puborectalis sling operation
  EXCLUDES *manual reduction of rectal prolapse (96.26)*
  DEF: Delorme repair of prolapsed rectum: Fixation of collapsed large intestine, rectal part.
  DEF: Proctosigmoidopexy: Suturing of twisted large intestine, rectal part.
  DEF: Puborectalis sling operation: Fixation of large intestine, rectal part by forming puborectalis muscle into sling.

48.79　Other repair of rectum
  Repair of old obstetric laceration of rectum
  EXCLUDES *anastomosis to:*
     large intestine (45.94)
     small intestine (45.92-45.93)
    repair of:
     current obstetrical laceration (75.62)
     vaginal rectocele (70.50, 70.52)

√4ᵗʰ **48.8　Incision or excision of perirectal tissue or lesion**
  INCLUDES pelvirectal tissue
     rectovaginal septum

48.81　Incision of perirectal tissue
  Incision of rectovaginal septum

48.82　Excision of perirectal tissue
  EXCLUDES *perirectal biopsy (48.26)*
     perirectofistulectomy (48.93)
     rectal fistulectomy (48.73)

√4ᵗʰ **48.9　Other operations on rectum and perirectal tissue**

48.91　Incision of rectal stricture

48.92　Anorectal myectomy
  DEF: Excision of anorectal muscle.

48.93　Repair of perirectal fistula
  EXCLUDES *that opening into rectum (48.73)*
  DEF: Closure of abdominal passage in tissue around large intestine, rectal part.
  AHA: 1Q, '07, 13
  TIP: Assign for Seton placement, which is a cord or stitch that is passed through the path of the fistula; it generates a fibrous reaction, allowing for tissue ingrowth over a period of time.

48.99　Other
  EXCLUDES *digital examination of rectum (89.34)*
     dilation of rectum (96.22)
     insertion of rectal tube (96.09)
     irrigation of rectum (96.38-96.39)
     manual reduction of rectal prolapse (96.26)
     proctoclysis (96.37)
     rectal massage (99.93)
     rectal packing (96.19)
     removal of:
      impacted feces (96.38)
      intraluminal foreign body from rectum without incision (98.05)
     rectal packing (97.59)
     transanal enema (96.39)

√3ʳᵈ **49　Operations on anus**
  Code also any application or administration of an adhesion barrier substance (99.77)

√4ᵗʰ **49.0　Incision or excision of perianal tissue**

49.01　Incision of perianal abscess
  AHA: 2Q, '05, 10

49.02　Other incision of perianal tissue
  Undercutting of perianal tissue
  EXCLUDES *anal fistulotomy (49.11)*

49.03　Excision of perianal skin tags

49.04　Other excision of perianal tissue
  EXCLUDES *anal fistulectomy (49.12)*
     biopsy of perianal tissue (49.22)
  AHA: 1Q, '01, 8

√4ᵗʰ **49.1　Incision or excision of anal fistula**
  EXCLUDES *closure of anal fistula (49.73)*

49.11　Anal fistulotomy

49.12　Anal fistulectomy

√4ᵗʰ **49.2　Diagnostic procedures on anus and perianal tissue**

49.21　Anoscopy

49.22　Biopsy of perianal tissue

49.23　Biopsy of anus

49.29　Other diagnostic procedures on anus and perianal tissue
  EXCLUDES *microscopic examination of specimen from anus (90.91-90.99)*

√4ᵗʰ **49.3　Local excision or destruction of other lesion or tissue of anus**
  Anal cryptotomy
  Cauterization of lesion of anus
  EXCLUDES *biopsy of anus (49.23)*
     control of (postoperative) hemorrhage of anus (49.95)
     hemorrhoidectomy (49.46)

49.31　Endoscopic excision or destruction of lesion or tissue of anus

49.39　Other local excision or destruction of lesion or tissue of anus
  EXCLUDES *that by endoscopic approach (49.31)*
  AHA: 1Q, '01, 8

√4ᵗʰ **49.4　Procedures on hemorrhoids**

49.41　Reduction of hemorrhoids
  DEF: Manual manipulation to reduce hemorrhoids.

49.42　Injection of hemorrhoids

49.43　Cauterization of hemorrhoids
  Clamp and cautery of hemorrhoids

49.44　Destruction of hemorrhoids by cryotherapy

49.45　Ligation of hemorrhoids

49.46　Excision of hemorrhoids
  Hemorrhoidectomy NOS
  AHA: 1Q, '07, 13

49.47　Evacuation of thrombosed hemorrhoids
  DEF: Removal of clotted material from hemorrhoid.

BI Bilateral Procedure **NC** Non-covered Procedure **LC** Limited Coverage Procedure ▶◀ Revised Text ● New Code ▲ Revised Code Title

134 – Volume 3   2010 ICD-9-CM

49.49   **Other procedures on hemorrhoids**
Lord procedure

√4th **49.5**   **Division of anal sphincter**

49.51   **Left lateral anal sphincterotomy**

49.52   **Posterior anal sphincterotomy**

49.59   **Other anal sphincterotomy**
Division of sphincter NOS

49.6   **Excision of anus**

√4th **49.7**   **Repair of anus**
EXCLUDES   *repair of current obstetric laceration (75.62)*

49.71   **Suture of laceration of anus**

49.72   **Anal cerclage**
DEF: Encircling anus with ring or sutures.

49.73   **Closure of anal fistula**
EXCLUDES   *excision of anal fistula (49.12)*

49.74   **Gracilis muscle transplant for anal incontinence**
DEF: Moving pubic attachment of gracilis muscle to restore anal control.

49.75   **Implantation or revision of artificial anal sphincter**
Removal with subsequent replacement
Replacement during same or subsequent operative episode
AHA: 4Q, '02, 105

49.76   **Removal of artificial anal sphincter**
Explantation or removal without replacement
EXCLUDES   *revision with implantation during same operative episode (49.75)*
AHA: 4Q, '02, 105

49.79   **Other repair of anal sphincter**
Repair of old obstetric laceration of anus
EXCLUDES   *anoplasty with synchronous hemorrhoidectomy (49.46)*
repair of current obstetric laceration (75.62)
AHA: 2Q, '98, 16; 1Q, '97, 9

√4th **49.9**   **Other operations on anus**
EXCLUDES   *dilation of anus (sphincter) (96.23)*

49.91   **Incision of anal septum**

49.92   **Insertion of subcutaneous electrical anal stimulator**

49.93   **Other incision of anus**
Removal of:
foreign body from anus with incision
seton from anus
EXCLUDES   *anal fistulotomy (49.11)*
removal of intraluminal foreign body without incision (98.05)

49.94   **Reduction of anal prolapse**
EXCLUDES   *manual reduction of rectal prolapse (96.26)*
DEF: Manipulation of displaced anal tissue to normal position.

Dynamic Graciloplasty

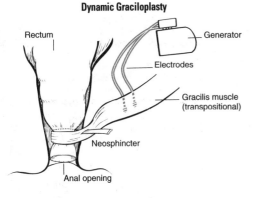

49.95   **Control of (postoperative) hemorrhage of anus**

49.99   **Other**

√3rd **50**   **Operations on liver**
Code also any application or administration of an adhesion barrier substance (99.77)

50.0   **Hepatotomy**
Incision of abscess of liver
Removal of gallstones from liver
Stromeyer-Little operation

√4th **50.1**   **Diagnostic procedures on liver**

50.11   **Closed (percutaneous) (needle) biopsy of liver**
Diagnostic aspiration of liver
AHA: 3Q, '05, 24; 4Q, '88, 12
TIP: When a laparotomy or other open procedure is performed and a needle biopsy of the liver is also performed, assign a separate code for the open procedure and code 50.11 for the needle biopsy.

50.12   **Open biopsy of liver**
Wedge biopsy
AHA: 3Q, '05, 24; 2Q, '05, 13

50.13   **Transjugular liver biopsy**
Transvenous liver biopsy
EXCLUDES   *closed (percutaneous) [needle] biopsy of liver (50.11)*
laparoscopic liver biopsy (50.14)
AHA: 4Q, '07, 113

50.14   **Laparoscopic liver biopsy**
EXCLUDES   *closed (percutaneous) [needle] biopsy of liver (50.11)*
open biopsy of liver (50.12)
transjugular liver biopsy (50.13)
AHA: 4Q, '07, 113

50.19   **Other diagnostic procedures on liver**
EXCLUDES   *laparoscopic liver biopsy (50.14)*
liver scan and radioisotope function study (92.02)
microscopic examination of specimen from liver (91.01-91.09)
transjugular liver biopsy (50.13)

Closed Liver Biopsy

Liver Biopsy (Open, Wedge)

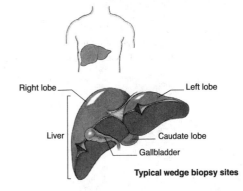

Typical wedge biopsy sites

Operations on the Digestive System

50.2–51.19

√4th **50.2 Local excision or destruction of liver tissue or lesion**

50.21 Marsupialization of lesion of liver

DEF: Exteriorizing lesion by incision and suturing cut edges to skin to create opening.

50.22 Partial hepatectomy

Wedge resection of liver

EXCLUDES   biopsy of liver (50.11-50.12)
hepatic lobectomy (50.3)

50.23 Open ablation of liver lesion or tissue

AHA: 4Q, '06, 124

50.24 Percutaneous ablation of liver lesion or tissue

AHA: 4Q, '06, 124

50.25 Laparoscopic ablation of liver lesion or tissue

AHA: 4Q, '06, 124

50.26 Other and unspecified ablation of liver lesion or tissue

AHA: 4Q, '06, 124

50.29 Other destruction of lesion of liver

Cauterization
Enucleation   } of hepatic lesion
Evacuation

EXCLUDES   ablation of liver lesion or tissue:
laparoscopic (50.25)
open (50.23)
other (50.26)
percutaneous (50.24)
▶laser interstitial thermal therapy [LITT]
of lesion or tissue of liver under
guidance (17.63)◀
percutaneous aspiration of lesion
(50.91)

AHA: 2Q, '03, 9

50.3 Lobectomy of liver

Total hepatic lobectomy with partial excision of other lobe

50.4 Total hepatectomy

AHA: 2Q, '08, 8

√4th **50.5 Liver transplant**

Note: To report donor source – see codes 00.91-00.93

50.51 Auxiliary liver transplant   NC

Auxiliary hepatic transplantation leaving patient's own liver in situ

50.59 Other transplant of liver   LC

AHA: 4Q, '08, 120; 2Q, '08, 8

√4th **50.6 Repair of liver**

50.61 Closure of laceration of liver

50.69 Other repair of liver

Hepatopexy

√4th **50.9 Other operations on liver**

EXCLUDES   lysis of adhesions (54.5)

50.91 Percutaneous aspiration of liver

EXCLUDES   percutaneous biopsy (50.11)

DEF: Incision into liver through body wall to withdraw fluid.

50.92 Extracorporeal hepatic assistance

Liver dialysis

DEF: Devices used outside body to assist liver function.

AHA: 2Q, '01, 21

50.93 Localized perfusion of liver

50.94 Other injection of therapeutic substance into liver

50.99 Other

√3rd **51 Operations on gallbladder and biliary tract**

INCLUDES   operations on:
ampulla of Vater
common bile duct
cystic duct
hepatic duct
intrahepatic bile duct
sphincter of Oddi

Code also any application or administration of an adhesion barrier substance (99.77)

√4th **51.0 Cholecystotomy and cholecystostomy**

51.01 Percutaneous aspiration of gallbladder

Percutaneous cholecystotomy for drainage
That by: needle or catheter

EXCLUDES   needle biopsy (51.12)

51.02 Trocar cholecystostomy

DEF: Creating opening in gallbladder with catheter.

AHA: 3Q, '89, 18

51.03 Other cholecystostomy

51.04 Other cholecystotomy

Cholelithotomy NOS

√4th **51.1 Diagnostic procedures on biliary tract**

EXCLUDES   that for endoscopic procedures classifiable to
51.64, 51.84-51.88, 52.14, 52.21, 52.93
-52.94, 52.97-52.98

AHA: 2Q, '97, 7

51.10 Endoscopic retrograde cholangiopancreatography [ERCP]

EXCLUDES   endoscopic retrograde:
cholangiography [ERC] (51.11)
pancreatography [ERP] (52.13)

DEF: Endoscopic and radioscopic exam of pancreatic and common bile ducts with contrast material injected in opposite direction of normal flow through catheter.

AHA: 4Q, '03, 118; 3Q, '03, 17; 1Q, '01, 8; 2Q, '99, 13

TIP: Do not assign separately if the ERCP was performed in conjunction with endoscopic sphincterotomy/papillotomy or other therapeutic biliary procedure.

51.11 Endoscopic retrograde cholangiography [ERC]

Laparoscopic exploration of common bile duct

EXCLUDES   endoscopic retrograde:
cholangiopancreatography [ERCP]
(51.10)
pancreatography [ERP] (52.13)

DEF: Endoscopic and radioscopic exam of common bile ducts with contrast material injected in opposite direction of normal flow through catheter.

AHA: 1Q, '96, 12; 3Q, '89, 18; 4Q, '88, 7

51.12 Percutaneous biopsy of gallbladder or bile ducts

Needle biopsy of gallbladder

51.13 Open biopsy of gallbladder or bile ducts

51.14 Other closed [endoscopic] biopsy of biliary duct or sphincter of Oddi

Brushing or washing for specimen collection
Closed biopsy of biliary duct or sphincter of Oddi by procedures classifiable to 51.10-51.11, 52.13

DEF: Endoscopic biopsy of muscle tissue around pancreatic and common bile ducts.

51.15 Pressure measurement of sphincter of Oddi

Pressure measurement of sphincter by procedures classifiable to 51.10-51.11, 52.13

DEF: Pressure measurement tests of muscle tissue surrounding pancreatic and common bile ducts.

51.19 Other diagnostic procedures on biliary tract

EXCLUDES   biliary tract x-ray (87.51-87.59)
microscopic examination of specimen
from biliary tract (91.01-91.09)

BI Bilateral Procedure   NC Non-covered Procedure   LC Limited Coverage Procedure   ▶◀ Revised Text   ● New Code   ▲ Revised Code Title

136 – Volume 3 • October 2009   2010 ICD-9-CM

Laparoscopic Cholecystectomy by Laser

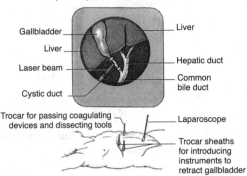

- Gallbladder
- Liver
- Laser beam
- Cystic duct
- Liver
- Hepatic duct
- Common bile duct
- Trocar for passing coagulating devices and dissecting tools
- Laparoscope
- Trocar sheaths for introducing instruments to retract gallbladder

√4th **51.2 Cholecystectomy**
AHA: 1Q, '93, 17; 4Q, '91, 26; 3Q, '89, 18

51.21 Other partial cholecystectomy
Revision of prior cholecystectomy
EXCLUDES that by laparoscope (51.24)
AHA: 4Q, '96, 69

51.22 Cholecystectomy
EXCLUDES laparoscopic cholecystectomy (51.23)
AHA: 4Q, '97, 52; 2Q, '91, 16

51.23 Laparoscopic cholecystectomy
That by laser
DEF: Endoscopic removal of gallbladder.
AHA: ▶4Q, '08, 174;◄ 3Q, '98, 10; 4Q, '97, 52; 1Q, '96, 12; 2Q, '95, 11; 4Q, '91, 26

51.24 Laparoscopic partial cholecystectomy
AHA: 4Q, '96, 69

√4th **51.3 Anastomosis of gallbladder or bile duct**
EXCLUDES resection with end-to-end anastomosis (51.61-51.69)

51.31 Anastomosis of gallbladder to hepatic ducts

51.32 Anastomosis of gallbladder to intestine

51.33 Anastomosis of gallbladder to pancreas

51.34 Anastomosis of gallbladder to stomach

51.35 Other gallbladder anastomosis
Gallbladder anastomosis NOS

51.36 Choledochoenterostomy
DEF: Connection of common bile duct to intestine.

51.37 Anastomosis of hepatic duct to gastrointestinal tract
Kasai portoenterostomy
DEF: Kaisi portoenterostomy: A duct to drain bile from the liver is formed by anastomosing the porta hepatis to a loop of bowel.
AHA: 2Q, '02, 12

51.39 Other bile duct anastomosis
Anastomosis of bile duct NOS
Anastomosis of unspecified bile duct to:
  intestine
  liver
  pancreas
  stomach

√4th **51.4 Incision of bile duct for relief of obstruction**

51.41 Common duct exploration for removal of calculus
EXCLUDES percutaneous extraction (51.96)
AHA: 1Q, '96, 12; 3Q, '89, 18; 4Q, '88, 7

51.42 Common duct exploration for relief of other obstruction
AHA: 3Q, '89, 18

51.43 Insertion of choledochohepatic tube for decompression
Hepatocholedochostomy
AHA: 3Q, '89, 18; 4Q, '88, 7

51.49 Incision of other bile ducts for relief of obstruction
AHA: 3Q, '89, 18

√4th **51.5 Other incision of bile duct**
EXCLUDES that for relief of obstruction (51.41-51.49)

51.51 Exploration of common duct
Incision of common bile duct
AHA: 2Q, '97, 16; 1Q, '96, 12

51.59 Incision of other bile duct
AHA: 2Q, '97, 16; 3Q, '89, 18

√4th **51.6 Local excision or destruction of lesion or tissue of biliary ducts and sphincter of Oddi**
Code also anastomosis other than end-to-end (51.31, 51.36-51.39)
EXCLUDES biopsy of bile duct (51.12-51.13)

51.61 Excision of cystic duct remnant
AHA: 3Q, '89, 18

51.62 Excision of ampulla of Vater (with reimplantation of common duct)

51.63 Other excision of common duct
Choledochectomy
EXCLUDES fistulectomy (51.72)

51.64 Endoscopic excision or destruction of lesion of biliary ducts or sphincter of Oddi
Excision or destruction of lesion of biliary duct by procedures classifiable to 51.10-51.11, 52.13

51.69 Excision of other bile duct
Excision of lesion of bile duct NOS
EXCLUDES fistulectomy (51.79)

√4th **51.7 Repair of bile ducts**

51.71 Simple suture of common bile duct

51.72 Choledochoplasty
Repair of fistula of common bile duct

51.79 Repair of other bile ducts
Closure of artificial opening of bile duct NOS
Suture of bile duct NOS
EXCLUDES operative removal of prosthetic device (51.95)

√4th **51.8 Other operations on biliary ducts and sphincter of Oddi**

51.81 Dilation of sphincter of Oddi
Dilation of ampulla of Vater
EXCLUDES that by endoscopic approach (51.84)
DEF: Dilation of muscle around common bile and pancreatic ducts; to mitigate constriction obstructing bile flow.

51.82 Pancreatic sphincterotomy
Incision of pancreatic sphincter
Transduodenal ampullary sphincterotomy
EXCLUDES that by endoscopic approach (51.85)
DEF: Pancreatic sphincterotomy: Division of muscle around common bile and pancreatic ducts.
DEF: Transduodenal ampullary sphincterotomy: Incision into muscle around common bile and pancreatic ducts; closing approach through first section of small intestine.

51.83 Pancreatic sphincteroplasty

51.84 Endoscopic dilation of ampulla and biliary duct
Dilation of ampulla and biliary duct by procedures classifiable to 51.10-51.11, 52.13

51.85 Endoscopic sphincterotomy and papillotomy
Sphincterotomy and papillotomy by procedures classifiable to 51.10-51.11, 52.13
DEF: Incision of muscle around common bile and pancreatic ducts and closing the duodenal papilla.
AHA: 4Q, '03, 118; 3Q, '03, 17; 2Q, '97, 7

51.86 Endoscopic insertion of nasobiliary drainage tube
Insertion of nasobiliary tube by procedures classifiable to 51.10-51.11, 52.13

Operations on the Digestive System

51.87–52.7

51.87 Endoscopic insertion of stent (tube) into bile duct
Endoprosthesis of bile duct
Insertion of stent into bile duct by procedures classifiable to 51.10-51.11, 52.13
EXCLUDES nasobiliary drainage tube (51.86)
replacement of stent (tube) (97.05)
AHA: 3Q, '03, 17

51.88 Endoscopic removal of stone(s) from biliary tract
Laparoscopic removal of stone(s) from biliary tract
Removal of biliary tract stone(s) by procedures classifiable to 51.10-51.11, 52.13
EXCLUDES percutaneous extraction of common duct stones (51.96)
AHA: 2Q, '00, 11; 2Q, '97, 7

51.89 Other operations on sphincter of Oddi

√4th **51.9 Other operations on biliary tract**
51.91 Repair of laceration of gallbladder
51.92 Closure of cholecystostomy
51.93 Closure of other biliary fistula
Cholecystogastroenteric fistulectomy
51.94 Revision of anastomosis of biliary tract
51.95 Removal of prosthetic device from bile duct
EXCLUDES nonoperative removal (97.55)
51.96 Percutaneous extraction of common duct stones
AHA: 4Q, '88, 7
51.98 Other percutaneous procedures on biliary tract
Percutaneous biliary endoscopy via existing T-tube or other tract for:
dilation of biliary duct stricture
removal of stone(s) except common duct stone
exploration (postoperative)
Percutaneous transhepatic biliary drainage
EXCLUDES percutaneous aspiration of gallbladder (51.01)
percutaneous biopsy and/or collection of specimen by brushing or washing (51.12)
percutaneous removal of common duct stone(s) (51.96)
AHA: 1Q, '97, 14; 3Q, '89, 18; N-D, '87, 1
51.99 Other
Insertion or replacement of biliary tract prosthesis
EXCLUDES biopsy of gallbladder (51.12-51.13)
irrigation of cholecystostomy and other biliary tube (96.41)
lysis of peritoneal adhesions (54.5)
nonoperative removal of:
cholecystostomy tube (97.54)
tube from biliary tract or liver (97.55)

√3rd **52 Operations on pancreas**
INCLUDES operations on pancreatic duct
Code also any application or administration of an adhesion barrier substance (99.77)

√4th **52.0 Pancreatotomy**
52.01 Drainage of pancreatic cyst by catheter
52.09 Other pancreatotomy
Pancreatolithotomy
EXCLUDES drainage by anastomosis (52.4, 52.96)
incision of pancreatic sphincter (51.82)
marsupialization of cyst (52.3)
DEF: Pancreatolithotomy: Incision into pancreas to remove stones.

√4th **52.1 Diagnostic procedures on pancreas**
52.11 Closed [aspiration] [needle] [percutaneous] biopsy of pancreas
52.12 Open biopsy of pancreas

52.13 Endoscopic retrograde pancreatography [ERP]
EXCLUDES endoscopic retrograde:
cholangiography [ERC] (51.11)
cholangiopancreatography [ERCP] (51.10)
that for procedures classifiable to 51.14-51.15, 51.64, 51.84-51.88, 52.14, 52.21, 52.92-52.94, 52.97-52.98

52.14 Closed [endoscopic] biopsy of pancreatic duct
Closed biopsy of pancreatic duct by procedures classifiable to 51.10-51.11, 52.13

52.19 Other diagnostic procedures on pancreas
EXCLUDES contrast pancreatogram (87.66)
endoscopic retrograde pancreatography [ERP] (52.13)
microscopic examination of specimen from pancreas (91.01-91.09)

√4th **52.2 Local excision or destruction of pancreas and pancreatic duct**
EXCLUDES biopsy of pancreas (52.11-52.12, 52.14)
pancreatic fistulectomy (52.95)
52.21 Endoscopic excision or destruction of lesion or tissue of pancreatic duct
Excision or destruction of lesion or tissue of pancreatic duct by procedures classifiable to 51.10-51.11, 52.13
52.22 Other excision or destruction of lesion or tissue of pancreas or pancreatic duct
52.3 Marsupialization of pancreatic cyst
EXCLUDES drainage of cyst by catheter (52.01)
DEF: Incision into pancreas and suturing edges to form pocket; promotes drainage and healing.
52.4 Internal drainage of pancreatic cyst
Pancreaticocystoduodenostomy
Pancreaticocystogastrostomy
Pancreaticocystojejunostomy
DEF: Withdrawing fluid from pancreatic cyst by draining it through a created passage to another organ.
DEF: Pancreaticocystoduodenostomy: Creation of passage from pancreatic cyst to first portion of small intestine.
DEF: Pancreaticocystogastrostomy: Creation of passage from pancreatic cyst to stomach.
DEF: Pancreaticocystojejunostomy: Creation of passage from pancreatic cyst to midsection of small intestine.

√4th **52.5 Partial pancreatectomy**
EXCLUDES pancreatic fistulectomy (52.95)
52.51 Proximal pancreatectomy
Excision of head of pancreas (with part of body)
Proximal pancreatectomy with synchronous duodenectomy
52.52 Distal pancreatectomy
Excision of tail of pancreas (with part of body)
52.53 Radical subtotal pancreatectomy
52.59 Other partial pancreatectomy
52.6 Total pancreatectomy
Pancreatectomy with synchronous duodenectomy
AHA: 4Q, '96, 71
52.7 Radical pancreaticoduodenectomy
One-stage pancreaticoduodenal resection with choledochojejunal anastomosis, pancreaticojejunal anastomosis, and gastrojejunostomy
Two-stage pancreaticoduodenal resection (first stage) (second stage)
Radical resection of the pancreas
Whipple procedure
EXCLUDES radical subtotal pancreatectomy (52.53)
DEF: Whipple procedure: pancreaticoduodenectomy involving the removal of the head of the pancreas and part of the small intestines; pancreaticojejunostomy, choledochojejunal anastomosis, and gastrojejunostomy included in the procedure.
AHA: 1Q, '01, 13

✓4ᵗʰ **52.8 Transplant of pancreas**
Note: To report donor source–see codes 00.91-00.93

10 **52.80 Pancreatic transplant, not otherwise specified** `NC` `LC`

52.81 Reimplantation of pancreatic tissue

10 **52.82 Homotransplant of pancreas** `NC` `LC`

52.83 Heterotransplant of pancreas `NC`

52.84 Autotransplantation of cells of islets of Langerhans
Homotransplantation of islet cells of pancreas
DEF: Transplantation of Islet cells from pancreas to another location of same patient.
AHA: 4Q, '96, 70, 71

52.85 Allotransplantation of cells of islets of Langerhans
Heterotransplantation of islet cells of pancreas
DEF: Transplantation of Islet cells from one individual to another.
AHA: 4Q, '96, 70, 71
TIP: Assign also code 55.69 Other kidney transplantation, if a renal transplant is performed simultaneously.

52.86 Transplantation of cells of islets of Langerhans, not otherwise specified
AHA: 4Q, '96, 70

✓4ᵗʰ **52.9 Other operations on pancreas**
DEF: Placement of tube into pancreatic duct, without an endoscope.

52.92 Cannulation of pancreatic duct
EXCLUDES   *that by endoscopic approach (52.93)*

52.93 Endoscopic insertion of stent (tube) into pancreatic duct
Insertion of cannula or stent into pancreatic duct by procedures classifiable to 51.10-51.11, 52.13
EXCLUDES   *endoscopic insertion of nasopancreatic drainage tube (52.97)*
replacement of stent (tube) (97.05)
AHA: 2Q, '97, 7

52.94 Endoscopic removal of stone(s) from pancreatic duct
Removal of stone(s) from pancreatic duct by procedures classifiable to 51.10-51.11, 52.13

52.95 Other repair of pancreas
Fistulectomy } of pancreas
Simple suture

52.96 Anastomosis of pancreas
Anastomosis of pancreas (duct) to:
    intestine
    jejunum
    stomach
EXCLUDES   *anastomosis to:*
    bile duct (51.39)
    gallbladder (51.33)

52.97 Endoscopic insertion of nasopancreatic drainage tube
Insertion of nasopancreatic drainage tube by procedures classifiable to 51.10-51.11, 52.13
EXCLUDES   *drainage of pancreatic cyst by catheter (52.01)*
replacement of stent (tube) (97.05)

52.98 Endoscopic dilation of pancreatic duct
Dilation of Wirsung's duct by procedures classifiable to 51.10-51.11, 52.13

52.99 Other
Dilation of pancreatic [Wirsung's] duct } by open approach
Repair of pancreatic [Wirsung's] duct
EXCLUDES   *irrigation of pancreatic tube (96.42)*
removal of pancreatic tube (97.56)

Indirect Repair of Hernia

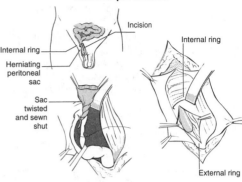

✓3ʳᵈ **53 Repair of hernia**
`INCLUDES`   hernioplasty
           herniorrhaphy
Code also any application or administration of an adhesion barrier substance (99.77)
EXCLUDES   *manual reduction of hernia (96.27)*
DEF: Repair of hernia: Restoration of abnormally protruding organ or tissue.
DEF: Herniorrhaphy: Repair of hernia.
DEF: Herniotomy: Division of constricted, strangulated, irreducible hernia.
AHA: 3Q, '94, 8

✓4ᵗʰ **53.0 Other unilateral repair of inguinal hernia**
EXCLUDES   *laparoscopic unilateral repair of inguinal hernia (17.11-17.13)*
AHA: ▶4Q, '08, 165-167◀

53.00 Unilateral repair of inguinal hernia, not otherwise specified
Inguinal herniorrhaphy NOS
AHA: 3Q, '03, 10

53.01 Other and open repair of direct inguinal hernia
Direct and indirect inguinal hernia
AHA: 4Q, '96, 66

53.02 Other and open repair of indirect inguinal hernia

53.03 Other and open repair of direct inguinal hernia with graft or prosthesis

53.04 Other and open repair of indirect inguinal hernia with graft or prosthesis

53.05 Repair of inguinal hernia with graft or prosthesis, not otherwise specified

✓4ᵗʰ **53.1 Other bilateral repair of inguinal hernia**
EXCLUDES   *laparoscopic bilateral repair of inguinal hernia (17.21-17.24)*
AHA: ▶4Q, '08, 165-167◀

53.10 Bilateral repair of inguinal hernia, not otherwise specified

53.11 Other and open bilateral repair of direct inguinal hernia

53.12 Other and open bilateral repair of indirect inguinal hernia

53.13 Other and open bilateral repair of inguinal hernia, one direct and one indirect

53.14 Other and open bilateral repair of direct inguinal hernia with graft or prosthesis

53.15 Other and open bilateral repair of indirect inguinal hernia with graft or prosthesis

53.16 Other and open bilateral repair of inguinal hernia, one direct and one indirect, with graft or prosthesis

53.17 Bilateral inguinal hernia repair with graft or prosthesis, not otherwise specified

---

10 Noncovered procedure unless reported with code 55.69 and a diagnosis code from 250.x0 or 250.x2 with 403.x1, 404.x2, 404.x3, 585.x, V42.0, or V42.89; or reported with a diagnosis code 250.x1 or 250.x3.

Operations on the Digestive System

53.2–54.12

✓4th **53.2 Unilateral repair of femoral hernia**

53.21 Unilateral repair of femoral hernia with graft or prosthesis

53.29 Other unilateral femoral herniorrhaphy

✓4th **53.3 Bilateral repair of femoral hernia**

53.31 Bilateral repair of femoral hernia with graft or prosthesis

53.39 Other bilateral femoral herniorrhaphy

✓4th **53.4 Repair of umbilical hernia**

EXCLUDES *repair of gastroschisis (54.71)*

AHA: ►4Q, '08, 165-168◄

53.41 Other and open repair of umbilical hernia with graft or prosthesis

53.42 Laparoscopic repair of umbilical hernia with graft or prosthesis

53.43 Other laparoscopic umbilical herniorrhaphy

53.49 Other open umbilical herniorrhaphy

EXCLUDES *other laparoscopic umbilical herniorrhaphy (53.43)*
repair of umbilical hernia with graft or prosthesis (53.41, 53.42)

✓4th **53.5 Repair of other hernia of anterior abdominal wall (without graft or prosthesis)**

53.51 Incisional hernia repair

AHA: 3Q, '03, 6

53.59 Repair of other hernia of anterior abdominal wall

Repair of hernia: Repair of hernia:
epigastric spigelian
hypogastric ventral

AHA: 2Q, '06, 10; 3Q, '03, 6; 3Q, '96, 15

✓4th **53.6 Repair of other hernia of anterior abdominal wall with graft or prosthesis**

AHA: ►4Q, '08, 165-168◄

53.61 Other open incisional hernia repair with graft or prosthesis

EXCLUDES *laparoscopic incisional hernia repair with graft or prosthesis (53.62)*

AHA: 3Q, '03, 11

53.62 Laparoscopic incisional hernia repair with graft or prosthesis

53.63 Other laparoscopic repair of other hernia of anterior abdominal wall with graft or prosthesis

53.69 Other and open repair of other hernia of anterior abdominal wall with graft or prosthesis

EXCLUDES *other laparoscopic repair of other hernia of anterior abdominal wall with graft or prosthesis (53.63)*

✓4th **53.7 Repair of diaphragmatic hernia, abdominal approach**

AHA: ►4Q, '08, 165-168◄

53.71 Laparoscopic repair of diaphragmatic hernia, abdominal approach

53.72 Other and open repair of diaphragmatic hernia, abdominal approach

53.75 Repair of diaphragmatic hernia, abdominal approach, not otherwise specified

EXCLUDES *laparoscopic repair of diaphragmatic hernia (53.71)*
other and open repair of diaphragmatic hernia (53.72)

✓4th **53.8 Repair of diaphragmatic hernia, thoracic approach**

DEF: Repair of diaphragmatic hernia though abdomen and thorax.

53.80 Repair of diaphragmatic hernia with thoracic approach, not otherwise specified

Thoracoabdominal repair of diaphragmatic hernia

53.81 Plication of the diaphragm

DEF: Tuck repair of diaphragmatic hernia.

53.82 Repair of parasternal hernia

DEF: Repair of hernia protruding into breastbone area.

53.83 Laparoscopic repair of diaphragmatic hernia, with thoracic approach

AHA: ►4Q, '08, 165-169◄

53.84 Other and open repair of diaphragmatic hernia, with thoracic approach

EXCLUDES *repair of diaphragmatic hernia with thoracic approach, NOS, (53.80)*

AHA: ►4Q, '08, 165-169◄

53.9 Other hernia repair

Repair of hernia:
ischiatic
ischiorectal
lumbar
obturator
omental
retroperitoneal
sciatic

EXCLUDES *relief of strangulated hernia with exteriorization of intestine (46.01, 46.03)*
repair of pericolostomy hernia (46.42)
repair of vaginal enterocele (70.92)

✓3rd **54 Other operations on abdominal region**

INCLUDES operations on:
epigastric region
flank
groin region
hypochondrium
inguinal region
loin region
mesentery
omentum
pelvic cavity
peritoneum
retroperitoneal tissue space

Code also any application or administration of an adhesion barrier substance (99.77)

EXCLUDES *hernia repair (53.00-53.9)*
obliteration of cul-de-sac (70.92)
retroperitoneal tissue dissection (59.00-59.09)
skin and subcutaneous tissue of abdominal wall (86.01-86.99)

54.0 Incision of abdominal wall

Drainage of:
abdominal wall
extraperitoneal abscess
retroperitoneal abscess

EXCLUDES *incision of peritoneum (54.95)*
laparotomy (54.11-54.19)

AHA: 2Q, '06, 23; 4Q, '05, 77; 1Q, '97, 11; N-D, '87, 12

TIP: Assign for incision and drainage (I&D) with debridement of abdominal wall surgical wound postoperative infection. Do not assign a separate debridement code; it's an integral component.

✓4th **54.1 Laparotomy**

DEF: Incision into abdomen.
AHA: 1Q, '92, 13

54.11 Exploratory laparotomy

EXCLUDES *exploration incidental to intra-abdominal surgery — omit code*

DEF: Exam of peritoneal cavity through incision into abdomen.

AHA: 3Q, '89, 14; 4Q, '88, 12

TIP: An exploratory procedure followed by definitive surgery is coded only to the definitive surgery performed, except for procedures involving biopsy and/or incidental appendectomy.

54.12 Reopening of recent laparotomy site

Reopening of recent laparotomy site for:
control of hemorrhage
exploration
incision of hematoma

BI Bilateral Procedure   NC Non-covered Procedure   LC Limited Coverage Procedure   ►◄ Revised Text   ● New Code   ▲ Revised Code Title

54.19 **Other laparotomy**
　　Drainage of intraperitoneal abscess or hematoma
　　EXCLUDES　*culdocentesis (70.0)*
　　　　　drainage of appendiceal abscess (47.2)
　　　　　exploration incidental to
　　　　　　intra-abdominal surgery —
　　　　　　omit code
　　　　　Ladd operation (54.95)
　　　　　percutaneous drainage of abdomen
　　　　　　(54.91)
　　　　　removal of foreign body (54.92)
　　AHA: 3Q, '03, 17

✓4th **54.2** **Diagnostic procedures of abdominal region**

54.21 **Laparoscopy**
　　Peritoneoscopy
　　EXCLUDES　*laparoscopic cholecystectomy (51.23)*
　　　　　that incidental to destruction of
　　　　　　fallopian tubes (66.21-66.29)
　　DEF: Endoscopic exam of peritoneal cavity through abdominal incision.

54.22 **Biopsy of abdominal wall or umbilicus**

54.23 **Biopsy of peritoneum**
　　Biopsy of:
　　　mesentery
　　　omentum
　　　peritoneal implant
　　　EXCLUDES　*closed biopsy of:*
　　　　　　omentum (54.24)
　　　　　　peritoneum (54.24)

54.24 **Closed [percutaneous] [needle] biopsy of intra-abdominal mass**
　　Closed biopsy of:
　　　omentum
　　　peritoneal implant
　　　peritoneum
　　　EXCLUDES　*that of:*
　　　　　　fallopian tube (66.11)
　　　　　　ovary (65.11)
　　　　　　uterine ligaments (68.15)
　　　　　　uterus (68.16)
　　AHA: 4Q, '97, 57

54.25 **Peritoneal lavage**
　　Diagnostic peritoneal lavage
　　EXCLUDES　*peritoneal dialysis (54.98)*
　　DEF: Irrigation of peritoneal cavity with siphoning of liquid contents for analysis.
　　AHA: 2Q, '98, 19; 4Q, '93, 28

54.29 **Other diagnostic procedures on abdominal region**
　　EXCLUDES　*abdominal lymphangiogram (88.04)*
　　　　　abdominal x-ray NEC (88.19)
　　　　　angiocardiography of venae cavae
　　　　　　(88.51)
　　　　　C.A.T. scan of abdomen (88.01)
　　　　　contrast x-ray of abdominal cavity
　　　　　　(88.11-88.15)
　　　　　intra-abdominal arteriography NEC
　　　　　　(88.47)
　　　　　microscopic examination of peritoneal
　　　　　　and retroperitoneal specimen
　　　　　　(91.11-91.19)
　　　　　phlebography of:
　　　　　　intra-abdominal vessels NEC
　　　　　　　(88.65)
　　　　　　portal venous system (88.64)
　　　　　sinogram of abdominal wall (88.03)
　　　　　soft tissue x-ray of abdominal wall NEC
　　　　　　(88.09)
　　　　　tomography of abdomen NEC (88.02)
　　　　　ultrasonography of abdomen and
　　　　　　retroperitoneum (88.76)

54.3 **Excision or destruction of lesion or tissue of abdominal wall or umbilicus**
　　Debridement of abdominal wall
　　Omphalectomy
　　EXCLUDES　*biopsy of abdominal wall or umbilicus (54.22)*
　　　　　size reduction operation (86.83)
　　　　　that of skin of abdominal wall (86.22, 86.26, 86.3)
　　AHA: 1Q, '89, 11

54.4 **Excision or destruction of peritoneal tissue**
　　Excision of:
　　　appendices epiploicae
　　　falciform ligament
　　　gastrocolic ligament
　　　lesion of:
　　　　mesentery
　　　　omentum
　　　　peritoneum
　　　presacral lesion NOS
　　　retroperitoneal lesion NOS
　　　EXCLUDES　*biopsy of peritoneum (54.23)*
　　　　　　endometrectomy of cul-de-sac (70.32)

✓4th **54.5** **Lysis of peritoneal adhesions**
　　Freeing of adhesions of:
　　　biliary tract
　　　intestines
　　　liver
　　　pelvic peritoneum
　　　peritoneum
　　　spleen
　　　uterus
　　　EXCLUDES　*lysis of adhesions of:*
　　　　　　bladder (59.11)
　　　　　　fallopian tube and ovary (65.81, 65.89)
　　　　　　kidney (59.02)
　　　　　　ureter (59.02-59.03)
　　AHA: 3Q, '94, 8; 4Q, '90, 18
　　TIP: Code separately only if the documentation specifies that the adhesions were significant, caused symptoms, and/or increased the difficulty of the procedure being performed.

54.51 **Laparoscopic lysis of peritoneal adhesions**
　　AHA: 4Q, '06, 134; 3Q, '03, 6-7; 4Q, '96, 65

54.59 **Other lysis of peritoneal adhesions**
　　AHA: 3Q, '06, 15; 3Q, '03, 11; 1Q, '03, 14; 4Q, '96, 66

✓4th **54.6** **Suture of abdominal wall and peritoneum**

54.61 **Reclosure of postoperative disruption of abdominal wall**

54.62 **Delayed closure of granulating abdominal wound**
　　Tertiary subcutaneous wound closure
　　DEF: Closure of outer layers of abdominal wound; follows procedure to close initial layers of wound.

54.63 **Other suture of abdominal wall**
　　Suture of laceration of abdominal wall
　　EXCLUDES　*closure of operative wound — omit code*

54.64 **Suture of peritoneum**
　　Secondary suture of peritoneum
　　EXCLUDES　*closure of operative wound — omit code*

✓4th **54.7** **Other repair of abdominal wall and peritoneum**

54.71 **Repair of gastroschisis**
　　DEF: Repair of congenital fistula of abdominal wall.
　　AHA: 2Q, '02, 9

54.72 **Other repair of abdominal wall**

54.73 **Other repair of peritoneum**
　　Suture of gastrocolic ligament

Operations on the Digestive System

54.74–54.99

54.74 **Other repair of omentum**
Epiplorrhaphy
Graft of omentum
Omentopexy
Reduction of torsion of omentum
EXCLUDES   *cardio-omentopexy (36.39)*
DEF: Epiplorrhaphy: Suture of abdominal serous membrane.
DEF: Graft of omentum: Implantation of tissue into abdominal serous membrane.
DEF: Omentopexy: Anchoring of abdominal serous membrane.
DEF: Reduction of torsion of omentum: Reduction of twisted abdominal serous membrane.
AHA: J-F, '87, 11

54.75 **Other repair of mesentery**
Mesenteric plication
Mesenteropexy
DEF: Creation of folds in mesentery for shortening.
DEF: Mesenteriopexy: Fixation of torn, incised mesentery.

✓4ᵗʰ **54.9** **Other operations of abdominal region**
EXCLUDES   *removal of ectopic pregnancy (74.3)*

54.91 **Percutaneous abdominal drainage**
Paracentesis
EXCLUDES   *creation of cutaneoperitoneal fistula (54.93)*
DEF: Puncture for removal of fluid.
AHA: 4Q, '07, 96; 3Q, '99, 9; 2Q, '99, 14; 3Q, '98, 12; 1Q, '92, 14; 2Q, '90, 25

54.92 **Removal of foreign body from peritoneal cavity**
AHA: 1Q, '89, 11

54.93 **Creation of cutaneoperitoneal fistula**
DEF: Creation of opening between skin and peritoneal cavity.
AHA: 2Q, '95, 10; N-D, '84, 6

54.94 **Creation of peritoneovascular shunt**
Peritoneovenous shunt
DEF: Peritoneal vascular shunt: Construction of shunt to connect peritoneal cavity with vascular system.
DEF: Peritoneovenous shunt: Construction of shunt to connect peritoneal cavity with vein.
AHA: 1Q, '94, 7; 1Q, '88, 9; S-O, '85, 6
TIP: Assign for insertion of a Denver shunt if it is described as a peritoneovascular shunt; if it is a Denver pleuroperitoneal shunt, assign instead 34.09.

54.95 **Incision of peritoneum**
Exploration of ventriculoperitoneal shunt at peritoneal site
Ladd operation
Revision of distal catheter of ventricular shunt
Revision of ventriculoperitoneal shunt at peritoneal site
EXCLUDES   *that incidental to laparotomy (54.11-54.19)*
DEF: Ladd operation: Peritoneal attachment of incompletely rotated cecum, obstructing duodenum.
AHA: 4Q, '95, 65
TIP: If a ventriculoperitoneal shunt is explored or revised at the ventricular site, assign instead code 02.41 or 02.42.

54.96 **Injection of air into peritoneal cavity**
Pneumoperitoneum
EXCLUDES   *that for:*
    collapse of lung (33.33)
    radiography (88.12-88.13, 88.15)

54.97 **Injection of locally-acting therapeutic substance into peritoneal cavity**
EXCLUDES   *peritoneal dialysis (54.98)*

54.98 **Peritoneal dialysis**
EXCLUDES   *peritoneal lavage (diagnostic) (54.25)*
DEF: Separation of blood elements by diffusion through membrane.
AHA: 4Q, '93, 28; N-D, '84, 6

54.99 **Other**
EXCLUDES   *removal of:*
    abdominal wall sutures (97.83)
    peritoneal drainage device (97.82)
    retroperitoneal drainage device (97.81)
AHA: 1Q, '99, 4

BI Bilateral Procedure   **NC** Non-covered Procedure   **LC** Limited Coverage Procedure   ▶◀ Revised Text   ● New Code   ▲ Revised Code Title

10. OPERATIONS ON THE URINARY SYSTEM (55-59)

√3rd **55 Operations on kidney**

INCLUDES operations on renal pelvis

Code also any application or administration of an adhesion barrier substance (99.77)

EXCLUDES perirenal tissue (59.00-59.09, 59.21-59.29, 59.91-59.92)

√4th **55.0 Nephrotomy and nephrostomy**

EXCLUDES drainage by:
anastomosis (55.86)
aspiration (55.92)

55.01 Nephrotomy

Evacuation of renal cyst
Exploration of kidney
Nephrolithotomy

DEF: Nephrotomy: Incision into kidney.

DEF: Evacuation of renal cyst: Draining contents of cyst.

DEF: Exploration of kidney: Exploration through incision.

DEF: Nephrolithotomy: Removal of kidney stone through incision.

55.02 Nephrostomy

AHA: 2Q, '97, 4

55.03 Percutaneous nephrostomy without fragmentation

Nephrostolithotomy, percutaneous (nephroscopic)
Percutaneous removal of kidney stone(s) by:
forceps extraction (nephroscopic)
basket extraction
Pyelostolithotomy, percutaneous (nephroscopic)
With placement of catheter down ureter

EXCLUDES percutaneous removal by fragmentation (55.04)
repeat nephroscopic removal during current episode (55.92)

DEF: Insertion of tube through abdominal wall without breaking up stones.

DEF: Nephrostolithotomy: Insertion of tube through the abdominal wall to remove stones.

DEF: Basket extraction: Removal, percutaneous of stone with grasping forceps.

DEF: Pyelostolithotomy: Removal, percutaneous of stones from funnel-shaped portion of kidney.

AHA: 2Q, '96, 5

55.04 Percutaneous nephrostomy with fragmentation

Percutaneous nephrostomy with disruption of kidney stone by ultrasonic energy and extraction (suction) through endoscope
With placement of catheter down ureter
With fluoroscopic guidance

EXCLUDES repeat fragmentation during current episode (59.95)

DEF: Insertion of tube through abdominal wall into kidney to break up stones.

AHA: 1Q, '89, 1; S-O, '86, 11

√4th **55.1 Pyelotomy and pyelostomy**

EXCLUDES drainage by anastomosis (55.86)
percutaneous pyelostolithotomy (55.03)
removal of calculus without incision (56.0)

55.11 Pyelotomy

Exploration of renal pelvis
Pyelolithotomy

55.12 Pyelostomy

Insertion of drainage tube into renal pelvis

√4th **55.2 Diagnostic procedures on kidney**

55.21 Nephroscopy

DEF: Endoscopic exam of renal pelvis; retrograde through ureter, percutaneous or open exposure.

55.22 Pyeloscopy

DEF: Fluoroscopic exam of kidney pelvis, calyces and ureters; follows IV or retrograde injection of contrast.

55.23 Closed [percutaneous] [needle] biopsy of kidney

Endoscopic biopsy via existing nephrostomy, nephrotomy, pyelostomy, or pyelotomy

55.24 Open biopsy of kidney

55.29 Other diagnostic procedures on kidney

EXCLUDES microscopic examination of specimen from kidney (91.21-91.29)
pyelogram:
intravenous (87.73)
percutaneous (87.75)
retrograde (87.74)
radioisotope scan (92.03)
renal arteriography (88.45)
tomography:
C.A.T scan (87.71)
other (87.72)

√4th **55.3 Local excision or destruction of lesion or tissue of kidney**

55.31 Marsupialization of kidney lesion

DEF: Exteriorization of lesion by incising anterior wall and suturing cut edges to create open pouch.

55.32 Open ablation of renal lesion or tissue

AHA: 4Q, '06, 124

55.33 Percutaneous ablation of renal lesion or tissue

AHA: 4Q, '06, 124

55.34 Laparoscopic ablation of renal lesion or tissue

AHA: 4Q, '06, 124

55.35 Other and unspecified ablation of renal lesion or tissue

AHA: 4Q, '06, 124

55.39 Other local destruction or excision of renal lesion or tissue

Obliteration of calyceal diverticulum

EXCLUDES ablation of renal lesion or tissue:
laparoscopic (55.34)
open (55.32)
other (55.35)
percutaneous (55.33)
biopsy of kidney (55.23-55.24)
partial nephrectomy (55.4)
percutaneous aspiration of kidney (55.92)
wedge resection of kidney (55.4)

55.4 Partial nephrectomy

Calycectomy
Wedge resection of kidney
Code also any synchronous resection of ureter (56.40-56.42)

DEF: Surgical removal of a part of the kidney.

DEF: Calycectomy: Removal of indentations in kidney.

√4th **55.5 Complete nephrectomy**

Code also any synchronous excision of:
adrenal gland (07.21-07.3)
bladder segment (57.6)
lymph nodes (40.3, 40.52-40.59)

55.51 Nephroureterectomy

Nephroureterectomy with bladder cuff
Total nephrectomy (unilateral)

EXCLUDES removal of transplanted kidney (55.53)

DEF: Complete removal of the kidney and all or portion of the ureter.

DEF: Nephroureterectomy with bladder cuff: Removal of kidney, ureter, and portion of bladder attached to ureter.

DEF: Total nephrectomy (unilateral): Complete excision of one kidney.

AHA: 2Q, '05, 4

55.52 Nephrectomy of remaining kidney

Removal of solitary kidney

EXCLUDES removal of transplanted kidney (55.53)

55.53 Removal of transplanted or rejected kidney

AHA: ▶4Q, 08, 83◀

√3rd √4th Additional Digit Required   Valid OR Procedure   Non-OR Procedure   Adjunct Code

Operations on the Urinary System

55.54–56.42

Symphysiostomy for Horseshoe Kidney

Inferior Vena Cava — Aorta
Ureter — Sutures

Horseshoe kidney joined at inferior poles

55.54   **Bilateral nephrectomy**
> *EXCLUDES*   *complete nephrectomy NOS (55.51)*
> **DEF:** Removal of both kidneys same operative session.

√4ᵗʰ **55.6**   **Transplant of kidney**
> Note: To report donor source – see codes 00.91-00.93

55.61   **Renal autotransplantation**

55.69   **Other kidney transplantation**   `LC`
> **AHA:** 4Q, '04, 117; 4Q, '96, 71

55.7   **Nephropexy**
> Fixation or suspension of movable [floating] kidney

√4ᵗʰ **55.8**   **Other repair of kidney**

55.81   **Suture of laceration of kidney**

55.82   **Closure of nephrostomy and pyelostomy**
> **DEF:** Removal of tube from kidney and closure of site of tube insertion.

55.83   **Closure of other fistula of kidney**

55.84   **Reduction of torsion of renal pedicle**
> **DEF:** Restoration of twisted renal pedicle into normal position.

55.85   **Symphysiotomy for horseshoe kidney**
> **DEF:** Division of congenitally malformed kidney into two parts.

55.86   **Anastomosis of kidney**
> Nephropyeloureterostomy
> Pyeloureterovesical anastomosis
> Ureterocalyceal anastomosis
> *EXCLUDES*   *nephrocystanastomosis NOS (56.73)*
> **DEF:** Nephropyeloureterostomy: Creation of passage between kidney and ureter.
> **DEF:** Pyeloureterovesical anastomosis: Creation of passage between kidney and bladder.
> **DEF:** Ureterocalyceal anastomosis: Creation of passage between ureter and kidney indentations.

55.87   **Correction of ureteropelvic junction**

55.89   **Other**

√4ᵗʰ **55.9**   **Other operations on kidney**
> *EXCLUDES*   *lysis of perirenal adhesions (59.02)*

55.91   **Decapsulation of kidney**
> Capsulectomy
> Decortication } of kidney

55.92   **Percutaneous aspiration of kidney (pelvis)**
> Aspiration of renal cyst
> Renipuncture
> *EXCLUDES*   *percutaneous biopsy of kidney (55.23)*
> **DEF:** Insertion of needle into kidney to withdraw fluid.
> **AHA:** N-D, '84, 20

55.93   **Replacement of nephrostomy tube**

55.94   **Replacement of pyelostomy tube**

55.95   **Local perfusion of kidney**
> **DEF:** Fluid passage through kidney.

55.96   **Other injection of therapeutic substance into kidney**
> Injection into renal cyst

55.97   **Implantation or replacement of mechanical kidney**

55.98   **Removal of mechanical kidney**

55.99   **Other**
> *EXCLUDES*   *removal of pyelostomy or nephrostomy tube (97.61)*

√3ʳᵈ **56**   **Operations on ureter**
> Code also any application or administration of an adhesion barrier substance (99.77)

56.0   **Transurethral removal of obstruction from ureter and renal pelvis**
> Removal of:
> blood clot
> calculus } from ureter or renal pelvis without incision
> foreign body
> *EXCLUDES*   *manipulation without removal of obstruction (59.8)*
> *that by incision (55.11,56.2)*
> *transurethral insertion of ureteral stent for passage of calculus (59.8)*
> **DEF:** Removal of obstruction by tube inserted through urethra to ureter.
> **AHA:** 1Q, '89, 1; S-O, '86, 12
> **TIP:** Assign for laser lithotripsy of the kidney or ureter, unless the documentation specifies extracorporeal shockwave lithotripsy (ESWL), see instead code 98.51.

56.1   **Ureteral meatotomy**
> **DEF:** Incision into ureteral meatus to enlarge passage.

56.2   **Ureterotomy**
> Incision of ureter for:
> drainage
> exploration
> removal of calculus
> *EXCLUDES*   *cutting of ureterovesical orifice (56.1)*
> *removal of calculus without incision (56.0)*
> *transurethral insertion of ureteral stent for passage of calculus (59.8)*
> *urinary diversion (56.51-56.79)*
> **AHA:** S-O, '86, 10

√4ᵗʰ **56.3**   **Diagnostic procedures on ureter**

56.31   **Ureteroscopy**

56.32   **Closed percutaneous biopsy of ureter**
> *EXCLUDES*   *endoscopic biopsy of ureter (56.33)*

56.33   **Closed endoscopic biopsy of ureter**
> Cystourethroscopy with ureteral biopsy
> Transurethral biopsy of ureter
> Ureteral endoscopy with biopsy through ureterotomy
> Ureteroscopy with biopsy
> *EXCLUDES*   *percutaneous biopsy of ureter (56.32)*

56.34   **Open biopsy of ureter**

56.35   **Endoscopy (cystoscopy) (looposcopy) of ileal conduit**
> **DEF:** Endoscopic exam of created opening between ureters and one end of small intestine; other end used to form artificial opening.

56.39   **Other diagnostic procedures on ureter**
> *EXCLUDES*   *microscopic examination of specimen from ureter (91.21-91.29)*

√4ᵗʰ **56.4**   **Ureterectomy**
> Code also anastomosis other than end-to-end (56.51-56.79)
> *EXCLUDES*   *fistulectomy (56.84)*
> *nephroureterectomy (55.51-55.54)*

56.40   **Ureterectomy, not otherwise specified**

56.41   **Partial ureterotomy**
> Excision of lesion of ureter
> Shortening of ureter with reimplantation
> *EXCLUDES*   *biopsy of ureter (56.32-56.34)*

56.42   **Total ureterectomy**

BI Bilateral Procedure   NC Non-covered Procedure   LC Limited Coverage Procedure   ▶◀ Revised Text   ● New Code   ▲ Revised Code Title

144 – Volume 3   **2010 ICD-9-CM**

√4ᵗʰ **56.5 Cutaneous uretero-ileostomy**

56.51 Formation of cutaneous uretero-ileostomy

Construction of ileal conduit
External ureteral ileostomy
Formation of open ileal bladder
Ileal loop operation
Ileoureterostomy (Bricker's) (ileal bladder)
Transplantation of ureter into ileum with external diversion

> **EXCLUDES** closed ileal bladder (57.87)
> replacement of ureteral defect by ileal segment (56.89)

> **DEF:** Creation of urinary passage by connecting the terminal end of small intestine to ureter then connected to opening through abdominal wall.
> **DEF:** Construction of ileal conduit: Formation of conduit from terminal end of small intestine.

56.52 Revision of cutaneous uretero-ileostomy

> **AHA:** 3Q, '96, 15; 4Q, '88, 7

√4ᵗʰ **56.6 Other external urinary diversion**

56.61 Formation of other cutaneous ureterostomy

Anastomosis of ureter to skin
Ureterostomy NOS

56.62 Revision of other cutaneous ureterostomy

Revision of ureterostomy stoma

> **EXCLUDES** nonoperative removal of ureterostomy tube (97.62)

√4ᵗʰ **56.7 Other anastomosis or bypass of ureter**

> **EXCLUDES** ureteropyelostomy (55.86)

56.71 Urinary diversion to intestine

Anastomosis of ureter to intestine
Internal urinary diversion NOS

Code also any synchronous colostomy (46.10-46.13)

> **EXCLUDES** external ureteral ileostomy (56.51)

56.72 Revision of ureterointestinal anastomosis

> **EXCLUDES** revision of external ureteral ileostomy (56.52)

56.73 Nephrocystanastomosis, not otherwise specified

> **DEF:** Connection of kidney to bladder.

56.74 Ureteroneocystostomy

Replacement of ureter with bladder flap
Ureterovesical anastomosis

> **DEF:** Transfer of ureter to another site in bladder.
> **DEF:** Ureterovesical anastomosis: Implantation of ureter into bladder.

56.75 Transureteroureterostomy

> **EXCLUDES** ureteroureterostomy associated with partial resection (56.41)

> **DEF:** Separating one ureter and joining the ends to the opposite ureter.

56.79 Other

√4ᵗʰ **56.8 Repair of ureter**

56.81 Lysis of intraluminal adhesions of ureter

> **EXCLUDES** lysis of periureteral adhesions (59.02-59.03)
> ureterolysis (59.02-59.03)

> **DEF:** Destruction of adhesions within urethral cavity.

56.82 Suture of laceration of ureter

56.83 Closure of ureterostomy

56.84 Closure of other fistula of ureter

56.85 Ureteropexy

56.86 Removal of ligature from ureter

56.89 Other repair of ureter

Graft of ureter
Replacement of ureter with ileal segment implanted into bladder
Ureteroplication

> **DEF:** Graft of ureter: Tissue from another site for graft replacement or repair of ureter.
> **DEF:** Replacement of ureter with ileal segment implanted into bladder and ureter replacement with terminal end of small intestine.
> **DEF:** Ureteroplication: Creation of tucks in ureter.

√4ᵗʰ **56.9 Other operations on ureter**

56.91 Dilation of ureteral meatus

56.92 Implantation of electronic ureteral stimulator

56.93 Replacement of electronic ureteral stimulator

56.94 Removal of electronic ureteral stimulator

> **EXCLUDES** that with synchronous replacement (56.93)

56.95 Ligation of ureter

56.99 Other

> **EXCLUDES** removal of ureterostomy tube and ureteral catheter (97.62)
> ureteral catheterization (59.8)

√3ʳᵈ **57 Operations on urinary bladder**

Code also any application or administration of an adhesion barrier substance (99.77)

> **EXCLUDES** perivesical tissue (59.11-59.29, 59.91-59.92)
> ureterovesical orifice (56.0-56.99)

57.0 Transurethral clearance of bladder

Drainage of bladder without incision
Removal of:
  blood clot
  calculus   } from bladder without incision
  foreign body

> **EXCLUDES** that by incision (57.19)

> **AHA:** S-O, '86, 11

> **DEF:** Insertion of device through urethra to cleanse bladder.

√4ᵗʰ **57.1 Cystotomy and cystostomy**

> **EXCLUDES** cystotomy and cystostomy as operative approach — omit code

> **DEF:** Cystotomy: Incision of bladder.
> **DEF:** Cystostomy: Creation of opening into bladder.

57.11 Percutaneous aspiration of bladder

57.12 Lysis of intraluminal adhesions with incision into bladder

> **EXCLUDES** transurethral lysis of intraluminal adhesions (57.41)

> **DEF:** Incision into bladder to destroy lesions.

57.17 Percutaneous cystostomy

Closed cystostomy
Percutaneous suprapubic cystostomy

> **EXCLUDES** removal of cystostomy tube (97.63)
> replacement of cystostomy tube (59.94)

> **DEF:** Incision through body wall into bladder to insert tube.
> **DEF:** Percutaneous (closed) suprapubic cystostomy: Incision above pubic arch, through body wall, into the bladder to insert tube.

57.18 Other suprapubic cystostomy

> **EXCLUDES** percutaneous cystostomy (57.17)
> removal of cystostomy tube (97.63)
> replacement of cystostomy tube (59.94)

57.19 Other cystotomy

Cystolithotomy

> **EXCLUDES** percutaneous cystostomy (57.17)
> suprapubic cystostomy (57.18)

> **AHA:** 4Q, '95, 73; S-O, '86, 11

Operations on the Urinary System

57.2–57.86

Transurethral Cystourethroscopy

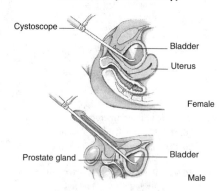

Cystoscope — Bladder — Uterus — Female

Prostate gland — Bladder — Male

✓4th **57.2 Vesicostomy**
> *EXCLUDES* *percutaneous cystostomy (57.17)*
> *suprapubic cystostomy (57.18)*

57.21 Vesicostomy
Creation of permanent opening from bladder to skin using a bladder flap
DEF: Creation of permanent opening from the bladder to the skin.

57.22 Revision or closure of vesicostomy
> *EXCLUDES* *closure of cystostomy (57.82)*

✓4th **57.3 Diagnostic procedures on bladder**

57.31 Cystoscopy through artificial stoma

57.32 Other cystoscopy
Transurethral cystoscopy
> *EXCLUDES* *cystourethroscopy with ureteral biopsy (56.33)*
> *retrograde pyelogram (87.74)*
> *that for control of hemorrhage (postoperative):*
> *bladder (57.93)*
> *prostate (60.94)*

AHA: 1Q, '01, 14

57.33 Closed [transurethral] biopsy of bladder

57.34 Open biopsy of bladder
AHA: 2Q, '05, 12

57.39 Other diagnostic procedures on bladder
> *EXCLUDES* *cystogram NEC (87.77)*
> *microscopic examination of specimen from bladder (91.31-91.39)*
> *retrograde cystourethrogram (87.76)*
> *therapeutic distention of bladder (96.25)*

✓4th **57.4 Transurethral excision or destruction of bladder tissue**
DEF: Destruction of bladder tissue with instrument inserted into urethra.

57.41 Transurethral lysis of intraluminal adhesions

57.49 Other transurethral excision or destruction of lesion or tissue of bladder
Endoscopic resection of bladder lesion
> *EXCLUDES* *transurethral biopsy of bladder (57.33)*
> *transurethral fistulectomy (57.83-57.84)*

✓4th **57.5 Other excision or destruction of bladder tissue**
> *EXCLUDES* *that with transurethral approach (57.41-57.49)*

57.51 Excision of urachus
Excision of urachal sinus of bladder
> *EXCLUDES* *excision of urachal cyst of abdominal wall (54.3)*

57.59 Open excision or destruction of other lesion or tissue of bladder
Endometrectomy of bladder
Suprapubic excision of bladder lesion
> *EXCLUDES* *biopsy of bladder (57.33-57.34)*
> *fistulectomy of bladder (57.83-57.84)*

DEF: Endometrectomy of bladder: Removal of inner lining.
DEF: Suprapubic excision of bladder lesion: Removal of lesion by excision above suprapubic bone arch.

57.6 Partial cystectomy
Excision of bladder dome   Wedge resection of bladder
Trigonectomy

✓4th **57.7 Total cystectomy**
> *INCLUDES* total cystectomy with urethrectomy

57.71 Radical cystectomy
Pelvic exenteration in male
Removal of bladder, prostate, seminal vesicles and fat
Removal of bladder, urethra, and fat in a female
Code also any:
lymph node dissection (40.3, 40.5)
urinary diversion (56.51-56.79)
> *EXCLUDES* *that as part of pelvic exenteration in female (68.8)*

DEF: Radical cystectomy: Removal of bladder and surrounding tissue.
DEF: Pelvic exenteration in male: Excision of bladder, prostate, seminal vessels and fat.

57.79 Other total cystectomy

✓4th **57.8 Other repair of urinary bladder**
> *EXCLUDES* *repair of:*
> *current obstetric laceration (75.61)*
> *cystocele (70.50-70.51)*
> *that for stress incontinence (59.3-59.79)*

57.81 Suture of laceration of bladder

57.82 Closure of cystostomy

57.83 Repair of fistula involving bladder and intestine
Rectovesicovaginal } fistulectomy
Vesicosigmoidovaginal

57.84 Repair of other fistula of bladder
Cervicovesical
Urethroperineovesical } fistulectomy
Uterovesical
Vaginovesical
> *EXCLUDES* *vesicoureterovaginal fistulectomy (56.84)*

57.85 Cystourethroplasty and plastic repair of bladder neck
Plication of sphincter of urinary bladder
V-Y plasty of bladder neck
DEF: Cystourethroplasty: Reconstruction of narrowed portion of bladder.
DEF: Plication of sphincter or urinary bladder: Creation of tuck in bladder sphincter.
DEF: V-Y plasty of bladder neck: Surgical reconstruction of the narrowed portion of bladder by V-Y technique.

57.86 Repair of bladder exstrophy
DEF: Surgical correction of a congenital bladder wall defect.

BI Bilateral Procedure   **NC** Non-covered Procedure   **LC** Limited Coverage Procedure   ▶◀ Revised Text   ● New Code   ▲ Revised Code Title

146 – Volume 3   **2010 ICD-9-CM**

57.87 Reconstruction of urinary bladder

Anastomosis of bladder with isolated segment of ileum

Augmentation of bladder

Replacement of bladder with ileum or sigmoid [closed ileal bladder]

Code also resection of intestine (45.50-45.52)

DEF: Anastomosis of bladder with isolated segment of ileum: Creation of connection between bladder and separated terminal end of small intestine.

AHA: 2Q, '05, 12; 2Q, '03, 11; 3Q, '00, 7

TIP: Assign for closed continent ileovesicostomy, along with code 45.51 Isolation of segment of small intestine, for the continent ileovesicostomy; the ileum and bladder anastomoses are included.

57.88 Other anastomosis of bladder

Anastomosis of bladder to intestine NOS

Cystocolic anastomosis

EXCLUDES   formation of closed ileal bladder (57.87)

57.89 Other repair of bladder

Bladder suspension, not elsewhere classified

Cystopexy NOS

Repair of old obstetric laceration of bladder

EXCLUDES   repair of current obstetric laceration (75.61)

✓4ᵗʰ **57.9 Other operations on bladder**

57.91 Sphincterotomy of bladder

Division of bladder neck

AHA: 2Q, '90, 26

57.92 Dilation of bladder neck

57.93 Control of (postoperative) hemorrhage of bladder

57.94 Insertion of indwelling urinary catheter

57.95 Replacement of indwelling urinary catheter

57.96 Implantation of electronic bladder stimulator   `NC`

57.97 Replacement of electronic bladder stimulator   `NC`

57.98 Removal of electronic bladder stimulator

EXCLUDES   that with synchronous replacement (57.97)

57.99 Other

EXCLUDES   irrigation of:

cystostomy (96.47)

other indwelling urinary catheter (96.48)

lysis of external adhesions (59.11)

removal of:

cystostomy tube (97.63)

other urinary drainage device (97.64)

therapeutic distention of bladder (96.25)

✓3ʳᵈ **58 Operations on urethra**

INCLUDES   operations on:

bulbourethral gland [Cowper's gland]

periurethral tissue

Code also any application or administration of an adhesion barrier substance (99.77)

58.0 Urethrotomy

Excision of urethral septum

Formation of urethrovaginal fistula

Perineal urethrostomy

Removal of calculus from urethra by incision

EXCLUDES   drainage of bulbourethral gland or periurethral tissue (58.91)

internal urethral meatotomy (58.5)

removal of urethral calculus without incision (58.6)

58.1 Urethral meatotomy

EXCLUDES   internal urethral meatotomy (58.5)

DEF: Incision of urethra to enlarge passage.

✓4ᵗʰ **58.2 Diagnostic procedures on urethra**

58.21 Perineal urethroscopy

58.22 Other urethroscopy

58.23 Biopsy of urethra

58.24 Biopsy of periurethral tissue

DEF: Removal for biopsy of tissue around urethra.

58.29 Other diagnostic procedures on urethra and periurethral tissue

EXCLUDES   microscopic examination of specimen from urethra (91.31-91.39)

retrograde cystourethrogram (87.76)

urethral pressure profile (89.25)

urethral sphincter electromyogram (89.23)

✓4ᵗʰ **58.3 Excision or destruction of lesion or tissue of urethra**

EXCLUDES   biopsy of urethra (58.23)

excision of bulbourethral gland (58.92)

fistulectomy (58.43)

urethrectomy as part of:

complete cystectomy (57.79)

pelvic evisceration (68.8)

radical cystectomy (57.71)

58.31 Endoscopic excision or destruction of lesion or tissue of urethra

Fulguration of urethral lesion

58.39 Other local excision or destruction of lesion or tissue of urethra

Excision of:

congenital valve

lesion   } of urethra

stricture

Urethrectomy

EXCLUDES   that by endoscopic appoach (58.31)

✓4ᵗʰ **58.4 Repair of urethra**

EXCLUDES   repair of current obstetric laceration (75.61)

58.41 Suture of laceration of urethra

58.42 Closure of urethrostomy

58.43 Closure of other fistula of urethra

EXCLUDES   repair of urethroperineovesical fistula (57.84)

58.44 Reanastomosis of urethra

Anastomosis of urethra

DEF: Repair of severed urethra.

58.45 Repair of hypospadias or epispadias

AHA: 3Q, '97, 6; 4Q, '96, 35

DEF: Repair of abnormal urethral opening.

58.46 Other reconstruction of urethra

Urethral construction

58.47 Urethral meatoplasty

DEF: Reconstruction of urethral opening.

58.49 Other repair of urethra

Benenenti rotation of bulbous urethra

Repair of old obstetric laceration of urethra

Urethral plication

EXCLUDES   repair of:

current obstetric laceration (75.61)

urethrocele (70.50-70.51)

AHA: ▶1Q, '09, 15◀

58.5 Release of urethral stricture

Cutting of urethral sphincter

Internal urethral meatotomy

Urethrolysis

AHA: 1Q, '97, 13

58.6 Dilation of urethra

Dilation of urethrovesical junction

Passage of sounds through urethra

Removal of calculus from urethra without incision

EXCLUDES   urethral calibration (89.29)

AHA: 1Q, '01, 14; 1Q, '97, 13

Operations on the Urinary System

58.9–59.8

✓4th **58.9** **Other operations on urethra and periurethral tissue**

    58.91 **Incision of periurethral tissue**
        Drainage of bulbourethral gland
        DEF: Incision of tissue around urethra.

    58.92 **Excision of periurethral tissue**
        EXCLUDES   biopsy of periurethral tissue (58.24)
                     lysis of periurethral adhesions
                      (59.11-59.12)

    58.93 **Implantation of artificial urinary sphincter [AUS]**
        Placement of inflatable:
           urethral sphincter
           bladder sphincter
        Removal with replacement of sphincter device [AUS]
        With pump and/or reservoir

    58.99 **Other**
        Repair of inflatable sphincter pump and/or reservoir
        Surgical correction of hydraulic pressure of inflatable sphincter device
        Removal of inflatable urinary sphincter without replacement
        EXCLUDES   removal of:
                      intraluminal foreign body from urethra without incision (98.19)
                      urethral stent (97.65)
        AHA: ▶1Q, '09, 15◀

✓3rd **59** **Other operations on urinary tract**
    Code also any application or administration of an adhesion barrier substance (99.77)

✓4th **59.0** **Dissection of retroperitoneal tissue**

    59.00 **Retroperitoneal dissection, not otherwise specified**

    59.02 **Other lysis of perirenal or periureteral adhesions**
        EXCLUDES   that by laparoscope (59.03)

    59.03 **Laparoscopic lysis of perirenal or periureteral adhesions**
        AHA: 4Q, '06, 134

    59.09 **Other incision of perirenal or periureteral tissue**
        Exploration of perinephric area
        Incision of perirenal abscess
        DEF: Exploration of the perinephric area: Exam of tissue around the kidney by incision.
        DEF: Incision of perirenal abscess: Incising abscess in tissue around kidney.

✓4th **59.1** **Incision of perivesical tissue**
    DEF: Incising tissue around bladder.

    59.11 **Other lysis of perivesical adhesions**

    59.12 **Laparoscopic lysis of perivesical adhesions**

    59.19 **Other incision of perivesical tissue**
        Exploration of perivesical tissue
        Incision of hematoma of space of Retzius
        Retropubic exploration

✓4th **59.2** **Diagnostic procedures on perirenal and perivesical tissue**

    59.21 **Biopsy of perirenal or perivesical tissue**

    59.29 **Other diagnostic procedures on perirenal tissue, perivesical tissue, and retroperitoneum**
        EXCLUDES   microscopic examination of specimen from:
                      perirenal tissue (91.21-91.29)
                      perivesical tissue (91.31-91.39)
                      retroperitoneum NEC (91.11-91.19)
                      retroperitoneal x-ray (88.14-88.16)

59.3 **Plication of urethrovesical junction**
    Kelly-Kennedy operation on urethra
    Kelly-Stoeckel urethral plication
    DEF: Suturing a tuck in tissues around urethra at junction with bladder; changes angle of junction and provides support.

59.4 **Suprapubic sling operation**
    Goebel-Frangenheim-Stoeckel urethrovesical suspension
    Millin-Read urethrovesical suspension
    Oxford operation for urinary incontinence
    Urethrocystopexy by suprapubic suspension
    DEF: Suspension of urethra from suprapubic periosteum to restore support to bladder and urethra.

59.5 **Retropubic urethral suspension**
    Burch procedure
    Marshall-Marchetti-Krantz operation
    Suture of periurethral tissue to symphysis pubis
    Urethral suspension NOS
    DEF: Suspension of urethra from pubic bone with suture placed from symphysis pubis to paraurethral tissues; elevates urethrovesical angle, restores urinary continence.
    AHA: 1Q, '97, 11

59.6 **Paraurethral suspension**
    Pereyra paraurethral suspension
    Periurethral suspension
    DEF: Suspension of bladder neck from fibrous membranes of anterior abdominal wall; upward traction applied; changes angle of urethra, improves urinary control.

✓4th **59.7** **Other repair of urinary stress incontinence**

    59.71 **Levator muscle operation for urethrovesical suspension**
        Cystourethropexy with levator muscle sling
        Gracilis muscle transplant for urethrovesical suspension
        Pubococcygeal sling

    59.72 **Injection of implant into urethra and/or bladder neck**
        Collagen implant
        Endoscopic injection of implant
        Fat implant
        Polytef implant
        DEF: Injection of collagen into submucosal tissues to increase tissue bulk and improve urinary control.
        AHA: 4Q, '95, 72, 73

    59.79 **Other**
        Anterior urethropexy
        Repair of stress incontinence NOS
        Tudor "rabbit ear" urethropexy
        DEF: Pubovaginal sling for treatment of stress incontinence: A strip of fascia is harvested and the vaginal epithelium is mobilized and then sutured to the midline at the urethral level to the rectus muscle to create a sling supporting the bladder.
        DEF: Vaginal wall sling with bone anchors for treatment of stress incontinence: A sling for the bladder is formed by a suture attachment of vaginal wall to the abdominal wall. In addition, a suture is run from the vagina to a bone anchor placed in the pubic bone.
        DEF: Transvaginal endoscopic bladder neck suspension for treatment of stress incontinence: Endoscopic surgical suturing of the vaginal epithelium and the pubocervical fascia at the bladder neck level on both sides of the urethra. Two supporting sutures are run from the vagina to an anchor placed in the pubic bone on each side.
        AHA: 2Q, '01, 20; 1Q, '00, 14, 15, 19

59.8 **Ureteral catheterization**
    Drainage of kidney by catheter
    Insertion of ureteral stent
    Ureterovesical orifice dilation
    Code also any ureterotomy (56.2)
    EXCLUDES   that for:
                retrograde pyelogram (87.74)
                transurethral removal of calculus or clot from ureter and renal pelvis (56.0)
    AHA: 2Q, '05, 12; 2Q, '03, 11; 3Q, '00, 7; 1Q, '89, 1; S-O, '86, 10
    TIP: Assign code twice if ureteral stents were placed bilaterally.

BI Bilateral Procedure   **NC** Non-covered Procedure   **LC** Limited Coverage Procedure   ▶◀ Revised Text   ● New Code   ▲ Revised Code Title

148 – Volume 3 • October 2009   **2010 ICD-9-CM**

✓4ᵗʰ **59.9** **Other operations on urinary system**
> *EXCLUDES*   *nonoperative removal of therapeutic device (97.61-97.69)*

59.91 **Excision of perienal or perivesical tissue**
> *EXCLUDES*   *biopsy of perirenal or perivesical tissue (59.21)*

59.92 **Other operations on perirenal or perivesical tissue**

59.93 **Replacement of ureterostomy tube**
> Change of ureterostomy tube
> Reinsertion of ureterostomy tube
> *EXCLUDES*   *nonoperative removal of ureterostomy tube (97.62)*

59.94 **Replacement of cystostomy tube**
> *EXCLUDES*   *nonoperative removal of cystostomy tube (97.63)*

59.95 **Ultrasonic fragmentation of urinary stones**
> Shattered urinary stones
> *EXCLUDES*   *percutaneous nephrostomy with fragmentation (55.04)*
> *shockwave disintegration (98.51)*

AHA: 1Q, '89, 1; S-O, '86, 11

59.99 **Other**
> *EXCLUDES*   *instillation of medication into urinary tract (96.49)*
> *irrigation of urinary tract (96.45-96.48)*

AHA: 2Q, '08, 14
TIP: Assign for removal of an infected pubovaginal sling.

Operations on the Male Genital Organs

60–60.95

11. OPERATIONS ON THE MALE GENITAL ORGANS (60-64)

√3rd **60** **Operations on prostate and seminal vesicles**

> **INCLUDES**   operations on periprostatic tissue
>
> Code also any application or administration of an adhesion barrier substance (99.77)
>
> **EXCLUDES**   *that associated with radical cystectomy (57.71)*

60.0 **Incision of prostate**   ♂

     Drainage of prostatic abscess

     Prostatolithotomy

> **EXCLUDES**   *drainage of periprostatic tissue only (60.81)*

√4th **60.1** **Diagnostic procedures on prostate and seminal vesicles**

  60.11 **Closed [percutaneous] [needle] biopsy**   ♂
             of prostate

         Approach:

            transrectal

            transurethral

         Punch biopsy

> **DEF:** Excision of prostate tissue by closed technique for biopsy.

  60.12 **Open biopsy of prostate**   ♂

  60.13 **Closed [percutaneous] biopsy of**   ♂
             seminal vesicles

         Needle biopsy of seminal vesicles

  60.14 **Open biopsy of seminal vesicles**   ♂

  60.15 **Biopsy of periprostatic tissue**   ♂

  60.18 **Other diagnostic procedures on**   ♂
             prostate and periprostatic tissue

> **EXCLUDES**   *microscopic examination of specimen from prostate (91.31-91.39)*
>   *x-ray of prostate (87.92)*

  60.19 **Other diagnostic procedures on**   ♂
             seminal vesicles

> **EXCLUDES**   *microscopic examination of specimen from seminal vesicles (91.31-91.39)*
>   *x-ray:*
>   *contrast seminal vesiculogram (87.91)*
>   *other (87.92)*

√4th **60.2** **Transurethral prostatectomy**

> **EXCLUDES**   *local excision of lesion of prostate (60.61)*
>
> **AHA:** 2Q, '94, 9; 3Q, '92, 13

  60.21 **Transurethral (ultrasound) guided laser**   ♂
             induced prostatectomy [TULIP]

         Ablation (contact) (noncontact) by laser

> **AHA:** 4Q, '95, 7

  60.29 **Other transurethral prostatectomy**   ♂

         Excision of median bar by transurethral approach

         Transurethral electrovaporization of prostate (TEVAP)

         Transurethral enucleative procedure

         Transurethral prostatectomy NOS

         Transurethral resection of prostate (TURP)

> **DEF:** Excision of median bar by transurethral approach: Removal of fibrous structure of prostate.
>
> **DEF:** Transurethral enucleative procedure: Transurethral prostatectomy.
>
> **AHA:** 3Q, '97, 3

60.3 **Suprapubic prostatectomy**   ♂

     Transvesical prostatectomy

> **EXCLUDES**   *local excision of lesion of prostate (60.61)*
>   *radical prostatectomy (60.5)*
>
> **DEF:** Resection of prostate through incision in abdomen above pubic arch.

60.4 **Retropubic prostatectomy**   ♂

> **EXCLUDES**   *local excision of lesion of prostate (60.61)*
>   *radical prostatectomy (60.5)*
>
> **DEF:** Removal of the prostate using an abdominal approach with direct cutting into prostatic capsule.

Transurethral Prostatectomy

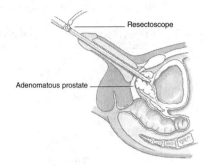

Resectoscope

Adenomatous prostate

60.5 **Radical prostatectomy**   ♂

     Prostatovesiculectomy

     Radical prostatectomy by any approach

> **EXCLUDES**   *cystoprostatectomy (57.71)*
>
> **DEF:** Removal of prostate, epididymis and vas ampullae.
>
> **DEF:** Prostatovesiculectomy: Removal of prostate and epididymis.
>
> **AHA:** 3Q, '93, 12

√4th **60.6** **Other prostatectomy**

  60.61 **Local excision of lesion of prostate**   ♂

> **EXCLUDES**   *biopsy of prostate (60.11-60.12)*
>   ▶*laser interstitial thermal therapy [LITT] of lesion or tissue of prostate under guidance (17.69)*◀

  60.62 **Perineal prostatectomy**   ♂

         Cryoablation of prostate

         Cryoprostatectomy

         Cryosurgery of prostate

         Radical cryosurcial ablation of prostate (RCSA)

> **EXCLUDES**   *local excision of lesion of prostate (60.61)*
>
> **DEF:** Excision of prostate tissue through incision between scrotum and anus.
>
> **AHA:** 4Q, '95, 71

  60.69 **Other**   ♂

√4th **60.7** **Operations on seminal vesicles**

  60.71 **Percutaneous aspiration of seminal**   ♂
             vesicle

> **EXCLUDES**   *needle biopsy of seminal vesicle (60.13)*

  60.72 **Incision of seminal vesicle**   ♂

  60.73 **Excision of seminal vesicle**   ♂

         Excision of Müllerian duct cyst

         Spermatocystectomy

> **EXCLUDES**   *biopsy of seminal vesicle (60.13-60.14)*
>   *prostatovesiculectomy (60.5)*

  60.79 **Other operations on seminal vesicles**   ♂

√4th **60.8** **Incision or excision of periprostatic tissue**

  60.81 **Incision of periprostatic tissue**   ♂

         Drainage of periprostatic abscess

  60.82 **Excision of periprostatic tissue**   ♂

         Excision of lesion of periprostatic tissue

> **EXCLUDES**   *biopsy of periprostatic tissue (60.15)*

√4th **60.9** **Other operations on prostate**

  60.91 **Percutaneous aspiration of prostate**   ♂

> **EXCLUDES**   *needle biopsy of prostate (60.11)*

  60.92 **Injection into prostate**   ♂

  60.93 **Repair of prostate**   ♂

  60.94 **Control of (postoperative) hemorrhage of**   ♂
             prostate

         Coagulation of prostatic bed

         Cystoscopy for control of prostatic hemorrhage

  60.95 **Transurethral balloon dilation of the**   ♂
             prostatic urethra

> **DEF:** Insertion and inflation of balloon to stretch prostate passage.
>
> **AHA:** 4Q, '91, 23

BI Bilateral Procedure   **NC** Non-covered Procedure   **LC** Limited Coverage Procedure   ▶◀ Revised Text   ● New Code   ▲ Revised Code Title

150 – Volume 3 • October 2009   2010 ICD-9-CM

60.96 **Transurethral destruction of prostate tissue by microwave thermotherapy**   ♂

Transurethral microwave thermotherapy [TUMT] of prostate

EXCLUDES *Prostatectomy:*
other (60.61-60.69)
radical (60.5)
retropubic (60.4)
suprapubic (60.3)
transurethral (60.21-60.29)

AHA: 4Q, '00, 67

60.97 **Other transurethral destruction of prostate tissue by other thermotherapy**   ♂

Radiofrequency thermotherapy
Transurethral needle ablation [TUNA] of prostate

EXCLUDES *Prostatectomy:*
other (60.61-60.69)
radical (60.5)
retropubic (60.4)
suprapubic (60.3)
transurethral (60.21-60.29)

AHA: 4Q, '00, 67

60.99 **Other**   ♂

EXCLUDES *prostatic massage (99.94)*

AHA: 3Q, '90, 12

✓3rd **61** **Operations on scrotum and tunica vaginalis**

61.0 **Incision and drainage of scrotum and tunica vaginalis**   ♂

EXCLUDES *percutaneous aspiration of hydrocele (61.91)*

✓4th **61.1** **Diagnostic procedures on scrotum and tunica vaginalis**

61.11 **Biopsy of scrotum or tunica vaginalis**   ♂

61.19 **Other diagnostic procedures on scrotum and tunica vaginalis**   ♂

61.2 **Excision of hydrocele (of tunica vaginalis)**   ♂

Bottle repair of hydrocele of tunica vaginalis

EXCLUDES *percutaneous aspiration of hydrocele (61.91)*

DEF: Removal of fluid collected in serous membrane of testes.

61.3 **Excision or destruction of lesion or tissue of scrotum**   ♂

Fulguration of lesion
Reduction of elephantiasis   } of scrotum
Partial scrotectomy

EXCLUDES *biopsy of scrotum (61.11)*
scrotal fistulectomy (61.42)

✓4th **61.4** **Repair of scrotum and tunica vaginalis**

61.41 **Suture of laceration of scrotum and tunica vaginalis**   ♂

61.42 **Repair of scrotal fistula**   ♂

61.49 **Other repair of scrotum and tunica vaginalis**   ♂

Reconstruction with rotational or pedicle flaps

✓4th **61.9** **Other operations on scrotum and tunica vaginalis**

61.91 **Percutaneous aspiration of tunica vaginalis**   ♂

Aspiration of hydrocele of tunica vaginalis

Hydrocelectomy

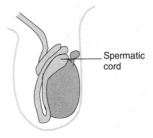

Scrotal skin incised
Sac opened
Fluid-filled sac mobilized
Excess tissue trimmed
Testis
Remaining sacular tissue folded back and sewn to itself to preclude recurrence ("bottle" procedure)

Orchiopexy with Detorsion of Testes

Spermatic cord

Torsion of testis

Testes after correction showing bilateral fixation

61.92 **Excision of lesion of tunica vaginalis other than hydrocele**   ♂

Excision of hematocele of tunica vaginalis

DEF: Removal of blood collected in tunica vaginalis.

61.99 **Other**   ♂

EXCLUDES *removal of foreign body from scrotum without incision (98.24)*

✓3rd **62** **Operations on testes**

62.0 **Incision of testis**   ♂

✓4th **62.1** **Diagnostic procedures on testes**

62.11 **Closed [percutaneous] [needle] biopsy of testis**   ♂

62.12 **Open biopsy of testis**

62.19 **Other diagnostic procedures on testes**   ♂

62.2 **Excision or destruction of testicular lesion**   ♂

Excision of appendix testis
Excision of cyst of Morgagni in the male
Excision of hydatid of Morgagni in the male

EXCLUDES *biopsy of testis (62.11-62.12)*

62.3 **Unilateral orchiectomy**   ♂

Orchidectomy (with epididymectomy) NOS

✓4th **62.4** **Bilateral orchiectomy**

Male castration
Radical bilateral orchiectomy (with epididymectomy)
Code also any synchronous lymph node dissection (40.3, 40.5)

DEF: Removal of both testes.

DEF: Radical bilateral orchiectomy (with epididymectomy): Excision of both testes and structures that store sperm.

62.41 **Removal of both testes at same operative episode**   ♂

Bilateral orchidectomy NOS

62.42 **Removal of remaining testis**   ♂

Removal of solitary testis

62.5 **Orchiopexy**   ♂

Mobilization and replacement of testis in scrotum
Orchiopexy with detorsion of testis
Torek (-Bevan) operation (orchidopexy) (first stage) (second stage)
Transplantation to and fixation of testis in scrotum

DEF: Fixation of testis in scrotum.

DEF: Orchiopexy with detorsion of testis: Fixation and placement of testis in scrotum after correcting angle.

DEF: Torek operation (first stage) (second stage): Transfer of congenitally undescended testis from inguinal canal to scrotum.

DEF: Transplantation to and fixation of testis in scrotum: Transfer of displaced testis to scrotum.

✓4th **62.6** **Repair of testes**

EXCLUDES *reduction of torsion (63.52)*

62.61 **Suture of laceration of testis**   ♂

62.69 **Other repair of testis**   ♂

Testicular graft

62.7 **Insertion of testicular prosthesis**   ♂

✓4th **62.9** **Other operations on testes**

62.91 **Aspiration of testis**   ♂

EXCLUDES *percutaneous biopsy of testis (62.11)*

Operations on the Male Genital Organs

62.92–64.95

Varicocelectomy

Ligated veins

Pampiniform plexus

Ligated veins

Vas deferens

Artery

62.92 Injection of therapeutic substance ♂
into testis

62.99 Other ♂

√3rd **63** **Operations on spermatic cord, epididymis, and vas deferens**

√4th **63.0** Diagnostic procedures on spermatic cord, epididymis, and vas deferens

    63.01 Biopsy of spermatic cord, epididymis, ♂
or vas deferens

    63.09 Other diagnostic procedures on spermatic ♂
cord, epididymis, and vas deferens

       EXCLUDES   *contrast epididymogram (87.93)*
contrast vasogram (87.94)
other x-ray of epididymis and vas
deferens (87.95)

63.1 Excision of varicocele and hydrocele of spermatic ♂
cord

High ligation of spermatic vein
Hydrocelectomy of canal of Nuck

DEF: Removal of a swollen vein and collected fluid from
spermatic cord.

DEF: High ligation of spermatic vein: Tying off of spermatic vein.

DEF: Hydrocelectomy of canal of Nuck: Removal of fluid
collected from serous membrane of inguinal canal.

63.2 Excision of cyst of epididymis ♂
Spermatocelectomy

63.3 Excision of other lesion or tissue of ♂
spermatic cord and epididymis

Excision of appendix epididymis
    EXCLUDES   *biopsy of spermatic cord or epididymis (63.01)*

63.4 Epididymectomy ♂
    EXCLUDES   *that synchronous with orchiectomy (62.3-62.42)*

√4th **63.5** Repair of spermatic cord and epididymis

    63.51 Suture of laceration of spermatic cord ♂
and epididymis

    63.52 Reduction of torsion of testis or ♂
spermatic cord
      EXCLUDES   *that associated with orchiopexy (62.5)*
      DEF: Correction of twisted testicle or spermatic cord.

    63.53 Transplantation of spermatic cord ♂

    63.59 Other repair of spermatic cord and ♂
epididymis

63.6 Vasotomy ♂
Vasostomy
DEF: Vasotomy: Incision of ducts carrying sperm from testicles.
DEF: Vasostomy: Creation of an opening into duct.

√4th **63.7** Vasectomy and ligation of vas deferens

    63.70 Male sterilization procedure, not NC ♂
otherwise specified

    63.71 Ligation of vas deferens NC ♂
Crushing of vas deferens
Division of vas deferens

    63.72 Ligation of spermatic cord NC ♂

    63.73 Vasectomy NC ♂
AHA: 2Q, '98, 13

√4th **63.8** Repair of vas deferens and epididymis

    63.81 Suture of laceration of vas ♂
deferens and epididymis

    63.82 Reconstruction of surgically ♂
divided vas deferens

    63.83 Epididymovasostomy ♂
      DEF: Creation of new connection between vas
deferens and epididymis.

    63.84 Removal of ligature from vas deferens ♂

    63.85 Removal of valve from vas deferens ♂

    63.89 Other repair of vas deferens and ♂
epididymis

√4th **63.9** Other operations on spermatic cord, epididymis, and vas
deferens

    63.91 Aspiration of spermatocele ♂
      DEF: Puncture of cystic distention of epididymis.

    63.92 Epididymotomy ♂
      DEF: Incision of epididymis.

    63.93 Incision of spermatic cord ♂
      DEF: Incision into sperm storage structure.

    63.94 Lysis of adhesions of spermatic cord ♂

    63.95 Insertion of valve in vas deferens ♂

    63.99 Other ♂

√3rd **64** **Operations on penis**

    INCLUDES   operations on:
       corpora cavernosa
       glans penis
       prepuce

64.0 Circumcision ♂
DEF: Removal of penis foreskin.

√4th **64.1** Diagnostic procedures on the penis

    64.11 Biopsy of penis ♂

    64.19 Other diagnostic procedures on penis ♂

64.2 Local excision or destruction of lesion of penis ♂
    EXCLUDES   *biopsy of penis (64.11)*

64.3 Amputation of penis ♂

√4th **64.4** Repair and plastic operation on penis

    64.41 Suture of laceration of penis ♂

    64.42 Release of chordee ♂
      DEF: Correction of downward displacement of penis.
      AHA: 4Q, '96, 34

    64.43 Construction of penis ♂

    64.44 Reconstruction of penis ♂

    64.45 Replantation of penis ♂
Reattachment of amputated penis

    64.49 Other repair of penis ♂
      EXCLUDES   *repair of epispadias and hypospadias*
(58.45)

64.5 Operations for sex transformation, not NC ♂
elsewhere classified

√4th **64.9** Other operations on male genital organs

    64.91 Dorsal or lateral slit of prepuce ♂

    64.92 Incision of penis ♂

    64.93 Division of penile adhesions ♂

    64.94 Fitting of external prosthesis of penis ♂
Penile prosthesis NOS

    64.95 Insertion or replacement of ♂
non-inflatable penile prosthesis

      Insertion of semi-rigid rod prosthesis into shaft of
penis

      EXCLUDES   *external penile prosthesis (64.94)*
inflatable penile prosthesis (64.97)
plastic repair, penis (64.43-64.49)
that associated with:
     construction (64.43)
     reconstruction (64.44)

BI Bilateral Procedure   NC Non-covered Procedure   LC Limited Coverage Procedure   ►◄ Revised Text   ● New Code   ▲ Revised Code Title

64.96   **Removal of internal prosthesis of**   ♂
            penis
            Removal without replacement of non-inflatable or
            inflatable penile prosthesis

64.97   **Insertion or replacement of inflatable**   ♂
            penile prosthesis
            Insertion of cylinders into shaft of penis and
            placement of pump and reservoir
            EXCLUDES   external penile prosthesis (64.94)
                        non-inflatable penile prosthesis (64.95)
                        plastic repair, penis (64.43-64.49)

64.98   **Other operations on penis**   ♂
            Corpora cavernosa-corpus spongiosum shunt
            Corpora-saphenous shunt
            Irrigation of corpus cavernosum
            EXCLUDES   removal of foreign body:
                          intraluminal (98.19)
                          without incision (98.24)
                        stretching of foreskin (99.95)

            DEF: Corpora cavernosa-corpus spongiosum shunt:
            Insertion of shunt between erectile tissues of penis.
            DEF: Corpora-saphenous shunt: Insertion of shunt
            between erectile tissue and vein of penis.
            DEF: Irrigation of corpus cavernosum: Washing of
            erectile tissue forming dorsum and side of penis.
            AHA: 3Q, '92, 9
            TIP: Assign for arterialization of deep dorsal vein of
            penis, which involves anastomosis of the common
            femoral artery via a saphenous vein graft to the deep
            dorsal penile vein.

64.99   **Other**   ♂
            EXCLUDES   collection of sperm for artificial
                        insemination (99.96)

Operations on the Female Genital Organs

65–66.11

12. OPERATIONS ON THE FEMALE GENITAL ORGANS (65-71)

√3rd **65**   **Operations on ovary**
Code also any application or administration of an adhesion barrier substance (99.77)

√4th **65.0**   **Oophorotomy**
Salpingo-oophorotomy
DEF: Incision into ovary.
DEF: Salpingo-oophorotomy: Incision into ovary and the fallopian tube.

   65.01   **Laparoscopic oophorotomy** ♀
   65.09   **Other oophorotomy** ♀

√4th **65.1**   **Diagnostic procedures on ovaries**

   65.11   **Aspiration biopsy of ovary** ♀
   65.12   **Other biopsy of ovary** ♀
   65.13   **Laparoscopic biopsy of ovary** ♀
      AHA: 4Q, '96, 67
   65.14   **Other laparoscopic diagnostic procedures on ovaries** ♀
   65.19   **Other diagnostic procedures on ovaries** ♀
      EXCLUDES   *microscopic examination of specimen from ovary (91.41-91.49)*

√4th **65.2**   **Local excision or destruction of ovarian lesion or tissue**

   65.21   **Marsupialization of ovarian cyst** ♀
      EXCLUDES   *that by laparoscope (65.23)*
      DEF: Exteriorized cyst to outside by incising anterior wall and suturing cut edges to create open pouch.
   65.22   **Wedge resection of ovary** ♀
      EXCLUDES   *that by laparoscope (65.24)*
   65.23   **Laparoscopic marsupialization of ovarian cyst** ♀
   65.24   **Laparoscopic wedge resection of ovary** ♀
   65.25   **Other laparoscopic local excision or destruction of ovary** ♀
   65.29   **Other local excision or destruction of ovary** ♀
      Bisection
      Cauterization } of ovary
      Parial excision
      EXCLUDES   *biopsy of ovary (65.11-65.13)*
                 that by laparoscope (65.25)

√4th **65.3**   **Unilateral oophorectomy**

   65.31   **Laparoscopic unilateral oophorectomy** ♀
   65.39   **Other unilateral oophorectomy** ♀
      EXCLUDES   *that by laparoscope (65.31)*
      AHA: 4Q, '96, 66

√4th **65.4**   **Unilateral salpingo-oophorectomy**

   65.41   **Laparoscopic unilateral salpingo-oophorectomy** ♀
      AHA: 4Q, '96, 67
   65.49   **Other unilateral salpingo-oophorectomy** ♀

√4th **65.5**   **Bilateral oophorectomy**

   65.51   **Other removal of both ovaries at same operative episode** ♀
      Female castration
      EXCLUDES   *that by laparoscope (65.53)*

      Oophorectomy

      Fallopian tube
      Fimbria
      Ovary
      Ovarian cyst

   65.52   **Other removal of remaining ovary** ♀
      Removal of solitary ovary
      EXCLUDES   *that by laparoscope (65.54)*
   65.53   **Laparoscopic removal of both ovaries at same operative episode** ♀
   65.54   **Laparoscopic removal of remaining ovary** ♀

√4th **65.6**   **Bilateral salpingo-oophorectomy**

   65.61   **Other removal of both ovaries and tubes at same operative episode** ♀
      EXCLUDES   *that by laparoscope (65.53)*
      AHA: 4Q, '96, 65
   65.62   **Other removal of remaining ovary and tube** ♀
      Removal of solitary ovary and tube
      EXCLUDES   *that by laparoscope (65.54)*
   65.63   **Laparoscopic removal of both ovaries and tubes at the same operative episode** ♀
      AHA: 4Q, '06, 133, 134; 4Q, '96, 68
   65.64   **Laparoscopic removal of remaining ovary and tube** ♀

√4th **65.7**   **Repair of ovary**
      EXCLUDES   *salpingo-oophorostomy (66.72)*

   65.71   **Other simple suture of ovary** ♀
      EXCLUDES   *that by laparoscope (65.74)*
   65.72   **Other reimplantation of ovary** ♀
      EXCLUDES   *that by laparoscope (65.75)*
      DEF: Grafting and repositioning of ovary at same site.
   65.73   **Other salpingo-oophoroplasty** ♀
      EXCLUDES   *that by laparoscope (65.76)*
   65.74   **Laparoscopic simple suture of ovary** ♀
   65.75   **Laparoscopic reimplantation of ovary** ♀
   65.76   **Laparoscopic salpingo-oophoroplasty** ♀
   65.79   **Other repair of ovary** ♀
      Oophoropexy

√4th **65.8**   **Lysis of adhesions of ovary and fallopian tube**

   65.81   **Laparoscopic lysis of adhesions of ovary and fallopian tube** ♀
      AHA: 4Q, '96, 67
   65.89   **Other lysis of adhesions of ovary and fallopian tube** ♀
      EXCLUDES   *that by laparoscope (65.81)*

√4th **65.9**   **Other operations on ovary**

   65.91   **Aspiration of ovary** ♀
      EXCLUDES   *aspiration biopsy of ovary (65.11)*
   65.92   **Transplantation of ovary** ♀
      EXCLUDES   *reimplantation of ovary (65.72, 65.75)*
   65.93   **Manual rupture of ovarian cyst** ♀
      DEF: Breaking up an ovarian cyst using manual technique or blunt instruments.
   65.94   **Ovarian denervation** ♀
      DEF: Destruction of nerve tracts to ovary.
   65.95   **Release of torsion of ovary** ♀
   65.99   **Other** ♀
      Ovarian drilling
      AHA: N-D, '86, 9

√3rd **66**   **Operations on fallopian tubes**
Code also any application or administration of an adhesion barrier substance (99.77)

√4th **66.0**   **Salpingotomy and salpingostomy**

   66.01   **Salpingotomy** ♀
   66.02   **Salpingostomy** ♀

√4th **66.1**   **Diagnostic procedures on fallopian tubes**

   66.11   **Biopsy of fallopian tube** ♀

BI Bilateral Procedure   **NC** Non-covered Procedure   **LC** Limited Coverage Procedure   ►◄ Revised Text   ● New Code   ▲ Revised Code Title

154 – Volume 3   2010 ICD-9-CM

66.19   **Other diagnostic procedures on fallopian tubes** ♀

> EXCLUDES   *microscopic examination of specimen from fallopian tubes (91.41-91.49)*
> *radiography of fallopian tubes (87.82-87.83, 87.85)*
> *Rubin's test (66.8)*

√4ᵗʰ 66.2 **Bilateral endoscopic destruction or occlusion of fallopian tubes**

> INCLUDES   bilateral endoscopic destruction or occlusion of fallopian tubes by:
> culdoscopy
> endoscopy
> hysteroscopy
> laparoscopy
> peritoneoscopy
> endoscopic destruction of solitary fallopian tube

DEF: Endoscopic blockage or destruction of both fallopian tubes.
DEF: Bilateral endoscopic destruction or occlusion of fallopian tubes by:
  Culdoscopy: Endoscopic insertion through posterior structure of vagina.
  Hysteroscopy: Endoscopic insertion through uterus.
  Laparoscopy: Endoscopic insertion through abdomen.
  Peritoneoscopy: Endoscopic insertion through abdominal serous membrane cavity.
  Endoscopic destruction of solitary fallopian tube: Endoscopic destruction of one fallopian tube.

66.21   **Bilateral endoscopic ligation and crushing of fallopian tubes** NC ♀

66.22   **Bilateral endoscopic ligation and division of fallopian tubes** NC ♀

66.29   **Other bilateral endoscopic destruction or occlusion of fallopian tubes** NC ♀

√4ᵗʰ 66.3 **Other bilateral destruction or occlusion of fallopian tubes**

for example - performed during c-section

> INCLUDES   destruction of solitary fallopian tube
> EXCLUDES   *endoscopic destruction or occlusion of fallopian tubes (66.21-66.29)*

66.31   **Other bilateral ligation and crushing of fallopian tubes** NC ♀

66.32   **Other bilateral ligation and division of fallopian tubes** NC ♀
          Pomeroy operation

66.39   **Other bilateral destruction or occlusion of fallopian tubes** NC ♀
          Female sterilization operation NOS

66.4   **Total unilateral salpingectomy** ♀

√4ᵗʰ 66.5 **Total bilateral salpingectomy**

> EXCLUDES   *bilateral partial salpingectomy for sterilization (66.39)*
> *that with oophorectomy (65.61-65.64)*

66.51   **Removal of both fallopian tubes at same operative episode** ♀

66.52   **Removal of remaining fallopian tube** ♀
          Removal of solitary fallopian tube

√4ᵗʰ 66.6 **Other salpingectomy**

> INCLUDES   salpingectomy by:
> cauterization
> coagulation
> electrocoagulation
> excision
> EXCLUDES   *fistulectomy (66.73)*

66.61   **Excision or destruction of lesion of fallopian tube** ♀

> EXCLUDES   *biopsy of fallopian tube (66.11)*

Endoscopic Ligation of Fallopian Tubes

Uterus — Ligated fallopian tube
Ovary
Monitor view

Laparoscopic procedure

66.62   **Salpingectomy with removal of tubal pregnancy** ♀
          Code also any synchronous oophorectomy (65.31, 65.39)
          AHA: 3Q, '95, 15; S-O, '85, 14
          TIP: If salpingectomy is not performed with removal of ectopic pregnancy, assign instead code 74.3 Removal of extratubal ectopic pregnancy.

66.63   **Bilateral partial salpingectomy, not otherwise specified** ♀

66.69   **Other partial salpingectomy** ♀

√4ᵗʰ 66.7 **Repair of fallopian tube**

66.71   **Simple suture of fallopian tube** ♀

66.72   **Salpingo-oophorostomy** ♀

66.73   **Salpingo-salpingostomy** ♀

66.74   **Salpingo-uterostomy** ♀

66.79   **Other repair of fallopian tube** ♀
          Graft of fallopian tube
          Reopening of divided fallopian tube
          Salpingoplasty
          DEF: Graft of fallopian: Repair of fallopian tube with implanted graft.
          DEF: Reopening of divided fallopian tube: Reconnection of severed fallopian tube to restore patency.
          DEF: Salpingoplasty: Plastic reconstruction of fallopian tube defect.
          AHA: 2Q, '95, 10
          TIP: When a patient is admitted for tubal ligation reversal, assign this diagnosis code V26.0 Tuboplasty or vasoplasty after previous sterilization, as the principal diagnosis.

66.8   **Insufflation of fallopian tube** ♀
          Insufflation of fallopian tube with:
          air
          dye
          gas
          saline
          Rubin's test

> EXCLUDES   *insufflation of therapeutic agent (66.95)*
> *that for hysterosalpingography (87.82-87.83)*

DEF: Forceful blowing of gas or liquid into fallopian tubes.
DEF: Rubin's test: Introduction of carbon dioxide gas into fallopian tubes.

√4ᵗʰ 66.9 **Other operations on fallopian tubes**

66.91   **Aspiration of fallopian tube** ♀

66.92   **Unilateral destruction or occlusion of fallopian tube** ♀

> EXCLUDES   *that of solitary tube (66.21-66.39)*

66.93   **Implantation or replacement of prosthesis of fallopian tube** ♀

66.94   **Removal of prosthesis of fallopian tube** ♀

66.95   **Insufflation of therapeutic agent into fallopian tubes** ♀

66.96   **Dilation of fallopian tube** ♀

√3ᵗʰ / √4ᵗʰ Additional Digit Required   Valid OR Procedure   Non-OR Procedure   Adjunct Code

Operations on the Female Genital Organs

66.97–68.16

66.97   **Burying of fimbriae in uterine wall**   ♀
> **DEF:** Implantation of fallopian tube, fringed edges into uterine wall.

66.99   **Other**   ♀
> **EXCLUDES**   *lysis of adhesions of ovary and tube (65.81, 65.89)*
>
> **AHA:** 2Q, '94, 11

√3rd **67**   **Operations on cervix**
> Code also any application or administration of an adhesion barrier substance (99.77)

67.0   **Dilation of cervical canal**   ♀
> **EXCLUDES**   *dilation and curettage (69.01-69.09)*
> *that for induction of labor (73.1)*

√4th **67.1**   **Diagnostic procedures on cervix**

67.11   **Endocervical biopsy**   ♀
> **EXCLUDES**   *conization of cervix (67.2)*

67.12   **Other cervical biopsy**   ♀
> Punch biopsy of cervix NOS
> **EXCLUDES**   *conization of cervix (67.2)*

67.19   **Other diagnostic procedures on cervix**   ♀
> **EXCLUDES**   *microscopic examination of specimen from cervix (91.41-91.49)*

67.2   **Conization of cervix**   ♀
> **EXCLUDES**   *that by:*
> *cryosurgery (67.33)*
> *electrosurgery (67.32)*
>
> **DEF:** Removal of cone-shaped section from distal cervix; cervical function preserved.

√4th **67.3**   **Other excision or destruction of lesion or tissue of cervix**

67.31   **Marsupialization of cervical cyst**   ♀
> **DEF:** Incision and then suturing open of a cyst in the neck of the uterus.

67.32   **Destruction of lesion of cervix by cauterization**   ♀
> Electroconization of cervix
> LEEP (loop electrosurgical excision procedure)
> LLETZ (large loop excision of the transformation zone)
> **DEF:** Destruction of lesion of uterine neck by applying intense heat.
> **DEF:** Electroconization of cervix: Electrocautery excision of multilayer cone-shaped section from uterine neck.
> **AHA:** 1Q, '98, 3

67.33   **Destruction of lesion of cervix by cryosurgery**   ♀
> Cryoconization of cervix
> **DEF:** Destruction of lesion of uterine neck by freezing.
> **DEF:** Cryoconization of cervix: Excision by freezing of multilayer cone-shaped section of abnormal tissue in uterine neck.

67.39   **Other excision or destruction of lesion or tissue of cervix**   ♀
> **EXCLUDES**   *biopsy of cervix (67.11-67.12)*
> *cervical fistulectomy (67.62)*
> *conization of cervix (67.2)*

67.4   **Amputation of cervix**   ♀
> Cervicectomy with synchronous colporrhaphy
> **DEF:** Excision of lower uterine neck.
> **DEF:** Cervicectomy with synchronous colporrhaphy: Excision of lower uterine neck with suture of vaginal stump.

√4th **67.5**   **Repair of internal cervical os**
> **DEF:** Repair of cervical opening defect.
> **AHA:** 4Q, '01, 63; 3Q, '00, 11

67.51   **Transabdominal cerclage of cervix**   ♀

[handwritten note:] Cerclage of the cervix is a surgical technique to reinforce the cervical muscle by placing sutures above the opening of the cervix to narrow the cervical canal.

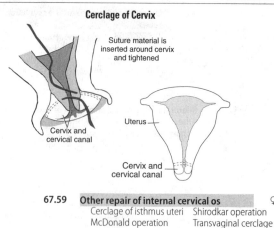

Cerclage of Cervix

Suture material is inserted around cervix and tightened

Cervix and cervical canal

Uterus

Cervix and cervical canal

67.59   **Other repair of internal cervical os**   ♀
> Cerclage of isthmus uteri   Shirodkar operation
> McDonald operation   Transvaginal cerclage
> **EXCLUDES**   *laparoscopically assisted supracervical hysterectomy [LASH] (68.31)*
> *transabdominal cerclage of cervix (67.51)*
>
> **DEF:** Cerclage of isthmus uteri: Placement of encircling suture between neck and body of uterus.
> **DEF:** Shirodkar operation: Placement of purse-string suture in internal cervical opening.
> **AHA:** ▶4Q, '08, 125◀

√4th **67.6**   **Other repair of cervix**
> **EXCLUDES**   *repair of current obstetric laceration (75.51)*

67.61   **Suture of laceration of cervix**   ♀

67.62   **Repair of fistula of cervix**   ♀
> Cervicosigmoidal fistulectomy
> **EXCLUDES**   *fistulectomy:*
> *cervicovesical (57.84)*
> *ureterocervical (56.84)*
> *vesicocervicovaginal (57.84)*
>
> **DEF:** Closure of fistula in lower uterus.
> **DEF:** Cervicosigmoidal fistulectomy: Excision of abnormal passage between uterine neck and torsion of large intestine.

67.69   **Other repair of cervix**   ♀
> Repair of old obstetric laceration of cervix

√3rd **68**   **Other incision and excision of uterus**
> Code also any application or administration of an adhesion barrier substance (99.77)

68.0   **Hysterotomy**   ♀
> Hysterotomy with removal of hydatidiform mole
> **EXCLUDES**   *hysterotomy for termination of pregnancy (74.91)*
> **DEF:** Incision into the uterus.

√4th **68.1**   **Diagnostic procedures on uterus and supporting structures**

68.11   **Digital examination of uterus**   ♀
> **EXCLUDES**   *pelvic examination, so described (89.26)*
> *postpartal manual exploration of uterine cavity (75.7)*

68.12   **Hysteroscopy**   ♀
> **EXCLUDES**   *that with biopsy (68.16)*

68.13   **Open biopsy of uterus**   ♀
> **EXCLUDES**   *closed biopsy of uterus (68.16)*

68.14   **Open biopsy of uterine ligaments**   ♀
> **EXCLUDES**   *closed biopsy of uterine ligaments (68.15)*

68.15   **Closed biopsy of uterine ligaments**   ♀
> Endoscopic (laparoscopy) biopsy of uterine adnexa, except ovary and fallopian tube

68.16   **Closed biopsy of uterus**   ♀
> Endoscopic (laparoscopy) (hysteroscopy) biopsy of uterus
> **EXCLUDES**   *open biopsy of uterus (68.13)*

■ BI Bilateral Procedure   ■ NC Non-covered Procedure   ■ LC Limited Coverage Procedure   ▶◀ Revised Text   ● New Code   ▲ Revised Code Title

156 – Volume 3 • February 2009   2010 ICD-9-CM

68.19 **Other diagnostic procedures on uterus and supporting structures** ♀

    EXCLUDES   *diagnostic:*
        aspiration curettage (69.59)
        dilation and curettage (69.09)
    microscopic examination of specimen
        from uterus (91.41-91.49)
    pelvic examination (89.26)
    radioisotope scan of:
        placenta (92.17)
        uterus (92.19)
    ultrasonography of uterus
        (88.78-88.79)
    x-ray of uterus (87.81-87.89)

√4ᵗʰ 68.2 Excision or destruction of lesion or tissue of uterus

68.21 **Division of endometrial synechiae** ♀
    Lysis of intraluminal uterine adhesions
    DEF: Separation of uterine adhesions.
    DEF: Lysis of intraluminal uterine adhesion: Surgical destruction of adhesive, fibrous structures inside uterine cavity.

68.22 **Incision or excision of congenital septum of uterus** ♀

68.23 **Endometrial ablation** ♀
    Dilation and curettage
    Hysteroscopic endometrial ablation
    DEF: Removal or destruction of uterine lining; usually by electrocautery or loop electrosurgical excision procedure (LEEP).
    AHA: 4Q, '96, 68
    TIP: The endometrium is ablated by a laser, radiofrequency electromagnetic energy, or electrocoagulation, via a roller ball or a U-shaped wire on the end of the hysteroscope.

68.29 **Other excision or destruction of lesion of uterus** ♀
    Uterine myomectomy
    EXCLUDES   *biopsy of uterus (68.13)*
                    uterine fistulectomy (69.42)
    AHA: 3Q, '06, 18; 1Q, '96, 14

√4ᵗʰ 68.3 Subtotal abdominal hysterectomy

68.31 **Laparoscopic supracervical hysterectomy [LSH]** ♀
    Classic infrafascial SEMM hysterectomy [CISH]
    Laparoscopically assisted supracervical hysterectomy [LASH]
    DEF: A hysterectomy that spares the cervix and maintains the integrity of the pelvic floor; SEMM version of the supracervical hysterectomy, also called the classic infrafascial Semm hysterectomy [CISH], the cardinal ligaments, or lateral cervical ligaments that merge with the pelvic diaphragm remain intact.
    AHA: 4Q, '03, 98-99

68.39 **Other and unspecified subtotal abdominal hysterectomy** ♀
    Supracervical hysterectomy
    EXCLUDES   *classic infrafascial SEMM hysterectomy [CISH] (68.31)*
                    laparoscopic supracervical hysterectomy [LSH] (68.31)
    AHA: 4Q, '03, 98

√4ᵗʰ 68.4 Total abdominal hysterectomy
    Code also any synchronous removal of tubes and ovaries (65.31-65.64)
    EXCLUDES   *laparoscopic total abdominal hysterectomy (68.41)*
                    radical abdominal hysterectomy, any approach (68.61-68.69)
    DEF: Complete excision of uterus and uterine neck through abdominal approach.
    AHA: 4Q, '96, 65

68.41 **Laparoscopic total abdominal hysterectomy** ♀
    Total laparoscopic hysterectomy [TLH]
    AHA: 4Q, '06, 130, 133

Vaginal Hysterectomy

Total hysterectomy (uterus only removed)   Total hysterectomy with bilateral salpingectomy (uterus and tubes removed)   Total hysterectomy with bilateral salpingo-oophorectomy (uterus, tubes, and ovaries removed)

68.49 **Other and unspecified total abdominal hysterectomy** ♀
    Hysterectomy:
        extended
    AHA: 4Q, '06, 130

√4ᵗʰ 68.5 Vaginal hysterectomy
    Code also any synchronous:
        removal of tubes and ovaries (65.31-65.64)
        repair of cystocele or rectocele (70.50-70.52)
        repair of pelvic floor (70.79)
    DEF: Complete excision of the uterus by a vaginal approach.

68.51 **Laparoscopically assisted vaginal hysterectomy [LAVH]** ♀
    AHA: 4Q, '96, 68

68.59 **Other and unspecified vaginal hysterectomy** ♀
    EXCLUDES   *laparoscopically assisted vaginal hysterectomy (68.51)*
                    radical vaginal hysterectomy (68.71-68.79)

√4ᵗʰ 68.6 Radical abdominal hysterectomy
    Code also any synchronous:
        lymph gland dissection (40.3, 40.5)
        removal of tubes and ovaries (65.31-65.64)
    EXCLUDES   *pelvic evisceration (68.8)*
    DEF: Excision of uterus, loose connective tissue and smooth muscle around uterus and vagina via abdominal approach.

68.61 **Laparoscopic radical abdominal hysterectomy** ♀
    Laparoscopic modified radical hysterectomy
    Total laparoscopic radical hysterectomy [TLRH]
    AHA: 4Q, '06, 130, 134

68.69 **Other and unspecified radical abdominal hysterectomy** ♀
    Modified radical hysterectomy
    Wertheim's operation
    EXCLUDES   *laparoscopic radical abdominal hysterectomy (68.61)*
                    laparoscopic total abdominal hysterectomy (68.41)
    AHA: 4Q, '06, 130

√4ᵗʰ 68.7 Radical vaginal hysterectomy
    Code also any synchronous:
        lymph gland dissection (40.3, 40.5)
        removal of tubes and ovaries (65.31-65.64)
    EXCLUDES   *abdominal hysterectomy, any approach (68.31-68.39, 68.41-68.49, 68.61-68.69, 68.9)*
    DEF: Excision of uterus, loose connective tissue and smooth muscle around uterus and vagina via vaginal approach.

68.71 **Laparoscopic radical vaginal hysterectomy [LRVH]** ♀
    AHA: 4Q, '06, 130

68.79 **Other and unspecified radical vaginal hysterectomy** ♀
    Hysterocolpectomy
    Schauta operation
    AHA: 4Q, '06, 130

√3ʳᵈ
√4ᵗʰ **Additional Digit Required**   **Valid OR Procedure**   **Non-OR Procedure**   **Adjunct Code**
2010 ICD-9-CM   **Volume 3 – 157**

68.8 Pelvic evisceration ♀
Removal of ovaries, tubes, uterus, vagina, bladder, and urethra (with removal of sigmoid colon and rectum)
Code also any synchronous:
colostomy (46.10-46.13)
lymph gland dissection (40.3, 40.5)
urinary diversion (56.51-56.79)

68.9 Other and unspecified hysterectomy ♀
Hysterectomy NOS
EXCLUDES abdominal hysterectomy, any approach (68.31-68.39, 68.41-68.49, 68.61-68.69)
vaginal hysterectomy, any approach (68.51-68.59, 68.71-68.79)

√3rd **69 Other operations on uterus and supporting structures**
Code also any application or administration of an adhesion barrier substance (99.77)

√4th **69.0 Dilation and curettage of uterus**
EXCLUDES aspiration curettage of uterus (69.51-69.59)
DEF: Stretching of uterine neck to scrape tissue from walls.
TIP: If the documentation indicates dilation with both curettage and suction, assign instead code 69.59.

69.01 Dilation and curettage for termination of pregnancy ♀
AHA: 1Q, '98, 4

69.02 Dilation and curettage following delivery or abortion ♀
AHA: 3Q, '93, 6

69.09 Other dilation and curettage ♀
Diagnostic D and C
AHA: 1Q, '98, 4
TIP: Assign for D&C of a blighted ovum, which is not considered a viable pregnancy.

√4th **69.1 Excision or destruction of lesion or tissue of uterus and supporting structures**

69.19 Other excision or destruction of uterus and supporting structures ♀
EXCLUDES biopsy of uterine ligament (68.14)

√4th **69.2 Repair of uterine supporting structures**

69.21 Interposition operation ♀
Watkins procedure

69.22 Other uterine suspension ♀
Hysteropexy
Manchester operation
Plication of uterine ligament
DEF: Hysteropexy: Fixation or anchoring of uterus.
DEF: Manchester operation: Fixation or anchoring of uterus with supportive banding tissue of uterine neck and vagina.
DEF: Plication of uterine ligament: Creation of tucks in suppurative uterine banding tissue.
DEF: Repositioning or realignment of bladder and uterus.

69.23 Vaginal repair of chronic inversion of uterus ♀
DEF: Repositioning of inverted uterus via vaginal approach.

69.29 Other repair of uterus and supporting structures ♀

69.3 Paracervical uterine denervation ♀

√4th **69.4 Uterine repair**
EXCLUDES repair of current obstetric laceration (75.50-75.52)

69.41 Suture of laceration of uterus ♀

69.42 Closure of fistula of uterus ♀
EXCLUDES uterovesical fistulectomy (57.84)

69.49 Other repair of uterus ♀
Repair of old obstetric laceration of uterus

√4th **69.5 Aspiration curettage of uterus**
EXCLUDES menstrual extraction (69.6)

69.51 Aspiration curettage of uterus for termination of pregnancy ♀
Therapeutic abortion NOS

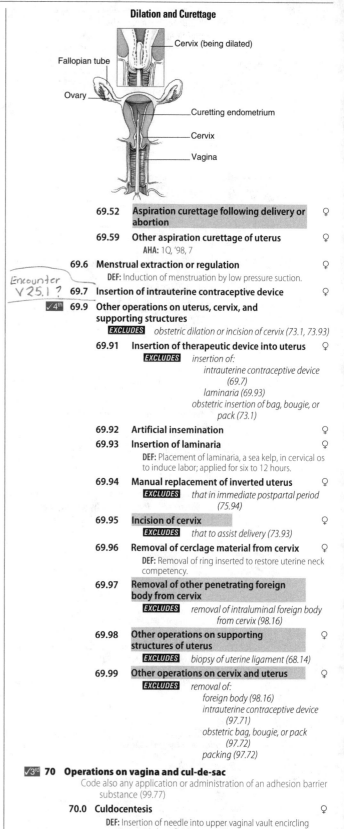

Dilation and Curettage

Cervix (being dilated)
Fallopian tube
Ovary
Curetting endometrium
Cervix
Vagina

69.52 Aspiration curettage following delivery or abortion ♀

69.59 Other aspiration curettage of uterus ♀
AHA: 1Q, '98, 7

69.6 Menstrual extraction or regulation ♀
DEF: Induction of menstruation by low pressure suction.

Encounter
V25.1 ? **69.7 Insertion of intrauterine contraceptive device** ♀

√4th **69.9 Other operations on uterus, cervix, and supporting structures**
EXCLUDES obstetric dilation or incision of cervix (73.1, 73.93)

69.91 Insertion of therapeutic device into uterus ♀
EXCLUDES insertion of:
intrauterine contraceptive device (69.7)
laminaria (69.93)
obstetric insertion of bag, bougie, or pack (73.1)

69.92 Artificial insemination ♀

69.93 Insertion of laminaria ♀
DEF: Placement of laminaria, a sea kelp, in cervical os to induce labor; applied for six to 12 hours.

69.94 Manual replacement of inverted uterus ♀
EXCLUDES that in immediate postpartal period (75.94)

69.95 Incision of cervix ♀
EXCLUDES that to assist delivery (73.93)

69.96 Removal of cerclage material from cervix ♀
DEF: Removal of ring inserted to restore uterine neck competency.

69.97 Removal of other penetrating foreign body from cervix ♀
EXCLUDES removal of intraluminal foreign body from cervix (98.16)

69.98 Other operations on supporting structures of uterus ♀
EXCLUDES biopsy of uterine ligament (68.14)

69.99 Other operations on cervix and uterus ♀
EXCLUDES removal of:
foreign body (98.16)
intrauterine contraceptive device (97.71)
obstetric bag, bougie, or pack (97.72)
packing (97.72)

√3rd **70 Operations on vagina and cul-de-sac**
Code also any application or administration of an adhesion barrier substance (99.77)

70.0 Culdocentesis ♀
DEF: Insertion of needle into upper vaginal vault encircling cervix to withdraw fluid.
AHA: 2Q, '90, 26
TIP: Assign for aspiration for sperm antibodies, which involves aspirating fluid from the female peritoneum or cul-de-sac area to check for the presence of sperm antibodies; assign separate codes for any tubal insufflation (66.8), and/or hysteroscopy (68.12).

√4th **70.1　Incision of vagina and cul-de-sac**

70.11　**Hymenotomy**　♀

70.12　**Culdotomy**　♀
DEF: Incision into pocket between terminal end of large intestine and posterior uterus.

70.13　**Lysis of intraluminal adhesions of vagina**　♀

70.14　**Other vaginotomy**　♀
Division of vaginal septum
Drainage of hematoma of vaginal cuff
DEF: Division of vaginal septum: Incision into partition of vaginal walls.
DEF: Drainage of hematoma of vaginal cuff: Incision into vaginal tissue to drain collected blood.

√4th **70.2　Diagnostic procedures on vagina and cul-de-sac**

70.21　**Vaginoscopy**　♀

70.22　**Culdoscopy**　♀
DEF: Endoscopic exam of pelvic viscera through incision in posterior vaginal wall.

70.23　**Biopsy of cul-de-sac**　♀

70.24　**Vaginal biopsy**　♀

70.29　**Other diagnostic procedures on vagina and cul-de-sac**　♀

√4th **70.3　Local excision or destruction of vagina and cul-de-sac**

70.31　**Hymenectomy**　♀

70.32　**Excision or destruction of lesion of cul-de-sac**
Endometrectomy of cul-de-sac
EXCLUDES biopsy of cul-de-sac (70.23)

70.33　**Excision or destruction of lesion of vagina**　♀
EXCLUDES biopsy of vagina (70.24)
vaginal fistulectomy (70.72-70.75)

70.4　Obliteration and total excision of vagina　♀
Vaginectomy
EXCLUDES obliteration of vaginal vault (70.8)
DEF: Vaginectomy: Removal of vagina.

√4th **70.5　Repair of cystocele and rectocele**

70.50　**Repair of cystocele and rectocele**　♀
EXCLUDES repair of cystocele and rectocele with graft or prosthesis (70.53)
DEF: Repair of anterior and posterior vaginal wall bulges.

70.51　**Repair of cystocele**　♀
Anterior colporrhaphy (with urethrocele repair)
EXCLUDES repair of cystocele and rectocele with graft or prosthesis (70.53)
repair of cystocele with graft or prosthesis (70.54)
AHA: N-D, '84, 20

70.52　**Repair of rectocele**　♀
Posterior colporrhaphy
EXCLUDES repair of cystocele and rectocele with graft or prosthesis (70.53)
repair of rectocele with graft or prosthesis (70.55)
STARR procedure (48.74)
AHA: 1Q, '06, 12

70.53　**Repair of cystocele and rectocele with graft or prosthesis**　♀
Use additional code for biological substance (70.94) or synthetic substance (70.95), if known
AHA: 4Q, '07, 114-115

70.54　**Repair of cystocele with graft or prosthesis**　♀
Anterior colporrhaphy (with urethrocele repair)
Use additional code for biological substance (70.94) or synthetic substance (70.95), if known
AHA: 4Q, '07, 114-115

70.55　**Repair of rectocele with graft or prosthesis**　♀
Posterior colporrhaphy
Use additional code for biological substance (70.94) or synthetic substance (70.95), if known
AHA: 4Q, '07, 114-115

√4th **70.6　Vaginal construction and reconstruction**

70.61　**Vaginal construction**　♀
AHA: 3Q, '06, 18

70.62　**Vaginal reconstruction**　♀
AHA: N-D, '84, 20

70.63　**Vaginal construction with graft or prosthesis**　♀
Use additional code for biological substance (70.94) or synthetic substance (70.95), if known
EXCLUDES vaginal construction (70.61)
AHA: 4Q, '07, 114-115

70.64　**Vaginal reconstruction with graft or prosthesis**　♀
Use additional code for biological substance (70.94) or synthetic substance (70.95), if known
EXCLUDES vaginal reconstruction (70.62)
AHA: 4Q, '07, 114-115

√4th **70.7　Other repair of vagina**
EXCLUDES lysis of intraluminal adhesions (70.13)
repair of current obstetric laceration (75.69)
that associated with cervical amputation (67.4)

70.71　**Suture of laceration of vagina**　♀
AHA: N-D, '84, 20

70.72　**Repair of colovaginal fistula**　♀
DEF: Correction of abnormal opening between midsection of large intestine and vagina.

70.73　**Repair of rectovaginal fistula**　♀
DEF: Correction of abnormal opening between last section of large intestine and vagina.

70.74　**Repair of other vaginoenteric fistula**　♀
DEF: Correction of abnormal opening between vagina and intestine; other than mid or last sections.

70.75　**Repair of other fistula of vagina**　♀
EXCLUDES repair of fistula:
rectovesicovaginal (57.83)
ureterovaginal (56.84)
urethrovaginal (58.43)
uterovaginal (69.42)
vesicocervicovaginal (57.84)
vesicosigmoidovaginal (57.83)
vesicoureterovaginal (56.84)
vesicovaginal (57.84)

70.76　**Hymenorrhaphy**　♀
DEF: Closure of vagina with suture of hymenal ring or hymenal remnant flaps.

70.77　**Vaginal suspension and fixation**　♀
DEF: Repair of vaginal protrusion, sinking or laxity by suturing vagina into position.

70.78　**Vaginal suspension and fixation with graft or prosthesis**　♀
Use additional code for biological substance (70.94) or synthetic substance (70.95), if known
AHA: 4Q, '07, 114-115

70.79　**Other repair of vagina**　♀
Colpoperineoplasty
Repair of old obstetric laceration of vagina

70.8　Obliteration of vaginal vault　♀
LeFort operation
DEF: LeFort operation: Uniting or sewing together vaginal walls.

Operations on the Female Genital Organs

70.9–71.9

√4th **70.9**   **Other operations on vagina and cul-de-sac**

    70.91   **Other operations on vagina**   ♀

      EXCLUDES   insertion of:
          diaphragm (96.17)
          mold (96.15)
          pack (96.14)
          pessary (96.18)
          suppository (96.49)
       removal of:
          diaphragm (97.73)
          foreign body (98.17)
          pack (97.75)
          pessary (97.74)
       replacement of:
          diaphragm (97.24)
          pack (97.26)
          pessary (97.25)
       vaginal dilation (96.16)
       vaginal douche (96.44)

    70.92   **Other operations on cul-de-sac**   ♀
      Obliteration of cul-de-sac
      Repair of vaginal enterocele

      AHA: 4Q, '94, 54

      DEF: Repair of vaginal enterocele: Elimination of herniated cavity within pouch between last part of large intestine and posterior uterus.

    70.93   **Other operations on cul-de-sac with graft or prosthesis**   ♀
      Repair of vaginal enterocele with graft or prosthesis
      Use additional code for biological substance (70.94) or synthetic substance (70.95), if known

      AHA: 4Q, '07, 114-115

    70.94   **Insertion of biological graft**   ♀
      Allogenic material or substance
      Allograft
      Autograft
      Autologous material or substance
      Heterograft
      Xenogenic material or substance
      Code first these procedures when done with graft or prosthesis:
        Other operations on cul-de-sac (70.93)
        Repair of cystocele (70.54)
        Repair of cystocele and rectocele (70.53)
        Repair of rectocele (70.55)
        Vaginal construction (70.63)
        Vaginal reconstruction (70.64)
        Vaginal suspension and fixation (70.78)

      AHA: 4Q, '07, 116

    70.95   **Insertion of synthetic graft or prosthesis**   ♀
      Artificial tissue
      Code first these procedures when done with graft or prosthesis:
        Other operations on cul-de-sac (70.93)
        Repair of cystocele (70.54)
        Repair of cystocele and rectocele (70.53)
        Repair of rectocele (70.55)
        Vaginal construction (70.63)
        Vaginal reconstruction (70.64)
        Vaginal suspension and fixation (70.78)

      AHA: 4Q, '07, 116

√3rd **71**   **Operations on vulva and perineum**
    Code also any application or administration of an adhesion barrier substance (99.77)

√4th **71.0**   **Incision of vulva and perineum**

    71.01   **Lysis of vulvar adhesions**   ♀

    71.09   **Other incision of vulva and perineum**   ♀
      Enlargement of introitus NOS
      EXCLUDES   removal of foreign body without incision (98.23)

√4th **71.1**   **Diagnostic procedures on vulva**

    71.11   **Biopsy of vulva**   ♀

    71.19   **Other diagnostic procedures on vulva**   ♀

√4th **71.2**   **Operations on Bartholin's gland**

    71.21   **Percutaneous aspiration of Bartholin's gland (cyst)**   ♀

    71.22   **Incision of Bartholin's gland (cyst)**   ♀

    71.23   **Marsupialization of Bartholin's gland (cyst)**   ♀
      DEF: Incision and suturing opening of a cyst in Bartholin's gland.

    71.24   **Excision or other destruction of Bartholin's gland (cyst)**   ♀

    71.29   **Other operations on Bartholin's gland**   ♀

   71.3   **Other local excision or destruction of vulva and perineum**   ♀
      Division of Skene's gland
      EXCLUDES   biopsy of vulva (71.11)
          vulvar fistulectomy (71.72)

      AHA: 4Q, '07, 91

   71.4   **Operations on clitoris**   ♀
      Amputation of clitoris   Female circumcision
      Clitoridotomy

      DEF: Amputation of clitoris: Removal of clitoris.
      DEF: Clitoridotomy: Incision into clitoris.
      DEF: Female circumcision: Incision of skin fold over clitoris.

   71.5   **Radical vulvectomy**   ♀
      Code also any synchronous lymph gland dissection (40.3, 40.5)

      DEF: Removal of over 80 percent of deep tissue from vulva, including tissue of abdomen, groin, labia minora, labia majora, clitoris, mons veneris, and terminal portions of urethra, vagina and other vulvar organs.

√4th **71.6**   **Other vulvectomy**

    71.61   **Unilateral vulvectomy**   ♀
      AHA: 2Q, '06, 19
      TIP: Assign for a partial radical vulvectomy.

    71.62   **Bilateral vulvectomy**   ♀
      Vulvectomy NOS

√4th **71.7**   **Repair of vulva and perineum**
      EXCLUDES   repair of current obstetric laceration (75.69)

    71.71   **Suture of laceration of vulva or perineum**   ♀

    71.72   **Repair of fistula of vulva or perineum**   ♀
      EXCLUDES   repair of fistula:
          urethroperineal (58.43)
          urethroperineovesical (57.84)
          vaginoperineal (70.75)

    71.79   **Other repair of vulva and perineum**   ♀
      Repair of old obstetric laceration of vulva or perineum

      AHA: 1Q, '97, 9

   71.8   **Other operations on vulva**   ♀
      EXCLUDES   removal of:
          foreign body without incision (98.23)
          packing (97.75)
          replacement of packing (97.26)

   71.9   **Other operations on female genital organs**   ♀
      AHA: 4Q, '04, 90; 1Q, '03, 13
      TIP: Assign for reversal of the type III female circumcision.

Marsupialization

Portion of cyst and overlying skin to be excised

Cyst "unroofed"

Cyst walls sutured to skin

BI Bilateral Procedure   NC Non-covered Procedure   LC Limited Coverage Procedure   ▶◀ Revised Text   ● New Code   ▲ Revised Code Title

160 – Volume 3   2010 ICD-9-CM

Low forceps - forceps are applied to a visable head after it has entered the pelvic floor,
mid forceps - applied to the head during its entry into the pelvic floor
High forceps - applied to the head before it enters the pelvic brim.

13. OBSTETRICAL PROCEDURES (72-75)

√3rd **72 Forceps, vacuum, and breech delivery**

72.0 Low forceps operation ♀
  Outlet forceps operation

72.1 Low forceps operation with episiotomy ♀
  Outlet forceps operation with episiotomy

√4th **72.2 Mid forceps operation**
  72.21 Mid forceps operation with episiotomy ♀
  72.29 Other mid forceps operation ♀

√4th **72.3 High forceps operation**
  72.31 High forceps operation with episiotomy ♀
  72.39 Other high forceps operation ♀

72.4 Forceps rotation of fetal head ♀
  DeLee maneuver
  Key-in-lock rotation
  Kielland rotation
  Scanzoni's maneuver
  Code also any associated forceps extraction (72.0-72.39)

√4th **72.5 Breech extraction**
  72.51 Partial breech extraction with forceps ♀
  to aftercoming head
  72.52 Other partial breech extraction ♀
  72.53 Total breech extraction with forceps to ♀
  aftercoming head
  72.54 Other total breech extraction ♀

72.6 Forceps application to aftercoming head ♀
  Piper forceps operation
  EXCLUDES partial breech extraction with forceps to
  aftercoming head (72.51)
  total breech extraction with forceps to
  aftercoming head (72.53)

√4th **72.7 Vacuum extraction**
  INCLUDES Malström's extraction
  72.71 Vacuum extraction with episiotomy ♀
  72.79 Other vacuum extraction ♀
  AHA: 2Q, '06, 5
  TIP: This code may be assigned with the appropriate
  code from category 74 Cesarean section and removal
  of fetus, when a vacuum is applied during cesarean
  surgery.

72.8 Other specified instrumental delivery ♀
72.9 Unspecified instrumental delivery ♀

√3rd **73 Other procedures inducing or assisting delivery**

√4th **73.0 Artificial rupture of membranes**
  73.01 Induction of labor by artificial rupture ♀
  of membranes
  Surgical induction NOS
  EXCLUDES artificial rupture of membranes after
  onset of labor (73.09)
  AHA: 3Q, '00, 5
  73.09 Other artificial rupture of membranes ♀
  Artificial rupture of membranes at time of delivery

Breech Extraction

Breech
presentation

Delivery
of legs

Baby rotated
for delivery
of arms

Umbilicus

73.1 Other surgical induction of labor ♀
  Induction by cervical dilation
  EXCLUDES injection for abortion (75.0)
  insertion of suppository for abortion (96.49)

√4th **73.2 Internal and combined version and extraction**
  73.21 Internal and combined version without ♀
  extraction
  Version NOS
  73.22 Internal and combined version with extraction ♀

73.3 Failed forceps ♀
  Application of forceps without delivery
  Trial forceps

73.4 Medical induction of labor ♀
  EXCLUDES medication to augment active labor —
  omit code

√4th **73.5 Manually assisted delivery**
  73.51 Manual rotation of fetal head ♀
  73.59 Other manually assisted delivery ♀
  Assisted spontaneous delivery
  Credé maneuver
  AHA: 4Q, '98, 76

If the episiotomy
extends
spontaneously to
become a perineal
laceration or tear, both
code 73.6 and
75.69 should
be
assigned.

73.6 Episiotomy ♀
  Episioproctotomy
  Episiotomy with subsequent episiorrhaphy
  EXCLUDES that with:
  high forceps (72.31)
  low forceps (72.1)
  mid forceps (72.21)
  outlet forceps (72.1)
  vacuum extraction (72.71)
  AHA: ▶4Q, '08, 192;◄ 1Q, '92, 10

73.8 Operations on fetus to facilitate delivery ♀
  Clavicotomy on fetus
  Destruction of fetus
  Needling of hydrocephalic head

√4th **73.9 Other operations assisting delivery**
  73.91 External version ♀
  73.92 Replacement of prolapsed umbilical cord ♀
  73.93 Incision of cervix to assist delivery ♀
  Dührssen's incisions
  73.94 Pubiotomy to assist delivery ♀
  Obstetrical symphysiotomy
  73.99 Other ♀
  EXCLUDES dilation of cervix, obstetrical, to induce
  labor (73.1)
  insertion of bag or bougie to induce
  labor (73.1)
  removal of cerclage material (69.96)

√3rd **74 Cesarean section and removal of fetus**
  Code also any synchronous:
  hysterectomy (68.3-68.4, 68.6, 68.8)
  myomectomy (68.29)
  sterilization (66.31-66.39, 66.63)
  AHA: 2Q, '06, 5
  74.0 Classical cesarean section *Abdominal peritoneal* ♀
  Transperitoneal classical cesarean section *approach*
  74.1 Low cervical cesarean section ♀
  Lower uterine segment cesarean section
  AHA: 1Q, '01, 11
  74.2 Extraperitoneal cesarean section ♀
  Supravesical cesarean section
  74.3 Removal of extratubal ectopic pregnancy ♀
  Removal of:
  ectopic abdominal pregnancy
  fetus from peritoneal or extraperitoneal cavity following
  uterine or tubal rupture
  EXCLUDES that by salpingostomy (66.02)
  that by salpingotomy (66.01)
  that with synchronous salpingectomy (66.62)
  AHA: 4Q, '92, 25; 2Q, '90, 25; 2Q, '90, 27; 1Q, '89, 11

Obstetrical Procedures

72–74.3

Amniocentesis

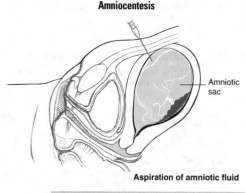

Amniotic sac

Aspiration of amniotic fluid

74.4   **Cesarean section of other specified type**   ♀
Peritoneal exclusion cesareansection
Transperitoneal cesarean section NOS
Vaginal cesarean section

✓4th **74.9**   **Cesarean section of unspecified type**
74.91   **Hysterotomy to terminate pregnancy**   ♀
Therapeutic abortion by hysterotomy

74.99   **Other cesarean section of unspecified type**   ♀
Cesarean section NOS
Obstetrical abdominouterotomy
Obstetrical hysterotomy

✓3rd **75**   **Other obstetric operations**
75.0   **Intra-amniotic injection for abortion**   ♀
Injection of:
prostaglandin
saline } for induction of abortion
Termination of pregnancy by intrauterine injection
EXCLUDES   *insertion of prostaglandin suppository for abortion (96.49)*

75.1   **Diagnostic amniocentesis**   ♀

75.2   **Intrauterine transfusion**   ♀
Exchange transfusion in utero
Insertion of catheter into abdomen of fetus for transfusion
Code also any hysterotomy approach (68.0)

✓4th **75.3**   **Other intrauterine operations on fetus and amnion**
Code also any hysterotomy approach (68.0)
75.31   **Amnioscopy**   ♀
Fetoscopy
Laparoamnioscopy
AHA: 3Q, '06, 16-17

75.32   **Fetal EKG (scalp)**   ♀

75.33   **Fetal blood sampling and biopsy**   ♀

75.34   **Other fetal monitoring**   ♀
Antepartum fetal nonstress test
Fetal monitoring, not otherwise specified
EXCLUDES   *fetal pulse oximetry (75.38)*

75.35   **Other diagnostic procedures on fetus and amnion**   ♀
Intrauterine pressure determination
EXCLUDES   *amniocentesis (75.1)*
diagnostic procedures on gravid uterus and placenta (87.81, 88.46, 88.78, 92.17)
AHA: 3Q, '06, 16-17

75.36   **Correction of fetal defect**   ♀

75.37   **Amnioinfusion**   ♀
Code also injection of antibiotic (99.21)
AHA: 4Q, '98, 76
TIP: This procedure involves the controlled instillation of sterile normal saline or lactated Ringers solution into the uterine cavity to replace the amniotic fluid.

75.38   **Fetal pulse oximetry**   ♀
Transcervical fetal oxygen saturation monitoring
Transcervical fetal SpO$_2$ monitoring
DEF: Single-use sensor inserted through the birth canal and positioned to rest against the fetal cheek, forehead, or temple; infrared beam of light aimed at the fetal skin is reflected back through the sensor for analysis.
AHA: 4Q, '01, 64

75.4   **Manual removal of retained placenta**   ♀
EXCLUDES   *aspiration curettage (69.52)*
dilation and curettage (69.02)
AHA: 3Q, '06, 11

✓4th **75.5**   **Repair of current obstetric laceration of uterus**
75.50   **Repair of current obstetric laceration of uterus, not otherwise specified**   ♀

75.51   **Repair of current obstetric laceration of cervix**   ♀

75.52   **Repair of current obstetric laceration of corpus uteri**   ♀
AHA: 2Q, '08, 8
TIP: Assign for B-Lynch procedure performed to control intraoperative hemorrhage during a cesarean section.

✓4th **75.6**   **Repair of other current obstetric laceration**
Code also episiotomy, if performed (73.6)
AHA: 1Q, '92, 11
75.61   **Repair of current obstetric laceration of bladder and urethra**   ♀

75.62   **Repair of current obstetric laceration of rectum and sphincter ani**   ♀

75.69   **Repair of other current obstetric laceration**   ♀
Episioperineorrhaphy
Repair of:
pelvic floor
perineum
Repair of:
vagina
vulva
Secondary repair of episiotomy
AHA: ▶4Q, '08, 192;◀ 4Q, '07, 12

75.7   **Manual exploration of uterine cavity, postpartum**   ♀

75.8   **Obstetric tamponade of uterus or vagina**   ♀
EXCLUDES   *antepartum tamponade (73.1)*

✓4th **75.9**   **Other obstetric operations**
75.91   **Evacuation of obstetrical incisional hematoma of perineum**   ♀
Evacuation of hematoma of:
episiotomy   perineorrhaphy

75.92   **Evacuation of other hematoma of vulva or vagina**   ♀

75.93   **Surgical correction of inverted uterus**   ♀
Spintelli operation
EXCLUDES   *vaginal repair of chronic inversion of uterus (69.23)*

75.94   **Manual replacement of inverted uterus**   ♀

75.99   **Other**   ♀
AHA: 3Q, '06, 16-17

14. OPERATIONS ON THE MUSCULOSKELETAL SYSTEM
(76-84)

√3ʳᵈ **76**   **Operations on facial bones and joints**
     EXCLUDES   *accessory sinuses (22.00-22.9)*
            nasal bones (21.00-21.99)
            skull (01.01-02.99)

√4ᵗʰ   **76.0**   **Incision of facial bone without division**

     76.01   **Sequestrectomy of facial bone**
          Removal of necrotic bone chip from facial bone

     76.09   **Other incision of facial bone**
          Reopening of osteotomy site of facial bone
          EXCLUDES   *osteotomy associated with*
                 orthognathic surgery
                 (76.61-76.69)
                 removal of internal fixation device
                 (76.97)

√4ᵗʰ   **76.1**   **Diagnostic procedures on facial bones and joints**

     76.11   **Biopsy of facial bone**

     76.19   **Other diagnostic procedures on facial bones and joints**
          EXCLUDES   *contrast arthrogram of*
                 temporomandibular joint
                 (87.13)
                 other x-ray (87.11-87.12, 87.14-87.16)
          AHA: N-D, '87, 12

   76.2   **Local excision or destruction of lesion of facial bone**
     EXCLUDES   *biopsy of facial bone (76.11)*
                excision of odontogenic lesion (24.4)

√4ᵗʰ   **76.3**   **Partial ostectomy of facial bone**

     76.31   **Partial mandibulectomy**
          Hemimandibulectomy
          EXCLUDES   *that associated with*
                 temporomandibular
                 arthroplasty (76.5)
          DEF: Excision, partial of lower jawbone.
          DEF: Hemimandibulectomy: Excision of one-half of lower jawbone.
          AHA: 2Q, '05, 8
          TIP: Assign for "composite resection," which includes the mandible and floor of the mouth, along with code 27.49 Other excision of mouth.

     76.39   **Partial ostectomy of other facial bone**
          Hemimaxillectomy (with bonegraft or prosthesis)
          DEF: Excision, partial of facial bone; other than lower jawbone.
          DEF: Hemimaxillectomy (with bone graft or prosthesis): Excision of one side of upper jawbone and restoration with bone graft or prosthesis.
          AHA: J-F, '87, 14

√4ᵗʰ   **76.4**   **Excision and reconstruction of facial bones**

     76.41   **Total mandibulectomy with synchronous reconstruction**

     76.42   **Other total mandibulectomy**

     76.43   **Other reconstruction of mandible**
          EXCLUDES   *genioplasty (76.67-76.68)*
                 that with synchronous total
                 mandibulectomy (76.41)
          AHA: 2Q, '03, 13

     76.44   **Total ostectomy of other facial bone with synchronous reconstruction**
          DEF: Excision, facial bone, total with reconstruction during same operative session.
          AHA: 3Q, '93, 6

     76.45   **Other total ostectomy of other facial bone**

     76.46   **Other reconstruction of other facial bone**
          EXCLUDES   *that with synchronous total ostectomy*
                 (76.44)

   76.5   **Temporomandibular arthroplasty**
     AHA: 4Q, '99, 20

√4ᵗʰ   **76.6**   **Other facial bone repair and orthognathic surgery**
     Code also any synchronous:
       bone graft (76.91)
       synthetic implant (76.92)
     EXCLUDES   *reconstruction of facial bones (76.41-76.46)*

     76.61   **Closed osteoplasty [osteotomy] of mandibular ramus**
          Gigli saw osteotomy
          DEF: Reshaping and restoration of lower jawbone projection; closed surgical field.
          DEF: Gigli saw osteotomy: Plastic repair using a flexible wire with saw teeth.

     76.62   **Open osteoplasty [osteotomy] of mandibular ramus**

     76.63   **Osteoplasty [osteotomy] of body of mandible**

     76.64   **Other orthognathic surgery on mandible**
          Mandibular osteoplasty NOS
          Segmental or subapical osteotomy
          AHA: 2Q, '04, 9, 10

     76.65   **Segmental osteoplasty [osteotomy] of maxilla**
          Maxillary osteoplasty NOS

     76.66   **Total osteoplasty [osteotomy] of maxilla**

     76.67   **Reduction genioplasty**
          Reduction mentoplasty
          DEF: Reduction of protruding chin or lower jawbone.

     76.68   **Augmentation genioplasty**
          Mentoplasty:
            NOS
            with graft or implant
          DEF: Extension of the lower jawbone to a functional position by means of plastic surgery.

     76.69   **Other facial bone repair**
          Osteoplasty of facial bone NOS

√4ᵗʰ   **76.7**   **Reduction of facial fracture**
     INCLUDES   internal fixation
     Code also any synchronous:
       bone graft (76.91)
       synthetic implant (76.92)
     EXCLUDES   *that of nasal bones (21.71-21.72)*

     76.70   **Reduction of facial fracture, not otherwise specified**

     76.71   **Closed reduction of malar and zygomatic fracture**

     76.72   **Open reduction of malar and zygomatic fracture**

     76.73   **Closed reduction of maxillary fracture**

     76.74   **Open reduction of maxillary fracture**

     76.75   **Closed reduction of mandibular fracture**

     76.76   **Open reduction of mandibular fracture**

     76.77   **Open reduction of alveolar fracture**
          Reduction of alveolar fracture with stabilization of teeth

     76.78   **Other closed reduction of facial fracture**
          Closed reduction of orbital fracture
          EXCLUDES   *nasal bone (21.71)*

     76.79   **Other open reduction of facial fracture**
          Open reduction of orbit rim or wall
          EXCLUDES   *nasal bone (21.72)*

√4ᵗʰ   **76.9**   **Other operations on facial bones and joints**

     76.91   **Bone graft to facial bone**
          Autogenous
          Bone bank   } graft to facial bone
          Heterogenous

     76.92   **Insertion of synthetic implant in facial bone**
          Alloplastic implant to facial bone

     76.93   **Closed reduction of temporomandibular dislocation**

     76.94   **Open reduction of temporomandibular dislocation**

Operations on the Musculoskeletal System

76.95–77.9

76.95	Other manipulation of temporomandibular joint
76.96	Injection of therapeutic substance into temporomandibular joint
76.97	Removal of internal fixation device from facial bone

> **EXCLUDES** removal of:
> dental wiring (97.33)
> external mandibular fixation device NEC (97.36)

76.99	Other

✓3rd 77 Incision, excision, and division of other bones

> **EXCLUDES** laminectomy for decompression (03.09)
> operations on:
> accessory sinuses (22.00-22.9)
> ear ossicles (19.0-19.55)
> facial bones (76.01-76.99)
> joint structures (80.00-81.99)
> mastoid (19.9-20.99)
> nasal bones (21.00-21.99)
> skull (01.01-02.99)

The following fourth-digit subclassification is for use with appropriate categories in section 77 to identify the site. Valid fourth-digit categories are in [brackets] under each code.

- 0 unspecified site
- 1 scapula, clavicle, and thorax [ribs and sternum]
- 2 humerus
- 3 radius and ulna
- 4 carpals and metacarpals
- 5 femur
- 6 patella
- 7 tibia and fibula
- 8 tarsals and metatarsals
- 9 other
  - Pelvic bones
  - Phalanges (of foot) (of hand)
  - Vertebrae

§ ✓4th 77.0 Sequestrectomy
[0-9]
DEF: Excision and removal of dead bone.

§ ✓4th 77.1 Other incision of bone without division
[0-9]
Reopening of osteotomy site

> **EXCLUDES** aspiration of bone marrow, (41.31, 41.91)
> removal of internal fixation device (78.60-78.69)

AHA: For code 77.17: 1Q, '02, 3

DEF: Incision into bone without division of site.

§ ✓4th 77.2 Wedge osteotomy
[0-9]
> **EXCLUDES** that for hallux valgus (77.51)

DEF: Removal of wedge-shaped piece of bone.

§ ✓4th 77.3 Other division of bone
[0-9]
Osteoarthrotomy

> **EXCLUDES** clavicotomy of fetus (73.8)
> laminotomy or incision of vertebra (03.01-03.09)
> pubiotomy to assist delivery (73.94)
> sternotomy incidental to thoracic operation — omit code

§ ✓4th 77.4 Biopsy of bone
[0-9]
AHA: 2Q, '98, 12; **For code 77.49:** 3Q, '06, 13

✓4th 77.5 Excision and repair of bunion and other toe deformities

77.51	**Bunionectomy with soft tissue correction and osteotomy of the first metatarsal**

DEF: Incision and removal of big toe bony prominence and reconstruction with soft tissue.

77.52	**Bunionectomy with soft tissue correction and arthrodesis**

DEF: Removal of big toe bony prominence and reconstruction with soft tissue and joint fixation.

77.53	**Other bunionectomy with soft tissue correction**

77.54	**Excision or correction of bunionette**
	That with osteotomy

DEF: Resection of fifth metatarsal head via exposure of joint; includes imbrication of capsule.

Repair of Hammer Toe

Corn
Callus
Hammertoe
Hemiphalengectomy
After

77.56	**Repair of hammer toe**
	Filleting
	Fusion } of hammer toe
	Phalangectomy (partial)

DEF: Repair of clawlike toe defect by joint fusion, or partial removal of toe via traction technique.

77.57	**Repair of claw toe**
	Capsulotomy
	Fusion
	Phalangectomy (partial) } of claw toe
	Tendon lenghening

DEF: Repair of clawlike toe defect by joint fusion, partial removal of toe, joint capsule incision or lengthening of fibrous muscle attachment.

77.58	**Other excision, fusion, and repair of toes**
	Cockup toe repair
	Overlapping toe repair
	That with use of prosthetic materials

77.59	**Other bunionectomy**
	Resection of hallux valgus joint with insertion of prosthesis

DEF: Resection of hallux valgus joint with insertion of prosthesis: Cutting away part of big toe with prosthesis insertion to correct bony prominence.

§ ✓4th 77.6 Local excision of lesion or tissue of bone
[0-9]
> **EXCLUDES** biopsy of bone (77.40-77.49)
> debridement of compound fracture (79.60-79.69)

AHA: For code 77.61: 3Q, '01, 9; **For code 77.65:** 4Q, '04, 128; S-O, '85, 4; **For code 77.67:** 1Q, '02, 3; 1Q, '99, 8; **For code 77.69:** 1Q, '08, 4; 2Q, '00, 18

TIP: Assign for debridement procedures that extend to bone.

§ ✓4th 77.7 Excision of bone for graft
[0-9]
AHA: 2Q, '07, 5; 4Q, '99, 11, 13; **For code 77.71:** 3Q, '03, 19; **For code 77.79:** 1Q, '08, 5; 2Q, '03, 13; 4Q, '02, 107, 109-110; 2Q, '02, 16; 2Q, '00 12, 13; 4Q, '99, 11, 13

§ ✓4th 77.8 Other partial ostectomy
[0-9]
Condylectomy

> **EXCLUDES** amputation (84.00-84.19, 84.91)
> arthrectomy (80.90-80.99)
> excision of bone ends associated with:
> arthrodesis (81.00-81.39, 81.62-81.66)
> arthroplasty (81.40-81.59, 81.71-81.85)
> excision of cartilage (80.5-80.6, 80.80-80.99)
> excision of head of femur with synchronous replacement (00.70-00.73, 81.51-81.53)
> hemilaminectomy (03.01-03.09)
> laminectomy (03.01-03.09)
> ostectomy for hallux valgus (77.51-77.59)
> partial amputation:
> finger (84.01)
> thumb (84.02)
> toe (84.11)
> resection of ribs incidental to thoracic operation — omit code
> that incidental to other operation — omit code

AHA: For code 77.89: 2Q, '02, 8

§ ✓4th 77.9 Total ostectomy
[0-9]
> **EXCLUDES** amputation of limb (84.00-84.19, 84.91)
> that incidental to other operation — omit code

---

§ Requires fourth digit. Valid digits are in [brackets] under each code. See category 77 for codes and definitions.

BI Bilateral Procedure   **NC** Non-covered Procedure   **LC** Limited Coverage Procedure   ►◄ Revised Text   ● New Code   ▲ Revised Code Title

164 – Volume 3   **2010 ICD-9-CM**

√3ʳᵈ **78 Other operations on bones, except facial bones**

EXCLUDES operations on:
   accessory sinuses (22.00-22.9)
   facial bones (76.01-76.99)
   joint structures (80.00-81.99)
   nasal bones (21.00-21.99)
   skull (01.01-02.99)

The following fourth-digit subclassification is for use with appropriate categories in section 78 to identify the site. Valid fourth-digit categories are in [brackets] under each code.

0 unspecified site
1 scapula, clavicle, and thorax [ribs and sternum]
2 humerus
3 radius and ulna
4 carpals and metacarpals
5 femur
6 patella
7 tibia and fibula
8 tarsals and metatarsals
9 other
   Pelvic bones
   Phalanges (of foot) (of hand)
   Vertebrae

§ √4ᵗʰ **78.0 Bone graft**
[0-9] Bone:
   bank graft
   graft (autogenous) (heterogenous)
That with debridement of bone graft site (removal of sclerosed, fibrous, or necrotic bone or tissue)
Transplantation of bone
Code also any excision of bone for graft (77.70-77.79)
EXCLUDES that for bone lengthening (78.30-78.39)
AHA: 2Q, '02, 11; 2Q, '98, 12; 3Q, '94, 10; 1Q, '91, 3
TIP: Assign a code from this subcategory whether the documentation indicates bone or bone marrow as the grafting material.

§ √4ᵗʰ **78.1 Application of external fixator device**
[0-9] Fixator with insertion of pins/wires/screws into bone
Code also any type of fixator device, if known (84.71-84.73)
EXCLUDES other immobilization, pressure, and attention to wound (93.51-93.59)
AHA: 2Q, '94, 4; **For code 78.12:** 4Q, '05, 129

§ √4ᵗʰ **78.2 Limb shortening procedures**
[0,2-5,7-9] Epiphyseal stapling
Open epiphysiodesis
Percutaneous epiphysiodesis
Resection/osteotomy

§ √4ᵗʰ **78.3 Limb lengthening procedures**
[0,2-5,7-9] Bone graft with or without internal fixation devices or osteotomy
Distraction technique with or without corticotomy/osteotomy
Code also any application of an external fixation device (78.10-78.19)

§ √4ᵗʰ **78.4 Other repair or plastic operations on bone**
[0-9] Other operation on bone NEC
Repair of malunion or nonunion fracture NEC
EXCLUDES application of external fixation device (78.10-78.19)
   limb lengthening procedures (78.30-78.39)
   limb shortening procedures (78.20-78.29)
   osteotomy (77.3)
   reconstruction of thumb (82.61-82.69)
   repair of pectus deformity (34.74)
   repair with bone graft (78.00-78.09)
AHA: 3Q, '91, 20; 4Q, '88, 11; **For code 78.41:** 2Q, '02, 16; **For code 78.47:** 3Q, '91, 20; **For code 78.49:** 3Q, '04, 9; 2Q, '03, 22; 3Q, '02, 12; 2Q, '02, 14, 15; 4Q, '99, 22; 1Q, '97, 5

§ √4ᵗʰ **78.5 Internal fixation of bone without fracture reduction**
[0-9] Internal fixation of bone (prophylactic)
Reinsertion of internal fixation device
Revision of displaced or broken fixation device
EXCLUDES arthroplasty and arthrodesis (81.00-81.85)
   bone graft (78.00-78.09)
   limb shortening procedures (78.20-78.29)
   that for fracture reduction (79.10-79.19, 79.30-79.59)
AHA: 2Q, '99, 11; 2Q, '94, 4; **For code 78.59:** 3Q, '04, 6; 2Q, '03, 15; 4Q, '99, 13

§ √4ᵗʰ **78.6 Removal of implanted devices from bone**
[0-9] External fixator device (invasive)
Internal fixation device
Removal of bone growth stimulator (invasive)
Removal of internal limb lengthening device
Removal of pedicle screw(s) used in spinal fusion
EXCLUDES removal of cast, splint, and traction device (Kirschner wire) (Steinmann pin) (97.88)
   removal of posterior spinal motion preservation (facet replacement, pedicle-based dynamic stabilization, interspinous process) device(s) (80.09)
   removal of skull tongs or halo traction device (02.95)
AHA: 1Q, '00, 15; **For code 78.67:** 2Q, '03, 14; **For code 78.69:** 4Q, '02, 110; 2Q, '00, 18

§ √4ᵗʰ **78.7 Osteoclasis**
[0-9] **DEF:** Surgical breaking or rebreaking of bone.

§ √4ᵗʰ **78.8 Diagnostic procedures on bone, not elsewhere classified**
[0-9] **EXCLUDES** biopsy of bone (77.40-77.49)
   magnetic resonance imaging (88.94)
   microscopic examination of specimen from bone (91.51-91.59)
   radioisotope scan (92.14)
   skeletal x-ray (87.21-87.29, 87.43, 88.21-88.33)
   thermography (88.83)

§ √4ᵗʰ **78.9 Insertion of bone growth stimulator**
[0-9] Insertion of:
   bone stimulator (electrical) to aid bone healing
   osteogenic electrodes for bone growth stimulation
   totally implanted device (invasive)
EXCLUDES non-invasive (transcutaneous) (surface) stimulator (99.86)

√3ʳᵈ **79 Reduction of fracture and dislocation**
INCLUDES application of cast or splint
reduction with insertion of traction device (Kirschner wire) (Steinmann pin)
Code also any:
   application of external fixator device (78.10-78.19)
   type of fixator device, if known (84.71-84.73)
EXCLUDES external fixation alone for immobilization of fracture (93.51-93.56, 93.59)
   internal fixation without reduction of fracture (78.50-78.59)
   operations on:
    facial bones (76.70-76.79)
    nasal bones (21.71-21.72)
    orbit (76.78-76.79)
    skull (02.02)
    vertebrae (03.53)
   removal of cast or splint (97.88)
   replacement of cast or splint (97.11-97.14)
   traction alone for reduction of fracture (93.41-93.46)

[handwritten: aka "manipulation"]
[handwritten: "Open" reduction involves surgical exposure of the bone. "Closed" reduction... alignment is achieved without incision to the fracture site.]

The following fourth-digit subclassification is for use with appropriate categories in section 79 to identify the site. Valid fourth-digit categories are in [brackets] under each code.

0 unspecified site
1 humerus
2 radius and ulna
   Arm NOS
3 carpals and metacarpals
   Hand NOS
4 phalanges of hand
5 femur
6 tibia and fibula
   Leg NOS
7 tarsals and metatarsals
   Foot NOS
8 phalanges of foot
9 other specified bone

§ √4ᵗʰ **79.0 Closed reduction of fracture without internal fixation**
[0-9] **EXCLUDES** that for separation of epiphysis (79.40-79.49)
DEF: Manipulative realignment of fracture; without incision or internal fixation.
AHA: 2Q, '94, 3; 3Q, '89, 17; 4Q, '88, 11; **For code 79.01:** 4Q, '05, 129; **For code 79.05:** 3Q, '89, 16

§ √4ᵗʰ **79.1 Closed reduction of fracture with internal fixation**
[0-9] **EXCLUDES** that for separation of epiphysis (79.40-79.49)
DEF: Manipulative realignment of fracture; with internal fixation but without incision.
AHA: 2Q, '94, 4; 4Q, '93, 35; 1Q, '93, 27

§ Requires fourth digit. Valid digits are in [brackets] under each code. See appropriate category for codes and definitions.

√3ʳᵈ/√4ᵗʰ Additional Digit Required   Valid OR Procedure   Non-OR Procedure   Adjunct Code

Operations on the Musculoskeletal System

79.2–80.50

§ ✓4th **79.2** **Open reduction of fracture without internal**
[0-9] **fixation**
  EXCLUDES *that for separation of epiphysis (79.50-79.59)*
  AHA: 2Q, '94, 3

§ ✓4th **79.3** **Open reduction of fracture with internal fixation**
[0-9] **EXCLUDES** *that for separation of epiphysis (79.50-79.59)*
  DEF: Realignment of fracture with incision and internal fixation.
  AHA: 2Q, '98, 12; 3Q, '94, 10; 2Q, '94, 3; 4Q, '93, 35; **For code 79.32:**
  1Q, '07, 7; **For code 79.35:** 1Q, '07, 4

§ ✓4th **79.4** **Closed reduction of separated epiphysis**
[0-2,5,6,9] Reduction with or without internal fixation
  DEF: Manipulative reduction of expanded joint end of long bone
  to normal position without incision.

§ ✓4th **79.5** **Open reduction of separated epiphysis**
[0-2,5,6,9] Reduction with or without internal fixation
  DEF: Reduction of expanded joint end of long bone with
  incision.

§ ✓4th **79.6** **Debridement of open fracture site**
[0-9] Debridement of compound fracture
  DEF: Removal of damaged tissue at fracture site.
  AHA: 3Q, '95, 12; 3Q, '89, 16
  TIP: Do not assign a skin/soft tissue debridement procedure
  code (e.g., 86.22) in addition to the open fracture debridement
  code; all debridement is included.

Included in codes for
reduction of open
fractures involving the
skull, nasal/orbital
bones, other facial
bones,
and vertebral
bones,

✓4th **79.7** **Closed reduction of dislocation**
  INCLUDES closed reduction (with external traction device)
  EXCLUDES *closed reduction of dislocation of*
  temporomandibular joint (76.93)
  DEF: Manipulative reduction of displaced joint without incision;
  with or without external traction.

  79.70 **Closed reduction of dislocation of unspecified**
  site
  79.71 **Closed reduction of dislocation of shoulder**
  79.72 **Closed reduction of dislocation of elbow**
  79.73 **Closed reduction of dislocation of wrist**
  79.74 **Closed reduction of dislocation of hand and**
  finger
  79.75 **Closed reduction of dislocation of hip**
  79.76 **Closed reduction of dislocation of knee**
    AHA: N-D, '86, 7
  79.77 **Closed reduction of dislocation of ankle**
  79.78 **Closed reduction of dislocation of foot and toe**
  79.79 **Closed reduction of dislocation of other**
  specified sites

✓4th **79.8** **Open reduction of dislocation**
  INCLUDES open reduction (with internal and external
  fixation devices)
  EXCLUDES *open reduction of dislocation of*
  temporomandibular joint (76.94)
  DEF: Reduction of displaced joint via incision; with or without
  internal and external fixation.

  79.80 **Open reduction of dislocation of unspecified**
  site
  79.81 **Open reduction of dislocation of shoulder**
  79.82 **Open reduction of dislocation of elbow**
  79.83 **Open reduction of dislocation of wrist**
  79.84 **Open reduction of dislocation of hand and**
  finger
  79.85 **Open reduction of dislocation of hip**
  79.86 **Open reduction of dislocation of knee**
  79.87 **Open reduction of dislocation of ankle**
  79.88 **Open reduction of dislocation of foot and toe**
  79.89 **Open reduction of dislocation of other**
  specified sites

§ ✓4th **79.9** **Unspecified operation on bone injury**
[0-9]

✓3rd **80** **Incision and excision of joint structures**
  INCLUDES operations on:
    capsule of joint
    cartilage
    condyle
    ligament
    meniscus
    synovial membrane
  EXCLUDES *cartilage of:*
    ear (18.01-18.9)
    nose (21.00-21.99)
    temporomandibular joint (76.01-76.99)

The following fourth-digit subclassification is for use with
appropriate categories in section 80 to identify the site:

0 unspecified site	**6** knee
1 shoulder	**7** ankle
2 elbow	**8** foot and toe
3 wrist	**9** other specified sites
4 hand and finger	Spine
5 hip	

▲ § ✓4th **80.0** **Arthrotomy for removal of prosthesis, without**
[0-9] **replacement**
  INCLUDES removal of posterior spinal motion preservation
  (dynamic stabilization, facet
  replacement, interspinous process)
  device(s)
  Code also any:
    insertion of (cement) (joint) (methylmethacrylate) spacer
    (84.56)
    removal of (cement) (joint) (methylmethacrylate) spacer
    (84.57)
  EXCLUDES *removal of pedicle screws used in spinal fusion*
  (78.69)
  DEF: Incision into joint to remove prosthesis.
  AHA: For code 80.05: 2Q, '08, 4, 5; **For code 80.06:** 2Q, '97, 10
  TIP: Assign 80.05 for a Girdlestone procedure, in which an
  infected hip prosthesis is removed without replacement, until
  the surgical site heals.

§ ✓4th **80.1** **Other arthrotomy**
[0-9] Arthrostomy
  EXCLUDES *that for:*
    arthrography (88.32)
    arthroscopy (80.20-80.29)
    injection of drug (81.92)
    operative approach — omit code
  DEF: Incision into joint; other than to remove prosthesis.
  DEF: Arthrostomy: Creation of opening into joint.
  AHA: For code 80.15: 3Q, '06, 22-23; **For code 80.16:** 3Q, '06, 23

§ ✓4th **80.2** **Arthroscopy**
[0-9] **AHA:** 3Q, '93, 5; 1Q, '93, 23

§ ✓4th **80.3** **Biopsy of joint structure**
[0-9] Aspiration biopsy
  AHA: For code 80.39: 3Q, '05, 13-14

§ ✓4th **80.4** **Division of joint capsule, ligament, or cartilage**
[0-9] Goldner clubfoot release
  Heyman-Herndon(-Strong) correction of metatarsus varus
  Release of:
    adherent or constrictive joint capsule
    joint
    ligament
  EXCLUDES *symphysiotomy to assist delivery (73.94)*
    that for:
      carpal tunnel syndrome (04.43)
      tarsal tunnel syndrome (04.44)
  DEF: Incision and separation of joint tissues, including capsule,
  fibrous bone attachment or cartilage.
  AHA: For code 80.49: 2Q, '02, 16

✓4th **80.5** **Excision, destruction and other repair of intervertebral**
disc

  80.50 **Excision, destruction and other repair of**
  intervertebral disc, unspecified
    Unspecified as to excision or destruction

---

§   Requires fourth digit. Valid digits are in [brackets] under each code. See appropriate category for codes and definitions.

B1 Bilateral Procedure   **NC** Non-covered Procedure   **LC** Limited Coverage Procedure   ▶◀ Revised Text   ● New Code   ▲ Revised Code Title

166 – Volume 3 • October 2009   **2010 ICD-9-CM**

80.51 **Excision of intervertebral disc**

Note: Requires additional code for any concomitant decompression of spinal nerve root at different level from excision site

Diskectomy
Level:
    cervical
    thoracic
    lumbar (lumbosacral)
Removal of herniated nucleus pulposus (H N P)
That by laminotomy or hemilaminectomy
That with decompression of spinal nerve root at same level

Code also any:
    concurrent spinal fusion (81.00-81.08)
    repair of the anulus fibrosus (80.53-80.54)

EXCLUDES   *intervertebral chemonucleolysis (80.52)*
    laminectomy for exploration of intraspinal canal (03.09)
    laminotomy for decompression of spinal nerve root only (03.09)
    that for insertion of (non-fusion) spinal disc replacement device (84.60-84.69)
    that with corpectomy, (vertebral) (80.99)

DEF: Diskectomy: Removal of intervertebral disc.
DEF: Removal of a herniated nucleus pulposus: (H N P) Removal of displaced intervertebral disc, central part.
AHA: ▶2Q, '09, 4-5;◀ 4Q, '08, 184; 2Q, '08, 14; 1Q, '08, 5; 1Q, '07, 9; 1Q, '06, 12; 4Q, '04, 133; 3Q, '03, 12; 1Q, '96, 7; 2Q, '95, 9; 2Q, '90, 27; S-O, '86, 12

80.52 **Intervertebral chemonucleolysis**

With aspiration of disc fragments
With diskography
Injection of proteolytic enzyme into intervertebral space (chymopapain)

EXCLUDES   *injection of anesthestic substance (03.91)*
    injection of other substances (03.92)

DEF: Destruction of intervertebral disc via injection of enzyme.

80.53 **Repair of the anulus fibrosus with graft or prosthesis**

INCLUDES   microsurgical suture repair with fascial autograft
    soft tissue re-approximation repair with tension bands
    surgical mesh repair

Anular disc repair
Closure (sealing) of the anulus fibrosus defect

Code also any:
    application or administration of adhesion barrier substance, if performed (99.77)
    intervertebral discectomy, if performed (80.51)
    locally harvested fascia for graft (83.43)

DEF: Adjunct procedure involving closure of defect in annulus fibrosis (ring of cartilage and fibrous tissue surrounding nucleus pulposus of IV disc) following discectomy surgery; prevents later disc herniation.
AHA: 4Q, '08, 183-184

80.54 **Other and unspecified repair of the anulus fibrosus**

Anular disc repair
Closure (sealing) of the anulus fibrosus defect
Microsurgical suture repair without fascial autograft
Percutaneous repair of the anulus fibrosus

Code also any:
    application or administration of adhesion barrier substance, if performed (99.77)
    intervertebral discectomy, if performed (80.51)

DEF: Adjunct procedure involving closure of defect in annulus fibrosis (ring of cartilage and fibrous tissue surrounding nucleus pulposus of IV disc) following discectomy surgery; prevents later disc herniation.
AHA: 4Q, '08, 183-184

80.59 **Other destruction of intervertebral disc**

Destruction NEC   That by laser
AHA: 3Q, '02, 10
TIP: Assign for intradiscal electrothermal therapy (IDET), whereby thermal energy (heat) is directed into the outer disc wall (annulus) and inner disc contents (nucleus) via a heating coil, decreasing the pressure inside the disc.

80.6 **Excision of semilunar cartilage of knee**

Excision of meniscus of knee
AHA: 2Q, '03, 18; 3Q, '00, 4; 2Q, '96, 3; 1Q, '93, 23

§ ✓4ᵗʰ **80.7** **Synovectomy**
[0-9]
Complete or partial resection of synovial membrane
EXCLUDES   *excision of Baker's cyst (83.39)*
DEF: Excision of inner membrane of joint capsule.

§ ✓4ᵗʰ **80.8** **Other local excision or destruction of lesion of joint**
[0-9]
AHA: For code 80.86: 1Q, '08, 7

§ ✓4ᵗʰ **80.9** **Other excision of joint**
[0-9]
EXCLUDES   *cheilectomy of joint (77.80-77.89)*
    excision of bone ends (77.80-77.89)
AHA: For code 80.99: 1Q, '07, 20

✓3ʳᵈ **81** **Repair and palstic operations on joint structures**

✓4ᵗʰ **81.0** **Spinal fusion**

INCLUDES   arthrodesis of spine with:
    bone graft
    internal fixation

Code also any:
    insertion of interbody spinal fusion device (84.51)
    insertion of recombinant bone morphogenetic protein (84.52)
    synchronous excision of (locally) harvested bone for graft (77.70-77.79)
Code also the total number of vertebrae fused (81.62-81.64)
EXCLUDES   *corrections of pseudarthrosis of spine (81.30-81.39)*
    refusion of spine (81.30-81.39)

DEF: Spinal fusion: Immobilization of spinal column.
DEF: Anterior interbody fusion: Arthrodesis by excising disc and cartilage end plates with bone graft insertion between two vertebrae.
DEF: Lateral fusion: Arthrodesis by decorticating and bone grafting lateral surface of zygapophysial joint, pars interarticularis and transverse process.
DEF: Posterior fusion: Arthrodesis by decorticating and bone grafting of neural arches between right and left zygapophysial joints.
DEF: Posterolateral fusion: Arthrodesis by decorticating and bone grafting zygapophysial joint, pars interarticularis and transverse processes
AHA: 4Q, '03, 99
TIP: Assign also code 03.53 if the fusion was performed for treatment of acute traumatic spinal fracture.

81.00 **Spinal fusion, not otherwise specified**

81.01 **Atlas-axis spinal fusion**

Craniocervical fusion   ⎫ by anterior transoral
C1–C2 fusion   ⎬ or posterior
Occiput C2 fusion   ⎭ technique

§   Requires fourth digit. Valid digits are in [brackets] under each code. See category 80 for codes and definitions.

✓3ʳᵈ/✓4ᵗʰ Additional Digit Required   Valid OR Procedure   Non-OR Procedure   Adjunct Code

2010 ICD-9-CM   **October 2009 • Volume 3 – 167**

Operations on the Musculoskeletal System

81.02–81.34

Types of Grafts for Anterior Arthrodesis

Anteroposterior   Anteroposterior   Anteroposterior

Lateral   Lateral   Lateral

Subtalar Joint Arthroereisis

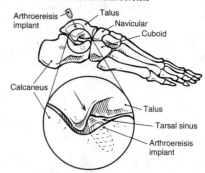

Arthroereisis implant — Talus — Navicular — Cuboid — Calcaneus — Talus — Tarsal sinus — Arthroereisis implant

---

81.02   **Other cervical fusion, anterior technique**
Arthrodesis of C2 level or below:
   anterior (interbody) technique
   anterolateral technique
AHA: 4Q, '03, 101; 1Q, '01, 6; 1Q, '96, 7

81.03   **Other cervical fusion, posterior technique**
Arthrodesis of C2 level or below:
   posterior (interbody) technique
   posterolateral technique

81.04   **Dorsal and dorsolumbar fusion, anterior technique**
Arthrodesis of thoracic or thoracolumbar region:
   anterior (interbody) technique
   anterolateral technique
AHA: 3Q, '03, 19

81.05   **Dorsal and dorsolumbar fusion, posterior technique**
Arthrodesis of thoracic or thoracolumbar region:
   posterior (interbody) technique
   posterolateral technique
AHA: 2Q, '02, 16; 4Q, '99, 11

81.06   **Lumbar and lumbosacral fusion, anterior technique**
Anterior lumbar interbody fusion (ALIF)
Arthrodesis of lumbar or lumbosacral region:
   anterior (interbody) technique
   anterolateral technique
AHA: 2Q, '08, 14; 1Q, '07, 20; 4Q, '05, 122; 4Q, '02, 107; 4Q, '99, 11

81.07   **Lumbar and lumbosacral fusion, lateral transverse process technique**
AHA: ▶2Q, '09, 4;◀ 4Q, '02, 108

81.08   **Lumbar and lumbosacral fusion, posterior technique**
Arthrodesis of lumbar or lumbosacral region:
   posterior (interbody) technique
   posterolateral technique
Posterior lumbar interbody fusion (PLIF)
Transforaminal lumbar interbody fusion (TLIF)
AHA: ▶2Q, '09, 4-5;◀ 1Q, '08, 5; 1Q, '06, 12, 13; 4Q, '05, 122-123; 4Q, '02, 107, 109; 2Q, '00, 12, 13; 4Q, '99, 13; 2Q, '95, 9

√4ᵗʰ **81.1**   **Arthrodesis and arthroereisis of foot and ankle**
    INCLUDES   arthrodesis of foot and ankle with:
       bone graft
       external fixation device
    DEF: Fixation of foot or ankle joints.

81.11   **Ankle fusion**
Tibiotalar fusion

81.12   **Triple arthrodesis**
Talus to calcaneus and calcaneus to cuboid and navicular

81.13   **Subtalar fusion**
    EXCLUDES   arthroereisis (81.18)

81.14   **Midtarsal fusion**

81.15   **Tarsometatarsal fusion**

81.16   **Metatarsophalangeal fusion**

81.17   **Other fusion of foot**

81.18   **Subtalar joint arthroereisis**
    DEF: Insertion of an endoprostheses to limit excessive valgus motion of the subtalar joint; nonfusion procedure to prevent pronation.
    AHA: 4Q, '05, 124

√4ᵗʰ **81.2**   **Arthrodesis of other joint**
    INCLUDES   arthrodesis with:
       bone graft
       external fixation device
       excision of bone ends and compression

81.20   **Arthrodesis of unspecified joint**

81.21   **Arthrodesis of hip**

81.22   **Arthrodesis of knee**

81.23   **Arthrodesis of shoulder**

81.24   **Arthrodesis of elbow**

81.25   **Carporadial fusion**

81.26   **Metacarpocarpal fusion**

81.27   **Metacarpophalangeal fusion**

81.28   **Interphalangeal fusion**

81.29   **Arthrodesis of other specified joints**

√4ᵗʰ **81.3**   **Refusion of spine**
    INCLUDES   arthrodesis of spine with:
       bone graft
       internal fixation
       correction of pseudarthrosis of spine
    Code also any:
      insertion of interbody spinal fusion device (84.51)
      insertion of recombinant bone morphogenetic protein (84.52)
      synchronous excision of (locally) harvested bone for graft (77.70-77.79)
    Code also the total number of vertebrae fused (81.62-81.64)
    AHA: 4Q, '03, 99; 4Q, '01, 64

81.30   **Refusion of spine, not otherwise specified**

81.31   **Refusion of atlas-axis spine**
Craniocervical fusion ⎫
C1-C2 fusion   ⎬ by anterior transoral or posterior technique
Occiput C2 fusion ⎭

81.32   **Refusion of other cervical spine, anterior technique**
Arthrodesis of C2 level or below:
   anterior (interbody) technique
   anterolateral technique

81.33   **Refusion of other cervical spine, posterior technique**
Arthrodesis of C2 level or below:
   posterior (interbody) technique
   posterolateral technique

81.34   **Refusion of dorsal and dorsolumbar spine, anterior technique**
Arthrodesis of thoracic or thoracolumbar region:
   anterior (interbody) technique
   anterolateral technique

B1 Bilateral Procedure   **NC** Non-covered Procedure   **LC** Limited Coverage Procedure   ▶◀ Revised Text   ● New Code   ▲ Revised Code Title

168 – Volume 3   **2010 ICD-9-CM**

81.35 Refusion of dorsal and dorsolumbar spine, posterior technique
Arthrodesis of thoracic or thoracolumbar region:
posterior (interbody) technique
posterolateral technique

81.36 Refusion of lumbar and lumbosacral spine, anterior technique
Anterior lumbar interbody fusion (ALIF)
Arthrodesis of lumbar or lumbosacral region:
anterior (interbody) technique
anterolateral technique
AHA: 4Q, '05, 122-123

81.37 Refusion of lumbar and lumbosacral spine, lateral transverse process technique

81.38 Refusion of lumbar and lumbosacral spine, posterior technique
Arthrodesis of lumbar or lumbosacral region:
posterior (interbody) technique
posterolateral technique
Posterior lumbar interbody fusion (PLIF)
Transforaminal lumbar interbody fusion (TLIF)
AHA: 4Q, '05, 122-123; 4Q, '02, 110

81.39 Refusion of spine, not elsewhere classified

√4ᵗʰ 81.4 Other repair of joint of lower extremity
INCLUDES arthroplasty of lower extremity with:
external traction or fixation
graft of bone (chips) or cartilage
internal fixation device
AHA: S-O, '85, 4

81.40 Repair of hip, not elsewhere classified

81.42 Five-in-one repair of knee
Medial meniscectomy, medial collateral ligament repair, vastus medialis advancement, semitendinosus advancement, and pes anserinus transfer

81.43 Triad knee repair
Medial meniscectomy with repair of the anterior cruciate ligament and the medial collateral ligament
O'Donoghue procedure

Total Hip Replacement

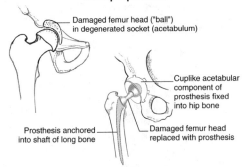
- Damaged femur head ("ball") in degenerated socket (acetabulum)
- Cuplike acetabular component of prosthesis fixed into hip bone
- Damaged femur head replaced with prosthesis
- Prosthesis anchored into shaft of long bone

Partial Hip Replacement

- Acetabulum remains intact
- Prosthesis

81.44 Patellar stabilization
Roux-Goldthwait operation for recurrent dislocation of patella
DEF: Roux-Goldthwait operation: Stabilization of patella via lateral ligament transposed at insertion beneath undisturbed medial insertion; excision of capsule ellipse and medial patella retinaculum; capsule reefed for lateral patella hold.

81.45 Other repair of the cruciate ligaments
AHA: M-A, '87, 12

81.46 Other repair of the collateral ligaments

81.47 Other repair of knee
AHA: 2Q, '06, 13; 2Q, '03, 18; 1Q, '00, 12, 13; 1Q, '96, 3; 3Q, '93, 5
TIP: Assign for Unispacer™ arthroplasty for degenerative arthritis of the knee; the device fits between the natural structures of the knee and helps to stabilize knee alignment.

81.49 Other repair of ankle
AHA: 2Q, '01, 15; 3Q, '00, 4

√4ᵗʰ 81.5 Joint replacement of lower extremity
▶Note: Removal of prior prothesis — omit code◀
INCLUDES arthroplasty of lower extremity with:
external traction or fixation
graft of bone (chips) or cartilage
internal fixation device or prosthesis
AHA: S-O, '85, 4

81.51 Total hip replacement Bl
Replacement of both femoral head and acetabulum by prosthesis
Total reconstruction of hip
Code also any type of bearing surface, if known (00.74-00.77)
DEF: Repair of both surfaces of hip joint with prosthesis.
AHA: ▶2Q, '09, 11;◀ 4Q, '04, 113; 2Q, '91, 18

81.52 Partial hip replacement Bl
Bipolar endoprosthesis
Code also any type of bearing surface, if known (00.74-00.77)
DEF: Repair of single surface of hip joint with prosthesis.
AHA: 2Q, '91, 18

81.53 Revision of hip replacement, not otherwise specified
Revision of hip replacement, not specified as to component(s) replaced, (acetabular, femoral or both)
Code also any:
removal of (cement) (joint) spacer (84.57)
type of bearing surface, if known (00.74-00.77)
EXCLUDES revision of hip replacement, components specified (00.70-00.73)
AHA: 4Q, '05, 125; 3Q, '97, 12

81.54 Total knee replacement Bl
Bicompartmental
▶Partial knee replacement◀
Tricompartmental
Unicompartmental (hemijoint)
DEF: Repair of a knee joint with prosthetic implant in one, two, or three compartments.

Total Knee Replacement

- Condyle component
- Femur
- Patella
- Plateau component
- Prosthesis
- Tibia

Operations on the Musculoskeletal System

81.55–81.85

Vertebroplasty

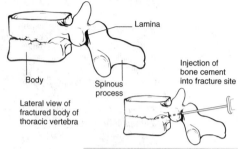

Lateral view of fractured body of thoracic vertebra

- Lamina
- Injection of bone cement into fracture site
- Body
- Spinous process

81.55   **Revision of knee replacement, not otherwise specified**

Code also any removal of (cement) (joint) spacer (84.57)

EXCLUDES   arthrodesis of knee (81.22)
revision of knee replacement, components specified (00.80–00.84)

AHA: 4Q, '05, 113; 2Q, '97, 10

81.56   **Total ankle replacement**   `BI`

81.57   **Replacement of joint of foot and toe**

81.59   **Revision of joint replacement of lower extremity, not elsewhere classified**

✓4ᵗʰ **81.6**   **Other procedures on spine**

Note: Number of vertebrae

The vertebral spine consists of 25 vertebrae in the following order and number:

Cervical: C1 (atlas), C2 (axis), C3, C4, C5, C6, C7
Thoracic or Dorsal: T1, T2, T3, T4, T5, T6, T7, T8, T9, T10, T11, T12
Lumbar and Sacral: L1, L2, L3, L4, L5, S1

Coders should report only one code from the series 81.62–81.64 to show the total number of vertebrae fused on the patient.

Code also the level and approach of the fusion or refusion (81.00–81.08, 81.30–81.39)

DEF: A combined posterior and anterior fusion performed by a surgeon through one incision: lateral transverse, posterior, or anterior.

AHA: 4Q, '03, 99

81.62   **Fusion or refusion of 2-3 vertebrae**

AHA: ▶2Q, '09, 4-5;◀2Q, '08, 14; 1Q, '08, 5; 1Q, '06, 12, 13; 4Q, '05, 123; 4Q, '03, 99

81.63   **Fusion or refusion of 4-8 vertebrae**

AHA: 1Q, '07, 20; 14Q, '03, 99-101

81.64   **Fusion or refusion of 9 or more vertebrae**

AHA: 4Q, '03, 99

81.65   **Percutaneous vertebroplasty**

Injection of bone void filler (cement) (polymethylmethacrylate) (PMMA) into the diseased or fractured vertebral body

EXCLUDES   kyphoplasty (81.66)
percutaneous vertebral augmentation (81.66)

AHA: 2Q, '08, 15

Percutaneous Vertebral Augmentation

- Spinal cord
- Vertebral body
- Tube
- Inflated balloon
- Fractured vertebra
- Disc
- The cavity is filled with bone cement

81.66   **Percutaneous vertebral augmentation**

Arcuplasty
Insertion of inflatable balloon, bone tamp, or other device displacing (removing) (compacting) bone to create a space (cavity) (void) prior to the injection of bone void filler (cement) (polymethylmethacrylate) (PMMA) or other substance
Kyphoplasty
SKyphoplasty
Spineoplasty

EXCLUDES   percutaneous vertebroplasty (81.65)

AHA: 1Q, '07, 5, 7; 3Q, '06, 13; 4Q, '04, 126

TIP: Assign a separate code from subcategory 77.4 for bone biopsy, if performed with percutaneous vertebral augmentation.

✓4ᵗʰ **81.7**   **Arthroplasty and repair of hand, fingers, and wrist**

`INCLUDES`   arthroplasty of hand and finger with:
external traction or fixation
graft of bone (chips) or cartilage
internal fixation device or prosthesis

EXCLUDES   operations on muscle, tendon, and fascia of hand (82.01–82.99)

DEF: Plastic surgery of hand, fingers and wrist joints.

81.71   **Arthroplasty of metacarpophalangeal and interphalangeal joint with implant**

81.72   **Arthroplasty of metacarpophalangeal and interphalangeal joint without implant**

AHA: 1Q, '93, 28

81.73   **Total wrist replacement**

81.74   **Arthroplasty of carpocarpal or carpometacarpal joint with implant**

81.75   **Arthroplasty of carpocarpal or carpometacarpal joint without implant**

AHA: 3Q, '93, 8

81.79   **Other repair of hand, fingers, and wrist**

✓4ᵗʰ **81.8**   **Arthroplasty and repair of shoulder and elbow**

`INCLUDES`   arthroplasty of upper limb NEC with:
external traction or fixation
graft of bone (chips) or cartilage
internal fixation device or prosthesis

81.80   **Total shoulder replacement**

AHA: 2Q, '08, 5

81.81   **Partial shoulder replacement**

81.82   **Repair of recurrent dislocation of shoulder**

AHA: 3Q, '95, 15

81.83   **Other repair of shoulder**

Revision of arthroplasty of shoulder

AHA: 1Q, '02, 9; 4Q, '01, 51; 2Q, '00, 14; 3Q, '93, 5

TIP: Assign for SLAP (superior labral anterior posterior—glenoid labrum lesion) repair.

81.84   **Total elbow replacement**

▶Partial elbow replacement◀

81.85   **Other repair of elbow**

Arthrocentesis

- Needle access into fluid filled knee joint
- Femur
- Patella (kneecap)
- Fluid-filled joint capsule
- Tibia

`BI` Bilateral Procedure   `NC` Non-covered Procedure   `LC` Limited Coverage Procedure   ▶◀ Revised Text   ● New Code   ▲ Revised Code Title

170 – Volume 3 · October 2009   **2010 ICD-9-CM**

✓4th **81.9**   **Other operations on joint structures**

     81.91   **Arthrocentesis**
         Joint aspiration
         EXCLUDES   *that for:*
                  arthrography (88.32)
                  biopsy of joint structure
                     (80.30-80.39)
                  injection of drug (81.92)
         DEF: Insertion of needle to withdraw fluid from joint.

     81.92   **Injection of therapeutic substance into joint or ligament**
         AHA: 2Q, '00, 14; 3Q, '89, 16

     81.93   **Suture of capsule or ligament of upper extremity**
         EXCLUDES   *that associated with arthroplasty*
                  (81.71-81.75, 81.80-81.81,
                  81.84)

     81.94   **Suture of capsule or ligament of ankle and foot**
         EXCLUDES   *that associated with arthroplasty*
                  (81.56-81.59)

     81.95   **Suture of capsule or ligament of other lower extremity**
         EXCLUDES   *that associated with arthroplasty*
                  (81.51-81.55, 81.59)

     81.96   **Other repair of joint**

     81.97   **Revision of joint replacement of upper extremity**
         Partial
         Removal of cement spacer
         Total
         AHA: 1Q, '04, 12

     81.98   **Other diagnostic procedures on joint structures**
         EXCLUDES   *arthroscopy (80.20-80.29)*
                  biopsy of joint structure (80.30-80.39)
                  microscopic examination of specimen
                     from joint (91.51-91.59)
                  thermography (88.83)
                  x-ray (87.21-87.29, 88.21-88.33)

     81.99   **Other**
         AHA: 4Q, '05, 124

✓3rd **82**   **Operations on muscle, tendon, and fascia of hand**

     INCLUDES   operations on:
         aponeurosis
         synovial membrane (tendon sheath)
         tendon sheath

✓4th **82.0**   **Incision of muscle, tendon, fascia, and bursa of hand**

     82.01   **Exploration of tendon sheath of hand**
         Incision of   }   tendon sheath of
         Removal of rice bodies in   hand
         EXCLUDES   *division of tendon (82.11)*
         DEF: Incision into and exploring the hand's muscle and its accompanying supportive, connective tissue, bands, and sacs.

     82.02   **Myotomy of hand**
         EXCLUDES   *myotomy for division (82.19)*
         DEF: Incision into hand muscle.

     82.03   **Bursotomy of hand**

     82.04   **Incision and drainage of palmar or thenar space**

     82.09   **Other incision of soft tissue of hand**
         EXCLUDES   *incision of skin and subcutaneous tissue alone (86.01-86.09)*
         AHA: N-D, '87, 10

✓4th **82.1**   **Division of muscle, tendon, and fascia of hand**

     82.11   **Tenotomy of hand**
         Division of tendon of hand

     82.12   **Fasciotomy of hand**
         Division of fascia of hand

     82.19   **Other division of soft tissue of hand**
         Division of muscle of hand

✓4th **82.2**   **Excision of lesion of muscle, tendon, and fascia of hand**

     82.21   **Excision or lesion of tendon sheath of hand**
         Ganglionectomy of tendon sheath (wrist)

     82.22   **Excision of lesion of muscle of hand**

     82.29   **Excision of other lesion of soft tissue of hand**
         EXCLUDES   *excision of lesion of skin and subcutaneous tissue (86.21-86.3)*

✓4th **82.3**   **Other excision of soft tissue of hand**
     Code also any skin graft (86.61-86.62, 86.73)
     EXCLUDES   *excision of skin and subcutaneous tissue (86.21-86.3)*

     82.31   **Bursectomy of hand**

     82.32   **Excision of tendon of hand for graft**
         DEF: Resection and excision of fibrous tissue connecting bone to hand muscle for grafting.

     82.33   **Other tenonectomy of hand**
         Tenosynovectomy of hand
         EXCLUDES   *excision of lesion of:*
                  tendon (82.29)
                  sheath (82.21)
         DEF: Removal of fibrous bands connecting muscle to bone of hand.
         DEF: Tenosynovectomy of hand: Excision of fibrous band connecting muscle and bone of hand and removal of coverings.

     82.34   **Excision of muscle or fascia of hand for graft**

     82.35   **Other fasciectomy of hand**
         Release of Dupuytren's contracture
         EXCLUDES   *excision of lesion of fascia (82.29)*
         DEF: Excision of fibrous connective tissue; other than for grafting or removing lesion.
         DEF: Release of Dupuytren's contracture: Excision of fibrous connective tissue to correct flexion of fingers.

     82.36   **Other myectomy of hand**
         EXCLUDES   *excision of lesion of muscle (82.22)*

     82.39   **Other excision of soft tissue of hand**
         EXCLUDES   *excision of skin (86.21-86.3)*
                  excision of soft tissue lesion (82.29)

✓4th **82.4**   **Suture of muscle, tendon, and fascia of hand**

     82.41   **Suture of tendon sheath of hand**

     82.42   **Delayed suture of flexor tendon of hand**
         DEF: Suture of fibrous band between flexor muscle and bone; following initial repair.

     82.43   **Delayed suture of other tendon of hand**

     82.44   **Other suture of flexor tendon of hand**
         EXCLUDES   *delayed suture of flexor tendon of hand (82.42)*

     82.45   **Other suture of other tendon of hand**
         EXCLUDES   *delayed suture of other tendon of hand (82.43)*

     82.46   **Suture of muscle or fascia of hand**

✓4th **82.5**   **Transplantation of muscle and tendon of hand**
         AHA: 1Q, '93, 28

     82.51   **Advancement of tendon of hand**
         DEF: Detachment of fibrous connective muscle band and bone with reattachment at advanced point of hand.

     82.52   **Recession of tendon of hand**
         DEF: Detachment of fibrous band of muscle and bone with reattachment at drawn-back point of hand.

     82.53   **Reattachment of tendon of hand**

     82.54   **Reattachment of muscle of hand**

     82.55   **Other change in hand muscle or tendon length**

     82.56   **Other hand tendon transfer or transplantation**
         EXCLUDES   *pollicization of thumb (82.61)*
                  transfer of finger, except thumb (82.81)
         AHA: 2Q, '99, 10; 4Q, '98, 40

Operations on the Musculoskeletal System

82.57–83.13

82.57   **Other hand tendon transposition**
> AHA: 1Q, '93, 28; 3Q, '93, 8

82.58   **Other hand muscle transfer or transplantation**

82.59   **Other hand muscle transposition**

✓4th **82.6**   **Reconstruction of thumb**
> INCLUDES   digital transfer to act as thumb
> Code also any amputation for digital transfer (84.01, 84.11)

82.61   **Pollicization operation carrying over nerves and blood supply**
> DEF: Creation or reconstruction of a thumb with another digit, commonly the index finger.

82.69   **Other reconstruction of thumb**
> "Cocked-hat" procedure [skin flap and bone]
> Grafts:
>   bone
>   skin (pedicle) } to thumb

✓4th **82.7**   **Plastic operation on hand with graft or implant**

82.71   **Tendon pulley reconstruction**
> Reconstruction for opponensplasty
> DEF: Reconstruction of fibrous band between muscle and bone of hand.

82.72   **Plastic operation on hand with graft of muscle or fascia**

82.79   **Plastic operation on hand with other graft or implant**
> Tendon graft to hand
> AHA: J-F, '87, 6

✓4th **82.8**   **Other plastic operations on hand**

82.81   **Transfer of finger, except thumb**
> EXCLUDES   pollicization of thumb (82.61)
> AHA: 2Q, '05, 7
> TIP: Assign this code, along with code 84.11 Amputation of toe, for a procedure in which a toe is transferred to the site of previous traumatic finger amputation.

82.82   **Repair of cleft hand**
> DEF: Correction of fissure defect of hand.

82.83   **Repair of macrodactyly**
> DEF: Reduction in size of abnormally large fingers.

82.84   **Repair of mallet finger**
> DEF: Repair of flexed little finger.

82.85   **Other tenodesis of hand**
> Tendon fixation of hand NOS
> DEF: Fixation of fibrous connective band between muscle and bone of hand.

82.86   **Other tenoplasty of hand**
> Myotenoplasty of hand
> DEF: Myotenoplasty of hand: Plastic repair of muscle and fibrous band connecting muscle to bone.

82.89   **Other plastic operations on hand**
> Plication of fascia
> Repair of fascial hernia
> EXCLUDES   that with graft or implant (82.71-82.79)

✓4th **82.9**   **Other operations on muscle, tendon, and fascia of hand**
> EXCLUDES   diagnostic procedures on soft tissue of hand (83.21-83.29)

82.91   **Lysis of adhesions of hand**
> Freeing of adhesions of fascia, muscle, and tendon of hand
> EXCLUDES   decompression of carpal tunnel (04.43)
>   that by stretching or manipulation only (93.26)

82.92   **Aspiration of bursa of hand**

82.93   **Aspiration of other soft tissue of hand**
> EXCLUDES   skin and subcutaneous tissue (86.01)

82.94   **Injection of therapeutic substance into bursa of hand**

82.95   **Injection of therapeutic substance into tendon of hand**

82.96   **Other injection of locally-acting therapeutic substance into soft tissue of hand**
> EXCLUDES   subcutaneous or intramuscular injection (99.11-99.29)

82.99   **Other operations on muscle, tendon, and fascia of hand**

✓3rd **83**   **Operations on muscle, tendon, fascia, and bursa, except hand**
> INCLUDES   operations on:
>   aponeurosis
>   synovial membrane of bursa and tendon sheaths
>   tendon sheaths
> EXCLUDES   diaphragm (34.81-34.89)
>   hand (82.01-82.99)
>   muscles of eye (15.01-15.9)

✓4th **83.0**   **Incision of muscle, tendon, fascia, and bursa**

83.01   **Exploration of tendon sheath**
> Incision of tendon sheath
> Removal of rice bodies from tendon sheath
> DEF: Incision of external covering of fibrous cord for exam.
> DEF: Removal of rice bodies from tendon sheath: Incision and removal of small bodies resembling grains of rice.

83.02   **Myotomy**
> EXCLUDES   cricopharyngeal myotomy (29.31)
> AHA: 4Q, '08, 135; 2Q, '89, 18

83.03   **Bursotomy**
> Removal of calcareous deposit of bursa
> EXCLUDES   aspiration of bursa (percutaneous) (83.94)

83.09   **Other incision of soft tissue**
> Incision of fascia
> EXCLUDES   incision of skin and subcutaneous tissue alone (86.01-86.09)
> AHA: ▶1Q, '09, 10◀

✓4th **83.1**   **Division of muscle, tendon, and fascia**

83.11   **Achillotenotomy**

83.12   **Adductor tenotomy of hip**
> DEF: Incision into fibrous attachment between adductor muscle and hip bone.

83.13   **Other tenotomy**
> Aponeurotomy   Tendon transection
> Division of tendon   Tenotomy for thoracic
> Tendon release   outlet decompression
> DEF: Aponeurotomy: Incision and separation of fibrous cords attaching a muscle to bone to aid movement.
> DEF: Division of tendon: Separation of fibrous band connecting muscle to bone.
> DEF: Tendon release: Surgical detachment of fibrous band from muscle and/or bone.
> DEF: Tendon transection: Incision across width of fibrous bands between muscle and bone.
> DEF: Tenotomy for thoracic outlet decompression: Incision of fibrous muscle with separation from bone to relieve compressed thoracic outlet.

BI Bilateral Procedure   NC Non-covered Procedure   LC Limited Coverage Procedure   ▶◀ Revised Text   ● New Code   ▲ Revised Code Title

172 – Volume 3 • October 2009   2010 ICD-9-CM

83.14   Fasciotomy
Division of fascia
Division of iliotibial band
Fascia stripping
Release of Volkmann's contracture by fasciotomy
DEF: Division of fascia: Incision to separate fibrous connective tissue.
DEF: Division of iliotibial band: Incision to separate fibrous band connecting tibial bone to muscle in flank.
DEF: Fascia stripping: Incision and lengthwise separation of fibrous connective tissue.
DEF: Release of Volkmann's contracture by fasciotomy: Divisional incision of connective tissue to correct defect in flexion of finger(s).
AHA: 4Q, '06, 102; 3Q, '98, 8
TIP: Assign for all fasciotomy procedures, regardless of whether the approach is open or endoscopic. For fasciotomy of hand, see code 82.12.

83.19   Other division of soft tissue
Division of muscle
Muscle release
Myotomy for thoracic outlet decompression
Myotomy with division
Scalenotomy
Transection of muscle

√4th **83.2   Diagnostic procedures on muscle, tendon, fascia, and bursa, including that of hand**

83.21   Biopsy of soft tissue
EXCLUDES   biopsy of chest wall (34.23)
biopsy of skin and subcutaneous tissue (86.11)

83.29   Other diagnostic procedures on muscle, tendon, fascia, and bursa, including that of hand
EXCLUDES   microscopic examination of specimen (91.51-91.-59)
soft tissue x-ray (87.09, 87.38-87.39, 88.09, 88.35, 88.37)
thermography of muscle (88.84)

√4th **83.3   Excision of lesion of muscle, tendon, fascia, and bursa**
EXCLUDES   biopsy of soft tissue (83.21)

83.31   Excision of lesion of tendon sheath
Excision of ganglion of tendon sheath, except of hand

83.32   Excision of lesion of muscle
Excision of:
heterotopic bone
muscle scar for release of Volkmann's contracture
myositis ossificans
DEF: Heterotopic bone: Bone lesion in muscle.
DEF: Muscle scar for release of Volkmann's contracture: Scarred muscle tissue interfering with finger flexion.
DEF: Myositis ossificans: Bony deposits in muscle.

83.39   Excision of lesion of other soft tissue
Excision of Baker's cyst
EXCLUDES   bursectomy (83.5)
excision of lesion of skin and subcutaneous tissue (86.3)
synovectomy (80.70-80.79)
AHA: 2Q, '05, 3; 2Q, '97, 6

√4th **83.4   Other excision of muscle, tendon, and fascia**
83.41   Excision of tendon for graft
83.42   Other tenonectomy
Excision of:
aponeurosis
tendon sheath
Tenosynovectomy
83.43   Excision of muscle or fascia for graft
83.44   Other fasciectomy
DEF: Excision of fascia; other than for graft.

83.45   Other myectomy
Debridement of muscle NOS
Scalenectomy
DEF: Scalenectomy: Removal of thoracic scaleni muscle tissue.
AHA: 1Q, '99, 8
TIP: Do not assign a skin/soft tissue debridement procedure code (e.g., 86.22) in addition to the muscle debridement (83.45) code; all more superficial debridement is included when multilayer debridement is performed at the same site.

83.49   Other excision of soft tissue

83.5   Bursectomy
AHA: 2Q, '06, 15; 2Q, '99, 11

√4th **83.6   Suture of muscle, tendon, and fascia**
83.61   Suture of tendon sheath
83.62   Delayed suture of tendon
83.63   Rotator cuff repair
DEF: Repair of musculomembranous structure around shoulder joint capsule.
AHA: 1Q, '06, 6; 2Q, '93, 8
83.64   Other suture of tendon
Achillorrhaphy
Aponeurorrhaphy
EXCLUDES   delayed suture of tendon (83.62)
DEF: Achillorrhaphy: Suture of fibrous band connecting Achilles tendon to heel bone.
DEF: Aponeurorrhaphy: Suture of fibrous cords connecting muscle to bone.
83.65   Other suture of muscle or fascia
Repair of diastasis recti

√4th **83.7   Reconstruction of muscle and tendon**
EXCLUDES   reconstruction of muscle and tendon associated with arthroplasty
83.71   Advancement of tendon
DEF: Detaching fibrous cord between muscle and bone with reattachment at advanced point.
83.72   Recession of tendon
DEF: Detaching fibrous cord between muscle and bone with reattachment at drawn-back point.
83.73   Reattachment of tendon
83.74   Reattachment of muscle
83.75   Tendon transfer or transplantation
83.76   Other tendon transposition
83.77   Muscle transfer or transplantation
Release of Volkmann's contracture by muscle transplantation
83.79   Other muscle transposition

√4th **83.8   Other plastic operations on muscle, tendon, and fascia**
EXCLUDES   plastic operations on muscle, tendon, and fascia associated with arthroplasty
83.81   Tendon graft
83.82   Graft of muscle or fascia
AHA: 3Q, '01, 9
83.83   Tendon pulley reconstruction
DEF: Reconstruction of fibrous cord between muscle and bone; at any site other than hand.
83.84   Release of clubfoot, not elsewhere classified
Evans operation on clubfoot
83.85   Other change in muscle or tendon length
Hamstring lengthening
Heel cord shortening
Plastic achillotenotomy
Tendon plication
DEF: Plastic achillotenotomy: Increase in heel cord length.
DEF: Tendon plication: Surgical tuck of tendon.
83.86   Quadricepsplasty
DEF: Correction of quadriceps femoris muscle.

Operations on the Musculoskeletal System

83.87–84.16

83.87 **Other plastic operations on muscle**
Musculoplasty
Myoplasty
AHA: 1Q, '97, 9

83.88 **Other plastic operations on tendon**
Myotenoplasty   Tenodesis
Tendon fixation   Tenoplasty

83.89 **Other plastic operations on fascia**
Fascia lengthening   Plication of fascia
Fascioplasty

√4th **83.9** **Other operations on muscle, tendon, fascia, and bursa**
EXCLUDES nonoperative:
manipulation (93.25-93.29)
stretching (93.27-93.29)

83.91 **Lysis of adhesions of muscle, tendon, fascia, and bursa**
EXCLUDES that for tarsal tunnel syndrome (04.44)
DEF: Separation of created fibrous structures from muscle, connective tissues, bands and sacs.

83.92 **Insertion or replacement of skeletal muscle stimulator**
Implantation, insertion, placement, or replacement of skeletal muscle:
electrodes
stimulator
AHA: 2Q, '99, 10

83.93 **Removal of skeletal muscle stimulator**

83.94 **Aspiration of bursa**

83.95 **Aspiration of other soft tissue**
EXCLUDES that of skin and subcutaneous tissue (86.01)

83.96 **Injection of therapeutic substance into bursa**

83.97 **Injection of therapeutic substance into tendon**

83.98 **Injection of locally-acting therapeutic substance into other soft tissue**
EXCLUDES subcutaneous or intramuscular injection (99.11-99.29)
AHA: 2Q, '06, 11

83.99 **Other operations on muscle, tendon, fascia, and bursa**
Suture of bursa

√3rd **84** **Other procedures on musculoskeletal system**

√4th **84.0** **Amputation of upper limb**
EXCLUDES revision of amputation stump (84.3)

84.00 **Upper limb amputation, not otherwise specified**
Closed flap amputation
Kineplastic amputation
Open or guillotine amputation } of upper limb NOS
Revision of current traumatic amputation

DEF: Closed flap amputation: Sewing a created skin flap over stump end of upper limb.
DEF: Kineplastic amputation: Amputation and preparation of stump of upper limb to permit movement.
DEF: Open or guillotine amputation: Straight incision across upper limb; used when primary closure is contraindicated.
DEF: Revision of current traumatic amputation: Reconstruction of traumatic amputation of upper limb to enable closure.

84.01 **Amputation and disarticulation of finger**
EXCLUDES ligation of supernumerary finger (86.26)

84.02 **Amputation and disarticulation of thumb**

84.03 **Amputation through hand**
Amputation through carpals

Amputation → **84.04** **Disarticulation of wrist**

84.05 **Amputation through forearm**
Forearm amputation

84.06 **Disarticulation of elbow**
DEF: Amputation of forearm through elbow joint.

84.07 **Amputation through humerus**
Upper arm amputation

84.08 **Disarticulation of shoulder**
DEF: Amputation of arm through shoulder joint.

84.09 **Interthoracoscapular amputation**
Forequarter amputation
DEF: Removal of upper arm, shoulder bone and collarbone.

√4th **84.1** **Amputation of lower limb**
EXCLUDES revision of amputation stump (84.3)

84.10 **Lower limb amputation, not otherwise specified**
Closed flap amputation
Kineplastic amputation
Open or guillotine amputation } of lower limb NOS
Revision of current traumatic amputation

DEF: Closed flap amputation: Sewing a created skin flap over stump of lower limb.
DEF: Kineplastic amputation: Amputation and preparation of stump of lower limb to permit movement.
DEF: Open or guillotine amputation: Straight incision across lower limb; used when primary closure is contraindicated.
DEF: Revision of current traumatic amputation: Reconstruction of traumatic amputation of lower limb to enable closure.

84.11 **Amputation of toe**
Amputation through metatarsophalangeal joint
Disarticulation of toe
Metatarsal head amputation
Ray amputation of foot (disarticulation of the metatarsal head of the toe extending across the forefoot, just proximal to the metatarsophalangeal crease)
EXCLUDES ligation of supernumerary toe (86.26)
AHA: 2Q, '05, 7; 4Q, '99, 19

84.12 **Amputation through foot**
Amputation of forefoot
Amputation through middle of foot
Chopart's amputation
Midtarsal amputation
Transmetatarsal amputation (amputation of the forefoot, including the toes)
EXCLUDES Ray amputation of foot (84.11)
DEF: Amputation of forefoot: Removal of foot in front of joint between toes and body of foot.
DEF: Chopart's amputation: Removal of foot with retention of heel, ankle and other associated ankle bones.
DEF: Midtarsal amputation: Amputation of foot through tarsals.
DEF: Transmetatarsal amputation: Amputation of foot through metatarsals.
AHA: 4Q, '99, 19

84.13 **Disarticulation of ankle**
DEF: Removal of foot through ankle bone.

84.14 **Amputation of ankle through malleoli of tibia and fibula**

84.15 **Other amputation below knee**
Amputation of leg through tibia and fibula NOS

84.16 **Disarticulation of knee**
Batch, Spitler, and McFaddin amputation
Mazet amputation
S.P. Roger's amputation
DEF: Removal of lower leg through knee joint.

BI Bilateral Procedure   NC Non-covered Procedure   LC Limited Coverage Procedure   ▶◀ Revised Text   ● New Code   ▲ Revised Code Title

174 – Volume 3   **2010 ICD-9-CM**

84.17 Amputation above knee
     Amputation of leg through femur
     Amputation of thigh
     Conversion of below-knee amputation into
         above-knee amputation
     Supracondylar above-knee amputation
     AHA: 1Q, '05, 16; 1Q, '05, 16; 3Q, '03, 14

84.18 Disarticulation of hip
     DEF: Removal of leg through hip joint.

84.19 Abdominopelvic amputation
     Hemipelvectomy
     Hindquarter amputation
     DEF: Removal of leg and portion of pelvic bone.
     DEF: Hemipelvectomy: Removal of leg and lateral
         pelvis.

√4ᵗʰ **84.2 Reattachment of extremity**
     AHA: 1Q, '95, 8

84.21 Thumb reattachment

84.22 Finger reattachment

84.23 Forearm, wrist, or hand reattachment

84.24 Upper arm reattachment
     Reattachment of arm NOS

84.25 Toe reattachment

84.26 Foot reattachment

84.27 Lower leg or ankle reattachment
     Reattachment of leg NOS

84.28 Thigh reattachment

84.29 Other reattachment

84.3 Revision of amputation stump
     Reamputation
     Secondary closure } of stump
     Trimming
     EXCLUDES revision of current traumatic amputation
         [revision by further amputation of current
         injury] (84.00-84.19, 84.91)
     AHA: 4Q, '99, 15; 2Q, '98, 15; 4Q, '88, 12
     TIP: Only assign if the documentation indicates that the
     amputation stump revision involves transecting the entire
     circumference of the bone.

√4ᵗʰ **84.4 Implantation or fitting of prosthetic limb device**

**84.40 Implantation or fitting of prosthetic limb
     device, not otherwise specified**

84.41 Fitting of prosthesis of upper arm and shoulder

84.42 Fitting of prosthesis of lower arm and hand

**84.43 Fitting of prosthesis of arm, not otherwise
     specified**

84.44 Implantation of prosthetic device of arm

84.45 Fitting of prosthesis above knee

84.46 Fitting of prosthesis below knee

**84.47 Fitting of prosthesis of leg, not otherwise
     specified**

84.48 Implantation of prosthetic device of leg

Spinal Fusion with Metal Cage

Metal cages
support spine
until fusion
occurs

Anterior view

Lateral view

Spinal fusion
with metal cages

Detail

√4ᵗʰ **84.5 Implantation of other musculoskeletal devices and
substances**
     EXCLUDES insertion of (non-fusion) spinal disc replacement
         device (84.60-84.69)

84.51 Insertion of interbody spinal fusion device
     Insertion of:
         cages (carbn, ceramic, metal, plastic or
            titanium)
         interbody fusion cage
         synthetic cages or spacers
         threaded bone dowels
     Code also refusion of spine (81.30-81.39)
     Code also spinal fusion (81.00-81.08)
     AHA: ▶2Q, '09, 5;◀ 2Q, '08, 14; 1Q, '07, 20; 4Q, '05, 123;
     1Q, '04, 21; 4Q, '02, 108-110

**84.52 Insertion of recombinant bone morphogenetic
protein**
     rhBMP
     That via collagen sponge, coral, ceramic and other
         carriers
     Code also primary procedure performed:
         fracture repair (79.00-79.99)
         spinal fusion (81.00-81.08)
         spinal refusion (81.30-81.39)
     DEF: Surgical implantation of bone morphogenetic
     proteins (BMP) and recombinant BMP (rhBMP) to
     induce new bone growth formation; clinical
     applications include delayed unions and nonunions,
     fractures, and spinal fusions.
     AHA: ▶2Q, '09, 4-5;◀ 4Q, '02, 110

**84.53 Implantation of internal limb lengthening
device with kinetic distraction**
     Code also limb lengthening procedure
         (78.30-78.39)

**84.54 Implantation of other internal limb lengthening
device**
     Implantation of internal limb lengthening device,
         not otherwise specified (NOS)
     Code also limb lengthening procedure
         (78.30-78.39)

84.55 Insertion of bone void filler
     Insertion of:
         acrylic cement (PMMA)
         bone void cement
         calcium based bone void filler
         polymethylmethacrylate (PMMA)
     EXCLUDES that with percutaneous vertebral
         augmentation (81.66)
         that with percutaneous vertebroplasty
         (81.65)
     AHA: 4Q, '04, 128

84.56 Insertion or replacement of (cement) spacer
     Insertion or replacement of joint
         (methylmethacrylate) spacer
     AHA: 2Q, '08, 4; 4Q, '05, 124

84.57 Removal of (cement) spacer
     Removal of joint (methylmethacrylate) spacer
     AHA: 2Q, '08, 4, 5; 4Q, '05, 113, 124-125

84.59 Insertion of other spinal devices
     EXCLUDES initial insertion of pedicle screws with
         spinal fusion — omit code
         insertion of facet replacement device(s)
         (84.84)
         insertion of interspinous process
         device(s) (84.80)
         insertion of pedicle-based dynamic
         stabilization device(s) (84.82)
     AHA: 1Q, '07, 9, 10

√3ᵗʰ
√4ᵗʰ Additional Digit Required   Valid OR Procedure   Non-OR Procedure   Adjunct Code
2010 ICD-9-CM   **October 2009 • Volume 3 – 175**

√4th **84.6**   **Replacement of spinal disc**

> **INCLUDES**   non-fusion arthroplasty of the spine with insertion of artificial disc prosthesis

84.60   **Insertion of spinal disc prosthesis, not otherwise specified**

> Replacement of spinal disc, NOS
> **INCLUDES**   diskectomy (discectomy)

84.61   **Insertion of partial spinal disc prosthesis, cervical**

> Nuclear replacement device, cervical
> Partial artificial disc prosthesis (flexible), cervical
> Replacement of nuclear disc (nucleus pulposus), cervical
> **INCLUDES**   diskectomy (discectomy)

84.62   **Insertion of total spinal disc prosthesis, cervical**

> Replacement of cervical spinal disc, NOS
> Replacement of total spinal disc, cervical
> Total artificial disc prosthesis (flexible), cervical
> **INCLUDES**   diskectomy (discectomy)

84.63   **Insertion of spinal disc prosthesis, thoracic**

> Artificial disc prosthesis (flexible), thoracic
> Replacement of thoracic spinal disc, partial or total
> **INCLUDES**   diskectomy (discectomy)

84.64   **Insertion of partial spinal disc prosthesis, lumbosacral**

> Nuclear replacement device, lumbar
> Partial artificial disc prosthesis (flexible), lumbar
> Replacement of nuclear disc (nucleus pulposus), lumbar
> **INCLUDES**   diskectomy (discectomy)

[11] **84.65**   **Insertion of total spinal disc prosthesis, lumbosacral**   **NC**

> Replacement of lumbar spinal disc, NOS
> Replacement of total spinal disc, lumbar
> Total artificial disc prosthesis (flexible), lumbar
> **INCLUDES**   diskectomy (discectomy)
> **AHA:** 4Q, '04, 133

84.66   **Revision or replacement of artificial spinal disc prosthesis, cervical**

> Removal of (partial) (total) spinal disc prosthesis with synchronous insertion of new (partial) (total) spinal disc prosthesis, cervical
> Repair of previously inserted spinal disc prosthesis, cervical

84.67   **Revision or replacement of artificial spinal disc prosthesis, thoracic**

> Removal of (partial) (total) spinal disc prosthesis with synchronous insertion of new (partial) (total) spinal disc prosthesis, thoracic
> Repair of previously inserted spinal disc prosthesis, thoracic

External Fixator Devices

Monoplanar   Ring system   Hybrid

84.68   **Revision or replacement of artificial spinal disc prosthesis, lumbosacral**

> Removal of (partial) (total) spinal disc prosthesis with synchronous insertion of new (partial) (total) spinal disc prosthesis, lumbosacral
> Repair of previously inserted spinal disc prosthesis, lumbosacral

84.69   **Revision or replacement of artificial spinal disc prosthesis, not otherwise specified**

> Removal of (partial) (total) spinal disc prosthesis with synchronous insertion of new (partial) (total) spinal disc prosthesis
> Repair of previously inserted spinal disc prosthesis

√4th **84.7**   **Adjunct codes for external fixator devices**

> Code also any primary procedure performed:
> application of external fixator device (78.10, 78.12-78.13, 78.15, 78.17-78.19)
> reduction of fracture and dislocation (79.00-79.89)
> **AHA:** 4Q, '05, 127-129

84.71   **Application of external fixator device, monoplanar system**

> **EXCLUDES**   *other hybrid device or system (84.73)*
> *ring device or system (84.72)*
> **DEF:** Instrumentation that provides percutaneous neutralization, compression, and /or distraction of bone in a single plane by applying force within that plane.
> **AHA:** 4Q, '05, 129

84.72   **Application of external fixator device, ring system**

> Ilizarov type
> Sheffield type
> **EXCLUDES**   *monoplanar device or system (84.71)*
> *other hybrid device or system (84.73)*
> **DEF:** Instrumentation that provides percutaneous neutralization, compression, and/or distraction of bone through 360 degrees of force application.

84.73   **Application of hybrid external fixator device**

> Computer (assisted) (dependent) external fixator device
> Hybrid system using both ring and monoplanar devices
> **EXCLUDES**   *monoplanar device or system, when used alone (84.71)*
> *ring device or system, when used alone (84.72)*
> **DEF:** Instrumentation that provides percutaneous neutralization, compression, and /or distraction of bone by applying multiple external forces using monoplanar and ring device combinations.

√4th **84.8**   **Insertion, replacement and revision of posterior spinal motion preservation device(s)**

> Dynamic spinal stabilization device(s)
> **INCLUDES**   any synchronous facetectomy (partial, total) performed at the same level
> Code also any synchronous surgical decompression (foraminotomy, laminectomy, laminotomy), if performed (03.09)
> **EXCLUDES**   *fusion of spine (81.00-81.08, 81.30-81.39)*
> *insertion of artificial disc prosthesis (84.60-84.69)*
> *insertion of interbody spinal fusion device (84.51)*
> **AHA:** 4Q, '07, 116-120

84.80   **Insertion or replacement of interspinous process device(s)**

> Interspinous process decompression device(s)
> Interspinous process distraction device(s)
> **EXCLUDES**   *insertion or replacement of facet replacement device (84.84)*
> *insertion or replacement of pedicle-based dynamic stabilization device (84.82)*

---

[11]   Noncovered except when patient is 60 years or less.

BI Bilateral Procedure   **NC** Non-covered Procedure   **LC** Limited Coverage Procedure   ▶◀ Revised Text   ● New Code   ▲ Revised Code Title

176 – Volume 3   **2010 ICD-9-CM**

Posterior Spinal Motion Preservation Devices

Interspinous devices　　　Dynamic stabilization　　　Facet replacement

84.81　Revision of interspinous process device(s)

Repair of previously inserted interspinous process device(s)

> **EXCLUDES**　　*revision of facet replacement device(s) (84.85)*
> *revision of pedicle-based dynamic stabilization device (84.83)*

84.82　Insertion or replacement of pedicle-based dynamic stabilization device(s)

> **EXCLUDES**　　*initial insertion of pedicle screws with spinal fusion — omit code*
> *insertion or replacement of facet replacement device(s) (84.84)*
> *insertion or replacement of interspinous process device(s) (84.80)*
> *replacement of pedicle screws used in spinal fusion (78.59)*

84.83　Revision of pedicle-based dynamic stabilization device(s)

Repair of previously inserted pedicle-based dynamic stabilization device(s)

> **EXCLUDES**　　*removal of pedicle screws used in spinal fusion (78.69)*
> *replacement of pedicle screws used in spinal fusion (78.59)*
> *revision of facet replacement device(s) (84.85)*
> *revision of interspinous process device(s) (84.81)*

84.84　Insertion or replacement of facet replacement device(s)

Facet arthroplasty

> **EXCLUDES**　　*initial insertion of pedicle screws with spinal fusion — omit code*
> *insertion or replacement of interspinous process device(s) (84.80)*
> *insertion or replacement of pedicle-based dynamic stabilization device(s) (84.82)*
> *replacement of pedicle screws used in spinal fusion (78.59)*

> **AHA:** 4Q, '07, 120

84.85　Revision of facet replacement device(s)

Repair of previously inserted facet replacement device(s)

> **EXCLUDES**　　*removal of pedicle screws used in spinal fusion (78.69)*
> *replacement of pedicle screws used in spinal fusion (78.59)*
> *revision of interspinous process device(s) (84.81)*
> *revision of pedicle-based dynamic stabilization device(s) (84.83)*

√4th **84.9　Other operations on musculoskeletal system**

> **EXCLUDES**　　*nonoperative manipulation (93.25-93.29)*

84.91　Amputation, not otherwise specified

84.92　Separation of equal conjoined twins

84.93　Separation of unequal conjoined twins

Separation of conjoined twins NOS

84.99　Other

Operations on the Integumentary System

85–85.44

15. OPERATIONS ON THE INTEGUMENTARY SYSTEM (85-86)

✓3ʳᵈ **85   Operations on the breast**

    INCLUDES   operations on the skin and subcutaneous tissue of:
      breast
      previous mastectomy site   } female or male
      revision of previous mastectomy site

85.0   Mastotomy
    Incision of breast (skin)   Mammotomy
    EXCLUDES   *aspiration of breast (85.91)*
               removal of implant (85.94)
    AHA: 1Q, '04, 3; 2Q, '90, 27

✓4ᵗʰ **85.1   Diagnostic procedures on breast**

    85.11   Closed [percutaneous] [needle] biopsy of breast
       DEF: Mammatome biopsy: Excision of breast tissue using a needle inserted through a small incision; followed by a full cut circle of tissue surrounding the core biopsy to obtain; multiple contiguous directional sampling for definitive diagnosis and staging of cancer.
       AHA: 2Q, '00, 10; 3Q, '89, 17

    85.12   Open biopsy of breast
       DEF: Excision of breast tissue for examination.
       AHA: 3Q, '89, 17; M-A, '86, 11
       TIP: If an entire breast lesion is excised, assign instead code 85.21 Local excision of lesion of breast.

    85.19   Other diagnostic procedures on breast
       EXCLUDES   *mammary ductogram (87.35)*
               mammography NEC (87.37)
               manual examination (89.36)
               microscopic examination of specimen
                  (91.61-91.69)
               thermography (88.85)
               ultrasonography (88.73)
               xerography (87.36)

✓4ᵗʰ **85.2   Excision or destruction of breast tissue**
    EXCLUDES   *mastectomy (85.41-85.48)*
               reduction mammoplasty (85.31-85.32)

    85.20   Excision or destruction of breast tissue, not otherwise specified
       EXCLUDES   ▶*laser interstitial thermal therapy [LITT] of lesion or tissue of breast under guidance (17.69)*◀

    85.21   Local excision of lesion of breast
       Lumpectomy
       Removal of area of fibrosis from breast
       EXCLUDES   *biopsy of breast (85.11-85.12)*
       AHA: 2Q, '90, 27; 3Q, '89, 17; M-A, '86, 11

    85.22   Resection of quadrant of breast

    85.23   Subtotal mastectomy
       EXCLUDES   *quadrant resection (85.22)*
       DEF: Excision of a large portion of breast tissue.
       AHA: 2Q, '92, 7

    85.24   Excision of ectopic breast tissue
       Excision of accessory nipple
       DEF: Excision of breast tissue outside normal breast region.

    85.25   Excision of nipple
       EXCLUDES   *excision of accessory nipple (85.24)*

Mastectomy

Partial mastectomy (lumpectomy): skin left intact

Lymph nodes

Simple mastectomy   Radical mastectomy

✓4ᵗʰ **85.3   Reduction mammoplasty and subcutaneous mammectomy**
    AHA: 4Q, '95, 79, 80

    85.31   Unilateral reduction mammoplasty
       Unilateral:
          amputative mammoplasty
          size reduction mammoplasty

    85.32   Bilateral reduction mammoplasty
       Amputative mammoplasty
       Biesenberger operation
       Reduction mammoplasty (for gynecomastia)

    85.33   Unilateral subcutaneous mammectomy with synchronous implant
       EXCLUDES   *that without synchronous implant (85.34)*
       DEF: Removal of mammary tissue, leaving skin and nipple intact with implant of prosthesis.

    85.34   Other unilateral subcutaneous mammectomy
       Removal of breast tissue with preservation of skin and nipple
       Subcutaneous mammectomy NOS
       DEF: Excision of mammary tissue, leaving skin and nipple intact.

    85.35   Bilateral subcutaneous mammectomy with synchronous implant
       EXCLUDES   *that without synchronous implant (85.36)*
       DEF: Excision of mammary tissue, both breasts, leaving skin and nipples intact; with prosthesis.

    85.36   Other bilateral subcutaneous mammectomy

✓4ᵗʰ **85.4   Mastectomy**

    85.41   Unilateral simple mastectomy
       Mastectomy:
          NOS
          complete
       DEF: Removal of one breast.

    85.42   Bilateral simple mastectomy
       Bilateral complete mastectomy
       DEF: Removal of both breasts.

    85.43   Unilateral extended simple mastectomy
       Extended simple mastectomy NOS
       Modified radical mastectomy
       Simple mastectomy with excision of regional lymph nodes
       DEF: Removal of one breast and lymph nodes under arm.
       AHA: 2Q, '92, 7; 3Q, '91, 24; 2Q, '91, 21

    85.44   Bilateral extended simple mastectomy
       AHA: 2Q, '92, 7; 3Q, '91, 24; 2Q, '91, 21

BI Bilateral Procedure   NC Non-covered Procedure   LC Limited Coverage Procedure   ▶◀ Revised Text   ● New Code   ▲ Revised Code Title

178 – Volume 3• October 2009   **2010 ICD-9-CM**

85.45   Unilateral radical mastectomy
Excision of breast, pectoral muscles, and regional
lymph nodes [axillary, clavicular,
supraclavicular]
Radical mastectomy NOS
DEF: Removal of one breast and regional lymph nodes,
pectoral muscle and adjacent tissue.
AHA: 2Q, '91, 21
TIP: Do not assign a separate code for lymph node
excision (subcategory 40.3 or 40.5); the service is
included in the radical mastectomy code.

85.46   Bilateral radical mastectomy
AHA: 2Q, '91, 21

85.47   Unilateral extended radical mastectomy
Excision of breast, muscles, and lymph nodes
[axillary, clavicular, supraclavicular, internal
mammary, and mediastinal]
Extended radical mastectomy NOS
DEF: Removal of one breast, regional and middle chest
lymph nodes, chest muscle and adjacent tissue.

85.48   Bilateral extended radical mastectomy
DEF: Removal of both breasts, regional and middle
chest lymph nodes, chest muscle and adjacent tissue.

√4ᵗʰ **85.5 Augmentation mammoplasty**
EXCLUDES *that associated with subcutaneous*
mammectomy (85.33, 85.35)
DEF: Plastic surgery to increase breast size.
AHA: 3Q, '97, 12; 4Q, '95, 76, 80

**85.50   Augmentation mammoplasty, not otherwise
specified**

**85.51   Unilateral injection into breast for
augmentation**

85.52   Bilateral injection into breast for augmentation
Injection into breast for augmentation NOS

85.53   Unilateral breast implant
AHA: 2Q, '00 18; 2Q, '98, 14

85.54   Bilateral breast implant
Breast implant NOS

85.6 Mastopexy
DEF: Anchoring of pendulous breast.

√4ᵗʰ **85.7 Total reconstruction of breast**
AHA: ▶4Q, '08, 185-187;◀ 4Q, '95, 77; 1Q, '93, 27
TIP: When a patient is admitted for breast reconstruction following mastectomy, assign diagnosis code V51.0 as the principal or
first-listed diagnosis.

**85.70   Total reconstruction of breast, not
otherwise specified**
Perforator flap, free

85.71   Latissimus dorsi myocutaneous flap

**85.72   Transverse rectus abdominis
myocutaneous [TRAM] flap, pedicled**
EXCLUDES *transverse rectus abdominis*
myocutaneous (TRAM) flap,
free (85.73)

**85.73   Transverse rectus abdominis
myocutaneous [TRAM] flap, free**
EXCLUDES *transverse rectus abdominis*
myocutaneous (TRAM) flap,
pedicled (85.72)

**85.74   Deep inferior epigastric artery perforator
[DIEP] flap, free**

**85.75   Superficial inferior epigastric artery [SIEA]
flap, free**

85.76   Gluteal artery perforator [GAP] flap, free

85.79   Other total reconstruction of breast
EXCLUDES *deep inferior epigastric artery*
perforator [DIEP] flap, free
(85.74)
gluteal artery perforator [GAP] flap,
free (85.76)
latissimus dorsi myocutaneous flap
(85.71)
perforator flap, free (85.70)
superficial inferior epigastric artery
[SIEA] flap, free (85.75)
total reconstruction of breast, not
otherwise specified (85.70)
transverse rectus abdominis
myocutaneous [TRAM] flap,
free (85.73)
transverse rectus abdominis
myocutaneous [TRAM] flap,
pedicled (85.72)

√4ᵗʰ **85.8 Other repair and plastic operations on breast**
EXCLUDES *that for:*
augmentation (85.50-85.54)
reconstruction (85.70-85.76, 85.79)
reduction (85.31-85.32)
AHA: 4Q, '95, 77

85.81   Suture of laceration of breast

85.82   Split-thickness graft to breast

85.83   Full-thickness graft to breast
AHA: 4Q, '95, 77

85.84   Pedicle graft to breast
DEF: Implantation of transferred muscle tissue still
connected to vascular source.
AHA: 4Q, '95, 77

85.85   Muscle flap graft to breast
DEF: Relocation of nipple.
AHA: 4Q, '95, 77

85.86   Transposition of nipple
AHA: 4Q, '95, 78

85.87   Other repair or reconstruction of nipple
AHA: 4Q, '95, 78

85.89   Other mammoplasty

√4ᵗʰ **85.9 Other operations on the breast**

85.91   Aspiration of breast
EXCLUDES *percutaneous biopsy of breast (85.11)*

85.92   Injection of therapeutic agent into breast
EXCLUDES *that for augmentation of breast*
(85.51-85.52)

85.93   Revision of implant of breast
AHA: 2Q, '98, 14; 4Q, '95, 76

85.94   Removal of implant of breast
AHA: 2Q, '98, 14; 3Q, '92, 4

85.95   Insertion of breast tissue expander
Insertion (soft tissue) of tissue expander (one or
more) under muscle or platysma to develop
skin flaps for donor use

85.96   Removal of breast tissue expander(s)
AHA: 2Q, '00, 18; 4Q, '95, 77

85.99   Other

√3rd **86**   **Operations on skin and subcutaneous tissue**

INCLUDES   operations on:
- hair follicles
- male perineum
- nails
- sebaceous glands
- subcutaneous fat pads
- sudoriferous glands
- superficial fossae

EXCLUDES   *those on skin of:*
- *anus (49.01-49.99)*
- *breast (mastectomy site) (85.0-85.99)*
- *ear (18.01-18.9)*
- *eyebrow (08.01-08.99)*
- *eyelid (08.01-08.99)*
- *female perineum (71.01-71.9)*
- *lips (27.0-27.99)*
- *nose (21.00-21.99)*
- *penis (64.0-64.99)*
- *scrotum (61.0-61.99)*
- *vulva (71.01-71.9)*

√4th **86.0**   **Incision of skin and subcutaneous tissue**

86.01   **Aspiration of skin and subcutaneous tissue**
Aspiration of:
- abscess
- hematoma } of nail, skin, or subcutaneous tissue
- seroma

AHA: 3Q, '89, 16

86.02   **Injection or tattooing of skin lesion or defect**
Insertion
Injection } of filling material
Pigmenting of skin
DEF: Pigmenting of skin: Adding color to skin.

86.03   **Incision of pilonidal sinus or cyst**
EXCLUDES   *marsupialization (86.21)*

86.04   **Other incision with drainage of skin and subcutaneous tissue**
EXCLUDES   *drainage of:*
- *fascial compartments of face and mouth (27.0)*
- *palmar or thenar space (82.04)*
- *pilonidal sinus or cyst (86.03)*

AHA: ▶1Q, '09, 11;◀ 4Q, '04, 76
TIP: If extensive debridement is performed along with the I&D procedure, assign instead code 86.22.

86.05   **Incision with removal of foreign body or device from skin and subcutaneous tissue**
Removal of carotid sinus baroreflex activation device
Removal of loop recorder
Removal of neurostimulator pulse generator (single array, dual array)
Removal of tissue expander(s) from skin or soft tissue other than breast tissue
EXCLUDES   *removal of foreign body without incision (98.20-98.29)*

AHA: 2Q, '96, 15; N-D, '87, 10; N-D, '86, 9

86.06   **Insertion of totally implantable infusion pump**
Code also any associated catheterization → 38.93(?)
EXCLUDES   *insertion of totally implantable vascular access device (86.07)*

AHA: 2Q, '99, 4; 4Q, '90, 14

[handwritten note: Pump is self-contained and completely implanted in the body. Laparotomy approach is not coded.]

86.07   **Insertion of totally implantable vascular access device [VAD]**
Totally implanted port
EXCLUDES   *insertion of totally implantable infusion pump (86.06)*

DEF: Placement of vascular access infusion catheter system under skin to allow for frequent manual infusions into blood vessel.
AHA: 1Q, '01, 13; 1Q, '96, 3; 2Q, '94, 11; 3Q, '91, 13; 4Q, '90, 15

[handwritten note: Not a pump but a port implanted in the body to provide easy access to the vascular system.]

86.09   **Other incision of skin and subcutaneous tissue**
Creation of thalamic stimulator pulse generator pocket, new site
Escharotomy
Exploration:
- sinus tract, skin
- superficial fossa
Relocation of subcutaneous device pocket NEC
Reopening subcutaneous pocket for device revision without replacement
Undercutting of hair follicle
EXCLUDES   *creation of loop recorder pocket, new site and insertion/relocation of device (37.79)*
creation of pocket for implantable, patient-activated cardiac event recorder and insertion/relocation of device (37.79)
removal of catheter from cranial cavity (01.27)
that for drainage (86.04)
that of:
- *cardiac pacemaker pocket, new site (37.79)*
- *fascial compartments of face and mouth (27.0)*

AHA: 1Q, '05, 17; 2Q, '04, 7, 8; 4Q, '00, 68; 4Q, '99, 21; 4Q, '97, 57; 3Q, '89, 17; N-D, '86, 1; N-D, '84, 6

√4th **86.1**   **Diagnostic procedures on skin and subcutaneous tissue**

86.11   **Biopsy of skin and subcutaneous tissue**
AHA: 4Q, '08, 99

86.19   **Other diagnostic procedures on skin and subcutaneous tissue**
EXCLUDES   *microscopic examination of specimen from skin and subcutaneous tissue (91.61-91.79)*

√4th **86.2**   **Excision or destruction of lesion or tissue of skin and subcutaneous tissue**

86.21   **Excision of pilonidal cyst or sinus**
Marsupialization of cyst
EXCLUDES   *incision of pilonidal cyst or sinus (86.03)*
DEF: Marsupialization of cyst: Incision of cyst and suturing edges to skin to open site.

86.22   **Excisional debridement of wound, infection, or burn**
Removal by excision of:
- devitalized tissue
- necrosis
- slough
EXCLUDES   *debridement of:*
- *abdominal wall (wound) (54.3)*
- *bone (77.60-77.69)*
- *muscle (83.45)*
- *of hand (82.36)*
- *nail (bed) (fold) (86.27)*
- *nonexcisional debridement of wound, infection, or burn (86.28)*
- *open fracture site (79.60-79.69)*
- *pedicle or flap graft (86.75)*

AHA: 3Q, '08, 8; 1Q, '08, 3-4; 3Q, '06, 19; 2Q, '06, 11; 1Q, '05, 14; 4Q, '04, 138; 3Q,'02, 23; 2Q, '00, 9; 1Q, '99, 8; 2Q, '92, 17; 3Q, '91, 18; 3Q, '89, 16; 4Q, '88, 5; N-D, '86, 1
TIP: Assign only if the debridement involves skin and subcutaneous tissues; any deeper structures (e.g., muscle, bone) are coded elsewhere.

86.23   **Removal of nail, nail bed, or nail fold**

86.24   **Chemosurgery of skin**
Chemical peel of skin
DEF: Chemicals applied to destroy skin tissue.
DEF: Chemical peel of skin: Chemicals used to peel skin layers.

BI Bilateral Procedure   **NC** Non-covered Procedure   **LC** Limited Coverage Procedure   ▶◀ Revised Text   ● New Code   ▲ Revised Code Title

180 – Volume 3 · October 2009   2010 ICD-9-CM

86.25 Dermabrasion
That with laser
EXCLUDES *dermabrasion of wound to remove embedded debris (86.28)*
DEF: Removal of wrinkled or scarred skin; with fine sandpaper, wire, brushes or laser.

86.26 Ligation of dermal appendage
EXCLUDES *excision of preauricular appendage (18.29)*
DEF: Tying off extra skin.

86.27 Debridement of nail, nail bed, or nail fold
Removal of:
necrosis
slough
EXCLUDES *removal of nail, nail bed, or nail fold (86.23)*

86.28 Nonexcisional debridement of wound, infection, or burn
Debridement NOS
Maggot therapy
Removal of devitalized tissue, necrosis, and slough by such methods as:
brushing
irrigation (under pressure)
scrubbing
washing
Water scalpel (jet)
DEF: Removal of damaged skin; by methods other than excision.
AHA: 1Q, '07, 10, 11; 1Q, '05, 14; 2Q, '04, 5, 6; 4Q, '03, 110; 2Q, '03, 15; 3Q, '02, 23; 2Q, '01, 18; 3Q, '91, 18; 4Q, '88, 5

86.3 Other local excision or destruction of lesion or tissue of skin and subcutaneous tissue
Destruction of skin by:
cauterization
cryosurgery
fulguration
laser beam
That with Z-plasty
EXCLUDES *adipectomy (86.83)*
biopsy of skin (86.11)
wide or radical excision of skin (86.4)
Z-plasty without excision (86.84)
AHA: 1Q, '96, 15; 2Q, '90, 27; 1Q, '89, 12; 3Q, '89, 18; 4Q, '88, 7

86.4 Radical excision of skin lesion
Wide excision of skin lesion involving underlying or adjacent structure
Code also any lymph node dissection (40.3-40.5)

√4ᵗʰ **86.5 Suture or other closure of skin and subcutaneous tissue**

86.51 Replantation of scalp

86.59 Closure of skin and subcutaneous tissue of other sites
Adhesives (surgical)(tissue)
Staples
Sutures
EXCLUDES *application of adhesive strips (butterfly) — omit code*
AHA: 4Q, '99, 23

√4ᵗʰ **86.6 Free skin graft**
INCLUDES excision of skin for autogenous graft
EXCLUDES *construction or reconstruction of:*
penis (64.43-64.44)
trachea (31.75)
vagina (70.61-70.64)
DEF: Transplantation of skin to another site.

86.60 Free skin graft, not otherwise specified

86.61 Full-thickness skin graft to hand
EXCLUDES *heterograft (86.65)*
homograft (86.66)

86.62 Other skin graft to hand
EXCLUDES *heterograft (86.65)*
homograft (86.66)

86.63 Full-thickness skin graft to other sites
EXCLUDES *heterograft (86.65)*
homograft (86.66)

86.64 Hair transplant
EXCLUDES *hair follicle transplant to eyebrow or eyelash (08.63)*

86.65 Heterograft to skin
Pigskin graft
Porcine graft
EXCLUDES *application of dressing only (93.57)*
DEF: Implantation of nonhuman tissue.
AHA: 3Q,'02, 23

86.66 Homograft to skin
Graft to skin of:
amnionic membrane ⎫
skin   ⎬ from donor
                                  ⎭
DEF: Implantation of tissue from human donor.

86.67 Dermal regenerative graft
Artificial skin, NOS
Creation of "neodermis"
Decellularized allodermis
Integumentary matrix implants
Prosthetic implant of dermal layer of skin
Regenerate dermal layer of skin
EXCLUDES *heterograft to skin (86.65)*
homograft to skin (86.66)
DEF: Replacement of dermis and epidermal layer of skin by cultured or regenerated autologous tissue; used to treat full-thickness or deep partial-thickness burns; also called cultured epidermal autograft (CEA).
AHA: 3Q, '06, 19; 4Q, '98, 76, 79

86.69 Other skin graft to other sites
EXCLUDES *heterograft (86.65)*
homograft (86.66)
AHA: 4Q, '99, 15

√4ᵗʰ **86.7 Pedicle grafts or flaps**
EXCLUDES *construction or reconstruction of:*
penis (64.43-64.44)
trachea (31.75)
vagina (70.61-70.64)
DEF: Full thickness skin and subcutaneous tissue partially attached to the body by a narrow strip of tissue so that it retains its blood supply. The unattached portion is sutured to the defect.

86.70 Pedicle or flap graft, not otherwise specified

86.71 Cutting and preparation of pedicle grafts or flaps
Elevation of pedicle from its bed
Flap design and raising
Partial cutting of pedicle or tube
Pedicle delay
EXCLUDES *pollicization or digital transfer (82.61,82.81)*
revision of pedicle (86.75)
DEF: Elevation of pedicle from its bed: Separation of tissue implanted from its bed.
DEF: Flap design and raising: Planing and elevation of tissue to be implanted.
DEF: Pedicle delay: Elevation and preparation of tissue still attached to vascular bed; delayed implant.
AHA: 4Q, '01, 66

86.72 Advancement of pedicle graft
AHA: 3Q, '99, 9, 10

86.73 Attachment of pedicle or flap graft to hand
EXCLUDES *pollicization or digital transfer (82.61, 82.81)*

√3ʳᵈ
√4ᵗʰ Additional Digit Required

Operations on the Integumentary System

86.25–86.73

86.74 **Attachment of pedicle or flap graft to other sites**

Attachment by:
advanced flap
double pedicled flap
pedicle graft
rotating flap
sliding flap
tube graft

DEF: Advanced flap: Sliding tissue implant into new position.

DEF: Double pedicle flap: Implant connected to two vascular beds.

DEF: Pedicle graft: Implant connected to vascular bed.

DEF: Rotating flap: Implant rotated along curved incision.

DEF: Sliding flap: Sliding implant to site.

DEF: Tube graft: Double tissue implant to form tube with base connected to original site.

AHA: 3Q, '99, 9; 1Q, '96, 15

86.75 **Revision of pedicle or flap graft**

Debridement
Defatting } of pedicle or flap graft

DEF: Connection of implant still attached to its vascular tissue.

✓4ᵗʰ **86.8** **Other repair and reconstruction of skin and subcutaneous tissue**

86.81 **Repair for facial weakness**

86.82 **Facial rhytidectomy**

Face lift

EXCLUDES *rhytidectomy of eyelid (08.86-08.87)*

DEF: Revision and tightening of excess, wrinkled facial skin.

86.83 **Size reduction plastic operation**

Liposuction
Reduction of adipose tissue of:
abdominal wall (pendulous)
arms (batwing)
buttock
thighs (trochanteric lipomatosis)

EXCLUDES *breast (85.31-85.32)*

DEF: Excision and plastic repair of excess skin and underlying tissue.

AHA: 2Q, '06, 10

TIP: Assign for abdominoplasty or panniculectomy performed after a morbid obesity surgical procedure and significant weight loss.

86.84 **Relaxation of scar or web contracture of skin**

Z-plasty of skin

EXCLUDES *Z-plasty with excision of lesion (86.3)*

86.85 **Correction of syndactyly**

DEF: Plastic repair of webbed fingers or toes.

86.86 **Onychoplasty**

DEF: Plastic repair of nail or nail bed.

86.89 **Other repair and reconstruction of skin and subcutaneous tissue**

EXCLUDES *mentoplasty (76.67-76.68)*

AHA: 4Q, '02, 107; 1Q, '00, 26; 2Q, '98, 20; 2Q, '93, 11; 2Q, '92, 17

✓4ᵗʰ **86.9** **Other operations on skin and subcutaneous tissue**

86.91 **Excision of skin for graft**

Excision of skin with closure of donor site

EXCLUDES *that with graft at same operative episode (86.60-86.69)*

86.92 **Electrolysis and other epilation of skin**

EXCLUDES *epilation of eyelid (08.91-08.93)*

86.93 **Insertion of tissue expander**

Insertion (subcutaneous) (soft tissue) of expander (one or more) in scalp (subgaleal space), face, neck, trunk except breast, and upper and lower extremities for development of skin flaps for donor use

EXCLUDES *flap graft preparation (86.71)*
tissue expander, breast (85.95)

86.94 **Insertion or replacement of single array neurostimulator pulse generator, not specified as rechargeable**

Pulse generator (single array, single channel) for intracranial, spinal, and peripheral neurostimulator

Code also any associated lead implantation (02.93, 03.93, 04.92)

EXCLUDES *insertion or replacement of single array rechargeable neurostimulator pulse generator (86.97)*

AHA: 4Q, '04, 135

86.95 **Insertion or replacement of dual array neurostimulator pulse generator, not specified as rechargeable**

Pulse generator (dual array, dual channel) for intracranial, spinal, and peripheral neurostimulator

Code also any associated lead implantation (02.93, 03.93, 04.92)

EXCLUDES *insertion or replacement of dual array rechargeable neurostimulator pulse generator (86.98)*

86.96 **Insertion or replacement of other neurostimulator pulse generator**

Code also any associated lead implantation (02.93, 03.93, 04.92)

EXCLUDES *insertion of dual array neurostimulator pulse generator (86.95, 86.98)*
insertion of single array neurostimulator pulse generator (86.94, 86.97)

AHA: 2Q, '07, 8; 2Q, '06, 5-6

86.97 **Insertion or replacement of single array rechargeable neurostimulator pulse generator**

Rechargeable pulse generator (single array, single channel) for intracranial, spinal, and peripheral neurostimulator

Code also any associated lead implantation (02.93, 03.93, 04.92)

AHA: 4Q, '05, 130

86.98 **Insertion or replacement of dual array rechargeable neurostimulator pulse generator**

Rechargeable pulse generator (dual array, dual channel) for intracranial, spinal, and peripheral neurostimulator

Code also any associated lead implantation (02.93, 03.93, 04.92)

AHA: 4Q, '05, 130

86.99 **Other**

EXCLUDES *removal of sutures from:*
abdomen (97.83)
head and neck (97.38)
thorax (97.43)
trunk NEC (97.84)
wound catheter:
irrigation (96.58)
replacement (97.15)

AHA: 4Q, '97, 57; N-D, '86, 1

BI Bilateral Procedure   **NC** Non-covered Procedure   **LC** Limited Coverage Procedure   ▶◀ Revised Text   ● New Code   ▲ Revised Code Title

182 – Volume 3   **2010 ICD-9-CM**

16. MISCELLANEOUS DIAGNOSTIC AND THERAPEUTIC PROCEDURES (87-99)

√3ʳᵈ 87 Diagnostic radiology

√4ᵗʰ 87.0 Soft tissue x-ray of face, head, and neck
EXCLUDES angiography (88.40-88.68)

87.01 Pneumoencephalogram
DEF: Radiographic exam of cerebral ventricles and subarachnoid spaces; with injection of air or gas for contrast.

87.02 Other contrast radiogram of brain and skull
Pneumocisternogram
Pneumoventriculogram
Posterior fossa myelogram
DEF: Pneumocisternogram: radiographic exam of subarachnoid spaces after injection of gas or contrast.
DEF: Pneumoventriculography: radiographic exam of cerebral ventricles after injection of gas or contrast.
DEF: Posterior fossa myelogram: radiographic exam of posterior channel of spinal cord after injection of gas or contrast.

87.03 Computerized axial tomography of head
C.A.T. scan of head
AHA: 3Q, '05, 12; 3Q, '99, 7

87.04 Other tomography of head

87.05 Contrast dacryocystogram
DEF: Radiographic exam of tear sac after injection of contrast.

87.06 Contrast radiogram of nasopharynx

87.07 Contrast laryngogram

87.08 Cervical lymphangiogram
DEF: Radiographic exam of lymph vessels of neck; with or without contrast.

87.09 Other soft tissue x-ray of face, head, and neck
Noncontrast x-ray of:
adenoid
larynx
nasolacrimal duct
nasopharynx
salivary gland
thyroid region
uvula
EXCLUDES x-ray study of eye (95.14)

√4ᵗʰ 87.1 Other x-ray of face, head, and neck
EXCLUDES angiography (88.40-88.68)

87.11 Full-mouth x-ray of teeth

87.12 Other dental x-ray
Orthodontic cephalogram or cephalometrics
Panorex examination of mandible
Root canal x-ray

87.13 Temporomandibular contrast arthrogram

87.14 Contrast radiogram of orbit

87.15 Contrast radiogram of sinus

87.16 Other x-ray of facial bones
X-ray of:
frontal area
mandible
maxilla
nasal sinuses
nose
orbit
supraorbital area
symphysis menti
zygomaticomaxillary complex

87.17 Other x-ray of skull
Lateral projection
Sagittal projection } of skull
Tangential projection
DEF: Lateral projection: Side to side view of head.
DEF: Sagittal projection: View of body in plane running midline from front to back.
DEF: Tangential projection: Views from adjacent skull surfaces.

√4ᵗʰ 87.2 X-ray of spine

87.21 Contrast myelogram
DEF: Radiographic exam of space between middle and outer spinal cord coverings after injection of contrast.

87.22 Other x-ray of cervical spine

87.23 Other x-ray of thoracic spine

87.24 Other x-ray of lumbosacral spine
Sacrococcygeal x-ray

87.29 Other x-ray of spine
Spinal x-ray NOS

√4ᵗʰ 87.3 Soft tissue x-ray of thorax
EXCLUDES angiocardiography (88.50-88.58)
angiography (88.40-88.68)

87.31 Endotracheal bronchogram
DEF: Radiographic exam of lung, main branch, with contrast introduced through windpipe.

87.32 Other contrast bronchogram
Transcricoid bronchogram
DEF: Transcricoid bronchogram: Radiographic exam of lung, main branch, with contrast introduced through cartilage of neck.

87.33 Mediastinal pneumogram
DEF: Radiographic exam of cavity containing heart, esophagus and adjacent structures.

87.34 Intrathoracic lymphangiogram
DEF: Radiographic exam of lymphatic vessels within chest; with or without contrast.

87.35 Contrast radiogram of mammary ducts
DEF: Radiographic exam of mammary ducts; with contrast.

87.36 Xerography of breast
DEF: Radiographic exam of breast via selenium-coated plates.

87.37 Other mammography
AHA: 3Q, '89, 17; 2Q, '90, 28; N-D, '87, 1
TIP: Assign as an additional code when mammographic localization is performed immediately prior to breast lesion biopsy or excision. Wire localization is included.

87.38 Sinogram of chest wall
Fistulogram of chest wall
DEF: Fistulogram of chest wall: Radiographic exam of abnormal opening in chest.

87.39 Other soft tissue x-ray of chest wall

√4ᵗʰ 87.4 Other x-ray of thorax
EXCLUDES angiocardiography (88.50-88.58)
angiography (88.40-88.68)

87.41 Computerized axial tomography of thorax
C.A.T. scan of heart
C.A.T. scan
Crystal linea scan of x-ray beam
Electronic subtraction } of thorax
Photoelectric response
Tomography with use of computer, x-rays, and camera

87.42 Other tomography of thorax
Cardiac tomogram
EXCLUDES C.A.T. scan of heart (87.41)
DEF: Radiographic exam of chest plane.

Diagnostic and Therapeutic Procedures

87.43–88.25

87.43   **X-ray of ribs, sternum, and clavicle**
Examination for:
   cervical rib
   fracture

87.44   **Routine chest x-ray, so described**
X-ray of chest NOS

87.49   **Other chest x-ray**
X-ray of: X-ray of:
   bronchus NOS   lung NOS
   diaphragm NOS   mediastinum NOS
   heart NOS   trachea NOS

√4th **87.5**   **Biliary tract x-ray**

87.51   **Percutaneous hepatic cholangiogram**
DEF: Radiographic exam of bile tract of gallbladder; with needle injection of contrast into bile duct of liver.
AHA: 2Q, '90, 28; N-D, '87, 1

87.52   **Intravenous cholangiogram**
DEF: Radiographic exam of bile ducts; with intravenous contrast injection.

87.53   **Intraoperative cholangiogram**
DEF: Radiographic exam of bile ducts; with contrast; following gallbladder removal.
AHA: 1Q, '96, 12; 2Q, '90, 28; 3Q, '89, 18; 4Q, '88, 7

87.54   **Other cholangiogram**

87.59   **Other biliary tract x-ray**
Cholecystogram

√4th **87.6**   **Other x-ray of digestive system**

87.61   **Barium swallow**

87.62   **Upper GI series**

87.63   **Small bowel series**

87.64   **Lower GI series**

87.65   **Other x-ray of intestine**

87.66   **Contrast pancreatogram**

87.69   **Other digestive tract x-ray**

√4th **87.7**   **X-ray of urinary system**
EXCLUDES   *angiography of renal vessels (88.45, 88.65)*

87.71   **Computerized axial tomography of kidney**
C.A.T. scan of kidney

87.72   **Other nephrotomogram**
DEF: Radiographic exam of kidney plane.

87.73   **Intravenous pyelogram**
Diuretic infusion pyelogram
DEF: Radiographic exam of lower kidney, with intravenous contrast injection.
DEF: Diuretic infusion pyelogram: Radiographic exam of lower kidney with diuretic contrast.

87.74   **Retrograde pyelogram**
TIP: The diagnostic cystoscopy service is included in the retrograde pyelogram code; do not assign 57.32 separately.

87.75   **Percutaneous pyelogram**

87.76   **Retrograde cystourethrogram**
DEF: Radiographic exam of bladder and urethra with contrast injected through catheter into bladder.

87.77   **Other cystogram**

87.78   **Ileal conduitogram**
DEF: Radiographic exam of passage created between ureter and artificial opening into abdomen.
AHA: M-J, '87, 11

87.79   **Other x-ray of the urinary system**
KUB x-ray

√4th **87.8**   **X-ray of female genital organs**

87.81   **X-ray of gravid uterus**   ♀
Intrauterine cephalometry by x-ray

87.82   **Gas contrast hysterosalpingogram**   ♀
DEF: Radiographic exam of uterus and fallopian tubes; with gas contrast.

87.83   **Opaque dye contrast hysterosalpingogram**   ♀

Ureteropyelography

Minor calyces · Fat and abdominal wall · Renal pelvis · Major calyces · Renal pelvis · Ureter · Kidney · Percutaneous injection · Cutaway schematic · Ureter · Bladder

87.84   **Percutaneous hysterogram**   ♀
DEF: Radiographic exam of uterus with contrast injected through body wall.

87.85   **Other x-ray of fallopian tubes and uterus**   ♀

87.89   **Other x-ray of female genital organs**   ♀

√4th **87.9**   **X-ray of male genital organs**

87.91   **Contrast seminal vesiculogram**   ♂

87.92   **Other x-ray of prostate and seminal vesicles**   ♂

87.93   **Contrast epididymogram**   ♂

87.94   **Contrast vasogram**   ♂

87.95   **Other x-ray of epididymis and vas deferens**   ♂

87.99   **Other x-ray of male genital organs**   ♂

√3rd **88**   **Other diagnostic radiology and related techniques**

√4th **88.0**   **Soft tissue x-ray of abdomen**
EXCLUDES   *angiography (88.40-88.68)*

88.01   **Computerized axial tomography of abdomen**
C.A.T. scan of abdomen
EXCLUDES   *C.A.T. scan of kidney (87.71)*
AHA: 2Q, '98, 13

88.02   **Other abdomen tomography**
EXCLUDES   *nephrotomogram (87.72)*

88.03   **Sinogram of abdominal wall**
Fistulogram of abdominal wall
DEF: Radiographic exam of abnormal abdominal passage.

88.04   **Abdominal lymphangiogram**
DEF: Radiographic exam of abdominal lymphatic vessels; with contrast.

88.09   **Other soft tissue x-ray of abdominal wall**

√4th **88.1**   **Other x-ray of abdomen**

88.11   **Pelvic opaque dye contrast radiography**

88.12   **Pelvic gas contrast radiography**
Pelvic pneumoperitoneum

88.13   **Other peritoneal pneumogram**

88.14   **Retroperitoneal fistulogram**

88.15   **Retroperitoneal pneumogram**

88.16   **Other retroperitoneal x-ray**

88.19   **Other x-ray of abdomen**
Flat plate of abdomen
AHA: 3Q, '99, 9

√4th **88.2**   **Skeletal x-ray of extremities and pelvis**
EXCLUDES   *contrast radiogram of joint (88.32)*

88.21   **Skeletal x-ray of shoulder and upper arm**

88.22   **Skeletal x-ray of elbow and forearm**

88.23   **Skeletal x-ray of wrist and hand**

88.24   **Skeletal x-ray of upper limb, not otherwise specified**

88.25   **Pelvimetry**
DEF: Imaging of pelvic bones to measure pelvic capacity.

BI Bilateral Procedure   NC Non-covered Procedure   LC Limited Coverage Procedure   ►◄ Revised Text   ● New Code   ▲ Revised Code Title

88.26   Other skeletal x-ray of pelvis and hip

88.27   Skeletal x-ray of thigh, knee, and lower leg

88.28   Skeletal x-ray of ankle and foot

88.29   Skeletal x-ray of lower limb, not otherwise specified

✓4ᵗʰ **88.3   Other x-ray**

88.31   **Skeletal series**
X-ray of whole skeleton

88.32   **Contrast arthrogram**
EXCLUDES   *that of temporomandibular joint (87.13)*

88.33   **Other skeletal x-ray**
EXCLUDES   *skeletal x-ray of:*
extremities and pelvis (88.21-88.29)
face, head, and neck (87.11-87.17)
spine (87.21-87.29)
thorax (87.43)

88.34   **Lymphangiogram of upper limb**

88.35   **Other soft tissue x-ray of upper limb**

88.36   **Lymphangiogram of lower limb**

88.37   **Other soft tissue x-ray of lower limb**
EXCLUDES   *femoral angiography (88.48, 88.66)*

88.38   **Other computerized axial tomography**
C.A.T. scan NOS
EXCLUDES   *C.A.T. scan of:*
abdomen (88.01)
head (87.03)
heart (87.41)
kidney (87.71)
thorax (87.41)
AHA: 3Q, '05, 13-14

88.39   **X-ray, other and unspecified**

✓4ᵗʰ **88.4   Arteriography using contrast material**
Note: The fourth-digit subclassification identifies the site to be viewed, not the site of injection.
INCLUDES   angiography of arteries
arterial puncture for injection of contrast material
radiography of arteries (by fluoroscopy)
retrograde arteriography
EXCLUDES   *arteriography using:*
radioisotopes or radionuclides (92.01-92.19)
ultrasound (88.71-88.79)
fluorescein angiography of eye (95.12)
DEF: Electromagnetic wave photography of arteries; with contrast.
AHA: N-D, '85, 14

[handwritten margin note: The same codes are assigned for digital subtraction angiography, which is the same procedure as standard angiography except for the manner in which the image is detected and stored.]

88.40   **Arteriography using contrast material, unspecified site**

88.41   **Arteriography of cerebral arteries**
Angiography of:
basilar artery
carotid (internal)
posterior cerebral circulation
vertebral artery
AHA: 1Q, '00, 16; 1Q, '99, 7; 1Q, '97, 3

88.42   **Aortography**
Arteriography of aorta and aortic arch
AHA: 1Q, '99, 17

88.43   **Arteriography of pulmonary arteries**

88.44   **Arteriography of other intrathoracic vessels**
EXCLUDES   *angiocardiography (88.50-88.58)*
arteriography of coronary arteries (88.55-88.57)

88.45   **Arteriography of renal arteries**

88.46   **Arteriography of placenta**   ♀
Placentogram using contrast material

88.47   **Arteriography of other intra-abdominal arteries**
AHA: ▶2Q, '09, 7;◀ 1Q, '00, 18; N-D, '87, 4

88.48   **Arteriography of femoral and other lower extremity arteries**
AHA: 2Q, '06, 23; 3Q, '03, 10; 1Q, '03, 17; 2Q, '96, 6; 2Q, '89, 17

88.49   **Arteriography of other specified sites**

✓4ᵗʰ **88.5   Angiocardiography using contrast material**
INCLUDES   arterial puncture and insertion of arterial catheter for injection of contrast material
cineangiocardiography
selective angiocardiography
Code also synchronous cardiac catheterization (37.21-37.23)
EXCLUDES   *angiography of pulmonary vessels (88.43, 88.62)*
DEF: Electromagnetic wave photography of heart and great vessels; with contrast.
AHA: 3Q, '08, 18; 3Q, '92, 10; M-J, '87, 11

88.50   **Angiocardiography, not otherwise specified**

88.51   **Angiocardiography of venae cavae**
Inferior vena cavography
Phlebography of vena cava (inferior) (superior)

88.52   **Angiocardiography of right heart structures**
Angiocardiography of:
pulmonary valve
right atrium
right ventricle (outflow tract)
EXCLUDES   *intra-operative fluorescence vascular angiography (88.59)*
that combined with left heart angiocardiography (88.54)
AHA: 1Q, '07, 16

88.53   **Angiocardiography of left heart structures**
Angiocardiography of:
aortic valve
left atrium
left ventricle (outflow tract)
EXCLUDES   *intra-operative fluorescence vascular angiography (88.59)*
that combined with right heart angiocardiography (88.54)
AHA: 1Q, '07, 11, 17; 4Q, '05, 71; 3Q, '05, 14; 1Q, '00, 20; 4Q, '88, 4

88.54   **Combined right and left heart angiocardiography**
EXCLUDES   *intra-operative fluorescence vascular angiography (88.59)*

88.55   **Coronary arteriography using a single catheter**
Coronary arteriography by Sones technique
Direct selective coronary arteriography using a single catheter
EXCLUDES   *intra-operative fluorescence vascular angiography (88.59)*
AHA: 2Q, '06, 25-26; 3Q, '02, 20

88.56   **Coronary arteriography using two catheters**
Coronary arteriography by:
Judkins technique
Ricketts and Abrams technique
Direct selective coronary arteriography using two catheters
EXCLUDES   *intra-operative fluorescence vascular angiography (88.59)*
AHA: 3Q, '06, 8; 1Q, '00, 20; 4Q, '88, 4

88.57   **Other and unspecified coronary arteriography**
Coronary arteriography NOS
EXCLUDES   *intra-operative fluorescence vascular angiography (88.59)*
AHA: 1Q, '07, 15; 2Q, '06, 25; 4Q, '05, 71; 3Q, '05, 14; 2Q, '05, 17; 1Q, '00, 21

88.58   **Negative-contrast cardiac roentgenography**
Cardiac roentgenography with injection of carbon dioxide

[right margin tab: Diagnostic and Therapeutic Procedures   88.26–88.58]

Allows for real-time evaluation of the coronary vasculature and cardiac chambers during CABG.

88.59   Intra-operative fluorescence vascular angiography
Intraoperative laser arteriogram (SPY)
SPY arteriogram
SPY arteriography

DEF: Coronary artery bypass grafting (CABG) procedure imaging technology; utilizes dye with high-speed digital infrared photography. Sequence is performed for each graft; provides information on graft patency, vessel size, blood flow velocities.

AHA: 4Q, '07, 121

✓4ᵗʰ **88.6   Phlebography**
Note: The fourth-digit subclassification (88.60-88.67) identifies the site to be viewed, not the site of injection.

INCLUDES   angiography of veins
radiography of veins (by fluoroscopy)
retrograde phlebography
venipuncture for injection of contrast material
venography using contrast material

EXCLUDES   *angiography using:*
radioisotopes or radionuclides (92.01-92.19)
ultrasound (88.71-88.79)
fluorescein angiography of eye (95.12)

DEF: Electromagnetic wave photography of veins; with contrast.

88.60   Phlebography using contrast material, unspecified site

88.61   Phlebography of veins of head and neck using contrast material

88.62   Phlebography of pulmonary veins using contrast material

88.63   Phlebography of other intrathoracic veins using contrast material
AHA: 3Q, '08, 18

88.64   Phlebography of the portal venous system using contrast material
Splenoportogram (by splenic arteriography)

88.65   Phlebography of other intra-abdominal veins using contrast material

88.66   Phlebography of femoral and other lower extremity veins using contrast material
AHA: 2Q, '06, 23

88.67   Phlebography of other specified sites using contrast material

88.68   Impedance phlebography

✓4ᵗʰ **88.7   Diagnostic ultrasound**
INCLUDES   echography
non-invasive ultrasound
ultrasonic angiography
ultrasonography

EXCLUDES   *intravascular imaging (adjunctive) (IVUS)*
(00.21-00.29)
therapeutic ultrasound (00.01-00.09)

DEF: Graphic recording of anatomical structures via high frequency, sound-wave imaging and computer graphics.

88.71   Diagnostic ultrasound of head and neck
Determination of midline shift of brain
Echoencephalography
EXCLUDES   *eye (95.13)*
AHA: 1Q, '02, 10; 1Q, '92, 11

88.72   Diagnostic ultrasound of heart
Echocardiography
Transesophageal echocardiography
EXCLUDES   *echocardiography of heart chambers (37.28)*
intracardiac echocardiography (ICE) (37.28)
intravascular (IVUS) imaging of coronary vessels (00.24)
AHA: 1Q, '07, 11; 3Q, '05, 14; 2Q, '05, 17; 4Q, '04, 121; 1Q, '04, 16; 1Q, '00, 20, 21; 1Q, '99, 6; 3Q, '98, 11
TIP: Assign also code 42.23 Esophagoscopy, NEC, when a transesophageal echocardiogram is performed.

88.73   Diagnostic ultrasound of other sites of thorax
Aortic arch
Breast   } ultrasonography
Lung

88.74   Diagnostic ultrasound of digestive system

88.75   Diagnostic ultrasound of urinary system

88.76   Diagnostic ultrasound of abdomen and retroperitoneum
AHA: 2Q, '99, 14

88.77   Diagnostic ultrasound of peripheral vascular system
Deep vein thrombosis ultrasonic scanning
EXCLUDES   *adjunct vascular system procedures (00.40-00.43)*
AHA: 4Q, '99, 17; 1Q, '99, 12; 1Q, '92, 11

88.78   Diagnostic ultrasound of gravid uterus ♀
Intrauterine cephalometry:
echo
ultrasonic
Placental localization by ultrasound
AHA: 4Q, '08, 125

88.79   Other diagnostic ultrasound
Ultrasonography of: Ultrasonography of:
multiple sites   total body
nongravid uterus

✓4ᵗʰ **88.8   Thermography**
DEF: Infrared photography to determine various body temperatures.

88.81   Cerebral thermography

88.82   Ocular thermography

88.83   Bone thermography
Osteoarticular thermography

88.84   Muscle thermography

88.85   Breast thermography

88.86   Blood vessel thermography
Deep vein thermography

88.89   Thermographay of other sites
Lymph gland thermography
Thermography NOS

✓4ᵗʰ **88.9   Other diagnostic imaging**

88.90   Diagnostic imaging, not elsewhere classified
AHA: 2Q, '06, 25-26

88.91   Magnetic resonance imaging of brain and brain stem
EXCLUDES   *intraoperative magnetic resonance imaging (88.96)*
▶*laser interstitial thermal therapy [LITT] of lesion or tissue of brain under guidance (17.61)*◀
real-time magnetic resonance imaging (88.96)

BI   Bilateral Procedure   NC   Non-covered Procedure   LC   Limited Coverage Procedure   ▶◀ Revised Text   ● New Code   ▲ Revised Code Title

186 – Volume 3 · October 2009   2010 ICD-9-CM

88.92 Magnetic resonance imaging of chest and myocardium
For evaluation of hilar and mediastinal lymphadenopathy
EXCLUDES ▶*laser interstitial thermal therapy [LITT] of lesion or tissue of breast under guidance (17.69)*
laser interstitial thermal therapy [LITT] of lesion or tissue of lung under guidance (17.69)◀

88.93 Magnetic resonance imaging of spinal canal
Spinal cord levels: Spinal cord
   cervical   Spine
   thoracic
   lumbar (lumbosacral)

88.94 Magnetic resonance imaging of musculoskeletal
Bone marrow blood supply
Extremities (upper) (lower)

88.95 Magnetic resonance imaging of pelvis, prostate, and bladder
EXCLUDES ▶*laser interstitial thermal therapy (LITT) of lesion or tissue of prostate under guidance (17.69)◀*

88.96 Other intraoperative magnetic resonance imaging
iMRI
Real-time magnetic resonance imaging
AHA: 4Q, '02, 111

88.97 Magnetic resonance imaging of other and unspecified sites
Abdomen
Eye orbit
Face
Neck
EXCLUDES ▶*laser interstitial thermal therapy (LITT) of lesion or tissue of other and unspecified site under guidance (17.69)◀*

88.98 Bone mineral density studies
Dual photon absorptiometry
Quantitative computed tomography (CT) studies
Radiographic densitometry
Single photon absorptiometry
DEF: Dual photon absorptiometry: Measurement of bone mineral density by comparing dissipation of emission from two separate photoelectric energy peaks.
DEF: Quantitative computed tomography (CT) studies: Computer assisted analysis of x-ray absorption through bone to determine density.
DEF: Radiographic densimetry: Measurement of bone mineral density by degree of bone radiopacity.
DEF: Single photon absorptiometry: Measurement of bone mineral density by degree of dissipation of emission from one photoelectric energy peaks emitted by gadolinium 153.

✓3rd **89 Interview, evaluation, consultation, and examination**

✓4th **89.0 Diagnostic interview, consultation, and evaluation**
EXCLUDES *psychiatric diagnostic interview (94.11-94.19)*

89.01 Interview and evaluation, described as brief
Abbreviated history and evaluation

89.02 Interview and evaluation, described as limited
Interval history and evaluation

89.03 Interview and evaluation, described as comprehensive
History and evaluation of new problem

89.04 Other interview and evaluation

89.05 Diagnostic interview and evaluation, not otherwise specified

89.06 Consultation, described as limited
Consultation on a single organ system

89.07 Consultation, described as comprehensive

89.08 Other consultation

89.09 Consulation, not otherwise specified

✓4th **89.1 Anatomic and physiologic measurements and manual examinations — nervous system and sense organs**
EXCLUDES *ear examination (95.41-95.49)*
eye examination (95.01-95.26)
the listed procedures when done as part of a general physical examination (89.7)

89.10 Intracarotid amobarbital test
Wada test
DEF: Amobarbital injections into internal carotid artery to induce hemiparalysis to determine the hemisphere that controls speech and language.

89.11 Tonometry
DEF: Pressure measurements inside eye.

89.12 Nasal function study
Rhinomanometry
DEF: Rhinomanometry: Measure of degree of nasal cavity obstruction.

89.13 Neurologic examination

89.14 Electroencephalogram
EXCLUDES *that with polysomnogram (89.17)*
DEF: Recording of electrical currents in brain via electrodes to detect epilepsy, lesions and other encephalopathies.
AHA: 3Q, '05, 12

89.15 Other nonoperative neurologic function tests
AHA: 3Q, '95, 5; 2Q, '91, 14; J-F, '87, 16; N-D, '84, 6

89.16 Transillumination of newborn skull
DEF: Light passed through newborn skull for diagnostic purposes.

89.17 Polysomnogram
Sleep recording
DEF: Graphic studies of sleep patterns.

89.18 Other sleep disorder function tests
Multiple sleep latency test [MSLT]

89.19 Video and radio-telemetered electroencephalographic monitoring
Radiographic   } EEG Monitoring
Video
AHA: 1Q, '92, 17; 2Q, '90, 27

✓4th **89.2 Anatomic and physiologic measurements and manual examinations — genitourinary system**
EXCLUDES *the listed procedures when done as part of a general physical examination (89.7)*
AHA: 1Q, '90, 27

89.21 Urinary manometry
Manometry through:
   indwelling ureteral catheter
   nephrostomy
   pyelostomy
   ureterostomy
DEF: Measurement of urinary pressure by:
   Indwelling urinary catheter: Semipermanent urinary catheter.
   Nephrostomy: Opening into pelvis of kidney.
   Pyelostomy: Opening in lower kidney.
   Ureterostomy: Opening into ureter.

89.22 Cystometrogram
DEF: Pressure recordings at various stages of bladder filling.

89.23 Urethral sphincter electromyogram

89.24 Uroflowmetry [UFR]
DEF: Continuous recording of urine flow.

89.25 Urethral pressure profile [UPP]

89.26 Gynecological examination   ♀
Pelvic examination

89.29 Other nonoperative genitourinary system measurements
Bioassay of urine   Urine chemistry
Renal clearance
AHA: N-D, '84, 6

✓3rd
✓4th Additional Digit Required   Valid OR Procedure   Non-OR Procedure   Adjunct Code
2010 ICD-9-CM   **October 2009 · Volume 3 – 187**

Diagnostic and Therapeutic Procedures

89.3–89.59

√4th **89.3 Other anatomic and physiologic measurements and manual examinations**

> EXCLUDES the listed procedures when done as part of a general physical examination (89.7)

89.31 Dental examination
Oral mucosal survey
Periodontal survey

89.32 Esophageal manometry
DEF: Measurement of esophageal fluid and gas pressures.
AHA: 3Q, '96, 13

89.33 Digital examination of enterostomy stoma
Digital examination of colostomy stoma

89.34 Digital examination of rectum

89.35 Transillumination of nasal sinuses

89.36 Manual examination of breast

89.37 Vital capacity determination
> EXCLUDES endoscopic pulmonary airway flow measurement (33.72)

DEF: Measurement of expelled gas volume after full inhalation.

89.38 Other nonoperative respiratory measurements
Plethysmography for measurement of respiratory function
Thoracic impedance plethysmography
> EXCLUDES endoscopic pulmonary airway flow measurement (33.72)

DEF: Plethysmography for measurement of respiratory function: Registering changes in respiratory function as noted in blood circulation.
AHA: S-O, '87, 6

89.39 Other nonoperative measurements and examinations
^{14}C-Urea breath test
Basal metabolic rate [BMR]
Gastric:
  analysis
  function NEC
> EXCLUDES body measurement (93.07)
> cardiac tests (89.41-89.69)
> fundus photography (95.11)
> limb length measurement (93.06)

AHA: 2Q, '01, 9; 3Q, '00, 9; 3Q, '96, 12; 1Q, '94, 18; N-D, '84, 6

TIP: Assign for Kinevac stimulation of the gallbladder, performed for analysis of function and examination of bile.

√4th **89.4 Cardiac stress tests, pacemaker and defibrillator checks**

89.41 Cardiovascular stress test using treadmill
AHA: 1Q, '88, 11

89.42 Masters' two-step stress test
AHA: 1Q, '88, 11

89.43 Cardiovascular stress test using bicycle ergometer
DEF: Electrocardiogram during exercise on bicycle with device capable of measuring muscular, metabolic and respiratory effects of exercise.
AHA: 1Q, '88, 11

89.44 Other cardiovascular stress test
Thallium stress test with or without transesophageal pacing

89.45 Artificial pacemaker rate check
Artificial pacemaker function check NOS
Bedside device check of pacemaker or cardiac resynchronization pacemaker [CRT-P]
Interrogation only without arrhythmia induction
> EXCLUDES catheter based invasive electrophysiologic testing (37.26)
> non-invasive programmed electrical stimulation [NIPS] (arrhythmia induction) (37.20)

AHA: 1Q, '02, 3

89.46 Artificial pacemaker artifact wave form check

89.47 Artificial pacemaker electrode impedance check

89.48 Artificial pacemaker voltage or amperage threshold check

89.49 Automatic implantable cardioverter/defibrillator (AICD) check
Bedside check of an AICD or cardiac resynchronization defibrillator [CRT-D]
Checking pacing thresholds of device
Interrogation only without arrhythmia induction
> EXCLUDES catheter based invasive electrophysiologic testing (37.26)
> non-invasive programmed electrical stimulation [NIPS] (arrhythmia induction) (37.20)

AHA: 4Q, '04, 136

√4th **89.5 Other nonoperative cardiac and vascular diagnostic procedures**
> EXCLUDES fetal EKG (75.32)

89.50 Ambulatory cardiac monitoring
Analog devices [Holter-type]
AHA: 4Q, '99, 21; 4Q, '91, 23

89.51 Rhythm electrocardiogram
Rhythm EKG (with one to three leads)

89.52 Electrocardiogram
ECG NOS
EKG (with 12 or more leads)
AHA: 1Q, '88, 11; S-O, '87, 6

89.53 Vectorcardiogram (with ECG)

89.54 Electrographic monitoring
Telemetry
> EXCLUDES ambulatory cardiac monitoring (89.50)
> electrographic monitoring during surgery — omit code

DEF: Evaluation of heart electrical activity by continuous screen monitoring.
DEF: Telemetry: Evaluation of heart electrical activity; with radio signals at distance from patient.
AHA: 4Q, '91, 23; 1Q, '88, 11

89.55 Phonocardiogram with ECG lead

89.56 Carotid pulse tracing with ECG lead
> EXCLUDES oculoplethysmography (89.58)

89.57 Apexcardiogram (with ECG lead)
AHA: J-F, '87, 16

89.58 Plethysmogram
Penile plethysmography with nerve stimulation
> EXCLUDES plethysmography (for):
> measurement of respiratory function (89.38)
> thoracic impedance (89.38)

DEF: Determination and recording of blood pressure variations present or passing through an organ.
AHA: S-O, '87, 7

89.59 Other nonoperative cardiac and vascular measurements
AHA: 3Q, '05, 21; 3Q, '03, 23; 2Q, '92, 12

Central Venous Pressure Monitoring

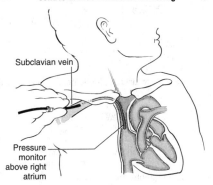

Subclavian vein

Pressure monitor above right atrium

√4ᵗʰ 89.6 Circulatory monitoring
> **EXCLUDES** *electrocardiographic monitoring during surgery — omit code*
> *implantation or replacement of subcutaneous device for intracardiac hemodynamic monitoring (00.57)*
> *insertion or replacement of implantable pressure sensor (lead) for intracardiac hemodynamic monitoring (00.56)*
>
> **AHA:** M-J, '87, 11

89.60 Continuous intra-arterial blood gas monitoring
> Insertion of blood gas monitoring system and continuous monitoring of blood gases through an intra-arterial sensor
>
> **AHA:** 4Q, '02, 111

89.61 Systemic arterial pressure monitoring
> **EXCLUDES** *intra-aneurysm sac pressure monitoring (intraoperative) (00.58)*
> *intravascular pressure measurement of intrathoracic arteries (00.67)*
> *intravascular pressure measurement of peripheral arteries (00.68)*

89.62 Central venous pressure monitoring
> **EXCLUDES** *intravascular pressure measurement, other specified and unspecified vessels (00.69)*

89.63 Pulmonary artery pressure monitoring
> **EXCLUDES** *pulmonary artery wedge monitoring (89.64)*

89.64 Pulmonary artery wedge monitoring
> Pulmonary capillary wedge [PCW] monitoring
> Swan-Ganz catheterization
>
> **DEF:** Monitoring pulmonary artery pressure via catheter inserted through right lower and upper heart chambers into pulmonary artery and advancing the balloon-tip to wedge it in the distal pulmonary artery branch.

89.65 Measurement of systemic arterial blood gases
> **EXCLUDES** *continuous intra-arterial blood gas monitoring (89.60)*

89.66 Measurement of mixed venous blood gases

89.67 Monitoring of cardiac output by oxygen consumption technique
> Fick method
>
> **DEF:** Fick method: Indirect measure of cardiac output through blood volume flow over pulmonary capillaries; determines oxygen absorption by measurement of arterial oxygen content versus venous oxygen content.

89.68 Monitoring of cardiac output by other technique
> Cardiac output monitor by thermodilution indicator
>
> **DEF:** Cardiac output monitor by thermodilution indicator: Injection of ice cold dextrose solution into right lower heart chamber; temperature sensitive catheter monitors disappearance from beat to beat to measure expelled blood volume.

89.69 Monitoring of coronary blood flow
> Coronary blood flow monitoring by coincidence counting technique
>
> **EXCLUDES** *intravascular pressure measurement of coronary arteries (00.59)*

89.7 General physical examination

89.8 Autopsy

√3ʳᵈ 90 Microscopic examination - I
> The following fourth-digit subclassification is for use with categories in section 90 to identify type of examination:
> 1 bacterial smear
> 2 culture
> 3 culture and sensitivity
> 4 parasitology
> 5 toxicology
> 6 cell block and Papanicolaou smear
> 9 other microscopic examination

§ **√4ᵗʰ 90.0 Microscopic examination of specimen from nervous**
[1-6,9] **system and of spinal fluid**

§ **√4ᵗʰ 90.1 Microscopic examination of specimen from endocrine**
[1-6,9] **gland, not elsewhere classified**

§ **√4ᵗʰ 90.2 Microscopic examination of specimen from eye**
[1-6,9]

§ **√4ᵗʰ 90.3 Microscopic examination of specimen from ear, nose,**
[1-6,9] **throat, and larynx**

§ **√4ᵗʰ 90.4 Microscopic examination of specimen from trachea,**
[1-6,9] **bronchus, pleura, lung, and other thoracic specimen, and of sputum**

§ **√4ᵗʰ 90.5 Microscopic examination of blood**
[1-6,9]

§ **√4ᵗʰ 90.6 Microscopic examination of specimen from spleen and of**
[1-6,9] **bone marrow**

§ **√4ᵗʰ 90.7 Microscopic examination of specimen from lymph node**
[1-6,9] **and of lymph**

§ **√4ᵗʰ 90.8 Microscopic examination of specimen from upper**
[1-6,9] **gastrointestinal tract and of vomitus**

§ **√4ᵗʰ 90.9 Microscopic examination of specimen from lower**
[1-6,9] **gastrointestinal tract and of stool**

√3ʳᵈ 91 Microscopic examination - II
> The following fourth-digit subclassification is for use with categories in section 91 to identify type of examination:
> 1 bacterial smear
> 2 culture
> 3 culture and sensitivity
> 4 parasitology
> 5 toxicology
> 6 cell block and Papanicolaou smear
> 9 other microscopic examination

§ **√4ᵗʰ 91.0 Microscopic examination of specimen from liver, biliary**
[1-6,9] **tract, and pancreas**

§ **√4ᵗʰ 91.1 Microscopic examination of peritoneal and**
[1-6,9] **retroperitoneal specimen**

§ **√4ᵗʰ 91.2 Microscopic examination of specimen from kidney,**
[1-6,9] **ureter, perirenal and periureteral tissue**

§ **√4ᵗʰ 91.3 Microscopic examination of specimen from bladder,**
[1-6,9] **urethra, prostate, seminal vesicle, perivesical tissue, and of urine and semen**

§ **√4ᵗʰ 91.4 Microscopic examination of specimen from** ♀
[1-6,9] **female genital tract**
> Amnionic sac
> Fetus

---

§   Requires fourth digit. Valid digits are in [brackets] under each code. See appropriate category for codes and definitions.

√3ʳᵈ
√4ᵗʰ **Additional Digit Required**   **Valid OR Procedure**   **Non-OR Procedure**   **Adjunct Code**

Diagnostic and Therapeutic Procedures

91.5–92.31

§ ✓4ᵗʰ **91.5 Microscopic examination of specimen from** [1-6,9] **musculoskeletal system and of joint fluid**
Microscopic examination of:
bone
bursa
cartilage
fascia
ligament
muscle
synovial membrane
tendon

§ ✓4ᵗʰ **91.6 Microscopic examination of specimen from skin and** [1-6,9] **other integument**
Microscopic examination of:
hair
nails
skin
EXCLUDES *mucous membrane — code to organ site*
that of operative wound (91.71-91.79)

§ ✓4ᵗʰ **91.7 Microscopic examination of specimen from operative** [1-6,9] **wound**

§ ✓4ᵗʰ **91.8 Microscopic examination of specimen from other site** [1-6,9]

§ ✓4ᵗʰ **91.9 Microscopic examination of specimen from unspecified** [1-6,9] **site**

✓3ʳᵈ **92 Nuclear medicine**

✓4ᵗʰ **92.0 Radioisotope scan and function study**

92.01 Thyroid scan and radioisotope function studies
Iodine-131 uptake
Protein-bound iodine
Radio-iodine uptake

92.02 Liver scan and radioisotope function study

92.03 Renal scan and radioisotope function study
Renal clearance study

92.04 Gastrointestinal scan and radioisotope function study
Radio-cobalt B₁₂ Schilling test
Radio-iodinated triolein study

92.05 Cardiovascular and hematopoietic scan and radioisotope function study
Bone marrow
Cardiac output
Circulation time
Radionuclide cardiac ventriculogram
Spleen
⎫
⎬ scan or function
⎭ study

AHA: 2Q, '92, 7; 1Q, '88, 11

92.09 Other radioisotope function studies

✓4ᵗʰ **92.1 Other radioisotope scan**

92.11 Cerebral scan
Pituitary

92.12 Scan of other sites of head
EXCLUDES *eye (95.16)*

92.13 Parathyroid scan

92.14 Bone scan

92.15 Pulmonary scan

92.16 Scan of lymphatic system

92.17 Placental scan ♀

92.18 Total body scan

92.19 Scan of other sites

✓4ᵗʰ **92.2 Therapeutic radiology and nuclear medicine**
EXCLUDES *that for:*
ablation of pituitary gland (07.64-07.69)
destruction of chorioretinal lesion
(14.26-14.27)
DEF: Radiation and nuclear isotope treatment of diseased tissue.
AHA: 3Q, '92, 5

92.20 Infusion of liquid brachytherapy radioisotope
I-125 radioisotope
Intracavitary brachytherapy
EXCLUDES *removal of radioisotope*
AHA: 4Q, '05, 117-118
TIP: Refer to codes 01.26 and 01.27 for placement or removal of balloon catheter used for liquid brachytherapy radioisotope infusion.

92.21 Superficial radiation
Contact radiation [up to 150 KVP]

92.22 Orthovoltage radiation
Deep radiation [200-300 KVP]

92.23 Radioisotopic teleradiotherapy
Teleradiotherapy using:
cobalt-60
iodine-125
radioactive cesium

92.24 Teleradiotherapy using photons
Megavoltage NOS
Supervoltage NOS
Use of:
Betatron
linear accelerator

92.25 Teleradiotherapy using electrons
Beta particles
EXCLUDES *intra-operative electron radiation*
therapy (92.41)

92.26 Teleradiotherapy of other particulate radiation
Neutrons
Protons NOS

92.27 Implantation or insertion of radioactive elements
Intravascular brachytherapy
Code also incision of site
EXCLUDES *infusion of liquid brachytherapy*
radioisotope (92.20)
AHA: 1Q, '04, 3-4; 1Q, '00, 11, 12; 3Q, '94, 11; 1Q, '88, 4

92.28 Injection or instillation of radioisotopes
Injection or infusion of radioimmunoconjugate
Intracavitary injection or instillation
Intravenous injection or instillation
Iodine-131 [I-131] tositumomab
Radioimmunotherapy
Ytrium-90 [Y-90] ibritumomab tiuxetan
EXCLUDES *infusion of liquid brachytherapy*
radioisotope (92.20)

92.29 Other radiotherapeutic procedure
AHA: 3Q, '06, 14-15

✓4ᵗʰ **92.3 Stereotactic radiosurgery**
Code also stereotactic head frame application (93.59)
EXCLUDES *stereotactic biopsy*
DEF: Ablation of deep intracranial lesions; single procedure; placement of head frame for 3-D analysis of lesion, followed by radiation treatment from helmet attached to frame.
AHA: 4Q, '98, 79; 4Q, '95, 70
TIP: Do not assign when stereotactic technique is used to obtain the coordinates for the exact location of a brain tumor, after which open craniotomy is performed. See instead subcategory 01.5.

92.30 Stereotactic radiosurgery, not otherwise specified

92.31 Single source photon radiosurgery
High energy x-rays
Linear accelerator (LINAC)

---

§ Requires fourth digit. Valid digits are in [brackets] under each code. See category 91 for codes and definitions.

| **B1** Bilateral Procedure | **NC** Non-covered Procedure | **LC** Limited Coverage Procedure | ▶◀ Revised Text | ● New Code | ▲ Revised Code Title |

92.32　Multi-source photon radiosurgery
　　　Cobalt 60 radiation
　　　Gamma irradiation
　　　AHA: 4Q, '04, 113

92.33　Particulate radiosurgery
　　　Particle beam radiation (cyclotron)
　　　Proton accelerator

92.39　Stereotactic radiosurgery, not elsewhere classified

✓4ᵗʰ **92.4　Intra-operative radiation procedures**

92.41　Intra-operative electron radiation therapy
　　　IOERT
　　　That using a mobile linear accelerator
　　　DEF: Use of a mobile linear accelerator unit that delivers precision electron radiation beam radiation to highly focused anatomic sites, protecting the normal surrounding tissues from exposure.
　　　AHA: 4Q, '07, 122

✓3ʳᵈ **93　Physical therapy, respiratory therapy, rehabilitation, and related procedures**

✓4ᵗʰ **93.0　Diagnostic physical therapy**
　　　AHA: N-D, '86, 7

93.01　Functional evaluation

93.02　Orthotic evaluation

93.03　Prosthetic evaluation

93.04　Manual testing of muscle function
　　　AHA: J-F, '87, 16

93.05　Range of motion testing
　　　AHA: J-F, '87, 16

93.06　Measurement of limb length

93.07　Body measurement
　　　Girth measurement
　　　Measurement of skull circumference

93.08　Electromyography
　　　EXCLUDES　　*eye EMG (95.25)*
　　　　　　　　that with polysomnogram (89.17)
　　　　　　　　urethral sphincter EMG (89.23)
　　　DEF: Graphic recording of electrical activity of muscle.
　　　AHA: J-F, '87, 16

93.09　Other diagnostic physical therapy procedure

✓4ᵗʰ **93.1　Physical therapy exercises**
　　　AHA: J-F, '87, 16; N-D, '86, 7

93.11　Assisting exercise
　　　EXCLUDES　　*assisted exercise in pool (93.31)*

93.12　Other active musculoskeletal exercise

93.13　Resistive exercise

93.14　Training in joint movements

93.15　Mobilization of spine

93.16　Mobilization of other joints
　　　EXCLUDES　　*manipulation of temporomandibular joint (76.95)*

93.17　Other passive musculoskeletal exercise

93.18　Breathing exercise

93.19　Exercise, not elsewhere classified

✓4ᵗʰ **93.2　Other physical therapy musculoskeletal manipulation**
　　　AHA: N-D, '86, 7

93.21　Manual and mechanical traction
　　　EXCLUDES　　*skeletal traction (93.43-93.44)*
　　　　　　　　skin traction (93.45-93.46)
　　　　　　　　spinal traction (93.41-93.42)

93.22　Ambulation and gait training

93.23　Fitting of orthotic device

93.24　Training in use of prosthetic or orthotic device
　　　Training in crutch walking

93.25　Forced extension of limb

93.26　Manual rupture of joint adhesions
　　　DEF: Therapeutic application of force to rupture adhesions restricting movement.

93.27　Stretching of muscle or tendon

93.28　Stretching of fascia

93.29　Other forcible correction of deformity
　　　AHA: N-D, '85, 11

✓4ᵗʰ **93.3　Other physical therapy therapeutic procedures**

93.31　Assisted exercise in pool

93.32　Whirlpool treatment

93.33　Other hydrotherapy

93.34　Diathermy

93.35　Other heat therapy
　　　Acupuncture with smouldering moxa
　　　Hot packs
　　　Hyperthermia NEC
　　　Infrared irradiation
　　　Moxibustion
　　　Paraffin bath
　　　EXCLUDES　　*hyperthermia for treatment of cancer (99.85)*
　　　DEF: Moxibustion: Igniting moxa, a Chinese plant, for counterirritation of skin.
　　　DEF: Paraffin bath: Hot wax treatment.

93.36　Cardiac retraining
　　　DEF: Cardiac rehabilitation regimen following myocardial infarction or coronary bypass graft procedure.

93.37　Prenatal training
　　　Training for natural childbirth

93.38　Combined physical therapy without mention of the components

93.39　Other physical therapy
　　　AHA: 2Q, '05, 6; 4Q, '03, 105 -106, 108-110; 3Q, '97, 12; 3Q, '91, 15

✓4ᵗʰ **93.4　Skeletal traction and other traction**

93.41　Spinal traction using skull device
　　　Traction using:
　　　　caliper tongs
　　　　Crutchfield tongs
　　　　halo device
　　　　Vinke tongs
　　　EXCLUDES　　*insertion of tongs or halo traction device (02.94)*
　　　DEF: Applying device to head to exert pulling force on spine.
　　　AHA: 3Q, '01, 8; 3Q, '96, 14; 2Q, '94, 3

93.42　Other spinal traction
　　　Cotrel's traction
　　　EXCLUDES　　*cervical collar (93.52)*
　　　DEF: Pulling force exerted on spine without skull device.

93.43　Intermittent skeletal traction

93.44　Other skeletal traction
　　　Bryant's ⎤
　　　Dunlop's ⎟ traction
　　　Lyman Smith ⎟
　　　Russell's ⎦

93.45　Thomas' splint traction
　　　DEF: Thomas splint: Placement of ring around thigh, attached to rods running length of leg for therapeutic purposes.

93.46　Other skin traction of limbs
　　　Adhesive tape traction
　　　Boot traction
　　　Buck's traction
　　　Gallows traction

✓4ᵗʰ **93.5　Other immobilization, pressure, and attention to wound**
　　　EXCLUDES　　*external fixator device (84.71-84.73)*
　　　　　　　　wound cleansing (96.58-96.59)

93.51　Application of plaster jacket
　　　EXCLUDES　　*Minerva jacket (93.52)*

Diagnostic and Therapeutic Procedures

93.52–93.95

93.52   **Application of neck support**
Application of:
    cervical collar
    Minerva jacket
    molded neck support

93.53   **Application of other cast**

93.54   **Application of splint**
Plaster splint
Tray splint
EXCLUDES   *periodontal splint (24.7)*

93.55   **Dental wiring**
EXCLUDES   *that for orthodontia (24.7)*

93.56   **Application of pressure dressing**
Application of:
    Gibney bandage
    Robert Jones' bandage
    Shanz dressing

93.57   **Application of other wound dressing**
Porcine wound dressing
AHA: 3Q, '02, 23

93.58   **Application of pressure trousers**
Application of:
    anti-shock trousers
    MAST trousers
    vasopneumatic device
AHA: 3Q, '96, 13

93.59   **Other immobilization, pressure, and attention to wound**
Elastic stockings
Electronic gaiter
Intermittent pressure device
Oxygenation of wound (hyperbaric)
Stereotactic head frame application
Strapping (non-traction)
Velpeau dressing
AHA: 3Q, '99, 7; 1Q, '99, 12, 13; 1Q, '91, 11; 1Q, '89, 12

☑4ᵗʰ **93.6**   **Osteopathic manipulative treatment**

93.61   **Osteopathic manipulative treatment for general mobilization**
General articulatory treatment

93.62   **Osteopathic manipulative treatment using high-velocity, low-amplitude forces**
Thrusting forces

93.63   **Osteopathic manipulative treatment using low-velocity, high-amplitude forces**
Springing forces

93.64   **Osteopathic manipulative treatment using isotonic, isometric forces**

93.65   **Osteopathic manipulative treatment using indirect forces**

93.66   **Osteopathic manipulative treatment to move tissue fluids**
Lymphatic pump

93.67   **Other specified osteopathic manipulative treatment**

☑4ᵗʰ **93.7**   **Speech and reading rehabilitation and rehabilitation of the blind**

93.71   **Dyslexia training**

93.72   **Dysphasia training**
DEF: Speech training to coordinate and arrange words in proper sequence.

93.73   **Esophageal speech training**
DEF: Speech training after voice box removal; sound is produced by vibration of air column in esophagus against the cricopharangeal sphincter.

93.74   **Speech defect training**

93.75   **Other speech training and therapy**
AHA: 4Q, '03, 105, 109; 4Q, '97, 36; 3Q, '97, 12

93.76   **Training in use of lead dog for the blind**

93.77   **Training in braille or Moon**

93.78   **Other rehabilitation for the blind**

☑4ᵗʰ **93.8**   **Other rehabilitation therapy**

93.81   **Recreational therapy**
Diversional therapy
Play therapy
EXCLUDES   *play psychotherapy (94.36)*

93.82   **Educational therapy**
Education of bed-bound children
Special schooling for the handicapped

93.83   **Occupational therapy**
Daily living activities therapy
EXCLUDES   *training in activities of daily living for the blind (93.78)*
AHA: 2Q, '05, 6; 4Q, '03, 105-106, 108, 110; 3Q, '97, 12

93.84   **Music therapy**

93.85   **Vocational rehabilitation**
Sheltered employment
Vocational:
    assessment
    retraining
    training

93.89   **Rehabilitation, not elsewhere classified**
AHA: 2Q, '05, 6

☑4ᵗʰ **93.9**   **Respiratory therapy**
EXCLUDES   *insertion of airway (96.01-96.05)*
other continuous invasive (through endotracheal tube or tracheostomy) mechanical ventilation (96.70-96.72)

93.90   **Non-invasive mechanical ventilation**
Note: Patients admitted on *non-invasive* mechanical ventilation that subsequently require *invasive* mechanical ventilation; code both types of mechanical ventilation

Bi-level airway pressure
BiPAP without (delivery through) endotracheal tube or tracheostomy
CPAP without (delivery through) endotracheal tube or tracheostomy
Mechanical ventilation NOS
Non-invasive positive pressure (NIPPV)
Non-invasive PPV
NPPV
That delivered by non-invasive interface:
    face mask
    nasal mask
    nasal pillow
    oral mouthpiece
    oronasal mask
EXCLUDES   *invasive (through endotracheal tube or tracheostomy) continuous mechanical ventilation (96.70-96.72)*
DEF: Noninvasive ventilation support system that augments the ability to breathe spontaneously without the insertion of an endotracheal tube or tracheostomy.
AHA: ▶4Q, '08, 187-189;◀ 1Q, '08, 8-9; 3Q, '04, 3; 1Q, '02, 12, 13; 3Q, '98, 14; 4Q, '91, 21

93.91   **Intermittent positive pressure breathing [IPPB]**
AHA: 4Q, '91, 21

93.93   **Nonmechanical methods of resuscitation**
Artificial respiration
Manual resuscitation
Mouth-to-mouth resuscitition
AHA: 2Q, '03, 17

93.94   **Respiratory medication administered by nebulizer**
Mist therapy

93.95   **Hyperbaric oxygenation**
EXCLUDES   *oxygenation of wound (93.59)*

BI Bilateral Procedure	**NC** Non-covered Procedure	**LC** Limited Coverage Procedure	▶◀ Revised Text	● New Code ▲ Revised Code Title

93.96 Other oxygen enrichment
Catalytic oxygen therapy
Cytoreductive effect
Oxygenators
Oxygen therapy
EXCLUDES *oxygenation of wound (93.59)*
SuperSaturated oxygen therapy (00.49)

93.97 Decompression chamber

93.98 Other control of atmospheric pressure and composition
Antigen-free air conditioning
Helium therapy
EXCLUDES *inhaled nitric oxide therapy (INO) (00.12)*
AHA: 1Q, '02, 14

93.99 Other respiratory procedures
Continuous negative pressure ventilation [CNP]
Postural drainage
AHA: 4Q, '03, 108; 3Q, '99, 11; 4Q, '91, 22

√3rd 94 Procedures related to the psyche

√4th 94.0 Psychologic evaluation and testing

94.01 Administration of intelligence test
Administration of:
Stanford-Binet
Wechsler Adult Intelligence Scale
Wechsler Intelligence Scale for Children

94.02 Administration of psychologic test
Administration of:
Bender Visual-Motor Gestalt Test
Benton Visual Retention Test
Minnesota Multiphasic Personality Inventory
Wechsler Memory Scale

94.03 Character analysis

94.08 Other psychologic evaluation and testing

94.09 Psychologic mental status determination, not otherwise specified

√4th 94.1 Psychiatric interviews, consultations, and evaluations

94.11 Psychiatric mental status determination
Clinical psychiatric mental status determination
Evaluation for criminal responsibility
Evaluation for testimentary capacity
Medicolegal mental status determination
Mental status determination NOS

94.12 Routine psychiatric visit, not otherwise specified

94.13 Psychiatric commitment evaluation
Pre-commitment interview

94.19 Other psychiatric interview and evaluation
Follow-up psychiatric interview NOS

√4th 94.2 Psychiatric somatotherapy
DEF: Biological treatment of mental disorders.

94.21 Narcoanalysis
Narcosynthesis

94.22 Lithium therapy

94.23 Neuroleptic therapy

94.24 Chemical shock therapy

94.25 Other psychiatric drug therapy
AHA: S-O, '86, 4

94.26 Subconvulsive electroshock therapy

94.27 Other electroshock therapy
Electroconvulsive therapy (ECT)
EST

94.29 Other psychiatric somatotherapy

√4th 94.3 Individual psychotherapy

94.31 Psychoanalysis

94.32 Hypnotherapy
Hypnodrome
Hypnosis

94.33 Behavior therapy
Aversion therapy
Behavior modification
Desensitization therapy
Relaxation training
Token economy
Extinction therapy

94.34 Individual therapy for psychosexual dysfunction
EXCLUDES *that performed in group setting (94.41)*

94.35 Crisis intervention

94.36 Play psychotherapy

94.37 Exploratory verbal psychotherapy

94.38 Supportive verbal psychotherapy

94.39 Other individual psychotherapy
Biofeedback

√4th 94.4 Other psychotherapy and counseling

94.41 Group therapy for psychosexual dysfunction

94.42 Family therapy

94.43 Psychodrama

94.44 Other group therapy

94.45 Drug addiction counseling

94.46 Alcoholism counseling

94.49 Other counseling

√4th 94.5 Referral for psychologic rehabilitation

94.51 Referral for psychotherapy

94.52 Referral for psychiatric aftercare
That in:
halfway house
outpatient (clinic) facility

94.53 Referral for alcoholism rehabilitation

94.54 Referral for drug addiction rehabilitation

94.55 Referral for vocational rehabilitation

94.59 Referral for other psychologic rehabilitation

√4th 94.6 Alcohol and drug rehabilitation and detoxification
AHA: 2Q, '91, 12

94.61 Alcohol rehabilitation
DEF: Program designed to restore social and physical functioning, free of the dependence of alcohol.

94.62 Alcohol detoxification
DEF: Treatment of physical symptoms during withdrawal from alcohol dependence.

94.63 Alcohol rehabilitation and detoxification

94.64 Drug rehabilitation
DEF: Program designed to restore social and physical functioning, free of the dependence of drugs.

94.65 Drug detoxification
DEF: Treatment of physical symptoms during withdrawal from drug dependence.

94.66 Drug rehabilitation and detoxification

94.67 Combined alcohol and drug rehabilitation

94.68 Combined alcohol and drug detoxification

94.69 Combined alcohol and drug rehabilitation and detoxification

√3rd 95 Ophthalmologic and otologic diagnosis and treatment

√4th 95.0 General and subjective eye examination

95.01 Limited eye examination
Eye examination with prescription of spectacles

95.02 Comprehensive eye examination
Eye examination covering all aspects of the visual system

95.03 Extended ophthalmologic work-up
Examination (for):
glaucoma
neuro-ophthalmology
retinal disease

95.04 Eye examination under anesthesia
Code also type of examination

Diagnostic and Therapeutic Procedures

95.05–96.25

95.05   **Visual field study**

95.06   **Color vision study**

95.07   **Dark adaptation study**
> **DEF:** Exam of eye's adaption to dark.

95.09   **Eye examination, not otherwise specified**
> Vision check NOS

√4th **95.1**   **Examinations of form and structure of eye**

95.11   **Fundus photography**

95.12   **Fluorescein angiography or angioscopy of eye**

95.13   **Ultrasound study of eye**

95.14   **X-ray study of eye**

95.15   **Ocular motility study**

95.16   **P_{32} and other tracer studies of eye**

√4th **95.2**   **Objective functional tests of eye**
> **EXCLUDES**   *that with polysomnogram (89.17)*

95.21   **Electroretinogram [ERG]**

95.22   **Electro-oculogram [EOG]**

95.23   **Visual evoked potential [VEP]**
> **DEF:** Measuring and recording evoked visual responses of body and senses.

95.24   **Electronystagmogram [ENG]**
> **DEF:** Monitoring of brain waves to record induced and spontaneous eye movements.

95.25   **Electromyogram of eye [EMG]**

95.26   **Tonography, provocative tests, and other glaucoma testing**

√4th **95.3**   **Special vision services**

95.31   **Fitting and dispensing of spectacles**

95.32   **Prescription, fitting, and dispensing of contact lens**

95.33   **Dispensing of other low vision aids**

95.34   **Ocular prosthetics**

95.35   **Orthoptic training**

95.36   **Ophthalmologic counselling and instruction**
> Counselling in:
> adaptation to visual loss
> use of low vision aids

√4th **95.4**   **Nonoperative procedures related to hearing**

95.41   **Audiometry**
> Békésy 5-tone audiometry
> Impedance audiometry
> Stapedial reflex response
> Subjective audiometry
> Tympanogram

95.42   **Clinical test of hearing**
> Tuning fork test
> Whispered speech test

95.43   **Audiological evaluation**
> Audiological evaluation by:
> Bárány noise machine
> blindfold test
> delayed feedback
> masking
> Weber lateralization

95.44   **Clinical vestibular function tests**
> Thermal test of vestibular function

95.45   **Rotation tests**
> Bárány chair
> **DEF:** Irrigation of ear canal with warm or cold water to evaluate vestibular function.

95.46   **Other auditory and vestibular function tests**

95.47   **Hearing examination, not otherwise specified**

95.48   **Fitting of hearing aid**
> **EXCLUDES**   *implantation of electromagnetic hearing device (20.95)*
> **AHA:** 4Q, '89, 5

95.49   **Other nonoperative procedures related to hearing**
> Adjustment (external components) of cochlear prosthetic device

√3rd **96**   **Nonoperative intubation and irrigation**

√4th **96.0**   **Nonoperative intubation of gastrointestinal and respiratory tracts**

96.01   **Insertion of nasopharyngeal airway**

96.02   **Insertion of oropharyngeal airway**

96.03   **Insertion of esophageal obturator airway**

96.04   **Insertion of endotracheal tube**
> **AHA:** ▶2Q, '09, 11;◀ 1Q, '07, 11; 2Q, '06, 8; 4Q, '05, 88; 3Q, '05, 10; 2Q, '05, 19

96.05   **Other intubation of respiratory tract**
> **EXCLUDES**   *endoscopic insertion or replacement of bronchial device or substance (33.71, 33.79)*
> **AHA:** 1Q, '97, 14

96.06   **Insertion of Sengstaken tube**
> Esophageal tamponade
> **DEF:** Insertion of Sengstaken tube: Nonsurgical emergency measure to stop esophageal bleeding using compression exerted by inflated balloons; additional tube ports to aspirate blood and clots.

96.07   **Insertion of other (naso-) gastric tube**
> Intubation for decompression
> **EXCLUDES**   *that for enteral infusion of nutritional substance (96.6)*
> **AHA:** 4Q, '08, 139

96.08   **Insertion of (naso-) intestinal tube**
> Miller-Abbott tube (for decompression)

96.09   **Insertion of rectal tube**
> Replacement of rectal tube

√4th **96.1**   **Other nonoperative insertion**
> **EXCLUDES**   *nasolacrimal intubation (09.44)*

96.11   **Packing of external auditory canal**

96.14   **Vaginal packing**   ♀

96.15   **Insertion of vaginal mold**   ♀

96.16   **Other vaginal dilation**   ♀

96.17   **Insertion of vaginal diaphragm**   ♀

96.18   **Insertion of other vaginal pessary**   ♀

96.19   **Rectal packing**

√4th **96.2**   **Nonoperative dilation and manipulation**

96.21   **Dilation of frontonasal duct**

96.22   **Dilation of rectum**

96.23   **Dilation of anal sphincter**

96.24   **Dilation and manipulation of enterostomy stoma**

96.25   **Therapeutic distention of bladder**
> Intermittent distention of bladder

Endotracheal Intubation

Laryngoscope

Larynx

Trachea

Balloon inflated above carina

 Bilateral Procedure   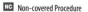 Non-covered Procedure   **LC** Limited Coverage Procedure   ▶◀ Revised Text   ● New Code   ▲ Revised Code Title

194 – Volume 3 · October 2009   **2010 ICD-9-CM**

96.26   Manual reduction of rectal prolapse

96.27   Manual reduction of hernia

96.28   Manual reduction of enterostomy prolapse
> AHA: N-D, '87, 11

96.29   Reduction of intussusception of alimentary tract
> With:
>   fluoroscopy
>   ionizing radiation enema
>   ultrasonography guidance
> Hydrostatic reduction
> Pneumatic reduction
> **EXCLUDES**   *intra-abdominal manipulation of intestine, not otherwise specified (46.80)*
>
> AHA: 4Q, '98, 82

√4th   **96.3**   **Nonoperative alimentary tract irrigation, cleaning, and local instillation**

96.31   Gastric cooling
> Gastric hypothermia
> **DEF:** Reduction of internal stomach temperature.

96.32   Gastric freezing

96.33   Gastric lavage

96.34   Other irrigation of (naso-)gastric tube

96.35   Gastric gavage
> **DEF:** Food forced into stomach.

96.36   Irrigation of gastrostomy or enterostomy

96.37   Proctoclysis
> **DEF:** Slow introduction of large amounts of fluids into lower large intestine.

96.38   Removal of impacted feces
> Removal of impaction:
>   by flushing manually

96.39   Other transanal enema
> Rectal irrigation
> **EXCLUDES**   *reduction of intussusception of alimentary tract by ionizing radiation enema (96.29)*

√4th   **96.4**   **Nonoperative irrigation, cleaning, and local instillation of other digestive and genitourinary organs**

96.41   Irrigation of cholecystostomy and other biliary tube

96.42   Irrigation of pancreatic tube

96.43   Digestive tract instillation, except gastric gavage

96.44   Vaginal douche   ♀

96.45   Irrigation of nephrostomy and pyelostomy

96.46   Irrigation of ureterostomy and ureteral catheter

96.47   Irrigation of cystostomy

96.48   Irrigation of other indwelling urinary catheter

96.49   Other genitourinary instillation
> Insertion of prostaglandin suppository
> AHA: 1Q, '01, 5

√4th   **96.5**   **Other nonoperative irrigation and cleaning**

96.51   Irrigation of eye
> Irrigation of cornea
> **EXCLUDES**   *irrigation with removal of foreign body (98.21)*

96.52   Irrigation of ear
> Irrigation with removal of cerumen

96.53   Irrigation of nasal passages

96.54   Dental scaling, polishing, and debridement
> Dental prophylaxis   Plaque removal

96.55   Tracheostomy toilette

96.56   Other lavage of bronchus and trachea
> **EXCLUDES**   *diagnostic bronchoalveolar lavage (BAL) (33.24)*
>   *whole lung lavage (33.99)*
> AHA: 3Q, '02, 18

96.57   Irrigation of vascular catheter
> AHA: 3Q, '93, 5

96.58   Irrigation of wound catheter

96.59   Other irrigation of wound
> Wound cleaning NOS
> **EXCLUDES**   *debridement (86.22, 86.27-86.28)*
> AHA: S-O, '85, 7

96.6   **Enteral infusion of concentrated-nutritional substances**

√4th   **96.7**   **Other continuous invasive mechanical ventilation**
> BiPAP delivered through endotracheal tube or tracheostomy (invasive interface)
> CPAP delivered through endotracheal tube or tracheostomy (invasive interface)
> Endotracheal respiratory assistance
> Invasive positive pressure ventilation [IPPV]
> Mechanical ventilation through invasive interface
> That by tracheostomy
> Weaning of an intubated (endotracheal tube) patient
> Code also any associated:
>   endotracheal tube insertion (96.04)
>   tracheostomy (31.1-31.29)
> **EXCLUDES**   *continuous negative pressure ventilation [CNP] (iron lung) (cuirass) (93.99)*
>   *intermittent positive pressure breathing [IPPB] (93.91)*
>   *non-invasive bi-level positive airway pressure [BiPAP] (93.90)*
>   *non-invasive continuous positive airway pressure [CPAP] (93.90)*
>   *non-invasive positive pressure (NIPPV) (93.90)*
>   *that by face mask (93.90-93.99)*
>   *that by nasal cannula (93.90-93.99)*
>   *that by nasal catheter (93.90-93.99)*

Note: Endotracheal intubation

To calculate the number of hours (duration) of continuous mechanical ventilation during a hospitalization, begin the count from the start of the (endotracheal) intubation. The duration ends with (endotracheal) extubation.

If a patient is intubated prior to admission, begin counting the duration from the time of the admission. If a patient is transferred (discharged) while intubated, the duration would end at the time of transfer (discharge).

For patients who begin on (endotracheal) intubation and subsequently have a tracheostomy performed for mechanical ventilation, the duration begins with the (endotracheal) intubation and ends when the mechanical ventilation is turned off (after the weaning period).

Tracheostomy

To calculate the number of hours of continuous mechanical ventilation during a hospitalization, begin counting the duration when mechanical ventilation is started. The duration ends when the mechanical ventilator is turned off (after the weaning period).

If a patient has received a tracheostomy prior to admission and is on mechanical ventilation at the time of admission, begin counting the duration from the time of admission. If a patient is transferred (discharged) while still on mechanical ventilation via tracheostomy, the duration would end at the time of the transfer (discharge).
> AHA: 4Q, '08, 187-190 3Q, '04, 3; 2Q, '92, 13; 4Q, '91, 16; 4Q, '91, 18; 4Q, '91, 21

TIP: Do not assign if the patient is not intubated or does not have a tracheostomy. Refer to subcategory 93.9 for noninvasive mechanical ventilation.

96.70   **Continuous invasive mechanical ventilation of unspecified duration**
> Invasive mechanical ventilation NOS

96.71   **Continuous invasive mechanical ventilation for less than 96 consecutive hours**
> AHA: ▶2Q, '09, 11;◀ 3Q, '07, 6; 2Q, '06, 8; 3Q, '05, 10; 3Q, '04, 11; 2Q, '02, 19; 1Q, '02, 12; 1Q, '01, 6

96.72   **Continuous invasive mechanical ventilation for 96 consecutive hours or more**
> AHA: 2Q, '05, 19; 1Q, '04, 23

Diagnostic and Therapeutic Procedures

97–97.69

√3rd **97   Replacement and removal of therapeutic appliances**

√4th **97.0   Nonoperative replacement of gastrointestinal appliance**

97.01   Replacement of (naso-)gastric or esophagostomy tube

97.02   Replacement of gastrostomy tube
AHA: 1Q, '97, 11

97.03   Replacement of tube or enterostomy device of small intestine
AHA: 1Q, '03, 10

97.04   Replacement of tube or enterostomy device of large intestine

97.05   Replacement of stent (tube) in biliary or pancreatic duct
AHA: 2Q, '99, 13

√4th **97.1   Nonoperative replacement of musculoskeletal and integumentary system appliance**

97.11   Replacement of cast on upper limb

97.12   Replacement of cast on lower limb

97.13   Replacement of other cast

97.14   Replacement of other device for musculoskeletal immobilization
Splinting
Strapping

97.15   Replacement of wound catheter

97.16   Replacement of wound packing or drain
EXCLUDES   repacking of:
dental wound (97.22)
vulvar wound (97.26)

√4th **97.2   Other nonoperative replacement**

97.21   Replacement of nasal packing

97.22   Replacement of dental packing

97.23   Replacement of tracheostomy tube
AHA: N-D, '87, 11

97.24   Replacement and refitting of vagina diaphragm   ♀

97.25   Replacement of other vaginal pessary   ♀

97.26   Replacement of vaginal or vulvar packing or drain   ♀

97.29   Other nonoperative replacements
AHA: 3Q, '99, 9; 3Q, '98, 12

√4th **97.3   Nonoperative removal of therapeutic device from head and neck**

97.31   Removal of eye prosthesis
EXCLUDES   removal of ocular implant (16.71)
removal of orbital implant (16.72)

97.32   Removal of nasal packing

97.33   Removal of dental wiring

97.34   Removal of dental packing

97.35   Removal of dental prosthesis

97.36   Removal of other external mandibular fixation device

97.37   Removal of tracheostomy tube

97.38   Removal of sutures from head and neck

97.39   Removal of other therapeutic device from head and neck
EXCLUDES   removal of skull tongs (02.94)

√4th **97.4   Nonoperative removal of therapeutic device from thorax**

97.41   Removal of thoracotomy tube or pleural cavity drain
AHA: 1Q, '99, 10

97.42   Removal of mediastinal drain

97.43   Removal of sutures from thorax

Intraaortic Balloon Pump

Transverse aorta
Descending aorta
Aorta
Balloon pump in inflated phase
Thoracic aorta
Femoral artery access
Diaphragm
Abdominal aorta

97.44   Nonoperative removal of heart assist system
Explantation [removal] of circulatory assist device
Explantation [removal] of percutaneous external heart assist device
Removal of extrinsic heart assist device
Removal of pVAD
Removal of percutaneous heart assist device
AHA: 4Q, '01, 65
DEF: Non-invasive removal of ventricular assist systems, or intraaortic balloon pump, which is a balloon catheter placed into the descending thoracic aorta and timed to inflate and deflate with the patient's own heart rhythm to aid in blood circulation.

97.49   Removal of other device from thorax
EXCLUDES   endoscopic removal of bronchial device(s) or substances (33.78)
AHA: N-D, '86, 9

√4th **97.5   Nonoperative removal of therapeutic device from digestive system**

97.51   Removal of gastrostomy tube

97.52   Removal of tube from small intestine

97.53   Removal of tube from large intestine or appendix

97.54   Removal of cholecystostomy tube

97.55   Removal of T-tube, other bile duct tube, or liver tube
Removal of bile duct stent
AHA: 1Q, '01, 8
TIP: Assign also code 51.10 if a biliary stent was removed via ERCP guidance.

97.56   Removal of pancreatic tube or drain

97.59   Removal of other device from digestive system
Removal of rectal packing

√4th **97.6   Nonoperative removal of therapeutic device from urinary system**

97.61   Removal of pyelostomy and nephrostomy tube
DEF: Nonsurgical removal of tubes from lower part of kidney.

97.62   Removal of ureterostomy tube and ureteral catheter

97.63   Removal of cystostomy tube

97.64   Removal of other urinary drainage device
Removal of indwelling urinary catheter

97.65   Removal of urethral stent

97.69   Removal of other device from urinary system

BI Bilateral Procedure   NC Non-covered Procedure   LC Limited Coverage Procedure   ▶◀ Revised Text   ● New Code   ▲ Revised Code Title

196 – Volume 3   **2010 ICD-9-CM**

✓4ᵗʰ **97.7** Nonoperative removal of therapeutic device from genital system

[handwritten: Encounter? V 25,42]

97.71 Removal of intrauterine contraceptive device ♀

97.72 Removal of intrauterine pack ♀

97.73 Removal of vaginal diaphragm ♀

97.74 Removal of other vaginal pessary ♀

97.75 Removal of vaginal or vulvar packing ♀

97.79 Removal of other device from genital tract
Removal of sutures

✓4ᵗʰ **97.8** Other nonoperative removal of therapeutic device

97.81 Removal of retroperitoneal drainage device

97.82 Removal of peritoneal drainage device
AHA: 2Q, '90, 28; S-O, '86, 12

97.83 Removal of abdominal wall sutures

97.84 Removal of sutures from trunk, not elsewhere classified

97.85 Removal of packing from trunk, not elsewhere classified

97.86 Removal of other device from abdomen

97.87 Removal of other device from trunk

97.88 Removal of external immobilization device
Removal of:
    brace
    cast
    splint

97.89 Removal of other therapeutic device

✓3ʳᵈ **98** Nonoperative removal of foreign body or calculus

✓4ᵗʰ **98.0** Removal of intraluminal foreign body from digestive system without incision
EXCLUDES *removal of therapeutic device (97.51-97.59)*
DEF: Retrieval of foreign body from digestive system lining without incision.

98.01 Removal of intraluminal foreign body from mouth without incision

98.02 Removal of intraluminal foreign body from esophagus without incision

98.03 Removal of intraluminal foreign body from stomach and small intestine without incision

98.04 Removal of intraluminal foreign body from large intestine without incision

98.05 Removal of intraluminal foreign body from rectum and anus without incision

✓4ᵗʰ **98.1** Removal of intraluminal foreign body from other sites without incision
EXCLUDES *removal of therapeutic device (97.31-97.49, 97.61-97.89)*

98.11 Removal of intraluminal foreign body from ear without incision

98.12 Removal of intraluminal foreign body from nose without incision

98.13 Removal of intraluminal foreign body from pharynx without incision

98.14 Removal of intraluminal foreign body from larynx without incision

98.15 Removal of intraluminal foreign body from trachea and bronchus without incision
EXCLUDES *endoscopic removal of bronchial device(s) or substances (33.78)*

98.16 Removal of intraluminal foreign body from uterus without incision ♀
EXCLUDES *removal of intrauterine contraceptive device (97.71)*

98.17 Removal of intraluminal foreign body from vagina without incision ♀

98.18 Removal of intraluminal foreign body from artificial stoma without incision

98.19 Removal of intraluminal foreign body from urethra without incision

✓4ᵗʰ **98.2** Removal of other foreign body without incision
EXCLUDES *removal of intraluminal foreign body (98.01-98.19)*

98.20 Removal of foreign body, not otherwise specified

98.21 Removal of superficial foreign body from eye without incision

98.22 Removal of other foreign body without incision from head and neck
Removal of embedded foreign body from eyelid or conjunctiva without incision

98.23 Removal of foreign body from vulva without incision ♀

98.24 Removal of foreign body from scrotum or penis without incision ♂

98.25 Removal of other foreign body without incision from trunk except scrotum, penis, or vulva

98.26 Removal of foreign body from hand without incision
AHA: N-D, '87, 10

98.27 Removal of foreign body without incision from upper limb, except hand

98.28 Removal of foreign body from foot without incision

98.29 Removal of foreign body without incision from lower limb, except foot

✓4ᵗʰ **98.5** Extracorporeal shockwave lithotripsy [ESWL]
Lithotriptor tank procedure
Disintegration of stones by extracorporeal induced shockwaves
That with insertion of stent
DEF: Breaking of stones with high voltage condenser device synchronized with patient R waves.

98.51 Extracorporeal shockwave lithotripsy [ESWL] of the kidney, ureter and/or bladder
AHA: 4Q, '95, 73; 1Q, '89, 2
TIP: If the lithotripsy is documented with an endoscopic approach (e.g., cystoscopic), assign instead 56.0 and 59.95; if by percutaneous nephrostomy, assign instead 55.04.

98.52 Extracorporeal shockwave lithotripsy [ESWL] of the gallbladder and/or bile duct `NC`

98.59 Extracorporeal shockwave lithotripsy of other sites `NC`

Extracorporeal Shock Wave Lithotripsy

Extracorporeal Shock Wave Lithotripsy

√3rd **99**   **Other nonoperative procedures**

√4th   **99.0**   **Transfusion of blood and blood components**
Use additional code for that done via catheter or cutdown (38.92-38.94)

99.00   **Perioperative autologous transfusion of whole blood or blood components**
Intraoperative blood collection
Postoperative blood collection
Salvage
DEF: Salvaging patient blood with reinfusion during perioperative period.
AHA: 4Q, '95, 69

99.01   **Exchange transfusion**
Transfusion:
   exsanguination
   replacement
DEF: Repetitive withdrawal of blood, replaced by donor blood.
AHA: 2Q, '89, 15

99.02   **Transfusion of previously collected autologous blood**
Blood component
DEF: Transfusion with patient's own previously withdrawn and stored blood.
AHA: 4Q, '95, 69; 1Q, '90, 10; J-A, '85, 16

99.03   **Other transfusion of whole blood**
Transfusion:
   blood NOS
   hemodilution
   NOS

99.04   **Transfusion of packed cells**

99.05   **Transfusion of platelets**
Transfusion of thrombocytes

99.06   **Transfusion of coagulation factors**
Transfusion of antihemophilic factor

99.07   **Transfusion of other serum**
Transfusion of plasma
EXCLUDES   injection [transfusion] of:
     antivenin (99.16)
     gamma globulin (99.14)

99.08   **Transfusion of blood expander**
Transfusion of Dextran

99.09   **Transfusion of other substance**
Transfusion of:
   blood surrogate
   granulocytes
EXCLUDES   transplantation [transfusion] of bone marrow (41.0)

√4th   **99.1**   **Injection or infusion of therapeutic or prophylactic substance**
INCLUDES   injection or infusion given:
     hypodermically
     intramuscularly } acting locally or
     intravenously   systemically

99.10   **Injection or infusion of thrombolytic agent**
Alteplase
Anistreplase
Reteplase
Streptokinase
Tenecteplase
Tissue plasminogen activator (TPA)
Urokinase
EXCLUDES   aspirin — omit code
     GP IIb/IIIa platelet inhibitors (99.20)
     heparin (99.19)
     SuperSaturated oxygen therapy (00.49)
     warfarin — omit code
AHA: 2Q, '06, 22; 4Q, '05, 101-103; 2Q, '01, 7-9, 23; 4Q, '98, 83
TIP: If a tPA infusion is started in another facility within 24 hours of transferring to the current facility, assign diagnosis code V45.88, whether or not the infusion is continued in the current facility.

99.11   **Injection of Rh immune globulin**
Injection of:
   Anti-D (Rhesus) globulin
   RhoGAM

99.12   **Immunization for allergy**
Desensitization

99.13   **Immunization for autoimmune disease**

99.14   **Injection or infusion of gamma globulin**
Injection of immune sera

99.15   **Parenteral infusion of concentrated nutritional substances**
Hyperalimentation
Total parenteral nutrition [TPN]
Peripheral parenteral nutrition [PPN]
DEF: Administration of greater than necessary amount of nutrients via other than the alimentary canal (e.g., infusion).
AHA: 4Q, '03, 104

99.16   **Injection of antidote**
Injection of:
   antivenin
   heavy metal antagonist

99.17   **Injection of insulin**

99.18   **Injection or infusion of electrolytes**

99.19   **Injection of anticoagulant**
EXCLUDES   infusion of drotrecogin alfa (activated) (00.11)

√4th   **99.2**   **Injection or infusion of other therapeutic or prophylactic substance**
INCLUDES   injection or infusion given:
     hypodermically
     intramuscularly } acting locally or
     intravenously   systemically
Use additional code for:
   injection (into):
     breast (85.92)
     bursa (82.94, 83.96)
     intraperitoneal (cavity) (54.97)
     intrathecal (03.92)
     joint (76.96, 81.92)
     kidney (55.96)
     liver (50.94)
     orbit (16.91)
     other sites — see Alphabetic Index
   perfusion:
     NOS (39.97)
     intestine (46.95, 46.96)
     kidney (55.95)
     liver (50.93)
     total body (39.96)
EXCLUDES   SuperSaturated oxygen therapy (00.49)

99.20   **Injection or infusion of platelet inhibitor**
Glycoprotein IIb/IIIa inhibitor
GP IIb-IIIa inhibitor
GP IIb/IIIa inhibitor
EXCLUDES   infusion of heparin (99.19)
     injection or infusion of thrombolytic agent (99.10)
AHA: 3Q, '06, 8; 2Q, '04, 3; 4Q, '02, 114; 4Q, '98, 85

99.21   **Injection of antibiotic**
EXCLUDES   injection or infusion of oxazolidinone class of antibiotics (00.14)
AHA: 4Q, '98, 76; 2Q, '90, 24; M-A, '87, 9

99.22   **Injection of other anti-infective**
EXCLUDES   injection or infusion of oxazolidinone class of antibiotics (00.14)

99.23   **Injection of steroid**
Injection of cortisone
Subdermal implantation of progesterone
AHA: 3Q, '00, 15; 1Q, '99, 8; 3Q, '96, 7; 3Q, '92, 9; S-O, '85, 7

99.24   **Injection of other hormone**
Includes insertion of viadur implant
AHA: 1Q, '06, 9

BI Bilateral Procedure   NC Non-covered Procedure   LC Limited Coverage Procedure   ►◄ Revised Text   ● New Code   ▲ Revised Code Title

198 – Volume 3   2010 ICD-9-CM

99.25 Injection or infusion of cancer chemotherapeutic substance
Chemoembolization
Injection or infusion of antineoplastic agent
Use additional code for disruption of blood brain barrier, if performed [BBBD] (00.19)
> EXCLUDES   immunotherapy, antineoplastic (00.15, 99.28)
> implantation of chemotherapeutic agent (00.10)
> injection of radioisotope (92.28)
> injection or infusion of biological response modifier [BRM] as an antineoplastic agent (99.28)
> ▶intravenous infusion of clofarabine (17.70)◀

AHA: 4Q, '08, 82; 4Q, '07, 104; 2Q, '03, 6, 16; 4Q, '02, 93; 1Q, '99, 4; 1Q, '98, 6; 3Q, '96, 11; 4Q, '95, 67; 2Q, '92, 7; 1Q, '92, 12; 1Q, '88, 8; N-D, '86, 11

99.26 Injection of tranquilizer

99.27 Iontophoresis
DEF: Iontophoresis: Introduction of soluble salts into tissues via electric current.

99.28 Injection or infusion of biological response modifier [BRM] as an antineoplastic agent
Immunotherapy, antineoplastic
Infusion of cintredekin besudotox
Interleukin therapy
Low-dose interleukin-2 [IL-2] therapy
Tumor vaccine
> EXCLUDES   high-dose infusion interleukin-2 [IL-2] (00.15)

AHA: 4Q, '06, 123; 4Q, '03, 92; 2Q, '99, 8; 2Q, '98, 10; 4Q, '94, 51

99.29 Injection or infusion of other therapeutic or prophylactic substance
> EXCLUDES   administration of neuroprotective agent (99.75)
> immunization (99.31-99.59)
> infusion of blood brain barrier disruption substance (00.19)
> injection of sclerosing agent into:
>   esophageal varices (42.33)
>   hemorrhoids (49.42)
>   veins (39.92)
> injection or infusion of:
>   human B-type natriuretic peptide (hBNP) (00.13)
>   nesiritide (00.13)
>   platelet inhibitor (99.20)
>   thrombolytic agent (99.10)

AHA: 1Q, '07, 11; 2Q, '03, 10; 3Q, '02, 19, 24; 1Q, '01, 15; 2Q, '00, 14; 1Q, '00, 8, 18, 23; 4Q, '99, 17; 3Q, '99, 21; 4Q, '98, 83; 2Q, '98, 17, 18, 23, 24; 1Q, '98, 6; 2Q, '97, 11; 1Q, '97, 3; 4Q, '95, 67; 2Q, '95, 12; 4Q, '90, 14; 2Q, '90, 23; 2Q, '89, 17; 1Q, '88, 9; N-D, '87, 4; S-O, '87, 11

✓4th **99.3 Prophylactic vaccination and inoculation against certain bacterial diseases**
DEF: Administration of a killed bacteria suspension to produce immunity.

99.31 Vaccination against cholera

99.32 Vaccination against typhoid and paratyphoid fever
Administration of TAB vaccine

99.33 Vaccination against tuberculosis
Administration of BCG vaccine

99.34 Vaccination against plague

99.35 Vaccination against tularemia

99.36 Administration of diphtheria toxoid
> EXCLUDES   administration of:
>   diphtheria antitoxin (99.58)
>   diphtheria-tetanus-pertussis, combined (99.39)

99.37 Vaccination against pertussis
> EXCLUDES   administration of diphtheria-tetanus-pertussis, combined (99.39)

99.38 Administration of tetanus toxoid
> EXCLUDES   administration of:
>   diphtheria-tetanus-pertussis, combined (99.39)
>   tetanus antitoxin (99.56)

99.39 Administration of diphtheria-tetanus- pertussis, combined

✓4th **99.4 Prophylactic vaccination and inoculation against certain viral diseases**
DEF: Administration of a killed virus suspension to produce immunity.

99.41 Administration of poliomyelitis vaccine

99.42 Vaccination against smallpox

99.43 Vaccination against yellow fever

99.44 Vaccination against rabies

99.45 Vaccination against measles
> EXCLUDES   administration of measles-mumps-rubella vaccine (99.48)

99.46 Vaccination against mumps
> EXCLUDES   administration of measles-mumps-rubella vaccine (99.48)

99.47 Vaccination against rubella
> EXCLUDES   administration of measles-mumps-rubella vaccine (99.48)

99.48 Administration of measles-mumps-rubella vaccine

✓4th **99.5 Other vaccination and inoculation**

99.51 Prophylactic vaccination against the common cold

99.52 Prophylactic vaccination against influenza

99.53 Prophylactic vaccination against arthropod-borne viral encephalitis

99.54 Prophylactic vaccination against other arthropod-borne viral diseases

99.55 Prophylactic administration of vaccine against other diseases
Vaccination against:
   anthrax
   brucellosis
   Rocky Mountain spotted fever
   Staphylococcus
   Streptococcus
   typhus
AHA: 2Q, '00, 9; 1Q, '94, 10

99.56 Administration of tetanus antitoxin

99.57 Administration of botulism antitoxin

99.58 Administration of other antitoxins
Administration of:
   diphtheria antitoxin
   gas gangrene antitoxin
   scarlet fever antitoxin

99.59 Other vaccination and inoculation
Vaccination NOS
> EXCLUDES   injection of:
>   gamma globulin (99.14)
>   Rh immune globulin (99.11)
> immunization for:
>   allergy (99.12)
>   autoimmune disease (99.13)

A temporary transmyocardial pacemaker in which a needle is inserted into the chest and into the myocardium with leads fed through the needle directly into the heart muscle and attached to an external pacing device is sometimes used in an effort of CPR (99.60) and no additional code is assigned.

Diagnostic and Therapeutic Procedures

99.6–99.99

✓4ᵗʰ **99.6   Conversion of cardiac rhythm**
> **EXCLUDES**   *open chest cardiac:*
> *electric stimulation (37.91)*
> *massage (37.91)*
> **DEF:** Correction of cardiac rhythm.

✳ **99.60   Cardiopulmonary resuscitation, not otherwise specified**
> **AHA:** 1Q, '94, 16

99.61   Atrial cardioversion
> **DEF:** Application of electric shock to upper heart chamber to restore normal heart rhythm.

99.62   Other electric countershock of heart
> Cardioversion:
> NOS
> external
> Conversion to sinus rhythm
> Defibrillation
> External electrode stimulation
> **AHA:** 1Q, '07, 17

99.63   Closed chest cardiac massage
> Cardiac massage NOS
> Manual external cardiac massage
> **DEF:** Application of alternating manual pressure over breastbone to restore normal heart rhythm.

99.64   Carotid sinus stimulation

99.69   Other conversion of cardiac rhythm
> **AHA:** 4Q, '88, 11

✓4ᵗʰ **99.7   Therapeutic apheresis or other injection, administration, or infusion of other therpeutic or prophylactic substance**

99.71   Therapeutic plasmapheresis
> **EXCLUDES**   *extracorporeal immunoadsorption [ECI] (99.76)*

99.72   Therapeutic leukopheresis
> Therapeutic leukocytapheresis

99.73   Therapeutic erythrocytapheresis
> Therapeutic erythropheresis
> **AHA:** 1Q, '94, 20

99.74   Therapeutic plateletpheresis

99.75   Administration of neuroprotective agent
> **DEF:** Direct application of neuroprotective agent (e.g., nimodipine) to miinimize ischemic injury by inhibiting toxic neurotransmitters, blocking free ions, removing free radicals, and causing vasodilation.
> **AHA:** 4Q, '00, 68

99.76   Extracorporeal immunoadsorption
> Removal of antibodies from plasma with protein A columns
> **AHA:** 4Q, '02, 112

99.77   Application or administration of adhesion barrier substance
> **AHA:** 4Q, '02, 113

99.78   Aquapheresis
> Plasma water removal
> Ultrafiltration [for water removal]
> **EXCLUDES**   *hemodiafiltration (39.95)*
> *hemodialysis (39.95)*
> *therapeutic plasmapheresis (99.71)*

99.79   Other
> Apheresis (harvest) of stem cells
> **AHA:** ▶3Q, '08, 19;◀1Q, '06, 12, 13; 1Q, '05, 16; 4Q, '97, 55

✓4ᵗʰ **99.8   Miscellaneous physical procedures**

99.81   Hypothermia (central) (local)
> **EXCLUDES**   *gastric cooling (96.31)*
> *gastric freezing (96.32)*
> *that incidental to open heart surgery (39.62)*

99.82   Ultraviolet light therapy
> Actinotherapy

99.83   Other phototherapy
> Phototherapy of the newborn
> **EXCLUDES**   *extracorporeal photochemotherapy (99.88)*
> *photocoagulation of retinal lesion (14.23-14.25, 14.33-14.35, 14.53-14.55)*
> **DEF:** Treating disease with light rays of various concentrations.
> **AHA:** 2Q, '89, 15

99.84   Isolation
> Isolation after contact with infectious disease
> Protection of individual from his surroundings
> Protection of surroundings from individual

99.85   Hyperthermia for treatment of cancer
> Hyperthermia (adjunct therapy) induced by microwave, ultrasound, low energy radio frequency, probes (interstitial), or other means in the treatment of cancer
>
> Code also any concurrent chemotherapy or radiation therapy
> **AHA:** 3Q, '96, 11; 3Q, '89, 17

99.86   Non-invasive placement of bone growth stimulator
> Transcutaneous (surface) placement of pads or patches for stimulation to aid bone healing
> **EXCLUDES**   *insertion of invasive or semi-invasive bone growth stimulators (device) (percutaneous electrodes) (78.90-78.99)*

99.88   Therapeutic photopheresis
> Extracorporeal photochemotherapy
> Extracorporeal photopheresis
> **EXCLUDES**   *other phototherapy (99.83)*
> *ultraviolet light therapy (99.82)*
> **DEF:** Extracorporeal photochemotherapy: Treating disease with drugs that react to ultraviolet radiation or sunlight.
> **AHA:** 2Q, '99, 7

✓4ᵗʰ **99.9   Other miscellaneous procedures**

99.91   Acupuncture for anesthesia

99.92   Other acupuncture
> **EXCLUDES**   *that with smouldering moxa (93.35)*

99.93   Rectal massage (for levator spasm)

99.94   Prostatic massage   ♂

99.95   Stretching of foreskin   ♂

99.96   Collection of sperm for artificial insemination   ♂

99.97   Fitting of denture

99.98   Extraction of milk from lactating breast   ♀

99.99   Other
> Leech therapy

BI Bilateral Procedure   **NC** Non-covered Procedure   **LC** Limited Coverage Procedure   ▶◀ Revised Text   ● New Code   ▲ Revised Code Title

DRG Mapping Table

The table below contains a map with the Medicare Severity (MS) DRGs (version 25.0) mapped back to their corresponding CMS DRGs, version 24.0. Please note that there are three alternative DRG cluster groupings in MS-DRGs: 1) three subgroups: with MCC, with CC, w/o CC/MCC; 2) two subgroups: with MCC, w/o MCC; or 3) two subgroups: with CC/MCC, w/o CC/MCC. There are several instances in which diagnosis codes were mapped to more than one MS-DRG cluster, which are denoted with footnotes. There are also several procedure codes that are always grouped to the highest weighted MS-DRG in the cluster, regardless of severity level; these are also designated with footnotes. This information was derived from the CMS Crosswalk from CMS-DRG to MS-DRG mapping file that can be found at http://www.cms.hhs.gov/AcuteInpatientPPS/FFD.

Note: This Table has not been updated to reflect any changes made to the MS-DRG system since version 26.0.

MDC	Med/Surg	CMS-DRG	MS-DRG	MS-DRG Title
PRE	S	103	001, 002	Heart transplant or implant of heart assist system w MCC, w/o MCC
PRE	S	541	003	ECMO or trach w MV 96+ hrs or PDX exc face, mouth & neck w maj O.R.
PRE	S	542	004	Trach w MV 96+ hrs or PDX exc face, mouth & neck w/o maj O.R.
PRE	S	480	005, 006	Liver transplant w MCC or intestinal transplant, w/o MCC
PRE	S	495	007	Lung transplant
PRE	S	512	008	Simultaneous pancreas/kidney transplant
PRE	S	481	009	Bone marrow transplant
PRE	S	513	010	Pancreas transplant
PRE	S	482	011, 012, 013	Tracheostomy for face,mouth & neck diagnoses w MCC, w CC, w/o CC/MCC
01	S	528	020, 021, 022	Intracranial vascular procedures w PDX hemorrhage w MCC, w CC, w/o CC/MCC
01	S	543	023, 024	Craniotomy w major device implant or acute complex CNS PDX w MCC or with chemo implant, w/o MCC
01	S	[1]001, [1]002, [1, 2]003	025, 026, 027	Craniotomy & endovascular intracranial procedures w MCC, w CC, w/o CC/MCC
01	S	531, 532	028, 029, 030	Spinal procedures w MCC, w CC or with spinal neurostimulators, w/o CC/MCC
01	S	529, 530	031, 032, 033	Ventricular shunt procedures w MCC, w CC, w/o CC/MCC
01	S	577	034, 035, 036	Carotid artery stent procedure w MCC, w CC, w/o CC/MCC
01	S	533, 534	037, 038, 039	Extracranial procedures w MCC, w CC, w/o CC/MCC
01	S	006, 007, 008	040, 041, 042	Periph & cranial nerve & other nerv syst proc w MCC, w CC or with peripheral neurostimulators, w/o CC/MCC
01	M	009	052, 053	Spinal disorders & injuries w CC/MCC, w/o CC/MCC
01	M	010, 011	054, 055	Nervous system neoplasms w MCC, w/o MCC
01	M	012	056, 057	Degenerative nervous system disorders w MCC, w/o MCC
01	M	013	058, 059, 060	Multiple sclerosis & cerebellar ataxia w MCC, w CC, w/o CC/MCC
01	M	559	061, 062, 063	Acute ischemic stroke w use of thrombolytic agent w MCC, w CC, w/o CC/MCC
01	M	014	064, 065, 066	Intracranial hemorrhage or cerebral infarction w MCC, w CC, w/o CC/MCC
01	M	015	067, 068	Nonspecific cva & precerebral occlusion w/o infarct w MCC, w/o MCC
01	M	524	069	Transient ischemia
01	M	016, 017	070, 071, 072	Nonspecific cerebrovascular disorders w MCC, w CC, w/o CC/MCC
01	M	018, 019	073, 074	Cranial & peripheral nerve disorders w MCC, w/o MCC
01	M	021	075, 076	Viral meningitis w CC/MCC, w/o CC/MCC
01	M	022	077, 078, 079	Hypertensive encephalopathy w MCC, w CC, w/o CC/MCC
01	M	023	080, 081	Nontraumatic stupor & coma w MCC, w/o MCC
01	M	027	082, 083, 084	Traumatic stupor & coma, coma >1 hr w MCC, w CC, w/o CC/MCC
01	M	031, 032, 033	088, 089, 090	Concussion w MCC, w CC, w/o CC/MCC
01	M	034, 035	091, 092, 093	Other disorders of nervous system w MCC, w CC, w/o CC/MCC
01	M	560	094, 095, 096	Bacterial & tuberculous infections of nervous system w MCC, w CC, w/o CC/MCC
01	M	561	097, 098, 099	Non-bacterial infect of nervous sys exc viral meningitis w MCC, w CC, w/o CC/MCC
01	M	[3]026, 562, 563	100, 101	Seizures w MCC, w/o MCC
01	M	564	102, 103	Headaches w MCC, w/o MCC

[1] Some procedures in these DRGs also group to MS-DRGs 131-132

[2] CMS-DRG 003 procedures are split between MS DRGs 025, 026, 027, 031, 032, 033

[3] CMS-DRG 026 PDX are split between MS-DRGs 100.01. 102, 103

DRG Mapping Table

MDC	Med/Surg	CMS-DRG	MS-DRG	MS-DRG Title
02	S	[1]037	113, 114	Orbital procedures w CC/MCC, w/o CC/MCC
02	S	040, 041	115	Extraocular procedures except orbit
02	S	036, 038, 039, 042	116, 117	Intraocular procedures w CC/MCC, w/o CC/MCC
02	M	044	121, 122	Acute major eye infections w CC/MCC, w/o CC/MCC
02	M	045	123	Neurological eye disorders
02	M	043, 046, 047, 048	124, 125	Other disorders of the eye w MCC, w/o MCC
03	S	049	129, 130	Major head & neck procedures w CC/MCC or with major device, w/o CC/MCC
03	S	001-003, 037, 063	[4]131, [4]132	Cranial/facial procedures w CC/MCC, w/o CC/MCC
03	S	052, 055-063	133, 134	Other ear, nose, mouth & throat O.R. procedures w CC/MCC, w/o CC/MCC
03	S	053, 054	135, 136	Sinus & mastoid procedures w CC/MCC, w/o CC/MCC
03	S	168, 169	137, 138	Mouth procedures w CC/MCC, w/o CC/MCC
03	S	050, 051	139	Salivary gland procedures
03	M	064	146, 147, 148	Ear, nose, mouth & throat malignancy w MCC, w CC, w/o CC/MCC
03	M	065	149	Dysequilibrium
03	M	066	150, 151	Epistaxis w MCC, w/o MCC
03	M	067-071	152, 153	Otitis media & URI w MCC, w/o MCC
03	M	072, 073, 074	154, 155, 156	Nasal trauma & deformity w MCC, w CC, w/o CC/MCC
03	M	185, 186, 187	157, 158, 159	Dental & oral diseases w MCC, w CC, w/o CC/MCC
04	S	075	163, 164, 165	Major chest procedures w MCC, w CC, w/o CC/MCC
04	S	076, 077	166, 167, 168	Other resp system O.R. procedures w MCC, w CC, w/o CC/MCC
04	M	078	175, 176	Pulmonary embolism w MCC, w/o MCC
04	M	079, 080, 081	177, 178, 179	Respiratory infections & inflammations w MCC, w CC, w/o CC/MCC
04	M	082	180, 181, 182	Respiratory neoplasms w MCC, w CC, w/o CC/MCC
04	M	083, 084	183, 184, 185	Major chest trauma w MCC, w CC, w/o CC/MCC
04	M	085, 086	186, 187, 188	Pleural effusion w MCC, w CC, w/o CC/MCC
04	M	087	189	Pulmonary edema & respiratory failure
04	M	088	190, 191, 192	Chronic obstructive pulmonary disease w MCC, w CC, w/o CC/MCC
04	M	089, 090, 091	193, 194, 195	Simple pneumonia & pleurisy w MCC, w CC, w/o CC/MCC
04	M	092, 093	196, 197, 198	Interstitial lung disease w MCC, w CC, w/o CC/MCC
04	M	094, 095	199, 200, 201	Pneumothorax w MCC, w CC, w/o CC/MCC
04	M	096, 097, 098	202, 203	Bronchitis & asthma w CC/MCC, w/o CC/MCC
04	M	099, 100	204	Respiratory signs & symptoms
04	M	101, 102	205, 206	Other respiratory system diagnoses w MCC, w/o MCC
04	M	565	207	Respiratory system diagnosis w ventilator support 96+ hours
04	M	566	208	Respiratory system diagnosis w ventilator support <96 hours
05	S	525	215	Other heart assist system implant
05	S	104	216, 217, 218	Cardiac valve & oth maj cardiothoracic proc w card cath w MCC, w CC, w/o CC/MCC
05	S	105	219, 220, 221	Cardiac valve & oth maj cardiothoracic proc w/o card cath w MCC, w CC, w/o CC/MCC
05	S	535	222, 223	Cardiac defib implant w cardiac cath w AMI/HF/shock w MCC, w/o MCC
05	S	536	224, 225	Cardiac defib implant w cardiac cath w/o AMI/HF/shock w MCC, w/o MCC
05	S	515	226, 227	Cardiac defibrillator implant w/o cardiac cath w MCC, w/o MCC
05	S	108	228, 229, 230	Other cardiothoracic procedures w MCC, w CC, w/o CC/MCC
05	S	106	231, 232	Coronary bypass w PTCA w MCC, w/o MCC
05	S	547, 548	233, 234	Coronary bypass w cardiac cath w MCC, w/o MCC
05	S	549, 550	235, 236	Coronary bypass w/o cardiac cath w MCC, w/o MCC
05	S	110, 111	237, 238	Major cardiovascular procedures w MCC or with thoracic aortic aneurysm repair, w/o MCC

[1] Some procedures in these DRGs also group to MS-DRGs 131-132

[4] Some procedures previously grouped to CMS-DRGs 001–003, 037, 063 are now also included in these MS-DRGs

MDC	Med/Surg	CMS-DRG	MS-DRG	MS-DRG Title
05	S	113	239, 240, 241	Amputation for circ sys disorders exc upper limb & toe w MCC, w CC, w/o CC/MCC
05	S	551, 552	242, 243, 244, 245, 265	Permanent cardiac pacemaker implant w MCC, w CC, w/o CC/MCC or AICD lead, genrtr proc
05	S	557, 558	246, 247	Percutaneous cardiovascular proc w drug-eluting stent w MCC or 4+ vessels/stents, w/o MCC
05	S	555, 556	248, 249	Percutaneous cardiovasc proc w non-drug-eluting stent w MCC or 4+ vessels/stents, w/o MCC
05	S	518	250, 251	Perc cardiovasc proc w/o coronary artery stent or AMI w MCC, w/o MCC
05	S	479, 553, 554	252, 253, 254	Other vascular procedures w MCC, w CC, w/o CC/MCC
05	S	114	255, 256, 257	Upper limb & toe amputation for circ system disorders w MCC, w CC, w/o CC/MCC
05	S	118	258, 259	Cardiac pacemaker device replacement w MCC, w/o MCC
05	S	117	260, 261, 262	Cardiac pacemaker revision except device replacement w MCC, w CC, w/o CC/MCC
05	S	119	263	Vein ligation & stripping
05	S	120	264	Other circulatory system O.R. procedures
05	M	121, 122	280, 281, 282	Acute myocardial infarction, discharged alive w MCC, w CC, w/o CC/MCC
05	M	123	283, 284, 285	Acute myocardial infarction, expired w MCC, w CC, w/o CC/MCC
05	M	124, 125	286, 287	Circulatory disorders except AMI, w card cath w MCC, w/o MCC
05	M	126	288, 289, 290	Acute & subacute endocarditis w MCC, w CC, w/o CC/MCC
05	M	127	291, 292, 293	Heart failure & shock w MCC, w CC, w/o CC/MCC
05	M	128	294, 295	Deep vein thrombophlebitis w CC/MCC, w/o CC/MCC
05	M	129	296, 297, 298	Cardiac arrest, unexplained w MCC, w CC, w/o CC/MCC
05	M	130, 131	299, 300, 301	Peripheral vascular disorders w MCC, w CC, w/o CC/MCC
05	M	132, 133	302, 303	Atherosclerosis w MCC, w/o MCC
05	M	134	304, 305	Hypertension w MCC, w/o MCC
05	M	135, 136, 137	306, 307	Cardiac congenital & valvular disorders w MCC, w/o MCC
05	M	138, 139	308, 309, 310	Cardiac arrhythmia & conduction disorders w MCC, w CC, w/o CC/MCC
05	M	140	311	Angina pectoris
05	M	141, 142	312	Syncope & collapse
05	M	143	313	Chest pain
05	M	144, 145	314, 315, 316	Other circulatory system diagnoses w MCC, w CC, w/o CC/MCC
06	S	155, 156, 567, 568	326, 327, 328	Stomach, esophageal & duodenal proc w MCC, w CC, w/o CC/MCC
06	S	149, 569, 570	329, 330, 331	Major small & large bowel procedures w MCC, w CC, w/o CC/MCC
06	S	146, 147	332, 333, 334	Rectal resection w MCC, w CC, w/o CC/MCC
06	S	150, 151	335, 336, 337	Peritoneal adhesiolysis w MCC, w CC, w/o CC/MCC
06	S	164, 165	338, 339, 340	Appendectomy w complicated principal diag w MCC, w CC, w/o CC/MCC
06	S	166, 167	341, 342, 343	Appendectomy w/o complicated principal diag w MCC, w CC, w/o CC/MCC
06	S	152, 153	344, 345, 346	Minor small & large bowel procedures w MCC, w CC, w/o CC/MCC
06	S	157, 158	347, 348, 349	Anal & stomal procedures w MCC, w CC, w/o CC/MCC
06	S	161, 162, [5]163	350, 351, 352	Inguinal & femoral hernia procedures w MCC, w CC, w/o CC/MCC
06	S	159, 160	353, 354, 355	Hernia procedures except inguinal & femoral w MCC, w CC, w/o CC/MCC
06	S	170, 171	356, 357, 358	Other digestive system O.R. procedures w MCC, w CC, w/o CC/MCC
06	M	571	368, 369, 370	Major esophageal disorders w MCC, w CC, w/o CC/MCC
06	M	572	371, 372, 373	Major gastrointestinal disorders & peritoneal infections w MCC, w CC, w/o CC/MCC
06	M	172, 173	374, 375, 376	Digestive malignancy w MCC, w CC, w/o CC/MCC
06	M	174, 175	377, 378, 379	G.I. hemorrhage w MCC, w CC, w/o CC/MCC
06	M	176	380, 381, 382	Complicated peptic ulcer w MCC, w CC, w/o CC/MCC
06	M	177, 178	383, 384	Uncomplicated peptic ulcer w MCC, w/o MCC
06	M	179	385, 386, 387	Inflammatory bowel disease w MCC, w CC, w/o CC/MCC
06	M	180, 181	388, 389, 390	G.I. obstruction w MCC, w CC, w/o CC/MCC
06	M	182, 183, 184	391, 392	Esophagitis, gastroent & misc digest disorders w MCC, w/o MCC

[5] CMS DRG 163 is split between MS-DRGs 350, 351, 352, 353, 354, 355

DRG Mapping Table

MDC	Med/Surg	CMS-DRG	MS-DRG	MS-DRG Title
06	M	188, 189, 190	393, 394, 395	Other digestive system diagnoses w MCC, w CC, w/o CC/MCC
07	S	191, 192	405, 406, 407	Pancreas, liver & shunt procedures w MCC, w CC, w/o CC/MCC
07	S	193, 194	408, 409, 410	Biliary tract proc except only cholecyst w or w/o c.d.e. w MCC, w CC, w/o CC/MCC
07	S	195, 196	411, 412, 413	Cholecystectomy w c.d.e. w MCC, w CC, w/o CC/MCC
07	S	197, 198	414, 415, 416	Cholecystectomy except by laparoscope w/o c.d.e. w MCC, w CC, w/o CC/MCC
07	S	493, 494	417, 418, 419	Laparoscopic cholecystectomy w/o c.d.e. w MCC, w CC, w/o CC/MCC
07	S	199, 200	420, 421, 422	Hepatobiliary diagnostic procedures w MCC, w CC, w/o CC/MCC
07	S	201	423, 424, 425	Other hepatobiliary or pancreas O.R. procedures w MCC, w CC, w/o CC/MCC
07	M	202	432, 433, 434	Cirrhosis & alcoholic hepatitis w MCC, w CC, w/o CC/MCC
07	M	203	435, 436, 437	Malignancy of hepatobiliary system or pancreas w MCC, w CC, w/o CC/MCC
07	M	204	438, 439, 440	Disorders of pancreas except malignancy w MCC, w CC, w/o CC/MCC
07	M	205, 206	441, 442, 443	Disorders of liver except malig,cirr,alc hepa w MCC, w CC, w/o CC/MCC
07	M	207, 208	444, 445, 446	Disorders of the biliary tract w MCC, w CC, w/o CC/MCC
08	S	496	453, 454, 455	Combined anterior/posterior spinal fusion w MCC, w CC, w/o CC/MCC
08	S	546	456, 457, 458	Spinal fusion exc cerv w spinal curvature/infection, malig or 9+ fusions w MCC, w CC, w/o CC/MCC
08	S	497, 498	459, 460	Spinal fusion except cervical w MCC, w/o MCC
08	S	471	461, 462	Bilateral or multiple major joint procs of lower extremity w MCC, w/o MCC
08	S	217	463, 464, 465	Wnd debrid & skn grft exc hand, for musculo-conn tiss dis w MCC, w CC, w/o CC/MCC
08	S	545	466, 467, 468	Revision of hip or knee replacement w MCC, w CC, w/o CC/MCC
08	S	544	469, 470	Major joint replacement or reattachment of lower extremity w MCC, w/o MCC
08	S	519, 520	471, 472, 473	Cervical spinal fusion w MCC, w CC, w/o CC/MCC
08	S	213	474, 475, 476	Amputation for musculoskeletal sys & conn tissue dis w MCC, w CC, w/o CC/MCC
08	S	216	477, 478, 479	Biopsies of musculoskeletal system & connective tissue w MCC, w CC, w/o CC/MCC
08	S	210, 211, 212	480, 481, 482	Hip & femur procedures except major joint w MCC, w CC, w/o CC/MCC
08	S	491	483, 484	Major joint & limb reattachment proc of upper extremity w CC/MCC, w/o CC/MCC
08	S	501, 502	485, 486, 487	Knee procedures w pdx of infection w MCC, w CC, w/o CC/MCC
08	S	503	488, 489	Knee procedures w/o pdx of infection w CC/MCC, w/o CC/MCC
08	S	499, 500	490, 491	Back & neck procedures except spinal fusion w CC/MCC or with disc devices/neurostimulators, w/o CC/MCC
08	S	218, 219, 220	492, 493, 494	Lower extrem & humer proc except hip,foot,femur w MCC, w CC, w/o CC/MCC
08	S	537, 538	495, 496, 497	Local excision & removal int fix devices exc hip & femur w MCC, w CC, w/o CC/MCC
08	S	230	498, 499	Local excision & removal int fix devices of hip & femur w CC/MCC, w/o CC/MCC
08	S	226, 227	500, 501, 502	Soft tissue procedures w MCC, w CC, w/o CC/MCC
08	S	225	503, 504, 505	Foot procedures w MCC, w CC, w/o CC/MCC
08	S	228	506	Major thumb or joint procedures
08	S	223	507, 508	Major shoulder or elbow joint procedures w CC/MCC, w/o CC/MCC
08	S	232	509	Arthroscopy
08	S	224	510, 511, 512	Shoulder,elbow or forearm proc,exc major joint proc w MCC, w CC, w/o CC/MCC
08	S	229	513, 514	Hand or wrist proc, except major thumb or joint proc w CC/MCC, w/o CC/MCC
08	S	233, 234	515, 516, 517	Other musculoskelet sys & conn tiss O.R. proc w MCC, w CC, w/o CC/MCC
08	M	235	533, 534	Fractures of femur w MCC, w/o MCC
08	M	236	535, 536	Fractures of hip & pelvis w MCC, w/o MCC
08	M	237	537, 538	Sprains, strains, & dislocations of hip, pelvis & thigh w CC/MCC, w/o CC/MCC
08	M	238	539, 540, 541	Osteomyelitis w MCC, w CC, w/o CC/MCC
08	M	239	542, 543, 544	Pathological fractures & musculoskelet & conn tiss malig w MCC, w CC, w/o CC/MCC
08	M	240, 241	545, 546, 547	Connective tissue disorders w MCC, w CC, w/o CC/MCC
08	M	242	548, 549, 550	Septic arthritis w MCC, w CC, w/o CC/MCC
08	M	243	551, 552	Medical back problems w MCC, w/o MCC
08	M	244, 245, 246	553, 554	Bone diseases & arthropathies w MCC, w/o MCC
08	M	247	555, 556	Signs & symptoms of musculoskeletal system & conn tissue w MCC, w/o MCC

MDC	Med/Surg	CMS-DRG	MS-DRG	MS-DRG Title
08	M	248	557, 558	Tendonitis, myositis & bursitis w MCC, w/o MCC
08	M	249	559, 560, 561	Aftercare, musculoskeletal system & connective tissue w MCC, w CC, w/o CC/MCC
08	M	250-255	562, 563	Fx, sprn, strn & disl except femur, hip, pelvis & thigh w MCC, w/o MCC
08	M	256	564, 565, 566	Other musculoskeletal sys & connective tissue diagnoses w MCC, w CC, w/o CC/MCC
09	S	263, 264	573, 574, 575	Skin graft &/or debrid for skn ulcer or cellulitis w MCC, w CC, w/o CC/MCC
09	S	265, 266	576, 577, 578	Skin graft &/or debrid exc for skin ulcer or cellulitis w MCC, w CC, w/o CC/MCC
09	S	267-270	579, 580, 581	Other skin, subcut tiss & breast proc w MCC, w CC, w/o CC/MCC
09	S	257, 258	582, 583	Mastectomy for malignancy w CC/MCC, w/o CC/MCC
09	S	259-262	584, 585	Breast biopsy, local excision & other breast procedures w CC/MCC, w/o CC/MCC
09	M	271	592, 593, 594	Skin ulcers w MCC, w CC, w/o CC/MCC
09	M	272, 273	595, 596	Major skin disorders w MCC, w/o MCC
09	M	274, 275	597, 598, 599	Malignant breast disorders w MCC, w CC, w/o CC/MCC
09	M	276	600, 601	Non-malignant breast disorders w CC/MCC, w/o CC/MCC
09	M	277, 278, 279	602, 603	Cellulitis w MCC, w/o MCC
09	M	280, 281, 282	604, 605	Trauma to the skin, subcut tiss & breast w MCC, w/o MCC
09	M	283, 284	606, 607	Minor skin disorders w MCC, w/o MCC
10	S	286	614, 615	Adrenal & pituitary procedures w CC/MCC, w/o CC/MCC
10	S	285	616, 617, 618	Amputat of lower limb for endocrine,nutrit,& metabol dis w MCC, w CC, w/o CC/MCC
10	S	288	619, 620, 621	O.R. procedures for obesity w MCC, w CC, w/o CC/MCC
10	S	287	622, 623, 624	Skin grafts & wound debrid for endoc, nutrit & metab dis w MCC, w CC, w/o CC/MCC
10	S	289, 290, 291	625, 626, 627	Thyroid, parathyroid & thyroglossal procedures w MCC, w CC, w/o CC/MCC
10	S	292, 293	628, 629, 630	Other endocrine, nutrit & metab O.R. proc w MCC, w CC, w/o CC/MCC
10	M	294, 295	637, 638, 639	Diabetes w MCC, w CC, w/o CC/MCC
10	M	296, 297, 298	640, 641	Nutritional & misc metabolic disorders w MCC, w/o MCC
10	M	299	642	Inborn errors of metabolism
10	M	300, 301	643, 644, 645	Endocrine disorders w MCC, w CC, w/o CC/MCC
11	S	302	652	Kidney transplant
11	S	573	653, 654, 655	Major bladder procedures w MCC, w CC, w/o CC/MCC
11	S	303	656, 657, 658	Kidney & ureter procedures for neoplasm w MCC, w CC, w/o CC/MCC
11	S	304, 305	659, 660, 661	Kidney & ureter procedures for non-neoplasm w MCC, w CC, w/o CC/MCC
11	S	308, 309	662, 663, 664	Minor bladder procedures w MCC, w CC, w/o CC/MCC
11	S	306, 307	665, 666, 667	Prostatectomy w MCC, w CC, w/o CC/MCC
11	S	310, 311	668, 669, 670	Transurethral procedures w MCC, w CC, w/o CC/MCC
11	S	312, 313, 314	671, 672	Urethral procedures w CC/MCC, w/o CC/MCC
11	S	315	673, 674, 675	Other kidney & urinary tract procedures w MCC, w CC, w/o CC/MCC
11	M	316	682, 683, 684	Renal failure w MCC, w CC, w/o CC/MCC
11	M	317	685	Admit for renal dialysis
11	M	318, 319	686, 687, 688	Kidney & urinary tract neoplasms w MCC, w CC, w/o CC/MCC
11	M	320, 321, 322	689, 690	Kidney & urinary tract infections w MCC, w/o MCC
11	M	323	691, 692	Urinary stones w esw lithotripsy w CC/MCC, w/o CC/MCC
11	M	324	693, 694	Urinary stones w/o esw lithotripsy w MCC, w/o MCC
11	M	325, 326, 327	695, 696	Kidney & urinary tract signs & symptoms w MCC, w/o MCC
11	M	328, 329, 330	697	Urethral stricture
11	M	331, 332, 333	698, 699, 700	Other kidney & urinary tract diagnoses w MCC, w CC, w/o CC/MCC
12	S	334, 335	707, 708	Major male pelvic procedures w CC/MCC, w/o CC/MCC
12	S	341	709, 710	Penis procedures w CC/MCC, w/o CC/MCC
12	S	338, 339, 340	711, 712	Testes procedures w CC/MCC, w/o CC/MCC
12	S	336, 337	713, 714	Transurethral prostatectomy w CC/MCC, w/o CC/MCC
12	S	344	715, 716	Other male reproductive system O.R. proc for malignancy w CC/MCC, w/o CC/MCC
12	S	345	717, 718	Other male reproductive system O.R. proc exc malignancy w CC/MCC, w/o CC/MCC

MDC	Med/Surg	CMS-DRG	MS-DRG	MS-DRG Title
		342,⁶343		Deleted
12	M	346, 347	722, 723, 724	Malignancy, male reproductive system w MCC, w CC, w/o CC/MCC
12	M	348, 349	725, 726	Benign prostatic hypertrophy w MCC, w/o MCC
12	M	350	727, 728	Inflammation of the male reproductive system w MCC, w/o MCC
12	M	351, 352	729, 730	Other male reproductive system diagnoses w CC/MCC, w/o CC/MCC
13	S	353	734, 735	Pelvic evisceration, rad hysterectomy & rad vulvectomy w CC/MCC, w/o CC/MCC
13	S	357	736, 737, 738	Uterine & adnexa proc for ovarian or adnexal malignancy w MCC, w CC, w/o CC/MCC
13	S	354, 355	739, 740, 741	Uterine,adnexa proc for non-ovarian/adnexal malig w MCC, w CC, w/o CC/MCC
13	S	358, 359	742, 743	Uterine & adnexa proc for non-malignancy w CC/MCC, w/oCC/MCC
13	S	361-364	744, 745	D&C, conization, laparoscopy & tubal interruption w CC/MCC, w/o CC/MCC
13	S	360	746, 747	Vagina, cervix & vulva procedures w CC/MCC, w/o CC/MCC
13	S	356	748	Female reproductive system reconstructive procedures
13	S	365	749, 750	Other female reproductive system O.R. procedures w CC/MCC, w/o CC/MCC
13	M	366, 367	754, 755, 756	Malignancy, female reproductive system w MCC, w CC, w/o CC/MCC
13	M	368	757, 758, 759	Infections, female reproductive system w MCC, w CC, w/o CC/MCC
13	M	369	760, 761	Menstrual & other female reproductive system disorders w CC/MCC, w/o CC/MCC
14	S	370, 371	765, 766	Cesarean section w CC/MCC, w/o CC/MCC
14	S	374	767	Vaginal delivery w sterilization &/or D&C
14	S	375	768	Vaginal delivery w O.R. proc except steril &/or D&C
14	S	377	769	Postpartum & post abortion diagnoses w O.R. procedure
14	S	381	770	Abortion w D&C, aspiration curettage or hysterotomy
14	M	372	774	Vaginal delivery w complicating diagnoses
14	M	373	775	Vaginal delivery w/o complicating diagnoses
14	M	376	776	Postpartum & post abortion diagnoses w/o O.R. procedure
14	M	378	777	Ectopic pregnancy
14	M	379	778	Threatened abortion
14	M	380	779	Abortion w/o D&C
14	M	382	780	False labor
14	M	383	781	Other antepartum diagnoses w medical complications
14	M	384	782	Other antepartum diagnoses w/o medical complications
15	M	385	789	Neonates, died or transferred to another acute care facility
15	M	386	790	Extreme immaturity or respiratory distress syndrome, neonate
15	M	387	791	Prematurity w major problems
15	M	388	792	Prematurity w/o major problems
15	M	389	793	Full term neonate w major problems
15	M	390	794	Neonate w other significant problems
15	M	391	795	Normal newborn
16	S	392, 393	799, 800, 801	Splenectomy w MCC, w CC, w/o CC/MCC
16	S	394	802, 803, 804	Other O.R. proc of the blood & blood forming organs w MCC, w CC, w/o CC/MCC
16	M	574	808, 809, 810	Major hematol/immun diag exc sickle cell crisis & coagul w MCC, w CC, w/o CC/MCC
16	M	395, 396	811, 812	Red blood cell disorders w MCC, w/o MCC
16	M	397	813	Coagulation disorders
16	M	398, 399	814, 815, 816	Reticuloendothelial & immunity disorders w MCC, w CC, w/o CC/MCC
17	S	539, 540	820, 821, 822	Lymphoma & leukemia w major O.R. procedure w MCC, w CC, w/o CC/MCC
17	S	401, 402	823, 824, 825	Lymphoma & non-acute leukemia w other O.R. proc w MCC, w CC, w/o CC/MCC
17	S	406, 407	826, 827, 828	Myeloprolif disord or poorly diff neopl w maj O.R. proc w MCC, w CC, w/o CC/MCC
17	S	408	829, 830	Myeloprolif disord or poorly diff neopl w other O.R. proc w CC/MCC, w/o CC/MCC
17	M	405, 473	834, 835, 836	Acute leukemia w/o major O.R. procedure w MCC, w CC, w/o CC/MCC

⁶ OR procedure 64.0 (Circumcision) changed to non-OR and DRGs 342 & 343 deleted

MDC	Med/Surg	CMS-DRG	MS-DRG	MS-DRG Title
17	M	[1,4]492	837, 838, 839	Chemo w acute leukemia as sdx or w high dose chemo agent w MCC, w CC, w/o CC/MCC (no high dose chemo)
17	M	403, 404	840, 841, 842	Lymphoma & non-acute leukemia w MCC, w CC, w/o CC/MCC
17	M	411-414	843, 844, 845	Other myeloprolif dis or poorly diff neopl diag w MCC, w CC, w/o CC/MCC
17	M	410	846, 847, 848	Chemotherapy w/o acute leukemia as secondary diagnosis w MCC, w CC, w/o CC/MCC
17	M	409	849	Radiotherapy
18	S	578	853, 854, 855	Infectious & parasitic diseases w O.R. procedure w MCC, w CC, w/o CC/MCC
18	S	579	856, 857, 858	Postoperative or post-traumatic infections w O.R. proc w MCC, w CC, w/o CC/MCC
18	M	418	862, 863	Postoperative & post-traumatic infections w MCC, w/o MCC
18	M	419, 420	864	Fever of unknown origin
18	M	421, [7]422	865, 866	Viral illness w MCC, w/o MCC
18	M	423	867, 868, 869	Other infectious & parasitic diseases diagnoses w MCC, w CC, w/o MCC
18	M	417, 575	870	Septicemia w MV 96+ hours
18	M	576	871, 872	Septicemia w/o MV 96+ hours w MCC, w/o MCC
19	S	424	876	O.R. procedure w principal diagnoses of mental illness
19	M	425	880	Acute adjustment reaction & psychosocial dysfunction
19	M	426	881	Depressive neuroses
19	M	427	882	Neuroses except depressive
19	M	428	883	Disorders of personality & impulse control
19	M	429	884	Organic disturbances & mental retardation
19	M	430	885	Psychoses
19	M	431	886	Behavioral & developmental disorders
19	M	432	887	Other mental disorder diagnoses
20	M	433	894	Alcohol/drug abuse or dependence, left ama
20	M	521, 522	895	Alcohol/drug abuse or dependence w rehabilitation therapy
20	M	523	896, 897	Alcohol/drug abuse or dependence w/o rehabilitation therapy w MCC, w/o MCC
21	S	440	901, 902, 903	Wound debridements for injuries w MCC, w CC, w/o CC/MCC
21	S	439	904, 905	Skin grafts for injuries w CC/MCC, w/o CC/MCC
21	S	441	906	Hand procedures for injuries
21	S	442, 443	907, 908, 909	Other O.R. procedures for injuries w MCC, w CC, w/o CC/MCC
21	M	444, 445, 446	913, 914	Traumatic injury w MCC, w/o MCC
21	M	447, 448	915, 916	Allergic reactions w MCC, w/o MCC
21	M	449, 450, 451	917, 918	Poisoning & toxic effects of drugs w MCC, w/o MCC
21	M	452, 453	919, 920, 921	Complications of treatment w MCC, w CC, w/o CC/MCC
21	M	454, 455	922, 923	Other injury, poisoning & toxic effect diag w MCC, w/o MCC
22	S	504	927	Extensive burns or full thickness burns w MV 96+ hrs w skin graft
22	S	506, 507	928, 929	Full thickness burn w skin graft or inhal inj w CC/MCC, w/o CC/MCC
22	M	505	933	Extensive burns or full thickness burns w MV 96+ hrs w/o skin graft
22	M	508, 509	934	Full thickness burn w/o skin grft or inhal inj
22	M	510, 511	935	Non-extensive burns
23	S	461	939, 940, 941	O.R. proc w diagnoses of other contact w health services w MCC, w CC, w/o CC/MCC
23	M	462	945, 946	Rehabilitation w CC/MCC, w/o CC/MCC
23	M	463, 464	947, 948	Signs & symptoms w MCC, w/o MCC
23	M	465, 466	949, 950	Aftercare w CC/MCC, w/o CC/MCC
23	M	467	951	Other factors influencing health status
24	S	484	955	Craniotomy for multiple significant trauma
24	S	485	956	Limb reattachment, hip & femur proc for multiple significant trauma
24	S	486	957, 958, 959	Other O.R. procedures for multiple significant trauma w MCC, w CC, w/o CC/MCC

[1] Some procedures in these DRGs also group to MS-DRGs 131-132

[4] Some procedures previously grouped to CMS-DRGs 001–003, 037, 063 are now also included in these MS-DRGs

[7] CMS DRG 422 is split between MS-DRGs 864, 865, 866

MDC	Med/Surg	CMS-DRG	MS-DRG	MS-DRG Title
24	M	487	963, 964, 965	Other multiple significant trauma w MCC, w CC, w/o CC/MCC
25	S	488	969, 970	HIV w extensive O.R. procedure w MCC, w/o MCC
25	M	489	974, 975, 976	HIV w major related condition w MCC, w CC, w/o CC/MCC
25	M	490	977	HIV w or w/o other related condition
	S	468	981, 982, 983	Extensive O.R. procedure unrelated to principal diagnosis w MCC, w CC, w/o CC/MCC
	S	476	984, 985, 986	Prostatic O.R. procedure unrelated to principal diagnosis w MCC, w CC, w/o CC/MCC
	S	477	987, 988, 989	Non-extensive O.R. proc unrelated to principal diagnosis w MCC, w CC, w/o CC/MCC
	*	469	998	Principal diagnosis invalid as discharge diagnosis
	*	470	999	Ungroupable

Diagnosis Code/MDC/DRG List

The following list provides the MDC and **Medical** DRG(s) to which the diagnosis code is assigned when listed as the principal diagnosis with the exception of principal diagnosis in combination with secondary diagnosis causing assignment to MDC 24 or the significant HIV related diagnosis causing assignment to MDC 25. The resources used to compile this list are the 3M Definitions Manual, Version 27.0, the Medicare Program; Changes to the Hospital Inpatient Prospective Payment System: Proposed Rule *Federal Register*, May 22, 2009.

DX....	MDC.....	DRG	DX....	MDC.....	DRG	DX....	MDC.....	DRG	DX....	MDC.....	DRG	DX....	MDC.....	DRG
Infectious and Parasitic Diseases			008.61	06	391-392	011.40	04	177-179	012.36	03	154-156	013.95	01	094-096
001.0	06	371-373	008.62	06	391-392	011.41	04	177-179	012.80	04	177-179	013.96	01	094-096
001.1	06	371-373	008.63	06	391-392	011.42	04	177-179	012.81	04	177-179	014.00	06	371-373
001.9	06	371-373	008.64	06	391-392	011.43	04	177-179	012.82	04	177-179	014.01	06	371-373
002.0	18	867-869	008.65	06	391-392	011.44	04	177-179	012.83	04	177-179	014.02	06	371-373
002.1	18	867-869	008.66	06	391-392	011.45	04	177-179	012.84	04	177-179	014.03	06	371-373
002.2	18	867-869	008.67	06	391-392	011.46	04	177-179	012.85	04	177-179	014.04	06	371-373
002.3	18	867-869	008.69	06	391-392	011.50	04	177-179	012.86	04	177-179	014.05	06	371-373
002.9	18	867-869	008.8	06	391-392	011.51	04	177-179	013.00	01	094-096	014.06	06	371-373
003.0	06	371-373	009.0	06	391-392	011.52	04	177-179	013.01	01	094-096	014.80	06	371-373
003.1	18	870-872	009.1	06	391-392	011.53	04	177-179	013.02	01	094-096	014.81	06	371-373
003.20	18	867-869	009.2	06	391-392	011.54	04	177-179	013.03	01	094-096	014.82	06	371-373
003.21	01	094-096	009.3	06	391-392	011.55	04	177-179	013.04	01	094-096	014.83	06	371-373
003.22	04	177-179	010.00	04	177-179	011.56	04	177-179	013.05	01	094-096	014.84	06	371-373
003.23	08	548-550	010.01	04	177-179	011.60	04	177-179	013.06	01	094-096	014.85	06	371-373
003.24	08	539-541	010.02	04	177-179	011.61	04	177-179	013.10	01	094-096	014.86	06	371-373
003.29	18	867-869	010.03	04	177-179	011.62	04	177-179	013.11	01	094-096	015.00	08	539-541
003.8	18	867-869	010.04	04	177-179	011.63	04	177-179	013.12	01	094-096	015.01	08	539-541
003.9	18	867-869	010.05	04	177-179	011.64	04	177-179	013.13	01	094-096	015.02	08	539-541
004.0	06	371-373	010.06	04	177-179	011.65	04	177-179	013.14	01	094-096	015.03	08	539-541
004.1	06	371-373	010.10	04	177-179	011.66	04	177-179	013.15	01	094-096	015.04	08	539-541
004.2	06	371-373	010.11	04	177-179	011.70	04	177-179	013.16	01	094-096	015.05	08	539-541
004.3	06	371-373	010.12	04	177-179	011.71	04	177-179	013.20	01	094-096	015.06	08	539-541
004.8	06	371-373	010.13	04	177-179	011.72	04	177-179	013.21	01	094-096	015.10	08	548-550
004.9	06	371-373	010.14	04	177-179	011.73	04	177-179	013.22	01	094-096	015.11	08	548-550
005.0	06	371-373	010.15	04	177-179	011.74	04	177-179	013.23	01	094-096	015.12	08	548-550
005.1	18	867-869	010.16	04	177-179	011.75	04	177-179	013.24	01	094-096	015.13	08	548-550
005.2	06	371-373	010.80	04	177-179	011.76	04	177-179	013.25	01	094-096	015.14	08	548-550
005.3	06	371-373	010.81	04	177-179	011.80	04	177-179	013.26	01	094-096	015.15	08	548-550
005.4	06	371-373	010.82	04	177-179	011.81	04	177-179	013.30	01	094-096	015.16	08	548-550
005.81	06	371-373	010.83	04	177-179	011.82	04	177-179	013.31	01	094-096	015.20	08	548-550
005.89	06	371-373	010.84	04	177-179	011.83	04	177-179	013.32	01	094-096	015.21	08	548-550
005.9	06	391-392	010.85	04	177-179	011.84	04	177-179	013.33	01	094-096	015.22	08	548-550
006.0	06	371-373	010.86	04	177-179	011.85	04	177-179	013.34	01	094-096	015.23	08	548-550
006.1	06	371-373	010.90	04	177-179	011.86	04	177-179	013.35	01	094-096	015.24	08	548-550
006.2	06	371-373	010.91	04	177-179	011.90	04	177-179	013.36	01	094-096	015.25	08	548-550
006.3	07	441-443	010.92	04	177-179	011.91	04	177-179	013.40	01	094-096	015.26	08	548-550
006.4	04	177-179	010.93	04	177-179	011.92	04	177-179	013.41	01	094-096	015.50	08	539-541
006.5	01	097-099	010.94	04	177-179	011.93	04	177-179	013.42	01	094-096	015.51	08	539-541
006.6	09	606-607	010.95	04	177-179	011.94	04	177-179	013.43	01	094-096	015.52	08	539-541
006.8	18	867-869	010.96	04	177-179	011.95	04	177-179	013.44	01	094-096	015.53	08	539-541
006.9	18	867-869	011.00	04	177-179	011.96	04	177-179	013.45	01	094-096	015.54	08	539-541
007.0	06	371-373	011.01	04	177-179	012.00	04	177-179	013.46	01	094-096	015.55	08	539-541
007.1	06	371-373	011.02	04	177-179	012.01	04	177-179	013.50	01	094-096	015.56	08	539-541
007.2	06	371-373	011.03	04	177-179	012.02	04	177-179	013.51	01	094-096	015.60	03	154-156
007.3	06	371-373	011.04	04	177-179	012.03	04	177-179	013.52	01	094-096	015.61	03	154-156
007.4	06	371-373	011.05	04	177-179	012.04	04	177-179	013.53	01	094-096	015.62	03	154-156
007.5	06	371-373	011.06	04	177-179	012.05	04	177-179	013.54	01	094-096	015.63	03	154-156
007.8	06	371-373	011.10	04	177-179	012.06	04	177-179	013.55	01	094-096	015.64	03	154-156
007.9	06	371-373	011.11	04	177-179	012.10	04	177-179	013.56	01	094-096	015.65	03	154-156
008.00	06	371-373	011.12	04	177-179	012.11	04	177-179	013.60	01	094-096	015.66	03	154-156
008.01	06	371-373	011.13	04	177-179	012.12	04	177-179	013.61	01	094-096	015.70	08	539-541
008.02	06	371-373	011.14	04	177-179	012.13	04	177-179	013.62	01	094-096	015.71	08	539-541
008.03	06	371-373	011.15	04	177-179	012.14	04	177-179	013.63	01	094-096	015.72	08	539-541
008.04	06	371-373	011.16	04	177-179	012.15	04	177-179	013.64	01	094-096	015.73	08	539-541
008.09	06	371-373	011.20	04	177-179	012.16	04	177-179	013.65	01	094-096	015.74	08	539-541
008.1	06	371-373	011.21	04	177-179	012.20	04	177-179	013.66	01	094-096	015.75	08	539-541
008.2	06	371-373	011.22	04	177-179	012.21	04	177-179	013.80	01	094-096	015.76	08	539-541
008.3	06	371-373	011.23	04	177-179	012.22	04	177-179	013.81	01	094-096	015.80	08	548-550
008.41	06	371-373	011.24	04	177-179	012.23	04	177-179	013.82	01	094-096	015.81	08	548-550
008.42	06	371-373	011.25	04	177-179	012.24	04	177-179	013.83	01	094-096	015.82	08	548-550
008.43	06	371-373	011.26	04	177-179	012.25	04	177-179	013.84	01	094-096	015.83	08	548-550
008.44	06	371-373	011.30	04	177-179	012.26	04	177-179	013.85	01	094-096	015.84	08	548-550
008.45	06	371-373	011.31	04	177-179	012.30	03	154-156	013.86	01	094-096	015.85	08	548-550
008.46	06	371-373	011.32	04	177-179	012.31	03	154-156	013.90	01	094-096	015.86	08	548-550
008.47	06	371-373	011.33	04	177-179	012.32	03	154-156	013.91	01	094-096	015.90	08	548-550
008.49	06	371-373	011.34	04	177-179	012.33	03	154-156	013.92	01	094-096	015.91	08	548-550
008.5	06	371-373	011.35	04	177-179	012.34	03	154-156	013.93	01	094-096	015.92	08	548-550
			011.36	04	177-179	012.35	03	154-156	013.94	01	094-096	015.93	08	548-550

DX	MDC	DRG	DX	MDC	DRG	DX	MDC	DRG	DX	MDC	DRG	DX	MDC	DRG
015.94	08	548-550	017.15	09	595-596	018.96	18	867-869	037	18	867-869	046.3	01	056-057
015.95	08	548-550	017.16	09	595-596	020.0	18	867-869	038.0	18	870-872	046.71	01	056-057
015.96	08	548-550	017.20	16	814-816	020.1	18	867-869	038.10	18	870-872	046.72	01	056-057
016.00	11	689-690	017.21	16	814-816	020.2	18	870-872	038.11	18	870-872	046.79	01	056-057
016.01	11	689-690	017.22	16	814-816	020.3	04	177-179	038.12	18	870-872	046.8	01	056-057
016.02	11	689-690	017.23	16	814-816	020.4	04	177-179	038.19	18	870-872	046.9	01	056-057
016.03	11	689-690	017.24	16	814-816	020.5	04	177-179	038.2	18	870-872	047.0	01	075-076
016.04	11	689-690	017.25	16	814-816	020.8	18	867-869	038.3	18	870-872	047.1	01	075-076
016.05	11	689-690	017.26	16	814-816	020.9	18	867-869	038.40	18	870-872	047.8	01	075-076
016.06	11	689-690	017.30	02	124-125	021.0	18	867-869	038.41	18	870-872	047.9	01	075-076
016.10	11	689-690	017.31	02	124-125	021.1	06	371-373	038.42	18	870-872	048	01	075-076
016.11	11	689-690	017.32	02	124-125	021.2	04	177-179	038.43	18	870-872	049.0	01	075-076
016.12	11	689-690	017.33	02	124-125	021.3	18	867-869	038.44	18	870-872	049.1	01	075-076
016.13	11	689-690	017.34	02	124-125	021.8	18	867-869	038.49	18	870-872	049.8	01	097-099
016.14	11	689-690	017.35	02	124-125	021.9	18	867-869	038.8	18	870-872	049.9	01	097-099
016.15	11	689-690	017.36	02	124-125	022.0	09	606-607	038.9	18	870-872	050.1	18	865-866
016.16	11	689-690	017.40	03	154-156	022.1	04	177-179	039.0	09	606-607	050.2	18	865-866
016.20	11	689-690	017.41	03	154-156	022.2	06	371-373	039.1	04	177-179	050.9	18	865-866
016.21	11	689-690	017.42	03	154-156	022.3	18	870-872	039.2	06	371-373	051.01	18	865-866
016.22	11	689-690	017.43	03	154-156	022.8	18	867-869	039.3	09	606-607	051.02	18	865-866
016.23	11	689-690	017.44	03	154-156	022.9	18	867-869	039.4	09	606-607	051.1	09	606-607
016.24	11	689-690	017.45	03	154-156	023.0	18	867-869	039.8	18	867-869	051.2	09	606-607
016.25	11	689-690	017.46	03	154-156	023.1	18	867-869	039.9	18	867-869	051.9	18	865-866
016.26	11	689-690	017.50	10	643-645	023.2	18	867-869	040.0	18	867-869	052.0	01	097-099
016.30	11	689-690	017.51	10	643-645	023.3	18	867-869	040.1	18	867-869	052.1	04	177-179
016.31	11	689-690	017.52	10	643-645	023.8	18	867-869	040.2	06	393-395	052.2	01	097-099
016.32	11	689-690	017.53	10	643-645	023.9	18	867-869	040.3	18	867-869	052.7	18	865-866
016.33	11	689-690	017.54	10	643-645	024	18	867-869	040.41	18	867-869	052.8	18	865-866
016.34	11	689-690	017.55	10	643-645	025	18	867-869	040.42	18	867-869	052.9	18	865-866
016.35	11	689-690	017.56	10	643-645	026.0	18	867-869	040.81	08	557-558	053.0	01	075-076
016.36	11	689-690	017.60	10	643-645	026.1	18	867-869	040.82	18	867-869	053.10	01	073-074
016.40	12	727-728	017.61	10	643-645	026.9	18	867-869	040.89	18	867-869	053.11	01	073-074
016.41	12	727-728	017.62	10	643-645	027.0	18	867-869	041.00	18	867-869	053.12	01	073-074
016.42	12	727-728	017.63	10	643-645	027.1	18	867-869	041.01	18	867-869	053.13	01	073-074
016.43	12	727-728	017.64	10	643-645	027.2	18	867-869	041.02	18	867-869	053.14	01	097-099
016.44	12	727-728	017.65	10	643-645	027.8	18	867-869	041.03	18	867-869	053.19	01	073-074
016.45	12	727-728	017.66	10	643-645	027.9	18	867-869	041.04	18	867-869	053.20	02	124-125
016.46	12	727-728	017.70	16	814-816	030.0	18	867-869	041.05	18	867-869	053.21	02	124-125
016.50	12	727-728	017.71	16	814-816	030.1	18	867-869	041.09	18	867-869	053.22	02	124-125
016.51	12	727-728	017.72	16	814-816	030.2	18	867-869	041.10	18	867-869	053.29	02	124-125
016.52	12	727-728	017.73	16	814-816	030.3	18	867-869	041.11	18	867-869	053.71	03	154-156
016.53	12	727-728	017.74	16	814-816	030.8	18	867-869	041.12	18	867-869	053.79	18	865-866
016.54	12	727-728	017.75	16	814-816	030.9	18	867-869	041.19	18	867-869	053.8	18	865-866
016.55	12	727-728	017.76	16	814-816	031.0	04	177-179	041.2	18	867-869	053.9	09	595-596
016.56	12	727-728	017.80	06	368-370	031.1	09	606-607	041.3	18	867-869	054.0	09	606-607
016.60	13	757-759	017.81	06	368-370	031.2	18	867-869	041.4	18	867-869	054.10	12	727-728
016.61	13	757-759	017.82	06	368-370	031.8	18	867-869	041.5	18	867-869	054.10	13	757-759
016.62	13	757-759	017.83	06	368-370	031.9	18	867-869	041.6	18	867-869	054.11	13	757-759
016.63	13	757-759	017.84	06	368-370	032.0	03	154-156	041.7	18	867-869	054.12	13	757-759
016.64	13	757-759	017.85	06	368-370	032.1	03	154-156	041.81	18	867-869	054.13	12	727-728
016.65	13	757-759	017.86	06	368-370	032.2	03	154-156	041.82	18	867-869	054.19	12	727-728
016.66	13	757-759	017.90	18	867-869	032.3	03	154-156	041.83	18	867-869	054.19	13	757-759
016.70	13	757-759	017.91	18	867-869	032.81	02	124-125	041.84	18	867-869	054.2	03	157-159
016.71	13	757-759	017.92	18	867-869	032.82	05	314-316	041.85	18	867-869	054.3	01	097-099
016.72	13	757-759	017.93	18	867-869	032.83	06	371-373	041.86	18	867-869	054.40	02	124-125
016.73	13	757-759	017.94	18	867-869	032.84	11	689-690	041.89	18	867-869	054.41	02	124-125
016.74	13	757-759	017.95	18	867-869	032.85	09	606-607	041.9	18	867-869	054.42	02	124-125
016.75	13	757-759	017.96	18	867-869	032.89	18	867-869	042	25	974-977	054.43	02	124-125
016.76	13	757-759	018.00	18	867-869	032.9	18	867-869	045.00	01	097-099	054.44	02	124-125
016.90	11	689-690	018.01	18	867-869	033.0	04	202-203	045.01	01	097-099	054.49	02	124-125
016.91	11	689-690	018.02	18	867-869	033.1	04	202-203	045.02	01	097-099	054.5	18	870-872
016.92	11	689-690	018.03	18	867-869	033.8	04	202-203	045.03	01	097-099	054.6	09	606-607
016.93	11	689-690	018.04	18	867-869	033.9	04	202-203	045.10	01	097-099	054.71	06	393-395
016.94	11	689-690	018.05	18	867-869	034.0	03	152-153	045.11	01	097-099	054.72	01	075-076
016.95	11	689-690	018.06	18	867-869	034.1	18	867-869	045.12	01	097-099	054.73	03	154-156
016.96	11	689-690	018.80	18	867-869	035	09	602-603	045.13	01	097-099	054.74	01	097-099
017.00	09	606-607	018.81	18	867-869	036.0	01	094-096	045.20	18	865-866	054.79	18	865-866
017.01	09	606-607	018.82	18	867-869	036.1	01	094-096	045.21	18	865-866	054.8	18	865-866
017.02	09	606-607	018.83	18	867-869	036.2	18	870-872	045.22	18	865-866	054.9	09	606-607
017.03	09	606-607	018.84	18	867-869	036.3	18	870-872	045.23	18	865-866	055.0	01	097-099
017.04	09	606-607	018.85	18	867-869	036.40	05	314-316	045.90	01	097-099	055.1	04	177-179
017.05	09	606-607	018.86	18	867-869	036.41	05	314-316	045.91	01	097-099	055.2	03	152-153
017.06	09	606-607	018.90	18	867-869	036.42	05	288-290	045.92	01	097-099	055.71	02	124-125
017.10	09	595-596	018.91	18	867-869	036.43	05	314-316	045.93	01	097-099	055.79	18	865-866
017.11	09	595-596	018.92	18	867-869	036.81	02	123	046.0	01	056-057	055.8	18	865-866
017.12	09	595-596	018.93	18	867-869	036.82	08	548-550	046.11	01	056-057	055.9	18	865-866
017.13	09	595-596	018.94	18	867-869	036.89	18	870-872	046.19	01	056-057	056.00	01	073-074
017.14	09	595-596	018.95	18	867-869	036.9	18	870-872	046.2	01	056-057	056.01	01	097-099

DX	MDC	DRG	DX	MDC	DRG	DX	MDC	DRG	DX	MDC	DRG	DX	MDC	DRG
056.09	01	097-099	070.44	07	441-443	080	18	867-869	091.82	09	606-607	098.59	08	548-550
056.71	08	553-554	070.49	07	441-443	081.0	18	867-869	091.89	18	867-869	098.6	03	152-153
056.79	18	865-866	070.51	07	441-443	081.1	18	867-869	091.9	18	867-869	098.7	06	393-395
056.8	18	865-866	070.52	07	441-443	081.2	18	867-869	092.0	18	867-869	098.81	02	124-125
056.9	18	865-866	070.53	07	441-443	081.9	18	867-869	092.9	18	867-869	098.82	01	094-096
057.0	18	865-866	070.54	07	441-443	082.0	18	867-869	093.0	05	306-307	098.83	05	314-316
057.8	18	865-866	070.59	07	441-443	082.1	18	867-869	093.1	05	306-307	098.84	05	288-290
057.9	18	865-866	070.6	07	441-443	082.2	18	867-869	093.20	05	288-290	098.85	05	314-316
058.10	18	865-866	070.70	07	441-443	082.3	18	867-869	093.21	05	306-307	098.86	06	371-373
058.11	18	865-866	070.71	07	441-443	082.40	18	867-869	093.22	05	306-307	098.89	18	867-869
058.12	18	865-866	070.9	07	441-443	082.41	18	867-869	093.23	05	306-307	099.0	12	727-728
058.21	01	097-099	071	01	097-099	082.49	18	867-869	093.24	05	306-307	099.0	13	757-759
058.29	01	097-099	072.0	12	727-728	082.8	18	867-869	093.81	05	314-316	099.1	12	727-728
058.81	09	606-607	072.1	01	075-076	082.9	18	867-869	093.82	05	314-316	099.1	13	757-759
058.82	09	606-607	072.2	01	097-099	083.0	18	867-869	093.89	05	314-316	099.2	12	727-728
058.89	09	606-607	072.3	07	438-440	083.1	18	867-869	093.9	05	314-316	099.2	13	757-759
059.00	18	865-866	072.71	07	441-443	083.2	18	867-869	094.0	01	056-057	099.3	08	545-547
059.01	18	865-866	072.72	01	073-074	083.8	18	867-869	094.1	01	056-057	099.40	12	727-728
059.09	18	865-866	072.79	18	865-866	083.9	18	867-869	094.2	01	097-099	099.40	13	757-759
059.10	18	865,866	072.8	18	865-866	084.0	18	867-869	094.3	01	097-099	099.41	12	727-728
059.11	18	865-866	072.9	18	865-866	084.1	18	867-869	094.81	01	097-099	099.41	13	757-759
059.12	18	865-866	073.0	04	177-179	084.2	18	867-869	094.82	01	056-057	099.49	12	727-728
059.19	18	865-866	073.7	18	865-866	084.3	18	867-869	094.83	02	124-125	099.49	13	757-759
059.21	18	865-866	073.8	18	865-866	084.4	18	867-869	094.84	02	124-125	099.50	12	727-728
059.22	18	865-866	073.9	18	865-866	084.5	18	867-869	094.85	01	056-057	099.50	13	757-759
059.29	18	865-866	074.0	03	152-153	084.6	18	867-869	094.86	03	154-156	099.51	03	152-153
059.8	18	865-866	074.1	04	193-195	084.7	18	867-869	094.87	01	091-093	099.52	06	393-395
059.9	18	865-866	074.20	05	314-316	084.8	18	867-869	094.89	01	056-057	099.53	12	727-728
060.0	18	865-866	074.21	05	314-316	084.9	18	867-869	094.9	01	056-057	099.53	13	757-759
060.1	18	865-866	074.22	05	306-307	085.0	18	867-869	095.0	02	124-125	099.54	11	689-690
060.9	18	865-866	074.23	05	314-316	085.1	09	606-607	095.1	04	177-179	099.55	12	727-728
061	18	865-866	074.3	18	865-866	085.2	09	606-607	095.2	06	371-373	099.55	13	757-759
062.0	01	097-099	074.8	18	865-866	085.3	09	606-607	095.3	07	441-443	099.56	06	393-395
062.1	01	097-099	075	18	865-866	085.4	09	606-607	095.4	11	689-690	099.59	12	727-728
062.2	01	097-099	076.0	02	124-125	085.5	09	606-607	095.5	08	539-541	099.59	13	757-759
062.3	01	097-099	076.1	02	124-125	085.9	18	867-869	095.6	08	557-558	099.8	12	727-728
062.4	01	097-099	076.9	02	124-125	086.0	05	314-316	095.7	08	557-558	099.8	13	757-759
062.5	01	097-099	077.0	02	124-125	086.1	18	867-869	095.8	18	867-869	099.9	12	727-728
062.8	01	097-099	077.1	02	124-125	086.2	18	867-869	095.9	18	867-869	099.9	13	757-759
062.9	01	097-099	077.2	02	124-125	086.3	18	867-869	096	18	867-869	100.0	18	867-869
063.0	01	097-099	077.3	02	124-125	086.4	18	867-869	097.0	18	867-869	100.81	01	097-099
063.1	01	097-099	077.4	02	124-125	086.5	18	867-869	097.1	18	867-869	100.89	01	097-099
063.2	01	097-099	077.8	02	124-125	086.9	18	867-869	097.9	18	867-869	100.9	18	867-869
063.8	01	097-099	077.98	02	124-125	087.0	18	867-869	098.0	12	727-728	101	03	152-153
063.9	01	097-099	077.99	02	124-125	087.1	18	867-869	098.0	13	757-759	102.0	09	606-607
064	01	097-099	078.0	09	606-607	087.9	18	867-869	098.10	12	727-728	102.1	09	606-607
065.0	18	865-866	078.10	09	606-607	088.0	18	867-869	098.10	13	757-759	102.2	09	606-607
065.1	18	865-866	078.11	09	606-607	088.81	18	867-869	098.11	11	689-690	102.3	09	606-607
065.2	18	865-866	078.12	09	606-607	088.82	18	867-869	098.12	12	727-728	102.4	09	606-607
065.3	18	865-866	078.19	09	606-607	088.89	18	867-869	098.13	12	727-728	102.5	03	154-156
065.4	18	865-866	078.2	18	865-866	088.9	18	867-869	098.14	12	727-728	102.6	08	548-550
065.8	18	865-866	078.3	16	814-816	090.0	18	867-869	098.15	13	757-759	102.7	18	867-869
065.9	18	865-866	078.4	18	865-866	090.1	18	867-869	098.16	13	757-759	102.8	18	867-869
066.0	18	865-866	078.5	18	865-866	090.2	18	867-869	098.17	13	757-759	102.9	18	867-869
066.1	18	865-866	078.6	11	689-690	090.3	02	124-125	098.19	12	727-728	103.0	09	606-607
066.2	01	097-099	078.7	18	865-866	090.40	01	097-099	098.19	13	757-759	103.1	09	606-607
066.3	18	865-866	078.81	01	091-093	090.41	01	097-099	098.2	12	727-728	103.2	18	867-869
066.40	18	865-866	078.82	06	391-392	090.42	01	097-099	098.2	13	757-759	103.3	09	606-607
066.41	18	865-866	078.88	18	865-866	090.49	01	097-099	098.30	11	689-690	103.9	18	867-869
066.42	18	865-866	078.89	18	865-866	090.5	18	867-869	098.31	11	689-690	104.0	18	867-869
066.49	18	865-866	079.0	18	865-866	090.6	18	867-869	098.32	12	727-728	104.8	18	867-869
066.8	18	865-866	079.1	18	865-866	090.7	18	867-869	098.33	12	727-728	104.9	18	867-869
066.9	18	865-866	079.2	18	865-866	090.9	18	867-869	098.34	12	727-728	110.0	09	606-607
070.0	07	441-443	079.3	18	865-866	091.0	12	727-728	098.35	13	757-759	110.1	09	606-607
070.71	07	441-443	079.4	18	865-866	091.0	13	757-759	098.36	13	757-759	110.2	09	606-607
070.1	07	441-443	079.50	18	865-866	091.1	06	393-395	098.37	13	757-759	110.3	09	606-607
070.20	07	441-443	079.51	18	865-866	091.2	18	867-869	098.39	12	727-728	110.4	09	606-607
070.21	07	441-443	079.52	18	865-866	091.3	09	606-607	098.39	13	757-759	110.5	09	606-607
070.22	07	441-443	079.53	18	865-866	091.4	16	814-816	098.40	02	124-125	110.6	09	606-607
070.23	07	441-443	079.59	18	865-866	091.50	02	124-125	098.41	02	124-125	110.8	09	606-607
070.30	07	441-443	079.6	18	865-866	091.51	02	124-125	098.42	02	124-125	110.9	09	606-607
070.31	07	441-443	079.81	18	865-866	091.52	02	124-125	098.43	02	124-125	111.0	09	606-607
070.32	07	441-443	079.83	18	865-866	091.61	08	539-541	098.49	02	124-125	111.1	09	606-607
070.33	07	441-443	079.88	18	865-866	091.62	07	441-443	098.50	08	548-550	111.2	09	606-607
070.41	07	441-443	079.89	18	865-866	091.69	06	393-395	098.51	08	548-550	111.3	09	606-607
070.42	07	441-443	079.98	18	865-866	091.7	18	867-869	098.52	08	548-550	111.8	09	606-607
070.43	07	441-443	079.99	18	865-866	091.81	01	097-099	098.53	08	539-541	111.9	09	606-607

Diagnosis Code/MDC/DRG List

DX	MDC	DRG
112.0	03	157-159
112.1	13	757-759
112.2	12	727-728
112.2	13	757-759
112.3	09	606-607
112.4	04	177-179
112.5	18	867-869
112.81	05	288-290
112.82	03	154-156
112.83	01	097-099
112.84	06	368-370
112.85	06	391-392
112.89	18	867-869
112.9	18	867-869
114.0	04	177-179
114.1	09	606-607
114.2	01	097-099
114.3	18	867-869
114.4	04	177-179
114.5	04	177-179
114.9	18	867-869
115.00	18	867-869
115.01	01	097-099
115.02	02	124-125
115.03	05	314-316
115.04	05	288-290
115.05	04	177-179
115.09	18	867-869
115.10	18	867-869
115.11	01	097-099
115.12	02	124-125
115.13	05	314-316
115.14	05	288-290
115.15	04	177-179
115.19	18	867-869
115.90	18	867-869
115.91	01	097-099
115.92	02	124-125
115.93	05	314-316
115.94	05	288-290
115.95	04	177-179
115.99	18	867-869
116.0	18	867-869
116.1	18	867-869
116.2	18	867-869
117.0	18	867-869
117.1	18	867-869
117.2	18	867-869
117.3	18	867-869
117.4	18	867-869
117.5	18	867-869
117.6	18	867-869
117.7	18	867-869
117.8	18	867-869
117.9	18	867-869
118	18	867-869
120.0	11	689-690
120.1	07	441-443
120.2	18	867-869
120.3	09	606-607
120.8	18	867-869
120.9	18	867-869
121.0	07	441-443
121.1	07	441-443
121.2	04	177-179
121.3	07	441-443
121.4	07	441-443
121.5	18	867-869
121.6	18	867-869
121.8	18	867-869
121.9	18	867-869
122.0	07	441-443
122.1	04	177-179
122.2	10	643-645
122.3	18	867-869
122.4	18	867-869
122.5	07	441-443
122.6	18	867-869
122.7	18	867-869
122.8	07	441-443
122.9	18	867-869
123.0	06	391-392
123.1	06	371-373
123.2	06	391-392
123.3	06	391-392
123.4	06	391-392
123.5	06	371-373
123.6	06	371-373
123.8	06	371-373
123.9	06	371-373
124	18	867-869
125.0	18	867-869
125.1	18	867-869
125.2	18	867-869
125.3	18	867-869
125.4	18	867-869
125.5	18	867-869
125.6	18	867-869
125.7	18	867-869
125.9	18	867-869
126.0	06	371-373
126.1	06	371-373
126.2	06	371-373
126.3	06	371-373
126.8	06	371-373
126.9	06	371-373
127.0	06	391-392
127.1	06	391-392
127.2	06	391-392
127.3	06	391-392
127.4	06	391-392
127.5	06	391-392
127.6	06	391-392
127.7	06	391-392
127.8	18	867-869
127.9	06	391-392
128.0	18	867-869
128.1	18	867-869
128.8	18	867-869
128.9	18	867-869
129	06	391-392
130.0	01	097-099
130.1	02	124-125
130.2	02	124-125
130.3	05	314-316
130.4	04	177-179
130.5	07	441-443
130.7	18	867-869
130.8	18	867-869
130.9	18	867-869
131.00	12	727-728
131.00	13	757-759
131.01	13	757-759
131.02	12	727-728
131.02	13	757-759
131.03	12	727-728
131.09	12	727-728
131.09	13	757-759
131.8	18	867-869
131.9	18	867-869
132.0	09	606-607
132.1	09	606-607
132.2	09	606-607
132.3	09	606-607
132.9	09	606-607
133.0	09	606-607
133.8	09	606-607
133.9	09	606-607
134.0	09	606-607
134.1	09	606-607
134.2	09	606-607
134.8	09	606-607
134.9	09	606-607
135	04	196-198
136.0	18	867-869
136.1	08	545-547
136.21	18	867-869
136.29	18	867-869
136.3	04	177-179
136.4	18	867-869
136.5	18	867-869
136.8	18	867-869
136.9	18	867-869
137.0	04	196-198
137.1	01	091-093
137.2	11	689-690
137.3	08	564-566
137.4	18	867-869
138	01	091-093
139.0	01	091-093
139.1	02	124-125
139.8	18	867-869

Neoplasms

DX	MDC	DRG
140.0	03	146-148
140.1	03	146-148
140.3	03	146-148
140.4	03	146-148
140.5	03	146-148
140.6	03	146-148
140.8	03	146-148
140.9	03	146-148
141.0	03	146-148
141.1	03	146-148
141.2	03	146-148
141.3	03	146-148
141.4	03	146-148
141.5	03	146-148
141.6	03	146-148
141.8	03	146-148
141.9	03	146-148
142.0	03	146-148
142.1	03	146-148
142.2	03	146-148
142.8	03	146-148
142.9	03	146-148
143.0	03	146-148
143.1	03	146-148
143.8	03	146-148
143.9	03	146-148
144.0	03	146-148
144.1	03	146-148
144.8	03	146-148
144.9	03	146-148
145.0	03	146-148
145.1	03	146-148
145.2	03	146-148
145.3	03	146-148
145.4	03	146-148
145.5	03	146-148
145.6	03	146-148
145.8	03	146-148
145.9	03	146-148
146.0	03	146-148
146.1	03	146-148
146.2	03	146-148
146.3	03	146-148
146.4	03	146-148
146.5	03	146-148
146.6	03	146-148
146.7	03	146-148
146.8	03	146-148
146.9	03	146-148
147.0	03	146-148
147.1	03	146-148
147.2	03	146-148
147.3	03	146-148
147.8	03	146-148
147.9	03	146-148
148.0	03	146-148
148.1	03	146-148
148.2	03	146-148
148.3	03	146-148
148.8	03	146-148
148.9	03	146-148
149.0	03	146-148
149.1	03	146-148
149.8	03	146-148
149.9	03	146-148
150.0	06	374-376
150.1	06	374-376
150.2	06	374-376
150.3	06	374-376
150.4	06	374-376
150.5	06	374-376
150.8	06	374-376
150.9	06	374-376
151.0	06	374-376
151.1	06	374-376
151.2	06	374-376
151.3	06	374-376
151.4	06	374-376
151.5	06	374-376
151.6	06	374-376
151.8	06	374-376
151.9	06	374-376
152.0	06	374-376
152.1	06	374-376
152.2	06	374-376
152.3	06	374-376
152.8	06	374-376
152.9	06	374-376
153.0	06	374-376
153.1	06	374-376
153.2	06	374-376
153.3	06	374-376
153.4	06	374-376
153.5	06	374-376
153.6	06	374-376
153.7	06	374-376
153.8	06	374-376
153.9	06	374-376
154.0	06	374-376
154.1	06	374-376
154.2	06	374-376
154.3	06	374-376
154.8	06	374-376
155.0	07	435-437
155.1	07	435-437
155.2	07	435-437
156.0	07	435-437
156.1	07	435-437
156.2	07	435-437
156.8	07	435-437
156.9	07	435-437
157.0	07	435-437
157.1	07	435-437
157.2	07	435-437
157.3	07	435-437
157.4	07	435-437
157.8	07	435-437
157.9	07	435-437
158.0	17	843-845
158.8	06	374-376
158.9	06	374-376
159.0	06	374-376
159.1	17	840-842
159.8	06	374-376
159.9	06	374-376
160.0	03	146-148
160.1	03	146-148
160.2	03	146-148
160.3	03	146-148
160.4	03	146-148
160.5	03	146-148
160.8	03	146-148
160.9	03	146-148
161.0	03	146-148
161.1	03	146-148
161.2	03	146-148
161.3	03	146-148
161.8	03	146-148
161.9	03	146-148
162.0	04	180-182
162.2	04	180-182
162.3	04	180-182
162.4	04	180-182
162.5	04	180-182
162.8	04	180-182
162.9	04	180-182
163.0	04	180-182
163.1	04	180-182
163.8	04	180-182
163.9	04	180-182
164.0	17	843-845
164.1	05	314-316
164.2	04	180-182
164.3	04	180-182
164.8	04	180-182
164.9	04	180-182
165.0	03	146-148
165.8	04	180-182
165.9	04	180-182
170.0	08	542-544
170.1	08	542-544
170.2	08	542-544
170.3	08	542-544
170.4	08	542-544
170.5	08	542-544
170.6	08	542-544
170.7	08	542-544
170.8	08	542-544
170.9	08	542-544
171.0	08	542-544
171.3	08	542-544
171.4	08	542-544
171.5	08	542-544
171.6	08	542-544
171.7	08	542-544
171.8	08	542-544
171.9	08	542-544
172.0	09	595-596
172.1	02	124-125
172.2	09	595-596
172.3	09	595-596
172.4	09	595-596
172.5	09	595-596
172.6	09	595-596
172.7	09	595-596
172.8	09	595-596
172.9	09	595-596
173.0	09	606-607
173.1	02	124-125
173.2	09	606-607
173.3	09	606-607
173.4	09	606-607
173.5	09	606-607
173.6	09	606-607
173.7	09	606-607
173.8	09	606-607
173.9	09	606-607
174.0	09	597-599
174.1	09	597-599
174.2	09	597-599
174.3	09	597-599
174.4	09	597-599
174.5	09	597-599
174.6	09	597-599
174.8	09	597-599
174.9	09	597-599
175.0	09	597-599
175.9	09	597-599
176.0	09	606-607
176.1	09	606-607
176.2	03	146-148
176.3	06	374-376
176.4	04	180-182
176.5	17	840-842
176.8	09	606-607

DX	MDC	DRG	DX	MDC	DRG	DX	MDC	DRG	DX	MDC	DRG	DX	MDC	DRG
176.9	09	606-607	192.8	01	054-055	200.28	17	840-842	201.24	17	840-842	202.30	17	840-842
179	13	754-756	192.9	01	054-055	200.30	17	840-842	201.25	17	840-842	202.31	17	840-842
180.0	13	754-756	193	10	643-645	200.31	17	840-842	201.26	17	840-842	202.32	17	840-842
180.1	13	754-756	194.0	10	643-645	200.32	17	840-842	201.27	17	840-842	202.33	17	840-842
180.8	13	754-756	194.1	10	643-645	200.33	17	840-842	201.28	17	840-842	202.34	17	840-842
180.9	13	754-756	194.3	10	643-645	200.34	17	840-842	201.40	17	840-842	202.35	17	840-842
181	13	754-756	194.4	01	054-055	200.35	17	840-842	201.41	17	840-842	202.36	17	840-842
182.0	13	754-756	194.5	01	054-055	200.36	17	840-842	201.42	17	840-842	202.37	17	840-842
182.1	13	754-756	194.6	01	054-055	200.37	17	840-842	201.43	17	840-842	202.38	17	840-842
182.8	13	754-756	194.8	10	643-645	200.38	17	840-842	201.44	17	840-842	202.40	17	840-842
183.0	13	754-756	194.9	10	643-645	200.30	17	840-842	201.45	17	840-842	202.41	17	840-842
183.2	13	754-756	195.0	03	146-148	200.41	17	840-842	201.46	17	840-842	202.42	17	840-842
183.3	13	754-756	195.1	04	180-182	200.42	17	840-842	201.47	17	840-842	202.43	17	840-842
183.4	13	754-756	195.2	06	374-376	200.43	17	840-842	201.48	17	840-842	202.44	17	840-842
183.5	13	754-756	195.3	12	722-724	200.44	17	840-842	201.50	17	840-842	202.45	17	840-842
183.8	13	754-756	195.3	13	754-756	200.45	17	840-842	201.51	17	840-842	202.46	17	840-842
183.9	13	754-756	195.4	17	843-845	200.46	17	840-842	201.52	17	840-842	202.47	17	840-842
184.0	13	754-756	195.5	17	843-845	200.47	17	840-842	201.53	17	840-842	202.48	17	840-842
184.1	13	754-756	195.8	17	843-845	200.48	17	840-842	201.54	17	840-842	202.50	17	843-845
184.2	13	754-756	196.0	17	840-842	200.50	17	840-842	201.55	17	840-842	202.51	17	843-845
184.3	13	754-756	196.1	17	840-842	200.51	17	840-842	201.56	17	840-842	202.52	17	843-845
184.4	13	754-756	196.2	17	840-842	200.52	17	840-842	201.57	17	840-842	202.53	17	843-845
184.8	13	754-756	196.3	17	840-842	200.53	17	840-842	201.58	17	840-842	202.54	17	843-845
184.9	13	754-756	196.5	17	840-842	200.54	17	840-842	201.60	17	840-842	202.55	17	843-845
185	12	722-724	196.6	17	840-842	200.55	17	840-842	201.61	17	840-842	202.56	17	843-845
186.0	12	722-724	196.8	17	840-842	200.56	17	840-842	201.62	17	840-842	202.57	17	843-845
186.9	12	722-724	196.9	17	840-842	200.57	17	840-842	201.63	17	840-842	202.58	17	843-845
187.1	12	722-724	197.0	04	180-182	200.58	17	840-842	201.64	17	840-842	202.60	17	840-842
187.2	12	722-724	197.1	04	180-182	200.60	17	840-842	201.65	17	840-842	202.61	17	840-842
187.3	12	722-724	197.2	04	180-182	200.61	17	840-842	201.66	17	840-842	202.62	17	840-842
187.4	12	722-724	197.3	04	180-182	200.62	17	840-842	201.67	17	840-842	202.63	17	840-842
187.5	12	722-724	197.4	06	374-376	200.63	17	840-842	201.68	17	840-842	202.64	17	840-842
187.6	12	722-724	197.5	06	374-376	200.64	17	840-842	201.70	17	840-842	202.65	17	840-842
187.7	12	722-724	197.6	06	374-376	200.65	17	840-842	201.71	17	840-842	202.66	17	840-842
187.8	12	722-724	197.7	07	435-437	200.66	17	840-842	201.72	17	840-842	202.67	17	840-842
187.9	12	722-724	197.8	06	374-376	200.67	17	840-842	201.73	17	840-842	202.68	17	840-842
188.0	11	686-688	198.0	11	686-688	200.68	17	840-842	201.74	17	840-842	202.70	17	840-842
188.1	11	686-688	198.1	11	686-688	200.70	17	840-842	201.75	17	840-842	202.71	17	840-842
188.2	11	686-688	198.2	09	597-599	200.71	17	840-842	201.76	17	840-842	202.72	17	840-842
188.3	11	686-688	198.3	01	054-055	200.72	17	840-842	201.77	17	840-842	202.73	17	840-842
188.4	11	686-688	198.4	01	054-055	200.73	17	840-842	201.78	17	840-842	202.74	17	840-842
188.5	11	686-688	198.5	08	542-544	200.74	17	840-842	201.90	17	840-842	202.75	17	840-842
188.6	11	686-688	198.6	13	754-756	200.75	17	840-842	201.91	17	840-842	202.76	17	840-842
188.7	11	686-688	198.7	10	643-645	200.76	17	840-842	201.92	17	840-842	202.77	17	840-842
188.8	11	686-688	198.81	09	597-599	200.77	17	840-842	201.93	17	840-842	202.78	17	840-842
188.9	11	686-688	198.82	12	722-724	200.78	17	840-842	201.94	17	840-842	202.80	17	840-842
189.0	11	686-688	198.82	13	754-756	200.80	17	840-842	201.95	17	840-842	202.81	17	840-842
189.1	11	686-688	198.89	17	843-845	200.81	17	840-842	201.96	17	840-842	202.82	17	840-842
189.2	11	686-688	199.0	17	843-845	200.82	17	840-842	201.97	17	840-842	202.83	17	840-842
189.3	11	686-688	199.1	17	843-845	200.83	17	840-842	201.98	17	840-842	202.84	17	840-842
189.4	11	686-688	199.2	17	843-845	200.84	17	840-842	202.00	17	840-842	202.85	17	840-842
189.8	11	686-688	200.00	17	840-842	200.85	17	840-842	202.01	17	840-842	202.86	17	840-842
189.9	11	686-688	200.01	17	840-842	200.86	17	840-842	202.02	17	840-842	202.87	17	840-842
190.0	02	124-125	200.02	17	840-842	200.87	17	840-842	202.03	17	840-842	202.88	17	840-842
190.1	02	124-125	200.03	17	840-842	200.88	17	840-842	202.04	17	840-842	202.90	17	840-842
190.2	02	124-125	200.04	17	840-842	201.00	17	840-842	202.05	17	840-842	202.91	17	840-842
190.3	02	124-125	200.05	17	840-842	201.01	17	840-842	202.06	17	840-842	202.92	17	840-842
190.4	02	124-125	200.06	17	840-842	201.02	17	840-842	202.07	17	840-842	202.93	17	840-842
190.5	02	124-125	200.07	17	840-842	201.03	17	840-842	202.08	17	840-842	202.94	17	840-842
190.6	02	124-125	200.08	17	840-842	201.04	17	840-842	202.10	17	840-842	202.95	17	840-842
190.7	02	124-125	200.10	17	840-842	201.05	17	840-842	202.11	17	840-842	202.96	17	840-842
190.8	02	124-125	200.11	17	840-842	201.06	17	840-842	202.12	17	840-842	202.97	17	840-842
190.9	02	124-125	200.12	17	840-842	201.07	17	840-842	202.13	17	840-842	202.98	17	840-842
191.0	01	054-055	200.13	17	840-842	201.08	17	840-842	202.14	17	840-842	203.00	17	840-842
191.1	01	054-055	200.14	17	840-842	201.10	17	840-842	202.15	17	840-842	203.01	17	840-842
191.2	01	054-055	200.15	17	840-842	201.11	17	840-842	202.16	17	840-842	203.02	17	840-842
191.3	01	054-055	200.16	17	840-842	201.12	17	840-842	202.17	17	840-842	203.10	17	840-842
191.4	01	054-055	200.17	17	840-842	201.13	17	840-842	202.18	17	840-842	203.11	17	840-842
191.5	01	054-055	200.18	17	840-842	201.14	17	840-842	202.20	17	840-842	203.12	17	840-842
191.6	01	054-055	200.20	17	840-842	201.15	17	840-842	202.21	17	840-842	203.80	17	840-842
191.7	01	054-055	200.21	17	840-842	201.16	17	840-842	202.22	17	840-842	203.81	17	840-842
191.8	01	054-055	200.22	17	840-842	201.17	17	840-842	202.23	17	840-842	203.82	17	840-842
191.9	01	054-055	200.23	17	840-842	201.18	17	840-842	202.24	17	840-842	204.00	17	834-836
192.0	01	054-055	200.24	17	840-842	201.20	17	840-842	202.25	17	840-842	204.01	17	834-836
192.1	01	054-055	200.25	17	840-842	201.21	17	840-842	202.26	17	840-842	204.02	17	834-839
192.2	01	054-055	200.26	17	840-842	201.22	17	840-842	202.27	17	840-842	204.10	17	840-842
192.3	01	054-055	200.27	17	840-842	201.23	17	840-842	202.28	17	840-842	204.11	17	840-842

DX	MDC	DRG
204.12	17	840-842
204.20	17	840-842
204.21	17	840-842
204.22	17	840-842
204.80	17	840-842
204.81	17	840-842
204.82	17	840-842
204.90	17	840-842
204.91	17	840-842
204.92	17	840-842
205.00	17	834-836
205.01	17	834-836
205.02	17	834-839
205.10	17	840-842
205.11	17	840-842
205.12	17	840-842
205.20	17	840-842
205.21	17	840-842
205.22	17	840-842
205.30	17	840-842
205.31	17	840-842
205.32	17	840-842
205.80	17	840-842
205.81	17	840-842
205.82	17	840-842
205.90	17	840-842
205.91	17	840-842
205.92	17	840-842
206.00	17	834-836
206.01	17	834-836
206.02	17	834-839
206.10	17	840-842
206.11	17	840-842
206.12	17	840-842
206.20	17	840-842
206.21	17	840-842
206.22	17	840-842
206.80	17	840-842
206.81	17	840-842
206.82	17	840-842
206.90	17	840-842
206.91	17	840-842
206.92	17	840-842
207.00	17	834-836
207.01	17	834-836
207.02	17	834-839
207.10	17	840-842
207.11	17	840-842
207.12	17	840-842
207.20	17	840-842
207.21	17	840-842
207.22	17	840-842
207.80	17	840-842
207.81	17	840-842
207.82	17	840-842
208.00	17	834-836
208.01	17	834-836
208.02	17	834-839
208.10	17	840-842
208.11	17	840-842
208.12	17	840-842
208.20	17	840-842
208.21	17	840-842
208.22	17	840-842
208.80	17	840-842
208.81	17	840-842
208.82	17	840-842
208.90	17	840-842
208.91	17	840-842
208.92	17	840-842
209.00	06	374-376
209.01	06	374-376
209.02	06	374-376
209.03	06	374-376
209.10	06	374-376
209.11	06	374-376
209.12	06	374-376
209.13	06	374-376
209.14	06	374-376
209.15	06	374-376
209.16	06	374-376
209.17	06	374-376
209.20	17	843-845
209.21	06	374-376
209.22	17	843-845
209.23	06	374-376
209.24	11	686-688
209.25	06	374-376
209.26	06	374-376
209.27	06	374-376
209.29	17	843-845
209.30	17	843-845
209.31	09	595-596
209.32	09	595-596
209.33	09	595-596
209.34	09	595-596
209.35	09	595-596
209.36	09	595-596
209.40	06	393-395
209.41	06	393-395
209.42	06	393-395
209.43	06	393-395
209.50	06	393-395
209.51	06	393-395
209.52	06	393-395
209.53	06	393-395
209.54	06	393-395
209.55	06	393-395
209.56	06	393-395
209.57	06	393-395
209.60	17	843-845
209.61	04	180-182
209.62	16	814-816
209.63	06	393-395
209.64	11	686-688
209.65	06	393-395
209.66	06	393-395
209.67	06	393-395
209.69	17	843-845
209.70	17	843-845
209.71	17	840-842
209.72	07	435-437
209.73	08	542-544
209.74	06	374-376
209.75	09	595-596
209.79	17	843-845
210.0	03	157-159
210.1	03	157-159
210.2	03	154-156
210.3	03	157-159
210.4	03	157-159
210.5	03	154-156
210.6	03	154-156
210.7	03	154-156
210.8	03	154-156
210.9	03	154-156
211.0	06	393-395
211.1	06	393-395
211.2	06	393-395
211.3	06	393-395
211.4	06	393-395
211.5	07	441-443
211.6	07	438-440
211.7	10	643-645
211.8	06	393-395
211.9	06	393-395
212.0	03	154-156
212.1	03	154-156
212.2	04	180-182
212.3	04	180-182
212.4	04	180-182
212.5	04	180-182
212.6	16	814-816
212.7	05	314-316
212.8	04	180-182
212.9	04	180-182
213.0	08	564-566
213.1	03	157-159
213.2	08	564-566
213.3	04	180-182
213.4	08	564-566
213.5	08	564-566
213.6	08	564-566
213.7	08	564-566
213.8	08	564-566
213.9	08	564-566
214.0	09	606-607
214.1	09	606-607
214.2	04	180-182
214.3	06	393-395
214.4	12	729-730
214.8	09	606-607
214.9	09	606-607
215.0	08	564-566
215.2	08	564-566
215.3	08	564-566
215.4	08	564-566
215.5	08	564-566
215.6	08	564-566
215.7	08	564-566
215.8	08	564-566
215.9	08	564-566
216.0	09	606-607
216.1	02	124-125
216.2	09	606-607
216.3	09	606-607
216.4	09	606-607
216.5	09	606-607
216.6	09	606-607
216.7	09	606-607
216.8	09	606-607
216.9	09	606-607
217	09	606-607
218.0	13	760-761
218.1	13	760-761
218.2	13	760-761
218.9	13	760-761
219.0	13	760-761
219.1	13	760-761
219.8	13	760-761
219.9	13	760-761
220	13	760-761
221.0	13	760-761
221.1	13	760-761
221.2	13	760-761
221.8	13	760-761
221.9	13	760-761
222.0	12	729-730
222.1	12	729-730
222.2	12	729-730
222.3	12	729-730
222.4	12	729-730
222.8	12	729-730
222.9	12	729-730
223.0	11	686-688
223.1	11	686-688
223.2	11	686-688
223.3	11	686-688
223.81	11	686-688
223.89	11	686-688
223.9	11	686-688
224.0	02	124-125
224.1	02	124-125
224.2	02	124-125
224.3	02	124-125
224.4	02	124-125
224.5	02	124-125
224.6	02	124-125
224.7	02	124-125
224.8	02	124-125
224.9	02	124-125
225.0	01	054-055
225.1	01	054-055
225.2	01	054-055
225.3	01	054-055
225.4	01	054-055
225.8	01	054-055
225.9	01	054-055
226	10	643-645
227.0	10	643-645
227.1	10	643-645
227.3	10	643-645
227.4	01	054-055
227.5	01	054-055
227.6	01	054-055
227.8	10	643-645
227.9	10	643-645
228.00	05	314-316
228.01	09	606-607
228.02	01	091-093
228.03	02	124-125
228.04	06	391-392
228.09	05	314-316
228.1	16	814-816
229.0	16	814-816
229.8	17	843-845
229.9	17	843-845
230.0	03	146-148
230.1	06	374-376
230.2	06	374-376
230.3	06	374-376
230.4	06	374-376
230.5	06	374-376
230.6	06	374-376
230.7	06	374-376
230.8	07	435-437
230.9	06	374-376
231.0	03	146-148
231.1	04	180-182
231.2	04	180-182
231.8	04	180-182
231.9	04	180-182
232.0	09	606-607
232.1	02	124-125
232.2	09	606-607
232.3	09	606-607
232.4	09	606-607
232.5	09	606-607
232.6	09	606-607
232.7	09	606-607
232.8	09	606-607
232.9	09	606-607
233.0	09	597-599
233.1	13	754-756
233.2	13	754-756
233.30	13	754-756
233.31	13	754-756
233.32	13	754-756
233.39	13	754-756
233.4	12	722-724
233.5	12	722-724
233.6	12	722-724
233.7	11	686-688
233.9	11	686-688
234.0	02	124-125
234.8	17	843-845
234.9	17	843-845
235.0	03	146-148
235.1	03	146-148
235.2	06	374-376
235.3	07	435-437
235.4	06	374-376
235.5	06	374-376
235.6	03	146-148
235.7	04	180-182
235.8	04	180-182
235.9	04	180-182
236.0	13	754-756
236.1	13	754-756
236.2	13	754-756
236.3	13	754-756
236.4	12	722-724
236.5	12	722-724
236.6	12	722-724
236.7	11	686-688
236.90	11	686-688
236.91	11	686-688
236.99	11	686-688
237.0	10	643-645
237.1	01	054-055
237.2	10	643-645
237.3	01	054-055
237.4	10	643-645
237.5	01	054-055
237.6	01	054-055
237.70	01	091-093
237.71	01	091-093
237.72	01	091-093
237.9	01	054-055
238.0	08	542-544
238.1	08	564-566
238.2	09	606-607
238.3	09	597-599
238.4	17	840-842
238.5	17	840-842
238.6	17	840-842
238.71	16	814-816
238.72	16	811-812
238.73	16	811-812
238.74	16	811-812
238.75	16	811-812
238.76	17	840-842
238.77	21	919-921
238.79	17	840-842
238.8	17	843-845
238.9	17	843-845
239.0	06	374-376
239.1	04	180-182
239.2	08	564-566
239.3	09	600-601
239.4	11	686-688
239.5	11	686-688
239.6	01	054-055
239.7	10	643-645
239.81	17	843-845
239.89	17	843-845
239.9	17	843-845

Endocrine, Nutritional and Metabolic Diseases, and Immunity Diseases

DX	MDC	DRG
240.0	10	643-645
240.9	10	643-645
241.0	10	643-645
241.1	10	643-645
241.9	10	643-645
242.00	10	643-645
242.01	10	643-645
242.10	10	643-645
242.11	10	643-645
242.20	10	643-645
242.21	10	643-645
242.30	10	643-645
242.31	10	643-645
242.40	10	643-645
242.41	10	643-645
242.80	10	643-645
242.81	10	643-645
242.90	10	643-645
242.91	10	643-645
243	10	643-645
244.0	10	643-645
244.1	10	643-645
244.2	10	643-645
244.3	10	643-645
244.8	10	643-645
244.9	10	643-645
245.0	10	643-645
245.1	10	643-645
245.2	10	643-645

DX	MDC	DRG
245.3	10	643-645
245.4	10	643-645
245.8	10	643-645
245.9	10	643-645
246.0	10	643-645
246.1	10	643-645
246.2	10	643-645
246.3	10	643-645
246.8	10	643-645
246.9	10	643-645
249.00	10	637-639
249.01	10	637-639
249.10	10	637-639
249.11	10	637-639
249.20	10	637-639
249.21	10	637-639
249.30	10	637-639
249.31	10	637-639
249.40	11	698-700
249.41	11	698-700
249.50	02	124-125
249.51	02	124-125
249.60	01	073-074
249.61	01	073-074
249.70	05	299-301
249.71	05	299-301
249.80	10	637-639
249.81	10	637-639
249.90	10	637-639
249.91	10	637-639
250.00	10	637-639
250.01	10	637-639
250.02	10	637-639
250.03	10	637-639
250.10	10	637-639
250.11	10	637-639
250.12	10	637-639
250.13	10	637-639
250.20	10	637-639
250.21	10	637-639
250.22	10	637-639
250.23	10	637-639
250.30	10	637-639
250.31	10	637-639
250.32	10	637-639
250.33	10	637-639
250.40	11	698-700
250.41	11	698-700
250.42	11	698-700
250.43	11	698-700
250.50	02	124-125
250.51	02	124-125
250.52	02	124-125
250.53	02	124-125
250.60	01	073-074
250.61	01	073-074
250.62	01	073-074
250.63	01	073-074
250.70	05	299-301
250.71	05	299-301
250.72	05	299-301
250.73	05	299-301
250.80	10	637-639
250.81	10	637-639
250.82	10	637-639
250.83	10	637-639
250.90	10	637-639
250.91	10	637-639
250.92	10	637-639
250.93	10	637-639
251.0	10	640-641
251.1	10	643-645
251.2	10	640-641
251.3	10	640-641
251.4	10	643-645
251.5	06	380-382
251.8	10	643-645
251.9	10	643-645
252.00	10	643-645
252.01	10	643-645
252.02	10	643-645
252.08	10	643-645
252.1	10	643-645
252.8	10	643-645
252.9	10	643-645
253.0	10	643-645
253.1	10	643-645
253.2	10	643-645
253.3	10	643-645
253.4	10	643-645
253.5	10	643-645
253.6	10	643-645
253.7	10	643-645
253.8	10	643-645
253.9	10	643-645
254.0	16	814-816
254.1	16	814-816
254.8	16	814-816
254.9	16	814-816
255.0	10	643-645
255.10	10	643-645
255.11	10	643-645
255.12	10	643-645
255.13	10	643-645
255.14	10	643-645
255.2	10	643-645
255.3	10	643-645
255.41	10	643-645
255.42	10	643-645
255.5	10	643-645
255.6	10	643-645
255.8	10	643-645
255.9	10	643-645
256.0	13	760-761
256.1	13	760-761
256.2	13	760-761
256.31	13	760-761
256.39	13	760-761
256.4	13	760-761
256.8	13	760-761
256.9	13	760-761
257.0	10	643-645
257.1	10	643-645
257.2	10	643-645
257.8	10	643-645
257.9	10	643-645
258.01	10	643-645
258.02	10	643-645
258.03	10	643-645
258.1	10	643-645
258.8	10	643-645
258.9	10	643-645
259.0	10	643-645
259.1	10	643-645
259.2	10	643-645
259.3	10	643-645
259.4	10	643-645
259.50	10	643-645
259.51	10	643-645
259.52	10	643-645
259.8	10	643-645
259.9	10	643-645
260	10	640-641
261	10	640-641
262	10	640-641
263.0	10	640-641
263.1	10	640-641
263.2	10	640-641
263.8	10	640-641
263.9	10	640-641
264.0	02	124-125
264.1	02	124-125
264.2	02	124-125
264.3	02	124-125
264.4	02	124-125
264.5	02	124-125
264.6	02	124-125
264.7	02	124-125
264.8	10	640-641
264.9	10	640-641
265.0	10	640-641
265.1	10	640-641
265.2	10	640-641
266.0	10	640-641
266.1	10	640-641
266.2	10	640-641
266.9	10	640-641
267	10	640-641
268.0	08	553-554
268.1	08	553-554
268.2	08	553-554
268.9	10	640-641
269.0	10	640-641
269.1	10	640-641
269.2	10	640-641
269.3	10	640-641
269.8	10	640-641
269.9	10	640-641
270.0	10	642
270.1	10	642
270.2	10	642
270.3	10	642
270.4	10	642
270.5	10	642
270.6	10	642
270.7	10	642
270.8	10	642
270.9	10	642
271.0	10	642
271.1	10	642
271.2	06	391-392
271.3	06	391-392
271.4	10	642
271.8	10	642
271.9	10	642
272.0	10	642
272.1	10	642
272.2	10	642
272.3	10	642
272.4	10	642
272.5	10	642
272.6	10	642
272.7	10	642
272.8	10	642
272.9	10	642
273.0	16	814-816
273.1	16	814-816
273.2	17	840-842
273.3	17	840-842
273.4	10	642
273.8	17	843-845
273.9	17	843-845
274.00	08	553-554
274.01	08	553-554
274.02	08	553-554
274.03	08	553-554
274.10	11	698-700
274.11	11	691-694
274.19	11	698-700
274.81	08	553-554
274.82	08	553-554
274.89	08	553-554
274.9	08	553-554
275.0	10	642
275.1	10	642
275.2	10	640-641
275.3	10	642
275.40	10	640-641
275.41	10	640-641
275.42	10	640-641
275.49	10	640-641
275.5	10	640-641
275.8	10	642
275.9	10	642
276.0	10	640-641
276.1	10	640-641
276.2	10	640-641
276.3	10	640-641
276.4	10	640-641
276.50	10	640-641
276.51	10	640-641
276.52	10	640-641
276.6	10	640-641
276.7	10	640-641
276.8	10	640-641
276.9	10	640-641
277.00	10	640-641
277.01	15	791, 793
277.02	04	177-179
277.03	06	393-395
277.09	10	640-641
277.1	10	642
277.2	10	642
277.30	08	545-547
277.31	08	545-547
277.39	08	545-547
277.4	07	441-443
277.5	10	642
277.6	10	642
277.7	10	642
277.81	10	642
277.82	10	642
277.83	10	642
277.84	10	642
277.85	10	642
277.86	10	642
277.87	10	642
277.88	11	682-684
277.89	10	642
277.9	10	642
278.00	10	640-641
278.01	10	640-641
278.02	10	640-641
278.1	10	640-641
278.2	10	640-641
278.3	10	640-641
278.4	10	640-641
278.8	10	640-641
279.00	16	814-816
279.01	16	814-816
279.02	16	814-816
279.03	16	814-816
279.04	16	814-816
279.05	16	814-816
279.06	16	814-816
279.09	16	814-816
279.10	16	814-816
279.11	16	808-810
279.12	16	808-810
279.13	16	808-810
279.19	16	808-810
279.2	16	808-810
279.3	16	814-816
279.41	08	545-547
279.49	08	545-547
279.50	16	808-810
279.51	16	808-810
279.52	16	808-810
279.53	16	808-810
279.8	16	814-816
279.9	16	814-816

Diseases of the Blood and Blood Forming Organs

DX	MDC	DRG
280.0	16	811-812
280.1	16	811-812
280.8	16	811-812
280.9	16	811-812
281.0	16	811-812
281.1	16	811-812
281.2	16	811-812
281.3	16	811-812
281.4	16	811-812
281.8	16	811-812
281.9	16	811-812
282.0	16	811-812
282.1	16	811-812
282.2	16	811-812
282.3	16	811-812
282.41	16	811-812
282.42	16	811-812
282.49	16	811-812
282.5	16	811-812
282.60	16	811-812
282.61	16	811-812
282.62	16	811-812
282.63	16	811-812
282.64	16	811-812
282.68	16	811-812
282.69	16	811-812
282.7	16	811-812
282.8	16	811-812
282.9	16	811-812
283.0	16	808-810
283.10	16	808-810
283.11	16	811-812
283.19	16	808-810
283.2	16	808-810
283.9	16	808-810
284.01	16	808-810
284.09	16	808-810
284.1	16	811-812
284.2	17	840-842
284.81	16	808-810
284.89	16	808-810
284.9	16	808-810
285.0	16	811-812
285.1	16	811-812
285.21	16	811-812
285.22	16	811-812
285.29	16	811-812
285.3	16	811-812
285.8	16	811-812
285.9	16	811-812
286.0	16	813
286.1	16	813
286.2	16	813
286.3	16	813
286.4	16	813
286.5	16	813
286.6	16	813
286.7	16	813
286.9	16	813
287.0	16	813
287.1	16	813
287.2	16	813
287.30	16	813
287.31	16	813
287.32	16	813
287.33	16	813
287.39	16	813
287.4	16	813
287.5	16	813
287.8	16	813
287.9	16	813
288.00	16	808-810
288.01	16	808-810
288.02	16	808-810
288.03	16	808-810
288.04	16	808-810
288.09	16	808-810
288.1	16	808-810
288.2	16	808-810
288.3	16	814-816
288.4	16	814-816

DX	MDC	DRG
288.50	16	814-816
288.51	16	814-816
288.59	16	814-816
288.60	16	814-816
288.61	16	814-816
288.62	16	814-816
288.63	16	814-816
288.64	16	814-816
288.65	16	814-816
288.66	16	814-816
288.69	16	814-816
288.8	16	814-816
288.9	16	814-816
289.0	16	814-816
289.1	16	814-816
289.2	06	393-395
289.3	16	814-816
289.4	16	814-816
289.50	16	814-816
289.51	16	814-816
289.52	16	814-816
289.53	16	814-816
289.59	16	814-816
289.6	16	814-816
289.7	16	811-812
289.81	16	814-816
289.82	16	814-816
289.83	17	840-842
289.84	16	813
289.89	16	814-816
289.9	16	814-816

Mental Disorders

DX	MDC	DRG
290.0	19	884
290.10	19	884
290.11	19	884
290.12	19	884
290.13	19	884
290.20	19	884
290.21	19	884
290.3	19	884
290.40	19	884
290.41	19	884
290.42	19	884
290.43	19	884
290.8	19	884
290.9	19	884
291.0	20	894-897
291.1	20	894-897
291.2	20	894-897
291.3	20	894-897
291.4	20	894-897
291.5	20	894-897
291.81	20	894-897
291.82	20	894-897
291.89	20	894-897
291.9	20	894-897
292.0	20	894-897
292.11	20	894-897
292.12	20	894-897
292.2	20	894-897
292.81	20	894-897
292.82	20	894-897
292.83	20	894-897
292.84	20	894-897
292.85	20	894-897
292.89	20	894-897
292.9	20	894-897
293.0	19	880
293.1	19	880
293.81	19	884
293.82	19	884
293.83	19	884
293.84	19	884
293.89	19	884
293.9	19	880
294.10	19	884
294.11	19	884
294.8	19	884
294.9	19	884
295.00	19	885
295.01	19	885
295.02	19	885
295.03	19	885
295.04	19	885
295.05	19	885
295.10	19	885
295.11	19	885
295.12	19	885
295.13	19	885
295.14	19	885
295.15	19	885
295.20	19	885
295.21	19	885
295.22	19	885
295.23	19	885
295.24	19	885
295.25	19	885
295.30	19	885
295.31	19	885
295.32	19	885
295.33	19	885
295.34	19	885
295.35	19	885
295.40	19	885
295.41	19	885
295.42	19	885
295.43	19	885
295.44	19	885
295.45	19	885
295.50	19	885
295.51	19	885
295.52	19	885
295.53	19	885
295.54	19	885
295.55	19	885
295.60	19	885
295.61	19	885
295.62	19	885
295.63	19	885
295.64	19	885
295.65	19	885
295.70	19	885
295.71	19	885
295.72	19	885
295.73	19	885
295.74	19	885
295.75	19	885
295.80	19	885
295.81	19	885
295.82	19	885
295.83	19	885
295.84	19	885
295.85	19	885
295.90	19	885
295.91	19	885
295.92	19	885
295.93	19	885
295.94	19	885
295.95	19	885
296.00	19	885
296.01	19	885
296.02	19	885
296.03	19	885
296.04	19	885
296.05	19	885
296.06	19	885
296.10	19	885
296.11	19	885
296.12	19	885
296.13	19	885
296.14	19	885
296.15	19	885
296.16	19	885
296.20	19	885
296.21	19	885
296.22	19	885
296.23	19	885
296.24	19	885
296.25	19	885
296.26	19	885
296.30	19	885
296.31	19	885
296.32	19	885
296.33	19	885
296.34	19	885
296.35	19	885
296.36	19	885
296.40	19	885
296.41	19	885
296.42	19	885
296.43	19	885
296.44	19	885
296.45	19	885
296.46	19	885
296.50	19	885
296.51	19	885
296.52	19	885
296.53	19	885
296.54	19	885
296.55	19	885
296.56	19	885
296.60	19	885
296.61	19	885
296.62	19	885
296.63	19	885
296.64	19	885
296.65	19	885
296.66	19	885
296.7	19	885
296.80	19	885
296.81	19	885
296.82	19	885
296.89	19	885
296.90	19	885
296.99	19	885
297.0	19	885
297.1	19	885
297.2	19	885
297.3	19	885
297.8	19	885
297.9	19	885
298.0	19	885
298.1	19	885
298.2	19	887
298.3	19	885
298.4	19	885
298.8	19	885
298.9	19	885
299.00	19	884
299.01	19	884
299.10	19	884
299.11	19	884
299.80	19	885
299.81	19	885
299.90	19	885
299.91	19	885
300.00	19	880
300.01	19	880
300.02	19	880
300.09	19	880
300.10	19	880
300.11	19	880
300.12	19	880
300.13	19	880
300.14	19	883
300.15	19	880
300.16	19	880
300.19	19	880
300.20	19	882
300.21	19	882
300.22	19	882
300.23	19	882
300.29	19	882
300.3	19	882
300.4	19	881
300.5	19	882
300.6	19	882
300.7	19	882
300.81	19	882
300.82	19	882
300.89	19	882
300.9	19	880
301.0	19	883
301.10	19	883
301.11	19	883
301.12	19	881
301.13	19	883
301.20	19	883
301.21	19	883
301.22	19	883
301.3	19	883
301.4	19	883
301.50	19	883
301.51	19	883
301.59	19	883
301.6	19	883
301.7	19	883
301.81	19	883
301.82	19	883
301.83	19	883
301.84	19	883
301.89	19	883
301.9	19	883
302.0	19	887
302.1	19	887
302.2	19	887
302.3	19	887
302.4	19	887
302.50	19	887
302.51	19	887
302.52	19	887
302.53	19	887
302.6	19	887
302.70	19	887
302.71	19	887
302.72	19	887
302.73	19	887
302.74	19	887
302.75	19	887
302.76	19	887
302.79	19	887
302.81	19	887
302.82	19	887
302.83	19	887
302.84	19	887
302.85	19	887
302.89	19	887
302.9	19	887
303.00	20	894-897
303.01	20	894-897
303.02	20	894-897
303.03	20	894-897
303.90	20	894-897
303.91	20	894-897
303.92	20	894-897
303.93	20	894-897
304.00	20	894-897
304.01	20	894-897
304.02	20	894-897
304.03	20	894-897
304.10	20	894-897
304.11	20	894-897
304.12	20	894-897
304.13	20	894-897
304.20	20	894-897
304.21	20	894-897
304.22	20	894-897
304.23	20	894-897
304.30	20	894-897
304.31	20	894-897
304.32	20	894-897
304.33	20	894-897
304.40	20	894-897
304.41	20	894-897
304.42	20	894-897
304.43	20	894-897
304.50	20	894-897
304.51	20	894-897
304.52	20	894-897
304.53	20	894-897
304.60	20	894-897
304.61	20	894-897
304.62	20	894-897
304.63	20	894-897
304.70	20	894-897
304.71	20	894-897
304.72	20	894-897
304.73	20	894-897
304.80	20	894-897
304.81	20	894-897
304.82	20	894-897
304.83	20	894-897
304.90	20	894-897
304.91	20	894-897
304.92	20	894-897
304.93	20	894-897
305.00	20	894-897
305.01	20	894-897
305.02	20	894-897
305.03	20	894-897
305.1	23	951
305.20	20	894-897
305.21	20	894-897
305.22	20	894-897
305.23	20	894-897
305.30	20	894-897
305.31	20	894-897
305.32	20	894-897
305.33	20	894-897
305.40	20	894-897
305.41	20	894-897
305.42	20	894-897
305.43	20	894-897
305.50	20	894-897
305.51	20	894-897
305.52	20	894-897
305.53	20	894-897
305.60	20	894-897
305.61	20	894-897
305.62	20	894-897
305.63	20	894-897
305.70	20	894-897
305.71	20	894-897
305.72	20	894-897
305.73	20	894-897
305.80	20	894-897
305.81	20	894-897
305.82	20	894-897
305.83	20	894-897
305.90	20	894-897
305.91	20	894-897
305.92	20	894-897
305.93	20	894-897
306.0	08	557-558
306.1	04	205-206
306.2	05	314-316
306.3	09	606-607
306.4	06	391-392
306.50	11	698-700
306.51	13	760-761
306.52	13	760-761
306.53	11	698-700
306.59	11	698-700
306.6	10	643-645
306.7	19	882
306.8	19	887
306.9	19	882
307.0	19	887
307.1	19	883

DX	MDC	DRG	DX	MDC	DRG	DX	MDC	DRG	DX	MDC	DRG	DX	MDC	DRG
307.20	01	091-093	312.9	19	886	324.1	01	094-096	333.83	01	091-093	339.84	01	102-103
307.21	01	091-093	313.0	19	882	324.9	01	094-096	333.84	01	091-093	339.85	01	102-103
307.22	01	091-093	313.1	19	882	325	01	091-093	333.85	01	091-093	339.89	01	102-103
307.23	01	091-093	313.21	19	886	326	01	091-093	333.89	01	091-093	340	01	058-060
307.3	19	887	313.22	19	886	327.00	19	887	333.90	01	056-057	341.0	01	058-060
307.40	19	887	313.23	19	886	327.01	19	887	333.91	01	091-093	341.1	01	058-060
307.41	19	887	313.3	19	886	327.02	19	887	333.92	01	091-093	341.20	01	097-099
307.42	19	887	313.81	19	886	327.09	19	887	333.93	01	091-093	341.21	01	097-099
307.43	19	887	313.82	19	886	327.10	19	887	333.94	01	056-057	341.22	01	097-099
307.44	19	887	313.83	19	886	327.11	19	887	333.99	01	056-057	341.8	01	058-060
307.45	19	887	313.89	19	886	327.12	19	887	334.0	01	058-060	341.9	01	058-060
307.46	19	887	313.9	19	886	327.13	19	887	334.1	01	058-060	342.00	01	056-057
307.47	19	887	314.00	19	886	327.14	19	887	334.2	01	058-060	342.01	01	056-057
307.48	19	887	314.01	19	886	327.15	19	887	334.3	01	058-060	342.02	01	056-057
307.49	19	887	314.1	19	886	327.19	19	887	334.4	01	058-060	342.10	01	056-057
307.50	19	887	314.2	19	886	327.20	03	154-156	334.8	01	058-060	342.11	01	056-057
307.51	19	887	314.8	19	886	327.21	01	091-093	334.9	01	058-060	342.12	01	056-057
307.52	19	886	314.9	19	886	327.22	04	204	335.0	01	056-057	342.80	01	056-057
307.53	19	882	315.00	19	886	327.23	03	154-156	335.10	01	056-057	342.81	01	056-057
307.54	19	882	315.01	19	886	327.24	03	154-156	335.11	01	056-057	342.82	01	056-057
307.59	19	887	315.02	19	886	327.25	01	091-093	335.19	01	056-057	342.90	01	056-057
307.6	19	886	315.09	19	886	327.26	03	154-156	335.20	01	056-057	342.91	01	056-057
307.7	19	886	315.1	19	886	327.27	01	091-093	335.21	01	056-057	342.92	01	056-057
307.80	19	882	315.2	19	886	327.29	03	154-156	335.22	01	056-057	343.0	01	052-053
307.81	01	100-103	315.31	19	886	327.30	01	091-093	335.23	01	056-057	343.1	01	052-053
307.89	19	882	315.32	19	886	327.31	01	091-093	335.24	01	056-057	343.2	01	052-053
307.9	19	884	315.34	19	886	327.32	01	091-093	335.29	01	056-057	343.3	01	091-093
308.0	19	880	315.39	19	886	327.33	01	091-093	335.8	01	056-057	343.4	01	052-053
308.1	19	880	315.4	19	886	327.34	01	091-093	335.9	01	056-057	343.8	01	091-093
308.2	19	880	315.5	19	886	327.35	01	091-093	336.0	01	056-057	343.9	01	091-093
308.3	19	880	315.8	19	886	327.36	01	091-093	336.1	01	091-093	344.00	01	052-053
308.4	19	880	315.9	19	886	327.37	01	091-093	336.2	01	091-093	344.01	01	052-053
308.9	19	880	316	19	884	327.39	01	091-093	336.3	01	091-093	344.02	01	052-053
309.0	19	881	317	19	884	327.40	03	154-156	336.8	01	091-093	344.03	01	052-053
309.1	19	881	318.0	19	884	327.41	01	091-093	336.9	01	091-093	344.04	01	052-053
309.21	19	882	318.1	19	884	327.42	03	154-156	337.00	01	073-074	344.09	01	052-053
309.22	19	882	318.2	19	884	327.43	01	091-093	337.01	01	073-074	344.1	01	052-053
309.23	19	882	319	19	884	327.44	03	154-156	337.09	01	073-074	344.2	01	052-053
309.24	19	882				327.49	03	154-156	337.1	01	073-074	344.30	01	091-093
309.28	19	882	**Diseases of the Nervous System and Sense Organs**			327.51	01	091-093	337.20	01	073-074	344.31	01	091-093
309.29	19	882	320.0	01	094-096	327.52	01	091-093	337.21	01	073-074	344.32	01	091-093
309.3	19	882	320.1	01	094-096	327.53	03	154-156	337.22	01	073-074	344.40	01	091-093
309.4	19	882	320.2	01	094-096	327.59	03	154-156	337.29	01	073-074	344.41	01	091-093
309.81	19	882	320.3	01	094-096	327.8	03	154-156	337.3	01	073-074	344.42	01	091-093
309.82	19	882	320.7	01	094-096	330.0	01	056-057	337.9	01	073-074	344.5	01	091-093
309.83	19	882	320.81	01	094-096	330.1	01	056-057	338.0	01	091-093	344.60	01	073-074
309.89	19	882	320.82	01	094-096	330.2	01	056-057	338.11	23	947-948	344.61	11	698-700
309.9	19	882	320.89	01	094-096	330.3	01	056-057	338.12	23	947-948	344.81	01	091-093
310.0	19	884	320.9	01	094-096	330.8	01	056-057	338.18	23	947-948	344.89	01	091-093
310.1	19	884	321.0	01	097-099	330.9	01	056-057	338.19	23	947-948	344.9	01	091-093
310.2	01	100-103	321.1	01	097-099	331.0	01	056-057	338.21	01	091-093	345.00	01	100-101
310.8	19	884	321.2	01	097-099	331.11	01	056-057	338.22	01	091-093	345.01	01	100-101
310.9	19	884	321.3	01	097-099	331.19	01	056-057	338.28	01	091-093	345.10	01	100-101
311	19	881	321.4	01	097-099	331.2	01	056-057	338.29	01	091-093	345.11	01	100-101
312.00	19	886	321.8	01	097-099	331.3	01	056-057	338.3	23	947-948	345.2	01	100-101
312.01	19	886	322.0	01	097-099	331.4	01	056-057	338.4	01	091-093	345.3	01	100-101
312.02	19	886	322.1	01	097-099	331.5	01	056-057	339.00	01	102-103	345.40	01	100-101
312.03	19	886	322.2	01	097-099	331.7	01	056-057	339.01	01	102-103	345.41	01	100-101
312.10	19	886	322.9	01	097-099	331.81	01	091-093	339.02	01	102-103	345.50	01	100-101
312.11	19	886	323.01	01	097-099	331.82	01	056-057	339.03	01	102-103	345.51	01	100-101
312.12	19	886	323.02	01	097-099	331.83	01	056-057	339.04	01	102-103	345.60	01	100-101
312.13	19	886	323.1	01	097-099	331.89	01	056-057	339.05	01	102-103	345.61	01	100-101
312.20	19	886	323.2	01	097-099	331.9	01	056-057	339.09	01	102-103	345.70	01	100-101
312.21	19	886	323.41	01	097-099	332.0	01	056-057	339.10	01	102-103	345.71	01	100-101
312.22	19	886	323.42	01	097-099	332.1	01	056-057	339.11	01	102-103	345.80	01	100-101
312.23	19	886	323.51	01	097-099	333.0	01	056-057	339.12	01	102-103	345.81	01	100-101
312.30	19	886	323.52	01	097-099	333.1	01	091-093	339.20	01	102-103	345.90	01	100-101
312.31	19	883	323.61	01	097-099	333.2	01	091-093	339.21	01	102-103	345.91	01	100-101
312.32	19	883	323.62	01	097-099	333.3	01	091-093	339.22	01	102-103	346.00	01	102-103
312.33	19	886	323.63	01	097-099	333.4	01	056-057	339.3	01	102-103	346.01	01	102-103
312.34	19	883	323.71	01	091-093	333.5	01	056-057	339.41	01	102-103	346.02	01	102-103
312.35	19	883	323.72	01	091-093	333.6	01	056-057	339.42	01	102-103	346.03	01	102-103
312.39	19	883	323.81	01	097-099	333.71	01	056-057	339.43	01	102-103	346.10	01	102-103
312.4	19	886	323.82	01	097-099	333.72	01	091-093	339.44	01	102-103	346.11	01	102-103
312.81	19	886	323.9	01	097-099	333.79	01	091-093	339.81	01	102-103	346.12	01	102-103
312.82	19	886	324.0	01	094-096	333.81	02	124-125	339.82	01	102-103	346.13	01	102-103
312.89	19	886				333.82	01	091-093	339.83	01	102-103	346.20	01	102-103

DX....	MDC....	DRG	DX....	MDC....	DRG	DX....	MDC....	DRG	DX....	MDC....	DRG	DX....	MDC....	DRG
346.21	01	102-103	354.0	01	073-074	360.33	02	124-125	362.37	02	123	364.00	02	124-125
346.22	01	102-103	354.1	01	073-074	360.34	02	124-125	362.40	02	124-125	364.01	02	124-125
346.23	01	102-103	354.2	01	073-074	360.40	02	124-125	362.41	02	124-125	364.02	02	124-125
346.30	01	102-103	354.3	01	073-074	360.41	02	124-125	362.42	02	124-125	364.03	02	124-125
346.31	01	102-103	354.4	01	073-074	360.42	02	124-125	362.43	02	124-125	364.04	02	124-125
346.32	01	102-103	354.5	01	073-074	360.43	02	124-125	362.50	02	124-125	364.05	02	124-125
346.33	01	102-103	354.8	01	073-074	360.44	02	124-125	362.51	02	124-125	364.10	02	124-125
346.40	01	102-103	354.9	01	073-074	360.50	02	124-125	362.52	02	124-125	364.11	02	124-125
346.41	01	102-103	355.0	01	073-074	360.51	02	124-125	362.53	02	124-125	364.21	02	124-125
346.42	01	102-103	355.1	01	073-074	360.52	02	124-125	362.54	02	124-125	364.22	02	124-125
346.43	01	102-103	355.2	01	073-074	360.53	02	124-125	362.55	02	124-125	364.23	02	124-125
346.50	01	102-103	355.3	01	073-074	360.54	02	124-125	362.56	02	124-125	364.24	02	124-125
346.51	01	102-103	355.4	01	073-074	360.55	02	124-125	362.57	02	124-125	364.3	02	124-125
346.52	01	102-103	355.5	01	073-074	360.59	02	124-125	362.60	02	124-125	364.41	02	124-125
346.53	01	102-103	355.6	01	073-074	360.60	02	124-125	362.61	02	124-125	364.42	02	124-125
346.60	01	102-103	355.71	01	073-074	360.61	02	124-125	362.62	02	124-125	364.51	02	124-125
346.61	01	102-103	355.79	01	073-074	360.62	02	124-125	362.63	02	124-125	364.52	02	124-125
346.62	01	102-103	355.8	01	073-074	360.63	02	124-125	362.64	02	124-125	364.53	02	124-125
346.63	01	102-103	355.9	01	073-074	360.64	02	124-125	362.65	02	124-125	364.54	02	124-125
346.70	01	102-103	356.0	01	073-074	360.65	02	124-125	362.66	02	124-125	364.55	02	124-125
346.71	01	102-103	356.1	01	073-074	360.69	02	124-125	362.70	02	124-125	364.56	02	124-125
346.72	01	102-103	356.2	01	073-074	360.81	02	124-125	362.71	02	124-125	364.57	02	124-125
346.73	01	102-103	356.3	01	091-093	360.89	02	124-125	362.72	02	124-125	364.59	02	124-125
346.80	01	102-103	356.4	01	073-074	360.9	02	124-125	362.73	02	124-125	364.60	02	124-125
346.81	01	102-103	356.8	01	073-074	361.00	02	124-125	362.74	02	124-125	364.61	02	124-125
346.82	01	102-103	356.9	01	073-074	361.01	02	124-125	362.75	02	124-125	364.62	02	124-125
346.83	01	102-103	357.0	01	094-096	361.02	02	124-125	362.76	02	124-125	364.63	02	124-125
346.90	01	102-103	357.1	01	073-074	361.03	02	124-125	362.77	02	124-125	364.64	02	124-125
346.91	01	102-103	357.2	01	073-074	361.04	02	124-125	362.81	02	124-125	364.70	02	124-125
347.00	01	091-093	357.3	01	073-074	361.05	02	124-125	362.82	02	124-125	364.71	02	124-125
347.01	01	091-093	357.4	01	073-074	361.06	02	124-125	362.83	02	124-125	364.72	02	124-125
347.10	01	091-093	357.5	01	073-074	361.07	02	124-125	362.84	02	124-125	364.73	02	124-125
347.11	01	091-093	357.6	01	073-074	361.10	02	124-125	362.85	02	124-125	364.74	02	124-125
348.0	01	091-093	357.7	01	073-074	361.11	02	124-125	362.89	02	124-125	364.75	02	124-125
348.1	01	091-093	357.81	01	073-074	361.12	02	124-125	362.9	02	124-125	364.76	02	124-125
348.2	01	102-103	357.82	01	073-074	361.13	02	124-125	363.00	02	124-125	364.77	02	124-125
348.30	01	070-072	357.89	01	073-074	361.14	02	124-125	363.01	02	124-125	364.81	02	124-125
348.31	01	070-072	357.9	01	073-074	361.19	02	124-125	363.03	02	124-125	364.82	02	124-125
348.39	01	070-072	358.00	01	056-057	361.2	02	124-125	363.04	02	124-125	364.89	02	124-125
348.4	01	080-081	358.01	01	056-057	361.30	02	124-125	363.05	02	124-125	364.9	02	124-125
348.5	01	080-081	358.1	01	056-057	361.31	02	124-125	363.06	02	124-125	365.00	02	124-125
348.81	01	070-072	358.2	01	073-074	361.32	02	124-125	363.07	02	124-125	365.01	02	124-125
348.89	01	070-072	358.8	01	073-074	361.33	02	124-125	363.08	02	124-125	365.02	02	124-125
348.9	01	070-072	358.9	01	073-074	361.81	02	124-125	363.10	02	124-125	365.03	02	124-125
349.0	01	102-103	359.0	01	091-093	361.89	02	124-125	363.11	02	124-125	365.04	02	124-125
349.1	01	091-093	359.1	01	091-093	361.9	02	124-125	363.12	02	124-125	365.10	02	124-125
349.2	01	091-093	359.21	01	091-093	362.01	02	124-125	363.13	02	124-125	365.11	02	124-125
349.31	21	919-921	359.22	01	091-093	362.02	02	124-125	363.14	02	124-125	365.12	02	123
349.39	21	919-921	359.23	01	091-093	362.03	02	124-125	363.15	02	124-125	365.13	02	124-125
349.81	01	091-093	359.24	01	091-093	362.04	02	124-125	363.20	02	124-125	365.14	02	124-125
349.82	01	091-093	359.29	01	091-093	362.05	02	124-125	363.21	02	124-125	365.15	02	124-125
349.89	01	070-072	359.3	01	091-093	362.06	02	124-125	363.22	02	124-125	365.20	02	124-125
349.9	01	070-072	359.4	01	091-093	362.07	02	124-125	363.30	02	124-125	365.21	02	124-125
350.1	01	073-074	359.5	01	091-093	362.10	02	124-125	363.31	02	124-125	365.22	02	124-125
350.2	01	073-074	359.6	01	091-093	362.11	02	124-125	363.32	02	124-125	365.23	02	124-125
350.8	01	073-074	359.71	08	545-547	362.12	02	124-125	363.33	02	124-125	365.24	02	124-125
350.9	01	073-074	359.79	08	545-547	362.13	02	124-125	363.34	02	124-125	365.31	02	124-125
351.0	01	073-074	359.81	01	091-093	362.14	02	124-125	363.35	02	124-125	365.32	02	124-125
351.1	01	073-074	359.89	01	091-093	362.15	02	124-125	363.40	02	124-125	365.41	02	124-125
351.8	01	073-074	359.9	01	091-093	362.16	02	124-125	363.41	02	124-125	365.42	02	124-125
351.9	01	073-074	360.00	02	121-122	362.17	02	124-125	363.42	02	124-125	365.43	02	124-125
352.0	01	073-074	360.01	02	121-122	362.18	02	124-125	363.43	02	124-125	365.44	02	124-125
352.1	01	073-074	360.02	02	121-122	362.20	02	124-125	363.50	02	124-125	365.51	02	124-125
352.2	01	073-074	360.03	02	124-125	362.21	02	124-125	363.51	02	124-125	365.52	02	124-125
352.3	01	073-074	360.04	02	121-122	362.22	02	124-125	363.52	02	124-125	365.59	02	124-125
352.4	01	073-074	360.11	02	124-125	362.23	02	124-125	363.53	02	124-125	365.60	02	124-125
352.5	01	073-074	360.12	02	124-125	362.24	02	124-125	363.54	02	124-125	365.61	02	124-125
352.6	01	073-074	360.13	02	121-122	362.25	02	124-125	363.55	02	124-125	365.62	02	124-125
352.9	01	073-074	360.14	02	124-125	362.26	02	124-125	363.56	02	124-125	365.63	02	124-125
353.0	01	073-074	360.19	02	121-122	362.27	02	124-125	363.57	02	124-125	365.64	02	124-125
353.1	01	073-074	360.20	02	124-125	362.29	02	124-125	363.61	02	124-125	365.65	02	124-125
353.2	01	073-074	360.21	02	124-125	362.30	02	123	363.62	02	124-125	365.81	02	124-125
353.3	01	073-074	360.23	02	124-125	362.31	02	123	363.63	02	124-125	365.82	02	124-125
353.4	01	073-074	360.24	02	124-125	362.32	02	123	363.70	02	124-125	365.83	02	124-125
353.5	01	073-074	360.29	02	124-125	362.33	02	123	363.71	02	124-125	365.89	02	124-125
353.6	01	073-074	360.30	02	124-125	362.34	02	123	363.72	02	124-125	365.9	02	124-125
353.8	01	073-074	360.31	02	124-125	362.35	02	123	363.8	02	124-125	366.00	02	124-125
353.9	01	073-074	360.32	02	124-125	362.36	02	123	363.9	02	124-125	366.01	02	124-125

DX	MDC	DRG	DX	MDC	DRG	DX	MDC	DRG	DX	MDC	DRG	DX	MDC	DRG
366.02	02	124-125	368.54	02	124-125	370.52	02	124-125	372.22	02	124-125	374.55	02	124-125
366.03	02	124-125	368.55	02	123	370.54	02	124-125	372.30	02	124-125	374.56	02	124-125
366.04	02	124-125	368.59	02	124-125	370.55	02	121-122	372.31	02	124-125	374.81	02	124-125
366.09	02	124-125	368.60	02	124-125	370.59	02	124-125	372.33	02	124-125	374.82	02	124-125
366.10	02	124-125	368.61	02	124-125	370.60	02	124-125	372.34	02	124-125	374.83	02	124-125
366.11	02	124-125	368.62	02	124-125	370.61	02	124-125	372.39	02	124-125	374.84	02	124-125
366.12	02	124-125	368.63	02	124-125	370.62	02	124-125	372.40	02	124-125	374.85	02	124-125
366.13	02	124-125	368.69	02	124-125	370.63	02	124-125	372.41	02	124-125	374.86	02	124-125
366.14	02	124-125	368.8	02	124-125	370.64	02	124-125	372.42	02	124-125	374.87	02	124-125
366.15	02	124-125	368.9	02	124-125	370.8	02	124-125	372.43	02	124-125	374.89	02	124-125
366.16	02	124-125	369.00	02	124-125	370.9	02	124-125	372.44	02	124-125	374.9	02	124-125
366.17	02	124-125	369.01	02	124-125	371.00	02	124-125	372.45	02	124-125	375.00	02	124-125
366.18	02	124-125	369.02	02	124-125	371.01	02	124-125	372.50	02	124-125	375.01	02	121-122
366.19	02	124-125	369.03	02	124-125	371.02	02	124-125	372.51	02	124-125	375.02	02	124-125
366.20	02	124-125	369.04	02	124-125	371.03	02	124-125	372.52	02	124-125	375.03	02	124-125
366.21	02	124-125	369.05	02	124-125	371.04	02	124-125	372.53	02	124-125	375.11	02	124-125
366.22	02	124-125	369.06	02	124-125	371.05	02	124-125	372.54	02	124-125	375.12	02	124-125
366.23	02	124-125	369.07	02	124-125	371.10	02	124-125	372.55	02	124-125	375.13	02	124-125
366.30	02	124-125	369.08	02	124-125	371.11	02	124-125	372.56	02	124-125	375.14	02	124-125
366.31	02	124-125	369.10	02	124-125	371.12	02	124-125	372.61	02	124-125	375.15	02	124-125
366.32	02	124-125	369.11	02	124-125	371.13	02	124-125	372.62	02	124-125	375.16	02	124-125
366.33	02	124-125	369.12	02	124-125	371.14	02	124-125	372.63	02	124-125	375.20	02	124-125
366.34	02	124-125	369.13	02	124-125	371.15	02	124-125	372.64	02	124-125	375.21	02	124-125
366.41	02	124-125	369.14	02	124-125	371.16	02	124-125	372.71	02	124-125	375.22	02	124-125
366.42	02	124-125	369.15	02	124-125	371.20	02	124-125	372.72	02	124-125	375.30	02	124-125
366.43	02	124-125	369.16	02	124-125	371.21	02	124-125	372.73	02	124-125	375.31	02	121-122
366.44	02	124-125	369.17	02	124-125	371.22	02	124-125	372.74	02	124-125	375.32	02	121-122
366.45	02	124-125	369.18	02	124-125	371.23	02	124-125	372.75	02	124-125	375.33	02	124-125
366.46	02	124-125	369.20	02	124-125	371.24	02	124-125	372.81	02	124-125	375.41	02	124-125
366.50	02	124-125	369.21	02	124-125	371.30	02	124-125	327.89	02	124-125	375.42	02	124-125
366.51	02	124-125	369.22	02	124-125	371.31	02	124-125	372.9	02	124-125	375.43	02	124-125
366.52	02	124-125	369.23	02	124-125	371.32	02	124-125	373.00	02	124-125	375.51	02	124-125
366.53	02	124-125	369.24	02	124-125	371.33	02	124-125	373.01	02	124-125	375.52	02	124-125
366.8	02	124-125	369.25	02	124-125	371.40	02	124-125	373.02	02	124-125	375.53	02	124-125
366.9	02	124-125	369.3	02	124-125	371.41	02	124-125	373.11	02	124-125	375.54	02	124-125
367.0	02	124-125	369.4	02	124-125	371.42	02	124-125	373.12	02	124-125	375.55	02	124-125
367.1	02	124-125	369.60	02	124-125	371.43	02	124-125	373.13	02	124-125	375.56	02	124-125
367.20	02	124-125	369.61	02	124-125	371.44	02	124-125	373.2	02	124-125	375.57	02	124-125
367.21	02	124-125	369.62	02	124-125	371.45	02	124-125	373.31	02	124-125	375.61	02	124-125
367.22	02	124-125	369.63	02	124-125	371.46	02	124-125	373.32	02	124-125	375.69	02	124-125
367.31	02	124-125	369.64	02	124-125	371.48	02	124-125	373.33	02	124-125	375.81	02	124-125
367.32	02	124-125	369.65	02	124-125	371.49	02	124-125	373.34	02	124-125	375.89	02	124-125
367.4	02	124-125	369.66	02	124-125	371.50	02	124-125	373.4	02	124-125	375.9	02	124-125
367.51	02	124-125	369.67	02	124-125	371.51	02	124-125	373.5	02	124-125	376.00	02	124-125
367.52	02	123	369.68	02	124-125	371.52	02	124-125	373.6	02	124-125	376.01	02	121-122
367.53	02	124-125	369.69	02	124-125	371.53	02	124-125	373.8	02	124-125	376.02	02	121-122
367.81	02	124-125	369.70	02	124-125	371.54	02	124-125	373.9	02	124-125	376.03	02	121-122
367.89	02	124-125	369.71	02	124-125	371.55	02	124-125	374.00	02	124-125	376.04	02	121-122
367.9	02	124-125	369.72	02	124-125	371.56	02	124-125	374.01	02	124-125	376.10	02	124-125
368.00	02	124-125	369.73	02	124-125	371.57	02	124-125	374.02	02	124-125	376.11	02	124-125
368.01	02	124-125	369.74	02	124-125	371.58	02	124-125	374.03	02	124-125	376.12	02	124-125
368.02	02	124-125	369.75	02	124-125	371.60	02	124-125	374.04	02	124-125	376.13	02	124-125
368.03	02	124-125	369.76	02	124-125	371.61	02	124-125	374.05	02	124-125	376.21	02	124-125
368.10	02	124-125	369.8	02	124-125	371.62	02	124-125	374.10	02	124-125	376.22	02	124-125
368.11	02	123	369.9	02	124-125	371.70	02	124-125	374.11	02	124-125	376.30	02	124-125
368.12	02	123	370.00	02	121-122	371.71	02	124-125	374.12	02	124-125	376.31	02	124-125
368.13	02	124-125	370.01	02	124-125	371.72	02	124-125	374.13	02	124-125	376.32	02	124-125
368.14	02	124-125	370.02	02	124-125	371.73	02	124-125	374.14	02	124-125	376.33	02	124-125
368.15	02	124-125	370.03	02	121-122	371.81	02	124-125	374.20	02	124-125	376.34	02	123
368.16	02	124-125	370.04	02	121-122	371.82	02	124-125	374.21	02	124-125	376.35	02	123
368.2	02	123	370.05	02	121-122	371.89	02	124-125	374.22	02	124-125	376.36	02	123
368.30	02	124-125	370.06	02	121-122	371.9	02	124-125	374.23	02	124-125	376.40	02	124-125
368.31	02	124-125	370.07	02	124-125	372.00	02	124-125	374.30	02	123	376.41	02	124-125
368.32	02	124-125	370.20	02	124-125	372.01	02	124-125	374.31	02	123	376.42	02	124-125
368.33	02	124-125	370.21	02	124-125	372.02	02	124-125	374.32	02	123	376.43	02	124-125
368.34	02	124-125	370.22	02	124-125	372.03	02	124-125	374.33	02	124-125	376.44	02	124-125
368.40	02	123	370.23	02	124-125	372.04	02	124-125	374.34	02	124-125	376.45	02	124-125
368.41	02	123	370.24	02	124-125	372.05	02	124-125	374.41	02	124-125	376.46	02	124-125
368.42	02	124-125	370.31	02	124-125	372.06	02	124-125	374.43	02	124-125	376.47	02	124-125
368.43	02	123	370.32	02	124-125	372.10	02	124-125	374.44	02	124-125	376.50	02	124-125
368.44	02	123	370.33	02	124-125	372.11	02	124-125	374.45	02	123	376.51	02	124-125
368.45	02	123	370.34	02	124-125	372.12	02	124-125	374.46	02	124-125	376.52	02	124-125
368.46	02	123	370.35	02	124-125	372.13	02	124-125	374.50	02	124-125	376.6	02	124-125
368.47	02	123	370.40	02	124-125	372.14	02	124-125	374.51	09	606-607	376.81	02	124-125
368.51	02	124-125	370.44	02	124-125	372.15	02	124-125	374.52	02	124-125	376.82	02	123
368.52	02	124-125	370.49	02	124-125	372.20	02	124-125	374.53	02	124-125	376.89	02	124-125
368.53	02	124-125	370.50	02	124-125	372.21	02	124-125	374.54	02	124-125	376.9	02	124-125

DX	MDC	DRG	DX	MDC	DRG	DX	MDC	DRG	DX	MDC	DRG	DX	MDC	DRG
377.00	01	091-093	378.55	02	123	380.12	03	154-156	384.9	03	154-156	388.61	01	091-093
377.01	01	091-093	378.56	02	123	380.13	03	154-156	385.00	03	154-156	388.69	03	154-156
377.02	02	124-125	378.60	02	124-125	380.14	03	154-156	385.01	03	154-156	388.70	03	154-156
377.03	02	124-125	378.61	02	124-125	380.15	03	154-156	385.02	03	154-156	388.71	03	154-156
377.04	01	091-093	378.62	02	124-125	380.16	03	154-156	385.03	03	154-156	388.72	03	154-156
377.10	02	123	378.63	02	124-125	380.21	03	154-156	385.09	03	154-156	388.8	03	154-156
377.11	02	123	378.71	02	124-125	380.22	03	154-156	385.10	03	154-156	388.9	03	154-156
377.12	02	123	378.72	02	123	380.23	03	154-156	385.11	03	154-156	389.00	03	154-156
377.13	02	124-125	378.73	02	123	380.30	03	154-156	385.12	03	154-156	389.01	03	154-156
377.14	02	124-125	378.81	02	124-125	380.31	03	154-156	385.13	03	154-156	389.02	03	154-156
377.15	02	123	378.82	02	124-125	380.32	03	154-156	385.19	03	154-156	389.03	03	154-156
377.16	02	123	378.83	02	124-125	380.39	03	154-156	385.21	03	154-156	389.04	03	154-156
377.21	02	123	378.84	02	124-125	380.4	03	154-156	385.22	03	154-156	389.05	03	154-156
377.22	02	124-125	378.85	02	124-125	380.50	03	154-156	385.23	03	154-156	389.06	03	154-156
377.23	02	124-125	378.86	01	091-093	380.51	03	154-156	385.24	03	154-156	389.08	03	154-156
377.24	02	123	378.87	02	123	380.52	03	154-156	385.30	03	154-156	389.10	03	154-156
377.30	02	123	378.9	02	124-125	380.53	03	154-156	385.31	03	154-156	389.11	03	154-156
377.31	02	123	379.00	02	124-125	380.81	03	154-156	385.32	03	154-156	389.12	03	154-156
377.32	02	123	379.01	02	124-125	380.89	03	154-156	385.33	03	154-156	389.13	03	154-156
377.33	02	123	379.02	02	124-125	380.9	03	154-156	385.35	03	154-156	389.14	03	154-156
377.34	02	123	379.03	02	124-125	381.00	03	152-153	385.82	03	154-156	389.15	03	154-156
377.39	02	123	379.04	02	124-125	381.01	03	152-153	385.83	03	154-156	389.16	03	154-156
377.41	02	123	379.05	02	124-125	381.02	03	152-153	385.89	03	154-156	389.17	03	154-156
377.42	02	123	379.06	02	124-125	381.03	03	152-153	385.9	03	154-156	389.18	03	154-156
377.43	02	123	379.07	02	124-125	381.04	03	152-153	386.00	03	149	389.20	03	154-156
377.49	02	123	379.09	02	124-125	381.05	03	152-153	386.01	03	149	389.21	03	154-156
377.51	01	091-093	379.11	02	124-125	381.06	03	152-153	386.02	03	149	389.22	03	154-156
377.52	01	091-093	379.12	02	124-125	381.10	03	152-153	386.03	03	149	389.7	03	154-156
377.53	01	091-093	379.13	02	124-125	381.19	03	152-153	386.04	03	149	389.8	03	154-156
377.54	01	091-093	379.14	02	124-125	381.20	03	152-153	386.10	03	149	389.9	03	154-156
377.61	01	091-093	379.15	02	124-125	381.29	03	152-153	386.11	03	149			
377.62	01	091-093	379.16	02	124-125	381.3	03	152-153	386.12	03	149			
377.63	01	091-093	379.19	02	124-125	381.4	03	152-153	386.19	03	149	**Diseases of the Circulatory System**		
377.71	01	091-093	379.21	02	124-125	381.50	03	152-153	386.2	03	149	390	08	545-547
377.72	01	091-093	379.22	02	124-125	381.51	03	152-153	386.30	03	149	391.0	05	314-316
377.73	01	091-093	379.23	02	124-125	381.52	03	152-153	386.31	03	149	391.1	05	306-307
377.75	01	091-093	379.24	02	124-125	381.60	03	154-156	386.32	03	149	391.2	05	314-316
377.9	01	091-093	379.25	02	124-125	381.61	03	154-156	386.33	03	149	391.8	05	314-316
378.00	02	124-125	379.26	02	124-125	381.62	03	154-156	386.34	03	149	391.9	05	314-316
378.01	02	124-125	379.29	02	124-125	381.63	03	154-156	386.35	03	149	392.0	05	314-316
378.02	02	124-125	379.31	02	124-125	381.7	03	154-156	386.40	03	154-156	392.9	05	314-316
378.03	02	124-125	379.32	02	124-125	381.81	03	154-156	386.41	03	154-156	393	05	314-316
378.04	02	124-125	379.33	02	124-125	381.89	03	154-156	386.42	03	154-156	394.0	05	306-307
378.05	02	124-125	379.34	02	124-125	381.9	03	154-156	386.43	03	154-156	394.1	05	306-307
378.06	02	124-125	379.39	02	124-125	382.00	03	152-153	386.48	03	154-156	394.2	05	306-307
378.07	02	124-125	379.40	02	123	382.01	03	152-153	386.50	03	149	394.9	05	306-307
378.08	02	124-125	379.41	02	123	382.02	03	152-153	386.51	03	149	395.0	05	306-307
378.10	02	124-125	379.42	02	123	382.1	03	152-153	386.52	03	149	395.1	05	306-307
378.11	02	124-125	379.43	02	123	382.2	03	152-153	386.53	03	149	395.2	05	306-307
378.12	02	124-125	379.45	01	056-057	382.3	03	152-153	386.54	03	149	395.9	05	306-307
378.13	02	124-125	379.46	02	123	382.4	03	152-153	386.55	03	149	396.0	05	306-307
378.14	02	124-125	379.49	02	123	382.9	03	152-153	386.56	03	149	396.1	05	306-307
378.15	02	124-125	379.50	02	123	383.00	03	152-153	386.58	03	149	396.2	05	306-307
378.16	02	124-125	379.51	02	124-125	383.01	03	152-153	386.8	03	149	396.3	05	306-307
378.17	02	124-125	379.52	02	123	383.02	03	152-153	386.9	03	149	396.8	05	306-307
378.18	02	124-125	379.53	02	124-125	383.1	03	152-153	387.0	03	154-156	396.9	05	306-307
378.20	02	124-125	379.54	02	123	383.20	03	152-153	387.1	03	154-156	397.0	05	306-307
378.21	02	124-125	379.55	02	123	383.21	03	152-153	387.2	03	154-156	397.1	05	306-307
378.22	02	124-125	379.56	02	124-125	383.22	03	152-153	387.8	03	154-156	397.9	05	306-307
378.23	02	124-125	379.57	02	123	383.30	03	154-156	387.9	03	154-156	398.0	05	314-316
378.24	02	124-125	379.58	02	123	383.31	03	154-156	388.00	03	154-156	398.90	05	314-316
378.30	02	124-125	379.59	02	124-125	383.32	03	154-156	388.01	03	154-156	398.91	05	291-293
378.31	02	124-125	379.60	02	124-125	383.33	03	154-156	388.02	03	154-156	398.99	05	314-316
378.32	02	124-125	379.61	02	124-125	383.81	03	154-156	388.10	03	154-156	401.0	05	304-305
378.33	02	124-125	379.62	02	124-125	383.89	03	154-156	388.11	03	154-156	401.1	05	304-305
378.34	02	124-125	379.63	02	124-125	383.9	03	152-153	388.12	03	154-156	401.9	05	304-305
378.35	02	124-125	379.8	02	124-125	384.00	03	152-153	388.2	03	154-156	402.00	05	304-305
378.40	02	124-125	379.90	02	124-125	384.01	03	152-153	388.30	03	154-156	402.01	05	291-293
378.41	02	124-125	379.91	02	124-125	384.09	03	152-153	388.31	03	154-156	402.10	05	304-305
378.42	02	124-125	379.92	02	124-125	384.1	03	152-153	388.32	03	154-156	402.11	05	291-293
378.43	02	124-125	379.93	02	124-125	384.20	03	154-156	388.40	03	154-156	402.90	05	304-305
378.44	02	124-125	379.99	02	124-125	384.21	03	154-156	388.41	03	154-156	402.91	05	291-293
378.45	02	124-125	380.00	03	152-153	384.22	03	154-156	388.42	03	154-156	403.00	11	682-684
378.50	02	123	380.01	08	564-566	384.23	03	154-156	388.43	03	154-156	403.01	11	682-684
378.51	02	123	380.02	08	564-566	384.24	03	154-156	388.44	03	154-156	403.10	11	682-684
378.52	02	123	380.03	08	564-566	384.25	03	154-156	388.45	19	886	403.11	11	682-684
378.53	02	123	380.10	03	154-156	384.81	03	154-156	388.5	03	154-156	403.90	11	682-684
378.54	02	123	380.11	03	154-156	384.82	03	154-156	388.60	03	154-156	403.91	11	682-684

DX	MDC	DRG	DX	MDC	DRG	DX	MDC	DRG	DX	MDC	DRG	DX	MDC	DRG
404.00	05	304-305	416.1	05	314-316	428.1	05	291-293	438.22	01	056-057	445.89	05	299-301
404.01	05	291-293	416.2	04	175-176	428.9	05	291-293	438.30	01	056-057	446.0	08	545-547
404.02	11	682-684	416.8	05	314-316	428.20	05	291-293	438.31	01	056-057	446.1	08	545-547
404.03	05	291-293	416.9	05	314-316	428.21	05	291-293	438.32	01	056-057	446.20	08	545-547
404.10	05	304-305	417.0	05	314-316	428.22	05	291-293	438.40	01	056-057	446.21	08	545-547
404.11	05	291-293	417.1	05	314-316	428.23	05	291-293	438.41	01	056-057	446.29	08	545-547
404.12	11	682-684	417.8	05	314-316	428.30	05	291-293	438.42	01	056-057	446.3	08	542-544
404.13	05	291-293	417.9	05	314-316	428.31	05	291-293	438.50	01	056-057	446.4	08	542-544
404.90	05	304-305	420.0	05	314-316	428.32	05	291-293	438.51	01	056-057	446.5	08	545-547
404.91	05	291-293	420.90	05	314-316	428.33	05	291-293	438.52	01	056-057	446.6	08	545-547
404.92	11	682-684	420.91	05	314-316	428.40	05	291-293	438.53	01	056-057	446.7	08	545-547
404.93	05	291-293	420.99	05	314-316	428.41	05	291-293	438.6	01	056-057	447.0	05	299-301
405.01	05	304-305	421.0	05	288-290	428.42	05	291-293	438.7	01	056-057	447.1	05	299-301
405.09	05	304-305	421.1	05	288-290	428.43	05	291-293	438.81	01	056-057	447.2	05	299-301
405.11	05	304-305	421.9	05	288-290	428.9	05	291-293	438.82	01	056-057	447.3	11	698-700
405.19	05	304-305	422.0	05	314-316	429.0	05	314-316	438.83	01	056-057	447.4	06	391-392
405.91	05	304-305	422.90	05	314-316	429.1	05	314-316	438.84	01	056-057	447.5	05	299-301
405.99	05	304-305	422.91	05	314-316	429.2	05	302-303	438.85	01	056-057	447.6	08	545-547
410.00	05	314-316	422.92	05	314-316	429.3	05	302-303	438.89	01	056-057	447.8	05	299-301
410.01	05	280-285	422.93	05	314-316	429.4	05	314-316	438.9	01	056-057	447.9	05	299-301
410.02	05	314-316	422.99	05	314-316	429.5	05	306-307	440.0	05	299-301	448.0	05	299-301
410.10	05	314-316	423.0	05	314-316	429.6	05	306-307	440.1	11	698-700	448.1	09	606-607
410.11	05	280-285	423.1	05	314-316	429.71	05	314-316	440.20	05	299-301	448.9	05	299-301
410.12	05	314-316	423.2	05	314-316	429.79	05	314-316	440.21	05	299-301	449	05	299-301
410.20	05	314-316	423.3	05	314-316	429.81	05	306-307	440.22	05	299-301	451.0	05	299-301
410.21	05	280-285	423.8	05	314-316	429.82	05	314-316	440.23	05	299-301	451.11	05	294-295
410.22	05	314-316	423.9	05	314-316	429.83	05	314-316	440.24	05	299-301	451.19	05	294-295
410.30	05	314-316	424.0	05	306-307	429.89	05	302-303	440.29	05	299-301	451.2	05	294-295
410.31	05	280-285	424.1	05	306-307	429.9	05	302-303	440.30	05	299-301	451.81	05	294-295
410.32	05	314-316	424.2	05	306-307	430	01	064-066	440.31	05	299-301	451.82	05	299-301
410.40	05	314-316	424.3	05	306-307	431	01	064-066	440.32	05	299-301	451.83	05	299-301
410.41	05	280-285	424.90	05	306-307	432.0	01	064-066	440.4	05	299-301	451.84	05	299-301
410.42	05	314-316	424.91	05	306-307	432.1	01	064-066	440.8	05	299-301	451.89	05	299-301
410.50	05	314-316	424.99	05	306-307	432.9	01	064-066	440.9	05	299-301	451.9	05	299-301
410.51	05	280-285	425.0	05	314-316	433.00	01	067-068	441.00	05	299-301	452	07	441-443
410.52	05	314-316	425.1	05	314-316	433.01	01	061-066	441.01	05	299-301	453.0	07	441-443
410.60	05	314-316	425.2	05	314-316	433.10	01	067-068	441.02	05	299-301	453.1	05	299-301
410.61	05	280-285	425.3	05	314-316	433.11	01	061-066	441.03	05	299-301	453.2	05	294-295
410.62	05	314-316	425.4	05	314-316	433.20	01	067-068	441.1	05	299-301	453.3	11	698-700
410.70	05	314-316	425.5	05	314-316	433.21	01	061-066	441.2	05	299-301	453.40	05	299-301
410.71	05	280-285	425.7	05	314-316	433.30	01	067-068	441.3	05	299-301	453.41	05	299-301
410.72	05	314-316	425.8	05	314-316	433.31	01	061-066	441.4	05	299-301	453.42	05	299-301
410.80	05	314-316	425.9	05	314-316	433.80	01	067-068	441.5	05	299-301	453.50	05	299-301
410.81	05	280-285	426.0	05	308-310	433.81	01	061-066	441.6	05	299-301	453.51	05	299-301
410.82	05	314-316	426.10	05	308-310	433.90	01	067-068	441.7	05	299-301	453.52	05	299-301
410.90	05	314-316	426.11	05	308-310	433.91	01	061-066	441.9	05	299-301	453.6	05	299-301
410.91	05	280-285	426.12	05	308-310	434.00	01	067-068	442.0	05	299-301	453.71	05	299-301
410.92	05	314-316	426.13	05	308-310	434.01	01	061-066	442.1	11	698-700	453.72	05	299-301
411.0	05	314-316	426.2	05	308-310	434.10	01	067-068	442.2	05	299-301	453.73	05	299-301
411.1	05	311	426.3	05	308-310	434.11	01	061-066	442.3	05	299-301	453.74	05	299-301
411.81	05	311	426.4	05	308-310	434.90	01	067-068	442.81	05	299-301	453.75	05	299-301
411.89	05	311	426.50	05	308-310	434.91	01	061-066	442.82	05	299-301	453.76	05	299-301
412	05	302-303	426.51	05	308-310	435.0	01	069	442.83	05	299-301	453.77	05	299-301
413.0	05	311	426.52	05	308-310	435.1	01	069	442.84	05	299-301	453.79	05	299-301
413.1	05	311	426.53	05	308-310	435.2	01	069	442.89	05	299-301	453.81	05	299-301
413.9	05	311	426.54	05	308-310	435.8	01	069	442.9	05	299-301	453.82	05	299-301
414.00	05	302-303	426.6	05	308-310	435.9	01	069	443.0	08	545-547	453.83	05	299-301
414.01	05	302-303	426.7	05	308-310	436	01	067-068	443.1	05	299-301	453.84	05	299-301
414.02	05	302-303	426.81	05	308-310	437.0	01	070-072	443.21	05	299-301	453.85	05	299-301
414.03	05	302-303	426.82	05	308-310	437.1	01	069	443.22	05	299-301	453.86	05	299-301
414.04	05	302-303	426.89	05	308-310	437.2	01	077-079	443.23	11	698-700	453.87	05	299-301
414.05	05	302-303	426.9	05	308-310	437.3	01	091-093	443.24	05	299-301	453.89	05	299-301
414.06	05	302-303	427.0	05	308-310	437.4	01	102-103	443.29	05	299-301	453.9	05	299-301
414.07	05	302-303	427.1	05	308-310	437.5	01	091-093	443.81	05	299-301	454.0	05	299-301
414.10	05	314-316	427.2	05	308-310	437.6	01	091-093	443.82	05	299-301	454.1	05	299-301
414.11	05	314-316	427.31	05	308-310	437.7	01	070-072	443.89	05	299-301	454.2	05	299-301
414.12	05	314-316	427.32	05	308-310	437.8	01	070-072	443.9	05	299-301	454.8	05	299-301
414.19	05	314-316	427.41	05	308-310	437.9	01	070-072	444.0	05	299-301	454.9	05	299-301
414.2	05	302-303	427.42	05	308-310	438.0	01	056-057	444.1	05	299-301	455.0	06	393-395
414.3	05	302-303	427.5	05	296-298	438.10	01	056-057	444.21	05	299-301	455.1	06	393-395
414.8	05	302-303	427.60	05	308-310	438.11	01	056-057	444.22	05	299-301	455.2	06	393-395
414.9	05	302-303	427.61	05	308-310	438.12	01	056-057	444.81	05	299-301	455.3	06	393-395
415.0	05	314-316	427.69	05	308-310	438.13	01	056-057	444.89	05	299-301	455.5	06	393-395
415.11	04	175-176	427.81	05	308-310	438.14	01	056-057	444.9	05	299-301	455.6	06	393-395
415.12	04	175-176	427.89	05	308-310	438.19	01	056-057	445.01	05	299-301	455.7	06	393-395
415.19	04	175-176	427.9	05	308-310	438.20	01	056-057	445.02	05	299-301	455.8	06	393-395
416.0	05	314-316	428.0	05	291-293	438.21	01	056-057	445.81	11	698-700			

Diagnosis Code/MDC/DRG List

DX	MDC	DRG
455.9	06	393-395
456.0	06	368-370
456.1	06	368-370
456.20	06	368-370
456.21	06	393-395
456.3	05	299-301
456.4	12	729-730
456.5	12	729-730
456.5	13	760-761
456.6	13	760-761
456.8	05	299-301
457.0	09	600-601
457.1	09	606-607
457.2	09	602-603
457.8	16	814-816
457.9	16	814-816
458.0	05	312
458.1	05	314-316
458.21	05	312
458.29	05	312
458.8	05	314-316
458.9	05	314-316
459.0	05	314-316
459.1	05	299-301
459.2	05	299-301
459.10	05	299-301
459.11	05	299-301
459.12	05	299-301
459.13	05	299-301
459.19	05	299-301
459.30	05	299-301
459.31	05	299-301
459.32	05	299-301
459.33	05	299-301
459.39	05	299-301
459.81	05	299-301
459.89	05	302-303
459.9	05	302-303

Diseases of the Respiratory System

DX	MDC	DRG
460	03	152-153
461.0	03	152-153
461.1	03	152-153
461.2	03	152-153
461.3	03	152-153
461.8	03	152-153
461.9	03	152-153
462	03	152-153
463	03	152-153
464.00	03	152-153
464.01	03	152-153
464.10	04	202-203
464.11	04	202-203
464.20	03	152-153
464.21	03	152-153
464.30	03	152-153
464.31	03	152-153
464.4	03	152-153
464.50	03	152-153
464.51	03	152-153
465.0	03	152-153
465.8	03	152-153
465.9	03	152-153
466.0	04	202-203
466.11	04	202-203
466.19	04	202-203
470	03	154-156
471.0	03	154-156
471.1	03	154-156
471.8	03	154-156
471.9	03	154-156
472.0	03	152-153
472.1	03	152-153
472.2	03	152-153
473.0	03	152-153
473.1	03	152-153
473.2	03	152-153
473.3	03	152-153
473.8	03	152-153
473.9	03	152-153
474.00	03	152-153
474.01	03	152-153
474.02	03	152-153
474.10	03	154-156
474.11	03	154-156
474.12	03	154-156
474.2	03	154-156
474.8	03	154-156
474.9	03	154-156
475	03	152-153
476.0	03	152-153
476.1	03	152-153
477.0	03	152-153
477.1	03	152-153
477.2	03	152-153
477.8	03	152-153
477.9	03	152-153
478.0	03	154-156
478.11	03	154-156
478.19	03	154-156
478.20	03	154-156
478.21	03	152-153
478.22	03	152-153
478.24	03	152-153
478.25	03	154-156
478.26	03	154-156
478.29	03	154-156
478.30	03	154-156
478.31	03	154-156
478.32	03	154-156
478.33	03	154-156
478.34	03	154-156
478.4	03	154-156
478.5	03	154-156
478.6	03	154-156
478.70	03	154-156
478.71	03	152-153
478.74	03	154-156
478.75	03	154-156
478.79	03	154-156
478.8	03	152-153
478.9	03	152-153
480.0	04	193-195
480.1	04	193-195
480.2	04	193-195
480.8	04	193-195
480.9	04	193-195
481	04	193-195
482.0	04	177-179
482.1	04	177-179
482.2	04	193-195
482.30	04	193-195
482.31	04	193-195
482.32	04	193-195
482.39	04	193-195
482.40	04	177-179
482.41	04	177-179
482.42	04	177-179
482.49	04	177-179
482.81	04	177-179
482.82	04	177-179
482.83	04	177-179
482.84	04	177-179
482.89	04	177-179
482.9	04	193-195
483.0	04	193-195
483.1	04	193-195
483.8	04	193-195
484.1	04	177-179
484.3	04	177-179
484.5	04	177-179
484.6	04	177-179
484.7	04	177-179
484.8	04	177-179
485	04	193-195
486	04	193-195
487.0	04	193-195
487.1	03	152-153
487.8	18	865-866
488.0	03	152-153
488.1	03	152-153
490	04	202-203
491.0	04	202-203
491.1	04	190-192
491.20	04	190-192
491.21	04	190-192
491.22	04	190-192
491.8	04	190-192
491.9	04	190-192
492.0	04	190-192
492.8	04	190-192
493.00	04	202-203
493.01	04	202-203
493.02	04	202-203
493.10	04	202-203
493.11	04	202-203
493.12	04	202-203
493.20	04	190-192
493.21	04	190-192
493.22	04	190-192
493.81	04	202-203
493.82	04	202-203
493.90	04	202-203
493.91	04	202-203
493.92	04	202-203
494.0	04	190-192
494.1	04	190-192
495.0	04	196-198
495.1	04	196-198
495.2	04	196-198
495.3	04	196-198
495.4	04	196-198
495.5	04	196-198
495.6	04	196-198
495.7	04	196-198
495.8	04	196-198
495.9	04	196-198
496	04	190-192
500	04	196-198
501	04	196-198
502	04	196-198
503	04	196-198
504	04	196-198
505	04	196-198
506.0	04	205-206
506.1	04	189
506.2	04	205-206
506.3	04	205-206
506.4	04	190-192
506.9	04	190-192
507.0	04	177-179
507.1	04	177-179
507.8	04	177-179
508.0	04	205-206
508.1	04	196-198
508.8	04	205-206
508.9	04	205-206
510.0	04	177-179
510.9	04	177-179
511.0	04	193-195
511.1	04	177-179
511.81	04	180-182
511.89	04	186-188
511.9	04	186-188
512.0	04	199-201
512.1	04	199-201
512.8	04	199-201
513.0	04	177-179
513.1	04	177-179
514	04	189
515	04	196-198
516.1	04	196-198
516.2	04	196-198
516.3	04	196-198
516.8	04	196-198
516.9	04	196-198
517.1	04	196-198
517.2	04	196-198
517.3	04	196-198
517.8	04	196-198
518.0	04	205-206
518.1	04	199-201
518.2	04	205-206
518.3	04	196-198
518.4	04	189
518.5	04	189
518.6	04	196-198
518.7	04	205-206
518.81	04	189
518.82	04	204
518.83	04	189
518.84	04	189
518.89	04	205-206
519.00	04	205-206
519.0	04	205-206
519.02	04	205-206
519.09	04	205-206
519.11	04	202-203
519.19	04	202-203
519.2	04	177-179
519.3	04	205-206
519.4	04	205-206
519.8	04	205-206
519.9	04	205-206

Diseases of the Digestive System

DX	MDC	DRG
520.0	03	157-159
520.1	03	157-159
520.2	03	157-159
520.3	03	157-159
520.4	03	157-159
520.5	03	157-159
520.6	03	157-159
520.7	03	157-159
520.8	03	157-159
520.9	03	157-159
521.00	03	157-159
521.01	03	157-159
521.02	03	157-159
521.03	03	157-159
521.04	03	157-159
521.06	03	157-159
521.07	03	157-159
521.08	03	157-159
521.09	03	157-159
521.10	03	157-159
521.11	03	157-159
521.12	03	157-159
521.13	03	157-159
521.14	03	157-159
521.15	03	157-159
521.20	03	157-159
521.21	03	157-159
521.22	03	157-159
521.23	03	157-159
521.24	03	157-159
521.25	03	157-159
521.30	03	157-159
521.31	03	157-159
521.32	03	157-159
521.33	03	157-159
521.34	03	157-159
521.35	03	157-159
521.40	03	157-159
521.41	03	157-159
521.42	03	157-159
521.49	03	157-159
521.5	03	157-159
521.6	03	157-159
521.7	03	157-159
521.81	03	157-159
521.89	03	157-159
521.9	03	157-159
522.0	03	157-159
522.1	03	157-159
522.2	03	157-159
522.3	03	157-159
522.4	03	157-159
522.5	03	157-159
522.6	03	157-159
522.7	03	157-159
522.8	03	157-159
522.9	03	157-159
523.00	03	157-159
523.01	03	157-159
523.10	03	157-159
523.11	03	157-159
523.20	03	157-159
523.21	03	157-159
523.23	03	157-159
523.24	03	157-159
523.25	03	157-159
523.30	03	157-159
523.31	03	157-159
523.32	03	157-159
523.33	03	157-159
523.40	03	157-159
523.41	03	157-159
523.42	03	157-159
523.5	03	157-159
523.6	03	157-159
523.8	03	157-159
523.9	03	157-159
524.00	03	157-159
524.01	03	157-159
524.02	03	157-159
524.03	03	157-159
524.04	03	157-159
524.05	03	157-159
524.06	03	157-159
524.07	03	157-159
524.09	03	157-159
524.10	03	157-159
524.11	03	157-159
524.12	03	157-159
524.19	03	157-159
524.20	03	157-159
524.21	03	157-159
524.22	03	157-159
524.23	03	157-159
524.24	03	157-159
524.25	03	157-159
524.26	03	157-159
524.27	03	157-159
524.28	03	157-159
524.29	03	157-159
524.30	03	157-159
524.31	03	157-159
524.32	03	157-159
524.33	03	157-159
524.34	03	157-159
524.35	03	157-159
524.36	03	157-159
524.37	03	157-159
524.39	03	157-159
524.4	03	157-159
524.50	03	157-159
524.51	03	157-159
524.52	03	157-159
524.53	03	157-159
524.54	03	157-159
524.55	03	157-159
524.56	03	157-159
524.57	03	157-159
524.59	03	157-159
524.60	03	157-159

Diagnosis Code/MDC/DRG List

Diagnosis Code/MDC/DRG List

DX	MDC	DRG	DX	MDC	DRG	DX	MDC	DRG	DX	MDC	DRG	DX	MDC	DRG
524.61	03	157-159	527.8	03	154-156	532.51	06	380-382	537.82	06	391-392	558.41	06	391-392
524.62	03	157-159	527.9	03	154-156	532.60	06	377-379	537.83	06	377-379	558.42	06	391-392
524.63	03	157-159	528.00	03	157-159	532.61	06	377-379	537.84	06	377-379	558.9	06	391-392
524.64	03	157-159	528.01	03	157-159	532.70	06	383-384	537.89	06	391-392	560.0	06	388-390
524.69	03	157-159	528.02	03	157-159	532.71	06	380-382	537.9	06	391-392	560.1	06	388-390
524.70	03	157-159	528.09	03	157-159	532.90	06	383-384	538	06	391-392	560.2	06	388-390
524.71	03	157-159	528.1	03	157-159	532.91	06	380-382	540.0	06	371-373	560.30	06	388-390
524.72	03	157-159	528.2	03	157-159	533.00	06	377-379	540.1	06	371-373	560.31	06	388-390
524.73	03	157-159	528.3	03	157-159	533.01	06	377-379	540.9	06	393-395	560.39	06	388-390
524.74	03	157-159	528.4	03	157-159	533.10	06	380-382	541	06	393-395	560.81	06	388-390
524.75	03	157-159	528.5	03	157-159	533.11	06	380-382	542	06	393-395	560.89	06	388-390
524.76	03	157-159	528.6	03	157-159	533.20	06	377-379	543.0	06	393-395	560.9	06	388-390
524.79	03	157-159	528.71	03	157-159	533.21	06	377-379	543.9	06	393-395	562.00	06	391-392
524.81	03	157-159	528.72	03	157-159	533.30	06	383-384	550.00	06	393-395	562.01	06	391-392
524.82	03	157-159	528.79	03	157-159	533.31	06	380-382	550.01	06	393-395	562.02	06	377-379
524.89	03	157-159	528.8	03	157-159	533.40	06	377-379	550.02	06	393-395	562.03	06	377-379
524.9	03	157-159	528.9	03	157-159	533.41	06	377-379	550.03	06	393-395	562.10	06	391-392
525.0	03	157-159	529.0	03	157-159	533.50	06	380-382	550.10	06	393-395	562.11	06	391-392
525.10	03	157-159	529.1	03	157-159	533.51	06	380-382	550.11	06	393-395	562.12	06	377-379
525.11	03	157-159	529.2	03	157-159	533.60	06	377-379	550.12	06	393-395	562.13	06	377-379
525.12	03	157-159	529.3	03	157-159	533.61	06	377-379	550.13	06	393-395	564.00	06	391-392
525.13	03	157-159	529.4	03	157-159	533.70	06	383-384	550.90	06	393-395	564.01	06	391-392
525.19	03	157-159	529.5	03	157-159	533.71	06	380-382	550.91	06	393-395	564.02	06	391-392
525.20	03	157-159	529.6	03	157-159	533.90	06	383-384	550.92	06	393-395	564.09	06	391-392
525.21	03	157-159	529.8	03	157-159	533.91	06	380-382	550.93	06	393-395	564.1	06	391-392
525.22	03	157-159	529.9	03	157-159	534.00	06	377-379	551.00	06	393-395	564.2	06	391-392
525.23	03	157-159	530.0	06	391-392	534.01	06	377-379	551.01	06	393-395	564.3	06	391-392
525.24	03	157-159	530.10	06	391-392	534.10	06	380-382	551.02	06	393-395	564.4	06	391-392
525.25	03	157-159	530.11	06	391-392	534.11	06	380-382	551.03	06	393-395	564.5	06	391-392
525.26	03	157-159	530.12	06	391-392	534.20	06	377-379	551.1	06	393-395	564.6	06	391-392
525.3	03	157-159	530.13	06	391-392	534.21	06	377-379	551.20	06	393-395	564.7	06	393-395
525.40	03	157-159	530.19	06	391-392	534.30	06	380-382	551.21	06	393-395	564.81	06	391-392
525.41	03	157-159	530.20	06	380-382	534.31	06	380-382	551.29	06	393-395	564.89	06	391-392
525.42	03	157-159	530.21	06	380-382	534.40	06	377-379	551.3	06	393-395	564.9	06	391-392
525.43	03	157-159	530.3	06	391-392	534.41	06	377-379	551.8	06	393-395	565.0	06	393-395
525.44	03	157-159	530.4	06	368-370	534.50	06	380-382	551.9	06	393-395	565.1	06	393-395
525.50	03	157-159	530.5	06	391-392	534.51	06	380-382	552.00	06	393-395	566	06	393-395
525.51	03	157-159	530.6	06	391-392	534.60	06	377-379	552.01	06	393-395	567.0	06	371-373
525.52	03	157-159	530.7	06	368-370	534.61	06	377-379	552.02	06	393-395	567.1	06	371-373
525.53	03	157-159	530.81	06	391-392	534.70	06	380-382	552.03	06	393-395	567.21	06	371-373
525.54	03	157-159	530.82	06	368-370	534.71	06	380-382	552.1	06	393-395	567.22	06	371-373
525.60	03	157-159	530.83	06	391-392	534.90	06	380-382	552.20	06	393-395	567.23	06	371-373
525.61	03	157-159	530.84	06	368-370	534.91	06	380-382	552.21	06	393-395	567.29	06	371-373
525.62	03	157-159	530.85	06	380-382	535.00	06	391-392	552.29	06	393-395	567.31	06	371-373
525.63	03	157-159	530.86	06	393-395	535.01	06	377-379	552.3	06	391-392	567.38	06	371-373
525.64	03	157-159	530.87	06	393-395	535.10	06	391-392	552.8	06	393-395	567.39	06	371-373
525.65	03	157-159	530.89	06	391-392	535.11	06	377-379	552.9	06	393-395	567.81	06	393-395
525.66	03	157-159	530.9	06	391-392	535.20	06	391-392	553.00	06	393-395	567.82	06	393-395
525.67	03	157-159	531.00	06	377-379	535.21	06	377-379	553.01	06	393-395	567.89	06	371-373
525.69	03	157-159	531.01	06	377-379	535.30	06	391-392	553.02	06	393-395	568.0	06	371-373
525.71	03	157-159	531.10	06	380-382	535.31	06	377-379	553.03	06	393-395	568.81	06	393-395
525.72	03	157-159	531.11	06	380-382	535.40	06	391-392	553.1	06	393-395	568.82	06	393-395
525.73	03	157-159	531.20	06	377-379	535.41	06	377-379	553.20	06	393-395	568.89	06	393-395
525.79	03	157-159	531.21	06	377-379	535.50	06	391-392	553.21	06	393-395	568.9	06	393-395
525.8	03	157-159	531.30	06	383-384	535.51	06	377-379	553.29	06	393-395	569.0	06	393-395
525.9	03	157-159	531.31	06	380-382	535.60	06	391-392	553.3	06	391-392	569.1	06	393-395
526.0	03	157-159	531.40	06	377-379	535.61	06	377-379	553.8	06	393-395	569.2	06	393-395
526.1	03	157-159	531.41	06	377-379	535.70	06	391-392	553.9	06	393-395	569.3	06	377-379
526.2	03	157-159	531.50	06	380-382	535.71	06	377-379	555.0	06	385-387	569.41	06	393-395
526.3	03	157-159	531.51	06	380-382	536.0	06	391-392	555.1	06	385-387	569.42	06	393-395
526.4	03	157-159	531.60	06	377-379	536.1	06	391-392	555.2	06	385-387	569.43	06	393-395
526.5	03	157-159	531.61	06	377-379	536.2	06	391-392	555.9	06	385-387	569.44	06	393-395
526.61	03	157-159	531.70	06	383-384	536.3	06	391-392	556.0	06	385-387	569.49	06	393-395
526.62	03	157-159	531.71	06	380-382	536.40	06	393-395	556.1	06	385-387	569.5	06	371-373
526.63	03	157-159	531.90	06	383-384	536.41	06	393-395	556.2	06	385-387	569.60	06	393-395
526.69	03	157-159	531.91	06	380-382	536.42	06	393-395	556.3	06	385-387	569.61	06	393-395
526.81	03	157-159	532.00	06	377-379	536.49	06	393-395	556.4	06	385-387	569.62	06	393-395
526.89	03	157-159	532.01	06	377-379	536.8	06	391-392	556.5	06	385-387	569.69	06	393-395
526.9	03	157-159	532.10	06	380-382	536.9	06	391-392	556.6	06	385-387	569.71	06	393-395
527.0	03	154-156	532.11	06	380-382	537.0	06	380-382	556.8	06	385-387	569.79	06	393-395
527.1	03	154-156	532.20	06	377-379	537.1	06	391-392	556.9	06	385-387	569.81	06	393-395
527.2	03	154-156	532.21	06	377-379	537.2	06	391-392	557.0	06	393-395	569.82	06	393-395
527.3	03	154-156	532.30	06	383-384	537.3	06	380-382	557.1	06	393-395	569.83	06	393-395
527.4	03	154-156	532.31	06	380-382	537.4	06	391-392	557.9	06	393-395	569.84	06	393-395
527.5	03	154-156	532.40	06	377-379	537.5	06	391-392	558.1	06	393-395	569.85	06	377-379
527.6	03	154-156	532.41	06	377-379	537.6	06	391-392	558.2	06	393-395	569.86	06	393-395
527.7	03	154-156	532.50	06	380-382	537.81	06	391-392	558.3	06	391-392			

DX	MDC	DRG	DX	MDC	DRG	DX	MDC	DRG	DX	MDC	DRG	DX	MDC	DRG
569.87	06	393-395	579.2	06	391-392	593.70	11	698-700	601.4	12	727-728	614.3	13	757-759
569.89	06	393-395	579.3	06	391-392	593.71	11	698-700	601.8	12	727-728	614.4	13	757-759
569.9	06	393-395	579.4	06	391-392	593.72	11	698-700	601.9	12	727-728	614.5	13	757-759
570	07	441-443	579.8	06	391-392	593.73	11	698-700	602.0	12	729-730	614.6	13	760-761
571.0	07	441-443	579.9	06	391-392	593.81	11	698-700	602.1	12	729-730	614.7	13	757-759
571.1	07	432-434				593.82	11	698-700	602.2	12	729-730	614.8	13	757-759
571.2	07	432-434	**Diseases of the Genitourinary System**			593.89	11	698-700	602.3	12	729-730	614.9	13	757-759
571.3	07	432-434	580.0	11	698-700	593.9	11	698-700	602.8	12	729-730	615.0	13	757-759
571.40	07	441-443	580.4	11	698-700	594.0	11	698-700	602.9	12	729-730	615.1	13	757-759
571.41	07	441-443	580.81	11	698-700	594.1	11	691-694	603.0	12	729-730	615.9	13	757-759
571.42	07	441-443	580.89	11	698-700	594.2	11	691-694	603.1	12	727-728	616.0	13	757-759
571.49	07	441-443	580.9	11	698-700	594.8	11	691-694	603.8	12	729-730	616.10	13	757-759
571.5	07	432-434	581.0	11	698-700	594.9	11	691-694	603.9	12	729-730	616.11	13	757-759
571.6	07	432-434	581.1	11	698-700	595.0	11	689-690	604.0	12	727-728	616.2	13	760-761
571.8	07	441-443	581.2	11	698-700	595.1	11	689-690	604.90	12	727-728	616.3	13	757-759
571.9	07	441-443	581.3	11	698-700	595.2	11	689-690	604.91	12	727-728	616.4	13	757-759
572.0	07	441-443	581.81	11	698-700	595.3	11	689-690	604.99	12	727-728	616.50	13	760-761
572.1	07	441-443	581.89	11	698-700	595.4	11	689-690	605	12	727-728	616.51	13	760-761
572.2	07	441-443	581.9	11	698-700	595.81	11	689-690	606.0	12	729-730	616.81	13	757-759
572.3	07	441-443	582.0	11	698-700	595.82	11	689-690	606.1	12	729-730	616.89	13	757-759
572.4	07	441-443	582.1	11	698-700	595.89	11	689-690	606.8	12	729-730	616.9	13	757-759
572.8	07	441-443	582.2	11	698-700	595.9	11	689-690	606.9	12	729-730	617.0	13	760-761
573.0	07	441-443	582.4	11	698-700	596.0	11	698-700	607.0	12	729-730	617.1	13	760-761
573.1	07	441-443	582.81	11	698-700	596.1	11	698-700	607.1	12	727-728	617.2	13	760-761
573.2	07	441-443	582.89	11	698-700	596.2	11	698-700	607.2	12	727-728	617.3	13	760-761
573.3	07	441-443	582.9	11	698-700	596.3	11	698-700	607.3	12	729-730	617.4	13	760-761
573.4	07	441-443	583.0	11	698-700	596.4	11	698-700	607.81	12	727-728	617.5	06	391-392
573.8	07	441-443	583.1	11	698-700	596.51	11	698-700	607.82	12	729-730	617.6	09	606-607
573.9	07	441-443	583.2	11	698-700	596.52	11	698-700	607.83	12	729-730	617.8	13	760-761
574.00	07	444-446	583.4	11	698-700	596.53	11	698-700	607.84	12	729-730	617.9	13	760-761
574.01	07	444-446	583.6	11	698-700	596.54	11	698-700	607.85	12	729-730	618.00	13	760-761
574.10	07	444-446	583.7	11	698-700	596.55	11	698-700	607.89	12	729-730	618.01	13	760-761
574.11	07	444-446	583.81	11	698-700	596.59	11	698-700	607.9	12	729-730	618.02	13	760-761
574.20	07	444-446	583.89	11	698-700	596.6	11	698-700	608.0	12	727-728	618.03	13	760-761
574.21	07	444-446	583.9	11	698-700	596.7	11	698-700	608.1	12	729-730	618.04	13	760-761
574.30	07	444-446	584.5	11	682-684	596.8	11	698-700	608.20	12	729-730	618.05	13	760-761
574.31	07	444-446	584.6	11	682-684	596.9	11	698-700	608.21	12	729-730	618.09	13	760-761
574.40	07	444-446	584.7	11	682-684	597.0	11	689-690	608.22	12	729-730	618.1	13	760-761
574.41	07	444-446	584.8	11	682-684	597.80	11	689-690	608.23	12	729-730	618.2	13	760-761
574.50	07	444-446	584.9	11	682-684	597.81	11	689-690	608.24	12	729-730	618.3	13	760-761
574.51	07	444-446	585.1	11	682-684	597.89	11	689-690	608.3	12	729-730	618.4	13	760-761
574.60	07	444-446	585.2	11	682-684	598.00	11	697	608.4	12	727-728	618.5	13	760-761
574.61	07	444-446	585.3	11	682-684	598.01	11	697	608.81	12	729-730	618.6	13	760-761
574.70	07	444-446	585.4	11	682-684	598.1	11	697	608.82	12	729-730	618.7	13	760-761
574.71	07	444-446	585.5	11	682-684	598.2	11	697	608.83	12	729-730	618.81	13	760-761
574.80	07	444-446	585.6	11	682-684	598.8	11	697	608.84	12	729-730	618.82	13	760-761
574.81	07	444-446	585.9	11	682-684	598.9	11	697	608.85	12	729-730	618.83	13	760-761
574.90	07	444-446	586	11	682-684	599.0	11	689-690	608.86	12	729-730	618.84	13	760-761
574.91	07	444-446	587	11	698-700	599.1	11	698-700	608.87	12	729-730	618.89	13	760-761
575.0	07	444-446	588.0	11	698-700	599.2	11	698-700	608.89	12	729-730	618.9	13	760-761
575.10	07	444-446	588.1	11	698-700	599.3	11	698-700	608.9	12	729-730	619.0	13	760-761
575.11	07	444-446	588.81	11	698-700	599.4	11	698-700	610.0	09	600-601	619.1	06	393-395
575.12	07	444-446	588.89	11	698-700	599.5	11	698-700	610.1	09	600-601	619.2	13	760-761
575.2	07	444-446	588.9	11	698-700	599.60	11	698-700	610.2	09	600-601	619.8	13	760-761
575.3	07	444-446	589.0	11	698-700	599.69	11	698-700	610.3	09	600-601	619.9	13	760-761
575.4	07	444-446	589.1	11	698-700	599.70	11	695-696	610.4	09	600-601	620.0	13	760-761
575.5	07	444-446	589.9	11	698-700	599.71	11	695-696	610.8	09	600-601	620.1	13	760-761
575.6	07	444-446	590.00	11	689-690	599.72	11	695-696	610.9	09	600-601	620.2	13	760-761
575.8	07	444-446	590.01	11	689-690	599.81	11	698-700	611.0	09	600-601	620.3	13	760-761
575.9	07	444-446	590.10	11	689-690	599.82	11	698-700	611.1	09	600-601	620.4	13	760-761
576.0	07	444-446	590.11	11	689-690	599.83	11	698-700	611.2	09	600-601	620.5	13	760-761
576.1	07	444-446	590.2	11	689-690	599.84	11	698-700	611.3	09	600-601	620.6	13	760-761
576.2	07	444-446	590.3	11	689-690	599.89	11	698-700	611.4	09	600-601	620.7	13	760-761
576.3	07	444-446	590.80	11	689-690	599.9	11	698-700	611.5	09	600-601	620.8	13	760-761
576.4	07	444-446	590.81	11	689-690	600.00	12	725-726	611.6	09	600-601	620.9	13	760-761
576.5	07	444-446	590.9	11	689-690	600.01	12	725-726	611.71	09	600-601	621.0	13	760-761
576.8	07	444-446	591	11	691-694	600.10	12	725-726	611.72	09	600-601	621.1	13	760-761
576.9	07	444-446	592.0	11	691-694	600.11	12	725-726	611.79	09	600-601	621.2	13	760-761
577.0	07	438-440	592.1	11	691-694	600.20	12	725-726	611.81	09	600-601	621.30	13	760-761
577.1	07	438-440	592.9	11	691-694	600.21	12	725-726	611.82	09	600-601	621.31	13	760-761
577.2	07	438-440	593.0	11	698-700	600.30	12	725-726	611.83	09	600-601	621.32	13	760-761
577.8	07	438-440	593.1	11	698-700	600.31	12	725-726	611.89	09	600-601	621.33	13	760-761
577.9	07	438-440	593.2	11	698-700	600.90	12	725-726	611.9	09	600-601	621.34	13	760-761
578.0	06	377-379	593.3	11	689-690	600.91	12	725-726	612.0	09	600-601	621.35	13	760-761
578.1	06	377-379	593.4	11	691-694	601.0	12	727-728	612.1	09	600-601	621.4	13	760-761
578.9	06	377-379	593.5	11	691-694	601.1	12	727-728	614.0	13	757-759	621.5	13	760-761
579.0	06	391-392	593.6	11	698-700	601.2	12	727-728	614.1	13	757-759	621.6	13	760-761
579.1	06	391-392				601.3	12	727-728	614.2	13	757-759	621.7	13	760-761

DX	MDC	DRG
621.8	13	760-761
621.9	13	760-761
622.0	13	760-761
622.10	13	760-761
622.11	13	760-761
622.12	13	760-761
622.2	13	760-761
622.3	13	760-761
622.4	13	760-761
622.5	13	760-761
622.6	13	760-761
622.7	13	760-761
622.8	13	760-761
622.9	13	760-761
623.0	13	760-761
623.1	13	760-761
623.2	13	760-761
623.3	13	760-761
623.4	13	760-761
623.5	13	760-761
623.6	13	760-761
623.7	13	760-761
623.8	13	760-761
623.9	13	760-761
624.01	13	760-761
624.02	13	760-761
624.09	13	760-761
624.1	13	760-761
624.2	13	760-761
624.3	13	760-761
624.4	13	760-761
624.5	13	760-761
624.6	13	760-761
624.8	13	760-761
624.9	13	760-761
625.0	13	760-761
625.1	13	760-761
625.2	13	760-761
625.3	13	760-761
625.4	13	760-761
625.5	13	760-761
625.6	13	760-761
625.70	13	760-761
625.71	13	757-759
625.79	13	760-761
625.8	13	760-761
625.9	13	760-761
626.0	13	760-761
626.1	13	760-761
626.2	13	760-761
626.3	13	760-761
626.4	13	760-761
626.5	13	760-761
626.6	13	760-761
626.7	13	760-761
626.8	13	760-761
626.9	13	760-761
627.0	13	760-761
627.1	13	760-761
627.2	13	760-761
627.3	13	760-761
627.4	13	760-761
627.8	13	760-761
627.9	13	760-761
628.0	13	760-761
628.1	13	760-761
628.2	13	760-761
628.3	13	760-761
628.4	13	760-761
628.8	13	760-761
628.9	13	760-761
629.0	13	760-761
629.1	13	760-761
629.20	13	760-761
629.21	13	760-761
629.22	13	760-761
629.23	13	760-761
629.29	13	760-761
629.81	13	760-761
629.89	13	760-761
629.9	13	760-761

Complications of Pregnancy, Childbirth and the Puerperium

DX	MDC	DRG
630	14	781-782
631	14	781-782
632	14	779
633.00	14	777
633.01	14	777
633.10	14	777
633.11	14	777
633.20	14	777
633.21	14	777
633.80	14	777
633.81	14	777
633.90	14	777
633.91	14	777
634.00	14	779
634.01	14	779
634.02	14	779
634.10	14	779
634.11	14	779
634.12	14	779
634.20	14	779
634.21	14	779
634.22	14	779
634.30	14	779
634.31	14	779
634.32	14	779
634.40	14	779
634.41	14	779
634.42	14	779
634.50	14	779
634.51	14	779
634.52	14	779
634.60	14	779
634.61	14	779
634.62	14	779
634.70	14	779
634.71	14	779
634.72	14	779
634.80	14	779
634.81	14	779
634.82	14	779
634.90	14	779
634.91	14	779
634.92	14	779
635.00	14	779
635.01	14	779
635.02	14	779
635.10	14	779
635.11	14	779
635.12	14	779
635.20	14	779
635.21	14	779
635.22	14	779
635.30	14	779
635.31	14	779
635.32	14	779
635.40	14	779
635.41	14	779
635.42	14	779
635.50	14	779
635.51	14	779
635.52	14	779
635.60	14	779
635.61	14	779
635.62	14	779
635.70	14	779
635.71	14	779
635.72	14	779
635.80	14	779
635.81	14	779
635.82	14	779
635.90	14	779
635.91	14	779
635.92	14	779
636.00	14	779
636.01	14	779
636.02	14	779
636.10	14	779
636.11	14	779
636.12	14	779
636.20	14	779
636.21	14	779
636.22	14	779
636.30	14	779
636.31	14	779
636.32	14	779
636.40	14	779
636.41	14	779
636.42	14	779
636.50	14	779
636.51	14	779
636.52	14	779
636.60	14	779
636.61	14	779
636.62	14	779
636.70	14	779
636.71	14	779
636.72	14	779
636.80	14	779
636.81	14	779
636.82	14	779
636.90	14	779
636.91	14	779
636.92	14	779
637.00	14	779
637.01	14	779
637.02	14	779
637.10	14	779
637.11	14	779
637.12	14	779
637.20	14	779
637.21	14	779
637.22	14	779
637.30	14	779
637.31	14	779
637.32	14	779
637.40	14	779
637.41	14	779
637.42	14	779
637.50	14	779
637.51	14	779
637.52	14	779
637.60	14	779
637.61	14	779
637.62	14	779
637.70	14	779
637.71	14	779
637.72	14	779
637.80	14	779
637.81	14	779
637.82	14	779
637.90	14	779
637.91	14	779
637.92	14	779
638.0	14	779
638.1	14	779
638.2	14	779
638.3	14	779
638.4	14	779
638.5	14	779
638.6	14	779
638.7	14	779
638.8	14	779
638.9	14	779
639.0	14	776
639.1	14	776
639.2	14	776
639.3	14	776
639.4	14	776
639.5	14	776
639.6	14	776
639.8	14	776
639.9	14	776
640.00	14	778
640.01	14	774-775
640.03	14	778
640.80	14	778
640.81	14	774-775
640.83	14	778
640.90	14	778
640.91	14	774-775
640.93	14	778
641.00	14	998
641.01	14	774
641.03	14	781-782
641.10	14	998
641.11	14	774
641.13	14	781-782
641.20	14	998
641.21	14	774
641.23	14	781-782
641.30	14	998
641.31	14	774
641.33	14	781
641.80	14	998
641.81	14	774
641.83	14	781-782
641.90	14	998
641.91	14	774
641.93	14	781-782
642.00	14	998
642.01	14	774
642.02	14	774
642.03	14	781
642.04	14	776
642.10	14	998
642.11	14	774
642.12	14	774
642.13	14	781
642.14	14	776
642.20	14	998
642.21	14	774
642.22	14	774
642.23	14	781
642.24	14	776
642.30	14	998
642.31	14	774-775
642.32	14	774-775
642.33	14	781-782
642.34	14	776
642.40	14	998
642.41	14	774
642.42	14	774
642.43	14	781
642.44	14	776
642.50	14	998
642.51	14	774
642.52	14	774
642.53	14	781
642.54	14	776
642.60	14	998
642.61	14	774
642.62	14	774
642.63	14	781
642.64	14	776
642.70	14	998
642.71	14	774
642.72	14	774
642.73	14	781
642.74	14	776
642.90	14	998
642.91	14	774
642.92	14	774
642.93	14	781
642.94	14	776
643.00	14	998
643.01	14	774-775
643.03	14	781
643.10	14	998
643.11	14	774-775
643.13	14	781
643.20	14	998
643.21	14	774-775
643.23	14	781
643.80	14	998
643.81	14	774-775
643.83	14	781
643.90	14	998
643.91	14	774-775
643.93	14	781
644.00	14	778
644.03	14	778
644.10	14	780
644.13	14	780
644.20	14	781-782
644.21	14	774-775
645.10	14	998
645.11	14	774-775
645.13	14	781-782
645.20	14	998
645.21	14	774-775
645.23	14	781-782
646.00	14	774-775
646.01	14	774-775
646.03	14	781-782
646.10	14	998
646.11	14	774-775
646.12	14	774-775
646.13	14	781
646.14	14	776
646.20	14	998
646.21	14	774-775
646.22	14	774-775
646.23	14	781
646.24	14	776
646.30	14	998
646.31	14	774-775
646.33	14	781-782
646.40	14	998
646.41	14	774-775
646.42	14	774-775
646.43	14	781
646.44	14	776
646.50	14	998
646.51	14	774-775
646.52	14	774-775
646.53	14	781-782
646.54	14	776
646.60	14	998
646.61	14	774-775
646.62	14	774-775
646.63	14	781
646.64	14	776
646.70	14	998
646.71	14	774-775
646.73	14	781
646.80	14	998
646.81	14	774-775
646.82	14	774-775
646.83	14	781
646.84	14	776
646.90	14	998
646.91	14	774-775
646.93	14	781-782
647.00	14	998
647.01	14	774
647.02	14	774
647.03	14	781
647.04	14	776
647.10	14	998
647.11	14	774

DX	MDC	DRG	DX	MDC	DRG	DX	MDC	DRG	DX	MDC	DRG	DX	MDC	DRG
647.12	14	774	648.80	14	998	652.01	14	774-775	654.41	14	774-775	656.61	14	774-775
647.13	14	781	648.81	14	774-775	652.03	14	781-782	654.42	14	774-775	656.63	14	781-782
647.14	14	776	648.82	14	774-775	652.10	14	998	654.43	14	781-782	656.70	14	998
647.20	14	998	648.83	14	781	652.11	14	774-775	654.44	14	776	656.71	14	774-775
647.21	14	774	648.84	14	776	652.13	14	781-782	654.50	14	998	656.73	14	781-782
647.22	14	774	648.90	14	998	652.20	14	998	654.51	14	774-775	656.80	14	998
647.23	14	781	648.91	14	774-775	652.21	14	774-775	654.52	14	774-775	656.81	14	774-775
647.24	14	776	648.92	14	774-775	652.23	14	781-782	654.53	14	781-782	656.83	14	781-782
647.30	14	998	648.93	14	781	652.30	14	998	654.54	14	776	656.90	14	998
647.31	14	774	648.94	14	776	652.31	14	774-775	654.60	14	998	656.91	14	774-775
647.32	14	774	649.00	14	998	652.33	14	781-782	654.61	14	774-775	656.93	14	781-782
647.33	14	781	649.01	14	774-775	652.40	14	998	654.62	14	774-775	657.00	14	998
647.34	14	776	649.02	14	774-775	652.41	14	774-775	654.63	14	781-782	657.01	14	774-775
647.40	14	998	649.03	14	781-782	652.43	14	781-782	654.64	14	776	657.03	14	781-782
647.41	14	774	649.04	14	776	652.50	14	998	654.70	14	998	658.00	14	998
647.42	14	774	649.10	14	998	652.51	14	774-775	654.71	14	774-775	658.01	14	774-775
647.43	14	781	649.11	14	774-775	652.53	14	781-782	654.72	14	774-775	658.03	14	781-782
647.44	14	776	649.12	14	774-775	652.60	14	998	654.73	14	781-782	658.10	14	774-775
647.50	14	998	649.13	14	781-782	652.61	14	774-775	654.74	14	776	658.11	14	774-775
647.51	14	774	649.14	14	776	652.63	14	781-782	654.80	14	998	658.13	14	781-782
647.52	14	774	649.20	14	998	652.70	14	998	654.81	14	774-775	658.20	14	774-775
647.53	14	781	649.21	14	774-775	652.71	14	774-775	654.82	14	774-775	658.21	14	774-775
647.54	14	776	649.22	14	774-775	652.73	14	781-782	654.83	14	781-782	658.23	14	781-782
647.60	14	998	649.23	14	781-782	652.80	14	998	654.84	14	776	658.30	14	774-775
647.61	14	774	649.24	14	776	652.81	14	774-775	654.90	14	998	658.31	14	774-775
647.62	14	774	649.30	14	998	652.83	14	781-782	654.91	14	774-775	658.33	14	781-782
647.63	14	781	649.31	14	774-775	652.90	14	998	654.92	14	774-775	658.40	14	774-775
647.64	14	776	649.32	14	774-775	652.91	14	774-775	654.93	14	781-782	658.41	14	774-775
647.80	14	998	649.33	14	781-782	652.93	14	781-782	654.94	14	776	658.43	14	781-782
647.81	14	774	649.34	14	776	653.00	14	998	655.00	14	998	658.80	14	998
647.82	14	774	649.40	14	998	653.01	14	774-775	655.01	14	774-775	658.81	14	774-775
647.83	14	781	649.41	14	774-775	653.03	14	781-782	655.03	14	781-782	658.83	14	781-782
647.84	14	776	649.42	14	774-775	653.10	14	998	655.10	14	998	658.90	14	998
647.90	14	998	649.43	14	781-782	653.11	14	774-775	655.11	14	774-775	658.91	14	774-775
647.91	14	774	649.44	14	776	653.13	14	781-782	655.13	14	781-782	658.93	14	781-782
647.92	14	774	649.50	14	998	653.20	14	998	655.20	14	998	659.00	14	774-775
647.93	14	781	649.51	14	774-775	653.21	14	774-775	655.21	14	774-775	659.01	14	774-775
647.94	14	776	649.53	14	781-782	653.23	14	781-782	655.23	14	781-782	659.03	14	781-782
648.00	14	998	649.60	14	998	653.30	14	998	655.30	14	998	659.10	14	774-775
648.01	14	774	649.61	14	774-775	653.31	14	774-775	655.31	14	774-775	659.11	14	774-775
648.02	14	774	649.62	14	774-775	653.33	14	781-782	655.33	14	781-782	659.13	14	781-782
648.03	14	781	649.63	14	781-782	653.40	14	998	655.40	14	998	659.20	14	774-775
648.04	14	776	649.64	14	776	653.41	14	774-775	655.41	14	774-775	659.21	14	774
648.10	14	998	649.70	14	998	653.43	14	781-782	655.43	14	781-782	659.23	14	774-775
648.11	14	774-775	649.71	14	774-775	653.50	14	998	655.50	14	998	659.30	14	774-775
648.12	14	774-775	649.73	14	781-782	653.51	14	774-775	655.51	14	774-775	659.31	14	774
648.13	14	781	650	14	774-775	653.53	14	781-782	655.53	14	781-782	659.33	14	781-782
648.14	14	776	651.00	14	998	653.60	14	998	655.60	14	998	659.40	14	998
648.20	14	998	651.01	14	774-775	653.61	14	774-775	655.61	14	774-775	659.41	14	774-775
648.21	14	774-775	651.03	14	781-782	653.63	14	781-782	655.63	14	781-782	659.43	14	781-782
648.22	14	774-775	651.10	14	998	653.70	14	998	655.70	14	998	659.50	14	774-775
648.23	14	781	651.11	14	774-775	653.71	14	774-775	655.71	14	774-775	659.51	14	774-775
648.24	14	776	651.13	14	781-782	653.73	14	781-782	655.73	14	781-782	659.53	14	781-782
648.30	14	998	651.20	14	998	653.80	14	998	655.80	14	998	659.60	14	774-775
648.31	14	774-775	651.21	14	774-775	653.81	14	774-775	655.81	14	774-775	659.61	14	774-775
648.32	14	774-775	651.23	14	781-782	653.83	14	781-782	655.83	14	781-782	659.63	14	781-782
648.33	14	781	651.30	14	998	653.90	14	998	655.90	14	998	659.70	14	774-775
648.34	14	776	651.31	14	774-775	653.91	14	774-775	655.91	14	774-775	659.71	14	774-775
648.40	14	998	651.33	14	781-782	653.93	14	781-782	655.93	14	781-782	659.73	14	781-782
648.41	14	774-775	651.40	14	998	654.00	14	998	656.00	14	998	659.80	14	774-775
648.42	14	774-775	651.41	14	774-775	654.01	14	774-775	656.01	14	774-775	659.81	14	774-775
648.43	14	781	651.43	14	781-782	654.02	14	774-775	656.03	14	781-782	659.83	14	781-782
648.44	14	776	651.50	14	998	654.03	14	781-782	656.10	14	998	659.90	14	774-775
648.50	14	998	651.51	14	774-775	654.04	14	776	656.11	14	774-775	659.91	14	774-775
648.51	14	774	651.53	14	781-782	654.10	14	998	656.13	14	781-782	659.93	14	781-782
648.52	14	774	651.60	14	998	654.11	14	774-775	656.20	14	998	660.00	14	774-775
648.53	14	781	651.61	14	774-775	654.12	14	774-775	656.21	14	774-775	660.01	14	774-775
648.54	14	776	651.63	14	781-782	654.13	14	781-782	656.23	14	781-782	660.03	14	781-782
648.60	14	998	651.70	14	998	654.14	14	776	656.30	14	774-775	660.10	14	774-775
648.61	14	774	651.71	14	774-775	654.20	14	998	656.31	14	774-775	660.11	14	774-775
648.62	14	774	651.73	14	781-782	654.21	14	774-775	656.33	14	781-782	660.13	14	781-782
648.63	14	781	651.80	14	998	654.23	14	781-782	656.40	14	774-775	660.20	14	774-775
648.64	14	776	651.81	14	774-775	654.30	14	998	656.41	14	774-775	660.21	14	774-775
648.70	14	998	651.83	14	781-782	654.31	14	774-775	656.43	14	781-782	660.23	14	781-782
648.71	14	774-775	651.90	14	998	654.32	14	774-775	656.50	14	998	660.30	14	774-775
648.72	14	774-775	651.91	14	774-775	654.33	14	781-782	656.51	14	774-775	660.31	14	774-775
648.73	14	781	651.93	14	781-782	654.34	14	776	656.53	14	781-782	660.33	14	781-782
648.74	14	776	652.00	14	998	654.40	14	998	656.60	14	998	660.40	14	774-775

Diagnosis Code/MDC/DRG List

DX	MDC	DRG	DX	MDC	DRG	DX	MDC	DRG	DX	MDC	DRG	DX	MDC	DRG
660.41	14	774-775	664.10	14	774-775	668.01	14	774	670.84	14	776	674.32	14	774
660.43	14	781-782	664.11	14	774-775	668.02	14	774	671.00	14	998	674.34	14	776
660.50	14	774-775	664.14	14	776	668.03	14	781-782	671.01	14	774-775	674.40	14	998
660.51	14	774-775	664.20	14	774-775	668.04	14	776	671.02	14	774-775	674.42	14	774-775
660.53	14	781-782	664.21	14	774-775	668.10	14	774-775	671.03	14	781-782	674.44	14	776
660.60	14	774-775	664.24	14	776	668.11	14	774	671.04	14	776	674.50	14	998
660.61	14	774-775	664.30	14	774-775	668.12	14	774	671.10	14	998	674.51	14	774
660.63	14	781-782	664.31	14	774-775	668.13	14	781-782	671.11	14	774-775	674.52	14	774
660.70	14	774-775	664.34	14	776	668.14	14	776	671.12	14	774-775	674.53	14	781-782
660.71	14	774-775	664.40	14	774-775	668.20	14	774-775	671.13	14	781-782	674.54	14	776
660.73	14	781-782	664.41	14	774-775	668.21	14	774	671.14	14	776	674.80	14	998
660.80	14	774-775	664.44	14	776	668.22	14	774	671.20	14	998	674.82	14	774
660.81	14	774-775	664.50	14	774-775	668.23	14	781-782	671.21	14	774-775	674.84	14	776
660.83	14	781-782	664.51	14	774-775	668.24	14	776	671.22	14	774-775	674.90	14	998
660.90	14	774-775	664.54	14	776	668.80	14	774-775	671.23	14	781-782	674.92	14	774-775
660.91	14	774-775	664.60	14	774-775	668.81	14	774	671.24	14	776	674.94	14	776
660.93	14	781-782	664.61	14	774-775	668.82	14	774	671.30	14	998	675.00	14	998
661.00	14	774-775	664.64	14	776	668.83	14	781-782	671.31	14	774	675.01	14	774
661.01	14	774-775	664.80	14	774-775	668.84	14	776	671.33	14	781-782	675.02	14	774
661.03	14	781-782	664.81	14	774-775	668.90	14	774-775	671.40	14	998	675.03	14	781-782
661.10	14	774-775	664.84	14	776	668.91	14	774	671.42	14	774	675.04	14	776
661.11	14	774-775	664.90	14	774-775	668.92	14	774	671.44	14	776	675.10	14	998
661.13	14	781-782	664.91	14	774-775	668.93	14	781-782	671.50	14	998	675.11	14	774
661.20	14	774-775	664.94	14	776	668.94	14	776	671.51	14	774	675.12	14	774
661.21	14	774-775	665.00	14	774-775	669.00	14	774-775	671.52	14	774	675.13	14	781-782
661.23	14	781-782	665.01	14	774-775	669.01	14	774-775	671.53	14	781-782	675.14	14	776
661.30	14	774-775	665.03	14	781-782	669.02	14	774-775	671.54	14	776	675.20	14	998
661.31	14	774-775	665.10	14	774-775	669.03	14	781-782	671.80	14	998	675.21	14	774
661.33	14	781-782	665.11	14	774-775	669.04	14	776	671.81	14	774-775	675.22	14	774
661.40	14	774-775	665.20	14	774-775	669.10	14	774-775	671.82	14	774-775	675.23	14	781-782
661.41	14	774-775	665.22	14	774-775	669.11	14	774	671.83	14	781-782	675.24	14	776
661.43	14	781-782	665.24	14	776	669.12	14	774	671.84	14	776	675.80	14	998
661.90	14	774-775	665.30	14	774-775	669.13	14	781-782	671.90	14	998	675.81	14	774-775
661.91	14	774-775	665.31	14	774-775	669.14	14	776	671.91	14	774-775	675.82	14	774-775
661.93	14	781-782	665.34	14	776	669.20	14	774-775	671.92	14	774-775	675.83	14	781-782
662.00	14	774-775	665.40	14	774-775	669.21	14	774-775	671.93	14	781-782	675.84	14	776
662.01	14	774-775	665.41	14	774-775	669.22	14	774-775	671.94	14	776	675.90	14	998
662.03	14	781-782	665.44	14	776	669.23	14	781-782	672.00	14	998	675.91	14	774-775
662.10	14	774-775	665.50	14	774-775	669.24	14	776	672.02	14	774	675.92	14	774-775
662.11	14	774-775	665.51	14	774-775	669.30	14	774-775	672.04	14	776	675.93	14	781-782
662.13	14	781-782	665.54	14	776	669.32	14	774	673.00	14	998	675.94	14	776
662.20	14	774-775	665.60	14	774-775	669.34	14	776	673.01	14	774	676.00	14	998
662.21	14	774-775	665.61	14	774-775	669.40	14	774-775	673.02	14	774	676.01	14	774-775
662.23	14	781-782	665.64	14	776	669.41	14	774	673.03	14	781-782	676.02	14	774-775
662.30	14	774-775	665.70	14	774-775	669.42	14	774	673.04	14	776	676.03	14	781-782
662.31	14	774-775	665.71	14	774-775	669.43	14	781-782	673.10	14	998	676.04	14	776
662.33	14	781-782	665.72	14	774-775	669.44	14	776	673.11	14	774	676.10	14	998
663.00	14	774-775	665.74	14	776	669.50	14	774-775	673.12	14	774	676.11	14	774-775
663.01	14	774-775	665.80	14	774-775	669.51	14	774-775	673.13	14	781-782	676.12	14	774-775
663.03	14	781-782	665.81	14	774-775	669.60	14	774-775	673.14	14	776	676.13	14	781-782
663.10	14	774-775	665.82	14	774-775	669.61	14	774-775	673.20	14	998	676.14	14	776
663.11	14	774-775	665.83	14	781-782	669.70	14	774-775	673.21	14	774	676.20	14	998
663.13	14	781-782	665.84	14	776	669.71	14	774-775	673.22	14	774	676.21	14	774-775
663.20	14	774-775	665.90	14	774-775	669.80	14	774-775	673.23	14	781-782	676.22	14	774-775
663.21	14	774-775	665.91	14	774-775	669.81	14	774-775	673.24	14	776	676.23	14	781-782
663.23	14	781-782	665.92	14	774-775	669.82	14	774-775	673.30	14	998	676.24	14	776
663.30	14	774-775	665.93	14	781-782	669.83	14	781-782	673.31	14	774	676.30	14	998
663.31	14	774-775	665.94	14	776	669.84	14	776	673.32	14	774	676.31	14	774-775
663.33	14	781-782	666.00	14	998	669.90	14	774-775	673.33	14	781-782	676.32	14	774-775
663.40	14	774-775	666.02	14	774	669.91	14	774-775	673.34	14	776	676.33	14	781-782
663.41	14	774-775	666.04	14	776	669.92	14	774-775	673.80	14	998	676.34	14	776
663.43	14	781-782	666.10	14	998	669.93	14	781-782	673.81	14	774	676.40	14	998
663.50	14	774-775	666.12	14	774	669.94	14	776	673.82	14	774	676.41	14	774-775
663.51	14	774-775	666.14	14	776	670.00	14	998	673.83	14	781-782	676.42	14	774-775
663.53	14	781-782	666.20	14	998	670.02	14	774	673.84	14	776	676.43	14	781-782
663.60	14	774-775	666.22	14	774	670.04	14	776	674.00	14	998	676.44	14	776
663.61	14	774-775	666.24	14	776	670.10	14	998	674.01	14	774	676.50	14	998
663.63	14	781-782	666.30	14	998	670.12	14	774	674.02	14	774	676.51	14	774-775
663.80	14	774-775	666.32	14	774	670.14	14	776	674.03	14	781-782	676.52	14	774-775
663.81	14	774-775	666.34	14	776	670.20	14	998	674.04	14	776	676.53	14	781-782
663.83	14	781-782	667.00	14	998	670.22	14	774	674.10	14	998	676.54	14	776
663.90	14	774-775	667.02	14	774	670.24	14	774	674.12	14	774	676.60	14	998
663.91	14	774-775	667.04	14	776	670.30	14	998	674.14	14	776	676.61	14	774-775
663.93	14	781-782	667.10	14	998	670.32	14	774	674.20	14	998	676.62	14	774-775
664.00	14	774-775	667.12	14	774	670.34	14	776	674.22	14	774	676.63	14	781-782
664.01	14	774-775	667.14	14	776	670.80	14	998	674.24	14	776	676.64	14	776
664.04	14	776	668.00	14	774-775	670.82	14	774	674.30	14	998	676.80	14	998

DX	MDC	DRG
676.81	14	774-775
676.82	14	774-775
676.83	14	781-782
676.84	14	776
676.90	14	998
676.91	14	774-775
676.92	14	774-775
676.93	14	781-782
676.94	14	776
677	14	998
678.00	14	998
678.01	14	774-775
678.03	14	781-782
678.10	14	998
678.11	14	774-775
678.13	14	781,782
679.00	14	774-775
679.01	14	774
679.02	14	774
679.03	14	781-782
679.04	14	776
679.10	14	998
679.11	14	774-775
679.12	14	774-775
679.13	14	781-782
679.14	14	776

Diseases of the Skin and Subcutaneous Tissue

DX	MDC	DRG
680.0	09	602-603
680.1	09	602-603
680.2	09	602-603
680.3	09	602-603
680.4	09	602-603
680.5	09	602-603
680.6	09	602-603
680.7	09	602-603
680.8	09	602-603
680.9	09	602-603
681.00	09	602-603
681.01	09	602-603
681.02	09	602-603
681.10	09	602-603
681.11	09	602-603
681.9	09	602-603
682.0	09	602-603
682.1	09	602-603
682.2	09	602-603
682.3	09	602-603
682.4	09	602-603
682.5	09	602-603
682.6	09	602-603
682.7	09	602-603
682.8	09	602-603
682.9	09	602-603
683	16	814-816
684	09	602-603
685.0	09	602-603
685.1	09	602-603
686.00	09	602-603
686.01	09	602-603
686.09	09	602-603
686.1	09	602-603
686.8	09	602-603
686.9	09	602-603
690.10	09	606-607
690.11	09	606-607
690.12	09	606-607
690.18	09	606-607
690.8	09	606-607
691.0	09	606-607
691.8	09	606-607
692.0	09	606-607
692.1	09	606-607
692.2	09	606-607
692.3	09	606-607
692.4	09	606-607
692.5	09	606-607
692.6	09	606-607
692.70	09	606-607
692.71	09	606-607
692.72	09	606-607
692.73	09	606-607
692.74	09	606-607
692.75	09	606-607
692.76	09	606-607
692.77	09	606-607
692.79	09	606-607
692.81	09	606-607
692.82	09	606-607
692.83	09	606-607
692.84	09	606-607
692.89	09	606-607
692.9	09	606-607
693.0	09	606-607
693.1	09	606-607
693.8	09	606-607
693.9	09	606-607
694.0	09	606-607
694.1	09	606-607
694.2	09	606-607
694.3	09	606-607
694.4	09	595-596
694.5	09	595-596
694.60	09	595-596
694.61	02	124-125
694.8	09	595-596
694.9	09	595-596
695.0	09	595-596
695.10	09	595-596
695.11	09	595-596
695.12	09	595-596
695.13	09	595-596
695.14	09	595-596
695.15	09	595-596
695.19	09	595-596
695.2	09	595-596
695.3	09	606-607
695.4	09	595-596
695.50	09	606-607
695.51	09	606-607
695.52	09	606-607
695.53	09	606-607
695.54	09	606-607
695.55	09	606-607
695.56	09	606-607
695.57	09	606-607
695.58	09	606-607
695.59	09	606-607
695.81	09	595-596
695.89	09	606-607
695.9	09	606-607
696.0	08	545-547
696.1	09	595-596
696.2	09	595-596
696.3	09	606-607
696.4	09	606-607
696.5	09	606-607
696.8	09	606-607
697.0	09	606-607
697.1	09	606-607
697.8	09	606-607
697.9	09	606-607
698.0	09	606-607
698.1	12	729-730
698.1	13	757-759
698.2	09	606-607
698.3	09	606-607
698.4	09	606-607
698.8	09	606-607
698.9	09	606-607
700	09	606-607
701.0	09	606-607
701.1	09	606-607
701.2	09	606-607
701.3	09	606-607
701.4	09	606-607
701.5	09	606-607
701.8	09	606-607
701.9	09	606-607
702.0	09	606-607
702.11	09	606-607
702.19	09	606-607
702.8	09	606-607
703.0	09	606-607
703.8	09	606-607
703.9	09	606-607
704.00	09	606-607
704.01	09	606-607
704.02	09	606-607
704.09	09	606-607
704.1	09	606-607
704.2	09	606-607
704.3	09	606-607
704.8	09	606-607
704.9	09	606-607
705.0	09	606-607
705.1	09	606-607
705.21	09	606-607
705.22	09	606-607
705.81	09	606-607
705.82	09	606-607
705.83	09	606-607
705.89	09	606-607
705.9	09	606-607
706.0	09	606-607
706.1	09	606-607
706.2	09	606-607
706.3	09	606-607
706.8	09	606-607
706.9	09	606-607
707.00	09	592-594
707.01	09	592-594
707.02	09	592-594
707.03	09	592-594
707.04	09	592-594
707.05	09	592-594
707.06	09	592-594
707.07	09	592-594
707.09	09	592-594
707.10	09	592-594
707.11	09	592-594
707.12	09	592-594
707.13	09	592-594
707.14	09	592-594
707.15	09	592-594
707.19	09	592-594
707.20	09	592-594
707.21	09	592-594
707.22	09	592-594
707.23	09	592-594
707.24	09	592-594
707.25	09	592-594
707.8	09	592-594
707.9	09	592-594
708.0	09	606-607
708.1	09	606-607
708.2	09	606-607
708.3	09	606-607
708.4	09	606-607
708.5	09	606-607
708.8	09	606-607
708.9	09	606-607
709.00	09	606-607
709.01	09	606-607
709.09	09	606-607
709.1	09	606-607
709.2	09	606-607
709.3	09	606-607
709.4	09	606-607
709.8	09	606-607
709.9	09	606-607

Diseases of the Musculoskeletal System and Connective Tissue

DX	MDC	DRG
710.0	08	545-547
710.1	08	545-547
710.2	08	545-547
710.3	08	545-547
710.4	08	545-547
710.5	08	545-547
710.8	08	545-547
710.9	08	545-547
711.00	08	548-550
711.01	08	548-550
711.02	08	548-550
711.03	08	548-550
711.04	08	548-550
711.05	08	548-550
711.06	08	548-550
711.07	08	548-550
711.08	08	548-550
711.09	08	548-550
711.10	08	545-547
711.11	08	545-547
711.12	08	545-547
711.13	08	545-547
711.14	08	545-547
711.15	08	545-547
711.16	08	545-547
711.17	08	545-547
711.18	08	545-547
711.19	08	545-547
711.20	08	545-547
711.21	08	545-547
711.22	08	545-547
711.23	08	545-547
711.24	08	545-547
711.25	08	545-547
711.26	08	545-547
711.27	08	545-547
711.28	08	545-547
711.29	08	545-547
711.30	08	553-554
711.31	08	553-554
711.32	08	553-554
711.33	08	553-554
711.34	08	553-554
711.35	08	553-554
711.36	08	553-554
711.37	08	553-554
711.38	08	553-554
711.39	08	553-554
711.40	08	548-550
711.41	08	548-550
711.42	08	548-550
711.43	08	548-550
711.44	08	548-550
711.45	08	548-550
711.46	08	548-550
711.47	08	548-550
711.48	08	548-550
711.49	08	548-550
711.50	08	553-554
711.51	08	553-554
711.52	08	553-554
711.53	08	553-554
711.54	08	553-554
711.55	08	553-554
711.56	08	553-554
711.57	08	553-554
711.58	08	553-554
711.59	08	553-554
711.60	08	548-550
711.61	08	548-550
711.62	08	548-550
711.63	08	548-550
711.64	08	548-550
711.65	08	548-550
711.66	08	548-550
711.67	08	548-550
711.68	08	548-550
711.69	08	548-550
711.70	08	548-550
711.71	08	548-550
711.72	08	548-550
711.73	08	548-550
711.74	08	548-550
711.75	08	548-550
711.76	08	548-550
711.78	08	548-550
711.79	08	548-550
711.80	08	548-550
711.81	08	548-550
711.82	08	548-550
711.83	08	548-550
711.84	08	548-550
711.85	08	548-550
711.86	08	548-550
711.87	08	548-550
711.88	08	548-550
711.89	08	548-550
711.90	08	548-550
711.91	08	548-550
711.92	08	548-550
711.93	08	548-550
711.94	08	548-550
711.95	08	548-550
711.96	08	548-550
711.97	08	548-550
711.98	08	548-550
711.99	08	548-550
712.10	08	553-554
712.11	08	553-554
712.12	08	553-554
712.13	08	553-554
712.14	08	553-554
712.15	08	553-554
712.16	08	553-554
712.17	08	553-554
712.18	08	553-554
712.19	08	553-554
712.20	08	553-554
712.21	08	553-554
712.22	08	553-554
712.23	08	553-554
712.24	08	553-554
712.25	08	553-554
712.26	08	553-554
712.27	08	553-554
712.28	08	553-554
712.29	08	553-554
712.30	08	553-554
712.31	08	553-554
712.32	08	553-554
712.33	08	553-554
712.34	08	553-554
712.35	08	553-554
712.36	08	553-554
712.37	08	553-554
712.38	08	553-554
712.39	08	553-554
712.80	08	553-554
712.81	08	553-554
712.82	08	553-554
712.83	08	553-554
712.84	08	553-554
712.85	08	553-554
712.86	08	553-554
712.87	08	553-554
712.88	08	553-554
712.89	08	553-554
712.90	08	553-554
712.91	08	553-554
712.92	08	553-554
712.93	08	553-554
712.94	08	553-554

DX	MDC	DRG	DX	MDC	DRG	DX	MDC	DRG	DX	MDC	DRG	DX	MDC	DRG
712.95	08	553-554	716.11	08	553-554	716.99	08	553-554	718.59	08	553-554	719.45	08	555-556
712.96	08	553-554	716.12	08	553-554	717.0	08	562-563	718.60	08	564-566	719.46	08	555-556
712.97	08	553-554	716.13	08	553-554	717.1	08	562-563	718.65	08	564-566	719.47	08	555-556
712.98	08	553-554	716.14	08	553-554	717.2	08	562-563	718.70	08	564-566	719.48	08	555-556
712.99	08	553-554	716.15	08	553-554	717.3	08	562-563	718.71	08	564-566	719.49	08	555-556
713.0	08	553-554	716.16	08	553-554	717.40	08	562-563	718.72	08	564-566	719.50	08	555-556
713.1	08	553-554	716.17	08	553-554	717.41	08	562-563	718.73	08	564-566	719.51	08	555-556
713.2	08	553-554	716.18	08	553-554	717.42	08	562-563	718.74	08	564-566	719.52	08	555-556
713.3	08	553-554	716.19	08	553-554	717.43	08	562-563	718.75	08	564-566	719.53	08	555-556
713.4	08	553-554	716.20	08	553-554	717.49	08	562-563	718.76	08	564-566	719.54	08	555-556
713.5	08	553-554	716.21	08	553-554	717.5	08	562-563	718.77	08	564-566	719.55	08	555-556
713.6	08	553-554	716.22	08	553-554	717.6	08	564-566	718.78	08	564-566	719.56	08	555-556
713.7	08	553-554	716.23	08	553-554	717.7	08	562-563	718.79	08	564-566	719.57	08	555-556
713.8	08	553-554	716.24	08	553-554	717.81	08	562-563	718.80	08	564-566	719.58	08	555-556
714.0	08	545-547	716.25	08	553-554	717.82	08	562-563	718.81	08	564-566	719.59	08	555-556
714.1	08	545-547	716.26	08	553-554	717.83	08	562-563	718.82	08	564-566	719.60	08	555-556
714.2	08	545-547	716.27	08	553-554	717.84	08	562-563	718.83	08	564-566	719.61	08	555-556
714.30	08	545-547	716.28	08	553-554	717.85	08	562-563	718.84	08	564-566	719.62	08	555-556
714.31	08	545-547	716.29	08	553-554	717.89	08	562-563	718.85	08	564-566	719.63	08	555-556
714.32	08	545-547	716.30	08	553-554	717.9	08	562-563	718.86	08	564-566	719.64	08	555-556
714.33	08	545-547	716.31	08	553-554	718.00	08	564-566	718.87	08	564-566	719.65	08	555-556
714.4	08	553-554	716.32	08	553-554	718.01	08	562-563	718.88	08	564-566	719.66	08	555-556
714.81	04	196-198	716.33	08	553-554	718.02	08	562-563	718.89	08	564-566	719.67	08	555-556
714.89	08	545-547	716.34	08	553-554	718.03	08	562-563	718.90	08	564-566	719.68	08	555-556
714.9	08	553-554	716.35	08	553-554	718.04	08	562-563	718.91	08	564-566	719.69	08	555-556
715.00	08	553-554	716.36	08	553-554	718.05	08	564-566	718.92	08	564-566	719.7	08	555-556
715.04	08	553-554	716.37	08	553-554	718.07	08	562-563	718.93	08	564-566	719.80	08	555-556
715.09	08	553-554	716.38	08	553-554	718.08	08	564-566	718.94	08	564-566	719.81	08	555-556
715.10	08	553-554	716.39	08	553-554	718.09	08	564-566	718.95	08	564-566	719.82	08	555-556
715.11	08	553-554	716.40	08	553-554	718.10	08	564-566	718.97	08	564-566	719.83	08	555-556
715.12	08	553-554	716.41	08	553-554	718.11	08	564-566	718.98	08	564-566	719.84	08	555-556
715.13	08	553-554	716.42	08	553-554	718.12	08	564-566	718.99	08	564-566	719.85	08	555-556
715.14	08	553-554	716.43	08	553-554	718.13	08	564-566	719.00	08	564-566	719.86	08	555-556
715.15	08	553-554	716.44	08	553-554	718.14	08	564-566	719.01	08	564-566	719.87	08	555-556
715.16	08	553-554	716.45	08	553-554	718.15	08	564-566	719.02	08	564-566	719.88	08	555-556
715.17	08	553-554	716.46	08	553-554	718.17	08	564-566	719.03	08	564-566	719.89	08	555-556
715.18	08	553-554	716.47	08	553-554	718.18	08	564-566	719.04	08	564-566	719.90	08	555-556
715.20	08	553-554	716.48	08	553-554	718.19	08	564-566	719.05	08	564-566	719.91	08	555-556
715.21	08	553-554	716.49	08	553-554	718.20	08	562-563	719.06	08	564-566	719.92	08	555-556
715.22	08	553-554	716.50	08	553-554	718.21	08	562-563	719.07	08	564-566	719.93	08	555-556
715.23	08	553-554	716.51	08	553-554	718.22	08	562-563	719.08	08	564-566	719.94	08	555-556
715.24	08	553-554	716.52	08	553-554	718.23	08	562-563	719.09	08	564-566	719.95	08	555-556
715.25	08	553-554	716.53	08	553-554	718.24	08	562-563	719.10	08	553-554	719.96	08	555-556
715.26	08	553-554	716.54	08	553-554	718.25	08	564-566	719.11	08	553-554	719.97	08	555-556
715.27	08	553-554	716.55	08	553-554	718.26	08	562-563	719.12	08	553-554	719.98	08	555-556
715.28	08	553-554	716.56	08	553-554	718.27	08	562-563	719.13	08	553-554	719.99	08	555-556
715.30	08	553-554	716.57	08	553-554	718.28	08	564-566	719.14	08	553-554	720.0	08	545-547
715.31	08	553-554	716.58	08	553-554	718.29	08	564-566	719.15	08	553-554	720.1	08	551-552
715.32	08	553-554	716.59	08	553-554	718.30	08	564-566	719.16	08	553-554	720.2	08	551-552
715.33	08	553-554	716.60	08	553-554	718.31	08	562-563	719.17	08	553-554	720.81	08	551-552
715.34	08	553-554	716.61	08	553-554	718.32	08	562-563	719.18	08	553-554	720.89	08	551-552
715.35	08	553-554	716.62	08	553-554	718.33	08	562-563	719.19	08	553-554	720.9	08	551-552
715.36	08	553-554	716.63	08	553-554	718.34	08	562-563	719.20	08	553-554	721.0	08	551-552
715.37	08	553-554	716.64	08	553-554	718.35	08	564-566	719.21	08	553-554	721.1	08	551-552
715.38	08	553-554	716.65	08	553-554	718.36	08	562-563	719.22	08	553-554	721.2	08	551-552
715.80	08	553-554	716.66	08	553-554	718.37	08	562-563	719.23	08	553-554	721.3	08	551-552
715.89	08	553-554	716.67	08	553-554	718.38	08	564-566	719.24	08	553-554	721.41	08	551-552
715.90	08	553-554	716.68	08	553-554	718.39	08	564-566	719.25	08	553-554	721.42	08	551-552
715.91	08	553-554	716.80	08	553-554	718.40	08	564-566	719.26	08	553-554	721.5	08	551-552
715.92	08	553-554	716.81	08	553-554	718.41	08	564-566	719.27	08	553-554	721.6	08	551-552
715.93	08	553-554	716.82	08	553-554	718.42	08	564-566	719.28	08	553-554	721.7	08	551-552
715.94	08	553-554	716.83	08	553-554	718.43	08	564-566	719.29	08	553-554	721.8	08	551-552
715.95	08	553-554	716.84	08	553-554	718.44	08	564-566	719.30	08	553-554	721.90	08	551-552
715.96	08	553-554	716.85	08	553-554	718.45	08	564-566	719.31	08	553-554	721.91	08	551-552
715.97	08	553-554	716.86	08	553-554	718.46	08	564-566	719.32	08	553-554	722.0	08	551-552
715.98	08	553-554	716.87	08	553-554	718.47	08	564-566	719.33	08	553-554	722.10	08	551-552
716.00	08	553-554	716.88	08	553-554	718.48	08	564-566	719.34	08	553-554	722.11	08	551-552
716.01	08	553-554	716.89	08	553-554	718.49	08	564-566	719.35	08	553-554	722.2	08	551-552
716.02	08	553-554	716.90	08	553-554	718.50	08	553-554	719.36	08	553-554	722.30	08	551-552
716.03	08	553-554	716.91	08	553-554	718.51	08	553-554	719.37	08	553-554	722.31	08	551-552
716.04	08	553-554	716.92	08	553-554	718.52	08	553-554	719.38	08	553-554	722.32	08	551-552
716.05	08	553-554	716.93	08	553-554	718.53	08	553-554	719.39	08	553-554	722.39	08	551-552
716.06	08	553-554	716.94	08	553-554	718.54	08	553-554	719.40	08	555-556	722.4	08	551-552
716.07	08	553-554	716.95	08	553-554	718.55	08	553-554	719.41	08	555-556	722.51	08	551-552
716.08	08	553-554	716.96	08	553-554	718.56	08	553-554	719.42	08	555-556	722.52	08	551-552
716.09	08	553-554	716.97	08	553-554	718.57	08	553-554	719.43	08	555-556	722.6	08	551-552
716.10	08	553-554	716.98	08	553-554	718.58	08	553-554	719.44	08	555-556	722.70	08	551-552

DX	MDC	DRG	DX	MDC	DRG	DX	MDC	DRG	DX	MDC	DRG	DX	MDC	DRG
722.71	08	551-552	727.42	08	557-558	730.14	08	539-541	733.12	08	542-544	737.12	08	551-552
722.72	08	551-552	727.43	08	557-558	730.15	08	539-541	733.13	08	542-544	737.19	08	551-552
722.73	08	551-552	727.49	08	557-558	730.16	08	539-541	733.14	08	542-544	737.20	08	551-552
722.80	08	551-552	727.50	08	557-558	730.17	08	539-541	733.15	08	542-544	737.21	08	551-552
722.81	08	551-552	727.51	08	557-558	730.18	08	539-541	733.16	08	542-544	737.22	08	551-552
722.82	08	551-552	727.59	08	557-558	730.19	08	539-541	733.19	08	542-544	737.29	08	551-552
722.83	08	551-552	727.60	08	557-558	730.20	08	539-541	733.20	08	553-554	737.30	08	551-552
722.90	08	551-552	727.61	08	557-558	730.21	08	539-541	733.21	08	553-554	737.31	08	551-552
722.91	08	551-552	727.62	08	557-558	730.22	08	539-541	733.22	08	553-554	737.32	08	551-552
722.92	08	551-552	727.63	08	557-558	730.23	08	539-541	733.29	08	553-554	737.33	08	551-552
722.93	08	551-552	727.64	08	557-558	730.24	08	539-541	733.3	08	564-566	737.34	08	551-552
723.0	08	551-552	727.65	08	557-558	730.25	08	539-541	733.40	08	553-554	737.39	08	551-552
723.1	08	551-552	727.66	08	557-558	730.26	08	539-541	733.41	08	553-554	737.40	08	551-552
723.2	01	073-074	727.67	08	557-558	730.27	08	539-541	733.42	08	553-554	737.41	08	551-552
723.3	01	073-074	727.68	08	557-558	730.28	08	539-541	733.43	08	553-554	737.42	08	551-552
723.4	01	073-074	727.69	08	557-558	730.29	08	539-541	733.44	08	553-554	737.43	08	551-552
723.5	08	551-552	727.81	08	557-558	730.30	08	553-554	733.45	08	553-554	737.8	08	551-552
723.6	09	606-607	727.82	08	557-558	730.31	08	553-554	733.49	08	553-554	737.9	08	551-552
723.7	08	551-552	727.83	08	557-558	730.32	08	553-554	733.5	08	553-554	738.0	03	154-156
723.8	08	551-552	727.89	08	557-558	730.33	08	553-554	733.6	04	205-206	738.10	08	564-566
723.9	08	551-552	727.9	08	557-558	730.34	08	553-554	733.7	08	564-566	738.11	08	564-566
724.00	08	551-552	728.0	08	557-558	730.35	08	553-554	733.81	08	564-566	738.12	08	564-566
724.01	08	551-552	728.10	08	557-558	730.36	08	553-554	733.82	08	564-566	738.19	08	564-566
724.02	08	551-552	728.11	08	557-558	730.37	08	564-566	733.90	08	564-566	738.2	08	564-566
724.09	08	551-552	728.12	08	557-558	730.38	08	564-566	733.91	08	564-566	738.3	08	564-566
724.1	08	551-552	728.13	08	557-558	730.39	08	564-566	733.92	08	553-554	738.4	08	551-552
724.2	08	551-552	728.19	08	557-558	730.70	08	564-566	733.93	08	542-544	738.5	08	551-552
724.3	08	551-552	728.2	08	557-558	730.71	08	564-566	733.94	08	542-544	738.6	08	564-566
724.4	08	551-552	728.3	08	557-558	730.72	08	564-566	733.95	08	542-544	738.7	03	154-156
724.5	08	551-552	728.4	08	557-558	730.73	08	564-566	733.96	08	542 544	738.8	08	564-566
724.6	08	551-552	728.5	08	557-558	730.74	08	564-566	733.97	08	542-544	738.9	08	564-566
724.70	08	551-552	728.6	08	557-558	730.75	08	564-566	733.98	08	542-544	739.0	08	555-556
724.71	08	551-552	728.71	08	557-558	730.76	08	564-566	733.99	08	564-566	739.1	08	551-552
724.79	08	551-552	728.79	08	557-558	730.77	08	564-566	734	08	564-566	739.2	08	551-552
724.8	08	551-552	728.81	08	557-558	730.78	08	564-566	735.0	08	564-566	739.3	08	551-552
724.9	08	551-552	728.82	08	557-558	730.79	08	564-566	735.1	08	564-566	739	08	551-552
725	08	545-547	728.83	08	557-558	730.80	08	539-541	735.2	08	564-566	739.5	08	555-556
726.0	08	557-558	728.84	08	557-558	730.81	08	539-541	735.3	08	564-566	739.6	08	555-556
726.10	08	557-558	728.85	08	555-556	730.82	08	539-541	735.4	08	564-566	739.7	08	555-556
726.11	08	557-558	728.86	08	557-558	730.83	08	539-541	735.5	08	564-566	739.8	08	555-556
726.12	08	557-558	728.87	08	555-556	730.84	08	539-541	735.8	08	564-566	739.9	08	555-556
726.19	08	557-558	728.88	08	557-558	730.85	08	539-541	735.9	08	564-566			
726.2	08	557-558	728.89	08	557-558	730.86	08	539-541	736.00	08	564-566	**Congenital Anomalies**		
726.30	08	557-558	728.9	08	557-558	730.87	08	539-541	736.01	08	564-566	740.0	01	091-093
726.31	08	557-558	729.0	08	555-556	730.88	08	539-541	736.02	08	564-566	740.1	01	091-093
726.32	08	557-558	729.1	08	555-556	730.89	08	539-541	736.03	08	564-566	740.2	01	091-093
726.33	08	557-558	729.2	01	073-074	730.90	08	539-541	736.04	08	564-566	741.00	01	091-093
726.39	08	557-558	729.30	09	606-607	730.91	08	539-541	736.05	01	073-074	741.01	01	091-093
726.4	08	557-558	729.31	09	606-607	730.92	08	539-541	736.06	01	073-074	741.02	01	091-093
726.5	08	557-558	729.39	09	606-607	730.93	08	539-541	736.07	01	073-074	741.03	01	091-093
726.60	08	557-558	729.4	08	557-558	730.94	08	539-541	736.09	08	564-566	741.90	01	091-093
726.61	08	557-558	729.5	08	555-556	730.95	08	539-541	736.1	08	564-566	741.91	01	091-093
726.62	08	557-558	729.6	08	564-566	730.96	08	539-541	736.20	08	564-566	741.92	01	091-093
726.63	08	557-558	729.71	08	557-558	730.97	08	539-541	736.21	08	564-566	741.93	01	091-093
726.64	08	557-558	729.72	08	557-558	730.98	08	539-541	736.22	08	564-566	742.0	01	091-093
726.65	08	557-558	729.73	08	557-558	730.99	08	539-541	736.29	08	564-566	742.1	01	091-093
726.69	08	557-558	729.79	08	557-558	731.0	08	553-554	736.30	08	564-566	742.2	01	091-093
726.70	08	557-558	729.81	08	555-556	731.1	08	553-554	736.31	08	564-566	742.3	01	091-093
726.71	08	557-558	729.82	08	555-556	731.2	08	553-554	736.32	08	564-566	742.4	01	091-093
726.72	08	557-558	729.89	08	555-556	731.3	08	553-554	736.39	08	564-566	742.51	01	091-093
726.73	08	564-566	729.90	08	555-556	731.8	08	553-554	736.41	08	564-566	742.53	01	091-093
726.79	08	557-558	729.91	08	555-556	732.0	08	553-554	736.42	08	564-566	742.59	01	091-093
726.8	08	557-558	729.92	08	555-556	732.1	08	553-554	736.5	08	564-566	742.8	01	091-093
726.90	08	557-558	729.99	08	555-556	732.2	08	553-554	736.6	08	564-566	742.9	01	091-093
726.91	08	557-558	730.00	08	539-541	732.3	08	553-554	736.70	08	564-566	743.00	02	124-125
727.00	08	557-558	730.01	08	539-541	732.4	08	553-554	736.71	08	564-566	743.03	02	124-125
727.01	08	557-558	730.02	08	539-541	732.5	08	553-554	736.72	08	564-566	743.06	02	124-125
727.02	08	564-566	730.03	08	539-541	732.6	08	553-554	736.73	08	564-566	743.10	02	124-125
727.03	08	557-558	730.04	08	539-541	732.7	08	553-554	736.74	01	073-074	743.11	02	124-125
727.04	08	557-558	730.05	08	539-541	732.8	08	553-554	736.75	08	564-566	743.12	02	124-125
727.05	08	557-558	730.06	08	539-541	732.9	08	553-554	736.76	08	564-566	743.20	02	124-125
727.06	08	557-558	730.07	08	539-541	733.00	08	553-554	736.79	08	564-566	743.21	02	124-125
727.09	08	557-558	730.08	08	539-541	733.01	08	553-554	736.81	08	564-566	743.22	02	124-125
727.1	08	564-566	730.09	08	539-541	733.02	08	553-554	736.89	08	564-566	743.30	02	124-125
727.2	08	557-558	730.10	08	539-541	733.03	08	553-554	736.9	08	564-566	743.31	02	124-125
727.3	08	557-558	730.11	08	539-541	733.09	08	553-554	737.0	08	551-552	743.32	02	124-125
727.40	08	557-558	730.12	08	539-541	733.10	08	542-544	737.10	08	551-552	743.33	02	124-125
727.41	08	557-558	730.13	08	539-541	733.11	08	542-544	737.11	08	551-552	743.34	02	124-125

DX	MDC	DRG	DX	MDC	DRG	DX	MDC	DRG	DX	MDC	DRG	DX	MDC	DRG
743.35	02	124-125	746.1	05	306-307	750.23	03	154-156	754.31	08	564-566	756.12	08	551-552
743.36	02	124-125	746.2	05	306-307	750.24	03	154-156	754.32	08	564-566	756.13	08	551-552
743.37	02	124-125	746.3	05	306-307	750.25	03	157-159	754.33	08	564-566	756.14	08	551-552
743.39	02	124-125	746.4	05	306-307	750.26	03	157-159	754.35	08	564-566	756.15	08	551-552
743.41	02	124-125	746.5	05	306-307	750.27	03	154-156	754.40	08	564-566	756.16	08	564-566
743.42	02	124-125	746.6	05	306-307	750.29	03	154-156	754.41	08	562-563	756.17	01	091-093
743.43	02	124-125	746.7	05	306-307	750.3	06	368-370	754.42	08	564-566	756.19	08	551-552
743.44	02	124-125	746.81	05	306-307	750.4	06	368-370	754.43	08	564-566	756.2	08	564-566
743.45	02	124-125	746.82	05	306-307	750.5	06	393-395	754.44	08	564-566	756.3	04	205-206
743.46	02	124-125	746.83	05	306-307	750.6	06	393-395	754.50	08	564-566	756.4	08	564-566
743.47	02	124-125	746.84	05	306-307	750.7	06	393-395	754.51	08	564-566	756.50	08	564-566
743.48	02	124-125	746.85	05	306-307	750.8	06	393-395	754.52	08	564-566	756.51	08	564-566
743.49	02	124-125	746.86	05	308-310	750.9	06	393-395	754.53	08	564-566	756.52	08	564-566
743.51	02	124-125	746.87	05	306-307	751.0	06	380-382	754.59	08	564-566	756.53	08	564-566
743.52	02	124-125	746.89	05	306-307	751.1	06	393-395	754.60	08	564-566	756.54	08	564-566
743.53	02	124-125	746.9	05	306-307	751.2	06	393-395	754.61	08	564-566	756.55	08	564-566
743.54	02	124-125	747.0	05	306-307	751.3	06	393-395	754.62	08	564-566	756.56	08	564-566
743.55	02	124-125	747.10	05	306-307	751.4	06	393-395	754.69	08	564-566	756.59	08	564-566
743.56	02	124-125	747.11	05	306-307	751.5	06	393-395	754.70	08	564-566	756.6	04	205-206
743.57	02	124-125	747.20	05	306-307	751.60	07	444-446	754.71	08	564-566	756.70	06	393-395
743.58	02	124-125	747.21	05	306-307	751.61	07	444-446	754.79	08	564-566	756.71	06	393-395
743.59	02	124-125	747.22	05	306-307	751.62	07	441-443	754.81	04	205-206	756.72	06	393-395
743.61	02	124-125	747.29	05	306-307	751.69	07	441-443	754.82	04	205-206	756.73	06	393-395
743.62	02	124-125	747.3	05	306-307	751.7	07	438-440	754.89	08	564-566	756.79	06	393-395
743.63	02	124-125	747.40	05	306-307	751.8	06	393-395	755.00	08	564-566	756.81	08	564-566
743.64	02	124-125	747.41	05	306-307	751.9	06	393-395	755.01	08	564-566	756.82	08	564-566
743.65	02	124-125	747.42	05	306-307	752.0	13	760-761	755.02	08	564-566	756.83	08	564-566
743.66	02	124-125	747.49	05	306-307	752.10	13	760-761	755.10	08	564-566	756.89	08	564-566
743.69	02	124-125	747.5	05	299-301	752.11	13	760-761	755.11	08	564-566	756.9	08	564-566
743.8	02	124-125	747.60	05	299-301	752.19	13	760-761	755.12	08	564-566	757.0	09	606-607
743.9	02	124-125	747.61	05	299-301	752.2	13	760-761	755.13	08	564-566	757.1	09	606-607
744.00	03	154-156	747.62	05	299-301	752.3	13	760-761	755.14	08	564-566	757.2	09	606-607
744.01	03	154-156	747.63	05	299-301	752.40	13	760-761	755.20	08	564-566	757.31	09	606-607
744.02	03	154-156	747.64	05	299-301	752.41	13	760-761	755.21	08	564-566	757.32	09	606-607
744.03	03	154-156	747.69	05	299-301	752.42	13	760-761	755.22	08	564-566	757.33	09	606-607
744.04	03	154-156	747.81	01	091-093	752.49	13	760-761	755.23	08	564-566	757.39	09	606-607
744.05	03	154-156	747.82	01	091-093	752.51	12	729-730	755.24	08	564-566	757.4	09	606-607
744.09	03	154-156	747.83	15	791-793	752.52	12	729-730	755.25	08	564-566	757.5	09	606-607
744.1	03	154-156	747.89	05	299-301	752.61	12	729-730	755.26	08	564-566	757.6	09	600-601
744.21	03	154-156	747.9	05	299-301	752.62	12	729-730	755.27	08	564-566	757.8	09	606-607
744.22	03	154-156	748.0	03	154-156	752.63	12	729-730	755.28	08	564-566	757.9	09	606-607
744.23	03	154-156	748.1	03	154-156	752.64	12	729-730	755.29	08	564-566	758.0	19	884
744.24	03	154-156	748.2	03	154-156	752.65	12	729-730	755.30	08	564-566	758.1	19	884
744.29	03	154-156	748.3	03	154-156	752.69	12	729-730	755.31	08	564-566	758.2	19	884
744.3	03	154-156	748.4	04	205-206	752.7	12	729-730	755.32	08	564-566	758.31	19	884
744.41	03	154-156	748.5	04	205-206	752.7	13	760-761	755.33	08	564-566	758.32	19	884
744.42	03	154-156	748.60	04	205-206	752.81	12	729-730	755.34	08	564-566	758.33	19	884
744.43	03	154-156	748.61	04	190-192	752.89	12	729-730	755.35	08	564-566	758.39	19	884
744.46	03	154-156	748.69	04	205-206	752.8	13	760-761	755.36	08	564-566	758.4	23	951
744.47	03	154-156	748.8	04	205-206	752.9	12	729-730	755.37	08	564-566	758.5	23	951
744.49	03	154-156	748.9	04	205-206	752.9	13	760-761	755.38	08	564-566	758.6	12	729-730
744.5	09	606-607	749.00	03	157-159	753.0	11	698-700	755.39	08	564-566	758.6	13	760-761
744.81	03	157-159	749.01	03	157-159	753.10	11	698-700	755.4	08	564-566	758.7	12	729-730
744.82	03	157-159	749.02	03	157-159	753.11	11	698-700	755.50	08	564-566	758.8	12	729-730
744.83	03	157-159	749.03	03	157-159	753.12	11	698-700	755.51	08	564-566	758.81	12	729-730
744.84	03	157-159	749.04	03	157-159	753.13	11	698-700	755.52	08	564-566	758.81	13	760-761
744.89	03	154-156	749.10	03	157-159	753.14	11	698-700	755.53	08	564-566	758.89	12	729-730
744.9	09	606-607	749.11	03	157-159	753.15	11	698-700	755.54	08	564-566	758.89	13	760-761
745.0	05	306-307	749.12	03	157-159	753.16	11	698-700	755.55	08	564-566	758.9	23	951
745.10	05	306-307	749.13	03	157-159	753.17	11	698-700	755.56	08	564-566	759.0	16	814-816
745.11	05	306-307	749.14	03	157-159	753.19	11	698-700	755.57	08	564-566	759.1	10	643-645
745.12	05	306-307	749.20	03	157-159	753.20	11	698-700	755.58	08	564-566	759.2	10	643-645
745.19	05	306-307	749.21	03	157-159	753.21	11	698-700	755.59	08	564-566	759.3	06	393-395
745.2	05	306-307	749.22	03	157-159	753.22	11	698-700	755.60	08	564-566	759.4	06	393-395
745.3	05	306-307	749.23	03	157-159	753.23	11	698-700	755.61	08	564-566	759.5	01	091-093
745.4	05	306-307	749.24	03	157-159	753.29	11	698-700	755.62	08	564-566	759.6	17	843-845
745.5	05	306-307	749.25	03	157-159	753.3	11	698-700	755.63	08	564-566	759.7	08	564-566
745.60	05	306-307	750.0	03	157-159	753.4	11	698-700	755.64	08	564-566	759.81	08	564-566
745.61	05	306-307	750.10	03	157-159	753.5	11	698-700	755.65	08	564-566	759.82	05	306-307
745.69	05	306-307	750.11	03	157-159	753.6	11	698-700	755.66	08	564-566	759.83	19	884
745.7	05	306-307	750.12	03	157-159	753.7	11	698-700	755.67	08	564-566	759.89	08	564-566
745.8	05	306-307	750.13	03	157-159	753.8	11	698-700	755.69	08	564-566	759.9	23	951
745.9	05	306-307	750.15	03	157-159	753.9	11	698-700	755.8	08	564-566			
746.00	05	306-307	750.16	03	157-159	754.0	08	564-566	755.9	08	564-566			
746.01	05	306-307	750.19	03	157-159	754.1	08	564-566	756.0	08	564-566			
746.02	05	306-307	750.21	03	154-156	754.2	08	564-566	756.10	08	551-552			
746.09	05	306-307	750.22	03	154-156	754.30	08	564-566	756.11	08	551-552			

Certain Conditions Originating in the Perinatal Period

DX	MDC	DRG
760.0	15	794

DX	MDC	DRG	DX	MDC	DRG	DX	MDC	DRG	DX	MDC	DRG	DX	MDC	DRG
760.1	15	794	764.24	15	791, 793	770.12	15	791, 793	776.2	15	791, 793	780.79	23	947-948
760.2	15	794	764.25	15	791, 793	770.13	15	791, 793	776.3	15	791, 793	780.8	09	606-607
760.3	15	794	764.26	15	791, 793	770.14	15	791, 793	776.4	15	794	780.91	23	947-948
760.4	15	794	764.27	15	791, 793	770.15	15	791, 793	776.5	15	794	780.92	23	947-948
760.5	15	794	764.28	15	791, 793	770.16	15	791, 793	776.6	15	791, 793	780.93	23	947-948
760.61	15	794	764.29	15	794	770.17	15	791, 793	776.7	15	794	780.94	23	947-948
760.62	15	794	764.90	15	794	770.18	15	791, 793	776.8	15	794	780.95	23	947-948
760.63	15	794	764.91	15	794	770.2	15	791, 793	776.9	15	794	780.96	23	947-948
760.64	15	794	764.92	15	794	770.3	15	791, 793	777.1	15	791, 793	780.97	23	947-948
760.70	15	794	764.93	15	794	770.4	15	791, 793	777.2	15	791, 793	780.99	23	947-948
760.71	15	794	764.93	15	794	770.5	15	794	777.3	15	794	781.0	01	091-093
760.72	15	794	764.94	15	794	770.6	15	794	777.4	15	794	781.1	01	091-093
760.73	15	794	764.95	15	794	770.7	04	196-198	777.50	15	791, 793	781.2	01	091-093
760.74	15	794	764.96	15	794	770.81	15	794	777.51	15	791, 793	781.3	01	091-093
760.75	15	794	764.97	15	794	770.82	15	794	777.52	15	791, 793	781.4	01	091-093
760.77	15	794	764.98	15	795	770.83	15	794	777.53	15	791, 793	781.5	04	205-206
760.78	15	794	764.99	15	795	770.84	15	791, 793	777.6	15	791, 793	781.6	01	091-093
760.79	15	794	765.00	15	791-792	770.85	15	791, 793	777.8	15	794	781.7	10	640-641
760.8	15	794	765.01	15	790	770.86	15	791, 793	777.9	15	794	781.8	01	091-093
760.9	15	794	765.02	15	790	770.87	15	794	778.0	15	791, 793	781.91	01	091-093
761.0	15	794	765.03	15	790	770.88	15	794	778.1	15	794	781.92	01	091-093
761.1	15	794	765.04	15	790	770.89	15	794	778.2	15	794	781.93	08	551-552
761.2	15	794	765.05	15	790	770.9	15	794	778.3	15	794	781.94	01	091-093
761.3	15	794	765.06	15	791-792	771.0	15	791, 793	778.4	15	794	781.99	01	091-093
761.4	15	794	765.07	15	791-792	771.1	15	791, 793	778.5	15	794	782.0	01	091-093
761.5	15	794	765.08	15	791-792	771.2	15	791, 793	778.6	15	794	782.1	09	606-607
761.6	15	794	765.09	15	999	771.3	15	794	778.7	15	794	782.2	09	606-607
761.7	15	794	765.10	15	791-792	771.4	15	791, 793	778.8	15	795	782.3	23	947-948
761.8	15	794	765.11	15	791-792	771.5	15	791, 793	778.9	15	794	782.4	07	441-443
761.9	15	794	765.12	15	791-792	771.6	15	794	779.0	15	791, 793	782.5	23	947-948
762.0	15	794	765.13	15	791-792	771.7	15	794	779.1	15	791, 793	782.61	23	947-948
762.1	15	794	765.14	15	791-792	771.8	15	791, 793	779.2	15	791, 793	782.62	23	947-948
762.2	15	794	765.15	15	791-792	771.81	15	791, 793	779.31	15	795	782.7	16	813
762.3	15	794	765.16	15	791-792	771.82	15	791, 793	779.32	15	791, 793	782.8	09	606-607
762.4	15	795	765.17	15	791-792	771.83	15	791, 793	779.33	15	795	782.9	09	606-607
762.5	15	795	765.18	15	791-792	771.89	15	791, 793	779.34	10	640-641	783.0	10	640-641
762.6	15	795	765.19	15	791-792	772.0	15	791, 793	779.4	15	791, 793	783.1	10	640-641
762.7	15	794	765.20	15	795	772.10	15	791, 793	779.5	15	791, 793	783.21	10	640-641
762.8	15	794	765.21	15	790	772.11	15	791, 793	779.6	15	794	783.22	10	640-641
762.9	15	794	765.22	15	790	772.12	15	791, 793	779.7	01	091-093	783.40	10	640-641
763.0	15	795	765.23	15	790	772.13	15	791, 793	779.81	15	794	783.41	10	640-641
763.1	15	795	765.24	15	791-792	772.14	15	791, 793	779.82	15	794	783.42	10	640-641
763.2	15	795	765.25	15	791-792	772.2	15	791, 793	779.83	15	795	783.43	10	640-641
763.3	15	795	765.26	15	791-792	772.3	15	794	779.84	15	794	783.5	10	640-641
763.4	15	791, 793	765.27	15	791-792	772.4	15	791, 793	779.85	15	791, 793	783.6	10	640-641
763.5	15	794	765.28	15	791-792	772.5	15	791, 793	779.89	15	794	783.7	10	640-641
763.6	15	795	765.29	15	795	772.6	15	795	779.9	15	794	783.9	10	640-641
763.7	15	794	766.0	15	795	772.8	15	794				784.0	01	102-103
763.81	15	794	766.1	15	795	772.9	15	794	**Symptoms, Signs and**			784.1	03	154-156
763.82	15	794	766.21	15	795	773.0	15	794	**Ill-defined Conditions**			784.2	09	606-607
763.83	15	794	766.22	15	795	773.1	15	794	780.01	01	080-081	784.3	01	091-093
763.84	15	794	767.0	15	791, 793	773.2	15	791, 793	780.02	19	884	784.40	03	154-156
763.89	15	794	767.11	15	791, 793	773.3	15	791, 793	780.03	01	080-081	784.41	03	154-156
763.9	15	795	767.19	15	795	773.4	15	791, 793	780.09	01	080-081	784.42	03	154-156
764.00	15	794	767.2	15	794	773.5	15	791, 793	780.1	19	880	784.43	03	154-156
764.01	15	794	767.3	15	794	774.0	15	794	780.2	05	312	784.44	03	154-156
764.02	15	794	767.4	15	791, 793	774.1	15	794	780.31	01	100-101	784.49	03	154-156
764.03	15	794	767.5	15	794	774.2	15	794	780.32	01	100-101	784.51	01	091-093
764.04	15	794	767.6	15	794	774.30	15	795	780.39	01	100-101	784.59	01	091-093
764.05	15	794	767.7	15	791, 793	774.31	15	795	780.4	03	149	784.60	19	887
764.06	15	794	767.8	15	794	774.39	15	795	780.50	19	887	784.61	19	886
764.07	15	794	767.9	15	794	774.4	15	791, 793	780.51	03	154-156	784.69	19	886
764.08	15	795	768.0	15	794	774.5	15	795	780.52	19	887	784.7	03	150-151
764.09	15	795	768.1	15	794	774.6	15	795	780.53	03	154-156	784.8	03	154-156
764.10	15	794	768.2	15	794	774.7	15	791, 793	780.54	19	887	784.91	03	154-156
764.11	15	791, 793	768.3	15	794	775.0	15	794	780.55	19	887	784.99	03	154-156
764.12	15	791, 793	768.4	15	794	775.1	15	791, 793	780.56	19	887	785.0	05	308-310
764.13	15	791, 793	768.5	15	791, 793	775.2	15	791, 793	780.57	03	154-156	785.1	05	308-310
764.14	15	791, 793	768.6	15	795	775.3	15	791, 793	780.58	19	887	785.2	05	306-307
764.15	15	791, 793	768.70	15	794	775.4	15	791, 793	780.59	19	887	785.3	05	314-316
764.16	15	791, 793	768.71	15	794	775.5	15	791, 793	780.60	18	864	785.4	05	299-301
764.17	15	791, 793	768.72	15	791, 793	775.6	15	791, 793	780.61	18	864	785.50	05	291-293
764.18	15	791, 793	768.73	15	791, 793	775.7	15	791, 793	780.62	18	864	785.51	05	291-293
764.19	15	794	768.9	15	794	775.81	15	794	780.63	18	864	785.52	18	870-872
764.20	15	794	769	15	790	775.89	15	794	780.64	23	947-948	785.59	18	870-872
764.21	15	791, 793	770.0	15	791, 793	775.9	15	794	780.65	23	947-948	785.6	16	814-816
764.22	15	791, 793	770.10	15	791, 793	776.0	15	791, 793	780.71	23	947-948	785.9	05	314-316
764.23	15	791, 793	770.11	15	791, 793	776.1	15	791, 793	780.72	01	052-053	786.00	04	204

DX	MDC	DRG
786.01	04	204
786.02	04	204
786.03	04	204
786.04	04	204
786.05	04	204
786.06	04	204
786.07	04	204
786.09	04	204
786.1	04	204
786.2	04	204
786.3	04	204
786.4	04	204
786.50	05	313
786.51	05	313
786.52	04	204
786.59	05	313
786.6	04	204
786.7	04	204
786.8	04	204
786.9	04	204
787.01	06	391-392
787.02	06	391-392
787.03	06	391-392
787.04	06	391-392
787.1	06	391-392
787.20	06	391-392
787.21	06	391-392
787.22	06	391-392
787.23	06	391-392
787.24	06	391-392
787.29	06	391-392
787.3	06	391-392
787.4	06	391-392
787.5	06	391-392
787.6	06	391-392
787.7	06	391-392
787.91	06	391-392
787.99	06	391-392
788.0	11	691-694
788.1	11	695-696
788.20	11	695-696
788.21	11	695-696
788.29	11	695-696
788.30	11	695-696
788.31	11	695-696
788.32	11	695-696
788.33	11	695-696
788.34	11	695-696
788.35	11	695-696
788.36	11	695-696
788.37	11	695-696
788.38	11	695-696
788.39	11	695-696
788.41	11	695-696
788.42	11	695-696
788.43	11	695-696
788.5	11	682-684
788.61	11	695-696
788.62	11	695-696
788.63	11	695-696
788.64	11	695-696
788.65	11	695-696
788.69	11	695-696
788.7	11	695-696
788.8	11	695-696
788.91	11	695-696
788.99	11	695-696
789.00	06	391-392
789.01	06	391-392
789.02	06	391-392
789.03	06	391-392
789.04	06	391-392
789.05	06	391-392
789.06	06	391-392
789.07	06	391-392
789.09	06	391-392
789.1	07	441-443
789.2	16	814-816
789.30	06	391-392
789.31	06	391-392
789.32	06	391-392
789.33	06	391-392
789.34	06	391-392
789.35	06	391-392
789.36	06	391-392
789.37	06	391-392
789.39	06	391-392
789.40	06	393-395
789.41	06	393-395
789.42	06	393-395
789.43	06	393-395
789.44	06	393-395
789.45	06	393-395
789.46	06	393-395
789.47	06	393-395
789.49	06	393-395
789.51	23	947-948
789.59	23	947-948
789.60	06	391-392
789.61	06	391-392
789.62	06	391-392
789.63	06	391-392
789.64	06	391-392
789.65	06	391-392
789.66	06	391-392
789.67	06	391-392
789.69	06	391-392
789.7	06	391-392
789.9	06	391-392
790.01	16	811-812
790.09	16	811-812
790.1	23	947-948
790.21	10	640-641
790.22	10	640-641
790.29	10	640-641
790.3	20	894-897
790.4	23	947-948
790.5	23	947-948
790.6	23	947-948
790.7	18	870-872
790.8	18	865-866
790.91	23	947-948
790.92	23	947-948
790.93	23	947-948
790.94	23	947-948
790.95	23	947-948
790.99	23	947-948
791.0	11	695-696
791.1	11	695-696
791.2	11	695-696
791.3	23	947-948
791.4	07	441-443
791.5	10	637-639
791.6	10	640-641
791.7	11	695-696
791.9	11	695-696
792.0	01	091-093
792.1	06	391-392
792.2	12	729-730
792.3	14	781-782
792.4	03	154-156
792.5	23	947-948
792.9	23	947-948
793.0	01	091-093
793.1	04	204
793.2	05	302-303
793.3	07	444-446
793.4	06	391-392
793.5	11	695-696
793.6	06	391-392
793.7	08	564-566
793.80	09	600-601
793.81	09	600-601
793.82	09	600-601
793.89	09	600-601
793.91	23	947-948
793.99	23	947-948
794.00	01	091-093
794.01	01	091-093
794.02	01	091-093
794.09	01	091-093
794.10	01	091-093
794.11	02	124-125
794.12	02	124-125
794.13	02	124-125
794.14	02	124-125
794.15	03	154-156
794.16	03	154-156
794.17	08	564-566
794.19	01	091-093
794.2	04	205-206
794.30	05	314-316
794.31	05	314-316
794.39	05	314-316
794.4	11	695-696
794.5	10	643-645
794.6	10	643-645
794.7	10	643-645
794.8	07	441-443
794.9	11	695-696
795.00	13	760-761
795.01	13	760-761
795.02	13	760-761
795.03	13	760-761
795.04	13	760-761
795.05	13	760-761
795.06	13	760-761
795.07	13	760-761
795.08	13	760-761
795.09	13	760-761
795.10	13	760-761
795.11	13	760-761
795.12	13	760-761
795.13	13	760-761
795.14	13	760-761
795.15	13	760-761
795.16	13	760-761
795.18	13	760-761
795.19	13	760-761
795.2	23	951
795.31	18	867-869
795.39	18	867-869
795.4	23	947-948
795.5	04	177-179
795.6	08	545-547
795.71	16	814-816
795.79	16	814-816
795.81	23	947-948
795.82	23	947-948
795.89	23	947-948
796.0	21	922-923
796.1	01	091-093
796.2	05	314-316
796.3	05	314-316
796.4	23	947-948
796.5	14	781-782
796.6	23	947-948
796.70	06	393-395
796.71	06	393-395
796.72	06	393-395
796.73	06	393-395
796.74	06	393-395
796.75	06	393-395
796.76	06	393-395
796.77	06	393-395
796.78	06	393-395
796.79	06	393-395
796.9	23	947-948
797	19	884
798.0	01	091-093
798.1	05	296-298
798.2	05	296-298
798.9	23	951
799.01	4	205-206
799.02	4	205-206
799.1	04	205-206
799.21	19	880
799.22	19	880
799.23	19	882
799.24	19	883
799.25	19	880
799.29	19	880
799.3	23	947-948
799.4	23	947-948
799.81	23	951
799.82	23	951
799.89	23	951
799.9	23	951

Injury and Poisoning

DX	MDC	DRG
800.00	01	082-087
800.01	01	082-087
800.02	01	082-087
800.03	01	082-084
800.04	01	082-084
800.05	01	082-084
800.06	01	082-087
800.09	01	082-087
800.10	01	082-087
800.11	01	082-087
800.12	01	082-087
800.13	01	082-084
800.14	01	082-084
800.15	01	082-084
800.16	01	082-084
800.19	01	082-087
800.20	01	082-087
800.21	01	082-087
800.22	01	082-087
800.23	01	082-084
800.24	01	082-084
800.25	01	082-084
800.26	01	082-084
800.29	01	082-087
800.30	01	082-087
800.31	01	082-087
800.32	01	082-087
800.33	01	082-084
800.34	01	082-084
800.35	01	082-084
800.36	01	082-084
800.39	01	082-087
800.40	01	082-087
800.41	01	082-087
800.42	01	082-087
800.43	01	082-084
800.44	01	082-084
800.45	01	082-084
800.46	01	082-084
800.49	01	082-087
800.50	01	082-087
800.51	01	082-087
800.52	01	082-087
800.53	01	082-084
800.54	01	082-084
800.55	01	082-084
800.56	01	082-084
800.59	01	082-087
800.60	01	082-087
800.61	01	082-087
800.62	01	082-087
800.63	01	082-084
800.64	01	082-084
800.65	01	082-084
800.66	01	082-084
800.69	01	082-087
800.70	01	082-087
800.71	01	082-087
800.72	01	082-087
800.73	01	082-084
800.74	01	082-084
800.75	01	082-084
800.76	01	082-084
800.79	01	082-087
800.80	01	082-087
800.81	01	082-087
800.82	01	082-087
800.83	01	082-087
800.84	01	082-084
800.85	01	082-084
800.86	01	082-084
800.89	01	082-087
800.90	01	082-087
800.91	01	082-087
800.92	01	082-087
800.93	01	082-084
800.94	01	082-084
800.95	01	082-084
800.96	01	082-084
800.99	01	082-087
801.00	01	082-087
801.01	01	082-087
801.02	01	082-087
801.03	01	082-084
801.04	01	082-087
801.05	01	082-084
801.06	01	082-084
801.09	01	082-087
801.10	01	082-087
801.11	01	082-087
801.12	01	082-087
801.13	01	082-087
801.14	01	082-084
801.15	01	082-084
801.16	01	082-084
801.19	01	082-087
801.21	01	082-087
801.22	01	082-087
801.23	01	082-084
801.24	01	082-084
801.25	01	082-087
801.26	01	082-084
801.29	01	082-087
801.30	01	082-087
801.31	01	082-087
801.32	01	082-087
801.33	01	082-084
801.34	01	082-084
801.35	01	082-084
801.36	01	082-084
801.39	01	082-087
801.40	01	082-087
801.41	01	082-087
801.42	01	082-087
801.43	01	082-084
801.44	01	082-084
801.45	01	082-084
801.46	01	082-084
801.49	01	082-087
801.50	01	082-087
801.51	01	082-087
801.52	01	082-087
801.53	01	082-084
801.54	01	082-084
801.55	01	082-084
801.56	01	082-084
801.59	01	082-087
801.60	01	082-087
801.61	01	082-084
801.62	01	082-087
801.63	01	082-084
801.64	01	082-084
801.65	01	082-084
801.66	01	082-084

Diagnosis Code/MDC/DRG List (left margin)

DX	MDC	DRG	DX	MDC	DRG	DX	MDC	DRG	DX	MDC	DRG	DX	MDC	DRG
801.69	01	082-087	803.31	01	082-087	804.29	01	082-087	805.5	08	551-552	807.3	04	183-185
801.70	01	082-087	803.32	01	082-087	804.30	01	082-087	805.6	08	551-552	807.4	04	183-185
801.71	01	082-087	803.33	01	082-084	804.31	01	082-087	805.7	08	551-552	807.5	03	154-156
801.72	01	082-087	803.34	01	082-084	804.32	01	082-087	805.8	08	551-552	807.6	03	154-156
801.73	01	082-084	803.35	01	082-084	804.33	01	082-084	805.9	08	551-552	808.0	08	535-536
801.74	01	082-084	803.36	01	082-084	804.34	01	082-084	806.00	01	052-053	808.1	08	535-536
801.75	01	082-084	803.39	01	082-087	804.35	01	082-084	806.01	01	052-053	808.2	08	535-536
801.76	01	082-084	803.40	01	082-087	804.36	01	082-084	806.02	01	052-053	808.3	08	535-536
801.79	01	082-087	803.41	01	082-087	804.39	01	082-087	806.03	01	052-053	808.41	08	535-536
801.80	01	082-087	803.42	01	082-087	804.40	01	082-087	806.04	01	052-053	808.42	08	535-536
801.81	01	082-087	803.43	01	082-084	804.41	01	082-087	806.05	01	052-053	808.43	08	535-536
801.82	01	082-087	803.44	01	082-084	804.42	01	082-087	806.06	01	052-053	808.49	08	535-536
801.83	01	082-084	803.45	01	082-084	804.43	01	082-084	806.07	01	052-053	808.51	08	535-536
801.84	01	082-084	803.46	01	082-084	804.44	01	082-084	806.08	01	052-053	808.52	08	535-536
801.85	01	082-084	803.49	01	082-087	804.45	01	082-084	806.09	01	052-053	808.53	08	535-536
801.86	01	082-084	803.50	01	082-087	804.46	01	082-084	806.10	01	052-053	808.59	08	535-536
801.89	01	082-087	803.51	01	082-087	804.49	01	082-087	806.11	01	052-053	808.8	08	535-536
801.90	01	082-087	803.52	01	082-087	804.50	01	082-087	806.12	01	052-053	808.9	08	535-536
801.91	01	082-087	803.53	01	082-084	804.51	01	082-087	806.13	01	052-053	809.0	08	564-566
801.92	01	082-087	803.54	01	082-084	804.52	01	082-087	806.14	01	052-053	809.1	08	564-566
801.93	01	082-084	803.55	01	082-084	804.53	01	082-084	806.15	01	052-053	810.00	08	562-563
801.94	01	082-084	803.56	01	082-084	804.54	01	082-084	806.16	01	052-053	810.01	08	562-563
801.95	01	082-084	803.59	01	082-087	804.55	01	082-084	806.17	01	052-053	810.02	08	562-563
801.96	01	082-084	803.60	01	082-087	804.56	01	082-084	806.18	01	052-053	810.03	08	562-563
801.99	01	082-087	803.61	01	082-087	804.59	01	082-087	806.19	01	052-053	810.10	08	562-563
802.0	03	154-156	803.62	01	082-087	804.60	01	082-087	806.20	01	052-053	810.11	08	562-563
802.1	03	154-156	803.63	01	082-084	804.61	01	082-087	806.21	01	052-053	810.12	08	562-563
802.20	03	157-159	803.64	01	082-084	804.62	01	082-087	806.22	01	052-053	810.13	08	562-563
802.21	03	157-159	803.65	01	082-084	804.63	01	082-084	806.23	01	052-053	811.00	08	562-563
802.22	03	157 159	803.66	01	082-084	804.64	01	082-084	806.24	01	052-053	811.01	08	562-563
802.23	03	157-159	803.69	01	082-087	804.65	01	082-084	806.25	01	052-053	811.02	08	562-563
802.24	03	157-159	803.70	01	082-087	804.66	01	082-084	806.26	01	052-053	811.03	08	562-563
802.25	03	157-159	803.71	01	082-087	804.69	01	082-087	806.27	01	052-053	811.09	08	564-566
802.26	03	157-159	803.72	01	082-087	804.70	01	082-087	806.28	01	052-053	811.10	08	562-563
802.27	03	157-159	803.73	01	082-084	804.71	01	082-087	806.29	01	052-053	811.11	08	562-563
802.28	03	157-159	803.74	01	082-084	804.72	01	082-087	806.30	01	052-053	811.12	08	562-563
802.29	03	157-159	803.75	01	082-084	804.73	01	082-084	806.31	01	052-053	811.13	08	562-563
802.30	03	157-159	803.76	01	082-084	804.74	01	082-084	806.32	01	052-053	811.19	08	564-566
802.31	03	157-159	803.79	01	082-087	804.75	01	082-084	806.33	01	052-053	812.00	08	562-563
802.32	03	157-159	803.80	01	082-087	804.76	01	082-084	806.34	01	052-053	812.01	08	562-563
802.33	03	157-159	803.81	01	082-087	804.79	01	082-087	806.35	01	052-053	812.02	08	562-563
802.34	03	157-159	803.82	01	082-087	804.80	01	082-087	806.36	01	052-053	812.03	08	562-563
802.35	03	157-159	803.83	01	082-084	804.81	01	082-087	806.37	01	052-053	812.09	08	562-563
802.36	03	157-159	803.84	01	082-084	804.82	01	082-087	806.38	01	052-053	812.10	08	562-563
802.37	03	157-159	803.85	01	082-084	804.83	01	082-084	806.39	01	052-053	812.11	08	562-563
802.38	03	157-159	803.86	01	082-084	804.84	01	082-084	806.4	01	052-053	812.12	08	562-563
802.39	03	157-159	803.89	01	082-087	804.85	01	082-084	806.5	01	052-053	812.13	08	562-563
802.4	03	157-159	803.90	01	082-087	804.86	01	082-084	806.60	01	052-053	812.19	08	562-563
802.5	03	157-159	803.91	01	082-087	804.89	01	082-087	806.61	01	052-053	812.20	08	562-563
802.6	02	124-125	803.92	01	082-087	804.90	01	082-087	806.62	01	052-053	812.21	08	562-563
802.7	02	124-125	803.93	01	082-084	804.91	01	082-087	806.69	01	052-053	812.30	08	562-563
802.8	08	564-566	803.94	01	082-084	804.92	01	082-087	806.70	01	052-053	812.31	08	562-563
802.9	08	564-566	803.95	01	082-084	804.93	01	082-084	806.71	01	052-053	812.40	08	562-563
803.00	01	082-087	803.96	01	082-084	804.94	01	082-084	806.72	01	052-053	812.41	08	562-563
803.01	01	082-087	803.99	01	082-087	804.95	01	082-084	806.79	01	052-053	812.42	08	562-563
803.02	01	082-087	804.00	01	082-087	804.96	01	082-084	806.8	01	052-053	812.43	08	562-563
803.03	01	082-084	804.01	01	082-087	804.99	01	082-087	806.9	01	052-053	812.44	08	562-563
803.04	01	082-084	804.02	01	082-087	805.00	08	551-552	807.00	04	205-206	812.49	08	562-563
803.05	01	082-084	804.03	01	082-084	805.01	08	551-552	807.01	04	205-206	812.50	08	562-563
803.06	01	082-084	804.04	01	082-084	805.02	08	551-552	807.02	04	205-206	812.51	08	562-563
803.09	01	082-087	804.05	01	082-084	805.03	08	551-552	807.03	04	183-185	812.52	08	562-563
803.10	01	082-087	804.06	01	082-084	805.04	08	551-552	807.04	04	183-185	812.53	08	562-563
803.11	01	082-087	804.09	01	082-087	805.05	08	551-552	807.05	04	183-185	812.54	08	562-563
803.12	01	082-087	804.10	01	082-087	805.06	08	551-552	807.06	04	183-185	812.59	08	562-563
803.13	01	082-084	804.11	01	082-087	805.07	08	551-552	807.07	04	183-185	813.00	08	562-563
803.14	01	082-084	804.12	01	082-087	805.08	08	551-552	807.08	04	183-185	813.01	08	562-563
803.15	01	082-084	804.13	01	082-084	805.10	08	551-552	807.09	04	183-185	813.02	08	562-563
803.16	01	082-084	804.14	01	082-084	805.11	08	551-552	807.10	04	183-185	813.03	08	562-563
803.19	01	082-087	804.15	01	082-084	805.12	08	551-552	807.11	04	183-185	813.04	08	562-563
803.20	01	082-087	804.16	01	082-084	805.13	08	551-552	807.12	04	183-185	813.05	08	562-563
803.21	01	082-087	804.19	01	082-087	805.14	08	551-552	807.13	04	183-185	813.06	08	562-563
803.22	01	082-087	804.20	01	082-087	805.15	08	551-552	807.14	04	183-185	813.07	08	562-563
803.23	01	082-084	804.21	01	082-087	805.16	08	551-552	807.15	04	183-185	813.08	08	562-563
803.24	01	082-084	804.22	01	082-087	805.17	08	551-552	807.16	04	183-185	813.10	08	562-563
803.25	01	082-084	804.23	01	082-084	805.18	08	551-552	807.17	04	183-185	813.11	08	562-563
803.26	01	082-084	804.24	01	082-084	805.2	08	551-552	807.18	04	183-185	813.12	08	562-563
803.29	01	082-087	804.25	01	082-084	805.3	08	551-552	807.19	04	183-185	813.13	08	562-563
803.30	01	082-087	804.26	01	082-084	805.4	08	551-552	807.2	04	183-185	813.14	08	562-563

DX	MDC	DRG
813.15	08	562-563
813.16	08	562-563
813.17	08	562-563
813.18	08	562-563
813.20	08	562-563
813.21	08	562-563
813.22	08	562-563
813.23	08	562-563
813.30	08	562-563
813.31	08	562-563
813.32	08	562-563
813.33	08	562-563
813.40	08	562-563
813.41	08	562-563
813.42	08	562-563
813.43	08	562-563
813.44	08	562-563
813.45	08	562-563
813.46	08	562-563
813.47	08	562-563
813.50	08	562-563
813.51	08	562-563
813.52	08	562-563
813.53	08	562-563
813.54	08	562-563
813.80	08	562-563
813.81	08	562-563
813.82	08	562-563
813.83	08	562-563
813.90	08	562-563
813.91	08	562-563
813.92	08	562-563
813.93	08	562-563
814.00	08	562-563
814.01	08	562-563
814.02	08	562-563
814.03	08	562-563
814.04	08	562-563
814.05	08	562-563
814.06	08	562-563
814.07	08	562-563
814.08	08	562-563
814.09	08	562-563
814.10	08	562-563
814.11	08	562-563
814.12	08	562-563
814.13	08	562-563
814.14	08	562-563
814.15	08	562-563
814.16	08	562-563
814.17	08	562-563
814.18	08	562-563
814.19	08	562-563
815.00	08	562-563
815.01	08	562-563
815.02	08	562-563
815.03	08	562-563
815.04	08	562-563
815.09	08	562-563
815.10	08	562-563
815.11	08	562-563
815.12	08	562-563
815.13	08	562-563
815.14	08	562-563
815.19	08	562-563
816.00	08	562-563
816.01	08	562-563
816.02	08	562-563
816.03	08	562-563
816.10	08	562-563
816.11	08	562-563
816.12	08	562-563
816.13	08	562-563
817.0	08	562-563
817.1	08	562-563
818.0	08	562-563
818.1	08	562-563
819.0	21	913-914
819.1	21	913-914
820.00	08	535-536
820.01	08	535-536
820.02	08	535-536
820.03	08	535-536
820.09	08	535-536
820.10	08	535-536
820.11	08	535-536
820.12	08	535-536
820.13	08	535-536
820.19	08	535-536
820.20	08	535-536
820.21	08	535-536
820.22	08	535-536
820.30	08	535-536
820.31	08	535-536
820.32	08	535-536
820.8	08	535-536
820.9	08	535-536
821.00	08	533-534
821.01	08	533-534
821.10	08	533-534
821.11	08	533-534
821.20	08	533-534
821.21	08	533-534
821.22	08	533-534
821.23	08	533-534
821.29	08	533-534
821.30	08	533-534
821.31	08	533-534
821.32	08	533-534
821.33	08	533-534
821.39	08	533-534
822.0	08	562-563
822.1	08	562-563
823.00	08	562-563
823.01	08	562-563
823.02	08	562-563
823.10	08	562-563
823.11	08	562-563
823.12	08	562-563
823.20	08	562-563
823.21	08	562-563
823.22	08	562-563
823.30	08	562-563
823.31	08	562-563
823.32	08	562-563
823.40	08	562-563
823.41	08	562-563
823.42	08	562-563
823.80	08	562-563
823.81	08	562-563
823.82	08	562-563
823.90	08	562-563
823.91	08	562-563
823.92	08	562-563
824.0	08	562-563
824.1	08	562-563
824.2	08	562-563
824.3	08	562-563
824.4	08	562-563
824.5	08	562-563
824.6	08	562-563
824.7	08	562-563
824.8	08	562-563
824.9	08	562-563
825.0	08	562-563
825.1	08	562-563
825.20	08	562-563
825.21	08	562-563
825.22	08	562-563
825.23	08	562-563
825.24	08	562-563
825.25	08	562-563
825.29	08	562-563
825.30	08	562-563
825.31	08	562-563
825.32	08	562-563
825.33	08	562-563
825.34	08	562-563
825.35	08	562-563
825.39	08	562-563
826.0	08	562-563
826.1	08	562-563
827.0	08	562-563
827.1	08	562-563
828.0	21	913-914
828.1	21	913-914
829.0	08	562-563
829.1	08	562-563
830.0	03	157-159
830.1	03	157-159
831.00	08	562-563
831.01	08	562-563
831.02	08	562-563
831.03	08	562-563
831.04	08	562-563
831.09	08	562-563
831.10	08	562-563
831.11	08	562-563
831.12	08	562-563
831.13	08	562-563
831.14	08	562-563
831.19	08	562-563
832.00	08	562-563
832.01	08	562-563
832.02	08	562-563
832.03	08	562-563
832.04	08	562-563
832.09	08	562-563
832.10	08	562-563
832.11	08	562-563
832.12	08	562-563
832.13	08	562-563
832.14	08	562-563
832.19	08	562-563
832.2	08	562-563
833.00	08	562-563
833.01	08	562-563
833.02	08	562-563
833.03	08	562-563
833.04	08	562-563
833.05	08	562-563
833.09	08	562-563
833.10	08	562-563
833.11	08	562-563
833.12	08	562-563
833.13	08	562-563
833.14	08	562-563
833.15	08	562-563
833.19	08	562-563
834.00	08	562-563
834.01	08	562-563
834.02	08	562-563
834.10	08	562-563
834.11	08	562-563
834.12	08	562-563
835.00	08	537-538
835.01	08	537-538
835.02	08	537-538
835.03	08	537-538
835.10	08	537-538
835.11	08	537-538
835.12	08	537-538
835.13	08	537-538
836.0	08	562-563
836.1	08	562-563
836.2	08	562-563
836.3	08	562-563
836.4	08	562-563
836.50	08	562-563
836.51	08	562-563
836.52	08	562-563
836.53	08	562-563
836.54	08	562-563
836.59	08	562-563
836.60	08	562-563
836.61	08	562-563
836.62	08	562-563
836.63	08	562-563
836.64	08	562-563
836.69	08	562-563
837.0	08	562-563
837.1	08	562-563
838.00	08	562-563
838.01	08	562-563
838.02	08	562-563
838.03	08	562-563
838.04	08	562-563
838.05	08	562-563
838.06	08	562-563
838.09	08	562-563
838.10	08	562-563
838.11	08	562-563
838.12	08	562-563
838.13	08	562-563
838.14	08	562-563
838.15	08	562-563
838.16	08	562-563
838.19	08	562-563
839.00	08	551-552
839.01	08	551-552
839.02	08	551-552
839.03	08	551-552
839.04	08	551-552
839.05	08	551-552
839.06	08	551-552
839.07	08	551-552
839.08	08	551-552
839.10	08	551-552
839.11	08	551-552
839.12	08	551-552
839.13	08	551-552
839.14	08	551-552
839.15	08	551-552
839.16	08	551-552
839.17	08	551-552
839.18	08	551-552
839.20	08	551-552
839.21	08	551-552
839.30	08	551-552
839.31	08	551-552
839.40	08	551-552
839.41	08	551-552
839.42	08	551-552
839.49	08	551-552
839.50	08	551-552
839.51	08	551-552
839.52	08	551-552
839.59	08	551-552
839.61	04	183-185
839.69	08	562-563
839.71	04	183-185
839.79	08	562-563
839.8	08	562-563
839.9	08	562-563
840.0	08	562-563
840.1	08	562-563
840.2	08	562-563
840.3	08	562-563
840.4	08	562-563
840.5	08	562-563
840.6	08	562-563
840.7	08	562-563
840.8	08	562-563
840.9	08	562-563
841.0	08	562-563
841.1	08	562-563
841.2	08	562-563
841.3	08	562-563
841.8	08	562-563
841.9	08	562-563
842.00	08	562-563
842.01	08	562-563
842.02	08	562-563
842.09	08	562-563
842.10	08	562-563
842.11	08	562-563
842.12	08	562-563
842.13	08	562-563
842.19	08	562-563
843.0	08	537-538
843.1	08	537-538
843.8	08	537-538
843.9	08	537-538
844.0	08	562-563
844.1	08	562-563
844.2	08	562-563
844.3	08	562-563
844.8	08	562-563
844.9	08	562-563
845.00	08	562-563
845.01	08	562-563
845.02	08	562-563
845.03	08	562-563
845.09	08	562-563
845.10	08	562-563
845.11	08	562-563
845.12	08	562-563
845.13	08	562-563
845.19	08	562-563
846.0	08	551-552
846.1	08	551-552
846.2	08	551-552
846.3	08	551-552
846.8	08	551-552
846.9	08	551-552
847.0	08	551-552
847.1	08	551-552
847.2	08	551-552
847.3	08	551-552
847.4	08	551-552
847.9	08	551-552
848.0	08	564-566
848.1	03	157-159
848.2	08	564-566
848.3	04	205-206
848.40	04	205-206
848.41	04	205-206
848.42	04	205-206
848.49	04	205-206
848.5	08	537-538
848.8	08	562-563
848.9	08	562-563
850.0	01	088-090
850.11	01	088-090
850.12	01	088-090
850.2	01	088-090
850.3	01	088-090
850.4	01	088-090
850.5	01	088-090
850.9	01	088-090
851.00	01	082-087
851.01	01	082-087
851.02	01	082-087
851.03	01	082-084
851.04	01	082-084
851.05	01	082-084
851.06	01	082-084
851.09	01	082-087
851.10	01	082-087
851.11	01	082-087
851.12	01	082-087
851.13	01	082-084
851.14	01	082-084
851.15	01	082-084
851.16	01	082-084

Diagnosis Code/MDC/DRG List

DX	MDC	DRG	DX	MDC	DRG	DX	MDC	DRG	DX	MDC	DRG	DX	MDC	DRG
851.19	01	082-087	852.15	01	082-084	861.11	05	314-316	865.11	16	814-816	873.21	03	154-156
851.20	01	082-087	852.16	01	082-084	861.12	05	314-316	865.12	16	814-816	873.22	03	154-156
851.21	01	082-087	852.19	01	082-087	861.13	05	314-316	865.13	16	814-816	873.23	03	154-156
851.22	01	082-087	852.20	01	082-087	861.20	04	205-206	865.14	16	814-816	873.29	03	154-156
851.23	01	082-084	852.21	01	082-087	861.21	04	205-206	865.19	16	814-816	873.30	03	154-156
851.24	01	082-084	852.22	01	082-087	861.22	04	183-185	866.00	11	698-700	873.31	03	154-156
851.25	01	082-084	852.23	01	082-084	861.30	04	205-206	866.01	11	698-700	873.32	03	154-156
851.26	01	082-084	852.24	01	082-084	861.31	04	205-206	866.02	11	698-700	873.33	03	154-156
851.29	01	082-087	852.25	01	082-084	861.32	04	183-185	866.03	11	698-700	873.39	03	154-156
851.30	01	082-087	852.26	01	082-084	862.0	04	183-185	866.10	11	698-700	873.40	09	604-605
851.31	01	082-084	852.29	01	082-087	862.1	04	183-185	866.11	11	698-700	873.41	09	604-605
851.32	01	082-087	852.30	01	082-087	862.21	04	183-185	866.12	11	698-700	873.42	09	604-605
851.33	01	082-084	852.31	01	082-087	862.22	06	368-370	866.13	11	698-700	873.43	03	157-159
851.34	01	082-084	852.32	01	082-087	862.29	04	205-206	867.0	11	698-700	873.44	03	157-159
851.35	01	082-084	852.33	01	082-084	862.31	04	183-185	867.1	11	698-700	873.49	09	604-605
851.36	01	082-084	852.34	01	082-084	862.32	06	393-395	867.2	11	698-700	873.50	09	604-605
851.39	01	082-087	852.35	01	082-084	862.39	04	205-206	867.3	11	698-700	873.51	09	604-605
851.40	01	082-087	852.36	01	082-084	862.8	21	913-914	867.4	13	760-761	873.52	09	604-605
851.41	01	082-087	852.39	01	082-087	862.9	21	913-914	867.5	13	760-761	873.53	03	157-159
851.42	01	082-087	852.40	01	082-087	863.0	06	393-395	867.6	12	729-730	873.54	03	157-159
851.43	01	082-084	852.41	01	082-087	863.1	06	393-395	867.6	13	760-761	873.59	09	604-605
851.44	01	082-084	852.42	01	082-087	863.20	06	393-395	867.7	12	729-730	873.60	03	157-159
851.45	01	082-087	852.43	01	082-084	863.21	06	393-395	867.7	13	760-761	873.61	03	157-159
851.46	01	082-084	852.44	01	082-084	863.29	06	393-395	867.8	12	729-730	873.62	03	157-159
851.49	01	082-087	852.45	01	082-084	863.30	06	393-395	867.8	13	760-761	873.63	03	157-159
851.50	01	082-087	852.46	01	082-084	863.31	06	393-395	867.9	12	729-730	873.64	03	157-159
851.51	01	082-087	852.49	01	082-087	863.39	06	393-395	867.9	13	760-761	873.65	03	157-159
851.52	01	082-087	852.50	01	082-087	863.40	06	393-395	868.00	06	393-395	873.69	03	157-159
851.53	01	082-084	852.51	01	082-087	863.41	06	393-395	868.01	10	643-645	873.70	03	157-159
851.54	01	082-084	852.52	01	082 087	863.42	06	393-395	868.02	07	444-446	873.71	03	157-159
851.55	01	082-084	852.53	01	082-084	863.43	06	393-395	868.03	06	393-395	873.72	03	157-159
851.56	01	082-087	852.54	01	082-084	863.44	06	393-395	868.04	11	698-700	873.73	03	157-159
851.59	01	082-087	852.55	01	082-084	863.45	06	393-395	868.09	21	913-914	873.74	03	157-159
851.60	01	082-087	852.56	01	082-084	863.46	06	393-395	868.10	06	393-395	873.75	03	157-159
851.61	01	082-087	852.59	01	082-087	863.49	06	393-395	868.11	10	643-645	873.79	03	157-159
851.62	01	082-087	853.00	01	082-087	863.50	06	393-395	868.12	07	444-446	873.8	09	604-605
851.63	01	082-084	853.01	01	082-087	863.51	06	393-395	868.13	06	393-395	873.9	09	604-605
851.64	01	082-084	853.02	01	082-087	863.52	06	393-395	868.14	11	698-700	874.00	03	154-156
851.65	01	082-084	853.03	01	082-084	863.53	06	393-395	868.19	21	913-914	874.01	03	154-156
851.66	01	082-084	853.04	01	082-084	863.54	06	393-395	869.0	21	913-914	874.02	04	183-185
851.69	01	082-087	853.05	01	082-084	863.55	06	393-395	869.1	21	913-914	874.10	03	154-156
851.70	01	082-087	853.06	01	082-084	863.56	06	393-395	870.0	02	124-125	874.11	03	154-156
851.71	01	082-087	853.09	01	082-087	863.59	06	393-395	870.1	02	124-125	874.12	04	183-185
851.72	01	082-087	853.10	01	082-087	863.80	06	393-395	870.2	02	124-125	874.2	10	643-645
851.73	01	082-084	853.11	01	082-087	863.81	07	438-440	870.3	02	124-125	874.3	10	643-645
851.74	01	082-084	853.12	01	082-087	863.82	07	438-440	870.4	02	124-125	874.4	03	154-156
851.75	01	082-084	853.13	01	082-084	863.83	07	438-440	870.8	02	124-125	874.5	03	154-156
851.76	01	082-084	853.14	01	082-084	863.84	07	438-440	870.9	02	124-125	874.8	09	604-605
851.79	01	082-087	853.15	01	082-084	863.85	06	393-395	871.0	02	124-125	874.9	09	604-605
851.80	01	082-087	853.16	01	082-084	863.89	06	393-395	871.1	02	124-125	875.0	09	604-605
851.81	01	082-087	853.19	01	082-087	863.90	06	393-395	871.2	02	124-125	875.1	21	913-914
851.82	01	082-087	854.00	01	082-087	863.91	07	438-440	871.3	02	124-125	876.0	09	604-605
851.83	01	082-084	854.01	01	082-087	863.92	07	438-440	871.4	02	124-125	876.1	09	604-605
851.84	01	082-084	854.02	01	082-087	863.93	07	438-440	871.5	02	124-125	877.0	09	604-605
851.85	01	082-084	854.03	01	082-084	863.94	07	438-440	871.6	02	124-125	877.1	09	604-605
851.86	01	082-084	854.04	01	082-084	863.95	06	393-395	871.7	02	124-125	878.0	12	729-730
851.89	01	082-087	854.05	01	082-084	863.99	06	393-395	871.9	02	124-125	878.1	12	729-730
851.90	01	082-087	854.06	01	082-084	864.00	07	441-443	872.00	03	154-156	878.2	12	729-730
851.91	01	082-087	854.09	01	082-087	864.01	07	441-443	872.01	03	154-156	878.3	12	729-730
851.92	01	082-087	854.10	01	082-087	864.02	07	441-443	872.02	03	154-156	878.4	13	760-761
851.93	01	082-084	854.11	01	082-087	864.03	07	441-443	872.10	03	154-156	878.5	13	760-761
851.94	01	082-084	854.12	01	082-087	864.04	07	441-443	872.11	03	154-156	878.6	13	760-761
851.95	01	082-084	854.13	01	082-084	864.05	07	441-443	872.12	03	154-156	878.7	13	760-761
851.96	01	082-084	854.14	01	082-084	864.09	07	441-443	872.61	03	154-156	878.8	12	729-730
851.99	01	082-087	854.15	01	082-084	864.10	07	441-443	872.62	03	154-156	878.8	13	760-761
852.00	01	082-087	854.16	01	082-084	864.11	07	441-443	872.63	03	154-156	878.9	12	729-730
852.01	01	082-087	854.19	01	082-087	864.12	07	441-443	872.64	03	154-156	878.9	13	760-761
852.02	01	082-087	860.0	04	199-201	864.13	07	441-443	872.69	03	154-156	879.0	09	604-605
852.03	01	082-084	860.1	04	199-201	864.14	07	441-443	872.71	03	154-156	879.1	09	604-605
852.04	01	082-084	860.2	04	199-201	864.15	07	441-443	872.72	03	154-156	879.2	09	604-605
852.05	01	082-084	860.3	04	199-201	864.19	07	441-443	872.73	03	154-156	879.3	21	913-914
852.06	01	082-084	860.4	04	199-201	865.00	16	814-816	872.74	03	154-156	879.4	09	604-605
852.09	01	082-087	860.5	04	199-201	865.01	16	814-816	872.79	03	154-156	879.5	21	913-914
852.10	01	082-087	861.00	05	314-316	865.02	16	814-816	872.8	03	154-156	879.6	09	604-605
852.11	01	082-087	861.01	05	314-316	865.03	16	814-816	872.9	03	154-156	879.7	21	913-914
852.12	01	082-087	861.02	05	314-316	865.04	16	814-816	873.0	09	604-605	879.8	09	604-605
852.13	01	082-084	861.03	05	314-316	865.09	16	814-816	873.1	09	604-605	879.9	21	913-914
852.14	01	082-084	861.10	05	314-316	865.10	16	814-816	873.20	03	154-156	880.00	09	604-605

DX	MDC	DRG	DX	MDC	DRG	DX	MDC	DRG	DX	MDC	DRG	DX	MDC	DRG
880.01	09	604-605	900.1	21	913-914	904.9	21	913-914	913.4	09	606-607	923.01	09	604-605
880.02	09	604-605	900.81	21	913-914	905.0	01	091-093	913.5	09	602-603	923.02	09	604-605
880.03	09	604-605	900.82	21	913-914	905.1	08	551-552	913.6	09	604-605	923.03	09	604-605
880.09	09	604-605	900.89	21	913-914	905.2	08	559-561	913.7	09	602-603	923.09	09	604-605
880.10	21	913-914	900.9	21	913-914	905.3	08	559-561	913.8	09	604-605	923.10	09	604-605
880.11	21	913-914	901.0	21	913-914	905.4	08	559-561	913.9	09	602-603	923.11	09	604-605
880.12	21	913-914	901.1	21	913-914	905.5	08	559-561	914.0	09	604-605	923.20	09	604-605
880.13	21	913-914	901.2	21	913-914	905.6	08	562-563	914.1	09	602-603	923.21	09	604-605
880.19	21	913-914	901.3	21	913-914	905.7	08	562-563	914.2	09	606-607	923.3	09	604-605
880.20	08	564-566	901.40	21	913-914	905.8	08	559-561	914.3	09	602-603	923.8	09	604-605
880.21	08	564-566	901.41	21	913-914	905.9	08	559-561	914.4	09	606-607	923.9	09	604-605
880.22	08	564-566	901.42	21	913-914	906.0	09	604-605	914.5	09	602-603	924.00	09	604-605
880.23	08	564-566	901.81	21	913-914	906.1	09	604-605	914.6	09	604-605	924.01	09	604-605
880.29	08	564-566	901.82	21	913-914	906.2	09	604-605	914.7	09	602-603	924.10	09	604-605
881.00	09	604-605	901.83	21	913-914	906.3	09	604-605	914.8	09	604-605	924.11	09	604-605
881.01	09	604-605	901.89	21	913-914	906.4	09	604-605	914.9	09	602-603	924.20	09	604-605
881.02	09	604-605	901.9	21	913-914	906.5	09	604-605	915.0	09	604-605	924.21	09	604-605
881.10	21	913-914	902.0	21	913-914	906.6	09	604-605	915.1	09	602-603	924.3	09	604-605
881.11	21	913-914	902.10	21	913-914	906.7	09	604-605	915.2	09	606-607	924.4	09	604-605
881.12	21	913-914	902.11	21	913-914	906.8	09	604-605	915.3	09	602-603	924.5	09	604-605
881.20	08	564-566	902.19	21	913-914	906.9	09	604-605	915.4	09	606-607	924.8	09	604-605
881.21	08	564-566	902.20	21	913-914	907.0	01	091-093	915.5	09	602-603	924.9	09	604-605
881.22	08	564-566	902.21	21	913-914	907.1	01	091-093	915.6	09	604-605	925.1	21	913-914
882.0	09	604-605	902.22	21	913-914	907.2	01	052-053	915.7	09	602-603	925.2	21	913-914
882.1	21	913-914	902.23	21	913-914	907.3	01	091-093	915.8	09	604-605	926.0	12	729-730
882.2	08	564-566	902.24	21	913-914	907.4	01	091-093	915.9	09	602-603	926.0	13	760-761
883.0	09	604-605	902.25	21	913-914	907.5	01	091-093	916.0	09	604-605	926.11	21	913-914
883.1	21	913-914	902.26	21	913-914	907.9	01	091-093	916.1	09	602-603	926.12	21	913-914
883.2	08	564-566	902.27	21	913-914	908.0	04	205-206	916.2	09	606-607	926.19	21	913-914
884.0	09	604-605	902.29	21	913-914	908.1	06	393-395	916.3	09	602-603	926.8	21	913-914
884.1	21	913-914	902.31	21	913-914	908.2	12	729-730	916.4	09	606-607	926.9	21	913-914
884.2	08	564-566	902.32	21	913-914	908.2	13	760-761	916.5	09	602-603	927.00	21	913-914
885.0	21	913-914	902.33	21	913-914	908.3	05	299-301	916.6	09	604-605	927.01	21	913-914
885.1	21	913-914	902.34	21	913-914	908.4	05	299-301	916.7	09	602-603	927.02	21	913-914
886.0	21	913-914	902.39	21	913-914	908.5	21	913-914	916.8	09	604-605	927.03	21	913-914
886.1	21	913-914	902.40	21	913-914	908.6	21	913-914	916.9	09	602-603	927.09	21	913-914
887.0	21	913-914	902.41	21	913-914	908.9	21	913-914	917.0	09	604-605	927.10	21	913-914
887.1	21	913-914	902.42	21	913-914	909.0	21	922-923	917.1	09	602-603	927.11	21	913-914
887.2	21	913-914	902.49	21	913-914	909.1	21	922-923	917.2	09	606-607	927.20	21	913-914
887.3	21	913-914	902.50	21	913-914	909.2	21	922-923	917.3	09	602-603	927.21	21	913-914
887.4	21	913-914	902.51	21	913-914	909.3	21	922-923	917.4	09	606-607	927.3	21	913-914
887.5	21	913-914	902.52	21	913-914	909.4	21	922-923	917.5	09	602-603	927.8	21	913-914
887.6	21	913-914	902.53	21	913-914	909.9	21	922-923	917.6	09	604-605	927.9	21	913-914
887.7	21	913-914	902.54	21	913-914	910.0	09	604-605	917.7	09	602-603	928.00	21	913-914
890.0	09	604-605	902.55	21	913-914	910.1	09	602-603	917.8	09	604-605	928.01	21	913-914
890.1	21	913-914	902.56	21	913-914	910.2	09	606-607	917.9	09	602-603	928.10	21	913-914
890.2	08	564-566	902.59	21	913-914	910.3	09	606-607	918.0	02	124-125	928.11	21	913-914
891.0	09	604-605	902.81	21	913-914	910.4	09	606-607	918.1	02	124-125	928.20	21	913-914
891.1	21	913-914	902.82	21	913-914	910.5	09	602-603	918.2	02	124-125	928.21	21	913-914
891.2	08	564-566	902.87	21	913-914	910.6	09	604-605	918.9	02	124-125	928.3	21	913-914
892.0	09	604-605	902.89	21	913-914	910.7	09	602-603	919.0	09	604-605	928.8	21	913-914
892.1	21	913-914	902.9	21	913-914	910.8	09	604-605	919.1	09	602-603	928.9	21	913-914
892.2	08	564-566	903.00	21	913-914	910.9	09	602-603	919.2	09	606-607	929.0	21	913-914
893.0	09	604-605	903.01	21	913-914	911.0	09	604-605	919.3	09	602-603	929.9	21	913-914
893.1	21	913-914	903.02	21	913-914	911.1	09	602-603	919.4	09	606-607	930.0	02	124-125
893.2	08	564-566	903.1	21	913-914	911.2	09	606-607	919.5	09	602-603	930.1	02	124-125
894.0	09	604-605	903.2	21	913-914	911.3	09	602-603	919.6	09	604-605	930.2	02	124-125
894.1	21	913-914	903.3	21	913-914	911.4	09	606-607	919.7	09	602-603	930.8	02	124-125
894.2	08	564-566	903.4	21	913-914	911.5	09	602-603	919.8	09	604-605	930.9	02	124-125
895.0	21	913-914	903.5	21	913-914	911.6	09	604-605	919.9	09	602-603	931	03	154-156
895.1	21	913-914	903.8	21	913-914	911.7	09	602-603	920.	09	604-605	932	03	154-156
896.0	21	913-914	903.9	21	913-914	911.8	09	604-605	921.0	02	124-125	933.0	03	154-156
896.1	21	913-914	904.0	21	913-914	911.9	09	602-603	921.1	02	124-125	933.1	03	154-156
896.2	21	913-914	904.1	21	913-914	912.0	09	604-605	921.2	02	124-125	934.0	04	205-206
896.3	21	913-914	904.2	21	913-914	912.1	09	602-603	921.3	02	124-125	934.1	04	205-206
897.0	21	913-914	904.3	21	913-914	912.2	09	604-605	921.9	02	124-125	934.8	04	205-206
897.1	21	913-914	904.40	21	913-914	912.3	09	602-603	922.0	09	604-605	934.9	04	205-206
897.2	21	913-914	904.41	21	913-914	912.4	09	606-607	922.1	09	604-605	935.0	03	157-159
897.3	21	913-914	904.42	21	913-914	912.5	09	602-603	922.2	09	604-605	935.1	06	393-395
897.4	21	913-914	904.50	21	913-914	912.6	09	604-605	922.31	09	604-605	935.2	06	393-395
897.5	21	913-914	904.51	21	913-914	912.7	09	602-603	922.32	09	604-605	936	06	393-395
897.6	21	913-914	904.52	21	913-914	912.8	09	604-605	922.33	09	604-605	937	06	393-395
897.7	21	913-914	904.53	21	913-914	912.9	09	602-603	922.4	12	729-730	938	06	393-395
900.00	21	913-914	904.54	21	913-914	913.0	09	604-605	922.4	13	760-761	939.0	11	698-700
900.01	21	913-914	904.6	21	913-914	913.1	09	602-603	922.8	09	604-605	939.1	13	760-761
900.02	21	913-914	904.7	21	913-914	913.2	09	606-607	922.9	09	604-605	939.2	13	760-761
900.03	21	913-914	904.8	21	913-914	913.3	09	602-603	923.00	09	604-605	939.3	12	729-730

Diagnosis Code/MDC/DRG List

DX	MDC	DRG	DX	MDC	DRG	DX	MDC	DRG	DX	MDC	DRG	DX	MDC	DRG
939.9	11	698-700	942.13	22	935	943.56	22	933-934	945.26	22	935	948.83	22	933
940.0	02	124-125	942.14	22	935	943.59	22	933-934	945.29	22	935	948.84	22	933
940.1	02	124-125	942.15	22	935	944.00	22	935	945.30	22	933-934	948.85	22	933
940.2	02	124-125	942.19	22	935	944.01	22	935	945.31	22	933-934	948.86	22	933
940.3	02	124-125	942.20	22	935	944.02	22	935	945.32	22	933-934	948.87	22	933
940.4	02	124-125	942.21	22	935	944.03	22	935	945.33	22	933-934	948.88	22	933
940.5	02	124-125	942.22	22	935	944.04	22	935	945.34	22	933-934	948.90	22	935
940.9	02	124-125	942.23	22	935	944.05	22	935	945.35	22	933-934	948.91	22	933
941.00	22	935	942.24	22	935	944.06	22	935	945.36	22	933-934	948.92	22	933
941.01	22	935	942.25	22	935	944.07	22	935	945.39	22	933-934	948.93	22	933
941.02	02	124-125	942.29	22	935	944.08	22	935	945.40	22	933-934	948.94	22	933
941.03	22	935	942.30	22	933-934	944.10	22	935	945.41	22	933-934	948.95	22	933
941.04	22	935	942.31	22	933-934	944.11	22	935	945.42	22	933-934	948.96	22	933
941.05	22	935	942.32	22	933-934	944.12	22	935	945.43	22	933-934	948.97	22	933
941.06	22	935	942.33	22	933-934	944.13	22	935	945.44	22	933-934	948.98	22	933
941.07	22	935	942.34	22	933-934	944.14	22	935	945.45	22	933-934	948.99	22	933
941.08	22	935	942.35	22	933-934	944.15	22	935	945.46	22	933-934	949.0	22	935
941.09	22	935	942.39	22	933-934	944.16	22	935	945.49	22	933-934	949.1	22	935
941.10	22	935	942.40	22	933-934	944.17	22	935	945.50	22	933-934	949.2	22	935
941.11	22	935	942.41	22	933-934	944.18	22	935	945.51	22	933-934	949.3	22	933-934
941.12	02	124-125	942.42	22	933-934	944.20	22	935	945.52	22	933-934	949.4	22	933-934
941.13	22	935	942.43	22	933-934	944.21	22	935	945.53	22	933-934	949.5	22	933-934
941.14	22	935	942.44	22	933-934	944.22	22	935	945.54	22	933-934	950.0	02	124-125
941.15	22	935	942.45	22	933-934	944.23	22	935	945.55	22	933-934	950.1	01	091-093
941.16	22	935	942.49	22	933-934	944.24	22	935	945.56	22	933-934	950.2	01	091-093
941.17	22	935	942.50	22	933-934	944.25	22	935	945.59	22	933-934	950.3	01	091-093
941.18	22	935	942.51	22	933-934	944.26	22	935	946.0	22	935	950.9	01	091-093
941.19	22	935	942.52	22	933-934	944.27	22	935	946.1	22	935	951.0	01	073-074
941.20	22	935	942.53	22	933-934	944.28	22	935	946.2	22	935	951.1	01	073-074
941.21	22	935	942.54	22	933-934	944.30	22	933-934	946.3	22	933-934	951.2	01	073-074
941.22	02	124-125	942.55	22	933-934	944.31	22	933-934	946.4	22	933-934	951.3	01	073-074
941.23	22	935	942.59	22	933-934	944.32	22	933-934	946.5	22	933-934	951.4	01	073-074
941.24	22	935	943.00	22	935	944.33	22	933-934	947.0	03	154-156	951.5	03	154-156
941.25	22	935	943.01	22	935	944.34	22	933-934	947.1	04	205-206	951.6	01	073-074
941.26	22	935	943.02	22	935	944.35	22	933-934	947.2	06	368-370	951.7	01	073-074
941.27	22	935	943.03	22	935	944.36	22	933-934	947.3	06	393-395	951.8	01	073-074
941.28	22	935	943.04	22	935	944.37	22	933-934	947.4	13	760-761	951.9	01	073-074
941.29	22	935	943.05	22	935	944.38	22	933-934	947.8	22	935	952.00	01	052-053
941.30	22	933-934	943.06	22	935	944.40	22	933-934	947.9	22	935	952.01	01	052-053
941.31	22	933-934	943.09	22	935	944.41	22	933-934	948.00	22	935	952.02	01	052-053
941.32	02	124-125	943.10	22	935	944.42	22	933-934	948.10	22	935	952.03	01	052-053
941.33	22	933-934	943.11	22	935	944.43	22	933-934	948.11	22	933-934	952.04	01	052-053
941.34	22	933-934	943.12	22	935	944.44	22	933-934	948.20	22	935	952.05	01	052-053
941.35	22	933-934	943.13	22	935	944.45	22	933-934	948.21	22	933	952.06	01	052-053
941.36	22	933-934	943.14	22	935	944.46	22	933-934	948.22	22	933	952.07	01	052-053
941.37	22	933-934	943.15	22	935	944.47	22	933-934	948.30	22	935	952.08	01	052-053
941.38	22	933-934	943.16	22	935	944.48	22	933-934	948.31	22	933	952.09	01	052-053
941.39	22	933-934	943.19	22	935	944.50	22	933-934	948.32	22	933	952.10	01	052-053
941.40	22	933-934	943.20	22	935	944.51	22	933-934	948.33	22	933	952.11	01	052-053
941.41	22	933-934	943.21	22	935	944.52	22	933-934	948.40	22	935	952.12	01	052-053
941.42	02	124-125	943.22	22	935	944.53	22	933-934	948.41	22	933	952.13	01	052-053
941.43	22	933-934	943.23	22	935	944.54	22	933-934	948.42	22	933	952.14	01	052-053
941.44	22	933-934	943.24	22	935	944.55	22	933-934	948.43	22	933	952.15	01	052-053
941.45	22	933-934	943.25	22	935	944.56	22	933-934	948.44	22	933	952.16	01	052-053
941.46	22	933-934	943.26	22	935	944.57	22	933-934	948.50	22	935	952.17	01	052-053
941.47	22	933-934	943.29	22	935	944.58	22	933-934	948.51	22	933	952.18	01	052-053
941.48	22	933-934	943.30	22	933-934	945.00	22	935	948.52	22	933	952.19	01	052-053
941.49	22	933-934	943.31	22	933-934	945.01	22	935	948.53	22	933	952.2	01	052-053
941.50	22	933-934	943.32	22	933-934	945.02	22	935	948.54	22	933	952.3	01	052-053
941.51	22	933-934	943.33	22	933-934	945.03	22	935	948.55	22	933	952.4	01	052-053
941.52	02	124-125	943.34	22	933-934	945.04	22	935	948.60	22	935	952.8	01	052-053
941.53	22	933-934	943.35	22	933-934	945.05	22	935	948.61	22	933	952.9	01	052-053
941.54	22	933-934	943.36	22	933-934	945.06	22	935	948.62	22	933	953.0	01	073-074
941.55	22	933-934	943.39	22	933-934	945.09	22	935	948.63	22	933	953.1	01	073-074
941.56	22	933-934	943.40	22	933-934	945.10	22	935	948.64	22	933	953.2	01	073-074
941.57	22	933-934	943.41	22	933-934	945.11	22	935	948.65	22	933	953.3	01	073-074
941.58	22	933-934	943.42	22	933-934	945.12	22	935	948.66	22	933	953.4	01	073-074
941.59	22	933-934	943.43	22	933-934	945.13	22	935	948.70	22	935	953.5	01	073-074
942.00	22	935	943.44	22	933-934	945.14	22	935	948.71	22	933	953.8	01	073-074
942.01	22	935	943.45	22	933-934	945.15	22	935	948.72	22	933	953.9	01	073-074
942.02	22	935	943.46	22	933-934	945.16	22	935	948.73	22	933	954.0	01	073-074
942.03	22	935	943.49	22	933-934	945.19	22	935	948.74	22	933	954.1	01	073-074
942.04	22	935	943.50	22	933-934	945.20	22	935	948.75	22	933	954.8	01	073-074
942.05	22	935	943.51	22	933-934	945.21	22	935	948.76	22	933	954.9	01	073-074
942.09	22	935	943.52	22	933-934	945.22	22	935	948.77	22	933	955.0	01	073-074
942.10	22	935	943.53	22	933-934	945.23	22	935	948.80	22	935	955.1	01	073-074
942.11	22	935	943.54	22	933-934	945.24	22	935	948.81	22	933	955.2	01	073-074
942.12	22	935	943.55	22	933-934	945.25	22	935	948.82	22	933	955.3	01	073-074

DX....	MDC.....	DRG	DX....	MDC.....	DRG	DX....	MDC.....	DRG	DX....	MDC.....	DRG	DX....	MDC.....	DRG
955.4	01	073-074	963.0	21	917-918	971.0	21	917-918	980.1	21	917-918	992.8	21	922-923
955.5	01	073-074	963.1	21	917-918	971.1	21	917-918	980.2	21	917-918	992.9	21	922-923
955.6	01	073-074	963.2	21	917-918	971.2	21	917-918	980.3	21	917-918	993.0	03	152-153
955.7	01	073-074	963.3	21	917-918	971.3	21	917-918	980.8	21	917-918	993.1	03	152-153
955.8	01	073-074	963.4	21	917-918	971.9	21	917-918	980.9	21	917-918	993.2	21	922-923
955.9	01	073-074	963.5	21	917-918	972.0	21	917-918	981	21	917-918	993.3	21	922-923
956.0	01	073-074	963.8	21	917-918	972.1	21	917-918	982.0	21	917-918	993.4	21	922-923
956.1	01	073-074	963.9	21	917-918	972.2	21	917-918	982.1	21	917-918	993.8	21	922-923
956.2	01	073-074	964.0	21	917-918	972.3	21	917-918	982.2	21	917-918	993.9	21	922-923
956.3	01	073-074	964.1	21	917-918	972.4	21	917-918	982.3	21	917-918	994.0	21	922-923
956.4	01	073-074	964.2	21	917-918	972.5	21	917-918	982.4	21	917-918	994.1	21	922-923
956.5	01	073-074	964.3	21	917-918	972.6	21	917-918	982.8	21	917-918	994.2	21	922-923
956.8	01	073-074	964.4	21	917-918	972.7	21	917-918	983.0	21	917-918	994.3	21	922-923
956.9	01	073-074	964.5	21	917-918	972.8	21	917-918	983.1	21	917-918	994.4	21	922-923
957.0	01	073-074	964.6	21	917-918	972.9	21	917-918	983.2	21	917-918	994.5	21	922-923
957.1	01	073-074	964.7	21	917-918	973.0	21	917-918	983.9	21	917-918	994.6	03	149
957.8	01	073-074	964.8	21	917-918	973.1	21	917-918	984.0	21	917-918	994.7	21	922-923
957.9	01	073-074	964.9	21	917-918	973.2	21	917-918	984.1	21	917-918	994.8	21	922-923
958.0	04	175-176	965.00	21	917-918	973.3	21	917-918	984.8	21	917-918	994.9	21	922-923
958.1	04	175-176	965.01	21	917-918	973.4	21	917-918	984.9	21	917-918	995.0	21	915-916
958.2	21	922-923	965.02	21	917-918	973.5	21	917-918	985.0	21	917-918	995.1	21	915-916
958.3	18	862-863	965.09	21	917-918	973.6	21	917-918	985.1	21	917-918	995.20	21	917-918
958.4	21	922-923	965.1	21	917-918	973.8	21	917-918	985.2	21	917-918	995.21	21	917-918
958.5	11	682-684	965.4	21	917-918	973.9	21	917-918	985.3	21	917-918	995.22	21	917-918
958.6	08	564-566	965.5	21	917-918	974.0	21	917-918	985.4	21	917-918	995.23	21	917-918
958.7	04	199-201	965.61	21	917-918	974.1	21	917-918	985.5	21	917-918	995.24	21	917-918
958.8	21	922-923	965.69	21	917-918	974.2	21	917-918	985.6	21	917-918	995.27	21	917-918
958.90	21	922-923	965.7	21	917-918	974.3	21	917-918	985.8	21	917-918	995.29	21	917-918
958.91	21	922-923	965.8	21	917-918	974.4	21	917-918	985.9	21	917-918	995.3	21	915-916
958.92	21	922-923	965.9	21	917-918	974.5	21	917-918	986	21	917-918	995.4	21	922-923
958.93	21	922-923	966.0	21	917-918	974.6	21	917-918	987.0	21	917-918	995.50	21	922-923
958.99	21	922-923	966.1	21	917-918	974.7	21	917-918	987.1	21	917-918	995.51	21	922-923
959.01	21	913-914	966.2	21	917-918	975.0	21	917-918	987.2	21	917-918	995.52	21	922-923
959.09	21	913-914	966.3	21	917-918	975.1	21	917-918	987.3	21	917-918	995.53	21	922-923
959.11	21	913-914	966.4	21	917-918	975.2	21	917-918	987.4	21	917-918	995.54	21	922-923
959.12	21	913-914	967.0	21	917-918	975.3	21	917-918	987.5	21	917-918	995.55	21	922-923
959.13	21	913-914	967.1	21	917-918	975.4	21	917-918	987.6	21	917-918	995.59	21	922-923
959.14	21	913-914	967.2	21	917-918	975.5	21	917-918	987.7	21	917-918	995.60	21	915-916
959.19	21	913-914	967.3	21	917-918	975.6	21	917-918	987.8	21	917-918	995.61	21	915-916
959.2	21	913-914	967.4	21	917-918	975.7	21	917-918	987.9	21	917-918	995.62	21	915-916
959.3	21	913-914	967.5	21	917-918	975.8	21	917-918	988.0	21	917-918	995.63	21	915-916
959.4	21	913-914	967.6	21	917-918	976.0	21	917-918	988.1	21	917-918	995.64	21	915-916
959.5	21	913-914	967.8	21	917-918	976.1	21	917-918	988.2	21	917-918	995.65	21	915-916
959.6	21	913-914	967.9	21	917-918	976.2	21	917-918	988.8	21	917-918	995.66	21	915-916
959.7	21	913-914	968.0	21	917-918	976.3	21	917-918	989.0	21	917-918	995.67	21	915-916
959.8	21	913-914	968.1	21	917-918	976.4	21	917-918	989.1	21	917-918	995.68	21	915-916
959.9	21	913-914	968.2	21	917-918	976.5	02	124-125	989.2	21	917-918	995.69	21	915-916
960.0	21	917-918	968.3	21	917-918	976.6	21	917-918	989.3	21	917-918	995.7	21	922-923
960.1	21	917-918	968.4	21	917-918	976.7	21	917-918	989.4	21	917-918	995.80	21	922-923
960.2	21	917-918	968.5	21	917-918	976.8	21	917-918	989.5	21	917-918	995.81	21	922-923
960.3	21	917-918	968.6	21	917-918	976.9	21	917-918	989.6	21	917-918	995.82	21	922-923
960.4	21	917-918	968.7	21	917-918	977.0	21	917-918	989.7	21	917-918	995.83	21	922-923
960.5	21	917-918	968.9	21	917-918	977.1	21	917-918	989.81	21	917-918	995.84	21	922-923
960.6	21	917-918	969.00	21	917-918	977.2	21	917-918	989.82	21	917-918	995.85	21	922-923
960.7	21	917-918	969.01	21	917-918	977.3	21	917-918	989.83	21	917-918	995.86	21	922-923
960.8	21	917-918	969.02	21	917-918	977.4	21	917-918	989.84	21	917-918	995.89	21	922-923
960.9	21	917-918	969.03	21	917-918	977.8	21	917-918	989.89	21	917-918	995.90	18	870-872
961.0	21	917-918	969.04	21	917-918	977.9	21	917-918	989.9	21	917-918	995.91	18	870-872
961.1	21	917-918	969.05	21	917-918	978.0	21	917-918	990	21	922-923	995.92	18	870-872
961.2	21	917-918	969.09	21	917-918	978.1	21	917-918	991.0	21	922-923	995.93	18	870-872
961.3	21	917-918	969.1	21	917-918	978.2	21	917-918	991.1	21	922-923	995.94	18	870-872
961.4	21	917-918	969.2	21	917-918	978.3	21	917-918	991.2	21	922-923	996.00	05	314-316
961.5	21	917-918	969.3	21	917-918	978.4	21	917-918	991.3	21	922-923	996.01	05	308-310
961.6	21	917-918	969.4	21	917-918	978.5	21	917-918	991.4	21	922-923	996.02	05	306-307
961.7	21	917-918	969.5	21	917-918	978.6	21	917-918	991.5	21	922-923	996.03	05	314-316
961.8	21	917-918	969.6	21	917-918	978.8	21	917-918	991.6	21	922-923	996.04	05	308-310
961.9	21	917-918	969.70	21	917-918	978.9	21	917-918	991.8	21	922-923	996.09	05	314-316
962.0	21	917-918	969.71	21	917-918	979.0	21	917-918	991.9	21	922-923	996.1	05	314-316
962.1	21	917-918	969.72	21	917-918	979.1	21	917-918	992.0	21	922-923	996.2	01	091-093
962.2	21	917-918	969.73	21	917-918	979.2	21	917-918	992.1	21	922-923	996.30	11	698-700
962.3	21	917-918	969.79	21	917-918	979.3	21	917-918	992.2	21	922-923	996.31	11	698-700
962.4	21	917-918	969.8	21	917-918	979.4	21	917-918	992.3	21	922-923	996.32	13	760-761
962.5	21	917-918	969.9	21	917-918	979.5	21	917-918	992.4	21	922-923	996.39	11	698-700
962.6	21	917-918	970.0	21	917-918	979.6	21	917-918	992.5	21	922-923	996.40	08	559-561
962.7	21	917-918	970.1	21	917-918	979.7	21	917-918	992.6	21	922-923	996.41	08	559-561
962.8	21	917-918	970.8	21	917-918	979.9	21	917-918	992.7	21	922-923	996.42	08	559-561
962.9	21	917-918	970.9	21	917-918	980.0	21	917-918				996.43	08	559-561

DX	MDC	DRG
996.44	08	559-561
996.45	08	559-561
996.46	08	559-561
996.47	08	559-561
996.49	08	559-561
996.51	02	124-125
996.52	21	919-921
996.53	02	124-125
996.54	09	600-601
996.55	21	919-921
996.56	21	919-921
996.57	21	919-921
996.59	21	919-921
996.60	21	919-921
996.61	05	314-316
996.62	05	314-316
996.63	01	091-093
996.64	11	698-700
996.65	11	698-700
996.66	08	559-561
996.67	08	559-561
996.68	21	919-921
996.69	21	919-921
996.70	21	919-921
996.71	05	314-316
996.72	05	314-315
996.73	05	314-316
996.74	05	314-316
996.75	01	091-093
996.76	11	698-700
996.77	08	559-561
996.78	08	559-561
996.79	21	919-921
996.80	21	919-921
996.81	11	698-700
996.82	07	441-443
996.83	05	314-316
996.84	04	205-206
996.85	16	808-810
996.86	07	438-440
996.87	21	919-921
996.89	21	919-921
996.90	08	559-561
996.91	08	559-561
996.92	08	559-561
996.93	08	559-561
996.94	08	559-561
996.95	08	559-561
996.96	08	559-561
996.99	08	559-561
997.00	01	091-093
997.01	01	091-093
997.02	01	091-093
997.09	01	091-093
997.1	05	314-316
997.2	05	299-301
997.31	04	205-206
997.39	04	205-206
997.4	06	393-395
997.5	11	698-700
997.60	08	564-566
997.61	08	564-566
997.62	08	564-566
997.69	08	564-566
997.71	06	393-395
997.72	11	698-700
997.79	05	299-301
997.91	21	919-921
997.99	21	919-921
998.0	21	919-921
998.11	21	919-921
998.12	21	919-921
998.13	21	919-921
998.2	21	919-921
998.30	21	919-921
998.31	21	919-921
998.32	21	919-921
998.33	21	919-921

DX	MDC	DRG
998.4	21	919-921
998.51	18	862-863
998.59	18	862-863
998.6	21	919-921
998.7	21	919-921
998.81	21	919-921
998.82	02	124-125
998.83	21	919-921
998.89	21	919-921
998.9	21	919-921
999.0	18	865-866
999.1	04	175-176
999.2	05	314-316
999.31	05	314-316
999.39	18	867-869
999.4	21	915-916
999.5	21	915-916
999.6	16	811-812
999.7	16	811-812
999.81	05	314-316
999.82	05	314-316
999.88	05	314-316
999.89	16	811-812
999.9	21	919-920

Supplementary Classification of Factors Influencing Health Status and Contact with Health Services

DX	MDC	DRG
V01.0	23	951
V01.1	23	951
V01.2	23	951
V01.3	23	951
V01.4	23	951
V01.5	23	951
V01.6	23	951
V01.71	23	951
V01.79	23	951
V01.81	15	795
V01.81	23	951
V01.83	23	951
V01.84	23	951
V01.89	23	951
V01.9	23	951
V02.0	23	951
V02.1	23	951
V02.2	23	951
V02.3	23	951
V02.4	23	951
V02.51	23	951
V02.52	23	951
V02.53	23	951
V02.54	23	951
V02.59	23	951
V02.60	07	441-443
V02.61	07	441-443
V02.62	07	441-443
V02.69	07	441-443
V02.7	23	951
V02.8	23	951
V02.9	23	951
V03.0	23	951
V03.1	23	951
V03.2	23	951
V03.3	23	951
V03.4	23	951
V03.5	23	951
V03.6	23	951
V03.7	23	951
V03.81	23	951
V03.82	23	951
V03.89	23	951
V03.9	23	951
V04.0	23	951
V04.1	23	951
V04.2	23	951
V04.3	23	951

DX	MDC	DRG
V04.4	23	951
V04.5	23	951
V04.6	23	951
V04.7	23	951
V04.81	23	951
V04.82	23	951
V04.89	23	951
V05.0	23	951
V05.1	23	951
V05.2	23	951
V05.3	23	951
V05.4	23	951
V05.8	23	951
V05.9	23	951
V06.0	23	951
V06.1	23	951
V06.2	23	951
V06.3	23	951
V06.4	23	951
V06.5	23	951
V06.6	23	951
V06.8	23	951
V06.9	23	951
V07.0	23	951
V07.1	23	951
V07.2	23	951
V07.31	23	951
V07.39	23	951
V07.4	23	951
V07.51	23	951
V07.52	23	951
V07.59	23	951
V07.8	23	951
V07.9	23	951
V08	18	865-866
V09.0	18	867-869
V09.1	18	867-869
V09.2	18	867-869
V09.3	18	867-869
V09.4	18	867-869
V09.50	18	867-869
V09.51	18	867-869
V09.6	18	867-869
V09.70	18	867-869
V09.71	18	867-869
V09.80	18	867-869
V09.90	18	867-869
V09.91	18	867-869
V10.00	17	843-845
V10.01	17	843-845
V10.02	17	843-845
V10.03	17	843-845
V10.04	17	843-845
V10.05	17	843-845
V10.06	17	843-845
V10.07	17	843-845
V10.09	17	843-845
V10.11	17	843-845
V10.12	17	843-845
V10.20	17	843-845
V10.21	17	843-845
V10.22	17	843-845
V10.29	17	843-845
V10.3	17	843-845
V10.40	17	843-845
V10.41	17	843-845
V10.42	17	843-845
V10.43	17	843-845
V10.44	17	843-845
V10.45	17	843-845
V10.46	17	843-845
V10.47	17	843-845
V10.48	17	843-845
V10.49	17	843-845
V10.50	17	843-845
V10.51	17	843-845
V10.52	17	843-845

DX	MDC	DRG
V10.53	17	843-845
V10.59	17	843-845
V10.60	17	843-845
V10.61	17	843-845
V10.62	17	843-845
V10.63	17	843-845
V10.69	17	843-845
V10.71	17	843-845
V10.72	17	843-845
V10.79	17	843-845
V10.81	17	843-845
V10.82	17	843-845
V10.83	17	843-845
V10.84	17	843-845
V10.85	17	843-845
V10.86	17	843-845
V10.87	17	843-845
V10.88	17	843-845
V10.89	17	843-845
V10.90	17	843-845
V10.91	17	843-845
V11.0	23	951
V11.1	23	951
V11.2	23	951
V11.3	23	951
V11.8	23	951
V11.9	23	951
V12.00	23	951
V12.01	23	951
V12.02	23	951
V12.03	23	951
V12.04	23	951
V12.09	23	951
V12.1	23	951
V12.2	23	951
V12.3	23	951
V12.40	23	951
V12.41	23	951
V12.42	23	951
V12.49	23	951
V12.50	23	951
V12.51	23	951
V12.52	23	951
V12.53	23	951
V12.54	23	951
V12.59	23	951
V12.60	23	951
V12.61	23	951
V12.69	23	951
V12.70	23	951
V12.71	23	951
V12.72	23	951
V12.79	23	951
V13.00	23	951
V13.01	23	951
V13.02	23	951
V13.03	23	951
V13.09	23	951
V13.1	23	951
V13.21	23	951
V13.22	17	843-845
V13.29	23	951
V13.3	23	951
V13.4	23	951
V13.51	23	951
V13.52	23	951
V13.59	23	951
V13.61	23	951
V13.69	23	951
V13.7	23	951
V13.8	23	951
V13.9	23	951
V14.0	23	951
V14.1	23	951
V14.2	23	951
V14.3	23	951
V14.4	23	951
V14.5	23	951

DX	MDC	DRG
V14.6	23	951
V14.7	23	951
V14.8	23	951
V14.9	23	951
V15.01	23	951
V15.02	23	951
V15.03	23	951
V15.04	23	951
V15.05	23	951
V15.06	23	951
V15.07	23	951
V15.08	23	951
V15.09	23	951
V15.1	23	951
V15.21	23	951
V15.22	23	951
V15.29	23	951
V15.3	23	951
V15.41	23	951
V15.42	23	951
V15.49	23	951
V15.51	23	951
V15.52	23	951
V15.59	23	951
V15.6	23	951
V15.7	23	951
V15.80	23	951
V15.81	23	951
V15.82	23	951
V15.83	23	951
V15.84	23	951
V15.85	23	951
V15.86	23	951
V15.87	23	951
V15.88	23	951
V15.89	23	951
V15.9	23	951
V16.0	23	951
V16.1	23	951
V16.2	23	951
V16.3	23	951
V16.40	23	951
V16.41	23	951
V16.42	23	951
V16.43	23	951
V16.49	23	951
V16.51	23	951
V16.52	23	951
V16.59	23	951
V16.6	23	951
V16.7	23	951
V16.8	23	951
V16.9	23	951
V17.0	23	951
V17.1	23	951
V17.2	23	951
V17.3	23	951
V17.41	23	951
V17.49	23	951
V17.5	23	951
V17.6	23	951
V17.7	23	951
V17.81	23	951
V17.89	23	951
V18.0	23	951
V18.11	23	951
V18.19	23	951
V18.2	23	951
V18.3	23	951
V18.4	23	951
V18.51	23	951
V18.59	23	951
V18.61	23	951
V18.69	23	951
V18.7	23	951
V18.8	23	951
V18.9	23	951
V19.0	23	951

DX	MDC	DRG	DX	MDC	DRG	DX	MDC	DRG	DX	MDC	DRG	DX	MDC	DRG
V19.1	23	951	V26.49	23	951	V41.3	23	951	V45.79	23	951	V52.1	08	559-561
V19.2	23	951	V26.51	23	951	V41.4	23	951	V45.81	23	951	V52.2	23	951
V19.3	23	951	V26.52	23	951	V41.5	23	951	V45.82	23	951	V52.3	23	951
V19.4	23	951	V26.81	23	951	V41.6	23	951	V45.83	23	951	V52.4	23	951
V19.5	23	951	V26.82	23	951	V41.7	23	951	V45.84	23	951	V52.8	23	945-946
V19.6	23	951	V26.89	23	951	V41.8	23	951	V45.85	23	951	V52.9	23	945-946
V19.7	23	951	V26.9	23	951	V41.9	23	951	V45.86	23	951	V53.01	01	091-093
V19.8	23	951	V27.0	23	951	V42.0	11	698-700	V45.87	23	951	V53.02	01	091-093
V20.0	23	951	V27.1	23	951	V42.1	05	314-316	V45.88	23	951	V53.09	01	091-093
V20.1	23	951	V27.2	23	951	V42.2	05	314-316	V45.89	23	951	V53.1	23	951
V20.2	23	951	V27.3	23	951	V42.3	09	606-607	V46.0	23	951	V53.2	23	951
V20.31	23	951	V27.4	23	951	V42.4	08	564-566	V46.11	23	951	V53.31	05	314-316
V20.32	23	951	V27.5	23	951	V42.5	02	124-125	V46.12	23	951	V53.32	05	314-316
V21.0	23	951	V27.6	23	951	V42.6	04	205-206	V46.13	23	951	V53.39	05	314-316
V21.1	23	951	V27.7	23	951	V42.7	07	441-443	V46.14	23	951	V53.4	23	951
V21.2	23	951	V27.9	23	951	V42.81	16	814-816	V46.2	23	951	V53.50	06	393-395
V21.30	23	951	V28.0	14	781-782	V42.82	16	814-816	V46.3	23	951	V53.51	06	393-395
V21.31	23	951	V28.1	14	781-782	V42.83	07	438-440	V46.8	23	951	V53.59	06	393-395
V21.32	23	951	V28.2	14	781-782	V42.84	07	951	V46.9	23	951	V53.6	11	698-700
V21.33	23	951	V28.3	23	951	V42.89	23	951	V47.0	23	951	V53.7	08	559-561
V21.34	23	951	V28.4	23	951	V42.9	23	951	V47.1	23	951	V53.8	23	951
V21.35	23	951	V28.5	23	951	V43.0	02	124-125	V47.2	23	951	V53.90	23	951
V21.8	23	951	V28.6	23	951	V43.1	02	124-125	V47.3	23	951	V53.91	23	951
V21.9	23	951	V28.81	23	951	V43.21	05	314-316	V47.4	23	951	V53.99	23	951
V22.0	23	951	V28.82	23	951	V43.22	05	314-316	V47.5	23	951	V54.01	08	559-561
V22.1	23	951	V28.89	23	951	V43.3	05	314-316	V47.9	23	951	V54.02	08	559-561
V22.2	23	951	V28.9	23	951	V43.4	05	314-316	V48.0	23	951	V54.09	08	559-561
V23.0	14	998	V29.0	23	951	V43.5	11	698-700	V48.1	23	951	V54.11	08	559-561
V23.1	14	998	V29.1	23	951	V43.60	08	564-566	V48.2	23	951	V54.12	08	559-561
V23.2	14	998	V29.2	23	951	V43.61	08	564-566	V48.3	23	951	V54.13	08	559-561
V23.3	14	998	V29.3	23	951	V43.62	08	564-566	V48.4	23	951	V54.14	08	559-561
V23.41	14	998	V29.8	23	951	V43.63	08	564-566	V48.5	23	951	V54.15	08	559-561
V23.49	14	998	V29.9	23	951	V43.64	08	564-566	V48.6	23	951	V54.16	08	559-561
V23.5	14	998	V30.00	15	795	V43.65	08	564-566	V48.7	23	951	V54.17	08	559-561
V23.7	14	998	V30.01	15	795	V43.66	08	564-566	V48.8	23	951	V54.19	08	559-561
V23.81	14	998	V30.1	15	795	V43.69	08	564-566	V48.9	23	951	V54.20	08	559-561
V23.82	14	998	V30.2	15	998	V43.7	08	564-566	V49.0	23	951	V54.21	08	559-561
V23.83	14	998	V31.00	15	795	V43.81	23	951	V49.1	23	951	V54.22	08	559-561
V23.84	14	998	V31.01	15	795	V43.82	23	951	V49.2	23	951	V54.23	08	559-561
V23.85	14	998	V31.1	15	795	V43.83	23	951	V49.3	23	951	V54.24	08	559-561
V23.86	14	998	V31.2	15	998	V43.89	23	951	V49.4	23	951	V54.25	08	559-561
V23.89	14	998	V32.00	15	795	V44.0	23	951	V49.5	23	951	V54.26	08	559-561
V23.9	14	998	V32.01	15	795	V44.1	23	951	V49.60	23	951	V54.27	08	559-561
V24.0	14	776	V32.1	15	795	V44.2	23	951	V49.61	23	951	V54.29	08	559-561
V24.1	23	951	V32.2	15	998	V44.3	23	951	V49.62	23	951	V54.81	08	559-561
V24.2	23	951	V33.00	15	795	V44.4	23	951	V49.63	23	951	V54.89	08	559-561
V25.01	23	951	V33.01	15	795	V44.50	23	951	V49.64	23	951	V54.9	08	559-561
V25.02	23	951	V33.1	15	795	V44.51	23	951	V49.65	23	951	V55.0	04	205-206
V25.03	23	951	V33.2	15	998	V44.52	23	951	V49.66	23	951	V55.1	06	393-395
V25.04	23	951	V34.00	15	795	V44.59	23	951	V49.67	23	951	V55.2	06	393-395
V25.09	23	951	V34.01	15	795	V44.6	23	951	V49.70	23	951	V55.3	06	393-395
V25.1	23	951	V34.1	15	795	V44.7	23	951	V49.71	23	951	V55.4	06	393-395
V25.2	12	729-730	V34.2	15	998	V44.8	23	951	V49.72	23	951	V55.5	11	698-700
V25.2	13	760-761	V35.00	15	795	V44.9	23	951	V49.73	23	951	V55.6	11	698-700
V25.3	13	760-761	V35.01	15	795	V45.00	23	951	V49.74	23	951	V55.7	13	760-761
V25.40	23	951	V35.1	15	795	V45.01	23	951	V49.75	23	951	V55.8	23	951
V25.41	23	951	V35.2	15	998	V45.02	23	951	V49.76	23	951	V55.9	23	951
V25.42	23	951	V36.00	15	795	V45.09	23	951	V49.77	23	951	V56.0	11	685
V25.43	23	951	V36.01	15	795	V45.11	23	951	V49.81	23	951	V56.1	11	685
V25.49	23	951	V36.1	15	795	V45.12	23	951	V49.82	23	951	V56.2	11	685
V25.5	23	951	V36.2	15	998	V45.2	23	951	V49.83	23	951	V56.31	11	685
V25.8	23	951	V37.00	15	795	V45.3	23	951	V49.84	23	951	V56.32	11	685
V25.9	23	951	V37.01	15	795	V45.4	23	951	V49.85	23	951	V56.8	11	685
V26.0	12	729-730	V37.1	15	795	V45.51	23	951	V49.89	23	951	V57.0	23	951
V26.0	13	760-761	V37.2	15	998	V45.52	23	951	V49.9	23	951	V57.1	23	945-946
V26.1	23	951	V39.00	15	795	V45.59	23	951	V50.0	09	606-607	V57.21	23	945-946
V26.21	23	951	V39.01	15	795	V45.61	23	951	V50.1	09	606-607	V57.22	23	945-946
V26.22	23	951	V39.1	15	795	V45.69	23	951	V50.2	12	727-728	V57.3	23	945-946
V26.29	23	951	V39.2	15	998	V45.71	23	951	V50.3	23	951	V57.4	23	951
V26.31	23	951	V40.0	23	951	V45.72	23	951	V50.41	9	600-601	V57.81	23	951
V26.32	23	951	V40.1	23	951	V45.73	23	951	V50.42	13	760-761	V57.89	23	945-946
V26.33	23	951	V40.2	23	951	V45.74	11	698-700	V50.49	23	951	V57.9	23	945-946
V26.34	23	951	V40.3	23	951	V45.75	23	951	V50.8	23	951	V58.0	17	849
V26.35	23	951	V40.9	23	951	V45.76	04	205-206	V50.9	23	951	V58.11	17	837-839, 846-848
V26.39	23	951	V41.0	23	951	V45.77	12	729-730	V51.0	09	606-607			
V26.41	23	951	V41.1	23	951	V45.77	13	760-761	V51.8	09	606-607			
V26.42	23	951	V41.2	23	951	V45.78	02	124-125	V52.0	08	559-561			

DX	MDC	DRG	DX	MDC	DRG	DX	MDC	DRG	DX	MDC	DRG	DX	MDC	DRG
V58.12	17	837-839, 846-848	V61.29	23	951	V67.3	23	951	V73.81	23	951	V81.4	23	951
V58.2	23	951	V61.3	23	951	V67.4	23	949-950	V73.88	23	951	V81.5	23	951
V58.30	23	951	V61.41	23	951	V67.51	23	951	V73.89	23	951	V81.6	23	951
V58.31	23	951	V61.42	23	951	V67.59	23	951	V73.98	23	951	V82.0	23	951
V58.32	23	951	V61.49	23	951	V67.6	23	951	V73.99	23	951	V82.1	23	951
V58.41	23	949-950	V61.5	13	760-761	V67.9	23	951	V74.0	23	951	V82.2	23	951
V58.42	23	949-950	V61.6	14	781-782	V68.01	23	951	V74.1	23	951	V82.3	23	951
V58.43	23	949-950	V61.7	14	779	V68.09	23	951	V74.2	23	951	V82.4	23	951
V58.44	23	949-950	V61.8	23	951	V68.1	23	951	V74.3	23	951	V82.5	23	951
V58.49	23	949-950	V61.9	23	951	V68.2	23	951	V74.4	23	951	V82.6	23	951
V58.5	23	949-950	V62.0	23	951	V68.81	23	951	V74.5	23	951	V82.71	23	951
V58.61	23	949-950	V62.1	23	951	V68.89	23	951	V74.6	23	951	V82.79	23	951
V58.62	23	949-950	V62.21	23	951	V68.9	23	951	V74.8	23	951	V82.81	23	951
V58.63	23	949-950	V62.22	23	951	V69.0	23	951	V74.9	23	951	V82.89	23	951
V58.64	23	949-950	V62.29	23	951	V69.1	23	951	V75.0	23	951	V82.9	23	951
V58.65	23	949-950	V62.3	23	951	V69.2	23	951	V75.1	23	951	V83.01	23	951
V58.66	23	949-950	V62.4	23	951	V69.3	23	951	V75.2	23	951	V83.02	23	951
V58.67	23	949-950	V62.5	23	951	V69.4	23	951	V75.3	23	951	V83.81	23	951
V58.69	23	949-950	V62.6	23	951	V69.5	23	951	V75.4	23	951	V83.89	23	951
V58.71	23	949-950	V62.81	23	951	V69.8	23	951	V75.5	23	951	V84.01	23	951
V58.72	23	949-950	V62.82	23	951	V69.9	23	951	V75.6	23	951	V84.02	23	951
V58.73	23	949-950	V62.83	23	951	V70.0	23	951	V75.7	23	951	V84.03	23	951
V58.74	23	949-950	V62.84	19	880	V70.1	23	951	V75.8	23	951	V84.04	23	951
V58.75	23	949-950	V62.89	23	951	V70.2	23	951	V75.9	23	951	V84.09	23	951
V58.76	23	949-950	V62.9	23	951	V70.3	23	951	V76.0	23	951	V84.81	23	951
V58.77	23	949-950	V63.0	23	951	V70.4	23	951	V76.10	23	951	V84.89	23	951
V58.78	23	949-950	V63.1	23	951	V70.5	23	951	V76.11	23	951	V85.0	23	951
V58.81	23	949-950	V63.2	23	951	V70.6	23	951	V76.12	23	951	V85.1	23	951
V58.83	23	949-950	V63.8	23	951	V70.7	23	951	V76.19	23	951	V85.21	23	951
V58.82	23	949-950	V63.9	23	951	V70.8	23	951	V76.2	23	951	V85.22	23	951
V58.89	23	949-950	V64.00	23	951	V70.9	23	951	V76.3	23	951	V85.23	23	951
V58.9	23	949-950	V64.01	23	951	V71.01	19	880	V76.41	23	951	V85.24	23	951
V59.01	23	951	V64.02	23	951	V71.02	19	880	V76.42	23	951	V85.25	23	951
V59.02	23	951	V64.03	23	951	V71.09	19	887	V76.43	23	951	V85.30	23	951
V59.09	23	951	V64.04	23	951	V71.1	17	843-845	V76.44	23	951	V85.31	23	951
V59.1	09	606-607	V64.05	23	951	V71.2	04	177-179	V76.45	23	951	V85.32	23	951
V59.2	08	564-566	V64.06	23	951	V71.3	21	922-923	V76.46	23	951	V85.33	23	951
V59.3	23	951	V64.07	23	951	V71.4	21	922-923	V76.47	23	951	V85.34	23	951
V59.4	11	698-700	V64.08	23	951	V71.5	23	951	V76.49	23	951	V85.35	23	951
V59.5	23	951	V64.09	23	951	V71.6	21	922-923	V76.50	23	951	V85.36	23	951
V59.6	07	441-443	V64.1	23	951	V71.7	05	313	V76.51	23	951	V85.37	23	951
V59.70	23	951	V64.2	23	951	V71.81	23	951	V76.52	23	951	V85.38	23	951
V59.71	23	951	V64.3	23	951	V71.82	23	951	V76.81	23	951	V85.39	23	951
V59.72	23	951	V64.41	23	951	V71.83	23	951	V76.89	23	951	V85.4	10	640-641
V59.73	23	951	V64.42	23	951	V71.89	23	951	V76.9	23	951	V85.51	23	951
V59.74	23	951	V64.43	23	951	V71.9	23	951	V77.0	23	951	V85.52	23	951
V59.8	23	951	V65.0	23	951	V72.0	23	951	V77.1	23	951	V85.53	23	951
V59.9	23	951	V65.11	23	951	V72.11	23	951	V77.2	23	951	V85.54	23	951
V60.0	23	951	V65.19	23	951	V72.12	23	951	V77.3	23	951	V86.0	23	951
V60.1	23	951	V65.2	23	951	V72.19	23	951	V77.4	23	951	V86.1	23	951
V60.2	23	951	V65.3	23	951	V72.2	23	951	V77.5	23	951	V87.01	23	951
V60.3	23	951	V65.40	23	951	V72.31	23	951	V77.6	23	951	V87.09	23	951
V60.4	23	951	V65.41	23	951	V72.32	23	951	V77.7	23	951	V87.11	23	951
V60.5	23	951	V65.42	23	951	V72.40	23	951	V77.8	23	951	V87.12	23	951
V60.6	23	951	V65.43	23	951	V72.41	23	951	V77.91	23	951	V87.19	23	951
V60.81	23	951	V65.44	23	951	V72.42	23	951	V77.99	23	951	V87.2	23	951
V60.89	23	951	V65.45	23	951	V72.5	23	951	V78.0	23	951	V87.31	23	951
V60.9	23	951	V65.46	23	951	V72.60	23	951	V78.1	23	951	V87.32	23	951
V61.01	23	951	V65.49	23	951	V72.61	23	951	V78.2	23	951	V87.39	23	951
V61.02	23	951	V65.5	23	951	V72.62	23	951	V78.3	23	951	V87.41	23	949-950
V61.03	23	951	V65.8	23	951	V72.63	23	951	V78.8	23	951	V87.42	23	949-950
V61.04	23	951	V65.9	23	951	V72.69	23	951	V78.9	23	951	V87.43	23	949-950
V61.05	23	951	V66.0	23	951	V72.7	23	951	V79.0	23	951	V87.44	23	949-950
V61.06	23	951	V66.1	23	951	V72.81	23	951	V79.1	23	951	V87.45	23	949-950
V61.07	23	951	V66.2	23	951	V72.82	23	951	V79.2	23	951	V87.46	23	949-950
V61.08	23	951	V66.3	23	951	V72.83	23	951	V79.3	23	951	V87.49	23	949-950
V61.09	23	951	V66.4	23	951	V72.84	23	951	V79.8	23	951	V88.01	13	760-761
V61.10	23	951	V66.5	23	951	V72.85	23	951	V79.9	23	951	V88.02	13	760-761
V61.11	23	951	V66.6	23	951	V72.86	23	951	V80.01	23	951	V88.03	13	760-761
V61.12	23	951	V66.7	23	951	V72.9	23	951	V80.09	23	951	V89.01	23	951
V61.20	23	951	V66.9	23	951	V73.0	23	951	V80.1	23	951	V89.02	23	951
V61.21	23	951	V67.00	23	949-950	V73.1	23	951	V80.2	23	951	V89.03	23	951
V61.22	23	951	V67.01	23	949-950	V73.2	23	951	V80.3	23	951	V89.04	23	951
V61.23	23	951	V67.09	23	949-950	V73.3	23	951	V81.0	23	951	V89.05	23	951
V61.24	23	951	V67.1	17	849	V73.4	23	951	V81.1	23	951	V89.09	23	951
V61.25	23	951	V67.2	17	837-839, 846-848	V73.5	23	951	V81.2	23	951			
						V73.6	23	951	V81.3	23	951			

Major Complication & Comorbidity (MCC) Code List

The following is the standards list of conditions considered to be major complications and comorbidities that when present as a secondary diagnosis may affect DRG assignment under the Medicare Severity DRG (MS-DRG) system version 27.0. An astersisk (*) indicates that a code range is represented.

003.1	072.2	286.6	431	*531.6	568.81	642.61	673.82
003.21	073.0	*320	432.0	531.71	569.83	642.62	673.83
003.22	084.0	*320.8	432.1	531.91	569.85	642.63	673.84
006.3	090.41	320.9	433.01	*532.0	569.86	642.64	674.01
006.4	090.42	*321	433.11	*532.1	570	642.71	674.50
006.5	091.81	322.0	433.21	*532.2	572.0	642.72	674.51
*011.6	094.2	322.1	433.31	532.31	572.1	642.73	674.52
*013.0	094.81	322.9	433.81	*532.4	572.2	642.74	674.53
*013.1	094.87	*323.0	433.91	*532.5	572.4	644.03	674.54
*013.2	098.82	323.1	434.01	*532.6	573.4	644.21	707.02
*013.3	098.83	323.2	434.11	532.71	574.81	648.01	707.03
*013.4	098.84	*323.4	434.91	532.91	575.4	648.02	707.04
*013.5	100.81	*323.5	*441.0	*533.0	576.2	654.51	707.05
*013.6	112.4	*323.6	441.1	*533.1	576.3	654.52	707.06
*013.8	112.5	*323.7	441.3	*533.2	577.0	654.53	707.07
*013.9	112.81	*323.8	441.5	533.31	580.0	654.54	728.86
*014.0	112.83	323.9	441.6	*533.4	580.4	658.41	740.0
*018.0	114.2	*324	*443.2	*533.5	580.81	658.43	740.1
*018.8	115.01	325	446.6	*533.6	580.89	659.31	740.2
*018.9	115.03	331.81	452	533.71	580.9	659.33	742.2
*020	115.04	333.92	453.0	533.91	583.4	665.01	745.0
022.1	115.05	336.1	453.2	*534.0	583.6	665.03	745.10
022.3	115.11	343.2	456.0	*534.1	*584	665.11	745.11
*036	115.13	*344.0	456.20	*534.2	585.6	669.11	745.19
037	115.14	344.81	464.01	534.31	590.11	669.12	745.2
038.0	115.15	345.2	464.11	*534.4	590.2	669.13	745.3
*038.1	115.91	345.3	464.21	*534.5	596.6	669.14	745.7
038.2	115.93	345.71	464.31	*534.6	614.5	669.21	746.01
038.3	115.94	*348.3	464.51	534.71	*634.3	669.22	746.1
*038.4	115.95	348.4	*480	534.91	*634.5	669.32	746.2
038.8	117.7	348.5	481	535.01	634.61	669.34	746.7
038.9	130.0	349.82	*482	535.11	634.62	670.02	746.81
040.0	130.3	358.01	*483	535.21	635.30	670.04	746.82
040.82	130.4	410.01	*484	535.31	635.31	670.22	746.84
042	130.8	410.11	485	535.41	635.32	670.24	746.86
*045.0	136.2	410.21	486	535.51	*635.5	670.32	747.11
*045.1	136.3	410.31	487.0	535.61	*635.6	670.34	747.3
052.0	242.01	410.41	506.1	537.83	*636.3	670.80	747.81
052.1	242.11	410.51	*507	537.84	*636.5	670.82	747.83
052.2	242.21	410.61	*510	540.0	*636.6	670.84	748.5
053.0	242.31	410.71	511.1	540.1	*637.3	671.31	750.3
053.14	242.41	410.81	511.8	*550.0	*637.5	671.33	751.61
054.3	242.81	410.91	512.0	*551.0	*637.6	671.42	755.55
054.5	242.91	414.12	513.0	551.1	638.3	671.44	756.6
054.72	*250.1	*415	513.1	*551.2	638.5	673.01	756.70
054.74	*250.2	421.0	518.4	551.3	638.6	673.02	756.71
055.0	*250.3	421.1	518.5	551.8	639.3	673.03	756.72
055.1	260	421.9	518.81	551.9	639.5	673.04	756.73
056.01	261	422.0	518.84	557.0	639.6	673.11	756.79
058.21	262	*422.9	519.2	560.2	641.11	673.12	758.32
058.29	277.01	*427.4	530.21	562.02	641.13	673.13	759.4
*062	277.02	427.5	530.4	562.03	641.21	673.14	767.0
*063	277.88	428.21	530.7	562.12	641.31	673.21	768.5
064	282.42	428.23	530.82	562.13	641.33	673.22	768.73
*066.4	282.62	428.31	530.84	567.0	642.11	673.23	769
070.0	282.64	428.33	*531.0	567.1	642.12	673.24	770.0
*070.2	282.69	428.41	*531.1	*567.2	642.42	673.31	770.12
*070.4	283.11	428.43	*531.2	*567.3	642.51	673.32	770.14
070.6	*284.8	429.5	531.31	567.81	642.52	673.33	770.16
070.71	286.0	429.6	*531.4	567.89	642.53	673.34	770.18
072.1	286.1	430	*531.5	567.9	642.54	673.81	770.2

770.3	*800.1	*803.8	807.4	*851.2	864.03	902.50	948.76
770.7	*800.2	*803.9	807.5	*851.3	864.04	902.51	948.77
770.84	*800.3	804.03	807.6	851.45	*864.1	902.52	948.81
770.86	800.43	804.04	808.0	*851.5	865.03	902.53	948.82
770.87	800.44	804.05	808.1	*851.6	865.04	902.54	948.83
771.1	800.45	*804.1	808.3	*851.7	*865.1	902.59	948.84
771.2	*800.5	*804.2	*808.5	*851.8	866.03	902.87	948.85
771.3	*800.6	*804.3	808.9	*851.9	866.10	*903.0	948.86
771.81	*800.7	804.43	809.1	*852.0	866.11	904.0	948.87
772.13	*800.8	804.44	*812.1	*852.1	866.12	904.1	948.88
772.14	*800.9	804.45	*812.3	*852.2	866.13	904.2	948.91
772.2	801.03	804.53	*812.5	*852.3	867.1	*904.4	948.92
772.4	801.04	804.54	*813.1	*852.4	867.3	948.21	948.93
773.3	801.05	804.55	*813.3	*852.5	867.5	948.22	948.94
773.4	*801.1	*804.6	*813.5	*853.0	867.7	948.31	948.95
774.4	*801.2	*804.7	*813.9	*853.1	867.9	948.32	948.96
774.7	*801.3	*804.8	*820	854.05	869.1	948.33	948.97
775.7	801.43	804.93	*821.0	*854.1	*868.1	948.41	948.98
776.1	801.44	804.94	*821.1	860.1	869.1	948.42	948.99
776.2	801.45	804.95	*821.3	860.2	*874.0	948.43	*952.0
776.7	*801.5	*805.1	*823.1	860.3	*874.1	948.44	*952.1
777.5	*801.6	805.3	*823.3	860.4	887.6	948.51	952.2
777.6	*801.7	805.5	*823.9	860.5	887.7	948.52	952.3
778.0	*801.8	805.7	828.0	861.02	896.2	948.53	952.4
779.0	*801.9	805.9	828.1	861.03	896.3	948.54	952.8
779.2	803.03	*806.0	835.10	*861.1	897.6	948.55	958.0
779.32	803.04	*806.1	835.11	861.22	897.7	948.61	958.1
779.7	803.05	*806.2	835.12	*861.3	901.0	948.62	958.4
779.85	*803.1	*806.3	835.13	862.1	901.1	948.63	958.5
780.01	*803.2	806.4	*839.1	862.21	901.2	948.64	995.91
785.51	*803.3	806.5	*839.3	862.22	901.3	948.65	995.92
785.52	803.43	*806.6	839.50	*862.3	*901.4	948.66	995.94
785.59	803.44	*806.7	839.59	862.9	901.83	948.71	999.1
799.1	803.45	806.8	839.71	863.1	902.0	948.72	
800.03	*803.5	806.9	850.4	*863.3	*902.1	948.73	
800.04	*803.6	*807.1	851.05	*863.5	*902.2	948.74	
800.05	*803.7	807.3	*851.1	*863.9	*902.3	948.75	
					*902.4		

Complication and Comorbidity (CC) Code List

The following is the standards list of conditions considered to be complications and comorbidities that when present as a secondary diagnosis may affect DRG assignment under the Medicare Severity DRG (MS-DRG) system version 27.0. An asterisk (*) indicates that a code range is represented.

*001	*017.3	*065	093.9	123.5	*205.0	277.5	295.22	301.51	359.4
*002	*017.4	066.0	094.0	123.6	*205.1	277.85	295.23	304.01	359.6
003.0	*017.5	066.1	094.1	123.8	*205.2	277.86	295.24	304.11	359.81
003.23	*017.6	066.2	094.3	124	*205.3	277.87	295.30	304.21	360.00
003.24	*017.7	066.3	094.82	*125	*205.8	277.89	295.31	304.41	360.01
003.29	*017.8	066.8	094.83	*126	*205.9	*279.0	295.32	304.51	360.02
003.8	*017.9	066.9	094.84	*127	*206.0	*279.1	295.33	304.61	360.04
003.9	*021	070.1	094.85	130.1	*206.1	279.2	295.34	304.71	360.11
004.0	022.0	070.30	094.86	130.2	*206.2	279.3	295.40	304.81	360.12
005.0	022.2	070.31	094.89	130.5	*206.8	*279.5	295.41	304.91	360.13
005.1	022.8	070.32	094.9	130.7	*206.9	282.8	295.42	307.1	360.19
005.2	022.9	070.33	095.0	130.9	*207.0	282.9	295.43	307.51	361.2
005.3	023.8	070.51	095.1	136.29	*207.1	283.0	295.44	318.1	*361.8
005.4	023.9	070.52	095.2	136.4	*207.2	283.10	295.53	318.2	361.9
005.81	024	070.53	095.3	136.5	*207.8	283.19	295.54	322.2	362.30
005.89	025	070.59	095.4	*150	*208.0	283.9	295.60	330.0	362.31
006.0	*026	070.9	095.5	*151	*208.1	*284.0	295.61	330.1	362.32
006.1	027.0	071	095.6	*152	*208.2	284.1	295.62	330.2	362.33
006.2	027.2	072.0	095.7	*153	*208.8	284.2	295.63	330.3	362.34
006.8	027.8	072.3	095.8	*154	*208.9	284.9	295.64	330.8	362.35
007.1	027.9	*072.7	095.9	*155	*209.0	285.1	295.71	330.9	362.40
007.2	*030	072.8	098.0	*156	*209.1	286.2	295.72	331.3	362.42
007.4	*031	073.7	*098.1	*157	*209.2	286.3	295.73	331.4	362.43
007.5	*032	073.8	*098.4	*158	*209.3	286.4	295.74	331.5	362.84
007.8	*033	073.9	*098.5	*162	209.71	286.5	295.80	332.1	*363.1
007.9	034.1	*074.2	098.81	*163	209.72	286.7	295.81	333.0	363.20
*008.0	*036.8	078.3	098.85	*164	209.73	286.9	295.82	333.4	363.63
008.1	036.9	078.5	098.86	*170	209.74	287.0	295.83	333.71	*363.7
008.2	*039	078.6	098.89	*171	209.79	287.31	295.84	333.72	364.00
008.3	040.2	078.7	099.56	*176	238.5	287.32	295.91	333.79	364.01
*008.4	040.3	079.51	100.0	183.0	238.6	287.33	295.92	333.90	364.02
008.5	040.41	079.52	100.89	*189	238.73	288.4	295.93	333.91	364.03
*008.6	040.42	079.53	100.9	*191	238.74	289.7	295.94	*334	364.22
009.0	040.81	*079.8	101	*192	238.76	289.81	296.00	*335	364.3
009.1	046.0	080	112.0	*194	238.77	289.82	296.01	336.0	365.22
009.2	*046.1	*081	112.2	*196	238.79	289.83	296.02	336.2	368.11
009.3	046.2	*082	112.82	*197	245.0	290.11	296.03	336.3	368.12
*010.0	046.3	*083	112.84	*198	246.3	290.12	296.04	336.8	376.01
*010.1	*046.7	084.1	112.85	199.0	251.0	290.13	296.10	336.9	376.02
*010.8	046.8	084.2	112.89	199.2	251.3	290.20	296.11	337.1	376.03
*010.9	046.9	084.3	114.0	*200.0	253.1	290.21	296.12	*337.2	377.00
*011.0	*047	084.4	114.1	*200.1	253.2	290.3	296.13	*341	377.01
*011.1	048	084.5	114.3	*200.2	253.5	290.41	296.14	*342	*377.3
*011.2	*049	084.6	114.4	*200.3	253.6	290.42	296.20	343.0	*377.5
*011.3	*050	084.7	114.5	*200.4	254.1	290.43	296.21	343.1	*377.6
*011.4	052.7	084.8	114.9	*200.5	255.0	290.8	296.22	343.4	377.71
*011.5	052.8	084.9	115.02	*200.6	255.3	290.9	296.23	344.1	377.72
*011.7	052.9	*085	115.09	*200.7	255.41	291.0	296.24	344.2	377.73
*011.8	053.10	*086	115.12	*200.8	255.42	291.2	296.30	344.60	380.14
*011.9	053.11	*087	115.19	*201.0	255.5	291.3	296.31	344.61	*383.0
*012.0	053.12	088.0	115.92	*201.1	255.6	291.81	296.32	345.01	388.61
*012.1	053.13	088.81	116.0	*201.2	259.2	291.89	296.33	345.11	*391
*012.2	053.19	088.82	116.1	*201.4	263.2	291.9	296.34	345.40	*392
*012.3	*053.2	090.0	117.3	*201.5	263.8	292.0	296.40	345.41	393
*012.8	053.71	090.2	117.4	*201.6	263.9	*292.1	296.41	345.50	398.0
*014.8	053.79	090.3	117.5	*201.7	265.0	292.81	296.42	345.51	398.91
*015.0	053.8	090.40	117.6	*201.9	265.1	292.82	296.43	345.60	401.0
*015.1	054.2	090.49	117.8	*202.0	266.0	293.0	296.44	345.61	*402.0
*015.2	054.40	090.5	117.9	*202.1	268.0	293.1	296.50	345.70	*403.0
*015.5	054.41	091.3	118	*202.2	*270	293.81	296.51	345.80	403.11
*015.6	054.42	091.4	*120	*202.3	271.0	293.82	296.52	345.81	403.91
*015.7	054.43	*091.5	121.0	*202.4	271.1	293.9	296.53	345.91	*404.0
*015.8	054.44	*091.6	121.1	*202.5	271.8	294.11	296.54	*346.6	404.11
*015.9	054.49	091.7	121.2	*202.6	274.11	295.00	296.60	348.1	404.12
*016.0	054.71	091.82	121.3	*202.7	276.0	295.01	296.61	349.1	404.13
*016.1	054.79	091.89	121.4	*202.8	276.1	295.02	296.62	349.31	404.91
*016.2	*055.7	091.9	121.5	*202.9	276.2	295.03	296.63	349.39	404.92
*016.3	056.00	093.0	121.6	*203.0	276.3	295.04	296.64	349.81	404.93
*016.4	056.09	093.1	121.8	*203.1	276.4	295.10	296.89	356.3	*405.0
*016.5	*056.7	093.20	*122	*203.8	277.00	295.11	296.99	357.0	*411
*016.6	057.0	093.21	123.0	*204.0	277.03	295.12	298.0	357.81	413.0
*016.7	059.01	093.22	123.1	*204.1	277.09	295.13	298.1	357.82	413.1
*016.9	059.21	093.23	123.2	*204.2	277.1	295.14	298.3	358.1	414.02
*017.0	*060	093.24	123.3	*204.8	277.2	295.20	298.4	359.0	414.03
*017.2	061	*093.8	123.4	*204.9	*277.3	295.21	*299	359.1	414.04

414.06	459.2	58.2	591	642.91	651.13	707.10	753.0	799.4	813.83
414.07	459.31	560.0	592.1	642.92	651.21	707.11	*753.1	800.00	*814.1
414.10	459.33	560.1	593.4	642.93	651.23	707.12	*753.2	800.01	*815.1
414.19	464.30	*560.3	593.5	642.94	651.41	707.13	753.5	800.02	*816.1
416.0	*466.1	*560.8	593.81	644.13	651.43	707.14	753.6	800.06	817.1
416.1	475	560.9	593.82	644.20	651.51	707.19	754.2	800.09	818.1
416.2	478.21	562.01	595.0	646.21	651.53	710.3	754.89	800.40	819.0
417.0	478.22	562.11	595.82	646.22	651.81	710.4	756.13	800.41	819.1
417.1	478.24	564.7	596.1	646.23	651.83	710.5	756.3	800.42	*821.2
420.0	478.34	564.81	596.2	646.24	656.13	710.8	756.51	800.46	822.0
420.90	478.71	566	596.7	646.31	656.31	*711.0	756.52	800.49	822.1
420.91	491.21	567.82	597.0	646.61	656.41	*711.1	756.83	801.00	823.00
420.99	491.22	568.82	599.0	646.62	656.43	*711.2	758.1	801.01	823.02
*423	493.01	569.3	599.1	646.63	656.51	*711.3	758.2	801.02	823.20
*424.9	493.02	569.41	601.0	646.64	657.01	*711.4	758.31	801.06	823.22
*425	493.11	569.5	601.2	646.71	658.01	*711.5	758.33	801.09	823.40
426.0	493.12	569.61	603.1	646.73	658.03	*711.6	758.39	801.40	823.42
426.12	493.21	569.62	604.0	647.01	658.81	*711.7	759.0	801.41	823.80
426.53	493.22	569.69	607.3	647.02	659.21	*711.8	759.3	801.42	823.82
426.54	493.91	569.71	607.82	647.03	660.03	*711.9	759.5	801.46	824.1
426.89	493.92	569.79	*608.2	647.04	662.11	714.31	759.6	801.49	824.3
427.0	494.1	569.81	614.0	647.11	664.21	*719.1	759.7	802.1	824.5
427.1	495.7	569.82	614.3	647.12	664.31	721.1	759.81	*802.2	824.7
427.32	495.8	572.3	614.7	647.13	664.61	*721.4	759.82	*802.3	824.9
428.1	495.9	573.1	615.0	647.14	664.64	721.7	759.89	802.4	825.1
428.20	506.0	573.2	616.3	647.21	665.22	721.91	767.11	802.5	*825.3
428.22	508.0	574.00	616.4	647.22	665.31	722.71	768.70	802.6	827.1
428.30	508.1	574.01	616.81	647.23	665.41	722.72	768.71	802.7	830.1
428.32	*511.8	574.10	*619	647.24	665.51	722.73	768.72	802.8	*831.1
428.40	511.9	574.11	620.5	647.31	665.61	728.0	770.4	802.9	*832.1
428.42	512.1	574.21	*633	647.32	665.71	728.88	770.5	803.00	*833.1
*429.7	512.8	574.30	*634.0	647.33	665.72	729.71	770.81	803.01	835.00
429.81	514	574.31	*634.2	647.34	666.02	729.72	770.82	803.02	835.01
429.82	*516	574.40	*634.4	647.41	666.04	729.73	770.83	803.06	835.02
429.83	517.1	574.41	634.60	647.42	666.12	729.79	771.0	803.09	835.03
432.9	517.2	574.51	634.70	647.43	666.14	*730.0	771.4	803.40	836.4
*435	517.3	574.60	634.71	647.44	666.22	*730.1	771.5	803.41	*836.6
436	518.0	574.61	634.72	647.51	666.24	*730.2	771.82	803.42	837.1
437.1	518.3	574.70	634.80	647.52	666.32	*730.8	771.83	803.46	*839.0
437.2	518.6	574.71	634.81	647.53	669.24	*730.9	771.89	803.49	839.51
437.4	518.7	574.80	634.82	647.54	*670.1	*733.1	772.10	804.00	839.52
437.5	518.82	574.91	*635.8	647.61	670.30	*733.4	772.11	804.01	839.61
437.6	518.83	575.0	*636.0	647.62	671.20	*733.8	772.12	804.02	839.79
*438.2	*519.0	575.12	*636.2	647.63	671.21	*741.0	772.5	804.06	839.9
440.24	522.0	575.2	*636.4	647.64	671.22	742.0	775.1	804.09	850.11
444.0	522.4	575.3	*636.7	647.81	671.23	742.4	775.2	804.40	850.12
444.1	527.3	575.5	*636.8	647.82	671.24	745.12	775.3	804.41	850.2
*444.2	527.4	576.1	*637.0	647.83	671.30	745.4	775.4	804.42	850.3
*444.8	528.3	576.4	*637.2	647.84	671.40	745.5	775.81	804.46	850.5
444.9	530.12	577.1	*637.4	647.91	*671.5	*745.6	775.89	804.49	851.02
*445.0	530.20	577.2	*637.7	647.92	*671.8	746.00	776.0	804.50	851.03
*445.8	530.86	578.0	*637.8	647.93	671.90	746.02	776.3	804.51	851.04
446.0	530.87	578.1	638.0	647.94	671.91	746.09	776.5	804.52	851.06
446.1	531.30	578.9	638.1	648.00	671.92	746.3	776.6	804.56	851.42
*446.2	532.30	579.1	638.2	648.03	672.02	746.4	777.4	804.59	851.43
446.3	533.30	579.2	638.4	648.04	672.04	746.5	778.1	804.90	851.44
446.4	534.30	579.3	638.7	648.31	673.30	746.6	778.5	804.91	851.46
446.7	536.1	579.4	638.8	648.32	674.02	746.83	779.4	804.92	854.02
447.2	536.41	579.8	639.0	648.33	674.03	746.85	779.5	804.96	854.03
447.4	536.42	579.9	639.1	648.34	674.04	746.87	780.03	804.99	854.04
447.5	537.0	581.0	639.2	648.51	675.11	747.0	780.1	*805.0	854.06
449	537.3	581.1	639.4	648.52	675.12	747.10	780.31	805.2	860
451.11	537.4	581.2	639.8	648.53	*682	*747.2	780.32	805.4	861.00
451.19	538	581.3	639.9	648.54	685.0	*747.4	781.4	805.6	861.01
451.81	540.9	581.81	640.01	648.61	686.01	747.82	781.6	805.8	861.20
451.83	550.10	581.89	640.03	648.62	694.4	747.89	781.7	*807.0	861.21
451.89	550.11	581.9	640.93	648.63	694.5	747.9	781.8	807.2	862.0
453.1	550.12	*582	641.01	648.64	695.0	748.3	782.4	808.2	862.29
453.3	550.13	583.0	641.03	648.71	695.12	748.4	784.3	*808.4	862.8
*453.4	*552.0	583.1	641.23	648.72	695.13	748.61	785.4	808.8	863.0
*453.5	552.1	583.2	642.01	648.73	695.14	750.4	785.50	809.0	*863.2
453.6	*552.2	583.7	642.02	648.74	695.15	751.1	786.04	*810.1	*863.4
*453.7	552.3	585.4	642.03	*649.3	695.53	751.2	786.3	*811.1	*863.8
*453.8	552.8	585.5	642.13	649.41	695.54	751.3	788.8	*812.0	864.00
453.9	552.9	588.1	642.14	649.42	695.55	751.4	*789.5	*812.2	864.01
454.2	*555	588.81	642.31	649.43	695.56	751.5	790.01	*812.4	864.02
456.1	*556	590.01	642.32	649.44	695.57	751.60	790.7	*813.2	864.05
456.21	557.1	590.10	642.41	*649.7	695.58	751.62	791.1	*813.4	864.09
459.11	557.9	590.3	642.43	651.01	695.59	751.69	791.3	813.80	865.00
459.13	558.1	*590.8	642.44	651.11		751.7	799.01	813.82	865.01

865.02	871.9	890.2	902.81	934.8	947.4	991.3	995.93	*997.3	V42.0
865.09	872.12	891.2	902.82	940.5	948.10	991.4	*996.0	997.4	V42.1
866.00	*872.6	892.2	902.89	*941.3	948.11	992.0	996.1	997.62	V42.6
866.01	*872.7	893.2	902.9	*941.4	948.20	993.3	996.2	*997.7	V42.7
866.02	873.23	894.2	903.1	*941.5	948.30	994.1	996.30	997.99	V42.81
867.0	873.33	896.0	903.2	*942.3	948.40	994.7	996.39	998.0	V42.82
867.2	874.2	896.1	903.3	*942.4	948.50	995.0	*996.4	*998.1	V42.83
867.4	874.3	897.0	903.4	*942.5	948.60	995.4	*996.5	998.2	V42.84
867.6	874.4	897.1	903.5	*943.3	948.70	995.50	*996.6	*998.3	*V43.2
867.8	874.5	897.2	903.8	*943.4	948.80	995.51	996.71	998.4	*V46.1
*868.0	875.0	897.3	903.9	*943.5	948.90	995.52	996.72	*998.5	V55.1
869.0	875.1	897.4	904.3	*944.3	949.3	995.53	996.73	998.6	V62.84
870.2	*880.2	897.5	*904.5	*944.4	949.4	995.54	996.74	998.7	V85.0
870.3	*881.2	*900.0	904.6	*944.5	949.5	995.55	996.75	998.83	V85.4
870.4	882.2	900.1	904.7	*945.3	*950	995.59	996.76	999.0	
870.8	883.2	*900.8	904.8	*945.4	*951	*995.6	996.77	999.2	
870.9	884.2	900.9	904.9	*945.5	958.2	995.80	996.78	*999.3	
871.0	887.0	901.81	925.1	946.3	958.3	995.81	996.79	999.4	
871.1	887.1	901.82	925.2	946.4	958.7	995.83	*996.8	999.5	
871.2	887.2	901.89	928.00	946.5	*958.9	995.84	*996.9	999.6	
871.3	887.3	901.9	928.01	947.1	991.0	995.85	*997.0	999.7	
871.5	887.4	902.55	934.0	947.2	991.1	995.86	997.1	999.81	
871.6	887.5	902.56	934.1	947.3	991.2	995.90	997.2	999.82	

Pharmacological Listings

Pharmacology Considerations
Medications are listed by classification and brand name for each of the chapters of ICD-9-CM. The list includes many of the common medications and should not be considered exhaustive. The pharmacology considerations that follow are presented as guidance only for the recognition of the link between implication of disease process and treatment.

Infectious and Parasitic Diseases (001-139)

AIDS Related Complex (ARC) Therapeutic Agents
Agenerase	Crixivan
Epivir	Fortovase
Hivid	Intron A
Invirase	Norvir
Pentam	Rescriptor
Retrovir	Rimactane
Roferon-A	Sustiva
Videx	Viracept
Vitravene	Zerit
Ziagen	Zovirax

Antibiotics
Achromycin-V	Amikin
Amoxicillin	Amoxil
Ampicillin	Ancef
Augmentin	Azactam
Bactrim	Bicillin
Biocef	Ceclor
Cefizox[2]	Cefobid
Cefotan	Ceftin
Chloromycetin	Cipro
Claforan	Cleocin
Duricef	E-Mycin
ERYC	Ery-Tab
Erythromycin	Factive
Floxin	Fortaz
Garamycin	Levaquin
Macrobid	Maxipime
Mefoxin	Minocin
Nebcin	Neo-fradin
PCE Dispertab	Penicillin G
Penicillin V	Pfizerpen
Pipracil	Primaxin
Proloprim	Septra
Spectrobid	Suprax
Synersid	Tazicef
Tazidime	Terramycin
Tetracycline HCl	Ticar
Timentin	Totacillin
Trimox	Trimpex
Unasyn	Unipen
Vancocin	Vibramycin
Vibra-Tabs	Wycillin
Zefazone	Zinacef
Zithromax	Zosyn
Zymar	

Antiparasitics
Antiminth	Aralen
Daraprim	Flagyl
G-well	Helidac
MepronnebuPent	Pentam 300
Penticarinat	Pin-X
Protostat	Vermox

Corticosteroids
Aristocort	Celestone
Cortastat	Cortef
Cortenema	Cortone Acetate
Dalalone	Decadron
Deltasone	Depo-Medrol
Florinef acetate	Hydeltrasol
Hydrocortisone	Hydrocortone
Medralone	Medrol
Orasone	Predalone
Prednisone	Prelone
Protocort	Solu-Cortef

Fungal Medications
Abelcet	AmBisome
Amphocin	Amphotec
Ancobon	Diflucan
Fulvicin P/G	Fungilin
Fungizone	Fungoid
Grifulvin	Grisactin
Gris-PEG	Lamisil
Lotrimin	Lotrisone
Monistat	Mycelex-G
Mycolog	Mycostatin
Nilstst	Nizoral
Spectazole	Sporanox

Tuberculosis Preparations
Capastat	INH Tablets
Lamprene	Laniazid
Myambutol	Mycobutin
Priftin	Pyrazinamide
Rifadin	Rifamate
Rimactane	Seromycin
Sodium P.A.S.	Streptomycin
Trecator-SC	

Viral Agents
Abreva	Agenerase
Combivir	Crixivan
Cytovene	Emtriva
Epivir	Famvir
Flumadine	Fortovase
Foscavir	Fuzeon
Herplex	Hepsera
Hivid	Invirase
Lexiva	Norvir
Relenza	Rescriptor
Retrovir	Reyataz
Sustiva	Symmetrel
Tamiflu	Valtrex
Videx	Viracept
Viramune	Virazole
Vistide	Vitravene
Zerit	Ziagen
Zovirax	

Neoplasms (140-239)

Adjunct
Anzemet	Arrestin
Compazine	Epogen
Ergamisol	Kytril
Leukine	Martinol
Metastron	Neumega
Neupogen	Procrit
Prokine	Quadramet
Reglan	Relcomide
Salagen	Sandostatin
Zinecard	Zofran

Androgen Inhibitor
Casodex	Eulexin
Lupron	Nilandron
Zoladex	

Antibiotic Derivatives
Adriamycin	Blenoxane
Cerubidine	Cosmegen
Doxorubicin	Idamycin
Mutamycin	Mithracin
Nipent	Novantrone
Pacis	Rubex
TheraCys	

Antiestrogen
Femara	Nolvadex

Antimetabolites
Adrucil	Cytarabine
Cytosar-U	Droxia
Efudex	Folex
Fludara	Fluoroplex
Fluorouracil	FUDR
Intron A	Leustatin
Methotrexate	Purinethol
Roferon-A	Thioguanine
Xeloda	

Cytotoxic Agents
Adriamycin	BiCNU
CeeNU	Cerubidine
Cytosar-U	Doxorubicin
Gemzar	Hexalen
Hydrea	Intron A
Matulane	Mutamycin
Myleran	Novantrone
Paraplatin	Platinol

Zanosar

Hormones
Arimidex	Aromasin
Depo-Provera	Eligard
Emcyt	Estinyl
Estradurin	Fareston
Lupron	Megace
Stilphostrol	Teslac
Zoladex	

Nitrogen Mustard Derivatives
Alkeran	Cytoxan
Leukeran	Mustargen
Neosar	Thiotepa

Steroids and Combinations
Celestone Soluspan

Other
Camptosar	DTIC-Dome
Elspar	Etopophos
Iressa	Navelbine
Oncaspar	Oncovin
Phosphocol P32	Photofrin
Proleukin	Rituxan
Semzar	Taxol
Taxotere	TICE
Velban	Velcade
VePesid	Vesanoid
Vumon	

Endocrine, Nutritional and Metabolic Diseases and Immunity Disorders (240-279)

Acidifier and Alkalinizers
Ammonium chloride	Citrocarbonate
Sodium bicarbonate	Sodium lactate
Tham	

Antigout Agents
Anturane	Benemid
Colchicine	Probalan
Zyloprim	

Antilipemics
atorvastatin calcium	crestor
fluvastatin sodium	Lescol
Lipitor	lovastatin
Mevacor	Pravachol
pravastatin sodium	simvastatin
Tricor	Vytorin
Zetia	Zocor

Antioxidants
Aquasol E	Calcium-D
Calcium Health Packs	Carotene-E
Carotene Health Packs	Glutathione
Performance Packs	Pure-E

Appetite Suppressants
Adipex-P	Adipost
Biphetamine	Bontril
Desoxyn	Didrex
Fastin	Ionamin
Mazanor	Meridia
Phentride	Plegine
Pondimin	Prelu-2
Sanorex	Tenuate

Diabetic Agents and Glucagon
Actos	Amaryl
Avandia	DiaBeta
Diabinese	Glucagon
Glucophage	Glucotrol
Glynase	Glyset
Humulin R	Iletin II
Januvia	Lantus
Lispro (Humalog)	Micronase
Novolin	NovoLog
Prandin	Precose
Rezulin	Riomet
Ultralente	Velosulin

Electrolytes and Replacement Solutions

Calcium acetate	Calcium carbonate
Calcium chloride	Calcium citrate
Calcium gluconate	Calcium lactate
Calcium phosphate, dibasic	Calcium phosphate, tribasic
Dextran	Gendex
Hespan	Magnesium chloride
Magnesium sulfate	Phoslo
Potassium acetate	

Potassium bicarbonate (K+ Care ET, Klor-Con/EF, K-Vescent)
Potassium chloride (Kaochlor, Kaon-Cl, Kato Powder, Kay Ciel, K-Lease, K-Lor, Klor-10%, Klor-Con, Klorvess, Klotrix, K-Lyte/Cl, K-Tab, Micro-K Extencaps,SK-Potassium Chloride, Slow-K, Ten-K)
Potassium gluconate (Glu-K, Kaon, Kayliker, K-G Elixir)

Slow-mag	Ringer's Injection

Hormones

Anadrol-50	Android
A.P.L.	Combipatch
Delatestryl	Depo-Provers
Estrace	Estraderm
Estratab	Estrovis
Factrel	Halotestin
Micronor	Norplant
Ogen	Ortho-Est
Ortho-Novum	Orvette
Pregnyl	premarin
Proscar	Provera
Testoderm	Testred

Parathyroid-like Agents

Aredia	Calcimar
Calderol	Cibacalcin
Didronel	E-Vista
Fosamax	Miacalcin
Osteocalcin	Rocaltrol
Salmonine	

Pituitary Hormones

ACTH	Acthar
Cortrosyn	Diapid
Genotropin	Humatrope
Pegvisomant	Pitressin
Protropin	Somavert
Stimate	

Thyroid Antagonists

Pima	Tapazole

Thyroid Hormones

Cytomel	Euthroid
Levothroid	Levoxine
Levoxyl	Triostat
Synthroid	Vitamins
Vitamin A	

Vitamin B complex (including cyanocobalamin, hydroxocobalamin, folic acid, leucovorin calcium, niacin, niacinamide, pyridoxine hydrochloride, riboflavin, thiamine hydrochloride)
Vitamin C
Vitamin D (cholecalciferol, ergocalciferol)
Vitamin E
Vitamin K analogs (menadione/menadiol sodium diphosphate, phytonadione, sodium fluoride)
Trace elements (chromium, copper, iodine, manganese, selenium, zinc)

Blood and Blood-Forming Organs (280-289)

Anticoagulants

abciximab	Aggrastat
cilostazol	clopidrogrel bisulfate
eptifibatide	Integrilin
Plavix	Pletal
RepPro	ticlopidine hydrochloride
Ticlid	tirofiban hydrochloride

Coagulants

AlphaNine Coagulation Factor
Profilate OSD Antihemophilic Factor
Trasylol

Hematinics

Ferrous fumarate:

Femiron	Feostat
Hemocyte	Ircon
Nephro-Fer	Novofumar
Vitron-C	

Ferrous gluconate:

Fergon	Feratab
Fer-Gen-Sol	

Ferrous sulfate:

ED-IN-SOL	Fe50
Feosol	Fer-In-Sol
Fer-Iron	Slow Fe

Iron dextran:

DexFerrum	INFeD

Others

Konyne-HT Factor IX Complex Nu-Iron
Monoclate-P Factor VIII:C, Antihemophilic Factor
Promacta: thrombopoeitin receptor antagonist

Mental Disorders (290-319)

Central Nervous System Stimulants

Adderall XR	Atomoxetine HCl
Concerta	Cylert
Desoxyn	Dexedrine
Dopram	Methylin
Provigil	Ritalin
Strattera	Vivarin
Vyranse	

Cerebral Metabolic Enhancer

Ergostat	Hydergine
Migranal	

Alzheimer's Dementia Agents

Aricept	Cognex
Exelon	Namenda
Reminyl	

Anti-anxiety

Atarax	Ativan
BuSpar	Libritabs
Librium	Miltown
Serax	Tranxene
Valium	Versed
Xanax	

Anti-depressants

Anafranil	Asendin
Aventyl	Celexa
Cymbalta	Desyryl
Effexor	Elavil
Lexapro	Nardil
Norpramin	Pamelor
Parnate	Paxil
Prozac	Remeron
Serzone	Sinequan
Surmontil	Tofranillbutrin
Trialodine	Wellbutrin
Yentreve	Zoloft

Anti-psychotics

Abilify	Clozaril
Etrafon	Haldol
Loxitane	Mellaril
Navane	Orap
Prolixin	Risperdal
Serentil	Seroquel
Serpasil	Stelazine
Thorazine	Triavil
Trilafon	Zyprexa

Sedatives

Ambien	Dalmane
Diprivan	Mebaral
Nembutal	Precedex
ProSom	Restoril
Seconal Sodium	Sonata
Tuinal	Unisom

Other Psychotrophics

Antabuse	Cibalith-S
Eskalith	Lithane
Lithium Carbonate	Lithobid
Luvox	Meridia
Methadone	Zomig
Zyban	

Nervous System and Sense Organs (320-389)

Antibiotics Central Nervous System Agents:

Amikin	Ancef
Cefizox	Fortaz
Garamycin	Kefurox

Nebcin	Rocephin
Tazidime	

Anticonvulsants

Banzel	Celontin
Cerebyx	Cholinesterase Inhibitor
Depakene	Depakote
Dilantin	Felbatol
Keppra	Klonopin
Lamictal	Mebaral
Mesantoin	Milontin
Mysoline	Neurontin
Peganone	Phenobarbital
Phenytoin	Phenurone
Rufinamide	Tegretol
Tranxene	Tridione
Vimpat	Zarontin

Cholinesterase Inhibitor

Aricept

Dopamine Receptor Agonist

Eldepryl	Mirapex
Parlodel	Permax
Requip	Sinemet
Stalevo	Symmetrel
Tasmar	

Miscellaneous Ophthalmics

Alphagan	Betoptic
Emadine	Iopidine
Lacrisert	Lumigan
Opticrom	OptiPranolol
OPTIVAR	Propine
Timoptic	Trusopt
Zaditor	

Migraine Agents

Amerge	Cafergot
Depakote	Ergostat
Imitrex	Inderal
Isocom	Maxalt
Midrin	Migranal
Relpax	Sansert
Treximet	Wigraine
Zomig	

Miotics

Carboptic	Miochol-E
Miostat	Pilocar
Pilostat	Phospholine Iodide

Mydriatics

AK-Dilate	AK-Nefrin
AK-Pentolate	Atropisol
Cyclogyl	Epifrin
Epinal	Eppy/N
Homatropine	Glaucon
Isopto Atropine	Isopto Frin
Isopto Homatropine	Isopto Hyoscine
Minims	Mydfrin
Mydriacyl	

Ophthalmic Antiinfectives

AK-Tracin	Bleph-10 Liqifilm
Chloromycetin	Ciloxan
Garamycin	Ilotycin
Polymyxin B Sulfate	Ocuflox
Sodium Sulamyd	Tobradex
Tobrex	Vigamox
Vira-A	Zymar

Ophthalmic Antiinflammatory Agents

Acular	Decadron Phosphate
Flarex	Fluor-Op
Maxidex	Ocufen
Voltarin	

Otics

Augmentin	Auro-Dri
Cerumex	Chloromycetin Otic
Coly-Mycin S	Cortisporin
Cotrim	LazerSporin-C
Murine Ear	OticTridesilon
PediOtic	Septra

Parasympathomimetics

Duvoid	Evoxac
Mestinon	Prostigmin
Tensilon	Urecholine

Parkinsonism Agents

Akineton	Artane

Benztropine
Comtan
Larodopa
Parlodel
Requip
Symmetrel

Cogentin
Dopar
Mirapex
Permax
Sinemet

Skeletal Muscle Relaxants
Dantrium
Lioresal
Zaraflex

Flexeril
Vanadom

Vertigo Agents
Antivert

Vergon

Circulatory System (390-459)

Alpha Adrenoceptor Agonists
Aldomet
Cardura
Catapres
Hytrin
Regitine
Wytensin

Alpha Receptor
 Blocking Agents
Combipres
Minipress
Trandate

Anginal Preparations
Calan
Cardizem
Inderal
Isordil
Nitro-Dur
Nitrogard
Procardia
Transderm-Nitro

Cardia XT
Dilitrate-SR
Isoptin
Nitro-Bid
Nitrodisc
Nitrostat IV
Sorbitrate

Angiotensin Converting Enzyme Inhibitors
Accupril
Avapro
Capozide
Lotensin
Monopril
Univasc
Zestril

Altace
Capoten
Cozaar
Mavik
Prinivil
Vasotec

Antihypertensives
Aldactazide
Aldomet
Atacard
Avapro
Calan
Cardizem
Catapres
Cozaar
HydroDIURIL
Hytrin
Inderal
Levatol
Minipress
Procardia
Temex
Teveten
Wytensin

Aldactone
Apresoline
Atenolol
Benicar HCT
Capoten
Cardura
Corlopam
Diuril
Hyperstat
Hyzaar
Isoptin
Lopressor
Monopril
Renese
Tenormin
Vasotec
Zestric

Arrhythmia Medications
Betapace
Cardioquin
Inderal
Mexitil
Procan
Quinaglute
Tonocard

Calan
Cordarone
Isoptin
Norpace
Pronestyl
Rythmol

Beta Blocking Agents
Blocadren
Coreg
Corzide
Kerlone
Lopressor
Sectral
Tenormin
Trandate
Zebeta

Cartrol
Corgard
Inderal
Levatol
Normodyne
Tenoretic
Toprol XL
Visken

Calcium Channel Blockers
Adalat
Cardene
Cardizem
Isoptin
Norvasc
Procardia
Vascor

Calan
Cardiac Glycosides
DynaCirc
Lanoxin (Digoxin)
Posicor
Sular
Verelan

Diuretics
Aldactazide
Bumex
Demadex
Dyazide
Esidrix
Furosemide
Rauzide
Zaroxolyn

Aldoril
Combipres
Diuril
Edecrin
Esimil
Lasix
Renese

Thrombolytic Enzymes
Abbokinase
Kabikinase
Streptase

Activase
Retavase

Vasodilators, Cerebral
Pavabid

Vasodilators, Coronary
Cardilate
Nitro-Bid
Nitrolingual Spray
Pavabid
Sorbitrate

Isordil
Nitro-Dur
Nitrostat IV
Peritrate
Transderm-Nitro

Vasodilators, Peripheral
Apresoline
Esimil
Loniten

Dibenzyline
Hyperstat IV
Pavabid

Respiratory System (460-519)

Allergy Relief Products
Antihist-1
Brexin
Clarinex
Naldecon
Trimeton

Benadryl
Bromphen
Dristan
Tavist

Antibiotics
Achromycin
Amoxicillin
Ampicillin
Augmentin
Bactrim
Bicillin
Cefizox
Cefotan
Cipro
Duricef
E-Mycin
ERYC
Factive
Fortaz
Geocillin
Iotycin
Keftab
Levaquin
Mefoxin
Mezlin
Nebcin
PCE Dispertab
Penicillin V
Primaxin
Rocephin
Spectrobid
Tazicef
Tetracycline HCl
Timentin
Wycillin
Zefazone
Zithromax

Amikin
Amoxil
Ancef
Azactam
Biaxin
Ceclor
Cefobid
Ceftin
Claforan
Dynabec
Ery-Tab
Erythromycin
Floxin
Garamycin
Ilosone
Keflex
Kefurox
Mandol
Meropen
Minocin
Netromycin
Penicillin G
Pipracil
Raxar
Septra
Suprax
Tazidime
Ticar
Trovan
Zagam
Zinacef

Antihistamines
Actifed
Allerest
Atarax
Bromphen
Claritin
Deconamine
Periactin
Triaminic

Allegra
Astepro
Benadryl
Chlor-Trimeton
Coricidin
Four-Way
Tavist
Zyrtec

Asthma Preparations
Accolate
Alupent
Beclovent
Bronkaid
Crolom
Flovent
Maxair
Primatene

AeroBid
Aminophylline
Brethine
Choledyl SA
Dilor
Intal
Metaprel
Proventil

Serevent
Symbicort
Tilade
Vanceril
Zyflo

Singulair
TheoDur
Tornalate
Ventolin

Bronchial Dilators
Accolate
Alupent
Asbron G
Brethaire Inhaler
Bronkephrine
Combivent
Isuprel
Marax
Medihaler-Iso
Primatene
Quadrinal
Serevent
Slo-bid
Theolair
Ventolin
Xopenex

Advair Diskus
Aminophylline
Atrovent
Bricanyl
Bronkometer
Choledyl
Lufyllin
Maxair
Prez-D
Proventil
Quibron
Singulair
Tedral
Tornalate
Xolair
Zyflo

Cold, Cough Preparations and Mucolytics
Calcidrine
Comtrex
Dimetane
Guaifed
Hycomine
Novahistine
Ornade
Quibron
Rondec
Rynatan
Sine-Aid
Tuss-Ornade
Tussionex

Cheracol
Dimetapp
Entex
Humibid
Naldecon
Nucofed
Quelidrine
Robitussin
Ru-Tuss
Rynatuss
Triaminic
Tussi-Organdin

Corticosteroids
Aristocort
Cortone Acetate
Depo-Medrol
Hydrocortone
Solu-Cortef

Celestone
Deltasone
Hydeltrasol
Prednisone
Solu-Medrol

Nasal Preparations
Adrenalin Chloride
Beconase
Dopram Injectable
Nasacort
Nasarel
Privine

Afrin
Decadron Phosphate
Flonase
Nasalide
Otrivin

Respiratory Stimulants
Rhinocort
Vancenase

Turbinaire

Respiratory Therapy Agents
Alupent
Survanta

Arm-a-Med
Isoetharine

Digestive System (520-579)

Anorectal Products
Analpram-HC
Rowasa

Proctofoam-HC

Antacids
Alka-Seltzer
Basaljel
Gaviscon
Mylanta
Riopan

Amphojel
Di-Gel
Maalox
Polycitra
Tums

Antibiotics and Antibacterials
Amikin
Azactam
Cefobid
Claforan
Furoxone
Mandol
Nebcin
Pipracil
Tazicef
Ticar
Vancocin

Ancef
Cefizox
Cefotan
Fortaz
Kefzol
Mefoxin
Netromycin
Primaxin
Tazidime
Unasyn
Zefazone

Antispasmodics and Anticholinergics
Bentyl
Donnatal
Librax

Darabid
Levsin
Prilosec

Pro-Banthine   Quarzan
Reglan   Robinul

Antiulcer
Asacol   cimetidine
esomeprazole magnesium   famotidine
iansoprazole   Nexium
omeprazole   Pepcid AC
Prevacid   Prilosec
ranitidine hydrochloride   Tagamet
Zantac

Corticosteroids
Alinia   Aristocort
Cortenema   Decadron
Deltasone   Depo-Medrol
Hydeltrasol   Hydrocortone
Prednisone   Solu-Cortef
Solu-Medrol

Diarrhea Medications
Alinia   Arco-Lase Plus
Charcoal Plus   Donnagel
Furoxone   Kaopectate
Kapectolin   Imodium
Lomotil   Mitrolan
Motofen   Pepto-Bismol

Digestants
Cotazym   Donnazyme
Entozyme   Ku-Zyme
Lactaid   Pancrease
Pancreatin   Ultrase
Viokase

Flatulence Relief
Flatulex   Gas-X
Kutrase   Mylicon
Phazyme

Gallstone Dissolution Agent
Actigall Capsules

Gastric Acid Secretion Inhibitor
Axid   Cytotec
Prevacid   Zantac

Gastrointestinal Antigranulomatous Disease
Azulfidine Tablets,   Dipentum Capsules
   EN-tabs   Mesasal
Pentasa   Remicade
Rowasa

Nausea and Vertigo Medications
Aloxi   Anzeme
Anfernet   Antivert
Aprepitant   Bonine
Bucladin-S Softab   Compazine
Dramamine   Emend
Kytril   Marinol
Reglan   Tigan
Torecan   Vergon
Zofran

Parasympatholytics
Bellergal-S   Bentyl
Cantil   Levsin
Robinul

Genitourinary System (580–629)

Alpha-adrenergic blockers
Flomax   Rapaflo
Tamsulosin HCL

Antibiotics
Achromycin   Ancef
Augmentin   Azactam
Azo Gantanol   Azo Gantrisin
Bactrim   Ceclor
Cefizox   Cefobid
Cefotan   Ceftin
Ceptaz   Cipro
Claforan   Duricef
E-Mycin   Ery-tab
Floxin   Fortaz
Garamycin   Keftab
Kefurox   Mefoxin
Mezlin   Monuril
Nebcin   Netromycin
Noroxin   PCE Dispertab
Penetrex   Primaxin

Rocephin   Septra
Sumycin   Suprax
Tazidime   Timentin
Unasyn   Zinacef

Gonadotropin Inhibitors
Antagon   Danocrine Capsules
Synarel Nasal Solution

Hormones

Androgen and estrogen combinations:
Estratest   Lybrel
Premarin with   Premphase
   Methyltestosterone   Prempro

Estrogens:
Climara   Estrace
Estraderm   Estrofem
Femring   Levolet
Menest   Ogen
Premarin   Seasonale

Gonadotropin:
Lutrepulse   Pregnyl
Profasi   Synarel

Menotropins:
Humegon   Pergonal
Repronex

Progesterone:
Cycrin   Provera

Progestogen:
Aygestin   Micronor

Urinary Tract Agents

Analgesics:
Pyridium   Rimso-50

Antibacterials:
Bactrim   Cipro
Furadantin   Gantanol
Gantrisin   Macrobid
Macrodantin   NegGram
Neosporin   Noroxin
Proloprim   Septra
Thiosulfil   Trimpex
Uroqid Acid No. 2

Antispasmodics:
Cystospaz   Levsin
Oxytrol   Urised
Urispas   UroXatral

Vaginal Preparations

Antifungal agents:
Betadine Douche   Femstat
Gyne-Lotrimin   Monistat
Mycelex   Terazol
Vagistat   Yeast-X

Capsules, tablets:
Mycelex-G   Sultrin

Creams:
Amino-Cerv   Estrace
Mycostatin   Nystex
Premarin   SCE-A
Trysul

Inserts, suppositories:
Terazol   Vagisec Plus

Jellies, ointments:
Aci-Jel

Pregnancy, Childbirth, Puerperium (630–679)

Antibiotics
Amikin   Ancef
Azactam   Ceclor
Cefizox   Cefobid
Cefotan   Claforan
E-Mycin   Fortaz
Garamycin   Keftab
Kefzol   Mefoxin
Nebcin   PCE Dispertab
Primaxin   Rocephin
Tazidime   Ticar
Timentin   Trobicin
Unasyn   Zefazone
Zolicef   Zyvox

Antihypertensives
Adalat   Aldactazide
Aldactone   Aldomet
Apresoline   Calan
Cardizem   Catapres
Deponit   Diuril
Esidrix   Hydralazine
HydroDIURIL   Hygroton
Hyperstat   Hytrin
Inderal   Isoptin
Levatol   Lopressor
Midamor   Minipress
Minoxidil   Nitrostat
Procardia   Renese
Tenormin   Tridil
Vasotec   Wytensin

Diuretics
Aldactazide   Aldactone
Aldoril   Bumex
Demadex   Diuril
Dyazide   Dyrenium
Edecrin   Esidrix
Esimil   HydroDIURIL
Lasix   Lozol
Maxzide   Rauzide
Renese   Zaroxolyn

Galactokinetic Agents
Syntocinon Nasal Spray

Nausea Medication
Antivert   Arrestin
Bonine   Compazine
Emetrol   Norzine
Tigan   Torecan

Oxytocics
Cervidil   Hemabate
Methergine   Oxytocin
Pitocin   Syntocinon
Uterine Relaxants   Yutopar

Skin and Subcutaneous Tissue (680–709)

Abradants
Ureacin

Acne Preparations
Accutane Tablets   Azelex
Benzac   Benzamycin
Cleocin   Clinda-Derm
Desquam   Emgel
Erycette   Novacet
Persa-Gel   Retin-A
Staticin   Sulfacet-R Acne
Theramycin Z   Xerac

Antibacterials, Antifungals and Combinations
Benzamycin   Fungi-Nail
Loprox   Lotrisone
Neosporin   Nizoral
Sporanox

Antibiotics
Amikin   Ancef
Azactam   Bactroban
Ceclor   Cefizox
Cefobid   Cefotan
Ceftin   Cipro
Cubicin   Duricef
ERYC   Erythromycin
Floxin   Furacin
Garamycin   Ilosone
Ilotycin   Keflex
Keftab   Kefzol
Mandol   Mefoxin
Mezlin   Netromycin
Pipracil   Primaxin
Rocephin   Silvadene
Spectrobid   Tazidime
Ticar   Timentin
Ultracef   Zefazone
Zinacef

Antiinflammatory Agents
Aclovate   Aristocort
Cortisporin   Cutivate
Cyclocort   Decadron
Diprolene   Elocon
Halog   Kenalog

Pharmacological Listings

Lidex
Mantadil
Nutracort
Synalar
Topicort
Ultravate

Lotrisone
NeoDecadron
Synacort
Temovate
Tridesilon
Westcort

Corticosteroids
Amcort
Cortef
Depo-Medrol
Solu-Cortef

Celestone
Deltasone
Hydeltrasol
Solu-Medrol

Depigmenting Agents
Benoquin Cream
Eldoquin

Eldopaque

Dermatologicals

Dermatitis Herpetiformis:
Dapsone USP

Dermatitis Relief:
Decaspray
Florone
Locoid
Psorcon

Elidel
Hytone
Mytrex

Epidermal and Cellular Growth:
Lazer Cream

Fungicides:
Amphotec
BAZA Cream
Exelderm
Grisactin
Lamisil
Lotrimin
Mycelex
Mycostatin

Abelcet
Clioquinol
Fungoid Creme
Halotex
Loprox
Lotrisone
Mycolog-11
Spectazole

Keratolytics:
Adrucil
Keralyt Gel

Fluoroplex
Occlusal-HP

Pruritis Medications:
Alphatrex
Dermoplast
Eurax
Hytone
Locoid
Periactin
Psorcon

Betatrex
Eldecort
Florone
Hyzine-50
Mytrex
Pramosone
Vistaril

Psoriasis Agents:
Amevive
Cormax
DHS Tar
Drithocreme
Enbrel
Pentrax
Tazorac
Zetar

Anthra-Derm
Denorex
Dovonex
Dritho-Scalp
Hunira
Raptiva
Temovate

Steroids and Combinations:
Neo-Synalar
Synalar
Vanoxide-HC

Psorcon
Synemol
Vytone

Wart Removers:
Compound W
LazerFormalyde
Podocon-25
Sal-Plant Gel
Trans-Ver-Sal
Verrex
Viranol Gel

Condylox
Occlusal
Sal-Acid Plasters
Trans-Plantar
Verr-Canth
Verrusol

Musculoskeletal System and Connective Tissue (710-739)

Analgesics
Advil
Anaprox
Ansaid
Bufferin
Clinoril
Darvon
Disalcid
Easprin
Empirin/Codeine
Esgic
Feldene
Hydrocodone

Anacin
Anexsia
Ascriptin
Butazolidin
Darvocet
Datril
Dolobid
Ecotrin
Equagesic
Exedrin
Flexeril
Indocin

Lortab/Lorcet
Medipren
Motrin
Naprosyn
Norgesic
Parafon Forte
Percodan
Ponstel
Salflex
Synalgos-DC
Talwin
Tolectin
Tylenol
Tylox
Wygesic

Meclomen
Mono-Gesic
Nalfon
Norflex
Orudis
Percocet
Phenaphen/Codeine
Rufen
Sarapin
Talacen
Tapentadol
Trilisate
Tylenol/Codeine
Vicodin

Antibiotics (Osteomyelitis Treatments)
Amikin
Cefizox
Cipro
Floxin
Garamycin
Keftab
Kefzol
Mefoxin
Pipracil
Timentin
Zinacef

Ancef
Cefotan
Clindamycin
Fortaz
Keflex
Kefurox
Mandol
Monocid
Rocephin
Vancocin

Antiinflammatory Agents, Steroids and Combinations
Aristocort
Celebrex
Decadron
Depo-Medrol
Hydeltrasol
Kenalog
Lexiva
Relafen
Voltren

Bextra
Cortone
Deltasone
Hydeltra-T.B.A.
Hydrocortone
Lodine
Medrol
Remicade

Antirheumatic, Disease Modifying Agent
Abatacept
Etanercept

Enbrel
Orencia

Calcium Preparations
Calcium-D
Caltrate
Dical-D
Nephro-Calci
Phos-Ex

Calphosan
Citracal
Neo-Calglucon
Os-Cal
Posture

Muscle Relaxants
Actonel
Forteo
Parafon Forte
Robaxisal
Soma
Valrelease

Flexeril
Paraflex
Robaxin
Skelaxin
Valium

Osteoporosis Preparations
Actonel
Boniva
Didronel
Fosamax
Lexiva

Aredia
Calcimar
Evista
Gerimed
Miacalcin

Congenital Anomalies (740-759)
A pharmacological reference list cannot be presented for this chapter because most conditions listed are treatable only by surgical methods and are not affected by medications.

Conditions in the Perinatal Period (760-779)

Antibiotics
Amoxicillin
Bicillin
Dicloxacillin
Fortaz
Kefzol
Mezlin
Rocephin
Tazicef
Ticar
Zithromax

Biaxin
Cloxacillin
E-Mycin
Garamycin
Mandol
Nebcin
Spectrobid
Tazidime
Vibramycin

Bronchodilators
Aerolate Jr.
Bronkephrine

Asbron G
Choledyl

Dilor
Quadrinal
Theolair

Proventil
Somophyllin
Ventolin

Corticosteroids
Aristocort
Cortone Acetate
Deltasone
Hydeltrasol
Solu-Cortef

Celeston
Decadron
Depo-Medrol
Prednisone
Solu-Medrol

Electrolytes
Infalyte
Pedialyte

Oralyte
Rehydralyte

Galactokinetics (Milk Flow Stimulants)
Syntocinon Nasal Spray

Galactorrhea (Lactation) Inhibitors
Parlodel

Neonatal Respiratory Distress Syndrome Agents
Exosurf

Survanta

Ophthalmic Ointments, Antibiotics
Ilotycin

Rh Hemolytic Disease-Related Agents
Gamulin Rh
HypRho-D Full Dose (for baby)
HypRho-D Mini-Dose (for mother)
Win Rho-SD

Uterine Contractants
Oxytocin

Vitamins
AquaMEPHYTON

Symptoms, Signs and Ill-Defined Conditions (780-799)

Analgesics

Acetaminophens and combinations:
Acetaminophen
Anexsia
Datril
Feverall
Midrin

Anacin–Aspirin-Free
Bufferin
Excedrin
Isocom
Tylenol

Aspirins:
Easprin
Forprin

Ecotrin

Aspirin combinations:
Anacin
Bufferin
Norgesic

Ascriptin A/D
Equagesic

Narcotics, synthetics and combinations:
Alfenta
Astramorph/PF
B&O Supprettes
Damason-P
Darvon
Dilaudid
Duramorph
Fioricet
Hydrocet
Levo-Dromoran
Lurline
Methadone-HCl
MSIR
Numorphan
Oramorph
Percodan
Phrenilin
Roxicodone
Stadol
Sufenta
Talacen
Tylox

Anexsia
Azdone
Dalgan
Darvocet-N
Demerol
Dolophine
Esgic
Fiorinal
Infumorph
Lortab
Mepergan
MS-Contin
Nubain
Oralet
Percocet
Phenaphen/Codeine
Roxanol
Sedapap
Sublimaze
Synalgos-DC
Talwin-NX
Vicodin

Nonsteroidal antiinflammatory drugs (NSAIDs):
Advil
Daypro
Feldene
Lodine
Medipren
Nalfon
Nuprin
Ponstel

Anaprox
Duract
Indocin
Meclomen
Motrin
Naprosyn
Orudis
Rufen

Tolectin   Toradol
Voltaren

Other:
Alka-Seltzer   Dolobid
Empirin/Codeine   Mono-Gesic
Norflex   Parafon Forte
Salflex   Sarapin
Trilisate

Antacids
Alka-Seltzer   Amphojel
Basaljel   Maalox
Mylanta   Riopan

Anticonvulsives
Depakane   Depakote
Dilantin   Jabatril
Lamictal   Nurontin
Phenobarbital   Tegretol
Topamax

Antiflatulents and Antigas Medications
Flatulex   Kutrase
Mylicon

Antipyretics
Acetaminophen   Ascriptin A/D
Feverall   PediaProfen
Rufen   Trilisate
Tylenol

Antispasmodics and Anticholinergics
Arco-Lase   Bentyl
Cantil   Darabid
Donnatal   Kinesed
Kutrase   Levsin
Levsinex   Librax
Prilosec   Pro-Banthine
Quarzan   Robinul
Valpin-50

Appetite Suppressants
Amphetamines:
Biphetamine   Desoxyn
Dexedrine   Didrex

Nonamphetamines:
Adipex-P   Bontril
Fastin   Ionamin
Plegine   Pondimin
Prelu-2   Redux
Sanorex   Tenuate

Digestives
Cotazym   Donnazyme
Ku-Zyme   Pancrease
Pancreatin   Viokase

Diuretics
Aldactazide   Aldactone
Bumex   Capozide
Corzide   Demadex
Diamox   Diulo
Diuril   Dyazide
Dyrenium   Edecrin
Enduron   Enduronyl
Esidrex   Exna
HydroDIURIL   Hydromox
Lasix   Lozol
Maxzide   Midamor
Moduretic   Naturetin
Oretic   Prinzide
Rauzide   Renese
Saluron   Thalitone
Vaseretic   Zestoretic

Nausea and Vertigo Agents
Aloxi   Antivert
Bonine   Compazine
Emend   Emetrol
Kytril   Norzine
Phenergan   Tigan
Torecan   Zofran

Sleep Aids
Ambien   Chloral hydrate
Dalmane   Doriden
Halcion   Lunesta
Restoril   Rozerem
Valmid

Hypnotics:
Butisol   Mebaral
Phenobarbital

Sedatives (barbiturates):
Benadryl   BufferinAF
Excedrin PM   Magonate
Mepergan   Phenergan
Tylenol PM   Unisom
Versed

Sedatives (nonbarbiturates):
Eldertonic   Niferex
Nu-Iron

Tonics
Inderal

Tremor Preparations
Eldertonic   Niferex
Nu-Iron   Inderal

Injury and Poisoning (800-999)

Agents Used in Poisonings
Amyl nitrate   Antilirium
Antizole   BAL
Benadryl   Desferal
Digibind   Ipecac Syrup
Narcan (Naloxone)   Penicillamine
Pralidoxime   Protopam Chloride
Revex   Romazicon
Sodium nitrite

Analgesics
Acetaminophens and combinations:
Acetaminophen   Anexsia
Aspirin-Free Anacin   Excedrin
Feverall   Isocom
Midrin   Tylenol
Tylenol with codeine

Aspirins:
Aspirin   Easprin
Ecotrin

Aspirin combinations:
Anacin   Ascriptin A/D
Bufferin   Equagesic
Norgesic

Narcotics, synthetics and combinations:
Alfenta   Anexsia
Astromorph PF   Azdone
B&O Supprettes   Dalgan
Damason-P   Darvocet-N
Darvon   Demerol
Dilaudid   Dolophine
Duramorph   Esgic
Fioricet   Fiorinal
Hydrocet   Infumorph
Levo-Dromoran   Lortab/Lorcet
Lurline   Mepergan
Methadone HCl   MS Contin
MSIR   Nubain
Numorphan   Oramorph
Percocet   Percodan
Phrenilin   Roxanol
Roxicodone   Sedapap
Stadol   Sublimaze
Sufenta   Synalgos-DC
Talacen   Talwin
Tegretol   Tylox
Vicodin   Wygesic
Zydone

Nonsteroidal antiinflammatory drugs (NSAIDs):
Advil   Anaprox
Ansaid   Cataflam
Clinoril   Daypro
Feldene   Ibuprofen
Lodine   Meclamen
Medipren   Motrin
Nalfon   Naprosyn
Nuprin   Orudis
Ponstel   Relafen
Rufen   Tolectin
Toradol   Voltaren

Antibiotics
Achromycin   Amikin
Amoxicillin   Amoxil
Ancef   Augmentin
Azactam   Ceclor
Cefizox   Cefobid
Cefotan   Cipro
Claforan   Floxin
Garamycin   Keflex
Keftab   Kefurox
Kefzol   Mefoxin
Mezlin   Nebcin
Netromycin   Pipracil
Tazidime   Timentin
Zefazone   Zinacef

Anticoagulants
Calciparine   Coumadin
Dicumarol   Fragmin
Heparin Sodium   Lovenox
Organan   Panwarfin

Antihistamines
Allegra   Atarax/Vistaril
Benadryl   Chlor-Trimeton
Claritin   Dimetap
Extendryl   Hismanal
Optimine   Seldane
Tacaryl   Temaril
Zyrtec

Antivertigo Medications
Antivert   Bonine
Bucladin-S   Meclizine
Vontrol

Burn Agents
Americaine   Aquaphor
Butesin Picrate   Chloresium
Collagenase Santyl   Dermoplast
Eucerin   Nupercainal
Panafil   Prophyllin
Silvadine   Sween Cream
Tronothane

Corticosteroids
Aristocort   Celestone
Decadron   Deltasone
Depo-Medrol   Hydeltrasol
Hydrocortone   Prednisone
Solu-Cortef   Solu-Medrol

Detoxifying Agents
Mesnex Injection

Skin Wound Preparations
Betadine   Debrisan
DuoDERM

Wound Dressings
Aquaphor   Chloresium
Critic-Aid   Debrisan
DuoDERM   Granulex
Lazer   Panafil
SSD

Valid Three-digit ICD-9-CM Codes

Three-digit ICD-9-CM codes are used to identify a condition or disease only when a fourth or fifth digit is not available. The following are the only ICD-9-CM codes that are valid without further specificity.

024	Glanders
025	Melioidosis
035	Erysipelas
037	Tetanus
042	Human immunodeficiency virus (HIV) disease
048	Other enterovirus diseases of central nervous system
061	Dengue
064	Viral encephalitis transmitted by other and unspecified arthropods
071	Rabies
075	Infectious mononucleosis
080	Louse-borne [epidemic] typhus
096	Late syphilis, latent
101	Vincent's angina
118	Opportunistic mycoses
124	Trichinosis
129	Intestinal parasitism, unspecified
135	Sarcoidosis
138	Late effects of acute poliomyelitis
179	Malignant neoplasm of uterus, part unspecified
181	Malignant neoplasm of placenta
185	Malignant neoplasm of prostate
193	Malignant neoplasm of thyroid gland
217	Benign neoplasm of breast
220	Benign neoplasm of ovary
226	Benign neoplasm of thyroid glands
243	Congenital hypothyroidism
260	Kwashiorkor
261	Nutritional marasmus
262	Other severe, protein-calorie malnutrition
267	Ascorbic acid deficiency
311	Depressive disorder, not elsewhere classified

316	Psychic factors associated with diseases classified elsewhere
317	Mild mental retardation
319	Unspecified mental retardation
325	Phlebitis and thrombophlebitis of intracranial venous sinuses
326	Late effects of intracranial abscess or pyogenic infection
340	Multiple sclerosis
390	Rheumatic fever without mention of heart involvement
393	Chronic rheumatic pericarditis
412	Old myocardial infarction
430	Subarachnoid hemorrhage
431	Intracerebral hemorrhage
436	Acute, but ill-defined, cerebrovascular disease
449	Septic arterial embolism
452	Portal vein thrombosis
460	Acute nasopharyngitis [common cold]
462	Acute pharyngitis
463	Acute tonsillitis
470	Deviated nasal septum
475	Peritonsillar abscess
481	Pneumococcal pneumonia [Streptococcus pneumoniae pneumonia]
485	Bronchopneumonia, organism unspecified
486	Pneumonia, organism unspecified
490	Bronchitis, not specified as acute or chronic
496	Chronic airway obstruction, not elsewhere classified
500	Coal workers' pneumoconiosis
501	Asbestosis
502	Pneumoconiosis due to other silica or silicates
503	Pneumoconiosis due to other inorganic dust
504	Pneumonopathy due to inhalation of other dust

505	Pneumoconiosis, unspecified
514	Pulmonary congestion and hypostasis
515	Postinflammatory pulmonary fibrosis
538	Gastrointestinal mucostitis (ulcerative)
541	Appendicitis, unqualified
542	Other appendicitis
566	Abscess of anal and rectal regions
570	Acute and subacute necrosis of liver
586	Renal failure, unspecified
587	Renal sclerosis, unspecified
591	Hydronephrosis
605	Redundant prepuce and phimosis
630	Hydatidiform mole
631	Other abnormal product of conception
632	Missed abortion
650	Normal delivery
677	Late effect of complication of pregnancy, childbirth, and the puerperium
683	Acute lymphadenitis
684	Impetigo
700	Corns and callosities
725	Polymyalgia rheumatica
734	Flat foot
769	Respiratory distress syndrome
797	Senility without mention of psychosis
920	Contusion of face, scalp, and neck except eye(s)
931	Foreign body in ear
932	Foreign body in nose
936	Foreign body in intestine and colon
937	Foreign body in anus and rectum
938	Foreign body in digestive system, unspecified
981	Toxic effect of petroleum products
986	Toxic effect of carbon monoxide
990	Effects of radiation, unspecified
V08	Asymptomatic HIV infection status

Present on Admission (POA) Tutorial

Background

The Deficit Reduction Act of 2005 (DRA), section 5001(C), requires that CMS implement Present on Admission (POA) indicators for all diagnoses and external causes of injury on Medicare claims for inpatient acute care discharges beginning October 1, 2007. Critical access hospitals, Maryland waiver hospitals, long term care hospitals, cancer hospitals, and children's inpatient facilities are exempt from this requirement.

Claim Submission Requirements

Beginning October 1, 2007, all inpatient acute care hospital discharges were required to be reported using POA indicators on all diagnoses and external cause of injury codes. The only exception is for a select group of codes that are designated as exempt from the POA regulations. This list of codes may be found at the end of this tutorial. Hospitals that failed to submit claims for discharges beginning January 1, 2008 with POA indicators received remittance advice remarks only. After April 1, 2008, claims were returned for completion with POA indicators.

CMS is also required to identify at least two conditions will be designated such that when the POA indicator reflects that they developed during the admission, they will not be recognized as major complication/comorbidity (MCC) or complication/comorbidity (CC) conditions under the DRG inpatient prospective payment system (IPPS). These conditions will have met the following criteria:

- high cost and/or high volume
- represent conditions that could have been avoided using evidence-based practice guidelines
- when present with other secondary diagnoses on the claim result in higher DRG payment weight

Effective October 1, 2008 (FY2009), hospitals will not receive additional payment for claims with codes that represent one of the selected conditions when not indicated as present on admission, meaning it developed during the acute care inpatient stay. The regulation effectively deactivates the CC or MCC status of the code, but hospital staff should be aware that other conditions on the case may carry valid CC or MCC status. Refer to page 60 of this tutorial, which provides a list of the eight conditions that CMS has designated as "Hospital Acquired Conditions" and will be included in the policy for FY2009.

General Guidelines

The POA indicator guidelines are not intended to replace the official ICD-9-CM reporting guidelines. Nor will the POA guidelines supersede the Uniform Hospital Discharge Data Set (UHDDS) definition of principal diagnosis. A principal diagnosis remains defined as the condition established after study to be chiefly responsible for occasioning the admission of the patient to the hospital. The definition of "Other Diagnoses' also remains the same. Coders must report all conditions that coexist at the time of admission, develop subsequently, or that affect the treatment received and/or the length of stay. This has significant impact on the practice of assigning the POA indicators.

Because the POA indicator selection should accurately reflect the patient's conditions upon admission, review of POA guidelines and official coding guidelines is required. Consistent, complete documentation in the medical record is of the utmost importance. Lack of complete documentation may impact DRG case grouping and reimbursement. It is incumbent upon the provider to resolve any documentation issues.

The following is a summary of the basic POA Indicator Guidelines:

- The POA indictor requirement applies only to acute care hospital inpatient admissions or other facilities, as required by regulation for public health reporting.

- A POA condition is defined not only as one that is clearly present at the time of admission, but also those that were clearly present, but not diagnosed until after the time of admission.

- Present on admission is defined as present at the time the order for an inpatient admission is made, regardless of whether the patient's episode of care originated in the emergency department, ambulatory surgery area, or other outpatient area. Conditions that develop during an outpatient encounter are considered present on admission.

- The POA guidelines are not intended to replace any of the other ICD-9-CM Official Guidelines for Coding and Reporting.

Guidelines are not intended to determine whether or not a condition should be coded, but rather how to apply the POA indicator.

The following options should be used to indicate whether a condition was POA:

Y	Yes
N	No
U	Unknown
W	Clinically undetermined

Unreported/not used – (Exempt from POA reporting) – CMS has developed a standard "exempt" list of conditions and external causes. For these codes the POA indicator is left blank, except on the UB-04 form where an indicator of "1" is indicated as the equivalent of a blank. On the UB-04 blanks are undesirable when submitting this data via the 4010A.

See Appendix 1 of the ICD-9-CM Official Coding Guidelines for Coding and Reporting and the end of this tutorial for the complete list of exempt codes.

When using the options listed above, the following definitions should be used:

Y	present at the time of inpatient admission
N	not present at the time of inpatient admission
U	documentation is insufficient to determine if condition is present on admission
W	Provider is unable to clinically determine whether condition was present on admission or not

Most ICD-9-CM diagnosis codes and E codes require POA indicator assignment. However, there are some diagnoses that are considered exempt from the POA reporting. To view exempt codes, refer to the ICD-9-CM Official Guidelines for Coding and Reporting and the end of this tutorial. The list reflects those conditions that either do not represent a current disease or are always considered POA.

Specific Guidelines

Before instituting a policy and procedure for assigning POA indicators, review and educational activities should be conducted, with ongoing feedback to the coders. Complete and accurate medical record documentation is a critical aspect of the review and training that must take place. The ICD-9-CM Official Guidelines for Coding and Reporting indicate that to achieve accurate and complete documentation, code assignment, and reporting of diagnoses and procedures, documentation must be a collaborative effort between healthcare provider and the coder. To assist the coder in determining which documentation in the medical record may be used for code selection, an Official Guidelines for Source Documentation Table is provided at the end of this section.

Assignment of POA indicators may be confusing for several types of cases, particularly if the documentation is not clear. The following are examples of POA guidelines and case scenarios illustrating various coding situations:

Note: As always, query the physician for a definitive diagnosis when documentation is inconsistent. The tips are presented as a guide to what information a coder might review in the process of verifying a diagnosis before assigning a POA indicator. The HIM department should work closely with the medical staff to develop a list of criteria for all conditions that are frequently queried.

- **Combination Codes:** Assign "N" if any part of the combination code was not present at the time of admission.

Example: Obstructive chronic bronchitis with acute exacerbation

Tips: The POA indicator "N" would be assigned if the exacerbation did not happen until after the admission (code 491.21).

Definition of acute exacerbation: the presence of one or more of the following findings are indications of acute exacerbation: increase in sputum purulence, increase in sputum volume, tightening of chest, fluid retention and worsening of dyspnea or shortness of breath and/or wheezing.

Indicators of an acute exacerbation of COPD might be the documentation of either of the following treatments:

- Bronchodilator: Nebulised beta2-agonist or ipratropium bromide. If no response, IV aminophylline or nebulised beta2-agonist and ipratropium bromide in combination
- Oxygen: Given in ambulance or on arrival, 24-28% by mask or 2 ltr/min by nasal prongs.

Source Documents: Laboratory report, physician orders, nursing notes

- **Impending Conditions:** If a threatened or impending condition is present prior to or at the time of admission, report "Y" for the POA indicator.

Example: An impending acute myocardial infarction (code 411.1)

Tips: Impending acute myocardial infarction is also documented as unstable angina. This condition is a type of acute chest pain that occurs when the heart does not get enough oxygen. Patients with atherosclerosis, which is the most common cause of unstable angina, may accelerate to unstable angina. Unstable angina is acute worsening of chest pain.

The chest pain that:

- Occurs without cause
- Lasts longer than 15 to 20 minutes
- Does not go away with nitroglycerine
- May occur along with a drop in blood pressure or significant shortness of breath

Tests to diagnose angina include:

- Blood tests to check the levels of creatine phosphokinase(CPK), myoglobin, and troponin I and T
- Coronary angiography
- ECG (transient ST- or T-wave changes that develop duringa symptomatic episode at rest and resolve when thepatient becomes asymptomatic strongly suggest unstableangina)
- Echocardiography

Drug treatment associated with Impending myocardial infarction:

- Aspirin: 324 mg
- Heparin: 80 units/kg IV bolus with constant IV infusion at18 units/kg/hr titrated to maintain a PTT between 46 and70 seconds
- Nitrates: Sublingual (1-3 tablets); IV (5-100 micro-g/min)
- Beta Blockers: Oral dose appropriate for specific drug: IVmetoprolol (1-5 m slow IV every 5 minutes to 15 mg total);IV propranolol 0.5 to 1.0 mg; IV atenolol 5 mg everyminute to 10 mg total
- Narcotics: Morphine sulfate 2 to 5 mg IV
- Source Documents: Laboratory reports, physician orders, EKG

- **Two or More Contrasting Conditions:** If the symptoms related to the two conditions were present at the time of admission, the POA indicators for both are "Y."

Example: Diverticulitis versus chronic appendicitis (codes 562.11, 542)

Tip: A patient may present with acute abdominal pain but mayimprove clinically and be discharged or transferred before a definitivedetermination of the final diagnosis can be made.

Tests to diagnose diverticulitis include:

- Abdominal palpation, which may indicate left lower quadrant mass
- CT scan may reveal thickening of the inflamed area orbowel spasm if irritable bowel syndrome accompaniesdiverticular disease
- Lab studies may indicate elevated white blood count

Diverticular disease may be diagnosed via barium enema or sigmoidoscopy or colonoscopy services, but these studies are typically not performed if the acute inflamed diverticulitis phase of the disease is present, since these procedures may cause bowel rupture or require strenuous bowel prep.

Tests to diagnose appendicitis include:

- Abdominal palpation, which may indicate right lower quadrant pain, which typically worsens when the patient is asked to cough or upon gentle percussion

- Lab studies may indicate a moderately elevated white blood count, with increased numbers of immature cells
- Enema studies with a contrast agent may be helpful; appendicitis is present if the appendix does not fill with contrast agent

In this example, the POA indicator for codes representing both the diverticulitis and the chronic appendicitis should be "Y," since it was thought that the presenting symptom was caused by one of these conditions.

Source Documents: Radiology reports, laboratory results, physician documentation of abdominal examination findings

- **Symptom Followed by Comparative or Contrasting Conditions:** If a symptom followed by comparative or contrasting conditions is present prior to or at the time of admission, all indicators are reported as "Y."

Example: Chills due to either pneumonia or urinary tract infection. (codes 780.99, 486, 599.0).

Tips: A patient may present with chills but may improve clinically and be discharged or transferred before a definitive determination of the final diagnosis can be made.

A patient presenting with chills is typically worked-up for an infectious disease process. Chest X-rays or other radiological studies may be performed to rule out the presence of pneumonia, but coders should be aware that in some cases, the first chest X-ray may not show any consolidation indicative of pneumonia. After the patient is admitted and hydrated, the follow-up chest X-ray may show signs of pneumonia, but this disease process may have been present at the time of admission. The determination must be made by the physician, who may have documented clinical signs of pneumonia in the initial physical examination.

The search for the underlying cause of an infectious disease process is also typically aided by laboratory studies, which may includes putum or urine cultures. The coder should not assign any diagnosis code based on laboratory findings only, but these findings are clues that help focus the clinical picture for each patient. Coders must also be aware that some cultures may contain contaminated material that does not represent an infectious process. This is particularly problematic with Staphylococcus aureus, which is a bacteria very commonly found on skin surfaces. Culture and sensitivity studies help determine which antibiotics would be most effective in treating the particular infection. Again, the coder may not assign any diagnosis code based on treatment options, but they can provide clues to the type of infectious process that may be present. For example, if a patient presents with fever and chills, is found to have consolidation on chest X-ray and is treated with Sporanox, an antifungal agent, this is indicative of a fungal pneumonia and the physician documentation should specify such.

Source Documents: physical examination, radiology reports, laboratory findings, including urine, sputum or blood cultures, sputum gram stain, biopsy results

In this example, codes for all the presenting diagnoses would be represented with a "Y" POA indicator.

- **Same Diagnosis Code for Two or More Conditions:** When the same ICD-9-CM diagnosis code applies to two or more conditions during the same encounter (e.g. bilateral condition, or two separate conditions classified to the same ICD-9-CM diagnosis code):

- Assign "Y" if all conditions represented by the single ICD-9-CM code were present on admission (e.g. bilateral fracture of the same bone, same site, and both fractures were present on admission)
- Assign "N" if any of the conditions represented by the single ICD-9-CM code was not present on admission (e.g. dehydration with hyponatremia is assigned to code 276.1, but only one of these conditions was present on admission).

- **External Cause of Injury Codes:** If an injury or poisoning occurred prior to or at the time of admission, both the code for the injury/poisoning and the corresponding E code are reported with POA indicator "Y."

Tips: Typically most trauma cases are very straight-forward and it is very clear which injuries were present at the time of admission. However, in cases of multiple trauma, one or several injuries may not be diagnosed initially, but may have been present at the time of admission. For example, if a patient suffers a closed head injury and internal abdominal injuries, a comparatively minor fractured extremity may not be diagnosed or treated initially, during the lifesaving treatment phase. But if the injury was sustained in the original injury, the POA indicator should remain "Y."

Coders should be extremely careful in assigning the appropriate POA indicator if a patient suffers an injury while an inpatient. For example, if a patient falls from the hospital bed and fractures a hip, the codes representing that injury (along with the appropriate E code) should be designated "N" in the corresponding POA indicator assignment.

Source Documents: Emergency Department reports, radiology reports, History and Physical report, consultation reports (particularly orthopedic), physician orders

The following guidelines may be helpful when assigning POA indicators for obstetrical patients.

Coders should also keep in mind that several of the obstetrical related codes (such as code 650, Normal delivery) are found on the POA exemption list and do not require POA indicator assignment.

- **Antepartum Conditions:** If an antepartum condition is present prior to or at the time of the current admission, report "Y" for the POA indicator.

Example: Pregnancy with fetal distress, antepartum (code 656.33).

Tip: Most obstetrical departments in acute care facilities use preprinted forms specifically designed for pregnant patients. These forms should include designations for labor-related conditions that were present at the time the patient was admitted. Other forms are used to detail a patient's course as she progresses from labor through delivery. Although nursing staff document most of the information on these forms, the physician should also document any complication of labor, along with treatment provided.

Source Documents: Obstetrical Intake Record, History & Physical, Labor Record

- **Pre-existing Chronic Conditions:** If a pregnant patient has a chronic condition that was present prior to or at the time of admission, the POA indicator is "Y."

Example: Pregnancy with pre-existing hypertension, delivered (code 642.01).

Tip: The POA guideline related to pre-existing chronic conditions for pregnant patients follows that for other patients. Any pre-existing chronic condition should be coded with POA indicator "Y," denoting that the condition was present before or at the time the patient was admitted. Coders should keep in mind that there may be a specific pregnancy related code for the condition.

Source Documents: Obstetrical Intake Record, History & Physical, Labor Record

- **Acute Conditions:** If a pregnant patient has an acute condition that develops during delivery and it was not present prior to or at the time of admission, the POA indicator is "N."

Example: Second degree perineal laceration, delivered (code 664.11);

Tip: Many of the conditions that are a result of the delivery process itself are, by their very definition, not present on admission. At admission, the pregnant patient has not progressed to the point of delivery or sustained a condition such as a perineal laceration. All conditions that develop as a result of the delivery process itself should be considered not present on admission and designated with POA indicator "N."

Source Documents: Obstetrical Intake Record, History & Physical, Labor Record, Delivery Record, Discharge Summary

- **Co-existing Conditions:** If a patient has a condition that is diagnosed on the current admission but the documentation does not indicate whether it was present at the time of admission, the provider should be queried. If no answer can be determined, the POA indicator is "U."

Example: Pregnant patient delivers and is also found to have a breast nipple abscess (code 675.01).

Tip: In only very limited circumstances should a POA indicator of "U" be assigned, and only if the physician cannot be reached for clarification. Conditions that are pregnancy related should be clearly documented concerning whether they were present at the time of admission. It is typically conditions related to other body systems that may not contain specific enough detail to determine whether they were present at the time of admission. Most acute care facilities have physician query processes in place to address these issues, but in some limited cases, a POA indicator of "U" must be assigned.

Source Documents: Obstetrical Intake Record, History & Physical, Labor Record, Delivery Record, Discharge Summary

The following guidelines may be helpful when assigning POA indicators for V codes:

- **Birth or Outcome of Delivery:** If a V code represents a birth or outcome of delivery (mother's record) for the current admission, the POA indicator is "Y."

Example: Normal single liveborn infant, born in hospital, delivered vaginally; single liveborn infant (outcome of delivery) (code V30.00 or V27.0).

Tip: The two V codes that represent either a birth or an outcome of delivery for the mother's medical record should always be considered "Y" for POA assignment. These are routine cases with expected outcomes.

Source Documents: Labor Record, Delivery Record, Discharge Summary

- **Reason for Encounter:** If a V code indicates the reason that the patient was admitted for the encounter, the POA indicator is "Y." Example: A patient is admitted for radiation therapy (code V58.0).

Tip: A V code representing a reason for a patient encounter would always be considered "Y" POA indicator since it was obviously a planned admission and the circumstances were known at the time of admission.

Source Documents: History & Physical, physician orders

- **Status or History:** When a V code represents a status or history at the time of the current admission, the POA indicator is Y. Example: Personal history of breast carcinoma or tracheostomy status (code V10.3 or V44.0).

Tip: V codes representing either history or patient status should always be considered "Y" POA indicator since the condition has already happened and was known at the time of admission.

Source Documents: History & Physical, physician orders

One of the most significant challenges to correct POA indicator assignment may be ensuring complete, consistent and appropriate physician documentation at the time of initial coding. While some cases, particularly those for surgical patients admitted for a specific procedure, are very straight-forward and it is clear which conditions were present at the time of admission, many other cases are much more vague. Coders should keep in mind that a patient may present to the hospital with ambiguous signs or symptoms of a disease that could take several days to accurately diagnose. If the presenting signs or symptoms were related to the subsequently diagnosed condition, the POA indicator should be "Y," but only the provider may make this connection and it must be clearly documented in the medical record. The POA Reporting Guidelines include: "Issues related to inconsistent, missing, conflicting or unclear documentation must still be resolved by the provider." This may involve physician queries either during or following the patient encounter; medical record documentation from any provider involved in the care and treatment of the patient may be used to support the determination of whether a condition was present on admission or not. To assist the coder in determining which documentation in the medical record may be used for code selection, the following Official Guidelines for Source Documentation Table was developed. The table includes AHA's *Coding Clinic for ICD-9-CM* official guidelines related to medical record documentation.

Selected Hospital Acquired Conditions for FY2009

In the IPPS Proposed Rule for FY2009, released on April 30, 2008, CMS designated the following eight conditions to be subject to the 'Hospital Acquired Conditions' provision affecting reimbursement, effective October 1, 2008 (FY2009):

Selected HACs	Code(s)
Foreign object retained after surgery	998.4, 998.7
Air embolism	999.1
Blood incompatibility	999.6
Stage III and IV pressure (decubitus) ulcers	707.23, 707.24
Falls and trauma: fractures, dislocations, intracranial injuries, crushing injuries, burns	MCCs and CCs within the code ranges: 800–829, 830–839, 850–854, 925–929, 940–949, 991–994
Catheter-associated urinary tract infection	996.64, and excludes any of the following from acting as a CC or MCC: 112.2, 590.10, 590.11, 590.2, 590.3, 590.80, 590.81, 595.0, 597.0, 599.0

Present on Admission (POA) Tutorial

Selected HACs	Code(s)
Vascular catheter-associated infection	999.31
Surgical site infection—Mediastinitis after coronary artery bypass graft (CABG)	519.2 and one of the following procedure codes: 36.10–36.19
Manifestations of poor glycemic control	250.10–250.13, 250.20–250.23, 251.0, 249.10–249.11, 249.20–249.21
Surgical site infection following certain orthopedic procedures	996.67, 998.59 and any one of the following procedure codes: 81.01–81.08, 81.23–81.24, 81.31–81.38, 81.83, 81.85
Surgical site infection following bariatric surgery for obesity	Principal diagnosis 278.01, secondary code 998.59 and one of the following procedure codes: 44.38, 44.39, 44.95
Deep vein thrombosis and pulmonary embolism following certain orthopedic procedures	415.11, 415.19, 453.40–453.42 and one of the following procedure codes: 81.51–81.52, 81.54

For more specific instructions on Medicare POA indicator reporting options, refer to:

http://www.cms.hhs.gov/HospitalAcqCond/02_Statute_Regulations_Program_Instructions.asp#TopOfPage

SOURCE DOCUMENTATION OFFICIAL GUIDELINES

Issues	Guideline	POA Impact	Coding Clinic Source
Internal Coding Guidelines	A facility's internal guidelines may not conflict with the *Official ICD-9-CM Guidelines for Coding & Reporting* and may not be used in place of actual physician documentation in the medical record used to substantiate code assignment.	A physician must be queried concerning the presence of a diagnosis if there are abnormal lab values or other documentation indicating the possibility of a condition either present on admission or developing later.	2Q, '04, 13-14; 3Q, '00, 6; 1Q, '00, 24
Coding Chronic Conditions	Chronic conditions such as, but not limited to, hypertension, Parkinson's disease, COPD, and diabetes mellitus are chronic systemic diseases that ordinarily should be coded even in the absence of documented intervention or further evaluation. Some chronic conditions affect the patient for the rest of his or her life and almost always require some form of continuous clinical evaluation or monitoring during hospitalization, and therefore should be coded.	If documentation is ambiguous or unclear concerning the presence of a chronic condition, the provider should be queried to determine whether the patient carries the diagnosis. This determination affects the POA indicator, which would be assigned as YES (Y) for most chronic conditions unless initially diagnosed during the present admission.	3Q, '07, 10-11
Information from MD other than attending physician	Code assignment may be based on information documented by another physician as long as it doesn't conflict with that from the attending physician.	Medical record documentation provided by any physician other than the attending physician should be carefully reviewed to ensure that all conditions present and treated are coded appropriately.	1Q, '04, 18-19
Mid-level provider documentation	Codes may be assigned based on documentation by nurse practitioners or physician assistants who provide diagnoses and provide care, if they are considered legally accountable for establishing a diagnosis within the regulations governing the provider and the facility.	Coders should be aware of the admitting and attending regulations for their facility and always review nurse practitioner and physician assistant medical record entries carefully for documentation of codable diagnoses.	4Q, '04, 138
Coding diagnoses from pathology reports (inpatient visits)	When a pathology report reflects a completely different diagnosis than the physician documented (e.g., CA breast vs breast mass), the coder must query the physician for additional clarifying information to resolve the conflict. If the pathology report adds greater detail to a diagnosis made by the attending physician, it may be used for coding purposes.	Coders should ensure that any postoperative diagnosis that is found on a pathology report is also documented elsewhere in the record by the physician. It should also be determined whether the condition in question was actually present on admission, even if the postoperative condition differs from the preoperative condition.	3Q, '08, 11; 1Q, '04, 20-21
Coding diagnoses from autopsy reports (inpatient visits)	The information provided on an autopsy report may be used for coding purposes if it clarifies, or provides greater detail or specificity to the diagnoses provided by the attending physician. The autopsy report is completed by a pathologist, who is a physician.	If an autopsy report is available at the time of coding, the coder must ensure that any diagnoses contained in it are substantiated by attending physician documentation. Any conflicts should be clarified by the attending physician.	1Q, '01, 5
Anesthesia record diagnosis documentation	An anesthesiologist is a physician and diagnostic information may be coded from the anesthesiology report unless it conflicts with information provided by the attending physician, in which case the attending should be queried.	Anesthesia reports should be regularly reviewed as part of the coding process. This evaluation can also be helpful in determining the onset of various diagnoses, pertinent in the assignment of the POA indicator.	2Q, '00, 15
Diagnoses found in the body of the medical record	Documentation of codable diagnoses is not limited to the final diagnostic statement, discharge summary, H&P or other specific report. If a physician has documented the diagnosis and it does not conflict with diagnostic information listed elsewhere, it may be coded.	Coders should not limit their review to only those medical record reports that most often contain diagnostic information. Codable diagnoses may be found in any area of the record that contains documentation by a physician or other licensed caregiver.	2Q, '00, 17-18
Adding specificity from radiology reports	When a physician has documented a general diagnosis and a radiology report adds specificity to that diagnosis, without any conflicting information concerning the original diagnosis, the specific information may be used in code selection.	Coders should review all diagnostic or therapeutic reports that carry diagnoses by a physician. If the diagnosis does not conflict with that provided by the attending physician, it may be used to aid in code specificity.	1Q, '99, 5

Present on Admission (POA) Tutorial

Issues	Guideline	POA Impact	Coding Clinic Source
Diagnoses based on physician orders	When a physician orders a prescribed medication for a patient without supporting documentation of a related diagnosis, he or she must be queried concerning the presence of a corresponding diagnosis.	Coders may not assign diagnosis codes based on documentation of physician orders for medications. The query process should include information related to asking the physician to document each condition treated and whether it was a long-standing, chronic or new condition.	3Q, '05, 18-20
Pneumonia coding	While laboratory results can aid in the diagnosis of pneumonia, it is the physician documentation of physical findings, along with supporting information, that substantiates the diagnosis for coding purposes. Coders may not assign a pneumonia code based on laboratory or radiology findings alone, or on treatment by antibiotics or antifungal medications.	Coders must review laboratory, radiology and treatment related documentation and may query the physician based on information contained in these reports. The physician must also document whether the patient had signs or symptoms of the disease process at the time of admission in order to assign the most appropriate POA indicator.	2Q, '98, 3-6
Abnormal lab values	The physician must substantiate that an abnormal lab value represents an actual condition before it may be coded. If the findings are outside the normal range and there is an indication that the physician has ordered further work-up or treatment, the physician should be queried.	No secondary diagnoses should be assigned based on lab values alone. The coder may review the lab and the dates on which the lab studies were performed in order to formulate a physician query to identify whether the patient has a particular condition and whether it was present on admission.	*Official Coding Guidelines* 11/15/06: Section III.B; 2Q, '90, 16
Documentation required for reporting body mass index (BMI)	BMI codes may be reported based on documentation by a dietitian's note, but the condition must follow UHDDS guidelines for reporting secondary diagnoses. Documentation of the underlying overweight, obesity or morbid obesity condition must be documented by a provider.	Coders should not report codes for BMI alone, without the underlying condition that reflects the clinical significance for the patient encounter.	4Q, '08, 191
Using a resident's documentation without attending physician sign-off	Code assignment may be based on other physician documentation (i.e., consultants, residents, etc.) as long as there is no conflicting information from the attending physician. Confirmation of a resident's documentation by the attending physician is dependent on medical staff by-laws, a hospital's internal policies, etc.	Coding management staff should ascertain whether there are specific documentation requirements for residents and their attending physicians and follow those guidelines accordingly.	3Q, '08, 3
Coding based solely on drug administration	It is inappropriate for coders to assign a diagnosis based solely on drug administration without the provider documenting the condition being treated.	When there is a question concerning whether a condition is present, the provider should be queried.	3Q, '08, 14
Clinical information found in *Coding Clinic*	Any clinical information found in *Coding Clinic* does not constitute clinical criteria for establishing a diagnosis, nor does it substitute for the provider's clinical judgment, or eliminate the need for clear and complete physician documentation.	Clinical information presented in *Coding Clinic* is provided as background material to aid the coder's understanding of disease process. When there is a question concerning a specific diagnosis or disease process, the provider should be queried	3Q, '08, 15-16
Required timeframe for physician documentation related to POA	There is no required timeframe concerning when a provider must identify or document a condition to be present on admission.	The coder may use all provider documentation in determining POA indicator assignment, regardless of when it was documented.	3Q, '08, 20
POA indicator requirement for E-codes	Some E-codes are exempt from POA reporting, but others do require POA indicator assignment if they are reported among the secondary diagnoses.	Coders should carefully review the "Categories & Codes Exempt from Diagnosis POA Reporting" section of the most current version of the *ICD-9-CM Official Guidelines for Coding and Reporting*. POA indicators should be assigned for all E-codes not found on the exempt list.	3Q, '08, 21
POA pressure ulcer clarification	A pressure ulcer is only coded and reported once at the highest stage.	If the pressure ulcer is present at the time of admission, the POA indicator is "Y," regardless of whether or not the ulcer progresses to a higher stage during the admission.	1Q, '09, 19

Categories and Codes Exempt from Diagnosis Present on Admission Requirement

Note: "Diagnosis present on admission" for these code categories are exempt because they represent circumstances regarding the healthcare encounter or factors influencing health status that do not represent a current disease or injury or are always present on admission

Categories & Codes	Description
137-139	Late effects of infectious and parasitic diseases
268.1	Rickets, late effect
326	Late effects of intracranial abscess or pyogenic infection
412	Old myocardial infarction
438	Late effects of cerebrovascular disease
650	Normal delivery
660.7	Failed forceps or vacuum extractor, unspecified
677	Late effect of complication of pregnancy, childbirth, and the puerperium
905-909	Late effects of injuries, poisonings, toxic effects, and other external causes
V02	Carrier or suspected carrier of infectious diseases
V03	Need for prophylactic vaccination and inoculation against bacterial diseases
V04	Need for prophylactic vaccination and inoculation against certain viral diseases
V05	Need for other prophylactic vaccination and inoculation against single diseases
V06	Need for prophylactic vaccination and inoculation against combinations of diseases
V07	Need for isolation and other prophylactic measures
V10	Personal history of malignant neoplasm
V11	Personal history of mental disorder
V12	Personal history of certain other diseases
V13	Personal history of other diseases
V14	Personal history of allergy to medicinal agents
V15.01-V15.09	Other personal history, Allergy, other than to medicinal agents
V15.1	Other personal history, Surgery to heart and great vessels
V15.2	Other personal history, Surgery to other major organs
V15.3	Other personal history, Irradiation
V15.4	Other personal history, Psychological trauma
V15.5	Other personal history, Injury
V15.6	Other personal history, Poisoning
V15.7	Other personal history, Contraception
V15.81	Other personal history, Noncompliance with medical treatment
V15.82	Other personal history, History of tobacco use
V15.88	Other personal history, History of fall
V15.89	Other personal history, Other
V15.9	Unspecified personal history presenting hazards to health
V16	Family history of malignant neoplasm

Categories & Codes	Description
V17	Family history of certain chronic disabling diseases
V18	Family history of certain other specific conditions
V19	Family history of other conditions
V20	Health supervision of infant or child
V21	Constitutional states in development
V22	Normal pregnancy
V23	Supervision of high-risk pregnancy
V24	Postpartum care and examination
V25	Encounter for contraceptive management
V26	Procreative management
V27	Outcome of delivery
V28	Antenatal screening
V29	Observation and evaluation of newborns for suspected condition not found
V30-V39	Liveborn infants according to type of birth
V42	Organ or tissue replaced by transplant
V43	Organ or tissue replaced by other means
V44	Artificial opening status
V45	Other postprocedural states
V46	Other dependence on machines
V49.60-V49.77	Upper and lower limb amputation status
V49.81-V49.84	Other specified conditions influencing health status
V50	Elective surgery for purposes other than remedying health states
V51	Aftercare involving the use of plastic surgery
V52	Fitting and adjustment of prosthetic device and implant
V53	Fitting and adjustment of other device
V54	Other orthopedic aftercare
V55	Attention to artificial openings
V56	Encounter for dialysis and dialysis catheter care
V57	Care involving use of rehabilitation procedures
V58	Encounter for other and unspecified procedures and aftercare
V59	Donors
V60	Housing, household, and economic circumstances
V61	Other family circumstances
V62	Other psychosocial circumstances
V64	Persons encountering health services for specific procedures, not carried out
V65	Other persons seeking consultation
V66	Convalescence and palliative care
V67	Follow-up examination
V68	Encounters for administrative purposes
V69	Problems related to lifestyle
V70	General medical examination
V71	Observation and evaluation for suspected condition not found
V72	Special investigations and examinations
V73	Special screening examination for viral and chlamydial diseases

Categories & Codes	Description
V74	Special screening examination for bacterial and spirochetal diseases
V75	Special screening examination for other infectious diseases
V76	Special screening for malignant neoplasms
V77	Special screening for endocrine, nutritional, metabolic, and immunity disorders
V78	Special screening for disorders of blood and blood-forming organs
V79	Special screening for mental disorders and developmental handicaps
V80	Special screening for neurological, eye, and ear diseases
V81	Special screening for cardiovascular, respiratory, and genitourinary diseases
V82	Special screening for other conditions
V83	Genetic carrier status
V84	Genetic susceptibility to disease
V85	Body Mass Index
V86	Estrogen receptor status
V87.4	Personal history of drug therapy
V88	Acquired absence of cervix and uterus
V89	Suspected maternal and fetal conditions not found
E000	External cause status
E001-E030	Activity
E800-E807	Railway accidents
E810-E819	Motor vehicle traffic accidents
E820-E825	Motor vehicle nontraffic accidents
E826-E829	Other road vehicle accidents
E830-E838	Water transport accidents
E840-E845	Air and space transport accidents
E846-E848	Vehicle accidents not elsewhere classifiable
E849.0-E849.6	Place of occurrence
E849.8-E849.9	Place of occurrence
E883.1	Accidental fall into well
E883.2	Accidental fall into storm drain or manhole
E884.0	Fall from playground equipment
E884.1	Fall from cliff
E885.0	Fall from (nonmotorized) scooter
E885.1	Fall from roller skates
E885.2	Fall from skateboard
E885.3	Fall from skis
E885.4	Fall from snowboard
E886.0	Fall on same level from collision, pushing, or shoving, by or with other person, In sports
E890.0-E890.9	Conflagration in private dwelling
E893.0	Accident caused by ignition of clothing, from controlled fire in private dwelling

Categories & Codes	Description
E893.2	Accident caused by ignition of clothing, from controlled fire not in building or structure
E894	Ignition of highly inflammable material
E895	Accident caused by controlled fire in private dwelling
E897	Accident caused by controlled fire not in building or structure
E898.0-E898.1	Accident caused by other specified fire and flames
E917.0	Striking against or struck accidentally by objects or persons, in sports without subsequent fall
E917.1	Striking against or struck accidentally by objects or persons, caused by a crowd, by collective fear or panic without subsequent fall
E917.2	Striking against or struck accidentally by objects or persons, in running water without subsequent fall
E917.5	Striking against or struck accidentally by objects or persons, object in sports with subsequent fall
E917.6	Striking against or struck accidentally by objects or persons, caused by a crowd, by collective fear or panic with subsequent fall
E919.0-E919.1	Accidents caused by machinery
E919.3-E919.9	Accidents caused by machinery
E921.0-E921.9	Accident caused by explosion of pressure vessel
E922.0-E922.9	Accident caused by firearm and air gun missile
E924.1	Caustic and corrosive substances
E926.2	Visible and ultraviolet light sources
E928.0-E928.8	Other and unspecified environmental and accidental causes
E929.0-E929.9	Late effects of accidental injury
E959	Late effects of self-inflicted injury
E970-E978	Legal intervention
E979	Terrorism
E981.0-E981.8	Poisoning by gases in domestic use, undetermined whether accidentally or purposely inflicted
E982.0-E982.9	Poisoning by other gases, undetermined whether accidentally or purposely inflicted
E985.0-E985.7	Injury by firearms air guns and explosives, undetermined whether accidentally or purposely inflicted
E987.0	Falling from high place, undetermined whether accidentally or purposely inflicted, residential premises
E987.2	Falling from high place, undetermined whether accidentally or purposely inflicted, natural sites
E989	Late effects of injury, undetermined whether accidentally or purposely inflicted
E990-E999	Injury resulting from operations of war

10 Steps to Correct Coding

Follow the 10 steps below to correctly code encounters for healthcare services.

Step 1: Identify the reason for the visit or encounter (i.e., a sign, symptom, diagnosis and/or condition).

The medical record documentation should accurately reflect the patient's condition, using terminology that includes specific diagnoses and symptoms, or clearly states the reasons for the encounter.

Choosing the main term that best describes the reason chiefly responsible for the service provided is the most important step in coding. If symptoms are present and documented, but a definitive diagnosis has not yet been determined, code the symptoms. **Do not code conditions that are referred to as "rule out," "suspected," "probable" or "questionable."** Diagnoses often are not established at the time of the initial encounter/visit. Two or more visits may be necessary to establish the diagnosis. Code only what is documented in the available records and only to the highest degree of certainty known at the time of the patient's visit.

Step 2: After selecting the reason for the encounter, always consult the Alphabetic Index, Volume 2, before verifying code selection in the Tabular section.

The most critical rule is to begin the code selection process in the *Alphabetic Index*. Never turn first to the Tabular List (Volume 1). The Index provides cross references, essential and non-essential modifiers, and inclusion terms not found in the Tabular List. To prevent coding errors, always use both the Alphabetic Index and the Tabular List when locating and assigning a code. Always verify the code found in the Alphabetic Index in the Tabular List. First, the Index does not include the important instructional notes found in the Tabular. Second, the advantage of a classification system is that like items are grouped together. A quick scan of the Tabular might provide coding options for the coder that would have been missed.

Step 3: Locate the main term entry.

The Alphabetic Index is a listing of conditions. Conditions may be expressed as nouns or eponyms, with critical use of adjectives. Some conditions have multiple entries under synonyms. Reasons for encounters may be located under general terms such as admission, encounter, and examination. Other general terms such as history of or status post are used to locate factors influencing health.

Step 4: Read and interpret any notes listed with the main term or the subterm.

Notes such as common fifth-digit references and cross references are identified by italicized type. Always check any cross-references to ensure that all alternative terms are researched.

Step 5: Review entries for modifiers.

Nonessential modifiers are the terms located within parentheses following the main term entry. These parenthetical terms are supplementary words or explanatory information that may either be present or absent in the diagnostic statement and do not affect code selection. The subterms listed under the main term are essential modifiers that do affect coding assignment. Each line of indent represents a more specific code entry.

Step 6: Interpret abbreviations, cross-references, fifth digits, and brackets.

The cross-references used are "see," "see category" and "see also" which indicate alternative term choices for code searches. The abbreviation NEC may follow main terms or subterms. NEC (not elsewhere classified) indicates that there is no specific code for the condition even though the medical documentation may be very specific. Is a fifth digit required? You MUST refer to the Tabular List to discover the correct code. Italicized brackets [ ] enclose a second code that must be used along with the code immediately preceding it, with the bracketed code sequenced as the secondary code. This is a mandatory multiple code situation. Both the underlying condition and the manifestation (code in the slanted bracket) must be reported.

Step 7: Choose a potential code and locate it in the Tabular List.

The coder must follow any Includes, Excludes notes, and other instructional notes, such as "Code first" and "Use additional code," listed in the Tabular for the chapter, category, subcategory, and subclassification level of code selection which direct the coder to use a different or additional code.

Any codes in the Tabular range, 001.0 through 999.9, may be used to identify the diagnostic reason for the encounter. The Tabular encompasses many codes describing disease and injury classifications (e.g., infectious and parasitic diseases, neoplasms, symptoms, signs and ill-defined conditions, etc.).

Codes that describe symptoms and signs, as opposed to definitive diagnoses, should be used for reporting purposes when an established diagnosis has not been made (confirmed) by the physician. Chapter 16 of the ICD-9-CM code book, "Symptoms, Signs, and Ill-Defined Conditions" (codes 780.01-799.9) contains many, but not all, codes for symptoms.

ICD-9-CM classifies encounters with health care providers for circumstances other than a disease or injury using codes in the Supplementary Classification of Factors Influencing Health Status and Contact with Health Services (V01.0-V89.09). There are many occasions when circumstances other than a disease or injury are recorded as chiefly responsible for the encounter.

Step 8: Determine whether the code is at the highest level of specificity.

A code is invalid if it has not been coded to the full number of digits (greatest level of specificity) required. A three-digit code is to be used only if the category is not further subdivided. Assign four-digit codes (subcategory codes) only if there are no five-digit codes for that category. Assign five-digit codes (fifth-digit subclassification codes) for those categories mandating the use of five digits.

Step 9: Assign the code.

Having reviewed all relevant information concerning the possible code choices, assign the code that most completely describes the condition.

Repeat steps one through nine for all additional documented conditions that meet the following criteria:

- Conditions that currently exist at the time of the visit
- Conditions that require or affect patient care, treatment or management.

Step 10: Sequence codes correctly

Sequencing is defined as the order in which the codes are listed on the claim. List first the ICD-9-CM code for the diagnosis, condition, problem or other reason for the encounter/visit, which is shown in the medical record to be chiefly responsible for the services provided. List additional codes that describe any coexisting conditions. Follow the official coding guidelines (See Section IV Diagnostic Coding and reporting Guidelines for Outpatient Services) concerning proper sequencing of codes.

Coding Examples

Diagnosis: Anorexia
- Step 1: The reason for the encounter was the condition, anorexia.
- Step 2: Consult the Index to Diseases.
- Step 3: Locate the main term "Anorexia," which indicates a code of 783.0.
- Step 4: There are no italicized instructional notes to interpret.
- Step 5: Note that there are two possible subterms (essential modifiers), "hysterical" and "nervosa," neither of which is documented in this instance and therefore cannot be used in code selection. The code listed next to the main term is called the default code selection.
- Step 6: There are no abbreviations, cross-references, fifth-digit notations, or brackets.
- Step 7: Turn to code 783.0 in the Tabular List and read the instructional notes. In this case the "Excludes" note indicates that anorexia determined to be of non-organic origin should be coded to Chapter 5. The diagnostic statement does not indicate non-organic origin.
- Step 8: There is no further division of the category past the fourth digit subcategory. Therefore, the subcategory code level is the highest level of specificity.
- Step 9: The default code, 783.0 is the correct code selection.
- Step 10: Since anorexia is listed as the chief reason for the healthcare encounter, the primary or principal diagnosis is 783.0.

Diagnosis: Acute bronchitis
- Step 1: The reason for the encounter was the condition, acute bronchitis.
- Step 2: Consult the Index to Diseases.
- Step 3: Locate the main term "Bronchitis."
- Step 4: There are no italicized instructional notes to interpret.

- Step 5: Review entries for modifiers. Since "acute" is not listed as a nonessential modifier, read past the "with" modifier until you find the subterm "acute or subacute" with code 466.0.
- Step 6: There are no abbreviations, cross-references, fifth digit notations, or brackets.
- Step 7: Since there are no more appropriate subterms, turn to code 466.0 in the Tabular List. The Includes note under category 466.0 does refer to possible infective organism, and other alternative terms for acute bronchitis. Note that inclusion term list is not exhaustive, but is only a representative selection of diagnoses that are included in the subcategory. At the beginning of chapter 8, "Diseases of the Respiratory System," you will notice the "use additional code" note that tells you to assign a code to identify the infectious organism. This instructional note applies to the entire chapter.
- Step 8: There is no further division of the category past the fourth- digit subcategory. Therefore, the subcategory code level is the highest level of specificity.
- Step 9: Assign code 466.0.
- Step 10: Repeat steps 1-9 for any additional code assignments.

Diagnosis: Acute bronchitis due to staphylococcus
- Step 1: The reason for the encounter was the condition, acute bronchitis due to staphylococcus.
- Step 2: Follow the steps listed in the above example for the diagnosis of acute bronchitis. You will now start the search for code identifying the underlying infectious organism, which in this case is staphylococcus.
- Step 3. Consult the Index to Diseases.
- Step 4: Locate the main term Staphylococcus, staphylococcal.
- Step 5: The italicized instructional notes states see condition. Locate the main term "Infection, infected, infective".
- Step 6: Review entries for modifiers. Locate the subterm "staphylococcal NEC," where you will find code 041.10 referenced. The abbreviation NEC indicates that a review of the medical record may be necessary to determine if there is documentation concerning the specific type of staphylococcus.
- Step 7: Verify code 041.10 in the Tabular List. The code title is Staphylococcus, unspecified. If there is additional information identifying the organism as aureus or other, assign the appropriate code, 041.11 or 041.19. Otherwise, assign code 041.10, Staphylococcus, unspecified, as an additional code.
- Step 8: There is no further division of the category past the fifth-digit subclassification level. Therefore, the subclassification code level is the highest level of specificity. The final code assignment would be 041.10.
- Step 9: Assign code 041.10.
- Step 10: Sequence codes as directed by the instructional note for category 466. Code first 466.0 and assign code 041.10 as additional.

Diagnosis: Traveler's diarrhea
- Step 1: The reason for the encounter was the condition, Traveler's diarrhea.
- Step 2. Consult the Index to Diseases.
- Step 3: Locate the main term "Diarrhea" in the Alphabetic Index.

- Step 4: There are no italicized instructional notes to interpret.
- Step 5: Review entries for modifiers. Note that the nonessential modifiers (in parentheses) after the main term do not include the term "Traveler's," which means that the coder should search the subterms for the term "Traveler's." The subterm "Traveler's" has a possible code selection, 009.2, and suggests the subterm "due to specified organism NEC 008.8." The diagnostic statement does not include the infectious agent; therefore, code 008.8 does not apply.
- Step 6: There are no abbreviations, cross-references, fifth-digit notations, or brackets.
- Step 7: Locate code 009.2 in the Tabular List and read all instructional notes under the main category and subcategories. The Includes notes does not list the term "Traveler's" under code 009.2. As instructed by the Alphabetic Index, you should code the condition to 009.2. The ICD-9-CM code book implies that "Traveler's diarrhea" is the same as infectious diarrhea when it is not attributed to any specified infectious agent.
- Step 8: There is no further division of the category past the fourth-digit subcategory level. Therefore, the subcategory code level is the highest level of specificity. The final code assignment would be 009.2.
- Step 9: Assign code 009.2.
- Step 10: Since infectious diarrhea is listed as the chief reason for the healthcare encounter, the primary or principal diagnosis is 009.2.

Diagnosis: Ingrown toenail, infected
- Step 1: The reason for the encounter was the condition, infected ingrown toenail.
- Step 2. Consult the Index to Diseases.
- Step 3: First you must decide what the searchable main term should be. Reminder: search for condition, not anatomical site. The Alphabetic Index helps you determine the main term. Refer to "toenail" in the Alphabetic Index; the closest match is "Toe," which includes the instruction "see condition." Locate the main term "Infection" in the Alphabetic Index. The subterm toe has a subterm "nail" which refers the coder to category 681, Cellulitis and abscess of finger and toe. This does not indicate the condition ingrown toenail. The main term, therefore, is "Ingrown." A review of the Alphabetic Index takes you to "Ingrowing."
- Step 4: There are no italicized instructional notes to interpret.
- Step 5: Review the subterms. The subterm "nail" appears and lists nonessential modifiers (in parentheses) as "finger," "toe" and "infected." These nonessential modifiers complete the diagnostic statement.
- Step 6: There are no abbreviations, cross-references, fifth-digit notations, or brackets.
- Step 7: Verify code 703.0 in the Tabular List Before assigning the code, review all instructional notes under category 703 and under code 703.0. The note, "Excludes: infection, nail NOS (681.9)," can be ignored because the diagnostic statement specifies the infection is due to the ingrowing nail.
- Step 8: Therefore, the subcategory code level is the highest level of specificity. The final code assignment would be 703.0.
- Step 9: The correct code choice is 703.0, Ingrowing nail with infection.
- Step 10: Since infectious infected ingrown toenail is listed as the chief reason for the healthcare encounter, the primary or principal diagnosis is 703.0.